Collins

Concise Dictionary & Thesaurus

Collins

Concise Dictionary & Thesaurus

Collins

An Imprint of HarperCollins*Publishers*

third edition 2003

HarperCollins Publishers
Westerhill Road, Bishopbriggs, Glasgow G64 2QT
Great Britain

www.collinsdictionaries.com

ISBN 0-00-716262-6

Acknowledgements

We would like to thank those authors and publishers who kindly gave permission for copyright material to be used in the Bank of English. We would also like to thank Times Newspapers Ltd for providing valuable data.

Note

Entered words that we have reason to believe constitute trademarks have been designated as such. However, neither the presence nor absence of such designation should be regarded as affecting the legal status of any trademark.

A catalogue record for this book is available from the British Library

Text typeset by Barbers Ltd, Wrotham, England

Supplement typeset by Wordcraft, Glasgow

Printed and bound in Great Britain by The Bath Press, Bath

EDITORIAL STAFF

Editor
Lorna Gilmour

Publishing Management
Elaine Higgleton

Series Editor
Lorna Sinclair Knight

Language in Action Supplement
Penny Hands and Jenny Kumar

Contributors

Ian Brookes
Patrick Drysdale
Sheila Ferguson
Alison Foy
Ian A Gordon
Ronald G Hardie
Andrew Holmes
Geoffrey Hughes
W A Krebs
Danielle McGinley
Mike Munro
Michael Murphy
Judith Scott
Elspeth Summers
G A Wilkes
Anne Young

BANK *of* ENGLISH

This dictionary has been compiled with constant reference to the Bank of English, a unique database containing over 524 million words of written and spoken English, enabling Collins lexicographers to analyse how the language is actually used and how it is changing. The Bank of English was set up as a joint initiative by HarperCollins Publishers and the University of Birmingham to be a resource for language research and lexicography. It contains a very wide range of material from books, newspapers, radio, TV, magazines, letters and talks, thereby reflecting the whole spectrum of English today. Its size and range make it an unequalled resource, and the purpose-built software for its analysis is unique to Collins dictionaries.

This ensures that Collins dictionaries accurately reflect English as it is used today in a way that is most helpful to the dictionary or thesaurus user.

CONTENTS

FOREWORD

Collins Concise Dictionary and Thesaurus provides two kinds of language help, arranged on the same page for quick and easy reference. In the top section of each page you will find a dictionary text which gives help with spellings and meanings, while the lower section of each page provides a thesaurus with a choice of synonyms.

A Dictionary

In the top part of each page is a dictionary text with over 68,000 references. Each word defined is given as a main entry in a single alphabetical sequence. Every definition is given in concise, straightforward English. Where a word has more than one sense, the one given first is the normal everyday meaning in today's language. Other senses of a word – for instance, historical or technical meanings – are explained after the main present-day meaning. Each sense is separately numbered.

In addition, the dictionary gives help with spelling. The text shows all plurals and verb parts where these are difficult, unusual, or likely to produce problems. It makes it clear, for instance, that in British English there are two "l"s in *travelling*, and that the plural of *larynx* can be either *larynges* or *larynxes*. Simple pronunciations are given for words which might be unfamiliar. Help is given with difficult or controversial points in the use of English. Particularly problematic words have notes after the entry showing the current view on their usage, especially in cases where this usage is changing.

The dictionary section was compiled using the Bank of English, a unique computer-based collection of over 520 million words of written and spoken English. Analysis of this material has enabled the authors to give the users of this dictionary the most up-to-date information about how English is spoken and written today. All of the examples of use given in the dictionary text are based on an examination of the uses recorded in the Bank of English.

A Thesaurus

In the bottom part of each page is the thesaurus section, which is also arranged in a single alphabetical listing of main words. At each of these main entries, you will find a list or lists of alternative words and phrases of the same or similar meaning. Even if an entry word has more than one meaning, synonyms for the different meanings will be found at the same entry, grouped in alphabetical lists according to the different senses of the main word. The different senses are arranged in the order that they are found in the dictionary entry.

Suppose, for instance, that you want to find another word for *difficult*. Perhaps you have used it already, or perhaps you feel it is not quite suited to the tone or context of what you want to write or say.

The entry for *difficult* in the thesaurus section of the page provides you with a choice of words, suited to all occasions, that can be used in its place. So from the many alternatives given you could, for example, substitute: an *onerous* task; *trying* circumstances; an *obstreperous* customer.

Not every word or sense in the dictionary section has an entry in the thesaurus. Terms denoting specific things often have no synonyms (*begonia*, *ankle*, and *oxygen*, for example). Such items are not included unless they have an alternative name or give rise to a figurative use. *Retina*, for instance, only appears in the dictionary; but *eye* is in the thesaurus in both literal and figurative senses, while *ear* is given figurative senses only.

A Dictionary and a Thesaurus together

The arrangement of the two texts in parallel format enables you to refer from dictionary to thesaurus entries and then back again with ease. All the information on any one word in all its aspects is contained at one place.

Collins Concise Dictionary and Thesaurus is thus a uniquely helpful book, providing spelling, meaning, and a wide choice of alternative words, all together at one place. The convenience of the matching texts makes it an invaluable reference book for many occasions, and an ideal companion for everyone who wants to increase their command of English.

Language in Action Supplement

The Language in Action Supplement provides further language help, with practical advice on how to write in a clear and persuasive style that will enable you to communicate effectively in any situation.

FEATURES OF THE DICTIONARY AND THESAURUS

Numbered definitions help you find the sense you want

Coverage of World English

Homonym numbers distinguish entry words with identical spelling but different meanings

Spelling help with changes in form of entry word

Tips on current English

Parts of speech

licit *adj Formal* lawful; permitted.

lick *vb* **1** to pass the tongue over in order to taste, wet, or clean. **2** to flicker over or round (something): *flames licked the gutters.* **3** *Informal* **a** to defeat. **b** to thrash. **4 lick into shape** to put into a satisfactory condition. **5 lick one's wounds** to retire after a defeat. ~*n* **6** an instance of passing the tongue over something. **7** a small amount: *a lick of paint.* **8** *Informal* a blow. **9** *Informal* a fast pace: *a pulsating rhythm taken at a lick.* **10 a lick and a promise** something hastily done, esp. a hurried wash.

licorice *n US & Canad* same as **liquorice.**

lid *n* **1** a removable or hinged cover: *a saucepan lid.* **2** short for **eyelid. 3 put the (tin) lid on** *Informal* to put an end to. **lidded** *adj*

lido (lee-doe) *n, pl* **-dos** *Brit* an open-air swimming pool or a part of a beach used by the public for swimming and sunbathing.

lie[1] *vb* **lying, lied 1** to speak untruthfully with the intention of deceiving. **2** to convey a false impression: *the camera cannot lie.* ~*n* **3** an untrue statement deliberately used to mislead. **4** something that is deliberately intended to deceive. **5 give the lie to a** to disprove. **b** to accuse of lying.

lie[2] *vb* **lying, lay, lain 1** (often foll. by *down*) to place oneself or be in a horizontal position. **2** to be situated: *I left the money lying on the table; Nepal became the only country lying between China and India.* **3** to be and remain (in a particular state or condition): *others of their species lie asleep.* **4** to stretch or extend: *an enormous task lies ahead.* **5** (usually foll. by *in*) to exist or comprise: *her charm lies in her inner beauty.* **6** (foll. by *with*) to rest (with): *the fault lies with the NHS.* ~*n* **7** the manner, place, or style in which something is situated. **8** an animal's lair. **9 lie of the land** the way in which a situation is developing. ~See also **lie down, lie in.**

➤ **Note that the past of *lie* is *lay*: *She lay on the beach all day.* Do not confuse with the main verb *lay* meaning "put".**

Liebfraumilch (leeb-frow-milk) *n* a sweet white wine from the German Rhine.

lied (leed) *n, pl* **lieder** *Music* a musical setting for solo voice and piano of a romantic or lyrical poem.

lie detector *n Informal* a device used to measure any increase in blood pressure, pulse rate, etc., of someone being questioned, which is thought to indicate that the person is lying.

lie down *vb* **1** to place oneself or be in a horizontal position in order to rest. **2** to yield to: *never take any attack on your candidate lying down.* ~*n* **lie-down 3** a rest.

liege (leej) *adj* **1** (of a lord) owed feudal allegiance:

THESA

Numbered lists help you find the sense you want

Homonym numbers

Parts of speech

dissoluteness, lechery, lewdness, libertinism, libidinousness, lust, lustfulness, profligacy, promiscuity, prurience, salaciousness, salacity, wantonness

lick *vb.* **1.** brush, lap, taste, tongue, touch, wash **2.** dart, flick, flicker, ignite, kindle, play over, ripple, touch **3.** *informal* **a.** beat, blow out of the water (*slang*), clobber (*slang*), defeat, master, overcome, rout, run rings around (*informal*), tank (*slang*), trounce, undo, vanquish, wipe the floor with (*informal*) **b.** beat, clobber (*slang*), flog, lambast(e), slap, spank, strike, thrash, wallop (*informal*) ~*n.* **4.** bit, brush, dab, little, sample, speck, stroke, taste, touch **5.** *informal* clip (*informal*), pace, rate, speed

lie[1] **1.** *vb.* dissimulate, equivocate, fabricate, falsify, fib, forswear oneself, invent, misrepresent, perjure, prevaricate, tell a lie, tell untruths **2.** *n.* deceit, fabrication, falsehood, falsification, falsity, fib, fiction, invention, mendacity, prevarication, untruth, white lie

their liege lord. **2** (of a vassal or subject) owing feudal allegiance: *a liege subject.* **3** faithful; loyal. ~*n* **4** a liege lord. **5** a subject.

lie in *vb* **1** to remain in bed late into the morning. ~*n* **lie-in 2** a long stay in bed in the morning.

Restrictive labels show context of use

lien *n* *Law* a right to retain possession of someone else's property until a debt is paid.

lieu **(lyew)** *n* **in lieu of** instead of.

Lieut. lieutenant.

lieutenant **(lef-ten-ant)** *n* **1** a junior officer in the army, navy, or the US police force. **2** a person who acts as principal assistant. **lieutenancy** *n*

Pronunciation help for all words that could cause confusion, with the stressed syllable in bold type

lieutenant colonel *n* an officer in an army, air force, or marine corps immediately junior to a colonel.

lieutenant commander *n* an officer in a navy immediately junior to a commander.

lieutenant general *n* a senior officer in an army, air force, or marine corps.

lieutenant governor *n* **1** a deputy governor. **2** (in Canada) the representative of the Crown in a province.

life *n, pl* **lives 1** the state or quality that identifies living beings, characterized chiefly by growth, reproduction, and response to stimuli. **2** the period between birth and death or between birth and the present time. **3** a living person or being: *riots which claimed 22 lives.* **4** the remainder or extent of one's life: *with that lady for the rest of her life.* **5** the process of living: *rituals gave his life stability.* **6** *Informal* a sentence of life imprisonment, usually approximating to fifteen years. **7** a characteristic state or mode of existence: *country life is best.* **8** the length of time that something is active or functioning: *the life of a battery.* **9** a present condition or mode of existence: *they are leading a joyous life.* **10** a biography. **11** the sum or course of human events and activities. **12** liveliness or high spirits: *full of life.* **13** a source of strength, animation, or vitality: *he was the life of the show.* **14** all living things collectively: *there is no life on Mars; marine life.* **15 a matter of life and death** a matter of extreme urgency. **16 as large as life** *Informal* real and living. **17 not on your life** *Informal* certainly not. **18 true to life** faithful to reality. **19 to the life** (of a copy of a painting or drawing) resembling the original exactly.

Example phrases show how words are actually used

Common phrases explained

life assurance *n* insurance that provides for a sum of money to be paid to the insured person at a certain age or to the spouse or children on the death of the insured. Also called: **life insurance**

Variant forms shown

life belt *n* an inflatable ring used to keep a person afloat when in danger of drowning.

lifeblood *n* **1** the blood vital to life. **2** something that is essential for existence, development, or success.

URUS

Homonym numbers

lie[2] *vb.* **1.** be prone, be prostrate, be recumbent, be supine, couch, loll, lounge, recline, repose, rest, sprawl, stretch out **2.** be, be buried, be found, be interred, be located, belong, be placed, be situated, exist, extend, remain **3.** *usually with* **in** be present, consist, dwell, exist, inhere, pertain

life 1. animation, being, breath, entity, growth, sentience, viability, vitality **2.** being, career, continuance, course, duration, existence, lifetime, span, time **3.** human, human being, individual, mortal, person, soul **4.** behaviour, conduct, life style, way of life **5.** autobiography, biography, career, confessions, history, life story, memoirs, story **6.** the human condition, the times, the world, this mortal coil, trials and tribulations, vicissitudes **7.** activity, animation, brio, energy, get-up-and-go *(informal)*, go *(informal)*, high spirits, liveliness, oomph *(informal)*, pep, sparkle, spirit, verve, vigour, vitality, vivacity, zest **8.** animating spirit,

Restrictive labels

ABBREVIATIONS USED IN THIS BOOK

abbrev.	abbreviation
adj	adjective
adv	adverb(ial)
Anat	Anatomy
Anthropol	Anthropology
Archaeol	Archaeology
Archit	Architecture
Astrol	Astrology
Astron	Astronomy
Austral	Australian
Bacteriol	Bacteriology
Biochem	Biochemistry
Biol	Biology
Bot	Botany
Brit	British
C	Celsius
Canad	Canadian
cap	capital
cent.	century
Chem	Chemistry
comp.	comparative
conj	conjunction
Crystallog	Crystallography
dim.	diminutive
E	East(ern)
Econ	Economics
esp.	especially
etc.	et cetera
F	Fahrenheit
fem	feminine
foll.	followed
Geog	Geography
Geol	Geology
Geom	Geometry
imit.	imitative
infl.	influence(d)
interj	interjection
lit.	literally
masc	masculine
Maths	Mathematics
Med	Medicine
Meteorol	Meteorology
Mil	Military
Myth	Mythology
n	noun
N	North(ern)
Naut	Nautical
NE	Northeast(ern)
NW	Northwest(ern)
NZ	New Zealand
obs.	obsolete
orig.	originally
Ornithol	Ornithology
Pathol	Pathology
Pharmacol	Pharmacology
Photog	Photography
Physiol	Physiology
pl	plural
pp	past participle
prep	preposition
prob.	probably
pron	pronoun
Psychoanal	Psychoanalysis
Psychol	Psychology
pt	past tense
RC	Roman Catholic
rel.	related
S	South(ern)
Scot	Scots, Scottish
SE	Southeast(ern)
sing	singular
SW	Southwest(ern)
Theol	Theology
ult.	ultimately
US	United States
var.	variant
vb	verb
W	West(ern)
Zool	Zoology

A

a *or* **A** *n, pl* **a's, A's,** *or* **As 1** the first letter of the English alphabet. **2 from A to B** from one place to another: *I just want a car that takes me from A to B.* **3 from A to Z** from start to finish.

a *adj* (*indefinite article*) **1** used preceding a singular count noun that has not been mentioned before: *a book; a great shame.* **2** used preceding a noun or adjective of quantity: *a litre of wine; a great amount has been written; I swim a lot and walk much more.* **3** each or every; per: *I saw him once a week for six weeks.*

A 1 *Music* the sixth note of the scale of C major. **2** ampere(s). **3** atomic: *an A-bomb.*

Å angstrom unit.

a- *or before a vowel* **an-** *prefix* not or without: *atonal; asocial; anaphrodisiac.*

A1, A-1, *or* **A-one** *adj Informal* first-class, excellent.

A4 *n* a standard paper size, 297 × 210 mm.

AA 1 Alcoholics Anonymous. **2** (in Britain) Automobile Association.

AAA *Brit* Amateur Athletic Association.

aardvark *n* an African mammal with long ears and snout.

AB 1 able-bodied seaman. **2** Alberta.

ab- *prefix* away from or opposite to: *abnormal.*

aback *adv* **taken aback** startled or disconcerted.

abacus (ab-a-cuss) *n* a counting device consisting of a frame holding beads on metal rods.

abaft *adv, adj Naut* closer to the stern of a ship.

abalone (ab-a-**lone**-ee) *n* an edible sea creature with a shell lined with mother-of-pearl.

abandon *vb* **1** to desert or leave: *he had already abandoned his first wife.* **2** to give up completely: *did you abandon all attempts at contact with the boy?* **3** to give oneself over completely to an emotion. *~n* **4 with abandon** uninhibitedly and without restraint. **abandonment** *n*

abandoned *adj* **1** no longer used or occupied: *four people were found dead in an abandoned vehicle.* **2** wild and uninhibited: *she made his aunt laugh, that fluffy abandoned laugh he so liked to hear.*

abase *vb* **abasing, abased abase oneself** to make oneself humble. **abasement** *n*

abashed *adj* embarrassed and ashamed.

abate *vb* **abating, abated** to make or become less strong: *the tension has abated in recent months.* **abatement** *n*

abattoir (**ab**-a-twahr) *n* a slaughterhouse.

abbacy *n, pl* **-cies** the office or jurisdiction of an abbot or abbess.

abbé (**ab**-bay) *n* a French abbot or other clergyman.

abbess *n* the nun in charge of a convent.

abbey *n* **1** a church associated with a community of monks or nuns. **2** a community of monks or nuns. **3** a building inhabited by monks or nuns.

abbot *n* the head of an abbey of monks.

abbreviate *vb* **-ating, -ated 1** to shorten a word by leaving out some letters. **2** to cut short. **abbreviation** *n*

ABC *n* **1** the alphabet. **2** an alphabetical guide. **3** the basics of something.

abdicate *vb* **-cating, -cated 1** to give up the throne formally. **2** to give up one's responsibilities. **abdication** *n*

abdomen *n* the part of the body that contains the stomach and intestines. **abdominal** *adj*

abduct *vb* to remove (a person) by force; kidnap. **abduction** *n* **abductor** *n*

abeam *adv, adj* at right angles to the length of a ship or aircraft.

Aberdeen Angus *n* a black hornless breed of beef cattle originating in Scotland.

aberrant *adj* not normal, accurate, or correct: *aberrant behaviour.*

aberration *n* **1** a sudden change from what is normal, accurate, or correct. **2** a brief lapse in control of one's thoughts or feelings: *he suddenly had a mental aberration.*

abet *vb* **abetting, abetted** to help or encourage in wrongdoing.

abeyance *n* **in abeyance** put aside temporarily.

abhor *vb* **-horring, -horred** to detest utterly.

THESAURUS

abandon *vb.* **1.** desert, evacuate, forsake, jilt, leave, leave behind, quit, vacate, withdraw from **2.** abdicate, cede, desist, discontinue, drop, forgo, give up, kick (*informal*), relinquish, renounce, resign, surrender, waive, yield *~n.* **3.** careless freedom, dash, recklessness, unrestraint, wantonness, wild impulse, wildness

abandoned 1. cast aside, cast away, cast out, derelict, deserted, discarded, forlorn, forsaken, left, neglected, rejected, relinquished, unoccupied, vacant **2.** uncontrolled, uninhibited, unrestrained, wild

abandonment 1. desertion, evacuation, forsaking, jilting, leaving, quitting, withdrawal from **2.** abdication, cession, desistance, discontinuation, dropping, giving up, relinquishment, renunciation, resignation, surrender, waiver

abbey cloister, convent, friary, monastery, nunnery, priory

abbreviate abridge, abstract, clip, compress, condense, contract, curtail, cut, précis, reduce, shorten, summarize, trim, truncate

abbreviation abridgment, abstract, clipping, compendium, compression, condensation, conspectus, contraction, curtailment, digest, epitome, précis, reduction, résumé, shortening, summary, synopsis, trimming, truncation

abdicate abandon, abjure, abnegate, cede, forgo, give up, quit, relinquish, renounce, resign, retire, step down (*informal*), surrender, vacate, waive, yield

abdication abandonment, abjuration, abnegation, cession, giving up, quitting, relinquishment, renunciation, resignation, retiral (*esp. Scot.*), retirement, surrender, waiver, yielding

abdominal gastric, intestinal, visceral

abduct carry off, kidnap, make off with, run away with, run off with, seize, snatch (*slang*)

abet aid, assist, condone, connive at, egg on, encourage, help, incite, support, urge

abeyance in abeyance hanging fire, on ice (*informal*), pending, shelved, suspended

abhor abominate, detest, execrate, hate, loathe, recoil from, regard with repugnance *or* horror, shrink from, shudder at

abhorrent abominable, detestable, disgusting, distasteful, execrable, hated, hateful, heinous, horrible,

abhorrent *adj* hateful or disgusting. **abhorrence** *n*
abide *vb* **1** to tolerate: *I can't abide stupid people.* **2** to last or exist for a long time: *these instincts, while subdued in the individual, may abide in the race.* **3 abide by** to act in accordance with: *he must abide by the findings of the report.* **4** *Archaic* to live.
abiding *adj* lasting for ever: *an abiding interest in history.*
ability *n, pl* **-ties 1** possession of the necessary skill or power to do something. **2** great skill or competence: *his ability as a speaker was legendary.*
abject *adj* **1** utterly miserable: *one Mexican in five lives in abject poverty.* **2** lacking all self-respect. **abjectly** *adv*
abjure *vb* **-juring, -jured** to renounce or deny under oath. **abjuration** *n*
ablation *n* **1** the surgical removal of an organ or part. **2** the wearing away of a rock or glacier. **3** the melting of a part, such as the heat shield of a space re-entry vehicle.
ablaze *adj* **1** on fire. **2** brightly illuminated: *the sky was ablaze with the stars shining bright.* **3** emotionally aroused: *his eyes were ablaze with anger.*
able *adj* **1** having the necessary power, skill, or opportunity to do something. **2** capable or talented.
-able *suffix forming adjectives* able to be acted upon as specified: *washable.* **-ably** *suffix forming adverbs* **-ability** *suffix forming nouns*
able-bodied *adj* strong and healthy.
able-bodied seaman *or* **able seaman** *n* a seaman who is trained in certain skills.
able rating *n* a seaman of the lowest rank in a navy.
ablutions *pl n* the act of washing: *after the nightly ablutions, I settled down to read.*
ably *adv* competently or skilfully.
ABM antiballistic missile.
abnegation *n* the act of giving something up.
abnormal *adj* differing from the usual or typical. **abnormality** *n* **abnormally** *adv*
aboard *adv, adj, prep* on, in, onto, or into (a ship, plane, or train).
abode *n* one's home.
abolish *vb* to do away with (laws, regulations, or customs).
abolition *n* **1** the act of doing away with something: *the abolition of slavery.* **2 Abolition** the ending of slavery. **abolitionist** *n, adj*
A-bomb *n* short for **atom bomb.**
abominable *adj* very bad or unpleasant: *what is being done here is utterly abominable.* **abominably** *adv*
abominable snowman *n* a large creature, like a man or an ape, that is said to live in the Himalayas.
abominate *vb* **-nating, -nated** to dislike intensely. **abomination** *n*
aboriginal *adj* existing in a place from the earliest known period.
Aboriginal *adj* **1** of the Aborigines of Australia. *~n* **2** an Aborigine.
aborigine (ab-or-**rij**-in-ee) *n* an original inhabitant of a country or region.
Aborigine *n* a member of a dark-skinned people who

THESAURUS

horrid, loathsome, obnoxious, obscene, odious, offensive, repellent, repugnant, repulsive, revolting, yucky *or* yukky (*slang*)
abide 1. accept, bear, brook, endure, put up with, stand, stomach, submit to, suffer, tolerate **2.** continue, endure, last, persist, remain, survive
abide by acknowledge, adhere to, agree to, carry out, comply with, conform to, discharge, follow, fulfil, hold to, keep to, obey, observe, persist in, stand by, submit to
abiding eternal, everlasting, immortal, permanent, unending
ability 1. aptitude, capability, capacity, endowment, facility, faculty, potentiality, power **2.** adeptness, competence, competency, craft, dexterity, expertise, flair, gift, knack, know-how (*informal*), proficiency, qualification, skill, talent
abject 1. deplorable, forlorn, hopeless, miserable, pitiable, wretched **2.** base, contemptible, cringing, debased, degraded, despicable, dishonourable, fawning, grovelling, humiliating, ignoble, ignominious, low, mean, servile, slavish, sordid, submissive, vile, worthless
ablaze 1. aflame, alight, blazing, burning, fiery, flaming, ignited, lighted, on fire **2.** aglow, brilliant, flashing, gleaming, glowing, illuminated, incandescent, luminous, radiant, sparkling **3.** angry, aroused, enthusiastic, excited, fervent, frenzied, fuming, furious, impassioned, incensed, passionate, raging, stimulated
able 1. adept, adequate, adroit, capable, clever, competent, effective, efficient, experienced, fit, fitted, powerful, practised, proficient, qualified, strong **2.** accomplished, expert, gifted, highly endowed, masterful, masterly, skilful, skilled, talented
able-bodied firm, fit, hale, hardy, healthy, hearty, lusty, powerful, robust, sound, staunch, stout, strapping, strong, sturdy, vigorous
abnormal aberrant, anomalous, atypical, curious, deviant, eccentric, erratic, exceptional, extraordinary, irregular, monstrous, odd, oddball (*informal*), outré, peculiar, queer, singular, strange, uncommon, unexpected, unnatural, untypical, unusual, weird
abnormality aberration, anomaly, atypicalness, bizarreness, deformity, deviation, eccentricity, exception, extraordinariness, flaw, irregularity, monstrosity, oddity, peculiarity, queerness, singularity, strangeness, uncommonness, unexpectedness, unnaturalness, untypicalness, unusualness, weirdness
abolish abrogate, annihilate, annul, axe (*informal*), blot out, cancel, destroy, do away with, eliminate, end, eradicate, expunge, exterminate, extinguish, extirpate, invalidate, nullify, obliterate, overthrow, overturn, put an end to, quash, repeal, repudiate, rescind, revoke, stamp out, subvert, suppress, terminate, vitiate, void, wipe out
abolition abrogation, annihilation, annulment, blotting out, cancellation, destruction, elimination, end, ending, eradication, expunction, extermination, extinction, extirpation, invalidation, nullification, obliteration, overthrow, overturning, quashing, repeal, repudiation, rescission, revocation, stamping out, subversion, suppression, termination, vitiation, voiding, wiping out, withdrawal
abominable abhorrent, accursed, atrocious, base, contemptible, despicable, detestable, disgusting, execrable, foul, godawful (*slang*), hateful, heinous, hellish, horrible, horrid, loathsome, nauseous, obnoxious, obscene, odious, repellent, reprehensible, repugnant, repulsive, revolting, terrible, vile, villainous, wretched, yucky *or* yukky (*slang*)
abominate abhor, detest, execrate, hate, loathe, recoil from, regard with repugnance, shudder at
abomination 1. abhorrence, antipathy, aversion, detestation, disgust, distaste, execration, hate, hatred, horror, loathing, odium, repugnance, revulsion **2.** anathema, *bête noire,* bugbear, curse, disgrace, evil, horror, plague, shame, torment

were already living in Australia when European settlers arrived.

abort *vb* **1** (of a pregnancy) to end before the fetus is viable. **2** to perform an abortion on a pregnant woman. **3** to end a plan or process before completion.

abortion *n* **1** an operation to end pregnancy. **2** the premature ending of a pregnancy when a fetus is expelled from the womb before it can live independently. **3** the failure of a mission or project. **4** *Informal* something that is grotesque. **abortionist** *n*

abortive *adj* failing to achieve its purpose.

abound *vb* **1** to exist in large numbers. **2 abound in** to have a large number of.

about *prep* **1** relating to or concerning. **2** near to. **3** carried on: *I haven't any money about me.* **4** on every side of. *~adv* **5** near in number, time, or degree; approximately. **6** nearby. **7** here and there: *there were some fifteen other people scattered about on the first floor.* **8** all around; on every side. **9** in or to the opposite direction. **10** in rotation: *turn and turn about.* **11** used to indicate understatement: *it's about time somebody told the truth on that subject.* **12 about to** on the point of; intending to: *she was about to get in the car.* **13 not about to** determined not to: *we're not about to help her out.* *~adj* **14** active: *he was off the premises well before anyone was up and about*

about-turn *or US* **about-face** *n* **1** a complete change of opinion or direction. **2** a reversal of the direction in which one is facing.

above *prep* **1** higher than; over. **2** greater than in quantity or degree: *above average.* **3** superior to or higher than in quality, rank, or ability. **4** too high-minded for: *he considered himself above the task of working.* **5** too respected for; beyond: *his flect was above suspicion.* **6** too difficult to be understood by: a *discussion that was way above my head.* **7** louder or higher than (other noise). **8** in preference to. **9 above all** most of all; especially. *~adv* **10** in or to a higher place: *the hills above* **11** in a previous place (in something written or printed). **12** higher in rank or position. *~n* **13 the above** something previously mentioned. *~adj* **14** appearing in a previous place (in something written or printed): *for a copy of the free brochure write to the above address.*

above board *adj* completely honest and open.

abracadabra *n* a word used in magic spells, which is supposed to possess magic powers.

abrasion *n* **1** a scraped area on the skin; graze. **2** *Geog* the erosion of rock by rock fragments scratching and scraping it.

abrasive *adj* **1** rude and unpleasant in manner. **2** tending to rub or scrape; rough. *~n* **3** a substance used for cleaning, smoothing, or polishing.

abreast *adj* **1** alongside each other and facing in the same direction: *the two cars were abreast.* **2 abreast of** up to date with.

abridge *vb* **abridging, abridged** to shorten a written work by taking out parts. **abridgment** *or* **abridgement** *n*

abroad *adv* **1** to or in a foreign country. **2** generally known or felt: *there is a new spirit abroad.*

abrogate *vb* **-gating, -gated** to cancel (a law or an agreement) formally. **abrogation** *n*

abrupt *adj* **1** sudden or unexpected: *an abrupt departure.* **2** rather rude in speech or manner. **abruptly** *adv* **abruptness** *n*

abscess (**ab**-sess) *n* **1** a swelling containing pus as a result of inflammation. *~vb* **2** to form a swelling containing pus. **abscessed** *adj*

abscissa *n, pl* **-scissas** *or* **-scissae** *Maths* (in a two-dimensional system of Cartesian coordinates) the distance from the vertical axis measured parallel to the horizontal axis.

abscond *vb* to run away unexpectedly.

abseil (**ab**-sale) *vb* **1** to go down a steep drop by a rope fastened at the top and tied around one's body. *~n* **2** an instance of abseiling.

THESAURUS

aboriginal ancient, earliest, first, indigenous, native, original, primary, primeval, primitive, primordial, pristine

abound be jammed with, be packed with, be plentiful, crowd, flourish, increase, infest, luxuriate, overflow, proliferate, superabound, swarm, swell, teem, thrive

about *prep.* **1.** as regards, concerned with, concerning, connected with, dealing with, on, re, referring to, regarding, relating to, relative to, respecting, touching, with respect to **2.** adjacent, beside, circa (*used with dates*), close to, near, nearby **3.** around, encircling, on all sides, round, surrounding *~adv.* **4.** almost, approaching, approximately, around, close to, more or less, nearing, nearly, roughly **5.** from place to place, here and there, hither and thither, to and fro *~adj.* **6.** active, around, astir, in motion, present, stirring

about to intending to, on the point of, on the verge *or* brink of, ready to

above *prep.* **1.** atop, beyond, exceeding, higher than, on top of, over, upon *~adv.* **2.** aloft, atop, in heaven, on high, overhead *~adj.* **3.** aforementioned, aforesaid, earlier, foregoing, preceding, previous, prior **4.** before, beyond, exceeding, prior to, superior to, surpassing

above board candid, fair and square, forthright, frank, guileless, honest, honourable, kosher (*informal*), legitimate, on the up and up, open, overt, square, straight, straightforward, true, trustworthy, truthful, upfront (*informal*), upright, veracious

abrasion chafe, graze, scrape, scratch, surface injury

abrasive *adj.* **1.** annoying, biting, caustic, cutting, galling, grating, hurtful, irritating, nasty, rough, sharp, unpleasant, vitriolic **2.** chafing, erosive, frictional, grating, rough, scraping, scratching, scratchy, scuffing

abreast **1.** alongside, beside, level, shoulder to shoulder, side by side **2.** **abreast of** acquainted, *au courant,* au fait, conversant, familiar, informed, in touch, knowledgeable, up to date

abridge abbreviate, abstract, compress, concentrate, condense, contract, cut, cut down, précis, shorten, summarize, trim

abridgment abbreviation, abstract, compendium, condensation, conspectus, contraction, curtailment, cutting, decrease, digest, diminishing, diminution, epitome, lessening, limitation, outline, précis, reduction, restraint, restriction, résumé, shortening, summary, synopsis

abroad **1.** beyond the sea, in foreign lands, out of the country, overseas **2.** about, at large, away, circulating, current, elsewhere, extensively, far, far and wide, forth, in circulation, out, out-of-doors, outside, publicly, widely, without

abrupt **1.** hasty, headlong, hurried, precipitate, quick, sudden, surprising, swift, unanticipated, unexpected, unforeseen **2.** blunt, brisk, brusque, curt, direct, discourteous, gruff, impatient, impolite, rough, rude, short, snappish, snappy, terse, unceremonious, uncivil, ungracious

abscond bolt, clear out, decamp, disappear, do a bunk (*Brit. slang*), escape, flee, flit (*informal*), fly, make off, run off, skedaddle (*informal*), slip away, sneak away, steal away, take it on the lam (*U.S. & Canad. slang*)

absence *n* **1** the state of being away. **2** the time during which a person or thing is away. **3** the fact of being without something.

absent *adj* **1** not present in a place or situation. **2** lacking. **3** not paying attention. *~vb* **4 absent oneself** to stay away. **absently** *adv*

absentee *n* a person who should be present but is not.

absenteeism *n* persistent absence from work or school.

absent-minded *adj* inattentive or forgetful. **absent-mindedly** *adv*

absinthe *n* a strong, green, alcoholic drink, originally containing wormwood.

absolute *adj* **1** total and complete: *he ordered an immediate and absolute ceasefire.* **2** with unrestricted power and authority: *she has absolute control with fifty per cent of the shares.* **3** undoubted or certain: *I was telling the absolute truth.* **4** not dependent on or relative to anything else. **5** pure; unmixed: *absolute alcohol.* *~n* **6** a principle or rule believed to be unfailingly correct. **7 the Absolute** *Philosophy* that which is totally unconditioned, perfect, or complete.

absolutely *adv* **1** completely or perfectly. *~interj* **2** yes indeed, certainly.

absolute majority *n* a number of votes totalling over 50 per cent, such as the total number of votes that beats the combined opposition.

absolute pitch *n* the ability to identify the pitch of a note, or to sing a given note, without reference to one previously sounded.

absolute zero *n Physics* the lowest temperature theoretically possible, at which the particles that make up matter would be at rest: equivalent to –273.15°C or –459.67°F.

absolution *n Christianity* a formal forgiveness of sin pronounced by a priest.

absolutism *n* a political system in which a monarch or dictator has unrestricted power.

absolve *vb* **-solving, -solved** to declare to be free from blame or sin.

absorb *vb* **1** to soak up a liquid. **2** to engage the interest of someone. **3** to receive the force of an impact. **4** *Physics* to take in radiant energy and retain it. **5** to take in or incorporate: *West Germany has absorbed almost one million refugees.* **absorbent** *adj* **absorbing** *adj*

absorption *n* **1** the process of absorbing something or the state of being absorbed. **2** *Physiol* the process by which nutrients enter the tissues of an animal or a plant. **absorptive** *adj*

abstain *vb* **1** to choose not to do something: *you will be asked to abstain from food prior to your general anaesthetic.* **2** to choose not to vote. **abstainer** *n*

abstemious (ab-**steem**-ee-uss) *adj* taking very little alcohol or food. **abstemiously** *adv* **abstemiousness** *n*

abstention *n* **1** the formal act of not voting. **2** the act of abstaining from something, such as drinking alcohol.

abstinence *n* the practice of choosing not to do something one would like. **abstinent** *adj*

abstract *adj* **1** referring to ideas or qualities rather than material objects: *an abstract noun.* **2** not applied or practical; theoretical: *he was frustrated by the highly abstract mathematics being taught.* **3** of art in which the subject is represented by shapes and patterns rather than by a realistic likeness. *~n* **4** a summary. **5** an abstract painting or sculpture. **6** an abstract word or idea. **7 in the abstract** without referring to specific

THESAURUS

absence **1.** absenteeism, nonappearance, nonattendance, truancy **2.** default, defect, deficiency, lack, need, nonexistence, omission, privation, unavailability, want

absent *adj.* **1.** away, elsewhere, gone, nonattendant, nonexistent, not present, out, truant, unavailable **2.** lacking, missing, wanting **3.** absent-minded, absorbed, abstracted, bemused, blank, daydreaming, distracted, dreamy, empty, faraway, heedless, inattentive, musing, oblivious, preoccupied, unaware, unconscious, unheeding, unthinking, vacant, vague *~vb.* **4. absent oneself** abscond, depart, keep away, play truant, remove, slope off (*informal*), stay away, truant, withdraw

absently absent-mindedly, abstractedly, bemusedly, blankly, distractedly, dreamily, emptily, heedlessly, inattentively, obliviously, on automatic pilot, unconsciously, unheedingly, vacantly, vaguely

absent-minded absent, absorbed, abstracted, bemused, distracted, dreaming, dreamy, engrossed, faraway, forgetful, heedless, inattentive, musing, oblivious, preoccupied, unaware, unconscious, unheeding, unthinking

absolute **1.** arrant, complete, consummate, deep-dyed (*usually derogatory*), downright, entire, out-and-out, outright, perfect, pure, sheer, thorough, total, unadulterated, unalloyed, unmitigated, unmixed, unqualified, utter **2.** full, supreme, unbounded, unconditional, unlimited, unqualified, unquestionable, unrestrained, unrestricted **3.** actual, categorical, certain, conclusive, decided, decisive, definite, exact, genuine, infallible, positive, precise, sure, unambiguous, unequivocal, unquestionable

absolutely completely, consummately, entirely, fully, perfectly, purely, thoroughly, totally, unmitigatedly, utterly, wholly

absolutism autarchy, authoritarianism, autocracy, despotism, dictatorship, totalitarianism, tyranny

absolve acquit, clear, exculpate, exonerate, vindicate

absorb **1.** captivate, engage, engross, fascinate, occupy, preoccupy, rivet **2.** assimilate, incorporate, receive, take in

absorbing arresting, captivating, engrossing, fascinating, gripping, interesting, intriguing, preoccupying, riveting, spellbinding

abstain avoid, cease, decline, deny (oneself), desist, forbear, forgo, give up, keep from, kick (*informal*), refrain, refuse, renounce, shun, stop, withhold

abstemious abstinent, ascetic, austere, moderate, self-denying, sober, sparing, temperate

abstention abstaining, abstinence, avoidance, desistance, eschewal, forbearance, nonindulgence, refraining, refusal, self-control, self-denial, self-restraint

abstinence abstemiousness, asceticism, avoidance, continence, forbearance, moderation, refraining, self-denial, self-restraint, sobriety, temperance

abstinent abstaining, abstemious, continent, forbearing, moderate, self-controlled, self-denying, self-restraining, sober, temperate

abstract *adj.* **1.** conceptual, hypothetical, intellectual, nonconcrete, notional, occult, philosophical, theoretic, theoretical, unpractical, unrealistic *~n.* **2.** abridgment, compendium, condensation, digest, epitome, essence, outline, précis, recapitulation, résumé, summary, synopsis *~vb.* **3.** abbreviate, abridge, condense, outline, précis, shorten, summarize **4.** detach, dissociate, extract, isolate, remove, separate, steal, take away, take out, withdraw

circumstances. ~*vb* **8** to summarize. **9** to remove or extract.

abstracted *adj* lost in thought; preoccupied. **abstractedly** *adv*

abstraction *n* **1** a general idea rather than a specific example: *these absurd philosophical abstractions continued to bother him.* **2** the quality of being abstract or abstracted.

abstruse *adj* not easy to understand.

absurd *adj* obviously senseless or illogical; ridiculous. **absurdity** *n* **absurdly** *adv*

abundance *n* **1** a great amount. **2** degree of plentifulness. **3 in abundance** in great amounts: *they had fish and fruit in abundance.* **abundant** *adj*

abundantly *adv* **1** very: *he made his disagreement with the prime minister abundantly clear.* **2** plentifully; in abundance.

abuse *n* **1** prolonged ill-treatment of or violence towards someone: *child abuse.* **2** insulting comments. **3** improper use: *an abuse of power.* ~*vb* **abusing, abused 4** to take advantage of dishonestly: *these two ministers had abused their position for financial gain.* **5** to ill-treat violently: *he had been sexually abused as a child.* **6** to speak insultingly or cruelly to. **abuser** *n*

abusive *adj* rude or insulting: *he was alleged to have used abusive language towards spectators.* **abusively** *adv*

abut *vb* **abutting, abutted** to be next to or touching.

abutment *n* a construction that supports the end of a bridge.

abysmal *adj Informal* extremely bad. **abysmally** *adv*

abyss *n* **1** a very deep hole in the ground. **2** a frightening or threatening situation: *the abyss of revolution and war ahead.*

Ac *Chem* actinium.

AC 1 alternating current. **2** athletic club.

a/c 1 account. **2** account current.

acacia (a-**kay**-sha) *n* a shrub or tree with small yellow or white flowers.

academic *adj* **1** relating to a college or university. **2** (of pupils) having an aptitude for study. **3** relating to studies such as languages and pure science rather than technical or professional studies. **4** of theoretical interest only: *the argument is academic.* ~*n* **5** a member of the teaching or research staff of a college or university. **academically** *adv*

academy *n, pl* **-mies 1** a society for the advancement of literature, art, or science. **2** a school for training in a particular skill: *sixteen hundred students would also spend their first year at the military academy.* **3** (in Scotland) a secondary school.

acanthus *n* **1** a plant with large spiny leaves and spikes of white or purplish flowers. **2** a carved ornament based on the leaves of the acanthus plant.

ACAS (in Britain) Advisory Conciliation and Arbitration Service.

acc. 1 *Grammar* accusative. **2** account.

accede *vb* **-ceding, -ceded accede to 1** to agree to. **2** to take up (an office or position): *he acceded to the throne after his Irish exile.*

accelerando *adv Music* with increasing speed.

accelerate *vb* **-ating, -ated 1** to move or cause to move more quickly. **2** to cause to happen sooner than expected.

acceleration *n* **1** the act of increasing speed. **2** the rate of increase of speed or the rate of change of velocity.

accelerator *n* **1** a pedal in a motor vehicle that is pressed to increase speed. **2** *Physics* a machine for increasing the speed and energy of charged particles.

accent *n* **1** the distinctive style of pronunciation of a person or group from a particular area, country, or social background. **2** a mark used in writing to indicate the prominence of a syllable or the way a vowel is pronounced. **3** particular emphasis: *there will be an*

THESAURUS

abstracted absent, absent-minded, bemused, daydreaming, dreamy, faraway, inattentive, preoccupied, remote, withdrawn

abstraction **1.** concept, formula, generality, generalization, hypothesis, idea, notion, theorem, theory, thought **2.** absent-mindedness, bemusedness, dreaminess, inattention, pensiveness, preoccupation, remoteness, woolgathering

abstruse arcane, complex, dark, deep, Delphic, enigmatic, esoteric, hidden, incomprehensible, mysterious, mystical, obscure, occult, perplexing, profound, puzzling, recondite, unfathomable, vague

absurd crazy (*informal*), daft (*informal*), farcical, foolish, idiotic, illogical, inane, incongruous, irrational, laughable, ludicrous, meaningless, nonsensical, preposterous, ridiculous, senseless, silly, stupid, unreasonable

absurdity craziness (*informal*), farce, farcicality, farcicalness, folly, foolishness, idiocy, illogicality, illogicalness, incongruity, irrationality, joke, ludicrousness, meaninglessness, nonsense, preposterousness, ridiculousness, senselessness, silliness, stupidity, unreasonableness

abundance ampleness, bounty, copiousness, exuberance, fullness, heap (*informal*), plenitude, plenteousness, plenty, profusion

abundant ample, bounteous, bountiful, copious, exuberant, filled, full, lavish, luxuriant, overflowing, plenteous, plentiful, profuse, rank, rich, teeming, well-provided, well-supplied

abuse *n.* **1.** harm, hurt, ill-treatment, maltreatment, oppression **2.** blame, calumniation, castigation, censure, character assassination, contumely, curses, cursing, defamation, derision, disparagement, insults, invective, libel, opprobrium, reproach, revilement, scolding, slander, swearing, tirade, traducement, upbraiding, vilification, vituperation **3.** exploitation, misapplication, misuse ~*vb.* **4.** exploit, misapply, misuse, take advantage of **5.** harm, hurt, ill-treat, maltreat, manhandle, oppress **6.** calumniate, castigate, curse, defame, disparage, insult, inveigh against, libel, malign, revile, scold, slander, smear, swear at, traduce, upbraid, vilify, vituperate

abusive calumniating, castigating, censorious, contumelious, defamatory, derisive, disparaging, insulting, invective, libellous, maligning, offensive, opprobrious, reproachful, reviling, rude, scathing, scolding, slanderous, traducing, upbraiding, vilifying, vituperative

abyss bottomless depth, chasm, crevasse, fissure, gorge, gulf, pit, void

academic *adj.* **1.** campus, college, collegiate, scholastic, school, university **2.** bookish, studious **3.** abstract, conjectural, hypothetical, impractical, notional, speculative, theoretical ~*n.* **4.** don, fellow, lecturer, master, professor, scholar, scholastic, tutor

accede **1.** accept, acquiesce, admit, agree, assent, comply, concede, concur, consent, endorse, grant, yield **2.** assume, attain, come to, enter upon, inherit, succeed, succeed to (*as heir*)

accelerate **1.** advance, forward, further, hasten, hurry, pick up speed, quicken, speed, speed up, spur, step up (*informal*), stimulate **2.** expedite, precipitate

acceleration expedition, hastening, hurrying, quickening, speeding up, spurring, stepping up (*informal*), stimulation

accent on sport and many will enjoy rowing. **4** the stress on a syllable or musical note. ~*vb* **5** to lay particular emphasis on.

accentuate *vb* **-ating, -ated** to stress or emphasize. **accentuation** *n*

accept *vb* **1** to take or receive something offered. **2** to agree to. **3** to consider something as true. **4** to tolerate or resign oneself to. **5** to take on the responsibilities of: *he asked if I would become his assistant and I accepted that position.* **6** to receive someone into a community or group. **7** to receive something as adequate or valid.

acceptable *adj* **1** able to be endured; tolerable: *in war killing is acceptable.* **2** good enough; adequate: *he found the article acceptable.* **acceptability** *n* **acceptably** *adv*

acceptance *n* **1** the act of accepting something. **2** favourable reception. **3** belief or agreement.

accepted *adj* commonly approved or recognized: *the accepted wisdom about old age.*

access *n* **1** a means of approaching or entering a place. **2** the condition of allowing entry, for example entry to a building by wheelchairs or prams. **3** the right or opportunity to use something or enter a place: *the bourgeoisie gained access to political power.* ~*vb* **4** to obtain information from a computer.

accessible *adj* **1** easy to approach, enter, or use. **2** easy to understand: *the most accessible opera by Wagner.* **accessibility** *n*

accession *n* the act of taking up an office or position: *the 40th anniversary of her accession to the throne.*

accessory *n, pl* **-ries 1** a supplementary part or object. **2** a small item, such as a bag or belt, worn or carried by someone to complete his or her outfit. **3** a person who is involved in a crime but who was not present when it took place.

access road *n* a road providing a way to a particular place or on to a motorway.

access time *n* the time required to retrieve a piece of stored information from a computer.

accident *n* **1** an unpleasant event that causes damage, injury, or death. **2** an unforeseen event or one without apparent cause: *they had met in town by accident.*

accidental *adj* **1** occurring by chance or unintentionally. ~*n* **2** *Music* a symbol denoting a sharp, flat, or natural that is not a part of the key signature. **accidentally** *adv*

accident-prone *adj* (of a person) often involved in accidents.

acclaim *vb* **1** to applaud or praise: *the highly acclaimed children's TV series.* **2** to acknowledge publicly: *he was immediately acclaimed the new prime minister.* ~*n* **3** an enthusiastic expression of approval.

acclamation *n* **1** an enthusiastic reception or display of approval. **2** *Canad* an instance of being elected without opposition. **3 by acclamation** by a majority without a ballot.

acclimatize *or* **-tise** *vb* **-tizing, -tized** *or* **-tising, -tised** to adapt to a new climate or environment. **acclimatization** *or* **-tisation** *n*

accolade *n* **1** an award, praise, or honour. **2** a touch on the shoulder with a sword conferring knighthood.

accommodate *vb* **-dating, -dated 1** to provide with lodgings. **2** to have room for. **3** to do a favour for. **4** to get used to (something).

THESAURUS

accent *n.* **1.** articulation, enunciation, inflection, intonation, modulation, pronunciation, timbre, tone **2.** beat, emphasis, force, stress ~*vb.* **3.** accentuate, emphasize, stress, underline, underscore

accentuate accent, draw attention to, emphasize, highlight, stress, underline, underscore

accept 1. acquire, gain, get, have, obtain, receive, secure, take **2.** accede, acquiesce, agree to, approve, concur with, consent to, cooperate with **3.** believe, buy (*slang*), swallow (*informal*) **4.** bear, bow to, brook, defer to, put up with, stand, submit to, suffer, take, yield to **5.** assume, bear, take on, undertake **6.** admit, adopt **7.** acknowledge, admit, recognize

acceptable adequate, all right, fair, moderate, passable, satisfactory, so-so (*informal*), standard

acceptance 1. accepting, acquiring, gaining, getting, having, obtaining, receipt, securing, taking **2.** approbation, approval, stamp *or* seal of approval **3.** acknowledgment, acquiescence, admission, affirmation, agreement, assent, assumption, avowal, belief, compliance, concession, concurrence, consensus, consent, cooperation, credence, O.K. *or* okay (*informal*), permission, recognition

accepted acknowledged, admitted, agreed, agreed upon, approved, authorized, common, confirmed, conventional, customary, established, normal, received, recognized, regular, sanctioned, standard, time-honoured, traditional, universal, usual

access 1. approach, avenue, course, door, entrée, entry, gateway, key, passage, passageway, path, road **2.** admission, admittance, entrance

accessibility approachability, attainability, availability, handiness, nearness, obtainability, possibility, readiness

accessible achievable, at hand, attainable, available, handy, near, nearby, obtainable, on hand, possible, reachable, ready

accessory *n.* **1.** accompaniment, addition, add-on, adjunct, adornment, appendage, attachment, component, decoration, extension, extra, frill, help, supplement, trim, trimming **2.** abettor, accomplice, assistant, associate (*in crime*), colleague, confederate, helper, partner

accident 1. blow, calamity, casualty, chance, collision, crash, disaster, misadventure, mischance, misfortune, mishap, pile-up (*informal*) **2.** chance, fate, fluke, fortuity, fortune, hazard, luck

accidental adventitious, casual, chance, contingent, fortuitous, haphazard, inadvertent, incidental, inessential, nonessential, random, uncalculated, uncertain, unessential, unexpected, unforeseen, unintended, unintentional, unlooked-for, unplanned, unpremeditated, unwitting

accidentally adventitiously, by accident, by chance, by mistake, casually, fortuitously, haphazardly, inadvertently, incidentally, randomly, unconsciously, undesignedly, unexpectedly, unintentionally, unwittingly

acclaim 1. *vb.* applaud, approve, celebrate, cheer, clap, commend, eulogize, exalt, extol, hail, honour, laud, praise, salute, welcome **2.** *n.* acclamation, applause, approbation, approval, celebration, cheering, clapping, commendation, eulogizing, exaltation, honour, laudation, plaudits, praise, welcome

acclamation acclaim, adulation, approbation, cheer, cheering, cheers, enthusiasm, laudation, loud homage, ovation, plaudit, praise, salutation, shouting, tribute

acclimatization adaptation, adjustment, habituation, inurement

acclimatize accommodate, accustom, adapt, adjust, become seasoned to, get used to, habituate, inure

accommodate 1. billet, board, entertain, harbour, house, lodge, put up, quarter, shelter **2.** aid, assist, help, oblige **3.** accustom, adapt, adjust, settle

➤ Note the double "c" and double "m". This word is very commonly misspelled.

accommodating *adj* willing to help; obliging.

accommodation *n* a place in which to sleep, live, or work.

accommodation address *n* an address on letters to a person who cannot or does not wish to receive mail at a permanent address.

accompaniment *n* **1** something that accompanies something else. **2** *Music* a supporting part for an instrument, a band, or an orchestra.

accompanist *n* a person who plays a musical accompaniment.

accompany *vb* **-nies, -nying, -nied 1** to go with (someone). **2** to happen or exist at the same time as. **3** to provide a musical accompaniment for.

accomplice *n* a person who helps someone else commit a crime.

accomplish *vb* **1** to manage to do; achieve: *most infants accomplish it immediately.* **2** to complete.

➤ The usual pronunciation of the syllable "com" in British English sounds like "kum", but the sound "kom" is increasingly used.

accomplished *adj* **1** expert or proficient: *an accomplished liar.* **2** successfully completed.

accomplishment *n* **1** the successful completion of something. **2** something successfully completed. **3 accomplishments** personal abilities or skills.

accord *n* **1** agreement or harmony. **2** a formal agreement between groups or nations: *the Paris peace accords.* **3 of one's own accord** voluntarily or willingly. **4 with one accord** unanimously. *~vb* **5** to grant: *she was at last accorded her true status.* **6 accord with** to fit in with or be consistent with.

➤ Do not confuse *of one's own accord* with *on one's own account* "for one's own benefit".

accordance *n* **in accordance with** conforming to or according to: *food is prepared in accordance with Jewish laws.*

according *adv* **1 according to a** as stated by: *according to her, they were once engaged.* **b** in conformity with: *work hours varied according to the tides.* **2 according as** depending on whether.

accordingly *adv* **1** in an appropriate manner. **2** consequently.

accordion *n* a box-shaped musical instrument played by moving the two sides apart and together, and pressing a keyboard or buttons to produce the notes. **accordionist** *n*

accost *vb* to approach, stop, and speak to.

account *n* **1** a report or description. **2** a person's money held in a bank. **3** a statement of financial transactions with the resulting balance. **4** part or behalf: *I am sorry that you suffered on my account.* **5 call someone to account** to demand an explanation from someone. **6 give a good** *or* **bad account of oneself** to perform well or fail to perform well. **7 of no account** of little importance or value. **8 on account of** because of. **9 take account of** *or* **take into account** to take into consideration; allow for. *~vb* **10** to consider as: *the evening was accounted a major step forward.*

accountable *adj* responsible to someone or for some action. **accountability** *n*

accountant *n* a person who maintains and audits business accounts. **accountancy** *n*

account for *vb* **1** to give reasons for. **2** to explain or count up what has been spent.

accounting *n* the skill or practice of maintaining and auditing business accounts.

accoutrements (ak-**koo**-tra-ments) *or US* **accouterments** (ak-**koo**-ter-ments) *pl n* clothing and equipment for a particular activity.

accredit *vb* **1** to give official recognition to. **2** to send (a diplomat) with official credentials to a particular country. **3** to certify as meeting required standards. **4**

THESAURUS

accommodating complaisant, considerate, co-operative, friendly, helpful, hospitable, kind, obliging, polite, unselfish, willing

accommodation board, digs (*Brit. informal*), harbouring, house, housing, lodging(s), quartering, quarters, shelter, sheltering

accompany 1. attend, chaperon, conduct, escort, go with, squire, usher **2.** coexist with, coincide with, come with, follow, go together with, join with, occur with, supplement

accomplice abettor, accessory, ally, assistant, associate, collaborator, colleague, confederate, helper, henchman, partner

accomplish 1. achieve, attain, bring about, bring off (*informal*), carry out, do, effect, effectuate, execute, fulfil, manage, perform, produce, realize **2.** complete, conclude, consummate, finish

accomplished 1. adept, consummate, cultivated, expert, gifted, masterly, polished, practised, proficient, skilful, skilled, talented **2.** achieved, attained, brought about, carried out, completed, concluded, consummated, done, effected, executed, finished, fulfilled, managed, performed, produced, realized

accomplishment 1. achievement, attainment, bringing about, carrying out, completion, conclusion, consummation, doing, effecting, execution, finishing, fulfilment, management, performance, production, realization **2.** achievement, act, attainment, coup, deed, exploit, feat, stroke, triumph **3.** ability, achievement, art, attainment, capability, craft, gift, proficiency, skill, talent

accord *n.* **1.** accordance, agreement, concert, concurrence, conformity, congruence, correspondence, harmony, rapport, sympathy, unanimity, unison *~vb.* **2.** allow, bestow, concede, confer, endow, give, grant, present, render, tender, vouchsafe **3.** agree, be in tune (*informal*), concur, conform, correspond, fit, harmonize, match, suit, tally

accordingly 1. appropriately, correspondingly, fitly, properly, suitably **2.** as a result, consequently, ergo, hence, in consequence, so, therefore, thus

according to 1. as maintained by, as stated by, on the authority of, on the report of **2.** after, after the manner of, consistent with, in accordance with, in compliance with, in conformity with, in harmony with, in keeping with, in line with, in obedience to, in step with, in the manner of, obedient to

account *n.* **1.** chronicle, description, detail, explanation, history, narration, narrative, recital, record, relation, report, statement, story, tale, version **2.** balance, bill, book, books, charge, computation, inventory, invoice, ledger, reckoning, register, score, statement, tally **3.** advantage, benefit, consequence, distinction, esteem, honour, import, importance, merit, note, profit, rank, repute, significance, standing, use, value, worth **4.** basis, cause, consideration, ground, grounds, interest, motive, reason, regard, sake, score *~vb.* **5.** appraise, assess, believe, calculate, compute, consider, count, deem, esteem, estimate, explain, gauge, hold, judge, rate, reckon, regard, think, value, weigh

accountability answerability, chargeability, culpability, liability, responsibility

to attribute (a quality or an action) to (a person). **5** *NZ* to pass (a candidate for university entrance) on school recommendation, without external examination. **accreditation** *n*

accretion (ak-**kree**-shun) *n* **1** a gradual increase in size, through growth or addition. **2** something added, such as an extra layer.

accrue *vb* **-cruing, -crued 1** (of money or interest) to increase gradually over a period of time. **2 accrue to** to fall naturally to: *some advantage must accrue to the weaker party.*

accumulate *vb* **-lating, -lated** to gather together in an increasing quantity; collect. **accumulative** *adj*

accumulation *n* **1** something that has been collected. **2** the collecting together of things.

accumulator *n* **1** a rechargeable device for storing electrical energy. **2** *Brit horse racing* a collective bet on successive races, with both stake and winnings being carried forward to accumulate progressively.

accuracy *n* faithful representation of the truth: *care is taken to ensure the accuracy of the content.*

accurate *adj* faithfully representing the truth: *all the information was accurate.* **accurately** *adv*

accursed (a-**curse**-id) *adj* **1** under a curse. **2** hateful or detestable.

accusation *n* **1** an allegation that a person is guilty of some wrongdoing. **2** a formal charge brought against a person. **accusatory** *adj*

accusative *n Grammar* a grammatical case in some languages that identifies the direct object of a verb.

accuse *vb* **-cusing, -cused** to charge a person with wrongdoing. **accuser** *n* **accusing** *adj* **accusingly** *adv*

accused *n* **the accused** *Law* the defendant appearing on a criminal charge.

accustom *vb* **accustom oneself to** to become familiar with or used to.

accustomed *adj* **1** usual or customary: *he parked his motorcycle in its accustomed place.* **2 accustomed to a** used to. **b** in the habit of.

ace *n* **1** a playing card with one symbol on it. **2** *Informal* an expert: *an American stock car ace.* **3** *Tennis* a winning serve that the opponent fails to reach. **4** a fighter pilot who has destroyed several enemy aircraft. ~*adj* **5** *Informal* superb or excellent: *an ace tennis player.*

acerbic (ass-**sir**-bik) *adj* harsh or bitter: *an acerbic critic.*

acerbity *n, pl* **-ties 1** bitter speech or temper. **2** bitterness of taste.

acetaldehyde (ass-it-**tal**-dee-hide) *n Chem* a colourless volatile liquid, used as a solvent.

acetate (**ass**-it-tate) *n* **1** *Chem* any salt or ester of acetic acid. **2** Also: **acetate rayon** a synthetic textile fibre made from cellulose acetate.

acetic (ass-**see**-tik) *adj Chem* of, containing, or producing acetic acid or vinegar.

acetic acid *n Chem* a strong-smelling colourless liquid used to make vinegar.

acetone (**ass**-it-tone) *n Chem* a strong-smelling colourless liquid used as a solvent for paints and lacquers.

acetylene (ass-**set**-ill-een) *n Chem* a colourless soluble flammable gas used in welding metals.

ache *vb* **aching, ached 1** to feel or be the source of a continuous dull pain. **2** to suffer mental anguish. ~*n* **3** a continuous dull pain.

achieve *vb* **achieving, achieved** to gain by hard work or effort. **achiever** *n*

➤ Note the "ie". This word is very commonly misspelled.

THESAURUS

accountable amenable, answerable, charged with, liable, obligated, obliged, responsible

account for answer for, clarify, clear up, elucidate, explain, illuminate, justify, rationalize

accredit 1. appoint, authorize, commission, depute, empower, entrust, sanction **2.** certify, endorse, guarantee, license, recognize, vouch for **3.** ascribe, assign, attribute, credit

accrue accumulate, amass, arise, be added, build up, collect, enlarge, ensue, flow, follow, grow, increase, issue, spring up

accumulate accrue, amass, build up, collect, cumulate, gather, grow, hoard, increase, pile up, stockpile, store

accumulation aggregation, augmentation, build-up, collection, conglomeration, gathering, growth, heap, hoard, increase, mass, pile, stack, stock, stockpile, store

accuracy authenticity, carefulness, closeness, correctness, exactitude, exactness, faithfulness, faultlessness, fidelity, meticulousness, niceness, nicety, precision, strictness, truth, truthfulness, veracity, verity

accurate authentic, careful, close, correct, exact, faithful, faultless, just, meticulous, nice, precise, proper, regular, right, scrupulous, spot-on (*Brit. informal*), strict, true, truthful, unerring, veracious

accurately authentically, carefully, closely, correctly, exactly, faithfully, faultlessly, justly, meticulously, nicely, precisely, properly, regularly, rightly, scrupulously, strictly, truly, truthfully, unerringly, veraciously

accursed 1. bedevilled, bewitched, condemned, cursed, damned, doomed, hopeless, ill-fated, ill-omened, jinxed, luckless, ruined, undone, unfortunate, unlucky, wretched **2.** abominable, despicable, detestable, execrable, hateful, hellish, horrible

accusation allegation, arraignment, attribution, charge, citation, complaint, denunciation, impeachment, imputation, incrimination, indictment, recrimination

accuse allege, arraign, attribute, blame, censure, charge, cite, denounce, impeach, impute, incriminate, indict, recriminate, tax

accustom acclimatize, acquaint, adapt, discipline, exercise, familiarize, habituate, inure, season, train

accustomed 1. common, conventional, customary, established, everyday, expected, fixed, general, habitual, normal, ordinary, regular, routine, set, traditional, usual, wonted **2.** acclimatized, acquainted, adapted, disciplined, exercised, familiar, familiarized, given to, habituated, in the habit of, inured, seasoned, trained, used

ace *n.* **1.** *Cards, dice, etc.* one, single point **2.** *informal* adept, buff (*informal*), champion, dab hand (*Brit. informal*), expert, genius, hotshot (*informal*), master, star, virtuoso, whizz (*informal*), winner, wizard (*informal*) ~*adj.* **3.** *informal* brilliant, champion, excellent, expert, fine, great, masterly, outstanding, superb, virtuoso

ache *vb.* **1.** hurt, pain, pound, smart, suffer, throb, twinge **2.** agonize, eat one's heart out, grieve, mourn, sorrow, suffer ~*n.* **3.** hurt, pain, pang, pounding, smart, smarting, soreness, suffering, throb, throbbing

achieve accomplish, acquire, attain, bring about, carry out, complete, consummate, do, earn, effect, execute, finish, fulfil, gain, get, obtain, perform, procure, reach, realize, win

achievement 1. accomplishment, acquirement, at-

achievement *n* **1** something that has been accomplished by hard work, ability, or heroism. **2** the successful completion of something.

Achilles heel (ak-**kill**-eez) *n* a small but fatal weakness.

Achilles tendon *n* the fibrous cord that connects the muscles of the calf to the heel bone.

achromatic *adj* **1** without colour. **2** refracting light without breaking it up into its component colours. **3** *Music* involving no sharps or flats. **achromatically** *adv*

acid *n* **1** *Chem* one of a class of compounds, corrosive and sour when dissolved in water, that combine with a base to form a salt. **2** *Slang* LSD. **3** a sour-tasting substance. *~adj* **4** *Chem* of, from, or containing acid. **5** sharp or sour in taste. **6** sharp in speech or manner. **acidly** *adv*

Acid House *or* **Acid** *n* a type of funk-based, electronically edited disco music of the late 1980s, which has hypnotic sound effects and which is associated with hippy culture and the use of the drug ecstasy.

acidic *adj* containing acid.

acidify *vb* **-fies, -fying, -fied** to convert into acid.

acidity *n* **1** the quality of being acid. **2** the amount of acid in a solution.

acid rain *n* rain containing pollutants released into the atmosphere by burning coal or oil.

acid test *n* a rigorous and conclusive test of worth or value.

acknowledge *vb* **-edging, -edged 1** to recognize or admit the truth of a statement. **2** to show recognition of a person by a greeting or glance. **3** to make known that a letter or message has been received. **4** to express gratitude for (a favour or compliment).

acknowledgment *or* **acknowledgement** *n* **1** the act of acknowledging something or someone. **2** something done or given as an expression of gratitude.

➤ The alternative spellings with or without an "e" between "g" and "m" are equally acceptable.

acme (**ak**-mee) *n* the highest point of achievement or excellence.

acne (**ak**-nee) *n* a skin disease in which pus-filled spots form on the face.

acolyte *n* **1** a follower or attendant. **2** *Christianity* a person who assists a priest.

aconite *n* **1** a poisonous plant with hoodlike flowers. **2** dried aconite root, used as a narcotic.

acorn *n* the fruit of the oak tree, consisting of a smooth nut in a cuplike base.

acoustic *adj* **1** of sound, hearing, or acoustics. **2** (of a musical instrument) without electronic amplification. **3** designed to absorb sound: *acoustic tiles.* **acoustically** *adv*

acoustics *n* **1** the scientific study of sound. *~pl n* **2** the characteristics of a room or auditorium determining how well sound can be heard within it.

acquaint *vb* **acquaint with** to make (someone) familiar with.

➤ The idiom is *acquaint* someone *with* something.

acquaintance *n* **1** a person whom one knows slightly. **2** slight knowledge of a person or subject. **3 make the acquaintance of** to come into social contact with. **4** the people one knows: *an actress of my acquaintance.*

acquainted *adj* **1** on terms of familiarity but not intimacy. **2 acquainted with** familiar with: *she became acquainted with the classics of Chinese literature.*

acquiesce (ak-wee-**ess**) *vb* **-escing, -esced** to agree to what someone wants. **acquiescence** *n* **acquiescent** *adj*

➤ The idiom is *acquiesce in* something.

acquire *vb* **-quiring, -quired** to get or develop (something such as an object, trait, or ability). **acquirement** *n*

acquired taste *n* **1** a liking for something at first considered unpleasant. **2** the thing liked.

acquisition *n* **1** something acquired, often to add to a collection. **2** the act of acquiring something.

acquisitive *adj* eager to gain material possessions. **acquisitively** *adv* **acquisitiveness** *n*

acquit *vb* **-quitting, -quitted 1** to pronounce someone not guilty: *he's been acquitted of negligence.* **2** to behave in a particular way: *she acquitted herself well in the meeting.* **acquittal** *n*

acre *n* **1** a unit of area equal to 4840 square yards

THESAURUS

tainment, deed, effort, exploit, feat, stroke **2.** accomplishment, completion, execution, fulfilment, performance, production, realization

acid 1. acerbic, biting, pungent, sharp, sour, tart, vinegarish, vinegary **2.** acerbic, acrid, biting, bitter, caustic, cutting, harsh, hurtful, mordant, pungent, sharp, stinging, trenchant, vitriolic

acidity 1. acerbity, acridity, acridness, bitterness, pungency, sharpness, sourness, tartness, vinegariness, vinegarishness **2.** acerbity, acridity, acridness, bitterness, causticity, causticness, harshness, hurtfulness, mordancy, pungency, sharpness, trenchancy

acknowledge 1. accede, accept, acquiesce, admit, allow, concede, confess, declare, grant, own, profess, recognize, yield **2.** address, greet, hail, notice, recognize, salute **3.** answer, reply to, respond to, return

acknowledgment 1. acceptance, accession, acquiescence, admission, allowing, confession, declaration, profession, realization, yielding **2.** addressing, greeting, hail, hailing, notice, recognition, salutation, salute **3.** answer, appreciation, Brownie points, credit, gratitude, reaction, recognition, reply, response, return, thanks

acme apex, climax, crest, crown, culmination, height, high point, optimum, peak, pinnacle, summit, top, vertex, zenith

acquaint advise, announce, apprise, disclose, divulge, enlighten, familiarize, inform, let (someone) know, notify, reveal, tell

acquaintance 1. associate, colleague, contact **2.** awareness, cognizance, experience, familiarity, knowledge, understanding **3.** association, social contact

acquainted alive to, apprised of, *au fait,* aware of, cognizant of, conscious of, conversant with, experienced in, familiar with, informed of, in on, knowledgeable about, privy to, versed in

acquiesce accede, accept, agree, allow, approve, assent, bow to, comply, concur, conform, consent, give in, go along with, submit, yield

acquiescence acceptance, accession, agreement, approval, assent, compliance, concurrence, conformity, consent, giving in, obedience, submission, yielding

acquire achieve, amass, attain, buy, collect, earn, gain, gather, get, obtain, pick up, procure, realize, receive, secure, win

acquisition 1. buy, gain, possession, prize, property, purchase **2.** achievement, acquirement, attainment, gaining, learning, obtainment, procurement, pursuit

acquisitive avaricious, covetous, grabbing, grasping, greedy, predatory, rapacious

acquisitiveness avarice, covetousness, greed, rapacity

(4046.86 square metres). **2 acres** *Informal* a large amount: *acres of skin.*

acreage (**ake**-er-rij) *n* land area in acres.

acrid (**ak**-rid) *adj* **1** unpleasantly strong-smelling. **2** sharp in speech or manner. **acridity** *n* **acridly** *adv*

acrimony *n* bitterness and resentment felt about something. **acrimonious** *adj*

acrobat *n* an entertainer who performs gymnastic feats requiring skill, agility, and balance. **acrobatic** *adj* **acrobatically** *adv*

acrobatics *pl n* the skills or feats of an acrobat.

acronym *n* a word made from the initial letters of other words, for example *UNESCO* for the *United Nations Educational, Scientific, and Cultural Organization.*

acrophobia *n* abnormal fear of being at a great height.

acropolis (a-**crop**-pol-liss) *n* the citadel of an ancient Greek city.

across *prep* **1** from one side to the other side of. **2** on or at the other side of. *~adv* **3** from one side to the other. **4** on or to the other side.

across-the-board *adj* affecting everyone in a particular group or place equally: *across-the-board tax cuts.*

acrostic *n* a number of lines of writing, such as a poem, in which the first or last letters form a word or proverb.

acrylic *adj* **1** made of acrylic. *~n* **2** a man-made fibre used for clothes and blankets. **3** a kind of paint made from acrylic acid.

acrylic acid *n Chem* a strong-smelling colourless corrosive liquid.

acrylic fibre *n* a man-made fibre used for clothes and blankets.

acrylic resin *n Chem* any of a group of polymers of acrylic acid, used as synthetic rubbers, in paints, and as plastics.

act *n* **1** something done. **2** a formal decision reached or law passed by a law-making body: *an act of parliament.* **3** a major division of a play or opera. **4** a short performance, such as a sketch or dance. **5** a pretended attitude: *she appeared calm but it was just an act.* **6 get in on the act** *Informal* to become involved in something in order to share the benefit. **7 get one's act together** *Informal* to organize oneself. *~vb* **8** to do something. **9** to perform (a part or role) in a play, film, or broadcast. **10** to present (a play) on stage. **11 act for** to be a substitute for: *Mr Lewis was acting for the head of the department.* **12 act as** to serve the function of: *she is acting as my bodyguard.* **13** to behave: *she acts as though she really hates you.* **14** to behave in an unnatural way. ~See also **act up.**

acting *n* **1** the art of an actor. *~adj* **2** temporarily performing the duties of: *the acting president has declared a state of emergency.*

actinide series *n Chem* a series of 15 radioactive elements with increasing atomic numbers from actinium to lawrencium.

actinium *n Chem* a radioactive element of the actinide series, occurring as a decay product of uranium. Symbol: Ac

action *n* **1** doing something for a particular purpose. **2** something done on a particular occasion. **3** a lawsuit. **4** movement during some physical activity. **5** the operating mechanism in a gun or machine. **6** the way in which something operates or works. **7** *Slang* the main activity in a place. **8** the events that form the plot of a story or play. **9** activity, force, or energy. **10** a minor battle. **11 actions** behaviour. **12 out of action** not functioning.

actionable *adj Law* giving grounds for legal action.

action painting *n* an art form in which paint is thrown, smeared, dripped, or spattered on the canvas.

action replay *n* the rerunning of a small section of a television tape, for example of a sporting event.

action stations *pl n* the positions taken up by individuals in preparation for battle or for some other activity.

activate *vb* **-vating, -vated 1** to make something active. **2** *Physics* to make something radioactive. **3** *Chem* to increase the rate of a reaction. **activation** *n*

active *adj* **1** busy and energetic. **2** energetically involved in or working hard for: *active in the peace movement.* **3** happening now and energetically: *the plan is under active discussion.* **4** functioning or causing a reaction: *the active ingredient is held within the capsule.* **5** (of a volcano) erupting periodically. **6** *Grammar* denoting a form of a verb used to indicate

THESAURUS

acquit 1. absolve, clear, exculpate, exonerate, vindicate **2.** bear, behave, comport, conduct, perform

acquittal absolution, clearance, exculpation, exoneration, vindication

acrid acrimonious, biting, bitter, caustic, cutting, harsh, mordant, nasty, sarcastic, sharp, trenchant, vitriolic

acrimonious bitter, rancorous, vitriolic

acrimony bitterness, ill will, rancour, virulence

act *n.* **1.** accomplishment, achievement, action, blow, deed, doing, execution, exertion, exploit, feat, move, operation, performance, step, stroke, undertaking **2.** bill, decree, edict, enactment, law, measure, ordinance, resolution, statute **3.** performance, routine, show, sketch, turn **4.** affectation, attitude, counterfeit, dissimulation, fake, feigning, front, performance, pose, posture, pretence, sham, show, stance *~vb.* **5.** carry out, do, enact, execute, function, go about, make, move, operate, perform, react, serve, strike, take effect, undertake, work **6.** act out, characterize, enact, impersonate, mime, mimic, perform, personate, personify, play, play *or* take the part of, portray, represent **7. act for** cover for, deputize for, fill in for, function in place of, replace, represent, serve, stand in for, substitute for, take the place of **8.** acquit, behave, comport, conduct **9.** affect, assume, counterfeit, dissimulate, feign, imitate, perform, pose, posture, pretend, put on, seem, sham

acting 1. *n.* characterization, dramatics, enactment, impersonation, performance, performing, playing, portrayal, portraying, stagecraft, theatre **2.** *adj.* interim, *pro tem,* provisional, substitute, surrogate, temporary

action 1. exercise, exertion, operation, undertaking **2.** accomplishment, achievement, act, blow, deed, exploit, feat, move, performance, step, stroke **3.** case, cause, lawsuit, litigation, proceeding, prosecution, suit **4.** activity, motion, movement **5.** functioning, operation, work, working **6.** activity, effort, energy, exertion, force, liveliness, power, spirit, vigour, vim, vitality **7.** affray, battle, clash, combat, contest, encounter, engagement, fight, fray, skirmish, sortie

actions bearing, behaviour, comportment, conduct, demeanour, deportment, manners, ways

activate actuate, animate, arouse, energize, galvanize, get going, impel, initiate, kick-start, mobilize, motivate, move, prod, prompt, propel, rouse, set going, set in motion, set off, start, stimulate, stir, switch on, trigger (off), turn on

active 1. alert, animated, bustling, busy, diligent, energetic, engaged, full, hard-working, industrious, lively, nimble, occupied, on the go (*informal*), on the

that the subject is performing the action, for example *kicked* in *The boy kicked the football*. *~n* **7** *Grammar* the active form of a verb. **actively** *adv*

active list *n Mil* a list of officers available for full duty.

active service *n* military duty in an operational area.

activist *n* a person who works energetically to achieve political or social goals. **activism** *n*

activity *n* **1** the state of being active. **2** lively movement. **3** (*pl* **-ties**) any specific action or pursuit: *he was engaged in political activities abroad.*

act of God *n Law* a sudden occurrence caused by natural forces, such as a flood.

actor *or fem* **actress** *n* a person who acts in a play, film, or broadcast.

actual *adj* existing in reality or as a matter of fact.
➤ Avoid using *actual* or *actually* when it adds nothing to the sense of the sentence. Compare: *It's an actual fact: It's a fact.*

actuality *n, pl* **-ties** reality.

actually *adv* as an actual fact; really.

actuary *n, pl* **-aries** a person qualified to calculate commercial risks and probabilities involving uncertain future events, esp. in such contexts as life assurance. **actuarial** *adj*

actuate *vb* **-ating, -ated 1** to start up a mechanical device. **2** to motivate someone.

act up *vb Informal* to behave in a troublesome way.

acuity (ak-**kew**-it-ee) *n* keenness of vision or thought.

acumen (**ak**-yew-men) *n* the ability to make good decisions.

acupuncture *n* a medical treatment involving the insertion of needles at various parts of the body to stimulate the nerve impulses. **acupuncturist** *n*

acute *adj* **1** severe or intense: *acute staff shortages.* **2** penetrating in perception or insight. **3** sensitive or keen: *it was amazing how acute your hearing got in the bush.* **4** (of a disease) sudden and severe. **5** *Maths* (of an angle) of less than 90°. *~n* **6** an acute accent. **acutely** *adv* **acuteness** *n*

acute accent *n* the mark (´), used in some languages to indicate that the vowel over which it is placed is pronounced in a certain way.

ad *n Informal* an advertisement.

A.D. *or* **AD** (indicating years numbered from the supposed year of the birth of Christ) in the year of the Lord.

ad- *prefix* **1** to or towards: *adverb.* **2** near or next to: *adrenal.*

Ada *n* a high-level computer programming language, used esp. for military systems.

adage (**ad**-ij) *n* a traditional saying that is generally accepted as being true.

adagietto *Music ~adv* **1** slowly, but more quickly than adagio. *~n, pl* **-tos 2** a movement or piece to be performed fairly slowly.

adagio (ad-**dahj**-yo) *Music ~adv* **1** slowly. *~n, pl* **-gios 2** a movement or piece to be performed slowly.

Adam *n* **not know someone from Adam** to not know someone at all.

adamant *adj* unshakable in determination or purpose. **adamantly** *adv*

Adam's apple *n* the projecting lump of thyroid cartilage at the front of a person's neck.

adapt *vb* **1** to adjust (something or oneself) to different conditions. **2** to change something to suit a new purpose. **adaptable** *adj* **adaptability** *n*

adaptation *n* **1** something that is produced by adapting something else: *a TV adaptation of a Victorian novel.* **2** the act of adapting.

adaptor *or* **adapter** *n* **1** a device used to connect

THESAURUS

move, quick, spirited, sprightly, spry, vibrant, vigorous, vital, vivacious **2.** committed, devoted, engaged, enthusiastic, hard-working, industrious, involved, militant, zealous **3.** astir, at work, effectual, functioning, in action, in force, in operation, live, moving, operative, running, stirring, working

activity 1. action, activeness, enterprise, exercise, exertion, labour, motion, movement, work **2.** animation, bustle, hurly-burly, hustle, life, liveliness, stir **3.** act, avocation, deed, endeavour, enterprise, hobby, interest, job, labour, occupation, pastime, project, pursuit, scheme, task, undertaking, venture, work

actor actress, dramatic artist, leading man, performer, play-actor, player, Thespian, tragedian, trouper

actress actor, dramatic artist, leading lady, performer, play-actor, player, starlet, Thespian, tragedienne, trouper

actual absolute, authentic, categorical, certain, concrete, confirmed, corporeal, definite, existent, factual, genuine, indisputable, indubitable, living, physical, positive, real, realistic, substantial, tangible, true, truthful, undeniable, unquestionable, verified

actually absolutely, as a matter of fact, de facto, essentially, indeed, in fact, in reality, in truth, literally, really, truly, veritably

actuate animate, arouse, cause, dispose, drive, excite, get going, impel, incite, induce, influence, inspire, instigate, motivate, move, prompt, quicken, rouse, set off, spur, stimulate, stir, urge

act up be naughty, carry on, cause trouble, give bother, give trouble, horse around (*informal*), malfunction, mess about, misbehave, play up (*Brit. informal*)

acumen acuteness, astuteness, cleverness, discernment, ingenuity, insight, intelligence, judgment, keenness, penetration, perception, perspicacity, sagacity, sharpness, shrewdness, smartness, wisdom, wit

acute 1. critical, crucial, dangerous, decisive, essential, fierce, grave, important, intense, overpowering, overwhelming, serious, severe, urgent, vital **2.** astute, canny, clever, discerning, discriminating, incisive, ingenious, insightful, intuitive, keen, observant, penetrating, perceptive, perspicacious, piercing, sensitive, sharp, smart, subtle

acuteness 1. criticality, criticalness, danger, dangerousness, decisiveness, fierceness, gravity, importance, intenseness, intensity, seriousness, severity, urgency **2.** acuity, astuteness, canniness, cleverness, discernment, discrimination, ingenuity, insight, intuition, intuitiveness, keenness, perception, perceptiveness, perspicacity, sensitivity, sharpness, smartness, subtleness, subtlety, wit

adamant determined, firm, fixed, immovable, inexorable, inflexible, insistent, intransigent, obdurate, relentless, resolute, rigid, set, stiff, stubborn, unbending, uncompromising, unrelenting, unshakable, unyielding

adapt acclimatize, accommodate, adjust, alter, apply, change, comply, conform, convert, familiarize, fashion, fit, habituate, harmonize, make, match, modify, prepare, qualify, remodel, shape, suit, tailor

adaptability changeability, flexibility, malleability, plasticity, pliability, pliancy, resilience, variability, versatility

adaptable adjustable, alterable, changeable, compliant, conformable, convertible, flexible, malleable, modifiable, plastic, pliant, resilient, variable, versatile

adaptation 1. adjustment, alteration, change, conversion, modification, refitting, remodelling, rework-

several electrical appliances to a single socket. **2** any device for connecting two parts of different sizes or types.

ADC aide-de-camp.

add *vb* **1** to combine (numbers or quantities) so as to make a larger number or quantity. **2** to join something to something else so as to increase its size, effect, or scope: *these new rules will add an extra burden on already overworked officials.* **3** to say or write something further. **4 add in** to include. ~See also **add up.**

addendum *n, pl* **-da** something added on, esp. an appendix to a book or magazine.

adder *n* a small poisonous snake with a black zigzag pattern along the back.

addict *n* **1** a person who is unable to stop taking narcotic drugs. **2** *Informal* a person who is devoted to something: *he's a telly addict.* **addictive** *adj*

addicted *adj* **1** dependent on a narcotic drug. **2** *Informal* devoted to something: *I'm a news freak and addicted to BBC Breakfast News.* **addiction** *n*

addition *n* **1** the act of adding. **2** a person or thing that is added. **3** a mathematical operation in which the total of two or more numbers or quantities is calculated. **4 in addition (to)** besides; as well (as). **additional** *adj* **additionally** *adv*

additive *n* any substance added to something, such as food, to improve it or prevent deterioration.

addled *adj* **1** confused or unable to think clearly. **2** (of eggs) rotten.

address *n* **1** the place at which someone lives. **2** the conventional form by which the location of a building is described. **3** a formal speech. **4** *Computers* a number giving the location of a piece of stored information. ~*vb* **5** to mark (a letter or parcel) with an address. **6** to speak to. **7** to direct one's attention to (a problem or an issue). **8 address oneself to a** to speak or write to. **b** to apply oneself to: *we have got to address ourselves properly to this problem.*

addressee *n* a person to whom a letter or parcel is addressed.

adduce *vb* **-ducing, -duced** to mention something as evidence.

add up *vb* **1** to calculate the total of (two or more numbers or quantities). **2** *Informal* to make sense: *there's something about it that doesn't add up.* **3 add up to** to amount to.

adenoidal *adj* having a nasal voice or impaired breathing because of enlarged adenoids.

adenoids (**ad**-in-oidz) *pl n* a mass of tissue at the back of the throat.

adept *adj* **1** proficient in something requiring skill. ~*n* **2** a person skilled in something. **adeptness** *n*

adequate *adj* just enough in amount or just good enough in quality. **adequacy** *n* **adequately** *adv*

à deux (ah **duh**) *adj, adv* of or for two people.

adhere *vb* **-hering, -hered 1** to stick to. **2** to act according to (a rule or agreement). **3** to be a loyal supporter of (something).

adherent *n* **1** a supporter or follower. ~*adj* **2** sticking or attached. **adherence** *n*

adhesion *n* **1** the quality or condition of sticking together. **2** *Pathol* the joining together of two structures or parts of the body that are normally separate, for example after surgery.

adhesive *n* **1** a substance used for sticking things together. ~*adj* **2** able or designed to stick to things.

ad hoc *adj, adv* for a particular purpose only.

adieu (**a-dew**) *interj, n, pl* **adieux** *or* **adieus** (**a-dewz**) goodbye.

THESAURUS

ing, shift, transformation, variation, version **2.** acclimatization, accustomedness, familiarization, habituation, naturalization

add 1. add up, compute, count up, reckon, sum up, total, tot up **2.** adjoin, affix, amplify, annex, append, attach, augment, enlarge by, include, increase by, supplement

addendum addition, adjunct, affix, appendage, appendix, attachment, augmentation, codicil, extension, extra, postscript, supplement

addict 1. junkie (*informal*), user (*informal*) **2.** adherent, buff (*informal*), devotee, enthusiast, fan, fiend (*informal*), follower, freak (*informal*), nut (*slang*)

addicted absorbed, accustomed, dedicated, dependent, devoted, disposed, fond, habituated, hooked (*slang*), inclined, obsessed, prone

addiction craving, dependence, enslavement, habit, obsession

addition 1. adding, adjoining, affixing, amplification, annexation, attachment, augmentation, enlargement, extension, inclusion, increasing **2.** addendum, additive, adjunct, affix, appendage, appendix, extension, extra, gain, increase, increment, supplement **3.** adding up, computation, counting up, reckoning, summation, summing up, totalling, totting up **4. in addition (to)** additionally, also, as well (as), besides, into the bargain, moreover, over and above, to boot, too, withal

additional added, add-on, affixed, appended, extra, fresh, further, increased, more, new, other, over-and-above, spare, supplementary

address *n.* **1.** abode, domicile, dwelling, home, house, location, lodging, pad (*slang*), place, residence, situation, whereabouts **2.** discourse, disquisition, dissertation, harangue, lecture, oration, sermon, speech, talk ~*vb.* **3.** accost, apostrophize, approach, greet, hail, invoke, salute, speak to, talk to **4. address (oneself) to** apply (oneself) to, attend to, concentrate on, devote (oneself) to, engage in, focus on, knuckle down to, look to, take care of, take up, turn to, undertake

adduce advance, allege, cite, designate, mention, name, offer, present, quote

add up 1. add, compute, count, count up, reckon, sum up, total, tot up **2.** be plausible, be reasonable, hold water, make sense, ring true, stand to reason **3.** amount, come to

adept 1. *adj.* able, accomplished, adroit, dexterous, expert, masterful, masterly, practised, proficient, skilful, skilled, versed **2.** *n.* buff (*informal*), dab hand (*Brit. informal*), expert, genius, hotshot (*informal*), master, whizz (*informal*)

adequacy capability, competence, fairness, sufficiency, suitability, tolerability

adequate capable, commensurate, competent, enough, fair, passable, requisite, satisfactory, sufficient, suitable, tolerable

adhere 1. attach, cement, cleave, cling, cohere, fasten, fix, glue, glue on, hold fast, paste, stick, stick fast, unite **2.** abide by, follow, fulfil, heed, keep, keep to, maintain, mind, obey, observe, respect, stand by **3.** be attached, be constant, be devoted, be faithful, be loyal, be true, cleave to, cling, support

adherent 1. *n.* admirer, advocate, devotee, disciple, fan, follower, hanger-on, henchman, partisan, protagonist, supporter, upholder, votary **2.** *adj.* adhering, adhesive, clinging, gluey, glutinous, gummy, holding, mucilaginous, sticking, sticky, tacky, tenacious

adhesive 1. *n.* cement, glue, gum, mucilage, paste **2.** *adj.* adhering, attaching, clinging, cohesive, gluey, glutinous, gummy, holding, mucilaginous, sticking, sticky, tacky, tenacious

ad infinitum *adv* endlessly: *we would not be able to sustain the currency ad infinitum.*
adipose *adj* of or containing fat; fatty: *adipose tissue.*
adj. adjective.
adjacent *adj* **1** near or next: *the schools were adjacent but there were separate doors.* **2** *Geom* (of a side of a right-angled triangle) lying between a specified angle and the right angle.
adjective *n* a word that adds information about a noun or pronoun. **adjectival** *adj*
adjoin *vb* to be next to and joined onto. **adjoining** *adj*
adjourn *vb* **1** to close a court at the end of a session. **2** to postpone or be postponed temporarily. **3** *Informal* to go elsewhere: *can we adjourn to the dining room?* **adjournment** *n*
adjudge *vb* **-judging, -judged** to declare someone to be something specified: *my wife was adjudged to be the guilty party.*
adjudicate *vb* **-cating, -cated 1** to give a formal decision on a dispute. **2** to serve as a judge, for example in a competition. **adjudication** *n* **adjudicator** *n*
adjunct *n* **1** something added that is not essential. **2** a person who is subordinate to another.
adjure *vb* **-juring, -jured 1** to command someone to do something. **2** to appeal earnestly to someone. **adjuration** *n*
adjust *vb* **1** to adapt to a new environment. **2** to alter slightly, so as to be accurate or suitable. **3** *Insurance* to determine the amount payable in settlement of a claim. **adjustable** *adj* **adjuster** *n*
adjustment *n* **1** a slight alteration. **2** the act of adjusting.
adjutant (**aj**-oo-tant) *n* an officer in an army who acts as administrative assistant to a superior.
ad-lib *vb* **-libbing, -libbed 1** to improvise a speech or piece of music without preparation. *~adj* **2** improvised: *ad-lib studio chat.* *~n* **3** an improvised remark. *~adv* **ad lib 4** spontaneously or freely.
Adm. Admiral.
adman *n, pl* **-men** *Informal* a man who works in advertising.
admin *n Informal* administration.
administer *vb* **1** to manage (an organization or estate). **2** to organize and put into practice: *anyone can learn to administer the test procedure.* **3** to give medicine to someone. **4** to supervise the taking of (an oath).
administrate *vb* **-trating, -trated** to manage an organization.
administration *n* **1** management of the affairs of an organization. **2** the people who administer an organization. **3** a government: *the Clinton administration.* **4** the act of administering something, such as medicine or an oath. **administrative** *adj*
administrator *n* a person who administers an organization or estate.
admirable (**ad**-mer-a-bl) *adj* deserving or inspiring admiration: *the boldness of the undertaking is admirable.* **admirably** *adv*
admiral *n* **1** Also called: **admiral of the fleet** a naval officer of the highest rank. **2** any of various brightly coloured butterflies.
Admiralty *n* the government department in charge of the Royal Navy.
admire *vb* **-miring, -mired** to respect and approve of (a person or thing). **admiration** *n* **admirer** *n* **admiring** *adj* **admiringly** *adv*
admissible *adj Law* allowed to be brought as evidence in court.

THESAURUS

adieu farewell, goodbye, leave-taking, parting, valediction
adjacent abutting, adjoining, alongside, beside, bordering, close, contiguous, near, neighbouring, next door, proximate, touching
adjoin abut, add, affix, annex, append, approximate, attach, border, combine, communicate with, connect, couple, impinge, interconnect, join, link, neighbour, touch, unite, verge
adjoining adjacent, contiguous, near, neighbouring, next door
adjourn defer, delay, discontinue, interrupt, postpone, prorogue, put off, suspend, take a rain check on (*informal*)
adjournment deferment, deferral, delay, interruption, postponement, prorogation, recess, stay, suspension
adjudge adjudicate, assign, award, decide, declare, decree, determine, judge, order, pronounce
adjudicate 1. adjudge, arbitrate, decide, determine, judge, mediate, settle **2.** referee, umpire
adjudication adjudgment, arbitration, conclusion, decision, determination, finding, judgment, pronouncement, ruling, settlement, verdict
adjust 1. acclimatize, accommodate, accustom, adapt, fit, harmonize, make conform, reconcile, settle **2.** adapt, alter, arrange, compose, convert, fix, modify, order, rectify, redress, regulate, remodel, set, tune (up)
adjustable adaptable, flexible, malleable, movable, tractable
adjustment 1. adaptation, alteration, arrangement, modification, ordering, rectification, redress, regulation **2.** acclimatization, orientation, reconciliation, settlement
ad-lib 1. *vb.* extemporize, improvise, make up, speak extemporaneously, speak impromptu, speak off the cuff, vamp, wing it (*informal*) **2.** *adj.* extemporaneous, extempore, impromptu, improvised, made up, off-the-cuff (*informal*), unprepared, unrehearsed **3.** *adv.* extemporaneously, extempore, impromptu, off the cuff, off the top of one's head (*informal*), without preparation, without rehearsal
administer 1. conduct, control, direct, govern, handle, manage, oversee, run, superintend, supervise **2.** apply, contribute, dispense, distribute, execute, give, impose, mete out, perform, provide
administration 1. application, conduct, control, direction, dispensation, distribution, execution, government, management, overseeing, performance, provision, running, superintendence, supervision **2.** executive, governing body, government, management, ministry, term of office
administrative directorial, executive, governmental, gubernatorial (*chiefly U.S.*), management, managerial, organizational, regulatory, supervisory
admirable choice, commendable, estimable, excellent, exquisite, fine, laudable, meritorious, praiseworthy, rare, sterling, superior, valuable, wonderful, worthy
admiration adoration, affection, amazement, appreciation, approbation, approval, astonishment, delight, esteem, pleasure, praise, regard, respect, surprise, veneration, wonder, wonderment
admire adore, appreciate, approve, esteem, idolize, look up to, praise, prize, respect, think highly of, value, venerate, worship

admission *n* **1** permission or the right to enter. **2** permission to join an organization. **3** the price charged for entrance. **4** a confession: *she was, by her own admission, not educated.*

admit *vb* **-mitting, -mitted 1** to confess or acknowledge (a crime or mistake). **2** to concede (the truth of something). **3** to allow (someone) to enter. **4** to take (someone) in to a hospital for treatment: *he was admitted for tests.* **5 admit to** to allow someone to participate in something. **6 admit of** to allow for: *these rules admit of no violation.*

admittance *n* **1** the right to enter. **2** the act of entering a place.

admittedly *adv* it must be agreed: *my research is admittedly incomplete.*

admixture *n* **1** a mixture. **2** an ingredient.

admonish *vb* to reprimand sternly. **admonition** *n* **admonitory** *adj*

ad nauseam (ad **naw**-zee-am) *adv* to a boring or sickening extent: *she went on and on ad nauseam about her divorce.*

ado *n* fuss: *without further ado.*

adobe (ad-**oh**-bee) *n* **1** a sun-dried brick. **2** the claylike material from which such bricks are made. **3** a building made of such bricks.

adolescence *n* the period between puberty and adulthood.

adolescent *adj* **1** of or relating to adolescence. **2** *Informal* (of behaviour) immature. *~n* **3** an adolescent person.

Adonis *n* a handsome young man.

adopt *vb* **1** *Law* to take someone else's child as one's own. **2** to choose (a plan or method). **3** to choose (a country or name) to be one's own. **adoption** *n*

adoptive *adj* **1** acquired or related by adoption: *an adoptive father.* **2** of or relating to adoption.

adorable *adj* very attractive; lovable.

adore *vb* **adoring, adored 1** to love intensely or deeply. **2** *Informal* to like very much: *I adore being in the country.* **3** to worship a god with religious rites. **adoration** *n* **adoring** *adj* **adoringly** *adv*

adorn *vb* to decorate; increase the beauty of. **adornment** *n*

ADP automatic data processing.

adrenal (ad-**reen**-al) *adj Anat* **1** on or near the kidneys. **2** of or relating to the adrenal glands.

adrenal glands *pl n Anat* two endocrine glands covering the upper surface of the kidneys.

adrenalin *or* **adrenaline** *n Biochem* a hormone secreted by the adrenal gland in response to stress. It increases heart rate, pulse rate, and blood pressure.

adrift *adj, adv* **1** drifting. **2** without a clear purpose. **3** *Informal* off course, wrong: *it was obvious that something had gone adrift.*

adroit *adj* quick and skilful in how one behaves or thinks. **adroitly** *adv* **adroitness** *n*

adsorb *vb* (of a gas or vapour) to condense and form a thin film on a surface. **adsorbent** *adj* **adsorption** *n*

ADT Atlantic Daylight Time.

adulation *n* uncritical admiration.

adult *n* **1** a mature fully grown person, animal, or plant. *~adj* **2** having reached maturity; fully developed. **3** suitable for or typical of adult people: *she had very adult features.* **4** sexually explicit: *adult films.* **adulthood** *n*

adulterate *vb* **-ating, -ated** to spoil something by adding inferior material. **adulteration** *n*

THESAURUS

admirer adherent, buff (*informal*), devotee, disciple, enthusiast, fan, follower, partisan, protagonist, supporter, votary, worshipper

admission 1. acceptance, access, admittance, entrance, entrée, entry, ingress, initiation, introduction **2.** acknowledgment, affirmation, allowance, avowal, concession, confession, declaration, disclosure, divulgence, profession, revelation

admit 1. acknowledge, affirm, avow, concede, confess, declare, disclose, divulge, own, profess, reveal **2.** accept, allow, allow to enter, give access, initiate, introduce, let in, receive, take in **3.** agree, allow, grant, let, permit, recognize

admittance acceptance, access, admitting, allowing, entrance, entry, letting in, passage, reception

admonish bawl out (*informal*), berate, carpet (*informal*), caution, censure, check, chide, give a rocket (*Brit. & N.Z. informal*), read the riot act, rebuke, reprimand, reprove, scold, tear into (*informal*), tear (someone) off a strip (*Brit. informal*), tell off (*informal*), upbraid, warn

admonition caution, rebuke, remonstrance, reprimand, reproach, reproof, scolding, telling off (*informal*), warning

admonitory cautionary, reproachful, warning

adolescence boyhood, girlhood, juvenescence, minority, teens, youth

adolescent *adj.* **1.** boyish, girlish, growing, teenage, young, youthful **2.** immature, juvenile, puerile *~n.* **3.** juvenile, minor, teenager, youngster, youth

adopt 1. foster, take in **2.** accept, approve, choose, embrace, endorse, espouse, follow, maintain, ratify, select, support, take over, take up **3.** assume, take on

adoption acceptance, approbation, approval, choice, endorsement, espousal, maintenance, ratification, selection, support

adorable appealing, attractive, captivating, charming, cute, darling, dear, delightful, fetching, lovable, pleasing, precious

adoration admiration, esteem, estimation, exaltation, glorification, honour, idolatry, idolization, love, reverence, veneration, worship

adore admire, bow to, cherish, dote on, esteem, exalt, glorify, honour, idolize, love, revere, venerate, worship

adorn array, beautify, bedeck, decorate, embellish, emblazon, enhance, enrich, festoon, garnish, grace, ornament, trim

adornment accessory, beautification, decorating, decoration, embellishment, festoon, frill, frippery, ornament, ornamentation, trimming

adrift 1. afloat, drifting, unanchored, unmoored **2.** aimless, directionless, goalless, purposeless **3.** amiss, astray, off course, wrong

adroit able, adept, apt, artful, clever, cunning, deft, dexterous, expert, ingenious, masterful, neat, nimble, proficient, quick-witted, skilful, skilled

adroitness ability, ableness, adeptness, aptness, artfulness, cleverness, craft, cunning, deftness, dexterity, expertise, ingeniousness, ingenuity, masterfulness, mastery, nimbleness, proficiency, quick-wittedness, skilfulness, skill

adulation blandishment, extravagant flattery, fawning, fulsome praise, servile flattery, sycophancy, worship

adulatory fawning, obsequious, servile, slavish, sycophantic

adult 1. *n.* grown *or* grown-up person (man *or* woman), grown-up, person of mature age **2.** *adj.* full

adulterer *or fem* **adulteress** *n* a person who has committed adultery.

adultery *n, pl* **-teries** sexual unfaithfulness of a husband or wife. **adulterous** *adj*

adv. adverb.

advance *vb* **-vancing, -vanced 1** to go or bring forward. **2** to make progress: *this student has advanced in reading and writing.* **3** to further a cause: *an association founded to advance the interests of ex-soldiers.* **4 advance on** to move towards someone in a threatening manner. **5** to present an idea for consideration. **6** to lend a sum of money. *~n* **7** a forward movement. **8** improvement or progress: *the greatest advance in modern medicine.* **9** a loan of money. **10** a payment made before it is legally due. **11** an increase in price: *any advance on fifty pounds?* **12 in advance** beforehand: *you have to pay in advance.* **13 in advance of** ahead of in time or development. *~adj* **14** done or happening before an event: *advance warning.* ~See also **advances.**

advanced *adj* **1** at a late stage in development. **2** not elementary: *the advanced class in economics.*

Advanced level *n* a formal name for **A level.**

advancement *n* promotion in rank or status.

advances *pl n* approaches made to a person with the hope of starting a romantic or sexual relationship.

advantage *n* **1** a more favourable position or state. **2** benefit or profit: *they could make this work to their advantage.* **3** *Tennis* the point scored after deuce. **4 take advantage of a** to use a person unfairly. **b** to use an opportunity. **5 to advantage** to good effect: *her hair was shaped to display to advantage her superb neck.*

advantaged *adj* in a superior social or financial position.

advantageous *adj* likely to bring benefits. **advantageously** *adv*

advection *n Physics* the transferring of heat in a horizontal stream of gas.

advent *n* an arrival: *the advent of the personal computer.*

Advent *n* the season that includes the four Sundays before Christmas.

Adventist *n* a member of a Christian group that believes in the imminent return of Christ.

adventitious *adj* added or appearing accidentally.

adventure *n* **1** a risky undertaking, the ending of which is uncertain. **2** exciting or unexpected events.

adventure playground *n Brit* a playground for children that contains building materials and other equipment to build with or climb on.

adventurer *or fem* **adventuress** *n* **1** a person who seeks money or power by unscrupulous means. **2** a person who seeks adventure.

adventurism *n* recklessness in politics or finance.

adventurous *adj* daring or enterprising.

adverb *n* a word that modifies a sentence, verb, adverb, or adjective, for example *easily, very,* and *happily* in *They could easily envy the very happily married couple.* **adverbial** *adj*

adversary (**ad**-verse-er-ree) *n, pl* **-saries** an opponent in a fight, disagreement, or sporting contest.

adverse *adj* **1** unfavourable to one's interests: *adverse effects.* **2** antagonistic or hostile. **adversely** *adv*

adversity *n, pl* **-ties** very difficult or hard circumstances.

advert *n Informal* an advertisement.

advertise *vb* **-tising, -tised 1** to present or praise (goods or a service) to the public, in order to encourage sales. **2** to make (a vacancy, an event, or an article for sale) publicly known. **advertiser** *n* **advertising** *n*

advertisement *n* any public announcement designed to sell goods or publicize an event

➤ Note that the standard pronunciation of *advertise-*

THESAURUS

grown, fully developed, fully grown, grown-up, mature, of age, ripe

adulterate attenuate, bastardize, contaminate, corrupt, debase, depreciate, deteriorate, devalue, make impure, mix with, thin, vitiate, water down, weaken

advance *vb.* **1.** accelerate, bring forward, bring up, come forward, elevate, go ahead, go forward, go on, hasten, move onward, move up, press on, proceed, progress, promote, send forward, speed, upgrade **2.** benefit, further, grow, improve, multiply, prosper, thrive **3.** present, proffer, put forward, submit, suggest *~n.* **4.** advancement, development, forward movement, headway, inroad, onward movement, progress **5.** advancement, amelioration, betterment, breakthrough, furtherance, gain, growth, improvement, progress, promotion, step **6.** prepayment, retainer **7.** increase (*in price*), rise (*in price*) **8. in advance** ahead, beforehand, earlier, in the forefront, in the lead, in the van, previously *~adj.* **9.** beforehand, early, foremost, forward, in front, leading, prior

advanced ahead, avant-garde, extreme, foremost, forward, higher, late, leading, precocious, progressive

advancement betterment, improvement, preferment, progress, promotion, rise

advances approach, approaches, moves, overtures, proposals, proposition

advantage 1. ascendancy, dominance, lead, precedence, pre-eminence, start, superiority, sway, upper hand **2.** aid, asset, assistance, avail, benefit, blessing, boon, convenience, gain, good, help, interest, profit, service, use, utility

advantageous beneficial, convenient, expedient, helpful, of service, profitable, useful, valuable, worthwhile

advent appearance, approach, arrival, coming, entrance, occurrence, onset, visitation

adventitious accidental, casual, chance, unexpected

adventure chance, contingency, enterprise, escapade, experience, exploit, hazard, occurrence, risk, speculation, undertaking, venture

adventurer 1. charlatan, fortune-hunter, gambler, mercenary, opportunist, rogue, speculator **2.** daredevil, hero, heroine, knight-errant, soldier of fortune, swashbuckler, traveller, venturer, voyager, wanderer

adventurous audacious, bold, dangerous, daredevil, daring, enterprising, foolhardy, have-a-go (*informal*), hazardous, headstrong, intrepid, rash, reckless, risky, venturesome

adversary antagonist, competitor, contestant, enemy, foe, opponent, rival

adverse 1. detrimental, disadvantageous, inexpedient, injurious, inopportune, negative, unfavourable, unfortunate, unpropitious **2.** antagonistic, conflicting, contrary, hostile, inimical, opposing, unfriendly, unwilling

adversity affliction, bad luck, calamity, catastrophe, disaster, distress, hardship, hard times, ill-fortune, ill-luck, misery, misfortune, mishap, reverse, sorrow, suffering, trial, trouble, woe, wretchedness

advertise 1. blazon, display, flaunt, plug (*informal*), praise, promote, promulgate, publicize, push (*informal*), tout **2.** advise, announce, apprise, declare, inform, make known, notify, proclaim, publish

advertisement ad (*informal*), advert (*Brit. infor-*

ment differs from *advertise*. The main stress is on "ver", while "tise" is pronounced "tiz".

advice *n* **1** recommendation as to an appropriate choice of action. **2** formal notification of facts.

advisable *adj* sensible and likely to achieve the desired result. **advisability** *n*

advise *vb* **-vising, -vised 1** to offer advice to. **2** to inform or notify. **adviser** *or* **advisor** *n*

advised *adj* thought-out: *ill-advised.*

advisedly (ad-**vize**-id-lee) *adv* deliberately; after careful consideration: *I use the word advisedly.*

advisory *adj* able to offer advice.

advocaat *n* a liqueur with a raw egg base.

advocacy *n* active support of a cause or course of action.

advocate *vb* **-cating, -cated 1** to recommend a course of action publicly. *~n* **2** a person who upholds or defends a cause or course of action. **3** a person who speaks on behalf of another in a court of law. **4** *Scots Law* a barrister.

adze *or US* **adz** *n* a tool with a blade at right angles to the handle, used for shaping timber.

AEA Atomic Energy Authority.

AEC *US* Atomic Energy Commission.

AEEU Amalgamated Engineering and Electrical Union.

aegis (**ee**-jiss) *n* **under the aegis of** with the sponsorship or protection of.

aeolian harp (ee-**oh**-lee-an) *n* a musical instrument that produces sounds when the wind passes over its strings.

aeon *or US* **eon** (**ee**-on) *n* **1** an immeasurably long period of time. **2** the longest division of geological time.

aerate *vb* **-ating, -ated** to put gas into a liquid, for example when making a fizzy drink. **aeration** *n*

aerial *n* **1** the metal pole or wire on a television or radio which transmits or receives signals. *~adj* **2** in, from, or operating in the air. **3** extending high into the air. **4** of or relating to aircraft.

aero-, aeri-, *or* **aer-** *combining form* **1** relating to aircraft. **2** relating to air, atmosphere, or gas.

aerobatics *n* spectacular manoeuvres, such as loops or rolls, performed by aircraft.

aerobic *adj* designed for or relating to aerobics: *aerobic exercise.*

aerobics *n* exercises to increase the amount of oxygen in the blood and strengthen the heart and lungs.

aerodrome *n* a small airport.

aerodynamics *n* the study of how air flows around moving objects. **aerodynamic** *adj*

aero engine *n* an engine for an aircraft.

aerofoil *n* a part of an aircraft, such as the wing, designed to give lift in flight.

aerogram *n* an air-mail letter on a single sheet of light paper that seals to form an envelope.

aeronautics *n* the study or practice of flight through the air. **aeronautical** *adj*

aeroplane *or US & Canad* **airplane** *n* a heavier-than-air powered flying vehicle with fixed wings.

aerosol *n* a small metal pressurized can from which a substance can be dispensed in a fine spray.

➤ Be careful not to confuse the spelling "aer-" with "air-".

aerospace *n* **1** the earth's atmosphere and space beyond. *~adj* **2** of rockets or space vehicles: *the aerospace industry.*

aesthete *or US* **esthete** (**eess**-theet) *n* a person who has or who pretends to have a highly developed appreciation of beauty.

aesthetic *or US* **esthetic** (iss-**thet**-ik) *adj* relating to the appreciation of art and beauty. **aesthetically** *or US* **esthetically** *adv* **aestheticism** *or US* **estheticism** *n*

aesthetics *or US* **esthetics** *n* **1** the branch of philosophy concerned with the study of the concepts of beauty and taste. **2** the study of the rules and principles of art.

aether *n* same as **ether** (senses 2, 3).

aetiology (ee-tee-**ol**-a-jee) *n* same as **etiology.**

a.f. audio frequency.

afar *n* **from afar** from or at a great distance.

affable *adj* showing warmth and friendliness. **affability** *n* **affably** *adv*

affair *n* **1** an event or happening: *the Irangate affair.* **2** a sexual relationship outside marriage. **3** a thing to be done or attended to: *my wife's career is her own affair.* **4** something previously specified: *lunch was a subdued affair.*

affairs *pl n* **1** personal or business interests. **2** matters of public interest: *foreign affairs.*

affect[1] *vb* **1** to influence (someone or something): *the very difficult conditions continued to affect our per-*

THESAURUS

mal), announcement, bill, blurb, circular, commercial, display, notice, placard, plug (*informal*), poster, promotion, publicity

advice 1. caution, counsel, guidance, help, opinion, recommendation, suggestion, view **2.** information, instruction, intelligence, notice, notification, warning, word

advisability appropriateness, aptness, desirability, expediency, fitness, judiciousness, profitability, propriety, prudence, seemliness, soundness, suitability, wisdom

advisable appropriate, apt, desirable, expedient, fit, fitting, judicious, politic, profitable, proper, prudent, recommended, seemly, sensible, sound, suggested, suitable, wise

advise 1. caution, commend, counsel, prescribe, recommend, suggest, urge **2.** acquaint, apprise, inform, make known, notify, report, tell, warn

adviser aide, authority, coach, confidant, consultant, counsel, counsellor, guide, helper, lawyer, mentor, right-hand man, solicitor, teacher, tutor

advocate *vb.* **1.** advise, argue for, campaign for, champion, countenance, defend, encourage, espouse, favour, hold a brief for (*informal*), justify, plead for, prescribe, press for, promote, propose, recommend, speak for, support, uphold, urge *~n.* **2.** apologist, apostle, backer, campaigner, champion, counsellor, defender, pleader, promoter, proponent, proposer, speaker, spokesman, supporter, upholder **3.** attorney, barrister, counsel, lawyer, solicitor

aegis advocacy, auspices, backing, favour, guardianship, patronage, protection, shelter, sponsorship, support, wing

affability amiability, amicability, approachability, benevolence, benignity, civility, congeniality, cordiality, courtesy, friendliness, geniality, good humour, good nature, graciousness, kindliness, mildness, obligingness, pleasantness, sociability, urbanity, warmth

affable amiable, amicable, approachable, benevolent, benign, civil, congenial, cordial, courteous, friendly, genial, good-humoured, good-natured, gracious, kindly, mild, obliging, pleasant, sociable, urbane, warm

affair 1. activity, business, circumstance, concern, episode, event, happening, incident, matter, occur-

formance. **2** (of pain or disease) to attack: *the virus can spread to affect the heart muscle.* **3** to move someone emotionally: *the experience has affected him deeply.*
➤ Note the difference between the verbs *affect* meaning "influence" and *effect* meaning "accomplish".

affect[2] *vb* **1** to put on a show of: *he affects a certain disinterest.* **2** to wear or use by preference: *he likes to be called captain John and affects a nautical cap.*

affectation *n* an attitude or manner put on to impress others.

affected *adj* **1** behaving or speaking in a manner put on to impress others. **2** pretended: *an affected indifference.*

affecting *adj* arousing feelings of pity; moving.

affection *n* **1** fondness or tenderness for a person or thing. **2 affections** feelings of love; emotions: *I was angry with her for playing with their affections.*

affectionate *adj* having or displaying tenderness, affection, or warmth. **affectionately** *adv*

affianced (af-**fie**-anst) *adj Old-fashioned* engaged to be married.

affidavit (af-fid-**dave**-it) *n Law* a written statement made under oath.

affiliate *vb* **-ating, -ated 1** (of a group) to link up with a larger group. ~*n* **2** a person or organization that is affiliated with another. **affiliation** *n*

affiliation order *n Law* an order that the father of an illegitimate child must contribute towards the child's maintenance.

affinity *n, pl* **-ties 1** a feeling of closeness to and understanding of a person. **2** a close similarity in appearance, structure, or quality. **3** a chemical attraction.

affirm *vb* **1** to declare to be true. **2** to state clearly one's support for (an idea or belief). **affirmation** *n*

affirmative *adj* **1** indicating agreement: *an affirmative answer.* ~*n* **2** a word or phrase indicating agreement, such as *yes.*

affix *vb* **1** to attach or fasten. ~*n* **2** a word or syllable added to a word to produce a derived or inflected form, such as *-ment* in *establishment.*

afflict *vb* to cause someone suffering or unhappiness.

affliction *n* **1** something that causes physical or mental suffering. **2** a condition of great distress or suffering.

affluent *adj* having plenty of money. **affluence** *n*

affluent society *n* a society in which the material benefits of prosperity are widely available.

afford *vb* **1 can afford** to be able to do or spare something without risking financial difficulties or undesirable consequences: *she can't afford to be choosy.* **2** to give or supply: *afford me an opportunity to judge for myself.* **affordable** *adj*

afforest *vb* to plant trees on. **afforestation** *n*

affray *n* a noisy fight in a public place.

affront *n* **1** a deliberate insult. ~*vb* **2** to hurt someone's pride or dignity.
➤ *Affront* is often followed by "to": *An affront to my feelings.*

Afghan *adj* **1** of Afghanistan. ~*n* **2** a person from Afghanistan. **3** the language of Afghanistan.

Afghan hound *n* a large slim dog with long silky hair.

aficionado (af-fish-yo-**nah**-do) *n, pl* **-dos** an enthusiastic fan of a sport or interest.

afield *adv* **far afield** far away: *they used to travel as far afield as Hungary.*

aflame *adv, adj* **1** in flames. **2** deeply aroused: *his face was aflame with self-contempt and embarrassment.*

THESAURUS

rence, proceeding, project, question, subject, transaction, undertaking **2.** amour, intrigue, liaison, relationship, romance

affect[1] **1.** act on, alter, bear upon, change, concern, impinge upon, influence, interest, involve, modify, prevail over, regard, relate to, sway, transform **2.** disturb, impress, move, overcome, perturb, stir, touch, upset

affect[2] adopt, aspire to, assume, contrive, counterfeit, feign, imitate, pretend, put on, sham, simulate

affectation act, affectedness, appearance, artificiality, assumed manners, façade, false display, insincerity, mannerism, pose, pretence, pretension, pretentiousness, sham, show, simulation, unnatural imitation

affected 1. camp (*informal*), conceited, la-di-da (*informal*), mannered, mincing, pompous, precious, pretentious, stiff **2.** artificial, counterfeit, feigned, insincere, phoney *or* phony (*informal*), pretended, put-on, sham, simulated, spurious, studied, unnatural

affecting moving, pathetic, piteous, pitiable, pitiful, poignant, sad, saddening, touching

affection amity, attachment, care, desire, feeling, fondness, friendliness, good will, inclination, kindness, liking, love, passion, tenderness, warmth

affectionate attached, caring, devoted, doting, fond, friendly, kind, loving, tender, warm, warm-hearted

affiliate ally, amalgamate, annex, associate, band together, combine, confederate, connect, incorporate, join, unite

affiliation alliance, amalgamation, association, coalition, combination, confederation, connection, incorporation, league, merging, relationship, union

affinity 1. attraction, fondness, inclination, leaning, liking, partiality, rapport, sympathy **2.** alliance, analogy, closeness, compatibility, connection, correspondence, kinship, likeness, relation, relationship, resemblance, similarity

affirm assert, asseverate, attest, aver, avouch, avow, certify, confirm, declare, maintain, pronounce, ratify, state, swear, testify

affirmation assertion, asseveration, attestation, averment, avouchment, avowal, certification, confirmation, declaration, oath, pronouncement, ratification, statement, testimony

affirmative consenting, corroborative, favourable, positive

afflict beset, burden, distress, grieve, harass, hurt, oppress, pain, plague, rack, smite, torment, trouble, try, wound

affliction adversity, calamity, cross, curse, depression, disease, distress, grief, hardship, misery, misfortune, ordeal, pain, plague, scourge, sickness, sorrow, suffering, torment, trial, tribulation, trouble, woe, wretchedness

affluence abundance, big money, exuberance, fortune, opulence, plenty, profusion, prosperity, riches, tidy sum (*informal*), wealth

affluent loaded (*slang*), moneyed, opulent, prosperous, rich, wealthy, well-heeled (*informal*), well-off, well-to-do

afford 1. bear, spare, stand, sustain **2.** bestow, furnish, give, grant, impart, offer, produce, provide, render, supply, yield

affront 1. *n.* abuse, indignity, injury, insult, offence, slap in the face (*informal*), slight, slur, wrong **2.** *vb.* abuse, insult, offend, pique, slight

aflame 1. ablaze, alight, blazing, burning, fiery, flam-

afloat *adj, adv* **1** floating. **2** free of debt: *his goal is to keep the company afloat.* **3** aboard ship; at sea.

afoot *adj, adv* happening; in operation: *I had no suspicion of what was afoot.*

afore *adv, prep, conj Old-fashioned or dialect* before.

aforementioned *adj* mentioned before.

aforesaid *adj* referred to previously.

aforethought *adj* premeditated: *malice aforethought.*

a fortiori (**eh** for-tee-**or**-rye) *adv* for similar but more convincing reasons.

afraid *adj* **1** feeling fear or apprehension. **2** regretful: *I'm afraid I lost my temper.*

afresh *adv* once more.

African *adj* **1** of Africa. ~*n* **2** a person from Africa.

Africana *n* objects of cultural or historical interest from Africa.

African-American *n* **1** an American of African descent. ~*adj* **2** of African-Americans, their history, or their culture.

Africander *n* a breed of humpbacked cattle originally from southern Africa.

African time *n S African slang* unpunctuality.

African violet *n* a flowering house plant with pink or purple flowers and hairy leaves.

Afrikaans *n* one of the official languages of South Africa, descended from Dutch.

Afrikaner *n* a White South African whose native language is Afrikaans.

Afro *n, pl* **-ros** a frizzy bushy hairstyle.

Afro- *combining form* indicating Africa or African: *Afro-Caribbean.*

Afro-American *n, adj* same as **African-American.**

aft *adv, adj* at or towards the rear of a ship or aircraft.

after *prep* **1** following in time or place. **2** in pursuit of: *he was after my mother's jewellery.* **3** concerning: *he asked after Laura.* **4** considering: *you seem all right after what happened last night.* **5** next in excellence or importance to. **6** in imitation of; in the manner of. **7** in accordance with: *a man after his own heart.* **8** the same name as: *the street is named after the designer of the church.* **9** *US* past (the hour of): *fifteen after twelve.* **10 after all a** in spite of everything: *I was, after all, a suspect.* **b** in spite of expectations or efforts. **11 after you** please go before me. ~*adv* **12** at a later time; afterwards. ~*conj* **13** at a time later than the time when: *she arrived after the reading had begun.* ~*adj* **14** *Naut* further aft: *the after cabin.*

afterbirth *n* the placenta and fetal membranes expelled from the mother's womb after childbirth.

aftercare *n* **1** the help and support given to a person discharged from a hospital or prison. **2** the regular care required to keep something in good condition.

afterdamp *n* a poisonous gas formed after the explosion of firedamp in a coal mine.

aftereffect *n* any result occurring some time after its cause.

afterglow *n* **1** the glow left after the source of a light has disappeared, for example after sunset. **2** a pleasant feeling remaining after an enjoyable experience.

afterlife *n* life after death.

aftermath *n* effects or results of an event considered collectively: *the aftermath of the weekend violence.*

afternoon *n* the period between noon and evening.

afterpains *pl n* pains caused by contraction of a woman's womb after childbirth.

afters *n Brit informal* the sweet course of a meal.

aftershave *n* a scented lotion applied to a man's face after shaving.

aftershock *n* one of a series of minor tremors occurring after the main shock of an earthquake.

aftertaste *n* a taste that lingers on after eating or drinking.

afterthought *n* **1** something thought of after the opportunity to use it has passed. **2** an addition to something already completed.

afterwards *or* **afterward** *adv* later.

Ag *Chem* silver.

again *adv* **1** another or a second time: *I want to look at that atlas again.* **2** once more in a previously experienced state or condition: *he pictured her again as she used to be.* **3** in addition to the original amount: *twice as much again.* **4** on the other hand. **5** moreover or furthermore: *she is beautiful and, again, intelligent.* **6 again and again** continually or repeatedly.

against *prep* **1** standing or leaning beside: *he leaned against a tree.* **2** opposed to or in disagreement with. **3** in contrast to: *his complexion was a sickly white against the black stubble of his beard.* **4** coming in contact with: *rain rattled against the window.* **5** having an unfavourable effect on: *the system works against you when you don't have money.* **6** as a protection from: *a safeguard against bacteria.* **7** in exchange for or in return for: *the dollar has gained very slightly against the yen.* **8 as against** as opposed to; as compared with.

agape *adj* **1** (of the mouth) wide open. **2** (of a person) very surprised.

agar (**ayg**-ar) *or* **agar-agar** *n* a jelly-like substance obtained from seaweed and used as a thickener in food.

agaric *n* any fungus with gills on the underside of the cap, such as a mushroom.

agate (**ag**-git) *n* a hard semiprecious form of quartz with striped colouring.

agave (a-**gave**-vee) *n* a tropical American plant with tall flower stalks and thick leaves.

age *n* **1** the length of time that a person or thing has existed. **2** a period or state of human life. **3** the latter part of human life. **4** a period of history marked by some feature. **5 ages** *Informal* a long time. **6 come of age** to become legally responsible for one's actions

THESAURUS

ing, ignited, lighted, lit, on fire **2.** afire, aroused, excited, fervent, impassioned, passionate, stimulated

afoot about, abroad, astir, brewing, circulating, current, going on, hatching, in preparation, in progress, in the wind, on the go (*informal*), operating, up (*informal*)

afraid 1. alarmed, anxious, apprehensive, cowardly, faint-hearted, fearful, frightened, intimidated, nervous, reluctant, scared, suspicious, timid, timorous **2.** regretful, sorry, unhappy

afresh again, anew, newly, once again, once more, over again

after afterwards, behind, below, following, later, subsequently, succeeding, thereafter

aftermath after-effects, consequences, effects, end, outcome, results, sequel, upshot

again 1. afresh, anew, another time, once more **2.** also, besides, furthermore, in addition, moreover, on the contrary, on the other hand

against 1. anti (*informal*), averse to, contra (*informal*), counter, hostile to, in contrast to, in defiance of, in opposition to, in the face of, opposed to, opposing, resisting, versus **2.** abutting, close up to, facing, fronting, in contact with, on, opposite to, touching, upon **3.**

(usually at 18 years). *~vb* **ageing *or* aging, aged 7** to become old. **8** to appear or cause to appear older: *the years had not aged her in any way; skin type changes as one ages.*

aged *adj* **1** (**ay**-jid) advanced in years; old. **2** (rhymes with **raged**) being at the age of: *a girl aged thirteen is missing.*

ageing *or* aging *n* **1** the fact or process of growing old. *~adj* **2** becoming or appearing older.

➤ Both spellings of *ageing,* with or without an "e", are equally acceptable.

ageless *adj* **1** apparently never growing old. **2** seeming to have existed for ever; eternal: *an ageless profession.*

agency *n, pl* **-cies 1** an organization providing a specific service: *an advertising agency.* **2** the business or functions of an agent. **3** *Old-fashioned* action or power by which something happens: *the intervention of a human agency in the sequence of events.*

agenda *n* a schedule or list of items to be attended to, for example at a meeting.

agent *n* **1** a person who arranges business for other people, esp. for actors or singers. **2** a spy. **3** a substance which causes change in other substances: *an emulsifying agent.* **4** someone or something which causes an effect: *the agent of change.*

agent provocateur (**azh**-on prov-vok-at-**tur**) *n, pl* **agents provocateurs** (**azh**-on prov-vok-at-**tur**) a person employed by the authorities to tempt people to commit illegal acts and so be discredited or punished.

age-old *adj* very old; ancient.

agglomerate *vb* **-ating, -ated 1** to form or be formed into a mass. *~n* **2** a volcanic rock consisting of fused angular fragments of rock.

agglomeration *n* a confused mass or cluster.

agglutinate *vb* **-nating, -nated** to stick as if with glue. **agglutination** *n*

aggrandize *or* -dise *vb* **-dizing, -dized *or* -dising, -dised** to make greater in size, power, or rank. **aggrandizement *or* -disement** *n*

aggravate *vb* **-vating, -vated 1** to make (a disease, situation or problem) worse. **2** *Informal* to annoy. **aggravating** *adj* **aggravation** *n*

➤ The longer-established meaning is "make worse". Some people regard the use of *aggravate* to mean "annoy" as poor usage but it is nevertheless widespread.

aggregate *n* **1** an amount or total formed from separate units. **2** *Geol* a rock, such as granite, consisting of a mixture of minerals. **3** the sand and stone mixed with cement and water to make concrete. *~adj* **4** formed of separate units collected into a whole. *~vb* **-gating, -gated 5** to combine or be combined into a whole. **6** to amount to (a particular number). **aggregation** *n*

aggression *n* **1** violent and hostile behaviour. **2** an unprovoked attack. **aggressor** *n*

aggressive *adj* **1** full of anger or hostility. **2** forceful or determined: *an aggressive salesman.* **aggressively** *adv* **aggressiveness** *n*

aggrieved *adj* upset and angry.

aggro *n Slang* aggressive behaviour.

aghast *adj* overcome with amazement or horror.

agile *adj* **1** quick in movement; nimble. **2** mentally quick or acute. **agility** *n*

agin *prep Dialect* against or opposed to: *he gave the usual line of talk agin the government.*

agitate *vb* **-tating, -tated 1** to excite, disturb, or

THESAURUS

in anticipation of, in expectation of, in preparation for, in provision for

age *n.* **1.** date, day(s), duration, epoch, era, generation, lifetime, period, span, time **2.** advancing years, decline (*of life*), majority, maturity, old age, senescence, senility, seniority *~vb.* **3.** decline, deteriorate, grow old, mature, mellow, ripen

aged age-old, ancient, antiquated, antique, elderly, getting on, grey, hoary, old, senescent, superannuated

agency 1. bureau, business, department, office, organization **2.** action, activity, auspices, efficiency, force, influence, intercession, intervention, means, mechanism, mediation, medium, operation, power, work

agenda calendar, diary, list, plan, programme, schedule, timetable

agent 1. advocate, deputy, emissary, envoy, factor, go-between, negotiator, rep (*informal*), representative, substitute, surrogate **2.** agency, author, cause, doer, executor, force, instrument, means, mover, operative, operator, performer, power, vehicle, worker

aggravate 1. exacerbate, exaggerate, heighten, increase, inflame, intensify, magnify, make worse, worsen **2.** *informal* annoy, be on one's back (*slang*), bother, exasperate, gall, get in one's hair (*informal*), get on one's nerves (*informal*), hassle (*informal*), irk, irritate, nark (*slang*), needle (*informal*), nettle, pester, piss one off (*taboo slang*), provoke, tease, vex

aggravation 1. exacerbation, exaggeration, heightening, increase, inflaming, intensification, magnification, worsening **2.** *informal* annoyance, exasperation, gall, hassle (*informal*), irksomeness, irritation, provocation, teasing, vexation

aggregate 1. *n.* accumulation, agglomeration, amount, assemblage, body, bulk, collection, combination, heap, lump, mass, mixture, pile, sum, total, whole **2.** *adj.* accumulated, added, assembled, collected, collective, combined, composite, corporate, cumulative, mixed, total **3.** *vb.* accumulate, amass, assemble, collect, combine, heap, mix, pile

aggression 1. aggressiveness, antagonism, belligerence, destructiveness, hostility, pugnacity **2.** assault, attack, encroachment, injury, invasion, offence, offensive, onslaught, raid

aggressive 1. belligerent, destructive, hostile, offensive, pugnacious, quarrelsome **2.** assertive, bold, dynamic, energetic, enterprising, forceful, militant, pushing, pushy (*informal*), vigorous, zealous

aggressor assailant, assaulter, attacker, invader

aggrieved afflicted, distressed, disturbed, harmed, hurt, ill-used, injured, peeved (*informal*), saddened, unhappy, woeful, wronged

aghast afraid, amazed, appalled, astonished, astounded, awestruck, confounded, frightened, horrified, horror-struck, shocked, startled, stunned, thunder-struck

agile 1. active, brisk, limber, lissom(e), lithe, lively, nimble, quick, sprightly, spry, supple, swift **2.** acute, alert, clever, quick, quick-witted, sharp

agility 1. activity, liveliness, quickness, sprightliness, suppleness, swiftness **2.** acuteness, alertness, cleverness, quickness, quick-wittedness, sharpness

agitate 1. alarm, arouse, confuse, disconcert, disquiet, distract, disturb, excite, faze, ferment, fluster, incite, inflame, perturb, rouse, ruffle, stimulate, trouble, unnerve, upset, work up, worry **2.** beat, churn, shake, stir, toss **3.** argue, debate, dispute, ventilate

agitation 1. alarm, arousal, clamour, commotion, confusion, discomposure, disquiet, distraction, disturbance, excitement, ferment, flurry, fluster, incitement, lather (*informal*), outcry, stimulation, trouble, tumult, turmoil, upheaval, upset, worry **2.** churning,

trouble. **2** to shake or stir (a liquid). **3** to attempt to stir up public opinion for or against something. **agitated** *adj* **agitatedly** *adv* **agitation** *n* **agitator** *n*

agitprop *n* political agitation and propaganda.

aglitter *adj* sparkling or glittering.

aglow *adj* glowing.

aglu *or* **agloo** *n Canad* a breathing hole made in ice by a seal.

AGM annual general meeting.

agnostic *n* **1** a person who believes that it is impossible to know whether God exists. **2** a person who claims that the answer to some specific question cannot be known with certainty. *~adj* **3** of or relating to agnostics. **agnosticism** *n*

ago *adv* in the past: *fifty years ago.*

agog *adj* eager or curious: *Marcia would be agog to hear his news.*

agonize *or* **-nise** *vb* **-nizing, -nized** *or* **-nising, -nised 1** to worry greatly. **2** to suffer agony. **agonizing** *or* **-nising** *adj* **agonizingly** *or* **-nisingly** *adv*

agony *n, pl* **-nies** acute physical or mental pain.

agony aunt *n* a person who replies to readers' letters in an agony column.

agony column *n* a newspaper or magazine feature offering advice on readers' personal problems.

agoraphobia *n* an illogical fear of open spaces. **agoraphobic** *adj, n*

AGR advanced gas-cooled reactor.

agrarian *adj* of or relating to land or agriculture. **agrarianism** *n*

agree *vb* **agreeing, agreed 1** to be of the same opinion. **2** to give assent; consent. **3** to reach a joint decision: *the ministers agreed on a strategy.* **4** to be consistent. **5 agree with** to be agreeable or suitable to (one's health or appearance): *marriage and motherhood must agree with you.* **6** to concede: *the unions have agreed that the results of appraisal are relevant.* **7** *Grammar* to be the same in number, gender, and case as a connected word.

➤ *Agree* is usually followed by a preposition. Use agree *on* something; agree *with* someone; agree *to* do something.

agreeable *adj* **1** pleasant and enjoyable. **2** prepared to consent: *I cannot say that she was agreeable to the project but she was resigned.* **agreeably** *adv*

agreement *n* **1** the act or state of agreeing. **2** a legally enforceable contract.

agriculture *n* the rearing of crops and livestock; farming. **agricultural** *adj* **agriculturalist** *n*

agrimony *n* a plant with small yellow flowers and bitter-tasting bristly fruits.

agronomy (ag-**ron**-om-mee) *n* the science of land cultivation, soil management, and crop production. **agronomist** *n*

aground *adv* onto the bottom of shallow water: *they felt a jolt as the ship ran aground.*

ague (**aig**-yew) *n* **1** *Old-fashioned* malarial fever with shivering. **2** a fit of shivering.

ah *interj* an exclamation expressing pleasure, pain, sympathy, etc.

aha *interj* an exclamation expressing triumph, surprise, etc.

ahead *adv* **1** at or in the front; before. **2** forwards: *go straight ahead.* **3 get ahead** to achieve success: *I was young and hungry to get ahead.* *~adj* **4** in a leading position: *he is ahead in the polls.*

ahem *interj* a clearing of the throat, used to attract attention or express doubt.

ahoy *interj Naut* a shout made to call a ship or to attract attention.

AI 1 artificial insemination. **2** artificial intelligence.

aid *n* **1** money, equipment, or services provided for people in need; assistance. **2** a person or device that helps or assists. *~vb* **3** to help financially or in other ways.

Aid *or* **-aid** *n combining form* denoting a charitable organization that raises money for a particular cause: *Band Aid.*

AID formerly, artificial insemination by donor.

aide *n* an assistant: *a senior aide to the Prime Minister.*

aide-de-camp (aid-de-**kom**) *n, pl* **aides-de-camp** (aid-de-**kom**) a military officer serving as personal assistant to a senior.

AIDS acquired immunodeficiency syndrome: a viral disease that destroys the body's ability to fight infection.

AIH artificial insemination by husband.

ail *vb Literary* **1** to trouble or afflict. **2** to feel unwell.

aileron (**ale**-er-on) *n* a hinged flap on the back of an aircraft wing which controls rolling.

ailing *adj* unwell or unsuccessful over a long period: *an ailing company.*

ailment *n* a slight illness.

aim *vb* **1** to point (a weapon or missile) or direct (a blow or remark) at a particular person or object. **2** to propose or intend: *they aim to provide full and equal*

THESAURUS

convulsion, disturbance, rocking, shake, shaking, stir, stirring, tossing, turbulence, upheaval **3.** argument, controversy, debate, dispute, ventilation

agitator agent provocateur, demagogue, firebrand, inciter, instigator, rabble-rouser, revolutionary, stirrer (*informal*), troublemaker

agog avid, curious, eager, enthralled, enthusiastic, excited, expectant, impatient, in suspense, keen

agony affliction, anguish, distress, misery, pain, pangs, suffering, throes, torment, torture, woe

agree 1. be of the same mind, comply, concur, see eye to eye, settle **2.** accede, acquiesce, allow, assent, consent, engage, grant, permit **3.** accord, answer, chime, coincide, conform, correspond, fit, get on (together), harmonize, match, square, suit, tally **4.** admit, concede, grant

agreeable 1. acceptable, congenial, delightful, enjoyable, gratifying, likable *or* likeable, pleasant, pleasing, pleasurable, satisfying, to one's liking, to one's taste **2.** acquiescent, amenable, approving, consenting, in accord, responsive, sympathetic, well-disposed, willing

agreement 1. accord, accordance, affinity, analogy, compatibility, compliance, concert, concord, concurrence, conformity, congruity, consistency, correspondence, harmony, similarity, suitableness, union, unison **2.** arrangement, bargain, compact, contract, covenant, deal (*informal*), pact, settlement, treaty, understanding

agriculture agronomy, cultivation, culture, farming, husbandry, tillage

aground ashore, beached, foundered, grounded, high and dry, on the rocks, stranded, stuck

ahead *adv.* **1.** before, in advance, in front, in the foreground, in the lead, in the vanguard, to the fore **2.** along, forwards, on, onwards *~adj.* **3.** at an advantage, at the head, in front, in the foreground, in the lead, in the vanguard, leading, to the fore, winning

aid *n.* **1.** assistance, benefit, encouragement, favour, help, promotion, relief, service, succour, support **2.**

rights to all groups. ~*n* **3** the action of directing something at an object. **4** intention or purpose. **5 take aim** to point a weapon or missile at a person or object.
➤ The idiom is *aim at* something or *aim to do* something.

aimless *adj* having no purpose or direction. **aimlessly** *adv*

ain't *Not standard* am not, is not, are not, have not, *or* has not: *it ain't fair.*

air *n* **1** the mixture of gases that forms the earth's atmosphere. It consists chiefly of nitrogen, oxygen, argon, and carbon dioxide. **2** the space above and around the earth; sky. **3** a distinctive quality, appearance, or manner: *I thought he had an air of elegance and celebrity about him.* **4** a simple tune. **5** transportation in aircraft: *I went off to Italy by air and train.* **6 in the air** in circulation; current: *a sense of expectation is in the air.* **7 into thin air** leaving no trace behind. **8 on the air** in the act of broadcasting on radio or television. **9 up in the air** uncertain. ~*vb* **10** to make known publicly: *these issues will be aired at a ministerial meeting.* **11** to expose to air to dry or ventilate. –See also **airs.**

air base *n* a centre from which military aircraft operate.

airborne *adj* **1** carried by air. **2** (of aircraft) flying; in the air.

air brake *n* a brake in heavy vehicles that is operated by compressed air.

airbrick *n Chiefly Brit* a brick with holes in it, put into the wall of a building for ventilation.

airbrush *n* an atomizer which sprays paint by means of compressed air.

air chief marshal *n* a very senior officer in an air force.

air commodore *n* a senior officer in an air force.

air conditioning *n* a system for controlling the temperature and humidity of the air in a building. **air-conditioned** *adj* **air conditioner** *n*

aircraft *n, pl* **craft** any machine capable of flying, such as a glider or aeroplane.

aircraft carrier *n* a warship with a long flat deck for the launching and landing of aircraft.

aircraftman *n, pl* **-men** a serviceman of the most junior rank in an air force. **aircraftwoman** *fem n*

air cushion *n* **1** an inflatable cushion. **2** the pocket of air that supports a hovercraft.

airfield *n* a place where aircraft can land and take off.

air force *n* the branch of a nation's armed services that is responsible for air warfare.

air gun *n* a gun fired by means of compressed air.

airhead *n Slang* a person who is stupid or incapable of serious thought.

air hostess *n* a stewardess on an airliner.

airily *adv* in a light-hearted and casual manner.

airing *n* **1** exposure to air or warmth for drying or ventilation. **2** exposure to public debate: *both these notions got an airing during the campaign.*

airing cupboard *n* a heated cupboard in which laundry is aired and kept dry.

airless *adj* lacking fresh air; stuffy.

air letter *n* same as **aerogram.**

airlift *n* **1** the transportation by air of troops or cargo when other routes are blocked. ~*vb* **2** to transport by an airlift.

airline *n* an organization that provides scheduled flights for passengers or cargo.

airliner *n* a large passenger aircraft.

airlock *n* **1** a bubble of air blocking the flow of liquid in a pipe. **2** an airtight chamber between places that do not have the same air pressure, such as in a spacecraft or submarine.

air mail *n* **1** the system of sending mail by aircraft. **2** mail sent by aircraft.

airman *or fem* **airwoman** *n, pl* **-men** *or* **-women** a person serving in an air force.

air marshal *n* **1** a senior Royal Air Force officer of equivalent rank to a vice admiral in the Royal Navy. **2** a Royal New Zealand Air Force officer of the highest rank when chief of defence forces.

airplane *n US & Canad* an aeroplane.

airplay *n* the broadcast performances of a record on radio.

air pocket *n* a small descending air current that causes an aircraft to lose height suddenly.

airport *n* a landing and taking-off area for civil aircraft, with facilities for aircraft maintenance and passenger arrival and departure.

air pump *n* a device for pumping air into or out of something.

air raid *n* an attack by enemy aircraft in which bombs are dropped.

air rifle *n* a rifle fired by means of compressed air.

airs *pl n* manners put on to impress people: *we're poor and we never put on airs.*

airship *n* a lighter-than-air self-propelled aircraft.

airsick *adj* nauseated from travelling in an aircraft.

airspace *n* the atmosphere above a particular country, regarded as its territory.

airspeed *n* the speed of an aircraft relative to the air in which it moves.

airstrip *n* a cleared area for the landing and taking-off of aircraft.

air terminal *n* a building in a city from which air passengers are transported to an airport.

airtight *adj* **1** sealed so that air cannot enter. **2** having no weak points: *your reasoning is airtight and your evidence sound.*

airtime *n* the time allocated to a particular pro-

THESAURUS

abettor, adjutant, aide, aide-de-camp, assistant, helper, second, supporter ~*vb.* **3.** abet, assist, befriend, encourage, favour, help, promote, relieve, second, serve, subsidize, succour, support, sustain

aim 1. *vb.* aspire, attempt, design, direct, endeavour, intend, level, mean, plan, point, propose, purpose, resolve, seek, set one's sights on, sight, strive, take aim (at), train, try, want, wish **2.** *n.* ambition, aspiration, course, design, desire, direction, end, goal, intent, intention, mark, object, objective, plan, purpose, scheme, target, wish

aimless chance, directionless, erratic, frivolous, goalless, haphazard, pointless, purposeless, random, stray, undirected, unguided, unpredictable, vagrant, wayward

air *n.* **1.** atmosphere, heavens, sky **2.** ambience, appearance, atmosphere, aura, bearing, character, demeanour, effect, feeling, flavour, impression, look, manner, mood, quality, style, tone, vibes (*slang*) **3.** aria, lay, melody, song, tune ~*vb.* **4.** circulate, communicate, declare, disclose, display, disseminate, divulge, exhibit, expose, express, give vent to, make known, make public, proclaim, publicize, reveal, tell, utter, ventilate, voice **5.** aerate, expose, freshen, ventilate

airing 1. aeration, drying, freshening, ventilation **2.** circulation, display, dissemination, exposure, expression, publicity, utterance, vent, ventilation

airless breathless, close, heavy, muggy, oppressive, stale, stifling, stuffy, suffocating, sultry, unventilated

gramme, topic, or type of material on radio or television.

air vice-marshal *n* a senior officer in an air force.

airwaves *pl n Informal* radio waves used in radio and television broadcasting.

airway *n* an air route used regularly by aircraft.

airworthy *adj* (of an aircraft) safe to fly. **airworthiness** *n*

airy *adj* **airier, airiest 1** spacious and well ventilated. **2** light-hearted and casual. **3** having little basis in reality; fanciful: *airy assurances.*

aisle (rhymes with **mile**) *n* a passageway separating seating areas in a church, theatre, or cinema, or separating rows of shelves in a supermarket.

aitchbone *n* a cut of beef from the rump bone.

ajar *adj, adv* (of a door) slightly open.

AK Alaska.

AK-47 *n Trademark* same as **kalashnikov.**

akimbo *adv* **(with) arms akimbo** with hands on hips and elbows turned outwards.

akin *adj* **akin to** similar or very close to: *the technique is akin to impressionist painting.*

Al *Chem* aluminium.

AL Alabama.

à la *prep* in the manner or style of: *laced with gothic allusion à la David Lynch.*

alabaster *n* a kind of white stone used for making statues and vases.

à la carte *adj, adv* (of a menu) having dishes individually priced.

alacrity *n* speed or eagerness: *I accepted the invitation with alacrity.*

à la mode *adj* fashionable.

alarm *n* **1** fear aroused by awareness of danger. **2** a noise warning of danger: *there had been no time to put on life jackets or to sound the alarm.* **3** a device that transmits a warning. **4** short for **alarm clock.** *~vb* **5** to fill with fear. **6** to fit or activate a burglar alarm on (a house, car, etc.). **alarming** *adj*

alarm clock *n* a clock that sounds at a set time to wake a person up.

alarmist *n* **1** a person who alarms others needlessly. *~adj* **2** causing needless alarm.

alas *adv* **1** unfortunately or regrettably: *the answer, alas, is that they cannot get any for the moment.* *~interj* **2** *Old-fashioned* an exclamation of grief or alarm.

alb *n* a long white linen robe worn by a Christian priest.

albacore *n* a tuna found in warm seas which is valued as a food fish.

Albanian *adj* **1** of Albania. *~n* **2** a person from Albania. **3** the language of Albania.

albatross *n* **1** a large sea bird with very long wings. **2** *Golf* a score of three strokes under par for a hole.

albeit *conj* even though: *these effects occur, albeit to a lesser degree.*

albino *n, pl* **-nos** a person or animal with white or almost white hair and skin and pinkish eyes. **albinism** *n*

Albion *n Poetic* Britain or England.

album *n* **1** a book with blank pages, for keeping photographs or stamps in. **2** a long-playing record.

albumen *n* **1** egg white. **2** *Biochem* same as **albumin.**

albumin *or* **albumen** *n Biochem* a water-soluble protein found in blood plasma, egg white, milk, and muscle.

alchemy *n* a medieval form of chemistry concerned with trying to change base metals into gold and to find an elixir to prolong life indefinitely. **alchemist** *n*

alcohol *n* **1** a colourless flammable liquid present in intoxicating drinks. **2** intoxicating drinks generally.

alcohol-free *adj* (of beer or wine) containing only a trace of alcohol.

alcoholic *n* **1** a person who is addicted to alcohol. *~adj* **2** of or relating to alcohol.

alcoholism *n* a condition in which dependence on alcohol harms a person's health and everyday life.

alcove *n* a recess in the wall of a room.

aldehyde *n Chem* any organic compound containing the group –CHO, derived from alcohol by oxidation.

alder *n* a tree with toothed leaves and conelike fruits, often found in damp places.

alderman *n, pl* **-men 1** (formerly, in England and Wales) a senior member of a local council, elected by other councillors. **2** (in the US and Canada) a member of the governing body of a city.

ale *n* **1** a beer that is made without hops. **2** *Chiefly Brit* any kind of beer.

alehouse *n Old-fashioned* a public house.

alembic *n* **1** an obsolete type of container used for distillation. **2** anything that distils or purifies things.

alert *adj* **1** watchful and attentive. **2** **alert to** aware of. *~n* **3** a warning or the period during which a warning remains in effect. **4** **on the alert** watchful. *~vb* **5** to warn of danger. **6** to make aware of a fact. **alertness** *n*

THESAURUS

airs affectation, arrogance, haughtiness, hauteur, pomposity, pretensions, superciliousness, swank (*informal*)

airy 1. light, open, spacious, uncluttered, well-ventilated **2.** blithe, buoyant, cheerful, cheery, chirpy (*informal*), debonair, frolicsome, gay, genial, graceful, happy, high-spirited, jaunty, light, light-hearted, lively, merry, nonchalant, sprightly, upbeat (*informal*) **3.** aerial, delicate, ethereal, fanciful, flimsy, illusory, imaginary, immaterial, incorporeal, insubstantial, light, vaporous, visionary, weightless, wispy

aisle alley, corridor, gangway, lane, passage, passageway, path

alarm *n.* **1.** anxiety, apprehension, consternation, dismay, distress, fear, fright, nervousness, panic, scare, terror, trepidation, unease, uneasiness **2.** alarm-bell, alert, bell, danger signal, distress signal, siren, tocsin, warning *~vb.* **3.** daunt, dismay, distress, frighten, give (someone) a turn (*informal*), panic, put the wind up (someone) (*informal*), scare, startle, terrify, unnerve

alarming daunting, dismaying, distressing, disturbing, dreadful, frightening, scaring, shocking, startling, terrifying, unnerving

alcoholic 1. *n.* boozer (*informal*), dipsomaniac, drunk, drunkard, hard drinker, inebriate, soak (*slang*), sot, sponge (*informal*), tippler, toper, wino (*informal*) **2.** *adj.* brewed, distilled, fermented, hard, inebriant, inebriating, intoxicating, spirituous, strong, vinous

alcove bay, bower, compartment, corner, cubbyhole, cubicle, niche, nook, recess

alert 1. *adj.* active, agile, attentive, brisk, careful, circumspect, heedful, lively, nimble, observant, on guard, on one's toes, on the ball (*informal*), on the lookout, on the watch, perceptive, quick, ready, spirited, sprightly, vigilant, wary, watchful, wide-awake **2.** *n.* alarm, signal, siren, warning **3.** *vb.* alarm, forewarn, inform, notify, signal, warn

alertness activeness, agility, attentiveness, brisk-

A level *n* **1** the advanced level of a subject taken for the General Certificate of Education. **2** a pass in a subject at A level.

alfalfa *n* a plant widely used for feeding farm animals.

alfresco *adj, adv* in the open air.

algae (**al**-jee) *pl n, sing* **alga** (**al**-ga) plants which grow in water or moist ground, and which have no true stems, roots, or leaves.

algebra *n* a branch of mathematics in which symbols are used to represent numbers. **algebraic** *adj*

ALGOL *n* a computer programming language designed for mathematical and scientific purposes.

algorism *n* the Arabic or decimal system of counting.

algorithm *n* a logical arithmetical or computational procedure for solving problems.

alias *adv* **1** also known as: *Ken Barlow, alias Bill Roache.* ~*n, pl* **-ases 2** a false name.

alibi *n, pl* **-bis 1** *Law* a plea of being somewhere else when a crime was committed. **2** *Informal* an excuse. ~*vb* **-biing, -bied 3** to provide someone with an alibi.

Alice band *n* a band worn across the head to hold the hair back from the face.

alien *adj* **1** foreign. **2** from another world. **3 alien to** repugnant or opposed to: *these methods are alien to the world of politics.* ~*n* **4** a person who is a citizen of a country other than the one in which he or she lives. **5** a being from another world. **6** a person who does not seem to fit in with his or her environment.

alienable *adj Law* able to be transferred to another owner.

alienate *vb* **-ating, -ated 1** to cause a friend to become unfriendly or hostile. **2** *Law* to transfer the ownership of property to another person. **alienation** *n*

alight[1] *vb* **alighting, alighted** *or* **alit 1** to step out of a vehicle or off a horse: *we alighted on Vladivostok station.* **2** to land: *we saw thirty goldfinches alighting on the ledge.*

alight[2] *adj, adv* **1** on fire. **2** illuminated: *the lamp on the desk was alight.*

align (**a-line**) *vb* **1** to bring (a person or group) into agreement with the policy of another. **2** to place (two objects) in a particular position in relation to each other. **alignment** *n*

alike *adj* **1** similar: *they were thought to be very alike.* ~*adv* **2** in the same way: *they even dressed alike.* **3** considered together: *players and spectators alike.*

alimentary *adj* of or relating to nutrition.

alimentary canal *n* the tubular passage in the body through which food is passed and digested.

alimony *n Law* an allowance paid under a court order by one spouse to another after separation.

A-line *adj* (of a skirt) slightly flared.

aliphatic *adj Chem* (of an organic compound) having an open chain structure.

aliquant *adj Maths* denoting or belonging to a number that is not an exact divisor of a given number.

aliquot *adj Maths* denoting or belonging to an exact divisor of a number.

alive *adj* **1** living; having life. **2** in existence: *he said that he would keep the company alive, no matter what.* **3** lively. **4 alive to** aware of. **5 alive with** swarming with: *the rocky shoreline was alive with birds.*

alkali (**alk**-a-lie) *n Chem* a substance that combines with acid and neutralizes it to form a salt.

alkaline *adj Chem* having the properties of or containing an alkali. **alkalinity** *n*

alkaloid *n Chem* any of a group of organic compounds containing nitrogen. Many are poisonous and some are used as drugs.

alkane *n Chem* any saturated hydrocarbon with the general formula C_nH_{2n+2}.

alkene *n Chem* any unsaturated hydrocarbon with the general formula C_nH_{2n}.

all *adj, adv* **1** the whole quantity or number (of): *all the banks agree; we're all to blame.* **2** every one of a class: *almost all animals sneeze.* **3** the greatest possible: *in all seriousness.* **4** any whatever: *I'm leaving out all question of motive for the time being.* **5 all along** since the beginning. **6 all but** nearly. **7 all in all** everything considered. **8 all over a** finished. **b** everywhere in or on: *we send them all over the world.* **c** *Informal* typically: *that's him all over.* **9 all the** so much (more or less) than otherwise: *the need for new drugs is all the more important.* **10 at all** used for emphasis: *my throat's no better at all.* **11 be all for** *Informal* to be strongly in favour of. **12 for all** in spite of: *for all his cynicism, he's at heart a closet idealist.* **13 in all**

THESAURUS

ness, carefulness, circumspection, heedfulness, liveliness, nimbleness, perceptiveness, promptitude, quickness, readiness, spiritedness, sprightliness, vigilance, wariness, watchfulness

alias 1. *adv.* also called, also known as, otherwise, otherwise known as **2.** *n.* assumed name, *nom de guerre,* nom de plume, pen name, pseudonym, stage name

alibi defence, excuse, explanation, justification, plea, pretext, reason

alien *adj.* **1.** exotic, foreign, not native, not naturalized, outlandish, remote, strange, unfamiliar **2.** adverse, conflicting, contrary, inappropriate, incompatible, incongruous, opposed, repugnant ~*n.* **3.** foreigner, newcomer, outsider, stranger

alienate 1. break off, disaffect, divert, divorce, estrange, make unfriendly, separate, set against, turn away, withdraw **2.** *Law* convey, transfer

alienation 1. breaking off, disaffection, diversion, divorce, estrangement, indifference, remoteness, rupture, separation, setting against, turning away, withdrawal **2.** *Law* conveyance, transfer

alight[1] *vb.* **1.** descend, disembark, dismount, get down, get off **2.** come down, come to rest, descend, land, light, perch, settle, touch down

alight[2] *adj.* **1.** ablaze, aflame, blazing, burning, fiery, flaming, flaring, ignited, lighted, lit, on fire **2.** bright, brilliant, illuminated, lit up, shining

align 1. affiliate, agree, ally, associate, cooperate, join, side, sympathize **2.** arrange in line, coordinate, even, even up, line up, make parallel, order, range, regulate, straighten

alignment 1. affiliation, agreement, alliance, association, cooperation, sympathy, union **2.** adjustment, arrangement, coordination, evening, evening up, line, lining up, order, ranging, regulating, sequence, straightening up

alike 1. *adj.* akin, analogous, corresponding, duplicate, equal, equivalent, even, identical, parallel, resembling, similar, the same, uniform **2.** *adv.* analogously, correspondingly, equally, evenly, identically, similarly, uniformly

alive 1. animate, breathing, having life, in the land of the living (*informal*), living, subsisting **2.** active, existent, existing, extant, functioning, in existence, in force, operative, unquenched **3.** active, alert, animated, awake, brisk, cheerful, chirpy (*informal*), eager, energetic, full of life, lively, quick, spirited, sprightly, spry, vigorous, vital, vivacious, zestful **4. alive to** alert to, awake to, aware of, cognizant of, eager for, sensible of, sensitive to, susceptible to

altogether: *there were five in all.* ~*adv* **14** (in scores of games) each: *the score was two all.* ~*n* **15 give one's all** to make the greatest possible effort.

Allah *n* the name of God in Islam.

allay *vb* to reduce (fear or anger).

all clear *n* a signal indicating that danger is over.

allegation *n* an unproved assertion or accusation.

allege *vb* **-leging, -leged** to state without proof.

alleged *adj* stated but not proved: *the spot where the alleged crime took place.* **allegedly** (al-**lej**-id-lee) *adv*

allegiance *n* loyalty or dedication to a person, cause, or belief.

allegory *n, pl* **-ries** a story, poem, or picture with an underlying meaning as well as the literal one. **allegorical** *adj* **allegorize** *or* **-rise** *vb*

allegretto *Music* ~*adv* **1** fairly quickly or briskly. ~*n, pl* **-tos 2** a piece or passage to be performed fairly quickly or briskly.

allegro *Music* ~*adv* **1** in a brisk lively manner. ~*n, pl* **-gros 2** a piece or passage to be performed in a brisk lively manner.

allele (al-**leel**) *n* any of two or more genes that are responsible for alternative characteristics, such as smooth or wrinkled seeds in peas.

alleluia *interj* praise the Lord!

allergen (**al**-ler-jen) *n* a substance capable of causing an allergic reaction. **allergenic** *adj*

allergic *adj* **1** having or caused by an allergy. **2 allergic to** *Informal* having a strong dislike of: *Father and son seemed to have been allergic to each other from the start.*

allergy *n, pl* **-gies 1** extreme sensitivity to a substance such as a food or pollen, which causes the body to react to any contact with it. **2** *Informal* a strong dislike for something.

alleviate *vb* **-ating, -ated** to lessen (pain or suffering). **alleviation** *n*

alley *n* **1** a narrow passage between or behind buildings. **2 a** a building containing lanes for tenpin bowling. **b** a long narrow wooden lane down which the ball is rolled in tenpin bowling. **3** a path in a garden, often lined with trees.

alleyway *n* a narrow passage with buildings or walls on both sides.

all found *adv* (of charges for accommodation) including meals, heating, and other living expenses.

Allhallows *n* same as **All Saints' Day.**

alliance *n* **1** the state of being allied. **2** a formal relationship between two or more countries or political parties to work together. **3** the countries or parties involved.

allied *adj* **1** united by a common aim or common characteristics: *the allied areas of telepathy and clairvoyance.* **2 Allied** relating to the countries that fought against Germany and Japan in the Second World War: *the Allied bombing of German cities.*

alligator *n* a large reptile of the southern US and China, similar to the crocodile but with a shorter broader snout.

all in *adj* **1** *Informal* exhausted. **2** (of wrestling) with no style forbidden. ~*adv* **3** with all expenses included.

alliteration *n* the use of the same sound at the start of words occurring together, as in *round the rugged rock the ragged rascal ran.* **alliterative** *adj*

allocate *vb* **-cating, -cated** to assign to someone or for a particular purpose. **allocation** *n*

allopathy (al-**lop**-ath-ee) *n Med* an orthodox method of treating disease, by using drugs that produce an effect opposite to the effect of the disease being treated, as contrasted with homeopathy. **allopathic** *adj*

allot *vb* **-lotting, -lotted** to assign as a share or for a particular purpose.

allotment *n* **1** *Brit* a small piece of land rented by a person to grow vegetables on. **2** a portion allotted. **3** distribution.

allotrope *n Chem* any of two or more physical forms in which an element can exist.

allotropy *n Chem* the existence of an element in two or more physical forms. **allotropic** *adj*

all-out *adj Informal* using one's maximum powers: *an all-out attack on inflation.*

THESAURUS

all *adj.* **1.** every bit of, the complete, the entire, the sum of, the totality of, the total of, the whole of **2.** each, each and every, every, every one of, every single **3.** complete, entire, full, greatest, perfect, total, utter **4. in all** altogether, completely, entirely, fully, totally, utterly, wholly

allegation accusation, affirmation, assertion, asseveration (*formal*), averment, avowal, charge, claim, declaration, deposition, plea, profession, statement

allege advance, affirm, assert, asseverate (*formal*), aver, avow, charge, claim, declare, depose, maintain, plead, profess, put forward, state

alleged affirmed, asserted, averred, declared, described, designated, ostensible, professed, purported, so-called, stated, supposed

allegorical emblematic, figurative, parabolic, symbolic, symbolizing

allegory emblem, fable, myth, parable, story, symbol, symbolism, tale

allergic 1. affected by, hypersensitive, sensitive, sensitized, susceptible **2. allergic to** *informal* antipathetic, averse, disinclined, hostile, loath, opposed

allergy 1. antipathy, hypersensitivity, sensitivity, susceptibility **2.** *informal* antipathy, aversion, disinclination, dislike, hostility, loathing, opposition

alley alleyway, backstreet, lane, passage, passageway, pathway, walk

alliance affiliation, affinity, agreement, association, coalition, combination, compact, concordat, confederacy, confederation, connection, federation, league, marriage, pact, partnership, treaty, union

allied affiliated, amalgamated, associated, bound, combined, confederate, connected, hand in glove (*informal*), in cahoots, in league, joined, joint, kindred, leagued, linked, married, related, unified, united, wed

allocate allot, apportion, appropriate, assign, budget, designate, earmark, mete, set aside, share out

allocation allotment, allowance, apportionment, appropriation, grant, lot, measure, portion, quota, ration, share, stint, stipend

allot allocate, apportion, appropriate, assign, budget, designate, earmark, mete, set aside, share out

allotment 1. kitchen garden, patch, plot, tract **2.** allocation, allowance, apportionment, appropriation, grant, lot, measure, portion, quota, ration, share, stint, stipend

all-out complete, determined, exhaustive, full, full-scale, maximum, optimum, outright, resolute, supreme, thorough, thoroughgoing, total, undivided, unlimited, unremitting, unrestrained, unstinted, utmost

allow 1. approve, authorize, bear, brook, endure, give leave, let, permit, put up with (*informal*), sanction, stand, suffer, tolerate **2.** allocate, allot, assign, deduct, give, grant, provide, remit, spare **3.** acknowledge, acquiesce, admit, concede, confess, grant, own **4. allow for** arrange for, consider, foresee, keep in mind, make allowances for, make concessions for, make provision

allow *vb* **1** to permit someone to do something. **2** to set aside: *I allowed plenty of time.* **3** to acknowledge (a point or claim). **4 allow for** to take into account. **allowable** *adj*

allowance *n* **1** an amount of money given at regular intervals. **2** (in Britain) an amount of a person's income that is not subject to income tax. **3 make allowances for a** to treat or judge someone less severely because he or she has special problems. **b** to take into account in one's plans.

alloy *n* **1** a mixture of two or more metals. *~vb* **2** to mix metals in order to obtain a substance with a desired property.

all-purpose *adj* useful for many purposes.

all right *adj* **1** acceptable or satisfactory: *Is everything all right?* **2** unharmed; safe: *I'm going to check if he's all right.* *~interj* **3** an expression of approval or agreement. *~adv* **4** satisfactorily. **5** safely. **6** without doubt: *it was him all right.*

all-round *adj* **1** having many skills; versatile: *an all-round player.* **2** of broad scope; comprehensive: *we cannot do without up-to-date and all-round training.*

all-rounder *n* a person with many skills and abilities.

All Saints' Day *n* a Christian festival celebrated on November 1 to honour all the saints.

All Souls' Day *n RC Church* a day of prayer (November 2) for the dead in purgatory.

allspice *n* a spice used in cooking, which comes from the berries of a tropical American tree.

all-time *adj Informal* unsurpassed at a particular time: *one of boxing's all-time greats.*

allude *vb* **-luding, -luded allude to** to refer indirectly to.

➤ *Allude* is followed by *to.* Be careful not to confuse this word with *elude* meaning "escape".

allure *n* attractiveness or appeal.

alluring *adj* extremely attractive.

allusion *n* an indirect reference.

➤ Be careful not to confuse *allusion* with *illusion* meaning "fallacy" or "fantasy".

alluvial *adj* **1** of or relating to alluvium. *~n* **2** same as **alluvium.**

alluvium *n, pl* **-via** a fertile soil consisting of mud, silt, and sand deposited by flowing water.

ally *n, pl* **-lies 1** a country, person, or group with an agreement to support another. *~vb* **-lies, -lying, -lied 2 ally oneself with** to agree to support another country, person, or group.

alma mater *n* the school, college, or university that one attended.

almanac *n* a yearly calendar with detailed information on matters like anniversaries and phases of the moon.

almighty *adj* **1** having power over everything. **2** *Informal* very great: *there was an almighty bang.* *~n* **3 the Almighty** God.

almond *n* an edible oval nut with a yellowish-brown shell, which grows on a small tree.

almoner *n Brit* a former name for a hospital social worker.

almost *adv* very nearly.

alms (**ahmz**) *pl n Old-fashioned* donations of money or goods to the poor.

almshouse *n Brit* (formerly) a house, financed by charity, which offered accommodation to the poor.

aloe *n* **1** a plant with fleshy spiny leaves. **2 aloes** a bitter drug made from aloe leaves.

aloe vera *n* a plant producing a juice which is used to treat skin and hair.

aloft *adv* **1** in the air. **2** *Naut* in the rigging of a ship.

alone *adj, adv* **1** without anyone or anything else. **2 leave someone** *or* **something alone** to refrain from annoying someone *or* interfering with something. **3 let alone** not to mention: *it looked inconceivable that he could run again, let alone be elected.*

along *prep* **1** over part or all of the length of: *we were going along the railway tracks.* *~adv* **2** moving forward: *they were roaring along at 40mph.* **3** in company with another or others: *let them go along for the ride.* **4 along with** together with: *I'm including the good days along with the bad.*

alongside *prep* **1** close beside. *~adv* **2** near the side of something.

➤ Avoid following *alongside* with *of.* Its use is unnecessary.

aloof *adj* distant or haughty in manner.

alopecia (al-loh-**pee**-sha) *n* loss of hair, usually due to illness.

aloud *adv* in an audible voice.

alp *n* **1** a high mountain. **2 the Alps** a high mountain range in S central Europe.

alpaca *n* **1** a South American mammal related to the

THESAURUS

for, plan for, provide for, set (something) aside for, take into account, take into consideration

allowable acceptable, admissible, all right, appropriate, approved, permissible, sanctionable, sufferable, suitable, tolerable

allowance allocation, allotment, amount, annuity, apportionment, grant, lot, measure, pension, portion, quota, ration, remittance, share, stint, stipend, subsidy

alloy **1.** *n.* admixture, amalgam, blend, combination, composite, compound, hybrid, meld, mixture **2.** *vb.* admix, amalgamate, blend, combine, compound, fuse, meld, mix

all right *adj.* **1.** acceptable, adequate, average, fair, O.K. *or* okay (*informal*), passable, satisfactory, standard, unobjectionable **2.** hale, healthy, safe, sound, unharmed, unimpaired, uninjured, well, whole *~adv.* **3.** acceptably, adequately, O.K. *or* okay (*informal*), passably, satisfactorily, unobjectionably, well enough

allure appeal, attraction, charm, enchantment, enticement, glamour, lure, persuasion, seductiveness, temptation

allusion casual remark, glance, hint, implication, indirect reference, innuendo, insinuation, intimation, mention, suggestion

ally **1.** *n.* abettor, accessory, accomplice, associate, coadjutor, collaborator, colleague, confederate, co-worker, friend, helper, partner **2.** *vb.* affiliate, associate, band together, collaborate, combine, confederate, connect, join, join forces, league, marry, unify, unite

almighty **1.** absolute, all-powerful, invincible, omnipotent, supreme, unlimited **2.** *informal* awful, desperate, enormous, excessive, great, intense, loud, severe, terrible

almost about, all but, approximately, as good as, close to, just about, nearly, not far from, not quite, on the brink of, practically, virtually, well-nigh

alone abandoned, apart, by itself, by oneself, deserted, desolate, detached, forlorn, forsaken, isolated, lonely, lonesome, only, separate, single, single-handed, sole, solitary, unaccompanied, unaided, unassisted, unattended, uncombined, unconnected, unescorted

aloof chilly, cold, cool, detached, distant, forbidding, formal, haughty, indifferent, remote, reserved, stand-

llama, with dark shaggy hair. **2** wool or cloth made from this hair.

alpenstock *n* a strong stick with an iron tip used by hikers and mountain climbers.

alpha *n* **1** the first letter in the Greek alphabet (Α, α). **2** *Brit* the highest grade in an examination or for a piece of academic work. **3 alpha and omega** the first and last.

alphabet *n* a set of letters in fixed conventional order, used in a writing system.

alphabetical *adj* in the conventional order of the letters of an alphabet. **alphabetically** *adv*

alphabetize *or* **-ise** *vb* **-izing, -ized** *or* **-ising, -ised** to put in alphabetical order. **alphabetization** *or* **-isation** *n*

alphanumeric *adj* consisting of alphabetical and numerical symbols.

alpha particle *n Physics* a positively charged particle, emitted during some radioactive transformations.

alpha ray *n Physics* a stream of alpha particles.

alpine *adj* **1** of high mountains. **2 Alpine** of the Alps. *~n* **3** a plant grown on or native to mountains.

alpinist *n* a mountain climber.

already *adv* **1** before the present time. **2** before an implied or expected time.

alright *adj, interj, adv Not universally accepted* same as **all right.**

➤ While this compact form is commonly acceptable, many people still regard it as an error and prefer *all right.*

Alsatian *n* a large wolflike dog.

also *adv* in addition; too.

also-ran *n* a loser in a race, competition, or election.

Alta. Alberta.

altar *n* **1** the table used for Communion in Christian churches. **2** a raised structure on which sacrifices are offered and religious rites performed.

altarpiece *n* a painting or a decorated screen set above and behind the altar in a Christian church.

alter *vb* to make or become different; change.

alteration *n* a change or modification.

altercation *n* a noisy argument.

alter ego *n* **1** a hidden side to one's personality. **2** a very close friend.

alternate *vb* **-nating, -nated 1** to occur by turns. **2** to interchange regularly or in succession. *~adj* **3** occurring by turns. **4** every second (one) of a series: *alternate days.* **5** being a second choice. **alternately** *adv* **alternation** *n*

alternate angles *pl n Geom* two angles at opposite ends and on opposite sides of a line intersecting two other lines.

alternating current *n* an electric current that reverses direction at frequent regular intervals.

alternative *n* **1** a possibility of choice between two or more things. **2** either or any of such choices. *~adj* **3** presenting a choice between two or more possibilities. **4** of a lifestyle etc. that is less conventional or materialistic than is usual. **alternatively** *adv*

➤ Although the strict meaning of *alternative,* "a choice between two things", is not usually observed nowadays, it is preferable to say *there are three choices* rather than *there are three alternatives.*

alternative energy *n* a form of energy obtained from natural resources like waves and wind.

alternative medicine *n* the treatment of disease by unconventional methods like homeopathy, and involving attention to the patient's emotional wellbeing.

alternator *n* an electrical machine that generates an alternating current.

although *conj* in spite of the fact that.

altimeter (al-**tim**-it-er) *n* an instrument that measures altitude.

altitude *n* height, esp. above sea level.

alto *n, pl* **-tos 1** short for **contralto. 2** the highest adult male voice. **3** a singer with an alto voice. **4** a musical instrument, for instance a saxophone, that is the second or third highest in its family. *~adj* **5** denoting such an instrument, singer, or voice: *an alto flute.*

altogether *adv* **1** completely: *an altogether different message.* **2** on the whole: *this is not altogether a bad thing.* **3** in total: *altogether, 25 aircraft took part. ~n* **4 in the altogether** *Informal* naked.

altruism *n* unselfish concern for the welfare of others. **altruist** *n* **altruistic** *adj*

alum *n Chem* a double sulphate of aluminium and potassium, used in manufacturing and in medicine.

aluminium *or US & Canad* **aluminum** *n Chem* a light malleable silvery-white metallic element that does not rust. Symbol: Al

aluminize *or* **-ise** *vb* **-nizing, -nized** *or* **-nising, -nised** to cover with aluminium.

alumnus (al-**lumm**-nuss) *or fem* **alumna** (al-**lumm**-na) *n, pl* **-ni** (-nie) *or* **-nae** (-nee) *Chiefly US & Canad* a graduate of a school or college.

alveolus (al-**vee**-ol-luss) *n, pl* **-li** (-lie) any small pit, cavity, or saclike dilation, such as a honeycomb cell, a tooth socket, or the tiny air sacs in the lungs.

always *adv* **1** without exception: *she was always at*

THESAURUS

offish, supercilious, unapproachable, unfriendly, uninterested, unresponsive, unsociable, unsympathetic

aloud audibly, clearly, distinctly, intelligibly, out loud, plainly

already as of now, at present, before now, by now, by that time, by then, by this time, even now, heretofore, just now, previously

also additionally, along with, and, as well, as well as, besides, further, furthermore, in addition, including, into the bargain, moreover, on top of that, plus, to boot, too

alter adapt, adjust, amend, change, convert, diversify, metamorphose, modify, recast, reform, remodel, reshape, revise, shift, transform, transmute, turn, vary

alteration adaptation, adjustment, amendment, change, conversion, difference, diversification, metamorphosis, modification, reformation, remodelling, reshaping, revision, shift, transformation, transmutation, variance, variation

alternate *vb.* **1.** act reciprocally, alter, change, fluctuate, follow in turn, follow one another, interchange, intersperse, oscillate, rotate, substitute, take turns, vary *~adj.* **2.** alternating, every other, every second, interchanging, rotating **3.** alternative, another, different, second, substitute

alternative 1. *n.* choice, option, other (*of two*), preference, recourse, selection, substitute **2.** *adj.* alternate, another, different, other, second, substitute

alternatively as an alternative, by way of alternative, if not, instead, on the other hand, or, otherwise

although albeit, despite the fact that, even if, even supposing, even though, notwithstanding, tho' (*U.S. or poetic*), though, while

altitude elevation, height, loftiness, peak, summit

altogether 1. absolutely, completely, fully, perfectly, quite, thoroughly, totally, utterly, wholly **2.** all in all, all things considered, as a whole, collectively, generally,

the top of her form in school work. **2** continually: *you're always shouting or whining.* **3** in any case: *they're all adults, they can always say no.*

alyssum *n* a garden plant with clusters of small white flowers.

Alzheimer's disease (**alts**-hime-erz) *n* a disorder of the brain resulting in a progressive decline in intellectual and physical abilities and eventual senility.

am *vb* (used with *I*) a form of the present tense of **be.**

Am *Chem* americium.

AM amplitude modulation.

Am. America(n).

a.m. before noon.

amah *n* (in the East, formerly) a nurse or maidservant.

amalgam *n* **1** a blend or combination. **2** an alloy of mercury with another metal: *dental amalgam.*

amalgamate *vb* **-ating, -mated 1** to combine or unite. **2** to alloy (a metal) with mercury. **amalgamation** *n*

amandla (a-**mand**-la) *n S African* a political slogan calling for power to the Black population.

amanuensis (am man-yew-**en**-siss) *n, pl* **-ses** (-seez) a person who copies manuscripts or takes dictation.

amaranth *n* **1** *Poetic* an imaginary flower that never fades. **2** a lily-like plant with small green, red, or purple flowers.

amaryllis *n* a lily-like plant with large red or white flowers and a long stalk.

amass *vb* to accumulate or collect: *the desire to amass wealth.*

amateur *n* **1** a person who engages in a sport or other activity as a pastime rather than as a profession. **2** a person unskilled in a subject or activity. *~adj* **3** doing something out of interest, not for money. **4** amateurish. **amateurism** *n*

amateurish *adj* lacking skill.

amatory *adj* of or relating to romantic or sexual love.

amaze *vb* **amazing, amazed** to fill with surprise; astonish. **amazement** *n* **amazing** *adj* **amazingly** *adv*

Amazon *n* **1** a strong and powerful woman. **2** *Greek myth* one of a race of women warriors of Scythia. **Amazonian** *adj*

ambassador *n* **1** a diplomat of the highest rank, sent to another country as permanent representative of his or her own country. **2** a representative or messenger: *he saw himself as an ambassador for the game.* **ambassadorial** *adj*

amber *n* **1** a yellow translucent fossilized resin, used in jewellery. *~adj* **2** brownish-yellow.

ambergris (**am**-ber-greece) *n* a waxy substance secreted by the sperm whale, which is used in making perfumes.

ambidextrous *adj* able to use both hands with equal ease.

ambience *or* **ambiance** *n* the atmosphere of a place.

ambient *adj* surrounding: *low ambient temperatures.*

ambiguity *n, pl* **-ties 1** the possibility of interpreting an expression in more than one way. **2** an ambiguous situation or expression: *the ambiguities of feminine identity.*

ambiguous *adj* having more than one possible interpretation. **ambiguously** *adv*

ambit *n* limits or boundary.

ambition *n* **1** strong desire for success. **2** something so desired; a goal.

ambitious *adj* **1** having a strong desire for success. **2** requiring great effort or ability: *ambitious plans.*

ambivalence (am-**biv**-a-lenss) *n* the state of feeling two conflicting emotions at the same time. **ambivalent** *adj*

amble *vb* **-bling, -bled 1** to walk at a leisurely pace. *~n* **2** a leisurely walk or pace.

ambrosia *n* **1** something delightful to taste or smell. **2** *Classical myth* the food of the gods.

ambulance *n* a motor vehicle designed to carry sick or injured people.

ambulatory *adj* **1** of or relating to walking. **2** able to walk. *~n, pl* **-ries 3** a place for walking in, such as a cloister.

ambush *n* **1** the act of waiting in a concealed position to make a surprise attack. **2** an attack from such a position. *~vb* **3** to attack suddenly from a concealed position.

THESAURUS

in general, *in toto,* on the whole **3.** all told, everything included, in all, in sum, *in toto,* taken together

always consistently, constantly, continually, eternally, ever, everlastingly, evermore, every time, forever, *in perpetuum,* invariably, perpetually, repeatedly, unceasingly, without exception

amalgamate alloy, ally, blend, coalesce, combine, commingle, compound, fuse, incorporate, integrate, intermix, meld, merge, mingle, unite

amalgamation admixture, alliance, alloy, amalgam, amalgamating, blend, coalition, combination, commingling, composite, compound, fusion, incorporation, integration, joining, meld, merger, mingling, mixing, mixture, union

amass accumulate, aggregate, assemble, collect, compile, garner, gather, heap up, hoard, pile up, rake up, scrape together

amateur dabbler, dilettante, layman, nonprofessional

amateurish amateur, bungling, clumsy, crude, inexpert, unaccomplished, unprofessional, unskilful

amaze alarm, astonish, astound, bewilder, bowl over (*informal*), confound, daze, dumbfound, electrify, flabbergast, shock, stagger, startle, stun, stupefy, surprise

amazement admiration, astonishment, bewilderment, confusion, marvel, perplexity, shock, stupefaction, surprise, wonder

ambassador agent, consul, deputy, diplomat, emissary, envoy, legate, minister, plenipotentiary, representative

ambiguity doubt, doubtfulness, dubiety, dubiousness, enigma, equivocacy, equivocality, equivocation, inconclusiveness, indefiniteness, indeterminateness, obscurity, puzzle, tergiversation, uncertainty, unclearness, vagueness

ambiguous cryptic, Delphic, doubtful, dubious, enigmatic, enigmatical, equivocal, inconclusive, indefinite, indeterminate, obscure, oracular, puzzling, uncertain, unclear, vague

ambition **1.** aspiration, avidity, desire, drive, eagerness, enterprise, get-up-and-go (*informal*), hankering, longing, striving, yearning, zeal **2.** aim, aspiration, desire, dream, end, goal, hope, intent, objective, purpose, wish

ambitious **1.** aspiring, avid, desirous, driving, eager, enterprising, hopeful, intent, purposeful, striving, zealous **2.** arduous, bold, challenging, demanding, difficult, elaborate, energetic, exacting, formidable, grandiose, hard, impressive, industrious, pretentious, severe, strenuous

ameliorate (am-**meal**-yor-rate) *vb* **-rating, -rated** to make (something) better. **amelioration** *n*

amen *interj* so be it: used at the end of a prayer.

amenable (a-**mean**-a-bl) *adj* likely or willing to cooperate.

amend *vb* to make small changes to something such as a piece of writing or a contract, in order to improve it.

amendment *n* an improvement or correction.

amends *pl n* **make amends for** to compensate for some injury or insult.

amenity *n, pl* **-ties** a useful or enjoyable feature: *all kinds of amenities including horse riding and golf.*

amenorrhoea *or esp US* **amenorrhea** (aim-men-or-**ree**-a) *n* abnormal absence of menstruation.

American *adj* **1** of the United States of America or the American continent. *~n* **2** a person from the United States of America or the American continent.

American football *n* a game similar to rugby, played by two teams of eleven players.

American Indian *n* **1** a member of any of the original peoples of America. *~adj* **2** of any of these peoples.

Americanism *n* an expression or custom that is characteristic of the people of the United States.

Americanize *or* **-ise** *vb* **-izing, -ized** *or* **-ising, -ised** to make American in outlook or form.

americium *n Chem* a white metallic element artificially produced from plutonium. Symbol: Am

amethyst (**am**-myth-ist) *n* **1** a purple or violet variety of quartz used as a gemstone. *~adj* **2** purple or violet.

Amharic *n* the official language of Ethiopia.

amiable *adj* having a pleasant nature; friendly. **amiability** *n* **amiably** *adv*

amicable *adj* characterized by friendliness: *ideally the parting should be amicable.* **amicability** *n* **amicably** *adv*

amid *or* **amidst** *prep* in the middle of; among.
➤ The meaning of *amid* overlaps with that of *among,* but the form *amidst* is old-fashioned. Nowadays use *amid* or *among.*

amide *n Chem* **1** any organic compound containing the group $-CONH_2$. **2** an inorganic compound having the general formula $M(NH_2)_x$, where M is a metal atom.

amidships *adv Naut* at, near, or towards the centre of a ship.

amine (am-**mean**) *n Chem* an organic base formed by replacing one or more of the hydrogen atoms of ammonia by organic groups.

amino acid (am-**mean**-oh) *n Chem* any of a group of organic compounds containing the **amino** group, $-NH_2$, and one or more carboxyl groups, $-COOH$, esp. one that is a component of protein.

amir (am-**meer**) *n* same as **emir.**

amiss *adv* **1** wrongly or badly: *anxious not to tread amiss.* **2 take something amiss** to be offended by something. *~adj* **3** wrong or faulty.

amity *n Formal* friendship.

ammeter *n* an instrument for measuring an electric current in amperes.

ammo *n Informal* ammunition.

ammonia *n* **1** a colourless strong-smelling gas containing hydrogen and nitrogen. **2** a solution of this in water.

ammonite *n* the fossilized spiral shell of an extinct sea creature.

ammonium *adj Chem* of or containing the chemical group NH_4- or the ion NH_4^+.

ammunition *n* **1** bullets, bombs, and shells that can be fired from or as a weapon. **2** facts that can be used in an argument.

amnesia *n* a partial or total loss of memory. **amnesiac** *adj, n*

amnesty *n, pl* **-ties 1** a general pardon for offences against a government. **2** a period during which a law is suspended, to allow people to confess to crime or give up weapons without fear of prosecution.

amniocentesis *n, pl* **-ses** removal of amniotic fluid from the womb of a pregnant woman in order to detect possible abnormalities in the fetus.

amnion *n, pl* **-nia** the innermost of two membranes enclosing an embryo. **amniotic** *adj*

amniotic fluid *n* the fluid surrounding the fetus in the womb.

amoeba *or US* **ameba** (am-**mee**-ba) *n, pl* **-bae** (-bee) *or* **-bas** a microscopic single-cell creature that is able to change its shape.

amok *or* **amuck** *adv* **run amok** to run about in a violent frenzy.

among *or* **amongst** *prep* **1** in the midst of: *she decided to dwell among the Greeks.* **2** in the group, class, or number of: *he is among the top trainers.* **3** to each of: *the stakes should be divided among the players.* **4** with one another within a group: *sort it out among*

THESAURUS

amble dawdle, meander, mosey (*informal*), ramble, saunter, stroll, walk, wander

ambush 1. *n.* concealment, cover, hiding, hiding place, lying in wait, retreat, shelter, trap, waylaying **2.** *vb.* ensnare, surprise, trap, waylay

amenable able to be influenced, acquiescent, agreeable, open, persuadable, responsive, susceptible, tractable

amend alter, better, change, correct, enhance, fix, improve, mend, modify, rectify, reform, remedy, repair, revise

amendment 1. alteration, amelioration, betterment, change, correction, emendation, enhancement, improvement, mending, modification, rectification, reform, remedy, repair, revision **2.** addendum, addition, adjunct, alteration, attachment, clarification

amends apology, atonement, compensation, expiation, indemnity, recompense, redress, reparation, requital, restitution, restoration, satisfaction

amenity advantage, comfort, convenience, facility, service

amiable affable, agreeable, attractive, benign, charming, cheerful, congenial, delightful, engaging, friendly, genial, good-humoured, good-natured, kind, kindly, likable *or* likeable, lovable, obliging, pleasant, pleasing, sociable, sweet-tempered, winning, winsome

amicable amiable, brotherly, civil, cordial, courteous, fraternal, friendly, good-humoured, harmonious, kind, kindly, neighbourly, peaceable, peaceful, polite, sociable

amid amidst, among, amongst, in the middle of, in the midst of, in the thick of, surrounded by

amiss 1. *adv.* **take something amiss** as an insult, as offensive **2.** *adj.* awry, confused, defective, erroneous, fallacious, false, faulty, improper, inaccurate, inappropriate, incorrect, mistaken, out of order, unsuitable, untoward, wrong

ammunition armaments, cartridges, explosives, materiel, munitions, powder, rounds, shells, shot, shot and shell

amnesty absolution, condonation, dispensation, forgiveness, general pardon, immunity, oblivion, remission (*of penalty*), reprieve

amok, amuck berserk, destructively, ferociously,

yourselves.
➤ *Among* is generally used when more than two things are mentioned: *It's hard to choose among friends.* The form *amongst* is rather old-fashioned.
amoral (aim-**mor**-ral) *adj* without moral standards or principles. **amorality** *n*
➤ *Amoral* should not be confused with *immoral,* "acting contrary to moral standards".
amorous *adj* feeling, displaying, or relating to sexual love or desire.
amorphous *adj* **1** lacking a definite shape. **2** of no recognizable character or type.
amortize *or* **-tise** *vb* **-tizing, -tized** *or* **-tising, -tised** *Finance* to pay off (a debt) gradually by periodic transfers to a sinking fund.
amount *n* **1** extent or quantity. *~vb* **2 amount to** to be equal or add up to.
amour *n* a secret love affair.
amour-propre (am-moor-**prop**-ra) *n* self-esteem.
amp *n* **1** an ampere. **2** *Informal* an amplifier.
amperage *n* the strength of an electric current measured in amperes.
ampere (**am**-pair) *n* the basic unit of electric current.
ampersand *n* the character &, meaning *and.*
➤ It is best to avoid using an *ampersand* (&) to replace the word *and* in formal writing
amphetamine (am-**fet**-am-mean) *n* a drug used as a stimulant.
amphibian *n* **1** an animal, such as a newt, frog, or toad, that lives on land but breeds in water. **2** a vehicle that can travel on both water and land.
amphibious *adj* **1** living or operating both on land and in or on water. **2** relating to a military attack launched from the sea against a shore.
amphitheatre *or US* **amphitheater** *n* a circular or oval building without a roof, in which tiers of seats rise from a central open arena.
amphora (**am**-for-ra) *n, pl* **-phorae** (-for-ree) an ancient Greek or Roman jar with two handles and a narrow neck.
ample *adj* **1** more than sufficient: *there is already ample evidence.* **2** large: *ample helpings of stewed pomegranates and pears.*
amplifier *n* an electronic device used to increase the strength of a current or sound signal.
amplify *vb* **-fies, -fying, -fied 1** *Electronics* to increase the strength of (a current or sound signal). **2** to explain in more detail. **3** to increase the size, extent, or effect of. **amplification** *n*
amplitude *n* **1** greatness of extent. **2** *Physics* the maximum displacement from the zero or mean position of a wave or oscillation.
amplitude modulation *n Electronics* a method of transmitting information using radio waves in which the amplitude of the carrier wave is varied in accordance with the amplitude of the input signal.
amply *adv* fully or generously: *she was amply rewarded for it.*
ampoule *or US* **ampule** *n Med* a small glass container in which liquids for injection are sealed.
ampulla *n, pl* **-pullae 1** *Anat* the dilated end part of certain tubes in the body. **2** *Christianity* a container for the wine and water, or the oil, used in church.
amputate *vb* **-tating, -tated** to cut off (a limb or part of a limb) for medical reasons. **amputation** *n*
amputee *n* a person who has had a limb amputated.
amuck *adv* same as **amok.**
amulet *n* a trinket or jewel worn as a protection against evil.
amuse *vb* **amusing, amused 1** to cause to laugh or smile. **2** to entertain or keep interested. **amusing** *adj* **amusingly** *adv*
amusement *n* **1** the state of being amused. **2** something that amuses or entertains someone.
amusement arcade *n* a large room with coin-operated electronic games and fruit machines.
amusement park *n* a large open-air entertainment area with rides and stalls.
amylase *n* an enzyme present in saliva that helps to change starch into sugar.
an *adj* (*indefinite article*) same as **a:** used before an initial vowel sound: *an old man; an hour.*
an- *prefix* See **a-**.
➤ This form of the indefinite article is also used with abbreviations which have a vowel sound when read aloud: *an MA.* It is old-fashioned to use *an* before words like *hotel* or *historic.*
Anabaptist *n* **1** a member of a 16th-century Protestant movement that believed in adult baptism. *~adj* **2** of this movement.
anabolic steroid *n* a synthetic steroid hormone used to stimulate muscle and bone growth.
anabolism *n Biol* a metabolic process in which body tissues are synthesized from food.

THESAURUS

frenziedly, in a frenzy, insanely, madly, maniacally, murderously, savagely, uncontrollably, violently, wildly
among, amongst 1. amid, amidst, in association with, in the middle of, in the midst of, in the thick of, midst, surrounded by, together with, with **2.** in the class of, in the company of, in the group of, in the number of, out of **3.** between, to each of **4.** by all of, by the joint action of, by the whole of, mutually, with one another
amorous affectionate, amatory, ardent, attached, doting, enamoured, erotic, fond, impassioned, in love, lovesick, loving, lustful, passionate, tender
amount 1. *n.* aggregate, bulk, entirety, expanse, extent, lot, magnitude, mass, measure, number, quantity, sum, sum total, supply, total, volume, whole **2.** *vb.* **amount to** add up to, aggregate, become, come to, develop into, equal, grow, mean, purport, total
ample 1. abounding, abundant, bountiful, copious, enough and to spare, generous, lavish, liberal, plenteous, plentiful, plenty, profuse, rich, unrestricted **2.** big, broad, capacious, commodious, expansive, extensive, full, great, large, roomy, spacious, substantial, voluminous, wide
amplify 1. elaborate, expatiate (*formal*), flesh out, go into detail **2.** augment, boost, deepen, develop, dilate, enlarge, expand, extend, heighten, increase, intensify, lengthen, magnify, raise, strengthen, stretch, supplement, widen
amply abundantly, bountifully, capaciously, completely, copiously, extensively, fully, generously, greatly, lavishly, liberally, plenteously, plentifully, profusely, richly, substantially, thoroughly, unstintingly, well, with a blank cheque, with a free hand, without stinting
amuck *see* AMOK
amuse 1. charm, cheer, delight, enliven, gladden, gratify, please, tickle **2.** divert, entertain, interest, occupy, please, regale
amusement 1. beguilement, cheer, delight, diversion, enjoyment, entertainment, fun, gladdening, gratification, hilarity, interest, laughter, merriment, mirth, pleasing, pleasure, recreation, regalement, sport **2.** distraction, diversion, entertainment, game, hobby, joke, lark, pastime, prank, recreation, sport
amusing 1. charming, cheerful, cheering, comical,

anachronism (an-**nak**-kron-iz-zum) *n* **1** the representation of something in a historical context in which it could not have occurred or existed. **2** a person or thing that seems to belong to another time. **anachronistic** *adj*

anaconda *n* a large S American snake which squeezes its prey to death.

anaemia *or US* **anemia** (an-**neem**-ee-a) *n* a deficiency of red blood cells or their haemoglobin content, resulting in paleness and lack of energy.

anaemic *or US* **anemic** *adj* **1** having anaemia. **2** pale and sickly-looking. **3** lacking vitality.

anaerobe *n Biol* an organism that does not require oxygen. **anaerobic** *adj*

anaesthesia *or US* **anesthesia** (an-niss-**theez**-ee-a) *n* loss of bodily feeling caused by disease or accident or by drugs such as ether: called **general anaesthesia** when consciousness is lost and **local anaesthesia** when only a specific area of the body is involved.

anaesthetic *or US* **anesthetic** (an-niss-**thet**-ik) *n* **1** a substance that causes anaesthesia. *~adj* **2** causing anaesthesia.

anaesthetist (an-**neess**-thet-ist) *n Brit* a doctor who administers anaesthetics.

anaesthetize, anaesthetise *or US* **anesthetize** *vb* **-tizing, -tized** *or* **-tising, -tised** to cause to feel no pain by administering an anaesthetic.

Anaglypta *n Trademark* a thick embossed wallpaper, designed to be painted.

anagram *n* a word or phrase made by rearranging the letters of another word or phrase.

anal (**ain**-al) *adj* of or relating to the anus.

analgesia *n* the absence of pain.

analgesic (an-nal-**jeez**-ik) *n* **1** a drug that relieves pain. *~adj* **2** pain-relieving.

analog *n US & computers* same as **analogue.**

analogize *or* **-gise** *vb* **-gizing, -gized** *or* **-gising, -gised 1** to use analogy in argument. **2** to reveal analogy between (one thing and another).

analogous *adj* similar in some respects.

analogue *or US* **analog** *n* **1** a physical object or quantity used to measure or represent another quantity. **2** something that is analogous to something else. *~adj* **3** displaying information by means of a dial: *analogue speedometers.*

analogy *n, pl* **-gies 1** a similarity, usually in a limited number of features. **2** a comparison made to show such a similarity. **analogical** *adj*

analyse *or US* **-lyze** (**an**-nal-lize) *vb* **-lysing, -lysed** *or* **-lyzing, -lyzed 1** to examine (something) in detail in order to discover its meaning or essential features. **2** to break (something) down into its components. **3** to psychoanalyse (someone).

analysis (an-**nal**-liss-iss) *n, pl* **-ses** (-seez) **1** the separation of a whole into its parts for study or interpretation. **2** a statement of the results of this. **3** short for **psychoanalysis.**

analyst *n* **1** a person who is skilled in analysis. **2** a psychoanalyst.

analytical *or* **analytic** *adj* relating to or using analysis. **analytically** *adv*

anarchism *n* a doctrine advocating the abolition of government and its replacement by a social system based on voluntary cooperation.

anarchist *n* **1** a person who advocates anarchism. **2** a person who causes disorder or upheaval. **anarchistic** *adj*

anarchy (**an**-ark-ee) *n* **1** general lawlessness and disorder. **2** the absence of government. **anarchic** *adj*

anastigmat *n* a lens corrected for astigmatism. **anastigmatic** *adj*

anathema (an-**nath**-im-a) *n* a detested person or thing: *the very colour was anathema to him.*

anathematize *or* **-tise** *vb* **-tizing, -tized** *or* **-tising, -tised** to curse: *he anathematized the world in general.*

anatomist *n* an expert in anatomy.

anatomy *n, pl* **-mies 1** the science of the physical structure of animals and plants. **2** the structure of an animal or plant. **3** *Informal* a person's body: *the male anatomy.* **4** a detailed analysis: *an anatomy of the massacre.* **anatomical** *adj*

ANC African National Congress: South African political movement opposed to apartheid.

ancestor *n* **1** a person in former times from whom one is descended. **2** a forerunner: *the immediate ancestor of rock and roll is rhythm and blues.*

ancestral *adj* of or inherited from ancestors.

ancestry *n, pl* **-tries 1** family descent: *of Japanese ancestry.* **2** origin or roots: *a vehicle whose ancestry dated back to the 1950s.*

THESAURUS

delightful, droll, enjoyable, facetious, funny, gladdening, gratifying, humorous, jocular, laughable, lively, merry, pleasant, pleasing, rib-tickling, witty **2.** diverting, entertaining, interesting, pleasing

anaemic 1. ashen, bloodless, colourless, pale, pallid, sickly, wan **2.** bloodless, characterless, dull, enervated, feeble, frail, infirm, weak

anaesthetic 1. *n.* analgesic, anodyne, narcotic, opiate, painkiller, sedative, soporific **2.** *adj.* analgesic, anodyne, deadening, dulling, narcotic, numbing, opiate, pain-killing, sedative, sleep-inducing, soporific

analogy agreement, comparison, correlation, correspondence, equivalence, homology, likeness, parallel, relation, resemblance, similarity, similitude

analyse 1. assay, estimate, evaluate, examine, interpret, investigate, judge, research, test, work over **2.** anatomize, break down, consider, dissect, dissolve, divide, resolve, separate, study, think through

analysis 1. anatomization, anatomy, assay, breakdown, dissection, dissolution, division, enquiry, examination, investigation, perusal, resolution, scrutiny, separation, sifting, test **2.** estimation, evaluation, finding, interpretation, judgment, opinion, reasoning, study

analytical, analytic detailed, diagnostic, discrete, dissecting, explanatory, expository, inquiring, inquisitive, interpretative, interpretive, investigative, logical, organized, problem-solving, questioning, rational, searching, studious, systematic, testing

anarchist insurgent, nihilist, rebel, revolutionary, terrorist

anarchy chaos, confusion, disorder, disorganization, lawlessness, misgovernment, misrule, rebellion, revolution, riot

anathema abomination, bane, *bête noire,* bugbear, enemy, pariah

anathematize abominate, ban, condemn, curse, damn, denounce, excommunicate, execrate, imprecate, proscribe

anatomy 1. build, composition, frame, framework, make-up, structure **2.** analysis, dismemberment, dissection, division, enquiry, examination, investigation, study

ancestor forebear, forefather, forerunner, precursor, predecessor, progenitor

anchor *n* **1** a hooked device attached to a boat by a cable and dropped overboard to fasten the boat to the sea bottom. **2** a source of stability or security: *a spiritual anchor.* ~*vb* **3** to use an anchor to hold (a boat) in one place. **4** to fasten securely: *we anchored his wheelchair to a huge stone.*

anchorage *n* a place where boats can be anchored.

anchorite *n* a person who chooses to live in isolation for religious reasons.

anchorman *or* **anchorwoman** *n* **1** a broadcaster in a central studio, who links up and presents items from outside camera units and reporters in other studios. **2** the last person to compete in a relay team.

anchovy (**an**-chov-ee) *n, pl* **-vies** a small marine food fish with a salty taste.

ancien régime (**on**-syan ray-**zheem**) *n* **1** the political and social system of France before the 1789 Revolution. **2** a former system.

ancient *adj* **1** dating from very long ago. **2** very old. **3** of the far past, esp. before the collapse of the Western Roman Empire (476 AD). ~*n* **4 ancients** people who lived very long ago, such as the Romans and Greeks.

ancillary *adj* **1** supporting the main work of an organization: *hospital ancillary workers.* **2** used as an extra or supplement: *I had a small ancillary sleeping tent.*

and *conj* **1** in addition to: *plants and birds.* **2** as a consequence: *she fell downstairs and broke her neck.* **3** afterwards: *she excused herself and left.* **4** used for emphasis or to indicate repetition or continuity: *they called again and again.* **5** used to express a contrast between instances of something: *there are jobs and jobs.* **6** *Informal* used in place of *to* in infinitives after verbs such as *try, go,* and *come: come and see us again.*

andante (an-**dan**-tay) *Music* ~*adv* **1** moderately slowly. ~*n* **2** a passage or piece to be performed moderately slowly.

andantino (an-dan-**tee**-noh) *Music* ~*adv* **1** slightly faster than andante. ~*n, pl* **-nos 2** a passage or piece to be performed in this manner.

andiron *n* either of a pair of metal stands for supporting logs in a fireplace.

and/or *conj Not universally accepted* either one or the other or both.

➤ Avoid using *and/or* where *or* alone will do. Its use generally suggests commercial and official correspondence.

androgynous *adj* having both male and female characteristics.

android *n* a robot resembling a human being.

anecdote *n* a short amusing account of an incident. **anecdotal** *adj*

anemia *n US* anaemia.

anemometer *n* an instrument for recording wind speed.

anemone (an-**nem**-on-ee) *n* a flowering plant with white, purple, or red flowers.

aneroid barometer *n* a device for measuring air pressure, consisting of a partially evacuated chamber, in which variations in pressure cause a pointer on the lid to move.

anesthesia *n US* anaesthesia.

aneurysm *or* **aneurism** (**an**-new-riz-zum) *n Med* a permanent swelling of a blood vessel.

anew *adv* **1** once more. **2** in a different way.

angel *n* **1** a spiritual being believed to be an attendant or messenger of God. **2** a conventional representation of an angel as a human being with wings. **3** *Informal* a person who is kind, pure, or beautiful. **4** *Informal* an investor in a theatrical production.

angel cake *or esp US* **angel food cake** *n* a very light sponge cake.

angelfish *n, pl* **-fish** *or* **-fishes** a South American aquarium fish with large fins.

angelic *adj* **1** very kind, pure, or beautiful. **2** of or relating to angels. **angelically** *adv*

angelica (an-**jell**-ik-a) *n* a plant whose candied stalks are used in cookery.

Angelus (**an**-jell-uss) *n RC Church* **1** prayers recited in the morning, at midday, and in the evening. **2** the bell signalling the times of these prayers.

anger *n* **1** a feeling of extreme annoyance or displeasure. ~*vb* **2** to make (someone) angry.

angina (an-**jine**-a) *or* **angina pectoris** (**peck**-tor-riss) *n* a sudden intense chest pain caused by momentary lack of adequate blood supply to the heart muscle.

angle[1] *n* **1** the space between or shape formed by two straight lines or surfaces that meet. **2** the divergence between two such lines or surfaces, measured in degrees. **3** a recess or corner. **4** point of view. ~*vb* **-gling, -gled 5** to move in or place at an angle. **6** to write (an article) from a particular point of view.

angle[2] *vb* **-gling, -gled 1** to fish with a hook and line. **2 angle for** to try to get by hinting: *he's just angling for sympathy.*

angler *n* a person who fishes with a hook and line.

Angles *pl n* a race from N Germany who settled in E and N England in the 5th and 6th centuries AD.

Anglican *adj* **1** of or relating to the Church of England. ~*n* **2** a member of the Anglican Church. **Anglicanism** *n*

THESAURUS

ancestry ancestors, antecedents, blood, derivation, descent, extraction, family, forebears, forefathers, genealogy, house, line, lineage, origin, parentage, pedigree, progenitors, race, stock

ancient aged, age-old, antediluvian, antiquated, antique, archaic, bygone, early, hoary, obsolete, old, olden, old-fashioned, outmoded, out-of-date, primeval, primordial, superannuated, timeworn

ancillary accessory, additional, auxiliary, contributory, extra, secondary, subordinate, subsidiary, supplementary

and along with, also, as well as, furthermore, in addition to, including, moreover, plus, together with

anecdote reminiscence, short story, sketch, story, tale, urban legend, yarn

anew afresh, again, another time, from scratch, from the beginning, once again, once more, over again

angel 1. archangel, cherub, divine messenger, guardian spirit, seraph, spiritual being **2.** *informal* beauty, darling, dear, dream, gem, ideal, jewel, paragon, saint, treasure

angelic 1. adorable, beatific, beautiful, entrancing, innocent, lovely, pure, saintly, virtuous **2.** celestial, cherubic, ethereal, heavenly, seraphic

anger 1. *n.* annoyance, antagonism, choler, displeasure, exasperation, fury, ill humour, ill temper, indignation, ire, irritability, irritation, outrage, passion, pique, rage, resentment, spleen, temper, vexation, wrath **2.** *vb.* affront, aggravate (*informal*), annoy, antagonize, be on one's back (*slang*), displease, enrage, exasperate, excite, fret, gall, get in one's hair (*informal*), get on one's nerves (*informal*), hassle (*informal*), incense, infuriate, irritate, madden, nark (*slang*), nettle, offend, outrage, pique, provoke, rile, vex

angle[1] **1.** bend, corner, crook, crotch, cusp, edge, elbow, intersection, knee, nook, point **2.** approach,

Anglicism *n* an expression or custom that is peculiar to the English.

anglicize *or* **-cise** *vb* **-cizing, -cized** *or* **-cising, -cised** to make or become English in outlook or form.

angling *n* the art or sport of fishing with a hook and line.

Anglo *n, pl* **-glos 1** *US* a White inhabitant of the US who is not of Latin extraction. **2** *Canad* an English-speaking Canadian whose ancestors came from Britain or Ireland.

Anglo- *combining form* English or British: *the Anglo-Irish agreement.*

Anglo-French *adj* **1** of England and France. **2** of the Anglo-French language. *~n* **3** the Norman-French language of medieval England.

Anglo-Indian *adj* **1** of England and India. **2** denoting or relating to Anglo-Indians. *~n* **3** a person of mixed British and Indian descent. **4** an English person who has lived for a long time in India.

Anglo-Norman *adj* **1** of or relating to the Norman conquerors of England or their language. *~n* **2** a Norman inhabitant of England after 1066. **3** the Anglo-French language.

Anglophile *n* a person who admires England or the English.

Anglo-Saxon *n* **1** a member of any of the West Germanic tribes that settled in Britain from the 5th century AD. **2** any White person whose native language is English. **3** same as **Old English. 4** *Informal* plain, blunt, and often rude English. *~adj* **5** of the Anglo-Saxons or the Old English language. **6** of the White Protestant culture of Britain and the US.

angora *n* **1** a variety of goat, cat, or rabbit with long silky hair. **2** the hair of the angora goat or rabbit. **3** cloth made from this hair.

Angostura Bitters *pl n Trademark* a bitter tonic, used as a flavouring in alcoholic drinks.

angry *adj* **-grier, -griest 1** feeling or expressing annoyance or rage. **2** severely inflamed: *he had angry welts on his forehead.* **3** dark and stormy: *angry waves.* **angrily** *adv*

angst *n* a feeling of anxiety.

angstrom *n* a unit of length equal to 10^{-10} metre, used to measure wavelengths.

anguish *n* great mental pain.

anguished *adj* feeling or showing great mental pain: *anguished cries.*

angular *adj* **1** lean and bony: *his angular face.* **2** having an angle or angles. **3** measured by an angle: *angular momentum.* **angularity** *n*

anhydrous *adj Chem* containing no water.

anil *n* a West Indian shrub which is a source of indigo.

aniline *n Chem* a colourless oily poisonous liquid, obtained from coal tar and used for making dyes, plastics, and explosives.

animal *n* **1** *Zool* any living being that is capable of voluntary movement and possesses specialized sense organs. **2** any living being other than a human being. **3** any living being with four legs. **4** a cruel or coarse person. **5** *Facetious* a person or thing: *there's no such animal.* *~adj* **6** of or from animals. **7** of or relating to physical needs or desires.

animalcule *n* a microscopic animal.

animal husbandry *n* the science of breeding, rearing, and caring for farm animals.

animalism *n* **1** preoccupation with physical matters; sensuality. **2** the doctrine that human beings lack a spiritual nature.

animality *n* **1** the animal instincts of human beings. **2** the state of being an animal.

animalize *or* **-ise** *vb* **-izing, -ized** *or* **-ising, -ised** to make (a person) brutal or sensual.

animal magnetism *n* the quality of being sexually attractive.

animal rights *pl n* the rights of animals to be protected from human abuse.

animal spirits *pl n* outgoing and boisterous enthusiasm.

animate *vb* **-mating, -mated 1** to give life to. **2** to make lively. **3** to produce (a story) as an animated cartoon. *~adj* **4** having life.

animated *adj* **1** interesting and lively. **2** (of a cartoon) made by using animation. **animatedly** *adv*

animated cartoon *n* a film produced by photographing a series of gradually changing drawings, which give the illusion of movement when the series is projected rapidly.

animation *n* **1** the techniques used in the production of animated cartoons. **2** liveliness and enthusiasm: *there's an animation in her that is new.*

animator *n* a person who makes animated cartoons.

animism *n* the belief that natural objects possess souls. **animist** *n, adj* **animistic** *adj*

animosity *n, pl* **-ties** a powerful dislike or hostility.

animus *n* intense dislike; hatred.

anion (**an**-eye-on) *n* an ion with negative charge. **anionic** *adj*

anise (**an**-niss) *n* a Mediterranean plant with liquorice-flavoured seeds.

THESAURUS

aspect, outlook, perspective, point of view, position, side, slant, standpoint, viewpoint

angle² cast, fish

angry annoyed, antagonized, choleric, cross, displeased, enraged, exasperated, furious, hacked (off) (*U.S. slang*), heated, hot, hot under the collar (*informal*), ill-tempered, incensed, indignant, infuriated, irascible, irate, ireful, irritable, irritated, mad (*informal*), nettled, outraged, passionate, piqued, pissed off (*taboo slang*), provoked, raging, resentful, riled, splenetic, tumultuous, uptight (*informal*), wrathful

anguish agony, distress, grief, heartache, heartbreak, misery, pain, pang, sorrow, suffering, throe, torment, torture, woe

angular bony, gaunt, lank, lanky, lean, rangy, rawboned, scrawny, skinny, spare

animal *n.* **1.** beast, brute, creature **2.** *Applied to a person* barbarian, beast, brute, monster, savage, wild man *~adj.* **3.** bestial, bodily, brutish, carnal, fleshly, gross, physical, sensual

animate 1. *vb.* activate, embolden, encourage, energize, enliven, excite, fire, gladden, impel, incite, inspire, inspirit, instigate, invigorate, kindle, move, prod, quicken, revive, rouse, spark, spur, stimulate, stir, urge, vitalize, vivify **2.** *adj.* alive, breathing, live, living, moving

animated active, airy, ardent, brisk, buoyant, dynamic, ebullient, elated, energetic, enthusiastic, excited, fervent, gay, lively, passionate, quick, sparky, spirited, sprightly, vibrant, vigorous, vital, vivacious, vivid, zealous, zestful

animation action, activity, airiness, ardour, brio, briskness, buoyancy, dynamism, ebullience, elation, energy, enthusiasm, excitement, exhilaration, fervour, gaiety, high spirits, life, liveliness, passion, pep, pizzazz *or* pizazz (*informal*), sparkle, spirit, sprightliness, verve, vibrancy, vigour, vitality, vivacity, zeal, zest, zing (*informal*)

aniseed *n* the liquorice-flavoured seeds of the anise plant, used for flavouring.

ankh *n* a T-shaped cross with a loop on the top, which symbolized eternal life in ancient Egypt.

ankle *n* **1** the joint connecting the leg and the foot. **2** the part of the leg just above the foot.

anklet *n* an ornamental chain worn round the ankle.

ankylosis (ang-kill-**loh**-siss) *n* abnormal immobility of a joint, caused by a fibrous growth within the joint.

anna *n* a former Indian coin worth one sixteenth of a rupee.

annals *pl n* **1** yearly records of events. **2** regular reports of the work of a society or other organization. **annalist** *n*

anneal *vb* to toughen (glass or metal) by heat treatment.

annelid *n* a worm with a segmented body, such as the earthworm.

annex *vb* **1** to seize (territory) by conquest or occupation. **2** to take without permission. **3** to join or add (something) to something larger. **annexation** *n*

annexe *or esp US* **annex** *n* **1** an extension to a main building. **2** a building used as an addition to a main one nearby.

annihilate *vb* **-lating, -lated 1** to destroy (a place or a group of people) completely. **2** *Informal* to defeat totally in an argument or a contest. **annihilation** *n*

anniversary *n, pl* **-ries 1** the date on which an event, such as a wedding, occurred in some previous year. **2** the celebration of this.

anno Domini *adv* in the year of our Lord.

annotate *vb* **-tating, -tated** to add critical or explanatory notes to a written work. **annotation** *n*

announce *vb* **-nouncing, -nounced 1** to make known publicly. **2** to proclaim. **3** to declare the arrival of (a person). **4** to be a sign of: *snowdrops announced the arrival of spring.* **announcement** *n*

announcer *n* a person who introduces programmes on radio or television.

annoy *vb* **1** to irritate or displease. **2** to harass sexually. **annoyance** *n* **annoying** *adj*

annual *adj* **1** occurring or done once a year: *the Labour Party's annual conference.* **2** lasting for a year: *the annual subscription is £42 a year.* ~*n* **3** a plant that completes its life cycle in one year. **4** a book published once every year. **annually** *adv*

annualize *or* **-ise** *vb* **-izing, -ized** *or* **-ising, -ised** to calculate (a rate) for or as if for a year.

annuity *n, pl* **-ties** a fixed sum payable at specified intervals over a period.

annul *vb* **-nulling, -nulled** to declare (a contract or marriage) invalid.

annular (**an**-new-lar) *adj* ring-shaped.

annular eclipse *n* an eclipse of the sun in which a ring of sunlight can be seen surrounding the shadow of the moon.

annulate (**an**-new-lit) *adj* having, composed of, or marked with rings.

annulment *n* the formal declaration that a contract or marriage is invalid.

Annunciation *n* **1 the Annunciation** the announcement by the angel Gabriel to the Virgin Mary of her conception of Christ. **2** the festival commemorating this, on March 25 (Lady Day).

anode *n Electronics* the positive electrode in an electrolytic cell or in an electronic valve or tube.

anodize *or* **-dise** *vb* **-dizing, -dized** *or* **-dising, -dised** *Chem* to coat (a metal) with a protective oxide film by electrolysis.

THESAURUS

animosity acrimony, animus, antagonism, antipathy, bad blood, bitterness, enmity, hate, hatred, hostility, ill will, malevolence, malice, malignity, rancour, resentment, virulence

annals accounts, archives, chronicles, history, journals, memorials, records, registers

annex 1. acquire, appropriate, arrogate, conquer, expropriate, occupy, seize, take over 2. add, adjoin, affix, append, attach, connect, fasten, join, subjoin, tack, unite

annexe extension, wing

annihilate abolish, destroy, eradicate, erase, exterminate, extinguish, extirpate, liquidate, nullify, obliterate, root out, wipe out

annihilation abolition, destruction, eradication, erasure, extermination, extinction, extinguishing, extirpation, liquidation, nullification, obliteration, rooting out, wiping out

annotate commentate, comment on, elucidate, explain, footnote, gloss, illustrate, interpret, make observations, note

annotation comment, commentary, elucidation, exegesis, explanation, explication, footnote, gloss, illustration, interpretation, note, observation

announce 1. advertise, blow wide open (*slang*), disclose, divulge, give out, intimate, make known, propound, publish, report, reveal, tell 2. broadcast, declare, proclaim, promulgate 3. augur, betoken, foretell, harbinger, herald, portend, presage, signal, signify

announcement advertisement, broadcast, bulletin, communiqué, declaration, disclosure, divulgence, intimation, proclamation, promulgation, publication, report, revelation, statement

announcer anchor man, broadcaster, commentator, master of ceremonies, newscaster, news reader, reporter

annoy aggravate (*informal*), anger, badger, bedevil, be on one's back (*slang*), bore, bother, bug (*informal*), displease, disturb, exasperate, gall, get (*informal*), get in one's hair (*informal*), get on one's nerves (*informal*), harass, harry, hassle (*informal*), incommode, irk, irritate, madden, molest, nark (*slang*), needle (*informal*), nettle, peeve, pester, plague, provoke, rile, ruffle, tease, trouble, vex

annoyance 1. aggravation, anger, bedevilment, bother, displeasure, disturbance, exasperation, harassment, hassle (*informal*), irritation, nuisance, provocation, trouble, vexation 2. bind (*informal*), bore, bother, drag (*informal*), gall, nuisance, pain (*informal*), pain in the arse (*taboo informal*), pain in the neck (*informal*), pest, plague, tease

annoying aggravating, bedevilling, boring, bothersome, displeasing, disturbing, exasperating, galling, harassing, irksome, irritating, maddening, peeving (*informal*), provoking, teasing, troublesome, vexatious

annual 1. once a year, yearly 2. yearlong

annually by the year, each year, every year, once a year, per annum, per year, year after year, yearly

annul abolish, abrogate, cancel, countermand, declare *or* render null and void, invalidate, negate, nullify, obviate, recall, repeal, rescind, retract, reverse, revoke, void

annulment abolition, abrogation, cancellation, countermanding, invalidation, negation, nullification, recall, repeal, rescindment, rescission, retraction, reversal, revocation, voiding

anodyne 1. *n.* analgesic, narcotic, painkiller, painreliever, palliative 2. *adj.* analgesic, deadening, dulling,

anodyne *n* **1** something that relieves pain or distress. *~adj* **2** neutral. **3** capable of relieving pain or distress.
anoint *vb* to smear with oil as a sign of consecration.
anointing of the sick *n RC Church* a sacrament in which a person who is dying is anointed by a priest.
anomalous *adj* different from the normal or usual order or type.
anomaly (an-**nom**-a-lee) *n, pl* **-lies** something that deviates from the normal; an irregularity.
anomie *or* **anomy** (**an**-oh-mee) *n Sociol* lack of social or moral standards.
anon *adv Old-fashioned or informal* soon: *you shall see him anon.*
anon. anonymous.
anonymous *adj* **1** by someone whose name is unknown or withheld: *an anonymous letter.* **2** having no known name: *an anonymous writer.* **3** lacking distinguishing characteristics: *an anonymous little town.* **anonymity** *n*
anorak *n* a waterproof hip-length jacket with a hood.
anorexia *or* **anorexia nervosa** *n* a psychological disorder characterized by fear of becoming fat and refusal to eat. **anorexic** *adj, n*
another *adj* **1** one more: *they don't have the right to demand another chance.* **2** different: *you'll have to find another excuse.* *~pron* **3** one more: *help yourself to another.* **4** a different one: *one way or another.*
answer *vb* **1** to reply or respond (to) by word or act. **2** to be responsible (to a person). **3** to reply correctly to (a question). **4** to respond or react: *a dog that answers to the name of Pugg.* **5** to meet the requirements of. **6** to give a defence of (a charge). *~n* **7** a reply to a question, request, letter, or article. **8** a solution to a problem. **9** a reaction or response.
answerable *adj* **answerable for** *or* **to** responsible for or accountable to.
answer back *vb* to reply rudely (to).
answering machine *n* a device for answering a telephone automatically and recording messages.
ant *n* a small often wingless insect, living in highly organized colonies.
antacid *Chem ~n* **1** a substance used to treat acidity in the stomach. *~adj* **2** having the properties of this substance.
antagonism *n* openly expressed hostility.
antagonist *n* an opponent or adversary. **antagonistic** *adj*
antagonize *or* **-nise** *vb* **-nizing, -nized** *or* **-nising, -nised** to arouse hostility in: *it was not prudent to antagonize a hired killer.*
antalkali (ant-**alk**-a-lie) *n Chem* a substance that neutralizes alkalis.
Antarctic *n* **1 the Antarctic** the area around the South Pole. *~adj* **2** of this region.
Antarctic Circle *n* the imaginary circle around the earth at latitude 66° 32′S.
ante *n* **1** the stake put up before the deal in poker by the players. **2** *Informal* a sum of money representing a person's share. *~vb* **-teing, -ted** *or* **-teed** **3** to place (one's stake) in poker. **4 ante up** *Informal* to pay.
ante- *prefix* before in time or position: *antediluvian; antechamber.*
anteater *n* a mammal with a long snout used for eating termites.
antecedent *n* **1** an event or circumstance that happens or exists before another. **2** *Grammar* a word or phrase to which a relative pronoun, such as *who*, refers. **3 antecedents** a person's ancestors and past history. *~adj* **4** preceding in time or order.
antechamber *n* an anteroom.
antedate *vb* **-dating, -dated** **1** to be or occur at an earlier date than. **2** to give (something) a date that is earlier than the actual date.
antediluvian *adj* **1** belonging to the ages before the biblical Flood. **2** old-fashioned.
antelope *n, pl* **-lopes** *or* **-lope** any of a group of graceful deerlike mammals of Africa and Asia, which have long legs and horns.
antenatal *adj* before birth; during pregnancy: *an antenatal clinic.*
antenna *n* **1** (*pl* **-nae**) one of a pair of mobile feelers on the heads of insects, lobsters, and certain other creatures. **2** (*pl* **-nas**) an aerial.
antepenultimate *adj* **1** third from last. *~n* **2** anything that is third from last.
anterior *adj* **1** at or towards the front. **2** earlier.

THESAURUS

narcotic, numbing, pain-killing, pain-relieving, palliative
anoint **1.** daub, embrocate, grease, oil, rub, smear, spread over **2.** bless, consecrate, hallow, sanctify
anomalous aberrant, abnormal, atypical, bizarre, deviating, eccentric, exceptional, incongruous, inconsistent, irregular, odd, oddball (*informal*), off-the-wall (*slang*), outré, peculiar, rare, unusual
anomaly aberration, abnormality, departure, deviation, eccentricity, exception, incongruity, inconsistency, irregularity, oddity, peculiarity, rarity
anonymous **1.** incognito, innominate, nameless, unacknowledged, unattested, unauthenticated, uncredited, unidentified, unknown, unnamed, unsigned **2.** characterless, nondescript, unexceptional
answer *vb.* **1.** acknowledge, explain, react, refute, rejoin, reply, resolve, respond, retort, return, solve **2.** conform, correlate, correspond, do, fill, fit, fulfil, measure up, meet, pass, qualify, satisfy, serve, suffice, suit, work *~n.* **3.** acknowledgment, comeback, counterattack, defence, explanation, plea, reaction, refutation, rejoinder, reply, report, resolution, response, retort, return, riposte, solution, vindication
answerable **1.** accountable, amenable, chargeable, liable, responsible, subject, to blame **2.** explainable, refutable, resolvable, solvable
answer back argue, be cheeky, be impertinent, cheek (*informal*), contradict, disagree, dispute, rebut, retort, talk back
antagonism antipathy, competition, conflict, contention, discord, dissension, friction, hostility, opposition, rivalry
antagonist adversary, competitor, contender, enemy, foe, opponent, opposer, rival
antagonistic adverse, antipathetic, at odds, at variance, averse, conflicting, contentious, hostile, ill-disposed, incompatible, in dispute, inimical, opposed, unfriendly
antagonize aggravate (*informal*), alienate, anger, annoy, be on one's back (*slang*), disaffect, estrange, gall, get in one's hair (*informal*), get on one's nerves (*informal*), hassle (*informal*), insult, irritate, nark (*slang*), offend, repel, rub up the wrong way (*informal*)
antecedent **1. antecedents** ancestors, ancestry, background, blood, descent, extraction, family, forebears, forefathers, genealogy, history, line, past, progenitors, stock **2.** anterior, earlier, foregoing, former, preceding, precursory, preliminary, previous, prior
antediluvian **1.** prehistoric, primeval, primitive, primordial **2.** ancient, antiquated, antique, archaic, ob-

anteroom *n* a small room leading into a larger room, often used as a waiting room.

anthem *n* 1 a song of loyalty or devotion: *a national anthem.* 2 a piece of music for a choir, usually set to words from the Bible.

anther *n Bot* the part of the stamen of a flower which contains the pollen.

ant hill *n* a mound of soil built by ants around the entrance to their nest.

anthology *n, pl* **-gies** a collection of poems or other literary pieces by various authors. **anthologist** *n*

anthracite *n* a hard coal that burns slowly with little smoke or flame but intense heat.

anthrax *n* a dangerous infectious disease of cattle and sheep, which can be passed to humans.

anthropocentric *adj* regarding the human being as the most important factor in the universe.

anthropoid *adj* 1 resembling a human being. *~n* 2 an ape, such as the chimpanzee, that resembles a human being.

anthropology *n* the study of human origins, institutions, and beliefs. **anthropological** *adj* **anthropologist** *n*

anthropomorphism *n* the attribution of human form or personality to a god, animal, or object. **anthropomorphic** *adj*

anthropomorphous *adj* shaped like a human being.

anti *Informal ~adj* 1 opposed to a party, policy, or attitude. *~n* 2 an opponent of a party, policy, or attitude.

anti- *prefix* 1 against or opposed to: *antiwar.* 2 opposite to: *anticlimax.* 3 counteracting or neutralizing: *antifreeze.*

anti-aircraft *adj* for defence against aircraft attack.

antiballistic missile *n* a missile designed to destroy a ballistic missile in flight.

antibiotic *n* 1 a chemical substance capable of destroying bacteria. *~adj* 2 of or relating to antibiotics

antibody *n, pl* **-bodies** a protein produced in the blood, which destroys bacteria.

Antichrist *n* 1 *New Testament* the chief enemy of Christ. 2 an enemy of Christ or Christianity.

anticipate *vb* **-pating, -pated** 1 to foresee and act in advance of: *he anticipated some probing questions.* 2 to look forward to. 3 to make use of (something, such as one's salary) before receiving it. 4 to mention (part of a story) before its proper time. **anticipatory** *adj*

anticipation *n* the act of anticipating; expectation, premonition, or foresight: *smiling in happy anticipation.*

anticlerical *adj* opposed to the power and influence of the clergy in politics.

anticlimax *n* a disappointing conclusion to a series of events. **anticlimactic** *adj*

anticline *n Geol* a fold of rock raised up into a broad arch so that the strata slope down on both sides.

anticlockwise *adv, adj* in the opposite direction to the rotation of the hands of a clock.

anticoagulant (an-tee-koh-**ag**-yew-lant) *n* a substance that prevents the clotting of blood.

antics *pl n* absurd acts or postures.

anticyclone *n Meteorol* an area of moving air of high pressure in which the winds rotate outwards.

antidepressant *n* 1 a drug used to treat depression. *~adj* 2 of or relating to such a drug.

antidote *n* 1 *Med* a substance that counteracts a poison. 2 anything that counteracts a harmful condition: *exercise may be a good antidote to insomnia.*

antifreeze *n* a liquid added to water to lower its freezing point, used in the radiator of a motor vehicle to prevent freezing.

antigen (**an**-tee-jen) *n* a substance, usually a toxin, that causes the body to produce antibodies.

antihero *n, pl* **-roes** a central character in a novel, play, or film, who lacks the traditional heroic virtues.

antihistamine *n* a drug that neutralizes the effects of histamine, used in the treatment of allergies.

antiknock *n* a substance added to motor fuel to reduce knocking in the engine caused by too rapid combustion.

antilogarithm *n Maths* a number corresponding to a given logarithm.

antimacassar *n* a cloth put over the back of a chair to prevent it getting dirty.

antimatter *n Physics* a hypothetical form of matter composed of antiparticles.

antimony (**an**-tim-mon-ee) *n Chem* a silvery-white metallic element that is added to alloys to increase their strength. Symbol: Sb

antinomy (**an**-tin-nom-ee) *n, pl* **-mies** contradiction between two laws or principles that are reasonable in themselves.

antinovel *n* a type of prose fiction in which conventional elements of the novel are rejected.

antinuclear *adj* opposed to nuclear weapons or nuclear power.

antiparticle *n Nuclear physics* an elementary particle that has the same mass as its corresponding particle, but opposite charge and opposite magnetism.

antipasto *n, pl* **-tos** an appetizer in an Italian meal.

antipathy (an-**tip**-a-thee) *n* a feeling of dislike or hostility. **antipathetic** *adj*

antipersonnel *adj* (of weapons or bombs) designed to be used against people rather than equipment.

antiperspirant *n* a substance applied to the skin to reduce or prevent perspiration.

antiphon *n* a hymn sung in alternate parts by two groups of singers.

antipodes (an-**tip**-pod-deez) *pl n* 1 any two places that are situated diametrically opposite one another

THESAURUS

solete, old-fashioned, out-of-date, out of the ark (*informal*), passé

anteroom antechamber, foyer, lobby, outer room, reception room, vestibule, waiting room

anthem 1. paean, song of praise 2. canticle, chant, chorale, hymn, psalm

anthology analects, choice, collection, compendium, compilation, digest, garland, miscellany, selection, treasury

anticipate 1. apprehend, await, count upon, expect, forecast, foresee, foretell, hope for, look for, look forward to, predict, prepare for 2. antedate, beat (someone) to it (*informal*), forestall, intercept, prevent

anticipation apprehension, awaiting, expectancy, expectation, foresight, foretaste, forethought, hope, preconception, premonition, prescience, presentiment

anticlimax bathos, comedown (*informal*), disappointment, letdown

antics buffoonery, capers, clowning, escapades, foolishness, frolics, larks, mischief, monkey tricks, playfulness, pranks, silliness, skylarking, stunts, tomfoolery, tricks

antidote antitoxin, corrective, countermeasure, cure, neutralizer, nostrum, preventive, remedy, specific

antipathy abhorrence, animosity, animus, antagonism, aversion, bad blood, contrariety, disgust, dislike,

on the earth's surface. **2 the Antipodes** Australia and New Zealand. **antipodean** *adj*

antipope *n* a pope set up in opposition to the one chosen by church laws.

antipyretic *adj* **1** reducing fever. *~n* **2** a drug that reduces fever.

antiquarian *adj* **1** collecting or dealing with antiquities or rare books. *~n* **2** an antiquary.

antiquary *n, pl* **-quaries** a person who collects, deals in, or studies antiques or ancient works of art.

antiquated *adj* obsolete or old-fashioned.

antique *n* **1** a decorative object or piece of furniture, of an earlier period, that is valued for its beauty, workmanship, and age. *~adj* **2** made in an earlier period. **3** *Informal* old-fashioned.

antiquity *n, pl* **-ties 1** great age. **2** the far distant past. **3 antiquities** objects dating from ancient times.

antiracism *n* the policy of challenging racism or promoting racial tolerance. **antiracist** *n, adj*

antirrhinum *n* a two-lipped flower of various colours, such as the snapdragon.

antiscorbutic *adj* preventing or curing scurvy.

anti-Semitic *adj* discriminating against Jews. **anti-Semite** *n* **anti-Semitism** *n*

antiseptic *adj* **1** preventing infection by killing germs. *~n* **2** an antiseptic substance.

antiserum *n* blood serum containing antibodies used to treat or provide immunity to a disease.

antisocial *adj* **1** avoiding the company of other people. **2** (of behaviour) annoying or harmful to other people.

antistatic *adj* reducing the effects of static electricity.

antitank *adj* (of weapons) designed to destroy military tanks.

antithesis (an-**tith**-iss-iss) *n, pl* **-ses** (-seez) **1** the exact opposite. **2** *Rhetoric* the placing together of contrasting ideas or words to produce an effect of balance, such as *where gods command, mere mortals must obey.* **antithetical** *adj*

antitoxin *n* an antibody that acts against a toxin. **antitoxic** *adj*

antitrades *pl n* winds blowing in the opposite direction from and above the trade winds.

antitrust *adj Chiefly US* (of laws) opposing business monopolies.

antler *n* one of a pair of branched horns on the heads of male deer.

antonym *n* a word that means the opposite of another.

antrum *n, pl* **-tra** *Anat* a natural cavity, esp. in a bone.

anus (**ain**-uss) *n* the opening at the end of the alimentary canal, through which faeces are discharged.

anvil *n* a heavy iron block on which metals are hammered into particular shapes.

anxiety *n, pl* **-ties 1** a state of uneasiness about what may happen. **2** eagerness: *she was uneasy with his mixture of diffidence and anxiety to please.*

anxious *adj* **1** worried and tense. **2** causing anxiety: *he was anxious about the enormity of the task ahead.* **3** intensely desiring: *both sides were anxious for a deal.* **anxiously** *adv*

any *adj, pron* **1** one, some, or several, no matter how much or what kind: *the jar opener fits over the top of any bottle or jar; have you left me any?* **2** even the smallest amount or even one: *we can't answer any questions; don't give her any.* **3** whatever or whichever: *police may board any bus or train.* **4** an indefinite or unlimited amount or number: *he would sign cheques for any amount of money.* *~adv* **5** to even the smallest extent: *the outcome wouldn't have been any different.*

anybody *pron* same as **anyone.**

anyhow *adv* same as **anyway.**

anyone *pron* **1** any person: *is anyone there?* **2** a person of any importance: *is he anyone?*

➤ It is acceptable to use *anyone* with a following plural form as in *Has anyone lost their purse?*

anything *pron* **1** any object, event, or action whatever: *they'll do anything to please you.* *~adv* **2** in any way: *it is not a computer nor anything like a computer.* **3 anything but** not at all: *the result is anything but simple.*

anyway *adv* **1** at any rate; nevertheless. **2** in any manner. **3** carelessly.

anywhere *adv* **1** in, at, or to any place. **2 get anywhere** to be successful: *we will not get anywhere by being negative.*

Anzac *n* (in the First World War) a soldier serving with the Australian and New Zealand Army Corps.

AOB (on the agenda for a meeting) any other business.

aorta (eh-**or**-ta) *n* the main artery of the body, which carries oxygen-rich blood from the heart.

apace *adv Literary* quickly: *repairs to the grid continued apace.*

Apache *n, pl* **Apaches** *or* **Apache** a member of a N American Indian people of the southwestern US and N Mexico.

apart *adj, adv* **1** to or in pieces: *he took a couple of cars apart and rebuilt them.* **2** separate in time, place, or position: *my father and myself stood slightly apart from them.* **3** individual or distinct: *a nation apart.* **4**

THESAURUS

distaste, enmity, hatred, hostility, ill will, incompatibility, loathing, odium, opposition, rancour, repugnance, repulsion

antiquated antediluvian, antique, archaic, dated, obsolete, old-fashioned, old hat, outmoded, out-of-date, outworn, passé

antique *n.* **1.** bygone, heirloom, object of virtu, relic *~adj.* **2.** antiquarian, classic, olden, vintage **3.** archaic, obsolete, old-fashioned, outdated

antiquity **1.** age, ancientness, elderliness, old age, oldness **2.** ancient times, distant past, olden days, time immemorial **3. antiquities** antiques, relics, ruins

antiseptic **1.** *adj.* aseptic, clean, germ-free, hygienic, pure, sanitary, sterile, uncontaminated, unpolluted **2.** *n.* disinfectant, germicide, purifier

antisocial **1.** alienated, asocial, misanthropic, reserved, retiring, uncommunicative, unfriendly, unsociable, withdrawn **2.** antagonistic, belligerent, disorderly, disruptive, hostile, menacing, rebellious

anxiety angst, apprehension, care, concern, disquiet, disquietude, distress, foreboding, fretfulness, misgiving, nervousness, restlessness, solicitude, suspense, tension, trepidation, unease, uneasiness, watchfulness, worry

anxious **1.** apprehensive, concerned, disquieted, distressed, disturbed, fearful, fretful, in suspense, nervous, overwrought, restless, solicitous, taut, tense, troubled, twitchy (*informal*), uneasy, unquiet (*chiefly literary*), watchful, wired (*slang*), worried **2.** ardent, avid, desirous, eager, expectant, impatient, intent, itching, keen, yearning

apart **1.** asunder, in bits, in pieces, into parts, to bits, to pieces **2.** afar, alone, aloof, aside, away, by itself, by oneself, cut off, distant, distinct, divorced, excluded, independent, independently, isolated, piecemeal, sepa-

not being taken into account: *early timing difficulties apart, they encountered few problems.* **5 apart from** other than: *apart from searching the house there is little more we can do.*

apartheid *n* (formerly) the official government policy of racial segregation in South Africa.

apartment *n* **1** any room in a building, usually one of several forming a suite, used as living accommodation. **2** *Chiefly US & Canad* a flat.

apathy *n* lack of interest or enthusiasm. **apathetic** *adj*

ape *n* **1** an animal, such as a chimpanzee or gorilla, which is closely related to human beings and the monkeys, and which has no tail. **2** a stupid, clumsy, or ugly man. *~vb* **aping, aped 3** to imitate. **apelike** *adj*

apeman *n, pl* **-men** an extinct primate thought to have been the forerunner of true humans.

aperient (ap-**peer**-ee-ent) *Med ~adj* **1** having a mild laxative effect. *~n* **2** a mild laxative.

aperitif (ap-per-rit-**teef**) *n* an alcoholic drink taken before a meal.

aperture *n* **1** a hole or opening. **2** an opening in a camera or telescope that controls the amount of light entering it.

apex *n* the highest point.

APEX Advance Purchase Excursion: a reduced fare for journeys booked a specified period in advance.

aphasia *n* a disorder of the central nervous system that affects the ability to use and understand words.

aphelion (ap-**heel**-lee-on) *n, pl* **-lia** (-lee-a) *Astron* the point in the orbit of a planet or comet when it is farthest from the sun.

aphid (**eh** fid) *or* **aphis** (**eh**-fiss) *n, pl* **aphids** *or* **aphides** (**eh**-fid-deez) a small insect which feeds by sucking the juices from plants.

aphorism *n* a short clever saying expressing a general truth.

aphrodisiac (af-roh-**diz**-zee-ak) *n* **1** a substance that arouses sexual desire. *~adj* **2** arousing sexual desire.

apiary (**ape**-yar-ee) *n, pl* **-aries** a place where bees are kept. **apiarist** *n*

apical (**ape**-ik-kl) *adj* of, at, or being an apex.

apiculture *n* the breeding and care of bees. **apiculturist** *n*

apiece *adv* each: *they had another cocktail apiece and then went down to dinner.*

apish (**ape**-ish) *adj* **1** stupid or foolish. **2** resembling an ape.

aplomb (ap-**plom**) *n* calm self-possession.

apocalypse *n* **1** the end of the world. **2** an event of great destructive violence. **apocalyptic** *adj*

Apocalypse *n* **the Apocalypse** *Bible* the Book of Revelation, the last book of the New Testament.

Apocrypha (ap-**pok**-rif-fa) *pl n* **the Apocrypha** the 14 books included as an appendix to the Old Testament, which are not accepted as part of the Hebrew scriptures.

apocryphal *adj* of questionable authenticity: *this apocryphal tale is common in Britain.*

apogee (**ap**-oh-jee) *n* **1** *Astron* the point in its orbit around the earth when the moon or a satellite is farthest from the earth. **2** the highest point: *the concept found its apogee in Renaissance Italy.*

apolitical *adj* not concerned with political matters.

apologetic *adj* showing or expressing regret. **apologetically** *adv*

apologetics *n* the branch of theology concerned with the reasoned defence of Christianity.

apologia *n* a formal written defence of a cause.

apologist *n* a person who offers a formal defence of a cause.

apologize *or* **-gise** *vb* **-gizing, -gized** *or* **-gising, -gised** to say that one is sorry for some wrongdoing.

apology *n, pl* **-gies 1** an expression of regret for some wrongdoing. **2** same as **apologia. 3 an apology for** a poor example of: *an apology for a man.*

apophthegm (**ap**-poth-em) *n* a short clever saying expressing a general truth.

apoplectic *adj* **1** of apoplexy. **2** *Informal* furious.

apoplexy *n Med* a stroke.

apostasy (ap-**poss**-stass-ee) *n, pl* **-sies** abandonment of one's religious faith, political party, or cause.

apostate *n* **1** a person who has abandoned his or her religion, political party, or cause. *~adj* **2** guilty of apostasy.

a posteriori (**eh** poss-steer-ee-**or**-rye) *adj Logic* involving reasoning from effect to cause.

apostle *n* **1** one of the twelve disciples chosen by Christ to preach his gospel. **2** an ardent supporter of a cause or movement.

apostolic (ap-poss-**stoll**-ik) *adj* **1** of or relating to the Apostles or their teachings. **2** of or relating to the pope.

Apostolic See *n* the see of the pope, at Rome.

apostrophe[1] (ap-**poss**-trof-fee) *n* the punctuation mark (') used to indicate the omission of a letter or letters, such as *he's* for *he has* or *he is,* and to form the possessive, as in *John's father.*

THESAURUS

rate, separated, separately, singly, to itself, to oneself, to one side **3. apart from** aside from, besides, but, except for, excluding, not counting, other than, save

apartment accommodation, chambers, compartment, flat, living quarters, penthouse, quarters, room, rooms, suite

apathetic cold, cool, emotionless, impassive, indifferent, insensible, listless, passive, phlegmatic, sluggish, stoic, stoical, torpid, unconcerned, unemotional, unfeeling, uninterested, unmoved, unresponsive

apathy coldness, coolness, emotionlessness, impassibility, impassivity, indifference, inertia, insensibility, listlessness, nonchalance, passiveness, passivity, phlegm, sluggishness, stoicism, torpor, unconcern, unfeelingness, uninterestedness, unresponsiveness

ape affect, caricature, copy, counterfeit, echo, imitate, mimic, mirror, mock, parody, parrot

aperture breach, chink, cleft, crack, eye, eyelet, fissure, gap, hole, interstice, opening, orifice, passage, perforation, rent, rift, slit, slot, space, vent

aphorism adage, apothegm, axiom, dictum, maxim, precept, proverb, saw (*old-fashioned*), saying

apiece each, for each, from each, individually, respectively, separately, severally, to each

aplomb balance, calmness, composure, confidence, coolness, equanimity, level-headedness, poise, sangfroid, self-assurance, self-confidence, self-possession, stability

apocryphal doubtful, dubious, equivocal, fictitious, legendary, mythical, questionable, spurious, unauthenticated, uncanonical, unsubstantiated, unverified

apologetic contrite, penitent, regretful, remorseful, rueful, sorry

apologize ask forgiveness, beg pardon, express regret, say one is sorry, say sorry

apology 1. acknowledgment, confession, defence, excuse, explanation, extenuation, justification, plea,

apostrophe[2] *n Rhetoric* a digression from a speech to address an imaginary or absent person or thing.

apostrophize *or* **-phise** *vb* **-phizing, -phized** *or* **-phising, -phised** *Rhetoric* to address an apostrophe to.

apothecary *n, pl* **-caries** *Old-fashioned* a chemist.

apotheosis (ap-poth-ee-**oh**-siss) *n, pl* **-ses** (-seez) **1** a perfect example: *it was the apotheosis of elitism.* **2** elevation to the rank of a god.

appal *or US* **appall** *vb* **-palling, -palled** to fill with horror; terrify.

appalling *adj* **1** causing dismay, horror, or revulsion. **2** very bad. **appallingly** *adv*

apparatus *n* **1** a collection of equipment used for a particular purpose. **2** any complicated device, system, or organization: *the whole apparatus of law enforcement.*

apparel (ap-**par**-rel) *n Old-fashioned* clothing.

apparent *adj* **1** readily seen or understood; obvious. **2** seeming as opposed to real: *he frowned in apparent bewilderment.* **apparently** *adv*

apparition *n* a ghost or ghostlike figure.

appeal *vb* **1** to make an earnest request. **2 appeal to** to attract, please, or interest. **3** *Law* to apply to a higher court to review (a case or issue decided by a lower court). **4** to resort to a higher authority to change a decision. **5** to call on in support of an earnest request: *he appealed for volunteers to help in relief work.* **6** *Cricket* to request the umpire to declare a batsman out. *~n* **7** an earnest request for money or help. **8** the power to attract, please, or interest people. **9** *Law* a request for a review of a lower court's decision by a higher court. **10** an application to a higher authority to change a decision that has been made. **11** *Cricket* a request to the umpire to declare the batsman out.

appealing *adj* attractive or pleasing.

appear *vb* **1** to come into sight. **2** to seem: *it appears that no one survived the crash.* **3** to come into existence: *a rash and small sores appeared around the shoulder and neck.* **4** to perform: *she hadn't appeared in a film for almost fifty years.* **5** to be present in court before a magistrate or judge: *two men have appeared in court in London charged with conspiracy.* **6** to be published or become available: *both books appeared in 1934.*

appearance *n* **1** a sudden or unexpected arrival of someone or something at a place. **2** the introduction or invention of something: *the appearance of credit cards.* **3** an act or instance of appearing: *it will be his fiftieth appearance for his country.* **4** the way a person or thing looks: *I spotted a man of extraordinary appearance.* **5 keep up appearances** to maintain the public impression of wellbeing or normality. **6 put in an appearance** to attend an event briefly. **7 to all appearances** apparently: *to all appearances they seemed enthralled by what he was saying.*

appease *vb* **-peasing, -peased** **1** to pacify (someone) by yielding to his or her demands. **2** to satisfy or relieve (a feeling). **appeasement** *n*

appellant *Law ~n* **1** a person who appeals to a higher court to review the decision of a lower court. *~adj* **2** same as **appellate.**

appellate (ap-**pell**-it) *adj Law* **1** of appeals. **2** (of a tribunal) having the power to review appeals.

appellation *n Formal* a name or title.

append *vb Formal* to add as a supplement: *a series of notes appended to his translation of the poems.*

appendage *n* a secondary part attached to a main part.

appendicectomy *or esp US & Canad* **appendectomy** *n, pl* **-mies** surgical removal of the appendix.

appendicitis *n* inflammation of the appendix, causing abdominal pain.

THESAURUS

vindication **2.** caricature, excuse, imitation, makeshift, mockery, stopgap, substitute, travesty

apostle advocate, champion, pioneer, propagandist, propagator, proponent

apotheosis deification, elevation, exaltation, glorification, idealization, idolization

appal alarm, astound, daunt, dishearten, dismay, frighten, harrow, horrify, intimidate, outrage, petrify, scare, shock, terrify, unnerve

appalling alarming, astounding, awful, daunting, dire, disheartening, dismaying, dreadful, fearful, frightening, frightful, ghastly, grim, harrowing, hideous, horrible, horrid, horrific, horrifying, intimidating, petrifying, scaring, shocking, terrible, terrifying, unnerving

apparatus **1.** appliance, contraption (*informal*), device, equipment, gear, implements, machine, machinery, materials, means, mechanism, outfit, tackle, tools, utensils **2.** bureaucracy, chain of command, hierarchy, network, organization, setup (*informal*), structure, system

apparent **1.** blatant, clear, conspicuous, discernible, distinct, evident, indubitable, manifest, marked, obvious, open, overt, patent, plain, understandable, unmistakable, visible **2.** ostensible, outward, seeming, specious, superficial

apparently it appears that, it seems that, on the face of it, ostensibly, outwardly, seemingly, superficially

apparition chimera, ghost, phantom, shade (*literary*), spectre, spirit, spook (*informal*), visitant, wraith

appeal *vb.* **1.** adjure, apply, ask, beg, beseech, call, call upon, entreat, implore, petition, plead, pray, refer, request, resort to, solicit, sue, supplicate **2. appeal to** allure, attract, charm, engage, entice, fascinate, interest, invite, please, tempt *~n.* **3.** adjuration, application, entreaty, invocation, petition, plea, prayer, request, solicitation, suit, supplication **4.** allure, attraction, attractiveness, beauty, charm, engagingness, fascination, interestingness, pleasingness

appear **1.** come forth, come into sight, come into view, come out, come to light, emerge, issue, loom, materialize, show (*informal*), show up (*informal*), surface **2.** look (like *or* as if), occur, seem, strike one as **3.** crop up (*informal*), develop, occur **4.** act, be exhibited, come on, come onstage, enter, perform, play, play a part, take part **5.** become available, be created, be developed, be invented, be published, come into being, come into existence, come out

appearance **1.** advent, appearing, arrival, coming, debut, emergence, introduction, presence, showing up (*informal*), turning up **2.** air, aspect, bearing, demeanour, expression, face, figure, form, image, look, looks, manner, mien (*literary*) **3.** front, guise, illusion, image, impression, outward show, pretence, semblance

appease **1.** conciliate, placate **2.** allay, alleviate, assuage, blunt, calm, compose, diminish, ease, lessen, lull, mitigate, mollify, pacify, quell, quench, quiet, satisfy, soften, soothe, subdue, tranquillize

appeasement **1.** acceding, accommodation, compromise, concession, conciliation, placation, propitiation **2.** abatement, alleviation, assuagement, blunting, easing, lessening, lulling, mitigation, mollification, pacification, quelling, quenching, quieting, satisfaction, softening, solace, soothing, tranquillization

append add, adjoin, affix, annex, attach, fasten, hang, join, subjoin, tack on, tag on

appendix (ap-**pen**-dix) *n, pl* **-dixes** *or* **-dices** (-diss-seez) **1** separate additional material at the end of a book. **2** *Anat* a short thin tube, closed at one end and attached to the large intestine at the other end.
➤ Extra sections at the end of a book are *appendices.* The plural *appendixes* is used in medicine.

appertain *vb* **appertain to** to belong to, relate to, or be connected with.

appetence *or* **appetency** *n, pl* **-tences** *or* **-tencies** a craving or desire.

appetite *n* **1** a desire for food or drink. **2** a liking or willingness: *he had an insatiable appetite for publicity.*

appetizer *or* **-iser** *n* a small amount of food or drink taken at the start of a meal to stimulate the appetite.

appetizing *or* **-ising** *adj* stimulating the appetite; looking or smelling delicious.

applaud *vb* **1** to show approval of by clapping one's hands. **2** to express approval of: *we applaud her determination and ambition.*

applause *n* appreciation shown by clapping one's hands.

apple *n* **1** a round firm fruit with red, yellow, or green skin and crisp whitish flesh, that grows on trees. **2 apple of one's eye** a person that one loves very much.

apple-pie bed *n* a bed made with the sheets folded so as to prevent the person from entering it.

apple-pie order *n* **in apple-pie order** *Informal* very tidy.

appliance *n* a machine or device that has a specific function.

applicable *adj* appropriate or relevant.

applicant *n* a person who applies for something, such as a job or grant.

application *n* **1** a formal request, for example for a job. **2** the act of applying something to a particular use: *you can make practical application of this knowledge to everyday living.* **3** concentrated effort: *success would depend on their talent and application.* **4** the act of putting something, such as a lotion or paint, on to a surface.

applicator *n* a device for applying cosmetics, medication, or some other substance.

applied *adj* put to practical use: *applied mathematics.*

appliqué (ap-**plee**-kay) *n* a kind of decoration in which one material is cut out and sewn or fixed onto another.

apply *vb* **-plies, -plying, -plied 1** to make a formal request for something, such as a job or a loan. **2** to put to practical use: *he applied his calligrapher's skill.* **3** to put on to a surface: *the hand lotion should be applied whenever possible throughout the day.* **4** to be relevant or appropriate: *he had been involved in research applied to flying wing aircraft.* **5 apply oneself** to concentrate one's efforts or faculties.

appoint *vb* **1** to assign officially to a job or position. **2** to fix or decide (a time or place for an event). **3** to equip or furnish: *It was a beautifully appointed room with rows and rows of books.* **appointee** *n*

appointment *n* **1** an arrangement to meet a person. **2** the act of placing someone in a job or position. **3** the person appointed. **4** the job or position to which a person is appointed. **5 appointments** fixtures or fittings.

apportion *vb* to divide out in shares.

apposite *adj* suitable or appropriate: *an apposite saying.*

apposition *n* a grammatical construction in which a

THESAURUS

appendage accessory, addendum, addition, adjunct, affix, ancillary, annexe, appendix, appurtenance, attachment, auxiliary, supplement

appendix addendum, addition, add-on, adjunct, appendage, codicil, postscript, supplement

appertain to apply, bear upon, be characteristic of, be connected, belong, be part of, be pertinent, be proper, be relevant, have to do with, inhere in, pertain, refer, relate, touch upon

appetite appetence, appetency, craving, demand, desire, hankering, hunger, inclination, liking, longing, passion, proclivity, propensity, relish, stomach, taste, willingness, yearning, zeal, zest

appetizer antipasto, apéritif, canapé, cocktail, hors d'oeuvre, titbit

appetizing appealing, delicious, inviting, mouthwatering, palatable, savoury, scrumptious (*informal*), succulent, tasty, tempting

applaud acclaim, approve, cheer, clap, commend, compliment, encourage, eulogize, extol, laud, magnify (*archaic*), praise

appliance apparatus, device, gadget, implement, instrument, machine, mechanism, tool

applicable apposite, appropriate, apropos, apt, befitting, fit, fitting, germane, pertinent, relevant, suitable, suited, to the point, to the purpose, useful

applicant aspirant, candidate, claimant, inquirer, petitioner, postulant, suitor, suppliant

application 1. appeal, claim, inquiry, petition, request, requisition, solicitation, suit **2.** exercise, function, practice, use **3.** assiduity, attention, attentiveness, commitment, dedication, diligence, effort, hard work, industry, perseverance, study **4.** balm, cream, dressing, emollient, lotion, ointment, poultice, salve, unguent

apply 1. appeal, claim, inquire, make application, petition, put in, request, requisition, solicit, sue **2.** administer, assign, bring into play, bring to bear, carry out, employ, engage, execute, exercise, exert, implement, practise, put to use, use, utilize **3.** anoint, bring into contact with, cover with, lay on, paint, place, put on, smear, spread on, touch to **4.** appertain, be applicable, be appropriate, bear upon, be fitting, be relevant, fit, pertain, refer, relate, suit **5.** address, be assiduous, be diligent, be industrious, buckle down (*informal*), commit, concentrate, dedicate, devote, direct, give, make an effort, pay attention, persevere, study, try, work hard

appoint 1. assign, choose, commission, delegate, elect, install, name, nominate, select **2.** allot, arrange, assign, choose, decide, designate, determine, establish, fix, set, settle **3.** equip, fit out, furnish, provide, supply

appointment 1. arrangement, assignation, consultation, date, engagement, interview, meeting, rendezvous, session, tryst (*archaic*) **2.** allotment, assignment, choice, choosing, commissioning, delegation, designation, election, installation, naming, nomination, selection **3.** appointee, candidate, delegate, nominee, office-holder, representative **4.** assignment, berth (*informal*), job, office, place, position, post, situation, station **5.** *plural* accoutrements, appurtenances, equipage, fittings, fixtures, furnishings, gear, outfit, paraphernalia, trappings

apportion allocate, allot, assign, deal, dispense, distribute, divide, dole out, measure out, mete out, parcel out, ration out, share

apposite appertaining, applicable, appropriate, apropos, apt, befitting, fitting, germane, pertinent,

noun or group of words is placed after another to modify its meaning, for example *my friend the mayor.*

appraisal *n* an assessment of the worth or quality of a person or thing.

appraise *vb* **-praising, -praised** to assess the worth, value, or quality of.

appreciable *adj* enough to be noticed; significant. **appreciably** *adv*

appreciate *vb* **-ating, -ated 1** to value highly: *we appreciate his music but can't afford £400 a seat.* **2** to be aware of and understand: *I can fully appreciate how desperate you must feel.* **3** to feel grateful for: *we do appreciate all you do for us.* **4** to increase in value.

appreciation *n* **1** gratitude. **2** awareness and understanding of a problem or difficulty. **3** sensitive recognition of good qualities, as in art. **4** an increase in value.

appreciative *adj* feeling or expressing appreciation. **appreciatively** *adv*

apprehend *vb* **1** to arrest and take into custody. **2** to grasp (something) mentally; understand.

apprehension *n* **1** anxiety or dread. **2** the act of arresting. **3** understanding.

apprehensive *adj* fearful or anxious about the future.

apprentice *n* **1** someone who works for a skilled person for a fixed period in order to learn his or her trade. *~vb* **-ticing, -ticed 2** to take or place as an apprentice. **apprenticeship** *n*

apprise *or* **-prize** *vb* **-prising, -prised** *or* **-prizing, -prized** to make aware: *I needed to apprise the students of the dangers that may be involved.*

appro *n* **on appro** *Informal* on approval.

approach *vb* **1** to come close or closer to. **2** to make a proposal or suggestion to. **3** to begin to deal with (a matter). *~n* **4** the act of coming close or closer. **5** a proposal or suggestion made to a person. **6** the way or means of reaching a place; access. **7** a way of dealing with a matter. **8** an approximation. **9** the course followed by an aircraft preparing for landing. **approachable** *adj*

approbation *n* approval.

appropriate *adj* **1** right or suitable. *~vb* **-ating, -ated 2** to take for one's own use without permission. **3** to put (money) aside for a particular purpose. **appropriately** *adv*

appropriation *n* **1** the act of putting money aside for a particular purpose. **2** money put aside for a particular purpose.

approval *n* **1** consent. **2** a favourable opinion. **3 on approval** (of articles for sale) with an option to be re-

THESAURUS

proper, relevant, suitable, suited, to the point, to the purpose

appraisal assay, assessment, estimate, estimation, evaluation, judgment, opinion, pricing, rating, recce (*slang*), reckoning, sizing up (*informal*), survey, valuation

appreciable ascertainable, clear-cut, considerable, definite, detectable, discernible, distinguishable, evident, marked, material, measurable, noticeable, obvious, perceivable, perceptible, pronounced, recognizable, significant, substantial, visible

appreciate 1. admire, cherish, enjoy, esteem, like, prize, rate highly, regard, relish, respect, savour, treasure, value **2.** acknowledge, be alive to, be aware (cognizant, conscious) of, comprehend, estimate, know, perceive, realize, recognize, sympathize with, take account of, understand **3.** be appreciative, be grateful for, be indebted, be obliged, be thankful for, give thanks for **4.** enhance, gain, grow, improve, increase, inflate, raise the value of, rise

appreciation 1. acknowledgment, gratefulness, gratitude, indebtedness, obligation, thankfulness, thanks **2.** appraisal, assessment, awareness, cognizance, comprehension, knowledge, perception, realization, recognition, regard, responsiveness, sensitivity, sympathy, understanding, valuation **3.** enhancement, gain, growth, improvement, increase, inflation, rise

appreciative 1. beholden, grateful, indebted, obliged, thankful **2.** aware, cognizant, conscious, enthusiastic, in the know (*informal*), knowledgeable, mindful, perceptive, regardful, respectful, responsive, sensitive, supportive, sympathetic, understanding

apprehend 1. arrest, bust (*informal*), capture, catch, collar (*informal*), lift (*slang*), nab (*informal*), nail (*informal*), nick (*slang*), pinch (*informal*), run in (*slang*), seize, take, take prisoner **2.** appreciate, believe, comprehend, conceive, grasp, imagine, know, perceive, realize, recognize, think, understand

apprehension 1. alarm, anxiety, apprehensiveness, concern, disquiet, doubt, dread, fear, foreboding, misgiving, mistrust, premonition, suspicion, trepidation, unease, uneasiness, worry **2.** arrest, capture, catching, seizure, taking **3.** awareness, comprehension, grasp, intellect, intelligence, ken, knowledge, perception, understanding

apprehensive afraid, alarmed, anxious, concerned, disquieted, doubtful, fearful, foreboding, mistrustful, nervous, suspicious, twitchy (*informal*), uneasy, worried

apprentice beginner, learner, neophyte, novice, probationer, pupil, student, trainee, tyro

approach *vb.* **1.** advance, catch up, come close, come near, come to, draw near, gain on, meet, move towards, near, push forward, reach **2.** appeal to, apply to, broach the matter with, make advances to, make a proposal to, make overtures to, sound out **3.** begin, begin work on, commence, embark on, enter upon, make a start, set about, undertake *~n.* **4.** access, advance, advent, arrival, avenue, coming, drawing near, entrance, nearing, passage, road, way **5.** advance, appeal, application, invitation, offer, overture, proposal, proposition **6.** attitude, course, manner, means, method, mode, modus operandi, procedure, style, technique, way **7.** approximation, likeness, semblance

approachable accessible, attainable, reachable

appropriate *adj.* **1.** adapted, applicable, apposite, appurtenant, apropos, apt, becoming, befitting, belonging, congruous, correct, felicitous, fit, fitting, germane, meet (*archaic*), opportune, pertinent, proper, relevant, right, seemly, suitable, to the point, to the purpose, well-suited, well-timed *~vb.* **2.** annex, arrogate, assume, commandeer, confiscate, embezzle, expropriate, filch, impound, misappropriate, pilfer, pocket, pre-empt, seize, steal, take, take over, take possession of, usurp **3.** allocate, allot, apportion, assign, devote, earmark, set apart

appropriation allocation, allotment, apportionment, assignment, earmarking, setting apart

approval 1. acquiescence, agreement, assent, authorization, blessing, compliance, concurrence, confirmation, consent, countenance, endorsement, imprimatur, leave, licence, mandate, O.K. *or* okay (*informal*), permission, ratification, recommendation, sanction, the go-ahead (*informal*), the green light, validation **2.** acclaim, admiration, applause, appreciation, approbation, commendation, esteem, favour, good opinion, liking, praise, regard, respect

approve 1. acclaim, admire, applaud, appreciate, be pleased with, commend, esteem, favour, have a good

turned without payment if unsatisfactory: *each volume in the collection will be sent to you on approval.*

approve *vb* **-proving, -proved 1 approve of** to consider fair, good, or right. **2** to authorize or agree to.

approx. approximate or approximately.

approximate *adj* **1** almost but not quite exact. *~vb* **-mating, -mated 2 approximate to a** to come close to. **b** to be almost the same as. **approximately** *adv* **approximation** *n*

appurtenances *pl n* minor or additional features or possessions.

Apr. April.

après-ski (ap-ray-**skee**) *n* social activities after a day's skiing.

apricot *n* **1** a yellowish-orange juicy fruit which resembles a small peach. *~adj* **2** yellowish-orange.

April *n* the fourth month of the year.

April fool *n* a victim of a practical joke played on the first of April (**April Fools' Day** *or* **All Fools' Day**).

a priori (**eh** pry-or-rye) *adj Logic* involving reasoning from cause to effect.

apron *n* **1** a garment worn over the front of the body to protect one's clothes. **2** a hard-surfaced area at an airport or hangar for manoeuvring and loading aircraft. **3** the part of a stage extending in front of the curtain. **4 tied to someone's apron strings** dependent on or dominated by someone.

apropos (ap-prop-**poh**) *adj* **1** appropriate. *~adv* **2** by the way; incidentally. **3 apropos of** with regard to.

apse *n* an arched or domed recess at the east end of a church.

apsis (**ap**-siss) *n, pl* **apsides** (**ap**-sid-deez) *Astron* either of two points lying at the extremities of the elliptical orbit of a planet or satellite.

apt *adj* **1** having a specified tendency: *they are apt to bend the rules.* **2** suitable or appropriate. **3** quick to learn: *she was turning out to be a more apt pupil than he had expected.* **aptly** *adv* **aptness** *n*

APT Advanced Passenger Train.

apteryx *n* same as **kiwi.**

aptitude *n* natural tendency or ability.

aqua *adj* short for **aquamarine.**

aqua fortis *n Obsolete* nitric acid.

aqualung *n* an apparatus for breathing underwater, consisting of a mouthpiece attached to air cylinders.

aquamarine *n* **1** a clear greenish-blue gemstone. *~adj* **2** greenish-blue.

aquaplane *n* **1** a board on which a person stands to be towed by a motorboat for sport. *~vb* **-planing, -planed 2** to ride on an aquaplane. **3** (of a motor vehicle) to skim uncontrollably on a thin film of water.

aqua regia (**ak**-wa **reej**-ya) *n* a mixture of nitric acid and hydrochloric acid.

aquarium *n, pl* **aquariums** *or* **aquaria 1** a tank in which fish and other underwater creatures are kept. **2** a building containing such tanks.

Aquarius *n Astrol* the eleventh sign of the zodiac: the Water Carrier.

aquatic *adj* **1** growing or living in water. **2** *Sport* performed in or on water. *~n* **3** an aquatic animal or plant. **4 aquatics** water sports.

aquatint *n* a print like a watercolour, produced by etching copper with acid.

aqua vitae (**ak**-wa **vee**-tie) *n Old-fashioned* brandy.

aqueduct *n* a structure, often a bridge, that carries water across a valley or river.

aqueous *adj* **1** of, like, or containing water. **2** produced by the action of water.

aqueous humour *n Physiol* the watery fluid in the eyeball, between the cornea and the lens.

aquifer *n* a deposit of rock, such as sandstone, containing water that can be used to supply wells.

aquiline *adj* **1** (of a nose) curved like an eagle's beak. **2** of or like an eagle.

A & R artists and repertoire.

Ar *Chem* argon.

AR Arkansas.

Arab *n* **1** a member of a Semitic people originally from Arabia. *~adj* **2** of the Arabs.

arabesque (ar-ab-**besk**) *n* **1** a ballet position in which one leg is raised behind and the arms are extended. **2** *Arts* an elaborate design of intertwined leaves, flowers, and scrolls. **3** an ornate piece of music.

Arabian *adj* **1** of Arabia or the Arabs. *~n* **2** same as **Arab.**

THESAURUS

opinion of, like, praise, regard highly, respect, think highly of **2.** accede to, accept, advocate, agree to, allow, assent to, authorize, bless, concur in, confirm, consent to, countenance, endorse, give the go-ahead (*informal*), give the green light, go along with, mandate, O.K. *or* okay (*informal*), pass, permit, ratify, recommend, sanction, second, subscribe to, uphold, validate

approximate 1. *adj.* almost accurate, almost exact, close, estimated, inexact, loose, near, rough **2.** *vb.* approach, border on, come close, come near, reach, resemble, touch, verge on

approximately about, almost, around, circa (*used with dates*), close to, generally, in the neighbourhood of, in the region of, in the vicinity of, just about, loosely, more or less, nearly, not far off, relatively, roughly

approximation 1. conjecture, estimate, estimation, guess, guesswork, rough calculation, rough idea **2.** approach, correspondence, likeness, resemblance, semblance

apron pinafore, pinny (*informal*)

apropos *adj.* **1.** applicable, apposite, appropriate, apt, befitting, belonging, correct, fit, fitting, germane, meet (*archaic*), opportune, pertinent, proper, related, relevant, right, seemly, suitable, to the point, to the purpose *~adv.* **2.** by the bye, by the way, incidentally, in passing, parenthetically, while on the subject *~prep.* **3. apropos of** in respect of, on the subject of, re, regarding, respecting, with reference to, with regard to, with respect to

apt 1. disposed, given, inclined, liable, likely, of a mind, prone, ready **2.** applicable, apposite, appropriate, apropos, befitting, correct, fit, fitting, germane, meet (*archaic*), pertinent, proper, relevant, seemly, suitable, timely, to the point, to the purpose **3.** astute, bright, clever, expert, gifted, ingenious, intelligent, prompt, quick, sharp, skilful, smart, talented, teachable

aptitude ability, aptness, bent, capability, capacity, cleverness, disposition, faculty, flair, gift, giftedness, inclination, intelligence, knack, leaning, predilection, proclivity, proficiency, proneness, propensity, quickness, talent, tendency

aptness 1. aptitude, bent, disposition, inclination, leaning, liability, likelihood, likeliness, predilection, proclivity, proneness, propensity, readiness, tendency **2.** applicability, appositeness, appropriateness, becomingness, congruousness, correctness, felicitousness, felicity, fitness, fittingness, germaneness, opportuneness, pertinence, properness, relevance, rightness, seemliness, suitability, timeliness, well-suitedness **3.**

Arabic *n* **1** the language of the Arabs. *~adj* **2** of this language, the Arabs, or Arabia.

Arabic numerals *pl n* the symbols 1,2,3,4,5,6,7,8,9,0, used to represent numbers.

arable *adj* (of land) suitable for growing crops on.

arachnid (ar-**rak**-nid) *n* an eight-legged insect-like creature, such as a spider, scorpion, or tick.

arak *n* same as **arrack.**

Aramaic *n* an ancient Semitic language spoken in parts of Syria and the Lebanon.

Aran *adj* (of knitwear) knitted in a complicated pattern traditional to the Aran Islands off the west coast of Ireland.

arbiter *n* **1** a person empowered to judge in a dispute. **2** a person with influential opinions about something: *the customer must be the ultimate arbiter of quality.*

arbitrary *adj* **1** not done according to any plan or for any particular reason. **2** without consideration for the wishes of others: *the arbitrary power of the king.* **arbitrarily** *adv*

arbitrate *vb* **-trating, -trated** to settle (a dispute) by arbitration. **arbitrator** *n*

arbitration *n* the hearing and settlement of a dispute by an impartial referee chosen by both sides.

arbor[1] *n US* same as **arbour.**

arbor[2] *n* a revolving shaft or axle in a machine.

arboreal (ahr-**bore**-ee-al) *adj* **1** of or resembling a tree. **2** living in or among trees.

arboretum (ahr-bore-**ee**-tum) *n, pl* **-ta** (-ta) a botanical garden where rare trees or shrubs are cultivated.

arboriculture *n* the cultivation of trees or shrubs.

arbor vitae (**ahr**-bore **vee**-tie) *n* an evergreen tree.

arbour *or US* **arbor** *n* a shelter in a garden shaded by trees or climbing plants.

arbutus (ar-**byew**-tuss) *n* an evergreen shrub with berries like strawberries.

arc *n* **1** something curved in shape. **2** *Maths* a section of a circle or other curve. **3** *Electricity* a stream of very bright light that forms when an electric current flows across a small gap between two electrodes. *~vb* **4** to form an arc.

ARC AIDS-related complex: relatively mild symptoms suffered in the early stages of infection with the AIDS virus.

arcade *n* **1** a covered passageway lined with shops. **2** a set of arches and their supporting columns.

Arcadian *Literary ~adj* **1** rural, in an idealized way. *~n* **2** a person who leads a quiet simple country life.

arcane *adj* very mysterious.

arch[1] *n* **1** a curved structure that spans an opening or supports a bridge or roof. **2** something curved. **3** the curved lower part of the foot. *~vb* **4** to form an arch.

arch[2] *adj* **1** knowing or superior. **2** coyly playful: *he gave an arch smile to indicate his pride.* **archly** *adv*

arch- *or* **archi-** *combining form* chief or principal: *archbishop; archenemy.*

archaeology *or* **archeology** *n* the study of ancient cultures by the scientific analysis of physical remains. **archaeological** *or* **archeological** *adj* **archaeologist** *or* **archeologist** *n*

archaeopteryx *n* an extinct primitive bird with teeth, a long tail, and well-developed wings.

archaic (ark-**kay**-ik) *adj* **1** of a much earlier period. **2** out of date or old-fashioned. **3** (of a word or phrase) no longer in everyday use. **archaically** *adv*

archaism (**ark**-kay-iz-zum) *n* an archaic word or style. **archaistic** *adj*

archangel (**ark**-ain-jell) *n* an angel of the highest rank.

archbishop *n* a bishop of the highest rank.

archbishopric *n* the rank, office, or diocese of an archbishop.

archdeacon *n* a church official ranking just below a bishop. **archdeaconry** *n*

archdiocese *n* the diocese of an archbishop.

archduchess *n* **1** a woman who holds the rank of archduke. **2** the wife or widow of an archduke.

archduchy *n, pl* **-duchies** the territory ruled by an archduke or archduchess.

archduke *n* a duke of high rank, esp. one from Austria.

archenemy *n, pl* **-mies** a chief enemy.

archeology *n* same as **archaeology.**

archer *n* a person who shoots with a bow and arrow.

archery *n* the art or sport of shooting with a bow and arrow.

archetype (**ark**-ee-type) *n* **1** a perfect or typical specimen. **2** an original model; prototype. **archetypal** *adj*

archidiaconal (ark-ee-die-**ak**-on-al) *adj* of an archdeacon or his office.

archiepiscopal (aek-ee-ip-**piss**-kop-al) *adj* of an archbishop or his office.

archipelago (ark-ee-**pel**-a-go) *n, pl* **-gos** **1** a group of islands. **2** a sea full of small islands.

architect *n* **1** a person qualified to design and supervise the construction of buildings. **2** any planner or creator: *you will be the architect of your own future.*

THESAURUS

ability, capability, capacity, cleverness, faculty, fitness, flair, gift, giftedness, intelligence, knack, proficiency, quickness, suitability, talent

arable cultivable, farmable, fecund, fertile, fruitful, ploughable, productive, tillable

arbiter **1.** adjudicator, arbitrator, judge, referee, umpire **2.** authority, controller, dictator, expert, governor, lord, master, pundit, ruler

arbitrary **1.** capricious, chance, discretionary, erratic, fanciful, inconsistent, optional, personal, random, subjective, unreasonable, whimsical, wilful **2.** absolute, autocratic, despotic, dictatorial, dogmatic, domineering, high-handed, imperious, magisterial, overbearing, peremptory, summary, tyrannical, tyrannous, uncontrolled, unlimited, unrestrained

arbitrate adjudge, adjudicate, decide, determine, judge, mediate, pass judgment, referee, settle, sit in judgment, umpire

arbitration adjudication, arbitrament, decision, determination, judgment, settlement

arbitrator adjudicator, arbiter, judge, referee, umpire

arc arch, bend, bow, crescent, curve, half-moon

arch[1] *n.* **1.** archway, curve, dome, span, vault **2.** arc, bend, bow, curvature, curve, hump, semicircle *~vb.* **3.** arc, bend, bow, bridge, curve, embow, span

arch[2] **1.** accomplished, chief, consummate, expert, finished, first, foremost, greatest, head, highest, lead, leading, main, major, master, pre-eminent, primary, principal, top **2.** artful, frolicsome, knowing, mischievous, pert, playful, roguish, saucy, sly, waggish, wily

archaic ancient, antiquated, antique, behind the times, bygone, obsolete, old, olden (*archaic*), old-fashioned, old hat, outmoded, out of date, passé, primitive, superannuated

archetype classic, exemplar, form, ideal, model, norm, original, paradigm, pattern, prime example, prototype, standard

architecture *n* **1** the style in which a building is designed and built: *Gothic architecture.* **2** the science of designing and constructing buildings. **3** the structure or design of anything: *computer architecture.* **architectural** *adj*

architrave (**ark**-ee-trave) *n Archit* **1** a beam that rests on top of columns. **2** a moulding around a doorway or window opening.

archive (**ark**-ive) *n* **1** a place where records or documents are kept. **2 archives** a collection of records or documents.

archivist (**ark**-iv-ist) *n* a person in charge of archives.

archway *n* a passageway under an arch.

arctic *adj Informal* very cold; freezing.

Arctic *n* **1 the Arctic** the area around the North Pole. *~adj* **2** of this region.

Arctic Circle *n* the imaginary circle around the earth at latitude 66° 32′N.

arctic hare *n* a large hare of the Canadian Arctic whose fur turns white in winter.

arctic willow *n* a low-growing shrub of the Canadian Arctic.

arc welding *n* a technique in which metal is welded by heat generated by an electric arc.

ardent *adj* **1** passionate. **2** intensely enthusiastic. **ardently** *adv*

ardour *or US* **ardor** *n* **1** emotional warmth; passion. **2** intense enthusiasm.

arduous *adj* difficult to accomplish; strenuous.

are[1] *vb* the plural form of the present tense of **be** and the singular form used with *you.*

are[2] *n* a unit of measure equal to one hundred square metres.

area *n* **1** a section, part, or region. **2** a part having a specified function: *reception area.* **3** the size of a two-dimensional surface. **4** a subject field: *the area of literature.* **5** a sunken area giving access to a basement. **6** any flat, curved, or irregular expanse of a surface. **7** range or scope.

arena *n* **1** a seated enclosure where sports events take place. **2** the area of an ancient Roman amphitheatre where gladiators fought. **3** a sphere of intense activity: *the political arena.*

aren't are not.

areola *n, pl* **-lae** *or* **-las** a small circular area, such as the coloured ring around the human nipple.

arête *n* a sharp ridge separating valleys.

Argentine *or* **Argentinian** *adj* **1** of Argentina. *~n* **2** a person from Argentina.

argon *n Chem* an unreactive odourless element of the rare gas series, forming almost 1 per cent of the atmosphere. Symbol: Ar

argosy *n, pl* **-sies** *Old-fashioned or poetic* a large merchant ship, or a fleet of such ships.

argot (**ahr**-go) *n* slang or jargon peculiar to a particular group.

argue *vb* **-guing, -gued 1** to try to prove by presenting reasons. **2** to debate. **3** to quarrel. **4** to persuade: *we argued her out of going.* **5** to suggest: *her looks argue despair.* **arguable** *adj* **arguably** *adv*

argument *n* **1** a quarrel. **2** a discussion. **3** a point presented to support or oppose a proposition.

argumentation *n* the process of reasoning methodically.

argumentative *adj* likely to argue.

argy-bargy *or* **argie-bargie** *n, pl* **-bargies** *Brit informal* a squabbling argument.

aria (**ah**-ree-a) *n* an elaborate song for solo voice in an opera or choral work.

arid *adj* **1** having little or no rain. **2** uninteresting. **aridity** *n*

Aries *n Astrol* the first sign of the zodiac: the Ram.

aright *adv* correctly or properly.

arise *vb* **arising, arose, arisen 1** to come into being:

THESAURUS

architect 1. designer, master builder, planner **2.** author, contriver, creator, deviser, engineer, founder, instigator, inventor, maker, originator, planner, prime mover, shaper

architecture 1. building, construction, design, planning **2.** construction, design, framework, make-up, structure, style

archive 1. museum, record office, registry, repository **2. archives** annals, chronicles, documents, papers, records, registers, rolls

arctic *informal* chilly, cold, freezing, frigid, frostbound, frosty, frozen, gelid, glacial, icy

ardent avid, eager, enthusiastic, fervent, fervid, fierce, fiery, flaming, hot, hot-blooded, impassioned, intense, keen, lusty, passionate, spirited, vehement, warm, warm-blooded, zealous

ardour avidity, devotion, eagerness, earnestness, enthusiasm, feeling, fervour, fierceness, fire, heat, intensity, keenness, passion, spirit, vehemence, warmth, zeal

arduous backbreaking, burdensome, difficult, exhausting, fatiguing, formidable, gruelling, hard, harsh, heavy, laborious, onerous, painful, punishing, rigorous, severe, steep, strenuous, taxing, tiring, toilsome, tough, troublesome, trying

area 1. district, domain, locality, neighbourhood, part, patch, plot, portion, realm, region, section, sector, sphere, stretch, territory, tract, turf (*informal*), zone **2.** arena, department, domain, field, province, realm, sphere, territory **3.** sunken space, yard **4.** ambit, breadth, compass, expanse, extent, range, scope, size, width

arena 1. amphitheatre, bowl, coliseum, field, ground, park (*U.S. & Canad.*), ring, stadium, stage **2.** area, domain, field, province, realm, scene, sector, sphere, territory, theatre

argot cant, dialect, idiom, jargon, lingo (*informal*), parlance, patois, slang, vernacular

argue 1. assert, claim, contend, controvert, debate, discuss, dispute, expostulate, hold, maintain, plead, question, reason, remonstrate **2.** altercate, bandy words, bicker, disagree, dispute, fall out (*informal*), feud, fight, have an argument, quarrel, squabble, wrangle **3.** convince, persuade, prevail upon, talk into, talk round **4.** denote, imply, indicate, suggest

argument 1. altercation, barney (*informal*), bickering, clash, controversy, difference of opinion, disagreement, dispute, falling out (*informal*), feud, fight, quarrel, row, squabble, wrangle **2.** contention, debate, discussion, dispute, expostulation, questioning **3.** argumentation, assertion, case, claim, contention, defence, dialectic, expostulation, ground(s), line of reasoning, logic, plea, polemic, reason, reasoning, remonstrance, remonstration

argumentative belligerent, combative, contentious, contrary, disputatious, litigious, opinionated, quarrelsome

arid 1. barren, desert, dried up, dry, moistureless, parched, sterile, torrid, waterless **2.** boring, colourless, dreary, dry, dull, flat, jejune, lifeless, spiritless, tedious, uninspired, uninteresting, vapid

aright accurately, appropriately, aptly, correctly, duly,

the opportunity for action did not arise. **2** to come into notice: *people can seek answers to their problems as and when they arise.* **3** **arise from** to happen as a result of. **4** *Old-fashioned* to get or stand up.

aristocracy *n, pl* **-cies** **1** a class of people of high social rank. **2** government by this class. **3** a group of people considered to be outstanding in a particular sphere of activity.

aristocrat *n* a member of the aristocracy.

aristocratic *adj* **1** of the aristocracy. **2** grand or elegant.

Aristotelian (ar-riss-tot-**eel**-ee-an) *adj* of Aristotle, 4th-century BC Greek philosopher, or to his philosophy.

arithmetic *n* **1** the branch of mathematics concerned with numerical calculations, such as addition, subtraction, multiplication, and division. **2** calculations involving numerical operations. **3** knowledge of or skill in arithmetic: *even simple arithmetic was beyond him.* *~adj also* **arithmetical** **4** of or using arithmetic. **arithmetically** *adv* **arithmetician** *n*

arithmetic mean *n* the average value of a set of terms, expressed as their sum divided by their number: *the arithmetic mean of 3, 4, and 8 is 5.*

arithmetic progression *n* a sequence, each term of which differs from the preceding term by a constant amount, such as 3,6,9,12.

ark *n Bible* the boat built by Noah, which survived the Flood.

Ark *n Judaism* **1** Also called: **Holy Ark** the cupboard in a synagogue in which the Torah scrolls are kept. **2** Also called: **Ark of the Covenant** a chest containing the laws of the Jewish religion, regarded as the most sacred symbol of God's presence among the Hebrew people.

arm[1] *n* **1** (in humans, apes, and monkeys) either of the upper limbs from the shoulder to the wrist. **2** the sleeve of a garment. **3** the side of a chair on which one's arm can rest. **4** a subdivision or section of an organization: *the London-based arm of a Swiss bank.* **5** something resembling an arm in appearance or function: *the arm of a record player.* **6** power or authority: *the long arm of the law.* **7** **arm in arm** with arms linked. **8** **at arm's length** at a distance. **9** **with open arms** with warmth and hospitality.

arm[2] *vb* **1** to supply with weapons. **2** to prepare (an explosive device) for use. **3** to provide (a person or thing) with something that strengthens, or protects: *you will be armed with all the information you will ever need.* ~See also **arms. armed** *adj*

armada *n* **1** a large number of ships. **2** **the Armada** the great fleet sent by Spain against England in 1588.

armadillo *n, pl* **-los** a small S American burrowing mammal covered in strong bony plates.

Armageddon *n* **1** *New Testament* the final battle between good and evil at the end of the world. **2** a catastrophic and extremely destructive conflict.

armament *n* **1** **armaments** the weapon equipment of a military vehicle, ship, or aircraft. **2** preparation for war.

armature *n* **1** a revolving structure in an electric motor or generator, wound with the coils that carry the current. **2** *Sculpture* a framework to support the clay or other material used in modelling.

armchair *n* **1** an upholstered chair with side supports for the arms. *~adj* **2** taking no active part: *we are, on the whole, a nation of armchair athletes.*

armed forces *pl n* all the military forces of a nation or nations.

armful *n* as much as can be held in the arms.

armhole *n* the opening in a piece of clothing through which the arm passes.

armistice (**arm**-miss-stiss) *n* an agreement between opposing armies to stop fighting.

Armistice Day *n* the anniversary of the signing of the armistice that ended the First World War, on November 11, 1918.

armlet *n* a band or bracelet worn around the arm.

armorial *adj* of or relating to heraldry or heraldic arms.

armour *or US* **armor** *n* **1** metal clothing worn by medieval warriors for protection in battle. **2** *Mil* armoured fighting vehicles in general. **3** the protective metal plates on a tank or warship. **4** protective covering, such as the shell of certain animals. **5** a quality or attitude that gives protection. *~vb* **6** to equip or cover with armour.

armoured *or US* **armored** *adj* **1** having a protective covering. **2** consisting of armoured vehicles: *an armoured brigade.*

armourer *or US* **armorer** *n* **1** a person who makes or mends arms and armour. **2** a person in charge of small arms in a military unit.

armour plate *n* a tough heavy steel for protecting warships and vehicles. **armour-plated** *adj*

armoury *or US* **armory** *n, pl* **-mouries** *or* **-mories** **1** a secure storage place for weapons. **2** military supplies. **3** resources on which to draw: *modern medicine*

THESAURUS

exactly, fitly, in due order, justly, properly, rightly, suitably, truly, without error

arise **1.** appear, begin, come into being, come to light, commence, crop up (*informal*), emanate, emerge, ensue, follow, happen, issue, occur, originate, proceed, result, set in, spring, start, stem **2.** *old-fashioned* get to one's feet, get up, go up, rise, stand up, wake up

aristocracy body of nobles, elite, gentry, *haut monde*, nobility, noblesse (*literary*), patricians, patriciate, peerage, ruling class, upper class, upper crust (*informal*)

aristocrat grandee, lady, lord, noble, nobleman, noblewoman, patrician, peer, peeress

aristocratic **1.** blue-blooded, elite, gentle (*archaic*), gentlemanly, highborn, lordly, noble, patrician, titled, upper-class, well-born **2.** courtly, dignified, elegant, fine, haughty, polished, refined, snobbish, stylish, well-bred

arm[1] *n.* **1.** appendage, limb, upper limb **2.** bough, branch, department, detachment, division, extension, offshoot, projection, section, sector **3.** authority, command, force, might, potency, power, strength, sway

arm[2] *vb.* **1.** accoutre, array, deck out, equip, furnish, issue with, outfit, provide, rig, supply **2.** brace, equip, forearm, fortify, gird one's loins, guard, make ready, outfit, prepare, prime, protect, strengthen

armada fleet, flotilla, navy, squadron

armaments ammunition, arms, guns, materiel, munitions, ordnance, weaponry, weapons

armed accoutred, arrayed, carrying weapons, equipped, fitted out, forearmed, fortified, furnished, girded, guarded, in arms, prepared, primed, protected, provided, ready, rigged out, strengthened, supplied, under arms

armistice ceasefire, peace, suspension of hostilities, truce

armour armour plate, covering, protection, sheathing, shield

has a large armoury of drugs for the treatment of mental illness.

armpit *n* the hollow beneath the arm where it joins the shoulder.

armrest *n* the part of a chair or sofa, that supports the arm.

arms *pl n* **1** weapons collectively. **2** military exploits: *prowess in arms.* **3** the heraldic symbols of a family or state. **4 take up arms** to prepare to fight. **5 under arms** armed and prepared for war. **6 up in arms** prepared to protest strongly.

army *n, pl* **-mies 1** the military land forces of a nation. **2** a large number of people or animals.

aroha *n NZ* love, compassion, or affection.

aroma *n* **1** a distinctive pleasant smell. **2** a subtle pervasive quality or atmosphere.

aromatherapy *n* massage with fragrant oils to relieve tension.

aromatic *adj* **1** having a distinctive pleasant smell. **2** *Chem* (of an organic compound) having an unsaturated ring of atoms, usually six carbon atoms. *~n* **3** something, such as a plant or drug, that gives off a fragrant smell.

arose *vb* the past tense of **arise.**

around *prep* **1** situated at various points in: *cameramen were positioned around the auditorium.* **2** from place to place in: *he had spent twenty-five minutes driving around Amsterdam.* **3** somewhere in or near. **4** approximately in: *around 1980.* *~adv* **5** in all directions from a point of reference: *there wasn't a house for miles around.* **6** in the vicinity, esp. restlessly but idly: *I couldn't hang around too long.* **7** in no particular place or direction: *a few tropical fish tanks dotted around.* **8** *Informal* present in some unknown or unspecified place. **9** *Informal* available: *cancer drugs have been around for years.* **10 have been around** *Informal* to have gained considerable experience of a worldly or social nature.

arouse *vb* **arousing, aroused 1** to produce (a reaction, emotion, or response). **2** to awaken from sleep. **arousal** *n*

arpeggio (arp-**pej**-ee-oh) *n, pl* **-gios** a chord whose notes are played or sung in rapid succession.

arquebus (**ark**-wee-bus) *n* a portable long-barrelled gun dating from the 15th century.

arrack *or* **arak** *n* a coarse alcoholic drink distilled in Eastern countries from grain or rice.

arraign (ar-**rain**) *vb* **1** to bring (a prisoner) before a court to answer a charge. **2** to accuse. **arraignment** *n*

arrange *vb* **-ranging, -ranged 1** to plan in advance: *my parents had arranged a surprise party.* **2** to arrive at an agreement: *they had arranged to go to the cinema.* **3** to put into a proper or systematic order. **4** to adapt (a musical composition) for performance in a certain way.

arrangement *n* **1** a preparation or plan made for an event: *travel arrangements.* **2** an agreement or a plan to do something. **3** a thing composed of various ordered parts: *a flower arrangement.* **4** the form in which things are arranged. **5** an adaptation of a piece of music for performance in a different way.

arrant *adj* utter or downright: *that's the most arrant nonsense I've ever heard.*

arras *n* a tapestry wall-hanging.

array *n* **1** an impressive display or collection. **2** an orderly arrangement, such as of troops in battle order. **3** *Computers* a data structure in which elements may be located by index numbers. **4** *Poetic* rich clothing. *~vb* **5** to arrange in order. **6** to dress in rich clothing.

arrears *pl n* **1** money owed. **2 in arrears** late in paying a debt.

arrest *vb* **1** to take (a person) into custody. **2** to slow or stop the development of. **3** to catch and hold (one's attention). *~n* **4** the act of taking a person into custody. **5 under arrest** being held in custody by the po-

THESAURUS

armoured armour-plated, bombproof, bulletproof, ironclad, mailed, protected, steel-plated

armoury ammunition dump, arms depot, arsenal, magazine, ordnance depot

arms 1. armaments, firearms, guns, instruments of war, ordnance, weaponry, weapons **2.** blazonry, crest, escutcheon, heraldry, insignia

army 1. armed force, host (*archaic*), land forces, legions, military, military force, soldiers, soldiery, troops **2.** array, horde, host, multitude, pack, swarm, throng, vast number

aroma bouquet, fragrance, odour, perfume, redolence, savour, scent, smell

aromatic balmy, fragrant, odoriferous, perfumed, pungent, redolent, savoury, spicy, sweet-scented, sweet-smelling

around *prep.* **1.** about, encircling, enclosing, encompassing, environing, on all sides of, on every side of, surrounding **2.** about, approximately, circa (*used with dates*), roughly *~adv.* **3.** about, all over, everywhere, here and there, in all directions, on all sides, throughout, to and fro **4.** at hand, close, close at hand, close by, near, nearby, nigh (*archaic, poetic*)

arouse agitate, animate, awaken, call forth, enliven, excite, foment, foster, goad, incite, inflame, instigate, kindle, move, prod, provoke, quicken, rouse, sharpen, spark, spur, stimulate, stir up, summon up, waken, wake up, warm, whet, whip up

arrange 1. adjust, agree to, come to terms, compromise, construct, contrive, determine, devise, fix up, organize, plan, prepare, project, schedule, settle **2.** align, array, class, classify, dispose, file, form, group, line up, marshal, order, organize, position, put in order, range, rank, set out, sort, sort out (*informal*), systematize, tidy **3.** adapt, instrument, orchestrate, score

arrangement 1. adjustment, agreement, compact, compromise, construction, deal, devising, organization, plan, planning, preparation, provision, schedule, settlement, terms **2.** alignment, array, classification, design, display, disposition, form, grouping, line-up, marshalling, order, ordering, organization, ranging, rank, setup (*informal*), structure, system **3.** adaptation, instrumentation, interpretation, orchestration, score, version

array *n.* **1.** arrangement, collection, display, disposition, exhibition, formation, line up, marshalling, muster, order, parade, show, supply **2.** *poetic* apparel, attire, clothes, dress, finery, garb, garments, raiment (*archaic or poetic*), regalia *~vb.* **3.** align, arrange, display, dispose, draw up, exhibit, form up, group, line up, marshal, muster, order, parade, place in order, range, set in line (*Military*), show **4.** accoutre, adorn, apparel (*archaic*), attire, bedeck, caparison, clothe, deck, decorate, dress, equip, festoon, fit out, garb, get ready, outfit, robe, supply, wrap

arrest *vb.* **1.** apprehend, bust (*informal*), capture, catch, collar (*informal*), detain, lay hold of, lift (*slang*), nab (*informal*), nail (*informal*), nick (*slang*), pinch (*informal*), run in (*slang*), seize, take, take into custody, take prisoner **2.** block, check, delay, end, halt, hinder, hold, inhibit, interrupt, obstruct, restrain, retard, slow, stall, stay, stop, suppress **3.** absorb, catch, engage, engross, fascinate, grip, hold, intrigue, occupy *~n.* **4.** apprehension, bust (*informal*), capture, cop (*slang*), detention, seizure **5.** blockage, check, delay, end, halt,

lice. **6** the slowing or stopping of something: *a cardiac arrest.*

arresting *adj* attracting attention; striking.

arrival *n* **1** the act of arriving. **2** a person or thing that has just arrived. **3** *Informal* a recently born baby.

arrive *vb* **-riving, -rived 1** to reach a place or destination. **2 arrive at** to come to (a conclusion, idea, or decision). **3** to occur: *the crisis he predicted then has now arrived.* **4** *Informal* to be born. **5** *Informal* to attain success.

arrivederci (ar-reeve-a-**der**-chee) *interj* goodbye.

arrogant *adj* having an exaggerated opinion of one's own importance or ability. **arrogance** *n* **arrogantly** *adv*

arrogate *vb* **-gating, -gated** to claim or seize without justification. **arrogation** *n*

arrow *n* **1** a long slender pointed weapon, with feathers at one end, that is shot from a bow. **2** an arrow-shaped sign or symbol used to show the direction to a place.

arrowhead *n* the pointed tip of an arrow.

arrowroot *n* an easily digestible starch obtained from the root of a West Indian plant.

arse *or US & Canad* **ass** *n Taboo* the buttocks or anus.

arsehole *or US & Canad* **asshole** *n Taboo* **1** the anus. **2** a stupid or annoying person.

arsenal *n* **1** a building in which arms and ammunition are made or stored. **2** a store of anything regarded as weapons: *this new weapon in the medical arsenal.*

arsenic *n* **1** a toxic metalloid element. Symbol: As **2** a nontechnical name for **arsenic trioxide**, a highly poisonous compound used as a rat poison and insecticide. *~adj also* **arsenical 3** of or containing arsenic.

arson *n* the crime of intentionally setting fire to property. **arsonist** *n*

art *n* **1** the creation of works of beauty or other special significance. **2** works of art collectively. **3** human creativity as distinguished from nature. **4** skill: *she was still new to the art of bargaining.* **5** any branch of the visual arts, esp. painting. **6 get something down to a fine art** to become proficient at something through practice.

Art Deco (art **deck**-oh) *n* a style of design, at its height in the 1930s, characterized by geometrical shapes.

artefact *or* **artifact** *n* something made by human beings, such as a tool or a work of art.

arterial *adj* **1** of or affecting an artery. **2** being a major route: *an arterial road.*

arteriosclerosis (art-ear-ee-oh-skler-**oh**-siss) *n* thickening and loss of elasticity of the walls of the arteries. Nontechnical name: **hardening of the arteries**

artery *n, pl* **-teries 1** any of the tubes that carry oxygenated blood from the heart to various parts of the body. **2** a major road or means of communication.

artesian well (art-**teez**-yan) *n* a well receiving water from a higher altitude, so the water is forced to flow upwards.

Artex *n Trademark* a type of coating for walls and ceilings that gives a textured finish.

art form *n* a recognized mode or medium of artistic expression.

artful *adj* **1** cunning. **2** skilful in achieving a desired end. **artfully** *adv*

arthritis *n* inflammation of a joint or joints, causing pain and stiffness. **arthritic** *adj, n*

arthropod *n* a creature, such as an insect or a spider, which has jointed legs and a hard case on its body.

artic *n Informal* an articulated lorry.

artichoke *n* **1** Also called: **globe artichoke** the flower head of a thistle-like plant, cooked as a vegetable. **2** same as **Jerusalem artichoke.**

article *n* **1** a written composition in a magazine or newspaper. **2** an item or object. **3** a clause in a written document. **4** *Grammar* any of the words *a, an,* or *the.*

articled *adj* bound by a written contract, such as one that governs a period of training: *an articled clerk.*

articular *adj* of or relating to joints.

articulate *adj* **1** able to express oneself fluently and coherently. **2** distinct, clear, or definite: *his amiable and articulate campaign attracted support.* **3** *Zool* possessing joints. *~vb* **-lating, -lated 4** to speak clearly and distinctly. **5** to express coherently in words. **articulately** *adv*

articulated truck *n* a large truck in two separate sections connected by a pivoted bar.

THESAURUS

hindrance, inhibition, interruption, obstruction, restraint, stalling, stay, stoppage, suppression

arresting conspicuous, engaging, extraordinary, impressive, noticeable, outstanding, remarkable, striking, stunning, surprising

arrival 1. advent, appearance, arriving, coming, entrance, happening, occurrence, taking place **2.** arriver, caller, comer, entrant, incomer, newcomer, visitant, visitor

arrive 1. appear, attain, befall, come, enter, get to, happen, occur, reach, show up (*informal*), take place, turn up **2.** *informal* achieve recognition, become famous, make good, make it (*informal*), make the grade (*informal*), reach the top, succeed

arrogance bluster, conceit, conceitedness, contemptuousness, disdainfulness, haughtiness, hauteur, high-handedness, imperiousness, insolence, loftiness, lordliness, overweeningness, pomposity, pompousness, presumption, pretension, pretentiousness, pride, scornfulness, superciliousness, swagger, uppishness (*Brit. informal*)

arrogant assuming, blustering, conceited, contemptuous, disdainful, haughty, high and mighty (*informal*), high-handed, imperious, insolent, lordly, overbearing, overweening, pompous, presumptuous, pretentious, proud, scornful, supercilious, swaggering, uppish (*Brit. informal*)

arrogation appropriation, assumption, commandeering, demand, expropriation, presumption, seizure, usurpation

arrow 1. bolt, dart, shaft **2.** indicator, pointer

arsenal ammunition dump, armoury, arms depot, magazine, ordnance depot, stock, stockpile, store, storehouse, supply

art adroitness, aptitude, artifice (*archaic*), artistry, craft, craftsmanship, dexterity, expertise, facility, ingenuity, knack, knowledge, mastery, method, profession, skill, trade, virtuosity

artful adept, adroit, clever, crafty, cunning, deceitful, designing, dexterous, foxy, ingenious, intriguing, masterly, politic, proficient, resourceful, scheming, sharp, shrewd, skilful, sly, smart, subtle, tricky, wily

article 1. composition, discourse, essay, feature, item, paper, piece, story, treatise **2.** commodity, item, object, piece, substance, thing, unit **3.** branch, clause, count, detail, division, head, heading, item, matter, paragraph, part, particular, passage, piece, point, portion, section

articulate 1. *adj.* clear, coherent, comprehensible, eloquent, expressive, fluent, intelligible, lucid, mean-

articulation *n* **1** the expressing of an idea in words. **2** the process of articulating a speech sound or the sound so produced. **3** a being jointed together. **4** *Zool* a joint between bones or arthropod segments.

artifact *n* same as **artefact.**

artifice *n* **1** a clever trick. **2** skill or cleverness.

artificer (**art**-tiff-iss-er) *n* a skilled craftsman.

artificial *adj* **1** man-made; not occurring naturally. **2** made in imitation of a natural product: *artificial flavourings.* **3** not sincere. **artificiality** *n* **artificially** *adv*

artificial insemination *n* introduction of semen into the womb by means other than sexual intercourse.

artificial intelligence *n* the branch of computer science aiming to produce machines which can imitate intelligent human behaviour.

artificial respiration *n* any method of restarting a person's breathing after it has stopped.

artillery *n* **1** large-calibre guns. **2** military units specializing in the use of such guns.

artisan *n* a skilled workman; craftsman.

artist *n* **1** a person who produces works of art such as paintings or sculpture. **2** a person who is skilled at something. **3** same as **artiste. artistic** *adj* **artistically** *adv*

artiste *n* a professional entertainer such as a singer or dancer.

artistry *n* **1** artistic ability. **2** great skill.

artless *adj* **1** free from deceit or cunning: *artless generosity.* **2** natural or unpretentious. **artlessly** *adv*

Art Nouveau (ahr noo-**voh**) *n* a style of art and architecture of the 1890s, characterized by sinuous outlines and stylized natural forms.

arts *pl n* **1 the arts** the nonscientific branches of knowledge. **2** See **fine art. 3** cunning schemes.

artwork *n* all the photographs and illustrations in a publication.

arty *adj* **artier, artiest** *Informal* having an affected interest in art. **artiness** *n*

arum lily *n* a plant with a white funnel-shaped leaf surrounding a yellow spike of flowers.

Aryan (**air**-ree-an) *n* **1** (in Nazi ideology) a non-Jewish person of the Nordic type. **2** a person supposedly descended from the Indo-Europeans. *~adj* **3** of Aryans.

as *conj* **1** while or when: *he arrived just as the band finished the song.* **2** in the way that: *they had talked and laughed as only the best of friends can.* **3** that which; what: *George did as he was asked.* **4** (of) which fact or event (referring to the previous statement): *to become wise, as we all know, is not easy.* **5 as it were** in a way; in a manner of speaking: *he was, as it were, on probation.* **6** since; seeing that. **7** for instance. *~adv, conj* **8** used to indicate amount or extent in comparisons: *he was as fat as his mum and dad. ~prep* **9** in the role of; being: *my task, as his physician, is to do the best that I can.* **10 as for** *or* **to** with reference to. **11 as if** *or* **though** as it would be if: *she felt as if she had been run over by a bulldozer.* **12 as (it) is** in the existing state of affairs.

As *Chem* arsenic.

ASA 1 Amateur Swimming Association. **2** Advertising Standards Authority.

asafoetida *n* a strong-smelling plant resin used as a spice in Eastern cookery.

a.s.a.p. as soon as possible.

asbestos *n* a fibrous mineral which does not burn, formerly widely used as a heat-resistant material.

asbestosis *n* inflammation of the lungs resulting from inhalation of asbestos fibre.

ascend *vb* **1** to go or move up. **2** to slope upwards. **3 ascend the throne** to become king or queen.

ascendancy *or* **ascendance** *n* the condition of being dominant.

ascendant *or* **ascendent** *adj* **1** dominant or influential. *~n* **2** *Astrol* the sign of the zodiac that is rising

THESAURUS

ingful, understandable, vocal, well-spoken **2.** *vb.* enounce, enunciate, express, pronounce, say, speak, state, talk, utter, verbalize, vocalize, voice

artifice 1. contrivance, device, dodge, expedient, hoax, machination, manoeuvre, ruse, stratagem, subterfuge, tactic, trick, wile **2.** adroitness, cleverness, deftness, facility, finesse, ingenuity, invention, inventiveness, skill

artificer artisan, craftsman, mechanic

artificial 1. man-made, manufactured, non-natural, plastic, synthetic **2.** bogus, counterfeit, ersatz, fake, imitation, mock, phoney *or* phony (*informal*), sham, simulated, specious, spurious **3.** affected, assumed, contrived, false, feigned, forced, hollow, insincere, meretricious, phoney *or* phony (*informal*), pretended, spurious, unnatural

artillery battery, big guns, cannon, cannonry, gunnery, ordnance

artisan artificer, craftsman, handicraftsman, journeyman, mechanic, skilled workman, technician

artistic aesthetic, beautiful, creative, cultivated, cultured, decorative, elegant, exquisite, graceful, imaginative, ornamental, refined, sensitive, sophisticated, stylish, tasteful

artistry accomplishment, art, artistic ability, brilliance, craft, craftsmanship, creativity, finesse, flair, genius, mastery, proficiency, sensibility, skill, style, talent, taste, touch, virtuosity, workmanship

artless 1. candid, direct, fair, frank, genuine, guileless, honest, open, plain, sincere, straightforward, true, undesigning, upfront (*informal*) **2.** humble, natural, plain, pure, simple, unadorned, unaffected, uncontrived, unpretentious

as *conj.* **1.** at the time that, during the time that, just as, when, while **2.** in the manner that, in the way that, like **3.** that which, what **4. as it were** in a manner of speaking, in a way, so to say, so to speak **5.** because, considering that, seeing that, since **6.** for instance, like, such as *~prep.* **7.** being, in the character of, in the role of, under the name of **8. as for** as regards, in reference to, on the subject of, with reference to, with regard to, with respect to

ascend climb, float up, fly up, go up, lift off, mount, move up, rise, scale, slope upwards, soar, take off, tower

ascendancy, ascendency authority, command, control, dominance, domination, dominion, hegemony, influence, mastery, power, predominance, pre-eminence, prevalence, reign, rule, sovereignty, superiority, supremacy, sway, upper hand

ascendant, ascendent 1. *adj.* authoritative, commanding, controlling, dominant, influential, powerful, predominant, pre-eminent, prevailing, ruling, superior, supreme, uppermost **2.** *n.* **in the ascendant** ascending, climbing, commanding, dominant, dominating, flourishing, growing, increasing, mounting, on the rise, on the way up, prevailing, rising, supreme, up-and-coming, uppermost, winning

ascent 1. ascending, ascension, clambering, climb, climbing, mounting, rise, rising, scaling, upward

on the eastern horizon at a particular moment. **3 in the ascendant** increasing in power or influence.
ascension *n* the act of ascending.
ascent *n* **1** the act of ascending. **2** an upward slope.
ascertain *vb* to find out definitely. **ascertainment** *n*
ascetic (ass-**set**-tik) *n* **1** a person who abstains from worldly comforts and pleasures. *~adj* **2** rigidly abstinent and self-denying.
ascorbic acid (ass-**core**-bik) *n* a vitamin that occurs in citrus fruits, tomatoes, and green vegetables, and which prevents and cures scurvy. Also called: **vitamin C**
ascribe *vb* **-cribing, -cribed 1** to attribute, as to a particular origin: *headaches which may be ascribed to stress.* **2** to consider that (a particular quality) is possessed by something or someone: *specific human qualities are ascribed to each of the four elements.* **ascription** *n*
aseptic (eh-**sep**-tik) *adj* free from harmful bacteria.
asexual (eh-**sex**-yew-al) *adj* **1** having no apparent sex or sex organs. **2** (of reproduction) not involving sexual activity. **asexually** *adv*
ash[1] *n* **1** the powdery substance formed when something is burnt. **2** fine particles of lava thrown out by an erupting volcano.
ash[2] *n* a tree with grey bark and winged seeds.
ashamed *adj* **1** overcome with shame or remorse. **2** unwilling through fear of humiliation or shame: *she'd be ashamed to admit to jealousy.*
ash can *n US* dustbin.
ashen *adj* pale with shock.
ashes *pl n* **1** remains after burning. **2** the remains of a human body after cremation.
Ashes *pl n* **the Ashes** a cricket trophy competed for by England and Australia since 1882.
ashlar *or* **ashler** *n* **1** a square block of cut stone for use in building. **2** a thin dressed stone used to face a wall.
ashore *adv* towards or on land.
ashram *n* a religious retreat where a Hindu holy man lives.
ashtray *n* a dish for tobacco ash and cigarette ends.
Ash Wednesday *n* the first day of Lent, named from the Christian custom of sprinkling ashes on penitents' heads.
ashy *adj* **ashier, ashiest 1** pale greyish. **2** covered with ash.
Asian *adj* **1** of Asia. **2** *Brit* of the Indian subcontinent. *~n* **3** a person from Asia. **4** *Brit* a person from the Indian subcontinent or a descendant of one.
➤ Use *Asian* for "someone who comes from Asia". *Asiatic* in this context can be offensive.
Asian pear *n* an apple-shaped pear with crisp juicy flesh.
Asiatic *adj* Asian.
➤ Use *Asian* for "someone who comes from Asia". *Asiatic* in this context can be offensive.
aside *adv* **1** to one side. **2** out of other people's hearing: *her mother took her aside for a serious talk.* **3** out of mind: *she pushed aside her fears of being beaten or killed.* **4** into reserve: *a certain amount must also be put aside for defence and government.* *~n* **5** a remark not meant to be heard by everyone present. **6** a remark that is not connected with the subject being discussed.
asinine (**ass**-in-nine) *adj* **1** obstinate or stupid. **2** of or like an ass.
ask *vb* **1** to say or write (something) in a form that requires an answer: *I asked him his name; "do you think we'll have trouble landing?" he asked.* **2** to make a request or demand: *the chairman asked for a show of hands.* **3** to invite. **4** to inquire about: *I pretended to be lost and asked for directions.* **5** to expect: *is that too much to ask?*
ask after *vb* to make polite inquiries about the health of: *he asked after you.*
askance (ass-**kanss**) *adv* **look askance at a** to look at with an oblique glance. **b** to regard with suspicion.
askew *adv, adj* towards one side; crooked.
ask for *vb* **1** to seek to speak to. **2** to request. **3** *Informal* to behave in a manner that is regarded as inviting (something): *you were asking for trouble there.*
asking price *n* the price suggested by a seller.
aslant *adv* **1** at a slant. *~prep* **2** slanting across.
asleep *adj* **1** in or into a state of sleep. **2** (of limbs) numb. **3** *Informal* not listening or paying attention.
ASLEF Associated Society of Locomotive Engineers and Firemen.
asp *n* a small viper of S Europe.
asparagus *n* the young shoots of a plant of the lily family, which can be cooked and eaten.
aspartame *n* an artificial sweetener.
aspect *n* **1** a distinct feature or element in a problem or situation. **2** a position facing a particular direction:

THESAURUS

movement **2.** acclivity, gradient, incline, ramp, rise, rising ground, upward slope
ascertain confirm, determine, discover, establish, ferret out, find out, fix, identify, learn, make certain, settle, suss (out) (*slang*), verify
ascetic 1. *n.* abstainer, anchorite, hermit, monk, nun, recluse, self-denier **2.** *adj.* abstemious, abstinent, austere, celibate, frugal, harsh, plain, puritanical, rigorous, self-denying, self-disciplined, severe, Spartan, stern
ascribe assign, attribute, charge, credit, impute, put down, refer, set down
ashamed abashed, bashful, blushing, chagrined, conscience-stricken, crestfallen, discomfited, distressed, embarrassed, guilty, humbled, humiliated, mortified, prudish, reluctant, remorseful, shamefaced, sheepish, shy, sorry
ashore aground, landwards, on dry land, on land, on the beach, on the shore, shorewards, to the shore
aside 1. *adv.* alone, alongside, apart, away, beside, in isolation, in reserve, on one side, out of mind, out of the way, privately, separately, to one side, to the side **2.** *n.* departure, digression, excursion, excursus, interpolation, interposition, parenthesis, tangent
asinine braindead (*informal*), brainless, daft (*informal*), dunderheaded, fatuous, foolish, goofy (*informal*), gormless (*Brit. informal*), halfwitted, idiotic, imbecile, imbecilic, inane, moronic, obstinate, senseless, silly, stupid, thickheaded, thick-witted
ask 1. inquire, interrogate, query, question, quiz **2.** appeal, apply, beg, beseech, claim, crave, demand, entreat, implore, petition, plead, pray, request, seek, solicit, sue, supplicate **3.** bid, invite, summon
askance a awry, indirectly, obliquely, out of the corner of one's eye, sideways, with a side glance **b** disapprovingly, distrustfully, doubtfully, dubiously, mistrustfully, sceptically, suspiciously
askew *adv./adj.* aslant, awry, cockeyed (*informal*), crooked, crookedly, lopsided, oblique, obliquely, off-centre, skewwhiff (*Brit. informal*), to one side
asleep dead to the world (*informal*), dormant, dozing, fast asleep, napping, sleeping, slumbering, snoozing (*informal*), sound asleep
aspect 1. angle, facet, feature, side **2.** bearing, direc-

due to the room's east-facing aspect, the existing fabrics had not faded. **3** appearance or look: *a room with a somewhat gloomy aspect.*

aspen *n* a poplar tree whose leaves quiver in the wind.

asperity (ass-**per**-rit-ee) *n, pl* **-ties** roughness or sharpness of temper.

aspersion *n* **cast aspersions on** to make disparaging or malicious remarks about.

asphalt *n* **1** a black tarlike substance used in road-surfacing and roofing materials. *~vb* **2** to cover with asphalt.

asphodel *n* a plant with clusters of yellow or white flowers.

asphyxia (ass-**fix**-ee-a) *n* unconsciousness or death caused by lack of oxygen.

asphyxiate *vb* **-ating, -ated** to smother or suffocate. **asphyxiation** *n*

aspic *n* a savoury jelly based on meat or fish stock, used as a mould for meat or vegetables.

aspidistra *n* a house plant with long tapered evergreen leaves.

aspirant *n* a person who aspires, such as to a powerful position.

aspirate *Phonetics* *vb* **-rating, -rated 1** to pronounce (a word or syllable) with an initial *h*. *~n* **2** the sound represented in English and several other languages as *h*.

aspiration *n* **1** a strong desire or aim. **2** *Phonetics* the pronunciation of an aspirated consonant. **aspirational** *adj*

aspirator *n* a device for removing fluids from a body cavity by suction.

aspire *vb* **-piring, -pired** to yearn for something or hope to do or be something: *it struck him as bizarre that somebody could aspire to be a dental technician.* **aspiring** *adj*

aspirin *n, pl* **-rin** *or* **-rins 1** a drug used to relieve pain and fever. **2** a tablet of aspirin.

ass[1] *n* **1** a mammal resembling the horse but with longer ears. **2** a foolish person.

ass[2] *n US & Canad taboo* same as **arse.**

assagai *n* same as **assegai.**

assail *vb* **1** to attack violently. **2** to criticize strongly. **3** to disturb: *he was assailed by a dizzy sensation.* **assailant** *n*

assassin *n* a murderer of a prominent person.

assassinate *vb* **-nating, -nated** to murder (a prominent person). **assassination** *n*

assault *n* **1** a violent attack, either physical or verbal. *~vb* **2** to attack violently.

assault and battery *n Criminal law* a threat of attack to another person followed by actual attack.

assault course *n* an obstacle course designed to give soldiers practice in negotiating hazards.

assay *vb* **1** to analyse (a substance, such as gold) to find out how pure it is. *~n* **2** an analysis of the purity of an ore or precious metal.

assegai *or* **assagai** *n, pl* **-gais** a sharp light spear used in southern Africa.

assemblage *n* **1** a collection or group of things. **2** the act of assembling.

assemble *vb* **-bling, -bled 1** to collect or gather together. **2** to put together the parts of (a machine).

assembler *n* **1** a person or thing that assembles. **2** a computer program that converts a set of low-level symbolic data into machine language.

assembly *n, pl* **-blies 1** a number of people gathered together for a meeting. **2** the act of assembling.

THESAURUS

tion, exposure, outlook, point of view, position, prospect, scene, situation, view **3.** air, appearance, attitude, bearing, condition, countenance, demeanour, expression, look, manner, mien (*literary*)

asperity acerbity, acrimony, bitterness, churlishness, crabbedness, crossness, harshness, irascibility, irritability, moroseness, peevishness, roughness, ruggedness, severity, sharpness, sourness, sullenness

asphyxiate choke, smother, stifle, strangle, strangulate, suffocate, throttle

aspirant applicant, aspirer, candidate, hopeful, postulant, seeker, suitor

aspiration aim, ambition, craving, desire, dream, eagerness, endeavour, goal, hankering, hope, longing, object, objective, wish, yearning

aspire aim, be ambitious, be eager, crave, desire, dream, hanker, hope, long, pursue, seek, wish, yearn

aspiring ambitious, aspirant, eager, endeavouring, hopeful, longing, striving, wishful, would-be

ass 1. donkey, jennet, moke (*Brit. slang*) **2.** airhead (*slang*), berk (*Brit. slang*), blockhead, bonehead (*slang*), charlie (*Brit. informal*), coot, daftie (*informal*), dickhead (*slang*), dipstick (*Brit. slang*), divvy (*Brit. slang*), dolt, dope (*informal*), dork (*slang*), dunce, dweeb (*U.S. slang*), fool, fuckwit (*taboo slang*), geek (*slang*), halfwit, idiot, jackass, jerk (*slang, chiefly U.S. & Canad.*), nerd *or* nurd (*slang*), nincompoop, ninny, nitwit (*informal*), numskull *or* numbskull, oaf, pillock (*Brit. slang*), plank (*Brit. slang*), plonker (*slang*), prat (*slang*), prick (*derogatory slang*), schmuck (*U.S. slang*), simpleton, twerp *or* twirp (*informal*), twit (*informal, chiefly Brit.*), wally (*slang*)

assail 1. assault, attack, belabour, beset, charge, encounter, fall upon, invade, lay into (*informal*), maltreat, set about, set upon **2.** abuse, berate, blast, criticize, impugn, lambast(e), malign, put down, revile, tear into (*informal*), vilify

assassin eliminator (*slang*), executioner, hatchet man (*slang*), hit man (*slang*), killer, liquidator, murderer, slayer

assassinate blow away (*slang, chiefly U.S.*), eliminate (*slang*), hit (*slang*), kill, liquidate, murder, slay, take out (*slang*)

assault 1. *n.* aggression, attack, charge, incursion, inroad, invasion, offensive, onset, onslaught, storm, storming, strike **2.** *vb.* assail, attack, belabour, beset, charge, fall upon, invade, lay into (*informal*), set about, set upon, storm, strike at

assay 1. *vb.* analyse, appraise, assess, evaluate, examine, inspect, investigate, prove, test, try, weigh **2.** *n.* analysis, examination, inspection, investigation, test, trial

assemble 1. accumulate, amass, bring together, call together, collect, come together, congregate, convene, convoke, flock, forgather, gather, marshal, meet, muster, rally, round up, summon **2.** build up, connect, construct, erect, fabricate, fit together, join, make, manufacture, piece together, put together, set up

assembly 1. accumulation, aggregation, assemblage, body, collection, company, conclave, conference, congregation, congress, convocation, council, crowd, diet, flock, gathering, group, house, mass, meeting, multitude, rally, synod, throng **2.** building up, connecting, construction, erection, fabrication, fitting together, joining, manufacture, piecing together, putting together, setting up

assent 1. *n.* acceptance, accession, accord, acquiescence, agreement, approval, compliance, concurrence,

assembly line *n* a sequence of machines and workers in a factory assembling a product.
assemblyman *n, pl* **-men** a member of a legislative assembly.
assent *n* **1** agreement, consent. *~vb* **2** to agree.
assert *vb* **1** to state or declare. **2** to insist upon (one's rights, etc.). **3 assert oneself** to speak and act forcefully.
assertion *n* **1** a positive statement, usually made without evidence. **2** the act of asserting.
assertive *adj* confident and direct in dealing with others. **assertively** *adv* **assertiveness** *n*
assess *vb* **1** to judge the worth or importance of. **2** to estimate the value of (income or property) for taxation purposes. **assessment** *n*
assessor *n* **1** a person who values property for taxation or insurance purposes. **2** a person with technical expertise called in to advise a court. **3** a person who evaluates the merits of something.
asset *n* **1** a thing or person that is valuable or useful. **2** any property owned by a person or company.
asset-stripping *n Commerce* the practice of taking over a failing company at a low price and then selling the assets piecemeal. **asset-stripper** *n*
asseverate *vb* **-ating, -ated** *Formal* to declare solemnly. **asseveration** *n*
assiduous *adj* **1** hard-working. **2** done with care. **assiduity** *n* **assiduously** *adv*
assign *vb* **1** to select (someone) for a post or task. **2** to give a task or duty (to someone). **3** to attribute to a specified cause. **4** to set apart (a place or time) for a particular function or event: *to assign a day for the meeting.* **5** *Law* to transfer (one's right, interest, or title to property) to someone else.
assignation (ass-sig-**nay**-shun) *n* a secret arrangement to meet, esp. one between lovers.
assignment *n* **1** something that has been assigned, such as a task. **2** the act of assigning. **3** *Law* the transfer to another person of a right, interest, or title to property.
assimilate *vb* **-lating, -lated 1** to learn (information) and understand it thoroughly. **2** to adjust or become adjusted: *they became assimilated to German culture.* **3** to absorb (food). **assimilable** *adj* **assimilation** *n*
assist *vb* to give help or support.
assistance *n* help or support.
assistant *n* **1** a helper or subordinate. **2** same as **shop assistant.** *~adj* **3** junior or deputy: *assistant manager.*
assizes *pl n* (formerly in England and Wales) the sessions of the principal court in each county.
assoc. association.
associate *vb* **-ating, -ated 1** to connect in the mind. **2** to mix socially: *addicts are driven to associate with criminals.* **3 be associated** *or* **associate oneself with** to be involved with (a group) because of shared views: *she had long been associated with the far right.* *~n* **4** a partner in business. **5** a companion or friend. *~adj* **6** having partial rights or subordinate status: *an associate member.* **7** joined with in business: *an associate director.*
association *n* **1** a group of people with a common interest. **2** the act of associating or the state of being

THESAURUS

consent, permission, sanction **2.** *vb.* accede, accept, acquiesce, agree, allow, approve, comply, concur, consent, fall in with, go along with, grant, permit, sanction, subscribe
assert 1. affirm, allege, asseverate, attest, aver, avouch (*archaic*), avow, contend, declare, maintain, predicate, profess, pronounce, state, swear **2.** claim, defend, insist upon, press, put forward, stand up for, stress, uphold, vindicate **3. assert oneself** exert one's influence, make one's presence felt, put oneself forward
assertion 1. affirmation, allegation, asseveration, attestation, avowal, contention, declaration, predication, profession, pronouncement, statement **2.** defence, insistence, maintenance, stressing, vindication
assertive aggressive, confident, decided, decisive, demanding, dogmatic, domineering, emphatic, feisty (*informal, chiefly U.S. & Canad.*), firm, forceful, forward, insistent, overbearing, positive, pushy (*informal*), self-assured, strong-willed
assess 1. appraise, compute, determine, estimate, evaluate, eye up, fix, gauge, judge, rate, size up (*informal*), value, weigh **2.** demand, evaluate, fix, impose, levy, rate, tax, value
assessment 1. appraisal, computation, determination, estimate, estimation, evaluation, judgment, rating, valuation **2.** charge, demand, duty, evaluation, fee, impost, levy, rate, rating, tariff, tax, taxation, toll, valuation
asset 1. advantage, aid, benefit, blessing, boon, help, resource, service **2.** *plural* capital, estate, funds, goods, holdings, means, money, possessions, property, reserves, resources, valuables, wealth
assiduous attentive, constant, diligent, hard-working, indefatigable, industrious, laborious, persevering, persistent, sedulous, steady, studious, unflagging, untiring, unwearied
assign 1. appoint, choose, delegate, designate, name, nominate, select **2.** allocate, allot, apportion, consign, distribute, give, give out, grant **3.** accredit, ascribe, attribute, put down **4.** appoint, appropriate, determine, fix, set apart, stipulate
assignment 1. appointment, charge, commission, duty, job, mission, position, post, responsibility, task **2.** allocation, allotment, appointment, apportionment, appropriation, ascription, attribution, choice, consignment, delegation, designation, determination, distribution, giving, grant, nomination, selection, specification, stipulation
assist abet, aid, back, benefit, boost, collaborate, cooperate, encourage, expedite, facilitate, further, help, promote, reinforce, relieve, second, serve, succour, support, sustain, work for, work with
assistance abetment, aid, backing, benefit, boost, collaboration, cooperation, encouragement, furtherance, help, helping hand, promotion, reinforcement, relief, service, succour, support, sustenance
assistant abettor, accessory, accomplice, aide, aider, ally, associate, auxiliary, backer, coadjutor (*rare*), collaborator, colleague, confederate, cooperator, helper, helpmate, henchman, partner, protagonist, right-hand man, second, supporter
associate *vb.* **1.** affiliate, ally, combine, confederate, conjoin, connect, correlate, couple, identify, join, league, link, lump together, mix, pair, relate, think of together, unite, yoke **2.** accompany, befriend, be friends, consort, fraternize, hang about, hang out (*informal*), hobnob, mingle, mix, run around (*informal*) *~n.* **3.** collaborator, colleague, confrère, co-worker **4.** ally, companion, comrade, friend, mate, partner
association 1. affiliation, alliance, band, clique, club, coalition, combine, company, confederacy, confederation, cooperative, corporation, federation, fraternity, group, league, order, organization, partnership, society, syndicate, union **2.** affinity, companionship, comradeship, familiarity, fellowship, fraternization,

associated. **3** friendship: *their association still had to remain a secret.* **4** a mental connection of ideas or feelings: *the place contained associations for her.*

association football *n* same as **soccer.**

associative *adj Maths* (of an operation such as multiplication or addition) producing the same answer regardless of the way the elements are grouped, for example $(2\times 3)\times 4 = 2\times(3\times 4)$.

assonance *n* the rhyming of vowel sounds but not consonants, as in *time* and *light.*

assorted *adj* **1** consisting of various kinds mixed together. **2** matched: *an ill-assorted childless couple.*

assortment *n* a collection of various things or sorts.

asst assistant.

assuage (ass-**wage**) *vb* **-suaging, -suaged** to relieve (grief, pain, or thirst).

assume *vb* **-suming, -sumed 1** to take to be true without proof. **2** to undertake or take on: *every general staff officer was able to assume control of the army.* **3** to make a pretence of: *the man had assumed a debonair attitude.* **4** to take on: *her eyes assumed a scared haunted look.*

assumed name *n* a false name used by someone to disguise his or her identity.

assuming *conj* if it is assumed or taken for granted: *assuming the first two phases were successful, the third phase would follow.*

assumption *n* **1** something that is taken for granted. **2** the act of assuming power or possession.

Assumption *n Christianity* the taking up of the Virgin Mary into heaven when her earthly life was ended.

assurance *n* **1** a statement or assertion intended to inspire confidence. **2** feeling of confidence; certainty. **3** *Chiefly Brit* insurance that provides for events that are certain to happen, such as death.

➤ When used in the context of business, *assurance* and *insurance* have the same meaning.

assure *vb* **-suring, -sured 1** to promise or guarantee. **2** to convince: *they assured me that they had not seen the document.* **3** to make (something) certain. **4** *Chiefly Brit* to insure against loss of life.

assured *adj* **1** confident or self-assured. **2** certain to happen. **3** *Chiefly Brit* insured. **assuredly** (a-**sure**-id-lee) *adv*

Assyrian *n* an inhabitant of ancient Assyria, a kingdom of Mesopotamia.

AST Atlantic Standard Time.

astatine *n Chem* a radioactive element occurring naturally in minute amounts or artificially produced by bombarding bismuth with alpha particles. Symbol: At

aster *n* a plant with white, blue, purple, or pink daisy-like flowers.

asterisk *n* **1** a star-shaped character (*) used in printing or writing to indicate a footnote etc. *~vb* **2** to mark with an asterisk.

astern *adv, adj Naut* **1** at or towards the stern of a ship. **2** backwards. **3** behind a vessel.

asteroid *n* any of the small planets that orbit the sun between Mars and Jupiter.

asthma (**ass**-ma) *n* an illness causing difficulty in breathing. **asthmatic** *adj, n*

astigmatic *adj* of, having, or correcting astigmatism.

astigmatism (eh-**stig**-mat-tiz-zum) *n* a defect of a lens, esp. of the eye, causing it not to focus properly.

astir *adj* **1** out of bed. **2** in motion.

astonish *vb* to surprise greatly. **astonishing** *adj* **astonishment** *n*

astound *vb* to overwhelm with amazement **astounding** *adj*

astraddle *prep* astride.

astrakhan *n* **1** a fur made of the dark curly fleece of lambs from Astrakhan in the former USSR. **2** a cloth resembling this.

astral *adj* **1** relating to or resembling the stars. **2** of the spirit world.

astray *adj, adv* out of the right or expected way

THESAURUS

friendship, intimacy, liaison, partnership, relations, relationship **3.** blend, bond, combination, concomitance, connection, correlation, identification, joining, juxtaposition, linkage, linking, lumping together, mixing, mixture, pairing, relation, tie, union, yoking

assorted different, diverse, diversified, heterogeneous, manifold, miscellaneous, mixed, motley, sundry, varied, variegated, various

assortment array, choice, collection, diversity, farrago, hotchpotch, jumble, medley, *mélange,* miscellany, mishmash, mixed bag (*informal*), mixture, potpourri, salmagundi, selection, variety

assume 1. accept, believe, expect, fancy, guess (*informal, chiefly U.S. & Canad.*), imagine, infer, presume, presuppose, suppose, surmise, suspect, take for granted, think **2.** accept, acquire, attend to, begin, don, embark upon, embrace, enter upon, put on, set about, shoulder, take on, take over, take responsibility for, take up, undertake **3.** adopt, affect, counterfeit, feign, imitate, impersonate, mimic, pretend to, put on, sham, simulate

assumption 1. acceptance, belief, conjecture, expectation, fancy, guess, hypothesis, inference, postulate, postulation, premise, premiss, presumption, presupposition, supposition, surmise, suspicion, theory **2.** acceptance, acquisition, adoption, appropriation, arrogation, embracing, entering upon, expropriation, preempting, putting on, seizure, shouldering, takeover, taking, taking on, taking up, undertaking, usurpation

assurance 1. affirmation, assertion, declaration, guarantee, oath, pledge, profession, promise, protestation, vow, word, word of honour **2.** assertiveness, assuredness, boldness, certainty, certitude, confidence, conviction, coolness, courage, faith, firmness, nerve, poise, positiveness, security, self-confidence, self-reliance, sureness

assure 1. affirm, attest, certify, confirm, declare confidently, give one's word to, guarantee, pledge, promise, swear, vow **2.** comfort, convince, embolden, encourage, hearten, persuade, reassure, soothe **3.** clinch, complete, confirm, ensure, guarantee, make certain, make sure, seal, secure

assured 1. assertive, audacious, bold, brazen, certain, complacent, confident, overconfident, poised, positive, pushy (*informal*), self-assured, self-confident, self-possessed, sure of oneself **2.** beyond doubt, clinched, confirmed, dependable, ensured, fixed, guaranteed, indubitable, irrefutable, made certain, sealed, secure, settled, sure, unquestionable

astonish amaze, astound, bewilder, confound, daze, dumbfound, flabbergast (*informal*), stagger, stun, stupefy, surprise

astonishing amazing, astounding, bewildering, breathtaking, brilliant, impressive, sensational (*informal*), staggering, striking, stunning, stupefying, surprising, wondrous (*archaic or literary*)

astonishment amazement, awe, bewilderment, confusion, consternation, stupefaction, surprise, wonder, wonderment

astounding amazing, astonishing, bewildering, breathtaking, brilliant, impressive, sensational (*informal*), staggering, striking, stunning, stupefying, surprising, wondrous (*archaic or literary*)

astride *adj* **1** with a leg on either side. **2** with legs far apart. ~*prep* **3** with a leg on either side of.

astringent *adj* **1** causing contraction of body tissue. **2** checking the flow of blood from a cut. **3** severe or harsh. ~*n* **4** an astringent drug or lotion. **astringency** *n*

astro- *combining form* indicating a star or stars: *astrology.*

astrolabe *n* an instrument formerly used to measure the altitude of stars and planets.

astrology *n* the study of the alleged influence of the stars, planets, sun, and moon on human affairs. **astrologer** *or* **astrologist** *n* **astrological** *adj*

astronaut *n* a person trained for travelling in space.

astronautics *n* the science and technology of space flight. **astronautical** *adj*

astronomical *or* **astronomic** *adj* **1** enormously large. **2** of astronomy. **astronomically** *adv*

astronomy *n* the scientific study of heavenly bodies. **astronomer** *n*

astrophysics *n* the study of the physical and chemical properties of celestial bodies. **astrophysical** *adj* **astrophysicist** *n*

astute *adj* quick to notice or understand. **astutely** *adv* **astuteness** *n*

asunder *adv, adj Literary* into parts or pieces; apart.

asylum *n* **1** refuge granted to a political refugee from a foreign country. **2** (formerly) a mental hospital.

asymmetry *n* lack of symmetry. **asymmetric** *or* **asymmetrical** *adj*

asymptote (**ass**-im-tote) *n* a straight line that is closely approached but never met by a curve. **asymptotic** *adj*

at *prep* **1** indicating location or position: *she had planted a vegetable garden at the back.* **2** towards; in the direction of: *she was staring at the wall behind him.* **3** indicating position in time: *we arrived at 12.30.* **4** engaged in: *the innocent laughter of children at play.* **5** during the passing of: *she works at night as a nurse's aide.* **6** for; in exchange for: *crude oil is selling at its lowest price since September.* **7** indicating the object of an emotion: *I'm angry at you because you were rude to me.*

At *Chem* astatine.

at. **1** atmosphere. **2** atomic.

atavism (**at**-a-viz-zum) *n* **1** the recurrence of primitive characteristics that were present in distant ancestors but not in more recent ones. **2** reversion to a former type. **atavistic** *adj*

ataxia *n Pathol* lack of muscular coordination. **ataxic** *adj*

ate *vb* the past tense of **eat.**

atelier (**at**-tell-yay) *n* an artist's studio.

atheism (**aith**-ee-iz-zum) *n* the belief that there is no God. **atheist** *n*

atherosclerosis *n, pl* **-ses** a disease in which deposits of fat cause the walls of the arteries to thicken. **atherosclerotic** *adj*

athlete *n* **1** a person trained to compete in sports or exercises. **2** *Chiefly Brit* a competitor in track-and-field events.

athlete's foot *n* a fungal infection of the skin of the foot.

athletic *adj* **1** physically fit or strong. **2** of or for an athlete or athletics. **athletically** *adv* **athleticism** *n*

athletics *pl n Chiefly Brit* track-and-field events.

at-home *n* a social gathering in a person's home.

athwart *prep* **1** across. ~*adv* **2** transversely; from one side to another.

Atlantic *adj* of the Atlantic Ocean, the world's second largest ocean, bounded by the Arctic, the Antarctic, America, and Europe and Africa.

Atlantis *n* (in ancient legend) a continent said to have sunk beneath the Atlantic west of Gibraltar.

atlas *n* a book of maps.

atmosphere *n* **1** the mass of gases surrounding the earth or any other heavenly body. **2** the air in a particular place. **3** a pervasive feeling or mood: *the atmosphere was tense.* **4** a unit of pressure equal to the normal pressure of the air at sea level. **atmospheric** *adj* **atmospherically** *adv*

atmospherics *pl n* radio interference caused by electrical disturbance in the atmosphere.

atoll *n* a circular coral reef surrounding a lagoon.

atom *n* **1** **a** the smallest unit of matter which can take part in a chemical reaction. **b** this entity as a source of nuclear energy. **2** a very small amount.

atom bomb *n* same as **atomic bomb.**

atomic *adj* **1** of or using atom bombs or atomic energy. **2** of atoms. **atomically** *adv*

atomic bomb *or* **atom bomb** *n* a type of bomb in which the energy is provided by nuclear fission.

atomic energy *n* same as **nuclear energy.**

atomic mass unit *n* a unit of mass that is equal to one twelfth of the mass of an atom of carbon-12.

atomic number *n* the number of protons in the nucleus of an atom of an element.

atomic theory *n* any theory in which matter is regarded as consisting of atoms.

THESAURUS

astray *adj./adv.* adrift, afield, amiss, into error, into sin, lost, off, off course, off the mark, off the right track, off the subject, to the bad, wrong

astronaut cosmonaut, spaceman, space pilot, space traveller, spacewoman

astute adroit, artful, bright, calculating, canny, clever, crafty, cunning, discerning, foxy, insightful, intelligent, keen, knowing, penetrating, perceptive, politic, sagacious, sharp, shrewd, sly, subtle, wily

astuteness acumen, adroitness, artfulness, brightness, canniness, cleverness, craftiness, cunning, discernment, foxiness, insight, intelligence, keenness, knowledge, penetration, perceptiveness, sagacity, sharpness, shrewdness, slyness, smarts (*slang, chiefly U.S.*), subtlety, suss (*slang*), wiliness

asylum **1.** harbour, haven, preserve, refuge, retreat, safety, sanctuary, shelter **2.** *old-fashioned* funny farm (*facetious*), hospital, institution, loony bin (*slang*), madhouse (*informal*), mental hospital, nuthouse (*slang*), psychiatric hospital

atheism disbelief, freethinking, godlessness, heathenism, infidelity, irreligion, nonbelief, paganism, scepticism, unbelief

atheist disbeliever, freethinker, heathen, infidel, irreligionist, nonbeliever, pagan, sceptic, unbeliever

athlete competitor, contender, contestant, games player, gymnast, player, runner, sportsman, sportswoman

athletic able-bodied, active, brawny, energetic, fit, herculean, husky (*informal*), lusty, muscular, powerful, robust, sinewy, strapping, strong, sturdy, vigorous, well-proportioned

athletics contests, exercises, games of strength, gymnastics, races, sports, track and field events

atmosphere **1.** aerosphere, air, heavens, sky **2.** air, ambience, aura, character, climate, environment, feel,

atomic weight *n* the ratio of the average mass per atom of an element to one twelfth of the mass of an atom of carbon-12.

atomize *or* **-ise** *vb* **-izing, -ized** *or* **-ising, -ised 1** to separate into free atoms. **2** to reduce to fine particles or spray. **3** to destroy by nuclear weapons.

atomizer *or* **-iser** *n* a device for reducing a liquid to a fine spray.

atonal (eh-**tone**-al) *adj* (of music) not written in an established key. **atonality** *n*

atone *vb* **atoning, atoned** to make amends (for sin or wrongdoing).

atonement *n* **1** something done to make amends for wrongdoing. **2** *Christian theol* the reconciliation of humankind with God through the sacrificial death of Christ.

atop *prep* on top of.

atrium *n, pl* **atria 1** *Anat* the upper chamber of each half of the heart. **2** a central hall that extends through several storeys in a modern building. **3** the open main court of an ancient Roman house. **atrial** *adj*

atrocious *adj* **1** extremely cruel or wicked. **2** horrifying or shocking. **3** *Informal* very bad. **atrociously** *adv*

atrocity *n* **1** behaviour that is wicked or cruel. **2** (*pl* **-ties**) an act of extreme cruelty.

atrophy (**at**-trof-fee) *n, pl* **-phies 1** a wasting away of a physical organ or part. **2** a failure to grow. *~vb* **-phies, -phying, -phied 3** to waste away.

atropine *n* a poisonous alkaloid obtained from deadly nightshade.

attach *vb* **1** to join, fasten, or connect. **2** to attribute or ascribe: *he attaches particular importance to the proposed sale.* **3 attach oneself** *or* **be attached to** to become associated with or join.

attaché (at-**tash**-shay) *n* a specialist attached to a diplomatic mission.

attaché case *n* a flat rectangular briefcase for carrying papers.

attached *adj* **1** married, engaged, or in an exclusive sexual relationship. **2 attached to** fond of.

attachment *n* **1** affection or regard for. **2** an accessory that can be fitted to a device to change what it can do.

attack *vb* **1** to launch a physical assault (against). **2** to criticize vehemently. **3** to set about (a job or problem) with vigour. **4** to affect adversely: *BSE attacks the animal's brain.* **5** to take the initiative in a game or sport. *~n* **6** the act of attacking. **7** any sudden appearance of a disease or symptoms: *a bad attack of mumps.* **attacker** *n*

attain *vb* **1** to manage to do or get (something): *the country attained economic growth.* **2** to reach. **attainable** *adj*

attainment *n* an achievement or the act of achieving something.

attar *n* a perfume made from damask roses.

attempt *vb* **1** to make an effort (to do or achieve something); try. *~n* **2** an endeavour to achieve something; effort. **3 attempt on someone's life** an attack on someone with the intention to kill.

attend *vb* **1** to be present at (an event). **2** to go regularly to a school, college, etc. **3** to look after: *the actors lounged in their canvas chairs, attended by sycophants.* **4** to pay attention. **5 attend to** to apply oneself to: *I've a few things I must attend to.*

THESAURUS

feeling, flavour, mood, quality, spirit, surroundings, tone, vibes (*slang*)

atom bit, crumb, dot, fragment, grain, iota, jot, mite, molecule, morsel, mote, particle, scintilla (*rare*), scrap, shred, speck, spot, tittle, trace, whit

atone answer for, compensate, do penance for, make amends for, make redress, make reparation for, make up for, pay for, recompense, redress

atrocious 1. barbaric, brutal, cruel, diabolical, fiendish, flagrant, godawful (*slang*), heinous, infamous, infernal, inhuman, monstrous, nefarious, ruthless, savage, vicious, villainous, wicked **2.** appalling, detestable, execrable, grievous, horrible, horrifying, shocking, terrible

atrocity 1. atrociousness, barbarity, barbarousness, brutality, cruelty, enormity, fiendishness, grievousness, heinousness, horror, infamy, inhumanity, monstrousness, nefariousness, ruthlessness, savagery, shockingness, viciousness, villainousness, wickedness **2.** abomination, act of savagery, barbarity, brutality, crime, cruelty, enormity, evil, horror, monstrosity, outrage, villainy

attach 1. add, adhere, affix, annex, append, bind, connect, couple, fasten, fix, join, link, make fast, secure, stick, subjoin, tie, unite **2.** ascribe, assign, associate, attribute, connect, impute, invest with, lay, place, put **3.** accompany, affiliate, associate, become associated with, combine, enlist, join, join forces with, latch on to, sign on with, sign up with, unite with

attached 1. accompanied, engaged, married, partnered, spoken for **2. attached to** affectionate towards, devoted, fond of, full of regard for, possessive

attachment 1. affection, affinity, attraction, bond, devotion, fidelity, fondness, friendship, liking, love, loyalty, partiality, possessiveness, predilection, regard, tenderness **2.** accessory, accoutrement, adapter, addition, add-on, adjunct, appendage, appurtenance, auxiliary, extension, extra, fitting, fixture, supplement, supplementary part

attack *vb.* **1.** assail, assault, charge, fall upon, invade, lay into (*informal*), raid, rush, set about, set upon, storm, strike (at) **2.** abuse, berate, blame, blast, censure, criticize, excoriate, impugn, lambast(e), malign, put down, revile, tear into (*informal*), vilify *~n.* **3.** aggression, assault, charge, foray, incursion, inroad, invasion, offensive, onset, onslaught, raid, rush, strike **4.** access, bout, convulsion, fit, paroxysm, seizure, spasm, spell, stroke

attacker aggressor, assailant, assaulter, intruder, invader, raider

attain accomplish, achieve, acquire, arrive at, bring off, complete, earn, effect, fulfil, gain, get, grasp, obtain, procure, reach, realize, reap, score (*slang*), secure, win

attainment accomplishment, achievement, acquirement, acquisition, arrival at, completion, feat, fulfilment, gaining, getting, obtaining, procurement, reaching, realization, reaping, winning

attempt 1. *vb.* endeavour, essay, experiment, have a crack (go (*informal*), shot (*informal*), stab (*informal*)) (*informal*), seek, strive, tackle, take on, try, try one's hand at, undertake, venture **2.** *n.* assault, attack, bid, crack (*informal*), effort, endeavour, essay, experiment, go (*informal*), shot (*informal*), stab (*informal*), trial, try, undertaking, venture

attend 1. appear, be at, be here, be present, be there, frequent, go to, haunt, make one (*archaic*), put in an appearance, show oneself, show up (*informal*), turn up, visit **2.** care for, look after, mind, minister to, nurse, take care of, tend **3.** follow, hear, hearken (*archaic*), heed, listen, look on, mark, mind, note, notice, observe, pay attention, pay heed, regard, take to heart, watch **4. attend to** apply oneself to, concentrate on, devote oneself to, get to work on, look after, occupy oneself with, see to, take care of

attendance *n* **1** the act of attending. **2** the number of people present. **3** regularity in attending.

attendant *n* **1** a person who assists, guides, or provides a service. *~adj* **2** associated: *nuclear power and its attendant dangers.* **3** being in attendance.

attention *n* **1** concentrated direction of the mind. **2** consideration, notice, or observation. **3** detailed care or treatment. **4** the alert position in military drill. **5 attentions** acts of courtesy: *the attentions of men seemed to embarrass her.*

attentive *adj* **1** paying close attention. **2** considerately helpful: *at society parties he is attentive to his wife.* **attentively** *adv* **attentiveness** *n*

attenuated *adj* **1** weakened. **2** thin and extended. **attenuation** *n*

attest *vb* **1** to affirm or prove the truth of. **2** to bear witness to (an act or event). **attestation** *n*

attested *adj Brit* (of cattle) certified to be free from a disease, such as tuberculosis.

attic *n* a space or room within the roof of a house.

attire *n* clothes, esp. fine or formal ones.

attired *adj* dressed in a specified way.

attitude *n* **1** the way a person thinks and behaves. **2** a position of the body. **3** *Informal* a hostile manner. **4** the orientation of an aircraft or spacecraft in relation to some plane or direction.

attitudinize *or* **-nise** *vb* **-nizing, -nized** *or* **-nising, -nised** to adopt a pose or opinion for effect.

attorney *n* **1** a person legally appointed to act for another. **2** *US* a lawyer.

attorney general *n, pl* **attorneys general** *or* **attorney generals** a chief law officer of some governments.

attract *vb* **1** to arouse the interest or admiration of. **2** (of a magnet) to draw (something) closer by exerting a force on it.

attraction *n* **1** the act or quality of attracting. **2** an interesting or desirable feature: *the Scottishness of Scott is an attraction, but by no means his only merit.* **3** an object or place that people visit for interest: *this carefully preserved tourist attraction.* **4** (of a magnet) a force by which one object attracts another.

attractive *adj* appealing to the senses or mind. **attractively** *adv* **attractiveness** *n*

attribute *vb* **-uting, -uted 1 attribute to** to regard as belonging to or produced by: *a play attributed to William Shakespeare.* *~n* **2** a quality or feature representative of a person or thing. **attributable** *adj* **attribution** *n*

attributive *adj Grammar* (of an adjective) coming before the noun modified.

attrition *n* constant wearing down to weaken or destroy: *a war of attrition.*

attune *vb* **-tuning, -tuned** to adjust or accustom (a person or thing).

atypical (eh-**tip**-ik-kl) *adj* not typical. **atypically** *adv*

Au *Chem* gold.

aubergine (**oh**-bur-zheen) *n* the dark purple fruit of a tropical plant, cooked and eaten as a vegetable.

aubrietia (aw-**bree**-sha) *n* a trailing purple-flowered rock plant.

auburn *adj* (of hair) reddish-brown.

auction *n* **1** a public sale at which articles are sold to the highest bidder. *~vb* **2** to sell by auction.

auctioneer *n* a person who conducts an auction.

audacious *adj* **1** recklessly bold or daring. **2** impudent or presumptuous. **audacity** *n*

audible *adj* loud enough to be heard. **audibility** *n* **audibly** *adv*

THESAURUS

attendance **1.** appearance, attending, being there, presence **2.** audience, crowd, gate, house, number present, turnout

attendant **1.** *n.* aide, assistant, auxiliary, chaperon, companion, custodian, escort, flunky, follower, guard, guide, helper, lackey, menial, servant, steward, underling, usher, waiter **2.** *adj.* accessory, accompanying, associated, concomitant, consequent, related

attention **1.** concentration, consideration, contemplation, deliberation, heed, heedfulness, intentness, mind, scrutiny, thinking, thought, thoughtfulness **2.** awareness, consciousness, consideration, notice, observation, recognition, regard **3.** care, concern, looking after, ministration, treatment **4.** *plural* assiduities, care, civility, compliment, consideration, courtesy, deference, gallantry, mindfulness, politeness, regard, respect, service

attentive **1.** alert, awake, careful, concentrating, heedful, intent, listening, mindful, observant, regardful, studious, watchful **2.** accommodating, civil, conscientious, considerate, courteous, devoted, gallant, gracious, kind, obliging, polite, respectful, thoughtful

attic *n.* garret, loft

attitude **1.** approach, disposition, frame of mind, mood, opinion, outlook, perspective, point of view, position, posture, stance, standing, view **2.** air, aspect, bearing, carriage, condition, demeanour, manner, mien (*literary*), pose, position, posture, stance

attract allure, appeal to, bewitch, captivate, charm, decoy, draw, enchant, endear, engage, entice, fascinate, incline, induce, interest, invite, lure, pull (*informal*), tempt

attraction allure, appeal, attractiveness, bait, captivation, charm, come-on (*informal*), draw, enchantment, endearment, enticement, fascination, inducement, interest, invitation, lure, magnetism, pull (*informal*), temptation, temptingness

attractive agreeable, alluring, appealing, beautiful, captivating, charming, comely, engaging, enticing, fair, fascinating, fetching, glamorous, good-looking, gorgeous, handsome, interesting, inviting, likable *or* likeable, lovely, magnetic, pleasant, pleasing, prepossessing, pretty, seductive, tempting, winning, winsome

attribute **1.** *vb.* apply, ascribe, assign, blame, charge, credit, impute, lay at the door of, put down to, refer, set down to, trace to **2.** *n.* aspect, character, characteristic, facet, feature, idiosyncrasy, indication, mark, note, peculiarity, point, property, quality, quirk, sign, symbol, trait, virtue

auburn chestnut-coloured, copper-coloured, henna, nutbrown, reddish-brown, russet, rust-coloured, tawny, Titian red

audacious **1.** adventurous, bold, brave, courageous, daredevil, daring, dauntless, death-defying, enterprising, fearless, intrepid, rash, reckless, risky, valiant, venturesome **2.** assuming, brazen, cheeky, defiant, disrespectful, forward, fresh (*informal*), impertinent, impudent, insolent, pert, presumptuous, rude, sassy (*U.S. informal*), shameless

audacity **1.** adventurousness, audaciousness, boldness, bravery, courage, daring, dauntlessness, enterprise, fearlessness, front, guts (*informal*), intrepidity, nerve, rashness, recklessness, valour, venturesomeness **2.** audaciousness, brass neck (*Brit. informal*), cheek, chutzpah (*U.S. & Canad. informal*), defiance, disrespectfulness, effrontery, forwardness, gall (*informal*), impertinence, impudence, insolence, neck (*informal*), nerve, pertness, presumption, rudeness, shamelessness

audience *n* **1** a group of spectators or listeners at a concert or play. **2** the people reached by a book, film, or radio or television programme. **3** a formal interview.

audio *adj* **1** of or relating to sound or hearing. **2** of or for the transmission or reproduction of sound.

audio frequency *n* a frequency in the range 20 hertz to 20 000 hertz, audible to the human ear.

audiometer (aw-dee-**om**-it-er) *n* an instrument for testing hearing.

audiotypist *n* a typist trained to type from a dictating machine. **audiotyping** *n*

audiovisual *adj* involving both hearing and sight: *audiovisual teaching aids.*

audit *n* **1** an official inspection of business accounts by a qualified accountant. **2** any thoroughgoing assessment or review: *an audit of their lifestyle.* ~*vb* **auditing, audited 3** to examine (business accounts) officially.

audition *n* **1** a test of a performer's or musician's ability for a particular role or job. ~*vb* **2** to test or be tested in an audition.

auditor *n* a person qualified to audit accounts.

auditorium *n, pl* **-toriums** *or* **-toria 1** the area of a concert hall or theatre in which the audience sits. **2** *US & Canada* a building for public meetings.

auditory *adj* of or relating to hearing.

au fait (oh **fay**) *adj* **1** fully informed. **2** expert.

auf Wiedersehen (owf **vee**-der-zay-en) *interj* goodbye.

Aug. August.

Augean (aw-**jee**-an) *adj* extremely dirty or corrupt.

auger *n* a pointed tool for boring holes.

aught *pron Old-fashioned or literary* anything whatever: *for aught I know.*

augment *vb* to make or become greater in number or strength. **augmentation** *n*

au gratin (oh **grat**-tan) *adj* cooked with a topping of breadcrumbs and sometimes cheese.

augur *vb* to be a good or bad sign of future events: *a double fault on the opening point did not augur well.*

augury *n* **1** the foretelling of the future. **2** (*pl* **-ries**) an omen.

august *adj* dignified and imposing.

August *n* the eighth month of the year.

Augustan *adj* **1** of the Roman emperor Augustus Caesar or the poets writing during his reign. **2** of any literary period noted for refinement and classicism.

auk *n* a northern sea bird with a heavy body, short wings, and black-and-white plumage.

auld lang syne *n* times past.

aunt *n* **1** a sister of one's father or mother. **2** the wife of one's uncle. **3** a child's term of address for a female friend of the parents.

auntie *or* **aunty** *n, pl* **-ies** *Informal* an aunt.

Aunt Sally *n, pl* **-lies** *Brit* **1** a figure used in fairgrounds as a target. **2** any target for insults or criticism.

au pair *n* a young foreign woman who does housework in return for board and lodging.

aura *n, pl* **auras** *or* **aurae 1** a distinctive air or quality associated with a person or thing. **2** any invisible emanation.

aural *adj* of or using the ears or hearing. **aurally** *adv*

aureate *adj Literary* **1** covered with gold. **2** (of a style of writing or speaking) excessively elaborate.

aureole *or* **aureola** *n* **1** a ring of light surrounding the head of a figure represented as holy; halo. **2** the sun's corona, visible as a faint halo during eclipses.

au revoir (oh riv-**vwahr**) *interj* goodbye.

auric *adj* of or containing gold in the trivalent state.

auricle *n* **1** the upper chamber of the heart. **2** the outer part of the ear. **auricular** *adj*

auricula *n, pl* **-lae** *or* **-las** an alpine primrose with leaves shaped like a bear's ear.

auriferous *adj* containing gold.

aurochs *n, pl* **-rochs** a recently extinct European wild ox.

aurora *n, pl* **-ras** *or* **-rae 1** an atmospheric phenomenon of bands of light sometimes seen in the polar regions. **2** *Poetic* the dawn.

aurora australis *n* the aurora seen around the South Pole.

aurora borealis *n* the aurora seen around the North Pole.

auscultation *n* the listening to of the internal sounds of the body, usually with a stethoscope, to help with medical diagnosis.

auspices (**aw**-spiss-siz) *pl n* **under the auspices of** with the support and approval of.

auspicious *adj* showing the signs of future success.

Aussie *n, adj Informal* Australian.

THESAURUS

audible clear, detectable, discernible, distinct, hearable, perceptible

audience 1. assemblage, assembly, congregation, crowd, gallery, gathering, house, listeners, onlookers, spectators, turnout, viewers **2.** devotees, fans, following, market, public **3.** consultation, hearing, interview, meeting, reception

au fait abreast of, *au courant,* clued-up (*informal*), conversant, expert, familiar, fully informed, in the know, in touch, knowledgeable, on the ball (*informal*), well-acquainted, well up

augment add to, amplify, boost, build up, dilate, enhance, enlarge, expand, extend, grow, heighten, increase, inflate, intensify, magnify, multiply, raise, reinforce, strengthen, swell

augmentation accession, addition, amplification, boost, build-up, dilation, enhancement, enlargement, expansion, extension, growth, heightening, increase, inflation, intensification, magnification, multiplication, reinforcement, rise, strengthening, swelling

augur be an omen of, bespeak (*archaic*), betoken, bode, foreshadow, harbinger, herald, portend, predict, prefigure, presage, promise, prophesy, signify

augury 1. divination, prediction, prophecy, soothsaying, sortilege **2.** auspice, forerunner, forewarning, harbinger, herald, omen, portent, precursor, presage, prognostication, promise, prophecy, sign, token, warning

august dignified, exalted, glorious, grand, high-ranking, imposing, impressive, kingly, lofty, magnificent, majestic, monumental, noble, regal, solemn, stately, superb

auspices advocacy, aegis, authority, backing, care, championship, charge, control, countenance, guidance, influence, patronage, protection, sponsorship, supervision, support

auspicious bright, encouraging, favourable, felicitous, fortunate, happy, hopeful, lucky, opportune, promising, propitious, prosperous, rosy, timely

austere 1. cold, exacting, forbidding, formal, grave, grim, hard, harsh, inflexible, rigorous, serious, severe, solemn, stern, stiff, strict, stringent, unfeeling, unrelenting **2.** abstemious, abstinent, ascetic, chaste, con-

austere *adj* **1** stern or severe: *his austere and serious attitude to events.* **2** self-disciplined or ascetic: *an extraordinarily austere and puritanical organization.* **3** severely simple or plain: *the austere backdrop of grey.*

austerity *n, pl* **-ties 1** the state of being austere. **2** reduced availability of luxuries and consumer goods.

austral *adj* of or from the south.

Austral. 1 Australasia. 2 Australia(n).

Australasian *adj* of Australia, New Zealand, and neighbouring islands.

Australian *adj* **1** of Australia. *~n* **2** a person from Australia.

Austrian *adj* **1** of Austria. *~n* **2** a person from Austria.

autarchy (**aw**-tar-kee) *n, pl* **-chies** absolute power or autocracy.

autarky (**aw**-tar-kee) *n, pl* **-kies** a policy of economic self-sufficiency.

authentic *adj* **1** of undisputed origin or authorship; genuine. **2** reliable or accurate. **authentically** *adv* **authenticity** *n*

authenticate *vb* **-cating, -cated** to establish as genuine. **authentication** *n*

author *n* **1** a person who writes a book, article, or other written work. **2** an originator or creator.

➤ The word *author* should be used for both male and female writers. The form *authoress* suggests a minor or amateur writer.

authoritarian *adj* **1** insisting on strict obedience to authority. *~n* **2** a person who insists on strict obedience to authority. **authoritarianism** *n*

authoritative *adj* **1** recognized as being reliable: *the authoritative book on Shakespeare.* **2** possessing authority; official. **authoritatively** *adv*

authority *n, pl* **-ties 1** the power to command, control, or judge others. **2** a person or group with this power: *a third escapee turned himself in to the authorities.* **3** a decision-making organization or government department: *the local authority.* **4** an expert in a particular field. **5** official permission: *he had no authority to negotiate.* **6** a position that has the power to command, control, or judge others: *people in authority.* **7 on good authority** from reliable evidence. **8** confidence resulting from expertise.

authorize *or* **-ise** *vb* **-izing, -ized** *or* **-ising, -ised 1** to give authority to. **2** to give official permission for. **authorization** *or* **-isation** *n*

Authorized Version *n* **the Authorized Version** an English translation of the Bible published in 1611.

authorship *n* **1** the origin or originator of a written work or plan. **2** the profession of writing.

autism *n Psychiatry* abnormal self-absorption, usually affecting children, characterized by lack of response to people and limited ability to communicate. **autistic** *adj*

auto *n, pl* **-tos** *US & Canad informal* short for **automobile.**

auto- *or sometimes before a vowel* **aut-** *combining form* **1** self; of or by the same one: *autobiography.* **2** self-propelling: *automobile.*

autobahn *n* a motorway in German-speaking countries.

autobiography *n, pl* **-phies** an account of a person's life written by that person. **autobiographer** *n* **autobiographical** *adj*

autoclave *n* an apparatus for sterilizing objects by steam under pressure.

autocracy *n, pl* **-cies** government by an individual with unrestricted authority.

autocrat *n* **1** a ruler with absolute authority. **2** a dictatorial person. **autocratic** *adj* **autocratically** *adv*

autocross *n* a sport in which cars race over a circuit of rough grass.

Autocue *n Trademark* an electronic television prompting device displaying a speaker's script, unseen by the audience.

auto-da-fé (aw-toe-da-**fay**) *n, pl* **autos-da-fé 1** *History* the ceremonial passing of sentence on heretics by the Spanish Inquisition. **2** the burning to death of heretics.

autogiro *or* **autogyro** *n, pl* **-ros** a self-propelled aircraft resembling a helicopter but with an unpowered rotor.

autograph *n* **1** a handwritten signature of a famous person. *~vb* **2** to write one's signature on or in.

automat *n US* a vending machine.

automate *vb* **-mating, -mated** to make (a manufacturing process) automatic.

THESAURUS

tinent, economical, exacting, puritanical, rigid, self-denying, self-disciplined, sober, solemn, Spartan, strait-laced, strict, unrelenting **3.** bleak, economical, harsh, plain, severe, simple, spare, Spartan, stark, subdued, unadorned, unornamented

austerity 1. coldness, exactingness, forbiddingness, formality, gravity, grimness, hardness, harshness, inflexibility, rigour, seriousness, severity, solemnity, sternness, stiffness, strictness **2.** abstemiousness, abstinence, asceticism, chasteness, chastity, continence, economy, exactingness, puritanism, rigidity, self-denial, self-discipline, sobriety, solemnity, Spartanism, strictness **3.** economy, plainness, severity, simplicity, spareness, Spartanism, starkness

authentic accurate, actual, authoritative, bona fide, certain, dependable, factual, faithful, genuine, legitimate, original, pure, real, reliable, simon-pure (*rare*), true, true-to-life, trustworthy, valid, veritable

authenticity accuracy, actuality, authoritativeness, certainty, dependability, factualness, faithfulness, genuineness, legitimacy, purity, realness, reliability, trustworthiness, truth, truthfulness, validity, veritableness, verity

author architect, composer, creator, designer, doer, fabricator, father, founder, framer, initiator, inventor, maker, mover, originator, parent, planner, prime mover, producer, writer

authoritarian 1. *adj.* absolute, autocratic, despotic, dictatorial, disciplinarian, doctrinaire, dogmatic, domineering, harsh, imperious, rigid, severe, strict, tyrannical, unyielding **2.** *n.* absolutist, autocrat, despot, dictator, disciplinarian, tyrant

authority 1. ascendancy, charge, command, control, direction, domination, dominion, force, government, influence, jurisdiction, might, power, prerogative, right, rule, say-so, strength, supremacy, sway, weight **2. the authorities** administration, government, management, officialdom, police, powers that be, the establishment **3.** arbiter, bible, connoisseur, expert, judge, master, professional, scholar, specialist, textbook **4.** authorization, justification, licence, permission, permit, sanction, say-so, warrant **5.** attestation, avowal, declaration, evidence, profession, say-so, statement, testimony, word

authorization 1. ability, authority, power, right, say-so, strength **2.** approval, credentials, leave, licence, permission, permit, sanction, say-so, warrant

authorize 1. accredit, commission, empower, enable, entitle, give authority **2.** accredit, allow, approve, confirm, countenance, give authority for, give leave, license, permit, ratify, sanction, vouch for, warrant

automatic *adj* **1** (of a device or mechanism) able to activate or regulate itself. **2** (of a process) performed by automatic equipment. **3** done without conscious thought. **4** (of a firearm) utilizing some of the force of each explosion to reload and fire continuously. **5** occurring as a necessary consequence: *the certificate itself carries no automatic legal benefits.* ~*n* **6** an automatic firearm. **7** a motor vehicle with automatic transmission. **automatically** *adv*

automatic pilot *n* **1** a device that automatically maintains an aircraft on a preset course. **2 on automatic pilot** repeating an action or process without thought.

automatic transmission *n* a transmission system in a motor vehicle in which the gears change automatically.

automation *n* the use of automatic, often electronic, methods to control industrial processes.

automaton *n, pl* **-tons** *or* **-ta** **1** a mechanical device operating under its own power. **2** a person who acts mechanically.

automobile *n US* a motorcar.

automotive *adj* **1** relating to motor vehicles. **2** self-propelling.

autonomous *adj* **1** having self-government. **2** independent of others.

autonomy *n, pl* **-mies** **1** the right or state of self-government. **2** freedom to determine one's own actions and behaviour.

autopilot *n* an automatic pilot.

autopsy *n, pl* **-sies** examination of a corpse to determine the cause of death.

autoroute *n* a motorway in French-speaking countries.

autostrada *n* a motorway in Italian-speaking countries.

autosuggestion *n* a process in which a person unconsciously supplies the means of influencing his or her own behaviour or beliefs.

autumn *n* **1** the season of the year between summer and winter. **2** a period of late maturity followed by a decline. **autumnal** *adj*

aux. auxiliary.

auxiliaries *pl n* foreign troops serving another nation.

auxiliary *adj* **1** secondary or supplementary. **2** supporting. ~*n, pl* **-ries** **3** a person or thing that supports or supplements.

auxiliary verb *n* a verb used to indicate the tense, voice, or mood of another verb, such as *will* in *I will go.*

AV (of the Bible) Authorized Version.

av. **1** average. **2** avoirdupois.

avail *vb* **1** to be of use, advantage, or assistance (to). **2 avail oneself of** to make use of. ~*n* **3** use or advantage: *to no avail.*

available *adj* **1** obtainable or accessible. **2** able to be contacted and willing to talk: *a spokesman insisted she was not available for comment.* **availability** *n* **availably** *adv*

avalanche *n* **1** a fall of large masses of snow and ice down a mountain. **2** a sudden or overwhelming quantity of anything.

avant-garde (av-ong-**gard**) *n* **1** those artists, writers or musicians, whose techniques and ideas are in advance of those generally accepted. ~*adj* **2** using ideas or techniques in advance of those generally accepted.

avarice (**av**-a-riss) *n* extreme greed for wealth. **avaricious** *adj*

avast *interj Naut* stop! cease!

avatar *n Hinduism* the appearance of a god in human or animal form.

Ave (**ah**-vay) *or* **Ave Maria** (ma-**ree**-a) *n* same as **Hail Mary.**

Ave. avenue.

avenge *vb* **avenging, avenged** to inflict a punishment in retaliation for (harm done) or on behalf of (the person harmed). **avenger** *n*

avenue *n* **1** a wide street. **2** a road bordered by two rows of trees. **3** a line of approach: *the United States was exhausting every avenue to achieve a diplomatic solution.*

aver (av-**vur**) *vb* **averring, averred** to state to be true. **averment** *n*

average *n* **1** the typical or normal amount or quality. **2** the result obtained by adding the numbers or quantities in a set and dividing the total by the number of members in the set. **3 on average** usually or typically. ~*adj* **4** usual or typical. **5** calculated as an average. **6** mediocre or inferior. ~*vb* **-aging, -aged** **7** to calculate

THESAURUS

autocrat absolutist, despot, dictator, tyrant

autocratic absolute, all-powerful, despotic, dictatorial, domineering, imperious, tyrannical, tyrannous, unlimited

automatic **1.** automated, mechanical, mechanized, push-button, robot, self-acting, self-activating, self-moving, self-propelling, self-regulating **2.** habitual, instinctive, instinctual, involuntary, kneejerk, mechanical, natural, perfunctory, reflex, routine, spontaneous, unconscious, unwilled

autonomous free, independent, self-determining, self-governing, self-ruling, sovereign

autonomy freedom, home rule, independence, self-determination, self-government, self-rule, sovereignty

autopsy dissection, postmortem, postmortem examination

auxiliary **1.** *adj.* accessory, aiding, ancillary, assisting, back-up, emergency, fall-back, helping, reserve, secondary, subsidiary, substitute, supplementary, supporting **2.** *n.* accessory, accomplice, ally, assistant, associate, companion, confederate, helper, henchman, partner, protagonist, reserve, subordinate, supporter

available accessible, applicable, at hand, at one's disposal, attainable, convenient, free, handy, obtainable, on hand, on tap, ready, ready for use, to hand, vacant

avalanche **1.** landslide, landslip, snow-slide, snow-slip **2.** barrage, deluge, flood, inundation, torrent

avant-garde *adj.* experimental, far-out (*slang*), ground-breaking, innovative, innovatory, pioneering, progressive, unconventional, way-out (*informal*)

avaricious acquisitive, close-fisted, covetous, grasping, greedy, mean, miserable, miserly, niggardly, parsimonious, penny-pinching, penurious, rapacious, stingy

avenge even the score for, get even for (*informal*), hit back, punish, repay, requite, retaliate, revenge, take satisfaction for, take vengeance

avenue access, alley, approach, boulevard, channel, course, drive, driveway, entrance, entry, pass, passage, path, pathway, road, route, street, thoroughfare, way

average *n.* **1.** common run, mean, medium, midpoint, norm, normal, par, rule, run, run of the mill, standard **2. on average** as a rule, for the most part, generally, normally, typically, usually ~*adj.* **3.** banal, common, commonplace, fair, general, indifferent, mediocre, middling, moderate, normal, not bad, ordinary, passable, regular, run-of-the-mill, so-so (*informal*), standard, tolerable, typical, undistinguished, unexceptional,

or estimate the average of. **8** to amount to or be on average.

averse *adj* opposed: *he's not averse to publicity, of the right kind.*

aversion *n* **1** extreme dislike or disinclination. **2** a person or thing that arouses this.

avert *vb* **1** to turn away: *he had to avert his eyes.* **2** to ward off: *a final attempt to avert war.*

Avesta *n* a collection of sacred writings of Zoroastrianism.

avian (**aiv**-ee-an) *adj* of or like a bird.

aviary *n, pl* **aviaries** a large enclosure in which birds are kept.

aviation *n* the art or science of flying aircraft.

aviator *n Old-fashioned* the pilot of an aircraft. **aviatrix** *fem n*

avid *adj* **1** very keen or enthusiastic: *he is an avid football fan.* **2** eager: *avid for economic development.* **avidity** *n* **avidly** *adv*

avocado *n, pl* **-dos** a pear-shaped tropical fruit with a leathery green skin and greenish-yellow flesh.

avocation *n Old-fashioned* **1** a person's regular job. **2** a hobby.

avocet *n* a long-legged shore bird with a long slender upward-curving bill.

avoid *vb* **1** to refrain from doing. **2** to prevent from happening. **3** to keep out of the way of. **avoidable** *adj* **avoidably** *adv* **avoidance** *n*

avoirdupois *or* **avoirdupois weight** (av-er-de-**poise**) *n* a system of weights based on the pound, which contains 16 ounces.

avow *vb* **1** to state or affirm. **2** to admit openly. **avowal** *n* **avowed** *adj* **avowedly** (a-**vow**-id-lee) *adv*

avuncular *adj* (of a man) friendly, helpful, and caring towards someone younger.

await *vb* **1** to wait for. **2** to be in store for.

awake *adj* **1** not sleeping. **2** alert or aware: *awake to the danger.* ~*vb* **awaking, awoke** *or* **awaked, awoken** *or* **awaked 3** to emerge or rouse from sleep. **4** to become or cause to become alert.

awaken *vb* **1** to awake. **2** to cause to be aware of: *anxieties awakened by reunification.*

awakening *n* the start of a feeling or awareness in someone: *a picture of an emotional awakening.*

award *vb* **1** to give (something) for merit. **2** *Law* to declare to be entitled, such as by decision of a court. ~*n* **3** something awarded, such as a prize. **4** *Law* the decision of an arbitrator or court.

aware *adj* **1 aware of** knowing about: *he's at least aware of the problem.* **2** informed: *they are becoming more politically aware every day.* **awareness** *n*

awash *adv, adj* washed over by water.

away *adv* **1** from a particular place: *I saw them walk away and felt absolutely desolated.* **2** in or to another, a usual, or a proper place: *he decided to put the car away in the garage.* **3** at a distance: *keep away from the windows.* **4** out of existence: *the pillars rotted away.* **5** indicating motion or distance from a normal or proper place: *the child shook her head and looked away.* **6** continuously: *he continued to scribble away.* ~*adj* **7** not present: *he had been away from home for years.* **8** distant: *the castle was farther away than he had thought.* **9** *Sport* played on an opponent's ground.

awayday *n* a day trip taken for pleasure.

awe *n* **1** wonder and respect mixed with dread. ~*vb* **awing, awed 2** to inspire with reverence or dread.

THESAURUS

usual **4.** intermediate, mean, median, medium, middle ~*vb.* **5.** balance out to, be on average, do on average, even out to, make on average

averse antipathetic, backward, disinclined, hostile, ill-disposed, indisposed, inimical, loath, opposed, reluctant, unfavourable, unwilling

aversion abhorrence, animosity, antipathy, detestation, disgust, disinclination, dislike, distaste, hate, hatred, horror, hostility, indisposition, loathing, odium, opposition, reluctance, repugnance, repulsion, revulsion, unwillingness

aviation aeronautics, flight, flying, powered flight

aviator aeronaut, airman, flier, pilot

avid ardent, devoted, eager, enthusiastic, fanatical, fervent, intense, keen, passionate, zealous

avoid avert, body-swerve (*Scot.*), bypass, circumvent, dodge, duck (out of) (*informal*), elude, escape, eschew, evade, fight shy of, keep aloof from, keep away from, prevent, refrain from, shirk, shun, sidestep, steer clear of

avoidance body swerve (*Scot.*), circumvention, dodging, eluding, escape, eschewal, evasion, keeping away from, prevention, refraining, shirking, shunning, steering clear of

avowed acknowledged, admitted, confessed, declared, open, professed, self-proclaimed, sworn

await 1. abide, anticipate, expect, look for, look forward to, stay for, wait for **2.** attend, be in readiness for, be in store for, be prepared for, be ready for, wait for

awake *adj.* **1.** alert, alive, aroused, attentive, awakened, aware, conscious, heedful, not sleeping, observant, on guard, on the alert, on the lookout, vigilant, wakeful, waking, watchful, wide-awake ~*vb.* **2.** awaken, rouse, wake, wake up **3.** activate, alert, animate, arouse, awaken, call forth, enliven, excite, fan, incite, kindle, provoke, revive, stimulate, stir up, vivify

awaken activate, alert, animate, arouse, awake, call forth, enliven, excite, fan, incite, kindle, provoke, revive, rouse, stimulate, stir up, vivify, wake

awakening activation, animating, arousal, awaking, birth, enlivening, incitement, kindling, provocation, revival, rousing, stimulation, stirring up, vivification, waking, waking up

award 1. *vb.* accord, adjudge, allot, apportion, assign, bestow, confer, decree, distribute, endow, gift, give, grant, hand out, present, render **2.** *n.* adjudication, allotment, bestowal, conferment, conferral, decision, decoration, decree, endowment, gift, grant, hand-out, order, presentation, prize, stipend, trophy, verdict

aware acquainted, alive to, appreciative, apprised, attentive, *au courant,* clued-up (*informal*), cognizant, conscious, conversant, enlightened, familiar, hip (*slang*), informed, knowing, knowledgeable, mindful, sensible, sentient, wise (*slang*)

awareness acquaintance, appreciation, attention, cognizance, consciousness, enlightenment, familiarity, knowledge, mindfulness, perception, realization, recognition, sensibility, sentience, understanding

away *adv.* **1.** abroad, elsewhere, from here, from home, hence, off **2.** aside, out of the way, to one side **3.** apart, at a distance, far, remote **4.** continuously, incessantly, interminably, relentlessly, repeatedly, uninterruptedly, unremittingly ~*adj.* **5.** abroad, absent, elsewhere, gone, not at home, not here, not present, not there, out

awe 1. *n.* admiration, amazement, astonishment, dread, fear, horror, respect, reverence, terror, veneration, wonder **2.** *vb.* amaze, astonish, cow, daunt, frighten, horrify, impress, intimidate, stun, terrify

awe-struck afraid, amazed, astonished, awed, awe-

aweigh *adj Naut* (of an anchor) no longer hooked into the bottom.

awesome *adj* **1** inspiring or displaying awe. **2** *Slang* excellent or outstanding.

awe-struck *adj* overcome or filled with awe.

awful *adj* **1** very bad or unpleasant. **2** *Informal* considerable or great: *that's an awful lot of money, isn't it?* **3** *Obsolete* inspiring reverence or dread. *~adv* **4** *Not standard* very: *I'm working awful hard on my lines.*

awfully *adv* **1** in an unpleasant way. **2** *Informal* very: *we were both awfully busy.*

awhile *adv* for a brief period.

awkward *adj* **1** clumsy or ungainly. **2** embarrassed: *he was awkward and nervous around girls.* **3** difficult to deal with: *the lawyer was in an awkward situation.* **4** difficult to use or handle: *it was small but heavy enough to make it awkward to carry.* **5** embarrassing: *there were several moments of awkward silence.* **awkwardly** *adv* **awkwardness** *n*

awl *n* a pointed hand tool for piercing wood, leather, etc.

awn *n* any of the bristles growing from the flowering parts of certain grasses and cereals.

awning *n* a canvas roof supported by a frame to give protection against the weather.

awoke *vb* a past tense and (now rare or dialectal) past participle of **awake.**

awoken *vb* a past participle of **awake.**

AWOL (**eh**-woll) *Mil* absent without leave but without intending to desert.

awry (a-**rye**) *adv, adj* **1** with a twist to one side; askew: *my neck was really awry after the journey.* **2** amiss or faulty: *if a gear gets stuck, the whole system goes awry.*

axe *or US* **ax** *n, pl* **axes** **1** a hand tool with one side of its head sharpened to a cutting edge, used for felling trees and splitting timber. **2 an axe to grind** a favourite topic one wishes to promote. **3** *Informal* a severe cut in spending or in the number of staff employed. *~vb* **axing, axed 4** *Informal* to dismiss (employees), restrict (expenditure), or terminate (a project).

axes[1] *n* the plural of **axis.**

axes[2] *n* the plural of **axe.**

axial *adj* **1** forming or of an axis. **2** in, on, or along an axis. **axially** *adv*

axil *n* the angle where the stalk of a leaf joins a stem.

axiom *n* **1** a generally accepted principle. **2** a self-evident statement.

axiomatic *adj* **1** containing axioms. **2** self-evident or obvious. **axiomatically** *adv*

axis (**ax**-iss) *n, pl* **axes** (**ax**-eez) **1** a real or imaginary line about which a body can rotate or about which an object or geometrical construction is symmetrical. **2** one of two or three reference lines used in coordinate geometry to locate a point in a plane or in space.

axle *n* a shaft on which a wheel or pair of wheels revolves.

axolotl *n* an aquatic salamander of N America.

ayah *n* (in parts of the former British Empire) a native maidservant or nursemaid.

ayatollah *n* one of a class of Islamic religious leaders in Iran.

aye *or* **ay** *interj* **1** yes. *~n* **2** an affirmative vote or voter.

Ayrshire *n* one of a breed of brown-and-white dairy cattle.

AZ Arizona.

azalea (az-**zale**-ya) *n* a garden shrub grown for its showy flowers.

azimuth *n* **1** the arc of the sky between the zenith and the horizon. **2** *Surveying* the horizontal angle of a bearing measured clockwise from the north.

Aztec *n* **1** a member of a Mexican Indian race who established a great empire, overthrown by the Spanish in the early 16th century. **2** the language of the Aztecs. *~adj* **3** of the Aztecs or their language.

azure *n* **1** the deep blue colour of a clear blue sky. **2** *Poetic* a clear blue sky. *~adj* **3** deep blue.

THESAURUS

inspired, cowed, daunted, dumbfounded, fearful, frightened, horrified, impressed, intimidated, shocked, struck dumb, stunned, terrified, wonder-stricken, wonder-struck

awful **1.** abysmal, alarming, appalling, deplorable, dire, distressing, dreadful, fearful, frightful, ghastly, gruesome, harrowing, hideous, horrendous, horrible, horrid, horrific, horrifying, nasty, shocking, terrible, tremendous, ugly, unpleasant, unsightly **2.** *obsolete* amazing, awe-inspiring, awesome, dread, fearsome, majestic, portentous, solemn

awfully **1.** badly, disgracefully, disreputably, dreadfully, inadequately, reprehensibly, shoddily, unforgivably, unpleasantly, wickedly, woefully, wretchedly **2.** *informal* badly, dreadfully, exceedingly, exceptionally, excessively, extremely, greatly, immensely, quite, terribly, very, very much

awhile briefly, for a little while, for a moment, for a short time, for a while

awkward **1.** all thumbs, artless, blundering, bungling, clownish, clumsy, coarse, gauche, gawky, graceless, ham-fisted, ham-handed, ill-bred, inelegant, inept, inexpert, lumbering, maladroit, oafish, rude, skill-less, stiff, uncoordinated, uncouth, ungainly, ungraceful, unpolished, unrefined, unskilful, unskilled **2.** embarrassed, ill at ease, uncomfortable **3.** delicate, difficult, inconvenient, inopportune, painful, perplexing, sticky (*informal*), thorny, ticklish, troublesome, trying, unpleasant, untimely **4.** cumbersome, difficult, inconvenient, troublesome, unhandy, unmanageable, unwieldy **5.** compromising, cringe-making (*Brit. informal*), embarrassing

awkwardness **1.** artlessness, clownishness, clumsiness, coarseness, gaucheness, gaucherie, gawkiness, gracelessness, ill-breeding, inelegance, ineptness, inexpertness, maladroitness, oafishness, rudeness, stiffness, uncoordination, uncouthness, ungainliness, unskilfulness, unskilledness **2.** delicacy, difficulty, discomfort, embarrassment, inconvenience, inopportuneness, painfulness, perplexingness, stickiness (*informal*), thorniness, ticklishness, unpleasantness, untimeliness **3.** cumbersomeness, difficulty, inconvenience, troublesomeness, unhandiness, unmanageability, unwieldiness

axe *n.* **1.** adze, chopper, hatchet **2. an axe to grind** grievance, personal consideration, pet subject, private ends, private purpose, ulterior motive **3.** *informal* cancellation, cutback, discharge, dismissal, termination, the boot (*slang*), the chop (*slang*), the (old) heave-ho (*informal*), the sack (*informal*), wind-up *~vb.* **4.** *informal* cancel, cut back, discharge, dismiss, dispense with, eliminate, fire (*informal*), get rid of, oust, relegate, remove, sack (*informal*), terminate, throw out, turn off (*informal*), wind up

axiom adage, aphorism, apophthegm, dictum, fundamental, gnome, maxim, postulate, precept, principle, truism

axiomatic **1.** aphoristic, apophthegmatic, epigrammatic, gnomic, pithy, terse **2.** absolute, accepted, apodictic, assumed, certain, fundamental, given, granted, indubitable, manifest, presupposed, self-evident, understood, unquestioned

axis axle, centre line, pivot, shaft, spindle

axle arbor, axis, mandrel, pin, pivot, rod, shaft, spindle

B

b *or* **B** *n, pl* **b's, B's,** *or* **Bs 1** the second letter of the English alphabet. **2 from A to B** See **a** (sense 2).

B 1 *Music* the seventh note of the scale of C major. **2** the second in a series, class, or rank. **3** *Chem* boron. **4** *Chess* bishop.

b. 1 born. **2** *Cricket* **a** bowled. **b** bye.

Ba *Chem* barium.

BA 1 Bachelor of Arts. **2** British Airways.

baa *vb* **baaing, baaed 1** (of a sheep) to make a characteristic bleating sound. *~n* **2** the cry made by a sheep.

baas *n S African* a boss.

baasskap *n* (in South Africa) control by Whites of non-Whites.

babble *vb* **-bling, -bled 1** to talk in a quick, foolish, or muddled way. **2** to make meaningless sounds: *children first gurgle and babble at random.* **3** to disclose secrets carelessly. **4** *Literary* (of streams) to make a low murmuring sound. *~n* **5** muddled or foolish speech. **6** a murmuring sound. **babbler** *n* **babbling** *n*

babe *n* **1** a baby. **2 babe in arms** *Informal* a naive or inexperienced person. **3** *Slang, chiefly US* a girl.

babel (**babe**-el) *n* **1** a confusion of noises or voices. **2** a scene of noise and confusion.

baboon *n* a medium-sized monkey with a long face, large teeth, and a fairly long tail.

baby *n, pl* **-bies 1** a newborn child. **2** the youngest or smallest of a family or group. **3** a recently born animal. **4** an immature person. **5** *Slang* a sweetheart. **6** a project of personal concern. **7 be left holding the baby** to be left with a responsibility. *~adj* **8** comparatively small of its type: *baby carrots.* *~vb* **-bies, -bying, -bied 9** to treat like a baby. **babyhood** *n* **babyish** *adj*

baby bonus *n Canad informal* Family Allowance.

baby-sit *vb* **-sitting, -sat** to act or work as a baby-sitter. **baby-sitting** *n, adj*

baby-sitter *n* a person who takes care of a child while the parents are out.

baccalaureate (back-a-**law**-ree-it) *n* the university degree of Bachelor of Arts.

baccarat (**back**-a-rah) *n* a card game in which the punters gamble against the banker.

bacchanalian (back-a-**nail**-ee-an) *adj Literary* (of a party) unrestrained and involving a great deal of drinking and sometimes sexual activity.

baccy *n Brit informal* tobacco.

bachelor *n* **1** an unmarried man. **2** a person who holds a first degree from a university or college. **bachelorhood** *n*

Bachelor of Arts *n* a person with a first degree from a university or college, usually in the arts.

bacillary *adj* of or caused by bacilli.

bacillus (bass-**ill**-luss) *n, pl* **-li** (-lie) a rod-shaped bacterium, esp. one causing disease.

back *n* **1** the rear part of the human body, from the neck to the pelvis. **2** the spinal column. **3** the part or side of an object opposite the front. **4** the part of anything less often seen or used. **5** *Ball games* a defensive player or position. **6 at the back of one's mind** not in one's conscious thoughts. **7 behind someone's back** secretly or deceitfully. **8 put** *or* **get someone's back up** to annoy someone. **9 turn one's back on someone** to refuse to help someone. *~vb* **10** to move or cause to move backwards. **11** to provide money for (a person or enterprise). **12** to bet on the success of: *to back a horse.* **13** to provide (a pop singer) with a musical accompaniment. **14** (foll. by *on* or *onto*) to have the back facing (towards): *his garden backs onto a school.* **15** (of the wind) to change direction anticlockwise. *~adj* **16** situated behind: *back garden.* **17** owing from an earlier date: *back rent.* **18** remote: *a back road.* *~adv* **19** at, to, or towards the rear. **20** to or towards the original starting point or condition: *I went back home.* **21** in reply or retaliation: *to hit someone back.* **22** in concealment or reserve: *to keep something back.* **23 back and forth** to and fro. **24 back to front a** in reverse. **b** in disorder. ~See also **back down, back out, back up.**

backbencher *n Brit, Austral, NZ, etc* a Member of Parliament who does not hold office in the government or opposition.

backbite *vb* **-biting, -bit; -bitten** *or* **-bit** to talk spitefully about an absent person. **backbiter** *n*

back boiler *n* a tank at the back of a fireplace for heating water.

backbone *n* **1** the spinal column. **2** strength of character.

backbreaking *adj* (of work) exhausting.

backburn *Austral & NZ ~vb* **1** to clear (an area of bush) by creating a fire that burns in the opposite direction from the wind. **2** to prevent a bush fire from spreading by clearing an area of land in front of it. *~n* **3** the act or result of backburning.

backchat *n Informal* impudent replies.

THESAURUS

babble 1. *vb.* blab, burble, cackle, chatter, gabble, gibber, gurgle, jabber, mumble, murmur, mutter, prate, prattle, rabbit (on) (*Brit. informal*), run off at the mouth (*slang*), waffle (*informal, chiefly Brit.*) **2.** *n.* burble, clamour, drivel, gabble, gibberish, murmur, waffle (*informal, chiefly Brit.*)

babe 1. baby, bairn (*Scot. & N English*), child, infant, nursling, rug rat (*slang*), sprog (*slang*), suckling **2.** babe in arms, ingenue, innocent

baby 1. *n.* ankle-biter (*Austral. slang*), babe, bairn (*Scot.*), child, infant, newborn child, rug rat (*slang*), sprog (*slang*) **2.** *adj.* diminutive, dwarf, little, midget, mini, miniature, minute, pygmy *or* pigmy, small, teensy-weensy, teeny-weeny, tiny, wee **3.** *vb.* coddle, cosset, humour, indulge, mollycoddle, overindulge, pamper, pet, spoil, spoon-feed

babyish baby, childish, foolish, immature, infantile, juvenile, namby-pamby, puerile, silly, sissy, soft (*informal*), spoiled

back *n.* **1.** backside, end, far end, hind part, hindquarters, posterior, rear, reverse, stern, tail end **2. behind one's back** covertly, deceitfully, secretly, sneakily, surreptitiously *~vb.* **3.** abet, advocate, assist, champion, countenance, encourage, endorse, espouse, favour, finance, promote, sanction, second, side with, sponsor, subsidize, support, sustain, underwrite *~adj.* **4.** *from an earlier time* delayed, earlier, elapsed, former, overdue, past, previous

backbone 1. *Medical* spinal column, spine, vertebrae, vertebral column **2.** bottle (*Brit. slang*), character, courage, determination, firmness, fortitude, grit, hardihood, mettle, moral fibre, nerve, pluck, resolution, resolve, stamina, steadfastness, strength of character, tenacity, toughness, will, willpower

backcloth *n* a painted curtain at the back of a stage set. Also called: **backdrop**
backcomb *vb* to comb (the hair) towards the roots to give more bulk to a hairstyle.
back country *n Austral & NZ* land far away from settled areas.
backdate *vb* **-dating, -dated** to make (a document) effective from a date earlier than its completion.
back door *n* a means of entry to a job or position that is secret or obtained through influence.
back down *vb* to withdraw an earlier claim.
backer *n* a person who gives financial or other support.
backfire *vb* **-firing, -fired 1** (of a plan or scheme) to fail to have the desired effect. **2** (of an internal-combustion engine) to make a loud noise as a result of an explosion of unburnt gases in the exhaust system.
backgammon *n* a game for two people played on a board with pieces moved according to throws of the dice.
background *n* **1** the events or circumstances that help to explain something. **2** a person's social class, education, or experience. **3** the part of a scene furthest from the viewer. **4** an inconspicuous position: *in the background.* **5** the space behind the chief figures or objects in a picture.
backhand *n* **1** *Tennis etc* a stroke made from across the body with the back of the hand facing the direction of the stroke. **2** the side on which backhand strokes are made.
backhanded *adj* **1** (of a blow or shot) performed with the arm moving from across the body. **2** ambiguous or implying criticism: *a backhanded compliment.*
backhander *n* **1** *Slang* a bribe. **2** a backhanded stroke or blow.
backing *n* **1** support. **2** something that forms or strengthens the back of something. **3** musical accompaniment for a pop singer.
backing dog *n NZ* a dog that moves a flock of sheep by jumping on their backs.
backlash *n* **1** a sudden and adverse reaction. **2** a recoil between interacting badly fitting parts in machinery.
backlog *n* an accumulation of things to be dealt with.
back number *n* **1** an old issue of a newspaper or magazine. **2** *Informal* a person or thing considered to be old-fashioned.
back off *vb* **1** to retreat. **2** to abandon (an intention or objective).
back out *vb* (often foll. by *of*) to withdraw from (an agreement).
backpack *n* **1** a rucksack. *~vb* **2** to go hiking with a backpack.
back passage *n* the rectum.
back-pedal *vb* **-pedalling, -pedalled** *or US* **-pedaling, -pedaled** to retract or modify a previous opinion or statement.
back room *n* **1** a place where secret research or planning is done. *~adj* **back-room 2** of or relating to secret research or planning: *back-room boys.*
back seat *n Informal* a less important or responsible position: *lyricism took a back seat to drama.*
back-seat driver *n Informal* a person who offers unwanted advice.
backside *n Informal* the buttocks.
backslide *vb* **-sliding, -slid** to relapse into former bad habits or vices. **backslider** *n*
backspace *vb* **-spacing, -spaced** to move a typewriter carriage or computer cursor backwards.
backspin *n Sport* a backward spin given to a ball to reduce its speed at impact.
backstage *adv* **1** behind the stage in a theatre. *~adj* **2** situated backstage.
backstairs *or* **backstair** *adj* underhand: *backstairs gossip.*
backstreet *n* **1** a street in a town far from the main roads. *~adj* **2** denoting secret or illegal activities: *a backstreet abortion.*
backstroke *n Swimming* a stroke performed on the back, using backward circular strokes of each arm.
backtrack *vb* **1** to go back along the same route one has just travelled. **2** to retract or reverse one's opinion or policy.
back up *vb* **1** to support. **2** *Computers* to make a copy of (a data file), esp. as a security copy. *~n* **backup 3** a support or reinforcement. **4** a reserve or substitute. *~adj* **backup 5** able to be substituted: *a backup copy.*
backward *adj* **1** directed towards the rear. **2** retarded in physical, material, or intellectual development. **3** reluctant or bashful. *~adv* **4** same as **backwards. backwardness** *n*
backwards *or* **backward** *adv* **1** towards the rear. **2** with the back foremost. **3** in the reverse of the usual direction. **4** into a worse state: *the Gothic novel's been going backwards since Radcliffe.* **5 bend over backwards** *Informal* to make a special effort to please someone.

THESAURUS

backbreaking arduous, crushing, exhausting, gruelling, hard, killing, laborious, punishing, strenuous, toilsome, wearing, wearying
back down accede, admit defeat, back-pedal, concede, give in, surrender, withdraw, yield
backer advocate, angel (*informal*), benefactor, patron, promoter, second, sponsor, subscriber, supporter, underwriter, well-wisher
backfire boomerang, disappoint, fail, flop (*informal*), miscarry, rebound, recoil
background 1. circumstances, history **2.** breeding, credentials, culture, education, environment, experience, grounding, milieu, preparation, qualifications, tradition, upbringing
backhanded ambiguous, double-edged, equivocal, indirect, ironic, oblique, sarcastic, sardonic, two-edged
backing abetment, advocacy, aid, assistance, championing, encouragement, endorsement, espousal, funds, grant, moral support, patronage, promotion, sanction, seconding, sponsorship, subsidy, support
backlash backfire, boomerang, counteraction, counterblast, kickback, reaction, recoil, repercussion, resentment, resistance, response, retaliation, retroaction
backlog accumulation, build-up, excess, hoard, reserve, reserves, resources, stock, supply
back out abandon, cancel, chicken out (*informal*), cop out (*slang*), give up, go back on, recant, renege, resign, retreat, withdraw
backslide fall from grace, go astray, go wrong, lapse, regress, relapse, renege, retrogress, revert, sin, slip, stray, weaken
backslider apostate, deserter, recidivist, recreant, renegade, turncoat
back up aid, assist, bolster, confirm, corroborate, reinforce, second, stand by, substantiate, support
backward *adj.* **1.** behind, behindhand, braindead (*informal*), dense, dozy (*Brit. informal*), dull, obtuse, retarded, slow, stupid, subnormal, underdeveloped, un-

backwash *n* **1** water washed backwards by the motion of oars or a ship. **2** an unpleasant aftereffect of an event or situation.

backwater *n* **1** an isolated or backward place or condition. **2** a body of stagnant water connected to a river.

backwoods *pl n* **1** any remote sparsely populated place. **2** partially cleared, sparsely populated forests. **backwoodsman** *n*

back yard *n* **1** a yard at the back of a house, etc. **2 in one's own back yard a** close at hand. **b** involving or implicating one.

bacon *n* **1** meat from the back and sides of a pig, dried, salted, and often smoked. **2 bring home the bacon** *Informal* **a** to achieve success. **b** to provide material support.

bacteria *pl n, sing* **-rium** a large group of microorganisms, many of which cause disease. **bacterial** *adj*
➤ Note that the word *bacteria* is already plural and does not need an "-s".

bacteriology *n* the study of bacteria. **bacteriologist** *n*

Bactrian camel *n* a two-humped camel.

bad *adj* **worse, worst 1** not good; of poor quality. **2** lacking skill or talent: *I'm so bad at that sort of thing.* **3** harmful: *smoking is bad for you.* **4** evil or immoral. **5** naughty or mischievous. **6** rotten or decayed: *a bad egg.* **7** severe: *a bad headache.* **8** incorrect or faulty: *bad grammar.* **9** sorry or upset: *I feel bad about saying no.* **10** unfavourable or distressing: *bad news.* **11** offensive or unpleasant: *bad language.* **12** not valid: *a bad cheque.* **13** not recoverable: *a bad debt.* **14** (**badder, baddest**) *Slang* good; excellent. **15 not bad** *or* **not so bad** *Informal* fairly good. **16 too bad** *Informal* (often used dismissively) regrettable. *~n* **17** unfortunate or unpleasant events: *you've got to take the good with the bad.* *~adv* **18** *Not standard* badly: *to want something bad.* **badness** *n*

bad blood *n* a feeling of intense hatred or hostility between people.

bade *or* **bad** *vb* a past tense of **bid.**

badge *n* **1** a distinguishing emblem or mark worn to show membership or achievement. **2** any revealing feature or mark.

badger *n* **1** a stocky burrowing mammal with a black and white striped head. *~vb* **2** to pester or harass.

badinage (**bad**-in-nahzh) *n* playful and witty conversation.

badly *adv* **worse, worst 1** poorly; inadequately. **2** unfavourably: *our plan worked out badly.* **3** severely: *badly damaged.* **4** very much: *he badly needed to improve his image.* **5 badly off** poor.

badminton *n* a game played with rackets and a shuttlecock which is hit back and forth across a high net.

baffle *vb* **-fling, -fled 1** to perplex. *~n* **2** a mechanical device to limit or regulate the flow of fluid, light, or sound. **bafflement** *n* **baffling** *adj*

bag *n* **1** a flexible container with an opening at one end. **2** the contents of such a container. **3** a piece of luggage. **4** a handbag. **5** a loose fold of skin under the eyes. **6** any sac in the body of an animal. **7** *Offensive slang* an ugly or bad-tempered woman: *an old bag.* **8** the amount of game taken by a hunter. **9 in the bag** *Slang* assured of succeeding. *~vb* **bagging, bagged 10** to put into a bag. **11** to bulge or cause to bulge. **12** to capture or kill, as in hunting. **13** *Brit informal* to secure the right to do or to have: *he bagged the best chair.* ~See also **bags.**

bagatelle *n* **1** something of little value. **2** a board game in which balls are struck into holes. **3** a short piece of music.

bagel (**bay**-gl) *n* a hard ring-shaped bread roll.

baggage *n* **1** suitcases packed for a journey. **2** an army's portable equipment.

baggy *adj* **-gier, -giest** (of clothes) hanging loosely. **bagginess** *n*

bag lady *n* a homeless woman who carries around all her possessions in shopping bags.

bagpipes *pl n* a musical wind instrument in which sounds are produced in reed pipes by air from an inflated bag.

bags *pl n* **1** *Informal* a lot. *~interj* **2** Also: **bags I** *Children's slang, Brit* an indication of the desire to do, be, or have something.

bah *interj* an expression of contempt or disgust.

bail[1] *Law ~n* **1** a sum of money deposited with the court as security for a person's reappearance in court. **2** the person giving such security. **3 jump bail** to fail to reappear in court after bail has been paid. **4 stand** *or* **go bail** to act as surety for someone. *~vb* **5** (foll. by *out*) to obtain the release of (a person) from custody by depositing money with the court.

bail[2] *or* **bale** *vb* **bail out** to remove water from (a boat). See also **bale out.**

THESAURUS

developed **2.** bashful, diffident, hesitating, late, reluctant, shy, sluggish, tardy, unwilling, wavering

backwards, backward *adv.* aback, behind, in reverse, rearward

backwoods *pl. n.* back of beyond, middle of nowhere, outback, sticks (*informal*)

bacteria bacilli, bugs (*slang*), germs, microbes, microorganisms, pathogens, viruses

bad 1. chickenshit (*U.S. slang*), defective, deficient, duff (*Brit. informal*), erroneous, fallacious, faulty, imperfect, inadequate, incorrect, inferior, of a sort *or* of sorts, pathetic, poor (*slang*), substandard, unsatisfactory **2.** damaging, dangerous, deleterious, detrimental, harmful, hurtful, injurious, ruinous, unhealthy **3.** base, corrupt, criminal, delinquent, evil, immoral, mean, sinful, vile, villainous, wicked, wrong **4.** disobedient, mischievous, naughty, unruly **5.** decayed, mouldy, off, putrid, rancid, rotten, sour, spoiled **6.** disastrous, distressing, grave, harsh, painful, serious, severe, terrible **7.** apologetic, conscience-stricken, contrite, guilty, regretful, remorseful, sad, sorry, upset **8.** adverse, discouraged, discouraging, distressed, distressing, gloomy, grim, melancholy, troubled, troubling, unfortunate, unpleasant **9. not bad** *also* **not so bad** all right, average, fair, fair to middling (*informal*), moderate, O.K. *or* okay (*informal*), passable, respectable, so-so (*informal*), tolerable

badge brand, device, emblem, identification, insignia, mark, sign, stamp, token

badger bend someone's ear (*informal*), bully, chivvy, goad, harass, harry, hound, importune, nag, pester, plague, torment

badly 1. carelessly, defectively, erroneously, faultily, imperfectly, inadequately, incorrectly, ineptly, poorly, shoddily, wrong, wrongly **2.** unfavourably, unfortunately, unsuccessfully **3.** acutely, deeply, desperately, exceedingly, extremely, gravely, greatly, intensely, painfully, seriously, severely

baffle amaze, astound, bewilder, confound, confuse, daze, disconcert, dumbfound, elude, flummox, mystify, nonplus, perplex, puzzle, stump, stun

bag *vb.* **1.** balloon, bulge, droop, sag, swell **2.** acquire, capture, catch, gain, get, kill, land, shoot, take, trap

baggage accoutrements, bags, belongings, equip-

bail[3] *n* **1** *Cricket* either of two small wooden bars across the tops of the stumps. **2** a partition between stalls in a stable or barn. **3** *Austral & NZ* a framework in a cow shed used to secure the head of a cow during milking. **4** a movable bar on a typewriter that holds the paper against the roller.

bailey *n* the outermost wall or court of a castle.

Bailey bridge *n* a temporary bridge that can be rapidly assembled.

bailiff *n* **1** *Brit* a sheriff's officer who serves writs and summonses. **2** the agent of a landlord or landowner.

bailiwick *n* **1** *Law* the area over which a bailiff has power. **2** a person's special field of interest.

bail out *vb* same as **bale out.**

bain-marie (ban-mar-ee) *n, pl* **bains-marie** a container for holding hot water, in which sauces and other dishes are gently cooked or kept warm.

bairn *n Scot & N English* a child.

bait *n* **1** something edible fixed to a hook or in a trap to attract fish or animals. **2** an enticement. ~*vb* **3** to put a piece of food on or in (a hook or trap). **4** to persecute or tease. **5** to set dogs upon (a bear or badger).

baize *n* a feltlike woollen fabric, usually green, which is used for the tops of billiard and card tables.

bake *vb* **baking, baked 1** to cook by dry heat in an oven. **2** to cook bread, pastry, or cakes. **3** to make or become hardened by heat. **4** *Informal* to be extremely hot.

baked beans *pl n* haricot beans, baked and tinned in tomato sauce.

baker *n* a person who makes or sells bread, cakes, etc.

baker's dozen *n* thirteen.

bakery *n, pl* **-eries** a place where bread, cakes, etc. are made or sold.

baking powder *n* a powdered mixture that contains sodium bicarbonate and cream of tartar: used in baking as a raising agent.

bakkie (buck-ee) *n S African* a small truck with an enclosed cab and an open goods area at the back.

baksheesh *n* (in some Eastern countries) money given as a tip or present.

Balaclava *or* **Balaclava helmet** *n* a close-fitting woollen hood that covers the ears and neck.

balalaika *n* a Russian musical instrument with a triangular body and three strings.

balance *n* **1** stability of mind or body: *lose one's balance.* **2** a state of being in balance. **3** harmony in the parts of a whole. **4** the power to influence or control: *the balance of power.* **5** something that remains: *the balance of what you owe.* **6** *Accounting* **a** the matching of debit and credit totals in an account. **b** a difference between such totals. **7** a weighing device. **8 in the balance** in an undecided condition. **9 on balance** after weighing up all the factors. ~*vb* **-ancing, -anced 10** to weigh in or as if in a balance. **11** to be or come into equilibrium. **12** to bring into or hold in equilibrium. **13** to compare the relative weight or importance of. **14** to arrange so as to create a state of harmony. **15** *Accounting* to compare or equalize the credit and debit totals of (an account).

balance of power *n* the equal distribution of military and economic power among countries.

balance of trade *n* the difference in value between exports and imports of goods.

balance sheet *n* a statement that shows the financial position of a business.

balcony *n, pl* **-nies 1** a platform projecting from a building with a balustrade along its outer edge, often with access from a door. **2** an upper tier of seats in a theatre or cinema.

bald *adj* **1** having no hair or fur, esp. of a man having no hair on the scalp. **2** lacking natural covering. **3** plain or blunt: *the bald facts.* **4** (of a tyre) having a worn tread. **baldly** *adv* **baldness** *n*

balderdash *n* stupid or illogical talk.

balding *adj* becoming bald.

bale[1] *n* **1** a large bundle of hay or goods bound by ropes or wires for storage or transportation. ~*vb* **baling, baled 2** to make (hay) or put (goods) into a bale or bales.

bale[2] *vb* **baling, baled** same as **bail**[2].

baleen *n* whalebone.

baleen whale *n* same as **whalebone whale**.

baleful *adj* harmful, menacing, or vindictive. **balefully** *adv*

bale out *or* **bail out** *vb* **1** *Informal* to help (a person

THESAURUS

ment, gear, impedimenta, luggage, paraphernalia, suitcases, things

baggy billowing, bulging, droopy, floppy, ill fitting, loose, oversize, roomy, sagging, slack

bail[1] *n.* bond, guarantee, guaranty, pledge, security, surety, warranty

bail[2], **bale bail out** *vb.* dip, drain off, ladle, scoop

bait 1. *n.* allurement, attraction, bribe, decoy, enticement, inducement, lure, snare, temptation **2.** *vb.* aggravate (*informal*), annoy, be on one's back (*slang*), bother, gall, get in one's hair (*informal*), get on one's nerves (*informal*), harass, hassle (*informal*), hound, irk, irritate, nark, needle (*informal*), persecute, piss one off (*taboo slang*), provoke, tease, torment, wind up (*Brit. slang*)

baked arid, desiccated, dry, parched, scorched, seared, sun-baked, torrid

balance *n.* **1.** composure, equanimity, poise, self-control, self-possession, stability, steadiness **2.** correspondence, equilibrium, equipoise, equity, equivalence, evenness, parity, symmetry **3.** difference, remainder, residue, rest, surplus ~*vb.* **4.** level, match, parallel, poise, stabilize, steady **5.** adjust, compensate for, counteract, counterbalance, counterpoise, equalize, equate, make up for, neutralize, offset **6.** assess, compare, consider, deliberate, estimate, evaluate, weigh **7.** calculate, compute, settle, square, tally, total

balanced disinterested, equitable, even-handed, fair, impartial, just, unbiased, unprejudiced

balance sheet account, budget, credits and debits, ledger, report, statement

balcony 1. terrace, veranda **2.** gallery, gods, upper circle

bald 1. baldheaded, baldpated, hairless **2.** barren, bleak, exposed, naked, stark, treeless, uncovered **3.** bare, blunt, direct, downright, forthright, outright, plain, severe, simple, straight, straightforward, unadorned, unvarnished, upfront (*informal*)

balderdash balls (*taboo slang*), bilge (*informal*), bosh (*informal*), bull (*slang*), bullshit (*taboo slang*), bunk (*informal*), bunkum *or* buncombe (*chiefly U.S.*), claptrap (*informal*), cobblers (*Brit. taboo slang*), crap (*slang*), drivel, eyewash (*informal*), garbage (*informal*), gibberish, guff (*slang*), hogwash, hokum (*slang, chiefly U.S. & Canad.*), hot air (*informal*), moonshine, nonsense, pap, piffle (*informal*), poppycock (*informal*), rot, rubbish, shit (*taboo slang*), tommyrot (*old-fashioned, informal*), trash, tripe (*informal*), twaddle

baldness 1. alopecia (*Pathology*), baldheadedness, baldpatedness, hairlessness **2.** barrenness, bleakness, nakedness, sparseness, starkness, treelessness **3.** aus-

or organization) out of a predicament. **2** to make an emergency parachute jump from an aircraft.

balk *or* **baulk** *vb* **1** to stop short: *the horse balked at the jump.* **2** to recoil: *France balked at the parliament having a veto.* **3** to thwart, check, or foil: *he was balked in his plans.*

Balkan *adj* of any of the countries of the Balkan Peninsula in SE Europe, between the Adriatic and Aegean Seas.

ball[1] *n* **1** a spherical or nearly spherical mass: *a ball of wool.* **2** a round or roundish object used in various games. **3** a single delivery of the ball in a game. **4** any more or less rounded part of the body: *the ball of the foot.* **5 have the ball at one's feet** to have the chance of doing something. **6 on the ball** *Informal* alert; informed. **7 play ball** *Informal* to cooperate. **8 start** *or* **keep the ball rolling** to initiate or maintain the progress of an action, discussion, or project. ~*vb* **9** to form into a ball. ~See also **balls, balls-up.**

ball[2] *n* **1** a lavish or formal social function for dancing. **2 have a ball** *Informal* to have a very enjoyable time.

ballad *n* **1** a narrative song or poem often with a chorus that is repeated. **2** a slow sentimental song.

ballade *n* **1** *Prosody* a verse form consisting of three stanzas and an envoy, all ending with the same line. **2** *Music* a romantic instrumental composition.

ball-and-socket joint *n Anat* a joint in which a rounded head fits into a rounded cavity, allowing a wide range of movement.

ballast *n* **1** a substance, such as sand, used to stabilize a ship when it is not carrying cargo. **2** crushed rock used for the foundation of a road or railway track. ~*vb* **3** to give stability or weight to.

ball bearing *n* **1** an arrangement of steel balls placed between moving parts of a machine in order to reduce friction. **2** a metal ball used in such an arrangement.

ball boy *or fem* **ball girl** *n* (in tennis) a person who retrieves balls that go out of play.

ball cock *n* a device consisting of a floating ball and valve for regulating the flow of liquid into a tank or cistern.

ballerina *n* a female ballet dancer.

ballet *n* **1** a classical style of expressive dancing based on precise conventional steps. **2** a theatrical representation of a story performed by ballet dancers. **balletic** *adj*

ball game *n* **1** *US & Canad* a game of baseball. **2** *Informal* a state of affairs: *a whole new ball game.*

ballistic missile *n* a launched weapon which is guided automatically in flight but falls freely at its target.

ballistics *n* the study of the flight of projectiles, often in relation to firearms. **ballistic** *adj*

ballocks *pl n, interj* same as **bollocks.**

balloon *n* **1** an inflatable rubber bag used as a plaything or party decoration. **2** a large bag inflated with a lighter-than-air gas, designed to rise and float in the atmosphere with a basket for carrying passengers. **3** an outline containing the words or thoughts of a character in a cartoon. ~*vb* **4** to fly in a balloon. **5** to swell or increase rapidly in size: *the cost of health care has ballooned.* **balloonist** *n*

ballot *n* **1** the practice of selecting a representative or course of action by voting. **2** the number of votes cast in an election. **3** the actual vote or paper indicating a person's choice. ~*vb* **-loting, -loted 4** to vote or ask for a vote from: *we balloted the members on this issue.* **5** to vote for or decide on something by ballot.

ballot box *n* a box into which voting papers are dropped on completion.

ballot paper *n* a paper used for voting.

ballpark *n* **1** *US & Canad* a stadium used for baseball games. **2** *Informal* approximate range: *in the right ballpark.*

ballpoint *or* **ballpoint pen** *n* a pen which has a small ball bearing as a writing point.

ballroom *n* a large hall for dancing.

ballroom dancing *n* social dancing in couples to music in conventional rhythms, such as the waltz.

balls *pl n Taboo slang* **1** the testicles. **2** nonsense. **3** courage and determination. **ballsy** *adj*

balls-up *Taboo slang* ~*n* **1** something botched or muddled. ~*vb* **balls up 2** to muddle or botch.

bally *adj, adv Brit old-fashioned, slang* extreme or extremely: *a bally nuisance; he's too bally charming for his own good.*

ballyhoo *n Informal* unnecessary or exaggerated fuss.

balm *n* **1** an aromatic substance obtained from certain tropical trees and used for healing and soothing. **2** something comforting or soothing: *her calmness was like a balm to my troubled mind.* **3** an aromatic herb, lemon balm.

balmy *adj* **balmier, balmiest 1** (of weather) mild and pleasant. **2** same as **barmy.**

baloney *or* **boloney** *n Informal* nonsense.

balsa (**bawl**-sa) *n* **1** a tree of tropical America which yields light wood. **2** Also: **balsawood** the light wood of this tree, used for making rafts, models, etc.

balsam *n* **1** an aromatic resin obtained from various trees and shrubs and used in medicines and perfumes. **2** any plant yielding balsam. **3** a flowering plant, such as busy lizzie.

Baltic (**bawl**-tik) *adj* of the Baltic Sea in N Europe or the states bordering it.

baluster *n* a set of posts supporting a rail.

balustrade *n* an ornamental rail supported by a set of posts.

bamboo *n* a tall treelike tropical grass with hollow stems which are used to make canes, furniture, etc.

THESAURUS

terity, bluntness, plainness, severity, simplicity, spareness

bale *see* BAIL2

balk, baulk 1. demur, dodge, evade, flinch, hesitate, jib, recoil, refuse, resist, shirk, shrink from **2.** baffle, bar, check, counteract, defeat, disconcert, foil, forestall, frustrate, hinder, obstruct, prevent, thwart

ball 1. drop, globe, globule, orb, pellet, sphere, spheroid **2. play ball** *informal* collaborate, cooperate, go along, play along, reciprocate, respond, show willing

ballast balance, counterbalance, counterweight, equilibrium, sandbag, stability, stabilizer, weight

balloon *vb.* belly, billow, bloat, blow up, dilate, distend, enlarge, expand, inflate, puff out, swell

ballot election, poll, polling, vote, voting

ballyhoo babble, build-up, commotion, fuss, hubbub, hue and cry, hullabaloo, hype, noise, racket, to-do

balm 1. balsam, cream, embrocation, emollient, lotion, ointment, salve, unguent (*literary*) **2.** anodyne, comfort, consolation, curative, palliative, restorative, solace

balmy 1. clement, mild, pleasant, summery, temperate **2.** *see* BARMY

bamboozle 1. cheat, con (*informal*), deceive, defraud, delude, dupe, fool, hoax, hoodwink, skin

bamboozle *vb* **-zling, -zled** *Informal* **1** to cheat; mislead. **2** to confuse. **bamboozlement** *n*

ban *vb* **banning, banned 1** to prohibit or forbid officially. *~n* **2** an official prohibition.

banal (ban-**nahl**) *adj* lacking originality. **banality** *n*

banana *n* a crescent-shaped fruit that grows on a tropical or subtropical treelike plant.

banana republic *n Informal* a small politically unstable country whose economy is dominated by foreign interests.

band[1] *n* **1** a group of musicians playing together, esp. on brass or percussion instruments. **2** a group of people having a common purpose: *a band of revolutionaries. ~vb* **3** (foll. by *together*) to unite.

band[2] *n* **1** a strip of some material, used to hold objects together: *a rubber band.* **2** a strip of fabric used as an ornament or to reinforce clothing. **3** a stripe of contrasting colour or texture. **4** a driving belt in machinery. **5** *Physics* a range of frequencies or wavelengths between two limits. **6** a section of a gramophone record, esp. formerly. *~vb* **7** to fasten or mark with a band.

bandage *n* **1** a piece of material used to dress a wound or wrap an injured limb. *~vb* **-aging, -aged 2** to cover or wrap with a bandage.

bandanna *or* **bandana** *n* a large brightly-coloured handkerchief or neckerchief.

b. and b. *or* **B & B** bed and breakfast.

bandbox *n* a lightweight usually cylindrical box for hats.

bandeau (**ban**-doe) *n, pl* **-deaux** (-doze) a narrow ribbon worn round the head.

banderole *n* **1** a narrow flag usually with forked ends. **2** a ribbon-like scroll bearing an inscription.

bandicoot *n* **1** an Australian marsupial with a long pointed muzzle and a long tail. **2 bandicoot rat** any of three burrowing rats of S and SE Asia.

bandit *n* a robber, esp. a member of an armed gang. **banditry** *n*

bandmaster *n* the conductor of a band.

bandolier *n* a shoulder belt with small pockets for cartridges.

band saw *n* a power-operated saw consisting of an endless toothed metal band running over two wheels.

bandsman *n, pl* **-men** a player in a musical band.

bandstand *n* a roofed outdoor platform for a band.

bandwagon *n* **climb** *or* **jump on the bandwagon** to join a popular party or movement that seems assured of success.

bandy *adj* **-dier, -diest 1** Also: **bandy-legged** having legs curved outwards at the knees. **2** (of legs) curved outwards at the knees. *~vb* **-dies, -dying, -died 3** to exchange (words), sometimes in a heated manner. **4 bandy about** to use (a name, term, etc.) frequently.

bane *n* a person or thing that causes misery or distress: *the bane of my life.* **baneful** *adj*

bang *n* **1** a short loud explosive noise, such as the report of a gun. **2** a hard blow or loud knock. **3** *Taboo slang* an act of sexual intercourse. **4 with a bang** successfully: *the party went with a bang. ~vb* **5** to hit or knock, esp. with a loud noise. **6** to close (a door) noisily. **7** to make or cause to make a loud noise, as of an explosion. **8** *Taboo slang* to have sexual intercourse with. *~adv* **9** with a sudden impact: *the car drove bang into a lamppost.* **10** precisely: *bang in the middle.*

banger *n Brit* **1** *Informal* an old decrepit car. **2** *Slang* a sausage. **3** a firework that explodes loudly.

Bangladeshi *adj* **1** of Bangladesh. *~n* **2** a person from Bangladesh.

bangle *n* a bracelet worn round the arm or sometimes round the ankle.

banian *n* same as **banyan.**

banish *vb* **1** to send into exile. **2** to drive away: *it's the only way to banish weeds from the garden.* **banishment** *n*

banisters *or* **bannisters** *pl n* the railing and supporting balusters on a staircase.

banjo *n, pl* **-jos** *or* **-joes** a stringed musical instrument with a long neck and a circular drumlike body. **banjoist** *n*

bank[1] *n* **1** an institution offering services, such as the safekeeping and lending of money at interest. **2** the building used by such an institution. **3** the funds held by a banker or dealer in some gambling games. **4** any supply, store, or reserve: *a data bank. ~vb* **5** to deposit

THESAURUS

(*slang*), swindle, trick **2.** baffle, befuddle, confound, confuse, mystify, perplex, puzzle, stump

ban 1. *vb.* banish, bar, black, blackball, block, boycott, debar, disallow, disqualify, exclude, forbid, interdict, outlaw, prohibit, proscribe, restrict, suppress **2.** *n.* block, boycott, censorship, embargo, interdict, interdiction, prohibition, proscription, restriction, stoppage, suppression, taboo

banal clichéd, cliché-ridden, commonplace, everyday, hackneyed, humdrum, mundane, old hat, ordinary, pedestrian, platitudinous, stale, stereotyped, stock, threadbare, tired, trite, unimaginative, unoriginal, vapid

banality bromide (*informal*), cliché, commonplace, platitude, triteness, trite phrase, triviality, truism, vapidity

band[1] *n.* **1.** combo, ensemble, group, orchestra **2.** assembly, association, bevy, body, camp, clique, club, company, coterie, crew (*informal*), gang, horde, party, posse (*informal*), society, troop

band[2] *n.* belt, binding, bond, chain, cord, fetter, fillet, ligature, manacle, ribbon, shackle, strap, strip, tie

bandage 1. *n.* compress, dressing, gauze, plaster **2.** *vb.* bind, cover, dress, swathe

bandit brigand, crook, desperado, footpad (*old-fashioned*), freebooter, gangster, gunman, highwayman, hijacker, marauder, outlaw, pirate, racketeer, robber, thief

bandy 1. *adj.* bandy-legged, bent, bowed, bow-legged, crooked, curved **2.** *vb.* barter, exchange, interchange, pass, shuffle, swap, throw, toss, trade

bane affliction, *bête noire,* blight, burden, calamity, curse, despair, destruction, disaster, downfall, misery, nuisance, pest, plague, ruin, scourge, torment, trial, trouble, woe

baneful baleful, calamitous, deadly, deleterious, destructive, disastrous, fatal, harmful, hurtful, injurious, noxious, pernicious, pestilential, ruinous, venomous

bang *n.* **1.** boom, burst, clang, clap, clash, detonation, explosion, peal, pop, report, shot, slam, thud, thump **2.** belt (*informal*), blow, box, bump, cuff, hit, knock, punch, smack, stroke, wallop (*informal*), whack *~vb.* **3.** bash (*informal*), beat, belt (*informal*), bump, clatter, crash, hammer, knock, pound, pummel, rap, slam, strike, thump **4.** boom, burst, clang, detonate, drum, echo, explode, peal, resound, thump, thunder *~adv.* **5.** abruptly, hard, headlong, noisily, precisely, slap, smack, straight, suddenly

banish 1. deport, drive away, eject, evict, exclude, excommunicate, exile, expatriate, expel, ostracize, outlaw, shut out, transport **2.** ban, cast out, discard, dislodge, dismiss, dispel, eliminate, eradicate, get rid of, oust, remove, shake off

(cash or a cheque) in a bank. **6** to transact business with a bank. ~See also **bank on.**

bank[2] *n* **1** a long raised mass, esp. of earth. **2** a slope, as of a hill. **3** the sloping side and ground on either side of a river. ~*vb* **4** to form into a bank or mound. **5** to cover (a fire) with ashes and fuel so that it will burn slowly. **6** (of an aircraft) to tip to one side in turning.

bank[3] *n* **1** an arrangement of similar objects in a row or in tiers. ~*vb* **2** to arrange in a bank.

bank account *n* an arrangement whereby a customer deposits money at a bank and may withdraw it when it is needed.

bank card *n* any plastic card issued by a bank, such as a cash card or a cheque card.

banker[1] *n* **1** a person who owns or manages a bank. **2** the keeper of the bank in various gambling games.

banker[2] *n Austral & NZ informal* a stream almost overflowing its banks: *the creek was running a banker.*

banker's order *n* same as **standing order** (sense 1).

bank holiday *n* (in Britain) a public holiday when banks are closed by law.

banking *n* the business engaged in by a bank.

banknote *n* a piece of paper money issued by a central bank.

bank on *vb* to rely on.

bankrupt *n* **1** a person, declared by a court to be unable to pay his or her debts, whose property is sold and the proceeds distributed among the creditors. **2** a person no longer having a particular quality: *a spiritual bankrupt.* ~*adj* **3** declared insolvent. **4** financially ruined. **5** no longer having a particular quality: *morally bankrupt.* ~*vb* **6** to make bankrupt. **bankruptcy** *n*

banner *n* **1** a long strip of material displaying a slogan, advertisement, etc. **2** a placard carried in a demonstration. **3** Also called: **banner headline** a large headline in a newspaper extending across the page.

bannock *n Scot* a round flat cake made from oatmeal or barley.

banns *pl n* the public announcement of a marriage that is planned.

banquet *n* **1** an elaborate formal dinner often followed by speeches. ~*vb* **-queting, -queted 2** to hold or take part in a banquet.

banshee *n* (in Irish folklore) a female spirit whose wailing warns of a coming death.

bantam *n* **1** a small breed of domestic fowl. **2** a small but aggressive person.

bantamweight *n* a professional boxer weighing up to 118 pounds (53.5 kg) or an amateur weighing up to 54 kg.

banter *vb* **1** to tease jokingly. ~*n* **2** teasing or joking conversation.

Bantu *n* **1** a group of languages of Africa. **2** (*pl* **-tu** *or* **-tus**) *Offensive* a Black speaker of a Bantu language. ~*adj* **3** of the Bantu languages or the peoples who speak them.

Bantustan *n Offensive* an area reserved for occupation by a Black African people.

banyan *or* **banian** *n* an Indian tree whose branches grow down into the soil forming additional trunks.

baobab (**bay**-oh-bab) *n* an African tree with a massive grey trunk, short angular branches, and large pulpy fruit.

bap *n Brit* a large soft bread roll.

baptism *n* a Christian religious rite in which a person is immersed in or sprinkled with water as a sign of being cleansed from sin and accepted as a member of the Church. **baptismal** *adj*

baptism of fire *n* **1** any introductory ordeal. **2** a soldier's first experience of battle.

Baptist *n* **1** a member of a Protestant denomination that believes in the necessity of adult baptism by immersion. **2 the Baptist** John the Baptist.

baptize *or* **-ise** *vb* **-tizing, -tized** *or* **-tising, -tised 1** *Christianity* to immerse (a person) in water or sprinkle water on (him or her) as part of the rite of baptism. **2** to give a name to.

bar[1] *n* **1** a rigid usually straight length of metal, wood, etc. used as a barrier or structural part. **2** a solid usually rectangular block of any material: *a bar of soap.* **3** anything that obstructs or prevents: *a bar to women's mobility.* **4** a counter or room where alcoholic drinks are served. **5** a narrow band or stripe, as of colour or light. **6** a heating element in an electric fire. **7** See **Bar. 8** the place in a court of law where the accused stands during trial. **9** *Music* a group of beats that is repeated with a consistent rhythm throughout a piece of music. **10** *Football etc* same as **crossbar. 11** *Heraldry* a narrow horizontal line across a shield. **12 behind bars** in prison. ~*vb* **barring, barred 13** to secure with a bar: *to bar the door.* **14** to obstruct: *the fallen tree barred the road.* **15** to exclude: *he was barred from membership of the club.* **16** to mark with a bar or bars. ~*prep* **17** except for.

bar[2] *n* a unit of pressure equal to 10^5 newtons per square metre.

THESAURUS

banishment deportation, exile, expatriation, expulsion, proscription, transportation

banisters, bannisters balusters, balustrade, handrail, rail, railing

bank[1] **1.** *n.* accumulation, depository, fund, hoard, repository, reserve, reservoir, savings, stock, stockpile, store, storehouse **2.** *vb.* deal with, deposit, keep, save, transact business with

bank[2] *n.* **1.** banking, embankment, heap, mass, mound, pile, ridge **2.** brink, edge, margin, shore, side ~*vb.* **3.** amass, heap, mass, mound, pile, stack **4.** camber, cant, heel, incline, pitch, slant, slope, tilt, tip

bank on assume, believe in, count on, depend on, lean on, look to, rely on, trust

bankrupt broke (*informal*), depleted, destitute, exhausted, failed, impoverished, insolvent, lacking, ruined, spent

bankruptcy disaster, exhaustion, failure, indebtedness, insolvency, lack, liquidation, ruin

banner banderole, colours, ensign, flag, pennant, pennon, standard, streamer

banquet dinner, feast, meal, repast, revel, treat

banter 1. *vb.* chaff, deride, jeer, jest, joke, josh (*slang, chiefly U.S. & Canad.*), kid (*informal*), make fun of, rib (*informal*), ridicule, taunt, tease, twit **2.** *n.* badinage, chaff, chaffing, derision, jeering, jesting, joking, kidding (*informal*), mockery, persiflage, pleasantry, raillery, repartee, ribbing (*informal*), ridicule, wordplay

baptism christening, immersion, purification, sprinkling

baptize, -ise 1. besprinkle, cleanse, immerse, purify **2.** call, christen, dub, name, title

bar *n.* **1.** batten, crosspiece, paling, palisade, pole, rail, rod, shaft, stake, stick **2.** barricade, barrier, block, deterrent, hindrance, impediment, obstacle, obstruction, rail, railing, stop **3.** boozer (*Brit., Austral., & N.Z. informal*), canteen, counter, inn, lounge, pub (*informal, chiefly Brit.*), public house, saloon, taproom (*old-fashioned*), tavern (*old-fashioned*), watering hole (*facetious slang*) **4.** *Law* barristers, body of lawyers, counsel, court, judgment, tribunal **5.** bench, court, courtroom, dock, law court ~*vb.* **6.** barricade, bolt,

Bar *n* **1 the Bar** barristers collectively. **2 be called to the Bar** *Brit* to become a barrister.

barb *n* **1** a cutting remark. **2** a point facing in the opposite direction to the main point of a fish-hook, harpoon, etc. **3** a beardlike growth, hair, or projection. *~vb* **4** to provide with a barb or barbs. **barbed** *adj*

barbarian *n* **1** a member of a primitive or uncivilized people. **2** a coarse or vicious person. *~adj* **3** uncivilized or brutal.

barbaric *adj* primitive or brutal.

barbarism *n* **1** a brutal, coarse, or ignorant act. **2** the condition of being backward, coarse, or ignorant. **3** a substandard word or expression.

barbarity *n, pl* **-ties 1** the state of being barbaric or barbarous. **2** a vicious act.

barbarous *adj* **1** uncivilized: *a barbarous and uninhabitable jungle.* **2** brutal or cruel: *the barbarous tortures inflicted on them.*

barbecue *n* **1** a grill on which food is cooked over hot charcoal, usually out of doors. **2** food cooked over hot charcoal, usually out of doors. **3** a party or picnic at which barbecued food is served. *~vb* **-cuing, -cued 4** to cook on a grill, usually over charcoal.

barbed wire *n* strong wire with sharp points protruding at close intervals.

barbel *n* **1** a long thin growth that hangs from the jaws of certain fishes, such as the carp. **2** a freshwater fish with such a growth.

barbell *n* a long metal rod to which heavy discs are attached at each end for weightlifting.

barber *n* a person whose business is cutting men's hair and shaving beards.

barberry *n, pl* **-ries** a shrub with orange or red berries.

barbican *n* a walled defence to protect a gate or drawbridge of a fortification.

barbiturate *n* a derivative of barbituric acid used in medicine as a sedative.

barbituric acid *n* a crystalline solid used in the preparation of barbiturate drugs.

barcarole *or* **barcarolle** *n* **1** a Venetian boat song. **2** an instrumental composition resembling this.

bar code *n* an arrangement of numbers and parallel lines on a package, which can be electronically scanned at a checkout to give the price of the goods.

bard *n* **1** *Archaic or literary* a poet. **2 a** (formerly) an ancient Celtic poet. **b** a poet who wins a verse competition at a Welsh eisteddfod. **3 the Bard** William Shakespeare, English playwright and poet.

bare *adj* **1** unclothed: used esp. of a part of the body. **2** without the natural, conventional, or usual covering: *bare trees.* **3** lacking appropriate furnishings, etc.: *a bare room.* **4** simple: *the bare facts.* **5** just sufficient: *the bare minimum.* *~vb* **baring, bared 6** to uncover. **bareness** *n*

bareback *adj, adv* (of horse-riding) without a saddle.

barefaced *adj* obvious or shameless: *a barefaced lie.*

barefoot *or* **barefooted** *adj, adv* with the feet uncovered.

bareheaded *adj, adv* with the head uncovered.

barely *adv* **1** only just: *barely enough.* **2** scantily: *barely furnished.*

➤ As *barely* already has a negative meaning, it should never be used with *not* or other negatives.

bargain *n* **1** an agreement establishing what each party will give, receive, or perform in a transaction. **2** something acquired or received in such an agreement. **3** something bought or offered at a low price. **4 drive a hard bargain** to forcefully pursue one's own profit in a transaction. **5 into the bargain** besides. *~vb* **6** to negotiate the terms of an agreement or transaction.

bargain for *vb* to anticipate.

bargain on *vb* to rely or depend on.

barge *n* **1** a flat-bottomed boat, used for transporting freight, esp. on canals. **2** a boat, often decorated, used in pageants, etc. *~vb* **barging, barged** *Informal* **3** (foll. by *into*) to bump into. **4** to push one's way violently. **5** (foll. by *into* or *in*) to interrupt rudely: *he barged into our conversation.*

bargee *n* a person in charge of a barge.

bargepole *n* **1** a long pole used to propel a barge. **2 not touch with a bargepole** *Informal* to refuse to have anything to do with.

bar graph *n* a diagram consisting of vertical or horizontal bars whose lengths are proportional to amounts or quantities.

baritone *n* **1** the second lowest adult male voice. **2** a singer with such a voice.

barium (**bare**-ee-um) *n Chem* a soft silvery-white metallic chemical element. Symbol: Ba

THESAURUS

fasten, latch, lock, secure **7.** ban, black, blackball, exclude, forbid, hinder, keep out, obstruct, prevent, prohibit, restrain

barb 1. affront, dig, gibe, insult, rebuff, sarcasm, scoff, sneer **2.** bristle, point, prickle, prong, quill, spike, spur, thorn

barbarian *n.* **1.** bigot, boor, ignoramus, illiterate, lowbrow, philistine **2.** brute, hooligan, lout, lowbrow, ned (*slang*), ruffian, savage, vandal, yahoo *~adj.* **3.** boorish, crude, lowbrow, philistine, primitive, rough, uncouth, uncultivated, uncultured, unsophisticated, vulgar, wild

barbaric barbarous, boorish, brutal, coarse, crude, cruel, fierce, inhuman, primitive, rude, savage, uncivilized, uncouth, vulgar, wild

barbarism 1. atrocity, barbarity, enormity, outrage **2.** coarseness, crudity, savagery, uncivilizedness **3.** corruption, misusage, misuse, solecism, vulgarism

barbarity brutality, cruelty, inhumanity, ruthlessness, savagery, viciousness

barbarous 1. barbarian, brutish, primitive, rough, rude, savage, uncivilized, uncouth, wild **2.** barbaric, brutal, cruel, ferocious, heartless, inhuman, monstrous, ruthless, vicious

bare 1. denuded, exposed, in the raw (*informal*), naked, naked as the day one was born (*informal*), nude, peeled, shorn, stripped, unclad, unclothed, uncovered, undressed, without a stitch on (*informal*) **2.** barren, blank, empty, lacking, mean, open, poor, scanty, scarce, unfurnished, vacant, void, wanting **3.** austere, bald, basic, cold, essential, hard, literal, plain, severe, sheer, simple, spare, spartan, stark, unadorned, unembellished, unvarnished

barefaced audacious, bald, blatant, bold, brash, brazen, flagrant, glaring, impudent, insolent, manifest, naked, obvious, open, palpable, patent, shameless, transparent, unconcealed

barely almost, hardly, just, scarcely

bargain *n.* **1.** agreement, arrangement, business, compact, contract, convention, engagement, negotiation, pact, pledge, promise, stipulation, transaction, treaty, understanding **2.** (cheap) purchase, discount, giveaway, good buy, good deal, good value, reduction, snip (*informal*), steal (*informal*) *~vb.* **3.** agree, barter, buy, contract, covenant, deal, haggle, negotiate, promise, sell, stipulate, trade, traffic, transact

bargain for anticipate, contemplate, expect, foresee, imagine, look for, plan for

bargain on assume, bank on, count on, plan on

barium meal *n* a preparation of barium sulphate, which is opaque to x-rays, used in x-ray examination of the alimentary canal.

bark[1] (**bark**) *n* **1** the loud harsh cry of a dog or certain other animals. ~*vb* **2** (of a dog or other animal) to make its typical cry. **3** to shout in an angry tone: *he barked an order.* **4 bark up the wrong tree** *Informal* to misdirect one's attention or efforts.

bark[2] *n* **1** an outer protective layer of dead corklike cells on the trunks of trees. ~*vb* **2** to scrape or rub off (skin), as in an injury. **3** to remove the bark from (a tree).

barker *n* a person at a fairground who loudly addresses passers-by to attract customers.

barley *n* **1** a tall grasslike plant with dense bristly flower spikes, widely cultivated for grain. **2** the grain of this grass used in making beer and whisky and for soups.

barleycorn *n* a grain of barley, or barley itself.

barley sugar *n* a brittle clear amber-coloured sweet.

barley water *n* a drink made from an infusion of barley.

barm *n* the yeasty froth on fermenting malt liquors.

barmaid *n* a woman who serves in a pub.

barman *n, pl* **-men** a man who serves in a pub.

bar mitzvah *Judaism* ~*n* **1** a ceremony marking the 13th birthday of a boy and his assumption of religious obligations. ~*adj* **2** (of a Jewish boy) having undergone this ceremony.

barmy *adj* **-mier, -miest** *Slang* insane.

barn *n* a large farm outbuilding, chiefly for storing grain, but also for livestock.

barnacle *n* a marine shellfish that lives attached to rocks, ship bottoms, etc. **barnacled** *adj*

barnacle goose *n* a goose with a black-and-white head and body.

barn dance *n* **1** *US & Canad* a party with square-dancing. **2** *Brit* a progressive round country dance.

barney *n Informal* a noisy fight or argument.

barn owl *n* an owl with a pale brown-and-white plumage and a heart-shaped face.

barnstorm *vb* **1** *Chiefly US & Canad* to tour rural districts making speeches in a political campaign. **2** to tour rural districts putting on shows. **barnstorming** *n, adj*

barnyard *n* a yard adjoining a barn.

barograph *n Meteorol* a barometer that automatically keeps a record of changes in atmospheric pressure.

barometer *n* an instrument for measuring atmospheric pressure, used to determine weather or altitude changes. **barometric** *adj*

baron *n* **1** a member of the lowest rank of nobility in the British Isles. **2** a powerful businessman or financier: *a press baron.* **baronial** *adj*

baroness *n* **1** a woman holding the rank of baron. **2** the wife or widow of a baron.

baronet *n* a commoner who holds the lowest hereditary British title. **baronetcy** *n*

barony *n, pl* **-nies** the domain or rank of a baron.

baroque (bar-**rock**) *n* **1** a highly ornate style of architecture and art, popular in Europe from the late 16th to the early 18th century. **2** a highly ornamented 17th-century style of music. ~*adj* **3** ornate in style.

barque (**bark**) *n* **1** a sailing ship, esp. one with three masts. **2** *Poetic* any boat.

barrack[1] *vb* to house (soldiers) in barracks.

barrack[2] *vb Informal* to criticize loudly or shout against (a team or speaker).

barracks *pl n* **1** a building or group of buildings used to accommodate military personnel. **2** a large and bleak building.

barracuda (bar-rack-**kew**-da) *n, pl* **-da** *or* **-das** a tropical fish which feeds on other fishes and attacks man.

barrage (**bar**-rahzh) *n* **1** a continuous delivery of questions, complaints, etc. **2** *Mil* the continuous firing of artillery over a wide area. **3** a construction built across a river to control the water level.

barrage balloon *n* a balloon tethered by cables, often with net suspended from it, used to deter low-flying air attack.

barre (**bar**) *n* a rail at hip height used for ballet practice.

barrel *n* **1** a cylindrical container usually with rounded sides and flat ends, and held together by metal hoops. **2** a unit of capacity of varying amount in different industries. **3** the tube through which the bullet of a firearm is fired. **4 over a barrel** *Informal* powerless. ~*vb* **-relling, -relled** *or US* **-reling, -reled 5** to put into a barrel or barrels.

barrel organ *n* a musical instrument played by turning a handle.

barren *adj* **1** incapable of producing offspring. **2** unable to support the growth of crops, fruit, etc.: *barren land.* **3** unprofitable or unsuccessful: *Real Madrid have had a barren two seasons.* **4** dull. **barrenness** *n*

barricade *n* **1** a barrier, esp. one erected hastily for defence. ~*vb* **-cading, -caded 2** to erect a barricade across (an entrance).

barrier *n* **1** anything that blocks a way or separates, such as a gate. **2** anything that prevents progress: *a barrier of distrust.* **3** anything that separates or hinders union: *a language barrier.*

barrier cream *n* a cream used to protect the skin.

THESAURUS

barge canal boat, flatboat, lighter, narrow boat, scow

barge in break in, burst in, butt in, infringe, interrupt, intrude, muscle in (*informal*)

bark[1] **1.** *n./vb.* bay, growl, howl, snarl, woof, yap, yelp **2.** *vb. figurative* bawl, bawl at, berate, bluster, growl, shout, snap, snarl, yell

bark[2] **1.** *n.* casing, cortex (*Anat., bot.*), covering, crust, husk, rind, skin **2.** *vb.* abrade, flay, rub, scrape, shave, skin, strip

barmy *or* **balmy** crackpot (*informal*), crazy, daft (*informal*), foolish, goofy (*informal*), idiotic, insane, loony (*slang*), loopy (*informal*), nuts (*slang*), nutty (*slang*), odd, off one's trolley (*slang*), out to lunch (*informal*), silly, stupid, up the pole (*informal*)

baroque bizarre, convoluted, elaborate, extravagant, flamboyant, florid, grotesque, ornate, overdecorated, rococo

barracks billet, camp, cantonment, encampment, garrison, quarters

barrage 1. assault, attack, burst, deluge, hail, mass, onslaught, plethora, profusion, rain, storm, stream, torrent **2.** battery, bombardment, cannonade, curtain of fire, fusillade, gunfire, salvo, shelling, volley

barren 1. childless, infertile, sterile, unprolific **2.** arid, desert, desolate, dry, empty, unfruitful, unproductive, waste **3.** boring, flat, fruitless, lacklustre, stale, uninformative, uninspiring, uninstructive, uninteresting, unrewarding, useless, vapid

barricade 1. *n.* barrier, blockade, bulwark, fence, obstruction, palisade, rampart, stockade **2.** *vb.* bar, block, blockade, defend, fortify, obstruct, protect, shut in

barrier 1. bar, barricade, block, blockade, boundary, ditch, fence, fortification, obstacle, obstruction, pale,

barrier reef *n* a long narrow ridge of coral, separated from the shore by deep water.
barring *prep* unless something occurs; except for.
barrister *n* a lawyer who is qualified to plead in the higher courts.
barrow[1] *n* **1** same as **wheelbarrow. 2** a handcart used by street traders.
barrow[2] *n* a heap of earth placed over a prehistoric tomb.
barrow boy *n Brit* a man who sells goods from a barrow.
Bart. Baronet.
barter *vb* **1** to trade goods or services in exchange for other goods or services, rather than for money. *~n* **2** trade by the exchange of goods.
baryon (**bar**-ree-on) *n* an elementary particle that has a mass greater than or equal to that of the proton.
baryta (bar-**rite**-a) *n* a compound of barium, such as barium oxide.
barytes (bar-**rite**-eez) *n* a colourless or white mineral: a source of barium.
basal *adj* **1** at, of, or constituting a base. **2** fundamental.
basalt (**bass**-awlt) *n* a dark volcanic rock. **basaltic** *adj*
bascule *n* a drawbridge that operates by a counterbalanced weight.
base[1] *n* **1** the bottom or supporting part of anything. **2** the fundamental principle or part: *agriculture was the economic base of the city's growth.* **3** a centre of operations, organization, or supply. **4** a starting point: *the new discovery became the base for further research.* **5** the main ingredient of a mixture: *to use rice as a base in cookery.* **6** *Chem* a compound that combines with an acid to form a salt. **7** the lower side or face of a geometric construction. **8** *Maths* the number of units in a counting system that is equivalent to one in the next higher counting place: *10 is the base of the decimal system.* **9** a starting or finishing point in any of various games. *~vb* **basing, based 10** (foll. by *on* or *upon*) to use as a basis for. **11** (foll. by *at* or *in*) to station, post, or place.
base[2] *adj* **1** dishonourable or immoral: *base motives.* **2** of inferior quality or value: *a base coin.* **3** debased; counterfeit: *base currency.*
baseball *n* **1** a team game in which the object is to score runs by batting the ball and running round all four bases. **2** the ball used in this game.
baseless *adj* not based on fact.
baseline *n* **1** a value or starting point on an imaginary scale with which other things are compared. **2** a line at each end of a tennis court that marks the limit of play.
basement *n* a partly or wholly underground storey of a building.
base metal *n* a common metal such as copper or lead, that is not a precious metal.
base rate *n* **1** the rate of interest used by a bank as a basis for its lending rates. **2** the rate at which the Bank of England lends to other financial organizations, which effectively controls interest rates throughout the UK.
bases[1] *n* the plural of **basis.**
bases[2] *n* the plural of **base**[1].
bash *Informal ~vb* **1** to strike violently or crushingly. **2** (foll. by *into*) to crash into. *~n* **3** a heavy blow. **4 have a bash** *Informal* to make an attempt.
bashful *adj* shy or modest. **bashfully** *adv*
-bashing *n and adj combining form Informal or slang* **a** indicating a malicious attack on members of a group: *union-bashing.* **b** indicating an activity undertaken energetically: *Bible-bashing.* **-basher** *n combining form*
basic *adj* **1** of or forming a base or basis. **2** elementary or simple: *a few basic facts.* **3** excluding additions or extras: *basic pay.* **4** *Chem* of or containing a base. *~n* **5 basics** fundamental principles, facts, etc. **basically** *adv*
BASIC *n* a computer programming language that uses common English terms.
basic slag *n* a slag produced in steel-making, containing calcium phosphate.
basil *n* an aromatic herb used for seasoning food.
basilica *n* **1** a Roman building, used for public administration, which is rectangular with two aisles and a rounded end. **2** a Christian church of similar design.
basilisk *n* (in classical legend) a serpent that could kill by its breath or glance.
basin *n* **1** a round wide container open at the top. **2** the amount a basin will hold. **3** a washbasin or sink. **4** any partially enclosed area of water where ships or boats may be moored. **5** the catchment area of a particular river. **6** a depression in the earth's surface.

THESAURUS

railing, rampart, stop, wall **2.** *figurative* check, difficulty, drawback, handicap, hindrance, hurdle, impediment, limitation, obstacle, restriction, stumbling block
barter bargain, exchange, haggle, sell, swap, trade, traffic
base[1] *n.* **1.** bed, bottom, foot, foundation, groundwork, pedestal, rest, stand, support **2.** basis, core, essence, essential, fundamental, heart, key, origin, principle, root, source **3.** camp, centre, headquarters, home, post, settlement, starting point, station *~vb.* **4.** build, construct, depend, derive, establish, found, ground, hinge, locate, station
base[2] **1.** abject, contemptible, corrupt, depraved, despicable, dishonourable, disreputable, evil, ignoble, immoral, infamous, scandalous, shameful, sordid, vile, villainous, vulgar, wicked **2.** downtrodden, grovelling, low, lowly, mean, menial, miserable, paltry, pitiful, poor, servile, slavish, sorry, subservient, worthless, wretched **3.** adulterated, alloyed, counterfeit, debased, fake, forged, fraudulent, impure, inferior, pinchbeck, spurious
baseless groundless, unconfirmed, uncorroborated, unfounded, ungrounded, unjustifiable, unjustified, unsubstantiated, unsupported
bash 1. belt (*informal*), biff (*slang*), break, crash, crush (*slang*), hit, lay one on (*slang*), punch, slosh (*Brit. slang*), smash, sock (*slang*), strike, wallop (*informal*) **2. have a bash** *informal* attempt, crack (*informal*), go (*informal*), shot (*informal*), stab (*informal*), try
bashful abashed, blushing, confused, constrained, coy, diffident, easily embarrassed, nervous, overmodest, reserved, reticent, retiring, self-conscious, self-effacing, shamefaced, sheepish, shrinking, shy, timid, timorous
basic bog-standard (*Brit. & Irish slang*), central, elementary, essential, fundamental, indispensable, inherent, intrinsic, key, necessary, primary, radical, underlying, vital
basically at bottom, at heart, essentially, firstly, fundamentally, inherently, in substance, intrinsically, mostly, primarily, radically
basics brass tacks (*informal*), core, essentials, facts, fundamentals, hard facts, necessaries, nitty-gritty (*in-*

basis *n, pl* **bases 1** something that underlies, supports, or is essential to an idea, belief, etc. **2** a principle on which something depends.

bask *vb* (foll. by *in*) **1** to lie in or be exposed (to pleasant warmth or sunshine). **2** to enjoy (approval or favourable conditions).

basket *n* **1** a container made of interwoven strips of wood or cane. **2** the amount a basket will hold. **3** *Basketball* **a** the high horizontal hoop through which a player must throw the ball to score points. **b** a point scored in this way.

basketball *n* a team game in which points are scored by throwing the ball through a high horizontal hoop.

basket weave *n* a weave of yarns, resembling that of a basket.

basketwork *n* same as **wickerwork.**

basking shark *n* a very large plankton-eating shark, which often floats at the sea surface.

basmati rice *n* a variety of long-grain rice with slender aromatic grains, used for savoury dishes.

basque *n* a tight-fitting bodice for women.

Basque *n* **1** a member of a people living in the W Pyrenees in France and Spain. **2** the language of the Basques. *~adj* **3** of the Basques.

bas-relief *n* sculpture in which the figures project slightly from the background.

bass[1] (**base**) *n* **1** the lowest adult male voice. **2** a singer with such a voice. **3** *Informal* same as **bass guitar** or **double bass.** *~adj* **4** of the lowest range of musical notes: *the system is engineered to give good bass sound from very small speakers.* **5** denoting a musical instrument that is lowest or second lowest in pitch in its family: *bass clarinet.* **6** of or relating to a bass guitar or double bass: *the band is unusual in that it has two bass players.* **7** of or written for a singer with the lowest adult male voice: *the bass soloist in next week's performance of Handel's "Messiah".*

bass[2] (rhymes with **gas**) *n* **1** an edible sea fish. **2** a European spiny-finned freshwater fish.

bass clef (**base**) *n* the clef that establishes F a fifth below middle C on the fourth line of the staff.

bass drum (**base**) *n* a large drum of low pitch.

basset hound *n* a smooth-haired dog with short legs and long ears.

bass guitar (**base**) *n* an electric guitar with the same pitch and tuning as a double bass.

bassinet *n* a wickerwork or wooden cradle or pram, usually hooded.

basso *n, pl* **-sos** *or* **-si** a singer with a bass voice.

bassoon *n* a woodwind instrument that produces a range of low sounds. **bassoonist** *n*

bastard *n* **1** *Informal, offensive* an obnoxious or despicable person. **2** a person born of parents not married to each other. **3** *Informal* something extremely difficult or unpleasant. *~adj* **4** illegitimate by birth. **5** counterfeit; spurious. **bastardy** *n*

bastardize *or* **-ise** *vb* **-izing, -ized** *or* **-ising, -ised 1** to debase. **2** to declare illegitimate.

baste[1] *vb* **basting, basted** to sew with loose temporary stitches.

baste[2] *vb* **basting, basted** to moisten (meat) during cooking with hot fat.

baste[3] *vb* **basting, basted** to thrash.

bastinado *n, pl* **-does 1** a punishment or torture by beating on the soles of the feet with a stick. *~vb* **-doing, -doed 2** to beat (a person) in this way.

bastion *n* **1** a projecting part of a fortification. **2** a thing or person regarded as defending a principle or way of life: *a bastion of anti-communism.*

bat[1] *n* **1** any of various types of club used to hit the ball in certain sports. **2** *Cricket* a batsman. **3 off one's own bat a** of one's own accord. **b** by one's own unaided efforts. *~vb* **batting, batted 4** to strike with or as if with a bat. **5** *Cricket etc* to take a turn at batting.

bat[2] *n* **1** a nocturnal mouselike flying animal with leathery wings. **2 blind as a bat** having extremely poor eyesight.

bat[3] *vb* **batting, batted 1** to flutter (one's eyelids). **2 not bat an eyelid** *Informal* to show no surprise.

batch *n* **1** a group of similar objects or people dispatched or dealt with at the same time. **2** the bread, cakes, etc. produced at one baking. *~vb* **3** to group (items) for efficient processing.

batch processing *n* a system by which the computer programs of several users are submitted as a single batch.

bated *adj* **with bated breath** in suspense or fear.

bath *n* **1** a large container in which to wash the body. **2** the act of washing in such a container. **3** the amount of water in a bath. **4** (*pl*) a public swimming pool. **5 a** a liquid in which something is immersed as part of a chemical process, such as developing photographs. **b** the vessel containing such a liquid. *~vb* **6** *Brit* to wash in a bath.

Bath chair *n* a wheelchair for invalids.

bath cube *n* a cube of soluble scented material for use in a bath.

bathe *vb* **bathing, bathed 1** to swim in open water for pleasure. **2** to apply liquid to (the skin or a wound) in order to cleanse or soothe. **3** *Chiefly US & Canad* to wash in a bath. **4** to spread over: *bathed in moonlight.* *~n* **5** *Brit* a swim in open water. **bather** *n*

bathos (**bay**-thoss) *n* a sudden ludicrous descent from exalted to ordinary matters in speech or writing. **bathetic** *adj*

bathrobe *n* **1** a loose-fitting garment for wear before or after a bath or swimming. **2** *US & Canad* a dressing gown.

THESAURUS

formal), nuts and bolts (*informal*), practicalities, principles, rudiments

basis 1. base, bottom, footing, foundation, ground, groundwork, support **2.** chief ingredient, core, essential, fundamental, heart, premise, principal element, principle, theory

bask in 1. laze, lie in, loll, lounge, relax, sunbathe, swim in, toast oneself, warm oneself **2.** delight in, enjoy, indulge oneself in, luxuriate in, relish, revel, savour, take pleasure in, wallow in

bass deep, deep-toned, grave, low, low-pitched, resonant, sonorous

bastard 1. *n.* illegitimate (child), love child, natural child **2.** *adj.* adulterated, baseborn, counterfeit, false, illegitimate, imperfect, impure, inferior, irregular, misbegotten, sham, spurious

bastion bulwark, citadel, defence, fastness, fortress, mainstay, prop, rock, stronghold, support, tower of strength

bat bang, hit, punch, rap, smack, strike, swat, thump, wallop (*informal*), whack

batch accumulation, aggregation, amount, assemblage, bunch, collection, crowd, group, lot, pack, quantity, set

bath 1. *n.* ablution, cleansing, douche, douse, scrubbing, shower, soak, soaping, sponging, tub, wash, washing **2.** *vb.* bathe, clean, douse, scrub down, shower, soak, soap, sponge, tub, wash

bathe 1. *vb.* cleanse, cover, dunk, flood, immerse,

bathroom *n* **1** a room with a bath or shower, washbasin, and toilet. **2** *US & Canad* a toilet.

bathyscaph *or* **bathyscaphe** *n* a deep-sea diving vessel for observation.

bathysphere *n* a strong steel deep-sea diving sphere, lowered by cable.

batik (bat-**teek**) *n* **a** a process of printing fabric in which areas not to be dyed are covered by wax. **b** fabric printed in this way.

batman *n, pl* **-men** an officer's servant in the armed forces.

baton *n* **1** a thin stick used by the conductor of an orchestra or choir. **2** *Athletics* a short bar transferred from one runner to another in a relay race. **3** a police officer's truncheon.

baton round *n* same as **plastic bullet.**

bats *adj Informal* mad or eccentric.

batsman *n, pl* **-men** *Cricket etc* a person who bats or specializes in batting.

battalion *n* a military unit comprised of three or more companies.

batten[1] *n* **1** a strip of wood used to strengthen something or make it secure. **2** a strip of wood used for holding a tarpaulin in place over a hatch on a ship. *~vb* **3** to strengthen or fasten with battens.

batten[2] *vb* (foll. by *on*) to thrive at the expense of (someone else).

batter[1] *vb* **1** to hit repeatedly. **2** to damage or injure, as by blows, heavy wear, etc. **3** to subject (someone, usually a close relative) to repeated physical violence. **battered** *adj* **batterer** *n* **battering** *n*

batter[2] *n* a mixture of flour, eggs, and milk, used in cooking.

batter[3] *n Baseball etc* a player who bats.

battering ram *n* (esp. formerly) a large beam used to break down fortifications.

battery *n, pl* **-teries 1** two or more primary cells connected to provide a source of electric current. **2** a number of similar things occurring together: *a battery of questions.* **3** *Criminal law* unlawful beating or wounding of a person. **4** *Chiefly Brit* a series of cages for intensive rearing of poultry. **5** a fortified structure on which artillery is mounted. *~adj* **6** kept in a series of cages for intensive rearing: *battery hens.*

battle *n* **1** a fight between large armed forces. **2** conflict or struggle. *~vb* **-tling, -tled 3** to fight in or as if in military combat: *shop stewards battling to improve conditions at work.* **4** to struggle: *she battled through the crowd.*

battle-axe *n* **1** a domineering woman. **2** (formerly) a large broad-headed axe.

battle cruiser *n* a high-speed warship with lighter armour than a battleship, but of the same size.

battle cry *n* **1** a slogan used to rally the supporters of a campaign, movement, etc. **2** a shout uttered by soldiers going into battle.

battledore *n* **1** Also called: **battledore and shuttlecock** an ancient racket game. **2** a light racket used in this game.

battledress *n* the ordinary uniform of a soldier.

battlefield *or* **battleground** *n* the place where a battle is fought.

battlement *n* a wall with gaps, originally for firing through.

battle royal *n* **1** a fight involving many combatants. **2** a long violent argument.

battleship *n* a large heavily armoured warship.

batty *adj* **-tier, -tiest** *Slang* **1** crazy. **2** eccentric.

bauble *n* a trinket of little value.

baulk *vb, n* same as **balk.**

bauxite *n* a claylike substance that is the chief source of aluminium.

bawdy *adj* **bawdier, bawdiest** (of language, writing, etc.) containing humorous references to sex. **bawdily** *adv* **bawdiness** *n*

bawdyhouse *n Archaic* a brothel.

bawl *vb* **1** to cry noisily. **2** to shout loudly. *~n* **3** a loud shout or cry. **bawling** *n*

bay[1] *n* a stretch of shoreline that curves inwards.

bay[2] *n* **1** a recess in a wall. **2** an area set aside for a particular purpose: *a sick bay; a loading bay.* **3** same

THESAURUS

moisten, rinse, soak, steep, suffuse, wash, wet **2.** *n.* dip, swim, wash

bathos anticlimax, false pathos, letdown, mawkishness, sentimentality

baton club, crook, mace, rod, sceptre, staff, stick, truncheon, wand

battalion army, brigade, company, contingent, division, force, horde, host, legion, multitude, regiment, squadron, throng

batten[1] board up, clamp down, cover up, fasten, fasten down, fix, nail down, secure, tighten

batten[2] fatten, flourish, gain, grow, increase, prosper, thrive, wax

batter 1. assault, bash (*informal*), beat, belabour, break, buffet, clobber (*slang*), dash against, lambast(e), lash, pelt, pound, pummel, smash, smite, thrash, wallop (*informal*) **2.** bruise, crush, deface, demolish, destroy, disfigure, hurt, injure, mangle, mar, maul, ruin, shatter, shiver, trash (*slang*)

battered beaten, beat-up (*informal*), broken-down, bruised, crushed, damaged, dilapidated, injured, ramshackle, squashed, weather-beaten

battery 1. chain, ring, sequence, series, set, suite **2.** assault, attack, beating, mayhem, onslaught, physical violence, thumping **3.** artillery, cannon, cannonry, gun emplacements, guns

battle *n.* **1.** action, attack, combat, encounter, engagement, fight, fray, hostilities, skirmish, war, warfare **2.** agitation, campaign, clash, conflict, contest, controversy, crusade, debate, disagreement, dispute, head-to-head (*informal*), strife, struggle *~vb.* **3.** agitate, argue, clamour, combat, contend, contest, dispute, feud, fight, strive, struggle, war

battle cry catchword, motto, slogan, war cry, war whoop, watchword

battlefield *or* **battleground** combat zone, field, field of battle, front

battleship capital ship, gunboat, man-of-war, ship of the line, warship

batty barking (*slang*), barking mad (*slang*), barmy (*slang*), bats (*slang*), bonkers (*slang, chiefly Brit.*), cracked (*slang*), crackers (*Brit. slang*), crackpot (*informal*), cranky (*informal*), crazy, daft (*informal*), dotty (*slang, chiefly Brit.*), eccentric, insane, loony (*slang*), loopy (*informal*), lunatic, mad, not the full shilling (*informal*), nuts (*slang*), nutty (*slang*), odd, oddball (*informal*), off one's rocker (*slang*), off one's trolley (*slang*), off-the-wall (*slang*), outré, out to lunch (*informal*), peculiar, potty (*Brit. informal*), queer (*informal*), screwy (*informal*), touched, up the pole (*informal*), wacko (*slang*)

bauble bagatelle, gimcrack, knick-knack, plaything, toy, trifle, trinket

bawdy blue, coarse, dirty, erotic, gross, indecent, indecorous, indelicate, lascivious, lecherous, lewd, libidinous, licentious, lustful, obscene, prurient, ribald,

as **bay window.** 4 an area off a road in which vehicles may park or unload. 5 a compartment in an aircraft: *the bomb bay.*

bay[3] *n* 1 a deep howl of a hound or wolf. 2 **at bay** a forced to turn and face attackers: *the stag at bay.* b at a safe distance: *to keep his mind blank and his despair at bay.* ~*vb* 3 to howl in deep prolonged tones.

bay[4] *n* 1 a Mediterranean laurel tree with glossy aromatic leaves. 2 **bays** a wreath of bay leaves.

bay[5] *adj* 1 reddish-brown. ~*n* 2 a reddish-brown horse.

bayberry *n, pl* **-ries** a tropical American tree that yields an oil used in making bay rum. Also: **bay**

bay leaf *n* the dried leaf of a laurel, used for flavouring in cooking.

bayonet *n* 1 a blade that can be attached to the end of a rifle and used as a weapon. ~*vb* **-neting, -neted** *or* **-netting, -netted** 2 to stab or kill with a bayonet.

bay rum *n* an aromatic liquid, used in medicines and cosmetics, which was originally obtained by distilling bayberry leaves with rum.

bay window *n* a window projecting from a wall.

bazaar *n* 1 a sale in aid of charity. 2 (esp. in the Orient) a market area, esp. a street of small stalls.

bazooka *n* a portable rocket launcher that fires a projectile capable of piercing armour.

BB Boys' Brigade.

BBC British Broadcasting Corporation.

BC 1 (indicating years numbered back from the supposed year of the birth of Christ) before Christ. 2 British Columbia.

BCG Bacillus Calmette-Guérin (antituberculosis vaccine).

BCNZ Broadcasting Corporation of New Zealand.

BD Bachelor of Divinity.

BDS Bachelor of Dental Surgery.

be *vb, present sing 1st person* **am;** *2nd person* **are;** *3rd person* **is.** *present pl* **are.** *past sing 1st person* **was;** *2nd person* **were;** *3rd person* **was.** *past pl* **were.** *present participle* **being.** *past participle* **been.** 1 to exist; live: *I think, therefore I am.* 2 to pay a visit; go: *have you been to Spain?* 3 to take place: *my birthday was last Thursday.* 4 used as a linking verb between the subject of a sentence and its complement: *John is a musician; honey is sweet; the dance is on Saturday.* 5 forms the progressive present tense: *the man is running.* 6 forms the passive voice of all transitive verbs: *a good film is being shown on television tomorrow.* 7 expresses intention, expectation, or obligation: *the president is to arrive at 9.30.*

Be *Chem* beryllium.

BE Bachelor of Engineering.

be- *prefix forming verbs mainly from nouns* 1 to surround or cover: *befog.* 2 to affect completely: *bedazzle.* 3 to consider as or cause to be: *befriend.* 4 to provide or cover with: *bejewel.* 5 (*from verbs*) at, for, against, on, or over: *bewail.*

beach *n* 1 an area of sand or pebbles sloping down to the sea or a lake. ~*vb* 2 to run or haul (a boat) onto a beach.

beachcomber *n* a person who searches shore debris for anything of worth.

beachhead *n Mil* an area of shore captured by an attacking army, on which troops and equipment are landed.

beacon *n* 1 a signal fire or light on a hill or tower, used formerly as a warning of invasion. 2 a lighthouse. 3 a radio or other signal marking a flight course in air navigation. 4 same as **Belisha beacon.**

bead *n* 1 a small pierced piece of glass, wood, or plastic that may be strung with others to form a necklace, rosary, etc. 2 a small drop of moisture. 3 a small metal knob acting as the sight of a firearm. ~*vb* 4 to decorate with beads. **beaded** *adj*

beading *n* a narrow rounded strip of moulding used for edging furniture.

beadle *n* 1 *Brit* (formerly) a minor parish official who acted as an usher. 2 *Scot* a church official who attends the minister.

beady *adj* **beadier, beadiest** small, round, and glittering: *beady eyes.*

beagle *n* a small hound with a smooth coat, short legs, and drooping ears.

beak[1] *n* 1 the projecting horny jaws of a bird. 2 *Slang* a person's nose. **beaky** *adj*

beak[2] *n Brit slang* a judge, magistrate, or headmaster.

beaker *n* 1 a tall drinking cup. 2 a lipped glass container used in laboratories.

beam *n* 1 a broad smile. 2 a ray of light. 3 a narrow flow of electromagnetic radiation or particles: *an electron beam.* 4 a long thick piece of wood, metal, etc. used in building. 5 the central shaft of a plough to which all the main parts are attached. 6 the breadth of a ship at its widest part. 7 **off (the) beam** *Informal* mistaken or irrelevant. ~*vb* 8 to smile broadly. 9 to send out or radiate. 10 to divert or aim (a radio signal, light, etc.) in a certain direction: *the concert was beamed live from Geneva.*

beam-ends *pl n* **on one's beam-ends** out of money.

bean *n* 1 the seed or pod of various climbing plants, eaten as a vegetable. 2 any of various beanlike seeds, such as coffee. 3 **full of beans** *Informal* full of energy and vitality. 4 **not have a bean** *Slang* to be without money.

beanbag *n* 1 a small cloth bag filled with dried beans and thrown in games. 2 a very large cushion filled with polystyrene granules and used as a seat.

bean curd *n* same as **tofu.**

THESAURUS

risqué, rude, salacious, smutty, steamy (*informal*), suggestive, vulgar

bawl 1. blubber, cry, sob, squall, wail, weep 2. bellow, call, clamour, halloo, howl, roar, shout, vociferate, yell

bay[1] bight, cove, gulf, inlet, natural harbour, sound

bay[2] alcove, compartment, embrasure, niche, nook, opening, recess

bay[3] 1. bark, clamour, cry, growl, howl, yelp 2. **at bay** caught, cornered, trapped

bayonet *vb.* impale, knife, run through, spear, stab, transfix

bazaar 1. bring-and-buy, fair, fête, sale of work 2. exchange, market, marketplace, mart

be 1. be alive, breathe, exist, inhabit, live 2. befall, come about, come to pass, happen, occur, take place, transpire (*informal*)

beach coast, lido, littoral, sands, seaboard (*chiefly U.S.*), seashore, seaside, shingle, shore, strand, water's edge

beachcomber loafer, scavenger, scrounger, tramp, vagabond, vagrant, wanderer

beacon beam, bonfire, flare, lighthouse, rocket, sign, signal, signal fire, smoke signal, watchtower

bead 1. *usually plural* chaplet, choker, necklace, necklet, pearls, pendant, rosary 2. blob, bubble, dot, drop, droplet, globule, pellet, pill, spherule

beak 1. bill, mandible, neb (*archaic or dialect*), nib 2. nose, proboscis, snout

beam *n.* 1. bar, emission, gleam, glimmer, glint, glow,

beanfeast *n Brit informal* any festive or merry occasion.

beano *n, pl* **beanos** *Brit old-fashioned, slang* a celebration or party.

beanpole *n Slang* a tall thin person.

beansprout *n* a small edible shoot grown from a bean seed, often used in Chinese dishes.

bear[1] *vb* **bearing, bore, borne 1** to support or hold up. **2** to bring: *to bear gifts.* **3** to accept the responsibility of: *to bear a heavier burden of taxation.* **4** (**born** in passive use except when foll. by *by*) to give birth to. **5** to produce by natural growth: *to bear fruit.* **6** to tolerate or endure. **7** to stand up to; sustain: *his story does not bear scrutiny.* **8** to hold in the mind: *to bear a grudge.* **9** to show or be marked with: *he still bears the scars.* **10** to have, be, or stand in (relation or comparison): *her account bears no relation to the facts.* **11** to move in a specified direction: *bear left.* **12 bring to bear** to bring into effect. ~See also **bear down on, bear on,** etc.

bear[2] *n, pl* **bears** *or* **bear 1** a large heavily-built mammal with a long shaggy coat. **2** a bearlike animal, such as the koala. **3** an ill-mannered person. **4** *Stock Exchange* a person who sells shares in anticipation of falling prices to make a profit on repurchase. **5 like a bear with a sore head** *Informal* bad-tempered, irritable.

bearable *adj* endurable; tolerable.

bear-baiting *n History* an entertainment in which dogs attacked a chained bear.

beard *n* **1** the hair growing on the lower parts of a man's face. **2** any similar growth in animals. ~*vb* **3** to oppose boldly: *I bearded my formidable employer in her den.* **bearded** *adj*

bear down on *vb* **1** to press down on. **2** to approach (someone) in a determined manner.

bearer *n* **1** a person or thing that carries, presents, or upholds something. **2** a person who presents a note or bill for payment.

bear hug *n* a rough tight embrace.

bearing *n* **1** (foll. by *on* or *upon*) relevance to: *it has no bearing on this problem.* **2** a part of a machine supporting another part, and usually reducing friction. **3** the act of producing fruit or young. **4** a person's general social conduct. **5** the angular direction of a point measured from a known position. **6** the position, as of a ship, fixed with reference to two or more known points. **7 bearings** a sense of one's relative position: *I lost my bearings in the dark.* **8** *Heraldry* a device on a heraldic shield.

bear on *vb* to be relevant to.

bear out *vb* to show to be truthful: *the witness will bear me out.*

bearskin *n* **1** the pelt of a bear. **2** a tall fur helmet worn by certain British Army regiments.

bear up *vb* to cope with hardships: *they are bearing up well under the pressure.*

bear with *vb* to be patient with.

beast *n* **1** a large wild animal. **2** a brutal or uncivilized person. **3** savage nature or characteristics: *the beast in man.*

beastly *adj Informal* **-lier, -liest** unpleasant; disagreeable.

beat *vb* **beating, beat; beaten** *or* **beat 1** to strike with a series of violent blows. **2** to move (wings) up and down. **3** to throb rhythmically. **4** *Cookery* to stir or whisk vigorously. **5** to shape (metal) by repeated blows. **6** *Music* to indicate (time) by one's hand or a baton. **7** to produce (a sound) by striking a drum. **8** to overcome or defeat: *he was determined to beat his illness.* **9** to form (a path or track) by repeated use. **10** to arrive, achieve, or finish before (someone or something): *she beat her team mate fair and square.* **11** (foll. by *back, down, off,* etc.) to drive, push, or thrust. **12** to scour (woodlands or undergrowth) to rouse game for shooting. **13** *Slang* to puzzle or baffle: *it beats me.* ~*n* **14** a stroke or blow. **15** the sound made by a stroke or blow. **16** a regular throb. **17** an assigned route, as of a policeman. **18** the basic rhythmic unit in a piece of music. **19** pop or rock music characterized

THESAURUS

radiation, ray, shaft, streak, stream **2.** girder, joist, plank, rafter, spar, support, timber ~*vb.* **3.** grin, laugh, smile **4.** broadcast, emit, glare, gleam, glitter, glow, radiate, shine, transmit

bear 1. cherish, entertain, exhibit, harbour, have, hold, maintain, possess, shoulder, support, sustain, uphold, weigh upon **2.** bring, carry, convey, hump (*Brit. slang*), move, take, tote (*informal*), transport **3.** beget, breed, bring forth, develop, engender, generate, give birth to, produce, yield **4.** abide, admit, allow, brook, endure, permit, put up with (*informal*), stomach, suffer, tolerate, undergo

bearable admissible, endurable, manageable, passable, sufferable, supportable, sustainable, tolerable

beard 1. *n.* bristles, five-o'clock shadow, stubble, whiskers **2.** *vb.* brave, confront, dare, defy, face, oppose, tackle

bearded bristly, bushy, hairy, hirsute, shaggy, stubbly, unshaven, whiskered

bear down on 1. burden, compress, encumber, press down, push, strain, weigh down **2.** advance on, approach, attack, close in, converge on, move in

bearer 1. agent, carrier, conveyor, messenger, porter, runner, servant **2.** beneficiary, consignee, payee

bearing 1. application, connection, import, pertinence, reference, relation, relevance, significance **2.** air, aspect, attitude, behaviour, carriage, demeanour, deportment, manner, mien, posture **3.** *Naut.* course, direction, point of compass **4.** *Plural* aim, course, direction, location, orientation, position, situation, track, way, whereabouts

bear on affect, appertain to, belong to, concern, involve, pertain to, refer to, relate to, touch upon

bear out confirm, corroborate, endorse, justify, prove, substantiate, support, uphold, vindicate

bear up bear the brunt, carry on, endure, grin and bear it (*informal*), persevere, suffer, withstand

bear with be patient, forbear, make allowances, put up with (*informal*), suffer, tolerate, wait

beast 1. animal, brute, creature **2.** barbarian, brute, fiend, ghoul, monster, ogre, sadist, savage, swine

beastly awful, disagreeable, foul, horrid, mean, nasty, rotten, shitty (*taboo slang*), terrible, unpleasant

beat *vb.* **1.** bang, batter, belt (*informal*), break, bruise, buffet, cane, chin (*slang*), clobber (*slang*), cudgel, deck (*slang*), flog, hit, knock, lambast(e), lash, lay one on (*slang*), lick (*informal*), maul, pelt, pound, punch, strike, thrash, thwack, whip **2.** flap, flutter, palpitate, pound, pulsate, pulse, quake, quiver, shake, throb, thump, tremble, vibrate **3.** fashion, forge, form, hammer, model, shape, work **4.** best, blow out of the water (*slang*), clobber (*slang*), conquer, defeat, excel, lick (*informal*), master, outdo, outrun, outstrip, overcome, overwhelm, run rings around (*informal*), subdue, surpass, tank (*slang*), undo, vanquish, wipe the floor with (*informal*) ~*n.* **5.** belt (*informal*), blow, hit, lash, punch, shake, slap, strike, swing, thump **6.** circuit, course, path, rounds, route, way **7.** accent, cadence,

by a heavy rhythmic beat. *~adj* **20** *Slang* totally exhausted. ~See also **beat down, beat up. beating** *n*

beatbox *n* same as **drum machine.**

beat down *vb* **1** (of the sun) to shine intensely. **2** *Informal* to force or persuade (a seller) to accept a lower price.

beater *n* **1** a device used for beating: *a carpet beater.* **2** a person who rouses wild game.

beatific *adj Literary* **1** displaying great happiness. **2** having a divine aura.

beatify (bee-at-if-fie) *vb* **-fies, -fying, -fied 1** *RC Church* to declare (a deceased person) to be among the blessed in heaven: the first step towards canonization. **2** to make extremely happy. **beatification** *n*

beatitude *n* supreme blessedness or happiness.

Beatitude *n Christianity* any of the blessings on the poor, meek, etc., in the Sermon on the Mount.

beatnik *n* a young person in the late 1950s who rebelled against conventional attitudes and styles of dress.

beat up *Informal ~vb* **1** to inflict severe physical damage on (someone) by striking or kicking repeatedly. *~adj* **beat-up 2** dilapidated.

beau (boh) *n, pl* **beaus** *or* **beaux (bohz) 1** *Chiefly US* a boyfriend. **2** a man who is greatly concerned with his appearance.

Beaufort scale *n Meteorol* a scale for measuring wind speeds, ranging from 0 (calm) to 12 (hurricane).

Beaujolais *n* a red or white wine from southern Burgundy in France.

beauteous *adj Poetic* beautiful.

beautician *n* a person who works in a beauty salon.

beautiful *adj* **1** being very attractive to look at. **2** highly enjoyable; very pleasant. **beautifully** *adv*

beautify *vb* **-fies, -fying, -fied** to make beautiful. **beautification** *n*

beauty *n, pl* **-ties 1** the combination of all the qualities of a person or thing that delight the senses and mind. **2** a very attractive woman. **3** *Informal* an outstanding example of its kind. **4** *Informal* an advantageous feature: *the beauty of this job is the short hours.*

beauty queen *n* a woman who has been judged the most beautiful in a contest.

beauty salon *or* **parlour** *n* an establishment that provides services such as hairdressing, facial treatment, and massage.

beauty spot *n* **1** a place of outstanding beauty. **2** a small dark-coloured spot formerly worn on a lady's face as decoration.

beaver *n* **1** a large amphibious rodent with soft brown fur, a broad flat tail, and webbed hind feet. **2** its fur. **3** a tall hat made of this fur. *~vb* **4 beaver away** to work very hard and steadily.

bebop *n* same as **bop.**

becalmed *adj* (of a sailing ship) motionless through lack of wind.

became *vb* the past tense of **become.**

because *conj* **1** on account of the fact that: *because it's so cold we'll go home.* **2 because of** on account of: *I lost my job because of her.*

➤ It is unnecessary to follow *because* with *the reason is/was: He was cold because the window was open* or *The reason he was cold was that the window was open.*

bechamel sauce (bay-sham-ell) *n* a thick white sauce flavoured with onion and seasonings.

beck[1] *n* **at someone's beck and call** having to be constantly available to do as someone asks.

beck[2] *n* (in N England) a stream.

beckon *vb* **1** to summon with a gesture. **2** to lure: *fame beckoned.*

become *vb* **-coming, -came, -come 1** to come to be: *he became Prime Minister in 1979.* **2** (foll. by *of*) to happen to: *what became of him?* **3** to suit: *that dress becomes you.*

becoming *adj* suitable or appropriate: *his conduct was not becoming to the rank of officer.*

becquerel (beck-a-**rell**) *n* the SI unit of activity of a radioactive source.

bed *n* **1** a piece of furniture on which to sleep. **2** a plot of ground in which plants are grown. **3** the bottom of a river, lake, or sea. **4** any underlying structure or part. **5** a layer of rock. **6 get out of bed on the wrong side** *Informal* to begin the day in a bad mood. **7 go to bed with** to have sexual intercourse with. *~vb* **bedding, bedded 8** (foll. by *down*) to go to or put into a place to sleep or rest. **9** to have sexual intercourse with. **10**

THESAURUS

measure (*Prosody*), metre, rhythm, stress, time **8.** flutter, palpitation, pulsation, pulse, throb *~adj.* **9.** *slang* clapped out (*Austral. & N.Z. informal*), exhausted, fatigued, tired, wearied, worn out, zonked (*slang*)

beaten 1. blended, foamy, frothy, mixed, stirred, whipped, whisked **2.** forged, formed, hammered, shaped, stamped, worked **3.** baffled, cowed, defeated, disappointed, disheartened, frustrated, overcome, overwhelmed, thwarted, vanquished **4.** much travelled, trampled, trodden, well-trodden, well-used, worn

beating 1. belting (*informal*), caning, chastisement, corporal punishment, flogging, pasting (*slang*), slapping, smacking, thrashing, whipping **2.** conquest, defeat, downfall, overthrow, pasting (*slang*), rout, ruin

beat up assault, attack, batter, beat the living daylights out of (*informal*), clobber (*slang*), do over (*Brit., Austral., & N.Z. slang*), duff up (*Brit. slang*), fill in (*Brit. slang*), knock about *or* around, lambast(e), put the boot in (*slang*), thrash

beau 1. admirer, boyfriend, escort, fancy man (*slang*), fiancé, guy (*informal*), lover, suitor, swain, sweetheart **2.** cavalier (*old-fashioned*), coxcomb (*informal*), dandy, fop, gallant (*Hist.*), ladies' man, popinjay, swell (*informal*)

beautiful alluring, appealing, attractive, charming, comely, delightful, drop-dead (*slang*), exquisite, fair, fine, glamorous, good-looking, gorgeous, graceful, handsome, lovely, pleasing, radiant, ravishing, stunning (*informal*)

beautify adorn, array, bedeck, deck, decorate, embellish, enhance, festoon, garnish, gild, glamorize, grace, ornament

beauty 1. allure, attractiveness, bloom, charm, comeliness, elegance, exquisiteness, fairness, glamour, grace, handsomeness, loveliness, pulchritude, seemliness, symmetry **2.** belle, charmer, cracker (*slang*), goddess, good-looker, lovely (*slang*), stunner (*informal*), Venus **3.** advantage, asset, attraction, benefit, blessing, boon, excellence, feature, good thing

becalmed motionless, settled, still, stranded, stuck

because as, by reason of, in that, on account of, owing to, since, thanks to

beckon 1. bid, gesticulate, gesture, motion, nod, signal, summon, wave at **2.** allure, attract, call, coax, draw, entice, invite, lure, pull, tempt

become 1. alter to, be transformed into, change into, develop into, evolve into, grow into, mature into, metamorphose into, ripen into **2.** embellish, enhance, fit, flatter, grace, harmonize, ornament, set off, suit

becoming 1. attractive, comely, enhancing, flattering, graceful, neat, pretty, tasteful **2.** appropriate, be-

to place firmly into position; embed: *the poles were bedded in concrete.* **11** *Geol* to form or be arranged in a distinct layer. **12** to plant in a bed of soil.
BEd Bachelor of Education.
bed and breakfast *n Chiefly Brit* overnight accommodation and breakfast.
bedaub *vb* to smear over with something sticky or dirty.
bedbug *n* a small blood-sucking wingless insect that infests dirty houses.
bedclothes *pl n* coverings for a bed.
bedding *n* **1** bedclothes, sometimes with a mattress. **2** litter, such as straw, for animals. **3** the distinct layered deposits of rocks.
bedeck *vb* to cover with decorations.
bedevil (bid-**dev**-ill) *vb* **-illing, -illed** *or US* **-iling, -iled 1** to harass or torment. **2** to throw into confusion. **bedevilment** *n*
bedfellow *n* **1** a temporary associate. **2** a person with whom one shares a bed.
bedlam *n* a noisy confused situation.
bed linen *n* sheets and pillowcases for a bed.
Bedouin *n* **1** (*pl* **-ins** *or* **-in**) a nomadic Arab tribesman of the deserts of Arabia, Jordan, and Syria. **2** a wanderer.
bedpan *n* a shallow container used as a toilet by people who are not well enough to leave bed.
bedraggled *adj* with hair or clothing that is untidy, wet, or dirty.
bedridden *adj* unable to leave bed because of illness.
bedrock *n* **1** the solid rock beneath the surface soil. **2** basic principles or facts.
bedroom *n* **1** a room used for sleeping. *~adj* **2** containing references to sex: *a bedroom comedy.*
Beds Bedfordshire.
bedside *n* **1** the area beside a bed. *~adj* **2** placed at or near the side of the bed: *the bedside table.*
bedsit *or* **bedsitter** *n* a furnished sitting room with a bed.
bedsore *n* an ulcer on the skin, caused by a lengthy period of lying in bed due to illness.
bedspread *n* a top cover on a bed.
bedstead *n* the framework of a bed.
bedstraw *n* a plant with small white or yellow flowers.
bed-wetting *n* involuntarily urinating in bed.
bee[1] *n* **1** a four-winged insect that collects nectar and pollen to make honey and wax. **2 have a bee in one's bonnet** to be obsessed with an idea.
bee[2] *n Chiefly US* a social gathering to carry out a communal task: *quilting bee.*
Beeb *n* **the Beeb** *Informal* the BBC.
beech *n* **1** a European tree with smooth greyish bark. **2** the hard wood of this tree. **3** See **copper beech.**
beechnut *n* the small brown triangular edible nut of the beech tree.
beef *n* **1** the flesh of a cow, bull, or ox. **2** *Slang* a complaint. *~vb* **3** *Slang* to complain. ~See also **beef up.**
beefburger *n* a flat fried or grilled cake of minced beef; hamburger.
beefcake *n Slang* musclemen as displayed in photographs.
beefeater *n* a yeoman warder of the Tower of London.
beef tea *n* a drink made by boiling pieces of lean beef.
beef tomato *or* **beefsteak tomato** *n* a type of large fleshy tomato.
beef up *vb Informal* to strengthen.
beefy *adj* **beefier, beefiest 1** *Informal* muscular. **2** like beef. **beefiness** *n*
beehive *n* a structure in which bees are housed.
beekeeper *n* a person who keeps bees for their honey. **beekeeping** *n*
beeline *n* **make a beeline for** to speedily take the most direct route to.
Beelzebub (bee-**ell**-zib-bub) *n* Satan or any devil.
been *vb* the past participle of **be.**
beep *n* **1** a high-pitched sound, like that of a car horn. *~vb* **2** to make or cause to make such a noise.
beer *n* **1** an alcoholic drink brewed from malt, sugar, hops, and water. **2** a glass, can, or bottle containing this drink.
beer and skittles *n Informal* enjoyment or pleasure.
beer parlour *n Canad* a licensed place in which beer is sold and drunk.
beery *adj* **beerier, beeriest** smelling or tasting of beer.
beeswax *n* **1** a wax produced by honeybees for making honeycombs. **2** this wax after refining, used in polishes, etc.
beet *n* a plant with an edible root and leaves, such as the sugar beet and beetroot.
beetle[1] *n* **1** an insect with a hard wing-case closed over its back for protection. *~vb* **-tling, -tled 2** (foll. by *along, off, etc.*) *Informal* to scuttle or scurry.

THESAURUS

fitting, *comme il faut,* compatible, congruous, decent, decorous, fit, fitting, in keeping, meet (*archaic*), proper, seemly, suitable, worthy
bed *n.* **1.** bedstead, berth, bunk, cot, couch, divan, pallet **2.** area, border, garden, patch, plot, row, strip **3.** base, bottom, foundation, groundwork, substratum *~vb.* **4.** base, embed, establish, fix, found, implant, insert, plant, settle, set up
bedclothes bedding, bed linen, blankets, coverlets, covers, duvets, eiderdowns, pillowcases, pillows, quilts, sheets
bedeck adorn, array, decorate, embellish, festoon, garnish, ornament, trim
bedevil afflict, aggravate (*informal*), annoy, be on one's back (*slang*), confound, distress, fret, frustrate, get in one's hair (*informal*), get on one's nerves (*informal*), harass, hassle (*informal*), irk, irritate, pester, plague, torment, torture, trouble, vex, worry
bedlam chaos, clamour, commotion, confusion, furore, hubbub, hullabaloo, madhouse (*informal*), noise, pandemonium, tumult, turmoil, uproar
bedraggled dirty, dishevelled, disordered, drenched, dripping, messy, muddied, muddy, sodden, soiled, stained, sullied, unkempt, untidy
bedridden confined, confined to bed, flat on one's back, incapacitated, laid up (*informal*)
bedrock 1. bed, bottom, foundation, nadir, rock bottom, substratum, substructure **2.** basics, basis, core, essentials, fundamentals, roots
beef 1. *informal* brawn, flesh, heftiness, muscle, physique, robustness, sinew, strength **2.** *slang* complaint, criticism, dispute, grievance, gripe (*informal*), grouch (*informal*), grouse, grumble, objection, protest, protestation
beefy *informal* **1.** brawny, bulky, burly, hulking, muscular, stalwart, stocky, strapping, sturdy, thickset **2.** chubby, corpulent, fat, fleshy, heavy, obese, overweight, paunchy, plump, podgy, portly, pudgy, rotund

beetle[2] *vb* **-tling, -tled** to overhang; jut: *the eaves of the roof beetled out over the windows.* **beetling** *adj*
beetle-browed *adj* having bushy or overhanging eyebrows.
beetroot *n* a variety of the beet plant with a dark red root that may be eaten as a vegetable, in salads, or pickled.
beet sugar *n* the sucrose obtained from sugar beet.
befall *vb* **-falling, -fell, -fallen** *Archaic or literary* to happen to.
befit *vb* **-fitting, -fitted** to be appropriate to or suitable for. **befitting** *adj*
before *conj* **1** earlier than the time when. **2** rather than: *she'll resign before she agrees to it.* ~*prep* **3** preceding in space or time; in front of; ahead of: *they stood before the altar.* **4** in the presence of: *to be brought before a judge.* **5** in preference to: *to put friendship before money.* ~*adv* **6** previously. **7** in front.
beforehand *adj, adv* early; in advance.
befriend *vb* to become a friend to.
befuddled *adj* stupefied or confused, as through alcoholic drink.
beg *vb* **begging, begged 1** to ask for money or food in the street. **2** to ask formally, humbly, or earnestly: *I beg forgiveness; I beg to differ.* **3 beg the question** to put forward an argument that assumes the very point it is supposed to establish, or that depends on some other questionable assumption. **4 go begging** to be unwanted or unused.
began *vb* the past tense of **begin.**
beget *vb* **-getting, -got** *or* **-gat; -gotten** *or* **-got** *Old-fashioned* **1** to cause or create: *repetition begets boredom.* **2** to father.
beggar *n* **1** a person who lives by begging. **2** *Chiefly Brit* a fellow: *lucky beggar!* ~*vb* **3 beggar description** to be impossible to describe. **beggarly** *adj*
begin *vb* **-ginning, -gan, -gun 1** to start (something). **2** to bring or come into being. **3** to start to say or speak. **4** to have the least capacity to do something: *it doesn't even begin to address the problem.* **beginner** *n*
beginner's luck *n* exceptional luck supposed to attend a beginner.
beginning *n* **1** a start. **2 beginnings** an early part or stage. **3** the place where or time when something starts. **4** an origin; source.
begone *interj* go away!
begonia *n* a tropical plant with ornamental leaves and waxy flowers.
begot *vb* a past tense and past participle of **beget.**
begotten *vb* a past participle of **beget.**
begrudge *vb* **-grudging, -grudged 1** to envy (someone) the possession of something. **2** to give or allow unwillingly: *he begrudged her an apology.*
beguile (big-**gile**) *vb* **-guiling, -guiled** to charm (someone) into doing something he or she would not normally do.
beguiling *adj* charming, often in a deceptive way.
beguine (big-**geen**) *n* **1** a dance of South American origin. **2** music for this dance.
begum (**bay**-gum) *n* (in certain Muslim countries) a woman of high rank.
begun *vb* the past participle of **begin.**
behalf *n* **on** *or US & Canad* **in behalf of** in the interest of or for the benefit of.
behave *vb* **-having, -haved 1** to act or function in a particular way. **2** to conduct oneself in a particular way: *the baby behaved very well.* **3** to conduct oneself properly.
behaviour *or US* **behavior** *n* **1** manner of behaving. **2** *Psychol* the response of an organism to a stimulus. **behavioural** *or US* **behavioral** *adj*
behavioural science *n* the scientific study of the behaviour of organisms.
behaviourism *or US* **behaviorism** *n* a school of psychology that regards objective observation of the

THESAURUS

beetle hang over, jut out, lean over, overhang, pendent, project, protrude, stick out, swell over
befall betide, chance, come to pass, ensue, fall, follow, happen, materialize, occur, supervene, take place, transpire (*informal*)
befitting apposite, appropriate, becoming, fit, fitting, meet (*archaic*), proper, right, seemly, suitable
before 1. *prep.* earlier than, in advance of, in front of, in the presence of, prior to **2.** *adv.* ahead, earlier, formerly, in advance, in front, previously, sooner
beforehand ahead of time, already, before, before now, earlier, in advance, in anticipation, previously, sooner
befriend advise, aid, assist, back, benefit, encourage, favour, help, patronize, side with, stand by, succour, support, sustain, uphold, welcome
befuddled confused, dazed, fuddled, groggy (*informal*), inebriated, intoxicated, muddled, woozy (*informal*)
beg 1. blag (*slang*), cadge, call for alms, mooch (*slang*), scrounge, seek charity, solicit charity, sponge on, touch (someone) for (*slang*) **2.** beseech, crave, desire, entreat, implore, importune, petition, plead, pray, request, solicit, supplicate **3.** *as in* **beg the question** avoid, dodge, duck (*informal*), equivocate, eschew, evade, fend off, flannel (*Brit. informal*), hedge, parry, shirk, shun, sidestep
beggar 1. *n.* bag lady (*chiefly U.S.*), bum (*informal*), cadger, down-and-out, mendicant, scrounger (*informal*), sponger (*informal*), supplicant, tramp, vagrant **2.** *vb. as in* **beggar description** baffle, challenge, defy, surpass
beggarly abject, base, contemptible, despicable, destitute, impoverished, inadequate, indigent, low, meagre, mean, miserly, needy, niggardly, pitiful, poor, poverty-stricken, stingy, vile, wretched
begin 1. commence, embark on, inaugurate, initiate, instigate, institute, prepare, set about, set on foot, start **2.** appear, arise, be born, come into being, come into existence, commence, crop up (*informal*), dawn, emerge, happen, originate, spring, start
beginner amateur, apprentice, cub, fledgling, freshman, greenhorn (*informal*), initiate, learner, neophyte, novice, recruit, starter, student, tenderfoot, trainee, tyro
beginning 1. birth, commencement, inauguration, inception, initiation, onset, opening, opening move, origin, outset, overture, preface, prelude, rise, rudiments, source, start, starting point **2.** embryo, fount, fountainhead, germ, root, seed
begrudge be jealous, be reluctant, be stingy, envy, grudge, resent
beguile charm, cheat, deceive, delude, dupe, fool, hoodwink, impose on, mislead, trick
beguiling alluring, attractive, bewitching, captivating, charming, diverting, enchanting, entertaining, enthralling, interesting, intriguing
behave 1. act, function, operate, perform, run, work **2.** act correctly, conduct oneself properly, mind one's manners

behaviour of organisms as the only valid subject for study. **behaviourist** *or US* **behaviorist** *adj, n*

behead *vb* to remove the head from.

beheld *vb* the past of **behold.**

behemoth (bee-**hee**-moth) *n* a huge person or thing.

behest *n* an order or earnest request: *I came at her behest.*

behind *prep* **1** in or to a position further back than. **2** in the past in relation to: *I want to leave the past behind me.* **3** late according to: *running behind schedule.* **4** concerning the circumstances surrounding: *the reasons behind his departure.* **5** supporting: *I'm right behind you in your application.* ~*adv* **6** in or to a position further back. **7** remaining after someone's departure: *she left her books behind.* **8** in arrears: *to fall behind with payments.* ~*adj* **9** in a position further back. ~*n* **10** *Informal* the buttocks.

behindhand *adj, adv* **1** in arrears. **2** backward. **3** late.

behold *vb* **-holding, -held** *Archaic or literary* to look (at); observe. **beholder** *n*

beholden *adj* indebted; obliged: *I am beholden to you.*

behove *vb* **-hoving, -hoved** *Archaic* to be necessary or fitting for: *it behoves me to warn you.*

beige *adj* pale creamy-brown.

being *n* **1** the state or fact of existing. **2** essential nature; self. **3** something that exists or is thought to exist: *a being from outer space.* **4** a human being.

bejewelled *or US* **bejeweled** *adj* decorated with jewels.

bel *n* a unit for comparing two power levels or measuring the intensity of a sound, equal to 10 decibels.

belabour *or US* **belabor** *vb* to attack verbally or physically.

belated *adj* late or too late: *belated greetings.* **belatedly** *adv*

belay *vb* **-laying, -layed 1** *Naut* to secure a line to a pin or cleat. **2** *Naut* to stop. **3** *Mountaineering* to secure (a climber) by fixing a rope round a rock or piton.

belch *vb* **1** to expel wind from the stomach noisily through the mouth. **2** to expel or be expelled forcefully: *smoke belching from factory chimneys.* ~*n* **3** an act of belching.

beleaguered *adj* **1** struggling against difficulties or criticism: *the beleaguered British film industry.* **2** besieged by an enemy: *the beleaguered capital city.*

belfry *n, pl* **-fries 1** the part of a tower or steeple in which bells are hung. **2** a tower or steeple.

Belgian *adj* **1** of Belgium. ~*n* **2** a person from Belgium.

Belial (**bee**-lee-al) *n* the devil or Satan.

belie *vb* **-lying, -lied 1** to show to be untrue: *the facts belied the theory.* **2** to misrepresent: *the score belied the closeness of the match.* **3** to fail to justify: *the promises were soon belied.*

belief *n* **1** trust or confidence: *belief in the free market.* **2** opinion; conviction: *it's my firm belief.* **3** a principle, etc., accepted as true, often without proof. **4** religious faith.

believe *vb* **-lieving, -lieved 1** to accept as true or real: *I believe God exists.* **2** to think, assume, or suppose: *I believe you know my father.* **3** to accept the statement or opinion of (a person) as true. **4** to have religious faith. **5 believe in** to be convinced of the truth or existence of: *I don't believe in ghosts.* **believable** *adj* **believer** *n*

Belisha beacon (bill-**lee**-sha) *n Brit* a flashing orange globe mounted on a striped post, indicating a pedestrian crossing.

belittle *vb* **-tling, -tled** to treat (something or someone) as having little value or importance.

bell *n* **1** a hollow, usually metal, cup-shaped instrument that emits a ringing sound when struck. **2** the sound made by such an instrument. **3** an electrical device that rings or buzzes as a signal. **4** something shaped like a bell. **5** *Brit slang* a telephone call. **6 ring a bell** to sound familiar; recall something previously experienced.

belladonna *n* **1** a drug obtained from deadly nightshade. **2** same as **deadly nightshade.**

THESAURUS

behaviour *or U.S.* **behavior 1.** actions, bearing, carriage, comportment, conduct, demeanour, deportment, manner, manners, ways **2.** action, functioning, operation, performance

behest bidding, charge, command, commandment, decree, dictate, direction, expressed desire, injunction, instruction, mandate, order, precept, wish

behind *prep.* **1.** after, at the back of, at the rear of, following, later than **2.** at the bottom of, causing, initiating, instigating, responsible for **3.** backing, for, in agreement, on the side of, supporting ~*adv.* **4.** after, afterwards, following, in the wake (of), next, subsequently **5.** behindhand, in arrears, in debt, overdue ~*n.* **6.** arse (*taboo slang*), ass (*U.S. & Canad. taboo slang*), bottom, bum (*Brit. slang*), butt (*U.S. & Canad. informal*), buttocks, posterior, rump, seat, tail (*informal*)

behindhand backward, behind time, dilatory, late, remiss, slow, tardy

behold check, check out (*informal*), clock (*Brit. slang*), consider, contemplate, discern, eye, eyeball (*U.S. slang*), get a load of (*informal*), look at, observe, perceive, recce (*slang*), regard, scan, survey, take a dekko at (*Brit. slang*), view, watch, witness

beholden bound, grateful, indebted, obligated, obliged, owing, under obligation

beige biscuit, buff, *café au lait*, camel, cinnamon, coffee, cream, ecru, fawn, khaki, mushroom, neutral, oatmeal, sand, tan

being 1. actuality, animation, existence, life, living, reality **2.** entity, essence, nature, soul, spirit, substance **3.** animal, beast, body, creature, human being, individual, living thing, mortal, thing

belabour *or U.S.* **belabor** attack, batter, beat, berate, blast, castigate, censure, clobber (*slang*), criticize, excoriate, flay, flog, lambast(e), lay into (*informal*), put down, tear into (*informal*), thrash, whip

belated behindhand, behind time, delayed, late, overdue, tardy

belch 1. burp (*informal*), eruct, eructate, hiccup **2.** discharge, disgorge, emit, erupt, give off, gush, spew forth, vent, vomit

beleaguered badgered, beset, besieged, bothered, harassed, nagged, persecuted, plagued, put upon, set upon, vexed

belief 1. admission, assent, assurance, confidence, conviction, credit, feeling, impression, judgment, notion, opinion, persuasion, presumption, reliance, theory, trust, view **2.** credence, credo, creed, doctrine, dogma, faith, ideology, principles, tenet

believable acceptable, authentic, credible, creditable, imaginable, likely, plausible, possible, probable, reliable, trustworthy, verisimilar

believe 1. accept, be certain of, be convinced of, buy (*slang*), count on, credit, depend on, have faith in, hold, place confidence in, presume true, rely on, swallow (*informal*), swear by, trust **2.** assume, conjecture, consider, gather, guess (*informal, chiefly U.S. &*

bell-bottoms *pl n* trousers that flare from the knee. **bell-bottomed** *adj*

belle *n* a beautiful woman, esp. the most attractive woman at a function: *the belle of the ball.*

belles-lettres (bell-**let**-tra) *n* literary works, particularly essays and poetry.

bellicose *adj* warlike; aggressive.

belligerence *n* the act or quality of being belligerent or warlike.

belligerent *adj* **1** marked by readiness to fight. **2** relating to or engaged in a war. ~*n* **3** a person or country engaged in war.

bell jar *n* a bell-shaped glass cover used to protect flower arrangements or cover apparatus to confine gases in experiments.

bellow *vb* **1** to make a loud deep cry like that of a bull. **2** to shout in anger. ~*n* **3** the characteristic noise of a bull. **4** a loud deep roar.

bellows *n* **1** a device consisting of an air chamber with flexible sides that is used to create and direct a stream of air. **2** a flexible corrugated part, such as that connecting the lens system of some cameras to the body.

bell pull *n* a handle or cord pulled to operate a bell.

bell push *n* a button pressed to operate an electric bell.

bell-ringer *n* a person who rings church bells or musical handbells. **bell-ringing** *n*

belly *n, pl* **-lies 1** the part of the body of a vertebrate containing the intestines and other organs. **2** the stomach. **3** the front, lower, or inner part of something. ~*vb* **-lies, -lying, -lied 4** to swell out; bulge.

bellyache *n* **1** *Informal* a pain in the abdomen. ~*vb* **-aching, -ached 2** *Slang* to complain repeatedly.

bellybutton *n Informal* the navel.

belly dance *n* **1** a sensuous dance performed by women, with undulating movements of the abdomen. ~*vb* **belly-dance, -dancing, -danced 2** to dance thus. **belly dancer** *n*

belly flop *n* **1** a dive into water in which the body lands horizontally. ~*vb* **belly-flop, -flopping, -flopped 2** to perform a belly flop.

bellyful *n* **1** *Slang* more than one can tolerate. **2** as much as one wants or can eat.

belly laugh *n* a loud deep hearty laugh.

belong *vb* **1** (foll. by *to*) to be the property of. **2** (foll. by *to*) to be bound to (a person, organization, etc.) by ties of affection, association, membership, etc.: *the nations concerned belonged to NATO.* **3** (foll. by *to, under, with,* etc.) to be classified with: *it belongs to a different class of comets.* **4** (foll. by *to*) to be a part of: *this lid belongs to that tin.* **5** to have a proper or usual place. **6** *Informal* to be acceptable, esp. socially.

belonging *n* a secure relationship: *they have a strong sense of belonging.*

belongings *pl n* the things that a person owns or has with him or her.

beloved *adj* **1** dearly loved. ~*n* **2** a person who is dearly loved.

below *prep* **1** at or to a position lower than; under. **2** less than. **3** unworthy of; beneath. ~*adv* **4** at or to a lower position. **5** at a later place in something written. **6** *Archaic* on earth or in hell.

belt *n* **1** a band of leather or cloth worn around the waist. **2** an area where a specific thing is found; zone: *a belt of high pressure.* **3** same as **seat belt. 4** a band of flexible material between rotating shafts or pulleys to transfer motion or transmit goods: *a fan belt; a conveyer belt.* **5** *Informal* a sharp blow. **6 below the belt** *Informal* unscrupulous or cowardly. **7 tighten one's belt** to reduce expenditure. **8 under one's belt** as part of one's experience: *he had a string of successes under his belt.* ~*vb* **9** to fasten with or as if with a belt. **10** to hit with a belt. **11** *Slang* to give (someone) a sharp blow. **12** (foll. by *along*) *Slang* to move very fast.

belt out *vb Informal* to sing (a song) loudly.

belt up *vb* **1** *Slang* to stop talking. **2** to fasten with a belt.

beluga (bill-**loo**-ga) *n* a large white sturgeon of the Black and Caspian Seas, from which caviar and isinglass are obtained.

belvedere *n* a building designed and situated to look out on pleasant scenery.

BEM British Empire Medal.

bemoan *vb* to lament: *he's always bemoaning his fate.*

bemused *adj* puzzled or confused.

ben *n Scot, Irish* a mountain peak: *Ben Lomond.*

bench *n* **1** a long seat for more than one person. **2 the bench a** a judge or magistrate sitting in court. **b** judges or magistrates collectively. **3** a long and strong worktable.

benchmark *n* **1** a mark on a fixed object, used as a reference point in surveying. **2** a criterion by which to measure something: *the speech was a benchmark of his commitment.*

bend[1] *vb* **bending, bent 1** to form a curve. **2** to turn from a particular direction: *the road bends right.* **3** (often foll. by *down,* etc.) to incline the body. **4** to

THESAURUS

Canad.), imagine, judge, maintain, postulate, presume, reckon, speculate, suppose, think

believer adherent, convert, devotee, disciple, follower, proselyte, protagonist, supporter, upholder, zealot

bellow bawl, bell, call, clamour, cry, howl, roar, scream, shout, shriek, yell

belly 1. *n.* abdomen, corporation (*informal*), gut, insides (*informal*), paunch, potbelly, stomach, tummy, vitals **2.** *vb.* billow, bulge, fill, spread, swell, swell out

belong 1. *with* **to** be at the disposal of, be held by, be owned by, be the property of **2.** *with* **to** be affiliated to, be allied to, be a member of, be associated with, be included in **3.** *with* **to** attach to, be connected with, be fitting, be part of, fit, go with, have as a proper place, pertain to, relate to

belonging acceptance, affiliation, affinity, association, attachment, fellowship, inclusion, kinship, loyalty, rapport, relationship

belongings accoutrements, chattels, effects, gear, goods, paraphernalia, personal property, possessions, stuff, things

beloved admired, adored, cherished, darling, dear, dearest, loved, pet, precious, prized, revered, sweet, treasured, worshipped

below *prep.* **1.** inferior, lesser, lesser than, subject, subordinate, unworthy of **2. below par** below average, imperfect, inferior, off colour, off form, poor, second-rate, unfit ~*adv.* **3.** beneath, down, lower, under, underneath

belt 1. band, cincture (*literary*), cummerbund, girdle, girth, sash, waistband **2.** *Geog.* area, district, layer, region, stretch, strip, tract, zone **3. below the belt** *informal* cowardly, foul, not playing the game (*informal*), unfair, unjust, unscrupulous, unsporting, unsportsmanlike

bemused absent-minded, at sea, bewildered, confused, dazed, engrossed, flummoxed, fuddled, half-drunk, muddled, nonplussed, perplexed, preoccupied, stunned, stupefied, tipsy

submit: *to bend before public opinion.* **5** to turn or direct (one's eyes, steps, or attention). **6 bend the rules** *Informal* to ignore or change rules to suit oneself. ~*n* **7** a curved part. **8** the act of bending. **9 round the bend** *Brit slang* mad. **bendy** *adj*

bend² *n Heraldry* a diagonal line across a shield.

bender *n Informal* a drinking bout.

bends *pl n* **the bends** *Informal* decompression sickness.

bend sinister *n Heraldry* a diagonal line across a shield, indicating a bastard line.

beneath *prep* **1** below; under. **2** too trivial for: *beneath his dignity.* ~*adv* **3** below; underneath.

Benedictine *n* **1** a monk or nun of the Christian order of Saint Benedict. **2** a liqueur first made by Benedictine monks. ~*adj* **3** of Saint Benedict or his order.

benediction *n* **1** a prayer for divine blessing. **2** a Roman Catholic service in which the congregation is blessed with the sacrament. **benedictory** *adj*

benefaction *n* **1** the act of doing good, particularly donating to charity. **2** the donation or help given.

benefactor *n* a person who supports a person or institution by giving money. **benefactress** *fem n*

benefice *n Christianity* a Church office that provides its holder with an income.

beneficent (bin-**eff**-iss-ent) *adj* charitable; generous. **beneficence** *n*

beneficial *adj* helpful or advantageous.

beneficiary *n, pl* **-ciaries 1** a person who gains or benefits. **2** *Law* a person entitled to receive funds or property under a trust, will, etc.

benefit *n* **1** something that improves or promotes. **2** advantage or sake: *I'm doing this for your benefit.* **3** a payment made by an institution or government to a person who is ill, unemployed, etc. **4** a theatrical performance or sports event to raise money for a charity. ~*vb* **-fiting, -fited** *or US* **-fitting, -fitted 5** to do or receive good; profit.

benefit society *n US* same as **friendly society.**

benevolence *n* **1** inclination to do good. **2** an act of kindness. **benevolent** *adj*

Bengali *n* **1** a member of a people living chiefly in Bangladesh and West Bengal. **2** the language of this people. ~*adj* **3** of Bengal or the Bengalis.

benighted *adj* lacking cultural, moral, or intellectual enlightenment.

benign (bin-**nine**) *adj* **1** showing kindliness. **2** favourable: *a stroke of benign fate.* **3** *Pathol* (of a tumour, etc.) able to be controlled. **benignly** *adv*

benignant *adj* **1** kind or gracious. **2** same as **benign** (senses 2, 3). **benignancy** *n*

benignity (bin-**nig**-nit-tee) *n, pl* **-ties** kindliness.

bent *adj* **1** not straight; curved. **2** *Slang* **a** dishonest; corrupt: *bent officials.* **b** *Offensive* homosexual. **3 bent on** determined to pursue (a course of action). ~*n* **4** personal inclination or aptitude: *he had a strong practical bent in his nature.*

Benthamism *n* the utilitarian philosophy of Jeremy Bentham, which holds that the ultimate goal of society should be to promote the greatest happiness of the greatest number. **Benthamite** *n, adj*

bentwood *n* **1** wood bent in moulds, used mainly for furniture. ~*adj* **2** made from such wood: *a bentwood chair.*

benumb *vb* **1** to make numb or powerless. **2** to stupefy (the mind, senses, will, etc.): *the work benumbed their minds and crushed their spirits.*

benzene *n* a flammable poisonous liquid used as a solvent, insecticide, etc.

benzine *n* a volatile liquid obtained from coal tar and used as a solvent.

bequeath *vb* **1** *Law* to dispose of (property) as in a will. **2** to hand down: *the author bequeaths no solutions.*

bequest *n* **1** the act of gifting money or property in a will. **2** money or property that has been gifted in a will.

berate *vb* **-rating, -rated** to scold harshly.

Berber *n* **1** a member of a Muslim people of N Africa. **2** the language of this people. ~*adj* **3** of the Berbers.

berberis *n* a shrub with red berries.

berceuse (bare-**suhz**) *n* **1** a lullaby. **2** an instrumental piece suggestive of this.

bereaved *adj* having recently lost a close relative or friend through death. **bereavement** *n*

bereft *adj* (foll. by *of*) deprived: *a government bereft of ideas.*

beret (**ber**-ray) *n* a round flat close-fitting brimless cap.

berg *n* short for **iceberg.**

bergamot *n* **1** a small Asian tree with sour pear-shaped fruit. **2 essence of bergamot** a fragrant essential oil from the fruit rind of this plant, used in perfumery.

beri-beri *n* a disease caused by a dietary deficiency of thiamine (vitamin B_1).

berk *or* **burk** *n Brit slang* a stupid person; fool.

berkelium *n Chem* an artificial radioactive element. Symbol: Bk

Berks Berkshire.

Bermuda shorts *pl n* shorts that come down to the knees.

THESAURUS

bench 1. form, pew, seat, settle, stall **2.** court, courtroom, judge, judges, judiciary, magistrate, magistrates, tribunal **3.** board, counter, table, trestle table, workbench, worktable

bend *vb.* **1.** arc, arch, bow, buckle, contort, crouch, curve, deflect, diverge, flex, incline, incurvate, lean, stoop, swerve, turn, twist, veer, warp **2.** compel, direct, influence, mould, persuade, shape, subdue, submit, sway, yield ~*n.* **3.** angle, arc, arch, bow, corner, crook, curve, hook, loop, turn, twist, zigzag

beneath 1. *prep.* below, inferior to, less than, lower than, unbefitting, underneath, unworthy of **2.** *adv.* below, in a lower place, underneath

beneficial advantageous, benign, expedient, favourable, gainful, healthful, helpful, profitable, salubrious, salutary, serviceable, useful, valuable, wholesome

benefit 1. *n.* advantage, aid, asset, assistance, avail, betterment, blessing, boon, favour, gain, good, help, interest, profit, use **2.** *vb.* advance, advantage, aid, ameliorate, assist, avail, better, enhance, further, improve, profit, promote, serve

bent *adj.* **1.** angled, arched, bowed, crooked, curved, hunched, stooped, twisted **2.** *with* **on** determined, disposed, fixed, inclined, insistent, predisposed, resolved, set ~*n.* **3.** ability, aptitude, bag (*slang*), cup of tea (*informal*), facility, faculty, flair, forte, inclination, knack, leaning, penchant, preference, proclivity, propensity, talent, tendency

bequeath bestow, commit, endow, entrust, give, grant, hand down, impart, leave to by will, pass on, transmit, will

bequest bequeathal, bestowal, dower (*archaic*), endowment, estate, gift, heritage, inheritance, legacy, settlement, trust

bereaved afflicted, deprived of kindred, dispos-

berry *n, pl* **-ries** a small round fruit that grows on bushes or trees and is often edible.

berserk *adj* **go berserk** to become violent or destructive.

berth *n* **1** a bunk in a ship or train. **2** *Naut* a place assigned to a ship at a mooring. **3** *Naut* sufficient room for a ship to manoeuvre. **4 give a wide berth to** to keep clear of. *~vb* **5** *Naut* to dock (a ship). **6** to provide with a sleeping place. **7** *Naut* to pick up a mooring in an anchorage.

beryl *n* a transparent hard mineral, used as a source of beryllium and as a gemstone.

beryllium *n* a toxic silvery-white metallic element. Symbol: Be

beseech *vb* **-seeching, -sought** *or* **-seeched** to ask earnestly; beg.

beset *vb* **-setting, -set 1** to trouble or harass constantly. **2** to surround or attack from all sides.

beside *prep* **1** next to; at, by, or to the side of. **2** as compared with. **3** away from: *beside the point.* **4 beside oneself** overwhelmed; overwrought: *beside oneself with grief.* *~adv* **5** at, by, to, or along the side of something or someone.

besides *adv* **1** in addition. *~prep* **2** apart from; even considering. *~conj* **3** anyway; moreover.

besiege *vb* **-sieging, -sieged 1** to surround with military forces to bring about surrender. **2** to hem in. **3** to overwhelm, as with requests.

besmirch *vb* to tarnish (someone's name or reputation).

besom *n* a broom made of a bundle of twigs tied to a handle.

besotted *adj* **1** having an irrational passion for a person or thing. **2** stupefied with alcohol.

besought *vb* a past of **beseech.**

bespatter *vb* **1** to splash with dirty water. **2** to dishonour or slander.

bespeak *vb* **-speaking, -spoke; -spoken** *or* **-spoke 1** to indicate or suggest: *imitation bespeaks admiration.* **2** to engage or ask for in advance: *she was bespoke to a family in the town.*

bespectacled *adj* wearing spectacles.

bespoke *adj Chiefly Brit* **1** (esp. of a suit) made to the customer's specifications. **2** making or selling such suits: *a bespoke tailor.*

best *adj* **1** the superlative of **good. 2** most excellent of a particular group, category, etc. **3** most suitable, desirable, etc. *~adv* **4** the superlative of **well. 5** in a manner surpassing all others; most attractively, etc. *~n* **6 the best** the most outstanding or excellent person, thing, or group in a category. **7** the utmost effort: *I did my best.* **8** a person's finest clothes. **9 at best a** in the most favourable interpretation. **b** under the most favourable conditions. **10 for the best a** for an ultimately good outcome. **b** with good intentions. **11 get the best of** to defeat or outwit. **12 make the best of** to cope as well as possible with. *~vb* **13** to defeat.

bestial *adj* **1** brutal or savage. **2** of or relating to a beast.

bestiality *n, pl* **-ties 1** brutal behaviour, character, or action. **2** sexual activity between a person and an animal.

bestiary *n, pl* **-aries** a medieval collection of descriptions of animals.

bestir *vb* **-stirring, -stirred** to cause (oneself) to become active.

best man *n* the male attendant of the bridegroom at a wedding.

bestow *vb* to present (a gift) or confer (an honour). **bestowal** *n*

bestrew *vb* **-strewing, -strewed; -strewn** *or* **-strewed** to scatter or lie scattered over (a surface).

bestride *vb* **-striding, -strode** to have or put a leg on either side of.

best seller *n* a book or other product that has sold in great numbers. **best-selling** *adj*

bet *n* **1** the act of staking a sum of money or other stake on the outcome of an event. **2** the stake risked. **3** a course of action: *your best bet is to go by train.* **4** *Informal* an opinion: *my bet is that you've been up to no good.* *~vb* **betting, bet** *or* **betted 5** to make or place a bet with (someone). **6** to stake (money, etc.) in a bet.

THESAURUS

sessed, divested, made destitute, stripped, taken away from, widowed

bereavement affliction, death, deprivation, loss, misfortune, tribulation

berth *n.* **1.** bed, billet, bunk, cot (*Naut.*), hammock **2.** anchorage, dock, harbour, haven, pier, port, quay, slip, wharf *~vb.* **3.** *Naut.* anchor, dock, drop anchor, land, moor, tie up

beseech adjure, ask, beg, call upon, crave, entreat, implore, importune, petition, plead, pray, solicit, sue, supplicate

beside 1. abreast of, adjacent to, alongside, at the side of, close to, near, nearby, neighbouring, next door to, next to, overlooking **2. beside oneself** apoplectic, berserk, crazed, delirious, demented, deranged, desperate, distraught, frantic, frenzied, insane, mad, out of one's mind, unbalanced, uncontrolled, unhinged

besides 1. *adv.* also, as well, further, furthermore, in addition, moreover, otherwise, too, what's more **2.** *prep.* apart from, barring, excepting, excluding, in addition to, other than, over and above, without

besiege 1. beleaguer, beset, blockade, confine, encircle, encompass, hedge in, hem in, lay siege to, shut in, surround **2.** badger, bend someone's ear (*informal*), bother, harass, harry, hassle (*informal*), hound, importune, nag, pester, plague, trouble

besotted 1. doting, hypnotized, infatuated, smitten, spellbound **2.** befuddled, bevvied (*dialect*), blitzed (*slang*), blotto (*slang*), bombed (*slang*), drunk, intoxicated, legless (*informal*), lit up (*slang*), out of it (*slang*), out to it (*Austral. & N.Z. slang*), paralytic (*informal*), pissed (*taboo slang*), smashed (*slang*), steamboats (*slang*), steaming (*slang*), stupefied, wasted (*slang*), wrecked (*slang*), zonked (*slang*)

best *adj.* **1.** chief, finest, first, first-class, first-rate, foremost, highest, leading, most excellent, outstanding, perfect, pre-eminent, principal, superlative, supreme, unsurpassed **2.** advantageous, apt, correct, golden, most desirable, most fitting, right **3.** greatest, largest, most *~adv.* **4.** advantageously, attractively, excellently, most fortunately **5.** extremely, greatly, most deeply, most fully, most highly *~n.* **6.** choice, cream, elite, favourite, finest, first, flower, pick, prime, top **7.** hardest, highest endeavour, utmost *~vb.* **8.** beat, blow out of the water (*slang*), conquer, defeat, get the better of, lick (*informal*), master, outclass, outdo, run rings around (*informal*), surpass, tank (*slang*), thrash, triumph over, trounce, undo, wipe the floor with (*informal*)

bestial animal, barbaric, barbarous, beastlike, beastly, brutal, brutish, carnal, degraded, depraved, gross, inhuman, low, savage, sensual, sordid, vile

bestow accord, allot, apportion, award, commit, confer, donate, entrust, give, grant, hand out, honour with, impart, lavish, present, render to

bestride bestraddle, bridge, dominate, extend, mount, span, step over, straddle, tower over

bet 1. *n.* ante, gamble, hazard, long shot, pledge, risk,

7 *Informal* to predict (a certain outcome): *I bet she doesn't turn up.* **8 you bet** *Informal* of course.

beta *n* 1 the second letter in the Greek alphabet (Β, β). 2 the second in a group or series.

beta-blocker *n* a drug that decreases the activity of the heart: used in the treatment of high blood pressure and angina pectoris.

beta-carotene *n Biochem* the most important form of the plant pigment carotene, which occurs in milk, vegetables, and other foods and, when eaten by man and animals, is converted in the body to vitamin A.

betake *vb* **-taking, -took, -taken betake oneself** *Formal* to go or move: *he betook himself to the public house.*

beta particle *n* a high-speed electron or positron emitted by a nucleus during radioactive decay or nuclear fission.

betatron *n* a type of particle accelerator for producing high-energy beams of electrons.

betel (bee-tl) *n* an Asian climbing plant, the leaves and nuts of which can be chewed.

bête noire (bet **nwahr**) *n, pl* **bêtes noires** a person or thing that one particularly dislikes or dreads.

betide *vb* **-tiding, -tided** to happen or happen to: *woe betide us if we're not ready on time.*

betoken *vb* to indicate; signify.

betray *vb* 1 to hand over or expose (one's nation, friend, etc.) treacherously to an enemy. 2 to disclose (a secret or confidence) treacherously. 3 to reveal unintentionally: *his singing voice betrays his origins.* **betrayal** *n* **betrayer** *n*

betroth *vb Archaic* to promise to marry or to give in marriage. **betrothal** *n*

betrothed *Old-fashioned* ~*adj* 1 engaged to be married. ~*n* 2 the person to whom one is engaged.

better *adj* 1 the comparative of **good.** 2 more excellent than others. 3 more suitable, attractive, etc. 4 improved or fully recovered in health. **5 the better part of** a large part of. ~*adv* 6 the comparative of **well.** 7 in a more excellent manner. 8 in or to a greater degree. **9 better off** in more favourable circumstances, esp. financially. **10 had better** would be sensible, etc. to: *I had better be off.* ~*n* **11 the better** something that is the more excellent, useful, etc. of two such things. **12 betters** people who are one's superiors, esp. in social standing. **13 get the better of** to defeat or outwit. ~*vb* 14 to improve upon.

better half *n Humorous* one's spouse.

betterment *n* improvement.

better-off *adj* reasonably wealthy: *Catalonia aims to attract better-off tourists.*

betting shop *n* (in Britain) a licensed bookmaker's premises not on a racecourse.

between *prep* 1 at a point intermediate to two other points in space, time, etc. 2 in combination; together: *between them, they saved enough money to buy a car.* 3 confined to: *between you and me.* 4 indicating a linking relation or comparison. 5 indicating alternatives, strictly only two alternatives. ~*adv also* **in between** 6 between one specified thing and another.

➤ *Between* is used when two people or things are mentioned: *the war between Iraq and Iran.* Otherwise use *among.*

betwixt *prep, adv* 1 *Archaic* between. **2 betwixt and between** in an intermediate or indecisive position.

bevel *n* 1 a slanting edge. ~*vb* **-elling, -elled** *or US* **-eling, -eled** 2 to be inclined; slope. 3 to cut a bevel on (a piece of timber, etc.).

bevel gear *n* a toothed gear meshed with another at an angle to it.

beverage *n* any drink other than water.

beverage room *n Canad* same as **beer parlour.**

bevvy *n, pl* **-vies** *Dialect* 1 an alcoholic drink. 2 a night of drinking.

bevy *n, pl* **bevies** a flock; a group.

bewail *vb* to express great sorrow over; lament.

beware *vb* **-waring, -wared** (often foll. by *of*) to be wary (of); be on one's guard (against).

THESAURUS

speculation, stake, venture, wager **2.** *vb.* chance, gamble, hazard, pledge, punt (*chiefly Brit.*), put money on, risk, speculate, stake, venture, wager

bête noire anathema, aversion, bane, bugbear, curse, pet hate

betide chance, come to pass, crop up (*informal*), ensue, happen, occur, overtake, supervene, take place, transpire (*informal*)

betoken augur, bespeak, bode, declare, denote, evidence, indicate, manifest, mark, portend, presage, prognosticate, promise, represent, signify, suggest, typify

betray 1. be disloyal (treacherous, unfaithful), break one's promise, break with, double-cross (*informal*), inform on *or* against, sell down the river (*informal*), sell out (*informal*), shop (*slang, chiefly Brit.*) **2.** blurt out, disclose, divulge, evince, expose, give away, lay bare, let slip, manifest, reveal, show, tell, tell on, uncover, unmask

betrayal 1. deception, disloyalty, double-cross (*informal*), double-dealing, duplicity, falseness, perfidy, sell-out (*informal*), treachery, treason, trickery, unfaithfulness **2.** blurting out, disclosure, divulgence, giving away, revelation, telling

better *adj.* **1.** bigger, excelling, finer, fitter, greater, higher quality, larger, more appropriate (desirable, expert, fitting, suitable, useful, valuable), preferable, superior, surpassing, worthier **2.** cured, fitter, fully recovered, healthier, improving, less ill, mending, more healthy, on the mend (*informal*), progressing, recovering, stronger, well ~*adv.* **3.** in a superior way, more advantageously (attractively, competently, completely, effectively, thoroughly), to a greater degree ~*n.* **4. get the better of** beat, best, defeat, get the upper hand, outdo, outsmart (*informal*), outwit, prevail over, score off, surpass, triumph over, worst ~*vb.* **5.** beat, cap (*informal*), clobber (*slang*), exceed, excel, improve on *or* upon, lick (*informal*), outdo, outstrip, run rings around (*informal*), surpass, top

between amidst, among, betwixt, halfway, in the middle of, mid

beverage bevvy (*dialect*), draught, drink, libation (*facetious*), liquid, liquor, potable, potation, refreshment

bevy band, bunch (*informal*), collection, company, covey, crowd, flight, flock, gathering, group, pack, troupe

bewail bemoan, cry over, deplore, express sorrow, grieve for, keen, lament, moan, mourn, regret, repent, rue, wail, weep over

beware avoid, be careful (cautious, wary), guard against, heed, look out, mind, refrain from, shun, steer clear of, take heed, watch out

bewilder baffle, befuddle, bemuse, confound, confuse, daze, flummox, mix up, mystify, nonplus, perplex, puzzle, stupefy

bewildered at sea, awed, baffled, bamboozled (*informal*), confused, disconcerted, dizzy, flummoxed, giddy, mystified, nonplussed, perplexed, puzzled,

bewilder *vb* to confuse utterly; puzzle. **bewildering** *adj* **bewilderment** *n*

bewitch *vb* **1** to attract and fascinate. **2** to cast a spell over. **bewitching** *adj*

bey *n* **1** (in modern Turkey) a title of address, corresponding to *Mr.* **2** (in the Ottoman Empire) a title given to provincial governors.

beyond *prep* **1** at or to a point on the other side of: *beyond those hills.* **2** outside the limits or scope of. *~adv* **3** at or to the other or far side of something. **4** outside the limits of something. *~n* **5 the beyond** the unknown, esp. life after death.

bezel *n* **1** the sloping edge of a cutting tool. **2** the slanting face of a cut gem. **3** a groove holding a gem, watch crystal, etc.

bezique *n* a card game for two or more players.

B/F *or* **b/f** *Book-keeping* brought forward.

BFPO British Forces Post Office.

bhaji *n, pl* **bhaji** *or* **bhajis** an Indian savoury made of chopped vegetables mixed in a spiced batter and deep-fried.

bhang *n* a preparation of Indian hemp used as a narcotic and intoxicant.

bhangra *n* a type of traditional Punjabi folk music combined with elements of Western pop music.

bhp brake horsepower.

Bi *Chem* bismuth.

bi- *combining form* **1** having two: *bifocal.* **2** occurring or lasting for two: *biennial.* **3** on both sides, directions, etc.: *bilateral.* **4** occurring twice during: *biweekly.* **5** *Chem* **a** denoting a compound containing two identical cyclical hydrocarbon systems: *biphenyl.* **b** indicating an acid salt of a dibasic acid: *sodium bicarbonate.*

biannual *adj* occurring twice a year. **biannually** *adv*

bias *n* **1** mental tendency, esp. prejudice. **2** a diagonal cut across the weave of a fabric. **3** *Bowls* a bulge or weight inside one side of a bowl that causes it to roll in a curve. *~vb* **-asing, -ased** *or* **-assing, -assed 4** to cause to have a bias; prejudice. **biased** *or* **biassed** *adj*

bias binding *n* a strip of material used for binding hems.

biaxial *adj* (esp. of a crystal) having two axes.

bib *n* **1** a piece of cloth or plastic worn to protect a very young child's clothes while eating. **2** the upper front part of some aprons, dungarees, etc.

bibcock *n* a tap with a nozzle bent downwards.

bibelot (**bib**-loh) *n* an attractive or curious trinket.

bibl. **1** bibliographical. **2** bibliography.

Bible *n* **1 the Bible** the sacred writings of the Christian religion, comprising the Old and New Testaments. **2 bible** a book regarded as authoritative: *this guide has long been regarded as the hill walkers' bible.* **biblical** *adj*

bibliography *n, pl* **-phies 1** a list of books on a subject or by a particular author. **2** a list of sources used in a book, etc. **3** the study of the history, etc., of literary material. **bibliographer** *n*

bibliophile *n* a person who collects or is fond of books.

bibulous *adj Literary* addicted to alcohol.

bicameral *adj* (of a legislature) consisting of two chambers.

bicarb *n* short for **bicarbonate of soda.**

bicarbonate *n* a salt of carbonic acid.

bicarbonate of soda *n* sodium bicarbonate used as medicine or a raising agent in baking.

bicentenary *or US* **bicentennial** *adj* **1** marking a 200th anniversary. *~n, pl* **-naries 2** a 200th anniversary.

biceps *n, pl* **-ceps** *Anat* a muscle with two origins, esp. the muscle that flexes the forearm.

bicker *vb* to argue over petty matters; squabble.

bicolour, bicoloured *or US* **bicolor, bicolored** *adj* two-coloured.

bicuspid *adj* **1** having two points. *~n* **2** a bicuspid tooth.

bicycle *n* **1** a vehicle with a metal frame and two wheels, one behind the other, pedalled by the rider. *~vb* **-cling, -cled 2** to ride a bicycle.

bid *vb* **bidding; bad, bade** *or* **bid; bidden** *or* **bid 1** to offer (an amount) in an attempt to buy something. **2** to say (a greeting): *to bid farewell.* **3** to order: *do as you are bid!* **4** *Bridge etc* to declare how many tricks one expects to make. *~n* **5 a** an offer of a specified amount. **b** the price offered. **6 a** the quoting by a seller of a price. **b** the price quoted. **7** an attempt, esp. to attain power. **8** *Bridge etc* the number of tricks a player undertakes to make. **bidder** *n*

biddable *adj* obedient.

bidding *n* **1** an order or command: *she had done his bidding.* **2** an invitation; summons: *he knew to knock and wait for bidding before he entered.* **3** the bids in an auction, card game, etc.

biddy *n, pl* **-dies** *Informal* a woman, esp. an old gossipy one.

bide *vb* **biding, bided** *or* **bode, bided 1** *Archaic or dialect* to remain. **2 bide one's time** to wait patiently for an opportunity.

bidet (**bee**-day) *n* a small low basin for washing the genital area.

biennial *adj* **1** occurring every two years. *~n* **2** a plant that completes its life cycle in two years.

bier *n* a stand on which a corpse or a coffin rests before burial.

biff *Slang ~n* **1** a blow with the fist. *~vb* **2** to give (someone) such a blow.

bifid *adj* divided into two by a cleft in the middle.

bifocal *adj* having two different focuses, esp. (of a lens) permitting near and distant vision.

THESAURUS

speechless, startled, stunned, surprised, taken aback, uncertain

bewitch absorb, allure, attract, beguile, captivate, charm, enchant, enrapture, entrance, fascinate, hypnotize, ravish, spellbind

beyond above, apart from, at a distance, away from, before, farther, out of range, out of reach, outwith (*Scot.*), over, past, remote, superior to, yonder

bias *n.* **1.** bent, bigotry, favouritism, inclination, intolerance, leaning, narrow-mindedness, one-sidedness, partiality, penchant, predilection, predisposition, prejudice, proclivity, proneness, propensity, tendency, turn, unfairness **2.** angle, cross, diagonal line, slant *~vb.* **3.** distort, influence, predispose, prejudice, slant, sway, twist, warp, weight

biased, biassed distorted, embittered, jaundiced, one-sided, partial, predisposed, prejudiced, slanted, swayed, twisted, warped, weighted

bicker argue, disagree, dispute, fight, quarrel, row (*informal*), scrap (*informal*), spar, squabble, wrangle

bid *vb.* **1.** offer, proffer, propose, submit, tender **2.** call, greet, say, tell, wish **3.** ask, call, charge, command, desire, direct, enjoin, instruct, invite, require, solicit, summon, tell *~n.* **4.** advance, amount, offer, price, proposal, proposition, submission, sum, tender **5.** attempt, crack (*informal*), effort, endeavour, go (*informal*), stab (*informal*), try, venture

bifocals *pl n* a pair of spectacles with bifocal lenses.

bifurcate *vb* **-cating, -cated 1** to fork into two branches. ~*adj* **2** forked into two branches. **bifurcation** *n*

big *adj* **bigger, biggest 1** of great or considerable size, weight, number, or capacity. **2** having great significance; important. **3** important through having power, wealth, etc. **4 a** elder: *my big brother.* **b** grown-up. **5** generous: *that's very big of you.* **6** extravagant; boastful: *big talk.* **7 too big for one's boots** conceited; unduly self-confident. **8** in an advanced stage of pregnancy: *big with child.* **9 in a big way** in a very grand or enthusiastic way. ~*adv Informal* **10** boastfully; pretentiously: *he talks big.* **11** on a grand scale: *think big.*

bigamy *n* the crime of marrying a person while still legally married to someone else. **bigamist** *n* **bigamous** *adj*

big-bang theory *n* a cosmological theory that suggests that the universe was created as the result of a massive explosion.

Big Brother *n* a person or organization that exercises total dictatorial control.

big business *n* large commercial organizations collectively.

big end *n Brit* the larger end of a connecting rod in an internal-combustion engine.

big game *n* large animals that are hunted or fished for sport.

bighead *n Informal* a conceited person. **big-headed** *adj*

bight *n* **1** a long curved shoreline. **2** the slack part or a loop in a rope.

bigot *n* a person who is intolerant, esp. regarding religion, politics, or race. **bigoted** *adj* **bigotry** *n*

big shot *n Informal* an important person.

Big Smoke *n* **the Big Smoke** *Informal* a big city, esp. London.

big stick *n Informal* force or the threat of force.

big time *n* **the big time** *Informal* the highest level of a profession, esp. entertainment. **big-timer** *n*

big top *n Informal* the main tent of a circus.

bigwig *n Informal* an important person.

bijou (bee-zhoo) *n, pl* **-joux** (-zhooz) **1** something small and delicately worked. ~*adj* **2** small but tasteful: *a bijou residence.*

bike *n Informal* a bicycle or motorcycle.

bikini *n* a woman's brief two-piece swimming costume.

bilateral *adj* affecting or undertaken by two parties; mutual.

bilberry *n, pl* **-ries** a blue or blackish edible berry that grows on a shrub.

bile *n* **1** a greenish fluid secreted by the liver to aid digestion of fats. **2** irritability or peevishness.

bilge *n* **1** *Informal* nonsense. **2** *Naut* the bottom of a ship's hull. **3** the dirty water that collects in a ship's bilge.

bilharzia (bill-**hart**-see-a) *n* a disease caused by infestation of the body with blood flukes.

biliary *adj* of bile, the ducts that convey bile, or the gall bladder.

bilingual *adj* **1** able to speak two languages. **2** expressed in two languages. **bilingualism** *n*

bilious *adj* **1** nauseous; sick: *a bilious attack.* **2** *Informal* bad-tempered; irritable: *the regime's most persistent and bilious critic.* **3** (of a colour) harsh and offensive.

bilk *vb* to cheat or deceive, esp. to avoid making payment to. **bilker** *n*

bill[1] *n* **1** a statement of money owed for goods or services supplied. **2** a draft of a proposed new law presented to a law-making body. **3** a printed notice or advertisement. **4** *US & Canad* a piece of paper money; note. **5** any list of items, events, etc. such as a theatre programme. ~*vb* **6** to send or present an account for payment to (a person). **7** to advertise by posters. **8** to schedule as a future programme: *next week they will discuss what are billed as new ideas for economic reform.* **9 fit** *or* **fill the bill** *Informal* to be suitable or adequate.

bill[2] *n* **1** the projecting jaws of a bird; beak. ~*vb* **2 bill and coo** (of lovers) to kiss and whisper amorously.

billabong *n Austral* a pool in the bed of a stream with an interrupted water flow.

billboard *n Chiefly US & Canad* a hoarding.

billet[1] *vb* **-leting, -leted 1** to assign a lodging to (a soldier). ~*n* **2** accommodation, esp. for a soldier, in civilian lodgings.

THESAURUS

bidding 1. beck, behest, call, canon, charge, command, demand, direction, injunction, instruction, invitation, order, request, summons **2.** auction, offer, offers, proposal, tender

big 1. bulky, burly, colossal, considerable, elephantine, enormous, extensive, gigantic, great, huge, hulking, humongous (*chiefly U.S. informal*), immense, large, mammoth, massive, ponderous, prodigious, sizable, spacious, substantial, vast, voluminous **2.** big-time (*informal*), eminent, important, influential, leading, main, major league (*informal*), momentous, paramount, powerful, prime, principal, prominent, serious, significant, valuable, weighty **3.** adult, elder, grown, grown-up, mature **4.** altruistic, benevolent, generous, gracious, heroic, magnanimous, noble, princely, unselfish **5.** arrogant, boastful, bragging, conceited, haughty, inflated, pompous, pretentious, proud

bigot dogmatist, fanatic, persecutor, sectarian, zealot

bigoted biased, dogmatic, illiberal, intolerant, narrow-minded, obstinate, opinionated, prejudiced, sectarian, twisted, warped

bigotry bias, discrimination, dogmatism, fanaticism, ignorance, injustice, intolerance, mindlessness, narrow-mindedness, pig-ignorance (*slang*), prejudice, provincialism, racialism, racism, sectarianism, sexism, unfairness

bigwig big shot (*informal*), celebrity, dignitary, heavyweight (*informal*), mogul, nob (*slang*), notability, notable, panjandrum, personage, somebody, V.I.P.

bile anger, bitterness, churlishness, ill humour, irascibility, irritability, nastiness, peevishness, rancour, spleen

bilious 1. liverish, nauseated, out of sorts, queasy, sick **2.** bad-tempered, cantankerous, crabby, cross, crotchety, edgy, grouchy (*informal*), grumpy, ill-humoured, ill-tempered, irritable, nasty, peevish, ratty (*Brit. & N.Z. informal*), short-tempered, testy, tetchy, touchy

bilk bamboozle (*informal*), cheat, con (*informal*), cozen, deceive, defraud, do (*slang*), fleece, rook (*old-fashioned slang*), skin (*slang*), swindle, trick

bill[1] *n.* **1.** account, charges, invoice, note of charge, reckoning, score, statement, tally **2.** measure, piece of legislation, projected law, proposal **3.** advertisement, broadsheet, bulletin, circular, handbill, handout, leaflet, notice, placard, playbill, poster **4.** agenda, card, catalogue, inventory, list, listing, programme, roster, schedule, syllabus ~*vb.* **5.** charge, debit, figure, in-

billet² *n* **1** a chunk of wood, esp. for fuel. **2** a small bar of iron or steel.

billet-doux (**bill**-ee-**doo**) *n, pl* **billets-doux** (**bill**-ee-**dooz**) *Old-fashioned or jocular* a love letter.

billhook *n* a tool with a hooked blade, used for chopping, etc.

billiards *n* a game in which a long cue is used to propel balls on a table.

billion *n, pl* **-lions** *or* **-lion 1** one thousand million: 1 000 000 000 or 10^9. **2** (in Britain, originally) one million million: 1 000 000 000 000 or 10^{12}. **3** (*often pl*) *Informal* an extremely large but unspecified number: *billions of dollars.* **billionth** *adj, n*

➤ Note that the use of the word *billion* has changed and may stand for different amounts according to the date of a book or article.

billionaire *n* a person who has money or property worth at least a billion pounds, dollars, etc.

bill of exchange *n* a document instructing a third party to pay a stated sum at a designated date or on demand.

bill of fare *n* a menu.

bill of health *n* **1** a certificate that confirms the health of a ship's company. **2 clean bill of health** *Informal* **a** a good report of one's physical condition. **b** a favourable account of a person's or a company's financial position.

bill of lading *n* a document containing full particulars of goods shipped.

billow *n* **1** a large sea wave. **2** a swelling or surging mass, as of smoke or sound. *~vb* **3** to rise up or swell out. **billowing** *adj, n* **billowy** *adj*

billy *or* **billycan** *n, pl* **-lies** *or* **-lycans** a metal can or pot for boiling water etc. over a campfire.

billy goat *n* a male goat.

biltong *n S African* strips of meat dried and cured in the sun.

bimbo *n, pl* **-bos** *Slang* an attractive but empty-headed young woman.

bimetallism *n* the use of two metals, esp. gold and silver, in fixed relative values as the standard of value and currency. **bimetallist** *n*

bin *n* **1** a container for rubbish, etc. **2** a large container for storing something in bulk, such as coal, grain, or bottled wine. *~vb* **binning, binned 3** to put in a rubbish bin: *I bin my junk mail without reading it.*

binary (**bine**-a-ree) *adj* **1** composed of two parts. **2** *Maths, computers* of or expressed in a system with two as its base. **3** *Chem* containing atoms of two different elements. *~n, pl* **-ries 4** something composed of two parts.

binary star *n* a system of two stars revolving around a common centre of gravity.

bind *vb* **binding, bound 1** to make secure, such as with a rope. **2** to unite with emotional ties or commitment. **3** to place (someone) under legal or moral obligation. **4** to place under certain constraints: *bound by the rules.* **5** to stick together or cause to stick: *egg binds fat and flour.* **6** to enclose and fasten (the pages of a book) between covers. **7** to provide (a garment) with an edging. **8** (foll. by *up*) to bandage. *~n* **9** *Informal* a difficult or annoying situation.

binder *n* **1** a firm cover for holding loose sheets of paper together. **2** a person who binds books. **3** something used to fasten or tie, such as rope or twine. **4** *Obsolete* a machine for cutting and binding grain into sheaves.

bindery *n, pl* **-eries** a place in which books are bound.

binding *n* **1** anything that binds or fastens. **2** the covering of a book. *~adj* **3** imposing an obligation or duty.

bind over *vb* to place (a person) under a legal obligation, esp. to keep the peace.

bindweed *n* a plant that twines around a support.

binge *n Informal* **1** a bout of excessive drinking. **2** excessive indulgence in anything.

bingo *n* a gambling game in which numbers called out are covered by players on their individual cards. The first to cover a given arrangement is the winner.

binnacle *n* a housing for a ship's compass.

binocular *adj* involving or intended for both eyes: *binocular vision.*

binoculars *pl n* an optical instrument for use with both eyes, consisting of two small telescopes joined together.

binomial *n* **1** a mathematical expression consisting of two terms, such as $3x + 2y$. *~adj* **2** referring to two names or terms.

binomial theorem *n* a general mathematical formula that expresses any power of a binomial without multiplying out, as in $(a+b)^2=a^2+2ab+b^2$.

bio- *combining form* indicating: **1** life or living organisms: *biogenesis.* **2** a human life or career: *biography.*

bioastronautics *n* the study of the effects of space flight on living organisms.

biochemistry *n* the study of the chemical compounds, reactions, etc., occurring in living organisms. **biochemical** *adj* **biochemist** *n*

biocoenosis *or US* **biocenosis** (bye-oh-see-**no**-siss) *n* the relationships between animals and plants subsisting together.

biodegradable *adj* (of sewage and packaging) capable of being decomposed by natural means. **biodegradability** *n*

biodiversity *n* the existence of a wide variety of plant and animal species in their natural environments.

bioengineering *n* the design and manufacture of aids, such as artificial limbs, to help people with disabilities.

biogenesis *n* the principle that a living organism must originate from a similar parent organism.

biography *n, pl* **-phies 1** an account of a someone's

THESAURUS

voice, reckon, record **6.** advertise, announce, give advance notice of, post

bill² beak, mandible, neb (*archaic or dialect*), nib

billet 1. *vb.* accommodate, berth, quarter, station **2.** *n.* accommodation, barracks, lodging, quarters

billow *n.* **1.** breaker, crest, roller, surge, swell, tide, wave **2.** cloud, deluge, flood, outpouring, rush, surge, wave *~vb.* **3.** balloon, belly, puff up, rise up, roll, surge, swell

billowy heaving, rippling, rolling, surging, swelling, swirling, undulating, waving, wavy

bind *vb.* **1.** attach, fasten, glue, hitch, paste, rope, secure, stick, strap, tie, tie up, truss, wrap **2.** compel, constrain, engage, force, necessitate, obligate, oblige, prescribe, require **3.** confine, detain, hamper, hinder, restrain, restrict **4.** border, edge, finish, hem, trim **5.** bandage, cover, dress, encase, swathe, wrap *~n.* **6.** *informal* bore, difficulty, dilemma, drag (*informal*), nuisance, pain in the arse (*taboo informal*), predicament, quandary, spot (*informal*), tight spot

binding *adj.* compulsory, conclusive, imperative, indissoluble, irrevocable, mandatory, necessary, obligatory, unalterable

life by another person. **2** such accounts collectively. **biographer** *n* **biographical** *adj*

biol. **1** biological. **2** biology.

biological *adj* **1** of or relating to biology. **2** (of a detergent) containing enzymes that remove natural stains, such as blood or grass. **biologically** *adv*

biological clock *n* an inherent timing mechanism that controls the rhythmic repetition of processes in living organisms, such as sleeping.

biological control *n* the control of destructive organisms, esp. insects, by nonchemical means, such as introducing a natural predator of the pest.

biological warfare *n* the use of living organisms or their toxic products to induce death or incapacity in humans.

biology *n* the study of living organisms. **biologist** *n*

biomedicine *n* **1** the medical and biological study of the effects of unusual environmental stress. **2** the study of herbal remedies.

bionic *adj* **1** of or relating to bionics. **2** (in science fiction) having physical functions augmented by electronic equipment.

bionics *n* **1** the study of biological functions in order to develop electronic equipment that operates similarly. **2** the replacement of limbs or body parts by artificial electronically powered parts.

biophysics *n* the physics of biological processes and the application of methods used in physics to biology. **biophysical** *adj* **biophysicist** *n*

biopic (**bye**-oh pick) *n Informal* a film based on the life of a famous person.

biopsy *n, pl* **-sies** examination of tissue from a living body to determine the cause or extent of a disease.

biorhythm *n* a complex recurring pattern of physiological states, believed to affect physical, emotional, and mental states.

bioscope *n* **1** a kind of early film projector. **2** *S African* a cinema.

biosphere *n* the part of the earth's surface and atmosphere inhabited by living things.

biosynthesis *n* the formation of complex compounds by living organisms. **biosynthetic** *adj*

biotechnology *n* the use of microorganisms, such as cells or bacteria, in industry and technology.

biotin *n* a vitamin of the B complex, abundant in egg yolk and liver.

bipartisan *adj* consisting of or supported by two political parties.

bipartite *adj* **1** consisting of or having two parts. **2** affecting or made by two parties: *a bipartite agreement.*

biped (**bye**-ped) *n* **1** any animal with two feet. *~adj also* **bipedal** **2** having two feet.

biplane *n* an aeroplane with two sets of wings, one above the other.

bipolar *adj* **1** having two poles. **2** having two extremes. **bipolarity** *n*

birch *n* **1** a tree with thin peeling bark and hard close-grained wood. **2 the birch** a bundle of birch twigs or a birch rod used, esp. formerly, for flogging offenders. *~vb* **3** to flog with the birch.

bird *n* **1** a two-legged creature with feathers and wings, which lays eggs and can usually fly. **2** *Slang, chiefly Brit* a girl or young woman. **3** *Informal* a person: *he's a rare bird.* **4 a bird in the hand** something definite or certain. **5 birds of a feather** people with the same ideas or interests. **6 kill two birds with one stone** to accomplish two things with one action.

birdie *n* **1** *Informal* a bird. **2** *Golf* a score of one stroke under par for a hole.

birdlime *n* a sticky substance smeared on twigs to catch small birds.

bird of paradise *n* a songbird of New Guinea, the male of which has brilliantly coloured plumage.

bird of prey *n* a bird, such as a hawk or owl, that hunts other animals for food.

birdseed *n* a mixture of various kinds of seeds for feeding cage birds.

bird's-eye view *n* **1** a view seen from above. **2** a general or overall impression of something.

bird-watcher *n* a person who studies wild birds in their natural surroundings.

biretta *n RC Church* a stiff square clerical cap.

Biro *n, pl* **-ros** *Trademark, Brit* a kind of ballpoint pen.

birth *n* **1** the process of bearing young; childbirth. **2** the act of being born. **3** the beginning of something; origin. **4** ancestry: *of noble birth.* **5 give birth to a** to bear (offspring). **b** to produce or originate (an idea, plan, etc.).

birth certificate *n* an official form stating the time and place of a person's birth.

birth control *n* limitation of child-bearing by means of contraception.

birthday *n* **1** an anniversary of the day of one's birth. **2** the day on which a person was born.

birthmark *n* a blemish on the skin formed before birth.

birthplace *n* the place where someone was born or where something originated.

birth rate *n* the ratio of live births to population, usually expressed per 1000 population per year.

birthright *n* privileges or possessions that a person has or is believed to be entitled to as soon as he or she is born.

biscuit *n* **1** *Brit* a small flat dry sweet or plain cake. **2** porcelain that has been fired but not glazed. *~adj* **3** pale brown or yellowish-grey.

bisect *vb* **1** *Maths* to divide into two equal parts. **2** to cut or split into two. **bisection** *n*

bisexual *adj* **1** sexually attracted to both men and women. **2** showing characteristics of both sexes. *~n* **3** a bisexual person. **bisexuality** *n*

bishop *n* **1** a clergyman having spiritual and administrative powers over a diocese. **2** a chessman capable of moving diagonally.

bishopric *n* the see, diocese, or office of a bishop.

bismuth *n Chem* a brittle pinkish-white metallic element. Some compounds are used in alloys and in medicine. Symbol: Bi

bison *n, pl* **-son** an animal of the cattle family with a massive head, shaggy forequarters, and a humped back.

bisque[1] *n* a thick rich soup made from shellfish.

bisque[2] *adj* **1** pink-to-yellowish-tan. *~n* **2** *Ceramics* same as **biscuit** (sense 2).

bistro *n, pl* **-tros** a small restaurant.

THESAURUS

binge beano (*Brit. old-fashioned slang*), bender (*informal*), bout, feast, fling, jag (*slang*), orgy, spree

biography account, curriculum vitae, CV, life, life history, life story, memoir, memoirs, profile, record

birth **1.** childbirth, delivery, nativity, parturition **2.** beginning, emergence, fountainhead, genesis, origin, rise, source **3.** ancestry, background, blood, breeding, derivation, descent, extraction, forebears, genealogy, line, lineage, nobility, noble extraction, parentage, pedigree, race, stock, strain

bisect bifurcate, cross, cut across, cut in half, cut in

bit[1] *n* **1** a small piece, portion, or quantity. **2** a short time or distance. **3 a bit** rather; somewhat: *a bit stupid.* **4 a bit of** rather: *a bit of a fool.* **5 bit by bit** gradually. **6 do one's bit** to make one's expected contribution.

bit[2] *n* **1** a metal mouthpiece on a bridle for controlling a horse. **2** a cutting or drilling tool, part, or head in a brace, drill, etc.

bit[3] *vb* the past tense of **bite.**

bit[4] *n Maths, computers* **1** a single digit of binary notation, represented either by 0 or by 1. **2** the smallest unit of information, indicating the presence or absence of a single feature.

bitch *n* **1** a female dog, fox, or wolf. **2** *Slang, offensive* a malicious or spiteful woman. **3** *Informal* a difficult situation or problem. *~vb* **4** *Informal* to complain; grumble.

bitchy *adj* **bitchier, bitchiest** *Informal* spiteful or malicious. **bitchiness** *n*

bite *vb* **biting, bit, bitten 1** to grip, cut off, or tear with the teeth or jaws. **2** (of animals or insects) to injure by puncturing (the skin) with the teeth or fangs. **3** (of corrosive material) to eat away or into. **4** to smart or cause to smart; sting. **5** *Angling* (of a fish) to take the bait or lure. **6** to take firm hold of or act effectively upon: *turn the screw till it bites the wood.* **7** *Slang* to annoy or worry: *what's biting her? ~n* **8** the act of biting. **9** a thing or amount bitten off. **10** a wound or sting inflicted by biting. **11** *Angling* an attempt by a fish to take the bait or lure. **12** a snack. **13** a stinging or smarting sensation. **biter** *n*

biting *adj* **1** piercing; keen: *a biting wind.* **2** sarcastic; incisive.

bit part *n* a very small acting role with few lines to speak.

bitten *vb* the past participle of **bite.**

bitter *adj* **1** having an unpalatable harsh taste, as the peel of an orange. **2** showing or caused by hostility or resentment. **3** difficult to accept: *a bitter blow.* **4** sarcastic: *bitter words.* **5** bitingly cold: *a bitter night. ~n* **6** *Brit* draught beer with a slightly bitter taste. **bitterly** *adv* **bitterness** *n*

bittern *n* a large wading marsh bird with a booming call.

bitters *pl n* bitter-tasting spirits flavoured with plant extracts.

bittersweet *adj* **1** tasting of or being a mixture of bitterness and sweetness. **2** pleasant but tinged with sadness.

bitty *adj* **-tier, -tiest** lacking unity; disjointed.

bitumen *n* a sticky or solid substance that occurs naturally in asphalt and tar and is used in road surfacing. **bituminous** *adj*

bituminous coal *n* a soft black coal that burns with a smoky yellow flame.

bivalve *n* **1** a sea creature, such as an oyster or mussel, that has a shell consisting of two hinged valves and breathes through gills. *~adj* **2** of these molluscs.

bivouac *n* **1** a temporary camp, as used by soldiers or mountaineers. *~vb* **-acking, -acked 2** to make a temporary camp.

biz *n Informal* business.

bizarre *adj* odd or unusual, esp. in an interesting or amusing way.

Bk *Chem* berkelium.

BL 1 Bachelor of Law. **2** Bachelor of Letters. **3** Barrister-at-Law.

blab *vb* **blabbing, blabbed** to divulge (secrets) indiscreetly.

blabber *n* **1** a person who blabs. *~vb* **2** to talk without thinking.

black *adj* **1** having no hue, owing to the absorption of all or almost all light; of the colour of coal. **2** without light. **3** without hope; gloomy: *the future looked black.* **4** dirty or soiled. **5** angry or resentful: *black looks.* **6** unpleasant in a cynical or macabre manner: *black comedy.* **7** (of coffee or tea) without milk or cream. **8** wicked or harmful: *a black lie. ~n* **9** the darkest colour; the colour of coal. **10** a dye or pigment producing this colour. **11** black clothing, worn esp. in mourning: *she was in black, as though in mourning.* **12** complete darkness: *the black of the night.* **13 in the black** in credit or without debt. *~vb* **14** same as **blacken. 15** to polish (shoes or boots) with blacking. **16** *Brit, Austral, & NZ* (of trade unionists) to organize a boycott of (specified goods, work, etc.). ~See also **blackout. blackness** *n* **blackish** *adj*

Black *n* **1** a member of a dark-skinned race. *~adj* **2** of

THESAURUS

two, divide in two, halve, intersect, separate, split, split down the middle

bishopric diocese, episcopacy, episcopate, primacy, see

bit[1] **1.** atom, chip, crumb, fragment, grain, iota, jot, mite, morsel, mouthful, part, piece, remnant, scrap, segment, slice, small piece, speck, tittle, whit **2.** instant, jiffy (*informal*), little while, minute, moment, period, second, spell, tick (*Brit. informal*), time

bit[2] brake, check, curb, restraint, snaffle

bitchy backbiting, catty (*informal*), cruel, malicious, mean, nasty, rancorous, shrewish, snide, spiteful, venomous, vicious, vindictive, vixenish

bite *vb.* **1.** champ, chew, clamp, crunch, crush, cut, gnaw, grip, hold, masticate, nibble, nip, pierce, pinch, rend, seize, snap, tear, wound **2.** burn, corrode, eat away, eat into, erode, smart, sting, tingle, wear away *~n.* **3.** itch, nip, pinch, prick, smarting, sting, tooth marks, wound **4.** food, light meal, morsel, mouthful, piece, refreshment, snack, taste

biting 1. bitter, blighting, cold, cutting, freezing, harsh, nipping, penetrating, piercing, sharp **2.** caustic, cutting, incisive, mordant, sarcastic, scathing, severe, sharp, stinging, trenchant, vitriolic, withering

bitter 1. acerbic, acid, acrid, astringent, sharp, sour, tart, unsweetened, vinegary **2.** acrimonious, begrudging, crabbed, embittered, hostile, morose, rancorous, resentful, sore, sour, sullen, with a chip on one's shoulder **3.** calamitous, cruel, dire, distressing, galling, grievous, harsh, heartbreaking, merciless, painful, poignant, ruthless, savage, vexatious **4.** biting, fierce, freezing, intense, severe, stinging

bitterness 1. acerbity, acidity, sharpness, sourness, tartness, vinegariness **2.** animosity, grudge, hostility, pique, rancour, resentment **3.** acrimoniousness, asperity, sarcasm, venom, virulence

bizarre abnormal, comical, curious, eccentric, extraordinary, fantastic, freakish, grotesque, ludicrous, odd, oddball (*informal*), off-beat, off-the-wall (*slang*), outlandish, outré, peculiar, queer, ridiculous, rum (*Brit. slang*), strange, unusual, wacko (*slang*), way-out (*informal*), weird, zany

blab blow wide open (*slang*), blurt out, disclose, divulge, gossip, let slip, reveal, shop (*slang, chiefly Brit.*), sing (*slang, chiefly U.S.*), spill one's guts (*slang*), tattle, tell, tell all, tell on

blabber 1. *n.* busybody, gossip, informer, rumourmonger, scandalmonger, talebearer, tattler, telltale **2.** *vb.* blather, blether (*Scot.*), chatter, gab (*informal*), jabber, prattle

black *adj.* **1.** coal-black, dark, dusky, ebony, inky, jet, murky, pitchy, raven, sable, starless, stygian, swarthy

or relating to a Black or Blacks.
➤ When *black* is used as a political or racial term it has a capital letter.

black-and-blue *adj* (of the skin) bruised, as from a beating.

black-and-white *n* **1** a photograph, film, etc., in black, white, and shades of grey, rather than in colour. **2 in black and white a** in print or writing. **b** in extremes: *he always sees things in black and white.*

black-backed gull *n* a large common black-and-white European gull.

blackball *vb* **1** to vote against. **2** to exclude (someone) from a group, etc.

black bear *n* **1** a bear inhabiting forests of North America. **2** a bear of central and E Asia.

black belt *n Judo, karate, etc* **a** a black belt that signifies that the wearer has reached a high standard in martial art. **b** a person entitled to wear this.

blackberry *n, pl* **-ries** a small blackish edible fruit that grows on a woody bush with thorny stems. Also called: **bramble**

blackbird *n* a common European thrush the male of which has black plumage and a yellow bill.

blackboard *n* a hard or rigid surface made of a smooth usually dark substance, used for writing or drawing on with chalk, esp. in teaching.

black box *n Informal* a flight recorder.

blackcap *n* a brownish-grey warbler, the male of which has a black crown.

blackcock *n* the male of the black grouse.

Black Country *n* **the Black Country** the heavily industrialized West Midlands of England.

blackcurrant *n* a very small blackish edible fruit that grows in bunches on a bush.

blackdamp *n* air that is low in oxygen content and high in carbon dioxide as a result of an explosion in a mine.

Black Death *n* **the Black Death** a form of bubonic plague in Europe and Asia during the 14th century.

black economy *n* that portion of the income of a nation that remains illegally undeclared.

blacken *vb* **1** to make or become black or dirty. **2** to damage (someone's reputation); discredit: *they planned to blacken my father's name.*

black eye *n* bruising round the eye.

Black Friar *n* a Dominican friar.

blackguard (**blag**-gard) *n* an unprincipled contemptible person.

blackhead *n* **1** a black-tipped plug of fatty matter clogging a pore of the skin. **2** a bird with black plumage on the head.

black hole *n Astron* a hypothetical region of space resulting from the collapse of a star and surrounded by a gravitational field from which neither matter nor radiation can escape.

black ice *n* a thin transparent layer of new ice on a road.

blacking *n* any preparation for giving a black finish to shoes, metals, etc.

blackjack[1] *n* pontoon or a similar card game.

blackjack[2] *n Chiefly US & Canad* a truncheon of leather-covered lead with a flexible shaft.

black lead *n* same as **graphite.**

blackleg *n Brit* **1** a person who continues to work or does another's job during a strike. ~*vb* **-legging, -legged 2** to refuse to join a strike.

blacklist *n* **1** a list of people or organizations considered untrustworthy or disloyal. ~*vb* **2** to put (someone) on a blacklist.

black magic *n* magic used for evil purposes.

blackmail *n* **1** the act of attempting to obtain money by threatening to reveal shameful information. **2** the use of unfair pressure in an attempt to influence someone. ~*vb* **3** to obtain or attempt to obtain money by intimidation. **4** to attempt to influence (a person) by unfair pressure. **blackmailer** *n*

Black Maria (mar-**rye**-a) *n* a police van for transporting prisoners.

black mark *n* a discredit noted against someone.

black market *n* a place or a system for buying or selling goods or currencies illegally, esp. in violation of controls or rationing. **black marketeer** *n*

black mass *n* a blasphemous travesty of the Christian Mass, used in black magic.

blackout *n* **1** (in wartime) the putting out or hiding of all lights as a precaution against a night air attack. **2** a momentary loss of consciousness, vision, or memory. **3** a temporary electrical power failure. **4** the prevention of information broadcasts: *a news blackout.* ~*vb* **black out 5** to put out (lights). **6** to lose vision, consciousness, or memory temporarily. **7** to stop (news, a television programme, etc.) from being broadcast.

black pepper *n* a dark-coloured hot seasoning made from the dried berries and husks of the pepper plant.

Black Power *n* a movement of Black people to obtain equality with Whites.

THESAURUS

2. *figurative* atrocious, depressing, dismal, distressing, doleful, foreboding, funereal, gloomy, hopeless, horrible, lugubrious, mournful, ominous, sad, sombre **3.** dingy, dirty, filthy, grimy, grubby, soiled, sooty, stained **4.** angry, furious, hostile, menacing, resentful, sullen, threatening **5.** bad, evil, iniquitous, nefarious, villainous, wicked **6. in the black** in credit, in funds, solvent, without debt ~*vb.* **7.** ban, bar, blacklist, boycott

blackball *vb.* ban, bar, blacklist, debar, drum out, exclude, expel, ostracize, oust, repudiate, snub, vote against

blacken 1. cloud, darken, grow black, make black, smudge, soil **2.** bad-mouth (*slang, chiefly U.S. & Canad.*), calumniate, decry, defame, defile, denigrate, dishonour, knock (*informal*), malign, rubbish (*informal*), slag (off) (*slang*), slander, smear, smirch, stain, sully, taint, tarnish, traduce, vilify

blackguard bad egg (*old-fashioned informal*), bastard (*offensive*), blighter (*Brit. informal*), bounder (*old-fashioned Brit. slang*), bugger (*taboo slang*), miscreant, rascal, rogue, scoundrel, scumbag (*slang*), shit (*taboo slang*), swine, villain, wretch

blacklist *vb.* ban, bar, blackball, boycott, debar, exclude, expel, ostracize, preclude, proscribe, reject, repudiate, snub, vote against

black magic black art, diabolism, necromancy, sorcery, voodoo, witchcraft, wizardry

blackmail 1. *n.* bribe, exaction, extortion, hush money (*slang*), intimidation, milking, pay-off (*informal*), protection (*informal*), ransom, slush fund **2.** *vb.* bleed (*informal*), bribe, coerce, compel, demand, exact, extort, force, hold to ransom, milk, squeeze, threaten

blackness darkness, duskiness, gloom, inkiness, melanism, murkiness, nigrescence, nigritude (*rare*), swarthiness

blackout *n.* **1.** power cut, power failure **2.** coma, faint, loss of consciousness, oblivion, swoon (*literary*), syncope (*Pathology*), unconsciousness **3.** censorship,

black pudding *n* a black sausage made from pig's blood, suet, etc.

Black Rod *n* (in Britain) the chief usher of the House of Lords and of the Order of the Garter.

black sheep *n* a person who is regarded as a disgrace or failure by his or her family or peer group.

Blackshirt *n* a member of the Italian Fascist party before and during the Second World War.

blacksmith *n* a person who works iron with a furnace, anvil, and hammer.

black spot *n* **1** a place on a road where accidents frequently occur. **2** an area where a particular situation is exceptionally bad: *an unemployment black spot.*

blackthorn *n* a thorny shrub with black twigs, white flowers, and small sour plumlike fruits.

black tie *n* **1** a black bow tie worn with a dinner jacket. *~adj* **black-tie 2** denoting an occasion when a dinner jacket should be worn.

Black Watch *n* **the Black Watch** the Royal Highland Regiment in the British Army.

black widow *n* an American spider the female of which is highly venomous and commonly eats its mate.

bladder *n* **1** *Anat* a membranous sac, usually containing liquid, esp. the urinary bladder. **2** a hollow bag made of leather, etc. which becomes round when filled with air or liquid. **3** a hollow saclike part in certain plants, such as seaweed. **bladdery** *adj*

blade *n* **1** the part of a sharp weapon, tool, or knife, that forms the cutting edge. **2** the thin flattish part of a propeller, oar, or fan. **3** the flattened part of a leaf, sepal, or petal. **4** the long narrow leaf of a grass or related plant.

blain *n* a blister, blotch, or sore on the skin.

blame *vb* **blaming, blamed 1** to consider (someone) responsible for: *I blame her for the failure.* **2** (foll. by *on*) to put responsibility for (something) on (someone): *she blames the failure on me.* **3 be to blame** to be at fault. *~n* **4** responsibility for something that is wrong: *they must take the blame for the failure.* **5** an expression of condemnation: *analysts lay the blame on party activists.* **blamable** *or* **blameable** *adj* **blameless** *adj*

blameworthy *adj* deserving blame. **blameworthiness** *n*

blanch *vb* **1** to whiten. **2** to become pale, as with sickness or fear. **3** to prepare (meat or vegetables) by plunging them in boiling water. **4** to cause (celery, chicory, etc.) to grow white from lack of light.

blancmange (blam-**monzh**) *n* a jelly-like dessert of milk, stiffened usually with cornflour.

bland *adj* **1** dull and uninteresting: *the bland British eating habits.* **2** smooth in manner: *he looked at his visitor with a bland smile.* **blandly** *adv*

blandish *vb* to persuade by mild flattery; coax.

blandishments *pl n* flattery intended to coax or cajole.

blank *adj* **1** (of a writing surface) not written on. **2** (of a form, etc.) with spaces left for details to be filled in. **3** without ornament or break: *a blank wall.* **4** empty or void: *a blank space.* **5** showing no interest or expression: *a blank look.* **6** lacking ideas or inspiration: *his mind went blank.* *~n* **7** an empty space. **8** an empty space for writing in. **9** the condition of not understanding: *my mind went a complete blank.* **10** a mark, often a dash, in place of a word. **11** same as **blank cartridge. 12 draw a blank** to get no results from something. *~vb* **13** (foll. by *out*) to cross out, blot, or obscure. **blankly** *adv*

blank cartridge *n* a cartridge containing powder but no bullet.

blank cheque *n* **1** a signed cheque on which the amount payable has not been specified. **2** complete freedom of action.

blanket *n* **1** a large piece of thick cloth for use as a bed covering. **2** a concealing cover, as of smoke, leaves, or snow. *~adj* **3** applying to or covering a wide group or variety of people, conditions, situations, etc.: *a blanket ban on all supporters travelling to away matches.* *~vb* **-keting, -keted 4** to cover as if with a blanket. **5** to cover a wide area; give blanket coverage to.

blanket stitch *n* a strong reinforcing stitch for the edges of blankets.

blank verse *n* unrhymed verse.

blare *vb* **blaring, blared 1** to sound loudly and harsh-

THESAURUS

noncommunication, radio silence, secrecy, suppression, withholding news

black out *vb.* **1.** conceal, cover, darken, eclipse, obfuscate, shade **2.** collapse, faint, flake out (*informal*), lose consciousness, pass out, swoon (*literary*)

black sheep disgrace, dropout, ne'er-do-well, outcast, prodigal, renegade, reprobate, wastrel (*literary*)

blame *vb.* **1.** accuse, admonish, blast, censure, charge, chide, condemn, criticize, disapprove, express disapprobation, find fault with, hold responsible, lambast(e), put down, reprehend, reproach, reprove, tax, tear into (*informal*), upbraid *~n.* **2.** accountability, culpability, fault, guilt, incrimination, liability, onus, rap (*slang*), responsibility **3.** accusation, castigation, censure, charge, complaint, condemnation, criticism, recrimination, reproach, reproof, stick (*slang*)

blameless above suspicion, clean, faultless, guiltless, immaculate, impeccable, innocent, in the clear, irreproachable, perfect, squeaky-clean, stainless, unblemished, unimpeachable, unoffending, unspotted, unsullied, untarnished, upright, virtuous

blameworthy discreditable, disreputable, indefensible, inexcusable, iniquitous, reprehensible, reproachable, shameful

bland 1. boring, dull, flat, humdrum, insipid, monotonous, tasteless, tedious, undistinctive, unexciting, uninspiring, uninteresting, unstimulating, vapid, weak **2.** affable, amiable, congenial, courteous, debonair, friendly, gentle, gracious, smooth, suave, unemotional, urbane

blandishments blarney, cajolery, coaxing, compliments, fawning, flattery, ingratiation, inveiglement, soft soap (*informal*), soft words, sweet talk (*informal*), wheedling, winning caresses

blank *adj.* **1.** bare, clean, clear, empty, plain, spotless, uncompleted, unfilled, unmarked, void, white **2.** deadpan, dull, empty, expressionless, hollow, impassive, inane, lifeless, poker-faced (*informal*), vacant, vacuous, vague **3.** at a loss, at sea, bewildered, confounded, confused, disconcerted, dumbfounded, flummoxed, muddled, nonplussed, uncomprehending *~n.* **4.** emptiness, empty space, gap, nothingness, space, vacancy, vacuity, vacuum, void

blanket *n.* **1.** afghan, cover, coverlet, rug **2.** carpet, cloak, coat, coating, covering, envelope, film, layer, mantle (*old-fashioned*), sheet, wrapper, wrapping *~adj.* **3.** across-the-board, all-inclusive, comprehensive, overall, sweeping, wide-ranging *~vb.* **4.** cloak, cloud, coat, conceal, cover, eclipse, hide, mask, obscure, suppress, surround

blare blast, boom, clamour, clang, honk, hoot, peal, resound, roar, scream, sound out, toot, trumpet

ly. **2** to proclaim loudly: *the newspaper headlines blared the news.* ~*n* **3** a loud harsh noise.

blarney *n* flattering talk.

blasé (blah-**zay**) *adj* indifferent or bored, esp. through familiarity.

blaspheme *vb* **-pheming, -phemed 1** to speak disrespectfully of (God or sacred things). **2** to utter curses. **blasphemer** *n*

blasphemy *n, pl* **-mies** behaviour or language that shows disrespect for God or sacred things. **blasphemous** *adj*

blast *n* **1** an explosion, such as that caused by dynamite. **2** the charge used in a single explosion. **3** a sudden strong gust of wind or air. **4** a sudden loud sound, such as that made by a trumpet. **5** a violent verbal outburst, esp. critical. **6** *US slang* a very enjoyable or thrilling experience: *the party was a blast.* **7 at full blast** at maximum speed, volume, etc. ~*interj* **8** *Slang* an exclamation of annoyance. ~*vb* **9** to blow up (a rock, tunnel, etc.) with explosives. **10** to make or cause to make a loud harsh noise. **11** to criticize severely.

blasted *adj, adv Slang* extreme or extremely: *a blasted idiot.*

blast furnace *n* a furnace for smelting using a blast of preheated air.

blastoff *n* **1** the launching of a rocket under its own power. ~*vb* **blast off 2** (of a rocket) to be launched.

blatant (**blay**-tant) *adj* **1** glaringly obvious: *a blatant lie.* **2** offensively noticeable: *their blatant disregard for my feelings.* **blatantly** *adv*

blather *vb, n* same as **blether.**

blaze[1] *n* **1** a strong fire or flame. **2** a very bright light or glare. **3** an outburst (of passion, patriotism, etc.). ~*vb* **blazing, blazed 4** to burn fiercely. **5** to shine brightly. **6** to become stirred, as with anger or excitement. **7 blaze away** to shoot continuously. ~See also **blazes.**

blaze[2] *n* **1** a mark, usually indicating a path, made on a tree. **2** a light-coloured marking on the face of an animal. ~*vb* **blazing, blazed 3** to mark (a tree, path, etc.) with a blaze. **4 blaze a trail** to explore new territories, areas of knowledge, etc.

blaze[3] *vb* **blazing, blazed blaze something abroad** to make something widely known.

blazer *n* a fairly lightweight jacket, often in the colours of a sports club, school, etc.

blazes *pl n Slang, euphemistic* hell.

blazon *vb* **1** to proclaim publicly: *the newspaper photographs were blazoned on the front pages.* **2** *Heraldry* to describe or colour (heraldic arms) conventionally. ~*n* **3** *Heraldry* a coat of arms.

bleach *vb* **1** to make or become white or colourless by exposure to sunlight, or by the action of chemical agents. ~*n* **2** a bleaching agent.

bleaching powder *n* a white powder consisting of chlorinated calcium hydroxide.

bleak *adj* **1** exposed and barren. **2** cold and raw. **3** offering little hope; dismal: *a bleak future.* **bleakly** *adv* **bleakness** *n*

bleary *adj* **blearier, bleariest 1** with eyes dimmed, by tears or tiredness. **2** indistinct or unclear. **blearily** *adv*

bleary-eyed *or* **blear-eyed** *adj* with eyes blurred, such as with old age or after waking.

bleat *vb* **1** (of a sheep, goat, or calf) to utter its plaintive cry. **2** to whine. ~*n* **3** the characteristic cry of sheep, goats, and calves. **4** a weak complaint or whine.

bleed *vb* **bleeding, bled 1** to lose or emit blood. **2** to remove or draw blood from (a person or animal). **3** (of plants) to exude (sap or resin), esp. from a cut. **4** *Informal* to obtain money, etc., from (someone), esp. by extortion. **5** to draw liquid or gas from (a container or enclosed system). **6 my heart bleeds for you** I am sorry for you: often used ironically.

bleeding *adj, adv Brit slang* extreme or extremely: *a bleeding fool.*

bleep *n* **1** a short high-pitched signal made by an electrical device. **2** same as **bleeper.** ~*vb* **3** to make a bleeping signal. **4** to call (someone) by means of a bleeper.

bleeper *n* a small portable radio receiver that makes a bleeping signal.

blemish *n* **1** a defect; flaw; stain. ~*vb* **2** to spoil or tarnish.

blench *vb* to shy away, as in fear.

blend *vb* **1** to mix or mingle (components). **2** to mix

THESAURUS

blarney blandishment, cajolery, coaxing, exaggeration, flattery, honeyed words, overpraise, soft soap (*informal*), spiel, sweet talk (*informal*), wheedling

blasé apathetic, bored, cloyed, glutted, indifferent, jaded, lukewarm, nonchalant, offhand, satiated, surfeited, unconcerned, unexcited, uninterested, unmoved, weary, world-weary

blaspheme abuse, anathematize, curse, damn, desecrate, execrate, profane, revile, swear

blasphemous godless, impious, irreligious, irreverent, profane, sacrilegious, ungodly

blasphemy cursing, desecration, execration, impiety, impiousness, indignity (*to God*), irreverence, profanation, profaneness, profanity, sacrilege, swearing

blast *n.* **1.** bang, blow-up, burst, crash, detonation, discharge, eruption, explosion, outburst, salvo, volley **2.** gale, gust, squall, storm, strong breeze, tempest **3.** blare, blow, clang, honk, peal, scream, toot, wail ~*vb.* **4.** blow up, break up, burst, demolish, destroy, explode, ruin, shatter **5.** attack, castigate, criticize, flay, lambast(e), put down, rail at, tear into (*informal*)

blastoff *n.* discharge, expulsion, firing, launch, launching, lift-off, projection, shot

blatant **1.** bald, brazen, conspicuous, flagrant, flaunting, glaring, naked, obtrusive, obvious, ostentatious, outright, overt, prominent, pronounced, sheer, unmitigated **2.** clamorous, deafening, ear-splitting, harsh, loud, noisy, piercing, strident

blaze *n.* **1.** bonfire, conflagration, fire, flame, flames **2.** beam, brilliance, flare, flash, glare, gleam, glitter, glow, light, radiance **3.** blast, burst, eruption, flare-up, fury, outbreak, outburst, rush, storm, torrent ~*vb.* **4.** beam, burn, fire, flame, flare, flash, glare, gleam, glow, shine **5.** boil, explode, flare up, fume, seethe

bleach blanch, etiolate, fade, grow pale, lighten, peroxide, wash out, whiten

bleak **1.** bare, barren, chilly, cold, desolate, exposed, gaunt, open, raw, unsheltered, weather-beaten, windswept, windy **2.** cheerless, comfortless, depressing, discouraging, disheartening, dismal, dreary, gloomy, grim, hopeless, joyless, sombre, unpromising

bleary blurred, blurry, dim, fogged, foggy, fuzzy, hazy, indistinct, misty, murky, rheumy, watery

bleed **1.** exude, flow, gush, lose blood, ooze, run, seep, shed blood, spurt, trickle, weep **2.** deplete, drain, draw *or* take blood, exhaust, extort, extract, fleece, leech, milk, reduce, sap, squeeze

blemish **1.** *n.* blot, blotch, blur, defect, demerit, disfigurement, disgrace, dishonour, fault, flaw, imperfection, mark, scar, smirch, smudge, speck, spot, stain,

(different varieties of tea, whisky, etc.). **3** to look good together; harmonize. **4** (esp. of colours) to shade gradually into each other. *~n* **5** a mixture produced by blending.

blende *n* a mineral consisting mainly of zinc sulphide: the chief source of zinc.

blender *n* an electrical kitchen appliance for pureeing vegetables etc.

blenny *n, pl* **-nies** a small fish of coastal waters with a tapering scaleless body and long fins.

bless *vb* **blessing, blessed** *or* **blest 1** to make holy by means of a religious rite. **2** to give honour or glory to (a person or thing) as holy. **3** to call upon God to protect. **4** to worship or adore (God). **5 be blessed with** to be endowed with: *she is blessed with immense energy.* **6 bless me!** an exclamation of surprise. **7 bless you!** said to a person who has just sneezed.

blessed *adj* **1** made holy. **2** *RC Church* (of a person) beatified by the pope. **3** bringing great happiness or good fortune: *he was blessed with good looks.* **4** *Euphemistic* damned: *I'm blessed if I know.*

blessing *n* **1** the act of invoking divine protection or aid. **2** approval; good wishes. **3** a happy event.

blest *vb* a past of **bless.**

blether *Scot ~vb* **1** to speak foolishly at length. *~n* **2** foolish talk. **3** a person who blethers.

blew *vb* the past tense of **blow.**

blight *n* **1** a person or thing that spoils or prevents growth. **2** any plant disease characterized by withering and shrivelling without rotting. **3** a fungus or insect that causes blight in plants. **4** an ugly urban district. *~vb* **5** to cause to suffer a blight. **6** to frustrate or disappoint: *blighted love.* **7** to destroy: *the event blighted her life.*

blighter *n Brit informal* a despicable or irritating person or thing.

Blighty *n Brit slang* (used esp. by troops serving abroad) **1** Britain; home. **2** (*pl* **Blighties**) (esp. in the First World War) a wound that causes the recipient to be sent home to Britain.

blimey *interj Brit slang* an exclamation of surprise or annoyance.

blimp[1] *n* **1** a small nonrigid airship. **2** *Films* a soundproof cover fixed over a camera during shooting.

blimp[2] *n Chiefly Brit* a person who is stupidly complacent and reactionary. Also called: **Colonel Blimp**

blind *adj* **1** unable to see. **2** unable or unwilling to understand: *she is blind to his faults.* **3** not determined by reason: *blind hatred.* **4** acting or performed without control or preparation. **5** done without being able to see, relying on instruments for information. **6** hidden from sight: *a blind corner.* **7** closed at one end: *a blind alley.* **8** completely lacking awareness or consciousness: *a blind stupor.* **9** having no openings: *a blind wall.* *~adv* **10** without being able to see ahead or using only instruments: *flying blind.* **11** without adequate information: *we bought the house blind.* **12 blind drunk** *Informal* very drunk. *~vb* **13** to deprive of sight permanently or temporarily. **14** to deprive of good sense, reason, or judgment. **15** to darken; conceal. **16** to overwhelm by showing detailed knowledge: *he tried to blind us with science.* *~n* **17** a shade for a window. **18** any obstruction or hindrance to sight, light, or air. **19** a person, action, or thing that serves to deceive or conceal the truth. **blinding** *adj* **blindly** *adv* **blindness** *n*

blind alley *n* **1** an alley open at one end only. **2** *Informal* a situation in which no further progress can be made.

blind date *n Informal* a prearranged social meeting between two people who have not met before.

blindfold *vb* **1** to prevent (a person or animal) from seeing by covering the eyes. *~n* **2** a piece of cloth used to cover the eyes. *~adj, adv* **3** having the eyes covered with a cloth.

blind man's buff *n* a game in which a blindfolded person tries to catch and identify the other players.

blind spot *n* **1** a small oval-shaped area of the retina which is unable to see. **2** a place where vision is obscured. **3** a subject about which a person is ignorant or prejudiced.

blindworm *n* same as **slowworm.**

blink *vb* **1** to close and immediately reopen (the eyes), usually involuntarily. **2** to shine intermittently or unsteadily. *~n* **3** the act or an instance of blinking. **4** a glance; glimpse. **5 on the blink** *Slang* not working properly.

blinker *vb* **1** to provide (a horse) with blinkers. **2** to obscure or be obscured with or as with blinkers.

THESAURUS

taint **2.** *vb.* blot, blotch, blur, damage, deface, disfigure, flaw, impair, injure, mar, mark, smirch, smudge, spoil, spot, stain, sully, taint, tarnish

blend *vb.* **1.** amalgamate, coalesce, combine, compound, fuse, intermix, meld, merge, mingle, mix, synthesize, unite **2.** complement, fit, go well, go with, harmonize, suit *~n.* **3.** alloy, amalgam, amalgamation, combination, composite, compound, concoction, fusion, meld, mix, mixture, synthesis, union

bless anoint, consecrate, dedicate, exalt, extol, give thanks to, glorify, hallow, invoke happiness on, magnify, ordain, praise, sanctify, thank

blessed 1. adored, beatified, divine, hallowed, holy, revered, sacred, sanctified **2.** endowed, favoured, fortunate, granted, jammy (*Brit. slang*), lucky

blessing 1. benediction, benison, commendation, consecration, dedication, grace, invocation, thanksgiving **2.** approbation, approval, backing, concurrence, consent, favour, good wishes, leave, permission, regard, sanction, support **3.** advantage, benefit, boon, bounty, favour, gain, gift, godsend, good fortune, help, kindness, profit, service, windfall

blight *n.* **1.** affliction, bane, contamination, corruption, curse, evil, plague, pollution, scourge, woe **2.** canker, decay, disease, fungus, infestation, mildew, pest, pestilence, rot *~vb.* **3.** *figurative* annihilate, crush, dash, disappoint, frustrate, mar, nullify, ruin, spoil, undo, wreck **4.** blast, destroy, injure, nip in the bud, ruin, shrivel, taint with mildew, wither

blind *adj.* **1.** destitute of vision, eyeless, sightless, stone-blind, unseeing, unsighted, visionless **2.** *figurative* careless, heedless, ignorant, inattentive, inconsiderate, indifferent, indiscriminate, injudicious, insensitive, morally darkened, neglectful, oblivious, prejudiced, thoughtless, unaware of, unconscious of, uncritical, undiscerning, unmindful of, unobservant, unreasoning **3.** hasty, impetuous, irrational, mindless, rash, reckless, senseless, uncontrollable, uncontrolled, unthinking, violent, wild **4.** closed, concealed, dark, dead-end, dim, hidden, leading nowhere, obscured, obstructed, without exit *~n.* **5.** camouflage, cloak, cover, façade, feint, front, mask, masquerade, screen, smoke screen

blindly 1. aimlessly, at random, confusedly, frantically, indiscriminately, instinctively, madly, purposelessly, wildly **2.** carelessly, heedlessly, impulsively, inconsiderately, passionately, recklessly, regardlessly, senselessly, thoughtlessly, unreasonably, wilfully

blink 1. bat, flutter, glimpse, nictate, nictitate, peer, squint, wink **2.** flash, flicker, gleam, glimmer, scintillate, shine, sparkle, twinkle, wink **3. on the blink**

blinkered *adj* **1** considering only a narrow point of view. **2** (of a horse) wearing blinkers.
blinkers *pl n Chiefly Brit* leather side pieces attached to a horse's bridle to prevent sideways vision.
blinking *adj, adv Informal* extreme or extremely: *a blinking idiot.*
blip *n* **1** a repetitive sound, such as the kind produced by an electronic device. **2** the spot of light on a radar screen indicating the position of an object. **3** a temporary irregularity in the performance of something.
bliss *n* **1** perfect happiness; serene joy. **2** the joy of heaven. **blissful** *adj* **blissfully** *adv*
blister *n* **1** a small bubble on the skin filled with a watery fluid. **2** a swelling containing air or liquid, such as on a painted surface. ~*vb* **3** to have or cause to have blisters. **4** to attack verbally with great scorn. **blistering** *adj*
blithe *adj* **1** heedless; casual and indifferent. **2** very happy or cheerful. **blithely** *adv*
blithering *adj Informal* stupid; foolish: *you blithering idiot.*
BLitt Bachelor of Letters.
blitz *n* **1** a violent and sustained attack by enemy aircraft. **2** any intensive attack or concerted effort. ~*vb* **3** to attack suddenly and intensively.
Blitz *n* **the Blitz** the systematic bombing of Britain in 1940–41 by the German Air Force.
blitzkrieg *n* a swift intensive military attack designed to defeat the opposition quickly.
blizzard *n* a blinding storm of wind and snow.
bloat *vb* **1** to cause to swell, as with a liquid or air. **2** to cause to be puffed up, as with conceit. **3** to cure (fish, esp. herring) by half drying in smoke. **bloated** *adj*
bloater *n* a herring that has been salted in brine, smoked, and cured.
blob *n* **1** a soft mass or drop. **2** a spot of colour, ink, etc. **3** an indistinct or shapeless form or object.
bloc *n* a group of people or countries combined by a common interest.
block *n* **1** a large solid piece of wood, stone, etc. **2** such a piece on which particular tasks may be done, as chopping, cutting, etc. **3** a large building of offices, flats, etc. **4** a group of buildings in a city bounded by intersecting streets on each side. **5** an obstruction or hindrance: *a writer with a block.* **6** one of a set of wooden or plastic cubes as a child's toy. **7** *Slang* a person's head. **8** *NZ* an area of bush reserved by licence for a trapper or hunter. **9** a piece of wood, metal, etc., engraved for printing. **10** a casing housing one or more freely rotating pulleys. See also **block and tackle. 11** a quantity considered as a single unit. ~*vb* **12** to obstruct or impede by introducing an obstacle: *lorry drivers had blocked the routes to Paris.* **13** to impede, retard, or prevent (an action or procedure). **14** to stamp (a title or design) on (a book cover, etc.). **15** *Cricket* to play (a ball) defensively. ~See also **block out. blockage** *n*
blockade *n* **1** *Mil* the closing off of a port or region to prevent the passage of goods. ~*vb* **-ading, -aded 2** to impose a blockade on.
block and tackle *n* a hoisting device in which a rope or chain is passed around a pair of blocks containing one or more pulleys.
blockbuster *n Informal* **1** a film, novel, etc. that has been or is expected to be highly successful. **2** a large bomb used to demolish extensive areas.
blockhead *n* a stupid person. **blockheaded** *adj*
block letter *n* a plain capital letter. Also called: **block capital**
block out *vb* **1** to plan or describe (something) in a general fashion. **2** to prevent the entry or consideration of (something).
bloke *n Brit informal* a man.
blonde *or masc* **blond** *adj* **1** (of hair) fair. **2** (of a person) having fair hair and a light complexion. ~*n* **3** a person having light-coloured hair and skin. **blondeness** *or masc* **blondness** *n*
blood *n* **1** a reddish fluid in vertebrates that is pumped by the heart through the arteries and veins. **2** bloodshed, esp. when resulting in murder: *they were responsible for the spilling of blood throughout the country.* **3** life itself; lifeblood. **4** relationship through being of the same family, race, or kind; kinship. **5 the blood** royal or noble descent: *a prince of the blood.* **6 flesh and blood a** near kindred or kinship, esp. that between a parent and child. **b** human nature: *it's more than flesh and blood can stand.* **7 in one's blood** as a natural or inherited characteristic or talent. **8** newcomers viewed as an invigorating force: *new*

THESAURUS

slang faulty, malfunctioning, not working (properly), on the fritz (*U.S. slang*), out of action, out of order, playing up
bliss beatitude, blessedness, blissfulness, ecstasy, euphoria, felicity, gladness, happiness, heaven, joy, paradise, rapture
blissful cock-a-hoop, delighted, ecstatic, elated, enchanted, enraptured, euphoric, happy, heavenly (*informal*), in ecstasies, joyful, joyous, over the moon (*informal*), rapt, rapturous
blister abscess, blain, boil, bubble, canker, carbuncle, cyst, pimple, pustule, sore, swelling, ulcer, welt, wen (*Pathology*)
blithe 1. careless, casual, heedless, indifferent, nonchalant, thoughtless, unconcerned, untroubled **2.** animated, buoyant, carefree, cheerful, cheery, chirpy (*informal*), debonair, gay, genial, gladsome (*archaic*), happy, jaunty, light-hearted, merry, mirthful, sprightly, sunny, upbeat (*informal*), vivacious
blitz assault, attack, blitzkrieg, bombardment, offensive, onslaught, raid, strike
blizzard blast, gale, snowstorm, squall, storm, tempest
bloat balloon, blow up, dilate, distend, enlarge, expand, inflate, puff up, swell
blob ball, bead, bubble, dab, dewdrop, drop, droplet, glob, globule, lump, mass, pearl, pellet, pill
bloc alliance, axis, cabal, clique, coalition, combine, entente, faction, group, league, ring, schism, union, wing
block *n.* **1.** bar, brick, cake, chunk, cube, hunk, ingot, lump, mass, piece, square **2.** bar, barrier, blockage, hindrance, impediment, jam, obstacle, obstruction, occlusion, stoppage ~*vb.* **3.** bung up (*informal*), choke, clog, close, obstruct, plug, stop up **4.** arrest, bar, check, deter, halt, hinder, impede, obstruct, stop, thwart
blockade barricade, barrier, block, closure, encirclement, hindrance, impediment, obstacle, obstruction, restriction, siege, stoppage
blockage block, blocking, impediment, obstruction, occlusion, stoppage, stopping up
blockhead berk (*Brit. slang*), charlie (*Brit. old-fashioned informal*), chump (*informal*), coot (*old-fashioned*), dolt, dullard (*old-fashioned*), dunce, fool, idiot, ignoramus, jerk (*slang, chiefly U.S. & Canad.*), nerd *or* nurd (*slang*), noodle, numskull *or* numbskull, pillock (*Brit. slang*), plonker (*slang*), prat (*slang*), prick (*derogatory slang*), thickhead, twit (*informal, chiefly Brit.*), wally (*slang*)

blood. **9 in cold blood** showing no passion; ruthlessly. **10 make one's blood boil** to cause to be angry or indignant. **11 make one's blood run cold** to fill with horror. *~vb* **12** *Hunting* to cause (young hounds) to taste the blood of a freshly killed quarry. **13** to initiate (a person) to war or hunting.

blood-and-thunder *adj* denoting melodramatic behaviour.

blood bank *n* a place where blood is stored until required for transfusion.

blood bath *n* a massacre.

blood brother *n* a man or boy who has sworn to treat another as his brother, often in a ceremony in which their blood is mingled.

blood count *n* determination of the number of red and white blood corpuscles in a specific sample of blood.

bloodcurdling *adj* terrifying.

blood donor *n* a person who gives blood to be used for transfusion.

blood group *n* any one of the various groups into which human blood is classified.

blood heat *n* the normal temperature of the human body, 98.4°F or 37°C.

bloodhound *n* a large hound, formerly used in tracking and police work.

bloodless *adj* **1** without blood: *bloodless surgery.* **2** conducted without violence: *a bloodless coup.* **3** anaemic-looking; pale. **4** lacking vitality; lifeless: *the bloodless ambience of supermarkets.*

blood-letting *n* **1** bloodshed, esp. in a feud. **2** the former medical practice of removing blood.

blood money *n* **1** money obtained by ruthlessly sacrificing others. **2** money paid to a hired murderer. **3** compensation paid to the relatives of a murdered person.

blood orange *n* a variety of orange the pulp of which is dark red when ripe.

blood poisoning *n* same as **septicaemia.**

blood pressure *n* the pressure exerted by the blood on the inner walls of the blood vessels.

blood relation *or* **relative** *n* a person related by birth.

bloodshed *n* slaughter; killing.

bloodshot *adj* (of an eye) inflamed.

blood sport *n* any sport involving the killing of an animal.

bloodstained *adj* discoloured with blood.

bloodstock *n* thoroughbred horses.

bloodstream *n* the flow of blood through the vessels of a living body.

bloodsucker *n* **1** an animal that sucks blood, esp. a leech. **2** *Informal* a person who preys upon another person, esp. by extorting money.

bloodthirsty *adj* **-thirstier, -thirstiest** taking pleasure in bloodshed or violence.

blood vessel *n* a tube through which blood travels in the body.

bloody *adj* **bloodier, bloodiest 1** covered with blood. **2** marked by much killing and bloodshed: *a bloody war.* **3** cruel or murderous: *a bloody tyrant. ~adj, adv* **4** *Slang* extreme or extremely: *a bloody fool; a bloody good idea. ~vb* **bloodies, bloodying, bloodied 5** to stain with blood.

Bloody Mary *n* a drink consisting of tomato juice and vodka.

bloody-minded *adj Brit informal* deliberately obstructive and unhelpful.

bloom *n* **1** a blossom on a flowering plant. **2** the state or period when flowers open. **3** a healthy or flourishing condition; prime. **4** a youthful or healthy glow. **5** a fine whitish coating on the surface of fruits or leaves. *~vb* **6** (of flowers) to open. **7** to bear flowers. **8** to flourish or grow. **9** to be in a healthy, glowing condition.

bloomer *n Brit informal* a stupid mistake; blunder.

bloomers *pl n* **1** *Informal* women's baggy knickers. **2** (formerly) loose trousers gathered at the knee worn by women.

blooming *adv, adj Brit informal* extreme or extremely: *blooming painful.*

blossom *n* **1** the flower or flowers of a plant, esp. producing edible fruit. **2** the period of flowering. *~vb* **3** (of plants) to flower. **4** to come to a promising stage.

blot *n* **1** a stain or spot, esp. of ink. **2** something that spoils. **3** a stain on one's character. *~vb* **blotting, blotted 4** to stain or spot. **5** to cause a blemish in or on: *he blotted his copybook by missing a penalty.* **6** to soak up (excess ink, etc.) by using blotting paper. **7 blot out a** to darken or hide completely: *the mist blotted out the sea.* **b** to block from one's mind: *to blot out the memories.*

blotch *n* **1** an irregular spot or discoloration. *~vb* **2** to become or cause to become marked by such discoloration. **blotchy** *adj*

blotter *n* a sheet of blotting paper.

blotting paper *n* a soft absorbent paper, used for soaking up surplus ink.

blotto *adj Slang* extremely drunk.

blouse *n* **1** a woman's shirtlike garment. **2** a waist-

THESAURUS

blonde *or masc.* **blond** fair, fair-haired, fair-skinned, flaxen, golden-haired, light, light-coloured, light-complexioned, tow-headed

blood 1. gore, lifeblood, vital fluid **2.** ancestry, birth, consanguinity, descendants, descent, extraction, family, kindred, kinship, lineage, noble extraction, relations

bloodcurdling appalling, chilling, dreadful, fearful, frightening, hair-raising, horrendous, horrifying, scaring, spine-chilling, terrifying

bloodless 1. anaemic, ashen, chalky, colourless, pale, pallid, pasty, sallow, sickly, wan **2.** cold, languid, lifeless, listless, passionless, spiritless, torpid, unemotional, unfeeling

bloodshed blood bath, bloodletting, butchery, carnage, gore, killing, massacre, murder, slaughter, slaying

bloodthirsty barbarous, brutal, cruel, ferocious, inhuman, murderous, ruthless, savage, vicious, warlike

bloody 1. bleeding, blood-soaked, blood-spattered, bloodstained, gaping, raw, unstaunched **2.** cruel, ferocious, fierce, sanguinary, savage

bloom *n.* **1.** blossom, blossoming, bud, efflorescence, flower, opening (*of flowers*) **2.** *figurative* beauty, blush, flourishing, flush, freshness, glow, health, heyday, lustre, perfection, prime, radiance, rosiness, vigour *~vb.* **3.** blossom, blow, bud, burgeon, open, sprout **4.** develop, fare well, flourish, grow, prosper, succeed, thrive, wax

blossom *n.* **1.** bloom, bud, floret, flower, flowers *~vb.* **2.** bloom, burgeon, flower **3.** *figurative* bloom, develop, flourish, grow, mature, progress, prosper, thrive

blot *n.* **1.** blotch, mark, patch, smear, smudge, speck, splodge, spot **2.** blemish, blur, defect, demerit, dis-

length belted jacket worn by soldiers. *~vb* **blousing, bloused 3** to hang or cause to hang in full loose folds.

blouson (**blew**-zon) *n* a short loose jacket with a tight-fitting waist.

blow[1] *vb* **blowing, blew, blown 1** (of a current of air, the wind, etc.) to be or cause to be in motion. **2** to move or be carried by or as if by wind. **3** to expel (air, etc.) through the mouth or nose. **4** to breathe hard; pant. **5** to inflate with air or the breath. **6** (of wind, etc.) to make a roaring sound. **7** to cause (a musical instrument) to sound by forcing air into it. **8** (often foll. by *up, down, in,* etc.) to explode, break, or disintegrate completely. **9** *Electronics* (of a fuse or valve) to burn out because of excessive current. **10** to shape (glass, etc.) by forcing air or gas through the material when molten. **11** *Slang* to spend (money) freely. **12** *Slang* to use (an opportunity) ineffectively. **13** *Slang* to expose or betray (a secret). **14** (*past participle* **blowed**) *Informal* same as **damn. 15 blow hot and cold** *Informal* to keep changing one's attitude towards someone or something. **16 blow one's top** *Informal* to lose one's temper. *~n* **17** the act or an instance of blowing. **18** the sound produced by blowing. **19** a blast of air or wind. ~See also **blow out, blow over,** etc.

blow[2] *n* **1** a powerful or heavy stroke with the fist, a weapon, etc. **2** a sudden setback: *the scheme was dealt a blow by the introduction of martial law.* **3** an attacking action: *a blow for freedom.* **4 come to blows a** to fight. **b** to result in a fight.

blow-by-blow *adj* explained in great detail: *a blow-by-blow account.*

blow-dry *vb* **-dries, -drying, -dried 1** to style (the hair) while drying it with a hand-held hair dryer. *~n* **2** this method of styling hair.

blower *n* **1** a mechanical device, such as a fan, that blows. **2** *Informal* a telephone.

blowfly *n, pl* **-flies** a fly that lays its eggs in meat.

blowhole *n* **1** the nostril of a whale. **2** a hole in ice through which seals, etc. breathe. **3** a vent for air or gas.

blown *vb* a past participle of **blow.**

blow out *vb* **1** (of a flame) to extinguish or be extinguished. **2** (of a tyre) to puncture suddenly. **3** (of an oil or gas well) to lose oil or gas in an uncontrolled manner. *~n* **blowout 4** a sudden burst in a tyre. **5** the uncontrolled escape of oil or gas from a well. **6** *Slang* a large filling meal.

blow over *vb* **1** to be forgotten. **2** to cease or be finished: *the crisis blew over.*

blowpipe *n* **1** a long tube from which poisoned darts, etc., are shot by blowing. **2** a tube for blowing air into a flame to intensify its heat. **3** an iron pipe used to blow glass into shape.

blowsy *adj* **blowsier, blowsiest** (of a woman) **1** slovenly or sluttish. **2** ruddy in complexion.

blowtorch *or* **blowlamp** *n* a small burner that produces a very hot flame, used to remove old paint, soften metal, etc.

blow up *vb* **1** to explode or cause to explode. **2** to inflate with air. **3** to increase the importance of (something): *an affair blown up out of all proportions.* **4** *Informal* to lose one's temper. **5** *Informal* to reprimand (someone). **6** *Informal* to enlarge (a photograph). **7** to come into existence with sudden force: *a crisis had blown up.* *~n* **blow-up 8** *Informal* an enlarged photograph.

blowy *adj* **blowier, blowiest** windy.

blubber *n* **1** the fatty tissue of aquatic mammals such as the whale. **2** *Informal* flabby body fat. *~vb* **3** to sob without restraint.

bludge *Austral & NZ informal ~vb* **bludging, bludged 1** (foll. by *on*) to scrounge from. **2** to evade work. *~n* **3** a very easy task.

bludgeon *n* **1** a stout heavy club, typically thicker at one end. *~vb* **2** to hit as if with a bludgeon. **3** to force; bully; coerce.

blue *n* **1** the colour of a clear unclouded sky. **2** anything blue, such as blue clothing or blue paint: *she is clothed in blue.* **3** a sportsman who represents or has represented Oxford or Cambridge University. **4** *Brit informal* a Tory. **5** *Austral & NZ slang* an argument or fight. **6** Also: **bluey** *Austral & NZ informal* a court summons. **7** *Austral & NZ informal* a mistake. **8 out of the blue** unexpectedly. *~adj* **bluer, bluest 9** of the colour blue; of the colour of a clear unclouded sky. **10** (of the flesh) having a purple tinge from cold. **11** depressed or unhappy. **12** pornographic: *blue movies.* *~vb* **blueing** *or* **bluing, blued 13** to make or become blue or bluer. **14** *Old-fashioned, informal* to spend extravagantly or wastefully: *I consoled myself by blueing my royalty cheque.* ~See also **blues. blueness** *n*

blue baby *n* a baby born with a bluish tinge to the skin because of lack of oxygen in the blood.

bluebell *n* a woodland plant with blue bell-shaped flowers.

THESAURUS

grace, fault, flaw, scar, smirch, spot, stain, taint *~vb.* **3.** bespatter, disfigure, disgrace, mark, smirch, smudge, spoil, spot, stain, sully, tarnish **4.** absorb, dry, soak up, take up **5. blot out** cancel, darken, destroy, efface, erase, expunge, obliterate, obscure, shadow

blow[1] *vb.* **1.** flow, rush, stream, whirl **2.** bear, buffet, drive, fling, flutter, sweep, waft, whirl, whisk **3.** blast, breathe, exhale, fan, pant, puff, waft **4.** blare, mouth, pipe, play, sound, toot, trumpet, vibrate **5. blow one's top** *informal* blow up (*informal*), do one's nut (*Brit. slang*), explode, fly into a temper, fly off the handle (*informal*), go spare (*Brit. slang*), have a fit (*informal*), lose one's temper, see red (*informal*), throw a tantrum *~n.* **6.** blast, draught, flurry, gale, gust, puff, strong breeze, tempest, wind

blow[2] *n.* **1.** bang, bash (*informal*), belt (*informal*), buffet, clomp (*slang*), clout (*informal*), clump (*slang*), knock, punch, rap, slosh (*Brit. slang*), smack, sock (*slang*), stroke, thump, wallop (*informal*), whack **2.** *figurative* affliction, bolt from the blue, bombshell, calamity, catastrophe, comedown (*informal*), disappointment, disaster, jolt, misfortune, reverse, setback, shock, upset

blow out 1. extinguish, put out, snuff **2.** burst, erupt, explode, rupture, shatter

blow over be forgotten, cease, die down, disappear, end, finish, pass, pass away, subside, vanish

blow up 1. bloat, distend, enlarge, expand, fill, inflate, puff up, pump up, swell **2.** blast, bomb, burst, detonate, dynamite, explode, go off, rupture, shatter **3.** enlarge, enlarge on, exaggerate, heighten, magnify, overstate **4.** *informal* become angry, become enraged, blow a fuse (*slang, chiefly U.S.*), crack up (*informal*), erupt, fly off the handle (*informal*), go off the deep end (*informal*), go up the wall (*slang*), hit the roof (*informal*), lose one's temper, rage, see red (*informal*)

bludgeon *n.* **1.** club, cosh (*Brit.*), cudgel, shillelagh, truncheon *~vb.* **2.** beat, beat up, club, cosh (*Brit.*), cudgel, knock down, strike **3.** browbeat, bulldoze (*informal*), bully, coerce, dragoon, force, hector, railroad (*informal*), steamroller

blue 1. azure, cobalt, navy, sapphire, sky-coloured, ultramarine **2.** *figurative* dejected, depressed, despondent, dismal, downcast, down-hearted, down in the dumps (*informal*), fed up, gloomy, glum, low, mel-

blueberry *n, pl* **-ries** a very small blackish edible fruit that grows on a North American shrub.
bluebird *n* a North American songbird with a blue plumage.
blue blood *n* royal or aristocratic descent.
bluebook *n* **1** (in Britain) a government publication, usually the report of a commission. **2** (in Canada) an annual statement of government accounts.
bluebottle *n* **1** a large fly with a dark-blue body; blowfly. **2** *Austral & NZ informal* a Portuguese man-of-war.
blue cheese *n* cheese containing a blue mould, such as Stilton or Danish blue.
blue chip *n* **1** *Finance* a stock considered reliable. *~adj* **blue-chip 2** denoting something considered to be a valuable asset.
blue-collar *adj* denoting manual industrial workers.
blue-eyed boy *n Informal, chiefly Brit* a favourite.
blue funk *n Slang* a state of great terror.
blue pencil *n* **1** deletion or alteration of the contents of a book or other work. *~vb* **blue-pencil, -cilling, -cilled** *or US* **-ciling, -ciled 2** to alter or delete parts of (a book, film, etc.).
blue peter *n* a signal flag of blue with a white square at the centre, displayed by a vessel about to leave port.
blueprint *n* **1** an original description of a plan or idea that explains how it is expected to work. **2** a photographic print of plans, technical drawings, etc. consisting of white lines on a blue background.
blue ribbon *n* **1** a badge awarded as the first prize in a competition. **2** (in Britain) a badge of blue silk worn by members of the Order of the Garter.
blues *pl n* **the blues 1** a feeling of depression or deep unhappiness. **2** a type of folk song originating among Black Americans.
bluestocking *n Usually disparaging* a scholarly or intellectual woman.
bluetit *n* a small European bird with a blue crown, wings, and tail and yellow underparts.
blue whale *n* a very large bluish-grey whale: the largest mammal.
bluff[1] *vb* **1** to pretend to be confident in order to influence (someone). *~n* **2** deliberate deception to create the impression of a strong position. **3 call someone's bluff** to challenge someone to give proof of his or her claims.
bluff[2] *n* **1** a steep promontory, bank, or cliff. **2** *Canad* a clump of trees on the prairie; copse. *~adj* **3** good-naturedly frank and hearty.
bluish *or* **blueish** *adj* slightly blue.
blunder *n* **1** a stupid or clumsy mistake. *~vb* **2** to make stupid or clumsy mistakes. **3** to act clumsily; stumble. **blundering** *n, adj*
blunderbuss *n* an obsolete gun with wide barrel and flared muzzle.
blunt *adj* **1** (esp. of a knife) lacking sharpness. **2** not having a sharp edge or point: *a blunt instrument.* **3** (of people, manner of speaking, etc.) straightforward and uncomplicated. *~vb* **4** to make less sharp. **5** to diminish the sensitivity or perception of: *prison life has blunted his mind.* **bluntly** *adv*
blur *vb* **blurring, blurred 1** to make or become vague or less distinct. **2** to smear or smudge. **3** to make (the judgment, memory, or perception) less clear; dim. *~n* **4** something vague, hazy, or indistinct. **5** a smear or smudge. **blurred** *adj* **blurry** *adj*
blurb *n* a promotional description, such as on the jackets of books.
blurt *vb* (foll. by *out*) to utter suddenly and involuntarily.
blush *vb* **1** to become suddenly red in the face, esp. from embarrassment or shame. *~n* **2** a sudden reddening of the face, esp. from embarrassment or shame. **3** a rosy glow. **4** same as **rosé.**
blusher *n* a cosmetic applied to the cheeks to give a rosy colour.
bluster *vb* **1** to speak loudly or in a bullying way. **2** (of the wind) to be gusty. *~n* **3** empty threats or protests. **blustery** *adj*
BM 1 Bachelor of Medicine. **2** British Museum.
BMA British Medical Association.
B-movie *n* a film originally made as a supporting film, now considered a genre in its own right.
BMus Bachelor of Music.
BMX *n* **1** bicycle motocross: stunt riding over an obstacle course on a bicycle. **2** a bicycle designed for bicycle motocross.
BO 1 *Informal* body odour. **2** box office.
boa *n* **1** a large nonvenomous snake of Central and South America that kills its prey by constriction. **2** a woman's long thin scarf of feathers or fur.
boa constrictor *n* a very large snake of tropical

THESAURUS

ancholy, sad, unhappy **3.** *informal* bawdy, dirty, indecent, lewd, naughty, near the knuckle (*informal*), obscene, risqué, smutty, vulgar
blueprint design, draft, layout, norm, outline, pattern, pilot scheme, plan, project, prototype, scheme, sketch
blues dejection, depression, despondency, doldrums, dumps (*informal*), gloom, gloominess, glumness, low spirits, melancholy, moodiness, the hump (*Brit. informal*)
bluff 1. *vb.* deceive, defraud, delude, fake, feign, humbug, lie, mislead, pretend, sham **2.** *n.* bluster, boast, bragging, bravado, deceit, deception, fake, feint, fraud, humbug, idle boast, lie, mere show, pretence, sham, show, subterfuge
blunder *n.* **1.** bloomer (*Brit. informal*), boob (*Brit. slang*), clanger (*informal*), error, fault, faux pas, gaffe, howler (*informal*), impropriety, inaccuracy, indiscretion, mistake, oversight, slip, slip-up (*informal*) *~vb.* **2.** bodge (*informal*), botch, bungle, err, slip up (*informal*) **3.** bumble, confuse, flounder, misjudge, stumble
blunt *adj.* **1.** dull, dulled, edgeless, pointless, rounded, unsharpened **2.** *figurative* bluff, brusque, discourteous, downright, explicit, forthright, frank, impolite, outspoken, plain-spoken, rude, straightforward, tactless, trenchant, uncivil, unpolished, upfront (*informal*) *~vb.* **3.** dampen, deaden, dull, numb, soften, take the edge off, water down, weaken
blur *vb.* **1.** cloud, darken, dim, fog, make hazy, make indistinct, make vague, mask, obscure, soften **2.** blot, smear, smudge, spot, stain *~n.* **3.** blear, blurredness, cloudiness, confusion, dimness, fog, haze, indistinctness, obscurity **4.** blot, smear, smudge, spot, stain
blurred bleary, blurry, faint, foggy, fuzzy, hazy, ill-defined, indistinct, lacking definition, misty, nebulous, out of focus, unclear, vague
blurt out babble, blab, cry, disclose, exclaim, gush, reveal, run off at the mouth (*slang*), spill, spill one's guts (*slang*), spill the beans (*informal*), spout (*informal*), sputter, tattle, tell all, utter suddenly
blush 1. *vb.* colour, crimson, flush, redden, turn red, turn scarlet **2.** *n.* colour, flush, glow, pink tinge, reddening, rosiness, rosy tint, ruddiness
bluster 1. *vb.* boast, brag, bulldoze, bully, domineer, hector, rant, roar, storm, swagger, swell, vaunt **2.** *n.* bluff, boasting, boisterousness, bombast, bragging, bravado, crowing, swagger, swaggering

America and the West Indies that kills its prey by constriction.

boar *n* **1** an uncastrated male pig. **2** a wild pig.

board *n* **1** a long wide flat piece of sawn timber. **2** a smaller flat piece of rigid material for a specific purpose: *ironing board.* **3 a** a group of people who officially administer a company, trust, etc. **b** any other official group, such as examiners or interviewers. **4** a person's meals, provided regularly for money. **5** stiff cardboard or similar material, used for the outside covers of a book. **6** a flat thin rectangular sheet of composite material, such as chipboard. **7** *Naut* the side of a ship. **8** a portable surface for indoor games such as chess or backgammon. **9 go by the board** *Informal* to be in disuse, neglected, or lost. **10 on board** on or in a ship, aeroplane, etc. **11 the boards** the stage. ~*vb* **12** to go aboard (a train or other vehicle). **13** to attack (a ship) by forcing one's way aboard. **14** (foll. by *up, in,* etc.) to cover with boards. **15** to receive meals and lodging in return for money. **16 board out** to arrange for (someone, esp. a child) to receive food and lodging away from home. **17** (in ice hockey and box lacrosse) to bodycheck an opponent against the boards. ~See also **boards.**

boarder *n* a pupil who lives at school during term time.

boarding *n* **1** the act of embarking on an aircraft, train, ship, etc. **2** a structure of boards. **3** timber boards collectively. **4** (in ice hockey and box lacrosse) an act of bodychecking an opponent against the boards.

boarding house *n* a private house that provides accommodation and meals for paying guests.

boarding school *n* a school providing living accommodation for pupils.

boardroom *n* a room where the board of directors of a company meets.

boards *pl n* a wooden wall forming the enclosure in which ice hockey or box lacrosse is played.

boast *vb* **1** to speak in excessively proud terms of one's possessions, talents, etc. **2** to possess (something to be proud of): *a team which boasts five current world record holders.* ~*n* **3** a bragging statement. **4** something that is bragged about: *this proved to be a false boast.*

boastful *adj* tending to boast.

boat *n* **1** a small vessel propelled by oars, paddle, sails, or motor. **2** *Informal* a ship. **3** See **gravy boat, sauce boat. 4 in the same boat** sharing the same problems. **5 miss the boat** to lose an opportunity. **6 rock the boat** *Informal* to cause a disturbance in the existing situation. ~*vb* **7** to travel or go in a boat, esp. as recreation.

boater *n* a stiff straw hat with a straight brim and flat crown.

boathouse *n* a shelter by the edge of a river, lake, etc., for housing boats.

boating *n* rowing, sailing, or cruising in boats as a form of recreation.

boatman *n, pl* **-men** a man who works on, hires out, or repairs boats.

boatswain (**boh**-sn) *n Naut* same as **bosun.**

boat train *n* a train scheduled to take passengers to or from a particular ship.

bob[1] *vb* **bobbing, bobbed 1** to move or cause to move up and down repeatedly, such as while floating in water. **2** to move or cause to move with a short abrupt movement, esp. of the head. **3 bob up** to appear or emerge suddenly. ~*n* **4** a short abrupt movement, as of the head.

bob[2] *n* **1** a hairstyle in which the hair is cut short evenly all round the head. **2** a dangling weight on a pendulum or plumb line. ~*vb* **bobbing, bobbed 3** to cut (the hair) in a bob.

bob[3] *n, pl* **bob** *Brit informal* (formerly) a shilling.

bobbejaan *n S African* **1** a baboon. **2** a large black spider. **3** a monkey wrench.

bobbin *n* a reel on which thread or yarn is wound.

bobble *n* a tufted ball, usually woollen, that is used for decoration.

bobby *n, pl* **-bies** *Informal* a British policeman.

bobby pin *n US, Canad, Austral, & NZ* a metal hairpin.

bobotie (ba-**boot**-ee) *n S African* a traditional Cape dish of curried minced meat.

bobsleigh *n* **1** a sledge for racing down a steeply banked ice-covered run. ~*vb* **2** to ride on a bobsleigh.

bobtail *n* **1** a docked tail. **2** an animal with such a tail. ~*adj also* **bobtailed 3** having the tail cut short.

Boche (**bosh**) *n Offensive slang* a German, esp. a German soldier.

bod *n Informal* a person: *he's a queer bod.*

bode[1] *vb* **boding, boded** to be an omen of (good or ill); portend.

bode[2] *vb* a past tense of **bide.**

bodega *n* a shop in a Spanish-speaking country that sells wine.

bodge *vb* **bodging, bodged** *Informal* to make a mess of; botch.

bodice *n* **1** the upper part of a woman's dress, from the shoulder to the waist. **2** a tight-fitting corset worn laced over a blouse, or (formerly) as a woman's undergarment.

bodily *adj* **1** relating to the human body. ~*adv* **2** by taking hold of the body: *he threw him bodily from the platform.* **3** in person; in the flesh.

bodkin *n* a blunt large-eyed needle.

body *n, pl* **bodies 1** the entire physical structure of an animal or human. **2** the trunk or torso. **3** a corpse. **4** a group regarded as a single entity: *a local voluntary body.* **5** the main part of anything: *the body of a car.* **6** a separate mass of water or land. **7** the flesh as opposed to the spirit. **8** the characteristic full quality of

THESAURUS

blustery blusterous, boisterous, gusty, inclement, squally, stormy, tempestuous, violent, wild

board *n.* **1.** panel, piece of timber, plank, slat, timber **2.** advisers, advisory group, committee, conclave, council, directorate, directors, panel, trustees **3.** daily meals, food, meals, provisions, victuals ~*vb.* **4.** embark, embus, enplane, enter, entrain, mount **5.** accommodate, feed, house, lodge, put up, quarter, room

boast *vb.* **1.** blow one's own trumpet, bluster, brag, crow, exaggerate, puff, strut, swagger, talk big (*slang*), vaunt **2.** be proud of, congratulate oneself on, exhibit, flatter oneself, possess, pride oneself on, show off ~*n.* **3.** avowal, brag, rodomontade (*literary*), swank (*informal*), vaunt **4.** gem, joy, pride, pride and joy, source of pride, treasure

boastful bragging, cocky, conceited, crowing, egotistical, puffed-up, swaggering, swanky (*informal*), swollen-headed, vainglorious, vaunting

bob bounce, duck, hop, jerk, leap, nod, oscillate, quiver, skip, waggle, weave, wobble

bode augur, betoken, foreshadow, foretell (*literary*), forewarn, impart, omen, portend, predict, presage, prophesy, signify, threaten

bodily 1. *adj.* actual, carnal, corporal, corporeal, fleshly, material, physical, substantial, tangible **2.** *adv.*

certain wines. **9** *Informal* a person: *all the important bodies from the council were present.* **10** a woman's one-piece undergarment. **11 keep body and soul together** to manage to survive.

body building *n* regular exercising designed to enlarge the muscles.

bodycheck *Ice hockey etc ~n* **1** obstruction of another player. *~vb* **2** to deliver a bodycheck to (an opponent).

bodyguard *n* a person or group of people employed to protect someone.

body language *n* the communication of one's thoughts or feelings by the position or movements of one's body rather than by words.

body politic *n* **the body politic** the people of a nation or the nation itself considered as a political entity.

body shop *n* a repair yard for vehicle bodywork.

body snatcher *n* (formerly) a person who robbed graves and sold the corpses for dissection.

body stocking *n* **1** a one-piece undergarment for women, covering the torso. **2** a tightly-fitting garment covering the whole of the body, worn esp. for dancing or exercising.

body warmer *n* a sleeveless quilted jerkin, worn as an outer garment.

bodywork *n* the external shell of a motor vehicle.

Boer *n* a descendant of any of the Dutch or Huguenot colonists who settled in South Africa.

boerbul (**boor**-bl) *n S African* a crossbred mastiff, often used as a watchdog.

boere- *combining form S African* rustic or country-style.

boerekos (**boor**-a-koss) *n S African* traditional Afrikaner food.

boeremeisie (**boor**-a-may-see) *n S African* a country girl of Afrikaans stock.

boereseun (**boor**-a-see-oon) *n S African* a country boy of Afrikaans stock.

boerewors (**boor**-a-vorss) *n S African* a traditional home-made farmer's sausage.

boffin *n Brit informal* a scientist.

bog *n* **1** a wet spongy area of land. **2** *Slang* a toilet. **boggy** *adj* **bogginess** *n*

bog down *vb* **bogging, bogged** to impede physically or mentally.

bogey *or* **bogy** *n* **1** an evil or mischievous spirit. **2** something that worries or annoys. **3** *Golf* **a** a score of one stroke over par on a hole. **b** *Old-fashioned* a standard score for a hole or course. **4** *Slang* a piece of dried mucus from the nose.

bogeyman *n, pl* **-men** a frightening person, real or imaginary, used as a threat, esp. to children.

boggle *vb* **-gling, -gled** **1** to be surprised, confused, or alarmed: *the mind boggles.* **2** to hesitate or be evasive when confronted with a problem.

bogie *or* **bogy** *n* an assembly of wheels forming a pivoted support at either end of a railway coach.

bog-standard *adj Brit & Irish slang* completely ordinary; run-of-the-mill.

bogus (**boh**-guss) *adj* not genuine.

bogy *n, pl* **-gies** same as **bogey** or **bogie.**

bohemian *n* **1** a person, esp. an artist or writer, who lives an unconventional life. *~adj* **2** unconventional in appearance, behaviour, etc. **Bohemianism** *n*

boil[1] *vb* **1** to change or cause to change from a liquid to a vapour so rapidly that bubbles of vapour are formed in the liquid. **2** to reach or cause to reach boiling point. **3** to cook or be cooked by the process of boiling. **4** to bubble and be agitated like something boiling: *the sea was boiling.* **5** to be extremely angry. *~n* **6** the state or action of boiling. ~See also **boil away, boil down, boil over.**

boil[2] *n* a red painful swelling with a hard pus-filled core caused by infection of the skin.

boil away *vb* to cause (liquid) to evaporate completely by boiling or (of liquid) to evaporate completely.

boil down *vb* **1** to reduce or be reduced in quantity by boiling. **2 boil down to** to be the essential element in.

boiler *n* **1** a closed vessel in which water is heated to provide steam to drive machinery. **2** a domestic device to provide hot water, esp. for central heating.

boilermaker *n* a person who works with metal in heavy industry.

boiler suit *n Brit* a one-piece overall.

boiling point *n* **1** the temperature at which a liquid boils. **2** *Informal* the condition of being angered or highly excited.

boil over *vb* **1** to overflow or cause to overflow while boiling. **2** to burst out in anger or excitement.

boisterous *adj* **1** noisy and lively; unruly. **2** (of the sea, etc.) turbulent or stormy.

bold *adj* **1** courageous, confident, and fearless. **2** im-

THESAURUS

altogether, as a body, as a group, collectively, completely, en masse, entirely, fully, totally, wholly

body **1.** build, figure, form, frame, physique, shape, torso, trunk **2.** cadaver (*Medical*), carcass, corpse, dead body, relics, remains, stiff (*slang*) **3.** association, band, bloc, collection, company, confederation, congress, corporation, society **4.** bulk, essence, main part, mass, material, matter, substance **5.** being, creature, human, human being, individual, mortal, person **6.** consistency, density, firmness, richness, solidity, substance

bog fen, marsh, marshland, mire, morass, moss (*Scot. & Northern English dialect*), peat bog, quagmire, slough, swamp, wetland

bog down delay, halt, impede, sink, slow down, slow up, stall, stick

bogey, bogy **1.** apparition, bogeyman, goblin, hobgoblin, imp, spectre, spirit, spook (*informal*), sprite **2.** *bête noire,* bugbear, nightmare

boggle **1.** be alarmed (confused, surprised, taken aback), shy, stagger, startle, take fright **2.** demur, dither (*chiefly Brit.*), doubt, equivocate, falter, hang back, hesitate, hover, jib, shillyshally (*informal*), shrink from, vacillate, waver

boggy fenny, marshy, miry, muddy, oozy, quaggy, soft, spongy, swampy, waterlogged, yielding

bogus artificial, counterfeit, dummy, ersatz, fake, false, forged, fraudulent, imitation, phoney *or* phony (*informal*), pseudo (*informal*), sham, spurious

bohemian **1.** *n.* beatnik, dropout, hippie, iconoclast, nonconformist **2.** *adj.* alternative, artistic, arty (*informal*), avant-garde, eccentric, exotic, nonconformist, oddball (*informal*), offbeat, off-the-wall (*slang*), outré, unconventional, unorthodox, way-out (*informal*)

boil[1] *vb.* **1.** agitate, bubble, churn, effervesce, fizz, foam, froth, seethe **2.** be angry, be indignant, blow a fuse (*slang, chiefly U.S.*), crack up (*informal*), fly off the handle (*informal*), foam at the mouth (*informal*), fulminate, fume, go off the deep end (*informal*), go up the wall (*slang*), rage, rave, see red (*informal*), storm

boil[2] *n.* blain, blister, carbuncle, pustule, tumour, ulcer

boisterous **1.** bouncy, clamorous, disorderly, impetuous, loud, noisy, obstreperous, riotous, rollicking, rowdy, rumbustious, unrestrained, unruly, uproarious,

modest or impudent: *she gave him a bold look.* **3** standing out distinctly; conspicuous: *a figure carved in bold relief.* **boldly** *adv* **boldness** *n*

bole *n* the trunk of a tree.

bolero *n, pl* **-ros 1** a Spanish dance, usually in triple time. **2** music for this dance. **3** a short open jacket not reaching the waist.

boll *n* the rounded seed capsule of flax, cotton, etc.

bollard *n* **1** *Brit* a small post marking a kerb or traffic island or barring cars from entering. **2** a strong wooden or metal post on a wharf, quay, etc., used for securing mooring lines.

bollocks *or* **ballocks** *Taboo slang ~pl n* **1** the testicles. *~n* **2** nonsense; rubbish. *~interj* **3** an exclamation of annoyance, disbelief, etc.

Bolshevik *n* **1** (formerly) a Russian Communist. **2** any Communist. **3** *Informal, offensive* any political radical, esp. a revolutionary. **Bolshevism** *n* **Bolshevist** *adj, n*

bolshie *or* **bolshy** *Brit informal ~adj* **1** difficult to manage; rebellious. **2** politically radical or left-wing. *~n, pl* **-shies 3** any political radical.

bolster *vb* **1** to support or strengthen: *the government were unwilling to bolster sterling. ~n* **2** a long narrow pillow. **3** any pad or support.

bolt[1] *n* **1** a bar that can be slid into a socket to lock a door, gate, etc. **2** a metal rod or pin that has a head and a screw thread to take a nut. **3** a flash (of lightning). **4** a sudden movement, esp. in order to escape. **5** an arrow, esp. for a crossbow. **6 a bolt from the blue** a sudden, unexpected, and usually unwelcome event. **7 shoot one's bolt** to exhaust one's efforts. *~vb* **8** to run away suddenly. **9** to secure or lock with or as if with a bolt. **10** to attach firmly one thing to another by means of a nut and bolt. **11** to eat hurriedly: *bolting your food may lead to indigestion.* **12** (of a horse) to run away without control. **13** (of vegetables) to produce flowers and seeds too soon. *~adv* **14 bolt upright** stiff and rigid.

bolt[2] *or* **boult** *vb* **1** to pass (flour, a powder, etc.) through a sieve. **2** to examine and separate.

bolt hole *n* a place of escape.

bomb *n* **1** a hollow projectile containing explosive, incendiary, or other destructive substance. **2** an object in which an explosive device has been planted: *a car bomb.* **3** *Brit slang* a large sum of money: *it cost a bomb.* **4** *US & Canad slang* a disastrous failure: *the new play was a total bomb.* **5 like a bomb** *Brit & NZ informal* with great speed or success. **6 the bomb** a hydrogen or an atom bomb considered as the ultimate destructive weapon. *~vb* **7** to attack with a bomb or bombs; drop bombs (on). **8** (foll. by *along*) *Informal* to move or drive very quickly. **9** *US & Canad slang* to fail disastrously. **bombing** *n*

bombard *vb* **1** to attack with concentrated artillery fire or bombs. **2** to attack persistently. **3** to attack verbally, esp. with questions. **4** *Physics* to direct high-energy particles or photons against (atoms, nuclei, etc.). **bombardment** *n*

bombardier *n* **1** *Brit* a noncommissioned rank in the Royal Artillery. **2** *US* the member of a bomber aircrew who releases the bombs. **3** *Canad trademark* a snow tractor, usually having caterpillar tracks at the rear and skis at the front.

bombast *n* pompous and flowery language. **bombastic** *adj*

Bombay duck *n* a fish that is eaten dried with curry dishes as a savoury.

bombazine *n* a twill fabric, usually of silk and worsted, formerly worn dyed black for mourning.

bomber *n* **1** a military aircraft designed to carry out bombing missions. **2** a person who plants bombs.

bombshell *n* a shocking or unwelcome surprise.

bona fide (bone-a **fide**-ee) *adj* **1** genuine: *a bona fide manuscript.* **2** undertaken in good faith: *a bona fide agreement.*

bonanza *n* **1** sudden and unexpected luck or wealth. **2** *US & Canad* a mine or vein rich in ore.

bonbon *n* a sweet.

bond *n* **1** something that binds, fastens, or holds together. **2** something that brings or holds people together; tie: *a bond of friendship.* **3 bonds** something that restrains or imprisons. **4** a written or spoken agreement, esp. a promise: *a marriage bond.* **5** *Chem* a means by which atoms are combined in a molecule. **6** *Finance* a certificate of debt issued in order to raise funds. **7** *Law* a written acknowledgment of an obligation to pay a sum or to perform a contract. **8 in bond** *Commerce* securely stored until duty is paid. *~vb* **9** to hold or be held together; bind. **10** to put or hold (goods) in bond.

bondage *n* **1** slavery. **2** subjection to some influence or duty. **3** a sexual practice in which one partner is tied or chained up.

bonded *adj* **1** *Finance* consisting of, secured by, or operating under a bond or bonds. **2** *Commerce* in bond.

bond paper *n* superior quality writing paper.

bondservant *n* a serf or slave.

bone *n* **1** any of the various structures that make up

THESAURUS

vociferous, wild **2.** blustery, gusty, raging, rough, squally, stormy, tempestuous, tumultuous, turbulent

bold 1. adventurous, audacious, brave, courageous, daring, dauntless, enterprising, fearless, gallant, gritty, heroic, intrepid, lion-hearted, valiant, valorous **2.** barefaced, brash, brazen, cheeky, confident, feisty (*informal, chiefly U.S. & Canad.*), forward, fresh (*informal*), impudent, insolent, pert, pushy (*informal*), rude, saucy, shameless **3.** bright, colourful, conspicuous, eye-catching, flashy, forceful, lively, loud, prominent, pronounced, showy, spirited, striking, strong, vivid

bolster aid, assist, augment, boost, brace, buoy up, buttress, cushion, help, hold up, maintain, pillow, prop, reinforce, shore up, stay, strengthen, support

bolt *n.* **1.** bar, catch, fastener, latch, lock, sliding bar **2.** peg, pin, rivet, rod **3.** bound, dart, dash, escape, flight, rush, spring, sprint **4.** arrow, dart, missile, projectile, shaft, thunderbolt *~vb.* **5.** abscond, bound, dash, decamp, do a runner (*slang*), escape, flee, fly, fly the coop (*U.S. & Canad. informal*), hurtle, jump, leap, make a break (for it), run, run for it, rush, skedaddle (*informal*), spring, sprint **6.** bar, fasten, latch, lock, secure **7.** cram, devour, gobble, gorge, gulp, guzzle, stuff, swallow whole, wolf

bomb 1. *n.* bombshell, charge, device, explosive, grenade, mine, missile, projectile, rocket, shell, torpedo **2.** *vb.* attack, blow up, bombard, destroy, shell, strafe, torpedo

bombard 1. assault, blast, blitz, bomb, cannonade, fire upon, open fire, pound, shell, strafe **2.** assail, attack, barrage, batter, beset, besiege, harass, hound, pester

bombardment assault, attack, barrage, blitz, bombing, cannonade, fire, flak, fusillade, shelling, strafe

bona fide actual, authentic, genuine, honest, kosher (*informal*), lawful, legal, legitimate, real, true

bond *n.* **1.** band, binding, chain, cord, fastening, fetter, ligature, link, manacle, shackle, tie **2.** affiliation, affinity, attachment, connection, link, relation, tie, union **3.** agreement, compact, contract, covenant,

the skeleton in most vertebrates. **2** the porous rigid tissue of which these parts are made. **3** something consisting of bone or a bonelike substance. **4 bones** the human skeleton. **5** a thin strip of plastic, etc. used to stiffen corsets and brassieres. **6 have a bone to pick** to have grounds for a quarrel. **7 make no bones about a** to be direct and candid about. **b** to have no scruples about. **8 near** *or* **close to the bone** risqué or indecent. **9 the bare bones** the essentials. ~*vb* **boning, boned 10** to remove the bones from (meat for cooking, etc.). **11** to stiffen (a corset, etc.) by inserting bones. ~See also **bone up on. boneless** *adj*

bone china *n* porcelain containing powdered bone.

bone-dry *adj Informal* completely dry.

bone-idle *adj* extremely lazy.

bone meal *n* dried and ground animal bones, used as a fertilizer or in stock feeds.

boneshaker *n Slang* a decrepit or rickety vehicle.

bone up on *vb Informal* to study intensively.

bonfire *n* a large outdoor fire.

bongo *n, pl* **-gos** *or* **-goes** a small bucket-shaped drum, usually one of a pair, played by beating with the fingers.

bonhomie (bon-om-**mee**) *n* exuberant friendliness.

bonk *vb Informal* **1** to have sexual intercourse. **2** to hit. **bonking** *n*

bonkers *adj Slang, chiefly Brit* mad; crazy.

bon mot (bon **moh**) *n, pl* **bons mots** a clever and fitting remark.

bonnet *n* **1** *Brit, Austral, NZ, & S African* the hinged metal cover over a motor vehicle's engine. **2** any of various hats tied with ribbons under the chin. **3** (in Scotland) a soft cloth cap.

bonny *adj* **-nier, -niest 1** *Scot & N English dialect* beautiful: *a bonny lass.* **2** good or fine.

bonsai *n, pl* **-sai** an ornamental tree or shrub grown in a small shallow pot in order to stunt its growth.

bonsela (bon-**sell**-a) *n S African informal* a small gift of money.

bonus *n* something given, paid, or received above what is due or expected.

bon voyage *interj* a phrase used to wish a traveller a pleasant journey.

bony *adj* **bonier, boniest 1** resembling or consisting of bone. **2** thin. **3** having many bones.

boo *interj* **1** a shout uttered to express dissatisfaction or contempt. **2** an exclamation uttered to startle someone. ~*vb* **booing, booed 3** to shout "boo" at (someone or something) as an expression of disapproval.

boob *Slang* ~*n* **1** *Brit* an embarrassing mistake; blunder. **2** a female breast. ~*vb* **3** *Brit* to make a blunder.

booby *n, pl* **-bies 1** an ignorant or foolish person. **2** a tropical marine bird related to the gannet.

booby prize *n* a mock prize given to the person with the lowest score in a competition.

booby trap *n* **1** a hidden explosive device primed so as to be set off by an unsuspecting victim. **2** a trap for an unsuspecting person, esp. one intended as a practical joke.

boodle *n Slang* money or valuables, esp. when stolen, counterfeit, or used as a bribe.

boogie *vb* **-gieing, -gied** *Slang* to dance to fast pop music.

boogie-woogie *n* a style of piano jazz using blues harmonies.

boohai *n* **up the boohai** *NZ informal* thoroughly lost.

boohoo *vb* **-hooing, -hooed 1** to sob or pretend to sob noisily. ~*n, pl* **-hoos 2** distressed or pretended sobbing.

book *n* **1** a number of printed pages bound together along one edge and protected by covers. **2** a written work or composition, such as a novel. **3** a number of sheets of paper bound together: *an account book.* **4 books** a record of the transactions of a business or society. **5** the libretto of an opera or musical. **6** a major division of a written composition, such as of a long novel or of the Bible. **7** a number of tickets, stamps, etc. fastened together along one edge. **8** a record of betting transactions. **9 a closed book** a subject that is beyond comprehension: *art remains a closed book to him.* **10 bring to book** to reprimand or require (someone) to give an explanation of his or her conduct. **11 by the book** according to the rules. **12 in someone's good** *or* **bad books** regarded by someone with favour (*or* disfavour). **13 throw the book at someone a** to charge someone with every relevant offence. **b** to inflict the most severe punishment on someone. ~*vb* **14** to reserve (a place, passage, etc.) or engage the services of (someone) in advance. **15** (of a police officer) to take the name and address of (a person) for an alleged offence with a view to prosecution. **16** (of a football referee) to take the name of (a player) who has broken the rules seriously. ~See also **book in.**

bookcase *n* a piece of furniture containing shelves for books.

book club *n* a club that sells books at low prices to members, usually by mail order.

book end *n* one of a pair of supports for holding a row of books upright.

bookie *n Informal* short for **bookmaker.**

book in *vb Chiefly Brit* to register one's arrival at a hotel.

booking *n* **1** *Chiefly Brit* a reservation, as of a table or seat. **2** *Theatre* an engagement of a performer.

bookish *adj* **1** fond of reading; studious. **2** forming opinions through reading rather than experience.

book-keeping *n* the skill or occupation of systematically recording business transactions. **book-keeper** *n*

booklet *n* a thin book with paper covers.

bookmaker *n* a person who as an occupation accepts bets, esp. on horse racing. **bookmaking** *n*

bookmark *n* a strip of some material put between the pages of a book to mark a place.

bookstall *n* a stall or stand where periodicals, newspapers, or books are sold.

bookworm *n* **1** a person devoted to reading. **2** a small insect that feeds on the binding paste of books.

Boolean algebra (**boo**-lee-an) *n* a system of sym-

THESAURUS

guarantee, obligation, pledge, promise, word ~*vb.* **4.** bind, connect, fasten, fix together, fuse, glue, gum, paste

bonny 1. beautiful, fair, handsome, lovely, pretty, sweet **2.** bouncing, buxom, chubby, fine, plump, rounded, shapely

bonus benefit, bounty, commission, dividend, extra, gift, gratuity, hand-out, honorarium, icing on the cake, perk (*Brit. informal*), plus, premium, prize, reward

bony angular, emaciated, gangling, gaunt, lanky, lean, rawboned, scrawny, skinny, thin

book *n.* **1.** hardback, manual, paperback, publication, roll, scroll, textbook, title, tome, tract, volume, work **2.** album, diary, exercise book, jotter, notebook, pad ~*vb.* **3.** arrange for, bill, charter, engage, line up, make reservations, organize, procure, programme, reserve, schedule **4.** enrol, enter, insert, list, log, mark down, note, post, put down, record, register, write down

bolic logic devised to codify nonmathematical logical operations: used in computers.

boom[1] *vb* **1** to make a loud deep echoing sound. **2** to prosper vigorously and rapidly: *business boomed.* ~*n* **3** a loud deep echoing sound. **4** a period of high economic growth.

boom[2] *n* **1** *Naut* a spar to which the foot of a sail is fastened to control its position. **2** a pole carrying an overhead microphone and projected over a film or television set. **3** a barrier across a waterway.

boomerang *n* **1** a curved wooden missile of Australian Aborigines which can be made to return to the thrower. **2** an action or statement that recoils on its originator. ~*vb* **3** (of a plan) to recoil unexpectedly, harming its originator.

boomslang *n* a large greenish venomous tree-living snake of southern Africa.

boon[1] *n* something extremely useful, helpful, or beneficial.

boon[2] *adj* close or intimate: *boon companion.*

boor *n* an ill-mannered, clumsy, or insensitive person. **boorish** *adj*

boost *n* **1** encouragement or help: *a boost to morale.* **2** an upward thrust or push. **3** an increase or rise. ~*vb* **4** to encourage or improve: *to boost morale.* **5** to cause to rise; increase: *we significantly boosted our market share.* **6** to advertise on a big scale.

booster *n* **1** a supplementary injection of a vaccine given to ensure that the first injection will remain effective. **2** a radio-frequency amplifier to strengthen signals. **3** the first stage of a multistage rocket.

boot[1] *n* **1** an outer covering for the foot that extends above the ankle. **2** *Brit, Austral, NZ, & S African* an enclosed compartment of a car for holding luggage. **3** *Informal* a kick: *he gave the door a boot.* **4 lick someone's boots** to behave flatteringly towards someone. **5 put the boot in** *Slang* **a** to kick a person when already down. **b** to finish something off with unnecessary brutality. **6 the boot** *Slang* dismissal from employment. ~*vb* **7** to kick. **8** to start up (a computer). **9 boot out** *Informal* **a** to eject forcibly. **b** to dismiss from employment.

boot[2] *n* **to boot** as well; in addition.

bootee *n* a soft boot for a baby, esp. a knitted one.

booth *n, pl* **booths 1** a small partially enclosed cubicle. **2** a stall, esp. a temporary one at a fair or market.

bootleg *vb* **-legging, -legged 1** to make, carry, or sell (illicit goods, esp. alcohol). ~*adj* **2** produced, distributed, or sold illicitly. **bootlegger** *n*

bootless *adj* of little or no use; vain; fruitless.

bootlicker *n Informal* one who seeks favour by grovelling to someone in authority.

boot sale *n* a sale of goods from car boots in a car park hired for the occasion.

booty *n, pl* **-ties** any valuable article or articles obtained as plunder.

booze *Informal* ~*n* **1** alcoholic drink. ~*vb* **boozing, boozed 2** to drink alcohol, esp. in excess. **boozy** *adj*

boozer *n Informal* **1** a person who is fond of drinking. **2** *Brit, Austral, & NZ* a bar or pub.

booze-up *n Brit, Austral, & NZ slang* a drinking spree.

bop *n* **1** a form of jazz with complex rhythms and harmonies. ~*vb* **bopping, bopped 2** *Informal* to dance to pop music. **bopper** *n*

boracic *adj* same as **boric.**

borage *n* a Mediterranean plant with star-shaped blue flowers.

borax *n* a white mineral in crystalline form used in making glass, soap, etc.

Bordeaux *n* a red or white wine produced around Bordeaux in SW France.

border *n* **1** the dividing line between political or geographic regions. **2** a band or margin around or along the edge of something. **3** a design around the edge of something. **4** a narrow strip of ground planted with flowers or shrubs: *a herbaceous border.* ~*vb* **5** to provide with a border. **6 a** to be adjacent to; lie along the boundary of. **b** to be nearly the same as; verge on: *a story that borders on the unbelievable.*

borderland *n* **1** land located on or near a boundary. **2** an indeterminate state or condition.

borderline *n* **1** a dividing line. **2** an indeterminate position between two conditions: *the borderline between love and friendship.* ~*adj* **3** on the edge of one category and verging on another: *a borderline failure.*

Borders *pl n* **the Borders** the area straddling the border between England and Scotland.

bore[1] *vb* **boring, bored 1** to produce (a hole) with a drill, etc. **2** to produce (a tunnel, mine shaft, etc.) by drilling. ~*n* **3** a hole or tunnel in the ground drilled in search of minerals, oil, etc. **4 a** the hollow of a gun barrel. **b** the diameter of this hollow; calibre.

bore[2] *vb* **boring, bored 1** to tire or make weary by being dull, repetitious, or uninteresting. ~*n* **2** a dull or repetitious person, activity, or state. **bored** *adj* **boring** *adj*

➤ *Bored* is followed by *with* or *by: ...bored by his conversation; ...bored with reading.* The usage *bored of* is

THESAURUS

bookish academic, donnish, erudite, intellectual, learned, literary, pedantic, scholarly, studious, well-read

boom *vb.* **1.** bang, blast, crash, explode, resound, reverberate, roar, roll, rumble, thunder **2.** develop, expand, flourish, gain, grow, increase, intensify, prosper, spurt, strengthen, succeed, swell, thrive ~*n.* **3.** bang, blast, burst, clap, crash, explosion, roar, rumble, thunder **4.** advance, boost, development, expansion, gain, growth, improvement, increase, jump, push, spurt, upsurge, upswing, upturn

boomerang backfire, come back, come home to roost, rebound, recoil, return, reverse, ricochet

boon[1] advantage, benefaction, benefit, blessing, donation, favour, gift, godsend, grant, gratuity, hand-out, present, windfall

boon[2] close, intimate, special

boorish awkward, barbaric, bearish, churlish, clownish, coarse, crude, gross, gruff, hick (*informal, chiefly U.S. & Canad.*), ill-bred, loutish, lubberly, oafish, rude, rustic, uncivilized, uncouth, uneducated, unrefined, vulgar

boost *n.* **1.** encouragement, help, hype, improvement, praise, promotion **2.** heave, hoist, lift, push, raise, shove, thrust **3.** addition, expansion, improvement, increase, increment, jump, rise ~*vb.* **4.** advance, advertise, assist, crack up (*informal*), encourage, foster, further, hype, improve, inspire, plug (*informal*), praise, promote, support, sustain **5.** elevate, heave, hoist, lift, push, raise, shove, thrust

boot *vb.* **1.** drive, drop-kick, kick, knock, punt, shove **2. boot out** *informal* dismiss, eject, expel, give the bum's rush (*slang*), give the heave *or* push (*informal*), kick out, oust, relegate, sack (*informal*), show one the door, throw out, throw out on one's ear (*informal*)

border *n.* **1.** borderline, boundary, frontier, line, march **2.** bound, boundary, bounds, brim, brink, confine, confines, edge, flange, hem, limit, limits, lip, margin, pale, rim, skirt, verge ~*vb.* **3.** bind, decorate, edge, fringe, hem, rim, trim

not fully accepted.

bore[3] *n* a high wave moving up a narrow estuary, caused by the tide.

bore[4] *vb* the past tense of **bear**[1].

boreal forest (**bore**-ee-al) *n* the forest of northern latitudes, esp. in Scandinavia, Canada, and Siberia, consisting mainly of spruce and pine.

boredom *n* the state of being bored.

boric *adj* of or containing boron.

boric acid *n* a white soluble crystalline solid used as a mild antiseptic.

born *vb* **1** a past participle of **bear**[1] (sense 4). **2 not have been born yesterday** not to be gullible or foolish. *~adj* **3** possessing certain qualities from birth: *a born musician.* **4** being in a particular social status at birth: *ignobly born.*

born-again *adj* **1** having experienced conversion, esp. to evangelical Christianity. **2** showing the enthusiasm of someone newly converted to any cause: *a born-again romantic.*

borne *vb* a past participle of **bear**[1].

boron *n Chem* a hard almost colourless crystalline metalloid element that is used in hardening steel. Symbol: B

borough *n* **1** a town, esp. (in Britain) one that forms the constituency of an MP or that was originally incorporated by royal charter. **2** any of the constituent divisions of Greater London or New York City.

borrow *vb* **1** to obtain (something, such as money) on the understanding that it will be returned to the lender. **2** to adopt (ideas, words, etc.) from another source. **borrower** *n* **borrowing** *n*

➤ *Borrow* is followed by *from: Borrow a pound from Frank.* The use of *borrow* followed by *off of* is nonstandard. Avoid confusing the meanings of *borrow* and *lend.*

borscht *or* **borsch** *n* a Russian soup based on beetroot.

borstal *n* (formerly in Britain) a prison for offenders aged 15 to 21.

borzoi *n* a tall dog with a narrow head and a long coat.

bosh *n Informal* meaningless talk or opinions; nonsense.

Bosnian *adj* **1** from Bosnia. *~n* **2** a person from Bosnia.

bosom *n* **1** the chest or breast of a person, esp. the female breasts. **2** a protective centre or part: *the bosom of the family.* **3** the breast considered as the seat of emotions. *~adj* **4** very dear: *a bosom friend.*

boss[1] *Informal ~n* **1** a person in charge of or employing others. *~vb* **2** to employ, supervise, or be in charge of. **3 boss around** *or* **about** to be domineering or overbearing towards.

boss[2] *n* a raised knob or stud, esp. an ornamental one on a vault, shield, etc.

bossa nova *n* **1** a dance similar to the samba, originating in Brazil. **2** music for this dance.

bossy *adj* **bossier, bossiest** *Informal* domineering, overbearing, or authoritarian. **bossiness** *n*

bosun *or* **boatswain** (**boh**-sn) *n* an officer who is responsible for the maintenance of a ship and its equipment.

bot. **1** botanical. **2** botany.

botany *n, pl* **-nies** the study of plants, including their classification, structure, etc. **botanical** *or* **botanic** *adj* **botanist** *n*

botch *vb* **1** to spoil through clumsiness or ineptitude. **2** to repair badly or clumsily. *~n also* **botch-up** **3** a badly done piece of work or repair.

both *adj* **1** two considered together: *both parents were killed during the war. ~pron* **2** two considered together: *both are to blame. ~conj* **3** not just one but also the other of two (people or things): *both Darren and Keith enjoyed the match.*

➤ After *both* the use of *of* is optional: *both of the boys* or *both (the) boys.*

bother *vb* **1** to take the time or trouble: *don't bother to come with me.* **2** to give annoyance, pain, or trouble to. **3** to trouble (a person) by repeatedly disturbing; pester. *~n* **4** a state of worry, trouble, or confusion. **5** a

THESAURUS

borderline *adj.* ambivalent, doubtful, equivocal, indecisive, indefinite, indeterminate, inexact, marginal, unclassifiable

bore[1] **1.** *vb.* burrow, drill, gouge out, mine, penetrate, perforate, pierce, sink, tunnel **2.** *n.* borehole, calibre, drill hole, hole, shaft, tunnel

bore[2] **1.** *vb.* annoy, be tedious, bother, exhaust, fatigue, jade, pall on, pester, send to sleep, tire, trouble, vex, wear out, weary, worry **2.** *n.* bother, drag (*informal*), dullard, dull person, headache (*informal*), nuisance, pain (*informal*), pain in the arse (*taboo informal*), pain in the neck (*informal*), pest, tiresome person, wearisome talker, yawn (*informal*)

boredom apathy, doldrums, dullness, ennui (*literary*), flatness, irksomeness, monotony, sameness, tediousness, tedium, weariness, world-weariness

boring dead, dull, flat, ho-hum (*informal*), humdrum, insipid, mind-numbing, monotonous, repetitious, routine, stale, tedious, tiresome, tiring, unexciting, uninteresting, unvaried, wearisome

borrow **1.** cadge, mooch (*slang*), scrounge (*informal*), take and return, take on loan, touch (someone) for (*slang*), use temporarily **2.** acquire, adopt, appropriate, copy, filch, imitate, obtain, pilfer, pirate, plagiarize, simulate, steal, take, use, usurp

bosom *n.* **1.** breast, bust, chest **2.** centre, circle, core, midst, protection, shelter **3.** affections, emotions, feelings, heart, sentiments, soul, spirit, sympathies *~adj.* **4.** boon, cherished, close, confidential, intimate, very dear

boss[1] **1.** *n.* administrator, chief, director, employer, executive, foreman, gaffer (*informal, chiefly Brit.*), governor (*informal*), head, kingpin, leader, manager, master, overseer, owner, superintendent, supervisor **2.** *vb.* administrate, command, control, direct, employ, manage, oversee, run, superintend, supervise, take charge

boss[2] knob, nub, nubble, point, protuberance, stud, tip

bossy arrogant, authoritarian, autocratic, despotic, dictatorial, domineering, hectoring, high-handed, imperious, lordly, overbearing, tyrannical

botch **1.** *vb.* balls up (*taboo slang*), blunder, bodge (*informal*), bungle, butcher, cobble, cock up (*Brit. slang*), fuck up (*offensive taboo slang*), fumble, mar, mess, mismanage, muff, patch, screw up (*informal*), spoil **2.** *n.* balls-up (*taboo slang*), blunder, bungle, bungling, cock-up (*Brit. slang*), failure, fuck-up (*offensive taboo slang*), fumble, hash, mess, miscarriage, pig's breakfast (*informal*), pig's ear (*informal*)

bother **1.** *vb.* alarm, annoy, bend someone's ear (*informal*), concern, dismay, distress, disturb, gall, harass, hassle (*informal*), inconvenience, irritate, molest, nag, nark, pester, plague, put out, trouble, upset, vex, worry **2.** *n.* aggravation, annoyance, bustle, difficulty, flurry, fuss, gall, hassle (*informal*), inconvenience, irri-

person or thing that causes fuss, trouble, or annoyance. **6** *Informal* a disturbance or fight: *a spot of bother.* ~*interj* **7** *Chiefly Brit* an exclamation of slight annoyance.

bothersome *adj* causing bother.

bothy *n, pl* **bothies** *Chiefly Scot* **1** a hut used for temporary shelter. **2** (formerly) a farm worker's quarters.

bottle *n* **1** a container, often of glass and usually cylindrical with a narrow neck, for holding liquids. **2** the amount such a container will hold. **3** *Brit slang* courage; nerve. **4 the bottle** *Informal* drinking of alcohol, esp. to excess. ~*vb* **-tling, -tled 5** to put or place in a bottle or bottles. ~See also **bottle up.**

bottle bank *n* a large container into which members of the public can throw glass bottles and jars for recycling.

bottle-feed *vb* **-feeding, -fed** to feed (a baby) with milk from a bottle.

bottle-green *adj* dark green.

bottleneck *n* **1** a narrow stretch of road or a junction at which traffic is or may be held up. **2** something that holds up progress.

bottlenose dolphin *n* a grey or greenish dolphin with a bottle-shaped snout.

bottle party *n* a party to which guests bring drink.

bottler *n Austral & NZ informal* an exceptional person or thing.

bottle store *n S African & NZ* an off-licence.

bottle up *vb* to restrain (powerful emotion).

bottom *n* **1** the lowest, deepest, or farthest removed part of a thing: *the bottom of a hill.* **2** the least important or successful position: *the bottom of a class.* **3** the ground underneath a sea, lake, or river. **4** the underneath part of a thing. **5** the buttocks. **6 at bottom** in reality; basically. **7 be at the bottom of** to be the ultimate cause of. **8 get to the bottom of** to discover the real truth about. ~*adj* **9** lowest or last.

bottomless *adj* **1** unlimited; inexhaustible: *bottomless resources.* **2** very deep: *bottomless valleys.*

bottom line *n* **1** the conclusion or main point of a process, discussion, etc. **2** the last line of a financial statement that shows the net profit or loss of a company or organization.

bottom out *vb* to reach the lowest point and level out: *consumer spending has bottomed out.*

botulism *n* severe food poisoning resulting from the toxin **botulin,** produced in imperfectly preserved food.

bouclé *n* a curled or looped yarn or fabric giving a thick knobbly effect.

boudoir (**boo**-dwahr) *n* a woman's bedroom or private sitting room.

bouffant (**boof**-fong) *adj* (of a hairstyle) having extra height and width through backcombing.

bougainvillea *n* a tropical climbing plant with flowers surrounded by showy red or purple bracts.

bough *n* any of the main branches of a tree.

bought *vb* the past of **buy.**

➤ Be careful not to confuse the past forms *bought* (from *buy*) with *brought* (from *bring*).

bouillon (**boo**-yon) *n* a thin clear broth or stock.

boulder *n* a smooth rounded mass of rock shaped by erosion.

boulder clay *n* an unstratified glacial deposit of fine clay, boulders, and pebbles.

boules (**bool**) *n* a game, popular in France, in which metal bowls are thrown to land as close as possible to a target ball.

boulevard *n* a wide usually tree-lined road in a city.

boult *vb* same as **bolt**².

bounce *vb* **bouncing, bounced 1** (of a ball, etc.) to rebound from an impact. **2** to cause (a ball, etc.) to hit a solid surface and spring back. **3** to move or cause to move suddenly; spring: *I bounced down the stairs.* **4** *Slang* (of a bank) to send (a cheque) back or (of a cheque) to be sent back unredeemed because of lack of funds in the account. ~*n* **5** the action of rebounding from an impact. **6** a leap or jump. **7** springiness. **8** *Informal* vitality; vigour. **bouncy** *adj*

bounce back *vb* to recover one's health, good spirits, confidence, etc., easily.

bouncer *n* **1** *Slang* a person employed at a club, disco, etc. to prevent unwanted people from entering and to eject drunks or troublemakers. **2** *Cricket* a ball bowled so that it bounces high on pitching.

bouncing *adj* vigorous and robust: *a bouncing baby.*

bound¹ *vb* **1** the past of **bind.** ~*adj* **2** tied as if with a rope. **3** restricted or confined: *housebound.* **4** certain: *it's bound to happen.* **5** compelled or obliged: *they agreed to be bound by the board's recommendations.* **6** (of a book) secured within a cover or binding. **7 bound up with** closely or inextricably linked with.

bound² *vb* **1** to move forwards by leaps or jumps. **2** to bounce; spring away from an impact. ~*n* **3** a jump upwards or forwards. **4** a bounce, as of a ball.

bound³ *vb* **1** to place restrictions on; limit: *ancient art is bound by tradition.* **2** to form a boundary of. ~*n* **3** See **bounds. boundless** *adj*

bound⁴ *adj* going or intending to go towards: *homeward bound.*

boundary *n, pl* **-ries 1** something that indicates the

THESAURUS

tation, molestation, nuisance, perplexity, pest, problem, strain, trouble, vexation, worry

bothersome aggravating, annoying, distressing, exasperating, inconvenient, irritating, tiresome, troublesome, vexatious, vexing

bottleneck block, blockage, congestion, hold-up, impediment, jam, obstacle, obstruction, snarl-up (*informal, chiefly Brit.*)

bottle up check, contain, curb, keep back, restrict, shut in, suppress, trap

bottom *n.* **1.** base, basis, bed, deepest part, depths, floor, foot, foundation, groundwork, lowest part, pedestal, support **2.** lower side, sole, underneath, underside **3.** arse (*taboo slang*), ass (*U.S. & Canad. taboo slang*), backside, behind (*informal*), bum (*Brit. slang*), butt (*U.S. & Canad. informal*), buttocks, posterior, rear, rear end, rump, seat ~*adj.* **4.** base, basement, basic, fundamental, ground, last, lowest, undermost

bottomless boundless, deep, fathomless, immeasurable, inexhaustible, infinite, unfathomable, unlimited

bounce *vb.* **1.** bob, bound, bump, jump, leap, rebound, recoil, ricochet, spring, thump ~*n.* **2.** bound, elasticity, give, rebound, recoil, resilience, spring, springiness **3.** animation, dynamism, energy, go (*informal*), life, liveliness, pep, vigour, vitality, vivacity, zip (*informal*)

bouncing blooming, bonny, healthy, robust, thriving, vigorous

bound¹ *adj.* **1.** cased, fastened, fixed, pinioned, secured, tied, tied up **2.** certain, destined, doomed, fated, sure **3.** beholden, committed, compelled, constrained, duty-bound, forced, obligated, obliged, pledged, required

bound² *vb./n.* bob, bounce, caper, frisk, gambol, hurdle, jump, leap, lope, pounce, prance, skip, spring, vault

farthest limit, such as of an area. **2** *Cricket* **a** the marked limit of the playing area. **b** a stroke that hits the ball beyond this limit, scoring four or six runs.

bounden *adj Old-fashioned* morally obligatory: *bounden duty.*

bounder *n Old-fashioned, Brit slang* a morally reprehensible person; cad.

bounds *pl n* **1** a limit; boundary: *their jealousy knows no bounds.* **2** something that restricts or controls, esp. the standards of a society: *within the bounds of good taste.*

bountiful *or* **bounteous** *adj Literary* **1** plentiful; ample: *a bountiful harvest.* **2** giving freely; generous.

bounty *n, pl* **-ties** **1** *Literary* generosity; liberality. **2** something provided in generous amounts: *nature's bounty.* **3** a reward or premium by a government.

bouquet *n* **1** a bunch of flowers, esp. a large carefully arranged one. **2** the aroma of wine.

bouquet garni *n, pl* **bouquets garnis** a bunch of herbs tied together and used for flavouring soups, stews, or stocks.

bourbon (**bur**-bn) *n* a whiskey distilled, chiefly in the US, from maize.

bourgeois (**boor**-zhwah) *Often disparaging* ~*adj* **1** characteristic of or comprising the middle class. **2** conservative or materialistic in outlook. **3** (in Marxist thought) dominated by capitalism. ~*n, pl* **-geois** **4** a member of the middle class, esp. one regarded as being conservative and materialistic.

bourgeoisie (boor-zhwah-**zee**) *n* **the bourgeoisie** **1** the middle classes. **2** (in Marxist thought) the capitalist ruling class.

bourn *n Chiefly S Brit* a stream.

bourrée (**boor**-ray) *n* **1** a traditional French dance in fast duple time. **2** music for this dance.

Bourse (**boorss**) *n* a stock exchange, esp. of Paris.

bout *n* **1** **a** a period of time spent doing something, such as drinking. **b** a period of illness: *a bad bout of flu.* **2** a boxing, wrestling or fencing match.

boutique *n* a small shop, esp. one that sells fashionable clothes.

bouzouki *n* a Greek long-necked stringed musical instrument related to the mandolin.

bovine *adj* **1** of or relating to cattle. **2** dull, sluggish, or ugly.

bow[1] *vb* **1** to lower (one's head) or bend (one's knee or body) as a sign of respect, greeting, agreement, or shame. **2** to comply or accept: *bow to the inevitable.* **3** **bow and scrape** to behave in a slavish manner. ~*n* **4** a lowering or bending of the head or body as a mark of respect, etc. **5** **take a bow** to acknowledge applause. ~See also **bow out.**

bow[2] *n* **1** a decorative knot usually having two loops and two loose ends. **2** a long stick across which are stretched strands of horsehair, used for playing a violin, viola, cello, etc. **3** a weapon for shooting arrows, consisting of an arch of flexible wood, plastic, etc. bent by a string fastened at each end. **4** something that is curved, bent, or arched. ~*vb* **5** to form or cause to form a curve or curves.

bow[3] *n* **1** *Chiefly naut* the front end or part of a vessel. **2** *Rowing* the oarsman at the bow.

bowdlerize *or* **-ise** *vb* **-izing, -ized** *or* **-ising, -ised** to remove passages or words regarded as indecent from (a play, novel, etc.). **bowdlerization** *or* **-isation** *n*

bowel *n* **1** an intestine, esp. the large intestine in man. **2** **bowels** entrails. **3** (*pl*) the innermost part: *the bowels of the earth.*

bower *n* a shady leafy shelter in a wood or garden.

bowerbird *n* a brightly coloured songbird of Australia and New Guinea.

bowie knife *n* a stout hunting knife.

bowl[1] *n* **1** a round container open at the top, used for holding liquid or serving food. **2** the amount a bowl will hold. **3** the hollow part of an object, esp. of a spoon or tobacco pipe.

bowl[2] *n* **1** **a** a wooden ball used in the game of bowls. **b** a large heavy ball with holes for gripping used in the game of bowling. ~*vb* **2** to roll smoothly or cause to roll smoothly along the ground. **3** *Cricket* **a** to send (a ball) from one's hand towards the batsman. **b** Also: **bowl out** to dismiss (a batsman) by delivering a ball that breaks his wicket. **4** to play bowls. **5** **bowl along** to move easily and rapidly, as in a car. ~See also **bowl over, bowls.**

bow-legged *adj* having legs that curve outwards at the knees.

bowler[1] *n* **1** a person who bowls in cricket. **2** a player at the game of bowls.

bowler[2] *n* a stiff felt hat with a rounded crown and narrow curved brim.

bowline *n Naut* **1** a line used to keep the sail taut against the wind. **2** a knot used for securing a loop that will not slip at the end of a piece of rope.

bowling *n* **1** a game in which a heavy ball is rolled

THESAURUS

bound[3] *vb.* circumscribe, confine, define, delimit, demarcate, encircle, enclose, hem in, limit, restrain, restrict, surround, terminate

boundary barrier, border, borderline, bounds, brink, confines, edge, extremity, fringe, frontier, limits, march, margin, pale, precinct, termination, verge

boundless endless, illimitable, immeasurable, immense, incalculable, inexhaustible, infinite, limitless, measureless, unbounded, unconfined, unending, unlimited, untold, vast

bounds border, boundary, confine, edge, extremity, fringe, limit, line, march, margin, pale, periphery, rim, termination, verge

bountiful *or* **bounteous** **1.** abundant, ample, bounteous, copious, exuberant, lavish, luxuriant, plenteous, plentiful, prolific **2.** beneficent, bounteous, generous, liberal, magnanimous, munificent, open-handed, princely, prodigal, unstinting

bouquet **1.** bunch of flowers, buttonhole, corsage, garland, nosegay, posy, spray, wreath **2.** aroma, fragrance, perfume, redolence, savour, scent

bourgeois conventional, hidebound, materialistic, middle-class, traditional

bout **1.** course, fit, period, round, run, session, spell, spree, stint, stretch, term, time, turn **2.** battle, boxing match, competition, contest, encounter, engagement, fight, head-to-head, match, set-to, struggle

bovine dense, dozy (*Brit. informal*), dull, slow, sluggish, stolid, stupid, thick

bow[1] *vb.* **1.** bend, bob, droop, genuflect, incline, make obeisance, nod, stoop **2.** accept, acquiesce, comply, concede, defer, give in, kowtow, relent, submit, succumb, surrender, yield ~*n.* **3.** bending, bob, genuflexion, inclination, kowtow, nod, obeisance, salaam

bow[2] *Naut.* fore, head, prow, stem

bowdlerize, -ise blue-pencil, censor, clean up, expurgate, mutilate

bowels **1.** entrails, guts, innards (*informal*), insides (*informal*), intestines, viscera, vitals **2.** belly, core, deep, depths, hold, inside, interior

bowl **1.** *n.* basin, deep dish, vessel **2.** *vb.* fling, hurl, pitch, revolve, roll, rotate, spin, throw, trundle, whirl

down a long narrow alley at a group of wooden pins. **2** *Cricket* the act of delivering the ball to the batsman.

bowl over *vb* **1** *Informal* to surprise (a person) greatly, in a pleasant way. **2** to knock down.

bowls *n* a game played on a very smooth area of grass in which opponents roll biased wooden bowls as near a small bowl (the jack) as possible.

bow out *vb* to retire or withdraw gracefully.

bowsprit *n Naut* a spar projecting from the bow of a sailing ship.

bowstring *n* the string of an archer's bow.

bow tie *n* a man's tie in the form of a bow.

bow window *n* a curved bay window.

bow-wow *n* **1** a child's word for **dog. 2** an imitation of the bark of a dog.

box[1] *n* **1** a container with a firm base and sides and sometimes a removable or hinged lid. **2** the contents of such a container. **3** a separate compartment for a small group of people, as in a theatre. **4** a compartment for a horse in a stable or a vehicle. **5** a section of printed matter on a page, enclosed by lines or a border. **6** a central agency to which mail is addressed and from which it is collected or redistributed: *a post-office box.* **7** same as **penalty box. 8 the box** *Brit informal* television. ~*vb* **9** to put into a box. ~See also **box in. boxlike** *adj*

box[2] *vb* **1** to fight (an opponent) in a boxing match. **2** to engage in boxing. **3** to hit (esp. a person's ears) with the fist. ~*n* **4** a punch with the fist, esp. on the ear.

box[3] *n* a slow-growing evergreen tree or shrub with small shiny leaves.

boxer *n* **1** a man who boxes. **2** a medium-sized dog with smooth hair and a short nose.

boxer shorts *or* **boxers** *pl n* men's underpants shaped like shorts but with a front opening.

box girder *n* a girder that is hollow and square or rectangular in shape.

box in *vb* to prevent from moving freely; confine.

boxing *n* the act, art, or profession of fighting with the fists.

Boxing Day *n Brit* the first weekday after Christmas, observed as a holiday.

box junction *n* (in Britain) a road junction marked with yellow crisscross lines which vehicles may only enter when their exit is clear.

box lacrosse *n Canad* lacrosse played indoors.

box number *n* a number used as an address for mail, esp. one used by a newspaper for replies to an advertisement.

box office *n* **1** an office at a theatre, cinema, etc. where tickets are sold. **2** the public appeal of an actor or production. ~*adj* **box-office 3** relating to the sales at the box office: *a box-office success.*

box pleat *n* a flat double pleat made by folding under the fabric on either side of it.

boxroom *n* a small room in which boxes, cases, etc. may be stored.

box spring *n* a coiled spring contained in a boxlike frame, used for mattresses, chairs, etc.

boxwood *n* the hard yellow wood of the box tree, used to make tool handles, etc. See **box**[3].

boy *n* **1** a male child. **2** a man regarded as immature or inexperienced. **3** *S African offensive* a Black male servant. **boyhood** *n* **boyish** *adj*

boycott *vb* **1** to refuse to deal with (an organization or country) as a protest against its actions or policy. ~*n* **2** an instance or the use of boycotting.

boyfriend *n* a male friend with whom a person is romantically or sexually involved.

Boyle's law *n* the principle that the pressure of a gas varies inversely with its volume at constant temperature.

boy scout *n* See **Scout.**

BP 1 blood pressure. **2** British Pharmacopoeia

bpi bits per inch (used of a computer tape).

Bq *Physics* becquerel.

Br *Chem* bromine.

Br. 1 Breton. **2** Britain. **3** British.

bra *n* a woman's undergarment for covering and supporting the breasts.

braaivleis (**brye-flayss**) *n S African* a barbecue. Also: **braai**

brace *n* **1** something that steadies, binds, or holds up another thing. **2** a beam or prop, used to stiffen a framework. **3** an appliance of metal bands and wires for correcting unevenness of teeth. **4** a hand tool for drilling holes. **5** a pair, esp. of game birds. **6** either of a pair of characters, { }, used for connecting lines of printing or writing. **7** See **braces.** ~*vb* **bracing, braced 8** to steady or prepare (oneself) before an impact. **9** to provide, strengthen, or fit with a brace.

brace and bit *n* a hand tool for boring holes, consisting of a cranked handle into which a drilling bit is inserted.

bracelet *n* an ornamental chain or band worn around the arm or wrist.

bracelets *pl n Slang* handcuffs.

braces *pl n Brit* a pair of straps worn over the shoulders for holding up the trousers.

brachiopod (**brake-ee-oh-pod**) *n* an invertebrate sea animal with a shell consisting of two valves.

brachium (**brake-ee-um**) *n, pl* **brachia** (**brake-ee-a**) *Anat* the arm, esp. the upper part.

bracing *adj* refreshing: *the bracing climate.*

THESAURUS

bowl over 1. amaze, astonish, astound, dumbfound, stagger, startle, stun, surprise **2.** bring down, fell, floor, knock down, overthrow, overturn

box[1] **1.** *n.* carton, case, casket, chest, container, pack, package, portmanteau (*old-fashioned*), receptacle, trunk **2.** *vb.* pack, package, wrap

box[2] *vb.* **1.** exchange blows, fight, spar **2.** belt (*informal*), buffet, butt, clout (*informal*), cuff, hit, lay one on (*slang*), punch, slap, sock (*slang*), strike, thwack, wallop (*informal*), whack ~*n.* **3.** belt (*informal*), blow, buffet, clout (*informal*), cuff, punch, slap, stroke, thumping, wallop (*informal*)

boxer fighter, prizefighter, pugilist, sparrer, sparring partner

box in cage, confine, contain, coop up, enclose, hem in, isolate, shut in, surround, trap

boxing prizefighting, pugilism, sparring, the fight game (*informal*), the ring

boy fellow, junior, lad, schoolboy, stripling, youngster, youth

boycott ban, bar, black, blackball, blacklist, embargo, exclude, ostracize, outlaw, prohibit, proscribe, refrain from, refuse, reject, spurn

boyfriend admirer, beau (*chiefly U.S.*), date, follower, lover, man, steady, suitor, swain (*archaic or poetic*), sweetheart, toy boy, young man

brace 1. *n.* bolster, bracket, buttress, prop, reinforcement, stanchion, stay, strut, support, truss **2.** *vb.* bandage, bind, bolster, buttress, fasten, fortify, hold up, prop, reinforce, shove, shove up, steady, strap, strengthen, support, tie, tighten

bracing brisk, chilly, cool, crisp, energizing, exhila-

bracken *n* **1** a fern with large fronds. **2** a clump of these ferns.

bracket *n* **1** a pair of characters, ( ), ( ), or { }, used to enclose a section of writing or printing. **2** a group or category falling within certain defined limits: *the lower income bracket.* **3** an L-shaped or other support fixed to a wall to hold a shelf, etc. *~vb* **-eting, -eted 4** to put (written or printed matter) in brackets. **5** to group or class together.

brackish *adj* (of water) slightly salty.

bract *n* a leaf, usually small and scaly, growing at the base of a flower.

brad *n* a small tapered nail with a small head.

brae *n Scot* a hill or slope.

brag *vb* **bragging, bragged 1** to speak arrogantly and boastfully. *~n* **2** boastful talk or behaviour. **3** a card game similar to poker.

braggart *n* a person who boasts loudly or exaggeratedly.

Brahma *n* **1** a Hindu god, the Creator. **2** same as **Brahman** (sense 2).

Brahman *n, pl* **-mans 1** Also: **Brahmin** a member of the highest or priestly caste in the Hindu caste system. **2** *Hinduism* the ultimate and impersonal divine reality of the universe. **Brahmanic** *adj*

braid *vb* **1** to interweave (hair, thread, etc.). **2** to decorate with an ornamental trim or border. *~n* **3** a length of hair that has been braided. **4** narrow ornamental tape of woven silk, wool, etc. **braiding** *n*

Braille *n* a system of writing for the blind consisting of raised dots interpreted by touch.

brain *n* **1** the soft mass of nervous tissue within the skull of vertebrates that controls and coordinates the nervous system. **2** (*often pl*) *Informal* intellectual ability: *he's got brains.* **3** *Informal* an intelligent person. **4 on the brain** *Informal* constantly in mind: *I had that song on the brain.* **5 the brains** *Informal* a person who plans and organizes something: *the brains behind the bid.* *~vb* **6** *Slang* to hit (someone) hard on the head.

brainchild *n Informal* an idea or plan produced by creative thought.

brain death *n* complete stoppage of breathing due to irreparable brain damage.

brain drain *n Informal* the emigration of scientists, technologists, academics, etc.

brainless *adj* stupid or foolish.

brainstorm *n* **1** *Brit informal* a sudden mental aberration. **2** a sudden and violent attack of insanity. **3** *US & Canad informal* same as **brainwave.**

brainstorming *n* a thorough discussion to solve problems or create ideas.

brains trust *n* a group of knowledgeable people who discuss topics in public or on radio or television.

brain-teaser *n Informal* a difficult problem.

brainwash *vb* to cause (a person) to alter his or her beliefs, by methods based on isolation, sleeplessness, etc. **brainwashing** *n*

brainwave *n Informal* a sudden idea or inspiration.

brain wave *n* a fluctuation of electrical potential in the brain.

brainy *adj* **brainier, brainiest** *Informal* clever; intelligent.

braise *vb* **braising, braised** to cook (food) slowly in a closed pan with a small amount of liquid.

brak[1] **(bruck)** *n S African* a crossbred dog; mongrel.

brak[2] **(bruck)** *adj S African* (of water) slightly salty; brackish.

brake[1] *n* **1** a device for slowing or stopping a vehicle. **2** something that slows down or stops progress: *he put a brake on my enthusiasm.* *~vb* **braking, braked 3** to slow down or cause to slow down, by or as if by using a brake.

brake[2] *n* an area of dense undergrowth; thicket.

brake horsepower *n* the rate at which an engine does work, measured by the resistance of an applied brake.

brake light *n* a red light at the rear of a motor vehicle that lights up when the brakes are applied.

brake lining *n* a renewable strip of asbestos riveted to a brake shoe to increase friction.

brake shoe *n* a curved metal casting that acts as a brake on a wheel.

bramble *n* **1** a prickly plant or shrub such as the blackberry. **2** *Scot & N English* a blackberry. **brambly** *adj*

bran *n* husks of cereal grain separated from the flour.

branch *n* **1** a secondary woody stem extending from the trunk or main branch of a tree. **2** one of a number of shops, offices, or groups that belongs to a central organisation: *he was transferred to their Japanese branch.* **3** a subdivision or subsidiary section of something larger or more complex: *branches of learning.* *~vb* **4** to divide, then develop in different directions. **branchlike** *adj*

branch off *vb* to diverge from the main way, road, topic, etc.

branch out *vb* to expand or extend one's interests.

brand *n* **1** a particular product or a characteristic that identifies a particular producer. **2** a particular kind or variety. **3** an identifying mark made, usually by burning, on the skin of animals as a proof of ownership. **4** an iron used for branding animals. **5** a mark of disgrace. **6** *Archaic or poetic* a flaming torch. *~vb* **7** to label, burn, or mark with or as if with a brand. **8** to label (someone): *he was branded a war criminal.*

brandish *vb* to wave (a weapon, etc.) in a triumphant or threatening way.

brand-new *adj* absolutely new.

THESAURUS

rating, fortifying, fresh, invigorating, lively, refreshing, restorative, reviving, rousing, stimulating, tonic, vigorous

brag blow one's own trumpet, bluster, boast, crow, swagger, talk big (*slang*), vaunt

braid entwine, interlace, intertwine, interweave, lace, plait, ravel, twine, weave

brain egghead (*informal*), genius, highbrow, intellect, intellectual, mastermind, prodigy, pundit, sage, scholar

brainless foolish, idiotic, inane, inept, mindless, senseless, stupid, thoughtless, unintelligent, witless

brainy bright, brilliant, clever, intelligent, smart

brake 1. *n.* check, constraint, control, curb, rein, restraint **2.** *vb.* check, decelerate, halt, moderate, reduce speed, slacken, slow, stop

branch 1. arm, bough, limb, offshoot, prong, ramification, shoot, spray, sprig **2.** chapter, department, division, local office, office, part, section, subdivision, subsection, wing

branch out add to, develop, diversify, enlarge, expand, extend, increase, multiply, proliferate, ramify, spread out

brand *n.* **1.** cast, class, grade, kind, make, quality, sort, species, type, variety **2.** emblem, hallmark, label, mark, marker, sign, stamp, symbol, trademark **3.** blot, disgrace, infamy, mark, reproach, slur, smirch, stain, stigma, taint *~vb.* **4.** burn, burn in, label, mark, scar,

brandy *n, pl* **-dies** an alcoholic spirit distilled from wine.

brandy snap *n* a crisp sweet biscuit, rolled into a cylinder.

brash *adj* **1** tastelessly or offensively loud, or showy: *brash modernization.* **2** impudent or bold: *I thought it was very brash of her to ask me.* **brashness** *n*

brass *n* **1** an alloy of copper and zinc. **2** an object, ornament, or utensil made of brass. **3 a** the large family of wind instruments including the trumpet, trombone, etc. made of brass. **b** instruments of this family forming a section in an orchestra. **4** same as **top brass. 5** *N English dialect* money. **6** *Brit* an engraved brass memorial tablet in a church. **7** *Informal* bold self-confidence; nerve.

brass band *n* a group of musicians playing brass and percussion instruments.

brasserie *n* a bar or restaurant serving drinks and cheap meals.

brass hat *n Brit informal* a top-ranking official, esp. a military officer.

brassica *n* any plant of the cabbage and turnip family.

brassiere *n* same as **bra.**

brass rubbing *n* an impression of an engraved brass tablet made by rubbing a paper placed over it with heelball or chalk.

brass tacks *pl n* **get down to brass tacks** *Informal* to discuss the realities of a situation.

brassy *adj* **brassier, brassiest 1** brazen or flashy. **2** like brass, esp. in colour. **3** (of sound) harsh and strident.

brat *n* a child, esp. one who is unruly.

bravado *n* an outward display of self-confidence.

brave *adj* **1** having or displaying courage, resolution, or daring. **2** fine; splendid: *a brave sight.* ~*n* **3** a warrior of a North American Indian tribe. ~*vb* **braving, braved 4** to confront with resolution or courage: *she braved the 21 miles of Lake Tahoe.* **bravery** *n*

bravo *interj* **1** well done! ~*n* **2** (*pl* **-vos**) a cry of "bravo". **3** (*pl* **-voes** *or* **-vos**) a hired killer or assassin.

bravura *n* **1** a display of boldness or daring. **2** *Music* brilliance of execution.

brawl *n* **1** a loud disagreement or fight. ~*vb* **2** to quarrel or fight noisily.

brawn *n* **1** strong well-developed muscles. **2** physical strength. **3** *Brit* a seasoned jellied loaf made from the head of a pig. **brawny** *adj*

bray *vb* **1** (of a donkey) to utter its characteristic loud harsh sound. **2** to utter something with a loud harsh sound. ~*n* **3** the loud harsh sound uttered by a donkey. **4** a similar loud sound.

braze *vb* **brazing, brazed** to join (two metal surfaces) by fusing brass between them.

brazen *adj* **1** shameless and bold. **2** made of or resembling brass. **3** having a ringing metallic sound. ~*vb* **4 brazen it out** to face and overcome a difficult or embarrassing situation boldly or shamelessly. **brazenly** *adv*

brazier[1] (**bray**-zee-er) *n* a portable metal container for burning charcoal or coal.

brazier[2] *n* a worker in brass.

brazil *n* **1** the red wood of various tropical trees of America. **2** same as **brazil nut.**

Brazilian *adj* **1** of Brazil. ~*n* **2** a person from Brazil.

brazil nut *n* a large three-sided nut of a tropical American tree.

breach *n* **1** a breaking of a promise, obligation, etc. **2** any serious disagreement or separation. **3** a crack, break, or gap. ~*vb* **4** to break (a promise, law, etc.). **5** to break through or make an opening or hole in.

breach of promise *n Law* (formerly) failure to carry out one's promise to marry.

breach of the peace *n Law* an offence against public order causing an unnecessary disturbance of the peace.

bread *n* **1** a food made from a dough of flour or meal mixed with water or milk, usually raised with yeast and then baked. **2** necessary food. **3** *Slang* money. ~*vb* **4** to cover (food) with breadcrumbs before cooking.

bread and butter *n Informal* a means of support; livelihood.

THESAURUS

stamp **5.** censure, denounce, discredit, disgrace, expose, mark, stigmatize

brandish display, exhibit, flaunt, flourish, parade, raise, shake, swing, wield

brash 1. audacious, foolhardy, hasty, impetuous, impulsive, indiscreet, precipitate, rash, reckless **2.** bold, brazen, cocky, forward, heedless, impertinent, impudent, insolent, pushy (*informal*), rude

brass audacity, brass neck (*Brit. informal*), cheek, effrontery, front, gall, impertinence, impudence, insolence, neck (*informal*), nerve (*informal*), presumption, rudeness

bravado bluster, boast, boastfulness, boasting, bombast, brag, swagger, swaggering, swashbuckling, vaunting

brave 1. *adj.* ballsy (*taboo slang*), bold, courageous, daring, dauntless, fearless, gallant, gritty, heroic, intrepid, plucky, resolute, undaunted, valiant, valorous **2.** *vb.* bear, beard, challenge, confront, dare, defy, endure, face, stand up to, suffer, tackle, withstand

bravery balls (*taboo slang*), boldness, bravura, courage, daring, dauntlessness, doughtiness, fearlessness, fortitude, gallantry, grit, guts (*informal*), hardihood, hardiness, heroism, indomitability, intrepidity, mettle, pluck, pluckiness, spirit, spunk (*informal*), valour

bravura animation, audacity, boldness, brilliance, daring, dash, display, élan, energy, exhibitionism, ostentation, panache, punch (*informal*), spirit, verve, vigour, virtuosity

brawl 1. *n.* affray (*Law*), altercation, argument, battle, clash, disorder, dispute, fight, fracas, fray, free-for-all (*informal*), melee *or* mêlée, punch-up (*Brit. informal*), quarrel, row (*informal*), rumpus, scrap (*informal*), scrimmage, scuffle, shindig (*informal*), shindy (*informal*), skirmish, squabble, tumult, uproar, wrangle **2.** *vb.* altercate, argue, battle, dispute, fight, quarrel, row (*informal*), scrap (*informal*), scuffle, tussle, wrangle, wrestle

brawn beef (*informal*), beefiness (*informal*), brawniness, flesh, might, muscle, muscles, muscularity, power, robustness, strength, vigour

brawny athletic, beefy (*informal*), bulky, burly, fleshy, hardy, hefty (*informal*), herculean, husky (*informal*), lusty, muscular, powerful, robust, sinewy, stalwart, strapping, strong, sturdy, thickset, vigorous, well-built

breach 1. contravention, disobedience, infraction, infringement, noncompliance, nonobservance, offence, transgression, trespass, violation **2.** alienation, difference, disaffection, disagreement, dissension, division, estrangement, falling-out (*informal*), parting of the ways, quarrel, schism, separation, severance, variance **3.** aperture, break, chasm, cleft, crack, fissure, gap, hole, opening, rent, rift, rupture, split

bread 1. aliment, diet, fare, food, necessities, nourishment, nutriment, provisions, subsistence, suste-

breadboard *n* **1** a wooden board on which bread is sliced. **2** an experimental arrangement of electronic circuits.

breadfruit *n, pl* **-fruits** *or* **-fruit** a tree of the Pacific Islands, whose edible round fruit has a texture like bread when baked.

breadline *n* **on the breadline** impoverished; living at subsistence level.

breadth *n* **1** the extent or measurement of something from side to side. **2** openness and lack of restriction, esp. of viewpoint or interest; liberality.

breadwinner *n* a person supporting a family with his or her earnings.

break *vb* **breaking, broke, broken 1** to separate or become separated into two or more pieces. **2** to damage or become damaged so as not to work. **3** to burst or cut the surface of (skin). **4** to fracture (a bone) in (a limb, etc.). **5** to fail to observe (an agreement, promise, or law): *they broke their promise.* **6** to reveal or be revealed: *she broke the news gently.* **7** (foll. by *with*) to separate oneself from. **8** to stop for a rest: *to break a journey.* **9** to bring or come to an end: *the winter weather broke at last.* **10** to weaken or overwhelm or be weakened or overwhelmed, as in spirit: *he felt his life was broken by his illness.* **11** to cut through or penetrate: *silence broken by shouts.* **12** to improve on or surpass: *she broke three world records.* **13** (often foll. by *in*) to accustom (a horse) to the bridle and saddle, to being ridden, etc. **14** (foll. by *of*) to cause (a person) to give up (a habit): *this cure will break you of smoking.* **15** to weaken the impact or force of: *this net will break his fall.* **16** to decipher: *to break a code.* **17** to lose the order of: *to break ranks.* **18** to reduce to poverty or the state of bankruptcy. **19** to come into being: *light broke over the mountains.* **20** (foll. by *into*) **a** to burst into (song, laughter, etc.). **b** to change to (a faster pace). **21** to open with explosives: *to break a safe.* **22** (of waves) **a** to strike violently against. **b** to collapse into foam or surf. **23** *Snooker* to scatter the balls at the start of a game. **24** *Boxing, wrestling* (of two fighters) to separate from a clinch. **25** (of the male voice) to undergo a change in register, quality, and range at puberty. **26** to interrupt the flow of current in (an electrical circuit). **27 break camp** to pack up and leave a camp. **28 break even** to make neither a profit nor a loss. **29 break the mould** to make a change that breaks an established habit or pattern. *~n* **30** the act or result of breaking; fracture. **31** a brief rest. **32** a sudden rush, esp. to escape: *they made a sudden break for freedom.* **33** any sudden interruption in a continuous action. **34** *Brit* a short period between classes at school. **35** *Informal* a fortunate opportunity, esp. to prove oneself. **36** *Informal* a piece of good or bad luck. **37** *Billiards, snooker* a series of successful shots during one turn. **38** *Snooker* the opening shot that scatters the placed balls. **39** a discontinuity in an electrical circuit. **40 break of day** the dawn. ~See also **breakaway, break down,** etc. **breakable** *adj*

breakage *n* **1** the act or result of breaking. **2** compensation or allowance for goods damaged while in use, transit, etc.

breakaway *n* **1** loss or withdrawal of a group of members from an association, club, etc. **2** *Austral* a stampede of cattle, esp. at the smell of water. *~adj* **3** dissenting: *a breakaway faction.* *~vb* **break away 4** to leave hastily or escape. **5** to withdraw or quit.

break dance *n* **1** an acrobatic dance style of the 1980s. *~vb* **break-dance, -dancing, -danced 2** to perform a break dance. **break dancing** *n*

break down *vb* **1** to cease to function; become ineffective. **2** to give way to strong emotion or tears. **3** to crush or destroy. **4** to have a nervous breakdown. **5** to separate into component parts: *with exercise the body breaks down fat to use as fuel.* **6** to separate or cause to separate into simpler chemical elements; decompose. **7** to analyse or be subjected to analysis. *~n* **breakdown 8** an act or instance of breaking down; collapse. **9** same as **nervous breakdown. 10** an analysis of something into its parts.

breaker *n* **1** a large sea wave with a white crest or one that breaks into foam on the shore. **2** a citizens' band radio operator.

breakfast *n* **1** the first meal of the day. *~vb* **2** to eat breakfast.

break in *vb* **1** to enter a building, illegally, esp. by force. **2** to interrupt. **3** to accustom (a person or animal) to normal duties or practice. **4** to use or wear (new shoes or new equipment) until comfortable or running smoothly. *~n* **break-in 5** the act of illegally entering a building, esp. by thieves.

breaking point *n* the point at which something or someone gives way under strain.

THESAURUS

nance, viands (*old-fashioned*), victuals (*old-fashioned*) **2.** *slang* cash, dosh (*Brit. & Austral. slang*), dough (*slang*), finance, funds, money, necessary (*informal*), needful (*informal*), shekels (*informal*), silver

breadth 1. beam (*of a ship*), broadness, latitude, span, spread, wideness, width **2.** broad-mindedness, freedom, latitude, liberality, open-mindedness, openness, permissiveness

break *vb.* **1.** batter, burst, crack, crash, demolish, destroy, disintegrate, divide, fracture, fragment, part, rend, separate, sever, shatter, shiver, smash, snap, splinter, split, tear, trash (*slang*) **2.** breach, contravene, disobey, disregard, infringe, renege on, transgress, violate **3.** announce, come out, disclose, divulge, impart, inform, let out, make public, proclaim, reveal, tell **4.** abandon, cut, discontinue, give up, interrupt, pause, rest, stop, suspend **5.** *of a record, etc.* beat, better, cap (*informal*), exceed, excel, go beyond, outdo, outstrip, surpass, top **6.** cow, cripple, demoralize, dispirit, enervate, enfeeble, impair, incapacitate, subdue, tame, undermine, weaken **7.** bust (*informal*), degrade, demote, discharge, dismiss, humiliate, impoverish, make bankrupt, reduce, ruin **8.** appear, burst out, come forth suddenly, emerge, erupt, happen, occur *~n.* **9.** breach, cleft, crack, division, fissure, fracture, gap, gash, hole, opening, rent, rift, rupture, split, tear **10.** breather (*informal*), halt, hiatus, interlude, intermission, interruption, interval, let-up (*informal*), lull, pause, recess, respite, rest, suspension **11.** *informal* advantage, chance, fortune, opening, opportunity, stroke of luck

breakable brittle, crumbly, delicate, flimsy, fragile, frail, frangible, friable

break away 1. decamp, escape, flee, fly, make a break for it, make a run for it (*informal*), make off, run away **2.** break with, detach, part company, secede, separate

break down be overcome, collapse, conk out (*informal*), crack up (*informal*), fail, give way, go kaput (*informal*), go to pieces, seize up, stop, stop working

breakdown 1. collapse, crackup (*informal*), disintegration, disruption, failure, mishap, stoppage **2.** analysis, categorization, classification, detailed list, diagnosis, dissection, itemization

break in 1. break and enter, burgle, invade, rob **2.** barge in, burst in, butt in, interfere, interject, interpose, interrupt, intervene, intrude **3.** accustom, condition, get used to, habituate, initiate, prepare, tame, train

breakneck *adj* (of speed or pace) excessively fast and dangerous.
break off *vb* 1 to sever or detach. 2 to end (a relationship or association). 3 to stop abruptly.
break out *vb* 1 to begin or arise suddenly: *fighting broke out between the two factions.* 2 to make an escape, esp. from prison. 3 **break out in** to erupt in (a rash or spots). *~n* **break-out** 4 an escape, esp. from prison.
break through *vb* 1 to penetrate. 2 to achieve success after lengthy efforts. *~n* **breakthrough** 3 a significant development or discovery.
break up *vb* 1 to separate or cause to separate. 2 to put an end to (a relationship) or (of a relationship) to come to an end. 3 to dissolve or cause to dissolve: *the meeting broke up at noon.* 4 *Brit* (of a school) to close for the holidays. *~n* **break-up** 5 a separation or disintegration.
breakwater *n* a massive wall built out into the sea to protect a shore or harbour from the force of waves.
bream *n, pl* **bream** 1 a freshwater fish covered with silvery scales. 2 a food fish of European seas.
breast *n* 1 either of the two soft fleshy milk-secreting glands on a woman's chest. 2 the front part of the body from the neck to the abdomen; chest. 3 the corresponding part in certain other mammals. 4 the source of human emotions. 5 the part of a garment that covers the breast. 6 **make a clean breast of something** to divulge truths about oneself. *~vb Literary* 7 to reach the summit of: *breasting the mountain top.* 8 to confront boldly; face: *breast the storm.*
breastbone *n* same as **sternum.**
breast-feed *vb* **-feeding, -fed** to feed (a baby) with milk from the breast; suckle.
breastplate *n* a piece of armour covering the chest.
breaststroke *n* a swimming stroke in which the arms are extended in front of the head and swept back on either side.
breastwork *n Fortifications* a temporary defensive work, usually breast-high.
breath *n* 1 the taking in and letting out of air during breathing. 2 a single instance of this. 3 the air taken in or let out during breathing. 4 the vapour, heat, or odour of air breathed out. 5 a slight gust of air. 6 a short pause or rest. 7 a suggestion or slight evidence; suspicion: *trembling at the least breath of scandal.* 8 a whisper or soft sound. 9 **catch one's breath a** to rest until breathing is normal. **b** to stop breathing momentarily from excitement, fear, etc. 10 **out of breath** gasping for air after exertion. 11 **save one's breath** to avoid useless talk. 12 **take someone's breath away** to overwhelm someone with surprise, etc. 13 **under one's breath** in a quiet voice or whisper.
Breathalyser *or* **-lyzer** *n Brit trademark* a device for estimating the amount of alcohol in the breath. **breathalyse** *or* **-lyze** *vb*
breathe *vb* **breathing, breathed** 1 to take in oxygen and give out carbon dioxide; respire. 2 to exist; be alive. 3 to rest to regain breath or composure. 4 (esp. of air) to blow lightly. 5 to exhale or emit: *the dragon breathed fire.* 6 to impart; instil: *a change that breathed new life into Polish industry.* 7 to speak softly; whisper. 8 **breathe again, freely** *or* **easily** to feel relief. 9 **breathe one's last** to die.
breather *n Informal* a short pause for rest.
breathing *n* 1 the passage of air into and out of the lungs to supply the body with oxygen. 2 the sound this makes.
breathing space *n* a short period during which a difficult situation temporarily becomes less severe: *the cut in interest rates creates a breathing space for struggling businesses.*
breathless *adj* 1 out of breath; gasping, etc. 2 holding one's breath or having it taken away by excitement, etc. 3 (esp. of the atmosphere) motionless and stifling. **breathlessness** *n*
breathtaking *adj* causing awe or excitement.
breath test *n Brit* a chemical test of a driver's breath to determine the amount of alcohol consumed.
bred *vb* the past of **breed.**
bredie (**breed**-ee) *n S African* a meat and vegetable stew.
breech *n* 1 the buttocks. 2 the part of a firearm behind the barrel.
breech delivery *n* birth of a baby with the feet or buttocks appearing first.
breeches *pl n* trousers extending to the knee or just below, worn for riding, etc.
breeches buoy *n* a pulley device with a life buoy and pair of breeches attached, which is used as a means of transference between ships or rescue from the sea.
breed *vb* **breeding, bred** 1 to produce new or improved strains of (domestic animals and plants). 2 to produce or cause to produce by mating. 3 to bear (offspring). 4 to bring up; raise: *she was city bred.* 5 to produce or be produced: *the agreement bred confi-*

THESAURUS

break-in breaking and entering, burglary, invasion, robbery
break off 1. detach, divide, part, pull off, separate, sever, snap off, splinter 2. cease, desist, discontinue, end, finish, halt, pause, stop, suspend, terminate
break out 1. appear, arise, begin, commence, emerge, happen, occur, set in, spring up, start 2. abscond, bolt, break loose, burst out, escape, flee, get free
breakthrough advance, development, discovery, find, finding, gain, improvement, invention, leap, progress, quantum leap, step forward
break up adjourn, disband, dismantle, disperse, disrupt, dissolve, divide, divorce, end, part, scatter, separate, sever, split, stop, suspend, terminate
break-up breakdown, breaking, crackup (*informal*), disintegration, dispersal, dissolution, divorce, ending, parting, rift, separation, split, splitting, termination, wind-up
breakwater groyne, jetty, mole, sea wall, spur
breast 1. boob (*slang*), bosom, bust, chest, front, teat, thorax, tit (*slang*), udder 2. being, conscience, core, emotions, feelings, heart, seat of the affections, sentiments, soul, thoughts
breath 1. air, animation, breathing, exhalation, gasp, gulp, inhalation, pant, respiration, wheeze 2. aroma, niff (*Brit. slang*), odour, smell, vapour, whiff 3. faint breeze, flutter, gust, puff, sigh, slight movement, waft, zephyr 4. break, breather, breathing-space, instant, moment, pause, respite, rest, second 5. hint, murmur, suggestion, suspicion, undertone, whisper
breathe 1. draw in, gasp, gulp, inhale and exhale, pant, puff, respire, wheeze 2. imbue, impart, infuse, inject, inspire, instil, transfuse 3. articulate, express, murmur, say, sigh, utter, voice, whisper
breathless 1. choking, exhausted, gasping, gulping, out of breath, panting, short-winded, spent, wheezing, winded 2. agog, anxious, astounded, avid, eager, excited, flabbergasted (*informal*), gobsmacked (*Brit. slang*), on tenterhooks, open-mouthed, thunderstruck, with bated breath
breathtaking amazing, astonishing, awe-inspiring, awesome, brilliant, exciting, heart-stirring, impressive,

dence between the two. ~*n* **6** a group of animals, esp. domestic animals, within a species, that have certain clearly defined characteristics. **7** a kind, sort, or group: *he was a gentleman, a breed not greatly admired.* **8** a lineage or race. **breeder** *n*

breeder reactor *n* a nuclear reactor that produces more fissionable material than it uses.

breeding *n* **1** the process of producing plants or animals by controlled methods of reproduction. **2** the process of bearing offspring. **3** the result of good upbringing or training.

breeze[1] *n* **1** a gentle or light wind. **2** *US & Canad informal* an easy task. ~*vb* **breezing, breezed 3** to move quickly or casually: *he breezed into the room.*

breeze[2] *n* ashes of coal, coke, or charcoal.

breeze block *n* a light building brick made from the ashes of coal, coke, etc. bonded together by cement.

breezy *adj* **breezier, breeziest 1** fresh; windy. **2** casual or carefree.

Bren gun *n* an air-cooled gas-operated light machine gun.

brent *or esp US* **brant** *n* a small goose with a dark grey plumage.

brethren *pl n Archaic except when referring to fellow members of a religion or society* a plural of **brother.**

Breton *adj* **1** of Brittany. ~*n* **2** a person from Brittany. **3** the Celtic language of Brittany.

breve *n* an accent (˘), placed over a vowel to indicate that it is short or is pronounced in a specified way.

breviary *n, pl* **-ries** *RC Church* a book of psalms, hymns, prayers, etc., to be recited daily.

brevity *n* **1** a short duration; brief time. **2** lack of verbosity.

brew *vb* **1** to make (beer, ale, etc.) from malt and other ingredients by steeping, boiling, and fermentation. **2** to prepare (a drink, such as tea) by infusing. **3** to devise or plan: *to brew a plot.* **4** to be in the process of being brewed. **5** to be about to happen or forming: *a rebellion was brewing.* ~*n* **6** a beverage produced by brewing, esp. tea or beer. **7** an instance of brewing: *last year's brew.* **brewer** *n*

brewery *n, pl* **-eries** a place where beer, ale, etc., is brewed.

briar[1] *or* **brier** *n* **1** a shrub of S Europe, with a hard woody root (briarroot). **2** a tobacco pipe made from this root.

briar[2] *n* same as **brier**[1].

bribe *vb* **bribing, bribed 1** to promise, offer, or give something, often illegally, to (a person) to receive services or gain influence. ~*n* **2** a reward, such as money or favour, given or offered for this purpose. **bribery** *n*

bric-a-brac *n* miscellaneous small ornamental objects.

brick *n* **1** a rectangular block of baked or dried clay, used in building construction. **2** the material used to make such blocks. **3** any rectangular block: *a brick of ice cream.* **4** bricks collectively. **5** *Informal* a reliable, trustworthy, or helpful person. **6 drop a brick** *Brit informal* to make a tactless or indiscreet remark. ~*vb* **7** (foll. by *in, up* or *over*) to construct, line, pave, fill, or wall up with bricks: *they bricked up access to the historic pillar.*

brickbat *n* **1** blunt criticism. **2** a piece of brick used as a weapon.

bricklayer *n* a person who builds with bricks.

brick-red *adj* reddish-brown.

bridal *adj* of a bride or a wedding.

bride *n* a woman who has just been or is about to be married.

bridegroom *n* a man who has just been or is about to be married.

bridesmaid *n* a girl or young woman who attends a bride at her wedding.

bridge[1] *n* **1** a structure that provides a way over a railway, river, etc. **2** a platform from which a ship is piloted and navigated. **3** the hard ridge at the upper part of the nose. **4** a dental plate containing artificial teeth that is secured to natural teeth. **5** a piece of wood supporting the strings of a violin, guitar, etc. ~*vb* **bridging, bridged 6** to build or provide a bridge over (something). **7** to connect or reduce the distance between: *talks aimed at bridging the gap between the two sides.*

bridge[2] *n* a card game for four players, based on whist, in which the trump suit is decided by bidding between the players.

THESAURUS

magnificent, moving, overwhelming, sensational, striking, stunning (*informal*), thrilling, wondrous (*old-fashioned or literary*)

breed *vb.* **1.** bear, beget (*old-fashioned*), bring forth, engender, generate, hatch, multiply, originate, procreate, produce, propagate, reproduce **2.** bring up, cultivate, develop, discipline, educate, foster, instruct, nourish, nurture, raise, rear **3.** arouse, bring about, cause, create, generate, give rise to, induce, make, occasion, originate, produce, stir up ~*n.* **4.** brand, class, extraction, family, ilk, kind, line, lineage, pedigree, progeny, race, sort, species, stamp, stock, strain, type, variety

breeding 1. ancestry, cultivation, development, lineage, nurture, raising, rearing, reproduction, training, upbringing **2.** civility, conduct, courtesy, cultivation, culture, gentility, manners, polish, refinement, sophistication, urbanity

breeze 1. *n.* air, breath of wind, capful of wind, current of air, draught, flurry, gust, light wind, puff of air, waft, whiff, zephyr **2.** *vb.* flit, glide, hurry, move briskly, pass, sail, sally, sweep, trip

breezy 1. airy, blowing, blowy, blusterous, blustery, fresh, gusty, squally, windy **2.** airy, animated, blithe, buoyant, carefree, casual, cheerful, chirpy (*informal*), debonair, easy-going, free and easy, genial, informal, jaunty, light, light-hearted, lively, sparkling, sparky, spirited, sprightly, sunny, upbeat (*informal*), vivacious

brevity briefness, conciseness, concision, condensation, crispness, curtness, economy, ephemerality, impermanence, pithiness, shortness, succinctness, terseness, transience, transitoriness

brew *vb.* **1.** boil, ferment, infuse (*tea*), make (*beer*), prepare by fermentation, seethe, soak, steep, stew **2.** breed, concoct, contrive, develop, devise, excite, foment, form, gather, hatch, plan, plot, project, scheme, start, stir up ~*n.* **3.** beverage, blend, concoction, distillation, drink, fermentation, infusion, liquor, mixture, preparation

bribe 1. *vb.* buy off, corrupt, get at, grease the palm *or* hand of (*slang*), influence by gifts, lure, oil the palm of (*informal*), pay off (*informal*), reward, suborn (*formal*) **2.** *n.* allurement, backhander (*slang*), boodle (*slang*), corrupting gift, enticement, graft (*informal*), hush money (*slang*), incentive, inducement, kickback (*U.S.*), pay-off (*informal*), payola (*informal*), reward for treachery, sop, sweetener (*slang*)

bribery buying off, corruption, graft (*informal*), inducement, palm-greasing (*slang*), payola (*informal*), protection, subornation

bridge 1. *n.* arch, flyover, overpass, span, viaduct **2.**

bridgehead *n Mil* a fortified or defensive position at the end of a bridge nearest to the enemy.

bridgework *n* a partial denture attached to the surrounding teeth.

bridging loan *n* a loan made to cover the period between two transactions, such as the buying of another house before the sale of the first is completed.

bridle *n* **1** headgear for controlling a horse, consisting of straps and a bit and reins. **2** something that curbs or restrains. *~vb* **-dling, -dled 3** to show anger or indignation: *he bridled at the shortness of her tone.* **4** to put a bridle on (a horse). **5** to restrain; curb.

bridle path *n* a path suitable for riding or leading horses.

Brie (**bree**) *n* a soft creamy white cheese.

brief *adj* **1** short in duration. **2** short in length or extent; scanty: *a brief bikini.* **3** terse or concise. *~n* **4** a condensed statement or written synopsis. **5** *Law* a document containing all the facts and points of law of a case by which a solicitor instructs a barrister to represent a client. **6** *RC Church* a papal letter that is less formal than a bull. **7** Also called: **briefing** instructions. **8 hold a brief for** to argue for; champion. **9 in brief** in short; to sum up. *~vb* **10** to prepare or instruct (someone) by giving a summary of relevant facts. **11** *English law* **a** to instruct (a barrister) by brief. **b** to retain (a barrister) as counsel. **briefly** *adv*

briefcase *n* a flat portable case for carrying papers, books, etc.

briefs *pl n* men's or women's underpants without legs.

brier[1] *or* **briar** *n* any of various thorny shrubs or other plants, such as the sweetbrier.

brier[2] *n* same as **briar**[1].

brig[1] *n Naut* a two masted square-rigged ship.

brig[2] *n Scot & N English* a bridge.

Brig. Brigadier.

brigade *n* **1** a military formation smaller than a division and usually commanded by a brigadier. **2** a group of people organized for a certain task: *a rescue brigade.*

brigadier *n* a senior officer in an army, usually commanding a brigade.

brigand *n* a bandit, esp. a member of a gang operating in mountainous areas.

brigantine *n* a two-masted sailing ship.

bright *adj* **1** emitting or reflecting much light; shining. **2** (of colours) intense or vivid. **3** full of promise: *a bright future.* **4** lively or cheerful. **5** quick-witted or clever. *~adv* **6** brightly: *the light burned bright in his office.* **brightly** *adv* **brightness** *n*

brighten *vb* **1** to make or become bright or brighter. **2** to make or become cheerful.

brill *n, pl* **brill** *or* **brills** a European flatfish similar to the turbot.

brilliance *or* **brilliancy** *n* **1** great brightness. **2** excellence in physical or mental ability. **3** splendour.

brilliant *adj* **1** shining with light; sparkling. **2** (of a colour) vivid. **3** splendid; magnificent: *a brilliant show.* **4** of outstanding intelligence or intellect. *~n* **5** a diamond cut with many facets to increase its sparkle.

brilliantine *n* a perfumed oil used to make the hair smooth and shiny.

brim *n* **1** the upper rim of a cup, bowl, etc. **2** a projecting edge of a hat. *~vb* **brimming, brimmed 3** to be full to the brim: *he saw the tears that brimmed in her eyes.* **brimless** *adj*

brimful *adj* (foll. by *of*) completely filled with.

brimstone *n Obsolete* sulphur.

brindled *adj* brown or grey streaked with a darker colour: *a brindled dog.*

brine *n* **1** a strong solution of salt and water, used for pickling. **2** *Literary* the sea or its water.

bring *vb* **bringing, brought 1** to carry, convey, or take (something or someone) to a designated place or

THESAURUS

vb. arch over, attach, bind, connect, couple, cross, cross over, extend across, go over, join, link, reach across, span, traverse, unite

bridle *n.* **1.** check, control, curb, rein, restraint, trammels *~vb.* **2.** be indignant, bristle, draw (oneself) up, get angry, get one's back up, raise one's hackles, rear up **3.** check, constrain, control, curb, govern, keep in check, master, moderate, rein, repress, restrain, subdue

brief *adj.* **1.** ephemeral, fast, fleeting, hasty, little, momentary, quick, quickie (*informal*), short, short-lived, swift, temporary, transitory **2.** compendious, compressed, concise, crisp, curt, laconic, limited, pithy, short, succinct, terse, thumbnail, to the point *~n.* **3.** abridgment, abstract, digest, epitome, outline, précis, sketch, summary, synopsis **4.** argument, case, contention, data, defence, demonstration *~vb.* **5.** advise, clue in (*informal*), explain, fill in (*informal*), gen up (*Brit. informal*), give (someone) a rundown, give (someone) the gen (*Brit. informal*), inform, instruct, prepare, prime, put (someone) in the picture (*informal*)

briefly abruptly, briskly, casually, concisely, cursorily, curtly, fleetingly, hastily, hurriedly, in a few words, in a nutshell, in brief, in outline, in passing, momentarily, precisely, quickly, shortly, temporarily

brigade band, body, camp, company, contingent, corps, crew, force, group, organization, outfit, party, squad, team, troop, unit

bright 1. beaming, blazing, brilliant, dazzling, effulgent, flashing, gleaming, glistening, glittering, glowing, illuminated, intense, lambent, luminous, lustrous, radiant, resplendent, scintillating, shimmering, shining, sparkling, twinkling, vivid **2.** auspicious, encouraging, excellent, favourable, golden, good, hopeful, optimistic, palmy, promising, propitious, prosperous, rosy **3.** cheerful, chirpy (*informal*), gay, genial, glad, happy, jolly, joyful, joyous, light-hearted, lively, merry, sparky, upbeat (*informal*), vivacious **4.** acute, astute, aware, brainy, brilliant, clear-headed, clever, ingenious, intelligent, inventive, keen, quick, quick-witted, sharp, smart, wide-awake

brighten 1. clear up, enliven, gleam, glow, illuminate, lighten, light up, make brighter, shine **2.** become cheerful, buck up (*informal*), buoy up, cheer, encourage, enliven, gladden, hearten, make happy, perk up

brilliance *or* **brilliancy 1.** blaze, brightness, dazzle, effulgence, gleam, glitter, intensity, luminosity, lustre, radiance, refulgence, resplendence, sheen, sparkle, vividness **2.** acuity, aptitude, braininess, cleverness, distinction, excellence, genius, giftedness, greatness, inventiveness, talent, wisdom **3.** éclat, gilt, glamour, gorgeousness, grandeur, illustriousness, magnificence, pizzazz *or* pizazz (*informal*), splendour

brilliant 1. ablaze, bright, coruscating, dazzling, glittering, glossy, intense, luminous, lustrous, radiant, refulgent, resplendent, scintillating, shining, sparkling, vivid **2.** celebrated, eminent, exceptional, famous, glorious, illustrious, magnificent, notable, outstanding, splendid, superb **3.** accomplished, acute, astute, brainy, clever, discerning, expert, gifted, intellectual, intelligent, inventive, masterly, penetrating, profound, quick, talented

brim 1. *n.* border, brink, circumference, edge, flange,

person. **2** to cause to happen: *responsibility brings maturity.* **3** to cause to come to mind: *it brought back memories.* **4** to cause to be in a certain state, position, etc.: *the punch brought him to his knees.* **5** to make (oneself): *she couldn't bring herself to do it.* **6** to sell for: *the painting brought £2000.* **7** *Law* **a** to institute (proceedings, charges, etc.). **b** to put (evidence, etc.) before a tribunal. ~See also **bring about, bring down,** etc.

bring about *vb* to cause to happen: *a late harvest brought about by bad weather.*

bring-and-buy sale *n Brit & NZ* an informal sale, often for charity, to which people bring items for sale and buy those that others have brought.

bring down *vb* to cause to fall.

bring forth *vb* to give birth to.

bring forward *vb* **1** to move (a meeting or event) to an earlier date or time. **2** to present or introduce (a subject) for discussion. **3** *Book-keeping* to transfer (a sum) to the top of the next page or column.

bring in *vb* **1** to yield (income, profit, or cash). **2** to introduce (a legislative bill, etc.). **3** to return (a verdict).

bring off *vb* to succeed in achieving (something difficult).

bring out *vb* **1** to produce, publish, or have (a book) published. **2** to expose, reveal, or cause to be seen: *he brought out the best in me.* **3** (foll. by *in*) to cause (a person) to become covered with (a rash, spots, etc.).

bring over *vb* to cause (a person) to change allegiances.

bring round *vb* **1** to restore (a person) to consciousness after a faint. **2** to convince (another person) of an opinion or point of view.

bring to *vb* to restore (a person) to consciousness: *the smelling salts brought her to.*

bring up *vb* **1** to care for and train (a child); rear. **2** to raise (a subject) for discussion; mention. **3** to vomit (food).

brinjal *n* (in India and Africa) same as **aubergine.**

brink *n* **1** the edge or border of a steep place. **2** the land at the edge of a body of water. **3 on the brink of** very near, on the point of: *on the brink of disaster.*

brinkmanship *n* the practice of pressing a dangerous situation to the limit of safety in order to win an advantage.

briny *adj* **brinier, briniest 1** of or like brine; salty. ~*n* **2 the briny** *Informal* the sea.

briquette *n* a small brick made of compressed coal dust, used for fuel.

brisk *adj* **1** lively and quick; vigorous: *brisk trade.* **2** invigorating or sharp: *brisk weather.* **3** practical and businesslike: *his manner was brisk.* **briskly** *adv*

brisket *n* beef from the breast of a cow.

brisling *n* same as **sprat.**

bristle *n* **1** any short stiff hair, such as on a pig's back. **2** something resembling these hairs: *toothbrush bristle.* ~*vb* **-tling, -tled 3** to stand up or cause to stand up like bristles. **4** to show anger or indignation: *she bristled at the suggestion.* **5** to be thickly covered or set: *the hedges bristled with blossom.* **bristly** *adj*

Brit *n Informal* a British person.

Brit. **1** Britain. **2** British.

➤ *Brit* used to be regarded as suggesting hostility, but it is now often used neutrally.

Britannia *n* a female warrior carrying a trident and wearing a helmet, personifying Great Britain.

Britannia metal *n* an alloy of tin with antimony and copper.

Britannic *adj* of Britain; British: *Her Britannic Majesty.*

britches *pl n* same as **breeches.**

British *adj* **1** of Britain or the British Commonwealth. **2** denoting the English language as spoken and written in Britain. ~*pl n* **3 the British** the people of Britain.

Briton *n* **1** a person from Britain. **2** *History* any of the early Celtic inhabitants of S Britain.

brittle *adj* **1** easily cracked or broken; fragile. **2** curt or irritable: *a brittle reply.* **3** hard or sharp in quality: *a brittle laugh.* **brittly** *adv*

broach *vb* **1** to initiate (a topic) for discussion. **2** to tap or pierce (a container) to draw off (a liquid). **3** to open in order to begin to use. ~*n* **4** a spit for roasting meat.

broad *adj* **1** having great breadth or width. **2** of vast extent: *broad plains.* **3** not detailed; general. **4** clear and open: *broad daylight.* **5** obvious: *broad hints.* **6** tolerant: *a broad view.* **7** extensive: *broad support.* **8**

THESAURUS

lip, margin, rim, skirt, verge **2.** *vb.* fill, fill up, hold no more, overflow, run over, spill, well over

brimful brimming, filled, flush, full, level with, overflowing, overfull, packed, running over

bring 1. accompany, bear, carry, conduct, convey, deliver, escort, fetch, gather, guide, import, lead, take, transfer, transport, usher **2.** cause, contribute to, create, effect, engender, inflict, occasion, produce, result in, wreak **3.** compel, convince, dispose, force, induce, influence, make, move, persuade, prevail on *or* upon, prompt, sway **4.** command, earn, fetch, gross, net, produce, return, sell for, yield

bring about accomplish, achieve, bring to pass, cause, compass, create, effect, effectuate, generate, give rise to, make happen, manage, occasion, produce, realize

bring down abase, cut down, drop, fell, floor, lay low, level, lower, overthrow, overturn, pull down, reduce, shoot down, undermine, upset

bring in accrue, bear, be worth, fetch, gross, produce, profit, realize, return, yield

bring off accomplish, achieve, bring home the bacon (*informal*), bring to pass, carry off, carry out, crack it (*informal*), cut it (*informal*), discharge, execute, perform, pull off, succeed

bring up 1. breed, develop, educate, form, nurture, raise, rear, support, teach, train **2.** advance, allude to, broach, introduce, mention, move, propose, put forward, submit

brink border, boundary, brim, edge, fringe, frontier, limit, lip, margin, point, rim, skirt, threshold, verge

brisk 1. active, agile, alert, animated, bustling, busy, energetic, lively, nimble, no-nonsense, quick, speedy, sprightly, spry, vigorous, vivacious **2.** biting, bracing, crisp, exhilarating, fresh, invigorating, keen, nippy, refreshing, sharp, snappy, stimulating

briskly actively, apace (*literary*), brusquely, coolly, decisively, efficiently, energetically, firmly, incisively, nimbly, posthaste, promptly, pronto (*informal*), quickly, rapidly, readily, smartly, vigorously

bristle *n.* **1.** barb, hair, prickle, spine, stubble, whisker ~*vb.* **2.** prickle, rise, stand on end, stand up **3.** be angry, be infuriated, be maddened, bridle, flare up, get one's dander up (*slang*), rage, see red, seethe, spit (*informal*) **4.** *with* **with** abound, be alive, be thick, crawl, hum, swarm, teem

brittle 1. breakable, crisp, crumbling, crumbly, delicate, fragile, frail, frangible, friable, shatterable, shivery **2.** curt, edgy, irritable, nervous, prim, stiff, stilted, tense, wired (*slang*)

vulgar or coarse. **9** strongly marked: *a broad Yorkshire accent.* ~*n* **10** *Slang, chiefly US & Canad* a woman. **11 the Broads** in East Anglia, a group of shallow lakes connected by a network of rivers. **broadly** *adv*

B-road *n* a secondary road in Britain.

broad bean *n* the large edible flattened seed of a Eurasian bean plant.

broadcast *n* **1** a transmission or programme on radio or television. ~*vb* **-casting, -cast** *or* **-casted 2** to transmit (announcements or programmes) on radio or television. **3** to take part in a radio or television programme. **4** to make widely known throughout an area: *to broadcast news.* **5** to scatter (seed, etc.). **broadcaster** *n* **broadcasting** *n*

broaden *vb* to make or become broad or broader; widen.

broad gauge *n* a railway track with a greater distance between the lines than the standard gauge of 56½.

broad-leaved *adj* denoting trees other than conifers; having broad rather than needle-shaped leaves.

broadloom *adj* of or designating carpets woven on a wide loom.

broad-minded *adj* **1** tolerant of opposing viewpoints; liberal. **2** not easily shocked.

broadsheet *n* a newspaper in a large format.

broadside *n* **1** a strong or abusive verbal or written attack. **2** *Naval* the simultaneous firing of all the guns on one side of a ship. **3** *Naut* the entire side of a ship. ~*adv* **4** with a broader side facing an object.

broadsword *n* a broad-bladed sword used for cutting rather than stabbing.

brocade *n* **1** a rich fabric woven with a raised design. ~*vb* **-cading, -caded 2** to weave with such a design.

broccoli *n* a variety of cabbage with greenish flower heads.

brochette (brosh-**ett**) *n* a skewer used for holding pieces of meat or vegetables while grilling.

brochure *n* a pamphlet or booklet, esp. one containing introductory information or advertising.

broderie anglaise *n* open embroidery on white cotton, fine linen, etc.

broekies (**brook**-eez) *pl n S African informal* underpants.

brogue[1] *n* a sturdy walking shoe, often with ornamental perforations.

brogue[2] *n* a broad gentle-sounding dialectal accent, esp. that used by the Irish in speaking English.

broil *vb US & Canad* same as **grill** (sense 1).

broiler *n* a young tender chicken suitable for roasting.

broke *vb* **1** the past tense of **break.** ~*adj* **2** *Informal* having no money.

broken *vb* **1** the past participle of **break.** ~*adj* **2** fractured, smashed, or splintered. **3** interrupted; disturbed: *broken sleep.* **4** not functioning. **5** (of a promise or contract) violated; infringed. **6** (of the speech of a foreigner) imperfectly spoken: *broken English.* **7** Also: **broken-in** made tame by training. **8** exhausted or weakened, as through ill-health or misfortune.

broken chord *n* same as **arpeggio.**

broken-down *adj* **1** worn out, as by age or long use; dilapidated. **2** not in working order.

brokenhearted *adj* overwhelmed by grief or disappointment.

broken home *n* a family which does not live together because the parents are separated or divorced.

broker *n* **1** an agent who buys or sells goods, securities, etc.: *insurance broker.* **2** same as **stockbroker. 3** a person who deals in second-hand goods.

brokerage *n* commission charged by a broker.

brolly *n, pl* **-lies** *Brit informal* an umbrella.

bromide *n* **1** *Chem* any compound of bromine with another element or radical. **2** a dose of sodium or potassium bromide given as a sedative. **3** a boring, meaningless, or obvious remark.

bromide paper *n* a type of photographic paper coated with an emulsion of silver bromide.

bromine *n Chem* a dark red liquid chemical element that gives off a pungent vapour. Symbol: Br

bronchial *adj* of or relating to both of the bronchi or the smaller tubes into which they divide.

bronchitis *n* inflammation of the bronchial tubes, causing coughing and difficulty in breathing.

bronchus (**bronk**-uss) *n, pl* **bronchi** (**bronk**-eye) either of the two main branches of the windpipe.

THESAURUS

broach 1. approach, bring up, hint at, introduce, mention, open up, propose, raise the subject, speak of, suggest, talk of, touch on **2.** crack, draw off, open, pierce, puncture, start, tap, uncork

broad 1. ample, beamy (*of a ship*), capacious, expansive, extensive, generous, large, roomy, spacious, vast, voluminous, wide, widespread **2.** all-embracing, catholic, comprehensive, encyclopedic, far-reaching, general, global, inclusive, nonspecific, sweeping, undetailed, universal, unlimited, wide, wide-ranging **3.** clear, full, obvious, open, plain, straightforward, undisguised **4.** broad-minded, liberal, open, permissive, progressive, tolerant, unbiased **5.** blue, coarse, gross, improper, indecent, indelicate, near the knuckle (*informal*), unrefined, vulgar

broadcast *n.* **1.** programme, show, telecast, transmission ~*vb.* **2.** air, beam, cable, put on the air, radio, relay, show, televise, transmit **3.** advertise, announce, circulate, disseminate, make public, proclaim, promulgate, publish, report, spread

broaden augment, develop, enlarge, expand, extend, fatten, increase, open up, spread, stretch, supplement, swell, widen

broad-minded catholic, cosmopolitan, dispassionate, flexible, free-thinking, indulgent, liberal, open-minded, permissive, responsive, tolerant, unbiased, unbigoted, undogmatic, unprejudiced

broadside abuse, assault, attack, battering, bombardment, censure, criticism, denunciation, diatribe, philippic, stick (*slang*)

brochure advertisement, booklet, circular, folder, handbill, hand-out, leaflet, mailshot, pamphlet

broke bankrupt, bust (*informal*), cleaned out (*slang*), down and out, flat broke (*informal*), impoverished, insolvent, on one's uppers, penniless, penurious, ruined, short, skint (*Brit. slang*), stony-broke (*Brit. slang*), without two pennies to rub together (*informal*)

broken 1. burst, demolished, destroyed, fractured, fragmented, rent, ruptured, separated, severed, shattered, shivered **2.** disconnected, discontinuous, disturbed, erratic, fragmentary, incomplete, intermittent, interrupted, spasmodic **3.** dishonoured, disobeyed, disregarded, forgotten, ignored, infringed, isolated, retracted, traduced, transgressed **4.** disjointed, halting, hesitating, imperfect, stammering

broken-down collapsed, dilapidated, in disrepair, inoperative, kaput (*informal*), not functioning, not in working order, old, on the blink (*slang*), out of commission, out of order, worn out

brokenhearted crestfallen, desolate, despairing, devastated, disappointed, disconsolate, grief-stricken,

bronco *n, pl* **-cos** (in the U.S. and Canada) a wild or partially tamed pony.

brontosaurus *n* a very large plant-eating four-footed dinosaur that had a long neck and long tail.

bronze *n* **1** an alloy of copper and smaller proportions of tin. **2** a statue, medal, or other object made of bronze. *~adj* **3** made of or resembling bronze. **4** yellowish-brown. *~vb* **bronzing, bronzed 5** (esp. of the skin) to make or become brown; tan.

Bronze Age *n* a phase of human culture, lasting in Britain from about 2000 to 500 BC during which weapons and tools were made of bronze.

bronze medal *n* a medal awarded as third prize.

brooch *n* an ornament with a hinged pin and catch, worn fastened to clothing.

brood *n* **1** a number of young animals, esp. birds, produced at one hatching. **2** all the children in a family: often used jokingly. *~vb* **3** (of a bird) to sit on or hatch eggs. **4** to think long and unhappily about something: *he brooded on his failure to avert the confrontation.* **brooding** *n, adj*

broody *adj* **broodier, broodiest 1** moody; introspective. **2** (of poultry) wishing to sit on or hatch eggs. **3** *Informal* (of a woman) wishing to have a baby.

brook[1] *n* a natural freshwater stream.

brook[2] *vb* to bear; tolerate: *she would brook no opposition.*

broom *n* **1** a type of long-handled sweeping brush. **2** a yellow-flowered shrub. **3 a new broom** a newly appointed official, etc., eager to make radical changes.

broomstick *n* the long handle of a broom.

bros. *or* **Bros.** brothers.

broth *n* a soup made by boiling meat, vegetables, etc. in water.

brothel *n* a house where men pay to have sexual intercourse with prostitutes.

brother *n* **1** a man or boy with the same parents as another person. **2** a man belonging to the same group, trade union, etc. as another or others; fellow member. **3** comrade; friend. **4** *Christianity* a member of a male religious order.

brotherhood *n* **1** fellowship. **2** an association, such as a trade union. **3** the state of being a brother.

brother-in-law *n, pl* **brothers-in-law 1** the brother of one's wife or husband. **2** the husband of one's sister.

brotherly *adj* of or like a brother, esp. in showing loyalty and affection.

brougham (**brew**-am) *n* a horse-drawn closed carriage with a raised open driver's seat in front.

brought *vb* the past of **bring.**

brouhaha *n* loud confused noise.

brow *n* **1** the part of the face from the eyes to the hairline; forehead. **2** same as **eyebrow. 3** the jutting top of a hill.

browbeat *vb* **-beating, -beat, -beaten** to frighten (someone) with threats.

brown *adj* **1** of the colour of wood or the earth. **2** (of bread) made from wheatmeal or wholemeal flour. **3** deeply tanned. *~n* **4** the colour of wood or the earth. **5** anything brown, such as brown paint or brown clothing: *clad in brown.* *~vb* **6** to make or become brown or browner, for example as a result of cooking. **brownish** *adj*

brown bear *n* a large ferocious brownish bear of N America, Europe and Asia.

brown coal *n* same as **lignite.**

browned-off *adj Informal, chiefly Brit* thoroughly bored and depressed.

brownie *n* **1** (in folklore) an elf said to do helpful work, esp. household chores, at night. **2** a small square nutty chocolate cake.

Brownie Guide *or* **Brownie** *n* a member of the junior branch of the Guides.

Brownie point *n* a notional mark to one's credit for being seen to do the right thing.

browning *n Brit* a substance used to darken gravies.

brown paper *n* a kind of coarse unbleached paper used for wrapping.

brown rice *n* unpolished rice, in which the grains retain the outer yellowish-brown layer (bran).

Brown Shirt *n* **1** (in Nazi Germany) a storm trooper. **2** a member of any fascist party or group.

brown trout *n* a common brownish trout that occurs in the rivers of N Europe.

browse *vb* **browsing, browsed 1** to look through (a book or articles for sale) in a casual leisurely manner. **2** (of deer, goats, etc.) to feed upon vegetation by continual nibbling. *~n* **3** an instance of browsing.

brucellosis *n* an infectious disease of cattle, goats, and pigs, caused by bacteria and transmittable to humans.

bruise *vb* **bruising, bruised 1** to injure (body tissue) without breaking the skin, usually with discoloration, or (of body tissue) to be injured in this way. **2** to hurt

THESAURUS

heartbroken, heart-sick, inconsolable, miserable, mournful, prostrated, sorrowful, wretched

broker agent, dealer, factor, go-between, intermediary, middleman, negotiator

bronze brownish, chestnut, copper, copper-coloured, metallic brown, reddish-brown, reddish-tan, rust, tan

brood *n.* **1.** breed, chicks, children, clutch, family, hatch, infants, issue, litter, offspring, progeny, young *~vb.* **2.** cover, hatch, incubate, set, sit upon **3.** agonize, dwell upon, eat one's heart out, fret, meditate, mope, mull over, muse, ponder, repine (*literary*), ruminate, think upon

brook beck, burn, gill (*dialect*), rill, rivulet, runnel (*literary*), stream, streamlet, watercourse

brother 1. blood brother, kin, kinsman, relation, relative, sibling **2.** associate, chum (*informal*), cock (*Brit. informal*), colleague, companion, compeer, comrade, confrère, fellow member, mate, pal (*informal*), partner **3.** cleric, friar, monk, regular, religious

brotherhood 1. brotherliness, camaraderie, companionship, comradeship, fellowship, friendliness, kinship **2.** alliance, association, clan, clique, community, coterie, fraternity, guild, league, order, society, union

brotherly affectionate, altruistic, amicable, benevolent, cordial, fraternal, friendly, kind, neighbourly, philanthropic, sympathetic

brow 1. air, appearance, aspect, bearing, countenance, eyebrow, face, forehead, front, mien (*literary*), temple **2.** brim, brink, crest, crown, edge, peak, rim, summit, tip, top, verge

browbeat badger, bulldoze (*informal*), bully, coerce, cow, domineer, dragoon, hector, intimidate, lord it over, oppress, overawe, overbear, threaten, tyrannize

brown 1. *adj.* auburn, bay, brick, bronze, bronzed, browned, brunette, chestnut, chocolate, coffee, dark, donkey brown, dun, dusky, ginger, hazel, rust, sunburnt, tan, tanned, tawny, toasted, umber **2.** *vb.* cook, fry, grill, sauté, seal, sear

browse 1. dip into, examine cursorily, flip through, glance at, leaf through, look round, look through, peruse, scan, skim, survey **2.** crop, eat, feed, graze, nibble, pasture

(someone's feelings). **3** to damage (fruit). ~*n* **4** a bodily injury without a break in the skin, usually with discoloration.

bruiser *n Informal* a strong tough person, esp. a boxer or a bully.

brunch *n* a meal eaten late in the morning, combining breakfast with lunch.

brunette *n* a girl or woman with dark brown hair.

brunt *n* the main force or shock of a blow, attack, etc.: *the town bore the brunt of the earthquake.*

brush[1] *n* **1** a device made of bristles, hairs, wires, etc. set into a firm back or handle: used to apply paint, groom the hair, etc. **2** the act of brushing. **3** a brief encounter, esp. an unfriendly one. **4** the bushy tail of a fox. **5** an electric conductor, esp. one made of carbon, that conveys current between stationary and rotating parts of a generator, motor, etc. ~*vb* **6** to clean, scrub, or paint with a brush. **7** to apply or remove with a brush or brushing movement. **8** to touch lightly and briefly. ~See also **brush aside, brush off, brush up.**

brush[2] *n* a thick growth of shrubs and small trees; scrub.

brush aside *or* **away** *vb* to dismiss (a suggestion or an idea) without consideration; disregard.

brushed *adj Textiles* treated with a brushing process to raise the nap and give a softer and warmer finish: *brushed nylon.*

brush off *Slang* ~*vb* **1** to dismiss and ignore (a person), esp. curtly. ~*n* **brushoff 2 give someone the brushoff** to reject someone.

brush up *vb* **1** (often foll. by *on*) to refresh one's knowledge or memory of (a subject). ~*n* **brush-up 2** *Brit* the act of tidying one's appearance: *have a wash and brush-up.*

brushwood *n* **1** cut or broken-off tree branches, twigs, etc. **2** same as **brush**[2].

brushwork *n* a characteristic manner of applying paint with a brush: *Rembrandt's brushwork.*

brusque *adj* blunt or curt in manner or speech. **brusquely** *adv* **brusqueness** *n*

Brussels sprout *n* a vegetable like a tiny cabbage.

brut (**broot**) *adj* (of champagne or sparkling wine) very dry.

brutal *adj* **1** cruel; vicious; savage. **2** extremely honest or frank in speech or manner. **brutality** *n* **brutally** *adv*

brutalism *n* an austere architectural style of the 1950s on, characterized by the use of exposed concrete and angular shapes.

brutalize *or* **-ise** *vb* **-izing, -ized** *or* **-ising, -ised 1** to make or become brutal. **2** to treat (someone) brutally. **brutalization** *or* **-isation** *n*

brute *n* **1** a brutal person. **2** any animal except man; beast. ~*adj* **3** wholly instinctive or physical, like that of an animal: *cricket is not a game of brute force.* **4** without reason or intelligence. **5** coarse and grossly sensual.

brutish *adj* **1** of or resembling a brute; animal. **2** coarse; cruel; stupid.

bryony *n, pl* **-nies** a climbing plant with greenish flowers and red or black berries.

Brythonic (brith-**on**-ik) *n* **1** the S group of Celtic languages, consisting of Welsh, Cornish, and Breton. ~*adj* **2** of this group of languages.

BS 1 Bachelor of Surgery. **2** British Standard(s).

BSc Bachelor of Science.

BSE bovine spongiform encephalopathy: a fatal virus disease of cattle.

BSI British Standards Institution.

B-side *n* the less important side of a gramophone record.

BST British Summer Time.

Bt Baronet.

BT British Telecom.

btu *or* **BThU** British thermal unit.

bubble *n* **1** a small globule of air or a gas in a liquid or a solid. **2** a thin film of liquid forming a ball around air or a gas: *a soap bubble.* **3** a dome, esp. a transparent glass or plastic one. **4** an unreliable scheme or enterprise. ~*vb* **-bling, -bled 5** to form bubbles. **6** to move or flow with a gurgling sound. **7 bubble over** to express an emotion freely: *she was bubbling over with excitement.*

bubble and squeak *n Brit* a dish of boiled cabbage and potatoes fried together.

bubble bath *n* **1** a substance used to scent, soften, and foam in bath water. **2** a bath with such a substance.

bubble car *n Brit* a small car of the 1950s with a transparent bubble-shaped top.

bubble gum *n* a type of chewing gum that can be blown into large bubbles.

bubbly *adj* **-blier, -bliest 1** lively; animated; excited. **2** full of or resembling bubbles. ~*n* **3** *Informal* champagne.

bubo (**byew**-boh) *n, pl* **-boes** *Pathol* inflammation and swelling of a lymph node, esp. in the armpit or groin. **bubonic** (bew-**bonn**-ik) *adj*

THESAURUS

bruise *vb.* **1.** blacken, blemish, contuse, crush, damage, deface, discolour, injure, mar, mark, pound, pulverize **2.** displease, grieve, hurt, injure, insult, offend, pain, sting, wound ~*n.* **3.** black-and-blue mark, black mark, blemish, contusion, discoloration, injury, mark, swelling

brunt burden, force, full force, impact, pressure, shock, strain, stress, thrust, violence

brush[1] *n.* **1.** besom, broom, sweeper **2.** clash, conflict, confrontation, encounter, fight, fracas, scrap (*informal*), set-to (*informal*), skirmish, slight engagement, spot of bother (*informal*), tussle ~*vb.* **3.** buff, clean, paint, polish, sweep, wash **4.** caress, contact, flick, glance, graze, kiss, scrape, stroke, sweep, touch

brush[2] *n.* brushwood, bushes, copse, scrub, shrubs, thicket, undergrowth, underwood

brush off *vb.* cold-shoulder, cut, deny, disdain, dismiss, disown, disregard, ignore, put down, rebuff, refuse, reject, repudiate, scorn, slight, snub, spurn

brushoff *n.* cold shoulder, cut, dismissal, knock-back (*slang*), rebuff, refusal, rejection, repudiation, repulse, slight, snub, the (old) heave-ho (*informal*)

brush up bone up on (*informal*), cram, go over, polish up, read up, refresh one's memory, relearn, revise, study

brutal 1. barbarous, bloodthirsty, cruel, ferocious, heartless, inhuman, merciless, pitiless, remorseless, ruthless, savage, uncivilized, vicious **2.** bearish, callous, gruff, harsh, impolite, insensitive, rough, rude, severe, uncivil, unfeeling, unmannerly

brute *n.* **1.** barbarian, beast, devil, fiend, ghoul, monster, ogre, sadist, savage, swine **2.** animal, beast, creature, wild animal ~*adj.* **3.** bodily, carnal, fleshly, instinctive, mindless, physical, senseless, unthinking **4.** bestial, coarse, depraved, gross, sensual

bubble *n.* **1.** air ball, bead, blister, blob, drop, droplet, globule, vesicle **2.** bagatelle, delusion, fantasy, illusion, toy, trifle, vanity ~*vb.* **3.** boil, effervesce, fizz, foam, froth, percolate, seethe, sparkle

bubonic plague *n* an acute infectious disease characterized by the formation of buboes.

buccaneer *n* a pirate, esp. in the Caribbean in the 17th and 18th centuries.

buck[1] *n* **1** the male of the goat, hare, kangaroo, rabbit, and reindeer. **2** *Archaic* a spirited young man. **3** the act of bucking. ~*vb* **4** (of a horse or other animal) to jump vertically, with legs stiff and back arched. **5** (of a horse, etc.) to throw (its rider) by bucking. **6** *Informal* to resist or oppose obstinately: *bucking the system.* ~See also **buck up.**

buck[2] *n US, Canad, & Austral slang* a dollar.

buck[3] *n* **pass the buck** *Informal* to shift blame or responsibility onto another.

bucket *n* **1** an open-topped cylindrical container with a handle. **2** the amount a bucket will hold. **3** a bucket-like part of a machine, such as the scoop on a mechanical shovel. **4 kick the bucket** *Slang* to die.

bucket down *vb* **-eting, -eted** (of rain) to fall very heavily.

bucket shop *n* **1** *Chiefly Brit* a travel agency specializing in cheap airline tickets. **2** an unregistered firm of stockbrokers that engages in fraudulent speculation.

buckle *n* **1** a clasp for fastening together two loose ends, esp. of a belt or strap. ~*vb* **-ling, -led 2** to fasten or be fastened with a buckle. **3** to bend or cause to bend out of shape, esp. as a result of pressure or heat.

buckle down *vb Informal* to apply oneself with determination.

buckler *n* a small round shield worn on the forearm.

Bucks Buckinghamshire.

buckshee *adj Brit slang* without charge; free.

buckshot *n* large lead pellets used for hunting game.

buckskin *n* **1** a strong greyish-yellow suede leather, originally made from deerskin. **2 buckskins** trousers made of buckskin.

buckteeth *pl n* projecting upper front teeth. **buck-toothed** *adj*

buckthorn *n* a thorny shrub whose berries were formerly used as a purgative.

buck up *vb Informal* **1** to make or become more cheerful or confident. **2** to make haste.

buckwheat *n* **1** a type of small black seed used as animal fodder and in making flour. **2** the flour obtained from such seeds.

bucolic (byew-**koll**-ik) *adj* **1** of the countryside or country life; rustic. **2** of or relating to shepherds; pastoral. ~*n* **3** a pastoral poem.

bud *n* **1** a swelling on the stem of a plant that develops into a flower or leaf. **2** a partially opened flower: *rosebud.* **3** any small budlike outgrowth: *taste buds.* **4 nip something in the bud** to put an end to something in its initial stages. ~*vb* **budding, budded 5** (of plants and some animals) to produce buds. **6** *Horticulture* to graft (a bud) from one plant onto another.

Buddhism *n* a religion founded by the Buddha that teaches that all suffering can be brought to an end by overcoming greed, hatred, and delusion. **Buddhist** *n, adj*

budding *adj* beginning to develop or grow: *a budding actor.*

buddleia *n* an ornamental shrub which has long spikes of purple flowers.

buddy *n, pl* **-dies 1** *Chiefly US & Canad informal* a friend. **2** a volunteer who helps and supports a person suffering from AIDS. ~*vb* **-dies, -dying, -died 3** to act as a buddy to (a person suffering from AIDS).

budge *vb* **budging, budged 1** to move slightly: *he refuses to budge off that chair.* **2** to change or cause to change opinions: *nothing would budge him from this idea.*

budgerigar *n* a small cage bird bred in many different-coloured varieties.

budget *n* **1** a plan of expected income and expenditure over a specified period. **2** the total amount of money allocated for a specific purpose during a specified period. ~*adj* **3** inexpensive: *a budget hotel.* ~*vb* **-eting, -eted 4** to enter or provide for in a budget. **5** to plan the expenditure of (money or time). **budgetary** *adj*

Budget *n* **the Budget** an annual estimate of British government expenditures and revenues and the financial plans for the following financial year.

budgie *n Informal* same as **budgerigar.**

buff[1] *n* **1** a soft thick flexible undyed leather. **2** a cloth or pad of material used for polishing. **3 in the buff** *Informal* completely naked. ~*adj* **4** dull yellowish-brown. ~*vb* **5** to clean or polish (a metal, floor, shoes, etc.) with a buff.

buff[2] *n Informal* an expert on or devotee of a given subject: *an opera buff.*

buffalo *n, pl* **-loes** *or* **-lo 1** a type of cattle with upward-curving horns. **2** same as **water buffalo. 3** *US & Canad* a bison.

buffer[1] *n* **1** one of a pair of spring-loaded steel pads at the ends of railway vehicles and railway tracks that reduces shock on impact. **2** a person or thing that lessens shock or protects from damaging impact, circumstances, etc. **3** *Chem* **a** a substance added to a solution to resist changes in its acidity or alkalinity. **b** Also called: **buffer solution** a solution containing such a substance. **4** *Computers* a device for temporarily storing data.

THESAURUS

bubbly 1. animated, bouncy, elated, excited, happy, lively, merry, sparky **2.** carbonated, curly, effervescent, fizzy, foamy, frothy, lathery, sparkling, sudsy

buccaneer corsair, freebooter, pirate, privateer, searover

buckle *n.* **1.** catch, clasp, clip, fastener, hasp ~*vb.* **2.** catch, clasp, close, fasten, hook, secure **3.** bend, bulge, cave in, collapse, contort, crumple, distort, fold, twist, warp

buckle down apply oneself, exert oneself, launch into, pitch in, put one's shoulder to the wheel, set to

buck up 1. brighten, cheer up, encourage, hearten, inspirit, perk up, rally, take heart **2.** get a move on, hasten, hurry up, shake a leg, speed up

bud 1. *n.* embryo, germ, shoot, sprout **2.** *vb.* burgeon, burst forth, develop, grow, pullulate, shoot, sprout

budding beginning, burgeoning, developing, embryonic, fledgling, flowering, germinal, growing, incipient, nascent (*formal*), potential, promising

budge 1. dislodge, give way, inch, move, propel, push, remove, roll, shift, slide, stir **2.** bend, change, convince, give way, influence, persuade, sway, yield

budget 1. *n.* allocation, allowance, cost, finances, financial statement, fiscal estimate, funds, means, resources **2.** *vb.* allocate, apportion, cost, cost out, estimate, plan, ration

buff[1] **1.** *n.* **in the buff** bare, buck naked (*slang*), in one's birthday suit (*informal*), in the altogether (*informal*), in the raw (*informal*), naked, nude, unclad, unclothed, with bare skin, without a stitch on (*informal*) **2.** *adj.* sandy, straw, tan, yellowish, yellowish-brown **3.** *vb.* brush, burnish, polish, rub, shine, smooth

buff[2] *informal* addict, admirer, aficionado, connoisseur, devotee, enthusiast, expert, fan, fiend (*informal*),

buffer² *n Brit informal* a stupid or bumbling person, esp. a man: *an old buffer.*

buffer state *n* a small and usually neutral state between two rival powers.

buffet¹ (**boof**-fay) *n* **1** a counter where light refreshments are served. **2** a meal at which guests help themselves from a number of dishes.

buffet² (**buff**-it) *vb* **-feting, -feted 1** to knock against or about; batter: *the ship was buffeted by strong winds.* **2** to hit, esp. with the fist. ~*n* **3** a blow, esp. with a hand.

buffet car (**boof**-fay) *n Brit* a railway coach where light refreshments are served.

buffoon *n* a person who amuses others by silly behaviour. **buffoonery** *n*

bug *n* **1** any of various insects having piercing and sucking mouthparts. **2** *Chiefly US & Canad* any insect. **3** *Informal* a minor illness caused by a germ or virus. **4** *Informal* an obsessive idea or hobby. **5** *Informal* a concealed microphone used for recording conversations in spying. ~*vb* **bugging, bugged** *Informal* **6** to irritate or upset (someone). **7** to conceal a microphone in (a room or telephone).

bugbear *n* a thing that causes obsessive anxiety.

bugger *n* **1** *Taboo slang* a person or thing considered to be unpleasant or difficult. **2** *Slang* a humorous or affectionate term for someone: *a friendly little bugger.* **3** a person who practises buggery. ~*vb* **4** *Slang* to tire; weary. **5** to practise buggery with. ~*interj* **6** *Taboo slang* an exclamation of annoyance or disappointment.

bugger about *or* **around** *vb Slang* **1** to fool about and waste time. **2** to create difficulties for: *they really buggered me about when I tried to get my money back.*

bugger off *vb Taboo slang* to go away; depart.

bugger up *vb Slang* to spoil or ruin (something).

buggery *n* anal intercourse.

buggy *n, pl* **-gies 1** a light horse-drawn carriage having two or four wheels. **2** a lightweight folding pram for babies or young children.

bugle *Music* ~*n* **1** a brass instrument used chiefly for military calls. ~*vb* **-gling, -gled 2** to play or sound (on) a bugle. **bugler** *n*

build *vb* **building, built 1** to make or construct by joining parts or materials: *more than 100 bypasses have been built in the past decade.* **2** to establish and develop: *it took ten years to build the business.* **3** to make in a particular way or for a particular purpose: *she's built for speed, not stamina.* **4** (often foll. by *up*) to increase in intensity. ~*n* **5** physical form, figure, or proportions: *he has an athletic build.*

builder *n* a person who constructs houses and other buildings.

building *n* **1** a structure, such as a house, with a roof and walls. **2** the business of building houses, etc.

building society *n* a cooperative banking enterprise where money can be invested and mortgage loans made available.

build up *vb* **1** to construct (something) gradually, systematically, and in stages. **2** to increase by degrees: *he steadily built up a power base.* **3** to prepare for or gradually approach a climax. ~*n* **build-up 4** a progressive increase in number or size: *the build-up of industry.* **5** a gradual approach to a climax. **6** extravagant publicity or praise, esp. as a campaign.

built *vb* the past of **build.**

built-in *adj* **1** included as an essential part: *a built-in cupboard.* **2** essential: *a built-in instinct.*

built-up *adj* **1** having many buildings: *a built-up area.* **2** increased by the addition of parts: *built-up heels.*

bulb *n* **1** same as **light bulb. 2** the onion-shaped base of the stem of some plants, which sends down roots. **3** a plant, such as a daffodil, which grows from a bulb. **4** any bulb-shaped thing. **bulbous** *adj*

Bulgarian *adj* **1** of Bulgaria. ~*n* **2** a person from Bulgaria. **3** the language of Bulgaria.

bulge *n* **1** a swelling or an outward curve on a normally flat surface. **2** a sudden increase in number, esp. of population. ~*vb* **bulging, bulged 3** to swell outwards. **bulging** *adj*

bulimia *n* a disorder characterized by compulsive overeating followed by vomiting.

bulk *n* **1** volume or size, esp. when great. **2** the main part: *he spends the bulk of his time abroad.* **3** a large body, esp. of a person. **4** the part of food which passes unabsorbed through the digestive system. **5 in bulk** in

THESAURUS

freak (*informal*), grandmaster, hotshot (*informal*), whiz (*informal*)

buffer bulwark, bumper, cushion, fender, intermediary, safeguard, screen, shield, shock absorber

buffet¹ *n.* café, cafeteria, cold table, counter, cupboard, refreshment-counter, salad bar, sideboard, snack bar

buffet² **1.** *vb.* bang, batter, beat, box, bump, clobber (*slang*), cuff, flail, knock, lambast(e), pound, pummel, punch, push, rap, shove, slap, strike, thump, wallop (*informal*) **2.** *n.* bang, blow, box, bump, cuff, jolt, knock, push, rap, shove, slap, smack, thump, wallop (*informal*)

buffoon clown, comedian, comic, droll, fool, harlequin, jester, joker, merry-andrew, silly billy (*informal*), wag

bug *n.* **1.** *informal* bacterium, disease, germ, infection, microorganism, virus **2.** craze, fad, mania, obsession, rage ~*vb.* **3.** *informal* aggravate (*informal*), annoy, badger, be on one's back (*slang*), bother, disturb, gall, get in one's hair (*informal*), get on one's nerves (*informal*), get on one's wick (*Brit. slang*), harass, hassle (*informal*), irk, irritate, nark, needle (*informal*), nettle, pester, piss one off (*taboo slang*), plague, vex **4.** eavesdrop, listen in, spy, tap, wiretap

bugbear anathema, bane, *bête noire,* bogey, devil, dread, fiend, horror, nightmare, pet hate

build *vb.* **1.** assemble, construct, erect, fabricate, form, make, put up, raise **2.** base, begin, constitute, establish, formulate, found, inaugurate, initiate, institute, originate, set up, start **3.** accelerate, amplify, augment, develop, enlarge, escalate, extend, improve, increase, intensify, strengthen ~*n.* **4.** body, figure, form, frame, physique, shape, structure

building **1.** domicile, dwelling, edifice, fabric, house, pile, structure **2.** architecture, construction, erection, fabricating, raising

build-up **1.** accumulation, development, enlargement, escalation, expansion, gain, growth, increase **2.** ballyhoo (*informal*), hype, plug (*informal*), promotion, publicity

built-in essential, implicit, in-built, included, incorporated, inherent, inseparable, integral, part and parcel of

bulge *n.* **1.** bump, hump, lump, projection, protrusion, protuberance, swelling **2.** boost, increase, intensification, rise, surge ~*vb.* **3.** bag, dilate, distend, enlarge, expand, project, protrude, puff out, sag, stand out, stick out, swell, swell out

bulk *n.* **1.** amplitude, bigness, dimensions, immensity, largeness, magnitude, massiveness, size, substance,

large quantities. *~vb* **6 bulk large** to be or seem important or prominent.

bulk buying *n* the purchase of goods in large amounts, often at reduced prices.

bulkhead *n* any upright partition in a ship or aeroplane.

bulky *adj* **bulkier, bulkiest** very large and massive, esp. so as to be unwieldy. **bulkiness** *n*

bull[1] *n* **1** a male of domestic cattle, esp. one that is sexually mature. **2** the male of various other animals including the elephant and whale. **3** a very large, strong, or aggressive person. **4** *Stock Exchange* a speculator who buys in anticipation of rising prices in order to make a profit on resale. **5** *Chiefly Brit* same as **bull's-eye** (senses 1, 2). **6 like a bull in a china shop** clumsy. **7 take the bull by the horns** to face and tackle a difficulty without shirking.

bull[2] *n* a ludicrously self-contradictory or nonsensical statement.

bull[3] *n* a formal document issued by the pope.

bulldog *n* a thickset dog with a broad head and a muscular body.

bulldog clip *n* a clip for holding papers together, consisting of two metal clamps and a spring.

bulldoze *vb* **-dozing, -dozed 1** to move, demolish, or flatten with a bulldozer. **2** *Informal* to coerce (someone) into doing something by intimidation.

bulldozer *n* a powerful tractor fitted with caterpillar tracks and a blade at the front, used for moving earth.

bullet *n* a small metallic missile used as the projectile of a gun or rifle.

bulletin *n* **1** a broadcast summary of the news. **2** an official statement on a matter of public interest. **3** a periodical published by an organization for its members.

bullfight *n* a public show, popular in Spain, in which a matador baits and usually kills a bull in an arena. **bullfighter** *n* **bullfighting** *n*

bullfinch *n* a common European songbird with a black head and, in the male, a pinkish breast.

bullfrog *n* any of various large frogs having a loud deep croak.

bullion *n* gold or silver in the form of bars and ingots.

bull-necked *adj* having a short thick neck.

bullock *n* a gelded bull; steer.

bullring *n* an arena for staging bullfights.

bull's-eye *n* **1** the small central disc of a target or a dartboard. **2** a shot hitting this. **3** *Informal* something that exactly achieves its aim. **4** a peppermint-flavoured boiled sweet. **5** a small circular window. **6** a thick disc of glass set into a ship's deck, etc. to admit light. **7** the glass boss at the centre of a sheet of blown glass. **8 a** a convex lens used as a condenser. **b** a lamp or lantern containing such a lens.

bullshit *Taboo slang ~n* **1** exaggerated or foolish talk; nonsense. *~vb* **-shitting, -shitted 2** to talk bullshit to: *don't bullshit me.*

bull terrier *n* a terrier with a muscular body and a short smooth coat.

bully *n, pl* **-lies 1** a person who hurts, persecutes, or intimidates weaker people. *~vb* **-lies, -lying, -lied 2** to hurt, intimidate, or persecute (a weaker or smaller person). *~interj* **3 bully for you, him,** etc.) *Informal* well done! bravo!: now usually used sarcastically.

bully beef *n* canned corned beef.

bully-off *Hockey ~n* **1** the method of starting play in which two opposing players stand with the ball between them and strike their sticks together three times before trying to hit the ball. *~vb* **bully off 2** to start play with a bully-off.

bulrush *n* **1** a tall reedlike marsh plant with brown spiky flowers. **2** *Bible* same as **papyrus** (sense 1).

bulwark *n* **1** a wall or similar structure used as a fortification; rampart. **2** a person or thing acting as a defence.

bum[1] *n Brit slang* the buttocks or anus.

bum[2] *Informal ~n* **1** a disreputable loafer or idler. **2** a tramp; hobo. *~vb* **bumming, bummed 3** to get by begging; cadge: *to bum a lift.* **4 bum around** to spend time to no good purpose; loaf. *~adj* **5** of poor quality; useless: *he hit a bum note.*

bumbag *n* a small bag worn on a belt around the waist.

bumble *vb* **-bling, -bled 1** to speak or do in a clumsy, muddled, or inefficient way. **2** to move in a clumsy or unsteady way. **bumbling** *adj, n*

bumblebee *n* a large hairy bee.

bumf *n* same as **bumph.**

bump *vb* **1** to knock or strike (someone or something) with a jolt. **2** to travel or proceed in jerks and jolts. **3** to hurt by knocking. *~n* **4** an impact; knock; jolt; collision. **5** a dull thud from an impact or collision. **6** a lump on the body caused by a blow. **7** a raised uneven part, such as on a road surface. ~See also **bump into, bump off, bump up. bumpy** *adj*

bumper[1] *n* a horizontal bar attached to the front and rear of a vehicle to protect against damage from impact.

bumper[2] *n* **1** a glass or tankard, filled to the brim, esp. as a toast. **2** an unusually large or fine example of something. *~adj* **3** unusually large, fine, or abundant: *a bumper crop.*

bumph *or* **bumf** *n Brit* **1** *Informal* official documents or forms. **2** *Slang* toilet paper.

THESAURUS

volume, weight **2.** better part, body, generality, lion's share, main part, majority, major part, mass, most, nearly all, plurality, preponderance *~vb.* **3. bulk large** be important, carry weight, dominate, loom, loom large, preponderate, stand out, threaten

bulldoze 1. demolish, flatten, level, raze **2.** browbeat, bully, coerce, cow, dragoon, hector, intimidate, railroad (*informal*)

bullet ball, missile, pellet, projectile, shot, slug

bulletin account, announcement, communication, communiqué, dispatch, message, news flash, notification, report, statement

bully 1. *n.* big bully, browbeater, bully boy, coercer, intimidator, oppressor, persecutor, ruffian, tormentor, tough **2.** *vb.* bluster, browbeat, bulldoze (*informal*), coerce, cow, domineer, hector, intimidate, oppress, overbear, persecute, push around (*slang*), ride roughshod over, swagger, terrorize, tyrannize **3.** *interj.* bravo, capital, good, grand, great, well done

bulwark 1. bastion, buttress, defence, embankment, fortification, outwork, partition, rampart, redoubt **2.** buffer, guard, mainstay, safeguard, security, support

bump *vb.* **1.** bang, collide (with), crash, hit, knock, slam, smash into, strike **2.** bounce, jar, jerk, jolt, jostle, jounce, rattle, shake *~n.* **3.** bang, blow, collision, crash, hit, impact, jar, jolt, knock, rap, shock, smash, thud, thump **4.** bulge, contusion, hump, knob, knot, lump, node, nodule, protuberance, swelling

bumper *adj.* abundant, bountiful, excellent, exceptional, jumbo (*informal*), massive, mega (*slang*), prodigal, spanking (*informal*), teeming, unusual, whacking (*informal, chiefly Brit.*), whopping (*informal*)

bump into *vb Informal* to meet (someone) by chance.
bumpkin *n* an awkward simple rustic person: *a country bumpkin.*
bump off *vb Slang* to murder (someone).
bumptious *adj* offensively self-assertive or conceited.
bump up *vb Informal* to increase (prices) by a large amount.
bun *n* **1** a small sweetened bread roll, often containing currants or spices. **2** a small round cake. **3** a hairstyle in which long hair is gathered into a bun shape at the back of the head.
bunch *n* **1** a number of things growing, fastened, or grouped together: *a bunch of grapes; a bunch of keys.* **2** a collection; group: *a bunch of queries.* **3** a group or company: *a bunch of cowards.* ~*vb* **4** to group or be grouped into a bunch.
bundle *n* **1** a number of things or a quantity of material gathered or loosely bound together: *a bundle of sticks.* **2** something wrapped or tied for carrying; package. **3** *Biol* a collection of strands of specialized tissue such as nerve fibres. **4** *Bot* a strand of conducting tissue within plants. ~*vb* **-dling, -dled 5** (foll. by *out, off, into,* etc.) to cause (someone) to go, esp. roughly or unceremoniously: *she bundled them unceremoniously out into the garden.* **6** to push or throw (something), esp. in a quick untidy way: *the soiled items were bundled into a black plastic bag.*
bundle up *vb* to make (something) into a bundle or bundles.
bun fight *n Brit slang* a tea party.
bung *n* **1** a stopper, esp. of cork or rubber, used to close something such as a cask or flask. **2** same as **bunghole.** ~*vb* **3** (foll. by *up*) *Informal* to close or seal (something) with or as if with a bung. **4** *Brit slang* to throw (something) somewhere in a careless manner; sling.
bungalow *n* a one-storey house.
bungee jumping *or* **bungy jumping** *n* a sport in which a person jumps from a high bridge, tower, etc., to which he or she is connected by a rubber rope.
bunghole *n* a hole in a cask or barrel through which liquid can be drained.
bungle *vb* **-gling, -gled 1** to spoil (an operation) through clumsiness or incompetence; botch. ~*n* **2** a clumsy or unsuccessful performance; blunder. **bungler** *n* **bungling** *adj, n*
bunion *n* an inflamed swelling of the first joint of the big toe.
bunk[1] *n* **1** a narrow shelflike bed fixed along a wall, esp. in a caravan or ship. **2** same as **bunk bed.**
bunk[2] *n Informal* same as **bunkum.**
bunk[3] *n* **do a bunk** *Brit slang* to make a hurried and secret departure.
bunk bed *n* one of a pair of beds constructed one above the other to save space.
bunker *n* **1** an obstacle on a golf course, usually a sand-filled hollow bordered by a ridge. **2** an underground shelter. **3** a large storage container for coal etc.
bunkum *n* empty talk; nonsense.
bunny *n, pl* **-nies** a child's word for **rabbit.**
bunny girl *n* a night-club hostess whose costume includes a rabbit-like tail and ears.
Bunsen burner *n* a gas burner consisting of a metal tube with an adjustable air valve at the base.
bunting[1] *n* decorative flags, pennants, and streamers.
bunting[2] *n* a songbird with a short stout bill.
buoy *n* **1** a brightly coloured floating object anchored to the sea bed for marking moorings, navigable channels, or obstructions in the water. ~*vb* **2** (foll. by *up*) to prevent from sinking: *the life belt buoyed him up.* **3** to raise the spirits of; hearten: *exports are on the increase, buoyed by a weak dollar.* **4** *Naut* to mark (a channel or obstruction) with a buoy or buoys.
buoyant *adj* **1** able to float in or rise to the surface of a liquid. **2** (of a liquid or gas) able to keep a body afloat. **3** cheerful or resilient. **buoyancy** *n*
bur *or* **burr** *n* **1** a seed case or flower head with hooks or prickles. **2** any plant that produces burs.
burble *vb* **-bling, -bled 1** to make or utter with a bubbling sound; gurgle. **2** to talk quickly and excitedly.
burbot *n, pl* **-bots** *or* **-bot** a freshwater fish of the cod family that has barbels around its mouth.
burden[1] *n* **1** something that is carried; load. **2** something that is difficult to bear. ~*vb* **3** to put or impose a

THESAURUS

bump into chance upon, come across, encounter, happen upon, light upon, meet, meet up with, run across, run into
bump off assassinate, dispatch, do away with, do in (*slang*), eliminate, finish off, kill, knock off (*slang*), liquidate, murder, remove, rub out (*U.S. slang*), take out (*slang*), wipe out (*informal*)
bumptious arrogant, boastful, brash, cocky, conceited, egotistic, forward, full of oneself, impudent, overbearing, overconfident, presumptuous, pushy (*informal*), self-assertive, showy, swaggering, vainglorious, vaunting
bunch *n.* **1.** assortment, batch, bouquet, bundle, clump, cluster, collection, heap, lot, mass, number, parcel, pile, quantity, sheaf, spray, stack, tuft **2.** band, bevy, crew (*informal*), crowd, flock, gang, gathering, group, knot, mob, multitude, party, posse (*informal*), swarm, team, troop ~*vb.* **3.** assemble, bundle, cluster, collect, congregate, cram together, crowd, flock, group, herd, huddle, mass, pack
bundle *n.* **1.** accumulation, assortment, batch, bunch, collection, group, heap, mass, pile, quantity, stack **2.** bag, bale, box, carton, crate, pack, package, packet, pallet, parcel, roll ~*vb.* **3.** *with* **out, off, into,** etc. hurry, hustle, push, rush, shove, throw, thrust
bundle up bale, bind, fasten, pack, package, palletize, tie, tie together, tie up, truss, wrap
bungle blow (*slang*), blunder, bodge (*informal*), botch, butcher, cock up (*Brit. slang*), foul up, fuck up (*offensive taboo slang*), fudge, louse up (*slang*), make a mess of, mar, mess up, miscalculate, mismanage, muff, ruin, screw up (*informal*), spoil
bungling awkward, blundering, botching, cack-handed (*informal*), clumsy, ham-fisted (*informal*), ham-handed (*informal*), incompetent, inept, maladroit, unskilful
bunk *or* **bunkum** balderdash, balls (*taboo slang*), baloney (*informal*), bilge (*informal*), bosh (*informal*), bullshit (*taboo slang*), cobblers (*Brit. taboo slang*), crap (*slang*), eyewash (*informal*), garbage (*informal*), guff (*slang*), havers (*Scot.*), hogwash, hokum (*slang, chiefly U.S. & Canad.*), hooey (*slang*), hot air (*informal*), moonshine, nonsense, piffle (*informal*), poppycock (*informal*), rot, rubbish, shit (*taboo slang*), stuff and nonsense, tomfoolery, tommyrot (*old-fashioned informal*), trash, tripe (*informal*), twaddle
buoy **1.** *n.* beacon, float, guide, marker, signal **2.** *vb.* *with* **up** boost, cheer, cheer up, encourage, hearten, keep afloat, lift, raise, support, sustain
buoyant **1.** afloat, floatable, floating, light, weightless

burden on; load. **4** to weigh down; oppress. **burdensome** *adj*

burden[2] *n* **1** a line of words recurring at the end of each verse of a song. **2** the theme of a speech, book, etc.

burdock *n* a weed with large heart-shaped leaves, and burlike fruits.

bureau (**byew**-roe) *n, pl* **-reaus** *or* **-reaux** (-rose) **1** an office or agency, esp. one providing services for the public. **2** *US* a government department. **3** *Chiefly Brit* a writing desk with pigeonholes and drawers against which the writing surface can be closed when not in use. **4** *US* a chest of drawers.

bureaucracy *n, pl* **-cies 1** a rigid system of administration based upon organization into bureaus, division of labour, a hierarchy of authority, etc. **2** government by such a system. **3** government officials collectively. **4** any administration in which action is impeded by unnecessary official procedures.

bureaucrat *n* **1** an official in a bureaucracy. **2** an official who adheres rigidly to bureaucracy. **bureaucratic** *adj*

burette *or US* **buret** *n* a graduated glass tube with a stopcock on one end for dispensing known volumes of fluids.

burgeon *vb* to develop or grow rapidly; flourish.

burger *n Informal* same as **hamburger.**

burgh *n* (in Scotland until 1975) a town with a degree of self-government.

burgher *n Archaic* a citizen, esp. one from the Continent.

burglar *n* a person who illegally enters a property to commit a crime.

burglary *n, pl* **-ries** the crime of entering a building as a trespasser to commit theft or another offence.

burgle *vb* **-gling, -gled** to break into (a house, shop, etc.).

burgomaster *n* the chief magistrate of a town in Austria, Belgium, Germany, or the Netherlands.

Burgundy *n* **1** a red or white wine produced in the Burgundy region, around Dijon in France. *~adj* **2 burgundy** dark purplish-red.

burial *n* the burying of a dead body.

burin (**byoor**-in) *n* a steel chisel used for engraving metal, wood, or marble.

burk *n Brit slang* same as **berk.**

burl *or* **birl** *n Informal* **1** *Scot, Austral, & NZ informal* an attempt; try: *give it a burl.* **2** *Austral & NZ* a ride in a car.

burlesque *n* **1** an artistic work, esp. literary or dramatic, satirizing a subject by caricaturing it. **2** *US & Canad theatre* a bawdy comedy show of the late 19th and early 20th centuries. *~adj* **3** of or characteristic of a burlesque.

burly *adj* **-lier, -liest** large and thick of build; sturdy.

burn[1] *vb* **burning, burnt** *or* **burned 1** to be or set on fire. **2** to destroy or be destroyed by fire. **3** to damage, injure, or mark by heat: *he burnt his hand.* **4** to die or put to death by fire. **5** to be or feel hot: *my forehead is burning.* **6** to smart or cause to smart: *brandy burns your throat.* **7** to feel strong emotion, esp. anger or passion. **8** to use for the purposes of light, heat, or power: *to burn coal.* **9** to form by or as if by fire: *to burn a hole.* **10** to char or become charred: *the toast is burning.* **11 burn one's boats** *or* **bridges** to commit oneself to a particular course of action with no possibility of turning back. **12 burn one's fingers** to suffer from having meddled or interfered. *~n* **13** an injury caused by exposure to heat, electrical, chemical, or radioactive agents. **14** a mark caused by burning. ~See also **burn out.**

➤ Either *burnt* or *burned* may be used as a past form.

burn[2] *n Scot* a small stream.

burner *n* the part of a stove or lamp that produces flame or heat.

burning *adj* **1** intense; passionate. **2** urgent; crucial: *a burning problem.*

burning glass *n* a convex lens for concentrating the sun's rays to produce fire.

burnish *vb* to make or become shiny or smooth by friction; polish.

burnous *n* a long circular cloak with a hood, worn esp. by Arabs.

burn out *vb* **1** to become or cause to become inoperative as a result of heat or friction: *the clutch burnt out.* *~n* **burnout 2** total exhaustion and inability to

THESAURUS

2. animated, blithe, bouncy, breezy, bright, carefree, cheerful, chirpy (*informal*), debonair, genial, happy, jaunty, joyful, light-hearted, lively, sunny, upbeat (*informal*), vivacious

burden *n.* **1.** *Naut.* cargo, freight, lading, tonnage **2.** affliction, anxiety, care, encumbrance, grievance, load, millstone, obstruction, onus, responsibility, sorrow, strain, stress, trial, trouble, weight, worry *~vb.* **3.** bother, encumber, handicap, load, oppress, overload, overwhelm, saddle with, strain, tax, weigh down, worry

bureau 1. agency, branch, department, division, office, service **2.** desk, writing desk

bureaucracy 1. administration, authorities, civil service, corridors of power, directorate, government, ministry, officialdom, officials, the system **2.** officialdom, officialese, red tape, regulations

bureaucrat administrator, civil servant, functionary, mandarin, minister, office-holder, officer, official, public servant

burglar cat burglar, housebreaker, pilferer, robber, sneak thief, thief

burglary break-in, breaking and entering, housebreaking, larceny, pilferage, robbery, stealing, theft, thieving

burial burying, entombment, exequies, funeral, inhumation, interment, obsequies, sepulture

buried 1. coffined, consigned to the grave, entombed, interred, laid to rest **2.** dead and buried, dead and gone, in the grave, long gone, pushing up the daisies, six feet under **3.** covered, forgotten, hidden, repressed, sunk in oblivion, suppressed **4.** cloistered, concealed, hidden, private, sequestered, tucked away **5.** caught up, committed, concentrating, devoted, engrossed, immersed, intent, lost, occupied, preoccupied, rapt

burlesque 1. *n.* caricature, mock, mockery, parody, satire, send-up (*Brit. informal*), spoof (*informal*), take-off (*informal*), travesty **2.** *adj.* caricatural, comic, farcical, hudibrastic, ironical, ludicrous, mock, mock-heroic, mocking, parodic, satirical, travestying

burly beefy (*informal*), big, brawny, bulky, hefty, hulking, muscular, powerful, stocky, stout, strapping, strong, sturdy, thickset, well-built

burn *vb.* **1.** be ablaze, be on fire, blaze, flame, flare, flash, flicker, glow, smoke **2.** brand, calcine, char, ignite, incinerate, kindle, light, parch, reduce to ashes, scorch, set on fire, shrivel, singe, toast, wither **3.** bite, hurt, pain, smart, sting, tingle **4.** be excited (angry, aroused, inflamed, passionate), blaze, desire, fume, seethe, simmer, smoulder, yearn

work effectively as a result of excessive demands or overwork.

burnt *vb* **1** a past of **burn**[1]. ~*adj* **2** affected by or as if by burning; charred.

burp *n* **1** *Informal* a belch. ~*vb* **2** *Informal* to belch. **3** to cause (a baby) to belch.

burr *n* **1** the soft trilling sound given to the letter (r) in some English dialects. **2** a whirring or humming sound. **3** a rough edge left on metal or paper after cutting. **4** a small hand-operated drill.

burrow *n* **1** a hole dug in the ground by a rabbit or other small animal. ~*vb* **2** to dig (a tunnel or hole) in, through, or under ground. **3** to move through a place by or as if by digging. **4** to delve deeply: *he burrowed into his coat pocket.* **5** to live in or as if in a burrow.

bursar *n* a treasurer of a school, college, or university.

bursary *n, pl* **-ries** a scholarship awarded esp. in Scottish and New Zealand schools and universities.

burst *vb* **bursting, burst 1** to break or cause to break open or apart suddenly and noisily; explode. **2** to come or go suddenly and forcibly: *he burst into the room.* **3** to be full to the point of breaking open: *bursting at the seams.* **4** (foll. by *into*) to give vent to (something) suddenly or loudly: *she burst into song.* ~*n* **5** an instance of breaking open suddenly; explosion. **6** a break; breach: *there was a burst in the pipe.* **7** a sudden increase of effort; spurt: *a burst of speed.* **8** a sudden and violent occurrence or outbreak: *a burst of applause.*

burton *n* **go for a burton** *Brit slang* **a** to be broken, useless, or lost. **b** to die.

bury *vb* **buries, burying, buried 1** to place (a corpse) in a grave. **2** to place (something) in the earth and cover it with soil. **3** to cover (something) from sight; hide. **4** to occupy (oneself) with deep concentration: *he buried himself in his work.* **5** to dismiss (a feeling) from the mind: *they decided to bury any hard feelings.*

bus *n* **1** a large motor vehicle designed to carry passengers between stopping places along a regular route. **2** *Informal* a car or aircraft that is old and shaky. **3** *Electronics, computers* an electrical conductor used to make a common connection between several circuits. ~*vb* **busing, bused** *or* **bussing, bussed 4** to travel or transport by bus. **5** *Chiefly US & Canad* to transport (children) by bus from one area to another in order to create racially integrated schools.

busby *n, pl* **-bies** a tall fur helmet worn by certain British soldiers.

bush[1] *n* **1** a dense woody plant, smaller than a tree, with many branches; shrub. **2** a dense cluster of such shrubs; thicket. **3** something resembling a bush, esp. in density: *a bush of hair.* **4 the bush** an uncultivated area covered with trees or shrubs in Australia, Africa, New Zealand, and Canada. **5** *Canad* an area on a farm on which timber is grown and cut. **6 beat about the bush** to avoid the point at issue.

bush[2] *n* **1** a thin metal sleeve or tubular lining serving as a bearing. ~*vb* **2** to fit a bush to (a casing or bearing).

bushbaby *n, pl* **-babies** a small agile tree-living mammal with large eyes and a long tail.

bushed *adj Informal* extremely tired; exhausted.

bushel *n Brit* an obsolete unit of dry or liquid measure equal to 8 gallons (36.4 litres).

bush jacket *n* a casual jacket with four patch pockets and a belt.

bush line *n* an airline operating in the bush country of Canada's northern regions.

bush lot *n Canad* same as **bush**[1] (sense 5).

bushman *n, pl* **-men** *Austral & NZ* a person who lives or travels in the bush.

Bushman *n, pl* **-men** a member of a hunting and gathering people of southern Africa.

bush pilot *n Canad* a pilot who operates in the bush country.

bush sickness *n NZ* a disease of animals caused by mineral deficiency in old bush country. **bush-sick** *adj*

bush telegraph *n* a means of spreading rumour or gossip.

bushveld *n S African* bushy countryside.

bushy *adj* **bushier, bushiest 1** (of hair) thick and shaggy. **2** covered or overgrown with bushes.

business *n* **1** the purchase and sale of goods and services. **2** a commercial or industrial establishment. **3** a trade or profession. **4** commercial activity; dealings: *firms that do business with Britain.* **5** proper or rightful concern or responsibility: *mind your own business.* **6** an affair; matter: *it's a dreadful business.* **7** serious work or activity: *get down to business.* **8** a difficult or complicated matter: *it's a business trying to see him.* **9 mean business** to be in earnest.

businesslike *adj* efficient and methodical.

businessman *or fem* **businesswoman** *n, pl* **-men** *or* **-women** a person engaged in commercial or industrial business, usually an owner or executive.

business park *n* an area specially designated to accommodate business offices, light industry, etc.

business school *n* an institution that offers

THESAURUS

burning 1. all-consuming, ardent, eager, earnest, fervent, fervid, flaming, frantic, frenzied, impassioned, intense, passionate, vehement, zealous **2.** acute, compelling, critical, crucial, essential, important, pressing, significant, urgent, vital

burrow 1. *n.* den, hole, lair, retreat, shelter, tunnel **2.** *vb.* delve, dig, excavate, hollow out, scoop out, tunnel

burst *vb.* **1.** blow up, break, crack, disintegrate, explode, fly open, fragment, puncture, rend asunder, rupture, shatter, shiver, split, tear apart **2.** barge, break, break out, erupt, gush forth, run, rush, spout ~*n.* **3.** bang, blast, blasting, blowout, blow-up, breach, break, crack, discharge, explosion, rupture, split **4.** eruption, fit, gush, gust, outbreak, outburst, outpouring, rush, spate, spurt, surge, torrent

bury 1. consign to the grave, entomb, inter, lay to rest, sepulchre **2.** drive in, embed, engulf, implant, sink, submerge **3.** conceal, cover, cover up, enshroud, hide, secrete, shroud, stash (*informal*), stow away **4.** absorb, engage, engross, immerse, interest, occupy

bush 1. hedge, plant, shrub, shrubbery, thicket **2.** backwoods, brush, scrub, scrubland, the wild, woodland

busily actively, assiduously, briskly, carefully, diligently, earnestly, energetically, industriously, intently, purposefully, speedily, strenuously

business 1. bargaining, commerce, dealings, industry, manufacturing, merchandising, selling, trade, trading, transaction **2.** company, concern, corporation, enterprise, establishment, firm, organization, venture **3.** calling, career, craft, employment, function, job, line, métier, occupation, profession, pursuit, trade, vocation, work **4.** affair, assignment, concern, duty, function, issue, matter, point, problem, question, responsibility, subject, task, topic

businesslike correct, efficient, matter-of-fact, methodical, orderly, organized, practical, professional, regular, routine, systematic, thorough, well-ordered, workaday

courses to managers in aspects of business, such as marketing, finance, and law.

busker *n* a person who entertains for money in streets or stations. **busk** *vb*

busman's holiday *n Informal* a holiday spent doing the same as one does at work.

bust[1] *n* **1** a woman's bosom. **2** a sculpture of the head, shoulders, and upper chest of a person.

bust[2] *Informal ~vb* **busting, busted** *or* **bust 1** to burst or break. **2** (of the police) to raid or search (a place) or arrest (someone). **3** *US & Canad* to demote in military rank. *~adj* **4** broken. **5 go bust** to become bankrupt.

bustle[1] *vb* **-tling, -tled 1** (often foll. by *about*) to hurry with a great show of energy or activity. *~n* **2** energetic and noisy activity. **bustling** *adj*

bustle[2] *n* a cushion or framework worn by women in the late 19th century at the back in order to expand the skirt.

bust-up *Informal ~n* **1** a serious quarrel, esp. one ending a relationship. **2** *Brit* a disturbance or brawl. *~vb* **bust up 3** to quarrel and part. **4** to disrupt (a meeting), esp. violently.

busy *adj* **busier, busiest 1** actively or fully engaged; occupied. **2** crowded with or characterized by activity. **3** *Chiefly US & Canad* (of a telephone line) in use; engaged. *~vb* **busies, busying, busied 4** to make or keep (someone, esp. oneself) busy; occupy. **busily** *adv*

busybody *n, pl* **-bodies** a meddlesome, prying, or officious person.

but *conj* **1** contrary to expectation: *he cut his hand but didn't cry.* **2** in contrast; on the contrary: *I like seafood but my husband doesn't.* **3** other than: *we can't do anything but wait.* **4** without it happening: *we never go out but it rains.* *~prep* **5** except: *they saved all but one.* **6 but for** were it not for: *but for you, we couldn't have managed.* *~adv* **7** only: *I can but try; he was but a child.* *~n* **8** an objection: *ifs and buts.*

but and ben *n Scot* a two-roomed cottage consisting of an outer room (**but**) and an inner room (**ben**).

butane (**byew**-tane) *n* a colourless gas used in the manufacture of rubber and fuels.

butch *adj Slang* (of a woman or man) markedly or aggressively masculine.

butcher *n* **1** a person who sells meat. **2** a person who kills animals for meat. **3** a brutal murderer. *~vb* **4** to kill and prepare (animals) for meat. **5** to kill (people) at random or brutally. **6** to make a mess of; botch.

butchery *n, pl* **-eries 1** senseless slaughter. **2** the business of a butcher.

butler *n* the head manservant of a household, in charge of the wines, table, etc.

butt[1] *n* **1** the thicker or blunt end of something, such as the stock of a rifle. **2** the unused end of a cigarette or cigar; stub. **3** *Chiefly US & Canad slang* the buttocks.

butt[2] *n* **1** a person or thing that is the target of ridicule or teasing. **2** *Shooting, archery* **a** a mound of earth behind the target. **b butts** the target range.

butt[3] *vb* **1** to strike (something or someone) with the head or horns. **2** (foll. by *in* or *into*) to intrude, esp. into a conversation; interfere. *~n* **3** a blow with the head or horns.

butt[4] *n* a large cask for collecting or storing liquids.

butte (**byewt**) *n US & Canad* an isolated steep flat-topped hill.

butter *n* **1** an edible fatty yellow solid made from cream by churning. **2** any substance with a butter-like consistency, such as peanut butter. *~vb* **3** to put butter on or in (something). ~See also **butter up. buttery** *adj*

butter bean *n* a large pale flat edible bean.

buttercup *n* a small bright yellow flower.

butterfingers *n Informal* a person who drops things by mistake or fails to catch things.

butterflies *pl n Informal* a nervous feeling in the stomach.

butterfly *n, pl* **-flies 1** an insect with a slender body and brightly coloured wings. **2** a swimming stroke in which the arms are plunged forward together in large circular movements. **3** a person who never settles with one interest or occupation for long.

butterfly nut *n* same as **wing nut.**

buttermilk *n* the sourish liquid remaining after the butter has been separated from milk.

butterscotch *n* a hard brittle toffee made with butter, brown sugar, etc.

butter up *vb* to flatter.

buttery *n, pl* **-teries** *Brit* (in some universities) a room in which food and drink are sold to students.

buttock *n* **1** either of the two large fleshy masses that

THESAURUS

businessman *or* **businesswoman** capitalist, employer, entrepreneur, executive, financier, *homme d'affaires,* industrialist, merchant, tradesman, tycoon

bust[1] bosom, breast, chest, torso

bust[2] *vb.* **1.** break, burst, fracture, rupture **2.** arrest, catch, collar (*informal*), cop (*slang*), feel one's collar (*slang*), lift (*slang*), nab (*informal*), nail (*informal*), raid, search *~adj.* **3. go bust** become insolvent, be ruined, break, fail, go bankrupt

bustle 1. *vb.* beetle, bestir, dash, flutter, fuss, hasten, hurry, rush, scamper, scramble, scurry, scuttle, stir, tear **2.** *n.* activity, ado, agitation, commotion, excitement, flurry, fuss, haste, hurly-burly, hurry, pother (*literary*), stir, to-do, tumult

busy *adj.* **1.** active, assiduous, brisk, diligent, employed, engaged, engrossed, hard at work, industrious, in harness, occupied, on duty, persevering, slaving, working **2.** active, energetic, exacting, full, hectic, hustling, lively, on the go (*informal*), restless, strenuous, tireless, tiring *~vb.* **3.** absorb, employ, engage, engross, immerse, interest, occupy

busybody eavesdropper, gossip, intriguer, intruder, meddler, nosy parker (*informal*), pry, scandalmonger, snoop, snooper, stirrer (*informal*), troublemaker

but *conj.* **1.** further, however, moreover, nevertheless, on the contrary, on the other hand, still, yet **2.** bar, barring, except, excepting, excluding, notwithstanding, save, with the exception of *~adv.* **3.** just, merely, only, simply, singly, solely

butcher *n.* **1.** destroyer, killer, murderer, slaughterer, slayer *~vb.* **2.** carve, clean, cut, cut up, dress, joint, prepare, slaughter **3.** assassinate, cut down, destroy, exterminate, kill, liquidate, massacre, put to the sword, slaughter, slay **4.** bodge (*informal*), botch, destroy, mess up, mutilate, ruin, spoil, wreck

butchery blood bath, blood-letting, bloodshed, carnage, killing, massacre, mass murder, murder, slaughter

butt[1] **1.** haft, handle, hilt, shaft, shank, stock **2.** base, end, fag end (*informal*), foot, leftover, stub, tail, tip

butt[2] Aunt Sally (*Brit.*), dupe, laughing stock, mark, object, point, subject, target, victim

butt[3] *vb./n.* **1.** *with or of the head or horns* buck, buffet, bump, jab, knock, poke, prod, punch, push, ram, shove, thrust *~vb.* **2.** *with* **in** *or* **into** chip in (*infor-

form the human rump. **2** the corresponding part in some mammals.

button *n* **1** a disc or knob of plastic, wood, etc., attached to a garment, which fastens two surfaces together by passing through a buttonhole. **2** a small disc that operates a door bell or machine when pressed. **3** a small round object, such as a sweet or badge. **4 not worth a button** *Brit* of no value; useless. *~vb* **5** to fasten (a garment) with a button or buttons.

buttonhole *n* **1** a slit in a garment through which a button is passed to fasten two surfaces together. **2** a flower worn pinned to the lapel or in the buttonhole. *~vb* **-holing, -holed 3** to detain (a person) in conversation.

button mushroom *n* an unripe mushroom.

button up *vb* **1** to fasten (a garment) with a button or buttons. **2** *Informal* to conclude (business) satisfactorily: *we've got it all buttoned up.*

buttress *n* **1** a construction, usually of brick or stone, built to support a wall. **2** any support or prop. *~vb* **3** to support (a wall) with a buttress. **4** to support or sustain: *his observations are buttressed by the most recent scholarly research.*

butty *n, pl* **-ties** *Chiefly N English dialect* a sandwich: *a jam butty.*

butyl (**byew**-tile) *adj* of or containing any of four isomeric forms of the group C_4H_9–: *butyl rubber.*

buxom *adj* (of a woman) healthily plump, attractive, and full-bosomed.

buy *vb* **buying, bought 1** to acquire (something) by paying a sum of money for it; purchase. **2** to be capable of purchasing: *money can't buy love.* **3** to acquire by any exchange or sacrifice: *the rise in interest rates was just to buy time until the weekend.* **4** to bribe (someone). **5** *Slang* to accept (something) as true. **6** (foll. by *into*) to purchase shares of (a company). *~n* **7** a purchase: *a good buy.* See also **buy in, buy into,** etc.

➤ Be careful not to confuse the past forms *bought* (from *buy*) with *brought* (from *bring*).

buyer *n* **1** a person who buys; customer. **2** a person employed to buy merchandise for a shop or factory.

buy in *vb* to purchase (goods) in large quantities.

buy off *vb* to pay (someone) to drop a charge or end opposition.

buy-out *n* **1** the purchase of a company, often by its former employees. *~vb* **buy out 2** to purchase the ownership of a company or property from (someone).

buy up *vb* **1** to purchase all that is available of (something). **2** to purchase a controlling interest in (a company).

buzz *n* **1** a rapidly vibrating humming sound, such as of a bee. **2** a low sound, such as of many voices in conversation. **3** *Informal* a telephone call. **4** *Informal* a sense of excitement. *~vb* **5** to make a vibrating sound like that of a prolonged *z*. **6** (of a place) to be filled with an air of excitement: *the city buzzed with the news.* **7** to summon (someone) with a buzzer. **8** *Informal* to fly an aircraft very low over (people, buildings, or another aircraft). **9 buzz about** *or* **around** to move around quickly and busily.

buzzard *n* a bird of prey with broad wings and tail and a soaring flight.

buzzer *n* an electronic device that produces a buzzing sound as a signal.

buzz off *vb Informal, chiefly Brit* to go away; depart.

buzz word *n Informal* a word, originally from a particular jargon, which becomes a popular vogue word.

by *prep* **1** used to indicate the performer of the action of a passive verb: *seeds eaten by the birds.* **2** used to indicate the person responsible for a creative work: *three songs by Britten.* **3** via; through: *enter by the back door.* **4** used to indicate a means used: *he frightened her by hiding behind the door.* **5** beside; next to; near: *a tree by the stream.* **6** passing the position of; past: *I drove by the place she works.* **7** not later than; before: *return the books by Tuesday.* **8** used to indicate extent: *it is hotter by five degrees.* **9** multiplied by: *four by three equals twelve.* **10** during the passing of: *by night.* **11** placed between measurements of the various dimensions of something: *a plank fourteen inches by seven.* *~adv* **12** near: *the house is close by.* **13** away; aside: *he put some money by each week.* **14** passing a point near something; past: *he drove by.* *~n, pl* **byes 15** same as **bye**[1].

by and by *adv* presently or eventually.

by and large *adv* in general; on the whole.

bye[1] *n* **1** *Sport* status of a player or team who wins a preliminary round by virtue of having no opponent. **2** *Cricket* a run scored off a ball not struck by the batsman. **3 by the bye** incidentally; by the way.

bye[2] *or* **bye-bye** *interj Informal* goodbye.

by-election *or* **bye-election** *n* an election held during the life of a parliament to fill a vacant seat.

bygone *adj* past; former: *a bygone age.*

bygones *pl n* **let bygones be bygones** to agree to forget past quarrels.

bylaw *or* **bye-law** *n* a rule made by a local authority.

by-line *n* **1** a line under the title of an article in a newspaper or magazine giving the author's name. **2** same as **touchline.**

BYO(G) *n Austral & NZ* an unlicensed restaurant at which diners may bring their own alcoholic drink.

bypass *n* **1** a main road built to avoid a city. **2** a secondary pipe, channel, or appliance through which the flow of a substance, such as gas or electricity, is redirected. **3** a surgical operation in which the blood flow is redirected away from a diseased or blocked part of the heart. *~vb* **4** to go around or avoid (a city, obstruction, problem, etc.). **5** to proceed without reference to (regulations or a superior); get round; avoid.

by-play *n* secondary action in a play, carried on apart while the main action proceeds.

by-product *n* **1** a secondary or incidental product of a manufacturing process. **2** a side effect.

THESAURUS

mal), cut in, interfere, interrupt, intrude, meddle, put one's oar in, put one's two cents in (*U.S. slang*), stick one's nose in

butt[4] barrel, cask, pipe

buttonhole *vb. figurative* accost, bore, catch, detain in talk, grab, importune, persuade importunately, take aside, waylay

buttress 1. *n.* abutment, brace, mainstay, pier, prop, reinforcement, shore, stanchion, stay, strut, support **2.** *vb.* augment, back up, bolster, brace, prop, prop up, reinforce, shore, shore up, strengthen, support, sustain, uphold

buy *vb.* **1.** acquire, get, invest in, obtain, pay for, procure, purchase, score (*slang*), shop for **2.** *often with* **off** bribe, corrupt, fix (*informal*), grease someone's palm (*slang*), square, suborn *~n.* **3.** acquisition, bargain, deal, purchase

by *prep.* **1.** through, through the agency of, under the aegis of **2.** along, beside, by way of, close to, near, next to, over, past, via *~adv.* **3.** aside, at hand, away, beyond, close, handy, in reach, near, past, to one side

by and by before long, eventually, in a while, in the course of time, one, presently, soon

byre *n Brit* a shelter for cows.
byroad *n* a secondary or side road.
bystander *n* a person present but not involved; onlooker; spectator.
byte *n Computers* a group of bits processed as one unit of data.
byway *n* a secondary or side road, esp. in the country.
byword *n* **1** a person or thing regarded as a perfect example of something: *their name is a byword for quality.* **2** a common saying; proverb.
Byzantine *adj* **1** of Byzantium, an ancient Greek city on the Bosphorus. **2** of the Byzantine Empire, the continuation of the Roman Empire in the East. **3** of the style of architecture developed in the Byzantine Empire, with massive domes, rounded arches, and mosaics. **4** (of attitudes, methods, etc.) inflexible or complicated. ~*n* **5** an inhabitant of Byzantium.

THESAURUS

bypass avoid, circumvent, depart from, detour round, deviate from, get round, go round, ignore, neglect, outflank, pass round
bystander eyewitness, looker-on, observer, onlooker, passer-by, spectator, viewer, watcher, witness

C

c 1 centi-. 2 cubic. 3 the speed of light in free space.

C 1 *Music* the first note of a major scale containing no sharps or flats (**C major**). 2 *Chem* carbon. 3 Celsius. 4 centigrade. 5 century: *C20.* 6 coulomb. 7 the Roman numeral for 100. 8 a high-level computer programming language.

c. 1 (Cricket) caught. 2 (used preceding a date) about: *c. 1800.*

Ca *Chem* calcium.

CA 1 California. 2 Chartered Accountant.

ca. (used preceding a date) about: *ca. 1930.*

cab *n* 1 a taxi. 2 the enclosed driver's compartment of a lorry, bus, or train.

cabal (kab-**bal**) *n* 1 a small group of political plotters. 2 a secret plot or conspiracy.

cabaret (**kab**-a-ray) *n* 1 a floor show of dancing and singing at a nightclub or restaurant. 2 a place providing such entertainment.

cabbage *n* 1 a vegetable with a large head of green or reddish-purple leaves. 2 *Informal* a person who is unable to move or think, as a result of brain damage: *he can only exist as a cabbage who must be cared for by his relatives.*

cabbage white *n* a large white butterfly whose larvae feed on cabbage leaves.

cabbie *or* **cabby** *n, pl* **-bies** *Informal* a taxi driver.

caber *n Scot* a heavy section of trimmed tree trunk tossed in competition at Highland games.

cabin *n* 1 a room used as living quarters in a ship or boat. 2 a small simple dwelling: *a log cabin.* 3 the enclosed part of an aircraft in which the passengers or crew sit.

cabin boy *n* a boy who waits on the officers and passengers of a ship.

cabin cruiser *n* a motorboat with a cabin.

cabinet *n* a piece of furniture containing shelves, cupboards, or drawers for storage or display: *a filing cabinet; a cocktail cabinet.*

Cabinet *n* a committee of senior government ministers or advisers to a president.

cabinet-maker *n* a person who makes fine furniture. **cabinet-making** *n*

cabin fever *n Canad* acute depression resulting from being isolated or sharing cramped quarters in the wilderness.

cable *n* 1 a strong thick rope of twisted hemp or wire. 2 a bundle of wires covered with plastic or rubber that conducts electricity. 3 a telegram sent abroad by submarine cable or telephone line. 4 Also called: **cable stitch** a knitted design which resembles a twisted rope. ~*vb* **-bling, -bled** 5 to send (someone) a message by cable.

cable car *n* a vehicle that is pulled up a steep slope by a moving cable.

cablegram *n* a more formal name for **cable** (sense 3).

cable television *n* a television service in which the subscriber's television is connected to a central receiver by cable.

caboodle *n* **the whole caboodle** *Informal* the whole lot.

caboose *n* 1 *US & Canad* a guard's van on a train. 2 *Canad* a mobile building used as the sleeping quarters of lumberjacks.

cabriolet (kab-ree-oh-**lay**) *n* a small two-wheeled horse-drawn carriage with a folding hood.

cacao (kak-**kah**-oh) *n* a tropical American tree with seed pods (**cacao beans**) from which cocoa and chocolate are prepared.

cachalot *n* the sperm whale.

cache (**kash**) *n* a hidden store of weapons, provisions, or treasure.

cachet (**kash**-shay) *n* prestige or distinction: *a Mercedes carries a certain cachet.*

cachou *n* a lozenge eaten to sweeten the breath.

cack-handed *adj Informal* clumsy: *I open cans in a very cack-handed way.*

cackle *vb* **-ling, -led** 1 to laugh shrilly. 2 (of a hen) to squawk with shrill broken notes. ~*n* 3 the sound of cackling. **cackling** *adj*

cacophony (kak-**koff**-on-ee) *n* harsh discordant sound: *a cacophony of barking.* **cacophonous** *adj*

cactus *n, pl* **-tuses** *or* **-ti** a thick fleshy desert plant with spines but no leaves.

cad *n Old-fashioned, informal* a man who behaves dishonourably. **caddish** *adj*

cadaver (kad-**dav**-ver) *n Med* a corpse.

cadaverous *adj* pale, thin, and haggard.

caddie *n* 1 a person who carries a golfer's clubs. ~*vb* **-dying, -died** 2 to act as a caddie.

caddis fly *n* an insect whose larva (the **caddis worm**) lives underwater in a protective case of silk, sand, and stones.

caddy[1] *n, pl* **-dies** *Chiefly Brit* a small container for tea.

caddy[2] *n, pl* **-dies**, *vb* **-dies, -dying, -died** same as **caddie.**

cadence (**kade**-enss) *n* 1 the rise and fall in the pitch of the voice. 2 the close of a musical phrase.

cadenza *n* a complex solo passage in a piece of music.

cadet *n* a young person training for the armed forces or the police.

cadge *vb* **cadging, cadged** *Informal* to get (something) from someone by taking advantage of his or her generosity. **cadger** *n*

cadi *n* a judge in a Muslim community.

cadmium *n Chem* bluish-white metallic element found in zinc ores and used in electroplating and alloys. Symbol: Cd

cadre (**kah**-der) *n* a small group of people selected and trained to form the core of a political organization or military unit.

caecum *or US* **cecum** (**seek**-um) *n, pl* **-ca** (-ka) the pouch at the beginning of the large intestine.

Caenozoic *adj* same as **Cenozoic.**

Caerphilly *n* a creamy white mild-flavoured cheese.

THESAURUS

cab hackney, minicab, taxi, taxicab

cabin 1. berth, compartment, quarters, room 2. bothy, chalet, cot (*literary or archaic*), cottage, hut, lodge, shack, shanty, shed

cabinet case, chiffonier, closet, cupboard, dresser, locker

Cabinet administration, assembly, council, counsellors, ministry

cad *old-fashioned informal* bounder (*old-fashioned*

Caesar (**seez**-ar) *n* **1** a Roman emperor. **2** any emperor or dictator.

Caesarean, Caesarian *or US* **Cesarean** (siz-**zair**-ee-an) *n* short for **Caesarean section.**

Caesarean section *n* surgical incision into the womb in order to deliver a baby.

caesium *or US* **cesium** *n Chem* a silvery-white metallic element used in photocells. Symbol: Cs

caesura (siz-**your**-ra) *n, pl* **-ras** *or* **-rae** (-ree) a pause in a line of verse.

café *n* **1** a small or inexpensive restaurant that serves drinks and snacks or light meals. **2** *S African* a corner shop.

cafeteria *n* a self-service restaurant.

caff *n Slang* a café.

caffeine *n* a stimulant found in tea, coffee, and cocoa.

caftan *n* same as **kaftan.**

cage *n* **1** an enclosure made of bars or wires, for keeping birds or animals in. **2** the enclosed platform of a lift in a mine. *~vb* **caging, caged 3** to confine in a cage. **caged** *adj*

cagey *adj* **cagier, cagiest** *Informal* reluctant to go into details; wary: *he is cagey about what he paid for the business.* **cagily** *adv*

cagoule (kag-**gool**) *n* a lightweight hooded waterproof jacket.

cahoots *pl n* **in cahoots** *Informal* conspiring together: *the loan sharks were in cahoots with the home-improvement companies.*

caiman *n, pl* **-mans** same as **cayman.**

cairn *n* a mound of stones erected as a memorial or marker.

cairngorm *n* a smoky yellow or brown quartz gemstone.

caisson (**kayss**-on) *n* a watertight chamber used to carry out construction work under water.

cajole *vb* **-joling, -joled** to persuade by flattery; coax: *he allowed himself to be cajoled into staying on.* **cajolery** *n*

cake *n* **1** a sweet food baked from a mixture of flour, sugar, eggs, etc. **2** a flat compact mass of something: *a cake of soap.* **3 have one's cake and eat it** to enjoy both of two incompatible alternatives. **4 piece of cake** *Informal* something that is easy to do. **5 sell like hot cakes** *Informal* to be sold very quickly: *books on the Royal Family are selling like hot cakes.* *~vb* **caking, caked 6** to form into a hardened mass or crust: *there was blood caked an inch thick on the walls.*

cal. calorie (small).

Cal. Calorie (large).

calabash *n* **1** a large round gourd that grows on a tropical American tree. **2** a bowl made from the dried hollow shell of a calabash.

calabrese (kal-lab-**bray**-zee) *n* a kind of green sprouting broccoli.

calamine *n* a pink powder consisting chiefly of zinc oxide, used to make soothing skin lotions and ointments.

calamitous *adj* resulting in or from disaster: *the country's calamitous economic decline.*

calamity *n, pl* **-ties** a disaster or misfortune.

calcareous (kal-**care**-ee-uss) *adj* of or containing calcium carbonate.

calciferol *n* a substance found in fish oils and used in the treatment of rickets. Also called: **vitamin D_2**

calciferous *adj* producing salts of calcium, esp. calcium carbonate.

calcify *vb* **-fies, -fying, -fied** to harden by the depositing of calcium salts. **calcification** *n*

calcine *vb* **-cining, -cined** to oxidize (a substance) by heating. **calcination** *n*

calcite *n* a colourless or white form of calcium carbonate.

calcium *n Chem* a soft silvery-white metallic element found in bones, teeth, limestone, and chalk. Symbol: Ca

calcium carbonate *n* a white crystalline salt found in limestone, chalk, and pearl, used to make cement.

calcium hydroxide *n* a white crystalline alkali used to make mortar and soften water.

calcium oxide *n* same as **quicklime.**

calculable *adj* able to be computed or estimated.

calculate *vb* **-lating, -lated 1** to solve or find out by a mathematical procedure or by reasoning. **2** to aim to have a particular effect: *this ad campaign is calculated to offend.*

calculated *adj* **1** undertaken after considering the likelihood of success: *a calculated gamble.* **2** carefully planned: *a calculated and callous murder.*

calculating *adj* selfishly scheming.

calculation *n* **1** the act or result of calculating. **2** selfish scheming: *there was an element of calculation in her insistence on arriving after dark.*

calculator *n* a small electronic device for doing mathematical calculations.

calculus *n* **1** the branch of mathematics dealing with infinitesimal changes to a variable number or quantity. **2** (*pl* **-li**) *Pathol* same as **stone** (sense 7).

Caledonian *adj* Scottish.

calendar *n* **1** a chart showing a year divided up into months, weeks, and days. **2** a system for determining the beginning, length, and divisions of years: *the Jewish calendar.* **3** a schedule of events or appointments: *concerts were an important part of the social calendar of the Venetian nobility.*

calender *n* **1** a machine in which paper or cloth is smoothed by passing it between rollers. *~vb* **2** to smooth in such a machine.

THESAURUS

Brit. slang), cur, heel (*slang*), knave (*archaic*), rat (*informal*), rotter (*old-fashioned slang*), scumbag (*slang*)

caddish despicable, ill-bred, low, ungentlemanly, unmannerly

café cafeteria, coffee bar, coffee shop, lunchroom (*U.S. & Canad.*), restaurant, snack bar, tearoom

cage 1. *n.* corral (*U.S.*), enclosure, pen, pound **2.** *vb.* confine, coop up, fence in, immure, impound, imprison, incarcerate, lock up, shut up

cajole beguile, coax, entice, flatter, inveigle, lure, seduce, sweet-talk (*informal*), tempt, wheedle

cake 1. *n.* bar, block, cube, loaf, lump, mass, slab **2.** *vb.* bake, encrust, harden, solidify

calamitous cataclysmic, catastrophic, devastating, dire, disastrous, ruinous, tragic, woeful

calamity adversity, cataclysm, catastrophe, disaster, hardship, misadventure, mischance, misfortune, mishap, reverse, tragedy, trial, tribulation, woe

calculate 1. compute, count, determine, enumerate, estimate, figure, reckon, work out **2.** aim, design, intend, plan

calculated considered, deliberate, intended, intentional, planned, premeditated, purposeful

calculating contriving, crafty, cunning, designing, devious, Machiavellian, manipulative, politic, scheming, sharp, shrewd, sly

calends *or* **kalends** *pl n* (in the ancient Roman calendar) the first day of each month.
calendula *n* a plant with orange-and-yellow rayed flowers.
calf[1] *n, pl* **calves 1** a young cow, bull, elephant, whale, or seal. **2** same as **calfskin.**
calf[2] *n, pl* **calves** the back of the leg between the ankle and the knee.
calf love *n* adolescent infatuation.
calfskin *n* fine leather made from the skin of a calf.
calibrate *vb* **-brating, -brated** to mark the scale or check the accuracy of (a measuring instrument). **calibration** *n*
calibre *or US* **caliber** (**kal**-lib-ber) *n* **1** a person's ability or worth: *a poet of Wordsworth's calibre.* **2** the diameter of the bore of a gun or of a shell or bullet.
calico *n* a white or unbleached cotton fabric.
californium *n Chem* a radioactive metallic element produced artificially. Symbol: Cf
caliper *n US* same as **calliper.**
caliph *n Islam* the title of the successors of Mohammed as rulers of the Islamic world.
caliphate *n* the office, jurisdiction, or reign of a caliph.
calisthenics *n* same as **callisthenics.**
call *vb* **1** to name: *a town called Eyemouth.* **2** to describe (someone or something) as being: *they called him a Hitler.* **3** to speak loudly so as to attract attention. **4** to telephone: *he left a message for Lynch to call him.* **5** to summon: *a doctor must be called immediately.* **6** to pay someone a visit: *the social worker called and she didn't answer the door.* **7** to arrange: *the meeting was called for the lunch hour.* **8 call someone's bluff** See **bluff**[1] (sense 3). ~*n* **9** a cry or shout. **10** the cry made by a bird or animal. **11** a communication by telephone. **12** a short visit: *I paid a call on an old friend.* **13** a summons or invitation: *the police and fire brigade continued to respond to calls.* **14** need, demand, or desire: *a call for economic sanctions.* **15** allure or fascination: *the call of the open road.* **16 on call** available when summoned: *there's a doctor on call in town.* ~See also **call for, call in,** etc. **caller** *n*
call box *n* a soundproof enclosure for a public telephone.
call for *vb* **1** to require: *appendicitis calls for removal of the appendix.* **2** to come and fetch.
call girl *n* a prostitute with whom appointments are made by telephone.
calligraphy *n* beautiful handwriting. **calligrapher** *n* **calligraphic** *adj*
call in *vb* **1** to summon to one's assistance: *she called in a contractor to make the necessary repairs.* **2** to pay a brief visit. **3** to demand payment of (a loan): *if the share price continues to drop, some banks may call in their loans.*
calling *n* **1** a strong urge to follow a particular profession or occupation, esp. a caring one. **2** a profession or occupation, esp. a caring one.
calliper *or US* **caliper** *n* **1** a metal splint for supporting the leg. **2** a measuring instrument consisting of two steel legs hinged together.
callisthenics *or* **calisthenics** *n* light exercises designed to promote general fitness. **callisthenic** *or* **calisthenic** *adj*
call off *vb* **1** to cancel or abandon: *the strike has now been called off.* **2** to order (a dog or a person) to stop attacking someone.
call on *or* **upon** *vb* to make an appeal or request to: *church leaders called on political leaders to resume the discussions.*
callous *adj* showing no concern for other people's feelings. **callously** *adv* **callousness** *n*
calloused *adj* covered in calluses.
call out *vb* **1** to shout loudly. **2** to summon to one's assistance: *the army and air force have been called out to help drop food packets.* **3** to order (workers) to strike.
callow *adj* young and inexperienced: *a callow youth.*
call up *vb* **1** to summon for active military service. **2** to cause one to remember. ~*n* **call-up 3** a general order to report for military service.
callus *n, pl* **-luses** an area of hard or thickened skin on the hand or foot.
calm *adj* **1** not showing or not feeling agitation or excitement. **2** not ruffled by the wind: *a flat calm sea.* **3** (of weather) windless. ~*n* **4** a peaceful state. ~*vb* **5** (often foll. by *down*) to make or become calm. **calmly** *adv* **calmness** *n*
Calor Gas *n Trademark* butane gas liquefied under pressure in portable containers for domestic use.
caloric (kal-**or**-ik) *adj* of heat or calories.
calorie *n* **1** a unit of measure for the energy value of food. **2** Also: **small calorie** the quantity of heat required to raise the temperature of 1 gram of water by 1°C.
Calorie *n* **1** Also: **large calorie** a unit of heat, equal to one thousand calories. **2** the amount of a food capable of producing one calorie of energy.
calorific *adj* of calories or heat.
calumniate *vb* **-ating, -ated** to make false or malicious statements about (someone).

THESAURUS

calculation 1. answer, computation, estimate, estimation, figuring, reckoning, result **2.** contrivance, craft, cunning, Machiavellianism, manipulation, shrewdness
calibre 1. ability, capacity, distinction, merit, quality, stature, talent, worth **2.** bore, diameter, gauge, measure
call *vb.* **1.** christen, denominate, designate, dub, entitle, name, style, term **2.** consider, describe as, estimate, judge, label, regard, think **3.** announce, cry, cry out, proclaim, shout, yell **4.** give (someone) a bell (*Brit. slang*), phone, ring up (*informal, chiefly Brit.*), telephone **5.** assemble, collect, convene, convoke (*formal*), gather, invite, muster, rally, summon **6.** appoint, arrange, order ~*n.* **7.** cry, scream, shout, yell **8.** command, demand, invitation, order, request, summons **9.** cause, claim, excuse, grounds, justification, need, occasion, reason, right
call for 1. demand, entail, involve, necessitate, need, require **2.** collect, fetch, pick up, uplift (*Scot.*)
calling business, career, employment, métier, occupation, profession, trade, vocation, work
call on *or* **call upon** appeal to, ask, entreat, invoke, request
callous case-hardened, cold, hard-bitten (*informal*), hard-boiled (*informal*), hardened, hardhearted, harsh, heartless, insensate, insensitive, obdurate, soulless, thick-skinned, uncaring, unfeeling, unsympathetic
calm *adj.* **1.** collected, composed, cool, equable, imperturbable, relaxed, sedate, self-possessed, undisturbed, unemotional, unexcitable, unexcited, unfazed (*informal*), unflappable (*informal*), unmoved, unruffled **2.** balmy, halcyon, mild, peaceful, placid, quiet, serene, smooth, still, tranquil, windless ~*n.* **3.** calmness, hush, peace, peacefulness, quiet, repose, serenity, stillness ~*vb.* **4.** hush, mollify, placate, quieten, relax, soothe

calumny *n, pl* **-nies** a false or malicious statement; slander.
Calvary *n Christianity* the place just outside the walls of Jerusalem where Jesus Christ was crucified.
calve *vb* **calving, calved** to give birth to a calf.
calves *n* the plural of **calf.**
Calvinism *n* the theological system of Calvin, the 16th-century French theologian, stressing predestination and salvation solely by God's grace. **Calvinist** *n, adj* **Calvinistic** *adj*
calypso *n, pl* **-sos** a West Indian song with improvised topical lyrics.
calyx (**kale**-ix) *n, pl* **calyxes** *or* **calyces** (**kal**-iss-seez) the outer leaves that protect the developing bud of a flower.
cam *n* a part of an engine that converts a circular motion into a to-and-fro motion.
camaraderie *n* familiarity and trust between friends.
camber *n* a slight upward curve to the centre of a road surface.
Cambodian *adj* **1** of Cambodia. ~*n* **2** a person from Cambodia.
Cambrian *adj Geol* of the period of geological time about 600 million years ago.
cambric *n* a fine white linen fabric.
Cambs Cambridgeshire.
camcorder *n* a combined portable video camera and recorder.
came *vb* the past tense of **come.**
camel *n* either of two humped mammals, the dromedary and Bactrian camel, that can survive long periods without food or water in desert regions.
camellia (kam-**meal**-ya) *n* an ornamental shrub with glossy leaves and white, pink, or red flowers.
camel's hair *or* **camelhair** *n* soft cloth, usually tan in colour, which is made from camel's hair and is used to make coats.
Camembert (**kam**-mem-bare) *n* a soft creamy cheese.
cameo *n, pl* **cameos 1** a brooch or ring with a profile head carved in relief. **2** a small but important part in a film or play played by a well-known actor or actress.
camera *n* **1** a piece of equipment used for taking photographs or pictures for television or cinema. **2 in camera** in private.
cameraman *n, pl* **-men** a man who operates a camera for television or cinema.
camera obscura *n* a darkened room with an opening through which images of outside objects are projected onto a flat surface.
camiknickers *pl n* a woman's undergarment consisting of knickers attached to a camisole top.
camisole *n* a woman's bodice-like garment with shoulder straps.
camomile *or* **chamomile** (**kam**-mo-mile) *n* an sweet-smelling plant used to make herbal tea.
camouflage (**kam**-moo-flahzh) *n* **1** the use of natural surroundings or artificial aids to conceal or disguise something. ~*vb* **-flaging, -flaged 2** to conceal by camouflage.
camp[1] *n* **1** a place where people stay in tents. **2** a collection of huts and other buildings used as temporary lodgings for military troops or for prisoners of war. **3** a group that supports a particular doctrine: *the socialist camp.* ~*vb* **4** to stay in a camp. **camper** *n* **camping** *n*
camp[2] *Informal* ~*adj* **1** effeminate or homosexual. **2** consciously artificial, vulgar, or affected. ~*vb* **3 camp it up** to behave in a camp manner.
campaign *n* **1** a series of coordinated activities designed to achieve a goal. **2** *Mil* a number of operations aimed at achieving a single objective. ~*vb* **3** to take part in a campaign: *he paid tribute to all those who'd campaigned for his release.* **campaigner** *n*
campanile (camp-an-**neel**-lee) *n* a bell tower, usually one not attached to another building.
campanology *n* the art of ringing bells. **campanologist** *n*
campanula *n* a plant with blue or white bell-shaped flowers.
camp bed *n* a lightweight folding bed.
camp follower *n* **1** a person who supports a particular group or organization without being a member of it. **2** a civilian who unofficially provides services to military personnel.
camphor *n* a sweet-smelling crystalline substance obtained from the wood of the **camphor tree**, which is used medicinally and in mothballs.
camphorated *adj* impregnated with camphor.
campion *n* a red, pink, or white European wild flower.
camp oven *n Austral & NZ* a heavy metal pot or box with a lid, used for baking over an open fire.
camp site *n* a place where people can stay in tents.
campus *n, pl* **-puses** the grounds and buildings of a university or college.
camshaft *n* a part of an engine consisting of a rod to which cams are attached.
can[1] *vb, past* **could 1** be able to: *make sure he can breathe easily.* **2** be allowed to: *you can swim in the large pool.*
can[2] *n* **1** a metal container, usually sealed, for food or liquids. ~*vb* **canning, canned 2** to put (something) into a can.
Can. 1 Canada. **2** Canadian.
Canada Day *n* (in Canada) July 1, a public holiday marking the anniversary of the day in 1867 when Canada became a dominion.
Canada goose *n* a greyish-brown North American goose with a black neck and head.
Canada jay *n* a grey jay of northern N America, notorious for stealing.
Canadian *adj* **1** of Canada. ~*n* **2** a person from Canada.
Canadiana *n* objects relating to Canadian history and culture.
Canadian football *n* a game like American football played on a grass pitch between teams of 12 players.
Canadianism *n* **1** the Canadian national character or spirit. **2** a linguistic feature peculiar to Canada or Canadians.
Canadianize *or* **-ise** *vb* **-izing, -ized** *or* **-ising, -ised** to make Canadian.
Canadian Shield *n* (in Canada) the wide area of Precambrian rock extending over most of central and E Canada: rich in minerals.

THESAURUS

calmness 1. composure, cool (*slang*), coolness, equanimity, imperturbability, sang-froid, self-possession **2.** calm, hush, peace, quiet, repose, serenity, smoothness, stillness, tranquillity
camouflage 1. *n.* blind, cloak, concealment, cover, disguise, false appearance, front, guise, mask, mimicry, protective colouring, screen **2.** *vb.* cloak, conceal, cover, disguise, hide, mask, obscure, screen, veil
camp[1] bivouac, camping ground, camp site, encampment, tents
camp[2] *informal* affected, artificial, camped up (*informal*), effeminate (*slang*), posturing

Canadien *or fem* **Canadienne** (kan-ad-**ee-en**) *n* a French Canadian.
canaille (kan-**nye**) *n* the masses or rabble.
canal *n* **1** an artificial waterway constructed for navigation or irrigation. **2** a passage or duct in a person's body: *the alimentary canal.*
canalize *or* **-lise** *vb* **-lizing, -lized** *or* **-lising, -lised** **1** to give direction to (a feeling or activity). **2** to convert into a canal. **canalization** *or* **-lisation** *n*
canapé (**kan**-nap-pay) *n* a small piece of bread or toast spread with a savoury topping.
canard *n* a false report.
canary *n, pl* **-naries** a small yellow songbird often kept as a pet.
canasta *n* a card game like rummy, played with two packs of cards.
cancan *n* a lively high-kicking dance performed by a female group.
cancel *vb* **-celling, -celled** *or US* **-celing, -celed** **1** to stop (something that has been arranged) from taking place. **2** to mark (a cheque or stamp) with an official stamp to prevent further use. **3 cancel out** to make ineffective by having the opposite effect: *economic vulnerability cancels out any possible political gain.* **cancellation** *n*
cancer *n* **1** a serious disease resulting from a malignant growth or tumour, caused by abnormal and uncontrolled cell division. **2** a malignant growth or tumour. **3** an evil influence that spreads dangerously: *their country would remain a cancer of instability.* **cancerous** *adj*
Cancer *n* **1** *Astrol* the fourth sign of the zodiac; the Crab. **2 tropic of Cancer** See **tropic** (sense 1).
candela (kan-**dee**-la) *n* the SI unit of luminous intensity (the amount of light a source gives off in a given direction).
candelabrum *or* **candelabra** *n, pl* **-bra, -brums,** *or* **-bras** a large branched holder for candles or overhead lights.
candid *adj* honest and straightforward in speech or behaviour. **candidly** *adv*
candidate *n* **1** a person seeking a job or position. **2** a person taking an examination. **3** a person or thing regarded as suitable or likely for a particular fate or position: *someone who smokes, drinks, or eats too much is a candidate for heart disease.* **candidacy** *or* **candidature** *n*
candied *adj* coated with or cooked in sugar: *candied peel.*
candle *n* **1** a stick or block of wax or tallow surrounding a wick, which is burned to produce light. **2 burn the candle at both ends** to exhaust oneself by doing too much.
candlelight *n* the light from a candle or candles. **candlelit** *adj*
Candlemas *n Christianity* February 2, the Feast of the Purification of the Virgin Mary.
candlepower *n* the luminous intensity of a source of light: now expressed in candelas.
candlestick *or* **candleholder** *n* a holder for a candle.
candlewick *n* cotton with a tufted pattern, used to make bedspreads and dressing gowns.
candour *or US* **candor** *n* honesty and straightforwardness of speech or behaviour.
candy *n, pl* **-dies** *Chiefly US & Canad* a sweet or sweets.
candyfloss *n Brit* a light fluffy mass of spun sugar, held on a stick.
candy-striped *adj* having narrow coloured stripes on a white background.
candytuft *n* a garden plant with clusters of white, pink, or purple flowers.
cane *n* **1** the long flexible stems of the bamboo or any similar plant. **2** strips of such stems, woven to make wickerwork. **3** a bamboo stem tied to a garden plant to support it. **4** a flexible rod used to beat someone. **5** a slender walking stick. *~vb* **caning, caned** **6** to beat with a cane.
cane sugar *n* sugar obtained from sugar cane.
canine (**kay**-nine) *adj* **1** of or like a dog. *~n* **2** a sharp-pointed tooth between the incisors and the molars.
canister *n* a metal container for dry food.
canker *n* **1** an ulceration or ulcerous disease. **2** something evil that spreads and corrupts.
cannabis *n* a drug obtained from the dried leaves and flowers of the hemp plant.
canned *adj* **1** preserved in a can. **2** *Informal* recorded in advance: *canned carols.*
cannelloni *or* **canneloni** *pl n* tubular pieces of pasta filled with meat or cheese.
cannery *n, pl* **-neries** a place where foods are canned.
cannibal *n* **1** a person who eats human flesh. **2** an animal that eats the flesh of other animals of its kind. **cannibalism** *n*
cannibalize *or* **-ise** *vb* **-izing, -ized** *or* **-ising, -ised** to use parts from (one machine or vehicle) to repair another.
canning *n* the process of sealing food in cans to preserve it.
cannon *n, pl* **-nons** *or* **-non** **1** a large gun consisting of a metal tube mounted on a carriage, formerly used in battles. **2** an automatic aircraft gun. **3** *Billiards* a shot in which the cue ball strikes two balls successively. *~vb* **4 cannon into** to collide with.
cannonade *n* continuous heavy gunfire.
cannonball *n* a heavy metal ball fired from a cannon.
cannon fodder *n* men regarded as expendable in war.
cannot *vb* can not.
canny *adj* **-nier, -niest** shrewd or cautious. **cannily** *adv*
canoe *n* a light narrow open boat, propelled by one or more paddles. **canoeist** *n*
canoeing *n* the sport of rowing or racing in a canoe.

THESAURUS

campaign attack, crusade, drive, expedition, movement, offensive, operation, push
cancel **1.** abolish, abort, abrogate, annul, call off, countermand, do away with, eliminate, repeal, rescind, revoke **2.** *usually with* **out** balance out, compensate for, counterbalance, make up for, neutralize, nullify, offset, redeem
cancellation abandonment, abolition, annulment, elimination, repeal, revocation
cancer **1.** carcinoma, growth, tumour **2.** blight, canker, corruption, evil, malignancy, rot
candid blunt, downright, forthright, frank, guileless, ingenuous, open, outspoken, plain, straightforward, truthful, upfront
candidate applicant, aspirant, competitor, contender, contestant, entrant, nominee, possibility
candour directness, frankness, honesty, openness, outspokenness, truthfulness

canon[1] *n* a priest serving in a cathedral.

canon[2] *n* **1** *Christianity* a Church decree regulating morals or religious practices. **2** a general rule or standard: *the Marx-Engels canon.* **3** a list of the works of an author that are accepted as authentic: *the Yeats canon.* **4** a piece of music in which a melody in one part is taken up in one or more other parts successively.

canonical *adj* **1** conforming with canon law. **2** included in a canon of writings.

canonical hour *n RC Church* one of the seven prayer times appointed for each day.

canonicals *pl n* the official clothes worn by clergy when taking services.

canonize *or* **-ise** *vb* **-izing, -ized** *or* **-ising, -ised** *RC Church* to declare (a dead person) to be a saint. **canonization** *or* **-isation** *n*

canon law *n* the body of laws of a Christian Church.

canoodle *vb* **-dling, -dled** *Slang* to kiss and cuddle.

canopied *adj* covered with a canopy: *canopied niches.*

canopy *n, pl* **-pies 1** an ornamental awning above a bed or throne. **2** a rooflike covering over an altar, niche, or door. **3** any large or wide covering: *the thick forest canopy.* **4** the part of a parachute that opens out. **5** the transparent hood of an aircraft cockpit.

cant[1] *n* **1** insincere talk concerning religion or morals. **2** specialized vocabulary of a particular group, such as thieves or lawyers. *~vb* **3** to use cant: *canting hypocrites.*

cant[2] *n* **1** a tilted position. *~vb* **2** to tilt or overturn: *the engine was canted to one side.*

can't *vb* can not.

cantabile (kan-**tah**-bill-lay) *adv Music* flowing and melodious.

cantaloupe *or* **cantaloup** *n* a kind of melon with sweet-tasting orange flesh.

cantankerous *adj* quarrelsome or bad-tempered.

cantata (kan-**tah**-ta) *n* a musical setting of a text, consisting of arias, duets, and choruses.

canteen *n* **1** a restaurant attached to a workplace or school. **2** a box containing a set of cutlery.

canter *n* **1** a gait of horses that is faster than a trot but slower than a gallop. *~vb* **2** (of a horse) to move at a canter.

canticle *n* a short hymn with words from the Bible.

cantilever *n* a beam or girder fixed at one end only.

cantilever bridge *n* a bridge made of two cantilevers which meet in the middle.

canto (**kan**-toe) *n, pl* **-tos** a main division of a long poem.

canton *n* a political division of a country, such as Switzerland.

Cantonese *adj* **1** of Canton, a port in SE China. *~n* **2** (*pl* **-nese**) a person from Canton. **3** the Chinese dialect of Canton.

cantonment (kan-**toon**-ment) *n* a permanent military camp in British India.

cantor *n Judaism* a man employed to lead synagogue services.

Canuck *n, adj US & Canad informal* Canadian.

canvas *n* **1** a heavy cloth of cotton, hemp, or jute, used to make tents and sails and for painting on in oils. **2** an oil painting done on canvas. **3 under canvas** in a tent: *sleeping under canvas.*

canvass *vb* **1** to try to persuade (people) to vote for a particular candidate or party in an election. **2** to find out the opinions of (people) by conducting a survey. *~n* **3** the activity of canvassing. **canvasser** *n* **canvassing** *n*

canyon *n* a deep narrow steep-sided valley.

caoutchouc (**cow**-chook) *n* same as **rubber**[1] (sense 1).

cap *n* **1** a soft close-fitting covering for the head. **2** *Sport* a cap given to someone selected for a national team. **3** a small flat lid: *petrol cap.* **4** a small amount of explosive enclosed in paper and used in a toy gun. **5** a contraceptive device placed over the mouth of the womb. **6 cap in hand** humbly. *~vb* **capping, capped 7** to cover or top with something: *a thick cover of snow capped the cars.* **8** *Sport* to select (a player) for a national team: *Australia's most capped player.* **9** to impose an upper level on (a tax): *charge capping.* **10** *Informal* to outdo or excel: *capping anecdote with anecdote.*

CAP (in the EU) Common Agricultural Policy.

cap. capital.

capability *n, pl* **-ties** the ability or skill to do something.

capable *adj* **1** having the ability or skill to do something: *a side capable of winning the championship.* **2** competent and efficient: *capable high achievers.* **capably** *adv*

capacious *adj* having a large capacity or area.

capacitance *n Physics* **1** the ability of a capacitor to store electrical charge. **2** a measure of this.

capacitor *n Physics* a device for storing a charge of electricity.

capacity *n, pl* **-ties 1** the ability to contain, absorb, or hold something. **2** the maximum amount something can contain or absorb: *filled to capacity.* **3** the ability to do something: *his capacity to elicit great loyalty.* **4** a

THESAURUS

canker 1. blister, cancer, infection, sore, ulcer **2.** bane, blight, cancer, corruption, rot, scourge

canny artful, careful, cautious, circumspect, clever, knowing, prudent, sharp, shrewd, subtle, wise, worldly-wise

canon 1. criterion, dictate, formula, precept, principle, rule, standard, yardstick **2.** catalogue, list

canopy awning, covering, shade, sunshade

cant[1] *n.* **1.** humbug, hypocrisy, insincerity, pretence, sanctimoniousness **2.** argot, jargon, lingo, slang, vernacular

cant[2] *vb.* angle, bevel, incline, rise, slant, slope, tilt

cantankerous bad-tempered, choleric, contrary, crabby, cranky (*informal*), crotchety (*informal*), crusty, difficult, disagreeable, grouchy (*informal*), grumpy, ill-humoured, irascible, irritable, liverish, peevish, quarrelsome, ratty (*Brit informal*), testy, tetchy

canting hypocritical, insincere, sanctimonious, two-faced

canvass *vb.* **1.** campaign, electioneer **2.** analyse, examine, inspect, investigate, poll, scan, scrutinize, study *~n.* **3.** examination, investigation, poll, scrutiny, survey

canyon gorge, gulch (*U.S. & Canad.*), gulf, gully, ravine

cap *vb.* **1.** cover, crown, top **2.** *informal* beat, better, clobber (*slang*), eclipse, exceed, lick (*informal*), outdo, outstrip, run rings around (*informal*), surpass, transcend

capability ability, capacity, competence, facility, faculty, means, power, proficiency, qualification, wherewithal

capable able, accomplished, adept, clever, competent, efficient, experienced, gifted, masterly, proficient, qualified, skilful, talented

position or function: *acting in an official capacity.* **5** the maximum output of which an industry or factory is capable: *the refinery had a capacity of three hundred thousand barrels a day.* **6** *Physics* same as **capacitance.** ~*adj* **7** of the maximum amount or number possible: *a capacity crowd.*

caparisoned (kap-**par**-riss-sond) *adj* (esp. of a horse) magnificently decorated or dressed.

cape[1] *n* a short sleeveless cloak.

cape[2] *n* a large piece of land that juts out into the sea.

Cape *n* **the 1** the Cape of Good Hope. **2** the SW region of South Africa's Cape Province.

caper *n* **1** a high-spirited escapade. ~*vb* **2** to skip about light-heartedly.

capercaillie *or* **capercailzie** (kap-per-**kale**-yee) *n* a large black European woodland grouse.

capers *pl n* the pickled flower buds of a Mediterranean shrub, used in making sauces.

capillarity *n Physics* a phenomenon caused by surface tension that results in the surface of a liquid rising or falling in contact with a solid.

capillary (kap-**pill**-a-ree) *n, pl* **-laries 1** *Anat* one of the very fine blood vessels linking the arteries and the veins. ~*adj* **2** (of a tube) having a fine bore. **3** *Anat* of the capillaries.

capital[1] *n* **1** the chief city of a country, where the government meets. **2** the total wealth owned or used in business by an individual or group. **3** wealth used to produce more wealth by investment. **4 make capital out of** to gain advantage from: *to make political capital out of the hostage situation.* **5** a capital letter. ~*adj* **6** *Law* involving or punishable by death: *a capital offence.* **7** denoting the large letter used as the initial letter in a sentence, personal name, or place name. **8** *Old-fashioned* excellent or first-rate: *a capital dinner.*

capital[2] *n* the top part of a column or pillar.

capital gain *n* profit from the sale of an asset.

capital goods *pl n Econ* goods that are themselves utilized in the production of other goods.

capitalism *n* an economic system based on the private ownership of industry.

capitalist *adj* **1** based on or supporting capitalism: *capitalist countries.* ~*n* **2** a supporter of capitalism. **3** a person who owns a business. **capitalistic** *adj*

capitalize *or* **-ise** *vb* **-izing, -ized** *or* **-ising, -ised 1 capitalize on** to take advantage of: *to capitalize on the available opportunities.* **2** to write or print (words) in capital letters. **3** to convert (debt or earnings) into capital stock. **capitalization** *or* **-isation** *n*

capital levy *n* a tax on capital or property as contrasted with a tax on income.

capitally *adv Old-fashioned* in an excellent manner; admirably.

capital punishment *n* the punishment of death for committing a serious crime.

capital stock *n* **1** the value of the total shares that a company can issue. **2** the total capital existing in an economy at a particular time.

capitation *n* a tax of a fixed amount per person.

capitulate *vb* **-lating, -lated** to surrender under agreed conditions. **capitulation** *n*

capo *n, pl* **-pos** a device fitted across the strings of a guitar or similar instrument so as to raise the pitch.

capon (**kay**-pon) *n* a castrated cock fowl fattened for eating.

cappuccino (kap-poo-**cheen**-oh) *n, pl* **-nos** coffee with steamed milk, usually sprinkled with powdered chocolate.

caprice (kap-**reess**) *n* **1** a sudden change of attitude or behaviour. **2** a tendency to have such changes.

capricious *adj* having a tendency to sudden unpredictable changes of attitude or behaviour. **capriciously** *adv*

Capricorn *n* **1** *Astrol* the tenth sign of the zodiac; the Goat. **2 tropic of Capricorn** See **tropic** (sense 1).

capriole *n* **1** an upward but not forward leap made by a horse. ~*vb* **-oling, -oled 2** to perform a capriole.

caps. capital letters.

capsicum *n* a kind of pepper used as a vegetable or ground to produce a spice.

capsize *vb* **-sizing, -sized** (of a boat) to overturn accidentally.

capstan *n* a vertical rotating cylinder round which a ship's rope or cable is wound.

capstone *n* same as **copestone** (sense 2).

capsule *n* **1** a soluble gelatine case containing a dose of medicine. **2** *Bot* a plant's seed case that opens when ripe. **3** *Anat* a membrane or sac surrounding an organ or part. **4** See **space capsule.** ~*adj* **5** very concise: *capsule courses.*

capsulize *or* **-ise** *vb* **-izing, -ized** *or* **-ising, -ised 1** to state (information) in a highly condensed form. **2** to enclose in a capsule.

Capt. Captain.

captain *n* **1** the person in charge of a ship, boat, or civil aircraft. **2** a middle-ranking naval officer. **3** a junior officer in the army. **4** the leader of a team or group. ~*vb* **5** to be captain of. **captaincy** *n*

caption *n* **1** a title, brief explanation, or comment accompanying a picture. ~*vb* **2** to provide with a caption.

captious *adj* tending to make trivial criticisms.

THESAURUS

capacious ample, broad, commodious, expansive, extended, extensive, generous, roomy, sizable, spacious, substantial, vast, voluminous, wide

capacity 1. amplitude, compass, dimensions, extent, magnitude, range, room, scope, size, space, volume **2.** ability, aptitude, capability, competence, competency, efficiency, facility, faculty, genius, gift, power **3.** appointment, function, office, position, post, role, sphere

cape head, headland, ness, peninsula, point, promontory

caper 1. *n.* escapade, high jinks, jape, jest, lark (*informal*), prank, sport **2.** *vb.* bound, cavort, dance, frisk, frolic, gambol, hop, jump, leap, romp, skip, spring, trip

capital 1. *n.* assets, cash, finance, finances, funds, investment, means, money, principal, property, resources, stock, wealth, wherewithal **2.** *adj.* excellent, fine, first-rate, prime, splendid, sterling, superb, world-class

capitalism free enterprise, private enterprise, private ownership

capitulate give in, give up, submit, succumb, surrender, yield

capitulation submission, surrender, yielding

caprice 1. fad, fancy, impulse, notion, quirk, vagary, whim, whimsy **2.** fickleness, inconstancy

capricious erratic, fanciful, fickle, impulsive, inconstant, mercurial, unpredictable, variable, wayward, whimsical

capsize invert, keel over, overturn, tip over, turn over, turn turtle, upset

capsule 1. lozenge, pill, tablet **2.** *Bot.* case, pericarp, pod, receptacle, sheath, shell

captivate *vb* **-vating, -vated** to attract and hold the attention of; enchant. **captivating** *adj*

captive *n* **1** a person who is kept in confinement. *~adj* **2** kept in confinement. **3** (of an audience) unable to leave.

captivity *n* the state of being kept in confinement.

captor *n* a person who captures a person or animal.

capture *vb* **-turing, -tured 1** to take by force. **2** to succeed in representing (something elusive) in words, pictures, or music: *the Guardian captures the tension of the crisis.* **3** *Physics* (of an atomic nucleus) to acquire (an additional particle). *~n* **4** the act of capturing or the state of being captured.

capuchin (**kap**-yew-chin) *n* a S American monkey with a cowl of thick hair on the top of its head.

Capuchin *n* **1** a friar belonging to a branch of the Franciscan Order founded in 1525. *~adj* **2** of this order.

capybara *n* the largest living rodent, found in S America.

car *n* **1** a motorized road vehicle designed to carry a small number of people. **2** the passenger compartment of a cable car, airship, lift, or balloon. **3** *US & Canad* a railway carriage.

caracal *n* a lynx with reddish fur, which inhabits deserts of N Africa and S Asia.

carafe (kar-**raff**) *n* a wide-mouthed bottle for water or wine.

carambola *n* a yellow edible star-shaped fruit that grows on a Brazilian tree.

caramel *n* **1** a chewy sweet made from sugar and milk. **2** burnt sugar, used for colouring and flavouring food.

caramelize *or* **-ise** *vb* **-izing, -ized** *or* **-ising, -ised** to turn into caramel.

carapace *n* the thick hard upper shell of tortoises and crustaceans.

carat *n* **1** a unit of weight of precious stones, equal to 0.20 grams. **2** a measure of the purity of gold in an alloy, expressed as the number of parts of gold in 24 parts of the alloy.

caravan *n* **1** *Brit* a large enclosed vehicle designed to be pulled by a car or horse and equipped to be lived in. **2** (in some Eastern countries) a company of traders or other travellers journeying together.

caravanning *n* *Brit* travelling or holidaying in a caravan.

caravanserai *n* (in some Eastern countries) a large inn enclosing a courtyard, providing accommodation for caravans.

caraway *n* a Eurasian plant with seeds that are used as a spice in cooking.

carbide *n* *Chem* a compound of carbon with a metal.

carbine *n* a type of light rifle.

carbohydrate *n* any of a large group of energy-producing compounds, including sugars and starches, that contain carbon, hydrogen, and oxygen.

carbolic acid *n* a disinfectant derived from coal tar.

carbon *n* **1** a nonmetallic element occurring in three forms, charcoal, graphite, and diamond, and present in all organic compounds. Symbol: C **2** short for **carbon paper** or **carbon copy.**

carbonaceous *adj* of, resembling, or containing carbon.

carbonate *n* a salt or ester of carbonic acid.

carbonated *adj* (of a drink) containing carbon dioxide; fizzy.

carbon black *n* powdered carbon produced by partial burning of natural gas or petroleum, used in pigments and ink.

carbon copy *n* **1** a duplicate obtained by using carbon paper. **2** *Informal* a person or thing that is identical or very similar to another.

carbon dating *n* a technique for finding the age of organic materials, such as wood, based on their content of radioactive carbon.

carbon dioxide *n* a colourless odourless incombustible gas formed during breathing, and used in fire extinguishers and in making fizzy drinks.

carbonic *adj* containing carbon.

carbonic acid *n* a weak acid formed when carbon dioxide combines with water.

carboniferous *adj* yielding coal or carbon.

Carboniferous *adj* *Geol* of the period of geological time about 330 million years ago, during which coal seams were formed.

carbonize *or* **-ise** *vb* **-izing, -ized** *or* **-ising, -ised 1** to turn into carbon as a result of partial burning. **2** to coat (a substance) with carbon. **carbonization** *or* **-isation** *n*

carbon monoxide *n* a colourless odourless poisonous gas formed by the incomplete burning of carbon compounds; part of the gases that come from a vehicle's exhaust.

carbon paper *n* a thin sheet of paper coated on one side with a dark waxy pigment, containing carbon, used to make a duplicate of something as it is typed or written.

carbon tetrachloride *n* a colourless nonflammable liquid used as a solvent, cleaning fluid, and insecticide.

Carborundum *n* *Trademark* an abrasive material consisting of silicon carbide.

carboxyl group *or* **radical** *n* *Chem* the chemical group –COOH: the functional group in organic acids.

carboy *n* a large bottle protected by a basket or box.

carbuncle *n* a large painful swelling under the skin like a boil.

carburettor *or* *US & Canad* **carburetor** *n* a device in an internal-combustion engine that mixes petrol with air and regulates the intake of the mixture into the engine.

carcass *or* **carcase** *n* **1** the dead body of an animal. **2** *Informal* a person's body: *ask that person to move his carcass.*

carcinogen *n* a substance that produces cancer. **carcinogenic** *adj*

carcinoma *n, pl* **-mas** *or* **-mata** a malignant tumour.

card[1] *n* **1** a piece of stiff paper or thin cardboard used for identification, reference, proof of membership, or sending greetings or messages: *a Christmas card.* **2** one of a set of small pieces of cardboard, marked with

THESAURUS

captain boss, chief, commander, head, leader, master, skipper

captivate absorb, allure, attract, beguile, bewitch, charm, dazzle, enchant, enthral, entrance, fascinate, hypnotize, mesmerize, ravish

captive 1. *n.* detainee, hostage, internee, prisoner **2.** *adj.* caged, confined, ensnared, imprisoned, incarcerated, locked up, penned

captivity bondage, confinement, custody, detention, imprisonment, incarceration, internment, slavery

capture 1. *vb.* apprehend, arrest, bag, catch, collar (*informal*), nab (*informal*), nail (*informal*), seize, take, take into custody, take prisoner **2.** *n.* apprehension, arrest, imprisonment, seizure, trapping

car auto (*U.S.*), automobile, jalopy (*informal*), machine, motor, motorcar, vehicle

figures or symbols, used for playing games or for fortune-telling. **3** a small rectangle of stiff plastic with identifying numbers for use as a credit card, cheque card, or charge card. **4** *Old-fashioned informal* a witty or eccentric person. ~See also **cards.**

card[2] *n* **1** a machine or tool for combing fibres of cotton or wool to disentangle them before spinning. ~*vb* **2** to process with such a machine or tool.

cardamom *n* a spice that is obtained from the seeds of a tropical plant.

cardboard *n* a thin stiff board made from paper pulp.

card-carrying *adj* being an official member of an organization: *a card-carrying Conservative.*

cardiac *adj* of or relating to the heart.

cardigan *n* a knitted jacket.

cardinal *n* **1** any of the high-ranking clergymen of the Roman Catholic Church who elect the pope and act as his chief counsellors. ~*adj* **2** fundamentally important; principal.

cardinal number *n* a number denoting quantity but not order in a group, for example one, two, or three.

cardinal points *pl n* the four main points of the compass: north, south, east, and west.

cardinal virtues *pl n* the most important moral qualities, traditionally justice, prudence, temperance, and fortitude.

card index *n* an index in which each item is separately listed on systematically arranged cards.

cardiogram *n* an electrocardiogram. See **electrocardiograph.**

cardiograph *n* an electrocardiograph. **cardiographer** *n* **cardiography** *n*

cardiology *n* the branch of medicine dealing with the heart and its diseases. **cardiologist** *n*

cardiovascular *adj* of or relating to the heart and the blood vessels.

cards *n* **1** any game played with cards, or card games generally. **2 lay one's cards on the table** to declare one's intentions openly. **3 on the cards** likely to take place: *a military coup was on the cards.* **4 play one's cards right** to handle a situation cleverly.

cardsharp *or* **cardsharper** *n* a professional card player who cheats.

card vote *n Brit* a vote by delegates in which each delegate's vote counts as a vote by all his or her constituents.

care *vb* **caring, cared 1** to be worried or concerned: *he does not care what people think about him.* **2** to like (to do something): *anybody care to go out?* **3 care for a** to look after or provide for: *it is still largely women who care for dependent family members.* **b** to like or be fond of: *he did not care for his concentration to be disturbed; I don't suppose you could ever care for me seriously.* **4 I couldn't care less** I am completely indifferent. ~*n* **5** careful or serious attention; caution: *treat all raw meat with extreme care to avoid food poisoning.* **6** protection or charge: *the children are now in the care of a state orphanage.* **7** trouble or worry: *his mind turned towards money cares.* **8 care of** (written on envelopes) at the address of. **9 in** *or* **into care** *Brit* (of a child) made the legal responsibility of a local authority by order of a court. **10 take care** to be careful. **11 take care of** to look after: *women have to take greater care of themselves during pregnancy.*

careen *vb* to tilt over to one side.

➤ Be careful not to confuse *careen,* "tilt", with *career,* "rush headlong".

career *n* **1** the series of jobs in a profession or occupation that a person has through his or her life: *he began his theatrical career in Cardiff.* **2** the part of a person's life spent in a particular occupation or type of work: *a school career punctuated with exams.* ~*vb* **3** to rush in an uncontrolled way. ~*adj* **4** having chosen to dedicate his or her life to a particular occupation: *a career soldier.*

➤ Do not confuse *career* "rush" with *careen* "tilt".

careerist *n* a person who seeks to advance his or her career by any means possible. **careerism** *n*

carefree *adj* without worry or responsibility.

careful *adj* **1** cautious in attitude or action. **2** very exact and thorough. **carefully** *adv* **carefulness** *n*

careless *adj* **1** done or acting with insufficient attention. **2** unconcerned in attitude or action. **carelessly** *adv* **carelessness** *n*

carer *n* a person who looks after someone who is ill or old, often a relative: *the group offers support for the carers of those with dementia.*

caress *n* **1** a gentle affectionate touch or embrace. ~*vb* **2** to touch gently and affectionately.

caret (**kar**-ret) *n* a symbol (‸) indicating a place in written or printed matter where something is to be inserted.

caretaker *n* **1** a person employed to look after a place or thing. ~*adj* **2** performing the duties of an office temporarily: *a caretaker administration.*

careworn *adj* showing signs of stress or worry: *her fatigued, careworn face.*

cargo *n, pl* **-goes** *or esp US* **-gos** goods carried by a ship, aircraft, or other vehicle.

THESAURUS

carcass body, cadaver (*Medical*), corpse, corse (*archaic*), dead body, remains

cardinal central, chief, essential, first, foremost, fundamental, greatest, highest, important, key, leading, main, paramount, pre-eminent, primary, prime, principal

care 1. attention, carefulness, caution, circumspection, heed (*formal*), meticulousness, pains, prudence, regard, vigilance, watchfulness **2.** charge, control, custody, guardianship, keeping, management, protection, supervision **3.** affliction, anxiety, burden, concern, hardship, pressure, stress, tribulation, trouble, woe, worry

career 1. *n.* calling, employment, livelihood, occupation, vocation **2.** *vb.* bolt, dash, hurtle, race, rush, speed, tear

care for 1. attend, foster, look after, mind, minister to, nurse, protect, provide for, tend, watch over **2.** be fond of, desire, enjoy, like, love, take to, want

carefree airy, blithe, breezy, buoyant, careless, cheerful, cheery, chirpy (*informal*), easy-going, happy, happy-go-lucky, insouciant, jaunty, light-hearted, sunny, untroubled

careful 1. cautious, chary, circumspect, discreet, heedful, prudent, thoughtful, vigilant, wary, watchful **2.** accurate, attentive, conscientious, fastidious, painstaking, precise, punctilious, scrupulous

careless 1. absent-minded, cursory, forgetful, hasty, heedless, incautious, irresponsible, lackadaisical, neglectful, negligent, offhand, remiss (*formal*), slapdash, slipshod, sloppy (*informal*), thoughtless, unconcerned, unthinking **2.** artless, casual, nonchalant, unstudied

carelessness inaccuracy, inattention, laxity, neglect, negligence, omission, slackness, sloppiness (*informal*), thoughtlessness

caress 1. *n.* cuddle, embrace, hug, pat, stroke **2.** *vb.* cuddle, embrace, fondle, hug, pet, stroke

caretaker 1. *n.* concierge, curator, custodian, janitor,

Carib *n* **1** (*pl* **-ibs** *or* **-ib**) a member of a group of American Indian peoples of NE South America and the S West Indies. **2** any of the languages of these peoples.
Caribbean *adj* of the Caribbean Sea, bounded by Central America, South America, and the West Indies, or the surrounding countries and islands.
caribou *n, pl* **-bous** *or* **-bou** a large North American reindeer.
caricature *n* **1** a drawing or description of a person which exaggerates characteristic features for comic effect. **2** a description or explanation of something that is so exaggerated or over-simplified that it is difficult to take seriously: *the caricature of Scotland found on postcards and shortbread tins.* ~*vb* **-turing, -tured** **3** to make a caricature of.
caries (**care**-reez) *n* tooth decay.
carillon (kar-**rill**-yon) *n* **1** a set of bells hung in a tower and played either from a keyboard or mechanically. **2** a tune played on such bells.
caring *adj* **1** feeling or showing care and compassion for other people. **2** of or relating to professional social or medical care: *the caring professions.*
carjack *vb* to attack (a driver in a car) in order to rob the driver or to steal the car for another crime.
Carmelite *n* **1** a Christian friar or nun belonging to the order of Our Lady of Carmel. ~*adj* **2** of this order.
carminative *adj* **1** able to relieve flatulence. ~*n* **2** a carminative drug.
carmine *adj* vivid red.
carnage *n* extensive slaughter of people.
carnal *adj* of a sexual or sensual nature: *carnal knowledge.* **carnality** *n*
carnation *n* a cultivated plant with clove-scented white, pink, or red flowers.
carnelian *n* a reddish-yellow variety of chalcedony, used as a gemstone.
carnet (**kar**-nay) *n* a customs licence permitting motorists to take their cars across certain frontiers.
carnival *n* **1** a festive period with processions, music, and dancing in the street. **2** a travelling funfair.
carnivore (**car**-niv-vore) *n* a meat-eating animal. **carnivorous** (car-**niv**-or-uss) *adj*
carob *n* the pod of a Mediterranean tree, used as a chocolate substitute.
carol *n* **1** a joyful religious song sung at Christmas. ~*vb* **-olling, -olled** *or US* **-oling, -oled** **2** to sing carols. **3** to sing joyfully.
carotene *n Biochem* any of four orange-red hydrocarbons, found in many plants, converted to vitamin A in the liver.
carotid (kar-**rot**-id) *n* **1** either of the two arteries that supply blood to the head and neck. ~*adj* **2** of either of these arteries.
carousal *n* a merry drinking party.
carouse *vb* **-rousing, -roused** to have a merry drinking party.
carousel (kar-roo-**sell**) *n* **1** a revolving conveyor for luggage at an airport or for slides for a projector. **2** *US & Canad* a merry-go-round.
carp[1] *n, pl* **carp** *or* **carps** a large freshwater food fish.
carp[2] *vb* to complain or find fault. **carping** *adj, n*
carpal *n* a wrist bone.
car park *n* an area or building reserved for parking cars.
carpel *n* the female reproductive organ of a flowering plant.
carpenter *n* a person who makes or repairs wooden structures.
carpentry *n* the skill or work of a carpenter.
carpet *n* **1** a heavy fabric for covering floors. **2** a covering like a carpet: *a carpet of leaves.* **3 on the carpet** *Informal* being or about to be reprimanded. **4 sweep something under the carpet** to conceal or keep silent about something that one does not want to be discovered. ~*vb* **-peting, -peted** **5** to cover with a carpet or a covering like a carpet.
carpetbag *n* a travelling bag made of carpeting.
carpetbagger *n* a politician who seeks office in a place where he or she has no connections.
carpeting *n* carpet material or carpets in general.
car phone *n* a telephone that operates by cellular radio for use in a car.
carport *n* a shelter for a car, consisting of a roof supported by posts.
carpus *n, pl* **-pi** the set of eight bones of the human wrist.
carrageen *n* an edible red seaweed of North America and N Europe.
carriage *n* **1** *Brit* one of the sections of a train for passengers. **2** the way a person holds and moves his or her head and body. **3** a four-wheeled horse-drawn passenger vehicle. **4** the moving part of a machine, such as a typewriter, that supports and shifts another part. **5** the charge made for conveying goods.
carriage clock *n* a style of portable clock, originally used by travellers.
carriageway *n Brit* the part of a road along which traffic passes in one direction: *the westbound carriageway of the M4.*
carrier *n* **1** a person, vehicle, or organization that carries something: *armoured personnel carriers.* **2** a person or animal that, without suffering from a disease, is capable of transmitting it to others. **3** short for **aircraft carrier.**
carrier bag *n Brit* a large plastic or paper bag for carrying shopping.
carrier pigeon *n* a homing pigeon used for carrying messages.
carrion *n* dead and rotting flesh.
carrion crow *n* a scavenging European crow with a completely black plumage and bill.
carrot *n* **1** a long tapering orange root vegetable. **2** something offered as an incentive.
carroty *adj* (of hair) reddish-orange.
carry *vb* **-ries, -rying, -ried** **1** to take from one place to another. **2** to have with one habitually, for example in one's pocket or handbag: *to carry a donor card.* **3** to transmit or be transmitted: *to carry disease.* **4** to have as a factor or result: *the charge of desertion carries a maximum penalty of twenty years.* **5** to be pregnant with: *women carrying Down's Syndrome babies.* **6** to

THESAURUS

keeper, porter, warden, watchman **2.** *adj.* acting, interim, short-term, temporary
cargo baggage, consignment, contents, freight, goods, lading, load, shipment
caricature **1.** *n.* burlesque, distortion, farce, lampoon, parody, satire, send-up (*Brit. informal*), takeoff (*informal*), travesty **2.** *vb.* distort, lampoon, parody, ridicule, satirize, send up (*Brit. informal*), take off (*informal*)
carnage blood bath, bloodshed, butchery, holocaust, massacre, mass murder, shambles (*old-fashioned*), slaughter
carnival celebration, fair, festival, fête, fiesta, gala, holiday, jamboree, Mardi Gras, merrymaking, revelry

hold (one's head or body) in a specified manner: *she always wears a sari and carries herself like an Indian.* **7** to secure the adoption of (a bill or motion): *the resolution was carried by fewer than twenty votes.* **8** (of a newspaper or television or radio station) to include in the contents: *several papers carried front-page pictures of the Russian president.* **9** *Maths* to transfer (a number) from one column of figures to the next. **10** to travel a certain distance or reach a specified point: *his faint voice carried no farther than the front few rows.* **11 carry the can** *Informal* to take all the blame for something. ~See also **carry away, carry forward,** etc.

carry away *vb* **be** *or* **get carried away** to be engrossed in or fascinated by something to the point of losing self-control: *he could be carried away by his own rhetoric.*

carrycot *n* a light portable bed for a baby, with handles and a hood, which usually also serves as the body of a pram.

carry forward *vb* to transfer (an amount) to the next column, page, or accounting period.

carry off *vb* **1** to lift and take (someone or something) away: *the German striker was carried off after snapping an Achilles tendon.* **2** to win: *who will carry off this year's honours is unclear.* **3** to handle (a situation) successfully: *he had the presence and social ability to carry off the job.* **4** to cause to die: *the circulatory disorder which carried off other members of his family.*

carry on *vb* **1** to continue: *we'll carry on exactly where we left off.* **2** to do, run, or take part in: *the vast trade carried on in the city.* **3** *Informal* to cause a fuss: *I don't want to carry on and make a big scene.* ~*n* **carry-on 4** *Informal, chiefly Brit* a fuss.

carry out *vb* **1** to follow (an order or instruction). **2** to accomplish (a task): *to carry out repairs.*

carry over *vb* to extend from one period or situation into another: *major debts carried over from last year.*

carry through *vb* to bring to completion: *these are difficult policies to carry through.*

carsick *adj* nauseated from riding in a car.

cart *n* **1** an open horse-drawn vehicle, usually with two wheels, used to carry goods or passengers. **2** any small vehicle that is pulled or pushed by hand. ~*vb* **3** to carry, usually with some effort: *men carted bricks and tiles and wooden boards.* ~See also **cart off.**

carte blanche *n* complete authority: *she's got carte blanche to redecorate.*

cartel *n* an association of competing firms formed in order to fix prices.

Cartesian *adj* of René Descartes, 17th-century French philosopher and mathematician, or his works.

Cartesian coordinates *pl n* a set of numbers that determine the location of a point in a plane or in space by its distance from two fixed intersecting lines.

carthorse *n* a large heavily built horse kept for pulling carts or for farm work.

Carthusian *n* **1** a Christian monk or nun belonging to a strict monastic order founded in 1084. ~*adj* **2** of this order.

cartilage (**kar**-till-ij) *n* a strong flexible tissue forming part of the skeleton. **cartilaginous** *adj*

cart off *vb* to take (someone) somewhere forcefully: *we had been carted off to the security police building.*

cartography *n* the art of making maps or charts. **cartographer** *n* **cartographic** *adj*

carton *n* **1** a cardboard box or container. **2** a container of waxed paper in which drinks are sold.

cartoon *n* **1** a humorous or satirical drawing in a newspaper or magazine. **2** same as **comic strip. 3** same as **animated cartoon. cartoonist** *n*

cartouche *n* **1** an ornamental tablet or panel in the form of a scroll. **2** (in ancient Egypt) an oblong or oval figure containing royal or divine names.

cartridge *n* **1** a metal casing containing an explosive charge and bullet for a gun. **2** the part of the pick-up of a record player that converts the movements of the stylus into electrical signals. **3** a sealed container of film or tape, or ink for a special kind of pen.

cartridge belt *n* a belt with loops or pockets for holding cartridges.

cartridge clip *n* a metallic container holding cartridges for an automatic gun.

cartridge paper *n* a type of heavy rough drawing paper.

cartwheel *n* **1** a sideways somersault supported by the hands with legs outstretched. **2** the large spoked wheel of a cart.

carve *vb* **carving, carved 1** to cut in order to form something: *carving wood.* **2** to form (something) by cutting: *the statue which was carved by Michelangelo.* **3** to slice (cooked meat). ~See also **carve out, carve up. carver** *n*

carve out *vb Informal* to make or create: *to carve out a political career.*

carvery *n, pl* **-veries** a restaurant where customers pay a set price for unrestricted helpings of carved meat and other food.

carve up *vb* **1** to divide or share out: *in 1705, Poland was carved up between three empires.* ~*n* **carve-up 2** the division or sharing out of something: *a territorial carve-up.*

carving *n* a figure or design produced by carving stone or wood.

carving knife *n* a long-bladed knife for carving cooked meat.

carwash *n* a place fitted with equipment for automatically washing cars.

caryatid (kar-ree-**at**-id) *n* a supporting column in the shape of a female figure.

Casanova *n* a promiscuous man.

casbah *n* the citadel of a North African city.

cascade *n* **1** a waterfall or series of waterfalls over rocks. **2** something flowing or falling like a waterfall: *a cascade of luxuriant hair.* ~*vb* **-cading, -caded 3** to flow or fall in a cascade: *rays of sunshine cascaded down.*

THESAURUS

carp beef (*slang*), cavil, complain, criticize, find fault, knock (*informal*), pick holes, quibble

carpenter cabinet-maker, joiner, woodworker

carriage 1. bearing, deportment, mien, posture **2.** cab, coach, conveyance, vehicle **3.** freight, transport

carry 1. bear, bring, convey, fetch, hump (*slang*), lug, move, relay, take, tote (*informal*), transfer, transmit, transport **2.** communicate, conduct, transmit

carry on 1. continue, keep going, last, maintain, perpetuate, persevere, persist **2.** manage, operate, run **3.** *informal* create (*Brit. slang*), make a fuss, misbehave

carry out accomplish, achieve, carry through, consummate, discharge, effect, execute, fulfil, implement, perform

carton box, case, container, pack, package, packet

cartoon 1. caricature **2.** comic strip **3.** animated cartoon, animated film, animation

cartridge 1. charge, magazine, round, shell **2.** capsule, case, cassette, container, cylinder

carve chisel, cut, engrave, fashion, form, hack, hew, incise, sculpt, sculpture, whittle

cascara *n* the bark of a N American shrub, used as a laxative.

case[1] *n* **1** a single instance or example of something: *cases of teenage pregnancies.* **2** a matter for discussion: *the case before the Ethics Committee.* **3** a specific condition or state of affairs: *a sudden-death play-off in the case of a draw.* **4** a set of arguments supporting an action or cause: *I put my case before the DSS.* **5** a person or problem dealt with by a doctor, social worker, or solicitor. **6 a** an action or lawsuit: *a rape case.* **b** the evidence offered in court to support a claim: *he will try to show that the case against his client is largely circumstantial.* **7** *Grammar* a form of a noun, pronoun, or adjective showing its relation to other words in the sentence: *the accusative case.* **8** *Informal* an amusingly eccentric person. **9 in any case** no matter what. **10 in case** so as to allow for the possibility that: *the President has ordered a medical team to stand by in case hostages are released.* **11 in case of** in the event of: *in case of a future conflict.*

case[2] *n* **1** a container, such as a box or chest. **2** a suitcase. **3** a protective outer covering. ~*vb* **casing, cased 4** *Slang* to inspect carefully (a place one plans to rob).

case-hardened *adj* having been made callous by experience: *a case-hardened senior policewoman.*

case history *n* a record of a person's background or medical history.

casein *n* a protein found in milk, which forms the basis of cheese.

case law *n* law established by following judicial decisions made in earlier cases.

caseload *n* the number of cases that someone like a doctor or social worker deals with at any one time.

casement *n* a window that is hinged on one side.

case study *n* an analysis of a group or person in order to make generalizations about a larger group or society as a whole.

casework *n* social work based on close study of the personal histories and circumstances of individuals and families. **caseworker** *n*

cash *n* **1** banknotes and coins, rather than cheques. **2** *Informal* money: *strapped for cash.* ~*adj* **3** of, for, or paid in cash: *cash hand-outs.* ~*vb* **4** to obtain or pay banknotes or coins for (a cheque or postal order). ~See also **cash in on.**

cash-and-carry *adj* operating on a basis of cash payment for goods that are taken away by the purchaser: *the-cash-and-carry wholesalers.*

cash-book *n Book-keeping* a journal in which all money transactions are recorded.

cash card *n* a card issued by a bank or building society which can be inserted into a cash dispenser in order to obtain money.

cash crop *n* a crop produced for sale rather than for subsistence.

cash desk *n* a counter or till in a shop where purchases are paid for.

cash discount *n* a discount granted to a purchaser who pays within a specified period.

cash dispenser *n* a computerized device outside a bank which supplies cash when a special card is inserted and the user's code number keyed in.

cashew *n* an edible kidney-shaped nut.

cash flow *n* the movement of money into and out of a business.

cashier[1] *n* a person responsible for handling cash in a bank, shop, or other business.

cashier[2] *vb* to dismiss with dishonour from the armed forces.

cash in on *vb Informal* to gain profit or advantage from: *trying to cash in on the dispute.*

cashmere *n* a very fine soft wool obtained from goats.

cash on delivery *n* a system involving cash payment to the carrier on delivery of merchandise.

cash register *n* a till that has a mechanism for displaying and adding the prices of the goods sold.

casing *n* a protective case or covering.

casino *n, pl* **-nos** a public building or room where gambling games are played.

cask *n* a strong barrel used to hold alcoholic drink.

casket *n* **1** a small box for valuables. **2** *US* a coffin.

Cassandra *n* someone whose prophecies of doom are unheeded.

cassava *n* a starch obtained from the root of a tropical American plant, used to make tapioca.

casserole *n* **1** a covered dish in which food is cooked slowly, usually in an oven, and served. **2** a dish cooked and served in this way: *beef casserole.* ~*vb* **-roling, -roled 3** to cook in a casserole.

cassette *n* a plastic case containing a reel of film or magnetic tape.

cassia *n* **1** a tropical plant whose pods yield a mild laxative. **2 cassia bark** a cinnamon-like spice obtained from the bark of a tropical Asian tree.

cassock *n* an ankle-length garment, usually black, worn by some Christian priests.

cassowary *n, pl* **-waries** a large flightless bird of Australia and New Guinea.

cast *n* **1** the actors in a play collectively. **2 a** an object made of material that has been shaped, while molten, by a mould. **b** the mould used to shape such an object. **3** *Surgery* a rigid casing made of plaster of Paris for immobilizing broken bones while they heal. **4** a sort, kind, or style: *people of an academic cast of mind.* **5** a slight squint in the eye. ~*vb* **casting, cast 6** to select (an actor) to play a part in a play or film. **7** to give or deposit (a vote). **8** to express (doubts or aspersions). **9** to cause to appear: *a shadow cast by the grandstand; the gloom cast by the recession.* **10 a** to shape (molten material) by pouring it into a mould. **b** to make (an object) by such a process. **11** to throw (a fishing line) into the water. **12** to throw with force: *cast into a bonfire.* **13** to direct (a glance): *he cast his eye over the horse-chestnut trees.* **14** to roll or throw (a dice). **15**

THESAURUS

cascade 1. *n.* cataract, deluge, falls, flood, fountain, outpouring, shower, torrent, waterfall **2.** *vb.* descend, flood, gush, overflow, pour, spill, tumble

case[1] **1.** example, instance, occasion, occurrence **2.** circumstance(s), condition, context, event, position, situation, state of affairs **3.** action, dispute, lawsuit, proceedings, suit, trial

case[2] **1.** box, cabinet, canister, capsule, carton, cartridge, casket, chest, container, crate, holder, receptacle, shell, trunk **2.** suitcase **3.** capsule, casing, cover, covering, envelope, integument, jacket, sheath, wrapper, wrapping

cash banknotes, brass (*Northern English dialect*), bread (*slang*), change, coin, coinage, dosh (*slang*), dough (*slang*), funds, money, necessary (*informal*), notes, ready (*informal*), ready money, shekels (*informal*), silver, specie

cashier[1] *n.* accountant, bank clerk, banker, bursar, clerk, purser, teller, treasurer

cashier[2] *vb.* discharge, dismiss, expel

casket Ark (*Judaism*), box, case, chest, coffer, jewel box

cast *n.* **1.** actors, characters, company, dramatis per-

cast aside to abandon or reject: *cast aside by her lover.* **16 cast a spell a** to perform magic. **b** to have an irresistible influence. ~See also **cast around, cast back,** etc.

castanets *pl n* a musical instrument, used by Spanish dancers, consisting of curved pieces of hollow wood, held between the fingers and thumb and clicked together.

cast around *or* **about** *vb* to make a mental or visual search: *he cast around for a job.*

castaway *n* a person who has been shipwrecked.

cast back *vb* to turn (the mind) to the past.

cast down *vb* to make (a person) feel discouraged or dejected.

caste *n* **1** any of the four major hereditary classes into which Hindu society is divided. **2** social rank.

castellated *adj* having turrets and battlements, like a castle.

caster *n* same as **castor.**

caster sugar *n* finely ground white sugar.

castigate *vb* **-gating, -gated** to find fault with or reprimand (a person) harshly. **castigation** *n*

casting *n* an object that has been cast in metal from a mould.

casting vote *n* the deciding vote used by the chairman of a meeting when an equal number of votes are cast on each side.

cast iron *n* **1** iron containing so much carbon that it is brittle and must be cast into shape rather than wrought. ~*adj* **cast-iron 2** made of cast iron. **3** definite or unchallengeable: *cast-iron guarantees.*

castle *n* **1** a large fortified building or set of buildings, often built as a residence for a ruler or nobleman in medieval Europe. **2** same as **rook**[2].

castle in the air *or* **in Spain** *n* a hope or desire unlikely to be realized.

cast-off *adj* **1** discarded because no longer wanted or needed: *cast-off clothing.* ~*n* **castoff 2** a person or thing that has been discarded because no longer wanted or needed. ~*vb* **cast off 3** to discard (something no longer wanted or needed). **4** to untie a ship from a dock. **5** to knot and remove (a row of stitches, esp. the final row) from the needle in knitting.

cast on *vb* to make (a row of stitches) on the needle in knitting.

castor *n* a small swivelling wheel fixed to a piece of furniture to enable it to be moved easily in any direction.

castor oil *n* an oil obtained from the seeds of an Indian plant, used as a lubricant and purgative.

castrate *vb* **-trating, -trated 1** to remove the testicles of. **2** to deprive of vigour or masculinity. **castration** *n*

casual *adj* **1** being or seeming careless or nonchalant: *he was casual about security.* **2** occasional or irregular: *casual workers.* **3** shallow or superficial: *casual relationships.* **4** for informal wear: *a casual jacket.* **5** happening by chance or without planning: *a casual comment.* ~*n* **6** an occasional worker. **casually** *adv*

casuals *pl n* **1** informal clothing. **2** young men wearing expensive casual clothes who go to football matches in order to start fights.

casualty *n, pl* **-ties 1** a person who is killed or injured in an accident or war. **2** the hospital department where victims of accidents are given emergency treatment. **3** a person or thing that has suffered as the result of a particular event or circumstance: *583 job losses with significant casualties among public-sector employees.*

casuistry *n* reasoning that is misleading or oversubtle. **casuist** *n*

cat *n* **1** a small domesticated mammal with thick soft fur and whiskers. **2** a wild animal related to the cat, such as the lynx, lion, or tiger. **3 let the cat out of the bag** to disclose a secret. **4 raining cats and dogs** raining very heavily. **5 set the cat among the pigeons** to stir up trouble. **catlike** *adj*

catabolism *n Biol* a metabolic process in which complex molecules are broken down into simple ones with the release of energy. **catabolic** *adj*

cataclysm (**kat**-a-kliz-zum) *n* **1** a violent upheaval of a social, political, or military nature: *the cataclysm of the Second World War.* **2** a disaster such as an earthquake or a flood. **cataclysmic** *adj*

catacombs (**kat**-a-koomz) *pl n* an underground burial place consisting of tunnels with side recesses for tombs.

catafalque (**kat**-a-falk) *n* a raised platform on which a body lies in state before or during a funeral.

Catalan *adj* **1** of Catalonia. ~*n* **2** a language of Catalonia in NE Spain. **3** a person from Catalonia.

catalepsy *n* a trancelike state in which the body is rigid. **cataleptic** *adj*

catalogue *or US* **catalog** *n* **1** a book containing details of items for sale. **2** a list of all the books of a library. **3** a list of events, qualities, or things considered as a group: *a catalogue of killings.* ~*vb* **-loguing, -logued** *or* **-loging, -loged 4** to enter (an item) in a catalogue. **5** to list a series of (events, qualities, or things): *the report catalogues two decades of human-rights violations.* **cataloguer** *n*

catalpa *n* tree of N America and Asia with bell-shaped whitish flowers.

catalyse *or US* **-lyze** *vb* **-lysing, -lysed** *or* **-lyzing, -lyzed** to influence (a chemical reaction) by catalysis.

catalysis *n* acceleration of a chemical reaction by the action of a catalyst. **catalytic** *adj*

catalyst *n* **1** a substance that speeds up a chemical reaction without itself undergoing any permanent chemical change. **2** a person or thing that causes an important change to take place.

catalytic converter *n* a device which uses catalysts to reduce the quantity of poisonous substances emitted by the exhaust of a motor vehicle.

catalytic cracker *n* a unit in an oil refinery in which mineral oils are converted into fuels by a catalytic process.

catamaran *n* a boat with twin parallel hulls.

THESAURUS

sonae, players, troupe **2.** complexion, manner, stamp, style, turn ~*vb.* **3.** allot, appoint, assign, choose, name, pick, select **4.** emit, give, shed, spread **5.** form, found, model, mould, set, shape **6.** chuck (*informal*), fling, hurl, impel, launch, lob, pitch, shy, sling, throw, toss

cast down deject, depress, desolate, discourage, dishearten, dispirit

caste class, estate (*History*), grade, order, rank, social order, station, status, stratum

castigate berate, blast, censure, chastise, criticize, excoriate (*literary*), give a rocket (*informal*), haul over the coals (*informal*), lambast(e), lash, read the riot act, rebuke, reprimand, scold, tear into (*informal*)

casual 1. blasé, cursory, indifferent, informal, insouciant, nonchalant, offhand, perfunctory, relaxed, unconcerned **2.** informal, sporty **3.** accidental, chance, fortuitous, incidental, random, unexpected, unforeseen, unintentional, unpremeditated

casualty loss, sufferer, victim

cat feline, moggy *or* mog (*Brit. slang*), puss (*informal*), pussy (*informal*)

catamite *n* a boy kept as a homosexual partner.

catapult *n* **1** a Y-shaped device with a loop of elastic fastened to the ends of the prongs, used by children for firing stones. **2** a device used to launch aircraft from a warship. *~vb* **3** to shoot forwards or upwards violently: *traffic catapulted forward with a roar.* **4** to cause (someone) suddenly to be in a particular situation: *catapulted to stardom.*

cataract *n* **1** *Pathol* **a** a condition in which the lens of the eye becomes partially or totally opaque. **b** the opaque area. **2** a large waterfall.

catarrh (kat-**tar**) *n* excessive mucus in the nose and throat, often experienced during or following a cold. **catarrhal** *adj*

catastrophe (kat-**ass**-trof-fee) *n* a great and sudden disaster or misfortune. **catastrophic** *adj*

catatonia *n* a form of schizophrenia in which the sufferer experiences stupor, with outbreaks of excitement. **catatonic** *adj*

cat burglar *n* a burglar who enters buildings by climbing through upper windows.

catcall *n* a shrill whistle or cry of disapproval or derision.

catch *vb* **catching, caught 1** to seize and hold. **2** to capture (a person or a fish or animal). **3** to surprise in an act: *two boys were caught stealing.* **4** to reach (a bus, train, or plane) in time to board it. **5** to see or hear: *fans desperate to catch Arsenal and Liverpool.* **6** to be infected with (an illness). **7** to entangle or become entangled. **8** to attract (someone's attention, imagination, or interest). **9** to comprehend or make out: *you have to work hard to catch his tone and meaning.* **10** to reproduce (a quality) accurately in a work of art. **11** (of a fire) to start burning. **12** *Cricket* to dismiss (a batsman) by catching a ball struck by him before it touches the ground. **13 catch at a** to attempt to grasp. **b** to take advantage of (an opportunity). **14 catch it** *Informal* to be punished. *~n* **15** a device such as a hook, for fastening a door, window, or box. **16** the total number of fish caught. **17** *Informal* a concealed or unforeseen drawback. **18** an emotional break in the voice. **19** *Informal* a person considered worth having as a husband or wife. **20** *Cricket* the act of catching a ball struck by a batsman before it touches the ground, resulting in him being out. ~See also **catch on, catch out, catch up.**

catch-22 *n* a situation in which a person is frustrated by a set of circumstances that prevent any attempt to escape from them.

catching *adj* infectious.

catchment *n* **1** a structure in which water is collected. **2** all the people served by a school or hospital in a particular catchment area.

catchment area *n* **1** the area of land draining into a river, basin, or reservoir. **2** the area served by a particular school or hospital.

catch on *vb Informal* **1** to become popular or fashionable. **2** to understand: *I was slow to catch on to what she was trying to tell me.*

catch out *vb Informal, chiefly Brit* to trap (someone) in an error or a lie.

catchpenny *adj* designed to have instant appeal without regard for quality.

catch phrase *n* a well-known phrase or slogan associated with a particular entertainer or other celebrity.

catch up *vb* **1 be caught up in** to be unwillingly or accidentally involved in: *hundreds of civilians have been caught up in the clashes.* **2 catch up on** *or* **with** to bring (something) up to date: *he had a lot of paperwork to catch up on.* **3 catch up with** to reach or pass (someone or something): *she ran to catch up with him.*

catchword *n* a well-known and frequently used phrase or slogan.

catchy *adj* **catchier, catchiest** (of a tune) pleasant and easily remembered.

catechism (**kat**-tik-kiz-zum) *n* instruction on the doctrine of a Christian Church by a series of questions and answers.

catechize *or* **-echise** *vb* **-echizing, -echized** *or* **-echising, -echised 1** to instruct in Christianity using a catechism. **2** to question (someone) thoroughly. **catechist** *n*

categorical *or* **categoric** *adj* absolutely clear and certain: *he was categorical in his denial.* **categorically** *adv*

categorize *or* **-rise** *vb* **-rizing, -rized** *or* **-rising, -rised** to put in a category. **categorization** *or* **-risation** *n*

category *n, pl* **-ries** a class or group of things or people with some quality or qualities in common.

cater *vb* **1** to provide what is needed or wanted: *operating theatres that can cater for open-heart surgery.* **2** to provide food or services: *they cater for vegetarians.*

caterer *n* a person whose job is to provide food for social events such as parties and weddings.

catering *n* the supplying of food for a social event.

caterpillar *n* **1** the wormlike larva of a butterfly or moth. **2** *Trademark* Also: **caterpillar track** an endless track, driven by cogged wheels, used to propel a heavy vehicle such as a bulldozer.

caterwaul *vb* **1** to make a yowling noise like a cat. *~n* **2** such a noise.

catfish *n, pl* **-fish** *or* **-fishes** a freshwater fish with whisker-like barbels around the mouth.

catgut *n* a strong cord made from dried animals' in-

THESAURUS

catalogue **1.** *n.* directory, index, inventory, list, record, register, roll **2.** *vb.* alphabetize, classify, file, index, inventory, list, register, tabulate

catapult **1.** *n.* sling **2.** *vb.* hurl, hurtle, pitch, propel, shoot, toss

cataract cascade, falls, torrent, waterfall

catastrophe blow, calamity, cataclysm, devastation, disaster, mischance, misfortune, mishap, reverse, tragedy

catcall *n.* boo, gibe, jeer, whistle

catch *vb.* **1.** clutch, get, grab, grasp, grip, lay hold of, seize, snatch, take **2.** apprehend, arrest, capture, ensnare, entrap, nab (*informal*), nail (*informal*), seize, snare **3.** detect, discover, find out, surprise, take unawares **4.** contract, develop, get, go down with **5.** bewitch, captivate, charm, delight, enchant, enrapture, fascinate **6.** apprehend, discern, feel, follow, get, grasp, perceive, recognize, sense, take in, twig (*Brit. informal*) *~n.* **7.** bolt, clasp, clip, fastener, hasp, hook, hook and eye, latch **8.** *informal* disadvantage, drawback, fly in the ointment, hitch, snag, stumbling block

catching communicable, contagious, infectious, transmittable

catch on comprehend, grasp, see, twig (*Brit. informal*), understand

catchword byword, motto, slogan, watchword

catchy captivating, haunting, memorable

catechize cross-examine, drill, examine, grill (*informal*), interrogate, question

categorical absolute, direct, downright, emphatic, explicit, express, positive, unambiguous, unequivocal, unqualified, unreserved

category class, classification, department, division,

testines, used to string musical instruments and sports rackets.

catharsis (kath-**thar**-siss) *n* **1** the relief of strong suppressed emotions, for example through drama or psychoanalysis. **2** evacuation of the bowels, esp. with the use of a laxative.

cathartic *adj* **1** causing catharsis. *~n* **2** a drug that causes catharsis.

Cathay *n* a literary or archaic name for China.

cathedral *n* the principal church of a diocese.

Catherine wheel *n* a firework that rotates, producing sparks and coloured flame.

catheter (**kath**-it-er) *n* a slender flexible tube inserted into a body cavity to drain fluid.

cathode *n Electronics* the negative electrode in an electrolytic cell or in an electronic valve or tube.

cathode rays *pl n* a stream of electrons emitted from the surface of a cathode in a vacuum tube.

cathode-ray tube *n* a vacuum tube in which a beam of electrons is focused onto a fluorescent screen to produce a visible image, used in television receivers and visual display units.

catholic *adj* (of tastes or interests) covering a wide range.

➤ Note that the meaning of *catholic* can change depending on whether it begins with a capital letter or not.

Catholic *Christianity ~adj* **1** of the Roman Catholic Church. *n* **2** a member of the Roman Catholic Church. **Catholicism** *n*

cation (**kat**-eye-on) *n* a positively charged ion.

catkin *n* a drooping flower spike found on trees such as the birch, hazel, and willow.

catmint *n* a Eurasian plant with scented leaves that attract cats. Also: **catnip**

catnap *n* **1** a short sleep or doze. *~vb* **-napping, -napped 2** to sleep or doze for a short time or intermittently.

cat-o'-nine-tails *n, pl* **-tails** a rope whip with nine knotted thongs, formerly used to inflict floggings as a punishment.

cat's cradle *n* a game played by making patterns with a loop of string between the fingers.

Catseyes *pl n Trademark, Brit* glass reflectors set into the road at intervals to indicate traffic lanes by reflecting light from vehicles' headlights.

cat's paw *n* a person used by someone else to do unpleasant things for him or her.

cattle *pl n* domesticated cows and bulls.

cattle-cake *n* concentrated food for cattle in the form of cakelike blocks.

cattle-grid *or NZ* **cattle-stop** *n* a grid covering a hole dug in a road to prevent livestock crossing while allowing vehicles to pass unhindered.

catty *adj* **-tier, -tiest** *Informal* spiteful: *her remarks were amusing and only slightly catty.* **cattiness** *n*

catwalk *n* **1** a narrow pathway over the stage of a theatre or along a bridge. **2** a narrow platform where models display clothes in a fashion show.

Caucasian *or* **Caucasoid** *adj* **1** of the predominantly light-skinned racial group of humankind. *~n* **2** a member of this group.

caucus *n, pl* **-cuses 1** a local committee or faction of a political party. **2** a political meeting to decide future plans.

caudal *adj Zool* at or near the tail or back part of an animal's body.

caught *vb* the past of **catch.**

caul *n Anat* a membrane sometimes covering a child's head at birth.

cauldron *or* **caldron** *n* a large pot used for boiling.

cauliflower *n* a vegetable with a large head of white flower buds surrounded by green leaves.

cauliflower ear *n* permanent swelling and distortion of the ear, caused by repeated blows usually received in boxing.

caulk *vb* to fill in (cracks) with paste or some other material.

causal *adj* of or being a cause: *a causal connection.* **causally** *adv*

causation *or* **causality** *n* **1** the production of an effect by a cause. **2** the relationship of cause and effect.

causative *adj* producing an effect: *bright lights seem to be a causative factor in some migraines.*

cause *n* **1** something that produces a particular effect. **2** grounds for action; justification: *there is cause for concern.* **3** an aim or principle which an individual or group is interested in and supports: *the Socialist cause. ~vb* **causing, caused 4** to be the cause of. **causeless** *adj*

cause célèbre (**kawz** sill-**leb**-ra) *n, pl* **causes célèbres** (**kawz** sill-**leb**-ras) a controversial legal case, issue, or person.

causeway *n* a raised path or road across water or marshland.

caustic *adj* **1** capable of burning or corroding by chemical action: *caustic soda.* **2** bitter and sarcastic: *caustic critics. ~n* **3** *Chem* a caustic substance. **caustically** *adv*

caustic soda *n* same as **sodium hydroxide.**

cauterize *or* **-ise** *vb* **-izing, -ized** *or* **-ising, -ised** to burn (a wound) with heat or a caustic agent to prevent infection. **cauterization** *or* **-isation** *n*

caution *n* **1** care or prudence, esp. in the face of danger. **2** warning: *a word of caution.* **3** *Law chiefly Brit* a formal warning given to a person suspected of an offence. *~vb* **4** to warn or advise: *he cautioned against an abrupt turnaround.* **cautionary** *adj*

THESAURUS

grade, grouping, heading, order, rank, section, sort, type

cater furnish, provide, purvey, supply

catholic all-embracing, all-inclusive, comprehensive, eclectic, general, universal, wide

cattle beasts, cows, kine (*archaic*), livestock, stock

catty backbiting, bitchy (*informal*), malevolent, malicious, mean, rancorous, shrewish, snide, spiteful, venomous

caucus assembly, congress, convention, meeting, session

cause *n.* **1.** agent, beginning, creator, genesis, mainspring, maker, origin, originator, prime mover, producer, root, source, spring **2.** basis, grounds, incentive, justification, motivation, motive, object, purpose, reason **3.** aim, belief, conviction, enterprise, ideal, movement, undertaking *~vb.* **4.** bring about, compel, create, effect, engender, generate, give rise to, incite, induce, lead to, motivate, occasion, precipitate, produce, provoke, result in

caustic 1. astringent, biting, burning, corrosive, vitriolic **2.** acrimonious, cutting, mordant, pungent, sarcastic, scathing, severe, stinging, trenchant, vitriolic

caution *n.* **1.** alertness, care, carefulness, circumspection, discretion, forethought, heed (*formal*), prudence, vigilance, watchfulness **2.** admonition, advice, counsel, injunction, warning *~vb.* **3.** admonish, advise, tip off, warn

cautious cagey (*informal*), careful, chary, circum-

cautious *adj* showing or having caution. **cautiously** *adv*
cavalcade *n* a procession of people on horseback or in cars.
cavalier *adj* **1** showing haughty disregard; offhand. *~n* **2** *Old-fashioned* a gallant or courtly gentleman.
Cavalier *n* a supporter of Charles I during the English Civil War.
cavalry *n* the part of an army originally mounted on horseback, but now often using fast armoured vehicles. **cavalryman** *n*
cave *n* a hollow in the side of a hill or cliff, or underground.
caveat (**kav**-vee-at) *n* **1** *Law* a formal notice requesting the court not to take a certain action without warning the person lodging the caveat. **2** a caution.
cave in *vb* **1** to collapse inwards. **2** *Informal* to yield completely under pressure: *the government caved in to the revolutionaries' demands. ~n* **cave-in 3** the sudden collapse of a roof or piece of ground.
cavel *n NZ* the drawing of lots among miners for a good place at the coalface.
caveman *n, pl* **-men 1** a prehistoric cave dweller. **2** *Informal* a man who is primitive or brutal in behaviour.
cavern *n* a large cave.
cavernous *adj* like a cavern in vastness, depth, or hollowness: *the cavernous building.*
caviar *or* **caviare** *n* the salted roe of the sturgeon, regarded as a delicacy and usually served as an appetizer.
cavil *vb* **-illing, -illed** *or US* **-iling, -iled 1** to raise annoying petty objections. *~n* **2** a petty objection.
caving *n* the sport of climbing in and exploring caves. **caver** *n*
cavity *n, pl* **-ties 1** a hollow space. **2** *Dentistry* a decayed area on a tooth.
cavort *vb* to skip about; caper.
caw *n* **1** the cry of a crow, rook, or raven. *~vb* **2** to make this cry.
cay *n* a small low island or bank of sand and coral fragments.
cayenne pepper *or* **cayenne** *n* a very hot red spice made from the dried seeds of capsicums.
cayman *or* **caiman** *n, pl* **-mans** a tropical American reptile similar to an alligator.
CB 1 Citizens' Band. **2** Commander of the Order of the Bath.
CBC Canadian Broadcasting Corporation.
CBE Commander of the Order of the British Empire.
CBI Confederation of British Industry.
cc *or* **c.c. 1** carbon copy. **2** cubic centimetre.
CC 1 County Council. **2** Cricket Club.
CCTV closed-circuit television.
cd candela.
Cd *Chem* cadmium.
CD compact disc.
CDI compact disc interactive: a system for storing a mix of software, data, audio, and compressed video for interactive use under processor control.
Cdn. Canadian.
CD player *n* a device for playing compact discs.
Cdr Commander.
CD-ROM compact disc read-only memory: a compact disc used with a computer system as a read-only optical disc.
CDT Central Daylight Time.
CD-video *n* a compact-disc player that, when connected to a television and a hi-fi, produces high-quality stereo sound and synchronized pictures from a compact disc.
Ce *Chem* cerium.
cease *vb* **ceasing, ceased 1** to bring or come to an end. *~n* **2 without cease** without stopping.
ceasefire *n* a temporary period of truce.
ceaseless *adj* without stopping. **ceaselessly** *adv*
cedar *n* **1** a coniferous tree with needle-like evergreen leaves and barrel-shaped cones. **2** the sweet-smelling wood of this tree.
cede *vb* **ceding, ceded** to transfer or surrender (territory or legal rights).
cedilla *n* a character (¸) placed underneath a *c*, esp. in French or Portuguese, indicating that it is to be pronounced (s), not (k).
Ceefax *n Trademark* the BBC teletext service.
ceilidh (**kay**-lee) *n* an informal social gathering in Scotland or Ireland with folk music and country dancing.
ceiling *n* **1** the inner upper surface of a room. **2** an upper limit set on something such as a payment or salary. **3** the upper altitude to which an aircraft can climb.
celandine *n* a wild plant with yellow flowers.
celebrant *n* a person who performs or takes part in a religious ceremony.
celebrate *vb* **-brating, -brated 1** to hold festivities to mark (a happy event, birthday, or anniversary). **2** to perform (a solemn or religious ceremony). **3** to praise

---

THESAURUS

spect, discreet, guarded, judicious, prudent, tentative, wary, watchful
cavalcade array, parade, procession, spectacle, train
cavalier 1. *adj.* arrogant, curt, disdainful, haughty, lofty, lordly, offhand, scornful, supercilious **2.** *n. old-fashioned* gallant, gentleman
cavalry horsemen, mounted troops
cave cavern, cavity, grotto, hollow, pothole
caveat admonition, caution, warning
cavern cave, hollow, pothole
cavernous concave, deep-set, hollow, sunken, yawning
cavil beef (*slang*), carp, complain, find fault, hypercriticize, object, quibble
cavity crater, dent, gap, hole, hollow, pit
cease break off, bring *or* come to an end, conclude, desist, die away, discontinue, end, finish, halt, leave off, stop, terminate
ceaseless constant, continual, continuous, endless, eternal, everlasting, incessant, interminable, never-ending, nonstop, perennial, perpetual, unending, unremitting
cede abandon, concede, convey (*Law*), grant, hand over, make over, relinquish, renounce, surrender, transfer, yield
celebrate 1. commemorate, drink to, honour, rejoice, toast **2.** bless, honour, keep, observe, perform, solemnize **3.** commend, crack up (*informal*), eulogize, exalt, extol, glorify, laud (*literary*), praise, proclaim, publicize
celebrated acclaimed, distinguished, eminent, famed, famous, glorious, illustrious, notable, outstanding, popular, pre-eminent, prominent, renowned, well-known
celebration 1. beano (*old-fashioned Brit. slang*), carousal, festival, festivity, gala, jollification, junketing,

publicly: *the novel is justly celebrated as a masterpiece.* **celebration** *n* **celebratory** *adj*
celebrated *adj* well known: *the celebrated musician.*
celebrity *n, pl* **-ties 1** a famous person. **2** the state of being famous.
celeriac (sill-**ler**-ree-ak) *n* a variety of celery with a large turnip-like root.
celerity (sill-**ler**-rit-tee) *n Formal* swiftness.
celery *n* a vegetable with long green crisp edible stalks.
celesta *n* an instrument like a small piano in which key-operated hammers strike metal plates.
celestial *adj* **1** heavenly or divine: *celestial music.* **2** of or relating to the sky or space: *celestial objects such as pulsars and quasars.*
celestial equator *n* an imaginary circle lying on the celestial sphere in a plane perpendicular to the earth's axis.
celestial sphere *n* an imaginary sphere of infinitely large radius enclosing the universe.
celibate *adj* **1** unmarried or abstaining from sex, esp. because of a religious vow of chastity. *~n* **2** a celibate person. **celibacy** *n*
cell *n* **1** *Biol* the smallest unit of an organism that is able to function independently. **2** a small simple room in a prison, convent, or monastery. **3** any small compartment, such as a cell of a honeycomb. **4** a small group operating as the core of a larger organization: *Communist cells.* **5** a device that produces electrical energy by chemical action.
cellar *n* **1** an underground room, usually used for storage. **2** a place where wine is stored. **3** a stock of bottled wines.
cellarage *n* **1** the area of a cellar. **2** a charge for storing goods in a cellar.
cello (**chell**-oh) *n, pl* **-los** a large low-pitched musical instrument of the violin family, held between the knees and played with a bow. **cellist** *n*
➤ It is not necessary to use an apostrophe before the word *cello.*
Cellophane *n Trademark* a thin transparent material made from cellulose that is used as a protective wrapping, esp. for food.
cellular *adj* **1** of, consisting of, or resembling a cell or cells: *cellular changes.* **2** woven with an open texture: *cellular blankets.* **3** designed for or using cellular radio: *cellular phones.*
cellular radio *n* radio communication, used esp. in car phones, based on a network of transmitters each serving a small area known as a cell.
cellulite *n* fat deposits under the skin alleged to resist dieting.
celluloid *n* **1** a kind of plastic made from cellulose nitrate and camphor, used to make toys and, formerly, photographic film. **2** the cinema or films generally: *a Shakespeare play committed to celluloid.*
cellulose *n* the main constituent of plant cell walls, used in making paper, rayon, and plastics.
cellulose acetate *n* a nonflammable material used to make film, lacquers, and artificial fibres.
cellulose nitrate *n* a compound used in plastics, lacquers, and explosives.
Celsius *adj* denoting a measurement on the Celsius scale.
Celsius scale *n* a scale of temperature in which 0° represents the melting point of ice and 100° represents the boiling point of water.
Celt (**kelt**) *n* **1** a person from Scotland, Ireland, Wales, Cornwall, or Brittany. **2** a member of a people who inhabited Britain, Gaul, and Spain in pre-Roman times.
Celtic (**kel**-tik, **sel**-tik) *n* **1** a group of languages that includes Gaelic, Welsh, and Breton. *~adj* **2** of the Celts or the Celtic languages.
cement *n* **1 a** a fine grey powder made of limestone and clay, mixed with water and sand to make mortar or concrete. **b** mortar or concrete. **2** something that unites, binds, or joins things or people: *bone cement; the cement of fear and hatred of the Left.* **3** *Dentistry* a material used for filling teeth. *~vb* **4** to join, bind, or cover with cement. **5** to make (a relationship) stronger: *this would cement a firm alliance between the army and rebels.*
cemetery *n, pl* **-teries** a place where dead people are buried.
cenotaph *n* a monument honouring soldiers who died in a war.
Cenozoic *or* **Caenozoic** (see-no-**zoh**-ik) *adj Geol* of the most recent geological era, beginning 65 million years ago, characterized by the development and increase of the mammals.
censer *n* a container for burning incense.
censor *n* **1** a person authorized to examine films, letters, or publications, in order to ban or cut anything considered obscene or objectionable. *~vb* **2** to ban or cut portions of (a film, letter, or publication).
censorious *adj* harshly critical.
censorship *n* the practice or policy of censoring films, letters, or publications.
censure *n* **1** severe disapproval. *~vb* **-suring, -sured 2** to criticize (someone or something) severely.
census *n, pl* **-suses** an official periodic count of a population including such information as sex, age, and occupation.
cent *n* a monetary unit worth one hundredth of the main unit of currency in many countries.
cent. 1 central. **2** century.
centaur *n Greek myth* a creature with the head, arms, and torso of a man, and the lower body and legs of a horse.
centenarian *n* a person who is at least 100 years old.

THESAURUS

merrymaking, party, rave (*slang*), revelry **2.** anniversary, commemoration, honouring, observance, performance, remembrance, solemnization
celebrity 1. big name, big shot (*informal*), bigwig (*informal*), dignitary, luminary, megastar (*informal*), name, personage, personality, star, superstar, V.I.P. **2.** distinction, eminence, fame, glory, honour, notability, pre-eminence, prestige, prominence, renown, reputation, repute, stardom
celestial 1. divine, elysian, eternal, ethereal, godlike, heavenly, immortal **2.** astral, heavenly
cell 1. chamber, compartment, cubicle **2.** caucus, group, nucleus, unit
cement 1. *n.* adhesive, glue, gum, paste, plaster, sealant **2.** *vb.* attach, bind, bond, glue, gum, join, plaster, seal, stick together, unite
cemetery burial ground, churchyard, graveyard, necropolis
censor blue-pencil, bowdlerize, cut, expurgate
censorious condemnatory, disapproving, disparaging, fault-finding, hypercritical, scathing, severe
censure 1. *n.* blame, castigation, condemnation, criticism, disapproval, dressing down (*informal*), obloquy (*formal*), rebuke, remonstrance, reprimand, reproach, reproof, stick (*slang*), stricture (*formal*) **2.** *vb.* abuse, bawl out (*informal*), berate, blame, blast, castigate, chide, condemn, criticize, denounce, excoriate (*literary*), give (someone) a rocket (*informal*), lam-

centenary (sen-**teen**-a-ree) *n, pl* **-naries** a 100th anniversary or the celebration of one. US equivalent: **centennial**

center *n, vb US* same as **centre.**

centesimal *n* **1** one hundredth. *~adj* **2** of or divided into hundredths.

centi- *prefix* **1** denoting one hundredth: *centimetre.* **2** a hundred: *centipede.*

centigrade *adj* same as **Celsius.**

➤ Scientists now use *Celsius* in preference to *centigrade.*

centigram *or* **centigramme** *n* one hundredth of a gram.

centilitre *or US* **centiliter** *n* a measure of volume equivalent to one hundredth of a litre.

centime (**son**-teem) *n* a monetary unit worth one hundredth of a franc.

centimetre *or US* **centimeter** *n* a unit of length equal to one hundredth of a metre.

centipede *n* a small wormlike creature with many legs.

central *adj* **1** of, at, or forming the centre of something: *eastern and central parts of the country.* **2** main or principal: *a central issue.* **centrally** *adv* **centrality** *n*

central bank *n* a national bank that acts as the government's banker, controls credit, and issues currency.

central government *n* the government of a whole country, as opposed to the smaller organizations that govern counties, towns, and districts.

central heating *n* a system for heating a building by means of radiators or air vents connected to a central source of heat. **centrally heated** *adj*

centralism *n* the principle of bringing a country or an organization under central control. **centralist** *adj*

centralize *or* **-ise** *vb* **-izing, -ized** *or* **-ising, -ised** to bring (a country or an organization) under central control. **centralization** *or* **-isation** *n*

central locking *n* a system by which all the doors of a motor vehicle are locked automatically when the driver's door is locked manually.

central nervous system *n* the part of the nervous system of vertebrates that consists of the brain and spinal cord.

central processing unit *n* the part of a computer that performs logical and arithmetical operations on the data.

central reservation *n Brit* the strip that separates the two sides of a motorway or dual carriageway.

centre *or US* **center** *n* **1** the middle point or part of something. **2** a place where a specified activity takes place: *a shopping centre.* **3** a person or thing that is a focus of interest: *the centre of a long-running dispute.* **4** a place of activity or influence: *the parliament building was the centre of resistance.* **5** a political party or group that favours moderation. **6** *Sport* a player who plays in the middle of the field rather than on a wing. *~vb* **-tring, -tred** *or US* **-tering, -tered 7** to put in the centre of something. **8 centre on** to have as a centre or main theme: *talks are likely to centre on arms control.*

centreboard *or US* **centerboard** *n* a supplementary keel for a sailing boat or dinghy.

centrefold *or US* **centerfold** *n* a large coloured illustration, often a photograph of a naked or scantily dressed young woman, folded to form the centre pages of a magazine.

centre forward *n Sport* the middle player in the forward line of a team.

centre half *or* **centre back** *n Soccer* a defender who plays in the middle of the defence.

centre of gravity *n* the point in an object around which its mass is evenly distributed.

centrepiece *or US* **centerpiece** *n* **1** the most important item of a group of things: *she was the centrepiece of this conference.* **2** an ornament for the centre of a table.

centrifugal (sent-**riff**-few-gl) *adj* **1** moving or tending to move away from a centre. **2** of or operated by centrifugal force: *centrifugal extractors.*

centrifugal force *n* a force that acts outwards on any body that rotates or moves along a curved path.

centrifuge *n* a machine that separates substances by the action of centrifugal force.

centripetal (sent-**rip**-it-al) *adj* moving or tending to move towards a centre.

centripetal force *n* a force that acts inwards on any body that rotates or moves along a curved path.

centrist *n* a person who holds moderate political views.

centurion *n* (in ancient Rome) the officer in command of a century.

century *n, pl* **-ries 1** a period of 100 years. **2** a score of 100 runs in cricket. **3** (in ancient Rome) a unit of foot soldiers, originally consisting of 100 men.

cephalopod (**seff**-a-loh-pod) *n* a sea mollusc with a head and tentacles, such as the octopus.

ceramic *n* **1** a hard brittle material made by heating clay to a very high temperature. **2** an object made of this material. *~adj* **3** made of ceramic: *ceramic tiles.*

ceramics *n* the art of producing ceramic objects. **ceramicist** *or* **ceramist** *n*

Cerberus (**sir**-ber-uss) *n Greek myth* a three-headed dog who guarded the entrance to Hades.

cere *n* a soft waxy swelling, containing the nostrils, at the base of the upper beak of a parrot.

cereal *n* **1** any grass that produces an edible grain, such as oat, wheat, or rice. **2** the grain produced by such a plant. **3** a breakfast food made from this grain, usually eaten mixed with milk.

cerebellum (serr-rib-**bell**-lum) *n, pl* **-lums** *or* **-la** (-la) the back part of the brain, which controls balance and muscular coordination.

cerebral (**serr**-rib-ral) *adj* **1** of the brain: *a cerebral haemorrhage.* **2** involving intelligence rather than emotions or instinct: *the cerebral joys of the literary world.*

cerebral palsy *n* a condition in which the limbs and muscles are permanently weak, caused by damage to the brain.

cerebrate (**serr**-rib-rate) *vb* **-brating, -brated** *Usually facetious* to use the mind; think. **cerebration** *n*

cerebrospinal *adj* of the brain and spinal cord: *cerebrospinal fluid.*

cerebrovascular (serr-rib-roh-**vass**-kew-lar) *adj* of the blood vessels and blood supply of the brain.

cerebrum (**serr**-rib-rum) *n, pl* **-brums** *or* **-bra** (-bra) the main part of the human brain, associated with thought, emotion, and personality.

THESAURUS

bast(e), put down (*slang*), read the riot act, rebuke, reprehend, reprimand, reproach, reprove, scold, tear into (*informal*), upbraid

central 1. inner, interior, mid, middle **2.** chief, essential, fundamental, key, main, primary, principal

centre *n.* **1.** core, heart, hub, kernel, mid, middle, midpoint, nucleus **2.** crux, focus, pivot

ceremonial *adj* 1 of ceremony or ritual. ~*n* 2 a system of formal rites; ritual. **ceremonially** *adv*
ceremonious *adj* excessively polite or formal. **ceremoniously** *adv*
ceremony *n, pl* **-nies** 1 a formal act or ritual performed for a special occasion: *a wedding ceremony.* 2 formally polite behaviour. 3 **stand on ceremony** to insist on or act with excessive formality.
cerise (ser-**reess**) *adj* cherry-red.
cerium *n Chem* a steel-grey metallic element found only in combination with other elements. Symbol: Ce
CERN Conseil Européen pour la Recherche Nucléaire: a European organization for research in high-energy particle physics.
cert *n* **a dead cert** *Informal* something that is certain to happen or to be successful.
cert. certificate.
certain *adj* 1 positive and confident about something: *he was certain they would agree.* 2 definitely known: *it is by no means certain the tomb still exists.* 3 sure or bound: *the cuts are certain to go ahead.* 4 some but not much: *a certain amount.* 5 particular: *certain aspects.* 6 named but not known: *a running commentary by a certain Mr Fox.* 7 **for certain** without doubt.
certainly *adv* without doubt: *he will certainly be back.*
certainty *n* 1 the condition of being certain. 2 (*pl* **-ties**) something established as inevitable.
certifiable *adj* considered to be legally insane.
certificate *n* an official document stating the details of something such as birth, death, or completion of an academic course.
certified *adj* 1 holding or guaranteed by a certificate: *a certified acupuncturist.* 2 declared legally insane.
certify *vb* **-fies, -fying, -fied** 1 to confirm or attest to. 2 to guarantee (that certain required standards have been met). 3 to declare legally insane. **certification** *n*
certitude *n Formal* confidence or certainty.
cervical smear *n Med* a smear taken from the neck (cervix) of the womb for detection of cancer.
cervix *n, pl* **cervixes** *or* **cervices** 1 the lower part of the womb that extends into the vagina. 2 *Anat* the neck. **cervical** *adj*
cesium *n US* same as **caesium.**
cessation *n* an ending or pause: *a cessation of hostilities.*
cession *n* the act of ceding territory or legal rights.
cesspool *or* **cesspit** *n* a covered tank or pit for collecting and storing sewage or waste water.
CET Central European Time.
cetacean (sit-**tay**-shun) *n* a sea creature such as a whale or dolphin, which belongs to a family of fish-shaped mammals and breathes through a blowhole.
cetane (**see**-tane) *n* a colourless liquid hydrocarbon, used as a solvent.
cetane number *n* a measure of the quality of a diesel fuel expressed as the percentage of cetane in it.
cf compare.
Cf *Chem* californium.
CF Canadian Forces.
CFB Canadian Forces Base.
CFC chlorofluorocarbon.
CFL Canadian Football League.
cg centigram.
cgs units *pl n* a metric system of units based on the centimetre, gram, and second: for scientific and technical purposes, replaced by SI units.
CH Companion of Honour (a Brit. title).
ch. 1 chapter. 2 church.
Chablis (**shab**-lee) *n* a dry white wine made around Chablis, France.
cha-cha *or* **cha-cha-cha** *n* 1 a modern ballroom dance from Latin America. 2 music for this dance.
chaconne *n* a musical form consisting of a set of variations on a repeated melodic bass line.
chafe *vb* **chafing, chafed** 1 to make sore or worn by rubbing. 2 to be annoyed or impatient: *the lower castes are chafing against 20 years of servitude.*
chafer *n* a large slow-moving beetle.
chaff[1] *n* 1 grain husks separated from the seeds during threshing. 2 something of little worth; rubbish: *you had to be a very perceptive listener to sort the wheat from the chaff of his discourse.*
chaff[2] *vb* to tease good-naturedly.
chaffinch *n* a small European songbird with black-and-white wings and, in the male, a reddish body and blue-grey head.
chafing dish *n* a dish with a heating apparatus beneath it, for cooking or keeping food warm at the table.
chagrin (**shag**-grin) *n* a feeling of annoyance and disappointment.
chagrined *adj* annoyed and disappointed.
chain *n* 1 a flexible length of metal links, used for fastening, binding, or connecting, or in jewellery. 2 **chains** anything that restricts or restrains someone: *bound by the chains of duty.* 3 a series of connected facts or events. 4 a number of establishments, such as hotels or shops, that have the same owner or management. 5 *Chem* a number of atoms or groups bonded together so that the resulting molecule, ion, or radical resembles a chain. 6 a row of mountains or islands. ~*vb* 7 to restrict, fasten or bind with or as if

THESAURUS

centrepiece cynosure (*literary*), focus, highlight, hub, star
ceremonial 1. *adj.* formal, ritual, ritualistic, solemn 2. *n.* ceremony, formality, rite, ritual, solemnity
ceremonious courteous, courtly, dignified, formal, punctilious (*formal*), solemn, starchy (*informal*), stately, stiff
ceremony 1. commemoration, function, observance, rite, ritual, service, solemnities 2. ceremonial, decorum, etiquette, form, formality, pomp, propriety, protocol
certain 1. assured, confident, convinced, positive, satisfied, sure 2. conclusive, definite, incontrovertible, indubitable, known, plain, true, undeniable, undoubted, unequivocal 3. bound, destined, fated, fixed, ineluctable (*formal*), inescapable, inevitable, inexorable, settled, sure 4. express, particular, precise, special, specific
certainty 1. assurance, certitude (*formal*), confidence, conviction, faith, positiveness, sureness, trust 2. fact, reality, sure thing (*informal*), truth
certificate credential(s), diploma, document, licence, voucher, warrant
certify assure, attest, authenticate, aver, avow, confirm, corroborate, endorse, guarantee, testify, validate, verify, vouch, witness
chafe 1. fret, gall, grate, irritate, rasp, rub, scrape, scratch 2. fret, fume
chaff[1] *n.* dregs, refuse, remains, rubbish, trash, waste
chaff[2] *vb.* banter, josh (*slang, chiefly U.S. & Canad.*), mock, rib (*informal*), take the piss out of (*taboo slang*), tease

with a chain: *the demonstrators chained themselves to railings.*

chain gang *n US* a group of convicted prisoners chained together.

chain letter *n* a letter, often with a request for or promise of money, that is sent to many people who are asked to send copies to other people.

chain mail *n* same as **mail**².

chain reaction *n* **1** a series of events, each of which causes the next. **2** a chemical or nuclear reaction in which the product of one step triggers the following step.

chain saw *n* a motor-driven saw in which the cutting teeth form links in a continuous chain.

chain-smoke *vb* **-smoking, -smoked** to smoke continuously, lighting one cigarette from the preceding one. **chain smoker** *n*

chair *n* **1** a seat with a back and four legs, for one person to sit on. **2** an official position of authority or the person holding it: *this lady is the chair of the Birkenhead constituency.* **3** a professorship. **4 in the chair** presiding over a meeting. **5 the chair** *Informal* the electric chair. ~*vb* **6** to preside over (a meeting).

chair lift *n* a series of chairs suspended from a moving cable for carrying people up a slope.

chairman *n, pl* **-men** a person who is in charge of a company's board of directors or a meeting. **chairwoman** *fem n* **chairmanship** *n*

➤ The use of *chairman* is sometimes felt to be sexist and the use of *chairperson* has been advocated. If this too is unacceptable, it may be better to use a different word, e.g. *President.*

chaise (**shaze**) *n* a light horse-drawn carriage with two wheels.

chaise longue (**long**) *n, pl* **chaise longues** *or* **chaises longues** a couch with a back and a single armrest.

chalcedony (kal-**sed**-don-ee) *n, pl* **-nies** a form of quartz composed of very fine crystals, often greyish or blue in colour.

chalet *n* **1** a type of Swiss wooden house with a steeply sloping roof. **2** a similar house used as a ski lodge or holiday home.

chalice (**chal**-liss) *n* **1** *Poetic* a drinking cup or goblet. **2** *Christianity* a gold or silver goblet containing the wine at communion.

chalk *n* **1** a soft white rock consisting of calcium carbonate. **2** a piece of chalk, either white or coloured, used for writing and drawing on blackboards. **3 as different as chalk and cheese** *Informal* totally different. **4 not by a long chalk** *Informal* by no means: *you haven't finished by a long chalk.* ~*vb* **5** to draw or mark with chalk. **chalky** *adj*

chalk up *vb Informal* **1** to score or register: *the home side chalked up a 9-1 victory.* **2** to charge or credit (money) to an account.

challenge *n* **1** a demanding or stimulating situation. **2** a call to engage in a contest, fight, or argument. **3** a questioning of a statement or fact. **4** a demand by a sentry for identification or a password. **5** *Law* a formal objection to a juror. ~*vb* **-lenging, -lenged 6** to invite or call (someone) to take part in a contest, fight, or argument. **7** to call (a decision or action) into question. **8** to order (a person) to stop and be identified. **9** *Law* to make formal objection to (a juror). **challenger** *n* **challenging** *adj*

chalybeate (kal-**lib**-bee-it) *adj* containing or impregnated with iron salts: *a natural chalybeate spring rises at the edge of the lake.*

chamber *n* **1** a meeting hall, usually one used for a legislative or judicial assembly. **2** a room equipped for a particular purpose: *a decompression chamber.* **3** a legislative or judicial assembly: *the Senate, the upper chamber of Canada's parliament.* **4** *Old-fashioned or poetic* a room in a house, esp. a bedroom. **5** a compartment or cavity: *the heart chambers.* **6** a compartment for a cartridge or shell in a gun. ~See also **chambers.**

chamberlain *n History* an officer who managed the household of a king or nobleman.

chambermaid *n* a woman employed to clean bedrooms in a hotel.

chamber music *n* classical music to be performed by a small group of musicians.

Chamber of Commerce *n* an organization of local business people to promote, regulate, and protect their interests.

chamber pot *n* a bowl for urine, formerly used in bedrooms.

chambers *pl n* **1** a judge's room for hearing private cases not taken in open court. **2** (in England) the set of rooms used as offices by a barrister.

chameleon (kam-**meal**-yon) *n* a small lizard that is able to change colour to blend in with its surroundings.

chamfer (**cham**-fer) *n* **1** a bevelled surface at an edge or corner. ~*vb* **2** to cut a chamfer on or in.

chamois *n, pl* **-ois 1** (**sham**-wah) a small mountain antelope of Europe and SW Asia. **2** (**sham**-ee) a soft suede leather made from the skin of this animal or from sheep or goats. **3** (**sham**-ee) Also: **chamois leather, shammy, chammy** a piece of such leather or similar material, used for cleaning and polishing.

chamomile (**kam**-mo-mile) *n* same as **camomile.**

champ¹ *vb* **1** to chew noisily. **2 champ at the bit** *Informal* to be restless or impatient to do something.

champ² *n Informal* short for **champion** (sense 1).

champagne *n* a white sparkling wine produced around Reims and Épernay, France.

champers (**sham**-perz) *n Slang* champagne.

champion *n* **1** a person, plant, or animal that has defeated all others in a competition: *the Olympic 100 metres champion.* **2** someone who defends a person or cause: *a champion of the downtrodden.* ~*vb* **3** to support: *he unceasingly championed equal rights and opportunities.* ~*adj* **4** *N English dialect* excellent. **championship** *n*

chance *n* **1** the extent to which something is likely to happen; probability. **2** an opportunity or occasion to do something: *a chance to escape rural poverty.* **3** a risk or gamble: *the government is not in the mood to take any more chances.* **4** the unknown and unpre-

THESAURUS

chain *n.* **1.** bond, fetter, link, manacle, shackle **2.** concatenation (*formal*), progression, sequence, series, set, string, succession, train ~*vb.* **3.** bind, confine, fetter, manacle, restrain, shackle, tether, trammel

chairman chairperson, chairwoman, director, master of ceremonies, president, presider, speaker, spokesman

challenge *n.* **1.** test, trial **2.** confrontation, dare, face-off (*slang*), ultimatum **3.** interrogation, question ~*vb.* **4.** call out, confront, dare, defy, face off (*slang*), throw down the gauntlet **5.** dispute, impugn, object to, question **6.** accost

chamber **1.** hall **2.** compartment, cubicle, enclosure, room **3.** assembly, council, legislative body, legislature **4.** apartment, bedroom **5.** cavity, compartment, hollow

champion *n.* **1.** conqueror, nonpareil, title holder, victor, winner **2.** backer, defender, guardian, hero, pa-

dictable element that causes something to happen in one way rather than another: *in Buddhism there is no such thing as chance or coincidence.* **5 by chance** without planning: *by chance she met an old school friend.* **6 on the off chance** acting on the slight possibility: *he had called on the agents on the off chance that he might learn something of value.* ~*vb* **chancing, chanced 7** to risk or hazard: *a few picnickers chanced the perilous footpath.* **8** to do something without planning to: *I chanced to look down.* **9 chance on** *or* **upon** to discover by accident: *I chanced upon a copy of this book.*

chancel *n* the part of a church containing the altar and choir.

chancellery *or* **chancellory** *n, pl* **-leries** *or* **-lories 1** the residence or office of a chancellor. **2** the office of an embassy or consulate.

chancellor *n* **1** the head of government in several European countries. **2** *US* the president of a university. **3** *Brit & Canad* the honorary head of a university. **chancellorship** *n*

Chancellor of the Exchequer *n Brit* the cabinet minister responsible for finance.

Chancery *n* (in England) the Lord Chancellor's court, a division of the High Court of Justice.

chancre (**shang**-ker) *n Pathol* a painless ulcer that develops as a primary symptom of syphilis.

chancy *adj* **chancier, chanciest** *Informal* uncertain or risky.

chandelier (shan-dill-**eer**) *n* an ornamental hanging light with branches and holders for several candles or bulbs.

chandler *n* a dealer in a specified trade or merchandise: *a ship's chandler.* **chandlery** *n*

change *n* **1** the fact of becoming different. **2** variety or novelty: *they wanted to print some good news for a change.* **3** a different set, esp. of clothes. **4** money exchanged for its equivalent in a larger denomination or in a different currency. **5** the balance of money when the amount paid is larger than the amount due. **6** coins of a small denomination. ~*vb* **changing, changed 7** to make or become different. **8** to replace with or exchange for another: *the Swedish Communist Party changed its name to the Left Party.* **9** to give and receive (something) in return: *slaves and masters changed places.* **10** to give or receive (money) in exchange for its equivalent sum in a smaller denomination or different currency. **11** to put on other clothes. **12** to get off one bus, train or airliner and on to another: *there's no direct train, so you'll need to change at York.* ~See also **change down, changeover, change up. changeless** *adj*

changeable *adj* changing often. **changeability** *n*

change down *vb* to select a lower gear when driving.

changeling *n* a child believed to have been exchanged by fairies for the parents' real child.

change of life *n* the menopause.

changeover *n* **1** a complete change from one system, attitude, or product to another. ~*vb* **change over 2** to swap places or activities: *the train crews changed over at the frontier.*

change up *vb* to select a higher gear when driving.

channel *n* **1** a band of radio frequencies assigned for the broadcasting of a radio or television signal. **2** a path for an electrical signal or computer data. **3** a means of access or communication: *reports coming through diplomatic channels.* **4** a broad strait connecting two areas of sea. **5** the bed or course of a river, stream, or canal. **6** a navigable course through an area of water. **7** a groove. ~*vb* **-nelling, -nelled** *or US* **-neling, -neled 8** to direct or convey through a channel or channels: *tunnels that channel the pilgrims into the area; to channel funds abroad.*

Channel *n* **the** the English Channel.

chant *vb* **1** to repeat (a slogan) over and over. **2** to sing or recite (a psalm). ~*n* **3** a rhythmic or repetitious slogan repeated over and over, usually by more than one person. **4** a religious song with a short simple melody in which several words or syllables are sung on one note.

chanter *n* the pipe on a set of bagpipes on which the melody is played.

chanticleer *n* a name for a cock, used in fables.

chanty *n, pl* **-ties** same as **shanty**[2].

Chanukah *or* **Hanukkah** (**hah**-na-ka) *n* an eight-day Jewish festival, held in December, commemorating the rededication of the temple by Judas Maccabaeus.

chaos *n* complete disorder or confusion. **chaotic** *adj* **chaotically** *adv*

chap *n Informal* a man or boy.

chapati *or* **chapatti** *n* (in Indian cookery) a kind of flat thin unleavened bread.

chapel *n* **1** a place of worship with its own altar, in a

THESAURUS

tron, protector, upholder ~*vb.* **3.** advocate, back, defend, encourage, espouse, fight for, promote, stick up for (*informal*), support, uphold

chance *n.* **1.** liability, likelihood, odds, possibility, probability **2.** occasion, opening, opportunity, prospect, scope, time, window **3.** accident, coincidence, destiny, fate, fortune, luck, providence ~*vb.* **4.** gamble, hazard, risk, stake, try, venture **5.** befall (*archaic or literary*), betide, come about, come to pass, happen, occur

chancy *informal* dangerous, dicey (*informal, chiefly Brit.*), dodgy (*Brit., Austral., & N.Z. informal*), hazardous, perilous, risky, uncertain

change *n.* **1.** alteration, difference, metamorphosis, modification, mutation, permutation, revolution, transformation, transition, transmutation, vicissitude **2.** break (*informal*), departure, diversion, novelty, variation, variety ~*vb.* **3.** alter, convert, diversify, fluctuate, metamorphose, moderate, modify, mutate, reform, remodel, reorganize, shift, transform, transmute, vary, veer **4.** convert, exchange, interchange, replace, substitute, swap (*informal*)

changeable capricious, erratic, fickle, fitful, fluid, inconstant, irregular, kaleidoscopic, mercurial, mutable, protean, shifting, temperamental, uncertain, unpredictable, unstable, unsteady, vacillating, variable, volatile, wavering

changeless abiding, consistent, constant, eternal, everlasting, fixed, immovable, immutable, permanent, perpetual, regular, settled, stationary, steadfast, steady, unalterable, unchanging, uniform, unvarying

channel *n.* **1.** approach, avenue, course, means, medium, path, route, way **2.** main, strait **3.** canal, conduit, duct, furrow, groove, gutter **4.** passage, route ~*vb.* **5.** conduct, convey, direct, guide, transmit

chant *vb.* **1.** chorus, intone, recite **2.** carol, chorus, croon, sing, warble ~*n.* **3.** carol, chorus, melody, psalm, song

chaos anarchy, bedlam, confusion, disorder, disorganization, entropy (*formal*), lawlessness, pandemonium, tumult

chaotic anarchic, confused, deranged, disordered, disorganized, lawless, topsy-turvy, tumultuous, uncontrolled

chap *informal* bloke (*Brit. informal*), character, cove

church or cathedral. **2** a similar place of worship in a large house or institution. **3** (in England and Wales) a Nonconformist place of worship. **4** (in Scotland) a Roman Catholic church. **5** the members of a trade union in a newspaper office, printing house, or publishing firm.

chaperone (**shap**-per-rone) *n* **1** an older person who accompanies and supervises a young person or young people on social occasions. *~vb* **-oning, -oned 2** to act as a chaperone to.

chaplain *n* a clergyman attached to a chapel, military body, or institution. **chaplaincy** *n*

chaplet *n* a garland worn on the head.

chapman *n, pl* **-men** *Old-fashioned* a travelling pedlar.

chapped *adj* (of the skin) raw and cracked, through exposure to cold.

chappie *n Informal* a man or boy.

chaps *pl n* leather leggings without a seat, worn by cowboys.

chapter *n* **1** a division of a book. **2** a period in a life or history: *the latest chapter in the long and complex tale of British brewing.* **3** a sequence of events: *a chapter of accidents.* **4** a branch of some societies or clubs. **5** a group of the canons of a cathedral. **6 chapter and verse** exact authority for an action or statement.

char[1] *vb* **charring, charred** to blacken by partial burning.

char[2] *Informal ~n* **1** short for **charwoman.** *~vb* **charring, charred 2** to clean other people's houses as a job.

char[3] *n Brit old-fashioned slang* tea.

char[4] *n, pl* **char** *or* **chars** a troutlike fish of cold lakes and northern seas.

charabanc (**shar**-rab-bang) *n Brit old-fashioned* a coach for sightseeing.

character *n* **1** the combination of qualities distinguishing an individual person, group of people, or place: *the British character.* **2** a distinguishing quality or characteristic: *bodily movements of a deliberate character.* **3** reputation, esp. good reputation: *a man of my Dad's character and standing in the community.* **4** an attractively unusual or interesting quality: *the little town was full of life and character.* **5** a person represented in a play, film, or story. **6** an unusual or amusing person: *quite a character.* **7** *Informal* a person: *a flamboyant character.* **8** a single letter, numeral, or symbol used in writing or printing. **9 in** *or* **out of character** typical *or* not typical of the apparent character of a person. **characterless** *adj*

character assassination *n* an attempt to destroy someone's good reputation by slander or deliberate misrepresentation of his or her views: *he described the accusation as "an appalling piece of character assassination".*

characteristic *n* **1** a distinguishing feature or quality. **2** *Maths* the integral part of a logarithm: *the characteristic of 2.4771 is 2.* *~adj* **3** typical or representative of someone or something: *the prime minister fought with characteristic passion.* **characteristically** *adv*

characterization *or* **-isation** *n* **1** the description or portrayal of a person by an actor or writer: *a novel full of rich characterization and complex plotting.* **2** the act or an instance of characterizing.

characterize *or* **-ise** *vb* **-izing, -ized** *or* **-ising, -ised 1** to be a characteristic of: *the violence that characterized the demonstrations.* **2** to describe: *we have made what I would characterize as outstanding progress.*

charade (shar-**rahd**) *n* an absurd pretence.

charades *n* a game in which one team acts out each syllable of a word or phrase, which the other team has to guess.

charcoal *n* **1** a black form of carbon made by partially burning wood or other organic matter. **2** a stick of this used for drawing. **3** a drawing done in charcoal. *~adj* **4** Also: **charcoal-grey** very dark grey.

charge *vb* **charging, charged 1** to ask (an amount of money) as a price. **2** to enter a debit against a person's account for (a purchase). **3** to accuse (someone) formally of a crime in a court of law. **4** to make a rush at or sudden attack upon. **5** to fill (a glass). **6** to cause (an accumulator or capacitor) to take and store electricity. **7** to fill or saturate with liquid or gas: *old mine workings charged with foul gas.* **8** to fill with a feeling or mood: *the emotionally charged atmosphere.* **9** *Formal* to command or assign: *the president has charged his foreign minister with trying to open talks.* *~n* **10** a price charged for something; cost. **11** a formal accusation of a crime in a court of law. **12** an onrush or attack. **13** custody or guardianship: *in the charge of the police.* **14** a person or thing committed to someone's care: *a nanny reported the cruel father of one of her charges to social workers.* **15 a** a cartridge or shell. **b** the explosive required to fire a gun. **16** *Physics* **a** the attribute of matter responsible for all electrical phenomena, existing in two forms, positive and negative. **b** the total amount of electricity stored in a capacitor or an accumulator. **17 in charge of** in control of and responsible for: *in charge of defence and foreign affairs.*

chargeable *adj* **1** liable to be taxed or charged. **2** liable to result in a legal charge.

charge card *n* a card issued by a chain store, shop, or organization, that enables customers to obtain goods and services for which they pay later.

THESAURUS

(*old-fashioned slang*), customer (*informal*), dude (*U.S. & Canad. informal*), fellow, guy (*informal*), individual, person, sort, type

chaperone 1. *n.* companion, duenna, escort **2.** *vb.* accompany, attend, escort, protect, safeguard, shepherd, watch over

chapter 1. episode, part, period, phase, stage **2.** branch, division, part, section

char carbonize, scorch, sear, singe

character 1. attributes, bent, calibre, cast, complexion, constitution, disposition, individuality, make-up, nature, personality, quality, temper, temperament, type **2.** honour, integrity, rectitude, uprightness **3.** part, persona, portrayal, role **4.** card (*informal*), eccentric, nut (*slang*), oddball (*informal*), oddity **5.** fellow, guy (*informal*), individual, person, sort, type **6.** device, emblem, figure, hieroglyph, letter, logo, mark, rune, sign, symbol, type

characteristic 1. *n.* attribute, faculty, feature, idiosyncrasy, mark, peculiarity, property, quality, quirk, trait **2.** *adj.* distinctive, distinguishing, idiosyncratic, individual, peculiar, representative, singular, special, specific, typical

characterize brand, distinguish, identify, indicate, inform, mark, represent, stamp, typify

charade fake, farce, pantomime, parody, pretence, travesty

charge *vb.* **1.** accuse, arraign, blame, impeach, incriminate, indict **2.** assail, assault, attack, rush, storm **3.** fill, instil, lade, load, suffuse **4.** *formal* bid, command, demand, enjoin, exhort, instruct, order *~n.* **5.** amount, cost, damage (*informal*), expenditure, expense, outlay, payment, price, rate **6.** accusation, alle-

chargé d'affaires (**shar**-zhay daf-**fair**) *n, pl* **chargés d'affaires** (**shar**-zhay daf-**fair**) **1** the temporary head of a diplomatic mission in the absence of the ambassador or minister. **2** the head of a small or unimportant diplomatic mission.

charge hand *n* a workman ranked just below a foreman.

charge nurse *n* a nurse in charge of a hospital ward.

charger *n* **1** a device for charging an accumulator. **2** (in the Middle Ages) a warhorse.

chariot *n* a two-wheeled horse-drawn vehicle used in ancient times for wars and races.

charioteer *n* a chariot driver.

charisma (kar-**rizz**-ma) *n* the quality or power of an individual to attract, influence, or inspire people. **charismatic** (kar-rizz-**mat**-ik) *adj*

charismatic movement *n Christianity* a group that believes in divine gifts such as instantaneous healing and uttering unintelligible sounds while in a religious ecstasy.

charitable *adj* **1** kind or lenient in one's attitude towards others. **2** of or for charity: *a charitable organization.* **charitably** *adv*

charity *n* **1** (*pl* **-ties**) an organization set up to provide help to those in need. **2** the giving of help, such as money or food, to those in need. **3** help given to those in need; alms. **4** a kindly attitude towards people.

charlady *n, pl* **-ladies** same as **charwoman.**

charlatan (**shar**-lat-tan) *n* a person who claims expertise that he or she does not have.

Charles' law *n Physics* the principle that the volume of a gas varies in proportion to its temperature at constant pressure.

charleston *n* a lively dance of the 1920s.

charlie *n Brit old-fashioned informal* a fool.

charlock *n* a weed with hairy leaves and yellow flowers.

charlotte *n* a dessert made with fruit and bread or cake crumbs: *apple charlotte.*

charm *n* **1** the quality of attracting, fascinating, or delighting people. **2** a trinket worn on a bracelet. **3** a small object worn for supposed magical powers. **4** a magic spell. *~vb* **5** to attract, fascinate, or delight. **6** to influence or obtain by personal charm: *you can easily be charmed into changing your mind.* **7** to protect as if by magic: *a charmed life.* **charmer** *n* **charmless** *adj*

charming *adj* delightful or attractive. **charmingly** *adv*

charnel house *n* (formerly) a building or vault for the bones of the dead.

charollais (**sharr**-ol-lay) *n* a breed of large white beef cattle.

chart *n* **1** a graph, table, or sheet of information in the form of a diagram. **2** a map of the sea or the stars. **3** **the charts** *Informal* the weekly lists of the best-selling pop records. *~vb* **4** to plot the course of. **5** to make a chart of. **6** to appear in the pop charts.

charter *n* **1** a formal document granting or demanding certain rights or liberties: *a children's charter.* **2** the fundamental principles of an organization: *the UN Charter.* **3** the hire or lease of transportation for private use. *~vb* **4** to lease or hire by charter. **5** to grant a charter to.

chartered accountant *n* (in Britain) an accountant who has passed the examinations of the Institute of Chartered Accountants.

Chartism *n English history* a movement (1838-48) for social and political reforms demand for which was presented to Parliament in charters. **Chartist** *n, adj*

chartreuse (shar-**truhz**) *n* a green or yellow liqueur made from herbs.

charwoman *n, pl* **-women** *Brit* a woman whose job is to clean other people's houses.

chary (**chair**-ee) *adj* **charier, chariest** wary or careful: *chary of interfering.*

Charybdis (kar-**rib**-diss) *n* **1** a ship-devouring monster in classical mythology, identified with a whirlpool off the coast of Sicily. **2** **between Scylla and Charybdis** See **Scylla.**

chase[1] *vb* **chasing, chased** **1** to pursue (a person or animal) persistently or quickly. **2** to force (a person or animal) to leave a place. **3** *Informal* to court (someone) in an unsubtle manner. **4** *Informal* to rush or run: *chasing around the world.* **5** *Informal* to pursue (something or someone) energetically in order to obtain results or information. *~n* **6** the act or an instance of chasing a person or animal.

chase[2] *vb* **chasing, chased** to engrave or emboss (metal).

chaser *n* a milder drink drunk after another stronger one, for example beer after whisky.

chasm (**kaz**-zum) *n* **1** a very deep crack in the ground. **2** a wide difference in interests or feelings: *a deep chasm separating science from politics.*

chassis (**shass**-ee) *n, pl* **chassis** (**shass**-eez) the steel frame, wheels, and mechanical parts of a vehicle.

chaste *adj* **1** abstaining from sex outside marriage or from all sexual intercourse. **2** (of conduct or speech)

THESAURUS

gation, imputation, indictment **7.** assault, attack, onset, onslaught, rush, sortie **8.** care, custody, guardianship, safekeeping, trust **9.** burden, concern, duty, office, responsibility

charitable **1.** broad-minded, considerate, favourable, forgiving, gracious, humane, indulgent, kindly, lenient, magnanimous, sympathetic, tolerant, understanding **2.** beneficent, benevolent, philanthropic

charity **1.** fund **2.** alms-giving, assistance, benefaction, philanthropy **3.** benefaction, contributions, donations, endowment, gift, hand-out, largess *or* largesse, relief **4.** affection, altruism, benevolence, bounty, compassion, fellow feeling, generosity, goodness, goodwill, humanity, indulgence, love, pity, tenderheartedness

charlatan cheat, con man (*informal*), fake, fraud, impostor, mountebank, phoney *or* phony (*informal*), pretender, quack, sham, swindler

charm *n.* **1.** allure, appeal, attraction, desirability, enchantment, fascination, magic, magnetism, sorcery, spell **2.** amulet, fetish, talisman, trinket *~vb.* **3.** absorb, allure, attract, beguile, bewitch, captivate, delight, enamour, enchant, enrapture, entrance, fascinate, mesmerize, please, ravish

charming appealing, attractive, bewitching, captivating, delectable, delightful, engaging, eye-catching, fetching, irresistible, likable *or* likeable, lovely, pleasant, pleasing, seductive, winning, winsome (*literary*)

chart **1.** *n.* blueprint, diagram, graph, map, plan, table, tabulation **2.** *vb.* delineate, draft, graph, map out, outline, plot, shape, sketch

charter *n.* **1.** bond, contract, deed, document, indenture, licence, permit *~vb.* **2.** commission, employ, hire, lease, rent **3.** authorize, sanction

chase *vb.* **1.** course, follow, hunt, pursue, run after, track **2.** drive away, expel, hound, put to flight *~n.* **3.** hunt, hunting, pursuit

chassis bodywork, frame, framework, fuselage, substructure

chaste **1.** decent, decorous, immaculate, innocent,

pure, decent, or modest: *a chaste kiss on the forehead.* **3** simple in style: *chaste furniture.* **chastely** *adv* **chastity** *n*

chasten (**chase**-en) *vb* to subdue (someone) by criticism.

chastise *vb* **-tising, -tised 1** to scold severely. **2** *Old-fashioned* to punish by beating. **chastisement** *n*

chasuble (**chazz**-yew-bl) *n Christianity* a long sleeveless robe worn by a priest when celebrating Mass.

chat *n* **1** an informal conversation. *~vb* **chatting, chatted 2** to have an informal conversation. ~See also **chat up.**

chateau (**shat**-toe) *n, pl* **-teaux** (-toe) *or* **-teaus** a French country house or castle.

chatelaine (**shat**-tell-lane) *n* (formerly) the mistress of a large house or castle.

chatline *n* a telephone service enabling callers to join in general conversation with each other.

chat show *n Brit* a television or radio show in which guests are interviewed informally.

chattels *pl n Old-fashioned* possessions.

chatter *vb* **1** to speak quickly and continuously about unimportant things. **2** (of birds or monkeys) to make rapid repetitive high-pitched noises. **3** (of the teeth) to click together rapidly through cold or fear. *~n* **4** idle talk or gossip. **5** the high-pitched repetitive noise made by a bird or monkey.

chatterbox *n Informal* a person who talks a great deal, usually about unimportant things.

chattering classes *n* **the chattering classes** *Informal, often derogatory* the members of the educated sections of society who enjoy discussion of political, social, and cultural issues.

chatty *adj* **-tier, -tiest 1** (of a person) fond of friendly, informal conversation; talkative. **2** (of a letter) informal and friendly; gossipy.

chat up *vb Brit informal* to talk flirtatiously to (someone) with a view to starting a romantic or sexual relationship.

chauffeur *n* **1** a person employed to drive a car for someone. *~vb* **2** to act as driver for (someone). **chauffeuse** *fem n*

chauvinism (**show**-vin-iz-zum) *n* an irrational belief that one's own country, race, group, or sex is superior: *male chauvinism.* **chauvinist** *n, adj* **chauvinistic** *adj*

cheap *adj* **1** costing relatively little; inexpensive. **2** of poor quality; shoddy: *planks of cheap, splintery pine.* **3** not valued highly; not worth much: *promises are cheap.* **4** *Informal* mean or despicable: *a cheap jibe.* *~n* **5 on the cheap** *Brit informal* at a low cost. *~adv* **6** at a low cost. **cheaply** *adv* **cheapness** *n*

cheapen *vb* **1** to lower the reputation of; degrade. **2** to reduce the price of.

cheap-jack *n Informal* a person who sells cheap and shoddy goods.

cheapskate *n Informal* a miserly person.

cheat *vb* **1** to act dishonestly in order to gain some advantage or profit. **2 cheat on** *Informal* to be unfaithful to (one's spouse or lover). *~n* **3** a person who cheats. **4** a fraud or deception.

check *vb* **1** to examine, investigate, or make an inquiry into. **2** to slow the growth or progress of. **3** to stop abruptly. **4** to correspond or agree: *that all checks with our data here.* *~n* **5** a test to ensure accuracy or progress. **6** a means to ensure against fraud or error. **7** a break in progress; stoppage. **8** *US* same as **cheque. 9** *Chiefly US & Canad* the bill in a restaurant. **10** a pattern of squares or crossed lines. **11** a single square in such a pattern. **12** *Chess* the state or position of a king under direct attack. **13 in check** under control or restraint. *~interj* **14** *Chiefly US & Canad* an expression of agreement. ~See also **check in, check out,** etc.

checked *adj* having a pattern of squares.

checker *n US & Canad* **1** same as **chequer. 2** same as **draughtsman** (sense 3).

checkered *adj US & Canad* same as **chequered.**

checkers *n US & Canad* same as **draughts.**

check in *vb* **1 a** to register one's arrival at a hotel or airport. **b** to register the arrival of (guests or passengers) at a hotel or airport. *~n* **check-in 2 a** the formal registration of arrival at a hotel or airport. **b** the place where one registers one's arrival at a hotel or airport.

check list *n* a list to be referred to for identification or verification.

checkmate *n* **1** *Chess* the winning position in which an opponent's king is under attack and unable to escape. **2** utter defeat. *~vb* **-mating, -mated 3** *Chess* to

THESAURUS

modest, moral, pure, uncontaminated, undefiled, unsullied, vestal, virginal, virtuous, wholesome **2.** austere, elegant, modest, neat, pure, quiet, refined, restrained, simple, unaffected

chasten castigate, chastise, correct, cow, discipline, humble, humiliate, repress, subdue, tame

chastise **1.** berate, castigate, censure, correct, scold, upbraid **2.** *old-fashioned* beat, discipline, flog, lash, lick (*informal*), punish, scourge, whip

chastity celibacy, continence, innocence, maidenhood, modesty, purity, virginity, virtue

chat **1.** *n.* chatter, chinwag (*Brit. informal*), confab (*informal*), gossip, heart-to-heart, natter, talk, tête-à-tête **2.** *vb.* chatter, chew the rag *or* fat (*slang*), gossip, jaw (*slang*), natter, talk

chatter *vb./n.* babble, blather, blether (*Scot.*), chat, gab (*informal*), gossip, jabber, natter, prate, prattle

chatty **1.** familiar, friendly, gossipy, talkative **2.** colloquial, friendly, gossipy, informal, newsy (*informal*)

cheap **1.** bargain, cheapo (*informal*), cut-price, economical, economy, inexpensive, keen, low-cost, low-priced, reasonable, reduced, sale **2.** common, crappy (*slang*), dime-a-dozen (*informal*), inferior, paltry, poor, second-rate, shoddy, tatty, tawdry, tinhorn (*U.S. slang*), two-bit (*U.S. & Canad. slang*), worthless **3.** *informal* base, contemptible, despicable, low, mean, scurvy (*old-fashioned*)

cheapen belittle, debase, degrade, demean, denigrate, depreciate, derogate, devalue, discredit, disparage, lower

cheat *vb.* **1.** bamboozle (*informal*), beguile, bilk, con (*informal*), cozen (*literary*), deceive, defraud, diddle (*informal*), do (*informal*), double-cross (*informal*), dupe, finagle (*informal*), fleece, fool, hoax, hoodwink, kid (*informal*), mislead, rip off (*slang*), skin (*slang*), sting (*informal*), swindle, take for a ride (*informal*), take in (*informal*), trick *~n.* **2.** charlatan, cheater, chiseller (*informal*), con man (*informal*), deceiver, double-crosser (*informal*), impostor, knave (*archaic*), rogue, shark, sharper, swindler, trickster **3.** artifice, deceit, deception, fraud, imposture, rip-off (*slang*), scam (*slang*), sting (*informal*), swindle, trickery

check *vb.* **1.** check out (*informal*), enquire into, examine, inspect, investigate, look at, look over, make sure, monitor, note, probe, research, scrutinize, study, take a dekko at (*Brit. slang*), test, verify, vet, work over **2.** arrest, bridle, control, curb, delay, halt, hinder, impede, inhibit, limit, nip in the bud, obstruct, pause, rein, repress, restrain, retard, stop, thwart *~n.* **3.** examination, inspection, investigation, research, scruti-

place the king of (one's opponent) in checkmate. **4** to thwart or defeat.

check out *vb* **1** to pay the bill and leave a hotel. **2** to investigate, examine, or look at: *he asked if he could check out the old man's theory; start the evening off by checking out one of the in bars in the city.* ~*n* **checkout 3** a counter in a supermarket, where customers pay.

checkpoint *n* a place where vehicles or travellers are stopped for identification or inspection.

checkup *n* a thorough examination to see if a person or thing is in good condition.

check up on *vb* to investigate the background of.

Cheddar *n* a firm orange or yellowy-white cheese.

cheek *n* **1** either side of the face below the eye. **2** *Informal* impudence, boldness, or lack of respect. **3** *Informal* a buttock. **4 cheek by jowl** close together. **5 turn the other cheek** to refuse to retaliate. ~*vb* **6** *Informal* to speak or behave disrespectfully to someone.

cheekbone *n* the bone at the top of the cheek, just below the eye.

cheeky *adj* **cheekier, cheekiest** disrespectful; impudent. **cheekily** *adv* **cheekiness** *n*

cheep *n* **1** the short weak high-pitched cry of a young bird. ~*vb* **2** to utter a cheep.

cheer *vb* **1** to applaud or encourage with shouts. **2 cheer up** to make or become happy or hopeful; comfort or be comforted. ~*n* **3** a shout of applause or encouragement. **4** a feeling of cheerfulness: *the news brought little cheer.*

cheerful *adj* **1** having a happy disposition. **2** pleasantly bright: *a cheerful colour.* **3** ungrudging: *a cheerful giver.* **cheerfully** *adv* **cheerfulness** *n*

cheerio *interj Informal, chiefly Brit* a farewell greeting.

cheerleader *n US & Canad* a person who leads a crowd in cheers, usually at sports events.

cheerless *adj* dreary or gloomy.

cheers *interj Informal, chiefly Brit* **1** a drinking toast. **2** a farewell greeting. **3** an expression of gratitude.

cheery *adj* **cheerier, cheeriest** cheerful. **cheerily** *adv*

cheese[1] *n* **1** a food made from coagulated milk curd. **2** a block of this. **cheesy** *adj*

cheese[2] *n* **big cheese** *Slang* an important person.

cheeseburger *n* a hamburger with a slice of cheese melted on top of it.

cheesecake *n* **1** a dessert with a biscuit-crumb base covered with a sweet cream-cheese mixture and sometimes with a fruit topping. **2** *Slang* magazine photographs of naked or scantily dressed women.

cheesecloth *n* a light, loosely woven cotton cloth.

cheesed off *adj Brit slang* bored, disgusted, or angry.

cheeseparing *adj* **1** mean or miserly. ~*n* **2** meanness or miserliness.

cheetah *n* a large fast-running wild cat of Africa and SW Asia, which has a light brown coat with black spots.

chef *n* a cook, usually the head cook, in a restaurant or hotel.

chef-d'oeuvre (shay-**durv**) *n, pl* **chefs-d'oeuvre** (shay-**durv**) a masterpiece.

Chelsea Pensioner *n* an inhabitant of the Chelsea Royal Hospital in SW London, a home for old and infirm soldiers.

chem. **1** chemical. **2** chemist. **3** chemistry.

chemical *n* **1** any substance used in or resulting from a reaction involving changes to atoms or molecules. ~*adj* **2** of or used in chemistry. **3** of, made from, or using chemicals: *a chemical additive found in many foods.* **chemically** *adv*

chemical engineering *n* the applications of chemistry in industrial processes. **chemical engineer** *n*

chemical warfare *n* warfare using weapons such as gases and poisons.

chemin de fer (shem-**man** de **fair**) *n* a gambling game, a variation of baccarat.

chemise (shem-**meez**) *n* a woman's old-fashioned loose-fitting slip or dress.

chemist *n* **1** *Brit* a shop selling medicines and cosmetics. **2** *Brit* a qualified dispenser of prescribed medicines. **3** a specialist in chemistry.

chemistry *n* the branch of science concerned with the composition, properties, and reactions of substances.

chemotherapy *n* the treatment of disease, often cancer, by means of chemicals.

chenille (shen-**neel**) *n* **1** a thick soft tufty yarn. **2** a fabric made of this.

cheque *or US* **check** *n* a written order to someone's bank to pay money from his or her account to the person to whom the cheque is made out.

cheque book *n* a book of detachable blank cheques issued by a bank.

cheque card *n* a plastic card issued by a bank guaranteeing payment of a customer's cheques.

chequer *or US* **checker** *n* a piece used in Chinese chequers. ~See also **chequers.**

chequered *or US* **checkered** *adj* **1** marked by varied fortunes: *a chequered career.* **2** marked with alternating squares of colour.

chequers *or US* **checkers** *n* the game of draughts.

THESAURUS

ny, test **4.** constraint, control, curb, damper, hindrance, impediment, inhibition, limitation, obstacle, obstruction, rein, restraint, stoppage

cheek *informal* audacity, brass neck (*Brit. informal*), brazenness, chutzpah (*U.S. & Canad. informal*), disrespect, effrontery, gall (*informal*), impertinence, impudence, insolence, lip (*slang*), neck (*informal*), nerve, sauce (*informal*), temerity

cheeky audacious, disrespectful, forward, fresh (*informal*), impertinent, impudent, insolent, insulting, pert, sassy (*U.S. informal*), saucy

cheer *vb.* **1.** acclaim, applaud, clap, hurrah **2.** *with* **up** animate, brighten, buoy up, cheer up, comfort, console, encourage, enliven, gladden, hearten, solace, uplift, warm ~*n.* **3.** acclamation, applause, ovation, plaudits **4.** animation, buoyancy, cheerfulness, comfort, gaiety, gladness, glee, joy, liveliness, merriment, solace

cheerful animated, blithe, bright, buoyant, cheery, chirpy (*informal*), gay, genial, glad, happy, hearty, jaunty, jolly, joyful, light-hearted, merry, sparkling, sunny, upbeat (*informal*)

cheerfulness buoyancy, exuberance, gaiety, geniality, gladness, good cheer, good humour, high spirits, jauntiness, joyousness, light-heartedness

cheerless austere, bleak, comfortless, dark, dejected, depressed, desolate, despondent, disconsolate, dismal, drab, dreary, dull, forlorn, funereal, gloomy, grim, joyless, melancholy, miserable, mournful, sad, sombre, sorrowful, sullen, unhappy, woebegone, woeful

cheery breezy, carefree, cheerful, chirpy (*informal*),

cherish *vb* **1** to cling to (an idea or feeling): *cherished notions.* **2** to care for.

Cherokee *n* **1** a member of a N American Indian people, formerly of the Appalachian mountains, now living chiefly in Oklahoma. **2** the language of this people.

cheroot (sher-**root**) *n* a cigar with both ends cut off squarely.

cherry *n, pl* **-ries 1** a small round soft fruit with red or blackish skin and a hard stone. **2** the tree on which this fruit grows. *~adj* **3** deep red.

cherry tomato *n* a miniature tomato, slightly bigger than a cherry.

cherub *n, pl* **cherubs** *or (for sense 1)* **cherubim 1** *Christianity* an angel, often represented as a winged child. **2** an innocent or sweet child. **cherubic** (chair-**roo**-bik) *adj*

chervil *n* an aniseed-flavoured herb.

Cheshire cheese *n* a mild white or pale orange cheese with a crumbly texture.

chess *n* a game of skill for two players using a chessboard on which chessmen are moved, with the object is of checkmating the opponent's king.

chessboard *n* a square board divided into 64 squares of two alternating colours, for playing chess.

chessman *n, pl* **-men** a piece used in chess.

chest *n* **1** the front of the body, from the neck to the waist. **2 get something off one's chest** *Informal* to unburden oneself of worries or secrets by talking about them. **3** a heavy box for storage or shipping: *a tea chest.*

chesterfield *n* a large couch with high padded sides and back.

chestnut *n* **1** a reddish-brown edible nut. **2** the tree that this nut grows on. **3** a horse of a reddish-brown colour. **4** *Informal* an old or stale joke. *~adj* **5** dark reddish-brown: *chestnut hair.*

chest of drawers *n* a piece of furniture consisting of a set of drawers in a frame.

chesty *adj* **chestier, chestiest** *Brit informal* suffering from or symptomatic of chest disease: *chesty colds.* **chestiness** *n*

cheval glass (shev-**val**) *n* a full-length mirror mounted so as to swivel within a frame.

chevalier (shev-a-**leer**) *n* **1** a member of the French Legion of Honour. **2** a chivalrous man.

Cheviot *n* a large British sheep with a heavy medium-length fleece.

chevron (**shev**-ron) *n* a V-shaped pattern, such as those worn on the sleeve of a military uniform to indicate rank.

chew *vb* **1** to work the jaws and teeth in order to grind (food). *~n* **2** the act of chewing. **3** something that is chewed, such as a sweet or a piece of tobacco.

chewing gum *n* a flavoured gum which is chewed but not swallowed.

chew over *vb* to consider carefully.

chewy *adj* **chewier, chewiest** of a consistency requiring a lot of chewing.

chez (**shay**) *prep* at the home of.

chianti (kee-**ant**-ee) *n* a dry red wine produced in Tuscany, Italy.

chiaroscuro (kee-ah-roh-**skew**-roh) *n, pl* **-ros** the distribution of light and shade in a picture.

chic (**sheek**) *adj* **1** stylish or elegant. *~n* **2** stylishness or elegance.

chicane (shik-**kane**) *n* an obstacle placed on a motor-racing circuit to slow the cars down.

chicanery *n* trickery or deception.

chick *n* **1** a baby bird, esp. a domestic fowl. **2** *Slang* a young woman.

chicken *n* **1** a domestic fowl bred for its flesh or eggs. **2** the flesh of this bird used for food. **3** *Slang* a coward. *~adj* **4** *Slang* cowardly.

chicken feed *n Slang* a trifling amount of money.

chicken-hearted *adj* easily frightened; cowardly.

chicken out *vb Informal* to fail to do something through cowardice.

chickenpox *n* an infectious viral disease, usually affecting children, which produces an itchy rash.

chicken wire *n* wire netting.

chickpea *n* an edible hard yellow pealike seed.

chickweed *n* a common garden weed with small white flowers.

chicory *n* **1** a plant grown for its leaves, which are used in salads, and for its roots. **2** the root of this plant, roasted, dried, and used as a coffee substitute.

chide *vb* **chiding, chided** *Old-fashioned* to rebuke or scold.

chief *n* **1** the head of a group or body of people. **2** the head of a tribe. *~adj* **3** most important: *the chief suspects.* **4** highest in rank: *the Chief Constable.*

chiefly *adv* **1** especially or essentially. **2** mainly or mostly.

chief petty officer *n* a senior noncommissioned officer in a navy.

chieftain *n* the leader of a tribe or clan.

chief technician *n* a noncommissioned officer in the Royal Air Force.

chiffchaff *n* a European warbler with a yellowish-brown plumage.

chiffon (**shif**-fon) *n* a fine see-through fabric of silk or nylon.

chiffonier *or* **chiffonnier** (shiff-on-**near**) *n* **1** a tall elegant chest of drawers. **2** a wide low open-fronted cabinet.

THESAURUS

genial, good-humoured, happy, jovial, lively, sunny, upbeat (*informal*)

cherish 1. cling to, encourage, entertain, foster, harbour, nurse, nurture, sustain **2.** care for, comfort, cosset, hold dear, nurse, prize, support, treasure

cherubic adorable, angelic, heavenly, innocent, lovable, seraphic, sweet

chest Ark (*Judaism*), box, case, casket, coffer, crate, strongbox, trunk

chew bite, champ, crunch, gnaw, grind, masticate, munch

chew over consider, deliberate upon, meditate, mull (over), muse on, ponder, reflect upon, ruminate

chic elegant, fashionable, modish, smart, stylish, trendy (*Brit. informal*), up-to-date

chide *old-fashioned* admonish, bawl out (*informal*), berate, blast, censure, check, criticize, find fault, give (someone) a rocket (*Brit. & N.Z. informal*), give (someone) a row (*informal*), lambast(e), lecture, read the riot act, rebuke, reprehend, reprimand, reproach, reprove, scold, tear into (*informal*), tell off (*informal*), upbraid

chief 1. *n.* boss (*informal*), captain, chieftain, commander, director, governor, head, leader, lord, manager, master, principal, ringleader, ruler, superintendent, suzerain **2.** *adj.* big-time (*informal*), capital, cardinal, central, especial, essential, foremost, grand, highest, key, leading, main, major league (*informal*), most important, outstanding, paramount, predominant, pre-eminent, premier, prevailing, primary, prime, principal, superior, supreme, uppermost, vital

chignon (**sheen**-yon) *n* a roll or knot of long hair pinned up at the back of the head.
chigoe (**chig**-go) *n* a tropical flea that burrows into the skin. Also: **chigger**
chihuahua (chee-**wah**-wah) *n* a tiny short-haired dog, originally from Mexico.
chilblain *n* an inflammation of the fingers or toes, caused by exposure to cold.
child *n, pl* **children 1** a young human being; boy or girl. **2** a son or daughter. **3** a childish or immature person. **4** the product of an influence or environment: *a child of the Army.* **5 with child** *Old-fashioned* pregnant. **childless** *adj* **childlessness** *n*
childbearing *n* **1** the process of giving birth to a child. *~adj* **2 of childbearing age** of an age when women are able to give birth to children.
child benefit *n Brit* a regular government payment to parents of children up to a certain age.
childbirth *n* the act of giving birth to a child.
childhood *n* the time or condition of being a child.
childish *adj* **1** immature or silly: *childish fighting over who did what.* **2** of or like a child: *childish illnesses.*
➤ Note that *childish* has overtones of *foolish* while *childlike* suggests an *innocent quality.*
childlike *adj* like a child, for example in being innocent or trustful.
child minder *n* a person who looks after children whose parents are working.
children *n* the plural of **child.**
child's play *n Informal* something that is easy to do.
chill *n* **1** a feverish cold. **2** a moderate coldness. **3** a feeling of coldness resulting from a cold or damp environment or from sudden fear. *~vb* **4** to make (something) cool or cold: *chilled white wine.* **5** to cause (someone) to feel cold or frightened. *~adj* **6** unpleasantly cold: *chill winds.* **chilling** *adj* **chillingly** *adv*
chiller *n* **1** short for **spine-chiller. 2** a cooling or refrigerating device.
chilli *or* **chili** *n* **1** (*pl* **chillies** *or* **chilies**) the small red or green hot-tasting pod of a type of capsicum, used in cookery, often in powdered form. **2** short for **chilli con carne.**
chilli con carne *n* a highly seasoned Mexican dish of meat, onions, beans, and chilli powder.
chill out *vb Slang, chiefly US* to relax or calm oneself.
chilly *adj* **-lier, -liest 1** causing or feeling moderately cold. **2** without warmth; unfriendly: *a chilly reception.*
chilly bin *n NZ informal* a portable insulated container for packing food and drink in ice.
Chiltern Hundreds *pl n* (in Britain) a nominal office that an MP applies for in order to resign his seat.
chime *n* **1** the musical ringing sound made by a bell or clock. *~vb* **chiming, chimed 2** (of a bell) to make a clear musical ringing sound. **3** (of a clock) to indicate (the time) by chiming.
chime in *vb* to say something, usually in agreement, just after someone else has spoken.
chimera (kime-**meer**-a) *n* **1** a wild and unrealistic dream or idea. **2** *Greek myth* a fire-breathing monster with the head of a lion, body of a goat, and tail of a serpent.
chimerical *adj* wildly fanciful or imaginary.
chime with *vb* to agree or be consistent with.
chimney *n* a hollow vertical structure that carries smoke or steam away from a fire or engine.
chimney breast *n* the walls surrounding the base of a chimney or fireplace.
chimneypot *n* a short pipe on the top of a chimney.
chimney stack *n* the part of a chimney sticking up above a roof.
chimney sweep *n* a person who cleans soot from chimneys.
chimp *n Informal* short for **chimpanzee.**
chimpanzee *n* an intelligent small black ape of central W Africa.
chin *n* the front part of the face below the mouth.
china[1] *n* **1** ceramic ware of a type originally from China. **2** dishes or ornamental objects made of china.
china[2] *n Brit & S African informal* a friend or companion.
china clay *n* same as **kaolin.**
Chinaman *n, pl* **-men** *Old-fashioned or offensive* a man from China.
Chinatown *n* a section of a town or city outside China with a mainly Chinese population.
chinchilla *n* **1** a small S American rodent bred in captivity for its soft silvery-grey fur. **2** the fur of this animal.
chine *n* **1** a cut of meat including part of the backbone. *~vb* **chining, chined 2** to cut (meat) along the backbone.
Chinese *adj* **1** of China. *~n* **2** (*pl* **-nese**) a person from China or a descendant of one. **3** any of the languages of China.
Chinese chequers *n* a game played with marbles or pegs on a six-pointed star-shaped board.
Chinese lantern *n* a collapsible lantern made of thin paper.
Chinese leaves *pl n* the edible leaves of a Chinese cabbage.
Chinese puzzle *n* a complicated puzzle or problem.
chink[1] *n* a small narrow opening: *a chink of light.*
chink[2] *vb* **1** to make a light ringing sound. *~n* **2** a light ringing sound.
chinless wonder *n Brit informal* a person, usually upper-class, lacking strength of character.
chinoiserie (sheen-**wahz**-a-ree) *n* **1** a style of decorative art based on imitations of Chinese motifs. **2** objects in this style.

THESAURUS

chiefly above all, especially, essentially, in general, in the main, largely, mainly, mostly, on the whole, predominantly, primarily, principally, usually
child babe, baby, bairn (*Scot.*), brat, descendant, infant, issue, juvenile, kid (*informal*), minor, nipper (*informal*), offspring, progeny, suckling, toddler, tot, youngster
childbirth child-bearing, confinement, delivery, labour, lying-in (*old-fashioned*), parturition
childhood boyhood, girlhood, immaturity, infancy, minority, schooldays, youth
childish 1. foolish, frivolous, immature, infantile, juvenile, puerile, silly, trifling **2.** boyish, girlish, immature, infantile, juvenile, puerile, young
childlike artless, credulous, guileless, ingenuous, innocent, naive, simple, trustful, trusting, unfeigned
chill *n.* **1.** bite, cold, coldness, coolness, crispness, frigidity, nip, rawness, sharpness *~vb.* **2.** cool, freeze, refrigerate **3.** deject, depress, discourage, dishearten, dismay *~adj.* **4.** biting, bleak, chilly, cold, freezing, frigid, parky (*Brit. informal*), raw, sharp, wintry
chilly 1. blowy, breezy, brisk, cool, crisp, draughty, fresh, nippy, parky (*Brit. informal*), penetrating, sharp **2.** frigid, hostile, unfriendly, unresponsive, unsympathetic, unwelcoming
chime *vb.* boom, clang, jingle, peal, ring, sound, strike, tinkle, toll

Chinook *n* **1** (*pl* **-nook** *or* **-nooks**) a member of a N American Indian people of the Pacific coast. **2** the language of this people.
Chinook salmon *n* a Pacific salmon valued as a food fish.
chinos (**chee**-nohz) *pl n* trousers made of a kind of hard-wearing cotton.
chintz *n* a printed patterned cotton fabric with a glazed finish, used for curtains and chair coverings.
chintzy *adj* **chintzier, chintziest 1** of or covered with chintz. **2** (of a room or house) decorated in an excessively fussy or twee way.
chinwag *n Brit informal* a chat.
chip *n* **1** a thin strip of potato fried in deep fat. **2** *US, Canad, & Austral* a potato crisp. **3** *Electronics* a tiny wafer of semiconductor material, such as silicon, processed to form an integrated circuit. **4** a counter used to represent money in gambling games. **5** a small piece removed by chopping, cutting, or breaking. **6** a mark left where a small piece has been broken off something. **7 chip off the old block** *Informal* a person who resembles one of his or her parents in personality. **8 have a chip on one's shoulder** *Informal* to be resentful or bear a grudge. **9 when the chips are down** *Informal* at a time of crisis. *~vb* **chipping, chipped 10** to break small pieces from.
chipboard *n* thin rigid board made of compressed wood particles.
chip in *vb Informal* **1** to contribute to a common fund. **2** to interrupt with a remark.
chipmunk *n* a squirrel-like striped burrowing rodent of North America and Asia.
chipolata *n Chiefly Brit* a small sausage.
Chippendale *adj* (of furniture) by or in the style of Thomas Chippendale, with Chinese and Gothic motifs, curved legs, and massive carving.
chiropodist (kir-**rop**-pod-ist) *n* a person who treats minor foot complaints like corns. **chiropody** *n*
chiropractic (kire-oh-**prak**-tik) *n* a system of treating bodily disorders by manipulation of the spine. **chiropractor** *n*
chirp *vb* **1** (of some birds and insects) to make a short high-pitched sound. **2** to speak in a lively fashion. *~n* **3** a chirping sound.
chirpy *adj* **chirpier, chirpiest** *Informal* lively and cheerful. **chirpiness** *n*
chirrup *vb* **1** (of some birds) to chirp repeatedly. *~n* **2** a chirruping sound.
chisel *n* **1** a metal tool with a sharp end for shaping wood or stone. *~vb* **-elling, -elled** *or US* **-eling, -eled 2** to carve or form with a chisel.
chiselled *or US* **chiseled** *adj* finely or sharply formed: *chiselled angular features.*
chit[1] *n* a short official note, such as a memorandum, requisition, or receipt. Also: **chitty**
chit[2] *n Old-fashioned* a pert or impudent girl.
chitchat *n* chat or gossip.
chitin (**kite**-in) *n* the tough substance forming the outer layer of the bodies of arthropods.
chitterlings *pl n* the intestines of a pig or other animal prepared as food.
chivalrous *adj* gallant or courteous. **chivalrously** *adv*
chivalry *n* **1** courteous behaviour, esp. by men towards women. **2** the medieval system and principles of knighthood. **chivalric** *adj*
chives *pl n* the long slender hollow leaves of a small Eurasian plant, used in cooking for their onion-like flavour.
chivvy *vb* **-vies, -vying, -vied** *Brit* to harass or nag.
chloral hydrate *n* a colourless crystalline solid used as a sedative.
chlorate *n Chem* any salt containing the ion ClO_3^-.
chloride *n Chem* **1** any compound of chlorine and another element and radical. **2** any salt or ester of hydrochloric acid.
chlorinate *vb* **-ating, -ated 1** to disinfect (water) with chlorine. **2** *Chem* to combine or treat (a substance) with chlorine: *chlorinated hydrocarbons.* **chlorination** *n*
chlorine *n* a poisonous strong-smelling greenish-yellow gaseous element, used in water purification and as a disinfectant, and, combined with sodium, to make common salt. Symbol: Cl
chloro- *combining form* green.
chlorofluorocarbon *n Chem* any of various gaseous compounds of carbon, hydrogen, chlorine, and fluorine, used as refrigerants and aerosol propellants, some of which break down the ozone in the atmosphere.
chloroform *n* a sweet-smelling liquid, used as a solvent and cleansing agent, and formerly as an anaesthetic.
chlorophyll *or US* **chlorophyl** *n* the green colouring matter of plants, which enables them to convert sunlight into energy.
chloroplast *n Biol* one of the parts of a plant cell that contains chlorophyll.
chock *n* **1** a block or wedge of wood used to prevent the sliding or rolling of a heavy object. *~vb* **2** to fit with or secure by a chock.
chock-a-block *adj* filled to capacity.
chock-full *adj* completely full.
chocolate *n* **1** a food made from roasted ground cacao seeds, usually sweetened and flavoured. **2** a sweet or drink made from this. *~adj* **3** deep brown. **chocolaty** *adj*
choice *n* **1** the act of choosing or selecting. **2** the opportunity or power of choosing: *parental choice.* **3** a person or thing chosen or that may be chosen: *the president's choice as the new head of the CIA.* **4** an alternative action or possibility: *they had no choice but to accept.* **5** a range from which to select: *a choice of weapons.* *~adj* **6** of high quality: *choice government jobs.*
choir *n* **1** an organized group of singers, usually for singing in church. **2** the part of a church, in front of the altar, occupied by the choir.
choirboy *n* a boy who sings in a church choir.

THESAURUS

china ceramics, crockery, porcelain, pottery, service, tableware
chink aperture, cleft, crack, cranny, crevice, cut, fissure, gap, opening, rift
chip *n.* **1.** flake, fragment, paring, scrap, scratch, shard, shaving, sliver, wafer **2.** dent, nick, notch *~vb.* **3.** chisel, gash, nick, whittle
chip in *informal* **1.** contribute, donate, go Dutch (*informal*), pay, subscribe **2.** interpose, interrupt
chivalrous bold, brave, courageous, courteous, courtly, gallant, gentlemanly, heroic, high-minded, honourable, intrepid, knightly, true, valiant
chivalry courtesy, courtliness, gallantry, gentlemanliness, politeness
chivvy *Brit.* annoy, badger, bug (*informal*), harass, hassle (*informal*), hound, nag, pester, plague, pressure, prod, torment
choice **1.** *n.* alternative, discrimination, election, op-

choke *vb* **choking, choked 1** to hinder or stop the breathing of (a person or animal) by strangling or smothering. **2** to have trouble in breathing, swallowing, or speaking. **3** to block or clog up: *the old narrow streets become choked to a standstill.* **4** to hinder the growth of: *weeds would outgrow and choke the rice crop.* ~*n* **5** a device in a vehicle's engine that enriches the petrol-air mixture by reducing the air supply.

choke back *vb* to suppress (tears or anger).

choked *adj Informal* disappointed or angry: *I still feel choked about him leaving.*

choker *n* a tight-fitting necklace.

choke up *vb* **1** to block completely. **2 choked up** *Informal* overcome with emotion.

choko *n, pl* **-kos** *Austral & NZ* the cucumber-like fruit of a tropical American vine.

choler (**kol**-ler) *n Archaic* anger or bad temper.

cholera (**kol**-ler-a) *n* a serious infectious disease causing severe diarrhoea and stomach cramps, caught from contaminated water or food.

choleric *adj* bad-tempered.

cholesterol (kol-**lest**-er-oll) *n* a fatty alcohol found in all animal fats, tissues, and fluids, an excess of which is thought to contribute to heart and artery disease.

chomp *vb* to chew (food) noisily.

chook *n Informal, chiefly Austral & NZ* a hen or chicken.

choose *vb* **choosing, chose, chosen 1** to select (a person, thing, or course of action) from a number of alternatives. **2** to like or please: *when she did choose to reveal her secret, the group were initially hushed.* **3** to consider it desirable or proper: *I don't choose to read that sort of book.*

choosy *adj* **choosier, choosiest** *Informal* fussy; hard to please.

chop[1] *vb* **chopping, chopped 1** (often foll. by *down* or *off*) to cut (something) with a blow from an axe or other sharp tool. **2** to cut into pieces. **3** *Boxing, karate* to hit (an opponent) with a short sharp blow. **4** *Brit informal* to dispense with or reduce. **5** *Sport* to hit (a ball) sharply downwards. ~*n* **6** a cutting blow. **7** a slice of mutton, lamb, or pork, usually including a rib. **8** *Sport* a sharp downward blow or stroke. **9 the chop** *Slang, chiefly Brit* dismissal from employment.

chop[2] *vb* **chopping, chopped 1 chop and change** to change one's mind repeatedly. **2 chop logic** to use excessively subtle or involved argument.

chop chop *adv Pidgin English* quickly.

chopper *n* **1** *Informal* a helicopter. **2** *Chiefly Brit* a small hand axe. **3** a butcher's cleaver. **4** a type of bicycle or motorcycle with very high handlebars. **5** *NZ* a child's bicycle.

choppy *adj* **-pier, -piest** (of the sea) fairly rough. **choppiness** *n*

chops *pl n* **1** the jaws or cheeks. **2 lick one's chops** *Informal* to anticipate something with pleasure.

chopsticks *pl n* a pair of thin sticks of ivory, wood, or plastic, used for eating Chinese or other East Asian food.

chop suey *n* a Chinese-style dish of chopped meat, bean sprouts, and other vegetables in a sauce.

choral *adj* of or for a choir.

chorale (kor-**rahl**) *n* **1** a slow stately hymn tune. **2** *Chiefly US* a choir or chorus.

chord[1] *n* **1** *Maths* a straight line connecting two points on a curve. **2** *Anat* same as **cord. 3 strike** *or* **touch a chord** to bring about an emotional response, usually of sympathy.

chord[2] *n* the simultaneous sounding of three or more musical notes.

chordate *n* any animal that has a long fibrous rod just above the gut to support the body, such as the vertebrates.

chore *n* **1** a small routine task. **2** an unpleasant task.

chorea (kor-**ree**-a) *n* a disorder of the nervous system characterized by uncontrollable brief jerky movements.

choreograph *vb* to compose the steps and dances for (a piece of music or ballet).

choreography *n* **1** the composition of steps and movements for ballet and other dancing. **2** the steps and movements of a ballet or dance. **choreographer** *n* **choreographic** *adj*

chorister *n* a singer in a church choir.

chortle *vb* **-tling, -tled 1** to chuckle with amusement. ~*n* **2** an amused chuckle.

chorus *n, pl* **-ruses 1** a large choir. **2** a piece of music to be sung by a large choir. **3** a part of a song repeated after each verse. **4** something expressed by many people at once: *a chorus of boos.* **5** the noise made by a group of birds or small animals: *the dawn chorus.* **6** a group of singers or dancers who perform together in a show. **7** (in ancient Greece) a group of actors who commented on the action of a play. **8** (in Elizabethan drama) the actor who spoke the prologue and epilogue. **9 in chorus** in unison. ~*vb* **10** to sing or say together.

chorus girl *n* a young woman who dances or sings in the chorus of a show or film.

chose *vb* the past tense of **choose.**

chosen *vb* **1** the past participle of **choose.** ~*adj* **2** selected for some special quality: *the chosen one.*

chough (**chuff**) *n* a large black bird of the crow family.

choux pastry (**shoo**) *n* a very light pastry made with eggs.

chow *n* **1** a thick-coated dog with a curled tail, originally from China. **2** *Informal* food.

chowder *n Chiefly US & Canad* a thick soup containing clams or fish.

THESAURUS

tion, pick, preference, say, selection, variety **2.** *adj.* bad (*slang*), best, crucial (*slang*), def (*slang*), elect, elite, excellent, exclusive, exquisite, prime, prize, rare, select, special, superior, valuable

choke 1. asphyxiate, gag, smother, stifle, strangle, suffocate, throttle **2.** bar, block, bung, clog, close, congest, constrict, dam, obstruct, occlude, stop

choleric angry, bad-tempered, cross, fiery, hasty, hot, hot-tempered, ill-tempered, irascible, irritable, petulant, quick-tempered, ratty (*Brit. & N.Z. informal*), testy, tetchy, touchy

choose 1. adopt, designate, elect, espouse, fix on, opt for, pick, select, settle upon, single out, take **2.** desire, prefer, see fit, wish

choosy *informal* discriminating, exacting, faddy, fastidious, finicky, fussy, particular, picky (*informal*), selective

chop *vb.* **1.** axe, cleave, cut, fell, hack, hew, lop, sever, shear, slash, truncate **2.** cube, dice, divide, fragment, mince ~*n.* **3. the chop** *slang, chiefly Brit.* dismissal, one's cards, sacking (*informal*), termination, the axe (*informal*), the boot (*slang*), the (old) heave-ho (*informal*), the order of the boot (*slang*), the sack (*informal*)

choppy blustery, rough, ruffled, squally, tempestuous

chow mein *n* a Chinese-American dish consisting of chopped meat or vegetables fried with noodles.

chrism *n* consecrated oil used for anointing in some churches.

Christ *n* **1** Jesus of Nazareth (Jesus Christ), regarded by Christians as the Messiah of Old Testament prophecies. **2** the Messiah of Old Testament prophecies. **3** an image or picture of Christ. *~interj* **4** *Taboo slang* an oath expressing annoyance or surprise.

christen *vb* **1** same as **baptize. 2** to give a name to (a person or thing). **3** *Informal* to use for the first time. **christening** *n*

Christendom *n* all Christian people or countries.

Christian *n* **1** a person who believes in and follows Jesus Christ. **2** *Informal* a person who displays the virtues of kindness and mercy encouraged in the teachings of Jesus Christ. *~adj* **3** of Jesus Christ, Christians, or Christianity. **4** kind or good.

Christian Era *n* the period beginning with the year of Christ's birth.

Christianity *n* **1** the religion based on the life and teachings of Christ. **2** Christian beliefs or practices. **3** same as **Christendom.**

Christianize *or* **-ise** *vb* **-izing, -ized** *or* **-ising, -ised 1** to convert to Christianity. **2** to fill with Christian principles, spirit, or outlook. **Christianization** *or* **-isation** *n*

Christian name *n Brit* a personal name formally given to Christians at baptism: loosely used to mean a person's first name.

Christian Science *n* the religious system founded by Mary Baker Eddy (1866), which emphasizes spiritual regeneration and healing through prayer. **Christian Scientist** *n*

Christmas *n* **1 a** *Christianity* a festival commemorating the birth of Christ, held by most Churches to have occurred on Dec. 25. **b** Also: **Christmas Day** Dec. 25, as a day of secular celebrations when gifts and greetings are exchanged. *~adj* **2** connected with or taking place at the time of year when this festival is celebrated: *the Christmas holidays.* **Christmassy** *adj*

Christmas box *n* a tip or present given at Christmas, esp. to postmen or tradesmen.

Christmas Eve *n* the evening or the whole day before Christmas Day.

Christmas pudding *n Brit* a rich steamed pudding containing suet, dried fruit, and spices.

Christmas rose *n* an evergreen plant with white or pink winter-blooming flowers.

Christmas tree *n* an evergreen tree or an imitation of one, decorated as part of Christmas celebrations.

chromate *n Chem* any salt or ester of chromic acid.

chromatic *adj* **1** of or in colour or colours. **2** *Music* **a** involving the sharpening or flattening of notes or the use of such notes. **b** of the chromatic scale. **chromatically** *adv*

chromatics *n* the science of colour.

chromatic scale *n* a twelve-note scale including all the semitones of the octave.

chromatin *n Biochem* the part of the nucleus of a cell that forms the chromosomes and can easily be dyed.

chromatography *n* the technique of separating and analysing the components of a mixture of liquids or gases by slowly passing it through an adsorbing material.

chrome *n* **1** same as **chromium. 2** anything plated with chromium. *~vb* **chroming, chromed 3** to plate or be plated with chromium.

chromite *n* a brownish-black mineral which is the only commercial source of chromium.

chromium *n Chem* a hard grey metallic element, used in steel alloys and electroplating to increase hardness and corrosion resistance. Symbol: Cr

chromosome *n* any of the microscopic rod-shaped structures that appear in a cell nucleus during cell division, consisting of units (genes) that are responsible for the transmission of hereditary characteristics.

chromosphere *n* a gaseous layer of the sun's atmosphere extending from the photosphere to the corona.

chronic *adj* **1** (of a disease) developing slowly or lasting for a long time. **2** (of a bad habit or bad behaviour) having continued for a long time; habitual: *chronic drug addiction.* **3** very serious or severe: *chronic food shortages.* **4** *Informal* very bad: *the play was chronic.* **chronically** *adv*

chronicle *n* **1** a record of events in chronological order. *~vb* **-cling, -cled 2** to record in or as if in a chronicle. **chronicler** *n*

chronological *adj* **1** (of a sequence of events) arranged in order of occurrence. **2** relating to chronology. **chronologically** *adv*

chronology *n, pl* **-gies 1** the arrangement of dates or events in order of occurrence. **2** the determining of the proper sequence of past events. **3** a table of events arranged in order of occurrence. **chronologist** *n*

chronometer *n* a timepiece designed to be accurate in all conditions.

chrysalis (**kriss**-a-liss) *n* an insect in the stage between larva and adult, when it is in a cocoon.

chrysanthemum *n* a garden plant with large round flowers made up of many petals.

chub *n, pl* **chub** *or* **chubs** a common freshwater game fish of the carp family with a dark greenish body.

chubby *adj* **-bier, -biest** plump and round. **chubbiness** *n*

chuck[1] *vb* **1** *Informal* to throw carelessly. **2** *Informal* (sometimes foll. by *in* or *up*) to give up; reject: *he chucked in his job.* **3** to pat (someone) affectionately under the chin. *~n* **4** a throw or toss. **5** a pat under the chin. ~See also **chuck off, chuck out.**

chuck[2] *n* **1** Also: **chuck steak** a cut of beef from the neck to the shoulder blade. **2** a device that holds a workpiece in a lathe or a tool in a drill.

chuck[3] *n W Canada* **1** a large body of water. **2** Also: **saltchuck** the sea.

THESAURUS

chore burden, duty, errand, fag (*informal*), job, task

chortle cackle, chuckle, guffaw

chorus 1. choir, choristers, ensemble, singers, vocalists **2.** burden, refrain, response, strain

christen baptize, call, designate, dub, name, style, term, title

chronic 1. confirmed, deep-rooted, deep-seated, habitual, incessant, incurable, ineradicable, ingrained, inveterate, persistent **2.** *informal* abysmal, appalling, atrocious, awful, dreadful

chronicle 1. *n.* account, annals, diary, history, journal, narrative, record, register, story **2.** *vb.* enter, narrate, put on record, record, recount, register, relate, report, set down, tell

chronicler annalist, diarist, historian, narrator, recorder, reporter, scribe

chronological consecutive, historical, in sequence, ordered, progressive, sequential

chubby buxom, flabby, fleshy, plump, podgy, portly, rotund, round, stout, tubby

chuckle *vb* **-ling, -led 1** to laugh softly or to oneself. *~n* **2** a partly suppressed laugh.

chuck off *vb* (often foll. by *at*) *Austral & NZ informal* to sneer.

chuck out *vb Informal* to throw out.

chuff *vb* to move while making a puffing sound, as a steam engine.

chuffed *adj Informal* pleased or delighted: *I suppose you're feeling pretty chuffed.*

chug *n* **1** a short dull sound like the noise of an engine. *~vb* **chugging, chugged 2** (esp. of an engine) to operate or move with this sound.

chukka *or* **chukker** *n Polo* a period of continuous play, usually 7½ minutes.

chum *n* **1** *Informal* a close friend. *~vb* **chumming, chummed 2 chum up with** to form a close friendship with.

chummy *adj* **-mier, -miest** *Informal* friendly. **chummily** *adv* **chumminess** *n*

chump *n* **1** *Informal* a stupid person. **2** a thick piece of meat. **3** a thick block of wood. **4 off one's chump** *Brit slang* crazy.

chunk *n* **1** a thick solid piece of something. **2** a considerable amount.

chunky *adj* **chunkier, chunkiest 1** thick and short. **2** containing thick pieces. **3** *Chiefly Brit* (of clothes, esp. knitwear) made of thick bulky material. **chunkiness** *n*

church *n* **1** a building for public Christian worship. **2** religious services held in a church. **3** a particular Christian denomination. **4** Christians collectively. **5** the clergy as distinguished from the laity. **6 Church** institutional religion as a political or social force: *conflict between Church and State.*

churchgoer *n* a person who attends church regularly.

churchman *n, pl* **-men** a clergyman.

Church of England *n* the reformed established state Church in England, with the sovereign as its temporal head.

Church of Scotland *n* the established Presbyterian church in Scotland.

churchwarden *n* **1** *Church of England, Episcopal Church* a lay assistant of a parish priest. **2** an old-fashioned long-stemmed tobacco pipe made of clay.

churchyard *n* the grounds round a church, used as a graveyard.

churl *n* **1** a surly ill-bred person. **2** *Archaic* a farm labourer.

churlish *adj* surly and rude.

churn *n* **1** a machine in which cream is shaken to make butter. **2** a large container for milk. *~vb* **3** to stir (milk or cream) vigorously in order to make butter. **4** to move about violently: *a hot tub of churning water.*

churn out *vb Informal* to produce (something) rapidly and in large numbers.

chute[1] **(shoot)** *n* a steep sloping channel or passage down which things may be dropped.

chute[2] *n Informal* short for **parachute.**

chutney *n* a pickle of Indian origin, made from fruit, vinegar, spices, and sugar: *mango chutney.*

chutzpah **(hhoots-pa)** *n US & Canad informal* unashamed self-confidence; impudence.

chyle *n* a milky fluid formed in the small intestine during digestion.

chyme *n* the thick fluid mass of partially digested food that leaves the stomach.

chypre **(sheep-ra)** *n* a perfume made from sandalwood.

Ci curie.

CI Channel Islands.

CIA Central Intelligence Agency; a U.S. bureau responsible for espionage and intelligence activities.

cicada (sik-**kah**-da) *n* a large broad insect, found in hot countries, that makes a high-pitched drone.

cicatrix **(sik-a-trix)** *n, pl* **cicatrices** (sik-a-**trice**-eez) the tissue that forms in a wound during healing; scar.

cicerone (siss-a-**rone**-ee) *n, pl* **-nes** *or* **-ni** *Literary* a person who guides and informs sightseers.

CID (in Britain) Criminal Investigation Department; the detective division of a police force.

cider *n* an alcoholic drink made from fermented apple juice.

cigar *n* a tube-like roll of cured tobacco leaves for smoking.

cigarette *n* a thin roll of shredded tobacco in thin paper, for smoking.

cilium *n, pl* **cilia** *Biol* **1** any of the short threads projecting from a cell or organism, whose rhythmic beating causes movement. **2** an eyelash. **ciliary** *adj*

C in C *Mil* Commander in Chief.

cinch **(sinch)** *n* **1** *Informal* an easy task. **2** *Slang* a certainty.

cinchona (sing-**kone**-a) *n* **1** a South American tree or shrub with medicinal bark. **2** its dried bark which yields quinine. **3** a drug made from cinchona bark.

cincture *n Literary* something, such as a belt or girdle, that goes around another thing.

cinder *n* **1** a piece of material that will not burn, left after burning coal or wood. **2 cinders** ashes.

Cinderella *n* a poor, neglected, or unsuccessful person or thing.

cine camera *n* a camera for taking moving pictures.

cinema *n* **1** a place designed for showing films. **2 the cinema a** the art or business of making films. **b** films collectively. **cinematic** *adj*

cinematograph *n Chiefly Brit* a combined camera, printer, and projector. **cinematographer** *n* **cinematographic** *adj*

cinematography *n* the technique of making films.

cineraria *n* a garden plant with daisy-like flowers.

cinerarium *n, pl* **-raria** a place for keeping the ashes of the dead after cremation. **cinerary** *adj*

cinnabar *n* **1** a heavy red mineral containing mercury. **2** a large red-and-black European moth.

cinnamon *n* the spice obtained from the aromatic bark of a tropical Asian tree.

cinquefoil *n* **1** a plant with five-lobed compound

THESAURUS

chuck *informal* cast, discard, fling, heave, hurl, pitch, shy, sling, throw, toss

chuckle chortle, giggle, laugh, snigger, titter

chum *informal* cock (*Brit. informal*), companion, comrade, crony, friend, mate (*informal*), pal (*informal*)

chunk block, dollop (*informal*), hunk, lump, mass, piece, portion, slab, wad, wodge (*Brit. informal*)

chunky beefy (*informal*), dumpy, stocky, stubby, thickset

churlish boorish, brusque, ill-tempered, impolite, loutish, morose, oafish, rude, sullen, surly, uncivil, uncouth, unmannerly, vulgar

churn *vb.* agitate, beat, boil, convulse, foam, froth, seethe, stir up, swirl, toss

cigarette cancer stick (*slang*), ciggy (*informal*), cof-

leaves. **2** an ornamental carving in the form of five arcs arranged in a circle.

Cinque Ports *pl n* an association of ports on the SE coast of England, with certain ancient duties and privileges.

cipher *or* **cypher** (**sife**-er) *n* **1** a method of secret writing using substitution of letters according to a key. **2** a secret message. **3** the key to a secret message. **4** a person or thing of no importance. **5** *Obsolete* the numeral zero. ~*vb* **6** to put (a message) into secret writing.

circa (**sir**-ka) *prep* (used with a date) approximately; about: *circa 1788.*

circadian *adj* of biological processes that occur regularly at 24-hour intervals.

circle *n* **1** a curved line surrounding a central point, every point of the line being the same distance from the centre. **2** the figure enclosed by such a curve. **3** something formed or arranged in the shape of a circle: *they ran round in little circles.* **4** a group of people sharing an interest, activity, or upbringing: *his judgment is well respected in diplomatic circles.* **5** *Theatre* the section of seats above the main level of the auditorium. **6** a process or chain of events or parts that forms a connected whole; cycle. **7 come full circle** to arrive back at one's starting point. ~*vb* **-cling, -cled 8** to move in a circle (around). **9** to enclose in a circle.

circlet *n* a small circle or ring, esp. a circular ornament worn on the head.

circuit *n* **1** a complete route or course, esp. one that is circular or that lies around an object. **2** a complete path through which an electric current can flow. **3 a** a periodical journey around an area, as made by judges or salesmen. **b** the places visited on such a journey. **4** a motor-racing track. **5** *Sport* a series of tournaments in which the same players regularly take part: *the professional golf circuit.* **6** a number of theatres or cinemas under one management.

circuit breaker *n* a device that stops the flow of current in an electrical circuit if there is a fault.

circuitous (sir-**kew**-it-uss) *adj* indirect and lengthy: *a circuitous route.*

circuitry (**sir**-kit-tree) *n* **1** the design of an electrical circuit. **2** the system of circuits used in an electronic device.

circular *adj* **1** of or in the shape of a circle. **2** travelling in a circle. **3** (of an arguments) not valid because a statement is used to prove the conclusion and the conclusion to prove the statement. **4** (of letters or announcements) intended for general distribution. ~*n* **5** a letter or advertisement sent to a large number of people at the same time. **circularity** *n*

circularize *or* **-ise** *vb* **-izing, -ized** *or* **-ising, -ised** to distribute circulars to.

circular saw *n* a power-driven saw in which a circular disc with a toothed edge is rotated at high speed.

circulate *vb* **-lating, -lated 1** to send, go, or pass from place to place or person to person: *rumours were circulating that the prime minister was about to resign.* **2** to move through a circuit or system, returning to the starting point: *regular exercise keeps the blood circulating around the body.* **3** to move around the guests at a party, talking to different people: *it wasn't like her not to circulate among all the guests.* **circulatory** *adj*

circulation *n* **1** the flow of blood from the heart through the arteries, and then back through the veins to the heart, where the cycle is renewed. **2** the number of copies of a newspaper or magazine that are sold. **3** the distribution of newspapers or magazines. **4** sending or moving around: *the circulation of air.* **5 in circulation a** (of currency) being used by the public. **b** (of people) active in a social or business context.

circum- *prefix* around; on all sides: *circumlocution.*

circumcise *vb* **-cising, -cised 1** to remove the foreskin of (a male). **2** to cut or remove the clitoris of (a female). **3** to perform such an operation as a religious rite on (someone). **circumcision** *n*

circumference *n* **1** the boundary of a specific area or figure, esp. of a circle. **2** the distance round this. **circumferential** *adj*

circumflex *n* a mark (ˆ) placed over a vowel to show that it is pronounced in a particular way, for instance as a long vowel in French.

circumlocution *n* **1** an indirect way of saying something. **2** an indirect expression. **circumlocutory** *adj*

circumnavigate *vb* **-gating, -gated** to sail, fly, or walk right around. **circumnavigation** *n*

circumscribe *vb* **-scribing, -scribed 1** *Formal* to limit or restrict within certain boundaries: *the President's powers are circumscribed by the Constitution.* **2** *Geom* to draw a geometric figure around (another figure) so that the two are in contact but do not intersect. **circumscription** *n*

circumspect *adj* cautious and careful not to take risks. **circumspection** *n* **circumspectly** *adv*

circumstance *n* **1** an occurrence or condition that accompanies or influences a person or event. **2** unplanned events and situations which cannot be controlled: *a victim of circumstance.* **3 pomp and circumstance** formal display or ceremony. **4 under** *or* **in no circumstances** in no case; never. **5 under the circumstances** because of conditions.

THESAURUS

fin nail (*slang*), fag (*Brit. slang*), gasper (*slang*), smoke (*informal*)

cinema big screen (*informal*), films, flicks (*slang*), motion pictures, movies, pictures

cipher 1. code, cryptograph **2.** nobody, nonentity **3.** *obsolete* nil, nothing, nought, zero

circle *n.* **1.** band, circumference, cordon, lap, loop, orb, revolution, ring, round, sphere, turn **2.** area, bounds, circuit, compass, domain, enclosure, field, orbit, province, range, realm, region, scene, sphere **3.** assembly, class, clique, club, company, coterie, crowd, fellowship, fraternity, group, order, school, set, society ~*vb.* **4.** belt, circumnavigate, circumscribe, curve, encircle, enclose, encompass, envelop, revolve, ring, rotate, surround, whirl

circuit area, compass, course, journey, lap, orbit, perambulation, revolution, round, route, tour, track

circuitous devious, indirect, labyrinthine, meandering, oblique, rambling, roundabout, tortuous, winding

circulate broadcast, diffuse, disseminate, distribute, issue, make known, promulgate, propagate, publicize, publish, spread

circulation currency, dissemination, distribution, spread, transmission

circumference border, boundary, bounds, circuit, edge, extremity, fringe, limits, outline, pale, perimeter, periphery, rim, verge

circumscribe *formal* bound, confine, delimit, delineate, demarcate, encircle, enclose, encompass, hem in, limit, mark off, restrain, restrict, surround

circumspect attentive, canny, careful, cautious, discreet, guarded, judicious, politic, prudent, sagacious, vigilant, wary, watchful

circumstance accident, condition, contingency, detail, element, event, fact, factor, happening, incident, item, occurrence, particular, position, respect, situation

circumstantial *adj* **1** (of evidence) strongly suggesting something but not proving it. **2** fully detailed.

circumstantiate *vb* **-ating, -ated** to prove by giving details.

circumvent *vb Formal* **1** to avoid or get round (a rule, restriction, etc.). **2** to outwit (a person). **circumvention** *n*

circus *n, pl* **-cuses 1** a travelling company of entertainers such as acrobats, clowns, trapeze artists, and trained animals. **2** a public performance given by such a company. **3** *Brit* an open place in a town where several streets meet. **4** *Informal* a hectic or well-published situation: *her second marriage turned into a media circus.* **5** (in ancient Rome) an open-air stadium for chariot races or public games. **6** a travelling group of professional sportsmen: *the Formula One circus.*

cirque (**sirk**) *n* a steep-sided semicircular hollow found in mountainous areas.

cirrhosis (sir-**roh**-siss) *n* a chronic progressive disease of the liver, often caused by drinking too much alcohol

cirrocumulus (sirr-oh-**kew**-myew-luss) *n, pl* **-li** (-lie) a high cloud of ice crystals grouped into small separate globular masses.

cirrostratus (sirr-oh-**strah**-tuss) *n, pl* **-ti** (-tie) a uniform layer of cloud above about 6000 metres.

cirrus *n, pl* **-ri 1** a thin wispy cloud found at high altitudes. **2** a plant tendril. **3** a slender tentacle in certain sea creatures.

CIS Commonwealth of Independent States.

cisalpine *adj* on this (the southern) side of the Alps, as viewed from Rome.

cisco *n, pl* **-coes** *or* **-cos** a whitefish, esp. the lake herring of cold deep lakes of North America.

cissy *n, pl* **-sies**, *adj* same as **sissy**.

Cistercian *n* **1** a Christian monk or nun belonging to an especially strict Benedictine order. *~adj* **2** of or relating to this order.

cistern *n* **1** a water tank, esp. one which holds water for flushing a toilet. **2** an underground reservoir.

citadel *n* a fortress in a city.

citation *n* **1** an official commendation or award, esp. for bravery. **2** the quoting of a book or author. **3** a quotation.

cite *vb* **citing, cited 1** to quote or refer to (a passage, book, or author). **2** to bring forward as proof. **3** to summon to appear before a court of law. **4** to mention or commend (someone) for outstanding bravery. **5** to enumerate: *the president cited the wonders of the American family.*

citified *adj Often disparaging* having the customs, manners, or dress of city people.

citizen *n* **1** a native or naturalized member of a state or nation. **2** an inhabitant of a city or town.

citizenry *n* citizens collectively.

Citizens' Band *n* a range of radio frequencies for use by the public for private communication.

citizenship *n* the condition or status of a citizen, with its rights and duties.

citrate *n* any salt or ester of citric acid.

citric *adj* of or derived from citrus fruits or citric acid.

citric acid *n* a weak acid found especially in citrus fruits and used as a flavouring (**E330**).

citron *n* **1** a lemon-like fruit of a small Asian tree. **2** the candied rind of this fruit.

citronella *n* **1** a tropical Asian grass with lemon-scented leaves. **2** the aromatic oil obtained from this grass.

citrus fruit *n* juicy, sharp-tasting fruit such as oranges, lemons, or limes.

city *n, pl* **cities 1** any large town. **2** (in Britain) a town that has received this title from the Crown. **3** the people of a city collectively. **4** (in the U.S. and Canada) a large town with its own government established by charter from the state or provincial government.

City *n* **the City 1** the area in central London in which the United Kingdom's major financial business is transacted. **2** the various financial institutions in this area.

city editor *n* (on a newspaper) **1** *Brit* the editor in charge of business news. **2** *US & Canad* the editor in charge of local news.

city-state *n Ancient history* a state consisting of a sovereign city and its dependencies.

civet (**siv**-vit) *n* **1** a spotted catlike mammal of Africa and S Asia. **2** the musky fluid produced by this animal, used in perfumes.

civic *adj* of a city or citizens. **civically** *adv*

civic centre *n Brit* a complex of public buildings, including recreational facilities and offices of local government.

civics *n* the study of the rights and responsibilities of citizenship.

civil *adj* **1** of or occurring within the state or between citizens: *civil unrest.* **2** of or relating to the citizen as an individual: *civil rights.* **3** not part of the military, legal or religious structures of a country: *civil aviation.* **4** polite or courteous: *he seemed very civil and listened politely.* **civilly** *adv*

civil defence *n* the organizing of civilians to deal with enemy attacks.

civil disobedience *n* a nonviolent protest, such as a refusal to obey laws or pay taxes.

civil engineer *n* a person qualified to design and construct public works, such as roads or bridges. **civil engineering** *n*

civilian *n* **1** a person who is not a member of the armed forces or police. *~adj* **2** not relating to the armed forces or police: *civilian clothes.*

civility *n, pl* **-ties 1** polite or courteous behaviour. **2 civilities** polite words or actions.

civilization *or* **-lisation** *n* **1** the total culture and way of life of a particular people, nation, region, or period. **2** a human society that has a complex cultural, political, and legal organization. **3** the races collective-

THESAURUS

circumstantial 1. founded on circumstances, incidental, indirect, inferential, presumptive, provisional 2. conjectural, contingent, detailed, particular, specific

cistern basin, sink, tank, vat

citadel fastness (*literary*), fortification, fortress, keep, stronghold, tower

citation 1. award, commendation, mention 2. excerpt, illustration, passage, quotation, quote, reference

cite 1. allude to, extract, mention, name, quote, specify 2. adduce, advance, evidence 3. *Law* call, subpoena, summon 4. enumerate

citizen burgher, denizen, dweller, inhabitant, ratepayer, resident, subject, townsman

city conurbation, megalopolis, metropolis, municipality

civic borough, communal, community, local, municipal, public

civil 1. civic, domestic, home, interior, municipal, political 2. civilized, courteous, courtly, polished, polite, refined, urbane, well-bred, well-mannered

civilization 1. customs, mores, way of life 2. community, nation, people, polity (*formal*), society 3. ad-

ly who have achieved such a state. **4** cities or populated areas, as contrasted with sparsely inhabited areas. **5** intellectual, cultural, and moral refinement.

civilize *or* **-lise** *vb* **-lizing, -lized** *or* **-lising, -lised 1** to bring out of barbarism into a state of civilization. **2** to refine, educate, or enlighten. **civilized** *or* **-lised** *adj*

civil law *n* **1** the law of a state, relating to private and civilian affairs. **2** a system of law based on that of ancient Rome.

civil liberties *pl n* a person's rights to freedom of speech and action.

civil list *n* (in Britain) the annual amount given by Parliament to the royal household and the royal family.

civil marriage *n Law* a marriage performed by an official other than a clergyman.

civil rights *pl n* the personal rights of the individual citizen to have equal treatment and equal opportunities.

civil servant *n* a member of the civil service.

civil service *n* the service responsible for the public administration of the government of a country.

civil war *n* war between people of the same country.

civvies *pl n Slang* civilian clothes as opposed to uniform.

civvy street *n Slang* civilian life.

cl centilitre.

Cl *Chem* chlorine.

clack *n* **1** the sound made by two hard objects striking each other. *~vb* **2** to make this sound.

clad *vb* a past of **clothe.**

cladding *n* **1** the material used to cover the outside of a building. **2** a protective metal coating attached to another metal.

cladistics *n* a method of grouping animals by measurable likenesses.

claim *vb* **1** to assert as a fact: *he had claimed to be too ill to return.* **2** to demand as a right or as one's property: *you can claim housing benefit to help pay your rent.* **3** to call for or need: *this problem claims our attention.* **4** to cause the death of: *violence which has claimed at least fifty lives.* **5** to succeed in obtaining; win: *she claimed her fifth European tour victory with a closing round of 64.* *~n* **6** an assertion of something as true or real. **7** an assertion of a right; a demand for something as due. **8** a right or just title to something: *a claim to fame.* **9** anything that is claimed, such as a piece of land staked out by a miner. **10 a** a demand for payment in connection with an insurance policy. **b** the sum of money demanded. **claimant** *n*

clairvoyance *n* the alleged power of perceiving things beyond the natural range of the senses.

clairvoyant *n* **1** a person claiming to have the power to foretell future events. *~adj* **2** of or possessing clairvoyance.

clam *n* an edible shellfish with a hinged shell. ~See also **clam up.**

clamber *vb* **1** to climb awkwardly, using hands and feet. *~n* **2** a climb performed in this manner.

clammy *adj* **-mier, -miest** unpleasantly moist and sticky. **clammily** *adv* **clamminess** *n*

clamour *or US* **clamor** *n* **1** a loud protest. **2** a loud and persistent noise or outcry. *~vb* **3 clamour for** to demand noisily. **4** to make a loud noise or outcry. **clamorous** *adj*

clamp[1] *n* **1** a mechanical device with movable jaws for holding things together tightly. **2** See **wheel clamp.** *~vb* **3** to fix or fasten with a clamp. **4** to immobilize (a car) by means of a wheel clamp.

clamp[2] *n* a mound of a harvested root crop, covered with straw and earth to protect it from winter weather.

clamp down *vb* **1 clamp down on a** to become stricter about. **b** to suppress (something regarded as undesirable). *~n* **clampdown 2** a sudden restriction placed on an activity.

clam up *vb* **clamming, clammed** *Informal* to keep or become silent.

clan *n* **1** a group of families with a common surname and a common ancestor, esp. among Scottish Highlanders. **2** an extended family related by ancestry or marriage: *America's leading political clan, the Kennedys.* **3** a group of people with common characteristics, aims, or interests. **clansman** *n*

clandestine *adj Formal* secret and concealed: *a base for clandestine activities.* **clandestinely** *adv*

clang *vb* **1** to make a loud ringing noise, as metal does when it is struck. *~n* **2** a ringing metallic noise.

clanger *n* **drop a clanger** *Informal* to make a very noticeable mistake.

clangour *or US* **clangor** *n* a loud continuous clanging sound. **clangorous** *adj*

clank *n* **1** an abrupt harsh metallic sound. *~vb* **2** to make such a sound.

clannish *adj* (of a group) tending to exclude outsiders: *the villagers can be very clannish.*

clap[1] *vb* **clapping, clapped 1** to applaud by striking the palms of one's hands sharply together. **2** to place or put quickly or forcibly: *in former times he would have been clapped in irons or shot.* **3** to strike (a person) lightly with an open hand as in greeting. **4** to make a sharp abrupt sound like two objects being struck together. **5 clap eyes on** *Informal* to catch sight of. *~n* **6** the act or sound of clapping. **7** a sharp abrupt sound, esp. of thunder. **8** a light blow.

clap[2] *n Slang* gonorrhoea.

clapped out *adj Informal* **1** *Brit, Austral, & NZ* worn out; dilapidated. **2** *Austral & NZ* extremely tired.

clapper *n* **1** a small piece of metal hanging inside a bell, which causes it to sound when struck against the side. **2 like the clappers** *Brit informal* extremely quickly: *he left, pedalling like the clappers.*

clapperboard *n* a pair of hinged boards clapped to-

THESAURUS

vancement, cultivation, culture, development, education, enlightenment, progress, refinement, sophistication

civilize cultivate, educate, enlighten, humanize, improve, polish, refine, sophisticate

civilized cultured, educated, enlightened, polite, sophisticated, urbane

claim *vb.* **1.** allege, assert, hold, insist, maintain, profess, uphold **2.** ask for, collect, demand, exact, pick up **3.** call for, need, require, take *~n.* **4.** affirmation, allegation, application, assertion, pretension, protestation **5.** call, demand, petition, request **6.** privilege, right, title

clamber claw, climb, scale, scrabble, scramble, shin

clamour babel, brouhaha, commotion, din, exclamation, hubbub, hullabaloo, noise, outcry, racket, shout, shouting, uproar, vociferation

clamp 1. *n.* bracket, fastener, grip, press, vice **2.** *vb.* brace, clinch, fasten, fix, make fast, secure

clan 1. family, house, sept, tribe **2.** band, brotherhood, clique, coterie, faction, fraternity, group, order, sect, set, society

gether during film shooting to help in synchronizing sound and picture.

claptrap *n Informal* foolish or pretentious talk: *pseudo-intellectual claptrap.*

claque *n Formal* **1** a group of people hired to applaud. **2** a group of fawning admirers.

claret (**klar**-rit) *n* **1** a dry red wine, esp. one from Bordeaux. ~*adj* **2** purplish-red.

clarify *vb* **-fies, -fying, -fied 1** to make or become clear or easy to understand. **2** to make or become free of impurities, esp. by heating: *clarified butter.* **clarification** *n*

clarinet *n* a keyed woodwind instrument with a single reed. **clarinettist** *n*

clarion *n* **1** an obsolete high-pitched trumpet. **2** its sound.

clarion call *n* strong encouragement to do something.

clarity *n* clearness.

clash *vb* **1** to come into conflict. **2** to be incompatible. **3** (of dates or events) to coincide. **4** (of colours or styles) to look ugly or incompatible together: *patterned fabrics which combine seemingly clashing shades to great effect.* **5** to make a loud harsh sound, esp. by striking together. ~*n* **6** a collision or conflict. **7** a loud harsh noise.

clasp *n* **1** a fastening, such as a catch or hook, for holding things together. **2** a firm grasp or embrace. ~*vb* **3** to grasp or embrace tightly. **4** to fasten together with a clasp.

clasp knife *n* a large knife with blades which fold into the handle.

class *n* **1** a group of people sharing a similar social and economic position. **2** the system of dividing society into such groups. **3** a group of people or things sharing a common characteristic. **4 a** a group of pupils or students who are taught together. **b** a meeting of a group of students for tuition. **5** a standard of quality or attainment: *second class.* **6** *Informal* excellence or elegance, esp. in dress, design, or behaviour: *a full-bodied red wine with real class.* **7** *Biol* one of the groups into which a phylum is divided, containing one or more orders. **8 in a class by oneself** *or* **in a class of its own** without an equal for ability, talent, etc. ~*vb* **9** to place in a class.

class-conscious *adj* aware of belonging to a particular social rank.

classic *adj* **1** serving as a standard or model of its kind; typical: *it is a classic symptom of iron deficiency.* **2** of lasting interest or significance because of excellence: *the classic work on Central America.* **3** characterized by simplicity and purity of form: *a classic suit.* ~*n* **4** an author, artist, or work of art of the highest excellence. **5** a creation or work considered as definitive. ➤ *Classic* and *classical* are synonyms except in the context of Greek and Roman culture, which is called *classical,* or highly rated art and literature, which is called *classic.*

classical *adj* **1** of or in a restrained conservative style: *it had been built in the eighteenth century in a severely classical style.* **2** *Music* **a** in a style or from a period marked by stability of form, intellectualism, and restraint. **b** denoting serious art music in general. **3** of or influenced by ancient Greek and Roman culture. **4** of the form of a language historically used for formal and literary purposes: *classical Chinese.* **5** (of an education) based on the humanities and the study of Latin and Greek. **classically** *adv*

classicism *n* **1** an artistic style based on Greek and Roman models, showing emotional restraint and regularity of form. **2** knowledge of the culture of ancient Greece and Rome. **classicist** *n*

classics *pl n* **1** the study of ancient Greek and Roman literature and culture. **2 the classics a** those works of literature regarded as great or lasting. **b** the ancient Greek and Latin languages.

classification *n* **1** placing things systematically in categories. **2** a division or category in a classifying system. **classificatory** *adj*

classified *adj* **1** arranged according to some system of classification. **2** *Government* (of information) not available to people outside a restricted group, esp. for reasons of national security.

classify *vb* **-fies, -fying, -fied 1** to arrange or order by classes. **2** *Government* to declare (information) to be officially secret. **classifiable** *adj*

classless *adj* **1** not belonging to a class. **2** distinguished by the absence of economic or social distinctions: *a classless society.*

classmate *n* a friend or contemporary in the same class of a school.

THESAURUS

clang 1. *vb.* chime, clank, clash, jangle, resound, reverberate, ring, toll **2.** *n.* clangour, knell, reverberation

clap *vb.* **1.** acclaim, applaud, cheer **2.** bang, pat, punch, slap, thwack, wallop (*informal*), whack

claptrap affectation, balls (*taboo slang*), bilge (*informal*), blarney, bombast, bosh (*informal*), bull (*slang*), bullshit (*taboo slang*), bunk (*informal*), bunkum *or* buncombe (*chiefly U.S.*), cobblers (*Brit. taboo slang*), crap (*slang*), drivel, eyewash (*informal*), flannel (*Brit. informal*), garbage (*informal*), guff (*slang*), hogwash, hokum (*slang, chiefly U.S. & Canad.*), hot air (*informal*), humbug, insincerity, moonshine, nonsense, pap, piffle (*informal*), poppycock (*informal*), rodomontade (*literary*), rot, rubbish, shit (*taboo slang*), tommyrot, tosh (*slang, chiefly Brit.*), tripe (*informal*)

clarification elucidation, explanation, exposition, illumination, interpretation, simplification

clarify 1. clear up, elucidate, explain, explicate (*formal*), illuminate, interpret, make plain, resolve, simplify, throw *or* shed light on **2.** cleanse, purify, refine

clarity 1. clearness, comprehensibility, explicitness, intelligibility, lucidity, obviousness, precision, simplicity **2.** clearness, limpidity, transparency

clash *vb.* **1.** conflict, cross swords, quarrel, war, wrangle **2.** bang, clang, clank, clatter, crash, jangle, jar, rattle ~*n.* **3.** brush, collision, conflict, confrontation, difference of opinion, disagreement, fight, showdown (*informal*)

clasp *n.* **1.** buckle, catch, clip, fastener, fastening, grip, hasp, hook, pin **2.** embrace, grasp, grip, hold, hug ~*vb.* **3.** clutch, embrace, enfold, grasp, grip, hold, hug, press, seize, squeeze **4.** connect, fasten, hold

class *n.* **1.** caste, rank, status **2.** category, classification, collection, denomination, department, division, genre, genus, grade, group, grouping, kind, league, order, set, sort, species, sphere, stamp, type, value ~*vb.* **3.** brand, categorize, classify, codify, designate, grade, group, label, rank, rate

classic *adj.* **1.** characteristic, regular, standard, typical, usual **2.** archetypal, definitive, exemplary, ideal, master, model, paradigmatic, quintessential, standard ~*n.* **3.** exemplar, masterpiece, masterwork, model, paradigm, prototype, standard

classical 1. elegant, harmonious, pure, refined, restrained, symmetrical, understated, well-proportioned **2.** Attic, Augustan, Grecian, Greek, Hellenic, Latin, Roman

classroom *n* a room in a school where lessons take place.

classy *adj* **classier, classiest** *Informal* stylish and sophisticated. **classiness** *n*

clatter *vb* **1** to make a rattling noise, as when hard objects hit each other. *~n* **2** a rattling sound or noise.

clause *n* **1** a section of a legal document such as a will or contract. **2** *Grammar* a group of words, consisting of a subject and a predicate including a finite verb, that does not necessarily constitute a sentence. **clausal** *adj*

claustrophobia *n* an abnormal fear of being in a confined space. **claustrophobic** *adj*

clavichord *n* an early keyboard instrument with a very soft tone.

clavicle *n* either of the two bones connecting the shoulder blades with the upper part of the breastbone; the collarbone.

claw *n* **1** a curved pointed nail on the foot of birds, some reptiles, and certain mammals. **2** a similar part in some invertebrates, such as a crab's pincer. *~vb* **3** to scrape, tear, or dig with claws or nails: *she clawed his face with her fingernails.* **4** to achieve (something) only after overcoming great difficulties: *he clawed his way to power and wealth; settlers attempting to claw a living from the desert.*

claw back *vb* **1** to get back (something) with difficulty. **2** to recover (a part of a grant or allowance) in the form of a tax or financial penalty.

clay *n* **1** a very fine-grained earth, soft when moist and hardening when baked, used to make bricks and pottery. **2** earth or mud. **3** *Poetic* the material of the human body. **clayey, clayish,** *or* **claylike** *adj*

claymore *n* a large two-edged broadsword used formerly by Scottish Highlanders.

clay pigeon *n* a disc of baked clay hurled into the air from a machine as a target for shooting.

CLC Canadian Labour Congress.

clean *adj* **1** free from dirt or impurities: *clean water.* **2** habitually hygienic and neat. **3** morally sound: *clean living.* **4** without objectionable language or obscenity: *good clean fun.* **5** without anything in it or on it: *a clean sheet of paper.* **6** causing little contamination or pollution: *rape seed oil may provide a clean alternative to petrol.* **7** recently washed; fresh. **8** thorough or complete: *a clean break with the past.* **9** skilful and done without fumbling; dexterous: *a clean catch.* **10** *Sport* played fairly and without fouls. **11** free from dishonesty or corruption: *clean government.* **12** simple and streamlined in design: *the clean lines and colourful simplicity of these ceramics.* **13** (esp. of a driving licence) showing or having no record of offences. **14** *Slang* **a** innocent. **b** not carrying illegal drugs, weapons, etc. *~vb* **15** to make or become free of dirt: *he wanted to help me clean the room.* *~adv* **16** in a clean way. **17** *Not standard* completely: *she clean forgot to face the camera.* **18 come clean** *Informal* to make a revelation or confession. *~n* **19** the act or an instance of cleaning: *the fridge could do with a clean.* ~See also **clean up.**

clean-cut *adj* **1** clearly outlined. **2** wholesome in appearance.

cleaner *n* **1** a person, device, or substance that removes dirt. **2** a shop or firm that provides a dry-cleaning service. **3 take someone to the cleaners** *Informal* to rob or defraud someone.

cleanly *adv* **1** easily or smoothly. **2** in a fair manner. *~adj* **-lier, -liest 3** habitually clean or neat. **cleanliness** *n*

cleanse *vb* **cleansing, cleansed 1** to remove dirt from. **2** to remove evil or guilt from. **cleanser** *n*

clean-shaven *adj* (of men) having the facial hair shaved off.

clean up *vb* **1** to make (something) free from dirt. **2** to make tidy or presentable. **3** to rid (a place) of undesirable people or conditions. **4** *Informal* to make a great profit. *~n* **cleanup 5** the process of cleaning up.

clear *adj* **1** free from doubt or confusion: *clear evidence of police thuggery.* **2** certain in the mind; sure: *I am still not clear about what they can and cannot do.* **3** easy to see or hear; distinct. **4** perceptive, alert: *clear thinking.* **5** evident or obvious: *it is not clear how he died.* **6** transparent: *clear glass doors.* **7** free from darkness or obscurity; bright. **8** (of sounds or the voice) not harsh or hoarse. **9** even and pure in tone or colour. **10** free of obstruction; open: *a clear path runs under the trees.* **11** (of weather) free from dullness or clouds. **12** without blemish or defect: *a clear skin.* **13** free of suspicion, guilt, or blame: *a clear conscience.* **14** (of money) without deduction; net. **15** free from debt or obligation. **16** without qualification or limitation; complete: *a clear lead.* *~adv* **17** in a clear or distinct manner. **18** completely. **19 clear of** out of the way of: *once we were clear of the harbour we headed east.* *~n* **20 in the clear** free of suspicion, guilt, or blame. *~vb* **21** to free from doubt or confusion. **22** to rid of objects or obstructions. **23** to make or form (a path) by removing obstructions. **24** to move or pass by or over without contact: *he cleared the fence easily.* **25** to make or become free from darkness or obscurity. **26** to rid (one's throat) of phlegm. **27 a** (of the weather) to become free from dullness, fog, or rain. **b** (of mist or fog) to disappear. **28** (of a cheque) to pass through one's bank and be charged against one's account. **29** to free from impurity or blemish. **30** to obtain or give (clearance). **31** to prove (someone) innocent of a crime or mistake. **32** to permit (someone) to see or handle classified information. **33** to make or

THESAURUS

classification arrangement, cataloguing, categorization, codification, grading, sorting, taxonomy

classify arrange, catalogue, categorize, codify, file, grade, pigeonhole, rank, sort, systematize, tabulate

clause article, chapter, item, paragraph, part, passage, point, section

claw 1. *n.* nail, pincer, talon **2.** *vb.* dig, graze, lacerate, mangle, maul, rip, scrabble, scrape, scratch, tear

clean *adj.* **1.** antiseptic, decontaminated, fresh, hygienic, immaculate, impeccable, pure, purified, sanitary, spotless, squeaky-clean, sterile, sterilized, unadulterated, unblemished, uncontaminated, unpolluted, unsoiled, unspotted, unstained, unsullied **2.** chaste, decent, exemplary, good, honourable, impeccable, innocent, moral, pure, respectable, undefiled, upright, virtuous **3.** fresh, laundered, washed **4.** complete, conclusive, decisive, entire, final, perfect, thorough, total, whole **5.** delicate, elegant, graceful, neat, simple, tidy, trim, uncluttered *~vb.* **6.** bath, cleanse, disinfect, launder, purge, purify, rinse, sanitize, scour, scrub, wash, wipe

clean-cut chiselled, clear, definite, etched, neat, outlined, sharp, trim, well-defined

cleanse 1. clean, clear, purge, purify, rinse, scour, scrub, wash **2.** absolve, purge, purify

cleanser detergent, disinfectant, purifier, scourer, soap, soap powder

clear *adj.* **1.** apparent, blatant, conspicuous, definite, distinct, evident, explicit, incontrovertible, manifest, obvious, palpable, patent, perceptible, plain, pronounced, unambiguous, unequivocal, unmistakable, unquestionable **2.** certain, convinced, decided, definite, positive, resolved, satisfied, sure **3.** crystalline,

gain (money) as profit. **34** to discharge or settle (a debt). **35 clear the air** to sort out a misunderstanding. ~See also **clear away, clear off,** etc. **clearly** *adv*

clearance *n* **1** the act of clearing: *slum clearance.* **2** permission for a vehicle or passengers to proceed. **3** official permission to have access to secret information or areas. **4** space between two parts in motion.

clearance sale *n* a sale in which a shop sells off unwanted goods at reduced prices.

clear away *vb* to remove (dishes, etc.) from the table after a meal.

clear-cut *adj* **1** easy to distinguish or understand: *there is no clear-cut distinction between safe and unsafe areas of the city.* **2** clearly outlined.

clearing *n* an area with few or no trees or shrubs in wooded or overgrown land.

clearing bank *n* (in Britain) any bank that makes use of the central clearing house in London.

clearing house *n* **1** *Banking* an institution where cheques and other commercial papers drawn on member banks are cancelled against each other so that only net balances are payable. **2** a central agency for the collection and distribution of information or materials.

clear off *vb Informal* to go away: often used as a command.

clear out *vb* **1** to remove and sort the contents of (a room or container). **2** *Informal* to go away: often used as a command.

clear up *vb* **1** to put (a place or thing that is disordered) in order. **2** to explain or solve (a mystery or misunderstanding). **3** (of an illness) to become better. **4** (of the weather) to become brighter.

clearway *n Brit* a stretch of road on which motorists may stop only in an emergency.

cleat *n* **1** a wedge-shaped block attached to a structure to act as a support. **2** a piece of wood or iron with two projecting ends round which ropes are fastened.

cleavage *n* **1** the space between a woman's breasts, as revealed by a low-cut dress. **2** a division or split. **3** (of crystals) the act of splitting or the tendency to split along definite planes so as to make smooth surfaces.

cleave[1] *vb* **cleaving; cleft, cleaved** *or* **clove; cleft, cleaved** *or* **cloven 1** to split apart: *cleave the stone along the fissures.* **2** to make by or as if by cutting: *a two-lane highway that cleaved its way through the northern extremities of the Everglades.*

cleave[2] *vb* **cleaving, cleaved** to cling or stick: *a farmhouse cleaved to the hill.*

cleaver *n* a heavy knife with a square blade, used for chopping meat.

cleavers *n* a plant with small white flowers and sticky fruits.

clef *n Music* a symbol placed at the beginning of each stave indicating the pitch of the music written after it.

cleft *n* **1** a narrow opening in a rock. **2** an indentation or split. ~*adj* **3 in a cleft stick** in a very difficult position. ~*vb* **4** a past of **cleave**[1].

cleft palate *n* a congenital crack in the mid line of the hard palate.

clematis *n* a climbing plant grown for its large colourful flowers.

clemency *n* mercy.

clement *adj* **1** (of the weather) mild. **2** merciful.

clementine *n* a citrus fruit resembling a tangerine.

clench *vb* **1** to close or squeeze together (the teeth or a fist) tightly. **2** to grasp or grip firmly. ~*n* **3** a firm grasp or grip.

clerestory (**clear**-store-ee) *n, pl* **-ries** a row of windows in the upper part of the wall of the nave of a church above the roof of the aisle.

clergy *n, pl* **-gies** priests and ministers as a group.

clergyman *n, pl* **-men** a member of the clergy.

cleric *n* a member of the clergy.

clerical *adj* **1** of clerks or office work: *a clerical job.* **2** of or associated with the clergy: *a Lebanese clerical leader.*

clerical collar *n* a stiff white collar with no opening at the front, worn by the clergy in certain Churches.

clerihew *n* a form of comic or satiric verse, consisting of two couplets and containing the name of a well-known person.

clerk *n* **1** an employee in an office, bank, or court who keeps records, files, and accounts. **2** *US & Canad* a hotel receptionist. **3** *Archaic* a scholar. ~*vb* **4** to work as a clerk. **clerkship** *n*

clerk of works *n* an employee who oversees building work.

clever *adj* **1** displaying sharp intelligence or mental alertness. **2** skilful with one's hands. **3** smart in a superficial way. **4** *Brit informal* sly or cunning. **cleverly** *adv* **cleverness** *n*

clianthus *n* a plant of Australia and New Zealand with clusters of ornamental scarlet flowers.

THESAURUS

glassy, limpid, pellucid (*literary*), see-through, translucent, transparent **4.** empty, free, open, smooth, unhampered, unhindered, unimpeded, unobstructed **5.** bright, cloudless, fair, fine, light, luminous, shining, sunny, unclouded, undimmed **6.** clean, guiltless, immaculate, innocent, pure, sinless, stainless, unblemished, undefiled, untarnished ~*vb.* **7.** disengage, disentangle, extricate, free, loosen, open, rid, unblock, unclog **8.** jump, leap, miss, pass over, vault **9.** break up, brighten, lighten **10.** clean, cleanse, purify, refine **11.** absolve, acquit, excuse, exonerate, justify, vindicate **12.** acquire, earn, gain, make, reap, secure

clearance 1. authorization, consent, endorsement, go-ahead (*informal*), green light, leave, O.K. *or* okay (*informal*), permission, sanction **2.** allowance, gap, headroom, margin

clear-cut definite, explicit, plain, precise, specific, straightforward, unambiguous, unequivocal

clearly beyond doubt, distinctly, evidently, incontestably, incontrovertibly, markedly, obviously, openly, overtly, undeniably, undoubtedly

clear out 1. empty, get rid of, sort, tidy up **2.** *informal* beat it (*slang*), decamp, depart, hook it (*slang*), leave, make oneself scarce, retire, slope off (*informal*), take oneself off, withdraw

clear up 1. order, rearrange, tidy (up) **2.** answer, clarify, elucidate, explain, resolve, solve, straighten out, unravel

cleave crack, divide, hew, open, part, rend, sever, slice, split, sunder, tear asunder

clergy churchmen, clergymen, clerics, ecclesiastics, ministry, priesthood

clergyman chaplain, cleric, curate, divine, man of God, minister, padre, parson, pastor, priest, rector, reverend (*informal*), vicar

clerical 1. book-keeping, office, secretarial **2.** ecclesiastical, pastoral, priestly, sacerdotal (*formal*)

clever 1. astute, brainy (*informal*), bright, intelligent, knowing, knowledgeable, quick, quick-witted, rational, sagacious, sensible, smart **2.** able, adroit, capable, dexterous, expert, gifted, skilful, talented **3.** *informal* canny, cunning, deep, shrewd

cleverness 1. astuteness, brains, brightness, intelligence, nous (*Brit. slang*), quickness, quick wits, sagacity, sense, sharpness, smartness, smarts (*slang, chiefly*

cliché (**klee**-shay) *n* an expression or idea that is no longer effective because of overuse. **clichéd** *or* **cliché'd** *adj*

click *n* **1** a short light often metallic sound. *~vb* **2** to make a clicking sound: *cameras clicked and whirred.* **3** Also: **click on** *Computers* to press and release (a button on a mouse) or select (a particular function) by pressing and releasing a button on a mouse. **4** *Informal* to become suddenly clear: *it wasn't until I saw the photograph that everything clicked into place.* **5** *Slang* (of two people) to get on well together: *I met him at a dinner party and we clicked straight away.* **6** *Slang* to be a great success: *the film cost so much that if it hadn't clicked at the box office we'd have been totally wiped out.*

client *n* **1** someone who uses the services of a professional person or organization. **2** a customer.

clientele (klee-on-**tell**) *n* customers or clients collectively.

cliff *n* a steep rock face, esp. along the seashore.

cliffhanger *n* a film, game, etc. which is exciting and full of suspense because its outcome is uncertain. **cliffhanging** *adj*

climacteric *n* **1** same as **menopause. 2** the period in the life of a man corresponding to the menopause, during which sexual drive and fertility diminish.

climate *n* **1** the typical weather conditions of an area. **2** an area with a particular kind of climate. **3** a prevailing trend: *the current economic climate.* **climatic** *adj* **climatically** *adv*

climax *n* **1** the most intense or highest point of an experience or of a series of events: *a striking climax to the year's efforts to promote tourism.* **2** a decisive moment in a dramatic or other work: *the film has a climax set atop a gale-swept lighthouse.* **3** an orgasm. *~vb* **4** *Not universally accepted* to reach or bring to a climax. **climactic** *adj*

climb *vb* **1** to go up or ascend (stairs, a mountain, etc.). **2** to move or go with difficulty: *she climbed through a window.* **3** to rise to a higher point or intensity: *I grew increasingly delirious as my temperature climbed.* **4** to increase in value or amount: *the shares climbed 7p to 151p.* **5** to ascend in social position: *he climbed the ranks of the organization.* **6** (of plants) to grow upwards by twining, using tendrils or suckers. **7** to incline or slope upwards: *the road climbed up through the foothills.* **8** **climb into** *Informal* to put on or get into: *I climbed into the van.* *~n* **9** the act or an instance of climbing. **10** a place or thing to be climbed, esp. a route in mountaineering. **climbable** *adj* **climber** *n* **climbing** *n, adj*

climb down *vb* **1** to retreat (from an opinion or position). *~n* **climb-down 2** a retreat from an opinion or position.

clime *n Poetic* a region or its climate.

clinch *vb* **1** to settle (an argument or agreement) decisively. **2** to secure (a nail) by bending the protruding point over. **3** to engage in a clinch, as in boxing or wrestling. *~n* **4** the act of clinching. **5** *Boxing, wrestling* a movement in which one or both competitors hold on to the other to avoid punches or regain wind. **6** *Slang* a lovers' embrace.

clincher *n Informal* something decisive, such as fact, argument, or point scored.

cling *vb* **clinging, clung 1** to hold fast or stick closely. **2** to be emotionally overdependent on. **3** to continue to do or believe in: *he clings to the belief that people are capable of change.* **clinging** *or* **clingy** *adj*

clingfilm *n* a thin polythene material used for wrapping food.

clinic *n* **1** a place in which outpatients are given medical treatment or advice. **2** a similar place staffed by specialist physicians or surgeons: *an antenatal clinic.* **3** *Brit* a private hospital or nursing home. **4** the teaching of medicine to students at the bedside.

clinical *adj* **1** of or relating to the observation and treatment of patients directly: *clinical trials of a new drug.* **2** of or relating to a clinic. **3** logical and unemotional: *they have a somewhat clinical attitude to their children's upbringing.* **4** (of a room or buildings) plain, simple, and usually unattractive. **clinically** *adv*

clinical thermometer *n* a thermometer for measuring the temperature of the body.

clink[1] *vb* **1** to make a light sharp metallic sound. *~n* **2** such a sound.

clink[2] *n Slang* prison.

clinker *n* the fused coal left over in a fire or furnace.

clinker-built *adj* (of a boat or ship) with a hull made from overlapping planks.

clip[1] *vb* **clipping, clipped 1** to cut or trim with scissors or shears. **2** to remove a short section from (a film or newspaper). **3** *Brit* to punch a hole in (something, esp. a ticket). **4** *Informal* to strike with a sharp, often slanting, blow. **5** to shorten (a word). *~n* **6** the act of clipping. **7** a short extract from a film. **8** something that has been clipped. **9** *Informal* a sharp, often slanting, blow: *a clip on the ear.* **10** *Informal* speed: *proceeding at a smart clip.* **11** *Austral & NZ* the total quantity of wool shorn, as in one place or season.

clip[2] *n* **1** a device for attaching or holding things together. **2** an article of jewellery that can be clipped onto a dress or hat. **3** short for **paperclip** or **car-**

THESAURUS

U.S.), suss (*slang*) **2.** ability, adroitness, dexterity, flair, gift, talent **3.** canniness, shrewdness

cliché banality, bromide, chestnut (*informal*), commonplace, platitude, stereotype, truism

click *n.* **1.** beat, clack, snap, tick *~vb.* **2.** beat, clack, snap, tick **3.** *informal* become clear, come home (to), fall into place, make sense **4.** *slang* be compatible, be on the same wavelength, get on, hit it off (*informal*), take to each other

client buyer, consumer, customer, habitué, patron, shopper

clientele business, clients, customers, following, market, patronage, regulars, trade

cliff bluff, crag, escarpment, face, overhang, precipice, rock face, scar, scarp

climactic climactical, critical, crucial, decisive, paramount, peak

climate 1. clime, temperature, weather **2.** country, region **3.** ambience, disposition, feeling, mood, temper, tendency, trend

climax 1. *n.* acme, apogee, crest, culmination, head, height, highlight, high spot (*informal*), pay-off (*informal*), peak, summit, top, zenith **2.** *vb.* come to a head, culminate, peak

climb ascend, clamber, mount, rise, scale, shin up, soar, top

climb down back down, eat one's words, retract, retreat

clinch 1. conclude, confirm, decide, determine, seal, secure, set the seal on, settle, sew up (*informal*), verify **2.** bolt, clamp, fasten, fix, make fast, nail, rivet, secure **3.** clutch, embrace, grasp, hug, squeeze

cling adhere, attach to, clasp, cleave to, clutch, embrace, fasten, grasp, grip, hug, stick, twine round

clip[1] **1.** *vb.* crop, cut, dock, pare, prune, shear, shorten, snip, trim **2.** *n./vb. informal* belt (*informal*), box, clout (*informal*), cuff, knock, punch, smack, thump,

tridge clip. ~*vb* **clipping, clipped 4** to attach or hold together with a clip.

clipboard *n* a portable writing board with a clip at the top for holding paper.

clip joint *n Slang* a nightclub in which customers are overcharged.

clipped *adj* (of speech) abrupt, clearly pronounced, and using as few words as possible.

clipper *n* a fast commercial sailing ship.

clippers *pl n* a tool used for clipping and cutting.

clippie *n Brit Old-fashioned informal* a bus conductress.

clipping *n* something cut out, esp. an article from a newspaper.

clique (**kleek**) *n* a small exclusive group of friends or associates. **cliquey cliquy** *or* **cliquish** *adj*

clitoris (**klit**-or-riss) *n* a small sexually sensitive organ at the front of the vulva. **clitoral** *adj*

Cllr councillor.

cloaca (kloh-**ake**-a) *n, pl* **-cae** a cavity in most animals, except higher mammals, into which the alimentary canal and the genital and urinary ducts open.

cloak *n* **1** a loose sleeveless outer garment, fastened at the throat and falling straight from the shoulders. **2** something that covers or conceals. ~*vb* **3** to hide or disguise. **4** to cover with or as if with a cloak.

cloak-and-dagger *adj* of or involving mystery and secrecy.

cloakroom *n* **1** a room in which coats may be left temporarily. **2** *Brit euphemistic* a toilet.

clobber[1] *vb Informal* **1** to batter. **2** to defeat utterly. **3** to criticize severely.

clobber[2] *n Brit informal* personal belongings, such as clothes.

cloche (**klosh**) *n* **1** a small glass or plastic cover for protecting young plants. **2** a woman's close-fitting hat.

clock[1] *n* **1** a device for showing the time, either through pointers that revolve over a numbered dial, or through a display of figures. **2** a device with a dial for recording or measuring. **3** the downy head of a dandelion that has gone to seed. **4** short for **time clock. 5** *Informal* same as **speedometer** or **mileometer. 6** *Brit slang* the face. **7 round the clock** all day and all night. ~*vb* **8** to record (time) with a stopwatch, esp. in the calculation of speed. **9** *Brit, Austral, & NZ slang* to strike, esp. on the face or head. **10** *Informal* to turn back the mileometer on (a car) illegally so that its mileage appears less. **11** *Brit slang* to see or notice.

clock[2] *n* an ornamental design on the side of a sock.

clock in *or* **on** *vb* to register one's arrival at work on an automatic time recorder.

clock out *or* **off** *vb* to register one's departure from work on an automatic time recorder.

clock up *vb* to record or reach (a total): *he has now clocked up over 500 games for the club.*

clockwise *adv, adj* in the direction in which the hands of a clock rotate.

clockwork *n* **1** a mechanism similar to that of a spring-driven clock, as in a wind-up toy. **2 like clockwork** with complete regularity and precision.

clod *n* **1** a lump of earth or clay. **2** a dull or stupid person. **cloddish** *adj*

clodhopper *n Informal* **1** a clumsy person. **2 clodhoppers** large heavy shoes.

clog *vb* **clogging, clogged 1** to obstruct or become obstructed with thick or sticky matter. **2** to encumber. **3** to stick in a mass. ~*n* **4** a wooden or wooden-soled shoe.

cloisonné (klwah-**zon**-nay) *n* a design made by filling in a wire outline with coloured enamel.

cloister *n* **1** a covered pillared walkway within a religious building. **2** a place of religious seclusion, such as a monastery. ~*vb* **3** to confine or seclude in or as if in a monastery.

cloistered *adj* sheltered or protected.

clomp *n, vb* same as **clump** (senses 2, 3).

clone *n* **1** a group of organisms or cells of the same genetic constitution that have been reproduced asexually from a single plant or animal. **2** *Informal* a person who closely resembles another. ~*vb* **cloning, cloned 3** to produce as a clone. **4** *Informal* to produce near copies of (a person). **cloning** *n*

clonk *vb* **1** to make a loud dull thud. **2** *Informal* to hit. ~*n* **3** a loud thud.

close[1] *vb* **closing, closed 1** to shut: *he lay back and closed his eyes.* **2** to bar, obstruct, or fill up (an entrance, a hole, etc.): *the blockades had closed major roads, railways and border crossings.* **3** to cease or cause to cease giving service: *both stores closed at 9 p.m.; the Shipping Company closed its offices in Bangkok.* **4** to end; terminate: *"Never," she said, so firmly that it closed the subject.* **5** (of agreements or deals) to complete or be completed successfully. **6** to come closer (to): *he was still in second place but closing fast on the leader.* **7** to take hold: *his small fingers closed around the coin.* **8** *Stock Exchange* to have a value at the end of a day's trading, as specified: *the pound closed four-and-a-half cents higher.* **9** to join the ends or edges of something: *to close a circuit.* ~*n* **10** the act of closing. **11** the end or conclusion: *the close of play.* **12** *Brit* a courtyard or quadrangle enclosed by buildings. **13** *Scot* the entry from the street to a tenement building. ~See also **close down, close in,** etc.

close[2] *adj* **1** near in space or time. **2** intimate: *we were such close friends in those days.* **3** near in relationship: *the dead man seems to have had no close relatives.* **4** careful, strict, or searching: *their research will not stand up to close scrutiny.* **5** having the parts near together: *a close formation.* **6** near to the surface; short: *an NCO's haircut, cropped close on top, shaved clean at sides and back.* **7** almost equal: *a close game.* **8** not deviating or varying greatly from something: *a close resemblance.* **9** confined or enclosed. **10** oppressive, heavy, or airless: *damp, close weather.* **11** strictly guarded: *he had been placed in close arrest.* **12** secretive or reticent. **13** miserly; not generous. **14** re-

THESAURUS

wallop (*informal*), whack **3.** *n. informal* gallop, lick (*informal*), rate, speed, velocity

clip[2] *vb.* attach, fasten, fix, hold, pin, staple

clique cabal, circle, clan, coterie, crew (*informal*), crowd, faction, gang, group, mob, pack, posse (*informal*), schism, set

cloak *n.* **1.** cape, coat, mantle, wrap **2.** blind, cover, front, mask, pretext, shield ~*vb.* **3.** camouflage, conceal, cover, disguise, hide, mask, obscure, screen, veil

clog *vb.* **1.** block, bung, congest, dam up, jam, obstruct, occlude, stop up **2.** burden, hamper, hinder, impede, shackle

cloistered confined, insulated, secluded, sequestered, sheltered, shielded, shut off, withdrawn

close[1] *vb.* **1.** bar, block, bung, choke, clog, cork, fill, lock, obstruct, plug, seal, secure, shut, shut up, stop up **2.** axe (*informal*), cease, conclude, discontinue, end, finish, shut down, terminate, wind up **3.** come together, connect, couple, join, unite ~*n.* **4.** cessation, completion, conclusion, culmination, denouement, end, ending, finale, finish, termination

close[2] **1.** adjacent, adjoining, approaching, at hand,

stricted as to public admission or membership. *~adv* **15** closely; tightly. **16** near or in proximity. **closely** *adv* **closeness** *n*

closed *adj* **1** blocked against entry. **2** only admitting a selected group of people; exclusive: *he had a fairly closed circle of friends.* **3** not open to question or debate. **4** *Maths* **a** (of a curve or surface) completely enclosing an area or volume. **b** (of a set) made up of members on which a specific operation, such as addition, gives as its result another existing member of the set.

closed circuit *n* a complete electrical circuit through which current can flow.

closed-circuit television *n* a television system used within a limited area such as a building.

close down *vb* **1** to stop operating or working: *the factory closed down many years ago.* *~n* **close-down** **2** *Brit radio, television* the end of a period of broadcasting.

closed shop *n* a place of work in which all workers must belong to a particular trade union.

close harmony *n* a type of singing in which all parts except the bass lie close together.

close in *vb* **1** (of days) to become shorter with the approach of winter. **2 close in on** to advance on so as to encircle or surround.

close quarters *pl n* **at close quarters a** engaged in hand-to-hand combat. **b** very near together.

close season *n* the period of the year when it is illegal to kill certain game or fish.

close shave *n Informal* a narrow escape.

closet *n* **1** *US* a small cupboard. **2** a small private room. **3** short for **water closet.** *~adj* **4** private or secret: *a closet homosexual.* *~vb* **-eting, -eted 5** to shut away in private, esp. in order to talk: *he was closeted with the President.*

close-up *n* **1** a photograph or film or television shot taken at close range. **2** a detailed or intimate view or examination. *~vb* **close up 3** to shut entirely: *every other shop front seemed to be closed up.* **4** to draw together: *the ranks closed up and marched on.* **5** (of wounds) to heal completely.

close with *vb* to engage in battle with (an enemy).

closure *n* **1** the act of closing or the state of being closed. **2** something that closes or shuts. **3** a procedure by which a debate may be stopped and an immediate vote taken.

clot *n* **1** a soft thick lump formed from liquid. **2** *Brit informal* a stupid person. *~vb* **clotting, clotted 3** to form soft thick lumps.

cloth *n, pl* **cloths 1** a fabric formed by weaving, felting, or knitting fibres. **2** a piece of such fabric used for a particular purpose. **3 the cloth** the clergy.

clothe *vb* **clothing, clothed** *or* **clad 1** to put clothes on. **2** to provide with clothes. **3** to cover or envelop (something) so as to change its appearance: *a small valley clothed in thick woodland.*

clothes *pl n* **1** articles of dress. **2** *Chiefly Brit* short for **bedclothes.**

clotheshorse *n* **1** a frame on which to hang laundry for drying or airing. **2** a person who is extremely concerned with his or her appearance.

clothesline *n* a piece of rope from which clean washing is hung to dry.

clothes peg *n* a small wooden or plastic clip for attaching washing to a clothesline.

clothier *n* a person who makes or sells clothes or cloth.

clothing *n* **1** garments collectively. **2** something that covers or clothes.

clotted cream *n Brit* a thick cream made from scalded milk.

cloud *n* **1** a mass of water or ice particles visible in the sky. **2** a floating mass of smoke, dust, etc. **3** a large number of insects or other small animals in flight. **4** something that darkens, threatens, or carries gloom. **5 in the clouds** not in contact with reality. **6 on cloud nine** *Informal* elated; very happy. **7 under a cloud a** under reproach or suspicion. **b** in a state of gloom or bad temper. *~vb* **8** to make or become more difficult to see through: *my glasses kept clouding up; mud clouded the water.* **9** to confuse or impair: *his judgment was no longer clouded by alcohol.* **10** to make or become gloomy or depressed: *insanity clouded the last years of his life.* ~See also **cloud over. cloudless** *adj*

cloudburst *n* a heavy fall of rain.

cloud chamber *n Physics* an apparatus for detecting high-energy particles by observing their tracks through a chamber containing a supersaturated vapour.

cloud-cuckoo-land *n* a place of fantasy or impractical ideas.

cloud over *vb* **1** (of the sky or weather) to become cloudy: *it was clouding over and we thought it would rain.* **2** (of a person's face or eyes) to suddenly look gloomy or depressed: *Grace's face clouded over and she turned away.*

cloudy *adj* **cloudier, cloudiest 1** covered with cloud or clouds. **2** (of liquids) opaque or muddy. **3** confused or unclear. **cloudily** *adv* **cloudiness** *n*

clout *n* **1** *Informal* a fairly hard blow. **2** power or influence. *~vb* **3** *Informal* to hit hard.

clove[1] *n* a dried closed flower bud of a tropical tree, used as a spice.

clove[2] *n* a segment of a bulb of garlic.

THESAURUS

handy, imminent, impending, near, nearby, neighbouring, nigh (*archaic or poetic*), upcoming **2.** attached, confidential, dear, devoted, familiar, inseparable, intimate, loving **3.** alert, assiduous, attentive, careful, concentrated, detailed, intense, intent, keen, minute, painstaking, rigorous, searching, thorough **4.** compact, congested, cramped, crowded, dense, impenetrable, jam-packed, packed, solid, thick, tight **5.** accurate, exact, faithful, literal, precise, strict **6.** airless, confined, frowsty, fuggy, heavy, humid, muggy, oppressive, stale, stifling, stuffy, suffocating, sweltering, thick, unventilated **7.** private, reticent, secret, secretive, taciturn, uncommunicative, unforthcoming **8.** illiberal, mean, mingy (*Brit. informal*), miserly, near, niggardly, parsimonious, penurious (*formal*), stingy, tight-fisted, ungenerous

closed 1. fastened, locked, sealed, shut **2.** exclusive, restricted **3.** concluded, decided, ended, finished, over, resolved, settled, terminated

cloth fabric, material, stuff, textiles

clothe array, attire, cover, deck, doll up (*slang*), drape, dress, equip, fit out, garb, get ready, outfit, rig, robe, swathe

clothes, clothing apparel, attire, clobber (*Brit. slang*), costume, dress, duds (*informal*), ensemble, garb, garments, gear (*informal*), get-up (*informal*), glad rags (*informal*), outfit, raiment (*archaic or poetic*), rigout (*informal*), togs (*informal*), vestments, wardrobe, wear

cloud *n.* **1.** billow, fog, haze, mist, nebula, vapour **2.** crowd, flock, horde, host, mass, multitude, shower, swarm, throng *~vb.* **3.** darken, dim, eclipse, obscure, overcast, overshadow, shade, shadow, veil **4.** confuse, disorient, distort, impair, muddle

clove[2] *vb* a past tense of **cleave**[1].

clove hitch *n* a knot used to fasten a rope to a spar or a larger rope.

cloven *vb* **1** a past participle of **cleave**[1]. *~adj* **2** split or divided.

cloven hoof *or* **foot** *n* the divided hoof of a pig, goat, cow, or deer.

clover *n* **1** a plant with three-lobed leaves and dense flower heads. **2 in clover** *Informal* in ease or luxury.

clown *n* **1** a comic entertainer, usually bizarrely dressed and made up, appearing in the circus. **2** an amusing person. **3** a clumsy rude person. *~vb* **4** to behave foolishly. **5** to perform as a clown. **clownish** *adj*

cloying *adj* so sweet or pleasurable that it ultimately becomes sickly: *cloying sentimentality.* **cloyingly** *adv*

club *n* **1** a group or association of people with common aims or interests. **2** the building used by such a group. **3** a stout stick used as a weapon. **4** a stick or bat used to strike the ball in various sports, esp. golf. **5** an establishment or regular event at which people dance to records; disco: *a new weekly club with resident DJ.* **6** a building in which members go to meet, dine, read, etc. **7** *Chiefly Brit* an organization, esp. in a shop, set up as a means of saving. **8** a playing card marked with one or more black trefoil symbols. **9** short for **Indian club.** *~vb* **clubbing, clubbed 10** to beat with a club. **11 club together** to combine resources or efforts for a common purpose.

club foot *n* a congenital deformity of the foot.

clubhouse *n* the premises of a sports or other club, esp. a golf club.

club root *n* a fungal disease of cabbages and related plants, in which the roots become thickened and distorted.

cluck *n* **1** the low clicking noise made by a hen. *~vb* **2** (of a hen) to make a clicking sound. **3** to express (a feeling) by making a similar sound: *the landlady was clucking feverishly behind them.*

clue *n* **1** something that helps to solve a problem or unravel a mystery. **2 not have a clue a** to be completely baffled. **b** to be ignorant or incompetent. *~adj* **3 clued-up** shrewd and well-informed.

clueless *adj Slang* helpless or stupid.

clump *n* **1** a small group of things or people together. **2** a dull heavy tread. *~vb* **3** to walk or tread heavily. **4** to form into clumps. **clumpy** *adj*

clumsy *adj* **-sier, -siest 1** lacking in skill or physical coordination. **2** badly made or done. **3** said or done without thought or tact: *I took the clumsy hint and left.* **clumsily** *adv* **clumsiness** *n*

clung *vb* the past of **cling.**

clunk *n* **1** a dull metallic sound. *~vb* **2** to make such a sound.

cluster *n* **1** a number of things growing, fastened, or occurring close together. **2** a number of people or things grouped together. *~vb* **3** to gather or be gathered in clusters.

clutch[1] *vb* **1** to seize with or as if with hands or claws. **2** to grasp or hold firmly. **3 clutch at** to attempt to get hold or possession of. *~n* **4** a device that enables two revolving shafts to be joined or disconnected, esp. one that transmits the drive from the engine to the gearbox in a vehicle. **5** the pedal which operates the clutch in a car. **6** a firm grasp. **7 clutches a** hands or claws in the act of clutching: *his free kick escaped the clutches of the rival goalkeeper.* **b** power or control: *rescued from the clutches of the Gestapo.*

clutch[2] *n* **1** a set of eggs laid at the same time. **2** a group, bunch, or cluster: *a clutch of gloomy economic reports.*

clutch bag *n* a handbag without handles.

clutter *vb* **1** to scatter objects about (a place) in an untidy manner. *~n* **2** an untidy heap or mass of objects. **3** a state of untidiness.

Clydesdale *n* a heavy powerful carthorse, originally from Scotland.

cm centimetre.

Cm *Chem* curium.

CND Campaign for Nuclear Disarmament.

CNS *Biol* central nervous system.

Co *Chem* cobalt.

CO 1 Colorado. **2** Commanding Officer.

Co.[1] *or* **co. 1** Company. **2 and co** *Informal* and the rest of them: *Harold and co.*

Co.[2] County.

co- *prefix* **1** together; joint or jointly: *coproduction.* **2** indicating partnership or equality: *co-star; copilot.* **3** to the same or a similar degree: *coextend.* **4** (in mathematics and astronomy) of the complement of an angle: *cosecant.*

c/o 1 care of. **2** *Book-keeping* carried over.

coach *n* **1** a large comfortable single-decker bus used for sightseeing or long-distance travel. **2** a railway carriage. **3** a large four-wheeled enclosed carriage, usually horse-drawn. **4** a trainer or instructor: *the coach of the Mexican national team.* **5** a tutor who prepares students for examinations. *~vb* **6** to train or teach. **coaching** *n*

coachman *n, pl* **-men** the driver of a horse-drawn coach or carriage.

coachwork *n* the body of a car.

coagulate (koh-**ag**-yew-late) *vb* **-lating, -lated** to

THESAURUS

cloudy 1. dark, dim, dismal, dull, dusky, gloomy, leaden, louring *or* lowering, overcast, sombre, sullen, sunless **2.** muddy, murky, opaque **3.** blurred, confused, hazy, indistinct, nebulous, obscure

clown *n.* **1.** buffoon, comedian, dolt, fool, harlequin, jester, joker, Pierrot, Punchinello **2.** boor, clodhopper (*informal*), yahoo *~vb.* **3.** act the fool, act the goat, jest, mess about, piss about (*taboo slang*), piss around (*taboo slang*)

club *n.* **1.** association, circle, clique, company, fraternity, group, guild, lodge, order, set, society, union **2.** bat, bludgeon, cosh (*Brit.*), cudgel, stick, truncheon *~vb.* **3.** bash, baste, batter, beat, bludgeon, clobber (*slang*), clout (*informal*), cosh (*Brit.*), hammer, pummel, strike

clue evidence, hint, indication, inkling, intimation, lead, pointer, sign, suggestion, tip, tip-off

clump 1. *n.* bunch, bundle, cluster, mass **2.** *vb.* clomp, lumber, plod, stamp, stomp, thud, thump, tramp

clumsy accident-prone, awkward, blundering, bumbling, bungling, butterfingered (*informal*), cack-handed (*informal*), gauche, gawky, ham-fisted (*informal*), ham-handed (*informal*), ill-shaped, inept, inexpert, klutzy (*U.S. & Canad. slang*), lumbering, maladroit, ponderous, uncoordinated, ungainly, unhandy, unskilful, unwieldy

cluster 1. *n.* assemblage, batch, bunch, clump, collection, gathering, group, knot **2.** *vb.* assemble, bunch, collect, flock, gather, group

clutch catch (up), clasp, cling to, embrace, fasten, grab, grasp, grip, seize, snatch

clutches 1. claws, grasp, grip, hands **2.** control, custody, hands, keeping, possession, power, sway

clutter 1. *vb.* litter, scatter, strew **2.** *n.* confusion, disarray, disorder, hotchpotch, jumble, litter, mess, muddle, untidiness

change from a liquid into a soft semisolid mass; clot. **coagulant** *n* **coagulation** *n*

coal *n* **1** a compact black or dark brown rock consisting largely of carbon formed from partially decomposed vegetation: a fuel and a source of coke, coal gas, and coal tar. **2** one or more lumps of coal. **3 coals to Newcastle** something supplied to a place where it is already plentiful.

coalesce (koh-a-**less**) *vb* **-lescing, -lesced** to unite or come together in one body or mass. **coalescence** *n* **coalescent** *adj*

coalface *n* the exposed seam of coal in a mine.

coalfield *n* an area rich in deposits of coal.

coal gas *n* a mixture of gases produced by the distillation of bituminous coal and used for heating and lighting.

coalition (koh-a-**lish**-un) *n* a temporary alliance, esp. between political parties.

coal scuttle *n* a container for holding coal for a domestic fire.

coal tar *n* a black tar, produced by the distillation of bituminous coal, used for making drugs and chemical products.

coal tit *n* a small songbird with a black head with a white patch on the nape.

coaming *n* a raised frame round a ship's hatchway for keeping out water.

coarse *adj* **1** rough in texture or structure. **2** unrefined or indecent: *coarse humour.* **3** of inferior quality. **coarsely** *adv* **coarseness** *n*

coarse fish *n* a freshwater fish that is not of the salmon family. **coarse fishing** *n*

coarsen *vb* to make or become coarse.

coast *n* **1** the place where the land meets the sea. **2 the coast is clear** *Informal* the obstacles or dangers are gone. *~vb* **3** to move by momentum or force of gravity, without the use of power. **4** to proceed without great effort: *they coasted to a 31-9 win in the pairs.* **coastal** *adj*

coaster *n* **1** a small mat placed under a bottle or glass to protect a table. **2** *Brit* a small ship used for coastal trade.

coastguard *n* **1** an organization which aids shipping, saves lives at sea, and prevents smuggling. **2** a member of this.

coastline *n* the outline of a coast.

coat *n* **1** an outer garment with sleeves, covering the body from the shoulders to below the waist. **2** the hair, wool, or fur of an animal. **3** any layer that covers a surface. *~vb* **4** to cover with a layer.

coat hanger *n* a curved piece of wood, wire, or plastic, fitted with a hook and used to hang up clothes.

coating *n* a layer or film spread over a surface.

coat of arms *n* the heraldic emblem of a family or organization.

coat of mail *n History* a protective garment made of linked metal rings or plates.

coax *vb* **1** to persuade (someone) gently. **2** to obtain (something) by persistent coaxing. **3** to work on (something) carefully and patiently so as to make it function as desired: *I watched him coax the last few drops of beer out of his glass.*

coaxial (koh-**ax**-ee-al) *adj* **1** *Electronics* (of a cable) transmitting by means of two concentric conductors separated by an insulator. **2** having a common axis.

cob *n* **1** a male swan. **2** a thickset type of horse. **3** the stalk of an ear of maize. **4** *Brit* a round loaf of bread. **5** *Brit* a hazel tree or hazelnut.

cobalt *n Chem* a brittle hard silvery-white metallic element used in alloys. Symbol: Co

cobber *n Austral & NZ* friend.

cobble *n* a cobblestone.

cobbled *adj* (of a street or road) paved with cobblestones.

cobbler *n* a person who makes or mends shoes.

cobblers *pl n Brit taboo slang* nonsense.

cobblestone *n* a rounded stone used for paving.

cobble together *vb* **-bling, -bled** to put together clumsily: *a coalition cobbled together from parties with widely differing aims.*

COBOL *n* a high-level computer programming language designed for general commercial use.

cobra *n* a highly venomous hooded snake of tropical Africa and Asia.

cobweb *n* **1** a web spun by certain spiders. **2** a single thread of such a web. **cobwebbed** *adj* **cobwebby** *adj*

cobwebs *pl n* mustiness, confusion, or obscurity: *her election dusted away the cobwebs that normally surround the presidency.*

coca *n* the dried leaves of a S American shrub which contain cocaine.

Coca-Cola *n Trademark* a carbonated soft drink.

cocaine *n* an addictive drug derived from coca leaves, used as a narcotic and local anaesthetic.

coccyx (**kok**-six) *n, pl* **coccyges** (kok-**sije**-eez) *Anat* a small triangular bone at the base of the spine in human beings and some apes.

cochineal *n* a scarlet dye obtained from a Mexican insect, used for colouring food.

cochlea (**kok**-lee-a) *n, pl* **-leae** (-lee-ee) *Anat* the spiral tube in the internal ear, which converts sound vibrations into nerve impulses.

cock *n* **1** a male bird, esp. of domestic fowl. **2** a stopcock. **3** *Taboo slang* a penis. **4** the hammer of a gun. **5** *Brit informal* friend: used as a term of address. *~vb* **6** to draw back the hammer of (a gun) so that it is ready

THESAURUS

coach *n.* **1.** bus, car, carriage, charabanc (*Brit. old-fashioned*), vehicle **2.** instructor, teacher, trainer, tutor *~vb.* **3.** drill, exercise, instruct, prepare, train, tutor

coalesce amalgamate, blend, cohere, combine, come together, commingle, consolidate, fuse, incorporate, integrate, meld, merge, mix, unite

coalition affiliation, alliance, amalgamation, association, bloc, combination, compact, confederacy, confederation, conjunction, fusion, integration, league, merger, union

coarse 1. coarse-grained, crude, homespun, rough-hewn, unfinished, unpolished, unrefined **2.** bawdy, boorish, brutish, earthy, foul-mouthed, immodest, impolite, improper, impure, indelicate, inelegant, loutish, offensive, raunchy (*slang*), ribald, rough, rude, smutty, vulgar

coarsen blunt, callous, deaden, desensitize, dull, harden, roughen

coarseness bawdiness, boorishness, crudity, earthiness, indelicacy, offensiveness, poor taste, ribaldry, roughness, smut, smuttiness

coast 1. *n.* beach, border, coastline, littoral, seaboard, seaside, shore, strand **2.** *vb.* cruise, drift, freewheel, get by, glide, sail, taxi

coat *n.* **1.** fleece, fur, hair, hide, pelt, skin, wool **2.** coating, covering, layer, overlay *~vb.* **3.** apply, cover, plaster, smear, spread

coating blanket, coat, covering, dusting, film, finish, glaze, lamination, layer, membrane, patina, sheet, skin, varnish, veneer

coax allure, beguile, cajole, entice, flatter, inveigle,

to fire. **7** to lift and turn (part of the body) in a particular direction. ~See also **cockup.**

cockabully *n* a small fresh-water fish of New Zealand.

cockade *n* a feather or rosette worn on the hat as a badge.

cock-a-hoop *adj* in very high spirits.

cock-a-leekie *n* a Scottish soup of chicken boiled with leeks.

cock-and-bull story *n Informal* an obviously improbable story, esp. one used as an excuse.

cockatoo *n, pl* **-toos 1** a light-coloured crested parrot of Australia and the East Indies. **2** *Austral & NZ* a small farmer or settler.

cockchafer *n* a large flying beetle.

cocked hat *n* **1** a hat with three corners and a turned-up brim. **2 knock into a cocked hat** *Slang* to outdo or defeat.

cockerel *n* a young domestic cock, less than a year old.

cocker spaniel *n* a small spaniel.

cockeyed *adj Informal* **1** crooked or askew. **2** foolish or absurd. **3** cross-eyed.

cockfight *n* a fight between two gamecocks fitted with sharp metal spurs.

cockle *n* **1** an edible bivalve shellfish. **2** its shell. **3 warm the cockles of one's heart** to make one feel happy.

cockleshell *n* **1** the rounded shell of the cockle. **2** a small light boat.

cockney *n* **1** a native of London, esp. of its East End. **2** the urban dialect of London or its East End. *~adj* **3** characteristic of cockneys or their dialect.

cockpit *n* **1** the compartment in an aircraft for the pilot and crew. **2** the driver's compartment in a racing car. **3** *Naut* a space in a small vessel containing the wheel and tiller. **4** the site of many battles or conflicts: *the south of the country is a cockpit of conflicting interests.* **5** an enclosure used for cockfights.

cockroach *n* a beetle-like insect which is a household pest.

cockscomb *n* same as **coxcomb.**

cocksure *adj* overconfident or arrogant.

cocktail *n* **1** a mixed alcoholic drink. **2** an appetizer of seafood or mixed fruits. **3** any combination of diverse elements: *Central America was a cocktail of death, poverty, and destruction.*

cockup *Brit slang ~n* **1** something done badly. *~vb* **cock up 2** to ruin or spoil.

cocky[1] *adj* **cockier, cockiest** excessively proud of oneself. **cockily** *adv* **cockiness** *n*

cocky[2] *n, pl* **cockies** *Austral & NZ informal* short for **cockatoo** (sense 2).

coco *n, pl* **-cos** the coconut palm.

cocoa *or* **cacao** *n* **1** a powder made by roasting and grinding cocoa beans. **2** a hot or cold drink made from cocoa powder.

cocoa bean *n* a cacao seed.

cocoa butter *n* a fatty solid obtained from cocoa beans and used for confectionery and toiletries.

coconut *n* **1** the fruit of a type of palm tree (**coconut palm**), which has a thick fibrous oval husk and a thin hard shell enclosing edible white flesh. The hollow centre is filled with a milky fluid (**coconut milk**). **2** the flesh of the coconut.

coconut matting *n* coarse matting made from the husk of the coconut.

cocoon *n* **1** a silky protective covering produced by a silkworm or other insect larva, in which the pupa develops. **2** a protective covering. *~vb* **3** to wrap in or protect as if in a cocoon.

cocotte *n* a small fireproof dish in which individual portions of food are cooked and served.

cod[1] *n, pl* **cod** *or* **cods** a large food fish found in the North Atlantic.

cod[2] *adj Brit slang* having the character of an imitation or parody: *the chorus were dressed in exuberant cod-medieval costumes.*

COD cash (in the US collect) on delivery.

coda (**kode**-a) *n Music* the final part of a musical movement or work.

coddle *vb* **-dling, -dled 1** to pamper or overprotect. **2** to cook (eggs) in water just below boiling point.

code *n* **1** a system of letters, symbols, or prearranged signals, by which information can be communicated secretly or briefly. **2** a set of principles or rules: *a code of practice.* **3** a system of letters or digits used for identification purposes: *area code; tax code.* *~vb* **coding, coded 4** to translate or arrange into a code.

codeine (**kode**-een) *n* a drug made mainly from morphine, used as a painkiller and sedative.

codex (**koh**-dex) *n, pl* **-dices** (-diss-seez) a volume of manuscripts of an ancient text.

codfish *n, pl* **-fish** *or* **-fishes** a cod.

codger *n Informal* an old man.

codicil (**cod**-iss-ill) *n Law* an addition to a will.

codify (**kode**-if-fie) *vb* **-fies, -fying, -fied** to organize or collect together (rules or procedures) systematically. **codification** *n*

codling *n* a young cod.

cod-liver oil *n* an oil extracted from fish, rich in vitamins A and D.

codpiece *n History* a bag covering the male genitals, attached to breeches.

codswallop *n Brit slang* nonsense.

coeducation *n* the education of boys and girls together. **coeducational** *adj*

coefficient *n* **1** *Maths* a number or constant placed before and multiplying another quantity: *the coefficient of the term 3xyz is 3.* **2** *Physics* a number or constant used to calculate the behaviour of a given substance under specified conditions.

coelacanth (**seel**-a-kanth) *n* a primitive marine fish, thought to be extinct until a living specimen was discovered in 1938.

coelenterate (seel-**lent**-a-rate) *n* any invertebrate that has a saclike body with a single opening, such as a jellyfish or coral.

coeliac disease (**seel**-ee-ak) *n* a disease which makes the digestion of food difficult.

coenobite (**seen**-oh-bite) *n* a member of a religious order in a monastic community.

coequal *adj, n* equal.

coerce (koh-**urss**) *vb* **-ercing, -erced** to compel or force. **coercion** *n*

coercive *adj* using force or authority to make a person do something against his or her will.

THESAURUS

persuade, prevail upon, soft-soap (*informal*), sweet-talk (*informal*), talk into, wheedle

cock 1. *n.* chanticleer, cockerel, rooster **2.** *vb.* perk up, prick, raise, stand up

cockeyed *informal* **1.** askew, asymmetrical, awry, crooked, lopsided, skewwhiff (*Brit. informal*), squint (*informal*) **2.** absurd, crazy, ludicrous, nonsensical, preposterous

cocky arrogant, brash, cocksure, conceited, egotistical, swaggering, swollen-headed, vain

coeval (koh-**eev**-al) *adj, n* contemporary. **coevally** *adv*

coexist *vb* **1** to exist together at the same time or in the same place. **2** to exist together in peace despite differences. **coexistence** *n* **coexistent** *adj*

coextensive *adj* covering the same area, either literally or figuratively: *the concepts of "the nation" and "the people" are not coextensive.*

C of E Church of England.

coffee *n* **1** a drink made from the roasted and ground seeds of a tall tropical shrub. **2** Also called: **coffee beans** the beanlike seeds of this shrub. **3** the shrub yielding these seeds. *~adj* **4** medium-brown.

coffee bar *n* a café; snack bar.

coffee house *n* a place where coffee is served, esp. one that was a fashionable meeting place in 18th-century London.

coffee mill *n* a machine for grinding roasted coffee beans.

coffee table *n* a small low table.

coffee-table book *n* a large expensive illustrated book.

coffer *n* **1** a chest for storing valuables. **2 coffers** a store of money. **3** an ornamental sunken panel in a ceiling or dome.

cofferdam *n* a watertight enclosure pumped dry to enable construction work or ship repairs to be done.

coffered *adj* (of a ceiling or dome) decorated with ornamental sunken panels.

coffin *n* a box in which a corpse is buried or cremated.

cog *n* **1** one of the teeth on the rim of a gearwheel. **2** a gearwheel, esp. a small one. **3** an unimportant person in a large organization or process.

cogent (**koh**-jent) *adj* forcefully convincing. **cogency** *n*

cogitate (**koj**-it-tate) *vb* **-tating, -tated** to think deeply about (something). **cogitation** *n* **cogitative** *adj*

cognac (**kon**-yak) *n* high-quality French brandy.

cognate *adj* **1** derived from a common original form: *cognate languages.* **2** related to or descended from a common ancestor. *~n* **3** a cognate word or language. **4** a relative. **cognation** *n*

cognition *n Formal* **1** the processes of getting knowledge, including perception, intuition and reasoning. **2** the results of such a process. **cognitive** *adj*

cognizance *or* **cognisance** *n Formal* **1** knowledge or understanding. **2 take cognizance of** to take notice of. **3** the range or scope of knowledge or understanding. **cognizant** *or* **cognisant** *adj*

cognomen (kog-**noh**-men) *n, pl* **-nomens** *or* **-nomina** (-**nom**-min-a) *Formal* **1** a nickname. **2** a surname. **3** an ancient Roman's third name or nickname.

cognoscenti (kon-yo-**shen**-tee) *pl n, sing* **-te** (-tee) connoisseurs.

cogwheel *n* same as **gearwheel.**

cohabit *vb* to live together as husband and wife without being married. **cohabitation** *n*

cohabitee *n* a person who lives with, and has a sexual and romantic relationship with, someone to whom he or she is not married.

cohere *vb* **-hering, -hered 1** to hold or stick firmly together. **2** to be logically connected or consistent.

coherent *adj* **1** logical and consistent. **2** capable of intelligible speech. **3** cohering or sticking together. **4** *Physics* (of two or more waves) having the same frequency and a constant fixed phase difference. **coherence** *n*

cohesion *n* **1** sticking together. **2** *Physics* the force that holds together the atoms or molecules in a solid or liquid. **cohesive** *adj*

cohort *n* **1** a band of associates. **2** a tenth part of an ancient Roman Legion.

coif *n* **1** a close-fitting cap worn in the Middle Ages. **2** a hairstyle. *~vb* **coiffing, coiffed 3** to arrange (the hair).

coiffeur *n* a hairdresser. **coiffeuse** *fem n*

coiffure *n* a hairstyle.

coil[1] *vb* **1** to wind or be wound into loops. **2** to move in a winding course. *~n* **3** something wound in a connected series of loops. **4** a single loop of such a series. **5** a contraceptive device in the shape of a coil, inserted in the womb. **6** an electrical conductor wound into a spiral, to provide inductance.

coil[2] *n* **mortal coil** the troubles of the world.

coin *n* **1** a metal disc used as money. **2** metal currency collectively. *~vb* **3** to invent (a new word or phrase). **4** to make or stamp (coins). **5 coin it in** *or* **coin money** *Informal* to make money rapidly.

coinage *n* **1** coins collectively. **2** the currency of a country. **3** a newly invented word or phrase. **4** the act of coining.

coincide *vb* **-ciding, -cided 1** to happen at the same time. **2** to agree or correspond exactly: *what she had said coincided exactly with his own thinking.* **3** to occupy the same place in space.

coincidence *n* **1** a chance occurrence of simultaneous or apparently connected events. **2** a coinciding.

coincident *adj* **1** having the same position in space or time. **2 coincident with** in exact agreement with.

coincidental *adj* resulting from coincidence; not intentional. **coincidentally** *adv*

coir *n* coconut fibre, used in making rope and matting.

coitus (**koh**-it-uss) *or* **coition** (koh-**ish**-un) *n* sexual intercourse. **coital** *adj*

coke[1] *n* **1** a solid fuel left after gas has been distilled

THESAURUS

code 1. cipher, cryptograph **2.** canon, convention, custom, ethics, etiquette, manners, maxim, regulations, rules, system

cogent compelling, conclusive, convincing, effective, forceful, influential, irresistible, potent, powerful, strong, weighty

cogitate consider, contemplate, deliberate, meditate, mull over, muse, ponder, reflect, ruminate, think

cogitation consideration, contemplation, deliberation, meditation, reflection, rumination, thought

cognate affiliated, akin, alike, allied, analogous, associated, connected, kindred, related, similar

cognition *formal* apprehension, awareness, comprehension, discernment, insight, intelligence, perception, reasoning, understanding

coherent 1. consistent, logical, lucid, meaningful, orderly, organized, rational, reasoned, systematic **2.** articulate, comprehensible, intelligible

coil curl, entwine, loop, snake, spiral, twine, twist, wind, wreathe

coin *n.* **1.** cash, change, copper, dosh (*Brit. & Austral. slang*), money, silver, specie *~vb.* **2.** conceive, create, fabricate, formulate, frame, invent, make up, originate, think up **3.** forge, mint, mould

coincide 1. be concurrent, coexist, occur simultaneously, synchronize **2.** accord, agree, concur, correspond, harmonize, match, square, tally

coincidence 1. accident, chance, eventuality, fluke,

from coal. ~*vb* **coking, coked 2** to become or convert into coke.

coke[2] *n Slang* cocaine.

Coke *n Trademark* short for **Coca-Cola.**

col *n* the lowest point of a ridge connecting two mountain peaks.

Col. Colonel.

cola *n* **1** a soft drink flavoured with an extract from the nuts of a tropical tree. **2** the W African tree whose nuts contain this extract.

colander *n* a bowl with a perforated bottom for straining or rinsing foods.

cold *adj* **1** low in temperature: *the cold March wind; cans of cold beer.* **2** not hot enough: *eat your food before it gets cold!* **3** lacking in affection or enthusiasm. **4** not affected by emotion: *the cold truth.* **5** dead. **6** (of a trail or scent in hunting) faint. **7** (of a colour) giving the impression of coldness. **8** *Slang* unconscious. **9** *Informal* (of a seeker) far from the object of a search. **10 cold comfort** little or no comfort. **11 have** *or* **get cold feet** to be or become fearful or reluctant. **12 in cold blood** deliberately and without mercy. **13 leave someone cold** *Informal* to fail to excite or impress someone. **14 throw cold water on** *Informal* to discourage. ~*n* **15** the absence of heat. **16** a viral infection of the nose and throat characterized by catarrh and sneezing. **17** the sensation caused by loss or lack of heat. **18 (out) in the cold** *Informal* neglected or ignored. ~*adv* **19** *Informal* unrehearsed or unprepared: *he played his part cold.* **coldly** *adv* **coldness** *n*

cold-blooded *adj* **1** callous or cruel. **2** *Zool* (of all animals except birds and mammals) having a body temperature that varies according to the temperature of the surroundings.

cold chisel *n* a toughened steel chisel.

cold cream *n* a creamy preparation used for softening and cleansing the skin.

cold frame *n* an unheated wooden frame with a glass top, used to protect young plants.

cold front *n Meteorol* the boundary line between a warm air mass and the cold air pushing it from beneath and behind.

cold-hearted *adj* lacking in feeling or warmth. **cold-heartedness** *n*

cold shoulder *Informal* ~*n* **1 give someone the cold shoulder** to snub someone. ~*vb* **cold-shoulder 2** to treat with indifference.

cold snap *n* a short period of cold and frosty weather.

cold sore *n* a cluster of blisters near the lips, caused by a virus.

cold storage *n* **1** the storage of things in a refrigerated place. **2** *Informal* a state of temporary disuse: *the idea has been in cold storage ever since.*

cold sweat *n Informal* coldness and sweating as a bodily reaction to fear or nervousness.

cold turkey *n Slang* a method of curing drug addiction by the sudden withdrawal of all doses.

cold war *n* a state of political hostility between two countries without actual warfare.

cole *n* any of various plants such as the cabbage and rape.

coleslaw *n* a salad dish of shredded raw cabbage in a dressing.

coley *n Brit* an edible fish with white or grey flesh.

colic *n* severe pains in the stomach and bowels. **colicky** *adj*

colitis (koh-**lie**-tiss) *n* inflammation of the colon, usually causing diarrhoea and lower abdominal pain.

collaborate *vb* **-rating, -rated 1** to work with another or others on a joint project. **2** to cooperate with an enemy invader. **collaboration** *n* **collaborative** *adj* **collaborator** *n*

collage (kol-**lahzh**) *n* **1** an art form in which various materials or objects are glued onto a surface to make a picture. **2** a picture made in this way. **collagist** *n*

collagen *n* a protein found in cartilage and bone that yields gelatine when boiled.

collapse *vb* **-lapsing, -lapsed 1** to fall down or cave in suddenly. **2** to fail completely: *a package holiday company which collapsed last year.* **3** to fall down from lack of strength, exhaustion, or illness: *he collapsed with an asthma attack.* **4** to sit down and rest because of tiredness or lack of energy: *she collapsed in front of the telly when she got home.* **5** to fold compactly, esp. for storage. ~*n* **6** the act of falling down or falling to pieces. **7** a sudden failure or breakdown.

collapsible *adj* able to be folded up for storage.

collar *n* **1** the part of a garment round the neck. **2** a band of leather, rope, or metal placed around an animal's neck. **3** *Biol* a ringlike marking around the neck of a bird or animal. **4** a cut of meat, esp. bacon, from the neck of an animal. **5** a ring or band around a pipe, rod, or shaft. ~*vb Informal* **6** to seize; arrest. **7** to catch in order to speak to. **8** to take for oneself.

collarbone *n* same as **clavicle.**

collate *vb* **-lating, -lated 1** to examine and compare carefully. **2** to gather together and put in order. **collator** *n*

collateral *n* **1** security pledged for the repayment of a loan. **2** a person, animal, or plant descended from the same ancestor as another but through a different line. ~*adj* **3** descended from a common ancestor but through different lines. **4** additional but subordinate: *a spokeswoman said that there was no collateral information to dispute the assurances the government had been given.* **5** situated or running side by side: *collateral ridges of mountains.*

collateral damage *n Mil* unintentional civilian

THESAURUS

luck **2.** concomitance, concurrence, conjunction, correlation, correspondence, synchronism

coincidental accidental, casual, chance, fluky (*informal*), fortuitous, unintentional, unplanned

cold *adj.* **1.** arctic, biting, bitter, bleak, chill, chilly, cool, freezing, frigid, frosty, frozen, harsh, icy, inclement, parky (*Brit. informal*), raw, wintry **2.** aloof, cold-blooded, distant, frigid, glacial, passionless, reserved, standoffish, stony, undemonstrative, unfeeling, unmoved, unresponsive, unsympathetic ~*n.* **3.** chill, chilliness, coldness, frigidity, frostiness, iciness, inclemency

cold-blooded barbarous, brutal, callous, cruel, heartless, inhuman, merciless, pitiless, ruthless, savage, stony-hearted, unfeeling

cold-hearted callous, frigid, hardhearted, harsh, heartless, inhuman, insensitive, stony-hearted, uncaring, unfeeling, unkind, unsympathetic

collaborate 1. cooperate, join forces, team up, work together **2.** collude, conspire, cooperate, fraternize

collaboration alliance, association, cooperation, partnership, teamwork

collaborator 1. associate, colleague, confederate, co-worker, partner, team-mate **2.** collaborationist, fraternizer, quisling, traitor, turncoat

collapse *vb.* **1.** cave in, crack up (*informal*), crumple, fall, give way, subside **2.** break down, come to noth-

casualties or damage to civilian property caused by military action: *to minimize collateral damage maximum precision in bombing is required.*

collation *n* **1** the act or result of collating. **2** *Formal* a light meal.

colleague *n* a fellow worker, esp. in a profession.

collect[1] *vb* **1** to gather together or be gathered together. **2** to gather (objects, such as stamps) as a hobby or for study. **3** to go to a place to fetch (a person or thing). **4** to receive payments of (taxes, dues, or contributions). **5** to regain control of (oneself or one's emotions).

collect[2] *n Christianity* a short prayer said during certain church services.

collected *adj* **1** calm and self-controlled. **2** brought together into one book or set of books: *the collected works of Dickens.*

collection *n* **1** things collected or accumulated. **2** the act or process of collecting. **3** a sum of money collected, as in church. **4** a regular removal of letters from a postbox.

collective *adj* **1** done by or characteristic of individuals acting as a group: *the army's collective wisdom regarding peacekeeping.* ~*n* **2** a group of people working together on an enterprise and sharing the benefits from it. **collectively** *adv*

collective bargaining *n* negotiation between a trade union and an employer on the wages and working conditions of the employees.

collective noun *n* a noun that is singular in form but that refers to a group of people or things, as *crowd* or *army.*

collectivism *n* the theory that the state should own all means of production. **collectivist** *adj*

collectivize *or* **-vise** *vb* **-vizing, -vized** *or* **-vising, -vised** to organize according to the theory of collectivism. **collectivization** *or* **-visation** *n*

collector *n* **1** a person who collects objects as a hobby. **2** a person employed to collect debts, rents, or tickets.

collector's item *n* an object highly valued by collectors for its beauty or rarity.

colleen *n Irish* a girl.

college *n* **1** an institution of higher or further education that is not a university. **2** a self-governing section of certain universities. **3** *Brit* a name given to some secondary schools. **4** an organized body of people with specific rights and duties: *the president is elected by an electoral college.* **5** a body organized within a particular profession, concerned with regulating standards. **6** the staff and students of a college.

collegian *n* a member of a college.

collegiate *adj* **1** of a college or college students. **2** (of a university) composed of various colleges.

collide *vb* **-liding, -lided 1** to crash together violently. **2** to conflict or disagree.

collie *n* a silky-haired dog used for herding sheep and cattle.

collier *n Chiefly Brit* **1** a coal miner. **2** a ship designed to carry coal.

colliery *n, pl* **-lieries** *Chiefly Brit* a coal mine and its buildings.

collision *n* **1** a violent crash between moving objects. **2** the conflict of opposed ideas or wishes.

collision course *n* **1** a trajectory of movement likely to result in a collision. **2** a course of action likely to result in a serious disagreement or confrontation: *the union is on an inevitable collision course with the government.*

collocate *vb* **-cating, -cated** (of words) to occur together regularly. **collocation** *n*

colloid *n* a mixture of particles of one substance suspended in a different substance. **colloidal** *adj*

collop *n* a small slice of meat.

colloquial *adj* suitable for informal speech or writing. **colloquially** *adv*

colloquialism *n* **1** a colloquial word or phrase. **2** the use of colloquial words and phrases.

colloquium *n, pl* **-quiums** *or* **-quia** an academic conference or seminar.

colloquy *n, pl* **-quies** *Formal* a conversation or conference. **colloquist** *n*

collude *vb* **-luding, -luded** to cooperate secretly or dishonestly with someone.

collusion *n* secret or illegal agreement or cooperation. **collusive** *adj*

collywobbles *pl n Slang* **1** an intense feeling of nervousness. **2** an upset stomach.

cologne *n* a perfumed toilet water.

colon[1] *n, pl* **-lons** the punctuation mark (:) used before an explanation or an example, a list, or an extended quotation.

colon[2] *n, pl* **-lons** *or* **-la** the part of the large intestine connected to the rectum. **colonic** *adj*

colonel *n* a senior commissioned officer in the army or air force. **colonelcy** *n*

colonial *adj* **1** of or inhabiting a colony or colonies. **2** of a style of architecture popular in North America in the 17th and 18th centuries: *a colonial mansion.* ~*n* **3** an inhabitant of a colony.

colonial goose *n NZ old-fashioned* stuffed roast mutton.

colonialism *n* the policy of acquiring and maintaining colonies, esp. for exploitation. **colonialist** *n, adj*

colonist *n* a settler in or inhabitant of a colony.

colonize *or* **-nise** *vb* **-nizing, -nized** *or* **-nising, -nised 1** to establish a colony in (an area). **2** to settle in (an area) as colonists. **colonization** *or* **-nisation** *n*

colonnade *n* a row of evenly spaced columns, usually supporting a roof. **colonnaded** *adj*

colony *n, pl* **-nies 1** a group of people who settle in a new country but remain under the rule of their homeland. **2** the territory occupied by such a settlement. **3** a group of people with the same nationality or interests,

THESAURUS

ing, fail, fold, founder ~*n.* **3.** cave-in, disintegration, downfall, subsidence **4.** breakdown, failure, flop

collar *vb. informal* apprehend, capture, catch, grab, lay hands on, nab (*informal*), nail (*informal*), seize

colleague associate, collaborator, fellow worker, partner, team-mate, workmate

collect 1. assemble, cluster, congregate, convene, converge, flock together, rally **2.** accumulate, aggregate, amass, assemble, gather, heap, hoard, save, stockpile

collected calm, composed, cool, placid, poised, sedate, self-possessed, serene, together (*slang*), unfazed (*informal*), unperturbed, unruffled

collection 1. accumulation, anthology, assemblage, assembly, assortment, cluster, compilation, gathering, group, heap, hoard, mass, pile, set, stockpile, store **2.** alms, contribution, offering, offertory

collide clash, conflict, crash, meet head-on

collision 1. accident, bump, crash, impact, pile-up (*informal*), prang (*old-fashioned slang*), smash **2.** clash, conflict, confrontation, opposition, skirmish

colloquial conversational, everyday, familiar, idiomatic, informal, vernacular

forming a community in a particular place: *an artists' colony.* **4** *Zool* a group of the same type of animal or plant living or growing together. **5** *Bacteriol* a group of microorganisms when grown on a culture medium.

colophon *n* a publisher's symbol on a book.

color *n, vb US* same as **colour.**

Colorado beetle *n* a black-and-yellow beetle that is a serious pest of potatoes.

coloration *or* **colouration** *n* arrangement of colours: *a red coloration of the eyes.*

coloratura *n Music* **1** a part for a solo singer which has much complicated ornamentation of the basic melody. **2** a soprano who specializes in such music.

colossal *adj* **1** very large in size: *the turbulent rivers and colossal mountains of New Zealand.* **2** very serious or significant: *a colossal legal blunder.*

colossus *n, pl* **-si** *or* **-suses 1** a very large statue. **2** a huge or important person or thing.

colostomy *n, pl* **-mies** an operation to form an opening from the colon onto the surface of the body, for emptying the bowel.

colour *or US* **color** *n* **1** a property of things that results from the particular wavelengths of light which they reflect or give out, producing a sensation in the eye. **2** a colour, such as a red or green, that possesses hue, as opposed to black, white, or grey. **3** a substance, such as a dye, that gives colour. **4** the skin complexion of a person. **5** the use of all the colours in painting, drawing, or photography. **6** the distinctive tone of a musical sound. **7** details which give vividness or authenticity: *I walked the streets and absorbed the local colour.* **8** semblance or pretext: *under colour of.* ~*vb* **9** to apply colour to (something). **10** to influence or distort: *anger coloured her judgment.* **11** to become red in the face, esp. when embarrassed or annoyed. **12** to give a convincing appearance to: *he coloured his account of what had happened.* ~See also **colours.**

colour bar *n* racial discrimination by whites against non-whites.

colour-blind *adj* unable to distinguish between certain colours, esp. red and green. **colour blindness** *n*

coloured *or US* **colored** *adj* having a colour or colours other than black or white: *coloured glass bottles; a peach-coloured outfit with matching hat.*

Coloured *or US* **Colored** *n* **1** *Old-fashioned* a person who is not White. **2** in South Africa, a person of racially mixed parentage or descent. ~*adj* **3** *S Africa* of mixed White and non-White parentage.

colourful *or US* **colorful** *adj* **1** with bright or richly varied colours. **2** vivid or distinctive in character.

colouring *or US* **coloring** *n* **1** the application of colour. **2** something added to give colour. **3** appearance with regard to shade and colour. **4** the colour of a person's complexion.

colourless *or US* **colorless** *adj* **1** without colour: *a colourless gas.* **2** dull and uninteresting: *a colourless personality.* **3** grey or pallid in tone or hue: *a watery sun hung low in the colourless sky.*

colours *or US* **colors** *pl n* **1** the flag of a country, regiment, or ship. **2** *Brit sport* a badge or other symbol showing membership of a team, esp. at a school or college. **3 nail one's colours to the mast** to commit oneself publicly to a course of action. **4 show one's true colours** to display one's true nature or character.

colour sergeant *n* a sergeant who carries the regimental, battalion, or national colours.

colour supplement *n Brit* an illustrated magazine accompanying a newspaper.

colt *n* **1** a young male horse or pony. **2** *Sport* a young and inexperienced player

coltsfoot *n, pl* **-foots** a weed with yellow flowers and heart-shaped leaves.

columbine *n* a plant that has brightly coloured flowers with five spurred petals.

column *n* **1** an upright pillar usually having a cylindrical shaft, a base, and a capital. **2** a form or structure in the shape of a column: *a column of smoke.* **3** a vertical division of a newspaper page. **4** a regular feature in a paper: *a cookery column.* **5** a vertical arrangement of numbers. **6** *Mil* a narrow formation in which individuals or units follow one behind the other. **columnar** *adj*

columnist *n* a journalist who writes a regular feature in a newspaper.

com- *or* **con-** *prefix* used with a main word to mean together; with; jointly: *commingle.*

coma *n* a state of unconsciousness from which a person cannot be aroused, caused by injury, disease, or drugs.

comatose *adj* **1** in a coma. **2** sound asleep.

comb *n* **1** a toothed instrument for disentangling or arranging hair. **2** a tool or machine that cleans and straightens wool or cotton. **3** a fleshy serrated crest on the head of a domestic fowl. **4** a honeycomb. ~*vb* **5** to use a comb on. **6** to search with great care: *police combed the streets for the missing girl.*

THESAURUS

collusion complicity, connivance, conspiracy, intrigue

colonize open up, people, pioneer, populate, settle

colony community, outpost, province, satellite state, settlement, territory

colossal elephantine, enormous, gargantuan, gigantic, ginormous (*informal*), herculean, huge, humongous (*informal, chiefly U.S.*), immense, mammoth, massive, monstrous, monumental, mountainous, prodigious, titanic, vast

colour *n.* **1.** dye, hue, paint, pigment, pigmentation, shade, tincture, tinge, tint **2.** bloom, blush, brilliance, flush, glow, rosiness, ruddiness, vividness **3.** appearance, disguise, excuse, facade, guise, plea, pretence, pretext, semblance ~*vb.* **4.** dye, paint, stain, tinge, tint **5.** disguise, distort, embroider, exaggerate, falsify, misrepresent, pervert, prejudice, slant, taint **6.** blush, burn, crimson, flush, go crimson, redden

colourful *or U.S.* **colorful 1.** bright, brilliant, Day-Glo (*Trademark*), intense, jazzy (*informal*), kaleidoscopic, motley, multicoloured, psychedelic, rich, variegated, vibrant, vivid **2.** characterful, distinctive, graphic, interesting, lively, picturesque, rich, unusual, vivid

colourless *or U.S.* **colorless 1.** achromatic, neutral **2.** characterless, dreary, insipid, lacklustre, tame, uninteresting, unmemorable, vacuous, vapid **3.** anaemic, ashen, bleached, drab, faded, sickly, wan, washed out

colours *or U.S.* **colors** banner, emblem, ensign, flag, standard

column 1. caryatid, obelisk, pilaster, pillar, post, shaft, support, upright **2.** file, line, rank, row, string, train

columnist correspondent, critic, editor, journalist, journo (*slang*), reporter, reviewer

coma insensibility, oblivion, stupor, torpor, trance, unconsciousness

comatose insensible, torpid, unconscious

comb *vb.* **1.** arrange, curry, dress, groom, untangle **2.** go through with a fine-tooth comb, hunt, ransack, scour, search, sift, sweep

combat 1. *n.* action, battle, conflict, contest, encoun-

combat *n* 1 a fight or struggle. ~*vb* **-bating, -bated 2** to fight: *a coordinated approach to combating the growing drugs problem.* **combative** *adj*

combatant *n* 1 a person taking part in a combat. ~*adj* 2 engaged in or ready for combat.

combe *n* same as **coomb.**

comber *n* a long curling wave.

combination *n* 1 the act of combining or state of being combined. 2 people or things combined. 3 the set of numbers or letters that opens a combination lock. 4 a motorcycle with a sidecar. 5 *Maths* an arrangement of the members of a set into specified groups without regard to order in the group.

combination lock *n* a lock that can only be opened when a set of dials is turned to show a specific sequence of numbers or letters.

combinations *pl n Brit* a one-piece undergarment with long sleeves and legs.

combine *vb* **-bining, -bined 1** to join together. 2 to form a chemical compound. ~*n* 3 an association of people or firms for a common purpose. 4 short for **combine harvester.**

combine harvester *n* a machine used to reap and thresh grain in one process.

combings *pl n* the loose hair or fibres removed by combing.

combining form *n* a part of a word that occurs only as part of a compound word, such as *anthropo-* in *anthropology.*

combo *n, pl* **-bos** a small group of jazz musicians.

combustible *adj* capable of igniting and burning easily.

combustion *n* 1 the process of burning. 2 a chemical reaction in which a substance combines with oxygen to produce heat and light.

come *vb* **coming, came, come 1** to move towards a place considered near to the speaker or hearer: *come and see me as soon as you can.* 2 to arrive or reach: *turn left and continue until you come to a cattle-grid; he came to Britain in the 1920s.* 3 to occur: *Christmas comes but once a year.* 4 to happen as a result: *no good will come of this.* 5 to occur to the mind: *the truth suddenly came to me.* 6 to reach a specified point, state, or situation: *a dull brown dress that came down to my ankles; he'd come to a decision.* 7 to be produced: *it also comes in other colours.* 8 **come from** to be or have been a resident or native (of): *my mother comes from Greenock.* 9 to become: *it was like a dream come true.* 10 *Slang* to have an orgasm. 11 *Brit informal* to play the part of: *don't come the innocent with me.* 12 (*subjunctive use*) when a specified time arrives: *come next August.* 13 **as ... as they come** the most characteristic example of a type: *he's an arrogant bastard and as devious as they come.* 14 **come again?** *Informal* what did you say? 15 **come to light** to be revealed. ~*interj* 16 an exclamation expressing annoyance or impatience: *come now!* ~See also **come about, come across,** etc.

come about *vb* to happen.

come across *vb* 1 to meet or find by accident. 2 to communicate the intended meaning or impression. 3 **come across as** to give a certain impression.

come at *vb* to attack: *he came at me with an axe.*

comeback *n Informal* 1 a return to a former position or status. 2 a response or retaliation. ~*vb* **come back** 3 to return, esp. to the memory. 4 to become fashionable again.

come between *vb* to cause the estrangement or separation of (two people).

come by *vb* to find or obtain, esp. accidentally: *Graham filled him in on how he came by the envelope.*

Comecon (**kom**-meek-on) *n* (formerly) an economic league of Soviet-oriented Communist nations.

comedian *or fem* **comedienne** *n* 1 an entertainer who tells jokes. 2 a person who performs in comedy.

comedown *n* 1 a decline in status or prosperity. 2 *Informal* a disappointment. ~*vb* **come down** 3 (of prices) to become lower. 4 to reach a decision: *a 1989 court ruling came down in favour of three councils who wanted Sunday trading banned.* 5 to be handed down by tradition or inheritance. 6 **come down with** to begin to suffer from (illness). 7 **come down on** to reprimand sharply. 8 **come down to** to amount to: *at the end the case came down to the one simple issue.* 9 **come down in the world** to lose status or prosperity.

comedy *n, pl* **-dies** 1 a humorous film, play, or

THESAURUS

ter, engagement, fight, skirmish, struggle, war, warfare 2. *vb.* battle, contend, contest, do battle with, fight, oppose, resist, withstand

combatant 1. *n.* adversary, antagonist, contender, fighter, opponent, soldier, warrior 2. *adj.* battling, belligerent, combating, conflicting, contending, fighting, opposing, warring

combination 1. amalgam, amalgamation, blend, coalescence, composite, meld, mix, mixture 2. alliance, association, cabal, cartel, coalition, compound, confederacy, confederation, consortium, federation, merger, syndicate, union

combine amalgamate, associate, bind, blend, bond, connect, cooperate, fuse, incorporate, integrate, join (together), link, marry, meld, merge, mix, pool, put together, unify, unite

come 1. advance, appear, approach, arrive, draw near, enter, move, move towards, near 2. appear, arrive, attain, enter, reach, show up (*informal*), turn up (*informal*) 3. fall, happen, occur, take place 4. arise, emanate, emerge, flow, issue, originate, result, turn out 5. extend, reach 6. be available (made, offered, on offer, produced)

come about arise, befall, come to pass, happen, occur, result, take place, transpire (*informal*)

come across bump into (*informal*), chance upon, discover, encounter, find, happen upon, hit upon, light upon, meet, notice, stumble upon, unearth

come at assail, assault, attack, charge, fall upon, fly at, go for, rush, rush at

comeback *informal* 1. rally, rebound, recovery, resurgence, return, revival, triumph 2. rejoinder, reply, response, retaliation, retort, riposte

come back reappear, recur, re-enter, return

come between alienate, divide, estrange, part, separate, set at odds

come by acquire, get, lay hold of, obtain, procure, score (*slang*), secure, take possession of, win

comedian *or fem.* **comedienne** card (*informal*), clown, comic, funny man *or* woman, humorist, jester, joker, laugh (*informal*), wag, wit

comedown 1. decline, demotion, humiliation, reverse 2. anticlimax, blow, deflation, disappointment, letdown

come down on bawl out (*informal*), blast, chew out (*U.S. & Canad. informal*), criticize, dress down (*informal*), give (someone) a rocket (*Brit. & N.Z. informal*), jump on (*informal*), lambast(e), put down, read the riot act, rebuke, reprimand, tear into (*informal*)

come down to amount to, boil down to, end up as, result in

come down with be stricken with, catch, contract,

broadcast. **2** such works as a genre. **3** the humorous aspect of life or of events. **4** (in classical literature) a play which ends happily.

come forward *vb* **1** to offer one's services. **2** to present oneself.

come-hither *adj Informal* flirtatious and seductive: *a come-hither look.*

come in *vb* **1** to prove to be: *it came in useful.* **2** to become fashionable or seasonable. **3** to finish a race (in a certain position). **4** to be received: *news is coming in of a fire in Hull.* **5** (of money) to be received as income. **6** to be involved in a situation: *where do I come in?* **7 come in for** to be the object of: *she came in for a lot of criticism.*

come into *vb* **1** to enter. **2** to inherit.

comely *adj* **-lier, -liest** *Old-fashioned* good-looking. **comeliness** *n*

come of *vb* to result from: *nothing came of it.*

come off *vb* **1** to emerge from a situation in a certain position: *the people to have come off worst are the poor.* **2** *Informal* to take place. **3** *Informal* to have the intended effect: *it was a gamble that didn't come off.*

come-on *n* **1** *Informal* a lure or enticement. *~vb* **come on 2** (of power or water) to start running or functioning. **3** to make progress: *my plants are coming on nicely.* **4** to begin: *I think I've got a cold coming on.* **5** to make an entrance on stage.

come out *vb* **1** to be made public or revealed: *it was only then that the truth came out.* **2** to be published or put on sale: *their latest album which came out last month.* **3** Also: **come out of the closet** to reveal something formerly concealed, esp. that one is a homosexual. **4** *Chiefly Brit* to go on strike. **5** to declare oneself: *the report has come out in favour of maintaining child benefit.* **6** to end up or turn out: *this wine consistently came out top in our tastings; the figures came out exactly right.* **7 come out in** to become covered with (a rash or spots). **8 come out with** to say or disclose: *she came out with a remark that left me speechless.* **9** to enter society formally.

come over *vb* **1** to influence or affect: *I don't know what's come over me.* **2** to communicate the intended meaning or impression. **3** to give a certain impression. **4** to change sides or opinions. **5** *Informal* to feel a particular sensation: *it makes him come over slightly queasy.*

come round *vb* **1** to recover consciousness. **2** to change one's opinion.

comestibles *pl n* food.

comet *n* a heavenly body that travels round the sun, leaving a long bright trail behind it.

come through *vb* to survive or endure (an illness or difficult situation) successfully.

come to *vb* **1** to regain consciousness. **2** to amount to (a total figure).

come up *vb* **1** to be mentioned or arise: *we hope that the difficulties that have arisen in the past will not keep coming up.* **2** to be about to happen: *the club has important games coming up at Leicester and Birmingham.* **3 come up against** to come into conflict with. **4 come up in the world** to rise in status. **5 come up to** to meet a standard. **6 come up with** to produce or propose: *he has a knack for coming up with great ideas.*

come upon *vb* to meet or encounter unexpectedly.

comeuppance *n Informal* deserved punishment.

comfit *n* a sugar-coated sweet.

comfort *n* **1** a state of physical ease or well-being. **2** relief from suffering or grief. **3** a person or thing that brings ease. **4 comforts** things that make life easier or more pleasant: *the comforts of home.* *~vb* **5** to soothe or console. **6** to bring physical ease to. **comforting** *adj*

comfortable *adj* **1** giving comfort; relaxing. **2** free from trouble or pain. **3** *Informal* well-off financially. **4** not afraid or embarrassed: *he was not comfortable expressing sympathy.* **comfortably** *adv*

comforter *n* **1** a person or thing that comforts. **2** a baby's dummy. **3** *Brit* a woollen scarf.

comfrey *n* a tall plant with bell-shaped blue, purple, or white flowers.

comfy *adj* **-fier, -fiest** *Informal* comfortable.

comic *adj* **1** humorous; funny. **2** of or relating to comedy. *~n* **3** a comedian. **4** a magazine containing comic strips.

comical *adj* causing amusement, often because of being ludicrous or ridiculous: *an enthusiasm comical to behold.* **comically** *adv*

comic opera *n* an opera with speech and singing that tells an amusing story.

comic strip *n* a sequence of drawings in a newspaper or magazine, telling a humorous story or an adventure.

coming *adj* **1** (of time or events) approaching or next: *in the coming weeks.* **2** likely to be important in the future: *he was regarded as a coming man at the*

THESAURUS

fall ill with, fall victim to, get, sicken for, take, take sick with

comedy **1.** farce, light entertainment, sitcom (*informal*), slapstick **2.** drollery, facetiousness, fun, hilarity, humour, jesting, joking, wisecracking, witticisms

come forward offer one's services, present *or* proffer oneself, volunteer

come in for bear the brunt of, endure, get, receive, suffer

come off *informal* go off, happen, occur, take place, transpire (*informal*)

come out **1.** appear, be published (announced, divulged, issued, released, reported, revealed) **2.** conclude, end, result, terminate

come round **1.** come to, rally, recover, regain consciousness, revive **2.** accede, acquiesce, mellow, relent, yield

come through endure, survive, withstand

come up arise, crop up, happen, occur, rise, spring up, turn up

comeuppance *informal* deserts, punishment, requital, retribution

come up to approach, compare with, equal, match, measure up to, meet, resemble, rival, stand *or* bear comparison with

come up with advance, create, discover, furnish, offer, present, produce, propose, provide, submit, suggest

comfort *n.* **1.** cosiness, creature comforts, ease, luxury, snugness, wellbeing **2.** compensation, consolation, help, relief, succour, support *~vb.* **3.** cheer, commiserate with, console, ease, gladden, hearten, reassure, solace, soothe, strengthen

comfortable **1.** cosy, easy, homely, relaxing, restful **2.** at ease, contented, gratified, happy, relaxed, serene **3.** *informal* affluent, prosperous, well-off, well-to-do

comforting cheering, consoling, heart-warming, reassuring, soothing

comic **1.** *adj.* amusing, comical, droll, facetious, farcical, funny, humorous, jocular, joking, light, waggish, witty **2.** *n.* buffoon, clown, comedian, funny man *or* woman, humorist, jester, wag, wit

Foreign Office. **3 have it coming to one** *Informal* to deserve what one is about to suffer. *~n* **4** arrival or approach.

comity *n, pl* **-ties** *Formal* friendly politeness, esp. between different countries.

comma *n* the punctuation mark (,) indicating a slight pause and used where there is a list of items or to separate the parts of a sentence.

command *vb* **1** to order or compel. **2** to have authority over. **3** to deserve and get: *a public figure who commands almost universal respect.* **4** to look down over: *the house commands a magnificent view of the sea and the islands.* *~n* **5** an authoritative instruction that something must be done. **6** the authority to command. **7** knowledge; control: *a fluent command of French.* **8** a military or naval unit with a specific function. **9** *Computers* a part of a program consisting of a coded instruction to the computer to perform a specified function.

commandant *n* an officer in charge of a place or group of people.

commandeer *vb* **1** to seize for military use. **2** to take as if by right: *he commandeered the one waiting taxi outside the station.*

commander *n* **1** an officer in command of a military group or operation. **2** a middle-ranking naval officer. **3** a high-ranking member of some orders of knights.

commander-in-chief *n, pl* **commanders-in-chief** the supreme commander of a nation's armed forces.

commanding *adj* **1** being in charge: *the commanding officer.* **2** in a position or situation where success looks certain: *a commanding lead.* **3** having the air of authority: *a commanding voice.* **4** having a wide view.

commandment *n* a divine command, esp. one of the Ten Commandments in the Old Testament.

commando *n, pl* **-dos** *or* **-does a** a military unit trained to make swift raids in enemy territory. **b** a member of such a unit.

commedia dell'arte (kom-**made**-ee-a dell-**art**-tay) *n* a form of improvised comedy popular in Italy in the 16th century, with stock characters and a stereotyped plot.

commemorate *vb* **-rating, -rated** to honour or keep alive the memory of: *a series of events to commemorate the end of the Second World War.* **commemoration** *n* **commemorative** *adj*

commence *vb* **-mencing, -menced** to begin.

commencement *n* **1** the beginning; start. **2** *US & Canad* a graduation ceremony.

commend *vb* **1** to praise in a formal manner: *the judge commended her bravery.* **2** to recommend: *he commended the scheme warmly.* **3** to entrust: *I commend my child to your care.* **commendable** *adj* **commendation** *n*

commensurable *adj* **1** measurable by the same standards. **2** *Maths* **a** having a common factor. **b** having units of the same dimensions and being related by whole numbers. **commensurability** *n*

commensurate *adj* **1** corresponding in degree, size, or value. **2** commensurable.

comment *n* **1** a remark, criticism, or observation. **2** a situation or event that expresses some feeling: *a sad comment on the nature of many relationships.* **3** talk or gossip. **4** a note explaining or criticizing a passage in a text. **5 no comment** I decline to say anything about the matter. *~vb* **6** to remark or express an opinion.

commentary *n, pl* **-taries** **1** a spoken accompaniment to an event, broadcast, or film. **2** a series of explanatory notes on a subject.

commentate *vb* **-tating, -tated** to act as a commentator.

commentator *n* **1** a person who provides a spoken commentary for a broadcast, esp. of a sporting event. **2** an expert who reports on and analyses a particular subject.

commerce *n* **1** the buying and selling of goods and services. **2** *Literary* social relations.

commercial *adj* **1** of or engaged in commerce: *commercial exploitation of sport.* **2** sponsored or paid for by an advertiser: *commercial radio.* **3** having profit as the main aim: *this is a more commercial, accessible album than its predecessor.* *~n* **4** a radio or television advertisement.

commercialism *n* **1** the principles and practices of

THESAURUS

comical absurd, amusing, comic, droll, farcical, funny, hilarious, humorous, laughable, ludicrous, priceless, ridiculous, risible, silly, whimsical

coming *adj.* **1.** approaching, at hand, due, forthcoming, future, imminent, impending, near, next, nigh, upcoming **2.** aspiring, future, promising, up-and-coming *~n.* **3.** advent, approach, arrival

command *vb.* **1.** bid, charge, compel, demand, direct, enjoin, order **2.** administer, control, dominate, govern, handle, head, lead, manage, reign over, rule, supervise *~n.* **3.** behest, bidding, canon, commandment, decree, demand, directive, edict, fiat, injunction, instruction, mandate, order **4.** authority, charge, control, direction, domination, dominion, government, management, mastery, power, rule, supervision, sway, upper hand

commandeer appropriate, confiscate, expropriate, requisition, seize

commander boss, captain, chief, C in C (*Military*), CO, commander-in-chief, commanding officer, director, head, leader, officer, ruler

commanding **1.** advantageous, controlling, dominant, dominating, superior **2.** assertive, authoritative, autocratic, compelling, forceful, imposing, peremptory

commemorate celebrate, honour, keep, observe, pay tribute to, remember

commemoration ceremony, honouring, memorial service, observance, remembrance, tribute

commence begin, embark on, enter upon, inaugurate, initiate, open, originate, start

commend **1.** acclaim, applaud, approve, compliment, extol, praise, recommend, speak highly of **2.** commit, consign, deliver, entrust, hand over

commendable admirable, creditable, estimable, exemplary, laudable, meritorious, praiseworthy, worthy

commendation acclaim, acclamation, approbation, approval, Brownie points, credit, encomium, good opinion, panegyric, praise, recommendation

commensurate coextensive, comparable, compatible, corresponding, equivalent, fit, fitting, proportionate

comment *n.* **1.** observation, remark, statement **2.** annotation, commentary, elucidation, explanation, exposition, illustration, note *~vb.* **3.** interpose, mention, note, observe, opine, point out, remark, say, utter

commentary **1.** description, narration, voice-over **2.** analysis, critique, exegesis, explanation, notes, review, treatise

commentator **1.** commenter, reporter, special correspondent, sportscaster **2.** annotator, critic, expositor, interpreter

commerce **1.** business, dealing, exchange, merchandising, trade, traffic **2.** *literary* communication, dealings, intercourse, relations, socializing

commerce. **2** exclusive or inappropriate emphasis on profit.

commercialize *or* **-ise** *vb* **-izing, -ized** *or* **-ising, -ised 1** to make commercial. **2** to exploit for profit, esp. at the expense of quality. **commercialization** *or* **-isation** *n*

commercial traveller *n* a travelling salesman.

commie *n, pl* **-mies,** *adj Informal & offensive* Communist.

commingle *vb* **-gling, -gled** to mix or be mixed.

commis *n, pl* **-mis** an apprentice waiter or chef.

commiserate *vb* **-ating, -ated** (usually foll. by *with*) to express sympathy or pity (for). **commiseration** *n*

commissar *n* formerly, an official responsible for political education in Communist countries.

commissariat *n* a military department in charge of food supplies.

commissary *n, pl* **-saries 1** *US* a shop supplying food or equipment, as in a military camp. **2** a representative or deputy.

commission *n* **1** an order for a piece of work, esp. a work of art or a piece of writing. **2** a duty given to a person or group to perform. **3** the fee or percentage paid to a salesperson for each sale made. **4** a group of people appointed to perform certain duties: *the Equal Opportunities Commission.* **5** the act of committing a sin or crime. **6** *Mil* the rank or authority officially given to an officer. **7** authority to perform certain duties. **8 in** *or* **out of commission** in *or* not in working order. ~*vb* **9** to place an order for: *a report commissioned by the United Nations; a new work commissioned by the BBC Symphony Orchestra.* **10** *Mil* to give a commission to. **11** to prepare (a ship) for active service. **12** to grant authority to.

commissionaire *n Chiefly Brit* a uniformed doorman at a hotel, theatre, or cinema.

commissioned officer *n* a military officer holding a rank by a commission.

commissioner *n* **1** an appointed official in a government department or other organization. **2** a member of a commission.

commit *vb* **-mitting, -mitted 1** to perform (a crime or error). **2** to hand over or allocate: *the British promised to commit four divisions to Europe.* **3** to pledge to a cause or a course of action. **4** to send (someone) to prison or hospital. **5 commit to memory** to memorize. **6 commit to paper** to write down.

commitment *n* **1** dedication to a cause or principle. **2** an obligation, responsibility, or promise that restricts freedom of action. **3** the act of committing or state of being committed.

committal *n* the official consignment of a person to a prison or mental hospital.

committed *adj* having pledged oneself to a particular belief or course of action: *a committed pacifist.*

committee *n* a group of people appointed to perform a specified service or function.

commode *n* **1** a chair with a hinged flap concealing a chamber pot. **2** a chest of drawers.

commodious *adj* with plenty of space.

commodity *n, pl* **-ties** something that can be bought or sold.

commodore *n* **1** *Brit* a senior commissioned officer in the navy. **2** the president of a yacht club.

common *adj* **1** frequently encountered: *a fairly common plant; this disease is most common in kittens and young cats.* **2** widespread among people in general: *common practice.* **3** belonging to two or more people: *we share common interests.* **4** belonging to the whole community: *common property.* **5** low-class, vulgar, or coarse. **6** *Maths* belonging to two or more: *the lowest common denominator.* **7** not belonging to the upper classes: *the common people.* **8 common or garden** *Informal* ordinary. ~*n* **9** a piece of open land belonging to all the members of a community. **10 in common** shared, in joint use. ~See also **Commons. commonly** *adv*

commonality *n, pl* **-ties 1** the sharing of common attributes. **2** the ordinary people.

commonalty *n, pl* **-ties 1** the ordinary people. **2** the members of an incorporated society.

common cold *n* same as **cold** (sense 16).

commoner *n* a person who does not belong to the nobility.

common fraction *n* same as **simple fraction.**

common law *n* **1** law based on judges' decisions and custom, as distinct from written laws. ~*adj* **common-law 2** (of a relationship) regarded as a marriage through being long-standing.

Common Market *n* same as **European Union.**

commonplace *adj* **1** so common or frequent as not to be worth commenting on: *foreign holidays have now become commonplace.* **2** dull or unoriginal: *a commonplace observation.* ~*n* **3** a cliché. **4** an ordinary thing.

common room *n Chiefly Brit* a sitting room for students or staff in schools or colleges.

commons *pl n* **1** *Brit* shared food or rations. **2 short commons** reduced rations.

THESAURUS

commercial 1. business, mercantile, profit-making, sales, trade, trading **2.** in demand, marketable, popular, profitable, profit-making, saleable

commission *n.* **1.** appointment, authority, charge, duty, employment, errand, function, mandate, mission, task, warrant **2.** allowance, brokerage, compensation, cut, fee, percentage, rake-off (*slang*), royalties **3.** board, body of commissioners, commissioners, committee, delegation, deputation, representatives ~*vb.* **4.** appoint, authorize, contract, delegate, depute, empower, engage, nominate, order, select

commit 1. carry out, do, enact, execute, perform, perpetrate **2.** commend, consign, deliver, deposit, engage, entrust, give, hand over **3.** align, bind, obligate, pledge, rank **4.** confine, imprison, put in custody

commitment 1. adherence, dedication, devotion, involvement, loyalty **2.** duty, engagement, liability, obligation, responsibility, tie **3.** assurance, guarantee, pledge, promise, undertaking, vow, word

common 1. average, commonplace, conventional, customary, daily, everyday, familiar, frequent, general, habitual, ordinary, plain, regular, routine, run-of-the-mill, simple, standard, stock, usual, workaday **2.** accepted, general, popular, prevailing, prevalent, universal, widespread **3.** collective, communal, community, popular, public **4.** coarse, inferior, low, plebeian, undistinguished, vulgar

commonplace 1. *adj.* banal, common, customary, everyday, humdrum, mundane, obvious, ordinary, pedestrian, stale, threadbare, trite, uninteresting, widespread, worn out **2.** *n.* banality, cliché, platitude, truism

common sense good sense, gumption (*Brit. informal*), horse sense, level-headedness, mother wit, native intelligence, nous (*Brit. slang*), practicality, pru-

Commons *n* **the Commons** same as **House of Commons.**

common sense *n* **1** good practical understanding. *~adj* **common-sense 2** inspired by or displaying this.

common time *n Music* a time signature with four crotchet beats to the bar; four-four time.

commonwealth *n* the people of a state or nation viewed politically.

Commonwealth *n* **the Commonwealth a** Official name: **the Commonwealth of Nations** an association of sovereign states that are or at some time have been ruled by Britain. **b** the official title of the federated states of Australia.

commotion *n* noisy disturbance.

communal *adj* **1** belonging to or used by a community as a whole. **2** of a commune. **communally** *adv*

commune[1] *n* **1** a group of people living together and sharing possessions and responsibilities. **2** the smallest district of local government in Belgium, France, Italy, and Switzerland.

commune[2] *vb* **-muning, -muned commune with a** to experience strong emotion for: *communing with nature.* **b** to talk intimately with.

communicable *adj* **1** capable of being communicated. **2** (of a disease) capable of being passed on easily.

communicant *n Christianity* a person who receives Communion.

communicate *vb* **-cating, -cated 1** to exchange (thoughts) or make known (information or feelings) by speech, writing, or other means. **2** (usually foll. by *to*) to transmit (to): *the reaction of the rapturous audience communicated itself to the performers.* **3** to have a sympathetic mutual understanding. **4** *Christianity* to receive Communion. **communicator** *n* **communicative** *adj*

communicating *adj* making or having a direct connection from one room to another: *the suite is made up of three communicating rooms; the communicating door.*

communication *n* **1** the exchange of information, ideas, or feelings. **2** something communicated, such as a message. **3 communications** means of travelling or sending messages.

communication cord *n Brit* a chain in a train which may be pulled by a passenger to stop the train in an emergency.

communion *n* **1** a sharing of thoughts, emotions, or beliefs. **2 communion with** strong feelings for: *private communion with nature.* **3** a religious group with shared beliefs and practices: *the Anglican communion.*

Communion *n Christianity* **1** a ritual commemorating Christ's Last Supper by the consecration of bread and wine. **2** the consecrated bread and wine. Also called: **Holy Communion**

communiqué (kom-**mune**-ik-kay) *n* an official announcement.

communism *n* the belief that private ownership should be abolished and all work and property should be shared by the community. **communist** *n, adj*

Communism *n* **1** a political movement based upon the writings of Karl Marx that advocates communism. **2** the political and social system established in countries with a ruling Communist Party. **Communist** *n, adj*

community *n, pl* **-ties 1** all the people living in one district. **2** a group of people with shared origins or interests: *the local Jewish community.* **3** a group of countries with certain interests in common. **4** the public; society. **5** a group of interdependent plants and animals inhabiting the same region.

community centre *n* a building used by a community for social gatherings or activities.

community charge *n* the formal name for **poll tax.**

community college *n US & Canad* a nonresidential college offering two-year courses of study.

community service *n* organized unpaid work intended for the good of the community: often used as a punishment for minor criminals.

commutative *adj Maths* giving the same result irrespective of the order of the numbers or symbols.

commutator *n* a device used to change alternating electric current into direct current.

commute *vb* **-muting, -muted 1** to travel some distance regularly between one's home and one's place of work. **2** *Law* to reduce (a sentence) to one less severe. **3** to substitute. **4** to pay (an annuity or pension) at one time, instead of in instalments. **commutable** *adj* **commutation** *n*

THESAURUS

dence, reasonableness, smarts (*slang, chiefly U.S.*), sound judgment, soundness, wit

common-sense *adj.* down-to-earth, hard-headed, judicious, level-headed, matter-of-fact, practical, realistic, reasonable, sane, sensible, shrewd, sound

commotion ado, agitation, brouhaha, bustle, disorder, disturbance, excitement, ferment, furore, fuss, hubbub, hullabaloo, hurly-burly, racket, riot, rumpus, to-do, tumult, turmoil, upheaval, uproar

communal collective, community, general, joint, neighbourhood, public, shared

commune[1] *n.* collective, community, cooperative, kibbutz

commune[2] *vb.* **1.** contemplate, meditate, muse, ponder, reflect **2.** communicate, confer, confide in, converse, discourse, discuss, parley

communicate 1. acquaint, announce, be in contact, be in touch, correspond, declare, disclose, disseminate, divulge, impart, inform, make known, pass on, phone, proclaim, publish, report, reveal, ring up (*informal, chiefly Brit.*), unfold **2.** convey, pass on, spread, transmit

communication 1. connection, contact, conversation, correspondence, dissemination, intercourse, link, transmission **2.** announcement, disclosure, dispatch, information, intelligence, message, news, report, statement, word

communications information technology, media, routes, telecommunications, transport, travel

communicative candid, chatty, expansive, forthcoming, frank, informative, loquacious, open, outgoing, talkative, unreserved, voluble

communion accord, affinity, agreement, closeness communing, concord, consensus, fellowship, harmony intercourse, participation, rapport, sympathy, togetherness, unity

Communion *Christianity* Eucharist, Lord's Supper Mass, Sacrament

communiqué announcement, bulletin, dispatch, news flash, report

communism Bolshevism, collectivism, Marxism, socialism, state socialism

communist Bolshevik, collectivist, Marxist, Red (*informal*), socialist

community 1. district, locality, people, populace, population, residents **2.** association, brotherhood, company, society **3.** body politic, commonwealth, state **4.** general public, people, public, society

commuter *n* a person who regularly travels a considerable distance to work.
compact[1] *adj* **1** closely packed together. **2** neatly fitted into a restricted space. **3** concise; brief. *~vb* **4** to pack closely together. *~n* **5** a small flat case containing a mirror and face powder. **compactly** *adv* **compactness** *n*
compact[2] *n* a contract or agreement.
compact disc *n* a small digital audio disc on which the sound is read by an optical laser system.
companion *n* **1** a person who associates with or accompanies someone: *a travelling companion.* **2** a woman paid to live or travel with another woman. **3** a guidebook or handbook. **4** one of a pair. **companionship** *n*
companionable *adj* friendly and pleasant to be with. **companionably** *adv*
companionway *n* a ladder from one deck to another in a ship.
company *n, pl* **-nies 1** a business organization. **2** a group of actors. **3** a small unit of troops. **4** the officers and crew of a ship. **5** the fact of being with someone: *I enjoy her company.* **6** a number of people gathered together. **7** a guest or guests. **8** a person's associates. **9 keep someone company** to accompany someone. **10 part company** to disagree or separate.
company sergeant-major *n Mil* the senior noncommissioned officer in a company.
comparable *adj* **1** worthy of comparison. **2** able to be compared (with). **comparability** *n*
comparative *adj* **1** relative: *despite the importance of his discoveries, he died in comparative poverty.* **2** involving comparison: *comparative religion.* **3** *Grammar* the form of an adjective or adverb that indicates that the quality denoted is possessed to a greater extent. In English the comparative is marked by the suffix *-er* or the word *more.* *~n* **4** the comparative form of an adjective or adverb. **comparatively** *adv*
compare *vb* **-paring, -pared 1** to examine in order to observe resemblances or differences: *the survey compared the health of three groups of children.* **2 compare to** to declare to be like: *one ambulance driver compared the carnage to an air crash.* **3** (usually foll. by *with*) to resemble: *his storytelling compares with the likes of Le Carré.* **4** to bear a specified relation when examined: *this full-flavoured white wine compares favourably with more expensive French wines.* **5 compare notes** to exchange opinions. *~n* **6 beyond compare** without equal.
comparison *n* **1** a comparing or being compared. **2** likeness or similarity: *there is no comparison at all between her and Catherine.* **3** *Grammar* the positive, comparative, and superlative forms of an adjective or adverb. **4 in comparison to** *or* **with** compared to. **5 bear** *or* **stand comparison with** to be able to be compared with (something else), esp. favourably: *his half-dozen best novels can stand comparison with anyone's.*
compartment *n* **1** one of the sections into which a railway carriage is sometimes divided. **2** a separate section: *filing the information away in some compartment of his mind.* **3** a small storage space: *the ice-making compartment of the fridge.*
compartmentalize *or* **-ise** *vb* **-izing, -ized** *or* **-ising, -ised** to put into categories or sections.
compass *n* **1** an instrument for finding direction, with a magnetized needle which points to magnetic north. **2** limits or range: *within the compass of a normal sized book such a comprehensive survey is not possible.* **3 compasses** an instrument used for drawing circles or measuring distances, that consists of two arms, joined at one end.
➤ The drawing instrument is technically *a pair of compasses* and some people insist on this usage.
compassion *n* a feeling of distress and pity for the suffering or misfortune of another.
compassionate *adj* showing or having compassion. **compassionately** *adv*
compassionate leave *n* leave from work granted on the grounds of family illness or bereavement.
compatible *adj* **1** able to exist together harmonious-

THESAURUS

commute 1. *Law: of penalties, etc.* alleviate, curtail, mitigate, modify, reduce, remit, shorten, soften **2.** barter, exchange, interchange, substitute, switch, trade
compact[1] *adj.* **1.** close, compressed, condensed, dense, firm, impenetrable, impermeable, pressed together, solid, thick **2.** brief, compendious, concise, epigrammatic, laconic, pithy, pointed, succinct, terse, to the point *~vb.* **3.** compress, condense, cram, pack down, stuff, tamp
compact[2] *n.* agreement, alliance, arrangement, bargain, bond, concordat, contract, covenant, deal, entente, pact, treaty, understanding
companion 1. accomplice, ally, associate, buddy (*informal*), colleague, comrade, confederate, consort, crony, friend, mate (*informal*), partner **2.** complement, counterpart, fellow, match, mate, twin
companionable affable, congenial, convivial, cordial, familiar, friendly, genial, gregarious, outgoing, sociable
companionship amity (*formal*), camaraderie, company, comradeship, conviviality, esprit de corps, fellowship, fraternity, friendship, rapport, togetherness
company 1. association, business, concern, corporation, establishment, firm, house, partnership, syndicate **2.** band, ensemble, troupe **3.** companionship, fellowship, presence, society **4.** assemblage, assembly, band, bevy, body, collection, community, concourse, convention, crowd, ensemble, gathering, group, league, party, society, throng **5.** callers, guests, visitors **6.** circle, coterie, crowd, set
comparable 1. a match for, as good as, commensurate, equal, equivalent, in a class with, on a par, proportionate, tantamount **2.** akin, alike, analogous, cognate, corresponding, related, similar
compare 1. balance, collate, contrast, juxtapose, set against, weigh **2.** *with* **to** correlate, equate, identify with, liken **3.** *usually with* **with** approach, approximate to, bear comparison, be in the same class as, be on a par with, come up to, compete with, equal, hold a candle to, match, vie
comparison analogy, comparability, correlation, likeness, resemblance, similarity
compartment 1. area, category, department, division, section, subdivision **2.** alcove, bay, berth, booth, cell, chamber, cubbyhole, cubicle, locker, niche, pigeonhole, section
compass area, bound, boundary, circle, circuit, circumference, enclosure, extent, field, limit, range, reach, realm, round, scope, sphere, stretch, zone
compassion charity, clemency, commiseration, condolence, fellow feeling, heart, humanity, kindness, mercy, pity, quarter, soft-heartedness, sympathy, tender-heartedness, tenderness
compassionate charitable, humane, humanitarian, kind-hearted, kindly, lenient, merciful, pitying, sympathetic, tender, tender-hearted, understanding
compatibility affinity, agreement, amity (*formal*), concord, congeniality, empathy, harmony, like-mindedness, rapport, single-mindedness, sympathy

ly. **2** consistent: *his evidence is fully compatible with the other data.* **3** (of pieces of equipment) capable of being used together. **compatibility** *n*

compatriot *n* a fellow countryman or countrywoman.

compel *vb* **-pelling, -pelled 1** to force (to be or do something). **2** to obtain by force: *his performance compelled attention.*

compelling *adj* **1** arousing strong interest: *a compelling new novel.* **2** convincing: *compelling evidence.*

compendious *adj* brief but comprehensive.

compendium *n, pl* **-diums** *or* **-dia 1** *Brit* a selection of different table games in one container. **2** a concise but comprehensive summary.

compensate *vb* **-sating, -sated 1** to make amends to (someone), esp. for loss or injury. **2** to cancel out the effects of (something): *the car's nifty handling fails to compensate for its many flaws.* **3** to serve as compensation for (injury or loss). **compensatory** *adj*

compensation *n* **1** payment made as reparation for loss or injury. **2** the act of making amends for something.

compere *Brit ~n* **1** a person who introduces a stage, radio, or television show. *~vb* **-pering, -pered 2** to be the compere of.

compete *vb* **-peting, -peted 1** to take part in (a contest or competition). **2** to strive (to achieve something or to be successful): *able to compete on the international market.*

competence *or* **competency** *n* **1** the ability to do something well or effectively. **2** a sufficient income to live on. **3** the state of being legally competent or qualified.

competent *adj* **1** having sufficient skill or knowledge: *he was a very competent engineer.* **2** suitable or sufficient for the purpose: *it was a competent performance, but hardly a remarkable one.* **3** having valid legal authority: *lawful detention after conviction by a competent court.*

competition *n* **1** the act of competing; rivalry: *competition for places was keen.* **2** an event in which people compete. **3** the opposition offered by competitors. **4** people against whom one competes.

competitive *adj* **1** involving rivalry: *the increasingly competitive computer industry.* **2** characterized by an urge to compete: *her naturally competitive spirit.* **3** of good enough value to be successful against commercial rivals: *we offer worldwide flights at competitive prices.* **competitiveness** *n*

competitor *n* a person, team, or firm that competes.

compile *vb* **-piling, -piled 1** to collect and arrange (information) from various sources. **2** *Computers* to convert (commands for a computer) from the language used by the person using it into machine code suitable for the computer, using a compiler. **compilation** *n*

compiler *n* **1** a person who compiles information. **2** a computer program which converts a high-level programming language into the machine language used by a computer.

complacency *n* extreme self-satisfaction. **complacent** *adj* **complacently** *adv*

complain *vb* **1** to express resentment or displeasure. **2 complain of** to state that one is suffering from a pain or illness: *he complained of breathing trouble and chest pains.* **3** to make a formal protest: *he complained to the police about his rowdy neighbours.*

complainant *n Law* a plaintiff.

complaint *n* **1** the act of complaining. **2** a reason for complaining. **3** a mild illness. **4** a formal protest.

complaisant (kom-**play**-zant) *adj* willing to please or oblige. **complaisance** *n*

complement *n* **1** a person or thing that completes something. **2** a complete amount or number: *a full complement of staff nurses and care assistants.* **3** the officers and crew needed to man a ship. **4** *Grammar* a word or words added to the verb to complete the meaning of the predicate in a sentence, as *a fool* in *He is a fool* or *that he would come* in *I hoped that he would come.* **5** *Maths* the angle that when added to a

THESAURUS

compatible 1. agreeable, congenial, harmonious, in harmony, like-minded **2.** accordant, congruent, congruous, consistent, in keeping, reconcilable

compel 1. bulldoze (*informal*), coerce, dragoon, drive, enforce, hustle (*slang*), impel, make, oblige, railroad (*informal*) **2.** enforce, exact, force, necessitate

compelling 1. enchanting, enthralling, gripping, hypnotic, irresistible, mesmeric, spellbinding **2.** cogent, conclusive, convincing, forceful, irrefutable, powerful, telling, weighty

compensate 1. atone, indemnify, make amends, make good, make restitution, recompense, refund, reimburse, remunerate, repay, requite, satisfy **2.** balance, cancel (out), counteract, counterbalance, make up for, offset, redress

compensation amends, atonement, damages, indemnification, indemnity, payment, recompense, reimbursement, remuneration, reparation, requital, restitution, satisfaction

compete be in the running, contend, contest, fight, pit oneself against, rival, strive, struggle, vie

competence *or* **competency** ability, adequacy, appropriateness, capability, capacity, competency, craft, expertise, fitness, proficiency, skill, suitability

competent able, adequate, appropriate, capable, clever, endowed, equal, fit, proficient, qualified, sufficient, suitable

competition 1. contention, contest, one-upmanship (*informal*), opposition, rivalry, strife, struggle **2.** championship, contest, event, head-to-head, tournament **3.** challengers, field, opposition, rivals

competitive aggressive, ambitious, antagonistic, at odds, combative, cutthroat, dog-eat-dog, opposing, rival, vying

competitor adversary, antagonist, challenger, competition, contestant, opponent, opposition, rival

compile accumulate, amass, collect, cull, garner, gather, marshal, organize, put together

complacency contentment, gratification, pleasure, satisfaction, self-satisfaction, smugness

complacent contented, gratified, pleased, pleased with oneself, satisfied, self-contented, self-satisfied, serene, smug, unconcerned

complain beef (*slang*), bellyache (*slang*), bemoan, bewail, bitch (*slang*), bleat, carp, deplore, find fault, fuss, grieve, gripe (*informal*), groan, grouch (*informal*), grouse, growl, grumble, kick up a fuss (*informal*), lament, moan, whine, whinge (*informal*)

complaint 1. accusation, beef (*slang*), bitch (*slang*), charge, criticism, fault-finding, grievance, gripe (*informal*), grouch (*informal*), grouse, grumble, lament, moan, plaint (*archaic*), protest, remonstrance **2.** affliction, ailment, disease, disorder, illness, indisposition, malady, sickness, upset

complement *n.* **1.** companion, completion, consummation, counterpart, finishing touch, rounding-off, supplement **2.** aggregate, capacity, entirety, quota, total, totality, wholeness *~vb.* **3.** cap (*informal*), complete, crown, round off, set off

specified angle produces a right angle. *~vb* **6** to complete or form a complement to.
complementary *adj* **1** forming a complete or balanced whole. **2** forming a complement.
complementary medicine *n* same as **alternative medicine.**
complete *adj* **1** thorough; absolute: *it was a complete shambles.* **2** perfect in quality or kind: *he is the complete modern footballer.* **3** finished. **4** having all the necessary parts. **5 complete with** having as an extra feature or part: *a mansion complete with swimming pool.* *~vb* **-pleting, -pleted 6** to finish. **7** to make whole or perfect. **completely** *adv* **completion** *n*
complex *adj* **1** made up of interconnected parts. **2** intricate or complicated. **3** *Maths* of or involving complex numbers. *~n* **4** a whole made up of related parts: *a leisure complex including a gymnasium, squash courts, and a 20-metre swimming pool.* **5** *Psychoanal* a group of unconscious feelings that influences a person's behaviour. **6** *Informal* an obsession or phobia: *I have never had a complex about my height.*
complex fraction *n Maths* a fraction in which the numerator or denominator or both contain fractions.
complexion *n* **1** the colour and general appearance of the skin of a person's face. **2** character or nature: *the political complexion of the government.*
complexity *n, pl* **-ties 1** the state or quality of being intricate or complex. **2** something complicated.
complex number *n* any number of the form $a + bi$, where a and b are real numbers and $i = \sqrt{-1}$.
compliance *n* **1** complying. **2** a tendency to do what others want. **compliant** *adj*
complicate *vb* **-cating, -cated** to make or become complex or difficult to deal with.
complicated *adj* difficult to understand or deal with.
complication *n* **1** something which makes a situation more difficult to deal with: *an added complication is the growing concern for the environment.* **2** a medical condition arising as a consequence of another.
complicity *n, pl* **-ties** the fact of being an accomplice in a crime.
compliment *n* **1** an expression of praise. **2 compliments** formal greetings. *~vb* **3** to express admiration for.
complimentary *adj* **1** expressing praise. **2** free of charge.
comply *vb* **-plies, -plying, -plied** to act in accordance (with a rule, order, or request).
component *n* **1** a constituent part or feature of a whole. **2** *Maths* one of a set of two or more vectors whose resultant is a given vector. *~adj* **3** forming or functioning as a part or feature.
comport *vb Formal* **1** to behave (oneself) in a specified way. **2 comport with** to suit or be appropriate to. **comportment** *n*
compose *vb* **-posing, -posed 1** to put together or make up. **2** to be the component elements of. **3** to create (a musical or literary work). **4** to calm (oneself). **5** to arrange artistically. **6** *Printing* to set up (type).
➤ For sense 2 the usual idiom is: *it is/was composed of.*
composed *adj* (of people) in control of their feelings.
composer *n* a person who writes music.
composite *adj* **1** made up of separate parts. **2** (of a plant) with flower heads made up of many small flow-

THESAURUS

complementary companion, completing, correlative, corresponding, fellow, interdependent, interrelating, matched, reciprocal
complete *adj.* **1.** absolute, consummate, deep-dyed (*usually derogatory*), dyed-in-the-wool, outright, perfect, thorough, thoroughgoing, total, utter **2.** accomplished, achieved, concluded, ended, finished **3.** all, entire, faultless, full, intact, integral, plenary, unabridged, unbroken, undivided, unimpaired, whole *~vb.* **4.** accomplish, achieve, close, conclude, discharge, do, end, execute, finalize, finish, fulfil, perform, realize, settle, terminate, wrap up (*informal*) **5.** cap, crown, fill in, perfect, round off
completely absolutely, altogether, down to the ground, en masse, entirely, from A to Z, from beginning to end, fully, heart and soul, hook, line and sinker, in full, *in toto,* perfectly, quite, root and branch, solidly, thoroughly, totally, utterly, wholly
completion accomplishment, attainment, close, conclusion, consummation, culmination, end, finalization, fruition, fulfilment, realization
complex *adj.* **1.** composite, compound, compounded, heterogeneous, manifold, multifarious, multiple **2.** circuitous, complicated, convoluted, intricate, involved, knotty, labyrinthine, tangled, tortuous *~n.* **3.** aggregate, composite, network, organization, scheme, structure, system **4.** fixation, fixed idea, *idée fixe,* obsession, phobia, preoccupation
complexion **1.** colour, colouring, hue, pigmentation, skin, skin tone **2.** appearance, aspect, cast, character, countenance, disposition, look, make-up, nature, stamp
complexity complication, convolution, elaboration, entanglement, intricacy, involvement, multiplicity, ramification
compliance acquiescence, agreement, assent, complaisance, concession, concurrence, conformity, consent, deference, obedience, observance, passivity, submission, submissiveness, yielding
complicate confuse, entangle, interweave, involve, make intricate, muddle, ravel, snarl up
complicated Byzantine (*of attitudes, etc.*), complex, convoluted, difficult, elaborate, intricate, involved, labyrinthine, perplexing, problematic, puzzling
complication aggravation, difficulty, drawback, factor, obstacle, problem, snag
complicity abetment, collaboration, collusion, connivance
compliment **1.** *n.* admiration, bouquet, commendation, congratulations, eulogy, flattery, honour, praise, tribute **2.** *vb.* commend, congratulate, extol, flatter, laud (*literary*), pay tribute to, praise, salute, sing the praises of, speak highly of
complimentary **1.** appreciative, approving, commendatory, eulogistic, flattering, laudatory, panegyrical **2.** courtesy, donated, free, free of charge, gratis, gratuitous, honorary, on the house
compliments good wishes, greetings, regards, respects, salutation
comply abide by, accede, accord, acquiesce, adhere, agree, conform, consent, defer to, follow, fulfil, obey, observe, perform, respect, satisfy, submit, yield
component **1.** *n.* constituent, element, ingredient, item, part, piece, unit **2.** *adj.* composing, constituent, inherent, intrinsic
compose **1.** build, compound, comprise, constitute, construct, fashion, form, make, make up, put together **2.** contrive, create, devise, frame, imagine, invent, produce, write **3.** calm, collect, control, quiet, soothe, still, tranquillize
composed at ease, calm, collected, confident, cool, imperturbable, laid-back (*informal*), level-headed,

ers, such as the dandelion. **3** *Maths* capable of being factorized: *a composite function.* *~n* **4** something composed of separate parts. **5** a composite plant.

Composite *adj* of a style of classical architecture which combines elements of the Ionic and Corinthian styles.

composite school *n Canad* a secondary school which offers both academic courses and vocational training.

composition *n* **1** the act of putting together or composing. **2** something composed. **3** the things or parts which make up a whole. **4** a work of music, art, or literature. **5** the harmonious arrangement of the parts of a work of art. **6** a written exercise; an essay. **7** *Printing* the act or technique of setting up type.

compositor *n* a person who arranges type for printing.

compos mentis *adj* sane.

compost *n* **1** a mixture of decaying plants and manure, used as a fertilizer. **2** soil mixed with fertilizer, used for growing plants. *~vb* **3** to make (vegetable matter) into compost.

composure *n* the state of being calm or unworried.

compote *n* fruit stewed with sugar or in a syrup.

compound[1] *n* **1** *Chem* a substance that contains atoms of two or more chemical elements held together by chemical bonds. **2** any combination of two or more parts, features, or qualities. **3** a word formed from two existing words or combining forms. *~vb* **4** to combine so as to create a compound. **5** to make by combining parts or features: *the film's score is compounded from surging strings, a heavenly chorus and jazzy saxophones.* **6** to intensify by an added element: *the problems of undertaking relief work are compounded by continuing civil war.* **7** *Law* to agree not to prosecute in return for payment: *to compound a crime.* *~adj* **8** composed of two or more parts or elements. **9** *Music* with a time in which the number of beats per bar is a multiple of three: *such tunes are usually in a form of compound time, for example six-four.* **compoundable** *adj*

compound[2] *n* a fenced enclosure containing buildings, such as a camp for prisoners of war.

compound fracture *n* a fracture in which the broken bone pierces the skin.

compound interest *n* interest paid on a sum and its accumulated interest.

comprehend *vb* **1** to understand. **2** to include. **comprehensible** *adj*

comprehension *n* **1** understanding. **2** inclusion.

comprehensive *adj* **1** of broad scope or content. **2** (of car insurance) providing protection against most risks, including third-party liability, fire, theft, and damage. **3** of the comprehensive school system. *~n* **4** a comprehensive school.

comprehensive school *n Chiefly Brit* a secondary school for children of all abilities.

compress *vb* **1** to squeeze together. **2** to condense. *~n* **3** a cloth or pad applied firmly to some part of the body to cool inflammation or relieve pain.

compression *n* **1** the act of compressing. **2** the reduction in volume and increase in pressure of the fuel mixture in an internal-combustion engine before ignition.

compressor *n* a device that compresses a gas.

comprise *vb* **-prising, -prised 1** to be made up of: *the group comprised six French diplomats, five Italians and three Bulgarians.* **2** to form or make up: *women comprised 57 per cent of all employees, but less than 10 per cent of managers.*

➤ *Comprise* is not followed by *of* but directly by its object.

compromise (**kom**-prom-mize) *n* **1** settlement of a dispute by concessions on each side: *everyone pleaded for compromise; the compromise was only reached after hours of hard bargaining.* **2** the terms of such a settlement. **3** something midway between different things. *~vb* **-mising, -mised 4** to settle (a dispute) by making concessions. **5** to put (oneself or another person) in a dishonourable position. *~adj* **6** being, or having the nature or, a compromise: *a compromise solution.* **compromising** *adj*

THESAURUS

poised, relaxed, sedate, self-possessed, serene, together (*slang*), tranquil, unfazed (*informal*), unflappable, unruffled, unworried

composite 1. *adj.* blended, combined, complex, compound, conglomerate, mixed **2.** *n.* amalgam, blend, compound, conglomerate, fusion, meld

composition 1. compilation, creation, fashioning, formation, formulation, invention, making, production **2.** arrangement, configuration, constitution, design, form, formation, layout, make-up, organization, structure **3.** arrangement, balance, concord, consonance (*formal*), harmony, proportion, symmetry **4.** creation, essay, exercise, literary work, opus, piece, study, treatise, work, writing

compost humus, mulch, organic fertilizer

composure aplomb, calm, calmness, collectedness, cool (*slang*), coolness, dignity, ease, equanimity, imperturbability, placidity, poise, sang-froid, sedateness, self-assurance, self-possession, serenity, tranquillity

compound *n.* **1.** alloy, amalgam, blend, combination, composite, composition, conglomerate, fusion, medley, meld, mixture, synthesis *~vb.* **2.** amalgamate, blend, coalesce, combine, concoct, fuse, intermingle, meld, mingle, mix, synthesize, unite **3.** add to, aggravate, augment, complicate, exacerbate, heighten, intensify, magnify, worsen *~adj.* **4.** complex, composite, conglomerate, intricate, multiple

comprehend 1. apprehend, assimilate, conceive, discern, fathom, grasp, know, make out, perceive, see, take in, understand **2.** comprise, contain, embody, embrace, enclose, encompass, include, involve, take in

comprehensible clear, coherent, conceivable, explicit, graspable, intelligible, plain, understandable, user-friendly

comprehension 1. conception, discernment, grasp, intelligence, knowledge, perception, realization, sense, understanding **2.** compass, domain, field, limits, province, range, reach, scope

comprehensive all-embracing, all-inclusive, blanket, broad, catholic, complete, encyclopedic, exhaustive, extensive, full, inclusive, sweeping, thorough, wide

compress 1. compact, concentrate, condense, constrict, contract, cram, crowd, crush, press, pucker, shorten, squash, squeeze, wedge **2.** abbreviate, shorten, summarize

compressed 1. compact, compacted, concentrated, constricted, flattened, reduced, shortened, squashed, squeezed **2.** concise, shortened

compression condensation, constriction, crushing, pressure, squeezing

comprise 1. be composed of, comprehend, consist of, contain, embrace, encompass, include, take in **2.** compose, constitute, form, make up

compromise *n.* **1.** accommodation, adjustment, agreement, concession, give-and-take, half measures, middle ground, settlement, trade-off *~vb.* **2.** adjust, agree, concede, give and take, go fifty-fifty (*informal*),

comptroller *n* a financial controller.
compulsion *n* **1** an irresistible urge to perform some action. **2** compelling or being compelled.
compulsive *adj* **1** resulting from or acting from a compulsion. **2** irresistible or absorbing. **compulsively** *adv*
compulsory *adj* required by regulations or laws.
compulsory purchase *n* the enforced purchase of a property by a local authority or government department.
compunction *n* a feeling of guilt or regret.
computation *n* a calculation involving numbers or quantities. **computational** *adj*
compute *vb* **-puting, -puted** to calculate (an answer or result), often by using a computer.
computer *n* an electronic device that processes data according to a set of instructions.
computer game *n* a game played on a home computer by manipulating a joystick or keys in response to the graphics on the screen.
computerize *or* **-ise** *vb* **-izing, -ized** *or* **-ising, -ised 1** to equip with a computer. **2** to control or perform (operations) by means of a computer. **computerization** *or* **-isation** *n*
computing *n* **1** the activity of using computers and writing programs for them. **2** the study of computers and their application.
comrade *n* **1** a fellow member of a union or a socialist political party. **2** a companion. **comradely** *adj* **comradeship** *n*
con[1] *Informal* ~*n* **1** same as **confidence trick.** ~*vb* **conning, conned 2** to swindle or defraud.
con[2] *n* See **pros and cons.**
con[3] *n Slang* a convict.
Con *Politics* Conservative.
con- *prefix* See **com-.**
concatenation *n Formal* a series of linked events.
concave *adj* curving inwards like the inside surface of a ball. **concavity** *n*
conceal *vb* **1** to cover and hide. **2** to keep secret. **concealment** *n*
concede *vb* **-ceding, -ceded 1** to admit (something) as true or correct. **2** to give up or grant (something, such as a right). **3** to acknowledge defeat in (a contest or argument).
conceit *n* **1** an excessively high opinion of oneself. **2** *Literary* a far-fetched or clever comparison.
conceited *adj* having an excessively high opinion of oneself. **conceitedness** *n*
conceivable *adj* capable of being understood, believed, or imagined. **conceivably** *adv*
conceive *vb* **-ceiving, -ceived 1** to imagine or think. **2** to consider in a certain way: *we must do what we conceive to be right.* **3** to form in the mind. **4** to become pregnant.
concentrate *vb* **-trating, -trated 1** to focus all one's attention, thoughts, or efforts on something: *she tried hard to concentrate, but her mind kept flashing back to the previous night.* **2** to bring or come together in large numbers or amounts in one place: *a flawed system that concentrates power in the hands of the few.* **3** to make (a liquid) stronger by removing water from it. ~*n* **4** a concentrated substance. **concentrated** *adj*
concentration *n* **1** intense mental application. **2** the act of concentrating. **3** something that is concentrated. **4** the amount or proportion of a substance in a mixture or solution.
concentration camp *n* a prison camp for civilian prisoners, as in Nazi Germany.
concentric *adj* having the same centre: *concentric circles.*
concept *n* an abstract or general idea: *one of the basic concepts of quantum theory.*
conception *n* **1** a notion, idea, or plan. **2** the fertilization of an egg by a sperm in the Fallopian tube followed by implantation in the womb. **3** origin or beginning: *the gap between the conception of an invention and its production.*

THESAURUS

meet halfway, settle, strike a balance **3.** discredit, dishonour, embarrass, implicate, prejudice, weaken
compulsion 1. drive, necessity, need, obsession, preoccupation, urge **2.** coercion, constraint, demand, duress, force, obligation, pressure, urgency
compulsive besetting, compelling, driving, irresistible, obsessive, overwhelming, uncontrollable, urgent
compulsory binding, *de rigueur,* forced, imperative, mandatory, obligatory, required, requisite
compute add up, calculate, cast up, count, enumerate, estimate, figure, figure out, measure, rate, reckon, tally, total
comrade ally, associate, buddy (*informal*), cock (*Brit. informal*), colleague, companion, compatriot, compeer, confederate, co-worker, crony, fellow, friend, mate (*informal*), pal (*informal*), partner
concave cupped, excavated, hollow, hollowed, indented, scooped, sunken
conceal 1. bury, camouflage, cover, disguise, hide, mask, obscure, screen, secrete, stash (*informal*) **2.** dissemble, hide, keep dark, keep secret
concealed covered, hidden, inconspicuous, masked, obscured, screened, secret, secreted, tucked away, unseen
concealment camouflage, cover, disguise, hiding, secrecy
concede 1. accept, acknowledge, admit, allow, confess, grant, own **2.** cede, give up, hand over, relinquish, surrender, yield
conceit 1. amour-propre, arrogance, complacency, egotism, narcissism, pride, self-importance, self-love, swagger, vainglory, vanity **2.** *literary* belief, fancy, fantasy, idea, image, notion, thought, whim, whimsy
conceited arrogant, bigheaded (*informal*), cocky, egotistical, immodest, narcissistic, puffed up, self-important, stuck-up (*informal*), swollen-headed, vain, vainglorious
conceivable believable, credible, imaginable, possible, thinkable
conceive 1. appreciate, apprehend, believe, comprehend, envisage, fancy, grasp, imagine, realize, suppose, understand **2.** contrive, create, design, develop, devise, form, formulate, produce, think up **3.** become impregnated, become pregnant
concentrate 1. be engrossed in, consider closely, focus attention on, give all one's attention to, put one's mind to, rack one's brains **2.** accumulate, centre, cluster, collect, congregate, converge, focus, gather, huddle
concentrated 1. all-out (*informal*), deep, hard, intense, intensive **2.** boiled down, condensed, evaporated, reduced, rich, thickened, undiluted
concentration 1. absorption, application, single-mindedness **2.** centralization, centring, convergence, focusing, intensification **3.** accumulation, aggregation, cluster, collection, convergence, horde, mass
concept abstraction, conception, conceptualization, hypothesis, idea, image, impression, notion, theory, view
conception 1. concept, design, idea, image, notion,

conceptual *adj* of or based on concepts.

conceptualize *or* **-ise** *vb* **-izing, -ized** *or* **-ising, -ised** to form a concept or idea of. **conceptualization** *or* **-isation** *n*

concern *n* **1** anxiety or worry: *the current concern over teenage pregnancies.* **2** something that is of interest or importance to a person. **3** regard or interest: *a scrupulous concern for client confidentiality.* **4** a business or firm. *~vb* **5** to worry or make anxious. **6** to involve or interest: *he had converted the building into flats without concerning himself with the niceties of planning permission.* **7** to be relevant or important to.

concerned *adj* **1** interested or involved: *I have spoken to the person concerned and he has no recollection of saying such a thing.* **2** worried or anxious: *we are increasingly concerned for her safety.*

concerning *prep* about; regarding.

concert *n* **1** a performance of music by players or singers in front of an audience. **2 in concert a** working together. **b** (of musicians or singers) performing live.

concerted *adj* decided or planned by mutual agreement: *a concerted effort.*

concertina *n* **1** a small musical instrument similar to an accordion. *~vb* **-naing, -naed 2** to collapse or fold up like a concertina.

concerto (kon-**chair**-toe) *n, pl* **-tos** *or* **-ti** (-tee) a large-scale composition for an orchestra and one or more soloists.

concert pitch *n* the internationally agreed pitch to which concert instruments are tuned for performance.

concession *n* **1** any grant of rights, land, or property by a government, local authority, or company. **2** a reduction in price for a certain category of person: *fare concessions for senior citizens.* **3** the act of yielding or conceding. **4** something conceded. **5** *Canad* **a** a land subdivision in a township survey. **b** same as **concession road. concessionary** *adj*

concessionaire *n* someone who holds a concession.

concession road *n Canad* one of a series of roads separating concessions in a township.

conch *n, pl* **conchs** *or* **conches 1** a marine mollusc with a large brightly coloured spiral shell. **2** its shell.

concierge (kon-see-**airzh**) *n* (in France) a caretaker in a block of flats.

conciliate *vb* **-ating, -ated** to try to end a disagreement with or pacify (somebody). **conciliation** *n* **conciliator** *n*

conciliatory *adj* intended to end a disagreement.

concise *adj* brief and to the point. **concisely** *adv* **conciseness** *or* **concision** *n*

conclave *n* **1** a secret meeting. **2** *RC Church* a private meeting of cardinals to elect a new pope.

conclude *vb* **-cluding, -cluded 1** to decide by reasoning: *the investigation concluded that key data for the paper were faked.* **2** to come or bring to an end: *the festival concludes on December 19th.* **3** to arrange or settle finally: *officials have refused to comment on the failure to conclude an agreement.*

conclusion *n* **1** a final decision, opinion, or judgment based on reasoning: *the obvious conclusion is that something is being covered up.* **2** end or ending. **3** outcome or result: *if you take that strategy to its logical conclusion you end up with communism.* **4 in conclusion** finally. **5 jump to conclusions** to come to a conclusion too quickly, without sufficient thought or evidence.

conclusive *adj* putting an end to doubt: *there is no conclusive proof of this.* **conclusively** *adv*

concoct *vb* **1** to make by combining different ingredients. **2** to invent or make up (a story or plan). **concoction** *n*

concomitant *adj* **1** existing or along with (something else). *~n* **2** something which is concomitant.

concord *n* **1** agreement or harmony. **2** peaceful relations between nations. **3** *Music* a harmonious combination of musical notes. **concordant** *adj*

concordance *n* **1** a state of harmony or agreement. **2** an alphabetical list of words in a literary work, with the context and often the meaning.

concordat *n Formal* a treaty or agreement, such as one between the Vatican and another state.

THESAURUS

plan **2.** fertilization, germination, impregnation, insemination **3.** beginning, birth, formation, inception, initiation, invention, launching, origin, outset

concern *n.* **1.** anxiety, apprehension, attention, care, consideration, disquiet, disquietude, distress, solicitude, worry **2.** affair, business, charge, department, field, interest, job, matter, mission, occupation, responsibility, task **3.** business, company, corporation, enterprise, establishment, firm, house, organization *~vb.* **4.** bother, disquiet, distress, disturb, make anxious, make uneasy, perturb, trouble, worry **5.** affect, apply to, bear on, be relevant to, interest, involve, pertain to, regard, touch

concerned 1. implicated, interested, involved, mixed up, privy to **2.** anxious, bothered, distressed, disturbed, exercised, troubled, uneasy, upset, worried

concerning about, apropos of, as regards, as to, in the matter of, on the subject of, re, regarding, relating to, respecting, touching, with reference to

concert in concert concertedly, in collaboration, in league, in unison, jointly, shoulder to shoulder, together, unanimously

concerted agreed upon, collaborative, combined, coordinated, joint, planned, prearranged, united

concession 1. acknowledgment, admission, assent, confession, surrender, yielding **2.** adjustment, allowance, boon, compromise, grant, indulgence, permit, privilege, sop

conciliate appease, mediate, mollify, pacify, placate, propitiate, reconcile, soothe, win over

conciliation appeasement, mollification, pacification, placation, propitiation, reconciliation, soothing

conciliatory appeasing, mollifying, pacific (*formal*), peaceable, placatory, propitiative

concise brief, compact, compressed, condensed, epigrammatic, laconic, pithy, short, succinct, summary, synoptic, terse, to the point

conclude 1. assume, decide, deduce, gather, infer, judge, reckon (*informal*), suppose, surmise **2.** bring down the curtain, cease, close, come to an end, complete, draw to a close, end, finish, round off, terminate, wind up **3.** accomplish, bring about, carry out, clinch, decide, determine, effect, establish, fix, pull off, resolve, settle, work out

conclusion 1. agreement, conviction, decision, deduction, inference, judgment, opinion, resolution, settlement, verdict **2.** close, completion, end, finale, finish, result, termination **3.** consequence, culmination, issue, outcome, result, sequel, upshot **4. in conclusion** finally, in closing, lastly, to sum up

conclusive clinching, convincing, decisive, definite, definitive, final, irrefutable, ultimate, unanswerable, unarguable

concoct 1. brew, cook up (*informal*), make up, manufacture, prepare **2.** contrive, design, devise, fab-

concourse *n* **1** a large open space in a public place, where people can meet: *a crowded concourse at Heathrow airport.* **2** a crowd.
concrete *n* **1** a building material made of cement, sand, stone and water that hardens to a stonelike mass. ~*vb* **-creting, -creted 2** to cover with concrete. ~*adj* **3** made of concrete. **4** specific as opposed to general. **5** relating to things that can be perceived by the senses, as opposed to abstractions.
concretion *n* **1** a solidified mass. **2** the act of solidifying.
concubine (**kon**-kew-bine) *n* **1** *Old-fashioned* a woman living with a man as his wife, but not married to him. **2** a secondary wife in polygamous societies. **concubinage** *n*
concupiscence (kon-**kew**-piss-enss) *n* *Formal* strong sexual desire. **concupiscent** *adj*
concur *vb* **-curring, -curred** to agree; be in accord.
concurrence *n* **1** agreement. **2** simultaneous occurrence.
concurrent *adj* **1** taking place at the same time or place. **2** meeting at, approaching, or having a common point: *concurrent lines.* **3** in agreement. **concurrently** *adv*
concuss *vb* to injure (the brain) by a fall or blow.
concussion *n* **1** a brain injury caused by a blow or fall, usually resulting in loss of consciousness. **2** violent shaking.
condemn *vb* **1** to express strong disapproval of. **2** to pronounce sentence on in a court of law. **3** to force into a particular state: *a system that condemns most of our youngsters to failure.* **4** to judge or declare (something) unfit for use. **5** to indicate the guilt of: *everything the man had said condemned him, morally if not technically.* **condemnation** *n* **condemnatory** *adj*
condensation *n* **1** anything that has condensed from a vapour, esp. on a window. **2** the act of condensing, or the state of being condensed.
condense *vb* **-densing, -densed 1** to express in fewer words. **2** to increase the density of; concentrate. **3** to change from a gas to a liquid or solid.
condensed milk *n* milk thickened by evaporation, with sugar added.
condenser *n* **1** an apparatus for reducing gases to their liquid or solid form by the removal of heat. **2** same as **capacitor. 3** a lens that concentrates light.
condescend *vb* **1** to behave patronizingly towards one's supposed inferiors. **2** to do something as if it were beneath one's dignity. **condescending** *adj* **condescension** *n*
condiment *n* any seasoning for food, such as salt, pepper, or sauces.
condition *n* **1** a particular state of being: *the human condition; the van is in very poor condition.* **2 conditions** circumstances: *worsening weather conditions; the government pledged to improve living and working conditions.* **3** a necessary requirement for something else to happen: *food is a necessary condition for survival.* **4** a restriction or a qualification. **5** a term of an agreement: *the conditions of the lease are set out.* **6** state of physical fitness, esp. good health: *she is in a serious condition in hospital; out of condition.* **7** an ailment: *a heart condition.* **8 on condition that** provided that. ~*vb* **9** to accustom or alter the reaction of (a person or animal) to a particular stimulus or situation. **10** to treat with a conditioner. **11** to make fit or healthy. **12** to influence or determine the form that something takes: *he argued that the failure of Latin American industry was conditioned by international economic structures.* **conditioning** *n, adj*
conditional *adj* **1** depending on other factors. **2** *Grammar* expressing a condition on which something else depends, for example "If he comes" is a conditional clause in the sentence "If he comes I shall go".
conditioner *n* a thick liquid used when washing to make hair or clothes feel softer.
condo *n, pl* **-dos** *US & Canad informal* a condominium building or apartment.

THESAURUS

ricate, formulate, hatch, invent, make up, manufacture, plot, think up, trump up
concoction blend, brew, combination, compound, creation, mixture, preparation
concrete *adj.* **1.** actual, definite, explicit, factual, real, specific **2.** material, real, sensible, substantial, tangible
concubine *old-fashioned* courtesan, kept woman, mistress, paramour
concur accord, agree, approve, assent, coincide, consent, cooperate, harmonize, join
concurrent 1. coexisting, coincident, concomitant, contemporaneous, simultaneous, synchronous **2.** confluent, convergent, converging, uniting **3.** agreeing, at one, compatible, consistent, cooperating, harmonious, in agreement, in rapport, like-minded, of the same mind
concussion clash, collision, crash, impact, jarring, jolt, jolting, shaking, shock
condemn 1. blame, censure, damn, denounce, disapprove, excoriate (*literary*), reprehend, reproach, reprobate, reprove, upbraid **2.** convict, damn, doom, pass sentence on, proscribe, sentence
condemnation 1. blame, censure, denouncement, denunciation, disapproval, reproach, reprobation, reproof, stricture (*formal*) **2.** conviction, doom, judgment, proscription, sentence
condensation abridgment, contraction, digest, précis, synopsis
condense 1. abbreviate, abridge, compact, compress, concentrate, contract, curtail, encapsulate, epitomize, précis, shorten, summarize **2.** boil down, concentrate, decoct, reduce, thicken
condensed 1. abridged, compressed, concentrated, curtailed, shortened, shrunken, summarized **2.** boiled down, concentrated, reduced, thickened
condescend 1. patronize, talk down to **2.** be courteous, bend, come down off one's high horse (*informal*), deign, humble *or* demean oneself, lower oneself, stoop, submit, unbend (*informal*), vouchsafe
condescending disdainful, lofty, lordly, patronizing, snobbish, snooty (*informal*), supercilious, superior, toffee-nosed (*slang, chiefly Brit.*)
condition *n.* **1.** case, circumstances, position, shape, situation, state, state of affairs, *status quo* **2.** prerequisite, requirement, requisite **3.** limitation, modification, qualification, restriction **4.** article, demand, provision, proviso, rider, rule, stipulation, terms **5.** fettle, fitness, health, kilter, order, shape, state of health, trim **6.** ailment, complaint, infirmity, malady, problem, weakness ~*vb.* **7.** accustom, adapt, educate, equip, habituate, make ready, prepare, ready, tone up, train, work out
conditional contingent, dependent, limited, provisional, qualified, subject to, with reservations
conditioned acclimatized, accustomed, adapted, adjusted, familiarized, habituated, inured, made ready, prepared, seasoned, trained, used
conditioning *n.* **1.** accustoming, familiarization,

condolence *n* sympathy expressed for someone in grief or pain. **condole** *vb*

condom *n* a rubber sheath worn on the penis or in the vagina during sexual intercourse to prevent conception or infection.

condominium *n, pl* **-ums 1** *US & Canad* **a** an apartment building in which each apartment is individually owned. **b** an apartment in such a building. **2** joint rule of a state by two or more other states.

condone *vb* **-doning, -doned** to overlook or forgive (an offence or wrongdoing).

condor *n* a very large rare S American vulture.

conducive *adj* (often foll. by *to*) likely to lead to or produce (a result).

conduct *n* **1** behaviour. **2** the management or handling of an activity or business. *~vb* **3** to carry out: *the police are conducting an investigation into the affair.* **4** to behave (oneself). **5** to control (an orchestra or choir) by the movements of the hands or a baton. **6** to accompany and guide (people or a party): *a conducted tour.* **7** to transmit (heat or electricity).

conductance *n* the ability of a specified body to conduct electricity.

conduction *n* the transmission of heat or electricity.

conductivity *n* the property of transmitting heat, electricity, or sound.

conductor *n* **1** a person who conducts an orchestra or choir. **2** an official on a bus who collects fares. **3** *US & Canad* a railway official in charge of a train. **4** something that conducts electricity or heat. **conductress** *fem n*

conduit (**kon**-dew-it) *n* **1** a route or system for transferring things from one place to another: *a conduit for smuggling cocaine into the United States.* **2** a channel or tube for carrying a fluid or electrical cables.

cone *n* **1** a geometric solid consisting of a circular or oval base, tapering to a point. **2** a cone-shaped wafer shell used to contain ice cream. **3** the scaly fruit of a conifer tree. **4** a plastic cone used as a temporary traffic marker on roads. **5** a type of cell in the retina, sensitive to colour and bright light.

coney *n* same as **cony.**

confab *n Informal* a conversation.

confabulation *n Formal* a conversation.

confection *n* **1** any sweet food, such as a cake or a sweet. **2** *Old-fashioned* an elaborate piece of clothing.

confectioner *n* a person who makes or sells confectionery.

confectionery *n, pl* **-eries 1** sweets and chocolates collectively. **2** the art or business of a confectioner.

confederacy *n, pl* **-cies** a union of states or people joined for a common purpose.

confederate *n* **1** a state or individual that is part of a confederacy. **2** an accomplice or conspirator. *~adj* **3** united; allied. *~vb* **-ating, -ated 4** to unite in a confederacy.

Confederate *adj* of or supporting those American states which withdrew from the USA in 1860-61, leading to the U.S. Civil War.

confederation *n* **1** a union or alliance of states or groups. **2** confederating or being confederated. **3** a federation.

confer *vb* **-ferring, -ferred 1** to discuss together. **2** to grant or give: *the power conferred by wealth.* **conferment** *n* **conferrable** *adj*

conference *n* a meeting for formal consultation or discussion.

confess *vb* **1** to admit (a fault or crime). **2** to admit to be true, esp. reluctantly. **3** *Christianity* to declare (one's sins) to God or to a priest, so as to obtain forgiveness.

confession *n* **1** something confessed. **2** an admission of one's faults, sins, or crimes. **3 confession of faith** a formal public statement of religious beliefs.

confessional *n* **1** *Christianity* a small room or enclosed stall in a church where a priest hears confessions. *~adj* **2** of or suited to a confession.

confessor *n* **1** *Christianity* a priest who hears confessions and gives spiritual advice. **2** *History* a person who demonstrates his Christian religious faith by the holiness of his life: *Edward the Confessor.*

confetti *n* small pieces of coloured paper thrown at weddings.

confidant *or fem* **confidante** *n* a person to whom private matters are confided.

confide *vb* **-fiding, -fided 1 confide in** to tell (something) in confidence to. **2** *Formal* to entrust into another's keeping.

confidence *n* **1** trust in a person or thing. **2** belief in one's own abilities. **3** trust or a trustful relationship: *she won first the confidence, then the admiration, of her bosses.* **4** something confided, such as a secret. **5 in confidence** as a secret.

THESAURUS

hardening, inurement **2.** grooming, preparation, readying, training

conditions circumstances, environment, milieu, situation, surroundings, way of life

condone disregard, excuse, forgive, let pass, look the other way, make allowance for, overlook, pardon, turn a blind eye to, wink at

conduct *n.* **1.** attitude, bearing, behaviour, carriage, comportment, demeanour, deportment, manners, mien (*literary*), ways **2.** administration, control, direction, guidance, leadership, management, organization, running, supervision *~vb.* **3.** administer, carry on, control, direct, govern, handle, lead, manage, organize, preside over, regulate, run, supervise **4.** acquit, act, behave, carry, comport, deport **5.** accompany, attend, convey, escort, guide, pilot, steer, usher

confederacy alliance, coalition, compact, confederation, covenant, federation, league, union

confederate 1. *n.* abettor, accessory, accomplice, ally, associate, colleague, partner **2.** *adj.* allied, associated, combined, federal, federated, in alliance **3.** *vb.* ally, amalgamate, associate, band together, combine, federate, merge, unite

confer 1. consult, converse, discourse, parley, talk **2.** accord, award, bestow, give, grant, hand out, present, vouchsafe

conference colloquium, congress, consultation, convention, convocation, discussion, forum, meeting, seminar, symposium, teach-in

confess 1. acknowledge, admit, blurt out, come clean (*informal*), confide, disclose, divulge, make a clean breast of, own up, sing (*slang, chiefly U.S.*), spill one's guts (*slang*) **2.** acknowledge, admit, allow, concede, grant, own, recognize

confession acknowledgment, admission, avowal, disclosure, divulgence, exposure, revelation

confidant *or fem.* **confidante** alter ego, bosom friend, close friend, crony, familiar, intimate

confide 1. admit, breathe, confess, disclose, divulge, impart, reveal, whisper **2.** *formal* commend, commit, consign, entrust

confidence 1. belief, credence, dependence, faith, reliance, trust **2.** aplomb, assurance, boldness, cour-

confidence trick *n* a swindle in which the swindler gains the victim's trust in order to cheat him or her.
confident *adj* **1** having or showing certainty: *we are now confident that this technique works.* **2** sure of oneself. **confidently** *adv*
confidential *adj* **1** spoken or given in confidence. **2** entrusted with another's secret affairs: *a confidential secretary.* **3** suggestive of intimacy: *a halting, confidential manner.* **confidentiality** *n* **confidentially** *adv*
confiding *adj* trusting: *a close and confiding relationship.* **confidingly** *adv*
configuration *n* **1** the arrangement of the parts of something. **2** the form or outline of such an arrangement.
confine *vb* **-fining, -fined 1** to keep within bounds. **2** to restrict the free movement of: *a nasty dose of flu which confined her to bed for days.* ~*n* **3 confines** boundaries or limits.
confinement *n* **1** being confined. **2** the period of childbirth.
confirm *vb* **1** to prove to be true or valid. **2** to reaffirm (something), so as to make (it) more definite: *she confirmed that she is about to resign as leader of the council.* **3** to strengthen: *this cruise confirmed my first impressions of the boat's performance.* **4** to formally make valid. **5** to administer the rite of confirmation to.
confirmation *n* **1** the act of confirming. **2** something that confirms. **3** a rite in several Christian churches that admits a baptized person to full church membership.
confirmed *adj* long-established in a habit or condition: *a confirmed bachelor.*
confiscate *vb* **-cating, -cated** to seize (property) by authority. **confiscation** *n*
conflagration *n* a large destructive fire.
conflate *vb* **-flating, -flated** to combine or blend into a whole. **conflation** *n*
conflict *n* **1** opposition between ideas or interests. **2** a struggle or battle. ~*vb* **3** to be incompatible. **conflicting** *adj*
confluence *n* **1** a place where rivers flow into one another. **2** a gathering. **confluent** *adj*
conform *vb* **1** to comply with accepted standards, rules, or customs. **2** to be like or in accordance with: *people tend to absorb ideas that conform with their existing beliefs, and reject those that do not.*
conformation *n* **1** the general shape of an object. **2** the arrangement of the parts of an object.
conformist *adj* **1 a** (of a person) behaving or thinking like most other people rather than in an original or unconventional way: *a shy and conformist type of boy.* **b** (of an organization or society) expecting everyone to behave in the same way: *the school was a dull, conformist place for staff and students alike.* ~*n* **2** a person who behaves or thinks like most other people rather than in an original or unconventional way.
conformity *n, pl* **-ities 1** compliance in actions or behaviour with certain accepted rules, customs, or standards. **2** likeness.
confound *vb* **1** to astound or bewilder. **2** to fail to distinguish between. **3 confound it!** damn it!
confounded *adj* **1** *Informal* damned: *what a confounded nuisance!* **2** bewildered; confused: *her silent, utterly confounded daughter.*
confrere (**kon-frair**) *n* a colleague.
confront *vb* **1** (of a problem or task) to present itself to. **2** to meet face to face in hostility or defiance. **3** to present (someone) with something, esp. in order to accuse or criticize: *she finally confronted him with her suspicions.*

THESAURUS

age, firmness, nerve, self-possession, self-reliance **3. in confidence** between you and me (and the gatepost), confidentially, in secrecy, privately
confident 1. certain, convinced, positive, satisfied, secure, sure **2.** assured, bold, dauntless, fearless, self-assured, self-reliant
confidential 1. classified, hush-hush (*informal*), intimate, off the record, private, privy (*archaic*), secret **2.** faithful, familiar, trusted, trustworthy, trusty
confidentially behind closed doors, between ourselves, in camera, in confidence, in secret, personally, privately, sub rosa
confine *vb.* bind, bound, circumscribe, close, enclose, hem in, hold back, immure, imprison, incarcerate, intern, keep, limit, repress, restrain, restrict, shut up, straiten
confined enclosed, limited, restricted
confinement 1. custody, detention, imprisonment, incarceration, internment, porridge (*slang*) **2.** childbed, childbirth, labour, lying-in, parturition, time, travail
confines boundaries, bounds, circumference, edge, limits, pale
confirm 1. approve, authenticate, bear out, corroborate, endorse, ratify, substantiate, validate, verify **2.** clinch, establish, fix, fortify, reinforce, settle, strengthen
confirmation authentication, corroboration, evidence, proof, ratification, substantiation, testimony, validation, verification
confirmed chronic, dyed-in-the-wool, habitual, hardened, ingrained, inveterate, long-established, rooted, seasoned
confiscate appropriate, commandeer, expropriate, impound, seize, sequester, sequestrate
confiscation appropriation, expropriation, impounding, seizure, sequestration, takeover
conflict *n.* **1.** antagonism, bad blood, difference, disagreement, discord, dissension, divided loyalties, friction, hostility, opposition, strife, variance **2.** battle, clash, collision, combat, contention, contest, encounter, engagement, fight, fracas, head-to-head, set-to (*informal*), strife, war, warfare ~*vb.* **3.** be at variance, clash, collide, combat, contend, contest, differ, disagree, fight, strive, struggle
conflicting antagonistic, clashing, contradictory, contrary, discordant, inconsistent, opposed, opposing, paradoxical
conform 1. adapt, adjust, comply, fall in with, follow, follow the crowd, obey, run with the pack, yield **2.** accord, agree, assimilate, correspond, harmonize, match, square, suit, tally
conformation 1. build, form, framework, outline, shape **2.** anatomy, arrangement, configuration, structure
conformist *n.* conventionalist, stick-in-the-mud (*informal*), traditionalist
conformity 1. compliance, conventionality, orthodoxy **2.** affinity, agreement, conformance, congruity, consonance, correspondence, harmony, likeness, resemblance, similarity
confound amaze, astonish, astound, baffle, bewilder, confuse, dumbfound, flabbergast (*informal*), flummox, mix up, mystify, nonplus, perplex, startle, surprise
confront accost, beard, brave, challenge, defy, encounter, face, face off (*slang*), face up to, oppose, stand up to, tackle

confrontation *n* a serious argument or fight.

Confucianism *n* the teachings of Confucius (551–479 BC), the ancient Chinese philosopher, which emphasize moral order. **Confucian** *n, adj* **Confucianist** *n*

confuse *vb* **-fusing, -fused 1** to fail to distinguish between one thing and another. **2** to perplex or disconcert. **3** to make unclear: *he confused his talk with irrelevant detail.* **4** to throw into disorder. **confusing** *adj* **confusingly** *adv*

confused *adj* **1** lacking a clear understanding of something. **2** disordered and difficult to understand or make sense of: *a confused dream.*

confusion *n* **1** mistaking one person or thing for another. **2** bewilderment. **3** lack of clarity. **4** disorder.

confute *vb* **-futing, -futed** to prove to be wrong. **confutation** *n*

conga *n* **1** a Latin American dance performed by a number of people in single file. **2** a large single-headed drum played with the hands. *~vb* **-gaing, -gaed 3** to dance the conga.

congeal *vb* to change from a liquid to a semisolid state.

congenial *adj* **1** friendly, pleasant, or agreeable: *he found the Botanic Gardens a most congenial place for strolling.* **2** having a similar disposition or tastes. **congeniality** *n*

congenital *adj* (of an abnormal condition) existing at birth but not inherited: *congenital heart disease.* **congenitally** *adv*

conger *n* a large sea eel.

congested *adj* **1** crowded to excess. **2** clogged or blocked. **congestion** *n*

conglomerate *n* **1** a large corporation made up of many different companies. **2** a thing composed of several different elements. **3** a type of rock consisting of rounded pebbles or fragments held together by silica or clay. *~vb* **-ating, -ated 4** to form into a mass. *~adj* **5** made up of several different elements. **6** (of rock) consisting of rounded pebbles or fragments held together by silica or clay. **conglomeration** *n*

congratulate *vb* **-lating, -lated 1** to express one's pleasure to (a person) at his or her success or good fortune. **2 congratulate oneself** to consider oneself clever or fortunate (as a result of): *she congratulated herself on her own business acumen.* **congratulatory** *adj*

congratulations *pl n, interj* expressions of pleasure or joy on another's success or good fortune.

congregate *vb* **-gating, -gated** to collect together in or as a crowd.

congregation *n* a group of worshippers. **congregational** *adj*

Congregationalism *n* a system of Protestant church government in which each church is self-governing. **Congregationalist** *adj, n*

congress *n* a formal meeting of representatives for discussion. **congressional** *adj*

Congress *n* the federal legislature of the US, consisting of the House of Representatives and the Senate. **Congressional** *adj* **Congressman** *n* **Congresswoman** *fem n*

congruent *adj* **1** agreeing or corresponding. **2** *Geom* identical in shape and size: *congruent triangles.* **congruence** *n*

congruous *adj Formal* **1** appropriate or in keeping: *an elegant, though not altogether congruous, wing was added to the house in 1735.* **2** corresponding or agreeing: *this finding is congruous with Adam's 1982 study.* **congruity** *n*

conical *adj* in the shape of a cone.

conic section *n* a figure, either a circle, ellipse, parabola, or hyperbola, formed by the intersection of a plane and a cone.

conifer *n* a tree or shrub bearing cones and evergreen leaves, such as the fir or larch. **coniferous** *adj*

THESAURUS

confrontation conflict, contest, crisis, encounter, face-off (*slang*), head-to-head, set-to (*informal*), show-down (*informal*)

confuse 1. confound, mistake, mix up, muddle **2.** baffle, bemuse, bewilder, discomfit, discompose, disconcert, discountenance, disorient, faze, flummox, fluster, mystify, nonplus, perplex, puzzle, rattle (*informal*), throw off balance, unnerve, upset **3.** disarrange, disorder, jumble, mix up, muddle, ravel, snarl up (*informal*), tangle

confused 1. at a loss, at sea, at sixes and sevens, baffled, bewildered, dazed, discombobulated (*informal, chiefly U.S. & Canad.*), disorientated, flummoxed, muddled, muzzy (*U.S. informal*), nonplussed, not with it (*informal*), perplexed, puzzled, taken aback, thrown off balance, upset **2.** at sixes and sevens, chaotic, disarranged, disarrayed, disordered, disorderly, disorganized, higgledy-piggledy (*informal*), huggermugger (*archaic*), in disarray, jumbled, mixed up, out of order, topsy-turvy, untidy

confusing ambiguous, baffling, complicated, contradictory, disconcerting, inconsistent, misleading, muddling, perplexing, puzzling, unclear

confusion 1. befuddlement, bemusement, bewilderment, disorientation, mystification, perplexity, puzzlement **2.** bustle, chaos, clutter, commotion, disarrangement, disarray, disorder, disorganization, hodgepodge (*U.S.*), hotchpotch, jumble, mess, muddle, pig's breakfast (*informal*), shambles, state, tangle, turmoil, untidiness, upheaval

congenial 1. adapted, affable, agreeable, companionable, complaisant, favourable, fit, friendly, genial, kindly, pleasant, pleasing, suitable **2.** compatible, kindred, like-minded, sympathetic, well-suited

congenital constitutional, inborn, inbred, inherent, innate, natural

congested 1. crammed, crowded, overcrowded, overfilled, overflowing, packed, teeming **2.** blocked-up, clogged, jammed, stuffed, stuffed-up

congestion 1. crowding, mass, overcrowding **2.** bottleneck, clogging, jam, snarl-up (*informal, chiefly Brit.*)

conglomerate 1. *n.* agglomerate, aggregate, multinational **2.** *vb.* accumulate, agglomerate, aggregate, cluster, coalesce, snowball **3.** *adj.* amassed, clustered, composite, heterogeneous, massed

conglomeration accumulation, aggregation, assortment, combination, composite, hotchpotch, mass, medley, miscellany, mishmash, potpourri

congratulate compliment, wish joy to

congratulations best wishes, compliments, felicitations, good wishes, greetings

congregate assemble, collect, come together, convene, converge, convoke, flock, foregather, gather, mass, meet, muster, rally, rendezvous, throng

congregation assembly, brethren, fellowship, flock, laity, parish, parishioners

congress assembly, conference, convention, convocation (*formal*), council, delegates, house, legislative assembly, legislature, meeting, parliament, representatives

conjecture *n* **1** the formation of conclusions from incomplete evidence. **2** a guess. ~*vb* **-turing, -tured 3** to form (an opinion or conclusion) from incomplete evidence. **conjectural** *adj*

conjugal (**kon**-jew-gal) *adj* of marriage: *conjugal rights.*

conjugate *vb* (**kon**-jew-gate) **-gating, -gated 1** *Grammar* to give the inflections of (a verb). **2** (of a verb) to undergo inflection according to a specific set of rules. **3** *Formal* to combine: *a country in which conjugating Marxism with Christianity has actually been tried.* ~*n* (**kon**-jew-git) **4** *Formal* something formed by conjugation: *haemoglobin is a conjugate of a protein with an iron-containing pigment.*

conjugation *n* **1** *Grammar* **a** inflection of a verb for person, number, tense, voice and mood. **b** the complete set of the inflections of a given verb. **2** a joining.

conjunction *n* **1** joining together. **2** simultaneous occurrence of events. **3** a word or group of words that connects words, phrases, or clauses; for example *and*, *if*, and *but*. **4** *Astron* the apparent nearness of two heavenly bodies to each other. **conjunctional** *adj*

conjunctiva *n, pl* **-vas** *or* **-vae** the delicate mucous membrane that covers the eyeball and inner eyelid. **conjunctival** *adj*

conjunctive *adj* **1** joining or joined. **2** used as a conjunction: *a conjunctive adverb.* ~*n* **3** a word or words used as a conjunction.

conjunctivitis *n* inflammation of the conjunctiva.

conjuncture *n* a combination of events, esp. one that leads to a crisis.

conjure *vb* **-juring, -jured 1** to perform tricks that appear to be magic. **2** to summon (a spirit or demon) by magic. **3** *Formal or literary* to appeal earnestly to: *I conjure you by all which you profess: answer me!* **conjuring** *n*

conjure up *vb* **1** to create an image in the mind: *the name Versailles conjures up a past of sumptuous grandeur.* **2** to produce as if from nowhere: *he conjured up a fabulous opening goal.*

conjuror *or* **conjurer** *n* a person who performs magic tricks for people's entertainment.

conk *Slang* ~*n* **1** the head or nose. ~*vb* **2** to strike (someone) on the head or nose.

conker *n* same as **horse chestnut** (sense 2).

conkers *n Brit* a game in which a player swings a horse chestnut (conker), threaded onto a string, against that of another player to try to break it.

conk out *vb Informal* **1** (of a machine or car) to break down. **2** to become tired or fall asleep suddenly.

con man *n Informal* a person who swindles someone by means of a confidence trick.

connect *vb* **1** to link or be linked: *high blood pressure is closely connected to heart disease.* **2** to put into telephone communication with. **3** (of two public vehicles) to have the arrival of one timed to occur just before the departure of the other, for the convenience of passengers. **4** to associate in the mind: *he had always connected sex with violence and attacks rather than loving and concern.* **5** to relate by birth or marriage: *she was distantly connected with the Wedgwood family.* **connective** *adj*

connection *or* **connexion** *n* **1** a relationship or association. **2** a link or bond. **3** a link between two components in an electric circuit. **4 a** an opportunity to transfer from one public vehicle to another. **b** the vehicle scheduled to provide such an opportunity. **5** an influential acquaintance. **6** a relative. **7** logical sequence in thought or expression. **8** a telephone link. **9** *Slang* a supplier of illegal drugs, such as heroin. **10 in connection with** with reference to: *a number of people have been arrested in connection with the explosion.*

connective tissue *n* body tissue that supports organs, fills the spaces between them, and forms tendons and ligaments.

conning tower *n* the raised observation tower containing the periscope on a submarine.

connivance *n* encouragement or permission of wrongdoing.

connive *vb* **-niving, -nived 1 connive at** to allow or encourage (wrongdoing) by ignoring it. **2** to conspire.

connoisseur (kon-noss-**sir**) *n* a person with special knowledge of the arts, food, or drink.

connotation *n* an additional meaning or association implied by a word: *the German term carries a connotation of elitism.* **connote** *vb*

connubial (kon-**new**-bee-al) *adj Formal* of marriage: *connubial bliss.*

conquer *vb* **1** to defeat (an opponent or opponents).

THESAURUS

conical cone-shaped, funnel-shaped, pointed, pyramidal, tapered, tapering

conjecture 1. *n.* assumption, conclusion, fancy, guess, guesswork, hypothesis, inference, notion, presumption, shot in the dark, speculation, supposition, surmise, theorizing, theory **2.** *vb.* assume, fancy, guess, hypothesize, imagine, infer, suppose, surmise, suspect, theorize

conjugal bridal, connubial (*formal*), marital, married, matrimonial, nuptial, wedded

conjunction association, coincidence, combination, concurrence, juxtaposition, union

conjure 1. call upon, charm, invoke, raise, summon up **2.** *formal or literary* adjure, appeal to, beg, beseech, crave, entreat, implore, pray, supplicate

conjure up 1. bring to mind, evoke, recall, recollect **2.** contrive, create, produce as by magic

conjuror, conjurer magician, sorcerer, wizard

connect 1. affix, cohere, combine, couple, fasten, join, link, unite **2.** ally, associate, couple, join, link, relate

connected 1. combined, coupled, joined, linked, united **2.** affiliated, akin, allied, associated, banded together, bracketed, coupled, joined, linked, related

connection *or* **connexion 1.** affiliation, affinity, alliance, association, attachment, commerce, communication, correlation, correspondence, interrelation, liaison, link, marriage, relation, relationship, relevance, tie, tie-in, union **2.** bond, coupling, fastening, junction, link, tie, union **3.** acquaintance, ally, associate, contact, friend, sponsor **4.** kin, kindred, kinsman, kith, relation, relative

connivance abetment, abetting, collusion, complicity, conspiring, tacit consent

connive 1. *with* **at** abet, aid, be an accessory to, be a party to, be in collusion with, blink at, disregard, lend oneself to, let pass, look the other way, overlook, pass by, shut one's eyes to, turn a blind eye to, wink at **2.** collude, conspire, cook up (*informal*), intrigue, plot, scheme

connoisseur aficionado, appreciator, arbiter, authority, buff (*informal*), cognoscente, devotee, expert, judge, specialist, whiz (*informal*)

conquer 1. beat, blow out of the water (*slang*), checkmate, clobber (*slang*), crush, defeat, discomfit, get the better of, humble, lick (*informal*), master, overcome, overpower, overthrow, quell, rout, run rings around (*informal*), subdue, subjugate, surmount, tank (*slang*), triumph, undo, vanquish, wipe the floor

2 to overcome (a difficulty or feeling). **3** to gain possession of (a place) by force or war. **conquering** *adj* **conqueror** *n*

conquest *n* **1** the act of conquering. **2** a person or thing that has been conquered. **3** a person whose affections have been won.

conquistador *n, pl* **-dors** *or* **-dores** one of the Spanish conquerors of Mexico and Peru in the 16th century.

Cons. Conservative.

consanguineous *adj Formal* related by birth. **consanguinity** *n*

conscience *n* **1** the sense of right and wrong that governs a person's thoughts and actions. **2** a feeling of guilt: *he showed no hint of conscience over the suffering he had inflicted.* **3 in (all) conscience** in fairness. **4 on one's conscience** causing feelings of guilt.

conscience-stricken *adj* feeling guilty because of having done something wrong.

conscientious *adj* **1** painstaking or thorough in one's work. **2** governed by conscience. **conscientiously** *adv* **conscientiousness** *n*

conscientious objector *n* a person who refuses to serve in the armed forces on moral or religious grounds.

conscious *adj* **1** alert and awake. **2** aware of one's surroundings and of oneself. **3** aware (of something): *he was conscious of a need to urinate.* **4** deliberate or intentional: *a conscious attempt.* **5** of the part of the mind that is aware of a person's self, surroundings, and thoughts, and that to a certain extent determines choices of action. *~n* **6** the conscious part of the mind. **consciously** *adv* **consciousness** *n*

conscript *n* **1** a person who is enrolled for compulsory military service. *~vb* **2** to enrol (someone) for compulsory military service.

conscription *n* compulsory military service.

consecrate *vb* **-crating, -crated** **1** to make or declare sacred or for religious use. **2** to devote or dedicate (something) to a specific purpose. **3** *Christianity* to sanctify (bread and wine) to be received as the body and blood of Christ. **consecration** *n*

consecutive *adj* following in order without interruption: *three consecutive nights of rioting.* **consecutively** *adv*

consensus *n* general or widespread agreement.

➤ Note the spelling of this word, often confused with that of *census.* In view of its meaning, it is redundant to say "a consensus of opinion".

consent *n* **1** agreement, permission, or approval. **2 age of consent** the age at which sexual intercourse is permitted by law. *~vb* **3** to permit or agree (to). **consenting** *adj*

consequence *n* **1** a logical result or effect. **2** significance or importance: *we said little of consequence to each other; a woman of little consequence.* **3 in consequence** as a result. **4 take the consequences** to accept whatever results from one's action.

consequent *adj* **1** following as an effect. **2** following as a logical conclusion.

consequential *adj* **1** important or significant. **2** following as a result.

consequently *adv* as a result; therefore.

conservancy *n* environmental conservation.

conservation *n* **1** protection and careful management of the environment and natural resources. **2** protection from change, loss, or injury. **3** *Physics* the principle that the quantity of a specified aspect of a system, such as momentum or charge, remains constant. **conservationist** *n*

conservative *adj* **1** favouring the preservation of established customs and values, and opposing change. **2** moderate or cautious: *a conservative estimate.* **3** conventional in style: *people in this area are conservative in their tastes.* *~n* **4** a conservative person. **conservatism** *n*

Conservative *adj* **1** of or supporting the Conservative Party, the major right-wing political party in Britain, which believes in private enterprise and capitalism. **2** of or supporting a similar right-wing party in other countries. *~n* **3** a supporter or member of the Conservative Party.

THESAURUS

with (*informal*) **2.** acquire, annex, obtain, occupy, overrun, seize, win

conqueror champion, conquistador, defeater, hero, lord, master, subjugator, vanquisher, victor, winner

conquest 1. defeat, discomfiture, mastery, overthrow, pasting (*slang*), rout, triumph, vanquishment, victory **2.** acquisition, annexation, appropriation, coup, invasion, occupation, subjection, subjugation, takeover **3.** acquisition, adherent, admirer, catch, fan, feather in one's cap, follower, prize, supporter, worshipper

conscience 1. moral sense, principles, scruples, sense of right and wrong, still small voice **2. in (all) conscience** certainly, fairly, honestly, in truth, rightly, truly

conscience-stricken ashamed, contrite, disturbed, guilty, penitent, remorseful, repentant, sorry, troubled

conscientious 1. careful, diligent, exact, faithful, meticulous, painstaking, particular, punctilious, thorough **2.** high-minded, high-principled, honest, honourable, incorruptible, just, moral, responsible, scrupulous, straightforward, strict, upright

conscious 1. alert, awake, aware, clued-up (*informal*), cognizant (*formal*), percipient (*formal*), responsive, sensible, sentient **2.** alive to, aware, sensible, wise to (*slang*) **3.** calculated, deliberate, intentional, knowing, premeditated, rational, reasoning, responsible, self-conscious, studied, wilful

consciousness apprehension, awareness, knowledge, realization, recognition, sensibility

consecrate dedicate, devote, exalt, hallow, ordain, sanctify, set apart, venerate

consecutive chronological, following, in sequence, in turn, running, sequential, succeeding, successive, uninterrupted

consensus agreement, assent, common consent, concord, concurrence, general agreement, harmony, unanimity, unity

consent 1. *n.* acquiescence, agreement, approval, assent, compliance, concurrence, go-ahead (*informal*), O.K. *or* okay (*informal*), permission, sanction **2.** *vb.* accede, acquiesce, agree, allow, approve, assent, comply, concur, permit, yield

consequence 1. effect, end, event, outcome, repercussion, result, sequel, upshot **2.** account, concern, import, importance, interest, moment, note, portent, significance, value, weight **3. in consequence** as a result, because, following

consequent ensuing, following, resultant, resulting, subsequent, successive

consequently accordingly, ergo, hence, necessarily, subsequently, therefore, thus

conservation custody, guardianship, husbandry, maintenance, preservation, protection, safeguarding, safekeeping, saving, upkeep

conservative *adj.* **1.** conventional, die-hard, hidebound, middle-of-the-road, reactionary, right-wing,

conservatoire (kon-**serv**-a-twahr) *n* a school of music.

conservatory *n, pl* **-tories 1** a greenhouse attached to a house. **2** a conservatoire.

conserve *vb* **-serving, -served 1** to protect from harm, decay, or loss. **2** to preserve (fruit or other food) with sugar. *~n* **3** fruit preserved by cooking in sugar.

consider *vb* **1** to be of the opinion that. **2** to think carefully about (a problem or decision). **3** to bear in mind: *Corsica is well worth considering for those seeking a peaceful holiday in beautiful surroundings.* **4** to have regard for or care about: *you must try to consider other people's feelings more.* **5** to discuss (something) in order to make a decision. **6** to look at: *he considered her and she forced herself to sit calmly under his gaze.*

considerable *adj* **1** large enough to reckon with: *a considerable number of people.* **2** a lot of: *he was in considerable pain.* **considerably** *adv*

considerate *adj* thoughtful towards other people.

consideration *n* **1** careful thought. **2** a fact to be taken into account when making a decision. **3** thoughtfulness for other people. **4** payment for a service. **5 take into consideration** to bear in mind. **6 under consideration** being currently discussed.

considered *adj* **1** presented or thought out with care: *a considered opinion.* **2** thought of in a specified way: *highly considered.*

considering *conj, prep* **1** taking (a specified fact) into account: *considering the mileage the car had done, it was lasting well.* *~adv* **2** *Informal* taking into account the circumstances: *it's not bad considering.*

consign *vb* **1** to give into the care or charge of. **2** to put irrevocably: *those events have been consigned to history.* **3** to put (in a specified place or situation): *only a few months ago such demands would have consigned the student leaders to prisons and labour camps.* **4** to address or deliver (goods): *a cargo of oil drilling equipment consigned to Saudi Arabia.* **consignee** *n* **consignor** *n*

consignment *n* **1** a shipment of goods. **2** the act or an instance of consigning: *the goods are sent to Hong Kong for onward consignment to customers in the area.*

consist *vb* **1 consist of** to be made up of. **2 consist in** to have as its main or only part: *his madness, if he is mad, consists in believing that he is a sundial.*

consistency *n, pl* **-encies 1** degree of thickness or smoothness. **2** being consistent.

consistent *adj* **1** holding to the same principles. **2** in agreement. **consistently** *adv*

consolation *n* **1** a person or thing that is a comfort in a time of sadness or distress. **2** a consoling or being consoled.

consolation prize *n* something given to console the loser of a game.

console[1] *vb* **-soling, -soled** to comfort (someone) in sadness or distress. **consolable** *adj*

console[2] *n* **1** a panel of controls for electronic equipment. **2** a cabinet for a television or audio equipment. **3** an ornamental bracket used to support a wall fixture. **4** the desklike case of an organ, containing the pedals, stops, and keys.

consolidate *vb* **-dating, -dated 1** to make or become stronger or more stable. **2** to combine into a whole. **consolidation** *n* **consolidator** *n*

consommé (kon-**som**-may) *n* a thin clear meat soup.

consonance *n Formal* agreement or harmony.

consonant *n* **1 a** a speech sound made by partially or completely blocking the breath streams, for example *b* or *f*. **b** a letter representing this. *~adj* **2 consonant with** in keeping or agreement with: *an individualistic style of religion, more consonant with liberal society.* **3** harmonious: *this highly-dissonant chord is followed by a more consonant one.*

consort *vb* **1 consort with** to keep company with. *~n* **2** a husband or wife of a reigning monarch. **3** a small group of voices or instruments.

consortium *n, pl* **-tia** an association of business firms.

THESAURUS

tory, traditional **2.** cautious, guarded, moderate *~n.* **3.** middle-of-the-roader, moderate, reactionary, right-winger, stick-in-the-mud (*informal*), tory, traditionalist

conservatory glasshouse, greenhouse, hothouse

conserve go easy on, hoard, husband, keep, preserve, protect, save, store up, take care of, use sparingly

consider 1. believe, deem, hold to be, judge, rate, regard as, think **2.** chew over, cogitate, contemplate, deliberate, examine, meditate, mull over, muse, ponder, reflect, revolve, ruminate, study, think about, turn over in one's mind, weigh **3.** bear in mind, keep in view, make allowance for, reckon with, regard, remember, respect, take into account

considerable abundant, ample, appreciable, goodly, great, large, lavish, marked, much, noticeable, plentiful, reasonable, sizable, substantial, tidy

considerably appreciably, greatly, markedly, noticeably, remarkably, significantly, substantially, very much

considerate attentive, concerned, forbearing, kind, kindly, obliging, tactful, thoughtful, unselfish

consideration 1. analysis, attention, cogitation, contemplation, deliberation, examination, perusal, reflection, regard, review, scrutiny, study, thought **2.** concern, factor, issue, point **3.** concern, considerateness, kindliness, kindness, respect, solicitude, tact, thoughtfulness **4.** fee, payment, perquisite, recompense, remuneration, reward, tip **5. take into consideration** bear in mind, make allowance for, take into account, weigh

considering all in all, all things considered, insomuch as, in the light of, in view of

consignment 1. batch, delivery, goods, shipment **2.** dispatch, distribution, handing over, sending, shipment, transmittal

consist 1. *with* **of** amount to, be composed of, be made up of, comprise, contain, embody, include, incorporate, involve **2.** *with* **in** be expressed by, be found *or* contained in, inhere, lie, reside

consistent 1. constant, dependable, persistent, regular, steady, true to type, unchanging, undeviating **2.** accordant, agreeing, all of a piece, coherent, compatible, congruous, consonant, harmonious, logical

consolation alleviation, assuagement, cheer, comfort, ease, encouragement, help, relief, solace, succour, support

console assuage, cheer, comfort, encourage, express sympathy for, relieve, solace, soothe

consolidate 1. fortify, reinforce, secure, stabilize, strengthen **2.** amalgamate, combine, fuse, join, unite

consolidation 1. fortification, reinforcement, strengthening **2.** amalgamation, fusion

consort 1. *vb. with* **with** associate, fraternize, go around with, hang about, around *or* out with, keep company, mingle, mix **2.** *n.* husband, partner, spouse, wife

conspectus *n Formal* a survey or summary.

conspicuous *adj* **1** clearly visible. **2** noteworthy or striking: *conspicuous bravery.* **conspicuously** *adv*

conspiracy *n, pl* **-cies 1** a secret plan to carry out an illegal or harmful act. **2** the act of making such plans.

conspire *vb* **-spiring, -spired 1** to plan a crime together in secret. **2** to act together as if by design: *the weather and the recession conspired to hit wine production and sales.* **conspirator** *n* **conspiratorial** *adj*

constable *n* a police officer of the lowest rank.

constabulary *n, pl* **-laries** *Chiefly Brit* the police force of an area.

constant *adj* **1** continuous: *she has endured constant criticism, mockery and humiliation.* **2** unchanging: *the average speed of the winds remained constant over this period.* **3** faithful. *~n* **4** *Maths, physics* a quantity or number which remains invariable: *the velocity of light is a constant.* **5** something that is unchanging. **constancy** *n* **constantly** *adv*

constellation *n* **1** a group of stars which form a pattern and are given a name. **2** a group of people or things: *the constellation of favourable circumstances.*

consternation *n* a feeling of anxiety or dismay.

constipated *adj* unable to empty one's bowels.

constipation *n* a condition in which emptying one's bowels is difficult.

constituency *n, pl* **-cies 1** the area represented by a Member of Parliament. **2** the voters in such an area.

constituent *n* **1** a person living in an MP's constituency. **2** a component part. *~adj* **3** forming part of a whole: *the constituent parts of the universe.* **4** having the power to make or change a constitution of a state: *a constituent assembly.*

constitute *vb* **-tuting, -tuted 1** to form or make up: *the amazing range of crags that constitute the Eglwyseg Mountains.* **2** to set up (an institution) formally.

constitution *n* **1** the principles on which a state is governed. **2 the Constitution** (in certain countries) the statute embodying such principles. **3** a person's state of health. **4** the make-up or structure of something: *changes in the very constitution of society.*

constitutional *adj* **1** of a constitution. **2** authorized by or in accordance with the Constitution of a nation: *constitutional monarchy.* **3** inherent in the nature of a person or thing: *a constitutional sensitivity to cold.* *~n* **4** a regular walk taken for the good of one's health. **constitutionally** *adv*

constitutive *adj* **1** forming a part of something. **2** with the power to appoint or establish.

constrain *vb* **1** to compel or force: *he felt constrained to apologize.* **2** to limit, restrict, or inhibit: *the mobility of workers is constrained by the serious housing shortage.*

constrained *adj* embarrassed or unnatural: *his constrained expression.*

constraint *n* **1** something that limits a person's freedom of action. **2** repression of natural feelings. **3** a forced unnatural manner.

constrict *vb* **1** to make smaller or narrower by squeezing. **2** to limit or restrict. **constrictive** *adj*

constriction *n* **1** a feeling of tightness in some part of the body, such as the chest. **2** a narrowing. **3** something that constricts.

constrictor *n* **1** a snake that coils around and squeezes its prey to kill it. **2** a muscle that contracts an opening.

construct *vb* **1** to build or put together. **2** *Geom* to draw (a figure) to specified requirements. **3** to compose (an argument or sentence). *~n* **4** a complex idea resulting from the combination of simpler ideas. **5** something formulated or built systematically. **constructor** *n*

construction *n* **1** the act of constructing or manner in which a thing is constructed. **2** something that has been constructed. **3** the business or work of building houses or other structures. **4** *Formal* an interpretation: *the financial markets will put the worst possible construction on any piece of news which might affect them.* **5** *Grammar* the way in which words are ar-

THESAURUS

conspicuous 1. apparent, blatant, clear, discernible, easily seen, evident, manifest, noticeable, obvious, patent, perceptible, visible **2.** eminent, notable, outstanding, prominent, remarkable, signal, striking

conspiracy cabal, collusion, confederacy, intrigue, league, plot, scheme

conspirator conspirer, intriguer, plotter, schemer

conspire 1. intrigue, manoeuvre, plot, scheme **2.** combine, concur, contribute, cooperate, work together

constancy 1. firmness, fixedness, permanence, regularity, stability, steadiness, uniformity **2.** devotion, fidelity, steadfastness

constant 1. ceaseless, continual, continuous, endless, eternal, everlasting, incessant, interminable, never-ending, nonstop, perpetual, persistent, relentless, sustained, uninterrupted, unrelenting, unremitting **2.** continual, even, firm, fixed, habitual, immovable, immutable, invariable, permanent, perpetual, regular, stable, steady, unalterable, unbroken, uniform, unvarying **3.** attached, dependable, devoted, faithful, loyal, stalwart, staunch, steadfast, tried-and-true, true, trustworthy, trusty, unfailing

constantly all the time, always, aye (*Scot.*), continually, continuously, endlessly, everlastingly, incessantly, interminably, invariably, morning, noon and night, night and day, nonstop, perpetually, persistently, relentlessly

consternation alarm, amazement, anxiety, bewilderment, confusion, dismay, distress, dread, fear, fright, horror, panic, shock, terror, trepidation

constituent *n.* **1.** elector, voter **2.** component, element, essential, factor, ingredient, part, unit *~adj.* **3.** basic, component, elemental, essential, integral

constitute 1. compose, comprise, form, make, make up **2.** appoint, create, establish, found, set up

constitution 1. build, health, physique **2.** character, composition, form, make-up, nature, structure **3.** composition, establishment, formation, organization

constitutional *adj.* **1.** chartered, statutory **2.** congenital, inborn, inherent, intrinsic *~n.* **3.** airing, stroll, turn, walk

constrain 1. coerce, compel, drive, force, impel, necessitate, oblige, pressure, pressurize **2.** check, confine, constrict, curb, hem in, rein, restrain, straiten

constrained embarrassed, forced, guarded, inhibited, reserved, subdued, unnatural

constraint 1. check, curb, damper, hindrance, limitation, rein, restriction **2.** bashfulness, diffidence, embarrassment, inhibition, repression, reservation, restraint, timidity

construct assemble, build, compose, create, design, engineer, erect, establish, fabricate, fashion, form, formulate, found, frame, make, manufacture, organize, put up, raise, set up, shape

construction 1. assembly, building, composition, creation, erection, fabric, fabrication, figure, form,

ranged in a sentence, clause, or phrase. **constructional** *adj*

constructive *adj* **1** useful and helpful: *constructive criticism.* **2** *Law* deduced by inference; not openly expressed. **constructively** *adv*

construe *vb* **-struing, -strued 1** to interpret the meaning of (something): *her indifference was construed as rudeness.* **2** to analyse the grammatical structure of (a sentence). **3** to combine (words) grammatically. **4** *Old-fashioned* to translate literally.

consul *n* **1** an official representing a state in a foreign country. **2** one of the two chief magistrates in ancient Rome. **consular** *adj* **consulship** *n*

consulate *n* **1** the workplace and official home of a consul. **2** the position or period of office of a consul.

consult *vb* **1** to ask advice from or discuss matters with (someone): *he never consults his wife about what he's about to do.* **2** to refer to for information: *he consulted his watch.*

consultant *n* **1** a specialist doctor with a senior position in a hospital. **2** a specialist who gives expert professional advice. **consultancy** *n*

consultation *n* **1** the act of consulting. **2** a meeting for discussion or the seeking of advice. **consultative** *adj*

consulting *adj* acting as an adviser on professional matters: *consulting engineers.*

consulting room *n* a room in which a doctor sees patients.

consume *vb* **-suming, -sumed 1** to eat or drink. **2** to use up. **3** to destroy: *the ship blew up and was consumed by flames.* **4** to obsess: *he was consumed with jealousy over the ending of their affair.* **consumable** *adj* **consuming** *adj*

consumer *n* a person who buys goods or uses services.

consumer durables *pl n* manufactured products that have a relatively long life, such as cars or televisions.

consumer goods *pl n* goods bought for personal needs rather than those required for the production of other goods or services.

consumerism *n* **1** the belief that a high level of consumer spending is desirable and beneficial to the economy: *the obsessive consumerism of the 80s.* **2** protection of the rights of consumers.

consummate *vb* (**kon**-sum-mate) **-mating, -mated 1** to make (a marriage) legal by sexual intercourse. **2** to complete or fulfil. ~*adj* (kon-**sum**-mit) **3** supremely skilled: *a consummate craftsman.* **4** complete or extreme: *consummate skill; consummate ignorance.* **consummation** *n*

consumption *n* **1** the quantity of something consumed or used: *for such a powerful car, fuel consumption is modest.* **2** the act of eating or drinking something: *this meat is unfit for human consumption.* **3** *Econ* purchase of goods and services for personal use. **4** *Old-fashioned* tuberculosis of the lungs.

consumptive *adj* **1** wasteful or destructive. **2** of tuberculosis of the lungs. ~*n* **3** a person with tuberculosis of the lungs.

cont. continued.

contact *n* **1** the state or act of communication: *the airport lost contact with the plane shortly before the crash.* **2** the state or act of touching: *rugby is a game of hard physical contact.* **3** an acquaintance who might be useful in business. **4** a connection between two electrical conductors in a circuit. **5** a person who has been exposed to a contagious disease. ~*vb* **6** to come or be in communication or touch with.

contact lens *n* a small lens placed on the eyeball to correct defective vision.

contagion *n* **1** the passing on of disease by contact. **2** a contagious disease. **3** a corrupting influence that tends to spread.

contagious *adj* **1** (of a disease) capable of being passed on by contact. **2** (of a person) capable of passing on a transmissible disease. **3** spreading from person to person: *contagious enthusiasm.*

contain *vb* **1** to hold or be capable of holding: *the bag contained a selection of men's clothing.* **2** to have as one of its ingredients or constituents: *tea and coffee both contain appreciable amounts of caffeine.* **3** to consist of: *the book contains 13 very different and largely separate chapters.* **4** to check or restrain (feelings or behaviour). **5** to prevent from spreading or going beyond fixed limits: *the blockade was too weak to contain the French fleet.* **containable** *adj*

container *n* **1** an object used to hold or store things in. **2** a large standard-sized box for transporting cargo by lorry or ship.

containerize *or* **-ise** *vb* **-izing, -ized** *or* **-ising, -ised 1** to pack (cargo) in large standard-sized containers. **2** to fit (a port, ship, or lorry) to carry goods in standard-sized containers. **containerization** *or* **-isation** *n*

containment *n* the prevention of the spread of something harmful.

THESAURUS

formation, shape, structure **2.** building, edifice, structure **3.** *formal* explanation, inference, interpretation, reading, rendering

constructive helpful, positive, practical, productive, useful, valuable

consult ask, ask advice of, compare notes with, confer, question, refer to, take counsel, turn to

consultant adviser, authority, specialist

consultation appointment, conference, council, deliberation, dialogue, discussion, hearing, interview, meeting, seminar, session

consume 1. devour, eat, eat up, gobble (up), guzzle, polish off (*informal*), put away, swallow **2.** absorb, deplete, dissipate, drain, eat up, employ, exhaust, expend, finish up, fritter away, lavish, spend, squander, use, use up, utilize, waste, wear out **3.** annihilate, demolish, destroy, devastate, lay waste, ravage **4.** *often passive* absorb, devour, dominate, eat up, engross, monopolize, obsess, preoccupy

consumer buyer, customer, purchaser, shopper, user

consuming absorbing, compelling, devouring, engrossing, gripping, immoderate, overwhelming

consummate *vb.* **1.** accomplish, achieve, carry out, complete, conclude, crown, effectuate, end, finish, perfect, perform ~*adj.* **2.** accomplished, polished, practised, skilled, superb, supreme **3.** absolute, complete, deep-dyed (*usually derogatory*), finished, matchless, perfect, supreme, total, transcendent, ultimate, unqualified, utter

consumption 1. consuming, decrease, depletion, use, using up, utilization **2.** *old-fashioned* T.B., tuberculosis

contact *n.* **1.** association, communication, connection **2.** acquaintance, connection ~*vb.* **3.** approach, call, communicate with, get hold of, get *or* be in touch with, phone, reach, ring (up) (*informal, chiefly Brit.*), speak to, write to

contagious catching, communicable, epidemic, infectious, pestilential, spreading, transmissible

contain 1. accommodate, enclose, have capacity for, hold, incorporate, seat **2.** comprehend, comprise, em-

contaminate *vb* **-nating, -nated 1** to make impure; pollute. **2** to make radioactive. **contaminant** *n* **contamination** *n*
contemn *vb Formal* to regard with contempt.
contemplate *vb* **-plating, -plated 1** to think deeply about. **2** to consider as a possibility. **3** to look at thoughtfully. **4** to meditate. **contemplation** *n*
contemplative *adj* **1** of or given to contemplation. *~n* **2** a person dedicated to religious contemplation.
contemporaneous *adj* happening at the same time. **contemporaneity** *n*
contemporary *adj* **1** existing or occurring at the present time. **2** living or occurring in the same period. **3** modern in style or fashion. **4** of approximately the same age. *~n, pl* **-raries 5** a person or thing living at the same time or of approximately the same age as another.
contempt *n* **1** scorn. **2 hold in contempt** to scorn or despise. **3** deliberate disrespect for the authority of a court of law: *contempt of court.*
contemptible *adj* deserving to be despised or hated: *a contemptible lack of courage.*
contemptuous *adj* showing or feeling strong dislike or disrespect. **contemptuously** *adv*
contend *vb* **1 contend with** to deal with. **2** to assert. **3** to compete or fight. **4** to argue earnestly. **contender** *n*
content[1] *n* **1 contents** everything inside a container. **2 contents** a list of chapters at the front of a book. **3** the meaning or substance of a piece of writing, often as distinguished from its style or form. **4** the amount of a substance contained in a mixture: *the high fat content of the British diet.*
content[2] *adj* **1** satisfied with things as they are. **2** willing to accept a situation or a proposed course of action. *~vb* **3** to satisfy (oneself or another person). *~n* **4** peace of mind. **contentment** *n*
contented *adj* satisfied with one's situation or life. **contentedly** *adv* **contentedness** *n*
contention *n* **1** disagreement or dispute. **2** a point asserted in argument. **3 bone of contention** a point of dispute.
contentious *adj* **1** causing disagreement. **2** tending to quarrel. **contentiousness** *n*
contest *n* **1** a game or match in which people or teams compete. **2** a struggle for power or control. *~vb* **3** to dispute: *he has said he will not contest the verdict.* **4** to take part in (a contest or struggle for power): *all parties which meet the legal requirements will be allowed to contest the election.* **contestable** *adj*
contestant *n* a person who takes part in a contest.
context *n* **1** the circumstances relevant to an event or fact. **2** the words before and after a word or passage in a piece of writing that contribute to its meaning: *taken out of context, lines like these sound ridiculous, but, as part of a scrupulously written play, they are just right.* **contextual** *adj*
contiguous *adj Formal* very near or touching.
continent[1] *n* one of the earth's large landmasses (Asia, Australia, Africa, Europe, North and South America, and Antarctica). **continental** *adj*

THESAURUS

body, embrace, include, involve **3.** control, curb, hold back, hold in, repress, restrain, stifle
container holder, receptacle, repository, vessel
contaminate adulterate, befoul, corrupt, defile, deprave, infect, pollute, smirch, soil, stain, sully, taint, tarnish
contamination adulteration, contagion, corruption, defilement, dirtying, filth, foulness, impurity, infection, poisoning, pollution, rottenness, taint
contemplate 1. brood over, consider, deliberate, meditate, meditate on, mull over, muse over, ponder, reflect upon, revolve *or* turn over in one's mind, ruminate (upon), study **2.** consider, have in view *or* in mind, intend, mean, plan, propose, think of **3.** examine, eye, eye up, gaze at, inspect, regard, scrutinize, stare at, survey, view, weigh
contemplation 1. cogitation, consideration, deliberation, meditation, musing, pondering, reflection, rumination, thought **2.** examination, gazing at, inspection, looking at, scrutiny, survey, viewing
contemplative deep *or* lost in thought, in a brown study, intent, introspective, meditative, musing, pensive, rapt, reflective, ruminative, thoughtful
contemporary *adj.* **1.** coeval, coexistent, coexisting, concurrent, contemporaneous, synchronous **2.** à la mode, current, happening (*informal*), in fashion, latest, modern, newfangled, present, present-day, recent, trendy (*Brit. informal*), ultramodern, up-to-date, up-to-the-minute, with it (*informal*) *~n.* **3.** compeer, fellow, peer
contempt contumely (*literary*), derision, disdain, disregard, disrespect, mockery, neglect, scorn
contemptible abject, base, cheap, despicable, detestable, ignominious, low, low-down (*informal*), mean, measly, paltry, pitiful, scurvy, shabby, shameful, vile, worthless
contemptuous arrogant, cavalier, condescending, derisive, disdainful, haughty, high and mighty, insolent, insulting, scornful, sneering, supercilious, withering
contend 1. affirm, allege, argue, assert, aver, avow, hold, maintain **2.** clash, compete, contest, cope, grapple, skirmish, strive, struggle, vie
content[1] **1.** burden, essence, gist, ideas, matter, meaning, significance, substance, thoughts **2.** capacity, load, measure, size, volume
content[2] *adj.* **1.** at ease, comfortable, contented, fulfilled, satisfied **2.** agreeable, satisfied, willing to accept *~vb.* **3.** appease, gladden, gratify, humour, indulge, mollify, placate, please, reconcile, sate, satisfy *~n.* **4.** comfort, contentment, ease, gratification, peace, peace of mind, pleasure, satisfaction
contented at ease, at peace, cheerful, comfortable, complacent, content, glad, gratified, happy, pleased, satisfied, serene
contention 1. discord, dispute, dissension, feuding, hostility, rivalry, row, strife, struggle, wrangling **2.** affirmation, allegation, argument, assertion, asseveration, belief, claim, declaration, idea, opinion, point, position, stand, view
contentious argumentative, bickering, captious, cavilling, pugnacious, quarrelsome, wrangling
contentment comfort, complacency, content, contentedness, ease, fulfilment, gladness, gratification, happiness, peace, pleasure, repletion, satisfaction, serenity
contest *n.* **1.** competition, game, head-to-head, match, tournament, trial **2.** affray, altercation, battle, combat, conflict, controversy, debate, discord, dispute, fight, struggle *~vb.* **3.** argue, call in *or* into question, challenge, debate, dispute, doubt, object to, oppose, question **4.** compete, contend, fight, fight over, strive, vie
contestant candidate, competitor, contender, entrant, participant, player
context background, circumstances, conditions,

continent[2] *adj* **1** able to control one's bladder and bowels. **2** sexually restrained. **continence** *n*
Continent *n* **the Continent** the mainland of Europe as distinct from the British Isles. **Continental** *adj*
continental breakfast *n* a light breakfast of coffee and rolls.
continental climate *n* a climate with hot summers, cold winters, and little rainfall, typical of the interior of a continent.
continental drift *n Geol* the theory that the earth's continents drift gradually over the surface of the planet, due to currents in its mantle.
continental quilt *n Brit* a large quilt used as a bed cover in place of the top sheet and blankets.
continental shelf *n* the gently sloping shallow sea bed surrounding a continent.
contingency *n, pl* **-cies 1** an unknown or unforeseen future event or condition. **2** something dependent on a possible future event.
contingent *n* **1** a group of people with a common interest, that represents a larger group: *a contingent of European scientists.* **2** a military group that is part of a larger force: *the force includes a contingent of the Foreign Legion.* ~*adj* **3** (foll. by *on* or *upon*) dependent on (something uncertain). **4** happening by chance.
continual *adj* **1** occurring without interruption. **2** recurring frequently. **continually** *adv*
continuance *n* **1** the act of continuing. **2** duration.
continuation *n* **1** the act of continuing. **2** a part or thing added, such as a sequel. **3** a renewal of an interrupted action or process.
continue *vb* **-tinuing, -tinued 1** to remain or cause to remain in a particular condition or place. **2** to carry on (doing something): *we continued kissing; heavy fighting continued until Thursday afternoon.* **3** to resume after an interruption: *we'll continue after lunch.* **4** to go on to a further place: *the road continues on up the hill.*
continuity *n, pl* **-ties 1** a smooth development or sequence. **2** the arrangement of scenes in a film so that they follow each other logically and without breaks.
continuo *n, pl* **-tinuos** *Music* a continuous bass accompaniment played usually on a keyboard instrument.
continuous *adj* **1** without end: *a continuous process.* **2** not having any breaks or gaps in it: *a continuous line of boats; continuous rain.* **continuously** *adv*
continuum *n, pl* **-tinua** *or* **-tinuums** a continuous series or whole, no part of which is noticeably different from the parts immediately next to it, although the ends or extremes of it are very different from each other: *the continuum from minor misbehaviour to major crime.*
contort *vb* to twist or bend out of shape. **contortion** *n*
contortionist *n* a performer who contorts his or her body to entertain others.
contour *n* **1** an outline. **2** same as **contour line.** ~*vb* **3** to shape so as to form or follow the contour of something.
contour line *n* a line on a map or chart joining points of equal height or depth.
contra- *prefix* **1** against or contrasting: *contraceptive.* **2** (in music) lower in pitch: *contrabass.*
contraband *n* **1** smuggled goods. ~*adj* **2** (of goods) smuggled.
contraception *n* the deliberate use of artificial or natural means to prevent pregnancy.
contraceptive *n* **1** a device, such as a condom, that is used to prevent pregnancy. ~*adj* **2** providing or relating to contraception: *the contraceptive pill.*
contract *n* **1** a formal agreement between two or more parties. **2** a document setting out a formal agreement. ~*vb* **3** to make a formal agreement with (a person or company) to do or deliver (something). **4** to enter into (a relationship or marriage) formally: *she had contracted an alliance with a wealthy man.* **5** to make or become smaller, narrower, or shorter. **6** to become affected by (an illness). **7** to draw (muscles) together or (of muscles) to be drawn together. **8** to shorten (a word or phrase) by omitting letters or syllables, usually indicated in writing by an apostrophe. **contractible** *adj*
contract bridge *n* the most common variety of bridge, in which only tricks bid and won count towards the game.
contraction *n* **1** a contracting or being contracted. **2** a shortening of a word or group of words, often marked by an apostrophe, for example *I've come* for *I have come.* **3 contractions** *Med* temporary shorten-

THESAURUS

connection, frame of reference, framework, relation, situation
continent abstemious, abstinent, ascetic, austere, celibate, chaste, self-restrained, sober
contingency accident, chance, emergency, event, eventuality, happening, incident, juncture, possibility
contingent *n.* **1.** body, bunch (*informal*), deputation, group, set ~*adj.* **2.** *with* **on** *or* **upon** conditional, controlled by, dependent, subject to **3.** accidental, casual, fortuitous, haphazard, random
continual 1. constant, continuous, endless, eternal, everlasting, incessant, interminable, perpetual, unceasing, uninterrupted, unremitting **2.** frequent, oft-repeated, recurrent, regular, repeated, repetitive
continually all the time, always, aye (*Scot.*), constantly, endlessly, eternally, everlastingly, forever, incessantly, interminably, nonstop, persistently, repeatedly
continuation 1. maintenance, perpetuation, prolongation **2.** addition, extension, furtherance, postscript, sequel, supplement **3.** renewal, resumption
continue 1. abide, carry on, endure, last, live on, persist, remain, stay, stay on, survive **2.** go on, keep at, keep on, keep up, maintain, persevere, persist in, prolong, stick at, stick to, sustain **3.** carry on, pick up where one left off, proceed, recommence, resume, return to, take up
continuing enduring, in progress, lasting, ongoing, sustained
continuity cohesion, connection, flow, interrelationship, progression, sequence, succession, whole
continuous constant, continued, extended, prolonged, unbroken, unceasing, undivided, uninterrupted
contour curve, figure, form, lines, outline, profile, shape
contraband *adj.* banned, black-market, bootleg, bootlegged, forbidden, hot (*informal*), illegal, illicit, interdicted, prohibited, smuggled, unlawful
contract *n.* **1.** agreement, arrangement, bargain, bond, compact, concordat, covenant, deal (*informal*), engagement, pact, settlement, understanding **2.** agreement, compact, concordat, convention, treaty ~*vb.* **3.** agree, arrange, bargain, clinch, close, come to terms, commit oneself, covenant, engage, enter into, pledge **4.** abbreviate, abridge, compress, condense, curtail, dwindle, epitomize, lessen, narrow, pucker, purse, reduce, shrink, shrivel, tighten, wither, wrinkle **5.** acquire, be afflicted with, catch, develop, get, go down with, incur
contraction 1. compression, constriction, diminu-

ing and tensing of the uterus during pregnancy and labour.

contractor *n* a person or firm that supplies materials or labour for other companies.

contract out *vb Brit* to agree not to take part in a scheme.

contractual *adj* of or in the nature of a contract.

contradict *vb* **1** to declare the opposite of (a statement) to be true. **2** (of a fact or statement) to suggest that (another fact or statement) is wrong. **contradiction** *n*

contradictory *adj* (of facts or statements) inconsistent.

contradistinction *n* a distinction made by contrasting different qualities. **contradistinctive** *adj*

contraflow *n* a flow of road traffic going alongside but in an opposite direction to the usual flow.

contralto *n, pl* **-tos** *or* **-ti** **1** the lowest female voice. **2** a singer with such a voice.

contraption *n Informal* a strange-looking device or gadget.

contrapuntal *adj Music* of or in counterpoint.

contrariwise *adv* **1** from a contrasting point of view. **2** in the opposite way.

contrary *n, pl* **-ries** **1 on** *or* **to the contrary** in opposition to what has just been said or implied. *~adj* **2** opposed; completely different: *a contrary view, based on equally good information.* **3** perverse; obstinate. **4** (of the wind) unfavourable. *~adv* **contrary to 5** in opposition or contrast to: *contrary to popular belief.* **6** in conflict with: *contrary to nature.* **contrariness** *n*

contrast *n* **1** a difference which is clearly seen when two things are compared. **2** a person or thing showing differences when compared with another. **3** the degree of difference between the colours in a photograph or television picture. *~vb* **4** to compare or be compared in order to show the differences between (things): *he contrasts that society with contemporary America.* **5 contrast with** to be very different from: *her speed of reaction contrasted with her husband's vagueness.* **contrasting** *adj*

contravene *vb* **-vening, -vened** *Formal* to break (a rule or law). **contravention** *n*

contretemps (**kon**-tra-tahn) *n, pl* **-temps** an embarrassing minor disagreement.

contribute *vb* **-uting, -uted** (often foll. by *to*) **1** to give (support or money) for a common purpose or fund. **2** to supply (ideas or opinions). **3 contribute to** to be partly responsible (for): *his own unconvincing play contributed to his defeat.* **4** to write (an article) for a publication. **contribution** *n* **contributory** *adj* **contributor** *n*

contrite *adj* full of guilt or regret. **contritely** *adv* **contrition** *n*

contrivance *n* **1** an ingenious device. **2** an elaborate or deceitful plan. **3** the act or power of contriving.

contrive *vb* **-triving, -trived** **1** to make happen: *he had already contrived the murder of King Alexander.* **2** to devise or construct ingeniously: *he contrived a plausible reason to fly back to London; he contrived a hook from a bent nail.*

control *n* **1** power to direct something: *the province is mostly under guerrilla control.* **2** a curb or check: *import controls.* **3 controls** instruments used to operate a machine. **4** a standard of comparison used in an experiment. **5** an experiment used to verify another by having all aspects identical except for the one that is being tested. *~vb* **-trolling, -trolled** **6** to have power over: *the gland which controls the body's metabolic rate.* **7** to limit or restrain: *he could not control his jealousy.* **8** to regulate or operate (a machine). **controllable** *adj*

controller *n* **1** a person who is in charge. **2** a person in charge of the financial aspects of a business.

control tower *n* a tall building at an airport from which air traffic is controlled.

controversy *n, pl* **-sies** argument or debate concerning a matter about which there is strong disagreement. **controversial** *adj*

THESAURUS

tion, drawing in, narrowing, reduction, shortening, shrinkage, shrivelling, tensing, tightening **2.** abbreviation, elision, shortening

contradict be at variance with, belie, challenge, contravene (*formal*), counter, counteract, deny, dispute, gainsay (*archaic or literary*), impugn, negate, oppose, rebut

contradiction conflict, confutation, contravention, denial, incongruity, inconsistency, negation, opposite

contradictory antithetical, conflicting, contrary, discrepant, incompatible, inconsistent, irreconcilable, opposed, opposite, paradoxical

contraption apparatus, contrivance, device, gadget, instrument, mechanism, rig

contrary *n.* **1. on** *or* **to the contrary** conversely, in contrast, not at all, on the other hand, quite the opposite *or* reverse *~adj.* **2.** adverse, antagonistic, clashing, contradictory, counter, discordant, hostile, inconsistent, inimical, opposed, opposite, paradoxical **3.** awkward, cantankerous, cussed (*informal*), difficult, disobliging, intractable, obstinate, perverse, stroppy (*Brit. slang*), unaccommodating, wayward, wilful

contrast 1. *n.* comparison, contrariety, difference, differentiation, disparity, dissimilarity, distinction, divergence, opposition **2.** *vb.* compare, differ, differentiate, distinguish, oppose, set in opposition, set off

contribute 1. add, afford, bestow, chip in (*informal*), donate, furnish, give, provide, subscribe, supply **2.** *with* **to** be conducive, be instrumental, be partly responsible for, conduce, help, lead, tend

contribution addition, bestowal, donation, gift, grant, input, offering, stipend, subscription

contributor 1. backer, bestower, conferrer, donor, giver, patron, subscriber, supporter **2.** correspondent, freelance, freelancer, journalist, journo (*slang*), reporter

contrite chastened, conscience-stricken, humble, in sackcloth and ashes, penitent, regretful, remorseful, repentant, sorrowful, sorry

contrivance 1. apparatus, appliance, contraption, device, equipment, gadget, implement, instrument, invention, machine, mechanism **2.** artifice, design, dodge, expedient, intrigue, machination, measure, plan, plot, ruse, scheme, stratagem, trick

contrive 1. arrange, bring about, effect, hit upon, manage, manoeuvre, succeed **2.** concoct, construct, create, design, devise, engineer, fabricate, frame, improvise, invent, manufacture

control *n.* **1.** authority, charge, command, direction, discipline, government, guidance, jurisdiction, management, mastery, rule, superintendence, supervision, supremacy **2.** brake, check, curb, limitation, regulation, restraint *~vb.* **3.** administer, boss (*informal*), call the tune, command, conduct, direct, dominate, govern, handle, have charge of, lead, manage, manipulate, oversee, pilot, reign over, rule, steer, superintend, supervise **4.** bridle, check, constrain, contain, curb, hold back, limit, master, rein in, repress, restrain, subdue

controls console, control panel, dash, dashboard, dials, instruments

➤ Note that the stress used always to be on the first syllable, "kon", but is now more often on the second syllable, "trov".

contumacy (**kon**-tume-mass-ee) *n, pl* **-cies** *Literary* obstinate disobedience. **contumacious** (kon-tume-**may**-shuss) *adj*

contumely (**kon**-tume-mill-ee) *n, pl* **-lies** *Literary* **1** scornful or insulting treatment. **2** a humiliating insult.

contusion *n Formal* a bruise. **contuse** *vb*

conundrum *n* **1** a puzzling question or problem. **2** a riddle whose answer contains a pun.

conurbation *n* a large heavily populated urban area formed by the growth and merging of towns.

convalesce *vb* **-lescing, -lesced** to recover health after an illness or operation.

convalescence *n* **1** gradual return to health after illness or an operation. **2** the period during which such recovery occurs. **convalescent** *n, adj*

convection *n* the transmission of heat caused by movement of molecules from cool regions to warmer regions of lower density.

convector *n* a heating device which gives out hot air.

convene *vb* **-vening, -vened** to gather or summon for a formal meeting.

convener *or* **convenor** *n* a person who calls or chairs a meeting: *the shop stewards' convener at the factory.*

convenience *n* **1** the quality of being suitable or convenient. **2 at your convenience** at a time suitable to you. **3** an object that is useful: *a house with every modern convenience.* **4** *Euphemistic, chiefly Brit* a public toilet.

convenience food *n* food that needs little preparation and can be used at any time.

convenient *adj* **1** suitable or opportune. **2** easy to use. **3** nearby.

convent *n* **1** a building where nuns live. **2** a school in which the teachers are nuns. **3** a community of nuns.

conventicle *n* a secret or unauthorized religious meeting.

convention *n* **1** the established view of what is thought to be proper behaviour. **2** an accepted rule or method: *a convention used by printers.* **3** a formal agreement or contract between people and nations. **4** a large formal assembly of a group with common interests.

conventional *adj* **1** following the accepted customs and lacking originality. **2** established by accepted usage or general agreement. **3** (of weapons or warfare) not nuclear. **conventionally** *adv*

conventionality *n, pl* **-ties 1** the quality of being conventional. **2** something conventional.

conventionalize *or* **-ise** *vb* **-izing, -ized** *or* **-ising, -ised** to make conventional.

converge *vb* **-verging, -verged 1** to move towards or meet at the same point. **2** (of opinions or effects) to move towards a shared conclusion or result. **convergence** *n* **convergent** *adj*

conversant *adj* **conversant with** having knowledge or experience of.

conversation *n* informal talk between two or more people.

conversational *adj* **1** of or used in conversation: *conversational French.* **2** resembling informal spoken language: *the author's easy, conversational style.*

conversationalist *n* a person with a specified ability at conversation: *a brilliant conversationalist.*

conversation piece *n* something, such as an unusual object, that provokes conversation.

converse[1] *vb* **-versing, -versed** to have a conversation.

converse[2] *adj* **1** reversed or opposite. –*n* **2** a statement or idea that is the opposite of another. **conversely** *adv*

conversion *n* **1** a change or adaptation. **2** *Maths* a calculation in which a weight, volume, or distance is worked out in a different system of measurement: *the conversion from Fahrenheit to Celsius.* **3** a change to another belief or religion. **4** *Rugby* a score made after a try by kicking the ball over the crossbar from a place kick.

convert *vb* **1** to change or adapt. **2** to cause (someone) to change in opinion or belief. **3** to change (a measurement) from one system of units to another. **4**

THESAURUS

controversial at issue, contended, contentious, debatable, disputable, disputed, open to question, polemic, under discussion

controversy altercation, argument, contention, debate, discussion, dispute, dissension, polemic, quarrel, row, squabble, strife, wrangle, wrangling

convalescence improvement, recovery, recuperation, rehabilitation, return to health

convalescent *adj.* getting better, improving, mending, on the mend, recovering, recuperating

convene assemble, bring together, call, come together, congregate, convoke, gather, meet, muster, rally, summon

convenience 1. accessibility, appropriateness, availability, fitness, handiness, opportuneness, serviceability, suitability, usefulness, utility **2.** *as in* **at your convenience** chance, leisure, opportunity, spare moment, spare time **3.** amenity, appliance, comfort, facility, help, labour-saving device

convenient 1. appropriate, fit, fitted, opportune, seasonable, suitable, suited, timely, well-timed **2.** adapted, beneficial, handy, helpful, labour-saving, serviceable, useful **3.** accessible, at hand, available, close at hand, handy, just round the corner, nearby, within reach

convent convent school, nunnery, religious community

convention 1. code, custom, etiquette, formality, practice, propriety, protocol, tradition, usage **2.** agreement, bargain, compact, concordat, contract, pact, protocol, treaty **3.** assembly, conference, congress, convocation, council, delegates, meeting, representatives

conventional 1. banal, bourgeois, commonplace, hackneyed, hidebound, pedestrian, prosaic, routine, run-of-the-mill, stereotyped, unoriginal **2.** accepted, common, correct, customary, expected, formal, habitual, normal, ordinary, orthodox, prevailing, prevalent, proper, regular, ritual, standard, traditional, usual, wonted

converge coincide, combine, come together, concentrate, focus, gather, join, meet, merge, mingle

conversant *with* **with** acquainted, *au fait,* experienced, familiar, knowledgeable, practised, proficient, skilled, versed, well-informed, well up in (*informal*)

conversation chat, chinwag (*Brit. informal*), colloquy (*formal*), communication, communion, confab (*informal*), confabulation, conference, converse, dialogue, discourse, discussion, exchange, gossip, intercourse, powwow, talk, tête-à-tête

converse 1. *adj.* contrary, counter, opposite, reverse, reversed, transposed **2.** *n.* antithesis, contrary, obverse, opposite, other side of the coin, reverse

conversion 1. adaptation, alteration, change, metamorphosis, modification, reconstruction, remodelling,

to change (money) into a different currency. **5** *Rugby* to make a conversion after (a try). *~n* **6** a person who has been converted to another belief or religion. **converter** *or* **convertor** *n*

convertible *adj* **1** capable of being converted. **2** *Finance* (of a currency) freely exchangeable into other currencies. *~n* **3** a car with a folding or removable roof.

convex *adj* curving outwards like the outside surface of a ball. **convexity** *n*

convey *vb* **1** to communicate (information). **2** to carry or transport from one place to another. **3** (of a channel or path) to transfer or transmit. **4** *Law* to transfer (the title to property). **conveyable** *adj* **conveyor** *n*

conveyance *n* **1** *Old-fashioned* a vehicle. **2** *Law* **a** a transfer of the legal title to property. **b** the document effecting such a transfer. **3** the act of conveying: *the conveyance of cycles on peak hour trains.* **conveyancer** *n*

conveyancing *n* the branch of law dealing with the transfer of ownership of property.

conveyor belt *n* an endless moving belt driven by rollers and used to transport objects, esp. in a factory.

convict *vb* **1** to declare (someone) guilty of an offence. *~n* **2** a person serving a prison sentence.

conviction *n* **1** a firmly held belief or opinion. **2** an instance of being found guilty of a crime: *he had several convictions for petty theft.* **3** a convincing or being convinced. **4 carry conviction** to be convincing.

convince *vb* **-vincing, -vinced** to persuade by argument or evidence. **convinced** *adj* **convincible** *adj* **convincing** *adj*

convivial *adj* sociable or lively: *a convivial atmosphere; convivial company.* **conviviality** *n*

convocation *n Formal* a large formal meeting.

convoke *vb* **-voking, -voked** *Formal* to call together.

convoluted *adj* **1** coiled or twisted. **2** (of an argument or sentence) complex and difficult to understand.

convolution *n* **1** a coil or twist. **2** an intricate or confused matter or condition. **3** a convex fold in the surface of the brain.

convolvulus *n, pl* **-luses** *or* **-li** a twining plant with funnel-shaped flowers and triangular leaves.

convoy *n* a group of vehicles or ships travelling together.

convulse *vb* **-vulsing, -vulsed 1** to shake or agitate violently. **2** (of muscles) to undergo violent spasms. **3** *Informal* to be overcome (with laughter or rage). **convulsive** *adj*

convulsion *n* **1** a violent muscular spasm. **2** a violent upheaval. **3 convulsions** *Informal* uncontrollable laughter: *I was in convulsions.*

cony *or* **coney** *n, pl* **-nies** *or* **-neys 1** a rabbit. **2** rabbit fur.

coo *vb* **cooing, cooed 1** (of a dove or pigeon) to make a soft murmuring sound. **2 bill and coo** to murmur softly or lovingly. *~n* **3** a cooing sound. *~interj* **4** *Brit slang* an exclamation of surprise or amazement. **cooing** *adj, n*

cooee *interj* a call used to attract attention.

cook *vb* **1** to prepare (food) by heating or (of food) to be prepared in this way. **2** *Slang* to alter or falsify (figures or accounts): *she had cooked the books.* *~n* **3** a person who prepares food for eating. ~See also **cook up.**

cook-chill *n* a method of food preparation used by caterers, in which cooked dishes are chilled rapidly and reheated as required.

cooker *n* **1** an apparatus for cooking heated by gas or electricity. **2** *Brit* an apple suitable for cooking but not for eating raw.

cookery *n* the art or practice of cooking.

cookery book *or* **cookbook** *n* a book containing recipes.

cookie *n, pl* **cookies 1** *US & Canad* a biscuit. **2 that's the way the cookie crumbles** *Informal* that is how things inevitably are. **3** *Informal* a person: *a real tough cookie.*

cook up *vb Informal* to invent (a story or scheme).

cool *adj* **1** moderately cold: *it should be served cool, even chilled.* **2** comfortably free of heat: *it was one of the few cool days that summer.* **3** calm and unemotional: *a cool head.* **4** indifferent or unfriendly: *the idea met with a cool response.* **5** calmly impudent. **6** *Informal* (of a large sum of money) without exaggeration: *a cool million.* **7** *Informal* sophisticated or elegant. **8** (of a colour) having violet, blue, or green pre-

THESAURUS

reorganization, transfiguration, transformation, transmogrification (*jocular*), transmutation **2.** change of heart, rebirth, reformation, regeneration

convert *vb.* **1.** adapt, alter, apply, change, interchange, metamorphose, modify, remodel, reorganize, restyle, revise, transform, transmogrify (*jocular*), transmute, transpose, turn **2.** baptize, bring to God, convince, proselytize, reform, regenerate, save *~n.* **3.** catechumen, disciple, neophyte, proselyte

convex bulging, outcurved, protuberant, rounded

convey 1. communicate, disclose, impart, make known, relate, reveal, tell **2.** bear, bring, carry, conduct, fetch, forward, guide, move, send, support, transmit, transport **3.** *Law* bequeath, cede, devolve, grant, lease, transfer, will

conveyance 1. *old-fashioned* transport, vehicle **2.** carriage, movement, transfer, transference, transmission, transport, transportation

convict 1. *vb.* condemn, find guilty, imprison, pronounce guilty, sentence **2.** *n.* con (*slang*), jailbird, lag (*slang*), prisoner

conviction 1. belief, creed, faith, opinion, principle, tenet, view **2.** assurance, certainty, certitude, confidence, earnestness, fervour, firmness

convince assure, bring round, gain the confidence of, persuade, prevail upon, prove to, satisfy, sway, win over

convincing cogent, conclusive, credible, impressive, incontrovertible, likely, persuasive, plausible, powerful, probable, telling

convulse 1. agitate, churn up, derange, disorder, disturb, shake **2.** twist, work

convulsion 1. contortion, contraction, cramp, fit, paroxysm, seizure, spasm, tremor **2.** agitation, commotion, disturbance, furore, shaking, tumult, turbulence, upheaval

cool *adj.* **1.** chilled, chilling, chilly, coldish, nippy, refreshing **2.** calm, collected, composed, dispassionate, imperturbable, laid-back (*informal*), level-headed, placid, quiet, relaxed, sedate, self-controlled, self-possessed, serene, together (*slang*), unemotional, unexcited, unfazed (*informal*), unruffled **3.** aloof, apathetic, distant, frigid, indifferent, lukewarm, offhand, reserved, standoffish, unenthusiastic, unfriendly, uninterested, unresponsive, unwelcoming **4.** audacious, bold, brazen, cheeky, impertinent, impudent, presump-

dominating. **9** *Informal, chiefly US & Canad* marvellous. ~*vb* **10** to make or become cooler. **11** to calm down. ~*n* **12** coolness: *in the cool of the evening.* **13** *Slang* calmness; composure: *he lost his cool and wantonly kicked the ball away.* **coolly** *adv* **coolness** *n*

coolant *n* a fluid used to cool machinery while it is working.

cool drink *n S African* a soft drink.

cooler *n* a container for making or keeping things cool.

coolie *n Old-fashioned, offensive* an unskilled Oriental labourer.

cooling tower *n* a tall hollow structure in a factory or power station, inside which hot water cools as it trickles down.

coomb *or* **coombe** *n* a short valley or deep hollow.

coon *n* **1** *Informal* short for **raccoon. 2** *Offensive slang* a Negro or Australian Aborigine. **3** *S African offensive* a person of mixed race.

coop[1] *n* **1** a cage or pen for poultry or small animals. ~*vb* **2 coop up** to confine in a restricted place.

coop[2] *or* **co-op** (**koh**-op) *n* a cooperative society or a shop run by a cooperative society.

cooper *n* a person who makes or repairs barrels or casks.

cooperate *or* **co-operate** *vb* **1** to work or act together. **2** to assist or be willing to assist. **cooperation** *or* **co-operation** *n*

cooperative *or* **co-operative** *adj* **1** willing to cooperate. **2** (of an enterprise or farm) owned and managed collectively. ~*n* **3** a cooperative organization.

cooperative society *n* a commercial enterprise owned and run by customers or workers, in which the profits are shared among the members.

coopt *or* **co-opt** (koh-**opt**) *vb* to add (someone) to a group by the agreement of the existing members.

coordinate *or* **co-ordinate** *vb* **-nating, -nated 1** to bring together and cause to work together efficiently. ~*n* **2** *Maths* any of a set of numbers defining the location of a point with reference to a system of axes. ~*adj* **3** of or involving coordination. **4** of or involving the use of coordinates: *coordinate geometry.* **coordination** *or* **co-ordination** *n* **coordinator** *or* **co-ordinator** *n*

coordinates *or* **co-ordinates** *pl n* clothes designed to be worn together.

coot *n* **1** a small black water bird. **2** *Old-fashioned* a foolish person.

cop *Slang* ~*n* **1** a policeman. **2 not much cop** of little value or worth. ~*vb* **copping, copped 3** to take or seize. **4 cop it** to get into trouble or be punished: *he copped it after he was spotted driving a car without a seat belt.* ~See also **cop out.**

copal *n* a resin used in varnishes.

copartner *n* a partner or associate. **copartnership** *n*

cope[1] *vb* **coping, coped 1** to deal successfully (with): *well-nourished people cope better with stress.* **2** to tolerate or endure: *the ability to cope with his pain.*

cope[2] *n* a large ceremonial cloak worn by some Christian priests.

cope[3] *vb* **coping, coped** to provide (a wall) with a coping.

copeck *n* same as **kopeck.**

Copernican (kop-**per**-nik-an) *adj* of the theory that the earth and the planets rotate round the sun.

copestone *n* **1** Also called: **coping stone** a stone used to form a coping. **2** the stone at the top of a building or wall.

copier *n* a person or machine that copies.

copilot *n* the second pilot of an aircraft.

coping *n* a layer of rounded or sloping bricks on the top of a wall.

coping saw *n* a handsaw with a U-shaped frame, used for cutting curves in wood.

copious (**kope**-ee-uss) *adj* existing or produced in large quantities. **copiously** *adv*

cop out *Slang* ~*vb* **1** to avoid taking responsibility or committing oneself. *n* **cop-out 2** a way or an instance of avoiding responsibility or commitment.

copper[1] *n* **1** a soft reddish metallic element, used in such alloys as brass and bronze. Symbol: Cu **2** *Informal* any copper or bronze coin. **3** *Chiefly Brit* a large metal container used to boil water. ~*adj* **4** reddish-brown.

copper[2] *n Slang* a policeman.

copper beech *n* a European beech with reddish leaves.

copper-bottomed *adj* financially reliable.

copperhead *n* a poisonous American snake with a reddish-brown head.

copperplate *n* **1** an elegant handwriting style. **2** a polished copper plate engraved for printing. **3** a print taken from such a plate.

copper sulphate *n* a blue crystalline copper salt used in electroplating and in plant sprays.

coppice *n* a small group of trees or bushes growing close together.

copra *n* the dried oil-yielding kernel of the coconut.

copse *n* same as **coppice.**

Copt *n* **1** a member of the Coptic Church, a part of the Christian Church which was founded in Egypt. **2** an Egyptian descended from the ancient Egyptians.

Coptic *n* **1** the language of the Copts, descended from Ancient Egyptian and surviving only in the Coptic Church. ~*adj* **2** of the Copts or the Coptic Church.

copula *n, pl* **-las** *or* **-lae** a verb, such as *be,* that is used to link the subject with the complement of a sentence, as in *he became king.*

copulate *vb* **-lating, -lated** to have sexual intercourse. **copulation** *n*

copy *n, pl* **copies 1** a thing made to look exactly like another. **2** a single specimen of a book, magazine, or

THESAURUS

tuous, shameless **5.** *informal* cosmopolitan, elegant, sophisticated, urbane ~*vb.* **6.** chill, cool off, freeze, lose heat, refrigerate ~*n.* **7.** *slang* calmness, composure, control, poise, self-control, self-discipline, self-possession

coop 1. *n.* box, cage, enclosure, hutch, pen, pound **2.** *vb. with* **up** cage, confine, impound, imprison, pen, pound, shut up

cooperate 1. collaborate, combine, conspire, coordinate, join forces, pool resources, pull together, work together **2.** abet, aid, assist, contribute, go along with, help, pitch in, play ball (*informal*)

cooperation 1. collaboration, combined effort, esprit de corps, teamwork, unity **2.** assistance, give-and-take, helpfulness, participation, responsiveness

cooperative accommodating, helpful, obliging, responsive, supportive

coordinate *vb.* correlate, harmonize, integrate, match, mesh, organize, relate, synchronize, systematize

cope carry on, contend (with), deal (with), get by (*informal*), handle, hold one's own, make out (*informal*), make the grade, manage, rise to the occasion, struggle through, survive

copious abundant, ample, bounteous, bountiful, ex-

record of which there are many others exactly the same. **3** written material for printing. **4** the text of an advertisement. **5** *Journalism informal* suitable material for an article: *disasters are always good copy.* ~*vb* **copies, copying, copied 6** to make a copy (of). **7** to act or try to be like another.

copybook *n* **1** a book of specimens of handwriting for imitation. **2 blot one's copybook** *Informal* to spoil one's reputation by a mistake or indiscretion. ~*adj* **3** done exactly according to the rules. **4** trite or unoriginal.

copycat *n Informal* a person who imitates or copies someone.

copyist *n* **1** a person who makes written copies. **2** an imitator: *although the songs are derivative, it is unfair to dismiss the band as mere copyists.*

copyright *n* **1** the exclusive legal right to reproduce and control an original literary, musical, or artistic work. ~*vb* **2** to take out a copyright on. ~*adj* **3** protected by copyright.

copy typist *n* a typist who types from written or typed drafts rather than dictation.

copywriter *n* a person employed to write advertising copy.

coquette *n* a woman who flirts. **coquetry** *n* **coquettish** *adj*

coracle *n* a small round boat made of wicker covered with skins.

coral *n* **1** the stony substance formed by the skeletons of marine animals called polyps, often forming an island or reef. **2** any of the polyps whose skeletons form coral. ~*adj* **3** orange-pink.

cor anglais *n, pl* **cors anglais** *Music* an alto woodwind instrument of the oboe family.

corbel *n Archit* a stone or timber support sticking out of a wall.

corbie *n Scot* a raven or crow.

cord *n* **1** string or thin rope made of twisted strands. **2** *Anat* a structure in the body resembling a rope: *the vocal cords.* **3** a ribbed fabric like corduroy. **4** *US & Canad* an electrical flex. **5** a unit for measuring cut wood, equal to 128 cubic feet. ~*adj* **6** (of fabric) ribbed. ~See also **cords.**

cordate *adj* heart-shaped.

corded *adj* **1** tied or fastened with cord. **2** (of a fabric) ribbed. **3** (of muscles) standing out like cords.

cordial *adj* **1** warm and friendly: *a cordial atmosphere.* **2** heartfelt or sincere: *I developed a cordial dislike for the place.* ~*n* **3** a drink with a fruit base: *lime cordial.* **cordially** *adv*

cordiality *n* warmth of feeling.

cordite *n* a smokeless explosive used in guns and bombs.

cordless *adj* (of an electrical appliance such as a kettle or telephone) powered by an internal battery or kept in a holder which is connected to the mains, so that there is no cable connecting the appliance itself to the electrical mains.

cordon *n* **1** a chain of police, soldiers, or vehicles guarding an area. **2** an ornamental braid or ribbon. **3** *Horticulture* a fruit tree trained to grow as a single stem bearing fruit. ~*vb* **4 cordon off** to put or form a cordon round.

cordon bleu (**bluh**) *adj* (of cookery or cooks) of the highest standard: *a cordon bleu chef.*

cordon sanitaire *n* **1** a line of buffer states shielding a country. **2** a guarded line isolating an infected area.

cords *pl n* trousers made of corduroy.

corduroy *n* a heavy cotton fabric with a velvety ribbed surface.

corduroys *pl n* trousers made of corduroy.

core *n* **1** the central part of certain fleshy fruits, containing the seeds. **2** the central or essential part of something: *the historic core of the city.* **3** a piece of magnetic soft iron inside an electromagnet or transformer. **4** *Geol* the central part of the earth. **5** a cylindrical sample of rock or soil, obtained by the use of a hollow drill. **6** *Physics* the region of a nuclear reactor containing the fissionable material. **7** *Computers* the main internal memory of a computer. ~*vb* **coring, cored 8** to remove the core from (fruit).

co-respondent *n Law* a person with whom someone being sued for divorce is claimed to have committed adultery.

corgi *n* a short-legged sturdy dog.

coriander *n* **1** a European plant, cultivated for its aromatic seeds. **2** the dried seeds of this plant used as a flavouring.

Corinthian *adj* **1** of Corinth, a port in S Greece. **2** of a style of classical architecture characterized by a bell-shaped capital with carved leaf-shaped ornaments. ~*n* **3** a person from Corinth.

cork *n* **1** the thick light porous outer bark of a Mediterranean oak. **2** a piece of cork used as a stopper. **3** *Bot* the outer bark of a woody plant. ~*vb* **4** to stop up (a bottle) with a cork.

corkage *n* a charge made at a restaurant for serving wine bought elsewhere.

corked *adj* (of wine) spoiled through being stored in a bottle with a decayed cork.

corker *n Old-fashioned slang* a splendid or outstanding person or thing.

corkscrew *n* **1** a device for pulling corks from bottles, usually consisting of a pointed metal spiral attached to a handle. ~*adj* **2** like a corkscrew in shape. ~*vb* **3** to move in a spiral or zigzag course.

corm *n* the scaly bulblike underground stem of certain plants.

cormorant *n* a large dark-coloured long-necked sea bird.

corn[1] *n* **1** a cereal plant such as wheat, oats, or barley. **2** the grain of such plants. **3** *US, Canad, & NZ* maize. **4** *Slang* something unoriginal or oversentimental.

corn[2] *n* a painful hardening of the skin of the toes, caused by pressure.

corncob *n* the core of an ear of maize, to which the kernels are attached.

corncrake *n* a brown bird with a harsh grating cry.

THESAURUS

tensive, exuberant (*of vegetation*), full, generous, lavish, liberal, luxuriant, overflowing, plenteous, plentiful, profuse, rich, superabundant

copy *n.* **1.** carbon copy, counterfeit, duplicate, facsimile, fake, fax, forgery, image, imitation, likeness, model, pattern, photocopy, Photostat (*Trademark*), print, replica, representation, reproduction, Xerox (*Trademark*) ~*vb.* **2.** counterfeit, duplicate, photocopy, Photostat (*Trademark*), replicate, reproduce, Xerox (*Trademark*) **3.** ape, echo, emulate, follow, follow suit, follow the example of, imitate, mimic, mirror, parrot, repeat, simulate

cordial 1. affable, affectionate, agreeable, cheerful, congenial, friendly, genial, hearty, sociable, warm, warm-hearted, welcoming **2.** earnest, heartfelt, hearty, sincere, wholehearted

cordiality affability, amiability, friendliness, geniality, heartiness, warmth

cordon 1. *n.* barrier, chain, line, ring **2.** *vb.* **cordon**

cornea (**korn**-ee-a) *n* the transparent membrane covering the eyeball. **corneal** *adj*

corned beef *n* cooked beef preserved in salt.

cornelian *n* same as **carnelian.**

corner *n* **1** the place or angle formed by the meeting of two converging lines or surfaces. **2** the space within the angle formed, as in a room. **3** the place where two streets meet. **4** a sharp bend in a road. **5** a remote place: *far-flung corners of the world.* **6** any secluded or private place. **7** *Sports* a free kick or shot taken from the corner of the field. **8 cut corners** to take the shortest or easiest way at the expense of high standards. **9 turn the corner** to pass the critical point of an illness or a difficult time. *~adj* **10** on or in a corner: *a corner seat.* *~vb* **11** to force (a person or animal) into a difficult or inescapable position. **12** (of a vehicle or its driver) to turn a corner. **13** to obtain a monopoly of.

corner shop *n* a small general shop serving a neighbourhood.

cornerstone *n* **1** an indispensable part or basis: *the food we eat is one of the cornerstones of good health.* **2** a stone at the corner of a wall.

cornet *n* **1** a brass instrument of the trumpet family. **2** *Brit* a cone-shaped ice-cream wafer. **cornetist** *n*

corn exchange *n* a building where corn is bought and sold.

cornflakes *pl n* a breakfast cereal made from toasted maize.

cornflour *n* a fine maize flour, used for thickening sauces.

cornflower *n* a small plant with blue flowers.

cornice (**korn**-iss) *n* **1** a decorative moulding round the top of a wall or building. **2** *Archit* the projecting mouldings at the top of a column.

Cornish *adj* **1** of Cornwall. *~n* **2** a Celtic language of Cornwall, extinct by 1800. *~pl n* **3 the Cornish** the people of Cornwall.

Cornish pasty *n* a pastry case with a filling of meat and vegetables.

cornucopia (korn-yew-**kope**-ee-a) *n* **1** a great abundance: *a cornucopia of rewards.* **2** a symbol of plenty, consisting of a horn overflowing with fruit and flowers.

corny *adj* **cornier, corniest** *Slang* unoriginal or oversentimental.

corolla *n* the petals of a flower collectively.

corollary (kor-**oll**-a-ree) *n, pl* **-laries 1** a proposition that follows directly from another that has been proved. **2** a natural consequence.

corona (kor-**rone**-a) *n, pl* **-nas** *or* **-nae** (-nee) **1** a circle of light around a luminous body, usually the moon. **2** the outermost part of the sun's atmosphere, visible as a faint halo during a total eclipse. **3** a long cigar with blunt ends. **4** *Bot* a crownlike part of some flowers on top of the seed or on the inner side of the corolla. **5** *Physics* an electrical glow appearing around the surface of a charged conductor.

coronary (**kor**-ron-a-ree) *adj* **1** *Anat* of the arteries that supply blood to the heart. *~n, pl* **-naries 2** a coronary thrombosis.

coronary thrombosis *n* a condition where the blood flow to the heart is blocked by a clot in a coronary artery.

coronation *n* the ceremony of crowning a monarch.

coroner *n* a public official responsible for the investigation of violent, sudden, or suspicious deaths.

coronet *n* **1** a small crown worn by princes or peers. **2** a band of jewels worn as a headdress.

corpora *pl n* the plural of **corpus.**

corporal[1] *n* a noncommissioned officer in an army.

corporal[2] *adj* of the body.

corporal punishment *n* physical punishment, such as caning.

corporate *adj* **1** relating to business corporations: *corporate finance.* **2** shared by a group. **3** forming a corporation; incorporated.

corporation *n* **1** a large business or company. **2** a city or town council. **3** *Informal* a large paunch. **corporative** *adj*

corporatism *n* organization of a state on the lines of a business enterprise, with substantial government management of the economy.

corporeal (kore-**pore**-ee-al) *adj* of the physical world rather than the spiritual.

corps (**kore**) *n, pl* **corps 1** a military unit with a specific function: *medical corps.* **2** an organized body of people: *the diplomatic corps.*

corps de ballet *n* the members of a ballet company.

corpse *n* a dead body, esp. of a human being.

corpulent *adj* fat or plump. **corpulence** *n*

corpus *n, pl* **-pora** a collection of writings, such as one by a single author or on a specific topic: *the rich corpus of British folk song.*

corpuscle *n* a red blood cell (see **erythrocyte**) or white blood cell (see **leucocyte**). **corpuscular** *adj*

corral *US & Canad ~n* **1** an enclosure for cattle or horses. *~vb* **-ralling, -ralled 2** to put in a corral.

corrasion *n Geol* erosion of rocks caused by fragments transported over them by water, wind, or ice.

correct *adj* **1** free from error; true: *the correct answer.* **2** in conformity with accepted standards: *in most cultures there is a strong sense of correct sexual conduct.* *~vb* **3** to make free from or put right errors. **4** to indicate the errors in (something). **5** to rebuke or

THESAURUS

off close off, encircle, enclose, fence off, isolate, separate, surround

core centre, crux, essence, gist, heart, kernel, nub, nucleus, pith

corner *n.* **1.** angle, bend, crook, joint **2.** cavity, cranny, hole, niche, nook, recess **3.** hideaway, hide-out, hidey-hole (*informal*), retreat *~vb.* **4.** bring to bay, run to earth, trap **5.** dominate, hog (*slang*), monopolize

cornerstone 1. basis, bedrock, key, starting point **2.** quoin

corny *slang* banal, commonplace, hackneyed, maudlin, mawkish, old-fashioned, old hat, sentimental, stale, stereotyped, trite

corporal anatomical, bodily, carnal, corporeal, physical, somatic

corporate collective, combined, communal, joint, merged, pooled, shared, united

corporation 1. association, corporate body, society **2.** civic authorities, council, municipal authorities, town council **3.** *informal* paunch, pot, potbelly, spare tyre

corps 1. company, contingent, detachment, division, regiment, squad, squadron, troop, unit **2.** band, body, company, contingent, crew, team, unit

corpse body, cadaver, carcass, remains, stiff (*slang*)

corpulent beefy (*informal*), bulky, burly, fat, fleshy, large, lusty, obese, overweight, plump, portly, roly-poly, rotund, stout, tubby, well-padded

correct *adj.* **1.** accurate, exact, faultless, flawless, O.K. *or* okay (*informal*), precise, right, strict, true **2.** acceptable, appropriate, diplomatic, fitting, just, ko-

punish in order to improve: *I stand corrected.* **6** to make conform to a standard. **correctly** *adv* **correctness** *n*

correction *n* **1** an act or instance of correcting. **2** an alteration correcting something: *corrections to the second proofs.* **3** a reproof or punishment. **correctional** *adj*

corrective *adj* intended to put right something that is wrong: *corrective action.*

correlate *vb* **-lating, -lated 1** to place or be placed in a mutual relationship: *water consumption is closely correlated to the number of people living in a house.* ~*n* **2** either of two things mutually related. **correlation** *n*

correlative *adj* **1** having a mutual relationship. **2** *Grammar* (of words, usually conjunctions) corresponding to each other and occurring regularly together, for example *neither* and *nor.*

correspond *vb* **1** to be consistent or compatible (with). **2** to be similar (to). **3** to communicate (with) by letter. **corresponding** *adj* **correspondingly** *adv*

correspondence *n* **1** communication by letters. **2** the letters exchanged in this way. **3** relationship or similarity.

correspondence course *n* a course of study conducted by post.

correspondent *n* **1** a person who communicates by letter. **2** a person employed by a newspaper or news service to report on a special subject or from a foreign country.

corridor *n* **1** a passage in a building or a train. **2** a strip of land or airspace that provides access through the territory of a foreign country. **3 corridors of power** the higher levels of government or the Civil Service.

corrie *n* (in Scotland) a circular hollow on the side of a hill.

corrigendum (kor-rij-**end**-um) *n, pl* **-da** (-da) **1** an error to be corrected. **2** a slip of paper inserted into a book after printing, listing corrections.

corroborate *vb* **-rating, -rated** to support (a fact or opinion) by giving proof. **corroboration** *n* **corroborative** *adj*

corroboree *n Austral* **1** a native gathering or dance of festive or warlike character. **2** any noisy gathering.

corrode *vb* **-roding, -roded 1** to eat away or be eaten away by chemical action or rusting. **2** to destroy gradually: *rumours corroding the public's affection for the royal family.*

corrosion *n* **1** the process by which something, esp. a metal, is corroded. **2** the result of corrosion. **corrosive** *adj*

corrugate *vb* **-gating, -gated** to fold into alternate grooves and ridges. **corrugation** *n*

corrugated iron *n* a thin sheet of iron or steel, formed with alternating ridges and troughs.

corrupt *adj* **1** open to or involving bribery or other dishonest practices: *corrupt practices.* **2** morally depraved. **3** (of a text or data) made unreliable by errors or alterations. ~*vb* **4** to make corrupt. **corruptive** *adj*

corruptible *adj* capable of being corrupted.

corruption *n* **1** dishonesty and illegal behaviour. **2** the act of corrupting morally or sexually. **3** the process of rotting or decaying. **4** an unintentional or unauthorized alteration in a text or data. **5** an altered form of a word.

corsage (kore-**sahzh**) *n* a small bouquet worn on the bodice of a dress.

corsair *n* **1** a pirate. **2** a pirate ship. **3** a privateer.

corse *n Archaic* a corpse.

corselet *n* **1** a woman's one-piece undergarment, combining corset and bra. **2** a piece of armour to cover the trunk.

corset *n* **1** a close-fitting undergarment worn by women to shape the torso. **2** a similar garment worn

THESAURUS

sher (*informal*), O.K. *or* okay (*informal*), proper, seemly, standard ~*vb.* **3.** adjust, amend, cure, emend, improve, rectify, redress, reform, regulate, remedy, right **4.** admonish, chasten, chastise, chide, discipline, punish, reprimand, reprove

correction 1. adjustment, alteration, amendment, emendation, improvement, modification, rectification, righting **2.** admonition, castigation, chastisement, discipline, punishment, reformation, reproof

correctly accurately, aright, perfectly, precisely, properly, right, rightly

correctness accuracy, exactitude, exactness, faultlessness, fidelity, preciseness, precision, truth

correlate *vb.* associate, compare, connect, coordinate, correspond, equate, interact, parallel, tie in

correlation correspondence, equivalence, interaction, interdependence, interrelationship, reciprocity

correspond 1. accord, agree, be consistent, coincide, complement, conform, correlate, dovetail, fit, harmonize, match, square, tally **2.** communicate, exchange letters, keep in touch, write

correspondence 1. communication, letters, mail, post, writing **2.** agreement, analogy, coincidence, comparability, comparison, concurrence, conformity, congruity, correlation, harmony, match, relation, similarity

correspondent 1. letter writer, pen friend *or* pal **2.** contributor, journalist, journo (*slang*), reporter, special correspondent

corresponding analogous, complementary, correlative, correspondent, equivalent, identical, interrelated, matching, reciprocal, similar, synonymous

corridor aisle, alley, hallway, passage, passageway

corroborate authenticate, back up, bear out, confirm, endorse, ratify, substantiate, support, sustain, validate

corrode 1. eat away, erode, oxidize, rust **2.** consume, corrupt, deteriorate, eat away, erode, gnaw, waste, wear away

corrosive consuming, corroding, erosive, wasting

corrugated channelled, creased, crinkled, fluted, furrowed, grooved, puckered, ridged, rumpled, wrinkled

corrupt *adj.* **1.** bent (*slang*), bribable, crooked (*informal*), dishonest, fraudulent, rotten, shady (*informal*), unethical, unprincipled, unscrupulous, venal **2.** abandoned, debased, defiled, degenerate, demoralized, depraved, dishonoured, dissolute, profligate, vicious **3.** adulterated, altered, distorted, doctored, falsified, tainted, tampered with ~*vb.* **4.** bribe, buy off, debauch, demoralize, deprave, entice, fix (*informal*), grease (someone's) palm (*slang*), lure, pervert, suborn, subvert

corruption 1. breach of trust, bribery, bribing, crookedness (*informal*), demoralization, dishonesty, extortion, fiddling (*informal*), fraud, fraudulency, graft (*informal*), jobbery, profiteering, shadiness, shady dealings (*informal*), unscrupulousness, venality **2.** baseness, decadence, degeneration, degradation, depravity, evil, immorality, impurity, iniquity, perversion, profligacy, sinfulness, turpitude, vice, viciousness, wickedness **3.** decay, foulness, infection, pollution, putrefaction, putrescence, rot, rottenness **4.** adultera-

by either sex to support and protect the back. **corsetry** *n*

cortege (kore-**tayzh**) *n* a funeral procession.

cortex (**kore**-tex) *n, pl* **-tices** (-tiss-seez) *Anat* the outer layer of the brain or some other internal organ. **cortical** *adj*

cortisone *n* a steroid hormone used in treating rheumatoid arthritis, allergies, and skin diseases.

corundum *n* a hard mineral used as an abrasive, and of which the ruby and sapphire are precious forms.

coruscate *vb* **-cating, -cated** *Formal* to emit flashes of light; sparkle. **coruscating** *adj* **coruscation** *n*

corvette *n* a lightly armed escort warship.

corymb *n Bot* a flat-topped flower cluster with the stems growing progressively shorter towards the centre.

cos[1] *or* **cos lettuce** *n* a lettuce with a long slender head and crisp leaves.

cos[2] cosine.

cosec (**koh**-sek) cosecant.

cosecant (koh-**seek**-ant) *n* (in trigonometry) the ratio of the length of the hypotenuse to that of the opposite side in a right-angled triangle.

cosh *Brit* ~*n* **1** a heavy blunt weapon, often made of hard rubber. ~*vb* **2** to hit on the head with a cosh.

cosignatory *n, pl* **-ries** a person or country that signs a document jointly with others.

cosine (**koh**-sine) *n* (in trigonometry) the ratio of the length of the adjacent side to that of the hypotenuse in a right-angled triangle.

cosmetic *n* **1** anything applied to the face or body in order to improve the appearance. ~*adj* **2** done or used to improve the appearance of the face or body. **3** improving in appearance only: *glossy brochures are part of a cosmetic exercise.*

cosmetic surgery *n* surgery performed to improve the appearance, rather than for medical reasons.

cosmic *adj* **1** of or relating to the whole universe: *the cosmic order.* **2** occurring in or coming from outer space: *cosmic dust.*

cosmogony *n, pl* **-nies** the study of the origin of the universe.

cosmology *n* the study of the origin and nature of the universe. **cosmological** *adj* **cosmologist** *n*

cosmonaut *n* the Russian name for an astronaut.

cosmopolitan *adj* **1** composed of people or elements from many different countries or cultures. **2** having lived and travelled in many countries. ~*n* **3** a cosmopolitan person. **cosmopolitanism** *n*

cosmos *n* the universe considered as an ordered system.

Cossack *n* **1** a member of a S Russian people, famous as horsemen and dancers. ~*adj* **2** of the Cossacks: *a Cossack dance.*

cosset *vb* **-seting, -seted** to pamper or pet.

cost *n* **1** the amount of money, time, or energy required to obtain or produce something. **2** suffering or sacrifice: *these were crucial truths which rugby never grasped, to its cost.* **3** the amount paid for a commodity by its seller: *to sell at cost.* **4 costs** *Law* the expenses of a lawsuit. **5 at all costs** regardless of any cost or effort involved. **6 at the cost of** at the expense of losing: *a man whose public triumphs were attained at the cost of private happiness.* ~*vb* **costing, cost 7** to be obtained or obtainable in exchange for: *calls cost 36p a minute cheap rate, 48p at other times.* **8** to involve the loss or sacrifice of: *a fall which almost cost him his life.* **9** to estimate the cost of producing something.

cost accounting *n* the recording and controlling of all the costs involved in running a business. **cost accountant** *n*

costal *adj* of the ribs.

cost-effective *adj* providing adequate financial return in relation to outlay.

costermonger *n Brit* a person who sells fruit and vegetables from a barrow in the street.

costive *adj Old-fashioned* having or causing constipation.

costly *adj* **-lier, -liest 1** expensive. **2** involving great loss or sacrifice: *a bitter and costly war.* **costliness** *n*

cost of living *n* the average cost of the basic necessities of life, such as food, housing, and clothing.

costume *n* **1** a style of dressing, including all the clothes and accessories, typical of a particular country or period. **2** the clothes worn by an actor or performer: *a jester's costume.* **3** short for **swimming costume.** ~*vb* **-tuming, -tumed 4** to provide with a costume: *she was costumed by many of the great Hollywood designers.* **costumed** *adj*

costume jewellery *n* inexpensive but attractive jewellery.

costumier *n* a make or supplier of theatrical or fancy dress costumes.

cosy *or US* **cozy** *adj* **-sier, -siest** *or US* **-zier, -ziest 1** warm and snug. **2** intimate and friendly: *a cosy chat.* ~*n, pl* **-sies** *or US* **-zies 3** a cover for keeping things warm: *a tea cosy.* **cosiness** *or US* **coziness** *n*

cot[1] *n* **1** a bed with high sides for a baby or very young child. **2** a small portable bed.

cot[2] *n* **1** *Literary or archaic* a small cottage. **2** a cote.

cot[3] cotangent.

cotangent *n* (in trigonometry) the ratio of the length of the adjacent side to that of the opposite side in a right-angled triangle.

cot death *n* the unexplained sudden death of a baby while asleep.

cote *or* **cot** *n* a small shelter for birds or animals.

coterie (**kote**-er-ee) *n* a small exclusive group of friends or people with common interests.

THESAURUS

tion, debasement, defilement, distortion, doctoring, falsification

corset belt, bodice, corselet, foundation garment, girdle, panty girdle, stays (*rare*)

cosmetic *adj.* beautifying, nonessential, superficial, surface, touching-up

cosmic huge, immense, infinite, limitless, measureless, universal

cosmonaut astronaut, spaceman, space pilot

cosmopolitan 1. *adj.* broad-minded, catholic, open-minded, sophisticated, universal, urbane, well-travelled, worldly, worldly-wise **2.** *n.* jetsetter, man *or* woman of the world, sophisticate

cost *n.* **1.** amount, charge, damage (*informal*), expenditure, expense, figure, outlay, payment, price, rate, worth **2.** damage, deprivation, detriment, expense, harm, hurt, injury, loss, penalty, sacrifice, suffering **3. at all costs** at any price, no matter what, regardless, without fail ~*vb.* **4.** come to, command a price of, sell at, set (someone) back (*informal*) **5.** do disservice to, harm, hurt, injure, lose, necessitate

costly 1. dear, excessive, exorbitant, expensive, extortionate, highly-priced, steep (*informal*), stiff, valuable **2.** catastrophic, damaging, deleterious, disastrous, harmful, loss-making, ruinous, sacrificial

costume apparel, attire, clothing, dress, ensemble, garb, get-up (*informal*), livery, national dress, outfit, robes, uniform

cotoneaster (kot-tone-ee-**ass**-ter) *n* a garden shrub with red berries.

cottage *n* a small simple house, usually in the country. **cottager** *n*

cottage cheese *n* a mild soft white cheese made from skimmed milk curds.

cottage industry *n* a craft industry in which employees work at home.

cottage pie *n* a dish of minced meat topped with mashed potato.

cotter[1] *n Machinery* a bolt or wedge that is used to secure parts of machinery.

cotter[2] *n Scot & history* a farm labourer occupying a cottage and land rent-free.

cotter pin *n Machinery* a split pin used to hold parts together and fastened by having the ends spread apart after it is inserted.

cotton *n* **1** the soft white downy fibre surrounding the seeds of a plant grown in warm climates, used to make cloth and thread. **2** cloth or thread made from cotton fibres. **cottony** *adj*

cotton bud *n* a small stick with cotton wool tips used for cleaning the ears, applying make-up, etc.

cotton on *vb Informal* to understand or realize the meaning (of): *it has taken the world 20 years to cotton on to this idea.*

cotton wool *n Chiefly Brit* absorbent fluffy cotton, used for surgical dressings and to apply creams to the skin.

cotyledon (kot-ill-**ee**-don) *n* the first leaf produced by a plant embryo.

couch *n* **1** a piece of upholstered furniture for seating more than one person. **2** a bed on which patients of a doctor or a psychoanalyst lie during examination or treatment. *~vb* **3** to express in a particular style of language: *a proclamation couched in splendidly archaic phraseology.* **4** *Archaic* (of an animal) to crouch, as when preparing to leap.

couchette (koo-**shett**) *n* a bed converted from seats on a train or ship.

couch grass *n* a grassy weed which spreads quickly.

couch potato *n Slang* a lazy person whose only hobby is watching television and videos.

cougar (**koo**-gar) *n* same as **puma.**

cough *vb* **1** to expel air abruptly and noisily from the lungs. **2** (of an engine or other machine) to make a sound similar to this. *~n* **3** an act or sound of coughing. **4** an illness which causes frequent coughing.

cough up *vb* **1** *Informal* to give up (money or information). **2** to bring up into the mouth by coughing: *to cough up blood.*

could *vb* used: **1** to make the past tense of **can**[1]. 2 to make the subjunctive mood of **can**[1], esp. in polite requests or conditional sentences: *could I have a word with you, please?* **3** to indicate the suggestion of a course of action: *we could make a fortune from selling players, but that would not be in the long term interests of the club.* **4** to indicate a possibility: *it could simply be a spelling mistake.*

couldn't could not.

coulis (**koo**-lee) *n* a thin purée of vegetables or fruit, usually served as a sauce surrounding a dish: *rum truffle cake with raspberry coulis.*

coulomb (**koo**-lom) *n* the SI unit of electric charge.

coulter (**kole**-ter) *n* a vertical blade on a plough in front of the ploughshare.

council *n* **1** a group meeting for discussion or consultation. **2** a legislative or advisory body: *the United Nations Security Council.* **3** *Brit* the local governing authority of a town or county. *~adj* **4** of or provided by a local council: *a council house.*

councillor *or US* **councilor** *n* a member of a council.

council tax *n* (in Britain) a tax based on the relative value of property levied to fund local council services.

counsel *n* **1** advice or guidance. **2** discussion or consultation: *when it was over they took counsel of their consciences.* **3** a barrister or group of barristers who conduct cases in court and advise on legal matters. *~vb* **-selling, -selled** *or US* **-seling, -seled 4** to give advice or guidance to. **5** to recommend or urge. **counselling** *or US* **counseling** *n*

counsellor *or US* **counselor** *n* **1** an adviser. **2** *US* a lawyer who conducts cases in court.

count[1] *vb* **1** to say numbers in ascending order up to and including: *count from one to ten.* **2** to add up or check (each thing in a group) in order to find the total: *he counted the money he had left.* **3** to be important: *it's the thought that counts.* **4** to consider: *he can count himself lucky.* **5** to take into account or include: *the time he'd spent in prison on remand counted towards his sentence.* **6 not counting** excluding. **7** *Music* to keep time by counting beats. *~n* **8** the act of counting. **9** the number reached by counting: *a high pollen count.* **10** *Law* one of a number of charges. **11 keep** *or* **lose count** to keep or fail to keep an accurate record of items or events. **12 out for the count** unconscious. ~See also **count against, countdown,** etc. **countable** *adj*

count[2] *n* a middle-ranking European nobleman.

count against *vb* to have an effect or influence that makes something more unlikely: *his age counts against him getting promotion.*

countdown *n* the act of counting backwards to zero to time exactly an operation such as the launching of a rocket.

countenance *n* **1** *Literary* the face or facial expression. *~vb* **-nancing, -nanced 2** to support or tolerate.

THESAURUS

cosy comfortable, comfy (*informal*), cuddled up, homely, intimate, secure, sheltered, snug, snuggled down, tucked up, warm

cottage but and ben (*Scot.*), cabin, chalet, cot, hut, lodge, shack

cough 1. *vb.* bark, clear one's throat, hack, hawk, hem **2.** *n.* bark, frog *or* tickle in one's throat, hack

cough up ante up (*informal, chiefly U.S.*), come across, deliver, fork out (*slang*), give up, hand over, pay up, shell out (*informal*), surrender

council assembly, board, cabinet, chamber, committee, conclave, conference, congress, convention, convocation, diet, governing body, house, ministry, panel, parliament, synod

counsel *n.* **1.** admonition, advice, caution, consideration, consultation, deliberation, direction, forethought, guidance, information, recommendation, suggestion, warning **2.** advocate, attorney, barrister, lawyer, legal adviser, solicitor *~vb.* **3.** admonish, advise, advocate, caution, exhort, instruct, prescribe, recommend, urge, warn

count *vb.* **1.** add (up), calculate, cast up, check, compute, enumerate, estimate, number, reckon, score, tally, tot up **2.** carry weight, cut any ice (*informal*), enter into consideration, matter, rate, signify, tell, weigh **3.** consider, deem, esteem, judge, look upon, rate, regard, think **4.** include, number among, take into account *or* consideration *~n.* **5.** calculation, computation, enumeration, numbering, poll, reckoning, sum, tally

countenance 1. *n.* appearance, aspect, expression,

counter[1] *n* **1** a long flat surface in a bank or shop, on which business is transacted. **2** a small flat disc used in board games. **3** a disc or token used as an imitation coin. **4 under the counter** (of the sale of goods) illegal.

counter[2] *n* an apparatus for counting things.

counter[3] *vb* **1** to say or do (something) in retaliation or response. **2** to oppose or act against. **3** to return the attack of (an opponent). ~*adv* **4** in an opposite or opposing direction or manner. **5 run counter to** to be in direct contrast with. ~*adj* **6** opposing or opposite. ~*n* **7** something that is contrary or opposite to something else. **8** an opposing action. **9** a return attack, such as a blow in boxing.

counter- *prefix* **1** against or opposite: *counterattack.* **2** complementary or corresponding: *counterpart.*

counteract *vb* to act against or neutralize. **counteraction** *n* **counteractive** *adj*

counterattack *n* **1** an attack in response to an attack. ~*vb* **2** to make a counterattack (against).

counterbalance *n* **1** a weight or influence that balances or neutralizes another. ~*vb* **-ancing, -anced 2** to act as a counterbalance to.

counterblast *n* an aggressive response to a verbal attack.

counterclockwise *adv, adj US & Canad* same as **anticlockwise.**

counterespionage *n* activities to counteract enemy espionage.

counterfeit *adj* **1** made in imitation of something genuine with the intent to deceive or defraud: *counterfeit currency.* **2** pretended: *counterfeit friendship.* ~*n* **3** an imitation designed to deceive or defraud. ~*vb* **4** to make a fraudulent imitation of. **5** to feign: *surprise is an easy emotion to counterfeit.*

counterfoil *n Brit* the part of a cheque or receipt kept as a record.

counterintelligence *n* activities designed to frustrate enemy espionage.

countermand *vb* to cancel (a previous order).

countermeasure *n* action taken to counteract some other action.

counterpane *n* a bed covering.

counterpart *n* **1** a person or thing complementary to or corresponding to another. **2** a duplicate of a legal document.

counterpoint *n* **1** the harmonious combining of two or more parts or melodies. **2** a melody or part combined in this way. ~*vb* **3** to set in contrast.

counterpoise *vb* **-poising, -poised** to oppose with something of equal weight or effect.

counterproductive *adj* having an effect opposite to the one intended.

countersign *vb* **1** to sign (a document already signed by another) as confirmation. ~*n* **2** the signature so written.

countersink *vb* **-sinking, -sank, -sunk** to drive (a screw) into a shaped hole so that its head is below the surface.

countertenor *n* **1** an adult male voice with an alto range. **2** a singer with such a voice.

countess *n* **1** a woman holding the rank of count or earl. **2** the wife or widow of a count or earl.

countless *adj* too many to count.

count noun *n* a noun that may be preceded by an indefinite article and can be used in the plural, such as *telephone* or *thing.*

count on *vb* to rely or depend on.

count out *vb* **1** *Informal* to exclude. **2** to declare (a boxer) defeated when he has not risen from the floor within ten seconds.

countrified *adj* having an appearance or manner associated with the countryside rather than a town.

country *n, pl* **-tries 1** an area distinguished by its people, culture, language, or government. **2** the territory of a nation or state. **3** the people of a nation or state. **4** the part of the land that is away from cities or industrial areas. **5** a person's native land. **6** same as **country and western. 7 across country** not keeping to roads. **8 go to the country** *Chiefly Brit* to dissolve Parliament and hold a general election.

country and western *or* **country music** *n* popular music based on American White folk music.

country club *n* a club in the country, which has sporting and social facilities.

country dance *n* a type of British folk dance performed in rows or circles.

countryman *n, pl* **-men 1** a person from one's own

THESAURUS

face, features, look, mien, physiognomy, visage **2.** *vb.* brook, endure, put up with (*informal*), stand for (*informal*), tolerate

counter 1. *vb.* answer, hit back, meet, offset, parry, resist, respond, retaliate, return, ward off **2.** *adv.* against, at variance with, contrarily, contrariwise, conversely, in defiance of, versus **3.** *adj.* adverse, against, conflicting, contradictory, contrary, contrasting, obverse, opposed, opposing, opposite

counteract annul, check, contravene, counterbalance, countervail, cross, defeat, foil, frustrate, hinder, invalidate, negate, neutralize, obviate, offset, oppose, resist, thwart

counterbalance balance, compensate, counterpoise, make up for, offset, set off

counterfeit 1. *adj.* bogus, copied, ersatz, faked, false, feigned, forged, fraudulent, imitation, phoney or phony (*informal*), sham, simulated, spurious, supposititious **2.** *n.* copy, fake, forgery, fraud, imitation, phoney *or* phony (*informal*), reproduction, sham **3.** *vb.* copy, fabricate, fake, feign, forge, imitate, impersonate, pretend, sham, simulate

countermand annul, cancel, override, repeal, rescind, retract, reverse, revoke

counterpart complement, copy, correlative, duplicate, equal, fellow, match, mate, opposite number, supplement, tally, twin

countless endless, immeasurable, incalculable, infinite, innumerable, legion, limitless, measureless, multitudinous, myriad, numberless, uncounted, untold

count on *or* **upon** bank on, believe (in), depend on, lean on, pin one's faith on, reckon on, rely on, take for granted, take on trust, trust

count out disregard, except, exclude, leave out, leave out of account, pass over

country *n.* **1.** commonwealth, kingdom, land, nation, people, realm, region, sovereign state, state, territory **2.** citizenry, citizens, community, electors, grass roots, inhabitants, nation, people, populace, public, society, voters **3.** backwoods, boondocks (*U.S. slang*), countryside, farmland, green belt, outback (*Austral. & N.Z.*), outdoors, provinces, rural areas, sticks (*informal*), the back of beyond, the bush, the middle of nowhere, wide open spaces (*informal*) **4.** fatherland, homeland, motherland, nationality, native land, one's native heath

countryman 1. bumpkin, country dweller, farmer, hick (*informal, chiefly U.S. & Canad.*), peasant, provincial, rustic, swain, yokel **2.** compatriot, fellow citizen

countryside country, farmland, green belt, outback

country. **2** a person who lives in the country. **countrywoman** *fem n*

countryside *n* land away from the cities.

county *n, pl* **-ties 1** a division of a country. *~adj* **2** *Brit informal* upper-class.

coup (**koo**) *n* **1** a brilliant and successful action. **2** a coup d'état.

coup de grâce (**koo** de **grahss**) *n, pl* **coups de grâce** (**koo** de **grahss**) a final or decisive action.

coup d'état (**koo** day-**tah**) *n, pl* **coups d'état** (**kooz** day-**tah**) a sudden violent or illegal overthrow of a government.

coupé (**koo**-pay) *n* a sports car with two doors and a sloping fixed roof.

couple *n* **1** two people who are married or romantically involved. **2** two partners in a dance or game. **3 a couple of a** a pair of: *a couple of guys.* **b** *Informal* a few: *a couple of weeks.* *~pron* **4 a couple a** two. **b** *Informal* a few: *give him a couple.* *~vb* **-pling, -pled 5** to connect or link: *an ingrained sense of shame, coupled with a fear of ridicule.* **6** *Literary* to have sexual intercourse.

couplet *n* two successive lines of verse, usually rhyming and of the same metre.

coupling *n* a device for connecting things, such as railway carriages.

coupon *n* **1** a piece of paper entitling the holder to a discount or free gift. **2** a detachable slip that can be used as a commercial order form. **3** *Brit* a football pools entry form.

courage *n* **1** the ability to face danger or pain without fear. **2 the courage of one's convictions** the confidence to act according to one's beliefs.

courageous *adj* showing courage. **courageously** *adv*

courgette *n* a type of small vegetable marrow.

courier *n* **1** a person who looks after and guides travellers. **2** a person paid to deliver urgent messages.

course *n* **1** a complete series of lessons or lectures: *a training course.* **2** a sequence of medical treatment prescribed for a period of time: *a course of antibiotics.* **3** an onward movement in time or space: *during the course of his career he worked with many leading actors.* **4** a route or direction taken: *the ships were blown off course by a gale.* **5** the path or channel along which a river moves. **6** an area on which a sport is played or a race is held: *a golf course.* **7** any of the successive parts of a meal. **8** a continuous, usually horizontal layer of building material, such as bricks or tiles, at one level in a building. **9** a mode of conduct or action: *the safest course of action was to do nothing.* **10** the natural development of a sequence of events: *allow the fever to run its course.* **11** a period of time: *over the course of the last two years.* **12 as a matter of course** as a natural or normal consequence or event. **13 in the course of** in the process of. **14 in due course** at the natural or appropriate time. **15 of course a** (*adv*) as expected; naturally. **b** (*interj*) certainly; definitely. *~vb* **coursing, coursed 16** (of a liquid) to run swiftly. **17** to hunt with hounds that follow the quarry by sight and not scent.

coursebook *n* a book that is used as part of an educational course.

courser[1] *n* **1** a person who courses hounds. **2** a hound trained for coursing.

courser[2] *n Literary* a swift horse; steed.

coursework *n* work done by a student and assessed as part of an educational course.

coursing *n* hunting with hounds trained to hunt game by sight.

court *n* **1** *Law* **a** a judicial body which hears and makes decisions on legal cases. **b** the room or building in which such a body meets. **2** a marked area used for playing a racket game. **3** an area of ground wholly or partly surrounded by walls or buildings. **4** a name given to some short street, blocks of flats, or large country houses as a part of their address: *Carlton Court.* **5** the residence or retinue of a sovereign. **6** any formal assembly held by a sovereign. **7 go to court** to take legal action. **8 hold court** to preside over a group of admirers. **9 out of court** without a trial or legal case. **10 pay court to** to give flattering attention to. *~vb* **11** to attempt to gain the love of. **12** to pay attention to (someone) in order to gain favour. **13** to try to obtain (something): *he has not courted controversy, but he has certainly attracted it.* **14** to make oneself open or vulnerable to: *courting disaster.*

court card *n* (in a pack of playing cards) a king, queen, or jack.

THESAURUS

(*Austral. & N.Z.*), outdoors, panorama, sticks (*informal*), view, wide open spaces (*informal*)

count up add, reckon up, sum, tally, total

county 1. *n.* province, shire **2.** *adj.* green-wellie, huntin', shootin', and fishin' (*informal*), plummy (*informal*), tweedy, upper-class, upper-crust (*informal*)

coup accomplishment, action, deed, exploit, feat, manoeuvre, masterstroke, stratagem, stroke, stroke of genius, stunt, *tour de force*

couple 1. *n.* brace, duo, item, pair, twosome **2.** *vb.* buckle, clasp, conjoin, connect, hitch, join, link, marry, pair, unite, wed, yoke

coupon card, certificate, detachable portion, slip, ticket, token, voucher

courage balls (*taboo slang*), boldness, bottle (*Brit. slang*), bravery, daring, dauntlessness, fearlessness, firmness, fortitude, gallantry, grit, guts (*informal*), hardihood, heroism, intrepidity, lion-heartedness, mettle, nerve, pluck, resolution, spunk (*informal*), valour

courageous audacious, ballsy (*taboo slang*), bold, brave, daring, dauntless, fearless, gallant, gritty, hardy, heroic, indomitable, intrepid, lion-hearted, plucky, resolute, stalwart, stouthearted, valiant, valorous

course *n.* **1.** classes, course of study, curriculum, lectures, programme, schedule, studies **2.** advance, advancement, continuity, development, flow, furtherance, march, movement, order, progress, progression, sequence, succession, unfolding **3.** channel, direction, duration, line, orbit, passage, path, road, route, tack, term, time, track, trail, trajectory, way **4.** circuit, field, ground, racecourse, stadium, track **5.** behaviour, conduct, manner, method, mode, plan, policy, procedure, programme, regimen **6. in due course** eventually, finally, in the course of time, in the end, in time, sooner or later **7. of course** certainly, definitely, indubitably, naturally, obviously, undoubtedly, without a doubt *~vb.* **8.** dash, flow, gush, move apace, race, run, scud, scurry, speed, stream, surge, tumble **9.** chase, follow, hunt, pursue

court *n.* **1.** bar, bench, court of justice, lawcourt, seat of judgment, tribunal **2.** cloister, courtyard, piazza, plaza, quad (*informal*), quadrangle, square, yard **3.** hall, manor, palace **4.** attendants, cortege, entourage, retinue, royal household, suite, train **5.** *as in* **pay court to** addresses, attention, homage, respects, suit *~vb.* **6.** chase, date, go (out) with, go steady with (*informal*), keep company with, make love to, archaic, pay court to, pay one's addresses to, pursue, run after, serenade, set one's cap at, take out, walk out with, woo **7.** cultivate, curry favour with, fawn upon, flatter, pander to, seek, solicit **8.** attract, bring about, incite, invite, prompt, provoke, seek

courteous affable, attentive, ceremonious, civil,

courteous *adj* polite and considerate in manner. **courteously** *adv* **courteousness** *n*
courtesan (kore-tiz-**zan**) *n History* a mistress or high-class prostitute.
courtesy *n, pl* **-sies 1** politeness; good manners. **2** a courteous act or remark. **3 by courtesy of** with the consent of.
courthouse *n* a public building in which courts of law are held.
courtier *n* an attendant at a royal court.
courtly *adj* **-lier, -liest 1** ceremoniously polite. **2** of or suitable for a royal court. **courtliness** *n*
court martial *n, pl* **court martials** *or* **courts martial 1** the trial of a member of the armed forces charged with breaking military law. *~vb* **court-martial, -tialling, -tialled** *or US* **-tialing, -tialed 2** to try by court martial.
courtship *n* the courting of an intended spouse or mate.
court shoe *n* a low-cut shoe for women, without laces or straps.
courtyard *n* an open area of ground surrounded by walls or buildings.
couscous (**kooss**-kooss) *n* **1** a type of semolina used in North African cookery. **2** a spicy North African dish, consisting of steamed semolina served with a stew.
cousin *n* the child of one's aunt or uncle. Also called: **first cousin**
couture (koo-**toor**) *n* high-fashion designing and dressmaking.
couturier *n* a person who designs fashion clothes for women.
covalency *or US* **covalence** *n Chem* **1** the ability to form a bond in which two atoms share a pair of electrons. **2** the number of covalent bonds which a particular atom can make with others. **covalent** *adj*
cove[1] *n* a small bay or inlet.
cove[2] *n Old-fashioned, slang* a fellow; chap.
coven (**kuv**-ven) *n* a meeting of witches.
covenant (**kuv**-ven-ant) *n* **1** a formal agreement to make an annual payment to charity. **2** *Law* a formal sealed agreement. **3** *Bible* God's promise to the Israelites and their commitment to worship him alone. *~vb* **4** to agree by a legal covenant. **covenanter** *n*
Covenanter *n Scot history* a person upholding either of two 17th-century covenants to establish and defend Presbyterianism.
Coventry *n* **send someone to Coventry** to punish someone by refusing to speak to him or her.
cover *vb* **1** to place something over so as to protect or conceal. **2** to put a garment on; clothe. **3** to extend over or lie thickly on the surface of: *the ground was covered with dry leaves.* **4** (sometimes foll. by *up*) to screen or conceal; hide from view. **5** to travel over. **6** to protect (an individual or group) by taking up a position from which fire may be returned if those being protected are fired upon. **7** to keep a gun aimed at. **8 a** to insure against loss or risk. **b** to provide for (loss or risk) by insurance. **9** to include or deal with: *the course covers accounting, economics, statistics, law and computer applications.* **10** to act as reporter or photographer on (a news event) for a newspaper or magazine. **11** (of a sum of money) to be enough to pay for (something). **12** *Music* to record a **cover version** of. **13** *Sport* to guard or obstruct (an opponent, team-mate, or area). **14 cover for** to deputize for (a person). **15** (foll. by *for* or *up for*) to provide an alibi (for): *can my men count on your friends at City Hall to cover for us?* *~n* **16** anything which covers. **17** a blanket or bedspread. **18** the outside of a book or magazine. **19** a pretext or disguise: *he claimed UN resolutions were being used as a cover for planned American aggression.* **20** an envelope or other postal wrapping: *under plain cover.* **21** an individual table setting. **22** insurance. **23** a cover version. **24 the covers** *Cricket* the area roughly at right angles to the pitch on the off side and about halfway to the boundary. **25 break cover** to come out from a shelter or hiding place. **26 take cover** to make for a place of safety or shelter. **27 under cover** protected or in secret. *~*See also **cover-up. covering** *adj, n*
coverage *n Journalism* the amount of reporting given to a subject or event.
cover charge *n* a fixed service charge added to the bill in a restaurant.
cover girl *n* an attractive woman whose picture appears on the cover of a magazine.
covering letter *n* an accompanying letter sent as an explanation.
coverlet *n* same as **bedspread.**

THESAURUS

courtly, elegant, gallant, gracious, mannerly, polished, polite, refined, respectful, urbane, well-bred, well-mannered
courtesy 1. affability, civility, courteousness, courtliness, elegance, gallantness, gallantry, good breeding, good manners, graciousness, polish, politeness, urbanity **2.** benevolence, consent, consideration, favour, generosity, indulgence, kindness
courtier attendant, follower, henchman, squire, trainbearer
courtly affable, aristocratic, ceremonious, chivalrous, civil, decorous, dignified, elegant, flattering, formal, gallant, highbred, lordly, obliging, polished, refined, stately, urbane
courtship courting, engagement, keeping company, pursuit, romance, suit, wooing
courtyard area, enclosure, peristyle, playground, quad, quadrangle, yard
cove anchorage, bay, bayou, creek, firth (*Scot.*), inlet, sound
covenant 1. *n.* arrangement, bargain, commitment, compact, concordat, contract, convention, pact, promise, stipulation, treaty, trust **2.** *vb.* agree, bargain, contract, engage, pledge, stipulate, undertake
cover *vb.* **1.** clothe, dress, put on **2.** canopy, clothe, coat, daub, encase, envelop, invest, layer, mantle, overlay, overspread, wrap **3.** camouflage, cloak, conceal, cover up, curtain, disguise, eclipse, enshroud, hide, hood, house, mask, obscure, screen, secrete, shade, shroud, veil **4.** cross, pass through *or* over, range, travel over, traverse **5.** defend, guard, protect, reinforce, shelter, shield, watch over **6.** comprehend, comprise, consider, contain, deal with, embody, embrace, encompass, examine, include, incorporate, involve, provide for, refer to, survey, take account of **7.** describe, detail, investigate, narrate, recount, relate, report, tell of, write up **8.** balance, compensate, counterbalance, insure, make good, make up for, offset *~n.* **9.** camouflage, canopy, cap, case, cloak, clothing, coating, concealment, covering, defence, disguise, dress, envelope, front, guard, hiding place, lid, mask, protection, refuge, sanctuary, screen, sheath, shelter, shield, smoke screen, top, undergrowth, veil, woods **10.** binding, jacket, wrapper **11.** camouflage, cover-up, facade, pretence, window-dressing **12.** compensation, indemnity, insurance, payment, protection, reimbursement
covering 1. *adj.* accompanying, descriptive, explan-

cover note *n Brit* a temporary certificate from an insurance company giving proof of a current policy.
covert *adj* **1** concealed or secret. ~*n* **2** a thicket or woodland providing shelter for game. **3** *Ornithol* any of the small feathers on the wings and tail of a bird that surround the bases of the larger feathers. **covertly** *adv*
cover-up *n* **1** concealment or attempted concealment of a mistake or crime. ~*vb* **cover up 2** to cover completely. **3** to attempt to conceal (a mistake or crime).
cover version *n* a version by a different artist of a previously recorded musical item.
covet *vb* **-eting, -eted** to long to possess (something belonging to another person).
covetous *adj* jealously longing to possess something. **covetously** *adv* **covetousness** *n*
covey (**kuv**-vee) *n* **1** a small flock of grouse or partridge. **2** a small group of people.
cow[1] *n* **1** the mature female of cattle. **2** the mature female of various other mammals, such as the elephant or whale. **3** *Not in technical use* any domestic species of cattle. **4** *Informal, offensive* a disagreeable woman.
cow[2] *vb* to frighten or subdue with threats.
coward *n* a person who is easily frightened and avoids dangerous or difficult situations. **cowardly** *adj*
cowardice *n* lack of courage.
cowbell *n* a bell hung around a cow's neck.
cowboy *n* **1** (in the U.S. and Canada) a ranch worker who herds and tends cattle, usually on horseback. **2** a conventional character of Wild West folklore or films. **3** *Informal* an irresponsible or unscrupulous worker or businessman. **cowgirl** *fem n*
cowcatcher *n* a fender on the front of a locomotive to clear the track of animals or other obstructions.
cow cocky *n Austral & NZ* a one-man dairy farmer.
cower *vb* to cringe or shrink in fear.
cowl *n* **1** a loose hood. **2** a monk's hooded robe. **3** a cover fitted to a chimney to increase ventilation and prevent draughts. **cowled** *adj*
cowlick *n* a tuft of hair which stands up over the forehead.
cowling *n* a streamlined detachable metal covering around an engine.
co-worker *n* a fellow worker.
cow parsley *n* a hedgerow plant with umbrella-shaped clusters of white flowers.
cowpat *n* a pool of cow dung.
cowpox *n* a contagious disease of cows, the virus of which is used to make smallpox vaccine.
cowrie *n, pl* **-ries** the glossy brightly-marked shell of a marine mollusc.
cowslip *n* a European wild plant with yellow flowers.
cox *n* **1** a coxswain. ~*vb* **2** to act as coxswain of (a boat).
coxcomb *or* **cockscomb** *n* **1** the comb of a domestic cock. **2** *Informal* a conceited dandy.
coxswain (**kok**-sn) *n* the person who steers a lifeboat or rowing boat.
coy *adj* **1** affectedly shy and modest. **2** unwilling to give information. **coyly** *adv* **coyness** *n*
coyote (koy-**ote**-ee) *n, pl* **-otes** *or* **-ote** a small wolf of the deserts and prairies of North America.
coypu *n, pl* **-pus** *or* **-pu** a beaver-like amphibious rodent, bred for its fur.
cozen *vb Literary* to cheat or trick. **cozenage** *n*
Cpl Corporal.
Cr *Chem* chromium.
crab *n* **1** an edible shellfish with five pairs of legs, the first pair modified into pincers. **2** short for **crab louse. 3 catch a crab** *Rowing* to make a stroke in which the oar misses the water or digs too deeply, causing the rower to fall backwards.
crab apple *n* a kind of small sour apple.
crabbed *adj* **1** (of handwriting) cramped and hard to read. **2** bad-tempered.
crabby *adj* **-bier, -biest** bad-tempered.
crab louse *n* a parasitic louse living in the pubic area of humans.
crack *vb* **1** to break or split without complete separation of the parts. **2** to break with a sudden sharp sound. **3** to make or cause to make a sudden sharp sound: *the coachman cracked his whip.* **4** (of the voice) to become harsh or change pitch suddenly. **5** *Informal* to fail or break down: *he had cracked under the strain of losing his job.* **6** to yield or cease to resist: *he had cracked under torture.* **7** to hit with a forceful or resounding blow. **8** to break into or force open: *it'll take me longer if I have to crack the safe myself.* **9** to solve or decipher (a code or problem). **10** *Informal* to tell (a joke). **11** to break (a molecule) into smaller molecules or radicals by heat or catalysis as in the distillation of petroleum. **12** to open (a bottle) for drinking. **13 crack it** *Informal* to achieve something. ~*n* **14** a sudden sharp noise. **15** a break or fracture without complete separation of the two parts. **16** a narrow opening or fissure. **17** *Informal* a sharp blow. **18 crack of dawn** daybreak. **19** a broken or cracked tone of voice. **20** *Informal* an attempt. **21** *Informal* a gibe or joke. **22** *Slang* a highly addictive form of cocaine. **23 a fair crack of the whip** *Informal* a fair

THESAURUS

atory, introductory **2.** *n.* blanket, casing, clothing, coating, cover, housing, layer, overlay, protection, shelter, top, wrap, wrapper, wrapping
cover-up complicity, concealment, conspiracy, front, smoke screen, whitewash (*informal*)
cover up 1. coat, cover, encrust, envelop, hide, plaster, swathe **2.** conceal, cover one's tracks, feign ignorance, hide, hush up, keep dark, keep secret, keep silent about, keep under one's hat (*informal*), repress, stonewall, suppress, whitewash (*informal*)
covet aspire to, begrudge, crave, desire, envy, fancy (*informal*), hanker after, have one's eye on, long for, lust after, thirst for, yearn for
covetous acquisitive, avaricious, close-fisted, envious, grasping, greedy, jealous, mercenary, rapacious, yearning
coward chicken (*slang*), craven, faint-heart, funk (*informal*), poltroon, recreant (*archaic*), scaredy-cat (*informal*), wimp (*informal*), yellow-belly (*slang*)
cowardly abject, base, chicken (*slang*), chicken-hearted, craven, dastardly, faint-hearted, fearful, gutless (*informal*), lily-livered, pusillanimous, recreant (*archaic*), scared, shrinking, soft, spineless, timorous, weak, weak-kneed (*informal*), white-livered, yellow (*informal*)
cowboy broncobuster (*U.S.*), cattleman, cowhand, cowpuncher (*U.S. informal*), drover, gaucho (*S. American*), herder, herdsman, rancher, ranchero (*U.S.*), stockman, wrangler (*U.S.*)
cower cringe, crouch, draw back, fawn, flinch, grovel, quail, shrink, skulk, sneak, tremble, truckle
coy arch, backward, bashful, coquettish, demure, evasive, flirtatious, kittenish, modest, overmodest, prudish, reserved, retiring, self-effacing, shrinking, shy, skittish, timid

chance or opportunity. *~adj* **24** *Slang* first-class or excellent: *crack troops.* ~See also **crack down, crack up.**

crackbrained *adj* idiotic or crazy: *a crackbrained scheme.*

crack down *vb* **1 crack down on** to take severe measures against. *~n* **crackdown 2** severe or repressive measures.

cracked *adj* **1** damaged by cracking. **2** harsh-sounding. **3** *Informal* crazy.

cracker *n* **1** a thin crisp unsweetened biscuit. **2** a decorated cardboard tube, pulled apart with a bang, containing a paper hat and a joke or a toy. **3** a small explosive firework. **4** *Brit, Austral, & NZ slang* an excellent or notable thing or person.

crackers *adj Brit slang* insane.

cracking *adj* **1 get cracking** *Informal* to start doing something immediately. **2 a cracking pace** *Informal* a high speed. *~adv, adj* **3** *Brit informal* first-class: *five cracking good saves.* *~n* **4** the oil-refining process in which heavy oils are broken down into smaller molecules by heat or catalysis.

crackle *vb* **-ling, -led 1** to make small sharp popping noises. *~n* **2** a crackling sound. **crackly** *adj*

crackling *n* **1** a series of small sharp popping noises. **2** the crisp browned skin of roast pork.

crackpot *Informal ~n* **1** an eccentric person. *~adj* **2** eccentric: *crackpot philosophies.*

crack up *vb* **1** *Informal* to have a physical or mental breakdown. **2** to begin to break into pieces: *there are worrying reports of buildings cracking up as the earth dries out and foundations move.* **3 not all it is cracked up to be** *Informal* not as good as people have claimed it to be. *~n* **crackup 4** *Informal* a physical or mental breakdown

-cracy *n combining form* indicating a type of government or rule: *plutocracy; mobocracy.* ~See also **-crat.**

cradle *n* **1** a baby's bed on rockers. **2** a place where something originates: *the cradle of civilization.* **3** a supporting framework or structure. **4** a platform or trolley in which workmen are suspended on the side of a building or ship. *~vb* **-dling, -dled 5** to hold gently as if in a cradle.

cradle-snatcher *n Informal* a person who marries or has a sexual relationship with someone much younger than himself or herself.

craft *n* **1** an occupation requiring skill or manual dexterity. **2** skill or ability. **3** cunning or guile. **4** (*pl* **craft**) a boat, ship, aircraft, or spacecraft. *~vb* **5** to make skilfully.

craftsman *or fem* **craftswoman** *n, pl* **-men** *or* **-women 1** a skilled worker. **2** a skilled artist. **craftsmanship** *n*

crafty *adj* **-tier, -tiest** skilled in deception. **craftily** *adv* **craftiness** *n*

crag *n* a steep rugged rock or peak. **craggy** *adj*

crake *n Zool* a bird of the rail family, such as the corncrake.

cram *vb* **cramming, crammed 1** to force (more people or things) into (a place) than it can hold. **2** to eat or feed to excess. **3** to study hard just before an examination.

crammer *n* a person or school that prepares pupils for an examination.

cramp[1] *n* **1** a sudden painful contraction of a muscle. **2** temporary stiffness of a muscle group from overexertion: *writer's cramp.* **3** severe stomach pain. **4** a clamp for holding masonry or timber together. *~vb* **5** to affect with a cramp.

cramp[2] *vb* **1** to confine or restrict. **2 cramp someone's style** *Informal* to prevent someone from im-

THESAURUS

crack *vb.* **1.** break, burst, chip, chop, cleave, crackle, craze, fracture, rive, snap, splinter, split **2.** burst, crash, detonate, explode, pop, ring, snap **3.** break down, collapse, give way, go to pieces, lose control, succumb, yield **4.** buffet, clip (*informal*), clout (*informal*), cuff, slap, thump, wallop (*informal*), whack **5.** decipher, fathom, get the answer to, solve, work out *~n.* **6.** burst, clap, crash, explosion, pop, report, snap **7.** breach, break, chink, chip, cleft, cranny, crevice, fissure, fracture, gap, interstice, rift **8.** *informal* buffet, clip (*informal*), clout (*informal*), cuff, slap, thump, wallop (*informal*), whack **9.** *informal* attempt, go (*informal*), opportunity, stab (*informal*), try **10.** *informal* dig, funny remark, gag (*informal*), insult, jibe, joke, quip, smart-alecky remark, wisecrack, witticism *~adj.* **11.** *slang* ace, choice, elite, excellent, first-class, first-rate, hand-picked, superior, world-class

cracked **1.** broken, chipped, crazed, damaged, defective, faulty, fissured, flawed, imperfect, split **2.** *slang* bats (*slang*), batty (*slang*), crackbrained, crackpot (*informal*), crazy (*informal*), daft (*informal*), eccentric, insane, loony (*slang*), loopy (*informal*), nuts (*slang*), nutty (*slang*), oddball (*informal*), off one's head *or* nut (*slang*), off one's trolley (*slang*), off-the-wall (*slang*), out of one's mind, outré, out to lunch (*informal*), round the bend (*slang*), touched, wacko (*slang*)

crack up **1.** break down, collapse, come apart at the seams (*informal*), freak out (*informal*), go ape (*slang*), go apeshit (*slang*), go berserk, go crazy (*informal*), go off one's rocker (*slang*), go out of one's mind, go to pieces, have a breakdown, throw a wobbly (*slang*) **2.** **not all it is cracked up to be** blown up, exaggerated, hyped (up), overpraised, overrated, puffed up

cradle *n.* **1.** bassinet, cot, crib, Moses basket **2.** beginning, birthplace, fount, fountainhead, origin, source, spring, wellspring *~vb.* **3.** hold, lull, nestle, nurse, rock, support

craft **1.** business, calling, employment, handicraft, handiwork, line, occupation, pursuit, trade, vocation, work **2.** ability, aptitude, art, artistry, cleverness, dexterity, expertise, expertness, ingenuity, knack, know-how (*informal*), skill, technique, workmanship **3.** artfulness, artifice, contrivance, craftiness, cunning, deceit, duplicity, guile, ruse, scheme, shrewdness, stratagem, subterfuge, subtlety, trickery, wiles **4.** aircraft, barque, boat, plane, ship, spacecraft, vessel

craftiness artfulness, astuteness, canniness, cunning, deviousness, duplicity, foxiness, guile, shrewdness, slyness, subtlety, trickiness, wiliness

craftsman artificer, artisan, maker, master, skilled worker, smith, technician, wright

craftsmanship artistry, expertise, mastery, technique, workmanship

crafty artful, astute, calculating, canny, cunning, deceitful, designing, devious, duplicitous, foxy, fraudulent, guileful, knowing, scheming, sharp, shrewd, sly, subtle, tricky, wily

crag bluff, peak, pinnacle, rock, tor

cram **1.** compact, compress, crowd, crush, fill to overflowing, force, jam, overcrowd, overfill, pack, pack in, press, ram, shove, squeeze, stuff **2.** glut, gorge, gormandize, guzzle, overeat, overfeed, pig out (*slang*), put *or* pack away, satiate, stuff **3.** bone up on (*informal*), mug up (*slang*), revise, study, swot, swot up

cramp[1] *n.* ache, contraction, convulsion, crick, pain, pang, shooting pain, spasm, stiffness, stitch, twinge

cramp[2] *vb.* check, circumscribe, clog, confine, con-

pressing another person or from behaving naturally: *shyness will cramp their style.*

cramped *adj* **1** closed in. **2** (of handwriting) small and irregular.

crampon *n* a spiked iron plate strapped to a boot for climbing on ice.

cranberry *n, pl* **-ries** a sour edible red berry.

crane *n* **1** a machine for lifting and moving heavy objects, usually by suspending them from a movable projecting arm. **2** a large wading bird with a long neck and legs. *~vb* **craning, craned 3** to stretch out (the neck) in order to see something.

crane fly *n* a fly with long legs, slender wings, and a narrow body.

cranesbill *n* a plant with pink or purple flowers.

cranial *adj* of or relating to the skull.

craniology *n* the scientific study of the human skull.

cranium *n, pl* **-niums** *or* **-nia** *Anat* **1** the skull. **2** the part of the skull that encloses the brain.

crank *n* **1** a device for transmitting or converting motion, consisting of an arm projecting at right angles from a shaft. **2** a handle incorporating a crank, used to start an engine or motor. **3** *Informal* an eccentric or odd person. *~vb* **4** to turn with a crank. **5** to start (an engine) with a crank.

crankcase *n* the metal case that encloses the crankshaft in an internal-combustion engine.

crankpin *n* a short cylindrical pin in a crankshaft, to which the connecting rod is attached.

crankshaft *n* a shaft with one or more cranks, to which the connecting rods are attached.

cranky *adj* **crankier, crankiest** *Informal* **1** eccentric. **2** bad-tempered. **crankiness** *n*

cranny *n, pl* **-nies** a narrow opening.

crap[1] *Slang ~n* **1** nonsense. **2** junk. **3** *Taboo* faeces. *~vb* **crapping, crapped 4** *Taboo* to defecate. **crappy** *adj*

crap[2] *n* same as **craps.**

crape *n* same as **crepe.**

craps *n* **1** a gambling game played with two dice. **2** **shoot craps** to play this game.

crapulent *or* **crapulous** *adj Literary* given to or resulting from excessive eating or drinking. **crapulence** *n*

crash *n* **1** a collision involving a vehicle or vehicles. **2** a sudden descent of an aircraft as a result of which it crashes. **3** a sudden loud noise. **4** a breaking and falling to pieces. **5** the sudden collapse of a business or stock exchange. *~vb* **6** to cause (a vehicle or aircraft) to collide with another vehicle, the ground, or some other object or (of vehicles or aircraft) to be involved in a collision. **7** to make or cause to make a loud smashing noise. **8** to drop with force and break into pieces with a loud noise. **9** to break or smash into pieces with a loud noise. **10** (of a business or stock exchange) to collapse or fail suddenly. **11** to move violently or noisily. **12** (of a computer system or program) to fail suddenly because of a malfunction. **13** *Brit informal* to gate-crash. *~adj* **14** requiring or using great effort in order to achieve results quickly: *a crash course.*

crash barrier *n* a safety barrier along the centre of a motorway, around a racetrack, or at the side of a dangerous road.

crash dive *n* **1** a sudden steep emergency dive by a submarine. *~vb* **crash-dive, -diving, -dived 2** to perform a crash dive.

crash helmet *n* a helmet worn by motorcyclists to protect the head in case of a crash.

crashing *adj Informal* extreme: *a crashing bore.*

crash-land *vb* (of an aircraft) to land in an emergency, causing damage. **crash-landing** *n*

crass *adj* stupid and insensitive: *the enquiry is crass and naive.* **crassly** *adv* **crassness** *n*

-crat *n combining form* indicating a supporter or member of a particular form of government: *autocrat; democrat.* **-cratic** *or* **-cratical** *adj combining form*

crate *n* **1** a large container made of wooden slats, used for packing goods. **2** *Slang* an old car or aeroplane. *~vb* **crating, crated 3** to put in a crate. **crateful** *n*

crater *n* **1** the bowl-shaped opening in a volcano or a geyser. **2** a cavity made by the impact of a meteorite or an explosion. **3** a roughly circular cavity on the surface of the moon and some planets. *~vb* **4** to make or form craters in (a surface, such as the ground). **cratered** *adj*

cravat *n* a scarf worn round the neck instead of a tie.

crave *vb* **craving, craved 1** to desire intensely: *a vulnerable, unhappy girl who craved affection.* **2** *Formal* to beg or plead for: *may I crave your lordship's indulgence?* **craving** *n*

craven *adj* **1** cowardly. *~n* **2** a coward.

craw *n* **1** the crop of a bird. **2** the stomach of an animal. **3 stick in one's craw** *Informal* to be difficult for one to agree with or accept.

crawfish *n, pl* **-fish** *or* **-fishes** same as **crayfish.**

THESAURUS

strain, encumber, hamper, hamstring, handicap, hinder, impede, inhibit, obstruct, restrict, shackle, stymie, thwart

cramped 1. awkward, circumscribed, closed in, confined, congested, crowded, hemmed in, jammed in, narrow, overcrowded, packed, restricted, squeezed, uncomfortable **2.** *esp. of handwriting* crabbed, indecipherable, irregular, small

cranky bizarre, capricious, eccentric, erratic, freakish, freaky *(slang)*, funny *(informal)*, idiosyncratic, odd, oddball *(informal)*, off-the-wall *(slang)*, outré, peculiar, queer, quirky, rum *(Brit. slang)*, strange, wacky *(slang)*

cranny breach, chink, cleft, crack, crevice, fissure, gap, hole, interstice, nook, opening, rift

crash *n.* **1.** accident, bump, collision, jar, jolt, pile-up *(informal)*, prang *(informal)*, smash, smash-up, thud, thump, wreck **2.** bang, boom, clang, clash, clatter, clattering, din, racket, smash, smashing, thunder **3.** bankruptcy, collapse, debacle, depression, downfall, failure, ruin, smash *~vb.* **4.** bang, bump (into), collide, crash-land *(an aircraft)*, drive into, have an accident, hit, hurtle into, plough into, run together, wreck **5.** come a cropper *(informal)*, dash, fall, fall headlong, give way, hurtle, lurch, overbalance, pitch, plunge, precipitate oneself, sprawl, topple **6.** break, break up, dash to pieces, disintegrate, fracture, fragment, shatter, shiver, smash, splinter **7.** be ruined, collapse, fail, fold, fold up, go broke *(informal)*, go bust *(informal)*, go to the wall, go under, smash *~adj.* **8.** *of a course of studies, etc.* emergency, immediate, intensive, round-the-clock, speeded-up, telescoped, urgent

crass asinine, blundering, boorish, bovine, coarse, dense, doltish, gross, indelicate, insensitive, lumpish, oafish, obtuse, stupid, unrefined, witless

crate 1. *n.* box, case, container, packing case, tea chest **2.** *vb.* box, case, encase, enclose, pack, pack up

crater depression, dip, hollow, shell hole

crave 1. be dying for, cry out for *(informal)*, desire, eat one's heart out over, fancy *(informal)*, hanker after, hope for, hunger after, long for, lust after, need, pant for, pine for, require, sigh for, thirst for, want, yearn for **2.** ask, beg, beseech, entreat, implore, petition, plead for, pray for, seek, solicit, supplicate

crawl *vb* **1** to move on one's hands and knees. **2** (of insects, worms or snakes) to creep slowly. **3** to move very slowly. **4** to act in a servile manner. **5** to be or feel as if covered with crawling creatures: *the kind of smile that made your hair stand on end and your flesh crawl.* ~*n* **6** a slow creeping pace or motion. **7** *Swimming* a stroke in which the feet are kicked like paddles while each arm in turn reaches forward and pulls back through the water.

crayfish *or esp US* **crawfish** *n, pl* **-fish** *or* **-fishes** an edible freshwater shellfish like a lobster.

crayon *n* **1** a small stick or pencil of coloured wax or clay. ~*vb* **2** to draw or colour with a crayon.

craze *n* **1** a short-lived fashion or enthusiasm. ~*vb* **crazing, crazed 2** to make mad. **3** *Ceramics, metallurgy* to develop or cause to develop fine cracks: *you must prevent the drill crazing the glazed surface of the tile.*

crazed *adj* **1** wild and uncontrolled in behaviour. **2** (of porcelain) having fine cracks.

crazy *adj* **-zier, -ziest** *Informal* **1** ridiculous. **2 crazy about** extremely fond of. **3** extremely annoyed or upset. **4** insane. **crazily** *adv* **craziness** *n*

crazy paving *n Brit* a form of paving on a path, made of irregular slabs of stone.

creak *vb* **1** to make or move with a harsh squeaking sound. ~*n* **2** a harsh squeaking sound. **creaky** *adj* **creakiness** *n*

cream *n* **1** the fatty part of milk, which rises to the top. **2** a cosmetic or medication that resembles cream in consistency. **3** any of various foods resembling or containing cream. **4** the best part of something. ~*adj* **5** yellowish-white. ~*vb* **6** to beat (foodstuffs) to a light creamy consistency. **7** to remove the cream from (milk). **8** to prepare or cook (foodstuffs) with cream or milk. **9 cream off** to take away the best part of. **creamy** *adj*

cream cheese *n* a type of very rich soft white cheese.

creamer *n* a powdered milk substitute for coffee.

creamery *n, pl* **-eries** a place where dairy products are made or sold.

cream of tartar *n* a purified form of the tartar produced in wine-making, an ingredient in baking powder.

crease *n* **1** a line made by folding or pressing. **2** a wrinkle or furrow, esp. on the face. **3** *Cricket* any of four lines near each wicket marking positions for the bowler or batsman. ~*vb* **creasing, creased 4** to make or become wrinkled or furrowed. **creasy** *adj*

create *vb* **-ating, -ated 1** to cause to come into existence. **2** to be the cause of. **3** to appoint to a new rank or position. **4** *Brit slang* to make an angry fuss.

creation *n* **1** a creating or being created. **2** something brought into existence or created.

Creation *n Christianity* **1** God's act of bringing the universe into being. **2** the universe as thus brought into being by God.

creative *adj* **1** having the ability to create. **2** imaginative or inventive. **creativity** *n*

creator *n* a person who creates.

THESAURUS

craving appetite, desire, hankering, hope, hunger, longing, lust, thirst, urge, yearning, yen (*informal*)

crawl 1. creep, drag, go on all fours, move on hands and knees, pull *or* drag oneself along, slither, worm one's way, wriggle, writhe **2.** advance slowly, creep, inch, move at a snail's pace **3.** abase oneself, cringe, fawn, grovel, humble oneself, pander to, toady, truckle **4.** be overrun (alive, full of, lousy (*slang*)), swarm, teem

craze 1. *n.* enthusiasm, fad, fashion, infatuation, mania, mode, novelty, passion, preoccupation, rage, the latest (*informal*), thing, trend, vogue **2.** *vb.* bewilder, confuse, dement, derange, distemper, drive mad, enrage, infatuate, inflame, madden, make insane, send crazy *or* berserk, unbalance, unhinge

crazy 1. absurd, bird-brained (*informal*), bizarre, cockeyed (*informal*), eccentric, fantastic, fatuous, foolhardy, foolish, half-baked (*informal*), idiotic, ill-conceived, impracticable, imprudent, inane, inappropriate, irresponsible, ludicrous, nonsensical, odd, oddball (*informal*), outrageous, peculiar, potty (*Brit. informal*), preposterous, puerile, quixotic, ridiculous, rum (*Brit. slang*), senseless, short-sighted, silly, strange, unrealistic, unwise, unworkable, wacky (*slang*), weird, wild **2.** *as in* **crazy about** ardent, beside oneself, devoted, eager, enamoured, enthusiastic, fanatical, hysterical, infatuated, into (*informal*), mad, passionate, smitten, very keen, wild (*informal*), zealous **3.** a bit lacking upstairs (*informal*), barking (*slang*), barking mad (*slang*), barmy (*slang*), batty (*slang*), berserk, bonkers (*slang, chiefly Brit.*), cracked (*slang*), crackpot (*informal*), crazed, cuckoo (*informal*), daft (*informal*), delirious, demented, deranged, idiotic, insane, loopy (*informal*), lunatic, mad, mad as a hatter, mad as a March hare, maniacal, mental (*slang*), not all there (*informal*), not the full shilling (*informal*), nuts (*slang*), nutty (*slang*), nutty as a fruitcake (*slang*), off one's head (*slang*), off one's trolley (*slang*), off-the-wall (*slang*), of unsound mind, out to lunch (*informal*), potty (*Brit. informal*), round the bend (*slang*), touched, unbalanced, unhinged

creak *vb.* grate, grind, groan, rasp, scrape, scratch, screech, squeak, squeal

cream *n.* **1.** cosmetic, emulsion, essence, liniment, lotion, oil, ointment, paste, salve, unguent **2.** best, *crème de la crème,* elite, flower, pick, prime ~*adj.* **3.** off-white, yellowish-white

creamy buttery, creamed, lush, milky, oily, rich, smooth, soft, velvety

crease 1. *n.* bulge, corrugation, fold, groove, line, overlap, pucker, ridge, ruck, tuck, wrinkle **2.** *vb.* corrugate, crimp, crinkle, crumple, double up, fold, pucker, ridge, ruck up, rumple, screw up, wrinkle

create 1. beget, bring into being *or* existence, coin, compose, concoct, design, develop, devise, dream up (*informal*), form, formulate, generate, give birth to, give life to, hatch, initiate, invent, make, originate, produce, spawn **2.** bring about, cause, lead to, occasion **3.** appoint, constitute, establish, found, install, invest, make, set up

creation 1. begetting, constitution, development, establishment, formation, foundation, generation, genesis, inception, institution, laying down, making, origination, procreation, production, setting up, siring **2.** achievement, brainchild (*informal*), *chef-d'oeuvre,* concept, concoction, handiwork, invention, *magnum opus, pièce de résistance,* production

Creation all living things, cosmos, life, living world, natural world, nature, universe, world

creative artistic, clever, fertile, gifted, imaginative, ingenious, inspired, inventive, original, productive, stimulating, visionary

creativity cleverness, fecundity, fertility, imagination, imaginativeness, ingenuity, inspiration, inventiveness, originality, productivity, talent

creator architect, author, begetter, designer, father, framer, God, initiator, inventor, maker, originator, prime mover

Creator *n* **the Creator** God.

creature *n* **1** an animal, bird, or fish. **2** a person. **3** a person or thing controlled by another.

crèche *n Chiefly Brit* a day nursery for very young children.

credence (**kreed**-enss) *n* belief in the truth or accuracy of a statement: *the question is, how much credence to give to their accounts?*

credentials *pl n* **1** something that entitles a person to credit or confidence. **2** a document giving evidence of the bearer's identity or qualifications.

credibility gap *n* the difference between claims or statements made and the true facts.

credible *adj* **1** capable of being believed; convincing: *there is no credible evidence.* **2** trustworthy or reliable: *the latest claim is the only one to involve a credible witness.* **credibility** *n*

credit *n* **1 a** the system of allowing customers to receive goods or services before payment. **b** the time allowed for paying for such goods or services. **2** reputation for trustworthiness in paying debts. **3 a** the positive balance in a person's bank account. **b** the sum of money that a bank makes available to a client in excess of any deposit. **4** a sum of money or equivalent purchasing power, available for a person's use. **5** *Accounting* **a** acknowledgment of a sum of money by entry on the right-hand side of an account. **b** an entry or total of entries on this side. **6** praise or approval, as for an achievement or quality: *you must give him credit for his perseverance.* **7** a person or thing who is a source of praise or approval: *he is a credit to his family.* **8** influence or reputation based on the good opinion of others: *he acquired credit within the community.* **9** belief or confidence in someone or something: *this theory is now gaining credit among the scientific community.* **10** *Education* **a** distinction awarded to an examination candidate obtaining good marks. **b** certification that a section of an examination syllabus has been satisfactorily completed. **11 on credit** with payment to be made at a future date. *~vb* **-iting, -ited** **12** *Accounting* **a** to enter (an item) as a credit in an account. **b** to acknowledge (a payer) by making such an entry. **13 credit with** to attribute to: *credit us with some intelligence.* **14** to believe. ~See also **credits.**

creditable *adj* deserving praise or honour. **creditably** *adv*

credit account *n Brit* a credit system in which shops allow customers to obtain goods and services before payment.

credit card *n* a card issued by banks or shops, allowing the holder to buy on credit.

creditor *n* a person or company to whom money is owed.

credit rating *n* an evaluation of the ability of a person or business to repay money lent.

credits *pl n* a list of people responsible for the production of a film, programme, or record.

creditworthy *adj* (of a person or a business) regarded as deserving credit on the basis of earning power and previous record of debt repayment. **creditworthiness** *n*

credo *n, pl* **-dos** a creed.

credulity *n* willingness to believe something on little evidence.

credulous *adj* **1** too willing to believe: *he has convinced only a few credulous American intellectuals.* **2** arising from or showing credulity: *credulous optimism.*

creed *n* **1** a system of beliefs or principles. **2** a formal statement of the essential parts of Christian belief.

creek *n* **1** a narrow inlet or bay. **2** *US, Canad, Austral & NZ* a small stream or tributary. **3 up the creek** *Slang* in a difficult position.

creel *n* a wickerwork basket used by fishermen.

creep *vb* **creeping, crept 1** to move quietly and cautiously. **2** to crawl with the body near to or touching the ground. **3** to have the sensation of something crawling over the skin, from fear or disgust: *she makes my flesh creep.* **4** (of plants) to grow along the ground or over rocks. *~n* **5** a creeping movement. **6** *Slang* an obnoxious or servile person.

creeper *n* **1** a plant, such as ivy, that grows by creeping. **2** *US & Canad* same as **tree creeper.**

THESAURUS

creature 1. animal, beast, being, brute, critter (*U.S. dialect*), dumb animal, living thing, lower animal, quadruped **2.** body, character, fellow, human being, individual, man, mortal, person, soul, woman **3.** dependant, hanger-on, hireling, instrument (*informal*), lackey, minion, puppet, retainer, tool

credentials attestation, authorization, card, certificate, deed, diploma, docket, letter of recommendation *or* introduction, letters of credence, licence, missive, passport, recommendation, reference(s), testament, testimonial, title, voucher, warrant

credibility believability, believableness, integrity, plausibility, reliability, tenability, trustworthiness

credible 1. believable, conceivable, imaginable, likely, plausible, possible, probable, reasonable, supposable, tenable, thinkable, verisimilar **2.** dependable, honest, reliable, sincere, trustworthy, trusty

credit *n.* **1.** acclaim, acknowledgment, approval, Brownie points, commendation, fame, glory, honour, kudos, merit, praise, recognition, thanks, tribute **2.** *as in* **be a credit to** feather in one's cap, honour, source of satisfaction *or* pride **3.** belief, confidence, credence, faith, reliance, trust **4. on credit** by deferred payment, by instalments, on account, on hire-purchase, on (the) H.P., on the slate (*informal*), on tick (*informal*) *~vb.* **5.** *with* **with** accredit, ascribe to, assign to, attribute to, chalk up to (*informal*), impute to, refer to **6.** accept, bank on, believe, buy (*slang*), depend on, fall for, have faith in, rely on, swallow (*informal*), trust

creditable admirable, commendable, deserving, estimable, exemplary, honourable, laudable, meritorious, praiseworthy, reputable, respectable, worthy

credulity blind faith, credulousness, gullibility, naiveté, silliness, simplicity, stupidity

credulous born yesterday (*informal*), dupable, green, gullible, naive, overtrusting, trustful, uncritical, unsuspecting, unsuspicious

creed articles of faith, belief, canon, catechism, confession, credo, doctrine, dogma, persuasion, principles, profession (*of faith*), tenet

creek 1. bay, bight, cove, firth (*Scot.*), inlet **2.** *U.S., Canad., Austral. & N.Z.* bayou, brook, burn (*Scot.*), rivulet, stream, streamlet, tributary, watercourse

creep *vb.* **1.** approach unnoticed, edge, inch, skulk, slink, sneak, steal, tiptoe **2.** crawl, crawl on all fours, glide, insinuate, slither, squirm, worm, wriggle, writhe *~n.* **3.** *slang* bootlicker (*informal*), sneak, sycophant, toady **4. give one the creeps** *or* **make one's flesh creep** disgust, frighten, horrify, make one flinch (quail, shrink, squirm, wince), make one's hair stand on end (*informal*), repel, repulse, scare, terrify, terrorize

creeper climber, climbing plant, rambler, runner, trailing plant, vine (*chiefly U.S.*)

creepy awful, direful, disgusting, disturbing, eerie,

creeps *pl n* **give someone the creeps** *Informal* to give someone a feeling of fear or disgust.

creepy *adj* **creepier, creepiest** *Informal* causing a feeling of fear or disgust. **creepiness** *n*

creepy-crawly *n, pl* **-crawlies** *Brit informal* a small crawling creature.

cremate *vb* **-mating, -mated** to burn (a corpse) to ash. **cremation** *n*

crematorium *n, pl* **-riums** *or* **-ria** a building where corpses are cremated.

crème de la crème *n* the very best: *the crème de la crème of cities.*

crème de menthe *n* a liqueur flavoured with peppermint.

crenellated *or US* **crenelated** *adj* having battlements. **crenellation** *or US* **crenelation** *n*

creole *n* **1** a language developed from a mixture of different languages which has become the main language of a place. *adj* **2** of or relating to a creole.

Creole *n* **1** (in the West Indies and Latin America) a native-born person of mixed European and African descent. **2** (in the Gulf States of the U.S.) a native-born person of French descent. **3** the French creole spoken in the Gulf States. *~adj* **4** of or relating to any of these peoples: *Creole cooking.*

creosote *n* **1** a thick dark liquid made from coal tar and used for preserving wood. **2** a colourless liquid made from wood tar and used as an antiseptic. *~vb* **-soting, -soted 3** to treat with creosote.

crepe (**krayp**) *n* **1** a thin light fabric with a crinkled texture. **2** a very thin pancake, often folded around a filling. **3** a type of rubber with a wrinkled surface, used for the soles of shoes.

crepe paper *n* paper with a crinkled texture, used for decorations.

crept *vb* the past of **creep.**

crepuscular *adj* **1** of or like twilight. **2** (of animals) active at twilight.

Cres. Crescent.

crescendo (**krish-end-oh**) *n, pl* **-dos 1** a gradual increase in loudness. **2** a musical passage that gradually gets louder. *~adv* **3** gradually getting louder.

crescent *n* **1** the curved shape of the moon when in its first or last quarter. **2** *Chiefly Brit* a crescent-shaped street. *~adj* **3** crescent-shaped.

cress *n* a plant with strong-tasting leaves, used in salads and as a garnish.

crest *n* **1** the top of a mountain, hill, or wave. **2** a tuft or growth of feathers or skin on the top of a bird's or animal's head. **3** a heraldic design or figure used on a coat of arms and elsewhere. **4** an ornamental plume or emblem on top of a helmet. *~vb* **5** to come or rise to a high point. **6** to lie at the top of. **7** to reach the top of (a hill or wave). **crested** *adj*

crestfallen *adj* disappointed or disheartened.

Cretaceous *adj Geol* of the period of geological time about 135 million years ago, at the end of which the dinosaurs died out.

cretin *n* **1** a person afflicted with cretinism. **2** *Informal* a very stupid person. **cretinous** *adj*

cretinism *n* physical and mental retardation caused by a thyroid deficiency.

cretonne *n* a heavy printed cotton or linen fabric, used in furnishings.

crevasse *n* a deep open crack in a glacier.

crevice *n* a narrow crack or gap in rock.

crew[1] *n* **1** the people who man a ship or aircraft. **2** a group of people working together: *a film crew.* **3** *Informal* any group of people. *~vb* **4** to serve as a crew member on a ship or boat.

crew[2] *vb Archaic* a past of **crow**[2].

crew cut *n* a closely cut haircut for men.

crewel *n* a loosely twisted worsted yarn, used in embroidery. **crewelwork** *n*

crew neck *n* a plain round neckline. **crew-neck** *or* **crew-necked** *adj*

crib *n* **1** a piece of writing stolen from elsewhere. **2** a translation or list of answers used by students, often dishonestly. **3** a baby's cradle. **4** a rack or manger for fodder. **5** a model of the manger scene at Bethlehem. **6** short for **cribbage.** *~vb* **cribbing, cribbed 7** to copy (someone's work) dishonestly. **8** to confine in a small space.

cribbage *n* a card game for two to four players, who each try to win a set number of points before the others.

crick *Informal ~n* **1** a painful muscle spasm or cramp in the neck or back. *~vb* **2** to cause a crick in.

cricket[1] *n* **1** a game played by two teams of eleven players using a ball, bats, and wickets. **2 not cricket** *Informal* not fair play. **cricketer** *n*

cricket[2] *n* a jumping insect like a grasshopper, which produces a chirping sound by rubbing together its forewings.

cried *vb* the past of **cry.**

crier *n* an official who makes public announcements.

crime *n* **1** an act prohibited and punished by law. **2** unlawful acts collectively. **3** *Informal* a disgraceful act: *to be a woman writing music is neither a crime against nature nor a freakish rarity.*

THESAURUS

forbidding, frightening, ghoulish, goose-pimply (*informal*), gruesome, hair-raising, horrible, macabre, menacing, nightmarish, ominous, scary (*informal*), sinister, terrifying, threatening, unpleasant, weird

crescent 1. *n.* half-moon, meniscus, new moon, old moon, sickle, sickle-shape **2.** *adj.* arched, bow-shaped, curved, semicircular, sickle-shaped

crest 1. apex, crown, head, height, highest point, peak, pinnacle, ridge, summit, top **2.** cockscomb, comb, crown, mane, plume, topknot, tuft **3.** *Heraldry* badge, bearings, charge, device, emblem, insignia, symbol

crestfallen chapfallen, dejected, depressed, despondent, disappointed, disconsolate, discouraged, disheartened, downcast, downhearted, sick as a parrot (*informal*)

crevice chink, cleft, crack, cranny, fissure, fracture, gap, hole, interstice, opening, rent, rift, slit, split

crew 1. hands, (ship's) company, (ship's) complement **2.** company, corps, gang, party, squad, team, working party **3.** *informal* assemblage, band, bunch (*informal*), camp, company, crowd, gang, herd, horde, lot, mob, pack, posse (*informal*), set, swarm, troop

crib *n.* **1.** key, translation **2.** bassinet, bed, cot, cradle **3.** bin, box, bunker, manger, rack, stall *~vb.* **4.** cheat, pass off as one's own work, pilfer, pirate, plagiarize, purloin, steal **5.** box up, cage, confine, coop, coop up, enclose, fence, imprison, limit, pen, rail, restrict, shut in

crime 1. atrocity, fault, felony, job (*informal*), malfeasance, misdeed, misdemeanour, offence, outrage, transgression, trespass, unlawful act, violation, wrong **2.** corruption, delinquency, guilt, illegality, iniquity, lawbreaking, malefaction, misconduct, sin, unrighteousness, vice, villainy, wickedness, wrong, wrongdoing

criminal *n.* **1.** con (*slang*), con man (*informal*), convict, crook (*informal*), culprit, delinquent, evildoer, felon, jailbird, lag (*slang*), lawbreaker, malefactor, of-

criminal *n* **1** a person guilty of a crime. *~adj* **2** of or relating to crime or its punishment. **3** *Informal* senseless or disgraceful. **criminally** *adv* **criminality** *n*

criminology *n* the scientific study of crime. **criminologist** *n*

crimp *vb* **1** to fold or press into ridges. **2** to curl (hair) tightly with curling tongs. **3** *Chiefly US informal* to restrict or hinder: *a slowdown in the US economy could crimp some big Swedish concerns' profits.* *~n* **4** the act or result of crimping.

Crimplene *n Trademark* a crease-resistant synthetic fabric.

crimson *adj* deep purplish-red.

cringe *vb* **cringing, cringed 1** to shrink or flinch in fear: *he cringed and shrank against the wall.* **2** to behave in a submissive or timid way: *women who cringe before abusive husbands.* **3** *Informal* to be very embarrassed: *I cringe every time I see that old photo of me.* *~n* **4** the act of cringing.

crinkle *vb* **-kling, -kled 1** to become slightly creased or folded. *~n* **2** a crease or fold. **crinkly** *adj*

crinoline *n* a petticoat stiffened with hoops to make the skirt stand out.

cripple *n* **1** a person who is lame or disabled. **2** a person with a mental or social problem: *an emotional cripple.* *~vb* **-pling, -pled 3** to make a cripple of. **4** to damage (something). **crippled** *adj* **crippling** *adj*

crisis *n, pl* **-ses 1** a crucial stage or turning point in the course of anything. **2** a time of extreme trouble or danger.

crisp *adj* **1** fresh and firm: *a crisp green salad.* **2** dry and brittle: *bake until crisp and golden brown.* **3** clean and neat: *crisp white cotton.* **4** (of weather) cold but invigorating: *a crisp autumn day.* **5** clear and sharp: *the telescope is designed to provide the first crisp images of distant galaxies.* **6** lively or brisk: *the service is crisp and efficient.* *~n* **7** *Brit* a very thin slice of potato fried till crunchy. *~vb* **8** to make or become crisp. **crisply** *adv* **crispness** *n*

crispbread *n* a thin dry biscuit made of wheat or rye.

crispy *adj* **crispier, crispiest** hard and crunchy. **crispiness** *n*

crisscross *vb* **1** to move in or mark with a crosswise pattern. *~adj* **2** (of lines) crossing one another in different directions.

criterion *n, pl* **-ria** *or* **-rions** a standard by which something can be judged or decided.

➤ It is incorrect to use *criteria* as a singular, though this use is often found.

critic *n* **1** a professional judge of art, music, or literature. **2** a person who finds fault and criticizes.

critical *adj* **1** very important or dangerous: *this was a critical moment in her career.* **2** so seriously ill or injured as to be in danger of dying: *he is in a critical condition in hospital.* **3** fault-finding or disparaging: *the article is highly critical of the government.* **4** examining and judging analytically and without bias: *he submitted the plans to critical examination.* **5** of a critic or criticism. **6** *Physics* denoting a constant value at which the properties of a system undergo an abrupt change: *the critical temperature above which the material loses its superconductivity.* **7** (of a nuclear power station or reactor) having reached a state in which a nuclear chain reaction becomes self-sustaining. **critically** *adv*

criticism *n* **1** fault-finding or censure. **2** an analysis of a work of art or literature. **3** the occupation of a critic. **4** a work that sets out to analyse.

criticize *or* **-cise** *vb* **-cizing, -cized** *or* **-cising, -cised 1** to find fault with. **2** to analyse (something).

critique *n* **1** a critical essay or commentary. **2** the act or art of criticizing.

THESAURUS

fender, sinner, transgressor, villain *~adj.* **2.** bent (*slang*), corrupt, crooked (*informal*), culpable, felonious, illegal, illicit, immoral, indictable, iniquitous, lawless, nefarious, under-the-table, unlawful, unrighteous, vicious, villainous, wicked, wrong **3.** *informal* deplorable, foolish, preposterous, ridiculous, scandalous, senseless

cringe 1. blench, cower, dodge, draw back, duck, flinch, quail, quiver, recoil, shrink, shy, start, tremble, wince **2.** bend, bow, crawl, creep, crouch, fawn, grovel, kneel, kowtow, pander to, sneak, stoop, toady, truckle

cripple *vb.* **1.** debilitate, disable, enfeeble, hamstring, incapacitate, lame, maim, mutilate, paralyse, weaken **2.** bring to a standstill, cramp, damage, destroy, halt, impair, put out of action, ruin, spoil, vitiate

crippled bedridden, deformed, disabled, enfeebled, handicapped, housebound, incapacitated, laid up (*informal*), lame, paralysed

crisis 1. climax, confrontation, critical point, crunch (*informal*), crux, culmination, height, moment of truth, point of no return, turning point **2.** catastrophe, critical situation, dilemma, dire straits, disaster, emergency, exigency, extremity, meltdown (*informal*), mess, panic stations (*informal*), plight, predicament, quandary, strait, trouble

crisp 1. brittle, crispy, crumbly, crunchy, firm, fresh, unwilted **2.** clean-cut, neat, orderly, smart, snappy, spruce, tidy, trig (*archaic or dialect*), well-groomed, well-pressed **3.** bracing, brisk, fresh, invigorating, refreshing

criterion bench mark, canon, gauge, measure, norm, par, principle, proof, rule, standard, test, touchstone, yardstick

critic 1. analyst, arbiter, authority, commentator, connoisseur, expert, expositor, judge, pundit, reviewer **2.** attacker, carper, caviller, censor, censurer, detractor, fault-finder, knocker (*informal*), reviler, vilifier

critical 1. all-important, crucial, dangerous, deciding, decisive, grave, hairy (*slang*), high-priority, momentous, perilous, pivotal, precarious, pressing, psychological, risky, serious, urgent, vital **2.** captious, carping, cavilling, censorious, derogatory, disapproving, disparaging, fault-finding, nagging, niggling, nit-picking (*informal*), scathing **3.** accurate, analytical, diagnostic, discerning, discriminating, fastidious, judicious, penetrating, perceptive, precise

criticism 1. animadversion, bad press, brickbats (*informal*), censure, character assassination, critical remarks, disapproval, disparagement, fault-finding, flak (*informal*), knocking (*informal*), panning (*informal*), slam (*slang*), slating (*informal*), stick (*slang*), stricture **2.** analysis, appraisal, appreciation, assessment, comment, commentary, critique, elucidation, evaluation, judgment, notice, review

criticize 1. blast, carp, censure, condemn, disapprove of, disparage, excoriate, find fault with, give (someone *or* something) a bad press, knock (*informal*), lambast(e), nag at, pan (*informal*), pass strictures upon, pick to pieces, put down, slam (*slang*), slate (*informal*), tear into (*informal*) **2.** analyse, appraise, assess, comment upon, evaluate, give an opinion, judge, pass judgment on, review

critique analysis, appraisal, assessment, commentary, essay, examination, review, treatise

croak *vb.* **1.** caw, gasp, grunt, squawk, utter *or* speak harshly (huskily, throatily), wheeze **2.** *slang* buy it (*U.S. slang*), check out (*U.S. slang*), die, expire, go

croak *vb* **1** (of a frog or crow) to make a low hoarse cry. **2** to utter or speak with a croak. **3** *Slang* to die. ~*n* **4** a low hoarse sound. **croaky** *adj*

Croatian (kroh-**ay**-shun) *adj* **1** of Croatia. ~*n* **2** a person from Croatia. **3** the dialect of Serbo-Croatian spoken in Croatia.

crochet (**kroh**-shay) *vb* **-cheting, -cheted 1** to make (a piece of needlework) by looping and intertwining thread with a hooked needle. ~*n* **2** work made by crocheting.

crock[1] *n* an earthenware pot or jar.

crock[2] *n* **old crock** *Slang, chiefly Brit* a person or thing that is old or broken-down.

crockery *n* china dishes or earthenware vessels collectively.

crocodile *n* **1** a large amphibious tropical reptile. **2** *Brit informal* a line of children walking two by two.

crocodile tears *pl n* an insincere show of grief.

crocus *n, pl* **-cuses** a plant with white, yellow, or purple flowers in spring.

croft *n* a small farm worked by one family in Scotland. **crofter** *n* **crofting** *adj, n*

croissant (**krwah**-son) *n* a flaky crescent-shaped bread roll.

cromlech *n* **1** a circle of prehistoric standing stones. **2** *No longer in technical use* a dolmen.

crone *n* a witchlike old woman.

crony *n, pl* **-nies** a close friend.

crook *n* **1** *Informal* a dishonest person. **2** a bent or curved place or thing: *she held the puppy in the crook of her arm.* **3** a bishop's or shepherd's staff with a hooked end. ~*vb* **4** to bend or curve.

crooked *adj* **1** bent or twisted. **2** set at an angle. **3** *Informal* dishonest or illegal. **crookedly** *adv* **crookedness** *n*

croon *vb* to sing, hum, or speak in a soft low tone. **crooner** *n*

crop *n* **1** a cultivated plant, such as a cereal, vegetable, or fruit plant. **2** the season's total yield of farm produce. **3** any group of things appearing at one time: *a remarkable crop of new Scottish plays.* **4** the handle of a whip. **5** short for **riding crop. 6** a pouchlike part of the gullet of a bird, in which food is stored or prepared for digestion. **7** a short cropped hairstyle. ~*vb* **cropping, cropped 8** to cut (something) very short. **9** to produce or harvest as a crop. **10** (of animals) to feed on (grass). **11** to clip part of (the ear or ears) of (an animal), esp. for identification. ~See also **crop up.**

cropper *n* **come a cropper** *Informal* **a** to fail completely. **b** to fall heavily.

crop up *vb Informal* to occur or appear unexpectedly.

croquet (**kroh**-kay) *n* a game played on a lawn in which balls are hit through hoops.

croquette (kroh-**kett**) *n* a fried cake of mashed potato, meat, or fish.

crosier *n* same as **crozier.**

cross *vb* **1** to move or go across (something): *she crossed the street to the gallery.* **2** to meet and pass: *further south, the way is crossed by Brewer Street.* **3** *Brit* to draw two parallel lines across (a cheque) and so make it payable only into a bank account. **4** to mark with a cross or crosses. **5** to cancel or delete with a cross or with lines: *she crossed out the first three words.* **6** to place across or crosswise: *he sat down and crossed his legs.* **7** to make the sign of the cross upon as a blessing. **8** to annoy or anger someone by challenging or opposing their wishes and plans. **9** to interbreed or cross-fertilize. **10** *Football* to pass (the ball) from a wing to the middle of the field. **11** (of each of two letters in the post) to be sent before the other is received. **12** (of telephone lines) to interfere with each other so that several callers are connected together at one time. **13 cross one's fingers** to fold one finger across another in the hope of bringing good luck. **14 cross one's heart** to promise by making the sign of a cross over one's heart. **15 cross one's mind** to occur to one briefly or suddenly. ~*n* **16** a structure, symbol, or mark consisting of two intersecting lines. **17** an upright post with a bar across it, used in ancient times as a means of execution. **18** a representation of the Cross on which Jesus Christ was executed as an emblem of Christianity. **19** a symbol (×) used as a signature or error mark. **20 the sign of the cross** a sign made with the hand by some Christians to represent the Cross. **21** a medal or monument in the shape of a cross. **22** the place in a town or village where a cross has been set up. **23** *Biol* **a** the process of crossing; hybridization. **b** a hybrid. **24** a mixture of two things. **25** a hindrance or misfortune: *we've all got our own cross to bear.* **26** *Football* a pass of the ball from a wing to the middle of the field. ~*adj* **27** angry. **28** lying or placed across: *a cross beam.* **crossly** *adv* **crossness** *n*

Cross *n* **the Cross a** the cross on which Jesus Christ was crucified. **b** Christianity.

cross- *combining form* **1** indicating action from one individual or group to another: *cross-cultural; cross-*

THESAURUS

belly-up (*slang*), hop the twig (*informal*), kick it (*slang*), kick the bucket (*informal*), pass away, peg it (*informal*), peg out (*informal*), perish, pop one's clogs (*informal*)

crook 1. *n. informal* cheat, criminal, knave (*archaic*), lag (*slang*), racketeer, robber, rogue, shark, swindler, thief, villain **2.** *vb.* angle, bend, bow, curve, flex, hook

crooked 1. bent, bowed, crippled, curved, deformed, deviating, disfigured, distorted, hooked, irregular, meandering, misshapen, out of shape, tortuous, twisted, twisting, warped, winding, zigzag **2.** angled, askew, asymmetric, at an angle, awry, lopsided, off-centre, skewwhiff (*Brit. informal*), slanted, slanting, squint, tilted, to one side, uneven, unsymmetrical **3.** *informal* bent (*slang*), corrupt, crafty, criminal, deceitful, dishonest, dishonourable, dubious, fraudulent, illegal, knavish, nefarious, questionable, shady (*informal*), shifty, treacherous, underhand, under-the-table, unlawful, unprincipled, unscrupulous

croon breathe, hum, purr, sing, warble

crop *n.* **1.** fruits, gathering, harvest, produce, reaping, season's growth, vintage, yield ~*vb.* **2.** clip, cut, dock, lop, mow, pare, prune, reduce, shear, shorten, snip, top, trim **3.** bring home, bring in, collect, garner, gather, harvest, mow, pick, reap **4.** browse, graze, nibble

crop up appear, arise, emerge, happen, occur, spring up, turn up

cross *vb.* **1.** bridge, cut across, extend over, ford, meet, pass over, ply, span, traverse **2.** crisscross, intersect, intertwine, lace, lie athwart of **3. cross out** *also* **off** blue-pencil, cancel, delete, eliminate, strike off *or* out **4.** block, deny, foil, frustrate, hinder, impede, interfere, obstruct, oppose, resist, thwart **5.** blend, crossbreed, cross-fertilize, cross-pollinate, hybridize, interbreed, intercross, mix, mongrelize ~*n.* **6.** crucifix, rood **7.** crossing, crossroads, intersection, junction **8.** crossbreed, cur, hybrid, hybridization, mongrel, mutt (*slang*) **9.** amalgam, blend, combination, mixture **10.** affliction, burden, grief, load, misery, misfortune, trial, tribulation, trouble, woe, worry ~*adj.* **11.** angry, annoyed, cantankerous, churlish, crotchety (*informal*), crusty, disagreeable, fractious, fretful, grouchy (*informal*), grumpy, ill-humoured, ill-

refer. **2** indicating movement or position across something: *crosscurrent; crosstalk.* **3** indicating a crosslike figure or intersection: *crossbones.*

crossbar *n* **1** a horizontal beam across a pair of goalposts. **2** the horizontal bar on a man's bicycle.

cross-bench *n Brit* a seat in Parliament for a member belonging to neither the government nor the opposition. **cross-bencher** *n*

crossbill *n* a finch that has a bill with crossed tips.

crossbow *n* a weapon consisting of a bow fixed across a wooden stock, which releases an arrow when the trigger is pulled.

crossbreed *vb* **-breeding, -bred 1** to produce (a hybrid animal or plant) by crossing two different species. *~n* **2** a hybrid animal or plant.

crosscheck *vb* **1** to check the accuracy of (something) by using a different method. *~n* **2** a crosschecking.

cross-country *adj, adv* **1** by way of open country or fields. *~n* **2** a long race held over open ground.

crosscut *vb* **-cutting, -cut 1** to cut across. *~adj* **2** cut across. *~n* **3** a transverse cut or course.

cross-examine *vb* **-examining, -examined 1** *Law* to question (a witness for the opposing side) in order to check his or her testimony. **2** to question closely or relentlessly. **cross-examination** *n* **cross-examiner** *n*

cross-eyed *adj* with one or both eyes turning inwards towards the nose.

cross-fertilize *vb* **-lizing** *or* **-lising, -lized** *or* **-lised** to fertilize (an animal or plant) by fusion of male and female reproductive cells from different individuals of the same species. **cross-fertilization** *or* **-lisation** *n*

crossfire *n* **1** *Mil* gunfire crossing another line of fire. **2** a lively exchange of ideas or opinions.

crosshatch *vb Drawing* to shade with two or more sets of parallel lines that cross one another.

crossing *n* **1** a place where a street, railway, or river may be crossed. **2** the place where one thing crosses another. **3** a journey across water.

cross-legged *adj* sitting with one leg crossed over the other.

crosspatch *n Informal* a bad-tempered person.

cross-ply *adj* (of a tyre) having the fabric cords in the outer casing running diagonally to stiffen the sidewalls.

cross-purposes *pl n* **at cross-purposes** misunderstanding each other in a discussion.

cross-question *vb* to cross-examine.

cross-refer *vb* **-referring, -referred** to refer from one part of something to another.

cross-reference *n* **1** a reference within a text to another part of the text. *~vb* **-referencing, -referenced 2** to cross-refer.

crossroad *n US & Canad* **1** a road that crosses another road. **2** a road that connects one main road to another.

crossroads *n* **1** the point at which roads cross one another. **2 at the crossroads** at the point at which an important choice has to be made.

cross section *n* **1** *Maths* a surface formed by cutting across a solid, usually at right angles to its longest axis. **2** a random sample regarded as representative. **cross-sectional** *adj*

cross-stitch *n* an embroidery stitch made from two crossing stitches.

crosstalk *n* **1** *Brit* rapid or witty talk. **2** unwanted signals transferred between communication channels.

crosswise *or* **crossways** *adj, adv* **1** across: *slice the celery crosswise.* **2** in the shape of a cross.

crossword puzzle *or* **crossword** *n* a puzzle in which vertically and horizontally crossing words suggested by clues are written into a grid of squares.

crotch *n* **1** the forked part of the human body between the legs. **2** the corresponding part of a pair of trousers or pants. **3** any forked part formed by the joining of two things: *the crotch of the tree.* **crotched** *adj*

crotchet *n Music* a note having the time value of a quarter of a semibreve.

crotchety *adj Informal* bad-tempered.

crouch *vb* **1** to bend low with the legs and body pulled close together. *~n* **2** this position.

croup[1] (**kroop**) *n* a throat disease of children, with a hoarse cough and laboured breathing.

croup[2] (**kroop**) *n* the hindquarters of a horse.

croupier (**kroop**-ee-ay) *n* a person who collects bets and pays out winnings at a gambling table.

crouton *n* a small piece of fried or toasted bread served in soup.

crow[1] *n* **1** a large black bird with a harsh call. **2 as the crow flies** in a straight line.

crow[2] *vb* **1** (*past* **crowed** *or* **crew**) (of a cock) to utter a shrill squawking sound. **2** to boast about one's superiority. **3** (of a baby) to utter cries of pleasure. *~n* **4** a crowing sound.

crowbar *n* a heavy iron bar used as a lever.

crowd *n* **1** a large number of things or people gathered together. **2** a particular group of people: *we got to know a French crowd from Lyons.* **3 the crowd** the masses. *~vb* **4** to gather together in large numbers. **5** to press together into a confined space. **6** to fill or occupy fully. **7** *Informal* to make (someone) uncomfortable by coming too close. **crowded** *adj*

crown *n* **1** a monarch's ornamental headdress, usually made of gold and jewels. **2** a wreath for the head, given as an honour. **3** the highest or central point of something arched or curved: *the crown of the head.* **4 a** the enamel-covered part of a tooth projecting beyond the gum. **b** a substitute crown, usually of gold or

THESAURUS

tempered, impatient, in a bad mood, irascible, irritable, liverish, out of humour, peeved (*informal*), peevish, pettish, petulant, pissed off (*taboo slang*), put out, querulous, ratty (*Brit. & N.Z. informal*), shirty (*slang, chiefly Brit.*), short, snappish, snappy, splenetic, sullen, surly, testy, tetchy, vexed, waspish **12.** crosswise, intersecting, oblique, transverse

cross-examine catechize, grill (*informal*), interrogate, pump, question, quiz

crotch crutch, groin

crotchety awkward, bad-tempered, cantankerous, contrary, crabby, cross, crusty, curmudgeonly, difficult, disagreeable, fractious, grumpy, irritable, liverish, obstreperous, peevish, ratty (*Brit. & N.Z. informal*), surly, testy, tetchy

crouch bend down, bow, duck, hunch, kneel, squat, stoop

crow bluster, boast, brag, drool, exult, flourish, gloat, glory in, strut, swagger, triumph, vaunt

crowd *n.* **1.** army, assembly, bevy, company, concourse, flock, herd, horde, host, mass, mob, multitude, pack, press, rabble, swarm, throng, troupe **2.** bunch (*informal*), circle, clique, group, lot, set **3. the crowd** hoi polloi, masses, mob, people, populace, proletariat, public, rabble, rank and file, riffraff, vulgar herd *~vb.* **4.** cluster, congregate, cram, flock, forgather, gather, huddle, mass, muster, press, push, stream, surge, swarm, throng **5.** bundle, congest, cram, pack, pile, squeeze **6.** batter, butt, elbow, jostle, shove

porcelain, fitted over a decayed or broken tooth. **5** a former British coin worth 25 pence. **6** the outstanding quality or achievement: *the last piece is the crown of the evening.* ~*vb* **7** to put a crown on the head of (someone), to proclaim him or her monarch. **8** to put on the top of. **9** to reward. **10** to form the topmost part of. **11** to put the finishing touch to (a series of events): *he crowned a superb display with three goals.* **12** to attach a crown to (a tooth). **13** *Slang* to hit over the head. **14** *Draughts* to promote (a draught) to a king by placing another draught on top of it.

Crown *n* **the Crown** the power or institution of the monarchy.

crown colony *n* a British colony controlled by the Crown.

crown court *n* a local criminal court in England and Wales.

Crown Derby *n* a type of fine porcelain made at Derby.

crown jewels *pl n* the jewellery used by a sovereign on ceremonial occasions.

crown prince *n* the male heir to a sovereign throne. **crown princess** *n*

crow's feet *pl n* wrinkles at the outer corners of the eye.

crow's nest *n* a lookout platform fixed at the top of a ship's mast.

crozier *or* **crosier** *n* a hooked staff carried by bishops as a symbol of office.

crucial *adj* **1** of exceptional importance. **2** *Slang* very good. **crucially** *adv*

crucible *n* a pot in which metals or other substances are melted.

crucifix *n* a model cross with a figure of Christ upon it.

crucifixion *n* a method of execution by fastening to a cross, normally by the hands and feet.

Crucifixion *n* **1 the Crucifixion** the crucifying of Christ. **2** a representation of this.

cruciform *adj* shaped like a cross.

crucify *vb* **-fies, -fying, -fied 1** to put to death by crucifixion. **2** to treat cruelly. **3** *Slang* to defeat or ridicule totally.

crud *n Slang* a sticky or encrusted substance. **cruddy** *adj*

crude *adj* **1** rough and simple: *crude farm implements.* **2** tasteless or vulgar. **3** in a natural or unrefined state. ~*n* **4** short for **crude oil. crudely** *adv* **crudity** *or* **crudeness** *n*

crude oil *n* unrefined petroleum.

crudités (**crew**-dit-tay) *pl n* a selection of raw vegetables often served with a variety of dips before a meal.

cruel *adj* **1** deliberately causing pain without pity. **2** causing pain or suffering. **cruelly** *adv* **cruelty** *n*

cruet *n* **1** a small container for pepper, salt, etc., at table. **2** a set of such containers on a stand.

cruise *n* **1** a sail taken for pleasure, stopping at various places. ~*vb* **cruising, cruised 2** to sail about from place to place for pleasure. **3** (of a vehicle, aircraft, or ship) to travel at a moderate and efficient speed. **4** to proceed steadily or easily: *they cruised into the final of the qualifying competition.*

cruise missile *n* a low-flying subsonic missile that is guided throughout its flight.

cruiser *n* **1** a large fast warship armed with medium-calibre weapons. **2** Also called: **cabin cruiser** a motorboat with a cabin.

cruiserweight *n Boxing* same as **light heavyweight.**

crumb *n* **1** a small fragment of bread or other dry food. **2** a small bit or scrap: *a crumb of comfort.*

crumble *vb* **-bling, -bled 1** to break into crumbs or fragments. **2** to fall apart or decay. ~*n* **3** a baked pud-

THESAURUS

crowded busy, congested, cramped, crushed, full, huddled, jam-packed, mobbed, overflowing, packed, populous, swarming, teeming, thronged

crown *n.* **1.** chaplet, circlet, coronal (*poetic*), coronet, diadem, tiara **2.** bays, distinction, garland, honour, kudos, laurels, laurel wreath, prize, trophy **3.** acme, apex, crest, head, perfection, pinnacle, summit, tip, top, ultimate, zenith ~*vb.* **4.** adorn, dignify, festoon, honour, invest, reward **5.** be the climax *or* culmination of, cap, complete, consummate, finish, fulfil, perfect, put the finishing touch to, round off, surmount, terminate, top **6.** *slang* belt (*informal*), biff (*slang*), box, cuff, hit over the head, punch

Crown the Crown emperor, empress, king, monarch, monarchy, queen, *rex,* royalty, ruler, sovereign, sovereignty

crucial central, critical, decisive, essential, high-priority, important, momentous, pivotal, pressing, psychological, searching, testing, trying, urgent, vital

crucify 1. execute, harrow, persecute, rack, torment, torture **2.** *slang* lampoon, pan (*informal*), ridicule, tear to pieces, wipe the floor with (*informal*)

crude 1. clumsy, makeshift, outline, primitive, rough, rough-hewn, rude, rudimentary, sketchy, undeveloped, unfinished, unformed, unpolished **2.** boorish, coarse, crass, dirty, gross, indecent, lewd, obscene, smutty, tactless, tasteless, uncouth, vulgar **3.** natural, raw, unmilled, unpolished, unprepared, unprocessed, unrefined

crudely bluntly, clumsily, coarsely, impolitely, indecently, pulling no punches (*informal*), roughly, rudely, sketchily, tastelessly, vulgarly

crudity 1. clumsiness, crudeness, primitiveness, roughness, rudeness **2.** coarseness, crudeness, impropriety, indecency, indelicacy, lewdness, loudness, lowness, obscenity, obtrusiveness, smuttiness, vulgarity

cruel atrocious, barbarous, bitter, bloodthirsty, brutal, brutish, callous, cold-blooded, depraved, excruciating, ferocious, fierce, flinty, grim, hard, hard-hearted, harsh, heartless, hellish, implacable, inexorable, inhuman, inhumane, malevolent, merciless, murderous, painful, pitiless, poignant, ravening, raw, relentless, remorseless, ruthless, sadistic, sanguinary, savage, severe, spiteful, stony-hearted, unfeeling, unkind, unnatural, unrelenting, vengeful, vicious

cruelly 1. barbarously, brutally, brutishly, callously, ferociously, fiercely, heartlessly, in cold blood, mercilessly, pitilessly, sadistically, savagely, spitefully, unmercifully, viciously **2.** bitterly, deeply, fearfully, grievously, monstrously, mortally, severely

cruelty barbarity, bestiality, bloodthirstiness, brutality, brutishness, callousness, depravity, ferocity, fiendishness, hardheartedness, harshness, heartlessness, inhumanity, mercilessness, murderousness, ruthlessness, sadism, savagery, severity, spite, spitefulness, venom, viciousness

cruise *n.* **1.** boat trip, sail, sea trip, voyage ~*vb.* **2.** coast, sail, voyage **3.** coast, drift, keep a steady pace, travel along

crumb atom, bit, grain, mite, morsel, particle, scrap, shred, sliver, snippet, *soupçon,* speck

ding consisting of stewed fruit with a crumbly topping: *rhubarb crumble.* **crumbly** *adj* **crumbliness** *n*

crumby *adj* **crumbier, crumbiest 1** full of crumbs. **2** same as **crummy.**

crummy *adj* **-mier, -miest** *Slang* **1** of very bad quality: *a crummy hotel.* **2** unwell: *I felt really crummy.*

crumpet *n Chiefly Brit* **1** a light soft yeast cake, eaten buttered. **2** *Slang* sexually attractive women collectively.

crumple *vb* **-pling, -pled 1** to crush or become crushed into untidy wrinkles or creases. **2** to collapse in an untidy heap: *her father lay crumpled on the floor.* ~*n* **3** an untidy crease or wrinkle. **crumply** *adj*

crunch *vb* **1** to bite or chew with a noisy crushing sound. **2** to make a crisp or brittle sound. ~*n* **3** a crunching sound. **4 the crunch** *Informal* the critical moment or situation. **crunchy** *adj* **crunchiness** *n*

crupper *n* **1** a strap that passes from the back of a saddle under a horse's tail. **2** the horse's rump.

crusade *n* **1** any of the medieval military expeditions undertaken by European Christians to recapture the Holy Land from the Muslims. **2** a vigorous campaign in favour of a cause. ~*vb* **-sading, -saded 3** to take part in a crusade. **crusader** *n*

cruse *n* a small earthenware container for liquids.

crush *vb* **1** to press or squeeze so as to injure, break, or put out of shape. **2** to break or grind into small pieces. **3** to control or subdue by force. **4** to extract (liquid) by pressing: *crush a clove of garlic.* **5** to defeat or humiliate utterly. **6** to crowd together. ~*n* **7** a dense crowd. **8** the act of crushing. **9** *Informal* an infatuation: *I had a teenage crush on my French teacher.* **10** a drink made by crushing fruit: *orange crush.*

crush barrier *n* a barrier put up to separate sections of large crowds and prevent crushing.

crust *n* **1** the hard outer part of bread. **2** the baked shell of a pie or tart. **3** any hard outer layer: *a thin crust of snow.* **4** the solid outer shell of the earth. ~*vb* **5** to cover with or form a crust.

crustacean *n* **1** an animal with a hard outer shell and several pairs of legs, which usually lives in water, such as a crab or lobster. ~*adj* **2** of crustaceans.

crusty *adj* **crustier, crustiest 1** having a crust. **2** rude or irritable. **crustiness** *n*

crutch *n* **1** a long staff with a rest for the armpit, used by a lame person to support the weight of the body. **2** something that supports. **3** *Brit* same as **crotch** (sense 1).

crutchings *pl n Austral & NZ* the wool clipped from a sheep's hindquarters.

crux *n, pl* **cruxes** *or* **cruces** a crucial or decisive point.

cry *vb* **cries, crying, cried 1** to shed tears. **2** to make a loud vocal sound, usually to express pain or fear or to appeal for help. **3** to utter loudly or shout. **4** (of an animal or bird) to utter loud characteristic sounds. **5 cry for** to appeal urgently for. ~*n, pl* **cries 6** a fit of weeping. **7** the act or sound of crying. **8** the characteristic utterance of an animal or bird. **9** an urgent appeal: *a cry for help.* **10** a public demand: *a cry for more law and order on the streets.* **11 a far cry from** something very different from. **12 in full cry a** in eager pursuit. **b** in the middle of talking or doing something. ~See also **cry off.**

crying *adj* **a crying shame** something that demands immediate attention.

cry off *vb Informal* to withdraw from an arrangement.

cryogenics *n* the branch of physics concerned with very low temperatures and their effects. **cryogenic** *adj*

crypt *n* a vault or underground chamber, such as one beneath a church, used as a burial place.

cryptic *adj* having a hidden or secret meaning; puzzling: *no-one knew what he meant by that cryptic remark.* **cryptically** *adv*

cryptogam *n Bot* a plant that reproduces by spores not seeds.

cryptography *n* the art of writing in and deciphering codes. **cryptographer** *n* **cryptographic** *adj*

crystal *n* **1** a solid with a regular internal structure and symmetrical arrangement of faces. **2** a single grain of a crystalline substance. **3** a very clear and brilliant glass. **4** something made of crystal. **5** crystal glass articles collectively. **6** *Electronics* a crystalline element used in certain electronic devices, such as a detector or oscillator. ~*adj* **7** bright and clear: *the crystal waters of the pool.*

crystal ball *n* the glass globe used in crystal gazing.

crystal gazing *n* **1** the act of staring into a crystal ball supposedly in order to see future events. **2** the act of trying to foresee or predict. **crystal gazer** *n*

crystalline *adj* **1** of or like crystal or crystals. **2** clear.

THESAURUS

crumble 1. bruise, crumb, crush, fragment, granulate, grind, pound, powder, pulverize **2.** break up, collapse, come to dust, decay, decompose, degenerate, deteriorate, disintegrate, fall apart, go to pieces, go to wrack and ruin, moulder, perish, tumble down

crumple 1. crease, crush, pucker, rumple, screw up, wrinkle **2.** break down, cave in, collapse, fall, give way, go to pieces

crunch 1. *vb.* champ, chew noisily, chomp, grind, masticate, munch **2.** *n.* **the crunch** *informal* crisis, critical point, crux, emergency, hour of decision, moment of truth, test

crusade campaign, cause, drive, holy war, jihad, movement, push

crusader advocate, campaigner, champion, reformer

crush *vb.* **1.** break, bruise, compress, contuse, crease, crumble, crumple, crunch, mash, pound, pulverize, rumple, smash, squeeze, wrinkle **2.** conquer, extinguish, overcome, overpower, overwhelm, put down, quell, stamp out, subdue, vanquish **3.** abash, browbeat, chagrin, dispose of, humiliate, mortify, put down (*slang*), quash, shame ~*n.* **4.** crowd, huddle, jam

crust caking, coat, coating, concretion, covering, encrustation, film, layer, outside, scab, shell, skin, surface

crusty 1. brittle, crisp, crispy, friable, hard, short, well-baked, well-done **2.** brusque, cantankerous, captious, choleric, crabby, cross, curt, gruff, ill-humoured, irritable, peevish, prickly, ratty (*Brit. & N.Z. informal*), short, short-tempered, snappish, snarling, splenetic, surly, testy, tetchy, touchy

cry *vb.* **1.** bawl, bewail, blubber, boohoo, greet (*Scot. or archaic*), howl one's eyes out, keen, lament, mewl, puie, shed tears, snivel, sob, wail, weep, whimper, whine, whinge (*informal*), yowl **2.** bawl, bellow, call, call out, ejaculate, exclaim, hail, halloo, holler (*informal*), howl, roar, scream, screech, shout, shriek, sing out, vociferate, whoop, yell **3.** *as in* **cry for** beg, beseech, clamour, entreat, implore, plead, pray ~*n.* **4.** bawling, blubbering, crying, greet (*Scot. or archaic*), howl, keening, lament, lamentation, snivel, snivelling, sob, sobbing, sorrowing, wailing, weep, weeping **5.** bawl, bell, bellow, call, ejaculation, exclamation, holler (*informal*), hoot, howl, outcry, roar, scream, screech, shriek, squawk, whoop, yell, yelp **6.** appeal, entreaty, petition, plea, prayer, supplication

crystallize, crystalize, *or* **-ise** *vb* **-izing, -ized** *or* **-ising, -ised 1** to make or become definite. **2** to form into crystals. **3** to preserve (fruit) in sugar. **crystallization, crystalization,** *or* **-isation** *n*
crystallography *n* the science of crystal structure.
crystalloid *n* a substance that in solution can pass through a membrane.
Cs *Chem* caesium.
CSE (formerly) Certificate of Secondary Education: an examination the first grade pass of which was an equivalent to a GCE O level.
CS gas *n* a gas causing tears and painful breathing, used to control civil disturbances.
CST Central Standard Time.
CT Connecticut.
CTV Canadian Television (Network Limited).
Cu *Chem* copper.
cu. cubic.
cub *n* **1** the young of certain mammals, such as the lion or bear. **2** a young or inexperienced person. *~vb* **cubbing, cubbed 3** to give birth to (cubs).
Cub *n* short for **Cub Scout.**
Cuban *adj* **1** from Cuba. *~n* **2** a person from Cuba.
cubbyhole *n* a small enclosed space or room.
cube *n* **1** an object with six equal square faces. **2** the product obtained by multiplying a number by itself twice: *the cube of 2 is 8.* *~vb* **cubing, cubed 3** to find the cube of (a number). **4** to cut into cubes.
cube root *n* the number or quantity whose cube is a given number or quantity: *2 is the cube root of 8.*
cubic *adj* **1 a** having three dimensions. **b** having the same volume as a cube with length, width, and depth each measuring the given unit: *a cubic metre.* **2** having the shape of a cube. **3** *Maths* involving the cubes of numbers.
cubicle *n* an enclosed part of a large room, screened for privacy.
cubic measure *n* a system of units for the measurement of volumes.
cubism *n* a style of art, begun in the early 20th century, in which objects are represented by geometrical shapes. **cubist** *adj, n*
cubit *n* an ancient measure of length based on the length of the forearm.
cuboid *adj* **1** shaped like a cube. *~n* **2** *Maths* a geometric solid whose six faces are rectangles.
Cub Scout *or* **Cub** *n* a member of the junior branch of the Scout Association.
cuckold *Literary or old-fashioned ~n* **1** a man whose wife has been unfaithful to him. *~vb* **2** to make a cuckold of.
cuckoo *n, pl* **cuckoos 1** a migratory bird with a characteristic two-note call, noted for laying its eggs in the nests of other birds. *~adj* **2** *Informal* insane or foolish.
cuckoopint *n* a plant with arrow-shaped leaves, purple flowers, and red berries.
cuckoo spit *n* a white frothy mass produced on plants by the larvae of some insects.
cucumber *n* **1** a long fruit with thin green rind and crisp white flesh, used in salads. **2 as cool as a cucumber** calm and self-possessed.
cud *n* **1** partially digested food which a ruminant brings back into its mouth to chew again. **2 chew the cud** to think deeply.
cuddle *vb* **-dling, -dled 1** to hug or embrace fondly. **2 cuddle up** to lie close and snug. *~n* **3** a fond hug. **cuddly** *adj*
cudgel *n* a short thick stick used as a weapon.
cue[1] *n* **1** a signal to an actor or musician to begin speaking or playing. **2** a signal or reminder. **3 on cue** at the right moment. *vb* **cueing, cued 4** to give a cue to.
cue[2] *n* **1** a long tapering stick used to hit the balls in billiards, snooker, or pool. *~vb* **cueing, cued 2** to hit (a ball) with a cue.
cuff[1] *n* **1** the end of a sleeve. **2** *US, Canad & Austral* a turn-up on trousers. **3 off the cuff** *Informal* impromptu: *he delivers many speeches off the cuff.*
cuff[2] *vb* **1** to strike with an open hand. *~n* **2** a blow with an open hand.
cuff link *n* one of a pair of decorative fastenings for shirt cuffs.
cuisine (quiz-**zeen**) *n* **1** a style of cooking: *Italian cuisine.* **2** the range of food served in a restaurant.
cul-de-sac *n, pl* **culs-de-sac** *or* **cul-de-sacs** a road with one end blocked off.
culinary *adj* of the kitchen or cookery.
cull *vb* **1** to choose or gather. **2** to remove or kill (the inferior or surplus) animals from a herd. *~n* **3** the act of culling.
culminate *vb* **-nating, -nated** to reach the highest point or climax: *the parade culminated in a memorial service.* **culmination** *n*
culottes *pl n* women's flared trousers cut to look like a skirt.
culpable *adj* deserving blame. **culpability** *n*
culprit *n* the person guilty of an offence or misdeed.
cult *n* **1** a specific system of religious worship. **2** a sect devoted to the beliefs of a cult. **3** devoted attachment to a person, idea, or activity. **4** a popular fashion: *the bungee-jumping cult.* *~adj* **5** very popular among a limited group of people: *a cult TV series.* •
cultivate *vb* **-vating, -vated 1** to prepare (land) to

THESAURUS

cry off back out, beg off, cop out (*slang*), excuse oneself, quit, withdraw, withdraw from
crypt catacomb, tomb, undercroft, vault
cub 1. offspring, whelp, young **2.** babe (*informal*), beginner, fledgling, greenhorn (*informal*), lad, learner, puppy, recruit, tenderfoot, trainee, whippersnapper, youngster
cuddle canoodle (*slang*), clasp, cosset, embrace, fondle, hug, nestle, pet, snuggle
cuddly buxom, cuddlesome, curvaceous, huggable, lovable, plump, soft, warm
cudgel baton, bludgeon, club, cosh (*Brit.*), shillelagh, stick, truncheon
cue catchword, hint, key, nod, prompt, reminder, sign, signal, suggestion
cuff off the cuff ad lib, extempore, impromptu, improvised, offhand, off the top of one's head, on the spur of the moment, spontaneous, spontaneously, unrehearsed
cul-de-sac blind alley, dead end
culminate climax, close, come to a climax, come to a head, conclude, end, end up, finish, terminate, wind up
culmination acme, apex, apogee, climax, completion, conclusion, consummation, crown, crowning touch, finale, height, *ne plus ultra*, peak, perfection, pinnacle, punch line, summit, top, zenith
culpable answerable, at fault, blamable, blameworthy, censurable, found wanting, guilty, in the wrong, liable, reprehensible, sinful, to blame, wrong
culprit criminal, delinquent, evildoer, felon, guilty party, malefactor, miscreant, offender, person responsible, rascal, sinner, transgressor, villain, wrongdoer
cult 1. body, church, clique, denomination, faction,

grow crops. **2** to grow (plants). **3** to develop or improve (something) by giving special attention to it: *he tried to cultivate a reputation for fairness.* **4** to try to develop a friendship with (a person).

cultivated *adj* well-educated: *a civilized and cultivated man.*

cultivation *n* **1** the act of cultivating. **2** culture or refinement.

cultivator *n* a farm implement used to break up soil and remove weeds.

culture *n* **1** the ideas, customs, and art of a particular society. **2** a particular civilization at a particular period. **3** a developed understanding of the arts. **4** development or improvement by special attention or training: *physical culture.* **5** the cultivation and rearing of plants or animals. **6** a growth of bacteria for study. *~vb* **-turing, -tured 7** to grow (bacteria) in a special medium. **cultural** *adj*

cultured *adj* **1** showing good taste or manners. **2** artificially grown or synthesized.

cultured pearl *n* a pearl artificially grown in an oyster shell.

culture shock *n Sociol* the feelings of isolation and anxiety experienced by a person on first coming into contact with a culture very different from his or her own.

culvert *n* a drain or pipe that crosses under a road or railway.

cum *prep* with: *a small living-cum-dining room.*

cumbersome *or* **cumbrous** *adj* **1** awkward because of size or shape. **2** difficult because of complexity: *the cumbersome appeals procedure.*

cumin *or* **cummin** *n* **1** the spicy-smelling seeds of a Mediterranean herb, used in cooking. **2** the plant from which these seeds are obtained.

cummerbund *n* a wide sash worn round the waist, esp. with a dinner jacket.

cumquat *n* same as **kumquat.**

cumulative (**kew**-myew-la-tiv) *adj* growing in amount, strength, or effect by small steps: *the cumulative effect of twelve years of war.*

cumulus (**kew**-myew-luss) *n, pl* **-li** (-lie) a thick or billowing white or dark grey cloud.

cuneiform (**kew**-nif-form) *n* **1** an ancient system of writing using wedge-shaped characters. *~adj* **2** written in cuneiform.

cunnilingus *n* the kissing and licking of a woman's genitals by her sexual partner.

cunning *adj* **1** clever at deceiving. **2** made with skill. *~n* **3** cleverness at deceiving. **4** skill or ingenuity.

cunt *n Taboo* **1** the female genitals. **2** *Offensive slang* a stupid or obnoxious person.

cup *n* **1** a small bowl-shaped drinking container with a handle. **2** the contents of a cup. **3** something shaped like a cup: *a bra with padded cups.* **4** a cup-shaped trophy awarded as a prize. **5** a sporting contest in which a cup is awarded to the winner. **6** a mixed drink with fruit juice or wine as a base: *claret cup.* **7** one's lot in life: *his cup of bitterness was full to overflowing.* **8 someone's cup of tea** *Informal* someone's chosen or preferred thing. *~vb* **cupping, cupped 9** to form (the hands) into the shape of a cup. **10** to hold in cupped hands.

cupboard *n* a piece of furniture or a recess with a door, for storage.

cupboard love *n* a show of love put on in order to gain something.

Cup Final *n* **1** the annual final of the FA or Scottish Cup soccer competition. **2** the final of any cup competition.

Cupid *n* **1** the Roman god of love, represented as a winged boy with a bow and arrow. **2** a picture or statue of Cupid.

cupidity (kew-**pid**-it-ee) *n Formal* strong desire for wealth or possessions.

cupola (**kew**-pol-la) *n* **1** a domed roof or ceiling. **2** a small dome on the top of a roof. **3** an armoured revolving gun turret on a warship.

cupreous (**kew**-pree-uss) *adj* of or containing copper.

cupric (**kew**-prick) *adj* of or containing copper in the divalent state.

cupronickel (kew-proh-**nik**-el) *n* a copper alloy containing up to 40 per cent nickel.

cup tie *n Sport* an eliminating match between two teams in a cup competition.

cur *n* **1** a vicious mongrel dog. **2** a contemptible person.

curable *adj* capable of being cured. **curability** *n*

curaçao (**kew**-rah-so) *n* an orange-flavoured liqueur.

curacy (**kew**-rah-see) *n, pl* **-cies** the work or position of a curate.

THESAURUS

faith, following, party, religion, school, sect **2.** admiration, devotion, idolization, reverence, veneration, worship **3.** craze, fad, fashion, mania, trend, vogue

cultivate 1. bring under cultivation, farm, fertilize, harvest, plant, plough, prepare, tend, till, work **2.** aid, devote oneself to, encourage, forward, foster, further, help, patronize, promote, pursue, support **3.** associate with, butter up, consort with, court, dance attendance upon, run after, seek out, seek someone's company *or* friendship, take trouble *or* pains with

cultivation 1. agronomy, farming, gardening, husbandry, planting, ploughing, tillage, tilling, working **2.** breeding, civility, civilization, culture, discernment, discrimination, education, enlightenment, gentility, good taste, learning, letters, manners, polish, refinement, sophistication, taste

cultural artistic, broadening, civilizing, developmental, edifying, educational, educative, elevating, enlightening, enriching, humane, humanizing, liberal, liberalizing

culture 1. civilization, customs, life style, mores, society, stage of development, the arts, way of life **2.** accomplishment, breeding, education, elevation, enlightenment, erudition, gentility, good taste, improvement, polish, politeness, refinement, sophistication, urbanity **3.** agriculture, agronomy, cultivation, farming, husbandry

cultured accomplished, advanced, educated, enlightened, erudite, genteel, highbrow, knowledgeable, polished, refined, scholarly, urbane, versed, well-bred, well-informed, well-read

culvert channel, conduit, drain, gutter, watercourse

cumbersome awkward, bulky, burdensome, clumsy, cumbrous, embarrassing, heavy, hefty (*informal*), incommodious, inconvenient, oppressive, unmanageable, unwieldy, weighty

cumulative accruing, accumulative, aggregate, amassed, collective, heaped, increasing, snowballing

cunning *adj.* **1.** artful, astute, canny, crafty, devious, foxy, guileful, knowing, Machiavellian, sharp, shifty, shrewd, subtle, tricky, wily **2.** adroit, deft, dexterous, imaginative, ingenious, skilful *~n.* **3.** artfulness, astuteness, craftiness, deceitfulness, deviousness, foxiness, guile, shrewdness, slyness, trickery, wiliness **4.** ability, adroitness, art, artifice, cleverness, craft, deftness, dexterity, finesse, ingenuity, skill, subtlety

curare (kew-**rah**-ree) *n* a poisonous resin obtained from a South American tree, used as a muscle relaxant in medicine.

curate *n* a clergyman who assists a vicar or parish priest.

curative *adj* **1** able to cure. ~*n* **2** something able to cure.

curator *n* the person in charge of a museum or art gallery. **curatorial** *adj* **curatorship** *n*

curb *n* **1** something that restrains or holds back. **2** a horse's bit with an attached chain or strap, used to check the horse. **3** a raised edge that strengthens or encloses. ~*vb* **4** to control or restrain. ~See also **kerb.**

curd *n* **1** coagulated milk, used in making cheese or as a food. **2** any similar substance: *bean curd.*

curd cheese *n* a mild smooth white cheese made from skimmed milk curds.

curdle *vb* **-dling, -dled 1** to turn into curd; coagulate. **2 make someone's blood curdle** to fill someone with horror.

cure *vb* **curing, cured 1** to get rid of (an ailment or problem). **2** to restore (someone) to health. **3** to preserve (meat or fish) by salting or smoking. **4** to preserve (leather or tobacco) by drying. **5** to vulcanize (rubber). ~*n* **6** a restoration to health. **7** medical treatment that restores health. **8** a means of restoring health or improving a situation. **9** a curacy.

cure-all *n* something supposed to cure all ailments or problems.

curette *or* **curet** *n* **1** a surgical instrument for scraping tissue from body cavities. ~*vb* **-retting, -retted 2** to scrape with a curette. **curettage** *n*

curfew *n* **1** a law which states that people must stay inside their houses after a specific time at night. **2** the time set as a deadline by such a law. **3** *History* the ringing of a bell at a fixed time, as a signal for putting out fires and lights.

Curia *n, pl* **-riae** the court and government of the Roman Catholic Church. **curial** *adj*

curie *n* the standard unit of radioactivity.

curio (**kew**-ree-oh) *n, pl* **-rios** a rare or unusual thing valued as a collector's item.

curiosity *n, pl* **-ties 1** eagerness to know or find out. **2** a rare or unusual thing.

curious *adj* **1** eager to learn or know. **2** eager to find out private details. **3** unusual or peculiar. **curiously** *adv*

curium (**kew**-ree-um) *n Chem* a silvery-white metallic radioactive element artificially produced from plutonium. Symbol: Cm

curl *vb* **1** to twist (hair) or (of hair) to grow in coils or ringlets. **2** to twist into a spiral or curve. **3** to play the game of curling. **4 curl one's lip** to show contempt by raising a corner of the lip. ~*n* **5** a coil of hair. **6** a curved or spiral shape. ~See also **curl up. curly** *adj*

curler *n* **1** a pin or small tube for curling hair. **2** a person who plays curling.

curlew *n* a large wading bird with a long downward-curving bill.

curlicue *n* an intricate ornamental curl or twist.

curling *n* a game played on ice, in which heavy stones with handles are slid towards a target circle.

curl up *vb* **1** to lie or sit with legs drawn up. **2** to be embarrassed or horrified.

curmudgeon *n* a bad-tempered or mean person. **curmudgeonly** *adj*

currant *n* **1** a small dried seedless raisin. **2** a small round acid berry, such as the redcurrant.

currency *n, pl* **-cies 1** the system of money or the actual coins and banknotes in use in a particular country. **2** general acceptance or use: *ideas that had gained currency during the early 1960s.*

current *adj* **1** of the immediate present: *current affairs; the current economic climate.* **2** most recent or up-to-date: *the current edition.* **3** commonly accepted: *current thinking on this issue.* **4** circulating and valid at present: *current coins.* ~*n* **5** a flow of water or air in a particular direction. **6** *Physics* a flow or rate of flow of electric charge through a conductor. **7** a general trend or drift: *two opposing currents of thought.* **currently** *adv*

current account *n* a bank account from which money may be drawn at any time using a chequebook or computerized card.

curriculum *n, pl* **-la** *or* **-lums 1** all the courses of study offered by a school or college. **2** a course of study in one subject at a school or college: *the sixth-form history curriculum.* **curricular** *adj*

curriculum vitae (**vee**-tie) *n, pl* **curricula vitae** an outline of someone's educational and professional history, prepared for job applications.

THESAURUS

cup beaker, chalice, cupful, demitasse, draught, drink, goblet, potion, teacup, trophy

cupboard cabinet, closet, locker, press

curb 1. *n.* brake, bridle, check, control, deterrent, limitation, rein, restraint **2.** *vb.* bite back, bridle, check, constrain, contain, control, hinder, impede, inhibit, moderate, muzzle, repress, restrain, restrict, retard, subdue, suppress

curdle clot, coagulate, condense, congeal, curd, solidify, thicken, turn sour

cure *vb.* **1.** alleviate, correct, ease, heal, help, make better, mend, rehabilitate, relieve, remedy, restore, restore to health **2.** dry, kipper, pickle, preserve, salt, smoke ~*n.* **3.** alleviation, antidote, corrective, healing, medicine, nostrum, panacea, recovery, remedy, restorative, specific, treatment

curiosity 1. inquisitiveness, interest, nosiness (*informal*), prying, snooping (*informal*) **2.** celebrity, freak, marvel, novelty, oddity, phenomenon, rarity, sight, spectacle, wonder

curious 1. inquiring, inquisitive, interested, puzzled, questioning, searching **2.** inquisitive, meddling, nosy (*informal*), peeping, peering, prying, snoopy (*informal*) **3.** bizarre, exotic, extraordinary, marvellous, mysterious, novel, odd, peculiar, puzzling, quaint, queer, rare, rum (*Brit. slang*), singular, strange, unconventional, unexpected, unique, unorthodox, unusual, wonderful

curl 1. *vb.* bend, coil, convolute, corkscrew, crimp, crinkle, crisp, curve, entwine, frizz, loop, meander, ripple, spiral, turn, twine, twirl, twist, wind, wreathe, writhe **2.** *n.* coil, curlicue, kink, ringlet, spiral, twist, whorl

curly corkscrew, crimped, crimpy, crinkly, crisp, curled, curling, frizzy, fuzzy, kinky, permed, spiralled, waved, wavy, winding

currency 1. bills, coinage, coins, dosh (*Brit. & Austral. slang*), medium of exchange, money, notes **2.** acceptance, circulation, exposure, popularity, prevalence, publicity, transmission, vogue

current *adj.* **1.** contemporary, fashionable, happening (*informal*), in, in fashion, in vogue, now (*informal*), present-day, trendy (*Brit. informal*), up-to-date, up-to-the-minute **2.** accepted, circulating, common, common knowledge, customary, general, going around, in circulation, in progress, in the air, in the news, ongoing, popular, present, prevailing, prevalent, rife, topical, widespread ~*n.* **3.** course, draught, flow, jet, progres-

curry[1] *n, pl* **-ries 1** a dish of Indian origin consisting of meat or vegetables in a hot spicy sauce. **2** curry seasoning or sauce. **3 curry powder** a mixture of spices for making curry. *~vb* **-ries, -rying, -ried 4** to prepare (food) with curry powder.

curry[2] *vb* **-ries, -rying, -ried 1** to groom (a horse). **2** to dress (leather) after it has been tanned. **3 curry favour** to ingratiate oneself with an important person.

currycomb *n* a ridged comb used for grooming horses.

curse *vb* **cursing, cursed 1** to swear or swear at (someone). **2** to call on supernatural powers to bring harm to (someone or something). *~n* **3** a profane or obscene expression, usually of anger. **4** an appeal to a supernatural power for harm to come to a person. **5** harm resulting from a curse. **6** something that causes great trouble or harm. **7 the curse** *Informal* menstruation or a menstrual period.

cursed *adj* **1** under a curse: *he is now sick after being cursed by the witch doctor.* **2 cursed with** having (something unfortunate or unwanted): *their new-born son had been cursed with a genetic defect.*

cursive *adj* **1** of handwriting or print in which letters are joined in a flowing style. *~n* **2** a cursive letter or printing type.

cursor *n* **1** a movable point of light that shows a specific position on a visual display unit. **2** the sliding part of a slide rule or other measuring instrument.

cursory *adj* hasty and usually superficial. **cursorily** *adv*

curt *adj* so blunt and brief as to be rude. **curtly** *adv* **curtness** *n*

curtail *vb* **1** to cut short: *the opening round was curtailed by heavy rain.* **2** to restrict: *a plan to curtail drinks advertising.* **curtailment** *n*

curtain *n* **1** a piece of material hung at an opening or window to shut out light or to provide privacy. **2** a hanging cloth that conceals all or part of a theatre stage from the audience. **3** the end of a scene or a performance in the theatre, marked by the fall or closing of the curtain. **4** the rise or opening of the curtain at the start of a performance. **5** something forming a barrier or screen: *a curtain of rain.* *~vb* **6** to shut off or conceal with a curtain. **7** to provide with curtains.

curtain call *n Theatre* a return to the stage by performers to receive applause.

curtain-raiser *n* **1** *Theatre* a short play performed before the main play. **2** a minor event happening before a major one.

curtains *pl n Informal* death or ruin; the end.

curtsy *or* **curtsey** *n, pl* **-sies** *or* **-seys 1** a woman's formal gesture of respect made by bending the knees and bowing the head. *~vb* **-sies, -sying, -sied** *or* **-seys, -seying, -seyed 2** to make a curtsy.

curvaceous *adj Informal* (of a woman) having a curved shapely body.

curvature *n* the state or degree of being curved.

curve *n* **1** a continuously bending line with no straight parts. **2** something that curves or is curved. **3** curvature. **4** *Maths* a system of points whose coordinates satisfy a given equation. **5** a line representing data on a graph. *~vb* **curving, curved 6** to form into or move in a curve. **curvy** *adj*

curvet *n* **1** a horse's low leap with all four feet off the ground. *~vb* **-vetting, -vetted** *or* **-veting, -veted 2** to make such a leap.

curvilinear *adj* consisting of or bounded by a curved line.

cushion *n* **1** a bag filled with a soft material, used to make a seat more comfortable. **2** something that provides comfort or absorbs shock. **3** the resilient felt-covered rim of a billiard table. *~vb* **4** to protect from injury or shock. **5** to lessen the effects of. **6** to provide with cushions. **cushiony** *adj*

cushy *adj* **cushier, cushiest** *Informal* easy: *a cushy job.*

cusp *n* **1** a small point on the grinding or chewing surface of a tooth. **2** a point where two curves meet. **3** *Astrol* any division between houses or signs of the zodiac. **4** *Astron* either of the points of a crescent moon.

cuss *Informal ~n* **1** a curse or oath. **2** an annoying person. *~vb* **3** to swear or swear at.

cussed (**kuss**-id) *adj Informal* **1** obstinate: *the older she got the more cussed she became.* **2** same as **cursed. cussedness** *n*

custard *n* **1** a sauce made of milk and sugar thickened with cornflour. **2** a baked sweetened mixture of eggs and milk.

custodian *n* the person in charge of a public building. **custodianship** *n*

custody *n, pl* **-dies 1** the act of keeping safe. **2** imprisonment prior to being tried. **custodial** *adj*

custom *n* **1** a long-established activity, action, or festivity: *the Scottish New Year custom of first-footing.* **2** the long-established habits or traditions of a society. **3**

THESAURUS

sion, river, stream, tide, tideway, undertow **4.** atmosphere, drift, feeling, inclination, mood, tendency, trend, undercurrent

curse *vb.* **1.** be foul-mouthed, blaspheme, cuss (*informal*), swear, take the Lord's name in vain, turn the air blue (*informal*), use bad language **2.** accurse, anathematize, damn, excommunicate, execrate, imprecate *~n.* **3.** blasphemy, expletive, oath, obscenity, swearing, swearword **4.** anathema, ban, denunciation, evil eye, excommunication, execration, hoodoo (*informal*), imprecation, jinx, malediction, malison (*archaic*) **5.** affliction, bane, burden, calamity, cross, disaster, evil, hardship, misfortune, ordeal, plague, scourge, torment, tribulation, trouble, vexation

cursed 1. accursed, bedevilled, blighted, cast out, confounded, damned, doomed, excommunicate, fey (*Scot.*), foredoomed, ill-fated, star-crossed, unholy, unsanctified **2.** *as in* **cursed with** afflicted, blighted, burdened, doomed, plagued, scourged, tormented, troubled, vexed

curt abrupt, blunt, brief, brusque, concise, gruff, offhand, pithy, rude, sharp, short, snappish, succinct, summary, tart, terse, unceremonious, uncivil, ungracious

curtail 1. abbreviate, abridge, cut, cut short, shorten, truncate **2.** contract, cut, cut back, decrease, dock, lessen, lop, pare down, reduce, retrench, trim

curtailment abbreviation, abridgment, contraction, cutback, cutting, cutting short, docking, retrenchment, truncation

curtain 1. *n.* drape (*chiefly U.S.*), hanging **2.** *vb.* conceal, drape, hide, screen, shroud, shut off, shutter, veil

curve 1. *n.* arc, bend, camber, curvature, half-moon, loop, trajectory, turn **2.** *vb.* arc, arch, bend, bow, coil, hook, inflect, spiral, swerve, turn, twist, wind

curved arced, arched, bent, bowed, crooked, humped, rounded, serpentine, sinuous, sweeping, turned, twisted

cushion 1. *n.* beanbag, bolster, hassock, headrest, pad, pillow, scatter cushion **2.** *vb.* bolster, buttress, cradle, dampen, deaden, muffle, pillow, protect, soften, stifle, support, suppress

custody 1. aegis, auspices, care, charge, custodianship, guardianship, keeping, observation, preservation,

a usual practice or habit: *she held his hand more tightly than was her custom in public.* **4** regular use of a shop or business. ~*adj* **5** made to the specifications of an individual customer: *a custom car; custom-tailored suits.* ~See also **customs.**

customary *adj* **1** usual. **2** established by custom. **customarily** *adv* **customariness** *n*

custom-built *or* **-made** *adj* made according to the specifications of an individual customer.

customer *n* **1** a person who buys goods or services. **2** *Informal* a person with whom one has to deal: *a tricky customer.*

custom house *n* a government office where customs are collected.

customize *or* **-ise** *vb* **-izing, -ized** *or* **-ising, -ised** to make (something) according to a customer's individual requirements.

customs *n* **1** duty charged on imports or exports. **2** the government department responsible for collecting this. **3** the area at a port, airport, or border where baggage and freight are examined for dutiable goods.

cut *vb* **cutting, cut 1** to open up or penetrate (a person or thing) with a sharp instrument. **2** (of a sharp instrument) to penetrate or open up (a person or thing). **3** to divide or be divided with or as if with a sharp instrument. **4** to trim. **5** to abridge or shorten. **6** to reduce or restrict: *cut your intake of fried foods.* **7** to form or shape by cutting. **8** to reap or mow. **9** *Sports* to hit (the ball) so that it spins and swerves. **10** to hurt the feelings of (a person): *her rudeness cut me to the core.* **11** *Informal* to pretend not to recognize. **12** *Informal* to absent oneself from without permission: *he found the course boring, and was soon cutting classes.* **13** to stop (doing something): *cut the nonsense.* **14** to dilute or adulterate: *heroin cut with talcum powder.* **15** to make a sharp or sudden change in direction: *the path cuts to the right just after you pass the quarry.* **16** to grow (teeth) through the gums. **17** *Films* **a** to call a halt to a shooting sequence. **b cut to** to move quickly to (another scene). **18** *Films* to edit (film). **19** to switch off (a light or engine). **20** to make (a commercial recording): *he cut his first solo album in 1971.* **21** *Cards* **a** to divide (the pack) at random into two parts after shuffling. **b** to pick cards from a spread pack to decide the dealer or who plays first. **22 cut a dash** to make a stylish impression. **23 cut a person dead** *Informal* to ignore a person completely. **24 cut and run** *Informal* to escape quickly from a difficult situation. **25 cut both ways a** to have both good and bad effects. **b** to serve both sides of an argument. **26 cut it fine** *Informal* to allow little margin of time or space. **27 cut no ice** *Informal* to fail to make an impression. **28 cut one's teeth on** *Informal* to get experience from. ~*n* **29** the act of cutting. **30** a stroke or incision made by cutting. **31** a piece cut off. **32** a channel or path cut or hollowed out. **33** a reduction: *a pay cut.* **34** a deletion in a text, film, or play. **35** *Informal* a portion or share. **36** the style in which hair or a garment is cut. **37** a direct route; short cut. **38** *Sports* a stroke which makes the ball spin and swerve. **39** *Films* an immediate transition from one shot to the next. **40** *Brit* a canal. **41 a cut above** *Informal* superior to; better than. ~*adj* **42** made or shaped by cutting. **43** reduced by cutting: *the shop has hundreds of suits, all at cut prices.* **44** adulterated or diluted. **45 cut and dried** *Informal* settled in advance. ~See also **cut across, cutback,** etc.

cut across *vb* **1** to go against (ordinary restrictions or expectations): *this dilemma has cut across class divisions.* **2** to cross or traverse.

cutaneous (kew-**tane**-ee-uss) *adj* of the skin.

cutaway *adj* (of a drawing or model) having part of the outside omitted to reveal the inside.

cutback *n* **1** a decrease or reduction. ~*vb* **cut back 2** to shorten by cutting. **3** to make a reduction: *we may cut back on other expenditure.*

cut down *vb* **1** to fell. **2** to make a reduction: *cut down on the amount of salt you eat.* **3** to kill. **4 cut someone down to size** to cause someone to feel less important or to be less conceited.

cute *adj* **1** appealing or attractive. **2** *Informal* clever or shrewd. **cuteness** *n*

cut glass *n* **1** glass with patterns cut into the surface. ~*adj* **cut-glass 2** upper-class; refined: *a cut-glass accent.*

cuticle (**kew**-tik-kl) *n* **1** hardened skin round the base of a fingernail or toenail. **2** same as **epidermis.**

cut in *vb* **1** to interrupt. **2** to move in front of another vehicle, leaving too little space.

THESAURUS

protection, safekeeping, supervision, trusteeship, tutelage, ward, watch **2.** arrest, confinement, detention, imprisonment, incarceration

custom 1. convention, etiquette, fashion, form, formality, matter of course, observance, observation, policy, practice, ritual, rule, style, tradition, unwritten law, usage, use **2.** habit, manner, mode, procedure, routine, way, wont **3.** customers, patronage, trade

customarily as a rule, commonly, generally, habitually, in the ordinary way, normally, ordinarily, regularly, traditionally, usually

customary accepted, accustomed, acknowledged, common, confirmed, conventional, established, everyday, familiar, fashionable, general, habitual, normal, ordinary, popular, regular, routine, traditional, usual, wonted

customer buyer, client, consumer, habitué, patron, prospect, purchaser, regular (*informal*), shopper

customs duty, import charges, tariff, taxes, toll

cut *vb.* **1.** chop, cleave, divide, gash, incise, lacerate, nick, notch, penetrate, pierce, score, sever, slash, slice, slit, wound **2.** *often with* **through, off,** *or* **across** bisect, carve, cleave, cross, dissect, divide, interrupt, intersect, part, segment, sever, slice, split, sunder **3.** carve, chip, chisel, chop, engrave, fashion, form, inscribe, saw, sculpt, sculpture, shape, whittle **4.** abbreviate, abridge, condense, curtail, delete, edit out, excise, precis, shorten **5.** contract, cut back, decrease, ease up on, lower, rationalize, reduce, slash, slim (down) **6.** clip, dock, fell, gather, hack, harvest, hew, lop, mow, pare, prune, reap, saw down, shave, trim **7.** avoid, cold-shoulder, freeze (someone) out (*informal*), grieve, hurt, ignore, insult, look straight through (someone), pain, put down, send to Coventry, slight, snub, spurn, sting, turn one's back on, wound ~*n.* **8.** gash, graze, groove, incision, laceration, nick, rent, rip, slash, slit, stroke, wound **9.** cutback, decrease, decrement, diminution, economy, fall, lowering, reduction, saving **10.** *informal* division, percentage, piece, portion, share, slice **11.** configuration, fashion, form, look, mode, shape, style **12. a cut above** *informal* better than, higher than, more efficient (capable, competent, reliable, trustworthy, useful) than, superior to ~*adj.* **13. cut and dried** *informal* automatic, fixed, organized, prearranged, predetermined, settled, sorted out (*informal*)

cutback cut, decrease, economy, lessening, reduction, retrenchment

cut down 1. fell, hew, level, lop, raze **2.** *sometimes with* **on** decrease, lessen, lower, reduce **3. cut (someone) down to size** abash, humiliate, make

cutlass *n* a curved one-edged sword formerly used by sailors.
cutler *n* a person who makes or sells cutlery.
cutlery *n* knives, forks, and spoons, used for eating.
cutlet *n* **1** a small piece of meat taken from the neck or ribs. **2** a flat croquette of chopped meat or fish.
cut off *vb* **1** to remove or separate by cutting. **2** to stop the supply of. **3** to interrupt (a person who is speaking), esp. during a telephone conversation. **4** to bring to an end. **5** to disinherit: *cut off without a penny.* **6** to intercept so as to prevent retreat or escape. *~n* **cutoff 7** the point at which something is cut off; limit. **8** *Chiefly US* a short cut. **9** a device to stop the flow of a fluid in a pipe.
cut out *vb* **1** to shape by cutting. **2** to delete or remove. **3** *Informal* to stop doing (something). **4** (of an engine) to cease to operate suddenly. **5** (of an electrical device) to switch off, usually automatically. **6 be cut out for** to be suited or equipped for: *you're not cut out for this job.* **7 have one's work cut out** to have as much work as one can manage. *~n* **cutout 8** a device that automatically switches off a circuit or engine as a safety device. **9** something that has been cut out from something else.
cut-price *or esp US* **cut-rate** *adj* **1** at a reduced price. **2** offering goods or services at prices below the standard price.
cutter *n* **1** a person or tool that cuts. **2** a small fast boat.
cutthroat *adj* **1** fierce or ruthless in competition: *the cutthroat world of international finance.* **2** (of a card game) played by three people: *cutthroat poker.* *~n* **3** a murderer. **4** *Brit* a razor with a long blade that folds into its handle.
cutting *n* **1** an article cut from a newspaper or magazine. **2** a piece cut from a plant for rooting or grafting. **3** a passage cut through high ground for a road or railway. **4** the editing process of a film. *~adj* **5** (of a remark) likely to hurt the feelings. **6** keen; piercing: *a cutting wind.* **7** designed for cutting: *the hatchet's blade is largely stone, but its cutting edge is made of copper.*
cutting edge *n* the leading position in any field; forefront: *the cutting edge of space technology.*
cuttlefish *n, pl* **-fish** *or* **-fishes** a flat squidlike mollusc which squirts an inky fluid when in danger.
cut up *vb* **1** to cut into pieces. **2 be cut up** *Informal* to be very upset. **3 cut up rough** *Brit informal* to become angry or violent.
CV curriculum vitae.
cwm (**koom**) *n* (in Wales) a valley.
cwt hundredweight.
cyanic acid *n* a colourless poisonous volatile liquid acid.
cyanide *n* any of a number of highly poisonous substances containing a carbon-nitrogen group of atoms.
cyanogen *n* a poisonous colourless flammable gas.
cyanosis *n Pathol* a blue discoloration of the skin, caused by a deficiency of oxygen in the blood.
cybernetics *n* the branch of science in which electronic and mechanical systems are studied and compared to biological systems. **cybernetic** *adj*
cyclamen (**sik**-la-men) *n* a plant with white, pink, or red flowers, with turned-back petals.
cycle *vb* **-cling, -cled 1** to ride a bicycle. **2** to occur in cycles. *~n* **3** a bicycle. **4** a motorcycle. **5** a complete series of recurring events. **6** the time taken or needed for one such series. **7** a single complete movement in an electrical, electronic, or mechanical process. **8** a set of plays, songs, or poems about a figure or event. **cycling** *n*
cyclical *or* **cyclic** *adj* **1** occurring in cycles. **2** *Chem* (of an organic compound) containing a closed ring of atoms.
cyclist *n* a person who rides a bicycle.
cyclo- *or before a vowel* **cycl-** *combining form* **1** indicating a circle or ring: *cyclotron.* **2** *Chem* denoting a cyclical compound: *cyclopropane.*
cyclometer (sike-**lom**-it-er) *n* a device that records the number of revolutions made by a wheel and the distance travelled.
cyclone *n* **1** a body of moving air below normal atmospheric pressure, which often brings rain. **2** a violent tropical storm. **cyclonic** *adj*
cyclopedia *or* **cyclopaedia** *n* same as **encyclopedia.**
Cyclops *n, pl* **Cyclopes** *or* **Cyclopses** *Classical myth* one of a race of giants having a single eye in the middle of the forehead.
cyclotron *n* an apparatus, used in atomic research, which accelerates charged particles by means of a strong vertical magnetic field.
cyder *n* same as **cider.**
cygnet *n* a young swan.
cylinder *n* **1** a solid or hollow body with circular equal ends and straight parallel sides. **2** a container or other object shaped like a cylinder. **3** the chamber in an internal-combustion engine within which the piston moves. **4** the rotating mechanism of a revolver, containing cartridge chambers. **cylindrical** *adj*
cymbal *n* a percussion instrument consisting of a round brass plate which is struck against another or hit with a stick. **cymbalist** *n*
cyme *n Bot* a flower cluster which has a single flower on the end of each stem and of which the central flower blooms first. **cymose** *adj*
Cymric (**kim**-rik) *adj* **1** of Wales. *~n* **2** the Celtic language of Wales.
cynic (**sin**-ik) *n* a person who believes that people always act selfishly.
Cynic *n* a member of an ancient Greek philosophical

THESAURUS

(someone) look small, take the wind out of (someone's) sails
cut in break in, butt in, interpose, interrupt, intervene, intrude, move in (*informal*)
cut off 1. isolate, separate, sever **2.** disconnect, intercept, interrupt **3.** bring to an end, discontinue, halt, obstruct, suspend **4.** disinherit, disown, renounce
cut out 1. cease, delete, extract, give up, kick (*informal*), refrain from, remove, sever, stop **2. cut out for** adapted, adequate, competent, designed, equipped, fitted, qualified, suitable, suited
cut-price bargain, cheap, cheapo (*informal*), cut-rate (*chiefly U.S.*), reduced, sale
cutthroat 1. *adj.* competitive, dog-eat-dog, fierce, merciless, relentless, ruthless, savage, unprincipled **2.** *n.* assassin, butcher, executioner, heavy (*slang*), hit man (*slang*), homicide, killer, liquidator, murderer, thug
cutting *adj.* **1.** acid, acrimonious, barbed, bitter, caustic, hurtful, malicious, pointed, sarcastic, sardonic, scathing, severe, trenchant, vitriolic, wounding **2.** biting, bitter, chill, keen, numbing, penetrating, piercing, raw, sharp, stinging
cut up *vb.* **1.** carve, chop, dice, divide, mince, slice **2. be cut up** *informal* agitated, dejected, desolated, distressed, disturbed, heartbroken, stricken, upset, wretched

school that had contempt for worldly things. **Cynicism** *n*

cynical *adj* **1** believing that people always act selfishly. **2** sarcastic or sneering. **cynically** *adv*

cynicism *n* the attitude or beliefs of a cynic.

cynosure (**sin**-oh-zyure) *n Literary* a centre of interest or attention.

cypher (**sife**-er) *n, vb* same as **cipher.**

cypress *n* **1** an evergreen tree with dark green leaves. **2** the wood of this tree.

Cypriot *adj* **1** of Cyprus. ~*n* **2** a person from Cyprus. **3** the dialect of Greek spoken in Cyprus.

Cyrillic *adj* of the Slavic alphabet devised supposedly by Saint Cyril, now used primarily for Russian and Bulgarian.

cyst (**sist**) *n* **1** *Pathol* an abnormal membranous sac containing fluid or diseased matter. **2** *Anat* any normal sac in the body.

cystic fibrosis *n* a congenital disease, usually affecting young children, which causes breathing disorders and malfunctioning of the pancreas.

cystitis (siss-**tite**-iss) *n* inflammation of the bladder, causing a desire to urinate frequently, accompanied by a burning sensation.

-cyte *n combining form* indicating a cell: *leucocyte.*

cytology (site-**ol**-a-jee) *n* the study of plant and animal cells. **cytological** *adj* **cytologist** *n*

cytoplasm *n* the protoplasm of a cell excluding the nucleus. **cytoplasmic** *adj*

czar (**zahr**) *n* same as **tsar.**

Czech *adj* **1** of the Czech Republic. ~*n* **2** a person from the Czech Republic. **3** the language of the Czech Republic.

Czechoslovak *or* **Czechoslovakian** *adj* **1** of the former Czechoslovakia. ~*n* **2** a person from the former Czechoslovakia.

THESAURUS

cycle aeon, age, circle, era, period, phase, revolution, rotation

cynic doubter, misanthrope, misanthropist, pessimist, sceptic, scoffer

cynical 1. distrustful, misanthropic, misanthropical, pessimistic **2.** contemptuous, derisive, ironic, mocking, sarcastic, sceptical, scoffing, scornful, sneering, unbelieving

cynicism disbelief, doubt, misanthropy, pessimism, sarcasm, sardonicism, scepticism

D

d 1 *Physics* density. 2 deci-.

D 1 *Music* the second note of the scale of C major. 2 *Chem* deuterium. 3 the Roman numeral for 500.

d. 1 *Brit* (before decimalization) penny *or* pennies. 2 died. 3 daughter.

dab[1] *vb* **dabbing, dabbed 1** to pat lightly and quickly. **2** to apply with short tapping strokes: *dabbing antiseptic on cuts.* ~*n* **3** a small amount of something soft or moist. **4** a light stroke or tap. **5 dabs** *Slang, chiefly Brit* fingerprints.

dab[2] *n* a small flatfish covered with rough toothed scales.

dabble *vb* **-bling, -bled 1** to be involved in an activity in a superficial way: *she dabbles in right-wing politics.* **2** to splash (one's toes or fingers) in water. **dabbler** *n*

dab hand *n Brit informal* a person who is particularly skilled at something: *a dab hand with a needle and thread.*

dace *n, pl* **dace** *or* **daces** a freshwater fish of the carp family.

dachshund *n* a small dog with short legs and a long body.

dactyl *n Prosody* a metrical foot of three syllables, one long followed by two short. **dactylic** *adj*

dad *or* **daddy** *n Informal* father.

Dada *or* **Dadaism** *n* an art movement of the early 20th century that systematically used arbitrary and absurd concepts. **Dadaist** *n, adj*

daddy-longlegs *n* a crane fly.

dado (**day**-doe) *n, pl* **-does** *or* **-dos 1** the lower part of an interior wall, often separated by a rail, that is decorated differently from the upper part. **2** *Archit* the part of a pedestal between the base and the cornice.

daemon (**deem**-on) *n* same as **demon.**

daffodil *n* **1** a spring plant with yellow trumpet-shaped flowers. ~*adj* **2** brilliant yellow.

daft *adj Informal, chiefly Brit* **1** foolish or crazy. **2 daft about** very enthusiastic about: *he's daft about football.*

dag *n Austral & NZ informal* a person with a good sense of humour.

dagga (**duhh**-a) *n S African* marijuana.

dagger *n* **1** a short knifelike weapon with a double-edged pointed blade. **2** a character (†) used to indicate a cross-reference. **3 at daggers drawn** in a state of open hostility. **4 look daggers** to glare with hostility.

daguerreotype (dag-**gair**-oh-type) *n* a type of early photograph produced on chemically treated silver.

dahlia (**day**-lya) *n* a garden plant with showy flowers.

Dáil Éireann (doil **air**-in) *or* **Dáil** *n* (in the Republic of Ireland) the lower chamber of parliament.

daily *adj* **1** occurring every day or every weekday: *there have been daily airdrops of food, blankets, and water.* **2** of or relating to a single day or to one day at a time: *her home help comes in on a daily basis; exercise has become part of our daily lives.* ~*adv* **3** every day. ~*n, pl* **-lies 4** a daily newspaper. **5** *Brit informal* a woman employed to clean someone's house.

dainty *adj* **-tier, -tiest 1** delicate, pretty, or elegant. ~*n, pl* **-ties 2** a small choice cake or sweet. **daintily** *adv*

daiquiri (**dak**-eer-ee) *n, pl* **-ris** an iced drink containing rum, lime juice, and sugar.

dairy *n, pl* **dairies 1** a company or shop that sells milk and milk products. **2** a place where milk and cream are stored or made into butter and cheese. ~*adj* **3** of milk or milk products: *dairy produce.*

dairy cattle *n* cows reared mainly for their milk.

dais (**day**-iss) *n* a raised platform in a hall or meeting place used by a speaker.

daisy *n, pl* **-sies** a small low-growing flower with a yellow centre and pinkish-white petals.

daisy chain *n* a string of daisies joined together by their stems to make a necklace.

daisywheel *n* a flat disc in a word processor with radiating spokes for printing characters.

dal[1] *n* same as **dhal.**

dal[2] decalitre(s).

Dalai Lama *n* the chief lama and (until 1959) ruler of Tibet.

dale *n* an open valley.

dalliance *n Old-fashioned* flirtation.

dally *vb* **-lies, -lying, -lied 1** *Old-fashioned* to waste time or dawdle. **2 dally with** to deal frivolously with: *to dally with someone's affections.*

Dalmatian *n* a large dog with a smooth white coat and black spots.

dam[1] *n* **1** a barrier built across a river to create a lake. **2** a lake created by such a barrier. ~*vb* **damming, dammed 3** to block up (a river) by a dam.

dam[2] *n* the female parent of an animal such as a sheep or horse.

dam[3] decametre(s).

damage *vb* **-aging, -aged 1** to harm or injure. ~*n* **2**

THESAURUS

dabble 1. dally, dip into, play at, potter, tinker, trifle (with) **2.** dip, moisten, paddle, splash, sprinkle, wet

dabbler amateur, dilettante, potterer, tinkerer, trifler

dab hand ace (*informal*), adept, buff (*informal*), past master, whizz (*informal*), wizard

dagger 1. bayonet, dirk, poniard, stiletto **2. at daggers drawn** at loggerheads, at odds, at war, on bad terms, up in arms **3. look daggers** frown, glare, glower, scowl

daily *adj.* **1.** circadian, diurnal, everyday, quotidian **2.** common, commonplace, day-to-day, everyday, ordinary, quotidian, regular, routine ~*adv.* **3.** constantly, day after day, day by day, every day, often, once a day, regularly

dainty *adj.* **1.** charming, delicate, elegant, exquisite, fine, graceful, neat, petite, pretty **2.** choice, delectable, delicious, palatable, savoury, tasty, tender, toothsome **3.** choosy, fastidious, finicky, fussy, nice, particular, picky (*informal*), scrupulous ~*n.* **4.** delicacy, sweetmeat, titbit

dale coomb, dell, dingle, glen, strath (*Scot.*), vale, valley

dam 1. *n.* barrage, barrier, embankment, wall, weir **2.** *vb.* barricade, block, block up, check, choke, confine, hold back, hold in, obstruct, restrict

damage *vb.* **1.** deface, harm, hurt, impair, incapacitate, injure, mar, mutilate, ruin, spoil, tamper with, undo, weaken, wreck ~*n.* **2.** destruction, detriment, devastation, harm, hurt, impairment, injury, loss, mischief, mutilation, suffering **3.** *informal* bill, charge, cost, expense, total

injury or harm caused to a person or thing. **3** *Informal* cost: *what's the damage?* **damaging** *adj*

damages *pl n Law* money awarded as compensation for injury or loss.

damask *n* a heavy fabric with a pattern woven into it, used for tablecloths, curtains, etc.

dame *n Slang* a woman.

Dame *n* (in Britain) the title of a woman who has been awarded the Order of the British Empire or another order of chivalry.

damn *interj* **1** *Slang* an exclamation of annoyance. *~adv, adj also* **damned 2** *Slang* extreme or extremely: *a damn good idea.* *~vb* **3** to condemn as bad or worthless. **4** to curse. **5** (of God) to condemn to hell or eternal punishment. **6** to prove (someone) guilty. **7 damn with faint praise** to praise so unenthusiastically that the effect is condemnation. *~n* **8 not give a damn** *Informal* not care. **damning** *adj*

damnable *adj* very unpleasant or annoying. **damnably** *adv*

damnation *interj* **1** an exclamation of anger. *~n* **2** *Theol* eternal punishment.

damned *adj* **1** condemned to hell. *~adv, adj Slang* **2** extreme or extremely: *a damned good try.* **3** used to indicate amazement or refusal: *I'm damned if I'll do it!*

damnedest *n* **do one's damnedest** *Informal* to do one's best: *I'm doing my damnedest to make myself clear.*

damp *adj* **1** slightly wet. *~n* **2** slight wetness; moisture. *~vb* **3** to make slightly wet. **4 damp down a** to reduce the intensity of (someone's emotions or reactions): *they attempted to damp down protests.* **b** to reduce the flow of air to (a fire) to make it burn more slowly. **damply** *adv* **dampness** *n*

dampcourse *or* **damp-proof course** *n* a layer of waterproof material built into the base of a wall to prevent moisture rising.

dampen *vb* **1** to reduce the intensity of. **2** to make damp.

damper *n* **1 put a damper on** to produce a depressing or inhibiting effect on. **2** a movable plate to regulate the draught in a stove or furnace. **3** the pad in a piano or harpsichord that deadens the vibration of each string as its key is released.

damsel *n Archaic or poetic* a young woman.

damson *n* a small blue-black edible plumlike fruit that grows on a tree.

dan *n Judo, karate* **1** any of the 10 black-belt grades of proficiency. **2** a competitor entitled to dan grading.

dance *vb* **dancing, danced 1** to move the feet and body rhythmically in time to music. **2** to perform (a particular dance): *to dance a tango.* **3** to skip or leap. **4** to move in a rhythmical way: *their reflection danced in the black waters.* **5 dance attendance on someone** to carry out someone's slightest wish in an overeager manner. *~n* **6** a social meeting arranged for dancing. **7** a series of rhythmical steps and movements in time to music. **8** a piece of music in the rhythm of a particular dance. **dancer** *n* **dancing** *n, adj*

D and C *n Med* dilatation of the cervix and curettage of the uterus: a minor operation to clear the womb or remove tissue for diagnosis.

dandelion *n* a wild plant with yellow rayed flowers and deeply notched leaves.

dander *n* **get one's dander up** *Slang* to become angry.

dandified *adj* dressed like or resembling a dandy.

dandle *vb* **-dling, -dled** to move (a young child) up and down on one's knee.

dandruff *n* loose scales of dry dead skin shed from the scalp.

dandy *n, pl* **-dies 1** a man who is greatly concerned with the elegance of his appearance. *~adj* **-dier, -diest 2** *Informal* very good or fine.

dandy-brush *n* a stiff brush used for grooming a horse.

Dane *n* a person from Denmark.

danger *n* **1** the possibility that someone may be injured or killed. **2** someone or something that may cause injury or harm. **3** a likelihood that something unpleasant will happen: *cities in China faced the danger of serious flooding.*

danger money *n* extra money paid to compensate for the risks involved in dangerous work.

dangerous *adj* likely or able to cause injury or harm. **dangerously** *adv*

THESAURUS

damages compensation, fine, indemnity, reimbursement, reparations, satisfaction

damaging deleterious, detrimental, disadvantageous, harmful, hurtful, injurious, prejudicial, ruinous

Dame baroness, dowager, *grande dame,* Lady, noblewoman, peeress

damn *vb.* **1.** anathematize, blast, castigate, censure, condemn, criticize, denounce, excoriate, inveigh against, lambast(e), pan (*informal*), put down, revile, slam (*slang*), slate (*informal*), tear into (*informal*) **2.** abuse, blaspheme, curse, execrate, imprecate, swear **3.** condemn, doom, sentence *~n.* **4.** brass farthing, hoot, iota, jot, tinker's curse *or* damn (*slang*), two hoots, whit **5. not give a damn** be indifferent, not care, not mind

damnable abominable, accursed, atrocious, culpable, cursed, despicable, detestable, execrable, hateful, horrible, offensive, wicked

damnation anathema, ban, condemnation, consigning to perdition, damning, denunciation, doom, excommunication, proscription, sending to hell

damned 1. accursed, anathematized, condemned, doomed, infernal, lost, reprobate, unhappy **2.** *slang* confounded, despicable, detestable, hateful, infamous, infernal, loathsome, revolting

damning accusatory, condemnatory, damnatory, dooming, implicating, incriminating

damp *adj.* **1.** clammy, dank, dewy, dripping, drizzly, humid, misty, moist, muggy, sodden, soggy, sopping, vaporous, wet *~n.* **2.** clamminess, dampness, dankness, dew, drizzle, fog, humidity, mist, moisture, vapour *~vb.* **3.** dampen, moisten, wet **4.** *as in* **damp down** allay, check, chill, cool, curb, dash, deaden, deject, depress, diminish, discourage, dispirit, dull, inhibit, moderate, restrain, stifle

damper chill, cloud, cold water (*informal*), curb, discouragement, gloom, hindrance, pall, restraint, wet blanket (*informal*)

dance 1. *vb.* bob up and down, caper, cut a rug (*informal*), frolic, gambol, hop, jig, prance, rock, skip, spin, sway, swing, trip, whirl **2.** *n.* ball, disco, discotheque, hop (*informal*), social

danger endangerment, hazard, insecurity, jeopardy, menace, peril, precariousness, risk, threat, vulnerability

dangerous alarming, breakneck, chancy (*informal*), exposed, hairy (*slang*), hazardous, insecure, menacing, nasty, parlous (*archaic*), perilous, precarious, risky, threatening, treacherous, ugly, unsafe

dangerously 1. alarmingly, carelessly, daringly, desperately, harmfully, hazardously, perilously, pre-

dangle *vb* **-gling, -gled 1** to hang loosely. **2** to display (something attractive) as an enticement.
Danish *adj* **1** of Denmark. *~n* **2** the language of Denmark.
Danish blue *n* a white cheese with blue veins and a strong flavour.
Danish pastry *n* a rich puff pastry filled with apple, almond paste, etc. and topped with icing.
dank *adj* (esp. of cellars or caves) unpleasantly damp and chilly.
dapper *adj* (of a man) neat in appearance and slight in build.
dappled *adj* **1** marked with spots of a different colour; mottled. **2** covered in patches of light and shadow.
dapple-grey *n* a horse with a grey coat and darker coloured spots.
Darby and Joan *n* a happily married elderly couple.
dare *vb* **daring, dared 1** to be courageous enough to try (to do something). **2** to challenge (someone) to do something risky. **3 I dare say a** it is quite possible. **b** probably. *~n* **4** a challenge to do something risky.
➤ When *dare* is used in a question or as a negative, it does not take an *-s: He dare not come.*
daredevil *n* **1** a recklessly bold person. *~adj* **2** recklessly bold or daring.
daring *adj* **1** willing to do things that may be dangerous. *~n* **2** the courage to do things that may be dangerous. **daringly** *adv*
dark *adj* **1** having little or no light. **2** (of a colour) reflecting little light: *dark brown.* **3** (of hair or skin) brown or black. **4** (of thoughts or ideas) gloomy or sad. **5** sinister or evil: *a dark deed.* **6** sullen or angry: *a dark scowl.* **7** secret or mysterious: *keep it dark.* *~n* **8** absence of light; darkness. **9** night or nightfall. **10 in the dark** in ignorance. **darkly** *adv* **darkness** *n*
dark age *n* a period of ignorance or barbarism.
Dark Ages *n* the period of European history between 500 and 1000 AD.
darken *vb* **1** to make or become dark or darker. **2** to make gloomy, angry, or sad.
dark horse *n* a person who reveals little about himself or herself, esp. someone who has unexpected talents.
darkroom *n* a darkened room in which photographs are developed.
darling *n* **1** a person very much loved: used as a term of address. **2** a favourite: *the darling of the gossip columns.* *~adj* **3** beloved. **4** pleasing: *a darling piano accompaniment.*
darn[1] *vb* **1** to mend a hole in (a knitted garment) with a series of interwoven stitches. *~n* **2** a patch of darned work on a garment.
darn[2] *interj, adj, adv, vb, n Euphemistic* same as **damn.**
darnel *n* a weed that grows in grain fields.
dart *n* **1** a small narrow pointed missile that is thrown or shot, as in the game of darts. **2** a sudden quick movement. **3** a tapered tuck made in dressmaking. *~vb* **4** to move or throw swiftly and suddenly. **darting** *adj*
dartboard *n* a circular board used as the target in the game of darts.
darts *n* a game in which darts are thrown at a dartboard.
Darwinism *or* **Darwinian theory** *n* the theory of the origin of animal and plant species by evolution. **Darwinian** *adj, n* **Darwinist** *n, adj*
dash *vb* **1** to move hastily; rush. **2** to hurl; crash: *deep-sea rollers dashing spray over jagged rocks.* **3** to frustrate: *prospects for peace have been dashed.* *~n* **4** a sudden quick movement. **5** a small amount: *a dash of milk.* **6** a mixture of style and courage: *the commander's dash did not impress him.* **7** the punctuation mark

THESAURUS

cariously, recklessly, riskily, unsafely, unsecurely **2.** critically, gravely, seriously, severely
dangle *vb.* **1.** flap, hang, hang down, sway, swing, trail **2.** brandish, flaunt, flourish, wave
dapper active, brisk, chic, dainty, natty (*informal*), neat, nice, nimble, smart, soigné *or* soignée, spruce, spry, stylish, trig (*archaic or dialect*), trim, well-groomed, well turned out
dappled brindled, checkered, flecked, freckled, mottled, piebald, pied, speckled, spotted, stippled, variegated
dare *vb.* **1.** brave, endanger, gamble, hazard, make bold, presume, risk, stake, venture **2.** challenge, defy, goad, provoke, taunt, throw down the gauntlet *~n.* **3.** challenge, defiance, provocation, taunt
daredevil 1. *n.* adventurer, desperado, exhibitionist, show-off (*informal*) **2.** *adj.* adventurous, audacious, bold, daring, death-defying, reckless
daring 1. *adj.* adventurous, audacious, ballsy (*taboo slang*), bold, brave, daredevil, fearless, game (*informal*), impulsive, intrepid, plucky, rash, reckless, valiant, venturesome **2.** *n.* audacity, balls (*taboo slang*), boldness, bottle (*Brit. slang*), bravery, courage, derring-do (*archaic*), fearlessness, grit, guts (*informal*), intrepidity, nerve (*informal*), pluck, rashness, spirit, spunk (*informal*), temerity
dark *adj.* **1.** cloudy, dim, dingy, indistinct, murky, overcast, pitch-black, pitchy, shadowy, shady, sunless, unlit **2.** black, brunette, dark-skinned, dusky, ebony, sable, swarthy **3.** bleak, cheerless, dismal, doleful, drab, gloomy, grim, joyless, morbid, morose, mournful, sombre **4.** atrocious, damnable, evil, foul, hellish, horrible, infamous, infernal, nefarious, satanic, sinful, sinister, vile, wicked **5.** abstruse, arcane, concealed, cryptic, deep, Delphic, enigmatic, hidden, mysterious, mystic, obscure, occult, puzzling, recondite, secret **6.** angry, dour, forbidding, frowning, glowering, glum, ominous, scowling, sulky, sullen, threatening *~n.* **7.** darkness, dimness, dusk, gloom, murk, murkiness, obscurity, semi-darkness **8.** evening, night, nightfall, night-time, twilight **9.** *figurative* concealment, ignorance, secrecy
darken 1. blacken, cloud up *or* over, deepen, dim, eclipse, make dark, make darker, make dim, obscure, overshadow, shade, shadow **2.** become angry, become gloomy, blacken, cast a pall over, cloud, deject, depress, dispirit, grow troubled, look black, sadden
darkness 1. blackness, dark, dimness, dusk, duskiness, gloom, murk, murkiness, nightfall, obscurity, shade, shadiness, shadows **2.** *figurative* blindness, concealment, ignorance, mystery, privacy, secrecy, unawareness
darling *n.* **1.** beloved, dear, dearest, love, sweetheart, truelove **2.** apple of one's eye, blue-eyed boy, fair-haired boy (*U.S.*), favourite, pet, spoilt child *~adj.* **3.** adored, beloved, cherished, dear, precious, treasured **4.** adorable, attractive, captivating, charming, cute, enchanting, lovely, sweet
darn 1. *vb.* mend, patch, repair, sew up, stitch **2.** *n.* invisible repair, mend, patch, reinforcement
dart 1. bound, dash, flash, flit, fly, race, run, rush, scoot, shoot, spring, sprint, start, tear, whistle, whizz **2.** cast, fling, hurl, launch, propel, send, shoot, sling, throw
dash *vb.* **1.** bolt, bound., dart, fly, haste, hasten, hurry, race, run, rush, speed, spring, sprint, tear **2.** cast, fling,

(—), used to indicate a change of subject. **8** the symbol (–), used in combination with the symbol *dot* (.) in Morse code. ~See also **dash off.**

dashboard *n* the instrument panel in a car, boat, or aircraft.

dasher *n Canad* the ledge along the top of the boards of an ice hockey rink.

dashing *adj* stylish and attractive: *a splendidly dashing character.*

dash off *vb* to write down or finish off hastily.

dassie *n S African* a hyrax, esp. a rock hyrax.

dastardly *adj Old-fashioned* mean and cowardly.

DAT digital audio tape.

dat. dative.

data *n* **1** a series of observations, measurements, or facts; information. **2** *Computers* the numbers, digits, characters, and symbols operated on by a computer. ➤ *Data* is a Latin plural word but it is generally used as a singular word in English.

database *n* a store of information in a form that can be easily handled by a computer.

data capture *n* a process for converting information into a form that can be handled by a computer.

data processing *n* a sequence of operations performed on data, esp. by a computer, in order to extract or interpret information.

date[1] *n* **1** a specified day of the month. **2** the particular day or year when an event happened. **3 a** an appointment, esp. with a person of the opposite sex. **b** the person with whom the appointment is made. **4 to date** up to now. ~*vb* **dating, dated 5** to mark (a letter or cheque) with the date. **6** to assign a date of occurrence or creation to. **7** to reveal the age of: *that dress dates her.* **8** to make or become old-fashioned: *it's the freshest look this year but may date quickly.* **9** *Informal, chiefly US & Canad* to be a boyfriend or girlfriend of. **10 date from** *or* **date back to** to have originated at (a specified time).

date[2] *n* the dark-brown, sweet tasting fruit of the date palm.

dated *adj* unfashionable; outmoded.

dateless *adj* likely to remain fashionable or interesting regardless of age.

dateline *n Journalism* information placed at the top of an article stating the time and place the article was written.

Date Line *n* short for **International Date Line.**

date palm *n* a tall palm grown in tropical regions for its fruit.

date rape *n* the act of a man raping a woman or pressuring her into having sex while they are on a date together.

dative *n Grammar* the grammatical case in certain languages that expresses the indirect object.

datum *n, pl* **-ta** a single piece of information usually in the form of a fact or statistic.

daub *vb* **1** to smear (paint or mud) quickly or carelessly over a surface. **2** to paint (a picture) clumsily or badly. ~*n* **3** a crude or badly done painting.

daughter *n* **1** a female child. **2** a girl or woman who comes from a certain place or is connected with a certain thing: *a daughter of the church.* ~*adj* **3** *Biol* denoting a cell, chromosome, etc. produced by the division of one of its own kind. **4** *Physics* (of a nuclide) formed from another nuclide by radioactive decay. **daughterly** *adj*

daughter-in-law *n, pl* **daughters-in-law** the wife of one's son.

daunting *adj* intimidating or worrying: *this project grows more daunting every day.*

dauntless *adj* fearless; not discouraged.

dauphin (**daw**-fin) *n* formerly, the eldest son of the king of France.

davenport *n* **1** *Chiefly Brit* a writing desk with drawers at the side. **2** *US & Canad* a large sofa.

davit (**dav**-vit) *n* a crane, usually one of a pair, on the side of a ship for lowering or hoisting a lifeboat.

Davy Jones's locker *n* the ocean's bottom, regarded as the grave of those lost or buried at sea.

Davy lamp *n* same as **safety lamp.**

dawdle *vb* **-dling, -dled** to walk slowly or lag behind.

dawn *n* **1** daybreak. **2** the beginning of something. ~*vb* **3** to begin to grow light after the night. **4** to begin to develop or appear. **5 dawn on** *or* **upon** to become apparent (to someone).

dawn chorus *n* the singing of birds at dawn.

day *n* **1** the period of 24 hours from one midnight to the next. **2** the period of light between sunrise and sunset. **3** the part of a day occupied with regular activity, esp. work. **4** a period or point in time: *in days gone by; in Shakespeare's day.* **5** a day of special observance: *Christmas Day.* **6** a time of success or recognition: *his day will come.* **7 all in a day's work** part of one's normal activity. **8 at the end of the day** in the

THESAURUS

hurl, slam, sling, throw **3.** blight, foil, frustrate, ruin, spoil, thwart, undo ~*n.* **4.** bolt, dart, haste, onset, race, run, rush, sprint, spurt **5.** bit, drop, flavour, hint, little, pinch, smack, *soupçon,* sprinkling, suggestion, tinge, touch **6.** brio, élan, flair, flourish, panache, spirit, style, verve, vigour, vivacity

dashing bold, daring, debonair, elegant, exuberant, flamboyant, gallant, lively, plucky, spirited, stylish, swashbuckling

data details, documents, dope (*informal*), facts, figures, info (*informal*), information, input, materials, statistics

date *n.* **1.** age, epoch, era, period, stage, time **2.** appointment, assignation, engagement, meeting, rendezvous, tryst **3.** escort, friend, partner, steady (*informal*) **4. to date** so far, up to now, up to the present, up to this point, yet ~*vb.* **5.** assign a date to, determine the date of, fix the period of, put a date on **6.** become obsolete, be dated, show one's age **7. date from** *also* **date back to** belong to, come from, exist from, originate in

dated antiquated, archaic, obsolete, old-fashioned, old hat, out, outdated, outmoded, out-of-date, passé, unfashionable

daub *vb.* bedaub, coat, cover, deface, dirty, paint, plaster, slap on (*informal*), smear, smudge, spatter, splatter, stain, sully

daunting *adj.* alarming, challenging, demoralizing, difficult, discouraging, dismaying, dispiriting, formidable, frightening, intimidating, off-putting, onerous, unnerving, worrying

dauntless bold, brave, courageous, daring, doughty, fearless, gallant, gritty, heroic, indomitable, intrepid, lion-hearted, resolute, stouthearted, undaunted, unflinching, valiant, valorous

dawdle dally, delay, dilly-dally (*informal*), hang about, idle, lag, loaf, loiter, potter, trail, waste time

dawn *n.* **1.** aurora (*poetic*), crack of dawn, daybreak, daylight, morning, sunrise, sunup **2.** advent, beginning, birth, dawning, emergence, genesis, inception, onset, origin, outset, rise, start, unfolding ~*vb.* **3.** break, brighten, gleam, glimmer, grow light, lighten **4.** appear, begin, develop, emerge, initiate, open, originate, rise, unfold **5. dawn on** *also* **dawn upon** come into one's

final reckoning. **9 call it a day** to stop work or other activity. **10 day in, day out** every day without changing. **11 that'll be the day a** that is most unlikely to happen. **b** I look forward to that.

daybreak *n* the time in the morning when light first appears.

day centre *n* a place that provides care where elderly or handicapped people can spend the day.

daydream *n* **1** a pleasant fantasy indulged in while awake. ~*vb* **2** to indulge in idle fantasy. **daydreamer** *n*

Day-Glo *adj* (of a colour) luminous in daylight: *Day-Glo pink.*

daylight *n* **1** light from the sun. **2** daytime. **3** daybreak. **4 see daylight** to realize that the end of a difficult task is approaching. ~See also **daylights.**

daylight robbery *n Informal* blatant overcharging.

daylights *pl n Informal* **1 beat the living daylights out of someone** to beat someone soundly. **2 scare the living daylights out of someone** to frighten someone greatly.

daylight-saving time *n* time set one hour ahead of the local standard time, to provide extra daylight in the evening in summer.

Day of Atonement *n* same as **Yom Kippur.**

day release *n Brit* a system whereby workers go to college one day a week for vocational training.

day return *n* a reduced fare for a train or bus journey travelling both ways in one day.

day room *n* a communal living room in a hospital or similar institution.

daytime *n* the time from sunrise to sunset.

day-to-day *adj* routine; everyday.

daze *vb* **dazing, dazed 1** to cause to be in a state of confusion or shock. ~*n* **2** a state of confusion or shock: *in a daze.* **dazed** *adj*

dazzle *vb* **-zling, -zled 1** to impress greatly: *she was dazzled by his wit.* **2** to blind for a short time by sudden excessive light: *he passed two cars and they dazzled him with their headlights.* ~*n* **3** bright light that dazzles. **dazzling** *adj* **dazzlingly** *adv*

dB *or* **db** decibel(s).

DC 1 direct current. **2** District of Columbia.

DD Doctor of Divinity.

D-day *n* the day selected for the start of some operation.

DDS *or* **DDSc** Doctor of Dental Surgery *or* Science.

DDT *n* dichlorodiphenyltrichloroethane; an insecticide, now banned in the United Kingdom.

DE Delaware.

de- *prefix* indicating: **1** removal: *dethrone.* **2** reversal: *declassify.* **3** departure from: *decamp.*

deacon *n Christianity* **1** (in episcopal churches) an ordained minister ranking immediately below a priest. **2** (in some Protestant churches) a lay official who assists the minister.

deactivate *vb* **-vating, -vated** to make (a bomb or other explosive device) harmless.

dead *adj* **1** no longer alive. **2** not endowed with life; inanimate. **3** no longer in use or finished: *a dead language; a dead match.* **4** unresponsive. **5** (of a limb) numb. **6** complete or absolute: *there was dead silence.* **7** *Informal* very tired. **8** (of a place) lacking activity. **9** *Electronics* **a** drained of electric charge. **b** not connected to a source of electric charge. **10** *Sport* (of a ball) out of play. **11 dead from the neck up** *Informal* stupid. **12 dead to the world** *Informal* fast asleep. ~*n* **13** a period during which coldness or darkness is most intense: *the dead of winter.* ~*adv* **14** *Informal* extremely: *dead easy.* **15** suddenly and abruptly: *stop dead.* **16 dead on** exactly right.

deadbeat *n Informal, chiefly US & Canad* a lazy or socially undesirable person.

dead beat *adj Informal* exhausted.

dead duck *n Slang* something that is doomed to failure.

deaden *vb* to make (something) less intense: *drugs deaden the pain; heavy curtains deadened the echo.* **deadening** *adj*

dead end *n* **1** a cul-de-sac. **2** a situation in which further progress is impossible: *efforts to free the hostages had reached a dead end.*

deadhead *n US & Canad* **1** *Informal* a person who does not pay on a bus, at a game, etc. **2** *Informal* a commercial vehicle travelling empty. **3** *Slang* a dull person. **4** a log sticking out of the water.

THESAURUS

head, come to mind, cross one's mind, flash across one's mind, hit, occur, register (*informal*), strike

day 1. daylight, daylight hours, daytime, twenty-four hours, working day **2.** age, ascendancy, cycle, epoch, era, generation, height, heyday, period, prime, time, zenith **3.** date, particular day, point in time, set time, time **4. call it a day** *informal* end, finish, knock off (*informal*), leave off, pack it in (*slang*), pack up (*informal*), shut up shop, stop

daybreak break of day, crack of dawn, dawn, first light, morning, sunrise, sunup

daydream 1. *n.* castle in the air *or* in Spain, dream, fancy, fantasy, figment of the imagination, fond hope, musing, pipe dream, reverie, vision, wish **2.** *vb.* dream, fancy, fantasize, imagine, muse

daydreamer dreamer, Walter Mitty, wishful thinker

daylight 1. light of day, sunlight, sunshine **2.** broad day, daylight hours, daytime

daze 1. *vb.* amaze, astonish, astound, benumb, bewilder, blind, confuse, dazzle, dumbfound, flabbergast (*informal*), flummox, nonplus, numb, paralyse, perplex, shock, stagger, startle, stun, stupefy, surprise **2.** *n.* bewilderment, confusion, distraction, shock, stupor, trance

dazed at sea, baffled, bemused, bewildered, confused, disorientated, dizzy, dopey (*slang*), flabbergasted (*informal*), flummoxed, fuddled, groggy (*informal*), light-headed, muddled, nonplussed, numbed, perplexed, punch-drunk, shocked, staggered, stunned, stupefied, woozy (*informal*)

dazzle *vb.* **1.** amaze, astonish, awe, bowl over (*informal*), fascinate, hypnotize, impress, overawe, overpower, overwhelm, strike dumb, stupefy **2.** blind, confuse, daze ~*n.* **3.** brilliance, flash, glitter, magnificence, razzle-dazzle (*slang*), razzmatazz (*slang*), sparkle, splendour

dazzling brilliant, glittering, glorious, radiant, ravishing, scintillating, sensational (*informal*), shining, sparkling, splendid, stunning, sublime, superb, virtuoso

dead *adj.* **1.** deceased, defunct, departed, extinct, gone, inanimate, late, lifeless, passed away, perished **2.** barren, inactive, inoperative, not working, obsolete, stagnant, sterile, still, unemployed, unprofitable, useless **3.** cold, dull, frigid, glassy, glazed, indifferent, inert, lukewarm, numb, paralysed, torpid, unresponsive, wooden **4.** *figurative* absolute, complete, downright, entire, outright, thorough, total, unqualified, utter **5.** *informal* dead beat (*informal*), exhausted, spent, tired, worn out **6.** boring, dull, flat, insipid, stale, uninteresting, vapid ~*n.* **7.** depth, middle, midst ~*adv.* **8.** absolutely, completely, directly, entirely, exactly, totally

deaden alleviate, anaesthetize, benumb, blunt,

dead heat *n* a tie for first place between two or more participants in a race or contest.

dead letter *n* **1** a letter that cannot be delivered or returned due to lack of information. **2** a law or rule that is no longer enforced.

deadline *n* a time or date by which a job or task must be completed.

deadlock *n* a point in a dispute at which no agreement can be reached.

deadlocked *adj* having reached a deadlock.

dead loss *n Informal* a useless person or thing.

deadly *adj* **-lier, -liest 1** likely to cause death: *deadly poison.* **2** *Informal* extremely boring. *~adv, adj* **3** like or suggestive of death: *deadly pale.* **4** extremely: *she was being deadly serious.*

deadly nightshade *n* a poisonous plant with purple bell-shaped flowers and black berries.

dead man's handle *or* **pedal** *n* a safety device which only allows equipment to operate when a handle or pedal is being pressed.

dead march *n* solemn funeral music played to accompany a procession.

dead marine *n Austral & NZ informal* an empty beer bottle.

dead-nettle *n* a plant with leaves like nettles but without stinging hairs.

deadpan *adj, adv* with a deliberately emotionless face or manner.

dead reckoning *n* a method of establishing one's position using the distance and direction travelled.

dead set *adv* firmly decided: *he is dead set on leaving.*

dead weight *n* **1** a heavy weight or load. **2** the difference between the loaded and the unloaded weights of a ship.

dead wood *n Informal* people or things that are no longer useful.

deaf *adj* **1** unable to hear. **2 deaf to** refusing to listen or take notice of. **deafness** *n*

deaf-and-dumb *adj Offensive* unable to hear or speak.

deafen *vb* to make deaf, esp. momentarily by a loud noise. **deafening** *adj*

deaf-mute *n* a person who is unable to hear or speak.

deal[1] *n* **1** an agreement or transaction. **2** a particular type of treatment received: *a fair deal.* **3** a large amount: *the land alone is worth a good deal.* **4** *Cards* a player's turn to distribute the cards. **5 big deal** *Slang* an important matter: often used sarcastically. *~vb* **dealing, dealt (delt) 6** to inflict (a blow) on. **7** *Slang* to sell any illegal drug. **8 deal in** to engage in commercially. **9 deal out** to apportion or distribute. ~See also **deal with.**

deal[2] *n* **1** a plank of softwood timber. **2** the sawn wood of various coniferous trees.

dealer *n* **1** a person or organization whose business involves buying and selling things. **2** *Slang* a person who sells illegal drugs. **3** *Cards* the person who distributes the cards.

dealings *pl n* business relations with a person or organization.

dealt *vb* the past of **deal**[1].

deal with *vb* **1** to take action on: *he was not competent to deal with the legal aspects.* **2** to be concerned with: *I do not wish to deal with specifics.* **3** to do business with.

dean *n* **1** the chief administrative official of a college or university faculty. **2** *Chiefly Church of England* the chief administrator of a cathedral or collegiate church.

deanery *n, pl* **-eries 1** a place where a dean lives. **2** the parishes presided over by a rural dean.

dear *n* **1** (often used in direct address) someone regarded with affection. *~adj* **2** beloved; precious. **3 a** highly priced. **b** charging high prices. **4** a form of address used at the beginning of a letter before the name of the recipient: *Dear Mr Anderson.* **5 dear to** important or close to. *~interj* **6** an exclamation of surprise or dismay: *oh dear, I've broken it.* *~adv* **7** dearly: *her errors have cost her dear.* **dearly** *adv*

dearth (**dirth**) *n* an inadequate amount; scarcity.

death *n* **1** the permanent end of life in a person or animal. **2** an instance of this: *his sudden death.* **3** ending or destruction. **4 at death's door** likely to die soon. **5 catch one's death (of cold)** *Informal* to contract a severe cold. **6 like death warmed up** *Informal* looking or feeling very ill or very tired. **7 put to death** to execute. **8 to death a** until dead. **b** very much: *I had probably scared him to death.*

deathbed *n* the bed in which a person dies or is about to die.

deathblow *n* a thing or event that destroys hope.

THESAURUS

check, cushion, damp, dampen, diminish, dull, hush, impair, lessen, muffle, mute, numb, paralyse, quieten, reduce, smother, stifle, suppress, weaken

deadlock dead heat, draw, full stop, halt, impasse, stalemate, standoff, standstill, tie

deadly 1. baleful, dangerous, death-dealing, deathly, destructive, fatal, lethal, malignant, mortal, noxious, pernicious, poisonous, venomous **2.** *informal* boring, dull, mind-numbing, monotonous, tedious, uninteresting, wearisome **3.** ashen, deathlike, deathly, ghastly, ghostly, pallid, wan, white **4.** accurate, effective, exact, on target, precise, sure, true, unerring, unfailing

deaf *adj.* **1.** hard of hearing, stone deaf, without hearing **2.** indifferent, oblivious, unconcerned, unhearing, unmoved

deafen drown out, make deaf, split *or* burst the eardrums

deafening booming, ear-piercing, ear-splitting, intense, overpowering, piercing, resounding, ringing, thunderous

deal *n.* **1.** *informal* agreement, arrangement, bargain, contract, pact, transaction, understanding **2.** amount, degree, distribution, extent, portion, quantity, share, transaction **3.** hand, round, shuffle *~vb.* **4.** bargain, buy and sell, do business, negotiate, sell, stock, trade, traffic, treat (with) **5.** allot, apportion, assign, bestow, dispense, distribute, divide, dole out, give, mete out, reward, share

dealer chandler, marketer, merchandiser, merchant, purveyor, supplier, trader, tradesman, wholesaler

dealings business, business relations, commerce, trade, traffic, transactions, truck

deal with 1. attend to, cope with, handle, manage, oversee, see to, take care of, treat **2.** be about, concern, consider, treat (of)

dear *n.* **1.** angel, baby, beloved, darling, honey (*U.S.*), loved one *~adj.* **2.** beloved, cherished, close, darling, esteemed, familiar, favourite, intimate, precious, prized, respected, treasured **3.** at a premium, costly, expensive, high-priced, overpriced, pricey (*informal*) *~adv.* **4.** at a heavy cost, at a high price, at great cost, dearly

dearly 1. extremely, greatly, profoundly, very much **2.** affectionately, devotedly, fondly, lovingly, tenderly **3.** at a heavy cost, at a high price, at great cost, dear

death 1. bereavement, curtains (*informal*), decease,

death certificate *n* a document signed by a doctor certifying the death of a person and stating the cause of death if known.
death duty *n* the former name for **inheritance tax.**
death knell *n* something that heralds death or destruction.
deathless *adj* everlasting because of fine qualities: *highbrow, deathless, and often endless prose.*
deathly *adj* **1** resembling death: *a deathly pallor.* **2** deadly.
death mask *n* a cast taken from the face of a person who has recently died.
death rate *n* the ratio of deaths in an area or group to the population of that area or group.
death row *n US* part of a prison where convicts awaiting execution are imprisoned.
death's-head *n* a human skull or a representation of one.
deathtrap *n* a place or vehicle considered very unsafe.
death warrant *n* **1** the official authorization for carrying out a sentence of death. **2 sign one's (own) death warrant** to cause one's own destruction.
deathwatch beetle *n* a beetle that bores into wood and produces a tapping sound.
deb *n Informal* a debutante.
debacle (day-**bah**-kl) *n* something that ends in a disastrous failure, esp. because it has not been properly planned.
debar *vb* **-barring, -barred** to prevent (someone) from doing something.
debase *vb* **-basing, -based** to lower in quality, character, or value. **debasement** *n*
debatable *adj* not absolutely certain: *her motives are highly debatable.*
debate *n* **1** a discussion. **2** a formal discussion, as in a parliament, in which opposing arguments are put forward. *~vb* **-bating, -bated 3** to discuss (something) formally. **4** to consider (possible courses of action).
debauch (dib-**bawch**) *vb* to make someone bad or corrupt, esp. sexually.
debauched *adj* immoral; sexually corrupt.
debauchery *n* corrupt or socially unacceptable behaviour.
debenture *n* a long-term bond, bearing fixed interest and usually unsecured, issued by a company or governmental agency. **debentured** *adj*
debenture stock *n* shares issued by a company, guaranteeing a fixed return at regular intervals.
debilitate *vb* **-tating, -tated** to make gradually weaker. **debilitation** *n* **debilitating** *adj*
debility *n, pl* **-ties** a state of weakness, esp. caused by illness.
debit *n* **1** the money, or a record of the money, withdrawn from a person's bank account. **2** *Accounting* **a** acknowledgment of a sum owing by entry on the left side of an account. **b** an entry or the total of entries on this side. *~vb* **-iting, -ited 3** to charge (an account) with a debt. **4** *Accounting* to record (an item) as a debit in an account.
debonair *or* **debonnaire** *adj* (of a man) confident, charming, and well-dressed.
debouch *vb* **1** (esp. of troops) to move into a more open space. **2** (of a river, glacier, etc.) to flow into a larger area or body. **debouchment** *n*
debrief *vb* to interrogate (a soldier, diplomat, etc.) on the completion of a mission. **debriefing** *n*
debris (**deb**-ree) *n* **1** fragments of something destroyed; rubble. **2** a mass of loose stones and earth.
debt *n* **1** a sum of money owed. **2 bad debt** a debt that is unlikely to be paid. **3 in debt** owing money. **4 in someone's debt** grateful to someone for his or her help: *I couldn't have managed without you – I'm in your debt.*
debt of honour *n* a debt that is morally but not legally binding.
debtor *n* a person who owes money.
debug *vb* **-bugging, -bugged** *Informal* **1** to locate and remove defects in (a computer program). **2** to remove concealed microphones from (a room or telephone).
debunk *vb Informal* to expose the falseness of: *many commonly held myths are debunked by the book.* **debunker** *n*
debut (**day**-byoo) *n* the first public appearance of a performer.

THESAURUS

demise, departure, dying, end, exit, loss, passing, quietus, release **2.** annihilation, destruction, downfall, eradication, extermination, extinction, finish, grave, obliteration, ruin, ruination, undoing
deathless eternal, everlasting, immortal, imperishable, incorruptible, timeless, undying
deathly 1. cadaverous, deathlike, gaunt, ghastly, grim, haggard, pale, pallid, wan **2.** deadly, extreme, fatal, intense, mortal, terrible
debacle catastrophe, collapse, defeat, devastation, disaster, downfall, fiasco, reversal, rout, ruin, ruination
debase bastardize, cheapen, contaminate, corrupt, defile, degrade, demean, devalue, disgrace, drag down, humble, humiliate, impair, lower, pollute, reduce, shame, taint, vitiate
debased 1. adulterated, devalued, impure, lowered, mixed, polluted, reduced **2.** abandoned, base, corrupt, debauched, degraded, depraved, fallen, low, perverted, sordid, vile
debasement 1. adulteration, contamination, depreciation, devaluation, pollution, reduction **2.** abasement, baseness, corruption, degradation, depravation, perversion
debatable arguable, borderline, controversial, disputable, doubtful, dubious, iffy (*informal*), in dispute, moot, open to question, problematical, questionable, uncertain, undecided, unsettled
debate *n.* **1.** argument, contention, controversy, discussion, disputation, dispute, polemic, row *~vb.* **2.** argue, contend, contest, discuss, dispute, question, wrangle **3.** cogitate, consider, deliberate, meditate upon, mull over, ponder, reflect, revolve, ruminate, weigh
debilitate enervate, enfeeble, exhaust, incapacitate, prostrate, sap, undermine, weaken, wear out
debility decrepitude, enervation, enfeeblement, exhaustion, faintness, feebleness, frailty, incapacity, infirmity, languor, malaise, sickliness, weakness
debonair affable, charming, cheerful, courteous, dashing, elegant, jaunty, light-hearted, refined, smooth, sprightly, suave, urbane, well-bred
debris bits, detritus, fragments, litter, pieces, remains, rubbish, rubble, ruins, waste, wreckage
debt 1. arrears, bill, claim, commitment, debit, due, duty, liability, obligation, score **2. in debt** accountable, in arrears, in hock (*informal, chiefly U.S.*), in the red (*informal*), liable, owing, responsible
debtor borrower, defaulter, insolvent, mortgagor

debutante (**day**-byoo-tont) *n* a young upper-class woman who is formally presented to society.

Dec. December.

decade *n* a period of ten years.

decadence (**deck**-a-denss) *n* a decline in morality or culture. **decadent** *adj*

decaf (**dee**-kaf) *Informal* ~*n* **1** decaffeinated coffee. ~*adj* **2** decaffeinated.

decaffeinated (dee-**kaf**-fin-ate-id) *adj* with the caffeine removed: *decaffeinated tea.*

decagon *n Geom* a figure with ten sides. **decagonal** *adj*

decahedron (deck-a-**heed**-ron) *n* a solid figure with ten plane faces. **decahedral** *adj*

decalitre *or US* **decaliter** *n* a measure of volume equivalent to 10 litres.

Decalogue *n* same as **Ten Commandments.**

decametre *or US* **decameter** *n* a unit of length equal to ten metres.

decamp *vb* to leave secretly or suddenly.

decant *vb* **1** to pour (a liquid, esp. wine) from one container to another. **2** to rehouse (people) while their homes are being renovated.

decanter *n* a stoppered bottle into which a drink is poured for serving.

decapitate *vb* **-tating, -tated** to behead. **decapitation** *n*

decapod *n* **1** a creature, such as a crab, with five pairs of walking limbs. **2** a creature, such as a squid, with eight short tentacles and two longer ones.

decarbonize *or* **-ise** *vb* **-izing, -ized** *or* **-ising, -ised** to remove carbon from (an internal-combustion engine). **decarbonization** *or* **-isation** *n*

decathlon *n* an athletic contest in which each athlete competes in ten different events. **decathlete** *n*

decay *vb* **1** to decline gradually in health, prosperity, or quality. **2** to rot or cause to rot. **3** *Physics* (of an atomic nucleus) to undergo radioactive disintegration. ~*n* **4** the process of something rotting: *too much sugar can cause tooth decay.* **5** the state brought about by this process. **6** *Physics* disintegration of a nucleus, occurring spontaneously or as a result of electron capture.

decease *n Formal* death.

deceased *adj Formal* **1** dead. ~*n* **2** a dead person: *the deceased.*

deceit *n* behaviour intended to deceive.

deceitful *adj* full of deceit.

deceive *vb* **-ceiving, -ceived 1** to mislead by lying. **2 deceive oneself** to refuse to acknowledge something one knows to be true. **3** to be unfaithful to (one's sexual partner).

decelerate *vb* **-ating, -ated** to slow down. **deceleration** *n*

December *n* the twelfth month of the year.

decencies *pl n* generally accepted standards of good behaviour.

decency *n* conformity to the prevailing standards of what is right.

decennial *adj* **1** lasting for ten years. **2** occurring every ten years.

decent *adj* **1** conforming to an acceptable standard or quality: *a decent living wage; he's made a few decent films.* **2** polite or respectable: *he's a decent man.* **3** fitting or proper: *that's the decent thing to do.* **4** conforming to conventions of sexual behaviour. **5** *Informal* kind; generous: *she was pretty decent to me.* **decently** *adv*

decentralize *or* **-ise** *vb* **-izing, -ized** *or* **-ising, -ised** to reorganize into smaller local units. **decentralization** *or* **-isation** *n*

THESAURUS

debunk cut down to size, deflate, disparage, expose, lampoon, mock, ridicule, show up

debut beginning, entrance, first appearance, inauguration, initiation, introduction, launching, presentation

decadence corruption, debasement, decay, decline, degeneration, deterioration, dissipation, dissolution, fall, perversion, retrogression

decadent corrupt, debased, debauched, decaying, declining, degenerate, degraded, depraved, dissolute, immoral, self-indulgent

decapitate behead, execute, guillotine

decay *vb.* **1.** atrophy, crumble, decline, degenerate, deteriorate, disintegrate, dissolve, dwindle, moulder, shrivel, sink, spoil, wane, waste away, wear away, wither **2.** corrode, decompose, mortify, perish, putrefy, rot ~*n.* **3.** atrophy, collapse, decadence, decline, degeneracy, degeneration, deterioration, dying, fading, failing, wasting, withering **4.** caries, decomposition, gangrene, mortification, perishing, putrefaction, putrescence, putridity, rot, rotting

decayed bad, corroded, decomposed, perished, putrefied, putrid, rank, rotten, spoiled, wasted, withered

decaying crumbling, deteriorating, disintegrating, gangrenous, perishing, rotting, wasting away, wearing away

decease *n.* death, demise, departure, dissolution, dying, release

deceased *adj.* dead, defunct, departed, expired, finished, former, gone, late, lifeless, lost

deceit artifice, cheating, chicanery, craftiness, cunning, deceitfulness, deception, dissimulation, double-dealing, duplicity, fraud, fraudulence, guile, hypocrisy, imposition, imposture, misrepresentation, pretence, ruse, scam (*slang*), slyness, stratagem, subterfuge, swindle, treachery, trick, trickery, underhandedness, wile

deceitful crafty, deceiving, deceptive, designing, dishonest, disingenuous, double-dealing, duplicitous, false, fraudulent, guileful, hypocritical, insincere, knavish (*archaic*), sneaky, treacherous, tricky, two-faced, underhand, untrustworthy

deceive 1. bamboozle (*informal*), beguile, betray, cheat, con (*informal*), cozen (*literary*), delude, disappoint, double-cross (*informal*), dupe, ensnare, entrap, fool, hoax, hoodwink, impose upon, kid (*informal*), lead (someone) on (*informal*), mislead, outwit, pull a fast one (*slang*), pull the wool over (someone's) eyes, sting (*informal*), swindle, take for a ride (*informal*), take in (*informal*), trick **2. be deceived by** be made a fool of, be taken in (by), be the dupe of, bite, fall for, fall into a trap, swallow (*informal*), swallow hook, line, and sinker (*informal*), take the bait

decency appropriateness, civility, correctness, courtesy, decorum, etiquette, fitness, good form, good manners, modesty, propriety, respectability, seemliness

decent 1. acceptable, adequate, ample, average, competent, fair, passable, reasonable, satisfactory, sufficient, tolerable **2.** appropriate, becoming, befitting, chaste, comely, decorous, delicate, fit, fitting, modest, nice, polite, presentable, proper, pure, respectable, seemly, suitable **3.** accommodating, courteous, friendly, generous, gracious, helpful, kind, obliging, thoughtful

deception 1. craftiness, cunning, deceit, deceitfulness, deceptiveness, dissimulation, duplicity, fraud, guile, hypocrisy, imposition, insincerity, legerdemain, treachery, trickery **2.** artifice, bluff, canard, cheat,

deception *n* **1** the act of deceiving someone or the state of being deceived. **2** something that deceives; trick.

deceptive *adj* likely or designed to deceive. **deceptively** *adv* **deceptiveness** *n*

deci- *combining form* denoting one tenth: *decimetre.*

decibel *n* a unit for comparing two power levels or measuring the intensity of a sound.

decide *vb* **-ciding, -cided 1** to reach a decision: *we must decide on suitable action; he decided to stay on.* **2** to cause to reach a decision. **3** to settle (a question): *possible profits decided the issue.* **4** to influence the outcome of (a contest) decisively: *the goal that decided the match came just before half-time.*

decided *adj* **1** definite or noticeable: *a decided improvement.* **2** strong and definite: *he has decided views on the matter.* **decidedly** *adv*

deciduous *adj* **1** (of a tree) shedding all leaves annually. **2** (of antlers or teeth) being shed at the end of a period of growth.

decilitre *or US* **deciliter** *n* a measure of volume equivalent to one tenth of a litre.

decimal *n* **1** a fraction written in the form of a dot followed by one or more numbers, for example $\cdot 2 = {}^2\!/_{10}$. *~adj* **2** relating to or using powers of ten. **3** expressed as a decimal.

decimal currency *n* a system of currency in which the units are parts or powers of ten.

decimalize *or* **-ise** *vb* **-izing, -ized** *or* **-ising, -ised** to change (a system or number) to the decimal system. **decimalization** *or* **-isation** *n*

decimal point *n* the dot between the unit and the fraction of a number in the decimal system.

decimal system *n* a number system with a base of ten, in which numbers are expressed by combinations of the digits 0 to 9.

decimate *vb* **-mating, -mated** to destroy or kill a large proportion of. **decimation** *n*

decimetre *or US* **decimeter** *n* a unit of length equal to one tenth of a metre.

decipher *vb* **1** to make out the meaning of (something obscure or illegible). **2** to convert from code into plain text. **decipherable** *adj*

decision *n* **1** a choice or judgment made about something. **2** the act of making up one's mind. **3** the ability to make quick and definite decisions.

decisive *adj* **1** having great influence on the result of something: *the decisive goal was scored in the closing minutes.* **2** having the ability to make quick decisions. **decisively** *adv* **decisiveness** *n*

deck *n* **1** an area of a ship that forms a floor, at any level. **2** a similar area in a bus. **3** same as **tape deck. 4** *US* a pack of playing cards. **5 clear the decks** *Informal* to prepare for action, as by removing obstacles.

deck chair *n* a folding chair with a wooden frame and a canvas seat.

deckle edge *n* a rough edge on paper, often left as ornamentation. **deckle-edged** *adj*

deck out *vb* to make more attractive by decorating: *the village was decked out in the blue-and-white flags.*

declaim *vb* **1** to speak loudly and dramatically. **2 declaim against** to protest against loudly and publicly. **declamation** *n* **declamatory** *adj*

declaration *n* **1** a firm, emphatic statement. **2** an official announcement or statement. **declaratory** *adj*

declare *vb* **-claring, -clared 1** to state firmly and forcefully. **2** to announce publicly or officially: *a state of emergency has been declared.* **3** to state officially that (someone or something) is as specified: *he was declared fit to play.* **4** to acknowledge (dutiable goods or income) for tax purposes. **5** *Cards* to decide (the trump suit) by making the winning bid. **6** *Cricket* to bring an innings to an end before the last batsman is out. **7 declare for** *or* **against** to state one's support or opposition for something.

declassify *vb* **-fies, -fying, -fied** to state officially that (information or a document) is no longer secret. **declassification** *n*

declension *n Grammar* changes in the form of nouns, pronouns, or adjectives to show case, number, and gender.

declination *n* **1** *Astron* the angular distance of a star or planet north or south from the celestial equator. **2** the angle made by a compass needle with the direction of the geographical north pole.

decline *vb* **-clining, -clined 1** to become smaller, weaker, or less important. **2** to politely refuse to ac-

THESAURUS

decoy, feint, fraud, hoax, hokum (*slang, chiefly U.S. & Canad.*), illusion, imposture, leg-pull (*Brit. informal*), lie, ruse, sham, snare, stratagem, subterfuge, trick, wile

deceptive ambiguous, deceitful, delusive, dishonest, fake, fallacious, false, fraudulent, illusory, misleading, mock, specious, spurious, unreliable

decide adjudge, adjudicate, choose, come to a conclusion, commit oneself, conclude, decree, determine, make a decision, make up one's mind, purpose, reach *or* come to a decision, resolve, settle

decided 1. absolute, categorical, certain, clear-cut, definite, distinct, express, indisputable, positive, pronounced, unambiguous, undeniable, undisputed, unequivocal, unquestionable **2.** assertive, decisive, deliberate, determined, emphatic, firm, resolute, strong-willed, unfaltering, unhesitating

decidedly absolutely, certainly, clearly, decisively, distinctly, downright, positively, unequivocally, unmistakably

decipher crack, decode, figure out (*informal*), interpret, make out, read, reveal, solve, understand, unfold, unravel

decision 1. arbitration, conclusion, finding, judgment, outcome, resolution, result, ruling, sentence, settlement, verdict **2.** decisiveness, determination, firmness, purpose, purposefulness, resoluteness, resolution, resolve, strength of mind *or* will

decisive 1. conclusive, critical, crucial, definite, definitive, fateful, final, influential, momentous, positive, significant **2.** decided, determined, firm, forceful, incisive, resolute, strong-minded, trenchant

deck out *vb.* adorn, beautify, bedeck, decorate, doll up (*slang*), dress, embellish, festoon, garland, grace, ornament, prettify, rig out, trick out

declaim 1. harangue, hold forth, lecture, proclaim, rant, recite, speak **2. declaim against** attack, decry, denounce, inveigh, rail

declamation address, harangue, lecture, oration, rant, recitation, speech, tirade

declaration 1. acknowledgment, affirmation, assertion, attestation, averment, avowal, deposition, disclosure, protestation, revelation, statement, testimony **2.** announcement, edict, manifesto, notification, proclamation, profession, promulgation, pronouncement

declare 1. affirm, announce, assert, asseverate, attest, aver, avow, certify, claim, confirm, maintain, proclaim, profess, pronounce, state, swear, testify, utter, validate **2.** confess, convey, disclose, make known, manifest, reveal, show

decline *vb.* **1.** decay, decrease, degenerate, deteriorate, diminish, drop, dwindle, ebb, fade, fail, fall, fall

cept or do (something). **3** *Grammar* to list the inflections of (a noun, pronoun, or adjective). ~*n* **4** a gradual weakening or loss.

declivity *n, pl* **-ties** a downward slope. **declivitous** *adj*

declutch *vb* to disengage the clutch of a motor vehicle.

decoct *vb* to extract the essence from (a substance) by boiling. **decoction** *n*

decode *vb* **-coding, -coded** to convert from code into ordinary language. **decoder** *n*

decoke *vb* **-coking, -coked** same as **decarbonize.**

décolletage (day-kol-**tahzh**) *n* a low-cut dress or neckline.

décolleté (day-**kol**-tay) *adj* (of a woman's garment) low-cut.

decommission *vb* to dismantle (an industrial plant or nuclear reactor) to an extent such that it can be safely abandoned.

decompose *vb* **-posing, -posed 1** to rot. **2** to break up or separate into constituent parts. **decomposition** *n*

decompress *vb* **1** to free from pressure. **2** to return (a diver) to normal atmospheric pressure. **decompression** *n*

decompression sickness *n* a disorder characterized by severe pain and difficulty in breathing caused by a sudden and sustained change in atmospheric pressure.

decongestant *n* a drug that relieves nasal congestion.

decontaminate *vb* **-nating, -nated** to make (a place or object) safe by removing poisons, radioactivity, etc. **decontamination** *n*

decor (**day**-core) *n* a style or scheme of interior decoration and furnishings in a room or house.

decorate *vb* **-rating, -rated 1** to make more attractive by adding some ornament or colour. **2** to paint or wallpaper. **3** to confer a mark of distinction, esp. a medal, upon. **decorative** *adj* **decorator** *n*

decoration *n* **1** an addition that makes something more attractive or ornate. **2** the way in which a room or building is decorated. **3** something, esp. a medal, conferred as a mark of honour.

decorous (**deck**-or-uss) *adj* polite, calm, and sensible in behaviour. **decorously** *adv* **decorousness** *n*

decorum (dik-**core**-um) *n* polite and socially correct behaviour.

decoy *n* **1** a person or thing used to lure someone into danger. **2** an image of a bird or animal, used to lure game into a trap or within shooting range. ~*vb* **3** to lure into danger by means of a decoy.

decrease *vb* **-creasing, -creased 1** to make or become less in size, strength, or quantity. ~*n* **2** a lessening; reduction. **3** the amount by which something has been diminished. **decreasing** *adj* **decreasingly** *adv*

decree *n* **1** a law made by someone in authority. **2** a judgment of a court. ~*vb* **decreeing, decreed 3** to order by decree.

decree absolute *n* the final decree in divorce proceedings, which leaves the parties free to remarry.

decree nisi *n* a provisional decree in divorce proceedings, which will later be made absolute unless cause is shown why it should not.

decrepit *adj* weakened or worn out by age or long use. **decrepitude** *n*

decretal *n RC Church* a papal decree.

decry *vb* **-cries, -crying, -cried** to express open disapproval of.

dedicate *vb* **-cating, -cated 1** to devote (oneself or one's time) wholly to a special purpose or cause. **2** to inscribe or address (a book, piece of music, etc.) to someone as a token of affection or respect. **3** to play

THESAURUS

off, flag, languish, lessen, pine, shrink, sink, wane, weaken, worsen **2.** abstain, avoid, deny, forgo, refuse, reject, say 'no', send one's regrets, turn down ~*n.* **3.** abatement, deterioration, diminution, downturn, drop, dwindling, falling off, lessening, recession, slump, weakening, worsening

decompose 1. break up, crumble, decay, fall apart, fester, putrefy, rot, spoil **2.** analyse, break down, break up, disintegrate, dissect, dissolve, distil, separate

decomposition breakdown, corruption, decay, disintegration, dissolution, division, putrefaction, putrescence, rot

decor colour scheme, decoration, furnishing style, ornamentation

decorate 1. adorn, beautify, bedeck, deck, embellish, enrich, festoon, grace, ornament, trim **2.** colour, do up (*informal*), paint, paper, renovate, wallpaper **3.** cite, honour, pin a medal on

decoration 1. adornment, beautification, elaboration, embellishment, enrichment, garnishing, ornamentation, trimming **2.** bauble, cartouche, curlicue, festoon, flounce, flourish, frill, furbelows, garnish, ornament, scroll, spangle, trimmings, trinket **3.** award, badge, colours, emblem, garter, medal, order, ribbon, star

decorative adorning, beautifying, enhancing, fancy, nonfunctional, ornamental, pretty

decorous appropriate, becoming, befitting, comely, correct, decent, dignified, fit, fitting, mannerly, polite, proper, refined, sedate, seemly, staid, suitable, well-behaved

decorum behaviour, breeding, courtliness, decency, deportment, dignity, etiquette, gentility, good grace, good manners, gravity, politeness, propriety, protocol, respectability, seemliness

decoy 1. *n.* attraction, bait, ensnarement, enticement, inducement, lure, pretence, trap **2.** *vb.* allure, bait, deceive, ensnare, entice, entrap, inveigle, lure, seduce, tempt

decrease 1. *vb.* abate, contract, curtail, cut down, decline, diminish, drop, dwindle, ease, fall off, lessen, lower, peter out, reduce, shrink, slacken, subside, wane **2.** *n.* abatement, contraction, cutback, decline, diminution, downturn, dwindling, ebb, falling off, lessening, loss, reduction, shrinkage, subsidence

decree 1. *n.* act, canon, command, demand, dictum, edict, enactment, law, mandate, order, ordinance, precept, proclamation, regulation, ruling, statute **2.** *vb.* command, decide, demand, determine, dictate, enact, establish, lay down, ordain, order, prescribe, proclaim, pronounce, rule

decrepit aged, antiquated, battered, beat-up (*informal*), broken-down, crippled, debilitated, deteriorated, dilapidated, doddering, effete, feeble, frail, incapacitated, infirm, ramshackle, rickety, run-down, superannuated, tumble-down, wasted, weak, weather-beaten, worn-out

decry abuse, belittle, blame, blast, censure, condemn, criticize, cry down, denounce, depreciate, derogate, detract, devalue, discredit, disparage, excoriate, lambast(e), put down, rail against, run down, tear into (*informal*), traduce

dedicate 1. commit, devote, give over to, pledge, surrender **2.** address, assign, inscribe, offer **3.** bless, consecrate, hallow, sanctify, set apart

(a record) on radio for someone as a greeting. **4** to set apart for sacred uses.

dedicated *adj* **1** devoted to a particular purpose or cause. **2** *Computers* designed to fulfil one function.

dedication *n* **1** wholehearted devotion. **2** an inscription in a book dedicating it to a person.

deduce *vb* **-ducing, -duced** to reach (a conclusion) by reasoning from evidence; work out. **deducible** *adj*

deduct *vb* to subtract (a number, quantity, or part).

deductible *adj* **1** capable of being deducted. **2** *US* tax-deductible.

deduction *n* **1** the act or process of subtracting. **2** something that is deducted. **3** *Logic* **a** a process of reasoning by which a conclusion necessarily follows from a set of general premises. **b** a conclusion reached by this process. **deductive** *adj*

deed *n* **1** something that is done. **2** a notable achievement. **3** action as opposed to words. **4** *Law* a legal document, esp. one concerning the ownership of property.

deed box *n* a strong box in which deeds and other documents are kept.

deed poll *n Law* a deed made by one party only, esp. to change one's name.

deejay *n Informal* a disc jockey.

deem *vb* to judge or consider: *common sense is deemed to be a virtue.*

deep *adj* **1** extending or situated far down from a surface: *a deep ditch.* **2** extending or situated far inwards, backwards, or sideways. **3** of a specified dimension downwards, inwards, or backwards: *six metres deep.* **4** coming from or penetrating to a great depth. **5** difficult to understand. **6** of great intensity: *deep doubts.* **7** **deep in** totally absorbed in: *deep in conversation.* **8** (of a colour) intense or dark. **9** low in pitch: *a deep laugh.* **10** **go off the deep end** *Informal* to lose one's temper. **11** **in deep water** *Informal* in a tricky position or in trouble. *~n* **12** any deep place on land or under water. **13** **the deep a** *Poetic* the ocean. **b** *Cricket* the area of the field relatively far from the pitch. **14** the most profound, intense, or central part: *the deep of winter.* *~adv* **15** late: *deep into the night.* **16** profoundly or intensely: *deep down I was afraid it was all my fault.* **deeply** *adv*

deepen *vb* to make or become deeper or more intense.

deep-freeze *n* **1** same as **freezer.** *~vb* **-freezing, -froze, -frozen 2** to freeze or keep in a deep-freeze.

deep-fry *vb* **-fries, -frying, -fried** to cook in hot oil deep enough to completely cover the food.

deep-laid *adj* (of a plan) carefully worked out and kept secret.

deep-rooted *or* **deep-seated** *adj* (of ideas, beliefs, etc.) firmly fixed or held.

deer *n, pl* **deer** *or* **deers** a large hoofed mammal that lives wild in parts of Britain.

deerstalker *n* a cloth hat with peaks at the front and back and earflaps.

de-escalate *vb* to reduce the intensity of (a problem or situation). **de-escalation** *n*

def *adj* **deffer, deffest** *Slang* very good.

deface *vb* **-facing, -faced** to deliberately spoil the surface or appearance of. **defacement** *n*

de facto *adv* **1** in fact. *~adj* **2** existing in fact, whether legally recognized or not.

defalcate *vb* **-cating, -cated** *Law* to make wrong use of funds entrusted to one. **defalcation** *n*

defame *vb* **-faming, -famed** to attack the good reputation of. **defamation** *n* **defamatory** (dif-**fam**-a-tree) *adj*

default *n* **1** a failure to do something, esp. to meet a financial obligation or to appear in court. **2** *Computers* an instruction to a computer to select a particular option unless the user specifies otherwise. **3** **by default** happening because something else has not happened: *they gained a colony by default because no other*

THESAURUS

dedicated committed, devoted, enthusiastic, given over to, purposeful, single-minded, sworn, wholehearted, zealous

dedication **1.** adherence, allegiance, commitment, devotedness, devotion, faithfulness, loyalty, single-mindedness, wholeheartedness **2.** address, inscription, message

deduce conclude, derive, draw, gather, glean, infer, reason, take to mean, understand

deduct decrease by, knock off (*informal*), reduce by, remove, subtract, take away, take from, take off, take out, withdraw

deduction **1.** abatement, allowance, decrease, diminution, discount, reduction, subtraction, withdrawal **2.** assumption, conclusion, consequence, corollary, finding, inference, reasoning, result

deed **1.** achievement, act, action, exploit, fact, feat, performance, reality, truth **2.** *Law* contract, document, indenture, instrument, title, title deed, transaction

deem account, believe, conceive, consider, esteem, estimate, hold, imagine, judge, reckon, regard, suppose, think

deep *adj.* **1.** abyssal, bottomless, far, profound, unfathomable, yawning **2.** abstract, abstruse, arcane, esoteric, hidden, mysterious, obscure, recondite, secret **3.** extreme, grave, great, intense, profound, unqualified **4.** absorbed, engrossed, immersed, lost, preoccupied, rapt **5.** *of a colour* dark, intense, rich, strong, vivid **6.** *of a sound* bass, booming, full-toned, low, low-pitched, resonant, sonorous *~n.* **7.** *usually preceded by* **the** briny (*informal*), high seas, main, ocean, sea **8.** culmination, dead, middle, mid point *~adv.* **9.** deeply, far down, far into, late

deepen dig out, dredge, excavate, grow, hollow, increase, intensify, magnify, reinforce, scoop out, scrape out, strengthen

deeply acutely, affectingly, completely, distressingly, gravely, intensely, mournfully, movingly, passionately, profoundly, seriously, severely, thoroughly, to the heart, to the quick

deep-rooted *or* **deep-seated** confirmed, entrenched, fixed, ineradicable, ingrained, inveterate, rooted, settled, subconscious, unconscious

deface blemish, deform, disfigure, impair, injure, mar, mutilate, obliterate, spoil, sully, tarnish, vandalize

defacement blemish, damage, destruction, disfigurement, distortion, impairment, injury, mutilation, vandalism

de facto **1.** *adv.* actually, in effect, in fact, in reality, really **2.** *adj.* actual, existing, real

defamation aspersion, calumny, character assassination, denigration, disparagement, libel, obloquy, opprobrium, scandal, slander, slur, smear, traducement, vilification

defamatory abusive, denigrating, derogatory, disparaging, injurious, insulting, libellous, slanderous, vilifying, vituperative

defame bad-mouth (*slang, chiefly U.S. & Canad.*), besmirch, blacken, calumniate, cast a slur on, cast aspersions on, denigrate, detract, discredit, disgrace, dishonour, disparage, knock (*informal*), libel, malign,

European power wanted it. **4 in default of** in the absence of. ~*vb* **5** to fail to fulfil an obligation, esp. to make payment when due. **defaulter** *n*

defeat *vb* **1** to win a victory over. **2** to thwart or frustrate: *this accident has defeated all his hopes of winning.* ~*n* **3** the act of defeating or state of being defeated.

defeatism *n* a ready acceptance or expectation of defeat. **defeatist** *n, adj*

defecate *vb* **-cating, -cated** to discharge waste from the body through the anus. **defecation** *n*

defect *n* **1** an imperfection or blemish. ~*vb* **2** to desert one's country or cause to join the opposing forces. **defection** *n* **defector** *n*

defective *adj* imperfect or faulty: *defective hearing.*

defence *or US* **defense** *n* **1** resistance against attack. **2** something that provides such resistance. **3** an argument or piece of writing in support of something that has been criticized or questioned. **4** a country's military resources. **5** *Law* a defendant's denial of the truth of a charge. **6** *Law* the defendant and his or her legal advisers collectively. **7** *Sport* the players in a team whose function is to prevent the opposing team from scoring. **8 defences** fortifications. **defenceless** *or US* **defenseless** *adj*

defend *vb* **1** to protect from harm or danger. **2** to support in the face of criticism: *I spoke up to defend her.* **3** to represent (a defendant) in court. **4** to protect (a title or championship) against a challenge. **defender** *n*

defendant *n* a person accused of a crime.

defensible *adj* capable of being defended because believed to be right. **defensibility** *n*

defensive *adj* **1** intended for defence. **2** guarding against criticism or exposure of one's failings: *he can be highly defensive and wary.* ~*n* **3 on the defensive** in a position of defence, as in being ready to reject criticism. **defensively** *adv*

defer[1] *vb* **-ferring, -ferred** to delay until a future time; postpone: *payment was deferred indefinitely.* **deferment** *or* **deferral** *n*

defer[2] *vb* **-ferring, -ferred defer to** to comply with the wishes (of).

deference *n* polite and respectful behaviour.

deferential *adj* showing respect. **deferentially** *adv*

defiance *n* open resistance to authority or opposition. **defiant** *adj*

deficiency *n, pl* **-cies 1** the state of being deficient. **2** a lack or shortage.

deficiency disease *n* any condition, such as scur-

THESAURUS

rubbish (*informal*), slag (off) (*slang*), slander, smear, speak evil of, stigmatize, traduce, vilify, vituperate

default 1. *n.* absence, defect, deficiency, dereliction, failure, fault, lack, lapse, neglect, nonpayment, omission, want **2.** *vb.* bilk, defraud, dodge, evade, fail, neglect, rat (*informal*), swindle, welsh (*slang*)

defaulter delinquent, embezzler, nonpayer, offender

defeat *vb.* **1.** beat, blow out of the water (*slang*), clobber (*slang*), conquer, crush, lick (*informal*), master, overpower, overthrow, overwhelm, quell, repulse, rout, run rings around (*informal*), subdue, subjugate, tank (*slang*), undo, vanquish, wipe the floor with (*informal*) **2.** baffle, balk, confound, disappoint, foil, frustrate, get the better of, ruin, thwart ~*n.* **3.** beating, conquest, debacle, disappointment, discomfiture, failure, frustration, overthrow, pasting (*slang*), rebuff, rout, setback, thwarting, trouncing, vanquishment

defeated balked, beaten, bested, checkmated, conquered, crushed, licked (*informal*), overcome, overpowered, overwhelmed, routed, thrashed, thwarted, trounced, vanquished, worsted

defeatist 1. *n.* pessimist, prophet of doom, quitter, submitter, yielder **2.** *adj.* pessimistic

defect 1. *n.* blemish, blotch, deficiency, error, failing, fault, flaw, foible, imperfection, inadequacy, mistake, shortcoming, spot, taint, want, weakness **2.** *vb.* break faith, change sides, desert, go over, rebel, revolt, tergiversate

defection abandonment, apostasy, backsliding, dereliction, desertion, rebellion, revolt, tergiversation

defective broken, deficient, faulty, flawed, imperfect, inadequate, incomplete, insufficient, not working, out of order, scant, short

defector apostate, deserter, rat (*informal*), recreant (*archaic*), renegade, tergiversator, turncoat

defence 1. armament, cover, deterrence, guard, immunity, protection, resistance, safeguard, security, shelter **2.** apologia, apology, argument, excuse, exoneration, explanation, extenuation, justification, plea, vindication **3.** *Law* alibi, case, declaration, denial, plea, pleading, rebuttal, testimony **4.** *often plural* barricade, bastion, buckler, bulwark, buttress, fastness, fortification, rampart, shield

defenceless endangered, exposed, helpless, naked, powerless, unarmed, unguarded, unprotected, vulnerable, wide open

defend 1. cover, fortify, guard, keep safe, preserve, protect, safeguard, screen, secure, shelter, shield, ward off, watch over **2.** assert, champion, endorse, espouse, justify, maintain, plead, speak up for, stand by, stand up for, stick up for (*informal*), support, sustain, uphold, vindicate

defendant appellant, defence, litigant, offender, prisoner at the bar, respondent, the accused

defender 1. bodyguard, escort, guard, protector **2.** advocate, champion, patron, sponsor, supporter, vindicator

defensible justifiable, pardonable, permissible, plausible, tenable, valid

defensive 1. averting, defending, opposing, protective, safeguarding, watchful, withstanding **2.** on the defensive, uptight (*informal*)

defensively at bay, in defence, in self-defence, on guard, on the defensive, suspiciously

defer[1] adjourn, delay, hold over, postpone, procrastinate, protract, put off, put on ice, put on the back burner (*informal*), set aside, shelve, suspend, take a rain check on (*chiefly U.S. & Canad. informal*)

defer[2] accede, bow, capitulate, comply, give in, give way to, respect, submit, yield

deference attention, civility, consideration, courtesy, esteem, homage, honour, obeisance, politeness, regard, respect, reverence, thoughtfulness, veneration

deferential civil, complaisant, considerate, courteous, dutiful, ingratiating, obedient, obeisant, obsequious, polite, regardful, respectful, reverential, submissive

deferment, deferral adjournment, delay, moratorium, postponement, putting off, stay, suspension

defiance challenge, confrontation, contempt, contumacy, disobedience, disregard, insolence, insubordination, opposition, provocation, rebelliousness, recalcitrance

defiant aggressive, audacious, bold, challenging, contumacious, daring, disobedient, insolent, insubordinate, mutinous, provocative, rebellious, recalcitrant, refractory, truculent

deficiency 1. defect, demerit, failing, fault, flaw,

vy, caused by a lack of vitamins or other essential substances.

deficient *adj* 1 lacking some essential. 2 inadequate in quantity or quality.

deficit *n* the amount by which a sum is lower than that expected or required.

defile[1] *vb* **-filing, -filed** 1 to make foul or dirty. 2 to make unfit for ceremonial use. **defilement** *n*

defile[2] *n* a narrow pass or gorge.

define *vb* **-fining, -fined** 1 to describe the nature of. 2 to state precisely the meaning of. 3 to show clearly the outline of: *the picture was sharp and cleanly defined.* 4 to fix with precision; specify: *define one's duties.* **definable** *adj*

definite *adj* 1 firm, clear, and precise: *I have very definite views on this subject.* 2 having precise limits or boundaries. 3 known for certain: *it's definite that they have won.* **definitely** *adv*

definite article *n Grammar* the word "the".

definition *n* 1 a statement of the meaning of a word or phrase. 2 a description of the essential qualities of something. 3 the quality of being clear and distinct. 4 sharpness of outline.

definitive *adj* 1 final and unable to be questioned or altered: *a definitive verdict.* 2 most complete, or the best of its kind: *the book was hailed as the definitive Dickens biography.* **definitively** *adv*

deflate *vb* **-flating, -flated** 1 to collapse or cause to collapse through the release of gas. 2 to take away the self-esteem or conceit from. 3 to cause deflation of (an economy).

deflation *n* 1 *Econ* a reduction in economic activity resulting in lower levels of output and investment. 2 a feeling of sadness following excitement. **deflationary** *adj*

deflect *vb* to turn or cause to turn aside from a course. **deflection** *n* **deflector** *n*

deflower *vb Literary* to deprive (a woman) of her virginity.

defoliate *vb* **-ating, -ated** to deprive (a plant) of its leaves. **defoliant** *n* **defoliation** *n*

deforestation *n* the cutting down or destruction of forests.

deform *vb* to put (something) out of shape or spoil its appearance.

deformed *adj* disfigured or misshapen.

deformity *n, pl* **-ties** 1 *Pathol* a distortion of an organ or part. 2 the state of being deformed.

defraud *vb* to cheat out of money, property, or a right to do something.

defray *vb* to provide money to cover costs or expenses. **defrayal** *n*

defrock *vb* to deprive (a priest) of ecclesiastical status.

defrost *vb* 1 to make or become free of frost or ice. 2 to thaw (frozen food) by removing from a deep-freeze.

deft *adj* quick and skilful in movement; dexterous. **deftly** *adv* **deftness** *n*

defunct *adj* no longer existing or working properly.

defuse *or US sometimes* **defuze** *vb* **-fusing, -fused** *or* **-fuzing, -fuzed** 1 to remove the fuse of (an explosive device). 2 to reduce the tension in (a difficult situation): *I said it in a bid to defuse the situation.*

defy *vb* **-fies, -fying, -fied** 1 to resist openly and boldly. 2 to elude in a baffling way: *his actions defy explanation.* 3 *Formal* to challenge (someone to do something).

degenerate *adj* 1 having deteriorated to a lower mental, moral, or physical level. ~*n* 2 a degenerate

THESAURUS

frailty, imperfection, shortcoming, weakness **2.** absence, dearth, deficit, inadequacy, insufficiency, lack, scantiness, scarcity, shortage

deficient **1.** defective, faulty, flawed, impaired, imperfect, incomplete, inferior, unsatisfactory, weak **2.** exiguous, inadequate, insufficient, lacking, meagre, pathetic, scant, scanty, scarce, short, skimpy, wanting

deficit arrears, default, deficiency, loss, shortage, shortfall

defiled besmirched, desecrated, dishonoured, impure, polluted, profaned, ravished, spoilt, tainted, unclean

define **1.** characterize, describe, designate, detail, determine, explain, expound, interpret, specify, spell out **2.** bound, circumscribe, delimit, delineate, limit, mark out, outline

definite **1.** clear, clear-cut, clearly defined, determined, exact, explicit, express, fixed, marked, obvious, particular, precise, specific **2.** assured, certain, decided, guaranteed, positive, settled, sure

definitely absolutely, beyond any doubt, categorically, certainly, clearly, decidedly, easily, far and away, finally, indubitably, obviously, plainly, positively, surely, undeniably, unequivocally, unmistakably, unquestionably, without doubt, without fail, without question

definition **1.** clarification, description, elucidation, explanation, exposition, statement of meaning **2.** delimitation, delineation, demarcation, determination, fixing, outlining, settling **3.** clarity, contrast, distinctness, focus, precision, sharpness

definitive absolute, authoritative, complete, conclusive, decisive, exhaustive, final, perfect, reliable, ultimate

deflate **1.** collapse, contract, empty, exhaust, flatten, puncture, shrink, void **2.** chasten, dash, debunk (*informal*), disconcert, dispirit, humble, humiliate, mortify, put down (*slang*), squash, take the wind out of (someone's) sails **3.** *Economics* decrease, depreciate, depress, devalue, diminish, reduce

deflect bend, deviate, diverge, glance off, ricochet, shy, sidetrack, slew, swerve, turn, turn aside, twist, veer, wind

deflection aberration, bend, bounce, declination, deviation, divergence, drift, refraction, ricochet, swerve, veer

deform buckle, contort, cripple, deface, disfigure, distort, gnarl, injure, maim, malform, mangle, misshape, mutilate, ruin, spoil, twist, warp

deformed bent, blemished, crippled, crooked, disfigured, distorted, maimed, malformed, mangled, marred, misbegotten, misshapen, twisted, warped

deformity abnormality, defect, disfigurement, distortion, irregularity, malformation, misproportion, misshapenness, ugliness

defraud beguile, bilk, cheat, con (*informal*), cozen, delude, diddle (*informal*), do (*slang*), dupe, embezzle, fleece, pilfer, pull a fast one on (*informal*), rip off (*slang*), rob, rook (*slang*), skin (*slang*), swindle, trick

deft able, adept, adroit, agile, clever, dexterous, expert, handy, neat, nimble, proficient, skilful

defunct a dead letter, bygone, dead, expired, inoperative, invalid, nonexistent, not functioning, obsolete, out of commission

defy **1.** beard, brave, challenge, confront, dare, disregard, face, flout, hurl defiance at, provoke, scorn, slight, spurn **2.** baffle, defeat, elude, foil, frustrate, repel, repulse, resist, thwart, withstand

degenerate **1.** *adj.* base, corrupt, debased, debauched, decadent, degenerated, degraded, depraved, deteriorated, dissolute, fallen, immoral, low, mean,

person. *~vb* **-ating, -ated 3** to become degenerate. **degeneracy** *n*

degeneration *n* **1** the process of degenerating. **2** *Biol* the loss of specialization or function by organisms.

degenerative *adj* (of a disease or condition) getting steadily worse.

degrade *vb* **-grading, -graded 1** to reduce to dishonour or disgrace. **2** to reduce in status or quality. **3** *Chem* to decompose into atoms or smaller molecules. **degradation** *n* **degrading** *adj*

degree *n* **1** a stage in a scale of relative amount or intensity: *this task involved a greater degree of responsibility.* **2** an academic award given by a university or college on successful completion of a course. **3** *Grammar* any of the forms of an adjective used to indicate relative amount or intensity. **4** a unit of temperature. Symbol: ° **5** a measure of angle equal to one three-hundred-and-sixtieth of the circumference of a circle. Symbol: ° **6** a unit of latitude or longitude. Symbol: ° **7 by degrees** little by little; gradually.

dehisce *vb* **-hiscing, -hisced** (of the seed capsules of some plants) to burst open spontaneously. **dehiscence** *n* **dehiscent** *adj*

dehumanize *or* **-ise** *vb* **-izing, -ized** *or* **-ising, -ised 1** to deprive of the qualities thought of as being best in human beings, such as kindness. **2** to make (an activity) mechanical or routine. **dehumanization** *or* **-isation** *n*

dehydrate *vb* **-drating, -drated 1** to remove water from (food) in order to preserve it. **2 be dehydrated** (of a person) to become weak or ill through losing too much water from the body. **dehydration** *n*

de-ice *vb* **de-icing, de-iced** to free of ice. **de-icer** *n*

deify (**day**-if-fie) *vb* **-fies, -fying, -fied** to treat or worship (someone or something) as a god. **deification** *n*

deign (**dane**) *vb* to do something that one considers beneath one's dignity: *she did not deign to reply.*

deindustrialization *or* **-sation** *n* a decline in the importance of a country's manufacturing industry.

deism (**dee**-iz-zum) *n* belief in the existence of God based only on natural reason, without reference to revelation. **deist** *n, adj* **deistic** *adj*

deity (**dee**-it-ee) *n, pl* **-ties 1** a god or goddess. **2** the state of being divine.

Deity *n* **the** God.

déjà vu (**day**-zhah **voo**) *n* a feeling of having experienced before something that is happening at the present moment.

dejected *adj* in low spirits; downhearted. **dejectedly** *adv* **dejection** *n*

de jure *adv* according to law.

deke *Canad slang ~vb* **deking, deked 1** (in ice hockey or box lacrosse) to draw (a defending player) out of position by faking a shot or movement. *~n* **2** such a shot or movement.

dekko *n Brit slang* **have a dekko** have a look.

delay *vb* **1** to put (something) off to a later time. **2** to slow up or cause to be late. **3 a** to hesitate in doing something. **b** to deliberately take longer than necessary to do something. *~n* **4** the act of delaying. **5** a period of inactivity or waiting before something happens or continues.

delectable *adj* delightful or very attractive.

delectation *n Formal* great pleasure and enjoyment.

delegate *n* **1** a person chosen to represent others at a conference or meeting. *~vb* **-gating, -gated 2** to entrust (duties or powers) to another person. **3** to appoint as a representative.

THESAURUS

perverted **2.** *vb.* decay, decline, decrease, deteriorate, fall off, lapse, regress, retrogress, rot, sink, slip, worsen

degeneration debasement, decline, degeneracy, descent, deterioration, dissipation, dissolution, regression

degradation 1. abasement, debasement, decadence, decline, degeneracy, degeneration, demotion, derogation, deterioration, downgrading, perversion **2.** discredit, disgrace, dishonour, humiliation, ignominy, mortification, shame

degrade 1. cheapen, corrupt, debase, demean, deteriorate, discredit, disgrace, dishonour, humble, humiliate, impair, injure, pervert, shame, vitiate **2.** adulterate, dilute, doctor, mix, thin, water, water down, weaken

degraded abandoned, base, corrupt, debased, debauched, decadent, depraved, despicable, disgraced, disreputable, dissolute, low, mean, profligate, sordid, vicious, vile

degrading cheapening, contemptible, debasing, demeaning, disgraceful, dishonourable, humiliating, infra dig (*informal*), lowering, shameful, undignified, unworthy

degree 1. calibre, class, extent, grade, intensity, level, order, position, proportion, quality, quantity, rank, scale, scope, standard, standing, station, status **2.** division, extent, gradation, grade, interval, limit, mark, measure, notch, point, rung, scale, stage, step, unit **3. by degrees** bit by bit, gently, gradually, imperceptibly, inch by inch, little by little, slowly, step by step

deign condescend, consent, deem worthy, lower oneself, see fit, stoop, think fit

deity celestial being, divine being, divinity, god, goddess, godhead, idol, immortal, supreme being

dejected blue, cast down, crestfallen, depressed, despondent, disconsolate, disheartened, dismal, doleful, down, downcast, downhearted, down in the dumps (*informal*), gloomy, glum, low, low-spirited, melancholy, miserable, morose, sad, sick as a parrot (*informal, usually facetious*), woebegone, wretched

dejection blues, depression, despair, despondency, doldrums, gloom, gloominess, heavy-heartedness, low spirits, melancholy, sadness, sorrow, the hump (*Brit. informal*), unhappiness

de jure according to the law, by right, legally, rightfully

delay *vb.* **1.** defer, hold over, postpone, procrastinate, prolong, protract, put off, put on the back burner (*informal*), shelve, stall, suspend, table, take a rain check on (*chiefly U.S. & Canad. informal*), temporize **2.** arrest, bog down, check, detain, halt, hinder, hold back, hold up, impede, obstruct, retard, set back, slow up, stop **3.** dawdle, dilly-dally (*informal*), drag, lag, linger, loiter, tarry *~n.* **4.** deferment, postponement, procrastination, stay, suspension **5.** check, detention, hindrance, hold-up, impediment, interruption, interval, obstruction, setback, stoppage, wait

delectable adorable, agreeable, appetizing, charming, dainty, delicious, delightful, enjoyable, enticing, gratifying, inviting, luscious, lush, pleasant, pleasurable, satisfying, scrumptious (*informal*), tasty, toothsome, yummy (*slang*)

delegate *n.* **1.** agent, ambassador, commissioner, deputy, envoy, legate, representative *~vb.* **2.** assign, consign, devolve, entrust, give, hand over, pass on, relegate, transfer **3.** accredit, appoint, authorize, commission, depute, designate, empower, mandate

delegation *n* **1** a group chosen to represent others. **2** the act of delegating.

delete *vb* **-leting, -leted** to remove or cross out (something printed or written). **deletion** *n*

deleterious (del-lit-**eer**-ee-uss) *adj Formal* harmful or injurious.

Delft *n* tin-glazed earthenware which originated in Delft in the Netherlands, typically with blue decoration on a white ground. Also: **delftware**

deliberate *adj* **1** carefully thought out in advance; intentional. **2** careful and unhurried: *a deliberate gait.* ~*vb* **-ating, -ated 3** to consider (something) deeply; think over. **deliberately** *adv* **deliberative** *adj*

deliberation *n* **1** careful consideration. **2** calmness and absence of hurry. **3 deliberations** formal discussions.

delicacy *n, pl* **-cies 1** fine or subtle quality, construction, etc.: *delicacy of craftsmanship.* **2** fragile or graceful beauty. **3** something that is considered particularly nice to eat. **4** frail health. **5** refinement of feeling, manner, or appreciation: *the delicacy of the orchestra's playing.* **6** requiring careful or tactful treatment.

delicate *adj* **1** fine or subtle in quality or workmanship. **2** having a fragile beauty. **3** (of colour, smell, or taste) pleasantly subtle. **4** easily damaged; fragile. **5** precise or sensitive in action: *the delicate digestive system.* **6** requiring tact: *a delicate matter.* **7** showing consideration for the feelings of other people. **delicately** *adv*

delicatessen *n* a shop selling unusual or imported foods, often already cooked or prepared.

delicious *adj* **1** very appealing to taste or smell. **2** extremely enjoyable. **deliciously** *adv*

delight *n* **1** extreme pleasure. **2** something or someone that causes this. ~*vb* **3** to please greatly. **4 delight in** to take great pleasure in. **delightful** *adj* **delightfully** *adv*

delighted *adj* greatly pleased.

delimit *vb* **-iting, -ited** to mark or lay down the limits of. **delimitation** *n*

delineate (dill-**lin**-ee-ate) *vb* **-ating, -ated 1** to show by drawing. **2** to describe in words. **delineation** *n*

delinquent *n* **1** someone, esp. a young person, who breaks the law. ~*adj* **2** repeatedly breaking the law. **delinquency** *n*

deliquesce *vb* **-quescing, -quesced** (esp. of certain salts) to dissolve in water absorbed from the air. **deliquescence** *n* **deliquescent** *adj*

delirious *adj* **1** suffering from delirium. **2** wildly excited and happy. **deliriously** *adv*

delirium *n* **1** a state of excitement and mental confusion, often with hallucinations. **2** violent excitement.

delirium tremens (**trem**-enz) *n* a severe condition characterized by delirium and trembling, caused by chronic alcoholism.

deliver *vb* **1** to carry (goods or mail) to a destination. **2** to hand over: *the tenants were asked to deliver up their keys.* **3** to aid in the birth of (offspring). **4** to present (a lecture or speech). **5** to release or rescue

THESAURUS

delegation 1. commission, contingent, deputation, embassy, envoys, legation, mission **2.** assignment, commissioning, committal, deputizing, devolution, entrustment, relegation

delete blot out, blue-pencil, cancel, cross out, cut out, edit, edit out, efface, erase, excise, expunge, obliterate, remove, rub out, strike out

deliberate *adj.* **1.** calculated, conscious, considered, designed, intentional, planned, prearranged, premeditated, purposeful, studied, thoughtful, wilful **2.** careful, cautious, circumspect, heedful, measured, methodical, ponderous, prudent, slow, thoughtful, unhurried, wary ~*vb.* **3.** cogitate, consider, consult, debate, discuss, meditate, mull over, ponder, reflect, think, weigh

deliberately by design, calculatingly, consciously, determinedly, emphatically, in cold blood, intentionally, knowingly, on purpose, pointedly, resolutely, studiously, wilfully, wittingly

deliberation 1. calculation, care, carefulness, caution, circumspection, cogitation, consideration, coolness, forethought, meditation, prudence, purpose, reflection, speculation, study, thought, wariness **2.** *usually plural* conference, consultation, debate, discussion

delicacy 1. accuracy, daintiness, elegance, exquisiteness, fineness, lightness, nicety, precision, subtlety **2.** dainty, luxury, relish, savoury, titbit, treat **3.** debility, flimsiness, fragility, frailness, frailty, infirmity, slenderness, tenderness, weakness **4.** discrimination, fastidiousness, finesse, purity, refinement, sensibility, sensitiveness, sensitivity, tact, taste

delicate 1. choice, dainty, delicious, elegant, exquisite, fine, graceful, savoury, tender **2.** faint, muted, pastel, soft, subdued, subtle **3.** ailing, debilitated, flimsy, fragile, frail, sickly, slender, slight, tender, weak **4.** accurate, deft, detailed, minute, precise, skilled **5.** critical, difficult, precarious, sensitive, sticky (*informal*), ticklish, touchy **6.** careful, considerate, critical, diplomatic, discreet, discriminating, fastidious, nice, prudish, pure, refined, scrupulous, sensitive, squeamish, tactful

delicately carefully, daintily, deftly, elegantly, exquisitely, fastidiously, finely, gracefully, lightly, precisely, sensitively, skilfully, softly, subtly, tactfully

delicious 1. appetizing, choice, dainty, delectable, luscious, mouthwatering, savoury, scrumptious (*informal*), tasty, toothsome, yummy (*slang*) **2.** agreeable, charming, delightful, enjoyable, entertaining, exquisite, pleasant, pleasing

delight *n.* **1.** ecstasy, enjoyment, felicity, gladness, gratification, happiness, joy, pleasure, rapture, transport ~*vb.* **2.** amuse, charm, cheer, divert, enchant, gratify, please, ravish, rejoice, satisfy, thrill **3.** *with* **in** appreciate, enjoy, feast on, glory in, indulge in, like, love, luxuriate in, relish, revel in, savour

delighted captivated, charmed, cock-a-hoop, ecstatic, elated, enchanted, gladdened, happy, joyous, jubilant, overjoyed, over the moon (*informal*), pleased, rapt, thrilled

delightful agreeable, amusing, captivating, charming, congenial, delectable, enchanting, engaging, enjoyable, entertaining, fascinating, gratifying, heavenly, pleasant, pleasing, pleasurable, rapturous, ravishing, thrilling

delinquency crime, fault, misbehaviour, misconduct, misdeed, misdemeanour, offence, wrongdoing

delinquent criminal, culprit, juvenile delinquent, lawbreaker, malefactor, miscreant, offender, villain, wrongdoer, young offender

delirious 1. crazy, demented, deranged, incoherent, insane, light-headed, mad, raving, unhinged **2.** beside oneself, carried away, ecstatic, excited, frantic, frenzied, hysterical, wild

delirium 1. derangement, hallucination, insanity, lunacy, madness, raving **2.** ecstasy, fever, frenzy, fury, hysteria, passion, rage

deliver 1. bear, bring, carry, cart, convey, distribute, transport **2.** cede, commit, give up, grant, hand over, make over, relinquish, resign, surrender, transfer, turn

(from captivity or danger). **6** to strike (a blow) suddenly. **7** *Informal* Also: **deliver the goods** to produce something promised. **deliverance** *n*

delivery *n, pl* **-eries 1 a** the act of delivering goods or mail. **b** something that is delivered. **2** the act of giving birth to a baby. **3** manner or style in public speaking: *her delivery was clear and humorous.* **4** *Cricket* the act or manner of bowling a ball.

dell *n* a small wooded hollow.

delouse *vb* **-lousing, -loused** to rid (a person or animal) of lice.

Delphic *adj* obscure or ambiguous, like the ancient Greek oracle at Delphi.

delphinium *n, pl* **-iums** *or* **-ia** a large garden plant with spikes of blue flowers.

delta *n* **1** the fourth letter in the Greek alphabet (Δ, δ). **2** the flat area at the mouth of some rivers where the main stream splits up into several branches.

delude *vb* **-luding, -luded** to make someone believe something that is not true.

deluge (**del**-lyooj) *n* **1** a great flood of water. **2** torrential rain. **3** an overwhelming number. ~*vb* **-uging, -uged 4** to flood. **5** to overwhelm.

Deluge *n* **the** same as the **Flood.**

delusion *n* **1** a mistaken idea or belief. **2** the state of being deluded. **delusive** *adj* **delusory** *adj*

de luxe *adj* rich or sumptuous; superior in quality: *a de luxe hotel.*

delve *vb* **delving, delved 1** to research deeply or intensively (for information). **2** *Old-fashioned* to dig.

demagnetize *or* **-ise** *vb* **-izing, -ized** *or* **-ising, -ised** to remove magnetic properties. **demagnetization** *or* **-isation** *n*

demagogue *or US sometimes* **demagog** *n* a political agitator who attempts to win support by appealing to the prejudice and passions of the mob. **demagogic** *adj* **demagogy** *n*

demand *vb* **1** to request forcefully. **2** to require as just, urgent, etc.: *the situation demands intervention.* **3** to claim as a right. ~*n* **4** a forceful request. **5** something that requires special effort or sacrifice: *demands upon one's time.* **6** *Econ* willingness and ability to purchase goods and services. **7 in demand** sought after; popular. **8 on demand** as soon as requested: *the funds will be available on demand.*

➤ The verb *demand* is followed by either *of* or *from*: *demand too much of them; demand an explanation from you.*

demanding *adj* requiring a lot of skill, time, or effort: *a demanding relationship.*

demarcation *n* the act of establishing limits or boundaries, esp. between the work performed by members of different trade unions.

demean *vb* to do something unworthy of one's status or character: *he will lose face with the boss by having to demean himself in this way.*

demeanour *or US* **demeanor** *n* the way a person behaves.

demented *adj* mad; insane. **dementedly** *adv*

dementia (dim-**men**-sha) *n* a state of serious mental deterioration.

demerara sugar *n* brown crystallized cane sugar from the West Indies.

demerit *n* **1** a fault or disadvantage. **2** *US & Canad* a mark given against a student for failure or misconduct.

demesne (dim-**mane**) *n* **1** land surrounding a house or manor. **2** *Property law* the possession of one's own property or land. **3** a region or district; domain.

demi- *combining form* **1** half: *demirelief.* **2** of less than full size, status, or rank: *demigod.*

demigod *n* **1 a** a being who is part mortal, part god. **b** a lesser deity. **2** a godlike person

demijohn *n* a large bottle with a short narrow neck, often encased in wickerwork.

demilitarize *or* **-rise** *vb* **-rizing, -rized** *or* **-rising, -rised** to remove all military forces from (an area): *demilitarized zone.* **demilitarization** *or* **-risation** *n*

demimonde *n* **1** (esp. in the 19th century) a class of women considered to be outside respectable society because of promiscuity. **2** any group considered not wholly respectable.

demise *n* **1** the eventual failure of something originally successful. **2** *Euphemistic, formal* death. **3** *Property law* a transfer of an estate by lease. ~*vb* **-mising, -mised 4** *Property law* to transfer for a limited period; lease.

THESAURUS

over, yield **3.** announce, declare, give, give forth, present, proclaim, pronounce, publish, read, utter **4.** acquit, discharge, emancipate, free, liberate, loose, ransom, redeem, release, rescue, save **5.** administer, aim, deal, direct, give, inflict, launch, strike, throw

deliverance emancipation, escape, liberation, ransom, redemption, release, rescue, salvation

delivery 1. consignment, conveyance, dispatch, distribution, handing over, surrender, transfer, transmission, transmittal **2.** *Medical* childbirth, confinement, labour, parturition **3.** articulation, elocution, enunciation, intonation, speech, utterance

delude bamboozle (*informal*), beguile, cheat, con (*informal*), cozen, deceive, dupe, fool, hoax, hoodwink, impose on, kid (*informal*), lead up the garden path (*informal*), mislead, take in (*informal*), trick

deluge *n.* **1.** downpour, flood, inundation, overflowing, spate, torrent **2.** *figurative* avalanche, barrage, flood, rush, spate, torrent ~*vb.* **3.** douse, drench, drown, flood, inundate, soak, submerge, swamp **4.** *figurative* engulf, inundate, overload, overrun, overwhelm, swamp

delusion deception, error, fallacy, false impression, fancy, hallucination, illusion, misapprehension, misbelief, misconception, mistake, self-deception

de luxe choice, costly, elegant, exclusive, expensive, gorgeous, grand, luxurious, opulent, palatial, plush (*informal*), rich, select, special, splendid, splendiferous (*informal*), sumptuous, superior

delve burrow, dig into, examine, explore, ferret out, investigate, look into, probe, ransack, research, rummage, search, unearth

demagogue agitator, firebrand, haranguer, rabble-rouser, soapbox orator, tub-thumper

demand *vb.* **1.** ask, challenge, inquire, interrogate, question, request **2.** call for, cry out for, entail, involve, necessitate, need, require, take, want **3.** claim, exact, expect, insist on, order ~*n.* **4.** bidding, inquiry, interrogation, order, question, request, requisition **5.** call, claim, market, necessity, need, requirement, want **6. in demand** fashionable, in vogue, needed, popular, requested, sought after

demanding challenging, difficult, exacting, exhausting, hard, taxing, tough, trying, wearing

demarcation delimitation, differentiation, distinction, division, separation

demean abase, debase, degrade, descend, humble, lower, stoop

demeanour air, bearing, behaviour, carriage, comportment, conduct, deportment, manner, mien

demented crackers (*Brit. slang*), crackpot (*informal*), crazed, crazy, daft (*informal*), deranged, distraught, dotty (*slang, chiefly Brit.*), foolish, frenzied, idiotic, insane, loopy (*informal*), lunatic, mad, mania-

demi-sec *adj* (of wines) medium-sweet.
demisemiquaver *n Music* a note with the time value of one thirty-second of a semibreve.
demist *vb* to make or become free of condensation. **demister** *n*
demo *n, pl* **-os** *Informal* **1** short for **demonstration** (sense 1). **2** a demonstration record or tape.
demob *vb* **-mobbing, -mobbed** *Brit informal* to demobilize.
demobilize *or* **-lise** *vb* **-lizing, -lized** *or* **-lising, -lised** to release from the armed forces. **demobilization** *or* **-lisation** *n*
democracy *n, pl* **-cies 1** a system of government or organization in which the citizens or members choose leaders or make other important decisions by voting. **2** a country in which the citizens choose their government by voting.
democrat *n* a person who believes in democracy.
Democrat *n US politics* a member or supporter of the Democratic Party, the more liberal of the two main political parties in the US. **Democratic** *adj*
democratic *adj* of or relating to a country, organization, or system in which leaders are chosen or decisions are made by voting. **democratically** *adv*
demodulation *n Electronics* the process by which an output wave or signal is obtained having the characteristics of the original modulating wave or signal.
demography *n* the study of population statistics, such as births and deaths. **demographic** *adj*
demolish *vb* **1** to tear down or break up (buildings). **2** to put an end to; destroy: *I demolished her argument in seconds.* **3** *Facetious* to eat up: *he demolished the whole cake.* **demolisher** *n* **demolition** *n*
demon *n* **1** an evil spirit. **2** a person, obsession, etc., thought of as evil or persistently tormenting. **3** a person extremely skilful in or devoted to a given activity: *a demon at cricket.* **demonic** *adj*
demonetize *or* **-tise** *vb* **-tizing, -tized** *or* **-tising, -tised** to withdraw from use as currency. **demonetization** *or* **-tisation** *n*
demoniac *or* **demoniacal** *adj* **1** appearing to be possessed by a devil. **2** suggesting inner possession or inspiration: *the demoniac fire of genius.* **3** frantic or frenzied: *demoniac activity.* **demoniacally** *adv*
demonolatry *n* the worship of demons.
demonology *n* the study of demons or demonic beliefs.
demonstrable *adj* able to be proved. **demonstrably** *adv*
demonstrate *vb* **-strating, -strated 1** to show or prove by reasoning or evidence. **2** to display and explain the workings of (a machine, product, etc.). **3** to reveal the existence of: *the adult literacy campaign demonstrated the scale of educational deprivation.* **4** to show support or opposition by public parades or rallies.
demonstration *n* **1** a march or public meeting to demonstrate opposition to something or support for something. **2** an explanation or demonstration showing how something works. **3** proof or evidence leading to proof.
demonstrative *adj* **1** tending to show one's feelings freely and openly. **2** *Grammar* denoting a word used to point out the person or thing referred to, such as *this* and *those.* **3 demonstrative of** giving proof of. **demonstratively** *adv*
demonstrator *n* **1** a person who demonstrates how a device or machine works. **2** a person who takes part in a public demonstration.
demoralize *or* **-ise** *vb* **-izing, -ized** *or* **-ising, -ised** to deprive (someone) of confidence or enthusiasm: *she had been demoralized and had just given up.* **demoralization** *or* **-isation** *n*
demote *vb* **-moting, -moted** to lower in rank or position. **demotion** *n*
demotic *adj* of or relating to the common people.
demur *vb* **-murring, -murred 1** to show reluctance; object. *~n* **2 without demur** without objecting.
demure *adj* quiet, reserved, and rather shy. **demurely** *adv* **demureness** *n*
demystify *vb* **-fies, -fying, -fied** to remove the mystery from: *he attempted to demystify the contemporary jargon of psychology.* **demystification** *n*
den *n* **1** the home of a wild animal; lair. **2** *Chiefly US* a small secluded room in a home, often used for a

THESAURUS

cal, manic, *non compos mentis,* not the full shilling (*informal*), off one's (rocker) trolley (*slang*), out to lunch (*informal*), unbalanced, unhinged
democracy commonwealth, government by the people, representative government, republic
democratic autonomous, egalitarian, popular, populist, representative, republican, self-governing
demolish 1. bulldoze, destroy, dismantle, flatten, knock down, level, pulverize, raze, ruin, tear down **2.** *figurative* annihilate, defeat, destroy, lick (*informal*), master, overthrow, overturn, tank (*slang*), undo, wipe the floor with (*informal*), wreck **3.** consume, devour, eat, gobble up, put away
demolition bulldozing, destruction, explosion, knocking down, levelling, razing, wrecking
demon 1. devil, evil spirit, fiend, ghoul, goblin, malignant spirit **2.** *figurative* devil, fiend, ghoul, monster, rogue, villain **3.** ace (*informal*), addict, fanatic, fiend, go-getter (*informal*), master, wizard
demonic, demoniac, demoniacal 1. devilish, diabolic, diabolical, fiendish, hellish, infernal, satanic **2.** crazed, frantic, frenetic, frenzied, furious, hectic, like one possessed, mad, maniacal, manic
demonstrable attestable, axiomatic, certain, evident, evincible, incontrovertible, indubitable, irrefutable, obvious, palpable, positive, provable, self-evident, undeniable, unmistakable, verifiable
demonstrate 1. display, establish, evidence, evince, exhibit, indicate, manifest, prove, show, testify to **2.** describe, explain, illustrate, make clear, show how, teach **3.** march, parade, picket, protest, rally
demonstration 1. march, mass lobby, parade, picket, protest, rally, sit-in **2.** affirmation, confirmation, display, evidence, exhibition, expression, illustration, manifestation, proof, substantiation, testimony, validation **3.** description, explanation, exposition, presentation, test, trial
demonstrative 1. affectionate, effusive, emotional, expansive, expressive, gushing, loving, open, unreserved, unrestrained **2.** evincive, explanatory, expository, illustrative, indicative, symptomatic
demoralize cripple, daunt, deject, depress, disconcert, discourage, dishearten, dispirit, enfeeble, rattle (*informal*), sap, shake, undermine, unnerve, weaken
demoralized broken, crushed, depressed, discouraged, disheartened, dispirited, downcast, sick as a parrot (*informal*), subdued, unnerved, weakened
demur 1. *vb.* balk, cavil, disagree, dispute, doubt, hesitate, object, pause, protest, refuse, take exception, waver **2.** *n.* compunction, dissent, hesitation, misgiving, objection, protest, qualm, scruple
demure bashful, coy, decorous, diffident, grave, modest, prim, reserved, reticent, retiring, sedate, shy, sober, staid, strait-laced, unassuming

hobby. **3** a place where people indulge in criminal or immoral activities: *a den of iniquity.*

denarius (din-**air**-ee-uss) *n, pl* **-narii** (-**nair**-ee-eye) a silver coin of ancient Rome, often called a penny in translation.

denary (**dean**-a-ree) *adj* calculated by tens; decimal.

denationalize *or* **-ise** *vb* **-izing, -ized** *or* **-ising, -ised** to transfer (an industry or a service) from public to private ownership. **denationalization** *or* **-isation** *n*

denature *vb* **-turing, -tured 1** to change the nature of. **2** to make (alcohol) unfit to drink by adding another substance.

dendrology *n* the study of trees.

dene, dean *n* a narrow wooded valley.

dengue (**deng**-gee) *n* a viral disease transmitted by mosquitoes, characterized by headache, fever, pains in the joints, and a rash.

denial *n* **1** a statement that something is not true. **2** a rejection of a request.

denier (**den**-yer) *n* a unit of weight used to measure the fineness of silk and man-made fibres.

denigrate *vb* **-grating, -grated** to criticize (someone or something) unfairly. **denigration** *n* **denigrator** *n*

denim *n* **1** a hard-wearing cotton fabric used for jeans, skirts, etc. **2 denims** jeans made of denim.

denizen *n* **1** a person, animal, or plant that lives or grows in a particular place. **2** an animal or plant established in a place to which it is not native.

denominate *vb* **-nating, -nated** to give a specific name to; designate.

denomination *n* **1** a group which has slightly different beliefs from other groups within the same faith. **2** a unit in a system of weights, values, or measures: *coins of small denomination have been withdrawn.* **3** a name given to a class or group; classification. **denominational** *adj*

denominator *n* the number below the line in a fraction, as 8 in ⅞.

denote *vb* **-noting, -noted 1** to be a sign or indication of: *these contracts denote movement on the widest possible scale.* **2** (of a word or phrase) to have as a literal or obvious meaning. **denotation** *n*

denouement (day-**noo**-mon) *n* the final outcome or solution in a play or other work.

denounce *vb* **-nouncing, -nounced 1** to condemn openly or vehemently. **2** to give information against.

dense *adj* **1** thickly crowded or closely packed. **2** difficult to see through: *dense clouds of smoke.* **3** *Informal* stupid or dull. **4** (of a film, book, etc.) difficult to follow or understand: *the content should be neither too dense nor too abstract.* **densely** *adv*

density *n, pl* **-ties 1** the degree to which something is filled or occupied: *an average population density.* **2** *Physics* a measure of the compactness of a substance, expressed as its mass per unit volume. **3** a measure of a physical quantity per unit of length, area, or volume.

dent *n* **1** a hollow in the surface of something. *~vb* **2** to make a dent in.

dental *adj* of or relating to the teeth or dentistry.

dental floss *n* a waxed thread used to remove particles of food from between the teeth.

dental surgeon *n* same as **dentist.**

dentate *adj* having teeth or toothlike notches.

dentifrice (**den**-tif-riss) *n* paste or powder for cleaning the teeth.

dentine (**den**-teen) *n* the hard dense tissue that forms the bulk of a tooth.

dentist *n* a person qualified to practise dentistry.

dentistry *n* the branch of medicine concerned with the teeth and gums.

dentition *n* the typical arrangement, type, and number of teeth in a species.

denture *n* (*often pl*) a partial or full set of artificial teeth.

denude *vb* **-nuding, -nuded 1** to make bare; strip: *the atrocious weather denuded the trees.* **2** *Geol* to expose (rock) by the erosion of the layers above. **denudation** *n*

denumerable *adj Maths* countable.

denunciation *n* open condemnation; denouncing.

deny *vb* **-nies, -nying, -nied 1** to declare (a statement) to be untrue. **2** to refuse to give or allow: *we have been denied permission.* **3** to refuse to acknowledge: *the baron denied his wicked son.*

deodar *n* a Himalayan cedar with drooping branches.

deodorant *n* a substance applied to the body to prevent or disguise the odour of perspiration.

deodorize *or* **-ise** *vb* **-izing, -ized** *or* **-ising, -ised** to remove or disguise the odour of. **deodorization** *or* **-isation** *n*

deoxyribonucleic acid *n* same as **DNA.**

depart *vb* **1** to leave. **2** to differ or deviate: *to depart from the original concept.*

departed *adj Euphemistic* dead.

department *n* **1** a specialized division of a large

THESAURUS

den 1. cave, cavern, haunt, hide-out, hole, lair, shelter **2.** *chiefly U.S.* cloister, cubbyhole, hideaway, retreat, sanctuary, sanctum, snuggery, study

denial contradiction, disavowal, disclaimer, dismissal, dissent, negation, prohibition, rebuff, refusal, rejection, renunciation, repudiation, retraction, veto

denigrate belittle, besmirch, blacken, calumniate, cast aspersions on, decry, defame, disparage, impugn, knock (*informal*), malign, revile, rubbish (*informal*), run down, slag (off) (*slang*), slander, vilify

denigration aspersion, backbiting, defamation, detraction, disparagement, obloquy, scandal, slander, vilification

denomination 1. belief, communion, creed, persuasion, religious group, school, sect **2.** grade, size, unit, value **3.** appellation, designation, label, name, style, term, title

denote betoken, designate, express, imply, import, indicate, mark, mean, show, signify, typify

denounce accuse, arraign, attack, brand, castigate, censure, condemn, declaim against, decry, excoriate, impugn, revile, stigmatize, vilify

dense 1. close, close-knit, compact, compressed, condensed, heavy, impenetrable, opaque, solid, substantial, thick, thickset **2.** crass, dozy (*Brit. informal*), dull, obtuse, slow, slow-witted, stolid, stupid, thick, thick-witted

density body, bulk, closeness, compactness, consistency, crowdedness, denseness, impenetrability, mass, solidity, thickness, tightness

dent 1. *n.* chip, concavity, crater, depression, dimple, dip, hollow, impression, indentation, pit **2.** *vb.* depress, hollow, imprint, make a dent in, make concave, press in, push in

denude bare, divest, expose, lay bare, strip, uncover

deny 1. contradict, disagree with, gainsay (*archaic or literary*), oppose, rebuff, rebut **2.** decline, disallow, forbid, refuse, reject, turn down, veto, withhold

deodorant air freshener, antiperspirant, disinfectant

depart 1. absent (oneself), decamp, disappear, escape, exit, go, go away, leave, migrate, quit, remove,

business organization, hospital, university, etc. **2** a major subdivision of the administration of a government. **3** an administrative division in several countries, such as France. **4** *Informal* a specialized sphere of activity: *wine-making is my wife's department.* **departmental** *adj*

department store *n* a large shop divided into departments selling many kinds of goods.

departure *n* **1** the act of departing. **2** a divergence from previous custom, rule, etc. **3** a course of action or venture: *the album represents a new departure for them.*

depend *vb* **depend on a** to put trust (in); rely (on). **b** to be influenced or determined (by): *the answer depends on four main issues.* **c** to rely (on) for income or support.

dependable *adj* reliable and trustworthy. **dependability** *n* **dependably** *adv*

dependant *n* a person who depends on another for financial support.

dependence *n* **1** the state of relying on something in order to be able to survive or operate properly. **2** reliance or trust: *they had a bond between them of mutual dependence and trust.*

dependency *n, pl* **-cies 1** a territory subject to a state on which it does not border. **2** *Psychol* overreliance on another person or on a drug.

dependent *adj* **1** depending on a person or thing for aid or support. **2 dependent on** *or* **upon** influenced or conditioned by.

depict *vb* **1** to represent by drawing, painting, etc. **2** to describe in words. **depiction** *n*

depilatory (dip-**pill**-a-tree) *adj* **1** able or serving to remove hair. *~n, pl* **-ries 2** a chemical used to remove hair.

deplete *vb* **-pleting, -pleted 1** to use up (supplies or money). **2** to reduce in number. **depletion** *n*

deplorable *adj* very bad or unpleasant. **deplorably** *adv*

deplore *vb* **-ploring, -plored** to express or feel strong disapproval of.

deploy *vb* to organize (troops or resources) into a position ready for immediate and effective action. **deployment** *n*

deponent *n Law* a person who makes a statement on oath.

depopulate *vb* **-lating, -lated** to cause to be reduced in population. **depopulation** *n*

deport *vb* **1** to remove forcibly from a country. **2 deport oneself** to behave in a specified manner.

deportation *n* the act of expelling someone from a country.

deportee *n* a person deported or awaiting deportation.

deportment *n* the way in which a person moves and stands: *she had the manners and deportment of a great lady.*

depose *vb* **-posing, -posed 1** to remove from an office or position of power. **2** *Law* to testify on oath.

deposit *vb* **-iting, -ited 1** to put down. **2** to entrust (money or valuables) for safekeeping. **3** to place (money) in a bank account or other savings account. **4** to lay down naturally: *the river deposits silt.* *~n* **5** a sum of money placed in a bank account or other savings account. **6** money given in part payment for goods or services. **7** an amount of a substance left on a surface as a result of chemical or geological process.

deposit account *n Brit* a bank account that earns interest.

depositary *n, pl* **-taries** a person or group to whom something is entrusted for safety.

THESAURUS

retire, retreat, set forth, start out, take (one's) leave, vanish, withdraw **2.** deviate, differ, digress, diverge, stray, swerve, turn aside, vary, veer

departed dead, deceased, expired, late

department 1. branch, bureau, division, office, section, station, subdivision, unit **2.** district, division, province, region **3.** area, domain, function, line, province, realm, responsibility, sector, speciality, sphere

departure 1. exit, exodus, going, going away, leave-taking, leaving, removal, retirement, withdrawal **2.** abandonment, branching off, deviation, digression, divergence, variation, veering **3.** branching out, change, difference, innovation, novelty, shift

depend depend on a bank on, build upon, calculate on, confide in, count on, lean on, reckon on, rely upon, trust in, turn to **b** be based on, be contingent on, be determined by, be subject to, be subordinate to, hang on, hinge on, rest on, revolve around

dependable faithful, reliable, reputable, responsible, staunch, steady, sure, trustworthy, trusty, unfailing

dependant *n.* child, client, hanger-on, henchman, minion, minor, protégé, relative, subordinate, vassal

dependent *adj.* **1.** counting on, defenceless, helpless, immature, reliant, relying on, vulnerable, weak **2.** conditional, contingent, depending, determined by, liable to, relative, subject to

depict 1. delineate, draw, illustrate, limn, outline, paint, picture, portray, render, reproduce, sculpt, sketch **2.** characterize, describe, detail, narrate, outline, sketch

deplete bankrupt, consume, decrease, drain, empty, exhaust, expend, impoverish, lessen, milk, reduce, use up

depleted consumed, decreased, depreciated, devoid of, drained, emptied, exhausted, lessened, out of, reduced, short of, spent, used (up), wasted, weakened, worn out

depletion consumption, decrease, deficiency, diminution, drain, dwindling, exhaustion, expenditure, lessening, lowering, reduction, using up

deplorable blameworthy, calamitous, dire, disastrous, disgraceful, dishonourable, disreputable, distressing, grievous, heartbreaking, lamentable, melancholy, miserable, opprobrious, pitiable, regrettable, reprehensible, sad, scandalous, shameful, unfortunate, wretched

deplore abhor, censure, condemn, denounce, deprecate, disapprove of, excoriate, object to

deploy arrange, dispose, extend, position, redistribute, set out, set up, spread out, station, use, utilize

deport 1. banish, exile, expatriate, expel, extradite, transport (*Hist.*) **2. deport oneself** acquit, act, bear, behave, carry, comport, conduct, hold

deportation banishment, eviction, exile, expatriation, expulsion, extradition, transportation

deportment air, appearance, aspect, bearing, behaviour, carriage, comportment, conduct, demeanour, manner, mien, posture, stance

depose 1. cashier, demote, dethrone, dismiss, displace, oust, overthrow, remove from office **2.** *Law* declare, make a deposition, testify

deposit *vb.* **1.** drop, lay, locate, place, precipitate, put, settle, sit down **2.** bank, consign, entrust, hoard, lodge, save, store *~n.* **3.** down payment, instalment, money (*in bank*), part payment, pledge, retainer, secu-

deposition *n* **1** *Law* the sworn statement of a witness used in court in his or her absence. **2** the act of deposing. **3** the act of depositing. **4** something deposited.

depositor *n* a person who places or has money on deposit in a bank or similar organization.

depository *n, pl* **-ries 1** a store where furniture, valuables, etc. can be kept for safety. **2** same as **depositary**.

depot (**dep**-oh) *n* **1** a place where goods and vehicles are kept when not in use. **2** *Chiefly US & Canad* a bus or railway station.

depraved *adj* morally bad; corrupt.

depravity *n, pl* **-ties** moral corruption.

deprecate *vb* **-cating, -cated** to express disapproval of. **deprecation** *n* **deprecatory** *adj*

depreciate *vb* **-ating, -ated 1** to decline in value or price. **2** to deride or criticize. **depreciatory** *adj*

depreciation *n* **1** *Accounting* the reduction in value of a fixed asset through use, obsolescence, etc. **2** a decrease in the exchange value of a currency. **3** the act or an instance of belittling.

depredation *n* plundering; pillage.

depress *vb* **1** to make sad and gloomy. **2** to lower (prices). **3** to push down. **depressing** *adj* **depressingly** *adv*

depressant *adj* **1** *Med* able to reduce nervous or functional activity; sedative. ~*n* **2** a depressant drug.

depressed *adj* **1** low in spirits; downcast. **2** suffering from economic hardship, such as unemployment: *the current depressed conditions.* **3** pressed down or flattened.

depression *n* **1** a mental state in which a person has feelings of gloom and inadequacy. **2** an economic condition in which there is substantial unemployment, low output and investment; slump. **3** *Meteorol* a mass of air below normal atmospheric pressure, which often causes rain. **4** a sunken place.

Depression *n* **the** the worldwide economic depression of the early 1930s.

depressive *adj* causing sadness and lack of energy.

deprive *vb* **-priving, -prived deprive of** to prevent from having or enjoying. **deprivation** *n*

deprived *adj* lacking adequate living conditions, education, etc.: *deprived ghettos.*

dept department.

depth *n* **1** the distance downwards, backwards, or inwards. **2** intensity of emotion or feeling. **3** the quality of having a high degree of knowledge, insight, and understanding. **4** intensity of colour. **5** lowness of pitch. **6 depths a** a remote inaccessible region: *the depths of the forest.* **b** the most severe part: *the depths of depression.* **c** a low moral state. **7 out of one's depth a** in water deeper than one is tall. **b** beyond the range of one's competence or understanding.

depth charge *n* a bomb used to attack submarines that explodes at a preset depth of water.

deputation *n* a body of people appointed to represent others.

depute *vb* **-puting, -puted** to appoint (someone) to act on one's behalf.

deputize *or* **-tise** *vb* **-tizing, -tized** *or* **-tising, -tised** to act as deputy.

deputy *n, pl* **-ties** a person appointed to act on behalf of another.

THESAURUS

rity, stake, warranty **4.** accumulation, alluvium, deposition, dregs, lees, precipitate, sediment, silt

deposition 1. *Law* affidavit, declaration, evidence, sworn statement, testimony **2.** dethronement, dismissal, displacement, ousting, removal

depository depot, repository, safe-deposit box, store, storehouse, warehouse

depot bus station, depository, garage, repository, storehouse, terminus, warehouse

deprave brutalize, corrupt, debase, debauch, degrade, demoralize, lead astray, pervert, seduce, subvert

depraved abandoned, corrupt, debased, debauched, degenerate, dissolute, evil, immoral, lascivious, lewd, licentious, perverted, profligate, shameless, sinful, vicious, vile, wicked

depravity baseness, corruption, criminality, debasement, debauchery, degeneracy, depravation, evil, immorality, iniquity, profligacy, sinfulness, turpitude, vice, viciousness, wickedness

depreciate 1. decrease, deflate, devaluate, devalue, lessen, lose value, lower, reduce **2.** belittle, decry, denigrate, deride, disparage, look down on, ridicule, run down, scorn, sneer at, traduce, underestimate, underrate, undervalue

depreciation 1. deflation, depression, devaluation, drop, fall, slump **2.** belittlement, deprecation, derogation, detraction, disparagement

depress 1. cast down, chill, damp, daunt, debilitate, deject, desolate, discourage, dishearten, dispirit, drain, enervate, exhaust, lower, make despondent, oppress, sadden, sap, weaken, weigh down **2.** cheapen, depreciate, devaluate, devalue, diminish, downgrade, impair, lessen, lower, reduce **3.** flatten, level, lower, press down, push down

depressed 1. blue, crestfallen, dejected, despondent, discouraged, dispirited, down, downcast, downhearted, down in the dumps (*informal*), fed up, glum, low, low-spirited, melancholy, moody, morose, pessimistic, sad, unhappy **2.** *of an area, circumstances* deprived, destitute, disadvantaged, distressed, grey, needy, poor, poverty-stricken, run-down **3.** concave, hollow, indented, recessed, set back, sunken

depressing black, bleak, daunting, dejecting, depressive, discouraging, disheartening, dismal, dispiriting, distressing, dreary, funereal, gloomy, harrowing, heartbreaking, hopeless, melancholy, sad, saddening, sombre

depression 1. dejection, despair, despondency, dolefulness, downheartedness, gloominess, hopelessness, low spirits, melancholia, melancholy, sadness, the blues, the dumps (*informal*), the hump (*Brit. informal*) **2.** *Commerce* economic decline, hard *or* bad times, inactivity, recession, slump, stagnation **3.** bowl, cavity, concavity, dent, dimple, dip, excavation, hollow, impression, indentation, pit, valley

deprivation 1. denial, dispossession, divestment, expropriation, removal, withdrawal, withholding **2.** destitution, detriment, disadvantage, distress, hardship, need, privation, want

deprive dispossess, divest, expropriate, rob, strip

deprived destitute, disadvantaged, forlorn, in need, in want, lacking, necessitous, needy, poor

depth 1. abyss, deepness, drop, extent, measure, profoundness, profundity **2.** *figurative* astuteness, discernment, insight, penetration, profoundness, profundity, sagacity, wisdom **3.** intensity, richness, strength **4.** *often plural* abyss, bowels of the earth, deepest (furthest, innermost, most intense, remotest) part, middle, midst, slough of despond

deputation commission, delegates, delegation, deputies, embassy, envoys, legation

deputize act for, stand in for, take the place of, understudy

derail *vb* to cause (a train) to go off the rails. **derailment** *n*
derailleur (dee-**rail**-yer) *n* a type of gear-change mechanism for bicycles.
deranged *adj* **1** mad, or behaving in a wild and uncontrolled way. **2** in a state of disorder. **derangement** *n*
derby *n, pl* **-bies** *US & Canad* a bowler hat.
Derby *n, pl* **-bies 1 the Derby** an annual horse race for three-year-olds, run at Epsom Downs, Surrey. **2 local derby** a sporting event between teams from the same area.
deregulate *vb* **-lating, -lated** to remove regulations or controls from. **deregulation** *n*
derelict *adj* **1** abandoned or unused and falling into ruins. *~n* **2** a social outcast or vagrant.
dereliction *n* **1** the state of being abandoned. **2 dereliction of duty** wilful neglect of one's duty.
derestrict *vb* to make (a road) free from speed limits. **derestriction** *n*
deride *vb* **-riding, -rided** to speak of or treat with contempt or ridicule. **derision** *n*
de rigueur (de rig-**gur**) *adj* required by fashion.
derisive *adj* mocking or scornful. **derisively** *adv*
derisory *adj* too small or inadequate to be considered seriously: *the shareholders have dismissed the offer as derisory.*
derivation *n* the origin or descent of something, such as a word.
derivative *adj* **1** based on other sources; not original. *~n* **2** a word, idea, etc., that is derived from another. **3** *Maths* the rate of change of one quantity with respect to another.
derive *vb* **-riving, -rived** to draw or be drawn (from) in source or origin.
dermatitis *n* inflammation of the skin.
dermatology *n* the branch of medicine concerned with the skin. **dermatologist** *n*
derogate *vb* **-gating, -gated derogate from** to cause to seem inferior; detract from. **derogation** *n*
derogatory (dir-**rog**-a-tree) *adj* expressing or showing a low opinion of someone or something.
derrick *n* **1** a simple crane that has lifting tackle slung from a boom. **2** the framework erected over an oil well to enable drill tubes to be raised and lowered.
derring-do *n Archaic or literary* a daring spirit or deed.
derv *n Brit* diesel oil, when used for road transport.
dervish *n* a member of a Muslim religious order noted for a frenzied, ecstatic, whirling dance.
desalination *n* the process of removing salt, esp. from sea water.
descale *vb* to remove the hard coating which sometimes forms inside kettles, pipes, etc.
descant *n* **1** a tune played or sung above a basic melody. *~adj* **2** of the highest member in a family of musical instruments: *a descant clarinet.*
descend *vb* **1** to move down (a slope, staircase, etc.). **2** to move or fall to a lower level, pitch, etc. **3 be descended from** to be connected by a blood relationship to. **4 descend on** to visit unexpectedly. **5** to stoop to (unworthy behaviour).
descendant *n* a person or animal descended from an individual, race, or species.
descendent *adj* descending.
descent *n* **1** the act of descending. **2** a downward slope. **3** a path or way leading downwards. **4** derivation from an ancestor; family origin. **5** a decline or degeneration.
describe *vb* **-scribing, -scribed 1** to give an account of (something or someone) in words. **2** to trace the outline of (a circle, etc.).
description *n* **1** a statement or account that describes someone or something. **2** the act of describing. **3** sort, kind, or variety: *antiques of every description.*
descriptive *adj* describing something: *it was a very descriptive account of the play.* **descriptively** *adv*
descry *vb* **-scries, -scrying, -scried 1** to catch sight of. **2** to discover by looking carefully.
desecrate *vb* **-crating, -crated** to violate the sacred character of (an object or place). **desecration** *n*
desegregate *vb* **-gating, -gated** to end racial segregation in (a school or other public institution). **desegregation** *n*
deselect *vb Brit politics* (of a constituency organiza-

THESAURUS

deputy agent, ambassador, commissioner, delegate, legate, lieutenant, nuncio, proxy, representative, second-in-command, substitute, surrogate, vicegerent
deranged berserk, crackpot (*informal*), crazed, crazy, delirious, demented, distracted, frantic, frenzied, insane, irrational, loopy (*informal*), lunatic, mad, maddened, unbalanced, unhinged
derelict 1. *adj.* abandoned, deserted, dilapidated, discarded, forsaken, neglected, ruined **2.** *n.* bag lady, bum (*informal*), down-and-out, good-for-nothing, ne'er-do-well, outcast, tramp, vagrant, wastrel
dereliction dereliction of duty evasion, failure, faithlessness, fault, neglect, negligence, nonperformance, remissness
deride chaff, contemn, disdain, disparage, gibe, insult, jeer, jibe, knock (*informal*), mock, pooh-pooh, ridicule, scoff, scorn, sneer at, take the piss out of (*taboo slang*), taunt
derisory contemptible, insulting, laughable, ludicrous, outrageous, preposterous, ridiculous
derivation ancestry, basis, beginning, descent, etymology, foundation, genealogy, origin, root, source
derivative 1. *adj.* copied, imitative, plagiaristic, plagiarized, rehashed, secondary, second-hand, uninventive, unoriginal **2.** *n.* by-product, derivation, descendant, offshoot, outgrowth, spin-off
derive 1. collect, deduce, draw, elicit, extract, follow, gain, gather, get, glean, infer, obtain, procure, receive, trace **2.** *with* **from** arise, descend, emanate, flow, issue, originate, proceed, spring from, stem from
derogatory belittling, damaging, defamatory, depreciative, detracting, discreditable, dishonouring, disparaging, injurious, offensive, slighting, uncomplimentary, unfavourable, unflattering
descend 1. alight, dismount, drop, fall, go down, move down, plummet, plunge, sink, subside, tumble **2.** dip, gravitate, incline, slant, slope **3.** *often with* **on** arrive, assail, assault, attack, come in force, invade, pounce, raid, swoop **4.** abase oneself, condescend, degenerate, deteriorate, lower oneself, stoop
descent 1. coming down, drop, fall, plunge, swoop **2.** declination, declivity, dip, drop, incline, slant, slope **3.** ancestry, extraction, family tree, genealogy, heredity, lineage, origin, parentage **4.** debasement, decadence, decline, degradation, deterioration
describe 1. characterize, define, depict, detail, explain, express, illustrate, narrate, portray, recount, relate, report, specify, tell **2.** delineate, draw, mark out, outline, trace
description 1. account, characterization, delineation, depiction, detail, explanation, narration, narrative, portrayal, report, representation, sketch **2.** brand,

tion) to refuse to select (an MP) for re-election. **deselection** *n*

desensitize *or* **-tise** *vb* **-tizing, -tized** *or* **-tising, -tised** to make insensitive or less sensitive: *the patient was desensitized to the allergen; to desensitize photographic film.*

desert[1] *n* a region that has little or no vegetation because of low rainfall.

desert[2] *vb* **1** to abandon (a person or place) without intending to return. **2** *Chiefly mil* to leave (a post or duty) with no intention of returning. **deserter** *n* **desertion** *n*

desertification *n* a process by which fertile land turns into desert.

desert island *n* a small uninhabited island in the tropics.

deserts *pl n* **get one's just deserts** get the punishment one deserves.

deserve *vb* **-serving, -served** to be entitled to or worthy of.

deserved *adj* rightfully earned. **deservedly** (diz-**zerv**-id-lee) *adv*

deserving *adj* worthy of a reward, help, or praise.

deshabille (day-zab-**beel**) *or* **dishabille** *n* the state of being partly dressed.

desiccate *vb* **-cating, -cated** to remove most of the water from; dry. **desiccated** *adj* **desiccation** *n*

design *vb* **1** to work out the structure or form of (something), by making a sketch or plans. **2** to plan and make (something) artistically. **3** to intend (something) for a specific purpose: *the move is designed to reduce travelling costs.* ~*n* **4** a sketch, plan, or preliminary drawing. **5** the arrangement or features of an artistic or decorative work: *he built it to his own design.* **6** a finished artistic or decorative creation. **7** the art of designing. **8** an intention; purpose. **9 have designs on** to plot to gain possession of.

designate (**dez**-zig-nate) *vb* **-nating, -nated 1** to give a name to; entitle. **2** to select (someone) for an office or duty; appoint. ~*adj* **3** appointed, but not yet in office: *a Prime Minister designate.*

designation *n* **1** something that designates, such as a name. **2** the act of designating.

designedly (dee-**zine**-id-lee) *adv* by intention.

designer *n* **1** a person who draws up original sketches or plans from which things are made. ~*adj* **2** designed by a well-known fashion designer: *designer clothes.* **3** having an appearance of fashionable trendiness: *designer stubble.*

designing *adj* cunning and scheming.

desirable *adj* **1** worth having or doing: *a desirable lifestyle.* **2** arousing sexual desire. **desirability** *n* **desirably** *adv*

desire *vb* **-siring, -sired 1** to want very much. **2** *Formal* to request: *we desire your company at the wedding of our daughter.* ~*n* **3** a wish or longing. **4** sexual appetite. **5** a person or thing that is desired.

desirous *adj* having a desire for: *desirous of living in London.*

desist *vb* to stop doing: *please desist from talking.*

desk *n* **1** a piece of furniture with a writing surface and usually drawers. **2** a service counter in a public building, such as a hotel. **3** the section of a newspaper or television station responsible for a particular subject: *the picture desk.*

deskill *vb* **1** to mechanize or computerize (a job) thereby reducing the skill required to do it. **2** to de-

THESAURUS

breed, category, class, genre, genus, ilk, kind, order, sort, species, type, variety

descriptive detailed, explanatory, expressive, graphic, illustrative, pictorial, picturesque, vivid

desert[1] *n.* solitude, waste, wasteland, wilderness, wilds

desert[2] *vb.* abandon, abscond, betray, decamp, defect, forsake, give up, jilt, leave, leave high and dry, leave (someone) in the lurch, leave stranded, maroon, quit, relinquish, renounce, resign

deserted abandoned, cast off, derelict, desolate, empty, forlorn, forsaken, godforsaken, isolated, left in the lurch, left stranded, lonely, neglected, solitary, unfriended, unoccupied, vacant

deserter absconder, fugitive, renegade, runaway, truant

desertion abandonment, absconding, apostasy, betrayal, defection, departure, dereliction, escape, evasion, flight, forsaking, relinquishment, truancy

deserve be entitled to, be worthy of, earn, gain, justify, merit, procure, rate, warrant, win

deserved appropriate, due, earned, fair, fitting, just, justifiable, justified, meet (*archaic*), merited, proper, right, rightful, suitable, warranted, well-earned

deserving commendable, estimable, laudable, meritorious, praiseworthy, righteous, worthy

design *vb.* **1.** delineate, describe, draft, draw, outline, plan, sketch, trace **2.** conceive, create, fabricate, fashion, invent, originate, think up **3.** aim, contrive, devise, intend, make, mean, plan, project, propose, purpose, scheme, tailor ~*n.* **4.** blueprint, delineation, draft, drawing, model, outline, plan, scheme, sketch **5.** arrangement, configuration, construction, figure, form, motif, organization, pattern, shape, style **6.** aim, end, goal, intent, intention, meaning, object, objective, point, purport, purpose, target, view **7.** *often plural* conspiracy, evil intentions, intrigue, machination, plot, scheme

designate 1. call, christen, dub, entitle, label, name, nominate, style, term **2.** allot, appoint, assign, choose, delegate, depute, nominate, select

designation 1. denomination, description, epithet, label, mark, name, title **2.** appointment, classification, delegation, indication, selection, specification

designer architect, artificer, couturier, creator, deviser, inventor, originator, stylist

designing artful, astute, conniving, conspiring, crafty, crooked (*informal*), cunning, deceitful, devious, intriguing, Machiavellian, plotting, scheming, sharp, shrewd, sly, treacherous, tricky, unscrupulous, wily

desirability advantage, benefit, merit, profit, usefulness, value, worth

desirable 1. advantageous, advisable, agreeable, beneficial, covetable, eligible, enviable, good, pleasing, preferable, profitable, worthwhile **2.** adorable, alluring, attractive, fascinating, fetching, glamorous, seductive, sexy (*informal*)

desire *vb.* **1.** aspire to, covet, crave, fancy, hanker after, hope for, long for, set one's heart on, thirst for, want, wish for, yearn for **2.** ask, entreat, importune, petition, request, solicit ~*n.* **3.** appetite, aspiration, craving, hankering, hope, longing, need, thirst, want, wish, yearning, yen (*informal*) **4.** appetite, concupiscence, lasciviousness, lechery, libido, lust, lustfulness, passion

desired accurate, appropriate, correct, exact, expected, express, fitting, necessary, particular, proper, required, right

desirous ambitious, anxious, aspiring, avid, craving, desiring, eager, hopeful, hoping, keen, longing, ready, willing, wishing, yearning

desist abstain, break off, cease, discontinue, end,

prive (employees) of the opportunity to use their skills.

desktop *adj* small enough to use at a desk: *a desktop computer.*

desktop publishing *n* a computer system which combines text and graphics and presents them in a professional-looking printed format.

desolate *adj* **1** uninhabited and bleak. **2** made uninhabitable; devastated. **3** without friends, hope, or encouragement. **4** gloomy or dismal; depressing. *~vb* **-lating, -lated 5** to deprive of inhabitants. **6** to make barren; devastate. **7** to make wretched or forlorn. **desolately** *adv* **desolateness** *n*

desolation *n* **1** ruin or devastation. **2** solitary misery; wretchedness.

despair *n* **1** total loss of hope. *~vb* **2** to lose or give up hope: *we must not despair of finding a peaceful solution.*

despatch *vb, n* same as **dispatch.**

desperado *n, pl* **-does** *or* **-dos** a reckless person ready to commit any violent illegal act.

desperate *adj* **1** willing to do anything to improve one's situation. **2** (of an action) undertaken as a last resort. **3** very grave: *in desperate agony.* **4** having a great need or desire: *I was desperate for a child.* **desperately** *adv*

desperation *n* **1** desperate recklessness. **2** the state of being desperate.

despicable *adj* deserving contempt. **despicably** *adv*

despise *vb* **-pising, -pised** to look down on with contempt.

despite *prep* in spite of.

despoil *vb Formal* to plunder. **despoliation** *n*

despondent *adj* dejected or depressed. **despondency** *n* **despondently** *adv*

despot *n* any person in power who acts tyrannically. **despotic** *adj* **despotically** *adv*

despotism *n* **1** absolute or tyrannical government. **2** tyrannical behaviour.

dessert *n* the sweet course served at the end of a meal.

dessertspoon *n* a spoon between a tablespoon and a teaspoon in size.

destination *n* the place to which someone or something is going.

destined (**dess**-tinnd) *adj* **1** certain to be or do something: *the school is destined to close this summer.* **2** heading towards a specific destination: *some of the oil was destined for Eastern Europe.*

destiny *n, pl* **-nies 1** the future destined for a person or thing. **2** the predetermined course of events. **3** the power that predetermines the course of events.

THESAURUS

forbear, give over (*informal*), give up, have done with, kick (*informal*), leave off, pause, refrain from, remit, stop, suspend

desolate *adj.* **1.** bare, barren, bleak, desert, dreary, godforsaken, ruined, solitary, unfrequented, uninhabited, waste, wild **2.** abandoned, bereft, cheerless, comfortless, companionless, dejected, depressing, despondent, disconsolate, dismal, downcast, forlorn, forsaken, gloomy, lonely, melancholy, miserable, wretched *~vb.* **3.** depopulate, despoil, destroy, devastate, lay low, lay waste, pillage, plunder, ravage, ruin **4.** daunt, deject, depress, discourage, dishearten, dismay, distress, grieve

desolation **1.** destruction, devastation, havoc, ravages, ruin, ruination **2.** anguish, dejection, despair, distress, gloom, gloominess, melancholy, misery, sadness, unhappiness, woe, wretchedness

despair **1.** *n.* anguish, dejection, depression, desperation, despondency, gloom, hopelessness, melancholy, misery, wretchedness **2.** *vb.* despond, give up, lose heart, lose hope

despairing anxious, broken-hearted, dejected, depressed, desperate, despondent, disconsolate, dismal, downcast, frantic, grief-stricken, hopeless, inconsolable, melancholy, miserable, suicidal, wretched

desperado bandit, criminal, cutthroat, gangster, gunman, heavy (*slang*), hoodlum (*chiefly U.S.*), lawbreaker, outlaw, ruffian, thug, villain

desperate **1.** audacious, dangerous, daring, death-defying, determined, foolhardy, frantic, furious, hasty, hazardous, headstrong, impetuous, madcap, precipitate, rash, reckless, risky, violent, wild **2.** acute, critical, dire, drastic, extreme, great, urgent, very grave

desperately badly, dangerously, gravely, perilously, seriously, severely

desperation **1.** defiance, foolhardiness, frenzy, heedlessness, impetuosity, madness, rashness, recklessness **2.** agony, anguish, anxiety, despair, despondency, distraction, heartache, hopelessness, misery, pain, sorrow, torture, trouble, unhappiness, worry

despicable abject, base, beyond contempt, cheap, contemptible, degrading, detestable, disgraceful, disreputable, hateful, ignominious, infamous, low, mean, pitiful, reprehensible, scurvy (*old-fashioned*), shameful, sordid, vile, worthless, wretched

despise abhor, contemn, deride, detest, disdain, disregard, loathe, look down on, neglect, revile, scorn, slight, spurn, undervalue

despite against, even with, in contempt of, in defiance of, in spite of, in the face of, in the teeth of, notwithstanding, regardless of, undeterred by

despoil destroy, devastate, dispossess, divest, loot, pillage, plunder, ravage, rifle, rob, vandalize, wreak havoc upon, wreck

despondency dejection, depression, despair, desperation, disconsolateness, discouragement, dispiritedness, downheartedness, gloom, hopelessness, low spirits, melancholy, misery, sadness, the hump (*Brit. informal*), wretchedness

despondent blue, dejected, depressed, despairing, disconsolate, discouraged, disheartened, dismal, dispirited, doleful, down, downcast, downhearted, gloomy, glum, hopeless, in despair, low, low-spirited, melancholy, miserable, morose, sad, sorrowful, woebegone, wretched

despot autocrat, dictator, oppressor, tyrant

despotic absolute, arbitrary, arrogant, authoritarian, autocratic, dictatorial, domineering, imperious, oppressive, tyrannical, unconstitutional

despotism absolutism, autarchy, autocracy, dictatorship, oppression, totalitarianism, tyranny

destination harbour, haven, journey's end, landing-place, resting-place, station, stop, terminus

destiny cup, divine decree, doom, fate, fortune, karma, kismet, lot, portion

destitute dirt-poor (*informal*), distressed, down and out, flat broke (*informal*), impecunious, impoverished, indigent, insolvent, moneyless, necessitous, needy, on one's uppers, on the breadline (*informal*), penniless, penurious, poor, poverty-stricken, short, without two pennies to rub together (*informal*)

destitution beggary, dire straits, distress, impecuniousness, indigence, neediness, pauperism, pennilessness, penury, privation, utter poverty, want

destroy annihilate, blow to bits, break down, crush,

destitute *adj* lacking the means to live; totally impoverished. **destitution** *n*
destroy *vb* **1** to ruin; demolish. **2** to put an end to. **3** to kill (an animal). **4** to crush or defeat.
destroyer *n* **1** a small heavily armed warship. **2** a person or thing that destroys.
destructible *adj* capable of being destroyed.
destruction *n* **1** the act of destroying something or state of being destroyed. **2** a cause of ruin.
destructive *adj* **1** causing or capable of causing harm, damage, or injury. **2** intended to discredit, esp. without positive suggestions or help: *destructive speeches against the platform.* **destructively** *adv*
desuetude (diss-**syoo**-it-tude) *n* the condition of not being in use.
desultory (**dez**-zl-tree) *adj* **1** passing or jumping from one thing to another; disconnected: *desultory conversation.* **2** occurring in a random way: *a desultory thought.* **desultorily** *adv*
detach *vb* **1** to disengage and separate. **2** *Mil* to send (a regiment, officer, etc.) on a special assignment. **detachable** *adj*
detached *adj* **1** separate or standing apart: *a detached farmhouse.* **2** showing no emotional involvement: *she continued to watch him in her grave and detached manner.*
detachment *n* **1** the state of not being personally involved in something. **2** *Mil* a small group of soldiers separated from the main group.
detail *n* **1** an item that is considered separately. **2** an item considered to be unimportant: *a mere detail.* **3** treatment of individual parts: *the census provides a considerable amount of detail.* **4** a small section of a work of art often enlarged to make the smaller features more distinct. **5** *Chiefly mil* **a** personnel assigned a specific duty. **b** the duty. **6 in detail** including all the important particulars. *~vb* **7** to list fully. **8** *Chiefly mil* to select (personnel) for a specific duty.
detailed *adj* having many details.
detain *vb* **1** to delay (someone). **2** to force (someone) to stay: *the police detained him for questioning.* **detainee** *n* **detainment** *n*
detect *vb* **1** to perceive or notice: *to detect a note of sarcasm.* **2** to discover the existence or presence of: *to detect alcohol in the blood.* **detectable** *adj* **detector** *n*
detection *n* **1** the act of noticing, discovering, or sensing something. **2** the act or process of extracting information.
detective *n* **a** a police officer who investigates crimes. **b** same as **private detective.**
detente (day-**tont**) *n* the easing of tension between nations.
detention *n* **1** imprisonment, esp. of a suspect awaiting trial. **2** a form of punishment in which a pupil is detained after school.
detention centre *n* a place where young people may be detained for short periods of time by order of a court.
deter *vb* **-terring, -terred** to discourage or prevent (someone) from doing something by instilling fear or doubt in them.
detergent *n* **1** a chemical substance used for washing clothes, dishes, etc. *~adj* **2** having cleansing power.
deteriorate *vb* **-rating, -rated** to become worse. **deterioration** *n*

THESAURUS

demolish, desolate, devastate, dismantle, dispatch, eradicate, extinguish, extirpate, gut, kill, ravage, raze, ruin, shatter, slay, smash, torpedo, trash (*slang*), waste, wipe out, wreck
destruction annihilation, crushing, demolition, devastation, downfall, end, eradication, extermination, extinction, havoc, liquidation, massacre, overthrow, overwhelming, ruin, ruination, shattering, slaughter, undoing, wreckage, wrecking
destructive **1.** baleful, baneful, calamitous, cataclysmic, catastrophic, damaging, deadly, deleterious, detrimental, devastating, fatal, harmful, hurtful, injurious, lethal, noxious, pernicious, ruinous **2.** adverse, antagonistic, contrary, derogatory, discouraging, discrediting, disparaging, hostile, invalidating, negative, opposed, undermining, vicious
detach cut off, disconnect, disengage, disentangle, disjoin, disunite, divide, free, isolate, loosen, remove, segregate, separate, sever, tear off, unbridle, uncouple, unfasten, unhitch
detached **1.** disconnected, discrete, disjoined, divided, free, loosened, separate, severed, unconnected **2.** aloof, disinterested, dispassionate, impartial, impersonal, neutral, objective, reserved, unbiased, uncommitted, uninvolved, unprejudiced
detachment **1.** aloofness, coolness, disinterestedness, fairness, impartiality, indifference, neutrality, nonchalance, nonpartisanship, objectivity, remoteness, unconcern **2.** *Military* body, detail, force, party, patrol, squad, task force, unit
detail *n.* **1.** aspect, component, count, element, fact, factor, feature, item, particular, point, respect, specific, technicality **2.** *plural* fine points, minutiae, niceties, particulars, parts, trivia, trivialities **3. in detail** comprehensively, exhaustively, inside out, item by item, point by point, thoroughly **4.** *Military* assignment, body, detachment, duty, fatigue, force, party, squad *~vb.* **5.** catalogue, delineate, depict, describe, enumerate, individualize, itemize, narrate, particularize, portray, recite, recount, rehearse, relate, specify, tabulate **6.** allocate, appoint, assign, charge, commission, delegate, detach, send
detailed blow by blow, circumstantial, comprehensive, elaborate, exact, exhaustive, full, intricate, itemized, meticulous, minute, particular, particularized, specific, thorough
detain **1.** check, delay, hinder, hold up, impede, keep, keep back, retard, slow up (*or* down), stay, stop **2.** arrest, confine, hold, intern, restrain
detect **1.** ascertain, catch, descry, distinguish, identify, note, notice, observe, recognize, scent, spot **2.** catch, disclose, discover, expose, find, reveal, track down, uncover, unmask
detection discovery, exposé, exposure, ferreting out, revelation, tracking down, uncovering, unearthing, unmasking
detective bizzy (*slang*), C.I.D. man, constable, cop (*slang*), copper (*slang*), dick (*slang, chiefly U.S.*), gumshoe (*U.S. slang*), investigator, private eye, private investigator, sleuth (*informal*), tec (*slang*)
detention confinement, custody, delay, hindrance, holding back, imprisonment, incarceration, keeping in, porridge (*slang*), quarantine, restraint, withholding
deter caution, check, damp, daunt, discourage, dissuade, frighten, hinder, inhibit from, intimidate, prevent, prohibit, put off, restrain, stop, talk out of
detergent **1.** *n.* cleaner, cleanser **2.** *adj.* cleaning, cleansing, purifying
deteriorate be the worse for wear (*informal*), crumble, decay, decline, decompose, degenerate, disintegrate, ebb, fade, fall apart, get worse, go downhill (*informal*), go to pot, go to the dogs (*informal*), lapse, retrogress, weaken, wear away, worsen
deterioration atrophy, corrosion, debasement, de-

determinant *adj* **1** serving to determine or affect. *~n* **2** a factor that controls or influences what will happen. **3** *Maths* a square array of elements that represents the sum of certain products of these elements.

determinate *adj* definitely limited or fixed.

determination *n* **1** the condition of being determined; resoluteness. **2** the act of making a decision.

determine *vb* **-mining, -mined 1** to settle (an argument or a question) conclusively. **2** to find out the facts about (something): *the tests determined it was in fact cancer.* **3** to fix in scope, extent, etc.: *to determine the degree of the problem.* **4** to make a decision.

determined *adj* firmly decided. **determinedly** *adv*

determiner *n Grammar* a word, such as a number, article, or personal pronoun, that determines the meaning of a noun phrase.

determinism *n* the theory that human choice is not free, but is decided by past events. **determinist** *n, adj*

deterrent *n* **1** something that deters. **2** a weapon or set of weapons held by one country to deter another country attacking. *~adj* **3** tending to deter. **deterrence** *n*

detest *vb* to dislike intensely. **detestable** *adj*

detestation *n* intense hatred.

dethrone *vb* **-throning, -throned** to remove from a throne or deprive of any high position. **dethronement** *n*

detonate *vb* **-nating, -nated** to make (an explosive device) explode or (of an explosive device) to explode. **detonation** *n*

detonator *n* a small amount of explosive or a device used to set off an explosion.

detour *n* a deviation from a direct route or course of action.

detoxify *vb* **-fies, -fying, -fied** to remove poison from. **detoxification** *n*

detract *vb* **detract from** to make (something) seem less good, valuable, or impressive: *I wouldn't want to detract from your triumph.* **detractor** *n* **detraction** *n*

detriment *n* disadvantage or damage. **detrimental** *adj* **detrimentally** *adv*

detritus (dit-**trite**-uss) *n* **1** a loose mass of stones and silt worn away from rocks. **2** debris. **detrital** *adj*

de trop (de **troh**) *adj* unwanted or unwelcome: *I know when I'm de trop, so I'll leave you two together.*

detumescence *n* the subsidence of a swelling.

deuce (**dyewss**) *n* **1** *Tennis* a tied score that requires one player to gain two successive points to win the game. **2** a playing card or dice with two spots.

deus ex machina *n* an unlikely development introduced into a play or film to resolve the plot.

deuterium *n* a stable isotope of hydrogen. Symbol: D or ^{2}H

deuterium oxide *n* same as **heavy water.**

Deutschmark (**doytch**-mark) *or* **Deutsche Mark** (**doytch**-a) *n* the standard monetary unit of Germany.

deutzia (**dyewt**-see-a) *n* a shrub with clusters of pink or white flowers.

devalue *vb* **-valuing, -valued 1** to reduce the exchange value of (a currency). **2** to reduce the value of (something or someone). **devaluation** *n*

devastate *vb* **-tating, -tated** to damage (a place) severely or destroy it. **devastation** *n*

devastated *adj* shocked and extremely upset. **devastating** *adj* **devastatingly** *adv*

develop *vb* **1** to grow or bring to a later, more elaborate, or more advanced stage. **2** to come or bring into existence: *the country has developed a consumer society.* **3** to make or become gradually clearer or more widely known. **4** to follow as a result of something: *Cubism developed from attempts to give painting a more intellectual concept of form.* **5** to contract (an illness). **6** to improve the value or change the use of

THESAURUS

cline, degeneration, degradation, depreciation, descent, dilapidation, disintegration, downturn, drop, fall, lapse, retrogression, slump, vitiation, worsening

determination backbone, constancy, conviction, dedication, doggedness, drive, firmness, fortitude, indomitability, perseverance, persistence, resoluteness, resolution, resolve, single-mindedness, steadfastness, tenacity, willpower

determine 1. arbitrate, conclude, decide, end, finish, fix upon, ordain, regulate, settle, terminate **2.** ascertain, certify, check, detect, discover, find out, learn, verify, work out **3.** affect, condition, control, decide, dictate, direct, govern, impel, impose, incline, induce, influence, lead, modify, regulate, rule, shape **4.** choose, decide, elect, establish, fix, make up one's mind, purpose, resolve

determined bent on, constant, dogged, firm, fixed, immovable, intent, persevering, persistent, purposeful, resolute, set on, single-minded, stalwart, steadfast, strong-minded, strong-willed, tenacious, unflinching, unwavering

deterrent *n.* check, curb, defensive measures, determent, discouragement, disincentive, hindrance, impediment, obstacle, restraint

detest abhor, abominate, despise, dislike intensely, execrate, feel aversion (disgust, hostility, repugnance) towards, hate, loathe, recoil from

detonate blast, blow up, discharge, explode, set off, touch off, trigger

detonation bang, blast, blow-up, boom, discharge, explosion, report

detour bypass, byway, circuitous route, deviation, diversion, indirect course, roundabout way

detract **detract from** devalue, diminish, lessen, lower, reduce, take away from

detraction abuse, aspersion, belittlement, calumny, defamation, denigration, deprecation, disparagement, innuendo, insinuation, misrepresentation, muckraking, running down, scandalmongering, scurrility, slander, traducement, vituperation

detractor backbiter, belittler, defamer, denigrator, disparager, muckraker, scandalmonger, slanderer, traducer

detriment damage, disadvantage, disservice, harm, hurt, impairment, injury, loss, mischief, prejudice

detrimental adverse, baleful, damaging, deleterious, destructive, disadvantageous, harmful, inimical, injurious, mischievous, pernicious, prejudicial, unfavourable

devastate demolish, desolate, despoil, destroy, lay waste, level, pillage, plunder, ravage, raze, ruin, sack, spoil, total (*slang*), trash (*slang*), waste, wreck

devastated confounded, discomfit, discomposed, disconcerted, floored (*informal*), gutted (*informal*), nonplussed, overpowered, overwhelmed, shocked, taken aback, upset

devastating caustic, cutting, deadly, destructive, effective, incisive, keen, mordant, overpowering, overwhelming, ravishing, sardonic, satirical, savage, stunning, trenchant, vitriolic, withering

devastation demolition, depredation, desolation, destruction, havoc, pillage, plunder, ravages, ruin, ruination, spoliation

(land). **7** to exploit the natural resources of (a country or region). **8** *Photog* to treat (a photographic plate or film) to produce a visible image.

developer *n* **1** a person who develops property. **2** *Photog* a chemical used to develop photographs or films.

developing country *n* a poor or nonindustrial country that is seeking to develop its resources by industrialization.

development *n* **1** the process of growing or developing. **2** the product of developing. **3** an event or incident that changes a situation. **4** an area of land that has been developed. **developmental** *adj*

development area *n* (in Britain) an area which has experienced economic depression and which is given government assistance to establish new industry.

deviant *adj* **1** deviating from what is considered acceptable behaviour. *~n* **2** a person whose behaviour deviates from what is considered to be acceptable. **deviance** *n*

deviate *vb* **-ating, -ated 1** to differ from others in belief or thought. **2** to depart from one's usual or previous behaviour. **deviation** *n*

device *n* **1** a machine or tool used for a particular purpose. **2** *Euphemistic* a bomb. **3** a scheme or plan. **4** a design or emblem. **5 leave someone to his** *or* **her own devices** to leave someone alone to do as he or she wishes.

devil *n* **1** *Theol* **the Devil** the chief spirit of evil and enemy of God. **2** any evil spirit. **3** a person regarded as wicked. **4** a person: *lucky devil.* **5** a person regarded as daring: *be a devil!* **6** *Informal* something difficult or annoying. **7 between the devil and the deep blue sea** between equally undesirable alternatives. **8 give the devil his due** to acknowledge the talent or success of an unpleasant person. **9 talk of the devil!** used when an absent person who has been the subject of conversation arrives unexpectedly. **10 the devil** used as an exclamation to show surprise or annoyance: *what the devil is she doing here? ~vb* **-illing, -illed** *or US* **-iling, -iled 11** to prepare (food) by coating with a highly flavoured spiced mixture. **12** *Chiefly Brit* to do routine literary work for a lawyer or author.

devilish *adj* **1** of or like a devil; fiendish. *~adv, adj* **2** *Informal* extreme or extremely: *devilish good food.* **devilishly** *adv*

devil-may-care *adj* happy-go-lucky; reckless.

devilment *n* mischievous conduct.

devilry *n* **1** reckless fun or mischief. **2** wickedness.

devil's advocate *n* a person who takes an opposing or unpopular point of view for the sake of argument.

devious *adj* **1** insincere and dishonest. **2** (of a route or course of action) indirect. **deviously** *adv*

devise *vb* **vising, vised** to work out (something) in one's mind.

devoid *adj* **devoid of** completely lacking in a particular quality: *she was a woman totally devoid of humour.*

devolution *n* a transfer of authority from a central government to regional governments. **devolutionist** *n, adj*

devolve *vb* **-volving, -volved** to pass or cause to pass to a successor or substitute, as duties or power.

Devonian *adj* **1** *Geol* of the period of geological time about 405 million years ago. **2** of or relating to Devon.

devote *vb* **-voting, -voted** to apply or dedicate (one's time, money, or effort) to a particular purpose.

devoted *adj* feeling or demonstrating loyalty or devotion: *he was clearly devoted to his family.* **devotedly** *adv*

THESAURUS

develop 1. advance, blossom, cultivate, evolve, flourish, foster, grow, mature, progress, promote, prosper, ripen **2.** acquire, begin, breed, commence, contract, establish, form, generate, invent, originate, pick up, start **3.** amplify, augment, broaden, dilate upon, elaborate, enlarge, expand, unfold, work out **4.** be a direct result of, break out, come about, ensue, follow, happen, result

development 1. advance, advancement, evolution, expansion, growth, improvement, increase, maturity, progress, progression, spread, unfolding, unravelling **2.** change, circumstance, event, happening, incident, issue, occurrence, outcome, phenomenon, result, situation, turn of events, upshot

deviant 1. *adj.* aberrant, abnormal, bent (*slang*), freaky (*slang*), heretical, kinky (*slang*), perverse, perverted, pervy (*slang*), queer (*informal, derogatory*), sick (*informal*), twisted, warped, wayward **2.** *n.* freak, misfit, odd type, pervert, queer (*informal, derogatory*)

deviate avert, bend, deflect, depart, differ, digress, diverge, drift, err, meander, part, stray, swerve, turn, turn aside, vary, veer, wander

deviation aberration, alteration, change, deflection, departure, digression, discrepancy, disparity, divergence, fluctuation, inconsistency, irregularity, shift, variance, variation

device 1. apparatus, appliance, contraption, contrivance, gadget, gimmick, gismo *or* gizmo (*slang, chiefly U.S. & Canad.*), implement, instrument, invention, tool, utensil **2.** artifice, design, dodge, expedient, gambit, improvisation, manoeuvre, plan, ploy, project, purpose, ruse, scheme, shift, stratagem, strategy, stunt, trick, wile **3.** badge, colophon, crest, design, emblem, figure, insignia, logo, motif, motto, symbol, token

devil 1. *sometimes cap.* Apollyon, archfiend, Beelzebub, Belial, demon, fiend, Lucifer, Old Harry (*informal*), Old Nick (*informal*), Old Scratch (*informal*), Prince of Darkness, Satan **2.** beast, brute, demon, fiend, ghoul, monster, ogre, rogue, savage, terror, villain **3.** beggar, creature, thing, unfortunate, wretch

devilish accursed, atrocious, damnable, detestable, diabolic, diabolical, execrable, fiendish, hellish, infernal, satanic, wicked

devilry 1. devilment, jiggery-pokery (*informal, chiefly Brit.*), knavery, mischief, mischievousness, monkey-business (*informal*), rascality, roguery **2.** cruelty, evil, malevolence, malice, vice, viciousness, villainy, wickedness

devious 1. calculating, crooked (*informal*), deceitful, dishonest, double-dealing, evasive, indirect, insidious, insincere, not straightforward, scheming, sly, surreptitious, treacherous, tricky, underhand, wily **2.** circuitous, confusing, crooked, deviating, erratic, excursive, indirect, misleading, rambling, roundabout, tortuous, wandering

devise arrange, conceive, concoct, construct, contrive, design, dream up, form, formulate, frame, imagine, invent, plan, plot, prepare, project, scheme, think up, work out

devoid barren, bereft, deficient, denuded, destitute, empty, free from, lacking, vacant, void, wanting, without

devolution decentralization, delegation

devolve be transferred, commission, consign, delegate, depute, entrust, fall upon *or* to, rest with, transfer

devote allot, apply, appropriate, assign, commit, concern oneself, consecrate, dedicate, enshrine, give, occupy oneself, pledge, reserve, set apart

devoted ardent, caring, committed, concerned, con-

devotee (dev-vote-**tee**) *n* **1** a person fanatically enthusiastic about a subject or activity. **2** a zealous follower of a religion.

devotion *n* **1** strong attachment to or affection for someone or something. **2** religious zeal; piety. **3 devotions** religious observance or prayers. **devotional** *adj*

devour *vb* **1** to eat up greedily. **2** to engulf and destroy. **3** to read avidly. **devouring** *adj*

devout *adj* **1** deeply religious. **2** sincere; heartfelt: *a devout confession.* **devoutly** *adv*

dew *n* drops of water that form on the ground or on a cool surface at night from vapour in the air. **dewy** *adj*

dewberry *n, pl* **-berries** a type of bramble with blue-black fruits.

dewclaw *n* a nonfunctional claw on a dog's leg.

Dewey Decimal System *n* a system of library book classification with ten main subject classes.

dewlap *n* a loose fold of skin hanging under the throat in cattle, dogs, etc.

dew-worm *n* a large earthworm used as fishing bait.

dewy-eyed *adj* innocent and inexperienced.

dexter *adj* of or on the right side of a shield, etc., from the bearer's point of view.

dexterity *n* **1** skill in using one's hands. **2** mental quickness.

dexterous *adj* possessing or done with dexterity. **dexterously** *adv*

dextrin *or* **dextrine** *n* a sticky substance obtained from starch: used as a thickening agent in food.

dextrose *n* a glucose occurring in fruit, honey, and in the blood of animals.

DFC Distinguished Flying Cross.

dg decigram.

DH *Brit* Department of Health.

dhal *or* **dal** *n* **1** the nutritious pealike seed of a tropical shrub. **2** a curry made from lentils or other pulses.

dharma *n* **1** *Hinduism* moral law or behaviour. **2** *Buddhism* ideal truth.

dhoti *n, pl* **-tis** a long loincloth worn by men in India.

DI Donor Insemination: a method of making a woman pregnant by transferring sperm from a man other than her husband or regular partner using artificial means.

di- *prefix* **1** twice; two; double: *dicotyledon.* **2** containing two specified atoms or groups of atoms: *carbon dioxide.*

diabetes (die-a-**beet**-eez) *n* a medical condition in which the body is unable to control the level of sugar in the blood.

diabetic *n* **1** a person who has diabetes. *~adj* **2** of or having diabetes. **3** suitable for people suffering from diabetes: *diabetic chocolate.*

diabolic *adj* of the Devil; satanic.

diabolical *adj Informal* **1** unpleasant or annoying: *the weather was diabolical.* **2** extreme: *diabolical cheek.* **3** same as **diabolic. diabolically** *adv*

diabolism *n* **a** witchcraft or sorcery. **b** worship of devils. **diabolist** *n*

diaconate *n* the position or period of office of a deacon. **diaconal** *adj*

diacritic *n* a sign placed above or below a character or letter to indicate phonetic value or stress.

diadem *n Old-fashioned* a small jewelled crown or headband, usually worn by royalty.

diaeresis *or esp US* **dieresis** (die-**air**-iss-iss) *n, pl* **-ses** (-seez) the mark (¨) placed over the second of two adjacent vowels to indicate that it is to be pronounced separately, as in naïve.

diagnose *vb* **-nosing, -nosed** to determine by diagnosis.

diagnosis (die-ag-**no**-siss) *n, pl* **-ses** (-seez) the discovery and identification of diseases from the examination of symptoms. **diagnostic** *adj*

diagonal *adj* **1** *Maths* connecting any two vertices in a polygon that are not adjacent. **2** slanting. *~n* **3** a diagonal line, plane, or pattern. **diagonally** *adv*

diagram *n* a sketch or plan showing the form or workings of something. **diagrammatic** *adj*

dial *n* **1** the face of a clock or watch, marked with divisions representing units of time. **2** the graduated disc on a measuring instrument. **3** the control on a radio or television set used to change the station. **4** a numbered disc on the front of some telephones. *~vb* **dialling, dialled** *or US* **dialing, dialed 5** to try to establish a telephone connection with (someone) by operating the dial or buttons on a telephone.

dialect *n* a form of a language spoken in a particular geographical area. **dialectal** *adj*

dialectic *n* **1** logical debate by question and answer

THESAURUS

stant, dedicated, devout, faithful, fond, loving, loyal, staunch, steadfast, true

devotee addict, adherent, admirer, aficionado, buff (*informal*), disciple, enthusiast, fan, fanatic, follower, supporter

devotion 1. adherence, affection, allegiance, ardour, attachment, commitment, consecration, constancy, dedication, earnestness, faithfulness, fidelity, fondness, intensity, love, loyalty, passion, zeal **2.** adoration, devoutness, godliness, holiness, piety, prayer, religiousness, reverence, sanctity, spirituality, worship **3.** *plural* church service, divine office, prayers, religious observance

devour 1. bolt, consume, cram, dispatch, eat, gobble, gorge, gulp, guzzle, pig out on (*slang*), polish off (*informal*), stuff, swallow, wolf **2.** annihilate, consume, destroy, ravage, spend, waste, wipe out **3.** absorb, appreciate, be engrossed by, be preoccupied, delight in, drink in, enjoy, feast on, go through, read compulsively *or* voraciously, relish, revel in, take in

devouring consuming, excessive, flaming, insatiable, intense, overwhelming, passionate, powerful

devout 1. godly, holy, orthodox, pious, prayerful, pure, religious, reverent, saintly **2.** ardent, deep, devoted, earnest, fervent, genuine, heartfelt, intense, passionate, profound, serious, sincere, zealous

devoutly fervently, heart and soul, profoundly, sincerely, with all one's heart

dexterity 1. adroitness, artistry, craft, deftness, effortlessness, expertise, facility, finesse, handiness, knack, mastery, neatness, nimbleness, proficiency, skill, smoothness, touch **2.** ability, address, adroitness, aptitude, aptness, art, cleverness, expertness, ingenuity, readiness, skilfulness, tact

diabolical appalling, atrocious, damnable, difficult, disastrous, dreadful, excruciating, fiendish, hellish, nasty, outrageous, shocking, tricky, unpleasant, vile

diagnose analyse, determine, distinguish, identify, interpret, investigate, pinpoint, pronounce, recognize

diagnosis analysis, examination, investigation, scrutiny

diagonal *adj.* angled, cross, crossways, crosswise, oblique, slanting

diagonally aslant, at an angle, crosswise, obliquely, on the bias, on the cross

diagram chart, drawing, figure, layout, outline, plan, representation, sketch

to resolve differences between two views. **2** the art of logical argument. **dialectical** *adj*

dialling tone *or US & Canad* **dial tone** *n* a continuous sound heard on picking up a telephone receiver, indicating that a number can be dialled.

dialogue *or US sometimes* **dialog** *n* **1** conversation between two people. **2** a conversation in a literary or dramatic work. **3** a discussion between representatives of two nations or groups.

dialysis (die-**al**-iss-iss) *n, pl* **-ses** (-seez) **1** *Med* the filtering of blood through a semipermeable membrane to remove waste products. **2** the separation of the particles in a solution by filtering through a semipermeable membrane. **dialyser** *or* **-lyzer** *n* **dialytic** *adj*

diamagnetism *n* the phenomenon exhibited by substances that are repelled by both poles of a magnet.

diamanté (die-a-**man**-tee) *adj* decorated with glittering bits of material, such as sequins.

diameter *n* **a** a straight line through the centre of a circle or sphere. **b** the length of such a line.

diametric *or* **diametrical** *adj* **1** of or relating to a diameter. **2** completely opposed: *the diametric opposition of the two camps.* **diametrically** *adv*

diamond *n* **1** a usually colourless exceptionally hard precious stone of crystallized carbon. **2** *Geom* a figure with four sides of equal length forming two acute and two obtuse angles. **3** a playing card marked with one or more red diamond-shaped symbols. **4** *Baseball* the playing field. *~adj* **5** (of an anniversary) the sixtieth: *diamond wedding.*

diapason (die-a-**pay**-zon) *n Music* **1** either of two stops found throughout the range of a pipe organ. **2** the range of an instrument or voice.

diaper *n US & Canad* a nappy.

diaphanous (die-**af**-fan-uss) *adj* (of fabrics) fine and translucent.

diaphoretic *n* **1** a drug that causes perspiration or sweat. *~adj* **2** relating to or causing perspiration or sweat.

diaphragm (**die**-a-fram) *n* **1** *Anat* the muscular partition that separates the abdominal cavity and chest cavity. **2 same as cap** (sense 5). **3** a device to control the amount of light entering an optical instrument. **4** a thin vibrating disc which converts sound to electricity or vice versa, as in a microphone or loudspeaker.

diapositive *n* a positive transparency; slide.

diarist *n* a person who writes a diary that is subsequently published.

diarrhoea *or esp US* **diarrhea** (die-a-**ree**-a) *n* frequent discharge of abnormally liquid faeces.

diary *n, pl* **-ries** **1** a book containing a record of daily events, appointments, or observations. **2** a written record of daily events, appointments, or observations.

Diaspora (die-**ass**-spore-a) *n* **1** the dispersion of the Jews after the Babylonian conquest of Palestine. **2** a dispersion of people originally belonging to one nation.

diastase (**die**-ass-stayss) *n* an enzyme that converts starch into sugar.

diastole (die-**ass**-stoh-lee) *n* dilation of the chambers of the heart. **diastolic** *adj*

diatom *n* a microscopic unicellular alga.

diatomic *adj* containing two atoms.

diatonic *adj* of or relating to any scale of five tones and two semitones produced by playing the white keys of a keyboard instrument.

diatribe *n* a bitter critical attack.

dibble *n* a small hand tool used to make holes in the ground for bulbs, seeds, or roots.

dice *n, pl* **dice** **1** a small cube, each of whose sides has a different number of spots (1 to 6), used in games of chance. *~vb* **dicing, diced** **2** to cut (food) into small cubes. **3 dice with death** to take a risk.

dicey *adj* **dicier, diciest** *Informal, chiefly Brit* dangerous or tricky.

dichotomy (die-**kot**-a-mee) *n, pl* **-mies** division into two opposed groups or parts. **dichotomous** *adj*

dichromatic *adj* having two colours.

dick *n Slang* **1** *Taboo* a penis. **2 clever dick** *Brit* an opinionated person.

dickens *n* **the dickens** *Informal* used as an exclamation to show surprise, confusion, or annoyance: *what the dickens do you think you're doing?*

Dickensian *adj* **1** of Charles Dickens (1812–70), British novelist. **2** denoting poverty, distress, and exploitation, as depicted in the novels of Dickens.

dicky[1] *n, pl* **dickies** a false shirt front.

dicky[2] *adj* **dickier, dickiest** *Brit informal* shaky or weak: *a dicky heart.*

dicky-bird *n* a child's word for a bird.

dicky-bow *n Brit* a bow tie.

dicotyledon (die-kot-ill-**leed**-on) *n* a flowering plant with two seed leaves.

dictate *vb* **-tating, -tated** **1** to say (words) aloud for another person to transcribe. **2** to seek to impose one's will on others. *~n* **3** an authoritative command. **4** a guiding principle: *the dictates of reason.*

dictation *n* **1** the act of dictating words to be taken down in writing. **2** the words dictated. **3** the act of giving authoritative commands.

dictator *n* **1** a ruler who has complete power. **2** a

THESAURUS

dialect accent, idiom, jargon, language, patois, pronunciation, speech, tongue, vernacular

dialectic *n. often plural* argumentation, contention, discussion, disputation, logic, polemics, ratiocination, reasoning

dialogue 1. colloquy, communication, confabulation (*formal*), conference, conversation, converse, discourse, discussion, duologue, interlocution **2.** conversation, lines, script, spoken part

diametric, diametrical antithetical, conflicting, contrary, contrasting, counter, opposed, opposite

diametrically absolutely, completely, entirely, utterly

diary appointment book, chronicle, daily record, day-to-day account, engagement book, Filofax (*Trademark*), journal, personal organizer

diatribe abuse, castigation, criticism, denunciation, disputation, harangue, invective, philippic, reviling, stream of abuse, stricture, tirade, verbal onslaught, vituperation

dicey chancy (*informal*), dangerous, difficult, hairy (*slang*), risky, ticklish, tricky

dicky *adj.* fluttery, queer, shaky, unreliable, unsound, unsteady, weak

dictate *vb.* **1.** read out, say, speak, transmit, utter **2.** command, decree, demand, direct, enjoin, establish, impose, lay down, ordain, order, prescribe, pronounce *~n.* **3.** behest, bidding, command, decree, demand, direction, edict, fiat, injunction, mandate, order, ordinance, requirement, statute, ultimatum, word **4.** canon, code, dictum, law, precept, principle, rule

dictator absolute ruler, autocrat, despot, oppressor, tyrant

dictatorial 1. absolute, arbitrary, autocratic, despotic, totalitarian, tyrannical, unlimited, unrestricted **2.**

person who behaves in a tyrannical manner. **dictatorship** *n*

dictatorial *adj* **1** of or pertaining to a dictator. **2** tyrannical; overbearing. **dictatorially** *adv*

diction *n* the manner of pronouncing words and sounds.

dictionary *n, pl* **-aries 1 a** a book that consists of an alphabetical list of words with their meanings. **b** a similar book giving equivalent words in two languages. **2** a reference book listing terms and giving information about a particular subject.

dictum *n, pl* **-tums** *or* **-ta 1** a formal statement; pronouncement. **2** a popular saying or maxim.

did *vb* the past tense of **do**[1].

didactic *adj* intended to teach or instruct people: *an Impressionist work can be as didactic in its way as a sermon.* **didactically** *adv* **didacticism** *n*

diddle *vb* **-dling, -dled** *Informal* to swindle. **diddler** *n*

didgeridoo *n* a native deep-toned Australian wind instrument.

didn't did not.

die[1] *vb* **dying, died 1** (of a person, animal, or plant) to cease all biological activity permanently. **2** (of something inanimate) to cease to exist. **3** to lose strength, power, or energy by degrees. **4** to stop working: *the engine died.* **5 be dying** to be eager (for something or to do something). **6 be dying of** *Informal* to be nearly overcome with (laughter, boredom, etc.). **7 die hard** to change or disappear only slowly: *old loyalties die hard.* ~See also **die down, die out.**

die[2] *n* **1** a shaped block used to cut or form metal. **2** a casting mould. **3** same as **dice** (sense 1). **4 the die is cast** an irrevocable decision has been taken.

die down *vb* **1** to lose strength or power by degrees. **2** to become calm: *the storm has died down now.*

die-hard *n* a person who resists change.

dieldrin *n* a highly toxic crystalline insecticide.

dielectric *n* **1** a substance of very low electrical conductivity; insulator. *~adj* **2** having the properties of a dielectric.

die out *or* **off** *vb* to become extinct or disappear after a gradual decline.

dieresis (die-air-iss-iss) *n, pl* **-ses** (-seez) same as **diaeresis.**

diesel *n* **1** same as **diesel engine. 2** a vehicle driven by a diesel engine. **3** *Informal* diesel oil.

diesel-electric *n* a locomotive with a diesel engine driving an electric generator.

diesel engine *n* an internal-combustion engine in which oil is ignited by compression.

diesel oil *or* **fuel** *n* a fuel obtained from petroleum distillation, used in diesel engines.

diet[1] *n* **1** the food that a person or animal regularly eats. **2** a specific allowance or selection of food, to control weight or for health reasons: *a high-fibre diet.* *~vb* **3** to follow a special diet so as to lose weight. *~adj* **4** suitable for eating with a weight-reduction diet: *diet soft drinks.* **dietary** *adj* **dieter** *n*

diet[2] *n* a legislative assembly in some countries.

dietary fibre *n* the roughage in fruits and vegetables that aid digestion.

dietetic *adj* prepared for special dietary requirements.

dietetics *n* the study of diet, nutrition, and the preparation of food.

dietician *n* a person qualified to advise people about healthy eating.

differ *vb* **1** to be dissimilar in quality, nature, or degree. **2** to disagree.

difference *n* **1** the state or quality of being unlike. **2** a disagreement or argument. **3** the result of the subtraction of one number or quantity from another. **4 make a difference** to have an effect. **5 split the difference a** to compromise. **b** to divide a remainder equally.

different *adj* **1** partly or completely unlike. **2** new or unusual. **3** not identical or the same; other: *he wears a different tie every day.* **differently** *adv*

➤ The accepted idiom is *different from* but *different to* is also used. *Different than* is an Americanism.

differential *adj* **1** of, relating to, or using a difference. **2** *Maths* involving differentials. *~n* **3** a factor that differentiates between two comparable things. **4** *Maths* a minute difference between values in a scale. **5** *Chiefly Brit* the difference between rates of pay for

THESAURUS

authoritarian, bossy (*informal*), dogmatical, domineering, imperious, iron-handed, magisterial, oppressive, overbearing

dictatorship absolute rule, absolutism, authoritarianism, autocracy, despotism, reign of terror, totalitarianism, tyranny

diction articulation, delivery, elocution, enunciation, fluency, inflection, intonation, pronunciation, speech

dictionary concordance, encyclopedia, glossary, lexicon, vocabulary, wordbook

die 1. breathe one's last, buy it (*U.S. slang*), croak (*slang*), decease, depart, expire, finish, give up the ghost, go belly-up (*slang*), kick it (*slang*), kick the bucket (*slang*), pass away, peg it (*informal*), peg out (*informal*), perish, pop one's clogs (*informal*), snuff it (*slang*) **2.** decay, decline, disappear, dwindle, ebb, end, fade, lapse, pass, sink, subside, vanish, wane, wilt, wither **3.** break down, fade out *or* away, fail, fizzle out, halt, lose power, peter out, run down, stop **4.** ache, be eager, desire, hunger, languish, long, pine for, swoon, yearn **5.** *usually with* **of** be overcome, collapse, succumb to

die-hard *n.* fanatic, intransigent, old fogy, reactionary, stick-in-the-mud (*informal*), ultraconservative, zealot

diet[1] *n.* **1.** aliment, comestibles, commons, edibles, fare, food, nourishment, nutriment, provisions, rations, subsistence, sustenance, viands, victuals **2.** abstinence, fast, regime, regimen *~vb.* **3.** abstain, eat sparingly, fast, lose weight, reduce, slim

diet[2] chamber, congress, convention, council, legislative assembly, legislature, meeting, parliament, sitting

differ 1. be dissimilar, be distinct, contradict, contrast, depart from, diverge, run counter to, stand apart, vary **2.** clash, contend, debate, demur, disagree, dispute, dissent, oppose, take issue

difference 1. alteration, change, contrast, deviation, differentiation, discrepancy, disparity, dissimilarity, distinction, distinctness, divergence, diversity, unlikeness, variation, variety **2.** argument, clash, conflict, contention, contrariety, contretemps, controversy, debate, disagreement, discordance, dispute, quarrel, row, set-to (*informal*), strife, tiff, wrangle **3.** balance, remainder, rest, result

different 1. altered, at odds, at variance, changed, clashing, contrasting, deviating, discrepant, disparate, dissimilar, divergent, diverse, inconsistent, opposed, unlike **2.** another story, atypical, bizarre, distinctive, extraordinary, out of the ordinary, peculiar, rare, singular, something else, special, strange, uncommon, unconventional, unique, unusual **3.** another, assorted, discrete, distinct, diverse, individual, manifold, many, miscellaneous, multifarious, numerous, other, separate, several, some, sundry, varied, various

different types of labour, esp. within a company or industry.

differential calculus *n* the branch of mathematics concerned with derivatives and differentials.

differential gear *n* the gear in the driving axle of a road vehicle that permits one driving wheel to rotate faster than the other when cornering.

differentiate *vb* **-ating, -ated 1** to perceive or show the difference (between). **2** to make (one thing) distinct from other such things. **3** *Maths* to determine the derivative of a function or variable. **differentiation** *n*

difficult *adj* **1** not easy to do, understand, or solve. **2** not easily pleased or satisfied: *a difficult patient.* **3** full of hardships or trials: *he had recently had a difficult time with his job as a self-employed builder.*

difficulty *n, pl* **-ties 1** the state or quality of being difficult. **2** a task or problem that is hard to deal with. **3** a troublesome or embarrassing situation: *in financial difficulties.* **4** an objection or obstacle: *you're just making difficulties.* **5** lack of ease; awkwardness: *he could run only with difficulty.*

diffident *adj* lacking self-confidence; shy. **diffidence** *n* **diffidently** *adv*

diffract *vb* to cause to undergo diffraction. **diffractive** *adj*

diffraction *n* **1** *Physics* a deviation in the direction of a wave at the edge of an obstacle in its path. **2** the formation of light and dark fringes by the passage of light through a small aperture.

diffuse *vb* **-fusing, -fused 1** to spread over a wide area. **2** *Physics* to cause to undergo diffusion. ~*adj* **3** spread out over a wide area. **4** lacking conciseness. **diffusible** *adj* **diffuser** *n*

diffusion *n* **1** the act of diffusing or the fact of being diffused; dispersion. **2** *Physics* the random thermal motion of atoms and molecules in gases, liquids, and some solids. **3** *Physics* the transmission or reflection of light, in which the radiation is scattered in many directions.

dig *vb* **digging, dug 1** to cut into, break up, and turn over or remove (earth), esp. with a spade. **2** to excavate (a hole or tunnel) by digging, usually with an implement or (of animals) with claws. **3** to obtain by digging: *dig out potatoes.* **4** to find by effort or searching: *he dug out a mini cassette from his pocket.* **5** *Informal* to like or understand. **6** (foll. by *in* or *into*) to thrust or jab. ~*n* **7** the act of digging. **8** an archaeological excavation. **9** a thrust or poke. **10** a cutting remark. ~See also **dig in.**

digest *vb* **1** to subject (food) to a process of digestion. **2** to absorb mentally. ~*n* **3** a shortened version of a book, report, or article. **digestible** *adj*

digestion *n* **1** the process of breaking down food into easily absorbed substances. **2** the body's system for doing this.

digestive *adj* relating to digestion.

digger *n* **1** a machine used for excavation. **2** *Austral & NZ informal* an Australian or New Zealander: often used as a friendly term of address.

dig in *vb* **1** to mix (compost or fertilizer) into the soil by digging. **2** *Informal* to begin to eat vigorously. **3** *Informal* (of soldiers) to dig a trench and prepare for an enemy attack. **4 dig one's heels in** *Informal* to refuse to move or be persuaded.

digit (**dij**-it) *n* **1** a finger or toe. **2** any numeral from 0 to 9.

digital *adj* **1** displaying information as numbers rather than with a dial. **2** representing data as a series of numerical values. **3** of or possessing digits. **digitally** *adv*

digital audio tape *n* magnetic tape on which sound is recorded digitally, giving high-fidelity reproduction.

digital clock *or* **watch** *n* a clock or watch in which

THESAURUS

differential 1. *adj.* diacritical, discriminative, distinctive, distinguishing **2.** *n.* amount of difference, difference, discrepancy, disparity

differentiate 1. contrast, discern, discriminate, distinguish, make a distinction, mark off, separate, set off or apart, tell apart **2.** adapt, alter, change, convert, make different, modify, transform

difficult 1. abstract, abstruse, arduous, baffling, burdensome, complex, complicated, delicate, demanding, formidable, hard, intricate, involved, knotty, laborious, no picnic (*informal*), obscure, onerous, painful, perplexing, problematical, strenuous, thorny, ticklish, toilsome, uphill, wearisome **2.** demanding, fastidious, fractious, fussy, hard to please, intractable, obstreperous, perverse, refractory, rigid, tiresome, troublesome, trying, unaccommodating, unamenable, unmanageable **3.** dark, full of hardship, grim, hard, straitened, tough, trying

difficulty 1. deep water, dilemma, distress, embarrassment, fix (*informal*), hot water (*informal*), jam (*informal*), mess, perplexity, pickle (*informal*), plight, predicament, quandary, spot (*informal*), straits, tight spot, trial, trouble **2.** *often plural* complication, hassle (*informal*), hindrance, hurdle, impediment, objection, obstacle, opposition, pitfall, problem, protest, snag, stumbling block **3.** arduousness, awkwardness, hardship, laboriousness, labour, pain, painfulness, strain, strenuousness, tribulation

diffidence backwardness, bashfulness, constraint, doubt, fear, hesitancy, hesitation, humility, insecurity, lack of self-confidence, meekness, modesty, reluctance, reserve, self-consciousness, sheepishness, shyness, timidity, timidness, timorousness, unassertiveness

diffident backward, bashful, constrained, distrustful, doubtful, hesitant, insecure, meek, modest, reluctant, reserved, self-conscious, self-effacing, sheepish, shrinking, shy, suspicious, timid, timorous, unassertive, unassuming, unobtrusive, unsure, withdrawn

diffuse *vb.* **1.** circulate, dispel, dispense, disperse, disseminate, dissipate, distribute, propagate, scatter, spread ~*adj.* **2.** dispersed, scattered, spread out, unconcentrated **3.** circumlocutory, copious, diffusive, digressive, discursive, long-winded, loose, maundering, meandering, prolix, rambling, vague, verbose, waffling (*informal*), wordy

diffusion circulation, dispersal, dispersion, dissemination, dissipation, distribution, expansion, propaganda, propagation, scattering, spread

dig *vb.* **1.** break up, burrow, delve, excavate, gouge, grub, hoe, hollow out, mine, penetrate, pierce, quarry, scoop, till, tunnel, turn over **2.** delve, dig down, go into, investigate, probe, research, search **3.** *with* **out** *or* **up** bring to light, come across, come up with, discover, expose, extricate, find, retrieve, root (*informal*), rootle, uncover, unearth **4.** *informal* appreciate, enjoy, follow, groove (*dated slang*), like, understand **5.** drive, jab, poke, prod, punch, thrust ~*n.* **6.** jab, poke, prod, punch, thrust **7.** barb, crack (*slang*), cutting remark, gibe, insult, jeer, quip, sneer, taunt, wisecrack (*informal*)

digest *vb.* **1.** absorb, assimilate, concoct, dissolve, incorporate, macerate **2.** absorb, assimilate, con, consider, contemplate, grasp, master, meditate, ponder, study, take in, understand ~*n.* **3.** abridgment, abstract, compendium, condensation, epitome, précis, résumé, summary, synopsis

the time is indicated by digits rather than by hands on a dial.

digital computer *n* a computer in which the input consists of numbers, letters, and other characters that are represented internally in binary notation.

digitalis *n* a drug made from foxglove leaves: used as a heart stimulant.

digital recording *n* a sound recording process that converts audio or analogue signals into a series of pulses.

digitate *adj* **1** (of leaves) having leaflets in the form of a spread hand. **2** (of animals) having digits.

digitize *or* **-ise** *vb* **-izing, -ized** *or* **-ising, -ised** to transcribe (data) into a digital form for processing by a computer. **digitizer** *or* **-iser** *n*

dignified *adj* calm, impressive, and worthy of respect.

dignify *vb* **-fies, -fying, -fied 1** to add distinction to: *the meeting was dignified by the minister.* **2** to add a semblance of dignity to by the use of a pretentious name or title: *she dignifies every plant with its Latin name.*

dignitary *n, pl* **-taries** a person of high official position or rank.

dignity *n, pl* **-ties 1** serious, calm, and controlled behaviour or manner. **2** the quality of being worthy of honour. **3** sense of self-importance: *he considered the job beneath his dignity.*

digraph *n* two letters used to represent a single sound, such as *gh* in *tough.*

digress *vb* to depart from the main subject in speech or writing. **digression** *n*

digs *pl n Brit informal* lodgings.

dihedral *adj* having or formed by two intersecting planes.

dilapidated *adj* (of a building) having fallen into ruin. **dilapidation** *n*

dilate *vb* **-lating, -lated** to make or become wider or larger: *her eyes dilated in the dark.* **dilation** *or* **dilatation** *n*

dilatory (dill-a-tree) *adj* tending or intended to waste time. **dilatorily** *adv* **dilatoriness** *n*

dildo *n, pl* **-dos** an object used as a substitute for an erect penis.

dilemma *n* a situation offering a choice between two equally undesirable alternatives.

➤ If a difficult choice involves more than two courses of action, it is preferable to speak of a *problem* or *difficulty.*

dilettante (dill-it-**tan**-tee) *n, pl* **-tantes** *or* **-tanti** a person whose interest in a subject is superficial rather than serious. **dilettantism** *n*

diligent *adj* **1** careful and persevering in carrying out tasks or duties. **2** carried out with care and perseverance: *a diligent approach to work.* **diligence** *n* **diligently** *adv*

dill *n* a sweet-smelling herb used for flavouring.

dilly-dally *vb* **-lies, -lying, -lied** *Informal* to dawdle or waste time.

dilute *vb* **-luting, -luted 1** to make (a liquid) less concentrated by adding water or another liquid. **2** to make (someone's power, idea, or role) weaker or less effective: *socialists used their majority in parliament to dilute legislation crucial to developing a market economy.* ~*adj* **3** *Chem* (of a solution) having a low concentration. **dilution** *n*

diluvian *adj* of a flood, esp. the great Flood described in the Old Testament.

dim *adj* **dimmer, dimmest 1** badly lit. **2** not clearly seen; faint: *a dim figure in the doorway.* **3** not seeing clearly: *eyes dim with tears.* **4** *Informal* mentally dull. **5** not clear in the mind; obscure: *a dim awareness.* **6** lacking in brightness or lustre: *a dim colour.* **7 take a dim view of** to disapprove of. ~*vb* **dimming, dimmed**

THESAURUS

digestion absorption, assimilation, conversion, incorporation, ingestion, transformation

dig in 1. *informal* begin, set about, start eating, tuck in (*informal*) **2.** defend, entrench, establish, fortify, maintain

dignified august, decorous, distinguished, exalted, formal, grave, honourable, imposing, lofty, lordly, noble, reserved, solemn, stately, upright

dignify adorn, advance, aggrandize, distinguish, elevate, ennoble, exalt, glorify, grace, honour, promote, raise

dignitary bigwig (*informal*), celeb (*informal*), high-up (*informal*), notable, personage, pillar of society (the church, the state), public figure, V.I.P., worthy

dignity 1. courtliness, decorum, grandeur, gravity, hauteur, loftiness, majesty, nobility, propriety, solemnity, stateliness **2.** elevation, eminence, excellence, glory, greatness, honour, importance, nobleness, rank, respectability, standing, station, status **3.** *amour-propre,* pride, self-esteem, self-importance, self-possession, self-regard, self-respect

digress be diffuse, depart, deviate, diverge, drift, get off the point *or* subject, go off at a tangent, meander, ramble, stray, turn aside, wander

digression apostrophe, aside, departure, detour, deviation, divergence, diversion, footnote, parenthesis, straying, wandering

dilapidated battered, beat-up (*informal*), broken-down, crumbling, decayed, decaying, decrepit, falling apart, gone to rack and ruin, in ruins, neglected, ramshackle, rickety, ruined, ruinous, run-down, shabby, shaky, tumbledown, uncared for, worn-out

dilate broaden, distend, enlarge, expand, extend, puff out, stretch, swell, widen

dilatory backward, behindhand, dallying, delaying, laggard, lingering, loitering, procrastinating, putting off, slack, slow, sluggish, snail-like, tardy, tarrying, time-wasting

dilemma difficulty, embarrassment, fix (*informal*), jam (*informal*), mess, pickle (*informal*), plight, predicament, problem, puzzle, quandary, spot (*informal*), strait, tight corner *or* spot

dilettante aesthete, amateur, dabbler, nonprofessional, trifler

diligence activity, application, assiduity, assiduousness, attention, attentiveness, care, constancy, earnestness, heedfulness, industry, intentness, laboriousness, perseverance, sedulousness

diligent active, assiduous, attentive, busy, careful, conscientious, constant, earnest, hard-working, indefatigable, industrious, laborious, painstaking, persevering, persistent, sedulous, studious, tireless

dilly-dally dally, dawdle, delay, dither (*chiefly Brit.*), falter, fluctuate, hesitate, hover, linger, loiter, potter, procrastinate, shillyshally (*informal*), trifle, vacillate, waver

dilute *vb.* **1.** adulterate, cut, make thinner, thin (out), water down, weaken **2.** attenuate, decrease, diffuse, diminish, lessen, mitigate, reduce, temper, weaken

dim *adj.* **1.** cloudy, dark, darkish, dusky, grey, overcast, poorly lit, shadowy, unilluminated **2.** bleary, blurred, faint, fuzzy, ill-defined, indistinct, obscured, shadowy, unclear **3.** braindead (*informal*), dense, doltish, dozy (*Brit. informal*), dull, dumb (*informal*), ob-

8 to become or cause to become dim. **9** to cause to seem less bright. **10** *US & Canad* same as **dip** (sense 4). **dimly** *adv* **dimness** *n*

dime *n* a coin of the US and Canada worth ten cents.

dimension *n* **1** an aspect or factor: *the attack brought a whole new dimension to the bombing campaign.* **2 dimensions** scope or extent. **3** (*often pl*) a measurement of the size of something in a particular direction. **dimensional** *adj*

dimer *n Chem* a molecule made up of two identical molecules bonded together.

diminish *vb* **1** to make or become smaller, fewer, or less. **2** *Music* to decrease (a minor interval) by a semitone. **3** to reduce in authority or status.

diminuendo *Music ~n, pl* **-dos 1 a** a gradual decrease in loudness. **b** a passage which gradually decreases in loudness. *~adv* **2** gradually decreasing in loudness.

diminution *n* reduction in size, volume, intensity, or importance.

diminutive *adj* **1** very small; tiny. **2** *Grammar* **a** denoting an affix added to a word to convey the meaning *small* or *unimportant* or to express affection, as for example, the suffix *-ette* in French. **b** denoting a word formed by the addition of a diminutive affix. *~n* **3** *Grammar* a diminutive word or affix. **diminutiveness** *n*

dimmer *n* **1** a device for dimming an electric light. **2** *US* **a** a dipped headlight on a road vehicle. **b** a parking light on a car.

dimple *n* **1** a small natural dent on the cheeks or chin. *~vb* **-pling, -pled 2** to produce dimples by smiling.

dimwit *n Informal* a stupid person. **dim-witted** *adj*

din *n* **1** a loud unpleasant confused noise. *~vb* **dinning, dinned 2 din something into someone** to instil something into someone by constant repetition.

dinar (**dee**-nahr) *n* a monetary unit of various Balkan, Middle Eastern, and North African countries.

dine *vb* **dining, dined 1** to eat dinner. **2 dine on** *or* **off** to make one's meal of: *the guests dined on roast beef.*

diner *n* **1** a person eating a meal in a restaurant. **2** *Chiefly US & Canad* a small cheap restaurant. **3** short for **dining car.**

dinette *n* an alcove or small area for use as a dining room.

ding-dong *n* **1** the sound of a bell. **2** a violent exchange of blows or words.

dinges (**ding**-uss) *n S African informal* a jocular word for something whose name is unknown or forgotten; thingumabob.

dinghy (**ding**-ee, **ding**-gee) *n, pl* **-ghies** a small boat, powered by sail, oars, or outboard motor.

dingle *n* a small wooded hollow or valley.

dingo *n, pl* **-goes** an Australian wild dog.

dingy (**din**-jee) *adj* **-gier, -giest 1** dull, neglected, and drab: *he waited in this dingy little outer office.* **2** shabby and discoloured: *she was wearing dingy white overalls.* **dinginess** *n*

dining car *n* a railway coach in which meals are served.

dining room *n* a room where meals are eaten.

dinkum *adj Austral & NZ informal* **1** genuine or right: *a fair dinkum offer.* **2 dinkum oil** the truth.

dinky *adj* **dinkier, dinkiest** *Brit informal* small and neat; dainty.

dinner *n* **1** the main meal of the day, eaten either in the evening or at midday. **2** a formal social occasion at which an evening meal is served.

dinner jacket *n* a man's semiformal black evening jacket without tails.

dinner service *n* a set of matching dishes suitable for serving a meal.

dinosaur *n* any of a large order of extinct prehistoric reptiles many of which were gigantic.

dint *n* **by dint of** by means of: *by dint of their own efforts.*

diocesan *adj* of or relating to a diocese.

diocese (**die**-a-siss) *n* the district over which a bishop has control.

diode *n* **1** a semiconductor device for converting alternating current to direct current. **2** an electronic valve with two electrodes between which a current can flow only in one direction.

dioecious (die-**eesh**-uss) *adj* (of plants) having the male and female reproductive organs on separate plants.

Dionysian (die-on-**niz**-zee-an) *adj* wild or orgiastic.

dioptre *or US* **diopter** (die-**op**-ter) *n* a unit for measuring the refractive power of a lens.

diorama *n* **1** a miniature three-dimensional scene, in which models of figures are seen against a background. **2** a picture made up of illuminated translucent curtains, viewed through an aperture.

dioxide *n* an oxide containing two oxygen atoms per molecule.

dip *vb* **dipping, dipped 1** to plunge or be plunged quickly or briefly into a liquid. **2** to put one's hands into something, esp. to obtain an object: *she dipped into her handbag looking for change.* **3** to slope downwards. **4** to switch (car headlights) from the main to the lower beam. **5** to undergo a slight decline, esp. temporarily: *sales dipped in November.* **6** to im-

THESAURUS

tuse, slow, slow on the uptake (*informal*), stupid, thick **4.** confused, hazy, imperfect, indistinct, intangible, obscure, remote, shadowy, vague **5.** dingy, dull, feeble, lacklustre, muted, opaque, pale, sullied, tarnished, weak **6. take a dim view** be displeased, be sceptical, disapprove, look askance, reject, suspect, take exception, view with disfavour *~vb.* **7.** bedim, blur, cloud, darken, dull, fade, lower, obscure, tarnish, turn down

dimension *often plural* **1.** amplitude, bulk, capacity, extent, measurement, proportions, size, volume **2.** bigness, extent, greatness, importance, largeness, magnitude, measure, range, scale, scope

diminish 1. abate, contract, curtail, cut, decline, decrease, die out, dwindle, ebb, fade away, lessen, lower, peter out, recede, reduce, retrench, shrink, shrivel, slacken, subside, wane, weaken **2.** belittle, cheapen, demean, depreciate, devalue

diminution abatement, contraction, curtailment, cut, cutback, decay, decline, decrease, deduction, lessening, reduction, retrenchment, weakening

diminutive *adj.* bantam, Lilliputian, little, midget, mini, miniature, minute, petite, pocket(-sized), pygmy *or* pigmy, small, teensy-weensy, teeny-weeny, tiny, undersized, wee

din 1. *n.* babel, clamour, clangour, clash, clatter, commotion, crash, hubbub, hullabaloo, noise, outcry, pandemonium, racket, row, shout, uproar **2.** *vb. usually with* **into** drum into, go on at, hammer into, inculcate, instil, instruct, teach

dine 1. banquet, eat, feast, lunch, sup **2.** *often with* **on** *or* **off** consume, eat, feed on

dingy bedimmed, colourless, dark, dim, dirty, discoloured, drab, dreary, dull, dusky, faded, gloomy, grimy, murky, obscure, seedy, shabby, soiled, sombre, tacky (*informal*)

merse (farm animals) briefly in a chemical to rid them of insects. **7** to lower or be lowered briefly: *she dipped her knee in a curtsy.* ~*n* **8** the act of dipping. **9** a brief swim. **10** a liquid chemical in which farm animals are dipped. **11** a depression, esp. in a landscape. **12** a momentary sinking down. **13** a creamy mixture into which pieces of food are dipped before being eaten. ~See also **dip into.**

Dip Ed (in Britain) Diploma in Education.

diphtheria (dif-**theer**-ree-a) *n* a contagious disease producing fever and difficulty in breathing and swallowing.

diphthong *n* a vowel sound, occupying a single syllable, in which the speaker's tongue moves continuously from one position to another, as in the pronunciation of *a* in *late.*

dip into *vb* **1** to draw upon: *he dipped into his savings.* **2** to read passages at random from (a book or journal).

diploid *adj Biol* denoting a cell or organism with pairs of homologous chromosomes.

diploma *n* a document conferring a qualification or recording successful completion of a course of study.

diplomacy *n* **1** the conduct of the relations between nations by peaceful means. **2** skill in the management of international relations. **3** tact or skill in dealing with people.

diplomat *n* an official, such as an ambassador, engaged in diplomacy.

diplomatic *adj* **1** of or relating to diplomacy. **2** skilled in negotiating between nations. **3** tactful in dealing with people. **diplomatically** *adv*

diplomatic immunity *n* the freedom from legal action and exemption from taxation which diplomats have in the country where they are working.

dipole *n* **1** two equal but opposite electric charges or magnetic poles separated by a small distance. **2** a molecule that has two such charges or poles. **dipolar** *adj*

dipper *n* **1** a ladle used for dipping. **2** a songbird that inhabits fast-flowing streams.

dipsomania *n* a compulsive desire to drink alcoholic beverages. **dipsomaniac** *n, adj*

dipstick *n* a rod with notches on it dipped into a container to indicate the fluid level.

dip switch *n* a device for dipping headlights on a vehicle.

dipterous *adj* having two wings or winglike parts.

diptych (**dip**-tik) *n* a painting on two hinged panels.

dire *adj* disastrous, urgent, or terrible: *he was now in dire financial straits.*

direct *adj* **1** shortest; straight: *a direct route.* **2** without intervening people: *they secretly arranged direct links to their commanders.* **3** honest; frank: *he was polite but very direct.* **4** diametric: *the direct opposite.* **5** in an unbroken line of descent: *a direct descendant.* ~*adv* **6** directly; straight. ~*vb* **7** to conduct or control the affairs of. **8** to give orders with authority to (a person or group). **9** to tell (someone) the way to a place. **10** to address (a letter, parcel, etc.). **11** to address (a look or remark) at someone: *the look she directed at him was one of unconcealed hatred.* **12 a** to provide guidance to (actors, cameramen, etc.) in (a play or film). **b** to supervise the making or staging of (a film or play). **directness** *n*

direct access *n* a method of reading data from a computer file without reading through the file from the beginning.

direct current *n* an electric current that flows in one direction only.

direct debit *n* an order given to a bank or other financial institution by an account holder to pay an amount of money from the account to a specified person or company at regular intervals.

direction *n* **1** the course or line along which a person or thing moves, points, or lies. **2** management or guidance: *the campaign was successful under his direction.* **3** the work of a stage or film director.

directional *adj* **1** of or showing direction. **2** *Electronics* (of an aerial) transmitting or receiving radio waves more effectively in some directions than in others.

directions *pl n* instructions for doing something or for reaching a place.

directive *n* an instruction; order.

THESAURUS

dinner banquet, beanfeast (*Brit. informal*), blowout (*slang*), collation, feast, main meal, meal, refection, repast, spread (*informal*)

dip *vb.* **1.** bathe, douse, duck, dunk, immerse, plunge, rinse, souse **2.** decline, descend, disappear, droop, drop (down), fade, fall, lower, sag, set, sink, slope, slump, subside, tilt ~*n.* **3.** douche, drenching, ducking, immersion, plunge, soaking **4.** bathe, dive, plunge, swim **5.** concoction, dilution, infusion, mixture, preparation, solution, suspension **6.** basin, concavity, depression, hole, hollow, incline, slope **7.** decline, drop, fall, lowering, sag, slip, slump

dip into 1. browse, dabble, glance at, peruse, play at, run over, sample, skim, try **2.** draw upon, reach into

diplomacy 1. international negotiation, statecraft, statesmanship **2.** artfulness, craft, delicacy, discretion, finesse, savoir-faire, skill, subtlety, tact

diplomat conciliator, go-between, mediator, moderator, negotiator, politician, public relations expert, tactician

diplomatic adept, discreet, polite, politic, prudent, sensitive, subtle, tactful

dire alarming, appalling, awful, calamitous, cataclysmic, catastrophic, critical, crucial, cruel, crying, desperate, disastrous, dismal, drastic, dreadful, exigent, extreme, fearful, gloomy, godawful (*slang*), grim, horrible, horrid, ominous, portentous, pressing, ruinous, terrible, urgent, woeful

direct *adj.* **1.** nonstop, not crooked, shortest, straight, through, unbroken, undeviating, uninterrupted **2.** face-to-face, first-hand, head-on, immediate, personal **3.** candid, downright, frank, honest, man-to-man, matter-of-fact, open, outspoken, plain-spoken, sincere, straight, straightforward, upfront (*informal*) ~*vb.* **4.** administer, advise, conduct, control, dispose, govern, guide, handle, lead, manage, mastermind, oversee, preside over, regulate, rule, run, superintend, supervise **5.** bid, charge, command, demand, dictate, enjoin, instruct, order **6.** guide, indicate, lead, point in the direction of, point the way, show **7.** address, label, mail, route, send **8.** address, aim, cast, fix, focus, intend, level, mean, point, train, turn

direction 1. aim, bearing, course, line, path, road, route, track, way **2.** administration, charge, command, control, government, guidance, leadership, management, order, oversight, superintendence, supervision

directions briefing, guidance, guidelines, indication, instructions, plan, recommendation, regulations

directive *n.* charge, command, decree, dictate, edict, fiat, imperative, injunction, instruction, mandate, notice, order, ordinance, regulation, ruling

directly 1. by the shortest route, candidly, exactly, face-to-face, honestly, in a beeline, in person, openly, overtly, personally, plainly, point-blank, precisely, straight, straightforwardly, truthfully, unequivocally, unswervingly, without deviation, without prevarica-

directly *adv* **1** in a direct manner. **2** at once; without delay. **3** immediately or very soon: *I'll do that directly.* ~*conj* **4** as soon as: *we left directly the money arrived.*

direct object *n Grammar* a noun, pronoun, or noun phrase denoting the person or thing receiving the direct action of a verb. For example, *a book* in *They bought Anne a book.*

director *n* **1** a person or thing that directs or controls. **2** a member of the governing board of a business, trust, etc. **3** the person responsible for the artistic and technical aspects of the making of a film or television programme. **directorial** *adj* **directorship** *n*

directorate *n* **1** a board of directors. **2** the position of director.

director-general *n, pl* **directors-general** a person in overall charge of certain large organizations.

directory *n, pl* **-ries 1** a book listing names, addresses, and telephone numbers of individuals or business companies. **2** *Computers* an area of a disk containing the names and locations of the files it currently holds.

direct speech *n* the reporting of what someone has said by quoting the exact words.

direct tax *n* a tax paid by the person or organization on which it is levied.

dirge *n* **1** a chant of lamentation for the dead. **2** any mournful song.

dirigible (**dir**-rij-jib-bl) *adj* **1** able to be steered. ~*n* **2** same as **airship.**

dirk *n* a dagger, formerly worn by Scottish Highlanders.

dirndl *n* **1** a woman's dress with a full gathered skirt and fitted bodice. **2** a gathered skirt of this kind.

dirt *n* **1** any unclean substance, such as mud; filth. **2** loose earth; soil. **3** packed earth, cinders, etc., used to make a racetrack. **4** obscene speech or writing. **5** *Informal* harmful gossip.

dirt-cheap *adj, adv* at an extremely low price.

dirt track *n* a racetrack made of packed earth or cinders.

dirty *adj* **dirtier, dirtiest 1** covered or marked with dirt; filthy. **2** causing one to become grimy: *a dirty job.* **3** (of a colour) not clear and bright. **4** unfair, dishonest, or unkind: *dirty tricks.* **5 a** obscene: *dirty jokes.* **b** sexually clandestine: *a dirty weekend.* **6** revealing dislike or anger: *a dirty look.* **7** (of weather) rainy or stormy. **8 dirty work** unpleasant or illicit activity. ~*n* **9 do the dirty on** *Informal* to behave meanly towards. ~*vb* **dirties, dirtying, dirtied 10** to make dirty; soil. **dirtiness** *n*

dis- *prefix* indicating: **1** reversal: *disconnect.* **2** negation or lack: *dissimilar; disgrace.* **3** removal or release: *disembowel.*

disability *n, pl* **-ties 1** a severe physical or mental illness that restricts the way a person lives his or her life. **2** something that disables someone.

disable *vb* **-abling, -abled** to make ineffective, unfit, or incapable. **disablement** *n*

disabled *adj* lacking one or more physical powers, such as the ability to walk or to coordinate one's movements.

disabuse *vb* **-abusing, -abused** to rid (someone) of a mistaken idea: *Arnold felt unable to disabuse her of her prejudices.*

disaccharide (die-**sack**-a-ride) *n* a sugar, such as sucrose, whose molecules consist of two linked monosaccharides.

disadvantage *n* **1** an unfavourable or harmful circumstance. **2 at a disadvantage** in a less favourable position than other people: *he continued to insist that he was at a disadvantage at the hearings.* **disadvantageous** *adj*

disadvantaged *adj* socially or economically deprived.

disaffected *adj* having lost loyalty to or affection for someone or something; alienated. **disaffection** *n*

disagree *vb* **-greeing, -greed 1** to have differing

THESAURUS

tion **2.** as soon as possible, at once, dead, due, forthwith, immediately, in a second, instantaneously, instantly, posthaste, presently, promptly, pronto (*informal*), quickly, right away, soon, speedily, straightaway

director administrator, boss (*informal*), chairman, chief, controller, executive, governor, head, leader, manager, organizer, principal, producer, supervisor

dirge coronach (*Scot. & Irish*), dead march, elegy, funeral song, lament, requiem, threnody

dirt 1. crap (*slang*), crud (*slang*), dust, excrement, filth, grime, grot (*slang*), gunge (*informal*), impurity, mire, muck, mud, shit (*taboo*), slime, tarnish **2.** clay, earth, loam, soil **3.** filth, indecency, obscenity, pornography, sleaze, smut

dirty *adj.* **1.** begrimed, filthy, foul, grimy, grotty (*slang*), grubby, grungy (*slang, chiefly U.S.*), messy, mucky, muddy, nasty, polluted, scuzzy (*slang, chiefly U.S.*), soiled, sullied, unclean **2.** clouded, dark, dull, miry, muddy, not clear **3.** base, beggarly, contemptible, corrupt, cowardly, crooked, despicable, dishonest, fraudulent, illegal, low, low-down (*informal*), mean, nasty, scurvy, shabby, sordid, squalid, treacherous, unfair, unscrupulous, unsporting, vile **4.** blue, filthy, indecent, obscene, off-colour, pornographic, risqué, salacious, sleazy, smutty, vulgar **5.** angry, annoyed, bitter, indignant, offended, resentful, scorching **6.** *of weather* gusty, louring *or* lowering, rainy, squally, stormy ~*vb.* **7.** begrime, blacken, defile, foul, mess up, muddy, pollute, smear, smirch, smudge, soil, spoil, stain, sully

disability 1. affliction, ailment, complaint, defect, disablement, disorder, handicap, impairment, infirmity, malady **2.** disqualification, impotency, inability, incapacity, incompetency, unfitness, weakness

disable cripple, damage, debilitate, enfeeble, hamstring, handicap, immobilize, impair, incapacitate, paralyse, prostrate, put out of action, render *hors de combat*, render inoperative, unfit, unman, weaken

disabled bedridden, crippled, differently abled (*euphemistic*), handicapped, incapacitated, infirm, lame, maimed, mangled, mutilated, paralysed, weak, weakened, wrecked

disadvantage 1. burden, damage, detriment, disservice, downside, drawback, flaw, fly in the ointment (*informal*), handicap, hardship, harm, hindrance, hurt, impediment, inconvenience, liability, loss, minus (*informal*), nuisance, prejudice, privation, snag, trouble, weakness, weak point **2. at a disadvantage** boxed in, cornered, handicapped, in a corner, vulnerable

disadvantageous adverse, damaging, deleterious, detrimental, harmful, hurtful, ill-timed, inconvenient, inexpedient, injurious, inopportune, prejudicial, unfavourable

disaffected alienated, antagonistic, discontented, disloyal, dissatisfied, estranged, hostile, mutinous, rebellious, seditious, uncompliant, unsubmissive

disaffection alienation, animosity, antagonism, antipathy, aversion, breach, disagreement, discontent, dislike, disloyalty, dissatisfaction, estrangement, hostility, ill will, repugnance, resentment, unfriendliness

disagree 1. argue, bicker, clash, contend, contest, debate, differ (in opinion), dispute, dissent, fall out

opinions or argue about (something). **2** to fail to correspond; conflict. **3** to cause physical discomfort to: *curry disagrees with me.*
disagreeable *adj* **1** (of an incident or situation) unpleasant. **2** (of a person) bad-tempered or disobliging. **disagreeably** *adv*
disagreement *n* **1** refusal or failure to agree. **2** a difference between results, totals, etc., which shows that they cannot all be true. **3** an argument.
disallow *vb* to reject as untrue or invalid; cancel.
disappear *vb* **1** to cease to be visible; vanish. **2** to go away or become lost, esp. without explanation. **3** to cease to exist: *the pain has disappeared.* **disappearance** *n*
disappoint *vb* **1** to fail to meet the expectations or hopes of; let down. **2** to prevent the fulfilment of (a plan, etc.); frustrate. **disappointed** *adj* **disappointing** *adj*
disappointment *n* **1** the feeling of being disappointed. **2** a person or thing that disappoints.
disapprobation *n* disapproval.
disapprove *vb* **-proving, -proved** to consider wrong or bad. **disapproval** *n* **disapproving** *adj*
disarm *vb* **1** to deprive of weapons. **2** to win the confidence or affection of. **3** (of a country) to decrease the size and capability of one's armed forces.
disarmament *n* the reduction of fighting capability by a country.
disarming *adj* removing hostility or suspicion. **disarmingly** *adv*
disarrange *vb* **-ranging, -ranged** to throw into disorder. **disarrangement** *n*
disarray *n* **1** confusion and lack of discipline. **2** extreme untidiness. *~vb* **3** to throw into confusion.
disassociate *vb* **-ating, -ated** same as **dissociate. disassociation** *n*
disaster *n* **1** an accident that causes great distress or destruction. **2** something, such as a project, that fails or has been ruined. **disastrous** *adj* **disastrously** *adv*
disavow *vb* to deny connection with or responsibility for (something). **disavowal** *n*
disband *vb* to stop or cause to stop functioning as a unit or group. **disbandment** *n*
disbelieve *vb* **-lieving, -lieved 1** to reject (a person or statement) as being untruthful. **2 disbelieve in** to have no faith or belief in: *to disbelieve in the supernatural.* **disbelief** *n*
disburse *vb* **-bursing, -bursed** to pay out. **disbursement** *n*
disc *n* **1** a flat circular object. **2** a gramophone record. **3** *Anat* a circular flat structure in the body, esp. between the vertebrae. **4** *Computers* same as **disk.**

THESAURUS

(*informal*), have words (*informal*), object, oppose, quarrel, take issue with, wrangle **2.** be discordant, be dissimilar, conflict, contradict, counter, depart, deviate, differ, diverge, run counter to, vary **3.** be injurious, bother, discomfort, distress, hurt, make ill, nauseate, sicken, trouble, upset
disagreeable 1. disgusting, displeasing, distasteful, horrid, nasty, objectionable, obnoxious, offensive, repellent, repugnant, repulsive, uninviting, unpalatable, unpleasant, unsavoury, yucky *or* yukky (*slang*) **2.** bad-tempered, brusque, churlish, contrary, cross, difficult, disobliging, ill-natured, irritable, nasty, peevish, ratty (*Brit. & N.Z. informal*), rude, surly, tetchy, unfriendly, ungracious, unlikable *or* unlikeable, unpleasant
disagreement 1. difference, discrepancy, disparity, dissimilarity, dissimilitude, divergence, diversity, incompatibility, incongruity, unlikeness, variance **2.** altercation, argument, clash, conflict, debate, difference, discord, dispute, dissent, division, falling out, misunderstanding, quarrel, row, squabble, strife, wrangle
disallow abjure, disavow, disclaim, dismiss, disown, rebuff, refuse, reject, repudiate
disappear 1. become invisible, drop out of sight, evanesce, fade away, vanish **2.** abscond, be lost to view, depart, ebb, escape, flee, fly, go, pass, recede, retire, vanish from sight, wane, withdraw **3.** cease, cease to be known, die out, dissolve, end, evaporate, expire, fade, leave no trace, melt away, pass away, perish, vanish
disappearance departure, desertion, disappearing, disappearing trick, eclipse, evanescence, evaporation, fading, flight, going, loss, melting, passing, vanishing, vanishing point
disappoint 1. dash, deceive, delude, disenchant, disgruntle, dishearten, disillusion, dismay, dissatisfy, fail, let down, sadden, vex **2.** baffle, balk, defeat, disconcert, foil, frustrate, hamper, hinder, thwart
disappointed balked, cast down, depressed, despondent, discontented, discouraged, disenchanted, disgruntled, disillusioned, dissatisfied, distressed, downhearted, foiled, frustrated, let down, saddened, thwarted, upset
disappointing depressing, disagreeable, disconcerting, discouraging, failing, inadequate, inferior, insufficient, lame, pathetic, sad, second-rate, sorry, unexpected, unhappy, unsatisfactory, unworthy, upsetting
disappointment 1. chagrin, discontent, discouragement, disenchantment, disillusionment, displeasure, dissatisfaction, distress, failure, frustration, ill-success, mortification, regret, unfulfilment **2.** blow, calamity, disaster, failure, fiasco, letdown, miscarriage, misfortune, setback, washout (*informal*)
disapproval censure, condemnation, criticism, denunciation, deprecation, disapprobation, displeasure, dissatisfaction, objection, reproach
disapprove blame, censure, condemn, deplore, deprecate, discountenance, dislike, find unacceptable, frown on, look down one's nose at (*informal*), object to, reject, take exception to
disarmament arms limitation, arms reduction, de-escalation, demilitarization, demobilization
disarming charming, irresistible, likable *or* likeable, persuasive, winning
disarrange confuse, derange, discompose, disorder, disorganize, disturb, jumble (up), mess (up), scatter, shake (up), shuffle, unsettle, untidy
disarray 1. confusion, discomposure, disharmony, dismay, disorder, disorderliness, disorganization, disunity, indiscipline, unruliness, upset **2.** chaos, clutter, dishevelment, hodgepodge (*U.S.*), hotchpotch, jumble, mess, mix-up, muddle, pig's breakfast (*informal*), shambles, state, tangle, untidiness
disaster accident, act of God, adversity, blow, calamity, cataclysm, catastrophe, misadventure, mischance, misfortune, mishap, reverse, ruin, ruination, stroke, tragedy, trouble
disastrous adverse, calamitous, cataclysmal, cataclysmic, catastrophic, destructive, detrimental, devastating, dire, dreadful, fatal, hapless, harmful, ill-fated, ill-starred, ruinous, terrible, tragic, unfortunate, unlucky, unpropitious, untoward
disbelief distrust, doubt, dubiety, incredulity, mistrust, scepticism, unbelief
disbelievingly askance, cynically, doubtingly, incredulously, mistrustfully, quizzically, sceptically, suspiciously, with a pinch of salt
discard abandon, axe (*informal*), cast aside, chuck (*informal*), dispense with, dispose of, ditch (*slang*),

discard *vb* to get rid of (something or someone) as useless or undesirable.

disc brake *n* a brake in which two pads rub against a flat disc.

discern *vb* to see or be aware of (something) clearly. **discernible** *adj*

discerning *adj* having or showing good judgment. **discernment** *n*

discharge *vb* **-charging, -charged 1** to release or allow to go. **2** to dismiss (someone) from duty or employment. **3** to fire (a gun). **4** to cause to pour forth: *the scar was red and swollen and began to discharge pus.* **5** to remove (the cargo) from a boat, etc.; unload. **6** to meet the demands of (a duty or responsibility). **7** to relieve oneself of (a debt). **8** *Physics* to take or supply electrical current from (a cell or battery). *~n* **9** something that is discharged. **10** dismissal or release from an office, job, etc. **11** a pouring out of a fluid; emission. **12** *Physics* a conduction of electricity through a gas

disciple (diss-**sipe**-pl) *n* **1** a follower of the doctrines of a teacher. **2** one of the personal followers of Christ during his earthly life.

disciplinarian *n* a person who practises strict discipline.

disciplinary *adj* of or imposing discipline; corrective.

discipline *n* **1** the practice of imposing strict rules of behaviour on other people. **2** the ability to behave and work in a controlled manner. **3** a particular area of academic study. *~vb* **-plining, -plined 4** to improve or attempt to improve the behaviour of (oneself or someone else) by training or rules. **5** to punish.

disciplined *adj* able to behave and work in a controlled way.

disc jockey *n* a person who announces and plays recorded pop records on a radio programme or at a disco.

disclaim *vb* **1** to deny (responsibility for or knowledge of something). **2** to give up (any claim to).

disclaimer *n* a statement denying responsibility for or knowledge of something.

disclose *vb* **-closing, -closed 1** to make (information) known. **2** to allow to be seen: *she agreed to disclose the contents of the box.* **disclosure** *n*

disco *n, pl* **-cos 1** a nightclub for dancing to amplified pop records. **2** an occasion at which people dance to amplified pop records. **3** mobile equipment for providing music for a disco.

discography *n, pl* **-phies** a classified list of gramophone records.

discolour *or US* **discolor** *vb* to change in colour; fade or stain. **discoloration** *n*

discomfit *vb* **-fiting, -fited** to make uneasy or confused. **discomfiture** *n*

discomfort *n* **1** a mild pain. **2** a feeling of worry or embarrassment. **3 discomforts** conditions that cause physical uncomfortableness: *the physical discomforts of pregnancy.*

discommode *vb* **-moding, -moded** to cause inconvenience. **discommodious** *adj*

discompose *vb* **-posing, -posed** to disturb or upset someone. **discomposure** *n*

disconcert *vb* to disturb the confidence or self-

THESAURUS

drop, dump (*informal*), get rid of, jettison, junk (*informal*), reject, relinquish, remove, repudiate, scrap, shed, throw away *or* out

discerning acute, astute, clear-sighted, critical, discriminating, ingenious, intelligent, judicious, knowing, penetrating, perceptive, percipient, perspicacious, piercing, sagacious, sensitive, sharp, shrewd, subtle, wise

discharge *vb.* **1.** absolve, acquit, allow to go, clear, exonerate, free, liberate, pardon, release, set free **2.** cashier, discard, dismiss, eject, expel, fire (*informal*), give (someone) the sack (*informal*), oust, remove, sack (*informal*) **3.** detonate, explode, fire, let off, set off, shoot **4.** dispense, emit, empty, excrete, exude, give off, gush, leak, ooze, pour forth, release, void **5.** disburden, lighten, off-load, remove, unburden, unload **6.** accomplish, carry out, do, execute, fulfil, observe, perform **7.** clear, honour, meet, pay, relieve, satisfy, settle, square up *~n.* **8.** demobilization, dismissal, ejection, the boot (*slang*), the (old) heave-ho (*informal*), the order of the boot (*slang*), the sack (*informal*) **9.** emission, emptying, excretion, flow, ooze, pus, secretion, seepage, suppuration, vent, voiding

disciple adherent, apostle, believer, convert, devotee, follower, learner, partisan, proselyte, pupil, student, supporter, votary

disciplinarian authoritarian, despot, drill sergeant, hard master, martinet, stickler, strict teacher, taskmaster, tyrant

discipline *n.* **1.** castigation, chastisement, correction, drill, exercise, method, practice, punishment, regimen, regulation, training **2.** conduct, control, orderliness, regulation, restraint, self-control, strictness **3.** area, branch of knowledge, course, curriculum, field of study, speciality, subject *~vb.* **4.** break in, bring up, check, control, drill, educate, exercise, form, govern, instruct, inure, prepare, regulate, restrain, train **5.** castigate, chasten, chastise, correct, penalize, punish, reprimand, reprove

disclaim 1. abjure, deny, disown, rebut, repudiate, retract **2.** abandon, abjure, abnegate, decline, forswear, reject, renounce

disclose 1. blow wide open (*slang*), broadcast, communicate, confess, divulge, impart, leak, let slip, make known, make public, publish, relate, reveal, spill one's guts about (*slang*), spill the beans about (*informal*), tell, unveil, utter **2.** bring to light, discover, exhibit, expose, lay bare, reveal, show, uncover, unveil

disclosure acknowledgment, admission, announcement, broadcast, confession, declaration, discovery, divulgence, exposé, exposure, leak, publication, revelation, uncovering

discolour fade, mar, mark, rust, soil, stain, streak, tarnish, tinge

discomfort *n.* **1.** ache, hurt, pain, soreness **2.** annoyance, disquiet, distress, hardship, hurt, inquietude, irritation, malaise, nuisance, trouble, uneasiness, unpleasantness, vexation

discomposure agitation, anxiety, confusion, discomfiture, disquiet, disquietude, distraction, disturbance, embarrassment, fluster, inquietude, malaise, nervousness, perturbation, trepidation, uneasiness

disconcert abash, agitate, bewilder, discompose, disturb, faze, flummox, flurry, fluster, nonplus, perplex, perturb, put out of countenance, rattle (*informal*), ruffle, shake up (*informal*), take aback, throw off balance, trouble, unbalance, unnerve, unsettle, upset, worry

disconcerted annoyed, at sea, bewildered, caught off balance, confused, distracted, disturbed, embarrassed, fazed, flummoxed, flurried, flustered, mixed-up, nonplussed, out of countenance, perturbed, rattled (*informal*), ruffled, shook up (*informal*), taken aback, thrown (*informal*), troubled, unsettled, upset

possession of; upset, embarrass, or take aback. **disconcerting** *adj*

disconnect *vb* **1** to undo or break the connection between (two things). **2** to stop the supply of (gas or electricity to a building). **disconnection** *n*

disconnected *adj* (of speech or ideas) not logically connected.

disconsolate *adj* sad beyond comfort. **disconsolately** *adv*

discontent *n* lack of contentment, as with one's condition or lot in life. **discontented** *adj* **discontentedly** *adv*

discontinue *vb* **-uing, -ued** to come or bring to an end; stop.

discontinuous *adj* characterized by interruptions; intermittent. **discontinuity** *n*

discord *n* **1** lack of agreement or harmony between people. **2** harsh confused sounds. **3** a combination of musical notes that lacks harmony.

discordant *adj* **1** at variance; disagreeing. **2** harsh in sound; inharmonious. **discordance** *n*

discotheque *n* same as **disco.**

discount *vb* **1** to leave (something) out of account as being unreliable, prejudiced, or irrelevant. **2** to deduct (an amount or percentage) from the price of something. *~n* **3** a deduction from the full amount of a price. **4 at a discount** below the regular price.

discountenance *vb* **-nancing, -nanced** to make (someone) ashamed or confused.

discourage *vb* **-aging, -aged 1** to deprive of the will or enthusiasm to persist in something. **2** to oppose by expressing disapproval. **discouragement** *n* **discouraging** *adj*

discourse *n* **1** conversation. **2** a formal treatment of a subject in speech or writing. *~vb* **-coursing, -coursed 3** to speak or write (about) at length.

discourteous *adj* showing bad manners; rude. **discourteously** *adv* **discourtesy** *n*

discover *vb* **1** to be the first to find or find out about. **2** to learn about for the first time. **3** to find after study or search. **discoverer** *n*

discovery *n, pl* **-eries 1** the act of discovering. **2** a person, place, or thing that has been discovered.

discredit *vb* **-iting, -ited 1** to damage the reputation

THESAURUS

disconcerting alarming, awkward, baffling, bewildering, bothersome, confusing, dismaying, distracting, disturbing, embarrassing, off-putting (*Brit. informal*), perplexing, upsetting

disconnect 1. detach, disengage, divide, part, separate, sever, take apart, uncouple **2.** cut off

disconnected confused, disjointed, garbled, illogical, incoherent, irrational, jumbled, mixed-up, rambling, uncoordinated, unintelligible, wandering

disconnection cessation, cut-off, cutting off, discontinuation, discontinuity, interruption, separation, severance, stoppage, suspension

disconsolate crushed, dejected, desolate, despairing, dismal, forlorn, gloomy, grief-stricken, heartbroken, hopeless, inconsolable, melancholy, miserable, sad, unhappy, woeful, wretched

discontent *n.* discontentment, displeasure, dissatisfaction, envy, fretfulness, regret, restlessness, uneasiness, unhappiness, vexation

discontented brassed off (*Brit. slang*), cheesed off (*Brit. slang*), complaining, disaffected, disgruntled, displeased, dissatisfied, exasperated, fed up, fretful, miserable, pissed off (*taboo slang*), unhappy, vexed, with a chip on one's shoulder (*informal*)

discontinue abandon, axe (*informal*), break off, cease, drop, end, finish, give up, halt, interrupt, kick (*informal*), leave off, pause, put an end to, quit, refrain from, stop, suspend, terminate

discontinued abandoned, ended, finished, given up *or* over, halted, no longer made, terminated

discord 1. clashing, conflict, contention, difference, disagreement, discordance, dispute, dissension, disunity, division, friction, incompatibility, lack of concord, opposition, row, rupture, strife, variance, wrangling **2.** cacophony, din, disharmony, dissonance, harshness, jangle, jarring, racket, tumult

discordant 1. at odds, clashing, conflicting, contradictory, contrary, different, disagreeing, divergent, incompatible, incongruous, inconsistent, opposite **2.** cacophonous, dissonant, grating, harsh, inharmonious, jangling, jarring, shrill, strident, unmelodious

discount *vb.* **1.** brush off (*slang*), disbelieve, disregard, ignore, leave out of account, overlook, pass over **2.** deduct, lower, mark down, rebate, reduce, take off *~n.* **3.** abatement, allowance, concession, cut, cut price, deduction, drawback, percentage (*informal*), rebate, reduction

discourage 1. abash, awe, cast down, cow, damp, dampen, dash, daunt, deject, demoralize, depress, dishearten, dismay, dispirit, frighten, intimidate, overawe, psych out (*informal*), put a damper on, scare, unman, unnerve **2.** check, curb, deprecate, deter, discountenance, disfavour, dissuade, divert from, hinder, inhibit, prevent, put off, restrain, talk out of, throw cold water on (*informal*)

discouraged crestfallen, dashed, daunted, deterred, disheartened, dismayed, dispirited, downcast, down in the mouth, glum, pessimistic, put off, sick as a parrot (*informal*)

discouragement 1. cold feet (*informal*), dejection, depression, despair, despondency, disappointment, discomfiture, dismay, downheartedness, hopelessness, loss of confidence, low spirits, pessimism **2.** constraint, curb, damper, deterrent, disincentive, hindrance, impediment, obstacle, opposition, rebuff, restraint, setback

discouraging dampening, daunting, depressing, disappointing, disheartening, dispiriting, off-putting (*Brit. informal*), unfavourable, unpropitious

discourse *n.* **1.** chat, communication, conversation, converse, dialogue, discussion, seminar, speech, talk **2.** address, disquisition, dissertation, essay, homily, lecture, oration, sermon, speech, talk, treatise *~vb.* **3.** confer, converse, debate, declaim, discuss, expatiate, hold forth, speak, talk

discourteous abrupt, bad-mannered, boorish, brusque, curt, disrespectful, ill-bred, ill-mannered, impolite, insolent, offhand, rude, uncivil, uncourteous, ungentlemanly, ungracious, unmannerly

discourtesy 1. bad manners, disrespectfulness, ill-breeding, impertinence, impoliteness, incivility, insolence, rudeness, ungraciousness, unmannerliness **2.** affront, cold shoulder, insult, rebuff, slight, snub

discover 1. bring to light, come across, come upon, dig up, find, light upon, locate, turn up, uncover, unearth **2.** ascertain, descry, detect, determine, discern, disclose, espy, find out, get wise to (*informal*), learn, notice, perceive, realize, recognize, reveal, see, spot, suss (out) (*slang*), turn up, uncover

discoverer author, explorer, founder, initiator, inventor, originator, pioneer

discovery 1. ascertainment, detection, disclosure, espial, exploration, finding, introduction, locating, location, origination, revelation, uncovering **2.** bonanza, breakthrough, coup, find, findings, godsend, innovation, invention, secret

of (someone). **2** to cause (an idea) to be disbelieved or distrusted. ~*n* **3** something that causes disgrace. **discreditable** *adj*

discreet *adj* **1** careful to avoid embarrassment when dealing with secret or private matters. **2** unobtrusive: *there was a discreet entrance down a side alley.* **discreetly** *adv*

discrepancy *n, pl* **-cies** a conflict or variation between facts, figures, or claims. **discrepant** *adj*

discrete *adj* separate or distinct. **discreteness** *n*

discretion (diss-**kresh**-on) *n* **1** the quality of behaving so as to avoid social embarrassment or distress. **2** freedom or authority to make judgments and to act as one sees fit: *at his discretion.* **discretionary** *adj*

discriminate *vb* **-nating, -nated 1** to make a distinction against or in favour of a particular person or group. **2** to recognize or understand a difference: *to discriminate between right and wrong.* **discriminating** *adj*

discrimination *n* **1** unfair treatment of a person, racial group, or minority. **2** subtle appreciation in matters of taste. **3** the ability to see fine distinctions.

discriminatory *adj* based on prejudice.

discursive *adj* passing from one topic to another.

discus *n Field sports* a disc-shaped object with a heavy middle, thrown by athletes.

discuss *vb* **1** to consider (something) by talking it over. **2** to treat (a subject) in speech or writing. **discussion** *n*

disdain *n* **1** a feeling of superiority and dislike; contempt. ~*vb* **2** to refuse or reject with disdain: *he disdained domestic conventions.* **disdainful** *adj* **disdainfully** *adv*

disease *n* an unhealthy condition in a person, animal, or plant which is caused by bacteria or infection. **diseased** *adj*

diseconomy *n Econ* a disadvantage, such as higher costs, resulting from the scale on which a business operates.

disembark *vb* to land or cause to land from a ship, aircraft, or other vehicle. **disembarkation** *n*

disembodied *adj* **1** lacking a body. **2** seeming not to be attached to or come from anyone. **disembodiment** *n*

disembowel *vb* **-elling, -elled** *or US* **-eling, -eled** to remove the entrails of. **disembowelment** *n*

disenchanted *adj* disappointed and disillusioned (with something). **disenchantment** *n*

disenfranchise *vb* **-chising, -chised** to deprive (someone) of the right to vote or of other rights of citizenship.

disengage *vb* **-gaging, -gaged 1** to release from a

THESAURUS

discredit *vb.* **1.** blame, bring into disrepute, censure, defame, degrade, detract from, disgrace, dishonour, disparage, reproach, slander, slur, smear, vilify **2.** challenge, deny, disbelieve, discount, dispute, distrust, doubt, mistrust, question ~*n.* **3.** aspersion, censure, disgrace, dishonour, disrepute, ignominy, ill-repute, imputation, odium, reproach, scandal, shame, slur, smear, stigma

discreditable blameworthy, degrading, disgraceful, dishonourable, humiliating, ignominious, improper, infamous, reprehensible, scandalous, shameful, unprincipled, unworthy

discredited brought into disrepute, debunked, discarded, exploded, exposed, obsolete, outworn, refuted, rejected

discreet careful, cautious, circumspect, considerate, diplomatic, discerning, guarded, judicious, politic, prudent, reserved, sagacious, sensible, tactful, wary

discrepancy conflict, contrariety, difference, disagreement, discordance, disparity, dissimilarity, dissonance, divergence, incongruity, inconsistency, variance, variation

discretion **1.** acumen, care, carefulness, caution, circumspection, consideration, diplomacy, discernment, good sense, judgment, judiciousness, maturity, prudence, sagacity, tact, wariness **2.** choice, disposition, inclination, liking, mind, option, pleasure, predilection, preference, responsibility, volition, will, wish

discretionary arbitrary (*Law*), elective, nonmandatory, open, open to choice, optional, unrestricted

discriminate **1.** disfavour, favour, show bias, show prejudice, single out, treat as inferior, treat differently, victimize **2.** assess, differentiate, discern, distinguish, draw a distinction, evaluate, segregate, separate, sift, tell the difference

discriminating acute, astute, critical, cultivated, discerning, fastidious, keen, particular, refined, selective, sensitive, tasteful

discrimination **1.** bias, bigotry, favouritism, inequity, intolerance, prejudice, unfairness **2.** acumen, acuteness, clearness, discernment, insight, judgment, keenness, penetration, perception, refinement, sagacity, subtlety, taste

discriminatory biased, favouring, inequitable, one-sided, partial, partisan, preferential, prejudiced, prejudicial, unjust, weighted

discuss argue, confer, consider, consult with, converse, debate, deliberate, examine, exchange views on, get together, go into, reason about, review, sift, talk about, thrash out, ventilate, weigh up the pros and cons

discussion analysis, argument, colloquy, confabulation, conference, consideration, consultation, conversation, debate, deliberation, dialogue, discourse, examination, exchange, review, scrutiny, seminar, symposium

disdain **1.** *n.* arrogance, contempt, contumely, derision, dislike, haughtiness, hauteur, indifference, scorn, sneering, snobbishness, superciliousness **2.** *vb.* belittle, contemn, deride, despise, disregard, look down on, look down one's nose at (*informal*), misprize, pooh-pooh, reject, scorn, slight, sneer at, spurn, undervalue

disdainful aloof, arrogant, contemptuous, derisive, haughty, high and mighty (*informal*), hoity-toity (*informal*), insolent, proud, scornful, sneering, supercilious, superior

disease affliction, ailment, complaint, condition, disorder, ill health, illness, indisposition, infection, infirmity, malady, sickness, upset

diseased ailing, infected, rotten, sick, sickly, tainted, unhealthy, unsound, unwell, unwholesome

disembark alight, arrive, get off, go ashore, land, step out of

disembodied bodiless, ghostly, immaterial, incorporeal, intangible, phantom, spectral, spiritual, unbodied

disenchanted blasé, cynical, disappointed, disillusioned, indifferent, jaundiced, let down, out of love, sick of, soured, undeceived

disenchantment disappointment, disillusion, disillusionment, revulsion, rude awakening

disengage detach, disconnect, disentangle, disunite, divide, ease, extricate, free, liberate, loosen, release, separate, set free, unbridle, undo, unloose, untie, withdraw

disengaged apart, detached, free, loose, out of gear,

connection. **2** *Mil* to withdraw from close action. **disengagement** *n*

disentangle *vb* **-gling, -gled 1** to release from entanglement or confusion. **2** to unravel or work out. **disentanglement** *n*

disequilibrium *n* a loss or absence of stability or balance.

disestablish *vb* to deprive (a church or religion) of established status. **disestablishment** *n*

disfavour *or US* **disfavor** *n* **1** disapproval or dislike. **2** the state of being disapproved of or disliked.

disfigure *vb* **-uring, -ured** to spoil the appearance or shape of. **disfigurement** *n*

disfranchise *vb* **-chising, -chised** same as **disenfranchise.**

disgorge *vb* **-gorging, -gorged 1** to vomit. **2** to discharge (contents).

disgrace *n* **1** a condition of shame, loss of reputation, or dishonour. **2** a shameful person or thing. **3** exclusion from confidence or trust: *he was sent home in disgrace.* ~*vb* **-gracing, -graced 4** to bring shame upon (oneself or others). **disgraceful** *adj* **disgracefully** *adv*

disgruntled *adj* sulky or discontented. **disgruntlement** *n*

disguise *vb* **-guising, -guised 1** to change the appearance or manner in order to conceal the identity of (someone or something). **2** to misrepresent (something) in order to obscure its actual nature or meaning. ~*n* **3** a mask, costume, or manner that disguises. **4** the state of being disguised. **disguised** *adj*

disgust *n* **1** a great loathing or distaste. ~*vb* **2** to sicken or fill with loathing. **disgusted** *adj* **disgusting** *adj*

dish *n* **1** a container used for holding or serving food, esp. an open shallow container. **2** the food in a dish. **3** a particular kind of food. **4** short for **dish aerial. 5** *Informal* an attractive person. ~See also **dish out, dish up.**

dishabille (diss-a-**beel**) *n* same as **deshabille.**

dish aerial *n Brit* a large disc-shaped aerial with a concave reflector, used to receive signals in radar, radio telescopes, and satellite broadcasting.

disharmony *n* lack of agreement or harmony. **disharmonious** *adj*

dishcloth *n* a cloth for washing dishes.

dishearten *vb* to weaken or destroy the hope, courage, or enthusiasm of. **disheartened** *adj* **disheartening** *adj*

dishevelled *or US* **disheveled** *adj* (of a person's hair, clothes, or general appearance) disordered and untidy.

dishonest *adj* not honest or fair. **dishonestly** *adv* **dishonesty** *n*

dishonour *or US* **dishonor** *vb* **1** to treat with disrespect. **2** to refuse to pay (a cheque). ~*n* **3** a lack of

THESAURUS

released, separate, unattached, unconnected, uncoupled

disengagement detachment, disconnection, disentanglement, division, separation, withdrawal

disentangle 1. detach, disconnect, disengage, extricate, free, loose, separate, sever, unfold, unravel, unsnarl, untangle, untwist **2.** clarify, clear (up), resolve, simplify, sort out, work out

disfavour 1. disapprobation, disapproval, dislike, displeasure **2.** *as in* **fall into disfavour** bad books (*informal*), discredit, disesteem, disgrace, doghouse (*informal*), shame, unpopularity

disfigure blemish, damage, deface, deform, disfeature, distort, injure, maim, make ugly, mar, mutilate, scar

disfigurement blemish, defacement, defect, deformity, distortion, impairment, injury, mutilation, scar, spot, stain

disgrace *n.* **1.** baseness, degradation, dishonour, disrepute, ignominy, infamy, odium, opprobrium, shame **2.** aspersion, blemish, blot, defamation, reproach, scandal, slur, stain, stigma ~*vb.* **3.** abase, bring shame upon, defame, degrade, discredit, disfavour, dishonour, disparage, humiliate, reproach, shame, slur, stain, stigmatize, sully, taint

disgraced branded, degraded, discredited, dishonoured, humiliated, in disgrace, in the doghouse (*informal*), mortified, shamed, stigmatized

disgraceful blameworthy, contemptible, degrading, detestable, discreditable, dishonourable, disreputable, ignominious, infamous, low, mean, opprobrious, scandalous, shameful, shocking, unworthy

disgruntled annoyed, cheesed off (*Brit. slang*), discontented, displeased, dissatisfied, grumpy, huffy, irritated, malcontent, peeved, peevish, petulant, pissed off (*taboo slang*), put out, sulky, sullen, testy, vexed

disguise *vb.* **1.** camouflage, cloak, conceal, cover, hide, mask, screen, secrete, shroud, veil **2.** deceive, dissemble, dissimulate, fake, falsify, fudge, gloss over, misrepresent ~*n.* **3.** camouflage, cloak, costume, cover, get-up (*informal*), mask, screen, veil **4.** deception, dissimulation, façade, front, pretence, semblance, trickery, veneer

disguised camouflaged, cloaked, covert, fake, false, feigned, incognito, in disguise, masked, pretend, undercover, unrecognizable

disgust 1. *n.* abhorrence, abomination, antipathy, aversion, detestation, dislike, distaste, hatefulness, hatred, loathing, nausea, odium, repugnance, repulsion, revulsion **2.** *vb.* cause aversion, displease, fill with loathing, gross out (*U.S. slang*), nauseate, offend, outrage, put off, repel, revolt, sicken, turn one's stomach

disgusted appalled, nauseated, offended, outraged, repelled, repulsed, scandalized, sick and tired of (*informal*), sickened, sick of (*informal*)

disgusting abominable, detestable, distasteful, foul, gross, grotty (*slang*), hateful, loathsome, nasty, nauseating, nauseous, objectionable, obnoxious, odious, offensive, repellent, repugnant, revolting, shameless, sickening, stinking, vile, vulgar, yucky *or* yukky (*slang*)

dish *n.* **1.** bowl, plate, platter, salver **2.** fare, food, recipe

dishearten cast down, crush, damp, dampen, dash, daunt, deject, depress, deter, discourage, dismay, dispirit, put a damper on

disheartened crestfallen, crushed, daunted, dejected, depressed, disappointed, discouraged, dismayed, dispirited, downcast, downhearted

dishevelled bedraggled, blowzy, disarranged, disarrayed, disordered, frowzy, hanging loose, messy, ruffled, rumpled, tousled, uncombed, unkempt, untidy

dishonest bent (*slang*), cheating, corrupt, crafty, crooked (*informal*), deceitful, deceiving, deceptive, designing, disreputable, double-dealing, false, fraudulent, guileful, knavish (*archaic*), lying, mendacious, perfidious, shady (*informal*), swindling, treacherous, unfair, unprincipled, unscrupulous, untrustworthy, untruthful

dishonesty cheating, chicanery, corruption, craft, criminality, crookedness, deceit, duplicity, falsehood, falsity, fraud, fraudulence, graft (*informal*), improbity,

honour or respect. **4** a state of shame or disgrace. **5** something that causes a loss of honour. **dishonourable** *adj* **dishonourably** *adv*

dish out *vb* **1** *Informal* to distribute. **2 dish it out** to inflict punishment.

dish up *vb* to serve (food).

dishwasher *n* a machine for washing and drying dishes, cutlery, etc.

dishwater *n* **1** water in which dishes have been washed. **2 like dishwater** (of tea) very weak.

dishy *adj* **dishier, dishiest** *Informal, chiefly Brit* good-looking.

disillusion *vb* **1** to destroy the illusions or false ideas of (someone). *~n also* **disillusionment 2** the state of being disillusioned.

disillusioned *adj* disappointed at finding out reality does not match one's ideals.

disincentive *n* something that discourages someone from behaving or acting in a particular way.

disinclined *adj* unwilling or reluctant. **disinclination** *n*

disinfect *vb* to rid of harmful germs by cleaning with a chemical substance. **disinfection** *n*

disinfectant *n* a substance that destroys harmful germs.

disinformation *n* false information intended to mislead.

disingenuous *adj* dishonest and insincere. **disingenuously** *adv*

disinherit *vb* **-iting, -ited** *Law* to deprive (an heir) of inheritance. **disinheritance** *n*

disintegrate *vb* **-grating, -grated 1** to lose cohesion; break up: *the business disintegrated.* **2** (of an object) to break into fragments; shatter. **3** *Physics* **a** to undergo nuclear fission or include nuclear fission in. **b** same as **decay** (sense 3). **disintegration** *n*

disinter *vb* **-terring, -terred 1** to dig up. **2** to bring to light; expose.

disinterested *adj* **1** free from bias; objective. **2** *Not universally accepted* feeling or showing a lack of interest; uninterested. **disinterest** *n*

➤ Distinguish *disinterested* from *uninterested,* meaning "apathetic, not caring": *We asked him to decide because he was a disinterested observer.*

disjointed *adj* having no coherence; disconnected: *a disjointed conversation.*

disjunctive *adj* serving to disconnect or separate.

disk *n* **1** *Chiefly US & Canad* same as **disc. 2** *Computers* a storage device, consisting of a stack of plates coated with a magnetic layer, which rotates rapidly as a single unit.

disk drive *n Computers* the unit that controls the mechanism for handling a floppy disk.

dislike *vb* **-liking, -liked 1** to consider unpleasant or disagreeable. *~n* **2** a feeling of not liking something or someone.

dislocate *vb* **-cating, -cated 1** to displace (a bone or joint) from its normal position. **2** to disrupt or shift out of place. **dislocation** *n*

dislodge *vb* **-lodging, -lodged** to remove (something) from a previously fixed position.

THESAURUS

mendacity, perfidy, sharp practice, stealing, treachery, trickery, unscrupulousness, wiliness

dishonour *vb.* **1.** abase, blacken, corrupt, debase, debauch, defame, defile, degrade, discredit, disgrace, shame, sully *~n.* **2.** abasement, degradation, discredit, disfavour, disgrace, disrepute, ignominy, infamy, obloquy, odium, opprobrium, reproach, scandal, shame **3.** abuse, affront, discourtesy, indignity, insult, offence, outrage, slight

dishonourable base, contemptible, corrupt, despicable, discreditable, disgraceful, disreputable, ignoble, ignominious, infamous, scandalous, shameful, shameless, treacherous, unprincipled, unscrupulous, untrustworthy

dish out allocate, distribute, dole out, hand out, inflict, mete out

dish up hand out, ladle, prepare, present, produce, scoop, serve, spoon

disillusion *vb.* break the spell, bring down to earth, disabuse, disenchant, open the eyes of, shatter one's illusions, undeceive

disillusioned disabused, disappointed, disenchanted, enlightened, indifferent, out of love, sadder and wiser, undeceived

disincentive damper, deterrent, discouragement, dissuasion, impediment

disinclination alienation, antipathy, aversion, demur, dislike, hesitance, lack of desire, lack of enthusiasm, loathness, objection, opposition, reluctance, repugnance, resistance, unwillingness

disinclined antipathetic, averse, balking, hesitating, indisposed, loath, not in the mood, opposed, reluctant, resistant, unwilling

disinfect clean, cleanse, decontaminate, deodorize, fumigate, purify, sanitize, sterilize

disinfectant antiseptic, germicide, sanitizer, sterilizer

disinherit cut off, cut off without a penny, disown, dispossess, oust, repudiate

disintegrate break apart, break up, crumble, disunite, fall apart, fall to pieces, reduce to fragments, separate, shatter, splinter

disinterest candidness, detachment, disinterestedness, dispassionateness, equity, fairness, impartiality, justice, neutrality, unbiasedness

disinterested candid, detached, dispassionate, equitable, even-handed, free from self-interest, impartial, impersonal, neutral, outside, unbiased, uninvolved, unprejudiced, unselfish

disjointed aimless, confused, disconnected, disordered, fitful, incoherent, loose, rambling, spasmodic, unconnected

dislike 1. *vb.* abhor, abominate, be averse to, despise, detest, disapprove, disfavour, hate, have no taste *or* stomach for, loathe, not be able to bear *or* abide, object to, scorn, shun **2.** *n.* animosity, animus, antagonism, antipathy, aversion, detestation, disapprobation, disapproval, disgust, disinclination, displeasure, distaste, enmity, hatred, hostility, loathing, odium, repugnance

dislocate 1. disarticulate, disconnect, disengage, disjoint, disunite, luxate (*Medical*), put out of joint, unhinge **2.** disorder, displace, disrupt, disturb, misplace, shift

dislocation 1. disarticulation, disconnection, disengagement, luxation (*Medical*), unhinging **2.** disarray, disorder, disorganization, disruption, disturbance, misplacement

disloyal apostate, disaffected, faithless, false, perfidious, seditious, subversive, traitorous, treacherous, treasonable, two-faced, unfaithful, unpatriotic, untrustworthy

disloyalty apostasy, betrayal of trust, breach of trust, breaking of faith, deceitfulness, double-dealing, falseness, falsity, inconstancy, infidelity, perfidy, treachery, treason, unfaithfulness

disloyal *adj* not loyal; deserting one's allegiance or duty. **disloyalty** *n*

dismal *adj* **1** gloomy and depressing. **2** *Informal* of poor quality. **dismally** *adv*

dismantle *vb* **-tling, -tled 1** to take apart piece by piece. **2** to cause (an organization or political system) to stop functioning by gradually reducing its power or purpose.

dismay *vb* **1** to fill with alarm or depression. ~*n* **2** a feeling of alarm or depression.

dismember *vb* **1** to remove the limbs of. **2** to cut to pieces. **dismemberment** *n*

dismiss *vb* **1** to remove (an employee) from a job. **2** to allow (someone) to leave. **3** to put out of one's mind; no longer think about. **4** (of a judge) to state that (a case) will not be brought to trial. **5** *Cricket* to bowl out (a side) for a particular number of runs. **dismissal** *n* **dismissive** *adj*

dismount *vb* to get off a horse or bicycle.

disobedient *adj* refusing to obey. **disobedience** *n*

disobey *vb* to neglect or refuse to obey (a person or an order).

disobliging *adj* unwilling to help.

disorder *n* **1** a state of untidiness and disorganization. **2** public violence or rioting. **3** an illness. **disordered** *adj*

disorderly *adj* **1** untidy and disorganized. **2** uncontrolled; unruly. **3** *Law* violating public peace.

disorganize *or* **-ise** *vb* **-izing, -ized** *or* **-ising, -ised** to disrupt the arrangement or system of. **disorganization** *or* **-isation** *n*

disorientate *or* **disorient** *vb* **-tating, -tated** *or* **-enting, -ented** to cause (someone) to lose his or her bearings. **disorientation** *n*

disown *vb* to deny any connection with (someone).

disparage *vb* **-aging, -aged** to speak contemptuously of. **disparagement** *n* **disparaging** *adj*

disparate *adj* utterly different in kind. **disparity** *n*

dispassionate *adj* not influenced by emotion; objective. **dispassionately** *adv*

dispatch *or* **despatch** *vb* **1** to send off to a destination or to perform a task. **2** to carry out (a duty or task) promptly. **3** to murder. ~*n* **4** an official communication or report, sent in haste. **5** a report sent to a newspaper by a correspondent. **6** murder. **7 with dispatch** quickly.

dispatch rider *n* a motorcyclist who carries dispatches.

dispel *vb* **-pelling, -pelled** to disperse or drive away.

dispensable *adj* not essential; expendable.

THESAURUS

dismal black, bleak, cheerless, dark, depressing, despondent, discouraging, dolorous, dreary, forlorn, funereal, gloomy, gruesome, lonesome, lowering *or* louring, lugubrious, melancholy, sad, sombre, sorrowful

dismay 1. *vb.* affright, alarm, appal, daunt, disappoint, discourage, dishearten, disillusion, dispirit, distress, fill with consternation, frighten, horrify, paralyse, put off, scare, terrify, unnerve **2.** *n.* agitation, alarm, anxiety, apprehension, chagrin, consternation, disappointment, discouragement, disillusionment, distress, dread, fear, fright, horror, panic, terror, trepidation, upset

dismember amputate, cut into pieces, dissect, divide, mutilate, rend, sever

dismiss 1. axe (*informal*), cashier, discharge, fire (*informal*), give notice to, lay off, oust, remove, sack (*informal*), send packing (*informal*) **2.** disband, disperse, dissolve, free, let go, release, send away **3.** banish, discard, dispel, disregard, drop, lay aside, pooh-pooh, put out of one's mind, reject, relegate, repudiate, set aside, shelve, spurn

dismissal 1. discharge, expulsion, marching orders (*informal*), notice, one's books *or* cards (*informal*), removal, the boot (*slang*), the (old) heave-ho (*informal*), the order of the boot (*slang*), the push (*slang*), the sack (*informal*) **2.** adjournment, end, freedom to depart, permission to go, release

disobedience contumacy, indiscipline, infraction, insubordination, mutiny, noncompliance, nonobservance, recalcitrance, revolt, unruliness, waywardness

disobedient contrary, contumacious, defiant, disorderly, insubordinate, intractable, mischievous, naughty, noncompliant, nonobservant, obstreperous, refractory, undisciplined, unruly, wayward, wilful

disobey contravene, defy, disregard, flout, go counter to, ignore, infringe, overstep, rebel, refuse to obey, resist, transgress, violate

disorderly 1. chaotic, confused, disorganized, higgledy-piggledy (*informal*), indiscriminate, irregular, jumbled, messy, shambolic (*informal*), unsystematic, untidy **2.** boisterous, disruptive, indisciplined, lawless, obstreperous, rebellious, refractory, riotous, rowdy, stormy, tumultuous, turbulent, ungovernable, unlawful, unmanageable, unruly

disorganize break up, confuse, derange, destroy, disarrange, discompose, disorder, disrupt, disturb, jumble, make a shambles of, muddle, turn topsy-turvy, unsettle, upset

disorganized chaotic, confused, disordered, haphazard, jumbled, muddled, shuffled, unmethodical, unorganized, unsystematic

disown abandon, cast off, deny, disallow, disavow, disclaim, rebut, refuse to acknowledge *or* recognize, reject, renounce, repudiate, retract

disparage bad-mouth (*slang, chiefly U.S. & Canad.*), belittle, blast, cast aspersions on, criticize, decry, defame, degrade, denigrate, deprecate, depreciate, deride, detract from, discredit, disdain, dismiss, knock (*informal*), lambast(e), malign, minimize, put down, ridicule, rubbish (*informal*), run down, scorn, slag (off) (*slang*), slander, tear into (*informal*), traduce, underestimate, underrate, undervalue, vilify

disparagement belittlement, condemnation, contempt, contumely, criticism, debasement, degradation, denunciation, depreciation, derision, discredit, disdain, impairment, lessening, prejudice, reproach, ridicule, scorn, slander, underestimation

dispassionate calm, candid, collected, composed, cool, detached, disinterested, fair, impartial, impersonal, imperturbable, indifferent, moderate, neutral, objective, quiet, serene, sober, temperate, unbiased, unemotional, unexcitable, unexcited, unfazed (*informal*), uninvolved, unmoved, unprejudiced, unruffled

dispatch, despatch *vb.* **1.** accelerate, consign, dismiss, express, forward, hasten, hurry, quicken, remit, send, transmit **2.** conclude, discharge, dispose of, expedite, finish, make short work of (*informal*), perform, settle **3.** assassinate, blow away (*slang, chiefly U.S.*), bump off (*slang*), butcher, eliminate (*slang*), execute, finish off, kill, murder, put an end to, slaughter, slay, take out (*slang*) ~*n.* **4.** account, bulletin, communication, communiqué, document, instruction, item, letter, message, missive, news, piece, report, story **5.** alacrity, celerity, expedition, haste, precipitateness, promptitude, promptness, quickness, rapidity, speed, swiftness

dispel allay, banish, chase away, dismiss, disperse, dissipate, drive away, eliminate, expel, resolve, rout, scatter

dispensary *n, pl* **-ries** a place where medicine is prepared and given out.

dispensation *n* **1** the act of distributing or dispensing. **2** *Chiefly RC Church* permission to dispense with an obligation of church law. **3** any exemption from an obligation. **4** the ordering of life and events by God.

dispense *vb* **-pensing, -pensed 1** to distribute in portions. **2** to prepare and distribute (medicine). **3** to administer (the law, etc.). **4 dispense with** to do away with or manage without. **dispenser** *n*

dispensing optician *n* See **optician** (sense 2).

disperse *vb* **-persing, -persed 1** to scatter over a wide area. **2** to leave or cause to leave a gathering. **3** to separate (light) into its different wavelengths. **4** to separate (particles) throughout a solid, liquid, or gas. **dispersal** *or* **dispersion** *n*

dispirit *vb* to make downhearted. **dispirited** *adj* **dispiriting** *adj*

displace *vb* **-placing, -placed 1** to move (something) from its usual place. **2** to remove (someone) from a post or position of authority.

displaced person *n* a person forced from his or her home or country, esp. by war or revolution.

displacement *n* **1** the act of displacing. **2** *Physics* the weight or volume of liquid displaced by an object submerged or floating in it. **3** *Maths* the distance measured in a particular direction from a reference point. Symbol: *s*

display *vb* **1** to show. **2** to reveal or make evident: *to display anger.* ~*n* **3** the act of exhibiting or displaying. **4** something displayed. **5** an exhibition. **6** *Electronics* a device capable of representing information visually, as on a screen. **7** *Zool* a pattern of behaviour by which an animal attracts attention while courting, defending its territory, etc.

displease *vb* **-pleasing, -pleased** to annoy or offend (someone). **displeasure** *n*

disport *vb* **disport oneself** to indulge oneself in pleasure.

disposable *adj* **1** designed for disposal after use: *disposable cigarette lighters.* **2** available for use if needed: *disposable capital.*

disposal *n* **1** the act or means of getting rid of something. **2 at one's disposal** available for use.

dispose *vb* **-posing, -posed 1 dispose of a** to throw away. **b** to give, sell, or transfer to another. **c** to deal with or settle: *I disposed of that problem right away.* **d** to kill. **2** to arrange or place in a particular way: *around them are disposed the moulded masks of witch doctors.*

disposed *adj* **1** willing or eager (to do something): *few would feel disposed to fault his judgment.* **2** having an inclination as specified (towards someone or something): *my people aren't too well disposed towards defectors.*

disposition *n* **1** a person's usual temperament. **2** a tendency or habit. **3** arrangement; layout.

dispossess *vb* to deprive (someone) of (a possession). **dispossessed** *adj* **dispossession** *n*

disproportion *n* lack of proportion or equality.

disproportionate *adj* out of proportion. **disproportionately** *adv*

disprove *vb* **-proving, -proved** to show (an assertion or claim) to be incorrect.

THESAURUS

dispensable disposable, expendable, inessential, needless, nonessential, superfluous, unnecessary, unrequired, useless

dispensation 1. allotment, appointment, apportionment, bestowal, conferment, consignment, dealing out, disbursement, distribution, endowment, supplying **2.** exception, exemption, immunity, indulgence, licence, permission, privilege, relaxation, relief, remission, reprieve

dispense 1. allocate, allot, apportion, assign, deal out, disburse, distribute, dole out, mete out, share **2.** measure, mix, prepare, supply **3.** administer, apply, carry out, direct, discharge, enforce, execute, implement, operate, undertake **4.** *with* **with** abolish, abstain from, brush aside, cancel, dispose of, disregard, do away with, do without, forgo, get rid of, give up, ignore, omit, pass over, relinquish, shake off, waive

disperse 1. broadcast, circulate, diffuse, disseminate, dissipate, distribute, scatter, spread, strew **2.** break up, disappear, disband, dismiss, dispel, dissolve, rout, scatter, send off, separate, vanish

dispirited crestfallen, dejected, depressed, despondent, discouraged, disheartened, down, downcast, gloomy, glum, in the doldrums, low, morose, sad

displace 1. disturb, misplace, move, shift, transpose **2.** cashier, depose, discard, discharge, dismiss, fire (*informal*), remove, sack (*informal*)

display *vb.* **1.** betray, demonstrate, disclose, evidence, evince, exhibit, expose, manifest, open, open to view, present, reveal, show, unveil ~*n.* **2.** array, demonstration, exhibition, exposition, exposure, manifestation, presentation, revelation, show **3.** flourish, ostentation, pageant, parade, pomp, show, spectacle

displease anger, annoy, disgust, dissatisfy, exasperate, gall, hassle (*informal*), incense, irk, irritate, nark (*Brit., Austral., & N.Z. slang*), nettle, offend, pique, piss one off (*taboo slang*), provoke, put out, rile, upset, vex

displeasure anger, annoyance, disapprobation, disapproval, disfavour, disgruntlement, dislike, dissatisfaction, distaste, indignation, irritation, offence, pique, resentment, vexation, wrath

disposable 1. biodegradable, compostable, decomposable, nonreturnable, paper, throwaway **2.** at one's service, available, consumable, expendable, free for use, spendable

disposal 1. clearance, discarding, dumping (*informal*), ejection, jettisoning, parting with, relinquishment, removal, riddance, scrapping, throwing away **2.** *as in* **at one's disposal** authority, conduct, control, determination, direction, discretion, government, management, ordering, regulation, responsibility

dispose 1. *with* **of** bin (*informal*), chuck (*informal*), destroy, discard, dump (*informal*), get rid of, jettison, junk (*informal*), scrap, throw out *or* away, unload **2.** *with* **of** bestow, give, make over, part with, sell, transfer **3.** *with* **of** deal with, decide, determine, end, finish with, settle **4.** adjust, arrange, array, determine, distribute, fix, group, marshal, order, place, put, range, rank, regulate, set, settle, stand

disposed apt, given, inclined, liable, likely, of a mind to, predisposed, prone, ready, subject, tending towards

disposition 1. character, constitution, make-up, nature, spirit, temper, temperament **2.** bent, bias, habit, inclination, leaning, predisposition, proclivity, proneness, propensity, readiness, tendency **3.** adjustment, arrangement, classification, disposal, distribution, grouping, ordering, organization, placement

disproportion asymmetry, discrepancy, disparity, imbalance, inadequacy, inequality, insufficiency, lopsidedness, unevenness, unsuitableness

disproportionate excessive, incommensurate, inordinate, out of proportion, too much, unbalanced, unequal, uneven, unreasonable

disprove confute, contradict, controvert, discredit,

dispute *n* **1** a disagreement between workers and their employer. **2** an argument between two or more people. *~vb* **-puting, -puted 3** to argue or quarrel about (something). **4** to doubt the validity of. **5** to fight over possession of. **6 beyond dispute** unable to be questioned or denied: *it's beyond dispute that tensions already existed between them.* **disputation** *n* **disputatious** *adj*

disqualify *vb* **-fies, -fying, -fied 1** to officially ban (someone) from doing something: *he was disqualified from driving for ten years.* **2** to make ineligible, as for entry to an examination. **disqualification** *n*

disquiet *n* **1** a feeling of anxiety or uneasiness. *~vb* **2** to make (someone) anxious. **disquieting** *adj* **disquietude** *n*

disquisition *n* a formal written or oral examination of a subject.

disregard *vb* **1** to give little or no attention to; ignore. *~n* **2** lack of attention or respect.

disrepair *n* the condition of being worn out or in poor working order.

disreputable *adj* having or causing a bad reputation. **disreputably** *adv*

disrepute *n* a loss or lack of good reputation.

disrespect *n* contempt or lack of respect. **disrespectful** *adj*

disrobe *vb* **-robing, -robed** *Literary* to undress.

disrupt *vb* to interrupt the progress of. **disruption** *n* **disruptive** *adj*

dissatisfied *adj* displeased or discontented. **dissatisfaction** *n*

dissect *vb* **1** to cut open (a corpse) to examine it. **2** to examine critically and minutely: *the above conclusion causes one to dissect that policy more closely.* **dissection** *n*

dissemble *vb* **-bling, -bled** to conceal one's real motives or emotions by pretence. **dissembler** *n*

disseminate *vb* **-nating, -nated** to spread (information, ideas, etc.) widely. **dissemination** *n*

dissension *n* disagreement and argument.

dissent *vb* **1** to disagree. **2** *Christianity* to reject the doctrines of an established church. *~n* **3** a disagree-

THESAURUS

expose, give the lie to, invalidate, negate, prove false, rebut, refute

disputation argumentation, controversy, debate, dispute, dissension, polemics

dispute *n.* **1.** altercation, argument, brawl, conflict, contention, controversy, debate, disagreement, discord, discussion, dissension, disturbance, feud, friction, quarrel, shindig (*slang*), shindy (*slang*), strife, wrangle *~vb.* **2.** argue, brawl, clash, contend, debate, discuss, quarrel, row, spar, squabble, wrangle **3.** challenge, contest, contradict, controvert, deny, doubt, impugn, question, rebut

disqualification 1. disability, disablement, incapacitation, incapacity, unfitness **2.** debarment, disenablement, disentitlement, elimination, exclusion, incompetence, ineligibility, rejection

disqualified debarred, eliminated, ineligible, knocked out, out of the running

disqualify ban, debar, declare ineligible, disentitle, forbid, invalidate, preclude, prohibit, rule out

disquiet 1. *n.* alarm, angst, anxiety, concern, disquietude, distress, disturbance, fear, foreboding, fretfulness, nervousness, restlessness, trepidation, trouble, uneasiness, unrest, worry **2.** *vb.* agitate, annoy, bother, concern, discompose, distress, disturb, fret, harass, hassle (*informal*), incommode, make uneasy, perturb, pester, plague, trouble, unsettle, upset, vex, worry

disquieting annoying, bothersome, disconcerting, distressing, disturbing, harrowing, irritating, perturbing, troubling, unnerving, unsettling, upsetting, vexing, worrying

disregard 1. *vb.* brush aside *or* away, cold-shoulder, discount, disdain, disobey, ignore, laugh off, leave out of account, make light of, neglect, overlook, pass over, pay no attention to, pay no heed to, slight, snub, take no notice of, turn a blind eye to **2.** *n.* contempt, disdain, disrespect, heedlessness, ignoring, inattention, indifference, neglect, negligence, oversight, slight, the cold shoulder

disrepair 1. collapse, decay, deterioration, dilapidation, ruination **2. in disrepair** broken, bust (*informal*), decayed, decrepit, kaput (*informal*), not functioning, on the blink (*slang*), out of commission, out of order, worn-out

disreputable base, contemptible, derogatory, dilapidated, dingy, discreditable, disgraceful, dishonourable, disorderly, down at heel, ignominious, infamous, louche, low, mean, notorious, opprobrious, scandalous, scruffy, seedy, shabby, shady (*informal*), shameful, shocking, threadbare, unprincipled, vicious, vile

disrepute discredit, disesteem, disfavour, disgrace, dishonour, ignominy, ill favour, ill repute, infamy, obloquy, shame, unpopularity

disrespect contempt, discourtesy, dishonour, disregard, impertinence, impoliteness, impudence, incivility, insolence, irreverence, lack of respect, lese-majesty, rudeness, unmannerliness

disrespectful bad-mannered, cheeky, contemptuous, discourteous, ill-bred, impertinent, impolite, impudent, insolent, insulting, irreverent, misbehaved, rude, uncivil

disrupt agitate, break up *or* into, confuse, disorder, disorganize, disturb, interfere with, interrupt, intrude, obstruct, spoil, throw into disorder, unsettle, upset

disruption confusion, disarray, disorder, disorderliness, disturbance, interference, interruption, stoppage

disruptive confusing, disorderly, distracting, disturbing, obstreperous, troublemaking, troublesome, unruly, unsettling, upsetting

dissatisfaction annoyance, chagrin, disappointment, discomfort, discontent, dislike, dismay, displeasure, distress, exasperation, frustration, irritation, regret, resentment, unhappiness

dissatisfied disappointed, discontented, disgruntled, displeased, fed up, frustrated, not satisfied, unfulfilled, ungratified, unhappy, unsatisfied

dissect 1. cut up *or* apart, dismember, lay open **2.** analyse, break down, explore, inspect, investigate, research, scrutinize, study

dissection 1. autopsy, dismemberment, necropsy, postmortem (examination) **2.** analysis, breakdown, examination, inspection, investigation, research, scrutiny

disseminate broadcast, circulate, diffuse, disperse, dissipate, distribute, proclaim, promulgate, propagate, publicize, publish, scatter, sow, spread

dissemination broadcasting, circulation, diffusion, distribution, promulgation, propagation, publication, publishing, spread

dissension conflict, conflict of opinion, contention, difference, disagreement, discord, discordance, dispute, dissent, friction, quarrel, row, strife, variance

dissent 1. *vb.* decline, differ, disagree, object, protest, refuse, withhold assent *or* approval **2.** *n.* difference, disagreement, discord, dissension, dissidence,

ment. **4** *Christianity* separation from an established church. **dissenter** *n* **dissenting** *adj*

Dissenter *n Christianity chiefly Brit* a Protestant who refuses to conform to the established church.

dissentient *adj* dissenting from the opinion of the majority.

dissertation *n* **1** a written thesis, usually required for a higher degree. **2** a long formal speech.

disservice *n* a harmful action.

dissident *n* **1** a person who disagrees with a government or a powerful organization. *~adj* **2** disagreeing or dissenting. **dissidence** *n*

dissimilar *adj* not alike; different. **dissimilarity** *n*

dissimulate *vb* **-lating, -lated** to conceal one's real feelings by pretence. **dissimulation** *n*

dissipate *vb* **-pating, -pated 1** to waste or squander. **2** to scatter or break up.

dissipated *adj* showing signs of overindulgence in alcohol or other physical pleasures.

dissipation *n* **1** the process of dissipating. **2** unrestrained indulgence in physical pleasures.

dissociate *vb* **-ating, -ated 1 dissociate oneself from** to deny or break an association with (a person or organization). **2** to regard or treat as separate. **dissociation** *n*

dissoluble *adj* same as **soluble. dissolubility** *n*

dissolute *adj* leading an immoral life.

dissolution *n* **1** the act of officially breaking up an organization or institution. **2** the act of officially ending a formal agreement, such as a marriage. **3** the formal ending of a meeting or assembly, such as a Parliament.

dissolve *vb* **-solving, -solved 1** to become or cause to become liquid; melt. **2** to officially break up (an organization or institution). **3** to formally end: *the campaign started as soon as Parliament was dissolved last month.* **4** to collapse emotionally: *she dissolved in loud tears.* **5** *Films, television* to fade out one scene and replace with another to make two scenes merge imperceptibly.

dissonance *n* a lack of agreement or harmony between things: *this dissonance of colours.* **dissonant** *adj*

dissuade *vb* **-suading, -suaded** to deter (someone) by persuasion from doing something or believing in something. **dissuasion** *n*

dissyllable *or* **disyllable** *n* a word of two syllables. **dissyllabic** *or* **disyllabic** *adj*

distaff *n* the rod on which wool, flax, etc., is wound for spinning.

distaff side *n* the female side of a family.

distance *n* **1** the space between two points or places. **2** the state of being apart. **3** a distant place. **4** remoteness in manner. **5 the distance** the most distant part of the visible scene. **6 go the distance** *Boxing* to complete a bout without being knocked out. **7 keep one's distance** to maintain a reserved attitude to another person. *~vb* **-tancing, -tanced 8 distance oneself** *or* **be distanced from** to separate oneself or be separated mentally from.

distant *adj* **1** far apart. **2** separated by a specified distance: *five kilometres distant.* **3** apart in relationship: *a distant cousin.* **4** going to a faraway place. **5** remote in manner; aloof. **6** abstracted: *a distant look entered her eyes.* **distantly** *adv*

THESAURUS

nonconformity, objection, opposition, refusal, resistance

dissenter dissident, nonconformist, objector, protestant

dissentient *adj.* conflicting, differing, disagreeing, dissenting, dissident, opposing, protesting

dissertation critique, discourse, disquisition, essay, exposition, thesis, treatise

disservice bad turn, disfavour, harm, ill turn, injury, injustice, unkindness, wrong

dissident 1. *n.* agitator, dissenter, nonconformist, protestor, rebel, recusant **2.** *adj.* differing, disagreeing, discordant, dissentient, dissenting, heterodox, nonconformist, schismatic

dissimilar different, disparate, divergent, diverse, heterogeneous, manifold, mismatched, not alike, not capable of comparison, not similar, unlike, unrelated, various

dissimilarity difference, discrepancy, disparity, dissimilitude, distinction, divergence, heterogeneity, incomparability, nonuniformity, unlikeness, unrelatedness

dissipate burn up, consume, deplete, disappear, dispel, disperse, dissolve, drive away, evaporate, expend, fritter away, indulge oneself, lavish, misspend, run through, scatter, spend, squander, vanish, waste

dissipated abandoned, debauched, dissolute, intemperate, profligate, rakish, self-indulgent

dissipation 1. disappearance, disintegration, dispersion, dissemination, dissolution, scattering, vanishing **2.** abandonment, debauchery, dissoluteness, drunkenness, excess, extravagance, indulgence, intemperance, lavishness, prodigality, profligacy, squandering, wantonness, waste

dissociate 1. break off, disband, disrupt, part company, quit **2.** detach, disconnect, distance, divorce, isolate, segregate, separate, set apart

dissolute abandoned, corrupt, debauched, degenerate, depraved, dissipated, immoral, lax, lewd, libertine, licentious, loose, profligate, rakish, unrestrained, vicious, wanton, wild

dissolution 1. breaking up, disintegration, division, divorce, parting, resolution, separation **2.** death, decay, decomposition, demise, destruction, dispersal, extinction, overthrow, ruin **3.** adjournment, conclusion, disbandment, discontinuation, dismissal, end, ending, finish, suspension, termination

dissolve 1. deliquesce, fuse, liquefy, melt, soften, thaw **2.** axe (*informal*), break up, destroy, discontinue, dismiss, end, overthrow, ruin, suspend, terminate, wind up

dissuade advise against, deter, discourage, disincline, divert, expostulate, persuade not to, put off, remonstrate, talk out of, urge not to, warn

distance *n.* **1.** absence, extent, gap, interval, lapse, length, range, reach, remoteness, remove, separation, space, span, stretch, width **2.** aloofness, coldness, coolness, frigidity, reserve, restraint, stiffness **3. go the distance** bring to an end, complete, finish, see through, stay the course **4. keep one's distance** avoid, be aloof (indifferent, reserved), keep (someone) at arm's length, shun **5. in the distance** afar, far away, far off, on the horizon, yonder *~vb.* **6.** dissociate oneself, put in proportion, separate oneself

distant 1. abroad, afar, far, faraway, far-flung, far-off, outlying, out-of-the-way, remote, removed **2.** apart, disparate, dispersed, distinct, scattered, separate **3.** aloof, ceremonious, cold, cool, formal, haughty, reserved, restrained, reticent, standoffish, stiff, unapproachable, unfriendly, withdrawn

distaste abhorrence, antipathy, aversion, detestation, disfavour, disgust, disinclination, dislike, displeasure, disrelish, dissatisfaction, horror, loathing, odium, repugnance, revulsion

distaste *n* a dislike of something offensive.

distasteful *adj* unpleasant or offensive. **distastefulness** *n*

distemper[1] *n* a highly contagious viral disease that can affect young dogs.

distemper[2] *n* **1** paint mixed with water, glue, etc. which is used for painting walls. ~*vb* **2** to paint with distemper.

distend *vb* to expand by pressure from within; swell. **distensible** *adj* **distension** *n*

distich (**diss**-stick) *n Prosody* a unit of two verse lines.

distil *or US* **distill** *vb* **-tilling, -tilled 1** to subject to or obtain by distillation. **2** to give off (a substance) in drops. **3** to extract the essence of.

distillation *n* **1** the process of evaporating a liquid and condensing its vapour. **2** Also: **distillate** a concentrated essence.

distiller *n* a person or company that makes spirits.

distillery *n, pl* **-eries** a place where alcoholic drinks are made by distillation.

distinct *adj* **1** not the same; different: *these two areas produce wines with distinct characteristics.* **2** clearly seen, heard, or recognized: *it is not possible to draw a distinct line between the two categories; there's a distinct smell of burning.* **3** clear and definite: *there is a distinct possibility of rain.* **4** obvious: *a distinct improvement.* **distinctly** *adv*

distinction *n* **1** the act of distinguishing or differentiating. **2** a distinguishing feature. **3** the state of being different or distinguishable. **4** special honour, recognition, or fame. **5** excellence of character. **6** a symbol of honour or rank.

distinctive *adj* easily recognizable; characteristic. **distinctively** *adv* **distinctiveness** *n*

distingué (diss-**tang**-gay) *adj* distinguished or noble.

distinguish *vb* **1** to make, show, or recognize a difference: *I have tried to distinguish between fact and theory.* **2** to be a distinctive feature of: *what distinguishes the good teenage reader from the less competent one?* **3** to make out by hearing, seeing, or tasting: *she listened but could distinguish nothing except the urgency of their discussion.* **4 distinguish oneself** to make oneself noteworthy. **distinguishable** *adj* **distinguishing** *adj*

distinguished *adj* **1** dignified in appearance or behaviour. **2** highly respected: *a distinguished historian.*

distort *vb* **1** to alter or misrepresent (facts). **2** to twist out of shape; deform. **3** *Electronics* to reproduce or amplify (a signal) inaccurately. **distorted** *adj* **distortion** *n*

distract *vb* **1** to draw (a person or his or her attention) away from something. **2** to amuse or entertain.

distracted *adj* unable to concentrate because one's mind is on other things.

distraction *n* **1** something that diverts the attention. **2** something that serves as an entertainment. **3** mental turmoil.

distrain *vb Law* to seize (personal property) to enforce payment of a debt. **distraint** *n*

distrait (diss-**tray**) *adj* absent-minded or abstracted.

distraught (diss-**trawt**) *adj* upset or agitated.

THESAURUS

distasteful abhorrent, disagreeable, displeasing, loathsome, nauseous, objectionable, obnoxious, obscene, offensive, repugnant, repulsive, undesirable, uninviting, unpalatable, unpleasant, unsavoury

distend balloon, bloat, bulge, dilate, enlarge, expand, increase, inflate, puff, stretch, swell, widen

distended bloated, dilated, enlarged, expanded, inflated, puffy, stretched, swollen, tumescent

distil condense, draw out, evaporate, express, extract, press out, purify, rectify, refine, sublimate, vaporize

distillation elixir, essence, extract, quintessence, spirit

distinct 1. detached, different, discrete, dissimilar, individual, separate, unconnected **2.** apparent, blatant, clear, clear-cut, decided, definite, evident, lucid, manifest, marked, noticeable, obvious, palpable, patent, plain, recognizable, sharp, unambiguous, unmistakable, well-defined

distinction 1. differentiation, discernment, discrimination, penetration, perception, separation **2.** characteristic, distinctiveness, feature, individuality, mark, particularity, peculiarity, quality **3.** contrast, difference, differential, division, separation **4.** account, celebrity, consequence, credit, eminence, excellence, fame, greatness, honour, importance, merit, name, note, prominence, quality, rank, renown, reputation, repute, superiority, worth

distinctive characteristic, different, distinguishing, extraordinary, idiosyncratic, individual, original, peculiar, singular, special, typical, uncommon, unique

distinctly clearly, decidedly, definitely, evidently, manifestly, markedly, noticeably, obviously, palpably, patently, plainly, precisely, sharply

distinguish 1. ascertain, decide, determine, differentiate, discriminate, judge, tell apart, tell between, tell the difference **2.** categorize, characterize, classify, individualize, make distinctive, mark, separate, set apart, single out **3.** discern, know, make out, perceive, pick out, recognize, see, tell **4.** celebrate, dignify, honour, immortalize, make famous, signalize

distinguishable clear, conspicuous, discernible, evident, manifest, noticeable, obvious, perceptible, plain, recognizable, well-marked

distinguished acclaimed, celebrated, conspicuous, eminent, famed, famous, illustrious, notable, noted, renowned, well-known

distinguishing characteristic, different, differentiating, distinctive, individualistic, marked, peculiar, typical

distort 1. bias, colour, falsify, garble, misrepresent, pervert, slant, twist **2.** bend, buckle, contort, deform, disfigure, misshape, twist, warp, wrench, wrest

distortion 1. bend, buckle, contortion, crookedness, deformity, malformation, twist, twistedness, warp **2.** bias, colouring, falsification, misrepresentation, perversion, slant

distract 1. divert, draw away, sidetrack, turn aside **2.** amuse, beguile, engross, entertain, occupy

distracted agitated, at sea, bemused, bewildered, confounded, confused, distraught, flustered, frantic, frenzied, grief-stricken, harassed, in a flap (*informal*), overwrought, perplexed, puzzled, troubled

distracting bewildering, bothering, confusing, disconcerting, dismaying, disturbing, off-putting (*Brit. informal*), perturbing

distraction 1. disturbance, diversion, interference, interruption **2.** amusement, beguilement, diversion, divertissement, entertainment, pastime, recreation **3.** abstraction, agitation, bewilderment, commotion, confusion, discord, disorder, disturbance

distress *n.* **1.** affliction, agony, anguish, anxiety, desolation, discomfort, grief, heartache, misery, pain, sadness, sorrow, suffering, torment, torture, woe, worry, wretchedness **2.** adversity, calamity, destitution, difficulties, hardship, indigence, misfortune, need, poverty, privation, straits, trial, trouble ~*vb.* **3.**

distress *n* **1** extreme unhappiness or worry. **2** great physical pain. **3** financial trouble. *~vb* **4** to upset badly. **5 in distress** in dire need of help. **distressing** *adj* **distressingly** *adv*

distressed *adj* **1** much troubled; upset. **2** in great physical pain. **3** in financial difficulties. **4** (of furniture or fabric) having signs of ageing artificially applied.

distributary *n, pl* **-taries** one of several outlet streams draining a river, esp. on a delta.

distribute *vb* **-uting, -uted 1** to hand out or deliver (leaflets, mail, etc.). **2** to share (something) among the members of a particular group.

distribution *n* **1** the delivering of leaflets, mail, etc., to individual people or organizations. **2** the sharing out of something among a particular group. **3** the arrangement or spread of anything over an area, space, or period of time: *the unequal distribution of wealth.* **4** *Commerce* the process of satisfying the demand for goods and services.

distributive *adj* **1** of or relating to distribution. **2** *Maths* of the rule that the same result is produced when multiplication is performed on a set of numbers as when performed on the members of the set individually.

distributor *n* **1** a wholesaler who distributes goods to retailers in a specific area. **2** the device in a petrol engine that sends the electric current to the sparking plugs.

district *n* **1** an area of land regarded as an administrative or geographical unit. **2** an area which has recognizable or special features: *an upper-class residential district.*

district high school *n* (in New Zealand) a school in a rural area providing both primary and secondary education.

district nurse *n* (in Britain) a nurse who attends to patients in their homes within a particular district.

distrust *vb* **1** to regard as untrustworthy. *~n* **2** a feeling of suspicion or doubt. **distrustful** *adj*

disturb *vb* **1** to intrude on; interrupt. **2** to upset or worry. **3** to disarrange; muddle. **4** to inconvenience. **disturbing** *adj* **disturbingly** *adv*

disturbance *n* **1** an interruption or intrusion. **2** an unruly outburst in public.

disturbed *adj Psychiatry* emotionally upset, troubled, or maladjusted.

disunite *vb* **-niting, -nited** to cause disagreement among. **disunion** *n* **disunity** *n*

disuse *n* the state of being neglected or no longer used; neglect.

disused *adj* no longer used.

disyllable *n* same as **dissyllable.**

ditch *n* **1** a narrow channel dug in the earth for drainage or irrigation. *~vb* **2** *Slang* to abandon or discard: *she ditched her boyfriend last month.*

dither *vb* **1** *Chiefly Brit* to be uncertain or indecisive. *~n* **2** *Chiefly Brit* a state of indecision or agitation. **ditherer** *n* **dithery** *adj*

dithyramb *n* (in ancient Greece) a passionate choral hymn in honour of Dionysus. **dithyrambic** *adj*

ditto *n, pl* **-tos 1** the above; the same: used in lists to avoid repetition, and represented by the mark („) placed under the thing repeated. *~adv* **2** in the same way.

ditty *n, pl* **-ties** a short simple song or poem.

diuretic (die-yoor-**et**-ik) *n* a drug that increases the flow of urine.

diurnal (die-**urn**-al) *adj* **1** happening during the day or daily. **2** (of animals) active during the day.

diva *n, pl* **-vas** *or* **-ve** a distinguished female singer; prima donna.

divalent *adj Chem* having two valencies or a valency of two. **divalency** *n*

divan *n* **a** a low bed with a thick base under the mattress. **b** a couch with no back or arms.

dive *vb* **diving, dived** *or US* **dove, dived 1** to plunge headfirst into water. **2** (of a submarine or diver) to submerge under water. **3** (of a bird or aircraft) to fly in a steep nose-down descending path. **4** to move quickly in a specified direction: *he dived for the door.* **5 dive**

THESAURUS

afflict, agonize, bother, disturb, grieve, harass, harrow, pain, perplex, sadden, torment, trouble, upset, worry, wound

distressed 1. afflicted, agitated, anxious, distracted, distraught, saddened, tormented, troubled, upset, worried, wretched **2.** destitute, indigent, needy, poor, poverty-stricken, straitened

distressing affecting, afflicting, distressful, disturbing, grievous, harrowing, heart-breaking, hurtful, lamentable, nerve-racking, painful, sad, upsetting, worrying

distribute 1. circulate, convey, deliver, hand out, pass round **2.** allocate, allot, apportion, assign, deal, dispense, dispose, divide, dole out, give, measure out, mete, share

distribution 1. circulation, diffusion, dispersal, dispersion, dissemination, propagation, scattering, spreading **2.** allocation, allotment, apportionment, dispensation, division, dole, partition, sharing **3.** arrangement, assortment, classification, disposition, grouping, location, organization, placement **4.** *Commerce* dealing, delivery, handling, mailing, marketing, trading, transport, transportation

district area, community, locale, locality, neighbourhood, parish, quarter, region, sector, vicinity, ward

distrust 1. *vb.* be sceptical of, be suspicious of, be wary of, disbelieve, discredit, doubt, misbelieve, mistrust, question, smell a rat (*informal*), suspect, wonder about **2.** *n.* disbelief, doubt, dubiety, lack of faith, misgiving, mistrust, qualm, question, scepticism, suspicion, wariness

disturb 1. bother, butt in on, disrupt, interfere with, interrupt, intrude on, pester, rouse, startle **2.** agitate, alarm, annoy, confound, discompose, distract, distress, excite, fluster, harass, hassle (*informal*), perturb, ruffle, shake, trouble, unnerve, unsettle, upset, worry **3.** confuse, derange, disarrange, disorder, disorganize, muddle, unsettle

disturbance 1. agitation, annoyance, bother, confusion, derangement, disorder, distraction, hindrance, interruption, intrusion, molestation, perturbation, upset **2.** bother (*informal*), brawl, commotion, disorder, fracas, fray, hubbub, riot, ruckus (*informal*), ruction (*informal*), shindig (*informal*), shindy (*informal*), tumult, turmoil, upheaval, uproar

disturbed *Psychiatry* disordered, maladjusted, neurotic, troubled, unbalanced, upset

disturbing alarming, disconcerting, discouraging, dismaying, disquieting, distressing, frightening, harrowing, perturbing, startling, threatening, troubling, unsettling, upsetting, worrying

disuse abandonment, decay, desuetude, idleness, neglect, non-employment, nonuse

ditch 1. *n.* channel, drain, dyke, furrow, gully, moat, trench, watercourse **2.** *vb. slang* abandon, axe (*informal*), bin (*informal*), chuck (*informal*), discard, dispose of, drop, dump (*informal*), get rid of, jettison, junk (*informal*), scrap, throw out *or* overboard

dither 1. *vb.* faff about (*Brit. informal*), falter, haver,

in *or* **into a** to put (one's hand) quickly or forcefully (into). **b** to start doing (something) enthusiastically. *~n* **6** a headlong plunge into water. **7** the act of diving. **8** a steep nose-down descent of a bird or aircraft. **9** *Slang* a disreputable bar or club.

dive bomber *n* a military aircraft designed to release bombs on a target during a dive. **dive-bomb** *vb*

diver *n* **1** a person who works or explores underwater. **2** a person who dives for sport. **3** a large diving bird of northern oceans with a straight pointed bill and webbed feet.

diverge *vb* **-verging, -verged 1** to separate and go in different directions. **2** to be at variance; differ: *the two books diverge in setting and in style.* **3** to deviate (from a prescribed course). **divergence** *n* **divergent** *adj*

diverse *adj* **1** having variety; assorted. **2** different in kind.

diversify *vb* **-fies, -fying, -fied 1** to create different forms of; vary. **2** (of an enterprise) to vary (products or operations) in order to expand or reduce the risk of loss. **diversification** *n*

diversion *n* **1** *Chiefly Brit* an official detour used by traffic when a main route is closed. **2** something that distracts someone's attention or concentration. **3** the act of diverting from a specified course. **4** a pleasant or amusing pastime or activity. **diversionary** *adj*

diversity *n* **1** the quality of being different or varied. **2** a point of difference.

divert *vb* **1** to change the course or direction of (traffic). **2** to distract the attention of. **3** to entertain or amuse.

diverticulitis *n* inflammation of pouches in the wall of the colon, causing lower abdominal pain.

divertimento *n, pl* **-ti** a piece of entertaining music in several movements.

divest *vb* **1** to strip (of clothes). **2** to deprive of a role, function, or quality: *the chairman felt duty-bound to stay with the company after it was divested of all its aviation interests.*

divide *vb* **-viding, -vided 1** to separate into parts. **2** to share or be shared out in parts. **3** to disagree or cause to disagree: *experts are divided over the plan.* **4** to keep apart or be a boundary between. **5** to categorize or classify. **6** to calculate how many times one number can be contained in another. *~n* **7** a division or split. **8** *Chiefly US & Canad* an area of high ground separating drainage basins.

dividend *n* **1** a portion of a company's profits paid to its shareholders. **2** an extra benefit: *Saudi progressives saw a dividend to the crisis.* **3** a number to be divided by another number.

divider *n* a screen placed so as to divide a room into separate areas.

dividers *pl n* compasses with two pointed arms, used for measuring or dividing lines.

divination *n* the art of discovering future events as though by supernatural powers.

divine *adj* **1** of God or a god. **2** godlike. **3** *Informal* splendid or perfect. *~n* **4** a priest who is learned in theology. *~vb* **-vining, -vined 5** to discover (something) by intuition or guessing. **divinely** *adv* **diviner** *n*

diving bell *n* a diving apparatus with an open bottom, supplied with compressed air from above.

diving board *n* a platform from which swimmers may dive.

diving suit *n* a waterproof suit used for diving with a detachable helmet and an air supply.

divining rod *n* a forked twig said to move when held over ground in which water or metal is to be found.

divinity *n, pl* **-ties 1** the study of religion. **2** a god or goddess. **3** the state of being divine.

divisible *adj* capable of being divided. **divisibility** *n*

division *n* **1** the separation of something into two or

THESAURUS

hesitate, oscillate, shillyshally (*informal*), swither (*Scot.*), teeter, vacillate, waver **2.** *n.* bother, flap (*informal*), fluster, flutter, pother, stew (*informal*), tizzy (*informal*), twitter (*informal*)

dive *vb.* **1.** descend, dip, disappear, drop, duck, fall, go underwater, jump, leap, nose-dive, pitch, plummet, plunge, submerge, swoop *~n.* **2.** dash, header (*informal*), jump, leap, lunge, nose dive, plunge, spring **3.** *slang* honky-tonk (*U.S. slang*), joint (*slang*), sleazy bar

diverge 1. bifurcate, branch, divaricate, divide, fork, part, radiate, separate, split, spread **2.** be at odds, be at variance, conflict, differ, disagree, dissent **3.** depart, deviate, digress, meander, stray, turn aside, wander

divergence branching out, deflection, departure, deviation, difference, digression, disparity, divagation, ramification, separation, varying

divergent conflicting, deviating, different, differing, disagreeing, dissimilar, diverging, diverse, separate, variant

diverse 1. assorted, diversified, manifold, miscellaneous, of every description, several, sundry, varied, various **2.** different, differing, discrete, disparate, dissimilar, distinct, divergent, separate, unlike, varying

diversify alter, assort, branch out, change, expand, mix, modify, spread out, transform, variegate, vary

diversion 1. alteration, change, deflection, departure, detour, deviation, digression, variation **2.** amusement, beguilement, delight, distraction, divertissement, enjoyment, entertainment, game, gratification, jollies (*slang*), pastime, play, pleasure, recreation, relaxation, sport

diversity assortment, difference, dissimilarity, distinctiveness, divergence, diverseness, diversification, heterogeneity, medley, multiplicity, range, unlikeness, variance, variegation, variety

divert 1. avert, deflect, redirect, switch, turn aside **2.** detract, distract, draw *or* lead away from, lead astray, sidetrack **3.** amuse, beguile, delight, entertain, gratify, recreate, regale

diverting amusing, beguiling, enjoyable, entertaining, fun, humorous, pleasant

divest 1. denude, disrobe, doff, remove, strip, take off, unclothe, undress **2.** deprive, dispossess, strip

divide 1. bisect, cleave, cut (up), detach, disconnect, part, partition, segregate, separate, sever, shear, split, subdivide, sunder **2.** allocate, allot, apportion, deal out, dispense, distribute, divvy (up) (*informal*), dole out, measure out, portion, share **3.** alienate, break up, cause to disagree, come between, disunite, estrange, set *or* pit against one another, set at variance *or* odds, sow dissension, split **4.** arrange, categorize, classify, grade, group, put in order, separate, sort

dividend bonus, cut (*informal*), divvy (*informal*), extra, gain, plus, portion, share, surplus

divine *adj.* **1.** consecrated, holy, religious, sacred, sanctified, spiritual **2.** angelic, celestial, godlike, heavenly, holy, spiritual, superhuman, supernatural **3.** *informal* beautiful, excellent, glorious, marvellous, perfect, splendid, superlative, wonderful *~n.* **4.** churchman, clergyman, cleric, ecclesiastic, minister, pastor, priest, reverend *~vb.* **5.** apprehend, conjecture, deduce, discern, foretell, guess, infer, intuit, perceive, prognosticate, suppose, surmise, suspect, understand

divinity 1. religion, religious studies, theology **2.** deity, god, goddess, guardian spirit, spirit **3.** deity, di-

more distinct parts. **2** the act of dividing or sharing out. **3** one of the parts into which something is divided. **4** the mathematical operation of dividing. **5** a difference of opinion. **6** a part of an organization that has been made into a unit for administrative or other reasons. **7** a formal vote in Parliament. **8** one of the groups of teams that make up a football or other sports league. **9** *Army* a major formation containing the necessary arms to sustain independent combat. **10** *Biol* one of the major groups into which the plant kingdom is divided, corresponding to a phylum. **divisional** *adj*

division sign *n* the symbol ÷, placed between two numbers to indicate that the first number should be divided by the second, as in 12 ÷ 6 = 2.

divisive (div-**vice**-iv) *adj* tending to cause disagreement: *he played an important role in defusing potentially divisive issues.*

divisor *n* a number to be divided into another number.

divorce *n* **1** the legal ending of a marriage. **2** a separation, esp. one that is permanent. *~vb* **-vorcing, -vorced 3** to separate or be separated by divorce. **4** to remove or separate.

divorcee *or masc* **divorcé** *n* a person who is divorced.

divot *n* a small piece of turf.

divulge *vb* **-vulging, -vulged** to make known: *I am not permitted to divulge his name.* **divulgence** *n*

divvy *vb* **-vies, -vying, -vied divvy up** *Informal* to divide and share.

Diwali (duh-**wah**-lee) *n* an annual Hindu festival honouring Lakshmi, the goddess of wealth.

Dixie *n* the southern states of the US. Also called: **Dixieland**

DIY *or* **d.i.y.** *Brit, Austral, & NZ* do-it-yourself.

dizzy *adj* **-zier, -ziest 1** feeling giddy. **2** unable to think clearly; confused. **3** tending to cause giddiness or confusion. *~vb* **-zies, -zying, -zied 4** to cause to feel giddy or confused. **dizzily** *adv* **dizziness** *n*

DJ *or* **dj** disc jockey.

djinni *or* **djinny** *n, pl* **djinn** same as **jinni**.

dl decilitre(s).

DLitt *or* **DLit 1** Doctor of Letters. **2** Doctor of Literature.

dm decimetre(s).

DM Deutschmark.

DMus Doctor of Music.

DNA deoxyribonucleic acid, the main constituent of the chromosomes of all organisms.

D-notice *n Brit* an official notice sent to newspapers prohibiting the publication of certain security information.

do[1] *vb* **does, doing, did, done 1** to perform or complete (a deed or action): *we do a fair amount of entertaining.* **2** to be adequate: *it's not what I wanted but it will have to do.* **3** to provide: *this hotel only does bed and breakfast.* **4** to make tidy or elegant: *he watched her do her hair.* **5** to improve: *that style does nothing for you.* **6** to find an answer to (a problem or puzzle). **7** to conduct oneself: *do as you want.* **8** to cause or produce: *herbal teas have active ingredients that can do good.* **9** to give or grant: *do me a favour.* **10** to work at as a course of study or a job. **11** to mimic. **12** to achieve a particular speed, amount, or rate: *this computer system can do 40 different cross checks; this car can do sixty miles to the gallon.* **13** used: **a** to form questions: *do you like it?* **b** to intensify positive statements and commands: *tensions do exist.* **c** to form negative statements or commands: *do not talk while I'm talking!* **d** to replace an earlier verb: *he drinks much more than I do.* **14** *Informal* to visit (a place) as a tourist: *we plan to do the States this year.* **15** *Slang* to serve (a period of time) as a prison sentence. **16** *Informal* to cheat or rob: *I was done out of ten pounds.* **17** *Slang* **a** to arrest. **b** to convict of a crime: *he was done for 3 years for housebreaking.* **18** *Slang, chiefly Brit* to assault. **19** *Slang* to take or use (drugs). **20 make do** to manage with whatever is available. *~n, pl* **dos** *or* **do's 21** *Informal, chiefly Brit & NZ* a party or other social event. **22 do's and don'ts** *Informal* rules. ~See also **do away with, do by,** etc.

do[2] *n, pl* **dos** *Music* same as **doh**.

do away with *vb* to get rid of (someone or something).

Doberman pinscher *or* **Doberman** *n* a large dog with a glossy black-and-tan coat.

THESAURUS

vine nature, godhead, godhood, godliness, holiness, sanctity

divisible dividable, fractional, separable, splittable

division 1. bisection, cutting up, detaching, dividing, partition, separation, splitting up **2.** allotment, apportionment, distribution, sharing **3.** branch, category, class, compartment, department, group, head, part, portion, section, sector, segment **4.** breach, difference of opinion, disagreement, discord, disunion, estrangement, feud, rupture, split, variance

divisive alienating, damaging, detrimental, discordant, disruptive, estranging, inharmonious, pernicious, troublesome, unsettling

divorce 1. *n.* annulment, breach, break, decree nisi, dissolution, disunion, rupture, separation, severance, split-up **2.** *vb.* annul, disconnect, dissociate, dissolve (*marriage*), disunite, divide, part, separate, sever, split up, sunder

divulge betray, blow wide open (*slang*), communicate, confess, declare, disclose, exhibit, expose, impart, leak, let slip, make known, proclaim, promulgate, publish, reveal, spill (*informal*), spill one's guts about (*slang*), tell, uncover

dizzy 1. faint, giddy, light-headed, off balance, reeling, shaky, staggering, swimming, vertiginous, weak at the knees, wobbly, woozy (*informal*) **2.** at sea, befuddled, bemused, bewildered, capricious, confused, dazed, dazzled, light-headed, muddled, scatterbrained

do *vb.* **1.** accomplish, achieve, act, carry out, complete, conclude, discharge, end, execute, perform, produce, transact, undertake, work **2.** answer, be adequate, be enough, be of use, be sufficient, pass muster, satisfy, serve, suffice, suit **3.** arrange, be responsible for, fix, get ready, look after, make, make ready, organize, prepare, see to, take on **4.** decipher, decode, figure out, puzzle out, resolve, solve, work out **5.** bear oneself, behave, carry oneself, comport oneself, conduct oneself **6.** bring about, cause, create, effect, produce **7.** *informal* cover, explore, journey through *or* around, look at, stop in, tour, travel, visit **8.** *informal* cheat, con (*informal*), cozen, deceive, defraud, diddle (*informal*), dupe, fleece, hoax, skin (*slang*), swindle, take (someone) for a ride (*informal*), trick *~n.* **9.** *informal* affair, event, function, gathering, occasion, party **10. do's and don'ts** *informal* code, customs, etiquette, instructions, regulations, rules, standards

do away with abolish, axe (*informal*), chuck (*informal*), discard, discontinue, eliminate, get rid of, junk (*informal*), put an end to, remove

docile amenable, biddable, compliant, manageable, obedient, pliant, submissive, tractable

do by *vb* to treat in the manner specified: *he felt badly done by.*
doc *n Informal* same as **doctor.**
docile *adj* (of a person or animal) easily controlled. **docilely** *adv* **docility** *n*
dock[1] *n* **1** an enclosed area of water where ships are loaded, unloaded, or repaired. **2** a wharf or pier. ~*vb* **3** to moor or be moored at a dock. **4** to link (two spacecraft) or (of two spacecraft) to be linked together in space.
dock[2] *vb* **1** to deduct (an amount) from (a person's wages). **2** to remove part of (an animal's tail) by cutting through the bone.
dock[3] *n* an enclosed space in a court of law where the accused person sits or stands.
dock[4] *n* a weed with broad leaves.
docker *n Brit* a person employed to load and unload ships.
docket *n* **1** *Chiefly Brit* a label on a package or other delivery, stating contents, delivery instructions, etc. ~*vb* **-eting, -eted 2** to fix a docket to (a package or other delivery).
dockyard *n* a place where ships are built or repaired.
Doc Martens *pl n Trademark* a brand of lace-up boots with thick lightweight resistant soles.
doctor *n* **1** a person licensed to practise medicine. **2** a person who has been awarded a doctorate. **3** *Chiefly US & Canad* a person licensed to practise dentistry or veterinary medicine. ~*vb* **4** to change in order to deceive: *she confessed to having doctored the figures.* **5** to poison or drug (food or drink). **6** to castrate (an animal). **doctoral** *adj*
doctorate *n* the highest academic degree in any field of knowledge.
doctrinaire *adj* stubbornly insistent on the application of a theory without regard to practicality.
doctrine (**dock**-trin) *n* **1** a body of teachings of a religious, political, or philosophical group. **2** a principle or body of principles that is taught or advocated. **doctrinal** *adj*
docudrama *n* a film or television programme based on true events, presented in a dramatized form.
document *n* **1** a piece of paper that provides an official record of something. ~*vb* **2** to record or report (something) in detail. **3** to support (a claim) with evidence.
documentary *n, pl* **-ries 1** a film or television programme presenting the facts about a particular subject. ~*adj* **2** of or based on documents: *vital documentary evidence has been found.*
documentation *n* documents supplied as proof or evidence of something.
dodder *vb* to move unsteadily. **dodderer** *n* **doddery** *adj*
doddle *n Brit informal* something easily accomplished: *the test turned out to be a doddle.*
dodecagon (doe-**deck**-a-gon) *n* a polygon with twelve sides.
dodecahedron (doe-deck-a-**heed**-ron) *n* a solid figure with twelve plane faces.
dodge *vb* **dodging, dodged 1** to avoid being hit, caught, or seen by moving suddenly. **2** to evade by cleverness or trickery: *the Government will not be able to dodge the issue.* ~*n* **3** a cunning and deceitful trick.
Dodgem *n Trademark* a small electric car driven and bumped against similar cars in a rink at a funfair.
dodger *n* a person who evades a duty or obligation.
dodgy *adj* **dodgier, dodgiest** *Brit, Austral, & NZ informal* **1** dangerous, risky, or unreliable: *he's in a very dodgy political position.* **2** untrustworthy: *they considered him a very dodgy character.*
dodo *n, pl* **dodos** *or* **dodoes 1** a large extinct bird that could not fly. **2 as dead as a dodo** no longer existing.
do down *vb* to belittle or humiliate: *the moderate constructionist does not wish to do science down.*
doe *n, pl* **does** *or* **doe** the female of the deer, hare, or rabbit.
DOE (in Britain) Department of the Environment.
doek (rhymes with **book**) *n S African informal* a square of cloth worn on the head by women.
doer *n* an active or energetic person.
does *vb* third person singular of the present tense of **do**[1].
doff *vb* to take off or lift (one's hat) in salutation.
do for *vb Informal* **1** to cause the ruin, death, or defeat of: *I'm done for if this error comes to light.* **2** to do housework for. **3 do well for oneself** to thrive or succeed.
dog *n* **1** a domesticated canine mammal occurring in many different breeds. **2** any other member of the dog family, such as the dingo or coyote. **3** the male of animals of the dog family. **4** *Informal* a person: *you lucky dog!* **5** *US & Canad informal* something unsatisfactory or inferior. **6 a dog's life** a wretched existence. **7 dog**

THESAURUS

docility amenability, biddableness, compliance, manageability, meekness, obedience, pliancy, submissiveness, tractability
dock *n.* **1.** harbour, waterfront **2.** jetty, pier, quay, wharf ~*vb.* **3.** anchor, berth, drop anchor, land, moor, put in, tie up **4.** *of spacecraft* couple, hook up, join, link up, rendezvous, unite
docket 1. *n.* bill, certificate, chit, chitty, counterfoil, label, receipt, tab, tag, tally, ticket **2.** *vb.* catalogue, file, index, label, mark, register, tab, tag, ticket
doctor *n.* **1.** general practitioner, G.P., medic (*informal*), medical practitioner, physician ~*vb.* **2.** alter, change, disguise, falsify, fudge, misrepresent, pervert, tamper with **3.** add to, adulterate, cut, dilute, mix with, spike, water down
doctrinaire biased, dogmatic, fanatical, inflexible, insistent, opinionated, rigid
doctrine article, article of faith, belief, canon, concept, conviction, creed, dogma, opinion, precept, principle, teaching, tenet
document 1. *n.* certificate, instrument, legal form, paper, record, report **2.** *vb.* authenticate, back up, certify, cite, corroborate, detail, give weight to, instance, particularize, substantiate, support, validate, verify
doddering aged, decrepit, doddery, faltering, feeble, floundering, infirm, senile, shaky, shambling, tottery, trembly, unsteady, weak
dodge *vb.* **1.** dart, duck, jink (*Scot.*), shift, sidestep, swerve, turn aside **2.** avoid, body-swerve (*Scot.*), deceive, elude, equivocate, evade, fend off, flannel (*Brit. informal*), fudge, get out of, hedge, parry, shirk, shuffle, trick ~*n.* **3.** contrivance, device, feint, flannel (*Brit. informal*), machination, ploy, ruse, scheme, stratagem, subterfuge, trick, wheeze (*Brit. slang*), wile
dodger evader, shifty so-and-so, shirker, slacker, slippery one, slyboots, trickster
doer achiever, active person, bustler, dynamo, go-getter (*informal*), live wire (*slang*), organizer, powerhouse (*slang*), wheeler-dealer (*informal*)
doff lift, raise, remove, take off, tip, touch
dog *n.* **1.** bitch, canine, cur, hound, man's best friend, mongrel, mutt (*slang*), pooch (*slang*), pup, puppy, tyke

eat dog ruthless competition. **8 like a dog's dinner** dressed smartly and ostentatiously. ~*vb* **dogging, dogged 9** to follow (someone) closely. **10** to trouble: *dogged by ill health.* ~See also **dogs.**

dog box *n Austral & NZ informal* same as **doghouse.**

dogcart *n* a light horse-drawn two-wheeled cart.

dog collar *n* **1** a collar for a dog. **2** *Informal* a clerical collar.

dog days *pl n* the hottest period of the summer.

doge (**doje**) *n* (formerly) the chief magistrate of Venice or Genoa.

dog-eared *adj* **1** (of a book) having pages folded down at the corner. **2** shabby or worn.

dog-end *n Informal* a cigarette end.

dogfight *n* **1** close-quarters combat between fighter aircraft. **2** any rough fight.

dogfish *n, pl* **-fish** *or* **-fishes** a small shark.

dogged (**dog**-gid) *adj* obstinately determined. **doggedly** *adv* **doggedness** *n*

doggerel *n* poorly written, usually comic, verse.

doggo *adv* **lie doggo** *Brit informal* to hide and keep quiet.

doggy *or* **doggie** *n, pl* **-gies 1** a child's word for a **dog.** ~*adj* **-gier, -giest 2** of or like a dog. **3** fond of dogs: *dogs are all right but doggy folk are real bores.*

doggy bag *n* a bag in which leftovers from a meal may be taken away, supposedly for the diner's dog.

doghouse *n* **1** *US & Canad* a kennel. **2 in the doghouse** *Informal* in disfavour.

dogie, dogy, *or* **dogey** (**dohg**-ee) *n, pl* **-gies** *or* **-geys** *US & Canad* a motherless calf.

dog in the manger *n* a person who prevents others from using something he has no use for.

dogleg *n* a sharp bend.

dogma *n* a doctrine or system of doctrines proclaimed by authority as true.

dogmatic *adj* habitually stating one's opinions in a forceful or arrogant manner. **dogmatically** *adv* **dogmatism** *n*

do-gooder *n Informal* a well-intentioned but naive or impractical person.

dog paddle *n* a swimming stroke in which the hands are paddled in imitation of a swimming dog.

dogs *pl n* **1 the dogs** *Brit informal* greyhound racing. **2 go to the dogs** *Informal* to go to ruin physically or morally. **3 let sleeping dogs lie** to leave things undisturbed.

dogsbody *n, pl* **-bodies** *Informal* a person who carries out boring or unimportant tasks for others.

dog-tired *adj Informal* exhausted.

dogwatch *n* either of two watches aboard ship, from four to six pm or from six to eight pm.

doh *or* **do** *n Music* (in tonic sol-fa) the first note of any ascending major scale.

doily *or* **doyley** *n, pl* **-lies** *or* **-leys** a decorative lace-like paper mat laid on a plate.

do in *vb Slang* **1** to kill. **2** to exhaust.

doings *pl n* **1** deeds or actions: *her brother's doings upset her terribly.* ~*n* **2** *Informal* anything of which the name is not known or is left unsaid: *do you have the doings to open this?*

do-it-yourself *n* the practice of constructing and repairing things oneself.

Dolby *n Trademark* a system used in tape recorders which reduces noise level on recorded or broadcast sound.

doldrums *n* **the doldrums 1 a** a feeling of depression. **b** a state of inactivity. **2** a belt of sea along the equator noted for absence of winds.

dole *n* **1 the dole** *Brit & Austral informal* money received from the state while unemployed. **2 on the dole** *Brit & Austral informal* receiving unemployment benefit. ~*vb* **doling, doled 3 dole out** to distribute in small quantities.

doleful *adj* dreary or mournful. **dolefully** *adv* **dolefulness** *n*

doll *n* **1** a small model of a human being, used as a toy. **2** *Slang* a pretty girl or young woman.

dollar *n* the standard monetary unit of the US, Canada, and various other countries.

dollop *n Informal* an amount of food served in a lump: *he shook the bottle and added a large dollop of ketchup.*

doll up *vb Slang* **get dolled up** to dress (oneself) in a stylish or showy manner.

dolly *n, pl* **-lies 1** a child's word for a **doll** (sense 1). **2** *Films, television* a wheeled support on which a camera may be mounted. **3** Also called: **dolly bird** *Slang, chiefly Brit* an attractive and fashionable girl.

dolman sleeve *n* a sleeve that is very wide at the armhole and tapers to a tight wrist.

dolmen *n* a prehistoric monument consisting of a horizontal stone supported by vertical stones, thought to be a tomb.

dolomite *n* a mineral consisting of calcium magnesium carbonate.

dolphin *n* a sea mammal of the whale family, with a long pointed snout.

THESAURUS

2. dog eat dog cutthroat, ferocious, fierce, ruthless, vicious, with no holds barred ~*vb.* **3.** haunt, hound, plague, pursue, shadow, tail (*informal*), track, trail, trouble

dogged determined, firm, immovable, indefatigable, obstinate, persevering, persistent, pertinacious, resolute, single-minded, staunch, steadfast, steady, stiff-necked, stubborn, tenacious, unflagging, unshakable, unyielding

doggedness bulldog tenacity, determination, endurance, obstinacy, perseverance, persistence, pertinacity, relentlessness, resolution, single-mindedness, steadfastness, steadiness, stubbornness, tenaciousness, tenacity

dogma article, article of faith, belief, credo, creed, doctrine, opinion, precept, principle, teachings, tenet

dogmatic arbitrary, arrogant, assertive, categorical, dictatorial, doctrinaire, downright, emphatic, imperious, magisterial, obdurate, opinionated, overbearing, peremptory

dogmatism arbitrariness, arrogance, dictatorialness, imperiousness, opinionatedness, peremptoriness, positiveness, presumption

dogs go to the dogs *informal* degenerate, deteriorate, go down the drain, go to pot, go to ruin

dogsbody drudge, general factotum, maid *or* man of all work, menial, skivvy (*chiefly Brit.*), slave

do in 1. blow away (*slang, chiefly U.S.*), butcher, dispatch, eliminate (*slang*), execute, kill, liquidate, murder, slaughter, slay, take out (*slang*) **2.** exhaust, fatigue, knacker (*slang*), shatter (*informal*), tire, wear out, weary

doings actions, affairs, concerns, dealings, deeds, events, exploits, goings-on (*informal*), handiwork, happenings, proceedings, transactions

doldrums apathy, blues, boredom, depression, dullness, dumps (*informal*), ennui, gloom, inertia, lassitude, listlessness, malaise, stagnation, tedium, the hump (*Brit. informal*), torpor

dole *usually with* **out** administer, allocate, allot, ap-

dolphinarium *n* an aquarium for dolphins, esp. one in which they give public displays.
dolt *n* a stupid person. **doltish** *adj*
domain *n* **1** a particular area of activity or interest. **2** land under one ruler or government.
dome *n* **1** a rounded roof built on a circular base. **2** something shaped like this.
domed *adj* shaped like a dome.
domestic *adj* **1** of one's own country or a specific country: *the domestic economy was generally better.* **2** of the home or family. **3** enjoying home or family life: *she was never a very domestic sort of person.* **4** intended for use in the home: *the kitchen was equipped with all the latest domestic appliances.* **5** (of an animal) bred or kept as a pet or for the supply of food. *~n* **6** a household servant. **domestically** *adv*
domesticate *vb* **-cating, -cated 1** to bring or keep (wild animals or plants) under control or cultivation. **2** to accustom (someone) to home life. **domestication** *n*
domesticity *n, pl* **-ties 1** home life. **2** devotion to home life.
domestic science *n* the study of cooking, needlework, and other household skills.
domicile (**dom**-miss-ile) *n* a person's regular dwelling place. **domiciliary** *adj*
domiciled *adj* living in a particular place: *the holding company was domiciled in Bermuda.*
dominant *adj* **1** having control, authority, or influence: *a dominant leader.* **2** main or chief: *coal, is still worldwide, the dominant fuel.* **3** *Genetics* (in a pair of genes) designating the gene that produces a particular character in an organism. **dominance** *n*
dominate *vb* **-nating, -nated 1** to control or govern. **2** to tower above (surroundings): *Dorchester is dominated by its abbey church.* **3** to predominate in. **dominating** *adj* **domination** *n*
dominee (**doom**-in-nee) *n S African* a minister of the Dutch Reformed Church.
domineering *adj* acting arrogantly or tyrannically.
Dominican *n* **1** a friar or nun of the Christian order founded by Saint Dominic. *~adj* **2** of the Dominican order.
dominion *n* **1** control or authority. **2** the land governed by one ruler or government. **3** (formerly) a self-governing division of the British Empire.
domino[1] *n, pl* **-noes** a small rectangular block marked with dots, used in dominoes.
domino[2] *n, pl* **-noes** *or* **-nos** a large hooded cloak worn with an eye mask at a masquerade.
dominoes *n* a game in which dominoes with matching halves are laid together.
don[1] *vb* **donning, donned** to put on (clothing).
don[2] *n* **1** *Brit* a member of the teaching staff at a university or college. **2** a Spanish gentleman or nobleman. **3** (in the Mafia) the head of a family.
donate *vb* **-nating, -nated** to give (something) to a charity or other organization.
donation *n* **1** the act of donating. **2** a contribution to a charity or other organization.
donder *S African slang ~vb* **1** to beat (someone) up. *~n* **2** a wretch; swine.
done *vb* **1** the past participle of **do**[1]. *~interj* **2** an expression of agreement: *sixty pounds seems reasonable, done!* *~adj* **3** (of a task) completed. **4** (of food) cooked enough. **5** used up: *the milk is done.* **6** socially acceptable: *the done thing.* **7** *Informal* cheated or tricked. **8** **done in** *or* **up** *Informal* exhausted.

THESAURUS

portion, assign, deal, dispense, distribute, divide, give, hand out, mete, share
dolt ass, berk (*Brit. slang*), blockhead, booby, charlie (*Brit. informal*), chump (*informal*), clot (*Brit. informal*), dimwit (*informal*), dope (*informal*), dullard, dunce, dweeb (*U.S. slang*), fool, idiot, ignoramus, jerk (*slang, chiefly U.S. & Canad.*), lamebrain (*informal*), nerd *or* nurd (*slang*), nitwit (*informal*), numskull *or* numbskull, oaf, plank (*Brit. slang*), plonker (*slang*), prat (*slang*), prick (*derogatory slang*), schmuck (*U.S. slang*), simpleton, thickhead, twit (*informal, chiefly Brit.*), wally (*slang*)
domestic *adj.* **1.** indigenous, internal, native, not foreign **2.** domiciliary, family, home, household, private **3.** domesticated, home-loving, homely, housewifely, stay-at-home **4.** domesticated, house, house-trained, pet, tame, trained *~n.* **5.** char (*informal*), charwoman, daily, daily help, help, maid, servant, woman (*informal*)
domesticate 1. break, gentle, house-train, tame, train **2.** acclimatize, accustom, familiarize, habituate, naturalize
domesticated 1. *of plants or animals* broken (in), naturalized, tame, tamed **2.** *of people* domestic, home-loving, homely, house-trained (*jocular*), housewifely
dominant 1. ascendant, assertive, authoritative, commanding, controlling, governing, leading, presiding, ruling, superior, supreme **2.** chief, influential, main, outstanding, paramount, predominant, pre-eminent, prevailing, prevalent, primary, principal, prominent
dominate 1. control, direct, domineer, govern, have the upper hand over, have the whip hand over, keep under one's thumb, lead, lead by the nose (*informal*), master, monopolize, overbear, rule, tyrannize **2.** bestride, loom over, overlook, stand head and shoulders above, stand over, survey, tower above
domination ascendancy, authority, command, control, influence, mastery, power, rule, superiority, supremacy, sway
domineering arrogant, authoritarian, autocratic, bossy (*informal*), bullying, coercive, despotic, dictatorial, hectoring, high-handed, imperious, iron-handed, magisterial, masterful, oppressive, overbearing, tyrannical
dominion 1. ascendancy, authority, command, control, domination, government, jurisdiction, mastery, power, rule, sovereignty, supremacy, sway **2.** country, domain, empire, kingdom, patch, province, realm, region, territory, turf (*U.S. slang*)
don clothe oneself in, dress in, get into, pull on, put on, slip on *or* into
donate bequeath, bestow, chip in (*informal*), contribute, gift, give, hand out, make a gift of, present, subscribe
donation alms, benefaction, contribution, gift, grant, gratuity, hand-out, largesse *or* largess, offering, present, stipend, subscription
done *interj.* **1.** agreed, it's a bargain, O.K. *or* okay (*informal*), settled, you're on (*informal*) *~adj.* **2.** accomplished, completed, concluded, consummated, ended, executed, finished, over, perfected, realized, terminated, through **3.** depleted, exhausted, finished, spent, used up **4.** acceptable, conventional, *de rigueur,* proper **5.** *informal* cheated, conned (*informal*), duped, taken for a ride (*informal*), tricked **6.** **done in** *or* **up** *informal* all in (*slang*), bushed (*informal*), clapped out (*Austral. & N.Z. informal*), dead (*informal*), dead beat (*informal*), dog-tired (*informal*), exhausted, fagged out (*informal*), knackered (*slang*), on one's last legs, ready

doner kebab *n* a dish of grilled minced lamb, served in a split slice of unleavened bread.

donga (**dong**-ga) *n S African, Austral, & NZ* a steep-sided gully created by soil erosion.

donjon *n* the heavily fortified central tower of a castle.

Don Juan *n* a successful seducer of women.

donkey *n* **1** a long-eared member of the horse family. **2** a person who is considered to be stupid or stubborn.

donkey jacket *n* a man's thick hip-length jacket with a waterproof panel across the shoulders.

donkey's years *pl n Informal* a long time.

donkey-work *n* uninteresting groundwork.

donnish *adj* resembling a university don; pedantic or fussy.

donor *n* **1** *Med* a person who gives blood or organs for use in the treatment of another person. **2** a person who makes a donation.

donor card *n* a card carried by someone to show that the body parts specified may be used for transplants after the person's death.

Don Quixote (**don** kee-**hoe**-tee) *n* an impractical idealist.

don't do not.

doodle *vb* **-dling, -dled 1** to scribble or draw aimlessly. *~n* **2** a shape or picture drawn aimlessly.

doom *n* **1** death or a terrible fate. *~vb* **2** to destine or condemn to death or a terrible fate.

doomsday *or* **domesday** *n* **1** the day on which the Last Judgment will occur. **2** any dreaded day.

door *n* **1** a hinged or sliding panel for closing the entrance to a building, room, or cupboard. **2** a doorway or entrance. **3** a means of access or escape: *the door to happiness.* **4 lay something at someone's door** to blame someone for something. **5 out of doors** in the open air.

doorjamb *n* one of the two vertical posts that form the sides of a door frame. Also called: **doorpost**

doorman *n, pl* **-men** a man employed to be on duty at the main entrance of a large building.

doormat *n* **1** a mat, placed at an entrance, for wiping dirt from shoes. **2** *Informal* a person who offers little resistance to being treated badly.

doorstep *n* **1** a step in front of a door. **2** *Informal* a thick slice of bread.

doorstop *n* a heavy object or one fixed to the floor, which prevents a door from closing or from striking a wall.

door-to-door *adj* **1** (of selling) from one house to the next. **2** (of a journey) direct.

doorway *n* an opening into a building or room.

dop *n S African informal* a tot or small drink, usually alcoholic.

dope *n* **1** *Slang* an illegal drug, such as cannabis. **2** a drug administered to a person or animal to affect performance in a race or other sporting competition. **3** *Informal* a slow-witted person. **4** confidential information. **5** a thick liquid, such as a lubricant. *~vb* **doping, doped 6** to administer a drug to.

dopey *or* **dopy** *adj* **dopier, dopiest 1** *Informal* half-asleep, as when under the influence of a drug. **2** *Slang* silly.

doppelgänger (**dop**-pl-geng-er) *n Legend* a ghostly duplicate of a living person.

Doppler effect *n* a change in the apparent frequency of a sound or light wave as a result of relative motion between the observer and the source.

Doric *adj* **1** of a style of classical architecture characterized by a heavy fluted column and a simple capital. *~n* **2** a rustic dialect, esp. a Scots one.

dormant *adj* **1** temporarily quiet, inactive, or not being used. **2** *Biol* alive but in a resting condition. **dormancy** *n*

dormer *or* **dormer window** *n* a window that is built upright in a sloping roof.

dormitory *n, pl* **-ries 1** a large room, esp. at a school, containing several beds. **2** *US* a building, esp. at a college, providing living accommodation. *~adj* **3** *Brit* denoting an area from which most of the residents commute to work: *the swelling suburban dormitory areas.*

Dormobile *n Trademark* a vanlike vehicle specially equipped for living in while travelling.

dormouse *n, pl* **-mice** a small rodent resembling a mouse with a furry tail.

dorp *n S African* a small town or village.

dorsal *adj Anat, zool* of or on the back.

dory *n, pl* **-ries** a spiny-finned food fish. Also called: **John Dory**

DOS *Computers* disk operating system.

dose *n* **1** a specific quantity of a medicine taken at one time. **2** *Informal* something unpleasant to experience: *a dose of the cold.* **3** the total energy of radiation absorbed. **4** *Slang* a sexually transmitted infection. *~vb* **dosing, dosed 5** to administer a quantity of medicine to (someone). **dosage** *n*

dosh *n Slang* money.

dosing strip *n* (in New Zealand) an area for treating dogs suspected of having hydatid disease.

doss down *vb Brit slang* to sleep on a makeshift bed.

THESAURUS

to drop, tired out, worn out, worn to a frazzle (*informal*), zonked (*slang*) **7. done for** *informal* beaten, broken, dashed, defeated, destroyed, doomed, finished, foiled, lost, ruined, undone, wrecked

donnish bookish, erudite, formalistic, pedagogic, pedantic, precise, scholarly, scholastic

donor almsgiver, benefactor, contributor, donator, giver, grantor (*Law*), philanthropist

doom 1. *n.* catastrophe, death, destiny, destruction, downfall, fate, fortune, lot, portion, ruin **2.** *vb.* condemn, consign, damn, decree, destine, foreordain, judge, predestine, preordain, sentence, threaten

doomed bedevilled, bewitched, condemned, cursed, fated, hopeless, ill-fated, ill-omened, luckless, star-crossed

Doomsday Armageddon, end of the world, Judgment Day, the Last Day, the Last Judgment, the last trump

door 1. doorway, egress, entrance, entry, exit, gate, gateway, ingress, opening, portal **2. lay something at someone's door** blame, censure, charge, hold responsible, impute to **3. out of doors** alfresco, in the air, out, outdoors, outside

dope *n.* **1.** drugs, narcotic, opiate **2.** berk (*Brit. slang*), blockhead, charlie (*Brit. informal*), dickhead (*slang*), dimwit (*informal*), dolt, dork (*slang*), dunce, fool, idiot, jerk (*slang, chiefly U.S. & Canad.*), lamebrain (*informal*), nerd *or* nurd (*slang*), nitwit (*informal*), numskull *or* numbskull, oaf, pillock (*Brit. slang*), prat (*slang*), prick (*derogatory slang*), schmuck (*U.S. slang*), simpleton, twit (*informal, chiefly Brit.*), wally (*slang*) **3.** details, facts, gen (*Brit. informal*), info (*informal*), information, inside information, lowdown (*informal*), news, tip *~vb.* **4.** anaesthetize, doctor, drug, inject, knock out, narcotize, sedate, stupefy

dormant asleep, comatose, fallow, hibernating, inac-

dosshouse *n Brit slang* a cheap lodging house for homeless people.

dossier (**doss**-ee-ay) *n* a collection of papers about a subject or person.

dot *n* **1** a small round mark. **2** the small round mark used to represent the short sound in Morse code. **3 on the dot** at exactly the arranged time. *~vb* **dotting, dotted 4** to mark with a dot. **5** to scatter or intersperse: *there are numerous churches dotted around Rome.* **6 dot one's i's and cross one's t's** *Informal* to pay meticulous attention to detail.

dotage *n* feebleness of mind as a result of old age.

dotard *n* a person who is feeble-minded through old age.

dote *vb* **doting, doted dote on** *or* **upon** to love (someone or something) to an excessive degree. **doting** *adj*

dotterel *n* a shore bird with reddish-brown underparts and white bands around the head and neck.

dottle *n* the tobacco left in a pipe after smoking.

dotty *adj* **-tier, -tiest** *Slang, chiefly Brit* slightly crazy. **dottiness** *n*

double *adj* **1** as much again in size, strength, number, etc.: *a double scotch.* **2** composed of two equal or similar parts. **3** designed for two users: *a double bed.* **4** folded in half: *the blanket had been folded double.* **5** stooping: *she was bent double over the flower bed.* **6** ambiguous: *a double meaning.* **7** false, deceitful, or hypocritical: *double standards.* **8** *Music* (of an instrument) sounding an octave lower: *a double bass.* *~adv* **9** twice over: *that's double the amount requested.* *~n* **10** twice the size, strength, number, etc. **11** a double measure of spirits. **12** a person who closely resembles another person. **13** a bet on two horses in different races in which any winnings from the first race are placed on the horse in the later race. **14 at** *or* **on the double** quickly or immediately. *~vb* **-bling, -bled 15** to make or become twice as much. **16** to bend or fold so that one part covers another. **17** to play two parts or serve two roles. **18** to turn sharply. **19** *Bridge* to make a call that will double certain scoring points if the preceding bid becomes the contract. **20 double for** to act as substitute. ~See also **double back, doubles, double up. doubler** *n*

double agent *n* a spy employed by two enemy countries at the same time.

double back *vb* to go back in the opposite direction: *I doubled back searching for the track.*

double-barrelled *or US* **-barreled** *adj* **1** (of a gun) having two barrels. **2** *Brit* (of surnames) having hyphenated parts.

double bass *n* a stringed instrument, the largest and lowest member of the violin family.

double-breasted *adj* (of a garment) having overlapping fronts.

double-check *vb* to make certain by checking again.

double chin *n* a fold of fat under the chin.

double cream *n Brit* thick cream with a high fat content.

double-cross *vb* **1** to cheat or betray. *~n* **2** an instance of double-crossing.

double-dealing *n* treacherous or deceitful behaviour.

double-decker *n* **1** *Chiefly Brit* a bus with two passenger decks one on top of the other. *~adj* **2** *Informal* having two layers: *a double-decker sandwich.*

double Dutch *n Brit informal* speech or writing that is difficult to understand: *it was double Dutch to me.*

double-edged *adj* **1** (of a remark) malicious in intent though apparently complimentary. **2** (of a knife) having a cutting edge on either side of the blade.

double entendre (**doob**-bl on-**tond**-ra) *n* a word or phrase with two interpretations, esp. with one meaning that is rude.

double entry *n* a book-keeping system in which a transaction is entered as a debit in one account and as a credit in another.

double glazing *n* a window consisting of two layers of glass separated by a space, fitted to reduce heat loss.

double Gloucester *n* a smooth orange-red cheese with a mild flavour.

double-jointed *adj* (of a person) having unusually flexible joints.

double knitting *n* a medium thickness of knitting wool.

double negative *n* a grammatical construction, considered incorrect, in which two negatives are used where one is needed, for example *I wouldn't never have believed it.*

double-park *vb* to park (a vehicle) alongside another vehicle, causing an obstruction.

double pneumonia *n* pneumonia affecting both lungs.

double-quick *adj* **1** very quick. *~adv* **2** in a very quick manner.

doubles *n* a game between two pairs of players.

double standard *n* a set of principles that allows greater freedom to one person or group than to another.

THESAURUS

tive, inert, inoperative, latent, quiescent, sleeping, sluggish, slumbering, suspended, torpid

dose dosage, draught, drench, measure, portion, potion, prescription, quantity

dot *n.* **1.** atom, circle, dab, fleck, full stop, iota, jot, mark, mite, mote, point, speck, speckle, spot **2. on the dot** exactly, on time, precisely, promptly, punctually, to the minute *~vb.* **3.** dab, dabble, fleck, speckle, spot, sprinkle, stipple, stud

dotage decrepitude, feebleness, old age, second childhood, senility, weakness

dote on *or* **upon** admire, adore, hold dear, idolize, lavish affection on, prize, treasure

doting adoring, devoted, fond, foolish, indulgent, lovesick

double *adj.* **1.** coupled, doubled, dual, duplicate, in pairs, paired, twice, twin, twofold **2.** deceitful, dishonest, false, hypocritical, insincere, Janus-faced, knavish (*archaic*), perfidious, treacherous, two-faced, vacillating *~n.* **3.** clone, copy, counterpart, dead ringer (*slang*), Doppelgänger, duplicate, fellow, impersonator, lookalike, mate, replica, ringer (*slang*), spitting image (*informal*), twin **4. at** *or* **on the double** at full speed, briskly, immediately, in double-quick time, posthaste, quickly, without delay *~vb.* **5.** duplicate, enlarge, grow, increase, magnify, multiply, plait, repeat **6.** fold, plait

double-cross betray, cheat, cozen, defraud, hoodwink, mislead, swindle, trick, two-time (*informal*)

double-dealer betrayer, cheat, con man (*informal*), deceiver, dissembler, double-crosser (*informal*), fraud, hypocrite, rogue, swindler, traitor, two-timer (*informal*)

double-dealing bad faith, betrayal, cheating, deceit, deception, dishonesty, duplicity, foul play, hypoc-

doublet (**dub**-lit) *n History* a man's close-fitting jacket, with or without sleeves.

double take *n* a delayed reaction by a person to a remark or situation: *she did a double take when he said he was leaving.*

double talk *n* deceptive or ambiguous talk.

doublethink *n* the acceptance of conflicting facts or principles at the same time.

double time *n* **1** a doubled wage rate sometimes paid for overtime work. **2** *Music* two beats per bar.

double up *vb* **1** to bend or cause to bend in two: *she was doubled up with stomach cramps.* **2** to share with other people: *we only took two cars, so we had to double up.*

doubloon *n* a former Spanish gold coin.

doubly *adv* **1** to or in a greater degree, quantity, or measure: *I have to be doubly careful.* **2** in two ways: *the defence debate was doubly complicated.*

doubt *n* **1** uncertainty about the truth, facts, or existence of something. **2** an unresolved difficulty or point. **3 give someone the benefit of the doubt** accept that someone is speaking the truth. **4 no doubt** almost certainly. *~vb* **5** to be inclined to disbelieve: *I doubt that we are late.* **6** to distrust or be suspicious of: *he doubted their motives.* **doubter** *n*

➤ If *doubt* is followed by a clause it is connected by *that* or *whether: I doubt whether she means it.* If it is used with a negative it is followed by *that: I don't doubt that he is sincere.*

doubtful *adj* **1** unlikely or improbable: *it's doubtful that I will marry again.* **2** unsure or uncertain: *I was doubtful about some of his ideas.* **doubtfully** *adv* **doubtfulness** *n*

doubtless *adv* probably or almost certainly: *somebody will know and doubtless somebody will ring us.*

douche (**doosh**) *n* **1** a stream of water directed onto or into the body for cleansing or medical purposes. **2** an instrument for applying a douche. *~vb* **douching, douched 3** to cleanse or treat by means of a douche.

dough *n* **1** a thick mixture of flour and water or milk, used for making bread, pastry, or biscuits. **2** *Slang* money.

doughnut *n* a small cake of sweetened dough cooked in hot fat.

doughty (**dowt**-ee) *adj* **-tier, -tiest** *Old-fashioned* brave and determined.

do up *vb* **1** to wrap and make into a bundle: *he did up the parcel.* **2** to fasten: *to do up one's blouse.* **3** to renovate or redecorate.

dour (**doo**-er) *adj* sullen and unfriendly. **dourness** *n*

douse *or* **dowse** (rhymes with **mouse**) *vb* **dousing, doused** *or* **dowsing, dowsed 1** to drench with water or other liquid. **2** to put out (a light).

dove *n* **1** a bird with a heavy body, small head, and short legs. **2** *Politics* a person opposed to war.

dovecote *or* **dovecot** *n* a box, shelter, or part of a house built for doves or pigeons to live in.

dove-grey *adj* greyish-brown.

dovetail *n* **1** Also called: **dovetail joint** a wedge-shaped joint used to fit two pieces of wood tightly together. *~vb* **2** to fit together closely or neatly: *her resignation dovetails well with the new structure.*

dowager *n* a woman possessing property or a title obtained from her dead husband.

dowdy *adj* **-dier, -diest** wearing dull and unfashionable clothes. **dowdily** *adv* **dowdiness** *n*

dowel *n* a wooden or metal peg that fits into two corresponding holes to join larger pieces of wood or metal together.

dower *n* **1** the life interest in a part of her husband's estate allotted to a widow by law. **2** *Archaic* a dowry.

dower house *n* a house for the use of a widow, often on her deceased husband's estate.

do with *vb* **1 could do with** need or would benefit from: *I could do with some royal treatment.* **2 have to do with** to be associated with: *his illness has a lot to do with his failing the exam.* **3 to do with** concerning; related to: *this book has to do with the occult.*

do without *vb* to manage without.

down[1] *prep* **1** from a higher to a lower position in or on. **2** at a lower or further level or position on, in, or along: *I wandered down the corridor.* *~adv* **3** at or to a lower level or position: *he bent down.* **4** indicating lowering or destruction: *to bring down an aircraft.* **5** indicating intensity or completion: *calm down and mind your manners.* **6** immediately: *cash down.* **7** on paper: *she copied it down.* **8** away from a more important place: *he came down from head office.* **9** reduced to a state of lack: *he was down to his last pound.* **10** lacking a specified amount: *down several pounds.* **11** lower in price. **12** from an earlier to a later time: *the ring was handed down from my grandmother.* **13** to a finer state: *to grind down.* **14** *Sport* being a specified number of points or goals behind an opponent. **15** (of a person) being inactive, owing to illness: *down with the cold.* *~adj* **16** depressed or unhappy: *he seems very down today.* **17** made in cash: *a down payment.* *~vb* **18** *Informal* to eat or drink quickly. *~n* **19 have a**

THESAURUS

risy, mendacity, perfidy, treachery, trickery, two-timing (*informal*)

double entendre ambiguity, double meaning, innuendo, play on words, pun

doubt *n.* **1.** dubiety, hesitancy, hesitation, indecision, irresolution, lack of conviction, scepticism, suspense, uncertainty, vacillation **2.** ambiguity, confusion, difficulty, dilemma, perplexity, problem, quandary **3. no doubt** admittedly, assuredly, certainly, doubtless, doubtlessly, probably, surely *~vb.* **4.** be dubious, be uncertain, demur, fluctuate, hesitate, scruple, vacillate, waver **5.** discredit, distrust, fear, lack confidence in, misgive, mistrust, query, question, suspect

doubter agnostic, disbeliever, doubting Thomas, questioner, sceptic, unbeliever

doubtful distrustful, hesitating, in two minds (*informal*), irresolute, leery (*slang*), perplexed, sceptical, suspicious, tentative, uncertain, unconvinced, undecided, unresolved, unsettled, unsure, vacillating, wavering

doubtless assuredly, certainly, clearly, indisputably, of course, precisely, surely, truly, undoubtedly, unquestionably, without doubt

dour dismal, dreary, forbidding, gloomy, grim, morose, sour, sullen, unfriendly

dovetail *vb.* accord, agree, coincide, conform, correspond, fit together, harmonize, interlock, join, link, match, tally

dowdy dingy, drab, frowzy, frumpish, frumpy, ill-dressed, old-fashioned, scrubby (*Brit. informal*), shabby, slovenly, tacky (*U.S. informal*), unfashionable

dower dowry, inheritance, legacy, portion, provision, share

do without abstain from, dispense with, forgo, get along without, give up, kick (*informal*), manage without

down 1. *adj.* blue, dejected, depressed, disheartened, dismal, downcast, low, miserable, sad, sick as a parrot (*informal*), unhappy **2.** *vb. informal* drain, drink (down), gulp, put away, swallow, toss off **3.** *n.* **have a down on** *informal* be antagonistic *or* hostile to, be

down on *Informal* to feel hostile towards: *you seem to have a down on the family tonight.*
down[2] *n* soft fine feathers. **downy** *adj*
down-and-out *n* **1** a person who is homeless and destitute. *~adj* **2** without any means of support; destitute.
downbeat *adj Informal* **1** depressed or gloomy: *she was in one of her downbeat moods.* **2** casual and restrained: *the chairman's statement was decidedly downbeat.* *~n* **3** *Music* the first beat of a bar.
downcast *adj* **1** sad and dejected. **2** (of the eyes) directed downwards.
downer *n Slang* **1** a barbiturate, tranquillizer, or narcotic. **2 on a downer** in a state of depression.
downfall *n* **1** a sudden loss of position or reputation. **2** the cause of this.
downgrade *vb* **-grading, -graded** to reduce in importance or value.
downhearted *adj* sad and discouraged.
downhill *adj* **1** going or sloping down. *~adv* **2** towards the bottom of a hill. **3 go downhill** *Informal* to deteriorate.
Downing Street *n* the British prime minister or the British government.
download *vb* to transfer (data) from the memory of one computer to that of another.
down-market *adj* cheap, popular, and of poor quality.
down payment *n* the deposit paid on an item purchased on hire-purchase, mortgage, etc.
downpour *n* a heavy continuous fall of rain.
downright *adv, adj* extreme or extremely: *it's just downright cruel.*
down-river *adj, adv* nearer the mouth of a river.
downs *pl n* an area of low grassy hills, esp. in S England.
downside *n* the disadvantageous aspect of a situation: *the downside of capitalism.*
downsize *vb* **1** to reduce the number of people employed by (a company). **2** to reduce the size of or produce a smaller version of (something).
Down's syndrome *n Pathol* a genetic disorder characterized by a flat face, slanting eyes, and mental retardation.
downstairs *adv* **1** down the stairs; to or on a lower floor. *~n* **2** a lower or ground floor.
downstream *adv, adj* in or towards the lower part of a stream; with the current.
downtime *n Commerce* time during which a computer or other machine is not working.
down-to-earth *adj* sensible or practical.
downtown *Chiefly US, Canad, & NZ ~n* **1** the central or lower part of a city, esp. the main commercial area. *~adv* **2** towards, to, or into this area.
downtrodden *adj* oppressed and lacking the will to resist.
downturn *n* a drop in the success of an economy or a business.
down under *Informal ~n* **1** Australia or New Zealand. *~adv* **2** in or to Australia or New Zealand.
downward *adj* **1** descending from a higher to a lower level, condition, or position. *~adv* **2** same as **downwards. downwardly** *adv*
downwards *or* **downward** *adv* **1** from a higher to a lower level, condition, or position. **2** from an earlier time or source to a later one.
downwind *adv, adj* in the same direction towards which the wind is blowing; with the wind from behind.
dowry *n, pl* **-ries** the property brought by a woman to her husband at marriage.
dowse (rhymes with **cows**) *vb* **dowsing, dowsed** to search for underground water or minerals using a divining rod. **dowser** *n*
doxology *n, pl* **-gies** a hymn or verse of praise to God.
doyen (**doy**-en) *n* the senior member of a group, profession, or society. **doyenne** (doy-**en**) *fem n*
doze *vb* **dozing, dozed 1** to sleep lightly or for a short period. **2 doze off** to fall into a light sleep. *~n* **3** a short sleep.
dozen *adj, n* twelve. **dozenth** *adj*
dozy *adj* **dozier, doziest 1** feeling sleepy. **2** *Brit informal* stupid and slow-witted.
DP displaced person.
DPP (in Britain) Director of Public Prosecutions.
Dr 1 Doctor. **2** Drive.
drab *adj* **drabber, drabbest 1** dull and dreary. **2** light olive-brown. **drabness** *n*
drachm (**dram**) *n Brit* a unit of liquid measure equal to one eighth of a fluid ounce (3.55 ml).
drachma *n, pl* **-mas** *or* **-mae** the standard monetary unit of Greece.
draconian *adj* severe or harsh: *draconian measures were taken by the government.*
draft *n* **1** a preliminary outline of a letter, book, or speech. **2** a written order for payment of money by a

THESAURUS

anti (*informal*), bear a grudge towards, be contra (*informal*), be prejudiced against, be set against, feel ill will towards, have it in for (*slang*)
down-and-out 1. *n.* bag lady (*chiefly U.S.*), beggar, bum (*informal*), derelict, dosser (*Brit. slang*), loser, outcast, pauper, tramp, vagabond, vagrant **2.** *adj.* derelict, destitute, dirt-poor (*informal*), flat broke (*informal*), impoverished, penniless, ruined, short, without two pennies to rub together (*informal*)
downcast cheerless, crestfallen, daunted, dejected, depressed, despondent, disappointed, disconsolate, discouraged, disheartened, dismal, dismayed, dispirited, miserable, sad, sick as a parrot (*informal*), unhappy
downfall breakdown, collapse, comedown, comeuppance (*slang*), debacle, descent, destruction, disgrace, fall, overthrow, ruin, undoing
downgrade degrade, demote, humble, lower *or* reduce in rank, take down a peg (*informal*)
downhearted blue, chapfallen, crestfallen, dejected, depressed, despondent, discouraged, disheartened, dismayed, dispirited, downcast, low-spirited, sad, sorrowful, unhappy
downpour cloudburst, deluge, flood, inundation, rainstorm, torrential rain
downright absolute(ly), arrant, blatant(ly), categorical(ly), clear(ly), complete(ly), deep-dyed (*usually derogatory*), explicit(ly), out-and-out, outright, plain(ly), positive(ly), simple, simply, thoroughgoing, total(ly), undisguised(ly), unequivocal(ly), unqualified(ly), utter(ly)
down-to-earth common-sense, hard-headed, matter-of-fact, mundane, no-nonsense, plain-spoken, practical, realistic, sane, sensible, unsentimental
downward *adj.* declining, descending, earthward, heading down, sliding, slipping
doze 1. *vb.* catnap, drop off (*informal*), drowse, kip (*Brit. slang*), nap, nod, nod off (*informal*), sleep, sleep lightly, slumber, snooze (*informal*) **2.** *n.* catnap, forty winks (*informal*), kip (*Brit. slang*), little sleep, nap, shuteye (*slang*), siesta, snooze (*informal*), zizz (*Brit. informal*)

bank. **3** *US & Austral* selection for compulsory military service. ~*vb* **4** to write a preliminary outline of a letter, book, or speech. **5** to send (personnel) from one place to another to carry out a specific job. **6** *US & Austral* to select for compulsory military service. ~*n, vb* **7** *US* same as **draught.**

drag *vb* **dragging, dragged 1** to pull with force along the ground. **2** to trail on the ground. **3** to persuade (someone) to go somewhere: *he didn't want to come so I had to drag him along.* **4** to move (oneself) slowly and with difficulty: *I had to drag myself out of bed this morning.* **5** to linger behind: *she dragged along behind her mother.* **6** to search (a river) with a dragnet or hook. **7** to draw (on a cigarette). **8** *Computers* to move (a graphics image) from one place to another on the screen by manipulating a mouse with its button held down. **9 drag away** *or* **from** to force (oneself) to come away from something interesting: *I was completely spellbound and couldn't drag myself away from the film.* **10 drag on** *or* **out** to last or be prolonged tediously: *winter dragged on.* **11 drag one's feet** *Informal* to act with deliberate slowness. ~*n* **12** a person or thing that slows up progress. **13** *Informal* a tedious or boring thing: *it was a drag having to walk 2 miles to the station every day.* **14** *Informal* a draw on a cigarette. **15** an implement, such as a dragnet, used for dragging. **16** *Aeronautics* the resistance to the motion of a body passing through air. **17 in drag** (of a man) wearing women's clothes, usually as a form of entertainment. See also **drag up.**

draggle *vb* **-gling, -gled** to make or become wet or dirty by trailing on the ground.

dragnet *n* a net used to scour the bottom of a pond or river when searching for something.

dragoman *n, pl* **-mans** *or* **-men** (in some Middle Eastern countries) a professional interpreter or guide.

dragon *n* **1** a mythical monster that resembles a large fire-breathing lizard. **2** *Informal* a fierce woman. **3 chase the dragon** *Slang* to smoke opium or heroin.

dragonfly *n, pl* **-flies** a brightly coloured insect with a long slender body and two pairs of wings.

dragoon *n* **1** a heavily armed cavalryman. ~*vb* **2** to coerce or force: *we were dragooned into participating in the competition.*

drag race *n* a race in which specially built or modified cars or motorcycles are timed over a measured course. **drag racing** *n*

drag up *vb Informal* to revive (an unpleasant fact or story).

drain *n* **1** a pipe that carries off water or sewage. **2** a cause of a continuous reduction in energy or resources: *the expansion will be a drain on resources.* **3** a metal grid on a road or pavement through which rainwater flows. **4 down the drain** wasted. ~*vb* **5** to draw off or remove (liquid) from. **6** to flow (away) or filter (off). **7** to dry or be emptied as a result of liquid running off or flowing away. **8** to drink the entire contents of (a glass or cup). **9** to make constant demands on (energy or resources); exhaust. **10** (of a river) to carry off the surface water from (an area).

drainage *n* **1** a system of pipes, drains, or ditches used to drain water or other liquids. **2** the process or a method of draining.

draining board *n* a grooved surface at the side of a sink, used for draining washed dishes.

drainpipe *n* a pipe for carrying off rainwater or sewage.

drake *n* the male of a duck.

dram *n* **1** a small amount of spirits, such as whisky. **2** a unit of weight equal to one sixteenth of an ounce (avoirdupois).

drama *n* **1** a serious play for theatre, television, or radio. **2** plays in general, as a form of literature. **3** the art of writing, producing, or acting in a play. **4** a situation that is exciting or highly emotional.

dramatic *adj* **1** of or relating to drama. **2** like a drama in suddenness or effectiveness: *the government's plan has had a dramatic effect on employment in television.* **3** acting or performed in a flamboyant way: *he spread his hands in a dramatic gesture of helplessness.* **dramatically** *adv*

dramatics *n* **1** the art of acting or producing plays. ~*pl n* **2** exaggerated, theatrical behaviour.

dramatis personae (**drah**-mat-tiss per-**soh**-nigh) *pl n* the characters in a play.

dramatist *n* a playwright.

dramatize *or* **-tise** *vb* **-tizing, -tized** *or* **-tising, -tised 1** to rewrite (a book or story) in a form suitable for performing on stage. **2** to express (something) in a dramatic or exaggerated way: *he dramatizes his illness.* **dramatization** *or* **-tisation** *n*

drank *vb* the past tense of **drink.**

drape *vb* **draping, draped 1** to cover with material or fabric. **2** to hang or arrange in folds. **3** to place

THESAURUS

drab cheerless, colourless, dingy, dismal, dreary, dull, flat, gloomy, grey, lacklustre, shabby, sombre, uninspired, vapid

draft *n.* **1.** abstract, delineation, outline, plan, preliminary form, rough, sketch, version **2.** bill (*of exchange*), cheque, order, postal order ~*vb.* **3.** compose, delineate, design, draw, draw up, formulate, outline, plan, sketch

drag *vb.* **1.** draw, haul, lug, pull, tow, trail, tug, yank **2.** crawl, creep, go slowly, inch, limp along, shamble, shuffle **3.** dawdle, draggle, lag behind, linger, loiter, straggle, trail behind **4.** *with* **on** *or* **out** draw out, extend, keep going, lengthen, persist, prolong, protract, spin out, stretch out **5. drag one's feet** *informal* block, hold back, obstruct, procrastinate, stall ~*n.* **6.** *slang* annoyance, bore, bother, nuisance, pain (*informal*), pain in the arse (*taboo informal*), pest

dragoon *vb.* browbeat, bully, coerce, compel, constrain, drive, force, impel, intimidate, railroad (*informal*)

drain *n.* **1.** channel, conduit, culvert, ditch, duct, outlet, pipe, sewer, sink, trench, wastepipe, watercourse **2.** depletion, drag, exhaustion, expenditure, reduction, sap, strain, withdrawal **3. down the drain** gone, gone for good, lost, ruined, wasted ~*vb.* **4.** bleed, draw off, dry, empty, evacuate, milk, pump off *or* out, remove, tap, withdraw **5.** discharge, effuse, exude, flow out, leak, ooze, seep, trickle, well out **6.** drink up, finish, gulp down, quaff, swallow **7.** consume, deplete, dissipate, empty, exhaust, sap, strain, tax, use up, weary

drainage bilge (water), seepage, sewage, sewerage, waste

dram drop, glass, measure, shot (*informal*), slug, snifter (*informal*), snort (*slang*), tot

drama 1. dramatization, play, show, stage play, stage show, theatrical piece **2.** acting, dramatic art, dramaturgy, stagecraft, theatre, Thespian art **3.** crisis, dramatics, excitement, histrionics, scene, spectacle, theatrics, turmoil

dramatic 1. dramaturgic, dramaturgical, theatrical, Thespian **2.** affecting, effective, expressive, impressive, moving, powerful, striking, vivid **3.** breathtaking, climactic, electrifying, emotional, exciting, melodramatic, sensational, shock-horror (*facetious*), startling, sudden, suspenseful, tense, thrilling

dramatist dramaturge, playwright, screen-writer, scriptwriter

casually: *he draped his arm across the back of the seat.* ~See also **drapes.**

draper *n Brit* a person who sells fabrics and sewing materials.

drapery *n, pl* **-peries 1** fabric or clothing arranged and draped. **2** fabrics and cloth collectively.

drapes *pl n Chiefly US & Canad* curtains.

drastic *adj* strong and severe: *the police are taking drastic measures against car thieves.* **drastically** *adv*

drat *interj Slang* an exclamation of annoyance.

draught *or US* **draft** *n* **1** a current of cold air, usually one coming into a room or vehicle. **2** a portion of liquid to be drunk, esp. a dose of medicine. **3** a gulp or swallow: *she took a deep draught then a sip.* **4 on draught** (of beer) drawn from a cask. **5** one of the flat discs used in the game of draughts. US and Canad. equivalent: **checker 6 feel the draught** to be short of money. *~adj* **7** (of an animal) used for pulling heavy loads: *horses are specialized draught animals.*

draught beer *n* beer stored in a cask.

draughtboard *n* a square board divided into 64 squares, used for playing draughts.

draughts *n* a game for two players using a draughtboard and 12 draughtsmen each.

draughtsman *or US* **draftsman** *n, pl* **-men 1** a person employed to prepare detailed scale drawings of equipment, machinery, or buildings. **2** a person skilled in drawing. **3** US and Canad. equivalent: **checker** *Brit* a flat disc used in the game of draughts. **draughtsmanship** *n*

draughty *or US* **drafty** *adj* **draughtier, draughtiest** *or US* **draftier, draftiest** exposed to draughts of air. **draughtily** *adv* **draughtiness** *n*

draw *vb* **drawing, drew, drawn 1** to sketch (a picture, pattern, or diagram) with a pen or pencil. **2** to cause (a person or thing) to move closer or further away from a place by pulling. **3** to bring, take, or pull (something) out of a container: *he drew a gun and laid it on the table.* **4** to take (something) from a particular source: *the inhabitants drew water from the well two miles away.* **5** to move in a specified direction: *he drew alongside me.* **6** to attract: *she drew enthusiastic audiences from all over the country.* **7** to formulate or decide: *he drew similar conclusions.* **8** to cause to flow: *the barman nodded and drew two pints.* **9** to choose or be given by lottery: *Brazil have drawn Spain in the semi-final of the Cup.* **10** (of two teams or contestants) to finish a game with an equal number of points. **11** *Archery* to bend (a bow) by pulling the string. **12** to cause (pus) to discharge from an abscess or wound. *~n* **13** a raffle or lottery. **14** *Informal* a person, place, show, or event that attracts a large audience. **15** a contest or game ending in a tie. ~See also **drawback, draw in,** etc.

drawback *n* **1** a disadvantage or hindrance. *~vb* **draw back 2** to move backwards: *the girl drew back as though in pain.* **3** to turn aside from an undertaking: *Labour drew back from a commitment to repeal legislation introducing the council tax.*

drawbridge *n* a bridge that may be raised to prevent access or to enable vessels to pass.

drawer *n* **1** a sliding box-shaped part of a piece of furniture used for storage. **2** a person or thing that draws.

drawers *pl n Old-fashioned* an undergarment worn on the lower part of the body.

draw in *vb* **1** (of a train) to arrive at a station. **2 the nights are drawing in** the hours of daylight are becoming shorter.

drawing *n* **1** a picture or plan made by means of lines on a surface. **2** the art of making drawings.

drawing pin *n Brit* a short tack with a broad smooth head used for fastening papers to a drawing board or other surface.

drawing room *n* a room where visitors are received and entertained.

drawl *vb* **1** to speak slowly with long vowel sounds. *~n* **2** the way of speech of someone who drawls. **drawling** *adj*

drawn *vb* **1** the past participle of **draw.** *~adj* **2** haggard, tired, or tense in appearance.

draw off *vb* to cause (a liquid) to flow from something.

draw on *vb* **1** to make use of from a source or fund: *they are able to draw on a repertoire of around 400 songs.* **2** (of a period of time) to come near or pass by: *summer draws on; time draws on.*

draw out *vb* **1** (of a train) to leave a station. **2** to encourage (someone) to talk freely: *therapy groups will continue to draw her out.* **3 draw out of** to find out (information) from.

drawstring *n* a cord run through a hem around an opening, so that when it is pulled tighter, the opening closes.

draw up *vb* **1** to prepare and write out: *the signatories drew up a draft agreement.* **2** (of a vehicle) to come to a halt.

THESAURUS

dramatize act, exaggerate, lay it on (thick) (*slang*), make a performance of, overdo, overstate, play-act, play to the gallery

drastic desperate, dire, extreme, forceful, harsh, radical, severe, strong

draught 1. *of air* current, flow, influx, movement, puff **2.** cup, dose, drink, potion, quantity

draw *vb.* **1.** delineate, depict, design, map out, mark out, outline, paint, portray, sketch, trace **2.** drag, haul, pull, tow, tug **3.** extort, extract, pull out, take out **4.** allure, attract, bring forth, call forth, elicit, engage, entice, evoke, induce, influence, invite, persuade **5.** deduce, derive, get, infer, make, take **6.** breathe in, drain, inhale, inspire, puff, pull, respire, suck **7.** choose, pick, select, single out, take *~n.* **8.** *informal* attraction, enticement, lure, pull (*informal*) **9.** dead heat, deadlock, impasse, stalemate, tie

drawback defect, deficiency, detriment, difficulty, disadvantage, downside, fault, flaw, fly in the ointment (*informal*), handicap, hindrance, hitch, impediment, imperfection, nuisance, obstacle, snag, stumbling block, trouble

draw back recoil, retract, retreat, shrink, start back, withdraw

drawing cartoon, delineation, depiction, illustration, outline, picture, portrayal, representation, sketch, study

drawl *vb. of speech sounds* drag out, draw out, extend, lengthen, prolong, protract

drawling dragging, drawly, droning, dull, twanging, twangy

drawn fatigued, fraught, haggard, harassed, harrowed, pinched, sapped, strained, stressed, taut, tense, tired, worn

draw on employ, exploit, extract, fall back on, have recourse to, make use of, rely on, take from, use

draw out drag out, extend, lengthen, make longer, prolong, prolongate, protract, spin out, stretch, string out

draw up 1. compose, draft, formulate, frame, pre-

dray *n* a low cart used for carrying heavy loads.
dread *vb* **1** to anticipate with apprehension or terror. ~*n* **2** great fear.
dreadful *adj* **1** extremely disagreeable or shocking. **2** extreme: *there were dreadful delays.* **dreadfully** *adv*
dreadlocks *pl n* hair worn in the Rastafarian style of tightly curled strands.
dream *n* **1** an imagined series of events experienced in the mind while asleep. **2** a daydream: *I dream of sailing in that sea, among those islands.* **3** a goal or aim: *his ultimate dream is to form a British team capable of winning the Tour de France.* **4** a wonderful person or thing: *her house is a dream.* ~*vb* **dreaming, dreamt** *or* **dreamed 5** to experience (a dream). **6** to indulge in daydreams. **7** to be unrealistic: *you're dreaming if you think we can win.* **8 dream of** to consider the possibility of: *she would not dream of taking his advice.* **9 dream of** *or* **about** to have an image of or fantasy about: *they often dream about what life will be like for them on the outside.* ~*adj* **10** beautiful or pleasing: *a dream kitchen.* **dreamer** *n*
dream up *vb* to formulate in the imagination: *a character dreamt up by a scriptwriter.*
dreamy *adj* **dreamier, dreamiest 1** vague or impractical: *she was wild-eyed and dreamy.* **2** relaxing or gentle: *I felt this dreamy contentment.* **3** *Informal* wonderful or impressive: *he drives a dreamy Jaguar.* **dreamily** *adv* **dreaminess** *n*
dreary *adj* **drearier, dreariest** dull or uninteresting: *there are long streets of dreary red houses spreading everywhere.* **drearily** *adv* **dreariness** *n*
dredge[1] *n* **1** a machine used to scoop or suck up silt or mud from a river bed or harbour. ~*vb* **dredging, dredged 2** to remove silt or mud from (a river bed or harbour) by means of a dredge. **3** to search for (a submerged object) with or as if with a dredge. **dredger** *n*
dredge[2] *vb* **dredging, dredged** to sprinkle (food) with a substance, such as flour. **dredger** *n*
dredge up *vb Informal* to remember (something obscure or half-forgotten): *I didn't retain you to dredge up unfortunate incidents from my past.*
dregs *pl n* **1** solid particles that settle at the bottom of some liquids. **2 the dregs** the worst or most despised elements: *the dregs of colonial society.*
drench *vb* **1** to make completely wet. **2** to give medicine to (an animal). **drenching** *n, adj*
Dresden *or* **Dresden china** *n* delicate and decorative porcelain made near Dresden, East Germany.
dress *n* **1** a one-piece garment worn by a woman or girl, with a skirt and bodice and sometimes sleeves. **2** complete style of clothing: *contemporary dress.* ~*adj* **3** suitable for a formal occasion: *he was wearing a dress shirt.* ~*vb* **4** to put clothes on. **5** to put on formal clothes. **6** to apply protective covering to (a wound). **7** to cover (a salad) with dressing. **8** to prepare (meat, poultry, or fish) for selling or cooking by cleaning or gutting. **9** to put a finish on (the surface of stone, metal, or other building material). ~See also **dress up.**
dressage (**dress**-ahzh) *n* **a** the method of training horses to perform manoeuvres as a display of obedience. **b** the manoeuvres performed.
dress circle *n* the first gallery in a theatre.
dresser[1] *n* **1** a piece of furniture with shelves and cupboards, used for storing or displaying dishes. **2** *US* a chest of drawers.
dresser[2] *n* **1** a person who dresses in a specified way: *a snappy dresser.* **2** *Theatre* a person employed to assist performers with their costumes.
dressing *n* **1** a sauce for food: *salad dressing.* **2** *US & Canad* same as **stuffing** (sense 1). **3** a covering for a wound. **4** manure or fertilizer spread on land. **5** a gluey material used for stiffening paper, textiles, etc.
dressing-down *n Informal* a severe reprimand.
dressing gown *n* a loose-fitting garment worn over one's pyjamas or nightdress.
dressing room *n* a room used for changing clothes and applying make-up, esp. a backstage room in a theatre.
dressing table *n* a piece of bedroom furniture with a mirror and a set of drawers.
dressmaker *n* a person who makes clothes for women. **dressmaking** *n*
dress rehearsal *n* **1** the last rehearsal of a play, opera, or show using costumes, lighting, and other effects. **2** any full scale practice: *astronauts are in the midst of a two day dress rehearsal of their launch countdown.*
dress shirt *n* a man's evening shirt, worn as part of formal evening dress.

THESAURUS

pare, write out **2.** bring to a stop, halt, pull up, run in, stop, stop short
dread 1. *vb.* anticipate with horror, cringe at, fear, have cold feet (*informal*), quail, shrink from, shudder, tremble **2.** *n.* affright, alarm, apprehension, aversion, awe, dismay, fear, fright, funk (*informal*), heebie-jeebies (*slang*), horror, terror, trepidation
dreadful alarming, appalling, awful, dire, distressing, fearful, formidable, frightful, ghastly, godawful (*slang*), grievous, hideous, horrendous, horrible, monstrous, shocking, terrible, tragic, tremendous
dream *n.* **1.** daydream, delusion, fantasy, hallucination, illusion, imagination, pipe dream, reverie, speculation, trance, vagary, vision **2.** ambition, aspiration, design, desire, goal, hope, notion, thirst, wish **3.** beauty, delight, gem, joy, marvel, pleasure, treasure ~*vb.* **4.** build castles in the air *or* in Spain, conjure up, daydream, envisage, fancy, fantasize, hallucinate, have dreams, imagine, stargaze, think, visualize
dreamer daydreamer, Don Quixote, fantasist, fantasizer, fantast, idealist, romancer, theorizer, utopian, visionary, Walter Mitty
dreamland cloud-cuckoo-land, cloudland, dream world, fairyland, fantasy, illusion, land of dreams, land of make-believe, land of Nod, never-never land (*informal*), sleep
dreamy 1. airy-fairy, dreamlike, fanciful, imaginary, impractical, quixotic, speculative, surreal, vague, visionary **2.** absent, abstracted, daydreaming, faraway, in a reverie, musing, pensive, preoccupied, with one's head in the clouds
dreary boring, colourless, drab, dull, ho-hum (*informal*), humdrum, lifeless, mind-numbing, monotonous, routine, tedious, uneventful, uninteresting, wearisome
dregs 1. deposit, draff, dross, grounds, lees, residue, residuum, scourings, scum, sediment, trash, waste **2.** *slang* down-and-outs, good-for-nothings, outcasts, rabble, ragtag and bobtail, riffraff, scum
drench drown, duck, flood, imbrue, inundate, saturate, soak, souse, steep, wet
dress *n.* **1.** apparel, attire, clothes, clothing, costume, ensemble, frock, garb, garment, garments, gear (*informal*), get-up (*informal*), guise, habiliment, outfit, raiment (*archaic or poetic*), rigout (*informal*), robe, suit, togs, vestment ~*vb.* **2.** attire, change, clothe, don, garb, put on, robe, slip on *or* into **3.** bandage, bind up, plaster, treat
dressing down carpeting (*informal*), castigation,

dress suit *n* a man's evening suit.
dress up *vb* **1** to put on glamorous or stylish clothes. **2** to put fancy dress on: *the guests dressed up like cowboys.* **3** to disguise (something) to make it more attractive or acceptable: *the offer was simply an old one dressed up in new terms.*
dressy *adj* **dressier, dressiest 1** (of clothes or occasions) elegant. **2** (of people) dressing stylishly. **dressiness** *n*
drew *vb* the past tense of **draw.**
drey *or* **dray** *n* a squirrel's nest.
dribble *vb* **-bling, -bled 1** to flow or allow to flow in a thin stream or drops. **2** to allow saliva to trickle from the mouth. **3** (in soccer, hockey, etc.) to propel (the ball) by kicking or tapping in quick succession. *~n* **4** a small quantity of liquid falling in drops or flowing in a thin stream. **5** a small supply: *there's only a dribble of milk left.* **6** an act or instance of dribbling. **dribbler** *n*
dribs and drabs *pl n Informal* small occasional amounts.
dried *vb* the past of **dry.**
drier[1] *adj* a comparative of **dry.**
drier[2] *n* same as **dryer**[1].
driest *adj* a superlative of **dry.**
drift *vb* **1** to be carried along by currents of air or water. **2** to move aimlessly from one place or activity to another. **3** to wander away from a fixed course or point. **4** (of snow) to pile up in heaps. *~n* **5** something piled up by the wind or current, as a snowdrift. **6** a general movement or development: *there has been a drift away from family control.* **7** the main point of an argument or speech: *I was beginning to get his drift.* **8** the extent to which a vessel or aircraft is driven off course by winds, etc. **9** a current of water created by the wind.
drifter *n* **1** a person who moves aimlessly from place to place. **2** a boat used for drift-net fishing.
drift net *n* a fishing net that is allowed to drift with the tide.
driftwood *n* wood floating on or washed ashore by the sea.
drill[1] *n* **1** a machine or tool for boring holes. **2** *Mil* training in procedures or movements, as for parades. **3** strict and often repetitious training. **4** *Informal* correct procedure: *he knows the drill as well as anybody.* *~vb* **5** to bore a hole in (something) with or as if with a drill. **6** to instruct or be instructed in military procedures or movements. **7** to teach by rigorous exercises or training.
drill[2] *n* **1** a machine for planting seeds in rows. **2** a furrow in which seeds are sown. **3** a row of seeds planted by means of a drill. *~vb* **4** to plant (seeds) by means of a drill.
drill[3] *n* a hard-wearing cotton cloth, used for uniforms.
drill[4] *n* a W African monkey, related to the mandrill.
drilling platform *n* an offshore structure that supports a drilling rig.
drilling rig *n* the complete machinery, equipment, and structures needed to drill an offshore oil well.
drily *or* **dryly** *adv* in a dry manner.
drink *vb* **drinking, drank, drunk 1** to swallow (a liquid). **2** to consume alcohol, esp. to excess. **3** to bring (oneself) into a specified condition by consuming alcohol: *he drank himself senseless every night.* **4 drink someone's health** to wish someone health or happiness with a toast. **5 drink in** to pay close attention to: *I drank in what the speaker said.* **6 drink to** to drink a toast: *I drank to their engagement.* *~n* **7** liquid suitable for drinking. **8** a portion of liquid for drinking. **9** alcohol, or the habit of drinking too much of it. **drinkable** *adj* **drinker** *n*
drink-driving *adj* of or relating to driving a car after drinking alcohol: *a drink-driving offence.*
drip *vb* **dripping, dripped 1** to fall or let fall in drops. *~n* **2** the falling of drops of liquid. **3** the sound made by falling drops. **4** *Informal* a weak or foolish person. **5** *Med* a device that administers a liquid drop by drop into a vein.
drip-dry *adj* **1** (of clothes or fabrics) designed to dry without creases if hung up when wet. *~vb* **-dries, -drying, -dried 2** to dry or become dry thus.
drip-feed *vb* **-feeding, -fed 1** to feed (someone) a liquid drop by drop, usually through a vein. *~n* **drip feed 2** same as **drip** (sense 5).
dripping *n* the fat that comes from meat while it is being roasted or fried.
drive *vb* **driving, drove, driven 1** to guide the movement of (a vehicle). **2** to transport or be transported in a vehicle. **3** to goad into a specified state: *the black despair that finally drove her to suicide.* **4** to push or propel: *he drove the nail into the wall with a hammer.* **5** *Sport* to hit (a ball) very hard and straight.

THESAURUS

rebuke, reprimand, reproof, rocket, scolding, telling off (*informal*), upbraiding
dressmaker couturier, modiste, seamstress, sewing woman, tailor
dress up 1. doll up (*slang*), dress for dinner, dress formally, put on one's best bib and tucker (*informal*), put on one's glad rags (*informal*) **2.** disguise, play-act, put on fancy dress, wear a costume **3.** camouflage, disguise, masquerade, pass off, pose
dribble 1. drip, drop, fall in drops, leak, ooze, run, seep, trickle **2.** drip saliva, drivel, drool, slaver, slobber
drift *vb.* **1.** be carried along, coast, float, go (aimlessly), meander, stray, waft, wander **2.** accumulate, amass, bank up, drive, gather, pile up *~n.* **3.** accumulation, bank, heap, mass, mound, pile **4.** course, current, direction, flow, impulse, movement, rush, sweep, trend **5.** aim, design, direction, gist, implication, import, intention, meaning, object, purport, scope, significance, tendency, tenor, thrust
drill *n.* **1.** bit, borer, boring-tool, gimlet, rotary tool **2.** discipline, exercise, instruction, practice, preparation, repetition, training *~vb.* **3.** coach, discipline, exercise, instruct, practise, rehearse, teach, train **4.** bore, penetrate, perforate, pierce, puncture, sink in
drink *vb.* **1.** absorb, drain, gulp, guzzle, imbibe, partake of, quaff, sip, suck, sup, swallow, swig (*informal*), swill, toss off, wash down, wet one's whistle (*informal*) **2.** bend the elbow (*informal*), bevvy (*dialect*), booze (*informal*), carouse, go on a binge *or* bender (*informal*), hit the bottle (*informal*), indulge, pub-crawl (*informal, chiefly Brit.*), revel, tipple, tope, wassail *~n.* **3.** beverage, liquid, potion, refreshment, thirst quencher **4.** cup, draught, glass, gulp, noggin, sip, snifter (*informal*), swallow, swig (*informal*), taste, tipple **5.** alcohol, bevvy (*dialect*), booze (*informal*), hooch *or* hootch (*informal, chiefly U.S. & Canad.*), liquor, spirits, the bottle (*informal*)
drinker alcoholic, bibber, boozer (*informal*), dipsomaniac, drunk, drunkard, guzzler, inebriate, lush (*slang*), soak (*slang*), sot, sponge (*informal*), tippler, toper, wino (*informal*)
drink in absorb, assimilate, be all ears (*informal*), be fascinated by, be rapt, hang on (someone's) words, hang on the lips of, pay attention
drink to pledge, pledge the health of, salute, toast
drip *vb.* **1.** dribble, drizzle, drop, exude, filter, plop,

6 *Golf* to strike (the ball) with a driver. **7** to chase (game) from cover. **8 drive home** to make (a point) clearly understood by emphasis. ~*n* **9** a journey in a driven vehicle. **10** a road for vehicles, esp. a private road leading to a house. **11** a special effort made by a group of people for a particular purpose: *a charity drive.* **12** energy, ambition, or initiative. **13** *Psychol* a motive or interest: *sex drive.* **14** a sustained and powerful military offensive. **15** the means by which power is transmitted in a machine. **16** *Sport* a hard straight shot or stroke.

drive at *vb Informal* to intend or mean: *he had no idea what she was driving at.*

drive-in *n* **1** a cinema, restaurant, etc. offering a service where people remain in their cars while using the service provided. ~*adj* **2** denoting a cinema, etc. of this kind.

drivel *n* **1** foolish talk. ~*vb* **-elling, -elled** *or US* **-eling, -eled 2** to speak foolishly. **3** to allow (saliva) to flow from the mouth.

driven *vb* the past participle of **drive.**

drive-thru *n* **1** a takeaway restaurant, bank, etc., designed so that customers can use it without leaving their cars. ~*adj* **2** denoting a restaurant etc. of this kind.

driveway *n* a path for vehicles connecting a building to a public road.

driving licence *n* an official document authorizing a person to drive a motor vehicle.

drizzle *n* **1** very light rain. ~*vb* **-zling, -zled 2** to rain lightly. **drizzly** *adj*

droll *adj* quaintly amusing. **drollery** *n* **drolly** *adv*

dromedary (**drom**-mid-er-ee) *n, pl* **-daries** a camel with a single hump.

drone[1] *n* **1** a male honeybee. **2** a person who lives off the work of others.

drone[2] *vb* **droning, droned 1** to make a monotonous low dull sound. **2 drone on** to talk in a monotonous tone without stopping. ~*n* **3** a monotonous low dull sound. **4** a single-reed pipe in a set of bagpipes.

drool *vb* **1 drool over** to show excessive enthusiasm for or pleasure in. **2** same as **drivel** (senses 2, 3).

droop *vb* **1** to sag, as from weakness or lack of support. **2** to be overcome by weariness: *her eyelids drooped as if she were falling asleep.* **drooping** *adj*

droopy *adj* hanging or sagging downwards: *a droopy moustache.*

drop *vb* **dropping, dropped 1** to fall or allow (something) to fall vertically. **2** to decrease in amount, strength, or value. **3** to fall to the ground, as from exhaustion. **4** to sink to a lower position, as on a scale. **5** to mention casually: *he dropped a hint.* **6** to set down (passengers or goods): *can you drop me at the hotel?* **7** *Informal* to send: *drop me a letter.* **8** to discontinue: *can we drop the subject?* **9** *Informal* to be no longer friendly with: *I dropped him when I discovered his political views.* **10** to leave out in speaking: *he has a tendency to drop his h's.* **11** (of animals) to give birth to (offspring). **12** *Sport* to omit (a player) from a team. **13** to lose (a game or point). **14 drop back** to progress more slowly than other people going in the same direction. **15 drop in** *or* **by** *Informal* to pay someone a casual visit. ~*n* **16** a small quantity of liquid forming a round shape. **17** a small quantity of liquid. **18** a small round sweet: *a lemon drop.* **19** a decrease in amount, strength, or value. **20** the vertical distance that anything may fall. **21** the act of unloading troops or supplies by parachute. ~See also **drop off, dropout, drops.**

drop curtain *n Theatre* a curtain that can be raised and lowered onto the stage.

droplet *n* a very small drop of liquid.

drop off *vb* **1** to set down (passengers or goods). **2**

THESAURUS

splash, sprinkle, trickle ~*n.* **2.** dribble, dripping, drop, leak, trickle **3.** *informal* milksop, mummy's boy (*informal*), namby-pamby, ninny, softy (*informal*), weakling, weed (*informal*), wet (*Brit. informal*), wimp (*Inf.*)

drive *vb.* **1.** direct, go, guide, handle, manage, motor, operate, ride, steer, travel **2.** actuate, coerce, compel, constrain, dragoon, force, goad, harass, impel, motivate, oblige, overburden, overwork, press, prick, prod, prompt, railroad (*informal*), rush, spur **3.** herd, hurl, impel, propel, push, send, urge ~*n.* **4.** excursion, hurl (*Scot.*), jaunt, journey, outing, ride, run, spin (*informal*), trip, turn **5.** action, advance, appeal, campaign, crusade, effort, push (*informal*), surge **6.** ambition, effort, energy, enterprise, get-up-and-go (*informal*), initiative, motivation, pep, pressure, push (*informal*), vigour, zip (*informal*)

drive at aim, allude to, get at, have in mind, hint at, imply, indicate, insinuate, intend, intimate, mean, refer to, signify, suggest

drivel *n.* **1.** balderdash, balls (*taboo slang*), bilge (*informal*), bosh (*informal*), bull (*slang*), bullshit (*taboo slang*), bunk (*informal*), bunkum *or* buncombe (*chiefly U.S.*), cobblers (*Brit. taboo slang*), crap (*slang*), dross, eyewash (*informal*), fatuity, garbage (*informal*), gibberish, guff (*slang*), hogwash, hokum (*slang, chiefly U.S. & Canad.*), hot air (*informal*), moonshine, nonsense, pap, piffle (*informal*), poppycock (*informal*), prating, rot, rubbish, shit (*taboo slang*), stuff, tommyrot, tosh (*slang, chiefly Brit.*), tripe (*informal*), twaddle, waffle (*informal, chiefly Brit.*) ~*vb.* **2.** babble, blether, gab (*informal*), gas (*informal*), maunder, prate, ramble, waffle (*informal, chiefly Brit.*) **3.** dribble, drool, slaver, slobber

drizzle 1. *n.* fine rain, Scotch mist, smir (*Scot.*) **2.** *vb.* mizzle (*dialect*), rain, shower, smir (*Scot.*), spot *or* spit with rain, spray, sprinkle

droll amusing, clownish, comic, comical, diverting, eccentric, entertaining, farcical, funny, humorous, jocular, laughable, ludicrous, odd, oddball (*informal*), off-the-wall (*slang*), quaint, ridiculous, risible, waggish, whimsical

drone[1] *n.* bludger (*Austral. & N.Z.*), idler, leech, loafer, lounger, parasite, scrounger (*informal*), skiver (*Brit. slang*), sluggard, sponger (*informal*)

drone[2] *vb.* **1.** buzz, hum, purr, thrum, vibrate, whirr **2.** *often with* **on** be boring, chant, drawl, intone, prose about, speak monotonously, spout, talk interminably ~*n.* **3.** buzz, hum, murmuring, purr, thrum, vibration, whirr, whirring

droop 1. bend, dangle, drop, fall down, hang (down), sag, sink **2.** decline, diminish, fade, faint, flag, languish, slump, wilt, wither

drop *vb.* **1.** decline, depress, descend, diminish, dive, droop, fall, lower, plummet, plunge, sink, tumble **2.** *sometimes with* **off** deposit, leave, let off, set down, unload **3.** abandon, axe (*informal*), cease, desert, discontinue, forsake, give up, kick (*informal*), leave, quit, relinquish, remit, terminate **4.** *informal* disown, ignore, jilt, reject, renounce, repudiate, throw over ~*n.* **5.** bead, bubble, driblet, drip, droplet, globule, pearl, tear **6.** dab, dash, mouthful, nip, pinch, shot (*informal*), sip, spot, taste, tot, trace, trickle **7.** cut, decline, decrease, deterioration, downturn, fall-off, lowering, reduction, slump **8.** abyss, chasm, declivity, descent, fall, plunge, precipice, slope

drop off 1. allow to alight, deliver, leave, let off, set down **2.** *informal* catnap, doze (off), drowse, fall

Informal to fall asleep. **3** to decrease or decline: *sales dropped off during our period of transition.*

dropout *n* **1** a person who rejects conventional society. **2** a student who does not complete a course of study. *~vb* **drop out 3** to abandon or withdraw (from an institution or group).

dropper *n* a small tube with a rubber part at one end for drawing up and dispensing drops of liquid.

droppings *pl n* the dung of certain animals, such as rabbits or birds.

drops *pl n* any liquid medication applied by means of a dropper.

drop scone *n* a flat spongy cake made by dropping a spoonful of batter on a hot griddle.

dropsy *n* an illness in which watery fluid collects in the body. **dropsical** *adj*

drosky *or* **droshky** *n, pl* **-kies** an open four-wheeled carriage, formerly used in Russia.

dross *n* **1** the scum formed on the surfaces of molten metals. **2** anything of inferior quality: *we can't publish this dross.*

drought *n* a prolonged period of time during which no rain falls.

drove[1] *vb* the past tense of **drive.**

drove[2] *n* **1** a herd of livestock being driven together. **2** a moving crowd of people.

drover *n* a person who drives sheep or cattle.

drown *vb* **1** to die or kill by immersion in liquid. **2** to drench thoroughly. **3** to make (a sound) impossible to hear by making a loud noise.

drowse *vb* **drowsing, drowsed** to be sleepy, dull, or sluggish.

drowsy *adj* **drowsier, drowsiest 1** feeling sleepy. **2** peaceful and quiet: *row upon row of windows looked out over drowsy parkland.* **drowsily** *adv* **drowsiness** *n*

drubbing *n* an utter defeat, as in a contest: *the Communists received a drubbing.*

drudge *n* **1** a person who works hard at an uninteresting task. *~vb* **drudging, drudged 2** to work at such tasks.

drudgery *n* uninteresting work that must be done.

drug *n* **1** any substance used in the treatment, prevention, or diagnosis of disease. **2** a chemical substance, such as a narcotic, taken for the effects it produces. *~vb* **drugging, drugged 3** to administer a drug to (a person or animal) in order to induce sleepiness or unconsciousness. **4** to mix a drug with (food or drink).

drug addict *n* a person who is dependent on narcotic drugs.

druggist *n US & Canad* a pharmacist.

drugstore *n US & Canad* a pharmacy where a wide variety of goods are available.

Druid *n* a member of an ancient order of Celtic priests. **Druidic** *or* **Druidical** *adj*

drum *n* **1** a percussion instrument sounded by striking a skin stretched across the opening of a hollow cylinder. **2** the sound produced by a drum. **3** an object shaped like a drum: *an oil drum.* **4** same as **eardrum.** *~vb* **drumming, drummed 5** to play (music) on a drum. **6** to tap rhythmically or regularly: *he drummed his fingers on the desk.* **7** to fix in someone's mind by constant repetition: *my father always drummed into us how privileged we were.* ~See also **drum up. drummer** *n*

drumbeat *n* the sound made by beating a drum.

drumhead *n* the part of a drum that is struck.

drum machine *n* a synthesizer programmed to reproduce the sound of percussion instruments.

drum major *n* the noncommissioned officer in the army who is in command of the drums and the band when paraded together.

drum majorette *n* a girl who marches at the head of a procession, twirling a baton.

drumstick *n* **1** a stick used for playing a drum. **2** the lower joint of the leg of a cooked fowl.

drum up *vb* to obtain (support or business) by making requests or canvassing.

drunk *vb* **1** the past participle of **drink.** *~adj* **2** intoxicated with alcohol to the extent of losing control over normal functions. **3** overwhelmed by strong influence or emotion: *he was half drunk with satisfaction at his*

THESAURUS

asleep, have forty winks (*informal*), nod (off), snooze (*informal*) **3.** decline, decrease, diminish, dwindle, fall off, lessen, slacken

drop out abandon, back out, cop out (*slang*), forsake, give up, leave, quit, renege, stop, withdraw

drought aridity, dehydration, dryness, dry spell, dry weather, parchedness

drove collection, company, crowd, flock, gathering, herd, horde, mob, multitude, press, swarm, throng

drown 1. deluge, drench, engulf, flood, go down, go under, immerse, inundate, sink, submerge, swamp **2.** *figurative* deaden, engulf, muffle, obliterate, overcome, overpower, overwhelm, stifle, swallow up, wipe out

drowse be drowsy, be lethargic, be sleepy, doze, drop off (*informal*), kip (*Brit. slang*), nap, nod, sleep, slumber, snooze (*informal*)

drowsy dazed, dopey (*slang*), dozy, drugged, half asleep, heavy, lethargic, nodding, sleepy, somnolent, tired, torpid

drubbing beating, clobbering (*slang*), defeat, flogging, hammering (*informal*), licking (*informal*), pasting (*slang*), pounding, pummelling, thrashing, trouncing, walloping (*informal*), whipping

drudge 1. *n.* dogsbody (*informal*), factotum, hack, maid *or* man of all work, menial, plodder, scullion (*archaic*), servant, skivvy (*chiefly Brit.*), slave, toiler, worker **2.** *vb.* grind (*informal*), keep one's nose to the grindstone, labour, plod, plug away (*informal*), slave, toil, work

drudgery chore, donkey-work, fag (*informal*), grind (*informal*), hack work, hard work, labour, menial labour, skivvying (*Brit.*), slavery, slog, sweat (*informal*), sweated labour, toil

drug *n.* **1.** medicament, medication, medicine, physic, poison, remedy **2.** dope (*slang*), narcotic, opiate, stimulant *~vb.* **3.** anaesthetize, deaden, knock out, numb, poison, stupefy

drum *vb.* **1.** beat, pulsate, rap, reverberate, tap, tattoo, throb **2.** *with* **into** din into, drive home, hammer away, harp on, instil, reiterate

drum up attract, bid for, canvass, obtain, petition, round up, solicit

drunk 1. *adj.* bacchic, bevvied (*dialect*), blitzed (*slang*), blotto (*slang*), bombed (*slang*), canned (*slang*), drunken, flying (*slang*), fu' (*Scot.*), fuddled, half seas over (*informal*), inebriated, intoxicated, legless (*informal*), lit up (*slang*), loaded (*slang, chiefly U.S. & Canad.*), maudlin, merry (*Brit. informal*), muddled, out of it (*slang*), out to it (*Austral. & N.Z. slang*), paralytic (*informal*), pickled (*informal*), pie-eyed (*slang*), pissed (*taboo slang*), plastered (*slang*), sloshed (*slang*), smashed (*slang*), soaked (*informal*), steamboats (*slang*), steaming (*slang*), stewed (*slang*), stoned (*slang*), tanked up (*slang*), tiddly (*slang, chiefly Brit.*), tight (*informal*), tipsy, tired and emotional

victory over the intruder. ~*n* **4** a person who is drunk or drinks habitually to excess.

drunkard *n* a person who is frequently or habitually drunk.

drunken *adj* **1** intoxicated with alcohol. **2** habitually drunk. **3** caused by or relating to alcoholic intoxication: *a drunken argument.* **drunkenly** *adv* **drunkenness** *n*

drupe *n* a fleshy fruit with a stone, such as the peach or cherry.

dry *adj* **drier, driest** *or* **dryer, dryest 1** lacking moisture. **2** having little or no rainfall. **3** having the water drained away or evaporated: *a dry gully for the most part of the year.* **4** not providing milk: *a dry cow.* **5** (of the eyes) free from tears. **6** *Informal* thirsty. **7** eaten without butter or jam: *a dry cracker.* **8** (of wine) not sweet. **9** dull and uninteresting: *a dry subject.* **10** (of humour) subtle and sarcastic. **11** prohibiting the sale of alcoholic liquor: *a dry district.* ~*vb* **dries, drying, dried 12** to make or become dry. **13** to preserve (food) by removing the moisture. ~See also **dry out, dry up. dryness** *n*

dry battery *n* a electric battery composed of dry cells.

dry cell *n* an electric cell in which the electrolyte is in the form of a paste to prevent it from spilling.

dry-clean *vb* to clean (clothes, etc.) with a solvent other than water. **dry-cleaner** *n* **dry-cleaning** *n*

dry dock *n* a dock that can be pumped dry to permit work on a ship's bottom.

dryer[1] *n* any device that removes moisture by heating or by hot air.

dryer[2] *adj* same as **drier**[1].

dry ice *n* solid carbon dioxide used as a refrigerant.

dryly *adv* same as **drily.**

dry out *vb* **1** to make or become dry. **2** to undergo or cause to undergo treatment for alcoholism or drug addiction.

dry rot *n* **1** crumbling and drying of timber, caused by certain fungi. **2** a fungus causing this decay.

dry run *n Informal* a rehearsal.

dry-stone *adj* (of a wall) made without mortar.

dry up *vb* **1** to make or become dry. **2** to dry (dishes, cutlery, etc.) with a tea towel after they have been washed. **3** (of a resource) to come to and end. **4** *Informal* to stop speaking: *she suddenly dried up in the middle of her speech.*

DSC *Mil* Distinguished Service Cross.

DSO *Brit mil* Distinguished Service Order.

DSS *Brit* Department of Social Security.

DSW (in New Zealand) Department of Social Welfare.

DTP *Computers* desktop publishing.

DT's *Informal* delirium tremens.

dual *adj* having two parts, functions, or aspects: *dual controls; dual nationality.* **duality** *n*

dual carriageway *n Brit* a road with a central strip of grass or concrete to separate traffic travelling in opposite directions.

dub[1] *vb* **dubbing, dubbed** to give (a person or place) a name or nickname: *he is dubbed a racist despite his strong denials.*

dub[2] *vb* **dubbing, dubbed 1** to provide (a film) with a new soundtrack in a different language. **2** to provide (a film or tape) with a soundtrack. ~*n* **3** *Music* a style of reggae record production involving exaggeration of instrumental parts, echo, etc.

dubbin *n Brit* a kind of thick grease applied to leather to soften it and make it waterproof.

dubious (**dew**-bee-uss) *adj* **1** not entirely honest, safe, or reliable: *this allegation was at best dubious and at worst an outright fabrication.* **2** unsure or undecided: *she felt dubious about the entire proposition.* **3** of doubtful quality or worth: *she had the dubious honour of being taken for his mother.* **dubiety** (dew-**by**-it-ee) *n* **dubiously** *adv*

ducal (**duke**-al) *adj* of a duke.

ducat (**duck**-it) *n* a former European gold or silver coin.

duchess *n* **1** a woman who holds the rank of duke. **2** the wife or widow of a duke.

duchy *n, pl* **duchies** the area of land owned or ruled by a duke or duchess.

duck[1] *n, pl* **ducks** *or* **duck 1** a water bird with short legs, webbed feet, and a broad blunt bill. **2** the flesh of this bird used for food. **3** the female of such a bird. **4** *Cricket* a score of nothing. **5 like water off a duck's back** without effect: *I reprimanded him but it was like water off a duck's back.*

duck[2] *vb* **1** to move (the head or body) quickly downwards, to escape being seen or avoid a blow. **2** to plunge suddenly under water. **3** *Informal* to dodge (a duty or responsibility).

duck-billed platypus *n* See **platypus.**

duckling *n* a young duck.

THESAURUS

(*euphemistic*), under the influence (*informal*), wasted (*slang*), well-oiled (*slang*), wrecked (*slang*), zonked (*slang*) **2.** *n.* boozer (*informal*), drunkard, inebriate, lush (*slang*), soak (*slang*), sot, toper, wino (*informal*)

drunkard alcoholic, dipsomaniac, drinker, drunk, lush (*slang*), soak (*slang*), sot, tippler, toper, wino (*informal*)

drunken 1. bevvied (*dialect*), bibulous, blitzed (*slang*), blotto (*slang*), bombed (*slang*), boozing (*informal*), drunk, flying (*slang*), (gin-)sodden, inebriate, intoxicated, legless (*informal*), lit up (*slang*), out of it (*slang*), out to it (*Austral. & N.Z. slang*), paralytic (*informal*), pissed (*taboo slang*), red-nosed, smashed (*slang*), sottish, steaming (*slang*), tippling, toping, under the influence (*informal*), wasted (*slang*), wrecked (*slang*), zonked (*slang*) **2.** bacchanalian, bacchic, boozy (*informal*), debauched, dionysian, dissipated, orgiastic, riotous, saturnalian

drunkenness alcoholism, bibulousness, dipsomania, inebriety, insobriety, intemperance, intoxication, sottishness, tipsiness

dry *adj.* **1.** arid, barren, dehydrated, desiccated, dried up, juiceless, moistureless, parched, sapless, thirsty, torrid, waterless **2.** *figurative* boring, dreary, dull, ho-hum (*informal*), monotonous, plain, tedious, tiresome, uninteresting **3.** *figurative* cutting, deadpan, droll, keen, low-key, quietly humorous, sarcastic, sharp, sly ~*vb.* **4.** dehumidify, dehydrate, desiccate, drain, make dry, parch, sear

dryness aridity, aridness, dehumidification, dehydration, drought, thirst, thirstiness

dry out *or* **dry up** become dry, become unproductive, harden, mummify, shrivel up, wilt, wither, wizen

dual binary, coupled, double, duplex, duplicate, matched, paired, twin, twofold

dub call, christen, denominate, designate, label, name, nickname, style, term

dubious 1. ambiguous, debatable, dodgy (*Brit., Austral., & N.Z. informal*), doubtful, equivocal, fishy (*informal*), questionable, shady (*informal*), suspect, suspicious, unclear, undependable, unreliable, unsettled, untrustworthy **2.** doubtful, hesitant, iffy (*informal*), leery (*slang*), sceptical, uncertain, unconvinced, undecided, unsure, wavering

duck 1. bend, bob, bow, crouch, dodge, drop, lower,

ducks and drakes *n* **1** a game in which a flat stone is bounced across the surface of water. **2 play ducks and drakes with** *Informal* to use recklessly: *he has played ducks and drakes with his life.*

duct *n* **1** a tube, pipe, or channel through which liquid or gas is sent. **2** a tube in the body through which liquid such as tears or bile can pass.

ductile *adj* (of a metal) able to be shaped into sheets or drawn out into threads. **ductility** *n*

dud *Informal* ~*n* **1** an ineffectual person or thing: *they had the foresight to pick on someone who was not a total dud.* ~*adj* **2** bad or useless: *a dud cheque.*

dude *n Informal* **1** *US & Canad* a man: *he was a black dude in his late twenties.* **2** *US & Canad old-fashioned* a dandy. **3** *Western US & Canad* a city dweller who spends his or her holiday on a ranch.

dudgeon *n* **in high dudgeon** angry or resentful: *the scientist departed in high dudgeon.*

due *adj* **1** expected to happen, be done, or arrive at a particular time: *he is due to return to Britain on Thursday.* **2** immediately payable: *the balance is now due.* **3** owed as a debt: *they finally agreed to pay her the money she was due.* **4** fitting or proper: *he was found guilty of driving without due care and attention.* **5 due to** happening or existing as a direct result of someone or something else: *the cause of death was chronic kidney failure due to diabetes.* ~*n* **6** something that is owed or required. **7 give someone his** *or* **her due** to acknowledge someone's good points: *I'll give him his due, he's resourceful.* ~*adv* **8** directly or exactly: *due west.*

➤ *Due to* is not synonymous with *because of* or *owing to.* If the words *due to* can be replaced by *attributable to,* it is generally appropriate to use *due to.*

duel *n* **1** a formal fight between two people using guns, swords, or other weapons to settle a quarrel. ~*vb* **duelling, duelled** *or US* **dueling, dueled 2** to fight in a duel. **duellist** *n*

duenna *n* (esp. in Spain) an elderly woman acting as chaperon to girls.

dues *pl n* membership fees paid to a club or organization: *union dues.*

duet *n* a piece of music sung or played by two people. **duettist** *n*

duff *adj* **1** *Brit, Austral, & NZ informal* broken or useless: *my car had a duff clutch.* ~*vb* **2** *Golf informal* to bungle (a shot). **3 duff up** *Brit slang* to beat (someone) severely.

duffel *or* **duffle** *n* same as **duffel coat.**

duffel bag *n* a cylinder-shaped canvas bag fastened with a drawstring.

duffel coat *n* a wool coat usually with a hood and fastened with toggles.

duffer *n Informal* a dull or incompetent person.

dug[1] *vb* the past of **dig.**

dug[2] *n* a teat or udder of a female animal.

dugong *n* a whalelike mammal found in tropical waters.

dugout *n* **1** a canoe made by hollowing out a log. **2** (at a sports ground) the covered bench where managers and substitutes sit. **3** *Mil* a covered shelter dug in the ground to provide protection.

duiker *or* **duyker** (**dike**-er) *n, pl* **-kers** *or* **-ker** a small African antelope.

duke *n* **1** a nobleman of the highest rank. **2** the prince or ruler of a small principality or duchy. **dukedom** *n*

dulcet (**dull**-sit) *adj* (of a sound) soothing or pleasant: *she smiled and, in dulcet tones, told me I would be next.*

dulcimer *n* a tuned percussion instrument consisting of a set of strings stretched over a sounding board and struck with hammers.

dull *adj* **1** not interesting: *the finished article would make dull reading.* **2** slow to learn or understand. **3** (of an ache) not intense: *I have a dull ache in the middle of my back.* **4** (of weather) not bright or clear. **5** not lively or energetic: *she appeared, looking dull and apathetic.* **6** (of colour) lacking brilliance. **7** (of the blade of a knife) not sharp. **8** (of a sound) not loud or clear: *his head fell back to the carpet with a dull thud.* ~*vb* **9** to make or become dull. **dullness** *n* **dully** *adv*

dullard *n Old-fashioned* a dull or stupid person.

dulse *n* a seaweed with large red edible fronds.

duly *adv* **1** in a proper manner: *my permit was duly stamped.* **2** at the proper time: *the photographer duly arrived.*

dumb *adj* **1** lacking the power to speak. **2** lacking the power of human speech: *the event was denounced as cruelty to dumb animals.* **3** temporarily unable to speak: *I was struck dumb when I heard the news.* **4**

THESAURUS

stoop **2.** dip, dive, douse, dunk, immerse, plunge, souse, submerge, wet **3.** *informal* avoid, body-swerve (*Scot.*), dodge, escape, evade, shirk, shun, sidestep

duct blood vessel, canal, channel, conduit, funnel, passage, pipe, tube

dud 1. *n.* failure, flop (*informal*), washout (*informal*) **2.** *adj.* broken, bust (*informal*), duff (*Brit. informal*), failed, inoperative, kaput (*informal*), not functioning, valueless, worthless

dudgeon in high dudgeon angry, fuming, indignant, offended, resentful, vexed

due *adj.* **1.** expected, expected to arrive, scheduled **2.** in arrears, outstanding, owed, owing, payable, unpaid **3.** appropriate, becoming, bounden, deserved, fit, fitting, just, justified, merited, obligatory, proper, requisite, right, rightful, suitable, well-earned ~*n.* **4.** comeuppance (*slang*), deserts, merits, prerogative, privilege, right(s) ~*adv.* **5.** dead, direct, directly, exactly, straight, undeviatingly

duel affair of honour, single combat

dues charge, charges, contribution, fee, levy, membership fee

duffer blunderer, booby, bungler, clod, clot (*Brit. informal*), galoot (*slang, chiefly U.S.*), lubber, lummox (*informal*), oaf

dull *adj.* **1.** banal, boring, commonplace, dozy, dreary, dry, flat, ho-hum (*informal*), humdrum, mind-numbing, monotonous, plain, prosaic, run-of-the-mill, tedious, tiresome, unimaginative, uninteresting, vapid **2.** dense, dim, dim-witted (*informal*), doltish, dozy (*Brit. informal*), obtuse, slow, stolid, stupid, thick, unintelligent **3.** cloudy, dim, dismal, gloomy, leaden, opaque, overcast, turbid **4.** apathetic, blank, callous, dead, empty, heavy, indifferent, insensible, insensitive, lifeless, listless, passionless, slow, sluggish, unresponsive, unsympathetic, vacuous **5.** drab, faded, feeble, indistinct, lacklustre, muffled, murky, muted, sombre, subdued, subfusc, toned-down **6.** blunt, blunted, edgeless, not keen, not sharp, unsharpened ~*vb.* **7.** allay, alleviate, assuage, blunt, cloud, dampen, darken, deject, depress, dim, discourage, dishearten, dispirit, fade, lessen, mitigate, moderate, obscure, palliate, paralyse, relieve, sadden, soften, stain, stupefy, sully, take the edge off, tarnish

dullard blockhead, clod, dimwit (*informal*), dolt, dope (*informal*), dunce, lamebrain (*informal*), nitwit (*informal*), numskull *or* numbskull, oaf

duly 1. accordingly, appropriately, befittingly, correctly, decorously, deservedly, fittingly, properly, rightfully, suitably **2.** at the proper time, on time, punctually

done or performed without speech: *I looked at her in dumb puzzlement.* **5** *Informal* stupid or slow to understand. **dumbly** *adv*

dumbbell *n* **1** a short bar with a heavy ball or disc at either end, used for physical exercise. **2** *Slang, chiefly US & Canad* a stupid person.

dumbfounded *adj* speechless with amazement: *she sat open-mouthed and dumbfounded.*

dumb show *n* meaningful gestures without speech.

dumbstruck *adj* temporarily speechless through shock or surprise.

dumbwaiter *n* **1** a lift for carrying food, etc. from one floor of a building to another. **2** *Brit* **a** a stand placed near a dining table to hold food. **b** a revolving circular tray placed on a table to hold food.

dumdum *or* **dumdum bullet** *n* a soft-nosed bullet that expands on impact and causes large and serious wounds.

dummy *n, pl* **-mies 1** a large model that looks like a human being, used for displaying clothes in a shop, as a target, etc. **2** a copy of an object, often lacking some essential feature of the original. **3** *Slang* a stupid person. **4** *Bridge* **a** the hand exposed on the table by the declarer's partner and played by the declarer. **b** the declarer's partner. **5** *Brit* a rubber teat for babies to suck. ~*adj* **6** imitation or substitute: *you can train them with dummy bombs and live ammunition.*

dummy run *n* a practice or test carried out to test if any problems remain: *we'll do a dummy run on the file to see if the program works.*

dump *vb* **1** to drop or let fall in a careless manner: *he dumped the books on the bed.* **2** *Informal* to abandon (someone or something) without proper care: *the unwanted babies were dumped in orphanages.* **3** to dispose of (nuclear waste). **4** *Commerce* to sell (goods) in bulk and at low prices, usually in another country, in order to keep prices high in the home market. **5** *Computers* to record (the contents of the memory) on a storage device at a series of points during a computer run. ~*n* **6** a place where rubbish is left. **7** *Informal* a dirty, unattractive place: *you're hardly in this dump out of choice.* **8** *Mil* a place where weapons or supplies are stored.

dumpling *n* **1** a small ball of dough cooked and served with stew. **2** a round pastry case filled with fruit: *an apple dumpling.*

dumps *pl n* **down in the dumps** *Informal* feeling depressed and miserable.

dumpy *adj* **dumpier, dumpiest** short and plump.

dun[1] *vb* **dunning, dunned 1** to press (a debtor) for payment. ~*n* **2** a demand for payment.

dun[2] *adj* brownish-grey.

dunce *n* a person who is stupid or slow to learn.

dunderhead *n* a slow-witted person.

dune *n* a mound or ridge of drifted sand.

dung *n* the faeces from large animals.

dungarees *pl n* trousers with a bib attached.

dungeon *n* a prison cell, often underground.

dunghill *n* a heap of dung.

dunk *vb* **1** to dip (a biscuit or piece of bread) in a drink or soup before eating it. **2** to put (something) in liquid: *dunk the garment in the dye for fifteen minutes.*

dunlin *n* a small sandpiper with a brown back.

dunnock *n* same as **hedge sparrow.**

duo *n, pl* **duos 1** two singers or musicians who sing or play music together as a pair. **2** *Informal* two people who have something in common or do something together: *when they're together they make an impressive duo.*

duodecimal *adj* relating to twelve or twelfths.

duodenum (dew-oh-**deen**-um) *n* the first part of the small intestine, just below the stomach. **duodenal** *adj*

duologue *or US sometimes* **duolog** *n* a part or all of a play in which the speaking roles are limited to two actors.

DUP (in Northern Ireland) Democratic Unionist Party.

dupe *vb* **duping, duped 1** to deceive or cheat: *you duped me into doing exactly what you wanted.* ~*n* **2** a person who is easily deceived.

duple *adj* **1** same as **double. 2** *Music* having two beats in a bar.

duplex *n* **1** *US & Canad* **a** an apartment on two floors. **b** a semidetached house. ~*adj* **2** having two parts.

duplicate *adj* **1** copied exactly from an original: *he had a duplicate key to the front door.* ~*n* **2** an exact copy. **3 in duplicate** in two exact copies: *submit the draft in duplicate, please.* ~*vb* **-cating, -cated 4** to

THESAURUS

dumb 1. at a loss for words, inarticulate, mum, mute, silent, soundless, speechless, tongue-tied, voiceless, wordless **2.** *informal* asinine, braindead (*informal*), dense, dim-witted (*informal*), dozy (*Brit. informal*), dull, foolish, obtuse, stupid, thick, unintelligent

dumbfounded, dumfounded amazed, astonished, astounded, at sea, bewildered, bowled over (*informal*), breathless, confounded, confused, dumb, flabbergasted (*informal*), flummoxed, gobsmacked (*Brit. slang*), knocked for six (*informal*), knocked sideways (*informal*), nonplussed, overcome, overwhelmed, speechless, staggered, startled, stunned, taken aback, thrown, thunderstruck

dummy *n.* **1.** figure, form, lay figure, manikin, mannequin, model **2.** copy, counterfeit, duplicate, imitation, sham, substitute **3.** *slang* berk (*Brit. slang*), blockhead, charlie (*Brit. informal*), coot, dickhead (*slang*), dimwit (*informal*), dipstick (*Brit. slang*), divvy (*Brit. slang*), dolt, dork (*slang*), dullard, dunce, dweeb (*U.S. slang*), fool, geek (*slang*), gonzo (*slang*), jerk (*slang, chiefly U.S. & Canad.*), lamebrain (*informal*), nerd *or* nurd (*slang*), nitwit (*informal*), numskull *or* numbskull, oaf, pillock (*Brit. slang*), plank (*Brit. slang*), plonker (*slang*), prat (*slang*), prick (*derogatory slang*), schmuck (*U.S. slang*), simpleton, wally (*slang*) ~*adj.* **4.** artificial, bogus, fake, false, imitation, mock, phoney *or* phony, practice (*informal*), sham, simulated, trial

dump *vb.* **1.** deposit, drop, fling down, let fall, throw down **2.** discharge, dispose of, ditch (*slang*), empty out, get rid of, jettison, scrap, throw away *or* out, tip, unload ~*n.* **3.** coup (*Scot.*), junkyard, refuse heap, rubbish heap, rubbish tip, tip **4.** *informal* hole (*informal*), hovel, joint (*slang*), mess, pigsty, shack, shanty, slum

dumps blues, dejection, depression, despondency, dolour, gloom, gloominess, low spirits, melancholy, mopes, sadness, the hump (*Brit. informal*), unhappiness, woe

dun *vb.* beset, importune, pester, plague, press, urge

dunce ass, blockhead, bonehead (*slang*), dimwit (*informal*), dolt, donkey, duffer (*informal*), dullard, dunderhead, goose (*informal*), halfwit, ignoramus, lamebrain (*informal*), loon (*informal*), moron, nincompoop, nitwit (*informal*), numskull *or* numbskull, oaf, simpleton, thickhead

dungeon cage, cell, donjon, lockup, oubliette, prison, vault

duplicate *adj.* **1.** corresponding, identical, matched, matching, twin, twofold ~*n.* **2.** carbon copy, clone, copy, double, facsimile, fax, likeness, lookalike, match, mate, photocopy, Photostat (*Trademark*), rep-

make an exact copy of. **5** to do again (something that has already been done). **duplication** *n* **duplicator** *n*

duplicity *n* deceitful behaviour: *he is a man of duplicity, who turns things to his advantage.*

durable *adj* strong and long-lasting: *the car's body was made of a light but durable plastic.* **durability** *n*

durable goods *pl n* goods that do not require frequent replacement. Also called: **durables**

duration *n* the length of time that something lasts.

durbar *n* (formerly) **a** the court of a native ruler or a governor in India. **b** a reception at such a court.

duress *n* physical or moral pressure used to force someone to do something: *confessions obtained under duress.*

during *prep* throughout or within the limit of (a period of time).

dusk *n* the time just before nightfall when it is almost dark.

dusky *adj* **duskier, duskiest 1** dark in colour: *her gold earings gleamed against her dusky cheeks.* **2** dim or shadowy: *the dusky room was crowded with absurd objects.* **duskily** *adv* **duskiness** *n*

dust *n* **1** small dry particles of earth, sand, or dirt. **2 bite the dust** to stop functioning: *my television has finally bitten the dust.* **3 shake the dust off one's feet** to depart angrily. **4 throw dust in someone's eyes** to confuse or mislead someone. *~vb* **5** to remove dust from (furniture) by wiping. **6** to sprinkle (something) with a powdery substance: *serve dusted with brown sugar and cinnamon.*

dustbin *n* a large container for household rubbish.

dust bowl *n* a dry area in which the surface soil is exposed to wind erosion.

dustcart *n* a lorry for collecting household rubbish.

dust cover *n* **1** same as **dustsheet. 2** same as **dust jacket.**

duster *n* a cloth used for dusting.

dust jacket *or* **cover** *n* a removable paper cover used to protect a book.

dustman *n, pl* **-men** *Brit* a man whose job is to collect household rubbish.

dustpan *n* a short-handled shovel into which dust is swept from floors.

dustsheet *n Brit* a large cloth cover used to protect furniture from dust.

dust-up *n Informal* a fight or argument.

dusty *adj* **dustier, dustiest 1** covered with dust. **2** (of a colour) tinged with grey.

Dutch *adj* **1** of the Netherlands. *~n* **2** the language of the Netherlands. *~pl n* **3 the Dutch** the people of the Netherlands. *~adv* **4 go Dutch** *Informal* to go on an outing where each person pays his or her own expenses.

Dutch auction *n* an auction in which the price is lowered by stages until a buyer is found.

Dutch barn *n Brit* a farm building with a steel frame and a curved roof.

Dutch courage *n* false courage gained from drinking alcohol.

Dutch elm disease *n* a fungal disease of elm trees.

Dutchman *or fem* **Dutchwoman** *n, pl* **-men** *or* **-women** a person from the Netherlands.

Dutch oven *n* **1** an iron or earthenware container with a lid, used for stews, etc. **2** a metal box, open in front, for cooking in front of an open fire.

Dutch treat *n Informal* an outing where each person pays his or her own expenses.

Dutch uncle *n Informal* a person who criticizes or scolds frankly and severely.

duteous *adj Formal or archaic* dutiful or obedient.

dutiable *adj* (of goods) requiring payment of duty.

dutiful *adj* doing what is expected: *she is a responsible and dutiful mother.* **dutifully** *adv*

duty *n, pl* **-ties 1** the work performed as part of one's job: *it is his duty to supervise the memorial services.* **2** a obligation to fulfil one's responsibilities: *it's my duty as a doctor to keep it confidential.* **3** a government tax on imports. **4 on** *or* **off duty** at (*or* not at) work.

duty-bound *adj* morally obliged to do something: *we are duty-bound to take whatever measures are necessary.*

duty-free *adj, adv* with exemption from customs or excise duties.

duty-free shop *n* a shop, esp. at an airport, that sells duty-free goods.

duvet (doo-vay) *n* same as **continental quilt.**

dwaal *n S African* a state of absent-mindedness; a daze.

dwarf *vb* **1** to cause (someone or something) to seem small by being much larger. *~adj* **2** (of an animal or plant) much below the average size for the species: *a dwarf evergreen shrub.* *~n, pl* **dwarfs** *or* **dwarves 3** a person who is smaller than average size. **4** (in folk-

THESAURUS

lica, reproduction, ringer (*slang*), twin, Xerox (*Trademark*) *~vb.* **3.** clone, copy, double, fax, photocopy, Photostat (*Trademark*), replicate, reproduce, Xerox (*Trademark*) **4.** echo, repeat

durability constancy, durableness, endurance, imperishability, lastingness, permanence, persistence

durable abiding, constant, dependable, enduring, fast, firm, fixed, hard-wearing, lasting, long-lasting, permanent, persistent, reliable, resistant, sound, stable, strong, sturdy, substantial, tough

duress coercion, compulsion, constraint, pressure, threat

dusk dark, evening, eventide, gloaming (*Scot. or poetic*), nightfall, sundown, sunset, twilight

dusky 1. dark, dark-complexioned, dark-hued, sable, swarthy **2.** cloudy, crepuscular, darkish, dim, gloomy, murky, obscure, overcast, shadowy, shady, twilight, twilit, veiled

dust *n.* **1.** dirt, earth, fine fragments, grime, grit, ground, particles, powder, powdery dirt, soil **2. bite the dust** *informal* die, drop dead, expire, fall in battle, pass away, perish **3. throw dust in the eyes of** con (*slang*), confuse, deceive, fool, have (someone) on, hoodwink, mislead, take in (*informal*) *~vb.* **4.** cover, dredge, powder, scatter, sift, spray, spread, sprinkle

dusty dirty, grubby, sooty, unclean, undusted, unswept

dutiful compliant, conscientious, deferential, devoted, docile, duteous (*archaic*), filial, obedient, punctilious, respectful, reverential, submissive

duty 1. assignment, business, calling, charge, engagement, function, mission, obligation, office, onus, province, responsibility, role, service, task, work **2.** customs, due, duty, excise, impost, levy, tariff, tax, toll **3. on duty** at work, busy, engaged **4. off duty** at leisure, free, off, off work, on holiday

dwarf *vb.* **1.** dim, diminish, dominate, minimize, overshadow, tower above *or* over *~adj.* **2.** baby, bonsai, diminutive, dwarfed, Lilliputian, miniature, petite, pocket, small, teensy-weensy, teeny-weeny, tiny, undersized *~n.* **3.** bantam, homunculus, hop-o'-my-thumb, Lilliputian, manikin, midget, pygmy *or* pigmy, Tom Thumb **4.** gnome, goblin

lore) a small ugly manlike creature, often possessing magical powers.

dwell *vb* **dwelling, dwelt** *or* **dwelled** *Formal, literary* to live as a permanent resident. **dweller** *n*

dwelling *n Formal, literary* a place of residence.

dwell on *or* **upon** *vb* to think, speak, or write at length about (something).

dwindle *vb* **-dling, -dled** to grow less in size, strength, or number.

Dy *Chem* dysprosium.

dye *n* **1** a colouring substance. **2** the colour produced by dyeing. *~vb* **dyeing, dyed 3** to colour (hair or fabric) by applying a dye. **dyer** *n*

dyed-in-the-wool *adj* having strong and unchanging attitudes or opinions: *he's a dyed-in-the-wool communist.*

dying *vb* **1** the present participle of **die**[1]. *~adj* **2** occurring at the moment of death: *in accordance with his dying wish.* **3** (of a person or animal) very ill and likely to die soon. **4** becoming less important or less current: *coal mining is a dying industry.*

dyke[1] *or esp US* **dike** *n* **1** a wall built to prevent flooding. **2** a ditch. **3** *Scot* a dry-stone wall.

dyke[2] *or* **dike** *n Slang* a lesbian.

dynamic *adj* **1** (of a person) full of energy, ambition, or new ideas. **2** relating to a force of society, history, or the mind that produces a change: *the government needs a more dynamic policy towards the poor.* **3** *Physics* relating to energy or forces that produce motion. **dynamically** *adv*

dynamics *n* **1** the branch of mechanics concerned with the forces that change or produce the motions of bodies. *~pl n* **2** those forces that produce change in any field or system. **3** *Music* the various degrees of loudness called for in a performance.

dynamism *n* great energy or enthusiasm.

dynamite *n* **1** an explosive made of nitroglycerine. **2** *Informal* a dangerous or exciting person or thing: *she's still dynamite.* *~vb* **-miting, -mited 3** to mine or blow (something) up with dynamite.

dynamo *n, pl* **-mos** a device for converting mechanical energy into electricity.

dynamoelectric *adj* of the conversion of mechanical energy into electricity or vice versa.

dynamometer (dine-a-**mom**-it-er) *n* an instrument for measuring mechanical power or force.

dynast *n* a hereditary ruler.

dynasty *n, pl* **-ties 1** a series of rulers of a country from the same family. **2** a period of time during which a country is ruled by the same family. **dynastic** *adj*

dysentery *n* infection of the intestine which causes severe diarrhoea.

dysfunction *n* **1** *Med* any disturbance or abnormality in the function of an organ or part. **2** (esp. of a family) failure to show the characteristics or fulfil the purposes accepted as normal or beneficial. **dysfunctional** *adj*

dyslexia *n* a developmental disorder that causes difficulty with reading. **dyslexic** *adj, n*

dysmenorrhoea *or esp US* **dysmenorrhea** *n* painful or difficult menstruation.

dyspepsia *n* indigestion. **dyspeptic** *adj, n*

dysprosium *n Chem* a metallic element of the lanthanide series. Symbol: Dy

dystrophy (**diss**-trof-fee) *n* See **muscular dystrophy.**

THESAURUS

dwell abide, establish oneself, hang out (*informal*), inhabit, live, lodge, quarter, remain, reside, rest, settle, sojourn, stay, stop

dwelling abode, domicile, dwelling house, establishment, habitation, home, house, lodging, pad (*slang*), quarters, residence

dwell on *or* **upon** be engrossed in, continue, elaborate, emphasize, expatiate, harp on, linger over, tarry over

dye 1. *n.* colorant, colour, colouring, pigment, stain, tinge, tint **2.** *vb.* colour, pigment, stain, tincture, tinge, tint

dyed-in-the-wool complete, confirmed, deep-dyed (*usually derogatory*), deep-rooted, die-hard, entrenched, established, inveterate, through-and-through

dying at death's door, ebbing, expiring, fading, failing, final, going, *in extremis*, moribund, mortal, passing, perishing, sinking

dynamic active, driving, electric, energetic, forceful, go-ahead, go-getting (*informal*), high-powered, lively, magnetic, powerful, vigorous, vital, zippy (*informal*)

dynasty ascendancy, dominion, empire, government, house, regime, rule, sovereignty, sway

E

e *Maths* a number used as the base of natural logarithms. Approximate value: 2.718 282...

E **1** *Music* the third note of the scale of C major. **2** East(ern). **3** English. **4** *Physics* **a** energy. **b** electromotive force. **5** the drug ecstasy.

E- *prefix* used with a number following it to indicate that something, such as a food additive, conforms to an EU standard.

each *adj* **1** every one of two or more people or things considered individually: *each year.* ~*pron* **2** every one of two or more people or things: *each had been given one room to design.* ~*adv* **3** for, to, or from each person or thing: *twenty pounds each.* **4 each other** (of two or more people) each one to or at the other or others; one another: *they stared at each other.*

➤ The expressions *each other* and *one another* are interchangeable.

eager *adj* very keen to have or do something. **eagerly** *adv* **eagerness** *n*

eagle *n* **1** a large bird of prey with broad wings and strong soaring flight. **2** *Golf* a score of two strokes under par for a hole.

eagle-eyed *adj* having very sharp eyesight.

eaglet *n* a young eagle.

ear[1] *n* **1** the part of the body with which a person or animal hears. **2** the external, visible part of the ear. **3** the ability to hear musical and other sounds and interpret them accurately: *a good ear for languages.* **4** willingness to listen: *they are always willing to lend an ear.* **5 be all ears** to be prepared to listen attentively to something. **6 fall on deaf ears** to be ignored: *his words fell on deaf ears.* **7 in one ear and out the other** heard but quickly forgotten or ignored. **8 out on one's ear** *Informal* dismissed suddenly and unpleasantly. **9 play by ear** to play without written music. **10 play it by ear** *Informal* to make up one's plan of action as one goes along. **11 turn a deaf ear to** to be deliberately unresponsive to: *many countries have turned a deaf ear to their cries for help.* **12 up to one's ears in** *Informal* deeply involved in.

ear[2] *n* the part of a cereal plant, such as wheat or barley, that contains the seeds.

earache *n* pain in the ear.

eardrum *n* the thin membrane separating the external ear from the middle ear.

earful *n Informal* a scolding or telling-off.

earl *n* (in Britain) a nobleman ranking below a marquess and above a viscount. **earldom** *n*

Earl Grey *n* a variety of China tea flavoured with oil of bergamot.

ear lobe *n* the soft hanging lowest part of the human ear.

early *adj, adv* **-lier, -liest 1** occurring or arriving before the correct or expected time. **2** in the first part of a period of time: *early April; early in the war.* **3** near the beginning of the development or history of something: *early Britain was very primitive; early models of this car rust easily.*

Early English *n* a style of architecture used in England in the 12th and 13th centuries, characterized by narrow pointed arches and ornamental intersecting stonework in windows.

earmark *vb* **1** to set (something) aside for a specific purpose. ~*n* **2** a feature that enables the nature of something to be identified: *it had all the earmarks of a disaster.*

earn *vb* **1** to gain or be paid (money) in return for work. **2** to acquire or deserve through one's behaviour or action: *you've earned a good night's sleep.* **3** to make (money) as interest or profit: *her savings earned 8% interest.* **earner** *n*

earnest[1] *adj* **1** serious and sincere, often excessively so. ~*n* **2 in earnest** with serious or sincere intentions. **earnestly** *adv* **earnestness** *n*

earnest[2] *n Old-fashioned* a part payment given in advance as a guarantee of the remainder, esp. to confirm a contract.

earnings *pl n* money earned.

earphone *n* a small device connected to a radio or tape recorder and worn over the ear, so that a person can listen to a broadcast or tape without anyone else hearing it.

ear-piercing *adj* extremely loud or shrill.

earplug *n* a piece of soft material placed in the ear to keep out noise or water.

earring *n* a piece of jewellery worn in or hanging from the ear lobe.

earshot *n* the range within which a sound can be heard: *out of earshot.*

ear-splitting *adj* extremely loud or shrill.

earth *n* **1** (*sometimes cap*) the planet that we live on, the third planet from the sun, the only one on which life is known to exist. **2** the part of the surface of this

THESAURUS

each **1.** *adj.* every **2.** *pron.* each and every one, each one, every one, one and all **3.** *adv.* apiece, for each, from each, individually, per capita, per head, per person, respectively, singly, to each

eager agog, anxious, ardent, avid, earnest, enthusiastic, fervent, fervid, greedy, hot, hungry, impatient, intent, keen, longing, raring, vehement, yearning, zealous

eagerness ardour, avidity, earnestness, enthusiasm, fervour, greediness, heartiness, hunger, impatience, impetuosity, intentness, keenness, longing, thirst, vehemence, yearning, zeal

ear **1.** appreciation, discrimination, musical perception, sensitivity, taste **2.** attention, consideration, hearing, heed, notice, regard **3. play it by ear** *informal* ad lib, extemporize, improvise, rise to the occasion, take it as it comes

early *adj./adv.* **1.** advanced, ahead of time, beforehand, forward, in advance, in good time, premature, prematurely, too soon, untimely **2.** primeval, primitive, primordial, undeveloped, young

earn **1.** bring in, collect, draw, gain, get, gross, make, net, obtain, procure, realize, reap, receive **2.** acquire, attain, be entitled to, be worthy of, deserve, merit, rate, warrant, win

earnest[1] **1.** *adj.* ardent, close, constant, determined, devoted, eager, enthusiastic, fervent, fervid, firm, fixed, grave, heartfelt, impassioned, intent, keen, passionate, purposeful, resolute, resolved, serious, sincere, solemn, stable, staid, steady, thoughtful, urgent, vehement, warm, zealous **2.** *n.* determination, reality, resolution, seriousness, sincerity, truth

earnest[2] *old-fashioned* assurance, deposit, down payment, foretaste, guarantee, pledge, promise, security, token

planet that is not water. **3** the soil in which plants grow. **4** the hole in which a fox lives. **5** a wire in a piece of electrical equipment through which electricity can escape into the ground if a fault develops. **6 come down to earth** to return to reality from a daydream or fantasy. **7 on earth** used for emphasis: *what on earth happened?* ~*vb* **8** to fit (a piece of electrical equipment) with an earth.

earthbound *adj* **1** unable to leave the surface of the earth. **2** lacking in imagination.

earthen *adj* made of earth or baked clay: *an earthen floor.*

earthenware *n* dishes and other objects made of baked clay.

earthly *adj* **-lier, -liest 1** of life on earth as opposed to any heavenly or spiritual state. **2** *Informal* conceivable or possible: *what earthly reason would they have for lying?*

earthquake *n* a series of vibrations at the earth's surface caused by movement of the earth's crust.

earth science *n* any science, such as geology, concerned with the structure, age, etc., of the earth.

earth-shattering *adj* very surprising or shocking: *an earth-shattering event.*

earthwards *adv* towards the earth.

earthwork *n* a large mound of earth built for defence.

earthworm *n* a common worm that burrows in the soil.

earthy *adj* **earthier, earthiest 1** open and direct in the treatment of sex, excretion, etc. **2** of or like earth: *earthy colours.* **earthiness** *n*

earwig *n* a thin brown insect with pincers at the tip of its abdomen.

ease *n* **1** lack of difficulty. **2** freedom from discomfort or worry. **3** rest, leisure, or relaxation. **4** freedom from poverty: *a life of leisure and ease.* **5 at ease a** *Mil* (of a soldier) standing in a relaxed position with the feet apart. **b** in a relaxed attitude or frame of mind. ~*vb* **easing, eased 6** to make or become less difficult or severe: *the pain gradually eased.* **7** to move into or out of a place or situation slowly and carefully. **8 ease off** *or* **up** to lessen or cause to lessen in severity, pressure, tension, or strain: *the rain eased off.*

easel *n* a frame on legs, used for supporting an artist's canvas, a display, or a blackboard.

easily *adv* **1** without difficulty. **2** without doubt; by far: *easily the most senior Chinese leader to visit the West.*

east *n* **1** one of the four cardinal points of the compass, at 90° clockwise from north. **2** the direction along a line of latitude towards the sunrise. **3 the east** any area lying in or towards the east. ~*adj* **4** situated in, moving towards, or facing the east. **5** (esp. of the wind) from the east. ~*adv* **6** in, to, or towards the east.

East *n* **1 the East a** the southern and eastern parts of Asia. **b** (esp. formerly) the countries in Eastern Europe and Asia which are or have been under Communist rule. ~*adj* **2** of or denoting the eastern part of a country or region.

eastbound *adj* going towards the east.

Easter *n* **1** *Christianity* a festival, in the spring, commemorating the Resurrection of Christ. ~*adj* **2** taking place at the time of the year when this festival is celebrated: *the Easter holidays.*

Easter egg *n* a chocolate egg given at Easter.

easterly *adj* **1** of or in the east. ~*adv, adj* **2** towards the east. **3** from the east: *an easterly breeze.*

eastern *adj* **1** situated in or towards the east. **2** facing or moving towards the east. **3** (*sometimes cap*) of or characteristic of the east or East. **easternmost** *adj*

Easterner *n* a person from the east of a country or region.

eastern hemisphere *n* the half of the globe that contains Europe, Asia, Africa, and Australia.

eastward *adj, adv also* **eastwards 1** towards the east. ~*n* **2** the eastward part or direction.

easy *adj* **easier, easiest 1** not difficult; simple: *the house is easy to keep clean.* **2** free from pain, care, or anxiety: *an easy life.* **3** tolerant and undemanding; easy-going. **4** defenceless or readily fooled: *easy prey.* **5** moderate and not involving any great effort: *an easy ride.* **6** *Informal* ready to fall in with any suggestion made: *he wanted to do something and I was easy about it.* **7** *Informal* pleasant and not involving any great effort to enjoy: *easy on the eye.* ~*adv* **8 go easy on a** to avoid using too much of: *he'd tried to go easy on the engines.* **b** to treat less severely than is deserved: *go easy on him, he's just a kid.* **9 take it easy**

THESAURUS

earnings emolument, gain, income, pay, proceeds, profits, receipts, remuneration, return, reward, salary, stipend, takings, wages

earth 1. globe, orb, planet, sphere, terrestrial sphere, world **2.** clay, clod, dirt, ground, land, loam, mould, sod, soil, topsoil, turf

earthenware ceramics, crockery, crocks, pots, pottery, terra cotta

earthly 1. base, carnal, fleshly, gross, human, low, material, materialistic, mortal, mundane, non-spiritual, physical, profane, secular, sensual, sordid, tellurian, temporal, terrestrial, vile, worldly **2.** *informal* conceivable, feasible, imaginable, likely, possible, practical

ease *n.* **1.** aplomb, composure, easiness, effortlessness, facility, flexibility, informality, liberty, naturalness, poise, readiness, simplicity, unaffectedness, unreservedness **2.** affluence, calmness, comfort, content, contentment, enjoyment, freedom, happiness, insouciance, leisure, nonchalance, peace, peace of mind, quiet, quietude, relaxation, relaxedness, repose, rest, restfulness, serenity, tranquillity ~*vb.* **3.** abate, aid, allay, alleviate, appease, assist, assuage, calm, comfort, expedite, facilitate, forward, further, lessen, lessen the labour of, lighten, make easier, mitigate, moderate, mollify, pacify, palliate, quiet, relax, relent, relieve, simplify, slacken, smooth, soothe, speed up, still, tranquillize **4.** edge, guide, inch, manoeuvre, move carefully, slide, slip, squeeze, steer

easily 1. comfortably, effortlessly, facilely, readily, simply, smoothly, with ease, without difficulty, without trouble **2.** absolutely, almost certainly, beyond question, by far, certainly, clearly, definitely, doubtlessly, far and away, indisputably, indubitably, plainly, probably, surely, undeniably, undoubtedly, unequivocally, unquestionably, well, without a doubt

easy 1. a piece of cake (*informal*), a pushover (*slang*), child's play (*informal*), clear, easy-peasy (*slang*), effortless, facile, light, no bother, not difficult, no trouble, painless, simple, smooth, straightforward, uncomplicated, undemanding **2.** calm, carefree, comfortable, contented, cushy (*informal*), easeful, leisurely, peaceful, pleasant, quiet, relaxed, satisfied, serene, tranquil, undisturbed, untroubled, unworried, well-to-do **3.** affable, casual, easy-going, flexible, friendly, gentle, graceful, gracious, indulgent, informal, laid-back (*informal*), lenient, liberal, light, mild, natural, open, permissive, pleasant, relaxed, smooth, tolerant, unaffected, unceremonious, unconstrained, undemanding, unforced, unoppressive, unpretentious **4.** accommodating, amenable, biddable, compliant, docile, gullible, manageable, pliant, soft, submissive, suggestible, sus-

to relax and avoid stress or undue hurry. **easiness** *n* ➤ *Easy* may be used as an adverb in set phrases like *take it easy.*

easy chair *n* a comfortable upholstered armchair.

easy-going *adj* relaxed in manner or attitude; very tolerant.

eat *vb* **eating, ate, eaten 1** to take (food) into the mouth and swallow it. **2** to have a meal: *sometimes we eat out of doors.* **3** *Informal* to make anxious or worried: *what's eating you?* **4 eat away, into** *or* **up** to destroy or use up partly or wholly: *inflation ate into the firm's profits.* ~See also **eat out, eat up. eater** *n*

eatable *adj* fit or suitable for eating.

eating *n* **1** food in relation to its quality or taste: *these add up to lots of vitamins and minerals, and good eating.* ~*adj* **2** suitable for eating uncooked: *eating apples.*

eat out *vb* to eat at a restaurant.

eat up *vb* **1** to eat or consume entirely: *eat up these potatoes.* **2** *Informal* to affect severely: *eaten up by jealousy.*

eau de Cologne (oh de kol-**lone**) *n* full form of **cologne.**

eau de vie (oh de **vee**) *n* brandy or a similar alcoholic drink.

eaves *pl n* the edge of a sloping roof that overhangs the walls.

eavesdrop *vb* **-dropping, -dropped** to listen secretly to a private conversation. **eavesdropper** *n*

ebb *vb* **1** (of the sea or the tide) to flow back from its highest point. **2** to fall away or decline: *her anger ebbed away.* ~*n* **3** the flowing back of the tide from high to low water. **4 at a low ebb** in a weak state: *her creativity was at a low ebb.*

ebony *n* **1** a very hard dark-coloured wood used to make furniture etc. ~*adj* **2** very deep black.

ebullient *adj* full of enthusiasm or excitement. **ebullience** *n*

EC European Community: a former name for the European Union.

eccentric *adj* **1** unconventional or odd. **2** (of circles) not having the same centre. ~*n* **3** a person who behaves unconventionally or oddly. **eccentrically** *adv*

eccentricity *n* **1** unconventional or odd behaviour. **2** (*pl* **-ties**) an unconventional or odd habit or act.

ecclesiastic *n* **1** a member of the clergy. ~*adj* **2** of or relating to the Christian Church or its clergy.

ecclesiastical *adj* of or relating to the Christian Church or its clergy.

ECG electrocardiogram.

echelon (**esh**-a-lon) *n* **1** a level of power or responsibility: *the upper echelons of society.* **2** *Mil* a formation in which units follow one another but are spaced out sideways to allow each a line of fire ahead.

echinoderm (ik-**kine**-oh-durm) *n* a sea creature with a five-part symmetrical body, such as a starfish or sea urchin.

echo *n, pl* **-oes 1 a** the reflection of sound by a solid object. **b** a sound reflected by a solid object. **2** a repetition or imitation of someone else's opinions. **3** something that brings back memories: *an echo of the past.* **4** the signal reflected back to a radar transmitter by an object. ~*vb* **-oing, -oed 5** (of a sound) to be reflected off an object in such a way that it can be heard again. **6** (of a place) to be filled with a sound and its echoes: *the church echoed with singing.* **7** (of people) to repeat or imitate (what someone else has said): *his conclusion echoed that of Jung.* **echoing** *adj*

echo chamber *n* a room with walls that reflect sound, used to create an echo effect in recording and broadcasting.

echolocation *n* the discovery of an object's position by measuring the time taken for an echo to return from it.

echo sounder *n* a navigation device that determines depth by measuring the time taken for a pulse of sound to reach the sea bed and for the echo to return.

éclair *n* a finger-shaped cake of choux pastry, filled with cream and coated with chocolate.

eclampsia *n Pathol* a serious condition that can develop towards the end of a pregnancy, causing high blood pressure, swelling, and convulsions.

eclectic *adj* **1** composed of elements selected from a wide range of styles, ideas, or sources: *the eclectic wine list includes bottles from all round the world.* **2** selecting elements from a wide range of styles, ideas, or sources: *an eclectic approach that takes the best from all schools of psychology.* ~*n* **3** a person who takes an eclectic approach. **eclecticism** *n*

eclipse *n* **1** the obscuring of one star or planet by another. A **solar eclipse** occurs when the moon passes

THESAURUS

ceptible, tractable, trusting, yielding **5.** comfortable, gentle, leisurely, light, mild, moderate, temperate, undemanding, unexacting, unhurried

easy-going amenable, calm, carefree, casual, complacent, easy, even-tempered, flexible, happy-go-lucky, indulgent, insouciant, laid-back (*informal*), lenient, liberal, mild, moderate, nonchalant, permissive, placid, relaxed, serene, tolerant, unconcerned, uncritical, undemanding, unhurried

eat 1. chew, consume, devour, gobble, ingest, munch, scoff (*slang*), swallow **2.** break bread, chow down (*slang*), dine, feed, have a meal, take food, take nourishment **3.** corrode, crumble, decay, dissolve, erode, rot, waste away, wear away

eavesdrop bug (*informal*), listen in, monitor, overhear, snoop (*informal*), spy, tap

ebb *vb.* **1.** abate, fall away, fall back, flow back, go out, recede, retire, retreat, sink, subside, wane, withdraw **2.** decay, decline, decrease, degenerate, deteriorate, diminish, drop, dwindle, fade away, fall away, flag, lessen, peter out, shrink, sink, slacken, weaken ~*n.* **3.** ebb tide, going out, low tide, low water, regression, retreat, subsidence, wane, waning, withdrawal

eccentric 1. *adj.* aberrant, abnormal, anomalous, bizarre, capricious, erratic, freakish, idiosyncratic, irregular, odd, oddball (*informal*), outlandish, outré, peculiar, queer (*informal*), quirky, rum (*Brit. slang*), singular, strange, uncommon, unconventional, weird, whimsical **2.** *n.* card (*informal*), case (*informal*), character (*informal*), crank (*informal*), freak (*informal*), kook (*U.S. & Canad. informal*), nonconformist, nut (*slang*), oddball (*informal*), oddity, screwball (*slang, chiefly U.S. & Canad.*), weirdo *or* weirdie (*informal*)

eccentricity 1. abnormality, bizarreness, capriciousness, freakishness, irregularity, nonconformity, oddity, oddness, outlandishness, peculiarity, queerness (*informal*), singularity, strangeness, unconventionality, waywardness, weirdness, whimsicality, whimsicalness **2.** aberration, anomaly, caprice, foible, idiosyncrasy, quirk

ecclesiastic 1. *n.* churchman, clergyman, cleric, divine, holy man, man of the cloth, minister, parson, pastor, priest **2.** *adj. Also* **ecclesiastical** church, churchly, clerical, divine, holy, pastoral, priestly, religious, spiritual

echo *n.* **1.** answer, repetition, reverberation, ringing **2.** copy, imitation, mirror image, parallel, reflection, reiteration, reproduction **3.** allusion, evocation, hint, intimation, memory, reminder, suggestion, trace ~*vb.*

between the sun and the earth; a **lunar eclipse** when the earth passes between the sun and the moon. **2** a loss of importance, power, or fame: *communism eventually went into eclipse.* ~*vb* **eclipsing, eclipsed 3** to overshadow or surpass. **4** (of a star or planet) to hide (another planet or star) from view.

ecliptic *n Astron* the great circle on the celestial sphere representing the apparent annual path of the sun relative to the stars.

eco- *combining form* denoting ecology or ecological: *ecotourism.*

ecological *adj* **1** of or relating to ecology. **2** tending or intended to benefit or protect the environment: *an ecological approach to agriculture.* **ecologically** *adv*

ecology *n* the study of the relationships between people, animals, and plants, and their environment. **ecologist** *n*

econ. economy.

economic *adj* **1** of or relating to an economy or economics. **2** *Brit* capable of being produced or operated for profit. **3** *Informal* inexpensive or cheap.

economical *adj* **1** not requiring a lot of money to use: *low fuel consumption makes this car very economical.* **2** (of a person) spending money carefully and sensibly. **3** using no more time, effort, or resources than is necessary. **economically** *adv*

economics *n* **1** the study of the production and consumption of goods and services and the commercial activities of a society. ~*pl n* **2** financial aspects: *the economics of health care.*

economist *n* a person who specializes in economics.

economize *or* **-mise** *vb* **-mizing, -mized** *or* **-mising, -mised** to reduce expense or waste: *people are being advised to economize on fuel use.*

economy *n, pl* **-mies 1** the system by which the production, distribution, and consumption of goods and services is organized in a country or community: *the rural economy.* **2** the ability of a country to generate wealth through business and industry: *unless the economy improves, more jobs will be lost.* **3** careful use of money or resources to save expense, time, or energy. **4** an instance of this: *we can make economies by reusing envelopes.* ~*adj* **5** denoting a class of air travel that is cheaper than first-class. **6** offering a larger quantity for a lower price: *an economy pack.*

ecosystem *n Ecology* the system of relationships between animals and plants and their environment.

ecru *adj* pale creamy-brown.

ecstasy *n, pl* **-sies 1** a state of extreme delight or joy. **2** *Slang* a strong drug that acts as a stimulant and can cause hallucinations. **ecstatic** *adj* **ecstatically** *adv*

ECT electroconvulsive therapy: the treatment of depression and some other mental disorders by passing a current of electricity through the brain, producing a convulsion.

ectoplasm *n* (in spiritualism) the substance that supposedly is emitted from the body of a medium during a trance.

ECU *n* European Currency Unit: a unit of currency based on the composite value of several different currencies in the European Union.

ecumenical *adj* **1** of or relating to the Christian Church throughout the world. **2** tending to promote unity among Christian churches.

ecumenicism *or* **ecumenism** *n* the aim of unity among Christian churches throughout the world.

eczema (**ek**-sim-a) *n Pathol* a condition in which the skin becomes inflamed and itchy.

ed. 1 edition. **2** editor.

Edam *n* a round yellow Dutch cheese with a red waxy covering.

eddy *n, pl* **-dies 1** a circular movement of air, water, or smoke. ~*vb* **-dies, -dying, -died 2** to move with a gentle circular motion; swirl gently.

edelweiss (**ade**-el-vice) *n* a small white alpine flower.

edema (id-**deem**-a) *n, pl* **-mata** same as **oedema.**

Eden *n* **1** Also called: **Garden of Eden** *Bible* the garden in which Adam and Eve were placed at the Creation. **2** a place of great delight or contentment.

edentate *n* **1** a mammal with few or no teeth, such as an armadillo or a sloth. ~*adj* **2** denoting such a mammal.

edge *n* **1** a border or line where something ends or begins: *the edge of the city.* **2** a line along which two faces or surfaces of a solid meet. **3** the sharp cutting side of a blade. **4** keenness, sharpness, or urgency: *there was a nervous edge to his voice.* **5 have the edge on** to have a slight advantage over. **6 on edge** nervous and irritable. **7 set someone's teeth on edge** to make someone acutely irritated. ~*vb* **edging, edged 8** to make, form, or be an edge or border for: *a pillow edged with lace.* **9** to move very gradually in a

THESAURUS

4. repeat, resound, reverberate, ring **5.** ape, copy, imitate, mirror, parallel, parrot, recall, reflect, reiterate, reproduce, resemble, second

eclipse *n.* **1.** darkening, dimming, extinction, obscuration, shading **2.** decline, diminution, failure, fall, loss ~*vb.* **3.** blot out, cloud, darken, dim, extinguish, obscure, overshadow, shroud, veil **4.** exceed, excel, outdo, outshine, surpass, transcend

economic 1. bread-and-butter (*informal*), budgetary, business, commercial, financial, fiscal, industrial, material, mercantile, monetary, money-making, pecuniary, productive, profitable, profit-making, remunerative, solvent, trade, viable **2.** *informal Also* **economical** cheap, fair, inexpensive, low, low-priced, modest, reasonable

economical 1. cost-effective, efficient, money-saving, sparing, time-saving, unwasteful, work-saving **2.** careful, economizing, frugal, prudent, saving, scrimping, sparing, thrifty **3.** *Also* **economic** cheap, fair, inexpensive, low, low-priced, modest, reasonable

economize be economical, be frugal, be sparing, cut back, husband, retrench, save, scrimp, tighten one's belt

economy frugality, husbandry, parsimony, providence, prudence, restraint, retrenchment, saving, sparingness, thrift, thriftiness

ecstasy bliss, delight, elation, enthusiasm, euphoria, exaltation, fervour, frenzy, joy, rapture, ravishment, rhapsody, seventh heaven, trance, transport

ecstatic blissful, cock-a-hoop, delirious, elated, enraptured, enthusiastic, entranced, euphoric, fervent, frenzied, in exaltation, in transports of delight, joyful, joyous, on cloud nine (*informal*), overjoyed, over the moon (*informal*), rapturous, rhapsodic, transported

eddy 1. *n.* counter-current, counterflow, swirl, undertow, vortex, whirlpool **2.** *vb.* swirl, whirl

edge *n.* **1.** border, bound, boundary, brim, brink, contour, flange, fringe, limit, line, lip, margin, outline, perimeter, periphery, rim, side, threshold, verge **2.** acuteness, animation, bite, effectiveness, force, incisiveness, interest, keenness, point, pungency, sharpness, sting, urgency, zest **3.** advantage, ascendancy, dominance, lead, superiority, upper hand **4. on edge** apprehensive, eager, edgy, excited, ill at ease, impatient, irritable, keyed up, nervous, on tenterhooks, tense, tetchy, twitchy (*informal*), uptight (*informal*),

particular direction: *I edged through to the front of the crowd.*

edgeways *or esp US & Canad* **edgewise** *adv* **1** with the edge forwards or uppermost. **2 get a word in edgeways** to interrupt a conversation in which someone else is talking continuously.

edging *n* anything placed along an edge for decoration.

edgy *adj* **edgier, edgiest** nervous, irritable, or anxious. **edginess** *n*

edible *adj* fit to be eaten; eatable. **edibility** *n*

edict (ee-dikt) *n* a decree or order given by any authority.

edifice (**ed**-if-iss) *n* **1** a large or impressive building. **2** an elaborate system of beliefs and institutions: *the crumbling edifice of Communist rule.*

edify (**ed**-if-fie) *vb* **-fies, -fying, -fied** to inform or instruct (someone) with a view to improving his or her morals or understanding. **edification** *n* **edifying** *adj*

edit *vb* **editing, edited 1** to prepare (text) for publication by checking and improving its accuracy or clarity. **2** to be in charge of (a newspaper or magazine). **3** to prepare (a film, tape, etc.) by rearranging or selecting material. **4 edit out** to remove (a section) from a text, film, etc.

edition *n* **1** a particular version of a book, newspaper, or magazine produced at one time: *the revised paperback edition.* **2** a single television or radio programme which forms part of a series: *tonight's edition of "Newsnight".*

editor *n* **1** a person who edits. **2** a person in overall charge of a newspaper or magazine. **3** a person in charge of one section of a newspaper or magazine: *the Political Editor.* **4** a person in overall control of a television or radio programme. **editorship** *n*

editorial *n* **1** an article in a newspaper expressing the opinion of the editor or publishers. *~adj* **2** of editing or editors: *an editorial meeting.* **3** relating to the contents and opinions of a magazine or newspaper: *the paper's editorial policy.* **editorially** *adv*

EDP electronic data processing.

EDT Eastern Daylight Time.

educate *vb* **-cating, -cated 1** to teach (someone) over a long period of time so that he or she acquires knowledge and understanding of a range of subjects. **2** to send (someone) to a particular educational establishment: *she was educated at Airdrie Academy.* **3** to teach (someone) about a particular matter: *a campaign to educate people to the dangers of smoking.* **educative** *adj*

educated *adj* **1** having an education, esp. a good one. **2** displaying culture, taste, and knowledge. **3 educated guess** a guess that is based on experience.

education *n* **1** the process of acquiring knowledge and understanding. **2** knowledge and understanding acquired through study and training: *education is the key to a good job.* **3** the process of teaching, esp. at a school, college, or university. **4** the theory of teaching and learning. **educational** *adj* **educationally** *adv* **educationalist** *or* **educationist** *n*

Edwardian *adj* of or in the reign of King Edward VII of Great Britain and Ireland (1901–10).

EEC European Economic Community: a former name for the European Union.

EEG electroencephalogram.

eel *n* a slimy snakelike fish.

e'er *adv Poetic* short for **ever.**

eerie *adj* **eerier, eeriest** strange and frightening. **eerily** *adv*

efface *vb* **-facing, -faced 1** to obliterate or make dim: *nothing effaced the memory.* **2** to rub out or erase. **3 efface oneself** to make oneself inconspicuous. **effacement** *n*

effect *n* **1** a change or state of affairs caused by something or someone: *the gales have had a serious effect on the crops.* **2** power to influence or produce a result: *the wine had little effect on him.* **3** the condition of being operative: *a new law has come into effect.* **4** the overall impression: *the whole effect is one of luxury.* **5** basic meaning or purpose: *words to that effect.* **6** an impression, usually a contrived one: *he paused for effect.* **7** a physical phenomenon: *the greenhouse effect.* **8 in effect** for all practical purposes: *in effect he has no choice.* **9 take effect** to begin to produce results. *~vb* **10** to cause (something) to take place: *a peace*

THESAURUS

wired (*slang*) *~vb.* **5.** bind, border, fringe, hem, rim, shape, trim **6.** creep, ease, inch, sidle, steal, work, worm

edgy anxious, ill at ease, irascible, irritable, keyed up, nervous, nervy (*Brit. informal*), on edge, restive, tense, tetchy, touchy, twitchy (*informal*), uptight (*informal*), wired (*slang*)

edible digestible, eatable, esculent, fit to eat, good, harmless, palatable, wholesome

edict act, canon, command, decree, demand, dictate, dictum, enactment, fiat, injunction, law, mandate, manifesto, order, ordinance, proclamation, pronouncement, regulation, ruling, statute

edifice building, construction, erection, habitation, house, pile, structure

edify educate, elevate, enlighten, guide, improve, inform, instruct, nurture, school, teach, uplift

edit 1. assemble, compose, put together, rearrange, reorder, select **2.** adapt, annotate, censor, check, condense, correct, emend, polish, rephrase, revise, rewrite

edition copy, impression, issue, number, printing, programme (*TV, Radio*), version, volume

educate civilize, coach, cultivate, develop, discipline, drill, edify, enlighten, exercise, foster, improve, indoctrinate, inform, instruct, mature, rear, school, teach, train, tutor

educated 1. coached, informed, instructed, nurtured, schooled, taught, tutored **2.** civilized, cultivated, cultured, enlightened, experienced, informed, knowledgeable, learned, lettered, literary, polished, refined, tasteful

education breeding, civilization, coaching, cultivation, culture, development, discipline, drilling, edification, enlightenment, erudition, improvement, indoctrination, instruction, knowledge, nurture, scholarship, schooling, teaching, training, tuition, tutoring

educational cultural, didactic, edifying, educative, enlightening, heuristic, improving, informative, instructive

educative didactic, edifying, educational, enlightening, heuristic, improving, informative, instructive

eerie awesome, creepy (*informal*), eldritch (*poetic*), fearful, frightening, ghostly, mysterious, scary (*informal*), spectral, spooky (*informal*), strange, uncanny, unearthly, uneasy, weird

efface 1. annihilate, blot out, cancel, cross out, delete, destroy, dim, eradicate, erase, excise, expunge, extirpate, obliterate, raze, rub out, wipe out **2.** *of oneself* be modest (bashful, diffident, retiring, timid, unassertive), humble, lower, make inconspicuous, withdraw

effect *n.* **1.** aftermath, conclusion, consequence, event, fruit, issue, outcome, result, upshot **2.** clout (*informal*), effectiveness, efficacy, efficiency, fact, force, influence, power, reality, strength, use, validity, vig-

treaty was effected.
➤ Note the difference between *effect* meaning "accomplish" and *affect* meaning "influence".
effective *adj* **1** producing a desired result: *an effective vaccine against HIV.* **2** officially coming into operation: *the new rates become effective at the end of May.* **3** impressive: *a highly effective speech.* **4** in reality, although not officially or in theory: *he is in effective control of the company.* **effectively** *adv* **effectiveness** *n*
effects *pl n* **1** personal belongings. **2** lighting, sounds, etc., to accompany a stage, film, or broadcast production.
effectual *adj* **1** producing the intended result. **2** (of a document etc.) having legal force. **effectually** *adv*
effeminate *adj* (of a man) displaying characteristics regarded as typical of a woman. **effeminacy** *n*
effervescent *adj* **1** (of a liquid) giving off bubbles of gas. **2** (of a person) lively and enthusiastic. **effervescence** *n*
effete **(if-feet)** *adj* weak, powerless, and decadent.
efficacious *adj* producing the intended result. **efficacy** *n*
efficient *adj* working or producing effectively without wasting effort, energy, or money. **efficiency** *n* **efficiently** *adv*
effigy **(ef-fij-ee)** *n, pl* **-gies** **1** a statue or carving of someone, often as a memorial: *a 14th-century wooden effigy of a knight.* **2** a crude representation of someone, used as a focus for contempt: *an effigy of the president was set on fire.*
efflorescence *n* **1** the blooming of flowers on a plant. **2** a brief period of high-quality artistic activity.
effluent *n* liquid discharged as waste, for instance from a factory or sewage works.
effluvium *n, pl* **-via** an unpleasant smell, such as the smell of decaying matter.
efflux *n* **1** the process of flowing out. **2** something that flows out.
effort *n* **1** physical or mental energy needed to do something. **2** a determined attempt to do something. **3** achievement or creation: *his earliest literary efforts.* **effortless** *adj* **effortlessly** *adv*
effrontery *n* insolence or boldness.
effusion *n* **1** an unrestrained verbal expression of emotions or ideas. **2** a sudden pouring out: *small effusions of blood.*
effusive *adj* enthusiastically showing pleasure, gratitude, or approval. **effusively** *adv* **effusiveness** *n*
EFL English as a Foreign Language.
EFTA European Free Trade Association.
EFTPOS electronic funds transfer at point of sale.
e.g. for example.
egalitarian *adj* **1** expressing or supporting the idea that all people should be equal. ~*n* **2** a person who believes that all people should be equal. **egalitarianism** *n*
egg *n* **1** the oval or round object laid by the females of

THESAURUS

our, weight **3.** action, enforcement, execution, force, implementation, operation **4.** drift, essence, impact, import, impression, meaning, purport, purpose, sense, significance, tenor **5. in effect** actually, effectively, essentially, for practical purposes, in actuality, in fact, in reality, in truth, really, to all intents and purposes, virtually **6. take effect** become operative, begin, come into force, produce results, work *~vb.* **7.** accomplish, achieve, actuate, bring about, carry out, cause, complete, consummate, create, execute, fulfil, give rise to, initiate, make, perform, produce
effective 1. able, active, adequate, capable, competent, effectual, efficacious, efficient, energetic, operative, productive, serviceable, useful **2.** active, actual, current, in effect, in execution, in force, in operation, operative, real **3.** cogent, compelling, convincing, emphatic, forceful, forcible, impressive, moving, persuasive, potent, powerful, striking, telling
effectiveness capability, clout *(informal)*, cogency, effect, efficacy, efficiency, force, influence, potency, power, strength, success, use, validity, vigour, weight
effects belongings, chattels, furniture, gear, goods, movables, paraphernalia, possessions, property, things, trappings
effeminacy delicacy, femininity, softness, tenderness, unmanliness, weakness, womanishness, womanliness
effeminate camp *(informal)*, delicate, feminine, sissy, soft, tender, unmanly, weak, wimpish *or* wimpy *(informal)*, womanish, womanlike, womanly
effervesce bubble, ferment, fizz, foam, froth, sparkle
effervescence 1. bubbling, ferment, fermentation, fizz, foam, foaming, froth, frothing, sparkle **2.** animation, buoyancy, ebullience, enthusiasm, excitedness, excitement, exhilaration, exuberance, gaiety, high spirits, liveliness, pizzazz *or* pizazz *(informal)*, vim *(slang)*, vitality, vivacity, zing *(informal)*
effervescent 1. bubbling, bubbly, carbonated, fermenting, fizzing, fizzy, foaming, foamy, frothing, frothy, sparkling **2.** animated, bubbly, buoyant, ebullient, enthusiastic, excited, exhilarated, exuberant, gay, in high spirits, irrepressible, lively, merry, vital, vivacious
effete burnt out, corrupt, debased, decadent, decayed, decrepit, degenerate, dissipated, drained, enervated, enfeebled, exhausted, feeble, ineffectual, overrefined, played out, spent, spoiled, used up, wasted, weak, worn out
efficacious active, adequate, capable, competent, effective, effectual, efficient, energetic, operative, potent, powerful, productive, serviceable, successful, useful
efficacy ability, capability, competence, effect, effectiveness, efficaciousness, efficiency, energy, force, influence, potency, power, strength, success, use, vigour, virtue, weight
efficiency ability, adeptness, capability, competence, economy, effectiveness, efficacy, power, productivity, proficiency, readiness, skilfulness, skill
efficient able, adept, businesslike, capable, competent, economic, effective, effectual, organized, powerful, productive, proficient, ready, skilful, well-organized, workmanlike
effigy dummy, figure, guy, icon, idol, image, likeness, picture, portrait, representation, statue
effluent discharge, effluvium, efflux, emanation, emission, exhalation, flow, issue, outflow, outpouring, pollutant, sewage, waste
effort 1. application, endeavour, energy, exertion, force, labour, pains, power, strain, stress, stretch, striving, struggle, toil, travail *(literary)*, trouble, work **2.** attempt, endeavour, essay, go, shot *(informal)*, stab *(informal)*, try **3.** accomplishment, achievement, act, creation, deed, feat, job, product, production
effortless easy, easy-peasy *(slang)*, facile, painless, simple, smooth, uncomplicated, undemanding, untroublesome
effusion 1. address, outpouring, speech, talk, utterance, writing **2.** discharge, effluence, efflux, emission, gush, issue, outflow, outpouring, shedding, stream
effusive demonstrative, ebullient, enthusiastic, ex-

birds, reptiles, and other creatures, containing a developing embryo. **2** a hen's egg used for food. **3** a type of cell produced in the body of a female animal which can develop into a baby if fertilized by a male reproductive cell. **4** **have egg on one's face** *Informal* to have been made to look ridiculous. **5** **put all one's eggs in one basket** to rely entirely on one action or decision, with no alternative in case of failure.

egg cup *n* a small cup for holding a boiled egg.

egghead *n Informal* an intellectual person.

eggnog *n* a drink made of raw eggs, milk, sugar, spice, and brandy or rum.

egg on *vb* to encourage (someone) to do something foolish or daring.

eggplant *n US, Canad, & Austral* same as **aubergine.**

eggshell *n* **1** the hard porous outer layer of a bird's egg. *~adj* **2** (of paint) having a very slight sheen.

ego *n, pl* **egos** **1** the part of a person's self that is able to recognize that person as being distinct from other people and things. **2** a person's opinion of his or her own worth: *men with fragile egos.*

egocentric *adj* thinking only of one's own interests and feelings. **egocentricity** *n*

egomania *n* an obsessive concern with fulfilling one's own needs and desires, regardless of the effect on other people. **egomaniac** *n*

egotism *or* **egoism** *n* concern only for one's own interests and feelings. **egotist** *or* **egoist** *n* **egotistical, egoistical,** *or* **egotistic, egoistic** *adj*

ego trip *n Informal* something that a person does in order to boost his or her self-image.

egregious (ig-**greej**-uss) *adj* shockingly bad: *egregious government waste.*

egress (**ee**-gress) *n Formal* **1** the act of going out. **2** a way out or exit.

egret (**ee**-grit) *n* a wading bird like a heron, with long white feathery plumes.

Egyptian *adj* **1** of Egypt. **2** of the ancient Egyptians. *~n* **3** a person from Egypt. **4** a member of an ancient people who established an advanced civilization in Egypt. **5** the language of the ancient Egyptians.

Egyptology *n* the study of the culture of ancient Egypt. **Egyptologist** *n*

eh *interj* an exclamation used to ask for repetition or confirmation.

eider *or* **eider duck** *n* a large sea duck of the N hemisphere.

eiderdown *n* a thick warm cover for a bed, filled with soft feathers, originally the breast feathers of the female eider duck.

Eid-ul-Adha (**eed**-ool-**ah**-da) *n* an annual Muslim festival, marking the end of the pilgrimage to Mecca.

Eid-ul-Fitr (**eed**-ool-**feet**-er) *n* an annual Muslim festival, marking the end of Ramadan.

eight *n* **1** the cardinal number that is the sum of one and seven. **2** a numeral, 8 or VIII, representing this number. **3** something representing or consisting of eight units. **4** *Rowing* **a** a light narrow boat rowed by eight people. **b** the crew of such a boat. *~adj* **5** amounting to eight: *eight apples.* **eighth** *adj, n*

eighteen *n* **1** the cardinal number that is the sum of ten and eight. **2** a numeral, 18 or XVIII, representing this number. **3** something representing or consisting of 18 units. *~adj* **4** amounting to eighteen: *eighteen months.* **eighteenth** *adj, n*

eightfold *adj* **1** having eight times as many or as much. **2** composed of eight parts. *~adv* **3** by eight times as many or as much.

eightsome reel *n* a lively Scottish country dance for eight people.

eighty *n, pl* **eighties** **1** the cardinal number that is the product of ten and eight. **2** a numeral, 80 or LXXX, representing this number. **3** something representing or consisting of 80 units. *~adj* **4** amounting to eighty: *eighty miles.* **eightieth** *adj, n*

eina (**ay**-na) *interj S African* an exclamation of pain.

einsteinium *n Chem* a radioactive metallic element artificially produced from plutonium. Symbol: Es

Eire *n* Ireland or the Republic or Ireland.

EIS Educational Institute of Scotland.

eisteddfod (ice-**sted**-fod) *n* a Welsh festival with competitions in music, poetry, drama, and art.

either *adj, pron* **1** one or the other (of two): *we were offered either fish or beef.* **2** both one and the other: *we sat at either end of a long settee.* *~conj* **3** used preceding two or more possibilities joined by *or*: *it must be stored either in the fridge or in a cool place.* *~adv* **4** likewise: *I don't eat meat and my husband doesn't either.* **5** used to qualify or modify a previous statement: *he wasn't exactly ugly, he wasn't an oil painting either.*

➤ When *either* is followed by a plural noun, it is acceptable to make the verb plural too: *Either of these books are useful.*

ejaculate *vb* **-lating, -lated** **1** to discharge semen from the penis while having an orgasm. **2** *Literary* to say or shout suddenly. **ejaculation** *n* **ejaculatory** *adj*

eject *vb* **1** to push or send out forcefully. **2** to compel (someone) to leave a place or position. **3** to leave an aircraft rapidly in mid-flight, using an ejector seat. **ejection** *n* **ejector** *n*

THESAURUS

pansive, extravagant, exuberant, free-flowing, fulsome, gushing, lavish, overflowing, profuse, talkative, unreserved, unrestrained, wordy

egg on encourage, exhort, goad, incite, prod, prompt, push, spur, urge

egocentric egoistic, egoistical, egotistic, egotistical, self-centred, selfish

egoism egocentricity, egomania, egotism, narcissism, self-absorption, self-centredness, self-importance, self-interest, selfishness, self-love, self-regard, self-seeking

egoist egomaniac, egotist, narcissist, self-seeker

egoistic, egoistical egocentric, egomaniacal, egotistic, egotistical, full of oneself, narcissistic, self-absorbed, self-centred, self-important, self-seeking

egotism conceitedness, egocentricity, egoism, egomania, narcissism, self-admiration, self-centredness, self-conceit, self-esteem, self-importance, self-love, self-praise, superiority, vainglory, vanity

egotist bighead (*informal*), boaster, braggart, egoist, egomaniac, self-admirer, swaggerer

egotistic, egotistical boasting, bragging, conceited, egocentric, egoistic, egoistical, egomaniacal, full of oneself, narcissistic, opinionated, self-admiring, self-centred, self-important, superior, vain, vainglorious

egress departure, emergence, escape, exit, exodus, issue, outlet, passage out, vent, way out, withdrawal

eject **1.** cast out, discharge, disgorge, emit, expel, spew, spout, throw out, vomit **2.** banish, boot out (*informal*), deport, discharge, dislodge, dismiss, dispossess, drive out, evacuate, evict, exile, expel, fire (*informal*), get rid of, kick out (*informal*), oust, relegate, remove, sack (*informal*), show one the door, throw out, throw out on one's ear (*informal*), turn out

ejection **1.** casting out, disgorgement, expulsion, spouting, throwing out **2.** banishment, deportation, discharge, dislodgement, dismissal, dispossession,

ejector seat *or* **ejection seat** *n* a seat in a military aircraft that throws the pilot out in an emergency.

eke out *vb* **eking, eked 1** to make (a supply) last for a long time by using as little as possible. **2** to manage to sustain (a living) despite having barely enough food or money.

elaborate *adj* **1** very complex because of having many different parts: *elaborate equipment.* **2** having a very complicated design: *elaborate embroidery.* ~*vb* **-rating, -rated 3 elaborate on** to describe in more detail: *he did not elaborate on his plans.* **4** to develop (a plan or theory) in detail. **elaborately** *adv* **elaboration** *n*

élan (ale-**an**) *n* style and liveliness.

eland (**eel**-and) *n* a large spiral-horned antelope of southern Africa.

elapse *vb* **elapsing, elapsed** (of time) to pass by.

elastane *n* a synthetic fibre that is able to return to its original shape after being stretched.

elastic *adj* **1** capable of returning to its original shape after stretching, compression, or other distortion. **2** capable of being adapted to meet the demands of a particular situation: *an elastic interpretation of the law.* **3** made of elastic. ~*n* **4** tape, cord, or fabric containing flexible rubber. **elastically** *adv* **elasticated** *adj* **elasticity** *n*

elastic band *n* a rubber band.

elated *adj* extremely happy and excited. **elatedly** *adv*

elation *n* a feeling of great happiness and excitement.

elbow *n* **1** the joint between the upper arm and the forearm. **2** the part of a garment that covers the elbow. ~*vb* **3** to push with one's elbow or elbows: *she elbowed him aside; he elbowed his way to the bar.*

elbow grease *n Facetious* vigorous physical labour, esp. hard rubbing.

elbow room *n* sufficient scope to move or to function.

elder[1] *adj* **1** (of one of two people) born earlier. ~*n* **2** an older person: *have some respect for your elders.* **3** a senior member of a tribe, who has authority. **4** (in certain Protestant Churches) a member of the church who has certain administrative, teaching, or preaching powers.

elder[2] *n* a shrub or small tree with clusters of small white flowers and dark purple berries.

➤ *Elder* (*eldest*) is used for age comparison in families, *older* for other age comparisons.

elderberry *n, pl* **-ries 1** the fruit of the elder. **2** same as **elder**[2].

elderly *adj* **1** rather old. ~*pl n* **2 the elderly** old people.

elder statesman *n* a respected influential older person, esp. a politician.

eldest *adj* (of a person, esp. a child) oldest.

El Dorado (el dor-**rah**-doe) *n* **1** a fabled city in South America, supposedly rich in treasure. **2** Also: **eldorado** any place of great riches or fabulous opportunity.

eldritch *adj Poetic, Scot* unearthly or weird.

elect *vb* **1** to choose (someone) to fill a position by voting for him or her: *she was elected President in 1990.* **2** to choose or decide: *those who elected to stay.* ~*adj* **3** voted into office but not yet having taken over from the current office-bearer: *the President elect.* ~*pl n* **4 the elect** any group of people specially chosen for some privilege. **electable** *adj*

election *n* **1 a** a process whereby people vote for a person or party to fill a position: *the Tory Party leadership election.* **b** short for **general election. 2** the gaining of political power or taking up of a position in an organization as a result of being voted for: *the election of a Labour government in 1945.*

electioneering *n* the act of taking an active part in a political campaign, for example by canvassing.

elective *adj* **1** of or based on selection by vote: *an elective office.* **2** not compulsory or necessary: *an elective hysterectomy.*

elector *n* **1** someone who is eligible to vote in an election. **2** (in the Holy Roman Empire) any of the German princes who were entitled to elect a new emperor: *the Elector of Hanover.*

electoral *adj* of or relating to elections: *the British electoral system.* **electorally** *adv*

electoral register *n* the official list of all the people in an area who are eligible to vote in elections.

electorate *n* **1** all the people in an area or country who have the right to vote in an election. **2** the rank or territory of an elector of the Holy Roman Empire.

electric *adj* **1** produced by, transmitting, or powered by electricity. **2** very tense or exciting: *the atmosphere was electric.* ~*n* **3 electrics** an electric circuit or electric appliances.

➤ Note that *electric* is an adjective. Avoid its use as a noun: *The electricity* (not *the electric*) *has failed.*

THESAURUS

evacuation, eviction, exile, expulsion, firing (*informal*), ouster (*Law*), removal, sacking (*informal*), the boot (*slang*), the sack (*informal*)

eke out be economical with, be frugal with, be sparing with, economize on, husband, stretch out

elaborate *adj.* **1.** careful, detailed, exact, intricate, laboured, minute, painstaking, perfected, precise, skilful, studied, thorough **2.** complex, complicated, decorated, detailed, extravagant, fancy, fussy, involved, ornamented, ornate, ostentatious, showy ~*vb.* **3.** add detail, amplify, complicate, decorate, develop, devise, embellish, enhance, enlarge, expand (upon), flesh out, garnish, improve, ornament, polish, produce, refine, work out

elapse glide by, go, go by, lapse, pass, pass by, roll by, roll on, slip away, slip by

elastic 1. ductile, flexible, plastic, pliable, pliant, resilient, rubbery, springy, stretchable, stretchy, supple, tensile, yielding **2.** accommodating, adaptable, adjustable, complaisant, compliant, flexible, supple, tolerant, variable, yielding

elated animated, blissful, cheered, cock-a-hoop, delighted, ecstatic, elevated, euphoric, excited, exhilarated, exultant, gleeful, in high spirits, joyful, joyous, jubilant, overjoyed, over the moon (*informal*), proud, puffed up, rapt, roused

elation bliss, delight, ecstasy, euphoria, exaltation, exhilaration, exultation, glee, high spirits, joy, joyfulness, joyousness, jubilation, rapture

elbow bump, crowd, hustle, jostle, knock, nudge, push, shoulder, shove

elbow room freedom, latitude, leeway, play, room, scope, space

elder *adj.* **1.** ancient, earlier born, first-born, older, senior ~*n.* **2.** older person, senior **3.** *Presbyterianism* church official, office bearer, presbyter

elect 1. *vb.* appoint, choose, decide upon, designate, determine, opt for, pick, pick out, prefer, select, settle on, vote **2.** *adj.* choice, chosen, elite, hand-picked, picked, preferred, select, selected

election appointment, choice, choosing, decision, determination, judgment, preference, selection, vote, voting

electrical *adj* of or relating to electricity. **electrically** *adv*

electrical engineering *n* the branch of engineering concerned with practical applications of electricity and electronics. **electrical engineer** *n*

electric blanket *n* a blanket fitted with an electric heating element, used to warm a bed.

electric chair *n* (in the US) a chair for executing criminals by passing a strong electric current through them.

electric eel *n* an eel-like South American freshwater fish, which can stun or kill its prey with a powerful electric shock.

electric field *n Physics* a region of space surrounding a charged particle within which another charged particle experiences a force.

electric guitar *n* an electrically amplified guitar.

electrician *n* a person trained to install and repair electrical equipment.

electricity *n* **1** a form of energy associated with stationary or moving electrons, ions, or other charged particles. **2** the supply of electricity to houses, factories, etc., for heating, lighting, etc.

electric shock *n* pain and muscular spasms caused by an electric current passing through the body.

electrify *vb* **-fies, -fying, -fied 1** to adapt or equip (a system or device) to work by electricity: *the railway line to London had been electrified.* **2** to provide (an area) with electricity. **3** to startle or excite intensely. **electrification** *n*

electrifying *adj* very exciting and surprising.

electro- *combining form* electric or electrically: *electroconvulsive.*

electrocardiograph *n* an instrument for making tracings (**electrocardiograms**) recording the electrical activity of the heart.

electrocute *vb* **-cuting, -cuted** to kill or injure by an electric shock. **electrocution** *n*

electrode *n* a small piece of metal used to take an electric current to or from a power source, piece of equipment, or living body.

electrodynamics *n* the branch of physics concerned with the interactions between electrical and mechanical forces.

electroencephalograph (ill-lek-tro-en-**sef**-a-loh-graf) *n* an instrument for making tracings (**electroencephalograms**) recording the electrical activity of the brain.

electrolysis (ill-lek-**troll**-iss-iss) *n* **1** the process of passing an electric current through a liquid in order to produce a chemical reaction in the liquid. **2** the destruction of living tissue, such as hair roots, by an electric current.

electrolyte *n* a solution or molten substance that conducts electricity. **electrolytic** *adj*

electromagnet *n* a magnet consisting of a coil of wire wound round an iron core through which a current is passed.

electromagnetic *adj* **1** of or operated by an electromagnet. **2** of or relating to electromagnetism. **electromagnetically** *adv*

electromagnetism *n* magnetism produced by an electric current.

electromotive *adj Physics* of or producing an electric current.

electromotive force *n Physics* **1** a source of energy that can cause current to flow in an electrical circuit. **2** the rate at which energy is drawn from such a source when a unit of current flows through the circuit, measured in volts.

electron *n Physics* an elementary particle in all atoms that has a negative electrical charge.

electronegative *adj Physics* **1** having a negative electric charge. **2** tending to gain or attract electrons.

electronic *adj* **1** (of a device, circuit, or system) containing transistors, silicon chips, etc., which control the current passing through it. **2** making use of electronic systems: *electronic surveillance devices.* **electronically** *adv*

electronic mail *n* the transmission of messages from one computer terminal to another.

electronic publishing *n* the publication of information on discs, magnetic tape, etc., so that it can be accessed by computer.

electronics *n* the technology concerned with the development, behaviour, and applications of devices and circuits, for example televisions and computers, which make use of electronic components such as transistors or silicon chips.

electron microscope *n* a powerful microscope that uses electrons, rather than light, to produce a magnified image.

electronvolt *n Physics* a unit of energy equal to the work done on an electron accelerated through a potential difference of 1 volt.

electroplate *vb* **-plating, -plated 1** to coat (an object) with metal by dipping it in a special liquid through which an electric current is passed. *~n* **2** electroplated articles collectively.

electropositive *adj Physics* **1** having a positive electric charge. **2** tending to release electrons.

electrostatics *n* the branch of physics concerned with static electricity. **electrostatic** *adj*

elegant *adj* **1** attractive and graceful or stylish. **2** cleverly simple and clear: *an elegant summary.* **elegance** *n* **elegantly** *adv*

elegiac *adj Literary* sad, mournful, or plaintive.

elegy (**el**-lij-ee) *n, pl* **-gies** a mournful poem or song, esp. a lament for the dead.

element *n* **1** one of the fundamental components making up a whole. **2** *Chem* any of the known substances that cannot be separated into simpler substances by chemical means. **3** a distinguishable section of a social group: *liberal elements in Polish society.* **4** a metal part in an electrical device, such as a kettle, that changes the electric current into heat. **5** one of the four substances (earth, air, water, and fire) formerly believed to make up the universe. **6 in one's element** in a situation in which one is happy and at

THESAURUS

elector chooser, constituent, selector, voter

electric *figurative* charged, dynamic, exciting, rousing, stimulating, stirring, tense, thrilling

electrify *figurative* amaze, animate, astonish, astound, excite, fire, galvanize, invigorate, jolt, rouse, shock, startle, stimulate, stir, take one's breath away, thrill

elegance, elegancy 1. beauty, courtliness, dignity, exquisiteness, gentility, grace, gracefulness, grandeur, luxury, polish, politeness, refinement, sumptuousness **2.** discernment, distinction, propriety, style, taste

elegant 1. à la mode, artistic, beautiful, chic, choice, comely, courtly, cultivated, delicate, exquisite, fashionable, fine, genteel, graceful, handsome, luxurious, modish, nice, polished, refined, stylish, sumptuous, tasteful **2.** appropriate, apt, clever, effective, ingenious, neat, simple

ease: *she was in her element behind the wheel.* **7 elements a** the basic principles of something. **b** weather conditions, esp. wind, rain, and cold: *only 200 braved the elements.*

elemental *adj* of or like basic and powerful natural forces or passions.

elementary *adj* **1** simple, basic, and straightforward: *elementary precautions.* **2** involving only the most basic principles of a subject: *elementary mathematics.*

elementary particle *n Physics* any of several entities, such as electrons, neutrons, or protons, that are less complex than atoms.

elementary school *n* **1** *Brit* same as **primary school. 2** *US & Canad* a state school for the first six to eight years of a child's education.

elephant *n* a very large four-legged animal that has a very long flexible nose called a trunk, large ears, and two ivory tusks, and lives in Africa or India.

elephantiasis (el-lee-fan-**tie**-a-siss) *n Pathol* a skin disease, caused by parasitic worms, in which the affected parts of the body become extremely enlarged.

elephantine *adj* like an elephant, esp. in being huge, clumsy, or ponderous.

elevate *vb* **-vating, -vated 1** to raise in rank or status: *she had elevated flirting to an art form.* **2** to lift to a higher place: *this action elevates the upper back.*

elevated *adj* **1** higher than normal: *elevated cholesterol levels.* **2** (of ideas or pursuits) on a high intellectual or moral level: *elevated discussions about postmodernism.* **3** (of land or part of a building) higher than the surrounding area.

elevation *n* **1** the act of elevating someone or something: *his elevation to the peerage.* **2** height above sea level. **3** a raised area. **4** a scale drawing of one side of a building.

elevator *n* **1** *US & Canad* a lift for carrying people. **2** a mechanical hoist.

eleven *n* **1** the cardinal number that is the sum of ten and one. **2** a numeral, 11 or XI, representing this number. **3** something representing or consisting of 11 units. **4** a team of 11 players in football, cricket, etc. *~adj* **5** amounting to eleven: *eleven years.* **eleventh** *adj, n*

eleven-plus *n* (in Britain, esp. formerly) an examination taken by children aged 10 or 11 that determines the type of secondary education they will be given.

elevenses *pl n Brit informal* a mid-morning snack.

eleventh hour *n* **1** the latest possible time. *~adj* **eleventh-hour 2** done at the latest possible time: *an eleventh-hour rescue.*

elf *n, pl* **elves** (in folklore) a small mischievous fairy.

elfin *adj* **1** small and delicate: *her elfin features.* **2** of or relating to elves.

elicit *vb* **1** to bring about (a response or reaction): *her remarks elicited a sharp retort.* **2** to draw out (information) from someone: *a phone call elicited the fact that she had just awakened.*

elide *vb* **eliding, elided** to omit (a syllable or vowel) from a spoken word.

eligible *adj* **1** meeting the requirements or qualifications needed: *eligible for unemployment benefit.* **2** *Old-fashioned* desirable as a spouse. **eligibility** *n*

eliminate *vb* **-nating, -nated 1** to get rid of (something or someone unwanted, unnecessary, or not meeting the requirements needed): *he can be eliminated from the list of suspects.* **2** to remove (a competitor or team) from a contest, esp. following a defeat: *United were eliminated in the third round.* **3** *Slang* to murder in cold blood: *Stalin had thousands of his former comrades eliminated.* **elimination** *n*

elision *n* omission of a syllable or vowel from a spoken word.

elite (ill-**eet**) *n* the most powerful, rich, or gifted members of a group or community.

elitism *n* **1** the belief that society should be governed by a small group of people who are superior to everyone else. **2** pride in being part of an elite. **elitist** *n, adj*

elixir (ill-**ix**-er) *n* **1** an imaginary substance that is supposed to be capable of prolonging life and changing base metals into gold. **2** a liquid medicine mixed with syrup.

Elizabethan *adj* **1** of or in the reign of Queen Elizabeth I of England (1558–1603). **2** a person who lived during the reign of Queen Elizabeth I.

elk *n* a very large deer of N Europe and Asia with broad flat antlers.

ellipse *n* an oval shape resembling a flattened circle.

ellipsis (ill-**lip**-siss) *n, pl* **-ses** (-seez) **1** the omission of a word or words from a sentence. **2** *Printing* three dots (...) indicating an omission.

ellipsoid *n Geom* a surface whose plane sections are ellipses or circles.

elliptical *or* **elliptic** *adj* **1** oval-shaped. **2** (of speech or writing) obscure or ambiguous.

elm *n* **1** a tall tree with broad leaves. **2** the hard heavy wood of this tree.

THESAURUS

elegy dirge, keen, lament, plaint (*archaic*), requiem, threnody

element 1. basis, component, constituent, essential factor, factor, feature, hint, ingredient, member, part, section, subdivision, trace, unit **2.** domain, environment, field, habitat, medium, milieu, sphere

elementary 1. clear, easy, facile, plain, rudimentary, simple, straightforward, uncomplicated **2.** basic, bog-standard (*informal*), elemental, fundamental, initial, introductory, original, primary, rudimentary

elements 1. basics, essentials, foundations, fundamentals, principles, rudiments **2.** atmospheric conditions, atmospheric forces, powers of nature, weather

elevate 1. advance, aggrandize, augment, boost, exalt, heighten, increase, intensify, magnify, prefer, promote, swell, upgrade **2.** heighten, hoist, lift, lift up, raise, uplift, upraise

elevated 1. greater, higher, upraised **2.** dignified, exalted, grand, high, high-flown, high-minded, inflated, lofty, noble, sublime

elevation 1. advancement, aggrandizement, exaltation, preferment, promotion, upgrading **2.** altitude, height **3.** eminence, height, hill, hillock, mountain, rise, rising ground

elicit bring about, bring forth, bring out, bring to light, call forth, cause, derive, draw out, evoke, evolve, exact, extort, extract, give rise to, obtain, wrest

eligible acceptable, appropriate, desirable, fit, preferable, proper, qualified, suitable, suited, worthy

eliminate 1. axe (*informal*), cut out, dispense with, dispose of, disregard, do away with, drop, eject, eradicate, exclude, expel, exterminate, get rid of, ignore, knock out, leave out, omit, put out, reject, remove, stamp out, take out, throw out **2.** *slang* annihilate, bump off (*slang*), kill, liquidate, murder, rub out (*U.S. slang*), slay, take out (*informal*), terminate

elite aristocracy, best, cream, *crème de la crème*, elect, flower, gentry, high society, nobility, pick, upper class

elocution articulation, declamation, delivery, diction, enunciation, oratory, pronunciation, public speaking,

elocution *n* the art of speaking clearly in public. **elocutionist** *n*

elongate (eel-long-gate) *vb* **-gating, -gated** to make or become longer. **elongation** *n*

elope *vb* **eloping, eloped** (of two people) to run away secretly to get married. **elopement** *n*

eloquence *n* the ability to speak or write in a skilful and convincing way.

eloquent *adj* **1** (of speech or writing) fluent and persuasive. **2** (of a person) able to speak in a fluent and persuasive manner. **3** visibly or vividly expressive: *he raised an eloquent eyebrow.* **eloquently** *adv*

else *adv* **1** in addition or more: *what else do you want to know?* **2** other or different: *it was unlike anything else that had happened.* **3 or else a** if not, then: *tell us soon or else we shall go mad.* **b** *Informal* or something terrible will result: used as a threat: *do it our way or else.*

elsewhere *adv* in or to another place.

ELT English Language Teaching.

elucidate *vb* **-dating, -dated** to make (something obscure or difficult) clear. **elucidation** *n*

elude *vb* **eluding, eluded 1** to avoid or escape from (someone or something). **2** to fail to be understood or remembered by: *the mysteries of commerce elude me.*

elusive *adj* **1** difficult to find or catch. **2** difficult to remember or describe. **elusiveness** *n*

elver *n* a young eel.

elves *n* the plural of **elf.**

Elysium (ill-liz-zee-um) *n* **1** *Greek myth* the dwelling place of the blessed after death. **2** a state or place of perfect bliss. **Elysian** *adj*

emaciated (im-**mace**-ee-ate-id) *adj* extremely thin through illness or lack of food. **emaciation** *n*

emanate (**em**-a-nate) *vb* **-nating, -nated** to come or seem to come from someone or something: *an aura of power emanated from him.* **emanation** *n*

emancipate *vb* **-pating, -pated** to free from social, political, or legal restrictions. **emancipation** *n*

emasculate *vb* **-lating, -lated** to deprive of power or strength. **emasculation** *n*

embalm *vb* to preserve (a corpse) by the use of chemicals and oils.

embankment *n* a man-made ridge of earth or stone that carries a road or railway or prevents a river or lake from overflowing.

embargo *n, pl* **-goes 1** an order by a government or international body prohibiting trade with a country: *the world trade embargo against Iraq.* ~*vb* **-going, -goed 2** to place an official prohibition on.

embark *vb* **1** to go on board (a ship or aircraft). **2 embark on** to begin (a new project or venture). **embarkation** *n*

embarrass *vb* **1** to make (someone) feel shy, ashamed, or guilty about something. **2** to cause political problems for (a government or party). **3** to cause to have financial difficulties. **embarrassed** *adj* **embarrassing** *adj* **embarrassingly** *adv* **embarrassment** *n*

embassy *n, pl* **-sies 1** the residence or place of business of an ambassador. **2** an ambassador and his or her assistants and staff.

embattled *adj* **1** (of a country) involved in fighting a war, esp. when surrounded by enemies. **2** facing many problems and difficulties: *the embattled Mayor.*

embed *vb* **-bedding, -bedded 1** to fix firmly in a surrounding solid mass: *the boy has shrapnel embedded in his spine.* **2** to fix (an attitude or idea) in a society or in someone's mind: *corruption was deeply embedded in the ruling party.*

embellish *vb* **1** to make (something) more attractive

THESAURUS

rhetoric, speech, speechmaking, utterance, voice production

elongate draw out, extend, lengthen, make longer, prolong, protract, stretch

elope abscond, bolt, decamp, disappear, escape, leave, run away, run off, slip away, steal away

eloquence expression, expressiveness, fluency, forcefulness, oratory, persuasiveness, rhetoric, way with words

eloquent 1. articulate, fluent, forceful, graceful, moving, persuasive, silver-tongued, stirring, well-expressed **2.** expressive, meaningful, pregnant, revealing, suggestive, telling, vivid

elsewhere abroad, absent, away, hence (*archaic*), in *or* to another place, not here, not present, somewhere else

elucidate annotate, clarify, clear up, explain, explicate, expound, gloss, illuminate, illustrate, interpret, make plain, shed *or* throw light upon, spell out, unfold

elucidation annotation, clarification, comment, commentary, explanation, explication, exposition, gloss, illumination, illustration, interpretation

elude 1. avoid, circumvent, dodge, duck (*informal*), escape, evade, flee, get away from, outrun, shirk, shun **2.** baffle, be beyond (someone), confound, escape, foil, frustrate, puzzle, stump, thwart

elusive 1. difficult to catch, shifty, slippery, tricky **2.** baffling, fleeting, indefinable, intangible, puzzling, subtle, transient, transitory

emaciated atrophied, attenuated, cadaverous, gaunt, haggard, lank, lean, meagre, pinched, scrawny, skeletal, thin, undernourished, wasted

emaciation atrophy, attenuation, gauntness, haggardness, leanness, meagreness, scrawniness, thinness, wasting away

emanate arise, come forth, derive, discharge, emerge, emit, exhale, flow, give off, give out, issue, originate, proceed, radiate, send forth, spring, stem

emanation arising, derivation, discharge, effluent, efflux, effusion, emergence, emission, exhalation, flow, origination, proceeding, radiation

emancipate deliver, discharge, enfranchise, free, liberate, manumit, release, set free, unbridle, unchain, unfetter, unshackle

emancipation deliverance, discharge, enfranchisement, freedom, liberation, liberty, manumission, release

embalm mummify, preserve

embargo 1. *n.* ban, bar, barrier, block, blockage, boycott, check, hindrance, impediment, interdict, interdiction, prohibition, proscription, restraint, restriction, stoppage **2.** *vb.* ban, bar, block, boycott, check, impede, interdict, prohibit, proscribe, restrict, stop

embark 1. board ship, go aboard, put on board, take on board, take ship **2.** *With* **on** *or* **upon** begin, broach, commence, engage, enter, initiate, launch, plunge into, set about, set out, start, take up, undertake

embarrass abash, chagrin, confuse, discomfit, discompose, disconcert, discountenance, distress, faze, fluster, mortify, shame, show up (*informal*)

embarrassing awkward, blush-making, compromising, cringe-making (*Brit. informal*), discomfiting, disconcerting, distressing, humiliating, mortifying, sensitive, shameful, shaming, touchy, tricky, uncomfortable

embarrassment awkwardness, bashfulness, chagrin, confusion, discomfiture, discomposure, distress,

by adding decorations. **2** to make (a story) more interesting by adding details which may not be true. **embellishment** *n*

ember *n* a smouldering piece of coal or wood remaining after a fire has died.

embezzle *vb* **-zling, -zled** to steal (money) that belongs to the company or organization that one works for. **embezzlement** *n* **embezzler** *n*

embittered *adj* feeling anger and despair as a result of misfortune: *embittered by poverty.* **embitterment** *n*

emblazon (im-**blaze**-on) *vb* **1** to decorate with a coat of arms, slogan, etc.: *a jacket emblazoned with his band's name.* **2** to proclaim or publicize: *I am not sure he would want his name emblazoned in my column.*

emblem *n* an object or design chosen to symbolize an organization or idea. **emblematic** *adj*

embody *vb* **bodies, -bodying, -bodied 1** to be an example of or express (an idea or other abstract concept). **2** to include as part of a whole: *the proposal has been embodied in a draft resolution.* **embodiment** *n*

embolden *vb* to make bold.

embolism *n Pathol* the blocking of a blood vessel by a blood clot, air bubble, etc.

embolus *n, pl* **-li** *Pathol* a blood clot, air bubble, or other stoppage that blocks a small blood vessel.

emboss *vb* to mould or carve a decoration on (a surface) so that it stands out from the surface.

embrace *vb* **-bracing, -braced 1** to clasp (someone) with one's arms as an expression of affection or a greeting. **2** to accept eagerly: *he has embraced the Islamic faith.* **3** to include or be made up of: *a church that embraces two cultures.* ~*n* **4** an act of embracing.

embrasure *n* **1** an opening for a door or window which is wider on the inside of the wall than on the outside. **2** an opening in a battlement or wall, for shooting through.

embrocation *n* a lotion rubbed into the skin to ease sore muscles.

embroider *vb* **1** to do decorative needlework on (a piece of cloth or a garment). **2** to add imaginary details to (a story). **embroiderer** *n*

embroidery *n* **1** decorative needlework, usually on cloth or canvas. **2** the act of adding imaginary details to a story.

embroil *vb* to involve (oneself or another person) in problems or difficulties. **embroilment** *n*

embryo (em-bree-oh) *n, pl* **-bryos 1** an unborn animal or human being in the early stages of development, in humans up to approximately the end of the second month of pregnancy. **2** something in an early stage of development: *the embryo of a serious comic novel.*

embryology *n* the scientific study of embryos.

embryonic *adj* **1** of or relating to an embryo. **2** in an early stage.

emend *vb* to make corrections or improvements to (a text). **emendation** *n*

emerald *n* **1** a green transparent variety of beryl highly valued as a gem. ~*adj* **2** bright green.

Emerald Isle *n Poetic* Ireland.

emerge *vb* **emerging, emerged 1** to come into view out of something: *two men emerged from the pub.* **2** to come out of a particular state of mind or way of existence: *she emerged from the trance.* **3** to come to the end of a particular event or situation: *no party emerged from the election with a clear majority.* **4** to become apparent, esp. as the result of a discussion or investigation: *it emerged that he had been drinking.* **5** to come into existence over a long period of time: *a new style of dance music emerged in the late 1980s.* **emergence** *n* **emergent** *adj*

emergency *n, pl* **-cies 1** an unforeseen or sudden occurrence, esp. of danger demanding immediate action. **2** *NZ* a reserve player in a sports team. **3 state of emergency** a time of crisis, declared by a government, during which normal laws and civil rights can be suspended. ~*adj* **4** for use in an emergency: *the emergency exit.* **5** made necessary because of an emergency: *emergency surgery.*

THESAURUS

humiliation, mortification, self-consciousness, shame, showing up (*informal*)

embellish adorn, beautify, bedeck, deck, decorate, dress up, elaborate, embroider, enhance, enrich, exaggerate, festoon, garnish, gild, grace, ornament, tart up (*slang*), varnish

embellishment adornment, decoration, elaboration, embroidery, enhancement, enrichment, exaggeration, gilding, ornament, ornamentation, trimming

embezzle appropriate, defalcate (*Law*), filch, have one's hand in the till (*informal*), misapply, misappropriate, misuse, peculate, pilfer, purloin, rip off (*slang*), steal

embezzlement appropriation, defalcation (*Law*), filching, fraud, larceny, misapplication, misappropriation, misuse, peculation, pilferage, pilfering, purloining, stealing, theft, thieving

emblazon **1.** adorn, blazon, colour, decorate, embellish, illuminate, ornament, paint **2.** extol, glorify, laud (*literary*), praise, proclaim, publicize, publish, trumpet

emblem badge, crest, device, figure, image, insignia, mark, representation, sign, symbol, token, type

embodiment **1.** bodying forth, epitome, example, exemplar, exemplification, expression, incarnation, incorporation, manifestation, personification, realization, reification, representation, symbol, type **2.** bringing together, codification, collection, combination, comprehension, concentration, consolidation, inclusion, incorporation, integration, organization, systematization

embolden animate, cheer, encourage, fire, hearten, inflame, inspirit, invigorate, nerve, reassure, rouse, stimulate, stir, strengthen, vitalize

embrace *vb.* **1.** clasp, cuddle, encircle, enfold, grasp, hold, hug, seize, squeeze, take *or* hold in one's arms **2.** accept, adopt, avail oneself of, espouse, grab, make use of, receive, seize, take up, welcome **3.** comprehend, comprise, contain, cover, deal with, embody, enclose, encompass, include, involve, provide for, subsume, take in, take into account ~*n.* **4.** canoodle (*slang*), clasp, clinch (*slang*), cuddle, hug, squeeze

embroil complicate, compromise, confound, confuse, disorder, disturb, encumber, enmesh, ensnare, entangle, implicate, incriminate, involve, mire, mix up, muddle, perplex, trouble

embryo beginning, germ, nucleus, root, rudiment

emend amend, correct, edit, improve, rectify, revise

emendation amendment, correction, editing, improvement, rectification, revision

emerge **1.** appear, arise, become visible, come forth, come into view, come out, come up, emanate, issue, proceed, rise, spring up, surface **2.** become apparent, become known, come out, come to light, crop up, develop, materialize, transpire, turn up

emergence advent, apparition, appearance, arrival, coming, dawn, development, disclosure, emanation, issue, materialization, rise

emeritus (im-**mer**-rit-uss) *adj* retired, but retaining one's title on an honorary basis: *a professor emeritus.*

emery *n* a hard greyish-black mineral used for smoothing and polishing.

emery board *n* a strip of cardboard coated with crushed emery, for filing one's fingernails.

emetic (im-**met**-ik) *n* **1** a substance that causes vomiting. *~adj* **2** causing vomiting.

EMF electromotive force.

emigrate *vb* **-grating, -grated** to leave one's native country to settle in another country. **emigrant** *n, adj* **emigration** *n*

émigré (**em**-mig-gray) *n* someone who has left his or her native country for political reasons.

eminence *n* **1** the state of being well-known and well-respected. **2** a piece of high ground.

Eminence *n* **Your** *or* **His Eminence** a title used to address or refer to a cardinal.

éminence grise (em-in-nonss **greez**) *n, pl* **éminences grises** a person who wields power and influence unofficially.

eminent *adj* well-known and well-respected.

eminently *adv* extremely: *eminently sensible.*

emir (em-**meer**) *n* an independent ruler in the Islamic world. **emirate** *n*

emissary *n, pl* **-saries** an agent sent on a mission by a government or head of state.

emission *n* **1** the act of giving out heat, light, a smell, etc. **2** energy or a substance given out by something: *exhaust emissions from motor vehicles.*

emit *vb* **emitting, emitted 1** to give or send forth (heat, light, a smell, etc.). **2** to produce (a sound).

Emmental (**em**-men-tahl) *n* a hard Swiss cheese with holes in it.

emollient *adj* **1** (of skin cream or lotion) having a softening effect. **2** helping to avoid confrontation; calming: *his emollient political style. ~n* **3** a cream or lotion that softens the skin.

emolument *n* fees or wages from employment.

emote *vb* **emoting, emoted** to display exaggerated emotion, as if acting.

emotion *n* **1** any strong feeling, such as joy or fear. **2** the part of a person's character based on feelings rather than thought: *the conflict between emotion and logic.*

emotional *adj* **1** of or relating to the emotions: *emotional abuse.* **2** influenced by feelings rather than rational thinking: *he was too emotional to be a good doctor.* **3** appealing to the emotions: *emotional appeals for public support.* **4** showing one's feelings openly, esp. when upset: *he became very emotional and burst into tears.* **emotionalism** *n* **emotionally** *adv*

emotive *adj* tending or designed to arouse emotion.

empathize *or* **-thise** *vb* **-thizing, -thized** *or* **-thising, -thised** to sense and understand someone else's feelings as if they were one's own.

empathy *n* the ability to sense and understand someone else's feelings as if they were one's own. **empathic** *adj*

emperor *n* a man who rules an empire.

emperor penguin *n* a very large Antarctic penguin with orange-yellow patches on its neck.

emphasis *n, pl* **-ses 1** special importance or significance given to something, such as an object or idea. **2** stress on a particular syllable, word, or phrase in speaking.

emphasize *or* **-sise** *vb* **-sizing, -sized** *or* **-sising, -sised** to give emphasis or prominence to.

emphatic *adj* **1** expressed, spoken, or done forcefully: *an emphatic denial of the allegations.* **2** forceful and positive: *he was emphatic about his desire for peace talks.* **emphatically** *adv*

emphysema (em-fiss-**see**-ma) *n Pathol* a condition in which the air sacs of the lungs are grossly enlarged, causing breathlessness.

empire *n* **1** a group of countries under the rule of a single person or sovereign state. **2** a large industrial

THESAURUS

emergency crisis, danger, difficulty, exigency, extremity, necessity, panic stations (*informal*), pinch, plight, predicament, quandary, scrape (*informal*), strait

emigrate migrate, move, move abroad, remove

emigration departure, exodus, migration, removal

eminence 1. celebrity, dignity, distinction, esteem, fame, greatness, illustriousness, importance, notability, note, pre-eminence, prestige, prominence, rank, renown, reputation, repute, superiority **2.** elevation, height, high ground, hill, hillock, knoll, rise, summit

eminent big-time (*informal*), celebrated, conspicuous, distinguished, elevated, esteemed, exalted, famous, grand, great, high, high-ranking, illustrious, important, notable, noted, noteworthy, outstanding, paramount, pre-eminent, prestigious, prominent, renowned, signal, superior, well-known

eminently conspicuously, exceedingly, exceptionally, extremely, greatly, highly, notably, outstandingly, prominently, remarkably, signally, strikingly, surpassingly, well

emission diffusion, discharge, ejaculation, ejection, emanation, exhalation, exudation, issue, radiation, shedding, transmission, utterance, venting

emit breathe forth, cast out, diffuse, discharge, eject, emanate, exhale, exude, give off, give out, give vent to, issue, radiate, send forth, send out, shed, throw out, transmit, utter, vent

emolument benefit, compensation, earnings, fee, gain, hire, pay, payment, profits, recompense, remuneration, return, reward, salary, stipend, wages

emotion agitation, ardour, excitement, feeling, fervour, passion, perturbation, sensation, sentiment, vehemence, warmth

emotional 1. demonstrative, excitable, feeling, hot-blooded, passionate, responsive, sensitive, sentimental, susceptible, temperamental, tender, warm **2.** affecting, emotive, exciting, heart-warming, moving, pathetic, poignant, sentimental, stirring, tear-jerking (*informal*), thrilling, touching **3.** ardent, enthusiastic, fervent, fervid, fiery, flaming, heated, impassioned, passionate, roused, stirred, zealous

emotive affecting, argumentative, controversial, delicate, emotional, exciting, heart-warming, moving, pathetic, poignant, sensitive, sentimental, stirring, tear-jerking (*informal*), thrilling, touching, touchy

emphasis accent, accentuation, attention, decidedness, force, importance, impressiveness, insistence, intensity, moment, positiveness, power, pre-eminence, priority, prominence, significance, strength, stress, underscoring, weight

emphasize accent, accentuate, dwell on, give priority to, highlight, insist on, lay stress on, play up, press home, put the accent on, stress, underline, underscore, weight

emphatic absolute, categorical, certain, decided, definite, direct, distinct, earnest, energetic, forceful, forcible, important, impressive, insistent, marked, momentous, positive, powerful, pronounced, resound-

organization that is controlled by one person: *the heiress to a jewellery empire.*

empire-builder *n Informal* a person who seeks extra power by increasing the number of his or her staff. **empire-building** *n, adj*

empirical *adj* derived from experiment, experience, and observation rather than from theory or logic: *there is no empirical data to support this claim.* **empirically** *adv*

empiricism *n Philosophy* the doctrine that all knowledge derives from experience. **empiricist** *n*

emplacement *n* a prepared position for an artillery gun.

employ *vb* **1** to hire (someone) to do work in return for money. **2** to keep busy or occupy: *she was busily employed cutting the grass.* **3** to use as a means: *you can employ various methods to cut your heating bills.* ~*n* **4 in the employ of** doing regular paid work for: *he is in the employ of The Sunday Times.* **employable** *adj*

employee *or US* **employe** *n* a person who is hired to work for someone in return for payment.

employer *n* a person or company that employs workers.

employment *n* **1** the act of employing or state of being employed. **2** a person's work or occupation. **3** the availability of jobs for the population of a town, country, etc.: *the party's commitment to full employment.*

emporium *n, pl* **-riums** *or* **-ria** *Old-fashioned* a large retail shop with a wide variety of merchandise.

empower *vb* to give (someone) the power or authority to do something.

empress *n* **1** a woman who rules an empire. **2** the wife or widow of an emperor.

empty *adj* **-tier, -tiest 1** containing nothing. **2** without inhabitants; unoccupied. **3** without purpose, substance, or value: *he contemplated yet another empty weekend.* **4** insincere or trivial: *empty words.* **5** *Informal* drained of energy or emotion. **6** *Maths, logic* (of a set or class) containing no members. ~*vb* **-ties, -tying, -tied 7** to make or become empty. **8** to remove from something: *they emptied out the remains of the tin of paint.* ~*n, pl* **-ties 9** an empty container, esp. a bottle. **emptiness** *n*

empty-handed *adj* having gained nothing: *the robbers ran off empty-handed.*

empty-headed *adj* silly or incapable of serious thought.

empyrean (em-pie-ree-an) *n Poetic* the sky or the heavens.

EMS European Monetary System: the system enabling EU members to coordinate their exchange rates by linking them to the ECU.

emu *n* a large Australian long-legged bird that cannot fly.

emulate *vb* **-lating, -lated** to imitate (someone) in an attempt to do as well as or better than him or her. **emulation** *n* **emulator** *n*

emulsifier *n* a substance that helps to combine two liquids, esp. a water-based liquid and an oil.

emulsify *vb* **-fies, -fying, -fied** to make or form into an emulsion.

emulsion *n* **1** a mixture of two liquids in which particles of one are suspended evenly throughout the other. **2** *Photog* a light-sensitive coating for paper or film. **3** a type of water-based paint.

enable *vb* **-abling, -abled 1** to provide (someone) with the means or opportunity to do something. **2** to make possible: *to enable the best possible chance of cure.*

enabling act *n* a legislative act giving certain powers to a person or organization.

enact *vb* **1** to establish by law: *plans to enact a bill of rights.* **2** to perform (a story or play) by acting. **enactment** *n*

enamel *n* **1** a coloured glassy coating on the surface of articles made of metal, glass, or pottery. **2** an enamel-like paint or varnish. **3** the hard white sub-

THESAURUS

ing, significant, striking, strong, telling, unequivocal, unmistakable, vigorous

empire commonwealth, domain, kingdom, realm

empirical, empiric experiential, experimental, first-hand, observed, practical, pragmatic

emplacement location, platform, position, site, situation, station

employ *vb.* **1.** commission, engage, enlist, hire, retain, take on **2.** engage, fill, keep busy, make use of, occupy, spend, take up, use up **3.** apply, bring to bear, exercise, exert, make use of, ply, put to use, use, utilize ~*n.* **4.** employment, engagement, hire, service

employee hand, job-holder, staff member, wage-earner, worker, workman

employer boss *(informal)*, business, company, establishment, firm, gaffer *(informal, chiefly Brit.)*, organization, outfit *(informal)*, owner, patron, proprietor

employment **1.** application, engagement, enlistment, exercise, exertion, hire, retaining, taking on, use, utilization **2.** avocation *(archaic)*, business, calling, craft, employ, job, line, métier, occupation, profession, pursuit, service, trade, vocation, work

emporium bazaar, market, mart, shop, store, warehouse

empower allow, authorize, commission, delegate, enable, entitle, license, permit, qualify, sanction, warrant

emptiness **1.** bareness, blankness, desertedness, desolation, destitution, vacancy, vacuum, void, waste **2.** aimlessness, banality, barrenness, frivolity, futility, hollowness, inanity, ineffectiveness, meaninglessness, purposelessness, senselessness, silliness, unreality, unsatisfactoriness, unsubstantiality, vainness, valuelessness, vanity, worthlessness **3.** cheapness, hollowness, idleness, insincerity, triviality, trivialness **4.** absentness, blankness, expressionlessness, unintelligence, vacancy, vacantness, vacuity, vacuousness

empty *adj.* **1.** bare, blank, clear, deserted, desolate, destitute, hollow, unfurnished, uninhabited, unoccupied, untenanted, vacant, void, waste **2.** aimless, banal, bootless, frivolous, fruitless, futile, hollow, inane, ineffective, meaningless, purposeless, senseless, silly, unreal, unsatisfactory, unsubstantial, vain, valueless, worthless **3.** cheap, hollow, idle, insincere, trivial ~*vb.* **4.** clear, consume, deplete, discharge, drain, dump, evacuate, exhaust, gut, pour out, unburden, unload, use up, vacate, void

empty-headed brainless, dizzy *(informal)*, featherbrained, flighty, frivolous, giddy, goofy *(informal)*, harebrained, inane, scatterbrained, silly, skittish, vacuous

enable allow, authorize, capacitate, commission, empower, entitle, facilitate, fit, license, permit, prepare, qualify, sanction, warrant

enact **1.** authorize, command, decree, establish, legislate, ordain, order, pass, proclaim, ratify, sanction **2.** act, act out, appear as, depict, perform, personate, play, play the part of, portray, represent

enactment **1.** authorization, command, commandment, decree, dictate, edict, law, legislation, order, or-

stance that covers teeth. ~*vb* **-elling, -elled** *or US* **-eling, -eled 4** to decorate or cover with enamel.

enamoured *or US* **enamored** *adj* **enamoured of a** in love with. **b** very fond of and impressed by: *he is not enamoured of Moscow.*

en bloc *adv* as a whole; all together.

enc. 1 enclosed. **2** enclosure.

encamp *vb Formal* to set up a camp. **encampment** *n*

encapsulate *vb* **-lating, -lated 1** to put in a concise form; summarize. **2** to enclose in, or as if in, a capsule. **encapsulation** *n*

encase *vb* **-casing, -cased** to enclose or cover completely: *her arms were encased in plaster.* **encasement** *n*

encephalitis (en-sef-a-**lite**-iss) *n* inflammation of the brain. **encephalitic** *adj*

encephalogram *n* an electroencephalogram.

enchant *vb* **1** to delight and fascinate. **2** to cast a spell on. **enchanted** *adj* **enchantment** *n* **enchanter** *n* **enchantress** *fem n*

enchilada (en-chill-**lah**-da) *n* a Mexican dish consisting of a tortilla filled with meat, served with chilli sauce.

encircle *vb* **-cling, -cled** to form a circle round. **encirclement** *n*

enclave *n* a part of a country entirely surrounded by foreign territory.

enclose *vb* **-closing, -closed 1** to surround completely: *the house enclosed a courtyard.* **2** to include along with something else: *he enclosed a letter with the parcel.*

enclosed *adj* kept separate from the normal everyday activities of the outside world: *an enclosed community of nuns.*

enclosure *n* **1** an area of land enclosed by a fence, wall, or hedge. **2** something, such as a cheque, enclosed with a letter.

encode *vb* **-coding, -coded** to convert (a message) into code.

encomium *n* a formal expression of praise.

encompass *vb* **1** to enclose within a circle; surround. **2** to include all of: *the programme encompasses the visual arts, music, literature, and drama.*

encore *interj* **1** again: used by an audience to demand a short extra performance. ~*n* **2** an extra song or piece performed at a concert in response to enthusiastic demand from the audience.

encounter *vb* **1** to meet (someone) unexpectedly. **2** to be faced with: *he had rarely encountered such suffering.* **3** to meet (an opponent or enemy) in a competition or battle. ~*n* **4** a casual or unexpected meeting. **5** a game or battle: *a fierce encounter between the army and armed rebels.*

encourage *vb* **-aging, -aged 1** to give (someone) the confidence to do something. **2** to stimulate (something or someone) by approval or help. **encouragement** *n* **encouraging** *adj*

encroach *vb* to intrude gradually on someone's rights or on a piece of land. **encroachment** *n*

encrust *vb* to cover (a surface) with a layer of something, such as jewels or ice. **encrustation** *n*

encumber *vb* **1** to hinder or impede: *neither was greatly encumbered with social engagements.* **2** to burden with a load or with debts.

encumbrance *n* something that impedes or is burdensome.

encyclical (en-**sik**-lik-kl) *n* a letter sent by the pope to all Roman Catholic bishops.

encyclopedia *or* **encyclopaedia** *n* a book or set of books, often in alphabetical order, containing facts

THESAURUS

dinance, proclamation, ratification, regulation, statute **2.** acting, depiction, performance, personation, play-acting, playing, portrayal, representation

enamoured bewitched, captivated, charmed, crazy about (*informal*), enchanted, enraptured, entranced, fascinated, fond, infatuated, in love, nuts on *or* about (*slang*), smitten, swept off one's feet, taken, wild about (*informal*)

encampment base, bivouac, camp, camping ground, campsite, quarters, tents

encapsulate, incapsulate abridge, compress, condense, digest, epitomize, précis, summarize, sum up

enchant beguile, bewitch, captivate, cast a spell on, charm, delight, enamour, enrapture, enthral, fascinate, hypnotize, mesmerize, ravish, spellbind

enchanter conjurer, magician, magus, necromancer, sorcerer, warlock, witch, wizard

enchantment 1. allure, allurement, beguilement, bliss, charm, delight, fascination, hypnotism, mesmerism, rapture, ravishment, transport **2.** charm, conjuration, incantation, magic, necromancy, sorcery, spell, witchcraft, wizardry

enchantress 1. conjurer, magician, necromancer, sorceress, witch **2.** charmer, *femme fatale*, seductress, siren, vamp (*informal*)

enclose, inclose 1. bound, circumscribe, cover, encase, encircle, encompass, environ, fence, hedge, hem in, pen, shut in, wall in, wrap **2.** include, insert, put in, send with

encompass 1. circle, circumscribe, encircle, enclose, envelop, environ, girdle, hem in, ring, surround **2.** admit, comprehend, comprise, contain, cover, embody, embrace, hold, include, incorporate, involve, subsume, take in

encounter *vb.* **1.** bump into (*informal*), chance upon, come upon, confront, experience, face, happen on *or* upon, meet, run across, run into (*informal*) **2.** attack, clash with, combat, come into conflict with, contend, cross swords with, do battle with, engage, fight, grapple with, strive, struggle ~*n.* **3.** brush, confrontation, meeting, rendezvous **4.** action, battle, clash, collision, combat, conflict, contest, dispute, engagement, fight, run-in (*informal*), set to (*informal*), skirmish

encourage 1. animate, buoy up, cheer, comfort, console, embolden, hearten, incite, inspire, inspirit, rally, reassure, rouse, stimulate **2.** abet, advance, advocate, aid, boost, egg on, favour, forward, foster, further, help, promote, prompt, spur, strengthen, succour, support, urge

encouragement advocacy, aid, boost, cheer, consolation, favour, help, incitement, inspiration, inspiritment, promotion, reassurance, stimulation, stimulus, succour, support, urging

encouraging bright, cheerful, cheering, comforting, good, heartening, hopeful, promising, reassuring, rosy, satisfactory, stimulating

encroach appropriate, arrogate, impinge, infringe, intrude, invade, make inroads, overstep, trespass, usurp

encroachment appropriation, arrogation, impingement, incursion, infringement, inroad, intrusion, invasion, trespass, usurpation, violation

encumber burden, clog, cramp, hamper, handicap, hinder, impede, incommode, inconvenience, make difficult, obstruct, oppress, overload, retard, saddle, slow down, trammel, weigh down

about many different subjects or about one particular subject.

encyclopedic *or* **encyclopaedic** *adj* (of knowledge or information) very full and thorough; comprehensive.

end *n* **1** one of the two extreme points of something such as a road. **2** the surface at one of the two extreme points of an object: *a pencil with a rubber at one end.* **3** the extreme extent or limit of something: *the end of the runway.* **4** the most distant place or time that can be imagined: *the ends of the earth.* **5** the act or an instance of stopping doing something or stopping something from continuing: *I want to put an end to all the gossip.* **6** the last part of something: *at the end of the story.* **7** a remnant or fragment: *cigarette ends.* **8** death or destruction. **9** the purpose of an action: *he will only use you to achieve his own ends.* **10** *Sport* either of the two defended areas of a playing field. **11 in the end** finally. **12 make ends meet** to have just enough money to meet one's needs. **13 no end** used for emphasis: *these moments give me no end of trouble.* **14 on end** *Informal* without pause or interruption: *for months on end.* **15 the end** *Slang* the worst, esp. beyond the limits of endurance. ~*vb* **16** to bring or come to a finish. **17 end it all** *Informal* to commit suicide. ~See also **end up**.

endanger *vb* to put in danger.

endangered *adj* (of a species of animal) in danger of becoming extinct.

endear *vb* to cause to be liked: *his wit endeared him to a great many people.* **endearing** *adj*

endearment *n* an affectionate word or phrase.

endeavour *or US* **endeavor** *Formal* ~*vb* **1** to try (to do something). ~*n* **2** an effort to do something.

endemic *adj* present within a localized area or only found in a particular group of people: *he found 100 species of plant endemic to that ridge.*

ending *n* **1** the last part or conclusion of something: *the film has a happy ending.* **2** the tip or end of something: *nerve endings.*

endive *n* a plant with crisp curly leaves, used in salads.

endless *adj* **1** having no end; eternal or infinite. **2** continuing too long or continually recurring: *an endless stream of visitors.* **endlessly** *adv*

endmost *adj* nearest the end.

endocrine *adj* of or denoting a gland that secretes hormones directly into the blood stream, or a hormone secreted by such a gland.

endogenous (en-**dodge**-in-uss) *adj Biol* developing or originating from within.

endometrium (end-oh-**meet**-tree-um) *n* the mucous membrane lining the womb. **endometrial** *adj*

endorphin *n* any of a group of chemicals found in the brain, which have an effect similar to morphine.

endorsation *n Canad* approval or support.

endorse *vb* **-dorsing, -dorsed 1** to give approval or support to. **2** to sign the back of (a cheque) to specify the payee. **3** *Chiefly Brit* to record a conviction on (a driving licence). **endorsement** *n*

endoskeleton *n Zool* an internal skeleton, such as the bony skeleton of vertebrates.

endothermic *adj* (of a chemical reaction) involving or requiring the absorption of heat.

endow *vb* **1** to provide with a source of permanent income, esp. by leaving money in a will. **2 endowed with** provided with or possessing (a quality or talent).

endowment *n* **1** the money given to an institution, such as a hospital. **2** a natural talent or quality.

endowment assurance *or* **insurance** *n* a kind of life insurance that pays a specified sum directly to the policyholder at a designated date or to his or her beneficiary should he or she die before this date.

THESAURUS

encumbrance burden, difficulty, drag, embarrassment, handicap, hindrance, impediment, inconvenience, liability, load, millstone, obstacle, obstruction

end *n.* **1.** bound, boundary, edge, extent, extreme, extremity, limit, point, terminus, tip **2.** attainment, cessation, close, closure, completion, conclusion, consequence, consummation, culmination, denouement, ending, expiration, expiry, finale, finish, issue, outcome, resolution, result, sequel, stop, termination, upshot, wind-up **3.** bit, butt, fragment, leftover, oddment, remainder, remnant, scrap, stub, tag end, tail end **4.** annihilation, death, demise, destruction, dissolution, doom, extermination, extinction, ruin, ruination **5.** aim, aspiration, design, drift, goal, intent, intention, object, objective, point, purpose, reason **6. the end** *slang* beyond endurance, insufferable, intolerable, the final blow, the last straw, the limit (*informal*), the worst, too much (*informal*), unbearable, unendurable ~*vb.* **7.** abolish, annihilate, axe (*informal*), bring to an end, cease, close, complete, conclude, culminate, destroy, dissolve, expire, exterminate, extinguish, finish, kill, put to death, resolve, ruin, stop, terminate, wind up

endanger compromise, hazard, imperil, jeopardize, put at risk, put in danger, risk, threaten

endear attach, attract, bind, captivate, charm, engage, win

endearing adorable, attractive, captivating, charming, cute, engaging, lovable, sweet, winning, winsome

endearment affectionate utterance, loving word, sweet nothing

endeavour 1. *vb.* aim, aspire, attempt, do one's best, do one's damnedest (*informal*), essay, give it one's all (*informal*), have a go (crack (*informal*), shot (*informal*), stab (*informal*)), knock oneself out (*informal*), labour, make an all-out effort (*informal*), make an effort, strive, struggle, take pains, try, undertake **2.** *n.* aim, attempt, crack (*informal*), effort, enterprise, essay, go (*informal*), shot (*informal*), stab (*informal*), trial, try, undertaking, venture

ending cessation, close, completion, conclusion, consummation, culmination, denouement, end, finale, finish, resolution, termination, wind-up

endless 1. boundless, ceaseless, constant, continual, continuous, eternal, everlasting, immortal, incessant, infinite, interminable, limitless, perpetual, unbounded, unbroken, undivided, undying, unending, uninterrupted, unlimited, whole **2.** interminable, monotonous, overlong

endorse 1. advocate, affirm, approve, authorize, back, champion, confirm, espouse, favour, prescribe, promote, ratify, recommend, sanction, subscribe to, support, sustain, vouch for, warrant **2.** countersign, sign, superscribe, undersign

endorsement 1. comment, countersignature, qualification, signature, superscription **2.** advocacy, affirmation, approbation, approval, authorization, backing, championship, confirmation, espousal, favour, fiat, O.K. *or* okay (*informal*), promotion, ratification, recommendation, sanction, seal of approval, subscription to, support, warrant

endow award, bequeath, bestow, confer, donate, enrich, favour, finance, fund, furnish, give, grant, invest, leave, make over, provide, purvey, settle on, supply, will

endowment 1. award, benefaction, bequest, bestowal, boon, donation, fund, gift, grant, hand-out, income, largess *or* largesse, legacy, presentation, prop-

endpaper *n* either of two leaves at the front and back of a book pasted to the inside of the cover.

end product *n* the final result of a process.

end up *vb* **1** to arrive at a place by a roundabout route or without intending to: *the van somehow ended up in Bordeaux.* **2** to arrive at a particular condition or situation without expecting to: *I thought I was going to hate it, but I ended up enjoying myself.*

endurance *n* the ability to withstand prolonged hardship.

endure *vb* **-during, -dured 1** to bear (hardship) patiently: *the children allegedly endured sexual abuse.* **2** to tolerate or put up with: *I cannot endure your disloyalty any longer.* **3** to last for a long time. **endurable** *adj*

enduring *adj* long-lasting.

endways *or esp US & Canad* **endwise** *adv* having the end forwards or upwards.

enema (**en**-im-a) *n Med* a quantity of fluid inserted into the rectum to empty the bowels, for example before an operation.

enemy *n, pl* **-mies 1** a person who is hostile or opposed to a person, group, or idea. **2** a hostile nation or people. **3** something that harms or opposes something: *oil is an enemy of the environment.* ~*adj* **4** of or belonging to an enemy: *enemy troops.*

energetic *adj* **1** having or showing energy and enthusiasm: *an energetic campaigner for democracy.* **2** involving a lot of movement and physical effort: *energetic exercise.* **energetically** *adv*

energize *or* **-ise** *vb* **-gizing, -gized** *or* **-gising, -gised** to stimulate or enliven.

energy *n, pl* **-gies 1** capacity for intense activity; vigour. **2** intensity or vitality of action or expression; forcefulness. **3** *Physics* the capacity to do work and overcome resistance. **4** a source of power, such as electricity.

enervate *vb* **-vating, -vated** to deprive of strength or vitality. **enervating** *adj* **enervation** *n*

enfant terrible (**on**-fon ter-**reeb**-la) *n, pl* **enfants terribles** a talented but unconventional or indiscreet person.

enfeeble *vb* **-bling, -bled** to make (someone or something) weak.

enfilade *Mil* ~*n* **1** a burst of gunfire sweeping from end to end along a line of troops. ~*vb* **-lading, -laded 2** to attack with an enfilade.

enfold *vb* **1** to cover (something) by, or as if by, wrapping something round it: *darkness enfolded the city.* **2** to embrace or hug.

enforce *vb* **-forcing, -forced 1** to ensure that (a law or decision) is obeyed. **2** to impose (obedience) by, or as if by, force. **enforceable** *adj* **enforcement** *n*

enfranchise *vb* **-chising, -chised** to grant (a person or group of people) the right to vote. **enfranchisement** *n*

Eng. 1 England. **2** English.

engage *vb* **-gaging, -gaged 1** Also: **be engaged** to take part or participate: *he engaged in criminal and illegal acts; they were engaged in espionage.* **2** to involve (a person or his or her attention) intensely: *there's nothing to engage the intellect in this film.* **3** to employ (someone) to do something. **4** to promise to do something. **5** *Mil* to begin a battle with. **6** to bring (part of a machine or other mechanism) into operation, esp. by causing components to interlock. **7 engage in conversation** to start a conversation with.

engaged *adj* **1** having made a promise to get married. **2** (of a telephone line or a toilet) already being used.

engagement *n* **1** a business or social appointment.

THESAURUS

erty, provision, revenue, stipend **2.** ability, aptitude, attribute, capability, capacity, faculty, flair, genius, gift, power, qualification, quality, talent

end up 1. arrive finally, come to a halt, fetch up (*informal*), finish up, stop, wind up **2.** become eventually, finish as, finish up, pan out (*informal*), turn out to be

endurable acceptable, bearable, sufferable, supportable, sustainable, tolerable

endurance bearing, fortitude, patience, perseverance, persistence, pertinacity, resignation, resolution, stamina, staying power, strength, submission, sufferance, tenacity, toleration

endure 1. bear, brave, cope with, experience, go through, stand, stick it out (*informal*), suffer, support, sustain, take it (*informal*), thole (*Scot.*), undergo, weather, withstand **2.** abide, allow, bear, brook, countenance, permit, put up with, stand, stick (*slang*), stomach, submit to, suffer, swallow, take patiently, tolerate **3.** abide, be durable, continue, hold, last, live, live on, persist, prevail, remain, stand, stay, survive, wear well

enduring abiding, continuing, durable, eternal, firm, immortal, immovable, imperishable, lasting, living, long-lasting, perennial, permanent, persistent, persisting, prevailing, remaining, steadfast, steady, surviving, unfaltering, unwavering

enemy adversary, antagonist, competitor, foe, opponent, rival, the opposition, the other side

energetic active, animated, brisk, dynamic, forceful, forcible, high-powered, indefatigable, lively, potent, powerful, spirited, strenuous, strong, tireless, vigorous

energy activity, animation, ardour, drive, efficiency, élan, exertion, fire, force, forcefulness, get-up-and-go (*informal*), go (*informal*), intensity, life, liveliness, pep, pluck, power, spirit, stamina, strength, strenuousness, verve, vigour, vim (*slang*), vitality, vivacity, zeal, zest, zip (*informal*)

enfold clasp, embrace, enclose, encompass, envelop, enwrap, fold, hold, hug, shroud, swathe, wrap, wrap up

enforce administer, apply, carry out, coerce, compel, constrain, exact, execute, implement, impose, insist on, oblige, prosecute, put in force, put into effect, reinforce, require, urge

enforcement 1. administration, application, carrying out, exaction, execution, implementation, imposition, prosecution, reinforcement **2.** coercion, compulsion, constraint, insistence, obligation, pressure, requirement

enfranchise give the vote to, grant suffrage to, grant the franchise to, grant voting rights to

enfranchisement giving the vote, granting suffrage *or* the franchise, granting voting rights

engage 1. embark on, enter into, join, partake, participate, practise, set about, take part, undertake **2.** absorb, busy, engross, grip, involve, occupy, preoccupy, tie up **3.** appoint, commission, employ, enlist, enrol, hire, retain, take on **4.** agree, bind, commit, contract, covenant, guarantee, obligate, oblige, pledge, promise, undertake, vouch, vow **5.** *Military* assail, attack, combat, come to close quarters with, encounter, fall on, fight with, give battle to, join battle with, meet, take on **6.** activate, apply, bring into operation, dovetail, energize, interact, interconnect, interlock, join, mesh, set going, switch on

engaged 1. affianced, betrothed (*archaic*), pledged, promised, spoken for **2.** absorbed, busy, committed,

2 the period when a couple has agreed to get married but the wedding has not yet taken place. **3** a limited period of employment, esp. in the performing arts. **4** a battle.

engagement ring *n* a ring worn by a woman engaged to be married.

engaging *adj* pleasant and charming. **engagingly** *adv*

engender *vb* to produce (a particular feeling, atmosphere, or situation).

engine *n* **1** any machine designed to convert energy into mechanical work, esp. one used to power a vehicle. **2** a railway locomotive.

engineer *n* **1** a person trained in any branch of engineering. **2** a person who repairs and maintains mechanical or electrical devices. **3** a soldier trained in engineering and construction work. **4** an officer responsible for a ship's engines. **5** *US & Canad* a train driver. ~*vb* **6** to cause or plan (an event or situation) in a clever or devious manner. **7** to design or construct as a professional engineer.

engineering *n* the profession of applying scientific principles to the design and construction of engines, cars, buildings, bridges, roads, and electrical machines.

English *adj* **1** of England or the English language. ~*n* **2** the official language of Britain, the US, most of the Commonwealth, and certain other countries. ~*pl n* **3** **the English** the people of England.

English breakfast *n* a breakfast including cooked food, such as bacon and eggs.

Englishman *or fem* **Englishwoman** *n, pl* **-men** *or* **-women** a person from England.

engorge *vb* **-gorging, -gorged** *Pathol* to clog or become clogged with blood. **engorgement** *n*

engrave *vb* **-graving, -graved 1** to carve or etch a design or inscription into (a surface). **2** to print (designs or characters) from a plate into which they have been cut or etched. **3** to fix deeply or permanently in the mind. **engraver** *n*

engraving *n* **1** a printing surface that has been engraved. **2** a print made from this.

engross (en-**groce**) *vb* to occupy the attention of (someone) completely. **engrossing** *adj*

engulf *vb* **1** to immerse, plunge, or swallow up: *engulfed by flames.* **2** to overwhelm: *a terrible fear engulfed her.*

enhance *vb* **-hancing, -hanced** to improve or increase in quality, value, or power: *grilling on the barbecue enhances the flavour.* **enhancement** *n* **enhancer** *n*

enigma *n* something or someone that is mysterious or puzzling. **enigmatic** *adj* **enigmatically** *adv*

enjoin *vb* **1** to order (someone) to do something. **2** to impose (a particular kind of behaviour) on someone: *the sect enjoins poverty on its members.* **3** *Law* to prohibit (someone) from doing something by an injunction.

enjoy *vb* **1** to receive pleasure from. **2** to have or experience (something, esp. something good): *many fat people enjoy excellent health.* **3** **enjoy oneself** to have a good time. **enjoyable** *adj* **enjoyably** *adv* **enjoyment** *n*

enlarge *vb* **-larging, -larged 1** to make or grow larger. **2** **enlarge on** to speak or write about in greater detail. **enlargement** *n* **enlarger** *n*

enlighten *vb* to give information or understanding to. **enlightening** *adj*

enlightened *adj* **1** rational and having beneficial ef-

THESAURUS

employed, engrossed, in use, involved, occupied, preoccupied, tied up, unavailable

engagement **1.** appointment, arrangement, commitment, date, meeting **2.** betrothal **3.** commission, employment, gig *(informal)*, job, post, situation, stint, work **4.** action, battle, combat, conflict, confrontation, contest, encounter, fight

engaging agreeable, appealing, attractive, captivating, charming, enchanting, fascinating, fetching *(informal)*, likable *or* likeable, lovable, pleasant, pleasing, winning, winsome

engender beget, breed, bring about, cause, create, excite, foment, generate, give rise to, hatch, incite, induce, instigate, lead to, make, occasion, precipitate, produce, provoke

engine **1.** machine, mechanism, motor **2.** locomotive

engineer bring about, cause, concoct, contrive, control, create, devise, effect, finagle *(informal)*, manage, manoeuvre, mastermind, originate, plan, plot, scheme, wangle *(informal)*

engrave **1.** carve, chase, chisel, cut, etch, inscribe **2.** impress, imprint, print **3.** embed, fix, impress, imprint, infix, ingrain, lodge

engraving **1.** block, carving, etching, inscription, plate, woodcut **2.** etching, impression, print

engross absorb, arrest, engage, engulf, hold, immerse, involve, occupy, preoccupy

engrossing absorbing, captivating, compelling, enthralling, fascinating, gripping, interesting, intriguing, riveting

enhance add to, augment, boost, complement, elevate, embellish, exalt, heighten, improve, increase, intensify, lift, magnify, raise, reinforce, strengthen, swell

enigma conundrum, mystery, problem, puzzle, riddle, teaser

enigmatic ambiguous, cryptic, Delphic, doubtful, equivocal, incomprehensible, indecipherable, inexplicable, inscrutable, mysterious, obscure, oracular, perplexing, puzzling, recondite, uncertain, unfathomable, unintelligible

enjoin **1.** advise, bid, call upon, charge, command, counsel, demand, direct, instruct, order, prescribe, require, urge, warn **2.** *Law* ban, bar, disallow, forbid, interdict, place an injunction on, preclude, prohibit, proscribe, restrain

enjoy **1.** appreciate, be entertained by, be pleased with, delight in, like, rejoice in, relish, revel in, take joy in, take pleasure in *or* from **2.** be blessed *or* favoured with, experience, have, have the benefit of, have the use of, own, possess, reap the benefits of, use **3.** **enjoy oneself** have a ball *(informal)*, have a good time, have fun, make merry

enjoyable agreeable, amusing, delectable, delicious, delightful, entertaining, gratifying, pleasant, pleasing, pleasurable, satisfying, to one's liking

enjoyment **1.** amusement, delectation, delight, diversion, entertainment, fun, gladness, gratification, gusto, happiness, indulgence, joy, pleasure, recreation, relish, satisfaction, zest **2.** advantage, benefit, exercise, ownership, possession, use

enlarge **1.** add to, amplify, augment, blow up *(informal)*, broaden, dilate, distend, elongate, expand, extend, grow, heighten, increase, inflate, lengthen, magnify, make *or* grow larger, multiply, stretch, swell, wax, widen **2.** amplify, develop, dilate, elaborate, expand, expatiate, give details

enlighten advise, apprise, cause to understand, civilize, counsel, edify, educate, inform, instruct, make aware, teach

enlightened aware, broad-minded, civilized, culti-

fects: *an enlightened approach to social welfare.* **2** (of a person) tolerant and unprejudiced.

enlightenment *n* the act of enlightening or the state of being enlightened.

enlist *vb* **1** to enter the armed forces. **2** to obtain (someone's help or support). **enlistment** *n*

enlisted *adj* (of a man or woman in the US Army or Navy) being below the rank of an officer.

enliven *vb* to make lively, cheerful, or bright. **enlivening** *adj*

en masse *adv* all together; as a group.

enmeshed *adj* deeply involved: *enmeshed in turmoil.*

enmity *n* a feeling of hostility or ill will.

ennoble *vb* **-bling, -bled 1** to make (someone) a member of the nobility. **2** to make (someone or his or her life) noble or dignified: *poverty does not ennoble people.*

ennui (on-**nwee**) *n Literary* boredom and dissatisfaction resulting from lack of activity or excitement.

enormity *n* **1** extreme wickedness. **2** (*pl* **-ties**) an act of great wickedness. **3** the vastness or extent of a problem or difficulty.

enormous *adj* unusually large in size, extent, or degree. **enormously** *adv*

enough *adj* **1** as much or as many as necessary. **2 that's enough!** used to stop someone behaving in a particular way. *~pron* **3** an adequate amount or number: *I don't know enough about the subject to be able to speak about it.* *~adv* **4** as much as necessary. **5** fairly or quite: *that's a common enough experience.* **6** very: used to give emphasis to the preceding word: *funnily enough.* **7** just adequately: *he sang well enough.*

en passant (on pass-**on**) *adv* in passing: *references made en passant.*

enquire *vb* **-quiring, -quired** same as **inquire. enquiry** *n*

enrage *vb* **-raging, -raged** to make extremely angry.

enraptured *adj* filled with delight and fascination.

enrich *vb* **1** to improve or increase the quality or value of: *his poetry has vastly enriched the English language.* **2** to improve in nutritional value, colour, or flavour: *a sauce enriched with beer.* **3** to make wealthy or wealthier. **enriched** *adj* **enrichment** *n*

enrol *or US* **enroll** *vb* **-rolling, -rolled** to become or cause to become a member. **enrolment** *or US* **enrollment** *n*

en route *adv* on or along the way.

ensconce *vb* **-sconcing, -sconced** to settle firmly or comfortably.

ensemble (on-**som**-bl) *n* **1** all the parts of something considered as a whole. **2** the complete outfit of clothes a person is wearing. **3** a group of musicians or actors performing together. **4** *Music* a passage in which all or most of the performers are playing or singing at once.

enshrine *vb* **-shrining, -shrined** to contain and protect (an idea or right) in a society, legal system, etc.: *the university's independence is enshrined in its charter.*

enshroud *vb* to cover or hide (an object) completely, as if by draping something over it: *fog enshrouded the forest.*

ensign *n* **1** a flag flown by a ship to indicate its nationality. **2** any flag or banner. **3** (in the US Navy) a commissioned officer of the lowest rank. **4** (formerly, in the British infantry) a commissioned officer of the lowest rank.

enslave *vb* **-slaving, -slaved** to make a slave of (someone). **enslavement** *n*

ensnare *vb* **-snaring, -snared 1** to trap or gain power over (someone) by dishonest or underhand means. **2** to catch (an animal) in a snare.

THESAURUS

vated, educated, informed, knowledgeable, liberal, literate, open-minded, reasonable, refined, sophisticated

enlightenment awareness, broad-mindedness, civilization, comprehension, cultivation, edification, education, information, insight, instruction, knowledge, learning, literacy, open-mindedness, refinement, sophistication, teaching, understanding, wisdom

enlist enrol, enter (into), gather, join, join up, muster, obtain, procure, recruit, register, sign up, volunteer

enliven animate, brighten, buoy up, cheer, cheer up, excite, exhilarate, fire, gladden, hearten, inspire, inspirit, invigorate, pep up, perk up, quicken, rouse, spark, stimulate, vitalize, vivify, wake up

enmity acrimony, animosity, animus, antagonism, antipathy, aversion, bad blood, bitterness, hate, hatred, hostility, ill will, malevolence, malice, malignity, rancour, spite, venom

ennoble aggrandize, dignify, elevate, enhance, exalt, glorify, honour, magnify, raise

ennui boredom, dissatisfaction, lassitude, listlessness, tedium, the doldrums

enormity **1.** atrociousness, atrocity, depravity, disgrace, evil, heinousness, monstrousness, nefariousness, outrageousness, turpitude, viciousness, vileness, villainy, wickedness **2.** abomination, atrocity, crime, disgrace, evil, horror, monstrosity, outrage, villainy **3.** enormousness, greatness, hugeness, immensity, magnitude, massiveness, vastness

enormous astronomic, colossal, elephantine, excessive, gargantuan, gigantic, gross, huge, humongous (*U.S. slang*), immense, jumbo (*informal*), mammoth, massive, monstrous, mountainous, prodigious, titanic, tremendous, vast

enough **1.** *adj.* abundant, adequate, ample, plenty, sufficient **2.** *n.* abundance, adequacy, ample supply, plenty, right amount, sufficiency **3.** *adv.* abundantly, adequately, amply, fairly, moderately, passably, reasonably, satisfactorily, sufficiently, tolerably

enquire *see* INQUIRE

enquiry *see* INQUIRY

enrage aggravate (*informal*), anger, exasperate, gall, incense, incite, inflame, infuriate, irritate, madden, make one's blood boil, make one see red (*informal*), nark (*Brit., Austral., & N.Z. slang*), provoke

enrich **1.** adorn, aggrandize, ameliorate, augment, cultivate, decorate, develop, embellish, endow, enhance, grace, improve, ornament, refine, supplement **2.** make rich, make wealthy

enrol accept, admit, engage, enlist, join up, matriculate, recruit, register, sign up *or* on, take on

enrolment acceptance, admission, engagement, enlistment, matriculation, recruitment, registration

en route in transit, on *or* along the way, on the road

ensemble *n.* **1.** aggregate, assemblage, collection, entirety, set, sum, total, totality, whole, whole thing **2.** costume, get-up (*informal*), outfit, suit **3.** band, cast, chorus, company, group, supporting cast, troupe

enshrine cherish, consecrate, dedicate, embalm, exalt, hallow, preserve, revere, sanctify, treasure

enshroud cloak, cloud, conceal, cover, enclose, enfold, envelop, enwrap, hide, obscure, pall, shroud, veil, wrap

ensign badge, banner, colours, flag, jack, pennant, pennon, standard, streamer

enslave bind, dominate, enchain, reduce to slavery, subjugate, yoke

ensue *vb* **-suing, -sued 1** to happen next. **2** to occur as a consequence: *if glaucoma is not treated, blindness can ensue.* **ensuing** *adj*

en suite *adv* (of a bathroom) connected to a bedroom and entered directly from it.

ensure *or esp US* **insure** *vb* **-suring, -sured 1** to make certain: *we must ensure that similar accidents do not happen again.* **2** to make safe or protect: *female athletes should take extra iron to ensure against anaemia.*

ENT *Med* ear, nose, and throat.

entablature *n Archit* the part of a classical building supported by the columns, consisting of an architrave, a frieze, and a cornice.

entail *vb* **1** to bring about or impose inevitably: *few women enter marriage knowing what it really entails.* **2** *Property law* to restrict the ability to inherit (a piece of property) to designated heirs.

entangle *vb* **-gling, -gled 1** to catch very firmly in something, such as a net or wire: *a fishing line had entangled his legs.* **2** to involve in a complicated series of problems or difficulties: *he entangles himself in contradictions.* **3** to involve in a troublesome relationship: *she kept getting entangled with unsuitable boyfriends.* **entanglement** *n*

entente (on-**tont**) *n* short for **entente cordiale.**

entente cordiale (cord-ee-**ahl**) *n* a friendly understanding between two or more countries.

enter *vb* **1** to come or go into (a particular place): *he entered the room.* **2** to join (a party or organization). **3** to become involved in or take part in: *1500 schools entered the competition.* **4** to become suddenly present or noticeable in: *a note of anxiety entered his voice.* **5** to record (an item) in a journal or list. **6** *Theatre* to come on stage: used as a stage direction: *enter Joseph.* **7** to begin (a new process or period of time): *the occupation of the square has entered its eleventh day.*

enteric (en-**ter**-ik) *adj* of the intestines.

enter into *vb* **1** to be an important factor in (a situation or plan): *money doesn't enter into it: it's a matter of principle.* **2** to start to do or be involved in (a process or series of events): *the government will not enter into negotiations with terrorists.*

enteritis (en-ter-**rite**-iss) *n* inflammation of the small intestine.

enterprise *n* **1** a business firm. **2** a project or undertaking, esp. one that requires boldness or effort. **3** boldness and energy.

enterprising *adj* full of boldness and initiative. **enterprisingly** *adv*

entertain *vb* **1** to provide amusement for (a person or audience). **2** to show hospitality to (guests). **3** to consider (an idea or suggestion).

entertainer *n* a person who entertains, esp. professionally.

entertaining *adj* **1** interesting, amusing, and enjoyable. ~*n* **2** the provision of hospitality to guests: *the small kitchen is perfect for entertaining.*

entertainment *n* **1** enjoyment and interest: *a match of top quality entertainment and goals.* **2** an act or show that entertains, or such acts and shows collectively.

enthral *or US* **enthrall** (en-**thrawl**) *vb* **-thralling, -thralled** to hold the attention or interest of. **enthralling** *adj* **enthralment** *or US* **enthrallment** *n*

enthrone *vb* **-throning, -throned 1** to place (a person) on a throne in a ceremony to mark the beginning of his or her new role as a monarch or bishop. **2** to give an important or prominent position to (something): *the religious fundamentalism now enthroned in American life.* **enthronement** *n*

enthuse *vb* **-thusing, -thused** to feel or cause to feel enthusiasm.

enthusiasm *n* ardent and lively interest or eagerness.

THESAURUS

ensue arise, attend, be consequent on, befall, come after, come next, derive, flow, follow, issue, proceed, result, stem, succeed, supervene, turn out *or* up

ensure, insure 1. certify, confirm, effect, guarantee, make certain, make sure, secure, warrant **2.** guard, make safe, protect, safeguard, secure

entail bring about, call for, cause, demand, encompass, give rise to, impose, involve, lead to, necessitate, occasion, require, result in

entangle 1. catch, compromise, embroil, enmesh, ensnare, entrap, foul, implicate, involve, knot, mat, mix up, ravel, snag, snare, tangle, trammel, trap **2.** bewilder, complicate, confuse, jumble, mix up, muddle, perplex, puzzle, snarl, twist

entanglement 1. complication, confusion, ensnarement, entrapment, imbroglio, involvement, jumble, knot, mesh, mess, mix-up, muddle, snare, snarl-up (*informal, chiefly Brit.*), tangle, toils, trap **2.** difficulty, embarrassment, imbroglio, involvement, liaison, predicament, tie

enter 1. arrive, come *or* go in *or* into, insert, introduce, make an entrance, pass into, penetrate, pierce **2.** become a member of, begin, commence, commit oneself to, embark upon, enlist, enrol, join, offer, participate in, present, proffer, put forward, register, set about, set out on, sign up, start, submit, take part in, take up, tender **3.** inscribe, list, log, note, record, register, set down, take down

enterprise 1. business, company, concern, establishment, firm, operation **2.** adventure, effort, endeavour, essay, operation, plan, programme, project, undertaking, venture **3.** activity, adventurousness, alertness, audacity, boldness, daring, dash, drive, eagerness, energy, enthusiasm, get-up-and-go (*informal*), gumption (*Informal*), initiative, pep, push (*informal*), readiness, resource, resourcefulness, spirit, vigour, zeal

enterprising active, adventurous, alert, audacious, bold, daring, dashing, eager, energetic, enthusiastic, go-ahead, intrepid, keen, ready, resourceful, spirited, stirring, up-and-coming, venturesome, vigorous, zealous

entertain 1. amuse, charm, cheer, delight, divert, occupy, please, regale **2.** accommodate, be host to, harbour, have company, have guests *or* visitors, lodge, put up, show hospitality to, treat **3.** cherish, cogitate on, conceive, consider, contemplate, foster, harbour, hold, imagine, keep in mind, maintain, muse over, ponder, support, think about, think over

entertaining amusing, charming, cheering, delightful, diverting, funny, humorous, interesting, pleasant, pleasing, pleasurable, witty

entertainment amusement, cheer, distraction, diversion, enjoyment, fun, good time, leisure activity, pastime, play, pleasure, recreation, satisfaction, sport, treat

enthral absorb, beguile, captivate, charm, enchant, enrapture, entrance, fascinate, grip, hold spellbound, hypnotize, intrigue, mesmerize, ravish, rivet, spellbind

enthralling beguiling, captivating, charming, compelling, compulsive, enchanting, entrancing, fascinating, gripping, hypnotizing, intriguing, mesmerizing, riveting, spellbinding

enthusiasm ardour, avidity, devotion, eagerness, earnestness, excitement, fervour, frenzy, interest,

enthusiast *n* a person who is very interested in and keen on something. **enthusiastic** *adj* **enthusiastically** *adv*

entice *vb* **-ticing, -ticed** to attract (someone) away from one place or activity to another. **enticement** *n* **enticing** *adj*

entire *adj* made up of or involving all of something, including every detail, part, or aspect. **entirely** *adv*

entirety *n, pl* **-ties 1** all of a person or thing: *you must follow this diet for the entirety of your life.* **2 in its entirety** as a whole.

entitle *vb* **-tling, -tled 1** to give (someone) the right to do or have something. **2** to give a name or title to (a book or film). **entitlement** *n*

entity *n, pl* **-ties** something that exists in its own right and not merely as part of a bigger thing.

entomb *vb* **1** to place (a corpse) in a tomb. **2** to bury or trap: *a circulatory system entombed in fat.* **entombment** *n*

entomology *n* the study of insects. **entomological** *adj* **entomologist** *n*

entourage (**on**-toor-ahzh) *n* a group of people who assist or travel with an important or well-known person.

entozoon (en-toe-**zoe**-on) *n, pl* **-zoa** (-**zoe**-a) a parasite, such as a tapeworm, that lives inside another animal.

entrails *pl n* **1** the internal organs of a person or animal; intestines. **2** the innermost parts of anything.

entrance[1] *n* **1** something, such as a door or gate, through which it is possible to enter a place. **2** the act of coming into a place, esp. with reference to the way in which it is done: *she made a sudden startling entrance.* **3** *Theatre* the act of appearing on stage. **4** the right to enter a place: *he refused her entrance because she was carrying her Scottie dog.* **5** ability or permission to join or become involved with a group or organization: *entrance to the profession should be open to men and women alike.* ~*adj* **6** necessary in order to enter something: *the entrance fee is £5.*

entrance[2] *vb* **-trancing, -tranced** to fill with delight. **entrancement** *n* **entrancing** *adj*

entrant *n* a person who enters a university, competition, etc.

entrap *vb* **-trapping, -trapped 1** to trick (someone) into danger or difficulty. **2** to catch in a trap. **entrapment** *n*

entreat *vb* to ask (someone) earnestly to do something.

entreaty *n, pl* **-treaties** an earnest request or plea.

entrecote (**on**-tra-coat) *n* a steak of beef cut from between the ribs.

entrée (**on**-tray) *n* **1** the right to enter a place. **2** a dish served before a main course. **3** *Chiefly US* the main course.

entrench *vb* **1** to fix or establish firmly: *the habit had become entrenched.* **2** *Mil* to fortify (a position) by digging trenches around it. **entrenchment** *n*

entrepreneur *n* the owner of a business who attempts to make money by risk and initiative. **entrepreneurial** *adj*

entropy (**en**-trop-ee) *n* **1** *Formal* lack of pattern or organization. **2** *Physics* a thermodynamic quantity that represents the amount of energy present in a system that cannot be converted into work because it is tied up in the atomic structure of the system.

entrust *vb* **1** to give (someone) a duty or responsibility: *Miss Conway, who was entrusted with the child's education.* **2** to put (something) into the care of someone: *he stole all the money we had entrusted to him.*

entry *n, pl* **-tries 1** something, such as a door or gate, through which it is possible to enter a place. **2** the act of coming in to a place, esp. with reference to the way in which it is done. **3** the right to enter a place: *he was refused entry to Britain.* **4** the act of joining an organization or group: *Britain's entry into the EC.* **5** a brief note, article, or group of figures in a diary, book, or computer file. **6** a quiz form, painting, etc., submitted in an attempt to win a competition. **7** a person, horse,

THESAURUS

keenness, passion, relish, vehemence, warmth, zeal, zest

enthusiast admirer, aficionado, buff (*informal*), devotee, fan, fanatic, fiend (*informal*), follower, freak (*informal*), lover, supporter, zealot

enthusiastic ardent, avid, devoted, eager, earnest, ebullient, excited, exuberant, fervent, fervid, forceful, hearty, keen, lively, passionate, spirited, unqualified, unstinting, vehement, vigorous, warm, wholehearted, zealous

entice allure, attract, beguile, cajole, coax, decoy, draw, inveigle, lead on, lure, persuade, prevail on, seduce, tempt, wheedle

entire absolute, complete, continuous, full, gross, integrated, outright, thorough, total, unbroken, undiminished, undivided, unified, unmitigated, unreserved, unrestricted, whole

entirely 1. absolutely, altogether, completely, fully, in every respect, perfectly, thoroughly, totally, unreservedly, utterly, wholly, without exception, without reservation **2.** exclusively, only, solely

entirety 1. aggregate, sum, total, unity, whole **2.** absoluteness, completeness, fullness, totality, undividedness, unity, wholeness

entitle 1. accredit, allow, authorize, empower, enable, enfranchise, fit for, license, make eligible, permit, qualify for, warrant **2.** call, characterize, christen, denominate, designate, dub, label, name, style, term, title

entity being, body, creature, existence, individual, object, organism, presence, quantity, substance, thing

entourage associates, attendants, companions, company, cortege, court, escort, followers, following, retainers, retinue, staff, suite, train

entrails bowels, guts, innards (*informal*), insides (*informal*), intestines, offal, viscera

entrance[1] *n.* **1.** access, avenue, door, doorway, entry, gate, ingress, inlet, opening, passage, portal, way in **2.** appearance, arrival, coming in, entry, ingress, introduction **3.** access, admission, admittance, entrée, entry, ingress, permission to enter

entrance[2] *vb.* absorb, bewitch, captivate, charm, delight, enchant, enrapture, enthral, fascinate, gladden, ravish, spellbind, transport

entrant candidate, competitor, contestant, entry, participant, player

entreaty appeal, earnest request, exhortation, importunity, petition, plea, prayer, request, solicitation, supplication

entrench 1. anchor, dig in, embed, ensconce, establish, fix, implant, ingrain, install, lodge, plant, root, seat, set, settle **2.** construct defences, dig in, dig trenches, fortify

entrust assign, authorize, charge, commend, commit, confide, consign, delegate, deliver, give custody of, hand over, invest, trust, turn over

entry 1. access, avenue, door, doorway, entrance, gate, ingress, inlet, opening, passage, passageway, portal, way in **2.** appearance, coming in, entering, entrance, initiation, introduction **3.** access, admission, entrance, entrée, free passage, permission to enter **4.**

car, etc., entering a competition. *~adj* **8** necessary in order to enter something: *entry fee.*

entwine *vb* **-twining, -twined** to twist together or round something else.

E number *n* any of a series of numbers with the prefix E- indicating a specific food additive recognized by the EU.

enumerate *vb* **-ating, -ated 1** to name or list one by one. **2** to count. **3** *Canad* to compile the voting list for an area. **enumeration** *n* **enumerator** *n*

enunciate *vb* **-ating, -ated 1** to pronounce (words) clearly. **2** to state precisely or formally. **enunciation** *n*

enuresis (en-yoo-**reece**-iss) *n* involuntary urination, esp. during sleep.

envelop *vb* to cover, surround, or enclose. **envelopment** *n*

envelope *n* **1** a flat covering of paper, that can be sealed, used to enclose a letter, etc. **2** any covering, wrapper, or enclosing structure: *an envelope of filo pastry.* **3** *Geom* a curve that is tangential to each one of a group of curves.

enviable *adj* so desirable or fortunate that it is likely to cause envy. **enviably** *adv*

envious *adj* feeling, showing, or resulting from envy. **enviously** *adv*

environment (en-**vire**-on-ment) *n* **1** the external conditions or surroundings in which people live: *working in a multicultural environment.* **2** *Ecology* the natural world of land, sea, air, plants, and animals: *nuclear waste must be prevented from leaking into the environment.* **environmental** *adj*

➤ Note the "n" before the "m" in the spelling of *environment.*

environmentalist *n* a person concerned with the protection and preservation of the natural environment.

environs *pl n* a surrounding area, esp. the outskirts of a city.

envisage *or US* **envision** *vb* **-aging, -aged** *or* **-ioning, -ioned** to believe to be possible or likely in the future: *the commission envisages a mix of government and private funding.*

envoy *n* **1** a messenger or representative. **2** a diplomat ranking next below an ambassador.

envy *n, pl* **-vies 1** a feeling of discontent aroused by someone else's possessions, achievements, or qualities. **2** something that causes envy: *their standards are the envy of the world.* *~vb* **-vies, -vying, -vied 3** to wish that one had the possessions, achievements, or qualities of (someone else). **envyingly** *adv*

enzyme *n* any of a group of complex proteins, that act as catalysts in specific biochemical reactions. **enzymatic** *adj*

Eocene (**ee**-oh-seen) *adj* of the epoch of geological time about 55 million years ago.

Eolithic *adj* of the early period of the Stone Age, when crude stone tools were used.

EP *n* an extended-play gramophone record, which is 7 inches in diameter and has a longer recording on each side than a single does.

epaulette *n* a piece of ornamental material on the shoulder of a garment, esp. a military uniform.

épée (**ep**-pay) *n* a straight-bladed sword used in fencing.

ephedrine (**eff**-fid-dreen) *n* an alkaloid used for the treatment of asthma and hay fever.

ephemera (if-**fem**-a-ra) *pl n* items designed to last only for a short time, such as programmes or posters.

ephemeral *adj* lasting only for a short time.

epic *n* **1** a long exciting book, poem, or film, usually telling of heroic deeds. **2** a long narrative poem telling of the deeds of a legendary hero. *~adj* **3** very large or grand: *a professional feud of epic proportions.*

epicene *adj* (esp. of a man) having characteristics or features which are not definitely male or female.

epicentre *or US* **epicenter** *n* the point on the earth's surface immediately above the origin of an earthquake.

epicure *n* a person who enjoys good food and drink. **epicurism** *n*

epicurean *adj* **1** devoted to sensual pleasures, esp. food and drink. *~n* **2** same as **epicure. epicureanism** *n*

epidemic *n* **1** a widespread occurrence of a disease. **2** a rapid development or spread of something: *an epidemic of rape.* *~adj* **3** (esp. of a disease) affecting

THESAURUS

account, item, jotting, listing, memo, memorandum, minute, note, record, registration **5.** attempt, candidate, competitor, contestant, effort, entrant, participant, player, submission

entwine braid, embrace, encircle, interlace, intertwine, interweave, knit, plait, ravel, surround, twine, twist, weave, wind

enumerate 1. cite, detail, itemize, list, mention, name, quote, recapitulate, recite, recount, rehearse, relate, specify, spell out, tell **2.** add up, calculate, compute, count, number, reckon, sum up, tally, total

enunciate 1. articulate, enounce, pronounce, say, sound, speak, utter, vocalize, voice **2.** declare, proclaim, promulgate, pronounce, propound, publish, state

envelop blanket, cloak, conceal, cover, embrace, encase, encircle, enclose, encompass, enfold, engulf, hide, obscure, sheathe, shroud, surround, swaddle, swathe, veil, wrap

envelope case, casing, coating, cover, covering, jacket, sheath, shell, skin, wrapper, wrapping

enviable advantageous, blessed, covetable, desirable, favoured, fortunate, lucky, much to be desired, privileged

envious begrudging, covetous, green-eyed, green with envy, grudging, jaundiced, jealous, malicious, resentful, spiteful

environment atmosphere, background, conditions, context, domain, element, habitat, locale, medium, milieu, scene, setting, situation, surroundings, territory

environs district, locality, neighbourhood, outskirts, precincts, purlieus, suburbs, surrounding area, vicinity

envisage anticipate, foresee, predict, see

envoy agent, ambassador, courier, delegate, deputy, diplomat, emissary, intermediary, legate, messenger, minister, plenipotentiary, representative

envy 1. *n.* covetousness, enviousness, grudge, hatred, ill will, jealousy, malice, malignity, resentfulness, resentment, spite, the green-eyed monster (*informal*) **2.** *vb.* be envious (of), begrudge, be jealous (of), covet, grudge, resent

ephemeral brief, evanescent, fleeting, flitting, fugitive, impermanent, momentary, passing, short, short-lived, temporary, transient, transitory

epicure *bon vivant,* epicurean, foodie, gastronome, gourmet

epicurean 1. *adj.* gluttonous, gourmandizing, hedonistic, libertine, luscious, lush, luxurious, pleasure-seeking, self-indulgent, sensual, sybaritic, voluptuous **2.** *n. bon vivant,* epicure, foodie, gastronome, gourmet

many people in an area: *stress has now reached epidemic proportions.*

epidemiology (ep-pid-deem-ee-**ol**-a-jee) *n* the branch of medical science concerned with epidemic diseases. **epidemiologist** *n*

epidermis *n* the thin protective outer layer of the skin. **epidermal** *adj*

epidural (ep-pid-**dure**-al) *adj* **1** on or over the outermost membrane covering the brain and spinal cord (**dura mater**). *~n* **2 a** an injection of anaesthetic into the space outside the outermost membrane enveloping the spinal cord. **b** anaesthesia produced by this method.

epiglottis *n* a thin flap of cartilage at the back of the mouth that covers the entrance to the larynx during swallowing.

epigram *n* **1** a witty remark. **2** a short poem with a witty ending. **epigrammatic** *adj*

epigraph *n* **1** a quotation at the beginning of a book. **2** an inscription on a monument or building.

epilepsy *n* a disorder of the central nervous system which causes periodic loss of consciousness and sometimes convulsions.

epileptic *adj* **1** of or having epilepsy. *~n* **2** a person who has epilepsy.

epilogue *n* a short concluding passage or speech at the end of a book or play.

episcopacy (ip-**piss**-kop-a-see) *n* **1** government of a Church by bishops. **2** (*pl* **-cies**) same as **episcopate.**

episcopal (ip-**piss**-kop-al) *adj* of or relating to bishops.

Episcopal Church *n* (in Scotland and the U.S.) a self-governing branch of the Anglican Church.

episcopalian *adj also* **episcopal 1** practising or advocating Church government by bishops. *~n* **2** an advocate of such Church government.

Episcopalian (ip-piss-kop-**pale**-ee-an) *adj* **1** of or relating to the Episcopal Church. *~n* **2** a member of this Church. **Episcopalianism** *n*

episcopate (ip-**piss**-kop-it) *n* **1** the office, status, or term of office of a bishop. **2** bishops collectively.

episiotomy (ip-peez-ee-**ot**-tom-ee) *n, pl* **-tomies** an operation involving cutting into the area between the genitals and the anus sometimes performed during childbirth to make the birth easier.

episode *n* **1** an event or series of events. **2** any of the sections into which a novel or a television or radio serial is divided.

episodic *adj* **1** resembling or relating to an episode. **2** occurring at irregular and infrequent intervals.

epistemology (ip-iss-stem-**ol**-a-jee) *n* the theory of knowledge, esp. the critical study of its validity, methods, and scope. **epistemological** *adj* **epistemologist** *n*

epistle *n* **1** *Formal or humorous* a letter. **2** a literary work in letter form, esp. a poem.

Epistle *n New Testament* any of the letters written by the apostles.

epistolary *adj* **1** of or relating to letters. **2** (of a novel) presented in the form of a series of letters.

epitaph *n* **1** a commemorative inscription on a tombstone. **2** a commemorative speech or written passage.

epithelium *n, pl* **-lia** *Anat* a cellular tissue covering the external and internal surfaces of the body. **epithelial** *adj*

epithet *n* a word or short phrase used to describe someone or something: *these tracks truly deserve that overworked epithet "classic".*

epitome (ip-**pit**-a-mee) *n* **1** a person or thing that is a typical example of a characteristic or class: *the epitome of rural tranquillity.* **2** a summary, esp. of a written work.

➤ Avoid the use of *epitome* to mean "the peak" of something.

epitomize *or* **-mise** *vb* **-mizing, -mized** *or* **-mising, -mised** to be or make a perfect or typical example of.

EPNS electroplated nickel silver.

epoch (ee-pok) *n* **1** a long period of time marked by some predominant characteristic: *the cold-war epoch.* **2** the beginning of a new or distinctive period: *the invention of nuclear weapons marked an epoch in the history of warfare.* **3** *Geol* a unit of time within a period during which a series of rocks is formed. **epochal** *adj*

epoch-making *adj* very important or significant.

eponymous (ip-**pon**-im-uss) *adj* **1** (of a person) being the person after whom a literary work, film, etc., is named: *the eponymous heroine in the film of Jane Eyre.* **2** (of a literary work, film, etc.) named after its central character or creator: *The Stooges' eponymous debut album.*

EPOS electronic point of sale.

epoxy *Chem ~adj* **1** of or containing an oxygen atom joined to two different groups that are themselves joined to other groups. **2** of or consisting of an epoxy resin. *~n, pl* **epoxies 3** an epoxy resin.

epoxy resin *n* a tough resistant thermosetting synthetic resin, used in laminates and adhesives.

Epsom salts *pl n* a medicinal preparation of hydrated magnesium sulphate, used to empty the bowels.

equable (**ek**-wab-bl) *adj* **1** even-tempered and reasonable. **2** (of a climate) not varying much throughout the year, and neither very hot nor very cold. **equably** *adv*

equal *adj* **1** identical in size, quantity, degree, or intensity. **2** having identical privileges, rights, or status. **3** applying in the same way to all people or in all circumstances: *equal rights.* **4 equal to** having the necessary strength, ability, or means for: *she was equal to any test the corporation put to her.* *~n* **5** a person or

THESAURUS

epidemic 1. *n.* contagion, growth, outbreak, plague, rash, spread, upsurge, wave **2.** *adj.* general, pandemic, prevailing, prevalent, rampant, rife, sweeping, wide-ranging, widespread

epigram aphorism, *bon mot,* quip, witticism

epilogue afterword, coda, concluding speech, conclusion, postscript

episode 1. adventure, affair, business, circumstance, escapade, event, experience, happening, incident, matter, occurrence **2.** chapter, instalment, part, passage, scene, section

epistle communication, letter, message, missive, note

epithet appellation, description, designation, name, nickname, sobriquet, tag, title

epitome 1. archetype, embodiment, essence, exemplar, norm, personification, quintessence, representation, type, typical example **2.** abbreviation, abridgment, abstract, compendium, condensation, conspectus, contraction, digest, précis, résumé, summary, synopsis

epitomize embody, exemplify, illustrate, incarnate, personify, represent, symbolize, typify

epoch age, date, era, period, time

equable 1. agreeable, calm, composed, easy-going, even-tempered, imperturbable, level-headed, placid, serene, temperate, unexcitable, unfazed (*informal*), unflappable (*informal*), unruffled **2.** consistent, con-

thing equal to another. ~*vb* **equalling, equalled** *or US* **equaling, equaled 6** to be equal to; match. **7** to make or do something equal to: *he has equalled his world record in the men's 100 metres.* **equally** *adv*

equality *n, pl* **-ties** the state of being equal.

equalize *or* **-ise** *vb* **-izing, -ized** *or* **-ising, -ised 1** to make equal or uniform. **2** (in a sport) to reach the same score as one's opponent or opponents. **equalization** *or* **-isation** *n* **equalizer** *or* **-iser** *n*

equal opportunity *n* the offering of employment or promotion equally to all, without discrimination as to sex, race, colour, etc.

equanimity *n* calmness of mind or temper; composure.

equate *vb* **equating, equated 1** to make or regard as equivalent. **2** *Maths* to form an equation from. **equatable** *adj*

equation *n* **1** a mathematical statement that two expressions are equal. **2** a situation or problem in which a number of different factors need to be considered: *this plan leaves human nature out of the equation.* **3** the act of equating. **4** *Chem* a representation of a chemical reaction using symbols of the elements.

equator *n* an imaginary circle around the earth at an equal distance from the North Pole and the South Pole.

equatorial *adj* of, like, or existing at or near the equator.

equerry (ek-kwer-ee) *n, pl* **-ries** an officer of the royal household who acts as a personal attendant to a member of the royal family.

equestrian *adj* **1** of or relating to horses and riding. **2** on horseback: *an equestrian statue of the Queen.* **equestrianism** *n*

equidistant *adj* equally distant. **equidistance** *n*

equilateral *adj* **1** having all sides of equal length. ~*n* **2** a geometric figure having all sides of equal length.

equilibrium *n, pl* **-ria 1** a stable condition in which forces cancel one another. **2** a state of mental and emotional balance; composure.

equine *adj* of or like a horse.

equinoctial *adj* **1** relating to or occurring at an equinox. ~*n* **2** a storm at or near an equinox.

equinox *n* either of the two occasions when day and night are of equal length, around March 21 and September 23.

equip *vb* **equipping, equipped 1** to provide with supplies, components, etc.: *the car comes equipped with a catalytic converter.* **2** to provide with abilities, understanding, etc.: *stress is something we are all equipped to cope with.*

equipment *n* **1** a set of tools or devices used for a particular purpose: *communications equipment.* **2** an act of equipping.

equipoise *n* the state of being perfectly balanced; equilibrium.

equitable *adj* fair and reasonable. **equitably** *adv*

equitation *n* riding and horsemanship

equities *pl n* same as **ordinary shares.**

equity *n, pl* **-ties 1** the quality of being impartial; fairness. **2** *Law* a system of using principles of natural justice and fair conduct to reach a judgment when common law is inadequate or inappropriate. **3** the difference in value between a person's debts and the value of the property on which they are secured: *negative equity.*

Equity *n Brit, Austral, & NZ* the actors' trade union.

equivalent *n* **1** something that has the same use or function as something else: *Denmark's equivalent to Silicon Valley.* ~*adj* **2** equal in value, quantity, significance, etc. **3** having the same or a similar effect or meaning. **equivalence** *n*

equivocal *adj* **1** capable of varying interpretations; ambiguous. **2** deliberately misleading or vague. **3** of doubtful character or sincerity: *the party's commitment to genuine reform is equivocal.* **equivocally** *adv*

equivocate *vb* **-cating, -cated** to use vague or am-

THESAURUS

stant, even, regular, smooth, stable, steady, temperate, tranquil, unchanging, uniform, unvarying

equal *adj.* **1.** alike, commensurate, equivalent, identical, like, one and the same, proportionate, tantamount, the same, uniform **2.** balanced, corresponding, egalitarian, equable, even, even-handed, evenly balanced, evenly matched, evenly proportioned, fair, fifty-fifty (*informal*), impartial, just, level pegging (*Brit. informal*), matched, regular, symmetrical, unbiased, uniform, unvarying **3.** able, adequate, capable, competent, fit, good enough, ready, strong enough, suitable, up to ~*n.* **4.** brother, counterpart, equivalent, fellow, match, mate, parallel, peer, rival, twin ~*vb.* **5.** agree with, amount to, balance, be equal to, be even with, be level with, be tantamount to, come up to, correspond to, equalize, equate, even, level, match, parallel, rival, square with, tally with, tie with

equality balance, correspondence, egalitarianism, equal opportunity, equivalence, evenness, fairness, identity, likeness, parity, sameness, similarity, uniformity

equalize balance, equal, equate, even up, level, make equal, match, regularize, smooth, square, standardize

equate agree, balance, be commensurate, compare, correspond with *or* to, equalize, liken, make *or* be equal, match, offset, pair, parallel, square, tally, think of together

equation agreement, balancing, comparison, correspondence, equality, equalization, equating, equivalence, likeness, match, pairing, parallel

equestrian *adj.* in the saddle, mounted, on horseback

equilibrium 1. balance, counterpoise, equipoise, evenness, rest, stability, steadiness, symmetry **2.** calm, calmness, collectedness, composure, coolness, equanimity, poise, self-possession, serenity, stability, steadiness

equip arm, array, attire, deck out, dress, endow, fit out, fit up, furnish, kit out, outfit, prepare, provide, rig, stock, supply

equipment accoutrements, apparatus, appurtenances, baggage, furnishings, furniture, gear, materiel, outfit, paraphernalia, rig, stuff, supplies, tackle, tools

equitable candid, disinterested, dispassionate, due, even-handed, fair, honest, impartial, just, nondiscriminatory, proper, proportionate, reasonable, right, rightful, unbiased, unprejudiced

equity disinterestedness, equitableness, even-handedness, fair-mindedness, fairness, fair play, honesty, impartiality, integrity, justice, reasonableness, rectitude, righteousness, uprightness

equivalence agreement, alikeness, conformity, correspondence, equality, evenness, identity, interchangeableness, likeness, match, parallel, parity, sameness, similarity

equivalent 1. *n.* correspondent, counterpart, equal, match, opposite number, parallel, peer, twin **2.** *adj.* alike, commensurate, comparable, correspondent, corresponding, equal, even, homologous, interchangeable, of a kind, same, similar, synonymous, tantamount

biguous language in order to deceive someone or to avoid telling the truth. **equivocation** *n* **equivocator** *n*

er *interj* a sound made when hesitating in speech.

Er *Chem* erbium.

ER Queen Elizabeth.

era *n* **1** a period of time considered as distinctive; epoch. **2** an extended period of time measured from a fixed point: *the Communist era.* **3** *Geol* a major division of time.

eradicate *vb* **-cating, -cated** to destroy or get rid of completely: *measures to eradicate racism.* **eradicable** *adj* **eradication** *n* **eradicator** *n*

erase *vb* **erasing, erased 1** to destroy all traces of: *he could not erase the memory of his earlier defeat.* **2** to rub or wipe out (something written). **3** to remove sound or information from (a magnetic tape or disk). **erasable** *adj*

eraser *n* an object, such as a piece of rubber, for erasing something written.

erasure *n* **1** an erasing. **2** the place or mark where something has been erased.

erbium *n Chem* a soft silvery-white element of the lanthanide series of metals. Symbol: Er

ere *conj, prep Poetic* before.

erect *vb* **1** to build. **2** to raise to an upright position. **3** to found or form: *the caricature of socialism erected by Lenin.* ~*adj* **4** upright in posture or position. **5** *Physiol* (of the penis, clitoris, or nipples) firm or rigid after swelling with blood, esp. as a result of sexual excitement. **erection** *n*

erectile *adj Physiol* (of an organ, such as the penis) capable of becoming erect.

eremite (**air**-rim-mite) *n* a Christian hermit.

ergo *conj* therefore.

ergonomic *adj* **1** designed to minimize effort and discomfort. **2** of or relating to ergonomics.

ergonomics *n* the study of the relationship between workers and their environment.

ergot *n* **1** a disease of a cereal, such as rye, caused by a fungus. **2** the dried fungus used in medicine.

Erin *n Archaic or poetic* Ireland.

ermine *n, pl* **-mines** *or* **-mine 1** the stoat in northern regions, where it has a white winter coat. **2** the fur of this animal, used to trim state robes of judges, nobles, etc.

erne *or* **ern** *n* a fish-eating sea eagle.

Ernie *n* (in Britain) a computer that randomly selects winning numbers of Premium Bonds.

erode *vb* **eroding, eroded 1** to wear down or away. **2** to deteriorate or cause to deteriorate.

erogenous (ir-**roj**-in-uss) *adj* sensitive to sexual stimulation: *an erogenous zone.*

erosion *n* **1** the wearing away of rocks or soil by the action of water, ice, or wind. **2** a gradual lessening or reduction: *an erosion of national sovereignty.* **erosive** *or* **erosional** *adj*

erotic *adj* of, concerning, or arousing sexual desire or giving sexual pleasure. **erotically** *adv*

erotica *pl n* explicitly sexual literature or art.

eroticism *n* **1** erotic quality or nature. **2** the use of sexually arousing symbolism in literature or art. **3** sexual excitement or desire.

err *vb* **1** to make a mistake. **2** to sin.

errand *n* **1** a short trip to get or do something for someone. **2 run an errand** to make such a trip.

errant *adj* **1** behaving in a way considered to be unacceptable: *an errant schoolboy.* **2** *Old-fashioned or literary* wandering in search of adventure: *a knight errant.* **errantry** *n*

erratic *adj* **1** irregular or unpredictable: *erratic behaviour.* ~*n* **2** *Geol* a rock that has been transported by glacial action. **erratically** *adv*

erratum *n, pl* **-ta** an error in writing or printing.

erroneous *adj* based on or containing an error or errors; incorrect. **erroneously** *adv*

error *n* **1** a mistake, inaccuracy, or misjudgment. **2** the act or state of being wrong or making a misjudgment: *the plane was shot down in error.* **3** the amount by which the actual value of a quantity might differ from an estimate: *a 3% margin of error.*

ersatz (**air**-zats) *adj* made in imitation of something more expensive: *ersatz coffee.*

Erse *n, adj* Gaelic.

erstwhile *adj* **1** former. ~*adv* **2** *Archaic* formerly.

eruct *or* **eructate** *vb Formal* to belch. **eructation** *n*

THESAURUS

equivocal ambiguous, ambivalent, doubtful, dubious, evasive, indefinite, indeterminate, misleading, oblique, obscure, oracular, prevaricating, questionable, suspicious, uncertain, vague

era aeon, age, cycle, date, day *or* days, epoch, generation, period, stage, time

eradicate abolish, annihilate, destroy, efface, eliminate, erase, excise, expunge, exterminate, extinguish, extirpate, obliterate, remove, root out, stamp out, uproot, weed out, wipe out

eradication abolition, annihilation, destruction, effacement, elimination, erasure, extermination, extinction, extirpation, obliteration, removal

erase blot, cancel, delete, efface, excise, expunge, obliterate, remove, rub out, scratch out, wipe out

erect *vb.* **1.** build, construct, elevate, lift, mount, pitch, put up, raise, rear, set up, stand up **2.** create, establish, form, found, initiate, institute, organize, set up ~*adj.* **3.** elevated, firm, perpendicular, pricked-up, raised, rigid, standing, stiff, straight, upright, vertical

erection 1. assembly, building, construction, creation, elevation, establishment, fabrication, manufacture **2.** building, construction, edifice, pile, structure

erode consume, corrode, destroy, deteriorate, disintegrate, eat away, grind down, spoil, wear down *or* away

erosion abrasion, attrition, consumption, corrasion, corrosion, destruction, deterioration, disintegration, eating away, grinding down, spoiling, wear, wearing down *or* away

erotic amatory, aphrodisiac, carnal, erogenous, lustful, rousing, seductive, sensual, sexy (*informal*), steamy (*informal*), stimulating, suggestive, titillating, voluptuous

err 1. be inaccurate, be incorrect, be in error, blunder, go astray, go wrong, make a mistake, misapprehend, miscalculate, misjudge, mistake, slip up (*informal*) **2.** do wrong, fall, go astray, lapse, misbehave, offend, sin, transgress, trespass

errand commission, job, mission, task

erratic aberrant, abnormal, capricious, changeable, desultory, eccentric, fitful, inconsistent, inconstant, irregular, shifting, uneven, unpredictable, unreliable, unstable, variable, wayward

erroneous amiss, fallacious, false, faulty, flawed, inaccurate, incorrect, inexact, invalid, mistaken, spurious, unfounded, unsound, untrue, wrong

error bloomer (*Brit. informal*), blunder, boob (*Brit. slang*), delusion, erratum, fallacy, fault, flaw, howler (*informal*), inaccuracy, misapprehension, miscalculation, misconception, mistake, oversight, slip, solecism

erstwhile bygone, ex (*informal*), former, late, old, once, one-time, past, previous, quondam, sometime

erudite (**air**-rude-ite) *adj* having or showing great academic knowledge. **erudition** *n*

erupt *vb* **1** (of a volcano) to throw out molten lava, ash, and steam in a sudden and violent way. **2** to burst forth suddenly and violently: *riots erupted across the country.* **3** (of a group of people) to suddenly become angry and aggressive: *the meeting erupted in fury.* **4** (of a blemish) to appear on the skin. **eruptive** *adj* **eruption** *n*

erysipelas (air-riss-**sip**-ill-ass) *n* an acute disease of the skin, with fever and raised purplish patches.

erythrocyte (ir-**rith**-roe-site) *n* a red blood cell that transports oxygen through the body.

Es *Chem* einsteinium.

escalate *vb* **-lating, -lated** to increase or be increased in size, seriousness, or intensity. **escalation** *n*

escalator *n* a moving staircase consisting of stair treads fixed to a conveyor belt.

escalope (**ess**-kal-lop) *n* a thin slice of meat, usually veal.

escapade *n* a mischievous act or adventure.

escape *vb* **-caping, -caped 1** to get away or break free from (confinement). **2** to manage to avoid (something dangerous, unpleasant, or difficult). **3** (of gases, liquids, etc.) to leak gradually. **4** to elude; be forgotten by: *those little round cakes whose name escapes me.* ~*n* **5** the act of escaping or state of having escaped. **6** a way of avoiding something difficult, dangerous, or unpleasant: *his frequent illnesses provided an escape from intolerable stress.* **7** a means of relaxation or relief: *he found temporary escape through the local cinema.* **8** a leakage of gas or liquid.

escapee *n* a person who has escaped from prison.

escapement *n* the mechanism in a clock or watch which connects the hands to the pendulum or balance.

escape road *n* a small road leading off a steep hill, into which a car can be driven if the brakes fail.

escape velocity *n* the minimum velocity necessary for a particle, space vehicle, etc. to escape from the gravitational field of the earth or other celestial body.

escapism *n* an inclination to retreat from unpleasant reality, for example through fantasy. **escapist** *n, adj*

escapologist *n* an entertainer who specializes in freeing himself or herself from chains, ropes, etc. **escapology** *n*

escarpment *n* the long continuous steep face of a ridge or mountain.

eschatology (ess-cat-**tol**-a-jee) *n* the branch of theology concerned with the end of the world. **eschatological** *adj*

escheat (**iss-cheat**) *Law* ~*n* **1** formerly, the return of property to the Crown or feudal lord in the absence of legal heirs. **2** the property so reverting. ~*vb* **3** to obtain (land) by escheat.

eschew (iss-**chew**) *vb* to avoid doing or being involved in (something disliked or harmful). **eschewal** *n*

escort *n* **1** people or vehicles accompanying another to protect or guard them. **2** a person who accompanies someone of the opposite sex on a social occasion. ~*vb* **3** to act as an escort to.

escritoire (ess-kree-**twahr**) *n* a writing desk with compartments and drawers.

escudo (ess-**kew**-doe) *n, pl* **-dos** the standard monetary unit of Portugal.

esculent *Formal* ~*adj* **1** edible. ~*n* **2** any edible substance.

escutcheon *n* **1** a shield displaying a coat of arms. **2 blot on one's escutcheon** a stain on one's honour.

Eskimo *n* **1** (*pl* **-mos** *or* **-mo**) a member of a group of peoples who live in N Canada, Greenland, Alaska, and E Siberia. **2** the language of these peoples. ~*adj* **3** of the Eskimos.

ESN educationally subnormal.

esoteric (ee-so-**ter**-rik) *adj* understood by only a small number of people, esp. because they have special knowledge. **esoterically** *adv*

ESP extrasensory perception.

esp. especially.

espadrille (**ess**-pad-drill) *n* a light canvas shoe with a braided cord sole.

espalier (ess-**pal**-yer) *n* **1** a shrub or fruit tree trained to grow flat. **2** the trellis on which such plants are grown.

esparto *or* **esparto grass** *n, pl* **-tos** any of various grasses of S Europe and N Africa, used to make ropes, mats, etc.

especial *adj Formal* same as **special.**

➤ *Special(ly)* is more common than *especial(ly)* and is always used in preference to *especial* when the sense is "out of the ordinary".

especially *adv* **1** particularly: *people are dying, especially children and babies.* **2** more than usually: *an especially virulent disease.*

Esperanto *n* an international artificial language. **Esperantist** *n, adj*

THESAURUS

erudite cultivated, cultured, educated, knowledgeable, learned, lettered, literate, scholarly, well-educated, well-read

erupt 1. be ejected, belch forth, blow up, break out, burst forth, burst into, burst out, discharge, explode, flare up, gush, pour forth, spew forth *or* out, spit out, spout, throw off, vent, vomit **2.** *Medical* appear, break out

eruption 1. discharge, ejection, explosion, flare-up, outbreak, outburst, sally, venting **2.** *Medical* inflammation, outbreak, rash

escalate amplify, ascend, be increased, enlarge, expand, extend, grow, heighten, increase, intensify, magnify, mount, raise, rise, step up

escapade adventure, antic, caper, fling, lark (*informal*), mischief, prank, romp, scrape (*informal*), spree, stunt, trick

escape *vb.* **1.** abscond, bolt, break free *or* out, decamp, do a bunk (*Brit. slang*), do a runner (*slang*), flee, fly, get away, make *or* effect one's escape, make one's getaway, run away *or* off, skedaddle (*informal*), skip, slip away **2.** avoid, circumvent, dodge, duck, elude, evade, pass, shun, slip **3.** discharge, drain, emanate, exude, flow, gush, issue, leak, pour forth, seep, spurt **4.** baffle, be beyond (someone), be forgotten by, elude, puzzle, stump ~*n.* **5.** bolt, break, break-out, decampment, flight, getaway **6.** avoidance, circumvention, elusion, evasion **7.** distraction, diversion, pastime, recreation, relief **8.** discharge, drain, effluence, efflux, emanation, emission, gush, leak, leakage, outflow, outpour, seepage, spurt

escort *n.* **1.** bodyguard, company, convoy, cortege, entourage, guard, protection, retinue, train **2.** attendant, beau, chaperon, companion, guide, partner, protector ~*vb.* **3.** accompany, chaperon, conduct, guard, guide, lead, partner, protect, shepherd, squire, usher

especial see SPECIAL

especially 1. exclusively, expressly, particularly, peculiarly, singularly, specifically, uniquely **2.** chiefly, conspicuously, exceptionally, extraordinarily, largely, mainly, markedly, notably, outstandingly, principally,

espionage (ess-pyon-ahzh) *n* **1** the use of spies to obtain secret information, esp. by governments. **2** the act of spying.

esplanade *n* a long open level stretch of ground, esp. beside the seashore or in front of a fortified place.

espousal *n* **1** adoption or support: *his espousal of the free market.* **2** *Old-fashioned* a marriage or engagement ceremony.

espouse *vb* **-pousing, -poused 1** to adopt or give support to (a cause, ideal, etc.). **2** *Old-fashioned* (esp. of a man) to marry.

espresso *n, pl* **-sos** coffee made by forcing steam or boiling water through ground coffee.

➤ Note that the second letter is "s" not "x".

esprit (ess-**pree**) *n* spirit, liveliness, or wit.

esprit de corps (de **kore**) *n* consciousness of and pride in belonging to a particular group.

espy *vb* **espies, espying, espied** to catch sight of.

Esq. esquire.

esquire *n* **1** *Chiefly Brit* a title of respect placed after a man's name and usually shortened to *Esq.*: *I Davies, Esquire.* **2** (in medieval times) the attendant of a knight.

essay *n* **1** a short literary composition on a single subject. **2** a short piece of writing on a subject done as an exercise by a student. **3** an attempt. ~*vb* **4** *Formal* to attempt: *he essayed a faint smile.*

essayist *n* a person who writes essays.

essence *n* **1** the most important and distinctive feature of something, which determines its identity. **2** a concentrated liquid used to flavour food. **3 in essence** essentially. **4 of the essence** vitally important.

essential *adj* **1** vitally important; absolutely necessary: *it is essential to get this finished on time.* **2** basic or fundamental: *she translated the essential points of the lecture into English.* ~*n* **3** something fundamental or indispensable. **essentially** *adv*

essential oil *n* any of various volatile oils in plants, which have the odour or flavour of the plant from which they are extracted.

EST 1 Eastern Standard Time. **2** electric-shock treatment.

est. 1 established. **2** estimate(d).

establish *vb* **1** to create or set up (an organization, link, etc.): *the regime wants to establish better relations with neighbouring countries.* **2** to make become firmly associated with a particular activity or reputation: *the play that established him as a major dramatist.* **3** to prove: *a test to establish if your baby has any chromosomal disorder.* **4** to cause (a principle) to be accepted: *our study establishes the case for further research.*

Established Church *n* a church, such as the Church of England, that is recognized as the official church of a country.

establishment *n* **1** the act of establishing or state of being established. **2 a** a business organization or other institution. **b** a place of business. **3** the people employed by an organization.

Establishment *n* **the Establishment** a group of people having authority within a society: usually seen as conservative.

estate *n* **1** a large piece of landed property, esp. in the country. **2** *Chiefly Brit* a large area of land with houses or factories built on it: *an industrial estate.* **3** *Law* property or possessions, esp. of a deceased person. **4** *History* any of the orders or classes making up a society.

estate agent *n Brit* a person whose job is to help people buy and sell houses and other property.

estate car *n Brit* a car which has a long body with a door at the back end and luggage space behind the rear seats.

estate duty *n* a former name for **inheritance tax.**

esteem *n* **1** admiration and respect. ~*vb* **2** to have great respect or high regard for (someone). **3** *Formal* to judge or consider: *I should esteem it a kindness.* **esteemed** *adj*

ester *n Chem* a compound produced by the reaction between an acid and an alcohol.

estimable *adj* worthy of respect.

estimate *vb* **-mating, -mated 1** to form an approximate idea of (size, cost, etc.); calculate roughly. **2** to form an opinion about; judge. **3** to submit an approxi-

THESAURUS

remarkably, signally, specially, strikingly, supremely, uncommonly, unusually

espionage counter-intelligence, intelligence, spying, surveillance, undercover work

espousal 1. adoption, advocacy, backing, championing, championship, defence, embracing, maintenance, promotion, support, taking up **2.** *archaic* betrothal, engagement, marriage, nuptials, plighting, wedding

espouse 1. adopt, advocate, back, champion, defend, embrace, maintain, promote, stand up for, support, take up **2.** *archaic* marry, take as spouse, take to wife, wed

essay article, composition, discourse, disquisition, dissertation, paper, piece, tract, treatise

essence 1. being, core, crux, entity, heart, kernel, life, lifeblood, meaning, nature, pith, principle, quiddity, quintessence, significance, soul, spirit, substance **2.** concentrate, distillate, elixir, extract, spirits **3. in essence** basically, essentially, fundamentally, in effect, in substance, in the main, materially, substantially, to all intents and purposes, virtually **4. of the essence** crucial, essential, indispensable, of the utmost importance, vital, vitally important

essential *adj.* **1.** crucial, important, indispensable, necessary, needed, requisite, vital **2.** basic, cardinal, constitutional, elemental, elementary, fundamental, inherent, innate, intrinsic, key, main, principal, radical ~*n.* **3.** basic, fundamental, must, necessity, prerequisite, principle, requisite, rudiment, *sine qua non,* vital part

establish 1. base, constitute, create, decree, enact, ensconce, entrench, fix, form, found, ground, implant, inaugurate, install, institute, organize, plant, root, secure, settle, set up, start **2.** authenticate, certify, confirm, corroborate, demonstrate, prove, ratify, show, substantiate, validate, verify

establishment 1. creation, enactment, formation, foundation, founding, inauguration, installation, institution, organization, setting up **2.** business, company, concern, corporation, enterprise, firm, house, institute, institution, organization, outfit (*informal*), setup (*informal*), structure, system **3.** building, factory, house, office, plant, quarters **4. the Establishment** established order, institutionalized authority, ruling class, the powers that be, the system

estate 1. area, demesne, domain, holdings, lands, manor, property **2.** *Property law* assets, belongings, effects, fortune, goods, possessions, property, wealth **3.** caste, class, order, rank

esteem *n.* **1.** admiration, consideration, credit, estimation, good opinion, honour, regard, respect, reverence, veneration ~*vb.* **2.** admire, be fond of, cherish, honour, like, love, prize, regard highly, respect, revere, reverence, think highly of, treasure, value, venerate **3.** *formal* account, believe, calculate, consider, deem, estimate, hold, judge, rate, reckon, regard, think, view

mate price for a job to a prospective client. ~*n* **4** an approximate calculation. **5** a statement of the likely charge for certain work. **6** an opinion. **estimator** *n*

estimation *n* **1** a considered opinion; judgment. **2** the act of estimating.

Estonian *adj* **1** from Estonia. ~*n* **2** a person from Estonia.

estranged *adj* **1** no longer living with one's husband or wife: *his estranged wife.* **2** having quarrelled and lost touch with one's family or friends: *he had become estranged from his daughter.* **estrangement** *n*

estuary *n, pl* **-aries** the widening channel of a river where it nears the sea. **estuarine** *adj*

ET *Brit* Employment Training: a government scheme offering training in technology and business skills for unemployed people.

ETA estimated time of arrival.

et al. **1** and elsewhere. **2** and others.

etc. et cetera.

➤ *Etc.* means "and the rest" so it is redundant to write *and etc.* Note the spelling; it comes from the Latin *et cetera.*

et cetera *or* **etcetera** (et **set**-ra) *n and vb substitute* **1** and the rest; and others; and so forth. **2** or the like; or something similar.

etceteras *pl n* miscellaneous extra things or people.

etch *vb* **1** to wear away the surface of a metal, glass, etc. by the action of an acid. **2** to cut a design or pattern into a printing plate with acid. **3** to imprint vividly: *the scene is etched on my mind.* **etcher** *n*

etching *n* **1** the art or process of preparing or printing etched designs. **2** a print made from an etched plate.

eternal *adj* **1** without beginning or end; lasting for ever. **2** unchanged by time: *eternal truths.* **3** seemingly unceasing: *his eternal whingeing.* **4** of or like God or a god: *the Eternal Buddha.* **eternally** *adv*

eternal triangle *n* an emotional or sexual relationship in which there are conflicts between a man and two women or a woman and two men.

eternity *n, pl* **-ties** **1** endless or infinite time. **2** a seemingly endless period of time: *it seemed an eternity before he could feel his heart beating again.* **3** the timeless existence after death. **4** the state of being eternal.

eternity ring *n* a ring given as a token of lasting affection, esp. one set all around with stones to symbolize continuity.

ethane *n* a flammable gaseous alkane obtained from natural gas and petroleum: used as a fuel.

ethanoic acid *n* same as **acetic acid.**

ethanol *n* same as **alcohol** (sense 1).

ethene *n* same as **ethylene.**

ether *n* **1** a colourless sweet-smelling liquid used as a solvent and anaesthetic. **2** the substance formerly believed to fill all space and to transmit electromagnetic waves. **3** the upper regions of the atmosphere; clear sky. Also (for senses 2 and 3): **aether**

ethereal (eth-**eer**-ee-al) *adj* **1** extremely delicate or refined. **2** heavenly or spiritual. **ethereally** *adv*

ethic *n* a moral principle or set of moral values held by an individual or group.

ethical *adj* **1** of or based on a system of moral beliefs about right and wrong. **2** in accordance with principles of professional conduct. **3** of or relating to ethics. **ethically** *adv*

ethics *pl n* **1** a code of behaviour, esp. of a particular group, profession, or individual. **2** the moral fitness of a decision, course of action, etc. ~*n* **3** the study of the moral value of human conduct.

Ethiopian *adj* **1** of Ethiopia. ~*n* **2** a person from Ethiopia.

ethnic *or* **ethnical** *adj* **1** of or relating to a human group with racial, religious, and linguistic characteristics in common. **2** characteristic of another culture, esp. a peasant one: *ethnic foodstuffs.* **ethnically** *adv*

ethnic cleansing *n* the practice, by the dominant ethnic group in an area, of removing other ethnic groups by expulsion or extermination.

ethnocentric *adj* of or relating to the belief that one's own nation, culture, or group is intrinsically superior. **ethnocentricity** *n*

ethnology *n* the branch of anthropology that deals with races and peoples and their relations to one another. **ethnological** *adj* **ethnologist** *n*

ethos (**eeth**-oss) *n* the distinctive spirit and attitudes of a people, culture, etc.

ethyl (**eth**-ill) *adj* of, consisting of, or containing the monovalent group C_2H_5–.

ethyl alcohol *n* same as **alcohol** (sense 1).

ethylene *or* **ethene** *n* a colourless flammable gaseous alkene used to make polythene and other chemicals.

etiolate (**ee**-tee-oh-late) *vb* **-lating, -lated** **1** *Formal* to become or cause to become weak. **2** *Bot* to make a green plant paler through lack of sunlight. **etiolation** *n*

etiology *n, pl* **-gies** **1** the study of causation. **2** the study of the cause of diseases. **etiological** *adj*

THESAURUS

estimate *vb.* **1.** appraise, assess, calculate roughly, evaluate, gauge, guess, judge, number, reckon, value **2.** assess, believe, conjecture, consider, form an opinion, guess, judge, rank, rate, reckon, surmise, think ~*n.* **3.** appraisal, appraisement, approximate calculation, assessment, evaluation, guess, guesstimate (*informal*), judgment, reckoning, valuation **4.** appraisal, appraisement, assessment, belief, conjecture, educated guess, estimation, judgment, opinion, surmise, thought(s)

estimation appraisal, appreciation, assessment, belief, consideration, considered opinion, estimate, evaluation, judgment, opinion, view

estrangement alienation, antagonization, breach, break-up, disaffection, dissociation, disunity, division, hostility, parting, separation, split, withdrawal, withholding

estuary creek, firth, fjord, inlet, mouth

et cetera and others, and so forth, and so on, and the like, and the rest, et al.

etch carve, corrode, cut, eat into, engrave, furrow, impress, imprint, incise, ingrain, inscribe, stamp

etching carving, engraving, impression, imprint, inscription, print

eternal abiding, ceaseless, constant, deathless, endless, enduring, everlasting, immortal, immutable, imperishable, indestructible, infinite, interminable, lasting, never-ending, perennial, permanent, perpetual, timeless, unceasing, undying, unending, unremitting, without end

eternity **1.** age, ages, endlessness, for ever, immortality, infinitude, infinity, perpetuity, timelessness, time without end **2.** *Theology* heaven, paradise, the afterlife, the hereafter, the next world

ethical conscientious, correct, decent, fair, fitting, good, honest, honourable, just, moral, principled, proper, right, righteous, upright, virtuous

ethics conscience, moral code, morality, moral philosophy, moral values, principles, rules of conduct, standards

etiquette *n* **1** the customs or rules of behaviour regarded as correct in social life. **2** a conventional code of practice in certain professions.

étude (**ay**-tewd) *n Music* a short composition for a solo instrument, esp. intended to be played as an exercise or to demonstrate virtuosity.

etymology *n, pl* **-gies 1** the study of the sources and development of words. **2** an account of the source and development of a word. **etymological** *adj* **etymologist** *n*

Eu *Chem* europium.

EU European Union.

eucalyptus *or* **eucalypt** *n, pl* **-lyptuses, -lyptus,** *or* **-lypts** any of a mostly Australian genus of trees, widely cultivated for timber and gum, and for the medicinal oil in their leaves (**eucalyptus oil**).

Eucharist (**yew**-kar-ist) *n* **1** the Christian sacrament commemorating Christ's Last Supper by the consecration of bread and wine. **2** the consecrated elements of bread and wine. **Eucharistic** *adj*

Euclidean *or* **Euclidian** (yew-**klid**-ee-an) *adj* denoting a system of geometry based on the rules of Euclid, 3rd-century BC Greek mathematician.

eugenics (yew-**jen**-iks) *n* the study of methods of improving the human race, esp. by selective breeding. **eugenic** *adj* **eugenically** *adv* **eugenicist** *n*

eulogize *or* **-gise** *vb* **-gizing, -gized** *or* **-gising, -gised** to praise (a person or thing) highly in speech or writing. **eulogistic** *adj*

eulogy *n, pl* **-gies 1** a speech or piece of writing praising a person or thing, esp. a person who has recently died. **2** high praise.

eunuch *n* a man who has been castrated, esp. (formerly) a guard in a harem.

euphemism *n* an inoffensive word or phrase substituted for one considered offensive or upsetting, such as *departed* for *dead.* **euphemistic** *adj* **euphemistically** *adv*

euphonious *adj* pleasing to the ear.

euphonium *n* a brass musical instrument with four valves, resembling a small tuba.

euphony *n, pl* **-nies** a pleasing sound, esp. in speech.

euphoria *n* a feeling of great but often unjustified or exaggerated happiness. **euphoric** *adj*

Eur. 1 Europe. **2** European.

Eurasian *adj* **1** of Europe and Asia. **2** of mixed European and Asian descent. *~n* **3** a person of mixed European and Asian descent.

eureka (yew-**reek**-a) *interj* an exclamation of triumph on discovering or solving something.

Euro- *combining form* Europe or European.

European *adj* **1** of Europe. *~n* **2** a person from Europe. **3** a person of European descent. **4** an advocate of closer links between the countries of Europe, esp. those in the European Union. **Europeanism** *n*

European Community *or* **European Economic Community** *n* a former name for **European Union.**

European Union *n* an economic organization of W European states, which have some shared monetary, social, and political goals.

europium *n Chem* a silvery-white element of the lanthanide series. Symbol: Eu

Eustachian tube *n* a tube that connects the middle ear with the pharynx and equalizes the pressure between the two sides of the eardrum.

euthanasia *n* the act of killing someone painlessly, esp. to relieve suffering from an incurable illness.

eV electronvolt.

evacuate *vb* **-ating, -ated 1** to send away from a dangerous place to a safe place: *200 people were evacuated from their homes because of the floods.* **2** to empty (a place) of people because it has become dangerous: *the entire street was evacuated until the fire was put out.* **3** *Physiol* to discharge waste from the body. **evacuation** *n* **evacuee** *n*

evade *vb* **evading, evaded 1** to get away from or avoid (imprisonment, captors, etc.). **2** to get around, shirk, or dodge (the law, a duty, etc.). **3** to avoid answering (a question).

evaluate *vb* **-ating, -ated** to find or judge the quality or value of something. **evaluation** *n*

evanesce *vb* **-nescing, -nesced** *Formal* to fade gradually from sight.

evanescent *adj Formal* quickly fading away; ephemeral or transitory. **evanescence** *n*

evangelical *Christianity ~adj* **1** of or following from the Gospels. **2** of certain Protestant sects which emphasize salvation through faith alone and a belief in the absolute authority of the Bible. *~n* **3** a member of an evangelical sect. **evangelicalism** *n* **evangelically** *adv*

evangelism *n* the practice of spreading the Christian gospel.

evangelist *n* a preacher, sometimes itinerant. **evangelistic** *adj*

Evangelist *n* any of the writers of the Gospels: Matthew, Mark, Luke, or John.

evangelize *or* **-lise** *vb* **-lizing, -lized** *or* **-lising, -lised** to preach the Christian gospel (to). **evangelization** *or* **-lisation** *n*

evaporate *vb* **-rating, -rated 1** to change from a liquid or solid to a vapour. **2** to become less and less and finally disappear: *faith in the government evapo-*

THESAURUS

ethnic cultural, folk, indigenous, national, native, racial, traditional

etiquette civility, code, convention, courtesy, customs, decorum, formalities, good *or* proper behaviour, manners, politeness, politesse, propriety, protocol, rules, usage

eulogy acclaim, acclamation, accolade, applause, commendation, compliment, encomium, exaltation, glorification, laudation, paean, panegyric, plaudit, praise, tribute

euphoria bliss, ecstasy, elation, exaltation, exhilaration, exultation, glee, high spirits, intoxication, joy, joyousness, jubilation, rapture, transport

evacuate 1. abandon, clear, decamp, depart, desert, forsake, leave, move out, pull out, quit, relinquish, remove, vacate, withdraw **2.** crap (*taboo slang*), defecate, discharge, eject, eliminate, empty, excrete, expel, shit (*taboo slang*), void

evade 1. avoid, circumvent, decline, dodge, duck, elude, escape, escape the clutches of, eschew, get away from, shirk, shun, sidestep, steer clear of **2.** equivocate, flannel (*Brit. informal*), fudge, hedge, prevaricate, quibble, waffle (*informal, chiefly Brit.*)

evaluate appraise, assay, assess, calculate, estimate, gauge, judge, rank, rate, reckon, size up (*informal*), value, weigh

evaluation appraisal, assessment, calculation, estimate, estimation, judgment, opinion, rating, valuation

evanescent brief, ephemeral, fading, fleeting, fugitive, impermanent, momentary, passing, short-lived, transient, transitory, vanishing

evangelical, evangelistic crusading, missionary, propagandizing, proselytizing, zealous

rated rapidly after the election. **evaporable** *adj* **evaporation** *n*

evaporated milk *n* thick unsweetened tinned milk from which some of the water has been removed.

evasion *n* **1** the act of evading something, esp. a duty or responsibility, by cunning or illegal means: *tax evasion.* **2** cunning or deception used to dodge a question, duty, etc.

evasive *adj* **1** seeking to evade; not straightforward: *an evasive answer.* **2** avoiding or seeking to avoid trouble or difficulties: *evasive action.* **evasively** *adv*

eve *n* **1** the evening or day before some special event. **2** the period immediately before an event: *on the eve of the Second World War.* **3** *Poetic or old-fashioned* evening.

even[1] *adj* **1** level and regular; flat. **2** on the same level: *make sure the surfaces are even with one another.* **3** regular and unvarying: *an even pace.* **4** equally balanced between two sides. **5** equal in number, quantity, etc. **6** (of a number) divisible by two. **7** denoting alternatives, events, etc., that have an equal probability: *they have a more than even chance of winning the next election.* **8** having scored the same number of points. **9 even money** *or* **evens** a bet in which the winnings are exactly the same as the amount staked. **10 get even with** *Informal* to exact revenge on; settle accounts with. *~adv* **11** used to suggest that the content of a statement is unexpected or paradoxical: *it's chilly in Nova Scotia, even in August.* **12** used to intensify a comparative adjective or adverb: *an even greater demand.* **13** used to introduce a word that is stronger and more accurate than one already used: *a normal, even inevitable aspect of ageing.* **14** used preceding a hypothesis to emphasize that whether or not the condition is fulfilled, the statement remains valid: *the remark didn't call for an answer even if he could have thought of one.* **15 even so** in spite of any assertion to the contrary; nevertheless. **16 even though** despite the fact that. ~See also **even out, even up. evenly** *adv* **evenness** *n*

even[2] *n Poetic or old-fashioned* **1** eve. **2** evening.

even-handed *adj* fair; impartial.

evening *n* **1** the latter part of the day, esp. from late afternoon until nightfall. *~adj* **2** of or in the evening: *the evening meal.*

evening dress *n* clothes for a formal occasion during the evening.

evening primrose *n* a plant with yellow flowers that open in the evening.

evening star *n* a planet, usually Venus, seen shining brightly in the west just after sunset.

even out *vb* to make or become even, by the removal of bumps, inequalities, etc.

evensong *n Church of England* the daily evening service. Also called: **Evening Prayer**

event *n* **1** anything that takes place, esp. something important. **2** a planned and organized occasion: *the wedding was one of the social events of the year.* **3** any one contest in a sporting programme. **4 at all events** *or* **in any event** whatever happens. **5 in the event** when it came to the actual or final outcome: *in the event, neither of them turned up.* **6 in the event of** if (such a thing) happens. **7 in the event that** if it should happen that.

even-tempered *adj* calm and not easily angered.

eventful *adj* full of exciting or important incidents.

eventide *n Archaic or poetic* evening.

eventing *n Chiefly Brit* riding competitions (esp. **three-day events**), usually involving cross-country riding, jumping, and dressage.

eventual *adj* happening or being achieved at the end of a situation or process: *the Fascists' eventual victory in the Spanish Civil War.* **eventually** *adv*

eventuality *n, pl* **-ties** a possible occurrence or result: *I was utterly unprepared for such an eventuality.*

THESAURUS

evaporate 1. dehydrate, desiccate, dry, dry up, vaporize **2.** dematerialize, disappear, dispel, disperse, dissipate, dissolve, evanesce, fade, fade away, melt, melt away, vanish

evaporation 1. dehydration, desiccation, drying, drying up, vaporization **2.** dematerialization, disappearance, dispelling, dispersal, dissipation, dissolution, evanescence, fading, fading away, melting, melting away, vanishing

evasion artifice, avoidance, circumvention, cop-out (*slang*), cunning, dodge, equivocation, escape, evasiveness, excuse, fudging, obliqueness, pretext, prevarication, ruse, shift, shirking, shuffling, sophism, sophistry, subterfuge, trickery, waffle (*informal, chiefly Brit.*)

evasive cagey (*informal*), cunning, deceitful, deceptive, devious, elusive, equivocating, indirect, misleading, oblique, prevaricating, shifty, slippery, sophistical, tricky

eve 1. day before, night before, vigil **2.** brink, edge, point, threshold, verge

even *adj.* **1.** flat, flush, horizontal, level, parallel, plane, plumb, smooth, steady, straight, true, uniform **2.** constant, metrical, regular, smooth, steady, unbroken, uniform, uninterrupted, unvarying, unwavering **3.** commensurate, comparable, drawn, equal, equalized, equally balanced, fifty-fifty (*informal*), identical, level, level pegging (*Brit. informal*), like, matching, neck and neck, on a par, parallel, similar, square, the same, tied, uniform **4.** balanced, disinterested, dispassionate, equitable, fair, fair and square, impartial, just, unbiased, unprejudiced **5. get even (with)** *informal* be revenged *or* revenge oneself, even the score, give tit for tat, pay back, reciprocate, repay, requite, return like for like, settle the score, take an eye for an eye, take vengeance *~adv.* **6.** all the more, much, still, yet **7.** despite, disregarding, in spite of, notwithstanding **8. even so** all the same, be that as it may, despite (that), however, in spite of (that), nevertheless, nonetheless, notwithstanding (that), still, yet *~vb.* **9.** *often followed by* **out** *or* **up** align, balance, become level, equal, equalize, flatten, level, match, regularize, smooth, square, stabilize, steady

even-handed balanced, disinterested, equitable, fair, fair and square, impartial, just, unbiased, unprejudiced

event 1. adventure, affair, business, circumstance, episode, escapade, experience, fact, happening, incident, matter, milestone, occasion, occurrence **2.** bout, competition, contest, game, tournament **3. at all events** at any rate, come what may, in any case, in any event, regardless, whatever happens

even-tempered calm, composed, cool, coolheaded, equable, imperturbable, level-headed, peaceful, placid, serene, steady, tranquil, unexcitable, unruffled

eventful active, busy, consequential, critical, crucial, decisive, dramatic, exciting, fateful, full, historic, important, lively, memorable, momentous, notable, noteworthy, remarkable, significant

eventual concluding, consequent, ensuing, final, future, later, overall, prospective, resulting, ultimate

eventuality case, chance, contingency, event, likelihood, possibility, probability

eventually after all, at the end of the day, finally, in

even up *vb* to make or become equal.

ever *adv* **1** at any time: *it was the fourth fastest time ever.* **2** always: *ever present.* **3** used to give emphasis: *tell him to put to sea as soon as ever he can.* **4 ever so** *or* **ever such** *Informal, chiefly Brit* used to give emphasis: *I'm ever so sorry.*

evergreen *adj* **1** (of certain trees and shrubs) bearing foliage throughout the year. ~*n* **2** an evergreen tree or shrub.

everlasting *adj* **1** never coming to an end; eternal. **2** lasting so long or occurring so often as to become tedious. **everlastingly** *adv*

evermore *adv* all time to come.

every *adj* **1** each without exception: *they were winning every battle.* **2** the greatest or best possible: *there is every reason to believe in the sincerity of their commitment.* **3** each: *every 20 years.* **4 every bit as** *Informal* just as: *she's every bit as clever as you.* **5 every other** each alternate: *every other month.*

everybody *pron* every person; everyone.
➤ *Everybody* and *everyone* are interchangeable. Although strict usage treats these pronouns as singular, modern practice is to use a plural after them: *Everyone nodded their head.*

everyday *adj* **1** commonplace or usual. **2** happening each day. **3** suitable for or used on ordinary days.

Everyman *n* the ordinary person; common man.

everyone *pron* every person; everybody.
➤ *Everybody* and *everyone* are interchangeable. Although strict usage treats these pronouns as singular, modern practice is to use a plural after them: *Everyone nodded their head.*

everything *pron* **1** the whole; all things: *everything had been carefully packed.* **2** the thing that is most important: *work was everything to her.*

everywhere *adv* to or in all parts or places.

evict *vb* to expel (someone) legally from his or her home or land. **eviction** *n*

evidence *n* **1** something which provides ground for belief or disbelief: *there is no evidence that depression is inherited.* **2** *Law* matter produced before a court of law in an attempt to prove or disprove a point in issue. **3 in evidence** on display; apparent. ~*vb* **-dencing, -denced 4** to show clearly; demonstrate: *you evidenced no talent for music.*

evident *adj* easy to see or understand. **evidently** *adv*

evidential *adj* of, serving as, or based on evidence. **evidentially** *adv*

evil *n* **1** a force or power that brings about wickedness and harm: *the battle between good and evil.* **2** a wicked or morally wrong act or thing: *the evil of racism.* ~*adj* **3** (of a person) deliberately causing great harm and misery; wicked: *an evil dictator.* **4** (of an act, idea, etc.) causing great harm and misery; morally wrong: *what you did was deeply evil.* **5** very unpleasant: *it was fascinating to see people vanish as if we had some very evil smell.* **evilly** *adv*

evildoer *n* a person who does evil. **evildoing** *n*

evil eye *n* **the evil eye** a look superstitiously supposed to have the power of inflicting harm.

evince *vb* **evincing, evinced** *Formal* to show or display (a quality or feeling) clearly: *a humility which he had never evinced in earlier days.*

eviscerate *vb* **-ating, -ated** to remove the internal organs of; disembowel. **evisceration** *n*

evocation *n* the act of evoking. **evocative** *adj*

evoke *vb* **evoking, evoked 1** to call or summon up (a memory or feeling) from the past. **2** to provoke or bring about: *his sacking evoked a huge public protest.*

evolution *n* **1** *Biol* a gradual change in the characteristics of a population of animals or plants over succes-

THESAURUS

the course of time, in the end, in the long run, one day, some day, some time, sooner or later, ultimately, when all is said and done

ever **1.** at all, at any time (period, point), by any chance, in any case, on any occasion **2.** always, at all times, aye (*Scot.*), constantly, continually, endlessly, eternally, everlastingly, evermore, for ever, incessantly, perpetually, relentlessly, to the end of time, unceasingly, unendingly

everlasting **1.** abiding, deathless, endless, eternal, immortal, imperishable, indestructible, infinite, interminable, never-ending, perpetual, timeless, undying **2.** ceaseless, constant, continual, continuous, endless, incessant, interminable, never-ending, unceasing, uninterrupted, unremitting

evermore always, eternally, ever, for ever, to the end of time

every all, each, each one, the whole number

everybody all and sundry, each one, each person, everyone, every person, one and all, the whole world

everyday **1.** accustomed, banal, common, common or garden (*informal*), commonplace, conventional, customary, dull, familiar, frequent, habitual, informal, mundane, ordinary, routine, run-of-the-mill, stock, unexceptional, unimaginative, usual, wonted, workaday **2.** daily, quotidian

everyone all and sundry, each one, each person, everybody, every person, one and all, the whole world

everything all, each thing, the aggregate, the entirety, the lot, the sum, the total, the whole caboodle (*informal*), the whole lot

everywhere all around, all over, far and wide *or* near, high and low, in each place, in every place, omnipresent, the world over, to *or* in all places, ubiquitous, ubiquitously

evict boot out (*informal*), chuck out (*informal*), dislodge, dispossess, eject, expel, kick out (*informal*), oust, put out, remove, show the door (to), throw on to the streets, throw out, turf out (*informal*), turn out

evidence **1.** *n.* affirmation, attestation, averment, confirmation, corroboration, data, declaration, demonstration, deposition, grounds, indication, manifestation, mark, proof, sign, substantiation, testimony, token, witness **2.** *vb.* demonstrate, denote, display, evince, exhibit, indicate, manifest, prove, reveal, show, signify, testify to, witness

evident apparent, blatant, clear, conspicuous, incontestable, incontrovertible, indisputable, manifest, noticeable, obvious, palpable, patent, perceptible, plain, tangible, unmistakable, visible

evidently **1.** clearly, doubtless, doubtlessly, incontestably, incontrovertibly, indisputably, manifestly, obviously, patently, plainly, undoubtedly, unmistakably, without question **2.** apparently, it seems, it would seem, ostensibly, outwardly, seemingly, to all appearances

evil *n.* **1.** badness, baseness, corruption, curse, depravity, heinousness, immorality, iniquity, maleficence, malignity, sin, sinfulness, turpitude, vice, viciousness, villainy, wickedness, wrong, wrongdoing ~*adj.* **2.** bad, base, corrupt, depraved, heinous, immoral, iniquitous, malevolent, malicious, malignant, nefarious, reprobate, sinful, vicious, vile, villainous, wicked, wrong **3.** foul, noxious, offensive, pestilential, putrid, unpleasant, vile

evoke arouse, awaken, call, excite, give rise to, induce, recall, rekindle, stimulate, stir up, summon up

sive generations. **2** a gradual development, esp. to a more complex form. **evolutionary** *adj*

evolve *vb* **evolving, evolved 1** to develop gradually. **2** (of animal or plant species) to undergo evolution.

ewe *n* a female sheep.

ewer *n* a large jug with a wide mouth.

ex[1] *prep Finance* excluding or without: *ex dividend.*

ex[2] *n, pl* **exes** *Informal* one's former wife or husband.

ex- *prefix* **1** out of, outside, or from: *exit.* **2** former: *ex-wife.*

exacerbate (ig-**zass**-er-bate) *vb* **-bating, -bated** to make (pain, emotion, or a situation) worse. **exacerbation** *n*

exact *adj* **1** correct in every detail; strictly accurate. **2** precise, as opposed to approximate. **3** based on measurement and the formulation of laws: *forecasting floods is not an exact science.* ~*vb* **4** to obtain or demand as a right, esp. through force or strength: *the rebels called for revenge to be exacted for the killings.*

exacting *adj* making rigorous or excessive demands.

exaction *n Formal* **1** the act of obtaining or demanding money as a right. **2** a sum or payment exacted.

exactitude *n* the quality of being exact; precision.

exactly *adv* **1** with complete accuracy and precision: *I don't know exactly where in York they live.* **2** in every respect: *he looks exactly like his father.* ~*interj* **3** just so! precisely!

exaggerate *vb* **-ating, -ated 1** to regard or represent as greater than is true. **2** to make greater or more noticeable. **exaggerated** *adj* **exaggeratedly** *adv* **exaggeration** *n*

exalt *vb* **1** to praise highly. **2** to raise to a higher rank. **exalted** *adj* **exaltation** *n*

exam *n* short for **examination.**

examination *n* **1** the act of examining. **2** *Education* exercises, questions, or tasks set to test a person's knowledge and skill. **3** *Med* physical inspection of a patient. **4** *Law* the formal questioning of a person on oath.

examine *vb* **-ining, -ined 1** to inspect carefully or in detail; investigate. **2** *Education* to test a person's knowledge of a subject by written or oral questions. **3** *Med* to investigate a patient's state of health. **4** *Law* to formally question someone on oath. **examinee** *n* **examiner** *n*

example *n* **1** a specimen that is typical of its group; sample: *a fine example of Georgian architecture.* **2** a particular event, object, or person that demonstrates a point or supports an argument, theory, etc.: *Germany is a good example of how federalism works in practice.* **3** a person, action, or thing that is worthy of imitation. **4** a punishment or the person punished regarded as a warning to others. **5 for example** as an illustration.

THESAURUS

evolution development, enlargement, expansion, growth, increase, maturation, progress, progression, unfolding, unrolling, working out

evolve develop, disclose, elaborate, enlarge, expand, grow, increase, mature, open, progress, unfold, unroll, work out

exact 1. *adj.* accurate, careful, correct, definite, explicit, express, faithful, faultless, identical, literal, methodical, meticulous, orderly, particular, precise, punctilious, right, rigorous, scrupulous, severe, specific, strict, true, unequivocal, unerring, veracious, very **2.** *vb.* call for, claim, command, compel, demand, extort, extract, force, impose, insist upon, require, squeeze, wrest, wring

exacting demanding, difficult, hard, harsh, imperious, oppressive, painstaking, rigid, rigorous, severe, stern, strict, stringent, taxing, tough, unsparing

exactly *adv.* **1.** accurately, carefully, correctly, definitely, explicitly, faithfully, faultlessly, literally, methodically, precisely, rigorously, scrupulously, severely, strictly, truly, truthfully, unequivocally, unerringly, veraciously **2.** absolutely, bang, explicitly, expressly, indeed, in every respect, just, particularly, precisely, quite, specifically ~*interj.* **3.** absolutely, assuredly, as you say, certainly, indeed, just so, of course, precisely, quite, quite so, spot-on (*Brit. informal*), truly

exactness accuracy, carefulness, correctness, exactitude, faithfulness, faultlessness, nicety, orderliness, painstakingness, preciseness, precision, promptitude, regularity, rigorousness, rigour, scrupulousness, strictness, truth, unequivocalness, veracity

exaggerate amplify, embellish, embroider, emphasize, enlarge, exalt, inflate, lay it on thick (*informal*), magnify, make a production (out) of (*informal*), overdo, overemphasize, overestimate, overstate

exaggerated amplified, exalted, excessive, extravagant, highly coloured, hyped, hyperbolic, inflated, overblown, overdone, overestimated, overstated, over the top (*informal*), pretentious, tall (*informal*)

exaggeration amplification, embellishment, emphasis, enlargement, exaltation, excess, extravagance, hyperbole, inflation, magnification, overemphasis, overestimation, overstatement, pretension, pretentiousness

exalt 1. acclaim, apotheosize, applaud, bless, extol, glorify, idolize, laud, pay homage to, pay tribute to, praise, reverence, set on a pedestal, worship **2.** advance, aggrandize, dignify, elevate, ennoble, honour, promote, raise, upgrade

exaltation 1. acclaim, acclamation, apotheosis, applause, blessing, extolment, glorification, glory, homage, idolization, laudation, lionization, magnification, panegyric, plaudits, praise, reverence, tribute, worship **2.** advancement, aggrandizement, dignity, elevation, eminence, ennoblement, grandeur, high rank, honour, loftiness, prestige, promotion, rise, upgrading

exalted 1. august, dignified, elevated, eminent, grand, high, high-ranking, honoured, lofty, prestigious **2.** elevated, high-minded, ideal, intellectual, lofty, noble, sublime, superior, uplifting

examination analysis, assay, catechism, checkup, exploration, inquiry, inquisition, inspection, interrogation, investigation, observation, perusal, probe, questioning, quiz, research, review, scrutiny, search, study, survey, test, trial

examine 1. analyse, appraise, assay, check, check out, consider, explore, go over *or* through, inspect, investigate, look over, peruse, ponder, pore over, probe, research, review, scan, scrutinize, sift, study, survey, take stock of, test, vet, weigh, work over **2.** catechize, cross-examine, grill (*informal*), inquire, interrogate, question, quiz

example 1. case, case in point, exemplification, illustration, instance, sample, specimen **2.** archetype, exemplar, ideal, illustration, model, norm, paradigm, paragon, pattern, precedent, prototype, standard **3.** admonition, caution, lesson, warning **4. for example** as an illustration, by way of illustration, e.g., *exempli gratia,* for instance, to cite an instance, to illustrate

exasperate aggravate (*informal*), anger, annoy, bug (*informal*), embitter, enrage, exacerbate, excite, gall, get (*informal*), get in one's hair (*informal*), get on one's nerves (*informal*), hassle (*informal*), incense, inflame, infuriate, irk, irritate, madden, nark (*Brit., Austral., & N.Z. slang*), needle (*informal*), nettle, peeve (*in-*

exasperate *vb* **-ating, -ated** to cause great irritation to. **exasperated** *adj* **exasperating** *adj* **exasperation** *n*
ex cathedra *adj, adv* **1** with the authority of one's official position. **2** *RC Church* (of doctrines of faith or morals) defined by the pope as infallibly true.
excavate *vb* **-vating, -vated 1** to unearth (buried objects) methodically to discover information about the past. **2** to make a hole in something by digging into it or hollowing it out: *one kind of shrimp excavates a hole for itself.* **excavation** *n* **excavator** *n*
exceed *vb* **1** to be greater in degree or quantity. **2** to go beyond the limit of (a restriction).
exceedingly *adv* very; extremely.
excel *vb* **-celling, -celled 1** to be better than; surpass. **2 excel in** *or* **at** to be outstandingly good at.
excellence *n* the quality of being exceptionally good.
Excellency *or* **Excellence** *n, pl* **-lencies** *or* **-lences Your, His** *or* **Her Excellency** a title used to address a high-ranking official, such as an ambassador.
excellent *adj* exceptionally good; outstanding.
except *prep* **1** Also: **except for** not including; apart from: *everyone except Jill laughed.* **2 except that** but for the fact that. *~vb* **3** to leave out or exclude.
excepting *prep* except.
exception *n* **1** anything excluded from or not conforming to a general rule or classification. **2 take exception to** to make objections to.
exceptionable *adj* open to objection.
exceptional *adj* **1** forming an exception. **2** having much more than average intelligence, ability, or skill. **exceptionally** *adv*
excerpt *n* **1** a passage taken from a book, speech, etc.; extract. *~vb* **2** to take a passage from a book, speech, etc.
excess *n* **1** the state or act of going beyond normal or permitted limits. **2** an immoderate or abnormal amount. **3** the amount, number, etc., by which one thing exceeds another. **4** behaviour regarded as too extreme or immoral to be acceptable: *a life of sex, drugs, and drunken excess.* **5 excesses** acts or actions that are unacceptably cruel or immoral: *one of the bloodiest excesses of a dictatorial regime.* **6 in excess of** more than. **7 to excess** to an extreme or unhealthy extent: *he had started to drink to excess.* *~adj* **8** more than normal, necessary, or permitted: *excess fat.* **excessive** *adj* **excessively** *adv*
excess luggage *or* **baggage** *n* luggage that is more in weight or number of pieces than an airline etc., will carry free.
exchange *vb* **-changing, -changed 1** (of two or more people, governments, etc.) to give each other (something similar) at the same time: *they nervously exchanged smiles.* **2** to replace (one thing) with another, esp. to replace unsatisfactory goods: *could I exchange this for a larger size, please?* *~n* **3** the act of exchanging. **4** anything given or received as an equivalent or substitute for something else. **5** an argument. **6** Also called: **telephone exchange** a centre in which telephone lines are interconnected. **7** a place where securities or commodities are traded, esp. by brokers or merchants. **8** a transfer of sums of money of equivalent value, as between different currencies. **9** the system by which commercial debts are settled, esp. by bills of exchange, without direct payment of money. **exchangeable** *adj*

THESAURUS

formal), pique, piss one off (*taboo slang*), provoke, rankle, rile (*informal*), rouse, try the patience of, vex
exasperation aggravation (*informal*), anger, annoyance, exacerbation, fury, ire (*literary*), irritation, passion, pique, provocation, rage, vexation, wrath
excavate burrow, cut, delve, dig, dig out, dig up, gouge, hollow, mine, quarry, scoop, trench, tunnel, uncover, unearth
excavation burrow, cavity, cut, cutting, dig, diggings, ditch, dugout, hole, hollow, mine, pit, quarry, shaft, trench, trough
exceed 1. beat, be superior to, better, cap (*informal*), eclipse, excel, go beyond, outdistance, outdo, outreach, outrun, outshine, outstrip, overtake, pass, surmount, surpass, top, transcend **2.** go beyond the bounds of, go over the limit of, go over the top, overstep
exceedingly enormously, especially, exceptionally, excessively, extraordinarily, extremely, greatly, highly, hugely, inordinately, superlatively, surpassingly, unusually, vastly, very
excel 1. beat, be superior, better, cap (*informal*), eclipse, exceed, go beyond, outdo, outrival, outshine, pass, surmount, surpass, top, transcend **2.** be good, be master of, be proficient, be skilful, be talented, predominate, shine, show talent, take precedence
excellence distinction, eminence, fineness, goodness, greatness, high quality, merit, perfection, pre-eminence, purity, superiority, supremacy, transcendence, virtue, worth
excellent A1 *or* A-one (*informal*), admirable, brill (*informal*), brilliant, capital, champion, choice, cracking (*Brit. informal*), crucial (*slang*), def (*slang*), distinguished, estimable, exemplary, exquisite, fine, first-class, first-rate, good, great, mean (*slang*), mega (*slang*), meritorious, notable, noted, outstanding, prime, select, sovereign, sterling, superb, superior, superlative, tiptop, topnotch (*informal*), world-class, worthy
except 1. *prep. Also* **except for** apart from, bar, barring, besides, but, excepting, excluding, exclusive of, omitting, other than, save (*archaic*), saving, with the exception of **2.** *vb.* ban, bar, disallow, exclude, leave out, omit, pass over, reject, rule out
exception 1. anomaly, departure, deviation, freak, inconsistency, irregularity, oddity, peculiarity, quirk, special case **2. take exception** be offended, be resentful, demur, disagree, object, quibble, take offence, take umbrage
exceptional 1. aberrant, abnormal, anomalous, atypical, deviant, extraordinary, inconsistent, irregular, odd, peculiar, rare, singular, special, strange, uncommon, unusual **2.** excellent, extraordinary, marvellous, notable, outstanding, phenomenal, prodigious, remarkable, special, superior
excess *n.* **1.** glut, leftover, overabundance, overdose, overflow, overload, plethora, remainder, superabundance, superfluity, surfeit, surplus, too much **2.** debauchery, dissipation, dissoluteness, exorbitance, extravagance, immoderation, intemperance, overindulgence, prodigality, unrestraint *~adj.* **3.** extra, leftover, redundant, remaining, residual, spare, superfluous, surplus
excessive disproportionate, enormous, exaggerated, exorbitant, extravagant, extreme, immoderate, inordinate, intemperate, needless, OTT (*slang*), overdone, overmuch, over the top (*slang*), prodigal, profligate, superfluous, too much, unconscionable, undue, unreasonable
exchange *vb.* **1.** bandy, barter, change, commute, convert into, interchange, reciprocate, swap (*informal*), switch, trade, truck *~n.* **2.** barter, dealing, inter-

exchange rate *n* the rate at which the currency unit of one country may be exchanged for that of another.

Exchequer *n Government* (in Britain and certain other countries) the accounting department of the Treasury.

excise[1] *n* **1** a tax on goods, such as spirits, produced for the home market. **2** *Brit* that section of the government service responsible for the collection of excise, now the Board of Customs and Excise.

excise[2] *vb* **-cising, -cised 1** to delete a passage from a book. **2** to remove an organ or part surgically. **excision** *n*

exciseman *n, pl* **-men** *Brit* (formerly) a government agent who collected excise and prevented smuggling.

excitable *adj* nervous and easily excited. **excitability** *n*

excite *vb* **-citing, -cited 1** to make (a person) feel so happy that he or she is unable to relax because he or she is looking forward eagerly to something: *he was excited at the long-awaited arrival of a son.* **2** to cause or arouse (an emotion, response, etc.): *the idea strongly excited his interest.* **3** to arouse sexually. **4** *Physiol* to cause a response in (an organ, tissue, or part). **5** *Physics* to raise (an atom, molecule, etc.) to a higher energy level. **excited** *adj* **excitedly** *adv*

excitement *n* **1** the state of being excited. **2** a person or thing that excites.

exciting *adj* causing excitement; stirring; stimulating. **excitingly** *adv*

exclaim *vb* to cry out or speak suddenly or excitedly, as from surprise, delight, horror, etc.

exclamation *n* **1** an abrupt or excited cry or utterance. **2** the act of exclaiming. **exclamatory** *adj*

exclamation mark *or US* **point** *n* the punctuation mark (!) used after exclamations and forceful commands.

exclude *vb* **-cluding, -cluded 1** to keep out; prevent from entering. **2** to leave out of consideration. **exclusion** *n*

excluding *prep* excepting.

exclusive *adj* **1** excluding or incompatible with anything else: *these two theories are mutually exclusive.* **2** not shared: *exclusive rights.* **3** used or lived in by a privileged minority, esp. a fashionable clique: *an exclusive skiing resort.* **4** not including the numbers, dates, etc., mentioned. **5 exclusive of** except for; not taking account of. **6 exclusive to** limited to; found only in. ~*n* **7** a story reported in only one newspaper. **exclusively** *adv* **exclusivity** *or* **exclusiveness** *n*

excommunicate *vb* **-cating, -cated** to expel (someone) from membership of a church and ban him or her from taking part in its services. **excommunication** *n*

excoriate *vb* **-ating, -ated 1** *Literary* to censure severely. **2** to strip skin from a person or animal. **excoriation** *n*

excrement *n* waste matter discharged from the body; faeces. **excremental** *adj*

excrescence *n* something that protrudes, esp. an outgrowth from a part of the body. **excrescent** *adj*

excreta (ik-**skree**-ta) *pl n* urine and faeces discharged from the body.

excrete *vb* **-creting, -creted** to discharge waste matter, such as urine, sweat, or faeces, from the body. **excretion** *n* **excretory** *adj*

excruciating *adj* **1** unbearably painful; agonizing. **2** hard to bear: *never had an afternoon passed with such excruciating slowness.* **excruciatingly** *adv*

exculpate *vb* **-pating, -pated** to free from blame or guilt.

excursion *n* a short outward and return journey, esp. for sightseeing, etc.; outing.

excuse *n* **1** an explanation offered to justify an action which has been criticized or as a reason for not fulfilling an obligation, etc. ~*vb* **-cusing, -cused 2** to put forward a reason or justification for (an action, fault, or offending person). **3** to pardon (a person) or overlook (a fault). **4** to free (someone) from having to

THESAURUS

change, quid pro quo, reciprocity, substitution, swap (*informal*), switch, tit for tat, trade, traffic, truck **3.** Bourse, market

excitable edgy, emotional, hasty, highly strung, hotheaded, hot-tempered, irascible, mercurial, nervous, passionate, quick-tempered, sensitive, susceptible, temperamental, testy, touchy, uptight (*informal*), violent, volatile

excite agitate, animate, arouse, awaken, discompose, disturb, electrify, elicit, evoke, fire, foment, galvanize, incite, inflame, inspire, instigate, kindle, move, provoke, quicken, rouse, stimulate, stir up, thrill, titillate, waken, whet

excited aflame, agitated, animated, aroused, awakened, discomposed, disturbed, enthusiastic, feverish, flurried, high (*informal*), hot and bothered (*informal*), moved, nervous, overwrought, roused, stimulated, stirred, thrilled, tumultuous, wild, worked up

excitement 1. action, activity, ado, adventure, agitation, animation, commotion, discomposure, elation, enthusiasm, ferment, fever, flurry, furore, heat, kicks (*informal*), passion, perturbation, thrill, tumult, warmth **2.** impulse, incitement, instigation, motivation, motive, provocation, stimulation, stimulus, urge

exciting dramatic, electrifying, exhilarating, inspiring, intoxicating, moving, provocative, rip-roaring (*informal*), rousing, sensational, sexy (*informal*), stimulating, stirring, thrilling, titillating

exclaim call, call out, cry, cry out, declare, ejaculate, proclaim, shout, utter, vociferate, yell

exclamation call, cry, ejaculation, expletive, interjection, outcry, shout, utterance, vociferation, yell

exclude 1. ban, bar, black, blackball, boycott, debar, disallow, embargo, forbid, interdict, keep out, ostracize, prohibit, proscribe, refuse, shut out, veto **2.** count out, eliminate, except, ignore, leave out, omit, pass over, preclude, reject, repudiate, rule out, set aside

exclusion 1. ban, bar, boycott, debarment, embargo, interdict, nonadmission, prohibition, proscription, refusal, veto **2.** elimination, exception, omission, rejection, repudiation

exclusive 1. absolute, complete, confined, entire, full, limited, only, peculiar, private, restricted, single, sole, total, undivided, unique, unshared, whole **2.** aristocratic, chic, choice, clannish, classy (*slang*), cliquish, closed, discriminative, elegant, fashionable, high-toned, limited, narrow, posh (*informal, chiefly Brit.*), private, restricted, restrictive, ritzy (*slang*), select, selfish, snobbish, swish (*informal, chiefly Brit.*), top-drawer, up-market **3.** debarring, except for, excepting, excluding, leaving aside, not counting, omitting, restricting, ruling out

excommunicate anathematize, ban, banish, cast out, denounce, eject, exclude, expel, proscribe, remove, repudiate

excruciating acute, agonizing, burning, exquisite, extreme, harrowing, insufferable, intense, piercing, racking, searing, severe, tormenting, torturous, unbearable, unendurable, violent

carry out a task, obligation, etc.: *a doctor's letter excusing him from games at school.* **5** to allow to leave. **6 be excused** *Euphemistic* to go to the toilet. **7 excuse me!** an expression used to catch someone's attention or to apologize for an interruption, disagreement, etc. **excusable** *adj*

ex-directory *adj Chiefly Brit* not listed in a telephone directory by request.

execrable (**eks**-sik-rab-bl) *adj* of very poor quality. **execrably** *adv*

execrate *vb* **-crating, -crated 1** to feel and express loathing and hatred of (someone or something). **2** to curse (a person or thing). **execration** *n*

execute *vb* **-cuting, -cuted 1** to put a condemned person to death. **2** to carry out or accomplish. **3** to produce or create (a work of art). **4** *Law* to render (a deed) effective, for example by signing it. **5** to carry out the terms of (a contract, will, etc.). **executer** *n*

execution *n* **1** the act of executing. **2** the carrying out or undergoing of a sentence of death. **3** the manner in which something is performed; technique.

executioner *n* a person whose job is to kill people who have been sentenced to death.

executive *n* **1** a person or group responsible for the administration of a project or business. **2** the branch of government responsible for carrying out laws, decrees, etc. *~adj* **3** having the function of carrying plans, orders, laws, etc., into effect: *the executive producer.* **4** of or for executives: *the executive car park.* **5** *Informal* very expensive or exclusive: *executive cars.*

executor *n Law* a person appointed by someone to ensure that the conditions set out in his or her will are carried out. **executorial** *adj* **executrix** *fem n*

exegesis (eks-sij-**jee**-siss) *n, pl* **-ses** (-seez) explanation of a text, esp. of the Bible.

exemplar *n* **1** a person or thing to be copied; model. **2** a typical specimen; example.

exemplary *adj* **1** so good as to be an example worthy of imitation. **2** (of a punishment) extremely harsh, so as to discourage others from committing a similar crime.

exemplify *vb* **-fies, -fying, -fied 1** to show by example. **2** to serve as an example of. **exemplification** *n*

exempt *adj* **1** not subject to an obligation, tax, etc. *~vb* **2** to release (someone) from an obligation, tax, etc. **exemption** *n*

exequies (**eks**-sik-weez) *pl n, sing* **-quy** funeral rites.

exercise *n* **1** physical exertion, esp. for training or keeping fit. **2** an activity planned to achieve a particular purpose: *the group's meeting was mainly an exercise in mutual reassurance.* **3** a set of movements, tasks, etc., designed to improve or test one's ability or fitness. **4** the use or practice of (a right, power, or authority). **5** *Mil* a manoeuvre or simulated combat operation. *~vb* **-cising, -cised 6** to put into use; make use of: *we urge all governments involved to exercise restraint.* **7** to take exercise or perform exercises. **8** to practise using in order to develop or train: *to exercise one's voice.* **9** to worry or vex: *Western governments have been exercised by the need to combat international terrorism.* **10** *Mil* to carry out simulated combat, manoeuvres, etc. **exerciser** *n*

exert *vb* **1** to use influence, authority, etc. forcefully or effectively. **2 exert oneself** to make a special effort.

THESAURUS

excursion airing, day trip, expedition, jaunt, journey, outing, pleasure trip, ramble, tour, trip

excusable allowable, defensible, forgivable, justifiable, minor, pardonable, permissible, slight, understandable, venial, warrantable

excuse *n.* **1.** apology, defence, explanation, grounds, justification, mitigation, plea, pretext, reason, vindication *~vb.* **2.** apologize for, condone, defend, explain, justify, mitigate, vindicate **3.** absolve, acquit, bear with, exculpate, exonerate, extenuate, forgive, indulge, make allowances for, overlook, pardon, pass over, tolerate, turn a blind eye to, wink at **4.** absolve, discharge, exempt, free, let off, liberate, release, relieve, spare

execrate abhor, abominate, anathematize, condemn, curse, damn, denounce, deplore, despise, detest, excoriate, hate, imprecate, loathe, revile, slam (*slang*), vilify

execration abhorrence, abomination, anathema, condemnation, contempt, curse, damnation, detestation, excoriation, hate, hatred, imprecation, loathing, malediction, odium, vilification

execute 1. behead, electrocute, guillotine, hang, kill, put to death, shoot **2.** accomplish, achieve, administer, bring off, carry out, complete, consummate, discharge, do, effect, enact, enforce, finish, fulfil, implement, perform, prosecute, put into effect, realize, render **3.** *Law* deliver, seal, serve, sign, validate

execution 1. accomplishment, achievement, administration, carrying out, completion, consummation, discharge, effect, enactment, enforcement, implementation, operation, performance, prosecution, realization, rendering **2.** capital punishment, hanging, killing **3.** delivery, manner, mode, performance, rendition, style, technique

executioner hangman, headsman

executive 1. *n.* administration, administrator, director, directorate, directors, government, hierarchy, leadership, management, manager, official **2.** *adj.* administrative, controlling, decision-making, directing, governing, managerial

exemplary 1. admirable, commendable, correct, estimable, excellent, fine, good, honourable, ideal, laudable, meritorious, model, praiseworthy, punctilious, sterling **2.** admonitory, cautionary, monitory, warning

exemplify demonstrate, depict, display, embody, evidence, exhibit, illustrate, instance, manifest, represent, serve as an example of, show

exempt 1. *adj.* absolved, clear, discharged, excepted, excused, favoured, free, immune, liberated, not liable, not subject, privileged, released, spared **2.** *vb.* absolve, discharge, except, excuse, exonerate, free, grant immunity, let off, liberate, release, relieve, spare

exemption absolution, discharge, dispensation, exception, exoneration, freedom, immunity, privilege, release

exercise *n.* **1.** action, activity, discipline, drill, drilling, effort, labour, toil, training, work, work-out **2.** drill, lesson, practice, problem, schooling, schoolwork, task, work **3.** accomplishment, application, discharge, employment, enjoyment, exertion, fulfilment, implementation, practice, use, utilization *~vb.* **4.** apply, bring to bear, employ, enjoy, exert, practise, put to use, use, utilize, wield **5.** discipline, drill, habituate, inure, practise, train, work out **6.** afflict, agitate, annoy, burden, distress, disturb, occupy, pain, perturb, preoccupy, trouble, try, vex, worry

exert 1. bring into play, bring to bear, employ, exercise, expend, make use of, put forth, use, utilize, wield **2. exert oneself** apply oneself, bend over backwards (*informal*), break one's neck (*informal*), bust a gut (*informal*), do one's best, do one's damnedest (*informal*), endeavour, give it one's all (*informal*), go for broke (*slang*), go for it (*informal*), knock oneself out (*infor-

exertion *n* **1** effort or exercise, esp. physical effort: *the sudden exertion of running for a bus.* **2** the act or an instance of using one's influence, powers, or authority: *the exertion of parental authority.*

exeunt (**eks**-see-unt) they go out: used as a stage direction.

exfoliate *vb* **-ating, -ated** to peel off in scales or layers. **exfoliation** *n*

ex-gratia (eks-**gray**-sha) *adj* given as a favour where no legal obligation exists: *an ex-gratia payment.*

exhale *vb* **-haling, -haled 1** to expel breath or smoke from the lungs; breathe out. **2** to give off or to be given off as gas, fumes, etc.: *the crater exhaled smoke.* **exhalation** *n*

exhaust *vb* **1** to tire out. **2** to use up totally. **3** to discuss a topic so thoroughly that no more remains to be said. *~n* **4** gases ejected from an engine as waste products. **5** the parts of an engine through which waste gases pass. **exhausted** *adj* **exhaustible** *adj*

exhaustion *n* **1** extreme tiredness. **2** the act of exhausting or state of being exhausted.

exhaustive *adj* very thorough; comprehensive. **exhaustively** *adv*

exhibit *vb* **1** to display (a work of art) to the public. **2** to show (a quality or feeling): *they exhibited extraordinary courage.* *~n* **3** an object exhibited to the public. **4** *Law* a document or object produced in court as evidence. **exhibitor** *n*

exhibition *n* **1** a public display of art, skills, etc. **2** the act of exhibiting or the state of being exhibited: *an exhibition of bad temper.* **3 make an exhibition of oneself** to behave so foolishly that one attracts public attention.

exhibitionism *n* **1** a compulsive desire to attract attention to oneself. **2** a compulsive desire to expose one's genitals publicly. **exhibitionist** *n*

exhilarate *vb* **-rating, -rated** to make (someone) feel lively and cheerful. **exhilaration** *n*

exhilarating *adj* causing strong feelings of excitement and happiness.

exhort *vb Formal* to urge (someone) earnestly. **exhortation** *n*

exhume (ig-**zyume**) *vb* **-huming, -humed** *Formal* to dig up something buried, esp. a corpse. **exhumation** *n*

exigency *n, pl* **-gencies** *Formal* **1** an urgent demand or need. **2** an emergency. **exigent** *adj*

exiguous *adj Formal* scanty or meagre. **exiguity** *n*

exile *n* **1** a prolonged, usually enforced absence from one's country. **2** a person banished or living away from his or her country. *~vb* **-iling, -iled 3** to expel (someone) from his or her country; banish.

exist *vb* **1** to have being or reality; be: *does God exist?* **2** to only just be able to keep oneself alive, esp. because of poverty or hunger. **3** to be living; live. **4** to be present under specified conditions or in a specified place. **existing** *adj*

existence *n* **1** the fact or state of being real, live, or actual. **2** a way of life, esp. a poor or hungry one. **3** everything that exists. **existent** *adj*

existential *adj* **1** of or relating to existence, esp. human existence. **2** of or relating to existentialism.

existentialism *n* a philosophical movement stressing personal experience and responsibility of the individual, who is seen as a free agent. **existentialist** *adj, n*

exit *n* **1** a way out. **2** the act of going out. **3** *Theatre* the act of going offstage. **4** *Brit* a point at which vehi-

THESAURUS

mal), labour, make an all-out effort (*informal*), make an effort, spare no effort, strain, strive, struggle, toil, try hard, work

exertion action, application, attempt, effort, employment, endeavour, exercise, industry, labour, pains, strain, stretch, struggle, toil, travail (*literary*), trial, use, utilization

exhaust 1. bankrupt, cripple, debilitate, disable, drain, enervate, enfeeble, fatigue, impoverish, prostrate, sap, tire, tire out, weaken, wear out **2.** consume, deplete, dissipate, expend, finish, run through, spend, squander, use up, waste

exhausted 1. all in (*slang*), beat (*slang*), clapped out (*Austral. & N.Z. informal*), crippled, dead (*informal*), dead beat (*informal*), dead tired, debilitated, disabled, dog-tired (*informal*), done in (*informal*), drained, enervated, enfeebled, fatigued, jaded, knackered (*slang*), out on one's feet (*informal*), prostrated, ready to drop, sapped, spent, tired out, wasted, weak, worn out, zonked (*slang*) **2.** at an end, consumed, depleted, dissipated, done, expended, finished, gone, spent, squandered, used up, wasted

exhaustion 1. debilitation, enervation, fatigue, feebleness, lassitude, prostration, tiredness, weariness **2.** consumption, depletion, emptying

exhaustive all-embracing, all-inclusive, all-out (*informal*), complete, comprehensive, encyclopedic, extensive, far-reaching, full, full-scale, in-depth, intensive, sweeping, thorough, thoroughgoing, total

exhibit 1. *vb.* air, demonstrate, disclose, display, evidence, evince, expose, express, flaunt, indicate, make clear *or* plain, manifest, offer, parade, present, put on view, reveal, show **2.** *n.* display, exhibition, illustration, model, show

exhibition airing, demonstration, display, exhibit, expo (*informal*), exposition, fair, manifestation, performance, presentation, representation, show, showing, spectacle

exhilarating breathtaking, cheering, enlivening, exalting, exciting, exhilarant, exhilarative, exhilaratory, gladdening, invigorating, stimulating, thrilling, vitalizing

exhort admonish, advise, beseech, bid, call upon, caution, counsel, encourage, enjoin, entreat, goad, incite, persuade, press, prompt, spur, urge, warn

exhortation admonition, advice, beseeching, bidding, caution, counsel, encouragement, entreaty, goading, incitement, lecture, persuasion, sermon, urging, warning

exhume dig up, disentomb, disinter, unbury, unearth

exigency 1. constraint, demand, necessity, need, requirement, wont **2.** crisis, difficulty, emergency, extremity, fix (*informal*), hardship, jam (*informal*), juncture, panic stations (*informal*), pass, pickle (*informal*), pinch, plight, predicament, quandary, scrape (*informal*), strait

exile *n.* **1.** banishment, deportation, expatriation, expulsion, ostracism, proscription, separation **2.** deportee, émigré, expatriate, outcast, refugee *~vb.* **3.** banish, deport, drive out, eject, expatriate, expel, ostracize, oust, proscribe

exist 1. abide, be, be extant, be living, be present, breathe, continue, endure, happen, last, live, obtain, occur, prevail, remain, stand, survive **2.** eke out a living, get along *or* by, stay alive, subsist, survive

existence actuality, animation, being, breath, continuance, continuation, duration, endurance, life, subsistence, survival

existent abiding, around, current, enduring, existing, extant, in existence, living, obtaining, present, prevailing, remaining, standing, surviving

cles may leave or join a motorway. ~*vb* **exiting, exited 5** to go away or out; depart. **6** *Theatre* to go offstage: used as a stage direction: *exit bleeding from the room.*

exocrine *adj* of or denoting a gland, such as the sweat gland, that discharges its product through a duct.

exodus (**eks**-so-duss) *n* the departure of a large number of people.

ex officio (**eks** off-**fish**-ee-oh) *adv, adj* by right of position or office.

exonerate *vb* **-ating, -ated** to clear (someone) of blame or a criminal charge. **exoneration** *n*

exorbitant *adj* (of prices, demands, etc.) excessively great or high: *an exorbitant rent.* **exorbitantly** *adv*

exorcize *or* **-cise** *vb* **-cizing, -cized** *or* **-cising, -cised** to expel (evil spirits) by prayers and religious rites. **exorcism** *n* **exorcist** *n*

exoskeleton *n Zool* the protective or supporting structure covering the outside of the body of many animals, for example insects or crabs.

exothermic *adj* (of a chemical reaction) involving or leading to the giving off of heat.

exotic *adj* **1** having a strange allure or beauty. **2** originating in a foreign country; not native. ~*n* **3** a non-native plant. **exotically** *adv*

exotica *pl n* exotic objects, esp. as a collection.

expand *vb* **1** to make or become greater in extent, size, or scope. **2** to spread out; unfold. **3 expand on** to go into more detail about (a story or subject). **4** to become increasingly relaxed, friendly, and talkative. **5** *Maths* to express a function or expression as the sum or product of terms. **expandable** *adj*

expanse *n* an uninterrupted wide area; stretch: *a large expanse of water.*

expansible *adj* able to expand or be expanded.

expansion *n* **1** the act of expanding. **2** an increase or development, esp. in the activities of a company.

expansionism *n* the practice of expanding the economy or territory of a country. **expansionist** *n, adj*

expansive *adj* **1** wide or extensive. **2** friendly, open, and talkative. **expansiveness** *n*

expat *adj, n* short for **expatriate.**

expatiate (iks-**pay**-shee-ate) *vb* **-ating, -ated expatiate on** *Formal* to speak or write at length on (a subject). **expatiation** *n*

expatriate (eks-**pat**-ree-it) *adj* **1** living away from one's native country: *an expatriate American.* **2** exiled. ~*n* **3** a person living away from his or her native country. **4** an exile. **expatriation** *n*

expect *vb* **1** to regard as likely. **2** to look forward to or be waiting for. **3** to require (something) as an obligation: *he expects an answer by January.* **4 be expecting** *Informal* to be pregnant.

expectancy *n* **1** something expected, esp. on the basis of a norm: *a life expectancy of 78.* **2** anticipation or expectation.

expectant *adj* **1** expecting or hopeful. **2 a** pregnant. **b** married to or living with a woman who is pregnant: *an expectant father.* **expectantly** *adv*

expectation *n* **1** the state of expecting or of being expected. **2** something looked forward to, whether feared or hoped for. **3** belief that someone should behave in a particular way: *women with expectations of old-fashioned gallantry.*

expectorant *Med* ~*adj* **1** helping to bring up phlegm from the respiratory passages. ~*n* **2** an expectorant medicine.

expectorate *vb* **-rating, -rated** *Formal* to cough up and spit out (phlegm from the respiratory passages). **expectoration** *n*

THESAURUS

exit *n.* **1.** door, egress, gate, outlet, passage out, vent, way out **2.** adieu, departure, evacuation, exodus, farewell, going, goodbye, leave-taking, retirement, retreat, withdrawal ~*vb.* **3.** bid farewell, depart, go away, go offstage (*Theatre*), go out, issue, leave, retire, retreat, say goodbye, take one's leave, withdraw

exodus departure, evacuation, exit, flight, going out, leaving, migration, retirement, retreat, withdrawal

exonerate absolve, acquit, clear, discharge, dismiss, exculpate, excuse, justify, pardon, vindicate

exorbitant enormous, excessive, extortionate, extravagant, extreme, immoderate, inordinate, outrageous, preposterous, ridiculous, unconscionable, undue, unreasonable, unwarranted

exorcise adjure, cast out, deliver (from), drive out, expel, purify

exorcism adjuration, casting out, deliverance, driving out, expulsion, purification

exotic 1. bizarre, colourful, curious, different, extraordinary, fascinating, glamorous, mysterious, outlandish, peculiar, strange, striking, unfamiliar, unusual **2.** alien, external, extraneous, extrinsic, foreign, imported, introduced, naturalized, not native

expand 1. amplify, augment, bloat, blow up, broaden, develop, dilate, distend, enlarge, extend, fatten, fill out, grow, heighten, increase, inflate, lengthen, magnify, multiply, prolong, protract, swell, thicken, wax, widen **2.** diffuse, open (out), outspread, spread (out), stretch (out), unfold, unfurl, unravel, unroll **3.** amplify, develop, dilate, elaborate, embellish, enlarge, expatiate, expound, flesh out, go into detail

expanse area, breadth, extent, field, plain, range, space, stretch, sweep, tract

expansion amplification, augmentation, development, diffusion, dilatation, distension, enlargement, expanse, growth, increase, inflation, magnification, multiplication, opening out, spread, swelling, unfolding, unfurling

expansive 1. all-embracing, broad, comprehensive, extensive, far-reaching, inclusive, thorough, voluminous, wide, wide-ranging, widespread **2.** affable, communicative, easy, effusive, free, friendly, garrulous, genial, loquacious, open, outgoing, sociable, talkative, unreserved, warm

expatiate amplify, descant, develop, dilate, dwell on, elaborate, embellish, enlarge, expound, go into detail

expatriate 1. *adj.* banished, emigrant, émigré, exiled, refugee **2.** *n.* emigrant, émigré, exile

expect 1. assume, believe, calculate, conjecture, forecast, foresee, imagine, presume, reckon, suppose, surmise, think, trust **2.** anticipate, await, bargain for, contemplate, envisage, hope for, look ahead to, look for, look forward to, predict, watch for **3.** call for, count on, demand, insist on, look for, rely upon, require, want, wish

expectancy anticipation, assumption, belief, conjecture, expectation, hope, looking forward, prediction, presumption, probability, supposition, surmise, suspense, waiting

expectant 1. anticipating, anxious, apprehensive, awaiting, eager, expecting, hopeful, in suspense, ready, watchful **2.** enceinte, expecting (*informal*), gravid, pregnant

expectation 1. assumption, assurance, belief, calculation, confidence, conjecture, forecast, likelihood, presumption, probability, supposition, surmise, trust **2.** anticipation, apprehension, chance, expectancy,

expediency *or* **expedience** *n, pl* **-encies** *or* **-ences 1** the use of methods that are advantageous rather than fair or just. **2** appropriateness or suitability.

expedient (iks-pee-dee-ent) *n* **1** something that achieves a particular purpose: *income controls were used only as a short-term expedient.* ~*adj* **2** useful or advantageous in a given situation: *they only talk about human rights when it is politically expedient.*

expedite *vb* **-diting, -dited** *Formal* **1** to hasten the progress of. **2** to do quickly.

expedition *n* **1** an organized journey or voyage, esp. for exploration. **2** the people and equipment comprising an expedition. **3** a pleasure trip or excursion: *an expedition to the seaside.* **expeditionary** *adj*

expeditious *adj* done quickly and efficiently.

expel *vb* **-pelling, -pelled 1** to drive out with force. **2** to dismiss from a school, club, etc., permanently.

expend *vb Formal* to spend or use up (time, energy, or money).

expendable *adj* **1** not worth preserving. **2** able to be sacrificed to achieve an objective, esp. a military one.

expenditure *n* **1** something expended, esp. money. **2** the amount expended.

expense *n* **1** a particular payment of money; expenditure. **2** the amount of money needed to buy or do something; cost. **3 expenses** money spent in the performance of a job, etc. **4** something requiring money for its purchase or upkeep. **5 at the expense of** to the detriment of.

expense account *n* **1** an arrangement by which an employee's expenses are refunded by his or her employer. **2** a record of such expenses.

expensive *adj* costing a great deal of money. **expensiveness** *n*

experience *n* **1** direct personal participation or observation of something: *his experience of prison life.* **2** a particular incident, feeling, etc., that a person has undergone. **3** accumulated knowledge, esp. of practical matters. ~*vb* **-encing, -enced 4** to participate in or undergo. **5** to be moved by; feel.

experienced *adj* skilful or knowledgeable as a result of having done something many times before.

experiential *adj Philosophy* relating to or derived from experience.

experiment *n* **1** a test or investigation to provide evidence for or against a theory. **2** the trying out of a new idea or method. ~*vb* **3** to carry out an experiment or experiments. **experimentation** *n* **experimenter** *n*

experimental *adj* **1** relating to, based on, or having the nature of an experiment. **2** trying out new ideas or methods. **experimentally** *adv*

expert *n* **1** a person who has extensive skill or knowledge in a particular field. ~*adj* **2** skilful or knowledgeable. **3** of, involving, or done by an expert. **expertly** *adv*

expertise (eks-per-teez) *n* special skill, knowledge, or judgment.

expiate *vb* **-ating, -ated** *Formal* to make amends for a sin or wrongdoing. **expiation** *n*

expiration *n* **1** the finish of something; expiry. **2** the

---

THESAURUS

fear, hope, looking forward, outlook, possibility, prediction, promise, prospect, suspense **3.** demand, insistence, reliance, requirement, trust, want, wish

expediency, expedience 1. contrivance, device, expedient, makeshift, manoeuvre, means, measure, method, resort, resource, scheme, shift, stopgap, stratagem, substitute **2.** advantageousness, advisability, appropriateness, aptness, benefit, convenience, desirability, effectiveness, fitness, helpfulness, judiciousness, meetness, practicality, pragmatism, profitability, properness, propriety, prudence, suitability, usefulness, utilitarianism, utility

expedient 1. *n.* contrivance, device, expediency, makeshift, manoeuvre, means, measure, method, resort, resource, scheme, shift, stopgap, stratagem, substitute **2.** *adj.* advantageous, advisable, appropriate, beneficial, convenient, desirable, effective, fit, helpful, judicious, meet, opportune, politic, practical, pragmatic, profitable, proper, prudent, suitable, useful, utilitarian, worthwhile

expedite accelerate, advance, assist, dispatch, facilitate, forward, hasten, hurry, precipitate, press, promote, quicken, rush, speed (up), urge

expedition 1. enterprise, excursion, exploration, journey, mission, quest, safari, tour, trek, trip, undertaking, voyage **2.** company, crew, explorers, team, travellers, voyagers, wayfarers

expel 1. belch, cast out, discharge, dislodge, drive out, eject, remove, spew, throw out **2.** ban, banish, bar, black, blackball, discharge, dismiss, drum out, evict, exclude, exile, expatriate, oust, proscribe, relegate, send packing, show one the door, throw out, throw out on one's ear (*informal*), turf out (*informal*)

expend consume, disburse, dissipate, employ, exhaust, fork out (*slang*), go through, lay out (*informal*), pay out, shell out (*informal*), spend, use (up)

expendable dispensable, inessential, nonessential, replaceable, unimportant, unnecessary

expenditure application, charge, consumption, cost, disbursement, expense, outgoings, outlay, output, payment, spending, use

expense charge, consumption, cost, disbursement, expenditure, loss, outlay, output, payment, sacrifice, spending, toll, use

expensive costly, dear, excessive, exorbitant, extravagant, high-priced, inordinate, lavish, overpriced, rich, steep (*informal*), stiff

experience *n.* **1.** contact, doing, evidence, exposure, familiarity, involvement, know-how (*informal*), knowledge, observation, participation, practice, proof, training, trial, understanding **2.** adventure, affair, encounter, episode, event, happening, incident, occurrence, ordeal, test, trial ~*vb.* **3.** apprehend, become familiar with, behold, encounter, endure, face, feel, go through, have, know, live through, meet, observe, participate in, perceive, sample, sense, suffer, sustain, taste, try, undergo

experienced accomplished, adept, capable, competent, expert, familiar, knowledgeable, master, practised, professional, qualified, seasoned, skilful, tested, trained, tried, veteran, well-versed

experiment 1. *n.* assay, attempt, examination, experimentation, investigation, procedure, proof, research, test, trial, trial and error, trial run, venture **2.** *vb.* assay, examine, investigate, put to the test, research, sample, test, try, verify

experimental empirical, exploratory, pilot, preliminary, probationary, provisional, speculative, tentative, test, trial, trial-and-error

expert 1. *n.* ace (*informal*), adept, authority, buff (*informal*), connoisseur, dab hand (*Brit. informal*), hotshot (*informal*), master, past master, pro (*informal*), professional, specialist, virtuoso, whiz (*informal*), wizard **2.** *adj.* able, adept, adroit, apt, clever, deft, dexterous, experienced, facile, handy, knowledgeable, master, masterly, practised, professional, proficient, qualified, skilful, skilled, trained, virtuoso

expertise ableness, adroitness, aptness, cleverness,

act, process, or sound of breathing out. **expiratory** *adj*

expire *vb* **-piring, -pired 1** to finish or run out; come to an end. **2** to breathe out air. **3** to die.

expiry *n, pl* **-ries** a coming to an end, esp. of the period of a contract.

explain *vb* **1** to make something easily understandable, esp. by giving a clear and detailed account of it. **2** to justify or attempt to justify oneself by giving reasons for one's actions. **3 explain away** to offer excuses or reasons for (mistakes).

explanation *n* **1** the reason or reasons why a particular event or situation happened: *there is no reasonable explanation for her behaviour.* **2** a detailed account or description: *a 90-minute explanation of his love of jazz.*

explanatory *adj* serving or intended to serve as an explanation.

expletive (iks-**plee**-tiv) *n* an exclamation or swearword expressing emotion rather than meaning.

explicable *adj* capable of being explained.

explicate *vb* **-cating, -cated** *Formal* to make clear; explain. **explication** *n*

explicit *adj* **1** precisely and clearly expressed, leaving nothing to implication: *an explicit commitment to democracy.* **2** leaving little to the imagination; graphically detailed: *the film contains some sexually explicit scenes.* **3** (of a person) expressing something in a precise and clear way, so as to leave no doubt about what is meant. **explicitly** *adv*

explode *vb* **-ploding, -ploded 1** to burst with great violence; blow up. **2** (of a gas) to undergo a sudden violent expansion as a result of a fast chemical or nuclear reaction. **3** to react suddenly or violently with emotion. **4** (esp. of a population) to increase rapidly. **5** to show (a theory, etc.) to be baseless.

exploit *vb* **1** to take advantage of a person or situation for one's own ends. **2** to make the best use of. *~n* **3** a notable deed or feat. **exploitation** *n* **exploiter** *n*

exploitative *adj* tending to take advantage of a person or situation for one's own ends.

explore *vb* **-ploring, -plored 1** to examine or investigate, esp. systematically. **2** to travel into an unfamiliar region, esp. for scientific purposes. **exploration** *n* **exploratory** *adj* **explorer** *n*

explosion *n* **1** an exploding. **2** a violent release of energy resulting from a rapid chemical or nuclear reaction. **3** a sudden or violent outburst of activity, noise, emotion, etc. **4** a rapid increase.

explosive *adj* **1** able or likely to explode. **2** potentially violent: *an explosive situation.* *~n* **3** a substance capable of exploding. **explosiveness** *n*

expo *n, pl* **-pos** short for **exposition** (sense 3).

exponent *n* **1** a person who advocates an idea, cause, etc.: *an exponent of free speech.* **2** a person who is a skilful performer of some activity: *one of the greatest modern exponents of the blues.* **3** *Maths* a number placed as a superscript to another number indicating how many times the number is to be used as a factor.

exponential *adj* **1** *Maths* of or involving numbers raised to an exponent. **2** *Informal* very rapid. **exponentially** *adv*

export *n* **1** the sale of goods and services to a foreign country: *a ban on the export of arms.* **2 exports** goods or services sold to a foreign country. *~vb* **3** to sell goods or services or transport goods to a foreign country. **exporter** *n*

expose *vb* **-posing, -posed 1** to uncover (something previously covered). **2** to reveal the truth about (someone or something), esp. when it is shocking or scandalous: *an MP whose private life was recently exposed in the press.* **3** to leave (a person or thing) unprotected in a potentially harmful situation: *workers were exposed to relatively low doses of radiation.* **4 expose someone to** to give someone an introduction to or experience of (something new). **5** *Photog* to sub-

THESAURUS

command, craft, deftness, dexterity, expertness, facility, judgment, knack, know-how (*informal*), knowledge, masterliness, mastery, proficiency, skilfulness, skill

expire 1. cease, close, come to an end, conclude, end, finish, lapse, run out, stop, terminate **2.** breathe out, emit, exhale, expel **3.** croak (*slang*), decease, depart, die, kick it (*slang*), kick the bucket (*informal*), pass away *or* on, peg out (*informal*), perish

explain 1. clarify, clear up, define, demonstrate, describe, disclose, elucidate, explicate (*formal*), expound, illustrate, interpret, make clear *or* plain, resolve, solve, teach, unfold **2.** account for, excuse, give an explanation for, give a reason for, justify

explanation 1. clarification, definition, demonstration, description, elucidation, explication, exposition, illustration, interpretation, resolution **2.** account, answer, cause, excuse, justification, meaning, mitigation, motive, reason, sense, significance, vindication

explanatory demonstrative, descriptive, elucidatory, explicative, expository, illuminative, illustrative, interpretive, justifying

explicit absolute, categorical, certain, clear, definite, direct, distinct, exact, express, frank, open, outspoken, patent, plain, positive, precise, specific, stated, straightforward, unambiguous, unequivocal, unqualified, unreserved, upfront (*informal*)

explode 1. blow up, burst, detonate, discharge, erupt, go off, set off, shatter, shiver **2.** belie, debunk, discredit, disprove, give the lie to, invalidate, refute, repudiate

exploit *vb.* **1.** abuse, impose upon, manipulate, milk, misuse, play on *or* upon, take advantage of **2.** capitalize on, cash in on (*informal*), make capital out of, make use of, profit by *or* from, put to use, turn to account, use, use to advantage, utilize *~n.* **3.** accomplishment, achievement, adventure, attainment, deed, escapade, feat, stunt

exploration 1. analysis, examination, inquiry, inspection, investigation, probe, research, scrutiny, search, study **2.** expedition, recce (*slang*), reconnaissance, survey, tour, travel, trip

exploratory analytic, experimental, fact-finding, investigative, probing, searching, trial

explore 1. analyse, examine, inquire into, inspect, investigate, look into, probe, prospect, research, scrutinize, search, work over **2.** case (*slang*), have *or* take a look around, range over, recce (*slang*), reconnoitre, scout, survey, tour, travel, traverse

explosion 1. bang, blast, burst, clap, crack, detonation, discharge, outburst, report **2.** eruption, fit, outbreak, outburst, paroxysm

explosive 1. unstable, volatile **2.** charged, dangerous; fiery, hazardous, overwrought, perilous, stormy, tense, touchy, ugly, vehement, violent

exponent 1. advocate, backer, champion, defender, promoter, propagandist, proponent, spokesman, spokeswoman, supporter, upholder **2.** executant, interpreter, performer, player, presenter

expose 1. display, exhibit, manifest, present, put on view, reveal, show, uncover, unveil **2.** air, betray, blow wide open (*slang*), bring to light, denounce, detect,

ject (a film) to light. **6 expose oneself** to display one's sexual organs in public.

exposé (iks-**pose**-ay) *n* the bringing of a scandal, crime, etc., to public notice.

exposed *adj* **1** not concealed; displayed for viewing: *the exposed soles of his shoes.* **2** without shelter from the elements. **3** vulnerable: *the enemy attacked our army's exposed flank.*

exposition *n* **1** a systematic explanation of a subject. **2** the act of expounding or setting out a viewpoint. **3** a large public exhibition. **4** *Music* the first statement of the themes of a movement.

expository *adj* explanatory.

ex post facto *adj* having retrospective effect.

expostulate *vb* **-lating, -lated expostulate with** to reason or argue with, esp. in order to dissuade or as a protest. **expostulation** *n* **expostulatory** *adj*

exposure *n* **1** the state of being exposed to, or lacking protection from, something: *the body cannot cope with sudden exposure to stress.* **2** the revealing of the truth about someone or something, esp. when it is shocking or scandalous: *the exposure of a loophole in the tax laws.* **3** the harmful effect on a person's body caused by lack of shelter from the weather, esp. the cold. **4** appearance before the public, as on television. **5** *Photog* **a** the act of exposing a film to light. **b** an area on a film that has been exposed. **6** *Photog* **a** the intensity of light falling on a film multiplied by the time for which it is exposed. **b** a combination of lens aperture and shutter speed used in taking a photograph.

exposure meter *n Photog* an instrument for measuring the intensity of light so that suitable camera settings can be chosen.

expound *vb* to explain a theory, belief, etc. in detail.

express *vb* **1** to state (an idea or feeling) in words; utter: *two record labels have expressed an interest in signing the band.* **2** to show (an idea or feeling): *his body and demeanour expressed distrust.* **3** to indicate through a symbol or formula. **4** to squeeze out (juice, etc.). **5 express oneself** to communicate one's thoughts or ideas. *~adj* **6** explicitly stated. **7** deliberate and specific: *she came with the express purpose of causing a row.* **8** of or for rapid transportation of people, mail, etc. *~n* **9** a fast train stopping at only a few stations. **10** *Chiefly US & Canad* a system for sending mail rapidly. *~adv* **11** using a system for rapid transportation of people, mail, etc.: *please send this letter express: it's very urgent!* **expressible** *adj*

expression *n* **1** the transforming of ideas into words. **2** a showing of emotion without words. **3** communication of emotion through music, painting, etc. **4** a look on the face that indicates mood or emotion. **5** a particular phrase used conventionally to express something. **6** *Maths* a variable, function, or some combination of these. **expressionless** *adj*

expressionism *n* an early 20th-century artistic and literary movement which sought to express emotions rather than to represent the physical world. **expressionist** *n, adj*

expression mark *n Music* one of a set of symbols indicating how a piece or passage is to be performed.

expressive *adj* **1** of or full of expression. **2 expressive of** showing or suggesting: *expressive of political tensions.*

expressly *adv* **1** definitely. **2** deliberately and specifically.

expressway *n* a motorway.

expropriate *vb* **-ating, -ated** (of a government or other official body) *Formal* to take (money or property) away from its owners. **expropriation** *n* **expropriator** *n*

expulsion *n* the act of expelling or the fact of being expelled. **expulsive** *adj*

expunge (iks-**sponge**) *vb* **-punging, -punged** *Formal* to remove all traces of: *he had tried to expunge his failure from his mind.*

THESAURUS

disclose, divulge, lay bare, let out, make known, reveal, show up, smoke out, uncover, unearth, unmask **3.** endanger, hazard, imperil, jeopardize, lay open, leave open, make vulnerable, risk, subject **4.** *With to* acquaint with, bring into contact with, familiarize with, introduce to, make conversant with

exposed **1.** bare, exhibited, laid bare, made manifest, made public, on display, on show, on view, revealed, shown, unconcealed, uncovered, unveiled **2.** open, open to the elements, unprotected, unsheltered **3.** in danger, in peril, laid bare, laid open, left open, liable, open, susceptible, vulnerable

exposition **1.** account, commentary, critique, description, elucidation, exegesis, explanation, explication, illustration, interpretation, presentation **2.** demonstration, display, exhibition, expo (*informal*), fair, presentation, show

expostulate argue (with), dissuade, protest, reason (with), remonstrate (with)

exposure **1.** baring, display, exhibition, manifestation, presentation, publicity, revelation, showing, uncovering, unveiling **2.** airing, betrayal, denunciation, detection, disclosure, divulgence, divulging, exposé, revelation, unmasking

expound describe, elucidate, explain, explicate (*formal*), illustrate, interpret, set forth, spell out, unfold

express *vb.* **1.** articulate, assert, asseverate, communicate, couch, declare, enunciate, phrase, pronounce, put, put across, put into words, say, speak, state, tell, utter, verbalize, voice, word **2.** bespeak, convey, denote, depict, designate, disclose, divulge, embody, evince, exhibit, indicate, intimate, make known, manifest, represent, reveal, show, signify, stand for, symbolize, testify **3.** extract, force out, press out, squeeze out *~adj.* **4.** accurate, categorical, certain, clear, definite, direct, distinct, exact, explicit, outright, plain, pointed, precise, unambiguous **5.** clearcut, especial, particular, singular, special **6.** direct, fast, high-speed, nonstop, quick, quickie (*informal*), rapid, speedy, swift

expression **1.** announcement, assertion, asseveration, communication, declaration, enunciation, mention, pronouncement, speaking, statement, utterance, verbalization, voicing **2.** demonstration, embodiment, exhibition, indication, manifestation, representation, show, sign, symbol, token **3.** air, appearance, aspect, countenance, face, look, mien (*literary*) **4.** idiom, locution, phrase, remark, set phrase, term, turn of phrase, word

expressive allusive, demonstrative, eloquent, emphatic, energetic, forcible, indicative, lively, meaningful, mobile, moving, poignant, pointed, pregnant, revealing, significant, striking, strong, suggestive, sympathetic, telling, thoughtful, vivid

expressly **1.** absolutely, categorically, clearly, decidedly, definitely, distinctly, explicitly, in no uncertain terms, manifestly, outright, plainly, pointedly, positively, unambiguously, unequivocally, unmistakably **2.** especially, exactly, intentionally, on purpose, particularly, precisely, purposely, specially, specifically

expropriate appropriate, arrogate, assume, commandeer, confiscate, impound, requisition, seize, take, take over

expulsion banishment, debarment, discharge, dis-

expurgate (**eks**-per-gate) *vb* **-gating, -gated** to amend a piece of writing by removing sections thought to be offensive. **expurgation** *n* **expurgator** *n*

exquisite *adj* **1** extremely beautiful or attractive. **2** showing unusual delicacy and craftsmanship. **3** sensitive or discriminating: *exquisite manners.* **4** intensely felt: *exquisite joy.* **exquisitely** *adv*

ex-serviceman *or fem* **ex-servicewoman** *n, pl* **-men** *or* **-women** a person who has served in the armed forces.

extant *adj* still in existence; surviving.
➤ *Extant* suggests that something still exists because it has survived: *The only example of this fossil extant.*

extemporaneous *adj* spoken or performed without preparation. **extemporaneously** *adv*

extempore (iks-**temp**-or-ee) *adv, adj* without planning or preparation.

extemporize *or* **-rise** *vb* **-rizing, -rized** *or* **-rising, -rised** to perform or speak without preparation. **extemporization** *or* **-risation** *n* **extemporizer** *or* **-riser** *n*

extend *vb* **1** to make bigger or longer than before: *they extended the house by building a conservatory.* **2** to reach to a certain distance or in a certain direction: *the suburbs extend for many miles.* **3** to last for a certain time: *in Norway maternity leave extends to 52 weeks.* **4** to include or affect more people or things than before: *the law was extended to ban all guns.* **5** to make something exist or be valid for longer than before: *her visa was extended for three months.* **6** to present or offer: *a tradition of extending asylum to refugees.* **7** to straighten or stretch out (part of the body): *she extended a hand in welcome.* **8 extend oneself** to make use of all one's ability or strength, often because forced to: *she'll have to really extend herself if she wants to win.* **extendable** *adj*

extended family *n* a social unit in which parents, children, grandparents, and other relatives live as a family unit.

extensible *adj* capable of being extended.

extension *n* **1** a room or rooms added to an existing building. **2** a development that includes or affects more people or things than before: *an extension of democracy within the EU.* **3** an additional telephone connected to the same line as another. **4** an extra period of time in which something continues to exist or be valid: *an extension of the contract for another 2 years.* ~*adj* **5** denoting something that can be extended or that extends another object: *an extension ladder.* **6** of or relating to the provision of teaching and other facilities by a school or college to people who cannot attend full-time courses.

extensive *adj* **1** covering a large area: *extensive moorland.* **2** very great in effect: *the bomb caused extensive damage.* **3** containing many details, ideas, or items on a particular subject: *an extensive collection of modern art.* **extensively** *adv*

extensor *n* any muscle that stretches or extends an arm, leg, or other part of the body.

extent *n* **1** the length, area, or size of something. **2** the scale or seriousness of a situation or difficulty: *the extent of the damage.* **3** the degree or amount to which something applies: *to a certain extent that's true.*

extenuate *vb Formal* **-ating, -ated** to make an offence or fault less blameworthy, by giving reasons that partly excuse it. **extenuating** *adj* **extenuation** *n*

exterior *n* **1** a part or surface that is on the outside. **2** the outward appearance of a person: *Jim's grumpy exterior concealed a warm heart.* **3** a film scene shot outside. ~*adj* **4** of, situated on, or suitable for the outside. **5** coming or acting from outside or abroad.

exterior angle *n* an angle of a polygon contained between one side extended and the adjacent side.

exterminate *vb* **-nating, -nated** to destroy a group or type of people, animals, or plants completely. **extermination** *n* **exterminator** *n*

external *adj* **1** of, situated on, or suitable for the outside: *the house's external walls.* **2** coming or acting from outside: *most ill health is caused by external influences.* **3** of or involving foreign nations: *Hong Kong's external trade.* **4** *Anat* situated on or near the outside of the body: *the external ear.* **5** brought into an organization to do a task which must be done impartially, esp. one involving testing or checking: *external examiners.* **6** of or relating to someone taking a university course, but not attending a university: *an ex-*

THESAURUS

lodgment, dismissal, ejection, eviction, exclusion, exile, expatriation, extrusion, proscription, removal

expurgate blue-pencil, bowdlerize, censor, clean up (*informal*), cut, purge, purify

exquisite **1.** attractive, beautiful, charming, comely, dainty, delicate, elegant, fine, lovely, pleasing, precious, striking **2.** admirable, choice, consummate, delicious, excellent, fine, flawless, incomparable, matchless, outstanding, peerless, perfect, rare, select, splendid, superb, superlative **3.** appreciative, consummate, cultivated, discerning, discriminating, fastidious, impeccable, meticulous, polished, refined, selective, sensitive **4.** acute, excruciating, intense, keen, piercing, poignant, sharp

extempore *adv./adj.* ad lib, extemporaneous, extemporary, freely, impromptu, improvised, offhand, off the cuff (*informal*), off the top of one's head, on the spot, spontaneously, unplanned, unpremeditated, unprepared

extemporize ad-lib, busk, improvise, make up, play (it) by ear, vamp, wing it (*informal*)

extend **1.** add to, amplify, augment, broaden, develop, dilate, enhance, enlarge, expand, increase, spread, supplement, widen **2.** amount to, attain, go as far as, reach, spread **3.** carry on, continue, go on, last, take **4.** carry on, continue, drag out, draw out, elongate, lengthen, make longer, prolong, protract, spin out, spread out, stretch, unfurl, unroll **5.** advance, bestow, confer, give, grant, hold out, impart, offer, present, proffer, put forth, reach out, stretch out, yield

extension **1.** addendum, addition, add-on, adjunct, annexe, appendage, appendix, branch, supplement, wing **2.** amplification, augmentation, broadening, continuation, delay, development, dilatation, distension, elongation, enlargement, expansion, extent, increase, lengthening, postponement, prolongation, protraction, spread, stretching, widening

extensive all-inclusive, broad, capacious, commodious, comprehensive, expanded, extended, far-flung, far-reaching, general, great, huge, humongous (*U.S. slang*), large, large-scale, lengthy, long, pervasive, prevalent, protracted, spacious, sweeping, thorough, universal, vast, voluminous, wholesale, wide, widespread

extent ambit, amount, amplitude, area, bounds, breadth, bulk, compass, degree, duration, expanse, expansion, length, magnitude, measure, play, quantity, range, reach, scope, size, sphere, stretch, sweep, term, time, volume, width

extenuating justifying, mitigating, moderating, qualifying, serving as an excuse

exterior *n.* **1.** appearance, aspect, coating, covering, façade, face, finish, outside, shell, skin, surface ~*adj.* **2.** external, outer, outermost, outside, outward, superficial, surface **3.** alien, exotic, external, extraneous, extrinsic, foreign, outside

ternal degree. ~*n* **7 externals** obvious circumstances or aspects, esp. superficial ones: *despite the war, the externals of life in the city remain normal.* **externality** *n* **externally** *adv*

externalize *or* **-ise** *vb* **-izing, -ized** *or* **-ising, -ised** to express (thoughts or feelings) in words or actions. **externalization** *or* **-isation** *n*

extinct *adj* **1** (of an animal or plant species) having died out. **2** no longer in existence, esp. because of social changes: *shipbuilding is virtually extinct in Scotland.* **3** (of a volcano) no longer liable to erupt.

extinction *n* **1** the dying out of a plant or animal species. **2** the end of a particular way of life or type of activity.

extinguish *vb* **1** to put out (a fire or light). **2** to remove or destroy entirely. **extinguishable** *adj* **extinguisher** *n*

extirpate (**eks**-ter-pate) *vb* **-pating, -pated** to remove or destroy completely: *the Romans attempted to extirpate the Celtic religion.* **extirpation** *n*

extol *or US* **extoll** *vb* **-tolling, -tolled** to praise lavishly.

extort *vb* to obtain money or favours by intimidation, violence, or the misuse of authority. **extortion** *n*

extortionate *adj* (of prices, profits, etc.) much higher than is fair. **extortionately** *adv*

extra *adj* **1** more than is usual, expected or needed; additional. ~*n* **2** a person or thing that is additional. **3** something for which an additional charge is made. **4** *Films* a person temporarily engaged, usually for crowd scenes. **5** *Cricket* a run not scored from the bat. **6** an additional edition of a newspaper. ~*adv* **7** unusually; exceptionally.

extra- *prefix* outside or beyond an area or scope: *extracellular; extraterrestrial.*

extract *vb* **1** to pull out or uproot by force. **2** to remove from a container. **3** to derive (pleasure, information, etc.) from some source. **4** *Informal* to obtain (money, information, etc.) from someone who is not willing to provide it: *a confession extracted by force.* **5** to obtain (a substance) from a material or the ground by mining, distillation, digestion, etc.: *oil extracted from shale.* **6** to copy out (an article, passage, etc.) from a publication. ~*n* **7** something extracted, such as a passage from a book, etc. **8** a preparation containing the concentrated essence of a substance. **extractive** *adj* **extractor** *n*

extraction *n* **1** the act or an instance of extracting. **2** the removal of a tooth by a dentist: *few patients need an extraction.* **3** the origin or ancestry of a person: *he is of German extraction.*

extractor fan *n* a fan used to remove stale air from a room.

extracurricular *adj* not part of the normal courses taken by students: *extracurricular sport.*

extradite *vb* **-diting, -dited** to hand over an alleged offender to the country where the crime took place for trial: *an agreement to extradite him to Hong Kong.* **extraditable** *adj* **extradition** *n*

extramarital *adj* occurring between a married person and a person other than his or her spouse: *an extramarital affair.*

extramural *adj* connected with but outside the normal courses of a university or college.

extraneous (iks-**train**-ee-uss) *adj* not essential or relevant to the situation or subject being considered.

extraordinary *adj* **1** very unusual or surprising: *the extraordinary sight of my grandfather wearing a dress.* **2** having some special or extreme quality: *an extraordinary first novel.* **3** (of a meeting, ambassador, etc.) specially called or appointed to deal with one particular topic. **extraordinarily** *adv*

extrapolate (iks-**trap**-a-late) *vb* **-lating, -lated 1** to infer something not known from the known facts, using logic and reason. **2** *Maths* to estimate the value

THESAURUS

exterminate abolish, annihilate, destroy, eliminate, eradicate, extirpate

external 1. apparent, exterior, outer, outermost, outside, outward, superficial, surface, visible **2.** alien, exotic, exterior, extramural, extraneous, extrinsic, foreign, independent, outside

extinct 1. dead, defunct, gone, lost, vanished **2.** abolished, defunct, ended, obsolete, terminated, void **3.** doused, extinguished, inactive, out, quenched, snuffed out

extinction abolition, annihilation, death, destruction, dying out, eradication, excision, extermination, extirpation, obliteration, oblivion

extinguish 1. blow out, douse, put out, quench, smother, snuff out, stifle **2.** abolish, annihilate, destroy, eliminate, end, eradicate, erase, expunge, exterminate, extirpate, kill, obscure, remove, suppress, wipe out

extol acclaim, applaud, celebrate, commend, cry up, eulogize, exalt, glorify, laud, magnify (*archaic*), panegyrize, pay tribute to, praise, sing the praises of

extort blackmail, bleed (*informal*), bully, coerce, exact, extract, force, squeeze, wrest, wring

extortion blackmail, coercion, compulsion, demand, exaction, force, oppression, rapacity, shakedown (*U.S. slang*)

extortionate excessive, exorbitant, extravagant, immoderate, inflated, inordinate, outrageous, preposterous, sky-high, unreasonable

extra 1. *adj.* accessory, added, additional, add-on, ancillary, auxiliary, excess, extraneous, fresh, further, inessential, leftover, more, needless, new, other, redundant, reserve, spare, supererogatory, superfluous, supernumerary, supplemental, supplementary, surplus, unnecessary, unneeded, unused **2.** *n.* accessory, addendum, addition, add-on, adjunct, affix, appendage, appurtenance, attachment, bonus, complement, extension, supernumerary, supplement **3.** *adv.* especially, exceptionally, extraordinarily, extremely, particularly, remarkably, uncommonly, unusually

extract *vb.* **1.** draw, extirpate, pluck out, pull, pull out, remove, take out, uproot, withdraw **2.** bring out, derive, draw, elicit, evoke, exact, gather, get, glean, obtain, reap, wrest, wring **3.** distil, draw out, express, obtain, press out, separate out, squeeze, take out **4.** abstract, choose, cite, copy out, cull, cut out, quote, select ~*n.* **5.** abstract, citation, clipping, cutting, excerpt, passage, quotation, selection **6.** concentrate, decoction, distillate, distillation, essence, juice

extraction 1. derivation, distillation, drawing, extirpation, pulling, removal, separation, taking out, uprooting, withdrawal **2.** ancestry, birth, blood, derivation, descent, family, lineage, origin, parentage, pedigree, race, stock

extraneous accidental, additional, adventitious, beside the point, extra, immaterial, impertinent, inadmissible, inapplicable, inapposite, inappropriate, inapt, incidental, inessential, irrelevant, needless, nonessential, off the subject, peripheral, redundant, superfluous, supplementary, unconnected, unessential, unnecessary, unneeded, unrelated

extraordinary amazing, bizarre, curious, exceptional, fantastic, marvellous, notable, odd, outstanding, particular, peculiar, phenomenal, rare, remarkable, singular, special, strange, surprising, uncommon, un-

of a function or measurement beyond the known values, by the extension of a curve. **extrapolation** *n*

extrasensory *adj* of or relating to extrasensory perception.

extrasensory perception *n* the supposed ability to obtain information without the use of normal senses of sight, hearing, etc.

extravagant *adj* **1** spending more than is reasonable or affordable. **2** costing more than is reasonable or affordable: *an extravagant gift.* **3** going beyond usual or reasonable limits: *extravagant expectations.* **4** (of behaviour or gestures) extreme, esp. in order to make a particular impression: *an extravagant display of affection.* **5** very elaborate and impressive: *extravagant costumes.* **extravagance** *n*

extravaganza *n* **1** an elaborate and lavish entertainment. **2** any fanciful display, literary composition, etc.

extravert *adj, n* same as **extrovert.**

extreme *adj* **1** of a high or the highest degree or intensity. **2** exceptionally severe or unusual: *people can survive extreme conditions.* **3** (of an opinion, political group, etc.) beyond the limits regarded as acceptable; fanatical. **4** farthest or outermost. *~n* **5** either of the two limits of a scale or range. **6 go to extremes** to be unreasonable in speech or action. **7 in the extreme** to the highest or further degree: *the effect was dramatic in the extreme.* **extremely** *adv*

extreme unction *n RC Church* a former name for **anointing of the sick.**

extremist *n* **1** a person who favours or uses extreme or violent methods, esp. to bring about political change. *~adj* **2** holding extreme opinions or using extreme methods. **extremism** *n*

extremity *n, pl* **-ties 1** the farthest point. **2** an unacceptable or extreme nature or degree: *the extremity of his views alienated other nationalists.* **3** an extreme condition, such as misfortune. **4 extremities** hands and feet.

extricate *vb* **-cating, -cated** to free from a difficult or complicated situation or place. **extricable** *adj* **extrication** *n*

extrinsic *adj* **1** not an integral or essential part. **2** originating or acting from outside. **extrinsically** *adv*

extroversion *n Psychol* the directing of one's interests outwards, esp. towards making social contacts.

extrovert *adj* **1** lively and outgoing. **2** *Psychol* concerned more with external reality than inner feelings. *~n* **3** a person who has these characteristics. **extroverted** *adj*

extrude *vb* **-truding, -truded 1** to squeeze or force out. **2** to produce moulded sections of plastic, metal, etc. by forcing through a shaped die. **extruded** *adj* **extrusion** *n*

exuberant *adj* **1** full of vigour and high spirits. **2** (of vegetation) growing thickly; flourishing. **exuberance** *n*

exude *vb* **-uding, -uded 1** (of a liquid or smell) to seep or flow out slowly and steadily. **2** to seem to have (a quality or feeling) to a great degree: *the Chancellor exuded confidence.* **exudation** *n*

exult *vb* to be joyful or jubilant. **exultation** *n* **exultant** *adj*

eye *n* **1** the organ of sight in humans and animals. **2** the external part of an eye, often including the area

THESAURUS

familiar, unheard-of, unique, unprecedented, unusual, unwonted, weird, wonderful, wondrous (*archaic or literary*)

extravagance 1. improvidence, lavishness, overspending, prodigality, profligacy, profusion, squandering, waste, wastefulness **2.** absurdity, dissipation, exaggeration, excess, exorbitance, folly, immoderation, outrageousness, preposterousness, recklessness, unreasonableness, unrestraint, wildness

extravagant 1. excessive, improvident, imprudent, lavish, prodigal, profligate, spendthrift, wasteful **2.** costly, excessive, exorbitant, expensive, extortionate, inordinate, overpriced, steep (*informal*), unreasonable **3.** absurd, exaggerated, excessive, exorbitant, fanciful, fantastic, foolish, immoderate, inordinate, OTT (*slang*), outrageous, over the top (*slang*), preposterous, reckless, unreasonable, unrestrained, wild **4.** fancy, flamboyant, flashy, garish, gaudy, grandiose, ornate, ostentatious, pretentious, showy

extreme *adj.* **1.** acute, great, greatest, high, highest, intense, maximum, severe, supreme, ultimate, utmost, uttermost, worst **2.** dire, Draconian, drastic, harsh, radical, rigid, severe, stern, strict, unbending, uncompromising **3.** downright, egregious, exaggerated, exceptional, excessive, extraordinary, extravagant, fanatical, immoderate, inordinate, intemperate, OTT (*slang*), out-and-out, outrageous, over the top (*slang*), radical, remarkable, sheer, uncommon, unconventional, unreasonable, unusual, utter, zealous **4.** faraway, far-off, farthest, final, last, most distant, outermost, remotest, terminal, ultimate, utmost, uttermost *~n.* **5.** acme, apex, apogee, boundary, climax, consummation, depth, edge, end, excess, extremity, height, limit, maximum, minimum, nadir, pinnacle, pole, termination, top, ultimate, zenith

extremely acutely, awfully (*informal*), exceedingly, exceptionally, excessively, extraordinarily, greatly, highly, inordinately, intensely, markedly, quite, severely, terribly, to *or* in the extreme, ultra, uncommonly, unusually, utterly, very

extremist die-hard, fanatic, radical, ultra, zealot

extremity 1. acme, apex, apogee, border, bound, boundary, brim, brink, edge, end, extreme, frontier, limit, margin, maximum, minimum, nadir, pinnacle, pole, rim, terminal, termination, terminus, tip, top, ultimate, verge, zenith **2.** adversity, crisis, dire straits, disaster, emergency, exigency, hardship, pinch, plight, setback, trouble **3.** *plural* fingers and toes, hands and feet, limbs

extricate clear, deliver, disembarrass, disengage, disentangle, free, get out, get (someone) off the hook (*slang*), liberate, release, relieve, remove, rescue, withdraw, wriggle out of

exuberance 1. animation, buoyancy, cheerfulness, eagerness, ebullience, effervescence, energy, enthusiasm, excitement, exhilaration, high spirits, life, liveliness, pep, spirit, sprightliness, vigour, vitality, vivacity, zest **2.** abundance, copiousness, lavishness, lushness, luxuriance, plenitude, profusion, rankness, richness, superabundance, teemingness

exuberant 1. animated, buoyant, cheerful, chirpy (*informal*), eager, ebullient, effervescent, elated, energetic, enthusiastic, excited, exhilarated, full of life, high-spirited, in high spirits, lively, sparkling, spirited, sprightly, upbeat (*informal*), vigorous, vivacious, zestful **2.** abundant, copious, lavish, lush, luxuriant, overflowing, plenteous, plentiful, profuse, rank, rich, superabundant, teeming

exult be delighted, be elated, be in high spirits, be joyful, be jubilant, be overjoyed, celebrate, jubilate, jump for joy, make merry, rejoice

exultant cock-a-hoop, delighted, elated, exulting, flushed, gleeful, joyful, joyous, jubilant, overjoyed, over the moon (*informal*), rapt, rejoicing, revelling, transported, triumphant

around it. 3 (*often pl*) the ability to see or record what is happening: *the eyes of an entire nation were upon us.* 4 a look, glance, or gaze. 5 attention or observation: *his new shirt caught my eye.* 6 the ability to judge or appreciate something: *his shrewd eye for talent.* 7 (*often pl*) opinion, judgment, or authority: *in the eyes of the law.* 8 a dark spot on a potato from which new shoots can grow. 9 a small hole, such as the one at the blunt end of a sewing needle. 10 a small area of calm in the centre of a storm, hurricane, or tornado. 11 **all eyes** *Informal* acutely vigilant. 12 **an eye for an eye** justice consisting of an equivalent action to the original wrong or harm. 13 **clap, lay** *or* **set eyes on** to see: *I never laid eyes on him again.* 14 **have eyes for** to be interested in. 15 **in one's mind's eye** imagined or remembered vividly. 16 **in the public eye** exposed to public curiosity. 17 **keep an eye on** to take care of. 18 **keep an eye open** *or* **out for** to watch with special attention for. 19 **keep one's eyes skinned** *or* **peeled** to watch vigilantly. 20 **look someone in the eye** to look openly and without embarrassment at someone. 21 **make eyes at someone** to look at someone in an obviously attracted manner. 22 **more than meets the eye** hidden motives, meanings, or facts. 23 **my eye!** *Old-fashioned informal* nonsense! 24 **see eye to eye with** to agree with. 25 **shut one's eyes to** *or* **turn a blind eye to** to pretend not to notice. 26 **up to one's eyes in** extremely busy with. 27 **with an eye to** with the intention of. 28 **with one's eyes open** in full knowledge of all the facts. *~vb* **eyeing** *or* **eying, eyed** 29 to look at carefully or warily. ~See also **eye up. eyeless** *adj* **eyelike** *adj*

eyeball *n* 1 the entire ball-shaped part of the eye. 2 **eyeball to eyeball** in close confrontation.

eyebrow *n* 1 the bony ridge over each eye. 2 the arch of hair on this ridge. 3 **raise an eyebrow** to show doubt or disapproval.

eye-catching *adj* very striking and tending to catch people's attention. **eye-catcher** *n*

eye dog *n NZ* a dog trained to control sheep by staring at them.

eyeful *n* 1 *Slang* a good look at or view of something. 2 *Slang* an attractive sight, esp. a woman. 3 an amount of liquid, dust, etc., that has got into someone's eye.

eyeglass *n* a lens for aiding defective vision.

eyelash *n* any of the short hairs that grow from the edge of the eyelids.

eyelet *n* 1 a small hole for a lace or cord to be passed through. 2 a small metal ring reinforcing such a hole.

eyelevel *adj* level with a person's eyes: *an eyelevel oven.*

eyelid *n* either of the two folds of skin that cover an eye when it is closed.

eyeliner *n* a cosmetic used to outline the eyes.

eye-opener *n Informal* something startling or revealing.

eyepiece *n* the lens in a microscope, telescope, etc., into which the person using it looks.

eye shadow *n* a coloured cosmetic worn on the upper eyelids.

eyesight *n* the ability to see: *poor eyesight.*

eyesore *n* something very ugly.

eyestrain *n* fatigue or irritation of the eyes, caused by tiredness or a failure to wear glasses.

eyetooth *n, pl* **-teeth** 1 either of the two canine teeth in the upper jaw. 2 **give one's eyeteeth for** to go to any lengths to achieve or obtain (something).

eye up *vb Informal* to look at (someone) in a way that indicates sexual interest.

eyewash *n* 1 a lotion for the eyes. 2 *Informal* nonsense; rubbish.

eyewitness *n* a person present at an event who can describe what happened.

eyrie *n* 1 the nest of an eagle, built in a high inaccessible place. 2 any high isolated place.

THESAURUS

exultation celebration, delight, elation, glee, high spirits, joy, joyousness, jubilation, merriness, rejoicing, transport

eye *n.* **1.** eyeball, optic (*informal*), orb (*poetic*), peeper (*slang*) **2.** appreciation, discernment, discrimination, judgment, perception, recognition, taste **3.** *often plural* belief, judgment, mind, opinion, point of view, viewpoint **4. keep an** *or* **one's eye on** guard, keep in view, keep tabs on (*informal*), keep under surveillance, look after, look out for, monitor, observe, pay attention to, regard, scrutinize, supervise, survey, watch, watch over **5. an eye for an eye** justice, reprisal, requital, retaliation, retribution, revenge, vengeance **6. lay, clap** *or* **set eyes on** behold, come across, encounter, meet, notice, observe, run into, see **7. see eye to eye** accord, agree, back, be in unison, coincide, concur, fall in, get on, go along, harmonize, jibe (*informal*), subscribe to **8. up to one's eyes** busy, caught up, engaged, flooded out, fully occupied, inundated, overwhelmed, up to here, up to one's elbows, wrapped up in *~vb.* **9.** check, check out (*informal*), clock (*Brit. slang*), contemplate, gaze at, get a load of (*informal*), glance at, have *or* take a look at, inspect, look at, peruse, recce (*slang*), regard, scan, scrutinize, stare at, study, survey, take a dekko at (*Brit. slang*), view, watch **10.** eye up, give (someone) the (glad) eye, leer at, make eyes at, ogle

eyesight observation, perception, range of vision, sight, vision

eyesore atrocity, blemish, blight, blot, disfigurement, disgrace, horror, mess, monstrosity, sight (*informal*), ugliness

eyewitness bystander, looker-on, observer, onlooker, passer-by, spectator, viewer, watcher, witness

F

f[1] *Physics* frequency.
f[2], **f/**, *or* **f:** f-number.
F **1** *Music* the fourth note of the scale of C major. **2** Fahrenheit. **3** farad(s). **4** *Chem* fluorine. **5** *Physics* force. **6** franc(s).
f. *or* **F.** **1** fathom(s). **2** female. **3** *Grammar* feminine. **4** (*pl* **ff.**) following (page).
fa *n Music* same as **fah.**
FA (in Britain) Football Association.
Fabian (**fay**-bee-an) *adj* **1** of the Fabian Society, which aims to establish socialism gradually and democratically. *~n* **2** a member of the Fabian Society. **Fabianism** *n*
fable *n* **1** a short story, often one with animals as characters, that illustrates a moral. **2** an unlikely story which is usually untrue. **3** a story about mythical characters or events.
fabled *adj* well-known from anecdotes and stories rather than experience: *the fabled Timbuktu.*
Fablon *n Trademark* a brand of adhesive-backed plastic used for covering surfaces.
fabric *n* **1** any cloth made from yarn or fibres by weaving or knitting. **2** the structure that holds a system together: *the fabric of British society.* **3** the walls, floor, and roof of a building.
fabricate *vb* **-cating, -cated** **1** to invent a story or lie: *fabricated reports about the opposition.* **2** to make or build. **fabrication** *n*
fabulous *adj* **1** *Informal* extremely good. **2** almost unbelievable: *a city of fabulous wealth.* **3** told of in fables and legends: *a fabulous horned creature.* **fabulously** *adv*
facade (fass-**sahd**) *n* **1** the front of a building. **2** a front or deceptive outer appearance.
face *n* **1** the front of the head from the forehead to the lower jaw. **2 a** one's expression: *as his eyes met hers his face sobered.* **b** a distorted expression to show disgust or defiance: *she was pulling a face at him.* **3** the front or main side of an object, building, etc. **4** the surface of a clock or watch that has the numbers or hands on it. **5** the functional side of an object, such as a tool or playing card. **6** the exposed area of a mine from which coal or metal can be mined. **7 in the face of** in spite of: *a determined character in the face of adversity.* **8 lose face** to lose one's credibility. **9 on the face of it** to all appearances. **10 put a good face** *or* **brave face on** to maintain a cheerful appearance despite misfortune. **11 save face** to keep one's good reputation. **12 set one's face against** to oppose with determination. **13 to someone's face** directly and openly. *~vb* **facing, faced** **14** to look towards. **15** to be opposite. **16** to be confronted by: *they were faced with the prospect of high inflation.* **17** to provide with a surface of a different material. ~See also **face up to.**
face card *n* a playing card showing a king, queen, or jack.
faceless *adj* without individual identity or character: *faceless government officials.*
face-lift *n* **1** cosmetic surgery for tightening sagging skin and smoothing wrinkles on the face. **2** an outward improvement designed to give a more modern appearance: *the stadium was given a face-lift.*
facer *n Brit old-fashioned informal* a difficulty or problem.
face-saving *adj* preventing damage to one's reputation. **face-saver** *n*
facet *n* **1** an aspect of something, such as a personality. **2** any of the surfaces of a cut gemstone.
facetious (fass-**see**-shuss) *adj* joking, or trying to be amusing, esp. at inappropriate times. **facetiously** *adv*
face up to *vb* to accept an unpleasant fact or reality.
face value *n* apparent worth or meaning: *only a fool would take it at face value.*
facia (**fay**-shee-a) *n, pl* **-ciae** (-shee-ee) same as **fascia.**
facial *adj* **1** of the face. *~n* **2** a beauty treatment for the face. **facially** *adv*
facile (**fass**-ile) *adj* **1** (of a remark, argument, etc.)

THESAURUS

fable **1.** allegory, parable **2.** fabrication, fairy story (*informal*), falsehood, fantasy, fib, fiction, figment, invention, lie, romance, tall story (*informal*), untruth, urban legend, white lie, yarn (*informal*) **3.** legend, myth, story, tale
fabric **1.** cloth, material, stuff, textile, web **2.** constitution, construction, foundations, framework, infrastructure, make-up, organization, structure
fabricate **1.** coin, concoct, devise, fake, falsify, feign, forge, form, invent, make up, trump up **2.** assemble, build, construct, erect, fashion, form, frame, make, manufacture, shape
fabrication **1.** cock-and-bull story (*informal*), concoction, fable, fairy story (*informal*), fake, falsehood, fiction, figment, forgery, invention, lie, myth, pork pie (*Brit. slang*), porky (*Brit. slang*), untruth **2.** assemblage, assembly, building, construction, erection, manufacture, production
fabulous **1.** *informal* brilliant, fantastic (*informal*), magic (*informal*), marvellous, out-of-this-world (*informal*), sensational (*informal*), spectacular, superb, wonderful **2.** amazing, astounding, breathtaking, fictitious, immense, inconceivable, incredible, legendary, phenomenal, unbelievable **3.** apocryphal, fantastic, fictitious, imaginary, invented, legendary, made-up, mythical, unreal
facade appearance, exterior, face, front, frontage, guise, mask, pretence, semblance, show, veneer
face *n.* **1.** clock (*Brit. slang*), countenance, dial (*Brit. slang*), features, kisser (*slang*), lineaments, mug (*slang*), physiognomy **2.** appearance, aspect, expression, frown, grimace, look, pout, scowl, smirk **3.** aspect, cover, exterior, facet, front, outside, right side, side, surface **4. on the face of it** apparently, at first sight, seemingly, to all appearances, to the eye **5. to someone's face** directly, in one's presence, openly, straight *~vb.* **6.** be opposite, front onto, give towards *or* onto, look onto, overlook **7.** be confronted by, brave, come up against, confront, cope with, deal with, defy, encounter, experience, meet, oppose, tackle **8.** clad, coat, cover, dress, finish, level, line, overlay, sheathe, surface
facet angle, aspect, face, part, phase, plane, side, slant, surface
facetious amusing, comical, droll, flippant, frivolous, funny, humorous, jesting, jocose, jocular, merry, playful, pleasant, tongue in cheek, unserious, waggish, witty
face up to accept, acknowledge, come to terms with, confront, cope with, deal with, meet head-on, tackle

overly simple and showing lack of real thought. **2** easily performed or achieved: *a facile winner of his only race this year.*

facilitate *vb* **-tating, -tated** to make easier the progress of: *the agreement helped facilitate trade between the countries.* **facilitation** *n*

facility *n, pl* **-ties 1 facilities** the means or equipment needed for an activity: *leisure and shopping facilities.* **2** the ability to do things easily and well. **3** skill or ease: *grown human beings can forget with remarkable facility.*

facing *n* **1** a piece of material used esp. to conceal the seam of a garment. **2 facings** contrasting collar and cuffs on a jacket. **3** an outer layer of material applied to the surface of a wall.

facsimile (fak-**sim**-ill-ee) *n* **1** an exact copy. **2** same as **fax** (senses 1, 2).

fact *n* **1** an event or thing known to have happened or existed. **2** a truth that can be proved from experience or observation. **3** a piece of information. **4 after** *or* **before the fact** *Criminal law* after or before the commission of the offence. **5 as a matter of fact** *or* **in fact** in reality or actuality. **6 fact of life** an inescapable truth, esp. an unpleasant one. See also **facts of life.**

faction[1] *n* **1** a small group of people within a larger body, but differing from it in certain aims and ideas. **2** strife within a group. **factional** *adj*

faction[2] *n* a dramatized presentation of actual events.

factitious *adj* artificial rather than natural.

factor *n* **1** an element that contributes to a result: *reliability was an important factor in the success of the car.* **2** *Maths* any whole number that will divide exactly into a given number, for example 2 and 3 are factors of 6. **3** a quantity by which an amount is multiplied or divided to become that number of times bigger or smaller: *production increased by a factor of 3.* **4** a level on a scale of measurement: *suntan oil with a factor of 5.* **5** (in Scotland) the manager of an estate.

factorial *Maths ~n* **1** the product of all the whole numbers from one to a given whole number. *~adj* **2** of factorials or factors.

factorize *or* **-rise** *vb* **-izing, -ized** *or* **-ising, -ised** *Maths* to resolve a whole number into factors. **factorization** *or* **-risation** *n*

factory *n, pl* **-ries** a building where goods are manufactured in large quantities.

factory farm *n* a farm in which animals are given foods that increase the amount of meat, eggs, or milk they yield. **factory farming** *n*

factory ship *n* a vessel that processes fish supplied by a fleet.

factotum *n* a person employed to do all kinds of work.

facts of life *pl n* the details of sexual behaviour and reproduction.

factual *adj* concerning facts rather than opinions or theories: *a factual report.* **factually** *adv*

faculty *n, pl* **-ties 1** one of the powers of the mind or body, such as memory, sight, or hearing. **2** any ability or power, either inborn or acquired: *his faculties of reasoning were considerable.* **3 a** a department within a university or college. **b** its staff. **c** *Chiefly US & Canad* all the staff of a university, school, or college.

fad *n Informal* **1** an intense but short-lived fashion: *the skateboard fad.* **2** a personal whim. **faddish** *adj*

faddy *adj* **-dier, -diest** unreasonably fussy, particularly about food.

fade *vb* **fading, faded 1** to lose brightness, colour, or strength. **2 fade away** *or* **out** to vanish slowly.

fade in *or* **out** *vb* (of vision or sound in a film or broadcast) to increase or decrease gradually.

faeces *or esp US* **feces** (**fee**-seez) *pl n* bodily waste matter discharged through the anus. **faecal** *or esp US* **fecal** (**fee**-kl) *adj*

Faeroese *or* **Faroese** (fair-oh-**eez**) *adj* **1** of the Faeroes, islands in the N Atlantic. *~n* **2** (*pl* **-ese**) a person from the Faeroes. **3** the language of the Faeroes.

THESAURUS

facile 1. cursory, glib, hasty, shallow, slick, superficial **2.** adept, adroit, dexterous, easy, effortless, fluent, light, proficient, quick, ready, simple, skilful, smooth, uncomplicated

facilitate assist the progress of, ease, expedite, forward, further, help, make easy, promote, smooth the path of, speed up

facility 1. *plural* amenities, equipment, means, resources **2.** ability, adroitness, craft, dexterity, ease, efficiency, effortlessness, expertness, fluency, gift, knack, proficiency, quickness, readiness, skilfulness, skill, smoothness, talent

facing cladding, coating, façade, false front, front, overlay, plaster, reinforcement, stucco, surface, trimming, veneer

facsimile carbon, carbon copy, copy, duplicate, fax (*Trademark*), photocopy, Photostat (*Trademark*), print, replica, reproduction, transcript, Xerox (*Trademark*)

fact 1. act, deed, event, *fait accompli*, happening, incident, occurrence, performance **2.** actuality, certainty, gospel (truth), naked truth, reality, truth **3.** circumstance, detail, feature, item, particular, point, specific **4. in fact** actually, indeed, in point of fact, in reality, in truth, really, truly

faction 1. bloc, cabal, camp, caucus, clique, coalition, combination, confederacy, contingent, coterie, division, gang, ginger group, group, junta, lobby, minority, party, pressure group, schism, section, sector, set, splinter group **2.** conflict, disagreement, discord, disharmony, dissension, disunity, division, divisiveness, friction, infighting, rebellion, sedition, strife, tumult, turbulence

factor 1. aspect, cause, circumstance, component, consideration, determinant, element, influence, item, part, point, thing **2.** *Scot.* agent, deputy, estate manager, middleman, steward

factory mill, plant, works

factotum Girl Friday, handyman, jack of all trades, Man Friday, man of all work, odd job man

facts data, details, gen (*Brit. informal*), info (*informal*), information, the lowdown (*informal*), the score (*informal*), the whole story

factual accurate, authentic, circumstantial, close, correct, credible, exact, faithful, genuine, literal, matter-of-fact, objective, precise, real, sure, true, true-to-life, unadorned, unbiased, veritable

faculties capabilities, intelligence, powers, reason, senses, wits

faculty 1. ability, adroitness, aptitude, bent, capability, capacity, cleverness, dexterity, facility, gift, knack, power, propensity, readiness, skill, talent, turn **2.** branch of learning, department, discipline, profession, school, teaching staff (*chiefly U.S.*)

fad affectation, craze, fancy, fashion, mania, mode, rage, trend, vogue, whim

fade 1. blanch, bleach, blench, dim, discolour, dull, grow dim, lose colour, lose lustre, pale, wash out **2.** decline, die away, die out, dim, disappear, disperse, dissolve, droop, dwindle, ebb, etiolate, evanesce, fail,

faff about *vb Brit informal* to dither or fuss.

fag[1] *n* **1** *Informal* a boring or tiring task: *weeding was a fag.* **2** *Brit* (esp. formerly) a young public school boy who performs menial chores for an older boy. *~vb* **fagging, fagged 3** *Brit* to do menial chores in a public school.

fag[2] *n Brit slang* a cigarette.

fag[3] *n Offensive slang, chiefly US & Canad* short for **faggot**[2].

fag end *n* **1** the last and worst part: *another dull game at the fag end of the football season.* **2** *Brit informal* the stub of a cigarette.

fagged *adj Informal* exhausted by hard work. Also: **fagged out**

faggot[1] *or esp US* **fagot** *n* **1** a ball of chopped liver bound with herbs and bread. **2** a bundle of sticks.

faggot[2] *n Offensive slang, chiefly US & Canad* a male homosexual.

fah *n Music* (in tonic sol-fa) the fourth note of any ascending major scale.

Fahrenheit (**far**-ren-hite) *adj* of or measured according to the scale of temperature in which 32° represents the melting point of ice and 212° the boiling point of water.

faïence (**fie**-ence) *n* tin-glazed earthenware.

fail *vb* **1** to be unsuccessful in an attempt. **2** to stop operating. **3** to judge or be judged as being below the officially accepted standard required in a course or examination. **4** to prove disappointing or useless to someone: *the government has failed the homeless.* **5** to neglect or be unable to do something: *he failed to repair the car.* **6** to go bankrupt. *~n* **7** a failure to attain the required standard. **8 without fail a** regularly or without exception: *use this shampoo once a week without fail.* **b** definitely: *they agreed to enforce the embargo without fail.*

failing *n* **1** a weak point. *~prep* **2 failing that** alternatively: *your doctor will normally be able to advise you or, failing that, one of the self-help agencies.*

fail-safe *adj* **1** designed to return to a safe condition in the event of a failure or malfunction. **2** safe from failure.

failure *n* **1** the act or an instance of failing. **2** someone or something that is unsuccessful: *he couldn't help but regard his own son as a failure.* **3** the fact of something required or expected not being done or not happening: *his failure to appear at the meeting.* **4** a halt in normal operation: *heart failure.* **5** a decline or loss of something: *crop failure.* **6** the fact of not reaching the required standard in an examination or test.

fain *adv Old-fashioned* gladly or willingly.

faint *adj* **1** lacking clarity, brightness, or volume: *her voice was very faint.* **2** feeling dizzy or weak. **3** lacking conviction or force: *a faint attempt to smile.* *~vb* **4** to lose consciousness. *~n* **5** a sudden loss of consciousness. **faintly** *adv*

faint-hearted *adj* lacking courage and confidence.

fair[1] *adj* **1** reasonable and just: *a move towards fair trade.* **2** in agreement with rules. **3** light in colour: *her fair skin.* **4** *Old-fashioned* young and beautiful: *a fair maiden.* **5** quite good: *a fair attempt at making a soufflé.* **6** quite large: *they made a fair amount of money.* **7** (of the tide or wind) favourable to the passage of a ship or plane. **8** fine or cloudless. **9 fair and square** in a correct or just way. *~adv* **10** in a fair way. **11** absolutely or squarely: *he was caught fair off his guard.* **fairness** *n*

fair[2] *n* **1** a travelling entertainment with sideshows, rides, and amusements. **2** an exhibition of goods pro-

THESAURUS

fall, flag, languish, melt away, perish, shrivel, vanish, vanish into thin air, wane, waste away, wilt, wither

faeces bodily waste, droppings, dung, excrement, excreta, ordure, stools

fail 1. be defeated, be found lacking *or* wanting, be in vain, be unsuccessful, break down, come a cropper (*informal*), come to grief, come to naught, come to nothing, fall, fall short, fall short of, fall through, fizzle out (*informal*), flop (*informal*), founder, go astray, go belly-up (*slang*), go down, go down like a lead balloon (*informal*), go up in smoke, meet with disaster, miscarry, misfire, miss, not make the grade (*informal*), run aground, turn out badly **2.** be on one's last legs (*informal*), cease, conk out (*informal*), cut out, decline, die, disappear, droop, dwindle, fade, give out, give up, gutter, languish, peter out, sicken, sink, stop working, wane, weaken **3.** abandon, break one's word, desert, disappoint, forget, forsake, let down, neglect, omit **4.** become insolvent, close down, crash, fold (*informal*), go bankrupt, go broke (*informal*), go bust (*informal*), go into receivership, go out of business, go to the wall, go under, smash **5. without fail** conscientiously, constantly, dependably, like clockwork, punctually, regularly, religiously, without exception

failing 1. *n.* blemish, blind spot, defect, deficiency, drawback, error, failure, fault, flaw, foible, frailty, imperfection, lapse, miscarriage, misfortune, shortcoming, weakness **2.** *prep.* in default of, in the absence of, lacking

failure 1. breakdown, collapse, defeat, downfall, fiasco, frustration, lack of success **2.** black sheep, dead duck (*slang*), disappointment, dud (*informal*), flop (*informal*), incompetent, loser, ne'er-do-well, no-good, no-hoper (*chiefly Austral.*), nonstarter **3.** default, deficiency, dereliction, neglect, negligence, nonobservance, nonperformance, nonsuccess, omission, remissness, shortcoming, stoppage **4.** breakdown, decay, decline, deterioration, failing, loss

faint *adj.* **1.** bleached, delicate, dim, distant, dull, faded, faltering, feeble, hazy, hushed, ill-defined, indistinct, light, low, muffled, muted, soft, subdued, thin, vague, whispered **2.** dizzy, drooping, enervated, exhausted, faltering, fatigued, giddy, languid, lethargic, light-headed, muzzy, vertiginous, weak, woozy (*informal*) **3.** faint-hearted, feeble, lily-livered, remote, slight, spiritless, timid, timorous, unenthusiastic, weak *~vb.* **4.** black out, collapse, fade, fail, flake out (*informal*), keel over (*informal*), lose consciousness, pass out, swoon (*literary*), weaken *~n.* **5.** blackout, collapse, swoon (*literary*), syncope (*Pathology*), unconsciousness

faint-hearted chickenshit (*U.S. slang*), cowardly, diffident, half-arsed, half-assed (*U.S. & Canad. slang*), half-hearted, irresolute, spineless, timid, timorous, weak, yellow

faintly 1. feebly, in a whisper, indistinctly, softly, weakly **2.** a little, dimly, slightly, somewhat

fair[1] *adj.* **1.** above board, according to the rules, clean, disinterested, dispassionate, equal, equitable, even-handed, honest, honourable, impartial, just, lawful, legitimate, objective, on the level (*informal*), proper, square, trustworthy, unbiased, unprejudiced, upright **2.** blond, blonde, fair-haired, flaxen-haired, light, light-complexioned **3.** *old-fashioned* beauteous, beautiful, bonny, comely, handsome, lovely, pretty, well-favoured **4.** adequate, all right, average, decent, mediocre, middling, moderate, not bad, O.K. *or* okay (*informal*), passable, reasonable, respectable, satisfactory, so-so (*informal*), tolerable **5.** bright, clear, clement, cloudless, dry, favourable, fine, sunny, sunshiny, unclouded

duced by a particular industry to promote business: *the Frankfurt book fair.*

fair copy *n* a neat copy, without mistakes or alterations, of a piece of writing.

fair game *n* a person regarded as a justifiable target for criticism or ridicule.

fairground *n* an open space used for a fair.

fairing *n* a metal structure fitted around parts of an aircraft, car, etc., to reduce drag.

Fair Isle *n* an intricate multicoloured knitted pattern.

fairly *adv* **1** to a moderate degree or extent: *in the Philippines labour is fairly cheap.* **2** to a great degree or extent: *the folder fairly bulged with documents.* **3** as deserved: *the pound was fairly valued against the Deutschmark.*

fair play *n* a conventional standard of honourable behaviour.

fair sex *n* **the** *Old-fashioned* women collectively.

fairway *n* **1** (on a golf course) the mown areas between tees and greens. **2** *Naut* a part of a river or sea on which ships may sail.

fair-weather *adj* not reliable in difficult situations: *a fair-weather friend.*

fairy *n, pl* **fairies 1** an imaginary supernatural being with magical powers. **2** *Offensive slang* a male homosexual.

fairy godmother *n* a generous friend who appears unexpectedly and offers help in time of trouble.

fairyland *n* **1** an imaginary place where fairies live. **2** an enchanted or wonderful place.

fairy lights *pl n* small coloured electric bulbs used as decoration, esp. on a Christmas tree.

fairy ring *n* a ring of dark grass caused by fungi.

fairy tale *or* **story** *n* **1** a story about fairies or magical events. **2** a highly improbable account: *his report was little more than a fairy tale.* ~*adj* **fairy-tale 3** of or like a fairy tale: *a fairy-tale wedding.* **4** highly improbable: *a fairy-tale account of his achievements.*

fait accompli (**fate ak-kom-plee**) *n* something already done and beyond alteration: *they had to accept the invasion as a fait accompli.*

faith *n* **1** strong belief in something, esp. without proof. **2** a specific system of religious beliefs. **3** complete confidence or trust, such as in a person or remedy. **4** allegiance to a person or cause. **5 bad faith** dishonesty. **6 good faith** honesty.

faithful *adj* **1** remaining true or loyal. **2** maintaining sexual loyalty to one's lover or spouse. **3** consistently reliable: *my old, but faithful, four cylinder car.* **4** accurate in detail: *a faithful translation of the book.* ~*pl n* **5 a** the believers in a religious faith. **b** loyal followers. **faithfully** *adv* **faithfulness** *n*

faith healing *n* treatment of a sick person through the power of religious faith. **faith healer** *n*

faithless *adj* treacherous or disloyal.

fake *vb* **faking, faked 1** to cause something not genuine to appear real or more valuable by fraud. **2** to pretend to have (an illness, emotion, etc.). ~*n* **3** an object, person, or act that is not genuine. ~*adj* **4** not genuine.

fakir (**fay-keer**) *n* **1** a member of any religious order of Islam. **2** a Hindu holy man.

falcon *n* a type of bird of prey that can be trained to hunt other birds and small animals.

falconry *n* **1** the art of training falcons to hunt. **2** the sport of hunting with falcons. **falconer** *n*

fall *vb* **falling, fell, fallen 1** to descend by the force of gravity from a higher to a lower place. **2** to drop suddenly from an upright position. **3** to collapse to the ground. **4** to become less or lower in number or quality: *inflation fell by one percentage point.* **5** to slope downwards. **6** to be badly wounded or killed. **7** to give in to attack: *in 1939 Barcelona fell to the Nationalists.* **8** to lose power or status. **9** to pass into a specified condition: *I fell asleep.* **10** to adopt a downhearted expression: *his face fell and he pouted like a child.* **11** (of night or darkness) to begin. **12** to occur at a specified time: *Christmas falls on a Sunday.* **13** to give in to temptation or sin. **14 fall apart a** to break owing to long use or poor construction: *the chassis is falling apart.* **b** to become disorganized and ineffective: *since you resigned, the office has fallen apart.* **15 fall short** to prove inadequate. **16 fall short of** to fail to reach (a standard). ~*n* **17** an instance of falling. **18** an amount of something, such as snow or soot, that has fallen. **19** a decrease in value or number. **20** a decline in status or importance: *the town's fall from prosperity.* **21** a capture or overthrow: *the fall of Budapest in February 1945.* **22** *Wrestling* a scoring move, pinning both shoulders of one's opponent to the floor for a

THESAURUS

fair[2] *n.* bazaar, carnival, expo (*informal*), exposition, festival, fête, gala, market, show

fair-and-square above board, correct, honest, just, kosher (*informal*), on the level (*informal*), straight

fairly 1. adequately, moderately, pretty well, quite, rather, reasonably, somewhat, tolerably **2.** absolutely, in a manner of speaking, positively, really, veritably **3.** deservedly, equitably, honestly, impartially, justly, objectively, properly, without fear or favour

fairness decency, disinterestedness, equitableness, equity, impartiality, justice, legitimacy, rightfulness, uprightness

fairy brownie, elf, hob, leprechaun, pixie, Robin Goodfellow, sprite

fairy tale *or* **fairy story 1.** folk tale, romance **2.** cock-and-bull story (*informal*), fabrication, fantasy, fiction, invention, lie, pork pie (*Brit. slang*), porky (*Brit. slang*), tall story, untruth

faith 1. belief, church, communion, creed, denomination, dogma, persuasion, religion **2.** assurance, confidence, conviction, credence, credit, dependence, reliance, trust **3.** allegiance, constancy, faithfulness, fealty, fidelity, loyalty, troth (*archaic*), truth, truthfulness **4.** *as in* **in good faith** honour, pledge, promise, sincerity, vow, word, word of honour

faithful 1. attached, constant, dependable, devoted, immovable, loyal, reliable, staunch, steadfast, true, true-blue, trusty, truthful, unswerving, unwavering **2.** accurate, close, exact, just, precise, strict, true **3.** *plural* adherents, believers, brethren, communicants, congregation, followers, the elect

faithfulness 1. adherence, constancy, dependability, devotion, fealty, fidelity, loyalty, trustworthiness **2.** accuracy, closeness, exactness, justice, strictness, truth

faithless disloyal, doubting, false, false-hearted, fickle, inconstant, perfidious, recreant (*archaic*), traitorous, treacherous, unbelieving, unfaithful, unreliable, untrue, untrustworthy, untruthful

fake 1. *vb.* affect, assume, copy, counterfeit, fabricate, feign, forge, pretend, put on, sham, simulate **2.** *n.* charlatan, copy, forgery, fraud, hoax, imitation, impostor, phoney *or esp. U.S.* phony (*informal*), reproduction, sham **3.** *adj.* affected, artificial, assumed, counterfeit, false, forged, imitation, mock, phoney *or esp. U.S.* phony (*informal*), pseudo (*informal*), reproduction, sham

fall *vb.* **1.** be precipitated, cascade, collapse, crash, descend, dive, drop, drop down, go head over heels, keel over, nose-dive, pitch, plummet, plunge, settle, sink,

specified period. **23** *Chiefly US & Canad* autumn. ~See also **fall about, fall away, falls,** etc.

Fall *n* **the Fall** *Theol* the state of mankind's innate sinfulness following Adam's sin of disobeying God.

fall about *vb* to laugh uncontrollably.

fallacy *n, pl* **-cies 1** an incorrect or misleading notion based on inaccurate facts or faulty reasoning: *the fallacy underlying the government's industrial policy.* **2** reasoning that is unsound. **fallacious** *adj*

fall away *vb* **1** to slope down: *the ground fell away sharply to the south.* **2** to decrease in size or intensity: *obstacles to all-party talks are falling away with amazing speed.*

fall back *vb* **1** to retreat. **2 fall back on** to have to choose (a less acceptable alternative): *they had to fall back on other lines of defence.*

fall behind *vb* **1** to fail to keep up. **2** to be in arrears, such as with a payment.

fall down *vb* **1** to drop suddenly or collapse. **2** to fail to meet requirements. **3** (of an argument or idea) to fail at a specific point: *in one area only did the comparison fall down.*

fallen *vb* **1** the past participle of **fall.** *~adj* **2** *Old-fashioned* (of a woman) having had sex outside marriage. **3** killed in battle.

fall for *vb* **1** to become strongly attracted to (someone). **2** to be deceived by (a lie or trick).

fall guy *n Informal* **1** the victim of a confidence trick. **2** *US* a person who is publicly blamed for something, though it may not be his or her fault.

fallible *adj* **1** (of a person) liable to make mistakes. **2** capable of error: *our all-too-fallible economic indicators.* **fallibility** *n*

fall in *vb* **1** to collapse. **2** to get into line or formation in a display, march, or procession. **3 fall in with a** to meet and join. **b** to agree with or support (a person or a suggestion).

falling star *n Informal* a meteor.

fall off *vb* **1** to drop unintentionally to the ground from (a bicycle, horse, etc.). **2** to decrease in size or intensity: *demand for beef began to fall off.*

fall on *vb* **1** to attack (an enemy). **2** to meet with (something unpleasant): *his family had fallen on hard times.* **3** to affect: *a horrified hush fell on the company.* **4 fall on one's feet** to emerge unexpectedly well from a difficult situation.

Fallopian tube *n* either of a pair of slender tubes through which eggs pass from the ovaries to the uterus in female mammals.

fallout *n* **1** radioactive material in the atmosphere following a nuclear explosion. **2** unpleasant circumstances following an event: *fallout from the Gulf crisis.* *~vb* **fall out 3** *Informal* to disagree and quarrel: *I hope we don't fall out over this issue.* **4** to leave a military formation.

fallow[1] *adj* (of land) left unseeded after being ploughed to regain fertility for a future crop.

fallow[2] *adj* light yellowish-brown.

fallow deer *n* a deer that has a reddish coat with white spots in summer.

falls *pl n* a waterfall.

fall through *vb* to fail before completion: *his transfer deal fell through.*

fall to *vb* **1** to become the responsibility of: *it fell to the Prime Minister to announce the plans.* **2** to begin (some activity, such as eating, working, or fighting).

false *adj* **1** not in accordance with the truth or facts: *false allegations.* **2** not real or genuine but intended to seem so: *false teeth.* **3** misleading or deceptive: *their false promises.* **4** forced or insincere: *false cheer.* **5** based on mistaken ideas. **falsely** *adv* **falseness** *n*

false alarm *n* a situation that appears to be dangerous but turns out not to be: *air-raid sirens sounded once but it turned out to be a false alarm.*

falsehood *n* **1** the quality of being untrue. **2** a lie.

false pretences *pl n* **under false pretences** so as to mislead people about one's true intentions.

false start *n Athletics & swimming* an occasion when one competitor starts a race before the starter's

THESAURUS

stumble, subside, topple, trip, trip over, tumble **2.** abate, become lower, decline, decrease, depreciate, diminish, drop, dwindle, ebb, fall off, flag, go down, lessen, slump, subside **3.** fall away, incline, incline downwards, slope **4.** be a casualty, be killed, be lost, be slain, die, meet one's end, perish **5.** be overthrown, be taken, capitulate, give in *or* up, give way, go out of office, pass into enemy hands, resign, succumb, surrender, yield **6.** become, befall, chance, come about, come to pass, fall out, happen, occur, take place **7.** backslide, err, go astray, lapse, offend, sin, transgress, trespass, yield to temptation **8. fall apart** break up, crumble, disband, disintegrate, disperse, dissolve, fall to bits, go *or* come to pieces, lose cohesion, shatter *~n.* **9.** descent, dive, drop, nose dive, plummet, plunge, slip, spill, tumble **10.** cut, decline, decrease, diminution, dip, drop, dwindling, falling off, lessening, lowering, reduction, slump **11.** capitulation, collapse, death, defeat, destruction, downfall, failure, overthrow, resignation, ruin, surrender

fallacy casuistry, deceit, deception, delusion, error, falsehood, faultiness, flaw, illusion, inconsistency, misapprehension, misconception, mistake, sophism, untruth

fall back on call upon, employ, have recourse to, make use of, press into service, resort to

fall behind be in arrears, drop back, get left behind, lag, lose one's place, trail

fall down disappoint, fail, fail to make the grade, fall short, go wrong, prove unsuccessful

fallen *adj.* **1.** collapsed, decayed, flat, on the ground, ruinous, sunken **2.** disgraced, dishonoured, immoral, loose, lost, ruined, shamed, sinful, unchaste **3.** dead, killed, lost, perished, slain, slaughtered

fall for 1. become infatuated with, desire, fall in love with, lose one's head over, succumb to the charms of **2.** accept, be deceived by (duped, fooled, taken in), buy (*slang*), give credence to, swallow (*informal*)

fallible erring, frail, ignorant, imperfect, mortal, prone to error, uncertain, weak

fall in cave in, collapse, come down about one's ears, sink

fall off *vb.* decelerate, decline, decrease, deteriorate, drop, slacken, slow down, slump, wane, worsen

fall out altercate, argue, clash, differ, disagree, fight, quarrel, squabble

fallow dormant, idle, inactive, inert, resting, uncultivated, undeveloped, unplanted, untilled, unused

fall through come to nothing, fail, fizzle out (*informal*)

false 1. concocted, erroneous, faulty, fictitious, improper, inaccurate, incorrect, inexact, invalid, mistaken, unfounded, unreal, wrong **2.** artificial, bogus, counterfeit, ersatz, fake, feigned, forged, imitation, mock, pretended, sham, simulated, spurious, synthetic **3.** deceitful, deceiving, deceptive, delusive, fallacious, fraudulent, hypocritical, lying, mendacious, misleading, trumped up, truthless, unreliable, unsound, untrue, untrustworthy, untruthful

falsehood 1. deceit, deception, dishonesty, dissimu-

signal has been given, which means that all competitors have to be recalled and the race restarted.

falsetto *n, pl* **-tos** a voice pitch higher than one's normal range.

falsies *pl n Informal* pads worn to exaggerate the size of a woman's breasts.

falsify *vb* **-fies, -fying, -fied** to make a report or evidence false by alteration in order to deceive. **falsification** *n*

falsity *n, pl* **-ties 1** the state of being false. **2** a lie.

falter *vb* **1** to be hesitant, weak, or unsure. **2** (of a machine) to lose power or strength in an uneven way: *the engine began to falter and the plane lost height.* **3** to speak nervously and without confidence. **4** to stop moving smoothly and start moving unsteadily: *as he neared the house his steps faltered.* **faltering** *adj*

fame *n* the state of being widely known or recognized.

famed *adj* extremely well-known: *the famed Michael Jackson.*

familial *adj Formal* of or relating to the family.

familiar *adj* **1** well-known. **2** frequent or common: *it was a familiar argument.* **3 familiar with** well acquainted with. **4** friendly and informal. **5** more intimate than is acceptable. *~n* **6** an animal or bird believed to share with a witch her supernatural powers. **7** a friend. **familiarly** *adv* **familiarity** *n*

familiarize *or* **-rise** *vb* **-izing, -ized** *or* **-ising, -ised** to make (oneself or someone else) fully aware of a particular subject. **familiarization** *or* **-risation** *n*

family *n, pl* **-lies 1** a social group consisting of parents and their offspring. **2** one's wife or husband and one's children. **3** one's children. **4** a group descended from a common ancestor. **5** all the people living together in one household. **6** any group of related objects or beings: *a family of chemicals.* **7** *Biol* one of the groups into which an order is divided, containing one or more genera: *the cat family.* *~adj* **8** of or suitable for a family or any of its members: *films for a family audience.* **9 in the family way** *Informal* pregnant.

Family Allowance *n* **1** (in Britain) a former name for **child benefit. 2** (in Canada) an allowance paid by the Federal Government to the parents of dependent children.

family benefit *n* (in New Zealand) a child allowance paid to the mothers of children under 18.

family credit *n* (in Britain) an allowance paid to families whose earnings from full-time work are low.

family man *n* **1** a man with a wife and children. **2** a man who loves his family and spends a lot of time with them.

family name *n* a surname, esp. when regarded as representing a family's good reputation.

family planning *n* the control of the number of children in a family by the use of contraceptives.

family support *n NZ* a top-up of family income in certain circumstances where there are dependent children.

family tree *n* a chart showing the relationships between individuals in a family over many generations.

famine *n* a severe shortage of food.

famish *vb* **be famished** *or* **famishing** to be very hungry.

famous *adj* known to or recognized by many people.

famously *adv* **1** well-known: *her famously relaxed manner.* **2** very well: *the two got on famously.*

fan[1] *n* **1** any device for creating a current of air, esp. a rotating machine of blades attached to a central hub. **2** a hand-held object, usu. made of paper, which creates a draught of cool air when waved. **3** something shaped like such a fan, such as the tail of certain birds. *~vb* **fanning, fanned 4** to create a draught of air in the direction of someone or something. **5 fan out** to spread out in the shape of a fan: *the troops fanned out along the beach.*

fan[2] *n* a person who admires or is enthusiastic about a

THESAURUS

lation, mendacity, perjury, prevarication, untruthfulness **2.** fabrication, fib, fiction, lie, misstatement, pork pie (*Brit. slang*), porky (*Brit. slang*), story, untruth

falsification adulteration, deceit, dissimulation, distortion, forgery, misrepresentation, perversion, tampering with

falsify alter, belie, cook (*slang*), counterfeit, distort, doctor, fake, forge, misrepresent, pervert, tamper with

falter break, hesitate, shake, speak haltingly, stammer, stumble, stutter, totter, tremble, vacillate, waver

faltering broken, hesitant, irresolute, stammering, tentative, timid, uncertain, weak

fame celebrity, eminence, glory, honour, illustriousness, prominence, public esteem, renown, reputation, repute, stardom

familiar 1. accustomed, common, common or garden (*informal*), conventional, customary, domestic, everyday, frequent, household, mundane, ordinary, recognizable, repeated, routine, stock, well-known **2. familiar with** abreast of, acquainted with, at home with, *au fait,* aware of, conscious of, conversant with, introduced, knowledgeable, no stranger to, on speaking terms with, versed in, well up in **3.** amicable, buddy-buddy (*slang, chiefly U.S. & Canad.*), chummy (*informal*), close, confidential, cordial, easy, free, free-and-easy, friendly, hail-fellow-well-met, informal, intimate, near, open, palsy-walsy (*informal*), relaxed, unceremonious, unconstrained, unreserved **4.** bold, disrespectful, forward, impudent, intrusive, overfree, presuming, presumptuous

familiarity 1. acquaintance, acquaintanceship, awareness, experience, grasp, understanding **2.** absence of reserve, closeness, ease, fellowship, freedom, friendliness, friendship, informality, intimacy, naturalness, openness, sociability, unceremoniousness **3.** boldness, disrespect, forwardness, liberties, liberty, presumption

familiarize accustom, bring into common use, coach, get to know (about), instruct, make conversant, make used to, prime, school, season, train

family 1. brood, children, descendants, folk (*informal*), household, issue, kin, kindred, kinsfolk, kinsmen, kith and kin, menage, offspring, one's nearest and dearest, one's own flesh and blood, people, progeny, relations, relatives **2.** ancestors, ancestry, birth, blood, clan, descent, dynasty, extraction, forebears, forefathers, genealogy, house, line, lineage, parentage, pedigree, race, sept, strain, tribe **3.** class, classification, genre, group, kind, network, subdivision, system

family tree ancestry, extraction, genealogy, line, lineage, line of descent, pedigree

famine dearth, destitution, hunger, scarcity, starvation

famous acclaimed, celebrated, conspicuous, distinguished, eminent, excellent, far-famed, glorious, honoured, illustrious, legendary, lionized, much-publicized, notable, noted, prominent, remarkable, renowned, signal, well-known

fan[1] *n.* **1.** air conditioner, blade, blower, propeller, punkah (*in India*), vane, ventilator *~vb.* **2.** air-condition, air-cool, blow, cool, refresh, ventilate, winnow (*rare*) **3.** *often figurative* add fuel to the flames, agitate, arouse, enkindle, excite, impassion, increase, provoke, rouse, stimulate, stir up, whip up, work up

pop star, actor, sport, or hobby: *he was a big fan of Woody Allen.*

fanatic *n* **1** a person whose enthusiasm for something, esp. a political or religious cause, is extreme. **2** *Informal* a person devoted to a particular hobby or pastime. *~adj also* **fanatical 3** excessively enthusiastic. **fanatically** *adv* **fanaticism** *n*

fan belt *n* the belt that drives a cooling fan in a car engine.

fancier *n* a person with a keen interest in the thing specified: *a pigeon fancier.*

fanciful *adj* **1** not based on fact. **2** made in a curious or imaginative way: *fanciful architecture.* **3** guided by unrestrained imagination: *fanciful tales of fairy folk.* **fancifully** *adv*

fan club *n* an organized group of admirers of a particular pop singer or star.

fancy *adj* **-cier, -ciest 1** special, unusual, and elaborate. **2** (often used ironically) superior in quality. **3** (of a price) higher than expected. *~n, pl* **-cies 4** a sudden spontaneous idea. **5** a sudden or irrational liking for a person or thing. **6** *Old-fashioned or literary* a person's imagination. *~vb* **-cies, -cying, -cied 7** *Brit informal* to be physically attracted to (another person). **8** *Informal* to have a wish for. **9** to picture in the imagination. **10** to think or suppose: *I fancy I am redundant here.* **11 fancy oneself** to have a high opinion of oneself. *~interj* **12** Also: **fancy that!** an exclamation of surprise. **fancily** *adv*

fancy dress *n* clothing worn for a party at which people dress up to look like a particular animal or character.

fancy-free *adj* free from commitments, esp. marriage.

fancy goods *pl n* small decorative gifts.

fancy man *n Old-fashioned slang* a woman's lover.

fancy woman *n Old-fashioned slang* a man's lover.

fancywork *n* ornamental needlework.

fandango *n, pl* **-gos 1** a lively Spanish dance. **2** music for this dance.

fanfare *n* a short rousing tune played on brass instruments.

fang *n* **1** the long pointed tooth of a poisonous snake through which poison is injected. **2** the canine tooth of a meat-eating mammal.

fanjet *n* same as **turbofan.**

fanlight *n* a semicircular window over a door or another window.

fanny *n, pl* **-nies** *Slang* **1** *Brit taboo* the female genitals. **2** *Chiefly US & Canad* the buttocks.

fantail *n* **1** a breed of domestic pigeon with a large tail like a fan. **2** a fly-catching bird of Australia, New Zealand, and SE Asia with a broad fan-shaped tail.

fantasia *n* **1** any musical work not composed in a strict form. **2** a mixture of popular tunes arranged as a continuous whole.

fantasize *or* **-sise** *vb* **-sizing, -sized** *or* **-sising, -sised** to imagine pleasant but unlikely events.

fantastic *adj* **1** *Informal* excellent. **2** *Informal* very large in degree or amount: *a fantastic amount of money.* **3** strange or exotic in appearance: *fantastic costumes.* **4** difficult to believe or unlikely to happen. **fantastically** *adv*

fantasy *n, pl* **-sies 1** a far-fetched idea. **2** imagination unrestricted by reality. **3** a daydream. **4** fiction with a large fantasy content. **5** *Music* same as **fantasia.**

fan vaulting *n Archit* vaulting with ribs that radiate like those of a fan from the top part of a pillar.

fanzine (**fan**-zeen) *n* a magazine produced by fans of a specific interest, football club, etc., for fellow fans.

far farther, farthest *or* **further, furthest** *adv* **1** at, to, or from a great distance. **2** at or to a remote time: *as far back as 1984.* **3** by a considerable degree: *far greater.* **4 as far as a** to the degree or extent that. **b** to the distance or place of. **c** *Informal* with reference to. **5 by far** by a considerable margin. **6 far and away** by a very great margin: *far and away the ugliest building in the city.* **7 far and wide** in a great many places over a large area. **8 go far a** to be successful. **b** to be sufficient or last long: *her wages didn't go far.* **9 go too far** to go beyond reasonable limits: *the press have gone too far this time.* **10 so far a** up to the present moment. **b** up to a certain point, extent, or degree. *~adj* **11** distant in space or time: *the far south.* **12** extending a great distance. **13** more distant: *over in the far corner.* **14 far from** by no means: *the battle is far*

THESAURUS

fan[2] adherent, admirer, aficionado, buff (*informal*), devotee, enthusiast, fiend (*informal*), follower, freak (*informal*), groupie (*slang*), love, supporter, zealot

fanatic *n.* activist, addict, bigot, buff (*informal*), devotee, enthusiast, extremist, militant, visionary, zealot

fanatical bigoted, burning, enthusiastic, extreme, fervent, frenzied, immoderate, mad, obsessive, overenthusiastic, passionate, rabid, visionary, wild, zealous

fanciful capricious, chimerical, curious, extravagant, fabulous, fairy-tale, fantastic, ideal, imaginary, imaginative, mythical, poetic, romantic, unreal, visionary, whimsical, wild

fancy *adj.* **1.** baroque, decorated, decorative, elaborate, elegant, embellished, extravagant, fanciful, intricate, ornamental, ornamented, ornate *~n.* **2.** caprice, desire, humour, idea, impulse, inclination, notion, thought, urge, whim **3.** fondness, hankering, inclination, liking, partiality, predilection, preference, relish, thirst *~vb.* **4.** *informal* be attracted to, be captivated by, desire, favour, go for, have an eye for, like, lust after, prefer, take a liking to, take to **5.** *informal* be attracted to, crave, desire, dream of, hanker after, have a yen for, hope for, long for, relish, thirst for, wish for, would like, yearn for **6.** be inclined to think, believe, conceive, conjecture, guess (*informal, chiefly U.S. & Canad.*), imagine, infer, reckon, suppose, surmise, think, think likely

fanfare ballyhoo, flourish, trumpet call

fantastic 1. *informal* boffo (*slang*), brill (*informal*), chillin' (*U.S. slang*), cracking (*Brit. informal*), crucial (*slang*), def (*slang*), excellent, first-rate, jim-dandy (*slang*), marvellous, mean (*slang*), mega (*slang*), out of this world (*informal*), sensational (*informal*), sovereign, superb, topping (*Brit. slang*), wonderful, world-class **2.** *informal* enormous, extreme, great, overwhelming, severe, tremendous **3.** comical, eccentric, exotic, fanciful, freakish, grotesque, imaginative, odd, oddball (*informal*), off-the-wall (*slang*), outlandish, outré, peculiar, phantasmagorical, quaint, queer, rococo, strange, unreal, weird, whimsical **4.** absurd, capricious, implausible, incredible, irrational, mad, preposterous, unlikely

fantasy 1. apparition, daydream, delusion, dream, fancy, figment of the imagination, flight of fancy, hallucination, illusion, mirage, nightmare, pipe dream, reverie, vision **2.** creativity, fancy, imagination, invention, originality

far *adv.* **1.** afar, a good way, a great distance, a long way, deep, miles **2.** considerably, decidedly, extremely, greatly, incomparably, much, very much **3. by far** by a long chalk (*informal*), by a long shot, by a long way, easily, far and away, immeasurably, incomparably, to a great degree, very much **4. far and wide** broadly, everywhere, extensively, far and near, here, there and everywhere, widely, worldwide **5. so far**

from over.
➤ *Farther* is often used, rather than *further,* when distance, not time or effort, is involved.
farad *n Physics* the SI unit of electric capacitance.
faraway *adj* **1** very distant. **2** dreamy or absent-minded: *a faraway look in his eyes.*
farce *n* **1** a humorous play involving characters in unlikely and ridiculous situations. **2** the style of comedy of this kind. **3** a ludicrous situation: *the game degenerated into farce.* **farcical** *adj*
fare *n* **1** the amount charged or paid for a journey in a bus, train, or plane. **2** a paying passenger. **3** a range of food and drink: *typical English fare.* ~*vb* **faring, fared 4** to get on (in a specified way): *he fared well in the exam.*
Far East *n* the countries of E Asia. **Far Eastern** *adj*
fare stage *n* **1** a section of a bus journey for which a set charge is made. **2** the bus stop marking the end of such a section.
farewell *interj* **1** *Old-fashioned* goodbye. ~*n* **2** the act of saying goodbye and leaving. ~*adj* **3** parting or closing: *the President's farewell speech.*
far-fetched *adj* unlikely to be true.
far-flung *adj* **1** distributed over a wide area. **2** far distant or remote.
farinaceous *adj* containing starch or having a starchy texture.
farm *n* **1** a tract of land, usually with a house and buildings, cultivated as a unit or used to rear livestock. **2** a unit of land or water devoted to the growing or rearing of some particular type of fruit, animal, or fish: *a salmon farm.* ~*vb* **3 a** to cultivate land. **b** to rear animals or fish on a farm. **4** to do agricultural work as a way of life. **5** to collect and keep the profits from a tax district or business. ~See also **farm out.**
farmer *n* a person who owns or manages a farm.
farm hand *n* a person who is hired to work on a farm.
farmhouse *n* a house attached to a farm.
farming *n* the business or skill of agriculture.
farmland *n* land that is used for or suitable for farming.
farm out *vb* **1** to send (work) to be done by another person or firm. **2** (of the state) to put a child into the care of a private individual.
farmstead *n* a farm and its main buildings.
farmyard *n* the small area of land enclosed by or around the farm buildings.
far-off *adj* distant in space or time: *a far-off land.*
far-out *adj* **1** very unusual or strange: *the idea was so far-out it was ludicrous.* **2** *Informal* wonderful.
farrago (far-**rah**-go) *n, pl* **-gos** *or* **-goes** a hotchpotch or mixture, esp. a ridiculous or unbelievable one: *a farrago of patriotic nonsense.*
far-reaching *adj* extensive in influence, effect, or range.
farrier *n Chiefly Brit* a person who shoes horses.
farrow *n* **1** a litter of piglets. ~*vb* **2** (of a sow) to give birth to a litter.
far-seeing *adj* having wise judgment.
far-sighted *adj* **1** able to look forward and plan ahead. **2** *US* long-sighted.
fart *Taboo* ~*n* **1** an emission of intestinal gas from the anus. ~*vb* **2** to break wind.
farther *adv* **1** to or at a greater distance in space or time. **2** in addition. ~*adj* **3** more distant or remote in space or time.
farthermost *adj* most distant or remote.
farthest *adv* **1** to or at the greatest distance in space or time. ~*adj* **2** most distant or remote in space or time.
farthing *n* a former British coin worth a quarter of an old penny.
farthingale *n* a hoop worn under skirts in the Elizabethan period.
fasces (**fass**-eez) *pl n, sing* **-cis** (-siss) (in ancient Rome) a bundle of rods containing an axe with its blade pointing out; a symbol of a magistrate's power.
fascia *or* **facia** (**fay**-shee-a) *n, pl* **-ciae** (-shee-ee) **1** the flat surface above a shop window. **2** *Archit* a flat band or surface. **3** *Brit* the outer panel which surrounds the instruments and dials of a motor vehicle.
fascinate *vb* **-nating, -nated** to attract and delight by arousing interest. **fascinating** *adj* **fascinatingly** *adv* **fascination** *n*
Fascism (**fash**-iz-zum) *n* **1** the authoritarian and nationalistic political movement in Italy (1922–43). **2** any ideology or movement like this. **Fascist** *n, adj*
fashion *n* **1** style in clothes, hairstyles, behaviour, etc., that is popular at a particular time. **2** the way that something happens or is done: *conversing in a very animated fashion.* **3 after a fashion** in some way, but

THESAURUS

thus far, to date, until now, up to now, up to the present ~*adj.* **6.** distant, faraway, far-flung, far-off, far-removed, long, outlying, out-of-the-way, remote, removed
faraway 1. beyond the horizon, distant, far, far-flung, far-off, far-removed, outlying, remote **2.** absent, abstracted, distant, dreamy, lost
farce 1. broad comedy, buffoonery, burlesque, comedy, satire, slapstick **2.** absurdity, joke, mockery, nonsense, parody, ridiculousness, sham, travesty
farcical absurd, amusing, comic, custard-pie, derisory, diverting, droll, funny, laughable, ludicrous, nonsensical, preposterous, ridiculous, risible, slapstick
fare *n.* **1.** charge, passage money, price, ticket money, transport cost **2.** passenger, pick-up (*informal*), traveller **3.** diet, eatables, feed, food, meals, menu, nosebag (*slang*), provisions, rations, sustenance, table, tack (*informal*), victuals ~*vb.* **4.** do, get along, get on, make out, manage, prosper
farewell adieu, adieux *or* adieus, departure, goodbye, leave-taking, parting, sendoff (*informal*), valediction
far-fetched doubtful, dubious, fantastic, hard to swallow (*informal*), implausible, improbable, incredible, preposterous, strained, unbelievable, unconvincing, unlikely, unnatural, unrealistic
farm 1. *n.* acreage, acres, croft (*Scot.*), farmstead, grange, holding, homestead, land, plantation, ranch (*chiefly North American*), smallholding, station (*Austral. & N.Z.*) **2.** *vb.* bring under cultivation, cultivate, operate, plant, practise husbandry, till the soil, work
farmer agriculturist, agronomist, husbandman, smallholder, yeoman
farming agriculture, agronomy, husbandry
far-reaching broad, extensive, important, momentous, pervasive, significant, sweeping, widespread
far-sighted acute, canny, cautious, discerning, far-seeing, judicious, politic, prescient, provident, prudent, sage, shrewd, wise
fascinate absorb, allure, beguile, bewitch, captivate, charm, delight, enamour, enchant, engross, enrapture, enravish, enthral, entrance, hold spellbound, hypnotize, infatuate, intrigue, mesmerize, ravish, rivet, spellbind, transfix
fascinating alluring, bewitching, captivating, compelling, enchanting, engaging, engrossing, enticing,

not very well: *he apologized, after a fashion, for his haste.* ~*vb* **4** to form, make, or shape: *he had fashioned a crude musical instrument.*

fashionable *adj* **1** popular with a lot of people at a particular time. **2** popular among well-off or famous people: *the fashionable Côte d'Azur.* **fashionably** *adv*

fast[1] *adj* **1** acting or moving quickly. **2** accomplished in or lasting a short time. **3** adapted to or allowing for rapid movement: *the fast lane.* **4** (of a clock or watch) indicating a time in advance of the correct time. **5** given to a life of expensive and exciting activities: *the desire for a fast life.* **6** firmly fixed, fastened, or shut. **7** (of colours and dyes) not likely to fade. **8** *Photog* very sensitive and able to be used in low-light conditions. **9 fast friends** devoted and loyal friends. **10 pull a fast one** *Informal* play an unscrupulous trick. ~*adv* **11** quickly. **12 fast asleep** in a deep sleep. **13** firmly and tightly: *stuck fast.* **14 play fast and loose** to behave in an insincere or unreliable manner.

fast[2] *vb* **1** to go without food for a period of time, esp. for religious reasons. ~*n* **2** a period of fasting.

fast-breeder reactor *n* a nuclear reactor that produces more fissionable material (plutonium) than it consumes for the purposes of generating electricity.

fasten *vb* **1** to make or become secure or joined. **2** to close by fixing firmly in place or locking. **3 fasten on a** to direct one's attention in a concentrated way towards: *the mind needs such imagery to fasten on to.* **b** to take a firm hold on. **fastener** *n*

fastening *n* something that fastens something, such as a clasp or lock.

fast food *n* food, such as hamburgers, that is prepared and served very quickly.

fastidious *adj* **1** paying great attention to neatness, detail, and order: *a fastidious dresser.* **2** excessively concerned with cleanliness. **fastidiously** *adv* **fastidiousness** *n*

fast lane *n* **1** the outside lane on a motorway for overtaking or travelling fast. **2** *Informal* the quickest but most competitive route to success: *the hectic pace of life in the corporate fast lane.*

fastness *n Literary* a stronghold or safe place that is hard to get to.

fast-track *adj* taking the quickest but most competitive route to success or personal advancement: *a fast-track marketer's dream.*

fat *adj* **fatter, fattest 1** having more flesh on the body than is thought necessary or desirable; overweight. **2** (of meat) containing a lot of fat. **3** thick or wide: *his obligatory fat cigar.* **4** profitable or productive: *fat years for the farmers are few and far between.* **5 a fat chance** *Slang* unlikely to happen. **6 a fat lot of good** *Slang* not at all good or useful. ~*n* **7** extra or unwanted flesh on the body. **8** a greasy or oily substance obtained from animals or plants and used in cooking. **9 the fat is in the fire** an action has been taken from which disastrous consequences are expected. **10 the fat of the land** the best that is obtainable. **fatless** *adj* **fatness** *n*

fatal *adj* **1** resulting in death: *a fatal accident.* **2** resulting in unfortunate consequences: *Gorbachov's second fatal mistake.* **fatally** *adv*

fatalism *n* the belief that all events are decided in advance by God or Fate so that human beings are powerless to alter their destiny. **fatalist** *n* **fatalistic** *adj* **fatalistically** *adv*

fatality *n, pl* **-ties** a death caused by an accident or disaster.

fate *n* **1** the ultimate force that supposedly predetermines the course of events. **2** the inevitable fortune that happens to a person or thing. **3** death or downfall: *Custer met his fate at Little Bighorn.*

fated *adj* **1** certain to be or do something: *he was always fated to be a musician.* **2** doomed to death or destruction.

fateful *adj* having important, and usually disastrous, consequences. **fatefully** *adv*

THESAURUS

gripping, intriguing, irresistible, ravishing, riveting, seductive

fascination allure, attraction, charm, enchantment, glamour, lure, magic, magnetism, pull, sorcery

fashion *n.* **1.** convention, craze, custom, fad, latest, latest style, look, mode, prevailing taste, rage, style, trend, usage, vogue **2.** attitude, demeanour, manner, method, mode, style, way **3. after a fashion** in a manner of speaking, in a way, moderately, somehow, somehow or other, to a degree, to some extent ~*vb.* **4.** construct, contrive, create, design, forge, form, make, manufacture, mould, shape, work

fashionable à la mode, all the go (*informal*), all the rage, chic, cool (*slang*), current, customary, happening (*informal*), hip (*slang*), in (*informal*), in vogue, latest, modern, modish, popular, prevailing, smart, stylish, trendsetting, trendy (*Brit. informal*), up-to-date, up-to-the-minute, usual, voguish (*informal*), with it (*informal*)

fast *adj.* **1.** accelerated, brisk, fleet, flying, hasty, hurried, mercurial, nippy (*Brit. informal*), quick, quickie (*informal*), rapid, speedy, swift, winged **2.** dissipated, dissolute, extravagant, gadabout (*informal*), giddy, immoral, intemperate, licentious, loose, profligate, promiscuous, rakish, reckless, self-indulgent, wanton, wild **3.** close, constant, fastened, firm, fixed, fortified, immovable, impregnable, lasting, loyal, permanent, secure, sound, stalwart, staunch, steadfast, tight, unwavering **4. pull a fast one** bamboozle (*informal*), cheat, con (*informal*), deceive, defraud, hoodwink, put one over on (*informal*), swindle, take advantage of, take for a ride (*informal*), trick ~*adv.* **5.** apace, hastily, hell for leather (*informal*), hotfoot, hurriedly, in haste, like a bat out of hell (*slang*), like a flash, like a shot (*informal*), posthaste, presto, quickly, rapidly, speedily, swiftly, with all haste **6.** deeply, firmly, fixedly, securely, soundly, tightly

fasten 1. affix, anchor, attach, bind, bolt, chain, connect, fix, grip, join, lace, link, lock, make fast, make firm, seal, secure, tie, unite **2.** *with* **on** aim, concentrate, direct, fix, focus, rivet

fat *adj.* **1.** beefy (*informal*), broad in the beam (*informal*), corpulent, elephantine, fleshy, gross, heavy, obese, overweight, plump, podgy, portly, roly-poly, rotund, solid, stout, tubby **2.** adipose, fatty, greasy, lipid, oily, oleaginous, suety **3.** affluent, cushy (*slang*), fertile, flourishing, fruitful, jammy (*Brit. slang*), lucrative, lush, productive, profitable, prosperous, rich, thriving ~*n.* **4.** beef (*informal*), blubber, bulk, cellulite, corpulence, fatness, flab, flesh, obesity, overweight, paunch, weight problem

fatal 1. deadly, destructive, final, incurable, killing, lethal, malignant, mortal, pernicious, terminal **2.** baleful, baneful, calamitous, catastrophic, disastrous, lethal, ruinous

fatality casualty, deadliness, death, disaster, fatal accident, lethalness, loss, mortality

fate 1. chance, destiny, divine will, fortune, nemesis, predestination, providence **2.** end, future, issue, outcome, upshot **3.** death, destruction, doom, downfall, end, ruin

fated destined, doomed, foreordained, ineluctable, inescapable, inevitable, marked down, predestined, pre-elected, preordained, sure, written

fathead *n Informal* a stupid person. **fatheaded** *adj*
father *n* **1** a male parent. **2** a person who founds a line or family; forefather. **3** a man who starts, creates, or invents something: *the father of democracy in Costa Rica.* **4** a leader of an association or council: *the city fathers.* *~vb* **5** (of a man) to be the biological cause of the conception and birth of (a child). **fatherhood** *n*
Father *n* **1** God. **2** a title used for Christian priests. **3** any of the early writers on Christian doctrine.
Father Christmas *n* same as **Santa Claus.**
father-in-law *n, pl* **fathers-in-law** the father of one's wife or husband.
fatherland *n* a person's native country.
fatherly *adj* kind or protective, like a father.
Father's Day *n* a day celebrated in honour of fathers.
fathom *n* **1** a unit of length, used in navigation, equal to six feet (1.83 metres). *~vb* **2** to understand by thinking carefully about: *I couldn't fathom his intentions.* **fathomable** *adj*
fathomless *adj* too deep or difficult to fathom.
fatigue (fat-**eeg**) *n* **1** extreme physical or mental tiredness. **2** the weakening of a material caused by repeated stress or movement. **3** the duties of a soldier that are not military. **4** **fatigues** a soldier's clothing for nonmilitary or battlefield duties. *~vb* **-tiguing, -tigued** **5** to make or become weary or exhausted.
fat stock *n* livestock fattened and ready for market.
fatten *vb* to grow or cause to grow fat or fatter. **fattening** *adj*
fatty *adj* **-tier, -tiest** **1** containing or derived from fat. **2** greasy or oily. *~n, pl* **-ties** **3** *Informal* a fat person.
fatty acid *n* any of a class of organic acids some of which, such as stearic acid, are found in animal or vegetable fats.
fatuity *n, pl* **-ties** **1** foolish thoughtlessness. **2** a fatuous remark.
fatuous *adj* foolish, inappropriate, and showing no thought. **fatuously** *adv*
faucet (**faw**-set) *n* **1** a tap fitted to a barrel. **2** *US & Canad* a tap.
fault *n* **1** responsibility for something wrong. **2** a defect or failing: *they shut the production line to remedy a fault.* **3** a weakness in a person's character. **4** *Geol* a fracture in the earth's crust with displacement of the rocks on either side. **5** *Tennis, squash, etc* a serve that bounces outside the proper service court or fails to get over the net. **6** (in showjumping) a penalty mark for failing to clear, or refusing, a fence. **7** **at fault** to be to blame for something wrong. **8** **find fault with** to seek out minor imperfections in. **9** **to a fault** more than is usual or necessary: *generous to a fault.* *~vb* **10** to criticize or blame. **11** *Geol* to undergo or cause to undergo a fault. **faultless** *adj* **faultlessly** *adv*
fault-finding *n* continual criticism.
faulty *adj* **faultier, faultiest** badly designed or not working properly: *a faulty toaster.*
faun *n* (in Roman legend) a creature with the head and torso of a man and the legs, ears, and horns of a goat.
fauna *n, pl* **-nas** *or* **-nae** all the animal life of a given place or time: *the fauna of the Arctic.*
faux pas (foe **pah**) *n, pl* **faux pas** (foe **pahz**) a socially embarrassing action or mistake.
favour *or US* **favor** *n* **1** an approving attitude: *the company looked with favour on his plan.* **2** an act done out of goodwill or generosity. **3** bias at the expense of others: *his fellow customs officers, showing no favour, demanded to see his luggage.* **4** **in** *or* **out of favour** regarded with approval or disapproval. **5** **in favour of** **a** approving. **b** to the benefit of. *~vb* **6** to prefer. **7** to show bias towards (someone) at the ex-

THESAURUS

fateful critical, crucial, deadly, decisive, destructive, disastrous, fatal, important, lethal, ominous, portentous, significant
father *n.* **1.** begetter, dad (*informal*), daddy (*informal*), old boy (*informal*), old man (*informal*), pa (*informal*), papa (*old-fashioned informal*), pater, patriarch, pop (*informal*), sire **2.** ancestor, forebear, forefather, predecessor, progenitor **3.** architect, author, creator, founder, inventor, maker, originator, prime mover **4.** city father, elder, leader, patriarch, patron, senator *~vb.* **5.** beget, get, procreate, sire
fatherland homeland, land of one's birth, land of one's fathers, motherland, native land, old country
fatherly affectionate, benevolent, benign, forbearing, indulgent, kind, kindly, paternal, patriarchal, protective, supportive, tender
fathom comprehend, get to the bottom of, grasp, interpret, understand
fatigue **1.** *n.* debility, ennui, heaviness, languor, lethargy, listlessness, overtiredness, tiredness **2.** *vb.* drain, drain of energy, exhaust, fag (out) (*informal*), jade, knacker (*slang*), overtire, poop (*informal*), take it out of (*informal*), tire, weaken, wear out, weary, whack (*Brit. informal*)
fatten broaden, coarsen, expand, gain weight, grow fat, put on weight, spread, swell, thicken, thrive
fatuous absurd, asinine, brainless, dense, dull, foolish, idiotic, inane, ludicrous, lunatic, mindless, moronic, puerile, silly, stupid, vacuous, weak-minded, witless
fault *n.* **1.** accountability, culpability, liability, responsibility **2.** blunder, boob (*Brit. slang*), error, error of judgment, inaccuracy, indiscretion, lapse, mistake, negligence, offence, omission, oversight, slip, slip-up **3.** blemish, defect, deficiency, drawback, failing, flaw, imperfection, infirmity, lack, shortcoming, snag, weakness, weak point **4.** **at fault** answerable, blamable, culpable, guilty, in the wrong, responsible, to blame **5.** **find fault with** carp at, complain, criticize, pick holes in, pull to pieces, quibble, take to task **6.** **to a fault** excessively, immoderately, in the extreme, needlessly, out of all proportion, overly (*U.S.*), overmuch, preposterously, ridiculously, unduly *~vb.* **7.** blame, call to account, censure, criticize, find fault with, find lacking, hold (someone) accountable (responsible, to blame), impugn
fault-finding carping, hairsplitting, nagging, niggling, nit-picking (*informal*)
faultless **1.** accurate, classic, correct, exemplary, faithful, flawless, foolproof, impeccable, model, perfect, unblemished **2.** above reproach, blameless, guiltless, immaculate, impeccable, innocent, irreproachable, pure, sinless, spotless, stainless, unblemished, unspotted, unsullied
faulty bad, blemished, broken, damaged, defective, erroneous, fallacious, flawed, impaired, imperfect, imprecise, inaccurate, incorrect, invalid, malfunctioning, not working, out of order, unsound, weak, wrong
faux pas bloomer (*Brit. informal*), blunder, boob (*Brit. slang*), breach of etiquette, clanger (*informal*), gaffe, impropriety, indiscretion, solecism
favour *n.* **1.** approbation, approval, backing, bias, championship, espousal, esteem, favouritism, friendliness, good opinion, goodwill, grace, kindness, kind regard, partiality, patronage, promotion, support **2.** benefit, boon, courtesy, good turn, indulgence, kindness, obligement (*Scot. or archaic*), service **3.** **in favour of** all for (*informal*), backing, for, on the side of, pro,

pense of others: *parents sometimes favour the youngest child in the family.* **8** to support or agree with (something): *he favours the abolition of capital punishment.* **favoured** *or US* **favored** *adj*

favourable *or US* **favorable** *adj* **1** advantageous, encouraging, or promising: *a favourable climate for business expansion.* **2** giving consent or approval. **favourably** *or US* **favorably** *adv*

favourite *or US* **favorite** *adj* **1** most liked. *~n* **2** a person or thing regarded with especial preference or liking. **3** *Sport* a competitor thought likely to win.

favouritism *or US* **favoritism** *n* the practice of giving special treatment to a person or group: *favouritism in the allocation of government posts.*

fawn[1] *n* **1** a young deer aged under one year. *~adj* **2** pale greyish-brown.

fawn[2] *vb* **fawn on 1** to seek attention from (someone) by insincere flattery: *it makes me sick to see the way you fawn on that awful woman.* **2** (of a dog) to try to please (someone) by a show of extreme friendliness. **fawning** *adj*

fax *n* **1** an electronic system for transmitting an exact copy of a document. **2** a document sent by this system. *~vb* **3** to send (a document) by this system.

FBI (in the U.S.) Federal Bureau of Investigation.

FD Defender of the Faith: the title of the British sovereign as head of the Church of England.

Fe *Chem* iron.

fealty *n, pl* **-ties** (in feudal society) the loyalty sworn to a lord by his tenant or servant.

fear *n* **1** a feeling of distress or alarm caused by danger or pain that is about to happen. **2** something that causes fear. **3** possibility or likelihood: *there is no fear of her agreeing to that.* **4 no fear** *Informal* certainly not. *~vb* **5** to be afraid of (someone or something). **6** *Formal* to be sorry: *I fear the children were not very good yesterday.* **7 fear for** to feel anxiety about something. **fearless** *adj* **fearlessly** *adv*

fearful *adj* **1** afraid and full of fear. **2** frightening or causing fear: *the ship hit a fearful storm.* **3** *Informal* very bad: *they were making a fearful noise.* **fearfully** *adv*

fearsome *adj* terrible or frightening.

feasible *adj* able to be done: *a manned journey to Mars is now feasible.* **feasibility** *n* **feasibly** *adv*

feast *n* **1** a large and special meal for many people. **2** something extremely pleasing: *a feast of colour.* **3** an annual religious celebration. *~vb* **4** to take part in a feast. **5** to give a feast to. **6 feast on** to eat a large amount of: *down come hundreds of vultures to feast on the remains.* **7 feast one's eyes on** to look at (someone or something) with a great deal of attention and pleasure.

Feast of Tabernacles *n* same as **Sukkoth.**

THESAURUS

supporting, to the benefit of *~vb.* **4.** advocate, approve, back, be in favour of, champion, choose, commend, countenance, encourage, espouse, fancy, incline towards, like, opt for, patronize, prefer, single out, support **5.** be partial to, esteem, have in one's good books, indulge, pamper, pull strings for (*informal*), reward, side with, smile upon, spoil, treat with partiality, value

favourable 1. advantageous, appropriate, auspicious, beneficial, convenient, encouraging, fair, fit, good, helpful, hopeful, opportune, promising, propitious, suitable, timely **2.** affirmative, agreeable, amicable, approving, benign, encouraging, enthusiastic, friendly, kind, positive, reassuring, sympathetic, understanding, welcoming, well-disposed

favourably 1. advantageously, auspiciously, conveniently, fortunately, opportunely, profitably, to one's advantage, well **2.** agreeably, approvingly, enthusiastically, genially, graciously, helpfully, in a kindly manner, positively, with approval (approbation, cordiality), without prejudice

favourite 1. *adj.* best-loved, choice, dearest, esteemed, favoured, preferred **2.** *n.* beloved, blue-eyed boy (*informal*), choice, darling, dear, idol, pet, pick, preference, teacher's pet, the apple of one's eye

favouritism bias, jobs for the boys (*informal*), nepotism, one-sidedness, partiality, partisanship, preference, preferential treatment

fawn[1] *vb. with* **on** be obsequious, be servile, bow and scrape, brown-nose (*taboo slang*), court, crawl, creep, cringe, curry favour, dance attendance, flatter, grovel, ingratiate oneself, kiss ass (*U S. & Canad. taboo slang*), kneel, kowtow, lick (someone's) boots, pander to, pay court, toady, truckle

fawn[2] *adj.* beige, buff, greyish-brown, neutral

fawning abject, bootlicking (*informal*), bowing and scraping, crawling, cringing, deferential, flattering, grovelling, obsequious, prostrate, servile, slavish, sycophantic

fear *n.* **1.** agitation, alarm, anxiety, apprehensiveness, awe (*informal*), consternation, cravenness, dismay, dread, fright, horror, panic, qualms, terror, timidity, tremors, trepidation, unease, uneasiness, worry **2.** *bête noire,* bogey, bugbear, horror, nightmare, phobia, spectre *~vb.* **3.** apprehend, be apprehensive (afraid, frightened, scared), dread, have a horror of, have a phobia about, have butterflies in one's stomach (*informal*), have qualms, live in dread of, shake in one's shoes, shudder at, take fright, tremble at **4.** *with* **for** be anxious about (concerned, distressed), be disquieted over, feel concern for, tremble for, worry about

fearful 1. afraid, alarmed, anxious, apprehensive, diffident, faint-hearted, frightened, hesitant, intimidated, jittery (*informal*), jumpy, nervous, nervy (*Brit. informal*), panicky, pusillanimous (*formal*), scared, shrinking, tense, timid, timorous, uneasy, wired (*slang*) **2.** appalling, atrocious, awful, dire, distressing, dreadful, frightful, ghastly, grievous, grim, gruesome, hair-raising, harrowing, hideous, horrendous, horrible, horrific, monstrous, shocking, terrible, unspeakable

fearfully 1. apprehensively, diffidently, in fear and trembling, nervously, timidly, timorously, uneasily, with many misgivings *or* forebodings, with one's heart in one's mouth **2.** awfully, exceedingly, excessively, frightfully, terribly, tremendously, very

fearless ballsy (*taboo slang*), bold, brave, confident, courageous, daring, dauntless, doughty, gallant, game (*informal*), gutsy (*slang*), heroic, indomitable, intrepid, lion-hearted, plucky, unabashed, unafraid, undaunted, unflinching, valiant, valorous

fearsome alarming, appalling, awe-inspiring, awesome, awful, baleful, daunting, dismaying, formidable, frightening, hair-raising, hellacious (*U.S. slang*), horrendous, horrifying, menacing, unnerving

feasibility expediency, practicability, usefulness, viability, workability

feasible achievable, attainable, likely, possible, practicable, realizable, reasonable, viable, workable

feast *n.* **1.** banquet, barbecue, beanfeast (*Brit. informal*), beano (*Brit. slang*), blowout (*slang*), carousal, carouse, dinner, entertainment, festive board, jollification, junket, repast, revels, slap-up meal (*Brit. informal*), spread (*informal*), treat **2.** celebration, festival, fête, gala day, holiday, holy day, saint's day *~vb.* **3.** eat one's fill, eat to one's heart's content, fare sumptuously, gorge, gormandize, indulge, overindulge, pig out (*slang*), stuff, stuff one's face (*slang*), wine and dine **4.**

feat *n* a remarkable, skilful, or daring action: *an extraordinary feat of engineering.*

feather *n* **1** any of the flat light structures that form the plumage of birds, each consisting of a shaft with soft thin hairs on either side. **2 feather in one's cap** a cause for pleasure at one's achievements. *~vb* **3** to fit, cover, or supply with feathers. **4** *Rowing* to turn an oar parallel to the water between strokes, in order to lessen wind resistance. **5 feather one's nest** to collect possessions and money to make one's life comfortable, often dishonestly. **feathered** *adj* **feathery** *adj*

feather bed *n* **1** a mattress filled with feathers or down. *~vb* **featherbed, -bedding, -bedded 2** to pamper or spoil (someone).

featherbedding *n* the practice of working in a factory or office deliberately slowly and inefficiently so that more workers are employed than are necessary.

featherbrain *n* an empty-headed or forgetful person. **featherbrained** *adj*

featherweight *n* **1** a professional or an amateur boxer weighing up to 126 pounds (57 kg). **2** something very light or of little importance: *a featherweight politician.*

feature *n* **1** any one of the parts of the face, such as the nose, chin, or mouth. **2** a prominent or distinctive part of something: *regular debates were a feature of our final year.* **3** the main film in a cinema programme. **4** an item appearing regularly in a newspaper or magazine. **5** a prominent story in a newspaper. *~vb* **-turing, -tured 6** to have as a feature or make a feature of: *this cooker features a fan-assisted oven.* **7** to give special prominence to: *the film features James Mason as Rommel.* **featureless** *adj*

Feb. February.

febrile (fee-brile) *adj Formal* **1** very active and nervous: *increasingly febrile activity at the Stock Exchange.* **2** of or relating to fever.

February *n, pl* **-aries** the second month of the year.

feckless *adj* irresponsible and lacking character and determination: *her feckless brother was always in debt.*

fecund *adj Literary* **1** fertile or capable of producing many offspring. **2** intellectually productive or creative: *an extraordinarily fecund year even by Mozart's standards.* **fecundity** *n*

fed *vb* the past of **feed.**

federal *adj* **1** of a form of government in which power is divided between one central and several regional governments. **2** of the central government of a federation. **federalism** *n* **federalist** *n, adj*

Federal *adj* of or supporting the Union government during the American Civil War.

Federal Government *n* the national government of a federated state, such as that of Canada located in Ottawa.

federalize *or* **-ise** *vb* **-izing, -ized** *or* **-ising, -ised 1** to unite in a federal union. **2** to subject to federal control. **federalization** *or* **-isation** *n*

federate *vb* **-ating, -ated** to unite in a federal union. **federative** *adj*

federation *n* **1** the union of several provinces, states, etc. **2** any alliance or association of organizations which have freely joined together for a common purpose: *a federation of twenty regional unions.*

fed up *adj Informal* annoyed or bored.

fee *n* **1** a charge paid to be allowed to do something: *the BBC licence fee.* **2** a payment asked by professional people for their services. **3** *Property law* an interest in land that can be inherited. The interest can be with unrestricted rights (**fee simple**) or restricted (**fee tail**).

feeble *adj* **1** lacking in physical or mental strength. **2** not effective or convincing: *feeble excuses for Scotland's latest defeat.* **feebly** *adv*

feeble-minded *adj* unable to think or understand effectively.

feed *vb* **feeding, fed 1** to give food to (a person or an animal). **2** to give (something) as food: *people feeding bread to their cattle.* **3** to eat food: *red squirrel feed in the pines.* **4** to supply or prepare food for. **5** to provide what is needed for the continued existence, operation, or growth of: *illustrations which will feed an older child's imagination; pools fed by waterfalls.* *~n* **6** the act of feeding. **7** food, esp. that given to animals or babies. **8** *Informal* a meal.

feedback *n* **1** information in response to an inquiry or experiment: *considerable feedback from the customers.* **2** the return of part of the output of an electronic circuit to its input. **3** the return of part of the sound output of a loudspeaker to the microphone, so that a high-pitched whine is produced.

feeder *n* **1** a device used to feed an animal, child, or

THESAURUS

entertain, hold a reception for, kill the fatted calf for, regale, treat, wine and dine

feat accomplishment, achievement, act, attainment, deed, exploit, performance

feathers down, plumage, plumes

feathery downy, feathered, fluffy, plumed, wispy

feature *n.* **1.** aspect, attribute, characteristic, facet, factor, hallmark, mark, peculiarity, point, property, quality, trait **2.** attraction, crowd puller (*informal*), draw, highlight, main item, special, special attraction, speciality, specialty **3.** article, column, comment, item, piece, report, story *~vb.* **4.** accentuate, call attention to, emphasize, give prominence to, give the full works (*slang*), headline, play up, present, promote, set off, spotlight, star

feckless aimless, feeble, futile, hopeless, incompetent, ineffectual, irresponsible, shiftless, useless, weak, worthless

federate *vb.* amalgamate, associate, combine, confederate, integrate, syndicate, unify, unite

federation alliance, amalgamation, association, *Bund,* coalition, combination, confederacy, copartnership, entente, federacy, league, syndicate, union

fed up annoyed, blue, bored, brassed off (*Brit. slang*), browned-off (*informal*), depressed, discontented, dismal, dissatisfied, down, gloomy, glum, hacked off (*U.S. slang*), pissed off (*taboo slang*), sick and tired of (*informal*), tired of, weary of

fee account, bill, charge, compensation, emolument, hire, honorarium, pay, payment, recompense, remuneration, reward, toll

feeble 1. debilitated, delicate, doddering, effete, enervated, enfeebled, etiolated (*formal*), exhausted, failing, faint, frail, infirm, languid, powerless, puny, sickly, weak, weakened, weedy (*informal*) **2.** flat, flimsy, inadequate, incompetent, indecisive, ineffective, ineffectual, inefficient, insignificant, insufficient, lame, paltry, pathetic, poor, slight, tame, thin, unconvincing, weak

feeble-minded bone-headed (*slang*), braindead (*informal*), deficient, dim-witted (*informal*), dozy (*Brit. informal*), dull, dumb (*informal*), half-witted, idiotic, imbecilic, lacking, moronic, obtuse, retarded, simple, slow on the uptake, slow-witted, soft in the head (*informal*), stupid, vacant, weak-minded

feed *vb.* **1.** cater for, nourish, provide for, provision, supply, sustain, wine and dine **2.** augment, bolster, encourage, foster, fuel, minister to, strengthen, supply *~n.* **3.** fodder, food, forage, pasturage, provender (*old-*

sick person. **2** an animal or a person who feeds: *these larvae are voracious feeders.* **3** a road, rail, or air service that links outlying areas to the main network. **4** a tributary or channel of a river.

feel *vb* **feeling, felt 1** to have a physical or emotional sensation of: *he felt a combination of shame and relief.* **2** to become aware of or examine by touching. **3** Also: **feel in one's bones** to sense by intuition. **4** to believe or think: *I felt I got off pretty lightly.* **5 feel for** to show compassion (towards). **6 feel like** to have an inclination (for something or doing something): *I feel like going to the cinema.* **7 feel up to** to be fit enough for (something or doing something). *~n* **8** the act of feeling. **9** an impression: *all this mixing and matching has a French feel to it.* **10** the sense of touch. **11** an instinctive ability: *a feel for art.*

➤ *Feel* is followed by an adjective when it refers back to the subject: *I feel sick.* Otherwise it is followed by an adverb: *She feels strongly about it.*

feeler *n* **1** an organ on an insect's head that is sensitive to touch. **2 put out feelers** to make informal suggestions or remarks designed to probe the reactions of others.

feeling *n* **1** an emotional reaction: *a feeling of discontent.* **2 feelings** emotional sensitivity: *I don't want to hurt your feelings.* **3** instinctive appreciation and understanding: *your feeling for language.* **4** an intuitive understanding that cannot be explained: *I began to have a sinking feeling that I was not going to get rid of her.* **5** opinion or view: *it was his feeling that the report was a misinterpretation of what had been said.* **6** capacity for sympathy or affection: *moved by feeling for his fellow citizens.* **7 a** the ability to experience physical sensations: *he has no feeling in his left arm.* **b** the sensation so experienced. **8** the impression or mood created by something: *a feeling of excitement in the air.* **9 bad feeling** resentment or anger between people, for example after an argument or an injustice: *his refusal may have triggered bad feeling between the two men.* **feelingly** *adv*

feet *n* **1** the plural of **foot. 2 be run** *or* **rushed off one's feet** to be very busy. **3 feet of clay** a weakness that is not widely known. **4 have** *or* **keep one's feet on the ground** to be practical and reliable. **5 put one's feet up** to take a rest. **6 stand on one's own feet** to be independent. **7 sweep off one's feet** to fill with enthusiasm.

feign **(fane)** *vb* to pretend to experience (a particular feeling): *he didn't have to feign surprise.* **feigned** *adj*

feint[1] **(faint)** *n* **1** a misleading movement designed to distract an opponent, such as in boxing or fencing. *~vb* **2** to make a feint.

feint[2] **(faint)** *n Printing* paper that has pale lines across it for writing on.

feisty **(fie-stee)** *adj* **feistier, feistiest** *Informal, chiefly US & Canad* showing courage or spirit.

feldspar *or* **felspar** *n* a hard mineral that is the main constituent of igneous rocks. **feldspathic** *or* **felspathic** *adj*

felicitations *pl n, interj* expressions of pleasure at someone's success or good fortune; congratulations.

felicitous *adj* appropriate and well-chosen: *a felicitous combination of architectural styles.*

felicity *n* **1** great happiness and pleasure. **2** the quality of being pleasant or desirable: *small moments of architectural felicity amidst acres of monotony.* **3** (*pl* **-ties**) an appropriate and well-chosen remark: *Nietzsche's verbal felicities are not lost in translation.*

feline *adj* **1** of or belonging to the cat family. **2** like a cat, esp. in stealth or grace. *~n* **3** any member of the cat family. **felinity** *n*

fell[1] *vb* the past tense of **fall.**

fell[2] *vb* **1** to cut down (a tree). **2** to knock down (a person), esp. in a fight.

fell[3] *adj* **in one fell swoop** in one single action or on one single occasion: *they arrested all the hooligans in one fell swoop.*

fell[4] *n Scot & N English* a mountain, hill, or moor.

fell[5] *n* an animal's skin or hide with its hair.

fellatio **(fill-lay-shee-oh)** *n* a sexual activity in which the penis is stimulated by the partner's mouth.

felloe *or* **felly** *n, pl* **-loes** *or* **-lies** a segment or the whole rim of a wooden wheel.

fellow *n* **1** *Old-fashioned* a man or boy. **2** comrade or associate. **3** a person in the same group or condition: *he earned the respect of his fellows at Dunkirk.* **4** a member of the governing body at any of various universities or colleges. **5** a postgraduate research student. *~adj* **6** in the same group or condition: *a conversation with a fellow passenger.*

Fellow *n* a senior member of an academic institution.

fellow feeling *n* sympathy existing between people who have shared similar experiences.

fellowship *n* **1** the state of sharing mutual interests or activities. **2** a society of people sharing mutual interests or activities. **3** companionship or friendship. **4** *Education* a financed research post providing study facilities.

THESAURUS

fashioned), silage **4.** *informal* feast, meal, nosh (*slang*), nosh-up (*Brit. slang*), repast, spread (*informal*), tuck-in (*informal*)

feel *vb.* **1.** be aware of, be sensible of, endure, enjoy, experience, go through, have, have a sensation of, know, notice, observe, perceive, suffer, take to heart, undergo **2.** caress, finger, fondle, handle, manipulate, maul, paw, run one's hands over, stroke, touch **3.** be convinced, feel in one's bones, have a hunch, have the impression, intuit, sense **4.** believe, be of the opinion that, consider, deem, hold, judge, think **5.** *with* **for** be moved by, be sorry for, bleed for, commiserate, compassionate, empathize, feel compassion for, pity, sympathize with **6. feel like** could do with, desire, fancy, feel inclined, feel the need for, feel up to, have the inclination, want *~n.* **7.** air, ambience, atmosphere, feeling, impression, quality, sense, vibes (*slang*) **8.** finish, surface, texture, touch

feeler 1. antenna, tentacle, whisker **2. put out feelers** approach, float a trial balloon, probe

feeling 1. *plural* ego, emotions, self-esteem, sensitivities, susceptibilities **2.** apprehension, consciousness, hunch, idea, impression, inkling, notion, presentiment, sense, suspicion **3.** inclination, instinct, opinion, point of view, view **4.** appreciation, compassion, concern, empathy, pity, sensibility, sensitivity, sympathy, understanding **5.** feel, perception, sensation, sense, sense of touch, touch **6.** air, ambience, atmosphere, aura, feel, mood, quality, vibes (*slang*) **7. bad feeling** anger, dislike, distrust, enmity, hostility, upset

feline 1. catlike, leonine **2.** graceful, sinuous, sleek, slinky, smooth, stealthy

fell *vb.* cut, cut down, demolish, flatten, floor, hew, knock down, level, prostrate, raze, strike down

fellow *n.* **1.** *old-fashioned* bloke (*Brit. informal*), boy, chap (*informal*), character, customer (*informal*), guy (*informal*), individual, man, person, punter (*informal*) **2.** associate, colleague, companion, compeer, comrade, co-worker, equal, friend, member, partner, peer *~adj.* **3.** affiliated, akin, allied, associate, associated, co-, like, related, similar

fellowship 1. amity, brotherhood, camaraderie, communion, companionability, companionship, fa-

fellow traveller *n History* a Communist sympathizer who was not a Communist Party member.
felon *n Criminal law* (formerly) a person who committed a serious crime.
felony *n, pl* **-nies** *Criminal law* (formerly) a serious crime, such as murder or arson. **felonious** *adj*
felspar *n* same as **feldspar.**
felt[1] *vb* the past of **feel.**
felt[2] *n* a matted fabric of wool, made by working the fibres together under pressure.
felt-tip pen *n* a pen with a writing point made from pressed fibres.
fem. **1** female. **2** feminine.
female *adj* **1** of the sex producing offspring. **2** of or characteristic of a woman. **3** (of reproductive organs such as the ovary and carpel) capable of producing reproductive cells (**gametes**) that are female. **4** (of flowers) not having parts in which pollen is produced (**stamens**). **5** (of a mechanical component) having an opening into which a projecting male component can be fitted. *~n* **6** a female animal or plant.
feminine *adj* **1** possessing qualities considered typical of or appropriate to a woman. **2** of women. **3** *Grammar* denoting a gender of nouns that includes some female animate things. **femininity** *n*
feminism *n* a doctrine or movement that advocates equal rights for women. **feminist** *n, adj*
femme fatale (**fam** fat-**tahl**) *n, pl* **femmes fatales** (**fam** fat-**tahlz**) an alluring or seductive woman who leads men into dangerous or difficult situations by her charm.
femto- *combining form* denoting 10^{-15}: *femtometer.*
femur (**fee**-mer) *n, pl* **femurs** *or* **femora** (**fee**-mer-ra) the thighbone. **femoral** *adj*
fen *n* low-lying flat marshy land.
fence *n* **1** a barrier that encloses an area such as a garden or field, usually made of posts connected by wire rails or boards. **2** an obstacle for a horse to jump in steeplechasing or showjumping. **3** *Slang* a dealer in stolen property. **4** *Machinery* a guard or guide, esp. in a circular saw or plane. **5** (**sit**) **on the fence** (to be) unwilling to commit oneself. *~vb* **fencing, fenced** **6** to construct a fence on or around (a piece of land). **7** **fence in** *or* **off** to close in or separate off with or as if with a fence. **8** to fight using swords or foils. **9** to argue cleverly but evasively: *they fenced for a while, weighing each other up.*
fencing *n* **1** the sport of fighting with swords or foils. **2** materials used for making fences.
fend *vb* **1** **fend for oneself** to look after oneself; be independent. **2** **fend off** to defend oneself against (verbal or physical attack).
fender *n* **1** a low metal barrier that stops coals from falling out of a fireplace. **2** a soft but solid object, such as a coil of rope, hung over the side of a vessel to prevent damage when docking. **3** *US & Canad* the wing of a car.
fenestration *n* the arrangement of windows in a building.
Fenian (**feen**-yan) *n* (formerly) a member of an Irish revolutionary organization founded to fight for an independent Ireland. **Fenianism** *n*
fenland *n* an area of low-lying flat marshy land.
fennel *n* a fragrant plant whose seeds, leaves, and root are used in cookery.
fenugreek *n* a Mediterranean plant grown for its heavily scented seeds.
feoff (**feef**) *n* same as **fief.**
feral *adj* **1** (of animals and plants) existing in a wild state, esp. after being domestic or cultivated. **2** savage.
ferment *n* **1** excitement and unrest caused by caused by change or uncertainty. **2** any substance, such as yeast, that causes fermentation. *~vb* **3** to undergo or cause to undergo fermentation.
fermentation *n* a chemical reaction in which an organic molecule splits into simpler substances, esp. the conversion of sugar to ethyl alcohol by yeast.
fermium *n Chem* an element artificially produced by neutron bombardment of plutonium. Symbol: Fm
fern *n* a flowerless plant with roots, stems, and long feathery leaves that reproduces by releasing spores. **ferny** *adj*
ferocious *adj* savagely fierce or cruel. **ferocity** *n*
ferret *n* **1** a small yellowish-white animal related to the weasel and bred for hunting rats and rabbits. *~vb* **-reting, -reted** **2** to hunt rabbits or rats with ferrets. **3** to search around. **4** **ferret out** **a** to drive from hiding. **b** to find by determined investigation: *she could ferret out little knowledge of his background.*
ferric *adj* of or containing iron in the trivalent state.
Ferris wheel *n* a large vertical fairground wheel with hanging seats for riding on.
ferroconcrete *n* same as **reinforced concrete.**
ferrous *adj* of or containing iron in the divalent state.
ferruginous (fur-**rooj**-in-uss) *adj* (of a mineral or rock) containing iron.
ferrule *n* a metal ring or cap placed over the end of a stick for added strength.
ferry *n, pl* **-ries** **1** a boat for transporting passengers and vehicles across a body of water, esp. as a regular service. **2** such a service. *~vb* **-ries, -rying, -ried** **3** to transport or go by ferry. **4** to transport (passengers or goods) on a regular basis. **ferryman** *n*
fertile *adj* **1** capable of producing offspring, crops, or

THESAURUS

miliarity, fraternization, intercourse, intimacy, kindliness, sociability **2.** association, brotherhood, club, fraternity, guild, league, order, sisterhood, society
feminine delicate, gentle, girlish, graceful, ladylike, modest, soft, tender, womanly
femme fatale charmer, enchantress, seductress, siren, vamp (*informal*)
fen bog, marsh, morass, quagmire, slough, swamp
fence *n.* **1.** barbed wire, barricade, barrier, defence, guard, hedge, paling, palisade, railings, rampart, shield, stockade, wall **2.** **on the fence** between two stools, irresolute, uncertain, uncommitted, undecided, vacillating *~vb.* **3.** **fence in** *or* **off** bound, circumscribe, confine, coop, defend, encircle, enclose, fortify, guard, hedge, impound, pen, pound, protect, restrict, secure, separate, surround **4.** beat about the bush, cavil, dodge, equivocate, evade, flannel (*Brit. informal*), hedge, parry, prevaricate, quibble, shift, stonewall
ferment *n.* **1.** *figurative* agitation, brouhaha, commotion, disruption, excitement, fever, frenzy, furore, glow, heat, hubbub, imbroglio, state of unrest, stew, stir, tumult, turbulence, turmoil, unrest, uproar **2.** bacteria, barm, fermentation agent, leaven, leavening, mother-of-vinegar, yeast *~vb.* **3.** boil, brew, bubble, concoct, effervesce, foam, froth, heat, leaven, rise, seethe, work
ferocious barbaric, barbarous, bloodthirsty, brutal, brutish, cruel, merciless, pitiless, relentless, ruthless, vicious
ferocity barbarity, bloodthirstiness, brutality, cruelty, ferociousness, fierceness, inhumanity, rapacity, ruthlessness, savageness, savagery, viciousness, wildness
ferret out bring to light, dig up, disclose, discover,

vegetation. **2** *Biol* capable of growth and development: *fertile seeds.* **3** highly productive: *a fertile imagination.* **4** *Physics* (of a substance) able to be transformed into fissile or fissionable material. **fertility** *n*

fertilize *or* **-lise** *vb* **-lizing, -lized** *or* **-lising, -lised 1** to provide (an animal or plant) with sperm or pollen to bring about fertilization. **2** to supply (soil) with nutrients. **fertilization** *or* **-lisation** *n*

fertilizer *or* **-liser** *n* any substance, such as manure, added to soil to increase its productivity.

fervent *or* **fervid** *adj* intensely sincere and passionate. **fervently** *adv*

fervour *or US* **fervor** *n* great intensity of feeling or belief.

fescue *n* a pasture and lawn grass with stiff narrow leaves.

fester *vb* **1** to grow worse and increasingly hostile: *the bitterness which had been festering beneath the surface.* **2** (of a wound) to form pus. **3** to rot and decay: *rubbish festered in the heat.*

festival *n* **1** an organized series of special events and performances: *the Edinburgh Festival.* **2** a day or period set aside for celebration.

festive *adj* of or like a celebration.

festivity *n, pl* **-ties 1** happy celebration: *a spirit of joy and festivity.* **2 festivities** celebrations.

festoon *vb* **1** to drape with decorations: *Christmas trees festooned with fairy lights.* ~*n* **2** a decorative chain of flowers or ribbons suspended in loops.

feta *n* a white Greek cheese made from sheep's or goat's milk.

fetch[1] *vb* **1** to go after and bring back. **2** to be sold for (a certain price): *Impressionist pictures fetch very high prices.* **3** *Informal* to give someone (a blow or slap). **4 fetch and carry** to perform menial tasks.

fetch[2] *n* the ghost or apparition of a living person.

fetching *adj Informal* attractive: *a fetching dress.*

fetch up *vb* **1** *Informal, Chiefly US* to arrive or end up. **2** *Slang* to vomit food.

fete (**fate**) *n* **1** an event, usually outdoors, with stalls, competitions, etc., held to raise money for charity. ~*vb* **feting, feted 2** to honour and entertain (someone) publicly: *the President was feted with an evening of music and dancing.*

fetid *or* **foetid** *adj* having a stale and unpleasant smell.

fetish *n* **1 a** a form of behaviour in which a person derives sexual satisfaction from handling an object. **b** any object that is involved in such behaviour. **2** any object, activity, etc., to which one is excessively devoted: *cleanliness is almost a fetish with her.* **3** an object that is believed to have magical powers. **fetishism** *n* **fetishist** *n*

fetlock *n* **1** the back part of a horse's leg, just behind the hoof. **2** the tuft of hair growing from this part.

fetter *n* **1 fetters** checks or restraints: *free from the fetters of religion.* **2** a chain fixed around a prisoner's ankle. ~*vb* **3** to prevent from behaving freely and naturally: *fettered by bureaucracy.* **4** to tie up in fetters.

fettle *n* **in fine fettle** in good spirits or health.

fetus *or* **foetus** (**fee-tuss**) *n, pl* **-tuses** the embryo of a mammal in the later stages of development. **fetal** *or* **foetal** *adj*

feu *n Scots Law* a right to the use of land in return for a fixed annual payment (**feu duty**).

feud *n* **1** long and bitter hostility between two families, clans, or individuals. ~*vb* **2** to carry on a feud.

feudal *adj* of or characteristic of feudalism.

feudalism *n* the legal and social system in medieval Europe, in which people were given land and protection by a lord in return for which they worked and fought for him. Also called: **feudal system**

fever *n* **1** an abnormally high body temperature, accompanied by a fast pulse rate, shivering, and nausea. **2** any disease characterized by a high temperature. **3**

THESAURUS

drive out, elicit, get at, nose out, root out, run to earth, search out, smell out, trace, track down, unearth

ferry **1.** *n.* ferryboat, packet, packet boat **2.** *vb.* carry, chauffeur, convey, run, ship, shuttle, transport

fertile abundant, fat, fecund, flowering, flowing with milk and honey, fruit-bearing, fruitful, generative, luxuriant, plenteous, plentiful, productive, prolific, rich, teeming, yielding

fertility abundance, fecundity, fruitfulness, luxuriance, productiveness, richness

fertilize **1.** fructify, impregnate, inseminate, make fruitful, make pregnant, pollinate **2.** compost, dress, enrich, feed, manure, mulch, top-dress

fertilizer compost, dressing, dung, guano, manure, marl

fervent, fervid animated, ardent, devout, eager, earnest, ecstatic, emotional, enthusiastic, excited, fiery, flaming, heartfelt, impassioned, intense, vehement, warm, zealous

fervour animation, ardour, eagerness, earnestness, enthusiasm, excitement, fervency, intensity, passion, vehemence, warmth, zeal

festival **1.** carnival, celebration, entertainment, festivities, fête, field day, gala, jubilee **2.** anniversary, commemoration, feast, fête, fiesta, holiday, holy day, saint's day

festive back-slapping, carnival, celebratory, cheery, Christmassy, convivial, festal, gala, gay, gleeful, happy, hearty, holiday, jolly, jovial, joyful, joyous, jubilant, light-hearted, merry, mirthful, sportive

festivity **1.** amusement, conviviality, fun, gaiety, jollification, joviality, joyfulness, merriment, merrymaking, mirth, pleasure, revelry, sport **2.** *often plural* beano (*Brit. slang*), carousal, celebration, entertainment, festival, festive event, festive proceedings, fun and games, jollification, party, rave (*Brit. slang*), rave-up (*Brit. slang*)

festoon **1.** *vb.* array, bedeck, deck, decorate, drape, garland, hang, swathe **2.** *n.* chaplet, garland, lei, swag, swathe, wreath

fetch **1.** bring, carry, conduct, convey, deliver, escort, get, go for, lead, obtain, retrieve, transport **2.** bring in, earn, go for, make, realize, sell for, yield

fetching alluring, attractive, captivating, charming, cute, enchanting, enticing, fascinating, intriguing, sweet, taking, winsome

fete **1.** *n.* bazaar, fair, festival, gala, garden party, sale of work **2.** *vb.* bring out the red carpet for (someone), entertain regally, hold a reception for (someone), honour, kill the fatted calf for (someone), lionize, make much of, treat, wine and dine

fetish **1.** fixation, *idée fixe,* mania, obsession, thing (*informal*) **2.** amulet, cult object, talisman

feud **1.** *n.* argument, bad blood, bickering, conflict, contention, disagreement, discord, dissension, enmity, estrangement, faction, falling out, grudge, hostility, quarrel, rivalry, row, strife, vendetta **2.** *vb.* be at daggers drawn, be at odds, bicker, brawl, clash, contend, dispute, duel, fall out, quarrel, row, squabble, war

fever *figurative* agitation, delirium, ecstasy, excitement, ferment, fervour, frenzy, heat, intensity, passion, restlessness, turmoil, unrest

intense nervous excitement: *she waited in a fever of anxiety.*

feverish *or* **fevered** *adj* **1** suffering from fever. **2** in a state of nervous excitement: *a feverish scramble to buy shares.* **feverishly** *adv*

fever pitch *n* a state of intense excitement.

few *adj* **1** hardly any: *few homes had telephones in Paris in the 1930s.* **2 a few** a small number of: *a few days ago.* **3 a good few** *Informal* several. **4 few and far between** scarce. **5 quite a few** *Informal* several.
➤ *Few(er)* is used of things that can be counted: *Fewer than five visits.* Compare *less,* which is used for quantity: *It uses less sugar.*

fey *adj* **1** vague and whimsically strange. **2** having the ability to look into the future.

fez *n, pl* **fezzes** a round red brimless hat with a flat top and a tassel hanging from it. Formerly worn by men in Turkey and some Arab countries.

ff. and the following (pages, lines, etc.).

fiancé *or fem* **fiancée** (fee-**on**-say) *n* a person who is engaged to be married.

fiasco *n, pl* **-cos** *or* **-coes** an action or attempt that fails completely in a ridiculous or disorganized way: *the invasion of Cuba ended in a fiasco.*

fiat (**fie**-at) *n* **1** an official order issued without the consultation of those expected to obey it: *the junta ruled by fiat.* **2** official permission.

fib *n* **1** a trivial and harmless lie. *~vb* **fibbing, fibbed** **2** to tell such a lie. **fibber** *n*

fibre *or US* **fiber** *n* **1** a natural or synthetic thread that may be spun into yarn. **2** a threadlike animal or plant tissue: *a simple network of nerve fibres.* **3** a fibrous substance that helps the body digest food: *fruits, vegetables, grains, lentils, and beans are high in fibre.* **4** strength of character: *moral fibre.* **5** essential substance or nature: *my every fibre sang out in sudden relief.* **fibrous** *adj*

fibreboard *n* a building material made of compressed wood.

fibreglass *n* **1** material consisting of matted fine glass fibres, used as insulation. **2** a light strong material made by bonding fibreglass with a synthetic resin, used for boats and car bodies.

fibre optics *n* the transmission of information by light along very thin flexible fibres of glass. **fibre optic** *adj*

fibril (**fibe**-rill) *n* a small fibre.

fibrillation *n* uncontrollable twitching of muscle fibres, esp. those of the heart.

fibrin *n* a white insoluble elastic protein formed when blood clots.

fibrinogen (fib-**rin**-no-jen) *n Biol* a soluble plasma protein involved in blood clotting.

fibroid (**fibe**-royd) *adj* **1** *Anat* (of structures or tissues) containing or resembling fibres. *~n* **2** a harmless tumour composed of fibrous connective tissue.

fibrosis (fibe-**roh**-siss) *n* the formation of an abnormal amount of fibrous tissue.

fibrositis (fibe-roh-**site**-iss) *n* inflammation of fibrous tissue, esp. of the back muscles, causing pain and stiffness.

fibula (**fib**-yew-la) *n, pl* **-lae** (-lee) *or* **-las** the outer and thinner of the two bones between the knee and ankle of the human leg. **fibular** *adj*

fiche (**feesh**) *n* a sheet of film for storing publications in miniature form.

fickle *adj* **1** changeable in purpose, affections, etc.: *notoriously fickle voters.* **2** (of the weather) changing often and suddenly. **fickleness** *n*

fiction *n* **1** literary works invented by the imagination, such as novels. **2** an invented story or explanation: *the fiction that the Baltic states freely joined the USSR.* **3** *Law* something assumed to be true for the sake of convenience, though probably false. **fictional** *adj*

fictionalize *or* **-ise** *vb* **-izing, -ized** *or* **-ising, -ised** to make into fiction.

fictitious *adj* **1** not genuine: *rumours of false accounting and fictitious loans had surrounded the bank for years.* **2** of or in fiction.

fiddle *n* **1** *Informal or disparaging* the violin. **2** a violin played as a folk instrument. **3** *Brit informal* a dishonest action or scheme. **4 on the fiddle** *Informal* engaged in an illegal or fraudulent undertaking. **5 fit as a fiddle** *Informal* in very good health. **6 play second fiddle** *Informal* to undertake a role that is less important or powerful than someone else's. *~vb* **-dling, -dled** **7** to play (a tune) on the fiddle. **8** *Informal* to do (something) by illegal or dishonest means. **9** *Informal*

THESAURUS

feverish 1. burning, febrile, fevered, flaming, flushed, hectic, hot, inflamed **2.** agitated, desperate, distracted, excited, frantic, frenetic, frenzied, impatient, obsessive, overwrought, restless

few 1. hardly any, inconsiderable, infrequent, insufficient, meagre, negligible, not many, rare, scant, scanty, scarce, scarcely any, scattered, sparse, sporadic, thin **2. few and far between** at great intervals, hard to come by, infrequent, in short supply, irregular, rare, scarce, scattered, seldom met with, uncommon, unusual, widely spaced

fiancé *or fem.* **fiancée** betrothed, intended, prospective spouse, wife- *or* husband-to-be

fiasco balls-up (*taboo slang*), catastrophe, cock-up (*Brit. slang*), debacle, disaster, failure, flap (*informal*), fuck-up (*offensive taboo slang*), mess, rout, ruin, washout (*informal*)

fib *n.* fiction, lie, pork pie (*Brit. slang*), porky (*Brit. slang*), prevarication, story, untruth, white lie, whopper (*informal*)

fibre 1. fibril, filament, pile, staple, strand, texture, thread, wisp **2.** *figurative as in* **moral fibre** resolution, stamina, strength, strength of character, toughness **3.** *figurative* essence, nature, quality, spirit, substance

fickle blowing hot and cold, capricious, changeable, faithless, fitful, flighty, inconstant, irresolute, mercurial, mutable, quicksilver, temperamental, unfaithful, unpredictable, unstable, unsteady, vacillating, variable, volatile

fickleness capriciousness, fitfulness, flightiness, inconstancy, mutability, unfaithfulness, unpredictability, unsteadiness, volatility

fiction 1. fable, fantasy, legend, myth, novel, romance, story, storytelling, tale, urban legend, work of imagination, yarn (*informal*) **2.** cock and bull story (*informal*), concoction, fabrication, falsehood, fancy, fantasy, figment of the imagination, imagination, improvisation, invention, lie, pork pie (*Brit. slang*), porky (*Brit. slang*), tall story, untruth

fictional imaginary, invented, legendary, made-up, nonexistent, unreal

fictitious apocryphal, artificial, assumed, bogus, counterfeit, fabricated, false, fanciful, feigned, imaginary, imagined, improvised, invented, made-up, make-believe, mythical, spurious, unreal, untrue

fiddle *n.* **1.** violin **2.** *informal* fix, fraud, graft (*informal*), piece of sharp practice, racket, scam (*slang*), sting (*informal*), swindle, wangle (*informal*) **3. fit as a fiddle** blooming, hale and hearty, healthy, in fine fettle, in good form, in good shape, in rude health, in the pink, sound, strong *~vb.* **4.** *informal* cheat, cook the books (*informal*), diddle (*informal*), finagle (*informal*),

to falsify (accounts). **10 fiddle with** to move or touch (something) restlessly or nervously. **11 fiddle about** *or* **around** *Informal* to waste time.

fiddle-faddle *interj Old-fashioned* nonsense.

fiddler *n* **1** a person who plays the fiddle. **2** a small burrowing crab. **3** *Informal* a person who dishonestly alters something or lies in order to get money.

fiddlesticks *interj* an expression of annoyance or disagreement.

fiddling *adj* small or unimportant.

fiddly *adj* **-dlier, -dliest** small and awkward to do or handle.

fidelity *n, pl* **-ties 1** faithfulness to one's spouse or lover. **2** loyalty to a person, belief, or cause. **3** accuracy in reporting detail: *an account of the invasion written with objectivity and fidelity.* **4** *Electronics* the degree to which an amplifier or radio accurately reproduces the input signal.

fidget *vb* **-eting, -eted 1** to move about restlessly. **2 fidget with** to make restless or uneasy movements with (something): *he broke off, fidgeting with the papers, unable to meet their gaze.* ~*n* **3** a person who fidgets. **4 the fidgets** a state of restlessness: *these youngsters are very highly strung and tend to get the fidgets.* **fidgety** *adj*

fiduciary (fid-**yewsh**-ya-ree) *Law* ~*n* **1** a person bound to act for someone else's benefit, as a trustee. ~*adj* **2** of or relating to a trust or trustee.

fie *interj Obsolete or facetious* an exclamation of disapproval.

fief (**feef**) *n* (in feudal Europe) land granted by a lord in return for military service.

field *n* **1** an area of uncultivated grassland; meadow. **2** a piece of cleared land used for pasture or growing crops. **3** a marked off area on which sports or athletic competitions are held. **4** an area that is rich in minerals or other natural resources: *an oil field.* **5 a** all the competitors in a competition. **b** the competitors in a competition excluding the favourite. **6** a battlefield. **7** *Cricket* the fielders collectively. **8** a wide expanse of land covered by some substance such as snow or lava. **9** an area of human activity or knowledge: *the most distinguished physicist in the field of quantum physics.* **10** a place away from the laboratory or classroom where practical work is done. **11** the surface or background of something, such as a flag. **12** *Physics* In full: **field of force** the region surrounding a body, such as a magnet, within which it can exert a force on another similar body not in contact with it. **13 play the field** *Informal* to have many romantic relationships before getting married. ~*adj* **14** *Mil* of equipment or personnel for operations in the field: *field guns.* ~*vb* **15** *Sport* to catch or return (the ball) as a fielder. **16** *Sport* to send (a player or team) onto the field to play. **17** *Sport* (of a player or team) to act or take turn as a fielder or fielders. **18** *Informal* to deal successfully with (a question or remark).

field day *n* **1** *Informal* an opportunity or occasion for unrestrained action, esp. if previously denied or restricted: *the revelations gave the press a field day.* **2** *Mil* a day devoted to manoeuvres or exercises.

fielder *n Cricket etc* a member of the fielding side.

field event *n* a competition, such as the discus, that takes place on a field as opposed to the track.

fieldfare *n* a type of large thrush.

field glasses *pl n* binoculars.

field hockey *n US & Canad* hockey played on a field, as distinguished from ice hockey.

field marshal *n* an officer holding the highest rank in certain armies.

fieldmouse *n, pl* **-mice** a nocturnal mouse that lives in woods and fields.

field officer *n* an officer holding the rank of major, lieutenant colonel, or colonel.

fieldsman *n, pl* **-men** *Cricket* a fielder.

field sports *pl n* sports carried on in the countryside, such as hunting or fishing.

field trip *n* an expedition, esp. by students, to study something at first hand.

fieldwork *n Mil* a temporary structure used in defending a place or position.

field work *n* an investigation made in the field as opposed to the classroom or laboratory. **field worker** *n*

fiend (**feend**) *n* **1** an evil spirit. **2** a cruel or wicked person. **3** *Informal* a person who is extremely interested in or fond of something: *a fitness fiend.* **fiendish** *adj* **fiendishly** *adv*

Fiend *n* **the Fiend** the devil.

fierce *adj* **1** very aggressive or angry: *a fierce dog.* **2** intense or strong: *a fierce wind.* **fiercely** *adv*

fiery (**fire**-ee) *adj* **fierier, fieriest 1** consisting of or like fire: *a fiery explosion.* **2** displaying strong passion, esp. anger: *a fiery speech.* **3** (of food) very spicy. **fierily** *adv* **fieriness** *n*

THESAURUS

fix, gerrymander, graft (*informal*), manoeuvre, racketeer, sting (*informal*), swindle, wangle (*informal*) **5. fiddle with** fidget, finger, interfere with, mess about *or* around, play, tamper with, tinker, toy, trifle

fiddling futile, insignificant, pettifogging, petty, trifling, trivial

fidelity 1. allegiance, constancy, dependability, devotedness, devotion, faith, faithfulness, fealty, integrity, loyalty, staunchness, troth (*archaic*), true-heartedness, trustworthiness **2.** accuracy, adherence, closeness, correspondence, exactitude, exactness, faithfulness, preciseness, precision, scrupulousness

fidget 1. *vb.* be like a cat on hot bricks (*informal*), bustle, chafe, fiddle (*informal*), fret, jiggle, jitter (*informal*), move restlessly, squirm, twitch, worry **2.** *n.* **the fidgets** fidgetiness, jitters (*informal*), nervousness, restlessness, unease, uneasiness

fidgety impatient, jerky, jittery (*informal*), jumpy, nervous, on edge, restive, restless, twitchy (*informal*), uneasy

field *n.* **1.** grassland, green, lea (*poetic*), meadow, pasture **2.** applicants, candidates, competition, competitors, contestants, entrants, possibilities, runners **3.** area, bounds, confines, department, discipline, domain, environment, limits, line, metier, pale, province, purview, range, scope, speciality, specialty, sphere of influence (activity, interest, study), territory ~*vb.* **4.** catch, pick up, retrieve, return, stop **5.** *figurative* deal with, deflect, handle, turn aside

fiend 1. demon, devil, evil spirit, hellhound **2.** barbarian, beast, brute, degenerate, ghoul, monster, ogre, savage **3.** *informal* addict, enthusiast, fanatic, freak (*informal*), maniac

fiendish accursed, atrocious, black-hearted, cruel, demoniac, devilish, diabolical, hellish, implacable, infernal, inhuman, malevolent, malicious, malignant, monstrous, satanic, savage, ungodly, unspeakable, wicked

fierce 1. baleful, barbarous, brutal, cruel, dangerous, feral, ferocious, fiery, menacing, murderous, passionate, savage, threatening, tigerish, truculent, uncontrollable, untamed, vicious, wild **2.** blustery, boisterous, furious, howling, inclement, powerful, raging, stormy, strong, tempestuous, tumultuous, uncontrollable, violent

fiercely ferociously, frenziedly, furiously, in a frenzy,

fiesta *n* (esp. in Spain and Latin America) a religious festival or carnival.

FIFA (fee-fa) International Association Football Federation.

fife *n* a small high-pitched flute, often used in military bands.

fifteen *n* **1** the cardinal number that is the sum of ten and five. **2** a numeral, 15 or XV, representing this number. **3** something representing or consisting of 15 units. **4** a Rugby Union team. ~*adj* **5** amounting to fifteen: *fifteen trees.* **fifteenth** *adj, n*

fifth *adj* **1** of or being number five in a series. ~*n* **2** one of five equal parts of something. **3** *Music* the interval between one note and the note three-and-a-half tones higher or lower than it. **4** an additional high gear fitted to some vehicles, esp. certain sports cars.

fifth column *n* any group that secretly helps the enemies of its own country or organization. **fifth columnist** *n*

fifty *n, pl* **-ties 1** the cardinal number that is the product of ten and five. **2** a numeral, 50 or L, representing this number. **3** something representing or consisting of 50 units. ~*adj* **4** amounting to fifty: *fifty bodies.* **fiftieth** *adj, n*

fifty-fifty *adj, adv Informal* **1** in equal parts. **2** just as likely to happen as not to happen: *a fifty-fifty chance of survival.*

fig *n* **1** a soft sweet fruit full of tiny seeds, which grows on a tree. **2 not care** *or* **give a fig** not to care at all: *he did not give a fig for his enemies.*

fig. **1** figurative(ly). **2** figure.

fight *vb* **fighting, fought 1** to struggle against (an enemy) in battle or physical combat. **2** to struggle to overcome or destroy: *to fight drug trafficking.* **3** to carry on (a battle or contest). **4** to make (one's way) somewhere with difficulty: *they fought their way upstream.* **5 fight for** to uphold (a cause) by struggling: *fight for your rights.* **6 fight it out** to struggle or compete until a decisive result is obtained. **7 fight shy of** to avoid: *they fought shy of direct involvement in the conflict.* ~*n* **8** a battle. **9** a quarrel or contest. **10** a boxing match. **11 put up a fight** to offer resistance. **fighting** *n*

fighter *n* **1** a professional boxer. **2** a person who has determination. **3** *Mil* an armed aircraft for destroying other aircraft.

fighting chance *n* a slight chance of success dependent on a struggle.

fight off *vb* **1** to drive away (an attacker). **2** to struggle to avoid: *to fight off infection.*

fig leaf *n* **1** a representation of a leaf of the fig tree used in sculpture to cover the genitals of nude figures. **2** anything used to conceal something thought to be shameful: *the agreement was a fig leaf for Hitler's violation of the treaty.*

figment *n* **a figment of one's imagination** something nonexistent and only imagined by someone.

figuration *n* ornamentation.

figurative *adj* **1** (of language) abstract, imaginative, or symbolic; not literal. **2** (of art) involving realistic representation of people and things. **figuratively** *adv*

figure *n* **1** a written symbol for a number. **2** an amount expressed in numbers. **3 figures** calculations with numbers. **4** visible shape or form; outline. **5** a slim bodily shape: *it's not good for your figure.* **6** a well known person: *a public figure.* **7** a representation in painting or sculpture, esp. of the human body. **8** an illustration or diagram in a text. **9** a decorative pattern. **10** a fixed set of movements in dancing or skating. **11** *Geom* any combination of points, lines, curves, or planes. **12** *Music* a characteristic short pattern of notes. **13 figure of fun** a person who is often laughed at by other people. ~*vb* **-uring, -ured 14** to calculate (sums or amounts). **15** *US, Canad, & NZ informal* to consider. **16** to be included or play a part: *a house which figures in several of White's novels.* **17** *Informal* to be consistent with expectation: *Small-time crook, earns most of his cash as an informer. – That figures.*

figured *adj* **1** decorated with a design: *a chair upholstered in figured velvet.* **2** *Music* ornamental.

figurehead *n* **1** a person who is formally the head of a movement or an organization, but has no real authority. **2** a carved bust on the bow of some sailing vessels.

figure of speech *n* an expression, such as a simile, in which words do not have their literal meaning.

figure out *vb Informal* to work out, solve, or understand.

figure skating *n* ice skating in which the skater traces outlines of selected patterns. **figure skater** *n*

figurine *n* a small carved or moulded figure.

filament *n* **1** the thin wire inside a light bulb that

THESAURUS

like cat and dog, menacingly, passionately, savagely, tempestuously, tigerishly, tooth and nail, uncontrolledly, viciously, with bared teeth, with no holds barred

fight *vb.* **1.** assault, battle, bear arms against, box, brawl, carry on war, clash, close, combat, come to blows, conflict, contend, cross swords, do battle, engage, engage in hostilities, exchange blows, feud, go to war, grapple, joust, row, scrap (*informal*), spar, struggle, take the field, take up arms against, tilt, tussle, wage war, war, wrestle **2.** contest, defy, dispute, make a stand against, oppose, resist, stand up to, strive, struggle, withstand **3.** carry on, conduct, engage in, prosecute, wage **4. fight shy of** avoid, duck out of (*informal*), keep aloof from, keep at arm's length, shun, steer clear of ~*n.* **5.** action, affray (*Law*), altercation, battle, bout, brawl, brush, clash, combat, conflict, contest, dispute, dissension, dogfight, duel, encounter, engagement, exchange of blows, fracas, fray, free-for-all (*informal*), head-to-head, hostilities, joust, melee, passage of arms, riot, row, rumble (*U.S. & N.Z. slang*), scrap (*informal*), scrimmage, scuffle, set-to (*informal*), shindig (*informal*), shindy (*informal*), skirmish, sparring match, struggle, tussle, war

fight down bottle up, control, curb, hold back, repress, restrain, suppress

fighter boxer, bruiser (*informal*), prize fighter, pugilist

fighting battle, bloodshed, blows struck, combat, conflict, hostilities, warfare

fight off beat off, keep *or* hold at bay, repel, repress, repulse, resist, stave off, ward off

figure *n.* **1.** character, cipher, digit, number, numeral, symbol **2.** amount, cost, price, sum, total, value **3.** form, outline, shadow, shape, silhouette **4.** body, build, frame, physique, proportions, shape, torso **5.** celebrity, character, dignitary, leader, notability, notable, personage, personality, presence, somebody, worthy **6.** depiction, design, device, diagram, drawing, emblem, illustration, motif, pattern, representation, sketch ~*vb.* **7.** add, calculate, compute, count, reckon, sum, tally, tot up, work out **8.** act, appear, be conspicuous, be featured, be included, be mentioned, contribute to, feature, have a place in, play a part

figurehead cipher, dummy, front man (*informal*), leader in name only, man of straw, mouthpiece, name, nonentity, puppet, titular *or* nominal head, token

figure of speech conceit, image, trope, turn of phrase

figure out calculate, comprehend, compute, decipher, fathom, make head or tail of (*informal*), make

emits light. 2 *Electronics* a high-resistance wire forming the cathode in some valves. 3 a single strand of fibre. 4 *Bot* the stalk of a stamen. **filamentary** *adj*

filbert *n* the brown edible nuts of the hazel.

filch *vb* to steal in small amounts.

file[1] *n* **1** a folder or box used to keep documents in order. **2** the documents, etc., kept in this way. **3** documents or information about a specific subject or person: *the doctor handed him his file.* **4** a line of people in marching formation, one behind another. **5** *Computers* an organized collection of related records. **6 on file** recorded for reference, as in a file. *~vb* **filing, filed 7** to place (a document) in a file. **8** to place (a legal document) on public or official record. **9** to bring a lawsuit, esp. for divorce. **10** to submit (a report or story) to a newspaper. **11** to march or walk in a line.

file[2] *n* **1** a hand tool consisting of a steel blade with small cutting teeth on its faces, used for shaping or smoothing. *~vb* **filing, filed 2** to shape or smooth (a surface) with a file.

filial *adj* of or suitable to a son or daughter: *filial duty.*

filibuster *n* **1** the process of obstructing legislation by means of long speeches so that time runs out and a vote cannot be taken. **2** a legislator who engages in such obstruction. *~vb* **3** to obstruct (legislation) with such delaying tactics.

filigree *n* **1** delicate ornamental work of gold or silver wire. *~adj* **2** made of filigree.

filings *pl n* shavings or particles removed by a file: *iron filings.*

Filipino (fill-lip-pee-no) *adj* **1** of the Philippines. *~n, pl* **-nos 2** Also (fem.): **Filipina** a person from the Philippines.

fill *vb* (often foll. by *up*) **1** to make or become full. **2** to occupy the whole of: *their supporters filled the entire stand.* **3** to plug (a gap or crevice). **4** to meet (a requirement or need) satisfactorily: *this book fills a major gap.* **5** to cover (a page or blank space) with writing or drawing. **6** to hold and perform the duties of (an office or position). **7** to appoint or elect an occupant to (an office or position). *~n* **8 one's fill** sufficient for one's needs or wants. ~See also **fill in, fill out, fill up.**

filler *n* **1** a paste used for filling in cracks or holes in a surface before painting. **2** *Journalism* an item to fill space between more important articles.

fillet *n* **1** a piece of boneless meat or fish. **2** a thin strip of ribbon or lace worn in the hair or around the neck. **3** *Archit* a narrow flat moulding. *~vb* **-leting, -leted 4** to cut or prepare (meat or fish) as a fillet.

fill in *vb* **1** to complete (a form). **2** to act as a substitute. **3** to put material into (a hole) so as to make it level with a surface. **4** *Informal* to give (a person) fuller details.

filling *n* **1** a substance or thing used to fill something: *a sandwich filling.* **2** *Dentistry* a substance that fills a gap or cavity of a tooth. *~adj* **3** (of food or a meal) substantial and satisfying.

filling station *n* a place where petrol and other supplies for motorists are sold.

fillip *n* **1** something that adds stimulation or enjoyment. **2** the action of holding a finger towards the palm with the thumb and suddenly releasing it with a snapping sound.

fill out *vb* **1** to fill in (a form or application). **2** to make or become plumper, thicker, or rounder. **3** to make more substantial: *he filled out his speech with a few jokes.*

fill up *vb* **1** to complete (a form or application). **2** to make or become full.

filly *n, pl* **-lies** a young female horse.

film *n* **1 a** a sequence of images projected onto a screen, creating the illusion of movement. **b** a form of entertainment in such a sequence of images. **2** a thin flexible strip of cellulose coated with a photographic emulsion, used to make negatives and slides. **3** a thin coating, covering, or layer: *a fine film of dust covered the floor.* **4** a thin sheet of any material, as of plastic for packaging. *~vb* **5 a** to photograph with a movie or video camera. **b** to make a film of (a screenplay or event). **6 film over** to cover or become covered with a thin layer. *~adj* **7** of or relating to films or the cinema.

film star *n* a popular film actor or actress.

film strip *n* a strip of film composed of different images projected separately as slides.

filmy *adj* **filmier, filmiest** very thin and almost transparent: *a shirt of filmy black chiffon.* **filmily** *adv* **filminess** *n*

filo *or* **filo pastry** (**feel**-o) *n* a type of flaky Greek pastry in very thin sheets.

Filofax *n Trademark* a type of loose-leaf ring binder, used as a portable personal filing system.

filter *n* **1** a substance, such as paper or sand, that allows fluid to pass but retains solid particles. **2** any device containing such a substance, esp. a tip on the mouth end of a cigarette. **3** any electronic or acoustic device that blocks signals of certain frequencies while allowing others to pass. **4** any transparent disc of gelatine or glass used to reduce the intensity of given frequencies from the light leaving a lamp or entering a

THESAURUS

out, reckon, resolve, see, suss (out) (*slang*), understand, work out

filament cilium (*Biol. & Zool.*), fibre, fibril, pile, staple, strand, string, thread, wire, wisp

filch abstract, crib (*informal*), embezzle, half-inch (*old-fashioned slang*), lift (*informal*), misappropriate, nick (*slang, chiefly Brit.*), pilfer, pinch (*informal*), purloin, rip off (*slang*), snaffle (*Brit. informal*), steal, swipe (*slang*), take, thieve, walk off with

file[1] *n.* **1.** case, data, documents, dossier, folder, information, portfolio **2.** column, line, list, queue, row, string *~vb.* **3.** document, enter, pigeonhole, put in place, record, register, slot in (*informal*) **4.** march, parade, troop

file[2] *vb.* burnish, furbish, polish, rasp, refine, rub, rub down, scrape, shape, smooth

filibuster 1. *n.* delay, hindrance, obstruction, postponement, procrastination **2.** *vb.* delay, hinder, obstruct, prevent, procrastinate, put off

fill 1. brim over, cram, crowd, furnish, glut, gorge, inflate, pack, pervade, replenish, sate, satiate, satisfy, stock, store, stuff, supply, swell **2.** block, bung, close, cork, plug, seal, stop **3.** assign, carry out, discharge, engage, execute, fulfil, hold, occupy, officiate, perform, take up **4. one's fill** all one wants, ample, a sufficiency, enough, plenty, sufficient

fill in 1. answer, complete, fill out, fill up **2.** deputize, replace, represent, stand in, sub, substitute, take the place of **3.** *informal* acquaint, apprise, bring up to date, give the facts *or* background, inform, put wise (*slang*)

filling 1. *n.* contents, filler, innards (*informal*), inside, insides, padding, stuffing, wadding **2.** *adj.* ample, heavy, satisfying, square, substantial

film *n.* **1.** flick (*slang*), motion picture, movie (*U.S. informal*) **2.** coat, coating, covering, dusting, gauze, integument, layer, membrane, pellicle, scum, skin, tissue *~vb.* **3.** photograph, shoot, take, video, videotape **4. film over** blear, blur, cloud, dull, haze, mist, veil

camera. **5** *Brit* a traffic signal which permits vehicles to turn either left or right when the main signals are red. ~*vb* **6** Also: **filter out** to remove or separate (particles) from (a liquid or gas) by a filter. **7** Also: **filter through** to pass through a filter or something like a filter.

filter out *or* **through** *vb* to become known gradually: *the crowd broke up when the news filtered through.*

filter paper *n* a porous paper used for filtering liquids.

filter tip *n* **1** an attachment to the mouth end of a cigarette for trapping impurities. **2** a cigarette with such an attachment. **filter-tipped** *adj*

filth *n* **1** disgusting dirt and muck. **2** offensive material or language. **filthiness** *n* **filthy** *adj*

filtrate *n* **1** a liquid or gas that has been filtered. ~*vb* **-trating, -trated 2** to filter. **filtration** *n*

fin *n* **1** any of the winglike projections from a fish's body enabling it to balance and swim. **2** *Brit* a vertical surface to which the rudder is attached at the rear of an aeroplane. **3** a swimmer's flipper. **finned** *adj*

fin. 1 finance. 2 financial.

finagle (fin-**nay**-gl) *vb* **-gling, -gled** *Informal* to use or achieve by craftiness or trickery.

final *adj* **1** of or occurring at the end; last. **2** having no possibility of further discussion, action, or change: *a final decision.* ~*n* **3** a deciding contest between the winners of previous rounds in a competition. ~See also **finals. finality** *n* **finally** *adv*

finale (fin-**nah**-lee) *n* the concluding part of a dramatic performance or musical composition.

finalist *n* a contestant who has reached the last stage of a competition.

finalize *or* **-ise** *vb* **-izing, -ized** *or* **-ising, -ised** to put into final form; settle: *finalized plans for Spain's entry into the EC.* **finalization** *or* **-isation** *n*

finals *pl n* **1** the deciding part of a competition. **2** *Education* the last examinations in an academic course.

finance *vb* **-nancing, -nanced 1** to provide or obtain funds for (a project or large purchase). ~*n* **2** the system of money, credit, and investment. **3** management of money, loans, or credits: *the dangerous political arena of public-sector finance.* **4** funds or the provision of funds. **5 finances** money resources: *the company's crumbling finances.*

financial *adj* **1** of or relating to finance, finances, or people who manage money. **2** *Austral & NZ informal* having money. **financially** *adv*

financial year *n Brit* any annual accounting period, such as that of the British Government which ends on April 5.

financier *n* a person who is engaged in large-scale financial operations

finch *n* a small songbird with a short strong beak.

find *vb* **finding, found 1** to discover by chance. **2** to discover by search or effort. **3** to realize or become aware: *I have found that if you make the effort then people will be more willing to help you.* **4** to consider (someone or something) to have a particular quality: *his business partner had found that odd.* **5** to experience (a particular feeling): *she found comfort in his words.* **6** *Law* to pronounce (the defendant) guilty or not guilty. **7** to reach (a target). **8** to provide, esp. with difficulty: *we'll find room for you too.* **9 find one's feet** to become capable or confident. ~*n* **10** a person or thing that is found, esp. a valuable discovery: *the archaeological find of the century.*

finder *n* **1** a small telescope fitted to a larger one. **2** a person or thing that finds. **3** *Photog* short for **viewfinder.**

finding *n* the conclusion reached after an inquiry or investigation.

THESAURUS

filmy chiffon, cobwebby, delicate, diaphanous, fine, finespun, flimsy, floaty, fragile, gauzy, gossamer, insubstantial, membranous, seethrough, sheer, transparent

filter *n.* **1.** gauze, membrane, mesh, riddle, sieve, strainer ~*vb.* **2.** *often with* **out** clarify, filtrate, purify, refine, screen, sieve, sift, strain, winnow **3.** *often with* **through** dribble, escape, exude, leach, leak, ooze, penetrate, percolate, seep, trickle, well

filth 1. carrion, contamination, crap (*slang*), crud (*slang*), defilement, dirt, dung, excrement, excreta, faeces, filthiness, foul matter, foulness, garbage, grime, grot (*slang*), muck, nastiness, ordure, pollution, putrefaction, putrescence, refuse, sewage, shit (*taboo slang*), slime, sludge, squalor, uncleanness **2.** corruption, dirty-mindedness, impurity, indecency, obscenity, pornography, smut, vileness, vulgarity

filthy 1. dirty, faecal, feculent, foul, nasty, polluted, putrid, scummy, slimy, squalid, unclean, vile **2.** begrimed, black, blackened, grimy, grubby, miry, mucky, muddy, mud-encrusted, smoky, sooty, unwashed **3.** bawdy, coarse, corrupt, depraved, dirty-minded, foul, foul-mouthed, impure, indecent, lewd, licentious, obscene, pornographic, smutty, suggestive

final 1. closing, concluding, end, eventual, last, last-minute, latest, terminal, terminating, ultimate **2.** absolute, conclusive, decided, decisive, definite, definitive, determinate, finished, incontrovertible, irrevocable, settled

finale climax, close, conclusion, crowning glory, culmination, dénouement, epilogue, finis, last act

finality certitude, conclusiveness, decidedness, decisiveness, definiteness, inevitableness, irrevocability, resolution, unavoidability

finalize agree, clinch, complete, conclude, decide, settle, sew up (*informal*), tie up, work out, wrap up (*informal*)

finally 1. at last, at length, at long last, at the last, at the last moment, eventually, in the end, in the long run, lastly, ultimately, when all is said and done **2.** in conclusion, in summary, to conclude **3.** beyond the shadow of a doubt, completely, conclusively, convincingly, decisively, for all time, for ever, for good, inescapably, inexorably, irrevocably, once and for all, permanently

finance 1. *vb.* back, bankroll (*U.S.*), float, fund, guarantee, pay for, provide security for, set up in business, subsidize, support, underwrite **2.** *n.* accounts, banking, business, commerce, economics, financial affairs, investment, money, money management

finances affairs, assets, capital, cash, financial condition, funds, money, resources, wherewithal

financial budgeting, economic, fiscal, monetary, money, pecuniary

find *vb.* **1.** catch sight of, chance upon, come across, come up with, descry, discover, encounter, espy, expose, ferret out, hit upon, lay one's hand on, light upon, locate, meet, recognize, run to earth, spot, stumble upon, track down, turn up, uncover, unearth **2.** arrive at, ascertain, become aware, detect, discover, experience, learn, note, notice, observe, perceive, realize, remark **3.** achieve, acquire, attain, earn, gain, get, obtain, procure, win **4.** be responsible for, bring, contribute, cough up (*informal*), furnish, provide, purvey,

find out *vb* **1** to learn something that one did not already know. **2 find someone out** to discover that someone has been dishonest or deceitful.

fine[1] *adj* **1** very good. **2** superior in skill: *a fine doctor.* **3** (of weather) clear and dry. **4** *Informal* quite well: *I felt fine.* **5** satisfactory: *as far as we can tell, everything is fine.* **6** of delicate or careful workmanship: *fine porcelain.* **7** subtle: *too fine a distinction.* **8** very thin or slender: *fine soft hair.* **9** very small: *fine print.* **10** (of edges or blades) sharp. **11** fancy, showy, or smart. **12** good-looking. **13** *Ironic* disappointing or terrible: *a fine mess!* ~*adv* **14** *Informal* very well: *that's what we've always done, and it suits us just fine.* ~*vb* **fining, fined 15** to make (something) finer or thinner. **16 fine down** to make (a theory or criticism) more precise or exact. **finely** *adv*

fine[2] *n* **1** a payment imposed as a penalty. ~*vb* **fining, fined 2** to impose a fine on.

fine art *n* **1** art produced chiefly to appeal to the sense of beauty. **2** any of the fields in which such art is produced, such as painting, sculpture, and engraving.

fine-drawn *adj* **1** (of arguments or distinctions) subtle. **2** (of wire) drawn out until very fine.

finery *n* elaborate or showy decoration, esp. clothing and jewellery.

fines herbes (feenz **airb**) *pl n* finely chopped mixed herbs, used to flavour omelettes.

finespun *adj* **1** spun or drawn out to a fine thread. **2** excessively subtle or concerned with minute detail: *a finespun theological debate.*

finesse (fin-**ness**) *n* **1** elegant and delicate skill. **2** subtlety and tact in handling difficult situations: *a lack of diplomatic finesse.* **3** *Bridge, whist* an attempt to win a trick when opponents hold a high card in the suit led by playing a lower card. ~*vb* **-nessing, -nessed 4** to bring about with finesse. **5** *Bridge, whist* to play (a card) as a finesse.

fine-tooth comb *or* **fine-toothed comb** *n* **1** a comb with fine teeth set closely together. **2 go over with a fine-tooth comb** to examine very thoroughly.

fine-tune *vb* **-tuning, -tuned** to make fine adjustments to (something) so that it works really well.

finger *n* **1** one of the four long jointed parts of the hand. **2** the part of a glove made to cover a finger. **3** something that resembles a finger in shape or function. **4** a quantity of liquid in a glass as deep as a finger is wide. **5 get one's finger out** *Brit informal* to begin or speed up activity, esp. after initial delay. **6 put one's finger on** to identify precisely. **7 put the finger on** *Informal* to inform on or identify, esp. for the police. **8 twist around one's little finger** to have easy and complete influence over. ~*vb* **9** to touch or manipulate with the fingers; handle. **10** to use one's fingers in playing (a musical instrument). **fingerless** *adj*

fingerboard *n* the long strip of hard wood on a violin, guitar, etc., upon which the strings are stopped by the fingers.

finger bowl *n* a small bowl of water for rinsing the fingers at table during a meal, esp. at a formal dinner.

fingering *n* **1** the technique of using one's fingers in playing a musical instrument. **2** the numerals in a musical part indicating this.

fingernail *n* a thin hard clear plate covering part of the upper surface of the end of each finger.

fingerprint *n* **1** an impression of the pattern of ridges on the inner surface of the end of each finger and thumb. ~*vb* **2** to take an inked impression of the fingerprints of (a person). **3** to take a sample of the DNA of (a person).

fingerstall *n* a protective covering for a finger.

fingertip *n* **1** the end of a finger. **2 have at one's fingertips** to know or understand thoroughly.

finicky *or* **finicking** *adj* **1** extremely fussy. **2** overelaborate or ornate: *finicky designer patterns.*

finis *n* the end: used at the end of books.

finish *vb* **1** to bring to an end; conclude or stop. **2** to be at or come to the end; use up. **3** to bring to a desired or complete condition. **4** to put a particular surface texture on (wood, cloth, or metal). **5 finish off a** to complete by doing the last part of: *he finished off his thesis last week.* **b** to destroy or defeat completely:

THESAURUS

supply ~*n.* **5.** acquisition, asset, bargain, catch, discovery, good buy

finding award, conclusion, decision, decree, judgment, pronouncement, recommendation, verdict

find out 1. detect, discover, learn, note, observe, perceive, realize **2. find someone out** bring to light, catch, detect, disclose, expose, reveal, rumble (*Brit. informal*), suss (out) (*slang*), uncover, unmask

fine[1] *adj.* **1.** accomplished, admirable, beautiful, choice, excellent, exceptional, exquisite, first-class, first-rate, great, magnificent, masterly, outstanding, rare, select, showy, skilful, splendid, sterling, superior, supreme, world-class **2.** balmy, bright, clear, clement, cloudless, dry, fair, pleasant, sunny **3.** acceptable, agreeable, all right, convenient, good, hunky-dory (*informal*), O.K. *or* okay (*informal*), satisfactory, suitable **4.** dainty, delicate, elegant, expensive, exquisite, fragile, quality **5.** abstruse, acute, critical, discriminating, fastidious, hairsplitting, intelligent, keen, minute, nice, precise, quick, refined, sensitive, sharp, subtle, tasteful, tenuous **6.** delicate, diaphanous, fine-grained, flimsy, gauzy, gossamer, light, lightweight, powdered, powdery, pulverized, sheer, slender, small, thin **7.** brilliant, cutting, honed, keen, polished, razor-sharp, sharp **8.** attractive, bonny, good-looking, handsome, lovely, smart, striking, stylish, well-favoured

fine[2] **1.** *n.* damages, forfeit, penalty, punishment **2.** *vb.* penalize, punish

finery decorations, frippery, gear (*informal*), gewgaws, glad rags (*informal*), ornaments, showiness, splendour, Sunday best, trappings, trinkets

finesse adeptness, adroitness, artfulness, cleverness, craft, delicacy, diplomacy, discretion, know-how (*informal*), polish, quickness, savoir-faire, skill, sophistication, subtlety, tact

finger *vb.* **1. put one's finger on** bring to mind, discover, find out, hit the nail on the head, hit upon, identify, indicate, locate, pin down, place, recall, remember **2.** feel, fiddle with (*informal*), handle, manipulate, maul, meddle with, paw (*informal*), play about with, touch, toy with

finish *vb.* **1.** accomplish, achieve, bring to a close *or* conclusion, carry through, cease, close, complete, conclude, culminate, deal with, discharge, do, end, execute, finalize, fulfil, get done, get out of the way, make short work of, put the finishing touch(es) to, round off, settle, stop, terminate, wind up, wrap up (*informal*) **2.** coat, face, gild, lacquer, polish, smooth off, stain, texture, veneer, wax **3.** *with* **off** administer *or* give the coup de grâce, annihilate, best, bring down, defeat, destroy, dispose of, drive to the wall, exterminate, get rid of, kill, overcome, overpower, put an end to, rout, ruin, worst ~*n.* **4.** cessation, close, closing, completion, conclusion, culmination, dénouement, end, ending, finale, last stage(s), termination, winding up (*informal*), wind-up **5.** annihilation, bankruptcy,

he finished off Faldo at the 16th hole. **6 finish with** to end a relationship with (someone). ~*n* **7** the final stage or part; end. **8** death or absolute defeat. **9** the surface texture of wood, cloth, or metal. **10** a thing or event that completes.

finishing school *n* a private school for girls that teaches social skills and polite behaviour.

finite (**fine**-ite) *adj* **1** having limits in size, space, or time: *finite supplies of fossil fuels.* **2** *Maths, logic* having a countable number of elements. **3** *Grammar* denoting any form of a verb inflected for person, number, and tense.

Finn *n* a person from Finland.

finnan haddock *or* **haddie** *n* a smoked haddock.

Finnish *adj* **1** of Finland. ~*n* **2** the language of Finland.

fino (**fee**-no) *n* a very dry sherry.

fiord (fee-**ord**) *n* same as **fjord.**

fipple flute *n* an end-blown flute with a plug (**fipple**) at the mouthpiece, such as the recorder or flageolet.

fir *n* a pyramid-shaped tree with needle-like leaves and erect cones.

fire *n* **1** the state of combustion producing heat, flames, and often smoke. **2** burning coal or wood, esp. in a hearth to heat a room. **3** a destructive uncontrolled burning that destroys building, crops, etc. **4** an electric or gas device for heating a room. **5** the act of shooting weapons. **6** passion and enthusiasm: *her questions brought new fire to the debate.* **7 catch fire** to start burning. **8 on fire a** burning. **b** ardent or eager. **9 open fire** to start firing a gun, artillery, etc. **10 play with fire** to be involved in something risky. **11 set fire to** *or* **set on fire a** to ignite. **b** to arouse or excite. **12 under fire** being attacked, such as by weapons or by harsh criticism. ~*vb* **firing, fired 13** to discharge (a firearm). **14** to detonate (an explosive device). **15** *Informal* to dismiss from employment. **16** to ask a lot of questions quickly in succession. **17** *Ceramics* to bake in a kiln to harden the clay. **18** to kindle or be kindled. **19** (of an internal-combustion engine) to produce an electrical spark which causes the fuel to burn and the engine to start. **20** to provide with fuel. **21** to arouse to strong emotion: *he fired his team mates with enthusiasm.*

fire alarm *n* a device to give warning of fire.

firearm *n* a weapon, such as a pistol, that fires bullets.

fireball *n* **1** ball-shaped lightning. **2** the hot ionized gas at the centre of a nuclear explosion. **3** a large bright meteor. **4** *Slang* an energetic person.

firebomb *n* a bomb that is designed to cause fires.

firebrand *n* a person who arouses passionate political feelings, often causing trouble.

firebreak *n* a strip of open land in a forest to stop the advance of a fire.

firebrick *n* a heat-resistant brick, used for lining furnaces, flues, and fireplaces.

fire brigade *n Chiefly Brit* an organized body of firefighters.

fire clay *n* a heat-resistant clay used in making firebricks and furnace linings.

firecracker *n* a firework which produces a loud bang.

firedamp *n* an explosive mixture of hydrocarbons, chiefly methane, formed in coal mines.

firedogs *pl n* two metal bars that support logs burning in a fire.

fire door *n* a door made of noncombustible material that prevents a fire spreading within a building.

fire drill *n* a rehearsal of procedures for escape from a fire.

fire-eater *n* **1** a performer who pretends to swallow flaming rods. **2** a very quarrelsome person.

fire engine *n* a vehicle that carries firefighters and firefighting equipment to a fire.

fire escape *n* a metal staircase or ladder on the outside of a building for escape in the event of fire.

fire-extinguisher *n* a portable device for spraying water, foam, or powder to extinguish a fire.

firefighter *n* a person whose job is to put out fires and rescue people endangered by them. **firefighting** *adj, n*

firefly *n, pl* **-flies** a beetle that glows in the dark.

fireguard *n* a screen made of wire mesh put before an open fire to protect against sparks.

fire hall *n Canad* a fire station.

fire hydrant *n* an outlet from a water main in the street, from which firefighters can draw water.

fire irons *pl n* a shovel, poker, and tongs for tending a domestic fire.

fireman *n, pl* **-men 1** a man whose job is to put out fires and rescue people endangered by them. **2** (on steam trains) the man who stokes the fire.

fireplace *n* an open recess at the base of a chimney for a fire; hearth.

fireplug *n Chiefly US & NZ* same as **fire hydrant.**

fire power *n Mil* the amount of fire that can be delivered by a unit or weapon.

fire raiser *n* a person who deliberately sets fire to property. **fire raising** *n*

fire ship *n History* a ship loaded with explosives, set on fire and left to drift among an enemy's warships.

fireside *n* the hearth.

fire station *n* a building where firefighting vehicles and equipment are stationed.

firetrap *n* a building that would burn easily or one without fire escapes.

firewater *n Informal* any alcoholic spirit.

firework *n* a device containing chemicals that is ignited to produce coloured sparks and sometimes bangs.

fireworks *pl n* **1** a show in which fireworks are let

THESAURUS

curtains (*informal*), death, defeat, end, end of the road, liquidation, ruin **6.** appearance, grain, lustre, patina, polish, shine, smoothness, surface, texture

finite bounded, circumscribed, conditioned, delimited, demarcated, limited, restricted, subject to limitations, terminable

fire *n.* **1.** blaze, combustion, conflagration, flames, inferno **2.** barrage, bombardment, cannonade, flak, fusillade, hail, salvo, shelling, sniping, volley **3.** *figurative* animation, ardour, brio, burning passion, dash, eagerness, élan, enthusiasm, excitement, fervency, fervour, force, heat, impetuosity, intensity, life, light, lustre, passion, pizzazz *or* pizazz (*informal*), radiance, scintillation, sparkle, spirit, splendour, verve, vigour, virtuosity, vivacity **4. on fire a.** ablaze, aflame, alight, blazing, burning, fiery, flaming, in flames **b.** ardent, eager, enthusiastic, excited, inspired, passionate ~*vb.* **5.** detonate, discharge, eject, explode, hurl, launch, let off, loose, pull the trigger, set off, shell, shoot, touch off **6.** *informal* cashier, discharge, dismiss, give marching orders, kiss off (*slang, chiefly U.S. & Canad.*), make redundant, sack (*informal*), show the door **7.** ignite, kindle, light, put a match to, set ablaze, set aflame, set alight, set fire to, set on fire **8.** *figurative* animate, arouse, electrify, enliven, excite, galvanize, impassion, incite, inflame, inspire, inspirit, irritate, quicken, rouse, stir

off. 2 *Informal* an outburst of temper. 3 an exciting an impressive performance, speech, or piece of writing: *Dickens' verbal fireworks.*

firing *n* 1 a discharge of a firearm. 2 the process of baking ceramics in a kiln. 3 something used as fuel.

firing line *n* 1 *Mil* the positions from which fire is delivered. 2 the leading or most vulnerable position in an activity: *the manager is in the firing line after a string of bad results.*

firing squad *n* a group of soldiers appointed to shoot a condemned criminal dead.

firm[1] *adj* 1 not soft or yielding to a touch or pressure. 2 securely in position. 3 definitely established: *a firm agreement.* 4 having determination or strength: *if you are firm and consistent she will come to see things your way.* ~*adv* 5 **stand firm** to refuse to give in. ~*vb* 6 to make or become firm. **firmly** *adv* **firmness** *n*

firm[2] *n* a business company.

firmament *n Literary* the sky or the heavens.

first *adj* 1 earliest in time or order. 2 rated, graded, or ranked above all other levels: *22 teams in the first division.* 3 denoting the lowest forward gear in a motor vehicle. 4 *Music* denoting the highest voice part in a chorus or one of the sections of an orchestra: *the first violin.* ~*n* 5 the person or thing coming before all others. 6 the beginning or outset. 7 *Education chiefly Brit* an honours degree of the highest class. 8 the lowest forward gear in a motor vehicle. ~*adv* 9 before anything else: *I would advise you to try surgery first.* 10 for the first time: *this story first came to public attention in January 1984.*

first aid *n* immediate medical assistance given in an emergency.

first-born *adj* 1 eldest of the children in a family. ~*n* 2 the eldest child in a family.

first class *n* 1 the class or grade of the best or highest value, rank, or quality. ~*adj* **first-class** 2 of the best or highest class or grade. 3 excellent. 4 denoting the most comfortable class of accommodation in a hotel, aircraft, or train. 5 denoting mail that is handled faster than second-class mail. ~*adv* **first-class** 6 by first-class mail, transport, etc.

first-day cover *n Philately* an envelope postmarked on the first day of the issue of its stamps.

first-degree burn *n* a burn in which the skin surface is red and painful.

first floor *n* 1 the storey of a building immediately above the one at ground level. 2 *US* the storey at ground level.

first-foot *Chiefly Scot* ~*n* 1 the first person to enter a household in the New Year. ~*vb* 2 to visit (someone) as first-foot. **first-footing** *n*

first fruits *pl n* 1 the first results or profits of an undertaking. 2 fruit that ripens first.

first-hand *adj, adv* 1 (obtained) directly from the original source. 2 **at first hand** directly.

First Lady *n* (in the US) the wife of the president.

firstly *adv* same as **first** (sense 9).

first mate *n* an officer second in command to the captain of a merchant ship.

first night *n* the first public performance of a play or other production.

first offender *n* a person convicted of a criminal offence for the first time.

first officer *n* same as **first mate.**

first person *n* the form of a pronoun or verb used by the speaker to refer to himself or herself, or a group including himself or herself.

first-rate *adj* of the best quality; excellent.

firth *n* a narrow inlet of the sea, esp. in Scotland.

fiscal *adj* 1 of or relating to government finances, esp. tax revenues. ~*n* 2 (in Scotland) same as **procurator fiscal.**

fish *n, pl* **fish** *or* **fishes** 1 a cold-blooded animal with a backbone, gills, and usually fins and a skin covered in scales, that lives in water. 2 the flesh of fish used as food. 3 **cold fish** a person who shows little emotion. 4 **drink like a fish** to drink alcohol to excess. 5 **have other fish to fry** to have other more important concerns. 6 **like a fish out of water** ill at ease in an unfamiliar situation. ~*vb* 7 to attempt to catch fish. 8 to fish in (a particular area of water): *the first trawler to fish these waters.* 9 to grope for and find with some difficulty: *he fished a cigarette from his pocket.* 10 **fish for** to seek (something) indirectly: *he was fishing for compliments.*

fish cake *n* a fried flattened ball of flaked fish mixed with mashed potatoes.

fisherman *n, pl* **-men** a person who fishes as a profession or for sport.

fishery *n, pl* **-eries** 1 **a** the industry of catching, pro-

THESAURUS

firebrand *figurative* agitator, demagogue, fomenter, incendiary, instigator, rabble-rouser, soapbox orator, tub-thumper

fireworks 1. illuminations, pyrotechnics 2. *figurative* fit of rage, hysterics, paroxysms, rage, rows, storm, temper, trouble, uproar

firm[1] *adj.* 1. close-grained, compact, compressed, concentrated, congealed, dense, hard, inelastic, inflexible, jelled, rigid, set, solid, solidified, stiff, unyielding 2. anchored, braced, cemented, embedded, fast, fastened, fixed, immovable, motionless, riveted, robust, rooted, secure, secured, stable, stationary, steady, strong, sturdy, taut, tight, unfluctuating, unmoving, unshakable 3. adamant, constant, definite, fixed, immovable, inflexible, obdurate, resolute, resolved, set on, settled, stalwart, staunch, steadfast, strict, true, unalterable, unbending, unfaltering, unflinching, unshakable, unshaken, unswerving, unwavering, unyielding

firm[2] *n.* association, business, company, concern, conglomerate, corporation, enterprise, house, organization, outfit (*informal*), partnership

firmly 1. enduringly, immovably, like a rock, motionlessly, securely, steadily, tightly, unflinchingly, unshakably 2. determinedly, resolutely, staunchly, steadfastly, strictly, through thick and thin, unchangeably, unwaveringly, with a rod of iron, with decision

firmness 1. compactness, density, fixedness, hardness, inelasticity, inflexibility, resistance, rigidity, solidity, stiffness 2. immovability, soundness, stability, steadiness, strength, tautness, tensile strength, tension, tightness 3. constancy, fixedness, fixity of purpose, inflexibility, obduracy, resolution, resolve, staunchness, steadfastness, strength of will, strictness

first *adj.* 1. earliest, initial, introductory, maiden, opening, original, premier, primeval, primitive, primordial, pristine 2. chief, foremost, head, highest, leading, pre-eminent, prime, principal, ruling ~*n.* 3. *as in* **from the first** beginning, commencement, inception, introduction, outset, start, starting point, word 'go' (*informal*) ~*adv.* 4. at the beginning, at the outset, before all else, beforehand, firstly, initially, in the first place, to begin with, to start with

first-hand direct, straight from the horse's mouth

first-rate admirable, A1 *or* A-one (*informal*), boffo (*slang*), brill (*informal*), chillin' (*U.S. slang*), crack (*slang*), cracking (*Brit. informal*), crucial (*slang*), def (*slang*), elite, excellent, exceptional, exclusive, first class, jim-dandy (*slang*), mean (*slang*), mega (*slang*),

cessing, and selling fish. **b** a place where this is carried on. **2** a place where fish are reared.

fish-eye lens *n Photog* a lens with a highly curved front that covers almost 180°.

fishfinger *n* an oblong piece of fish coated in breadcrumbs.

fishing *n* the occupation of catching fish.

fishing rod *n* a long tapered flexible pole for use with a fishing line and, usually, a reel.

fish meal *n* ground dried fish used as feed for farm animals or as a fertilizer.

fishmonger *n Chiefly Brit* a seller of fish.

fishnet *n* an open mesh fabric resembling netting, sometimes used for tights or stockings.

fishplate *n* a flat piece of metal joining one rail or beam to the next, esp. on railway tracks.

fishtail *n* a nozzle having a long narrow slot at the top, placed over a Bunsen burner to produce a thin fanlike flame.

fishwife *n, pl* **-wives** a coarse or bad-tempered woman with a loud voice.

fishy *adj* **fishier, fishiest 1** of or suggestive of fish. **2** *Informal* suspicious or questionable: *something a bit fishy about his explanation.* **fishily** *adv*

fissile *adj* **1** *Brit* capable of undergoing nuclear fission. **2** tending to split.

fission *n* **1** the act or process of splitting into parts. **2** *Biol* a form of asexual reproduction involving a division into two or more equal parts. **3** the splitting of atomic nuclei with the release of a large amount of energy. **fissionable** *adj*

fissure (**fish**-er) *n* any long narrow cleft or crack, esp. in a rock.

fist *n* a hand with the fingers clenched into the palm.

fisticuffs *pl n* fighting with the fists.

fistula (**fist**-yew-la) *n Pathol* a long narrow ulcer.

fit[1] *vb* **fitting, fitted 1** to be appropriate or suitable for. **2** to be of the correct size or shape (for). **3** to adjust in order to make appropriate. **4** to try clothes (on) and note any adjustments needed. **5** to make competent or ready: *the experience helped to fit him for the task.* **6** to correspond with the facts or circumstances: *this part doesn't fit in with the rest of his theory.* ~*adj* **fitter, fittest 7** appropriate. **8** in good health. **9** worthy or suitable: *houses fit for human habitation.* ~*n* **10** the manner in which something fits: *the suit was an excellent fit.* ~See also **fit in, fit out. fitly** *adv* **fitness** *n*

fit[2] *n* **1** a sudden attack or convulsion, such as an epileptic seizure. **2** a sudden short burst or spell: *fits of laughter; a fit of pique.* **3 by** *or* **in fits and starts** in spasmodic spells. **4 have a fit** *Informal* to become very angry.

fitful *adj* occurring in irregular spells. **fitfully** *adv*

fit in *vb* **1** to give a place or time to (someone or something). **2** to belong or conform, esp. after adjustment.

fitment *n* **1** an accessory attached to a machine. **2** *Chiefly Brit* a detachable part of the furnishings of a room.

fit out *vb* to equip: *he started to fit out a ship in secret.*

fitted *adj* **1** designed for excellent fit: *a fitted suit.* **2** (of a carpet) covering a floor completely. **3 a** (of furniture) built to fit a particular space. **b** (of a kitchen, bathroom, etc.) having equipment and furniture built or selected to suit the measurements of the room. **4** (of sheets) having ends that are elasticated to fit tightly over a mattress.

fitter *n* **1** a person who is skilled in the installation and adjustment of machinery. **2** a person who fits garments.

fitting *adj* **1** appropriate or proper. ~*n* **2** an accessory or part. **3** the trying-on of clothes so that they can be adjusted to fit. **4 fittings** furnishings or accessories in a building. **fittingly** *adv*

five *n* **1** the cardinal number that is the sum of one and four. **2** a numeral, 5 or V, representing this number. **3** something representing or consisting of five units. ~*adj* **4** amounting to five: *five years.* ~See also **fives.**

five-eighth *n Austral & NZ* a rugby player positioned between the halfbacks and three-quarters.

fivefold *adj* **1** having five times as many or as much. **2** composed of five parts. ~*adv* **3** by five times as many or as much.

fivepins *n* a bowling game played esp. in Canada.

fiver *n Brit informal* a five-pound note.

fives *n* a ball game similar to squash but played with bats or the hands.

fix *vb* **1** to make or become firm, stable, or secure. **2** to repair. **3** to attach or place permanently: *fix the mirror to the wall.* **4** to settle definitely or decide upon: *the meeting is fixed for the 12th.* **5** to direct (the eyes etc.)

THESAURUS

outstanding, prime, second to none, sovereign, superb, superlative, tiptop, top, topnotch (*informal*), topping (*Brit. slang*), tops (*slang*), world-class

fishy 1. fishlike, piscatorial, piscatory, piscine **2.** *informal* dodgy (*Brit., Austral., & N.Z. informal*), doubtful, dubious, funny (*informal*), implausible, improbable, odd, queer, questionable, rum (*Brit. slang*), suspect, suspicious, unlikely

fissure breach, break, chink, cleavage, cleft, crack, cranny, crevice, fault, fracture, gap, hole, interstice, opening, rent, rift, rupture, slit, split

fit[1] *vb.* **1.** accord, agree, be consonant, belong, concur, conform, correspond, dovetail, go, interlock, join, match, meet, suit, tally **2.** adapt, adjust, alter, arrange, dispose, fashion, modify, place, position, shape ~*adj.* **3.** able, adapted, adequate, apposite, appropriate, apt, becoming, capable, competent, convenient, correct, deserving, equipped, expedient, fitted, fitting, good enough, prepared, proper, qualified, ready, right, seemly, suitable, trained, well-suited, worthy **4.** able-bodied, hale, healthy, in good condition, in good shape, in good trim, robust, strapping, toned up, trim, well

fit[2] *n.* **1.** attack, bout, convulsion, paroxysm, seizure, spasm **2.** bout, burst, outbreak, outburst, spell **3. by** *or* **in fits and starts** erratically, fitfully, intermittently, irregularly, on and off, spasmodically, sporadically, unsystematically

fitful broken, desultory, disturbed, erratic, flickering, fluctuating, haphazard, impulsive, inconstant, intermittent, irregular, spasmodic, sporadic, uneven, unstable, variable

fitfully desultorily, erratically, in fits and starts, in snatches, intermittently, interruptedly, irregularly, off and on, spasmodically, sporadically

fitness 1. adaptation, applicability, appropriateness, aptness, competence, eligibility, pertinence, preparedness, propriety, qualifications, readiness, seemliness, suitability **2.** good condition, good health, health, robustness, strength, vigour

fit out accommodate, arm, equip, fit out, kit out, outfit, prepare, provide, rig out

fitted 1. adapted, cut out for, equipped, fit, qualified, right, suitable, tailor-made **2.** built-in, permanent

fitting 1. *adj.* apposite, appropriate, becoming, cor-

steadily: *she fixed her eyes upon the jewels.* **6** *Informal* to unfairly influence the outcome of: *the fight was fixed by the promoter.* **7** *Informal* to put a stop to the activities of (someone): *the Party was determined to fix him.* **8** *Informal, chiefly US & Canad* to prepare: *let me fix you a drink.* **9** *Photog* to treat (a film, plate, or paper) with fixer to make the image permanent. **10** to convert (atmospheric nitrogen) into nitrogen compounds. **11** *Slang* to inject a narcotic drug. *~n* **12** *Informal* a difficult situation. **13** the reckoning of a navigational position of a ship by radar, etc. **14** *Slang* an injection of a narcotic. ~See also **fix up.**

fixation *n* **1** an obsessive interest in something. **2** *Psychol* a strong attachment of a person to another person or an object in early life. **3** *Chem* the conversion of nitrogen in the air into a compound, esp. a fertilizer. **fixated** *adj*

fixative *n* **1** a fluid sprayed over drawings to prevent smudging. **2** a liquid used to hold objects, esp. dentures, in place. **3** a substance added to a perfume to make it less volatile.

fixed *adj* **1** attached or placed so as to be immovable. **2** stable: *fixed rates.* **3** unchanging and appearing artificial: *a fixed smile.* **4** established as to relative position: *a fixed point.* **5** always at the same time. **6** (of ideas) firmly maintained. **7** *Informal* equipped or provided for, esp. with money or possessions. **8** *Informal* illegally arranged: *a fixed trial.* **fixedly** (**fix**-id-lee) *adv*

fixed star *n* an extremely distant star that appears to be almost stationary.

fixer *n* **1** *Photog* a solution used to make an image permanent. **2** *Slang* a person who makes arrangements, esp. illegally.

fixity *n, pl* **-ties** the state or quality of a person's gaze, attitude, or concentration not changing or weakening: *a remarkable fixity of purpose.*

fixture *n* **1** an object firmly fixed in place, esp. a household appliance. **2** something or someone regarded as fixed in a particular place or position: *the diplomatic wife seems a fixture of international politics.* **3** *Chiefly Brit* **a** a sports match. **b** the date of it.

fix up *vb* **1** to arrange. **2 fix up with** to provide with: *can you fix me up with tickets?*

fizz *vb* **1** to make a hissing or bubbling sound. **2** (of a drink) to produce bubbles of carbon dioxide. *~n* **3** a hissing or bubbling sound. **4** releasing of small bubbles of gas by a liquid. **5** any effervescent drink. **fizzy** *adj* **fizziness** *n*

fizzle *vb* **-zling, -zled 1** to make a hissing or bubbling sound. **2 fizzle out** *Informal* to fail or die out, esp. after a promising start.

fjord (fee-**ord**) *n* a long narrow inlet of the sea between high cliffs, esp. in Norway.

FL Florida.

fl. fluid.

flab *n* unsightly or unwanted fat on the body.

flabbergasted *adj Informal* completely astonished.

flabby *adj* **-bier, -biest 1** having flabby flesh. **2** loose or limp. **3** weak and lacking purpose: *flabby hesitant leaders.* **flabbiness** *n*

flaccid (**flak**-sid) *adj* soft and limp. **flaccidity** *n*

flag[1] *n* **1** a piece of cloth often attached to a pole, used as an emblem or for signalling. **2** *Brit, Austral, & NZ* the part of a taximeter that is raised when a taxi is for hire. **3** a code inserted into a computer file to distinguish certain information. *~vb* **flagging, flagged 4** to mark with a tag or sticker. **5 flag down** to signal (a vehicle) to stop.

flag[2] *n* same as **iris** (sense 2).

flag[3] *vb* **flagging, flagged 1** to lose enthusiasm or energy. **2** to become limp. **flagging** *adj*

flag[4] *n* short for **flagstone.**

flag day *n Brit* a day on which money is collected by a charity and small stickers are given to contributors.

flagellate *vb* (**flaj**-a-late) **-lating, -lated 1** to whip, esp. in religious penance or for sexual pleasure. *~adj* (**flaj**-a-lit) **2** possessing one or more flagella. **3** like a whip. **flagellation** *n*

flagellum (flaj-**jell**-lum) *n, pl* **-la** (-la) *or* **-lums 1** *Biol* a long whiplike outgrowth that acts as an organ of movement. **2** *Bot* a long thin shoot or runner.

flageolet (flaj-a-**let**) *n* a high-pitched musical instrument of the recorder family.

flagged *adj* paved with flagstones.

flag of convenience *n* a foreign flag flown by a ship registered in that country to gain financial or legal advantage.

THESAURUS

rect, decent, decorous, desirable, proper, right, seemly, suitable **2.** *n.* accessory, attachment, component, connection, part, piece, unit

fix *vb.* **1.** anchor, embed, establish, implant, install, locate, place, plant, position, root, set, settle **2.** adjust, correct, mend, patch up, put to rights, regulate, repair, see to, sort **3.** attach, bind, cement, connect, couple, fasten, glue, link, make fast, pin, secure, stick, tie **4.** agree on, appoint, arrange, arrive at, conclude, decide, define, determine, establish, limit, name, resolve, set, settle, specify **5.** direct, focus, level at, rivet **6.** *informal* bribe, fiddle (*informal*), influence, manipulate, manoeuvre, pull strings (*informal*), rig **7.** *slang* cook (someone's) goose (*informal*), get even with (*informal*), get revenge on, pay back, settle (someone's) hash (*informal*), sort (someone) out (*informal*), take retribution on, wreak vengeance on *~n.* **8.** *informal* difficult situation, difficulty, dilemma, embarrassment, hole (*slang*), hot water (*informal*), jam (*informal*), mess, pickle (*informal*), plight, predicament, quandary, spot (*informal*), tight spot

fixation complex, hang-up (*informal*), *idée fixe*, infatuation, mania, obsession, preoccupation, thing (*informal*)

fixed 1. anchored, attached, established, immovable, made fast, permanent, rigid, rooted, secure, set **2.** *informal* framed, manipulated, packed, put-up, rigged

fix up 1. agree on, arrange, fix, organize, plan, settle, sort out **2.** *with* **with** accommodate, arrange for, bring about, furnish, lay on, provide

fizz bubble, effervesce, fizzle, froth, hiss, sparkle, sputter

fizzle out abort, collapse, come to nothing, die away, end in disappointment, fail, fall through, fold (*informal*), miss the mark, peter out

fizzy bubbling, bubbly, carbonated, effervescent, gassy, sparkling

flabbergasted abashed, amazed, astonished, astounded, bowled over (*informal*), confounded, dazed, disconcerted, dumbfounded, gobsmacked (*Brit. slang*), nonplussed, overcome, overwhelmed, rendered speechless, speechless, staggered, struck dumb, stunned

flag[1] *n.* **1.** banderole, banner, colours, ensign, gonfalon, jack, pennant, pennon, standard, streamer *~vb.* **2.** docket, indicate, label, mark, note, tab **3.** *with* **down** hail, salute, signal, warn, wave

flag[2] *vb.* abate, decline, die, droop, ebb, fade, fail, faint, fall, fall off, feel the pace, languish, peter out,

flag of truce *n* a white flag indicating an invitation to an enemy to negotiate.

flagon *n* **1** a large bottle of wine, cider, etc. **2** a narrow-necked jug for containing liquids.

flagpole *or* **flagstaff** *n* a pole on which a flag is flown.

flagrant (**flayg**-rant) *adj* openly outrageous: *flagrant violation of international law.* **flagrancy** *n*

flagship *n* **1** a ship aboard which the commander of a fleet is quartered. **2** the most important ship belonging to a shipping company. **3** the most modern or impressive product or asset of an organization: *"Panorama" was the flagship of BBC Television's current affairs.*

flagstone *n* a flat slab of hard stone for paving.

flag-waving *n Informal* an emotional appeal to patriotic feeling.

flail *n* **1** a tool formerly used for threshing grain by hand. *~vb* **2** to wave about wildly: *arms flailing, they staggered about.* **3** to beat with or as if with a flail.

flair *n* **1** natural ability. **2** originality and stylishness.

flak *n* **1** anti-aircraft fire. **2** severe criticism: *most of the flak was directed at the umpire.*

flake *n* **1** a small thin piece chipped off an object or substance. **2** a small piece: *flakes of snow. ~vb* **flaking, flaked 3** to peel or cause to peel off in flakes. **4** to break into small thin pieces: *bake for 30 minutes, or until the fish is firm and flakes easily.* **flaky** *adj*

flake out *vb Informal* to collapse or fall asleep from exhaustion.

flak jacket *n* a reinforced sleeveless jacket for protection against gunfire or shrapnel.

flambé (**flahm**-bay) *vb* **flambéeing, flambéed** to cook or serve (food) in flaming brandy.

flamboyant *adj* **1** behaving in a very noticeable, extravagant way: *a flamboyant jazz pianist.* **2** very bright and showy. **flamboyance** *n*

flame *n* **1** a hot luminous body of burning gas coming in flickering streams from burning material. **2 flames** the state of burning: *half the building was in flames.* **3** intense passion: *the flame of love. ~vb* **flaming, flamed 4** to burn brightly. **5** to become red or fiery: *colour flamed in Sally's cheeks.* **6** to become angry or excited.

flamenco *n, pl* **-cos 1** a rhythmical Spanish dance accompanied by a guitar and vocalist. **2** music for this dance.

flame-thrower *n* a weapon that ejects a stream or spray of burning fluid.

flaming *adj* **1** burning with flames. **2** glowing brightly. **3** very angry and heated: *a flaming row. ~adj, adv* **4** *Informal* extreme or extremely damned: *what the flaming hell do you think you're doing?; I was flaming mad about what happened.*

flamingo *n, pl* **-gos** *or* **-goes** a large pink wading bird with a long neck and legs.

flammable *adj* easily set on fire; inflammable. **flammability** *n*

➤ This now replaces *inflammable* in labelling and packaging because *inflammable* was often mistaken to mean "not flammable".

flan *n* an open sweet or savoury tart.

flange *n* a projecting collar or rim on an object for strengthening it or for attaching it to another object.

flank *n* **1** the side of a man or animal between the ribs and the hip. **2** a cut of beef from the flank. **3** the side of a naval or military formation. *~vb* **4** to be positioned at the side of (a person or thing).

flannel *n* **1** *Brit* a small piece of towelling cloth used to wash the face. **2** a soft light woollen fabric used for clothing. **3 flannels** trousers made of flannel. **4** *Brit informal* evasive talk that avoids giving any commitment or direct answer. *~vb* **-nelling, -nelled** *or US* **-neling, -neled 5** *Brit informal* to flatter or talk evasively.

flannelette *n* a cotton imitation of flannel, used to make sheets and nightdresses.

flap *vb* **flapping, flapped 1** to move backwards and forwards or up and down, like a bird's wings in flight. *~n* **2** the action of or noise made by flapping. **3** a piece of material attached at one edge and usually used to cover an opening, such as on a pocket. **4** a hinged section of an aircraft wing that is raised or lowered to control the aircraft's speed. **5** *Informal* a state of panic or agitation.

flapjack *n* a chewy biscuit made with rolled oats.

flapper *n* (in the 1920s) a lively young woman who dressed and behaved unconventionally.

flare *vb* **flaring, flared 1** to burn with an unsteady or sudden bright flame. **2** (of temper, violence, or trouble) to break out suddenly. **3** to spread outwards from a narrow to a wider shape. *~n* **4** an unsteady flame. **5** a sudden burst of flame. **6 a** a blaze of light used to il-

THESAURUS

pine, sag, sink, slump, succumb, taper off, wane, weaken, weary, wilt

flagging declining, decreasing, deteriorating, ebbing, fading, failing, faltering, giving up, sinking, slowing down, tiring, waning, weakening, wilting

flagrant arrant, atrocious, awful, barefaced, blatant, bold, brazen, crying, dreadful, egregious, enormous, flaunting, glaring, heinous, immodest, infamous, notorious, open, ostentatious, out-and-out, outrageous, scandalous, shameless, undisguised

flagstone block, flag, paving stone, slab

flail *vb.* beat, thrash, thresh, windmill

flair 1. ability, accomplishment, aptitude, faculty, feel, genius, gift, knack, mastery, talent **2.** chic, dash, discernment, elegance, panache, style, stylishness, taste

flake 1. *n.* disk, lamina, layer, peeling, scale, shaving, sliver, wafer **2.** *vb.* blister, chip, peel (off), scale (off)

flamboyant 1. actorly, baroque, camp (*informal*), elaborate, extravagant, florid, ornate, ostentatious, over the top (*informal*), rich, rococo, showy, theatrical **2.** brilliant, colourful, dashing, dazzling, exciting, glamorous, glitzy (*slang*), swashbuckling

flame *n.* **1.** blaze, brightness, fire, light **2.** *figurative* affection, ardour, enthusiasm, fervency, fervour, fire, intensity, keenness, passion, warmth *~vb.* **3.** blaze, burn, flare, flash, glare, glow, shine

flaming 1. ablaze, afire, blazing, brilliant, burning, fiery, glowing, ignited, in flames, raging, red, red-hot **2.** angry, ardent, aroused, frenzied, hot, impassioned, intense, raging, scintillating, vehement, vivid

flank *n.* **1.** ham, haunch, hip, loin, quarter, side, thigh **2.** side, wing *~vb.* **3.** border, bound, edge, fringe, line, screen, skirt, wall

flannel *figurative* **1.** *n.* baloney (*informal*), blarney, equivocation, flattery, hedging, prevarication, soft soap (*informal*), sweet talk (*U.S. informal*), waffle (*informal, chiefly Brit.*), weasel words (*informal, chiefly U.S.*) **2.** *vb.* blarney, butter up, equivocate, flatter, hedge, prevaricate, pull the wool over (someone's) eyes, soft-soap (*informal*), sweet-talk (*informal*), waffle (*informal, chiefly Brit.*)

flap *vb.* **1.** agitate, beat, flail, flutter, shake, swing, swish, thrash, thresh, vibrate, wag, wave *~n.* **2.** bang, banging, beating, flutter, shaking, swinging, swish, waving **3.** apron, cover, fly, fold, lapel, lappet, overlap, skirt, tab, tail **4.** *informal* agitation, commotion, flus-

luminate, signal distress, alert, etc. **b** the device producing such a blaze. **7 flares** trousers with legs that flare out at the bottom. **flared** *adj*

flare up *vb* **1** to burst suddenly into fire. **2** *Informal* to burst into anger.

flash *n* **1** a sudden short blaze of intense light or flame. **2** a sudden occurrence of a particular emotion or experience: *a flash of anger.* **3** a very brief time: *in a flash he was inside and locked the door behind him.* **4** a short unscheduled news announcement. **5** *Chiefly Brit* an emblem on a uniform or vehicle to identify its military formation. **6** *Photog* short for **flashlight. 7 flash in the pan** a project, person, etc., that enjoys only short-lived success. *~adj* **8** *Informal* ostentatious or vulgar. **9** brief and rapid: *a flash fire.* *~vb* **10** to burst or cause to burst suddenly into flame. **11** to shine with a bright light suddenly or repeatedly. **12** to move very fast. **13** to come rapidly (into the mind or vision). **14 a** to signal very fast: *a warning was flashed onto a computer screen in the cockpit.* **b** to signal by use of a light, such as car headlights. **15** *Informal* to display in a boastful and extravagant way: *flashing banknotes around.* **16** *Informal* to show briefly. **17** *Brit slang* to expose oneself indecently. **flasher** *n*

flashback *n* a scene in a book, play, or film that shows earlier events.

flashbulb *n Photog* a small light bulb that produces a bright flash of light.

flash flood *n* a sudden short-lived flood.

flashing *n* a weatherproof material used to cover the joins in a roof.

flashlight *n* **1** *Photog* the brief bright light emitted by a flashbulb. **2** *Chiefly US & Canad* a torch.

flash point *n* **1** a critical time beyond which a situation will inevitably erupt into violence. **2** the lowest temperature at which the vapour above a liquid can be ignited.

flashy *adj* **flashier, flashiest** showy in a vulgar way: *a loud and flashy tie.* **flashily** *adv* **flashiness** *n*

flask *n* **1** same as **vacuum flask. 2** a small flat container for alcoholic drink designed to be carried in a pocket. **3** a bottle with a narrow neck, esp. used in a laboratory.

flat[1] *adj* **flatter, flattest 1** horizontal or level: *roofs are now flat instead of slanted.* **2** even or smooth: *a flat surface.* **3** lying stretched out at full length. **4** (of a tyre) deflated. **5** (of shoes) having an unraised heel. **6** without qualification; total: *a flat rejection.* **7** fixed: *a flat rate.* **8** unexciting: *a picture curiously flat in tone.* **9** without variation or emotion: *a flat voice.* **10** (of drinks) no longer fizzy. **11** (of a battery) fully discharged. **12** (of paint) without gloss. **13** *Music* **a** denoting a note that has been lowered in pitch by one chromatic semitone: *B flat.* **b** (of an instrument, voice, etc.) out of tune by being too low in pitch. *~adv* **14** in or into a level or flat position: *the boat was knocked almost flat.* **15** completely: *flat broke.* **16** exactly: *in three months flat.* **17** *Music* **a** lower than a standard pitch. **b** too low in pitch: *singing flat.* **18 fall flat (on one's face)** to fail to achieve a desired effect. **19 flat out** *Informal* with maximum speed and effort. *~n* **20** a flat object or part. **21** low-lying land, esp. a marsh. **22** a mud bank exposed at low tide. **23** *Music* **a** an accidental that lowers the pitch of a note by one semitone. Symbol: ♭ **b** a note affected by this accidental. **24** *Theatre* a wooden frame covered with painted canvas, used to form part of a stage setting. **25** a punctured car tyre. **26 the flat** *Chiefly Brit* the season of flat racing. **flatly** *adv*

flat[2] *n* a set of rooms forming a home entirely on one floor of a building.

flatboat *n* a flat-bottomed boat for transporting goods on a canal.

flatfish *n, pl* **-fish** *or* **-fishes** a sea fish, such as the sole, which has a flat body with both eyes on the uppermost side.

flat-footed *adj* **1** having less than the usual degree of arching in the insteps of the feet. **2** *Informal* clumsy or insensitive.

flatiron *n* (formerly) an iron for pressing clothes that was heated by being placed on a stove.

flatlet *n* a small flat.

flatmate *n* a person with whom one shares a flat.

flat racing *n* the racing of horses on racecourses without jumps.

flat spin *n* **1** an aircraft spin in which the longitudinal axis is more nearly horizontal than vertical. **2** *Informal* a state of confusion.

flatten *vb* **1** to make or become flat or flatter. **2** *Informal* **a** to knock down or injure. **b** to crush or subdue.

THESAURUS

ter, panic, state (*informal*), stew (*informal*), sweat (*informal*), tizzy (*informal*), twitter (*informal*)

flare *vb.* **1.** blaze, burn up, dazzle, flicker, flutter, glare, waver **2.** broaden, spread out, widen *~n.* **3.** blaze, burst, dazzle, flame, flash, flicker, glare

flare up blaze, blow one's top (*informal*), boil over, break out, explode, fire up, fly off the handle (*informal*), lose control, lose one's cool (*informal*), lose one's temper, throw a tantrum

flash *n.* **1.** blaze, burst, coruscation, dazzle, flare, flicker, gleam, ray, scintillation, shaft, shimmer, spark, sparkle, streak, twinkle **2.** burst, demonstration, display, manifestation, outburst, show, sign, touch **3.** instant, jiffy (*informal*), moment, second, shake, split second, trice, twinkling, twinkling of an eye, two shakes of a lamb's tail (*informal*) *~adj.* **4.** *informal* cheap, glamorous, naff (*Brit. slang*), ostentatious, tacky (*informal*), tasteless, vulgar *~vb.* **5.** blaze, coruscate, flare, flicker, glare, gleam, glint, glisten, glitter, light, scintillate, shimmer, sparkle, twinkle **6.** bolt, burn rubber (*informal*), dart, dash, fly, race, shoot, speed, sprint, streak, sweep, whistle, zoom **7.** display, exhibit, expose, flaunt, flourish, show

flashy brash, cheap, cheap and nasty, flamboyant, flaunting, garish, gaudy, glittery, glitzy (*slang*), in poor taste, jazzy (*informal*), loud, meretricious, naff (*Brit. slang*), ostentatious, over the top (*informal*), showy, snazzy (*informal*), tacky (*informal*), tasteless, tawdry, tinselly

flat[1] *adj.* **1.** even, horizontal, level, levelled, low, planar, plane, smooth, unbroken **2.** laid low, lying full length, outstretched, prone, prostrate, reclining, recumbent, supine **3.** blown out, burst, collapsed, deflated, empty, punctured **4.** absolute, categorical, direct, downright, explicit, final, fixed, out-and-out, peremptory, plain, positive, straight, unconditional, unequivocal, unmistakable, unqualified **5.** boring, dead, dull, flavourless, ho-hum (*informal*), insipid, jejune, lacklustre, lifeless, monotonous, pointless, prosaic, spiritless, stale, tedious, uninteresting, vapid, watery, weak *~adv.* **6.** absolutely, categorically, completely, exactly, point blank, precisely, utterly **7. flat out** all out, at full gallop, at full speed, at full tilt, for all one is worth, hell for leather (*informal*), posthaste, under full steam *~n.* **8.** *often plural* lowland, marsh, mud flat, plain, shallow, shoal, strand, swamp

flat[2] apartment, rooms

flatly absolutely, categorically, completely, positively, unhesitatingly

flatten **1.** compress, even out, iron out, level, plaster,

flatter *vb* **1** to praise insincerely, esp. in order to win favour. **2** to show to advantage: *she wore a simple green cotton dress which she knew flattered her.* **3** to make (a person) appear more attractive than in reality: *a portrait that flattered him.* **4** to cater to the vanity of (a person): *I was flattered by her praise.* **5 flatter oneself** to believe, perhaps mistakenly, something good about oneself. **flatterer** *n*

flattery *n, pl* **-teries** excessive or insincere praise.

flatulent *adj* suffering from or caused by too much gas in the stomach or intestines. **flatulence** *n*

flatworm *n* a worm, such as a tapeworm, with a flattened body.

flaunt *vb* to display (oneself or one's possessions) arrogantly: *flaunting his new car.*

➤ Be careful not to confuse this with *flout* meaning "disobey".

flautist (**flaw**-tist) *n* a flute player.

flavour *or US* **flavor** *n* **1** taste perceived in food or liquid in the mouth. **2** a distinctive quality or atmosphere: *Rome has its own particular flavour.* ~*vb* **3** to give flavour to: *salmon flavoured with dill.* **flavourless** *or US* **flavorless** *adj*

flavouring *or US* **flavoring** *n* a substance used to flavour food.

flaw *n* **1** an imperfection or blemish. **2** a mistake in something that makes it invalid: *a flaw in the system.* **flawed** *adj* **flawless** *adj*

flax *n* **1** a plant that has blue flowers and is cultivated for its seeds and the fibres of its stems. **2** its fibres, made into linen fabrics. **3** *NZ* a swamp plant producing a fibre that is used by Maoris for decorative work and weaving baskets.

flaxen *adj* **1** of flax. **2** (of hair) pale yellow.

flay *vb* **1** to strip off the skin of, esp. by whipping. **2** to criticize severely.

flea *n* **1** a small wingless jumping insect feeding on the blood of mammals and birds. **2 flea in one's ear** *Informal* a sharp rebuke.

fleabite *n* **1** the bite of a flea. **2** a slight annoyance or discomfort.

flea-bitten *adj* **1** bitten by or infested with fleas. **2** *Informal* shabby or decrepit: *a flea-bitten hotel.*

flea market *n* an open-air market selling cheap second-hand goods.

fleapit *n Informal* a shabby cinema or theatre.

fleck *n* **1** a small marking or streak. **2** a small or tiny piece of something: *a fleck of grit.* ~*vb* **3** to speckle: *a grey suit flecked with white.*

fled *vb* the past of **flee.**

fledged *adj* **1** (of young birds) able to fly. **2** qualified and competent: *a fully fledged doctor.*

fledgling *or* **fledgeling** *n* **1** a young bird that has grown feathers. ~*adj* **2** new or inexperienced: *Poland's fledgling market economy.*

flee *vb* **fleeing, fled 1** to run away from (a place, danger, etc.). **2** to run or move quickly.

fleece *n* **1** the coat of wool that covers a sheep. **2** the wool removed from a sheep at one shearing. **3** sheepskin or a fabric with soft pile, used as a lining for coats, etc. ~*vb* **fleecing, fleeced 4** to defraud or overcharge. **5** same as **shear** (sense 1). **fleecy** *adj*

fleecie *n NZ* a person who collects fleeces after shearing and prepares them for baling.

fleet[1] *n* **1** a number of warships organized as a tactical unit. **2** all the ships of a nation or company: *the British merchant fleet.* **3** a number of vehicles under the same ownership.

fleet[2] *adj* rapid in movement.

fleet chief petty officer *n* a noncommissioned officer in a navy.

fleeting *adj* rapid and soon passing: *a fleeting moment.* **fleetingly** *adv*

Fleet Street *n* **1** the street in London where many newspaper offices were formerly situated. **2** British national newspapers collectively: *Fleet Street's obsession with the Royal Family.*

Fleming *n* a person from Flanders or Flemish-speaking Belgium.

Flemish *adj* **1** of Flanders, in Belgium. ~*n* **2** one of the two official languages of Belgium. ~*pl n* **3 the Flemish** people from Flanders or Flemish-speaking Belgium.

flesh *n* **1** the soft part of the body of an animal or human, esp. muscular tissue. **2** *Informal* excess weight; fat. **3** the meat of animals as opposed to that of fish or, sometimes, fowl. **4** the thick soft part of a fruit or vegetable. **5 the flesh** sexuality or sensuality: *pleasures of the flesh.* **6 flesh and blood** human beings or human nature: *it is almost more than flesh and*

THESAURUS

raze, roll, smooth off, squash, trample **2.** bowl over, crush, fell, floor, knock down, knock off one's feet, prostrate, subdue

flatter 1. blandish, butter up, cajole, compliment, court, fawn, flannel (*Brit. informal*), humour, inveigle, lay it on (thick) (*slang*), pander to, praise, puff, soft-soap (*informal*), sweet-talk (*informal*), wheedle **2.** become, do something for, enhance, set off, show to advantage, suit

flattery adulation, blandishment, blarney, cajolery, false praise, fawning, flannel (*Brit. informal*), fulsomeness, honeyed words, obsequiousness, servility, soft-soap (*informal*), sweet-talk (*informal*), sycophancy, toadyism

flavour *n.* **1.** aroma, essence, extract, flavouring, odour, piquancy, relish, savour, seasoning, smack, tang, taste, zest, zing (*informal*) **2.** aspect, character, essence, feel, feeling, property, quality, soupçon, stamp, style, suggestion, tinge, tone, touch ~*vb.* **3.** ginger up, imbue, infuse, lace, leaven, season, spice

flavouring essence, extract, spirit, tincture, zest

flaw 1. blemish, defect, disfigurement, failing, fault, imperfection, scar, speck, spot, weakness, weak spot **2.** fault, mistake, snag, weak point

flawed blemished, broken, chipped, cracked, damaged, defective, erroneous, faulty, imperfect, unsound

flawless 1. faultless, impeccable, perfect, spotless, unblemished, unsullied **2.** intact, sound, unbroken, undamaged, whole

flee abscond, avoid, beat a hasty retreat, bolt, cut and run (*informal*), decamp, depart, do a runner (*slang*), escape, fly, fly the coop (*U.S. & Canad. informal*), get away, hook it (*slang*), leave, make a quick exit, make off, make oneself scarce (*informal*), make one's escape, make one's getaway, run away, scarper (*Brit. slang*), skedaddle (*informal*), slope off, split (*slang*), take a powder (*U.S. & Canad. slang*), take flight, take it on the lam (*U.S. & Canad. slang*), take off (*informal*), take to one's heels, vanish

fleece 1. *figurative* bleed (*informal*), cheat, con (*informal*), cozen (*literary*), defraud, despoil, diddle (*informal*), overcharge, plunder, rifle, rip off (*slang*), rob, rook (*slang*), skin (*slang*), soak (*U.S. & Canad. slang*), steal, stiff (*slang*), swindle, take for a ride (*informal*), take to the cleaners (*slang*) **2.** clip, shear

fleet *n.* argosy (*archaic*), armada, flotilla, naval force, navy, sea power, squadron, task force, vessels, warships

blood can bear. **7 in the flesh** in person; actually present. **8 one's own flesh and blood** one's own family.

flesh-coloured *adj* yellowish-pink.

fleshly *adj* **-lier, -liest 1** relating to sexuality or sensuality: *the fleshly implications of their love.* **2** worldly as opposed to spiritual.

flesh out *vb* to expand on or give more details to: *further meetings will be needed to flesh out the agreement.*

fleshpots *pl n* places, such as brothels and strip clubs, where sexual desires are catered to.

flesh wound *n* a wound affecting superficial tissues.

fleshy *adj* **fleshier, fleshiest 1** plump. **2** resembling flesh. **3** *Bot* (of some fruits) thick and pulpy. **fleshiness** *n*

fleur-de-lys *or* **fleur-de-lis** (**flur**-de-lee) *n, pl* **fleurs-de-lys** *or* **fleurs-de-lis** (**flur**-de-leez) a representation of a lily with three distinct petals.

flew *vb* the past tense of **fly**[1].

flews *pl n* the fleshy hanging upper lip of a bloodhound or similar dog.

flex *n* **1** *Brit* a flexible insulated electric cable. *~vb* **2** to bend. **3** to bend and stretch (a muscle).

flexible *adj* **1** able to be bent easily without breaking. **2** adaptable to changing circumstances: *flexible working arrangements.* **flexibility** *n* **flexibly** *adv*

flexitime *n* a system permitting flexibility of working hours at the beginning or end of the day, provided an agreed total is worked.

flibbertigibbet *n Old-fashioned* an irresponsible, silly, gossipy person.

flick *vb* **1** to touch or move with the finger or hand in a quick jerky movement. **2** to move with a short sudden movement, often repeatedly: *the windscreen wipers flicked back and forth.* **3 flick through** to look at (a book or magazine) quickly or idly. *~n* **4** a tap or quick stroke.

flicker *vb* **1** to give out an unsteady or irregular light. **2** to move quickly to and fro. *~n* **3** an unsteady or brief light. **4** a brief or faint indication of emotion: *a flicker of fear in his voice.*

flick knife *n* a knife with a retractable blade that springs out when a button is pressed.

flicks *pl n Slang, old-fashioned* the cinema.

flier *n* same as **flyer.**

flight[1] *n* **1** a journey by aircraft. **2** the act or manner of flying. **3** a group of flying birds or aircraft. **4** an aircraft flying on a scheduled journey. **5** a set of stairs between one landing and the next. **6 flight of fancy** an idea that is imaginative but not practical. **7** small plastic or feather fins at the rear of an arrow or dart which make it stable in flight.

flight[2] *n* **1** the act of running away, esp. from danger. **2 put to flight** to cause to run away. **3 take (to) flight** to run away.

flight deck *n* **1** the crew compartment in an airliner. **2** the upper deck of an aircraft carrier from which aircraft take off.

flightless *adj* (of certain birds and insects) unable to fly.

flight lieutenant *n* a junior commissioned officer in an air force.

flight recorder *n* an electronic device in an aircraft for storing information concerning its performance in flight. It is often used to determine the cause of a crash. Also called: **black box**

flight sergeant *n* a noncommissioned officer in an air force.

flighty *adj* **flightier, flightiest** frivolous and not very reliable or serious. **flightiness** *n*

flimsy *adj* **-sier, -siest 1** not strong or substantial. **2** light and thin: *a flimsy gauze mask.* **3** not very convincing: *flimsy evidence.* **flimsily** *adv* **flimsiness** *n*

flinch *vb* **1** to draw back suddenly from pain or something unpleasant. **2 flinch from** to avoid: *I wouldn't flinch from saying that to his face.*

fling *vb* **flinging, flung 1** to throw with force. **2** to move or go hurriedly or violently: *she flung her arms open wide.* **3** to put or send without warning: *they used to fling me in jail.* **4** to put (something) somewhere hurriedly or carelessly. **5 fling oneself into** to apply oneself with enthusiasm to. *~n* **6** a short spell of self-indulgent enjoyment. **7** a brief romantic or sexual relationship. **8** a vigorous Scottish country dance: *a Highland fling.*

flint *n* **1** a very hard stone that produces sparks when struck with steel. **2** any piece of flint, esp. one used as

THESAURUS

fleeting brief, ephemeral, evanescent, flitting, flying, fugacious, fugitive, here today, gone tomorrow, momentary, passing, short, short-lived, temporary, transient, transitory

flesh 1. beef (*informal*), body, brawn, fat, fatness, food, meat, tissue, weight **2.** animality, body, carnality, flesh and blood, human nature, physicality, physical nature, sensuality **3. flesh and blood** homo sapiens, humankind, human race, living creatures, man, mankind, mortality, people, race, stock, world **4. one's own flesh and blood** blood, family, kin, kindred, kinsfolk, kith and kin, relations, relatives

flex *vb.* angle, bend, contract, crook, curve, tighten

flexibility adaptability, adjustability, complaisance, elasticity, give (*informal*), pliability, pliancy, resilience, springiness, tensility

flexible 1. bendable, ductile, elastic, limber, lissom(e), lithe, mouldable, plastic, pliable, pliant, springy, stretchy, supple, tensile, whippy, willowy, yielding **2.** adaptable, adjustable, discretionary, open, variable

flick *vb.* **1.** dab, fillip, flip, hit, jab, peck, rap, strike, tap, touch **2.** *with* **through** browse, flip, glance, skim, skip, thumb *~n.* **3.** fillip, flip, jab, peck, rap, tap, touch

flicker *vb.* **1.** flare, flash, glimmer, gutter, shimmer, sparkle, twinkle **2.** flutter, quiver, vibrate, waver *~n.* **3.** flare, flash, gleam, glimmer, spark **4.** atom, breath, drop, glimmer, iota, spark, trace, vestige

flight[1] **1.** *of air travel* journey, trip, voyage **2.** aeronautics, aviation, flying, mounting, soaring, winging **3.** flock, formation, squadron, swarm, unit, wing

flight[2] **1.** departure, escape, exit, exodus, fleeing, getaway, retreat, running away **2. put to flight** chase off, disperse, drive off, rout, scare off, scatter, send packing, stampede **3. take (to) flight** abscond, beat a retreat, bolt, decamp, do a bunk (*Brit. slang*), do a runner (*slang*), flee, fly the coop (*U.S. & Canad. informal*), make a hasty retreat, run away *or* off, skedaddle (*informal*), take it on the lam (*U.S. & Canad. slang*), withdraw hastily

flimsy 1. delicate, fragile, frail, gimcrack, insubstantial, makeshift, rickety, shaky, shallow, slight, superficial, unsubstantial **2.** chiffon, gauzy, gossamer, light, sheer, thin, transparent **3.** feeble, frivolous, implausible, inadequate, pathetic, poor, thin, transparent, trivial, unconvincing, unsatisfactory, weak

flinch baulk, blench, cower, cringe, draw back, duck, flee, quail, recoil, retreat, shirk, shrink, shy away, start, swerve, wince, withdraw

fling *vb.* **1.** cast, catapult, chuck (*informal*), heave, hurl, jerk, let fly, lob (*informal*), pitch, propel, send, shy, sling, throw, toss *~n.* **2.** bash, beano (*Brit. slang*),

a primitive tool. **3** a small piece of an iron alloy, used in cigarette lighters. **flinty** *adj*

flintlock *n* an obsolete gun in which the powder was lit by a spark produced by a flint.

flip *vb* **flipping, flipped 1** to throw (something light or small) carelessly. **2** to turn (something) over: *flip the fish on its back.* **3** to turn (a device or machine) on or off by quickly pressing a switch. **4** to throw (an object such as a coin) so that it turns in the air. **5 flip through** to look at (a book or magazine) idly. **6** Also: **flip one's lid** *Slang* to fly into an emotional outburst. ~*n* **7** a snap or tap, usually with the fingers. ~*adj* **8** *Informal* flippant or pert.

flipchart *n* a large pad of paper mounted on a stand, used in giving lectures, etc.

flip-flop *n* a rubber-soled sandal attached to the foot by a thong between the big toe and the next toe.

flippant *adj* treating serious matters with inappropriate light-heartedness or lack of respect. **flippancy** *n*

flipper *n* **1** the flat broad limb of seals, whales, and other aquatic animals specialized for swimming. **2** either of a pair of rubber paddle-like devices worn on the feet as an aid in swimming.

flirt *vb* **1** to behave as if sexually attracted to someone. **2 flirt with** to consider lightly; toy with: *he had often flirted with the idea of emigrating.* ~*n* **3** a person who flirts. **flirtation** *n* **flirtatious** *adj*

flit *vb* **flitting, flitted 1** to fly or move along rapidly and lightly. **2** to pass quickly: *a shadow flitted across his face.* **3** *Scot & N English dialect* to move house. **4** *Brit informal* to leave hurriedly and stealthily in order to avoid debts. ~*n* **5** the act of flitting.

flitch *n* a side of pork salted and cured.

flitter *vb Rare* same as **flutter.**

float *vb* **1** to rest on the surface of a fluid without sinking. **2** to move lightly or freely across a surface or through air or water. **3** to move about aimlessly, esp. in the mind: *a pleasant image floated into his mind.* **4 a** to launch (a commercial enterprise, etc.). **b** to offer for sale on the stock market. **5** *Finance* to allow (a currency) to fluctuate against other currencies. ~*n* **6** an inflatable object that helps people learning to swim stay afloat. **7** *Angling* an indicator attached to a baited line that moves when a fish bites. **8** a long rigid boatlike structure, of which there are usually two, attached to an aircraft instead of wheels so that it can land on and take off from water. **9** a decorated lorry that is part of a procession. **10** a small delivery vehicle: *milk floats.* **11** *Austral & NZ* a vehicle for transporting horses. **12** a sum of money used to cover small expenses or provide change. **13** the hollow floating ball of a ball cock.

floatation *n* same as **flotation.**

floating *adj* **1** (of a population) moving about; not settled. **2** (of an organ or part) displaced or abnormally movable: *a floating kidney.* **3** (of a voter) not committed to one party. **4** *Finance* **a** (of capital) available for current use. **b** (of a currency) free to fluctuate against other currencies.

floating rib *n* a lower rib not attached to the breastbone.

floats *pl n Theatre* footlights.

flocculent *adj* like tufts of wool. **flocculence** *n*

flock[1] *n* **1** a group of animals of one kind, esp. sheep or birds. **2** a large number of people. **3** a congregation of Christians regarded as the responsibility of a clergyman. ~*vb* **4** to gather together or move in large numbers.

flock[2] *n* **1** waste from fabrics such as cotton or wool, used for stuffing mattresses. ~*adj* **2** (of wallpaper) having a velvety raised pattern.

floe *n* a sheet of floating ice.

flog *vb* **flogging, flogged 1** to beat harshly, esp. with a whip or stick. **2** *Brit slang* to sell. **3 flog a dead horse** *Chiefly Brit* to waste one's energy. **flogging** *n*

flood *n* **1** an overflowing of water on an area that is normally dry. **2** a large amount of water. **3** the rising of the tide from low to high water. **4** a large amount: *a flood of letters.* **5** *Theatre* short for **floodlight.** ~*vb* **6** to cover or become covered with water. **7** to fill to overflowing. **8** to put a large number of goods on sale on (a market) at the same time, often at a cheap price: *the US was flooded with cheap televisions.* **9** to flow or surge: *the memories flooded back.* **10** to supply excess petrol to (a petrol engine) so that it cannot work properly. **11** to bleed profusely from the womb. **flooding** *n*

Flood *n* **the Flood** *Old Testament* the flood from which Noah and his family and livestock were saved in the ark (Genesis 7–8).

floodgate *n* **1** a gate used to control the flow of water. **2 floodgates** controls against an outpouring of emotion: *it had opened the floodgates of her anxiety.*

floodlight *n* **1** a lamp that casts a broad intense light, used in the theatre or to illuminate sports grounds or the exterior of buildings. ~*vb* **-lighting, -lit 2** to illuminate by floodlight.

THESAURUS

binge (*informal*), bit of fun, good time, indulgence, party, rave (*Brit. slang*), rave-up (*Brit. slang*), spree **3.** affair, amour, intrigue, liaison, relationship, romance

flip *vb./n.* cast, flick, jerk, pitch, snap, spin, throw, toss, twist

flippancy cheek (*informal*), cheekiness, disrespectfulness, frivolity, impertinence, irreverence, levity, pertness, sauciness

flippant cheeky, disrespectful, frivolous, glib, impertinent, impudent, irreverent, offhand, pert, rude, saucy, superficial

flirt *vb.* **1.** chat up (*informal*), coquet, dally, lead on, make advances, make eyes at, philander **2.** *with* **with** consider, dabble in, entertain, expose oneself to, give a thought to, play with, toy with, trifle with ~*n.* **3.** coquette, heart-breaker, philanderer, tease, trifler, wanton

flirtation coquetry, dalliance, intrigue, philandering, teasing, toying, trifling

flirtatious amorous, come-hither, come-on (*informal*), coquettish, coy, enticing, flirty, provocative, sportive, teasing

float *vb.* **1.** be buoyant, be *or* lie on the surface, displace water, hang, hover, poise, rest on water, stay afloat **2.** bob, drift, glide, move gently, sail, slide, slip along **3.** get going, launch, promote, push off, set up

floating fluctuating, free, migratory, movable, unattached, uncommitted, unfixed, variable, wandering

flock *n.* **1.** colony, drove, flight, gaggle, herd, skein **2.** assembly, bevy, collection, company, congregation, convoy, crowd, gathering, group, herd, host, mass, multitude, throng ~*vb.* **3.** collect, congregate, converge, crowd, gather, group, herd, huddle, mass, throng, troop

flog beat, castigate, chastise, flagellate, flay, lambast(e), lash, scourge, thrash, trounce, whack, whip

flogging beating, caning, flagellation, hiding (*informal*), horsewhipping, lashing, scourging, thrashing, trouncing, whipping

flood *n.* **1.** deluge, downpour, flash flood, freshet, inundation, overflow, spate, tide, torrent **2.** abundance,

flood plain *n Geog* a flat area bordering a river, made of sediment deposited during flooding.

floor *n* **1** the lower surface of a room. **2** a storey of a building. **3** a flat bottom surface: *the ocean floor.* **4** that part of a legislative hall in which debate is conducted. **5** a minimum limit: *a 12% floor for British interest rates.* **6 have the floor** to have the right to speak in a debate or discussion. *~vb* **7** to knock to the ground. **8** *Informal* to disconcert or defeat.

floorboard *n* one of the boards forming a floor.

floored *adj* covered with a floor: *an attic floored with pine planks.*

flooring *n* **1** the material used in making a floor. **2** a floor.

floor plan *n* a scale drawing of the arrangement of rooms on one floor of a building.

floor show *n* a series of entertainments, such as singing and dancing, in a nightclub.

floozy, floozie, *or* **floosie** *n, pl* **-zies** *or* **-sies** *Slang, old-fashioned* a woman considered to be disreputable or immoral.

flop *vb* **flopping, flopped 1** to bend, fall, or collapse loosely or carelessly. **2** *Informal* to fail: *his first big film flopped.* **3** to fall or move with a sudden noise. *~n* **4** *Informal* a complete failure. **5** the act of flopping. **floppy** *adj*

floppy disk *n* a flexible magnetic disk that stores data in the memory of a digital computer.

flora *n* all the plant life of a given place or time.

floral *adj* decorated with or consisting of flowers or patterns of flowers.

Florentine *adj* **1** of Florence, a city in central Italy. *~n* **2** a person from Florence.

floret (**flaw**-ret) *n* a small flower forming part of a composite flower head.

floribunda *n* a type of rose whose flowers grow in large clusters.

florid *adj* **1** having a red or flushed complexion. **2** very ornate and extravagant: *florid prose.*

florin *n* a former British coin, equivalent to ten pence.

florist *n* a person or shop selling flowers.

floss *n* **1** fine silky fibres, such as those obtained from silkworm cocoons. **2** See **dental floss. flossy** *adj*

flotation *or* **floatation** *n* the launching or financing of a commercial enterprise by bond or share issues.

flotilla *n* a small fleet or a fleet of small ships.

flotsam *n* **1** floating wreckage from a ship. **2 flotsam and jetsam a** odds and ends. **b** homeless or vagrant people.

flounce[1] *vb* **flouncing, flounced 1** to move or go with emphatic movements. *~n* **2** the act of flouncing.

flounce[2] *n* an ornamental frill on a garment or tablecloth.

flounder[1] *vb* **1** to struggle to move or stay upright, esp. in water or mud. **2** to behave or speak in an awkward, confused way.

flounder[2] *n, pl* **-der** *or* **-ders** an edible flatfish.

flour *n* **1** a powder prepared by grinding grain, esp. wheat. *~vb* **2** to sprinkle (food or utensils) with flour. **floury** *adj*

flourish *vb* **1** to be active, successful, or widespread; prosper. **2** to be at the peak of development. **3** to wave (something) dramatically. *~n* **4** a dramatic waving or sweeping movement: *he created a flourish with an imaginary wand.* **5** an ornamental curly line in writing. **6** a fancy or extravagant action or part of something: *he took his tie off with a flourish.* **flourishing** *adj*

flout (rhymes with **out**) *vb* to deliberately disobey (a rule, law, etc.).

➤ Be careful not to confuse this with *flaunt* meaning "display".

flow *vb* **1** (of liquids) to move in a stream. **2** (of blood, electricity, etc.) to circulate. **3** to move steadily and smoothly: *a golf club with rich-looking cars flowing into it.* **4** to be produced effortlessly: *words flowed from him in a steady stream.* **5** to hang freely: *her hair loose and flowing down her back.* **6** to be abundant: *at the buffet lunch, wine flowed like water.* **7** (of tide water) to rise. *~n* **8** the act, rate, or manner of flowing: *the abundant flow of water through domestic sprinklers.* **9** a continuous stream or discharge. **10** the advancing of the tide.

flow chart *or* **sheet** *n* a diagram showing a sequence of operations in an industrial process, computer program, etc.

flower *n* **1** the part of a plant that is, usually, brightly coloured, and quickly fades, producing seeds. **2** a

THESAURUS

flow, glut, multitude, outpouring, profusion, rush, stream, torrent *~vb.* **3.** brim over, deluge, drown, immerse, inundate, overflow, pour over, submerge, swamp **4.** choke, fill, glut, oversupply, saturate **5.** engulf, flow, gush, overwhelm, surge, swarm, sweep

floor 1. *n.* level, stage, storey, tier **2.** *vb. figurative* baffle, beat, bewilder, bowl over (*informal*), confound, conquer, defeat, discomfit, disconcert, dumbfound, faze, knock down, nonplus, overthrow, perplex, prostrate, puzzle, stump, throw (*informal*)

flop *vb.* **1.** collapse, dangle, droop, drop, fall, hang limply, sag, slump, topple, tumble **2.** *informal* bomb (*U.S. & Canad. slang*), close, come to nothing, fail, fall flat, fall short, fold (*informal*), founder, go belly-up (*slang*), go down like a lead balloon (*informal*), misfire *~n.* **3.** *informal* cockup (*Brit. slang*), debacle, disaster, failure, fiasco, loser, nonstarter, washout (*informal*)

floral flower-patterned, flowery

florid 1. blowzy, flushed, high-coloured, high-complexioned, rubicund, ruddy **2.** baroque, busy, embellished, euphuistic, figurative, flamboyant, flowery, fussy, grandiloquent, high-flown, ornate, overelaborate

flotsam debris, detritus, jetsam, junk, odds and ends, sweepings, wreckage

flounder *vb.* be in the dark, blunder, fumble, grope, muddle, plunge, struggle, stumble, thrash, toss, tumble, wallow

flourish *vb.* **1.** bear fruit, be in one's prime, be successful, be vigorous, bloom, blossom, boom, burgeon, develop, do well, flower, get ahead, get on, go great guns (*slang*), go up in the world, grow, grow fat, increase, prosper, succeed, thrive **2.** brandish, display, flaunt, flutter, shake, sweep, swing, swish, twirl, vaunt, wag, wave, wield *~n.* **3.** curlicue, decoration, embellishment, ornamentation, plume, sweep **4.** brandishing, dash, display, fanfare, parade, shaking, show, showy gesture, twirling, wave

flourishing blooming, burgeoning, doing well, going strong, in the pink, in top form, lush, luxuriant, mushrooming, on the up and up (*informal*), prospering, rampant, successful, thriving

flout defy, deride, gibe at, insult, jeer at, laugh in the face of, mock, outrage, ridicule, scoff at, scorn, show contempt for, sneer at, spurn, take the piss out of (*taboo slang*), taunt, treat with disdain

flow *vb.* **1.** circulate, course, glide, gush, move, pour, purl, ripple, roll, run, rush, slide, surge, sweep, swirl, whirl **2.** cascade, deluge, flood, inundate, issue, overflow, pour, run, run out, spew, spill, spurt, squirt, stream, teem, well forth **3.** arise, emanate, emerge, issue, pour, proceed, result, spring *~n.* **4.** course, cur-

plant grown for its colourful flowers. **3** the best or finest part: *in the flower of her youth.* **4 in flower** with flowers open. *~vb* **5** to produce flowers; bloom. **6** to reach full growth or maturity: *liberty only flowers in times of peace.*

flowered *adj* decorated with flowers or a floral design.

flowerpot *n* a pot in which plants are grown.

flowery *adj* **1** decorated with flowers or floral patterns. **2** (of language or style) containing elaborate literary expressions. **floweriness** *n*

flown *vb* the past participle of **fly**[1].

fl. oz. fluid ounce(s).

flu *n Informal* short for **influenza.**

fluctuate *vb* **-ating, -ated** to change frequently and erratically: *share prices fluctuated wildly throughout the day.* **fluctuation** *n*

flue *n* a passage or pipe in a chimney, used to carry off smoke, gas, or hot air.

fluent *adj* **1** able to speak or write with ease: *they spoke fluent English; fluent in French.* **2** spoken or written with ease. **fluency** *n* **fluently** *adv*

fluff *n* **1** soft light particles, such as the down of cotton or wool. **2** *Informal* a mistake, esp. in speaking or reading lines. *~vb* **3** to make or become soft and puffy. **4** *Informal* to make a mistake in performing. **fluffy** *adj* **fluffiness** *n*

fluid *n* **1** a substance, such as a liquid or gas, that can flow and has no fixed shape. *~adj* **2** capable of flowing and easily changing shape. **3** constantly changing or apt to change. **fluidity** *n*

fluid ounce *n* **1** *Brit* a unit of liquid measure equal to one twentieth of an Imperial pint (28.4 ml). **2** *US* a unit of liquid measure equal to one sixteenth of a US pint (29.6 ml).

fluke[1] *n* an accidental stroke of luck. **fluky** *adj*

fluke[2] *n* **1** the flat triangular point of an anchor. **2** either of the two lobes of the tail of a whale.

fluke[3] *n* any parasitic flatworm, such as the liver fluke.

flume *n* **1** a narrow sloping channel for water. **2** an enclosed water slide at a swimming pool.

flummery *n Informal* silly or trivial talk.

flummox *vb* to puzzle or confuse.

flung *vb* the past of **fling.**

flunk *vb Informal, chiefly US, Canad, & NZ* to fail (an examination, course, etc.).

flunky *or* **flunkey** *n, pl* **flunkies** *or* **flunkeys** **1** a manservant who wears ceremonial dress. **2** a person who performs small unimportant tasks for a powerful or important person in the hope of being rewarded.

fluor (**flew**-or) *n* same as **fluorspar.**

fluoresce *vb* **-rescing, -resced** to exhibit fluorescence.

fluorescence *n* **1** *Physics* the emission of light from atoms or molecules that are bombarded by particles, such as electrons, or by radiation from a separate source. **2** the radiation emitted as a result of fluorescence. **fluorescent** *adj*

fluorescent lamp *n* a lamp in which ultraviolet radiation from an electrical gas discharge causes a thin layer of phosphor on a tube's inside surface to fluoresce.

fluoridate *vb* **-dating, -dated** to add fluoride to (water) as protection against tooth decay. **fluoridation** *n*

fluoride *n Chem* any compound containing fluorine and another element or radical.

fluorinate *vb* **-nating, -nated** to treat or combine with fluorine. **fluorination** *n*

fluorine *n Chem* a poisonous strong-smelling pale yellow gas that is the most reactive of all the elements. Symbol: F

fluoroscopy (floor-**oss**-kop-ee) *n* same as **radioscopy.**

fluorspar, fluor *or US & Canad* **fluorite** *n* a white or colourless mineral, consisting of calcium fluoride in crystalline form: the chief ore of fluorine.

flurry *n, pl* **-ries** **1** a short rush of vigorous activity or movement. **2** a light gust of wind or rain or fall of snow. *~vb* **-ries, -rying, -ried** **3** to confuse or bewilder.

flush[1] *vb* **1** to blush or cause to blush. **2** to send water quickly through (a pipe or a toilet) so as to clean it. **3** to elate: *she was flushed with excitement.* *~n* **4** a rosy colour, esp. in the cheeks. **5** a sudden flow, such as of water. **6** a feeling of elation: *in the flush of victory.* **7** freshness: *in the first flush of youth.* **flushed** *adj*

flush[2] *adj* **1** level with another surface. **2** *Informal* having plenty of money. *~adv* **3** so as to be level.

THESAURUS

rent, drift, flood, flux, gush, issue, outflow, outpouring, spate, stream, tide, tideway, undertow **5.** abundance, deluge, effusion, emanation, outflow, outpouring, plenty, plethora, succession, train

flower *n.* **1.** bloom, blossom, efflorescence **2.** *figurative* best, choicest part, cream, elite, freshness, greatest *or* finest point, height, pick, vigour *~vb.* **3.** bloom, blossom, blow, burgeon, flourish, mature, open, unfold

flowery baroque, embellished, fancy, figurative, florid, high-flown, ornate, overwrought, rhetorical

fluctuate alter, alternate, change, ebb and flow, go up and down, hesitate, oscillate, rise and fall, seesaw, shift, swing, undulate, vacillate, vary, veer, waver

fluctuation alternation, change, fickleness, inconstancy, instability, oscillation, shift, swing, unsteadiness, vacillation, variation, wavering

fluency articulateness, assurance, command, control, ease, facility, glibness, readiness, slickness, smoothness, volubility

fluent articulate, easy, effortless, facile, flowing, glib, natural, ready, smooth, smooth-spoken, voluble, well-versed

fluff **1.** *n.* down, dust, dustball, fuzz, lint, nap, oose (*Scot.*), pile **2.** *vb. informal* bungle, cock up (*Brit. slang*), foul up (*informal*), fuck up (*offensive taboo slang*), make a mess off, mess up (*informal*), muddle, screw up (*informal*), spoil

fluid *n.* **1.** liquid, liquor, solution *~adj.* **2.** aqueous, flowing, in solution, liquefied, liquid, melted, molten, running, runny, watery **3.** adaptable, adjustable, changeable, flexible, floating, fluctuating, indefinite, mercurial, mobile, mutable, protean, shifting

flurry *n.* **1.** *figurative* ado, agitation, bustle, commotion, disturbance, excitement, ferment, flap, fluster, flutter, furore, fuss, hurry, stir, to-do, tumult, whirl **2.** burst, gust, outbreak, spell, spurt, squall *~vb.* **3.** agitate, bewilder, bother, bustle, confuse, disconcert, disturb, faze, fluster, flutter, fuss, hassle (*informal*), hurry, hustle, rattle (*informal*), ruffle, unnerve, unsettle, upset

flush[1] *vb.* **1.** blush, burn, colour, colour up, flame, glow, go red, redden, suffuse **2.** cleanse, douche, drench, eject, expel, flood, hose down, rinse out, swab, syringe, wash out *~n.* **3.** bloom, blush, colour, freshness, glow, redness, rosiness

flush[2] *adj.* **1.** even, flat, level, plane, square, true **2.** abundant, affluent, full, generous, lavish, liberal, overflowing, prodigal **3.** *informal* in funds, in the money (*informal*), moneyed, rich, rolling (*slang*), wealthy, well-heeled (*informal*), well-off, well-supplied *~adv.* **4.**

flush[3] *vb* to drive out of a hiding place.

flush[4] *n* (in poker and similar games) a hand containing only one suit.

fluster *vb* 1 to make or become nervous or upset. ~*n* 2 a nervous or upset state.

flute *n* 1 a wind instrument consisting of a tube of wood or metal with holes in the side stopped either by the fingers or keys. The breath is directed across a mouth hole in the side. 2 a tall narrow wineglass, used esp. for champagne. ~*vb* **fluting, fluted** 3 to utter in a high-pitched tone. **fluty** *adj*

fluted *adj* having decorated grooves.

fluting *n* a design or decoration of flutes on a column.

flutter *vb* 1 to wave rapidly. 2 (of birds or butterflies) to flap the wings. 3 to move with an irregular motion. 4 *Pathol* (of the heart) to beat abnormally rapidly. 5 to move about restlessly. ~*n* 6 a quick flapping or vibrating motion. 7 a state of nervous excitement or confusion. 8 excited interest. 9 *Brit informal* a modest bet. 10 *Pathol* an abnormally rapid beating of the heart. 11 *Electronics* a slow variation in pitch in a sound-reproducing system.

fluvial (**flew**-vee-al) *adj* of or relating to a river.

flux *n* 1 continuous change or instability. 2 a flow or discharge. 3 a substance mixed with a metal oxide to assist in fusion. 4 *Physics* **a** the rate of flow of particles, energy, or a fluid. **b** the strength of a field in a given area: *magnetic flux.*

fly[1] *vb* **flies, flying, flew, flown** 1 to move through the air on wings or in an aircraft. 2 to control the flight of (an aircraft). 3 to float, flutter, display, or be displayed in the air: *the Red Cross flag flew at each corner of the compound.* 4 to transport or be transported through the air by aircraft, wind, etc. 5 to move very quickly or suddenly: *the front door flew open.* 6 to pass quickly: *how time flies.* 7 to escape from (an enemy or a place). 8 **fly a kite** to release information or take a step in order to test public opinion. 9 **fly at** to attack (someone). 10 **fly high** *Informal* to have a high aim. 11 **let fly** *Informal* to lose one's temper: *a young child letting fly at you in a sudden moment of temper.* ~*n, pl* **flies** 12 Also: **flies** a closure that conceals a zip, buttons, or other fastening, as on trousers. 13 a flap forming the entrance to a tent. 14 **flies** *Theatre* the space above the stage, used for storing scenery.

fly[2] *n, pl* **flies** 1 a small insect with two pairs of wings. 2 any of various similar but unrelated insects, such as the dragonfly. 3 *Angling* a lure made from a fish-hook attached with feathers to resemble a fly. 4 **fly in the ointment** *Informal* a slight flaw that detracts from value or enjoyment. 5 **fly on the wall** a person who watches others, while not being noticed himself or herself. 6 **there are no flies on him** *or* **her** *Informal* he *or* she is no fool.

fly[3] *adj Slang, chiefly Brit* sharp and cunning.

flyaway *adj* 1 (of hair) very fine and soft. 2 frivolous or light-hearted: *a flyaway remark.*

flyblown *adj* 1 covered with blowfly eggs. 2 in a dirty and bad condition.

fly-by-night *Informal* ~*adj* 1 unreliable or untrustworthy, esp. in money matters. ~*n* 2 an untrustworthy person.

flycatcher *n* a small insect-eating songbird.

flyer *or* **flier** *n* 1 a small advertising leaflet. 2 a person or thing that flies or moves very fast. 3 *Old-fashioned* an aircraft pilot.

fly-fishing *n Angling* fishing using artificial flies as lures.

flying *n* 1 the act of piloting, navigating, or travelling in an aircraft. ~*adj* 2 hurried and brief: *a flying visit.* 3 fast or built for speed: *Australia's flying fullback.* 4 hanging, waving, or floating freely: *flags flying proudly.*

flying boat *n* a seaplane in which the fuselage consists of a hull that provides buoyancy.

flying buttress *n* an arch and vertical column that supports a wall from the outside.

flying colours *pl n* conspicuous success; triumph: *they passed with flying colours.*

flying fish *n* a fish of warm and tropical seas, with winglike fins used for gliding above the water.

flying fox *n* 1 a large fruit bat of tropical Africa and Asia. 2 *Austral & NZ* a cable mechanism used for transportation across a river, gorge, etc.

flying officer *n* a junior commissioned officer in an air force.

flying saucer *n* an unidentified disc-shaped flying object alleged to come from outer space.

flying squad *n* a small group of police or soldiers ready to move into action quickly.

flying start *n* 1 any promising beginning. 2 a start to a race in which the competitor is already travelling at speed as he or she passes the starting line.

THESAURUS

even with, hard against, in contact with, level with, squarely, touching

flushed blushing, burning, crimson, embarrassed, feverish, glowing, hot, red, rosy, rubicund, ruddy

fluster **1.** *vb.* agitate, bother, bustle, confound, confuse, disturb, excite, flurry, hassle (*informal*), heat, hurry, make nervous, perturb, rattle (*informal*), ruffle, throw off balance, unnerve, upset **2.** *n.* agitation, bustle, commotion, disturbance, dither (*chiefly Brit.*), flap (*informal*), flurry, flutter, furore, perturbation, ruffle, state (*informal*), turmoil

flutter *vb.* **1.** agitate, bat, beat, flap, flicker, flit, flitter, fluctuate, hover, palpitate, quiver, ripple, ruffle, shiver, tremble, vibrate, waver ~*n.* **2.** palpitation, quiver, quivering, shiver, shudder, tremble, tremor, twitching, vibration **3.** agitation, commotion, confusion, dither (*chiefly Brit.*), excitement, flurry, fluster, state (*informal*), state of nervous excitement, tremble, tumult

fly *vb.* **1.** flit, flutter, hover, mount, sail, soar, take to the air, take wing, wing **2.** aviate, be at the controls, control, manoeuvre, operate, pilot **3.** display, flap, float, flutter, show, wave **4.** barrel (along) (*informal, chiefly U.S. & Canad.*), be off like a shot (*informal*), bolt, burn rubber (*informal*), career, dart, dash, hare (*Brit. informal*), hasten, hurry, race, rush, scamper, scoot, shoot, speed, sprint, tear, whiz (*informal*), zoom **5.** elapse, flit, glide, pass, pass swiftly, roll on, run its course, slip away **6.** abscond, avoid, beat a retreat, clear out (*informal*), cut and run (*informal*), decamp, disappear, do a runner (*slang*), escape, flee, fly the coop (*U.S. & Canad. informal*), get away, hasten away, hightail (*informal, chiefly U.S.*), light out (*informal*), make a getaway, make a quick exit, make one's escape, run, run for it, run from, show a clean pair of heels, shun, skedaddle (*informal*), take flight, take it on the lam (*U.S. & Canad. slang*), take off, take to one's heels **7. fly at** assail, assault, attack, belabour, fall upon, get stuck into (*informal*), go for, have a go at (*informal*), lay about, pitch into (*informal*), rush at **8. let fly** burst forth, give free reign, keep nothing back, lash out, let (someone) have it, lose one's temper, tear into (*informal*), vent

fly-by-night cowboy (*informal*), dubious, questionable, shady, undependable, unreliable, untrustworthy

flying *adj.* **1.** brief, fleeting, fugacious, hasty, hurried, rushed, short-lived, transitory **2.** express, fast, fleet, mercurial, mobile, rapid, speedy, winged **3.** airborne,

flying wing *n* (in Canadian football) the twelfth player, who has a variable position behind the scrimmage line.

flyleaf *n, pl* **-leaves** the inner leaf of the endpaper of a book.

flyover *n Brit* an intersection of two roads at which one is carried over the other by a bridge.

flypaper *n* paper with a sticky and poisonous coating, hung up to trap flies.

fly-past *n* a ceremonial flight of aircraft over a given area.

fly sheet *n* a piece of canvas drawn over the ridgepole of a tent to form an outer roof.

fly spray *n* a liquid used to destroy flies, sprayed from an aerosol.

flyweight *n* a professional or an amateur boxer weighing up to 112 pounds (51 kg).

flywheel *n* a heavy wheel that regulates the speed of a machine.

Fm *Chem* fermium.

FM frequency modulation.

f-number *n Photog* the ratio of the effective diameter of a lens to its focal length.

foal *n* **1** the young of a horse or related animal. *~vb* **2** to give birth to (a foal).

foam *n* **1** a mass of small bubbles of gas formed on the surface of a liquid. **2** frothy saliva. **3** a light spongelike solid used for insulation, packing, etc. *~vb* **4** to produce or cause to produce foam. **5 foam at the mouth** to be very angry. **foamy** *adj*

fob *n* **1** a chain by which a pocket watch is attached to a waistcoat. **2** a small pocket in a man's waistcoat, for holding a watch.

f.o.b. *or* **FOB** *Commerce* free on board.

fob off *vb* **fobbing, fobbed 1** to pretend to satisfy (a person) with lies or excuses. **2** to sell or pass off (inferior goods) as valuable.

focal *adj* **1** of or relating to a focus. **2** situated at or measured from the focus.

focal length *n* the distance from the focal point of a lens or mirror to the surface of the mirror or the centre of the lens.

focal point *n* **1** the point where the rays of light from a lens or mirror meet. **2** the centre of attention or interest: *a focal point for high-technology industries.*

focus (foe-kuss) *vb* **-cusing, -cused** *or* **-cussing, -cussed 1** to adjust one's eyes or an instrument on an object so that its image is clear. **2** to concentrate. *~n, pl* **-cuses** *or* **-ci** (-sigh) **3** a point of convergence of light or sound waves, or a point from which they appear to diverge. **4 in focus** (of an object or image being viewed) clear and sharp. **5 out of focus** (of an object or image being viewed) blurred and fuzzy. **6** same as **focal point** or **focal length. 7** *Optics* the state of an optical image when it is distinct or the state of an instrument producing this image. **8** a point upon which attention or activity is concentrated: *the focus was on health and education.* **9** *Geom* a fixed reference point on the concave side of a conic section, used when defining its eccentricity.

fodder *n* bulk feed for livestock, esp. hay or straw.

foe *n Formal or literary* an enemy.

FoE *or* **FOE** Friends of the Earth.

foetid *adj* same as **fetid.**

foetus *n, pl* **-tuses** same as **fetus.**

fog *n* **1** a mass of droplets of condensed water vapour suspended in the air, often greatly reducing visibility. **2** *Photog* a blurred area on a developed negative, print, or transparency. *~vb* **fogging, fogged 3** to envelop or become enveloped with or as if with fog. **foggy** *adj*

fog bank *n* a distinct mass of fog, esp. at sea.

fogbound *adj* prevented from operating by fog.

fogey *or* **fogy** *n, pl* **-geys** *or* **-gies** an extremely old-fashioned person: *a stick-in-the-mud old fogey.* **fogeyish** *or* **fogyish** *adj*

foghorn *n* a large horn sounded at intervals as a warning to ships in fog.

foible *n* a slight peculiarity or minor weakness: *he was intolerant of other people's foibles.*

foil[1] *vb* to baffle or frustrate (a person or an attempt).

foil[2] *n* **1** metal in the form of very thin sheets. **2** a person or thing setting off another thing to advantage: *mint sauce is an excellent foil to lamb.*

foil[3] *n* a light slender flexible sword tipped by a button, used in fencing.

foist *vb* **foist on** to force (someone) to have or experience (something): *the economic policies which have been foisted on the developing world.*

fold[1] *vb* **1** to bend double so that one part covers another. **2** to bring together and intertwine (the arms or legs). **3 fold up** to enclose in a surrounding material. **4** *Literary* to clasp (a person) in one's arms. **5** Also: **fold in** to mix (ingredients) by gently turning one over the other with a spoon. **6** *Informal* (of a business, organization, or project) to fail or go bankrupt. *~n* **7** a piece or section that has been folded. **8** a mark, crease, or hollow made by folding. **9** a bend in stratified rocks that results from movements within the earth's crust.

THESAURUS

flapping, floating, fluttering, gliding, hovering, in the air, soaring, streaming, volitant, waving, wind-borne, winging

fly in the ointment difficulty, drawback, flaw, hitch, problem, rub, small problem, snag

foam 1. *n.* bubbles, froth, head, lather, spray, spume, suds **2.** *vb.* boil, bubble, effervesce, fizz, froth, lather

focus *vb.* **1.** aim, bring to bear, centre, concentrate, converge, direct, fix, join, meet, pinpoint, rivet, spotlight, zero in (*informal*), zoom in *~n.* **2.** bull's eye, centre, centre of activity, centre of attraction, core, cynosure (*literary*), focal point, headquarters, heart, hub, meeting place, target **3. in focus** clear, distinct, sharp-edged, sharply defined **4. out of focus** blurred, fuzzy, ill-defined, indistinct, muzzy, unclear

foe adversary, antagonist, enemy, opponent, rival

fog 1. *n.* gloom, miasma, mist, murk, murkiness, peasouper (*informal*), smog **2.** *vb.* becloud, bedim, befuddle, bewilder, blind, cloud, confuse, darken, daze, dim, mist over *or* up, muddle, obfuscate, obscure, perplex, steam up, stupefy

foggy 1. blurred, cloudy, dim, grey, hazy, indistinct, misty, murky, nebulous, obscure, smoggy, soupy, vaporous **2.** *figurative* befuddled, bewildered, clouded, cloudy, confused, dark, dazed, dim, indistinct, muddled, obscure, stupefied, stupid, unclear, vague

foil *vb.* baffle, balk, check, checkmate, circumvent, counter, defeat, disappoint, elude, frustrate, nip in the bud, nullify, outwit, put a spoke in (someone's) wheel (*Brit.*), stop, thwart

foist fob off, get rid of, impose, insert, insinuate, interpolate, introduce, palm off, pass off, put over, sneak in, unload

fold *vb.* **1.** bend, crease, crumple, dog-ear, double, double over, gather, intertwine, overlap, pleat, tuck, turn under **2. fold up** do up, enclose, enfold, entwine, envelop, wrap, wrap up **3.** *informal* be ruined, close, collapse, crash, fail, go bankrupt, go belly-up (*slang*), go bust (*informal*), go down like a lead balloon (*in-*

fold[2] *n* **1** a small enclosure for sheep. **2** a church or the members of it.

folder *n* a binder or file for holding loose papers.

folding door *n* a door with two or more vertical hinged leaves that can be folded one against another.

foliaceous *adj* **1** like a leaf. **2** *Geol* consisting of thin layers.

foliage *n* **1** the green leaves of a plant. **2** leaves together with the stems, twigs, and branches they are attached to, esp. when used for decoration.

foliation *n* **1** *Bot* **a** the process of producing leaves. **b** the state of being in leaf. **2** a leaflike decoration.

folio *n, pl* **-lios 1** a sheet of paper folded in half to make two leaves for a book. **2** a book of the largest common size made up of such sheets. **3 a** a leaf of paper numbered on the front side only. **b** the page number of a book. *~adj* **4** of or made in the largest book size, common esp. in early centuries of European printing: *the entire series is being reissued, several in the original folio format.*

folk *pl n* **1** people in general, esp. those of a particular group or class: *ordinary folk.* **2** Also: **folks** *Informal* members of one's family; relatives. *~n* **3** *Informal* short for **folk music. 4** a people or tribe. *~adj* **5** originating from or traditional to the common people of a country: *folk art.*

folk dance *n* **1** a traditional country dance. **2** music for such a dance.

folk etymology *n* the gradual change in the form of a word through the influence of a more familiar word, as for example *crayfish* from its Middle English form *crevis.*

folklore *n* the traditional beliefs of a people as expressed in stories and songs.

folk music *n* **1** music that is passed on from generation to generation. **2** a piece written in the style of this music.

folk song *n* **1** a song handed down among the common people. **2** a modern song like this. **folk singer** *n*

folksy *adj* **-sier, -siest** simple and unpretentious, sometimes in an artificial way.

follicle *n* any small sac or cavity in the body, esp. one from which a hair grows. **follicular** *adj*

follow *vb* **1** to go or come after. **2** to accompany: *he followed Isabel everywhere.* **3** to be a logical or natural consequence of. **4** to keep to the course or track of. **5** to act in accordance with: *follow the rules below and it will help you a great deal.* **6** to accept the ideas or beliefs of. **7** to understand (an explanation). **8** to have a keen interest in: *he's followed the singer's career for more than 25 years.* ~See also **follow-on, follow through, follow up.**

follower *n* **1** a person who accepts the teachings of another: *a follower of Nietzsche.* **2** a supporter, such as of a sport or team.

following *adj* **1** about to be mentioned. **2** next in time. **3** (of winds or currents) moving in the same direction as a vessel. *~prep* **4** as a result of: *uncertainty following the collapse of communism. ~n* **5** a group of supporters or enthusiasts.

follow-on *Cricket ~n* **1** an immediate second innings forced on a team scoring a prescribed number of runs fewer than its opponents in the first innings. *~vb* **follow on 2** to play a follow-on.

follow through *vb* **1** to continue an action or series of actions until finished. **2** *Sport* to continue a stroke, kick, etc., after striking the ball. *~n* **follow-through 3** *Sport* continuation of a kick, stroke, etc., after striking the ball: *Faldo's controlled follow-through.*

follow up *vb* **1** to investigate (a person, evidence, etc.) closely. **2** to continue (action) after a beginning, esp. to increase its effect. *~n* **follow-up 3** something done to reinforce an initial action: *a routine follow-up to his operation.*

folly *n, pl* **-lies 1** the quality of being foolish. **2** a foolish action, idea, etc. **3** an imitation castle, temple, etc., built as a decoration in a large garden or park.

foment (foam-**ent**) *vb* to encourage or stir up (trouble). **fomentation** *n*

fond *adj* **1 fond of** having a liking for. **2** loving and affectionate: *his fond parents.* **3** (of hopes or wishes) cherished but unlikely to be realized. **fondly** *adv* **fondness** *n*

fondant *n* (a sweet made from) a thick flavoured paste of sugar and water.

fondle *vb* **-dling, -dled** to touch or stroke tenderly.

fondue *n* a Swiss dish, consisting of melted cheese into which small pieces of bread are dipped.

font[1] *n* a large bowl in a church for baptismal water.

font[2] *n Printing chiefly US & Canad* same as **fount**[2].

THESAURUS

formal), go to the wall, go under, shut down *~n.* **4.** bend, crease, double thickness, folded portion, furrow, knife-edge, layer, overlap, pleat, turn, wrinkle

folder binder, envelope, file, portfolio

folk clan, ethnic group, family, kin, kindred, people, race, tribe

follow 1. come after, come next, step into the shoes of, succeed, supersede, supplant, take the place of **2.** accompany, attend, bring up the rear, come after, come *or* go with, escort, tag along, tread on the heels of **3.** arise, be consequent, develop, emanate, ensue, flow, issue, proceed, result, spring, supervene **4.** act in accordance with, be guided by, comply, conform, give allegiance to, heed, mind, note, obey, observe, regard, watch **5.** adopt, copy, emulate, imitate, live up to, pattern oneself upon, take as example **6.** appreciate, catch, catch on (*informal*), comprehend, fathom, get, get the picture, grasp, keep up with, realize, see, take in, understand **7.** be a devotee *or* supporter of, be devoted to, be interested in, cultivate, keep abreast of, support

follower 1. adherent, admirer, apostle, backer, believer, convert, devotee, disciple, fancier, habitué, henchman, partisan, protagonist, pupil, representative, votary, worshipper **2.** fan, fanatic, supporter

following 1. *adj.* coming, consequent, consequential, ensuing, later, next, specified, subsequent, succeeding, successive **2.** *n.* audience, circle, clientele, coterie, entourage, fans, patronage, public, retinue, suite, support, supporters, train

follow up 1. check out, find out about, investigate, look into, make inquiries, pursue, research **2.** consolidate, continue, make sure, reinforce

folly absurdity, daftness (*informal*), fatuity, foolishness, idiocy, imbecility, imprudence, indiscretion, irrationality, lunacy, madness, nonsense, preposterousness, rashness, recklessness, silliness, stupidity

fond 1. *with* **of** addicted to, attached to, enamoured of, have a liking (fancy, soft spot, taste) for, hooked on, into (*informal*), keen on, partial to, predisposed towards **2.** adoring, affectionate, amorous, caring, devoted, doting, indulgent, loving, tender, warm **3.** absurd, credulous, deluded, delusive, delusory, empty, foolish, naive, overoptimistic, vain

fondle caress, cuddle, dandle, pat, pet, stroke

fondly 1. affectionately, dearly, indulgently, lovingly, possessively, tenderly, with affection **2.** credulously, foolishly, naively, stupidly, vainly

fondness 1. attachment, fancy, liking, love, partial-

fontanelle *or esp US* **fontanel** *n Anat* a soft membranous gap between the bones of a baby's skull.

food *n* any substance that can be taken into the body by a living organism and changed into energy and body tissue.

food chain *n Ecology* a series of organisms in a community, each member of which feeds on another in the chain and is in turn eaten.

foodie *n Informal* a person with a keen interest in food and cookery.

food poisoning *n* an acute illness caused by food that is contaminated by bacteria.

food processor *n* a machine for chopping, mixing, or liquidizing food.

foodstuff *n* any substance that can be used as food.

fool[1] *n* **1** a person who lacks sense or judgment. **2** a person who is made to appear ridiculous. **3** (formerly) a professional jester living in a royal or noble household. **4 act** *or* **play the fool** to deliberately act foolishly. *~vb* **5** to deceive (someone), esp. in order to make them look ridiculous. **6 fool around** *or* **about with** *Informal* to act or play with irresponsibly or aimlessly. **7** to speak or act in a playful or jesting manner.

fool[2] *n Chiefly Brit* a dessert made from a puree of fruit with cream.

foolery *n* foolish behaviour.

foolhardy *adj* **-hardier, -hardiest** recklessly adventurous. **foolhardily** *adv* **foolhardiness** *n*

foolish *adj* very silly, unwise, or absurd. **foolishly** *adv* **foolishness** *n*

foolproof *adj Informal* **1** incapable of going wrong; infallible: *a foolproof identification system.* **2** (of machines etc.) guaranteed to function as intended despite human misuse or error.

foolscap *n Chiefly Brit* a standard paper size, 34.3 × 43.2 cm.

fool's errand *n* a fruitless undertaking.

fool's gold *n* a yellow-coloured mineral, such as pyrite, that is sometimes mistaken for gold.

fool's paradise *n* a state of happiness based on false hopes or beliefs.

foot *n, pl* **feet 1** the part of the leg below the ankle joint that is in contact with the ground during standing and walking. **2** the part of a garment covering a foot. **3** a unit of length equal to 12 inches (0.3048 metre). **4** the bottom, base, or lower end of something: *at the foot of the hill; the foot of the page.* **5** *Old-fashioned* infantry. **6** *Prosody* a group of two or more syllables in which one syllable has the major stress, forming the basic unit of poetic rhythm. **7 one foot in the grave** *Informal* near to death. **8 on foot** walking. **9 put one's best foot forward** to try to do one's best. **10 put one's foot down** *Informal* to act firmly. **11 put one's foot in it** *Informal* to make an embarrassing and tactless mistake. **12 under foot** on the ground. *~vb* **13 foot it** *Informal* to travel on foot. **14 foot the bill** to pay the entire cost of something. ~See also **feet. footless** *adj*

footage *n* **1** a length of film. **2** the sequences of filmed material: *footage of refugees leaving the city.*

foot-and-mouth disease *n* a highly infectious viral disease of cattle, pigs, sheep, and goats, in which blisters form in the mouth and on the feet.

football *n* **1** any of various games played with a ball in which two teams compete to kick, head, or propel the ball into each other's goal. **2** the ball used in any of these games. **footballer** *n*

football pools *pl n* same as **pools.**

footbridge *n* a narrow bridge for the use of pedestrians.

THESAURUS

ity, penchant, predilection, preference, soft spot, susceptibility, taste, weakness **2.** affection, attachment, devotion, kindness, love, tenderness

food 1. aliment, board, bread, chow (*informal*), comestibles, commons, cooking, cuisine, diet, eatables (*slang*), eats (*slang*), edibles, fare, feed, foodstuffs, grub (*slang*), larder, meat, menu, nosebag (*slang*), nosh (*slang*), nourishment, nutriment, nutrition, provender, provisions, rations, refreshment, scoff (*slang*), stores, subsistence, sustenance, table, tack (*informal*), tuck (*informal*), viands (*old-fashioned*), victuals (*old-fashioned*) **2.** *Cattle, etc.* feed, fodder, forage, provender

fool *n.* **1.** ass, berk (*Brit. slang*), bird-brain (*informal*), blockhead, bonehead (*slang*), charlie (*Brit. informal*), chump (*informal*), clot (*Brit. informal*), coot, dickhead (*slang*), dimwit (*informal*), dipstick (*Brit. slang*), divvy (*Brit. slang*), dolt, dope (*informal*), dork (*slang*), dunce, dunderhead, dweeb (*U.S. slang*), fathead (*informal*), fuckwit (*taboo slang*), geek (*slang*), gonzo (*slang*), goose (*informal*), halfwit, idiot, ignoramus, illiterate, imbecile (*informal*), jackass, jerk (*slang, chiefly U.S. & Canad.*), lamebrain (*informal*), loon, mooncalf, moron, nerd *or* nurd (*slang*), nincompoop, ninny, nit (*informal*), nitwit (*informal*), numbskull *or* numskull, oaf, pillock (*Brit. slang*), plank (*Brit. slang*), plonker (*slang*), prat (*slang*), prick (*derogatory slang*), sap (*slang*), schmuck (*U.S. slang*), silly, simpleton, twerp *or* twirp (*informal*), twit (*informal, chiefly Brit.*), wally (*slang*) **2.** butt, chump (*informal*), dupe, easy mark (*informal*), fall guy (*informal*), greenhorn (*informal*), laughing stock, mug (*Brit. slang*), stooge (*slang*), sucker (*slang*) **3.** buffoon, clown, comic, harlequin, jester, merry-andrew, motley, pierrot, punchinello **4. act** *or* **play the fool** act up, be silly, cavort, clown, cut capers, frolic, lark about (*informal*), mess about, piss about (*taboo slang*), piss around (*taboo slang*), play the goat, show off (*informal*) *~vb.* **5.** bamboozle, beguile, bluff, cheat, con (*informal*), deceive, delude, dupe, have (someone) on, hoax, hoodwink, kid (*informal*), make a fool of, mislead, play a trick on, put one over on (*informal*), stiff (*slang*), take in, trick **6.** *with* **around** *or* **about with** fiddle (*informal*), meddle, mess, monkey, piss about (*taboo slang*), piss around (*taboo slang*), play, tamper, toy, trifle **7.** act the fool, cut capers, feign, jest, joke, kid (*informal*), make believe, piss about (*taboo slang*), piss around (*taboo slang*), pretend, tease

foolery antics, capers, carry-on (*informal, chiefly Brit.*), childishness, clowning, folly, fooling, horseplay, larks, mischief, nonsense, practical jokes, pranks, shenanigans (*informal*), silliness, tomfoolery

foolhardy adventurous, bold, hot-headed, impetuous, imprudent, incautious, irresponsible, madcap, precipitate, rash, reckless, venturesome, venturous

foolish absurd, asinine, crackpot (*informal*), crazy, daft (*informal*), fatuous, goofy (*informal*), half-baked (*informal*), half-witted, harebrained, idiotic, ill-advised, ill-considered, ill-judged, imbecilic, imprudent, inane, incautious, indiscreet, injudicious, loopy (*informal*), ludicrous, moronic, nonsensical, potty (*Brit. informal*), ridiculous, senseless, short-sighted, silly, unintelligent, unwise

foolishly absurdly, idiotically, ill-advisedly, imprudently, incautiously, indiscreetly, injudiciously, like a fool, mistakenly, short-sightedly, stupidly, unwisely, without due consideration

foolishness absurdity, folly, idiocy, imprudence, inanity, indiscretion, irresponsibility, silliness, stupidity, weakness

footfall *n* the sound of a footstep.

foothills *pl n* relatively low hills at the foot of a mountain.

foothold *n* **1** a secure position from which further progress may be made: *a firm foothold in Europe's telecommunications market.* **2** a ledge or other place where a foot can be securely positioned, as during climbing.

footing *n* **1** basis or foundation: *on a sound financial footing.* **2** the relationship between two people or groups: *on an equal footing.* **3** a secure grip by or for the feet.

footle *vb* **-ling, -led** *Informal* to loiter aimlessly. **footling** *adj*

footlights *pl n Theatre* lights set in a row along the front of the stage floor.

footloose *adj* free to go or do as one wishes.

footman *n, pl* **-men** a male servant in uniform.

footnote *n* a note printed at the bottom of a page.

footpad *n Old-fashioned* a highwayman, on foot rather than horseback.

footpath *n* a narrow path for walkers only.

footplate *n Chiefly Brit* a platform in the cab of a locomotive on which the crew stand to operate the controls.

footprint *n* an indentation or outline of the foot on a surface.

footsie *n Informal* flirtation involving the touching together of feet.

footsore *adj* having sore or tired feet, esp. from much walking.

footstep *n* **1** a step in walking. **2** the sound made by walking. **3** a footmark. **4 follow in someone's footsteps** to continue the example of another.

footstool *n* a low stool used for supporting the feet of a seated person.

footwear *n* anything worn to cover the feet.

footwork *n* the way in which the feet are used, for example in sports or dancing: *nimble footwork.*

fop *n* a man who is excessively concerned with fashion. **foppery** *n* **foppish** *adj*

for *prep* **1** directed or belonging to: *a bottle of beer for himself.* **2** to the advantage of: *he spelt it out for her.* **3** in the direction of: *he headed for the door.* **4** over a span of (time or distance): *she considered him coolly for a moment.* **5** in favour of: *support for the war.* **6** in order to get: *for a bit of company.* **7** designed to meet the needs of: *the instructions are for right-handed players.* **8** at a cost of: *two dishes for $28.50.* **9** in place of: *she had to substitute for her mother because they woke late.* **10** because of: *dancing for joy.* **11** regarding the usual characteristics of: *unusually warm for the time of year.* **12** concerning: *our idea for the last scene.* **13** as being: *do you take me for an idiot?* **14** at (a specified time): *multiparty elections are planned for next year.* **15** to do or take part in: *two guests for dinner.* **16** in the duty or task of: *that's for you to decide.* **17** in relation to; as it affects: *it's too hard for me.* **18** in order to preserve or retain: *fighting for survival.* **19** as a direct equivalent to: *word for word.* **20** in order to become or enter: *training for the priesthood.* **21** in exchange for: *the cash was used to pay for food, shelter, and medical supplies.* **22 for all** See **all** (sense 12). **23 for it** *Brit informal* liable for punishment or blame: *you'll be for it if you get caught.* ~*conj* **24** *Formal* because or seeing that: *implausibility cries aloud, and this is a pity, for much of the narrative is entertaining.*

forage (**for**-ridge) *vb* **-aging, -aged 1** to search for food. **2** to obtain by searching about: *she foraged for her shoes.* ~*n* **3** food for horses or cattle, esp. hay or straw. **4** the act of searching for food or provisions.

forage cap *n* a cap with a flat round crown and a visor, worn by soldiers when not in battle or on parade.

foramen (for-**ray**-men) *n, pl* **-ramina** (-**ram**-in-a) *or* **-ramens** *Anat* a natural hole, esp. one in a bone through which nerves pass.

forasmuch as *conj Old-fashioned or legal* seeing that or since.

foray *n* **1** a short raid or incursion. **2** a first attempt or new undertaking: *an initial foray into unit trust investment.*

forbade *or* **forbad** *vb* the past tense of **forbid.**

forbear[1] *vb* **-bearing, -bore, -borne** to cease or refrain (from doing something). **forbearance** *n*

forbear[2] *n* same as **forebear.**

forbid *vb* **-bidding, -bade** *or* **-bad, -bidden** *or* **-bid** to prohibit or refuse to allow.

forbidding *adj* severe and threatening in appearance or manner.

forbore *vb* the past tense of **forbear**[1].

forborne *vb* the past participle of **forbear**[1].

force[1] *n* **1** strength or power: *the force of the impact had thrown him into the fireplace.* **2** exertion or the use of exertion against a person or thing that resists: *they used force and repression against those who opposed their policies.* **3** *Physics* an influence that changes a body from a state of rest to one of motion or changes its rate of motion. Symbol: ***F*** **4 a** intellectual or moral influence: *the Superintendent acknowledged the force of the Chief Constable's argument.* **b** a person or thing with such influence: *Hitler quickly became the decisive force behind German foreign policy.* **5** drive or intensity: *he reacted with frightening speed and force.* **6** a group of people organized for particular duties or tasks: *a UN peacekeeping force.* **7 in force a** (of a law) having legal validity. **b** in great strength or

THESAURUS

foolproof certain, guaranteed, infallible, never-failing, safe, sure-fire (*informal*), unassailable, unbreakable

footing 1. basis, establishment, foot-hold, foundation, ground, groundwork, installation, settlement **2.** condition, grade, position, rank, relations, relationship, standing, state, status, terms

footling fiddling, fussy, hairsplitting, immaterial, insignificant, irrelevant, minor, nickel-and-dime (*U.S. slang*), niggly, petty, pointless, silly, time-wasting, trifling, trivial, unimportant

footstep 1. footfall, step, tread **2.** footmark, footprint, trace, track

forage 1. *vb.* cast about, explore, hunt, look round, plunder, raid, ransack, rummage, scavenge, scour, scrounge (*informal*), search, seek **2.** *n. Cattle, etc.* feed, fodder, food, foodstuffs, provender

forbear abstain, avoid, cease, decline, desist, eschew, hold back, keep from, omit, pause, refrain, resist the temptation to, restrain oneself, stop, withhold

forbearance 1. indulgence, leniency, lenity, longanimity (*rare*), long-suffering, mildness, moderation, patience, resignation, restraint, self-control, temperance, tolerance **2.** abstinence, avoidance, refraining

forbearing clement, easy, forgiving, indulgent, lenient, long-suffering, merciful, mild, moderate, patient, tolerant

forbid ban, debar, disallow, exclude, hinder, inhibit, interdict, outlaw, preclude, prohibit, proscribe, rule out, veto

numbers. ~*vb* **forcing, forced 8** to compel (a person, group, etc.) to do something through effort, superior strength, etc.: *forced into an arranged marriage.* **9** to acquire or produce through effort, superior strength, etc.: *he forced a smile.* **10** to propel or drive despite resistance. **11** to break down or open (a lock, door, etc.). **12** to impose or inflict: *a series of opposition strikes forced the appointment of a coalition government.* **13** to cause (plants or farm animals) to grow at an increased rate.

force[2] *n* (in N England) a waterfall.

forced *adj* **1** done because of force: *forced labour.* **2** false or unnatural: *forced jollity.* **3** due to an emergency: *a forced landing.*

force-feed *vb* **-feeding, -fed** to force (a person or animal) to swallow food.

forceful *adj* **1** strong, emphatic, and confident: *a forceful speech.* **2** effective. **forcefully** *adv*

forcemeat *n* a mixture of chopped ingredients used for stuffing.

forceps *n, pl* **-ceps** a surgical instrument in the form of a pair of pincers.

forcible *adj* **1** involving physical force. **2** convincing or effective: *a strong shrewd mind and a steady forcible manner.* **forcibly** *adv*

ford *n* **1** a shallow area in a river that can be crossed by car, on horseback, etc. ~*vb* **2** to cross (a river) over a shallow area. **fordable** *adj*

fore *adj* **1** at, in, or towards the front: *the fore foot.* ~*n* **2** the front part. **3 fore and aft** located at both ends of a vessel: *two double cabins fore and aft.* **4 to the fore** to the front or prominent position. ~*interj* **5** a golfer's shouted warning to a person in the path of a flying ball.

fore- *prefix* **1** before in time or rank: *foregoing.* **2** at or near the front: *foreground.*

forearm[1] *n* the part of the arm from the elbow to the wrist.

forearm[2] *vb* to prepare or arm beforehand.

forebear *or* **forbear** *n* an ancestor.

foreboding *n* a strong feeling that something bad is about to happen.

forecast *vb* **-casting, -cast** *or* **-casted 1** to predict or calculate (weather, events, etc.), in advance. ~*n* **2** a statement predicting the weather. **3** a prediction. **forecaster** *n*

forecastle, fo'c's'le, *or* **fo'c'sle** (**foke**-sl) *n* the raised front part of a ship.

foreclose *vb* **-closing, -closed** *Law* to take possession of property bought with borrowed money because repayment has not been made: *the banks have been reluctant to foreclose on troubled borrowers.* **foreclosure** *n*

forecourt *n* a courtyard in front of a building, such as one in a filling station.

forefather *n* an ancestor.

forefinger *n* the finger next to the thumb. Also called: **index finger**

forefoot *n, pl* **-feet** either of the front feet of an animal.

forefront *n* **1** the most active or prominent position: *at the forefront of medical research.* **2** the very front.

foregather *or* **forgather** *vb* to gather together or assemble.

forego[1] *vb* **-going, -went, -gone** to precede in time, place, etc.

forego[2] *vb* **-going, -went, -gone** same as **forgo.**

foregoing *adj* (esp. of writing or speech) going before; preceding.

foregone conclusion *n* an inevitable result.

foreground *n* **1** the part of a view, esp. in a picture, nearest the viewer. **2** an important or prominent position.

forehand *Tennis, squash, etc* ~*adj* **1** (of a stroke) made with the palm of the hand facing the direction of the stroke. ~*n* **2** a forehand stroke.

forehead *n* the part of the face between the natural hairline and the eyes.

➤ The pronunciation "**for**-rid" is traditional but "**for**-hed" is also acceptable.

foreign *adj* **1** of, located in, or coming from another

THESAURUS

forbidden banned, outlawed, out of bounds, prohibited, proscribed, taboo, *verboten,* vetoed

forbidding baleful, daunting, foreboding, frightening, grim, hostile, menacing, ominous, sinister, threatening, unfriendly

force *n.* **1.** dynamism, energy, impact, impulse, life, might, momentum, muscle, potency, power, pressure, stimulus, strength, stress, vigour **2.** arm-twisting (*informal*), coercion, compulsion, constraint, duress, enforcement, pressure, violence **3.** bite, cogency, effect, effectiveness, efficacy, influence, persuasiveness, power, punch (*informal*), strength, validity, weight **4.** drive, emphasis, fierceness, intensity, persistence, vehemence, vigour **5.** army, battalion, body, corps, detachment, division, host, legion, patrol, regiment, squad, squadron, troop, unit **6. in force a.** binding, current, effective, in operation, on the statute book, operative, valid, working **b.** all together, in full strength, in great numbers ~*vb.* **7.** bring pressure to bear upon, coerce, compel, constrain, dragoon, drive, impel, impose, make, necessitate, obligate, oblige, overcome, press, press-gang, pressure, pressurize, put the squeeze on (*informal*), railroad (*informal*), strong-arm (*informal*), urge **8.** blast, break open, prise, propel, push, thrust, use violence on, wrench, wrest

forced 1. compulsory, conscripted, enforced, involuntary, mandatory, obligatory, slave, unwilling **2.** affected, artificial, contrived, false, insincere, laboured, stiff, strained, unnatural, wooden

forceful cogent, compelling, convincing, dynamic, effective, persuasive, pithy, potent, powerful, telling, vigorous, weighty

forcible 1. aggressive, armed, coercive, compulsory, drastic, violent **2.** active, cogent, compelling, effective, efficient, energetic, forceful, impressive, mighty, potent, powerful, strong, telling, valid, weighty

forcibly against one's will, by force, by main force, compulsorily, under compulsion, under protest, willy-nilly

forebear ancestor, father, forefather, forerunner, predecessor, progenitor

forebode augur, betoken, foreshadow, foreshow, foretell, foretoken, forewarn, indicate, portend, predict, presage, prognosticate, promise, warn of

foreboding anxiety, apprehension, apprehensiveness, chill, dread, fear, misgiving, premonition, presentiment

forecast 1. *vb.* anticipate, augur, calculate, divine, estimate, foresee, foretell, plan, predict, prognosticate, prophesy **2.** *n.* anticipation, conjecture, foresight, forethought, guess, outlook, planning, prediction, prognosis, projection, prophecy

forefather ancestor, father, forebear, forerunner, predecessor, primogenitor, procreator, progenitor

foregoing above, antecedent, anterior, former, preceding, previous, prior

country, area, or people. **2** dealing or concerned with another country, area, or people: *the Foreign Minister.* **3** not familiar; strange. **4** in an abnormal place or position: *a foreign body in the food.*

foreigner *n* **1** a person from a foreign country. **2** an outsider.

foreign minister *or* **secretary** *n* a cabinet minister who is responsible for a country's dealings with other countries.

foreign office *n* the ministry of a country that is concerned with dealings with other states.

foreknowledge *n* knowledge of something before it actually happens.

foreleg *n* either of the front legs of an animal.

forelock *n* a lock of hair growing or falling over the forehead.

foreman *n, pl* **-men 1** a person who supervises other workmen. **2** *Law* the leader of a jury.

foremast *n* the mast nearest the bow of a ship.

foremost *adj, adv* first in time, place, or importance: *Germany's foremost conductor.*

forenoon *n* the daylight hours before noon.

forensic (for-**ren**-sik) *adj* used in or connected with a court of law. **forensically** *adv*

forensic medicine *n* the application of medical knowledge for the purposes of the law, such as in determining the cause of death.

foreordain *vb* to determine (events, etc.) in the future.

forepaw *n* either of the front feet of a land mammal that does not have hooves.

foreplay *n* sexual stimulation before intercourse.

forerunner *n* **1** a person or thing that existed or happened before another and is similar in some way: *a forerunner of the surrealist painters.* **2** a person or thing that is a sign of what will happen in the future.

foresail *n* the main sail on the foremast of a ship.

foresee *vb* **-seeing, -saw, -seen** to see or know beforehand. **foreseeable** *adj*

foreshadow *vb* to show, indicate, or suggest in advance.

foreshore *n* the part of the shore between high- and low-tide marks.

foreshorten *vb* to see or draw (an object) from such an angle that it appears to be shorter than it really is.

foresight *n* **1** the ability to anticipate and provide for future needs. **2** the front sight on a firearm.

foreskin *n Anat* the fold of skin covering the tip of the penis.

forest *n* **1** a large wooded area with a thick growth of trees and plants. **2** a group of narrow or tall objects standing upright: *a forest of waving arms.* **3** *NZ* an area planted with pines or other trees that are not native to the country. **forested** *adj*

forestall *vb* to delay, stop, or guard against beforehand: *an action forestalling any further talks.*

forestation *n* the planting of trees over a wide area.

forester *n* a person skilled in forestry or in charge of a forest.

forestry *n* the science or skill of growing and maintaining trees in a forest, esp. to obtain wood.

foretaste *n* an early but limited experience of something to come.

foretell *vb* **-telling, -told** *Literary* to correctly predict (an event, a result, etc.) beforehand.

forethought *n* thoughtful planning for future events: *a little forethought can avoid a lot of problems later.*

foretoken *n* a sign of a future event.

for ever *or* **forever** *adv* **1** without end. **2** at all times. **3** *Informal* for a long time: *I could go on for ever about similar incidents.*

forewarn *vb* to warn beforehand.

foreword *n* an introductory statement to a book.

forfeit (**for**-fit) *n* **1** something lost or given up as a penalty for a fault, mistake, etc. *~vb* **2** to lose as a forfeit. *~adj* **3** lost as a forfeit. **forfeiture** *n*

forgather *vb* same as **foregather.**

forgave *vb* the past tense of **forgive.**

forge[1] *n* **1** a place in which metal is worked by heating and hammering; smithy. **2** a furnace used for heating metal. *~vb* **forging, forged 3** to shape (metal) by heating and hammering. **4** to make a fraudulent imitation of (a signature, money, a painting, etc.). **5** to create (an alliance, relationship, etc.). **forger** *n*

forge[2] *vb* **forging, forged 1** to move at a steady pace. **2 forge ahead** to increase speed or progress; take the lead.

THESAURUS

foreground centre, forefront, front, limelight, prominence

foreign 1. alien, borrowed, distant, exotic, external, imported, outlandish, outside, overseas, remote, strange, unfamiliar, unknown **2.** extraneous, extrinsic, incongruous, irrelevant, unassimilable, uncharacteristic, unrelated

foreigner alien, immigrant, incomer, newcomer, outlander, stranger

foremost chief, first, front, highest, inaugural, initial, leading, paramount, pre-eminent, primary, prime, principal, supreme

forerunner 1. ancestor, announcer, envoy, forebear, foregoer, harbinger, herald, precursor, predecessor, progenitor, prototype **2.** augury, foretoken, indication, omen, portent, premonition, prognostic, sign, token

foresee anticipate, divine, envisage, forebode, forecast, foretell, predict, prophesy, vaticinate (*rare*)

foreshadow adumbrate, augur, betoken, bode, forebode, imply, indicate, portend, predict, prefigure, presage, promise, prophesy, signal

foresight anticipation, care, caution, circumspection, far-sightedness, forethought, precaution, premeditation, preparedness, prescience, prudence

forestry arboriculture, dendrology (*Bot.*), silviculture, woodcraft, woodmanship

foretell adumbrate, augur, bode, forebode, forecast, foreshadow, foreshow, forewarn, portend, predict, presage, prognosticate, prophesy, signify, soothsay

forethought anticipation, far-sightedness, foresight, precaution, providence, provision, prudence

for ever *or* **forever 1.** always, evermore, for all time, for good and all (*informal*), for keeps, in perpetuity, till Doomsday, till the cows come home (*informal*), till the end of time, world without end **2.** all the time, constantly, continually, endlessly, eternally, everlastingly, incessantly, interminably, perpetually, unremittingly

forewarn admonish, advise, alert, apprise, caution, dissuade, give fair warning, put on guard, put on the qui vive, tip off

foreword introduction, preamble, preface, preliminary, prolegomenon, prologue

forfeit 1. *n.* damages, fine, forfeiture, loss, mulct, penalty **2.** *vb.* be deprived of, be stripped of, give up, lose, relinquish, renounce, surrender

forfeiture confiscation, giving up, loss, relinquishment, sequestration (*Law*), surrender

forge *vb.* **1.** construct, contrive, create, devise, fabri-

forgery *n, pl* **-geries 1** an illegal copy of a painting, banknote, antique, etc. **2** the crime of making a fraudulent imitation.

forget *vb* **-getting, -got, -gotten 1** to fail to remember (someone or something once known). **2** to neglect, either by mistake or on purpose. **3** to leave behind by mistake. **4 forget oneself** to act in an uncharacteristically unrestrained or unacceptable manner: *I might forget myself and slap your wrists.* **forgettable** *adj*

forgetful *adj* **1** tending to forget. **2 forgetful of** inattentive to or neglectful of: *Fiona, forgetful of the time, was still in bed.* **forgetfully** *adv*

forget-me-not *n* a low-growing plant with clusters of small blue flowers.

forgive *vb* **-giving, -gave, -given 1** to stop feeling anger and resentment towards (a person) or at (an action that has caused upset or harm). **2** to pardon (a mistake). **3** to free from (a debt).

forgiveness *n* the act of forgiving or the state of being forgiven.

forgiving *adj* willing to forgive.

forgo *or* **forego** *vb* **-going, -went, -gone** to give up or do without.

forgot *vb* **1** the past tense of **forget**. **2** *Old-fashioned or dialect* a past participle of **forget.**

forgotten *vb* a past participle of **forget.**

fork *n* **1** a small tool with long thin prongs on the end of a handle, used for lifting food to the mouth. **2** a larger similar-shaped gardening tool, used for lifting or digging. **3 forks** the part of a bicycle that links the handlebars to the front wheel. **4** (of a road, river, etc.) **a** a division into two or more branches. **b** the point where the division begins. **c** such a branch. *~vb* **5** to pick up, dig, etc., with a fork. **6** to be divided into two or more branches. **7** to take one or other branch at a fork in a road, etc.

forked *adj* **1** having a fork or forklike parts. **2** zigzag: *forked lightning.*

fork-lift truck *n* a vehicle with two moveable arms at the front that can be raised and lowered for transporting and unloading goods.

fork out *vb Slang* to pay, esp. with reluctance.

forlorn *adj* **1** lonely, unhappy, and uncared-for. **2** (of a place) having a deserted appearance. **3** desperate and without any expectation of success: *a final, apparently forlorn attempt to save the war-torn country.* **forlornly** *adv*

forlorn hope *n* **1** a hopeless enterprise. **2** a faint hope.

form *n* **1** the shape or appearance of something. **2** a visible person or animal. **3** the particular mode in which a thing or person appears: *wood in the form of paper.* **4** a type or kind: *abortion was widely used as a form of birth control.* **5** physical or mental condition. **6** a printed document, esp. one with spaces in which to fill details or answers. **7** the previous record of a horse, athlete, etc. **8** *Brit slang* a criminal record. **9** *Education chiefly Brit* a group of children who are taught together. **10** manners and etiquette: *it is considered bad form not to wear a tie.* **11** the structure and arrangement of a work of art or piece of writing as distinguished from its content. **12** a bench. **13** a hare's nest. **14** any of the various ways in which a word may be spelt or inflected. *~vb* **15** to give shape to or take shape, esp. a particular shape. **16** to come or bring into existence: *glaciers dammed the valley bottoms with debris behind which lakes have formed.* **17** to make or construct or be made or constructed. **18** to train or mould by instruction or example. **19** to acquire or develop: *they've formed this impression; we formed a bond.* **20** to be an element of: *they had formed part of a special murder unit.*

formal *adj* **1** of or following established conventions: *formal talks; a formal announcement.* **2** characterized by conventional forms of ceremony and behaviour: *a small formal dinner party.* **3** suitable for occasions organized according to conventional ceremony: *formal*

THESAURUS

cate, fashion, form, frame, hammer out, invent, make, mould, shape, work **2.** coin, copy, counterfeit, fake, falsify, feign, imitate

forger coiner, counterfeiter, falsifier

forgery 1. counterfeit, fake, falsification, imitation, phoney *or esp. U.S.* phony *(informal)*, sham **2.** coining, counterfeiting, falsification, fraudulence, fraudulent imitation

forget 1. consign to oblivion, dismiss from one's mind, let bygones be bygones, let slip from the memory **2.** leave behind, lose sight of, omit, overlook

forgetful absent-minded, apt to forget, careless, dreamy, heedless, inattentive, lax, neglectful, negligent, oblivious, slapdash, slipshod, unmindful

forgive absolve, accept (someone's) apology, acquit, bear no malice, condone, excuse, exonerate, let bygones be bygones, let off *(informal)*, pardon, remit

forgiveness absolution, acquittal, amnesty, condonation, exoneration, mercy, overlooking, pardon, remission

forgiving clement, compassionate, forbearing, humane, lenient, magnanimous, merciful, mild, softhearted, tolerant

forgo, forego abandon, abjure, cede, do without, give up, kick *(informal)*, leave alone *or* out, relinquish, renounce, resign, sacrifice, surrender, waive, yield

forgotten blotted out, buried, bygone, consigned to oblivion, gone (clean) out of one's mind, left behind *or* out, lost, obliterated, omitted, past, past recall, unremembered

fork *vb.* bifurcate, branch, branch off, diverge, divide, go separate ways, part, split

forked angled, bifurcate(d), branched, branching, divided, pronged, split, tined, zigzag

forlorn abandoned, bereft, cheerless, comfortless, deserted, desolate, destitute, disconsolate, forgotten, forsaken, friendless, helpless, homeless, hopeless, lonely, lost, miserable, pathetic, pitiable, pitiful, unhappy, woebegone, wretched

form *n.* **1.** appearance, cast, configuration, construction, cut, fashion, formation, model, mould, pattern, shape, stamp, structure **2.** anatomy, being, body, build, figure, frame, outline, person, physique, shape, silhouette **3.** arrangement, character, description, design, guise, kind, manifestation, manner, method, mode, order, practice, semblance, sort, species, stamp, style, system, type, variety, way **4.** condition, fettle, fitness, good condition, good spirits, health, shape, trim **5.** application, document, paper, sheet **6.** class, grade, rank **7.** behaviour, ceremony, conduct, convention, custom, done thing, etiquette, formality, manners, procedure, protocol, ritual, rule **8.** format, framework, harmony, order, orderliness, organization, plan, proportion, structure, symmetry *~vb.* **9.** arrange, combine, design, dispose, draw up, frame, organize, pattern, plan, think up **10.** accumulate, appear, become visible, come into being, crystallize, grow, materialize, rise, settle, show up *(informal)*, take shape **11.** assemble, bring about, build, concoct, construct, contrive, create, devise, establish, fabricate, fashion, forge, found, invent, make, manufacture, model, mould, produce, put together, set up, shape, stamp **12.** bring up, discipline, educate, in-

cocktail frocks. **4** methodical and organized: *a formal approach.* **5** (of education and training) given officially at a school, college, etc.: *he had no formal training in maths.* **6** symmetrical in form: *a formal garden.* **7** relating to the form or structure of something as distinguished from its substance or content: *they addressed the formal elements of the structure of police work.* **8** *Philosophy* logically deductive rather than based on facts and observation. **formally** *adv*

formaldehyde (for-**mal**-de-hide) *n* a colourless poisonous strong-smelling gas, used as formalin and in synthetic resins. Also: **methanal**

formalin *n* a solution of formaldehyde in water, used as a disinfectant and as a preservative for biological specimens.

formalism *n* concerned with outward appearances and structure at the expense of content. **formalist** *n*

formality *n, pl* **-ties** **1** something done as a requirement of custom or good manners: *he dealt with the formalities regarding the cremation.* **2** a necessary procedure without real effect: *trials were often a mere formality with the verdict decided beforehand.* **3** strict observance of ceremony.

formalize *or* **-ise** *vb* **-izing, -ized** *or* **-ising, -ised** **1** to make official or valid. **2** to give a definite form to. **formalization** *or* **-isation** *n*

format *n* **1** the shape, size, and general appearance of a publication. **2** style or arrangement, such as of a television programme: *a chat-show format.* **3** *Computers* the arrangement of data on disk or magnetic tape to comply with a computer's input device. *~vb* **-matting, -matted** **4** to arrange in a specified format.

formation *n* **1** the act of having or taking form or existence. **2** something that is formed. **3** the manner in which something is arranged. **4** an arrangement of people or things acting as a unit, such as a troop of soldiers. **5** a series of rocks or clouds of a particular structure or shape.

formative *adj* **1** of or relating to formation, development, or growth: *formative years at school.* **2** shaping or moulding: *the formative influence on his life.*

former *adj* **1** belonging to or occurring in an earlier time: *a grotesque parody of a former greatness.* **2** having been at a previous time: *the former prime minister.* *~n* **3** **the former** the first or first mentioned of two.

formerly *adv* in the past.

Formica *n Trademark* a hard laminated plastic used esp. for heat-resistant surfaces.

formic acid *n* an acid derived from ants.

formidable *adj* **1** frightening because very difficult to deal with or overcome: *the Finnish winter presents formidable problems to drivers.* **2** extremely impressive: *a formidable Juventus squad.* **formidably** *adv*

formless *adj* without a definite shape or form.

formula (**form**-yew-la) *n, pl* **-las** *or* **-lae** (-lee) **1** a group of letters, numbers, or other symbols which represents a mathematical or scientific rule. **2** a plan or set of rules for doing or producing something: *a formula for peace in the Middle East.* **3** an established form of words, as used in religious ceremonies, legal proceedings, etc. **4** *US & Canad* a powder used to make a milky drink for babies. **5** *Motor racing* the category in which a car competes, judged according to engine size. **formulaic** *adj*

formulary *n, pl* **-laries** a book of prescribed formulas.

formulate *vb* **-lating, -lated** **1** to express in a formula. **2** to plan or describe precisely and clearly: *formulating plans for a Scottish super league.* **formulation** *n*

fornicate *vb* **-cating, -cated** to have sexual intercourse without being married. **fornicator** *n*

fornication *n* voluntary sexual intercourse outside marriage.

forsake *vb* **-saking, -sook, -saken** **1** to withdraw support or friendship from. **2** to give up (something valued or enjoyed).

forsooth *adv Old-fashioned* in truth or indeed.

forswear *vb* **-swearing, -swore, -sworn** **1** to reject or renounce with determination. **2** to testify falsely in a court of law.

forsythia (for-**syth**-ee-a) *n* a shrub with yellow flowers which appear in spring before the leaves.

fort *n* **1** a fortified building or position. **2** **hold the fort** *Informal* to keep things in operation during someone's absence.

forte[1] (**for**-tay) *n* something at which a person excels: *cooking is his forte.*

forte[2] *adv Music* loudly.

THESAURUS

struct, rear, school, teach, train **13.** acquire, contract, cultivate, develop, get into (*informal*), pick up **14.** compose, comprise, constitute, make, make up, serve as

formal **1.** approved, ceremonial, explicit, express, fixed, lawful, legal, methodical, official, prescribed, *pro forma,* regular, rigid, ritualistic, set, solemn, strict **2.** affected, aloof, ceremonious, conventional, correct, exact, precise, prim, punctilious, reserved, starched, stiff, unbending

formality **1.** ceremony, convention, conventionality, custom, form, gesture, matter of form, procedure, red tape, rite, ritual **2.** ceremoniousness, correctness, decorum, etiquette, politesse, protocol

formation **1.** accumulation, compilation, composition, constitution, crystallization, development, establishment, evolution, forming, generation, genesis, manufacture, organization, production **2.** arrangement, configuration, design, disposition, figure, grouping, pattern, rank, structure

formative **1.** impressionable, malleable, mouldable, pliant, sensitive, susceptible **2.** determinative, developmental, influential, moulding, shaping

former *adj.* **1.** antecedent, anterior, earlier, erstwhile, ex-, late, one-time, previous, prior, quondam (*formal*) **2.** ancient, bygone, departed, long ago, long gone, of yore, old, old-time, past *~n.* **3.** above, aforementioned, aforesaid, first mentioned, foregoing, preceding

formerly aforetime (*archaic*), already, at one time, before, heretofore, lately, once, previously

formidable **1.** appalling, baleful, dangerous, daunting, dismaying, dreadful, fearful, frightful, horrible, intimidating, menacing, shocking, terrifying, threatening **2.** awesome, great, impressive, indomitable, mighty, powerful, puissant, redoubtable, terrific, tremendous

formula **1.** form of words, formulary, rite, ritual, rubric **2.** blueprint, method, modus operandi, precept, prescription, principle, procedure, recipe, rule, way

formulate **1.** codify, define, detail, express, frame, give form to, particularize, set down, specify, systematize **2.** coin, develop, devise, evolve, forge, invent, map out, originate, plan, work out

forsake **1.** abandon, cast off, desert, disown, jettison, jilt, leave, leave in the lurch, quit, repudiate, throw over **2.** abdicate, forgo, forswear, give up, have done with, kick (*informal*), relinquish, renounce, set aside, surrender, turn one's back on, yield

fort **1.** blockhouse, camp, castle, citadel, fastness, fortification, fortress, garrison, redoubt, station, stronghold **2.** **hold the fort** carry on, keep things moving,

forth *adv* **1** *Formal or old-fashioned* forward, out, or away: *running back and forth across the street; Christopher Columbus set forth on his epic voyage of discovery.* **2 and so forth** and so on.

forthcoming *adj* **1** about to appear or happen: *the forthcoming elections.* **2** given or made available. **3** (of a person) willing to give information.

forthright *adj* direct and outspoken.

forthwith *adv* at once.

fortification *n* **1** the act of fortifying. **2 fortifications** walls, mounds, etc., used to strengthen the defences of a place.

fortified wine *n* wine mixed with a small amount of brandy or alcohol, such as port or sherry.

fortify *vb* **-fies, -fying, -fied 1** to make (a place) defensible, such as by building walls. **2** to strengthen physically, mentally, or morally: *the news fortified their resolve to succeed.* **3** to increase the nutritious value of (a food), such as by adding vitamins.

fortissimo *adv Music* very loudly.

fortitude *n* calm and patient courage in trouble or pain.

fortnight *n* a period of 14 consecutive days.

fortnightly *Chiefly Brit* ~*adj* **1** occurring or appearing once each fortnight. ~*adv* **2** once a fortnight.

FORTRAN *n* a high-level computer programming language designed for mathematical and scientific purposes.

fortress *n* a large fort or fortified town.

fortuitous (for-**tyew**-it-uss) *adj* happening by chance, esp. by a lucky chance. **fortuitously** *adv*

fortunate *adj* **1** having good luck. **2** occurring by good luck. **fortunately** *adv*

fortune *n* **1** luck, esp. when favourable. **2** a person's destiny. **3** a power regarded as being responsible for human affairs. **4** wealth or material prosperity.

fortune-teller *n* a person who claims to predict events in other people's lives.

forty *n, pl* **-ties 1** the cardinal number that is the product of ten and four. **2** a numeral, 40 or XL, representing this number. **3** something representing or consisting of 40 units. ~*adj* **4** amounting to forty: *forty pages.* **fortieth** *adj, n*

forty winks *n Informal* a short light sleep.

forum *n* **1** a meeting or medium for the open discussion of subjects of public interest. **2** (in ancient Roman cities) an open space serving as a marketplace and centre of public business.

forward *adj* **1** directed or moving ahead. **2** at, in, or near the front. **3** overfamiliar or disrespectful. **4** well developed or advanced. **5** of or relating to the future or favouring change. ~*n* **6** an attacking player in any of various sports, such as soccer. ~*adv* **7** same as **forwards**. ~*vb* **8** to send (a letter, etc.) on to an ultimate destination. **9** to advance or promote: *the veneer of street credibility he had used to forward his career.*

forwards *or* **forward** *adv* **1** towards or at a place ahead or in advance, esp. in space but also in time. **2** towards the front.

fosse *or* **foss** *n* a ditch or moat, esp. one dug as a fortification.

fossick *vb Austral & NZ* **1** to search for gold or precious stones in abandoned workings, rivers, etc. **2** to search for (something).

fossil *n* **1** remains of a plant or animal that existed in a past geological age, occurring in the form of mineralized bones, shells, etc. ~*adj* **2** of, like, or being a fossil.

fossil fuel *n* fuel, such as coal or oil, formed from the decayed remains of prehistoric animals and plants.

fossilize *or* **-ise** *vb* **-izing, -ized** *or* **-ising, -ised 1** to convert or be converted into a fossil. **2** to become out-of-date or inflexible: *fossilized political attitudes.*

foster *adj* **1** of or involved in the bringing up of a

THESAURUS

keep things on an even keel, maintain the status quo, stand in, take over the reins

forte gift, long suit (*informal*), métier, speciality, strength, strong point, talent

forth ahead, away, forward, into the open, onward, out, out of concealment, outward

forthcoming 1. approaching, coming, expected, future, imminent, impending, prospective, upcoming **2.** accessible, at hand, available, in evidence, obtainable, on tap (*informal*), ready **3.** chatty, communicative, expansive, free, informative, open, sociable, talkative, unreserved

forthright above-board, blunt, candid, direct, downright, frank, open, outspoken, plain-spoken, straightforward, straight from the shoulder (*informal*), upfront (*informal*)

forthwith at once, directly, immediately, instantly, quickly, right away, straightaway, *tout de suite*, without delay

fortification 1. embattlement, reinforcement, strengthening **2.** *plural* bastion, bulwark, castle, citadel, defence, fastness, fort, fortress, keep, protection, stronghold

fortify 1. augment, brace, buttress, embattle, garrison, protect, reinforce, secure, shore up, strengthen, support **2.** brace, cheer, confirm, embolden, encourage, hearten, invigorate, reassure, stiffen, strengthen, sustain

fortitude backbone, braveness, courage, determination, endurance, fearlessness, firmness, grit, guts (*informal*), intrepidity, patience, perseverance, pluck, resolution, staying power, stoutheartedness, strength, strength of mind, valour

fortress castle, citadel, fastness, fort, redoubt, stronghold

fortunate 1. born with a silver spoon in one's mouth, bright, favoured, golden, happy, having a charmed life, in luck, jammy (*Brit. slang*), lucky, prosperous, rosy, sitting pretty (*informal*), successful, well-off **2.** advantageous, auspicious, convenient, encouraging, expedient, favourable, felicitous, fortuitous, helpful, opportune, profitable, promising, propitious, providential, timely

fortunately by a happy chance, by good luck, happily, luckily, providentially

fortune 1. accident, chance, contingency, destiny, fate, fortuity, hazard, kismet, luck, providence **2.** affluence, big bucks (*informal, chiefly U.S.*), big money, gold mine, megabucks (*U.S. & Canad. slang*), opulence, possessions, pretty penny (*informal*), property, prosperity, riches, tidy sum (*informal*), treasure, wad (*U.S. & Canad. slang*), wealth

forward *adj.* **1.** advance, first, fore, foremost, front, head, leading **2.** assuming, bare-faced, bold, brash, brass-necked (*Brit. informal*), brazen, brazen-faced, cheeky, confident, familiar, fresh (*informal*), impertinent, impudent, overassertive, overweening, pert, presuming, presumptuous, pushy (*informal*), sassy (*U.S. informal*) **3.** advanced, advancing, early, forward-looking, onward, precocious, premature, progressive, well-developed ~*adv.* **4.** *Also* **forwards** ahead, forth, on, onward ~*vb.* **5.** dispatch, freight, post, route, send, send on, ship, transmit **6.** advance, aid, assist, back,

child not one's own: *foster care.* ~*vb* **2** to bring up (a child not one's own). **3** to promote the growth or development of: *Catherine fostered knowledge and patronized the arts.* **fostering** *n*

fought *vb* the past of **fight.**

foul *adj* **1** offensive or loathsome: *a foul deed.* **2** stinking or dirty. **3** full of dirt or offensive matter. **4** (of language) obscene or vulgar. **5** unfair: *by fair or foul means.* **6** (of weather) unpleasant. **7** very bad-tempered and irritable: *he was in a foul mood.* **8** *Informal* disgustingly bad. ~*n* **9** *Sport* a violation of the rules. ~*vb* **10** to make dirty or polluted. **11** to make or become entangled. **12** to make or become clogged. **13** *Sport* to commit a foul against (an opponent). ~*adv* **14** **fall foul of** to come into conflict with.

foul-mouthed *adj* habitually using swearwords and bad language.

foul play *n* **1** violent activity esp. murder. **2** a violation of the rules in a game.

foul up *vb* **1** *Informal* to mismanage or bungle. **2** to contaminate. **3** to block or choke. ~*n* **foul-up** **4** a state of disorder resulting from mistakes or carelessness: *a foul-up by their computers.*

found[1] *vb* the past of **find.**

found[2] *vb* **1** to bring into being or establish (something, such as an institution). **2** to lay the foundation of. **3** **founded on** to have a basis in: *a political system founded on fear.* **founder** *n* **founding** *adj*

found[3] *vb* **1** to cast (metal or glass) by melting and pouring into a mould. **2** to make (articles) in this way. **founder** *n*

foundation *n* **1** the basic experience, idea, or attitude on which a way of life or belief is based: *respect for the law is the foundation of commercial society.* **2** a construction below the ground that distributes the load of a building, wall, etc. **3** the base on which something stands. **4** the act of founding. **5** an endowment for the support of an institution, such as a college. **6** an institution supported by an endowment. **7** a cosmetic used as a base for make-up.

foundation stone *n* a stone laid at a ceremony to mark the foundation of a new building.

founder *vb* **1** to break down or fail: *his negotiations have foundered on economic grounds.* **2** (of a ship) to sink. **3** to sink into or become stuck in soft ground. **4** (of a horse) to stumble or go lame.

foundling *n* an abandoned baby whose parents are not known.

foundry *n, pl* **-ries** a place where metal is melted and cast.

fount[1] *n* **1** *Poetic* a spring or fountain. **2** a source or supply: *a fount of knowledge.*

fount[2] *n* *Printing* a complete set of type of one style and size.

fountain *n* **1** an ornamental feature in a pool or lake consisting of a jet of water forced into the air by a pump. **2** a jet or spray of water. **3** a natural spring of water. **4** a source or supply: *a fountain of many new ideas about the causes of cancer.* **5** a cascade of sparks, lava, etc.

fountainhead *n* a principal or original source.

fountain pen *n* a pen supplied with ink from a container inside it.

four *n* **1** the cardinal number that is the sum of one and three. **2** a numeral, 4 or IV, representing this number. **3** something representing or consisting of four units. **4** *Cricket* a score of four runs, obtained by hitting the ball so that it crosses the boundary after hitting the ground. **5** *Rowing* **a** a rowing boat propelled by four oarsmen. **b** the crew of such a rowing boat. ~*adj* **6** amounting to four: *four zones.*

fourfold *adj* **1** having four times as many or as much. **2** composed of four parts. ~*adv* **3** by four times as many or as much.

four-in-hand *n* a carriage drawn by four horses and driven by one driver.

four-letter word *n* any of several short English words referring to sex or excrement: regarded generally as offensive or obscene.

four-poster *n* a bed with posts at each corner supporting a canopy and curtains.

fourscore *adj* *Old-fashioned* eighty.

foursome *n* **1** a group of four people. **2** *Golf* a game between two pairs of players.

foursquare *adv* **1** squarely or firmly. ~*adj* **2** solid and strong. **3** forthright and uncompromising.

four-stroke *adj* designating an internal-combustion engine in which the piston makes four strokes for every explosion.

fourteen *n* **1** the cardinal number that is the sum of ten and four. **2** a numeral, 14 or XIV, representing this number. **3** something representing or consisting of 14

THESAURUS

encourage, expedite, favour, foster, further, hasten, help, hurry, promote, speed, support

foster **1.** bring up, mother, nurse, raise, rear, take care of **2.** cultivate, encourage, feed, foment, nurture, promote, stimulate, support, uphold

foul *adj.* **1.** abhorrent, abominable, base, despicable, detestable, disgraceful, dishonourable, egregious, hateful, heinous, infamous, iniquitous, nefarious, notorious, offensive, scandalous, shameful, shitty (*taboo slang*), vicious, vile, wicked **2.** contaminated, dirty, disgusting, fetid, filthy, grotty (*slang*), grungy (*slang, chiefly U.S.*), impure, loathsome, malodorous, mephitic, nasty, nauseating, noisome, offensive, olid, polluted, putrid, rank, repulsive, revolting, rotten, scuzzy (*slang, chiefly U.S.*), squalid, stinking, sullied, tainted, unclean, yucky *or* yukky (*slang*) **3.** abusive, blasphemous, blue, coarse, dirty, filthy, foul-mouthed, gross, indecent, lewd, low, obscene, profane, scatological, scurrilous, smutty, vulgar **4.** crooked, dirty, dishonest, fraudulent, inequitable, shady (*informal*), underhand, unfair, unjust, unscrupulous, unsportsmanlike **5.** bad, blustery, disagreeable, foggy, murky, rainy, rough, stormy, wet, wild ~*vb.* **6.** begrime, besmear, besmirch, contaminate, defile, dirty, pollute, smear, smirch, soil, stain, sully, taint **7.** block, catch, choke, clog, ensnare, entangle, jam, snarl, twist

foul play chicanery, corruption, crime, deception, dirty work, double-dealing, duplicity, fraud, perfidy, sharp practice, skulduggery, treachery, villainy

found **1.** bring into being, constitute, construct, create, endow, erect, establish, fix, inaugurate, institute, organize, originate, plant, raise, settle, set up, start **2.** **founded on** based on, built on, grounded on, rooted in, sustained by

foundation **1.** base, basis, bedrock, bottom, footing, groundwork, substructure, underpinning **2.** endowment, establishment, inauguration, institution, organization, setting up, settlement

founder *vb.* **1.** abort, break down, collapse, come to grief, come to nothing, fail, fall through, go belly-up (*slang*), go down like a lead balloon (*informal*), miscarry, misfire **2.** be lost, go down, go to the bottom, sink, submerge **3.** collapse, fall, go lame, lurch, sprawl, stagger, stumble, trip

foundling orphan, outcast, stray, waif

fountain **1.** font, fount, jet, reservoir, spout, spray,

units. *~adj* **4** amounting to fourteen: *fourteen points.* **fourteenth** *adj, n*

fourth *adj* **1** of or being number four in a series. **2** denoting the highest forward gear in a motor vehicle. *~n* **3** the highest forward gear in a motor vehicle.

fourth dimension *n* **1** the dimension of time, which in addition to three spatial dimensions specifies the position of a point or particle. **2** the concept in science fiction of an extra dimension. **fourth-dimensional** *adj*

fourth estate *n* the press.

fowl *n* **1** a domesticated bird such as a hen. **2** any other bird that is used as food or hunted as game. **3** the meat of fowl. **4** *Old-fashioned* a bird. *~vb* **5** to hunt or snare wild birds.

fox *n, pl* **foxes** *or* **fox** **1** a doglike wild animal with a pointed muzzle and a bushy tail. **2** its reddish-brown or grey fur. **3** a person who is cunning and sly. *~vb* **4** *Informal* to confuse or puzzle.

foxglove *n* a tall plant with purple or white flowers.

foxhole *n Mil* a small pit dug to provide shelter against enemy fire.

foxhound *n* a breed of short-haired terrier, originally kept for hunting foxes.

fox-hunting *n* the activity of hunting foxes with hounds.

foxtrot *n* **1** a ballroom dance with slow and quick steps. **2** music for this. *~vb* **-trotting, -trotted** **3** to perform this dance.

foxy *adj* **foxier, foxiest** **1** of or resembling a fox, esp. in craftiness. **2** reddish-brown. **foxily** *adv* **foxiness** *n*

foyer (**foy**-ay) *n* an entrance hall in a hotel, theatre, or cinema.

fp forte-piano.

FP **1** fire plug. **2** freezing point

Fr **1** *Christianity* **a** Father. **b** Frater. **2** *Chem* francium.

fr. **1** franc. **2** from.

fracas (**frak**-ah) *n* a noisy quarrel or fight.

fraction *n* **1** *Maths* a numerical quantity that is not a whole number. **2** any part or subdivision. **3** a very small proportion or amount of something. **4** *Chem* a component of a mixture separated by distillation. **fractional** *adj* **fractionally** *adv*

fractional distillation *or* **fractionation** *n Chem* the process of separating the constituents of a liquid mixture by heating it and condensing the components separately according to their different boiling points.

fractious *adj* (esp. of children) easily upset and angered, often due to tiredness.

fracture *n* **1** breaking, esp. the breaking or cracking of a bone. *~vb* **-turing, -tured** **2** to break. **fractural** *adj*

fragile *adj* **1** able to be broken or damaged easily. **2** in a weakened physical state: *you're looking a bit fragile this morning.* **fragility** *n*

fragment *n* **1** a piece broken off. **2** an incomplete piece: *fragments of information.* *~vb* **3** to break into small pieces or different parts. **fragmentation** *n*

fragmentary *adj* made up of small or unconnected pieces: *fragmentary evidence to support his theory.*

fragrance *n* **1** a pleasant smell. **2** a perfume or scent.

fragrant *adj* having a pleasant smell.

frail *adj* **1** physically weak and delicate. **2** easily damaged: *the frail aircraft.* **3** easily tempted.

frailty *n* **1** physical or moral weakness. **2** (*pl* **-ties**) an inadequacy or fault resulting from moral weakness.

frame *n* **1** an open structure that gives shape and support to something, such as a building. **2** an enclosing case or border into which something is fitted: *the window frame.* **3** the system around which something is built up: *caught up in the frame of the revolution.* **4** the structure of the human body. **5** one of a series of exposures on film used in making motion pictures. **6** a television picture scanned by electron beams at a particular frequency. **7** *Snooker* **a** a single game in a match. **b** a wooden triangle used to arrange the red balls in formation before the start of a game. **8** short for **cold frame.** **9** *Slang* a frame-up. **10** **frame of mind** a state of mind: *in a complacent frame of mind.* *~vb* **framing, framed** **11** to construct by fitting parts together. **12** to create and develop (plans or a policy). **13** to construct (a statement) in a particular kind of language. **14** to provide or enclose with a frame. **15** *Slang* to conspire to incriminate (someone) on a false charge.

frame of reference *n* **1** a set of standards that determines behaviour. **2** any set of planes or curves, such as the three coordinate axes, used to locate a point in space.

THESAURUS

spring, well **2.** beginning, cause, commencement, derivation, fount, fountainhead, genesis, origin, rise, source, wellhead, wellspring

foxy artful, astute, canny, crafty, cunning, devious, guileful, knowing, sharp, shrewd, sly, tricky, wily

foyer antechamber, anteroom, entrance hall, lobby, reception area, vestibule

fracas affray (*Law*), aggro (*slang*), brawl, disturbance, fight, free-for-all (*informal*), melee, quarrel, riot, row, rumpus, scrimmage, scuffle, shindig (*informal*), shindy (*informal*), skirmish, trouble, uproar

fractious awkward, captious, crabby, cross, fretful, froward, grouchy (*informal*), irritable, peevish, pettish, petulant, querulous, ratty (*Brit. & N.Z. informal*), refractory, testy, tetchy, touchy, unruly

fracture **1.** *n.* breach, break, cleft, crack, fissure, gap, opening, rent, rift, rupture, schism, split **2.** *vb.* break, crack, rupture, splinter, split

fragile breakable, brittle, dainty, delicate, feeble, fine, flimsy, frail, frangible, infirm, slight, weak

fragment **1.** *n.* bit, chip, fraction, morsel, oddment, part, particle, piece, portion, remnant, scrap, shiver, sliver **2.** *vb.* break, break up, come apart, come to pieces, crumble, disintegrate, disunite, divide, shatter, shiver, splinter, split, split up

fragmentary bitty, broken, disconnected, discrete, disjointed, incoherent, incomplete, partial, piecemeal, scattered, scrappy, sketchy, unsystematic

fragrance aroma, balm, bouquet, fragrancy, perfume, redolence, scent, smell, sweet odour

fragrant ambrosial, aromatic, balmy, odoriferous, odorous, perfumed, redolent, sweet-scented, sweet-smelling

frail breakable, brittle, decrepit, delicate, feeble, flimsy, fragile, frangible, infirm, insubstantial, puny, slight, tender, unsound, vulnerable, weak, wispy

frailty **1.** fallibility, feebleness, frailness, infirmity, peccability, puniness, susceptibility, weakness **2.** blemish, defect, deficiency, failing, fault, flaw, foible, imperfection, peccadillo, shortcoming, vice, weak point

frame *n.* **1.** casing, construction, fabric, form, framework, scheme, shell, structure, system **2.** mount, mounting, setting **3.** anatomy, body, build, carcass, morphology, physique, skeleton **4. frame of mind** attitude, disposition, fettle, humour, mood, outlook, spirit, state, temper *~vb.* **5.** assemble, build, constitute, construct, fabricate, fashion, forge, form, institute, invent, make, manufacture, model, mould, put together, set up **6.** block out, compose, conceive, concoct, contrive, cook up, devise, draft, draw up, form, formulate,

frame-up *n Slang* a conspiracy to incriminate someone on a false charge.

framework *n* **1** a particular set of beliefs, ideas, or rules referred to in order to solve a problem: *a moral framework.* **2** a structure supporting something.

franc *n* the standard monetary unit of France, Switzerland, Belgium, and various African countries.

franchise *n* **1** the right to vote, esp. for a member of parliament. **2** any exemption, privilege, or right granted by a public authority. **3** *Commerce* authorization granted to a distributor to sell a company's goods. ~*vb* **-chising, -chised 4** *Commerce chiefly US & Canad* to grant (a person, firm, etc.) a franchise.

Franciscan *n* **1** a member of a Christian religious order of friars or nuns founded by Saint Francis of Assisi. ~*adj* **2** of this order.

francium *n Chem* an unstable radioactive element of the alkali-metal group. Symbol: Fr

Franco- *combining form* indicating France or French: *the Franco-Prussian war.*

frank *adj* **1** honest and straightforward in speech or attitude. ~*vb* **2** *Chiefly Brit* to put a mark on (a letter), ensuring free carriage. ~*n* **3** an official mark stamped to a letter ensuring free delivery. **frankly** *adv* **frankness** *n*

Frank *n* a member of the West Germanic peoples who in the late 4th century AD gradually conquered most of Gaul.

Frankenstein *n* a creation or monster that brings disaster and is beyond the control of its creator. Also called: **Frankenstein's monster**

frankfurter *n* a smoked sausage of pork or beef.

frankincense *n* an aromatic gum resin burnt as incense.

Frankish *n* **1** the ancient West Germanic language of the Franks. ~*adj* **2** of the Franks or their language.

frantic *adj* **1** distracted with fear, pain, joy, etc. **2** hurried and disorganized: *frantic activity.* **frantically** *adv*

frappé *adj* (esp. of drinks) chilled.

fraternal *adj* **1** of a brother; brotherly. **2** designating twins that developed from two separate fertilized ova. **fraternally** *adv*

fraternity *n, pl* **-ties 1** a body of people united in interests, aims, etc. **2** friendship between groups of people. **3** *US & Canad* a society of male students.

fraternize *or* **-nise** *vb* **-nizing, -nized** *or* **-nising, -nised** to associate on friendly terms: *fraternizing with the customers is off-limits.* **fraternization** *or* **-nisation** *n*

fratricide *n* **1** the act of killing one's brother. **2** a person who kills his or her brother. **fratricidal** *adj*

Frau (rhymes with **how**) *n, pl* **Frauen** *or* **Fraus** a German form of address equivalent to *Mrs* or *Ms.*

fraud *n* **1** deliberate deception or cheating intended to gain an advantage. **2** an act of such deception. **3** *Informal* a person who acts in a false or deceitful way.

fraudster *n* a person who commits a fraud; swindler.

fraudulent *adj* **1** acting with intent to deceive. **2** proceeding from fraud. **fraudulence** *n*

fraught (**frawt**) *adj* **1 fraught with** involving or filled with: *we expected the trip to be fraught with difficulties.* **2** tense or anxious.

Fräulein (**froy**-line) *n, pl* **-lein** *or* **-leins** a German form of address equivalent to *Miss.*

fray[1] *n* **1** a noisy quarrel or brawl. **2 the fray** any challenging conflict: *Woosnam returned to the fray with a win over Stadler.*

fray[2] *vb* **1** to wear away into loose threads, esp. at an edge. **2** to make or become strained or irritated.

frazil (**fray**-zil) *n* small pieces of ice that form in water moving turbulently enough to prevent the formation of a sheet of ice.

frazzle *n Informal* the state of being exhausted: *worn to a frazzle.*

freak *n* **1** a person, animal, or plant that is abnormal or deformed. **2** an object, event, etc., that is abnormal: *a statistical freak.* **3** *Informal* a person whose appearance or behaviour is very unusual. **4** *Informal* a person who is very enthusiastic about something specified: *a health freak.* ~*adj* **5** abnormal or unusual: *a freak accident.* **freakish** *adj* **freaky** *adj*

THESAURUS

hatch, map out, plan, shape, sketch **7.** case, enclose, mount, surround

frame-up fabrication, fit-up (*slang*), put-up job, trumped-up charge

framework core, fabric, foundation, frame, frame of reference, groundwork, plan, schema, shell, skeleton, structure, the bare bones

franchise authorization, charter, exemption, freedom, immunity, prerogative, privilege, right, suffrage, vote

frank artless, blunt, candid, direct, downright, forthright, free, honest, ingenuous, open, outright, outspoken, plain, plain-spoken, sincere, straightforward, straight from the shoulder (*informal*), transparent, truthful, unconcealed, undisguised, unreserved, unrestricted, upfront (*informal*)

frankly bluntly, candidly, directly, freely, honestly, in truth, openly, overtly, plainly, straight, to be honest, without reserve

frankness absence of reserve, bluntness, candour, forthrightness, ingenuousness, openness, outspokenness, plain speaking, truthfulness

frantic at one's wits' end, berserk, beside oneself, desperate, distracted, distraught, fraught (*informal*), frenetic, frenzied, furious, hectic, mad, overwrought, raging, raving, uptight (*informal*), wild

fraternity association, brotherhood, camaraderie, circle, clan, club, companionship, company, comradeship, fellowship, guild, kinship, league, order, set, sodality, union

fraternize associate, concur, consort, cooperate, go around with, hang out (*informal*), hobnob, keep company, mingle, mix, socialize, sympathize, unite

fraud **1.** artifice, canard, cheat, chicane, chicanery, craft, deceit, deception, double-dealing, duplicity, guile, hoax, humbug, imposture, scam (*slang*), sharp practice, spuriousness, sting (*informal*), stratagems, swindling, treachery, trickery **2.** bluffer, charlatan, cheat, counterfeit, double-dealer, fake, forgery, hoax, hoaxer, impostor, mountebank, phoney *or esp. U.S.* phony (*informal*), pretender, quack, sham, swindler

fraudulent counterfeit, crafty, criminal, crooked (*informal*), deceitful, deceptive, dishonest, double-dealing, duplicitous, false, knavish, phoney *or esp. U.S* phony (*informal*), sham, spurious, swindling, treacherous

fray *vb.* become threadbare, chafe, fret, rub, wear, wear away, wear thin

freak *n.* **1.** aberration, abnormality, abortion, anomaly, grotesque, malformation, monster, monstrosity, mutant, oddity, queer fish (*Brit. informal*), weirdo (*informal*) **2.** caprice, crotchet, fad, fancy, folly, humour, irregularity, quirk, turn, twist, vagary, whim, whimsy **3.** *slang* addict, aficionado, buff (*informal*), devotee, enthusiast, fan, fanatic, fiend (*informal*), nut (*slang*) ~*adj.* **4.** aberrant, abnormal, atypical, bizarre, erratic,

freak out *vb Informal* to be or cause to be in a heightened emotional state.

freckle *n* **1** a small brownish spot on the skin. *~vb* **-ling, -led 2** to mark or become marked with freckles. **freckled** *adj*

free *adj* **freer, freest 1** able to act at will; not under compulsion or restraint. **2** not enslaved or confined. **3** (of a country) independent. **4** (of a translation) not exact or literal. **5** provided without charge: *free school meals.* **6** not occupied or in use; available: *is this seat free?* **7** (of a person) not busy. **8** open or available to all. **9** not fixed or joined; loose: *the free end.* **10** without obstruction or blockage: *the free flow of capital.* **11** *Chem* chemically uncombined: *free nitrogen.* **12** **free and easy** casual or tolerant. **13 free from** not subject to: *free from surveillance.* **14 free with** using or giving (something) a lot: *he was free with his tongue.* **15 make free with** to behave too familiarly towards. *~adv* **16** in a free manner. **17** without charge or cost. *~vb* **freeing, freed 18** to release or liberate. **19** to remove obstructions or impediments from. **20** to make available or usable: *capital freed by the local authority.* **21 free of** *or* **from** to relieve or rid of (obstacles, pain, etc.). **freely** *adv*

➤ *Free of* means "not subject to": *free of charge. Free from* suggests a change of circumstances: *They were free from danger.*

-free *adj combining form* free from: *duty-free; nuclear – free zones.*

freebie *n Slang* something provided without charge.

freeboard *n* the space or distance between the deck of a vessel and the water line.

freebooter *n* a pirate.

freeborn *adj History* not born in slavery.

Free Church *n Chiefly Brit* any Protestant Church other than the Established Church.

freedman *n, pl* **-men** *History* a man freed from slavery.

freedom *n* **1** the state of being free, esp. to enjoy political and civil liberties. **2** exemption or immunity: *freedom from government control.* **3** liberation, such as from slavery. **4** the right or privilege of unrestricted access: *freedom of the skies.* **5** self-government or independence. **6** the power to order one's own actions. **7** ease or frankness of manner.

free enterprise *n* an economic system in which commercial organizations compete for profit with little state control.

free fall *n* **1** the part of a parachute descent before the parachute opens. **2** free descent of a body in which gravity is the only force acting on it.

free-for-all *n Informal* a disorganized brawl or argument involving all those present.

free hand *n* **1** unrestricted freedom to act: *the president must be able to deal with foreign hostilities with a free hand. ~adj, adv* **freehand 2** (done) by hand without the use of guiding instruments.

freehold *Property law ~n* **1** tenure of property for life without restrictions. *~adj* **2** of or held by freehold. **freeholder** *n*

free house *n Brit* a public house not bound to sell only one brewer's products.

free kick *n Soccer* an unopposed kick of the ball awarded for a foul or infringement.

freelance *n* **1** a self-employed person doing specific pieces of work for various employers. *~vb* **-lancing, -lanced 2** to work as a freelance. *~adj, adv* **3** of or as a freelance.

freeloader *n Slang* a person who habitually depends on others for food, accommodation, etc.

free love *n Old-fashioned* the practice of having sexual relationships outside marriage, often several relationships at the same time.

freeman *n, pl* **-men** a person who has been given the freedom of a city as an honour in return for public service.

free-market *adj* denoting an economic system which allows supply and demand to regulate prices and wages.

Freemason *n* a member of a widespread secret order whose members are pledged to help each other. Also called: **Mason Freemasonry** *n*

free-range *adj Chiefly Brit* kept or produced in natural conditions: *free-range eggs.*

freesia *n* a plant with fragrant tubular flowers.

free space *n* a region that has no gravitational and electromagnetic fields.

freestanding *adj* not attached to or supported by another object.

freestyle *n* **1** a competition, such as in swimming, in which each participant may use a style of his or her

THESAURUS

exceptional, fluky (*informal*), fortuitous, odd, queer, unaccountable, unexpected, unforeseen, unparalleled, unpredictable, unusual

free *adj.* **1.** at large, at liberty, footloose, independent, liberated, loose, off the hook (*slang*), on the loose, uncommitted, unconstrained, unengaged, unfettered, unrestrained **2.** autarchic, autonomous, democratic, emancipated, independent, self-governing, self-ruling, sovereign **3.** buckshee (*Brit. slang*), complimentary, for free (*informal*), for nothing, free of charge, gratis, gratuitous, on the house, unpaid, without charge **4.** able, allowed, clear, disengaged, loose, open, permitted, unattached, unengaged, unhampered, unimpeded, unobstructed, unregulated, unrestricted, untrammelled **5.** at leisure, available, empty, extra, idle, not tied down, spare, unemployed, uninhabited, unoccupied, unused, vacant **6.** *with* **from** above, beyond, deficient in, devoid of, exempt from, immune to, lacking (in), not liable to, safe from, unaffected by, unencumbered by, untouched by, without **7. free and easy** casual, easy-going, informal, laid-back (*informal*), lax, lenient, liberal, relaxed, tolerant, unceremonious *~adv.* **8.** abundantly, copiously, freely, idly, loosely **9.** at no cost, for love, gratis, without charge *~vb.* **10.** clear, cut loose, deliver, disengage, disentangle, exempt, extricate, ransom, redeem, relieve, rescue, rid, unburden, undo, unshackle **11.** deliver, discharge, disenthrall, emancipate, let go, let out, liberate, loose, manumit, release, set at liberty, set free, turn loose, unbridle, uncage, unchain, unfetter, unleash, untie

freedom 1. autonomy, deliverance, emancipation, home rule, independence, liberty, manumission, release, self-government **2.** exemption, immunity, impunity, privilege **3.** ability, blank cheque, carte blanche, discretion, elbowroom, facility, flexibility, free rein, latitude, leeway, licence, opportunity, play, power, range, scope **4.** abandon, candour, directness, ease, familiarity, frankness, informality, ingenuousness, lack of restraint *or* reserve, openness, unconstraint

free-for-all affray (*Law*), brawl, dust-up (*informal*), fight, fracas, melee, riot, row, scrimmage, shindig (*informal*), shindy (*informal*)

free hand *n.* authority, blank cheque, carte blanche, discretion, freedom, latitude, liberty, scope

freely 1. of one's own accord, of one's own free will, spontaneously, voluntarily, willingly, without prompting **2.** candidly, frankly, openly, plainly, unreservedly, without reserve **3.** as you please, unchallenged, without let or hindrance, without restraint **4.** abundantly, amply, bountifully, copiously, extravagantly, lavishly,

choice. **2** Also called: **all-in wrestling** a style of professional wrestling with no internationally agreed set of rules.

freethinker *n* a person who forms his or her ideas independently of authority, esp. in matters of religion.

free trade *n* international trade that is free of such government interference as protective tariffs.

free verse *n* unrhymed verse without a fixed rhythm.

freeway *n US* a motorway.

freewheel *vb* **1** to travel downhill on a bicycle without pedalling. **2** *~n* a device in the rear hub of a bicycle wheel that permits it to rotate freely while the pedals are stationary.

freewheeling *adj* behaving in a relaxed spontaneous manner, without any long-term plans or commitments: *he had to change his freewheeling lifestyle after his son was born.*

free will *n* **1** the ability to make a choice without outside coercion or pressure: *you walked in here of your own free will.* **2** *Philosophy* the belief that human behaviour is an expression of personal choice and is not determined by physical forces, Fate, or God.

Free World *n* the non-Communist countries collectively.

freeze *vb* **freezing, froze, frozen 1** to change from a liquid to a solid by the reduction of temperature, such as water to ice. **2** to preserve (food) by subjection to extreme cold. **3** to cover or become covered with ice. **4** to fix fast or become fixed (to something) because of frost. **5** to feel or cause to feel the effects of extreme cold. **6** to die of extreme cold. **7** to become motionless through fear, shock, etc. **8** to cause (moving film) to stop at a particular frame. **9** to fix (prices, incomes, etc.) at a particular level. **10** to forbid by law the exchange or collection of (loans, assets, etc.). *~n* **11** the act of freezing or state of being frozen. **12** *Meteorol* a spell of temperatures below freezing point. **13** the fixing of incomes, prices, etc., by legislation.

freeze-dry *vb* **-dries, -drying, -dried** to preserve (food) by rapid freezing and drying in a vacuum.

freeze out *vb* to prevent (someone) from being involved in an activity, conversation, etc., by being unfriendly or reserved.

freezer *n* an insulated cabinet for cold-storage of perishable foods.

freezing point *n* the temperature below which a liquid turns into a solid.

freezing works *n Austral & NZ* a slaughterhouse at which animal carcasses are frozen for export.

freight **(frate)** *n* **1 a** commercial transport of goods. **b** the cargo transported. **c** the cost of this. **2** *Chiefly Brit* a ship's cargo or part of it. *~vb* **3** to transport (goods) by freight. **4** to load with goods for transport.

freighter *n* a ship or aircraft designed for transporting cargo.

French *adj* **1** of France. *~n* **2** the official language of France and an official language of Switzerland, Belgium, Canada, and certain other countries. *~pl n* **3 the French** the people of France.

French beans *pl n* green beans, the pods of which are eaten.

French bread *n* white bread in a long, thin, crusty loaf.

French Canadian *n* a Canadian citizen whose native language is French.

French chalk *n* a variety of talc used to mark cloth or remove grease stains.

French dressing *n* a salad dressing made from oil and vinegar with seasonings.

French fries *pl n Chiefly US & Canad* potato chips.

French horn *n Music* a valved brass wind instrument with a coiled tube.

Frenchify *vb* **-fies, -fying, -fied** *Informal* to make or become French in appearance, etc.

French letter *n Brit slang* a condom.

Frenchman *or fem* **Frenchwoman** *n, pl* **-men** *or* **-women** a person from France.

French polish *n* a shellac varnish for wood, giving a high gloss.

French seam *n* a seam in which the edges are enclosed.

French windows *pl n Brit* a window extending to floor level, used as a door.

frenetic (frin-**net**-ik) *adj* wild, excited, and uncontrolled. **frenetically** *adv*

frenzy *n, pl* **-zies 1** violent or wild and uncontrollable behaviour. **2** excited or agitated activity: *a frenzy of speculation.* **frenzied** *adj*

Freon *n Trademark* any of a group of gas or liquid chemical compounds of methane with chlorine and fluorine: used in propellants, aerosols, and solvents.

frequency *n, pl* **-cies 1** the number of times that an event occurs within a given period. **2** the state of being frequent. **3** *Physics* the number of times a wave repeats itself in a given time.

frequency distribution *n* statistical data arranged to show the frequency with which the possible values of a variable occur.

frequency modulation *n* a method of transmitting information by varying the frequency of the carrier wave in accordance with the amplitude of the input signal.

frequent *adj* **1** happening often. **2** habitual. *~vb* **3** to visit often: *a spa town frequented by the Prussian nobility.* **frequently** *adv*

frequentative *Grammar ~adj* **1** denoting a verb or

THESAURUS

liberally, like water, open-handedly, unstintingly, with a free hand **5.** cleanly, easily, loosely, readily, smoothly

freethinker agnostic, deist, doubter, infidel, sceptic, unbeliever

freeze 1. benumb, chill, congeal, glaciate, harden, ice over *or* up, stiffen **2.** fix, hold up, inhibit, peg, stop, suspend

freight *n.* **1.** carriage, conveyance, shipment, transportation **2.** bales, bulk, burden, cargo, consignment, contents, goods, haul, lading, load, merchandise, payload, tonnage

French Gallic

frenzied agitated, all het up (*informal*), convulsive, distracted, distraught, excited, feverish, frantic, frenetic, furious, hysterical, mad, maniacal, rabid, uncontrolled, wild

frenzy 1. aberration, agitation, delirium, derangement, distraction, fury, hysteria, insanity, lunacy, madness, mania, paroxysm, passion, rage, seizure, transport, turmoil **2.** bout, burst, convulsion, fit, outburst, paroxysm, spasm

frequency constancy, frequentness, periodicity, prevalence, recurrence, repetition

frequent 1. *adj.* common, constant, continual, customary, everyday, familiar, habitual, incessant, numerous, persistent, recurrent, recurring, reiterated, repeated, usual **2.** *vb.* attend, be a regular customer of, be found at, hang out at (*informal*), haunt, patronize, resort, visit

frequently commonly, customarily, habitually, many

an affix meaning repeated action. ~*n* **2** a frequentative verb or affix.

fresco *n, pl* **-coes** *or* **-cos 1** a method of wall-painting using watercolours on wet plaster. **2** a painting done in this way.

fresh *adj* **1** newly made, acquired, etc. **2** not thought of before; novel: *fresh ideas.* **3** most recent: *fresh allegations.* **4** further or additional: *a fresh supply.* **5** (of food) not canned or frozen. **6** (of water) not salty. **7** bright and clear: *a fresh morning.* **8** (of a wind) cold and fairly strong. **9** not tired; alert. **10** not worn or faded: *the fresh colours of spring.* **11** having a healthy or ruddy appearance. **12** having recently come (from somewhere): *cakes fresh from the oven.* **13** youthful or inexperienced. **14** *Informal* overfamiliar or disrespectful. ~*adv* **15** recently: *a delicious fresh-baked cake.* **freshly** *adv* **freshness** *n*

freshen *vb* **1** to make or become fresh or fresher. **2** (of the wind) to become stronger. **3 freshen up** to wash and tidy up one's appearance.

fresher *or* **freshman** *n, pl* **-ers** *or* **-men** a first-year student at college or university.

freshet *n* **1** the sudden overflowing of a river. **2** a stream of fresh water emptying into the sea.

freshwater *adj* of or living in fresh water.

fret[1] *vb* **fretting, fretted 1** to worry: *he would fret about the smallest of problems.* **2** to rub or wear away. **3** to feel or give annoyance. ~*n* **4** a state of irritation or anxiety.

fret[2] *n* **1** a repetitive geometrical figure used for ornamentation. ~*vb* **fretting, fretted 2** to ornament with fret or fretwork.

fret[3] *n* a small metal bar set across the fingerboard of a musical instrument, such as a guitar, as a guide to fingering.

fretful *adj* irritable or upset. **fretfully** *adv*

fret saw *n* a fine-toothed saw with a long thin narrow blade, used for cutting designs in thin wood or metal.

fretwork *n* decorative geometrical carving in wood.

Freudian (**froy**-dee-an) *adj* of or relating to Sigmund Freud (1856–1939), Austrian psychiatrist, or his ideas. **Freudianism** *n*

Freudian slip *n* a slip of the tongue that may reveal an unconscious wish.

Fri. Friday.

friable (**fry**-a-bl) *adj* easily broken up. **friability** *n*

friar *n* a member of a male Roman Catholic religious order.

friar's balsam *n* a compound with a camphor-like smell, used as an inhalant to relieve bronchitis.

friary *n, pl* **-aries** a house of friars.

fricassee *n* stewed meat, esp. chicken or veal, served in a thick white sauce.

fricative *n* **1** a consonant produced by friction of breath through a partly closed mouth, such as (f) or (z). ~*adj* **2** relating to or being a fricative.

friction *n* **1** a resistance encountered when one body moves relative to another body with which it is in contact. **2** the act of rubbing one object against another. **3** disagreement or conflict. **frictional** *adj*

Friday *n* the sixth day of the week.

fridge *n* a cabinet for keeping food and drink cool. In full: **refrigerator**

fried *vb* the past of **fry**[1].

friend *n* **1** a person known well to another and regarded with liking, affection, and loyalty. **2** an ally in a fight or cause. **3** a patron or supporter: *our cause has many friends in Europe.* **4 make friends (with)** to become friendly (with). **friendless** *adj* **friendship** *n*

Friend *n* a member of the Society of Friends; Quaker.

friendly *adj* **-lier, -liest 1** showing or expressing liking, goodwill, or trust. **2** on the same side; not hostile. **3** tending to help or support. ~*n, pl* **-lies 4** *Sport* a match played for its own sake and not as part of a competition. **friendliness** *n*

-friendly *adj combining form* helpful, easy, or good

THESAURUS

a time, many times, much, not infrequently, oft (*archaic or poetic*), often, over and over again, repeatedly, thick and fast, very often

fresh 1. different, latest, modern, modernistic, new, new-fangled, novel, original, recent, this season's, unconventional, unusual, up-to-date **2.** added, additional, auxiliary, extra, further, more, other, renewed, supplementary **3.** crude, green, natural, raw, uncured, undried, unprocessed, unsalted **4.** bracing, bright, brisk, clean, clear, cool, crisp, invigorating, pure, refreshing, spanking, sparkling, stiff, sweet, unpolluted **5.** alert, bouncing, bright, bright-eyed and bushy-tailed (*informal*), chipper (*informal*), energetic, full of vim and vigour (*informal*), invigorated, keen, like a new man, lively, refreshed, rested, restored, revived, sprightly, spry, vigorous, vital **6.** dewy, undimmed, unfaded, unwearied, unwithered, verdant, vivid **7.** blooming, clear, fair, florid, glowing, good, hardy, healthy, rosy, ruddy, wholesome **8.** artless, callow, green, inexperienced, natural, new, raw, uncultivated, untrained, untried, youthful **9.** *informal* bold, brazen, cheeky, disrespectful, familiar, flip (*informal*), forward, impudent, insolent, pert, presumptuous, sassy (*U.S. informal*), saucy, smart-alecky (*informal*)

freshen 1. air, purify, ventilate **2. freshen up** enliven, liven up, refresh, restore, revitalize, rouse, spruce up, titivate

freshness 1. innovativeness, inventiveness, newness, novelty, originality **2.** bloom, brightness, cleanness, clearness, dewiness, glow, shine, sparkle, vigour, wholesomeness

fret 1. affront, agonize, anguish, annoy, brood, chagrin, goad, grieve, harass, irritate, lose sleep over, provoke, ruffle, torment, upset *or* distress oneself, worry **2.** agitate, bother, distress, disturb, gall, irk, nag, nettle, peeve (*informal*), pique, rankle with, rile, trouble, vex

fretful captious, complaining, cross, crotchety (*informal*), edgy, fractious, irritable, out of sorts, peevish, petulant, querulous, ratty (*Brit. & N.Z. informal*), short-tempered, splenetic, testy, tetchy, touchy, uneasy

friction 1. abrasion, attrition, chafing, erosion, fretting, grating, irritation, rasping, resistance, rubbing, scraping, wearing away **2.** animosity, antagonism, bad blood, bad feeling, bickering, conflict, disagreement, discontent, discord, disharmony, dispute, dissension, hostility, incompatibility, opposition, resentment, rivalry, wrangling

friend 1. alter ego, boon companion, bosom friend, buddy (*informal*), china (*Brit. slang*), chum (*informal*), companion, comrade, confidant, crony, familiar, intimate, mate (*informal*), pal, partner, playmate, soul mate **2.** adherent, advocate, ally, associate, backer, benefactor, partisan, patron, protagonist, supporter, well-wisher

friendless abandoned, alienated, all alone, alone, cut off, deserted, estranged, forlorn, forsaken, isolated, lonely, lonesome, ostracized, shunned, solitary, unattached, with no one to turn to, without a friend in the world, without ties

friendliness affability, amiability, companionability, congeniality, conviviality, geniality, kindliness, matey-

for the person or thing specified: *a user-friendly computer system; an environment-friendly means of transport.*

friendly society *n Brit* an association of people who pay regular dues in return for old-age pensions, sickness benefits, etc.

frier *n* a fryer.

fries *pl n* short for **French fries.**

Friesian (**free**-zhan) *n* any of several breeds of black-and-white dairy cattle.

frieze (**freeze**) *n* **1** a sculptured or decorated band on a wall. **2** *Archit* the horizontal band between the architrave and cornice of a classical temple.

frigate (**frig**-it) *n* **1** *Brit* a fast warship, smaller than a destroyer. **2** a medium-sized warship of the 18th and 19th centuries.

fright *n* **1** sudden fear or alarm. **2** a sudden alarming shock. **3** *Informal* a very strange or unattractive person or thing.

frighten *vb* **1** to terrify or scare. **2** to force (someone) to do something from fear. **frightening** *adj*

frightful *adj* **1** very alarming or horrifying. **2** annoying or disagreeable: *a frightful pair of socks.* **3** *Informal* extreme: *a frightful mess.* **frightfully** *adv*

frigid (**frij**-id) *adj* **1** (esp. of a woman) lacking sexual responsiveness. **2** very cold: *the frigid air.* **3** formal or stiff in behaviour or temperament. **frigidity** *n*

frill *n* **1** a long narrow strip of fabric with many folds in it attached at one edge of something as a decoration. **2** an unnecessary part of something added to make it more attractive or interesting: *no fuss, no frills, just a purity of sound and clarity of vision.* **frilly** *or* **frilled** *adj*

fringe *n* **1** hair cut short and hanging over the forehead. **2** an ornamental edge of hanging threads, tassels, etc. **3** an outer edge: *London's southern fringe.* **4** the minor and less important parts of an activity or organization: *two agents on the fringes of espionage activity.* **5** a small group of people within a larger body, but differing from it in certain aims and ideas: *the radical fringe of the Green Party.* ~*adj* **6** (of theatre) unofficial or unconventional. ~*vb* **fringing, fringed 7** to form a border for: *sandy paths fringing the water's edge.* **8** to decorate with a fringe: *tinsel fringed the desk.*

fringe benefit *n* a benefit given in addition to a regular salary or wage.

fringed *adj* **1** (of clothes, curtains, etc.) decorated with a fringe. **2 fringed with** *or* **by** bordered with or by: *a field fringed with trees.*

frippery *n, pl* **-peries 1** showy but useless ornamentation. **2** unimportant or trivial matters.

Frisian (**free**-zhan) *n* **1** a language spoken in the NW Netherlands. **2** a speaker of this language. ~*adj* **3** of this language or its speakers.

frisk *vb* **1** to leap, move about, or act in a playful manner. **2** *Informal* to search (someone) by feeling for concealed weapons, etc. ~*n* **3** a playful movement. **4** *Informal* an instance of frisking a person.

frisky *adj* **friskier, friskiest** lively, high-spirited, or playful. **friskily** *adv*

frisson (**freess**-on) *n* a short sudden feeling of fear or excitement.

THESAURUS

ness (*Brit. informal*), neighbourliness, open arms, sociability, warmth

friendly affable, affectionate, amiable, amicable, attached, attentive, auspicious, beneficial, benevolent, benign, buddy-buddy (*slang, chiefly U.S. & Canad.*), chummy (*informal*), close, clubby, companionable, comradely, conciliatory, confiding, convivial, cordial, familiar, favourable, fond, fraternal, genial, good, helpful, intimate, kind, kindly, matey (*Brit. informal*), neighbourly, on good terms, on visiting terms, outgoing, palsy-walsy (*informal*), peaceable, propitious, receptive, sociable, sympathetic, thick (*informal*), welcoming, well-disposed

friendship affection, affinity, alliance, amity, attachment, benevolence, closeness, concord, familiarity, fondness, friendliness, good-fellowship, goodwill, harmony, intimacy, love, rapport, regard

fright 1. alarm, apprehension, (blue) funk (*informal*), cold sweat, consternation, dismay, dread, fear, fear and trembling, horror, panic, quaking, scare, shock, terror, the shivers, trepidation **2.** *informal* eyesore, frump, mess (*informal*), scarecrow, sight (*informal*)

frighten alarm, appal *or U.S.* appall, cow, daunt, dismay, freeze one's blood, intimidate, make one's blood run cold, make one's hair stand on end (*informal*), make (someone) jump out of his skin (*informal*), petrify, put the wind up (someone) (*informal*), scare, scare (someone) stiff, scare the living daylights out of (someone) (*informal*), shock, startle, terrify, terrorize, throw into a fright, throw into a panic, unman, unnerve

frightened abashed, afraid, alarmed, cowed, dismayed, frozen, in a cold sweat, in a panic, in fear and trepidation, numb with fear, panicky, petrified, scared, scared shitless (*taboo slang*), scared stiff, shit-scared (*taboo slang*), startled, terrified, terrorized, terror-stricken, unnerved

frightening alarming, appalling, baleful, blood-curdling, daunting, dismaying, dreadful, fearful, fearsome, hair-raising, horrifying, intimidating, menacing, scary (*informal*), shocking, spooky (*informal*), terrifying, unnerving

frightful 1. alarming, appalling, awful, dire, dread, dreadful, fearful, ghastly, godawful (*slang*), grim, grisly, gruesome, harrowing, hellacious (*U.S. slang*), hideous, horrendous, horrible, horrid, lurid, macabre, petrifying, shocking, terrible, terrifying, traumatic, unnerving, unspeakable **2.** annoying, awful, disagreeable, dreadful, extreme, great, insufferable, terrible, terrific, unpleasant

frigid 1. arctic, chill, cold, cool, frost-bound, frosty, frozen, gelid, glacial, hyperboreal, icy, Siberian, wintry **2.** aloof, austere, cold-hearted, forbidding, formal, icy, lifeless, passionless, passive, repellent, rigid, stiff, unapproachable, unbending, unfeeling, unloving, unresponsive

frigidity aloofness, austerity, chill, cold-heartedness, coldness, frostiness, iciness, impassivity, lack of response, lifelessness, passivity, unapproachability, unresponsiveness, wintriness

frill *often plural* addition, affectation, bits and pieces, decoration, dressing up, embellishment, extra, fanciness, finery, frilliness, frippery, fuss, gewgaw, jazz (*slang*), mannerism, nonsense, ornamentation, ostentation, superfluity, tomfoolery, trimmings

fringe *n.* **1.** binding, border, edging, hem, tassel, trimming **2.** borderline, edge, limits, march, marches, margin, outskirts, perimeter, periphery ~*adj.* **3.** unconventional, unofficial, unorthodox ~*vb.* **4.** border, edge, enclose, skirt, surround, trim

frisk 1. bounce, caper, cavort, dance, frolic, gambol, hop, jump, play, prance, rollick, romp, skip, sport, trip **2.** *informal* check, inspect, run over, search, shake down (*U.S. slang*)

frisky bouncy, coltish, frolicsome, full of beans (*informal*), full of joie de vivre, high-spirited, in high spir-

fritter *n* a piece of food, such as apple, that is dipped in batter and fried in deep fat.

fritter away *vb* to waste: *he did not fritter away his energy on trivialities.*

frivolous *adj* **1** not serious or sensible in content, attitude, or behaviour. **2** unworthy of serious or sensible treatment: *frivolous distractions.* **frivolity** *n*

frizz *vb* **1** (of hair) to form or cause (hair) to form tight curls. *~n* **2** hair that has been frizzed. **frizzy** *adj*

frizzle[1] *vb* **-zling, -zled 1** to form (hair) into tight crisp curls. *~n* **2** a tight curl.

frizzle[2] *vb* **-zling, -zled** to cook or heat until crisp or shrivelled up.

frock *n Old-fashioned* **1** a girl's or woman's dress. **2** a loose garment, formerly worn by peasants.

frock coat *n* a man's skirted coat, as worn in the 19th century.

frog[1] *n* **1** a smooth-skinned tailless amphibian with long back legs used for jumping. **2 a frog in one's throat** phlegm on the vocal cords, hindering speech.

frog[2] *n* a military style fastening on a coat consisting of a button and a loop. **frogging** *n*

frog[3] *n* horny material in the centre of the sole of a horse's foot.

frogman *n, pl* **-men** a swimmer equipped with a rubber suit, flippers, and breathing equipment for working underwater.

frogmarch *Chiefly Brit ~n* **1** a method of carrying a resisting person in which each limb is held and the victim is face downwards. *~vb* **2** to carry in a frogmarch or cause to move forward unwillingly.

frogspawn *n* a jelly-like substance containing a frog's eggs.

frolic *vb* **-icking, -icked 1** to run and play in a lively way. *~n* **2** lively and merry behaviour. **3** a light hearted occasion.

frolicsome *adj* merry and playful.

from *prep* **1** indicating the original location, situation, etc.: *from America.* **2** in a period of time starting at: *from 1950 to the current year.* **3** indicating the distance between two things or places: *60 miles from the Iraqi border.* **4** indicating a lower amount: *from 5 to 6.* **5** showing the model of: *drawn from life.* **6** used with a verbal noun to denote prohibition, etc.: *she was banned from smoking at meetings.* **7** because of: *five hundred horses collapsed from exhaustion.*

➤ The use of *off* to mean *from* is very informal: *They bought milk from* (rather than *off*) *a farmer.*

fromage frais (**from**-ahzh **fray**) *n* a low-fat soft cheese with a smooth light texture.

frond *n* **1** the compound leaf of a fern. **2** the leaf of a palm.

front *n* **1** that part or side that is forward, or most often seen or used. **2** a position or place directly before or ahead. **3** the beginning, opening, or first part. **4** the position of leadership. **5** a promenade at a seaside resort. **6** *Mil* **a** the total area in which opposing armies face each other. **b** the space in which a military unit is operating. **7** *Meteorol* the dividing line between two different air masses. **8** an outward appearance: *he put on a bold front.* **9** *Informal* a business or other activity serving as a respectable cover for another, usually criminal, organization. **10** Also called: **front man** a nominal leader of an organization. **11** a particular field of activity: *on the economic front.* **12** a group of people with a common goal: *the National Liberation Front.* *~adj* **13** of, at, or in the front. *~vb* **14** to face (onto). **15** to be a front of or for. **16** to appear as a presenter in (a television show). **17** to be the leader of (a band) on stage.

frontage *n* **1** the facade of a building or the front of a plot of ground. **2** the extent of the front of a shop, plot of land, etc.

frontal *adj* **1** of, at, or in the front. **2** of or relating to the forehead.

front bench *n* the leadership of either the Government or Opposition in the House of Commons or in various other legislative assemblies. **front-bencher** *n*

frontier *n* **1** the region of a country bordering on another or a line marking such a boundary. **2** the edge of the settled area of a country. **3 frontiers** the limit of knowledge in a particular field: *twenty years ago, laser spectroscopy was on the frontiers of chemical research.*

frontispiece *n* an illustration facing the title page of a book.

frontrunner *n Informal* the leader or a favoured contestant in a race or election.

frost *n* **1** a white deposit of ice particles. **2** an atmospheric temperature of below freezing point, producing this deposit. *~vb* **3** to cover with frost. **4** to kill or damage (plants) with frost.

frostbite *n* destruction of tissues, esp. of the fingers, ears, toes, and nose, by freezing. **frostbitten** *adj*

frosted *adj* (of glass) having the surface roughened so that it cannot be seen through clearly.

frosting *n Chiefly US & Canad* icing.

frosty *adj* **frostier, frostiest 1** characterized by frost: *the frosty air.* **2** covered by frost. **3** unfriendly or disapproving: *a frosty reception from the bank manager.* **frostily** *adv* **frostiness** *n*

THESAURUS

its, kittenish, lively, playful, rollicking, romping, spirited, sportive

fritter (away) dally away, dissipate, fool away, idle (away), misspend, run through, spend like water, squander, waste

frivolity childishness, flightiness, flippancy, flummery (*informal*), folly, frivolousness, fun, gaiety, giddiness, jest, levity, light-heartedness, lightness, nonsense, puerility, shallowness, silliness, superficiality, trifling, triviality

frivolous 1. childish, dizzy, empty-headed, flighty, flip (*informal*), flippant, foolish, giddy, idle, ill-considered, juvenile, light-minded, nonserious, puerile, silly, superficial **2.** extravagant, footling (*informal*), impractical, light, minor, nickel-and-dime (*U.S. slang*), niggling, paltry, peripheral, petty, pointless, shallow, trifling, trivial, unimportant

frizzle crisp, fry, hiss, roast, scorch, sizzle, sputter

frolic *vb.* **1.** caper, cavort, cut capers, frisk, gambol, lark, make merry, play, rollick, romp, sport *~n.* **2.** antic, escapade, gambol, game, lark, prank, revel, romp, spree **3.** amusement, drollery, fun, fun and games, gaiety, high jinks, merriment, skylarking (*informal*), sport

frolicsome coltish, frisky, gay, kittenish, lively, merry, playful, rollicking, sportive, sprightly

front *n.* **1.** anterior, exterior, façade, face, facing, foreground, forepart, frontage, obverse **2.** beginning, fore, forefront, front line, head, lead, top, van, vanguard **3.** air, appearance, aspect, bearing, countenance, demeanour, expression, exterior, face, manner, mien, show **4.** blind, cover, cover-up, disguise, façade, mask, pretext, show *~adj.* **5.** first, foremost, head, headmost, lead, leading, topmost *~vb.* **6.** face (onto), look over *or* onto, overlook

frontier borderland, borderline, bound, boundary, confines, edge, limit, marches, perimeter, verge

frost freeze, freeze-up, hoarfrost, Jack Frost, rime

froth *n* **1** a mass of small bubbles of air or a gas in a liquid. **2** a mixture of saliva and air bubbles formed at the lips in certain diseases, such as rabies. **3** trivial but superficially attractive ideas or entertainment. *~vb* **4** to produce or cause to produce froth. **frothy** *adj*

frown *vb* **1** to wrinkle one's brows in worry, anger, or concentration. **2 frown on** to disapprove of: *smoking at work is frowned on.* *~n* **3** the act of frowning. **4** a look of disapproval or displeasure.

frowsty *adj* **frowstier, frowstiest** stale or musty.

frowzy *or* **frowsy** *adj* **frowzier, frowziest** *or* **frowsier, frowsiest 1** slovenly or unkempt in appearance. **2** musty and stale.

froze *vb* the past tense of **freeze.**

frozen *vb* **1** the past participle of **freeze.** *~adj* **2** turned into or covered with ice. **3** killed or stiffened by extreme cold. **4** (of food) preserved by a freezing process. **5 a** (of prices or wages) officially fixed at a certain level. **b** (of business assets) not convertible into cash. **6** motionless: *she was frozen in horror.*

FRS (in Britain) Fellow of the Royal Society.

fructify *vb* **-fies, -fying, -fied** to bear or cause to bear fruit.

fructose *n* a crystalline sugar occurring in honey and many fruits.

frugal (**froo**-gl) *adj* **1** economical in the use of money or resources; thrifty. **2** meagre and inexpensive: *a frugal meal.* **frugality** *n* **frugally** *adv*

fruit *n* **1** any fleshy part of a plant that supports the seeds and is edible, such as the strawberry. **2** *Bot* the ripened ovary of a flowering plant, containing one or more seeds. **3** any plant product useful to man, including grain and vegetables. **4 fruits** the results of an action or effort, esp. if pleasant: *they have enjoyed the fruits of a complete victory.* *~vb* **5** to bear fruit.

fruiterer *n Chiefly Brit* a person who sells fruit.

fruitful *adj* **1** producing good and useful results: *a fruitful relationship.* **2** bearing much fruit. **fruitfully** *adv*

fruition (froo-**ish**-on) *n* **1** the fulfilment of something worked for or desired. **2** the act or condition of bearing fruit.

fruitless *adj* **1** producing nothing of value: *a fruitless debate.* **2** without fruit. **fruitlessly** *adv*

fruit machine *n Brit* a coin-operated gambling machine that pays out money when a particular combination of diagrams, usually of fruit, appear on a screen.

fruit salad *or* **cocktail** *n* a dish consisting of pieces of different kinds of fruit.

fruit sugar *n* same as **fructose.**

fruity *adj* **fruitier, fruitiest 1** of or like fruit. **2** (of a voice) mellow or rich. **3** *Informal, chiefly Brit* referring humorously to things relating to sex. **fruitiness** *n*

frump *n* a woman who dresses in a dull and old-fashioned way. **frumpy** *or* **frumpish** *adj*

frustrate *vb* **-trating, -trated 1** to upset or anger (a person) by presenting difficulties that cannot be overcome: *his lack of ambition frustrated me.* **2** to hinder or prevent (the efforts, plans, or desires) of. **frustrating** *adj* **frustration** *n*

frustrated *adj* dissatisfied or unfulfilled.

frustum *n, pl* **-tums** *or* **-ta** *Geom* the part of a solid, such as a cone or pyramid, contained between the base and a plane parallel to the base that intersects the solid.

fry[1] *vb* **fries, frying, fried 1** to cook or be cooked in fat or oil, usually over direct heat. *~n, pl* **fries 2** Also: **fry-up** *Brit informal* a dish of mixed fried food. ~See also **fries. fryer** *or* **frier** *n*

fry[2] *pl n* **1** the young of various species of fish. **2** See **small fry.**

frying pan *n* **1** a long-handled shallow pan used for frying. **2 out of the frying pan into the fire** from a bad situation to a worse one.

FSH *Biol* follicle-stimulating hormone: a hormone secreted by the pituitary gland.

f-stop *n Photog* any of the lens aperture settings of a camera.

ft. foot or feet.

fuchsia (**fyew**-sha) *n* an ornamental shrub with hanging purple, red, or white flowers.

fuck *Taboo ~vb* **1** to have sexual intercourse with (someone). *~n* **2** an act of sexual intercourse. **3** *Slang* a partner in sexual intercourse. **4 not give a fuck** not to care at all. *~interj* **5** *Offensive* an expression of strong disgust or anger. **fucking** *n, adj, adv*

fuck off *vb Offensive taboo slang* to go away.

THESAURUS

frosty 1. chilly, cold, frozen, hoar (*rare*), ice-capped, icicled, icy, parky (*Brit. informal*), rimy, wintry **2.** discouraging, frigid, off-putting (*Brit. informal*), standoffish, unenthusiastic, unfriendly, unwelcoming

froth 1. *n.* bubbles, effervescence, foam, head, lather, scum, spume, suds **2.** *vb.* bubble over, come to a head, effervesce, fizz, foam, lather

frothy foaming, foamy, spumescent, spumous, spumy, sudsy

frown 1. give a dirty look, glare, glower, knit one's brows, look daggers, lower *or* lour, scowl **2.** *with* **on** disapprove of, discountenance, discourage, dislike, look askance at, not take kindly to, show disapproval *or* displeasure, take a dim view of, view with disfavour

frowsty close, fuggy, fusty, ill-smelling, musty, stale, stuffy

frozen 1. arctic, chilled, chilled to the marrow, frigid, frosted, icebound, ice-cold, ice-covered, icy, numb **2.** fixed, pegged (*of prices*), petrified, rooted, stock-still, stopped, suspended, turned to stone

frugal abstemious, careful, cheeseparing, economical, meagre, niggardly, parsimonious, penny-wise, provident, prudent, saving, sparing, thrifty

fruit 1. crop, harvest, produce, product, yield **2.** *plural* advantages, benefits, consequences, effects, outcomes, profits, results, returns, rewards

fruitful 1. advantageous, beneficial, effective, gainful, productive, profitable, rewarding, successful, useful, well-spent, worthwhile **2.** abundant, copious, fecund, fertile, flush, plenteous, plentiful, productive, profuse, prolific, rich, spawning

fruition actualization, attainment, completion, consummation, enjoyment, fulfilment, materialization, maturation, maturity, perfection, realization, ripeness

fruitless abortive, barren, futile, idle, ineffectual, in vain, pointless, profitless, to no avail, to no effect, unavailing, unfruitful, unproductive, unprofitable, unprolific, unsuccessful, useless, vain

fruity 1. full, mellow, resonant, rich **2.** *informal* bawdy, blue, hot, indecent, indelicate, juicy, near the knuckle (*informal*), racy, ripe, risqué, salacious, sexy, smutty, spicy (*informal*), suggestive, titillating, vulgar

frustrate 1. depress, discourage, dishearten **2.** baffle, balk, block, check, circumvent, confront, counter, defeat, disappoint, foil, forestall, inhibit, neutralize, nullify, render null and void, stymie, thwart

frustrated carrying a chip on one's shoulder (*informal*), disappointed, discontented, discouraged, disheartened, embittered, foiled, irked, resentful, sick as a parrot (*informal*)

frustration 1. annoyance, disappointment, dissatisfaction, grievance, irritation, resentment, vexation **2.**

fuck up *vb Offensive taboo slang* to make a mess of (something).

fuddle *vb* **-dling, -dled 1** to cause to be confused or intoxicated. *~n* **2** a confused state. **fuddled** *adj*

fuddy-duddy *n, pl* **-dies** *Informal* a person, esp. an elderly one, who is extremely conservative or dull.

fudge[1] *n* a soft sweet made from sugar, butter, and milk.

fudge[2] *vb* **fudging, fudged 1** to make (an issue or problem) less clear deliberately. **2** to avoid making a firm statement or decision.

fuel *n* **1** any substance burned for heat or power, such as coal or petrol. **2** the material that produces energy by fission in a nuclear reactor. **3 add fuel to** to make (a difficult situation) worse. *~vb* **fuelling, fuelled** *or US* **fueling, fueled 4** to supply with or receive fuel. **5** to intensify or make worse (a feeling or situation): *the move is bound to fuel speculation.*

fuel cell *n* a cell in which chemical energy is converted directly into electrical energy.

fug *n Chiefly Brit* a hot stale atmosphere. **fuggy** *adj*

fugitive (**fyew**-jit-iv) *n* **1** a person who flees, esp. from arrest or pursuit. *~adj* **2** fleeing. **3** not permanent; fleeting.

fugue (**fyewg**) *n* a musical form consisting of a theme repeated above or below the continuing first statement. **fugal** *adj*

Führer *n* a leader: the title used by Hitler as Nazi dictator.

-ful *adj suffix* **1** full of or characterized by: *painful, restful.* **2** able or tending to: *useful.* *~n suffix* **3** as much as will fill the thing specified: *mouthful.*

fulcrum *n, pl* **-crums** *or* **-cra** the pivot about which a lever turns.

fulfil *or US* **fulfill** *vb* **filling, filled 1** to bring about the achievement of (a desire or promise). **2** to carry out (a request or order). **3** to satisfy (demands or conditions). **4 fulfil oneself** to achieve one's potential. **fulfilment** *or US* **fulfillment** *n*

full[1] *adj* **1** holding as much or as many as possible. **2** abundant in supply: *full of enthusiasm.* **3** having consumed enough food or drink. **4** (of the face or figure) rounded or plump. **5** complete: *the full amount.* **6** with all privileges or rights: *full membership.* **7** *Music* powerful or rich in volume and sound. **8** (of a garment) containing a large amount of fabric. **9 full of** engrossed with: *she had been full of her own plans lately.* **10 full of oneself** full of pride or conceit. **11 full up** filled to capacity. *~adv* **12** completely or entirely. **13** directly or right: *she hit him full in the face.* **14 full well** very or extremely well: *we knew full well that she was watching every move we made.* *~n* **15 in full** without omitting or shortening. **16 to the full** thoroughly or fully. **fullness** *or esp US* **fulness** *n*

full[2] *vb* to make (cloth) more compact during manufacture through shrinking and beating.

fullback *n Soccer, hockey, & rugby* a defensive player.

full-blooded *adj* **1** vigorous or enthusiastic. **2** (esp of horses) having ancestors of a single race or breed.

full-blown *adj* fully developed.

full board *n* the daily provision by a hotel of bed, breakfast, and midday and evening meals.

full-bodied *adj* having a full rich flavour or quality: *a full-bodied vintage port.*

fuller's earth *n* a natural absorbent clay used for fulling cloth.

full-frontal *adj Informal* exposing the genitals to full view.

full house *n* **1** a theatre filled to capacity. **2** (in bingo) the set of numbers needed to win.

full-length *adj* **1** (of a mirror, portrait, etc.) showing the complete human figure. **2** not abridged.

full moon *n* the phase of the moon when it is visible as a fully illuminated disc.

full-scale *adj* **1** (of a plan) of actual size. **2** using all resources; all-out.

full stop *n* the punctuation mark (.) used at the end

THESAURUS

blocking, circumvention, contravention, curbing, failure, foiling, nonfulfilment, nonsuccess, obstruction, thwarting

fuddled bevvied (*dialect*), blitzed (*slang*), blotto (*slang*), bombed (*slang*), confused, drunk, flying (*slang*), inebriated, intoxicated, legless (*informal*), lit up (*slang*), muddled, muzzy, out of it (*slang*), out to it (*Austral. & N.Z. slang*), paralytic (*informal*), pissed (*taboo slang*), smashed (*slang*), sozzled (*informal*), steamboats (*slang*), steaming (*slang*), stupefied, tipsy, tired and emotional, wasted (*slang*), woozy (*informal*), wrecked (*slang*), zonked (*slang*)

fuddy-duddy back number (*informal*), conservative, dinosaur, dodo (*informal*), fossil, museum piece, (old) fogy, square (*informal*), stick-in-the-mud (*informal*), stuffed shirt (*informal*)

fudge *vb.* avoid, cook (*slang*), dodge, equivocate, evade, fake, falsify, flannel (*Brit. informal*), hedge, misrepresent, patch up, shuffle, slant, stall

fuel *vb.* charge, fan, feed, fire, incite, inflame, nourish, stoke up, sustain

fugitive 1. *n.* deserter, escapee, refugee, runaway **2.** *adj.* brief, ephemeral, evanescent, fleeing, fleeting, flitting, flying, momentary, passing, short, short-lived, temporary, transient, transitory, unstable

fulfilment accomplishment, achievement, attainment, carrying out *or* through, completion, consummation, crowning, discharge, discharging, effecting, end, implementation, observance, perfection, realization

fulfil *or U.S.* **fulfill** accomplish, achieve, answer, bring to completion, carry out, complete, comply with, conclude, conform to, discharge, effect, execute, fill, finish, keep, meet, obey, observe, perfect, perform, realise, satisfy

full 1. brimful, brimming, chock-a-block, chock-full, complete, crammed, crowded, entire, filled, gorged, intact, loaded, packed, replete, sated, satiated, satisfied, saturated, stocked, sufficient **2.** abundant, adequate, all-inclusive, ample, broad, comprehensive, copious, detailed, exhaustive, extensive, generous, maximum, plenary, plenteous (*literary*), plentiful, thorough, unabridged **3.** baggy, balloonlike, buxom, capacious, curvaceous, large, loose, plump, puffy, rounded, voluminous, voluptuous **4.** clear, deep, distinct, loud, resonant, rich, rounded **5. in full** completely, in its entirety, in total, *in toto*, without exception **6. to the full** completely, entirely, fully, thoroughly, to the utmost, without reservation

full-blooded ballsy (*taboo slang*), gutsy (*slang*), hearty, lusty, mettlesome, red-blooded, vigorous, virile

full-grown adult, developed, full-fledged, grown-up, in one's prime, marriageable, mature, nubile, of age, ripe

fullness 1. abundance, adequateness, ampleness, copiousness, fill, glut, plenty, profusion, repletion, satiety, saturation, sufficiency **2.** broadness, completeness, comprehensiveness, entirety, extensiveness, plenitude, totality, vastness, wealth, wholeness **3.** clearness, loudness, resonance, richness, strength **4.** curvaceousness, dilation, distension, enlargement, roundness, swelling, tumescence, voluptuousness

full-scale all-encompassing, all-out, comprehensive,

of a sentence and after abbreviations. Also called (esp. US and Canad.): **period**

full-time *adj* **1** for all of the normal working week: *a full-time job.* ~*adv* **full time 2** on a full-time basis: *she worked full time until she was 72.* ~*n* **full time 3** *Soccer, rugby, & hockey* the end of the game.

full toss *or* **pitch** *n Cricket* a bowled ball that reaches the batsman without bouncing.

fully *adv* **1** to the greatest degree or extent. **2** amply or adequately. **3** at least: *fully a hundred people.*

fully-fashioned *adj* (of stockings or knitwear) shaped and seamed so as to fit closely.

fulmar *n* a heavily-built Arctic sea bird with a short tail.

fulminate *vb* **-nating, -nated fulminate against** to criticize or denounce angrily. **fulmination** *n*

fulsome *adj* exaggerated and elaborate, and often sounding insincere: *fulsome praise.*

fumble *vb* **-bling, -bled 1** to use the hands clumsily or grope about blindly: *fumbling for a cigarette.* **2** to say or do awkwardly. ~*n* **3** the act of fumbling.

fume *vb* **fuming, fumed 1** to be overcome with anger or fury. **2** to give off (fumes) or (of fumes) to be given off, esp. during a chemical reaction. **3** to treat with fumes. ~*n* **4** a pungent or toxic vapour, gas, or smoke.

fumigate (**fyew**-mig-gate) *vb* **-gating, -gated** to treat (something contaminated) with fumes. **fumigation** *n*

fun *n* **1** pleasant, enjoyable, and light-hearted activity or amusement. **2 for** *or* **in fun** for amusement or as a joke. **3 make fun of** *or* **poke fun at** to ridicule or tease. ~*adj* **4** (of a person) amusing and likeable. **5** (of a place or activity) amusing and enjoyable.

function *n* **1** the intended role or purpose of a person or thing. **2** an official or formal social gathering. **3** a factor, the precise nature of which depends upon another thing in some way: *muscle breakdown is a function of vitamin E deficiency.* **4** *Maths* a quantity, the value of which depends on the varying value of another quantity. **5** a sequence of operations that a computer or calculator performs when a specified key is pressed. ~*vb* **6** to operate or work. **7 function as** to perform the action or role of (something or someone else).

functional *adj* **1** of or performing a function. **2** practical rather than decorative. **3** in working order. **4** *Med* affecting a function of an organ without structural change. **functionally** *adv*

functionalism *n* the theory that the form of a thing should be determined by its use. **functionalist** *n, adj*

functionary *n, pl* **-aries** a person acting in an official capacity, such as for a government; official.

fund *n* **1** a reserve of money set aside for a certain purpose. **2** a supply or store of something. ~*vb* **3** to provide money to. **4** *Finance* to convert (short-term debt) into long-term debt bearing fixed interest. ~See also **funds.**

fundamental *adj* **1** essential or primary: *fundamental mathematical concepts.* **2** basic: *a fundamental error.* ~*n* **3 fundamentals** the most important and basic parts of a subject or activity. **4** the lowest note of a harmonic series. **fundamentally** *adv*

fundamentalism *n* **1** *Christianity* the view that the Bible is literally true. **2** *Islam* a movement favouring strict observance of Islamic law. **fundamentalist** *n, adj*

fundamental particle *n Physics* same as **elementary particle.**

THESAURUS

exhaustive, extensive, full-dress, in-depth, major, proper, sweeping, thorough, thoroughgoing, wide-ranging

fully 1. absolutely, altogether, completely, entirely, every inch, from first to last, heart and soul, in all respects, intimately, perfectly, positively, thoroughly, totally, utterly, wholly **2.** abundantly, adequately, amply, comprehensively, enough, plentifully, satisfactorily, sufficiently **3.** at least, quite, without (any) exaggeration, without a word of a lie (*informal*)

fulmination condemnation, denunciation, diatribe, excoriation, invective, obloquy, philippic, reprobation, tirade

fulsome adulatory, cloying, excessive, extravagant, fawning, gross, immoderate, ingratiating, inordinate, insincere, nauseating, overdone, saccharine, sickening, smarmy (*Brit. informal*), sycophantic, unctuous

fumble 1. bumble, feel around, flounder, grope, paw (*informal*), scrabble **2.** bodge (*informal*), botch, bungle, cock up (*Brit. slang*), fuck up (*offensive taboo slang*), make a hash of (*informal*), mess up, misfield, mishandle, mismanage, muff, spoil

fume *figurative vb.* blow a fuse (*slang, chiefly U.S.*), boil, chafe, champ at the bit (*informal*), crack up (*informal*), fly off the handle (*informal*), get hot under the collar (*informal*), get steamed up about (*slang*), go off the deep end (*informal*), go up the wall (*slang*), rage, rant, rave, see red (*informal*), seethe, smoulder, storm

fumes effluvium, exhalation, exhaust, gas, haze, miasma, pollution, reek, smog, smoke, stench, vapour

fumigate clean out *or* up, cleanse, disinfect, purify, sanitize, sterilize

fuming all steamed up (*slang*), angry, at boiling point (*informal*), enraged, foaming at the mouth, in a rage, incensed, raging, roused, seething, up in arms

fun *n.* **1.** amusement, cheer, distraction, diversion, enjoyment, entertainment, frolic, gaiety, good time, high jinks, jollification, jollity, joy, junketing, living it up, merriment, merrymaking, mirth, play, pleasure, recreation, romp, sport, treat, whoopee (*informal*) **2. for** *or* **in fun** facetiously, for a joke, for a laugh, in jest, jokingly, light-heartedly, mischievously, playfully, roguishly, teasingly, tongue in cheek, with a gleam *or* twinkle in one's eye, with a straight face **3. make fun of** *or* **poke fun at** deride, hold up to ridicule, lampoon, laugh at, make a fool of, make game of, make sport of, make the butt of, mock, parody, poke fun at, rag, rib (*informal*), ridicule, satirize, scoff at, send up (*Brit. informal*), sneer at, take off, take the piss out of (*taboo slang*), taunt ~*adj.* **4.** amusing, convivial, diverting, enjoyable, entertaining, lively, witty

function *n.* **1.** activity, business, capacity, charge, concern, duty, employment, exercise, job, mission, occupation, office, operation, part, post, province, purpose, raison d'être, responsibility, role, situation, task **2.** affair, do (*informal*), gathering, reception, social occasion ~*vb.* **3.** act, act the part of, behave, be in commission, be in operation *or* action, be in running order, do duty, go, officiate, operate, perform, run, serve, serve one's turn, work

functional hard-wearing, operative, practical, serviceable, useful, utilitarian, utility, working

fund *n.* **1.** capital, endowment, fall-back, foundation, kitty, pool, reserve, stock, store, supply **2.** hoard, mine, repository, reserve, reservoir, source, storehouse, treasury, vein ~*vb.* **3.** capitalize, endow, finance, float, pay for, promote, stake, subsidize, support

fundamental 1. *adj.* basic, bog-standard (*informal*), cardinal, central, constitutional, crucial, elementary, essential, first, important, indispensable, integral, intrinsic, key, necessary, organic, primary, prime, principal, radical, rudimentary, underlying, vital **2.** *n.* plu-

fundi (**foon**-dee) *n S African* an expert.
funding *n* **1** the provision of money for a project or organization. **2** the amount of money provided.
fundraiser *n* **1** a person involved in organizing fundraising activities. **2** an event held to raise money for a cause.
fundraising *n* **1** the activity involved in raising money for a cause. *~adj* **2** of, for, or relating to fundraising: *a fundraising disco.*
funds *pl n* money that is readily available.
funeral *n* **1** a ceremony at which a dead person is buried or cremated. **2 it's your funeral** *Informal* a mistake has been made and you alone will be responsible for its consequences. *~adj* **3** of or for a funeral. **funerary** *adj*
funeral director *n* an undertaker.
funeral parlour *n* a place where the dead are prepared for burial or cremation.
funereal (fyew-**neer**-ee-al) *adj* suggestive of a funeral; gloomy or sombre. **funereally** *adv*
funfair *n Brit* an amusement park with machines to ride on and stalls.
fungicide *n* a substance used to destroy fungi.
fungoid *adj* resembling a fungus.
fungous *adj* appearing suddenly and spreading quickly like a fungus.
fungus *n, pl* **fungi** *or* **funguses** a plant without leaves, flowers, or roots, that reproduce by spores, including moulds, yeasts, and mushrooms. **fungal** *adj*
funicular (fyew-**nik**-yew-lar) *n* a railway up the side of a mountain, consisting of two cars at either end of a cable passing round a driving wheel at the summit. Also called: **funicular railway**
funk[1] *Old-fashioned, Brit ~n* **1** a state of nervousness, fear, or depression. **2** a coward. *~vb* **3** to avoid doing (something) through fear.
funk[2] *n* a type of Black dance music with a strong beat.
funky *adj* **-kier, -kiest** (of jazz or pop) having a strong beat.
funnel *n* **1** a tube with a wide mouth tapering to a small hole, used for pouring liquids into narrow openings. **2** a chimney of a ship or steam train. *~vb* **-nelling, -nelled** *or US* **-neling, -neled 3** to move or cause to move through or as if through a funnel.
funny *adj* **-nier, -niest 1** causing amusement or laughter; humorous. **2** peculiar or odd. **3** *Informal* faint or ill: *this smell is making me feel a bit funny.* **4**
funny business *Informal* suspicious or dubious behaviour. **funnily** *adv* **funniness** *n*
funny bone *n* a sensitive area near the elbow where the nerve is close to the surface of the skin.
fur *n* **1** the dense coat of fine silky hairs on many mammals. **2** the skin of certain animals, with the hair left on. **3** a garment made of fur. **4 make the fur fly** to cause a scene or disturbance. **5** *Informal* a whitish coating on the tongue, caused by illness. **6** *Brit* a deposit on the insides of water pipes or kettles, caused by hard water. *~vb* **furring, furred 7** Also: **fur up** to cover or become covered with a furlike deposit.
furbelow *n Old-fashioned* **1** a pleated or gathered piece of material used as a decoration on a woman's garment; ruffle. **2 furbelows** showy ornamentation.
furbish *vb Formal* to brighten up or renovate.
furcate *vb* **-cating, -cated 1** to divide into two parts. *~adj* **2** forked: *furcate branches.* **furcation** *n*
Furies *pl n, sing* **Fury** *Classical myth* the goddesses of vengeance, who pursued unpunished criminals.
furious *adj* **1** extremely angry or annoyed. **2** violent or unrestrained, such as in speed or energy: *fast and furious dance routines.* **furiously** *adv*
furl *vb* to roll up (an umbrella, flag, or sail) neatly and securely.
furlong *n* a unit of length equal to 220 yards (201.168 metres).
furlough (**fur**-loh) *n* leave of absence from military duty.
furnace *n* **1** an enclosed chamber in which heat is produced to destroy refuse or smelt ores. **2** *Informal* a very hot place.
furnish *vb* **1** to provide (a house or room) with furniture, etc. **2** to supply or provide. **furnished** *adj*
furnishings *pl n* furniture, carpets, and fittings with which a room or house is furnished.
furniture *n* the large movable articles, such as chairs and tables, that equip a room or house.
furore (fyew-**ror**-ee) *n* a very angry or excited reaction by people to something: *the furore over "The Satanic Verses".*
furrier *n* a person who makes or sells fur garments.
furrow *n* **1** a long narrow trench made in the ground by a plough. **2** any long deep groove, esp. a deep wrinkle on the forehead. *~vb* **3** to become wrinkled. **4** to make furrows in (land).
furry *adj* **-rier, -riest** like or covered with fur or something furlike.
further *adv* **1** in addition. **2** to a greater degree or ex-

THESAURUS

ral axioms, cornerstones, essentials, first principles, laws, principles, rudiments, rules
fundamentally at bottom, at heart, basically, essentially, intrinsically, primarily, radically
funds ackers (*slang*), brass (*Northern English dialect*), bread (*slang*), capital, cash, dibs (*slang*), dosh (*Brit. & Austral. slang*), dough (*slang*), finance, hard cash, money, necessary (*informal*), needful (*informal*), ready money, resources, rhino (*Brit. slang*), savings, shekels (*informal*), silver, spondulicks (*slang*), the ready (*informal*), the wherewithal, tin (*slang*)
funeral burial, inhumation, interment, obsequies
funnel *vb.* channel, conduct, convey, direct, filter, move, pass, pour
funny 1. absurd, amusing, a scream (card (*informal*), caution (*informal*)) (*informal*), comic, comical, diverting, droll, entertaining, facetious, farcical, hilarious, humorous, jocose, jocular, jolly, killing (*informal*), laughable, ludicrous, rich, ridiculous, riotous, risible, side-splitting, silly, slapstick, waggish, witty **2.** curious, dubious, mysterious, odd, peculiar, perplexing, puzzling, queer, remarkable, rum (*Brit. slang*), strange, suspicious, unusual, weird
furious 1. angry, beside oneself, boiling, cross, enraged, frantic, frenzied, fuming, incensed, infuriated, in high dudgeon, livid (*informal*), mad, maddened, on the warpath (*informal*), raging, up in arms, wrathful, wroth (*old-fashioned*) **2.** agitated, boisterous, fierce, impetuous, intense, savage, stormy, tempestuous, tumultuous, turbulent, ungovernable, unrestrained, vehement, violent, wild
furnish 1. appoint, decorate, equip, fit (out, up), outfit, provide, provision, purvey, rig, stock, store, supply **2.** afford, bestow, endow, give, grant, hand out, offer, present, provide, reveal, supply
furniture appliances, appointments, chattels (*old-fashioned*), effects, equipment, fittings, furnishings, goods, household goods, movable property, movables, possessions, things (*informal*)
furore commotion, disturbance, excitement, flap (*in-*

tent. **3** to or at a more advanced point. **4** to or at a greater distance in time or space. *~adj* **5** additional. **6** more distant or remote in time or space. *~vb* **7** to assist the progress of (something). **furtherance** *n*

further education *n* (in Britain) formal education beyond school other than at a university or polytechnic.

furthermore *adv* in addition.

furthest *adv* **1** to the greatest degree or extent. **2** to or at the greatest distance in time or space; farthest. *~adj* **3** most distant in time or space; farthest.

furtive *adj* sly, cautious, and secretive. **furtively** *adv*

fury *n, pl* **-ries 1** violent anger. **2** uncontrolled violence: *the fury of the sea.* **3** an outburst of violent anger. **4** a person with a violent temper. **5 like fury** *Old-fashioned* with great energy, strength, or power.

Fury *n, pl* **-ries** See **Furies.**

furze *n* gorse. **furzy** *adj*

fuse[1] *or US* **fuze** *n* **1** a lead containing an explosive for detonating a bomb. *~vb* **fusing, fused** *or* **fuzing, fuzed 2** to equip with such a fuse. **fuseless** *adj*

fuse[2] *n* **1** a protective device for safeguarding electric circuits, containing a wire that melts and breaks the circuit when the current exceeds a certain value. *~vb* **fusing, fused 2** *Brit* to fail or cause to fail as a result of a fuse blowing. **3** to equip (a plug or circuit) with a fuse. **4** to join or become combined: *the two ideas fused in his mind.* **5** to unite or become united by melting. **6** to become or cause to become liquid, esp. by the action of heat.

fuselage (**fyew**-zill-lahzh) *n* the main body of an aircraft.

fusible *adj* capable of being melted.

fusilier (fyew-zill-**leer**) *n* (formerly) an infantryman armed with a light musket: a term still used in the names of certain British regiments.

fusillade (fyew-zill-**lade**) *n* **1** a rapid continual discharge of firearms. **2** a sudden outburst of criticism, questions, etc.

fusion *n* **1** the act or process of melting together. **2** something produced by fusing. **3** a kind of popular music that is a blend of two or more styles, such as jazz and funk. **4** something new created by a mixture of qualities, ideas, or things. **5** See **nuclear fusion.**

fuss *n* **1** needless activity and worry. **2** complaint or objection: *it was silly to make a fuss over seating arrangements.* **3** an exhibition of affection or admiration: *when I arrived my nephews made a big fuss of me.* *~vb* **4** to worry unnecessarily. **5** to be excessively concerned over trivial matters. **6** to bother (a person). **7 fuss over** to show great or excessive concern or affection for.

fusspot *n Brit informal* a person who is difficult to please and complains often.

fussy *adj* **fussier, fussiest 1** inclined to fuss. **2** very particular about detail. **3** overelaborate: *a fussy, overdecorated palace.* **fussily** *adv*

fustian *n* **1** (formerly) a hard-wearing fabric of cotton mixed with flax or wool. **2** pompous talk or writing.

fusty *adj* **-tier, -tiest 1** smelling of damp or mould. **2** old-fashioned. **fustiness** *n*

futile (**fyew**-tile) *adj* **1** useless or having no chance of success. **2** foolish and of no value: *her futile remarks began to annoy me.* **futility** *n*

futon (**foo**-tonn) *n* a Japanese padded quilt, laid on the floor as a bed.

future *n* **1** the time yet to come. **2** undetermined events that will occur in that time. **3** the condition of a person or thing at a later date. **4** prospects: *he had faith in its future.* **5** *Grammar* a tense of verbs used when the action specified has not yet taken place. **6 in future** from now on. *~adj* **7** that is yet to come or be. **8** of or expressing time yet to come. **9** destined to become. **10** *Grammar* in or denoting the future as a tense of verbs. ~See also **futures.**

future perfect *Grammar ~adj* **1** denoting a tense of verbs describing an action that will have been performed by a certain time. *~n* **2** the future perfect tense.

futures *pl n* commodities bought or sold at an agreed price for delivery at a specified future date.

futurism *n* an early 20th-century artistic movement making use of the characteristics of the machine age. **futurist** *n, adj*

futuristic *adj* **1** of design or technology that appears to belong to some future time. **2** of futurism.

futurity *n, pl* **-ties 1** future. **2** a future event.

THESAURUS

formal), frenzy, fury, hullabaloo, outburst, outcry, stir, to-do, uproar

further 1. *adv.* additionally, also, as well as, besides, furthermore, in addition, moreover, on top of, over and above, to boot, what's more, yet **2.** *adj.* additional, extra, fresh, more, new, other, supplementary **3.** *vb.* advance, aid, assist, champion, contribute to, encourage, expedite, facilitate, forward, foster, hasten, help, lend support to, patronize, plug (*informal*), promote, push, speed, succour, work for

furtherance advancement, advocacy, backing, boosting, carrying-out, championship, promotion, prosecution, pursuit

furthest extreme, farthest, furthermost, most distant, outermost, outmost, remotest, ultimate, uttermost

furtive clandestine, cloaked, conspiratorial, covert, hidden, secret, secretive, skulking, slinking, sly, sneaking, sneaky, stealthy, surreptitious, underhand, under-the-table

fury 1. anger, frenzy, impetuosity, ire, madness, passion, rage, wrath **2.** ferocity, fierceness, force, intensity, power, savagery, severity, tempestuousness, turbulence, vehemence, violence **3.** hag, hellcat, shrew, spitfire, termagant, virago, vixen

fuss *n.* **1.** ado, agitation, bother, bustle, commotion, confusion, excitement, fidget, flap (*informal*), flurry, fluster, flutter, hurry, palaver, pother, stir, storm in a teacup (*Brit.*), to-do, upset, worry **2.** altercation, argument, bother, complaint, difficulty, display, furore, hassle (*informal*), objection, row, squabble, trouble, unrest, upset *~vb.* **3.** bustle, chafe, fidget, flap (*informal*), fret, fume, get in a stew (*informal*), get worked up, labour over, make a meal of (*informal*), make a thing of (*informal*), niggle, take pains, worry

fussy 1. choosy (*informal*), dainty, difficult, discriminating, exacting, faddish, faddy, fastidious, finicky, hard to please, nit-picking (*informal*), old-maidish, old womanish, overparticular, particular, pernickety, picky (*informal*), squeamish **2.** busy, cluttered, overdecorated, overelaborate, overembellished, overworked, rococo

futile 1. abortive, barren, bootless, empty, forlorn, fruitless, hollow, ineffectual, in vain, nugatory, profitless, sterile, to no avail, unavailing, unproductive, unprofitable, unsuccessful, useless, vain, valueless, worthless **2.** idle, pointless, trifling, trivial, unimportant

futility 1. emptiness, fruitlessness, hollowness, ineffectiveness, uselessness **2.** pointlessness, triviality, unimportance, vanity

future 1. *n.* expectation, hereafter, outlook, prospect, time to come **2.** *adj.* approaching, coming, destined,

futurology *n* the study or prediction of the future of mankind.

fuzz[1] *n* a mass or covering of fine or curly hairs, fibres, etc.

fuzz[2] *n Slang* the police or a policeman.

fuzzy *adj* **fuzzier, fuzziest 1** of, like, or covered with fuzz. **2** unclear, blurred, or distorted. **3** (of hair) tightly curled. **fuzzily** *adv* **fuzziness** *n*

fwd forward.

THESAURUS

eventual, expected, fated, forthcoming, impending, in the offing, later, prospective, subsequent, to be, to come, ultimate, unborn

G

g 1 gallon(s). 2 gram(s). 3 acceleration due to gravity.
G 1 *Music* the fifth note of the scale of C major. 2 gravity. 3 good. 4 giga-. 5 *Slang* grand (a thousand pounds or dollars).
Ga *Chem* gallium.
GA Georgia.
gab *Informal ~vb* **gabbing, gabbed** 1 to talk a lot, esp. about unimportant things. *~n* 2 idle talk. 3 **gift of the gab** the ability to talk easily and persuasively.
gabardine *or* **gaberdine** *n* 1 a strong twill cloth used esp. for raincoats. 2 a coat made of this cloth.
gabble *vb* **-bling, -bled** 1 to speak rapidly and indistinctly. *~n* 2 rapid and indistinct speech.
gable *n* the triangular upper part of a wall between the sloping ends of a ridged roof. **gabled** *adj*
gad *vb* **gadding, gadded** (often foll. by *about* or *around*) to go about in search of pleasure.
gadabout *n Informal* a person who restlessly seeks amusement.
gadfly *n, pl* **-flies** 1 a large fly that bites livestock. 2 a constantly irritating person.
gadget *n* a small mechanical device or appliance. **gadgetry** *n*
gadoid (**gay**-doid) *adj* 1 of or belonging to the cod family of marine fishes. *~n* 2 any gadoid fish.
gadolinium *n Chem* a silvery-white metallic element of the rare-earth group. Symbol: Gd
gadzooks *interj Archaic* a mild oath.
Gael (**gayl**) *n* a Gaelic-speaker of Scotland, Ireland, or the Isle of Man. **Gaeldom** *n*
Gaelic (**gal**-lik, **gay**-lik) *n* 1 any of the closely related Celtic languages of Scotland, Ireland, or the Isle of Man. *~adj* 2 of the Celtic people of Scotland, Ireland, or the Isle of Man, or their language.
gaff[1] *n* 1 *Angling* a pole with a hook attached for landing large fish. 2 *Naut* a spar hoisted to support a fore-and-aft sail.
gaff[2] *n* **blow the gaff** *Brit slang* to give away a secret.
gaffe *n* something said or done that is socially upsetting or incorrect.
gaffer *n* 1 *Informal, chiefly Brit* a boss or foreman. 2 an old man: often used affectionately. 3 *Informal* the senior electrician on a television or film set.
gag[1] *vb* **gagging, gagged** 1 to choke as if about to vomit or as if struggling for breath. 2 to stop up (a person's mouth), usually with a piece of cloth, to prevent them from speaking or crying out. 3 to deprive of free speech. *~n* 4 something, usually a piece of cloth, stuffed into or tied across the mouth. 5 any restraint on free speech. 6 a device for keeping the jaws apart: *a dentist's gag.*
gag[2] *Informal ~n* 1 a joke, usually one told by a professional comedian. *~vb* **gagging, gagged** 2 to tell jokes.
gaga (**gah**-gah) *adj Informal* 1 confused and suffering some memory loss as a result of old age. 2 foolishly doting: *she's gaga over him.*
gage[1] *n* (formerly) a glove or other object thrown down to indicate a challenge to fight.
gage[2] *n, vb* **gaging, gaged** *US* same as **gauge.**
gaggle *n* 1 *Informal* a group of people gathered together. 2 a flock of geese.
gaiety *n, pl* **-ties** 1 a state of lively good spirits. 2 festivity; merrymaking.
gaily *adv* 1 in a lively manner; cheerfully. 2 with bright colours.
gain *vb* 1 to acquire (something desirable). 2 to increase, improve, or advance: *the shares gained 4p.* 3 **gain on** to get nearer to or catch up on. 4 to get to; reach: *gaining the top of one of the hills.* 5 (of a watch or clock) to become or be too fast. *~n* 6 something won or acquired; profit; advantage: *a clear gain would result.* 7 an increase in size or amount. 8 *Electronics* the ratio of the output signal of an amplifier to the input signal, usually measured in decibels.
gainful *adj* useful or profitable. **gainfully** *adv*
gainsay *vb* **-saying, -said** *Archaic or literary* to deny or contradict.
gait *n* 1 manner of walking. 2 (of horses and dogs) the pattern of footsteps at a particular speed, such as a trot.
gaiters *pl n* cloth or leather coverings for the legs or ankles.

THESAURUS

gadabout gallivanter, pleasure-seeker, rambler, rover, wanderer
gad (about *or* **around)** gallivant, ramble, range, roam, rove, run around, stravaig (*Scot., & northern English dialect*), stray, traipse (*informal*), wander
gadget appliance, contraption (*informal*), contrivance, device, gimmick, gizmo (*slang, chiefly U.S.*), instrument, invention, novelty, thing, tool
gaffe bloomer (*informal*), blunder, boob (*Brit. slang*), boo-boo (*informal*), clanger (*informal*), faux pas, gaucherie, howler, indiscretion, mistake, slip, solecism
gaffer 1. *informal* boss (*informal*), foreman, ganger, manager, overseer, superintendent, supervisor **2.** granddad, greybeard, old boy (*informal*), old fellow, old man, old-timer (*U.S.*)
gag[1] *vb.* **1.** *slang* barf *slang* choke (*slang*), disgorge, gasp, heave, pant, puke (*slang*), retch, spew, struggle for breath, throw up (*informal*), vomit **2.** curb, muffle, muzzle, quiet, silence, stifle, still, stop up, suppress, throttle
gag[2] crack (*slang*), funny (*informal*), hoax, jest, joke, wisecrack (*informal*), witticism
gaiety 1. animation, blitheness, blithesomeness (*literary*), cheerfulness, effervescence, elation, exhilaration, glee, good humour, high spirits, hilarity, *joie de vivre*, jollity, joviality, joyousness, light-heartedness, liveliness, merriment, mirth, sprightliness, vivacity **2.** celebration, conviviality, festivity, fun, jollification, merrymaking, revelry, revels
gaily 1. blithely, cheerfully, gleefully, happily, joyfully, light-heartedly, merrily **2.** brightly, brilliantly, colourfully, flamboyantly, flashily, gaudily, showily
gain *vb.* **1.** acquire, bring in, clear, earn, get, make, net, obtain, produce, realize, win, yield **2.** achieve, acquire, advance, attain, bag, build up, capture, collect, enlist, gather, get, glean, harvest, improve, increase, net, obtain, pick up, procure, profit, realize, reap, score (*slang*), secure, win, win over **3.** *usually with* **on** approach, catch up with, close with, get nearer, narrow the gap, overtake **4.** arrive at, attain, come to, get to, reach *~n.* **5.** accretion, achievement, acquisition, advance, advancement, advantage, attainment, benefit, dividend, earnings, emolument, growth, headway, improvement, income, increase, increment, lucre, proceeds, produce, profit, progress, return, rise, winnings, yield

gal *n Old-fashioned, slang* a girl.

gala (**gah**-la) *n* **1** a special social occasion, esp. a special performance. **2** *Chiefly Brit* a sporting occasion with competitions in several events: *next week's sports gala.*

galactic *adj* of the Galaxy or other galaxies.

galaxy *n, pl* **-axies 1** a star system held together by gravitational attraction. **2** a collection of brilliant people or things: *a galaxy of legal talent.*

Galaxy *n* **the Galaxy** the spiral galaxy that contains the solar system. Also called: **Milky Way**

gale *n* **1** a strong wind, specifically one of force 8 on the Beaufort scale. **2 gales** a loud outburst: *gales of laughter.*

galena *or* **galenite** *n* a soft bluish-grey mineral consisting of lead sulphide: the chief source of lead.

Galia melon *n* a kind of melon with a raised network texture on the skin and sweet flesh.

gall[1] (**gawl**) *n* **1** *Informal* bold impudence: *she was stunned I had the gall to ask.* **2** a feeling of great bitterness. **3** *Physiol obsolete* same as **bile.**

gall[2] (**gawl**) *vb* **1** to annoy or irritate. **2** to make the skin sore by rubbing. *~n* **3** something that causes annoyance. **4** a sore on the skin caused by rubbing.

gall[3] (**gawl**) *n* an abnormal outgrowth on a tree or plant caused by parasites.

gallant *adj* **1** persistent and courageous in the face of overwhelming odds: *a gallant fight.* **2** (of a man) making a show of polite attentiveness to women. **3** having a reputation for bravery: *Police Medal for gallant and meritorious services.* *~n* **4** *History* a young man who tried to impress women with his fashionable clothes or daring acts. **gallantly** *adv*

gallantry *n* **1** showy, attentive treatment of women. **2** great bravery in war or danger.

gall bladder *n* a muscular sac, attached to the liver, that stores bile.

galleon *n* a large, three-masted sailing ship used from the 15th to the 18th centuries.

gallery *n, pl* **-leries 1** a room or building for displaying works of art. **2** a balcony running along or around the inside wall of a church, hall, or other building. **3** *Theatre* **a** an upper floor that projects from the rear and contains the cheapest seats. **b** the audience seated there. **4** an underground passage in a mine or cave. **5** a group of spectators, for instance at a golf match. **6 play to the gallery** to try to gain approval by appealing to popular taste.

galley *n* **1** the kitchen of a ship, boat, or aircraft. **2** a ship propelled by oars or sails, used in ancient or medieval times.

galley slave *n* **1** a criminal or slave forced to row in a galley. **2** *Informal* a drudge.

Gallic *adj* **1** French. **2** of ancient Gaul or the Gauls.

Gallicism *n* a word or idiom borrowed from French.

gallinaceous *adj* of an order of birds, including poultry, pheasants, and grouse, that have a heavy rounded body.

galling (**gawl**-ing) *adj* annoying or bitterly humiliating.

gallium *n Chem* a silvery metallic element used in high-temperature thermometers and low-melting alloys. Symbol: Ga

gallivant *vb* to go about in search of pleasure.

gallon *n* **1** *Brit* a unit of liquid measure equal to 4.55 litres. **2** *US* a unit of liquid measure equal to 3.79 litres.

gallop *vb* **1** (of a horse) to run fast with a two-beat stride in which all four legs are off the ground at once. **2** to ride (a horse) at a gallop. **3** to move or progress rapidly. *~n* **4** the fast two-beat gait of horses. **5** a galloping.

gallows *n, pl* **-lowses** *or* **-lows 1** a wooden structure consisting of two upright posts with a crossbeam, used for hanging criminals. **2 the gallows** execution by hanging.

gallstone *n* a small hard mass formed in the gall bladder or its ducts.

Gallup Poll *n* a sampling of the views of a representative cross section of the population, usually used to forecast voting.

galop *n* **1** a 19th-century dance in quick duple time. **2** music for this dance.

galore *adj* in abundance: *there were bargains galore.*

galoshes *pl n* a pair of waterproof overshoes.

THESAURUS

gainsay contradict, contravene, controvert, deny, disaffirm, disagree with, dispute, rebut, retract

gait bearing, carriage, pace, step, stride, tread, walk

gala *n.* beano (*Brit. slang*), carnival, celebration, festival, festivity, fête, jamboree, pageant, party, rave (*Brit. slang*), rave-up (*Brit. slang*)

gale 1. blast, cyclone, hurricane, squall, storm, tempest, tornado, typhoon **2.** *informal* burst, eruption, explosion, fit, howl, outbreak, outburst, peal, shout, shriek

gall[1] **1.** *informal* brass (*informal*), brass neck (*Brit. informal*), brazenness, cheek (*informal*), chutzpah (*U.S. & Canad. informal*), effrontery, impertinence, impudence, insolence, neck (*informal*), nerve (*informal*), sauciness **2.** acrimony, animosity, animus, antipathy, bad blood, bile, bitterness, enmity, hostility, malevolence, malice, malignity, rancour, sourness, spite, spleen, venom

gall[2] *vb.* **1.** aggravate (*informal*), annoy, be on one's back (*slang*), bother, exasperate, fret, get in one's hair (*informal*), get on one's nerves (*informal*), harass, hassle (*informal*), irk, irritate, nag, nark (*Brit., Austral., & N.Z. slang*), nettle, peeve (*informal*), pester, piss one off (*taboo slang*), plague, provoke, rankle, rile (*informal*), rub up the wrong way, ruffle, vex **2.** abrade, bark, chafe, excoriate, fret, graze, irritate, rub raw, scrape, skin *~n.* **3.** aggravation (*informal*), annoyance, bother, botheration (*informal*), exasperation, harassment, irritant, irritation, nuisance, pest, provocation, vexation **4.** abrasion, chafe, excoriation, raw spot, scrape, sore, sore spot, wound

gallant *adj.* **1.** bold, brave, courageous, daring, dashing, dauntless, doughty, fearless, game (*informal*), heroic, high-spirited, honourable, intrepid, lion-hearted, manful, manly, mettlesome, noble, plucky, valiant, valorous **2.** attentive, chivalrous, courteous, courtly, gentlemanly, gracious, noble, polite *~n.* **3.** adventurer, beau, blade (*archaic*), buck, cavalier, champion (*informal*), dandy, daredevil, fop, hero, knight, ladies' man, lady-killer (*informal*), man about town, man of fashion

gallantry 1. attentiveness, chivalry, courteousness, courtesy, courtliness, elegance, gentlemanliness, graciousness, nobility, politeness **2.** audacity, boldness, bravery, courage, courageousness, daring, dauntlessness, derring-do (*archaic*), fearlessness, heroism, intrepidity, manliness, mettle, nerve, pluck, prowess, spirit, valiance, valour

galling aggravating (*informal*), annoying, bitter, bothersome, exasperating, harassing, humiliating, irksome, irritating, nettlesome, plaguing, provoking, rankling, vexatious, vexing

gallop barrel (along) (*informal, chiefly U.S. & Canad.*), bolt, career, dart, dash, fly, hasten, hie (*archaic*), hurry, race, run, rush, scud, shoot, speed, sprint, tear along, zoom

galumph *vb Informal* to leap or move about clumsily or joyfully.

galvanic *adj* **1** of or producing an electric current by chemical means, such as in a battery. **2** *Informal* stimulating, startling, or energetic.

galvanize *or* **-nise** *vb* **-nizing, -nized** *or* **-nising, -nised 1** to stimulate into action. **2** to cover (metal) with a protective zinc coating. **3** to stimulate by an electric current. **galvanization** *or* **-nisation** *n*

galvanometer *n* a sensitive instrument for detecting or measuring small electric currents.

gambit *n* **1** an opening remark or action intended to gain an advantage. **2** *Chess* an opening move in which a piece, usually a pawn, is sacrificed to gain an advantageous position.

gamble *vb* **-bling, -bled 1** to play games of chance to win money or prizes. **2** to risk or bet (something) on the outcome of an event or sport. **3 gamble on** to act with the expectation of: *she has gambled on proving everyone wrong.* **4 gamble away** to lose by gambling. *~n* **5** a risky act or venture. **6** a bet or wager. **gambler** *n* **gambling** *n*

gamboge (gam-**boje**) *n* a gum resin obtained from a tropical Asian tree, used as a yellow pigment and as a purgative.

gambol -bolling, -bolled *or US* **-boling, -boled 1** to jump about playfully; frolic. *~n* **2** playful jumping about; frolicking.

game[1] *n* **1** an amusement for children. **2** a competitive activity with rules. **3** a single period of play in such an activity. **4** (in some sports) the score needed to win. **5** a single contest in a series; match. **6** short for **computer game. 7** style or ability in playing a game: *Swansea's game suddenly loosened.* **8** an activity that seems to operate according to unwritten rules: *the political game of power.* **9** an activity undertaken in a spirit of playfulness: *people who regard life as a game.* **10** wild animals, birds, or fish, hunted for sport or food. **11** the flesh of such animals, used as food. **12** an object of pursuit: *fair game.* **13** *Informal* a trick or scheme: *what's his game?* **14 games** an event consisting of various sporting contests, usually in athletics: *Commonwealth Games.* **15 on the game** *Slang, chiefly Brit* working as a prostitute. **16 give the game away** to reveal one's intentions or a secret. **17 play the game** to behave fairly. **18 the game is up** the scheme or trick has been found out and so cannot succeed. *~adj* **19** *Informal* full of fighting spirit; plucky. **20** *Informal* prepared or willing: *I'm always game for a new sensation. ~vb* **gaming, gamed 21** to play games of chance for money; gamble. **gamely** *adv* **gameness** *n*

game[2] *adj* lame: *he had a game leg.*

gamekeeper *n* a person employed to take care of game on an estate.

gamesmanship *n Informal* the art of winning by cunning practices without actually cheating.

gamester *n* a gambler.

gamete (**gam**-eet) *n* a cell that can fuse with another in reproduction. **gametic** *adj*

gamey *or* **gamy** *adj* **gamier, gamiest** having the smell or flavour of game.

gamin *n* a street urchin.

gamine (**gam**-een) *n* a slim and boyish girl or young woman.

gaming *n* gambling.

gamma *n* the third letter in the Greek alphabet (Γ, γ).

gamma radiation *n* electromagnetic radiation of shorter wavelength and higher energy than x-rays.

gamma rays *pl n* streams of gamma radiation.

gammon *n* **1** cured or smoked ham. **2** the hindquarter of a side of bacon.

gammy *adj* **-mier, -miest** *Brit slang* (of the leg) lame.

gamp *n Brit informal* an umbrella.

gamut *n* **1** entire range or scale: *a rich gamut of facial expressions.* **2** *Music* **a** a scale. **b** the whole range of notes.

gamy *adj* same as **gamey.**

gander *n* **1** a male goose. **2** *Informal* a quick look: *have a gander.*

gang[1] *n* **1** a group of people who go around together, often to commit crime. **2** an organized group of workmen. *~vb* **3** to become or act as a gang. ~See also **gang up on.**

gang[2] *vb Scot* to go or walk.

gangland *n* the criminal underworld.

gangling *or* **gangly** *adj* lanky and awkward in movement.

ganglion *n, pl* **-glia** *or* **-glions** a collection of nerve cells outside the brain and spinal cord. **ganglionic** *adj*

gangplank *n Naut* a portable bridge for boarding and leaving a ship.

gangrene *n* decay of body tissue caused by the blood supply being interrupted by disease or injury. **gangrenous** *adj*

gangsta rap *n* a style of rap music portraying life in

THESAURUS

galore (*informal*), all over the place, aplenty, everywhere, in abundance, in great quantity, in numbers, in profusion, to spare

galvanize arouse, awaken, electrify, excite, fire, inspire, invigorate, jolt, kick-start, move, prod, provoke, quicken, shock, spur, startle, stimulate, stir, thrill, wake

gamble *vb.* **1.** back, bet, game, have a flutter (*informal*), lay *or* make a bet, play, punt, stake, try one's luck, wager **2.** back, chance, hazard, put one's faith *or* trust in, risk, speculate, stake, stick one's neck out (*informal*), take a chance, venture *~n.* **3.** chance, leap in the dark, lottery, risk, speculation, uncertainty, venture **4.** bet, flutter (*informal*), punt, wager

gambol 1. *vb.* caper, cavort, curvet, cut a caper, frisk, frolic, hop, jump, prance, rollick, skip **2.** *n.* antic, caper, frolic, hop, jump, prance, skip, spring

game *n.* **1.** amusement, distraction, diversion, entertainment, frolic, fun, jest, joke, lark, merriment, pastime, play, recreation, romp, sport **2.** competition, contest, event, head-to-head, match, meeting, round, tournament **3.** chase, prey, quarry, wild animals **4.** *informal* design, device, plan, plot, ploy, scheme, stratagem, strategy, tactic, trick **5. play the game** conform, follow the rules, go along with, keep in step, play by the rules, play fair, toe the line *~adj.* **6.** ballsy (*taboo slang*), bold, brave, courageous, dauntless, dogged, fearless, feisty (*informal, chiefly U.S. & Canad.*), gallant, gritty, have-a-go (*informal*), heroic, intrepid, persevering, persistent, plucky, resolute, spirited, unflinching, valiant, valorous **7.** desirous, disposed, eager, inclined, interested, prepared, ready, willing

gamut area, catalogue, compass, field, range, scale, scope, series, sweep

gang band, bevy, camp, circle, clique, club, company, coterie, crew (*informal*), crowd, group, herd, horde, lot, mob, pack, party, posse (*slang*), ring, set, shift, squad, team, troupe

gangling *or* **gangly** angular, awkward, lanky, loose-jointed, rangy, rawboned, skinny, spindly, tall

gangster bandit, brigand, crook (*informal*), despera-

Black ghettos in the U.S. and featuring lyrics that are anti-authority and derogatory to women.

gangster *n* a member of an organized gang of criminals.

gangue *n* valueless material in an ore.

gang up on *or* **against** *vb Informal* to combine in a group against.

gangway *n* **1** *Brit* an aisle between rows of seats. **2** same as **gangplank. 3** an opening in a ship's side to take a gangplank.

gannet *n* **1** a heavily built white sea bird. **2** *Slang* a greedy person.

ganoid *adj* **1** (of the scales of certain fishes) consisting of an inner bony layer covered with an enamel-like substance. **2** (of a fish) having such scales. *~n* **3** a ganoid fish.

gantry *n, pl* **-tries** a large metal framework used to support something, such as a travelling crane, or to position a rocket on its launching pad.

gaol (**jayl**) *n, vb Brit* same as **jail. gaoler** *n*

gap *n* **1** a break or opening in something. **2** an interruption or interval. **3** a difference in ideas or viewpoint: *the generation gap.* **gappy** *adj*

gape *vb* **gaping, gaped 1** to stare in wonder with the mouth open. **2** to open the mouth wide, as in yawning. **3** to be or become wide open: *a hole gaped in the roof.* **gaping** *adj*

garage *n* **1** a building used to keep cars. **2** a place where cars are repaired and petrol is sold. *~vb* **-aging, -aged 3** to put or keep a car in a garage.

garage sale *n* a sale of household items held at a person's home, usually in the garage.

garb *n* **1** clothes, usually the distinctive dress of an occupation or group: *modern military garb. ~vb* **2** to clothe.

garbage *n* **1** *US* household waste. **2** worthless rubbish or nonsense.

garbled *adj* (of a story, message, etc.) jumbled and confused.

garçon (**garss**-on) *n* a waiter.

garda *n, pl* **gardaí** a member of the police force of the Republic of Ireland.

garden *n* **1** *Brit* an area of land usually next to a house, for growing flowers, fruit, or vegetables. **2** Also: **gardens** a cultivated area of land open to the public: *Kensington Gardens.* **3 lead someone up the garden path** *Informal* to mislead or deceive someone. *~vb* **4** to work in or take care of a garden. **gardener** *n* **gardening** *n*

garden centre *n* a place where plants and gardening tools and equipment are sold.

garden city *n Brit* a planned town of limited size surrounded by countryside.

gardenia (gar-**deen**-ya) *n* **1** a large fragrant waxy white flower. **2** the evergreen shrub on which it grows.

gargantuan *adj* huge or enormous.

gargle *vb* **-gling, -gled 1** to rinse the mouth and throat with (a liquid) by slowly breathing out through the liquid. *~n* **2** the liquid used for gargling. **3** the act or sound of gargling.

gargoyle *n* (on ancient buildings) a waterspout below the roof carved in the form of a grotesque face or figure.

garish *adj* crudely bright or colourful. **garishly** *adv* **garishness** *n*

garland *n* **1** a wreath of flowers and leaves worn round the head or neck or hung up. *~vb* **2** to decorate with a garland or garlands.

garlic *n* the bulb of a plant of the onion family, with a strong taste and smell, made up of small segments which are used in cooking. **garlicky** *adj*

garment *n* an article of clothing.

garner *vb* to collect or gather: *the financial rewards garnered by his book.*

garnet *n* a red semiprecious gemstone.

garnish *vb* **1** to decorate (food) with something to add to its appearance or flavour. *~n* **2** a decoration for food.

garret *n* an attic in a house.

garrison *n* **1** soldiers who guard a base or fort. **2** the place itself. *~vb* **3** to station (soldiers) in (a fort or base).

garrotte *or* **garotte** *n* **1** a Spanish method of execution by strangling. **2** a cord, wire, or iron collar, used

THESAURUS

do, gang member, heavy (*slang*), hood (*U.S. slang*), hoodlum (*chiefly U.S.*), mobster (*U.S. slang*), racketeer, robber, ruffian, thug, tough

gap 1. blank, breach, break, chink, cleft, crack, cranny, crevice, discontinuity, divide, entr'acte, hiatus, hole, interlude, intermission, interruption, interstice, interval, lacuna, lull, opening, pause, recess, rent, respite, rift, space, vacuity, void **2.** difference, disagreement, disparity, divergence, inconsistency

gape 1. gawk, gawp (*Brit. slang*), goggle, stare, wonder **2.** crack, open, split, yawn

gaping broad, cavernous, great, open, vast, wide, wide open, yawning

garbage 1. bits and pieces, debris, detritus, dreck (*slang, chiefly U.S.*), dross, filth, junk, litter, muck, odds and ends, offal, refuse, rubbish, scourings, scraps, slops, sweepings, swill, trash (*chiefly U.S.*), waste **2.** balderdash, balls (*taboo slang*), bilge (*informal*), bosh (*informal*), bull (*slang*), bullshit (*taboo slang*), bunkum (*chiefly U.S.*), claptrap (*informal*), cobblers (*Brit. taboo slang*), codswallop (*Brit. slang*), crap (*slang*), drivel, eyewash (*informal*), gibberish, guff (*slang*), havers (*Scot.*), hogwash, hokum (*slang, chiefly U.S. & Canad.*), horsefeathers (*U.S. slang*), hot air (*informal*), moonshine, nonsense, pap, piffle (*informal*), poppycock (*informal*), rot, shit (*taboo slang*), stuff and nonsense, tommyrot, tosh (*informal*), tripe (*informal*), twaddle

garbled confused, corrupted, distorted, jumbled, misinterpreted, misquoted, misreported, misrepresented, misstated, mixed up, twisted

garish brash, brassy, cheap, flash (*informal*), flashy, flaunting, gaudy, glaring, glittering, loud, meretricious, naff (*Brit. slang*), raffish, showy, tacky (*informal*), tasteless, tawdry, vulgar

garland 1. *n.* bays, chaplet, coronal, crown, festoon, honours, laurels, wreath **2.** *vb.* adorn, crown, deck, festoon, wreathe

garments apparel, array, articles of clothing, attire, clothes, clothing, costume, dress, duds (*informal*), garb, gear (*slang*), habiliments, habit, outfit, raiment (*archaic*), robes, togs, uniform, vestments, wear

garner accumulate, amass, assemble, collect, deposit, gather, hoard, husband, lay in *or* up, put by, reserve, save, stockpile, store, stow away, treasure

garnish 1. *vb.* adorn, beautify, bedeck, deck, decorate, embellish, enhance, festoon, grace, ornament, set off, trim **2.** *n.* adornment, decoration, embellishment, enhancement, festoon, garniture, ornament, ornamentation, trim, trimming

garrison *n.* **1.** armed force, command, detachment, troops, unit **2.** base, camp, encampment, fort, fortifica-

to strangle someone. ~*vb* **-rotting, -rotted 3** to execute with a garrotte.

garrulous *adj* constantly chattering; talkative. **garrulousness** *n*

garter *n* **1** a band, usually of elastic, worn round the leg to hold up a sock or stocking. **2** *US & Canad* a suspender.

Garter *n* **the Order of the Garter** the highest order of British knighthood.

garter stitch *n* knitting in which all the rows are knitted in plain stitch.

gas *n, pl* **gases** *or* **gasses 1** an airlike substance that is neither liquid nor solid at room temperature and atmospheric pressure. **2** a fossil fuel in the form of a gas, used as a source of heat. **3** an anaesthetic in the form of a gas. **4** *Mining* firedamp or the explosive mixture of firedamp and air. **5** *US, Canad, Austral, NZ* petrol. **6** a poisonous gas used in war. **7** *Informal* idle talk or boasting. **8** *Slang* an entertaining person or thing: *Monterey was a gas for musicians and fans alike.* ~*vb* **gases** *or* **gasses, gassing, gassed 9** to subject to gas fumes so as to make unconscious or to suffocate. **10** *Informal* to talk a lot; chatter.

gasbag *n Informal* a person who talks too much.

gas chamber *n* an airtight room which is filled with poison gas to kill people.

gaseous *adj* of or like a gas.

gash *n* **1** a long deep cut. ~*vb* **2** to make a long deep cut in.

gasholder *n* a large tank for storing gas before distributing it to users.

gasify *vb* **-fies, -fying, -fied** to change into a gas. **gasification** *n*

gasket *n* a piece of paper, rubber, or metal sandwiched between the faces of a metal joint to provide a seal.

gaslight *n* **1** a lamp in which light is produced by burning gas. **2** the light produced by such a lamp.

gasman *n, pl* **-men** a man employed to read household gas meters and install or repair gas fittings, etc.

gas mask *n* a mask fitted with a chemical filter to protect the wearer from breathing in harmful gases.

gas meter *n* a device for measuring and recording the amount of gas passed through it.

gasoline *or* **gasolene** *n US & Canad* petrol.

gasometer (gas-**som**-it-er) *n* same as **gasholder.**

gasp *vb* **1** to draw in the breath sharply or with difficulty. **2** to utter breathlessly. ~*n* **3** a short convulsive intake of breath.

gas ring *n* a circular metal pipe with several holes in it fed with gas for cooking.

gassy *adj* **-sier, -siest** filled with, containing, or like gas. **gassiness** *n*

gastric *adj* of the stomach.

gastric juice *n* a digestive fluid secreted by the stomach.

gastric ulcer *n* an ulcer on the lining of the stomach.

gastritis *n* inflammation of the lining of the stomach, causing vomiting or gastric ulcers.

gastroenteritis *n* inflammation of the stomach and intestine, causing vomiting and diarrhoea.

gastronomy *n* the art of good eating. **gastronomic** *adj*

gastropod *n* a mollusc, such as a snail or whelk that has a single flat muscular foot, eyes on stalks, and usually a spiral shell.

gasworks *n* a factory in which coal gas is made.

gate *n* **1** a movable barrier, usually hinged, for closing an opening in a wall or fence. **2 a** the number of people admitted to a sporting event or entertainment. **b** the total entrance money received from them. **3** an exit at an airport by which passengers get to an aircraft. **4** *Electronics* a circuit with one or more input terminals and one output terminal, the output being determined by the combination of input signals. **5** a slotted metal frame that controls the positions of the gear lever in a motor vehicle.

gateau (**gat**-toe) *n, pl* **-teaux** (-toes) a large rich layered cake.

gate-crash *vb Informal* to gain entry to (a party) without invitation. **gate-crasher** *n*

gatehouse *n* a building at or above a gateway.

gate-leg table *or* **gate-legged table** *n* a table with leaves supported by hinged legs that can swing back to let the leaves hang from the frame.

gateway *n* **1** an entrance that may be closed by a gate. **2** a means of entry or access: *his only gateway to the outside world.*

gather *vb* **1** to come or bring together. **2** to increase gradually in (pace, speed, or momentum). **3** to prepare oneself for a task or challenge by collecting one's thoughts, strength, or courage. **4** to learn from information given; conclude: *this is pretty important, I gather.* **5** to draw (fabric) into small folds or tucks. **6** to pick or harvest (crops). ~*n* **7 gathers** small folds or tucks in fabric.

gathering *n* a group of people, usu. meeting for some particular purpose.

GATT General Agreement on Tariffs and Trade.

gauche (**gohsh**) *adj* socially awkward.

gaucho (**gow**-choh) *n, pl* **-chos** a cowboy of the South American pampas.

gaudy *adj* **gaudier, gaudiest** vulgarly bright or colourful. **gaudily** *adv* **gaudiness** *n*

gauge (**gayj**) *vb* **gauging, gauged 1** to estimate or judge (people's feelings or reactions). **2** to measure using a gauge. ~*n* **3** an instrument for measuring quantities: *a petrol gauge.* **4** a scale or standard of meas-

THESAURUS

tion, fortress, post, station, stronghold ~*vb.* **3.** assign, mount, position, post, put on duty, station

garrulous babbling, chattering, chatty, effusive, gabby (*informal*), glib, gossiping, gushing, loquacious, mouthy, prating, prattling, talkative, verbose, voluble

gash 1. *n.* cleft, cut, gouge, incision, laceration, rent, slash, slit, split, tear, wound **2.** *vb.* cleave, cut, gouge, incise, lacerate, rend, slash, slit, split, tear, wound

gasp 1. *vb.* blow, catch one's breath, choke, fight for breath, gulp, pant, puff **2.** *n.* blow, gulp, pant, puff

gate access, barrier, door, doorway, egress, entrance, exit, gateway, opening, passage, port (*Scot.*), portal

gather 1. accumulate, amass, assemble, bring *or* get together, collect, congregate, convene, flock, forgather, garner, group, heap, hoard, marshal, mass, muster, pile up, round up, stack up, stockpile **2.** assume, be led to believe, conclude, deduce, draw, hear, infer, learn, make, surmise, understand **3.** crop, cull, garner, glean, harvest, pick, pluck, reap, select **4.** fold, pleat, pucker, ruffle, shirr, tuck

gathering assemblage, assembly, company, conclave, concourse, congregation, congress, convention, convocation, crowd, flock, get-together (*informal*), group, knot, meeting, muster, party, rally, throng, turnout

gauche awkward, clumsy, graceless, ignorant, ill-bred, ill-mannered, inelegant, inept, insensitive, lacking in social graces, maladroit, tactless, uncultured, unpolished, unsophisticated

gaudy brash, bright, brilliant, flash (*informal*), flashy,

urement. **5** a standard for estimating people's feelings or reactions: *a gauge of public opinion.* **6** the diameter of the barrel of a gun. **7** the distance between the rails of a railway track.

Gaul *n* a native of ancient Gaul.

gaunt *adj* **1** bony and emaciated in appearance. **2** (of a place) bleak or desolate: *the gaunt disused flour mill.* **gauntness** *n*

gauntlet[1] *n* **1** a long heavy protective glove. **2** a medieval armoured glove. **3 take up the gauntlet** to accept a challenge.

gauntlet[2] *n* **run the gauntlet** to be exposed to criticism or harsh treatment.

gauss (rhymes with **mouse**) *n, pl* **gauss** the cgs unit of magnetic flux density.

gauze *n* a transparent, loosely woven cloth, often used for surgical dressings. **gauzy** *adj*

gave *vb* the past tense of **give.**

gavel (gav-vl) *n* a small hammer used by a judge, auctioneer, or chairman to call for order or attention.

gavotte *n* **1** an old formal dance in quadruple time. **2** music for this dance.

gawk *vb* **1** to stare stupidly. *~n* **2** a clumsy stupid person.

gawky *adj* **gawkier, gawkiest** clumsy and awkward.

gawp *vb Slang* to stare stupidly.

gay *adj* **1** homosexual. **2** carefree and merry: *with gay abandon.* **3** bright and cheerful: *smartly dressed in gay colours.* *~n* **4** a homosexual, esp. a homosexual man: *solidarity amongst lesbians and gays.*

➤ The meaning "homosexual" is now the most frequent use of *gay,* which retains the meaning "happy" only in older books.

gayness *n* homosexuality.

gaze *vb* **gazing, gazed 1** to look long and steadily at someone or something. *~n* **2** a long steady look.

gazebo (gaz-zee-boh) *n, pl* **-bos** a summerhouse or pavilion with a good view.

gazelle *n* a small graceful fawn-coloured antelope of Africa and Asia.

gazette *n* an official newspaper that gives lists of announcements, for instance in legal or military affairs.

gazetteer *n* a book or section of a book that lists and describes places.

gazump *vb Brit informal* to raise the price of a house after agreeing a price verbally with an intending buyer.

gazunder *vb Brit informal* to reduce an offer on a house immediately before exchanging contracts, having earlier agreed a higher price with (the seller).

GB Great Britain.

GBH grievous bodily harm.

GC George Cross (a Brit. award for bravery).

GCE (in Britain) **1** General Certificate of Education. **2** *Informal* a pass in a GCE examination.

GCSE (in Britain) **1** General Certificate of Secondary Education; an examination in specified subjects which replaced the GCE O level and CSE. **2** *Informal* a pass in a GCSE examination.

Gd *Chem* gadolinium.

GDP gross domestic product.

Ge *Chem* germanium.

gear *n* **1** a set of toothed wheels that engages with another or with a rack in order to change the speed or direction of transmitted motion. **2** a mechanism for transmitting motion by gears. **3** the setting of a gear to suit engine speed or direction: *a higher gear; reverse gear.* **4** clothing or personal belongings. **5** equipment for a particular task: *police in riot gear.* **6 in** or **out of gear** with the gear mechanism engaged or disengaged. *~vb* **7** to prepare or organize for something: *a population geared for war.* ~See also **gear up.**

gearbox *n* the metal casing enclosing a set of gears in a motor vehicle.

gearing *n* a system of gears designed to transmit motion.

gear lever *or US & Canad* **gearshift** *n* a lever used to engage or change gears in a motor vehicle.

gear up *vb* to prepare for an activity: *to gear up for a massive relief operation.*

gearwheel *n* one of the toothed wheels in the gears of a motor vehicle.

gecko *n, pl* **geckos** a small tropical lizard.

gee *interj US & Canad informal* a mild exclamation of surprise, admiration, etc. Also: **gee whiz**

geese *n* the plural of **goose**[1].

geezer *n Informal* a man.

Geiger counter (guy-ger) *or* **Geiger-Müller counter** *n* an instrument for detecting and measuring radiation.

geisha (gay-sha) *n* a professional female companion for men in Japan, trained in music, dancing, and conversation.

gel (jell) *n* **1** a thick jelly-like substance, esp. one used to keep a hairstyle in shape. *~vb* **gelling, gelled 2** to become a gel. **3** same as **jell. 4** to apply gel to (one's hair).

gelatine (jell-a-teen) *or* **gelatin** *n* a clear water-

THESAURUS

florid, garish, gay, glaring, loud, meretricious, naff (*Brit. slang*), ostentatious, raffish, showy, tacky (*informal*), tasteless, tawdry, vulgar

gauge *vb.* **1.** adjudge, appraise, assess, estimate, evaluate, guess, judge, rate, reckon, value **2.** ascertain, calculate, check, compute, count, determine, measure, weigh *~n.* **3.** bore, capacity, degree, depth, extent, height, magnitude, measure, scope, size, span, thickness, width **4.** basis, criterion, example, exemplar, guide, guideline, indicator, measure, meter, model, par, pattern, rule, sample, standard, test, touchstone, yardstick

gaunt 1. angular, attenuated, bony, cadaverous, emaciated, haggard, lank, lean, meagre, pinched, rawboned, scraggy, scrawny, skeletal, skinny, spare, thin, wasted **2.** bare, bleak, desolate, dismal, dreary, forbidding, forlorn, grim, harsh

gawky awkward, clumsy, gauche, loutish, lumbering, lumpish, maladroit, oafish, uncouth, ungainly

gay *adj.* **1.** homosexual, lesbian, poofy (*offensive slang*), queer (*offensive slang*) **2.** animated, blithe, carefree, cheerful, debonair, glad, gleeful, happy, hilarious, insouciant, jolly, jovial, joyful, joyous, lighthearted, lively, merry, sparkling, sunny, vivacious **3.** bright, brilliant, colourful, flamboyant, flashy, fresh, garish, gaudy, rich, showy, vivid *~n.* **4.** dyke (*offensive slang*), faggot (*U.S. offensive slang*), fairy (*offensive slang*), homosexual, invert, lesbian, poof (*offensive slang*), queer (*offensive slang*)

gaze 1. *vb.* contemplate, eyeball (*U.S. slang*), gape, look, look fixedly, regard, stare, view, watch, wonder **2.** *n.* fixed look, look, stare

gazette journal, newspaper, news-sheet, organ, paper, periodical

gear *n.* **1.** cog, cogwheel, gearwheel, toothed wheel **2.** cogs, gearing, machinery, mechanism, works **3.** *slang* apparel, array, attire, baggage, belongings, clothes, clothing, costume, dress, effects, garb, garments, habit, kit, luggage, outfit, rigout, stuff, things (*informal*), togs, wear **4.** accessories, accoutrements, appa-

soluble protein made by boiling animal hides and bones, used in cooking, photography, etc.

gelatinous (jill-**at**-in-uss) *adj* with a thick, semi-liquid consistency.

geld *vb* **gelding, gelded** *or* **gelt** to castrate (a horse or other animal).

gelding *n* a castrated male horse.

gelignite *n* a type of dynamite used for blasting.

gem *n* **1** a precious stone used for decoration. **2** a person or thing regarded as precious or special: *a perfect gem of a hotel.*

Gemini *n Astrol* the third sign of the zodiac; the Twins.

gemsbok (**hemss**-bok) *n S African* same as **oryx.**

gemstone *n* a precious or semiprecious stone, esp. one which has been cut and polished.

gen *n Brit, Austral & NZ informal* information: *I want to get as much gen as I can about the American market.* ~See also **gen up on.**

Gen. General.

gendarme (**zhahn**-darm) *n* a member of the French police force.

gender *n* **1** the state of being male, female, or neuter. **2** the classification of nouns in certain languages as masculine, feminine, or neuter.

gene (**jean**) *n* a unit composed of DNA forming part of a chromosome, by which inherited characteristics are transmitted from parent to offspring.

genealogy (jean-ee-**al**-a-jee) *n* **1** the direct descent of an individual or group from an ancestor. **2** (*pl* **-gies**) a chart showing the descent of an individual or group. **genealogical** *adj* **genealogist** *n*

genera (**jen**-er-a) *n* a plural of **genus.**

general *adj* **1** common or widespread: *general goodwill.* **2** of, affecting, or including all or most of the members of a group. **3** not specialized or specializing: *a general hospital.* **4** including various or miscellaneous items: *general knowledge.* **5** not definite; vague: *the examples used will give a general idea.* **6** highest in authority or rank: *the club's general manager.* ~*n* **7** a very senior military officer. **8 in general** generally; mostly or usually.

general anaesthetic *n* a substance that causes general anaesthesia. See **anaesthesia.**

general election *n* an election in which representatives are chosen in all constituencies of a state.

generalissimo *n, pl* **-mos** a supreme commander of combined armed forces.

generality *n* **1** (*pl* **-ties**) a general principle or observation: *speaking in generalities.* **2** *Old-fashioned* the majority: *the generality of mankind.*

generalization *or* **-isation** *n* a principle or statement based on specific instances but applied generally: *the argument sinks to generalizations and name-calling.*

generalize *or* **-ise** *vb* **-izing, -ized** *or* **-ising, -ised 1** to form general principles or conclusions from specific instances. **2** to speak in generalities. **3** to make widely used or known: *generalized violence.*

generally *adv* **1** usually; as a rule: *these protests have generally been peaceful.* **2** commonly or widely: *it's generally agreed he has performed well.* **3** not specifically; broadly: *what are your thoughts generally about the war?*

general practitioner *n* a doctor who does not specialize but has a general medical practice in which he or she treats all illnesses.

general-purpose *adj* having a variety of uses: *general-purpose cooking oil.*

general staff *n* officers who assist commanders in the planning and execution of military operations.

general strike *n* a strike by all or most of the workers of a country.

generate *vb* **-ating, -ated** to produce or create.

generation *n* **1** all the people of approximately the same age: *the younger generation.* **2** a successive stage in descent of people or animals: *passed on from generation to generation.* **3** the average time between two generations of a species, about 35 years for humans: *an alliance which has lasted a generation.* **4** a specified stage of development: *the next generation of fighter aircraft.* **5** production, esp. of electricity or heat.

generation gap *n* the difference in outlook and the lack of understanding between people of different generations.

generative *adj* capable of producing or originating something.

generator *n* a device for converting mechanical energy into electrical energy.

generic (jin-**ner**-ik) *adj* of a whole class, or group, or genus. **generically** *adv*

generous *adj* **1** ready to give freely; unselfish. **2** free

THESAURUS

ratus, equipment, harness, instruments, outfit, paraphernalia, rigging, supplies, tackle, tools, trappings ~*vb.* **5.** adapt, adjust, equip, fit, rig, suit, tailor

gelatinous gluey, glutinous, gummy, jelly-like, sticky, viscid, viscous

gem **1.** jewel, precious stone, semiprecious stone, stone **2.** flower, jewel, masterpiece, pearl, pick, prize, treasure

genealogy ancestry, blood line, derivation, descent, extraction, family tree, line, lineage, pedigree, progeniture, stemma, stock, strain

general **1.** accepted, broad, common, extensive, popular, prevailing, prevalent, public, universal, widespread **2.** across-the-board, all-inclusive, blanket, broad, catholic, collective, comprehensive, encyclopedic, generic, indiscriminate, miscellaneous, panoramic, sweeping, total, universal **3.** accustomed, conventional, customary, everyday, habitual, normal, ordinary, regular, typical, usual **4.** approximate, ill-defined, imprecise, inaccurate, indefinite, inexact, loose, undetailed, unspecific, vague

generality abstract principle, generalization, loose statement, sweeping statement, vague notion

generally **1.** almost always, as a rule, by and large, conventionally, customarily, for the most part, habitually, in most cases, largely, mainly, normally, on average, on the whole, ordinarily, regularly, typically, usually **2.** commonly, extensively, popularly, publicly, universally, widely **3.** approximately, broadly, chiefly, for the most part, in the main, largely, mainly, mostly, on the whole, predominantly, principally

generate beget, breed, bring about, cause, create, engender, form, give rise to, initiate, make, originate, produce, propagate, spawn

generation **1.** age group, breed, crop **2.** age, day, days, epoch, era, period, time, times **3.** begetting, breeding, creation, engenderment, formation, genesis, origination, procreation, production, propagation, reproduction

generic all-encompassing, blanket, collective, common, comprehensive, general, inclusive, sweeping, universal, wide

generosity **1.** beneficence, benevolence, bounteousness, bounty, charity, kindness, largesse *or* largess, liberality, munificence, open-handedness **2.** disinterestedness, goodness, high-mindedness, magnanimity, nobleness, unselfishness

from pettiness in character and mind. **3** large or plentiful: *a generous donation.* **generously** *adv* **generosity** *n*

genesis (**jen**-iss-iss) *n, pl* **-ses** (-seez) the beginning or origin of anything.

genetic (jin-**net**-tik) *adj* of genetics, genes, or the origin of something. **genetically** *adv*

genetic code *n Biochem* the order in which the four nucleic acid bases of DNA are arranged in the molecule for transmitting genetic information to the cells.

genetic engineering *n* alteration of the genetic structure of an organism in order to produce more desirable traits.

genetic fingerprinting *n* the use of a person's unique pattern of DNA, which can be obtained from blood, saliva, or tissue, as a means of identification. **genetic fingerprint** *n*

genetics *n* the study of heredity and variation in organisms. **geneticist** *n*

genial (**jean**-ee-al) *adj* cheerful, easy-going, and friendly. **geniality** *n* **genially** *adv*

genie (**jean**-ee) *n* (in fairy tales) a servant who appears by magic and fulfils a person's wishes.

genital *adj* of the sexual organs or reproduction.

genitals *or* **genitalia** (jen-it-**ail**-ya) *pl n* the external sexual organs.

genitive *n Grammar* a grammatical case in some languages used to indicate a relation of ownership or association.

genius (**jean**-yuss) *n, pl* **-uses 1** a person with exceptional ability in a particular subject or activity. **2** such ability. **3** a person considered as exerting influence of a certain sort: *the evil genius behind the drug-smuggling empire.*

genocide (**jen**-no-side) *n* the deliberate killing of a people or nation. **genocidal** *adj*

genre (**zhahn**-ra) *n* **1** a kind or type of literary, musical, or artistic work: *the mystery and supernatural genres.* **2** a kind of painting depicting incidents from everyday life.

gent *n Old-fashioned, informal* short for **gentleman.**

genteel *adj* **1** overly concerned with being polite. **2** respectable, polite, and well-bred. **genteelly** *adv*

gentian (**jen**-shun) *n* a mountain plant with blue or purple flowers.

gentian violet *n* a violet-coloured solution used as an antiseptic and in the treatment of burns.

Gentile *n* **1** a person who is not a Jew. *~adj* **2** not Jewish.

gentility *n, pl* **-ties 1** noble birth or ancestry. **2** respectability and good manners.

gentle *adj* **1** kind and calm in character. **2** temperate or moderate: *gentle autumn rain.* **3** soft; not sharp or harsh: *gentle curves.* **gentleness** *n* **gently** *adv*

gentlefolk *pl n Old-fashioned* people regarded as being of good breeding.

gentleman *n, pl* **-men 1** a cultured, courteous, and well-bred man. **2** a man who comes from a family of high social position. **3** a polite name for a man. **gentlemanly** *adj*

gentrification *n* a process by which the character of a traditionally working class area is made fashionable by middle class people. **gentrify** *vb*

gentry *n Brit old-fashioned* people just below the nobility in social rank.

gents *n Brit informal* a men's public toilet.

genuflect *vb* to bend the knee as a sign of reverence or deference, esp. in church. **genuflection** *n*

genuine *adj* **1** real and exactly what it appears to be: *a genuine antique.* **2** sincerely felt: *genuine concern.* **3** (of a person) honest and without pretence. **genuinely** *adv* **genuineness** *n*

gen up on *vb* **genning, genned** *Brit informal* to become, or make someone else, fully informed about.

genus (**jean**-uss) *n, pl* **genera** *or* **genuses 1** *Biol* one of the groups into which a family is divided, containing one or more species. **2** a class or group.

geocentric *adj* **1** having the earth as a centre. **2** measured as from the centre of the earth.

geodesic *adj* **1** relating to the geometry of curved surfaces. *~n* **2** the shortest line between two points on a curved surface.

geodesy *n* the study of the shape and size of the earth.

geography *n* **1** the study of the earth's surface, including physical features, climate, and population. **2**

THESAURUS

generous 1. beneficent, benevolent, bounteous, bountiful, charitable, free, hospitable, kind, lavish, liberal, munificent, open-handed, princely, prodigal, ungrudging, unstinting **2.** big-hearted, disinterested, good, high-minded, lofty, magnanimous, noble, unselfish **3.** abundant, ample, copious, full, lavish, liberal, overflowing, plentiful, rich, unstinting

genesis beginning, birth, commencement, creation, dawn, engendering, formation, generation, inception, origin, outset, propagation, root, source, start

genial affable, agreeable, amiable, cheerful, cheery, congenial, convivial, cordial, easygoing, enlivening, friendly, glad, good-natured, happy, hearty, jolly, jovial, joyous, kind, kindly, merry, pleasant, sunny, warm, warm-hearted

geniality affability, agreeableness, amiability, cheerfulness, cheeriness, congenialness, conviviality, cordiality, friendliness, gladness, good cheer, good nature, happiness, heartiness, jollity, joviality, joy, joyousness, kindliness, kindness, mirth, pleasantness, sunniness, warm-heartedness, warmth

genius 1. adept, brain (*informal*), brainbox, buff (*informal*), expert, hotshot (*informal*), intellect (*informal*), maestro, master, mastermind, virtuoso, whiz (*informal*) **2.** ability, aptitude, bent, brilliance, capacity, creative power, faculty, flair, gift, inclination, knack, propensity, talent, turn

genteel aristocratic, civil, courteous, courtly, cultivated, cultured, elegant, fashionable, formal, gentlemanly, ladylike, mannerly, polished, polite, refined, respectable, sophisticated, stylish, urbane, well-bred, well-mannered

gentility 1. blue blood, gentle birth, good family, high birth, nobility, rank **2.** breeding, civility, courtesy, courtliness, cultivation, culture, decorum, elegance, etiquette, formality, good breeding, good manners, mannerliness, polish, politeness, propriety, refinement, respectability, sophistication, urbanity

gentle 1. amiable, benign, bland, compassionate, humane, kind, kindly, lenient, meek, merciful, mild, peaceful, placid, quiet, soft, sweet-tempered, tender **2.** balmy, calm, clement, easy, light, low, mild, moderate, muted, placid, quiet, serene, slight, smooth, soft, soothing, temperate, tranquil, untroubled **3.** easy, gradual, imperceptible, light, mild, moderate, slight, slow

gentlemanly civil, civilized, courteous, cultivated, debonair, gallant, genteel, gentlemanlike, honourable, mannerly, noble, obliging, polished, polite, refined, reputable, suave, urbane, well-bred, well-mannered

genuine 1. actual, authentic, bona fide, honest, le-

the physical features of a region. **geographer** *n* **geographical** *or* **geographic** *adj* **geographically** *adv*

geology *n* **1** the study of the origin, structure, and composition of the earth. **2** the geological features of an area. **geologist** *n* **geological** *adj* **geologically** *adv*

geometric *or* **geometrical** *adj* **1** of geometry. **2** consisting of shapes used in geometry, such as circles, triangles, and straight lines: *geometric design.* **geometrically** *adv*

geometric progression *n* a sequence of numbers, each of which differs from the succeeding one by a constant ratio, for example 1, 2, 4, 8.

geometry *n* the branch of mathematics concerned with points, lines, curves, and surfaces. **geometrician** *n*

geophysics *n* the study of the earth's physical properties and the physical forces which affect it. **geophysical** *adj* **geophysicist** *n*

Geordie *Brit* ~*n* **1** a person from Tyneside. **2** the Tyneside dialect. ~*adj* **3** of Tyneside: *a Geordie accent.*

George Cross *n* a British award for bravery, usu. awarded to civilians.

georgette (jor-**jet**) *n* a thin crepe dress material.

Georgian *adj* **1** of or in the reigns of any of the kings of Great Britain and Ireland called George. **2** denoting a style of architecture or furniture prevalent in Britain in the 18th century: *an elegant Georgian terrace in Edinburgh.*

geostationary *adj* (of a satellite) orbiting so as to remain over the same point on the earth's surface.

geothermal *adj* of or using the heat in the earth's interior.

geranium *n* a cultivated plant with scarlet, pink, or white flowers.

gerbil (**jur**-bill) *n* a small rodent with long back legs, often kept as a pet.

geriatric *adj* **1** of geriatrics or old people. ~*n* **2** an old person, esp. as a patient.

geriatrics *n* the branch of medicine concerned with illnesses affecting old people.

germ *n* **1** a tiny living thing, esp. one that causes disease: *a diphtheria germ.* **2** the beginning from which something may develop: *the germ of a book.*

German *adj* **1** of Germany. ~*n* **2** a person from Germany. **3** the official language of Germany, Austria, and parts of Switzerland.

germane *adj* relevant: *the studies provided some evidence germane to these questions.*

Germanic *n* **1** the ancient language from which English, German, and the Scandinavian languages developed. ~*adj* **2** of this ancient language or the languages that developed from it. **3** characteristic of German people or things: *Germanic-looking individuals.*

germanium *n Chem* a brittle grey metalloid element that is a semiconductor and is used in transistors. Symbol: Ge

German measles *n* same as **rubella.**

German shepherd dog *n* same as **Alsatian.**

germ cell *n* a sexual reproductive cell.

germicide *n* a substance used to destroy germs.

germinal *adj* **1** of or in the earliest stage of development: *the germinal phases of the case.* **2** of germ cells.

germinate *vb* **-nating, -nated** to grow or cause to grow. **germination** *n*

germ warfare *n* the military use of disease-spreading bacteria against an enemy.

gerontology *n* the scientific study of ageing and the problems of old people. **gerontologist** *n*

gerrymandering *n* the practice of dividing the constituencies of a voting area so as to give one party an unfair advantage.

gerund (**jer**-rund) *n* a noun formed from a verb, ending in *-ing,* denoting an action or state, for example *running.*

gesso (**jess**-oh) *n* plaster used for painting or in sculpture.

Gestapo *n* the secret state police of Nazi Germany.

gestation *n* **1** the process of carrying and developing babies in the womb during pregnancy, or the time during which this process takes place. **2** the process of developing a plan or idea in the mind.

gesticulate *vb* **-lating, -lated** to make expressive movements with the hands and arms, usually while talking. **gesticulation** *n*

gesture *n* **1** a movement of the hands, head, or body to express or emphasize an idea or emotion. **2** something said or done to indicate intention, or as a formality: *a gesture of goodwill.* ~*vb* **-turing, -tured 3** to make expressive movements with the hands and arms.

get *vb* **getting, got 1** to come into possession of. **2** to bring or fetch. **3** to catch (an illness). **4** to become: *they get frustrated and angry.* **5** to cause to be done or to happen: *he got a wart removed; to get steamed up.* **6** to hear or understand: *did you get that joke?* **7** to reach (a place or point): *we could not get to the airport in time.* **8** to catch (a bus or train). **9** to persuade: *she trying to get him to give secrets away.* **10** *Informal* to annoy: *you know what really gets me?* **11** *Informal* to baffle: *now you've got me.* **12** *Informal* to hit: *a bit of grenade got me on the left hip.* **13** *Informal* to be revenged on. **14** *Informal* to start: *we got talking about it; it got me thinking.* ~*n* **15** *Brit slang* same as **git.** ~See also **get about, get across,** etc.

THESAURUS

gitimate, natural, original, pure, real, sound, sterling, true, unadulterated, unalloyed, veritable **2.** artless, candid, earnest, frank, heartfelt, honest, sincere, unaffected, unfeigned

germ 1. bacterium, bug (*informal*), microbe, microorganism, virus **2.** beginning, bud, cause, embryo, origin, root, rudiment, seed, source, spark

germane akin, allied, apposite, appropriate, apropos, apt, cognate, connected, fitting, kindred, material, pertinent, proper, related, relevant, suitable, to the point *or* purpose

germinate bud, develop, generate, grow, originate, shoot, sprout, swell, vegetate

gestation development, evolution, incubation, maturation, pregnancy, ripening

gesticulate gesture, indicate, make a sign, motion, sign, signal, wave

gesture 1. *n.* action, gesticulation, indication, motion, sign, signal **2.** *vb.* gesticulate, indicate, motion, sign, signal, wave

get 1. achieve, acquire, attain, bag, bring, come by, come into possession of, earn, fall heir to, fetch, gain, glean, inherit, make, net, obtain, pick up, procure, realize, reap, receive, score (*slang*), secure, succeed to, win **2.** be afflicted with, become infected with, be smitten by, catch, come down with, contract, fall victim to, take **3.** become, come to be, grow, turn, wax **4.** arrange, contrive, fix, manage, succeed, wangle (*informal*) **5.** catch, comprehend, fathom, follow, hear, notice, perceive, see, suss (out) (*slang*), take in, understand, work out **6.** arrive, come, make it (*informal*), reach **7.** coax, convince, induce, influence, persuade, prevail upon, sway, talk into, wheedle, win over **8.** *informal* annoy, bother, bug (*informal*), gall, get (someone's) goat (*slang*), irk, irritate, nark (*Brit., Aus-*

get about *or* **around** *vb* **1** to be socially active. **2** (of news or a rumour) to circulate.
get across *vb* to make (something) understood.
get at *vb* **1** to gain access to: *to get at the information on these disks.* **2** to imply or mean: *it is hard to see quite what he is getting at.* **3** to annoy or criticize persistently: *people who know they're being got at.*
get away *vb* **1** to escape or leave. **2** **get away with** to do (something wrong) without being caught or punished. *~interj* **3** an exclamation of disbelief. *~n* **getaway** **4** the act of escaping, usually by criminals. *~adj* **getaway** **5** used to escape: *the getaway car was abandoned.*
get back *vb* **1** to have (something) returned to one. **2** to return to a former state or activity: *get back to normal.* **3** **get back at** to retaliate against. **4** **get one's own back** *Informal* to get one's revenge.
get by *vb Informal* to manage in spite of difficulties: *he saw for himself what people did to get by.*
get in *vb* **1** to arrive. **2** to be elected. **3** **get in on** to join in (an activity).
get off *vb* **1** to leave (a bus or train or a place). **2** to escape the consequences of or punishment for an action: *the real culprits have got off scot-free.* **3** **get off with** *Brit informal* to begin a romantic or sexual relationship with.
get on *vb* **1** to enter (a bus or train). **2** to have a friendly relationship: *he had a flair for getting on with people.* **3** to grow old: *he was getting on in years.* **4** (of time) to elapse: *the time was getting on.* **5** to make progress: *how are the children getting on?* **6** **get on with** to continue to do: *you can get on with whatever you were doing before.* **7** **getting on for** approaching (a time, age, or amount): *getting on for half a century ago.*
get out *vb* **1** to leave or escape. **2** to become known. **3** to gain something of significance or value: *that's all I got out of it.* **4** **get out of** to avoid: *to get out of doing the dishes.*
get over *vb* **1** to recover from (an illness or unhappy experience). **2** to overcome (a problem). **3** **get over with** to bring (something necessary but unpleasant) to an end: *better to get it over with.*
get round *vb* **1** to overcome (a problem or difficulty). **2** (of news or a rumour) to circulate. **3** *Informal* to gain the indulgence of (someone) by praise or flattery: *a child who learned to get round everybody and have her own way.* **4** **get round to** to come to (a task) eventually: *I will get round to paying the bill.*
get through *vb* **1** to complete (a task or process). **2** to use up (money or supplies). **3** to succeed in (an examination or test). **4** **get through to a** to succeed in making (someone) understand. **b** to contact (someone) by telephone.
get-together *n* **1** *Informal* a small informal social gathering. *~vb* **get together** **2** to meet socially or in order to have a discussion.
get up *vb* **1** to get out of bed. **2** **get up to** *Informal* to be involved in: *I don't know what those guys got up to down there.* *~n* **get-up** **3** *Informal* a costume or outfit.
get-up-and-go *n Informal* energy or drive.
geyser (**geez**-er) *n* **1** a spring that discharges steam and hot water. **2** *Brit* a domestic gas water heater.
ghastly *adj* **-lier, -liest** **1** *Informal* very unpleasant. **2** deathly pale. **3** horrible: *a ghastly accident.*
ghat *n* (in India) **1** stairs leading down to a river. **2** a mountain pass.
ghee (**gee**) *n* clarified butter, used in Indian cookery.
gherkin *n* a small pickled cucumber.
ghetto *n, pl* **-tos** *or* **-toes** an area that is inhabited by people of a particular race, religion, nationality, or class.
ghetto blaster *n Informal* a large portable cassette recorder with built-in speakers.
ghillie *n* same as **gillie.**
ghost *n* **1** the disembodied spirit of a dead person, supposed to haunt the living. **2** a faint trace: *the ghost of a smile.* **3** a faint secondary image in an optical instrument or a television screen. *~vb* **4** short for **ghostwrite.**
ghostly *adj* **-lier, -liest** frightening in appearance or effect: *ghostly noises.*

THESAURUS

tral., & N.Z. slang), pique, rub (someone) up the wrong way, upset, vex **9.** baffle, confound, mystify, nonplus, perplex, puzzle, stump
get across bring home to, communicate, convey, get (something) through to, impart, make clear *or* understood, put over, transmit
get at **1.** acquire, attain, come to grips with, gain access to, get, get hold of, reach **2.** hint, imply, intend, lead up to, mean, suggest **3.** annoy, attack, be on one's back (*slang*), blame, carp, criticize, find fault with, hassle (*informal*), irritate, nag, nark (*Brit., Austral., & N.Z. slang*), pick on, taunt
getaway break, break-out, decampment, escape, flight
get away abscond, break free, break out, decamp, depart, disappear, escape, flee, leave, make good one's escape, slope off
get back **1.** recoup, recover, regain, repossess, retrieve **2.** arrive home, come back *or* home, return, revert, revisit **3.** *with* **at** be avenged, get even with, hit back, retaliate, settle the score with, take vengeance on
get by *informal* contrive, cope, exist, fare, get along, make both ends meet, manage, subsist, survive
get in alight, appear, arrive, come, land
get off alight, depart, descend, disembark, dismount, escape, exit, leave
get on **1.** ascend, board, climb, embark, mount **2.** agree, be compatible, be friendly, concur, get along, harmonize, hit it off (*informal*) **3.** advance, cope, cut it (*informal*), fare, get along, make out (*informal*), manage, progress, prosper, succeed
get out alight, break out, clear out (*informal*), decamp, escape, evacuate, extricate oneself, free oneself, leave, vacate, withdraw
get out of avoid, body-swerve (*Scot.*), dodge, escape, evade, shirk
get over **1.** come round, get better, mend, pull through, rally, recover from, revive, survive **2.** defeat, get the better of, master, overcome, shake off
get round *informal* cajole, coax, convert, persuade, prevail upon, talk round, wheedle, win over
get together accumulate, assemble, collect, congregate, convene, converge, gather, join, meet, muster, rally, unite
get up arise, rise, stand
ghastly ashen, cadaverous, deathlike, deathly pale, dreadful, frightful, godawful (*slang*), grim, grisly, gruesome, hideous, horrendous, horrible, horrid, livid, loathsome, pale, pallid, repellent, shocking, spectral, terrible, terrifying, wan
ghost **1.** apparition, phantasm, phantom, revenant, shade (*literary*), soul, spectre, spirit, spook (*informal*),

ghost town *n* a town that used to be busy but is now deserted.

ghostwrite *vb* **-writing, -wrote, -written** to write (an article or book) on behalf of a person who is then credited as author. **ghostwriter** *n*

ghoul (**gool**) *n* **1** a person who is interested in morbid or disgusting things. **2** a demon that eats corpses. **ghoulish** *adj* **ghoulishly** *adv*

GHQ *Mil* General Headquarters.

GI *n, pl* **GIs** *or* **GI's** *US informal* a soldier in the US Army.

giant *n* **1** a mythical figure of superhuman size and strength. **2** a person or thing of exceptional size, ability, or importance: *industrial giants.* ~*adj* **3** remarkably large. **4** (of an atom or ion or its structure) having large numbers of particles present in a crystal lattice, with each particle exerting a strong force of attraction on those near to it.

giant panda *n* See **panda.**

gibber (**jib**-ber) *vb* to talk in a fast and unintelligible manner.

gibberish *n* rapid incomprehensible talk; nonsense.

gibbet (**jib**-bit) *n* a gallows.

gibbon (**gib**-bon) *n* a small agile ape of the forests of S Asia.

gibbous *adj* (of the moon) more than half but less than fully illuminated.

gibe (**jibe**) *n, vb* **gibing, gibed** same as **jibe**[1].

giblets (**jib**-lits) *pl n* the gizzard, liver, heart, and neck of a fowl.

gidday *interj Austral & NZ informal* same as **good day.**

giddy *adj* **-dier, -diest 1** feeling weak and unsteady on one's feet, as if about to faint. **2** happy and excited: *a state of giddy expectation.* **giddiness** *n*

gift *n* **1** something given to someone: *a birthday gift.* **2** a special ability or power: *a gift for caricature.*

gifted *adj* having natural talent or aptitude: *that era's most gifted director.*

giftwrap *vb* **-wrapping, -wrapped** to wrap (a gift) in decorative wrapping paper.

gig[1] *n* **1** a single performance by jazz or pop musicians. ~*vb* **gigging, gigged 2** to play gigs.

gig[2] *n* a light open two-wheeled one-horse carriage.

giga- *prefix* **1** denoting 10^9: *gigavolt.* **2** *Computers* denoting 2^{30}: *gigabyte.*

gigantic *adj* extremely large.

giggle *vb* **-gling, -gled 1** to laugh nervously or foolishly. ~*n* **2** a nervous or foolish laugh. **3** *Informal* an amusing person or thing. **giggly** *adj*

gigolo (**jig**-a-lo) *n, pl* **-los** a man who is paid by an older woman to be her escort or lover.

gigot *n* a leg of lamb or mutton.

gild *vb* **gilding, gilded** *or* **gilt 1** to cover with a thin layer of gold. **2** to make (something) appear golden: *the morning sun gilded the hills.* **3 gild the lily a** to adorn unnecessarily something already beautiful. **b** to praise someone excessively.

gill (**jill**) *n* a unit of liquid measure equal to one quarter of a pint (0.14 litres).

gillie *or* **ghillie** *n Scot* a sportsman's attendant or guide for hunting or fishing.

gills (**gillz**) *pl n* the breathing organs of fish and other water creatures.

gilt *vb* **1** a past of **gild.** ~*adj* **2** covered with a thin layer of gold. ~*n* **3** a thin layer of gold, used as decoration.

gilt-edged *adj* denoting government securities on which interest payments and final repayments are guaranteed.

gilts *pl n* gilt-edged securities.

gimcrack (**jim**-krak) *adj* showy but cheap; shoddy.

gimlet (**gim**-let) *n* **1** a small hand tool with a pointed spiral tip, used for boring holes in wood. ~*adj* **2** penetrating or piercing: *gimlet eyes.*

gimmick *n Informal* something designed to attract attention or publicity. **gimmicky** *adj* **gimmickry** *n*

gin[1] *n* an alcoholic drink distilled from malted grain and flavoured with juniper berries.

gin[2] *n* a noose of thin strong wire for catching small mammals.

ginger *n* **1** the root of a tropical plant, powdered and used as a spice or sugared and eaten as a sweet. ~*adj* **2** light reddish-brown: *ginger hair.* **gingery** *adj*

ginger ale *n* a nonalcoholic fizzy drink flavoured with ginger extract.

ginger beer *n* a drink made by fermenting a mixture of syrup and root ginger.

gingerbread *n* a moist brown cake flavoured with ginger.

THESAURUS

wraith **2.** glimmer, hint, possibility, semblance, shadow, suggestion, trace

ghostly eerie, ghostlike, illusory, insubstantial, phantasmal, phantom, spectral, spooky (*informal*), supernatural, uncanny, unearthly, weird, wraithlike

giant 1. *n.* behemoth, colossus, Hercules, leviathan, monster, ogre, titan **2.** *adj.* colossal, elephantine, enormous, gargantuan, gigantic, huge, humongous (*U.S. informal*), immense, jumbo (*informal*), large, mammoth, monstrous, prodigious, titanic, vast

gibberish babble, balderdash, balls (*taboo slang*), bilge (*informal*), blather, bosh (*informal*), bull (*slang*), bullshit (*taboo slang*), bunkum *or* buncombe (*chiefly U.S.*), cobblers (*Brit. taboo slang*), crap (*slang*), double talk, drivel, eyewash (*informal*), gabble, garbage (*informal*), gobbledegook (*informal*), guff (*slang*), hogwash, hokum (*slang, chiefly U.S. & Canad.*), horsefeathers (*U.S. slang*), hot air (*informal*), jabber, jargon, mumbo jumbo, nonsense, pap, piffle (*informal*), poppycock (*informal*), prattle, shit (*taboo slang*), tommyrot, tosh (*slang, chiefly Brit.*), tripe (*informal*), twaddle, yammer (*informal*)

gibe, jibe 1. *n.* barb, crack (*slang*), cutting remark, derision, dig, jeer, mockery, ridicule, sarcasm, scoffing, sneer, taunt **2.** *vb.* deride, flout, jeer, make fun of, mock, poke fun at, ridicule, scoff, scorn, sneer, take the piss out of (*slang*), taunt, twit

giddiness dizziness, faintness, light-headedness, vertigo

giddy dizzy, dizzying, faint, light-headed, reeling, unsteady, vertiginous

gift 1. benefaction, bequest, bonus, boon, bounty, contribution, donation, grant, gratuity, hand-out, largesse *or* largess, legacy, offering, present **2.** ability, aptitude, attribute, bent, capability, capacity, faculty, flair, genius, knack, power, talent, turn

gifted able, accomplished, adroit, brilliant, capable, clever, expert, ingenious, intelligent, masterly, skilled, talented

gigantic colossal, elephantine, enormous, gargantuan, giant, herculean, huge, humongous (*U.S. informal*), immense, mammoth, monstrous, prodigious, stupendous, titanic, tremendous, vast

giggle *vb./n.* cackle, chortle, chuckle, laugh, snigger, tee-hee, titter, twitter

gild adorn, beautify, bedeck, brighten, coat, deck,

ginger group *n* a group within a larger group that agitates for a more active policy.
gingerly *adv* carefully or cautiously: *she sat gingerly on the edge of the chair.*
ginger nut *or* **snap** *n* a hard biscuit flavoured with ginger.
gingham *n* a cotton fabric with a checked or striped design.
gingivitis (jin-jiv-**vite**-iss) *n* inflammation of the gums.
ginormous *adj Informal* very large.
gin rummy *n* a version of rummy in which a player may finish if the odd cards in his hand total less than ten points.
ginseng (**jin**-seng) *n* the root of a plant of China and N America, believed to have tonic and energy-giving properties.
gip (**jip**) *n* same as **GYP**
Gipsy *n, pl* **-sies** same as **Gypsy.**
giraffe *n* a cud-chewing African mammal with a very long neck and long legs and a spotted yellowy skin.
gird *vb* **girding, girded** *or* **girt 1** to put a belt or girdle around. **2 gird up one's loins** to prepare oneself for action.
girder *n* a large steel or iron beam used in the construction of bridges and buildings.
girdle *n* **1** a woman's elastic corset that covers the stomach and hips. **2** anything that surrounds something or someone: *his girdle of supporters.* **3** *Anat* an encircling arrangement of bones: *the shoulder girdle.* ~*vb* **-dling, -dled 4** to surround: *a ring of volcanic ash girdling the earth.*
girl *n* **1** a female child. **2** a young woman. **girlhood** *n* **girlish** *adj*
girlfriend *n* **1** a female friend with whom a person is romantically or sexually involved. **2** any female friend.
Girl Guide *n* a former name for **Guide.**
girlie *adj Informal* featuring naked or scantily dressed women: *girlie magazines.*
giro (**jire**-oh) *n, pl* **-ros 1** a system of transferring money within a bank or post office, directly from one account into another. **2** *Brit informal* a social security payment by giro cheque.
girt *vb* a past of **gird.**
girth *n* **1** the measurement around something. **2** a band fastened round a horse's middle to keep the saddle in position.
gist (**jist**) *n* the main point or meaning of something: *the gist of letter.*
git *n Brit slang* a contemptible person.
give *vb* **giving, gave, given 1** to present or hand (something) to someone. **2** to pay (an amount of money) for a purchase. **3** to grant or provide: *to give an answer.* **4** to utter (a shout or cry). **5** to perform, make, or do: *the prime minister gave a speech.* **6** to host (a party). **7** to sacrifice or devote: *comrades who gave their lives for their country.* **8** to concede: *he was very efficient, I have to give him that.* **9** to yield or break under pressure: *something has got to give.* **10 give or take** plus or minus: *about one hundred metres, give or take five.* ~*n* **11** a tendency to yield under pressure; elasticity. ~See also **give away, give in,** etc. **giver** *n*
give-and-take *n* **1** mutual concessions and cooperation. **2** a smoothly flowing exchange of ideas and talk: *a relaxed give-and-take about their past involvement.*
give away *vb* **1** to donate as a gift. **2** to reveal (a secret). **3** to present (a bride) formally to her husband in a marriage ceremony. ~*n* **giveaway 4** something that reveals hidden feelings or intentions. ~*adj* **giveaway 5** very cheap or free: *a giveaway rent.*
give in *vb* to admit defeat.
given *vb* **1** the past participle of **give.** ~*adj* **2** specific or previously stated: *priorities within the given department.* **3** to be assumed: *any given place on the earth.* **4 given to** inclined to: *a man not given to undue optimism.*
give off *vb* to send out (heat, light, or a smell).
give out *vb* **1** to hand out: *the bloke that was giving out those tickets.* **2** to send out (heat, light, or a smell). **3** to make known: *the man who gave out the news.* **4** to fail: *the engine gave out.*
give over *vb* **1** to set aside for a specific purpose: *the amount of space given over to advertisements.* **2** *Informal* to stop doing something annoying: *tell him to give over.*
give up *vb* **1** to stop (doing something): *I did give up smoking.* **2** to resign from (a job or position). **3** to admit defeat or failure. **4** to abandon (hope). **5 give oneself up a** to surrender to the police or other authorities. **b** to devote oneself completely: *she gave herself up to her work.*
gizzard *n* the part of a bird's stomach in which hard food is broken up.

THESAURUS

dress up, embellish, embroider, enhance, enrich, garnish, grace, ornament
gimmick dodge, ploy, scheme, stratagem, stunt, trick
gingerly carefully, cautiously, charily, circumspectly, daintily, delicately, fastidiously, hesitantly, reluctantly, squeamishly, suspiciously, timidly, warily
gird 1. belt, bind, girdle **2.** brace, fortify, make ready, prepare, ready, steel
girdle 1. *n.* band, belt, cummerbund, sash, waistband **2.** *vb.* bind, bound, encircle, enclose, encompass, engird, environ, gird, hem, ring, surround
girl bird (*slang*), chick (*slang*), colleen (*Irish*), damsel (*archaic*), daughter, female child, lass, lassie (*informal*), maid (*archaic*), maiden (*archaic*), miss, wench
girth bulk, circumference, measure, size
gist core, drift, essence, force, idea, import, meaning, nub, pith, point, quintessence, sense, significance, substance
give 1. accord, administer, allow, award, bestow, commit, confer, consign, contribute, deliver, donate, entrust, furnish, grant, hand over *or* out, make over, permit, present, provide, purvey, supply, vouchsafe **2.** announce, be a source of, communicate, emit, impart, issue, notify, pronounce, publish, render, transmit, utter **3.** cause, do, engender, lead, make, occasion, perform, produce **4.** allow, cede, concede, devote, grant, hand over, lend, relinquish, surrender, yield **5.** bend, break, collapse, fall, recede, retire, sink
give away betray, disclose, divulge, expose, inform on, leak, let out, let slip, reveal, shop (*slang, chiefly Brit.*), uncover
give in admit defeat, capitulate, collapse, comply, concede, quit, submit, succumb, surrender, yield
given addicted, apt, disposed, inclined, liable, likely, prone
give off discharge, emit, exhale, exude, produce, release, send out, smell of, throw out, vent
give out 1. discharge, emit, exhale, exude, produce, release, send out, smell of, throw out, vent **2.** announce, broadcast, communicate, disseminate, impart, make known, notify, publish, transmit, utter
give up abandon, capitulate, cease, cede, cut out, de-

glacé (**glass**-say) *adj* preserved in a thick sugary syrup: *glacé cherries.*
glacial *adj* **1** of glaciers or ice. **2** extremely cold. **3** cold and unfriendly: *a glacial stare.*
glacial period *n* same as **Ice Age.**
glaciation *n* the process of covering part of the earth's surface with glaciers or masses of ice. **glaciated** *adj*
glacier *n* a slowly moving mass of ice formed by an accumulation of snow.
glad *adj* **gladder, gladdest 1** happy and pleased. **2** very willing: *he was only too glad to help.* **3** *Archaic* causing happiness: *glad tidings.* **gladly** *adv* **gladness** *n* **gladden** *vb*
glade *n* an open space in a forest.
gladiator *n* (in ancient Rome) a man trained to fight in arenas to provide entertainment. **gladiatorial** *adj*
gladiolus (glad-ee-**oh**-luss) *n, pl* **-li** (-lie) a garden plant with brightly coloured funnel-shaped flowers.
glad rags *pl n Informal* one's best clothes.
gladsome *adj Old-fashioned* joyous or cheerful.
glamorous *adj* attractive or fascinating.
glamour *or US* **glamor** *n* exciting or alluring charm or beauty. **glamorize** *or* **-ise** *vb*
glance *n* **1** a quick look. ~*vb* **glancing, glanced 2** to look quickly at something. **3** to be deflected off an object at an oblique angle: *the ball glanced off a spectator.* **glancing** *adj*
gland *n* **1** an organ that synthesizes and secretes chemical substances for the body to use or eliminate. **2** a similar organ in plants.
glandular *adj* of or affecting a gland or glands.
glandular fever *n* an acute infectious viral disease that causes fever, sore throat, and painful swollen lymph nodes.
glare *vb* **glaring, glared 1** to stare angrily. **2** (of light or colour) to be too bright. ~*n* **3** an angry stare. **4** a dazzling light or brilliance. **5 in the glare of publicity** receiving a lot of attention from the media or the public.
glaring *adj* conspicuous or obvious: *glaring inconsistencies.* **glaringly** *adv*
glasnost *n* a policy of public frankness and accountability, developed in the USSR in the 1980s under Mikhail Gorbachov.
glass *n* **1** a hard brittle transparent solid, consisting of metal silicates or similar compounds. **2** a drinking vessel made of glass. **3** the amount contained in a drinking glass: *a glass of wine.* **4** objects made of glass, such as drinking glasses and bowls.
glass-blowing *n* the process of shaping a mass of molten glass by blowing air into it through a tube. **glass-blower** *n*
glasses *pl n* a pair of lenses for correcting faulty vision, in a frame that rests on the nose and hooks behind the ears.
glasshouse *n Brit* same as **greenhouse.**
glassy *adj* **glassier, glassiest 1** smooth, clear, and shiny, like glass: *the glassy sea.* **2** expressionless: *that glassy look.*
Glaswegian (glaz-**weej**-an) *adj* **1** of Glasgow, a city in W Scotland. ~*n* **2** a person from Glasgow. **3** the Glasgow dialect.
glaucoma *n* an eye disease in which increased pressure in the eyeball causes gradual loss of sight.
glaze *vb* **glazing, glazed 1** to fit or cover with glass. **2** to cover (a piece of pottery) with a protective shiny coating. **3** to cover (food) with beaten egg or milk before cooking, in order to produce a shiny coating. ~*n* **4** a protective shiny coating applied to a piece of pottery. **5** a shiny coating of beaten egg or milk applied to food. ~See also **glaze over. glazed** *adj* **glazing** *n*
glaze over *vb* to become dull through boredom or inattention: *the listener's eyes glaze over.*
glazier *n* a person who fits windows or doors with glass.
gleam *n* **1** a small beam or glow of light. **2** a brief or dim indication: *a gleam of anticipation in his eye.* ~*vb* **3** to shine. **gleaming** *adj*
glean *vb* **1** to gather (information) bit by bit. **2** to gather the useful remnants of (a crop) after harvesting. **gleaner** *n*
gleanings *pl n* pieces of information that have been gleaned.
glebe *n Brit* land granted to a clergyman as part of his benefice.

THESAURUS

sist, despair, forswear, hand over, kick (*informal*), leave off, quit, relinquish, renounce, resign, step down (*informal*), stop, surrender, throw in the towel, waive
glad 1. blithesome (*literary*), cheerful, chuffed (*slang*), contented, delighted, gay, gleeful, gratified, happy, jocund, jovial, joyful, overjoyed, pleased, willing **2.** *archaic* animated, cheerful, cheering, cheery, delightful, felicitous, gratifying, joyous, merry, pleasant, pleasing
gladden cheer, delight, elate, enliven, exhilarate, gratify, hearten, please, rejoice
gladly cheerfully, freely, gaily, gleefully, happily, jovially, joyfully, joyously, merrily, readily, willingly, with (a) good grace, with pleasure
gladness animation, blitheness, cheerfulness, delight, felicity, gaiety, glee, happiness, high spirits, hilarity, jollity, joy, joyousness, mirth, pleasure
glamorous alluring, attractive, beautiful, bewitching, captivating, charming, dazzling, elegant, enchanting, entrancing, exciting, fascinating, glittering, glitzy (*slang*), glossy, lovely, prestigious, smart
glamour allure, appeal, attraction, beauty, bewitchment, charm, enchantment, fascination, magnetism, prestige
glance *n.* **1.** brief look, butcher's (*Brit. slang*), dekko (*slang*), gander (*informal*), glimpse, look, peek, peep, quick look, shufti (*Brit. slang*), squint, view ~*vb.* **2.** check, check out (*informal*), clock (*Brit. informal*), gaze, glimpse, look, peek, peep, scan, take a dekko at (*Brit. slang*), view **3.** bounce, brush, graze, rebound, ricochet, skim
glare *vb.* **1.** frown, give a dirty look, glower, look daggers, lour *or* lower, scowl, stare angrily **2.** blaze, dazzle, flame, flare ~*n.* **3.** angry stare, black look, dirty look, frown, glower, lour *or* lower, scowl **4.** blaze, brilliance, dazzle, flame, flare, glow
glaring audacious, blatant, conspicuous, egregious, flagrant, gross, manifest, obvious, open, outrageous, outstanding, overt, patent, rank, unconcealed, visible
glassy 1. clear, glossy, icy, shiny, slick, slippery, smooth, transparent **2.** blank, cold, dazed, dull, empty, expressionless, fixed, glazed, lifeless, vacant
glaze 1. *vb.* burnish, coat, enamel, furbish, gloss, lacquer, polish, varnish **2.** *n.* coat, enamel, finish, gloss, lacquer, lustre, patina, polish, shine, varnish
gleam *n.* **1.** beam, flash, glimmer, glow, ray, sparkle **2.** flicker, glimmer, hint, inkling, ray, suggestion, trace ~*vb.* **3.** coruscate, flare, flash, glance, glimmer, glint, glisten, glitter, glow, scintillate, shimmer, shine, sparkle
glee cheerfulness, delight, elation, exhilaration, exuberance, exultation, fun, gaiety, gladness, hilarity,

glee *n* great merriment or joy, esp. caused by the misfortune of another person.

gleeful *adj* merry or joyful, esp. over someone else's mistake or misfortune. **gleefully** *adv*

glen *n* a deep narrow mountain valley.

glengarry *n, pl* **-ries** a brimless Scottish cap with a crease down the crown.

glib *adj* **glibber, glibbest** fluent and easy, often in an insincere or deceptive way: *there were no glib or easy answers.* **glibly** *adv* **glibness** *n*

glide *vb* **gliding, glided 1** to move easily and smoothly. **2** (of an aircraft) to land without engine power. **3** to fly a glider. **4** to float on currents of air.

glider *n* an aircraft that does not use an engine, but flies by floating on air currents.

glide time *n NZ* same as **flexitime.**

gliding *n* the sport of flying in a glider.

glimmer *vb* **1** (of a light) to glow faintly or flickeringly. *~n* **2** a faint indication: *a glimmer of hope.* **3** a glow or twinkle.

glimpse *n* **1** a brief view: *a glimpse of a rare snow leopard.* **2** a vague indication: *glimpses of insecurity.* *~vb* **glimpsing, glimpsed 3** to catch sight of momentarily.

glint *vb* **1** to gleam brightly. *~n* **2** a bright gleam.

glissade *n* **1** a gliding step in ballet. **2** a controlled slide down a snow slope. *~vb* **-sading, -saded 3** to perform a glissade.

glissando *n, pl* **-dos** *Music* a slide between two notes in which all intermediate notes are played.

glisten *vb* (of a wet or glossy surface) to gleam by reflecting light: *sweat glistened above his eyes.*

glitch *n* a small problem that stops something from working properly.

glitter *vb* **1** (of a surface) to reflect light in bright flashes. **2** (of light) to be reflected in bright flashes. **3** to be brilliant in a showy way: *she glitters socially.* *~n* **4** a sparkling light. **5** superficial glamour: *the trappings and glitter of the European aristocracy.* **6** tiny pieces of shiny decorative material. **7** *Canad* ice formed from freezing rain. **glittering** *adj* **glittery** *adj*

glitzy *adj* **glitzier, glitziest** *Slang* showily attractive.

gloaming *n Scot poetic* twilight; dusk.

gloat *vb* to regard one's own good fortune or the misfortune of others with smug or malicious pleasure.

glob *n Informal* a rounded mass of thick fluid.

global *adj* **1** of or applying to the whole earth: *global environmental problems.* **2** of or applying to the whole of something: *a global total for local-authority revenue.* **globally** *adv*

global warming *n* an increase in the overall temperature worldwide believed to be caused by the greenhouse effect.

globe *n* **1** a sphere on which a map of the world is drawn. **2 the globe** the earth. **3** a spherical object, such as a glass lamp shade or fishbowl. **4** *S African* an electric light bulb.

globetrotter *n* a habitual worldwide traveller. **globetrotting** *n, adj*

globular *adj* shaped like a globe or globule.

globule *n* a small round drop of liquid.

globulin *n* a simple protein found in living tissue.

glockenspiel *n* a percussion instrument consisting of tuned metal plates played with a pair of small hammers.

gloom *n* **1** depression or melancholy. **2** partial or total darkness.

gloomy *adj* **gloomier, gloomiest 1** despairing or sad. **2** causing depression or gloom: *gloomy economic forecasts.* **3** dark or dismal. **gloomily** *adv*

glorify *vb* **-fies, -fying, -fied 1** to make (something) seem more important than it really is: *computers are just glorified adding machines.* **2** to praise: *few coun-*

THESAURUS

jocularity, jollity, joviality, joy, joyfulness, joyousness, liveliness, merriment, mirth, sprightliness, triumph, verve

gleeful cheerful, chirpy (*informal*), cock-a-hoop, delighted, elated, exuberant, exultant, gay, gratified, happy, jocund, jovial, joyful, joyous, jubilant, merry, mirthful, overjoyed, over the moon (*informal*), pleased, rapt, triumphant

glib artful, easy, fast-talking, fluent, garrulous, insincere, plausible, quick, ready, slick, slippery, smooth, smooth-tongued, suave, talkative, voluble

glide coast, drift, float, flow, fly, roll, run, sail, skate, skim, slide, slip, soar

glimmer *vb.* **1.** blink, flicker, gleam, glisten, glitter, glow, shimmer, shine, sparkle, twinkle *~n.* **2.** flicker, gleam, grain, hint, inkling, ray, suggestion, trace **3.** blink, flicker, gleam, glow, ray, shimmer, sparkle, twinkle

glimpse 1. *n.* brief view, butcher's (*Brit. slang*), gander (*informal*), glance, look, peek, peep, quick look, shufti (*Brit. slang*), sight, sighting, squint **2.** *vb.* catch sight of, clock (*Brit. informal*), descry, espy, sight, spot, spy, view

glint 1. *vb.* flash, gleam, glimmer, glitter, shine, sparkle, twinkle **2.** *n.* flash, gleam, glimmer, glitter, shine, sparkle, twinkle, twinkling

glisten coruscate, flash, glance, glare, gleam, glimmer, glint, glitter, scintillate, shimmer, shine, sparkle, twinkle

glitter *vb.* **1.** coruscate, flare, flash, glare, gleam, glimmer, glint, glisten, scintillate, shimmer, shine, sparkle, twinkle *~n.* **2.** beam, brightness, brilliance, flash, glare, gleam, lustre, radiance, scintillation, sheen, shimmer, shine, sparkle **3.** display, gaudiness, gilt, glamour, pageantry, show, showiness, splendour, tinsel

gloat crow, drool, exult, glory, relish, revel in, rub it in (*informal*), triumph, vaunt

global 1. international, pandemic, planetary, universal, world, worldwide **2.** all-encompassing, all-inclusive, all-out, comprehensive, encyclopedic, exhaustive, general, thorough, total, unbounded, unlimited

globe ball, earth, orb, planet, round, sphere, world

globule bead, bubble, drop, droplet, particle, pearl, pellet

gloom 1. blues, dejection, depression, desolation, despair, despondency, downheartedness, low spirits, melancholy, misery, sadness, sorrow, unhappiness, woe **2.** blackness, cloud, cloudiness, dark, darkness, dimness, dullness, dusk, duskiness, gloominess, murk, murkiness, obscurity, shade, shadow, twilight

gloomy 1. blue, chapfallen, cheerless, crestfallen, dejected, despondent, dismal, dispirited, down, downcast, downhearted, down in the dumps (*informal*), down in the mouth, glum, in low spirits, melancholy, miserable, moody, morose, pessimistic, sad, saturnine, sullen **2.** bad, black, cheerless, comfortless, depressing, disheartening, dismal, dispiriting, dreary, funereal, joyless, sad, saddening, sombre **3.** black, crepuscular, dark, dim, dismal, dreary, dull, dusky, murky, obscure, overcast, shadowy, sombre

glorify 1. aggrandize, augment, dignify, elevate, enhance, ennoble, lift up, raise **2.** celebrate, crack up (*informal*), cry up (*informal*), eulogize, extol, hymn, laud, lionize, magnify, panegyrize, praise, sing *or* sound the

tries have glorified success in business more than the United States. **3** to worship (God). **glorification** *n*

glorious *adj* **1** brilliantly beautiful: *in glorious colour.* **2** delightful or enjoyable: *the glorious summer weather.* **3** having or full of glory: *glorious successes.* **gloriously** *adv*

glory *n, pl* **-ries 1** fame, praise, or honour: *tales of glory.* **2** splendour: *the glory of the tropical day.* **3** something worthy of praise: *the Lady Chapel is the great glory of Lichfield.* **4** adoration or worship: *the greater glory of God.* ~*vb* **-ries, -rying, -ried 5 glory in** to take great pleasure in: *the workers were glorying in their new-found freedom.*

glory box *n Austral & NZ* a box in which a young woman stores her trousseau.

glory hole *n* an untidy cupboard or storeroom.

Glos Gloucestershire.

gloss[1] *n* **1** a bright shine on a surface. **2** a superficially attractive appearance. **3** a paint with a shiny finish. **4** a cosmetic used to give a shiny appearance: *lip gloss.* ~*vb* **5** to paint with gloss. **6 gloss over** to conceal (an error, failing, or awkward moment) by minimizing it: *don't try to gloss over bad news.*

gloss[2] *n* **1** an explanatory comment added to the text of a book. ~*vb* **2** to add a gloss or glosses to.

glossary *n, pl* **-ries** an alphabetical list of technical or specialist words in a book, with explanations.

glossy *adj* **glossier, glossiest 1** smooth and shiny: *glossy black hair.* **2** superficially attractive or sophisticated: *his glossy Manhattan flat.* **3** (of a magazine) produced on expensive shiny paper.

glottal stop *n Phonetics* a speech sound produced by tightly closing and then opening the glottis.

glottis *n* the opening at the top of the windpipe, between the vocal cords.

glove *n* **1** a shaped covering for the hand with individual sheaths for each finger and the thumb. **2** a protective hand covering worn in sports such as boxing.

glove compartment *n* a small storage area in the dashboard of a car.

gloved *adj* covered by a glove or gloves: *a gloved hand.*

glow *n* **1** light produced as a result of great heat. **2** a steady light without flames. **3** brightness of complexion. **4** a feeling of wellbeing or satisfaction. ~*vb* **5** to produce a steady light without flames. **6** to shine intensely. **7** to experience a feeling of wellbeing or satisfaction: *she glowed with pleasure.* **8** (of the complexion) to have a strong bright colour: *his pale face glowing at the recollection.*

glower (rhymes with **power**) *vb* **1** to stare angrily. ~*n* **2** an angry stare.

glowing *adj* full of praise: *a glowing tribute.*

glow-worm *n* a European beetle, the females and larvae of which have organs producing a soft greenish light.

gloxinia *n* a plant with white, red, or purple bell-shaped flowers.

glucose *n* a white crystalline sugar found in plant and animal tissues.

glue *n* **1** a substance used for sticking things together. ~*vb* **gluing** *or* **glueing, glued 2** to join or stick together with glue. **3 glued to** paying full attention to: *golf fans will be glued to their televisions today for the Open Championship.* **gluey** *adj*

glue ear *n* an accumulation of fluid in the middle ear of children, caused by infection and causing deafness.

glue-sniffing *n* the practice of inhaling glue fumes to produce intoxicating or hallucinatory effects. **glue-sniffer** *n*

glum *adj* **glummer, glummest** gloomy and quiet, usu. because of a disappointment. **glumly** *adv*

glut *n* **1** an excessive supply. ~*vb* **glutting, glutted 2** to supply (a market) with a commodity in excess of the demand for it. **3 glut oneself** to eat or drink more than one really needs.

gluten (**gloo**-ten) *n* a sticky protein found in cereal grains, such as wheat.

glutinous (**gloo**-tin-uss) *adj* gluelike in texture.

glutton *n* **1** someone who eats and drinks too much.

THESAURUS

praises of **3.** adore, apotheosize, beatify, bless, canonize, deify, enshrine, exalt, honour, idolize, pay homage to, revere, sanctify, venerate, worship

glorious 1. beautiful, bright, brilliant, dazzling, divine, effulgent, gorgeous, radiant, resplendent, shining, splendid, splendiferous (*facetious*), superb **2.** delightful, enjoyable, excellent, fine, gorgeous, great, heavenly (*informal*), marvellous, pleasurable, splendid, splendiferous (*facetious*), wonderful **3.** celebrated, distinguished, elevated, eminent, excellent, famed, famous, grand, honoured, illustrious, magnificent, majestic, noble, noted, renowned, sublime, triumphant

glory *n.* **1.** celebrity, dignity, distinction, eminence, exaltation, fame, honour, illustriousness, immortality, kudos, praise, prestige, renown **2.** beauty, brilliance, éclat, gorgeousness, grandeur, greatness, lustre, magnificence, majesty, nobility, pageantry, pomp, radiance, resplendence, splendour, sublimity, triumph **3.** adoration, benediction, blessing, gratitude, homage, laudation, praise, thanksgiving, veneration, worship ~*vb.* **4.** boast, crow, drool, exult, gloat, pride oneself, relish, revel, take delight, triumph

gloss[1] *n.* **1.** brightness, brilliance, burnish, gleam, lustre, polish, sheen, shine, varnish, veneer **2.** appearance, façade, front, mask, semblance, show, surface ~*vb.* **3.** burnish, finish, furbish, glaze, lacquer, polish, shine, varnish, veneer **4.** camouflage, conceal, cover up, disguise, hide, mask, smooth over, veil, whitewash (*informal*)

gloss[2] **1.** *n.* annotation, comment, commentary, elucidation, explanation, footnote, interpretation, note, translation **2.** *vb.* annotate, comment, construe, elucidate, explain, interpret, translate

glossy bright, brilliant, burnished, glassy, glazed, lustrous, polished, shining, shiny, silken, silky, sleek, smooth

glow *n.* **1.** burning, gleam, glimmer, incandescence, lambency, light, luminosity, phosphorescence **2.** brightness, brilliance, effulgence, radiance, splendour, vividness **3.** bloom, blush, flush, reddening, rosiness ~*vb.* **4.** brighten, burn, gleam, glimmer, redden, shine, smoulder **5.** be suffused, blush, colour, flush, radiate

glower 1. *vb.* frown, give a dirty look, glare, look daggers, lour *or* lower, scowl **2.** *n.* angry stare, black look, dirty look, frown, glare, lour *or* lower, scowl

glowing adulatory, complimentary, ecstatic, enthusiastic, eulogistic, laudatory, rave (*informal*), rhapsodic

glue 1. *n.* adhesive, cement, gum, paste **2.** *vb.* affix, cement, fix, gum, paste, seal, stick

glum chapfallen, churlish, crabbed, crestfallen, crusty, dejected, doleful, down, gloomy, gruff, grumpy, huffy, ill-humoured, low, moody, morose, pessimistic, saturnine, sour, sulky, sullen, surly

glut *n.* **1.** excess, overabundance, oversupply, plethora, saturation, superabundance, superfluity, surfeit, surplus ~*vb.* **2.** choke, clog, deluge, flood, inundate, overload, oversupply, saturate **3.** cram, fill, gorge, overfeed, satiate, stuff

2 a person who has a great capacity for something: *a glutton for work.* **gluttonous** *adj*

gluttony *n* the practice of eating too much.

glycerine (**gliss**-ser-reen) *or* **glycerin** *n* a nontechnical name for **glycerol.**

glycerol (**gliss**-ser-ol) *n* a colourless odourless syrupy liquid obtained from animal and vegetable fats, used as a solvent, antifreeze, and sweetener, and in explosives.

glycogen (**glike**-oh-jen) *n* a starchlike carbohydrate stored in the liver and muscles of humans and animals.

glycolysis (glike-**kol**-iss-iss) *n Biochem* the breakdown of glucose by enzymes, with the release of energy.

gm gram.

G-man *n, pl* **G-men** *US slang* an FBI agent.

GMB General, Municipal and Boilermakers (Trade Union).

GMT Greenwich Mean Time.

gnarled *adj* rough, twisted, and knobbly, usually through age.

gnash *vb* to grind (the teeth) together in pain or anger.

gnat *n* a small biting two-winged insect.

gnaw *vb* **1** to bite or chew constantly so as to wear away bit by bit. **2 gnaw at** to cause constant distress or anxiety to: *uneasiness gnawed at his mind.* **gnawing** *adj*

gneiss *n* a coarse-grained layered metamorphic rock.

gnome *n* **1** an imaginary creature in fairy tales that looks like a little old man. **2** a small statue of a gnome in a garden.

gnomic (**no**-mik) *adj Literary* of or containing short clever sayings: *gnomic pronouncements.*

Gnosticism (**noss**-tiss-siz-zum) *n* a religious movement involving belief in intuitive spiritual knowledge. **Gnostic** *n, adj*

GNP gross national product.

gnu (**noo**) *n, pl* **gnus** *or* **gnu** a sturdy African antelope with an oxlike head.

go *vb* **going, went, gone 1** to move or proceed to or from a place: *go forward.* **2** to be in regular attendance at (work, church, or a place or learning). **3** to lead to a particular place: *the path that goes right along the bank.* **4** to be kept in a particular place: *where does this go?* **5** to do or become as specified: *he went white; the gun went bang.* **6** to be or continue to be in a specified state: *to go to sleep.* **7** to operate or function: *the car wouldn't go.* **8** to follow a specified course; fare: *I'd hate the meeting to go badly.* **9** to be allotted to a particular purpose or recipient: *a third of the total budget goes on the army.* **10** to be sold: *the portrait went for £231,000 to a telephone bidder.* **11** (of words or music) to be expressed or sung: *the song goes like this.* **12** to fail or break down: *my eyesight is going; he was on lap nineteen when the engine went.* **13** to die: *he went quickly at the end.* **14** to be spent or finished: *all tension and all hope had gone.* **15** to proceed up to or beyond certain limits: *I think this is going too far.* **16** to carry authority: *what Daddy says goes.* **17** to endure or last out: *they go for eight or ten hours without resting.* **18** *Nonstandard* to say: *then she goes, "shut up".* **19 anything goes** anything is acceptable. **20 be going to** to intend or be about to: *she was afraid of what was going to happen next.* **21 let go** to relax one's hold on; release. **22 let oneself go a** to act in an uninhibited manner. **b** to lose interest in one's appearance. **23 to go** remaining: *two days to go till the holidays.* ~*n, pl* **goes 24** an attempt: *he had a go at the furniture business.* **25** a verbal or physical attack: *he couldn't resist having another go at me.* **26** a turn to do something in a game: *"Your go now!" I shouted.* **27** *Informal* the quality of being active and energetic: *a grand old man, full of go and determination.* **28 from the word go** *Informal* from the very beginning. **29 make a go of** *Informal* to be successful in (a business venture or a relationship). **30 on the go** *Informal* active and energetic. ~See also **go about, go against,** etc.

go about *vb* **1** to tackle (a problem or task): *he went about it in the wrong way.* **2** to busy oneself with: *people have been going about their business as usual.*

goad *vb* **1** to provoke (someone) to take some kind of action, usually in anger. ~*n* **2** something that provokes someone to take some kind of action. **3** a sharp pointed stick for driving cattle.

go against *vb* **1** to conflict with (someone's wishes or beliefs). **2** to be unfavourable to (a person): *a referendum would almost certainly go against them.*

go-ahead *n* **1 give the go-ahead** *Informal* to give permission to proceed. ~*adj* **2** enterprising or ambitious: *prosperous and go-ahead republics.*

goal *n* **1** *Sport* the space into which players try to propel the ball or puck to score. **2** *Sport* **a** a successful attempt at scoring. **b** the score so made. **3** an aim or purpose: *a unitary nonracial South Africa is the ANC's accepted goal.* **goalless** *adj*

goalie *n Informal* a goalkeeper.

goalkeeper *n Sport* a player whose duty is to prevent the ball or puck from entering the goal.

goal line *n Sport* the line marking each end of the pitch, on which the goals stand.

goalpost *n* **1** either of two uprights supporting the

THESAURUS

glutton gannet (*slang*), gobbler, gorger, gourmand, pig (*informal*)

gluttony gourmandism, greed, greediness, piggishness, rapacity, voraciousness, voracity

gnarled contorted, knotted, knotty, knurled, leathery, rough, rugged, twisted, weather-beaten, wrinkled

gnaw 1. bite, chew, munch, nibble, worry **2.** distress, fret, harry, haunt, nag, plague, prey on one's mind, trouble, worry

go *vb.* **1.** advance, decamp, depart, fare (*archaic*), journey, leave, make for, move, move out, pass, proceed, repair, set off, slope off, travel, withdraw **2.** connect, extend, fit, give access, lead, reach, run, span, spread, stretch **3.** function, move, operate, perform, run, work **4.** develop, eventuate, fall out, fare, happen, pan out (*informal*), proceed, result, turn out, work out **5.** buy it (*U.S. slang*), check out (*U.S. slang*), croak (*slang*), die, expire, give up the ghost, go belly-up (*slang*), kick it (*slang*), kick the bucket (*slang*), pass away, peg it (*informal*), peg out (*informal*), perish, pop one's clogs (*informal*) **6.** elapse, expire, flow, lapse, pass, slip away ~*n.* **7.** attempt, bid, crack (*informal*), effort, essay, shot (*informal*), stab (*informal*), try, turn, whack (*informal*), whirl (*informal*) **8.** *informal* activity, animation, brio, drive, energy, force, get-up-and-go (*informal*), life, oomph (*informal*), pep, spirit, verve, vigour, vitality, vivacity

goad 1. *vb.* annoy, arouse, be on one's back (*slang*), drive, egg on, exhort, harass, hassle (*informal*), hound, impel, incite, instigate, irritate, nark (*Brit., Austral., & N.Z. slang*), prick, prod, prompt, spur, stimulate, sting, urge, worry **2.** *n.* impetus, incentive, incitement, irritation, motivation, pressure, spur, stimulation, stimulus, urge

go-ahead 1. *n. informal* assent, authorization, consent, green light, leave, O.K. *or* okay (*informal*), per-

crossbar of a goal. **2 move the goalposts** to change the aims of an activity to ensure the desired results.

goat *n* **1** an agile cud-chewing mammal with hollow horns. **2 act the goat** *Informal* to behave in a silly manner. **3 get someone's goat** *Slang* to annoy someone.

goatee *n* a small pointed beard that does not cover the cheeks.

goatherd *n* a person who looks after a herd of goats.

goatskin *n* leather made from the skin of a goat.

goatsucker *n US & Canad* same as **nightjar.**

go-away bird *n S African* a grey lourie.

gob[1] *n* a thick mass of a soft substance.

gob[2] *n Slang, chiefly Brit* the mouth.

go back on *vb* to fail to fulfil (a promise).

gobbet *n* a chunk or lump.

gobble[1] *vb* **-bling, -bled** to eat quickly and greedily.

gobble[2] *n* **1** the loud rapid gurgling sound made by a turkey. ~*vb* **-bling, -bled 2** to make this sound.

gobbledegook *or* **gobbledygook** *n* pretentious or unintelligible language.

gobbler *n Informal* a turkey.

go-between *n* a person who acts as a messenger between two people or groups.

goblet *n* a drinking vessel with a base and stem but without handles.

goblin *n* a small grotesque creature in fairy tales that causes trouble for people.

gobsmacked *adj Brit slang* astonished and astounded.

goby *n, pl* **-by** *or* **-bies** a small spiny-finned fish.

go by *vb* **1** to pass: *as time goes by.* **2** to be guided by: *if my experience is anything to go by.*

go-cart *n* same as **go-kart.**

god *n* **1** a supernatural being, worshipped as the controller of the universe or some aspect of life or as the personification of some force. **2** an image of such a being. **3** a person or thing to which excessive attention is given: *the All Blacks are gods in New Zealand.* **4 the gods** the top balcony in a theatre. **goddess** *fem n*

God *n* **1** the sole Supreme Being, Creator and ruler of all, in religions such as Christianity, Judaism, and Islam. ~*interj* **2** an oath or exclamation of surprise or annoyance.

godchild *n, pl* **-children** a person who is sponsored by godparents at baptism.

goddaughter *n* a female godchild.

godetia *n* a garden plant with showy flowers.

godfather *n* **1** a male godparent. **2** the head of a Mafia family or other criminal ring.

God-fearing *adj* deeply religious.

godforsaken *adj* desolate or dreary: *some godforsaken village in the Himalayas.*

Godhead *n* the nature and condition of being God.

godless *adj* **1** wicked or unprincipled. **2** not religious. **godlessness** *n*

godly *adj* **-lier, -liest** deeply religious. **godliness** *n*

godmother *n* a female godparent.

godparent *n* a person who promises at a person's baptism to look after his or her religious upbringing.

godsend *n* a person or thing that comes unexpectedly but is very welcome.

godson *n* a male godchild.

Godspeed *interj* an expression of good wishes for a person's safe journey and success.

goer *n* a person who attends something regularly: a *church goer.*

go for *vb* **1** to choose: *any politician will go for the soft option.* **2** *Informal* to like very much. **3** to attack. **4** to apply equally to: *the same might go for the other woman.*

go-getter *n Informal* an ambitious enterprising person. **go-getting** *adj*

gogga (**hohh**-a) *n S African informal* an insect.

goggle *vb* **-gling, -gled** to stare with wide-open eyes. ~See also **goggles. goggle-eyed** *adj*

gogglebox *n Brit slang* a television set.

goggles *pl n* close-fitting protective spectacles.

go-go *adj* of a type of dancing performed to pop music by young women wearing few clothes: *go-go club.*

Goidelic *n* **1** the group of Celtic languages, consisting of Irish Gaelic, Scottish Gaelic, and Manx. ~*adj* **2** of this group of languages.

go in for *vb* **1** to enter (a competition). **2** to take up or take part in (an activity).

going *n* **1** the condition of the ground with regard to walking or riding: *the going for the cross-country is perfect.* **2** *Informal* speed or progress: *not bad going for a lad of 58.* ~*adj* **3** thriving: *the racecourse was a going concern.* **4** current or accepted: *this is the going rate for graduates.*

going-over *n, pl* **goings-over** *Informal* **1** a thorough examination or investigation. **2** a physical beating.

goings-on *pl n Informal* mysterious or shady activities.

go into *vb* to describe or investigate in detail.

goitre *or US* **goiter** (**goy**-ter) *n Pathol* a swelling of the thyroid gland in the neck.

go-kart *n* a small four-wheeled motor vehicle, used for racing.

gold *n* **1** a bright yellow precious metal, used as a monetary standard and in jewellery and plating. Symbol: Au **2** jewellery or coins made of this metal. **3** short for **gold medal.** ~*adj* **4** deep yellow.

goldcrest *n* a small bird with a bright yellow-and-black crown.

THESAURUS

mission **2.** *adj.* ambitious, enterprising, go-getting (*informal*), pioneering, progressive, up-and-coming

goal aim, ambition, design, destination, end, intention, limit, mark, object, objective, purpose, target

go back change one's mind, desert, forsake, renege, repudiate, retract

gobble bolt, cram, devour, gorge, gulp, guzzle, pig out on (*U.S. & Canad. slang*), stuff, swallow, wolf

go-between agent, broker, dealer, factor, intermediary, liaison, mediator, medium, middleman

go by 1. elapse, exceed, flow on, move onward, pass, proceed **2.** adopt, be guided by, follow, heed, judge from, observe, take as guide

godforsaken abandoned, backward, bleak, deserted, desolate, dismal, dreary, forlorn, gloomy, lonely, neglected, remote, wretched

godless atheistic, depraved, evil, impious, irreligious, profane, ungodly, unprincipled, unrighteous, wicked

godly devout, god-fearing, good, holy, pious, religious, righteous, saintly

godsend blessing, boon, manna, stroke of luck, windfall

go for 1. admire, be attracted to, be fond of, choose, favour, hold with, like, prefer **2.** assail, assault, attack, launch oneself at, rush upon, set about *or* upon, spring upon

go in (for) adopt, embrace, engage in, enter, espouse, practise, pursue, take up, undertake

gold-digger *n Informal* a woman who marries or has a relationship with a man for his money.

gold dust *n* **1** gold in the form of small particles or powder. **2 like gold dust** in great demand because difficult to obtain: *kidney machines were like gold dust.*

golden *adj* **1** made of gold: *golden bangles.* **2** of the colour of gold: *golden corn.* **3** *Informal* very successful or destined for success: *the golden girl of British athletics.* **4** excellent or valuable: *a golden opportunity for peace.* **5** (of an anniversary) the fiftieth: *golden wedding; Golden Jubilee.*

golden age *n* the most flourishing and outstanding period in the history of an art or nation: *the golden age of Dixieland jazz.*

golden eagle *n* a large mountain eagle of the N hemisphere with golden-brown feathers.

golden handshake *n Informal* money given to an employee either on retirement or to compensate for loss of employment.

golden mean *n* the middle course between extremes.

golden retriever *n* a retriever with silky wavy gold-coloured hair.

goldenrod *n* a tall plant with spikes of small yellow flowers.

golden rule *n* an important principle: *the golden rule is to start with the least difficult problems.*

golden syrup *n Brit* a light golden-coloured treacle.

goldfinch *n* a European finch the male of which has yellow-and-black wings.

goldfish *n, pl* **-fish** *or* **-fishes** a gold or orange-red freshwater fish, often kept as a pet.

gold foil *n* thin gold sheet that is thicker than gold leaf.

gold leaf *n* very thin gold sheet made by rolling or hammering gold and used for gilding.

gold medal *n* a medal made of gold, awarded to the winner of a race or competition.

gold-plated *adj* covered with a very thin coating of gold.

gold rush *n* a large-scale migration of people to a territory where gold has been found.

goldsmith *n* a person who makes gold jewellery and other articles.

gold standard *n* a monetary system in which the basic currency unit equals a specified weight of gold.

golf *n* **1** a game in which a ball is struck with clubs into a series of eighteen holes in a grassy course. *~vb* **2** to play golf. **golfer** *n*

golf club *n* **1** a long-shafted club used to strike a golf ball. **2 a** an association of golf players. **b** the premises of such an association.

golf course *or* **links** *n* an area of ground laid out for golf.

golliwog *n* a soft doll with a black face, usually made of cloth.

golly *interj* an exclamation of mild surprise.

gonad *n* an organ in which reproductive cells are produced, such as a testis or ovary.

gondola *n* **1** a long narrow flat-bottomed boat with a high ornamented stem, traditionally used on the canals of Venice. **2** a moving cabin suspended from a cable, used as a ski lift.

gondolier *n* a person who propels a gondola.

gone *vb* **1** the past participle of **go.** *~adj* **2** no longer present or no longer in existence.

goner *n Slang* a person who is about to die or who is beyond help.

gong *n* **1** a flat circular metal disc that is hit with a hammer to give out a loud sound. **2** *Brit slang* a medal.

gonorrhoea *or esp US* **gonorrhea** (gon-or-**ree**-a) *n* a sexually transmitted disease that causes inflammation and a discharge from the genital organs.

goo *n Informal* a sticky substance.

good *adj* **better, best 1** having admirable, pleasing, or superior qualities: *a good listener.* **2** morally excellent; virtuous: *a good person.* **3** beneficial: *exercise is good for the heart.* **4** kindly or generous: *he is so good to us.* **5** competent or talented: *she's good at physics.* **6** obedient or well-behaved: *a good boy.* **7** reliable or recommended: *a good make.* **8** complete or thorough: *she went to have a good look round.* **9** appropriate or opportune: *a good time to clear the air.* **10** satisfying or enjoyable: *a good holiday.* **11** newest or of the best quality: *keep the good dishes for guests.* **12** fairly large, extensive, or long: *they contain a good amount of protein.* **13 as good as** virtually or practically: *the war was as good as over.* *~n* **14** advantage or benefit: *what is the good of it all?* **15** positive moral qualities; virtue. **16 for good** for ever; permanently: *his political career was over for good.* ~See also **goods.**

➤ Note that *good* is an adjective. To modify a verb, use *well: She did well.*

goodbye *interj* **1** an expression used on parting. *~n* **2** the act of saying goodbye: *he said his goodbyes.*

THESAURUS

go into analyse, consider, delve into, discuss, examine, inquire into, investigate, look into, probe, pursue, research, review, scrutinize, study, work over

golden 1. blond *or* blonde, bright, brilliant, flaxen, resplendent, shining, yellow **2.** best, blissful, delightful, flourishing, glorious, happy, joyful, joyous, precious, prosperous, rich, successful **3.** advantageous, auspicious, excellent, favourable, opportune, promising, propitious, rosy, valuable

gone absent, astray, away, dead, deceased, defunct, departed, elapsed, ended, extinct, finished, lacking, lost, missing, no more, over, past, vanished

good *adj.* **1.** acceptable, admirable, agreeable, bad (*slang*), capital, choice, commendable, crucial (*slang*), excellent, fine, first-class, first-rate, great, hunky-dory (*informal*), pleasant, pleasing, positive, precious, satisfactory, splendid, super (*informal*), superior, tiptop, valuable, wicked (*slang*), world-class, worthy **2.** admirable, estimable, ethical, exemplary, honest, honourable, moral, praiseworthy, right, righteous, trustworthy, upright, virtuous, worthy **3.** adequate, advantageous, auspicious, beneficial, convenient, favourable, fit, fitting, healthy, helpful, opportune, profitable, propitious, salubrious, salutary, suitable, useful, wholesome **4.** altruistic, approving, beneficent, benevolent, charitable, friendly, gracious, humane, kind, kind-hearted, kindly, merciful, obliging, well-disposed **5.** able, accomplished, adept, adroit, capable, clever, competent, dexterous, efficient, expert, first-rate, proficient, reliable, satisfactory, serviceable, skilled, sound, suitable, talented, thorough, useful **6.** decorous, dutiful, mannerly, obedient, orderly, polite, proper, seemly, well-behaved, well-mannered **7.** agreeable, cheerful, congenial, convivial, enjoyable, gratifying, happy, pleasant, pleasing, pleasurable, satisfying **8.** best, fancy, finest, newest, nicest, precious, smartest, special, valuable **9.** adequate, ample, complete, considerable, entire, extensive, full, large, long, sizable, solid, substantial, sufficient, whole *~n.* **10.** advantage, avail, behalf, benefit, gain, interest, profit, service, use, usefulness, welfare, wellbeing, worth **11.** excellence, goodness, merit, morality, probity, rectitude, right, righteousness, uprightness, virtue, worth

good day *interj* an expression of greeting or farewell used during the day.
good-for-nothing *n* **1** an irresponsible or worthless person. *~adj* **2** irresponsible or worthless.
Good Friday *n Christianity* the Friday before Easter, observed as a commemoration of the Crucifixion of Jesus Christ.
goodies *pl n* any things considered particularly desirable.
goodly *adj* **-lier, -liest** fairly large: *a goodly number of children.*
good morning *interj* an expression of greeting or farewell used in the morning.
good-natured *adj* tolerant and kindly.
goodness *n* **1** the quality of being good. *~interj* **2** an exclamation of surprise.
good night *interj* an expression of farewell used in the evening or at night.
goods *pl n* **1** articles produced to be sold: *consumer goods.* **2** movable personal property: *houses and goods are insured from fire.* **3 deliver the goods** *Informal* to do what is expected or required. **4 have the goods on someone** *US & Canad slang* to know something incriminating about someone.
Good Samaritan *n* a person who helps someone in difficulty or distress.
good-tempered *adj* tolerant and kindly.
good turn *n* a helpful and friendly act.
goodwill *n* **1** kindly feelings towards other people. **2** the popularity and good reputation of a well-established business, considered as a valuable asset.
goody *interj* **1** a child's exclamation of pleasure. *~n, pl* **goodies 2** *Informal* the hero in a film or book. **3** See **goodies.**
goody-goody *Informal ~n, pl* **-goodies 1** a person who behaves well in order to please people in authority. *~adj* **2** behaving well in order to please people in authority.
gooey *adj* **gooier, gooiest** *Informal* **1** sticky, soft, and often sweet. **2** sentimental: *one knows the whole gooey performance is an act.*
goof *vb Informal* **1** to bungle or botch. **2 goof off** to spend time in a lazy or foolish way: *he's goofing off on the Costa del Sol.*
go off *vb* **1** to stop functioning: *the heating went off.* **2** to make a sudden loud noise: *a bomb went off.* **3** to occur as specified: *the actual launch went off perfectly.* **4** *Brit informal* (of food) to become stale or rotten. **5** *Brit informal* to stop liking.
goofy *adj* **goofier, goofiest** *Informal* silly or ridiculous.
googly *n, pl* **-lies** *Cricket* a ball bowled like a leg break but spinning from off to leg on pitching.
goon *n* **1** a stupid person. **2** *US informal* a hired thug.
go on *vb* **1** to continue or proceed. **2** to take place: *there's a war going on.* **3** to talk at length and annoyingly.
goosander *n* a duck of Europe and North America with a dark head and white body.
goose[1] *n, pl* **geese 1** a fairly large web-footed long-necked migratory bird. **2** the female of such a bird. **3** the flesh of the goose used for food. **4** *Informal* a silly person.
goose[2] *vb* **goosing, goosed** *Slang* to prod (someone) playfully in the bottom.
gooseberry *n, pl* **-ries 1** a small edible green berry with tiny hairs on the skin. **2 play gooseberry** *Brit informal* to be an unwanted single person accompanying a couple.
goose flesh *n* the bumpy condition of the skin due to cold or fear, in which the muscles at the base of the hair follicles contract, making the hair bristle. Also: **goose pimples**
goose-step *vb* **-stepping, -stepped** to march raising the legs high alternately while keeping the legs straight.
go out *vb* **1** to go to entertainments or social functions. **2 go out with** to have a romantic relationship with. **3** to be extinguished or cease to function: *the lights went out.* **4** (of information) to be released publicly. **5** (of a broadcast) to be transmitted.
go over *vb* **1** to examine very carefully. **2 go over to** to change to: *he went over to the Free Orthodox Church.*
gopher (**go**-fer) *n* an American burrowing rodent with wide cheek pouches.
Gordian knot *n* **cut the Gordian knot** to solve a complicated problem by bold or forceful action.
gore[1] *n* blood shed from a wound.
gore[2] *vb* **goring, gored** (of an animal) to pierce or stab (a person or another animal) with a horn or tusk.
gore[3] *n* a tapering piece of material in a garment, sail, or umbrella.
gorge *n* **1** a deep narrow steep-sided valley. **2 one's gorge rises** one feels disgusted or nauseated. *~vb*

THESAURUS

12. for good finally, for ever, irrevocably, never to return, once and for all, permanently, *sine die*
goodbye adieu, farewell, leave-taking, parting
good-for-nothing 1. *n.* black sheep, idler, layabout, ne'er-do-well, profligate, rapscallion, skiver (*Brit. slang*), waster, wastrel **2.** *adj.* feckless, idle, irresponsible, useless, worthless
goodly ample, considerable, large, significant, sizable, substantial, tidy (*informal*)
good-natured agreeable, benevolent, friendly, good-hearted, helpful, kind, kindly, tolerant, warm-hearted, well-disposed, willing to please
goodness beneficence, benevolence, excellence, friendliness, generosity, goodwill, graciousness, honesty, honour, humaneness, integrity, kind-heartedness, kindliness, kindness, mercy, merit, morality, obligingness, quality, rectitude, righteousness, superiority, uprightness, value, virtue, wholesomeness, worth
goods 1. commodities, merchandise, stock, stuff, wares **2.** appurtenances, belongings, chattels, effects, furnishings, furniture, gear, movables, paraphernalia, possessions, property, things, trappings
goodwill amity, benevolence, favour, friendliness, friendship, heartiness, kindliness, zeal
go off 1. blow up, detonate, explode, fire **2.** happen, occur, take place **3.** *informal* go bad, go stale, rot
go on 1. continue, endure, happen, last, occur, persist, proceed, stay **2.** blether, carry on, chatter, prattle, rabbit (*Brit. informal*), ramble on, waffle (*informal, chiefly Brit.*), witter (on) (*informal*)
go out be extinguished, die out, expire, fade out
go over examine, inspect, rehearse, reiterate, review, revise, study, work over
gorge 1. *n.* canyon, cleft, clough (*dialect*), defile, fissure, pass, ravine **2.** *vb.* bolt, cram, devour, feed, fill, glut, gobble, gulp, guzzle, overeat, pig out (*U.S. & Canad. slang*), sate, satiate, stuff, surfeit, swallow, wolf
gorgeous 1. beautiful, brilliant, dazzling, drop-dead (*slang*), elegant, glittering, grand, luxuriant, magnifi-

gorging, gorged 3 Also: **gorge oneself** to eat greedily.

gorgeous *adj* **1** strikingly beautiful or attractive. **2** *Informal* warm, sunny, and very pleasant: *a gorgeous day.* **gorgeously** *adv*

Gorgon *n* **1** *Greek myth* one of three monstrous sisters who had live snakes for hair, and were so horrifying that anyone who looked at them was turned to stone. **2** *Informal* a terrifying or repulsive woman.

Gorgonzola *n* a sharp-flavoured blue-veined Italian cheese.

gorilla *n* a very large W African ape with coarse black hair.

gormless *adj Brit informal* stupid or dull-witted.

go round *vb* to be sufficient: *there wasn't enough money to go round.*

gorse *n* an evergreen shrub with small yellow flowers and prickles, which grows wild in the countryside.

gory *adj* **gorier, goriest 1** horrific or bloodthirsty: *the gory details.* **2** bloody: *gory remains.*

gosh *interj* an exclamation of mild surprise or wonder.

goshawk *n* a large swift short-winged hawk.

gosling *n* a young goose.

go-slow *n Brit* a deliberate slowing of the rate of production by workers as a tactic in industrial conflict.

gospel *n* **1 a** the teachings of Jesus Christ. **b** the story of Christ's life and teachings. **2** a doctrine held to be of great importance: *the gospel of self-help.* **3** Also called: **gospel truth** unquestionable truth: *gross inaccuracies which are sometimes taken as gospel.* ~*adj* **4** denoting a kind of religious music originating in the churches of the Black people in the Southern US.

Gospel *n Christianity* any of the first four books of the New Testament, namely Matthew, Mark, Luke, and John, which tell the story of Jesus Christ.

gossamer *n* **1** a very fine fabric. **2** a filmy cobweb often seen on foliage or floating in the air.

gossip *n* **1** idle talk, usually about other people's private lives, esp. of a disapproving or malicious nature: *office gossip.* **2** an informal conversation, esp. about other people's private lives: *to have a gossip and a giggle.* **3** a person who habitually talks about other people, usually maliciously. ~*vb* **4** to talk idly or maliciously, esp. about other people's private lives. **gossipy** *adj*

got *vb* **1** the past of **get. 2 have got** to possess. **3 have got to** must: *you have got to be prepared to work hard.*

Gothic *adj* **1** of a style of architecture used in W Europe from the 12th to the 16th centuries, characterized by pointed arches, ribbed vaults, and flying buttresses. **2** of a literary style featuring stories of gloom, horror, and the supernatural, popular in the late 18th century. **3** of or in a heavy ornate script typeface. ~*n* **4** Gothic architecture or art.

go through *vb* **1** to experience (a difficult time or process). **2** to name or describe: *the president went through a list of government ministers.* **3** to qualify for the next stage of a competition: *Linford Christie went through as a heat winner to the second-round stage.* **4** to be approved: *the bill went through parliament.* **5 go through with** to bring to a successful conclusion, often by persistence.

gotten *vb Chiefly US* a past participle of **get.**

gouache *n* opaque watercolour paint bound with glue.

Gouda *n* a round mild-flavoured Dutch cheese.

gouge (**gowj**) *vb* **gouging, gouged 1** to scoop or force (something) out of its position. **2** to cut (a hole or groove) in something with a pointed object. ~*n* **3** a mark or groove made by gouging.

goulash (**goo**-lash) *n* a rich stew seasoned with paprika, originating in Hungary.

gourd (**goord**) *n* **1** a large hard-shelled fruit similar to a cucumber or marrow. **2** a container made from a dried gourd shell.

gourmand (**goor**-mand) *n* a person devoted to eating and drinking, usually to excess.

gourmet (**goor**-may) *n* an expert on good food and drink.

gout (**gowt**) *n* a disease that causes painful inflammation of certain joints, for example of the big toe. **gouty** *adj*

govern *vb* **1** to direct and control the policy and affairs of (a country or an organization). **2** to control or determine: *the international organizations governing athletics and rugby.* **governable** *adj*

governance *n* government, control, or authority.

governess *n* a woman employed in a private household to teach the children.

government *n* **1** the executive policy-making body of a country or state. **2** the state and its administration: *the assembled heads of state and government.* **3** the system by which a country or state is ruled: *the old hard-line government.* **governmental** *adj*

governor *n* **1** the chief political administrator of a region, such as a US state or a colony. **2** *Brit* the senior administrator of a school, prison, or other institution. **3** *Brit informal* one's employer or father. **governorship** *n*

governor general *n, pl* **governors general** *or* **governor generals** the chief representative of the British government in a Commonwealth country.

THESAURUS

cent, opulent, ravishing, resplendent, showy, splendid, splendiferous (*facetious*), stunning (*informal*), sumptuous, superb **2.** *informal* bright, delightful, enjoyable, exquisite, fine, glorious, lovely

gory blood-soaked, bloodstained, bloodthirsty, bloody, murderous, sanguinary

gospel 1. credo, creed, doctrine, message, news, revelation, tidings **2.** certainty, fact, the last word, truth, verity

gossamer *adj.* airy, delicate, diaphanous, fine, flimsy, gauzy, light, sheer, silky, thin, transparent

gossip *n.* **1.** blether, chinwag (*Brit. informal*), chitchat, dirt (*U.S. slang*), gen (*Brit. informal*), hearsay, idle talk, jaw (*slang*), latest (*informal*), newsmongering (*old-fashioned*), prattle, scandal, small talk, tittle-tattle **2.** babbler, blether, busybody, chatterbox (*informal*), chatterer, flibbertigibbet, gossipmonger, newsmonger (*old-fashioned*), prattler, scandalmonger, tattler, telltale ~*vb.* **3.** blather, blether, chat, gabble, jaw (*slang*), prate, prattle, tattle

go through bear, brave, endure, experience, suffer, tolerate, undergo, withstand

govern 1. administer, be in power, command, conduct, control, direct, guide, handle, hold sway, lead, manage, order, oversee, pilot, reign, rule, steer, superintend, supervise **2.** bridle, check, contain, control, curb, decide, determine, direct, discipline, get the better of, guide, hold in check, influence, inhibit, master, regulate, restrain, rule, subdue, sway, tame, underlie

government 1. administration, executive, ministry, powers-that-be, regime **2.** administration, authority, dominion, execution, governance, law, polity, rule, sovereignty, state, statecraft

governor administrator, boss (*informal*), chief,

go with *vb* **1** to blend or harmonize with: *the style goes well with modern art.* **2** to be linked with: *respect goes with age.*

go without *vb Chiefly Brit* to be denied or deprived of: *no soldier should go without a pension.*

gown *n* **1** a woman's long formal dress. **2** a surgeon's overall. **3** a loose wide official robe worn by clergymen, judges, lawyers, and academics.

goy *n, pl* **goyim** *or* **goys** a Jewish word for a **Gentile.**

GP general practitioner.

GPMU Graphical, Paper and Media Union.

GPO general post office.

grab *vb* **grabbing, grabbed 1** to seize hold of. **2** to take (food, drink, or rest) hurriedly. **3** to take (an opportunity) eagerly. **4** to seize illegally or unscrupulously: *land grabbing.* **5** *Informal* to interest or impress. *~n* **6** the act of grabbing.

grace *n* **1** elegance and beauty of movement, form, or expression. **2** a pleasing or charming quality: *architecture with few redeeming graces.* **3** courtesy or decency: *at least she had the grace to laugh.* **4** a delay granted for the completion of a task or payment of a debt: *another year's grace.* **5** *Christian theol* the free and unmerited favour of God shown towards humankind. **6** a short prayer of thanks for a meal. **7 airs and graces** an affected manner. **8 with bad grace** unwillingly or grudgingly: *independence was granted with bad grace.* **9 with good grace** willingly or ungrudgingly: *to accept with good grace.* *~vb* **gracing, graced 10** to honour or favour: *graced by the presence of Henry Fonda.* **11** to decorate or make more attractive: *bedsit walls graced by Che Guevara and James Dean.*

Grace *n* **Your, His** *or* **Her Grace** a title used to address or refer to a duke, duchess, or archbishop.

graceful *adj* having beauty of movement, style, or form. **gracefully** *adv* **gracefulness** *n*

graceless *adj* **1** lacking elegance. **2** lacking manners.

grace note *n Music* a note that ornaments a melody.

Graces *pl n Greek myth* the three sister goddesses of charm and beauty.

gracious *adj* **1** showing kindness and courtesy. **2** characterized by elegance, ease, and indulgence: *gracious living.* *~interj* **3** an expression of mild surprise or wonder. **graciously** *adv* **graciousness** *n*

gradation *n* **1** a series of systematic stages; gradual progression. **2** a stage in such a series or progression.

grade *n* **1** a place on a scale of quality, rank, or size. **2** a mark or rating indicating a student's level of achievement. **3** a rank or level of importance in a company or organization. **4** *US & Canad* a class or year in a school. **5 make the grade** *Informal* to be successful by reaching a required standard. *~vb* **grading, graded 6** to arrange according to quality or rank: *passes are graded from A down to E.* **7** to give a grade to: *senior secretaries will need shorthand and be graded accordingly.*

gradient *n* **1** Also (esp. US): **grade** a sloping part of a railway, road, or path. **2** Also (esp. US): **grade** a measure of the steepness of such a slope. **3** a measure of the change in something, such as the angle of a curve, over a specified distance.

gradual *adj* occurring, developing, or moving in small stages: *a gradual handover of power.* **gradually** *adv*

gradualism *n* the policy of changing something gradually. **gradualist** *adj*

graduate *n* **1** a person who holds a university or college degree. **2** *US & Canad* a student who has completed a course of studies at a high school and received a diploma. **3** same as **postgraduate.** *~vb* **-ating, -ated 4** to receive a degree or diploma. **5** to change by degrees: *the winds graduate from tropical storms to cyclones.* **6** to mark (a measuring flask or instrument) with units of measurement.

graduation *n* **1** the act of graduating from university or college. **2** *US & Canad* the act of graduating from high school. **3** the ceremony at which degrees and diplomas are given to graduating students. **4** a mark indicating measure on an instrument or container.

Graeco-Roman *or esp US* **Greco-Roman** (greek-oh-**rome**-an) *adj* of, or showing the influence of, both Greek and Roman cultures.

graffiti (graf-**fee**-tee) *n* drawings or words scribbled or sprayed on walls or posters.

➤ English does not have a singular form for this word and tends to use *graffiti* for both singular and multiple examples.

THESAURUS

commander, comptroller, controller, director, executive, head, leader, manager, overseer, ruler, superintendent, supervisor

go with accompany, agree, blend, complement, concur, correspond, fit, harmonize, match, suit

go without abstain, be denied, be deprived of, deny oneself, do without, go short, lack, want

gown costume, dress, frock, garb, garment, habit, robe

grab bag, capture, catch *or* take hold of, catch (up), clutch, grasp, grip, latch on to, nab (*informal*), nail (*informal*), pluck, seize, snap up, snatch

grace *n.* **1.** attractiveness, beauty, charm, comeliness, ease, elegance, finesse, gracefulness, loveliness, pleasantness, poise, polish, refinement, shapeliness, tastefulness **2.** benefaction, beneficence, benevolence, favour, generosity, goodness, goodwill, kindliness, kindness **3.** breeding, consideration, courtesy, cultivation, decency, decorum, etiquette, mannerliness, manners, propriety, tact **4.** charity, clemency, compassion, forgiveness, indulgence, leniency, lenity, mercy, pardon, quarter, reprieve **5.** benediction, blessing, prayer, thanks, thanksgiving *~vb.* **6.** adorn, beautify, bedeck, deck, decorate, dignify, distinguish, elevate, embellish, enhance, enrich, favour, garnish, glorify, honour, ornament, set off

graceful agile, beautiful, becoming, charming, comely, easy, elegant, fine, flowing, natural, pleasing, smooth, symmetrical, tasteful

gracious accommodating, affable, amiable, beneficent, benevolent, benign, benignant, charitable, chivalrous, civil, compassionate, considerate, cordial, courteous, courtly, friendly, hospitable, indulgent, kind, kindly, lenient, loving, merciful, mild, obliging, pleasing, polite, well-mannered

grade *n.* **1.** brand, category, class, condition, degree, echelon, group, level, mark, notch, order, place, position, quality, rank, rung, size, stage, station, step **2. make the grade** *informal* come through with flying colours, come up to scratch (*informal*), measure up, measure up to expectations, pass muster, prove acceptable, succeed, win through **3.** *U.S.* acclivity, bank, declivity, gradient, hill, incline, rise, slope *~vb.* **4.** arrange, brand, class, classify, evaluate, group, order, range, rank, rate, sort, value

gradient acclivity, bank, declivity, grade, hill, incline, rise, slope

gradual continuous, even, gentle, graduated, moderate, piecemeal, progressive, regular, slow, steady, successive, unhurried

gradually bit by bit, by degrees, drop by drop, evenly, gently, little by little, moderately, piece by piece,

graft[1] *n* **1** *Surgery* a piece of tissue transplanted to an area of the body in need of the tissue. **2** a small piece of tissue from one plant that is joined to another plant so that they grow together as one. *~vb* **3** to transplant (tissue) to an area of the body in need of the tissue. **4** to join (part of one plant) onto another plant so that they grow together as one. **5** to attach or incorporate: *to graft Japanese production methods onto the American talent for innovation.*

graft[2] *n* **1** *Informal* hard work. **2** the practice of obtaining money by taking advantage of one's position. *~vb* **3** *Informal* to work hard.

Grail *n* See **Holy Grail.**

grain *n* **1** the small hard seedlike fruit of a cereal plant. **2** a mass of such fruits gathered for food. **3** cereal plants in general. **4** a small hard particle: *a grain of salt.* **5** a very small amount: *a grain of compassion.* **6 a** the arrangement of the fibres, layers, or particles in wood, leather, or stone. **b** the pattern or texture resulting from this. **7 go against the grain** to be contrary to one's natural inclinations. **grainy** *adj*

gram *or* **gramme** *n* a metric unit of weight equal to one thousandth of a kilogram.

graminivorous *adj* (of an animal) grass-eating.

grammar *n* **1** the rules of a language, that show how sentences are formed, or how words area inflected. **2** the way in which grammar is used: *the teacher found errors of spelling and grammar.* **3** a book on the rules of grammar.

grammarian *n* a person who studies or writes about grammar for a living.

grammar school *n* **1** *Brit* (esp. formerly) a secondary school for children of high academic ability. **2** *US* same as **elementary school. 3** *Austral* a private school, usually one controlled by a church. **4** *NZ* a secondary school forming part of the public education system.

grammatical *adj* **1** of grammar. **2** (of a sentence) following the rules of grammar. **grammatically** *adv*

gramme *n* same as **gram.**

gramophone *n* an old-fashioned type of record player.

grampus *n, pl* **-puses** a dolphin-like mammal with a blunt snout.

gran *n Informal* a grandmother.

granary *n, pl* **-ries 1** a building for storing threshed grain. **2** a region that produces a large amount of grain.

Granary *adj Trademark* (of bread or flour) containing malted wheat grain.

grand *adj* **1** large or impressive in size or appearance; magnificent: *the grand hall.* **2** ambitious or important: *grand themes.* **3** dignified or haughty. **4** *Informal* excellent or wonderful. **5** comprehensive or complete: *the grand total.* *~n* **6** (*pl* **grand**) *Slang* a thousand pounds or dollars. **7** short for **grand piano. grandly** *adv*

grandad, granddad *or US* **granddaddy** *n, pl* **-dads** *or* **-daddies** *Informal* a grandfather.

grandchild *n, pl* **-children** a son or daughter of one's son or daughter.

granddad *or US* **granddaddy** *n Informal* See **grandad.**

granddaughter *n* a daughter of one's son or daughter.

grand duke *n* a prince or nobleman who rules a territory, state, or principality. **grand duchess** *fem n* **grand duchy** *n*

grande dame (grond **dam**) *n* a woman regarded as the most prominent or respected member of her profession or group: *the grande dame of international fashion.*

grandee *n* **1** a high-ranking Spanish nobleman. **2** a person who has a high rank or position: *the Party's grandees.*

grandeur *n* **1** personal greatness, dignity, or nobility: *delusions of grandeur.* **2** magnificence or splendour: *cathedral-like grandeur.*

grandfather *n* the father of one's father or mother.

grandfather clock *n* an old-fashioned clock in a tall wooden case that stands on the floor.

grandiloquent *adj* using pompous or unnecessarily complicated language. **grandiloquence** *n*

grandiose *adj* impressive, or meant to impress: *grandiose plans for constructing a new stadium.*

grand jury *n Law chiefly US* a jury that investigates accusations of crime to decide whether the evidence is adequate to bring a prosecution.

grandma *or* **grandmama** *n Informal* a grandmother.

grand mal *n* a form of epilepsy in which there is loss of consciousness and violent convulsions.

grandmaster *n* a person who is exceptionally good at a particular activity or skill, especially chess.

grandmother *n* the mother of one's father or mother.

Grand National *n* an annual steeplechase for horses, run at Aintree, Liverpool.

grandnephew *n* same as **great-nephew.**

grandniece *n* same as **great-niece.**

grand opera *n* an opera that has a serious plot and no spoken dialogue.

grandpa *or* **grandpapa** *n Informal* a grandfather.

grandparent *n* the father or mother of one's father or mother.

grand piano *n* a large piano in which the strings are arranged horizontally.

Grand Prix (gron **pree**) *n* **1** an international formula motor race. **2** a very important international competitive event in other sports, such as athletics.

THESAURUS

piecemeal, progressively, slowly, steadily, step by step, unhurriedly

graduate *vb.* calibrate, grade, mark off, measure out, proportion, regulate

graft 1. *n.* bud, implant, scion, shoot, splice, sprout **2.** *vb.* affix, implant, ingraft, insert, join, splice, transplant

grain 1. grist, kernel, seed **2.** cereals, corn **3.** atom, bit, crumb, fragment, granule, iota, jot, mite, modicum, molecule, morsel, ounce, particle, piece, scrap, spark, speck, trace, whit **4.** fibre, nap, pattern, surface, texture, weave

grand 1. ambitious, august, dignified, elevated, eminent, exalted, fine, glorious, gorgeous, grandiose, great, haughty, illustrious, imposing, impressive, large, lofty, lordly, luxurious, magnificent, majestic, monumental, noble, opulent, ostentatious, palatial, pompous, pretentious, princely, regal, splendid, splendiferous (*facetious*), stately, striking, sublime, sumptuous, superb **2.** *informal* admirable, excellent, fine, first-class, first-rate, great (*informal*), hunky-dory (*informal*), marvellous (*informal*), outstanding, smashing (*informal*), splendid, splendiferous (*facetious*), super (*informal*), superb, terrific (*informal*), very good, wonderful, world-class

grandeur augustness, dignity, greatness, importance, loftiness, magnificence, majesty, nobility, pomp, splendour, state, stateliness, sublimity

grandiose affected, ambitious, bombastic, extrava-

grandsire *n Old-fashioned* a grandfather.

grand slam *n* **1** the achievement of winning all the games or major tournaments in a sport in one season. **2** See **slam**².

grandson *n* a son of one's son or daughter.

grandstand *n* the main block of seats giving the best view at a sports ground.

grand tour *n* **1** (formerly) an extended tour of continental Europe. **2** *Informal* a tour of inspection: *a grand tour of the house.*

grange *n Chiefly Brit* a farmhouse or country house with its farm buildings.

granite (**gran**-nit) *n* a very hard rock consisting of quartz and feldspars that is widely used for building.

granivorous *adj* (of an animal) grain-eating.

granny *or* **grannie** *n, pl* **-nies** *Informal* a grandmother.

granny flat *n* a flat in or joined on to a house, suitable for an elderly relative to live in.

granny knot *n* a reef knot with the ends crossed the wrong way, making it liable to slip or jam.

grant *vb* **1** to give (a sum of money or a right) formally: *to grant a thirty-eight per cent pay rise; only the President can grant a pardon.* **2** to consent to perform or fulfil: *granting the men's request for sanctuary.* **3** to admit that (something) is true: *I grant that her claims must be true.* **4 take for granted a** to accept that something is true without requiring proof. **b** to take advantage of (someone or something) without showing appreciation. *~n* **5** a sum of money provided by a government or public fund to a person or organization for a specific purpose: *student grants.*

Granth (**grunt**) *n* the sacred scripture of the Sikhs.

granular *adj* of, like, or containing granules: *granular materials such as powders.*

granulated *adj* (of sugar) in the form of coarse grains.

granule *n* a small grain of something: *gravy granules.*

grape *n* a small round sweet juicy fruit with a purple or green skin, which can be eaten raw, dried to make raisins, currants, or sultanas, or used to make wine.

grapefruit *n, pl* **-fruit** *or* **-fruits** a large round yellow juicy citrus fruit with a slightly bitter taste.

grapeshot *n* ammunition for cannons consisting of a cluster of iron balls that scatter after firing.

grapevine *n* **1** a vine grown for its grapes. **2** *Informal* an unofficial means of passing on information from person to person: *he'd doubtless heard rumours on the grapevine.*

graph *n* a diagram showing the relation between certain sets of numbers or quantities by means of a series of dots or lines plotted with reference to a set of axes.

-graph *n combining form* **1** an instrument that writes or records: *tachograph.* **2** a writing or record: *autograph.* **-graphic** *or* **-graphical** *adj combining form* **-graphically** *adv combining form*

graphic *adj* **1** vividly described: *a graphic account of her three days in captivity.* **2** of the graphic arts: *graphic design.* **3** Also: **graphical** *Maths* of or using a graph: *a graphic presentation.* **graphically** *adv*

graphic arts *pl n* the visual arts based on drawing or the use of line.

graphics *n* **1** the art of drawing in accordance with mathematical rules. *~pl n* **2** the illustrations in a magazine or book, or in a television or film production. **3** *Computers* information displayed in the form of diagrams or graphs.

graphite *n* a soft black form of carbon used in pencils, as a lubricant, and in some nuclear reactors.

graphology *n* the study of handwriting, usually to analyse the writer's character. **graphologist** *n*

graph paper *n* paper printed with a design of small squares for drawing graphs or diagrams on.

-graphy *n combining form* indicating: **1** a form of writing or representing things: *calligraphy; photography.* **2** an art or descriptive science: *choreography; topography.*

grapnel *n* a device with several hooks at one end, which is used to grasp or secure an object, esp. in sailing.

grapple *vb* **-pling, -pled grapple with a** to try to cope with: *a difficult concept to grapple with.* **b** to come to grips with (someone) in hand-to-hand combat.

grappling iron *n* same as **grapnel.**

grasp *vb* **1** to grip firmly. **2** to understand: *his failure to grasp the gravity of the crisis.* *~n* **3** a very firm grip. **4** understanding or comprehension: *a good grasp of detail.* **5 within someone's grasp** almost certain to be accomplished or won: *he now has that prize within his grasp.*

grasping *adj* greedy for money.

grass *n* **1** a very common green plant with jointed stems and long narrow leaves, eaten by animals such as sheep and cows, and used for lawns and sports fields. **2** a particular kind of grass, such as bamboo. **3** a lawn. **4** *Slang* marijuana. **5** *Brit slang* a person who informs, usually on criminals. *~vb* **6 grass on** *Brit slang* to inform on (someone) to the police or some other authority. **7 grass over** to cover with grass. **grassy** *adj*

grass hockey *n* (in W Canada) field hockey, as contrasted with ice hockey.

grasshopper *n* an insect with long hind legs which it uses for leaping.

grassland *n* **1** land covered with grass. **2** pasture land.

grass roots *pl n* **1** ordinary members of a group or organization, as distinct from its leaders. *~adj*

THESAURUS

gant, flamboyant, grand, high-flown, imposing, impressive, lofty, magnificent, majestic, monumental, ostentatious, pompous, pretentious, showy, stately

grant *vb.* **1.** allocate, allot, assign, award, bestow, confer, donate, give, hand out, impart, present **2.** accede to, accord, acknowledge, admit, agree to, allow, cede, concede, consent to, permit, vouchsafe, yield *~n.* **3.** admission, allocation, allotment, allowance, award, benefaction, bequest, boon, bounty, concession, donation, endowment, gift, hand-out, present, stipend, subsidy

granule atom, crumb, fragment, grain, iota, jot, molecule, particle, scrap, speck

graphic 1. clear, descriptive, detailed, explicit, expressive, forcible, illustrative, lively, lucid, picturesque, striking, telling, vivid, well-drawn **2.** delineated, diagrammatic, drawn, illustrative, pictorial, representational, seen, visible, visual

grapple catch, clasp, clutch, come to grips, fasten, grab, grasp, grip, hold, hug, lay *or* take hold, seize, wrestle

grasp *vb.* **1.** catch (up), clasp, clinch, clutch, grab, grapple, grip, hold, lay *or* take hold of, seize, snatch **2.** catch on, catch *or* get the drift of, comprehend, follow, get, realize, see, take in, understand *~n.* **3.** clasp, clutches, embrace, grip, hold, possession, tenure **4.** awareness, comprehension, ken, knowledge, mastery, perception, realization, understanding

grasping acquisitive, avaricious, close-fisted, covetous, greedy, mean, miserly, niggardly, penny-pinching

grassroots 2 of the ordinary members of a group or organization: *at grassroots level.*

grass snake *n* a harmless European snake with a brownish-green body.

grass widow *n* a woman whose husband is regularly absent for a time.

grate[1] *vb* **grating, grated 1** to reduce to shreds by rubbing against a rough surface: *grated cheese.* **2** to produce a harsh rasping sound by scraping against an object or surface: *the clutch plates grated.* **3 grate on** to annoy: *his manner always grated on me.*

grate[2] *n* **1** a framework of metal bars for holding coal or wood in a fireplace. **2** same as **grating**[1].

grateful *adj* feeling or showing thanks. **gratefully** *adv*

grater *n* a tool with a sharp surface for grating food.

gratify *vb* **-fies, -fying, -fied 1** to satisfy or please (someone). **2** to yield to (a desire or whim): *all his wishes were to be gratified.* **gratification** *n*

grating[1] *n* a framework of metal bars covering an opening in a wall or in the ground.

grating[2] *adj* **1** (of a sound) rough or unpleasant. **2** annoying or irritating: *his cringing obsequiousness was grating.*

gratis *adv, adj* without payment; free: *what I did for you was free, gratis.*

gratitude *n* a feeling of being grateful for gifts or favours.

gratuitous (grat-**tyoo**-it-uss) *adj* **1** unjustified or unreasonable: *gratuitous violence.* **2** given or received without charge or obligation: *his gratuitous voluntary services.* **gratuitously** *adv*

gratuity (grat-**tyoo**-it-ee) *n, pl* **-ties** money given for services rendered; tip.

grave[1] *adj* (rhymes with **save**) **1** serious and worrying: *grave concern.* **2** serious and solemn in appearance or behaviour: *the man looked grave and respectful.* **3** (rhymes with **halve**) denoting an accent (`) over a vowel in some languages, such as French, which indicates that the vowel is pronounced in a particular way. ~*n* (rhymes with **halve**) **4** a grave accent. **gravely** *adv*

grave[2] (rhymes with **save**) *n* **1** a place where a dead person is buried. **2** death: *people are smoking themselves to an early grave.* **3 make someone turn in his or her grave** to do something that would have shocked a person who is now dead.

gravel *n* **1** a mixture of rock fragments and pebbles that is coarser than sand. **2** *Pathol* small rough stones in the kidneys or bladder. ~*vb* **-elling, -elled** *or US* **-eling, -eled 3** to cover with gravel.

gravelly *adj* **1** covered with gravel. **2** (of a voice or sound) harsh and grating.

graven image *n Chiefly Bible* a carved image used as an idol.

gravestone *n* a stone marking a grave.

graveyard *n* a place where dead people are buried.

gravid (**grav**-id) *adj Med* pregnant.

gravimeter (grav-**vim**-it-er) *n* **1** an instrument for measuring the force of gravity. **2** an instrument for measuring relative density.

gravitas (**grav**-vit-tass) *n* seriousness or solemnity.

gravitate *vb* **-tating, -tated 1 gravitate towards** to be attracted or influenced by: *the mathematically inclined often gravitate towards computers.* **2** *Physics* to move under the influence of gravity.

gravitation *n Physics* **1** the force of attraction that bodies exert on one another as a result of their mass. **2** the process or result of this interaction. **gravitational** *adj*

gravity *n, pl* **-ties 1** *Physics* **a** the force that attracts bodies towards the centre of the earth, a moon, or any planet **b** same as **gravitation. 2** seriousness or importance: *the gravity of the situation.* **3** seriousness or solemnity of appearance or behaviour: *his priestly gravity.*

gravy *n, pl* **-vies a** the juices that come from meat during cooking. **b** the sauce made by thickening and flavouring these juices.

gravy boat *n* a small boat-shaped dish with a spout, used for serving gravy or sauce.

gravy train *n Slang* a job or scheme that produces a lot of money for little effort.

gray *adj, n, vb Chiefly US* grey.

graze[1] *vb* **grazing, grazed a** (of an animal) to eat (grass or other growing plants). **b** to feed (animals) on grass or other growing plants.

graze[2] *vb* **grazing, grazed 1** to break the skin of (a

THESAURUS

(*informal*), rapacious, selfish, stingy, tight-arsed (*taboo slang*), tight as a duck's arse (*slang*), tight-assed (*U.S. taboo slang*), tightfisted, usurious, venal

grate *vb.* **1.** mince, pulverize, shred **2.** creak, grind, rasp, rub, scrape, scratch **3.** aggravate (*informal*), annoy, chafe, exasperate, fret, gall, get one down, get on one's nerves (*informal*), irk, irritate, jar, nark (*Brit., Austral., & N.Z. slang*), nettle, peeve, rankle, rub one up the wrong way, set one's teeth on edge, vex

grateful appreciative, beholden, indebted, obliged, thankful

gratify cater to, delight, favour, feed, fulfil, give pleasure, gladden, humour, indulge, pander to, please, recompense, requite, satisfy, thrill

grating *adj.* annoying, disagreeable, discordant, displeasing, grinding, harsh, irksome, irritating, jarring, offensive, rasping, raucous, scraping, squeaky, strident, unpleasant, vexatious

gratis buckshee (*Brit. slang*), for nothing, free, freely, free of charge, gratuitously, on the house, unpaid

gratitude appreciation, gratefulness, indebtedness, obligation, recognition, sense of obligation, thankfulness, thanks

gratuitous 1. assumed, baseless, causeless, groundless, irrelevant, needless, superfluous, uncalled-for, unfounded, unjustified, unmerited, unnecessary, unprovoked, unwarranted, wanton **2.** buckshee (*Brit. slang*), complimentary, free, spontaneous, unasked-for, unpaid, unrewarded, voluntary

gratuity baksheesh, benefaction, bonus, boon, bounty, donation, gift, largesse *or* largess, perquisite, present, recompense, reward, tip

grave[1] **1.** acute, critical, crucial, dangerous, exigent, hazardous, important, life-and-death, momentous, of great consequence, perilous, pressing, serious, severe, significant, threatening, urgent, vital, weighty **2.** dignified, dour, dull, earnest, gloomy, grim-faced, heavy, leaden, long-faced, muted, quiet, sedate, serious, sober, solemn, sombre, staid, subdued, thoughtful, unsmiling

grave[2] *n.* burying place, crypt, last resting place, mausoleum, pit, sepulchre, tomb, vault

graveyard boneyard (*informal*), burial ground, cemetery, charnel house, churchyard, necropolis

gravitate 1. *with* **to** *or* **towards** be influenced (attracted, drawn, pulled), incline, lean, move, tend **2.** be precipitated, descend, drop, fall, precipitate, settle, sink

gravity 1. acuteness, consequence, exigency, hazardousness, importance, moment, momentousness, perilousness, seriousness, severity, significance, urgency,

part of the body) by scraping. **2** to brush against someone gently in passing. *~n* **3** an injury on the skin caused by scraping.

grazier *n* a rancher or farmer who keeps cattle or sheep on grazing land.

grazing *n* land where grass is grown for farm animals to feed upon.

grease *n* **1** soft melted animal fat. **2** a thick oily substance, such as the kind put on machine parts to make them work smoothly. *~vb* **greasing, greased 3** to apply grease to: *lightly grease a baking tin.* **4 grease someone's palm** *Slang* to bribe someone.

greasepaint *n* theatrical make-up.

greaseproof paper *n* any paper that is resistant to penetration by grease and oil, esp. one used for lining baking dishes or wrapping food.

greasy *adj* **greasier, greasiest 1** covered with or containing grease. **2** excessively pleasant or flattering in an insincere manner. **greasiness** *n*

great *adj* **1** large in size. **2** large in number or amount: *the great majority.* **3** larger than others of its kind: *the great white whale.* **4** extreme or more than usual: *great difficulty.* **5** of importance or consequence: *a great discovery.* **6** of exceptional talents or achievements: *a great artist.* **7** skilful: *he's a great storyteller; they are great at problem solving.* **8** *Informal* excellent. *~n* **9 the greats** the most successful people in a particular field: *the all-time greats of golf.* **greatly** *adv* **greatness** *n*

great- *prefix* (in expressing relationship) one generation older or younger than: *great-grandmother.*

great auk *n* an extinct large auk that could not fly.

great-aunt *n* an aunt of one's father or mother.

Great Britain *n* the mainland part of the British Isles; England, Scotland, and Wales.

great circle *n Maths* a circular section of a sphere that has a radius equal to the sphere's radius.

greatcoat *n* a heavy overcoat.

Great Dane *n* a very large dog with short smooth hair.

great-nephew *n* a son of one's nephew or niece.

great-niece *n* a daughter of one's nephew or niece.

Greats *pl n* (at Oxford University) **1** the Honours course in classics and philosophy. **2** the final examinations at the end of this course.

great-uncle *n* an uncle of one's father or mother.

Great War *n* same as **World War I.**

greave *n* a piece of armour for the shin.

grebe *n* a diving water bird.

Grecian (**gree**-shan) *adj* of ancient Greece.

greed *n* excessive desire for something, such as food or money.

greedy *adj* **greedier, greediest** having an excessive desire for something, such as food or money: *greedy for personal possessions.* **greedily** *adv*

Greek *adj* **1** of Greece. *~n* **2** a person from Greece. **3** the language of Greece.

Greek cross *n* a cross with each of the four arms of the same length.

green *adj* **1** of a colour between yellow and blue; of the colour of grass. **2** covered with grass, plants, or trees: *green fields.* **3** of or concerned with conservation and improvement of the environment: used in a political context: *green issues.* **4** (of fruit) fresh, raw, or unripe. **5** pale and sick-looking. **6** inexperienced or gullible. **7 green with envy** very envious. *~n* **8** a colour between yellow and blue. **9** anything green, such as green clothing or green ink: *printed in green.* **10** a small area of grassy land: *the village green.* **11** an area of smooth turf kept for a special purpose: *putting greens.* **12 greens** the leaves and stems of certain plants, eaten as a vegetable: *turnip greens.* **13 Green** a person who supports environmentalist issues. **greenish** *or* **greeny** *adj* **greenness** *n*

green beans *pl n* long narrow green beans that are cooked and eaten as a vegetable.

THESAURUS

weightiness **2.** demureness, dignity, earnestness, gloom, gravitas, grimness, reserve, sedateness, seriousness, sobriety, solemnity, thoughtfulness

graze *vb.* **1.** abrade, bark, chafe, scrape, scratch, skin **2.** brush, glance off, kiss, rub, scrape, shave, skim, touch *~n.* **3.** abrasion, scrape, scratch

greasy 1. fatty, oily, slick, slimy, slippery **2.** fawning, glib, grovelling, ingratiating, oily, slick, smarmy (*Brit. informal*), smooth, sycophantish, toadying, unctuous

great 1. big, bulky, colossal, elephantine, enormous, extensive, gigantic, huge, humongous (*U.S. slang*), immense, large, mammoth, prodigious, stupendous, tremendous, vast, voluminous **2.** considerable, decided, excessive, extended, extravagant, extreme, grievous, high, inordinate, lengthy, long, prodigious, prolonged, pronounced, protracted, strong **3.** big-time (*informal*), capital, chief, grand, head, lead, leading, main, major, major league (*informal*), paramount, primary, principal, prominent, superior **4.** consequential, critical, crucial, grave, heavy, important, momentous, serious, significant, weighty **5.** celebrated, distinguished, eminent, exalted, excellent, famed, famous, glorious, illustrious, notable, noteworthy, outstanding, prominent, remarkable, renowned, superb, superlative, talented, world-class **6.** able, adept, adroit, crack (*slang*), expert, good, masterly, proficient, skilful, skilled **7.** *informal* admirable, boffo (*slang*), brill (*informal*), chillin' (*U.S. slang*), cracking (*Brit. informal*), crucial (*slang*), def (*informal*), excellent, fantastic (*informal*), fine, first-rate, good, hunky-dory (*informal*), jim-dandy (*slang*), marvellous (*informal*), mean (*slang*), mega (*slang*), sovereign, superb, terrific (*informal*), topping (*Brit. slang*), tremendous (*informal*), wonderful

greatly abundantly, by leaps and bounds, by much, considerably, enormously, exceedingly, extremely, highly, hugely, immensely, markedly, mightily, much, notably, powerfully, remarkably, tremendously, vastly, very much

greatness 1. bulk, enormity, hugeness, immensity, largeness, length, magnitude, mass, prodigiousness, size, vastness **2.** amplitude, force, high degree, intensity, potency, power, strength **3.** gravity, heaviness, import, importance, moment, momentousness, seriousness, significance, urgency, weight **4.** celebrity, distinction, eminence, fame, glory, grandeur, illustriousness, lustre, note, renown

greed, greediness 1. gluttony, hunger, insatiableness, ravenousness, voracity **2.** acquisitiveness, avarice, avidity, covetousness, craving, cupidity, desire, eagerness, graspingness, longing, rapacity, selfishness

greedy 1. gluttonous, hoggish, hungry, insatiable, piggish, ravenous, voracious **2.** acquisitive, avaricious, avid, covetous, craving, desirous, eager, grasping, hungry, impatient, rapacious, selfish

Greek 1. *adj.* Hellenic **2.** *n.* Hellene

green *adj.* **1.** blooming, budding, flourishing, fresh, grassy, leafy, new, undecayed, verdant, verdurous **2.** conservationist, ecological, environment-friendly, non-polluting **3.** fresh, immature, new, raw, recent, unripe **4.** ill, nauseous, pale, sick, unhealthy, wan **5.** callow, credulous, gullible, ignorant, immature, inexperienced, inexpert, ingenuous, innocent, naive, new, raw, unpol-

green belt *n* a protected zone of parkland or open country surrounding a town or city.

Green Cross Code *n Brit* a road-safety code for children.

greenery *n* green leaves or growing plants: *lush greenery.*

green-eyed monster *n* jealousy.

greenfinch *n* a European finch the male of which has olive-green feathers.

green fingers *pl n* skill in growing plants.

greenfly *n, pl* **-flies** a green aphid commonly occurring as a pest on plants.

greengage *n* a green sweet variety of plum.

greengrocer *n Brit* a shopkeeper who sells fruit and vegetables.

greenhorn *n* an inexperienced person; novice.

greenhouse *n* **1** a building with glass walls and roof where plants are grown under controlled conditions. *~adj* **2** relating to or contributing to the greenhouse effect: *greenhouse gases such as carbon dioxide.*

greenhouse effect *n* the gradual rise in temperature in the earth's atmosphere due to heat being absorbed from the sun and being trapped by gases such as carbon dioxide in the air around the earth.

greenkeeper *n* a person responsible for maintaining a golf course or bowling green.

green light *n* **1** a signal to go. **2** permission to proceed with a project.

green paper *n* (in Britain) a government document containing policy proposals to be discussed.

green pepper *n* the green unripe fruit of the sweet pepper, eaten as a vegetable.

greenroom *n* (esp. formerly) a backstage room in a theatre where performers rest or receive visitors.

greenstick fracture *n* a fracture in which the bone is partly bent and splinters only on the outer side of the bend.

greensward *n Archaic or literary* an area of fresh green turf.

green tea *n* tea made from leaves that have been dried quickly without fermenting.

Greenwich Mean Time (**gren**-itch) *n* the local time of the 0° meridian passing through Greenwich, England: a basis for calculating times throughout most of the world.

greet[1] *vb* **1** to address or meet with expressions of friendliness or welcome. **2** to receive in a specified manner: *a direct request would be greeted coolly.* **3** to be immediately noticeable to: *the scene of devastation which greeted him.*

greet[2] *vb Scot* to weep.

greeting *n* the act or words of welcoming on meeting.

greetings *interj* an expression of friendly salutation.

gregarious *adj* **1** enjoying the company of others. **2** (of animals) living together in herds or flocks.

Gregorian calendar *n* the revision of the calendar introduced in 1582 by Pope Gregory XIII and still widely used.

Gregorian chant *n* same as **plainsong.**

gremlin *n* an imaginary imp jokingly blamed for malfunctions in machinery.

grenade *n* a small bomb filled with explosive or gas, thrown by hand or fired from a rifle.

grenadier *n Mil* **1** (in the British Army) a member of the senior regiment of infantry in the Household Brigade (the **Grenadier Guards**). **2** (formerly) a soldier trained to throw grenades.

grenadine (gren-a-**deen**) *n* a syrup made from pomegranate juice, often used as an ingredient in cocktails.

grew *vb* the past tense of **grow.**

grey *or US* **gray** *adj* **1** of a colour between black and white; of the colour of ashes. **2 a** (of hair) having partly turned white. **b** (of a person) having grey hair. **3** dismal, dark, or gloomy: *a grey and misty morning.* **4** dull or boring: *in 1948 life generally was grey.* *~n* **5** a colour between black and white. **6** anything grey, such as grey paint or grey clothing: *available in grey or brown.* **7** a grey or whitish horse. **greyness** *n* **greyish** *adj*

grey area *n* a situation or area that has no clearly defined characteristics or that falls somewhere between two categories.

Grey Friar *n* a Franciscan friar.

greyhound *n* a tall slender dog that can run very fast and is used for racing.

greying *adj* becoming grey: *greying hair.*

greylag *or* **greylag goose** *n* a large grey Eurasian goose.

grey matter *n Informal* intellect or brains.

grey squirrel *n* a grey-furred squirrel, native to E North America but now common in Britain.

grid *n* **1** a network of crossing parallel lines on a map, plan, or graph paper for locating points. **2 the grid** the national network of cables or pipes by which electricity, gas, or water is distributed. **3** *Electronics* an electrode that controls the flow of electrons between the cathode and anode of a valve.

griddle *n* a thick round iron plate placed on top of a cooker and used to cook food.

gridiron *n* **1** a utensil of parallel metal bars, used to grill food. **2 a** the field of play in American football. **b** *Informal* same as **American football.**

grief *n* **1** deep or intense sorrow. **2 come to grief** to have an unfortunate or unsuccessful end or outcome.

grief-stricken *adj* deeply affected by sorrow.

grievance *n* **1** a real or imaginary cause for complaint. **2** a feeling of resentment at having been unfairly treated.

THESAURUS

ished, unpractised, unskilful, unsophisticated, untrained, unversed, wet behind the ears (*informal*) **6.** covetous, envious, grudging, jealous, resentful *~n.* **7.** common, grassplot, lawn, turf

greet accost, address, compliment, hail, meet, nod to, receive, salute, tip one's hat to, welcome

greeting 1. address, hail, reception, salutation, salute, welcome **2.** *plural* best wishes, compliments, good wishes, regards, respects, salutations

gregarious affable, companionable, convivial, cordial, friendly, outgoing, sociable, social

grey 1. ashen, bloodless, colourless, livid, pale, pallid, wan **2.** cheerless, cloudy, dark, depressing, dim, dismal, drab, dreary, dull, foggy, gloomy, misty, murky, overcast, sunless

grief 1. affliction, agony, anguish, bereavement, dejection, distress, grievance, hardship, heartache, heartbreak, misery, mournfulness, mourning, pain, regret, remorse, sadness, sorrow, suffering, trial, tribulation, trouble, woe **2. come to grief** *informal* come unstuck, fail, meet with disaster, miscarry

grievance affliction, beef (*slang*), complaint, damage, distress, grief, gripe (*informal*), hardship, injury, injustice, protest, resentment, sorrow, trial, tribulation, trouble, unhappiness, wrong

grieve ache, afflict, agonize, bemoan, bewail, break the heart of, complain, crush, deplore, distress, hurt,

grieve *vb* **grieving, grieved** to feel or cause to feel great sorrow or distress. **grieved** *adj* **grieving** *adj*

grievous *adj* **1** very severe or painful: *grievous injuries.* **2** very serious or worrying: *a grievous loss.* **grievously** *adv*

grievous bodily harm *n Criminal law* serious injury caused by one person to another.

griffin, griffon, *or* **gryphon** *n* a mythical winged monster with an eagle's head and a lion's body.

griffon *n* **1** a large vulture with a pale feathers and black wings. **2** a small wire-haired breed of dog.

grill *vb* **1** to cook by direct heat under a grill or over a hot fire. **2** *Informal* to subject to relentless questioning: *the jury pool was grilled for signs of prejudice.* ~*n* **3** a device on a cooker that radiates heat downwards for grilling food. **4** a gridiron for cooking food. **5** a dish of grilled food. **6** See **grillroom. grilled** *adj* **grilling** *n*

grille *or* **grill** *n* a metal or wooden grating, used as a screen or partition.

grillroom *n* a restaurant specializing in grilled foods.

grilse (**grillss**) *n, pl* **grilses** *or* **grilse** a salmon on its first return from the sea to fresh water.

grim *adj* **grimmer, grimmest 1** unfavourable and worrying: *grim figures on unemployment.* **2** harsh and unpleasant: *grim conditions in the detention centres.* **3** stern or resolute: *a grim determination to fight on.* **4** *Informal* unpleasant or disagreeable. **grimly** *adv* **grimness** *n*

grimace *n* **1** an ugly or distorted facial expression of disgust, pain, or displeasure. ~*vb* **-macing, -maced 2** to make a grimace.

grime *n* **1** ingrained dirt. ~*vb* **griming, grimed 2** to make very dirty: *sweat-grimed faces.* **grimy** *adj*

grin *vb* **grinning, grinned 1** to smile broadly, showing one's teeth. **2 grin and bear it** *Informal* to suffer hardship without complaint. ~*n* **3** a broad smile. **grinning** *adj*

grind *vb* **grinding, ground 1** to reduce to small particles by pounding or rubbing: *grinding coffee.* **2** to smooth, sharpen, or polish by friction. **3** (of two objects) to scrape together with a harsh rasping sound. **4 an axe to grind** See **axe** (sense 2). **5 grind one's teeth** to rub one's upper and lower teeth against each other, as if chewing. **6 grind to a halt** to come to an end or a standstill: *without enzymes life would grind to a halt.* ~*n* **7** *Informal* hard or tedious work: *the grind of everyday life.* ~See also **grind down.**

grind down *vb* to treat harshly so as to suppress resistance: *to grind down the opposition.*

grinder *n* a device for grinding substances: *a coffee grinder.*

grindstone *n* **1** a revolving stone disc used for sharpening, grinding, or polishing things. **2 keep one's nose to the grindstone** to work hard and steadily.

grip *n* **1** a very tight hold: *he felt a grip at his throat.* **2** the style or manner of holding something, such as a golf club or tennis racket. **3** power or control over a situation, person, or activity: *rebel forces tighten their grip around the capital; families in the grip of the moneylenders.* **4 get** *or* **come to grips with** to face up to and deal with (a problem or subject). **5** a travelling bag or holdall. **6** a hairgrip. **7** a handle. **8** a person who manoeuvres the cameras in a film or television studio. ~*vb* **gripping, gripped 9** to take a tight hold of. **10** to affect strongly: *sudden panic gripped her.* **11** to hold the interest or attention of: *gripped by the intensity of the film; the story gripped him.*

gripe *vb* **griping, griped 1** *Informal* to complain persistently. **2** to cause sudden intense pain in the bowels. ~*n* **3** *Informal* a complaint. **4 the gripes** a sudden intense pain in the bowels.

grippe *n* a former name for **influenza.**

gripping *adj* very interesting and exciting: *a gripping story.*

grisly *adj* **-lier, -liest** causing horror or dread: *grisly murders.*

grist *n* **1** grain that is to be or that has been ground. **2 grist to the mill** anything that can be turned to profit or advantage.

gristle *n* tough stringy animal tissue found in meat. **gristly** *adj*

grit *n* **1** small hard particles of sand, earth, or stone. **2** courage and determination. ~*vb* **gritting, gritted 3** to cover (an icy road) with grit. **4 grit one's teeth a** to rub one's upper and lower teeth against each other, as if chewing. **b** to decide to carry on in a difficult situation: *he urged the Cabinet to grit its teeth and continue cutting public spending.*

grits *pl n* coarsely ground grain, a popular dish in the Southern US.

THESAURUS

injure, lament, make one's heart bleed, mourn, pain, regret, rue, sadden, sorrow, suffer, wail, weep, wound

grievous 1. afflicting, calamitous, damaging, distressing, dreadful, grave, harmful, heavy, hurtful, injurious, lamentable, oppressive, painful, severe, wounding **2.** appalling, atrocious, deplorable, dreadful, heinous, intolerable, lamentable, monstrous, shameful, shocking, unbearable

grim cruel, ferocious, fierce, forbidding, formidable, frightful, ghastly, godawful (*slang*), grisly, gruesome, hard, harsh, hideous, horrible, horrid, implacable, merciless, morose, relentless, resolute, ruthless, severe, shocking, sinister, stern, sullen, surly, terrible, unrelenting, unyielding

grimace 1. *n.* face, frown, mouth, scowl, sneer **2.** *vb.* frown, lour *or* lower, make a face *or* faces, mouth, scowl, sneer

grime dirt, filth, grot (*slang*), smut, soot

grimy begrimed, besmeared, besmirched, dirty, filthy, foul, grubby, smutty, soiled, sooty, unclean

grind *vb.* **1.** abrade, crush, granulate, grate, mill, pound, powder, pulverize **2.** file, polish, sand, sharpen, smooth, whet **3.** gnash, grate, grit, scrape ~*n.* **4.** *informal* chore, drudgery, hard work, labour, sweat (*informal*), task, toil

grind down afflict, harass, hold down, hound, oppress, persecute, plague, trouble, tyrannize (over)

grip *n.* **1.** clasp, handclasp (*U.S.*), purchase **2.** clutches, comprehension, control, domination, grasp, hold, influence, keeping, mastery, perception, possession, power, tenure, understanding **3. come** *or* **get to grips (with)** close with, confront, contend with, cope with, deal with, encounter, face up to, grapple with, grasp, handle, meet, tackle, take on, undertake ~*vb.* **4.** clasp, clutch, grasp, hold, latch on to, seize, take hold of **5.** absorb, catch up, compel, engross, enthral, entrance, fascinate, hold, involve, mesmerize, rivet, spellbind

gripping compelling, compulsive, engrossing, enthralling, entrancing, exciting, fascinating, riveting, spellbinding, thrilling, unputdownable (*informal*)

grisly abominable, appalling, awful, dreadful, frightful, ghastly, grim, gruesome, hellacious (*U.S. slang*), hideous, horrible, horrid, macabre, shocking, sickening, terrible, terrifying

grit *n.* **1.** dust, gravel, pebbles, sand **2.** backbone, balls (*taboo slang*), courage, determination, doggedness,

gritter *n* a vehicle that spreads grit on the roads in icy weather.

gritty *adj* **-tier, -tiest 1** courageous and tough. **2** covered with grit.

grizzle *vb* **-zling, -zled** *Informal, chiefly Brit* to whine or complain.

grizzled *adj* **1** (of hair) streaked or mixed with grey. **2** (of a person) having grey hair.

grizzly *n, pl* **-zlies** a large fierce greyish-brown bear of N America. In full: **grizzly bear**

groan *n* **1** a long deep cry of pain, grief, or disapproval. **2** *Informal* a grumble or complaint. *~vb* **3** to give a long deep cry of pain, grief, or disapproval. **4** *Informal* to complain or grumble. **5 groan under** to be weighed down by: *chemists' shelves groan under the weight of slimming aids.* **groaning** *adj, n*

groat *n* a former British coin worth four old pennies.

groats *pl n* the crushed grain of various cereals.

grocer *n* a shopkeeper who sells food and other household supplies.

groceries *pl n* food and other household supplies.

grocery *n, pl* **-ceries** the business or premises of a grocer.

grog *n* **1** an alcoholic drink, usually rum, diluted with water. **2** *Austral & NZ informal* any alcoholic drink.

groggy *adj* **-gier, -giest** *Informal* faint, weak, or dizzy.

groin *n* **1** the part of the body where the abdomen joins the legs. **2** *Archit* a curved edge formed where two intersecting vaults meet.

grommet *n* **1** a rubber, plastic, or metal ring or eyelet. **2** *Med* a small tube inserted into the eardrum to drain fluid from the middle ear.

groom *n* **1** a person employed to clean and look after horses. **2** short for **bridegroom.** *~vb* **3** to clean and smarten (a horse or other animal). **4** to keep (oneself or one's appearance) clean and tidy: *carefully groomed hair.* **5** to train (someone) for a particular task or occupation: *groomed for future leadership.* **grooming** *n*

groove *n* **1** a long narrow furrow cut into a surface. **2** the spiral channel in a gramophone record. **grooved** *adj*

groovy *adj* **groovier, grooviest** *Old-fashioned slang* attractive, fashionable, or exciting.

grope *vb* **groping, groped 1** to feel about uncertainly for something. **2** to find (one's way) by groping. **3** to search uncertainly for a solution or expression: *the new democracies are groping for stability.* **4** *Slang* to fondle (someone) in a rough sexual way. *~n* **5** an instance of groping.

gros point (**groh**) *n* **1** a cross-stitch in embroidery. **2** work done in this stitch.

gross *adj* **1** outrageously wrong: *gross violations of human rights.* **2** very coarse or vulgar: *gross bad taste.* **3** *Slang* disgusting or repulsive: *I think beards are gross.* **4** repulsively fat. **5** with no deductions for tax or the weight of the container; total: *gross income; a gross weight of 20,000 lbs.* *~n* **6** (*pl* **gross**) twelve dozen (144). **7** the entire amount or weight. *~vb* **8** to earn as total revenue, before deductions. **grossly** *adv*

gross domestic product *n* the total value of all goods and services produced domestically by a nation during a year.

gross national product *n* the total value of all final goods and services produced annually by a nation: equivalent to gross domestic product plus net investment income from abroad.

gross profit *n Accounting* the difference between total revenue from sales and the total cost of purchases or materials.

grotesque (groh-**tesk**) *adj* **1** strangely distorted or bizarre: *a grotesque and pervasive personality cult.* **2** ugly or repulsive. *~n* **3** a grotesque person or thing. **4** an artistic style in which parts of human, animal, and plant forms are distorted and mixed, or a work of art in this style. **grotesquely** *adv*

grotto *n, pl* **-toes** *or* **-tos** a small picturesque cave.

grotty *adj* **-tier, -tiest** *Brit slang* **1** nasty or unattractive. **2** in bad condition.

grouch *Informal ~vb* **1** to complain or grumble. *~n* **2** a person who is always complaining. **3** a persistent complaint.

grouchy *adj* **grouchier, grouchiest** bad-tempered.

ground[1] *n* **1** the land surface. **2** earth or soil. **3** an area used for a particular purpose: *a cricket ground.* **4** a matter for consideration or discussion: *there is no need to cover the same ground.* **5** an advantage in an argument or competition: *neither side seems willing to give ground in this trial of strength.* **6** the background colour of a painting. **7** *US & Canad* an electrical earth. **8 grounds a** the land around a building. **b** reason or justification: *the hostages should be freed on humanitarian grounds.* **c** sediment or dregs: *coffee grounds.* **9 break new ground** to do something that has not been done before. **10 common ground** an agreed basis for identifying issues in an argument. **11 get something**

THESAURUS

fortitude, gameness, guts (*informal*), hardihood, mettle, nerve, perseverance, pluck, resolution, spirit, tenacity, toughness *~vb.* **3.** clench, gnash, grate, grind

gritty 1. ballsy (*taboo slang*), brave, courageous, determined, dogged, feisty (*informal, chiefly U.S. & Canad.*), game, hardy, mettlesome, plucky, resolute, spirited, steadfast, tenacious, tough **2.** abrasive, dusty, grainy, granular, gravelly, rasping, rough, sandy

groan *n.* **1.** cry, moan, sigh, whine **2.** *informal* beef (*slang*), complaint, gripe (*informal*), grouse, grumble, objection, protest *~vb.* **3.** cry, moan, sigh, whine **4.** *informal* beef (*slang*), bemoan, bitch (*slang*), complain, gripe (*informal*), grouse, grumble, lament, moan, object

groggy befuddled, confused, dazed, dizzy, faint, punch-drunk, reeling, shaky, staggering, stunned, stupefied, unsteady, weak, wobbly, woozy (*informal*)

groom *n.* **1.** currier (*rare*), hostler *or* ostler (*archaic*), stableboy, stableman *~vb.* **2.** brush, clean, curry, rub down, tend **3.** clean, dress, get up (*informal*), preen, primp, smarten up, spruce up, tidy, turn out **4.** coach, drill, educate, make ready, nurture, prepare, prime, ready, train

groove channel, cut, cutting, flute, furrow, gutter, hollow, indentation, rebate, rut, score, trench

grope cast about, feel, finger, fish, flounder, fumble, grabble, scrabble, search

gross *adj.* **1.** apparent, arrant, blatant, downright, egregious, flagrant, glaring, grievous, heinous, manifest, obvious, outrageous, plain, rank, serious, shameful, sheer, shocking, unmitigated, unqualified, utter **2.** boorish, callous, coarse, crass, crude, dull, ignorant, improper, impure, indecent, indelicate, insensitive, lewd, low, obscene, offensive, ribald, rude, sensual, smutty, tasteless, uncultured, undiscriminating, unfeeling, unrefined, unseemly, unsophisticated, vulgar **3.** big, bulky, corpulent, dense, fat, great, heavy, hulking, large, lumpish, massive, obese, overweight, thick **4.** aggregate, before deductions, before tax, entire, total, whole *~vb.* **5.** bring in, earn, make, rake in (*informal*), take

grotesque absurd, bizarre, deformed, distorted, ex-

off the ground to get something started: *to get the peace conference off the ground.* **12 into the ground** to exhaustion or excess: *he was running himself into the ground.* **13 suit someone down to the ground** *Brit informal* to be totally suitable or appropriate for someone. *~adj* **14** on the ground: *ground troops.* *~vb* **15** to confine (an aircraft or pilot) to the ground. **16** *Naut* to move (a ship) onto the bottom of shallow water, so that it cannot move. **17** to instruct in the basics of a subject: *the student who is not grounded in the elements cannot understand the advanced teaching.* **18** to provide a basis for; establish: *a scientifically grounded documentation.* **19** *US & Canad* to connect (a circuit or electrical device) to an earth.

ground[2] *vb* **1** the past of **grind.** *~adj* **2** reduced to fine particles by grinding: *ground glass.*

ground bass *n Music* a short melodic bass line that is repeated over and over again.

ground beef *n* finely chopped beef, sometimes used to make hamburgers.

ground-breaking *adj* innovative.

ground control *n* the people and equipment on the ground that monitor the progress of aircraft or spacecraft.

ground cover *n* dense low plants that spread over the surface of the ground.

ground floor *n* the floor of a building that is level, or almost level, with the ground.

grounding *n* a foundation, esp. the basic general knowledge of a subject.

groundless *adj* without reason or justification: *the scare turned out to be groundless.*

groundnut *n* same as **peanut.**

groundsel (**grounce**-el) *n* a yellow-flowered weed.

groundsheet *n* a waterproof sheet placed on the ground in a tent to keep out damp.

groundsman *n, pl* **-men** a person employed to maintain a sports ground or park.

groundswell *n* a rapidly developing general feeling or opinion.

groundwork *n* preliminary work as a foundation or basis.

group *n* **1** a number of people or things considered as a unit. **2** a small band of players or singers, esp. of popular music. **3** an association of business firms that have the same owner. **4** *Chem* two or more atoms that are bound together in a molecule and behave as a single unit: *a methyl group* $-CH_3$. **5** *Chem* a vertical column of elements in the periodic table that all have similar properties: *the halogen group.* *~vb* **6** to put into or form into a group.

group captain *n* a middle-ranking officer in some air forces.

groupie *n Slang* an ardent fan of a celebrity or of a sport or activity: *a polo groupie.*

grouping *n* a set of people or organizations who act or work together to achieve a shared aim: *a pro-democracy grouping within China.*

group therapy *n Psychol* the treatment of people by bringing them together to share their problems in group discussion.

grouse[1] *n, pl* **grouse 1** a game bird with a stocky body and feathered legs and feet. **2** the flesh of this bird used for food.

grouse[2] *vb* **grousing, groused 1** to complain or grumble. *~n* **2** a persistent complaint.

grouse[3] *adj Austral & NZ slang* fine or excellent.

grout *n* **1** a thin mortar for filling joints between tiles or masonry. *~vb* **2** to fill with grout.

grove *n* a small wood or group of trees: *orange groves.*

grovel (**grov**-el) *vb* **-elling, -elled** *or US* **-eling, -eled 1** to behave excessively humbly towards someone, esp. a superior, in an attempt to win his or her favour. **2** to crawl on the floor, often in search of something: *grovelling on the floor for missing cards.* **grovelling** *or US* **groveling** *adj, n*

grow *vb* **growing, grew, grown 1** (of a person or animal) to increase in size and develop physically. **2** (of a plant) to exist and increase in size: *an ancient meadow where wild flowers grow.* **3** to produce (a plant) by planting seeds, bulbs, or cuttings, and looking after it: *many farmers have expressed a wish to grow more cotton.* **4** to let (one's hair or nails) develop: *to grow a beard.* **5** to increase in size or degree: *the gulf between rich and poor is growing.* **6** to originate or develop: *Melbourne grew from a sheep-farming outstation and occasional port to a city.* **7** to become increasingly as specified: *as the night wore on the audience grew more intolerant.* ~See also **grow on, grow out of,** etc. **growing** *adj* **grower** *n*

growing pains *pl n* **1** pains in muscles or joints sometimes experienced by growing children. **2** diffi-

THESAURUS

travagant, fanciful, fantastic, freakish, incongruous, ludicrous, malformed, misshapen, odd, outlandish, preposterous, ridiculous, strange, unnatural, weird, whimsical

ground *n.* **1.** clod, dirt, dry land, dust, earth, field, land, loam, mould, sod, soil, terra firma, terrain, turf **2.** arena, field, park (*informal*), pitch, stadium **3.** *often plural* area, country, district, domain, estate, fields, gardens, habitat, holding, land, property, realm, terrain, territory, tract **4.** *usually plural* account, argument, base, basis, call, cause, excuse, factor, foundation, inducement, justification, motive, occasion, premise, pretext, rationale, reason **5.** *usually plural* deposit, dregs, grouts, lees, sediment, settlings *~vb.* **6.** acquaint with, coach, familiarize with, inform, initiate, instruct, prepare, teach, train, tutor **7.** base, establish, fix, found, set, settle

groundless baseless, empty, false, idle, illusory, imaginary, unauthorized, uncalled-for, unfounded, unjustified, unprovoked, unsupported, unwarranted

groundwork base, basis, cornerstone, footing, foundation, fundamentals, preliminaries, preparation, spadework, underpinnings

group 1. *n.* aggregation, assemblage, association, band, batch, bevy, bunch, camp, category, circle, class, clique, clump, cluster, collection, company, congregation, coterie, crowd, faction, formation, gang, gathering, organization, pack, party, posse (*slang*), set, troop **2.** *vb.* arrange, assemble, associate, assort, band together, bracket, class, classify, cluster, congregate, consort, dispose, fraternize, gather, get together, marshal, order, organize, put together, range, sort

grouse 1. *vb.* beef (*slang*), bellyache (*slang*), bitch (*slang*), bleat, carp, complain, find fault, gripe (*informal*), grouch (*informal*), grumble, moan, whine, whinge (*informal*) **2.** *n.* beef (*slang*), complaint, grievance, gripe (*informal*), grouch (*informal*), grumble, moan, objection, protest

grovel abase oneself, bootlick (*informal*), bow and scrape, brown-nose (*taboo slang*), cower, crawl, creep, cringe, crouch, demean oneself, fawn, flatter, humble oneself, kiss ass (*taboo slang*), kowtow, pander to, sneak, toady

grow 1. develop, enlarge, expand, extend, fill out, get bigger, get taller, heighten, increase, multiply, spread, stretch, swell, thicken, widen **2.** develop, flourish, germinate, shoot, spring up, sprout, vegetate **3.** breed, cultivate, farm, nurture, produce, propagate, raise **4.**

culties experienced in the early stages of a new enterprise.

growl *vb* **1** (of a dog or other animal) to make a low rumbling sound, usually in anger. **2** to say in a gruff or angry manner: *"You're late," he growled.* **3** to make a deep rumbling sound: *his stomach growled.* ~*n* **4** the act or sound of growling.

grown *adj* developed or advanced: *fully grown; a grown man.*

grown-up *adj* **1** having reached maturity; adult. **2** of or suitable for an adult. ~*n* **3** an adult.

grow on *vb* to become progressively more acceptable or pleasant to: *I didn't like that programme at first but it has grown on me.*

grow out of *vb* to become too big or mature for: *I used to be into the 'fifties scene but grew out of it.*

growth *n* **1** the process of growing. **2** an increase in size, number, or significance: *the growth of drug trafficking.* **3** something grown or growing: *a thick growth of ivy.* **4** any abnormal tissue, such as a tumour. ~*adj* **5** of or relating to growth: *growth hormone.*

grow up *vb* to reach maturity; become adult.

groyne *n* a wall or breakwater built out from a shore to control erosion.

grub *n* **1** *Slang* food. **2** the short legless larva of certain insects, such as beetles. ~*vb* **grubbing, grubbed 3** to search carefully for something by digging or by moving things about. **4 grub up** to dig (roots or plants) out of the ground.

grubby *adj* **-bier, -biest 1** rather dirty. **2** unsavoury or morally unacceptable: *grubby activities.* **grubbiness** *n*

grudge *n* **1** a persistent feeling of resentment against a person who has caused harm or upset. ~*vb* **grudging, grudged 2** to give unwillingly: *the rich men who grudged pennies for the poor.* **3** to resent or envy the success or possessions of: *none of their guests grudged them this celebration.* ~*adj* **4** planned or carried out in order to settle a grudge: *a grudge match.*

grudging *adj* felt or done unwillingly: *grudging admiration for his opponent.* **grudgingly** *adv*

gruel *n* thin porridge made by boiling oatmeal in water or milk.

gruelling *or US* **grueling** *adj* extremely severe or tiring: *a gruelling journey.*

gruesome *adj* inspiring horror and disgust.

gruff *adj* **1** rough or surly in manner or speech. **2** (of a voice) low and throaty. **gruffly** *adv* **gruffness** *n*

grumble *vb* **-bling, -bled 1** to complain in a nagging way: *his neighbour grumbled about the long wait.* **2** to make low rumbling sounds: *the storm grumbled in the distance.* ~*n* **3** a complaint. **4** a low rumbling sound: *a distant grumble of artillery fire.* **grumbling** *adj, n*

grumpy *adj* **grumpier, grumpiest** sulky and bad-tempered. **grumpily** *adv*

grunge *n* **1** a style of rock music with a fuzzy guitar sound. **2** a deliberately untidy and uncoordinated fashion style.

grunt *vb* **1** to make a low short gruff noise, such as the sound made by a pig, or by a person to express annoyance. **2** to express (something) gruffly: *he grunted his thanks.* ~*n* **3** a low short gruff noise, such as the sound made by a pig, or by a person to express annoyance.

Gruyere (**grew**-yair) *n* a hard flat pale yellow cheese with holes.

gryphon *n* same as **griffin.**

G-string *n* a strip of cloth worn between the legs and attached to a waistband.

G-suit *n* a close-fitting pressurized garment that is worn by the crew of high-speed aircraft.

GT gran turismo: a touring car, usually a fast sports car with a hard fixed roof.

guano (**gwah**-no) *n* the dried manure of sea birds, used as a fertilizer.

guarantee *n* **1** a formal assurance in writing that a product or service will meet certain standards or specifications. **2** something that makes a specified condition or outcome certain: *there was no guarantee that there would not be another military coup.* **3** same as **guaranty.** ~*vb* **-teeing, -teed 4** to promise or make certain: *to guarantee absolute loyalty.* **5** (of a company) to provide a guarantee in writing for (a

THESAURUS

advance, expand, flourish, improve, progress, prosper, succeed, thrive **5.** arise, issue, originate, spring, stem **6.** become, come to be, develop (into), get, turn, wax

grown-up 1. *adj.* adult, fully-grown, mature, of age **2.** *n.* adult, man, woman

growth 1. aggrandizement, augmentation, development, enlargement, evolution, expansion, extension, growing, heightening, increase, multiplication, proliferation, stretching, thickening, widening **2.** advance, advancement, expansion, improvement, progress, prosperity, rise, success **3.** crop, cultivation, development, germination, produce, production, shooting, sprouting, vegetation **4.** *Medicine* excrescence, lump, tumour

grub *n.* **1.** *slang* eats (*slang*), feed, food, nosebag (*slang*), nosh (*slang*), rations, sustenance, tack (*informal*), victuals, vittles (*obsolete or dialect*) **2.** caterpillar, larva, maggot ~*vb.* **3.** ferret, forage, hunt, rummage, scour, search, uncover, unearth **4.** burrow, dig up, probe, pull up, root (*informal*), rootle (*Brit.*), search for, uproot

grubby besmeared, dirty, filthy, frowzy, grimy, manky (*Scot. dialect*), mean, messy, mucky, scruffy, scuzzy (*slang*), seedy, shabby, slovenly, smutty, soiled, sordid, squalid, unkempt, untidy, unwashed

grudge 1. *n.* animosity, animus, antipathy, aversion, bitterness, dislike, enmity, grievance, hard feelings, hate, ill will, malevolence, malice, pique, rancour, resentment, spite, venom **2.** *vb.* begrudge, be reluctant, complain, covet, envy, hold back, mind, resent, stint

gruelling arduous, backbreaking, brutal, crushing, demanding, difficult, exhausting, fatiguing, fierce, grinding, hard, harsh, laborious, punishing, severe, stiff, strenuous, taxing, tiring, trying

gruesome abominable, awful, fearful, ghastly, grim, grisly, hellacious (*U.S. slang*), hideous, horrendous, horrible, horrid, horrific, horrifying, loathsome, macabre, obscene, repugnant, repulsive, shocking, spine-chilling, terrible

gruff 1. bad-tempered, bearish, blunt, brusque, churlish, crabbed, crusty, curt, discourteous, grouchy (*informal*), grumpy, ill-humoured, ill-natured, impolite, rough, rude, sour, sullen, surly, uncivil, ungracious, unmannerly **2.** croaking, guttural, harsh, hoarse, husky, low, rasping, rough, throaty

grumble *vb.* **1.** beef (*slang*), bellyache (*slang*), bitch (*slang*), bleat, carp, complain, find fault, gripe (*informal*), grouch (*informal*), grouse, moan, repine, whine, whinge (*informal*) **2.** growl, gurgle, murmur, mutter, roar, rumble ~*n.* **3.** beef (*slang*), complaint, grievance, gripe (*informal*), grouch (*informal*), grouse, moan, objection, protest **4.** growl, gurgle, murmur, muttering, roar, rumble

guarantee 1. *n.* assurance, bond, certainty, collateral, covenant, earnest, guaranty, pledge, promise, security, surety, undertaking, warranty, word, word of

product or service). **6** to take responsibility for the debts or obligations of (another person).

guarantor *n* a person who gives or is bound by a guarantee or guaranty.

guaranty *n, pl* **-ties 1** a pledge of responsibility for fulfilling another person's obligations in case of that person's default. **2** a thing given or taken as security for a guaranty.

guard *vb* **1** to watch over or shield from danger or harm; protect: *US marines who guard the American embassy.* **2** to keep watch over (a prisoner) to prevent escape. **3** to protect (a right or privilege). **4** to take precautions: *to guard against a possible coup attempt.* ~*n* **5** a person or group of people who protect or watch over people or things. **6** *Brit* the official in charge of a train. **7** a device or part of a machine designed to protect the user against injury. **8** anything that provides protection: *a guard against future shocks.* **9 off guard** having one's defences down; unprepared: *England were caught off guard as the Dutch struck two telling blows.* **10 on guard** on duty to protect or watch over people or things. **11 on one's guard** prepared to face danger or difficulties: *parents have been warned to be on their guard against kidnappers.* **12 stand guard** (of a sentry) to keep watch.

guarded *adj* cautious and avoiding any commitment: *a guarded welcome.* **guardedly** *adv*

guardhouse *or* **guardroom** *n Mil* a military police office in which prisoners can be detained.

guardian *n* **1** one who looks after, protects, or defends someone or something: *the nation's moral guardians.* **2** someone legally appointed to manage the affairs of another person, such as a child or a person who is mentally ill. **guardianship** *n*

guardsman *n, pl* **-men** *Mil* a member of a regiment responsible for ceremonial duties.

guard's van *n Brit & NZ* a small railway carriage in which the guard travels.

guava (**gwah**-va) *n* a round tropical fruit with yellow skin and pink pulp.

gubernatorial *adj Chiefly US* of or relating to a governor.

gudgeon[1] *n* a small slender European freshwater fish, used as bait by anglers.

gudgeon[2] *n* the socket of a hinge, which fits round the pin.

guelder rose (**geld**-er) *n* a Eurasian shrub with clusters of white flowers.

Guernsey (**gurn**-zee) *n* a breed of dairy cattle that produces rich creamy milk, originating from Guernsey, in the Channel Islands.

guerrilla *or* **guerilla** *n* a member of an irregular, politically motivated, armed force that fights regular forces.

guess *vb* **1** to form an estimate or conclusion about (something), without proper knowledge: *a competition to guess the weight of the cake.* **2** to arrive at a correct estimate of (something) by guessing: *I had a notion that he guessed my thoughts.* **3** *Informal, chiefly US & Canad* to think or suppose: *I guess he must have been a great athlete.* ~*n* **4** an estimate or conclusion arrived at by guessing: *around 30 million pounds is the guess.*

guesswork *n* the process of arriving at conclusions or estimates by guessing.

guest *n* **1** a person who receives hospitality at someone else's home. **2** a person who is taken out socially by someone else who pays all the expenses. **3** a performer or speaker taking part in an event, show, or film by special invitation. **4** a person who is staying in a hotel. ~*vb* **5** to be a guest in an event, show, or film: *he guested in concert with Eric Clapton.*

guesthouse *n* a private home or boarding house offering accommodation.

guest of honour *n* a famous or important person who is the most important guest at a dinner or other social occasion.

guff *n Slang* ridiculous talk; nonsense.

guffaw *vb* **1** to laugh loudly and raucously. ~*n* **2** a loud raucous laugh.

guidance *n* help, advice, or instruction, usually from someone more experienced or more qualified: *marriage guidance.*

guide *n* **1** a person who conducts parties of tourists around places of interest, such as museums. **2** a person who leads travellers to a place, usually in a dangerous area: *a mountain guide.* **3** something that can be used to gauge something or to help in planning one's actions: *starting salary was not an accurate guide to future earnings.* **4** same as **guidebook. 5** a book that explains the basics of a subject or skill: *a guide to higher education.* ~*vb* **guiding, guided 6** to lead the way for (tourists or travellers). **7** to control the movement or course of; steer. **8** to direct the affairs of (a person, team, or country): *he will stay with the club he guided to promotion to the First Division.*

THESAURUS

honour **2.** *vb.* answer for, assure, certify, ensure, insure, maintain, make certain, pledge, promise, protect, secure, stand behind, swear, vouch for, warrant

guard *vb.* **1.** cover, defend, escort, keep, mind, oversee, patrol, police, preserve, protect, safeguard, save, screen, secure, shelter, shield, supervise, tend, watch, watch over ~*n.* **2.** convoy, custodian, defender, escort, lookout, patrol, picket, protector, sentinel, sentry, warder, watch, watchman **3.** buffer, bulwark, bumper, defence, pad, protection, rampart, safeguard, screen, security, shield **4. off guard** napping, unprepared, unready, unwary, with one's defences down **5. on guard** alert, cautious, circumspect, on the alert, on the lookout, prepared, ready, vigilant, wary, watchful

guarded cagey (*informal*), careful, cautious, circumspect, discreet, leery (*slang*), noncommittal, prudent, reserved, restrained, reticent, suspicious, wary

guardian attendant, champion, curator, custodian, defender, escort, guard, keeper, preserver, protector, trustee, warden, warder

guerrilla freedom fighter, irregular, member of the underground *or* resistance, partisan, underground fighter

guess *vb.* **1.** conjecture, estimate, fathom, hypothesize, penetrate, predict, solve, speculate, work out **2.** *informal, chiefly US & Canad* believe, conjecture, dare say, deem, divine, fancy, hazard, imagine, judge, reckon, suppose, surmise, suspect, think ~*n.* **3.** conjecture, feeling, hypothesis, judgment, notion, prediction, reckoning, speculation, supposition, surmise, suspicion, theory

guesswork conjecture, estimation, presumption, speculation, supposition, surmise, suspicion, theory

guest boarder, caller, company, lodger, visitant, visitor

guidance advice, auspices, conduct, control, counsel, counselling, direction, government, help, instruction, intelligence, leadership, management, teaching

guide *n.* **1.** adviser, attendant, chaperon, cicerone, conductor, controller, counsellor, director, dragoman, escort, leader, mentor, monitor, pilot, steersman, teacher, usher **2.** criterion, example, exemplar, ideal, inspiration, lodestar, master, model, par, paradigm,

9 to influence (a person) in his or her actions or opinions: *to be guided by the law.* **guiding** *adj*

Guide *n* a member of an organization for girls that encourages discipline and practical skills.

guidebook *n* a book which gives tourist information on a place.

guided missile *n* a missile whose course is controlled electronically.

guide dog *n* a dog that has been trained to lead a blind person.

guideline *n* a principle put forward to set standards or determine a course of action: *guidelines for arms exporting.*

guild *n* **1** an organization or club for people with shared interests. **2** (in Medieval Europe) an association of men in the same trade or craft.

guilder *n, pl* **-ders** *or* **-der** the standard monetary unit of the Netherlands.

guildhall *n Brit* a hall where members of a guild meet.

guile (**gile**) *n* craftiness or deviousness. **guileless** *adj*

guillemot (**gil**-lee-mot) *n* a black-and-white diving sea bird.

guillotine *n* **1** a device formerly used, esp. in France, for beheading people, consisting of a weighted blade between two upright posts, which was dropped on the neck. **2** a device with a blade for cutting paper. *~vb* **-tining, -tined 3** to behead with a guillotine.

guilt *n* **1** the fact or state of having done wrong: *the court was unable to establish guilt.* **2** remorse or self-reproach caused by feeling that one has done something wrong: *he feels no guilt about the planned cutbacks.*

guiltless *adj* free of all responsibility for wrongdoing or crime; innocent.

guilty *adj* **guiltier, guiltiest 1** *Law* judged to have committed a crime: *she has been found guilty of drug trafficking.* **2** responsible for doing something wrong: *students who are guilty of cheating.* **3** showing, feeling, or indicating guilt: *guilty conscience.* **guiltily** *adv*

guinea *n* a former British unit of currency worth £1.05 (21 shillings), sometimes still used in quoting professional fees.

guinea fowl *n* a domestic bird with a heavy rounded body and speckled feathers.

guinea pig *n* **1** a tailless S American rodent, commonly kept as a pet or used in scientific experiments. **2** a person used in an experiment.

guipure (geep-**pure**) *n* heavy lace that has its pattern connected by threads, rather than supported on a net mesh.

guise (rhymes with **size**) *n* **1** a false appearance: *in the guise of a wood-cutter.* **2** general appearance or form: *haricot beans are best known in Britain in their popular guise of baked beans.*

guitar *n* a stringed instrument with a flat back and a long neck with a fretted fingerboard, which is played by plucking or strumming. **guitarist** *n*

Gulag *n* a system or department that silences dissidents, esp. in the former Soviet Union.

gulch *n US & Canad* a narrow ravine with a stream running through it.

gulf *n* **1** a large deep bay. **2** something that divides or separates people, such as a lack of understanding: *gradually the gulf between father and son has lessened.*

gull *n* a large sea bird with white feathers tipped with black or grey.

gullet *n* the muscular tube through which food passes from the throat to the stomach.

gullible *adj* easily tricked; too trusting. **gullibility** *n*

gully *or* **gulley** *n, pl* **-lies** *or* **-leys 1** a channel or small valley originally worn away by running water. **2** *Cricket* a fielding position on the off side, between the slips and point.

gulp *vb* **1** to swallow (a drink or food) rapidly in large mouthfuls. **2** to gasp or breathe in violently, for example when nervous or when swimming. **3 gulp back** to stifle or suppress: *he gulped back the tears as he said his goodbyes.* *~n* **4** the act of gulping. **5** the quantity taken in a gulp.

gum[1] *n* **1** a sticky substance obtained from certain plants, which hardens on exposure to air and dissolves in water. **2** a substance used for sticking things together. **3** short for **chewing gum** or **bubble gum. 4** *Chiefly Brit* a gumdrop. *~vb* **gumming, gummed 5** to stick with gum. ~**See also gum up**.

gum[2] *n* the fleshy tissue that covers the bases of the teeth.

gum arabic *n* a gum obtained from certain acacia trees, used to make ink, food thickeners, and pills.

gumboil *n* an abscess on the gum.

gumboots *pl n Old-fashioned* same as **Wellington boots.**

gumdrop *n* a small hard fruit-flavoured jelly-like sweet.

THESAURUS

standard **3.** catalogue, directory, guidebook, handbook, instructions, key, manual, vade mecum *~vb.* **4.** accompany, attend, conduct, convoy, direct, escort, lead, pilot, shepherd, show the way, steer, usher **5.** command, control, direct, handle, manage, manoeuvre, steer **6.** advise, counsel, educate, govern, influence, instruct, oversee, regulate, rule, superintend, supervise, sway, teach, train

guild association, brotherhood, club, company, corporation, fellowship, fraternity, league, lodge, order, organization, society, union

guile art, artfulness, artifice, cleverness, craft, craftiness, cunning, deceit, deception, duplicity, gamesmanship (*informal*), knavery, ruse, sharp practice, slyness, treachery, trickery, trickiness, wiliness

guilt 1. blame, blameworthiness, criminality, culpability, delinquency, guiltiness, iniquity, misconduct, responsibility, sinfulness, wickedness, wrong, wrongdoing **2.** bad conscience, contrition, disgrace, dishonour, guiltiness, guilty conscience, infamy, regret, remorse, self-condemnation, self-reproach, shame, stigma

guiltless blameless, clean (*slang*), clear, immaculate, impeccable, innocent, irreproachable, pure, sinless, spotless, squeaky-clean, unimpeachable, unsullied, untainted, untarnished

guilty 1. at fault, blameworthy, convicted, criminal, culpable, delinquent, erring, evil, felonious, iniquitous, offending, reprehensible, responsible, sinful, to blame, wicked, wrong **2.** ashamed, conscience-stricken, contrite, hangdog, regretful, remorseful, rueful, shamefaced, sheepish, sorry

gulf 1. bay, bight, sea inlet **2.** abyss, breach, chasm, cleft, gap, opening, rent, rift, separation, split, void

gullibility credulity, innocence, naïveté, simplicity, trustingness

gullible born yesterday, credulous, easily taken in, foolish, green, innocent, naive, silly, simple, trusting, unsceptical, unsophisticated, unsuspecting

gully channel, ditch, gutter, watercourse

gulp *vb.* **1.** bolt, devour, gobble, guzzle, knock back (*informal*), quaff, swallow, swig (*informal*), swill, wolf

gummy[1] *adj* **-mier, -miest 1** sticky or tacky. **2** producing gum.
gummy[2] *adj* **-mier, -miest** toothless.
gumption *n Brit informal* common sense or initiative.
gumtree *n* **1** any of various trees that yield gum, such as the eucalyptus. **2 up a gumtree** *Brit informal* in an awkward position; in difficulties.
gum up *vb* **gum up the works** *Informal* to spoil a plan or hinder progress.
gun *n* **1** a weapon with a metallic tube or barrel from which a missile is fired, usually by force of an explosion. **2** a device used to force out (a substance, such as grease or paint) under pressure: *a spray gun.* **3 jump the gun** *Informal* to act prematurely. **4 stick to one's guns** *Informal* to stand by one's opinions or intentions in spite of opposition. *~vb* **gunning, gunned 5 gun down** to shoot (someone) with a gun. **6** to press hard on the accelerator of (a vehicle's engine). ~See also **gun for.**
gunboat *n* a small ship carrying mounted guns.
gunboat diplomacy *n* diplomacy conducted by threats of military intervention.
guncotton *n* a form of cellulose nitrate used as an explosive.
gun dog *n* **1** a dog trained to locate or retrieve birds or animals that have been shot in a hunt. **2** a dog belonging to any breed traditionally used for these activities.
gunfire *n* the repeated firing of guns.
gun for *vb Informal* to search for (someone) in order to harm him or her in some way.
gunge *n Informal* a sticky or congealed substance. **gungy** *adj*
gunk *n Informal* a slimy, oily, or dirty substance.
gunman *n, pl* **-men** a man who uses a gun to commit a crime.
gunmetal *n* **1** a type of bronze containing copper, tin, and zinc. *~adj* **2** dark grey.
gunnel (**gun**-nel) *n* same as **gunwale.**
gunner *n* a member of the armed forces who works with, uses, or specializes in guns.
gunnery *n* the art and science of the efficient design and use of large guns.
gunny *n Chiefly US* a coarse hard-wearing fabric, made from jute and used for sacks.
gunpoint *n* **at gunpoint** being under or using the threat of being shot: *eight tourists have been kidnapped at gunpoint by unidentified men.*
gunpowder *n* an explosive mixture of potassium nitrate, charcoal, and sulphur, used to make fireworks.
gunrunning *n* the practice of smuggling guns and ammunition into a country. **gunrunner** *n*
gunshot *n* **1** bullets fired from a gun. **2** the sound of a gun being fired. **3** the firing range of a gun: *within gunshot.*
gunslinger *n Slang* a person who can shoot very accurately and has been involved in many fights using guns, esp. in the frontier days of the American West.
gunstock *n* the wooden handle to which the barrel of a rifle is attached.
gunwale *n Naut* the top of the side of a ship.
guppy *n, pl* **-pies** a small brightly coloured tropical fish, often kept in aquariums in people's homes.
gurgle *vb* **-gling, -gled 1** (of water) to make low bubbling noises when flowing. **2** to make low throaty bubbling noises: *the baby gurgled in delight.* *~n* **3** the sound of gurgling.
Gurkha *n* **1** a member of a Hindu people living mainly in Nepal. **2** a member of a Gurkha regiment in the Indian or British Army.
gurnard *n, pl* **-nard** *or* **-nards** a sea fish with a spiny head and long finger-like pectoral fins.
guru *n* **1** a Hindu or Sikh religious teacher or leader. **2** a leader or adviser of a person or group of people: *marketing gurus.*
Guru Granth Sahib *n* same as **Granth.**
gush *vb* **1** to pour out suddenly and profusely. **2** to speak or behave in an overenthusiastic manner. *~n* **3** a sudden large flow of liquid. **4** a sudden surge of strong feeling: *she felt a gush of pure affection for her mother.*
gusher *n* **1** a person who gushes. **2** a spurting oil well.
gushing *adj* behaving in an overenthusiastic manner: *gushing television commentators.*
gusset *n* a piece of material sewn into a garment to strengthen it.
gust *n* **1** a sudden blast of wind. **2** a sudden surge of strong feeling: *a gust of joviality.* *~vb* **3** to blow in gusts. **gusty** *adj*
gusto *n* vigorous enjoyment: *he downed a pint with gusto.*
gut *n* **1** same as **intestine. 2** *Slang* a stomach, esp. a fat one. **3** short for **catgut. 4** a silky fibrous substance extracted from silkworms and used in the manufacture of fishing tackle. *~vb* **gutting, gutted 5** to remove the internal organs from (a dead animal or fish). **6** (of a fire) to destroy the inside of (a building). *~adj* **7** *Informal* basic, essential, or natural: *I have a gut feeling she's after something.* ~See also **guts.**
gutless *adj Informal* lacking courage or determination.

THESAURUS

2. choke, gasp, stifle, swallow *~n.* **3.** draught, mouthful, swallow, swig (*informal*)
gum 1. *n.* adhesive, cement, glue, paste, resin **2.** *vb.* affix, cement, glue, paste, stick
gumption acumen, astuteness, cleverness, common sense, discernment, enterprise, get-up-and-go (*informal*), horse sense, initiative, mother wit, nous (*Brit. slang*), resourcefulness, sagacity, savvy (*slang*), shrewdness, spirit, wit(s)
gunman assassin, bandit, bravo, desperado, gangster, gunslinger (*U.S. slang*), heavy (*slang*), hit man (*slang*), killer, mobster (*U.S. slang*), murderer, terrorist, thug
gurgle 1. *vb.* babble, bubble, burble, lap, murmur, plash, ripple, splash **2.** *n.* babble, murmur, ripple
guru authority, guiding light, leader, maharishi, mahatma, master, mentor, sage, swami, teacher, tutor
gush *vb.* **1.** burst, cascade, flood, flow, issue, jet, pour, run, rush, spout, spurt, stream **2.** babble, blather, chatter, effuse, enthuse, jabber, overstate, spout *~n.* **3.** burst, cascade, flood, flow, issue, jet, outburst, outflow, rush, spout, spurt, stream, torrent
gust *n.* **1.** blast, blow, breeze, flurry, gale, puff, rush, squall **2.** burst, eruption, explosion, fit, gale, outburst, paroxysm, passion, storm, surge *~vb.* **3.** blast, blow, puff, squall
gusto appetite, appreciation, brio, delight, enjoyment, enthusiasm, exhilaration, fervour, liking, pleasure, relish, savour, verve, zeal, zest
gut *n.* **1.** *often plural* belly, bowels, entrails, innards (*informal*), insides (*informal*), intestines, inwards, paunch, stomach, viscera **2.** *plural informal* audacity, backbone, boldness, bottle (*slang*), courage, daring, forcefulness, grit, hardihood, mettle, nerve, pluck, spirit, spunk (*informal*), willpower *~vb.* **3.** clean, disembowel, draw, dress, eviscerate *~adj.* **4.** *informal*

guts *pl n* **1** the internal organs of a person or an animal. **2** *Informal* courage, willpower, or daring. **3** *Informal* the inner or essential part: *the new roads have torn apart the guts of the city.*

gutsy *adj* **gutsier, gutsiest** *Slang* **1** bold or courageous: *the gutsy kid who lost a leg to cancer.* **2** robust or vigorous: *a gutsy rendering of "Bobby Shaftoe".*

gutta-percha *n* a whitish rubber substance, obtained from a tropical Asian tree and used in electrical insulation and dentistry.

gutted *adj Brit informal* disappointed and upset: *the supporters will be absolutely gutted if the manager leaves the club.*

gutter *n* **1** a channel on the roof of a building or alongside a kerb, used to collect and carry away rainwater. **2** *Tenpin bowling* one of the channels on either side of an alley. **3 the gutter** a poverty-stricken, degraded, or criminal environment: *he rose from the gutter.* ~*vb* **4** (of a candle) to flicker and be about to go out. **guttering** *n*

gutter press *n Informal* the section of the popular press that concentrates on the sensational aspects of the news.

guttersnipe *n* a child who spends most of his or her time in the streets, usually in a slum area.

guttural (**gut**-ter-al) *adj* **1** *Phonetics* pronounced at the back of the throat. **2** harsh-sounding.

guy[1] *n* **1** *Informal* a man or boy. **2** *Chiefly US* a person of either sex: *it's been very nice talking to you guys again.* **3** *Brit* a crude model of Guy Fawkes, that is burnt on top of a bonfire on Guy Fawkes Day (November 5).

guy[2] *n* a rope or chain for steadying or securing something such as a tent. Also: **guyrope**

guzzle *vb* **-zling, -zled** to eat or drink quickly or greedily.

gybe *or* **jibe** (**jibe**) *Naut* ~*vb* **gybing, gybed** *or* **jibing, jibed 1** (of a fore-and-aft sail) to swing suddenly from one side of a ship to the other. **2** to change the course of (a ship) by letting the sail gybe. ~*n* **3** an instance of gybing.

gym *n* short for **gymnasium** or **gymnastics.**

gymkhana (jim-**kah**-na) *n Chiefly Brit* an event in which horses and riders take part in various races and contests.

gymnasium *n* a large room containing equipment such as bars, weights, and ropes, for physical exercise.

gymnast *n* a person who is skilled or trained in gymnastics.

gymnastics *n* **1** practice or training in exercises that develop physical strength and agility. ~*pl n* **2** such exercises. **gymnastic** *adj*

gym shoes *pl n* same as **plimsolls.**

gymslip *n* a tunic formerly worn by schoolgirls as part of school uniform.

gynaecology *or US* **gynecology** (guy-nee-**kol**-la-jee) *n* the branch of medicine concerned with diseases and conditions specific to women. **gynaecological** *or US* **gynecological** *adj* **gynaecologist** *or US* **gynecologist** *n*

gyp *or* **gip** *n* **give someone gyp** *Brit & NZ slang* to cause someone severe pain.

gypsophila *n* a garden plant with small white flowers.

gypsum *n* a mineral used in making plaster of Paris.

Gypsy *or* **Gipsy** *n, pl* **-sies** a member of a travelling people scattered throughout Europe and North America.

gyrate (**jire-rate**) *vb* **-rating, -rated** to turn round and round in a circle. **gyration** *n*

gyrfalcon (**jur**-fawl-kon) *n* a very large rare falcon of northern regions.

gyro *n, pl* **-ros** short for **gyroscope.**

gyrocompass *n* a nonmagnetic compass that uses a motor-driven gyroscope to indicate true north.

gyroscope (**jire**-oh-skope) *n* a device containing a disc rotating on an axis that can turn freely in any direction, so that the disc maintains the same position regardless of the movement of the surrounding structure.

THESAURUS

basic, deep-seated, emotional, heartfelt, innate, instinctive, intuitive, involuntary, natural, spontaneous, unthinking, visceral

gutter channel, conduit, ditch, drain, duct, pipe, sluice, trench, trough, tube

guttural deep, gravelly, gruff, hoarse, husky, low, rasping, rough, thick, throaty

guy *informal* bloke (*Brit. informal*), cat (*slang*), chap, fellow, lad, man, person, youth

guzzle bolt, cram, devour, drink, gobble, gorge, knock back (*informal*), pig out (*U.S. & Canad. slang*), quaff, stuff (oneself), swill, tope, wolf

Gypsy, Gipsy Bohemian, nomad, rambler, roamer, Romany, rover, traveller, vagabond, vagrant, wanderer

H

H 1 *Chem* hydrogen. 2 *Physics* henry.
h. *or* **H.** 1 height. 2 hour.
ha[1] *or* **hah** *interj* an exclamation expressing triumph, surprise, or scorn.
ha[2] hectare.
Ha *Chem* hahnium.
habeas corpus (**hay**-bee-ass **kor**-puss) *n Law* a writ ordering a person to be brought before a judge, so as to decide whether his or her detention is lawful.
haberdasher *n Brit* a dealer in small articles used for sewing. **haberdashery** *n*
Haber process (**hah**-ber) *n Chem* a method of making ammonia by reacting nitrogen with hydrogen at high pressure in the presence of a catalyst.
habiliments *pl n* clothes.
habit *n* **1** a tendency to act in a particular way. **2** established custom or use: *the English habit of taking tea in the afternoon.* **3** an addiction to a drug. **4** mental disposition or attitude: *deference was a deeply ingrained habit of mind.* **5** the costume of a nun or monk. **6** a woman's riding costume.
habitable *adj* fit to be lived in. **habitability** *n*
habitant *n* an early French settler in Canada or Louisiana or a descendant of one, esp. a farmer.
habitat *n* the natural home of an animal or plant.
habitation *n* **1** occupation of a dwelling place: *unfit for human habitation.* **2** *Formal* a dwelling place.
habit-forming *adj* tending to become a habit or addiction.
habitual *adj* **1** done regularly and repeatedly: *habitual behaviour patterns.* **2** by habit: *a habitual criminal.* **habitually** *adv*
habituate *vb* **-ating, -ated** to accustom; get used to: *habituated to failure.* **habituation** *n*
habitué (hab-**it**-yew-ay) *n* a frequent visitor to a place.
hachure (**hash**-yoor) *n* shading of short lines drawn on a map to indicate the degree of steepness of a hill.
hacienda (hass-ee-**end**-a) *n* (in Spanish-speaking countries) a ranch or large estate with a house on it.
hack[1] *vb* **1** to chop roughly or violently. **2** to cut and clear (a way) through undergrowth. **3** (in sport) to foul (an opposing player) by kicking his or her shins. *~n* **4** a cut or gash. **5** a tool, such as a pick. **6** a chopping blow. **7** a kick on the shins, such as in rugby.
hack[2] *n* **1** a writer or journalist who produces work fast and on a regular basis. **2** a horse kept for riding, often one for hire. **3** *Brit* a country ride on horseback. *~vb* **4** *Brit* to ride (a horse) cross-country for pleasure. *~adj* **5** unoriginal or of a low standard: *clumsily contrived hack verse.*
hacker *n Slang* a computer enthusiast, esp. one who through a personal computer breaks into the computer system of a company or government. **hacking** *or* **hackery** *n*
hacking *adj* (of a cough) dry, painful and harsh-sounding.
hacking jacket *n* a jacket with vents at the side and sloping pockets, orig. designed for wearing on horseback.
hackles *pl n* **1 make one's hackles rise** make one feel angry or hostile. **2** the hairs or feathers on the back of the neck of certain animals or birds, which rise when they are angry.
hackney *n* **1** a taxi. **2** same as **hack**[2] (sense 2).
hackneyed (**hak**-need) *adj* (of a word or phrase) unoriginal and overused.
hacksaw *n* a small saw for cutting metal.
had *vb* the past of **have.**
haddock *n, pl* **-dock** a North Atlantic food fish.
hadedah *or* **hadeda** (**hah**-dee-dah) *n* a large grey-green S African ibis.
Hades (**hay**-deez) *n Greek myth* the underworld home of the souls of the dead.
hadj *n* same as **hajj.**
hadji *n, pl* **hadjis** same as **hajji.**
hadn't had not.
haemal *or US* **hemal** (**heem**-al) *adj* of the blood.
haematic *or US* **hematic** (hee-**mat**-ik) *adj* relating to or containing blood.
haematite *n* a type of iron ore which is reddish-brown when powdered.
haematology *or US* **hematology** *n* the branch of medical science concerned with the blood. **haematologist** *or US* **hematologist** *n*
haemoglobin *or US* **hemoglobin** (hee-moh-**globe**-in) *n* a protein in red blood cells that carries oxygen from the lungs to the tissues.
haemophilia *or US* **hemophilia** (hee-moh-**fill**-lee-a) *n* a hereditary disorder, usually affecting males, in which the blood does not clot properly. **haemophiliac** *n*
haemorrhage *or US* **hemorrhage** (**hem**-or-ij) *n* **1**

THESAURUS

habit *n.* **1.** bent, custom, disposition, manner, mannerism, practice, proclivity, propensity, quirk, tendency, way **2.** convention, custom, mode, practice, routine, rule, second nature, tradition, usage, wont **3.** addiction, dependence, fixation, obsession, weakness **4.** constitution, disposition, frame of mind, make-up, nature **5.** apparel, dress, garb, garment, habiliment, riding dress
habitation 1. inhabitance, inhabitancy, occupancy, occupation, tenancy **2.** abode, domicile, dwelling, dwelling house, home, house, living quarters, lodging, pad (*slang*), quarters, residence
habitual 1. accustomed, common, customary, familiar, fixed, natural, normal, ordinary, regular, routine, standard, traditional, usual, wonted **2.** chronic, confirmed, constant, established, frequent, hardened, ingrained, inveterate, persistent, recurrent
habituate acclimatize, accustom, break in, condition, discipline, familiarize, harden, inure, make used to, school, season, train
habitué constant customer, frequenter, frequent visitor, regular (*informal*), regular patron
hack[1] **1.** *vb.* chop, cut, gash, hew, kick, lacerate, mangle, mutilate, notch, slash **2.** *n.* chop, cut, gash, notch, slash
hack[2] *n.* **1.** Grub Street writer, literary hack, penny-a-liner, scribbler **2.** crock, hired horse, horse, jade, nag, poor old tired horse *~adj.* **3.** banal, mediocre, pedestrian, poor, stereotyped, tired, undistinguished, uninspired, unoriginal
hackles make one's hackles rise anger, annoy, bridle at, cause resentment, get one's dander up (*slang*), infuriate, make one see red (*informal*)
hackneyed banal, clichéd, common, commonplace,

heavy bleeding from ruptured blood vessels. ~*vb* **-rhaging, -rhaged 2** to bleed heavily.

haemorrhoids *or US* **hemorrhoids** (**hem**-or-oydz) *pl n Pathol* swollen veins in the wall of the anus.

haeremai (**hire**-a-my) *interj NZ* an expression of greeting or welcome.

hafnium *n Chem* a metallic element found in zirconium ores. Symbol: Hf

haft *n* the handle of an axe, knife, or dagger.

hag *n* **1** an unpleasant or ugly old woman. **2** a witch. **haggish** *adj*

haggard *adj* looking tired and ill.

haggis *n* a Scottish dish made from sheep's or calf's offal, oatmeal, suet, and seasonings boiled in a skin made from the animal's stomach.

haggle *vb* **-gling, -gled** to bargain or wrangle (over a price).

hagiography *n, pl* **-phies** the writing of lives of the saints. **hagiographer** *n*

hagiology *n, pl* **-gies** literature about the lives and legends of saints.

hag-ridden *adj* distressed or worried.

hah *interj* same as **ha**[1].

ha-ha[1] *or* **haw-haw** *interj* a written representation of the sound of laughter.

ha-ha[2] *n* a wall set in a ditch so as not to interrupt a view of the landscape.

hahnium *n Chem* a transuranic element artificially produced from californium. Symbol: Ha

haiku (**hie**-koo) *n, pl* **-ku** a Japanese verse form in 17 syllables.

hail[1] *n* **1** small pellets of ice falling from thunderclouds. **2** words, ideas, missiles, etc., directed with force and in great quantity: *a hail of abuse.* ~*vb* **3** to fall as hail: *it's hailing.* **4** to fall like hail: *blows hailed down on him.*

hail[2] *vb* **1** to call out to; greet: *a voice from behind hailed him.* **2** to praise, acclaim, or acknowledge: *his crew had been hailed as heroes.* **3** to stop (a taxi) by shouting or gesturing. **4 hail from** to come originally from: *she hails from Nova Scotia.* ~*n* **5 within hailing distance** within hearing range. ~*interj* **6** *Poetic* an exclamation of greeting.

hail-fellow-well-met *adj* genial and familiar in an offensive way.

Hail Mary *n RC Church* a prayer to the Virgin Mary.

hailstone *n* a pellet of hail.

hailstorm *n* a storm during which hail falls.

hair *n* **1** any of the threadlike outgrowths on the skin of mammals. **2** a mass of such outgrowths, such as on a person's head or an animal's body. **3** *Bot* a threadlike growth from the outer layer of a plant. **4** a very small distance or margin: *missed death by a hair.* **5 get in someone's hair** *Informal* to annoy someone. **6 hair of the dog** an alcoholic drink taken as a cure for a hangover. **7 let one's hair down** to enjoy oneself without restraint. **8 not turn a hair** to show no reaction. **9 split hairs** to make petty and unnecessary distinctions. **hairless** *adj*

hairdo *n, pl* **-dos** *Informal* the style of a person's hair.

hairdresser *n* **1** a person who cuts and styles hair. **2** a hairdresser's premises. **hairdressing** *n*

hairgrip *n Chiefly Brit* a small bent clasp used to fasten the hair.

hairline *n* **1** the edge of hair at the top of the forehead. ~*adj* **2** very fine or narrow: *a hairline crack.*

hairpiece *n* a section of false hair added to a person's real hair.

hairpin *n* a thin U-shaped pin used to fasten the hair.

hairpin bend *n* a bend in the road that curves very sharply.

hair-raising *adj* very frightening or exciting.

hair's-breadth *n* an extremely small margin or distance.

hair shirt *n* a shirt made of horsehair cloth worn against the skin as a penance.

hair slide *n* a decorative clasp used to fasten the hair.

hairsplitting *n* **1** the act of making petty distinctions. ~*adj* **2** characterized by petty distinctions.

hairspring *n* a fine spring in some clocks and watches which regulates the timekeeping.

hairstyle *n* the cut and arrangement of a person's hair. **hairstylist** *n*

hair trigger *n* a trigger that responds to the slightest pressure.

hairy *adj* **hairier, hairiest 1** covered with hair. **2** *Slang* dangerous, exciting, and difficult. **hairiness** *n*

hajj *or* **hadj** *n* the pilgrimage a Muslim makes to Mecca.

hajji *or* **hadji** *n, pl* **hajjis** *or* **hadjis** a Muslim who has made a pilgrimage to Mecca.

haka *n NZ* **1** a Maori war chant accompanied by actions. **2** a similar chant by a sports team.

hake *n, pl* **hake** *or* **hakes** an edible fish of the cod family.

halal *or* **hallal** *n* meat from animals that have been slaughtered according to Muslim law.

halberd *n History* a tall spear that includes an axe blade and a pick.

THESAURUS

overworked, pedestrian, played out (*informal*), run-of-the-mill, stale, stereotyped, stock, threadbare, time-worn, tired, trite, unoriginal, worn-out

hag beldam (*archaic*), crone, fury, harridan, Jezebel, shrew, termagant, virago, vixen, witch

haggard careworn, drawn, emaciated, gaunt, ghastly, hollow-eyed, pinched, shrunken, thin, wan, wasted, wrinkled

haggle bargain, barter, beat down, bicker, dispute, quarrel, squabble, wrangle

hail[1] **1.** *n.* barrage, bombardment, pelting, rain, shower, storm, volley **2.** *vb.* barrage, batter, beat down upon, bombard, pelt, rain, rain down on, shower, storm, volley

hail[2] **1.** accost, address, call, flag down, halloo, shout to, signal to, sing out, speak to, wave down **2.** acclaim, acknowledge, applaud, cheer, exalt, glorify, greet, honour, salute, welcome **3. hail from** be a native of, be born in, come from, originate in

hair 1. head of hair, locks, mane, mop, shock, tresses **2. get in someone's hair** aggravate (*informal*), annoy, be on someone's back (*slang*), exasperate, get on someone's nerves (*informal*), harass, hassle (*informal*), irritate, nark (*slang*), pester, plague **3. let one's hair down** chill out (*slang, chiefly U.S.*), let it all hang out (*informal*), let off steam (*informal*), let oneself go, relax **4. not turn a hair** keep one's cool (*slang*), not bat an eyelid, remain calm **5. split hairs** cavil, find fault, overrefine, pettifog, quibble

hair-raising alarming, bloodcurdling, breathtaking, creepy, exciting, frightening, horrifying, petrifying, scary, shocking, spine-chilling, startling, terrifying, thrilling

hair's-breadth fraction, hair, jot, narrow margin, whisker

hairsplitting *adj.* captious, carping, cavilling, fault-finding, fine, finicky, nice, niggling, nit-picking (*informal*), overrefined, pettifogging, quibbling, subtle

halcyon (**hal**-see-on) *adj* **1** peaceful, gentle, and calm. **2 halcyon days** a time, usually in the past, of greatest happiness or success.

hale *adj* healthy and robust: *hale and hearty.*

half *n, pl* **halves 1** either of two equal or corresponding parts that together make up a whole. **2** the fraction equal to one divided by two. **3** half a pint, esp. of beer. **4** *Sport* one of two equal periods of play in a game. **5** a half-price ticket. **6 by halves** without being thorough: *in Italy they rarely do things by halves.* **7 go halves** to share expenses. *~adj* **8** denoting one of two equal parts: *a half chicken.* *~adv* **9** half in degree or quantity: *half as much.* **10** partially; to an extent: *half hidden in the trees.* **11 by half** to an excessive degree: *too clever by half.* **12 not half** *Informal* **a** *Brit* very; indeed: *it isn't half hard to look at these charts.* **b** yes, indeed.

half-and-half *adj* half one thing and half another thing.

halfback *n Rugby* a player positioned immediately behind the forwards.

half-baked *adj Informal* poorly planned: *half-baked policies.*

half board *n* the daily provision by a hotel of bed, breakfast, and evening meal.

half-bottle *n* a bottle of spirits or wine that contains half the quantity of a standard bottle.

half-breed *n Often offensive* a person whose parents are of different races.

half-brother *n* the son of either one's mother or father by another partner.

half-caste *n* a person whose parents are of different races.

half-cock *n* **go off at half-cock** *or* **half-cocked** to fail because of lack of preparation.

half-crown *or* **half-a-crown** *n* a former British coin worth two shillings and sixpence (12½p).

half-cut *adj Brit slang* rather drunk.

half-day *n* a day when one works only in the morning or only in the afternoon.

half-dozen *n* six.

half-hearted *adj* without enthusiasm or determination. **half-heartedly** *adv*

half-hitch *n* a knot made by passing the end of a piece of rope around itself and through the loop so made.

half-hour *n* **1** a period of 30 minutes. **2** the point of time 30 minutes after the beginning of an hour. **half-hourly** *adv, adj*

half-life *n* the time taken for radioactive material to lose half its radioactivity.

half-light *n* a dim light, such as at dawn or dusk.

half-mast *n* the halfway position of a flag on a mast as a sign of mourning.

half measures *pl n* inadequate actions or solutions: *the education system cannot be reformed by half measures.*

half-moon *n* **1** the moon when half its face is illuminated. **2** the time at which a half-moon occurs. **3** something shaped like a half-moon.

half-nelson *n* a wrestling hold in which a wrestler places an arm under his opponent's arm from behind and exerts pressure with his palm on the back of his opponent's neck.

halfpenny *or* **ha'penny** (**hayp**-nee) *n, pl* **-pennies** a former British coin worth half a penny.

half-pie *adj NZ informal* badly planned; not properly thought out: *a half-pie scheme.*

half-price *adj, adv* for half the normal price: *special half-price tickets; jeans bought half-price in a sale.*

half-sister *n* the daughter of either one's mother or father by another partner.

half term *n Brit education* a short holiday midway through a term.

half-timbered *adj* (of a building) having an exposed timber framework filled with brick or plaster.

half-time *n Sport* an interval between the two halves of a game.

half-title *n* the first right-hand page of a book, with only the title on it.

halftone *n* a photographic illustration in which the image is composed of a large number of black and white dots.

half-track *n* a vehicle with moving tracks on the rear wheels.

half-truth *n* a partially true statement. **half-true** *adj*

half volley *n Sport* **1** a stroke or shot in which the ball is hit immediately after it bounces. *~vb* **half-volley 2** to hit or kick (a ball) immediately after it bounces.

halfway *adv, adj* **1** at or to half the distance. **2** at or towards the middle of a period of time or of an event or process: *he only managed to get halfway up the hill.* **3 meet someone halfway** to compromise with someone.

halfway house *n* **1** a place to rest midway on a journey. **2** the halfway stage in any process: *a halfway house between the theatre and cinema is possible.*

halfwit *n* a foolish or feeble-minded person. **half-witted** *adj*

halibut *n* a large edible flatfish.

halitosis *n* bad-smelling breath.

THESAURUS

hairy 1. bearded, bushy, fleecy, furry, hirsute, shaggy, stubbly, unshaven, woolly **2.** *slang* dangerous, difficult, hazardous, perilous, risky, scaring

halcyon 1. calm, gentle, mild, pacific, peaceful, placid, quiet, serene, still, tranquil, undisturbed, unruffled **2. halcyon days** carefree, flourishing, golden, happy, palmy, prosperous

hale able-bodied, blooming, fit, flourishing, healthy, hearty, in fine fettle, in the pink, robust, sound, strong, vigorous, well

half 1. *n.* bisection, division, equal part, fifty per cent, fraction, hemisphere, portion, section **2.** *adj.* divided, fractional, halved, incomplete, limited, moderate, partial **3.** *adv.* after a fashion, all but, barely, inadequately, incompletely, in part, partially, partly, pretty nearly, slightly **4. by half** considerably, excessively, very much

half-baked ill-conceived, ill-judged, impractical, poorly planned, short-sighted, unformed, unthought out *or* through

half-hearted apathetic, cool, indifferent, lacklustre, listless, lukewarm, neutral, passive, perfunctory, spiritless, tame, unenthusiastic, uninterested

halfway *adv./adj.* **1.** midway, to *or* in the middle, to the midpoint **2. meet someone halfway** accommodate, come to terms, compromise, concede, give and take, strike a balance, trade off

halfwit airhead (*slang*), berk (*Brit. slang*), charlie (*Brit. informal*), coot (*old-fashioned*), dimwit (*informal*), dolt, dork (*slang*), dullard, dunce, dunderhead, fool, idiot, imbecile (*informal*), jerk (*slang, chiefly U.S. & Canad.*), mental defective, moron, nerd *or* nurd (*slang*), nitwit (*informal*), numskull *or* numbskull, oaf, pillock (*Brit. slang*), plonker (*slang*), prat (*slang*), prick (*derogatory slang*), simpleton, twit (*informal, chiefly Brit.*), wally (*slang*)

halfwitted barmy (*slang*), batty (*slang*), crazy, dolt-

hall *n* **1** an entry area to other rooms in a house. **2** a building or room for public meetings, dances, etc. **3** a residential building in a college or university. **4** a great house of an estate; manor. **5** a large dining room in a college or university. **6** the large room of a castle or stately home.

hallelujah, halleluiah (hal-ee-**loo**-ya) *or* **alleluia** *interj* an exclamation of praise to God.

hallmark *n* **1** a typical feature: *secrecy became the hallmark of government.* **2** *Brit* an official seal stamped on gold, silver, or platinum articles to guarantee purity and date of manufacture. **3** a mark of authenticity or excellence. *~vb* **4** to stamp with a hallmark.

hallo *interj, n* same as **hello.**

halloo *interj* a shout used to call hounds at a hunt.

hallowed *adj* **1** regarded as holy: *hallowed ground.* **2** respected and revered because of age, importance, or reputation: *the hallowed pitch at Lord's.*

Hallowe'en *or* **Halloween** *n* October 31, celebrated by children by dressing up as ghosts, witches, etc.

hallucinate *vb* **-nating, -nated** to seem to see something that is not really there.

hallucination *n* the experience of seeming to see something that is not really there. **hallucinatory** *adj*

hallucinogen *n* any drug that causes hallucinations. **hallucinogenic** *adj*

hallway *n* an entrance area.

halo (**hay**-loh) *n, pl* **-loes** *or* **-los 1** a ring of light around the head of a sacred figure. **2** a circle of refracted light around the sun or moon. *~vb* **-loes** *or* **-los, -loing, -loed 3** to surround with a halo.

halogen (**hal**-oh-jen) *n Chem* any of the nonmetallic chemical elements fluorine, chlorine, bromine, iodine, and astatine which form salts when combined with metal.

halt *vb* **1** to come to a stop or bring (someone or something) to a stop. *~n* **2** a temporary standstill. **3** a military command to stop. **4** *Chiefly Brit* a minor railway station without a building. **5 call a halt to** to put an end to.

halter *n* **1** a strap around a horse's head with a rope to lead it with. *~vb* **2** to put a halter on (a horse).

halterneck *n* a woman's top or dress which fastens behind the neck, leaving the back and arms bare.

halting *adj* hesitant or uncertain: *she spoke halting Italian.*

halve *vb* **halving, halved 1** to divide (something) into two equal parts. **2** to reduce (the size or amount of something) by half. **3** *Golf* to draw with one's opponent on (a hole or round).

halyard *n Naut* a line for hoisting or lowering a ship's sail or flag.

ham[1] *n* smoked or salted meat from a pig's thigh.

ham[2] *n* **1** *Informal* an amateur radio operator. **2** *Theatre informal* an actor who overacts and exaggerates the emotions and gestures of a part. *~adj* **3** (of actors or their performances) exaggerated and overstated. *~vb* **hamming, hammed 4 ham it up** *Informal* to overact.

hamba *interj S African usually offensive* go away.

hamburger *n* a flat round of minced beef, often served in a bread roll.

ham-fisted *or* **ham-handed** *adj Informal* very clumsy or awkward.

hamlet *n* a small village.

hammer *n* **1** a hand tool consisting of a heavy metal head on the end of a handle, used for driving in nails, beating metal, etc. **2** the part of a gun that causes the bullet to shoot when the trigger is pulled. **3** *Athletics* **a** a heavy metal ball attached to a flexible wire: thrown in competitions. **b** the sport of throwing the hammer. **4** an auctioneer's mallet. **5** the part of a piano that hits a string when a key is pressed. **6 come** *or* **go under the hammer** to be on sale at auction. **7 hammer and tongs** with great effort or energy. *~vb* **8** to hit with or as if with a hammer. **9 hammer in** *or* **into** to force (facts or ideas) into someone through repetition. **10 hammer away at** to work at (something) constantly: *the paper hammered away at the same theme all the way through the campaign.* **11** *Brit* to criticize severely. **12** *Informal* to defeat heavily. **13** to feel or sound like hammering: *his heart was hammering.*

hammer and sickle *n* the emblem on the flag of the former Soviet Union, representing the industrial workers and the peasants.

hammerhead *n* a shark with a wide flattened head.

hammer out *vb* to settle (differences) with great effort.

hammertoe *n* a condition in which the toe is permanently bent at the joint.

hammock *n* a hanging bed made of canvas or net.

hamper[1] *vb* to make it difficult for (someone or something) to move or progress.

hamper[2] *n* **1** a large basket with a lid. **2** *Brit* a selection of food and drink packed as a gift.

hamster *n* a small rodent with a stocky body, short

THESAURUS

ish, dull, dull-witted, feeble-minded, foolish, goofy (*informal*), idiotic, moronic, nurdish (*slang*), obtuse, silly, simple, simple-minded, stupid

hall 1. corridor, entrance hall, entry, foyer, hallway, lobby, passage, passageway, vestibule **2.** assembly room, auditorium, chamber, concert hall, meeting place

hallmark authentication, device, endorsement, mark, seal, sign, signet, stamp, symbol

hallucination aberration, apparition, delusion, dream, fantasy, figment of the imagination, illusion, mirage, phantasmagoria, vision

halo aura, aureole *or* aureola, corona, nimbus, radiance, ring of light

halt *vb.* **1.** arrest, block, break off, bring to an end, call it a day, cease, check, close down, come to an end, curb, cut short, desist, draw up, end, hold back, impede, obstruct, pull up, rest, stand still, staunch, stem, stop, wait **2.** terminate *~n.* **3.** arrest, break, close, end, impasse, interruption, pause, stand, standstill, stop, stoppage, termination

halting awkward, faltering, hesitant, imperfect, laboured, stammering, stumbling, stuttering

halve bisect, cut in half, divide equally, reduce by fifty per cent, share equally, split in two

hammer *vb.* **1.** bang, beat, drive, hit, knock, lambast(e), strike, tap **2.** beat out, fashion, forge, form, make, shape **3. hammer in** *or* **into** din into, drive home, drub into, drum into, grind into, impress upon, instruct, repeat **4. hammer away at** beaver away (*Brit. informal*), drudge, grind, keep on, peg away (*chiefly Brit.*), persevere, persist, plug away (*informal*), pound away, stick at, work **5.** *informal* beat, blow out of the water (*slang*), clobber (*slang*), defeat, drub, lick (*informal*), master, run rings around (*informal*), slate (*informal*), tank (*slang*), thrash, trounce, undo, wipe the floor with (*informal*), worst

hammer out accomplish, bring about, come to a conclusion, complete, excogitate, finish, form a resolution, make a decision, negotiate, produce, settle, sort out, thrash out, work out

hamper *vb.* bind, cramp, curb, embarrass, encumber,

tail, and cheek pouches.

➤ Note the spelling. There is no "p".

hamstring *n* **1** one of the tendons at the back of the knee. *~vb* **-stringing, -strung 2** to make it difficult for someone to take any action.

hand *n* **1** the part of the body at the end of the arm, consisting of a thumb, four fingers, and a palm. **2** a person's style of writing: *scrolls written in her own hand.* **3** the influence a person or thing has over a particular situation: *the hand of the military in shaping policy was obvious.* **4** a part in some activity: *I remember with gratitude Fortune's hand in starting my collection.* **5** assistance: *give me a hand with the rice.* **6** a round of applause: *give a big hand to the most exciting duo in the game.* **7** consent to marry someone: *he asked for her hand in marriage.* **8** a manual worker. **9** a member of a ship's crew. **10** a pointer on a dial or gauge, esp. on a clock. **11 a** the cards dealt in one round of a card game. **b** one round of a card game. **12** a position indicated by its location to the side of an object or the observer: *on the right hand.* **13** a contrasting aspect or condition: *on the other hand.* **14** source: *I had experienced at first hand many management styles.* **15** a person who creates something: *a good hand at baking.* **16** a unit of length equalling four inches, used for measuring the height of horses. **17 by hand a** by manual rather than mechanical means. **b** by messenger: *the letter was delivered by hand.* **18 from hand to mouth** with no food or money in reserve: *living from hand to mouth.* **19 hand in glove** in close association. **20 hand over fist** steadily and quickly: *losing money hand over fist.* **21 in hand a** under control. **b** receiving attention: *the business in hand.* **c** available in reserve: *Rangers had a game in hand.* **22 keep one's hand in** to continue to practise something. **23 (near) at hand** very close. **24 on hand** close by; available. **25 out of hand a** beyond control. **b** decisively, without possible reconsideration: *he dismissed the competition out of hand.* **26 show one's hand** to reveal one's plans. **27 to hand** accessible. *~vb* **28** to pass or give by the hand or hands. **29 hand it to someone** to give credit to someone. ~See also **hand down, hand on, hands,** etc. **handless** *adj*

handbag *n* a woman's small bag carried to contain personal articles.

handball *n* a game in which players strike a ball against a wall with their hands.

handbill *n* a small printed notice for distribution by hand.

handbook *n* a reference manual giving practical information on a subject.

handbrake *n* a brake in a motor vehicle operated by a hand lever.

handcart *n* a simple cart pushed or pulled by hand, used for transporting goods.

handcrafted *adj* made by handicraft.

handcuff *n* **1** (*pl*) a linked pair of locking metal rings used for securing prisoners. *~vb* **2** to put handcuffs on (a person).

hand down *vb* **1** to pass on (knowledge, possessions, or skills) to a younger generation. **2** to pass (outgrown clothes) on from one member of a family to a younger one. **3** *US & Canad Law* to announce (a verdict).

handful *n, pl* **-fuls 1** the amount that can be held in the hand. **2** a small number: *a handful of parents.* **3** *Informal* a person or animal that is difficult to control: *as a child she was a real handful.*

handicap *n* **1** a physical or mental disability. **2** something that makes progress difficult. **3 a** a contest in which competitors are given advantages or disadvantages in an attempt to equalize their chances. **b** the advantage or disadvantage given. **4** *Golf* the number of strokes by which a player's averaged score exceeds par for the course. *~vb* **-capping, -capped 5** to make it difficult for (someone) to do something.

handicapped *adj* physically or mentally disabled.

handicraft *n* **1** a skill performed with the hands, such as weaving. **2** the objects produced by people with such skills.

handiwork *n* **1** the result of someone's work or activity. **2** work produced by hand.

handkerchief *n* a small square of fabric used to wipe the nose.

handle *n* **1** the part of an object that is held or operated in order that it may be used. **2** a small lever used to open and close a door or window. **3** *Slang* a person's name. **4** a reason for doing something: *trying to get a handle on why companies borrow money.* **5 fly off the handle** *Informal* to become suddenly extremely angry. *~vb* **-dling, -dled 6** to hold, move, operate or touch with the hands. **7** to have responsibility for: *she handles all their affairs personally.* **8** to manage successfully: *I can handle this challenge.* **9** to discuss (a subject). **10** to deal with in a specified way: *the affair was neatly handled.* **11** to trade or deal in (specified merchandise): *we handle 1800 properties in Nor-*

THESAURUS

entangle, fetter, frustrate, hamstring, handicap, hinder, hold up, impede, interfere with, obstruct, prevent, restrain, restrict, slow down, thwart, trammel

hand *n.* **1.** fist, hook, meathook (*slang*), mitt (*slang*), palm, paw (*informal*) **2.** calligraphy, chirography, handwriting, longhand, penmanship, script **3.** agency, direction, influence, part, participation, share **4.** aid, assistance, help, support **5.** clap, ovation, round of applause **6.** employee, hired man, labourer, operative, worker, workman **7.** artificer, artisan, craftsman **8. from hand to mouth** by necessity, improvidently, in poverty, insecurely, on the breadline (*informal*), precariously, uncertainly **9. hand in glove** allied, in cahoots (*informal*), in league, in partnership **10. hand over fist** by leaps and bounds, easily, steadily, swiftly **11. in hand a.** in order, receiving attention, under control **b.** available for use, in reserve, put by, ready **12. on hand** approaching, available, close, handy, imminent, near, nearby, on tap (*informal*), ready, within reach *~vb.* **13.** deliver, hand over, pass

handbook guide, guidebook, instruction book, manual, vade mecum

handcuff 1. *n. plural* bracelets (*slang*), cuffs (*informal*), fetters, manacles, shackles **2.** *vb.* fetter, manacle, shackle

hand down *or* **on** bequeath, give, grant, pass on *or* down, transfer, will

handful few, small number, small quantity, smattering, sprinkling

handicap *n.* **1.** defect, disability, impairment **2.** barrier, block, disadvantage, drawback, encumbrance, hindrance, impediment, limitation, millstone, obstacle, restriction, shortcoming, stumbling block **3.** advantage, edge, head start, odds, penalty, upper hand *~vb.* **4.** burden, encumber, hamper, hamstring, hinder, hold back, impede, limit, place at a disadvantage, restrict, retard

handicraft art, artisanship, craft, craftsmanship, handiwork, skill, workmanship

handiwork 1. achievement, artefact, creation, design, invention, product, production, result **2.** craft, handicraft, handwork

handle *n.* **1.** grip, haft, handgrip, helve, hilt, knob, stock *~vb.* **2.** feel, finger, fondle, grasp, hold, maul, paw (*informal*), pick up, poke, touch **3.** control, direct,

mandy. **12** to react or respond in a specified way to operation or control: *it's light and handles well.* **handling** *n*

handlebars *pl n* a metal tube with handles at each end, used for steering a bicycle or motorcycle.

handler *n* **1** a person who trains and controls an animal. **2** a person who handles something: *a baggage handler.*

handmade *adj* made by hand, not by machine.

handmaiden *or* **handmaid** *n* **1** *Old-fashioned* a female servant. **2** a person or thing that serves a useful but lesser purpose: *these policies resulted in agriculture becoming the poor handmaiden of industry.*

hand-me-down *n Informal* an item of clothing that someone has finished with and passed on to someone else.

hand on *vb* to pass (something) to the next person in a succession.

hand out *n* **1** clothing, food, or money given to a needy person. **2** a leaflet, free sample, etc., given out to publicize something. **3** a piece of written information given out to the audience at a talk, lecture, etc. ~*vb* **hand out 4** to distribute.

hand over *vb* to give up possession of or transfer (something).

hand-pick *vb* to select (a person) with great care, such as for a special job. **hand-picked** *adj*

handrail *n* a rail alongside a stairway, to provide support.

hands *pl n* **1 in someone's hands** in someone's control or power: *that's in the hands of the courts.* **2 change hands** to pass from the possession of one person to another. **3 have one's hands full** to be completely occupied. **4 off one's hands** no longer one's responsibility. **5 on one's hands** for which one is responsible: *what a problem case I've got on my hands.* **6 wash one's hands of** to have nothing more to do with. **7 win hands down** to win easily.

handset *n* a telephone mouthpiece and earpiece in a single unit.

handshake *n* the act of grasping and shaking a person's hand, such as in greeting or when agreeing on a deal.

handsome *adj* **1** (esp. of a man) good-looking. **2** (of a building, garden, etc.) large, well-made, and with an attractive appearance: *a handsome building.* **3** (of an amount of money) generous or large: *a handsome dividend.* **handsomely** *adv*

hands-on *adj* involving practical experience of equipment: *Navy personnel joined the 1986 expedition for hands-on operating experience.*

handspring *n* a gymnastic exercise in which a person leaps forwards or backwards into a handstand and then onto his or her feet.

handstand *n* the act of supporting the body on the hands in an upside-down position.

hand-to-hand *adj, adv* (of combat) at close quarters, with fists or knives.

hand-to-mouth *adj, adv* with barely enough money or food to live on.

handwork *n* work done by hand rather than by machine.

handwriting *n* **1** writing by hand rather than by typing or printing. **2** a person's characteristic writing style. **handwritten** *adj*

handy *adj* **handier, handiest 1** conveniently within reach. **2** easy to handle or use. **3** good at manual work. **handily** *adv*

handyman *n, pl* **-men** a man skilled at odd jobs.

hang *vb* **hanging, hung 1** to fasten or be fastened from above. **2** to place (something) in position, for instance by a hinge, so as to allow free movement: *to hang a door.* **3** to be suspended so as to allow movement from the place where it is attached: *her long hair hung over her face.* **4** to decorate with something suspended, such as pictures. **5** (of cloth or clothing) to fall or flow in a particular way: *the fine gauge knit hangs loosely with graceful femininity.* **6** (*pt & pp* **hanged**) to suspend or be suspended by the neck until dead. **7** to hover: *clouds hung over the mountains.* **8** to fasten to a wall: *to hang wallpaper.* **9** to exhibit or be exhibited in an art gallery. **10 hang over** to threaten or overshadow: *the threat of war hung over the Middle East.* **11** (*pt & pp* **hanged**) *Slang* to damn: used in mild curses or interjections. **12 hang fire** to put off doing something. ~*n* **13** the way in which something hangs. **14 get the hang of something** *Informal* to understand the technique of doing something. ~See also **hang about, hang back,** etc.

hang about *or* **around** *vb* **1** to stand about idly

THESAURUS

guide, manage, supervise **4.** cope with, deal with, manage, take care of **5.** discourse, discuss, treat **6.** administer, conduct, control, direct, guide, manage, manipulate, manoeuvre, operate, steer, treat **7.** carry, deal in, market, sell, stock, trade, traffic in

handling administration, approach, conduct, direction, management, manipulation, running, treatment

hand-out *n.* **1.** alms, charity, dole **2.** bulletin, circular, free sample, leaflet, literature (*informal*), mailshot, press release ~*vb.* **3. hand out** deal out, disburse, dish out (*informal*), dispense, disseminate, distribute, give out, mete

hand over deliver, donate, fork out *or* up (*slang*), present, release, surrender, transfer, turn over, yield

hand-picked choice, chosen, elect, elite, recherché, select, selected

hands 1. authority, care, charge, command, control, custody, disposal, guardianship, keeping, possession, power, supervision **2. wash one's hands of** abandon, accept no responsibility for, give up on, have nothing to do with, leave to one's own devices **3. hands down** easily, effortlessly, with no contest, with no trouble

handsome 1. admirable, attractive, becoming, comely, dishy (*informal, chiefly Brit.*), elegant, fine, good-looking, gorgeous, graceful, majestic, personable, stately, well-proportioned **2.** abundant, ample, bountiful, considerable, generous, gracious, large, liberal, magnanimous, plentiful, sizable

handsomely abundantly, amply, bountifully, generously, liberally, magnanimously, munificently, plentifully, richly

handwriting calligraphy, fist, hand, longhand, penmanship, scrawl, script

handy 1. accessible, at *or* on hand, available, close, convenient, near, nearby, within reach **2.** convenient, easy to use, helpful, manageable, neat, practical, serviceable, useful, user-friendly **3.** adept, adroit, clever, deft, dexterous, expert, nimble, proficient, ready, skilful, skilled

hang *vb.* **1.** be pendent, dangle, depend, droop, incline, suspend **2.** attach, fasten, fix **3.** cover, deck, decorate, drape, furnish **4.** execute, gibbet, send to the gallows, string up (*informal*) **5.** be poised, drift, float, hover, remain, swing **6. hang over** be imminent, impend, loom, menace, threaten **7. hang fire** be slow, be suspended, delay, hang back, procrastinate, stall, stick, vacillate ~*n.* **8. get the hang of** comprehend, get the knack *or* technique, grasp, understand

hang about *or* **around 1.** dally, linger, loiter,

somewhere. 2 (foll. by *with*) to spend a lot of time in the company (of someone).

hangar *n* a large building for storing aircraft.

hang back *vb* to be reluctant to do something.

hangdog *adj* dejected, ashamed, or guilty in appearance or manner.

hanger *n* same as **coat hanger.**

hanger-on *n, pl* **hangers-on** an unwanted follower, esp. of a rich or famous person.

hang-glider *n* an unpowered aircraft consisting of a large cloth wing stretched over a light framework from which the pilot hangs in a harness. **hang-gliding** *n*

hangi (**hung**-ee) *n NZ* **1** an open-air cooking pit. **2** the food cooked in it. **3** the social gathering at the resultant meal.

hanging *n* **1** the act or practice of putting a person to death by suspending the body by the neck. **2** a large piece of cloth hung on a wall as a decoration.

hanging valley *n Geog* a tributary valley that enters a main valley high up because the main valley has been deepened through erosion by a glacier.

hangman *n, pl* **-men** an official who carries out a sentence of hanging.

hangnail *n* a piece of skin partly torn away from the base or side of a fingernail.

hang on *vb* **1** *Informal* to wait: *hang on a minute, will you?* **2** to continue or persist with effort or difficulty. **3** to grasp or hold. **4** to depend on: *a lot hangs on its success.* **5** to listen attentively to: *she hangs on to every word our leader says.*

hang out *vb* **1** to suspend, be suspended, or lean. **2** *Informal* to live or spend a lot of time in a place: *fishermen hang out in waterfront bars.* **3 let it all hang out** *Informal, chiefly US* to relax completely; act or speak freely. ~*n* **hang-out 4** *Informal* a place where someone spends a lot of time.

hangover *n* a feeling of sickness and headache after drinking too much alcohol.

hang together *vb* **1** to be united. **2** to be consistent: *the story simply did not hang together.*

hang up *vb* **1** to replace (a telephone receiver) at the end of a conversation. **2** to put on a hook or hanger. ~*n* **hang-up 3** *Informal* an emotional or psychological problem.

hank *n* a loop or coil, esp. of yarn.

hanker *vb* (foll. by *for* or *after*) to have a great desire for. **hankering** *n*

hanky *or* **hankie** *n, pl* **hankies** *Informal* short for **handkerchief.**

hanky-panky *n Informal* **1** casual sexual relations. **2** mischievous behaviour.

Hanoverian (han-no-**veer**-ee-an) *adj* of or relating to the British royal house ruling from 1714 to 1901.

Hansard *n* the official report of the proceedings of the British or Canadian parliament.

Hanseatic League (han-see-**at**-ik) *n History* a commercial organization of towns in N Germany formed in the 14th century to protect and control trade.

hansom *n* formerly, a two-wheeled one-horse carriage with a fixed hood. Also called: **hansom cab**

Hants Hampshire.

Hanukkah *n* same as **Chanukah.**

haphazard *adj* not organized or planned. **haphazardly** *adv*

hapless *adj* unlucky: *the hapless victim of a misplaced murder attempt.*

haploid *adj Biol* denoting a cell or organism with unpaired chromosomes.

happen *vb* **1** to take place; occur. **2** to chance (to be or do something): *I happen to know him.* **3** to be the case, esp. by chance: *it happens that I know him.* **4 happen to** (of some unforeseen event, such as death) to be the experience or fate of: *if anything happens to me you will know.*

happening *n* an event that often occurs in a way that is unexpected or hard to explain: *some strange happenings in the village recently.*

happy *adj* **-pier, -piest 1** feeling or expressing joy. **2** causing joy or gladness: *the happiest day of my life.* **3**

THESAURUS

roam, tarry, waste time **2.** *with* **with** associate with, frequent, hang out (*informal*), haunt, resort

hang back be backward, be reluctant, demur, hesitate, hold back, recoil

hangdog abject, browbeaten, cowed, cringing, defeated, downcast, furtive, guilty, shamefaced, sneaking, wretched

hanger-on dependant, follower, freeloader (*slang*), lackey, leech, minion, parasite, sponger (*informal*), sycophant

hang on 1. *informal* hold on, hold the line, remain, stop, wait **2.** carry on, continue, endure, go on, hold on, hold out, persevere, persist, remain **3.** cling, clutch, grasp, grip, hold fast **4.** be conditional upon, be contingent on, be dependent on, be determined by, depend on, hinge, rest, turn on **5.** be rapt, give ear, listen attentively

hangover aftereffects, crapulence (*literary*), morning after (*informal*)

hang-up *informal* block, difficulty, inhibition, obsession, preoccupation, problem, thing (*informal*)

hank coil, length, loop, piece, roll, skein

hanker *with* **for** *or* **after** covet, crave, desire, eat one's heart out over, hope, hunger, itch, long, lust, pine, thirst, want, wish, yearn, yen (*informal*)

hankering craving, desire, hope, hunger, itch, longing, pining, thirst, urge, wish, yearning, yen (*informal*)

haphazard accidental, aimless, arbitrary, careless, casual, chance, disorderly, disorganized, fluky (*informal*), hit or miss (*informal*), indiscriminate, random, slapdash, slipshod, unmethodical, unsystematic

happen 1. appear, arise, come about, come off (*informal*), come to pass, crop up (*informal*), develop, ensue, eventuate, follow, materialize, occur, present itself, result, take place, transpire (*informal*) **2.** chance, fall out, have the fortune to be, pan out (*informal*), supervene, turn out **3. happen to** become of, befall, betide

happening accident, adventure, affair, case, chance, episode, escapade, event, experience, incident, occasion, occurrence, phenomenon, proceeding, scene

happily 1. agreeably, blithely, cheerfully, contentedly, delightedly, enthusiastically, gaily, gladly, gleefully, heartily, joyfully, joyously, merrily, with pleasure **2.** auspiciously, favourably, fortunately, luckily, opportunely, propitiously, providentially, seasonably **3.** freely, gladly, willingly, with pleasure

happiness beatitude, blessedness, bliss, cheer, cheerfulness, cheeriness, contentment, delight, ecstasy, elation, enjoyment, exuberance, felicity, gaiety, gladness, high spirits, joy, jubilation, light-heartedness, merriment, pleasure, prosperity, satisfaction, well-being

happy 1. blessed, blest, blissful, blithe, cheerful, cock-a-hoop, content, contented, delighted, ecstatic, elated, glad, gratified, jolly, joyful, joyous, jubilant, merry, overjoyed, over the moon (*informal*), pleased, rapt, sunny, thrilled, walking on air (*informal*) **2.** ad-

fortunate or lucky: *it was a happy coincidence.* **4** satisfied or content: *he seems happy to let things go on as they are.* **5** willing: *I'll be happy to arrange a loan for you.* **happily** *adv* **happiness** *n*

happy-go-lucky *adj* carefree or easy-going.

hara-kiri *n* (formerly, in Japan) ritual suicide by disembowelment when disgraced or under sentence of death.

harangue *vb* **-ranguing, -rangued 1** to address (a person or group) in an angry or forcefully persuasive way. *~n* **2** a forceful or angry speech.

harass *vb* to trouble or annoy (someone) by repeated attacks, questions, or problems. **harassed** *adj* **harassment** *n*

harbinger (**har**-binge-er) *n Literary* a person or thing that announces or indicates the approach of something: *a harbinger of death.*

harbour *or US* **harbor** *n* **1** a sheltered port. **2** a place of refuge or safety. *~vb* **3** to maintain secretly in the mind: *he might be harbouring a death wish.* **4** to give shelter or protection to: *the government accused her of harbouring criminals.*

harbour master *n* an official in charge of a harbour.

hard *adj* **1** firm, solid, or rigid. **2** difficult to do or understand: *a hard sum.* **3** showing or requiring a lot of effort or application: *hard work.* **4** unkind or unfeeling: *she's very hard, no pity for anyone.* **5** causing pain, sorrow, or hardship: *the hard life of a northern settler.* **6** tough or violent: *a hard man.* **7** forceful: *a hard knock.* **8** cool or uncompromising: *we took a long hard look at our profit factor.* **9** indisputable and proven to be true: *hard facts.* **10** (of water) containing calcium salts which stop soap lathering freely. **11** practical, shrewd, or calculating: *he is a hard man in business.* **12** harsh: *hard light.* **13** (of currency) high and stable in exchange value. **14** (of alcoholic drink) being a spirit rather than a wine or beer. **15** (of a drug) highly addictive. **16** hard-core. **17** *Phonetics* denoting the consonants *c* and *g* when they are pronounced **as** in *cat* and *got.* **18** politically extreme: *the hard left.* **19** **hard of hearing** slightly deaf. **20** **hard up** *Informal* in need of money. *~adv* **21** with great energy or force: *they fought so hard and well in Spain.* **22** with great intensity: *thinking hard about the conversation.* **23** **hard by** very close to: *Cleveland Place, hard by Bruntsfield Square.* **24** **hard put (to it)** scarcely having the capacity (to do something). *~n* **25** **have a hard on** *Taboo slang* to have an erection of the penis. **hardness** *n*

hard-and-fast *adj* (of rules) fixed and not able to be changed.

hardback *n* **1** a book with stiff covers. *~adj* **2** of or denoting a hardback.

hard-bitten *adj Informal* tough and determined.

hardboard *n* stiff board made in thin sheets of compressed sawdust and wood chips.

hard-boiled *adj* **1** (of an egg) boiled until solid. **2** *Informal* tough, realistic, and unemotional.

hard cash *n* money or payment in money, as opposed to payment by cheque, credit, etc.

hard copy *n* computer output printed on paper.

hard core *n* **1** the members of a group who most resist change. **2** broken stones used to form a foundation for a road. *~adj* **hard-core 3** (of pornography) showing sexual acts in explicit detail.

hard disk *n Computers* an inflexible disk in a sealed container.

harden *vb* **1** to make or become hard; freeze, stiffen, or set. **2** to make or become tough or unfeeling: *life in the camp had hardened her considerably.* **3** to make or become stronger or firmer: *they hardened defences.* **4** to make or become more determined or resolute: *the government has hardened its attitude to the crisis.* **5**

THESAURUS

vantageous, appropriate, apt, auspicious, befitting, convenient, enviable, favourable, felicitous, fortunate, lucky, opportune, promising, propitious, satisfactory, seasonable, successful, timely, well-timed

happy-go-lucky blithe, carefree, casual, devil-may-care, easy-going, heedless, improvident, insouciant, irresponsible, light-hearted, nonchalant, unconcerned, untroubled

harangue 1. *vb.* address, declaim, exhort, hold forth, lecture, rant, spout (*informal*) **2.** *n.* address, declamation, diatribe, exhortation, lecture, oration, philippic, screed, speech, spiel (*informal*), tirade

harass annoy, badger, bait, beleaguer, be on one's back (*slang*), bother, chivvy (*Brit.*), devil (*informal*), disturb, exasperate, exhaust, fatigue, harry, hassle (*informal*), hound, perplex, persecute, pester, plague, tease, tire, torment, trouble, vex, weary, worry

harassed careworn, distraught, harried, hassled (*informal*), plagued, strained, tormented, troubled, under pressure, under stress, vexed, worried

harassment aggravation (*informal*), annoyance, badgering, bedevilment, bother, hassle (*informal*), irritation, molestation, nuisance, persecution, pestering, torment, trouble, vexation

harbour *n.* **1.** anchorage, destination, haven, port **2.** asylum, covert, haven, refuge, retreat, sanctuary, sanctum, security, shelter *~vb.* **3.** believe, brood over, cherish, cling to, entertain, foster, hold, imagine, maintain, nurse, nurture, retain **4.** conceal, hide, lodge, protect, provide refuge, relieve, secrete, shelter, shield

hard *adj.* **1.** compact, dense, firm, impenetrable, inflexible, rigid, rocklike, solid, stiff, stony, strong, tough, unyielding **2.** baffling, complex, complicated, difficult, intricate, involved, knotty, perplexing, puzzling, tangled, thorny, unfathomable **3.** arduous, backbreaking, burdensome, exacting, exhausting, fatiguing, formidable, Herculean, laborious, rigorous, strenuous, toilsome, tough, uphill, wearying **4.** callous, cold, cruel, exacting, grim, hardhearted, harsh, implacable, obdurate, pitiless, ruthless, severe, stern, strict, stubborn, unfeeling, unjust, unkind, unrelenting, unsparing, unsympathetic **5.** calamitous, dark, disagreeable, disastrous, distressing, grievous, grim, intolerable, painful, unpleasant **6.** driving, fierce, forceful, heavy, powerful, strong, violent **7.** *of truth or facts* actual, bare, cold, definite, indisputable, plain, undeniable, unvarnished, verified **8.** **hard up** bankrupt, broke (*informal*), bust (*informal*), cleaned out (*slang*), dirt-poor (*informal*), down and out, flat broke (*informal*), impecunious, impoverished, in the red (*informal*), on one's uppers (*informal*), out of pocket, penniless, poor, short, short of cash *or* funds, skint (*Brit. slang*), without two pennies to rub together (*informal*) *~adv.* **9.** energetically, fiercely, forcefully, forcibly, heavily, intensely, powerfully, severely, sharply, strongly, vigorously, violently, with all one's might, with might and main **10.** assiduously, determinedly, diligently, doggedly, earnestly, industriously, intently, persistently, steadily, strenuously, untiringly

hard and fast binding, immutable, incontrovertible, inflexible, invariable, rigid, set, strict, stringent, unalterable

hard-bitten *or* **hard-boiled** case-hardened, cynical, down-to-earth, hard-headed, hard-nosed (*informal*), matter-of-fact, practical, realistic, shrewd, tough, unsentimental

hard-core explicit, obscene

harden 1. anneal, bake, cake, freeze, set, solidify,

Commerce (of prices or a market) to cease to fluctuate.

hardened *adj* toughened by experience: *a hardened criminal.*

hard-headed *adj* tough, realistic, or shrewd, esp. in business.

hardhearted *adj* unsympathetic and uncaring.

hardihood *n* courage or daring.

hard labour *n* difficult and tiring physical work: used as a punishment for a crime in some countries.

hard line *n* **1** an uncompromising policy. ~*adj* **hard-line 2** tough and uncompromising: *a hard-line attitude to the refugee problem.* **hardliner** *n*

hardly *adv* **1** scarcely; barely: *he'd hardly sipped his whisky.* **2** *Ironic* not at all: *it was hardly in the Great Train Robbery league.* **3** with difficulty: *their own families would hardly recognize them.*

➤ *Hardly* already has a negative sense and is not used with *no* or *not.*

hard pad *n* (in dogs) an abnormal increase in the thickness of the foot pads: a sign of distemper.

hard palate *n* the bony front part of the roof of the mouth.

hard-pressed *adj* **1** under a great deal of strain and worry: *hard-pressed companies having to cut costs.* **2** closely pursued.

hard science *n* one of the natural or physical sciences, such as physics, chemistry, or biology.

hard sell *n* an aggressive insistent technique of selling.

hardship *n* **1** conditions of life that are difficult to endure. **2** something that causes suffering.

hard shoulder *n Brit* a surfaced verge running along the edge of a motorway for emergency stops.

hardtack *n* a kind of hard saltless biscuit, formerly eaten by sailors.

hardware *n* **1** metal tools or implements, esp. cutlery or cooking utensils. **2** *Computers* the physical equipment used in a computer system. **3** heavy military equipment, such as tanks and missiles.

hard-wired *adj* (of a circuit or instruction) permanently wired into a computer.

hardwood *n* the wood of a deciduous tree such as oak, beech, or ash.

hardy *adj* **-dier, -diest 1** able to stand difficult conditions. **2** (of plants) able to live out of doors throughout the winter. **hardiness** *n*

hare *n, pl* **hares** *or* **hare 1** a mammal like a large rabbit, with longer ears and legs. ~*vb* **haring, hared 2** (foll. by *off* or *after*) *Brit informal* to run fast or wildly.

harebell *n* a blue bell-shaped flower.

harebrained *adj* foolish or impractical: *harebrained schemes.*

harelip *n* a slight split in the mid line of the upper lip.

harem *n* **1** a Muslim man's wives and concubines collectively. **2** the part of an Oriental house reserved for wives and concubines.

haricot bean *or* **haricot** (**har**-rik-oh) *n* a white edible bean, which can be dried.

hark *vb Old-fashioned* to listen; pay attention: *hark, the cocks are crowing.*

hark back *vb* to return (to an earlier subject in speech or thought): *he keeps harking back to his music-hall days.*

harlequin *n* **1** *Theatre* a stock comic character, usually wearing a diamond-patterned multicoloured costume and a black mask. ~*adj* **2** in varied colours.

harlequinade *n Theatre* a play in which harlequin has a leading role.

harlot *n Literary* a prostitute. **harlotry** *n*

harm *vb* **1** to injure physically, morally, or mentally. ~*n* **2** physical, moral, or mental injury.

harmful *adj* causing or tending to cause harm, esp. to a person's health.

harmless *adj* **1** safe to use, touch, or be near. **2** unlikely to annoy or worry people: *a harmless habit.*

harmonic *adj* **1** of, producing, or characterized by harmony; harmonious. ~*n* **2** *Music* an overtone of a musical note produced when that note is played, but not usually heard as a separate note. ~See also **harmonics. harmonically** *adv*

harmonica *n* a small wind instrument in which reeds enclosed in a narrow oblong box are made to vibrate by blowing and sucking.

harmonics *n* the science of musical sounds.

harmonious *adj* **1** (esp. of colours or sounds) consisting of parts which blend together well. **2** showing

THESAURUS

stiffen **2.** accustom, brutalize, case-harden, habituate, inure, season, train **3.** brace, buttress, fortify, gird, indurate, nerve, reinforce, steel, strengthen, toughen

hardened accustomed, habituated, inured, seasoned, toughened

hard-headed astute, cool, hard-boiled (*informal*), level-headed, practical, pragmatic, realistic, sensible, shrewd, tough, unsentimental

hardhearted callous, cold, cruel, hard, heartless, indifferent, inhuman, insensitive, intolerant, merciless, pitiless, stony, uncaring, unfeeling, unkind, unsympathetic

hard-line definite, inflexible, intransigent, tough, uncompromising, undeviating, unyielding

hardly 1. almost not, barely, faintly, infrequently, just, only, only just, scarcely **2.** by no means, not at all, not quite, no way **3.** with difficulty

hard-pressed harried, hotly pursued, in difficulties, pushed (*informal*), under attack, under pressure, up against it (*informal*), with one's back to the wall

hardship adversity, affliction, austerity, burden, calamity, destitution, difficulty, fatigue, grievance, labour, misery, misfortune, need, oppression, persecution, privation, suffering, toil, torment, trial, tribulation, trouble, want

hardy firm, fit, hale, healthy, hearty, in fine fettle, lusty, robust, rugged, sound, stalwart, stout, strong, sturdy, tough, vigorous

hark back look back, recall, recollect, regress, remember, revert, think back

harlot *literary* call girl, fallen woman, hussy, loose woman, pro (*slang*), prostitute, scrubber (*slang*), streetwalker, strumpet, tart (*informal*), tramp (*slang*), whore

harm 1. *vb.* abuse, blemish, damage, hurt, ill-treat, ill-use, impair, injure, maltreat, mar, molest, ruin, spoil, wound **2.** *n.* abuse, damage, detriment, disservice, hurt, ill, impairment, injury, loss, mischief, misfortune

harmful baleful, baneful, damaging, deleterious, destructive, detrimental, disadvantageous, evil, hurtful, injurious, maleficent, noxious, pernicious

harmless 1. innoxious, nontoxic, not dangerous, safe **2.** gentle, innocent, innocuous, inoffensive, unobjectionable

harmonious 1. agreeable, compatible, concordant, congruous, consonant, coordinated, correspondent, dulcet, euphonic, euphonious, harmonic, harmonizing,

agreement, peacefulness, and friendship: *a harmonious relationship.* **3** tuneful or melodious.

harmonium *n* a musical keyboard instrument in which air from pedal-operated bellows causes the reeds to vibrate.

harmonize *or* **-nise** *vb* **-nizing, -nized** *or* **-nising, -nised 1** to sing or play in harmony, such as with another singer or player. **2** to make or become harmonious.

harmony *n, pl* **-nies 1** a state of peaceful agreement and cooperation. **2** *Music* a pleasant combination of two or more notes sounded at the same time. **3** the way parts combine well together or into a whole.

harness *n* **1** an arrangement of straps for attaching a horse to a cart or plough. **2** something resembling this, for attaching something to a person's body: *a parachute harness.* **3 in harness** at one's routine work. *~vb* **4** to put a harness on (a horse or other animal). **5** to control something in order to make use of it: *learning to harness the power of your own mind.*

harp *n* **1** a large upright triangular stringed instrument played by plucking the strings with the fingers. *~vb* **2 harp on** to speak in a persistent and tedious manner (about a subject). **harpist** *n*

harpoon *n* **1** a barbed spear attached to a long rope and thrown or fired when hunting whales, etc. *~vb* **2** to spear with a harpoon.

harpsichord *n* a keyboard instrument, resembling a small piano, with strings that are plucked mechanically.

harpy *n, pl* **-pies** a violent, unpleasant, or greedy woman.

harridan *n* a scolding old woman; nag.

harrier[1] *n* a cross-country runner.

harrier[2] *n* a bird of prey with broad wings and long legs and tail.

harrow *n* **1** an implement used to break up clods of soil. *~vb* **2** to draw a harrow over (land).

harrowing *adj* very upsetting or disturbing.

harry *vb* **-ries, -rying, -ried** keep asking (someone) to do something; pester.

harsh *adj* **1** severe and difficult to cope with: *harsh winters.* **2** unkind and showing no understanding: *the Judge was very harsh on the demonstrators.* **3** excessively hard, bright, or rough: *harsh sunlight.* **4** (of sounds) unpleasant and grating. **harshly** *adv* **harshness** *n*

hart *n, pl* **harts** *or* **hart** the male of the deer, esp. the red deer.

hartebeest *n* a large African antelope with curved horns and a fawn-coloured coat.

harum-scarum *adj* **1** reckless. *~adv* **2** recklessly. *~n* **3** an impetuous person.

harvest *n* **1** the gathering of a ripened crop. **2** the crop itself. **3** the season for gathering crops. **4** the product of an effort or action. *~vb* **5** to gather (a ripened crop).

harvester *n* **1** a harvesting machine, esp. a combine harvester. **2** a person who harvests.

harvest festival *n* **1** a Christian church service held every year to thank God for the harvest. **2** any of various ceremonies celebrating the harvest in other religions.

harvest moon *n* the full moon occurring nearest to the autumn equinox.

harvest mouse *n* a very small reddish-brown mouse that lives in cornfields or hedgerows.

has *vb* third person singular of the present tense of **have.**

has-been *n Informal* a person who is no longer popular or successful.

hash[1] *n* **1** a dish of diced cooked meat, vegetables, etc., reheated: *corned-beef hash.* **2** a reworking of old material. **3 make a hash of** *Informal* to mess up or destroy.

hash[2] *n Slang* short for **hashish.**

hashish (**hash**-eesh) *n* a drug made from the hemp plant, smoked for its intoxicating effects.

hasn't has not.

hasp *n* a clasp which fits over a staple and is secured by a pin, bolt, or padlock, used as a fastening.

THESAURUS

matching, mellifluous, melodious, musical, sweet-sounding, symphonious (*literary*), tuneful **2.** agreeable, amicable, compatible, concordant, congenial, cordial, *en rapport,* fraternal, friendly, in accord, in harmony, in unison, of one mind, sympathetic

harmonize accord, adapt, agree, arrange, attune, be in unison, be of one mind, blend, chime with, cohere, compose, coordinate, correspond, match, reconcile, suit, tally, tone in with

harmony 1. accord, agreement, amicability, amity, assent, compatibility, concord, conformity, consensus, cooperation, friendship, goodwill, like-mindedness, peace, rapport, sympathy, unanimity, understanding, unity **2.** euphony, melodiousness, melody, tune, tunefulness, unison **3.** balance, compatibility, concord, congruity, consistency, consonance, coordination, correspondence, fitness, parallelism, suitability, symmetry

harness *n.* **1.** equipment, gear, tack, tackle, trappings **2. in harness** active, at work, busy, in action, working *~vb.* **3.** couple, hitch up, put in harness, saddle, yoke **4.** apply, channel, control, employ, exploit, make productive, mobilize, render useful, turn to account, utilize

harp *with* **on** *or* **upon** dwell on, go on, labour, press, reiterate, renew, repeat

harrowing agonizing, alarming, chilling, distressing, disturbing, excruciating, frightening, heartbreaking, heart-rending, nerve-racking, painful, racking, scaring, terrifying, tormenting, traumatic

harry annoy, badger, bedevil, be on one's back (*slang*), bother, chivvy, disturb, fret, get in one's hair (*informal*), harass, hassle (*informal*), molest, persecute, pester, plague, tease, torment, trouble, vex, worry

harsh 1. abusive, austere, bitter, bleak, brutal, comfortless, cruel, dour, Draconian, drastic, grim, hard, pitiless, punitive, relentless, ruthless, severe, sharp, Spartan, stern, stringent, unfeeling, unkind, unpleasant, unrelenting **2.** coarse, croaking, crude, discordant, dissonant, glaring, grating, guttural, jarring, rasping, raucous, rough, strident, unmelodious

harshly brutally, cruelly, grimly, roughly, severely, sharply, sternly, strictly

harshness acerbity, acrimony, asperity, austerity, bitterness, brutality, churlishness, coarseness, crudity, hardness, ill-temper, rigour, roughness, severity, sourness, sternness

harvest *n.* **1.** harvesting, harvest-time, ingathering, reaping **2.** crop, produce, yield **3.** consequence, effect, fruition, product, result, return *~vb.* **4.** gather, mow, pick, pluck, reap

hash 1. balls-up (*taboo slang*), cock-up (*Brit. slang*), confusion, fuck-up (*offensive taboo slang*), hodgepodge (*U.S.*), hotchpotch, jumble, mess, mishmash, mix-up, muddle, pig's breakfast (*informal*), pig's ear (*informal*), shambles, state **2. make a hash of** *infor-*

hassle *Informal* ~*n* **1** a great deal of trouble. **2** a prolonged argument. ~*vb* **-sling, -sled 3** to cause annoyance or trouble to (someone).

hassock *n* a cushion for kneeling on in church.

haste *n* **1** speed, esp. in an action. **2** the act of hurrying in a careless manner. **3 make haste** to hurry or rush. ~*vb* **hasting, hasted 4** *Poetic* to hasten.

hasten *vb* **1** to hurry or cause to hurry. **2** to be anxious (to say something).

hasty *adj* **-tier, -tiest 1** done or happening suddenly or quickly. **2** done too quickly and without thought; rash. **hastily** *adv*

hat *n* **1** a head covering, often with a brim, usually worn to give protection from the weather. **2** *Informal* a role or capacity: *I'm wearing my honorary consul's hat.* **3 keep something under one's hat** to keep something secret. **4 pass the hat round** to collect money for a cause. **5 take off one's hat to someone** to admire or congratulate someone.

hatband *n* a band or ribbon around the base of the crown of a hat.

hatch[1] *vb* **1** to cause (the young of various animals, esp. birds) to emerge from the egg or (of young birds, etc.) to emerge from the egg. **2** (of eggs) to break and release the young animal within. **3** to devise (a plot or plan).

hatch[2] *n* **1** a hinged door covering an opening in a floor or wall. **2 a** short for **hatchway. b** a door in an aircraft or spacecraft. **3** Also called: **serving hatch** an opening in a wall between a kitchen and a dining area. **4** *Informal* short for **hatchback.**

hatch[3] *vb Drawing, engraving, etc* to mark (a figure, etc.) with fine parallel or crossed lines to indicate shading. **hatching** *n*

hatchback *n* a car with a single lifting door in the rear.

hatchet *n* **1** a short axe used for chopping wood, etc. **2** ~*adj* narrow and sharp: *a hatchet face.* **3 bury the hatchet** to make peace or resolve a disagreement.

hatchet job *n Informal* a malicious verbal or written attack.

hatchet man *n Informal* a person who carries out unpleasant tasks on behalf of an employer.

hatchway *n* an opening in the deck of a vessel to provide access below.

hate *vb* **hating, hated 1** to dislike (someone or something) intensely. **2** to be unwilling (to do something): *I hate to trouble you.* ~*n* **3** intense dislike. **4** *Informal* a person or thing that is hated: *my own pet hate is restaurants.*

hateful *adj* causing or deserving hate.

hatred *n* intense dislike.

hatter *n* **1** a person who makes and sells hats. **2 mad as a hatter** eccentric.

hat trick *n* **1** *Cricket* the achievement of a bowler in taking three wickets with three successive balls. **2** any achievement of three successive goals, victories, etc.

hauberk *n History* a long sleeveless coat of mail.

haughty *adj* **-tier, -tiest** having or showing excessive pride or arrogance. **haughtily** *adv* **haughtiness** *n*

haul *vb* **1** to drag or pull (something) with effort. **2** to transport, such as in a lorry. **3** *Naut* to alter the course of (a vessel). ~*n* **4** the act of dragging with effort. **5** a quantity of something obtained: *a good haul of fish; a huge haul of stolen goods.* **6 long haul a** a long journey. **b** a long difficult process.

haulage *n* **1** the business of transporting goods. **2** a charge for transporting goods.

haulier *n Brit* a person or firm that transports goods by road.

haulm **(hawm)** *n* the stalks of beans, peas, or potatoes collectively.

haunch *n* **1** the human hip or fleshy hindquarter of an animal. **2** the leg and loin of an animal, used for food.

THESAURUS

mal bodge (*informal*), botch, bungle, cock up (*Brit. slang*), fuck up (*offensive taboo slang*), jumble, mess up, mishandle, mismanage, mix, muddle

hassle *n.* **1.** bother, difficulty, inconvenience, problem, struggle, trial, trouble, upset **2.** altercation, argument, bickering, disagreement, dispute, fight, quarrel, row, squabble, tussle, wrangle ~*vb.* **3.** annoy, badger, be on one's back (*slang*), bother, bug (*informal*), get in one's hair (*informal*), get on one's nerves (*informal*), harass, harry, hound, pester

haste 1. alacrity, briskness, celerity, dispatch, expedition, fleetness, nimbleness, promptitude, quickness, rapidity, rapidness, speed, swiftness, urgency, velocity **2.** bustle, hastiness, helter-skelter, hurry, hustle, impetuosity, precipitateness, rashness, recklessness, rush

hasten accelerate, advance, barrel (along) (*informal, chiefly U.S. & Canad.*), beetle, bolt, burn rubber (*informal*), dash, dispatch, expedite, fly, goad, haste, hurry (up), make haste, precipitate, press, push forward, quicken, race, run, rush, scurry, scuttle, speed, speed (up), sprint, step on it (*informal*), step up (*informal*), tear (along), urge

hastily 1. apace, double-quick, fast, hotfoot, posthaste, promptly, pronto (*informal*), quickly, rapidly, speedily, straightaway **2.** heedlessly, hurriedly, impetuously, impulsively, on the spur of the moment, precipitately, rashly, recklessly, too quickly

hasty 1. brief, brisk, cursory, eager, expeditious, fast, fleet, fleeting, hurried, passing, perfunctory, prompt, rapid, rushed, short, speedy, superficial, swift, urgent **2.** foolhardy, headlong, heedless, impetuous, impulsive, indiscreet, precipitate, rash, reckless, thoughtless, unduly quick

hatch 1. breed, bring forth, brood, incubate **2.** conceive, concoct, contrive, cook up (*informal*), design, devise, dream up (*informal*), manufacture, plan, plot, project, scheme, think up, trump up

hatchet man assassin, bravo, calumniator, cutthroat, debunker, defamer, destroyer, detractor, gunman, heavy (*slang*), hired assassin, hit man (*slang*), killer, murderer, smear campaigner, thug, traducer

hate *vb.* **1.** abhor, abominate, be hostile to, be repelled by, be sick of, despise, detest, dislike, execrate, have an aversion to, loathe, recoil from **2.** be loath, be reluctant, be sorry, be unwilling, dislike, feel disinclined, have no stomach for, shrink from ~*n.* **3.** abhorrence, abomination, animosity, animus, antagonism, antipathy, aversion, detestation, dislike, enmity, execration, hatred, hostility, loathing, odium

hateful abhorrent, abominable, despicable, detestable, disgusting, execrable, forbidding, foul, heinous, horrible, loathsome, obnoxious, obscene, odious, offensive, repellent, repugnant, repulsive, revolting, vile

hatred abomination, animosity, animus, antagonism, antipathy, aversion, detestation, dislike, enmity, execration, hate, ill will, odium, repugnance, revulsion

haughty arrogant, assuming, conceited, contemptuous, disdainful, high, high and mighty (*informal*), hoity-toity (*informal*), imperious, lofty, overweening, proud, scornful, snobbish, snooty (*informal*), stuck-up (*informal*), supercilious, uppish (*Brit. informal*)

haul *vb.* **1.** drag, draw, hale, heave, lug, pull, tow, trail, tug **2.** carry, cart, convey, hump (*Brit. slang*), move,

haunt *vb* **1** to visit (a person or place) in the form of a ghost. **2** to remain in the memory or thoughts of: *it was a belief which haunted her.* **3** to visit (a place) frequently. ~*n* **4** a place visited frequently.
haunted *adj* **1** (of a place) frequented or visited by ghosts. **2** (of a person) obsessed or worried.
haunting *adj* having a quality of great beauty or sadness so as to be memorable: *a haunting melody.*
hautboy (**oh**-boy) *n Old-fashioned* an oboe.
haute couture (**oat** koo-**ture**) *n* high fashion.
hauteur (oat-**ur**) *n* haughtiness.
Havana *n* a fine-quality cigar.
have *vb* **has, having, had 1** to possess: *he has a massive collection of old movies; I have an iron constitution.* **2** to receive, take, or obtain: *I had a long letter.* **3** to hold in the mind: *she always had a yearning to be a schoolteacher.* **4** to possess a knowledge of: *I have no German.* **5** to experience or be affected by: *a good way to have a change.* **6** to suffer from: *to have a blood pressure problem.* **7** to gain control of or advantage over: *you have me on that point.* **8** *Slang* to cheat or outwit: *I've been had.* **9** to show: *have mercy on me.* **10** to take part in; hold: *I had a telephone conversation.* **11** to cause to be done: *have my shoes mended by Friday.* **12 have to** used to express compulsion or necessity: *you'd have to wait six months.* **13** to eat or drink. **14** *Taboo slang* to have sexual intercourse with. **15** to tolerate or allow: *I won't have all this noise.* **16** to receive as a guest: *we have visitors.* **17** to be pregnant with or give birth to (offspring). **18** used to form past tenses: *I have gone; I had gone.* **19 have had it** *Informal* **a** to be exhausted or killed. **b** to have lost one's last chance. **20 have it off** *Taboo, Brit slang* to have sexual intercourse. ~*n* **21 haves** *Informal* people who have wealth, security, etc.: *the haves and the have-nots.* ~See also **have on, have out,** etc.
haven *n* **1** a place of safety. **2** a harbour for shipping.
haven't have not.
have on *vb* **1** to wear: *he'd got a long pair of trousers on.* **2** to have a commitment: *what do you have on this afternoon?* **3** *Informal* to trick or tease: *he's having you on.* **4** to have (information, esp. when incriminating) about (a person): *she's got something on him.*
have out *vb* to settle (a matter), esp. by fighting or by frank discussion: *I went to Carl's office to have it out with him.*
haver *vb* **1** *Scot & N English dialect* to talk nonsense. **2** to be unsure and hesitant; dither.
haversack *n* a canvas bag carried on the back or shoulder.
have up *vb* to bring to trial: *what, and get me had up for kidnapping?*
havoc *n* **1** *Informal* chaos, disorder, and confusion. **2 play havoc with** to cause a great deal of damage or confusion to.
haw[1] *n* the fruit of the hawthorn.
haw[2] *vb* **hum** *or* **hem and haw** to hesitate in speaking.
hawk[1] *n* **1** a bird of prey with short rounded wings and a long tail. **2** a supporter or advocate of warlike policies. ~*vb* **3** to hunt with falcons or hawks. **hawkish** *adj* **hawklike** *adj*
hawk[2] *vb* to offer (goods) for sale in the street or door-to-door.
hawk[3] *vb* **1** to clear the throat noisily. **2** to force (phlegm) up from the throat.
hawker *n* a person who travels from place to place selling goods.
hawk-eyed *adj* having extremely keen eyesight.
hawser *n Naut* a large heavy rope.
hawthorn *n* a thorny tree or shrub with white or pink flowers and reddish fruits.
hay *n* **1** grass cut and dried as fodder. **2 hit the hay** *Slang* to go to bed. **3 make hay while the sun shines** to take full advantage of an opportunity.
hay fever *n* an allergic reaction to pollen, which causes sneezing, runny nose, and watery eyes.
haystack *or* **hayrick** *n* a large pile of hay built in the open and covered with thatch.
haywire *adj* **go haywire** *Informal* to stop functioning properly.
hazard *n* **1** a thing likely to cause injury, loss, etc. **2 at hazard** at risk. **3** risk or likelihood of injury, loss, etc.: *evaluate the level of hazard in a situation.* **4** *Golf* an obstacle such as a bunker. ~*vb* **5** to risk: *hazarding the health of his crew.* **6 hazard a guess** to make a guess.
hazard lights *or* **hazard warning lights** *n* a device on a motor vehicle which when switched on causes all the direction indicator lights to flash simultaneously.
hazardous *adj* involving great risk.
haze *n* **1** *Meteorol* reduced visibility as a result of condensed water vapour, dust, etc., in the air. **2** confused or unclear understanding or feeling.
hazel *n* **1** a shrub with edible rounded nuts. ~*adj* **2** greenish-brown: *hazel eyes.*
hazelnut *n* the nut of a hazel shrub, which has a smooth shiny hard shell.

THESAURUS

transport ~*n.* **3.** drag, heave, pull, tug **4.** booty, catch, find, gain, harvest, loot, spoils, takings, yield
haunt *vb.* **1.** visit, walk **2.** beset, come back, obsess, plague, possess, prey on, recur, stay with, torment, trouble, weigh on **3.** frequent, hang around *or* about, repair, resort, visit ~*n.* **4.** den, gathering place, hangout (*informal*), meeting place, rendezvous, resort, stamping ground
haunted 1. cursed, eerie, ghostly, jinxed, possessed, spooky (*informal*) **2.** obsessed, plagued, preoccupied, tormented, troubled, worried
haunting disturbing, eerie, evocative, indelible, nostalgic, persistent, poignant, recurrent, recurring, unforgettable
have 1. hold, keep, obtain, occupy, own, possess, retain **2.** accept, acquire, gain, get, obtain, procure, receive, secure, take **3.** endure, enjoy, experience, feel, meet with, suffer, sustain, undergo **4.** *slang* cheat, deceive, dupe, fool, outwit, stiff (*slang*), swindle, take in (*informal*), trick **5.** comprehend, comprise, contain, embody, include, take in **6. have to** be bound, be compelled, be forced, be obliged, have got to, must, ought, should **7.** allow, consider, entertain, permit, put up with (*informal*), think about, tolerate **8.** bear, beget, bring forth, bring into the world, deliver, give birth to **9. have had it** *informal* be defeated, be exhausted, be finished, be out, be past it (*informal*), be pooped (*U.S. slang*)
haven 1. asylum, refuge, retreat, sanctuary, sanctum, shelter **2.** anchorage, harbour, port
have on 1. be clothed in, be dressed in, wear **2.** be committed to, be engaged to, have on the agenda, have planned **3.** deceive, kid (*informal*), play a joke on, tease, trick, wind up (*Brit. slang*)
havoc 1. *informal* chaos, confusion, disorder, disruption, mayhem, shambles **2. play havoc with** bring into chaos, confuse, demolish, destroy, devastate, disorganize, disrupt, wreck
hawk market, peddle, sell, tout (*informal*), vend
hazardous dangerous, dicey (*informal, chiefly Brit.*),

hazy *adj* **-zier, -ziest 1** (of the sky or a view) unable to be seen clearly because of dust or heat. **2** dim or vague: *my memory is a little hazy on this.* **hazily** *adv* **haziness** *n*

Hb haemoglobin.

HB *Brit* (of pencil lead) hard-black: denoting a medium-hard lead.

H-bomb *n* short for **hydrogen bomb.**

h & c hot and cold (water).

he *pron* refers to: **1** a male person or animal. **2** a person or animal of unknown or unspecified sex: *a member may vote as he sees fit.* ~*n* **3** a male person or animal: *a he-goat.*

➤ Try to avoid the use of *he* as a pronoun of general reference. It can appear sexist if the reference is to both men and women.

He *Chem* helium.

HE His *or* Her Excellency.

head *n* **1** the upper or front part of the body that contains the brain, eyes, mouth, nose, and ears. **2** a person's mind and mental abilities: *I haven't any head for figures.* **3** the most forward part of a thing: *the head of a queue.* **4** the highest part of a thing; upper end: *the head of the pass.* **5** something resembling a head in form or function, such as the top of a tool. **6** the position of leadership or command. **7** the person commanding most authority within a group or an organization. **8** *Bot* the top part of a plant, where the leaves or flowers grow in a cluster. **9** a culmination or crisis: *the matter came to a head in December 1928.* **10** the froth on the top of a glass of beer. **11** the pus-filled tip of a pimple or boil. **12** part of a computer or tape recorder that can read, write, or erase information. **13** the source of a river or stream. **14** the side of a coin that usually bears a portrait of the head of a monarch, etc. **15** a headland or promontory: *Beachy Head.* **16** pressure of water or steam in an enclosed space. **17** (*pl* **head**) a person or animal considered as a unit: *the cost per head of Paris's refuse collection; six hundred head of cattle.* **18** a headline or heading. **19** *Informal* short for **headmaster, headmistress** or **head teacher. 20** *Informal* short for **headache. 21 give someone his head** to allow someone greater freedom or responsibility. **22 go to one's head a** (of an alcoholic drink) to make one slightly drunk. **b** to make one conceited: *success has gone to his head.* **23 head over heels (in love)** very much (in love). **24 keep one's head** to remain calm. **25 not make head nor tail of** not to understand (a problem, etc.). **26 off one's head** *Slang* very foolish or insane. **27 on one's own head** at a one's own risk. **28 over someone's head a** to a higher authority: *the taboo of going over the head of their immediate boss.* **b** beyond a person's understanding. **29 put our, your,** *or* **their heads together** *Informal* to consult together. **30 turn someone's head** to make someone conceited. ~*vb* **31** to be at the front or top of: *Barnes headed the list.* **32** to be in charge of. **33** (often foll. by *for*) to go or cause to go (towards): *to head for the Channel ports.* **34** *Soccer* to propel (the ball) by striking it with the head. **35** to provide with a heading. ~See also **head off, heads.**

headache *n* **1** a continuous pain in the head. **2** *Informal* any cause of worry, difficulty, or annoyance.

head-banger *n Slang* **1** a person who shakes his head violently to the beat of heavy-metal music. **2** a crazy or stupid person.

headboard *n* a vertical board at the head of a bed.

headdress *n* any decorative head covering.

headed *adj* **1** having a head or heads: *two-headed; bald-headed.* **2** having a heading: *headed notepaper.*

header *n* **1** *Soccer* the action of striking a ball with the head. **2** *Informal* a headlong fall or dive.

headfirst *adv* **1** with the head foremost. **2** quickly and without thinking carefully: *she jumped into marriage headfirst.*

headgear *n* hats collectively.

head-hunting *n* **1** (of companies) the practice of actively searching for new high-level personnel, often from rival companies. **2** the practice among certain peoples of removing the heads of enemies they have killed and preserving them as trophies. **head-hunter** *n*

heading *n* **1** a title for a page, chapter, etc. **2** a main division, such as of a speech. **3** *Mining* a horizontal tunnel.

headland *n* a narrow area of land jutting out into a sea.

headlight *or* **headlamp** *n* a powerful light on the front of a vehicle.

headline *n* **1** a phrase in heavy large type at the top of a newspaper or magazine article indicating the subject. **2** (*pl*) the main points of a television or radio news broadcast.

headlong *adv, adj* **1** with the head foremost; headfirst. **2** with great haste and without much thought: *they rushed headlong into buying a house.*

THESAURUS

difficult, fraught with danger, hairy (*slang*), insecure, perilous, precarious, risky, unsafe

haze cloud, dimness, film, fog, mist, obscurity, smog, smokiness, steam, vapour

hazy 1. blurry, cloudy, dim, dull, faint, foggy, misty, nebulous, obscure, overcast, smoky, veiled **2.** fuzzy, ill-defined, indefinite, indistinct, loose, muddled, muzzy, nebulous, uncertain, unclear, vague

head *n.* **1.** conk (*slang*), cranium, crown, noddle (*informal, chiefly Brit.*), noggin, nut (*slang*), pate, skull **2.** ability, aptitude, brain, brains (*informal*), capacity, faculty, flair, intellect, intelligence, mentality, mind, talent, thought, understanding **3.** beginning, fore, forefront, front, start **4.** cutting edge, first place, fore, forefront, van, vanguard **5.** apex, crest, crown, height, peak, pitch, summit, tip, top, vertex **6.** boss (*informal*), captain, chief, chieftain, commander, director, headmaster, headmistress, head teacher, leader, manager, master, principal, superintendent, supervisor **7.** climax, conclusion, crisis, culmination, end, turning point **8.** cape, foreland, headland, point, promontory **9.** branch, category, class, department, division, heading, section, subject, topic **10. go to one's head** dizzy, excite, intoxicate, make conceited, puff up **11. head over heels** completely, intensely, thoroughly, uncontrollably, utterly, wholeheartedly **12. put our, your, or their heads together** *informal* confab (*informal*), confabulate, confer, consult, deliberate, discuss, palaver, powwow, talk over ~*vb.* **13.** be *or* go first, cap, crown, lead, lead the way, precede, top **14.** be in charge of, command, control, direct, govern, guide, lead, manage, rule, run, supervise **15.** *often with* **for** aim, go to, make a beeline for, make for, point, set off for, set out, start towards, steer, turn

headache 1. head (*informal*), migraine, neuralgia **2.** *informal* bane, bother, inconvenience, nuisance, problem, trouble, vexation, worry

headfirst 1. *adj./adv.* diving, headlong, head-on **2.** *adv.* carelessly, hastily, head over heels, precipitately, rashly, recklessly

heading 1. caption, headline, name, rubric, title **2.** category, class, division, section

headlong 1. *adj./adv.* headfirst, headforemost, head-on **2.** *adj.* breakneck, dangerous, hasty, impetuous, impulsive, inconsiderate, precipitate, reckless,

headmaster *or fem* **headmistress** *n* the principal of a school.
head off *vb* **1** to intercept and force to change direction: *police head off New Age travellers.* **2** to prevent or avert: *trying to head off the prospect of civil war.*
head-on *adv, adj* **1** front foremost: *a head-on collision.* **2** with directness or without compromise: *a head-on confrontation with the unions.*
headphones *pl n* two small loudspeakers held against the ears by a strap, worn to listen to the radio or recorded music without other people hearing it.
headquarters *pl n* any centre from which operations are directed.
headroom *or* **headway** *n* the space below a roof or bridge which allows an object to pass or stay underneath it without touching it.
heads *adv* with the side of a coin uppermost which has a portrait of a head on it.
headship *n* the position or state of being a leader, esp. the head teacher of a school.
headshrinker *n Slang* a psychiatrist.
headstall *n* the part of a bridle that fits round a horse's head.
head start *n* an initial advantage in a competitive situation.
headstone *n* a memorial stone at the head of a grave.
headstrong *adj* determined to do something in one's own way and ignoring the advice of others.
head teacher *n* the principal of a school.
head-to-head *adv, adj Informal* in direct competition.
headwaters *pl n* the tributary streams of a river in the area in which it rises.
headway *n* **1** progress towards achieving something: *have the police made any headway?* **2** motion forward: *we felt our way out to the open sea, barely making headway.* **3** same as **headroom.**
headwind *n* a wind blowing directly against the course of an aircraft or ship.
heady *adj* **headier, headiest 1** (of an experience or period of time) extremely exciting. **2** (of alcoholic drink, atmosphere, etc.) strongly affecting the physical senses: *a powerful, heady scent of cologne.* **3** rash and impetuous.
heal *vb* **1** (of a wound) to repair by natural processes, such as by scar formation. **2** to restore (someone) to health. **3** to repair (a rift in a personal relationship or an emotional wound). **healer** *n* **healing** *n, adj*
health *n* **1** the general condition of body and mind: *better health.* **2** the state of being bodily and mentally vigorous and free from disease. **3** the condition of an organization, society, etc.: *the economic health of the republics.*
health centre *n* the surgery and offices of the doctors in a district.
health farm *n* a residential establishment for people wishing to improve their health by losing weight, exercising, etc.
health food *n* natural food, organically grown and free from additives.
healthful *adj* same as **healthy** (senses 1, 2, 3).
health visitor *n* (in Britain) a nurse employed to visit mothers, their preschool children, and the elderly in their homes.
healthy *adj* **healthier, healthiest 1** having or showing good health. **2** likely to produce good health: *healthy seaside air.* **3** functioning well or being sound: *this is a very healthy business to be in.* **4** *Informal* considerable: *healthy profits.* **5** sensible: *a healthy scepticism about his promises.* **healthily** *adv* **healthiness** *n*
heap *n* **1** a pile of things lying one on top of another. **2** (*often pl*) *Informal* a large number or quantity. *~adv* **3 heaps** much: *he was heaps better.* *~vb* **4** to collect into a pile. **5** to give freely (to): *film roles were heaped on her.*
hear *vb* **hearing, heard 1** to perceive (a sound) with the sense of hearing. **2** to listen to: *I didn't want to hear what he had to say.* **3** to be informed (of something); receive information (about something): *I hear you mean to join the crusade.* **4** *Law* to give a hearing to (a case). **5 hear of** to allow: *she wouldn't hear of it.* **6 hear from** to receive a letter or telephone call from. **7 hear! hear!** an exclamation of approval. **hearer** *n*
hearing *n* **1** the sense by which sound is perceived. **2** an opportunity for someone to be listened to. **3** the

THESAURUS

thoughtless **3.** *adv.* hastily, heedlessly, helter-skelter, hurriedly, pell-mell, precipitately, rashly, thoughtlessly, wildly
head off 1. block off, cut off, deflect, divert, intercept, interpose, intervene **2.** avert, fend off, forestall, parry, prevent, stop, ward off
headstrong contrary, foolhardy, froward, heedless, imprudent, impulsive, intractable, mulish, obstinate, perverse, pig-headed, rash, reckless, self-willed, stiff-necked, stubborn, ungovernable, unruly, wilful
headway advance, improvement, progress, progression, way
heady 1. exciting, exhilarating, intoxicating, overwhelming, stimulating, thrilling **2.** inebriating, intoxicating, potent, spirituous, strong **3.** hasty, impetuous, impulsive, inconsiderate, precipitate, rash, reckless, thoughtless
heal 1. cure, make well, mend, regenerate, remedy, restore, treat **2.** alleviate, ameliorate, compose, conciliate, harmonize, patch up, reconcile, settle, soothe
healing 1. curative, medicinal, remedial, restorative, restoring, sanative, therapeutic **2.** assuaging, comforting, emollient, gentle, lenitive, mild, mitigative, palliative, soothing
health 1. fitness, good condition, haleness, healthiness, robustness, salubrity, soundness, strength, vigour, wellbeing **2.** condition, constitution, fettle, form, shape, state, tone
healthy 1. active, blooming, fit, flourishing, hale, hale and hearty, hardy, hearty, in fine feather, in fine fettle, in fine form, in good condition, in good shape (*informal*), in the pink, physically fit, robust, sound, strong, sturdy, vigorous, well **2.** beneficial, bracing, good for one, healthful, health-giving, hygienic, invigorating, nourishing, nutritious, salubrious, salutary, wholesome
heap *n.* **1.** accumulation, aggregation, collection, hoard, lot, mass, mound, mountain, pile, stack, stockpile, store **2.** *often plural informal* abundance, a lot, great deal, lashings (*Brit. informal*), load(s) (*informal*), lots (*informal*), mass, mint, ocean(s), oodles (*informal*), plenty, pot(s) (*informal*), quantities, stack(s), tons *~vb.* **3.** accumulate, amass, augment, bank, collect, gather, hoard, increase, mound, pile, stack, stockpile, store **4.** assign, bestow, burden, confer, load, shower upon
hear 1. attend, be all ears (*informal*), catch, eavesdrop, give attention, hark, hearken (*archaic*), heed, listen in, listen to, overhear **2.** ascertain, be informed, be told of, discover, find out, gather, get wind of (*informal*), hear tell (*dialect*), learn, pick up, understand **3.** *Law* examine, investigate, judge, try
hearing 1. ear, perception **2.** audience, audition,

range within which sound can be heard; earshot. **4** the investigation of a matter by a court of law.

hearing aid *n* a small amplifier worn by a partially deaf person in or behind the ear to improve hearing.

hearken *vb Archaic* to listen.

hearsay *n* gossip or rumour.

hearse *n* a large car used to carry a coffin at a funeral.

heart *n* **1** a hollow muscular organ whose contractions pump the blood throughout the body. **2** this organ considered as the centre of emotions, esp. love. **3** tenderness or pity: *my heart went out to her.* **4** courage or spirit. **5** the most central part or important part: *at the heart of Italian motor racing.* **6** (of vegetables, such as cabbage) the inner compact part. **7** the breast: *she held him to her heart.* **8** a shape representing the heart, with two rounded lobes at the top meeting in a point at the bottom. **9 a** a red heart-shaped symbol on a playing card. **b** a card with one or more of these symbols or (*when pl.*) the suit of cards so marked. **10 break someone's heart** to cause someone to grieve very deeply, esp. by ending a love affair. **11 by heart** by memorizing. **12 have a change of heart** to experience a profound change of outlook or attitude. **13 have one's heart in one's mouth** to be full of apprehension, excitement, or fear. **14 have the heart** to have the necessary will or callousness (to do something): *I didn't have the heart to tell him.* **15 set one's heart on something** to have something as one's ambition. **16 take heart** to become encouraged. **17 take something to heart** to take something seriously or be upset about something. **18 wear one's heart on one's sleeve** to show one's feelings openly. **19 with all one's heart** deeply and sincerely.

heartache *n* very great sadness and emotional suffering.

heart attack *n* a sudden severe malfunction of the heart.

heartbeat *n* one complete pulsation of the heart.

heartbreak *n* intense and overwhelming grief, esp. after the end of a love affair. **heartbreaking** *adj* **heartbroken** *adj*

heartburn *n* a burning sensation in the chest caused by indigestion.

hearten *vb* to encourage or make cheerful. **heartening** *adj*

heart failure *n* **1** a condition in which the heart is unable to pump an adequate amount of blood to the tissues. **2** sudden stopping of the heartbeat, resulting in death.

heartfelt *adj* sincerely and strongly felt: *heartfelt thanks.*

hearth *n* **1** the floor of a fireplace. **2** this as a symbol of the home.

heartland *n* **1** the central region of a country or continent: *we headed west towards the heartland of Tibet.* **2** the area where the thing specified is most common or strongest: *Germany's industrial heartland.*

heartless *adj* unkind or cruel. **heartlessly** *adv*

heart-rending *adj* causing great sadness and pity: *a heart-rending story.*

heart-searching *n* examination of one's feelings or conscience.

heartstrings *pl n Often facetious* deep emotions: *tugging our heartstrings with pictures of suffering.*

heart-throb *n* a man, esp. a film or pop star, who is attractive to a lot of women or girls.

heart-to-heart *adj* **1** (of a talk) concerned with personal problems or intimate feelings. *~n* **2** an intimate conversation.

heart-warming *adj* inspiring feelings of happiness: *the heart-warming spectacle of family reunion.*

heartwood *n* the central core of dark hard wood in tree trunks.

hearty *adj* **heartier, heartiest 1** warm, friendly, and enthusiastic. **2** strongly felt: *a hearty dislike.* **3** (of a meal) substantial and nourishing. **heartily** *adv*

heat *vb* **1** to make or become hot or warm. *~n* **2** the state of being hot. **3** the energy transferred as a result of a difference in temperature. **4** hot weather: *he loves the heat of Africa.* **5** intensity of feeling: *the heat of*

THESAURUS

chance to speak, interview **3.** auditory range, earshot, hearing distance, range, reach, sound **4.** industrial tribunal, inquiry, investigation, review, trial

hearsay buzz, dirt (*U.S. slang*), gossip, grapevine (*informal*), idle talk, mere talk, report, rumour, talk, talk of the town, tittle-tattle, word of mouth

heart 1. character, disposition, emotion, feeling, inclination, nature, sentiment, soul, sympathy, temperament **2.** affection, benevolence, compassion, concern, humanity, love, pity, tenderness, understanding **3.** balls (*taboo slang*), boldness, bravery, courage, fortitude, guts (*informal*), mettle, mind, nerve, pluck, purpose, resolution, spirit, spunk (*informal*), will **4.** central part, centre, core, crux, essence, hub, kernel, marrow, middle, nucleus, pith, quintessence, root **5. at heart** *au fond,* basically, essentially, fundamentally, in essence, in reality, really, truly **6. by heart** by memory, by rote, off pat, parrot-fashion (*informal*), pat, word for word **7. take heart** be comforted, be encouraged, be heartened, brighten up, buck up (*informal*), cheer up, perk up, revive **8. with all one's heart** deeply, devoutly, fervently, heart and soul, heartily, sincerely

heartbreaking agonizing, bitter, desolating, disappointing, distressing, grievous, harrowing, heart-rending, pitiful, poignant, sad, tragic

heartbroken brokenhearted, crestfallen, crushed, dejected, desolate, despondent, disappointed, disconsolate, disheartened, dismal, dispirited, downcast, grieved, heartsick, miserable, sick as a parrot (*informal*)

heartfelt ardent, cordial, deep, devout, earnest, fervent, genuine, hearty, honest, profound, sincere, unfeigned, warm, wholehearted

heartily 1. cordially, deeply, feelingly, genuinely, profoundly, sincerely, unfeignedly, warmly **2.** eagerly, earnestly, enthusiastically, resolutely, vigorously, zealously

heartless brutal, callous, cold, cold-blooded, cold-hearted, cruel, hard, hardhearted, harsh, inhuman, merciless, pitiless, uncaring, unfeeling, unkind

heart-rending affecting, distressing, harrowing, heartbreaking, moving, pathetic, piteous, pitiful, poignant, sad, tragic

heart-to-heart 1. *adj.* candid, intimate, open, personal, sincere, unreserved **2.** *n.* cosy chat, tête-à-tête

heart-warming affecting, cheering, encouraging, heartening, moving, touching, warming

hearty 1. affable, ardent, back-slapping, cordial, eager, ebullient, effusive, enthusiastic, friendly, generous, genial, jovial, unreserved, warm **2.** earnest, genuine, heartfelt, honest, real, sincere, true, unfeigned, wholehearted **3.** ample, filling, nourishing, sizable, solid, square, substantial

heat *vb.* **1.** become warm, chafe, flush, glow, grow hot, make hot, reheat, warm up *~n.* **2.** fever, fieriness, high temperature, hotness, hot spell, sultriness, swelter, torridity, warmness, warmth **3.** agitation, ardour,

their argument. **6** the most intense part: *in the heat of an election campaign.* **7** *Sport* a preliminary eliminating contest in a competition. **8** **in** *or* **on heat** (of some female mammals) ready for mating. **heating** *n*

heated *adj* impassioned or highly emotional: *a heated debated.* **heatedly** *adv*

heater *n* a device for supplying heat.

heath *n* **1** *Brit* a large open area, usually with sandy soil, low shrubs, and heather. **2** a low-growing evergreen shrub with small bell-shaped pink or purple flowers.

heathen *n, pl* **-thens** *or* **-then** *Old-fashioned* **1** a person who does not believe in an established religion; pagan. *~adj* **2** of or relating to heathen peoples.

heather *n* a shrub with small bell-shaped flowers growing on heaths and mountains.

Heath Robinson *adj* (of a mechanical device) absurdly complicated in design for a simple function.

heatstroke *n* same as **sunstroke.**

heat wave *n* a spell of unusually hot weather.

heave *vb* **heaving, heaved** *or* **hove** **1** to lift or move (something) with a great effort. **2** to throw (something heavy) with effort. **3** to utter (a sigh) noisily or unhappily. **4** to rise and fall heavily. **5** (*pt & pp* **hove**) *Naut* **a** to move in a specified direction: *heave her bows around and head north.* **b** (of a vessel) to pitch or roll. **6** to vomit or retch. *~n* **7** the act of heaving.

heaven *n* **1** the place where God is believed to live and where those leading good lives are believed to go when they die. **2** a place or state of happiness. **3** **heavens** the sky. **4** Also: **heavens** God or the gods, used in exclamatory phrases: *for heaven's sake!*

heavenly *adj* **1** *Informal* wonderful or very enjoyable: *a heavenly meal.* **2** of or occurring in space: *a heavenly body.* **3** of or relating to heaven.

heave to *vb* to stop (a ship) or (of a ship) to stop.

heavy *adj* **heavier, heaviest** **1** of comparatively great weight. **2** with a relatively high density: *lead is a heavy metal.* **3** great in degree or amount: *heavy traffic.* **4** considerable: *heavy emphasis.* **5** hard to fulfil: *an exceptionally heavy demand for this issue.* **6** using or consuming a lot of something quickly: *a heavy drinker.* **7** deep and loud: *heavy breathing.* **8** clumsy and slow: *a heavy lumbering trot.* **9** (of a movement or action) with great downward force or pressure: *a heavy blow with a club.* **10** solid or fat: *mountain animals acquire a heavy layer of fat.* **11** not easily digestible: *a heavy meal.* **12** (of cakes or bread) insufficiently raised. **13** (of soil) with a high clay content. **14** sad or dejected: *you feel heavy or sad afterwards.* **15** (of facial features) looking sad and tired. **16** (of a situation) serious and causing anxiety or sadness. **17** cloudy or overcast: *heavy clouds obscured the sun.* **18** (of an industry) engaged in the large-scale manufacture of large objects or extraction of raw materials. **19** *Mil* (of guns, etc.) large and powerful. **20** dull and uninteresting: *Diana finds his friends very heavy going.* **21** (of music, literature, etc.) difficult to understand or not immediately appealing. **22** *Slang* (of rock music) loud and having a powerful beat. **23** *Slang* using, or prepared to use, violence or brutality. *n, pl* **heavies** **24** *Slang* a large strong man hired to threaten violence or deter others by his presence. **25** **a** a villainous role. **b** an actor who plays such a part. **26** **the heavies** *Informal* serious newspapers. *~adv* **27** heavily: *time hung heavy.* **heavily** *adv* **heaviness** *n*

heavy-duty *adj* made to withstand hard wear, bad weather, etc.

heavy-handed *adj* acting forcefully and without care and thought.

heavy-hearted *adj* sad and discouraged.

heavy hydrogen *n* same as **deuterium.**

heavy metal *n* a type of very loud rock music featuring guitar riffs.

heavy water *n* water formed of oxygen and deuterium.

heavyweight *n* **1** a professional boxer weighing over 175 pounds (79 kg) or an amateur weighing over 81 kg. **2** a person who is heavier than average. **3** *Informal* an important or highly influential person.

Heb. *or* **Hebr.** Hebrew (language).

THESAURUS

earnestness, excitement, fervour, fever, fury, impetuosity, intensity, passion, vehemence, violence, warmth, zeal

heated angry, bitter, excited, fierce, fiery, frenzied, furious, impassioned, intense, passionate, raging, stormy, tempestuous, vehement, violent

heathen *old-fashioned* **1.** *n.* idolater, idolatress, infidel, pagan, unbeliever **2.** *adj.* godless, heathenish, idolatrous, infidel, irreligious, pagan

heave 1. drag (up), elevate, haul (up), heft (*informal*), hoist, lever, lift, pull (up), raise, tug **2.** cast, fling, hurl, pitch, send, sling, throw, toss **3.** breathe heavily, groan, puff, sigh, sob, utter wearily **4.** billow, breathe, dilate, exhale, expand, palpitate, pant, rise, surge, swell, throb **5.** be sick, gag, retch, spew, throw up (*informal*), vomit

heaven 1. abode of God, bliss, Elysium (*Greek myth*), happy hunting ground (*Amerind legend*), hereafter, life everlasting, life to come, next world, nirvana (*Buddhism, Hinduism*), paradise, Valhalla (*Norse myth*), Zion (*Christianity*) **2.** bliss, dreamland, ecstasy, enchantment, felicity, happiness, paradise, rapture, seventh heaven, sheer bliss, transport, utopia **3. heavens** empyrean (*poetic*), ether, firmament, sky

heavenly 1. *informal* alluring, beautiful, blissful, delightful, divine (*informal*), entrancing, exquisite, glorious, lovely, rapturous, ravishing, sublime, wonderful **2.** angelic, beatific, blessed, blest, celestial, cherubic, divine, empyrean (*poetic*), extraterrestrial, godlike, holy, immortal, paradisaical, seraphic, superhuman, supernal (*literary*), supernatural

heavily 1. closely, compactly, densely, fast, hard, thick, thickly **2.** a great deal, considerably, copiously, excessively, frequently, to excess, very much **3.** deep, deeply, profoundly, sound, soundly **4.** awkwardly, clumsily, ponderously, weightily **5.** dejectedly, dully, gloomily, sluggishly, woodenly

heaviness 1. gravity, heftiness, ponderousness, weight **2.** arduousness, burdensomeness, grievousness, onerousness, oppressiveness, severity, weightiness **3.** deadness, dullness, languor, lassitude, numbness, sluggishness, torpor **4.** dejection, depression, despondency, gloom, gloominess, glumness, melancholy, sadness, seriousness

heavy 1. bulky, hefty, massive, ponderous, portly, weighty **2.** abundant, considerable, copious, excessive, large, profuse **3.** crestfallen, dejected, depressed, despondent, disconsolate, downcast, gloomy, grieving, melancholy, sad, sorrowful **4.** burdensome, difficult, grievous, hard, harsh, intolerable, laborious, onerous, oppressive, severe, tedious, vexatious, wearisome **5.** dull, gloomy, leaden, louring *or* lowering, overcast **6.** apathetic, drowsy, dull, inactive, indolent, inert, listless, slow, sluggish, stupid, torpid, wooden **7.** complex, deep, difficult, grave, profound, serious, solemn, weighty

heavy-handed autocratic, awkward, bungling, clumsy, domineering, graceless, ham-fisted (*informal*), ham-handed (*informal*), harsh, inconsiderate, inept,

Hebraic (hib-**ray**-ik) *adj* of the Hebrews or their language or culture.

Hebrew *n* **1** the ancient language of the Hebrews, revived as the official language of Israel. **2** a member of an ancient Semitic people; an Israelite. *~adj* **3** of the Hebrews or their language.

heck *interj* a mild exclamation of surprise, irritation, etc.

heckle *vb* **-ling, -led** to interrupt (a public speaker) with comments, questions, or taunts. **heckler** *n*

hectare *n* a unit of measure equal to one hundred ares (10 000 square metres or 2.471 acres).

hectic *adj* involving a lot of rushed activity.

hector *vb* **1** to bully or torment. *~n* **2** a blustering bully.

he'd he had *or* he would.

hedge *n* **1** a row of shrubs or bushes forming a boundary. **2** a barrier or protection against something, esp. against the risk of loss on an investment. *~vb* **hedging, hedged 3** to avoid making a decision by making noncommittal statements. **4 hedge against** to guard against the risk of loss in (a bet or disagreement), by supporting the opposition as well.

hedgehog *n* a small mammal with a protective covering of spines.

hedgehop *vb* **-hopping, -hopped** (of an aircraft) to fly close to the ground, such as in crop spraying. **hedge-hopping** *n*

hedgerow *n* a hedge of shrubs or low trees bordering a field.

hedge sparrow *n* a small brownish songbird.

hedonism *n* the doctrine that the pursuit of pleasure is the most important thing in life. **hedonist** *n* **hedonistic** *adj*

heebie-jeebies *pl n* **the heebie-jeebies** *Slang* nervous apprehension.

heed *Formal ~n* **1** careful attention: *he must have taken heed of her warning. ~vb* **2** to pay close attention to (a warning or piece of advice).

heedless *adj* taking no notice; careless or thoughtless. **heedlessly** *adv*

heehaw *interj* a representation of the braying sound of a donkey.

heel[1] *n* **1** the back part of the foot. **2** the part of a stocking or sock designed to fit the heel. **3** the part of a shoe supporting the heel. **4** *Slang* a contemptible person. **5 at one's heels** following closely behind one. **6 cool** *or* **kick one's heels** to be kept waiting. **7 down at heel** untidy and in poor condition. **8 take to one's heels** to run off. **9 to heel** under control, such as a dog walking by a person's heel. *~vb* **10** to repair or replace the heel of (a shoe or boot).

heel[2] *vb* to lean to one side.

heelball *n* **a** a mixture of beeswax and lampblack used by shoemakers. **b** a similar substance used to take brass rubbings.

hefty *adj* **heftier, heftiest** *Informal* **1** large in size, weight, or amount. **2** forceful and vigorous: *a hefty slap on the back.* **3** involving a large amount of money: *a hefty fine.*

hegemony (hig-**em**-on-ee) *n, pl* **-nies** domination of one state, country, or class within a group of others.

Hegira *n* the starting point of the Muslim era the flight of Mohammed from Mecca to Medina in 622 AD, regarded as being the starting point of the Muslim era.

heifer (**hef**-fer) *n* a young cow.

height *n* **1** the vertical distance from the bottom of something to the top. **2** the vertical distance of a place above sea level. **3** relatively great distance from bottom to top. **4** the topmost point; summit. **5** the period of greatest intensity: *the height of the shelling.* **6** an extreme example: *the height of luxury.* **7 heights** extremes: *dizzy heights of success.*

heighten *vb* to make or become higher or more intense. **heightened** *adj*

height of land *n US & Canad* a ridge of high ground dividing two river basins.

heinous *adj* evil and shocking.

heir *n* the person legally succeeding to the property of a deceased person. **heiress** *fem n*

heir apparent *n, pl* **heirs apparent 1** *Law* a person whose right to succeed to certain property cannot be defeated. **2** a person whose succession to a role or position is extremely likely: *heir apparent to the England captaincy.*

heirloom *n* an object that has been in a family for generations.

heir presumptive *n Property law* a person who ex-

THESAURUS

inexpert, insensitive, like a bull in a china shop (*informal*), maladroit, oppressive, overbearing, tactless, thoughtless, unhandy

heckle bait, barrack (*informal*), boo, disrupt, interrupt, jeer, pester, shout down, taunt

hectic animated, boisterous, chaotic, excited, fevered, feverish, flurrying, flustering, frantic, frenetic, frenzied, furious, heated, riotous, rumbustious, tumultuous, turbulent, wild

hector bluster, boast, browbeat, bully, bullyrag, harass, huff and puff, intimidate, menace, provoke, ride roughshod over, roister, threaten, worry

hedge *n.* **1.** hedgerow, quickset **2.** compensation, counterbalance, guard, insurance cover, protection *~vb.* **3.** beg the question, be noncommittal, dodge, duck, equivocate, evade, flannel (*Brit. informal*), prevaricate, pussyfoot (*informal*), quibble, sidestep, temporize, waffle (*informal, chiefly Brit.*)

heed **1.** *n.* attention, care, caution, consideration, ear, heedfulness, mind, note, notice, regard, respect, thought, watchfulness **2.** *vb.* attend, bear in mind, be guided by, consider, follow, give ear to, listen to, mark, mind, note, obey, observe, pay attention to, regard, take notice of, take to heart

heedless careless, foolhardy, imprudent, inattentive, incautious, neglectful, negligent, oblivious, precipitate, rash, reckless, thoughtless, unmindful, unobservant, unthinking

heel[1] *n.* **1.** *slang* blackguard, bounder (*old-fashioned Brit. slang*), cad (*Brit informal*), rotter (*slang, chiefly Brit.*), scoundrel, scumbag (*slang*), swine **2. down at heel** dowdy, impoverished, out at elbows, run-down, seedy, shabby, slipshod, slovenly, worn **3. take to one's heels** escape, flee, hook it (*slang*), run away *or* off, show a clean pair of heels, skedaddle (*informal*), take flight, vamoose (*slang, chiefly U.S.*)

heel[2] cant, careen, incline, keel over, lean over, list, tilt

hefty **1.** ample, beefy (*informal*), big, brawny, bulky, burly, colossal, heavy, hulking, husky (*informal*), large, massive, muscular, ponderous, robust, strapping, strong, tremendous, weighty **2.** forceful, heavy, powerful, thumping (*slang*), vigorous **3.** colossal, heavy, large, massive, substantial

height **1.** altitude, elevation, highness, loftiness, stature, tallness **2.** apex, apogee, crest, crown, elevation, hill, mountain, peak, pinnacle, summit, top, vertex, zenith **3.** climax, culmination, extremity, limit, maximum, *ne plus ultra,* ultimate, utmost degree, uttermost

heighten add to, aggravate, amplify, augment, el-

pects to succeed to an estate but whose right may be defeated by the birth of an heir nearer in blood to the ancestor.

held *vb* the past of **hold**[1].

helical *adj* of or like a helix.

helicopter *n* an aircraft, powered by rotating overhead blades, that is capable of hovering, vertical flight, and horizontal flight in any direction.

heliograph *n* an instrument with mirrors and a shutter used for sending messages in Morse code by reflecting the sun's rays.

heliotrope *n* a plant with small fragrant purple flowers.

heliport *n* an airport for helicopters.

helium (**heel**-ee-um) *n Chem* a very light colourless odourless inert gas. Symbol: He

helix (**heel**-iks) *n, pl* **helices** (**hell**-iss-seez) *or* **helixes** a spiral.

hell *n* **1** (in Christianity and some other religions) the place or state of eternal punishment of the wicked after death. **2** (in various religions and cultures) the abode of the spirits of the dead. **3** *Informal* a situation that causes suffering or extreme difficulty: *war is hell.* **4 come hell or high water** *Informal* whatever difficulties may arise. **5 for the hell of it** *Informal* for the fun of it. **6 from hell** *Informal* denoting a person or thing that is particularly bad or alarming: *the neighbour from hell.* **7 give someone hell** *Informal* **a** to give someone a severe reprimand or punishment. **b** to be a torment to someone. **8 hell for leather** at great speed. **9 the hell** *Informal* **a** used for emphasis: *what the hell.* **b** an expression of strong disagreement: *the hell you do!* ~*interj* **10** *Informal* an exclamation of anger or surprise.

he'll he will *or* he shall.

hellbent *adj Informal* rashly intent: *hellbent on revenge.*

hellebore *n* a plant with white flowers that bloom in winter.

Hellene *n* a Greek.

Hellenic *adj* **1** of the Greeks or their language. **2** of or relating to ancient Greece during the classical period (776–323 BC).

Hellenism *n* **1** the principles and ideals of classical Greek civilization. **2** the spirit or national character of the Greeks. **Hellenist** *n*

Hellenistic *adj* of Greek civilization during the period 323–30 BC.

hellfire *n* the torment of hell, imagined as eternal fire.

hellish *adj Informal* very unpleasant.

hello, hallo, *or* **hullo** *interj* **1** an expression of greeting or surprise. **2** a call used to attract attention. ~*n, pl* **-los 3** the act of saying "hello".

Hell's Angel *n* a member of a motorcycle gang noted for their lawless behaviour.

helm *n* **1** *Naut* the tiller or wheel for steering a ship. **2 at the helm** in a position of leadership or control. **helmsman** *n*

helmet *n* a piece of protective headgear worn by motorcyclists, soldiers, policemen, divers, etc.

helot *n* (in ancient Greece) a serf or slave.

help *vb* **1** to assist (someone to do something). **2** to contribute to: *to help Latin America's economies.* **3** to improve a situation: *a felt or rubber underlay will help.* **4 a** to refrain from: *I couldn't help feeling foolish.* **b** to be responsible for: *you must not blame him, he simply can't help it.* **5** to serve (a customer). **6 help oneself** to take something, esp. food or drink, for oneself, without being served. ~*n* **7** the act of helping. **8** a person or thing that helps, esp. a farm worker or domestic servant. **9** a remedy: *there's no help for it.* ~*interj* **10** used to call for assistance. ~See also **help out. helper** *n*

helpful *adj* giving help. **helpfully** *adv* **helpfulness** *n*

helping *n* a single portion of food.

helpless *adj* **1** unable to manage independently. **2** made weak: *it reduced her to helpless laughter.* **helplessly** *adv* **helplessness** *n*

helpline *n* a telephone line set aside for callers to contact an organization for help with a problem.

helpmate *or* **helpmeet** *n* a companion and helper, esp. a husband or wife.

help out *vb* to assist (someone) by sharing the burden or cost of something.

helter-skelter *adj* **1** hurried or disorganized. ~*adv* **2** in a hurried or disorganized manner. ~*n* **3** *Brit* a high spiral slide at a fairground.

hem[1] *n* **1** the bottom edge of a garment, folded under and stitched down. ~*vb* **hemming, hemmed 2** to provide (a garment) with a hem. ~See also **hem in.**

hem[2] *n* **1** a representation of the sound of clearing the

THESAURUS

evate, enhance, ennoble, exalt, improve, increase, intensify, magnify, raise, sharpen, strengthen, uplift

heir beneficiary, heiress (*fem.*), inheritor, inheritress *or* inheritrix (*fem.*), next in line, scion, successor

hell 1. abode of the damned, abyss, bottomless pit, fire and brimstone, Hades (*Greek myth*), hellfire, infernal regions, inferno, lower world, nether world, underworld **2.** *informal* affliction, agony, anguish, martyrdom, misery, nightmare, ordeal, suffering, torment, trial, wretchedness **3. hell for leather** at the double, full-tilt, headlong, hotfoot, hurriedly, like a bat out of hell (*slang*), pell-mell, posthaste, quickly, speedily, swiftly

helm 1. *Nautical* rudder, steering gear, tiller, wheel **2. at the helm** at the wheel, directing, in charge, in command, in control, in the driving seat, in the saddle

help *vb.* **1.** abet, aid, assist, back, befriend, cooperate, encourage, lend a hand, promote, relieve, save, second, serve, stand by, succour, support **2.** alleviate, ameliorate, cure, ease, facilitate, heal, improve, mitigate, relieve, remedy, restore **3.** abstain, avoid, control, eschew, forbear, hinder, keep from, prevent, refrain from, resist, shun, withstand ~*n.* **4.** advice, aid, assistance, avail, benefit, cooperation, guidance, helping hand, promotion, service, support, use, utility **5.** assistant, employee, hand, helper, worker **6.** balm, corrective, cure, relief, remedy, restorative, salve, succour

helper abettor, adjutant, aide, aider, ally, assistant, attendant, auxiliary, coadjutor, collaborator, colleague, deputy, helpmate, henchman, mate, partner, protagonist, right-hand man, second, subsidiary, supporter

helpful accommodating, advantageous, beneficent, beneficial, benevolent, caring, considerate, constructive, cooperative, favourable, fortunate, friendly, kind, neighbourly, practical, productive, profitable, serviceable, supportive, sympathetic, timely, useful

helping dollop (*informal*), piece, plateful, portion, ration, serving

helpless 1. abandoned, defenceless, dependent, destitute, exposed, forlorn, incapable, incompetent, infirm, paralysed, powerless, unprotected, vulnerable **2.** debilitated, disabled, feeble, impotent, infirm, paralysed, powerless, unfit, weak

helter-skelter 1. *adj.* anyhow, confused, disordered, haphazard, higgledy-piggledy (*informal*), hit-or-miss, jumbled, muddled, random, topsy-turvy **2.** *adv.* care-

throat, used to gain attention. *~vb* **hemming, hemmed** **2** to make this sound. **3 hem and haw** See **haw**[2].

he-man *n, pl* **-men** *Informal* a strong man, esp. one who shows off his strength.

hemi- *prefix* half: *hemisphere.*

hem in *vb* to surround and prevent from moving.

hemipterous *adj* of an order of insects with sucking or piercing mouthparts.

hemisphere *n* one half of a sphere, esp. of the earth (**northern** and **southern hemisphere**) or of the brain. **hemispherical** *adj*

hemline *n* the level to which the hem of a skirt or dress hangs.

hemlock *n* a poisonous drug derived from a plant with spotted stems and small white flowers.

hemp *n* **1** an Asian plant with tough fibres. **2** the fibre of this plant, used to make canvas and rope. **3** a narcotic drug obtained from this plant. **hempen** *adj*

hen *n* the female of any bird, esp. the domestic fowl.

henbane *n* a poisonous plant with sticky hairy leaves.

hence *adv* **1** for this reason; therefore. **2** from this time: *two weeks hence.* **3** *Archaic* from here.

henceforth *or* **henceforward** *adv* from now on.

henchman *n, pl* **-men** a person employed by someone powerful to carry out orders.

henge *n* a circular monument, often containing a circle of stones, dating from the Neolithic and Bronze Ages.

henna *n* **1** a reddish dye, obtained from a shrub or tree of Asia and N Africa which is used to colour hair. *~vb* **2** to dye (the hair) with henna.

hen party *n Informal* a party at which only women are present.

henpecked *adj* (of a man) harassed by the persistent nagging of his wife.

henry *n, pl* **-ry, -ries,** *or* **-rys** the SI unit of electric inductance.

hepatic *adj* of the liver.

hepatitis *n* inflammation of the liver, causing fever, jaundice, and weakness.

hepta- *combining form* seven: *heptameter.*

heptagon *n Geom* a figure with seven sides. **heptagonal** *adj*

heptathlon *n* an athletic contest for women in which athletes compete in seven different events.

her *pron* refers to: **1** a female person or animal: *he loves her.* **2** things personified as feminine, such as ships and nations. *~adj* **3** of, belonging to, or associated with her: *her hair.*

herald *n* **1** a person who announces important news. **2** *Often literary* a forerunner. *~vb* **3** to announce or signal the approach of: *his arrival was heralded by excited barking.* **heraldic** *adj*

heraldry *n, pl* **-ries** the study of coats of arms and family trees.

herb *n* **1** an aromatic plant that is used for flavouring in cookery, and in medicine. **2** *Bot* a seed-bearing plant whose parts above ground die back at the end of the growing season. **herbal** *adj* **herby** *adj*

herbaceous *adj* designating plants that are soft-stemmed rather than woody.

herbaceous border *n* a flower bed that contains perennials rather than annuals.

herbage *n* herbaceous plants collectively, esp. those on which animals graze.

herbalist *n* a person who grows or specializes in the use of medicinal herbs.

herbicide *n* a substance used to destroy plants, esp. weeds.

herbivore (**her**-biv-vore) *n* an animal that feeds only on plants. **herbivorous** (her-**biv**-or-uss) *adj*

herculean (her-kew-**lee**-an) *adj* **1** (of a task) requiring tremendous effort or strength. **2** resembling Hercules, hero of classical myth, in strength or courage.

herd *n* **1** a large group of mammals, esp. cattle living and feeding together. **2** *Often disparaging* a large group of people. *~vb* **3** to collect or be collected into or as if into a herd.

herd instinct *n Psychol* the inborn tendency to associate with others and follow the group's behaviour.

herdsman *n, pl* **-men** *Chiefly Brit* a man who looks after a herd of animals.

here *adv* **1** in, at, or to this place, point, case, or respect: *I am pleased to be back here.* **2 here and there** at several places in or throughout an area. **3 here's to** a convention used in proposing a toast. **4 neither here nor there** of no relevance. *~n* **5** this place: *they leave here tonight.*

hereabouts *or* **hereabout** *adv* in this region.

hereafter *adv* **1** *Formal or law* in a subsequent part of this document, matter, or case. **2** at some time in the future. *~n* **3 the hereafter a** life after death. **b** the future.

hereby *adv* (used in official statements and documents) by means of or as a result of this.

hereditable *adj* same as **heritable.**

hereditary *adj* **1** passed on genetically from one generation to another. **2** *Law* passed on to succeeding generations by inheritance.

heredity (hir-**red**-it-ee) *n, pl* **-ties** the passing on from one generation to another of genetic factors that determine individual characteristics.

Hereford *n* a hardy breed of beef cattle which has a reddish body with white markings.

THESAURUS

lessly, hastily, headlong, hurriedly, pell-mell, rashly, recklessly, wildly

hem border, edge, fringe, margin, trimming

hem in beset, border, circumscribe, confine, edge, enclose, environ, hedge in, restrict, shut in, skirt, surround

hence ergo, for this reason, on that account, therefore, thus

henceforth *or* **henceforward** from now on, from this day forward, hence, hereafter, hereinafter (*formal or law*), in the future

henpecked browbeaten, bullied, cringing, dominated, led by the nose, meek, subject, subjugated, timid, treated like dirt

herald *n.* **1.** bearer of tidings, crier, messenger **2.** forerunner, harbinger, indication, omen, precursor, sign, signal, token *~vb.* **3.** advertise, announce, broadcast, pave the way, precede, proclaim, publicize, publish, show, trumpet, usher in

herd 1. *n. often disparaging* assemblage, collection, crowd, crush, drove, flock, horde, mass, mob, multitude, populace, press, rabble, riffraff, swarm, the hoi polloi, the masses, the plebs, throng **2.** *vb.* assemble, associate, collect, congregate, drive, flock, gather, goad, guide, huddle, lead, muster, rally, shepherd, spur

hereafter 1. *adv.* after this, from now on, hence, henceforth, henceforward, in future **2.** *n.* **the hereafter** afterlife, future life, life after death, next world, the beyond

hereditary 1. family, genetic, inborn, inbred, inheritable, transmissible **2.** *Law* ancestral, bequeathed,

herein *adv Formal or law* in this place, matter, or document.
hereinafter *adv Formal or law* from this point on in this document, matter, or case.
hereof *adv Formal or law* of or concerning this.
heresy (**herr**-iss-ee) *n, pl* **-sies 1** an opinion contrary to the principles of a religion. **2** any belief thought to be contrary to official or established theory.
heretic (**herr**-it-ik) *n* **1** *Now chiefly RC Church* a person who maintains beliefs contrary to the established teachings of the Church. **2** a person who holds unorthodox opinions in any field. **heretical** (hir-**ret**-ik-kl) *adj*
hereto *adv Formal or law* to this place, matter, or document.
heretofore *adv Formal or law* until now.
hereupon *adv* following immediately after this; at this stage.
herewith *adv Formal* together with this: *a schedule of the event is appended herewith.*
heritable *adj* capable of being inherited.
heritage *n* **1** something inherited at birth. **2** anything that has been carried over from the past or handed down by tradition. **3** the evidence of the past, such as historical sites, considered as the inheritance of present-day society.
hermaphrodite (her-**maf**-roe-dite) *n* an animal, flower, or person that has both male and female reproductive organs. **hermaphroditic** *adj*
hermetic *adj* sealed so as to be airtight. **hermetically** *adv*
hermit *n* a person living in solitude, esp. for religious reasons.
hermitage *n* **1** the home of a hermit. **2** any retreat.
hermit crab *n* a small crab that lives in the empty shells of other shellfish.
hernia *n* protrusion of an organ or part through the lining of the body cavity in which it is normally situated.
hero *n, pl* **-roes 1** the principal male character in a novel, play, etc. **2** a man of exceptional courage, nobility, etc. **3** a man who is idealized for having superior qualities in any field.
heroic *adj* **1** brave and courageous: *heroic work by the army engineers.* **2** of, like, or befitting a hero. **heroically** *adv*
heroics *pl n* behaviour or language considered too melodramatic or extravagant for the particular situation in which they are used.
heroin *n* a highly addictive drug derived from morphine.
heroine *n* **1** the principal female character in a novel, play, etc. **2** a woman of exceptional courage, nobility, etc. **3** a woman who is idealized for having superior qualities in any field.
heroism (**herr**-oh-izz-um) *n* great courage and bravery.
heron *n* a wading bird with a long neck, long legs, and grey or white feathers.
heronry *n, pl* **-ries** a colony of breeding herons.
hero worship *n* admiration for heroes or idealized people.
herpes (**her**-peez) *n* any of several inflammatory skin diseases, including shingles and cold sores.
herpes simplex *n* an acute viral disease causing clusters of watery blisters.
herpes zoster *n* same as **shingles**.
Herr (**hair**) *n, pl* **Herren** a German form of address equivalent to *Mr.*
herring *n, pl* **-rings** *or* **-ring** a food fish of northern seas, with a long silver-coloured body.
herringbone *n* a zigzag pattern consisting of short lines of V shapes, used esp. in fabrics.
herring gull *n* a common gull that has a white feathers with black-tipped wings.
hers *pron* **1** something belonging to her: *hers is the highest paid part-time job; the money which is rightfully hers.* **2 of hers** belonging to her.
herself *pron* **1 a** the reflexive form of *she* or *her*: *she busied herself at the stove.* **b** used for emphasis: *none other than The Great Mother herself.* **2** her normal self: *she hasn't been herself all week.*
Herts Hertfordshire.
hertz *n, pl* **hertz** the SI unit of frequency, equal to one cycle per second.
he's he is *or* he has.
hesitant *adj* doubtful and unsure in speech or action. **hesitancy** *n* **hesitantly** *adv*
hesitate *vb* **-tating, -tated 1** to be slow and uncertain in acting. **2** to be reluctant (to do something): *I hesitate to use the word "squandered".* **3** to pause during speech because of uncertainty. **hesitation** *n*

THESAURUS

handed down, inherited, patrimonial, traditional, transmitted, willed
heredity congenital traits, constitution, genetic make-up, genetics, inheritance
heresy apostasy, dissidence, error, heterodoxy, iconoclasm, impiety, revisionism, schism, unorthodoxy
heretic apostate, dissenter, dissident, nonconformist, renegade, revisionist, schismatic, sectarian, separatist
heretical freethinking, heterodox, iconoclastic, idolatrous, impious, revisionist, schismatic, unorthodox
heritage bequest, birthright, endowment, estate, inheritance, legacy, lot, patrimony, portion, share, tradition
hermit anchorite, eremite, monk, recluse, solitary, stylite
hero 1. lead actor, leading man, male lead, principal male character, protagonist **2.** celeb (*informal*), celebrity, champion, conqueror, exemplar, great man, heartthrob (*Brit.*), idol, man of the hour, megastar (*informal*), popular figure, star, superstar, victor
heroic bold, brave, courageous, daring, dauntless, doughty, fearless, gallant, intrepid, lion-hearted, stouthearted, undaunted, valiant, valorous
heroine 1. diva, female lead, lead actress, leading lady, prima donna, principal female character, protagonist **2.** celeb (*informal*), celebrity, goddess, ideal, megastar (*informal*), woman of the hour
heroism boldness, bravery, courage, courageousness, daring, fearlessness, fortitude, gallantry, intrepidity, prowess, spirit, valour
hero worship admiration, adoration, adulation, idealization, idolization, putting on a pedestal, veneration
hesitant diffident, doubtful, half-hearted, halting, hanging back, hesitating, irresolute, lacking confidence, reluctant, sceptical, shy, timid, uncertain, unsure, vacillating, wavering
hesitate 1. be uncertain, delay, dither (*chiefly Brit.*), doubt, haver (*Brit.*), pause, shillyshally (*informal*), swither (*Scot.*), vacillate, wait, waver **2.** balk, be reluctant, be unwilling, boggle, demur, hang back, scruple, shrink from, think twice **3.** falter, fumble, hem and haw, stammer, stumble, stutter
hesitation 1. delay, doubt, dubiety, hesitancy, inde-

hessian *n* a coarse jute fabric similar to sacking.

hetero- *combining form* other, another, or different: *heterosexual.*

heterodox *adj* different from established or accepted doctrines or beliefs. **heterodoxy** *n*

heterodyne *Electronics ~vb* **-dyning, -dyned 1** to combine (two alternating signals) so as to produce two signals with frequencies corresponding to the sum and the difference of the original frequencies. *~adj* **2** produced or operating by heterodyning two signals.

heterogeneous (het-er-oh-**jean**-ee-uss) *adj* varied in content; composed of different parts: *a heterogeneous collection of European art.* **heterogeneity** *n*

heteromorphic *adj Biol* **1** differing from the normal form. **2** (esp. of insects) having different forms at different stages of the life cycle. **heteromorphism** *n*

heterosexual *n* **1** a person who is sexually attracted to members of the opposite sex. *~adj* **2** (of a person) sexually attracted to members of the opposite sex. **3** (of a sexual relationship) between a man and a woman. **heterosexuality** *n*

het up *adj Informal* agitated or excited: *he was very het up about the traffic.*

heuristic (**hew**-rist-ik) *adj* (of a method of teaching) allowing students to learn things for themselves by trial and error.

hew *vb* **hewing, hewed, hewed** *or* **hewn 1** to chop or cut with an axe. **2** to carve (something) from a substance: *a tunnel hewn out of the living rock.*

hex *n* **1** short for **hexadecimal notation.** *~adj* **2** of or relating to hexadecimal notation: *hex code.*

hexa- *combining form* six: *hexameter.*

hexadecimal notation *n* a number system with a base of 16, the numbers 10–15 being represented by the letters A–F.

hexagon *n Geom* a figure with six sides. **hexagonal** *adj*

hexagram *n Geom* a star formed by extending the sides of a regular hexagon to meet at six points.

hexameter (hek-**sam**-it-er) *n Prosody* a verse line consisting of six metrical feet.

hey *interj* **1** an expression of surprise or for catching attention. **2 hey presto!** an exclamation used by conjurors at the climax of a trick.

heyday *n* the time of most power, popularity, or success: *Bette Davis in her heyday.*

Hf *Chem* hafnium.

Hg *Chem* mercury.

HGV (in Britain, formerly) heavy goods vehicle.

HH 1 His (*or* Her) Highness. **2** His Holiness (title of the Pope).

hi *interj Informal* hello.

HI Hawaii.

hiatus (hie-**ay**-tuss) *n, pl* **-tuses** *or* **-tus** a pause or an interruption in continuity: *diplomatic relations restored after a four-year hiatus.*

hiatus hernia *n* protrusion of the stomach through the diaphragm at the hole for the gullet.

hibernate *vb* **-nating, -nated** (of some animals) to pass the winter in a resting state in which heartbeat, temperature, and breathing rate are very low. **hibernation** *n*

Hibernia *n Poetic* Ireland. **Hibernian** *adj, n*

hibiscus *n, pl* **-cuses** a tropical plant with large brightly coloured flowers.

hiccup *n* **1** a spasm of the breathing organs with a sharp coughlike sound. **2** (*pl*) the state of having such spasms. **3** *Informal* a minor difficulty. *~vb* **-cuping, -cuped** *or* **-cupping, -cupped 4** to make a hiccup or hiccups. Also: **hiccough**

hick *n Informal, chiefly US & Canad* an unsophisticated country person.

hickory *n, pl* **-ries 1** a North American tree with edible nuts. **2** the hard wood of this tree.

hidden *vb* **1** a past participle of **hide**[1]. *~adj* **2** not easily noticed or obscure: *hidden dangers.* **3** difficult to find.

hidden agenda *n* a set of motives or intentions concealed from others who might object to them.

hide[1] *vb* **hiding, hid, hidden** *or* **hid 1** to conceal (oneself or an object) from view or discovery: *in an attempt to hide from his wife.* **2** to keep (information or one's feelings) secret. **3** to obscure or cover (something) from view: *the collar hid his face.* *~n* **4** *Brit* a place of concealment, disguised to appear as part of its surrounding, used by hunters, bird-watchers, etc.

hide[2] *n* the skin of an animal, either tanned or raw.

hide-and-seek *n* a game in which one player covers his or her eyes while the others hide, and that player then tries to find them.

hideaway *n* a hiding place or secluded spot.

hidebound *adj* restricted by petty rules and unwilling to accept new ideas.

hideous (**hid**-ee-uss) *adj* extremely ugly or unpleasant.

hide-out *n* a hiding place.

hiding[1] *n* **1** a state of concealment: *in hiding.* **2 hiding place** a place of concealment.

hiding[2] *n Informal* a severe beating.

hie *vb* **hieing** *or* **hying, hied** *Archaic or poetic* to hurry.

hierarchy (**hire**-ark-ee) *n, pl* **-chies 1** a system of

THESAURUS

cision, irresolution, uncertainty, vacillation **2.** demurral, misgiving(s), qualm(s), reluctance, scruple(s), unwillingness **3.** faltering, fumbling, hemming and hawing, stammering, stumbling, stuttering

hew 1. axe, chop, cut, hack, lop, split **2.** carve, fashion, form, make, model, sculpt, sculpture, shape, smooth

heyday bloom, flowering, pink, prime, prime of life, salad days

hiatus aperture, blank, breach, break, chasm, discontinuity, entr'acte, gap, interruption, interval, lacuna, lapse, opening, respite, rift, space

hidden abstruse, clandestine, close, concealed, covered, covert, cryptic, dark, hermetic, hermetical, masked, mysterious, mystic, mystical, obscure, occult, recondite, secret, shrouded, ulterior, unrevealed, unseen, veiled

hide[1] **1.** cache, conceal, go into hiding, go to ground, go underground, hole up, lie low, secrete, stash (*informal*), take cover **2.** hush up, keep secret, suppress, withhold **3.** blot out, bury, camouflage, cloak, conceal, cover, disguise, eclipse, mask, obscure, screen, shelter, shroud, veil

hide[2] fell, pelt, skin

hidebound brassbound, conventional, narrow, narrow-minded, rigid, set, set in one's ways, strait-laced, ultraconservative

hideous abominable, appalling, awful, detestable, disgusting, dreadful, ghastly, grim, grisly, grotesque, gruesome, horrendous, horrible, horrid, loathsome, macabre, monstrous, obscene, odious, repulsive, revolting, shocking, sickening, terrible, terrifying, ugly, unsightly

hide-out den, hideaway, hiding place, lair, secret place, shelter

hiding *informal* beating, caning, drubbing, flogging,

people or things arranged in a graded order. **2 the hierarchy** the people in power in any organization. **hierarchical** *adj*

hieroglyphic (hire-oh-**gliff**-ik) *adj* **1** of or relating to a form of writing using picture symbols, as used in ancient Egypt. *~n also* **hieroglyph 2** a symbol that is difficult to decipher. **3** a picture or symbol representing an object, idea, or sound.

hieroglyphics *n* **1** a form of writing, as used in ancient Egypt, in which pictures or symbols are used to represent objects, ideas, or sounds. **2** writing that is difficult to decipher.

hi-fi *n Informal* **1** a set of high-quality sound-reproducing equipment. **2** short for **high fidelity.** *~adj* **3** producing high-quality sound: *a hi-fi amplifier.*

higgledy-piggledy *adj, adv Informal* in a muddle.

high *adj* **1** being a relatively great distance from top to bottom: *a high stone wall.* **2** being at a relatively great distance above sea level: *a high village.* **3** being a specified distance from top to bottom: *three feet high.* **4** coming up to a specified level: *waist-high.* **5** being at its peak: *high summer.* **6** of greater than average height: *a high ceiling.* **7** greater than usual in intensity or amount: *high blood pressure; high fees.* **8** (of a sound) acute in pitch. **9** (of food) slightly decomposed, regarded as enhancing the flavour of game. **10** towards the top of a scale of importance or quality: *high fashion.* **11** intensely emotional: *high drama.* **12** very cheerful: *high spirits.* **13** *Informal* under the influence of alcohol or drugs. **14** luxurious or extravagant: *high life.* **15** advanced in complexity: *high finance.* **16** formal and elaborate: *High Mass.* **17 high and dry** abandoned in a difficult situation. **18 high and mighty** *Informal* too confident and full of self-importance. **19 high opinion** a favourable opinion. *~adv* **20** at or to a height: *flying high.* *~n* **21** a high level. **22** same as **anticyclone. 23 on a high** *Informal* **a** in a state of intoxication by alcohol or drugs. **b** in a state of great excitement and happiness.

High Arctic *n* the regions of Canada, esp. the northern islands, within the Arctic Circle.

highball *n Chiefly US* a long iced drink consisting of whisky with soda water or ginger ale.

highbrow *Often disparaging ~adj* **1** concerned with serious, intellectual subjects. *~n* **2** a person with such tastes.

highchair *n* a long-legged chair with a table-like tray, used for a child at meal times.

High Church *n* **1** the movement within the Church of England stressing the importance of ceremony and ritual. *~adj* **High-Church 2** of or relating to this movement.

high commissioner *n* the senior diplomatic representative sent by one Commonwealth country to another.

high country *n* **the high country** *NZ* sheep pastures in the foothills of the Southern Alps.

High Court *n* (in England, Wales, Australia, and New Zealand) the supreme court dealing with civil law cases.

Higher *n* (in Scotland) **1** the advanced level of the Scottish Certificate of Education. **2** a pass in a subject at this level: *she has got four Highers.*

higher education *n* education and training at colleges, universities, and polytechnics.

higher-up *n Informal* a person of higher rank.

highest common factor *n* the largest number that divides equally into each member of a group of numbers.

high explosive *n* an extremely powerful chemical explosive, such as TNT or gelignite.

highfalutin (hie-fa-loot-in) *adj Informal* (of behaviour) excessively grand or pompous.

high fidelity *n* **1** the electronic reproduction of sound with little or no distortion. *~adj* **2** able to produce sound with little or no distortion: *high-fidelity stereo earphones.*

high-flown *adj* extravagant or pretentious: *high-flown language.*

high-flyer *or* **high-flier** *n* **1** a person who is extremely ambitious. **2** a person of great ability in a career. **high-flying** *adj, n*

high frequency *n* a radio frequency between 30 and 3 megahertz.

High German *n* the standard German language.

high-handed *adj* using authority in an unnecessarily forceful way. **high-handedness** *n*

high jump *n* **the high jump a** an athletic event in which competitors have to jump over a high bar. **b** *Brit informal* a severe reprimand or punishment: *I was for the high jump again.*

Highland *adj* of or denoting the Highlands, a mountainous region of NW Scotland. **Highlander** *n*

Highland cattle *n* a breed of cattle with shaggy reddish-brown hair and long horns.

Highland fling *n* an energetic Scottish solo dance.

highlands *n* relatively high ground.

high-level language *n* a computer-programming language that is close to human language.

highlight *n* **1** Also called: **high spot** the most exciting or memorable part of something. **2** an area of the lightest tone in a painting or photograph. **3** a lightened

THESAURUS

larruping (*Brit. dialect*), lathering (*informal*), licking (*informal*), spanking, tanning (*slang*), thrashing, walloping (*informal*), whaling, whipping

hierarchy grading, pecking order, ranking

hieroglyphic enigmatical, figurative, indecipherable, obscure, runic, symbolical

high *adj.* **1.** elevated, lofty, soaring, steep, tall, towering **2.** excessive, extraordinary, extreme, great, intensified, sharp, strong **3.** acute, high-pitched, penetrating, piercing, piping, sharp, shrill, soprano, strident, treble **4.** arch, big-time (*informal*), chief, consequential, distinguished, eminent, exalted, important, influential, leading, major league (*informal*), notable, powerful, prominent, ruling, significant, superior **5.** boisterous, bouncy (*informal*), cheerful, elated, excited, exhilarated, exuberant, joyful, light-hearted, merry, strong, tumultuous, turbulent **6.** *informal* delirious, euphoric, hyped up (*old-fashioned slang*), inebriated, intoxicated, on a trip (*informal*), spaced-out (*informal*), stoned (*slang*), zonked (*slang*) **7.** extravagant, grand, lavish, luxurious, rich **8. high and dry** abandoned, bereft, destitute, helpless, stranded **9. high and mighty** *informal* arrogant, cavalier, conceited, disdainful, haughty, imperious, overbearing, self-important, snobbish, stuck-up (*informal*), superior *~adv.* **10.** aloft, at great height, far up, way up *~n.* **11.** apex, crest, height, peak, record level, summit, top **12.** *informal* delirium, ecstasy, euphoria, intoxication, trip (*informal*)

highbrow *often disparaging* **1.** *adj.* bookish, brainy (*informal*), cultivated, cultured, deep, highbrowed, intellectual, sophisticated **2.** *n.* aesthete, brain (*informal*), brainbox (*slang*), egghead (*informal*), intellectual, mastermind, savant, scholar

high-flown elaborate, exaggerated, extravagant, florid, grandiose, highfalutin (*informal*), inflated, lofty, magniloquent, overblown, pretentious

high-handed arbitrary, autocratic, bossy (*informal*),

streak in the hair produced by bleaching. ~*vb* **4** to give emphasis to: *the prime minister repeatedly highlighted the need for lower pay.*

highlighter *n* **1** a cosmetic cream or powder applied to the face to highlight the cheekbones or eyes. **2** a fluorescent felt-tip pen used as a marker to emphasize a section of text without obscuring it.

highly *adv* **1** extremely: *highly desirable.* **2** towards the top of a scale of importance, admiration, or respect: *highly paid doctors.*

highly strung *or US & Canad* **high-strung** *adj* tense and easily upset.

High Mass *n* a solemn and elaborate Mass.

high-minded *adj* having high moral principles.

Highness *n* (preceded by *Your, His* or *Her*) a title used to address or refer to a royal person.

high-pitched *adj* (of a sound, esp. a voice) pitched high in tone.

high-powered *adj* **1** (of machinery or equipment) powerful, advanced, and sophisticated. **2** important, successful, or influential: *a high-powered business contact.*

high-pressure *adj Informal* (of selling) persuasive in an aggressive and persistent manner.

high priest *n* the head of a cult or movement. **high priestess** *fem n*

high-rise *adj* of or relating to a building that has many storeys: *a high-rise block.*

high-risk *adj* denoting a group or area that is particularly subject to a danger.

highroad *n* a main road.

high school *n* a secondary school.

high seas *pl n* the open seas, which are outside the authority of any one nation.

high season *n* the most popular time of year at a holiday resort, etc.

high-spirited *adj* lively and wishing to have fun and excitement.

high tea *n Brit* an early evening meal consisting of a cooked dish, bread, cakes, and tea.

high-tech *adj* same as **hi-tech.**

high technology *n* any type of sophisticated industrial process, esp. one involving electronics.

high-tension *adj* (of electricity cable) carrying a powerful current.

high tide *n* the sea at its highest level on the coast.

high time *adv Informal* the latest possible time: *it was high time she got married.*

high treason *n* a serious crime directly affecting a sovereign or state.

high-water mark *n* **1** the level reached by sea water at high tide or a river in flood. **2** the highest or most successful stage: *the high-water mark of the British Empire.*

highway *n* **1** a public road that everyone may use. **2** *Chiefly US & Canad* a main road, esp. one that connects towns.

Highway Code *n* (in Britain) a booklet of regulations and recommendations for all road users.

highwayman *n, pl* **-men** (formerly) a robber, usually on horseback, who held up travellers on public roads.

hijack *vb* **1** to seize control of or divert (a vehicle or aircraft) while travelling. ~*n* **2** an instance of hijacking. **hijacker** *n*

hike *vb* **hiking, hiked 1** to walk a long way in the country, usually for pleasure. **2** to raise (prices). **3** to pull up with a quick movement: *he hiked up his trouser legs.* ~*n* **4** a long walk. **5** a rise in price. **hiker** *n*

hilarious *adj* very funny. **hilariously** *adv* **hilarity** *n*

hill *n* **1** a natural elevation of the earth's surface, less high than a mountain. **2** a heap or mound. **3** an incline or slope. **hilly** *adj*

hillbilly *n, pl* **-lies 1** *Usually disparaging* an unsophisticated person from the mountainous areas in the southeastern US. **2** same as **country and western.**

hillock *n* a small hill or mound.

hilt *n* **1** the handle or shaft of a sword, dagger, or knife. **2 to the hilt** to the full: *he plays the role to the hilt.*

hilum *n, pl* **-la** *Bot* a scar on a seed marking its point of attachment to the seed vessel.

him *pron* refers to a male person or animal: *I greeted him at the hotel; I must send him a note of congratulation.*

himself *pron* **1 a** the reflexive form of *he* or *him*: *he secretly asked himself.* **b** used for emphasis: *approved of by the Creator himself.* **2** his normal self: *he was almost himself again.*

THESAURUS

despotic, dictatorial, domineering, imperious, inconsiderate, oppressive, overbearing, peremptory, self-willed, tyrannical, wilful

highlight 1. *n.* best part, climax, feature, focal point, focus, high point, high spot, main feature, memorable part, peak **2.** *vb.* accent, accentuate, bring to the fore, emphasize, feature, focus attention on, give prominence to, play up, set off, show up, spotlight, stress, underline

highly decidedly, eminently, exceptionally, extraordinarily, extremely, greatly, immensely, supremely, tremendously, vastly, very, very much

highly strung easily upset, edgy, excitable, irascible, irritable, nervous, nervy (*Brit. informal*), neurotic, restless, sensitive, stressed, taut, temperamental, tense, tetchy, twitchy (*informal*), wired (*slang*)

high-minded elevated, ethical, fair, good, honourable, idealistic, magnanimous, moral, noble, principled, pure, righteous, upright, virtuous, worthy

high-pressure *informal* aggressive, bludgeoning, coercive, compelling, forceful, high-powered, importunate, insistent, intensive, persistent, persuasive, pushy (*informal*)

high-spirited animated, boisterous, bold, bouncy, daring, dashing, ebullient, effervescent, energetic, exuberant, frolicsome, full of life, fun-loving, gallant, lively, mettlesome, sparky, spirited, spunky (*old-fashioned*) (*informal*), vibrant, vital, vivacious

hijack commandeer, expropriate, seize, skyjack, take over

hike *vb.* **1.** back-pack, hoof it (*slang*), leg it (*informal*), ramble, tramp, walk **2.** hitch up, jack up, lift, pull up, raise ~*n.* **3.** journey on foot, march, ramble, tramp, trek, walk

hilarious amusing, comical, convivial, entertaining, exhilarated, funny, gay, happy, humorous, jolly, jovial, joyful, joyous, merry, mirthful, noisy, rollicking, side-splitting, uproarious

hilarity amusement, boisterousness, cheerfulness, conviviality, exhilaration, exuberance, gaiety, glee, high spirits, jollification, jollity, joviality, joyousness, laughter, levity, merriment, mirth

hill 1. brae (*Scot.*), down (*archaic*), elevation, eminence, fell, height, hillock, hilltop, knoll, mound, mount, prominence, tor **2.** drift, heap, hummock, mound, pile, stack **3.** acclivity, brae (*Scot.*), climb, gradient, incline, rise, slope

hillock barrow, hummock, knoll, mound

hind[1] *adj* **hinder, hindmost** situated at the back: *a hind leg.*

hind[2] *n, pl* **hinds** *or* **hind** the female of the deer, esp. the red deer.

hinder[1] *vb* to get in the way of (someone or something).

hinder[2] *adj* situated at the back.

Hindi *n* **1** a language or group of dialects of N central India. **2** a formal literary dialect of this language, the official language of India.

hindmost *adj* furthest back; last.

hindquarters *pl n* the rear of a four-legged animal.

hindrance *n* **1** an obstruction or snag. **2** the act of hindering.

hindsight *n* the ability to understand, after something has happened, what should have been done.

Hindu *n, pl* **-dus** **1** a person who practises Hinduism. *~adj* **2** of Hinduism.

Hinduism *n* the dominant religion of India, which involves the worship of many gods and belief in reincarnation.

Hindustani *n* a group of northern Indian languages that includes Hindi and Urdu.

hinge *n* **1** a device for holding together two parts, such as a door and its frame, so that one can swing freely. *~vb* **hinging, hinged** **2 hinge on** to depend on: *billions of dollars of western aid hinged on the outcome of the talks.* **3** to join or open (something) by means of a hinge. **hinged** *adj*

hinny *n, pl* **-nies** the offspring of a male horse and a female donkey.

hint *n* **1** a suggestion given in an indirect or subtle manner. **2** a helpful piece of advice. **3** a small amount: *a hint of irony. ~vb* **4** (sometimes foll. by *at*) to suggest indirectly: *a solution has been hinted at by a few politicians.*

hinterland *n* **1** land lying behind a coast or the shore of a river. **2** an area near and dependent on a large city, esp. a port.

hip[1] *n* either side of the body below the waist and above the thigh.

hip[2] *n* the berry-like brightly coloured fruit of a rose bush. Also called: **rosehip**

hip[3] *interj* an exclamation used to introduce cheers: *hip, hip, hurrah.*

hip[4] *adj* **hipper, hippest** *Slang* aware of or following the latest trends.

hip bath *n* a portable bath in which the bather sits.

hipbone *n* either of the two bones that form the sides of the pelvis.

hip flask *n* a small metal flask for whisky, brandy, etc.

hip-hop *n* a US pop-culture movement originating in the 1980s, comprising rap music, graffiti, and break dancing.

hippie *n* same as **hippy**[2].

hippo *n, pl* **-pos** *Informal* short for **hippopotamus.**

Hippocratic oath *n* an oath taken by a doctor to observe a code of medical ethics.

hippodrome *n* **1** a music hall, variety theatre, or circus. **2** (in ancient Greece or Rome) an open-air course for horse and chariot races.

hippopotamus *n, pl* **-muses** *or* **-mi** a very large mammal with thick wrinkled skin and short legs, which lives around the rivers of tropical Africa.

hippy[1] *adj* **-pier, -piest** *Informal* having large hips.

hippy[2] *or* **hippie** *n, pl* **-pies** (esp. during the 1960s) a person whose behaviour and dress imply a rejection of conventional values.

hipsters *pl n Brit* trousers cut so that the top encircles the hips.

hire *vb* **hiring, hired** **1** to acquire the temporary use of (a thing) or the services of (a person) in exchange for payment. **2** to employ (a person) for wages. **3** to provide (something) or the services of (oneself or others) for payment. **4 hire out** *Chiefly Brit* to pay independent contractors for (work to be done). *~n* **5** the act of hiring. **6 for hire** available to be hired.

hireling *n Disparaging* a person who works only for money.

hire-purchase *n Brit* a system in which a buyer takes possession of merchandise on payment of a deposit and completes the purchase by paying a series of instalments while the seller retains ownership until the final instalment is paid.

hirsute (**her**-suit) *adj* hairy.

his *adj* **1** of, belonging to, or associated with him: *his birthday. ~pron* **2** something belonging to him: *his is on the left; that book is his.* **3 of his** belonging to him.

Hispanic *adj* **1** of or derived from Spain or the Spanish. *~n* **2** *US* a US citizen of Latin-American descent.

hiss *n* **1** a sound like that of a prolonged *s.* **2** such a sound as an expression of dislike or disapproval. *~vb* **3** to utter a hiss. **4** to express with a hiss: *she hissed the name.* **5** to show dislike or disapproval towards (a speaker or performer) by hissing.

histamine (**hiss**-ta-meen) *n* a chemical compound released by the body tissues in allergic reactions.

histogram *n* a statistical graph that represents the frequency of values of a quantity by vertical bars of varying heights and widths.

THESAURUS

hilt **1.** grip, haft, handgrip, handle, helve **2. to the hilt** completely, entirely, fully, totally, wholly

hind after, back, caudal (*Zoology*), hinder, posterior, rear

hinder arrest, block, check, debar, delay, deter, encumber, frustrate, hamper, hamstring, handicap, hold up *or* back, impede, interrupt, obstruct, oppose, prevent, retard, slow down, stop, stymie, thwart, trammel

hindmost concluding, final, furthest, furthest behind, last, most remote, rearmost, terminal, trailing, ultimate

hindrance bar, barrier, block, check, deterrent, difficulty, drag, drawback, encumbrance, handicap, hitch, impediment, interruption, limitation, obstacle, obstruction, restraint, restriction, snag, stoppage, stumbling block, trammel

hinge be contingent, be subject to, depend, hang, pivot, rest, revolve around, turn

hint *n.* **1.** allusion, clue, implication, indication, inkling, innuendo, insinuation, intimation, mention, reminder, suggestion, tip-off, word to the wise **2.** advice, help, pointer, suggestion, tip, wrinkle (*informal*) **3.** breath, dash, *soupçon*, speck, suggestion, suspicion, taste, tinge, touch, trace, undertone, whiff, whisper *~vb.* **4.** allude, cue, imply, indicate, insinuate, intimate, let it be known, mention, prompt, suggest, tip off

hippy beatnik, bohemian, dropout, flower child, New Age traveller

hire appoint, charter, commission, employ, engage, lease, let, rent, sign up, take on

hiss *n.* **1.** buzz, hissing, sibilance, sibilation **2.** boo, catcall, contempt, derision, jeer, raspberry *~vb.* **3.** rasp, shrill, sibilate, wheeze, whirr, whistle, whiz **4.** blow a raspberry, boo, catcall, condemn, damn, decry, deride, hoot, jeer, mock, revile, ridicule

histology *n* the study of the tissues of an animal or plant.
historian *n* a person who writes or studies history.
historic *adj* important in history, or likely to be seen as important in the future.
historical *adj* **1** occurring in the past. **2** describing or representing situations or people that existed in the past: *a historical novel.* **3** belonging to or typical of the study of history: *historical perspective.* **historically** *adv*
historicism *n* **1** the belief that natural laws govern historical events. **2** excessive respect for historical institutions, such as traditions or laws.
historicity *n* historical authenticity.
historiographer *n* a historian employed to write the history of a group or public institution. **historiography** *n*
history *n, pl* **-ries 1** a record or account of past events and developments. **2** all that is preserved of the past, esp. in written form. **3** the study of interpreting past events. **4** the past events or previous experiences of a place, thing, or person: *he knew the whole history of the place.* **5** a play that depicts historical events.
histrionic *adj* **1** very dramatic and full of exaggerated emotion: *histrionic bursts of invective.* ~*n* **2** (*pl*) behaviour of this kind. **histrionically** *adv*
hit *vb* **hitting, hit 1** to strike or touch (a person or thing) forcefully. **2** to come into violent contact with: *a helicopter hit a Volvo.* **3** to propel (a ball) by striking. **4** *Cricket* to score (runs). **5** to affect (a person, place, or thing) badly: *the airline says that its revenue will be hit.* **6** to reach (a point or place): *the ERM hit new heights.* **7 hit the bottle** *Slang* to start drinking excessive amounts of alcohol. **8 hit the road** *Informal* to set out on a journey. ~*n* **9** an impact or collision. **10** a shot or blow that reaches its target. **11** *Informal* a person or thing that gains wide appeal: *those early collections made her a hit with the club set.* ~See also **hit off, hit on, hit out at.**
hit-and-run *adj* denoting a motor-vehicle accident in which the driver does not stop to give assistance or inform the police.
hitch *n* **1** a temporary or minor problem or difficulty. **2** a knot that can be undone by pulling against the direction of the strain that holds it. ~*vb* **3** *Informal* to obtain (a ride) by hitchhiking. **4** to fasten with a knot or tie. **5 get hitched** *Slang* to get married. **6 hitch up** to pull up (one's trousers etc.) with a quick jerk.
hitchhike *vb* **-hiking, -hiked** to travel by getting free lifts in motor vehicles. **hitchhiker** *n*
hi-tech *adj* using sophisticated, esp. electronic, technology.
hither *adv Old-fashioned* to or towards this place: *come hither.*
hitherto *adv Formal* until this time: *fundamental questions which have hitherto been ignored.*
hit list *n Informal* **1** a list of people to be murdered. **2** a list of targets to be eliminated: *the Treasury draws up a hit list for spending cuts.*
hit man *n* a person hired by terrorists or gangsters to murder someone.
hit off *vb* **hit it off** *Informal* to have a good relationship with someone.
hit on *or* **upon** *vb* to think of (an idea or a solution).
hit-or-miss *adj Informal* unplanned or unpredictable: *hit-or-miss service.* Also: **hit-and-miss**
hit out at *vb* **1** to direct blows forcefully and vigorously at (someone). **2** to make a verbal attack upon (someone).
HIV human immunodeficiency virus, the cause of AIDS.
hive *n* **1** a structure in which bees live. **2 hive of activity** a busy place with many people working hard.
hive off *vb* to transfer (part of a business, esp. the profitable part of a nationalized industry) to new ownership.
hives *n Pathol* an allergic reaction in which itchy red or whitish raised patches develop on the skin.
HM Her (*or* His) Majesty.
HMI (in Britain) Her (*or* His) Majesty's Inspector; a government official who examines and supervises schools.
H.M.S. *or* **HMS** Her (*or* His) Majesty's Ship.
HMSO (in Britain) Her (*or* His) Majesty's Stationery Office.
HNC (in Britain) Higher National Certificate; a qualification recognized by many national technical and professional institutions.
HND (in Britain) Higher National Diploma; a qualification in a technical subject equivalent to an ordinary degree.
Ho *Chem* holmium.

THESAURUS

historian annalist, biographer, chronicler, historiographer, recorder
historic celebrated, consequential, epoch-making, extraordinary, famous, momentous, notable, outstanding, red-letter, remarkable, significant
historical actual, archival, attested, authentic, chronicled, documented, factual, real, verifiable
history account, annals, autobiography, biography, chronicle, memoirs, narration, narrative, recapitulation, recital, record, relation, saga, story
hit *vb.* **1.** bang, bash (*informal*), batter, beat, belt (*informal*), chin (*slang*), clip (*informal*), clobber (*slang*), clout (*informal*), cuff, deck (*slang*), flog, knock, lambast(e), lay one on (*slang*), lob, punch, slap, smack, smite (*archaic*), sock (*slang*), strike, swat, thump, wallop (*informal*), whack **2.** bang into, bump, clash with, collide with, crash against, meet head-on, run into, smash into **3.** affect, damage, devastate, impinge on, influence, leave a mark on, make an impact *or* impression on, move, overwhelm, touch **4.** accomplish, achieve, arrive at, attain, gain, reach, secure, strike, touch ~*n.* **5.** belt (*informal*), blow, bump, clash, clout (*informal*), collision, cuff, impact, knock, rap, shot, slap, smack, stroke, swipe (*informal*), wallop (*informal*) **6.** *informal* sellout, sensation, smash (*informal*), success, triumph, winner
hitch *n.* **1.** catch, check, delay, difficulty, drawback, hassle (*informal*), hindrance, hold-up, impediment, mishap, obstacle, problem, snag, stoppage, trouble ~*vb.* **2.** *informal* hitchhike, thumb a lift **3.** attach, connect, couple, fasten, harness, join, make fast, tether, tie, unite, yoke **4. hitch up** hoick, jerk, pull, tug, yank
hither close (*old-fashioned*), closer, here, near, nearer, nigh (*archaic, poetic*), over here, to this place
hitherto *formal* heretofore, previously, so far, thus far, till now, until now, up to now
hit it off *informal* be on good terms, click (*slang*), get on (well) with, take to, warm to
hit on *or* **upon** arrive at, chance upon, come upon, discover, guess, invent, light upon, realize, strike upon, stumble on, think up
hit or miss *informal* aimless, casual, cursory, disorganized, haphazard, indiscriminate, perfunctory, random, undirected, uneven
hit out at assail, attack, castigate, condemn, de-

hoar *n* short for **hoarfrost.**

hoard *n* **1** a store of money, food, etc., hidden away for future use. *~vb* **2** to save or store (money, food, etc.). **hoarder** *n*

hoarding *n* a large board at the side of a road, used for displaying advertising posters.

hoarfrost *n* a white layer of ice crystals formed on the ground by condensation at temperatures below freezing point.

hoarse *adj* **1** (of a voice) rough and unclear through illness or too much shouting. **2** having a rough and unclear voice. **hoarsely** *adv* **hoarseness** *n*

hoary *adj* **hoarier, hoariest 1** having grey or white hair. **2** very old: *a hoary old problem.*

hoax *n* **1** a deception, esp. a practical joke. *~vb* **2** to deceive or play a joke on (someone).

hob *n* the flat top part of a cooker, or a separate flat surface, containing hotplates or burners.

hobble *vb* **-bling, -bled 1** to walk with a lame awkward movement. **2** to tie the legs of (a horse) together in order to restrict its movement.

hobby *n, pl* **-bies** an activity pursued in one's spare time for pleasure or relaxation.

hobbyhorse *n* **1** a favourite topic about which a person likes to talk at every opportunity: *public transport is his hobbyhorse.* **2** a toy consisting of a stick with a figure of a horse's head at one end. **3** a figure of a horse attached to a performer's waist in a morris dance.

hobgoblin *n* a small, mischievous creature in fairy stories.

hobnail boots *n Old-fashioned* heavy boots with short nails in the soles to lessen wear and tear.

hobnob *vb* **-nobbing, -nobbed** to socialize or talk informally: *hobnobbing with the rich.*

hobo *n, pl* **-boes** *or* **-bos** *Chiefly US & Canad* a tramp or vagrant.

Hobson's choice *n* the choice of taking what is offered or nothing at all.

hock[1] *n* the joint in the leg of a horse or similar animal that corresponds to the human ankle.

hock[2] *n* a white wine from the German Rhine.

hock[3] *Informal ~vb* **1** to pawn or pledge. *~n* **2 in hock a** in debt. **b** in pawn.

hockey *n* **1** a game played on a field by two teams of 11 players who try to hit a ball into their opponents' goal using long sticks curved at the end. **2** *US* ice hockey.

hocus-pocus *n Informal* something said or done in oder to confuse or trick someone.

hod *n* an open wooden box attached to a pole, for carrying bricks or mortar.

hodgepodge *n Chiefly US & Canad* same as **hotchpotch.**

Hodgkin's disease *n* a malignant disease that causes enlargement of the lymph nodes, spleen, and liver.

hoe *n* **1** a long-handled implement used to loosen the soil or to weed. *~vb* **hoeing, hoed 2** to scrape or weed with a hoe.

hog *n* **1** a castrated male pig. **2** *US & Canad* any mammal of the pig family. **3** *Informal* a greedy person. **4 go the whole hog** *Slang* to do something in the most complete way possible. *~vb* **hogging, hogged 5** *Slang* to take more than one's share of (something).

Hogmanay *n* New Year's Eve in Scotland.

hogshead *n* a large cask for storing alcoholic drinks.

hogwash *n Informal* nonsense.

ho-ho *interj* a written representation of the sound of a deep laugh.

hoick *vb* to raise abruptly and sharply.

hoi polloi *n* the ordinary people when compared to the rich or well-educated.

hoist *vb* **1** to raise or lift up, esp. by mechanical means. *~n* **2** any apparatus or device for lifting things.

hoity-toity *adj Informal* arrogant or haughty.

hokonui (hoke-a-**noo**-ee) *n NZ* illegally distilled whisky.

hokum *n Slang, chiefly US & Canad* **1** nonsense; bunk. **2** obvious sentimental material in a play or film.

hold[1] *vb* **holding, held 1** to keep (an object or a person) with or within the hands or arms. **2** to support: *a rope made from 1000 hairs would hold a large adult.* **3** to maintain in a specified state or position: *his reputation continued to hold secure.* **4** to have the capacity for: *trains designed to hold more than 400.* **5** to set aside or reserve: *they will hold our tickets until tomorrow.* **6** to restrain or keep back: *designed to hold dangerous criminals.* **7** to remain unbroken: *if the elastic holds.* **8** (of the weather) to remain dry and bright. **9** to keep (the attention of): *a writer holds a reader by his temperament.* **10** to arrange and cause to take place: *we must hold an inquiry.* **11** to have the ownership or possession of: *she holds a degree in Egyptology.* **12** to have responsibility for: *she cannot hold an elective office.* **13** to be able to control the outward effects of drinking (alcohol): *he can't hold his liquor.* **14** to (cause to) remain committed to (a promise, etc.). **15** to claim or believe: *some Sufis hold that all religious leaders were prophets.* **16** to remain valid or true: *the categories are not the same and equivalency does not hold.* **17** to consider in a specified manner: *philosophies which we hold so dear.* **18** to defend successfully: *the Russians were holding the Volga front.* **19** *Music* to sustain the sound of (a note). *~n* **20** a way of holding something or the act of holding it. **21** some-

THESAURUS

nounce, inveigh against, lash out, rail against, strike out at

hoard 1. *n.* accumulation, cache, fall-back, fund, heap, mass, pile, reserve, stockpile, store, supply, treasure-trove **2.** *vb.* accumulate, amass, buy up, cache, collect, deposit, garner, gather, hive, lay up, put away, put by, save, stash away (*informal*), stockpile, store, treasure

hoarder collector, magpie (*Brit.*), miser, niggard, saver, squirrel (*informal*)

hoarse croaky, discordant, grating, gravelly, growling, gruff, guttural, harsh, husky, rasping, raucous, rough, throaty

hoary 1. frosty, grey, grey-haired, grizzled, hoar, silvery, white, white-haired **2.** aged, ancient, antiquated, antique, old, venerable

hoax 1. *n.* canard, cheat, con (*informal*), deception, fast one (*informal*), fraud, imposture, joke, practical joke, prank, ruse, spoof (*informal*), swindle, trick **2.** *vb.* bamboozle (*informal*), bluff, con (*slang*), deceive, delude, dupe, fool, hoodwink, kid (*informal*), swindle, take in (*informal*), take (someone) for a ride (*informal*), trick, wind up (*Brit. slang*)

hobby diversion, favourite occupation, (leisure) activity, leisure pursuit, pastime, relaxation, sideline

hobnob associate, consort, fraternize, hang about, hang out (*informal*), keep company, mingle, mix, socialize

hoi polloi canaille, commonalty, riffraff, the (common) herd, the common people, the lower orders, the masses, the plebs, the populace, the proles (*offensive*

thing to hold onto for support. **22** controlling influence: *drugs will take a hold.* **23 with no holds barred** with all limitations removed. ~See also **hold back, hold down,** etc. **holder** *n*

hold[2] *n* the space in a ship or aircraft for storing cargo.

holdall *n Brit* a large strong travelling bag.

hold back *vb* **1** to restrain (someone) or refrain from doing something: *managers declined to hold back the crowds; buyers held back in the expectation of further price decreases.* **2** to withhold: *holding back the wages they owe.*

hold down *vb* **1** to restrain or control someone. **2** *Informal* to manage to keep (a job). **3** to prevent (wages, prices, etc.) from rising much.

hold forth *vb* to speak for a long time.

hold in *vb* to control or conceal (one's feelings).

holding *n* **1** land held under a lease. **2** property to which the holder has legal title, such as land, stocks, or shares.

holding company *n* a company that holds the controlling shares in one or more other companies.

holding paddock *n Austral & NZ* a paddock in which cattle or sheep are kept temporarily, such as when awaiting sale.

hold off *vb* **1** to keep (an attacker or attacking force) at a distance. **2** to put off (doing something): *he held off distributing weapons.*

hold on *vb* **1** to maintain a firm grasp (of something or someone). **2 hold on to** to keep: *he held on to his world No. 1 ranking.* **3** *Informal* to wait, esp. on the telephone.

hold out *vb* **1** to offer (something). **2** to last: *I could hold out until we return home.* **3** to continue to stand firm and manage to resist opposition. **4 hold out for** to wait patiently for (the fulfilment of one's wishes). **5 hold out on someone** *Informal* to keep from telling someone some important information.

hold over *vb* to postpone: *several cases had to be held over pending further investigation.*

hold-up *n* **1** an armed robbery. **2** a delay: *a traffic hold-up.* ~*vb* **hold up 3** to delay. **4** to support (an object). **5** to stop and rob (someone), using a weapon. **6** to exhibit or present (something) as an example: *he was held up as a model professional.*

hold with *vb* approve of: *I don't hold with divorce.*

hole *n* **1** an area hollowed out in a solid. **2** an opening in or through something. **3** an animal's burrow. **4** *Informal* a fault or error: *this points to a very big hole in parliamentary security.* **5 pick holes in** to point out faults in. **6** *Informal* an unattractive town or other place. **7 in a hole** *Slang* in a difficult and embarrassing situation. **8** (on a golf course) any one of the divisions of a course (usually 18) represented by the distance between the tee and the sunken cup on the green into which the ball is to be played. **9 make a hole in** *Informal* to use a great amount of (one's money or food supply). ~*vb* **holing, holed 10** to make a hole or holes in (something). **11** to hit (a golf ball) into a hole. **holey** *adj*

hole-and-corner *adj Informal* furtive or secretive.

hole in the heart *n* a congenital defect of the heart, in which there is an abnormal opening in the partition between the left and right halves.

hole up *vb Informal* to go into hiding.

Holi (**holl**-lee) *n* an annual Hindu spring festival, honouring Krishna.

holiday *n* **1** a period of time spent away from home for enjoyment and relaxation. **2** (*often pl*) *Chiefly Brit* a period in which a break is taken from work or studies for rest or recreation. **3** a day on which work is

THESAURUS

slang, chiefly Brit.), the proletariat, the rabble, the third estate, the underclass

hoist 1. *vb.* elevate, erect, heave, lift, raise, rear, upraise **2.** *n.* crane, elevator, lift, tackle, winch

hold *vb.* **1.** adhere, clasp, cleave, clinch, cling, clutch, cradle, embrace, enfold, grasp, grip, stick **2.** bear, brace, carry, prop, shoulder, support, sustain, take **3.** continue, endure, last, persevere, persist, remain, resist, stay, wear **4.** accommodate, comprise, contain, have a capacity for, seat, take **5.** arrest, bind, check, confine, curb, detain, impound, imprison, pound, restrain, stay, stop, suspend **6.** assemble, call, carry on, celebrate, conduct, convene, have, officiate at, preside over, run, solemnize **7.** have, keep, maintain, occupy, own, possess, retain **8.** assume, believe, consider, deem, entertain, esteem, judge, maintain, presume, reckon, regard, think, view **9.** apply, be in force, be the case, exist, hold good, operate, remain true, remain valid, stand up ~*n.* **10.** clasp, clutch, grasp, grip **11.** anchorage, foothold, footing, leverage, prop, purchase, stay, support, vantage **12.** ascendancy, authority, clout (*informal*), control, dominance, dominion, influence, mastery, pull (*informal*), sway

hold back 1. check, control, curb, inhibit, rein, repress, restrain, suppress **2.** desist, forbear, keep back, refuse, withhold

holder 1. case, container, cover, housing, receptacle, sheath **2.** bearer, custodian, incumbent, keeper, occupant, owner, possessor, proprietor, purchaser

hold forth declaim, descant, discourse, go on, harangue, lecture, orate, preach, speak, speechify, spiel (*informal*), spout (*informal*)

hold off 1. fend off, keep off, rebuff, repel, repulse, stave off **2.** avoid, defer, delay, keep from, postpone, put off, refrain

hold out 1. extend, give, offer, present, proffer **2.** carry on, continue, endure, hang on, last, persevere, persist, stand fast, withstand

hold over adjourn, defer, delay, postpone, put off, suspend, waive

hold-up 1. burglary, mugging (*informal*), robbery, steaming (*informal*), stick-up (*slang, chiefly U.S.*), theft **2.** bottleneck, delay, difficulty, hitch, obstruction, setback, snag, stoppage, traffic jam, trouble, wait

hold up 1. delay, detain, hinder, impede, retard, set back, slow down, stop **2.** bolster, brace, buttress, jack up, prop, shore up, support, sustain **3.** mug (*informal*), rob, stick up (*slang, chiefly U.S.*), waylay **4.** display, exhibit, flaunt, present, show

hold with agree to *or* with, approve of, be in favour of, countenance, subscribe to, support, take kindly to

hole 1. cave, cavern, cavity, chamber, depression, excavation, hollow, pit, pocket, scoop, shaft **2.** aperture, breach, break, crack, fissure, gap, opening, orifice, outlet, perforation, puncture, rent, split, tear, vent **3.** burrow, covert, den, earth, lair, nest, retreat, shelter **4.** defect, discrepancy, error, fallacy, fault, flaw, inconsistency, loophole **5. pick holes in** asperse, badmouth (*slang, chiefly U.S. & Canad.*), cavil, crab (*informal*), criticize, denigrate, disparage, disprove, find fault, knock (*informal*), niggle, pull to pieces, put down, rubbish (*informal*), run down, slag (off) (*slang*), slate (*informal*) **6.** *informal* dive (*slang*), dump (*informal*), hovel, joint (*slang*), slum

holiday 1. break, leave, recess, time off, vacation **2.** anniversary, bank holiday, celebration, feast, festival, festivity, fête, gala, public holiday, saint's day

suspended by law or custom, such as a bank holiday. *~vb* **4** *Chiefly Brit* to spend a holiday.

holier-than-thou *adj* offensively self-righteous.

Holiness *n* (preceded by *His* or *Your*) a title reserved for the pope.

holism *n* **1** the view that a whole is greater than the sum of its parts. **2** (in medicine) consideration of the complete person in the treatment of disease. **holistic** *adj*

hollandaise sauce *n* a rich sauce of egg yolks, butter, vinegar, and lemon juice.

holler *Informal ~vb* **1** to shout or yell. *~n* **2** a shout or yell.

hollow *adj* **1** having a hole or space within; not solid. **2** curving inwards: *hollow cheeks.* **3** (of sounds) as if echoing in a hollow place. **4** without any real value or worth: *a hollow enterprise, lacking purpose, and lacking soul. ~adv* **5 beat someone hollow** *Brit informal* to defeat someone thoroughly. *~n* **6** a cavity or space in something. **7** a dip in the land. *~vb* **8** (often foll. by *out*) to form a hole or cavity in. **hollowly** *adv*

holly *n* an evergreen tree with prickly leaves and bright red berries, used for Christmas decorations.

hollyhock *n* a tall garden plant with spikes of colourful flowers.

holmium *n Chem* a silver-white metallic element, the compounds of which are highly magnetic. Symbol: Ho

holm oak *n* an evergreen oak tree with prickly leaves like holly.

holocaust *n* **1** destruction or loss of life on a massive scale. **2 the Holocaust** mass murder of the Jews in Europe by the Nazis (1940–45).

Holocene *adj* of the current geological epoch, which began about 10 000 years ago.

hologram *n* a three-dimensional photographic image produced by means of a split laser beam.

holograph *n* a book or document handwritten by its author.

holography *n* the science of using lasers to produce holograms. **holographic** *adj* **holographically** *adv*

hols *pl n Brit school slang* holidays.

holster *n* a sheathlike leather case for a pistol, worn attached to a belt.

holt *n* the lair of an otter.

holy *adj* **-lier, -liest 1** of or associated with God or a deity. **2** (of a person) religious and leading a virtuous life. **holiness** *n*

Holy Communion *n Christianity* a church service in which people take bread and wine in remembrance of Christ's Last Supper and His atonement for the sins of the world.

Holy Ghost *n* **the Holy Ghost** same as **Holy Spirit.**

Holy Grail *n* **the Holy Grail** (in medieval legend) the bowl used by Jesus at the Last Supper.

Holy Land *n* **the Holy Land** Palestine.

holy of holies *n* **1** any sacred place or a place considered as if it were sacred: *the Long Room at Lord's, English cricket's holy of holies.* **2** the innermost chamber of a Jewish temple.

holy orders *pl n* the status of an ordained Christian minister.

Holy See *n* **the Holy See** *RC Church* the see of the pope as bishop of Rome.

Holy Spirit *n* **the Holy Spirit** *Christianity* one of the three aspects of God.

Holy Week *n Christianity* the week before Easter Sunday.

homage *n* a public show of respect or honour towards someone or something: *the master's jazzy-classical homage to Gershwin.*

homburg *n* a man's soft felt with a dented crown and a stiff upturned brim.

home *n* **1** the place where one lives. **2** the country or area of one's birth. **3** a building or organization set up to care for people in a certain category, such as orphans or the aged. **4** the place where something is invented or started: *the home of the first aircraft.* **5** *Sport* a team's own ground: *the match is at home.* **6** *Baseball, rounders, etc* the objective towards which a player runs after striking the ball. **7 at home a** in one's own home or country. **b** at ease: *he felt more at home with the Russians.* **c** receiving visitors. **8 home and dry** *Brit slang* definitely safe or successful. *~adj* **9** of one's home, birthplace, or native country. **10** (of an activity) done in one's house: *home movies.* **11** *Sport* played on one's own ground: *a home game. ~adv* **12** to or at home: *I came home.* **13** to or on the point: *the message struck home.* **14** to the fullest extent: *they drove their spears home.* **15 bring something home to someone** to make something clear to someone. *~vb* **homing, homed 16 home in on** to be directed towards (a goal or target). **17** (of birds) to return home accurately from a distance.

homeboy *n Slang, chiefly US* **1** a close friend. **2** a member of a gang.

home-brew *n* beer or other alcoholic drink brewed at home.

homecoming *n* a return home, esp. after a long absence.

Home Counties *pl n* the counties surrounding London.

home economics *n* the study of diet, budgeting, child care, and other subjects concerned with running a home.

THESAURUS

holier-than-thou goody-goody (*informal*), pietistic, pietistical, priggish, religiose, sanctimonious, self-righteous, self-satisfied, smug, squeaky-clean, unctuous

holiness blessedness, devoutness, divinity, godliness, piety, purity, religiousness, righteousness, sacredness, saintliness, sanctity, spirituality, virtuousness

hollow *adj.* **1.** empty, not solid, unfilled, vacant, void **2.** cavernous, concave, deep-set, depressed, indented, sunken **3.** deep, dull, expressionless, flat, low, muffled, muted, reverberant, rumbling, sepulchral, toneless **4.** empty, fruitless, futile, meaningless, pointless, Pyrrhic, specious, unavailing, useless, vain, worthless **5. beat (someone) hollow** *Brit. informal* defeat, hammer (*informal*), outdo, overcome, rout, thrash, trounce, worst *~n.* **6.** basin, bowl, cave, cavern, cavity, concavity, crater, cup, den, dent, depression, dimple, excavation, hole, indentation, pit, trough **7.** bottom, dale, dell, dingle, glen, valley *~vb.* **8.** channel, dig, dish, excavate, furrow, gouge, groove, pit, scoop

holocaust annihilation, carnage, conflagration, destruction, devastation, genocide, massacre, mass murder

holy 1. blessed, consecrated, dedicated, hallowed, sacred, sacrosanct, sanctified, venerable, venerated **2.** devout, divine, faithful, god-fearing, godly, hallowed, pious, pure, religious, righteous, saintly, sublime, virtuous

home *n.* **1.** abode, domicile, dwelling, dwelling place, environment, habitation, hearth, home ground, homestead, home town, house, pad (*slang*), residence **2. at home a.** available, in, present **b.** at ease, comfortable, familiar, relaxed **c.** entertaining, giving a party, having guests, receiving *~adj.* **3.** central, domestic, familiar,

home farm *n Brit* a farm that belonged to and provided food for a large country house.

Home Guard *n* a part-time military force of volunteers recruited for the defence of the United Kingdom in the Second World War.

home help *n Brit* a person employed by a local authority to do housework in an elderly or disabled person's home.

homeland *n* **1** the country from which the ancestors of a person or group came. **2** the official name in S Africa for a **Bantustan.**

homeless *adj* **1** having nowhere to live. *~pl n* **2** people who have nowhere to live: *night shelters for the homeless.* **homelessness** *n*

homely *adj* **-lier, -liest 1** simple, ordinary, and comfortable. **2** (of a person) **a** *Brit* warm and friendly. **b** *Chiefly US & Canad* plain or unattractive. **homeliness** *n*

home-made *adj* (esp. of foods) made at home or on the premises.

Home Office *n Brit government* the department responsible for law and order, immigration, and other domestic affairs.

homeopathy *or* **homoeopathy** (home-ee-**op**-ath-ee) *n* a method of treating disease by the use of small amounts of a drug that produces symptoms of the disease in healthy people. **homeopath** *or* **homoeopath** (**home**-ee-oh-path) *n* **homeopathic** *or* **homoeopathic** *adj*

homeostasis *or* **homoeostasis** (hom-ee-oh-**stass**-iss) *n* the tendency of an organism to achieve a stable metabolic state by compensating automatically for violent changes in the environment and other disruptions.

homeowner *n* a person who owns the home in which he or she lives.

Homeric (home-**mer**-rik) *adj* of or relating to Homer, Greek epic poet (circa 800 BC).

home rule *n* self-government in domestic affairs.

Home Secretary *n Brit government* the head of the Home Office.

homesick *adj* depressed by being away from home and family. **homesickness** *n*

homespun *adj* (of philosophies or opinions) plain and unsophisticated.

homestead *n* **1** a farmhouse and the adjoining land. **2** (in the western U.S. & Canada) a house and adjoining tract of land (originally often 160 acres) that was granted by the government for development as a farm. Homesteads are exempt from seizure or sale for debt.

homesteader *n* (in the western U.S. & Canada) a person who lives on and farms a homestead.

homestead law *n* (in the western U.S. & Canada) any of various laws granting certain privileges to owners of homesteads.

home truths *pl n* unpleasant facts told to a person about himself or herself.

home unit *n Austral & NZ* a self-contained residence which is part of a block of such residences.

homeward *adj* **1** going home. *~adv also* **homewards 2** towards home.

homework *n* **1** school work done at home. **2** research or preparation.

homicide *n* **1** the act of killing someone. **2** a person who kills someone. **homicidal** *adj*

homily *n, pl* **-lies** a moralizing talk or piece of writing. **homiletic** *adj*

homing *adj* **1** *Zool* denoting the ability to return home after travelling great distances. **2** (of a missile) capable of guiding itself onto a target.

homing pigeon *n* a pigeon developed for its homing instinct, used for racing.

hominid *n* **1** any member of the family of primates that includes modern man and the extinct forerunners of man. *~adj* **2** of or belonging to this family.

hominoid *adj* **1** of or like man; manlike. *~n* **2** a manlike animal.

hominy *n Chiefly US* coarsely ground maize prepared as a food by boiling in milk or water.

homo- *combining form* same or like: *homologous.*

homogeneous (home-oh-**jean**-ee-uss) *adj* having parts or members which are all the same or which consist of only one substance: *the Arabs are not a single, homogeneous nation.* **homogeneity** *n*

homogenize *or* **-nise** *vb* **-nizing, -nized** *or* **-nising, -nised 1** to break up the fat globules in (milk or cream) so that they are evenly distributed. **2** to make different elements the same or similar: *homogenized products for a mass market.*

homogenous (hom-**oj**-in-uss) *adj* having a similar structure because of common ancestry.

homograph *n* a word spelt the same as another, but having a different meaning, such as *bear* (to carry) and *bear* (the animal).

homologous (hom-**ol**-log-uss) *adj* **1** having a related or similar position or structure. **2** *Biol* (of organs and parts) having the same origin but different functions: *the wing of a bat and the arm of a monkey are homologous.*

homology (hom-**ol**-a-jee) *n* the condition of being homologous.

homonym *n* a word pronounced and spelt the same as another, but having a different meaning, such as *novel* (a book) and *novel* (new).

homophobia *n* intense hatred or fear of homosexuals.

homophone *n* a word pronounced the same as another, but having a different meaning or spelling or both, such as *bear* and *bare.*

Homo sapiens (**home**-oh **sap**-ee-enz) *n* the name for modern man as a species.

homosexual *n* **1** a person who is sexually attracted to members of the same sex. *~adj* **2** (of a person) sex-

THESAURUS

family, household, inland, internal, local, national, native *~adv.* **4. bring home to** drive home, emphasize, impress upon, make clear, press home

homeland country of origin, fatherland, mother country, motherland, native land

homeless 1. *adj.* abandoned, destitute, displaced, dispossessed, down-and-out, exiled, forlorn, forsaken, outcast, unsettled **2.** *pl. n.* dossers (*Brit. slang*), squatters, vagrants

homely comfortable, comfy (*informal*), cosy, domestic, everyday, familiar, friendly, homespun, homy, informal, modest, natural, ordinary, plain, simple, unaffected, unassuming, unpretentious, welcoming

homespun artless, coarse, homely, home-made, inelegant, plain, rough, rude, rustic, unpolished, unsophisticated

homicidal deadly, death-dealing, lethal, maniacal, mortal, murderous

homicide 1. bloodshed, killing, manslaughter, murder, slaying **2.** killer, murderer, slayer

homogeneity analogousness, comparability, consistency, correspondence, identicalness, oneness, sameness, similarity, uniformity

homogeneous akin, alike, analogous, cognate,

ually attracted to members of the same sex. **3** (of a sexual relationship) between members of the same sex. **homosexuality** *n*

homy *or esp US* **homey** *adj* **homier, homiest** like a home; pleasant and cosy.

Hon. Honourable (title).

hone *vb* **honing, honed 1** to develop and improve (a quality or ability): *a workshop to hone interview techniques.* **2** to sharpen (a tool). ~*n* **3** a fine whetstone used for sharpening edged tools and knives.

honest *adj* **1** truthful and moral in behaviour; trustworthy. **2** open and sincere in relationships and attitudes; without pretensions. **3** gained or earned fairly: *an honest income.*

honestly *adv* **1** in an honest manner. **2** truly: *honestly, that's all I can recall.*

honesty *n, pl* **-ties 1** the quality of being truthful and trustworthy. **2** a plant with flattened silvery pods which are used for indoor decoration.

honey *n* **1** a sweet edible sticky substance made by bees from nectar. **2** *Chiefly US & Canad* a term of affection. **3** *Informal, chiefly US & Canad* something very good of its kind: *a honey of a picture about American family life.*

honeybee *n* a bee widely domesticated as a source of honey and beeswax.

honeycomb *n* a waxy structure, constructed by bees in a hive, that consists of many six-sided cells in which honey is stored.

honeydew *n* a sugary substance excreted by aphids and similar insects.

honeydew melon *n* a melon with yellow skin and sweet pale flesh.

honeyed *adj Poetic* flattering or soothing: *honeyed words.*

honeymoon *n* **1** a holiday taken by a newly married couple. **2** the early period of an undertaking or activity, such as the start of new government's term of office, when an attitude of goodwill prevails. ~*vb* **3** to take a honeymoon. **honeymooner** *n*

honeysuckle *n* a climbing shrub with sweet-smelling white, yellow, or pink flowers.

honk *n* **1** the sound made by a motor horn. **2** the sound made by a goose. ~*vb* **3** to make or cause (something) to make a honking sound.

honky-tonk *n* **1** *US & Canad slang* a cheap disreputable nightclub or dance hall. **2** a style of ragtime piano-playing, esp. on a tinny-sounding piano.

honorarium *n, pl* **-iums** *or* **-ia** a voluntary fee paid for a service which is usually free.

honorary *adj* **a** held or given as a mark of respect, without the usual qualifications, payment, or work: *an honorary degree.* **b** (of a secretary, treasurer, etc.) unpaid.

honorific *adj* showing respect: *an honorific title.*

honour *or US* **honor** *n* **1** a person's good reputation and the respect they are given by other people. **2 a** fame or glory. **b** a person who wins fame or glory for his or her country, school, etc.: *he was an honour to his nation.* **3** great respect or esteem, or an outward sign of this. **4** a privilege or pleasure: *it was an honour to meet him.* **5** *Old-fashioned* a woman's virginity. **6** *Bridge, whist* any of the top four or five cards in a suit. **7** *Golf* the right to tee off first. **8 in honour of** out of respect for. **9 on one's honour** under a moral obligation. ~*vb* **10** to hold someone in respect. **11** to give (someone) special praise, attention, or an award. **12** to accept and then pay (a cheque or bill). **13** to keep (one's promise); fulfil (a previous agreement).

Honour *n* (preceded by *Your, His* or *Her*) a title used to address or refer to certain judges.

honourable *or US* **honorable** *adj* worthy of respect or esteem. **honourably** *adv*

Honourable *adj* **the Honourable** a title of respect placed before a name: used of various officials, of the children of certain peers, and in Parliament by one member speaking of another.

honours *or US* **honors** *pl n* **1** (in a university degree course) a rank or mark of the highest academic standard: *an honours degree.* **2** observances of respect, esp. at a funeral. **3 do the honours** to serve as host or hostess by serving food or pouring drinks.

hooch (rhymes with **smooch**) *n Informal* alcoholic drink, esp. illegally distilled spirits.

hood[1] *n* **1** a loose head covering either attached to a coat or made as a separate garment. **2** *US & Canad* the bonnet of a car. **3** the folding roof of a convertible car or a pram. ~*vb* **4** to cover with or as if with a hood. **hoodlike** *adj*

hood[2] *n Slang* short for **hoodlum.**

hooded *adj* **1** (of a garment) having a hood. **2** (of eyes) having heavy eyelids that appear to be half-closed.

THESAURUS

comparable, consistent, identical, kindred, similar, uniform, unvarying

homosexual bent (*slang*), camp (*informal*), gay, homoerotic, lesbian, queer (*informal, derogatory*), sapphic

honest 1. conscientious, decent, ethical, high-minded, honourable, law-abiding, reliable, reputable, scrupulous, trustworthy, trusty, truthful, upright, veracious, virtuous **2.** candid, direct, forthright, frank, ingenuous, open, outright, plain, sincere, straightforward, undisguised, unfeigned, upfront (*informal*) **3.** above board, authentic, bona fide, genuine, honest to goodness, on the level (*informal*), on the up and up, proper, real, straight, true

honestly 1. by fair means, cleanly, ethically, honourably, in good faith, lawfully, legally, legitimately, on the level (*informal*), with clean hands **2.** candidly, frankly, in all sincerity, in plain English, plainly, straight (out), to one's face, truthfully

honesty bluntness, candour, equity, faithfulness, fidelity, frankness, genuineness, honour, incorruptibility, integrity, morality, openness, outspokenness, plainness, probity, rectitude, reputability, scrupulousness, sincerity, straightforwardness, straightness, trustworthiness, truthfulness, uprightness, veracity, virtue

honorary complimentary, ex officio, formal, in name *or* title only, nominal, titular, unofficial, unpaid

honour *n.* **1.** credit, dignity, distinction, elevation, eminence, esteem, fame, glory, high standing, prestige, rank, renown, reputation, repute **2.** acclaim, accolade, adoration, Brownie points, commendation, deference, homage, kudos, praise, recognition, regard, respect, reverence, tribute, veneration **3.** compliment, credit, favour, pleasure, privilege, source of pride *or* satisfaction **4.** chastity, innocence, modesty, purity, virginity, virtue ~*vb.* **5.** acclaim, celebrate, commemorate, commend, compliment, crack up (*informal*), decorate, dignify, exalt, glorify, laud, lionize, praise **6.** accept, acknowledge, cash, clear, credit, pass, pay, take **7.** be as good as (*informal*), be faithful to, be true to, carry out, discharge, fulfil, keep, live up to, observe

honourable creditable, distinguished, eminent, estimable, great, illustrious, noble, notable, noted, pres-

hooded crow *n* a crow that has a grey body and black head, wings, and tail.

hoodlum *n* a violent criminal, esp. one who is a member of a gang.

hoodoo *n, pl* **-doos 1** *Informal* bad luck. **2** *Informal* a person or thing that brings bad luck. **3** *Chiefly US* same as **voodoo.**

hoodwink *vb* to trick or deceive.

hooey *n Slang* nonsense.

hoof *n, pl* **hooves** *or* **hoofs 1** the horny covering of the end of the foot in the horse, deer, and certain other mammals. ~*vb* **2 hoof it** *Slang* to walk. **hoofed** *adj*

hoo-ha *n* a noisy commotion or fuss.

hook *n* **1** a curved piece of metal or plastic used to hang, hold, or pull something. **2** something resembling a hook, such as a sharp bend in a river or a sharply curved strip of land. **3** *Boxing* a short swinging blow with the elbow bent. **4** *Cricket, golf* a shot that causes the ball to go to the player's left. **5 by hook or by crook** by any means: *get into the charts by hook or by crook.* **6 hook, line, and sinker** *Informal* completely: *we fell for it hook, line, and sinker.* **7 let someone off the hook** *Slang* to free someone from an obligation or a difficult situation. **8 sling one's hook** *Brit slang* to leave. ~*vb* **9** to fasten with or as if with a hook. **10** to catch (a fish) on a hook. **11** *Cricket, golf* to play (a ball) with a hook. **12** *Rugby* to obtain and pass (the ball) backwards from a scrum, using the feet.

hookah *n* an oriental pipe for smoking marijuana or tobacco, with a long flexible stem connected to a container of water through which smoke is drawn and cooled.

hooked *adj* **1** bent like a hook. **2 hooked on a** *Slang* addicted to: *hooked on drugs.* **b** obsessed with: *hooked on football.*

hooker *n* **1** *Slang* a prostitute. **2** *Rugby* a player who uses his feet to get the ball in a scrum.

hook-up *n* the linking of broadcasting equipment or stations to transmit a special programme.

hookworm *n* a blood-sucking worm with hooked mouthparts.

hooligan *n Slang* a young person who behaves in a noisy and violent way in public. **hooliganism** *n*

hoop *n* **1** a rigid circular band of metal, plastic, or wood. **2** a child's toy shaped like a hoop and rolled on the ground or whirled around the body. **3** *Croquet* any of the iron arches through which the ball is driven. **4** a large ring through which performers or animals jump. **5 go** *or* **be put through the hoops** to go through an ordeal or test. ~*vb* **6** to surround (something) with a hoop. **hooped** *adj*

hoopla *n Brit* a fairground game in which hoops are thrown over objects in an attempt to win them.

hoopoe (**hoop**-oo) *n* a bird with pinkish-brown plumage with black-and-white wings and a fanlike crest.

hooray *interj, n* same as **hurrah.**

Hooray Henry *n, pl* **Hooray Henries** *or* **-rys** a young upper-class man with an affectedly loud and cheerful manner.

hoot[1] *n* **1** the sound of a car horn. **2** the cry of an owl. **3** a high-pitched noise showing disapproval. **4** *Informal* an amusing person or thing. ~*vb* **5** *Brit* to blow (a car horn). **6** to make a hoot. **7** to jeer or yell contemptuously at someone. **8** to drive (speakers or performers on stage) off by hooting.

hoot[2] *n Austral & NZ slang* money.

hooter *n Chiefly Brit* **1** a device that hoots, such as a car horn. **2** *Slang* a nose.

Hoover *n* **1** *Trademark* a vacuum cleaner. ~*vb* **2 hoover** to vacuum-clean (a carpet).

hooves *n* a plural of **hoof.**

hop[1] *vb* **hopping, hopped 1** to jump forwards or upwards on one foot. **2** (of frogs, birds, etc.) to move forwards in short jumps. **3** to jump over something. **4** *Informal* to move quickly (in, on, out of, etc.): *hop into bed.* **5 hop it** *Brit slang* to go away. ~*n* **6** an instance of hopping. **7** *Informal* an informal dance. **8** *Informal* a short journey, usually in an aircraft. **9 on the hop** *Informal* **a** active or busy: *he keeps me on the hop.* **b** *Brit* unawares or unprepared: *you caught me on the hop.*

hop[2] *n* a climbing plant with green conelike flowers. See also **hops.**

hope *vb* **hoping, hoped 1** to desire (something), usually with some possibility of fulfilment: *you would hope for their cooperation.* **2** to trust or believe: *I hope I've arranged that.* ~*n* **3** a feeling of desire for something, usually with confidence in the possibility of its fulfilment: *the news was greeted by some as hope for further interest rate cuts.* **4** a reasonable ground for this feeling: *there is hope for you yet.* **5** the person, thing, situation, or event that gives cause for hope or is desired: *the young are a symbol of hope for the future.*

hopeful *adj* **1** having, inspiring, or expressing hope. ~*n* **2** a person considered to be on the brink of success: *a young hopeful.*

hopefully *adv* **1** in a hopeful manner. **2** *Informal* it is hoped: *hopefully I've got a long career ahead of me.*
➤ Although many people dislike the use of *hopefully* as in *I'll see you in June, hopefully,* it is now well established.

THESAURUS

tigious, proper, renowned, reputable, respectable, respected, right, righteous, venerable, virtuous

honours adornments, awards, decorations, dignities, distinctions, laurels, titles

hoodwink bamboozle (*informal*), befool, cheat, con (*informal*), cozen, deceive, delude, dupe, fool, gull (*archaic*), hoax, impose, kid (*informal*), lead up the garden path (*informal*), mislead, pull a fast one on (*informal*), rook (*slang*), swindle, trick

hook *n.* **1.** catch, clasp, fastener, hasp, holder, link, lock, peg **2. by hook or by crook** by any means, by fair means or foul, somehow, somehow or other, someway **3. hook, line, and sinker** *informal* completely, entirely, thoroughly, through and through, totally, utterly, wholly ~*vb.* **4.** catch, clasp, fasten, fix, hasp, secure **5.** catch, ensnare, entrap, snare, trap

hooligan *slang* casual, delinquent, hoodlum, lager lout, ned (*slang*), rowdy, ruffian, tough, vandal, yob *or* yobbo (*Brit. slang*)

hoop band, circlet, girdle, loop, ring, wheel

hoot *n.* **1.** call, cry, toot **2.** boo, catcall, hiss, jeer, yell **3.** *informal* card (*informal*), laugh (*informal*), scream (*informal*) ~*vb.* **4.** cry, scream, shout, shriek, toot, whoop, yell **5.** boo, catcall, condemn, decry, denounce, execrate, hiss, howl down, jeer, yell at

hop 1. *vb.* bound, caper, dance, jump, leap, skip, spring, trip, vault **2.** *n.* bounce, bound, jump, leap, skip, spring, step, vault

hope 1. *vb.* anticipate, aspire, await, believe, contemplate, count on, desire, expect, foresee, long, look forward to, rely, trust **2.** *n.* ambition, anticipation, assumption, belief, confidence, desire, dream, expectancy, expectation, faith, longing

hopeful anticipating, assured, auspicious, bright, buoyant, cheerful, confident, encouraging, expectant, heartening, looking forward to, optimistic, promising, propitious, reassuring, rosy, sanguine

hopefully 1. confidently, expectantly, optimistically,

hopeless *adj* **1** having or offering no hope. **2** impossible to solve. **3** *Informal* without skill or ability: *I'm hopeless at maths.* **hopelessly** *adv* **hopelessness** *n*

hopper *n* a funnel-shaped device from which solid materials can be discharged into a receptacle below.

hops *pl n* the dried flowers of the hop plant, used to give a bitter taste to beer.

hopscotch *n* a children's game in which a player throws a stone to land in one of a pattern of squares marked on the ground and then hops over to it to pick it up.

horde *n* a very large crowd, often frightening or unpleasant.

horehound *n* a plant that produces a bitter juice formerly used as a cough medicine.

horizon *n* **1** the apparent line that divides the earth and the sky. **2** (*pl*) the limits of a person's interests and activities: *seeking to broaden his horizons at college.* **3 on the horizon** almost certainly going to happen or be done in the future: *a new type of computer is on the horizon.*

horizontal *adj* **1** flat and level with the ground or with a line considered as a base. **2** affecting or happening at one level in a system or organization: *a horizontal division of labour.* ~*n* **3** a horizontal plane, position, or line. **horizontally** *adv*

hormone *n* **1** a chemical substance produced in an endocrine gland and transported in the blood to a certain tissue, on which it has a specific effect. **2** a similar substance produced by a plant that is essential for growth. **3** a synthetic substance having the same effects. **hormonal** *adj*

horn *n* **1** either of a pair of permanent bony outgrowths on the heads of animals such as cattle and antelopes. **2** any hornlike projection, such as the eyestalk of a snail. **3** the antler of a deer. **4** the hard substance of which horns are made. **5** a musical wind instrument made from horn. **6** any musical instrument consisting of a pipe or tube of brass fitted with a mouthpiece. **7** a device, such as on a vehicle, for producing a warning or signalling noise. **horned** *adj*

hornbeam *n* a tree with smooth grey bark.

hornbill *n* a tropical bird with a bony growth on its large beak.

hornblende *n* a green-to-black mineral containing aluminium, calcium, sodium, magnesium, and iron.

hornet *n* **1** a large wasp that can inflict a severe sting. **2 hornet's nest** a very unpleasant situation that is difficult to deal with: *you'll stir up a hornet's nest.*

horn of plenty *n* same as **cornucopia.**

hornpipe *n* **1** a solo dance, traditionally performed by sailors. **2** music for this dance.

horny *adj* **hornier, horniest 1** of, like, or hard as horn. **2** *Slang* sexually aroused.

horology *n* the art of making clocks and watches or of measuring time. **horological** *adj*

horoscope *n* **1** the prediction of a person's future based on the positions of the planets, sun, and moon at the time of birth. **2** a diagram showing the positions of the planets, sun, and moon at a particular time and place.

horrendous *adj* very unpleasant or shocking.

horrible *adj* **1** disagreeable and unpleasant: *a horrible hotel room.* **2** causing fear, shock, or disgust: *he died a horrible death.* **horribly** *adv*

horrid *adj* **1** disagreeable or unpleasant: *it had been a horrid day at school.* **2** *Informal* (of a person) unkind and nasty: *her horrid parents.*

horrific *adj* provoking horror: *horrific injuries.* **horrifically** *adv*

horrify *vb* **-fies, -fying, -fied** to cause feelings of horror in (someone); shock (someone) greatly.

horror *n* **1** extreme fear or terror. **2** intense hatred: *she had a horror of violence.* **3** a thing or person causing fear, loathing, or distaste. ~*adj* **4** having a frightening subject, usu. concerned with the supernatural: *a horror film.*

horrors *pl n* **the horrors** *Slang* a fit of nervousness or anxiety.

hors d'oeuvre (or **durv**) *n, pl* **hors d'oeuvre** *or* **hors d'oeuvres** (or **durv**) an appetizer, usually served before the main meal.

horse *n* **1** a four-footed mammal with hooves, a mane, and a tail, used for riding and pulling carts, etc. **2** the adult male of this species; stallion. **3 the horses** *Informal* horse races on which bets may be placed: *an occasional flutter on the horses.* **4** *Gymnastics* a padded apparatus on legs, used for vaulting. **5 be** *or* **get on one's high horse** *Informal* to act in a haughty manner. **6 the horse's mouth** the most reliable source: *I'll tell you straight from the horse's mouth.*

horse around *or* **about** *vb Informal* to play roughly or boisterously.

horseback *n* a horse's back: *on horseback.*

horsebox *n Brit* a van or trailer used for transporting horses.

horse brass *n* a decorative brass ornament, originally attached to a horse's harness.

horse chestnut *n* **1** a tree with broad leaves and brown shiny inedible nuts enclosed in a spiky case. **2** the nut of this tree.

horseflesh *n* **1** horses collectively: *Ascot's annual parade of fashion and horseflesh.* **2** the flesh of a horse as food.

horsefly *n, pl* **-flies** a large fly which sucks the blood of horses, cattle, and people.

THESAURUS

sanguinely **2.** *informal* all being well, conceivably, expectedly, feasibly, probably

hopeless 1. defeatist, dejected, demoralized, despairing, desperate, despondent, disconsolate, downhearted, forlorn, helpless, incurable, in despair, irremediable, irreparable, irreversible, lost, past remedy, pessimistic, remediless, woebegone **2.** forlorn, futile, impossible, impracticable, pointless, unachievable, unattainable, useless, vain **3.** *informal* inadequate, incompetent, ineffectual, inferior, no good, pathetic, poor, useless (*informal*)

horde band, crew, crowd, drove, gang, host, mob, multitude, pack, press, swarm, throng, troop

horizon 1. field of vision, skyline, vista **2.** *plural* ambit, compass, ken, perspective, prospect, purview, range, realm, scope, sphere, stretch

horrible 1. *informal* awful, beastly (*informal*), cruel, disagreeable, dreadful, ghastly (*informal*), horrid, mean, nasty, terrible, unkind, unpleasant **2.** abhorrent, abominable, appalling, awful, dreadful, fearful, frightful, ghastly, grim, grisly, gruesome, heinous, hellacious (*U.S. slang*), hideous, horrid, loathsome, obscene, repulsive, revolting, shameful, shocking, terrible, terrifying

horrid 1. awful, disagreeable, disgusting, dreadful, horrible, nasty, obscene, offensive, terrible, unpleasant, yucky *or* yukky (*slang*) **2.** *informal* beastly (*informal*), cruel, mean, nasty, unkind

horrify affright, alarm, appal, disgust, dismay, frighten, intimidate, outrage, petrify, scare, shock, sicken, terrify, terrorize

horror 1. alarm, apprehension, awe, consternation,

horsehair *n* hair from the tail or mane of a horse, used in upholstery.
horse laugh *n* a loud and coarse laugh.
horseman *n, pl* **-men 1** a man who is skilled in riding. **2** a man riding a horse. **horsemanship** *n* **horsewoman** *fem n*
horseplay *n* rough or rowdy play.
horsepower *n* a unit of power (equivalent to 745.7 watts), used to measure the power of an engine.
horseradish *n* a plant with a white strong-tasting root, which is used to make a sauce.
horse sense *n* same as **common sense.**
horseshoe *n* **1** a piece of iron shaped like a U, nailed to the bottom of a horse's hoof to protect the foot. **2** an object of similar shape: often regarded as a symbol of good luck.
horsetail *n* a plant with small dark toothlike leaves.
horsewhip *n* **1** a whip with a long thong, used for managing horses. *~vb* **-whipping, -whipped 2** to beat (a person or animal) with such a whip.
horsey *or* **horsy** *adj* **horsier, horsiest 1** of or relating to horses: *a horsey smell.* **2** devoted to horses: *the horsey set.* **3** like a horse: *a horsey face.*
hortatory *or* **hortative** *adj Formal* encouraging.
horticulture *n* the art or science of cultivating gardens. **horticultural** *adj* **horticulturalist** *or* **horticulturist** *n*
hosanna *interj* an exclamation of praise to God.
hose[1] *n* **1** a flexible pipe, for conveying a liquid or gas. *~vb* **hosing, hosed 2** to wash or water (a person or thing) with a hose.
hose[2] *n* **1** *Old-fashioned* stockings, socks, and tights collectively. **2** *History* a man's garment covering the legs and reaching up to the waist.
hosiery *n* stockings, socks, and knitted underclothing collectively.
hospice (**hoss**-piss) *n* **1** a nursing home that specializes in caring for the terminally ill. **2** *Archaic* a place of shelter for travellers, esp. one kept by a religious order.
hospitable *adj* generous, friendly, and welcoming to guests or strangers. **hospitably** *adv*
hospital *n* an institution for the medical or psychiatric care and treatment of patients.
hospitality *n, pl* **-ties** kindness in welcoming strangers or guests.
hospitalize *or* **-ise** *vb* **-izing, -ized** *or* **-ising, -ised** to admit or send (a person) into a hospital. **hospitalization** *or* **-isation** *n*
hospitaller *or US* **hospitaler** *n* a member of a religious order dedicated to hospital work, ambulance services, etc.
host[1] *n* **1** a person who receives or entertains guests, esp. in his own home. **2** the organization or country providing the facilities for a function or event: *Barcelona, host of the 1992 Olympic Games.* **3** the compere of a radio or television programme. **4** *Biol* an animal or plant in or on which a parasite lives. **5** *Old-fashioned* the owner or manager of an inn. *~vb* **6** to be the host of (a party, programme, or event): *he's hosting a radio show.*
host[2] *n* a great number; multitude.
Host *n Christianity* the bread used in Holy Communion.
hostage *n* a person who is illegally held prisoner until certain demands are met by other people.
hostel *n* **1** a building providing overnight accommodation at a low cost for particular groups of people, such as the homeless. **2** same as **youth hostel. 3** *Brit* a supervised lodging house for nurses, students, etc. **hosteller** *or US* **hosteler** *n*
hostelry *n, pl* **-ries** *Archaic or facetious* an inn.
hostel school *n Canad* same as **residential school.**
hostess *n* **1** a woman who receives and entertains guests, esp. in her own house. **2** a woman who receives and entertains patrons of a club, restaurant, or dance hall.
hostile *adj* **1** unfriendly and aggressive. **2** opposed (to): *hostile to the referendum.* **3** relating to or involving the enemies of a country.
hostility *n, pl* **-ties 1** unfriendly and aggressive feelings or behaviour. **2** (*pl*) acts of warfare.
hot *adj* **hotter, hottest 1** having a relatively high temperature. **2** having a temperature higher than desirable. **3** spicy or causing a burning sensation on the tongue: *hot chillies.* **4** (of a temper) quick to flare up. **5** (of a contest or conflict) intense. **6** recent or new: *hot from the press.* **7** much favoured: *a hot favourite.* **8** *Informal* having a dangerously high level of radioactivity. **9** *Slang* stolen or otherwise illegally obtained. **10** (of a colour) intense; striking: *hot pink.* **11** following closely: *this LP appeared hot on the heels of the debut smash.* **12** *Informal* dangerous or unpleasant: *they're making it hot for me here.* **13** (in various games) very near the answer. **14 hot on** *Informal* **a** strict about: *they are extremely hot on sloppy language.* **b** particu-

THESAURUS

dismay, dread, fear, fright, panic, terror **2.** abhorrence, abomination, antipathy, aversion, detestation, disgust, hatred, loathing, odium, repugnance, revulsion
horseman cavalier, cavalryman, dragoon, equestrian, horse-soldier, rider
horseplay buffoonery, clowning, fooling around, high jinks, pranks, romping, rough-and-tumble, roughhousing (*slang*), skylarking (*informal*)
horse sense *see* COMMON SENSE
hospitable amicable, bountiful, cordial, friendly, generous, genial, gracious, kind, liberal, sociable, welcoming
hospitality cheer, conviviality, cordiality, friendliness, heartiness, hospitableness, neighbourliness, sociability, warmth, welcome
host[1] *n.* **1.** entertainer, innkeeper, landlord, master of ceremonies, proprietor **2.** anchor man, compere (*Brit.*), presenter *~vb.* **3.** compere (*Brit.*), front (*informal*), introduce, present
host[2] army, array, drove, horde, legion, multitude, myriad, swarm, throng
hostage captive, gage, pawn, pledge, prisoner, security, surety
hostile adverse, alien, antagonistic, anti (*informal*), bellicose, belligerent, contrary, ill-disposed, inhospitable, inimical, malevolent, opposed, opposite, rancorous, unfriendly, unkind, unpropitious, unsympathetic, unwelcoming, warlike
hostility 1. abhorrence, animosity, animus, antagonism, antipathy, aversion, detestation, enmity, hatred, ill will, malevolence, malice, opposition, resentment, unfriendliness **2.** *plural* conflict, fighting, state of war, war, warfare
hot 1. blistering, boiling, burning, fiery, flaming, heated, piping hot, roasting, scalding, scorching, searing, steaming, sultry, sweltering, torrid, warm **2.** acrid, biting, peppery, piquant, pungent, sharp, spicy **3.** animated, ardent, excited, fervent, fervid, fierce, fiery, flaming, impetuous, inflamed, intense, irascible, lustful, passionate, raging, stormy, touchy, vehement, violent

larly knowledgeable about. **15 hot under the collar** *Informal* aroused with anger, annoyance, or resentment. **16 in hot water** *Informal* in trouble. ~See also **hot up. hotly** *adv*

hot air *n Informal* empty and usually boastful talk.

hotbed *n* a place offering ideal conditions for the growth of an idea or activity: *a hotbed of resistance.*

hot-blooded *adj* passionate or excitable.

hotchpotch *or esp US & Canad* **hodgepodge** *n* a jumbled mixture.

hot cross bun *n* a yeast bun marked with a cross and traditionally eaten on Good Friday.

hot dog *n* a long roll split lengthways with a hot sausage inside.

hotel *n* a commercially run establishment providing lodging and meals for guests.

hotelier *n* an owner or manager of a hotel.

hotfoot *adv* with all possible speed: *hotfoot to the accident.*

hot-gospeller *n Informal* a revivalist preacher with a highly enthusiastic delivery.

hot-headed *adj* impetuous, rash, or hot-tempered. **hot-headedness** *n*

hothouse *n* a greenhouse in which the temperature is maintained at a fixed level.

hot line *n* a direct telephone link between heads of government for emergency use.

hot money *n* capital that is transferred from one financial centre to another seeking the best opportunity for short-term gain.

hotplate *n* **1** a heated metal surface on an electric cooker. **2** a portable device on which food can be kept warm.

hotpot *n Brit* a casserole of meat and vegetables covered with a layer of potatoes.

hot rod *n* a car with an engine that has been modified to produce increased power.

hot seat *n* **1 in the hot seat** *Informal* in a difficult and responsible position. **2** *US slang* the electric chair.

hot spot *n* **1** a place where there is a lot of exciting activity or entertainment: *Birmingham's fashionable hot spots.* **2** an area where there is fighting or political unrest: *a political hot spot in the Caucasus.* **3** a small area of abnormally high temperature or radioactivity.

hot stuff *n Informal* **1** a person, object, or activity considered attractive, exciting, or important. **2** pornographic or erotic books, plays, films, etc.

Hottentot *n* **1** a race of indigenous people of South Africa which is now almost extinct. **2** a member of this race. **3** Also called: **Khoi Khoi** the language of this race.

hotting *n* the performing of high-speed stunts in a stolen car. **hotter** *n*

hot up *vb* **hotting, hotted** *Informal* to make or become more active and exciting.

hot-water bottle *n* a rubber container, designed to be filled with hot water and used for warming a bed.

hound *n* **1** a dog used for hunting: *to ride with the hounds.* **2** a despicable person. ~*vb* **3** to pursue, disturb, or criticize relentlessly: *hounded by the press.*

hour *n* **1** a period of time equal to 60 minutes; $1/_{24}$ of a day. **2** any of the points on the face of a clock or watch that indicate intervals of 60 minutes: *in my hurry I mistook the hour.* **3** the time of day. **4** the time allowed for or used for something: *a three and a half hour test.* **5** the distance covered in an hour: *an hour from the heart of Tokyo.* **6** a special moment: *the decisive hour.* ~See also **hours.**

hourglass *n* a device consisting of two transparent sections linked by a narrow channel, containing a quantity of sand that takes an hour to trickle from one section to the other.

houri *n, pl* **-ris** (in Muslim belief) any of the nymphs of Paradise.

hourly *adj* **1** of, occurring, or done once every hour. **2** measured by the hour: *hourly charges.* **3** frequent. ~*adv* **4** once every hour. **5** by the hour: *hourly paid.* **6** frequently. **7** at any moment: *the arrival of the men was hourly expected.*

hours *pl n* **1** an indefinite time: *they play on their bikes for hours.* **2** a period regularly appointed for work or business. **3** one's times of rising and going to bed: *you keep very late hours.* **4** *RC Church* prayers recited at seven specified times of the day.

house *n, pl* **houses 1** a building used as a home; dwelling. **2** the people in a house. **3** a building for some specific purpose: *beach house.* **4** a family or dynasty: *the House of Windsor.* **5** a commercial company: *auction house.* **6** a law-making body or the hall where it meets. **7** a division of a large school: *he was captain of the house rugby team.* **8** the audience in a theatre or cinema. **9** *Astrol* any of the 12 divisions of the zodiac. **10** *Informal* a brothel. **11 get on like a house on fire** *Informal* (of people) to get on very well together. **12 on the house** (usually of drinks) paid for by the management. **13 put one's house in order** to settle or organize one's affairs. ~*adj* **14** (of wine) sold unnamed by a restaurant, at a lower price than wines specified on the wine list: *house red.* ~*vb* **housing, housed 15** to give accommodation to. **16** to contain or cover (something).

house arrest *n* confinement to one's own home rather than in prison.

houseboat *n* a stationary boat used as a home.

housebound *adj* unable to leave one's house, usually because of illness.

housebreaking *n Criminal law* the act of entering a

THESAURUS

4. fresh, just out, latest, new, recent, up to the minute **5.** approved, favoured, in demand, in vogue, popular, sought-after **6.** close, following closely, in hot pursuit, near

hot air blather, blether, bombast, bosh (*informal*), bunkum *or* buncombe (*chiefly U.S.*), claptrap (*informal*), empty talk, gas (*informal*), guff (*slang*), rant, tall talk (*informal*), verbiage, wind

hotbed breeding ground, den, forcing house, nest, nursery, seedbed

hot-blooded ardent, excitable, fervent, fiery, heated, impulsive, passionate, rash, spirited, temperamental, wild

hotchpotch conglomeration, farrago, gallimaufry, hash, jumble, medley, *mélange,* mess, miscellany, mishmash, mixture, olio, olla podrida, potpourri

hotfoot hastily, helter-skelter, hurriedly, pell-mell, posthaste, quickly, speedily

hot-headed fiery, foolhardy, hasty, hot-tempered, impetuous, precipitate, quick-tempered, rash, reckless, unruly, volatile

hound *vb.* badger, chase, drive, give chase, goad, harass, harry, hunt, hunt down, impel, persecute, pester, prod, provoke

house *n.* **1.** abode, building, domicile, dwelling, edifice, habitation, home, homestead, pad (*slang*), residence **2.** family, household, ménage **3.** ancestry, clan, dynasty, family tree, kindred, line, lineage, race, tribe **4.** business, company, concern, establishment, firm, organization, outfit (*informal*), partnership **5.** assembly, Commons, legislative body, parliament **6. on the house** for nothing, free, gratis, without expense ~*vb.*

building as a trespasser for an unlawful purpose. **housebreaker** *n*

housecoat *n* a woman's loose robelike garment for casual wear.

housefly *n, pl* **-flies** a common fly often found in houses.

household *n* **1** all the people living together in one house. **2** *~adj* relating to the running of a household: *household budget.*

householder *n* a person who owns or rents a house.

household name *or* **word** *n* a person or thing that is very well known.

housekeeper *n* a person employed to run someone else's household.

housekeeping *n* **1** the running of a household. **2** money allotted for this.

house lights *pl n* the lights in the auditorium of a theatre or cinema.

housemaid *n* (esp. formerly) a female servant employed to do housework.

housemaid's knee *n* a fluid-filled swelling of the kneecap.

houseman *n, pl* **-men** *Med* a junior doctor in a hospital.

house martin *n* a swallow with a slightly forked tail.

House music *or* **House** *n* a type of disco music of the late 1980s, based on funk, with fragments of other recordings edited in electronically.

House of Commons *n* (in Britain and Canada) the lower chamber of Parliament.

House of Keys *n* the lower chamber of the lawmaking body of the Isle of Man.

House of Lords *n* (in Britain) the upper chamber of Parliament, composed of the peers of the realm.

house party *n* **1** a party, usually in a country house, at which guests are invited to stay for several days. **2** the guests who are invited.

house-proud *adj* excessively concerned with the appearance, cleanliness, and tidiness of one's house.

houseroom *n* **not give something houseroom** not to want to have something in one's house.

housetops *pl n* **shout** *or* **proclaim something from the housetops** to announce something publicly.

house-train *vb Brit* to train (a pet) to urinate and defecate outside.

house-warming *n* a party given after moving into a new home.

housewife *n, pl* **-wives** a woman who runs her own household and does not have a paid job. **housewifely** *adj*

housework *n* the work of running a home, such as cleaning, cooking, and shopping.

housing *n* **1** houses collectively. **2** the job of providing people with accommodation. **3** a part designed to contain and support a component or mechanism: *the inspection panel in the concrete housing.*

hove *vb Chiefly naut* a past of **heave.**

hovel *n* a small house or hut that is dirty or badly in need of repair.

hover *vb* **1** (of a bird, insect, or helicopter) to remain suspended in one place in the air. **2** to linger uncertainly in a place. **3** to be in an unsettled or uncertain situation or frame of mind: *hovering between two options.*

hovercraft *n* a vehicle that is able to travel across both land and water on a cushion of air.

how *adv* **1** in what way, by what means: *how did you spend the evening?; observing how elderly people coped.* **2** to what extent: *they don't know how tough I am.* **3** how good, how well, what ... like: *how good are the copies?; so that's how things are.* **4 how about?** used to suggest something: *how about some tea?* **5 how are you?** what is your state of health? **6 how's that? a** what is your opinion?: *we'll go out for a late-night supper – how's that?* **b** *Cricket* Also written: **howzat** (an appeal to the umpire) is the batsman out?

howdah *n* a seat for riding on an elephant's back.

however *adv* **1** still; nevertheless: *the book does, however, almost get funny.* **2** by whatever means: *get there however you can.* **3** (*with an adjective or adverb*) no matter how: *however low we plunge, there is always hope.*

howitzer *n* a large gun that fires shells at a steep angle.

howl *n* **1** the long, loud wailing noise made by a wolf or a dog. **2** a similar cry of pain or sorrow. **3** a loud burst of laughter. *~vb* **4** to express (something) in a howl or utter such cries. **5** (of the wind, etc.) to make a wailing noise.

howl down *vb* to prevent (a speaker) from being heard by shouting disapprovingly.

howler *n Informal* a glaring mistake.

howling *adj Informal* great: *a howling success.*

hoy *interj* a cry used to attract someone's attention.

hoyden *n Old-fashioned* a wild boisterous girl; tomboy. **hoydenish** *adj*

HP *or* **h.p. 1** *Brit* hire-purchase. **2** horsepower.

HQ *or* **h.q.** headquarters.

hr hour.

HRH Her (*or* His) Royal Highness.

HRT hormone replacement therapy.

hub *n* **1** the central portion of a wheel, through which the axle passes. **2** the central, most important, or active part of a place or organization.

hubble-bubble *n* **1** same as **hookah. 2** *Archaic* turmoil or confusion.

hubbub *n* **1** a confused noise of many voices. **2** great confusion or excitement.

THESAURUS

7. accommodate, billet, board, domicile, harbour, lodge, put up, quarter, take in **8.** contain, cover, keep, protect, sheathe, shelter, store

household 1. *n.* family, home, house, ménage **2.** *adj.* domestic, domiciliary, family, ordinary, plain

householder homeowner, occupant, resident, tenant

housekeeping home economy, homemaking (*U.S.*), housecraft, household management, housewifery

housing 1. accommodation, dwellings, homes, houses **2.** case, casing, container, cover, covering, enclosure, sheath

hovel cabin, den, hole, hut, shack, shanty, shed

hover 1. be suspended, drift, float, flutter, fly, hang, poise **2.** hang about, linger, wait nearby **3.** alternate, dither (*chiefly Brit.*), falter, fluctuate, haver (*Brit.*), oscillate, pause, seesaw, swither (*Scot. dialect*), vacillate, waver

however after all, anyhow, be that as it may, but, even though, nevertheless, nonetheless, notwithstanding, on the other hand, still, though, yet

howl 1. *n.* bawl, bay, bell, bellow, clamour, cry, groan, hoot, outcry, roar, scream, shriek, ululation, wail, yelp, yowl **2.** *vb.* bawl, bell, bellow, cry, cry out, lament, quest (*used of hounds*), roar, scream, shout, shriek, ululate, wail, weep, yell, yelp

howler *informal* bloomer (*Brit. informal*), blunder, boner (*slang*), boob (*Brit. slang*), booboo (*informal*),

hubby *n, pl* **-bies** *Informal* a husband.
hubcap *n* a metal disc that fits on to and protects the hub of a wheel, esp. on a car.
hubris (**hew**-briss) *n Formal* pride or arrogance. **hubristic** *adj*
huckster *n* **1** a person who uses aggressive methods of selling. **2** *Now rare* a person who sells small articles or fruit in the street.
huddle *n* **1** a small group of people or things standing or lying close together. **2 go into a huddle** *Informal* to have a private conference. *~vb* **-dling, -dled 3** (of a group of people) to crowd or nestle closely together. **4** to curl up one's arms and legs close to one's body through cold or fear.
hue *n* **1** the feature of colour that enables an observer to classify it as red, blue, etc. **2** a shade of a colour.
hue and cry *n* a loud public outcry.
huff *n* **1** a passing mood of anger or resentment: *in a huff.* *~vb* **2** to blow or puff heavily. **3** *Draughts* to remove (an opponent's draught) from the board for failure to make a capture. **4 huffing and puffing** empty threats or objections. **huffy** *adj* **huffily** *adv*
hug *vb* **hugging, hugged 1** to clasp (someone or something) tightly, usually with affection. **2** to keep close to (a shore or the kerb). *~n* **3** a tight or fond embrace.
huge *adj* extremely large. **hugely** *adv*
huggermugger *Archaic ~n* **1** confusion or secrecy. *~adj, adv* **2** in confusion.
Huguenot (**hew**-gan-oh) *n* a French Calvinist of the 16th or 17th centuries.
huh *interj* an exclamation of derision, bewilderment, or inquiry.
hui (**hoo**-ee) *n NZ* **1** a Maori social gathering. **2** any party.
hula *n* a Hawaiian dance performed by a woman.
Hula-Hoop *n Trademark* a plastic hoop swung round the body by wriggling the hips.
hulk *n* **1** the body of an abandoned ship. **2** *Disparaging* a large ungainly person or thing.
hulking *adj* big and ungainly.
hull *n* **1** the main body of a boat. **2** the outer covering of a fruit or seed such as a pea or bean. **3** the leaves round the stem of a strawberry, raspberry, or similar fruit. *~vb* **4** to remove the hulls from (fruit or seeds).
hullabaloo *n, pl* **-loos** a loud confused noise or commotion.
hullo *interj, n* same as **hello.**
hum *vb* **humming, hummed 1** to make a low continuous vibrating sound. **2** (of a person) to sing with the lips closed. **3** to utter an indistinct sound when hesitating. **4** *Informal* to be in a state of feverish activity: *the town hums with activity and life.* **5** *Slang* to smell unpleasant. **6 hum and haw** See **haw**[2]. *~n* **7** a low continuous murmuring sound. **8** an unpleasant smell. *~interj, n* **9** an indistinct sound of hesitation.
human *adj* **1** of or relating to people: *human occupants.* **2** having the qualities of people as opposed to animals, divine beings, or machines: *human nature.* **3** kind or considerate. *~n* **4** a human being.
human being *n* a man, woman, or child.
humane *adj* **1** showing kindness and sympathy. **2** inflicting as little pain as possible: *a humane method of killing minke whales.* **3** considered to have a civilizing effect on people: *the humane tradition of a literary education.*
humanism *n* the rejection of religion in favour of a belief in the advancement of humanity by its own efforts. **humanist** *n, adj* **humanistic** *adj*
humanitarian *adj* **1** having the interests of mankind at heart. *~n* **2** a person who has the interests of mankind at heart. **humanitarianism** *n*
humanity *n, pl* **-ties 1** the human race. **2** the quality of being human. **3** kindness or mercy. **4** (*pl*) the study of literature, philosophy, and the arts.
humanize *or* **-ise** *vb* **-izing, -ized** *or* **-ising, -ised** to make human or humane. **humanization** *or* **-isation** *n*
humankind *n* the human race; humanity.
humanly *adv* by human powers or means: *as fast as is humanly possible.*
humanoid *adj* **1** like a human being in appearance. *~n* **2** (in science fiction) a robot or creature resembling a human being.
human race *n* all men, women and children collectively.

THESAURUS

bull (*slang*), clanger (*informal*), error, malapropism, mistake, schoolboy howler
hub centre, core, focal point, focus, heart, middle, nerve centre, pivot
huddle *n.* **1.** confusion, crowd, disorder, heap, jumble, mass, mess, muddle *~vb.* **2.** cluster, converge, crowd, flock, gather, press, throng **3.** crouch, cuddle, curl up, hunch up, make oneself small, nestle, snuggle
hue 1. colour, dye, shade, tincture, tinge, tint, tone **2.** aspect, cast, complexion, light
hue and cry brouhaha, clamour, furore, hullabaloo, much ado, outcry, ruction (*informal*), rumpus, uproar
hug *vb.* **1.** clasp, cuddle, embrace, enfold, hold close, squeeze, take in one's arms **2.** cling to, follow closely, keep close, stay near *~n.* **3.** bear hug, clasp, clinch (*slang*), embrace, squeeze
huge bulky, colossal, elephantine, enormous, extensive, gargantuan, giant, gigantic, ginormous (*informal*), great, humongous (*informal, chiefly U.S.*), immense, jumbo (*informal*), large, mammoth, massive, mega (*slang*), monumental, mountainous, prodigious, stupendous, titanic, tremendous, vast
hulk 1. derelict, frame, hull, shell, shipwreck, wreck **2.** *disparaging* lout, lubber, lump (*informal*), oaf
hull *n.* **1.** body, casing, covering, frame, framework, skeleton **2.** husk, peel, pod, rind, shell, shuck, skin *~vb.* **3.** husk, peel, shell, shuck, skin, trim
hum 1. buzz, croon, drone, mumble, murmur, purr, sing, throb, thrum, vibrate, whir **2.** *informal* be active, be busy, bustle, buzz, move, pulsate, pulse, stir, vibrate
human *adj.* **1.** anthropoid, fleshly, manlike, mortal **2.** approachable, compassionate, considerate, fallible, forgivable, humane, kind, kindly, natural, understandable, understanding, vulnerable *~n.* **3.** body, child, creature, human being, individual, man, mortal, person, soul, woman
humane benevolent, benign, charitable, clement, compassionate, forbearing, forgiving, gentle, good, good-natured, kind, kind-hearted, kindly, lenient, merciful, mild, sympathetic, tender, understanding
humanitarian 1. *adj.* altruistic, beneficent, benevolent, charitable, compassionate, humane, philanthropic, public-spirited **2.** *n.* altruist, benefactor, Good Samaritan, philanthropist
humanitarianism beneficence, benevolence, charity, generosity, goodwill, humanism, philanthropy
humanity 1. flesh, Homo sapiens, humankind, human race, man, mankind, men, mortality, people **2.** human nature, humanness, mortality **3.** benevolence, benignity, brotherly love, charity, compassion, fellow feeling, kind-heartedness, kindness, mercy, philanthropy, sympathy, tenderness, tolerance, understand-

human rights *pl n* the basic rights of individuals to liberty, justice, etc.

humble *adj* **1** conscious of one's failings. **2** modest and unpretentious: *humble domestic objects.* **3** ordinary or not very important: *humble beginnings. ~vb* **-bling, -bled 4** to cause to become humble; humiliate. **humbly** *adv*

humble pie *n* **eat humble pie** to be forced to behave humbly; be humiliated.

humbug *n* **1** *Brit* a hard peppermint sweet with a striped pattern. **2** a speech or piece of writing that is obviously untrue, dishonest, or nonsense. **3** a dishonest person.

humdinger *n Slang* an excellent person or thing.

humdrum *adj* ordinary, dull, and uninteresting.

humerus (**hew**-mer-uss) *n, pl* **-meri** (-mer-rye) the bone from the shoulder to the elbow. **humeral** *adj*

humid *adj* (of the weather) damp and warm.

humidex (**hew**-mid-ex) *n Canad* a system of measuring discomfort showing the combined effect of humidity and temperature.

humidify *vb* **-fies, -fying, -fied** to make the air in (a room) more humid or damp. **humidifier** *n*

humidity *n* **1** dampness. **2** a measure of the amount of moisture in the air.

humiliate *vb* **-ating, -ated** to hurt the dignity or pride of: *the English cricket team was humiliated by Australia.* **humiliating** *adj* **humiliation** *n*

humility *n* the quality of being humble and modest.

hummingbird *n* a very small brightly-coloured American bird with a long slender bill, and powerful wings that hum as they vibrate.

hummock *n* a very small hill or a mound.

humongous (hew-**mung**-gus) *adj Informal, chiefly US* very large; enormous.

humorist *n* a person who speaks or writes in a humorous way.

humorous *adj* amusing, esp. in a witty or clever way. **humorously** *adv*

humour *or US* **humor** *n* **1** the quality of being funny. **2** the ability to appreciate or express things that are humorous: *a sense of humour.* **3** situations, speech, or writings that are humorous. **4** a state of mind; mood: *in astoundingly good humour.* **5** *Archaic* any of various fluids in the body: *aqueous humour. ~vb* **6** to be kind and indulgent to: *he decided the patient needed to be humoured.* **humourless** *adj*

hump *n* **1** a rounded lump on the ground. **2** a rounded deformity of the back. **3** a rounded lump on the back of a camel or related animal. **4 the hump** *Brit informal* a fit of sulking: *you've got the hump today. ~vb* **5** *Slang* to carry or heave.

humpback *n* **1** same as **hunchback. 2** Also called: **humpback whale** a large whalebone whale with a hump on its back. **3** Also called: **humpback bridge** *Brit* a road bridge with a sharp slope on either side. **humpbacked** *adj*

humph *interj* an exclamation of annoyance or indecision.

humus (**hew**-muss) *n* a dark brown or black mass of partially decomposed plant and animal matter in the soil.

Hun *n, pl* **Huns** *or* **Hun 1** a member of any of several Asiatic peoples who invaded the Roman Empire in the 4th and 5th centuries AD. **2** *Offensive, informal* (esp. in World War I) a German.

hunch *n* **1** a feeling or suspicion not based on facts. **2** same as **hump.** *~vb* **3** to draw (oneself or one's shoulders) up or together.

hunchback *n* a person who has an abnormal curvature of the spine. **hunchbacked** *adj*

hundred *n, pl* **-dreds** *or* **-dred 1** the cardinal number that is the product of ten and ten. **2** a numeral, 100 or C, representing this number. **3** (*often pl*) a large but

THESAURUS

ing **4.** *plural* classical studies, classics, liberal arts, literae humaniores

humanize civilize, cultivate, educate, enlighten, improve, mellow, polish, reclaim, refine, soften, tame

humble *adj.* **1.** meek, modest, self-effacing, submissive, unassuming, unostentatious, unpretentious **2.** common, commonplace, insignificant, low, low-born, lowly, mean, modest, obscure, ordinary, plebeian, poor, simple, undistinguished, unimportant, unpretentious *~vb.* **3.** abase, abash, break, bring down, chagrin, chasten, crush, debase, degrade, demean, disgrace, humiliate, lower, mortify, put down (*slang*), reduce, shame, sink, subdue, take down a peg (*informal*)

humbug 1. baloney (*informal*), cant, charlatanry, claptrap (*informal*), eyewash (*informal*), gammon (*Brit. informal*), hypocrisy, nonsense, quackery, rubbish **2.** charlatan, cheat, con man (*informal*), faker, fraud, impostor, phoney *or* phony (*informal*), quack, swindler, trickster

humdrum banal, boring, commonplace, dreary, dull, ho-hum (*informal*), mind-numbing, monotonous, mundane, ordinary, repetitious, routine, tedious, tiresome, uneventful, uninteresting, unvaried, wearisome

humid clammy, damp, dank, moist, muggy, steamy, sticky, sultry, watery, wet

humidity clamminess, damp, dampness, dankness, dew, humidness, moistness, moisture, mugginess, sogginess, wetness

humiliate abase, abash, bring low, chagrin, chasten, crush, debase, degrade, discomfit, disgrace, embarrass, humble, make (someone) eat humble pie, mortify, put down (*slang*), shame, subdue, take down a peg (*informal*)

humiliating cringe-making (*Brit. informal*), crushing, degrading, disgracing, embarrassing, humbling, ignominious, mortifying, shaming

humiliation abasement, affront, chagrin, condescension, degradation, disgrace, dishonour, embarrassment, humbling, ignominy, indignity, loss of face, mortification, put-down, resignation, self-abasement, shame, submission, submissiveness

humility diffidence, humbleness, lack of pride, lowliness, meekness, modesty, self-abasement, servility, submissiveness, unpretentiousness

humorist card (*informal*), comedian, comic, eccentric, funny man, jester, joker, wag, wit

humorous amusing, comic, comical, droll, entertaining, facetious, farcical, funny, hilarious, jocose, jocular, laughable, ludicrous, merry, playful, pleasant, side-splitting, waggish, whimsical, witty

humour *n.* **1.** amusement, comedy, drollery, facetiousness, fun, funniness, jocularity, ludicrousness, wit **2.** comedy, farce, gags (*informal*), jesting, jests, jokes, joking, pleasantry, wisecracks (*informal*), wit, witticisms, wittiness **3.** disposition, frame of mind, mood, spirits, temper *~vb.* **4.** accommodate, cosset, favour, feed, flatter, go along with, gratify, indulge, mollify, pamper, pander to, spoil

hump *n.* **1.** bulge, bump, hunch, knob, lump, mound, projection, protrusion, protuberance, swelling **2. the hump** *Brit. informal* the blues, the doldrums, the dumps (*informal*), the mopes, the sulks *~vb.* **3.** *slang* carry, heave, hoist, lug, shoulder

unspecified number. ~*adj* **4** amounting to a hundred: *a hundred yards.* **hundredth** *adj, n*

hundreds and thousands *pl n* tiny beads of coloured sugar, used in decorating cakes.

hundredweight *n, pl* **-weights** *or* **-weight 1** *Brit* a unit of weight equal to 112 pounds or 50.802kg. **2** *US & Canad* a unit of weight equal to 100 pounds or 45.359kg. **3** a metric unit of weight equal to 50 kilograms.

hung *vb* **1** the past of **hang** (except in the sense of *to execute*) ~*adj* **2** (of a parliament or jury) with no side having a clear majority. **3 hung over** *Informal* suffering the effects of a hangover.

Hungarian *adj* **1** of Hungary. ~*n* **2** a person from Hungary. **3** the language of Hungary.

hunger *n* **1** a feeling of emptiness or weakness caused by lack of food. **2** a lack of food that causes suffering or death: *refugees dying of hunger and disease.* **3** desire or craving: *Europe's hunger for bullion.* ~*vb* **4 hunger for** to have a great desire (for).

hunger strike *n* a refusal of all food, usually by a prisoner, as a means of protest.

hungry *adj* **-grier, -griest 1** desiring food. **2** (foll. by *for*) having a craving, desire, or need for: *hungry for revenge.* **3** expressing greed, craving, or desire: *the media's hungry search for impact.* **hungrily** *adv*

hunk *n* **1** a large piece: *a hunk of bread.* **2** *Slang* a sexually attractive man.

hunkers *pl n* haunches.

hunt *vb* **1** to seek out and kill (animals) for food or sport. **2 hunt for** to search for: *Western companies are hunting for opportunities to invest.* **3 hunt down** to track in an attempt to capture (someone): *hunting down villains.* ~*n* **4** the act or an instance of hunting. **5** a party organized for the pursuit of wild animals for sport. **6** the members of such a party. **hunting** *n*

hunter *n* **1** a person or animal that seeks out and kills or captures game. **2** a person who looks carefully for something: *a house hunter.* **3** a horse or dog bred for hunting. **4** a watch with a hinged metal lid or case to protect the glass.

huntsman *n, pl* **-men 1** a person who hunts. **2** a person who trains hounds and manages them during a hunt.

hurdle *n* **1** *Athletics* one of a number of light barriers over which runners leap in certain events. **2** a difficulty or problem: *the main technical hurdle is the environment.* **3 hurdles** a race involving hurdles. ~*vb* **-dling, -dled 4** to jump over (a hurdle or other obstacle). **hurdler** *n*

hurdy-gurdy *n, pl* **hurdy-gurdies** a mechanical musical instrument, such as a barrel organ.

hurl *vb* **1** to throw (something) with great force. **2** to utter (something) with force; yell: *onlookers hurled abuse at them.*

hurling *or* **hurley** *n* a traditional Irish game resembling hockey.

hurly-burly *n* great noise and activity; commotion.

hurrah *or* **hooray** *interj, n* a cheer of joy or victory.

hurricane *n* a severe, often destructive storm, esp. a tropical cyclone.

hurricane lamp *n* a paraffin lamp with a glass covering.

hurried *adj* done quickly or too quickly. **hurriedly** *adv*

hurry *vb* **-ries, -rying, -ried 1** to move or act or cause to move or act in great haste: *the umpires hurried the players off the ground.* **2** to speed up the completion or progress of: *eat a small snack rather than hurry a main meal.* ~*n* **3** haste. **4** urgency or eagerness. **5 in a hurry** *Informal* **a** easily: *striking old guy, not the sort you'd forget in a hurry.* **b** willingly: *he would not ease interest rates again in a hurry.*

hurt *vb* **hurting, hurt 1** to cause physical or mental injury to: *is she badly hurt?* **2** to cause someone to feel pain: *my head hurt.* **3** *Informal* to feel pain: *she was hurting.* ~*n* **4** physical or mental pain or suffering. ~*adj* **5** injured or pained: *his hurt head; a hurt expression.* **hurtful** *adj*

hurtle *vb* **-ling, -led** to move very quickly or violently.

THESAURUS

hunch 1. *n.* feeling, idea, impression, inkling, intuition, premonition, presentiment, suspicion **2.** *vb.* arch, bend, crouch, curve, draw in, huddle, hump, squat, stoop, tense

hunger *n.* **1.** appetite, emptiness, esurience, famine, hungriness, ravenousness, starvation, voracity **2.** appetence, appetite, craving, desire, greediness, itch, lust, thirst, yearning, yen (*informal*) ~*vb.* **3. hunger for** crave, desire, hanker, hope, itch, long, pine, starve, thirst, want, wish, yearn

hungry 1. empty, famished, famishing, hollow, peckish (*informal, chiefly Brit.*), ravenous, sharp-set, starved, starving, voracious **2.** athirst, avid, covetous, craving, desirous, eager, greedy, keen, yearning

hunk block, chunk, gobbet, lump, mass, piece, slab, wedge, wodge (*Brit. informal*)

hunt *vb.* **1. hunt for** ferret about, forage, go in quest of, look, look high and low, rummage through, scour, search, seek, try to find **2. hunt down** chase, gun for, hound, pursue, stalk, track, trail ~*n.* **3.** chase, hunting, investigation, pursuit, quest, search

hurdle *n.* **1.** barricade, barrier, block, fence, hedge, wall **2.** barrier, block, complication, difficulty, handicap, hindrance, impediment, obstacle, obstruction, snag, stumbling block

hurl cast, chuck (*informal*), fire, fling, heave, launch, let fly, pitch, project, propel, send, shy, sling, throw, toss

hurly-burly bedlam, brouhaha, chaos, commotion, confusion, disorder, furore, hubbub, pandemonium, tumult, turbulence, turmoil, upheaval, uproar

hurricane cyclone, gale, storm, tempest, tornado, typhoon, windstorm

hurried breakneck, brief, cursory, hasty, hectic, perfunctory, precipitate, quick, quickie (*informal*), rushed, short, slapdash, speedy, superficial, swift

hurry *vb.* **1.** burn rubber (*informal*), dash, fly, get a move on (*informal*), lose no time, make haste, rush, scoot, scurry, step on it (*informal*) **2.** accelerate, expedite, goad, hasten, hustle, push on, quicken, speed (up), urge ~*n.* **3.** bustle, celerity, commotion, dispatch, expedition, flurry, haste, precipitation, promptitude, quickness, rush, speed, urgency

hurt *vb.* **1.** bruise, damage, disable, harm, impair, injure, mar, spoil, wound **2.** afflict, aggrieve, annoy, cut to the quick, distress, grieve, pain, sadden, sting, upset, wound **3.** *informal* ache, be sore, be tender, burn, pain, smart, sting, throb ~*n.* **4.** discomfort, distress, pain, pang, soreness, suffering ~*adj.* **5.** aggrieved, bruised, crushed, cut, damaged, grazed, harmed, injured, miffed (*informal*), offended, pained, piqued, rueful, sad, scarred, scraped, scratched, wounded

hurtful cruel, cutting, damaging, destructive, detrimental, disadvantageous, distressing, harmful, injurious, maleficent, malicious, mean, mischievous, nasty, pernicious, prejudicial, spiteful, unkind, upsetting, wounding

husband *n* **1** a woman's partner in marriage. *~vb* **2** to use (resources, finances, etc.) economically.
husbandry *n* **1** the art or skill of farming. **2** management of resources.
hush *vb* **1** to make or be silent. *~n* **2** stillness or silence. *~interj* **3** a plea or demand for silence. **hushed** *adj*
hush-hush *adj Informal* (esp. of official work) secret and confidential.
hush money *n Slang* money given to a person to ensure that something is kept secret.
hush up *vb* to suppress information or rumours about (something).
husk *n* **1** the outer covering of certain fruits and seeds. *~vb* **2** to remove the husk from.
husky[1] *adj* **huskier, huskiest 1** (of a voice) slightly hoarse. **2** *Informal* (of a man) big and strong. **huskily** *adv*
husky[2] *n, pl* **huskies** an Arctic sledge dog with thick hair and a curled tail.
hussar (hoo-**zar**) *n History* a member of a light cavalry regiment.
hussy *n, pl* **-sies** *Old-fashioned* a woman considered sexually immoral or improper.
hustings *pl n* the campaigns and speeches at a parliamentary election.
hustle *vb* **-tling, -tled 1** to make (someone) move by pushing or jostling them: *he hustled her away.* **2** to deal with (something) hurriedly: *they did not heedlessly hustle the tempo.* **3** *US & Canad slang* (of a prostitute) to solicit clients. *~n* **4** lively activity and excitement.
hustler *n US informal* a person who tries to make money or gain an advantage from every situation, often by immoral or dishonest means.
hut *n* a small house or shelter.
hutch *n* a cage for small animals.
hyacinth *n* a plant with bell-shaped sweet-smelling flowers.
hyaena *n* same as **hyena.**
hybrid *n* **1** an animal or plant resulting from a cross between two different types of animal or plant. **2** anything that is a mixture of two different things. *~adj* **3** of mixed origin: *a hybrid electric car.*
hybridize *or* **-ise** *vb* **-izing, -ized** *or* **-ising, -ised** to produce or cause (species) to produce hybrids; crossbreed. **hybridization** *or* **-isation** *n*
hydatid disease (**hide**-at-id) *n* a condition caused by the presence of bladder-like cysts (**hydatids**) in the liver, lungs, or brain.
hydra *n* **1** a mythical many-headed serpent. **2** a persistent problem: *killing the hydra of drug production is impossible.* **3** a microscopic freshwater creature with a slender tubular body and tentacles around the mouth.
hydrangea *n* an ornamental shrub with large clusters of white, pink, or blue flowers.
hydrant *n* an outlet from a water main, from which water can be tapped for fighting fires.
hydrate *Chem ~n* **1** a compound containing water chemically combined with a substance: *chloral hydrate.* *~vb* **-drating, -drated 2** to treat or impregnate (a substance) with water. **hydration** *n*
hydraulic *adj* operated by pressure transmitted through a pipe by a liquid, such as water or oil. **hydraulically** *adv*
hydraulics *n* the study of the mechanical properties of fluids as they apply to practical engineering.
hydride *n Chem* a compound of hydrogen with another element.
hydro[1] *n, pl* **-dros** *Brit* a hotel offering facilities for hydropathic treatment.
hydro[2] *adj* short for **hydroelectric.**
hydro- *or before a vowel* **hydr-** *combining form* **1** indicating water or fluid: *hydrodynamics.* **2** *Chem* indicating hydrogen in a chemical compound: *hydrochloric acid.*
hydrocarbon *n Chem* a compound containing only carbon and hydrogen.
hydrocephalus *n* accumulation of fluid in the cavities of the brain, causing enlargement of the head in children. **hydrocephalic** *adj*
hydrochloric acid *n Chem* a solution of hydrogen chloride in water: a strong acid used in many industrial and laboratory processes.
hydrodynamics *n* the branch of science concerned with the mechanical properties of fluids.
hydroelectric *adj* **1** generated by the pressure of falling water: *hydroelectric power.* **2** of the generation of electricity by water pressure: *a hydroelectric scheme.* **hydroelectricity** *n*
hydrofoil *n* **1** a fast light vessel the hull of which is raised out of the water on one or more pairs of fins. **2** any of these fins.
hydrogen *n Chem* a colourless gas that burns easily and is the lightest element in the universe. It occurs in water and in most organic compounds. Symbol: H **hydrogenous** *adj*
hydrogenate (hide-**roj**-in-nate) *vb* **-ating, -ated** *Chem* to combine (a substance) with hydrogen: *hydrogenated vegetable oil.* **hydrogenation** *n*
hydrogen bomb *n* an extremely powerful bomb in which energy is released by fusion of hydrogen nuclei to give helium nuclei.
hydrogen peroxide *n* a colourless oily unstable liquid chemical used as a hair bleach and as an antiseptic.
hydrogen sulphide *n* a colourless poisonous gas with an odour of rotten eggs.
hydrography (hide-**rog**-ra-fee) *n* the study of the oceans, seas, and rivers. **hydrographer** *n* **hydrographic** *adj*
hydrology *n* the study of the distribution, conservation, and use of the water of the earth and its atmosphere.
hydrolysis (hide-**rol**-iss-iss) *n Chem* a process of decomposition in which a compound reacts with water to produce other compounds.
hydrometer (hide-**rom**-it-er) *n* an instrument for measuring the density of a liquid.

THESAURUS

husband budget, conserve, economize, hoard, manage thriftily, save, store, use sparingly
husbandry 1. agriculture, agronomy, cultivation, farming, land management, tillage **2.** careful management, economy, frugality, good housekeeping, thrift
hush 1. *vb.* mute, muzzle, quieten, shush, silence, still, suppress **2.** *n.* calm, peace, peacefulness, quiet, silence, still (*poetic*), stillness, tranquillity
hush-hush *informal* classified, confidential, restricted, secret, top-secret
husk bark, chaff, covering, glume, hull, rind, shuck
husky 1. croaking, croaky, gruff, guttural, harsh, hoarse, rasping, raucous, rough, throaty **2.** *informal* beefy (*informal*), brawny, burly, hefty, muscular, powerful, rugged, stocky, strapping, thickset
hustle bustle, crowd, elbow, force, haste, hasten, hurry, impel, jog, jostle, push, rush, shove, thrust

hydropathy *n* a method of treating disease by the use of large quantities of water both internally and externally. **hydropathic** *adj*

hydrophilic *adj Chem* tending to dissolve in or mix with water: *a hydrophilic layer.*

hydrophobia *n* **1** same as **rabies. 2** (esp. of a person with rabies) a fear of drinking fluids. **hydrophobic** *adj*

hydroplane *n* **1** a motorboat that raises its hull out of the water at high speeds. **2** a fin on the hull of a submarine for controlling its vertical motion.

hydroponics *n* a method of growing plants in gravel, etc., through which water containing the necessary nutrients is pumped.

hydrosphere *n* the watery part of the earth's surface.

hydrostatics *n* the branch of science concerned with the properties and behaviour of fluids that are not in motion. **hydrostatic** *adj*

hydrotherapy *n Med* the treatment of certain diseases by exercise in water.

hydrous *adj* containing water.

hydroxide *n Chem* a compound containing a hydroxyl group or ion.

hydroxyl *adj Chem* of or containing the monovalent group –OH or the ion OH^-: *forming a hydroxyl radical.*

hyena *or* **hyaena** *n* a meat-eating doglike mammal of Africa and S Asia.

hygiene *n* **1** the principles and practices of health and cleanliness: *personal hygiene.* **2** Also called: **hygienics** the science concerned with the maintenance of health. **hygienic** *adj* **hygienically** *adv* **hygienist** *n*

hygrometer (**hie-grom**-it-er) *n* an instrument for measuring humidity.

hygroscope *n* any device that indicates the humidity of the air without necessarily measuring it, such as an animal or vegetable fibre which contracts with moisture.

hygroscopic *adj* (of a substance) tending to absorb water from the air.

hymen *n Anat* a membrane that partly covers the entrance to the vagina and is usually ruptured when sexual intercourse takes place for the first time.

hymenopterous *adj* of or belonging to an order of insects with two pairs of membranous wings.

hymn *n* a Christian song of praise sung to God or a saint.

hymnal *n* a book of hymns. Also: **hymn book**

hymnody *n* **1** the composition or singing of hymns. **2** hymns collectively.

hymnology *n* the study of hymn composition. **hymnologist** *n*

hype *Slang* ~*n* **1** intensive or exaggerated publicity or sales promotion. ~*vb* **hyping, hyped 2** to market or promote (a commodity) using intensive or exaggerated publicity.

hyped up *adj Old-fashioned slang* stimulated or excited by or as if by drugs.

hyper *adj Informal* overactive or overexcited.

hyper- *prefix* above, over, or in excess: *hypercritical.*

hyperactive *adj* (of a person) unable to relax and always in a state of restless activity.

hyperbola (hie-**per**-bol-a) *n Geom* a curve produced when a cone is cut by a plane at a steeper angle to its base than its side.

hyperbole (hie-**per**-bol-ee) *n* a deliberate exaggeration of speech or writing used for effect, such as *he embraced her a thousand times.*

hyperbolic *or* **hyperbolical** *adj* of a hyperbola or a hyperbole.

hypercritical *adj* excessively critical.

hyperglycaemia *or US* **hyperglycemia** (hie-per-glice-**seem**-ee-a) *n Pathol* an abnormally large amount of sugar in the blood.

hypermarket *n* a huge self-service store.

hypersensitive *adj* **1** unduly emotionally vulnerable. **2** abnormally sensitive to an allergen, a drug, or high or low temperatures.

hypersonic *adj* having a speed of at least five times the speed of sound.

hypertension *n Pathol* abnormally high blood pressure.

hypertrophy (hie-**per**-trof-fee) *n, pl* **-phies** enlargement of an organ or part resulting from an increase in the size of the cells.

hyperventilation *n* an increase in the rate of breathing at rest, sometimes resulting in cramp and dizziness. **hyperventilate** *vb*

hyphen *n* the punctuation mark (-), used to separate parts of compound words and between syllables of a word split between two consecutive lines.

hyphenate *vb* **-ating, -ated** to separate (words) with a hyphen. **hyphenation** *n*

hyphenated *adj* having two words or syllables connected by a hyphen.

hypnosis *n* an artificially induced state of relaxation in which the mind is more than usually receptive to suggestion.

hypnotherapy *n* the use of hypnosis in the treatment of emotional and mental problems.

hypnotic *adj* **1** of or producing hypnosis or sleep. **2** having an effect resembling hypnosis: *the film makes for hypnotic viewing.* ~*n* **3** a drug that induces sleep. **hypnotically** *adv*

hypnotism *n* the practice of or process of inducing hypnosis. **hypnotist** *n*

hypnotize *or* **-tise** *vb* **-tizing, -tized** *or* **-tising, -tised 1** to induce hypnosis in (a person). **2** to hold the attention of (someone) completely; fascinate; mesmerize: *hypnotized by her beauty.*

hypo- *or before a vowel* **hyp-** *prefix* beneath; less than: *hypodermic.*

hypoallergenic *adj* not likely to cause an allergic reaction.

hypocaust *n* an ancient Roman heating system in which hot air circulated under the floor and between double walls.

THESAURUS

hut cabin, den, hovel, lean-to, refuge, shanty, shed, shelter

hybrid amalgam, composite, compound, cross, crossbreed, half-blood, half-breed, mixture, mongrel, mule

hygiene cleanliness, hygienics, sanitary measures, sanitation

hygienic aseptic, clean, disinfected, germ-free, healthy, pure, salutary, sanitary, sterile

hype *slang* ballyhoo (*informal*), brouhaha, build-up, plugging (*informal*), promotion, publicity, puffing, racket, razzmatazz (*slang*)

hyperbole amplification, enlargement, exaggeration, magnification, overstatement

hypercritical captious, carping, cavilling, censorious, fault-finding, finicky, fussy, hairsplitting, niggling, overcritical, overexacting, overscrupulous, pernickety (*informal*), strict

hypnotic mesmeric, mesmerizing, narcotic, opiate,

hypochondria *n* abnormal anxiety concerning one's health.

hypochondriac *n* a person abnormally concerned about his or her health.

hypocrisy (hip-**ok**-rass-ee) *n, pl* **-sies 1** the practice of claiming to have standards or beliefs that are contrary to one's real character or actual behaviour. **2** an act or instance of this.

hypocrite (**hip**-oh-krit) *n* a person who pretends to be what he or she is not. **hypocritical** *adj*

hypodermic *adj* **1** used for injecting. ~*n* **2** a hypodermic syringe or needle.

hypodermic syringe *n Med* a syringe consisting of a hollow cylinder, a piston, and a hollow needle, used for withdrawing blood samples or injecting drugs under the skin.

hypotension *n Pathol* abnormally low blood pressure.

hypotenuse (hie-**pot**-a-news) *n* the side in a right-angled triangle that is opposite the right angle.

hypothermia *n Pathol* an abnormally low body temperature, as a result of exposure to cold weather.

hypothesis (hie-**poth**-iss-iss) *n, pl* **-ses** (-seez) a suggested explanation for a group of facts, accepted either as a basis for further verification or as likely to be true. **hypothesize** *or* **-ise** *vb*

hypothetical *adj* based on assumption rather than fact or reality. **hypothetically** *adv*

hyrax (**hire**-ax) *n, pl* **hyraxes** *or* **hyraces** (**hire**-a-seez) a genus of hoofed rodent-like animals.

hyssop *n* **1** an aromatic plant used in herbal medicine. **2** a Biblical plant, used for sprinkling in the ritual practices of the Hebrews.

hysterectomy *n, pl* **-mies** surgical removal of the womb.

hysteria *n* **1** a mental disorder marked by emotional outbursts and, often, symptoms such as paralysis. **2** any uncontrolled emotional state, such as of panic, anger, or excitement.

hysteric *n* a hysterical person.

hysterical *adj* **1** in a state of uncontrolled panic, anger, or excitement: *a crazy hysterical adolescent.* **2** *Informal* wildly funny. **hysterically** *adv*

hysterics *n* **1** an attack of hysteria. **2** *Informal* wild uncontrollable bursts of laughter.

Hz hertz.

THESAURUS

sleep-inducing, somniferous, soothing, soporific, spellbinding

hypnotize 1. mesmerize, put in a trance, put to sleep **2.** absorb, entrance, fascinate, magnetize, spellbind

hypocrisy cant, deceit, deceitfulness, deception, dissembling, duplicity, falsity, imposture, insincerity, pretence, sanctimoniousness, speciousness, two-facedness

hypocrite charlatan, deceiver, dissembler, fraud, Holy Willie, impostor, pharisee, phoney *or* phony (*informal*), pretender

hypocritical canting, deceitful, deceptive, dissembling, duplicitous, false, fraudulent, hollow, insincere, phoney *or* phony (*informal*), sanctimonious, specious, spurious, two-faced

hypothesis assumption, postulate, premise, premiss, proposition, supposition, theory, thesis

hypothetical academic, assumed, conjectural, imaginary, putative, speculative, supposed, theoretical

hysteria agitation, delirium, frenzy, hysterics, madness, panic, unreason

hysterical 1. berserk, beside oneself, convulsive, crazed, distracted, distraught, frantic, frenzied, mad, overwrought, raving, uncontrollable **2.** *informal* comical, farcical, hilarious, screaming, side-splitting, uproarious, wildly funny

I

i the imaginary number $\sqrt{-1}$.

I[1] *pron* used by a speaker or writer to refer to himself or herself as the subject of a verb.

I[2] **1** *Chem* iodine. **2** the Roman numeral for one.

I. **1** Independent. **2** Institute. **3** International. **4** Island; Isle.

IA Iowa.

iamb (eye-am) *or* **iambus** *n, pl* **iambs** *or* **iambuses** *Prosody* a metrical foot of two syllables, a short one followed by a long one.

iambic (eye-**am**-bik) *Prosody ~adj* **1** written in metrical units of one short and one long syllable. *~n* **2** an iambic foot, line, or stanza.

IBA (in Britain) Independent Broadcasting Authority.

Iberian *adj* **1** of Iberia, the peninsula made up of Spain and Portugal. *~n* **2** a person from Iberia.

ibex (**ibe**-eks) *n, pl* **ibexes** *or* **ibex** a wild mountain goat with large backward-curving horns.

ibid. in the same place: used to refer to a book, page, or passage previously cited.

ibis (**ibe**-iss) *n, pl* **ibises** *or* **ibis** a large wading bird with a long thin curved bill.

Ibo (**ee**-boh) *n* **1** (*pl* **Ibos** *or* **Ibo**) a member of an African people of S Nigeria. **2** their language.

ICBM intercontinental ballistic missile.

ice *n* **1** water that has frozen and become solid. **2** a portion of ice cream. **3** **break the ice** to relax the atmosphere, esp. between strangers. **4** **on ice** in readiness or reserve. **5** **on thin ice** in an dangerous situation: *he knew he was on thin ice. ~vb* **icing, iced** **6** (foll. by *up* or *over*) to become covered with ice. **7** to cover with icing. **8** to cool or chill with ice.

Ice Age *n* any period of time during which a large part of the earth's surface was covered with ice, caused by the advance of glaciers.

iceberg *n* **1** a large mass of ice floating in the sea. **2** **tip of the iceberg** the small visible part of a problem that is much larger.

iceberg lettuce *n* a type of lettuce with very crisp pale leaves tightly enfolded.

icebox *n* **1** *US & Canad* a refrigerator. **2** a compartment in a refrigerator for making or storing ice. **3** a container packed with ice for keeping food cold.

icebreaker *n* a ship designed to break a channel through ice.

icecap *n* a thick mass of glacial ice that permanently covers an area.

ice cream *n* a sweet frozen food, made from cream, milk, or a custard base, flavoured in various ways.

iced *adj* **1** served very cold. **2** covered with icing.

ice field *n* a large expanse of floating sea ice.

ice floe *n* a sheet of ice floating in the sea.

ice hockey *n* a game like hockey played on ice by two teams wearing skates.

Icelander *adj* a person from Iceland.

Icelandic *adj* **1** of Iceland. *~n* **2** the official language of Iceland.

ice lolly *n Brit informal* a water ice or an ice cream on a stick.

ice pack *n* **1** a bag or folded cloth containing crushed ice, applied to a part of the body to reduce swelling. **2** same as **pack ice.**

ice skate *n* **1** a boot with a steel blade fitted to the sole which enables the wearer to glide over ice. *~vb* **ice-skate, -skating, -skated** **2** to glide over ice on ice skates. **ice-skater** *n*

I Ching *n* an ancient Chinese book of divination and a source of Confucian and Taoist philosophy.

ichneumon (ik-**new**-mon) *n* a greyish-brown mongoose.

ichthyology (ik-thi-**ol**-a-jee) *n* the study of fishes. **ichthyological** *adj* **ichthyologist** *n*

icicle *n* a tapering spike of ice hanging where water has dripped.

icing *n* **1** Also (esp. US and Canad.): **frosting** a mixture of sugar and water or egg whites used to cover and decorate cakes. **2** **icing on the cake** any unexpected extra or bonus. **3** the formation of ice on a ship or aircraft.

icing sugar *n Brit* a very finely ground sugar used for making icing or sweets.

icon *or* **ikon** *n* **1** a picture of Christ, the Virgin Mary, or a saint, venerated in the Orthodox Church. **2** a picture on a computer screen representing a computer function that can be activated by moving the cursor over it.

iconoclast *n* **1** a person who attacks established or traditional ideas or principles. **2** a destroyer of religious images or objects. **iconoclastic** *adj* **iconoclasm** *n*

icosahedron (ike-oh-sa-**heed**-ron) *n, pl* **-drons** *or* **-dra** (-dra) a solid figure with 20 faces.

icy *adj* **icier, iciest** **1** freezing or very cold. **2** covered with ice: *an icy runway.* **3** cold or reserved in manner. **icily** *adv* **iciness** *n*

id *n Psychoanal* the primitive instincts and energies in the unconscious mind that underlie all psychological impulses.

ID **1** Idaho. **2** identification.

I'd I had *or* I would.

idea *n* **1** any product of mental activity; thought. **2** a scheme, intention, or plan. **3** the thought of something: *the idea excites me.* **4** a belief or opinion. **5** a vague notion; inkling: *they had no idea of the severity of my injuries.* **6** a person's conception of something: *his idea of integrity is not the same as mine.* **7** aim or purpose: *the idea is to economize on transport.* **8** *Philosophy* (in Plato) a universal model of which all things in the same class are only imperfect imitations.

THESAURUS

ice **1.** **break the ice** begin, initiate the proceedings, kick off (*informal*), lead the way, make a start, start *or* set the ball rolling (*informal*), take the plunge (*informal*) **2.** **on thin ice** at risk, in jeopardy, open to attack, out on a limb, sticking one's neck out (*informal*), unsafe, vulnerable

icy **1.** arctic, biting, bitter, chill, chilling, chilly, cold, freezing, frost-bound, frosty, frozen over, ice-cold, parky (*Brit. informal*), raw **2.** glacial, glassy, like a sheet of glass, slippy (*informal or dialect*) **3.** *figurative* aloof, cold, distant, forbidding, frigid, frosty, glacial, hostile, indifferent, steely, stony, unfriendly, unwelcoming

idea **1.** abstraction, concept, conception, conclusion, fancy, impression, judgment, perception, thought, understanding **2.** design, hypothesis, plan, recommendation, scheme, solution, suggestion, theory **3.** belief, conviction, doctrine, interpretation, notion, opinion, teaching, view, viewpoint **4.** approximation, clue, estimate, guess, hint, impression, inkling, intimation, no-

ideal *n* **1** a conception of something that is perfect. **2** a person or thing considered to represent perfection. **3** something existing only as an idea. *~adj* **4** most suitable: *they seem to have adopted an ideal man as their candidate.* **5** of, involving, or existing only as an idea; imaginary: *an ideal world.* **ideally** *adv*

idealism *n* **1** belief in or striving towards ideals. **2** the tendency to represent things in their ideal forms, rather than as they are. **3** *Philosophy* the doctrine that material objects and the external world do not exist in reality, but are creations of the mind. **idealist** *n* **idealistic** *adj*

idealize *or* **-ise** *vb* **-izing, -ized** *or* **-ising, -ised** to consider or represent (something) as ideal or more nearly perfect than is true. **idealization** *or* **-isation** *n*

idée fixe (ee-day **feeks**) *n, pl* **idées fixes** (ee-day **feeks**) an idea with which a person is obsessed.

idem *pron, adj* the same: used to refer to an article, chapter, or book already quoted.

identical *adj* **1** that is the same: *they got the identical motel room as last year.* **2** exactly alike or equal. **3** (of twins) developed from a single fertilized ovum that has split into two, and thus of the same sex and very much alike. **identically** *adv*

identification parade *n* a group of people, including one suspected of a crime, assembled to discover whether a witness can identify the suspect.

identify *vb* **-fies, -fying, -fied 1** to prove or recognize as being a certain person or thing; determine the identity of. **2** (often foll. by *with*) to understand and sympathize with a person or group because one regards oneself as being similar or similarly situated. **3** to consider or treat as the same. **4** to connect or associate closely: *he was closely identified with the community charge.* **identifiable** *adj* **identification** *n*

Identikit *n Trademark* a composite picture, assembled from descriptions given, of a person wanted by the police.

identity *n, pl* **-ties 1** the state of being a specified person or thing: *the identity of his murderers was not immediately established.* **2** the individual characteristics by which a person or thing is recognized. **3** the state of being the same. **4** *Maths* Also called: **identity element** a member of a set that when combined with any other member of the set, leaves it unchanged: the identity for multiplication of numbers is 1.

ideo- *combining form* of or indicating ideas: *ideology.*

ideogram *or* **ideograph** *n* a character or symbol that directly represents a concept or thing, rather than the sounds that form its name.

ideology *n, pl* **-gies** the body of ideas and beliefs of a person, group, or nation. **ideological** *adj* **ideologically** *adv* **ideologist** *n*

ides *n* (in the ancient Roman calendar) the 15th day in March, May, July, and October and the 13th of the other months.

idiocy *n, pl* **-cies 1** utter stupidity. **2** a foolish act or remark.

idiom *n* **1** a group of words which, when used together, have a different meaning from the one suggested by the individual words, e.g. *it was raining cats and dogs.* **2** linguistic usage that is grammatical and natural to native speakers. **3** the characteristic vocabulary or usage of a person or group. **4** the characteristic artistic style of an individual or school. **idiomatic** *adj*

idiosyncrasy *n, pl* **-sies** a personal peculiarity of mind, habit, or behaviour; quirk. **idiosyncratic** *adj*

idiot *n* **1** a foolish or senseless person. **2** a person with severe mental retardation. **idiotic** *adj* **idiotically** *adv*

idle *adj* **1** not doing anything. **2** not operating or being used. **3** not wanting to work; lazy. **4** ineffective or useless: *it would be idle to look for a solution at this stage.* **5** frivolous or trivial: *idle pleasures.* **6** without

THESAURUS

tion, suspicion **5.** aim, end, import, intention, meaning, object, objective, plan, purpose, *raison d'être,* reason, sense, significance

ideal *n.* **1.** archetype, criterion, epitome, example, exemplar, last word, model, nonpareil, paradigm, paragon, pattern, perfection, prototype, standard, standard of perfection *~adj.* **2.** archetypal, classic, complete, consummate, model, optimal, perfect, quintessential, supreme **3.** abstract, conceptual, hypothetical, intellectual, mental, notional, theoretical, transcendental **4.** fanciful, imaginary, impractical, ivory-tower, unattainable, unreal, Utopian, visionary

idealist *n.* dreamer, romantic, Utopian, visionary

idealistic impracticable, optimistic, perfectionist, quixotic, romantic, starry-eyed, Utopian, visionary

ideally all things being equal, if one had one's way, in a perfect world, under the best of circumstances

identical alike, corresponding, duplicate, equal, equivalent, indistinguishable, interchangeable, like, matching, selfsame, the same, twin

identification 1. cataloguing, classifying, establishment of identity, labelling, naming, pinpointing, recognition **2.** association, connection, empathy, fellow feeling, involvement, rapport, relationship, sympathy **3.** credentials, ID, identity card, letters of introduction, papers

identify 1. catalogue, classify, diagnose, flag, label, make out, name, pick out, pinpoint, place, put one's finger on (*informal*), recognize, single out, spot, tag **2.** *often with* **with** ally, associate, empathize, feel for, put in the same category, put oneself in the place *or* shoes of, relate to, respond to, see through another's eyes, think of in connection (with)

identity 1. distinctiveness, existence, individuality, oneness, particularity, personality, self, selfhood, singularity, uniqueness **2.** accord, correspondence, empathy, rapport, sameness, unanimity, unity

idiocy abject stupidity, cretinism, fatuity, fatuousness, foolishness, imbecility, inanity, insanity, lunacy, senselessness, tomfoolery

idiom 1. expression, locution, phrase, set phrase, turn of phrase **2.** jargon, language, mode of expression, parlance, style, talk, usage, vernacular

idiomatic dialectal, native, vernacular

idiosyncrasy affectation, characteristic, eccentricity, habit, mannerism, oddity, peculiarity, personal trait, quirk, singularity, trick

idiot airhead (*slang*), ass, berk (*Brit. slang*), blockhead, booby, charlie (*Brit. old-fashioned informal*), coot (*old-fashioned*), cretin, dimwit (*informal*), dunderhead, fool, halfwit, imbecile, jerk (*slang, chiefly U.S. & Canad.*), moron, nerd *or* nurd (*slang*), nincompoop (*informal*), nitwit (*informal*), numskull *or* numbskull, oaf, pillock (*slang*), plonker (*slang*), prat (*slang*), prick (*offensive slang*), simpleton, twit (*informal, chiefly Brit.*), wally (*slang*)

idiotic asinine, crackpot (*informal*), crazy, daft (*informal*), dumb (*informal*), fatuous, foolhardy, foolish, halfwitted, harebrained, imbecile, imbecilic, inane, insane, loopy (*informal*), lunatic, moronic, senseless, stupid, unintelligent

idle *adj.* **1.** dead, empty, gathering dust, inactive, jobless, mothballed, out of action *or* operation, out-of-work, redundant, stationary, ticking over, unemployed, unoccupied, unused, vacant **2.** indolent, lackadaisical, lazy, shiftless, slothful, sluggish **3.** abor-

basis; unfounded: *idle rumours.* ~*vb* **idling, idled 7** (often foll. by *away*) to waste or pass (time) in idleness. **8** (of an engine) to run at low speed without transmitting any power. **idleness** *n* **idler** *n* **idly** *adv*

idol (eye-dl) *n* **1** an object of excessive devotion or admiration. **2** an image of a god used as an object of worship.

idolatry (ide-**ol**-a-tree) *n* **1** the worship of idols. **2** excessive devotion or reverence. **idolater** *n* **idolatrous** *adj*

idolize *or* **-ise** *vb* **-izing, -ized** *or* **-ising, -ised 1** to love or admire excessively. **2** to worship as an idol. **idolization** *or* **-isation** *n*

idyll *or US sometimes* **idyl** (**id**-ill) *n* **1** a scene or time of peace and happiness. **2** a poem or prose work describing a charming rural scene or episode. **idyllic** *adj*

i.e. that is to say.

if *conj* **1** in the event that, or on condition that: *if you work hard you'll succeed.* **2** used to introduce an indirect question to which the answer is either *yes* or *no*, whether: *it doesn't matter if the play is any good or not.* **3** even though: *a splendid if slightly decaying house.* **4** used to introduce an unfulfilled wish, with *only*: *if only you had told her.* ~*n* **5** a condition or stipulation: *there are no hidden ifs or buts.*

iffy *adj Informal* full of uncertainty.

igloo *n, pl* **-loos** a dome-shaped Eskimo house, built of blocks of solid snow.

igneous (**ig**-nee-uss) *adj* **1** (of rocks) formed as molten rock cools and hardens. **2** of or like fire.

ignis fatuus (**ig**-niss **fat**-yew-uss) *n, pl* **ignes fatui** (**ig**-neez **fat**-yew-eye) same as **will-o'-the-wisp**.

ignite *vb* **-niting, -nited** to catch fire or set fire to. **ignitable** *adj*

ignition *n* **1** the system used to ignite the fuel in an internal-combustion engine. **2** an igniting or the process of igniting.

ignoble *adj* **1** dishonourable. **2** of low birth or origins. **ignobly** *adv*

ignominy (**ig**-nom-in-ee) *n, pl* **-minies** disgrace or public shame. **ignominious** *adj*

ignoramus *n, pl* **-muses** an ignorant person.

ignorance *n* lack of knowledge or education.

ignorant *adj* **1** lacking in knowledge or education. **2** rude through lack of knowledge of good manners: *an ignorant remark.* **3 ignorant of** lacking in awareness or knowledge of: *ignorant of Asian culture.*

ignore *vb* **-noring, -nored** to refuse to notice; disregard deliberately.

iguana *n* a large tropical tree lizard of the W Indies and S America with a spiny back.

ikebana (eek-a-**bah**-na) *n* the Japanese art of flower arrangement.

ikon *n* same as **icon**.

IL Illinois.

il- *prefix* same as **in-**[1] or **in-**[2].

ileum *n* the third and lowest part of the small intestine.

ilex *n* **1** a genus of trees or shrubs that includes holly. **2** same as **holm oak**.

ilium *n, pl* **-ia** the uppermost and widest of the three sections of the hipbone.

ilk *n* a type or class: *three or four others of the same ilk.*

ill *adj* **worse, worst 1** not in good health. **2** bad, harmful, or hostile: *ill effects.* **3** promising an unfavourable outcome: *ill omen.* **4 ill at ease** unable to relax. ~*n* **5** evil or harm. ~*adv* **6** badly, wrongly: *the title ill befits*

THESAURUS

tive, bootless, fruitless, futile, groundless, ineffective, of no avail, otiose, pointless, unavailing, unproductive, unsuccessful, useless, vain, worthless **4.** frivolous, insignificant, irrelevant, nugatory (*formal*), superficial, trivial, unhelpful, unnecessary ~*vb.* **5.** *often with* **away** dally, dawdle, fool, fritter, hang out (*informal*), kill time, laze, loiter, lounge, potter, waste, while

idleness 1. inaction, inactivity, leisure, time on one's hands, unemployment **2.** hibernation, inertia, laziness, shiftlessness, sloth, sluggishness, torpor, vegetating **3.** dilly-dallying (*informal*), lazing, loafing, pottering, skiving (*Brit. slang*), time-wasting, trifling

idol 1. *figurative* beloved, darling, favourite, hero, pet, pin-up (*slang*), superstar **2.** deity, god, graven image, image, pagan symbol

idolize, -ise admire, adore, apotheosize, bow down before, deify, dote upon, exalt, glorify, hero-worship, look up to, love, revere, reverence, venerate, worship, worship to excess

if 1. *conj.* admitting, allowing, assuming, granting, in case, on condition that, on the assumption that, provided, providing, supposing, though, whenever, wherever, whether **2.** *n.* condition, doubt, hesitation, stipulation, uncertainty

ignite burn, burst into flames, catch fire, fire, flare up, inflame, kindle, light, put a match to (*informal*), set alight, set fire to, take fire

ignominious abject, despicable, discreditable, disgraceful, dishonourable, disreputable, humiliating, indecorous, inglorious, mortifying, scandalous, shameful, sorry, undignified

ignominy bad odour, contempt, discredit, disgrace, dishonour, disrepute, humiliation, infamy, mortification, obloquy, odium, opprobrium, reproach, shame, stigma

ignorance benightedness, blindness, greenness, illiteracy, inexperience, innocence, lack of education, mental darkness, nescience (*literary*), oblivion, unawareness, unconsciousness, unenlightenment, unfamiliarity, unintelligence

ignorant 1. benighted, blind to, inexperienced, innocent, in the dark about, oblivious, unaware, unconscious, unenlightened, uninformed, uninitiated, unknowing, unschooled, unwitting **2.** crass, crude, gross, half-baked (*informal*), insensitive, rude, shallow, superficial, uncomprehending, unscholarly **3.** green, illiterate, naive, unaware, uncultivated, uneducated, unknowledgeable, unlearned, unlettered, unread, untaught, untrained, untutored

ignore be oblivious to, bury one's head in the sand, cold-shoulder, cut (*informal*), discount, disregard, give the cold shoulder to, neglect, overlook, pass over, pay no attention to, reject, send (someone) to Coventry, shut one's eyes to, take no notice of, turn a blind eye to, turn a deaf ear to, turn one's back on

ill *adj.* **1.** ailing, dicky (*Brit. informal*), diseased, funny (*informal*), indisposed, infirm, laid up (*informal*), not up to snuff (*informal*), off-colour, on the sick list (*informal*), out of sorts (*informal*), poorly (*informal*), queasy, queer, seedy (*informal*), sick, under the weather (*informal*), unhealthy, unwell, valetudinarian **2.** bad, damaging, deleterious, detrimental, evil, foul, harmful, iniquitous, injurious, ruinous, unfortunate, unlucky, vile, wicked, wrong **3.** disturbing, foreboding, inauspicious, ominous, sinister, threatening, unfavourable, unhealthy, unlucky, unpromising, unpropitious, unwholesome **4. ill at ease** anxious, awkward, disquieted, disturbed, edgy, faltering, fidgety, hesitant, nervous, on edge, on pins and needles (*informal*), on tenterhooks, out of place, restless, self-conscious, strange, tense, twitchy (*informal*), uncomfortable, un-

him. **7** with difficulty; hardly: *we can ill afford another scandal.*

ill. **1** illustrated. **2** illustration.

I'll I will *or* I shall.

ill-advised *adj* **1** (of a plan or action) badly thought out. **2** (of a person) acting without reasonable care or thought.

ill-bred *adj* lacking good manners. **ill-breeding** *n*

ill-disposed *adj* unfriendly or unsympathetic.

illegal *adj* against the law. **illegally** *adv* **illegality** *n*

illegible *adj* unable to be read or deciphered. **illegibility** *n*

illegitimate *adj* **1** born of parents who were not married to each other at the time. **2** illegal; unlawful. **illegitimacy** *n*

ill-fated *adj* doomed or unlucky.

ill-favoured *adj* ugly or unattractive.

ill-founded *adj* not based on proper proof or evidence.

ill-gotten *adj* obtained dishonestly or illegally: *ill-gotten gains.*

ill-health *n* the condition of being unwell.

illiberal *adj* **1** narrow-minded or intolerant. **2** not generous; mean. **3** lacking in culture or refinement. **illiberality** *n*

illicit *adj* **1** same as **illegal.** **2** forbidden or disapproved of by society: *an illicit kiss.*

illiterate *adj* **1** unable to read and write. **2** uneducated or ignorant: *linguistically illiterate.* ~*n* **3** an illiterate person. **illiteracy** *n*

ill-mannered *adj* having bad manners.

illness *n* **1** a disease or indisposition. **2** a state of ill health.

illogical *adj* **1** senseless or unreasonable. **2** not following logical principles. **illogicality** *n* **illogically** *adv*

ill-starred *adj* very unlucky or unfortunate.

ill-tempered *adj* having a bad temper.

ill-timed *adj* done or happening at an unsuitable time.

ill-treat *vb* to treat cruelly or harshly. **ill-treatment** *n*

illuminant *n* **1** something that gives off light. ~*adj* **2** giving off light.

illuminate *vb* **-nating, -nated** **1** to light up. **2** to make easily understood; explain: *the report obscures rather than illuminates the most relevant facts.* **3** to decorate with lights. **4** to decorate (an initial letter or manuscript) with designs of gold, silver, or bright colours. **illuminating** *adj* **illuminative** *adj*

illumination *n* **1** an illuminating or being illuminated. **2** a source of light. **3** **illuminations** *Chiefly Brit* lights used as decorations in streets or towns. **4** the decoration in colours, gold, or silver used on some manuscripts.

illumine *vb* **-mining, -mined** *Literary* same as **illuminate.**

illusion *n* **1** a false appearance or deceptive impres-

THESAURUS

easy, unquiet, unrelaxed, unsettled, unsure, wired (*slang*) ~*n.* **5.** affliction, hardship, harm, hurt, injury, misery, misfortune, pain, trial, tribulation, trouble, unpleasantness, woe ~*adv.* **6.** badly, hard, inauspiciously, poorly, unfavourably, unfortunately, unluckily **7.** barely, by no means, hardly, insufficiently, scantily

ill-advised foolhardy, foolish, ill-considered, ill-judged, impolitic, imprudent, inappropriate, incautious, indiscreet, injudicious, misguided, overhasty, rash, reckless, short-sighted, thoughtless, unseemly, unwise, wrong-headed

ill-bred bad-mannered, boorish, churlish, coarse, crass, discourteous, ill-mannered, impolite, indelicate, rude, uncivil, uncivilized, uncouth, ungallant, ungentlemanly, unladylike, unmannerly, unrefined, vulgar

ill-disposed against, antagonistic, anti (*informal*), antipathetic, averse, disobliging, down on (*informal*), hostile, inimical, opposed, uncooperative, unfriendly, unwelcoming

illegal actionable (*Law*), banned, black-market, bootleg, criminal, felonious, forbidden, illicit, lawless, outlawed, prohibited, proscribed, unauthorized, unconstitutional, under-the-counter, under-the-table, unlawful, unlicensed, unofficial, wrongful

illegality crime, criminality, felony, illegitimacy, illicitness, lawlessness, unlawfulness, wrong, wrongness

illegible crabbed, faint, hard to make out, hieroglyphic, indecipherable, obscure, scrawled, undecipherable, unreadable

illegitimate **1.** baseborn (*archaic*), bastard, born on the wrong side of the blanket, born out of wedlock, fatherless, misbegotten (*literary*), natural **2.** illegal, illicit, improper, unauthorized, unconstitutional, under-the-table, unlawful, unsanctioned

ill-fated blighted, doomed, hapless, ill-omened, ill-starred, luckless, star-crossed, unfortunate, unhappy, unlucky

ill-founded baseless, empty, groundless, idle, unjustified, unproven, unreliable, unsubstantiated, unsupported

illicit **1.** *see* ILLEGAL **2.** clandestine, forbidden, furtive, guilty, immoral, improper, wrong

illiteracy benightedness, ignorance, illiterateness, lack of education

illiterate benighted, ignorant, uncultured, uneducated, unlettered, untaught, untutored

ill-mannered badly behaved, boorish, churlish, coarse, discourteous, ill-behaved, ill-bred, impolite, insolent, loutish, rude, uncivil, uncouth, unmannerly

illness affliction, ailment, attack, complaint, disability, disease, disorder, ill health, indisposition, infirmity, malady, malaise, poor health, sickness

illogical absurd, fallacious, faulty, inconclusive, inconsistent, incorrect, invalid, irrational, meaningless, senseless, sophistical, specious, spurious, unreasonable, unscientific, unsound

ill-starred doomed, ill-fated, ill-omened, inauspicious, star-crossed, unfortunate, unhappy, unlucky

ill-tempered annoyed, bad-tempered, choleric, cross, curt, grumpy, impatient, irascible, irritable, liverish, ratty (*Brit. informal*), sharp, spiteful, testy, tetchy, touchy

ill-timed awkward, inappropriate, inconvenient, inept, inopportune, unseasonable, untimely, unwelcome

ill-treat abuse, damage, handle roughly, harass, harm, harry, ill-use, injure, knock about *or* around, maltreat, mishandle, misuse, oppress, wrong

ill-treatment abuse, damage, harm, ill-use, injury, mistreatment, misuse, rough handling

illuminate **1.** brighten, illumine (*literary*), irradiate, light, light up **2.** clarify, clear up, elucidate, enlighten, explain, explicate, give insight into, instruct, interpret, make clear, shed light on **3.** adorn, decorate, illustrate, ornament

illuminating enlightening, explanatory, helpful, informative, instructive, revealing

illumination **1.** awareness, clarification, edification, enlightenment, insight, inspiration, instruction, perception, revelation, understanding **2.** beam, brighten-

sion of reality: *her upswept hair gave the illusion of above average height.* **2** a false or misleading idea or belief: *we may suffer from the illusion that we are special.*

illusionist *n* a conjuror.

illusory *or* **illusive** *adj* seeming to be true, but actually false: *the economic benefits of such reforms were largely illusory.*

illustrate *vb* **-trating, -trated 1** to clarify or explain by use of examples or comparisons. **2** to provide (a book or text) with pictures. **3** to be an example of. **illustrative** *adj* **illustrator** *n*

illustration *n* **1** a picture or diagram used to explain or decorate a text. **2** an example: *an illustration of the brutality of the regime.* **3** the art of illustrating.

illustrious *adj* famous and distinguished.

ill will *n* unkind feeling; hostility.

I'm I am.

im- *prefix* same as **in-**[1] or **in-**[2].

image *n* **1** a mental picture of someone or something produced by the imagination or memory. **2** the appearance or impression given to the public by a person or organization. **3** a simile or metaphor. **4** a representation of a person or thing in a work of art or literature. **5** an optical reproduction of an object, formed by the lens of an eye or camera or by a mirror. **6** a person or thing that resembles another closely. **7** a personification of a specified quality; epitome: *the image of good breeding.* ~*vb* **-aging, -aged 8** to picture in the mind. **9** to mirror or reflect an image of. **10** to portray or describe.

imagery *n, pl* **-ries 1** figurative or descriptive language in a literary work. **2** mental images. **3** images collectively, esp. statues or carvings.

imaginary *adj* **1** existing only in the imagination. **2** *Maths* relating to the square root of a negative number.

imagination *n* **1** the faculty or action of producing mental images of what is not present or in one's experience. **2** creative mental ability.

imaginative *adj* **1** produced by or showing a creative imagination. **2** having a vivid imagination.

imagine *vb* **-ining, -ined 1** to form a mental image of. **2** to think, believe, or guess: *I would imagine they'll be here soon.* **imaginable** *adj*

imaginings *pl n* speculative thoughts about what might be the case or what might happen; fantasies: *the morbid imaginings of the frustrated lover.*

imago (im-**may**-go) *n, pl* **imagoes** *or* **imagines** (im-**maj**-in-eez) a sexually mature adult insect.

imam *n Islam* **1** a leader of congregational prayer in a mosque. **2** the title of some Muslim leaders.

imbalance *n* a lack of balance, for instance in emphasis or proportion: *a chemical imbalance in the brain.*

imbecile (**im**-biss-eel) *n* **1** *Informal* an extremely stupid person. **2** *Old-fashioned* a person of abnormally low intelligence. ~*adj* **3** stupid or senseless: *imbecile fanaticism.* **imbecility** *n*

imbed *vb* **-bedding, -bedded** same as **embed.**

imbibe *vb* **-bibing, -bibed** *Formal* **1** to drink (alcoholic drinks). **2** to take in or assimilate (ideas): *values she had imbibed as a child.*

THESAURUS

ing, brightness, light, lighting, lighting up, lights, radiance, ray

illusion 1. deception, delusion, error, fallacy, false impression, fancy, misapprehension, misconception **2.** chimera, daydream, fantasy, figment of the imagination, hallucination, ignis fatuus, mirage, mockery, phantasm, semblance, will-o'-the-wisp

illusory *or* **illusive** apparent, beguiling, chimerical, deceitful, deceptive, delusive, fallacious, false, hallucinatory, misleading, mistaken, seeming, sham, unreal, untrue

illustrate 1. bring home, clarify, demonstrate, elucidate, emphasize, exemplify, exhibit, explain, explicate, instance, interpret, make clear, make plain, point up, show **2.** adorn, decorate, depict, draw, ornament, picture, sketch

illustrated decorated, embellished, graphic, illuminated, pictorial, picture, pictured, with illustrations

illustration 1. adornment, decoration, figure, picture, plate, sketch **2.** analogy, case, case in point, clarification, demonstration, elucidation, example, exemplification, explanation, instance, interpretation, specimen

illustrious brilliant, celebrated, distinguished, eminent, exalted, famed, famous, glorious, great, noble, notable, noted, prominent, remarkable, renowned, resplendent, signal, splendid

ill will acrimony, animosity, animus, antagonism, antipathy, aversion, bad blood, dislike, enmity, envy, grudge, hard feelings, hatred, hostility, malevolence, malice, no love lost, rancour, resentment, spite, unfriendliness, venom

image 1. appearance, effigy, figure, icon, idol, likeness, picture, portrait, reflection, representation, statue **2.** chip off the old block (*informal*), counterpart, (dead) ringer (*slang*), doppelgänger (*legend*), double, facsimile, replica, similitude, spit (*informal, chiefly Brit.*), spitting image *or* spit and image (*informal*)

imaginable believable, comprehensible, conceivable, credible, likely, plausible, possible, supposable, thinkable, under the sun, within the bounds of possibility

imaginary assumed, chimerical, dreamlike, fancied, fanciful, fictional, fictitious, hallucinatory, hypothetical, ideal, illusive, illusory, imagined, invented, legendary, made-up, mythological, nonexistent, phantasmal, shadowy, supposed, suppositious, supposititious, unreal, unsubstantial, visionary

imagination 1. creativity, enterprise, fancy, ingenuity, insight, inspiration, invention, inventiveness, originality, resourcefulness, vision, wit, wittiness **2.** chimera, conception, idea, ideality, illusion, image, invention, notion, supposition, unreality

imaginative clever, creative, dreamy, enterprising, fanciful, fantastic, ingenious, inspired, inventive, original, poetical, visionary, vivid, whimsical

imagine 1. conceive, conceptualize, conjure up, create, devise, dream up (*informal*), envisage, fantasize, form a mental picture of, frame, invent, picture, plan, project, scheme, see in the mind's eye, think of, think up, visualize **2.** apprehend, assume, believe, conjecture, deduce, deem, fancy, gather, guess (*informal, chiefly U.S. & Canad.*), infer, realize, suppose, surmise, suspect, take for granted, take it, think

imbecile 1. *n.* berk (*Brit. slang*), bungler, charlie (*Brit. old-fashioned informal*), coot (*old-fashioned*), cretin, dickhead (*slang*), dolt, dotard, fool, halfwit, idiot, jerk (*slang, chiefly U.S. & Canad.*), moron, nerd *or* nurd (*slang*), numskull *or* numbskull, pillock (*slang*), plonker (*slang*), prat (*slang*), prick (*derogatory slang*), thickhead, twit (*informal, chiefly Brit.*), wally (*slang*) **2.** *adj.* asinine, fatuous, feeble-minded, foolish, idiotic, imbecilic, inane, ludicrous, moronic, simple, stupid, thick, witless

imbecility asininity, childishness, cretinism, fatuity, foolishness, idiocy, inanity, incompetency, stupidity

imbroglio (imb-**role**-ee-oh) *n, pl* **-glios** a confusing and complicated situation.

imbue *vb* **-buing, -bued** to fill or inspire (with ideals or principles).

IMF International Monetary Fund.

imitate *vb* **-tating, -tated 1** to copy the manner or style of or take as a model: *he remains rock's most imitated guitarist.* **2** to mimic or impersonate, esp. for amusement. **3** to make a copy or reproduction of; duplicate. **imitable** *adj* **imitator** *n*

imitation *n* **1** a copy of an original or genuine article. **2** an instance of imitating someone: *her Coward imitations were not the best thing she did.* **3** behaviour modelled on the behaviour of someone else: *to learn by imitation.* ~*adj* **4** made to resemble something which is usually superior or more expensive: *imitation leather.*

imitative *adj* **1** imitating or tending to copy. **2** copying or reproducing an original, esp. in an inferior manner: *imitative painting.* **3** onomatopoeic.

immaculate *adj* **1** completely clean or tidy: *an immaculate pinstripe suit.* **2** completely flawless: *his equestrian pedigree is immaculate.* **immaculately** *adv*

immanent *adj* **1** present within and throughout something. **2** (of God) present throughout the universe. **immanence** *n*

immaterial *adj* **1** of no real importance or relevance. **2** not formed of matter.

immature *adj* **1** not fully grown or developed. **2** lacking wisdom, insight, or stability because of youth. **immaturity** *n*

immeasurable *adj* too great to be measured. **immeasurably** *adv*

immediate *adj* **1** taking place without delay: *an immediate cut in interest rates.* **2** next or nearest in space, time, or relationship: *our immediate neighbour.* **3** present; current: *they had no immediate plans to close it.* **immediacy** *n* **immediately** *adv*

immemorial *adj* having existed or happened for longer than anyone can remember: *this has been the custom since time immemorial.*

immense *adj* **1** huge or vast. **2** *Informal* very great. **immensely** *adv* **immensity** *n*

immerse *vb* **-mersing, -mersed 1** to plunge or dip into liquid. **2** to involve deeply: *he immersed himself in the history of Rome.* **3** to baptize by dipping the whole body into water. **immersion** *n*

immersion heater *n* an electrical device in a domestic hot-water tank for heating water.

immigrant *n* a person who comes to a foreign country in order to settle there.

immigration *n* the act of coming to a foreign country in order to settle there. **immigrate** *vb*

imminent *adj* likely to happen soon. **imminence** *n*

THESAURUS

imbibe 1. consume, drink, knock back (*informal*), quaff, sink (*informal*), suck, swallow, swig (*informal*) **2.** *literary* absorb, acquire, assimilate, gain, gather, ingest, receive, take in

imitate affect, ape, burlesque, caricature, copy, counterfeit, do (*informal*), do an impression of, duplicate, echo, emulate, follow, follow in the footsteps of, follow suit, impersonate, mimic, mirror, mock, parody, personate, repeat, send up (*Brit. informal*), simulate, spoof (*informal*), take a leaf out of (someone's) book, take off (*informal*), travesty

imitation *n.* **1.** fake, forgery, impersonation, impression, mockery, parody, reflection, replica, reproduction, sham, substitution, takeoff (*informal*), travesty **2.** aping, copy, counterfeit, counterfeiting, duplication, echoing, likeness, mimicry, resemblance, simulation ~*adj.* **3.** artificial, dummy, ersatz, man-made, mock, phoney *or* phony (*informal*), pseudo (*informal*), repro, reproduction, sham, simulated, synthetic

imitative copied, copycat (*informal*), copying, derivative, echoic, mimetic, mimicking, mock, onomatopoeic, parrotlike, plagiarized, pseudo (*informal*), put-on, second-hand, simulated, unoriginal

imitator aper, copier, copycat (*informal*), echo, follower, impersonator, impressionist, mimic, parrot, shadow

immaculate 1. clean, impeccable, neat, neat as a new pin, spick-and-span, spruce, squeaky-clean, trim, unexceptionable **2.** above reproach, faultless, flawless, guiltless, impeccable, incorrupt, innocent, perfect, pure, sinless, spotless, squeaky-clean, stainless, unblemished, uncontaminated, undefiled, unpolluted, unsullied, untarnished, virtuous

immaterial 1. a matter of indifference, extraneous, impertinent, inapposite, inconsequential, inconsiderable, inessential, insignificant, irrelevant, of little account, of no consequence, of no importance, trifling, trivial, unimportant, unnecessary **2.** airy, disembodied, ethereal, ghostly, incorporeal, metaphysical, spiritual, unembodied, unsubstantial

immature 1. adolescent, crude, green, imperfect, premature, raw, undeveloped, unfinished, unfledged, unformed, unripe, unseasonable, untimely, young **2.** babyish, callow, childish, inexperienced, infantile, jejune, juvenile, puerile, wet behind the ears (*informal*)

immaturity 1. crudeness, crudity, greenness, imperfection, rawness, unpreparedness, unripeness **2.** babyishness, callowness, childishness, inexperience, juvenility, puerility

immeasurable bottomless, boundless, endless, illimitable, immense, incalculable, inestimable, inexhaustible, infinite, limitless, measureless, unbounded, unfathomable, unlimited, vast

immediate 1. instant, instantaneous **2.** adjacent, close, contiguous, direct, near, nearest, next, primary, proximate, recent **3.** actual, current, existing, extant, on hand, present, pressing, up to date, urgent

immediately 1. at once, before you could say Jack Robinson (*informal*), directly, forthwith, instantly, now, posthaste, promptly, pronto (*informal*), right away, right now, straight away, this instant, this very minute, unhesitatingly, without delay, without hesitation **2.** at first hand, closely, directly, nearly

immemorial age-old, ancient, archaic, fixed, long-standing, of yore, olden (*archaic or poetic*), rooted, time-honoured, traditional

immense colossal, elephantine, enormous, extensive, giant, gigantic, ginormous (*informal*), great, huge, humongous (*informal, chiefly U.S.*), illimitable, immeasurable, infinite, interminable, jumbo (*informal*), large, mammoth, massive, mega (*slang*), monstrous, monumental, prodigious, stupendous, titanic, tremendous, vast

immensity bulk, enormity, expanse, extent, greatness, hugeness, infinity, magnitude, massiveness, scope, size, sweep, vastness

immersion 1. baptism, bathe, dip, dipping, dousing, ducking, dunking, plunging, submerging **2.** *figurative* absorption, concentration, involvement, preoccupation

immigrant incomer, newcomer, settler

imminent at hand, brewing, close, coming, fast-approaching, forthcoming, gathering, impending, in the air, in the offing, looming, menacing, near, nigh

immiscible *adj* (of liquids) incapable of being mixed: *oil and water are immiscible.* **immiscibility** *n*

immobile *adj* **1** not moving. **2** not able to move or be moved. **immobility** *n*

immobilize *or* **-lise** *vb* **-lizing, -lized** *or* **-lising, -lised** to make unable to move or work: *a device for immobilizing steering wheels.* **immobilization** *or* **-lisation** *n*

immoderate *adj* excessive or unreasonable: *immoderate consumption of alcohol.* **immoderately** *adv*

immodest *adj* **1** behaving in an indecent or improper manner. **2** behaving in a boastful or conceited manner. **immodesty** *n*

immolate *vb* **-lating, -lated** *Literary* to kill or offer as a sacrifice. **immolation** *n*

immoral *adj* **1** morally wrong; corrupt. **2** sexually depraved or promiscuous. **immorality** *n*

➤ Do not confuse *immoral* with *amoral,* which means "having no moral standards".

immortal *adj* **1** not subject to death or decay. **2** famous for all time. **3** everlasting. ~*n* **4** a person whose fame will last for all time. **5** an immortal being. **immortality** *n*

immortalize *or* **-ise** *vb* **-izing, -ized** *or* **-ising, -ised** **1** to give everlasting fame to: *a name immortalized by countless writers.* **2** to give immortality to.

immovable *or* **immoveable** *adj* **1** unable to be moved. **2** unwilling to change one's opinions or beliefs. **3** not affected by feeling; emotionless. **4** unchanging. **5** *Law* (of property) consisting of land or houses. **immovability** *or* **immoveability** *n* **immovably** *or* **immoveably** *adv*

immune *adj* **1** protected against a specific disease by inoculation or as the result of natural resistance. **2** **immune to** secure against: *football is not immune to economic recession.* **3** exempt from obligation or penalty.

immunity *n, pl* **-ties** **1** the ability of an organism to resist disease. **2** freedom from prosecution, tax, etc.

immunize *or* **-nise** *vb* **-nizing, -nized** *or* **-nising, -nised** to make (someone) immune to a disease, esp. by inoculation. **immunization** *or* **-nisation** *n*

immunodeficiency *n* a deficiency in or breakdown of a person's ability to fight diseases.

immunology *n* the branch of medicine concerned with the study of immunity. **immunological** *adj* **immunologist** *n*

immure *vb* **-muring, -mured** **1** *Archaic or literary* to imprison. **2** to shut (oneself) away from society.

immutable (im-**mute**-a-bl) *adj* unchangeable or unchanging: *the immutable sequence of night and day.* **immutability** *n*

imp *n* **1** a small demon. **2** a mischievous child.

imp. **1** imperative. **2** imperfect.

impact *n* **1** the effect or impression made by something. **2** the act of one object striking another; collision. **3** the force of a collision. ~*vb* **4** to press firmly against or into. **impaction** *n*

impacted *adj* (of a tooth) unable to grow out because of being wedged against another tooth below the gum.

impair *vb* to damage or weaken in strength or quality. **impairment** *n*

impala (imp-**ah**-la) *n, pl* **-las** *or* **-la** an African antelope with lyre-shaped horns.

impale *vb* **-paling, -paled** to pierce through or fix with a sharp object: *they impaled his severed head on a spear.* **impalement** *n*

impalpable *adj* *Formal* **1** not able to be felt by

THESAURUS

(*archaic*), on the horizon, on the way, threatening, upcoming

immobile at a standstill, at rest, fixed, frozen, immobilized, immovable, like a statue, motionless, rigid, riveted, rooted, stable, static, stationary, stiff, still, stockstill, stolid, unmoving

immobility absence of movement, firmness, fixity, immovability, inertness, motionlessness, stability, steadiness, stillness

immobilize, -ise bring to a standstill, cripple, disable, freeze, halt, lay up (*informal*), paralyse, put out of action, render inoperative, stop, transfix

immoderate egregious, enormous, exaggerated, excessive, exorbitant, extravagant, extreme, inordinate, intemperate, OTT (*Brit slang*), over the odds (*informal*), over the top (*slang*), profligate, steep (*informal*), uncalled-for, unconscionable, uncontrolled, undue, unjustified, unreasonable, unrestrained, unwarranted, wanton

immodesty **1.** bawdiness, coarseness, impurity, indecorousness, indelicacy, lewdness, obscenity **2.** audacity, balls (*taboo slang*), boldness, brass neck (*Brit. informal*), forwardness, gall (*informal*), impudence, shamelessness, temerity

immoral abandoned, bad, corrupt, debauched, degenerate, depraved, dishonest, dissolute, evil, impure, indecent, iniquitous, lewd, licentious, nefarious, obscene, of easy virtue, pornographic, profligate, reprobate, sinful, unchaste, unethical, unprincipled, vicious, vile, wicked, wrong

immorality badness, corruption, debauchery, depravity, dissoluteness, evil, iniquity, licentiousness, profligacy, sin, turpitude, vice, wickedness, wrong

immortal *adj.* **1.** abiding, constant, death-defying, deathless, endless, enduring, eternal, everlasting, imperishable, incorruptible, indestructible, lasting, perennial, perpetual, timeless, undying, unfading ~*n.* **2.** genius, great (*usually plural*), hero, paragon **3.** god, goddess, Olympian

immortality **1.** deathlessness, endlessness, eternity, everlasting life, incorruptibility, indestructibility, perpetuity, timelessness **2.** celebrity, fame, glorification, gloriousness, glory, greatness, renown

immortalize, -ise apotheosize, celebrate, commemorate, enshrine, eternalize, eternize, exalt, glorify, perpetuate, solemnize

immovable, immoveable **1.** fast, firm, fixed, immutable, jammed, rooted, secure, set, stable, stationary, stuck, unbudgeable **2.** adamant, constant, impassive, inflexible, obdurate, resolute, steadfast, stonyhearted, unchangeable, unimpressionable, unshakable, unshaken, unwavering, unyielding

immune clear, exempt, free, insusceptible, invulnerable, let off (*informal*), not affected, not liable, not subject, proof (against), protected, resistant, safe, unaffected

immunity **1.** immunization, protection, resistance **2.** amnesty, charter, exemption, exoneration, franchise, freedom, indemnity, invulnerability, liberty, licence, prerogative, privilege, release, right

immunize, -nise inoculate, protect, safeguard, vaccinate

imp brat, demon, devil, gamin, minx, pickle (*Brit. informal*), rascal, rogue, scamp, sprite, urchin

impact *n.* **1.** bang, blow, bump, collision, concussion, contact, crash, force, jolt, knock, shock, smash, stroke, thump **2.** brunt, burden, consequences, effect, full force, impression, influence, meaning, power, repercussions, significance, thrust, weight ~*vb.* **3.** clash, collide, crash, crush, hit, strike

impair blunt, damage, debilitate, decrease, deterio-

touching: *impalpable shadows.* **2** difficult to understand. **impalpability** *n*

impart *vb* **1** to communicate (information or knowledge). **2** to give (a specified quality): *flavouring to impart a sweet taste.*

impartial *adj* not favouring one side or the other. **impartiality** *n* **impartially** *adv*

impassable *adj* (of terrain or roads) not able to be travelled through or over. **impassability** *n*

impasse (**am**-pass) *n* a situation in which progress or escape is impossible.

impassible *adj* **1** *Rare* not susceptible to pain or injury. **2** impassive; unmoved. **impassibility** *or* **impassibleness** *n*

impassioned *adj* full of emotion: *an impassioned plea to the United Nations.*

impassive *adj* not showing or feeling emotion. **impassively** *adv* **impassivity** *n*

impasto *n* the technique of applying paint thickly, so that brush marks are evident.

impatient *adj* **1** irritable at any delay or difficulty. **2** restless to have or do something. **impatience** *n* **impatiently** *adv*

impeach *vb* **1** *Chiefly US* to charge (a public official) with an offence committed in office. **2** *Brit criminal law* to accuse of treason or serious crime. **3** to challenge or question (a person's honesty or honour). **impeachable** *adj* **impeachment** *n*

impeccable *adj* without flaw or error: *impeccable manners.* **impeccably** *adv*

impecunious *adj Formal* without money; penniless.

impedance (imp-**eed**-anss) *n Electricity* the total effective resistance in an electric circuit to the flow of an alternating current.

impede *vb* **-peding, -peded** to block or make progress or action difficult.

impediment *n* **1** a hindrance or obstruction. **2** a physical disability that makes speech or walking difficult.

impedimenta *pl n* any objects that impede progress, esp. the baggage and equipment carried by an army.

impel *vb* **-pelling, -pelled 1** to urge or force (a person) to do something. **2** to push, drive, or force into motion.

impending *adj* (esp. of something bad) about to happen.

impenetrable *adj* **1** impossible to get through: *an impenetrable barrier.* **2** impossible to understand. **3** not receptive to ideas or influence: *impenetrable ignorance.* **impenetrability** *n* **impenetrably** *adv*

impenitent *adj* not sorry or penitent. **impenitence** *n*

imperative *adj* **1** extremely urgent; essential. **2** commanding or authoritative: *an imperative tone of*

THESAURUS

rate, diminish, enervate, enfeeble, harm, hinder, injure, lessen, mar, reduce, spoil, undermine, vitiate, weaken, worsen

impart 1. communicate, convey, disclose, discover, divulge, make known, pass on, relate, reveal, tell **2.** accord, afford, bestow, confer, contribute, give, grant, lend, offer, yield

impartial detached, disinterested, equal, equitable, even-handed, fair, just, neutral, nondiscriminating, nonpartisan, objective, open-minded, unbiased, unprejudiced, without fear or favour

impartiality detachment, disinterest, disinterestedness, dispassion, equality, equity, even-handedness, fairness, lack of bias, neutrality, nonpartisanship, objectivity, open-mindedness

impassable blocked, closed, impenetrable, obstructed, pathless, trackless, unnavigable

impasse blind alley (*informal*), dead end, deadlock, stalemate, standoff, standstill

impassioned animated, ardent, blazing, excited, fervent, fervid, fiery, flaming, furious, glowing, heated, inflamed, inspired, intense, passionate, rousing, stirring, vehement, violent, vivid, warm, worked up

impatience 1. haste, hastiness, heat, impetuosity, intolerance, irritability, irritableness, quick temper, rashness, shortness, snappiness, vehemence, violence **2.** agitation, anxiety, avidity, disquietude, eagerness, edginess, fretfulness, nervousness, restiveness, restlessness, uneasiness

impatient 1. abrupt, brusque, curt, demanding, edgy, hasty, hot-tempered, indignant, intolerant, irritable, quick-tempered, snappy, sudden, testy, vehement, violent **2.** agog, chafing, eager, fretful, headlong, impetuous, like a cat on hot bricks (*informal*), restless, straining at the leash

impeach 1. accuse, arraign, blame, censure, charge, criminate (*rare*), denounce, indict, tax **2.** call into question, cast aspersions on, cast doubt on, challenge, disparage, impugn, question

impeachment accusation, arraignment, indictment

impeccable above suspicion, blameless, exact, exquisite, faultless, flawless, immaculate, incorrupt, innocent, irreproachable, perfect, precise, pure, sinless, stainless, unblemished, unerring, unimpeachable

impecunious broke (*informal*), cleaned out (*slang*), destitute, down and out, flat broke (*informal*), indigent, insolvent, penniless, poverty-stricken, short, skint (*Brit. slang*), stony-broke (*Brit. slang*), strapped (*slang*), without two pennies to rub together (*informal*)

impede bar, block, brake, check, clog, curb, delay, disrupt, hamper, hinder, hold up, obstruct, restrain, retard, slow (down), stop, throw a spanner in the works (*Brit. informal*), thwart

impediment bar, barrier, block, check, clog, curb, defect, difficulty, encumbrance, hindrance, obstacle, obstruction, snag, stumbling block

impedimenta accoutrements, baggage, belongings, effects, equipment, gear, junk (*informal*), luggage, movables, odds and ends, paraphernalia, possessions, stuff, things, trappings, traps

impel actuate, chivvy, compel, constrain, drive, force, goad, incite, induce, influence, inspire, instigate, motivate, move, oblige, power, prod, prompt, propel, push, require, spur, stimulate, urge

impending approaching, brewing, coming, forthcoming, gathering, hovering, imminent, in the offing, looming, menacing, near, nearing, on the horizon, threatening, upcoming

impenetrable 1. dense, hermetic, impassable, impermeable, impervious, inviolable, solid, thick, unpierceable **2.** arcane, baffling, dark, enigmatic, enigmatical, hidden, incomprehensible, indiscernible, inexplicable, inscrutable, mysterious, obscure, unfathomable, unintelligible

imperative 1. compulsory, crucial, essential, exigent, indispensable, insistent, obligatory, pressing, urgent, vital **2.** authoritative, autocratic, commanding, dictatorial, domineering, high-handed, imperious, lordly, magisterial, peremptory

imperceptible faint, fine, gradual, impalpable, inappreciable, inaudible, indiscernible, indistinguishable, infinitesimal, insensible, invisible, microscopic, min-

voice. **3** *Grammar* denoting a mood of verbs used in commands. ~*n* **4** *Grammar* the imperative mood.
imperceptible *adj* too slight, subtle, or gradual to be noticed. **imperceptibly** *adv*
imperfect *adj* **1** having faults or errors. **2** not complete. **3** *Grammar* denoting a tense of verbs describing continuous, incomplete, or repeated past actions. ~*n* **4** *Grammar* the imperfect tense. **imperfectly** *adv*
imperfection *n* **1** the state of being imperfect. **2** a fault or defect.
imperial *adj* **1** of an empire, emperor, or empress. **2** majestic; commanding. **3** exercising supreme authority; imperious. **4** (of weights or measures) conforming to the standards of a system formerly official in Great Britain. ~*n* **5** a wine bottle holding the equivalent of eight normal bottles.
imperialism *n* **1** the policy or practice of extending a country's influence over other territories by conquest, colonization, or economic domination. **2** an imperial system, authority, or government. **imperialist** *adj, n* **imperialistic** *adj*
imperil *vb* **-illing, -illed** *or US* **-iling, -iled** *Formal* to put in danger.
imperious *adj* used to being obeyed; domineering. **imperiously** *adv*
imperishable *adj* unable to disappear or be destroyed.
impermanent *adj* not permanent; fleeting. **impermanence** *n*
impermeable *adj* (of a substance) not allowing fluid to pass through: *an impermeable layer.* **impermeability** *n*
impermissible *adj* not allowed.
impersonal *adj* **1** without reference to any individual person; objective: *Buddhism began as a very impersonal doctrine.* **2** without human warmth or sympathy: *an impersonal manner.* **3** *Grammar* **a** (of a verb) having no subject, as in *it is raining.* **b** (of a pronoun) not referring to a person. **impersonality** *n* **impersonally** *adv*
impersonate *vb* **-ating, -ated 1** to pretend to be (another person). **2** to imitate the character or mannerisms of (another person) for entertainment. **impersonation** *n* **impersonator** *n*
impertinent *adj* disrespectful or rude. **impertinence** *n*
imperturbable *adj* not easily upset; calm. **imperturbability** *n* **imperturbably** *adv*
impervious *adj* **1** not letting water etc. through. **2** not influenced by a feeling, argument, etc.
impetigo (imp-it-**tie**-go) *n* a contagious skin disease causing spots or pimples.
impetuous *adj* **1** acting without consideration. **2** done rashly or hastily. **impetuosity** *n*
impetus (**imp**-it-uss) *n, pl* **-tuses 1** an incentive or impulse. **2** *Physics* the force that starts a body moving or that tends to resist changes in its speed or direction once it is moving.
impi *n, pl* **-pi** *or* **-pies** a group of Zulu warriors.
impiety *n* lack of respect or religious reverence.
impinge *vb* **-pinging, -pinged** to encroach, affect or restrict: *international economic forces impinging on the local economy.* **impingement** *n*
impious (**imp**-euss) *adj* showing a lack of respect or religious reverence.
impish *adj* mischievous. **impishness** *n*

THESAURUS

ute, shadowy, slight, small, subtle, tiny, undetectable, unnoticeable
imperceptibly by a hair's-breadth, inappreciably, indiscernibly, invisibly, little by little, slowly, subtly, unnoticeably, unobtrusively, unseen
imperfect broken, damaged, defective, deficient, faulty, flawed, immature, impaired, incomplete, inexact, limited, partial, patchy, rudimentary, sketchy, undeveloped, unfinished
imperfection blemish, defect, deficiency, failing, fallibility, fault, flaw, foible, frailty, inadequacy, incompleteness, infirmity, insufficiency, peccadillo, scar, shortcoming, stain, taint, weakness, weak point
imperial 1. kingly, majestic, princely, queenly, regal, royal, sovereign 2. august, exalted, grand, great, high, imperious, lofty, magnificent, noble, superior, supreme
imperil endanger, expose, hazard, jeopardize, risk
imperishable abiding, enduring, eternal, everlasting, immortal, indestructible, perennial, permanent, perpetual, undying, unfading, unforgettable
impersonal aloof, bureaucratic, businesslike, cold, detached, dispassionate, formal, inhuman, neutral, remote
impersonate act, ape, caricature, do (*informal*), do an impression of, enact, imitate, masquerade as, mimic, parody, pass oneself off as, personate, pose as (*informal*), take off (*informal*)
impersonation caricature, imitation, impression, mimicry, parody, takeoff (*informal*)
impertinence assurance, audacity, backchat (*informal*), boldness, brass neck (*Brit. informal*), brazenness, cheek (*informal*), disrespect, effrontery, forwardness, front, impudence, incivility, insolence, neck (*informal*), nerve (*informal*), pertness, presumption, rudeness, sauce (*informal*)
impertinent bold, brazen, cheeky (*informal*), discourteous, disrespectful, flip (*informal*), forward, fresh (*informal*), impolite, impudent, insolent, interfering, pert, presumptuous, rude, saucy (*informal*), uncivil, unmannerly
imperturbable calm, collected, complacent, composed, cool, nerveless, sedate, self-possessed, serene, stoical, tranquil, undisturbed, unexcitable, unfazed (*informal*), unflappable (*informal*), unmoved, unruffled
impervious 1. hermetic, impassable, impenetrable, impermeable, imperviable, invulnerable, resistant, sealed 2. closed to, immune, invulnerable, proof against, unaffected by, unmoved by, unreceptive, unswayable, untouched by
impetuosity haste, hastiness, impulsiveness, precipitancy, precipitateness, rashness, vehemence, violence
impetuous ardent, eager, fierce, furious, hasty, headlong, impassioned, impulsive, passionate, precipitate, rash, spontaneous, spur-of-the-moment, unbridled, unplanned, unpremeditated, unreflecting, unrestrained, unthinking, vehement, violent
impetus 1. catalyst, goad, impulse, impulsion, incentive, motivation, push, spur, stimulus 2. energy, force, momentum, power
impiety godlessness, iniquity, irreligion, irreverence, profaneness, profanity, sacrilege, sinfulness, ungodliness, unholiness, unrighteousness, wickedness
impinge affect, bear upon, encroach, have a bearing on, influence, infringe, invade, make inroads, obtrude, relate to, touch, touch upon, trespass, violate
impious blasphemous, godless, iniquitous, irreligious, irreverent, profane, sacrilegious, sinful, ungodly, unholy, unrighteous, wicked
impish devilish, elfin, mischievous, prankish, puckish, rascally, roguish, sportive, waggish
implacability implacableness, inexorability, inflexibility, intractability, mercilessness, pitilessness, re-

implacable *adj* **1** incapable of being appeased or pacified. **2** unyielding. **implacability** *n* **implacably** *adv*

implant *vb* **1** to fix firmly in the mind: *to implant sound moral principles.* **2** to plant or embed. **3** *Surgery* to graft or insert (a tissue or hormone) into the body. *~n* **4** anything implanted in the body, such as a tissue graft. **implantation** *n*

implausible *adj* not easy to believe. **implausibility** *n*

implement *vb* **1** to carry out (instructions etc.): *she refused to implement the agreed plan.* *~n* **2** a tool or other piece of equipment. **implementation** *n*

implicate *vb* **-cating, -cated 1** to show (someone) to be involved, esp. in a crime. **2** to imply.

implication *n* **1** something that is suggested or implied. **2** an act or instance of suggesting or implying or being implied.

implicit *adj* **1** expressed indirectly: *an implicit agreement.* **2** absolute and unquestioning: *implicit trust.* **3** contained in, although not stated openly: *this view of the mind was implicit in all his work.* **implicitly** *adv*

implied *adj* hinted at or suggested: *an implied criticism.*

implode *vb* **-ploding, -ploded** to collapse inwards.

implore *vb* **-ploring, -plored** to beg desperately.

imply *vb* **-plies, -plying, -plied 1** to express or indicate by a hint; suggest. **2** to suggest or involve as a necessary consequence: *a spending commitment implies a corresponding tax imposition.*

impolite *adj* discourteous; rude. **impoliteness** *n*

impolitic *adj* ill-advised; unwise.

imponderable *adj* **1** unable to be weighed or assessed. *~n* **2** something difficult or impossible to assess.

import *vb* **1** to bring in (goods) from another country. **2** *Formal* to signify; mean: *to import doom.* *~n* **3** something imported. **4** *Formal* importance: *his new work is of great import.* **5** meaning. **6** *Canad slang* a sportsman who is not native to the area where he plays. **importer** *n* **importation** *n*

important *adj* **1** of great significance, value, or consequence. **2** of social significance: *an important man in the company hierarchy.* **3** of great concern: *it was important to me to know.* **importance** *n* **importantly** *adv*

importunate *adj Formal* persistent or demanding.

importune *vb* **-tuning, -tuned** *Formal* to harass with persistent requests. **importunity** *n*

impose *vb* **-posing, -posed 1** to establish (a rule, condition, etc.) as something to be obeyed or complied with. **2** to take advantage of (a person or quality): *she imposed on her kindness.* **3** to force (oneself) on others. **4** *Printing* to arrange (pages) in the correct order for printing. **5** to pass off (something) deceptively on someone.

THESAURUS

lentlessness, ruthlessness, unforgivingness, vengefulness

implacable cruel, inexorable, inflexible, intractable, merciless, pitiless, rancorous, relentless, remorseless, ruthless, unappeasable, unbending, uncompromising, unforgiving, unrelenting, unyielding

implant 1. inculcate, infix, infuse, inseminate, instil, sow **2.** embed, fix, graft, ingraft, insert, place, plant, root, sow

implement 1. *vb.* bring about, carry out, complete, effect, enforce, execute, fulfil, perform, put into action *or* effect, realize **2.** *n.* agent, apparatus, appliance, device, gadget, instrument, tool, utensil

implementation accomplishment, carrying out, discharge, effecting, enforcement, execution, fulfilment, performance, performing, realization

implicate associate, compromise, concern, embroil, entangle, imply, include, incriminate, inculpate, involve, mire, tie up with

implicated incriminated, involved, suspected, under suspicion

implication 1. association, connection, entanglement, incrimination, involvement **2.** conclusion, inference, innuendo, meaning, overtone, presumption, ramification, significance, signification, suggestion

implicit 1. contained, implied, inferred, inherent, latent, tacit, taken for granted, undeclared, understood, unspoken **2.** absolute, constant, entire, firm, fixed, full, steadfast, total, unhesitating, unqualified, unreserved, unshakable, unshaken, wholehearted

implicitly absolutely, completely, firmly, unconditionally, unhesitatingly, unreservedly, utterly, without reservation

implied hinted at, implicit, indirect, inherent, insinuated, suggested, tacit, undeclared, unexpressed, unspoken, unstated

implore beg, beseech, conjure, crave, entreat, go on bended knee to, importune, plead with, pray, solicit, supplicate

imply 1. connote, give (someone) to understand, hint, insinuate, intimate, signify, suggest **2.** betoken, denote, entail, evidence, import, include, indicate, involve, mean, point to, presuppose

impolite bad-mannered, boorish, churlish, discourteous, disrespectful, ill-bred, ill-mannered, indecorous, indelicate, insolent, loutish, rough, rude, uncivil, uncouth, ungallant, ungentlemanly, ungracious, unladylike, unmannerly, unrefined

impoliteness bad manners, boorishness, churlishness, discourtesy, disrespect, incivility, indelicacy, insolence, rudeness, unmannerliness

import *vb.* **1.** bring in, introduce, land *~n.* **2.** bottom, consequence, importance, magnitude, moment, significance, substance, weight **3.** bearing, drift, gist, implication, intention, meaning, message, purport, sense, significance, thrust

importance 1. bottom, distinction, eminence, esteem, influence, mark, pre-eminence, prestige, prominence, standing, status, usefulness, worth **2.** concern, consequence, import, interest, moment, momentousness, significance, substance, value, weight

important 1. far-reaching, grave, large, material, meaningful, momentous, of substance, primary, salient, serious, signal, significant, substantial, urgent, weighty **2.** big-time (*informal*), eminent, foremost, high-level, high-ranking, influential, leading, major league (*informal*), notable, noteworthy, of note, outstanding, powerful, pre-eminent, prominent, seminal **3.** *usually with* **to** basic, essential, of concern *or* interest, relevant, valuable, valued

importunate burning, clamant, clamorous, demanding, dogged, earnest, exigent, insistent, persistent, pertinacious, pressing, solicitous, troublesome, urgent

impose 1. decree, establish, exact, fix, institute, introduce, lay, levy, ordain, place, promulgate, put, set **2.** appoint, charge with, dictate, enforce, enjoin, inflict, prescribe, saddle (someone) with **3.** *with* **on** *or* **upon a.** abuse, exploit, play on, take advantage of, use **b.** con (*informal*), deceive, dupe, hoodwink, pull the wool over (somebody's) eyes, trick **4.** *with* **on** *or* **upon** butt in, encroach, foist, force oneself, gate-crash

imposing *adj* grand or impressive: *an imposing building.*
imposition *n* **1** the act of imposing. **2** something imposed, esp. unfairly on someone. **3** the arrangement of pages for printing. **4** *Old-fashioned* a task set as a school punishment.
impossibility *n, pl* **-ties** **1** the state or quality of being impossible. **2** something that is impossible.
impossible *adj* **1** not able to be done or to happen. **2** absurd or unreasonable. **3** *Informal* intolerable or outrageous: *those children are impossible.* **impossibly** *adv*
imposter *or* **impostor** *n* a person who cheats or swindles by pretending to be someone else.
imposture *n Formal* deception, esp. by pretending to be someone else.
impotent (**imp**-a-tent) *adj* **1** not having the power to influence people or events. **2** (of a man) incapable of sexual intercourse. **impotence** *n*
impound *vb* **1** to take legal possession of; confiscate. **2** to confine (an animal) in a pound.
impoverish *vb* to make (someone) poor or weaken the quality of something. **impoverished** *adj* **impoverishment** *n*
impracticable *adj* **1** not able to be put into practice. **2** unsuitable for a desired use. **impracticability** *n*
impractical *adj* **1** not sensible or workable: *the use of force was viewed as impractical.* **2** not having practical skills. **impracticality** *n*
imprecation *n Formal* a curse. **imprecate** *vb*
imprecise *adj* inexact or inaccurate. **imprecision** *n*
impregnable *adj* **1** unable to be broken into or taken by force: *an impregnable fortress.* **2** unable to be affected or overcome: *a confident, impregnable person.* **impregnability** *n*
impregnate *vb* **-nating, -nated** **1** to saturate, soak, or fill throughout. **2** to make pregnant. **3** to imbue or permeate: *the party has been impregnated with an enthusiasm for reform.* **impregnation** *n*
impresario *n, pl* **-sarios** a person who runs theatre performances, concerts, etc.
impress *vb* **1** to make a strong, lasting, or favourable impression on: *he was impressed by the standard of play.* **2** to stress or emphasize. **3** to imprint or stamp by pressure: *a pattern impressed in paint on the rock.* ~*n* **4** an impressing. **5** a mark produced by impressing. **impressible** *adj*
impression *n* **1** an effect produced in the mind by a person or thing: *she was keen to create a relaxed impression.* **2** a vague idea or belief: *he only had a vague impression of how it worked.* **3** a strong, favourable, or remarkable effect. **4** an impersonation for entertainment. **5** an imprint or mark produced by pressing. **6** *Printing* the number of copies of a publication printed at one time.
impressionable *adj* easily impressed or influenced: *the promotion of smoking to the impressionable young.* **impressionability** *n*
Impressionism *n* a style of painting developed in 19th-century France, with the aim of reproducing the immediate impression or mood of things, especially the effects of light and atmosphere, rather than form or structure.
impressionist *n* **1** **Impressionist** an artist who

THESAURUS

(*informal*), intrude, obtrude, presume, take liberties, trespass
imposing august, commanding, dignified, effective, grand, impressive, majestic, stately, striking
imposition **1.** application, decree, introduction, laying on, levying, promulgation **2.** cheek (*informal*), encroachment, intrusion, liberty, presumption
impossibility hopelessness, impracticability, inability, inconceivability
impossible **1.** beyond one, beyond the bounds of possibility, hopeless, impracticable, inconceivable, not to be thought of, out of the question, unachievable, unattainable, unobtainable, unthinkable **2.** absurd, inadmissible, insoluble, intolerable, ludicrous, outrageous, preposterous, unacceptable, unanswerable, ungovernable, unreasonable, unsuitable, unworkable
imposter, impostor charlatan, cheat, deceiver, fake, fraud, hypocrite, impersonator, knave (*archaic*), phoney *or* phony (*informal*), pretender, quack, rogue, sham, trickster
impotence disability, enervation, feebleness, frailty, helplessness, inability, inadequacy, incapacity, incompetence, ineffectiveness, inefficacy, inefficiency, infirmity, paralysis, powerlessness, uselessness, weakness
impotent disabled, emasculate, enervated, feeble, frail, helpless, incapable, incapacitated, incompetent, ineffective, infirm, nerveless, paralysed, powerless, unable, unmanned, weak
impoverish bankrupt, break, deplete, diminish, drain, exhaust, pauperize, reduce, ruin, sap, use up, wear out
impoverished **1.** bankrupt, destitute, distressed, impecunious, indigent, in reduced *or* straitened circumstances, necessitous, needy, on one's uppers, penurious, poverty-stricken, ruined, straitened **2.** barren, denuded, depleted, drained, empty, exhausted, played out, reduced, spent, sterile, worn out
impracticability futility, hopelessness, impossibility, impracticality, unsuitableness, unworkability, uselessness
impracticable **1.** impossible, out of the question, unachievable, unattainable, unfeasible, unworkable **2.** awkward, impractical, inapplicable, inconvenient, unserviceable, unsuitable, useless
impractical **1.** impossible, impracticable, inoperable, nonviable, unrealistic, unserviceable, unworkable, visionary, wild **2.** idealistic, romantic, starry-eyed, unbusinesslike, unrealistic, visionary
impracticality hopelessness, impossibility, inapplicability, romanticism, unworkability
imprecise ambiguous, blurred round the edges, careless, equivocal, estimated, fluctuating, hazy, ill-defined, inaccurate, indefinite, indeterminate, inexact, inexplicit, loose, rough, sloppy (*informal*), vague, wide of the mark, woolly
impregnable immovable, impenetrable, indestructible, invincible, invulnerable, secure, strong, unassailable, unbeatable, unconquerable, unshakable
impregnate **1.** fill, imbue, infuse, percolate, permeate, pervade, saturate, seep, soak, steep, suffuse **2.** fertilize, fructify, get with child, inseminate, make pregnant
impress **1.** affect, excite, grab (*informal*), influence, inspire, make an impression, move, stir, strike, sway, touch **2.** *often with* **on** *or* **upon** bring home to, emphasize, fix, inculcate, instil into, stress **3.** emboss, engrave, imprint, indent, mark, print, stamp
impression **1.** effect, feeling, impact, influence, reaction, sway **2.** belief, concept, conviction, fancy, feeling, funny feeling (*informal*), hunch, idea, memory, notion, opinion, recollection, sense, suspicion **3.** imitation, impersonation, parody, send-up (*Brit. informal*), takeoff (*informal*) **4.** brand, dent, hollow, impress, imprint, indentation, mark, outline, stamp, stamping **5.** edition, imprinting, issue, printing

painted in the style of Impressionism. **2** a person who imitates the character or mannerisms of another person for entertainment.

impressionistic *adj* **1 Impressionistic** of or about Impressionism. **2** based on subjective observations or impressions rather than systematic study or facts.

impressive *adj* capable of impressing, esp. by size, magnificence, or importance. **impressively** *adv*

imprimatur (imp-rim-**ah**-ter) *n* official approval for something to be printed, usually given by the Roman Catholic Church.

imprint *n* **1** a mark or impression produced by pressing, printing, or stamping. **2** the publisher's name and address, often with the date of publication, printed on the title page of a book. ~*vb* **3** to produce (a mark) by pressing, printing, or stamping: *T-shirts imprinted with slogans.* **4** to establish firmly; impress: *he couldn't dislodge the images imprinted on his brain.*

imprison *vb* to confine in or as if in prison. **imprisonment** *n*

improbable *adj* not likely or probable. **improbability** *n* **improbably** *adv*

improbity *n, pl* **-ties** *Formal* dishonesty or wickedness.

impromptu *adj* **1** without planning or preparation; improvised. ~*adv* **2** in a spontaneous or improvised way: *he spoke impromptu.* ~*n* **3** a short piece of instrumental music resembling improvisation. **4** something that is impromptu.

improper *adj* **1** indecent. **2** irregular or incorrect. **improperly** *adv*

improper fraction *n* a fraction in which the numerator is greater than the denominator, as $\frac{7}{6}$.

impropriety (imp-roe-**pry**-a-tee) *n, pl* **-ties** *Formal* unsuitable or slightly improper behaviour.

improve *vb* **-proving, -proved 1** to make or become better in quality. **2 improve on** to achieve a better standard or quality in comparison with: *both had improved on their previous performance.* **improvable** *adj*

improvement *n* **1** the act of improving or the state of being improved. **2** a change that makes something better or adds to its value. **3** *Austral & NZ* a building on a piece of land, adding to its value.

improvident *adj* **1** not providing for the future. **2** incautious or rash. **improvidence** *n*

improvise *vb* **-vising, -vised 1** to do or make quickly from whatever is available, without previous planning. **2** to make up (a piece of music, speech, etc.) as one goes along. **improvisation** *n*

imprudent *adj* not carefully thought out; rash. **imprudence** *n*

impudent *adj* impertinent or insolent. **impudence** *n* **impudently** *adv*

impugn (imp-**yoon**) *vb Formal* to challenge or attack as false. **impugnment** *n*

impulse *n* **1** a sudden desire or whim. **2** an instinctive drive; urge: *the mothering impulse.* **3** *Physics* **a** the product of a force acting on a body and the time for which it acts. **b** the change in the momentum of a body as a result of a force acting upon it. **4** *Physiol* a stimulus transmitted in a nerve or muscle.

impulsive *adj* **1** tending to act without thinking first:

THESAURUS

impressionable feeling, gullible, ingenuous, open, receptive, responsive, sensitive, suggestible, susceptible, vulnerable

impressive affecting, exciting, forcible, moving, powerful, stirring, striking, touching

imprint 1. *n.* impression, indentation, mark, print, sign, stamp **2.** *vb.* engrave, establish, etch, fix, impress, print, stamp

imprison confine, constrain, detain, immure, incarcerate, intern, jail, lock up, put away, put under lock and key, send down (*informal*), send to prison

imprisonment confinement, custody, detention, duress, incarceration, internment, porridge (*slang*)

improbability doubt, doubtfulness, dubiety, uncertainty, unlikelihood

improbable doubtful, dubious, fanciful, far-fetched, implausible, questionable, unbelievable, uncertain, unconvincing, unlikely, weak

impromptu 1. *adj.* ad-lib, extemporaneous, extempore, extemporized, improvised, offhand, off the cuff (*informal*), spontaneous, unpremeditated, unprepared, unrehearsed, unscripted, unstudied **2.** *adv.* ad lib, off the cuff (*informal*), off the top of one's head (*informal*), on the spur of the moment, spontaneously, without preparation

improper 1. impolite, indecent, indecorous, indelicate, off-colour, risqué, smutty, suggestive, unbecoming, unfitting, unseemly, untoward, vulgar **2.** abnormal, erroneous, false, inaccurate, incorrect, irregular, wrong

impropriety bad taste, immodesty, incongruity, indecency, indecorum, unsuitability, vulgarity

improve advance, ameliorate, amend, augment, better, correct, develop, enhance, face-lift, gain strength, help, increase, look up (*informal*), make strides, mend, perk up, pick up, polish, progress, rally, rectify, reform, rise, take a turn for the better (*informal*), take on a new lease of life (*informal*), touch up, upgrade

improvement 1. advancement, amelioration, amendment, augmentation, betterment, correction, face-lift, gain, rectification **2.** advance, development, enhancement, furtherance, increase, progress, rally, recovery, reformation, rise, upswing

improvisation ad-lib, ad-libbing, expedient, extemporizing, impromptu, invention, makeshift, spontaneity

improvise 1. concoct, contrive, devise, make do, throw together **2.** ad-lib, busk, coin, extemporize, invent, play it by ear (*informal*), speak off the cuff (*informal*), vamp, wing it (*informal*)

improvised ad-lib, extemporaneous, extempore, extemporized, makeshift, off the cuff (*informal*), spontaneous, spur-of-the-moment, unprepared, unrehearsed

imprudent careless, foolhardy, foolish, heedless, ill-advised, ill-considered, ill-judged, impolitic, improvident, incautious, inconsiderate, indiscreet, injudicious, irresponsible, overhasty, rash, reckless, unthinking, unwise

impudence assurance, audacity, backchat (*informal*), boldness, brass neck (*Brit. informal*), brazenness, bumptiousness, cheek (*informal*), chutzpah (*U.S. & Canad. informal*), effrontery, face (*informal*), front, impertinence, insolence, lip (*slang*), neck (*informal*), nerve (*informal*), pertness, presumption, rudeness, sauciness, shamelessness

impudent audacious, bold, bold-faced, brazen, bumptious, cheeky (*informal*), cocky (*informal*), forward, fresh (*informal*), immodest, impertinent, insolent, pert, presumptuous, rude, saucy (*informal*), shameless

impulse 1. *figurative* caprice, drive, feeling, incitement, inclination, influence, instinct, motive, notion, passion, resolve, urge, whim, wish **2.** catalyst, force, impetus, momentum, movement, pressure, push, stimulus, surge, thrust

impulsive devil-may-care, emotional, hasty, head-

an impulsive man. **2** done without thinking first. **3** forceful or impelling.

impunity (imp-**yoon**-it-ee) *n* **with impunity** without punishment or unpleasant consequences.

impure *adj* **1** having unwanted substances mixed in. **2** immoral or obscene: *impure thoughts.* **3** dirty or unclean.

impurity *n, pl* **-ties 1** an impure element or thing: *impurities in the water.* **2** the quality of being impure.

impute *vb* **-puting, -puted 1** to attribute (blame or a crime) to a person. **2** to attribute to a source or cause: *I impute your success to nepotism.* **imputation** *n*

in *prep* **1** inside; within: *in the room.* **2** at a place where there is: *in the shade.* **3** indicating a state, situation, or condition: *in silence.* **4** when (a period of time) has elapsed: *come back in one year.* **5** using: *written in code.* **6** wearing: *the man in the blue suit.* **7** with regard to (a specified activity or occupation): *in journalism.* **8** while performing the action of: *in crossing the street he was run over.* **9** having as purpose: *in honour of the president.* **10** (of certain animals) pregnant with: *in calf.* **11** into: *he fell in the water.* **12 have it in one** to have the ability (to do something). **13 in that** *or* **in so far as** because or to the extent that: *it was of great help in that it gave me more confidence.* ~*adv* **14** in or into a particular place; indoors: *come in.* **15** at one's home or place of work: *he's not in at the moment.* **16** fashionable or popular: *long skirts are in this year.* **17** in office or power: *the Conservatives got in at the last election.* **18** so as to enclose: *block in.* **19** (in certain games) so as to take one's turn of the play: *you have to get the other side out before you go in.* **20** *Brit* (of a fire) alight. **21** indicating prolonged activity, esp. by a large number: *teach-in; sit-in.* **22 in for** about to experience (something, esp. something unpleasant): *they're in for a shock.* **23 in on** acquainted with or sharing in: *I was in on all his plans.* **24 in with** friendly with. **25 have got it in for** *Informal* to wish or intend harm towards. ~*adj* **26** fashionable; modish: *the in thing to do.* ~*n* **27 ins and outs** the detailed points or facts (of a situation).

In *Chem* indium.

IN Indiana.

in. inch(es).

in-[1], **il-, im-,** *or* **ir-** *prefix* **a** not; non: *incredible; illegal; imperfect; irregular.* **b** lack of: *inexperience.*

in-[2], **il-, im-,** *or* **ir-** *prefix* in; into; towards; within; on: *infiltrate.*

inability *n* the fact of not being able to do something.

in absentia *adv* in the absence of (someone indicated).

inaccessible *adj* **1** impossible or very difficult to reach. **2** unable to be used or seen: *his works are inaccessible to English speaking readers.* **3** difficult to understand or appreciate: *Webern's music is still considered inaccessible.* **inaccessibility** *n*

inaccuracy *n, pl* **-cies 1** lack of accuracy; imprecision. **2** an error or mistake. **inaccurate** *adj*

inaction *n* lack of action; inertia.

inactive *adj* **1** idle; not active. **2** *Chem* (of a substance) having little or no reactivity. **inactivity** *n*

inadequacy *n, pl* **-cies 1** lack or shortage. **2** the state of being or feeling inferior. **3** a weakness or failing: *their own failures or inadequacies.*

inadequate *adj* **1** not enough; insufficient. **2** not good enough. **inadequately** *adv*

inadmissible *adj* not allowable or acceptable.

THESAURUS

long, impetuous, instinctive, intuitive, passionate, precipitate, quick, rash, spontaneous, unconsidered, unpredictable, unpremeditated

impure 1. admixed, adulterated, alloyed, debased, mixed, unrefined 2. carnal, coarse, corrupt, gross, immodest, immoral, indecent, indelicate, lascivious, lewd, licentious, lustful, obscene, prurient, ribald, salacious, smutty, unchaste, unclean 3. contaminated, defiled, dirty, filthy, foul, infected, polluted, sullied, tainted, unclean, unwholesome, vitiated

impurity 1. admixture, adulteration, mixture 2. *often plural* bits, contaminant, dirt, dross, foreign body, foreign matter, grime, marks, pollutant, scum, spots, stains 3. carnality, coarseness, corruption, grossness, immodesty, immorality, indecency, lasciviousness, lewdness, licentiousness, obscenity, prurience, salaciousness, smuttiness, unchastity, vulgarity 4. contamination, defilement, dirtiness, filth, foulness, infection, pollution, taint, uncleanness

imputation accusation, ascription, aspersion, attribution, blame, censure, charge, insinuation, reproach, slander, slur

impute accredit, ascribe, assign, attribute, credit, lay at the door of, refer, set down to

inability disability, disqualification, impotence, inadequacy, incapability, incapacity, incompetence, ineptitude, powerlessness

inaccessible impassable, out of reach, out of the way, remote, unapproachable, unattainable, un-get-at-able (*informal*), unreachable

inaccuracy 1. erroneousness, imprecision, incorrectness, inexactness, unfaithfulness, unreliability 2. blunder, boob (*Brit. slang*), corrigendum, defect, erratum, error, fault, howler (*informal*), literal (*Printing*), miscalculation, mistake, slip, typo (*informal, printing*)

inaccurate careless, defective, discrepant, erroneous, faulty, imprecise, incorrect, in error, inexact, mistaken, out, unfaithful, unreliable, unsound, wide of the mark, wild, wrong

inaction dormancy, idleness, immobility, inactivity, inertia, rest, torpidity, torpor

inactive abeyant, dormant, dull, idle, immobile, indolent, inert, inoperative, jobless, kicking one's heels, latent, lazy, lethargic, low-key (*informal*), mothballed, out of service, out-of-work, passive, quiet, sedentary, slothful, slow, sluggish, somnolent, torpid, unemployed, unoccupied, unused

inactivity dilatoriness, dormancy, dullness, heaviness, hibernation, immobility, inaction, indolence, inertia, inertness, lassitude, laziness, lethargy, passivity, quiescence, sloth, sluggishness, stagnation, torpor, unemployment, vegetation

inadequacy 1. dearth, deficiency, inadequateness, incompleteness, insufficiency, meagreness, paucity, poverty, scantiness, shortage, skimpiness 2. defectiveness, faultiness, inability, inaptness, incapacity, incompetence, incompetency, ineffectiveness, inefficacy, unfitness, unsuitableness 3. defect, failing, imperfection, lack, shortage, shortcoming, weakness

inadequate 1. defective, deficient, faulty, imperfect, incommensurate, incomplete, insubstantial, insufficient, meagre, niggardly, scant, scanty, short, sketchy, skimpy, sparse 2. found wanting, inapt, incapable, incompetent, not up to scratch (*informal*), unequal, unfitted, unqualified

inadequately imperfectly, insufficiently, meagrely, poorly, scantily, sketchily, skimpily, sparsely, thinly

inadmissible immaterial, improper, inappropriate, incompetent, irrelevant, unacceptable, unallowable, unqualified, unreasonable

inadvertently 1. carelessly, heedlessly, in an unguarded moment, negligently, thoughtlessly, unguardedly, unthinkingly 2. accidentally, by accident, by mis-

inadvertent *adj* done unintentionally. **inadvertence** *n* **inadvertently** *adv*
inadvisable *adj* unwise; not sensible.
inalienable *adj* not able to be taken away or transferred to another: *the inalienable rights of the citizen.*
inamorata *or masc* **inamorato** *n, pl* **-tas** *or masc* **-tos** *Literary* a sweetheart or lover.
inane *adj* senseless or silly: *inane remarks.* **inanity** *n*
inanimate *adj* lacking the qualities of living beings: *inanimate objects.*
inanition *n Formal* exhaustion or weakness, as from lack of food.
inapplicable *adj* not suitable or relevant.
inapposite *adj* not suitable or appropriate. **inappositeness** *n*
inappropriate *adj* not suitable or proper. **inappropriately** *adv*
inapt *adj* **1** not apt or fitting. **2** lacking skill. **inaptitude** *n*
inarticulate *adj* unable to express oneself clearly or well.
inasmuch as *conj* **1** since; because. **2** in so far as.
inattentive *adj* not paying attention. **inattention** *n*
inaudible *adj* not loud enough to be heard. **inaudibly** *adv*
inaugural *adj* **1** of or for an inauguration. *~n* **2** *US* a speech made at an inauguration.
inaugurate *vb* **-rating, -rated 1** to open or celebrate the first public use of ceremonially: *British Rail's newest electrified line was inaugurated today.* **2** to formally establish (a new leader) in office. **3** to begin officially or formally. **inauguration** *n* **inaugurator** *n*
inauspicious *adj* unlucky; suggesting an unfavourable outcome.
inboard *adj* **1** (of a boat's motor or engine) situated within the hull. **2** situated close to the fuselage of an aircraft. *~adv* **3** within the sides of or towards the centre of a vessel or aircraft.
inborn *adj* existing from birth: *an inborn sense of sudden danger.*
inbred *adj* **1** produced as a result of inbreeding. **2** inborn or ingrained: *inbred good manners.*
inbreed *vb* **-breeding, -bred** to breed from closely related individuals.
inbreeding *n* breeding from closely related individuals.
inbuilt *adj* (of a quality or feeling) present from the beginning: *an inbuilt fear of strangers.*
Inc. *US* (of a company) incorporated.
Inca *n* **1** (*pl* **Inca** *or* **Incas**) a member of a S American Indian people whose empire, centred on Peru, lasted until the early 1530s. **2** the language of this people.
incalculable *adj* impossible to estimate or predict. **incalculability** *n*
in camera *adv* in private session: *the proceedings were held in camera.*
incandescent *adj* **1** glowing with heat. **2** (of artificial light) produced by a glowing filament. **incandescence** *n*
incandescent lamp *n* a lamp that contains a filament which is electrically heated to incandescence.
incantation *n* **1** ritual chanting of magic words or sounds. **2** a magic spell. **incantatory** *adj*
incapable *adj* **1 incapable of** lacking the ability to. **2** helpless: *drunk and incapable.*

THESAURUS

take, involuntarily, mistakenly, unintentionally, unwittingly
inadvisable ill-advised, impolitic, imprudent, inexpedient, injudicious, unwise
inane asinine, daft (*informal*), devoid of intelligence, empty, fatuous, frivolous, futile, goofy (*informal*), idiotic, imbecilic, mindless, puerile, senseless, silly, stupid, trifling, unintelligent, vacuous, vain, vapid, worthless
inanimate cold, dead, defunct, extinct, inactive, inert, insensate, insentient, lifeless, quiescent, soulless, spiritless
inapplicable inapposite, inappropriate, inapt, irrelevant, unsuitable, unsuited
inappropriate disproportionate, ill-fitted, ill-suited, ill-timed, improper, incongruous, out of place, tasteless, unbecoming, unbefitting, unfit, unfitting, unseemly, unsuitable, untimely
inapt **1.** ill-fitted, ill-suited, inapposite, inappropriate, infelicitous, unsuitable, unsuited **2.** awkward, clumsy, dull, gauche, incompetent, inept, inexpert, maladroit, slow, stupid
inarticulate blurred, dumb, faltering, halting, hesitant, incoherent, incomprehensible, indistinct, muffled, mumbled, mute, poorly spoken, silent, speechless, tongue-tied, unclear, unintelligible, unspoken, unuttered, unvoiced, voiceless, wordless
inattention absent-mindedness, carelessness, daydreaming, disregard, forgetfulness, heedlessness, inadvertence, inattentiveness, indifference, neglect, preoccupation, thoughtlessness, woolgathering
inattentive absent-minded, careless, distracted, distrait, dreamy, heedless, inadvertent, neglectful, negligent, preoccupied, regardless, remiss, slapdash, slipshod, thoughtless, unheeding, unmindful, unobservant, vague
inaudible indistinct, low, mumbling, out of earshot, stifled, unheard
inaugural dedicatory, first, initial, introductory, maiden, opening
inaugurate **1.** begin, commence, get under way, initiate, institute, introduce, kick off (*informal*), launch, originate, set in motion, set up, usher in **2.** induct, install, invest **3.** commission, dedicate, open, ordain
inauguration **1.** initiation, institution, launch, launching, opening, setting up **2.** induction, installation, investiture
inauspicious bad, black, discouraging, ill-omened, ominous, unfavourable, unfortunate, unlucky, unpromising, unpropitious, untoward
inborn congenital, hereditary, inbred, ingrained, inherent, inherited, innate, instinctive, intuitive, native, natural
inbred constitutional, deep-seated, ingrained, inherent, innate, native, natural
incalculable boundless, countless, enormous, immense, incomputable, inestimable, infinite, innumerable, limitless, measureless, numberless, uncountable, untold, vast, without number
incantation abracadabra, chant, charm, formula, invocation, spell
incapable **1.** feeble, inadequate, incompetent, ineffective, inept, inexpert, insufficient, not equal to, not up to, unfit, unfitted, unqualified, weak **2.** helpless, impotent, powerless, unable, unfit
incapacitate cripple, disable, disqualify, immobilize, lay up (*informal*), paralyse, prostrate, put out of action (*informal*), scupper (*Brit. slang*)
incapacitated disqualified, immobilized, indisposed, laid up (*informal*), out of action (*informal*), unfit

incapacitate *vb* **-tating, -tated** to deprive (a person) of strength, power, or ability; disable.
incapacity *n, pl* **-ties 1** lack of power, strength, or ability. **2** *Law* legal disqualification or ineligibility.
incarcerate *vb* **-ating, -ated** *Formal* to confine or imprison. **incarceration** *n*
incarnate *adj* **1** possessing human form: *a devil incarnate.* **2** personified or typified: *stupidity incarnate.* *~vb* **-nating, -nated 3** to give a bodily or concrete form to. **4** to be representative or typical of.
incarnation *n* **1** the act of embodying or state of being embodied in human form. **2** a person or thing that typifies some quality or idea.
Incarnation *n Christian theol* God's coming to earth in human form as Jesus Christ.
incautious *adj* (of a person or action) careless or rash.
incendiary (in-**send**-ya-ree) *adj* **1** (of bombs etc.) designed to cause fires. **2** tending to create strife or violence. **3** relating to the illegal burning of property or goods. *~n, pl* **-aries 4** a bomb that is designed to start fires. **5** a person who illegally sets fire to property or goods. **incendiarism** *n*
incense[1] *n* **1** an aromatic substance burnt for its fragrant odour, esp. in religious ceremonies. **2** the odour or smoke so produced. *~vb* **-censing, -censed 3** to burn incense to (a deity). **4** to perfume or fumigate with incense.
incense[2] *vb* **-censing, -censed** to make very angry. **incensed** *adj*
incentive *n* **1** something that encourages effort or action. **2** an additional payment made to employees to increase production. *~adj* **3** encouraging greater effort: *an incentive scheme for workers.*
inception *n* the beginning of a project.
incessant *adj* never stopping. **incessantly** *adv*
incest *n* sexual intercourse between two people who are too closely related to marry. **incestuous** *adj*
inch *n* **1** a unit of length equal to one twelfth of a foot (2.54cm). **2** *Meteorol* the amount of rain or snow that would cover a surface to a depth of one inch. **3** a very small distance, degree, or amount: *neither side was prepared to give an inch.* **4 every inch** in every way: *she arrived looking every inch a star.* **5 inch by inch** gradually. **6 within an inch of one's life** almost to death. *~vb* **7** to move very slowly or gradually: *I inched my way to the bar.*
inchoate (in-**koe**-ate) *adj Formal* just begun and not yet properly developed.
incidence *n* **1** extent or frequency of occurrence: *the rising incidence of car fires.* **2** *Physics* the arrival of a beam of light or particles at a surface. **3** *Geom* the partial overlapping of two figures or a figure and a line.
incident *n* **1** an occurrence or event, esp. a minor one. **2** a relatively insignificant event that might have serious consequences. **3** a public disturbance. *~adj* **4** *Physics* (of a beam of light or particles) arriving at or striking a surface. **5 incident to** *Formal* likely to occur in connection with: *the dangers are incident to a policeman's job.*
incidental *adj* **1** happening in connection with or resulting from something more important. **2** secondary or minor: *incidental expenses.* **incidentally** *adv*
incidental music *n* background music for a film or play.
incidentals *pl n* minor expenses, events, or action.
incinerate *vb* **-ating, -ated** to burn up completely. **incineration** *n*
incinerator *n* a furnace for burning rubbish.
incipient *adj Formal* just starting to be or happen.
incise *vb* **-cising, -cised** to cut into with a sharp tool.
incision *n* a cut, esp. one made during a surgical operation.

THESAURUS

incapacity disqualification, feebleness, impotence, inability, inadequacy, incapability, incompetency, ineffectiveness, powerlessness, unfitness, weakness
incarcerate commit, confine, coop up, detain, gaol, immure, impound, imprison, intern, jail, lock up, put under lock and key, restrain, restrict, send down (*Brit.*), throw in jail
incarnate 1. in bodily form, in human form, in the flesh, made flesh **2.** embodied, personified, typified
incarnation avatar (*Hinduism*), bodily form, embodiment, epitome, exemplification, impersonation, manifestation, personification, type
incautious careless, hasty, heedless, ill-advised, ill-judged, improvident, imprudent, impulsive, inconsiderate, indiscreet, injudicious, negligent, precipitate, rash, reckless, thoughtless, unguarded, unthinking, unwary
incendiary 1. *adj.* dissentious, inflammatory, provocative, rabble-rousing, seditious, subversive **2.** *n.* arsonist, firebug (*informal*), fire raiser, pyromaniac
incense[1] *n.* aroma, balm, bouquet, fragrance, perfume, redolence, scent
incense[2] *vb.* anger, enrage, exasperate, excite, gall, get one's hackles up, inflame, infuriate, irritate, madden, make one's blood boil (*informal*), make one see red (*informal*), make one's hackles rise, nark (*Brit., Austral., & N.Z. slang*), provoke, raise one's hackles, rile (*informal*)
incensed angry, cross, enraged, exasperated, fuming, furious, indignant, infuriated, irate, mad (*informal*), maddened, on the warpath (*informal*), steamed up (*slang*), up in arms, wrathful
incentive bait, carrot (*informal*), encouragement, enticement, goad, impetus, impulse, inducement, lure, motivation, motive, spur, stimulant, stimulus
inception beginning, birth, commencement, dawn, inauguration, initiation, kickoff (*informal*), origin, outset, rise, start
incessant ceaseless, constant, continual, continuous, endless, eternal, everlasting, interminable, never-ending, nonstop, perpetual, persistent, relentless, unbroken, unceasing, unending, unrelenting, unremitting
incessantly all the time, ceaselessly, constantly, continually, endlessly, eternally, everlastingly, interminably, nonstop, perpetually, persistently, without a break
incident 1. adventure, circumstance, episode, event, fact, happening, matter, occasion, occurrence **2.** brush, clash, commotion, confrontation, contretemps, disturbance, mishap, scene, skirmish
incidental 1. accidental, casual, chance, fortuitous, odd, random **2.** ancillary, minor, nonessential, occasional, secondary, subordinate, subsidiary
incidentally accidentally, by chance, casually, fortuitously
incidentals contingencies, extras, minutiae, odds and ends
incinerate burn up, carbonize, char, consume by fire, cremate, reduce to ashes
incipient beginning, commencing, developing, embryonic, inceptive, inchoate (*formal*), nascent (*formal*), originating, starting
incise carve, chisel, cut (into), engrave, etch, inscribe
incision cut, gash, notch, opening, slash, slit
incisive acid, acute, biting, caustic, cutting, keen,

incisive *adj* direct and forceful: *witty and incisive comments.*

incisor *n* a sharp cutting tooth at the front of the mouth.

incite *vb* **-citing, -cited** to stir up or provoke to action. **incitement** *n*

incivility *n, pl* **-ties 1** rudeness. **2** an impolite act or remark.

incl. 1 including. **2** inclusive.

inclement *adj Formal* (of weather) stormy or severe. **inclemency** *n*

inclination *n* **1** a liking, tendency, or preference: *he showed no inclination to change his routine.* **2** the degree of slope from a horizontal or vertical plane. **3** a slope or slant. **4** *Surveying* the angular distance of the horizon below the plane of observation.

incline *vb* **-clining, -clined 1** to veer from a vertical or horizontal plane; slope or slant. **2** to have or cause to have a certain tendency or disposition: *that does not incline me to think that you are right.* **3** to bend or lower (part of the body, esp. the head). **4 incline one's ear** to listen favourably. *~n* **5** an inclined surface or slope. **inclined** *adj*

inclined plane *n* a sloping plane used to enable a load to be raised or lowered by pushing or sliding, which requires less force than lifting.

include *vb* **-cluding, -cluded 1** to have as part of the whole. **2** to put in as part of a set, group, or category.

inclusion *n* **1** an including or being included. **2** something included.

inclusive *adj* **1** including everything: *capital inclusive of profit.* **2** including the limits specified: *Monday to Friday inclusive.* **3** comprehensive.

incognito (in-kog-**nee**-toe) *adv, adj* **1** under an assumed name or appearance. *~n, pl* **-tos 2** a false identity. **3** a person who is incognito.

incognizant *adj* **incognizant of** unaware of. **incognizance** *n*

incoherent *adj* **1** unable to express oneself clearly. **2** not logically connected or ordered. **incoherence** *n*

income *n* the total amount of money earned from work or obtained from other sources over a given period of time.

income support *n* (in Britain) an allowance paid by the government to people with a very low income.

income tax *n* a personal tax levied on annual income.

incoming *adj* **1** about to arrive. **2** about to come into office.

incommensurable *adj* **1** not able to be judged, measured, or compared. **2** *Maths* not having a common divisor other than 1, such as 2 and $\sqrt{-5}$. **incommensurability** *n*

incommensurate *adj* **1** inadequate or disproportionate: *gains incommensurate with the risk involved.* **2** incommensurable.

incommode *vb* **-moding, -moded** *Formal* to bother, disturb, or inconvenience.

incommodious *adj Formal* inconveniently small; cramped.

incommunicado *adv, adj* not allowed to communicate with other people, for instance while in solitary confinement.

incomparable *adj* so excellent as to be beyond or above comparison. **incomparably** *adv*

incompatible *adj* not able to exist together in harmony; conflicting or inconsistent. **incompatibility** *n*

incompetent *adj* **1** not having the necessary ability

THESAURUS

mordacious, mordant, penetrating, perspicacious, piercing, sarcastic, sardonic, satirical, severe, sharp, trenchant, vitriolic

incite agitate for *or* against, animate, drive, egg on, encourage, excite, foment, goad, impel, inflame, instigate, prod, prompt, provoke, put up to, rouse, set on, spur, stimulate, stir up, urge, whip up

incitement agitation, encouragement, goad, impetus, impulse, inducement, instigation, motivation, motive, prompting, provocation, spur, stimulus

incivility bad manners, boorishness, discourteousness, discourtesy, disrespect, ill-breeding, impoliteness, rudeness, unmannerliness

inclemency bitterness, boisterousness, rawness, rigour, roughness, severity, storminess

inclement bitter, boisterous, foul, harsh, intemperate, rigorous, rough, severe, stormy, tempestuous

inclination 1. affection, aptitude, bent, bias, desire, disposition, fancy, fondness, leaning, liking, partiality, penchant, predilection, predisposition, prejudice, proclivity, proneness, propensity, stomach, taste, tendency, thirst, turn, turn of mind, wish **2.** bending, bow, bowing, nod **3.** angle, bend, bending, deviation, gradient, incline, leaning, pitch, slant, slope, tilt

incline *vb.* **1.** bend, bevel, cant, deviate, diverge, heel, lean, slant, slope, tend, tilt, tip, veer **2.** be disposed *or* predisposed, bias, influence, persuade, predispose, prejudice, sway, tend, turn **3.** bend, bow, lower, nod, stoop *~n.* **4.** ascent, declivity, descent, dip, grade, gradient, ramp, rise, slope

inclined apt, disposed, given, liable, likely, minded, of a mind (*informal*), predisposed, prone, willing

include 1. comprehend, comprise, contain, cover, embody, embrace, encompass, incorporate, involve, subsume, take in, take into account **2.** add, allow for, build in, count, enter, insert, introduce, number among

including as well as, containing, counting, inclusive of, plus, together with, with

inclusion addition, incorporation, insertion

inclusive across-the-board, all-embracing, all in, all together, blanket, comprehensive, full, general, global, *in toto,* overall, sweeping, umbrella, without exception

incognito disguised, in disguise, under an assumed name, unknown, unrecognized

incoherence disconnectedness, disjointedness, inarticulateness, unintelligibility

incoherent confused, disconnected, disjointed, disordered, inarticulate, inconsistent, jumbled, loose, muddled, rambling, stammering, stuttering, unconnected, uncoordinated, unintelligible, wandering, wild

income earnings, gains, interest, means, pay, proceeds, profits, receipts, revenue, salary, takings, wages

incoming approaching, arriving, entering, homeward, landing, new, returning, succeeding

incomparable beyond compare, inimitable, matchless, paramount, peerless, superlative, supreme, transcendent, unequalled, unmatched, unparalleled, unrivalled

incomparably beyond compare, by far, easily, eminently, far and away, immeasurably

incompatibility antagonism, conflict, discrepancy, disparateness, incongruity, inconsistency, irreconcilability, uncongeniality

incompatible antagonistic, antipathetic, conflicting, contradictory, discordant, discrepant, disparate, ill-assorted, incongruous, inconsistent, inconsonant, irreconcilable, mismatched, uncongenial, unsuitable, unsuited

incompetence inability, inadequacy, incapability, incapacity, incompetency, ineffectiveness, ineptitude, ineptness, insufficiency, unfitness, uselessness

or skill to do something. **2** *Law* not legally qualified: *an incompetent witness.* ~*n* **3** an incompetent person. **incompetence** *n*

incomplete *adj* not finished or whole.

incomprehension *n* inability to understand. **incomprehensible** *adj*

inconceivable *adj* so unlikely to be true as to be unthinkable. **inconceivability** *n*

inconclusive *adj* not giving a final decision or result.

incongruous *adj* out of place; inappropriate: *an incongruous figure among the tourists.* **incongruously** *adv* **incongruity** *n*

inconnu (in-kon-new) *n Canad* a whitefish of arctic waters.

inconsequential *or* **inconsequent** *adj* **1** unimportant or insignificant. **2** not following logically as a consequence. **inconsequentially** *adv*

inconsiderable *adj* **1 not inconsiderable** fairly large: *he gets not inconsiderable royalties from his musicals.* **2** not worth considering; insignificant. **inconsiderably** *adv*

inconsiderate *adj* lacking in care or thought for others; thoughtless. **inconsiderateness** *n*

inconsistent *adj* **1** unstable or changeable in behaviour or mood. **2** containing contradictory elements: *an inconsistent argument.* **3** not in accordance: *actions inconsistent with high office.* **inconsistency** *n*

inconsolable *adj* very distressed. **inconsolably** *adv*

inconspicuous *adj* not easily noticed or seen.

inconstant *adj* **1** liable to change one's loyalties or opinions. **2** variable: *their household income is inconstant.* **inconstancy** *n*

incontestable *adj* impossible to deny or argue with.

incontinent *adj* **1** unable to control the bladder and bowels. **2** lacking self-restraint, esp. sexually. **incontinence** *n*

incontrovertible *adj* absolutely certain; undeniable. **incontrovertibly** *adv*

inconvenience *n* **1** a state or instance of trouble or difficulty. ~*vb* **-iencing, -ienced 2** to cause trouble or difficulty to (someone). **inconvenient** *adj*

incorporate *vb* **-rating, -rated 1** to include or be included as part of a larger unit. **2** to form a united whole or mass. **3** to form into a corporation. ~*adj* **4** incorporated. **incorporated** *adj* **incorporation** *n*

incorporeal *adj* without material form, substance, or existence.

incorrect *adj* **1** wrong: *an incorrect answer.* **2** not proper: *incorrect behaviour.* **incorrectly** *adv*

incorrigible *adj* (of a person or behaviour) beyond

THESAURUS

incompetent bungling, cowboy (*informal*), floundering, incapable, incapacitated, ineffectual, inept, inexpert, insufficient, skill-less, unable, unfit, unfitted, unskilful, useless

incomplete broken, defective, deficient, fragmentary, imperfect, insufficient, lacking, partial, short, unaccomplished, undeveloped, undone, unexecuted, unfinished, wanting

incomprehensible above one's head, all Greek to (*informal*), baffling, beyond comprehension, beyond one's grasp, enigmatic, impenetrable, inconceivable, inscrutable, mysterious, obscure, opaque, perplexing, puzzling, unfathomable, unimaginable, unintelligible, unthinkable

inconceivable beyond belief, impossible, incomprehensible, incredible, mind-boggling, not to be thought of, out of the question, staggering (*informal*), unbelievable, unheard-of, unimaginable, unknowable, unthinkable

inconclusive ambiguous, indecisive, indeterminate, open, uncertain, unconvincing, undecided, unsettled, up in the air (*informal*), vague

incongruity conflict, discrepancy, disparity, inappropriateness, inaptness, incompatibility, inconsistency, inharmoniousness, unsuitability

incongruous absurd, conflicting, contradictory, contrary, disconsonant, discordant, extraneous, improper, inappropriate, inapt, incoherent, incompatible, inconsistent, out of keeping, out of place, unbecoming, unsuitable, unsuited

inconsiderable exiguous (*formal*), inconsequential, insignificant, light, minor, negligible, petty, slight, small, small-time (*informal*), trifling, trivial, unimportant

inconsiderate careless, indelicate, insensitive, intolerant, rude, self-centred, selfish, tactless, thoughtless, uncharitable, ungracious, unkind, unthinking

inconsistency **1.** disagreement, discrepancy, disparity, divergence, incompatibility, incongruity, inconsonance, paradox, variance **2.** fickleness, instability, unpredictability, unreliability, unsteadiness

inconsistent **1.** capricious, changeable, erratic, fickle, inconstant, irregular, uneven, unpredictable, unstable, unsteady, variable **2.** at odds, at variance, conflicting, contradictory, contrary, discordant, discrepant, incoherent, incompatible, in conflict, incongruous, inconstant, irreconcilable, out of step

inconsolable brokenhearted, desolate, despairing, heartbroken, heartsick, prostrate with grief, sick at heart

inconspicuous camouflaged, hidden, insignificant, modest, muted, ordinary, plain, quiet, retiring, unassuming, unnoticeable, unobtrusive, unostentatious

incontestable beyond doubt, beyond question, certain, incontrovertible, indisputable, indubitable, irrefutable, self-evident, sure, undeniable, unquestionable

incontinent **1.** unbridled, unchecked, uncontrollable, uncontrolled, ungovernable, ungoverned, unrestrained **2.** debauched, lascivious, lecherous, lewd, loose (*old-fashioned*), lustful, profligate, promiscuous, unchaste, wanton

incontrovertible beyond dispute, certain, established, incontestable, indisputable, indubitable, irrefutable, positive, sure, undeniable, unquestionable, unshakable

inconvenience **1.** *n.* annoyance, awkwardness, bother, cumbersomeness, difficulty, disadvantage, disruption, disturbance, downside, drawback, fuss, hassle (*informal*), hindrance, nuisance, trouble, uneasiness, unfitness, unhandiness, unsuitableness, untimeliness, unwieldiness, upset, vexation **2.** *vb.* bother, discommode, disrupt, disturb, give (someone) bother *or* trouble, hassle (*informal*), irk, make (someone) go out of his way, put out, put to trouble, trouble, upset

inconvenient annoying, awkward, bothersome, cumbersome, difficult, disadvantageous, disturbing, embarrassing, inopportune, tiresome, troublesome, unhandy, unmanageable, unseasonable, unsuitable, untimely, unwieldy, vexatious

incorporate absorb, amalgamate, assimilate, blend, coalesce, combine, consolidate, embody, fuse, include, integrate, meld, merge, mix, subsume (*formal*), unite

incorrect **1.** erroneous, false, faulty, flawed, inaccurate, inappropriate, inexact, mistaken, out, specious, untrue, wide of the mark (*informal*), wrong **2.** improper, unfitting, unsuitable

correction or reform; incurably bad. **incorrigibility** *n* **incorrigibly** *adv*

incorruptible *adj* **1** too honest to be bribed or corrupted. **2** not prone to decay or disintegration. **incorruptibility** *n*

increase *vb* **-creasing, -creased 1** to make or become greater in size, degree, or frequency. *~n* **2** a rise in size, degree, or frequency. **3** the amount by which something increases. **4 on the increase** becoming more common. **increasingly** *adv*

incredible *adj* **1** unbelievable. **2** *Informal* marvellous; amazing. **incredibility** *n* **incredibly** *adv*

incredulity *n* unwillingness to believe.

incredulous *adj* not prepared or willing to believe something.

increment *n* **1** the amount by which something increases. **2** a regular salary increase. **3** *Maths* a small positive or negative change in a variable or function. **incremental** *adj*

incriminate *vb* **-nating, -nated 1** to make (someone) seem guilty of a crime. **2** to charge (someone) with a crime. **incrimination** *n* **incriminatory** *adj*

incrust *vb* same as **encrust.**

incubate (**in**-cube-ate) *vb* **-bating, -bated 1** (of birds) to hatch (eggs) by sitting on them. **2** to cause (bacteria) to develop, esp. in an incubator or culture medium. **3** (of disease germs) to remain inactive in an animal or human before causing disease. **4** to develop gradually. **incubation** *n*

incubator *n* **1** *Med* a heated enclosed apparatus for rearing premature babies. **2** an apparatus for hatching birds' eggs or growing bacterial cultures.

incubus (**in**-cube-uss) *n, pl* **-bi** *or* **-buses 1** a demon believed in folklore to have sexual intercourse with sleeping women. **2** a nightmarish burden or worry.

inculcate *vb* **-cating, -cated** to fix in someone's mind by constant repetition. **inculcation** *n*

inculpate *vb* **-pating, -pated** *Formal* to incriminate.

incumbency *n, pl* **-cies** the office, duty, or tenure of an incumbent.

incumbent *Formal ~n* **1** a person who holds a particular office or position. *~adj* **2** morally binding as a duty: *it is incumbent on cricketers to respect the umpire's impartiality.*

incur *vb* **-curring, -curred** to bring (something undesirable) upon oneself.

incurable *adj* **1** not able to be cured: *an incurable tumour.* **2** not able to be changed: *he is an incurable romantic.* *~n* **3** a person with an incurable disease. **incurability** *n* **incurably** *adv*

incurious *adj* showing no curiosity or interest. **incuriously** *adv*

incursion *n* **1** a sudden or brief invasion. **2** an inroad or encroachment: *a successful incursion into the American book-shop market.* **incursive** *adj*

ind. **1** independent. **2** index. **3** indicative. **4** indirect. **5** industrial.

Ind. **1** Independent. **2** India. **3** Indian. **4** Indies.

indaba (in-**dah**-ba) *n* **1** (among native peoples of southern Africa) a meeting to discuss a serious topic. **2** *S African informal* a matter of concern or for discussion.

indebted *adj* **1** owing gratitude for help or favours. **2** owing money. **indebtedness** *n*

indecent *adj* **1** morally or sexually offensive. **2** unseemly or improper: *indecent haste.* **indecency** *n* **indecently** *adv*

indecent assault *n* a sexual attack which does not include rape.

indecent exposure *n* the showing of one's genitals in public.

THESAURUS

incorrigible hardened, hopeless, incurable, intractable, inveterate, irredeemable, unreformed

incorruptibility honesty, honour, integrity, justness, uprightness

incorruptible **1.** above suspicion, honest, honourable, just, straight, trustworthy, unbribable, upright **2.** everlasting, imperishable, undecaying

increase *vb.* **1.** add to, advance, aggrandize, amplify, augment, boost, build up, develop, dilate, enhance, enlarge, escalate, expand, extend, grow, heighten, inflate, intensify, magnify, mount, multiply, proliferate, prolong, raise, snowball, spread, step up (*informal*), strengthen, swell, wax *~n.* **2.** addition, augmentation, boost, development, enlargement, escalation, expansion, extension, gain, growth, increment, intensification, rise, upsurge, upturn **3. on the increase** developing, escalating, expanding, growing, increasing, multiplying, on the rise, proliferating, spreading

increasingly more and more, progressively, to an increasing extent

incredible **1.** absurd, beyond belief, far-fetched, implausible, impossible, improbable, inconceivable, preposterous, unbelievable, unimaginable, unthinkable **2.** *informal* ace (*informal*), amazing, astonishing, astounding, awe-inspiring, brilliant, def (*slang*), extraordinary, far-out (*informal*), great, marvellous, mega (*slang*), prodigious, sensational (*informal*), superhuman, wonderful

incredulity disbelief, distrust, doubt, scepticism, unbelief

incredulous disbelieving, distrustful, doubtful, doubting, dubious, mistrustful, sceptical, suspicious, unbelieving, unconvinced

increment accretion, accrual, addition, advancement, augmentation, enlargement, gain, increase, step (up), supplement

incriminate accuse, arraign, blacken the name of, blame, charge, impeach, implicate, inculpate, indict, involve, point the finger at (*informal*), stigmatize

incumbent binding, compulsory, mandatory, necessary, obligatory

incur arouse, bring (upon oneself), contract, draw, earn, expose oneself to, gain, induce, lay oneself open to, meet with, provoke

incurable *adj.* **1.** fatal, inoperable, irrecoverable, irremediable, remediless, terminal **2.** dyed-in-the-wool, hopeless, incorrigible, inveterate

indebted beholden, grateful, in debt, obligated, obliged, under an obligation

indecency bawdiness, coarseness, crudity, foulness, grossness, immodesty, impropriety, impurity, indecorum, indelicacy, lewdness, licentiousness, obscenity, outrageousness, pornography, smut, smuttiness, unseemliness, vileness, vulgarity

indecent **1.** blue, coarse, crude, dirty, filthy, foul, gross, immodest, improper, impure, indelicate, lewd, licentious, pornographic, salacious, scatological, smutty, vile **2.** ill-bred, improper, in bad taste, indecorous, offensive, outrageous, tasteless, unbecoming, unseemly, vulgar

indecipherable crabbed, illegible, indistinguishable, unintelligible, unreadable

indecision *or* **indecisiveness** ambivalence, dithering (*chiefly Brit.*), doubt, hesitancy, hesitation, indecisiveness, irresolution, shilly-shallying (*informal*), uncertainty, vacillation, wavering

indecisive **1.** dithering (*chiefly Brit.*), doubtful, fal-

indecipherable *adj* impossible to read.

indecisive *adj* **1** unable to make decisions. **2** not decisive or conclusive: *an indecisive argument.* **indecision** *or* **indecisiveness** *n*

indeed *adv* **1** certainly; actually: *indeed, the sea featured heavily in his poems.* **2** truly, very: *it has become a dangerous place indeed.* **3** in fact; what is more: *it is necessary, indeed indispensable.* ~*interj* **4** an expression of doubt or surprise.

indefatigable *adj* never getting tired or giving up: *Mitterrand was an indefatigable organizer.* **indefatigably** *adv*

indefensible *adj* **1** (of behaviour or statements) unable to be justified or supported. **2** (of places or buildings) impossible to defend against attack. **indefensibility** *n*

indefinable *adj* difficult to describe or explain completely.

indefinite *adj* **1** without exact limits: *an indefinite number.* **2** vague or unclear. **indefinitely** *adv*

indefinite article *n Grammar* either of the words "a" or "an".

indelible *adj* **1** impossible to erase or remove. **2** making indelible marks: *indelible ink.* **indelibly** *adv*

indelicate *adj* **1** offensive, embarrassing, or tasteless. **2** coarse, crude, or rough. **indelicacy** *n*

indemnify *vb* **-fies, -fying, -fied 1** to secure against loss, damage, or liability. **2** to compensate for loss or damage. **indemnification** *n*

indemnity *n, pl* **-ties 1** insurance against loss or damage. **2** compensation for loss or damage. **3** legal exemption from penalties incurred.

indent *vb* **1** to start (a line of writing) further from the margin than the other lines. **2** to order (goods) using a special order form. **3** to notch (an edge or border). **4** to write out (a document) in duplicate. **5** to bind (an apprentice) by indenture. ~*n* **6** *Chiefly Brit* an official order for goods, esp. foreign merchandise.

indentation *n* **1** a hollow, notch, or cut, as on an edge or on a coastline. **2** an indenting or being indented. **3** Also: **indention** the leaving of space or the amount of space left between a margin and the start of an indented line.

indenture *n* **1** a contract, esp. one binding an apprentice to his or her employer. ~*vb* **-turing, -tured 2** to bind (an apprentice) by indenture. **3** to enter into an agreement by indenture.

independent *adj* **1** free from the influence or control of others. **2** not dependent on anything else for function or validity. **3** not relying on the support, esp. financial support, of others. **4** capable of acting for oneself or on one's own. **5** of or having a private income large enough to enable one to live without working: *independent means.* **6** *Maths* (of a variable) not dependent on another variable. ~*n* **7** an independent person or thing. **8** a politician who does not represent any political party. **independence** *n* **independently** *adv*

independent school *n* (in Britain) a school that is neither financed nor controlled by the government or local authorities.

in-depth *adj* detailed or thorough: *an in-depth analysis.*

indescribable *adj* too intense or extreme for words. **indescribably** *adv*

indestructible *adj* not able to be destroyed.

indeterminate *adj* **1** uncertain in extent, amount, or nature. **2** left doubtful; inconclusive: *an indeterminate reply.* **3** *Maths* **a** having no numerical meaning, as $0/0$. **b** (of an equation) having more than one variable and an unlimited number of solutions. **indeterminable** *adj* **indeterminacy** *n*

index (in-dex) *n, pl* **-dexes** *or* **-dices 1** an alphabetical list of names or subjects dealt with in a book, indicating where they are referred to. **2** a file or catalogue in a library which enables a book or reference to be found. **3** a number indicating the level of wages or prices as compared with some standard value. **4** an

THESAURUS

tering, hesitating, in two minds (*informal*), irresolute, pussyfooting (*informal*), tentative, uncertain, undecided, undetermined, vacillating, wavering **2.** inconclusive, indefinite, indeterminate, unclear, undecided

indeed actually, certainly, doubtlessly, in point of fact, in truth, positively, really, strictly, to be sure, truly, undeniably, undoubtedly, verily (*literary*), veritably

indefensible faulty, inexcusable, insupportable, unforgivable, unjustifiable, unpardonable, untenable, unwarrantable, wrong

indefinable dim, hazy, impalpable, indescribable, indistinct, inexpressible, nameless, obscure, unrealized, vague

indefinite ambiguous, confused, doubtful, equivocal, evasive, general, ill-defined, imprecise, indeterminate, indistinct, inexact, loose, obscure, oracular, uncertain, unclear, undefined, undetermined, unfixed, unknown, unlimited, unsettled, vague

indefinitely ad infinitum, continually, endlessly, for ever, *sine die*

indelible enduring, indestructible, ineffaceable, ineradicable, inexpungible, inextirpable, ingrained, lasting, permanent

indelicacy bad taste, coarseness, crudity, grossness, immodesty, impropriety, indecency, obscenity, offensiveness, rudeness, smuttiness, suggestiveness, tastelessness, vulgarity

indelicate blue, coarse, crude, embarrassing, gross, immodest, improper, indecent, indecorous, low, near the knuckle (*informal*), obscene, off-colour, offensive, risqué, rude, suggestive, tasteless, unbecoming, unseemly, untoward, vulgar

indemnify 1. endorse, guarantee, insure, protect, secure, underwrite **2.** compensate, pay, reimburse, remunerate, repair, repay, requite, satisfy

indemnity 1. guarantee, insurance, protection, security **2.** compensation, redress, reimbursement, remuneration, reparation, requital, restitution, satisfaction **3.** *Law* exemption, immunity, impunity, privilege

indent *vb.* **1.** ask for, order, request, requisition **2.** cut, mark, nick, notch, pink, scallop, score, serrate

independence autarchy, autonomy, freedom, home rule, liberty, self-determination, self-government, self-reliance, self-rule, self-sufficiency, separation, sovereignty

independent 1. absolute, free, liberated, separate, unconnected, unconstrained, uncontrolled, unrelated **2.** autarchic, autarchical, autonomous, decontrolled, nonaligned, self-determining, self-governing, separated, sovereign **3.** bold, individualistic, liberated, self-contained, self-reliant, self-sufficient, self-supporting, unaided, unconventional

independently alone, autonomously, by oneself, individually, on one's own, separately, solo, unaided

indescribable beggaring description, beyond description, beyond words, incommunicable, indefinable, ineffable, inexpressible, unutterable

indestructible abiding, durable, enduring, everlasting, immortal, imperishable, incorruptible, indelible, indissoluble, lasting, nonperishable, permanent, unbreakable, unfading

indication or sign: *national birth rate was once an index of military power.* **5** *Maths* **a** same as **exponent. b** a superscript number placed to the left of a radical sign indicating the root to be extracted: *the index of* $\sqrt[3]{8}$ *is 3.* **6** a number or ratio indicating a specific characteristic or property: *refractive index.* ~*vb* **7** to put an index in (a book). **8** to enter (a word or item) in an index. **9** to make index-linked.

indexation *or* **index-linking** *n* the act of making wages, pensions, or interest rates index-linked.

index finger *n* the finger next to the thumb. Also called: **forefinger**

index-linked *adj* (of pensions, wages, or interest rates) rising and falling in line with the cost of living.

Indiaman *n, pl* **-men** (formerly) a merchant ship engaged in trade with India.

Indian *adj* **1** of India. **2** of the original inhabitants of the American continent. ~*n* **3** a person from India. **4** a person descended from the original inhabitants of the American continent.

Indian club *n* a heavy bottle-shaped club, usually swung in pairs for exercise.

Indian corn *n* same as **maize.**

Indian file *n* same as **single file.**

Indian hemp *n* same as **hemp.**

Indian ink *or esp US & Canad* **India ink** *n* a black ink made from a fine black soot.

Indian list *n Informal* (in Canada) a list of people to whom spirits may not be sold.

Indian summer *n* **1** a period of warm sunny weather in autumn. **2** a period of tranquillity or of renewed productivity towards the end of a person's life or career.

India paper *n* a thin soft opaque printing paper originally made in the Orient.

Indic *adj* **1** of a branch of Indo-European consisting of many of the languages of India, including Sanskrit, Hindi, and Urdu. ~*n* **2** this group of languages.

indicate *vb* **-cating, -cated 1** to be or give a sign or symptom of: *to concede 18 goals in 7 games indicates a serious malaise.* **2** to point out or show. **3** to state briefly. **4** to switch on the indicators in a motor vehicle to show that one is changing direction. **5** (of measuring instruments) to show a reading of. **6** (*usually passive*) to recommend or require: *surgery seems to be indicated for this patient.* **indication** *n*

indicative (in-**dik**-a-tiv) *adj* **1 indicative of** suggesting: *the symptoms aren't indicative of anything serious.* **2** *Grammar* denoting a mood of verbs used to make a statement. ~*n* **3** *Grammar* the indicative mood.

indicator *n* **1** something that acts as a sign or indication: *an indicator of the moral decline of our society.* **2** a device for indicating that a motor vehicle is about to turn left or right, esp. two pairs of lights that flash. **3** an instrument, such as a gauge, that registers or measures something. **4** *Chem* a substance used to indicate the completion of a chemical reaction, usually by a change of colour.

indices (**in**-diss-seez) *n* a plural of **index.**

indict (in-**dite**) *vb* to charge (a person) formally with a crime, esp. in writing. **indictable** *adj*

indictment *n* **1** *Criminal law* a formal charge of crime, esp. in writing. **2** a serious criticism: *a scathing indictment of faith healing.*

indie *n Informal* an independent record company.

indifference *n* **1** lack of concern or interest: *elite indifference to mass opinion.* **2** lack of importance: *a matter of indifference to me.*

indifferent *adj* **1** showing no concern or interest: *he was indifferent to politics.* **2** of only average standard or quality. **3** not at all good. **4** unimportant. **5** showing or having no preferences.

indigenous (in-**dij**-in-uss) *adj* originating or occurring naturally in a country or area: *the indigenous population.*

indigent *adj Formal* so poor as to lack even necessities. **indigence** *n*

indigestible *adj* difficult or impossible to digest. **indigestibility** *n*

indigestion *n* difficulty in digesting food, accompanied by stomach pain, heartburn, and belching.

indignant *adj* feeling or showing indignation. **indignantly** *adv*

indignation *n* anger aroused by something felt to be unfair or wrong.

indignity *n, pl* **-ties** embarrassing or humiliating treatment.

THESAURUS

indeterminate imprecise, inconclusive, indefinite, inexact, uncertain, undefined, undetermined, unfixed, unspecified, unstipulated, vague

index clue, guide, indication, mark, sign, symptom, token

indicate 1. add up to (*informal*), bespeak, be symptomatic of, betoken, denote, evince, imply, manifest, point to, reveal, show, signify, suggest **2.** designate, point out, point to, specify **3.** display, express, mark, read, record, register, show

indication clue, evidence, explanation, forewarning, hint, index, inkling, intimation, manifestation, mark, note, omen, portent, sign, signal, suggestion, symptom, warning

indicative exhibitive, indicatory, indicial, pointing to, significant, suggestive, symptomatic

indicator display, gauge, guide, index, mark, marker, meter, pointer, sign, signal, signpost, symbol

indictment accusation, allegation, charge, impeachment, prosecution, summons

indifference 1. absence of feeling, aloofness, apathy, callousness, carelessness, coldness, coolness, detachment, disinterestedness, dispassion, disregard, equity, heedlessness, impartiality, inattention, lack of interest, negligence, neutrality, nonchalance, objectivity, stoicalness, unconcern **2.** insignificance, irrelevance, triviality, unimportance

indifferent 1. aloof, apathetic, callous, careless, cold, cool, detached, distant, heedless, impervious, inattentive, regardless, uncaring, unconcerned, unimpressed, uninterested, unmoved, unresponsive, unsympathetic **2.** average, fair, mediocre, middling, moderate, ordinary, passable, perfunctory, so-so (*informal*), undistinguished, uninspired **3.** immaterial, insignificant, of no consequence, unimportant **4.** disinterested, dispassionate, equitable, impartial, neutral, nonaligned, nonpartisan, objective, unbiased, uninvolved, unprejudiced

indigestion dyspepsia, heartburn, upset stomach

indignant angry, annoyed, disgruntled, exasperated, fuming (*informal*), furious, heated, huffy (*informal*), in a huff, incensed, in high dudgeon, irate, livid (*informal*), mad (*informal*), miffed (*informal*), narked (*Brit., Austral., & N.Z. slang*), peeved (*informal*), pissed off (*taboo slang*), provoked, resentful, riled, scornful, seeing red (*informal*), sore (*informal*), up in arms (*informal*), wrathful

indignation anger, exasperation, fury, ire (*literary*), pique, rage, resentment, righteous anger, scorn, umbrage, wrath

indignity abuse, affront, contumely, dishonour, dis-

indigo *adj* **1** deep violet-blue. ~*n, pl* **-gos** *or* **-goes 2** a dye of this colour originally obtained from plants.

indirect *adj* **1** done or caused by someone or something else: *indirect benefits.* **2** not going in a direct course or line: *he took the indirect route home.* **3** not coming straight to the point: *an indirect question.* **indirectly** *adv*

indirect object *n Grammar* the person or thing indirectly affected by the action of a verb and its direct object, as *John* in the sentence *I bought John a newspaper.*

indirect speech *n* same as **reported speech.**

indirect tax *n* a tax levied on goods or services which is paid indirectly by being added to the price.

indiscernible *adj* not able or scarcely able to be seen.

indiscipline *n* lack of discipline.

indiscreet *adj* incautious or tactless in revealing secrets.

indiscretion *n* **1** the lack of discretion. **2** an indiscreet act or remark.

indiscriminate *adj* lacking discrimination or careful choice: *an indiscriminate bombing campaign.* **indiscriminately** *adv* **indiscrimination** *n*

indispensable *adj* absolutely necessary: *an indispensable guide for any traveller.* **indispensability** *n*

indisposed *adj* **1** sick or ill. **2** unwilling. **indisposition** *n*

indisputable *adj* beyond doubt.

indissoluble *adj* permanent: *joining a political party is not an indissoluble marriage.*

indistinct *adj* unable to be seen or heard clearly. **indistinctly** *adv*

indistinguishable *adj* so similar as to be difficult to tell apart.

indium *n Chem* a rare soft silvery metallic element. Symbol: In

individual *adj* **1** of, relating to, or meant for a single person or thing: *small sums from individual donors.* **2** separate or distinct from others of its kind: *please mark the individual pages.* **3** characterized by unusual and striking qualities. ~*n* **4** a single person, esp. when regarded as distinct from others: *respect for the individual.* **5** *Informal* a person: *a most annoying individual.* **6** *Biol* a single animal or plant, esp. as distinct from a species. **individually** *adv*

individualism *n* **1** the principle of leading one's life in one's own way. **2** same as **laissez faire. 3** egotism. **individualist** *n* **individualistic** *adj*

individuality *n, pl* **-ties 1** distinctive or unique character or personality: *a house of great individuality.* **2** the qualities that distinguish one person or thing from another. **3** a separate existence.

individualize *or* **-ise** *vb* **-izing, -ized** *or* **-ising, -ised** to make individual or distinctive in character.

indivisible *adj* **1** unable to be divided. **2** *Maths* leaving a remainder when divided by a given number.

indoctrinate *vb* **-nating, -nated** to teach (someone) systematically to accept a doctrine or opinion uncritically. **indoctrination** *n*

Indo-European *adj* **1** of a family of languages spoken in most of Europe and much of Asia, including

THESAURUS

respect, humiliation, injury, insult, obloquy, opprobrium, outrage, reproach, slap in the face (*informal*), slight, snub

indirect 1. ancillary, collateral, contingent, incidental, secondary, subsidiary, unintended **2.** backhanded, circuitous, circumlocutory, crooked, devious, long-drawn-out, meandering, oblique, periphrastic, rambling, roundabout, tortuous, wandering, winding, zigzag

indirectly by implication, in a roundabout way, obliquely, second-hand

indiscernible hidden, impalpable, imperceptible, indistinct, indistinguishable, invisible, unapparent, undiscernible

indiscreet foolish, hasty, heedless, ill-advised, ill-considered, ill-judged, impolitic, imprudent, incautious, injudicious, naive, rash, reckless, tactless, undiplomatic, unthinking, unwise

indiscretion bloomer (*Brit. informal*), boob (*Brit. slang*), error, faux pas, folly, foolishness, gaffe, imprudence, mistake, rashness, recklessness, slip, slip of the tongue, tactlessness

indiscriminate aimless, careless, chaotic, confused, desultory, general, haphazard, higgledy-piggledy (*informal*), hit or miss (*informal*), jumbled, mingled, miscellaneous, mixed, mongrel, motley, promiscuous, random, sweeping, uncritical, undiscriminating, undistinguishable, unmethodical, unselective, unsystematic, wholesale

indispensable crucial, essential, imperative, key, necessary, needed, needful, requisite, vital

indisposed 1. ailing, confined to bed, ill, laid up (*informal*), on the sick list (*informal*), poorly (*informal*), sick, unwell **2.** averse, disinclined, loath, reluctant, unwilling

indisposition 1. ailment, ill health, illness, sickness **2.** aversion, disinclination, dislike, distaste, hesitancy, reluctance, unwillingness

indisputable absolute, beyond doubt, certain, evident, incontestable, incontrovertible, indubitable, irrefutable, positive, sure, unassailable, undeniable, unquestionable

indissoluble abiding, binding, enduring, eternal, fixed, imperishable, incorruptible, indestructible, inseparable, lasting, permanent, solid, unbreakable

indistinct ambiguous, bleary, blurred, confused, dim, doubtful, faint, fuzzy, hazy, ill-defined, indefinite, indeterminate, indiscernible, indistinguishable, misty, muffled, obscure, out of focus, shadowy, unclear, undefined, unintelligible, vague, weak

indistinguishable alike, identical, imperceptible, indiscernible, invisible, like as two peas in a pod (*informal*), obscure, (the) same, twin

individual 1. *adj.* characteristic, discrete, distinct, distinctive, exclusive, identical, idiosyncratic, own, particular, peculiar, personal, personalized, proper, respective, separate, several, single, singular, special, specific, unique **2.** *n.* being, body (*informal*), character, creature, mortal, party, person, personage, soul, type, unit

individualism egocentricity, egoism, freethinking, independence, originality, self-direction, self-interest, self-reliance

individualist freethinker, independent, loner, lone wolf, maverick, nonconformist, original

individuality character, discreteness, distinction, distinctiveness, originality, peculiarity, personality, separateness, singularity, uniqueness

individually apart, independently, one at a time, one by one, personally, separately, severally, singly

indoctrinate brainwash, drill, ground, imbue, initiate, instruct, school, teach, train

indoctrination brainwashing, drilling, grounding, inculcation, instruction, schooling, training

indolent idle, inactive, inert, lackadaisical, languid,

English, Russian, and Hindi. ~*n* **2** the Indo-European family of languages.

indolent *adj* lazy; idle. **indolence** *n*

indomitable *adj* too strong to be defeated or discouraged: *an indomitable work ethic.*

Indonesian *adj* **1** of Indonesia. ~*n* **2** a person from Indonesia.

indoor *adj* situated, happening, or used inside a building: *an indoor pool.*

indoors *adv, adj* inside or into a building.

indrawn *adj* drawn or pulled in: *he heard her indrawn breath.*

indubitable (in-**dew**-bit-a-bl) *adj* beyond doubt; definite. **indubitably** *adv*

induce *vb* **-ducing, -duced 1** to persuade or use influence on. **2** to cause or bring about. **3** *Med* to cause (labour) to begin by the use of drugs or other means. **4** *Logic obsolete* to draw (a general conclusion) from particular instances. **5** to produce (an electromotive force or electrical current) by induction. **6** to transmit (magnetism) by induction. **inducible** *adj*

inducement *n* **1** something that encourages someone to do something. **2** the act of inducing.

induct *vb* **1** to bring in formally or install in a job, rank, or position. **2** to initiate in knowledge of (a group or profession): *boys are inducted into the world of men.*

inductance *n* the property of an electric circuit as a result of which an electromotive force is created by a change of current in the same or in a neighbouring circuit.

induction *n* **1** *Logic* a process of reasoning by which a general conclusion is drawn from particular instances. **2** *Med* the process of inducing labour. **3** the process by which electrical or magnetic properties are transferred, without physical contact, from one circuit or body to another. **4** a formal introduction or entry into an office or position. **5** (in an internal-combustion engine) the drawing in of mixed air and fuel from the carburettor to the cylinder. **inductional** *adj*

induction coil *n* a transformer for producing a high voltage from a low voltage. It consists of a soft-iron core, a primary coil of few turns, and a concentric secondary coil of many turns.

induction course *n* a training course to help familiarize someone with a new job.

inductive *adj* **1** *Logic* of or using induction: *inductive reasoning.* **2** of or operated by electrical or magnetic induction.

inductor *n* a device designed to create inductance in an electrical circuit.

indulge *vb* **-dulging, -dulged 1** (often foll. by *in*) to yield to or gratify (a whim or desire for): *to indulge in new clothes.* **2** to allow (someone) to have or do everything he or she wants: *he had given her too much, indulged her in everything.* **3** to allow (oneself) the pleasure of something: *he indulged himself.* **4** *Informal* to take alcoholic drink.

indulgence *n* **1** something that is allowed because it gives pleasure. **2** the act of indulging oneself or someone else. **3** liberal or tolerant treatment. **4** something granted as a favour or privilege. **5** *RC Church* a remission of the temporal punishment for sin after its guilt has been forgiven.

indulgent *adj* kind or lenient, often to excess. **indulgently** *adv*

industrial *adj* **1** of, used in, or employed in industry. **2** with an economy relying heavily on industry: *northern industrial cities.*

industrial action *n Brit* action, such as a strike or work-to-rule, by which workers complain about their conditions.

industrial estate *n Brit* an area of land set aside for factories and warehouses.

industrialism *n* an organization of society characterized by large-scale manufacturing industry rather than trade or farming.

industrialist *n* a person who owns or controls large amounts of money or property in industry.

industrialize *or* **-ise** *vb* **-izing, -ized** *or* **-ising, -ised** to develop industry on a large scale in (a country or region). **industrialization** *or* **-isation** *n*

industrial relations *pl n* the relations between management and workers.

Industrial Revolution *n* **the Industrial Revolution** the transformation in the 18th and 19th centuries of Britain and other countries into industrial nations.

industrious *adj* hard-working.

industry *n, pl* **-tries 1** the work and process involved in manufacture: *Japanese industry increased output considerably last year.* **2** a branch of commercial enterprise concerned with the manufacture of a specified product: *the steel industry.* **3** the quality of working hard.

THESAURUS

lazy, lethargic, listless, lumpish, slack, slothful, slow, sluggish, torpid, workshy

indomitable bold, invincible, resolute, staunch, steadfast, unbeatable, unconquerable, unflinching, untameable, unyielding

indubitable certain, evident, incontestable, incontrovertible, indisputable, irrefutable, obvious, sure, unarguable, undeniable, undoubted, unquestionable, veritable

induce 1. actuate, convince, draw, encourage, get, impel, incite, influence, instigate, move, persuade, press, prevail upon, prompt, talk into **2.** bring about, cause, effect, engender, generate, give rise to, lead to, occasion, produce, set in motion, set off

inducement attraction, bait, carrot (*informal*), cause, come-on (*informal*), consideration, encouragement, impulse, incentive, incitement, influence, lure, motive, reward, spur, stimulus, urge

indulge 1. *with* **in** bask in, give free rein to, give oneself up to, luxuriate in, revel in, wallow in **2.** baby, coddle, cosset, favour, foster, give in to, go along with, humour, mollycoddle, pamper, pet, spoil **3.** cater to, feed, give way to, gratify, pander to, regale, satiate, satisfy, treat oneself to, yield to

indulgence 1. appeasement, fulfilment, gratification, satiation, satisfaction **2.** excess, fondness, immoderation, intemperance, intemperateness, kindness, leniency, pampering, partiality, permissiveness, profligacy, profligateness, spoiling **3.** courtesy, forbearance, goodwill, patience, tolerance, understanding **4.** extravagance, favour, luxury, privilege, treat

indulgent compliant, easy-going, favourable, fond, forbearing, gentle, gratifying, kind, kindly, lenient, liberal, mild, permissive, tender, tolerant, understanding

industrialist baron, big businessman, boss, capitalist, captain of industry, financier, magnate, manufacturer, producer, tycoon

industrious active, assiduous, busy, conscientious, diligent, energetic, hard-working, laborious, persevering, persistent, productive, purposeful, sedulous, steady, tireless, zealous

industry 1. business, commerce, commercial enterprise, manufacturing, production, trade **2.** activity, application, assiduity, determination, diligence, effort,

inebriate *n* 1 a person who is habitually drunk. *~adj* 2 drunk, esp. habitually. **inebriation** *n*
inebriated *adj* drunk.
inedible *adj* not fit to be eaten.
ineducable (in-**ed**-yuke-a-bl) *adj* incapable of being educated, esp. on account of mental retardation.
ineffable *adj* too great or intense to be expressed in words. **ineffably** *adv*
ineffective *adj* having no effect or an inadequate effect.
ineffectual *adj* having no effect or an inadequate effect: *the raids were costly and ineffectual.*
inefficient *adj* not performing a task or function to the best advantage. **inefficiency** *n*
inelegant *adj* lacking elegance or refinement.
ineligible *adj* not qualified for or entitled to something.
ineluctable *adj Formal* impossible to avoid: *the ineluctable collapse of the coalition.*
inept *adj* 1 awkward, clumsy, or incompetent. 2 not suitable or fitting; out of place. **ineptitude** *n*
inequable *adj* 1 unfair. 2 not uniform.
inequality *n, pl* **-ties** 1 the state or quality of being unequal. 2 an instance of this. 3 lack of smoothness or regularity of a surface. 4 *Maths* a statement indicating that the value of one quantity or expression is not equal to another.
inequitable *adj* unjust or unfair.
inequity *n, pl* **-ties** 1 injustice or unfairness. 2 something which is unjust or unfair.
ineradicable *adj* impossible to remove or root out: *an ineradicable distrust of foreigners.*
inert *adj* 1 without the power to move or to resist motion. 2 inactive or lifeless. 3 having only a limited ability to react chemically.
inertia *n* 1 feeling of unwillingness to do anything. 2 *Physics* the tendency of a body to remain still or continue moving unless a force is applied to it. **inertial** *adj*
inertia selling *n* the illegal practice of sending unrequested goods to householders, followed by a bill for the goods if they do not return them.
inescapable *adj* not able to be avoided.
inessential *adj* 1 not necessary. *~n* 2 an unnecessary thing.
inestimable *adj* too great to be calculated.
inevitable *adj* 1 unavoidable; sure to happen. 2 *Informal* so regular as to be predictable: *the inevitable guitar solo.* *~n* 3 (often preceded by *the*) something that is unavoidable. **inevitability** *n* **inevitably** *adv*
inexact *adj* not exact or accurate.
inexcusable *adj* too bad to be justified or tolerated.
inexhaustible *adj* incapable of being used up; endless.
inexorable *adj* unable to be prevented from continuing or progressing: *an inexorable trend.* **inexorably** *adv*
inexpensive *adj* not costing a lot of money.

THESAURUS

labour, perseverance, persistence, tirelessness, toil, vigour, zeal
inebriated befuddled, blind drunk, blotto (*slang*), drunk, half-cut (*Brit. slang*), inebriate, intoxicated, legless (*slang*), merry (*Brit. informal*), paralytic (*informal*), pie-eyed (*slang*), pissed (*Brit. taboo slang*), plastered (*slang*), sozzled (*informal*), stoned (*slang*), the worse for drink, tight (*informal*), tipsy, under the influence (*informal*), under the weather (*informal*), zonked (*slang*)
ineffective barren, bootless, feeble, fruitless, futile, idle, impotent, inadequate, ineffectual, inefficacious, inefficient, unavailing, unproductive, useless, vain, weak, worthless
ineffectual abortive, bootless, emasculate, feeble, fruitless, futile, idle, impotent, inadequate, incompetent, ineffective, inefficacious, inefficient, inept, lame, powerless, unavailing, useless, vain, weak
inefficiency carelessness, disorganization, incompetence, muddle, slackness, sloppiness
inefficient cowboy (*informal*), disorganized, feeble, incapable, incompetent, ineffectual, inefficacious, inept, inexpert, slipshod, sloppy, wasteful, weak
ineligible disqualified, incompetent (*Law*), objectionable, ruled out, unacceptable, undesirable, unequipped, unfit, unfitted, unqualified, unsuitable
inept 1. awkward, bumbling, bungling, cack-handed (*informal*), clumsy, cowboy (*informal*), gauche, incompetent, inexpert, maladroit, unhandy, unskilful, unworkmanlike 2. absurd, improper, inappropriate, inapt, infelicitous, meaningless, out of place, pointless, ridiculous, unfit, unsuitable
ineptitude 1. clumsiness, incapacity, incompetence, inexpertness, unfitness, unhandiness 2. absurdity, inappropriateness, pointlessness, uselessness
inequality bias, difference, disparity, disproportion, diversity, imparity, irregularity, lack of balance, preferentiality, prejudice, unevenness
inequitable biased, discriminatory, one-sided, partial, partisan, preferential, prejudiced, unfair, unjust
inert dead, dormant, dull, idle, immobile, inactive, inanimate, indolent, lazy, leaden, lifeless, motionless, passive, quiescent, slack, slothful, sluggish, static, still, torpid, unmoving, unreactive, unresponsive
inertia apathy, deadness, disinclination to move, drowsiness, dullness, idleness, immobility, inactivity, indolence, languor, lassitude, laziness, lethargy, listlessness, passivity, sloth, sluggishness, stillness, stupor, torpor, unresponsiveness
inescapable certain, destined, fated, ineluctable, inevitable, inexorable, sure, unavoidable
inestimable beyond price, immeasurable, incalculable, invaluable, precious, priceless, prodigious
inevitable assured, certain, decreed, destined, fixed, ineluctable, inescapable, inexorable, necessary, ordained, settled, sure, unavoidable, unpreventable
inevitably as a necessary consequence, as a result, automatically, certainly, necessarily, of necessity, perforce (*formal*), surely, unavoidably, willy-nilly
inexcusable indefensible, inexpiable, outrageous, unforgivable, unjustifiable, unpardonable, unwarrantable
inexhaustible bottomless, boundless, endless, illimitable, infinite, limitless, measureless, never-ending, unbounded
inexorable adamant, cruel, hard, harsh, immovable, implacable, ineluctable, inescapable, inflexible, merciless, obdurate, pitiless, relentless, remorseless, severe, unappeasable, unbending, unrelenting, unyielding
inexorably implacably, inevitably, irresistibly, relentlessly, remorselessly, unrelentingly
inexpensive bargain, budget, cheap, economical, low-cost, low-priced, modest, reasonable
inexperience greenness, ignorance, newness, inexpertness, unfamiliarity
inexperienced amateur, callow, fresh, green, immature, new, raw, unaccustomed, unacquainted, unfamiliar, unfledged, unpractised, unschooled, unseasoned,

inexperienced *adj* having no knowledge or experience of a particular situation, activity, etc. **inexperience** *n*

inexpert *adj* lacking skill.

inexpiable *adj* (of sin) incapable of being atoned for; unpardonable.

inexplicable *adj* impossible to explain.

inexpressible *adj* (of a feeling) too strong to be expressed in words.

in extremis *adv* **1** in dire straits. **2** at the point of death.

inextricable *adj* **1** impossible to escape from: *an inextricable dilemma.* **2** impossible to disentangle or separate: *an inextricable mass of broken and twisted chassis.* **inextricably** *adv*

inf. **1** infantry. **2** infinitive. **3** informal. **4** information.

infallible *adj* **1** incapable of error. **2** always successful: *an infallible cure.* **3** (of the Pope) incapable of error in setting forth matters of doctrine on faith and morals. **infallibility** *n* **infallibly** *adv*

infamous (**in**-fam-uss) *adj* well-known for something bad.

infamy *n, pl* **-mies** **1** the state of being infamous. **2** an infamous act or event.

infancy *n, pl* **-cies** **1** the state or period of being an infant. **2** an early stage of growth or development: *virtual reality is in its infancy.* **3** *Law* the state or period of being a minor.

infant *n* **1** a very young child; baby. **2** *Law* same as **minor** (sense 4). **3** *Brit* a young school child. *~adj* **4** of, relating to, or designed for young children: *infant school.* **5** in an early stage of development: *an infant democracy.*

infanta *n* **1** (formerly) a daughter of a king of Spain or Portugal. **2** the wife of an infante.

infante *n* (formerly) any son of a king of Spain or Portugal, except the heir to the throne.

infanticide *n* **1** the act of killing an infant. **2** a person who kills an infant.

infantile *adj* **1** childishly immature. **2** of infants or infancy.

infantile paralysis *n* same as **poliomyelitis.**

infantry *n, pl* **-tries** soldiers who fight on foot.

infant school *n Brit* a school for children aged between 5 and 7.

infatuate *vb* **-ating, -ated** to inspire or fill with an intense and unreasoning passion. **infatuation** *n*

infatuated *adj* (often foll. by *with*) carried away by an intense and unreasoning passion for someone.

infect *vb* **1** to contaminate (a person or thing) with a germ or virus or its consequent disease. **2** to taint or contaminate. **3** to affect with an opinion or feeling as if by contagion: *even she was infected by the excitement.*

infection *n* **1** an infectious disease. **2** contamination of a person or thing by a germ or virus or its consequent disease.

infectious *adj* **1** (of a disease) capable of being transmitted without actual contact. **2** causing or transmitting infection. **3** spreading from one person to another: *infectious laughter.*

infectious mononucleosis *n* same as **glandular fever.**

infelicity *n, pl* **-ties** *Formal* **1** something, esp. a remark or expression, that is inapt. **2** the state or quality of being unhappy or unfortunate. **infelicitous** *adj*

infer *vb* **-ferring, -ferred** **1** to conclude by reasoning from evidence; deduce. **2** *Not universally accepted* to imply or suggest.

➤ Someone *infers* something by "reading between the lines" of a remark. Do not confuse with *imply,* which means "to hint".

inference *n* **1** the act or process of reaching a conclusion by reasoning from evidence. **2** an inferred conclusion or deduction.

inferential *adj* of or based on inference.

inferior *adj* **1** lower in quality, quantity, or usefulness. **2** lower in rank, position, or status. **3** of poor quality. **4**

THESAURUS

unskilled, untrained, untried, unused, unversed, wet behind the ears (*informal*)

inexpert amateurish, awkward, bungling, cack-handed (*informal*), clumsy, inept, maladroit, skill-less, unhandy, unpractised, unprofessional, unskilful, unskilled, unworkmanlike

inexplicable baffling, beyond comprehension, enigmatic, incomprehensible, inscrutable, insoluble, mysterious, mystifying, strange, unaccountable, unfathomable, unintelligible

inexpressible incommunicable, indefinable, indescribable, ineffable, unspeakable, unutterable

inextricably indissolubly, indistinguishably, inseparably, intricately, irretrievably, totally

infallibility **1.** faultlessness, impeccability, irrefutability, omniscience, perfection, supremacy, unerringness **2.** dependability, reliability, safety, sureness, trustworthiness

infallible **1.** faultless, impeccable, omniscient, perfect, unerring, unimpeachable **2.** certain, dependable, foolproof, reliable, sure, sure-fire (*informal*), trustworthy, unbeatable, unfailing

infamous abominable, atrocious, base, detestable, disgraceful, dishonourable, disreputable, egregious, hateful, heinous, ignominious, ill-famed, iniquitous, loathsome, monstrous, nefarious, notorious, odious, opprobrious, outrageous, scandalous, scurvy, shameful, shocking, vile, villainous, wicked

infancy **1.** babyhood, early childhood **2.** beginnings, cradle, dawn, early stages, emergence, inception, origins, outset, start

infant **1.** *n.* babe, baby, bairn (*Scot. & N English*), child, little one, neonate, newborn child, suckling, toddler, tot **2.** *adj.* baby, dawning, developing, early, emergent, growing, immature, initial, nascent, newborn, unfledged, young

infantile babyish, childish, immature, puerile, tender, weak, young

infatuate beguile, bewitch, captivate, delude, enchant, enrapture, fascinate, make a fool of, mislead, obsess, stupefy, sweep one off one's feet, turn (someone's) head

infatuated beguiled, besotted, bewitched, captivated, carried away, crazy about (*informal*), enamoured, enraptured, fascinated, head over heels in love with, inflamed, intoxicated, obsessed, possessed, smitten (*informal*), spellbound, swept off one's feet, under the spell of

infatuation crush (*informal*), fixation, folly, foolishness, madness, obsession, passion, thing (*informal*)

infect affect, blight, contaminate, corrupt, defile, influence, poison, pollute, spread to *or* among, taint, touch, vitiate

infection contagion, contamination, corruption, defilement, poison, pollution, septicity, virus

infectious catching, communicable, contagious, contaminating, corrupting, defiling, infective, pestilential, poisoning, polluting, spreading, transmittable, virulent, vitiating

infer conclude, conjecture, deduce, derive, gather, presume, read between the lines, surmise, understand

lower in position. **5** *Printing* (of a character) printed at the foot of an ordinary character. ~*n* **6** a person inferior to another, esp. in rank. **inferiority** *n*

inferiority complex *n Psychiatry* a disorder arising from a feeling of inferiority to others, characterized by aggressiveness or extreme shyness.

infernal *adj* **1** of or relating to hell. **2** *Informal* irritating: *stop that infernal noise.*

inferno *n, pl* **-nos** **1** an intense raging fire. **2** a place or situation resembling hell, because it is crowded and noisy. **3 the inferno** hell.

infertile *adj* **1** not capable of producing offspring. **2** (of soil) not productive; barren. **infertility** *n*

infest *vb* to inhabit or overrun (a place, plant, etc.) in unpleasantly large numbers: *the area was infested with moles.* **infestation** *n*

infidel *n* **1** a person who has no religious belief. **2** a person who rejects a specific religion, esp. Christianity or Islam. ~*adj* **3** of unbelievers or unbelief.

infidelity *n, pl* **-ties** **1** sexual unfaithfulness to one's husband, wife, or lover. **2** an act or instance of unfaithfulness.

infield *n* **1** *Cricket* the area of the field near the pitch. **2** *Baseball* the area of the playing field enclosed by the base lines. **infielder** *n*

infighting *n* **1** rivalry or quarrelling between members of the same group or organization. **2** *Boxing* combat at close quarters.

infiltrate *vb* **-trating, -trated** **1** to enter (an organization, area, etc.) gradually and in secret, so as to gain influence or control: *they infiltrated the party structure.* **2** to pass (a liquid or gas) through (a substance) by filtering or (of a liquid or gas) to pass through (a substance) by filtering. **infiltration** *n* **infiltrator** *n*

infinite (**in**-fin-it) *adj* **1** having no limits or boundaries in time, space, extent, or size. **2** extremely or immeasurably great or numerous: *infinite wealth.* **3** *Maths* having an unlimited or uncountable number of digits, factors, or terms. **infinitely** *adv*

infinitesimal *adj* **1** extremely small. **2** *Maths* of or involving a small change in the value of a variable that approaches zero as a limit. ~*n* **3** *Maths* an infinitesimal quantity.

infinitive (in-**fin**-it-iv) *n Grammar* a form of the verb which in most languages is not inflected for tense or person and is used without a particular subject: in English, the infinitive usually consists of the word *to* followed by the verb.

infinitude *n Literary* **1** the state or quality of being infinite. **2** an infinite extent or quantity.

infinity *n, pl* **-ties** **1** an infinitely great number or amount. **2** endless time, space, or quantity. **3** *Maths* the concept of a value greater than any finite numerical value.

infirm *adj* physically or mentally weak, esp. from old age.

infirmary *n, pl* **-ries** a place for the treatment of the sick or injured; hospital.

infirmity *n, pl* **-ties** **1** the state of being infirm. **2** physical weakness or frailty.

infix *vb* **1** to fix firmly in. **2** to instil or impress on the mind by repetition. **infixation** *or* **infixion** *n*

in flagrante delicto (in flag-**grant**-ee dee-**lick**-toe) *adv Chiefly law* while committing the offence.

inflame *vb* **-flaming, -flamed** **1** to make angry or excited. **2** to increase or intensify; aggravate. **3** to produce inflammation in or become inflamed. **4** to set or be set on fire.

inflammable *adj* **1** liable to catch fire. **2** easily aroused to anger or passion. **inflammability** *n*

➤ *Inflammable* means the same as *flammable* but is falling out of general use as it was often mistaken to mean "not flammable". It is still used in metaphors: *an inflammable situation.*

inflammation *n* **1** the reaction of living tissue to injury or infection, characterized by heat, redness, swelling, and pain. **2** an inflaming or being inflamed.

inflammatory *adj* **1** likely to provoke anger. **2** characterized by or caused by inflammation.

THESAURUS

inference assumption, conclusion, conjecture, consequence, corollary, deduction, presumption, reading, surmise

inferior *adj.* **1.** bad, crappy (*slang*), duff (*Brit. Austral. & N.Z. informal*), imperfect, indifferent, low-grade, mean, mediocre, of a sort *or* of sorts, poor, poorer, second-class, second-rate, shoddy, substandard, worse **2.** junior, lesser, lower, menial, minor, secondary, subordinate, subsidiary, under, underneath ~*n.* **3.** junior, menial, subordinate, underling

inferiority **1.** badness, deficiency, imperfection, inadequacy, insignificance, meanness, mediocrity, shoddiness, unimportance, worthlessness **2.** abasement, inferior status *or* standing, lowliness, subordination, subservience

infernal **1.** lower, nether, Stygian (*chiefly literary*), underworld **2.** accursed, damnable, damned, demonic, devilish, diabolical, fiendish, hellish, malevolent, malicious, satanic

infertile barren, nonproductive, sterile, unfruitful, unproductive

infertility barrenness, sterility, unfruitfulness, unproductiveness

infest beset, flood, invade, overrun, penetrate, permeate, ravage, swarm, throng

infiltrate creep in, filter through, insinuate oneself, penetrate, percolate, permeate, pervade, sneak in (*informal*), work *or* worm one's way into

infinite absolute, all-embracing, bottomless, boundless, enormous, eternal, everlasting, illimitable, immeasurable, immense, inestimable, inexhaustible, interminable, limitless, measureless, never-ending, numberless, perpetual, stupendous, total, unbounded, uncounted, untold, vast, wide, without end, without number

infinitesimal atomic, inappreciable, insignificant, microscopic, minuscule, minute, negligible, teeny, tiny, unnoticeable, wee

infinity boundlessness, endlessness, eternity, immensity, infinitude, perpetuity, vastness

infirm ailing, debilitated, decrepit, doddery, enfeebled, failing, faltering, feeble, frail, indecisive, insecure, irresolute, lame, shaky, unsound, unstable, vacillating, wavering, wobbly

infirmity **1.** debility, decrepitude, deficiency, feebleness, frailty, ill health, imperfection, sickliness, vulnerability **2.** ailment, defect, disorder, failing, fault, malady, sickness, weakness

inflame **1.** agitate, anger, arouse, embitter, enrage, exasperate, excite, fire, foment, heat, ignite, impassion, incense, infuriate, intoxicate, kindle, madden, provoke, rile, rouse, stimulate **2.** aggravate, exacerbate, exasperate, increase, intensify, worsen

inflamed angry, chafing, festering, fevered, heated, hot, infected, red, septic, sore, swollen

inflammable combustible, flammable, incendiary

inflammation burning, heat, painfulness, rash, redness, sore, soreness, tenderness

inflatable *adj* 1 capable of being inflated. ~*n* 2 a plastic or rubber object which can be inflated.

inflate *vb* **-flating, -flated** 1 to expand or cause to expand by filling with gas or air. 2 to give an impression of greater importance than is justified: *something to inflate their self-esteem.* 3 to cause or undergo economic inflation.

inflation *n* 1 an inflating or being inflated. 2 *Econ* a progressive increase in the general level of prices brought about by an increase in the amount of money in circulation or by increases in costs. 3 *Informal* the rate of increase of prices. **inflationary** *adj*

inflect *vb* 1 to change (the voice) in tone or pitch. 2 *Grammar* to change (the form of a word) by inflection. 3 to bend or curve. **inflective** *adj*

inflection *or* **inflexion** *n* 1 change in the pitch of the voice. 2 *Grammar* a change in the form of a word, signalling change in such grammatical functions as tense or number. 3 an angle or bend. 4 an inflecting or being inflected. 5 *Maths* a change in curvature from concave to convex or vice versa. **inflectional** *or* **inflexional** *adj*

inflexible *adj* 1 unwilling to be persuaded; obstinate. 2 (of a rule etc.) firmly fixed: *inflexible schedules.* 3 incapable of being bent: *inflexible joints.* **inflexibility** *n*

inflict *vb* 1 to impose (something unpleasant) on. 2 to deliver (a blow or wound). **infliction** *n* **inflictor** *n*

in-flight *adj* happening or provided during flight in an aircraft: *in-flight meals.*

inflorescence *n Bot* 1 the arrangement of the flowers on the stalks. 2 the part of a plant that consists of the flower-bearing stalks. 3 the process of flowering; blossoming.

inflow *n* 1 something, such as a liquid or gas, that flows in. 2 the act of flowing in; influx.

influence *n* 1 an effect of one person or thing on another. 2 the power of a person or thing to have such an effect. 3 power resulting from ability, wealth, or position. 4 a person or thing with influence. 5 **under the influence** *Informal* drunk. ~*vb* **-encing, -enced** 6 to have an effect upon (actions or events). 7 to persuade or induce.

influential *adj* having or exerting influence.

influenza *n* a highly contagious viral disease characterized by fever, muscular pains, and catarrh.

influx *n* 1 the arrival or entry of many people or things. 2 the act of flowing in.

info *n Informal* short for **information.**

inform *vb* 1 to give information to; tell: *he informed me that he would be free after lunch.* 2 to make knowledgeable (about) or familiar (with): *he'll be informed of his rights.* 3 to give incriminating information to the police. 4 to impart some essential or formative characteristic to. 5 to animate or inspire. **informed** *adj*

informal *adj* 1 relaxed and friendly: *an informal interview.* 2 appropriate to everyday life or use rather than formal occasions: *informal clothes.* 3 (of speech or writing) appropriate to ordinary conversation rather than to formal written language. **informality** *n* **informally** *adv*

informant *n* a person who gives information.

information *n* 1 knowledge acquired in any manner; facts. 2 *Computers* **a** the meaning given to data by the way it is interpreted. **b** same as **data** (sense 2).

information technology *n* the production, stor-

THESAURUS

inflammatory anarchic, demagogic, explosive, fiery, incendiary, inflaming, instigative, insurgent, intemperate, provocative, rabble-rousing, rabid, riotous, seditious

inflate aerate, aggrandize, amplify, balloon, bloat, blow up, boost, dilate, distend, enlarge, escalate, exaggerate, expand, increase, puff up *or* out, pump up, swell

inflated bombastic, exaggerated, grandiloquent, ostentatious, overblown, swollen

inflation aggrandizement, blowing up, distension, enhancement, enlargement, escalation, expansion, extension, increase, intensification, puffiness, rise, spread, swelling

inflection, inflexion 1. accentuation, bend, bow, crook, curvature, intonation, modulation 2. *Grammar* conjugation, declension 3. angle, arc, arch

inflexibility 1. hardness, immovability, inelasticity, rigidity, stiffness, stringency 2. fixity, intransigence, obduracy, obstinacy, steeliness

inflexible 1. adamant, dyed-in-the-wool, firm, fixed, hard and fast, immovable, immutable, implacable, inexorable, intractable, iron, obdurate, obstinate, relentless, resolute, rigorous, set, set in one's ways, steadfast, steely, stiff-necked, strict, stringent, stubborn, unadaptable, unbending, unchangeable, uncompromising, unyielding 2. hard, hardened, inelastic, nonflexible, rigid, stiff, taut

inflict administer, apply, deliver, exact, impose, levy, mete *or* deal out, visit, wreak

infliction 1. administration, exaction, imposition, perpetration, wreaking 2. affliction, penalty, punishment, trouble, visitation, worry

influence *n.* 1. agency, ascendancy, authority, control, credit, direction, domination, effect, guidance, magnetism, mastery, power, pressure, rule, spell, sway, weight 2. clout (*informal*), connections, good offices, hold, importance, leverage, power, prestige, pull (*informal*), weight ~*vb.* 3. act *or* work upon, affect, arouse, bias, control, count, direct, dispose, guide, impel, impress, incite, incline, induce, instigate, lead to believe, manipulate, modify, move, persuade, predispose, prompt, rouse, sway 4. bring pressure to bear upon, carry weight with, make oneself felt, pull strings (*informal*)

influential authoritative, controlling, effective, efficacious, forcible, guiding, important, instrumental, leading, meaningful, momentous, moving, persuasive, potent, powerful, significant, telling, weighty

influx arrival, convergence, flow, incursion, inflow, inrush, inundation, invasion, rush

inform 1. acquaint, advise, apprise, communicate, enlighten, give (someone) to understand, instruct, leak to, let know, make conversant (with), notify, put (someone) in the picture (*informal*), send word to, teach, tell, tip off 2. *often with* **against** *or* **on** betray, blab, blow the whistle on (*informal*), denounce, grass (*Brit. slang*), incriminate, inculpate, rat (*informal*), shop (*slang, chiefly Brit.*), sing (*slang, chiefly U.S.*), snitch (*slang*), spill one's guts (*slang*), squeal (*slang*), tell all, tell on (*informal*) 3. animate, characterize, illuminate, imbue, inspire, permeate, suffuse, typify

informal casual, colloquial, cosy, easy, familiar, natural, relaxed, simple, unceremonious, unconstrained, unofficial

informality casualness, ease, familiarity, lack of ceremony, naturalness, relaxation, simplicity

information advice, blurb, counsel, data, dope (*informal*), facts, gen (*Brit. informal*), info (*informal*), inside story, instruction, intelligence, knowledge, latest

age, and communication of information using computers and electronic technology.
information theory *n* the study of the processes of communication and the transmission of information.
informative *adj* giving useful information.
informer *n* a person who informs to the police.
infra dig *adj Informal* beneath one's dignity.
infrared *adj* **1** of or using rays with a wavelength just beyond the red end of the visible spectrum. ~*n* **2** the infrared part of the spectrum.
infrasonic *adj* having a frequency below the range audible to the human ear.
infrastructure *n* **1** the basic structure of an organization or system. **2** the stock of facilities, services, and equipment in a country, including factories, roads, and schools, that are needed for it to function properly.
infrequent *adj* not happening often. **infrequently** *adv*
infringe *vb* **-fringing, -fringed 1** to violate or break (a law or agreement) **2 infringe on** *or* **upon** to encroach or trespass on: *the press infringed on their privacy.* **infringement** *n*
infuriate *vb* **-ating, -ated** to make very angry. **infuriating** *adj* **infuriatingly** *adv*
infuse *vb* **-fusing, -fused 1** to fill with (an emotion or quality). **2** to soak or be soaked in order to extract flavour.
infusible *adj* unable to be fused or melted. **infusibility** *n*
infusion *n* **1** the act of infusing. **2** a liquid obtained by infusing.
ingenious (in-**jean**-ee-uss) *adj* showing cleverness and originality.
ingenue (**an**-jay-new) *n* an innocent or inexperienced young woman, esp. as a role played by an actress.
ingenuity (in-jen-**new**-it-ee) *n* cleverness at inventing things.
ingenuous (in-**jen**-new-uss) *adj* **1** unsophisticated and trusting. **2** frank and straightforward.
ingest *vb* to take (food or liquid) into the body. **ingestion** *n*
ingle *n Archaic or dialect* a fire in a room or a fireplace.
inglenook *n Brit* a corner by a fireplace.
inglorious *adj* dishonourable or shameful.
ingoing *adj* going in; entering.
ingot *n* a piece of metal cast in a form suitable for storage, usually a bar.
ingrained *or* **engrained** *adj* **1** (of a habit, feeling, or belief) deeply impressed or instilled. **2** (of dirt) worked into or through the fibre or pores.
ingratiate *vb* **-ating, -ated** to act in order to bring (oneself) into favour (with someone). **ingratiating** *adj*
ingratitude *n* lack of gratitude or thanks.
ingredient *n* a component of a mixture or compound, esp. in cooking.
ingress *n Formal* **1** the act of going or coming in. **2** the right or permission to enter.
ingrowing *adj* (esp. of a toenail) growing abnormally into the flesh. **ingrown** *adj*
inhabit *vb* to live or dwell in. **inhabitable** *adj*
inhabitant *n* a person or animal that is a permanent resident of a particular place or region.
inhalant (in-**hale**-ant) *n* a medicinal preparation inhaled to help breathing problems.
inhale *vb* **-haling, -haled** to breathe in (air, smoke, or vapour). **inhalation** *n*
inhaler *n* a container used to administer an inhalant.
inharmonious *adj* lacking harmony; discordant; disagreeing.
inhere *vb* **-hering, -hered inhere in** to be an inseparable part (of).
inherent *adj* existing as an inseparable part. **inherently** *adv*
inherit *vb* **1** to receive money, property, or a title from someone who has died. **2** to receive (a characteristic)

THESAURUS

(*informal*), lowdown (*informal*), material, message, news, notice, report, tidings, word
informative chatty, communicative, edifying, educational, enlightening, forthcoming, gossipy, illuminating, instructive, newsy, revealing
informed abreast, acquainted, *au fait*, briefed, conversant, enlightened, erudite, expert, familiar, genned up (*Brit. informal*), in the know (*informal*), knowledgeable, learned, posted, primed, reliable, up, up to date, versed, well-read
informer accuser, betrayer, grass (*Brit. slang*), Judas, nark, sneak, squealer (*slang*), stool pigeon
infrequent few and far between, occasional, rare, sporadic, uncommon, unusual
infringe 1. break, contravene, disobey, transgress, violate 2. *with* **on** *or* **upon** encroach, intrude, trespass
infringement breach, contravention, infraction, noncompliance, nonobservance, transgression, trespass, violation
infuriate anger, be like a red rag to a bull, enrage, exasperate, gall, get one's back up, get one's goat (*slang*), incense, irritate, madden, make one's blood boil, make one see red (*informal*), make one's hackles rise, nark, provoke, raise one's hackles, rile
infuriating aggravating (*informal*), annoying, exasperating, galling, irritating, maddening, mortifying, pestilential, provoking, vexatious
ingenious adroit, bright, brilliant, clever, crafty, creative, dexterous, fertile, inventive, masterly, original, ready, resourceful, shrewd, skilful, subtle
ingenuity adroitness, cleverness, faculty, flair, genius, gift, ingeniousness, inventiveness, knack, originality, resourcefulness, sharpness, shrewdness, skill, turn
ingenuous artless, candid, childlike, frank, guileless, honest, innocent, naive, open, plain, simple, sincere, trustful, trusting, unreserved, unsophisticated, unstudied
inglorious discreditable, disgraceful, dishonourable, disreputable, failed, humiliating, ignoble, ignominious, infamous, obscure, shameful, unheroic, unknown, unsuccessful, unsung
ingratiate be a yes man, blandish, crawl, curry favour, fawn, flatter, get in with, get on the right side of, grovel, insinuate oneself, lick (someone's) boots, pander to, play up to, rub (someone) up the right way (*informal*), seek the favour (of someone), suck up to (*informal*), toady, worm oneself into (someone's) favour
ingratiating bootlicking (*informal*), crawling, fawning, flattering, humble, obsequious, servile, sycophantic, timeserving, toadying, unctuous
ingratitude thanklessness, unappreciativeness, ungratefulness
ingredient component, constituent, element, part
inhabit abide, dwell (*formal & literary*), live, lodge, make one's home, occupy, people, populate, possess, reside, take up residence in, tenant
inhabitant aborigine, citizen, denizen, dweller (*formal & literary*), inmate, native, occupant, occupier, resident, tenant
inhale breathe in, draw in, gasp, respire, suck in

from an earlier generation by heredity. **3** to receive (a position or situation) from a predecessor: *the Chancellor has inherited a miserable economic outlook.* **inheritor** *n*

inheritable *adj* **1** capable of being transmitted by heredity from one generation to a later one. **2** capable of being inherited.

inheritance *n* **1** *Law* **a** hereditary succession to an estate or title. **b** the right of an heir to succeed on the death of an ancestor. **2** something inherited or to be inherited. **3** the act of inheriting. **4** the fact of receiving characteristics from an earlier generation by heredity.

inheritance tax *n* (in Britain) a tax consisting of a percentage levied on the part of an inheritance that exceeds a specified allowance.

inhibit *vb* **1** to restrain or hinder (an impulse or desire). **2** to prohibit or prevent: *an attempt to inhibit nuclear proliferation.* **3** *Chem* to stop, prevent, or decrease the rate of (a chemical reaction). **inhibited** *adj* **inhibitor** *n*

inhibition *n* **1** *Psychol* a feeling of fear or embarrassment that stops one from behaving naturally. **2** an inhibiting or being inhibited. **3** the process of stopping or retarding a chemical reaction.

inhospitable *adj* **1** not welcoming; unfriendly. **2** (of a place or climate) not easy to live in; harsh.

inhuman *adj* **1** cruel or brutal. **2** not human.

inhumane *adj* extremely cruel or brutal.

inhumanity *n, pl* **-ties 1** lack of kindness or compassion. **2** an inhumane act.

inimical *adj* **1** adverse or unfavourable: *inimical to change.* **2** unfriendly or hostile.

inimitable *adj* impossible to imitate. **inimitably** *adv*

iniquity *n, pl* **-ties 1** injustice or wickedness. **2** a wicked act. **iniquitous** *adj*

initial *adj* **1** of or at the beginning. *~n* **2** the first letter of a word, esp. a person's name. **3** *Printing* a large letter set at the beginning of a chapter or work. *~vb* **-tialling, -tialled** *or US* **-tialing, -tialed 4** to sign with one's initials, esp. to indicate approval. **initially** *adv*

initiate *vb* **-ating, -ated 1** to begin or set going: *more women initiate divorce today.* **2** to accept (new members) into a group, often through secret ceremonies. **3** to teach the fundamentals of a skill or knowledge to (someone). *~n* **4** a person who has been initiated, esp. recently. **5** a beginner. **initiation** *n* **initiator** *n*

initiative *n* **1** a first step; commencing move: *a peace initiative.* **2** the right or power to initiate something: *it forced local people to take the initiative.* **3** enterprise: *the drive and initiative to create new products.* **4 on one's own initiative** without being prompted.

inject *vb* **1** *Med* to put (a fluid) into the body with a syringe. **2** to introduce (a new element): *to inject a dose of realism into the assessment.* **injection** *n*

injudicious *adj* showing poor judgment; unwise.

injunction *n* **1** *Law* a court order not to do something. **2** an authoritative command. **injunctive** *adj*

injure *vb* **-juring, -jured 1** to hurt physically or men-

THESAURUS

inherent basic, congenital, essential, hereditary, inborn, inbred, inbuilt, ingrained, inherited, innate, instinctive, intrinsic, native, natural

inherit accede to, be bequeathed, be left, come into, fall heir to, succeed to

inheritance bequest, birthright, heritage, legacy, patrimony

inhibit arrest, bar, bridle, check, constrain, cramp (someone's) style (*informal*), curb, debar, discourage, forbid, frustrate, hinder, hold back *or* in, impede, obstruct, prevent, prohibit, restrain, stop

inhibited constrained, frustrated, guarded, repressed, reserved, reticent, self-conscious, shy, subdued, uptight (*informal*), withdrawn

inhibition bar, block, check, embargo, hang-up (*informal*), hindrance, interdict, mental blockage, obstacle, prohibition, reserve, restraint, restriction, reticence, self-consciousness, shyness

inhospitable 1. cool, uncongenial, unfriendly, ungenerous, unkind, unreceptive, unsociable, unwelcoming, xenophobic **2.** bare, barren, bleak, desolate, empty, forbidding, godforsaken, hostile, lonely, sterile, unfavourable, uninhabitable

inhuman animal, barbaric, barbarous, bestial, brutal, cold-blooded, cruel, diabolical, fiendish, heartless, merciless, pitiless, remorseless, ruthless, savage, unfeeling, vicious

inhumane brutal, cruel, heartless, pitiless, uncompassionate, unfeeling, unkind, unsympathetic

inhumanity atrocity, barbarism, brutality, brutishness, cold-bloodedness, cold-heartedness, cruelty, hardheartedness, heartlessness, pitilessness, ruthlessness, unkindness, viciousness

inimical adverse, antagonistic, antipathetic, contrary, destructive, disaffected, harmful, hostile, hurtful, ill-disposed, injurious, noxious, opposed, pernicious, repugnant, unfavourable, unfriendly, unwelcoming

inimitable consummate, incomparable, matchless, nonpareil, peerless, supreme, unequalled, unexampled, unique, unmatched, unparalleled, unrivalled, unsurpassable

iniquitous abominable, accursed, atrocious, base, criminal, evil, heinous, immoral, infamous, nefarious, reprehensible, reprobate, sinful, unjust, unrighteous, vicious, wicked

iniquity abomination, baseness, crime, evil, evildoing, heinousness, infamy, injustice, misdeed, offence, sin, sinfulness, unrighteousness, wickedness, wrong, wrongdoing

initial *adj.* beginning, commencing, early, first, inaugural, inceptive, inchoate (*formal*), incipient, introductory, opening, primary

initially at first, at *or* in the beginning, at the outset, at the start, first, firstly, in the early stages, originally, primarily, to begin with

initiate *vb.* **1.** begin, break the ice, commence, get under way, inaugurate, institute, kick off (*informal*), kick-start, launch, lay the foundations of, open, originate, pioneer, set going, set in motion, set the ball rolling, start **2.** coach, familiarize with, indoctrinate, induct, instate, instruct, introduce, invest, teach, train *~n.* **3.** beginner, convert, entrant, learner, member, novice, probationer, proselyte, tyro

initiation admission, commencement, debut, enrolment, entrance, inauguration, inception, induction, installation, instatement, introduction, investiture

initiative 1. advantage, beginning, commencement, first move, first step, lead **2.** ambition, drive, dynamism, enterprise, get-up-and-go (*informal*), inventiveness, leadership, originality, push (*informal*), resource, resourcefulness

inject 1. inoculate, jab (*informal*), shoot (*informal*), vaccinate **2.** bring in, infuse, insert, instil, interject, introduce

injection 1. inoculation, jab (*informal*), shot (*informal*), vaccination, vaccine **2.** dose, infusion, insertion, interjection, introduction

injudicious foolish, hasty, ill-advised, ill-judged, ill-

tally. **2** to do wrong to (a person), esp. by an injustice: *the injured party.* **3** to damage: *an opportunity to injure your reputation.* **injured** *adj*

injurious *adj* **1** causing harm. **2** abusive, slanderous, or libellous.

injury *n, pl* **-ries 1** physical hurt. **2** a specific instance of this: *a leg injury.* **3** harm done to the feelings. **4** damage: *inflict no injury on the wealth of the nation.*

injury time *n Sport* playing time added at the end of a match to compensate for time spent treating injured players.

injustice *n* **1** unfairness. **2** an unfair action.

ink *n* **1** a black or coloured liquid used for printing, writing, and drawing. **2** a dark brown fluid squirted for self-concealment by an octopus or cuttlefish. *~vb* **3** to mark or cover with ink.

inkling *n* a vague idea or suspicion.

inkstand *n* a stand or tray for holding writing tools and containers for ink.

inkwell *n* a small container for ink, often fitted into the surface of a desk.

inky *adj* **inkier, inkiest 1** dark or black, like ink. **2** stained with ink. **inkiness** *n*

inlaid *adj* **1** set in another material so that the surface is smooth, such as a design in wood. **2** made in this way: *an inlaid table-top.*

inland *adj* **1** of or in the interior of a country or region, away from a sea or border. **2** *Chiefly Brit* operating within a country or region; domestic: *inland trade.* *~n* **3** the interior of a country or region. *~adv* **4** towards or into the interior of a country or region.

Inland Revenue *n* (in Britain and New Zealand) a government department that collects major direct taxes, such as income tax.

in-law *n* **1** a relative by marriage. *~adj* **2** related by marriage: *his brother-in-law.*

inlay *vb* **-laying, -laid 1** to decorate (an article, esp. of furniture) by inserting pieces of wood, ivory, or metal so that the surfaces are smooth and flat. *~n* **2** decoration made by inlaying. **3** an inlaid article. **4** *Dentistry* a filling shaped to fit a cavity.

inlet *n* **1** a narrow strip of water extending from the sea into the land. **2** a passage or valve through which a liquid or gas enters a machine.

in loco parentis (par-**rent**-iss) in place of a parent: said of a person acting for a parent.

inmate *n* a person who is confined to an institution such as a prison or hospital.

inmost *adj* same as **innermost.**

inn *n* a pub or small hotel providing food and accommodation.

innards *pl n Informal* **1** the internal organs of the body, esp. the entrails. **2** the working parts of a machine.

innate *adj* existing from birth, rather than acquired; inborn: *his innate decency.* **innately** *adv*

inner *adj* **1** happening or located inside or further inside: *the door to the inner office.* **2** of the mind or spirit: *her inner self.* **3** exclusive or private: *the inner sanctum of the party secretariat.* **4** more profound; less apparent: *the inner meaning.* *~n* **5** *Archery* **a** the red innermost ring on a target. **b** a shot which hits this ring.

inner city *n* the parts of a city in or near its centre, where there are often social and economic problems.

inner man *or fem* **inner woman** *n* **1** the mind or soul. **2** *Jocular* the stomach.

innermost *adj, adj* **1** most intimate or private: *innermost secrets.* **2** furthest within.

inner tube *n* an inflatable rubber tube inside a pneumatic tyre casing.

inning *n Baseball* a division of the game consisting of a turn at batting and a turn in the field for each side.

innings *n* **1** *Cricket* **a** the batting turn of a player or team. **b** the runs scored during such a turn. **2** a period of opportunity or action.

innkeeper *n* an owner or manager of an inn.

innocence *n* the quality or state of being innocent.

innocent *adj* **1** not guilty of a particular crime. **2** without experience of evil. **3** harmless or innocuous. **4** **innocent of** without or lacking: *innocent of prejudice.* *~n* **5** an innocent person, esp. a young child or a naive adult. **innocently** *adv*

innocuous *adj* having no adverse or harmful effect.

innovate *vb* **-vating, -vated** to introduce new ideas

THESAURUS

timed, impolitic, imprudent, incautious, inconsiderate, indiscreet, inexpedient, rash, unthinking, unwise

injunction admonition, command, dictate, exhortation, instruction, mandate, order, precept, ruling

injure abuse, blemish, blight, break, damage, deface, disable, harm, hurt, impair, maltreat, mar, ruin, spoil, tarnish, undermine, vitiate, weaken, wound, wrong

injured **1.** broken, disabled, hurt, lamed, undermined, weakened, wounded **2.** cut to the quick, disgruntled, displeased, hurt, long-suffering, put out, reproachful, stung, unhappy, upset, wounded **3.** abused, blackened, blemished, defamed, ill-treated, maligned, maltreated, offended, tarnished, vilified, wronged

injury abuse, damage, detriment, disservice, evil, grievance, harm, hurt, ill, injustice, mischief, ruin, wound, wrong

injustice bias, discrimination, favouritism, inequality, inequity, iniquity, one-sidedness, oppression, partiality, partisanship, prejudice, unfairness, unjustness, unlawfulness, wrong

inkling clue, conception, faintest *or* foggiest idea, glimmering, hint, idea, indication, intimation, notion, suggestion, suspicion, whisper

inland *adj.* domestic, interior, internal, upcountry

inlet arm (of the sea), bay, bight, cove, creek, entrance, firth *or* frith (*Scot.*), ingress (*formal*), passage, sea loch (*Scot.*)

inmost *see* INNERMOST

innate congenital, constitutional, essential, inborn, inbred, indigenous, ingrained, inherent, inherited, instinctive, intrinsic, intuitive, native, natural

inner **1.** central, essential, inside, interior, internal, intestinal, inward, middle **2.** emotional, mental, psychological, spiritual **3.** esoteric, hidden, intimate, personal, private, repressed, secret, unrevealed

innermost **1.** intimate, personal, private, secret **2.** basic, buried, central, deep, deepest, essential

innkeeper host, hostess, hotelier, landlady, landlord, publican

innocence **1.** blamelessness, chastity, clean hands, guiltlessness, incorruptibility, probity, purity, righteousness, sinlessness, stainlessness, uprightness, virginity, virtue **2.** artlessness, credulousness, freshness, guilelessness, gullibility, inexperience, ingenuousness, naiveté, simplicity, unsophistication, unworldliness **3.** harmlessness, innocuousness, innoxiousness, inoffensiveness **4.** ignorance, lack of knowledge, nescience (*literary*), unawareness, unfamiliarity

innocent *adj.* **1.** blameless, clear, faultless, guiltless, honest, in the clear, not guilty, uninvolved, unoffending **2.** artless, childlike, credulous, frank, guileless, gullible, ingenuous, naive, open, simple, unsuspicious,

or methods. **innovative** *or* **innovatory** *adj* **innovator** *n*

innovation *n* **1** something newly introduced, such as a new method or device. **2** the act of innovating.

innuendo *n, pl* **-dos** *or* **-does** an indirect or subtle reference to something rude or unpleasant.

Innuit (in-new-it) *n* same as **Inuit**.

innumerable *adj* too many to be counted. **innumerably** *adv*

innumerate *adj* having no understanding of mathematics or science. **innumeracy** *n*

inoculate *vb* **-lating, -lated 1** to protect against disease by injecting with a vaccine. **2** to introduce (microorganisms, esp. bacteria) into (a culture medium). **inoculation** *n*

inoffensive *adj* causing no harm or annoyance.

inoperable *adj Surgery* unable to be safely operated on: *an inoperable tumour.*

inoperative *adj* not working or functioning: *continued shelling has rendered the ceasefire inoperative.*

inopportune *adj* badly timed or inappropriate.

inordinate *adj* **1** excessive: *an inordinate amount of time spent arguing.* **2** unrestrained, as in behaviour or emotion: *inordinate anger.* **inordinately** *adv*

inorganic *adj* **1** not having the structure or characteristics of living organisms. **2** *Chem* of or denoting chemical compounds that do not contain carbon. **3** not resulting from or produced by growth; artificial: *inorganic fertilizers.*

inorganic chemistry *n* the branch of chemistry concerned with the elements and compounds which do not contain carbon.

inpatient *n* a patient who stays in a hospital for treatment.

input *n* **1** resources, such as money, labour, or power, put into a project. **2** *Computers* the data fed into a computer. *~vb* **-putting, -put 3** to enter (data) in a computer.

inquest *n* **1** an official inquiry into an unexplained, sudden, or violent death, held by a coroner. **2** *Informal* an investigation or discussion.

inquietude *n Formal* restlessness or anxiety.

inquire *or* **enquire** *vb* **-quiring, -quired 1** to seek information (about). **2 inquire into** to make an investigation. **3 inquire after** to ask about the health or progress of (a person). **4 inquire of** to ask (a person) for information: *I'll inquire of my aunt when she is coming.* **inquirer** *or* **enquirer** *n*

inquiry *or* **enquiry** *n, pl* **-ries 1** a question. **2** an investigation.

inquisition *n* **1** a thorough investigation. **2** an official inquiry, esp. one held by a jury before an officer of the Crown. **inquisitional** *adj*

Inquisition *n History* an organization within the Catholic Church (1232–1820) for suppressing heresy.

inquisitive *adj* **1** excessively curious about other people's business. **2** eager to learn. **inquisitively** *adv* **inquisitiveness** *n*

inquisitor *n* **1** a person who inquires, esp. deeply or ruthlessly. **2 Inquisitor** an officer of the Inquisition.

inquisitorial *adj* **1** of or like an inquisition or an inquisitor. **2** offensively curious. **inquisitorially** *adv*

inquorate *adj* without enough people present to make a quorum.

in re (in **ray**) *prep* in the matter of; concerning.

INRI Jesus of Nazareth, king of the Jews (the inscription placed over Christ's head during the Crucifixion).

inroads *pl n* **make inroads into** to start affecting or reducing: *my gambling has made great inroads into my savings.*

inrush *n* a sudden and overwhelming inward flow.

ins. **1** inches. **2** insurance.

THESAURUS

unworldly, wet behind the ears (*informal*) **3.** harmless, innocuous, inoffensive, unmalicious, unobjectionable, well-intentioned, well-meant *~n.* **4.** babe (in arms) (*informal*), child, greenhorn (*informal*), ingenue (*fem.*)

innovation alteration, change, departure, introduction, modernism, modernization, newness, novelty, variation

innuendo aspersion, hint, implication, imputation, insinuation, intimation, overtone, suggestion, whisper

innumerable beyond number, countless, incalculable, infinite, many, multitudinous, myriad, numberless, numerous, unnumbered, untold

inoffensive harmless, humble, innocent, innocuous, innoxious, mild, neutral, nonprovocative, peaceable, quiet, retiring, unobjectionable, unobtrusive, unoffending

inoperative broken, broken-down, defective, ineffective, ineffectual, inefficacious, invalid, nonactive, null and void, out of action, out of commission, out of order, out of service, unserviceable, unworkable, useless

inopportune ill-chosen, ill-timed, inappropriate, inauspicious, inconvenient, malapropos, mistimed, unfavourable, unfortunate, unpropitious, unseasonable, unsuitable, untimely

inordinate disproportionate, excessive, exorbitant, extravagant, immoderate, intemperate, preposterous, unconscionable, undue, unreasonable, unrestrained, unwarranted

inorganic artificial, chemical, man-made, mineral

inquest inquiry, inquisition, investigation, probe

inquire *or* **enquire 1.** ask, query, question, request information, seek information **2.** *with* **into** conduct an inquiry, examine, explore, inspect, investigate, look into, make inquiries, probe, research, scrutinize, search

inquiring analytical, curious, doubtful, inquisitive, interested, investigative, nosy (*informal*), outward-looking, probing, questioning, searching, wondering

inquiry *or* **enquiry 1.** query, question **2.** examination, exploration, inquest, interrogation, investigation, probe, research, scrutiny, search, study, survey

inquisition cross-examination, examination, grilling (*informal*), inquest, inquiry, investigation, question, quizzing, third degree (*informal*)

inquisitive curious, inquiring, intrusive, nosy (*informal*), nosy-parkering (*informal*), peering, probing, prying, questioning, scrutinizing, snooping (*informal*), snoopy (*informal*)

inroads **make inroads into** consume, eat away, eat up *or* into, encroach upon, use up

insane 1. barking (*slang*), barking mad (*slang*), crackpot (*informal*), crazed, crazy, demented, deranged, loopy (*informal*), mad, mentally disordered, mentally ill, *non compos mentis,* not the full shilling (*informal*), off one's trolley (*slang*), of unsound mind, out of one's mind, out to lunch (*informal*), unhinged, up the pole (*informal*) **2.** bizarre, daft (*informal*), fatuous, foolish, idiotic, impractical, inane, irrational, irresponsible, lunatic, preposterous, senseless, stupid

insanitary contaminated, dirtied, dirty, disease-ridden, feculent, filthy, impure, infected, infested, insalubrious, noxious, polluted, unclean, unhealthy, unhygienic

insane *adj* **1** mentally ill. **2** stupidly irresponsible: *acting on an insane impulse.* **insanely** *adv*

insanitary *adj* dirty or unhealthy.

insanity *n, pl* **-ties 1** the state of being insane. **2** stupidity.

insatiable (in-**saysh**-a-bl) *adj* impossible to satisfy. **insatiability** *n* **insatiably** *adv*

inscribe *vb* **-scribing, -scribed 1** to mark or engrave with (words, symbols, or letters). **2** to write one's name, and sometimes a brief dedication, on (a book) before giving to someone. **3** to enter (a name) on a list. **4** *Geom* to draw (a geometric construction) inside another construction so that the two are in contact at as many points as possible but do not intersect.

inscription *n* **1** something inscribed, esp. words carved or engraved on a coin, tomb, or ring. **2** a signature or brief dedication in a book or on a work of art.

inscrutable *adj* mysterious or enigmatic. **inscrutability** *n*

insect *n* **1** a small animal that has six legs and usually has wings, such as an ant, fly or butterfly. **2** (loosely) any similar invertebrate, such as a spider, tick, or centipede.

insecticide *n* a substance used to destroy insects.

insectivore *n* **1** a small mammal, such as a hedgehog or a shrew, that eats invertebrates. **2** a plant or animal that eats insects. **insectivorous** *adj*

insecure *adj* **1** anxious or uncertain. **2** not adequately protected: *low-paid or insecure employment.* **3** unstable or shaky. **insecurity** *n*

inseminate *vb* **-nating, -nated** to impregnate (a female) with semen. **insemination** *n*

insensate *adj* **1** lacking sensation or consciousness. **2** insensitive or unfeeling. **3** foolish.

insensible *adj* **1** unconscious. **2** without feeling. **3 insensible of** *or* **to** unaware of or indifferent to: *insensible to suffering.* **4** imperceptible. **insensibility** *n*

insensitive *adj* unaware of or ignoring other people's feelings. **insensitivity** *n*

inseparable *adj* **1** constantly together because of mutual liking: *they became inseparable companions.* **2** too closely connected to be separated. **inseparably** *adv*

insert *vb* **1** to place or fit (something) inside something else. **2** to introduce (a clause or comment) into text or a speech. *~n* **3** something inserted, esp. an advertisement in between the pages of a magazine.

insertion *n* **1** the act of inserting. **2** something inserted, such as an advertisement in a newspaper.

in-service *adj* denoting training that is given to employees during the course of employment: *an in-service course.*

inset *vb* **-setting, -set 1** to place in or within; insert. *~n* **2** something inserted. **3** *Printing* a small map or diagram set within the borders of a larger one. *~adj* **4** decorated with something inserted.

inshore *adj* **1** in or on the water, but close to the shore: *inshore fishermen. ~adv, adj* **2** towards the shore from the water: *the boat was forced inshore; a strong wind blowing inshore.*

inside *prep* **1** in or to the interior of: *a bomb had gone off inside the parliament building.* **2** in a period of time less than: *they took the lead inside seven minutes. ~adj* **3** on or of the inside: *some houses in Britain still lack an inside toilet.* **4** by or from someone within an organization, esp. illicitly: *inside information.* **5** of or being the lane in a road which is nearer the side than other lanes going in the same direction: *all the lorries were in the inside lane. ~adv* **6** on, in, or to the inside; indoors: *when the rain started we took our drinks inside.* **7** *Slang* in or into prison. *~n* **8** the inner side, surface, or part of something. **9 inside out** with the inside facing outwards. **10 know inside out** to know thoroughly. ~See also **insides.**

➤ Avoid using the expression *inside of,* as the second preposition *of* is superfluous.

inside job *n Informal* a crime committed with the assistance of someone employed by or trusted by the victim.

insider *n* a member of a group or organization who therefore has exclusive information about it.

insider dealing *n* the illegal practice of a person on the stock exchange or in the civil service taking ad-

THESAURUS

insanity **1.** aberration, craziness, delirium, dementia, frenzy, madness, mental derangement, mental disorder, mental illness **2.** folly, irresponsibility, lunacy, preposterousness, senselessness, stupidity

insatiable gluttonous, greedy, intemperate, rapacious, ravenous, unappeasable, unquenchable, voracious

inscribe **1.** carve, cut, engrave, etch, impress, imprint **2.** address, dedicate **3.** engross, enlist, enrol, enter, record, register, write

inscription dedication, engraving, label, legend, lettering, saying, words

inscrutable blank, deadpan, enigmatic, hidden, impenetrable, inexplicable, mysterious, poker-faced (*informal*), sphinxlike, undiscoverable, unexplainable, unfathomable, unreadable

insecure **1.** afraid, anxious, uncertain, unconfident, unsure **2.** dangerous, defenceless, exposed, hazardous, ill-protected, open to attack, perilous, unguarded, unprotected, unsafe, unshielded, vulnerable **3.** built upon sand, flimsy, frail, insubstantial, loose, on thin ice, precarious, rickety, rocky, shaky, unreliable, unsound, unstable, unsteady, weak, wobbly

insecurity **1.** anxiety, fear, uncertainty, unsureness, worry **2.** danger, defencelessness, hazard, peril, risk, uncertainty, vulnerability, weakness **3.** dubiety, frailness, instability, precariousness, shakiness, uncertainty, unreliability, unsteadiness, weakness

insensibility **1.** inertness, numbness, unconsciousness **2.** apathy, callousness, dullness, indifference, inertia, insensitivity, lethargy, thoughtlessness, torpor

insensible **1.** anaesthetized, benumbed, dull, inert, insensate, numbed, senseless, stupid, torpid **2.** apathetic, callous, cold, deaf, hard-hearted, impassive, impervious, indifferent, oblivious, unaffected, unaware, unconscious, unfeeling, unmindful, unmoved, unresponsive, unsusceptible, untouched **3.** imperceivable, imperceptible, minuscule, negligible, unnoticeable

insensitive callous, crass, hardened, imperceptive, indifferent, obtuse, tactless, thick-skinned, tough, uncaring, unconcerned, unfeeling, unresponsive, unsusceptible

inseparable **1.** bosom, close, devoted, intimate **2.** inalienable, indissoluble, indivisible, inseverable

insert embed, enter, implant, infix, interject, interpolate, interpose, introduce, place, pop in (*informal*), put, set, stick in, tuck in, work in

insertion addition, implant, inclusion, insert, inset, interpolation, introduction, supplement

inside *adj.* **1.** inner, innermost, interior, internal, intramural, inward **2.** classified, confidential, esoteric, exclusive, internal, limited, private, restricted, secret *~adv.* **3.** indoors, under cover, within *~n.* **4.** contents, inner part, interior

vantage of early confidential information in order to deal in shares for personal profit.

insides *pl n Informal* the stomach and bowels.

insidious *adj* working in a subtle or apparently harmless way, but nevertheless dangerous or deadly: *an insidious virus.* **insidiously** *adv* **insidiousness** *n*

insight *n* **1** a penetrating understanding, as of a complex situation or problem. **2** the ability to perceive clearly or deeply the inner nature of things.

insignia (in-**sig**-nee-a) *n, pl* **-nias** *or* **-nia** a badge or emblem of membership, office, or honour.

insignificant *adj* having little or no importance. **insignificance** *n*

insincere *adj* pretending what one does not feel. **insincerely** *adv* **insincerity** *n*

insinuate *vb* **-ating, -ated 1** to suggest indirectly by allusion, hints, or innuendo. **2** to get (someone, esp. oneself) into a position by gradual manoeuvres: *she insinuated herself into the conversation.*

insinuation *n* **1** an indirect or devious hint or suggestion. **2** an act or the practice of insinuating.

insipid *adj* **1** dull and boring. **2** lacking flavour. **insipidity** *n*

insist *vb* (often foll. by *on* or *upon*) **1** to make a determined demand (for): *he insisted on his rights.* **2** to express a convinced belief (in) or assertion (of): *she insisted that she had been given permission.*

insistent *adj* **1** making continual and persistent demands. **2** demanding attention: *the chirruping of an insistent bird.* **insistence** *n* **insistently** *adv*

in situ *adv, adj* in the original position.

in so far as *or US* **insofar as** *prep* to the degree or extent that.

insole *n* **1** the inner sole of a shoe or boot. **2** a loose inner sole used to give extra warmth or to make a shoe fit.

insolent *adj* rude and disrespectful. **insolence** *n* **insolently** *adv*

insoluble *adj* **1** impossible to solve. **2** not able to be dissolved. **insolubility** *n*

insolvent *adj* **1** unable to pay one's debts. *~n* **2** a person who is insolvent. **insolvency** *n*

insomnia *n* inability to sleep. **insomniac** *n, adj*

insomuch *adv* **1** (foll. by *as* or *that*) to such an extent or degree. **2** (foll. by *as*) because of the fact (that).

insouciant *adj* carefree or unconcerned. **insouciance** *n*

inspan *vb* **-spanning, -spanned** *Chiefly S African* **1** to harness (animals) to (a vehicle); yoke. **2** to press (people) into service.

inspect *vb* **1** to examine closely, esp. for faults or errors. **2** to examine officially. **inspection** *n*

inspector *n* **1** an official who checks that things or

THESAURUS

insides *informal* belly, bowels, entrails, gut, guts, innards (*informal*), internal organs, stomach, viscera, vitals

insidious artful, crafty, crooked, cunning, deceitful, deceptive, designing, disingenuous, intriguing, Machiavellian, slick, sly, smooth, sneaking, stealthy, subtle, surreptitious, treacherous, tricky, wily

insight acumen, awareness, comprehension, discernment, intuition, intuitiveness, judgment, observation, penetration, perception, perspicacity, understanding, vision

insignia badge, crest, decoration, distinguishing mark, earmark, emblem, ensign, symbol

insignificance immateriality, inconsequence, irrelevance, meaninglessness, negligibility, paltriness, pettiness, triviality, unimportance, worthlessness

insignificant flimsy, immaterial, inconsequential, inconsiderable, irrelevant, meagre, meaningless, measly, minor, negligible, nondescript, nonessential, not worth mentioning, nugatory, of no account (consequence, moment), paltry, petty, scanty, trifling, trivial, unimportant, unsubstantial

insincere deceitful, deceptive, devious, dishonest, disingenuous, dissembling, dissimulating, double-dealing, evasive, faithless, false, hollow, hypocritical, lying, mendacious, perfidious (*literary*), pretended, two-faced, unfaithful, untrue, untruthful

insincerity deceitfulness, deviousness, dishonesty, disingenuousness, dissimulation, duplicity, faithlessness, hypocrisy, lip service, mendacity, perfidy, pretence, untruthfulness

insinuate 1. allude, hint, imply, indicate, intimate, suggest **2.** curry favour, get in with, ingratiate, worm *or* work one's way in

insinuation 1. allusion, aspersion, hint, implication, innuendo, slur, suggestion **2.** infiltration, infusion, ingratiating, injection, instillation, introduction

insipid 1. anaemic, banal, bland, characterless, colourless, drab, dry, dull, flat, jejune, lifeless, limp, pointless, prosaic, prosy, spiritless, stale, stupid, tame, tedious, trite, unimaginative, uninteresting, vapid, weak, wearisome, wishy-washy (*informal*) **2.** bland, flavourless, savourless, tasteless, unappetizing, watered down, watery, wishy-washy (*informal*)

insipidity 1. banality, colourlessness, dullness, flatness, lack of imagination, pointlessness, staleness, tameness, tediousness, triteness, uninterestingness, vapidity **2.** blandness, flavourlessness, lack of flavour, tastelessness

insist 1. be firm, brook no refusal, demand, lay down the law, not take no for an answer, persist, press (someone), require, stand firm, stand one's ground, take *or* make a stand, urge **2.** assert, asseverate, aver, claim, contend, hold, maintain, reiterate, repeat, swear, urge, vow

insistence assertion, contention, demands, emphasis, importunity, insistency, persistence, pressing, reiteration, stress, urging

insistent demanding, dogged, emphatic, exigent, forceful, importunate, incessant, peremptory, persevering, persistent, pressing, unrelenting, urgent

insolence abuse, audacity, backchat (*informal*), boldness, cheek (*informal*), chutzpah (*U.S. & Canad. informal*), contemptuousness, contumely, disrespect, effrontery, front, gall (*informal*), impertinence, impudence, incivility, insubordination, offensiveness, pertness, rudeness, sauce (*informal*), uncivility

insolent abusive, bold, brazen-faced, contemptuous, fresh (*informal*), impertinent, impudent, insubordinate, insulting, pert, rude, saucy, uncivil

insoluble baffling, impenetrable, indecipherable, inexplicable, mysterious, mystifying, obscure, unaccountable, unfathomable, unsolvable

insolvency bankruptcy, failure, liquidation, ruin

insolvent bankrupt, broke (*informal*), failed, gone bust (*informal*), gone to the wall, in queer street (*informal*), in receivership, in the hands of the receivers, on the rocks (*informal*), ruined

insomnia sleeplessness, wakefulness

inspect audit, check, check out (*informal*), examine, give (something *or* someone) the once-over (*informal*), go over *or* through, investigate, look over, oversee, recce (*slang*), research, scan, scrutinize, search, superintend, supervise, survey, take a dekko at (*Brit. slang*), vet, work over

places meet certain regulations and standards. **2** a police officer ranking below a superintendent and above a sergeant.

inspectorate *n* **1** a group of inspectors. **2** the position or duties of an inspector.

inspiration *n* **1** stimulation of the mind or feelings to activity or creativity. **2** a person or thing that causes this state. **3** an inspired idea or action. **inspirational** *adj*

inspire *vb* **-spiring, -spired 1** to stimulate (a person) to activity or creativity. **2** to arouse (an emotion or a reaction): *he inspires confidence.*

inspired *adj* **1** brilliantly creative: *his most inspired compositions.* **2** very clever and accurate: *an inspired guess.*

inst. instant (this month).

instability *n* lack of steadiness or reliability.

install *vb* **1** to put in and prepare (equipment) for use. **2** to place (a person) formally in a position or rank. **3** to settle (a person, esp. oneself) in a position or state: *Tony installed himself in an armchair.*

installation *n* **1** installing. **2** equipment that has been installed. **3** a place containing equipment for a particular purpose: *radar installation.*

installment plan *n US* same as **hire-purchase.** Also (Canad.): **instalment plan**

instalment *or US* **installment** *n* **1** one of the portions into which a debt is divided for payment at regular intervals. **2** a portion of something that is issued, broadcast, or published in parts.

instance *n* **1** a case or particular example. **2 for instance** as an example. **3 in the first instance** in the first place; initially. **4** urgent request or order: *at the instance of.* ~*vb* **-stancing, -stanced 5** to mention as an example.

instant *n* **1** a very brief time; moment. **2** a particular moment: *at the same instant.* ~*adj* **3** immediate. **4** (of foods) able to be prepared very quickly and easily: *instant coffee.* **5** urgent or pressing. **6** of the present month: *a letter of the 7th instant.*

instantaneous *adj* happening at once: *the applause was instantaneous.* **instantaneously** *adv*

instantly *adv* immediately.

instead *adv* **1** as a replacement or substitute for the person or thing mentioned. **2 instead of** in place of or as an alternative to.

instep *n* **1** the middle part of the foot forming the arch between the ankle and toes. **2** the part of a shoe or stocking covering this.

instigate *vb* **-gating, -gated 1** to cause to happen: *to instigate rebellion.* **2** to urge on to some action. **instigation** *n* **instigator** *n*

instil *or US* **instill** *vb* **-stilling, -stilled 1** to introduce (an idea or feeling) gradually in someone's mind. **2** *Rare* to pour in or inject drop by drop. **instillation** *n* **instiller** *n*

THESAURUS

inspection check, checkup, examination, investigation, look-over, once-over (*informal*), recce (*slang*), review, scan, scrutiny, search, superintendence, supervision, surveillance, survey

inspector censor, checker, critic, examiner, investigator, overseer, scrutineer, scrutinizer, superintendent, supervisor

inspiration 1. arousal, awakening, encouragement, influence, muse, spur, stimulus **2.** creativity, elevation, enthusiasm, exaltation, genius, illumination, insight, revelation, stimulation

inspire 1. animate, be responsible for, encourage, enliven, fire *or* touch the imagination of, galvanize, hearten, imbue, influence, infuse, inspirit, instil, rouse, spark off, spur, stimulate **2.** arouse, excite, give rise to, produce, quicken, rouse, stir

inspired 1. brilliant, dazzling, enthralling, exciting, impressive, memorable, of genius, outstanding, superlative, thrilling, wonderful **2.** *of a guess* instinctive, instinctual, intuitive

inspiring affecting, encouraging, exciting, exhilarating, heartening, moving, rousing, stimulating, stirring, uplifting

instability capriciousness, changeableness, disequilibrium, fickleness, fitfulness, fluctuation, fluidity, frailty, imbalance, impermanence, inconstancy, insecurity, irresolution, mutability, oscillation, precariousness, restlessness, shakiness, transience, unpredictability, unsteadiness, vacillation, variability, volatility, wavering, weakness

install 1. fix, lay, lodge, place, position, put in, set up, station **2.** establish, inaugurate, induct, instate, institute, introduce, invest, set up **3.** ensconce, position, settle

installation 1. establishment, fitting, inauguration, induction, instalment, instatement, investiture, placing, positioning, setting up **2.** equipment, machinery, plant, system **3.** *Military* base, establishment, post, station

instalment *or U.S.* **installment** chapter, division, episode, part, portion, repayment, section

instance *n.* **1.** case, case in point, example, illustration, occasion, occurrence, precedent, situation, time **2.** application, behest, demand, entreaty, importunity, impulse, incitement, insistence, instigation, pressure, prompting, request, solicitation, urging ~*vb.* **3.** adduce, cite, mention, name, quote, specify

instant *n.* **1.** flash, jiffy (*informal*), moment, second, shake (*informal*), split second, tick (*Brit. informal*), trice, twinkling, twinkling of an eye (*informal*), two shakes of a lamb's tail (*informal*) **2.** juncture, moment, occasion, point, time ~*adj.* **3.** direct, immediate, instantaneous, on-the-spot, prompt, quick, quickie (*informal*), split-second, urgent **4.** convenience, fast, precooked, ready-mixed **5.** burning, exigent, imperative, importunate, pressing, urgent

instantaneous direct, immediate, instant, on-the-spot

instantaneously at once, forthwith, immediately, in a fraction of a second, instantly, in the same breath, in the twinkling of an eye (*informal*), like greased lightning (*informal*), on the instant, on the spot, posthaste, promptly, pronto (*informal*), quick as lightning, straight away, then and there

instantly at once, directly, forthwith, immediately, instantaneously, instanter (*Law*), now, on the spot, posthaste, pronto (*informal*), right away, right now, straight away, there and then, this minute, *tout de suite,* without delay

instead 1. alternatively, in lieu, in preference, on second thoughts, preferably, rather **2.** *with* **of** as an alternative *or* equivalent to, in lieu of, in place of, rather than

instigate actuate, bring about, encourage, foment, get going, impel, incite, influence, initiate, kick-start, kindle, move, persuade, prod, prompt, provoke, rouse, set off, set on, spur, start, stimulate, stir up, trigger, urge, whip up

instigation behest, bidding, encouragement, incentive, incitement, prompting, urging

instigator agitator, firebrand, fomenter, goad, incendiary, inciter, leader, mischief-maker, motivator, prime mover, ringleader, spur, stirrer (*informal*), troublemaker

instinct *n* **1** the inborn tendency to behave in a particular way without the need for thought: *maternal instinct.* **2** natural reaction: *my first instinct was to get out of the car.* **3** intuition: *he knew at once, by instinct, it wouldn't work.*

instinctive *or* **instinctual** *adj* done or happening without any logical thought: *an instinctive understanding of people.* **instinctively** *or* **instinctually** *adv*

institute *n* **1** an organization set up for a specific purpose, especially research or teaching. **2** the building where such an organization is situated. **3** a rule, custom, or precedent. ~*vb* **-tuting, -tuted 4** to start or establish. **5** to install in a position or office.

institution *n* **1** a large important organization such as a university or bank. **2** a hospital etc. for people with special needs. **3** an established custom, law, or principle: *the institution of marriage.* **4** *Informal* a well-established person or feature: *the programme has become an institution.* **5** an instituting or being instituted.

institutional *adj* **1** of or relating to an institution: *institutional care.* **2** dull, routine, and uniform: *institutional meals.* **institutionalism** *n*

institutionalize *or* **-ise** *vb* **-izing, -ized** *or* **-ising, -ised 1** (*often passive*) to subject (a person) to institutional life, often causing apathy and dependence on routine. **2** to make or become an institution: *institutionalized religion.* **3** to place in an institution.

instruct *vb* **1** to order to do something. **2** to teach (someone) how to do something. **3** to brief (a solicitor or barrister).

instruction *n* **1** a direction or order. **2** the process or act of teaching. **instructional** *adj*

instructions *pl n* information on how to do or use something: *the plane had ignored instructions from air traffic controllers.*

instructive *adj* informative or helpful.

instructor *n* **1** a person who teaches something. **2** *US & Canad* a college teacher ranking below assistant professor.

instrument *n* **1** a tool or implement, esp. one used for precision work. **2** *Music* any of various devices that can be played to produce musical sounds. **3** a measuring device to show height, speed, etc.: *the pilot's eyes never left his instruments.* **4** *Informal* a person used by another to gain an end. **5** an important factor in something: *her evidence was an instrument in his arrest.* **6** a formal legal document.

instrumental *adj* **1** helping to cause. **2** played by or composed for musical instruments. **3** of or done with an instrument: *instrumental error.*

instrumentalist *n* a person who plays a musical instrument.

instrumentation *n* **1** a set of instruments in a car etc. **2** the arrangement of music for instruments. **3** the list of instruments needed for a piece of music.

instrument panel *n* a panel holding the instruments in a vehicle or on a machine.

insubordinate *adj* not submissive to authority. **insubordination** *n*

insubstantial *adj* **1** flimsy, fine, or slight. **2** imaginary or unreal.

THESAURUS

instil *or U.S.* **instill** engender, engraft, imbue, implant, impress, inculcate, infix, infuse, insinuate, introduce

instinct aptitude, faculty, feeling, gift, gut feeling (*informal*), gut reaction (*informal*), impulse, intuition, knack, natural inclination, predisposition, proclivity, sixth sense, talent, tendency, urge

instinctive *or* **instinctual** automatic, inborn, inherent, innate, instinctual, intuitional, intuitive, involuntary, mechanical, native, natural, reflex, spontaneous, unlearned, unpremeditated, unthinking, visceral

instinctively *or* **instinctually** automatically, by instinct, intuitively, involuntarily, naturally, without thinking

institute *n.* **1.** academy, association, college, conservatory, foundation, guild, institution, school, seat of learning, seminary, society **2.** custom, decree, doctrine, dogma, edict, law, maxim, precedent, precept, principle, regulation, rule, tenet ~*vb.* **3.** appoint, begin, bring into being, commence, constitute, enact, establish, fix, found, induct, initiate, install, introduce, invest, launch, ordain, organize, originate, pioneer, put into operation, set in motion, settle, set up, start

institution 1. constitution, creation, enactment, establishment, formation, foundation, initiation, introduction, investiture, investment, organization **2.** academy, college, establishment, foundation, hospital, institute, school, seminary, society, university **3.** convention, custom, fixture, law, practice, ritual, rule, tradition

institutional 1. accepted, bureaucratic, conventional, established, establishment (*informal*), formal, organized, orthodox, societal **2.** cheerless, clinical, cold, drab, dreary, dull, forbidding, formal, impersonal, monotonous, regimented, routine, uniform, unwelcoming

instruct 1. bid, canon, charge, command, direct, enjoin, order, tell **2.** coach, discipline, drill, educate, enlighten, ground, guide, inform, school, teach, train, tutor **3.** acquaint, advise, apprise, brief, counsel, inform, notify, tell

instruction 1. briefing, command, demand, direction, directive, injunction, mandate, order, ruling **2.** apprenticeship, coaching, discipline, drilling, education, enlightenment, grounding, guidance, information, lesson(s), preparation, schooling, teaching, training, tuition, tutelage

instructions advice, directions, guidance, information, key, orders, recommendations, rules

instructive cautionary, didactic, edifying, educational, enlightening, helpful, illuminating, informative, instructional, revealing, useful

instructor adviser, coach, demonstrator, exponent, guide, handler, master, mentor, mistress, pedagogue, preceptor (*rare*), schoolmaster, schoolmistress, teacher, trainer, tutor

instrument 1. apparatus, appliance, contraption (*informal*), contrivance, device, gadget, implement, mechanism, tool, utensil **2.** agency, agent, channel, factor, force, means, mechanism, medium, organ, vehicle **3.** *informal* cat's-paw, dupe, pawn, puppet, tool

instrumental active, assisting, auxiliary, conducive, contributory, helpful, helping, influential, involved, of help *or* service, subsidiary, useful

insubordinate contumacious, defiant, disobedient, disorderly, fractious, insurgent, mutinous, rebellious, recalcitrant, refractory, riotous, seditious, turbulent, undisciplined, ungovernable, unruly

insubordination defiance, disobedience, indiscipline, insurrection, mutinousness, mutiny, rebellion, recalcitrance, revolt, riotousness, sedition, ungovernability

insufferable detestable, dreadful, enough to test the patience of a saint, enough to try the patience of Job, impossible, insupportable, intolerable, more than flesh and blood can stand, outrageous, past bearing, too much, unbearable, unendurable, unspeakable

insufferable *adj* unbearable. **insufferably** *adv*
insufficient *adj* not enough for a particular purpose. **insufficiency** *n* **insufficiently** *adv*
insular *adj* **1** not open to change or new ideas. **2** of or like an island. **insularity** *n*
insulate *vb* **-lating, -lated 1** to prevent or reduce the transfer of electricity, heat, or sound by surrounding or lining with a nonconducting material. **2** to isolate or set apart. **insulator** *n*
insulation *n* **1** material used to insulate something. **2** the act of insulating.
insulin (**in**-syoo-lin) *n* a hormone produced in the pancreas which controls the amount of sugar in the blood.
insult *vb* **1** to treat or speak to rudely. ~*n* **2** an offensive remark or action. **3** a person or thing producing the effect of an insult: *their explanation is an insult to our intelligence.*
insuperable *adj* impossible to overcome; insurmountable. **insuperability** *n*
insupportable *adj* **1** impossible to tolerate. **2** incapable of being upheld or justified: *an insupportable accusation.*
insurance *n* **1** the agreement by which one makes regular payments to a company who pay an agreed sum if damage, loss, or death occurs. **2** the money paid for insurance or by an insurance company. **3** a means of protection: *sensible insurance against heart attacks.*
insurance policy *n* a contract of insurance.
insure *vb* **-suring, -sured 1** to guarantee or protect (against risk or loss). **2** (often foll. by *against*) to issue (a person) with an insurance policy or take out an insurance policy (on): *the players were insured against accidents.* **3** *Chiefly US* same as **ensure**. **insurable** *adj* **insurability** *n*
insured *n* **the insured** the person covered by an insurance policy.
insurer *n* a person or company that sells insurance.
insurgent *adj* **1** rebellious or in revolt against an established authority. ~*n* **2** a person who takes part in a rebellion. **insurgency** *n*
insurmountable *adj* impossible to overcome: *insurmountable problems.*
insurrection *n* the act of rebelling against an established authority. **insurrectionist** *n, adj*
int. **1** internal. **2** Also: **Int** international.
intact *adj* not changed or damaged in any way.
intaglio (in-**tah**-lee-oh) *n, pl* **-lios** *or* **-li 1** a seal or gem decorated with an engraved design. **2** an engraved design. **intagliated** *adj*
intake *n* **1** a thing or a quantity taken in: *an intake of students.* **2** the act of taking in. **3** the opening through which fluid or gas enters a pipe or engine.
intangible *adj* **1** difficult for the mind to grasp: *intangible ideas.* **2** incapable of being felt by touch. **intangibility** *n*
integer *n* any positive or negative whole number or zero, as opposed to a number with fractions or decimals.
integral *adj* **1** being an essential part of a whole. **2** whole or complete. **3** *Maths* **a** of or involving an integral. **b** involving or being an integer. ~*n* **4** *Maths* the sum of a large number of minute quantities, summed either between stated limits (**definite integral**) or in the absence of limits (**indefinite integral**).
integral calculus *n Maths* the branch of calculus concerned with the determination of integrals and their use in solving differential equations.
integrand *n Maths* a mathematical function to be integrated.
integrate *vb* **-grating, -grated 1** to make or be made into a whole. **2** to amalgamate (a racial or religious group) with an existing community. **3** to designate (an institution) for use by all races or groups. **4** *Maths* to determine the integral of a function or variable. **integration** *n*
integrated circuit *n* a tiny electronic circuit on a silicon chip.
integrity *n* **1** honesty. **2** the quality of being whole or united: *respect for a state's territorial integrity.* **3** the quality of being unharmed or sound: *the integrity of the cell membrane.*
integument *n* any natural protective covering, such as a skin, rind, or shell.

THESAURUS

insufficient deficient, inadequate, incapable, incommensurate, incompetent, lacking, scant, short, unfitted, unqualified
insular *figurative* blinkered, circumscribed, closed, contracted, cut off, illiberal, inward-looking, isolated, limited, narrow, narrow-minded, parish-pump, parochial, petty, prejudiced, provincial
insulate *figurative* close off, cocoon, cushion, cut off, isolate, protect, sequester, shield, wrap up in cotton wool
insult **1.** *vb.* abuse, affront, call names, give offence to, injure, miscall (*dialect*), offend, outrage, put down, revile, slag (off) (*slang*), slander, slight, snub **2.** *n.* abuse, affront, aspersion, contumely, indignity, insolence, offence, outrage, put-down, rudeness, slap in the face (*informal*), slight, snub
insuperable impassable, insurmountable, invincible, unconquerable
insupportable **1.** insufferable, intolerable, past bearing, unbearable, unendurable **2.** indefensible, unjustifiable, untenable
insurance assurance, cover, coverage, guarantee, indemnification, indemnity, protection, provision, safeguard, security, something to fall back on (*informal*), warranty
insure assure, cover, guarantee, indemnify, underwrite, warrant
insurgent **1.** *adj.* disobedient, insubordinate, insurrectionary, mutinous, rebellious, revolting, revolutionary, riotous, seditious **2.** *n.* insurrectionist, mutineer, rebel, resister, revolter, revolutionary, revolutionist, rioter
insurmountable hopeless, impassable, impossible, insuperable, invincible, overwhelming, unconquerable
insurrection coup, insurgency, mutiny, putsch, rebellion, revolt, revolution, riot, rising, sedition, uprising
intact all in one piece, complete, entire, perfect, scatheless, sound, together, unbroken, undamaged, undefiled, unharmed, unhurt, unimpaired, uninjured, unscathed, untouched, unviolated, virgin, whole
integral **1.** basic, component, constituent, elemental, essential, fundamental, indispensable, intrinsic, necessary, requisite **2.** complete, entire, full, intact, undivided, whole
integrate accommodate, amalgamate, assimilate, blend, coalesce, combine, fuse, harmonize, incorporate, intermix, join, knit, meld, merge, mesh, unite
integration amalgamation, assimilation, blending, combining, commingling, fusing, harmony, incorporation, mixing, unification
integrity **1.** candour, goodness, honesty, honour, incorruptibility, principle, probity, purity, rectitude,

intellect *n* **1** the ability to understand, think, and reason. **2** a particular person's mind or intelligence, esp. a brilliant one: *his intellect is wasted on that job.* **3** *Informal* a person who has a brilliant mind.

intellectual *adj* **1** of, involving, or appealing to the intellect: *intellectual literature.* **2** clever or intelligent. ~*n* **3** a person who has a highly developed intellect. **intellectuality** *n* **intellectually** *adv*

intelligence *n* **1** the ability to understand, learn, and think things out quickly. **2** the collection of secret information, esp. for military purposes. **3** a group or department collecting military information. **4** *Old-fashioned* news or information.

intelligence quotient *n* a measure of the intelligence of a person calculated by dividing the person's mental age by his or her actual age and multiplying the result by 100.

intelligent *adj* **1** having or showing intelligence: *an intelligent child; an intelligent guess.* **2** (of a computerized device) able to initiate or modify action in the light of ongoing events. **intelligently** *adv*

intelligentsia *n* **the intelligentsia** the educated or intellectual people in a society.

intelligible *adj* able to be understood. **intelligibility** *n*

intemperate *adj* **1** unrestrained or uncontrolled: *intemperate remarks.* **2** drinking alcohol too much or too often. **3** extreme or severe: *an intemperate climate.* **intemperance** *n*

intend *vb* **1** to propose or plan (something or to do something). **2** have as one's purpose. **3** to mean to express or indicate: *no criticism was intended.* **4** (often foll. by *for*) to design or destine (for a certain purpose or person): *the plane was never intended for combat.*

intended *adj* **1** planned or future. ~*n* **2** *Informal* a person whom one is to marry.

intense *adj* **1** of very great force, strength, degree, or amount: *intense heat.* **2** characterized by deep or forceful feelings: *an intense person.* **intensely** *adv* **intenseness** *n*

intensifier *n* a word, esp. an adjective or adverb, that intensifies the meaning of the word or phrase that it modifies, for example, *very* or *extremely.*

intensify *vb* **-fies, -fying, -fied** to make or become intense or more intense. **intensification** *n*

intensity *n, pl* **-ties 1** the state or quality of being intense. **2** extreme force, degree, or amount. **3** *Physics* the amount or degree of strength of electricity, heat, light, or sound per unit area of volume.

intensive *adj* **1** of or needing concentrated effort or resources: *intensive training.* **2** using one specified factor more than others: *labour-intensive.* **3** *Agriculture* designed to increase production from a particular area: *intensive farming.* **4** *Grammar* of a word giving emphasis, for example, *very* in *the very same.* **intensively** *adv* **intensiveness** *n*

intensive care *n* thorough, continuously supervised treatment of an acutely ill patient in a hospital.

intent *n* **1** something that is intended. **2** *Law* the will or purpose to commit a crime: *loitering with intent.* **3 to all intents and purposes** in almost every respect; virtually. ~*adj* **4** having one's attention firmly fixed: *an intent look.* **5 intent on** *or* **upon** strongly resolved on: *intent on winning the election.* **intently** *adv* **intentness** *n*

THESAURUS

righteousness, uprightness, virtue **2.** coherence, cohesion, completeness, soundness, unity, wholeness

intellect 1. brains (*informal*), intelligence, judgment, mind, reason, sense, understanding **2.** *informal* brain (*informal*), egghead (*informal*), genius, intellectual, intelligence, mind, thinker

intellectual 1. *adj.* bookish, cerebral, highbrow, intelligent, mental, rational, scholarly, studious, thoughtful **2.** *n.* academic, egghead (*informal*), highbrow, thinker

intelligence 1. acumen, alertness, aptitude, brain power, brains (*informal*), brightness, capacity, cleverness, comprehension, discernment, grey matter (*informal*), intellect, mind, nous (*Brit. slang*), penetration, perception, quickness, reason, smarts (*slang, chiefly U.S.*), understanding **2.** advice, data, disclosure, facts, findings, gen (*Brit. informal*), information, knowledge, low-down (*informal*), news, notice, notification, report, rumour, tidings, tip-off, word

intelligent acute, alert, apt, brainy (*informal*), bright, clever, discerning, enlightened, instructed, knowing, penetrating, perspicacious, quick, quick-witted, rational, sharp, smart, thinking, well-informed

intelligentsia the intelligentsia eggheads (*informal*), highbrows, illuminati, intellectuals, literati, masterminds, the learned

intelligibility clarity, clearness, comprehensibility, distinctness, explicitness, lucidity, plainness, precision, simplicity

intelligible clear, comprehensible, distinct, lucid, open, plain, understandable

intemperate excessive, extravagant, extreme, immoderate, incontinent, inordinate, intoxicated, OTT (*slang*), over the top (*slang*), passionate, prodigal, profligate, self-indulgent, severe, tempestuous, unbridled, uncontrollable, ungovernable, unrestrained, violent, wild

intend 1. aim, be resolved *or* determined, contemplate, determine, have in mind *or* view, mean, meditate, plan, propose, purpose, scheme **2.** *often with* **for** aim, consign, design, destine, earmark, mark out, mean, set apart

intense 1. acute, agonizing, close, concentrated, deep, drastic, excessive, exquisite, extreme, fierce, forceful, great, harsh, intensive, powerful, profound, protracted, severe, strained, unqualified **2.** ardent, burning, consuming, eager, earnest, energetic, fanatical, fervent, fervid, fierce, flaming, forcible, heightened, impassioned, keen, passionate, speaking, vehement

intensely deeply, extremely, fiercely, passionately, profoundly, strongly

intensify add fuel to the flames (*informal*), add to, aggravate, augment, boost, concentrate, deepen, emphasize, enhance, escalate, exacerbate, heighten, increase, magnify, quicken, redouble, reinforce, set off, sharpen, step up (*informal*), strengthen, whet

intensity ardour, concentration, depth, earnestness, emotion, energy, excess, extremity, fanaticism, fervency, fervour, fierceness, fire, force, intenseness, keenness, passion, potency, power, severity, strain, strength, tension, vehemence, vigour

intensive all-out, comprehensive, concentrated, demanding, exhaustive, in-depth, thorough, thorough-going

intent *n.* **1.** aim, design, end, goal, intention, meaning, object, objective, plan, purpose **2. to all intents and purposes** as good as, practically, virtually ~*adj.* **3.** absorbed, alert, attentive, committed, concentrated, determined, eager, earnest, engrossed, fixed, industrious, intense, occupied, piercing, preoccupied, rapt, resolute, resolved, steadfast, steady, watchful, wrapped up **4.** *with* **on** *or* **upon** bent, hellbent (*informal*), set

intention aim, design, end, end in view, goal, idea, in-

intention *n* something intended; a plan, idea, or purpose: *he had no intention of resigning.*

intentional *adj* done on purpose. **intentionally** *adv*

inter (in-ter) *vb* **-terring, -terred** to bury (a corpse).

inter- *prefix* 1 between or among: *international.* 2 together, mutually, or reciprocally: *interdependent.*

interact *vb* to act on or in close relation with each other. **interaction** *n* **interactive** *adj*

inter alia (in-ter ale-ya) *adv* among other things.

interbreed *vb* **-breeding, -bred** 1 to breed within a related group so as to produce particular characteristics in the offspring. 2 same as **crossbreed** (sense 1).

intercede *vb* **-ceding, -ceded** 1 to plead in favour of. 2 to act as a mediator in order to end a disagreement: *Egypt interceded in the confrontation between Iraq and Israel.*

intercept *vb* 1 to stop or seize on the way from one place to another. 2 *Maths* to mark off or include (part of a line, curve, plane, or surface) between two points or lines. *~n* 3 *Maths* **a** a point at which two figures intersect. **b** the distance from the origin to the point at which a line, curve, or surface cuts a coordinate axis. **interception** *n* **interceptor** *n*

intercession *n* 1 the act of interceding. 2 a prayer offered to God on behalf of others. **intercessor** *n*

interchange *vb* **-changing, -changed** 1 to change places or cause to change places. *~n* 2 the act of interchanging. 3 a motorway junction of interconnecting roads and bridges designed to prevent streams of traffic crossing one another. **interchangeable** *adj* **interchangeably** *adv*

intercom *n* an internal communication system with loudspeakers.

intercommunicate *vb* **-cating, -cated** 1 to communicate mutually. 2 (of two rooms) to interconnect. **intercommunication** *n*

intercommunion *n* association between Churches, involving mutual reception of Holy Communion.

interconnect *vb* to connect with one another. **interconnected** *adj* **interconnection** *n*

intercontinental *adj* travelling between or linking continents.

intercourse *n* 1 the act of having sex. 2 communication or dealings between individuals or groups.

interdenominational *adj* among or involving more than one denomination of the Christian Church.

interdepartmental *adj* of or between different departments.

interdependent *adj* dependent on one another. **interdependence** *n*

interdict *n* 1 *Law* an official prohibition or restraint. 2 *RC Church* the exclusion of a person or place from certain sacraments, although not from communion. *~vb* 3 to prohibit or forbid. **interdiction** *n* **interdictory** *adj*

interdisciplinary *adj* involving more than one branch of learning.

interest *n* 1 curiosity or concern about something or someone. 2 the power of causing this: *to have great interest.* 3 something in which one is interested; a hobby or pursuit. 4 (*often pl*) advantage: *in one's own interests.* 5 money paid for the use of credit or borrowed money: *she borrowed money at 25 per cent interest.* 6 (*often pl*) a right, share, or claim, esp. in a business or property. 7 (*often pl*) a group of people with common aims: *foreign interests.* *~vb* 8 to arouse the curiosity or concern of. 9 to cause to become interested or involved in something.

interested *adj* 1 showing or having interest. 2 involved in or affected by: *a consultation paper sent to interested parties.*

interesting *adj* causing interest. **interestingly** *adv*

interface *n* 1 an area where two things interact or link: *the interface between Islamic culture and Western modernity.* 2 an electrical circuit linking one device, esp. a computer, with another. 3 *Physics, chem* a surface that forms the boundary between two liquids or chemical phases that cannot be mixed. *~vb* **-facing, -faced** 4 to connect or be connected with by interface.

interfacing *n* 1 a piece of fabric sewn beneath the facing of a garment to give shape and firmness. 2 same as **interlining.**

interfere *vb* **-fering, -fered** 1 to try to influence other people's affairs where one is not involved or wanted. 2 **interfere with a** to clash with or hinder.

THESAURUS

tent, meaning, object, objective, point, purpose, scope, target, view

intentional calculated, deliberate, designed, done on purpose, intended, meant, planned, prearranged, preconcerted, premeditated, purposed, studied, wilful

intentionally by design, deliberately, designedly, on purpose, wilfully

intently attentively, closely, fixedly, hard, keenly, searchingly, steadily, watchfully

inter bury, entomb, inhume, inurn, lay to rest, sepulchre

intercede advocate, arbitrate, interpose, intervene, mediate, plead, speak

intercept arrest, block, catch, check, cut off, deflect, head off, interrupt, obstruct, seize, stop, take

intercession advocacy, entreaty, good offices, intervention, mediation, plea, pleading, prayer, solicitation, supplication

interchange 1. *vb.* alternate, bandy, barter, exchange, reciprocate, swap (*informal*), switch, trade 2. *n.* alternation, crossfire, exchange, give and take, intersection, junction, reciprocation

interchangeable commutable, equivalent, exchangeable, identical, reciprocal, synonymous, the same, transposable

intercourse 1. carnal knowledge, coition, coitus, copulation, intimacy, sex (*informal*), sexual act, sexual intercourse, sexual relations 2. association, commerce, communication, communion, connection, contact, converse, correspondence, dealings, intercommunication, trade, traffic, truck

interest *n.* 1. affection, attention, attentiveness, attraction, concern, curiosity, notice, regard, suspicion, sympathy 2. concern, consequence, importance, moment, note, relevance, significance, weight 3. activity, diversion, hobby, leisure activity, pastime, preoccupation, pursuit, relaxation 4. *often plural* advantage, benefit, gain, good, profit 5. authority, claim, commitment, influence, investment, involvement, participation, portion, right, share, stake 6. *often plural* affair, business, care, concern, matter *~vb.* 7. amuse, arouse one's curiosity, attract, divert, engross, fascinate, hold the attention of, intrigue, move, touch 8. affect, concern, engage, involve

interested 1. affected, attentive, attracted, curious, drawn, excited, fascinated, intent, into (*informal*), keen, moved, responsive, stimulated 2. biased, concerned, implicated, involved, partial, partisan, predisposed, prejudiced

interesting absorbing, amusing, appealing, attractive, compelling, curious, engaging, engrossing, entertaining, gripping, intriguing, pleasing, provocative, stimulating, suspicious, thought-provoking, unusual

interfere 1. butt in, get involved, intervene, intrude, meddle, poke one's nose in (*informal*), stick one's oar

child-bearing may interfere with your career. **b** *Euphemistic* to abuse sexually. **3** *Physics* to produce or cause to produce interference. **interfering** *adj*

interference *n* **1** the act of interfering. **2** any undesired signal that interferes with the reception of radio waves. **3** *Physics* the meeting of two waves which reinforce or neutralize each other depending on whether they are in or out of phase.

interferon *n Biochem* a protein made by cells that stops the development of an invading virus.

interfuse *vb* **-fusing, -fused 1** to mix or become mixed. **2** to blend or fuse together. **interfusion** *n*

intergalactic *adj* occurring or located between different galaxies.

interim *adj* **1** temporary or provisional: *an interim government.* ~*n* **2 in the interim** during the intervening time.

interior *n* **1** a part or region that is on the inside: *the interior of the earth.* **2** the inside of a building or room, with respect to design and decoration. **3** the central area of a country or continent, furthest from the sea. **4** a picture of the inside of a room or building. ~*adj* **5** of, situated on, or suitable for the inside. **6** mental or spiritual: *interior development.* **7** coming or acting from within. **8** of a nation's domestic affairs.

interior angle *n* an angle of a polygon contained between two adjacent sides.

interior decoration *n* **1** the decoration and furnishings of the interior of a room or house. **2** Also called: **interior design** the art or business of planning this. **interior decorator** *n*

interj. interjection.

interject *vb* to make (a remark) suddenly or as an interruption.

interjection *n* a word or phrase which is used on its own and which expresses sudden emotion.

interlace *vb* **-lacing, -laced** to join by lacing or weaving together: *interlaced fingers.*

interlard *vb* to insert in or occur throughout: *to interlard one's writing with foreign phrases.*

interlay *vb* **-laying, -laid** to insert (layers) between: *to interlay gold among the silver.*

interleaf *n, pl* **-leaves** an extra leaf which is inserted.

interleave *vb* **-leaving, -leaved** to insert, as blank leaves in a book, between other leaves.

interleukin (in-ter-**loo**-kin) *n Biochem* a substance obtained from white blood cells that stimulates their activity against infection and may by used to fight some forms of cancer.

interline[1] *vb* **-lining, -lined** to write or print (matter) between the lines of (a text or book).

interline[2] *vb* **-lining, -lined** to provide (a part of a garment) with a second lining.

interlining *n* the material used to interline parts of garments.

interlink *vb* to connect together.

interlock *vb* **1** to join or be joined firmly together. ~*n* **2** a device used to prevent a mechanism from operating independently or unsafely.

interlocutor (in-ter-**lock**-yew-ter) *n Formal* a person who takes part in a conversation.

interlocutory (in-ter-**lock**-yew-tree) *adj* **1** *Law* pronounced during the course of legal proceedings; provisional: *an interlocutory injunction.* **2** *Formal* of dialogue; conversational.

interloper (**in**-ter-lope-er) *n* a person in a place or situation where he or she has no right to be.

interlude *n* **1** a period of time or different activity between longer periods or events. **2 a** a pause between the acts of a play. **b** a brief piece of music or other entertainment performed during this pause.

intermarry *vb* **-ries, -rying, -ried 1** (of different races, religions, or social groups) to become connected by marriage. **2** to marry within one's own family or tribe. **intermarriage** *n*

intermediary *n, pl* **-aries 1** a person who tries to bring about agreement between others. **2** a messenger. ~*adj* **3** acting as an intermediary. **4** intermediate.

intermediate *adj* **1** occurring between two points or extremes. ~*n* **2** something intermediate. **3** *Chem* a substance formed between the first and final stages of a chemical process. **intermediation** *n*

interment *n* a burial.

intermezzo (in-ter-**met**-so) *n, pl* **-zos** *or* **-zi 1** a short piece of instrumental music performed between the acts of a play or opera. **2 a** a short composition between two longer movements in an extended musical work. **b** a similar composition intended for independent performance.

interminable *adj* seemingly endless because boring: *an interminable, rambling anecdote.* **interminably** *adv*

intermingle *vb* **-gling, -gled** to mix together.

intermission *n* an interval between parts of a play, film, etc.

intermittent *adj* occurring at intervals. **intermittently** *adv*

THESAURUS

in (*informal*), tamper **2. interfere with** be a drag upon (*informal*), block, clash, collide, conflict, cramp, frustrate, get in the way of, hamper, handicap, hinder, impede, inhibit, obstruct, trammel

interference clashing, collision, conflict, impedance, intermeddling, intervention, intrusion, meddlesomeness, meddling, obstruction, opposition, prying

interim 1. *adj.* acting, caretaker, improvised, intervening, makeshift, pro tem, provisional, stopgap, temporary **2.** *n.* interregnum, interval, meantime, meanwhile, respite

interior *n.* **1.** bosom, centre, contents, core, heart, innards (*informal*), inside **2.** *Geog.* centre, heartland, upcountry ~*adj.* **3.** inner, inside, internal, inward **4.** *Geog.* central, inland, remote, upcountry **5.** hidden, inner, intimate, mental, personal, private, secret, spiritual **6.** *Politics* domestic, home

interjection cry, ejaculation, exclamation, interpolation, interposition

interloper gate-crasher (*informal*), intermeddler, intruder, meddler, trespasser, uninvited guest, unwanted visitor

interlude break, breathing space, delay, episode, halt, hiatus, intermission, interval, pause, respite, rest, spell, stop, stoppage, wait

intermediary *n.* agent, broker, entrepreneur, go-between, mediator, middleman

intermediate halfway, in-between (*informal*), intermediary, interposed, intervening, mean, mid, middle, midway, transitional

interment burial, burying, funeral, inhumation, sepulture

interminable boundless, ceaseless, dragging, endless, everlasting, immeasurable, infinite, limitless, long, long-drawn-out, long-winded, never-ending, perpetual, protracted, unbounded, unlimited, wearisome

intermingle amalgamate, blend, combine, commingle, fuse, interlace, intermix, interweave, meld, merge, mix

intermission break, cessation, interlude, interrup-

intern *vb* **1** to imprison, esp. during wartime. ~*n* **2** *Chiefly US* a trainee doctor in a hospital. **internment** *n*

internal *adj* **1** of, situated on, or suitable for the inside. **2** *Anat* affecting or relating to the inside of the body: *internal bleeding*. **3** of a nation's domestic affairs: *internal politics*. **4** coming or acting from within an organization: *an internal reorganization*. **5** spiritual or mental: *internal conflict*. **internally** *adv*

internal-combustion engine *n* an engine in which power is produced by the explosion of a fuel-and-air mixture within the cylinders.

international *adj* **1** of or involving two or more nations. **2** controlling or legislating for several nations: *an international court*. **3** available for use by all nations: *international waters*. ~*n* **4** *Sport* **a** a game or match between the national teams of different countries. **b** a member of a national team. **internationally** *adv*

International *n* any of several international socialist organizations.

International Date Line *n* the line approximately following the 180° meridian from Greenwich on the east side of which the date is one day earlier than on the west.

internationalism *n* the ideal or practice of cooperation and understanding for the good of all nations. **internationalist** *n*

International Phonetic Alphabet *n* a series of signs and letters for the representation of human speech sounds.

internecine *adj Formal* destructive to both sides: *internecine war*.

internee *n* a person who is interned.

internist *n* a physician who specializes in internal medicine.

interpenetrate *vb* **-trating, -trated 1** to penetrate (something) thoroughly. **2** to penetrate each other or one another mutually. **interpenetration** *n*

interpersonal *n* of or relating to relationship between people: *interpersonal conflict at work*.

interplanetary *adj* of or linking planets.

interplay *n* the action and reaction of things upon each other.

Interpol International Criminal Police Organization: an association of over 100 national police forces, devoted chiefly to fighting international crime.

interpolate (in-ter-pole-ate) *vb* **-lating, -lated 1** to insert (a comment or passage) into (a conversation or text). **2** *Maths* to estimate (a value of a function) between the values already known. **interpolation** *n*

interpose *vb* **-posing, -posed 1** to place (something) between or among other things. **2** to interrupt (with comments or questions). **3** to put forward so as to interrupt: *he ended the discussion by interposing a veto*. **interposition** *n*

interpret *vb* **1** to explain the meaning of. **2** to work out the significance of: *his remarks were widely interpreted as a promise not to raise taxes*. **3** to convey the meaning of (a poem, song, etc.) in performance. **4** to act as an interpreter. **interpretive** *adj*

interpretation *n* **1** the act or result of interpreting or explaining. **2** the particular way in which a performer expresses his or her view of a composition: *an interpretation of Mahler's fourth symphony*. **3** explanation, as of a historical site, provided by the use of original objects, visual display material, etc.

interpreter *n* **1** a person who translates orally from one language into another. **2** *Computers* a program that translates a statement in a source program to machine language and executes it before translating and executing the next statement.

interpretive centre *n* a building situated at a place of interest, such as a country park or historical site, that provides information about the site by showing videos, exhibiting objects, etc.

interracial *adj* between or among people of different races.

interregnum *n, pl* **-nums** *or* **-na** a period between the end of one ruler's reign and the beginning of the next. **interregnal** *adj*

interrelate *vb* **-lating, -lated** to connect (two or more things) or (of two or more things) to become connected to each other. **interrelation** *n* **interrelationship** *n*

interrogate *vb* **-gating, -gated** to question (someone) closely. **interrogation** *n* **interrogator** *n*

interrogative (in-ter-rog-a-tiv) *adj* **1** used in asking a question: *an interrogative pronoun*. **2** of or like a question: *an interrogative look*. ~*n* **3** an interrogative word, phrase, sentence, or construction.

interrogatory (in-ter-rog-a-tree) *adj* **1** expressing or involving a question. ~*n, pl* **-tories 2** a question or interrogation.

interrupt *vb* **1** to break into (a conversation or discussion) by questions or comment. **2** to stop (a pro-

THESAURUS

tion, interval, let-up (*informal*), lull, pause, recess, respite, rest, stop, stoppage, suspense, suspension

intermittent broken, discontinuous, fitful, irregular, occasional, periodic, punctuated, recurrent, recurring, spasmodic, sporadic, stop-go (*informal*)

intern confine, detain, hold, hold in custody

internal 1. inner, inside, interior, intimate, private, subjective 2. civic, domestic, home, in-house, intramural

international cosmopolitan, ecumenical (*rare*), global, intercontinental, universal, worldwide

interpolate add, insert, intercalate, introduce

interpolation addition, aside, insert, insertion, intercalation, interjection, introduction

interpose 1. come *or* place between, intercede, interfere, intermediate, intervene, intrude, mediate, step in 2. insert, interject, interrupt (with), introduce, put forth

interpret adapt, clarify, construe, decipher, decode, define, elucidate, explain, explicate, expound, make sense of, paraphrase, read, render, solve, spell out, take, throw light on, translate, understand

interpretation analysis, clarification, construction, diagnosis, elucidation, exegesis, explanation, explication, exposition, meaning, performance, portrayal, reading, rendering, rendition, sense, signification, translation, understanding, version

interpreter annotator, commentator, exponent, scholiast, translator

interrogate ask, catechize, cross-examine, cross-question, enquire, examine, give (someone) the third degree (*informal*), grill (*informal*), inquire, investigate, pump, put the screws on (*informal*), question, quiz

interrogation cross-examination, cross-questioning, enquiry, examination, grilling (*informal*), inquiry, inquisition, probing, questioning, third degree (*informal*)

interrogative curious, inquiring, inquisitive, inquisitorial, questioning, quizzical

interrupt barge in (*informal*), break, break in, break off, break (someone's) train of thought, check, cut, cut off, cut short, delay, disconnect, discontinue, disjoin, disturb, disunite, divide, hinder, hold up, interfere

cess or activity) temporarily. **interrupted** *adj* **interruptive** *adj*

interrupter *or* **interruptor** *n* a device for opening and closing an electric circuit.

interruption *n* **1** something that interrupts, such as a comment or question. **2** an interval or intermission. **3** the act of interrupting or the state of being interrupted.

interscholastic *adj* occurring between two or more schools: *an interscholastic competition.*

intersect *vb* **1** (of roads or lines) to cross (each other). **2** to divide or mark off (a place, area, or surface) by passing through or across.

intersection *n* **1** a point at which things intersect, esp. a road junction. **2** the act of intersecting or the state of being intersected. **3** *Maths* **a** a point or set of points common to two or more geometric figures. **b** the set of elements that are common to two sets. **intersectional** *adj*

intersperse *vb* **-spersing, -spersed 1** to scatter among, between, or on. **2** to mix (something) with other things scattered here and there. **interspersion** *n*

interstellar *adj* between or among stars.

interstice (in-ter-stiss) *n* (*usually pl*) **1** a small gap or crack between things. **2** *Physics* the space between adjacent atoms in a crystal lattice.

intertwine *vb* **-twining, -twined** to twist together.

interval *n* **1** the period of time between two events. **2** *Brit* a short period between parts of a play, concert, etc. **3** *Music* the difference of pitch between two notes. **4 at intervals a** now and then: *turn the chicken at intervals.* **b** with a certain amount of space between: *the poles were placed at intervals of twenty metres.*

intervene *vb* **-vening, -vened 1** (often foll. by *in*) to involve oneself in a situation, esp. to prevent conflict. **2** to interrupt a conversation. **3** to happen so as to stop something: *he hoped to play but a serious injury intervened.* **4** to come or be among or between: *ten years had intervened since he had seen Joe.*

intervention *n* the act of intervening, esp. to influence or alter a situation in some way. **interventionist** *n, adj*

interview *n* **1** a formal discussion, esp. one in which an employer assesses a job applicant. **2** a conversation in which a well-known person is asked about his or her views, career, etc., by a reporter. *~vb* **3** to question (someone). **interviewee** *n* **interviewer** *n*

interwar *adj* of or happening in the period between World War I and World War II.

interweave *vb* **-weaving, -wove** *or* **-weaved, -woven** *or* **-weaved** to weave together.

intestate *adj* **1** (of a person) not having made a will. *~n* **2** a person who dies without having made a will. **intestacy** *n*

intestine *n* the part of the alimentary canal between the stomach and the anus. See **large intestine, small intestine. intestinal** *adj*

intifada (in-tiff-**ah**-da) *n* the Palestinian uprising against Israel in the West Bank and Gaza Strip.

intimacy *n, pl* **-cies 1** close or warm friendship. **2** (*often pl*) intimate words or acts within a close relationship.

intimate[1] *adj* **1** characterized by a close or warm personal relationship: *an intimate friend.* **2** deeply personal, private, or secret. **3** (of knowledge) extensive and detailed. **4** *Euphemistic* having sexual relations. **5** having a friendly quiet atmosphere: *an intimate nightclub.* *~n* **6** a close friend. **intimately** *adv*

intimate[2] *vb* **-mating, -mated** *Formal* **1** to make (something) known in an indirect way: *he has intimated his intention to retire.* **2** to announce. **intimation** *n*

intimidate *vb* **-dating, -dated** to subdue or influence

THESAURUS

(with), intrude, lay aside, obstruct, punctuate, separate, sever, stay, stop, suspend

interrupted broken, cut off, disconnected, discontinuous, disturbed, incomplete, intermittent, uneven

interruption break, cessation, disconnection, discontinuance, disruption, dissolution, disturbance, disuniting, division, halt, hiatus, hindrance, hitch, impediment, intrusion, obstacle, obstruction, pause, separation, severance, stop, stoppage, suspension

intersect bisect, crisscross, cross, cut, cut across, divide, meet

intersection crossing, crossroads, interchange, junction

interval break, delay, distance, entr'acte, gap, hiatus, interim, interlude, intermission, meantime, meanwhile, opening, pause, period, playtime, respite, rest, season, space, spell, term, time, wait

intervene 1. arbitrate, intercede, interfere, interpose oneself, intrude, involve oneself, mediate, step in (*informal*), take a hand (*informal*) **2.** befall, come to pass, ensue, happen, occur, succeed, supervene, take place

intervention agency, intercession, interference, interposition, intrusion, mediation

interview 1. *n.* audience, conference, consultation, dialogue, evaluation, meeting, oral (examination), press conference, talk **2.** *vb.* examine, interrogate, question, sound out, talk to

interviewer examiner, interlocutor, interrogator, investigator, questioner, reporter

interwoven blended, connected, entwined, inmixed, interconnected, interlaced, interlocked, intermingled, knit

intestinal abdominal, coeliac, duodenal, gut (*informal*), inner, stomachic, visceral

intimacy closeness, confidence, confidentiality, familiarity, fraternization, understanding

intimate[1] *adj.* **1.** bosom, cherished, close, confidential, dear, friendly, near, nearest and dearest, thick (*informal*), warm **2.** confidential, personal, private, privy, secret **3.** deep, detailed, exhaustive, experienced, first-hand, immediate, in-depth, penetrating, personal, profound, thorough **4.** comfy (*informal*), cosy, friendly, informal, snug, tête-à-tête, warm *~n.* **5.** bosom friend, buddy (*informal*), china (*Brit. & S African informal*), chum (*informal*), close friend, cock (*Brit. informal*), comrade, confidant, confidante, (constant) companion, crony, familiar, friend, mate (*informal*), pal

intimate[2] *vb.* allude, announce, communicate, declare, drop a hint, give (someone) to understand, hint, impart, imply, indicate, insinuate, let it be known, make known, remind, state, suggest, tip (someone) the wink (*Brit. informal*), warn

intimately 1. affectionately, closely, confidentially, confidingly, familiarly, personally, tenderly, very well, warmly **2.** fully, in detail, inside out, thoroughly, through and through, to the core, very well

intimation 1. allusion, hint, indication, inkling, insinuation, reminder, suggestion, warning **2.** announcement, communication, declaration, notice

intimidate alarm, appal, browbeat, bully, coerce, cow, daunt, dishearten, dismay, dispirit, frighten, lean on (*informal*), overawe, scare, scare off (*informal*), subdue, terrify, terrorize, threaten, twist someone's arm (*informal*)

(someone) through fear. **intimidating** *adj* **intimidation** *n*

into *prep* **1** to the inner part of: *they went into the house.* **2** to the middle of so as to be surrounded by: *into the bushes.* **3** against; up against: *he drove into a wall.* **4** used to indicate the result of a change: *they turned the theatre into a garage.* **5** *Maths* used to indicate division: *three into six is two.* **6** *Informal* interested in: *I'm really into healthy food.*

intolerable *adj* more than can be endured. **intolerably** *adv*

intolerant *adj* refusing to accept practices and beliefs that differ from one's own. **intolerance** *n*

intonation *n* **1** the sound pattern produced by variations in the voice. **2** the act of intoning. **3** *Music* the ability to play or sing in tune. **intonational** *adj*

intone *vb* **-toning, -toned 1** to speak or recite in a monotonous tone. **2** to speak with a particular tone.

in toto *adv* totally or entirely.

intoxicant *n* **1** something, such as an alcoholic drink, that causes intoxication. *~adj* **2** causing intoxication.

intoxicate *vb* **-cating, -cated 1** (of an alcoholic drink) to make (a person) drunk. **2** to stimulate or excite to a point beyond self-control. **intoxicated** *adj* **intoxicating** *adj*

intoxication *n* **1** the state of being drunk. **2** great excitement and exhilaration.

intractable *adj* **1** (of a person) difficult to influence or direct. **2** (of a problem or illness) difficult to solve or cure. **intractability** *n* **intractably** *adv*

intramural *adj Chiefly US & Canad* operating within or involving those within a school or college: *intramural sports.*

intransigent *adj* **1** refusing to change one's attitude. *~n* **2** an intransigent person, esp. in politics. **intransigence** *n*

intransitive *adj* (of a verb) not taking a direct object. **intransitively** *adv*

intrapreneur *n* a person who while remaining within a larger organization uses entrepreneurial skills to develop new services or systems as a subsidiary of the organization.

intrauterine *adj* situated within the womb.

intrauterine device *n* a contraceptive device in the shape of a coil, inserted into the womb.

intravenous (in-tra-vee-nuss) *adj Anat* into a vein: *intravenous drug users.* **intravenously** *adv*

in-tray *n* a tray used in offices for incoming letters or documents requiring attention.

intrepid *adj* fearless or bold. **intrepidity** *n* **intrepidly** *adv*

intricate *adj* **1** difficult to sort out: *an intricate problem.* **2** full of complicated detail: *intricate Arab mosaics.* **intricacy** *n* **intricately** *adv*

intrigue *vb* **-triguing, -trigued 1** to make interested or curious: *a question which has intrigued him for years.* **2** to plot secretly or dishonestly. *~n* **3** secret plotting. **4** a secret love affair. **intriguing** *adj* **intriguingly** *adv*

intrinsic *adj* **1** essential to the real nature of a thing: *hedgerows are an intrinsic part of the countryside.* **2** *Anat* situated within or peculiar to a part: *intrinsic muscles.* **intrinsically** *adv*

intro *n, pl* **-tros** *Informal* short for **introduction.**

introduce *vb* **-ducing, -duced 1** to present (someone) by name (to another person). **2** to present (a radio or television programme). **3** to present for consideration or approval: *he introduced the bill to Parliament in 1967.* **4** to bring into use: *Latvia has introduced its own rouble into circulation.* **5 introduce to** to cause to experience for the first time: *his father introduced him to golf.* **6** to insert. **7 introduce with**

THESAURUS

intimidation arm-twisting (*informal*), browbeating, bullying, coercion, fear, menaces, pressure, terror, terrorization, threat(s)

intolerable beyond bearing, excruciating, impossible, insufferable, insupportable, more than flesh and blood can stand, not to be borne, painful, unbearable, unendurable

intolerance bigotry, chauvinism, discrimination, dogmatism, fanaticism, illiberality, impatience, jingoism, narrow-mindedness, narrowness, prejudice, racialism, racism, xenophobia

intolerant bigoted, chauvinistic, dictatorial, dogmatic, fanatical, illiberal, impatient, narrow, narrow-minded, one-sided, prejudiced, racialist, racist, small-minded, uncharitable, xenophobic

intone chant, croon, intonate, recite, sing

intoxicate 1. addle, befuddle, fuddle, go to one's head, inebriate, put (someone) under the table (*informal*), stupefy **2.** *figurative* elate, excite, exhilarate, inflame, make one's head spin, stimulate

intoxicated 1. blotto (*slang*), drunk, drunken, fuddled, high (*informal*), inebriated, legless (*slang*), paralytic (*Brit. informal*), pissed (*Brit. taboo slang*), plastered (*slang*), sozzled (*informal*), stewed (*slang*), stoned (*slang*), the worse for drink, tight (*informal*), tipsy, under the influence., zonked (*slang*) **2.** *figurative* dizzy, elated, enraptured, euphoric, excited, exhilarated, high (*informal*), infatuated, sent (*slang*), stimulated

intoxicating 1. alcoholic, inebriant, intoxicant, spirituous, strong **2.** *figurative* exciting, exhilarating, heady, sexy (*informal*), stimulating, thrilling

intoxication 1. drunkenness, inebriation, inebriety, insobriety, tipsiness **2.** *figurative* delirium, elation, euphoria, exaltation, excitement, exhilaration, infatuation

intransigent hardline, immovable, intractable, obdurate, obstinate, stiff-necked, stubborn, tenacious, tough, unbending, unbudgeable, uncompromising, unyielding

intrepid audacious, bold, brave, courageous, daring, dauntless, doughty, fearless, gallant, game (*informal*), heroic, lion-hearted, nerveless, plucky, resolute, stalwart, stouthearted, unafraid, undaunted, unflinching, valiant, valorous

intricacy complexity, complication, convolutions, elaborateness, entanglement, intricateness, involution, involvement, knottiness, obscurity

intricate baroque, Byzantine, complex, complicated, convoluted, difficult, elaborate, fancy, involved, knotty, labyrinthine, obscure, perplexing, rococo, sophisticated, tangled, tortuous

intrigue *vb.* **1.** arouse the curiosity of, attract, charm, fascinate, interest, pique, rivet, tickle one's fancy, titillate **2.** connive, conspire, machinate, manoeuvre, plot, scheme *~n.* **3.** cabal, chicanery, collusion, conspiracy, double-dealing, knavery, machination, manipulation, manoeuvre, plot, ruse, scheme, sharp practice, stratagem, trickery, wile **4.** affair, amour, intimacy, liaison, romance

intriguing beguiling, compelling, diverting, exciting, fascinating, interesting, tantalizing, titillating

intrinsic basic, built-in, central, congenital, constitutional, elemental, essential, fundamental, genuine, inborn, inbred, inherent, native, natural, radical, real, true, underlying

introduce 1. acquaint, do the honours, familiarize, make known, make the introduction, present **2.** begin,

to start: *he introduced his talk with some music.* **introducible** *adj*

introduction *n* **1** the act of introducing something or someone. **2** a preliminary part, as of a book or musical composition. **3** a book that explains the basic facts about a particular subject to a beginner. **4** a presentation of one person to another or others.

introductory *adj* serving as an introduction.

introit *n* **1** *RC Church* a short prayer said or sung as the celebrant is entering the sanctuary to celebrate Mass. **2** *Church of England* a hymn or psalm sung at the beginning of a service.

introspection *n* the examining of one's own thoughts, impressions, and feelings. **introspective** *adj*

introversion *n Psychol* the directing of interest inwards towards one's own thoughts and feelings rather than towards the external world or making social contacts.

introvert *adj* **1** shy and quiet. **2** *Psychol* concerned more with inner feelings than with external reality. *~n* **3** such a person. **introverted** *adj*

intrude *vb* **-truding, -truded** to come in or join in without being invited.

intruder *n* a person who enters a place without permission.

intrusion *n* **1** the act of intruding; an unwelcome visit, etc.: *an intrusion into her private life.* **2** *Geol* **a** the forcing of molten rock into spaces in the overlying strata. **b** molten rock formed in this way. **intrusive** *adj*

intrust *vb* same as **entrust.**

intuition *n* instinctive knowledge of or belief about something without conscious reasoning: *intuition told her something was wrong.* **intuitional** *adj*

intuitive *adj* of, possessing, or resulting from intuition: *an intuitive understanding.* **intuitively** *adv*

Inuit *n, pl* **-it** *or* **-its** an Eskimo of North America or Greenland.

Inuktitut *n* the language of the Inuit.

inundate *vb* **-dating, -dated 1** to cover completely with water. **2** to overwhelm, as if with a flood: *the police were inundated with calls.* **inundation** *n*

inured *adj* able to tolerate something unpleasant because one has become accustomed to it: *he became inured to the casual brutality of his captors.* **inurement** *n*

invade *vb* **-vading, -vaded 1** to enter (a country or territory) by military force. **2** to enter in large numbers: *the town was invaded by rugby supporters.* **3** to disturb (privacy, etc.). **invader** *n*

invalid[1] *n* **1** a person who is disabled or chronically ill. *~adj* **2** sick or disabled. *~vb* **3** *Chiefly Brit* to dismiss (a soldier etc.) from active service because of illness. **invalidism** *n*

invalid[2] *adj* **1** having no legal force: *an invalid cheque.* **2** (of an argument, result, etc.) not valid because it has been based on a mistake. **invalidity** *n* **invalidly** *adv*

invalidate *vb* **-dating, -dated 1** to make or show (an argument) to be invalid. **2** to take away the legal force of (a contract). **invalidation** *n*

invaluable *adj* having great value that is impossible to calculate.

invariable *adj* unchanging. **invariably** *adv*

invasion *n* **1** the act of invading with armed forces. **2** any intrusion: *an invasion of privacy.* **invasive** *adj*

invective *n* abusive speech or writing.

inveigh (in-**vay**) *vb Formal* **inveigh against** to make harsh criticisms against.

THESAURUS

bring in, commence, establish, found, inaugurate, initiate, institute, launch, organize, pioneer, set up, start, usher in **3.** add, inject, insert, interpolate, interpose, put in, throw in (*informal*)

introduction 1. baptism, debut, establishment, first acquaintance, inauguration, induction, initiation, institution, launch, pioneering, presentation **2.** commencement, foreword, intro (*informal*), lead-in, opening, opening passage, opening remarks, overture, preamble, preface, preliminaries, prelude, proem, prolegomena, prolegomenon, prologue

introductory early, elementary, first, inaugural, initial, initiatory, opening, precursory, prefatory, preliminary, preparatory, starting

introspective brooding, contemplative, inner-directed, introverted, inward-looking, meditative, pensive, subjective

introverted indrawn, inner-directed, introspective, inward-looking, self-centred, self-contained, withdrawn

intrude butt in, encroach, infringe, interfere, interrupt, meddle, obtrude, push in, thrust oneself in *or* forward, trespass, violate

intruder burglar, gate-crasher (*informal*), infiltrator, interloper, invader, prowler, raider, snooper (*informal*), squatter, thief, trespasser

intrusion encroachment, infringement, interference, interruption, invasion, trespass, violation

intrusive disturbing, forward, impertinent, importunate, interfering, invasive, meddlesome, nosy (*informal*), officious, presumptuous, pushy (*informal*), uncalled-for, unwanted

intuition discernment, hunch, insight, instinct, perception, presentiment, sixth sense

intuitive innate, instinctive, instinctual, involuntary, spontaneous, unreflecting, untaught

inundate deluge, drown, engulf, flood, glut, immerse, overflow, overrun, overwhelm, submerge, swamp

invade 1. assail, assault, attack, burst in, descend upon, encroach, infringe, make inroads, occupy, raid, violate **2.** infect, infest, overrun, overspread, penetrate, permeate, pervade, swarm over

invader aggressor, alien, attacker, looter, plunderer, raider, trespasser

invalid[1] **1.** *n.* convalescent, patient, valetudinarian **2.** *adj.* ailing, bedridden, disabled, feeble, frail, ill, infirm, poorly (*informal*), sick, sickly, valetudinarian, weak

invalid[2] *adj.* baseless, fallacious, false, ill-founded, illogical, inoperative, irrational, not binding, nugatory, null, null and void, unfounded, unscientific, unsound, untrue, void, worthless

invalidate abrogate, annul, cancel, nullify, overrule, overthrow, quash, render null and void, rescind, undermine, undo, weaken

invaluable beyond price, costly, inestimable, precious, priceless, valuable

invariable changeless, consistent, constant, fixed, immutable, inflexible, regular, rigid, set, unalterable, unchangeable, unchanging, unfailing, uniform, unvarying, unwavering

invariably always, consistently, customarily, day in, day out, ever, every time, habitually, inevitably, on every occasion, perpetually, regularly, unfailingly, without exception

invasion 1. aggression, assault, attack, foray, incursion, inroad, irruption, offensive, onslaught, raid **2.** breach, encroachment, infiltration, infraction, infringement, intrusion, overstepping, usurpation, violation

inveigle *vb* **-gling, -gled** to coax or manipulate (someone) into an action or situation. **inveiglement** *n*

invent *vb* **1** to think up or create (something new). **2** to make up (a story, excuse, etc.). **inventor** *n*

invention *n* **1** something that is invented. **2** the act of inventing. **3** creative power; inventive skill. **4** *Euphemistic* a lie: *his story is a malicious invention.*

inventive *adj* creative and resourceful.

inventory (in-ven-tree) *n, pl* **-tories 1** a detailed list of the objects in a particular place. *~vb* **-tories, -torying, -toried 2** to make a list of.

inverse *adj* **1** opposite in effect, sequence, direction, etc. **2** *Maths* linking two variables in such a way that one increases as the other decreases. *~n* **3** the exact opposite: *the inverse of this image.* **4** *Maths* an inverse element.

inversion *n* **1** the act of inverting or state of being inverted. **2** something inverted, esp. a reversal of order, functions, etc.: *an inversion of their previous relationship.* **inversive** *adj*

invert *vb* **1** to turn upside down or inside out. **2** to reverse in effect, sequence, or direction. *~n* **3** a homosexual. **invertible** *adj*

invertebrate *n* **1** any animal without a backbone, such as an insect, worm, or octopus. *~adj* **2** of or designating invertebrates.

inverted commas *pl n* same as **quotation marks.**

invest *vb* **1** (often foll. by *in*) to put (money) into an enterprise with the expectation of profit. **2** (often foll. by *in*) to devote (time or effort to a project). **3 invest in** to buy: *she invested in some barbecue equipment.* **4** to give power or authority to: *invested with the powers of government.* **5** (often foll. by *in*) to install someone (in an official position). **6** (foll. by *with* or *in*) to credit or provide (a person with qualities): *he was invested with great common sense.* **7 invest with** *Usually poetic* to cover, as if with a coat: *when spring invests the trees with leaves.* **investor** *n*

investigate *vb* **-gating, -gated** to inquire into (a situation or problem) thoroughly in order to discover the truth: *the police are currently investigating the case.* **investigative** *adj* **investigator** *n*

investigation *n* a careful search or examination in order to discover facts.

investiture *n* the formal installation of a person in an office or rank.

investment *n* **1** the act of investing. **2** money invested. **3** something in which money is invested.

investment trust *n* a financial enterprise that invests its subscribed capital in a wide range of securities for its investors' benefit.

inveterate *adj* **1** deep-rooted or ingrained: *an inveterate enemy of Marxism.* **2** confirmed in a habit or practice: *an inveterate gambler.* **inveteracy** *n*

invidious *adj* likely to cause resentment or unpopularity.

invigilate (in-vij-il-late) *vb* **-lating, -lated** *Brit* to supervise people who are sitting an examination. **invigilation** *n* **invigilator** *n*

invigorate *vb* **-ating, -ated** to give energy to or refresh. **invigorating** *adj*

invincible *adj* incapable of being defeated: *an army of invincible strength.* **invincibility** *n* **invincibly** *adv*

inviolable *adj* that must not be broken or violated: *an inviolable oath.* **inviolability** *n*

inviolate *adj* free from harm or injury. **inviolacy** *n*

invisible *adj* **1** not able to be seen by the eye: *invis-*

THESAURUS

invective abuse, berating, castigation, censure, contumely, denunciation, diatribe, obloquy, philippic(s), reproach, sarcasm, tirade, tongue-lashing, vilification, vituperation

invent 1. coin, come up with *(informal)*, conceive, contrive, create, design, devise, discover, dream up *(informal)*, formulate, imagine, improvise, originate, think up **2.** concoct, cook up *(informal)*, fabricate, feign, forge, make up, manufacture

invention 1. brainchild *(informal)*, contraption, contrivance, creation, design, development, device, discovery, gadget, instrument **2.** coinage, creativeness, creativity, genius, imagination, ingenuity, inspiration, inventiveness, originality, resourcefulness **3.** deceit, fabrication, fake, falsehood, fantasy, fib *(informal)*, fiction, figment *or* product of (someone's) imagination, forgery, lie, prevarication, sham, story, tall story *(informal)*, untruth, yarn

inventive creative, fertile, gifted, ground-breaking, imaginative, ingenious, innovative, inspired, original, resourceful

inventor architect, author, coiner, creator, designer, father, framer, maker, originator

inventory *n.* account, catalogue, file, list, record, register, roll, roster, schedule, stock book

inverse *adj.* contrary, converse, inverted, opposite, reverse, reversed, transposed

inversion antipode, antithesis, contraposition, contrariety, contrary, opposite, reversal, transposal, transposition

invert capsize, introvert, invaginate, overset, overturn, reverse, transpose, turn inside out, turn turtle, turn upside down, upset, upturn

invest 1. advance, devote, lay out, put in, sink, spend **2.** authorize, charge, empower, license, sanction, vest **3.** adopt, consecrate, enthrone, establish, inaugurate, induct, install, ordain **4.** *usually poetic* array, bedeck, clothe, deck, drape, dress, robe

investigate consider, enquire into, examine, explore, go into, inquire into, inspect, look into, make enquiries, probe, put to the test, recce *(slang)*, research, scrutinize, search, sift, study, work over

investigation analysis, enquiry, examination, exploration, fact finding, hearing, inquest, inquiry, inspection, probe, recce *(slang)*, research, review, scrutiny, search, study, survey

investigator examiner, inquirer, (private) detective, private eye *(informal)*, researcher, reviewer, sleuth *or* sleuthhound *(informal)*

investiture admission, enthronement, inauguration, induction, installation, instatement, investing, investment, ordination

investment 1. asset, investing, speculation, transaction, venture **2.** ante *(informal)*, contribution, stake

inveterate chronic, confirmed, deep-rooted, deep-seated, dyed-in-the-wool, entrenched, established, habitual, hard-core, hardened, incorrigible, incurable, ineradicable, ingrained, long-standing, obstinate

invidious discriminatory, hateful, obnoxious, odious, offensive, repugnant, slighting, undesirable

invigorate animate, brace, buck up *(informal)*, energize, enliven, exhilarate, fortify, freshen (up), galvanize, harden, liven up, nerve, pep up, perk up, put new heart into, quicken, refresh, rejuvenate, revitalize, stimulate, strengthen

invincible impregnable, indestructible, indomitable, inseparable, insuperable, invulnerable, unassailable, unbeatable, unconquerable, unsurmountable, unyielding

inviolable hallowed, holy, inalienable, sacred, sacrosanct, unalterable

ible radiation. **2** concealed from sight. **3** *Econ* relating to services, such as insurance and freight, rather than goods: *invisible earnings.* **invisibility** *n* **invisibly** *adv*

invitation *n* **1** a request to attend a dance, meal, etc. **2** the card or paper on which an invitation is written.

invite *vb* **-viting, -vited 1** to ask (a person) in a friendly or polite way (to do something, attend an event, etc.). **2** to make a request for, esp. publicly or formally: *we invite applications for six scholarships.* **3** to bring on or provoke: *his theory invites disaster.* **4** to tempt. *~n* **5** *Informal* an invitation.

inviting *adj* tempting or attractive.

in vitro *adv, adj* (of biological processes or reactions) happening outside the body of the organism in an artificial environment.

invocation *n* **1** the act of invoking. **2** a prayer to God or another deity asking for help, forgiveness, etc. **invocatory** *adj*

invoice *n* **1** a bill for goods and services supplied. *~vb* **-voicing, -voiced 2** to present (a customer) with an invoice.

invoke *vb* **-voking, -voked 1** to put (a law or penalty) into use: *chapter 8 of the UN charter was invoked.* **2** to bring about: *the hills invoked a feeling of serenity.* **3** to call on (God or another deity) for help, inspiration, etc. **4** to summon (a spirit) by uttering magic words.

involuntary *adj* **1** carried out without one's conscious wishes; unintentional. **2** *Physiol* (esp. of a movement or muscle) performed or acting without conscious control. **involuntarily** *adv*

involute *adj also* **involuted 1** complex, intricate, or involved. **2** rolled inwards or curled in a spiral. *~n* **3** *Geom* the curve described by the free end of a thread as it is wound around another curve on the same plane.

involve *vb* **-volving, -volved 1** to include as a necessary part. **2** to have an effect on: *around fifty riders were involved and some were hurt.* **3** to implicate: *several people were involved in the crime.* **4** to make complicated: *the situation was further involved by her disappearance.* **involvement** *n*

involved *adj* **1** complicated. **2 involved in** concerned in.

invulnerable *adj* not able to be wounded or damaged. **invulnerability** *n*

inward *adj* **1** directed towards the middle of something. **2** situated within. **3** of the mind or spirit: *inward meditation.* **4** of one's own country or a specific country: *inward investment.* *~adv* **5** same as **inwards.**

inwardly *adv* **1** within the private thoughts or feelings: *inwardly troubled, he kept smiling.* **2** not aloud: *to laugh inwardly.* **3** in or on the inside.

inwards *or* **inward** *adv* towards the inside or middle of something.

inwrought *adj* worked or woven into material, esp. decoratively.

Io *Chem* ionium.

iodide *n Chem* a compound containing an iodine atom, such as methyl iodide.

iodine *n Chem* a bluish-black element found in seaweed and used in medicine, photography, and dyeing. Symbol: I

iodize *or* **-dise** *vb* **-dizing, -dized** *or* **-dising, -dised** to treat with iodine. **iodization** *or* **-disation** *n*

IOM Isle of Man.

ion *n* an electrically charged atom or group of atoms formed by the loss or gain of one or more electrons.

ion exchange *n* the process in which ions are exchanged between a solution and an insoluble solid. It is used to soften water.

ionic *adj* of or in the form of ions.

Ionic *adj* of a style of classical architecture characterized by fluted columns with scroll-like ornaments on the capital.

ionize *or* **-ise** *vb* **-izing, -ized** *or* **-ising, -ised** to change or become changed into ions. **ionization** *or* **-isation** *n*

ionosphere *n* a region of ionized layers of air in the earth's upper atmosphere, which reflects radio waves. **ionospheric** *adj*

iota (eye-**oh**-ta) *n* **1** the ninth letter in the Greek alphabet (Ι, ι). **2** a very small amount: *I don't feel one iota of guilt.*

IOU *n* a written promise or reminder to pay a debt.

IOW Isle of Wight.

IPA International Phonetic Alphabet.

THESAURUS

inviolate entire, intact, pure, sacred, stainless, unbroken, undefiled, undisturbed, unhurt, unpolluted, unstained, unsullied, untouched, virgin, whole

invisible 1. imperceptible, indiscernible, out of sight, unperceivable, unseen **2.** concealed, disguised, hidden, inappreciable, inconspicuous, infinitesimal, microscopic

invitation asking, begging, bidding, call, invite (*informal*), request, solicitation, summons, supplication

invite 1. ask, beg, bid, call, request, request the pleasure of (someone's) company, solicit, summon **2.** allure, ask for (*informal*), attract, bring on, court, draw, encourage, entice, lead, leave the door open to, provoke, solicit, tempt, welcome

inviting alluring, appealing, attractive, beguiling, captivating, delightful, engaging, enticing, fascinating, intriguing, magnetic, mouthwatering, pleasing, seductive, tempting, warm, welcoming, winning

invocation appeal, beseeching, entreaty, petition, prayer, supplication

invoke 1. apply, call in, have recourse to, implement, initiate, put into effect, resort to, use **2.** adjure, appeal to, beg, beseech, call upon, conjure, entreat, implore, petition, pray, solicit, supplicate

involuntary automatic, blind, conditioned, instinctive, instinctual, reflex, spontaneous, unconscious, uncontrolled, unintentional, unthinking

involve 1. comprehend, comprise, contain, cover, embrace, include, incorporate, number among, take in **2.** affect, associate, compromise, concern, connect, draw in, implicate, incriminate, inculpate, mix up (*informal*), touch **3.** complicate, embroil, enmesh, entangle, link, mire, mix up, snarl up, tangle

involved 1. Byzantine, complex, complicated, confusing, convoluted, difficult, elaborate, intricate, knotty, labyrinthine, sophisticated, tangled, tortuous **2.** caught (up), concerned, implicated, in on (*informal*), mixed up in *or* with, occupied, participating, taking part

involvement 1. association, commitment, concern, connection, dedication, interest, participation, responsibility **2.** complexity, complication, difficulty, embarrassment, entanglement, imbroglio, intricacy, problem, ramification

invulnerable impenetrable, indestructible, insusceptible, invincible, proof against, safe, secure, unassailable

inwardly at heart, deep down, in one's head, in one's inmost heart, inside, privately, secretly, to oneself, within

inwards *or* **inward** *adj.* **1.** entering, inbound, incom-

ipecacuanha (ip-pee-kak-yew-**ann**-a) *or* **ipecac** (**ip**-pee-kak) *n* a drug made from the dried roots of a S American plant, used to cause vomiting.

ipso facto *adv* by that very fact or act.

IQ intelligence quotient.

Ir *Chem* iridium.

IRA Irish Republican Army.

Iranian *adj* **1** of Iran. ~*n* **2** a person from Iran. **3** a branch of the Indo-European family of languages, including Persian.

Iraqi *adj* **1** of Iraq. ~*n* **2** a person from Iraq.

irascible *adj* easily angered. **irascibility** *n* **irascibly** *adv*

irate *adj* very angry.

ire *n Literary* anger.

iridaceous (ir-rid-**day**-shuss) *adj* of or belonging to the iris family.

iridescent *adj* having shimmering changing colours like a rainbow. **iridescence** *n*

iridium *n Chem* a hard yellowish-white chemical element that occurs in platinum ores and is used as an alloy with platinum. Symbol: Ir

iris *n* **1** the coloured muscular membrane in the eye that surrounds and controls the size of the pupil. **2** a tall plant with long pointed leaves and large flowers.

Irish *adj* **1** of Ireland. ~*n* **2** same as **Irish Gaelic. 3** the dialect of English spoken in Ireland. ~*pl n* **4 the Irish** the people of Ireland.

Irish coffee *n* hot coffee mixed with Irish whiskey and topped with double cream.

Irish Gaelic *n* the Celtic language of Ireland.

Irishman *or fem* **Irishwoman** *n, pl* **-men** *or* **-women** a person from Ireland.

Irish moss *n* same as **carrageen.**

irk *vb* to irritate or vex.

irksome *adj* annoying or tiresome.

iron *n* **1** a strong silvery-white metallic element, widely used for structural and engineering purposes. Symbol: Fe **2** a tool made of iron. **3** a small electrically heated device with a weighted flat bottom for pressing clothes. **4** *Golf* a club with an angled metal head. **5** a splintlike support for a malformed leg. **6** great strength or resolve: *a will of iron.* **7 strike while the iron is hot** to act at a suitable moment. ~*adj* **8** made of iron. **9** very hard or merciless: *iron determination.* **10** very strong: *an iron constitution.* ~*vb* **11** to smooth (clothes or fabric) by removing (creases) with an iron. See also **iron out, irons.**

Iron Age *n* a phase of human culture that began in the Middle East about 1100 BC during which iron tools and weapons were used.

ironclad *adj* **1** covered or protected with iron: *an ironclad warship.* **2** unable to be contradicted: *ironclad proof.* ~*n* **3** *History* a large wooden 19th-century warship with armoured plating.

Iron Curtain *n* (formerly) the guarded border between the countries of the Soviet bloc and the rest of Europe.

ironic *or* **ironical** *adj* of, characterized by, or using irony. **ironically** *adv*

ironing *n* clothes to be ironed.

ironing board *n* a narrow cloth-covered board, usually with folding legs, on which to iron clothes.

iron lung *n* an airtight metal cylinder enclosing the entire body up to the neck and providing artificial respiration.

iron maiden *n* a medieval instrument of torture, consisting of a hinged case (often shaped in the form of a woman) lined with iron spikes.

ironmaster *n Brit history* a manufacturer of iron.

ironmonger *n Brit* a shopkeeper or shop dealing in hardware. **ironmongery** *n*

iron out *vb* to settle (a problem or difficulty) through negotiation or discussion.

iron pyrites *n* same as **pyrite.**

iron rations *pl n* emergency food supplies, esp. for military personnel in action.

irons *pl n* **1** fetters or chains. **2 have several irons in the fire** to have several projects or plans at once.

ironstone *n* **1** any rock consisting mainly of iron ore. **2** a tough durable earthenware.

ironwood *n* **1** any of various trees, such as hornbeam, with exceptionally hard wood. **2** the wood of any of these trees.

ironwork *n* work done in iron, esp. decorative work.

ironworks *n* a building in which iron is smelted, cast, or wrought.

irony *n, pl* **-nies 1** the mildly sarcastic use of words to imply the opposite of what they normally mean. **2** a situation or result that is the direct opposite of what was expected or intended.

irradiate *vb* **-ating, -ated 1** *Physics* to subject to or treat with light or other electromagnetic radiation. **2** to make clear or bright intellectually or spiritually. **3** to light up; illuminate. **irradiation** *n*

irrational *adj* **1** not based on logical reasoning. **2** incapable of reasoning. **3** *Maths* (of an equation or expression) involving radicals or fractional exponents. **irrationality** *n* **irrationally** *adv*

irrational number *n Maths* any real number that cannot be expressed as the ratio of two integers, such as π.

THESAURUS

ing, inflowing, ingoing, inpouring, penetrating **2.** confidential, hidden, inmost, inner, innermost, inside, interior, internal, personal, private, privy, secret

Irish green, Hibernian

irksome aggravating, annoying, boring, bothersome, burdensome, disagreeable, exasperating, irritating, tedious, tiresome, troublesome, uninteresting, unwelcome, vexatious, vexing, wearisome

iron *adj.* **1.** chalybeate, ferric, ferrous, irony **2.** *figurative* adamant, cruel, hard, heavy, immovable, implacable, indomitable, inflexible, obdurate, rigid, robust, steel, steely, strong, tough, unbending, unyielding

ironic *or* **ironical** double-edged, mocking, mordacious, sarcastic, sardonic, satirical, scoffing, sneering, wry

iron out clear up, eliminate, eradicate, erase, expedite, get rid of, harmonize, put right, reconcile, resolve, settle, simplify, smooth over, sort out, straighten out, unravel

irons bonds, chains, fetters, manacles, shackles

irony 1. mockery, sarcasm, satire **2.** contrariness, incongruity, paradox

irrational 1. absurd, crackpot (*informal*), crazy, foolish, illogical, injudicious, loopy (*informal*), nonsensical, preposterous, silly, unreasonable, unreasoning, unsound, unthinking, unwise **2.** aberrant, brainless, crazy, demented, insane, mindless, muddle-headed, raving, senseless, unstable, wild

irrationality absurdity, brainlessness, illogicality, insanity, lack of judgment, lunacy, madness, preposterousness, senselessness, unreasonableness, unsoundness

irreconcilable clashing, conflicting, diametrically opposed, incompatible, incongruous, inconsistent, opposed

irreconcilable *adj* not able to be resolved or settled: *irreconcilable differences.* **irreconcilability** *n*

irrecoverable *adj* not able to be recovered.

irredeemable *adj* **1** not able to be reformed, improved, or corrected. **2** (of bonds or shares) not able to be bought back directly or paid off. **3** (of paper money) not able to be converted into coin. **irredeemably** *adv*

irredentist *n* a person in favour of seizing territory that was once part of his or her country. **irredentism** *n*

irreducible *adj* impossible to put in a reduced or simpler form. **irreducibility** *n*

irrefutable *adj* impossible to deny or disprove.

irregular *adj* **1** uneven in shape, position, arrangement, etc. **2** not conforming to accepted practice or routine. **3** (of a word) not following the usual pattern of formation in a language. **4** not occurring at expected or equal intervals: *an irregular pulse.* **5** (of troops) not belonging to regular forces. *~n* **6** a soldier not in a regular army. **irregularity** *n* **irregularly** *adv*

irrelevant *adj* not connected with the matter in hand. **irrelevance** *or* **irrelevancy** *n*

irreligious *adj* **1** lacking religious faith. **2** indifferent or opposed to religion.

irremediable *adj* not able to be improved or cured.

irremovable *adj* not able to be removed. **irremovably** *adv*

irreparable *adj* not able to be repaired or put right: *irreparable damage to his reputation.* **irreparably** *adv*

irreplaceable *adj* impossible to replace: *acres of irreplaceable moorland were devastated.*

irrepressible *adj* not capable of being repressed, controlled, or restrained. **irrepressibility** *n* **irrepressibly** *adv*

irreproachable *adj* blameless or faultless. **irreproachability** *n*

irresistible *adj* **1** not able to be resisted or refused: *irresistible pressure from the financial markets.* **2** extremely attractive: *an irresistible woman.* **irresistibility** *n* **irresistibly** *adv*

irresolute *adj* unable to make decisions. **irresolution** *n*

irrespective *adj* **irrespective of** without taking account of.

irresponsible *adj* **1** not showing or done with due care for the consequences of one's actions or attitudes; reckless. **2** not capable of accepting responsibility. **irresponsibility** *n* **irresponsibly** *adv*

irretrievable *adj* impossible to put right or make good. **irretrievability** *n* **irretrievably** *adv*

irreverence *n* **1** lack of due respect. **2** a disrespectful remark or act. **irreverent** *adj*

irreversible *adj* not able to be reversed or put right again: *irreversible loss of memory.* **irreversibly** *adv*

irrevocable *adj* not possible to change or undo. **irrevocably** *adv*

THESAURUS

irrecoverable gone for ever, irreclaimable, irredeemable, irremediable, irreparable, irretrievable, lost, unregainable, unsalvageable, unsavable

irrefutable beyond question, certain, incontestable, incontrovertible, indisputable, indubitable, invincible, irrefragable, irresistible, sure, unanswerable, unassailable, undeniable, unquestionable

irregular *adj.* **1.** asymmetrical, broken, bumpy, craggy, crooked, elliptic, elliptical, holey, jagged, lopsided, lumpy, pitted, ragged, rough, serrated, unequal, uneven, unsymmetrical **2.** abnormal, anomalous, capricious, disorderly, eccentric, exceptional, extraordinary, immoderate, improper, inappropriate, inordinate, odd, peculiar, queer, quirky, rum (*Brit. slang*), unconventional, unofficial, unorthodox, unsuitable, unusual **3.** desultory, disconnected, eccentric, erratic, fitful, fluctuating, fragmentary, haphazard, inconstant, intermittent, nonuniform, occasional, out of order, patchy, random, shifting, spasmodic, sporadic, uncertain, uneven, unmethodical, unpunctual, unsteady, unsystematic, variable, wavering *~n.* **4.** guerrilla, partisan, volunteer

irregularity 1. asymmetry, bumpiness, crookedness, jaggedness, lack of symmetry, lopsidedness, lumpiness, patchiness, raggedness, roughness, spottiness, unevenness **2.** aberration, abnormality, anomaly, breach, deviation, eccentricity, freak, malfunction, malpractice, oddity, peculiarity, singularity, unconventionality, unorthodoxy **3.** confusion, desultoriness, disorderliness, disorganization, haphazardness, lack of method, randomness, uncertainty, unpunctuality, unsteadiness

irrelevance, irrelevancy inappositeness, inappropriateness, inaptness, inconsequence, non sequitur

irrelevant beside the point, extraneous, immaterial, impertinent, inapplicable, inapposite, inappropriate, inapt, inconsequent, neither here nor there, unconnected, unrelated

irreparable beyond repair, incurable, irrecoverable, irremediable, irreplaceable, irretrievable, irreversible

irreplaceable indispensable, invaluable, priceless, unique, vital

irrepressible boisterous, bubbling over, buoyant, ebullient, effervescent, insuppressible, uncontainable, uncontrollable, unmanageable, unquenchable, unrestrainable, unstoppable

irreproachable beyond reproach, blameless, faultless, guiltless, impeccable, inculpable, innocent, irreprehensible, irreprovable, perfect, pure, unblemished, unimpeachable

irresistible 1. compelling, imperative, overmastering, overpowering, overwhelming, potent, urgent **2.** alluring, beckoning, enchanting, fascinating, ravishing, seductive, tempting

irresolute doubtful, fickle, half-hearted, hesitant, hesitating, indecisive, infirm, in two minds, tentative, undecided, undetermined, unsettled, unstable, unsteady, vacillating, wavering, weak

irrespective of apart from, despite, discounting, in spite of, notwithstanding, regardless of, without reference to, without regard to

irresponsible careless, featherbrained, flighty, giddy, harebrained, harum-scarum, ill-considered, immature, reckless, scatter-brained, shiftless, thoughtless, undependable, unreliable, untrustworthy, wild

irreverence cheek (*informal*), cheekiness (*informal*), chutzpah (*U.S. & Canad. informal*), derision, disrespect, flippancy, impertinence, impudence, lack of respect, mockery, sauce (*informal*)

irreverent cheeky (*informal*), contemptuous, derisive, disrespectful, flip (*informal*), flippant, fresh (*informal*), iconoclastic, impertinent, impious, impudent, mocking, saucy, tongue-in-cheek

irreversible final, incurable, irreparable, irrevocable, unalterable

irrevocable changeless, fated, fixed, immutable, invariable, irremediable, irretrievable, irreversible, predestined, predetermined, settled, unalterable, unchangeable, unreversible

irrigate flood, inundate, moisten, water, wet

irrigate *vb* **-gating, -gated 1** to supply (land) with water through ditches or pipes in order to encourage the growth of crops. **2** *Med* to bathe (a wound or part of the body). **irrigation** *n* **irrigator** *n*

irritable *adj* **1** easily annoyed or angered. **2** *Pathol* abnormally sensitive. **3** *Biol* (of all living organisms) capable of responding to such stimuli as heat, light, and touch. **irritability** *n*

irritant *n* **1** something that annoys or irritates. **2** a substance that causes a part of the body to become tender or inflamed. ~*adj* **3** causing irritation.

irritate *vb* **-tating, -tated 1** to annoy or anger (someone). **2** *Pathol* to cause (an organ or part of the body) to become inflamed or tender. **3** *Biol* to stimulate (an organ) to respond in a characteristic manner. **irritation** *n*

irrupt *vb* to enter forcibly or suddenly. **irruption** *n* **irruptive** *adj*

is *vb* third person singular of the present tense of **be.**

isallobar (ice-**sal**-oh-bar) *n* a line on a map connecting places with equal pressure changes.

ISBN International Standard Book Number.

isinglass (**ize**-ing-glass) *n* **1** a gelatine made from the air bladders of freshwater fish. **2** same as **mica.**

Isl. **1** Island. **2** Isle.

Islam *n* **1** the Muslim religion teaching that there is only one God and that Mohammed is his prophet. **2** Muslim countries and civilization. **Islamic** *adj*

island *n* **1** a piece of land that is completely surrounded by water. **2** something isolated, detached, or surrounded: *a traffic island.*

islander *n* a person who lives on an island.

isle *n Poetic except when part of place name* an island.

islet *n* a small island.

ism *n Informal, often used to show contempt* a doctrine, system, or practice, esp. one whose name ends in *-ism*, such as *communism* or *fascism.*

-ism *n suffix* indicating: **1** a political or religious belief: *socialism; Judaism.* **2** a characteristic quality: *heroism.* **3** an action: *exorcism.* **4** prejudice on the basis specified: *sexism.*

isn't is not.

iso- *or before a vowel* **is-** *combining form* equal or identical: *isomagnetic.*

isobar (**ice**-oh-bar) *n* **1** a line on a map connecting places of equal atmospheric pressure. **2** *Physics* any of two or more atoms that have the same mass number but different atomic numbers. **isobaric** *adj* **isobarism** *n*

isochronal *or* **isochronous** *adj* **1** equal in length of time. **2** occurring at equal time intervals. **isochronism** *n*

isohel *n* a line on a map connecting places with an equal period of sunshine.

isohyet (ice-oh-**hie**-it) *n* a line on a map connecting places having equal rainfall.

isolate *vb* **-lating, -lated 1** to place apart or alone. **2** *Chem* to obtain (a substance) in an uncombined form. **3** *Med* to quarantine (a person or animal) with a contagious disease. **isolation** *n*

isomer (**ice**-oh-mer) *n Chem* a substance whose molecules contain the same atoms as another but in a different arrangement. **isomeric** *adj*

isometric *adj* **1** having equal dimensions or measurements. **2** *Physiol* relating to muscular contraction that does not produce shortening of the muscle. **3** (of a three-dimensional drawing) having the three axes equally inclined and all lines drawn to scale. **isometrically** *adv*

isometrics *n* a system of isometric exercises.

isomorphism *n* **1** *Biol* similarity of form, as in different generations of the same life cycle. **2** *Chem* the existence of two or more substances of different composition in a similar crystalline form. **3** *Maths* a one-to-one correspondence between the elements of two or more sets. **isomorph** *n* **isomorphic** *or* **isomorphous** *adj*

isosceles triangle (ice-**soss**-ill-eez) *n* a triangle with two sides of equal length.

isotherm (**ice**-oh-therm) *n* a line on a map linking places of equal temperature.

isotope (**ice**-oh-tope) *n* one of two or more atoms with the same number of protons in the nucleus but a different number of neutrons. **isotopic** *adj* **isotopy** *n*

isotropic *or* **isotropous** *adj* having uniform physical properties, such as elasticity or conduction in all directions. **isotropy** *n*

Israeli *adj* **1** of Israel. ~*n, pl* **-lis** *or* **-li 2** a person from Israel.

Israelite *n Bible* a member of the ethnic group claiming descent from Jacob; a Hebrew.

issue *n* **1** a topic of interest or discussion. **2** an important subject requiring a decision. **3** a particular edition of a magazine or newspaper. **4** a consequence or result. **5** *Law* the descendants of a person. **6** the act of sending or giving out something. **7** the act of emerging; outflow. **8** something flowing out, such as a river. **9 at issue a** under discussion. **b** in disagreement. **10 force the issue** to compel decision on some matter. **11 join issue** to join in controversy. **12 take issue** to disagree. ~*vb* **-suing, -sued 13** to make (a statement

THESAURUS

irritability bad temper, ill humour, impatience, irascibility, peevishness, petulance, prickliness, testiness, tetchiness, touchiness

irritable bad-tempered, cantankerous, choleric, crabbed, crabby, cross, crotchety (*informal*), edgy, exasperated, fiery, fretful, hasty, hot, ill-humoured, ill-tempered, irascible, narky (*slang*), out of humour, oversensitive, peevish, petulant, prickly, ratty (*Brit. informal*), snappish, snappy, snarling, tense, testy, tetchy, touchy

irritate 1. aggravate (*informal*), anger, annoy, bother, drive one up the wall (*slang*), enrage, exasperate, fret, gall, get in one's hair (*informal*), get one's back up, get one's hackles up, get on one's nerves (*informal*), harass, incense, inflame, infuriate, nark (*slang*), needle (*informal*), offend, pester, piss one off (*taboo slang*), provoke, raise one's hackles, rankle with, rub up the wrong way (*informal*), ruffle, try one's patience, vex **2.** aggravate, chafe, fret, inflame, intensify, pain, rub

irritated angry, annoyed, bothered, cross, displeased, exasperated, flustered, harassed, impatient, irritable, nettled, out of humour, peeved (*informal*), piqued, pissed off (*taboo slang*), put out, ruffled, vexed

irritating aggravating (*informal*), annoying, displeasing, disquieting, disturbing, galling, infuriating, irksome, maddening, nagging, pestilential, provoking, thorny, troublesome, trying, upsetting, vexatious, worrisome

irritation aggravation, annoyance, gall, goad, irritant, nuisance, pain (*informal*), pain in the arse (*taboo informal*), pain in the neck (*informal*), pest, provocation, tease, thorn in one's flesh

isolate cut off, detach, disconnect, divorce, insulate, quarantine, segregate, separate, sequester, set apart

isolation aloofness, detachment, disconnection, exile, insularity, insulation, loneliness, quarantine, re-

etc.) publicly. **14** to supply officially (with). **15** to send out or distribute. **16** to publish. **17** to come forth or emerge. **issuable** *adj*

isthmus (**iss**-muss) *n* a narrow strip of land connecting two relatively large land areas.

it *pron* **1** refers to a nonhuman, animal, plant, or inanimate thing, or sometimes to a small baby. **2** refers to something unspecified or implied or to a previous or understood clause, phrase, or word: *I knew it.* **3** used to represent human life or experience in respect of the present situation: *how's it going?* **4** used as the subject of impersonal verbs: *it is snowing; it's Friday.* **5** *Informal* the crucial or ultimate point: *the steering failed and I thought that was it.* ~*n* **6** *Informal* **a** sexual intercourse. **b** sex appeal. **7** a desirable quality or ability.

IT information technology.

ITA initial teaching alphabet: a partly phonetic alphabet used to teach reading.

Italian *adj* **1** of Italy. ~*n* **2** a person from Italy. **3** the official language of Italy and one of the official languages of Switzerland.

Italianate *adj* Italian in style or character.

italic *adj* **1** of a style of printing type in which the characters slant to the right. ~*pl n* **2** **italics** italic type or print, used for emphasis.

italicize *or* **-cise** *vb* **-cizing, -cized** *or* **-cising, -cised** to print (text) in italic type. **italicization** *or* **-cisation** *n*

itch *n* **1** a skin irritation causing a desire to scratch. **2** a restless desire. **3** any skin disorder, such as scabies, characterized by intense itching. ~*vb* **4** to feel an irritating or tickling sensation. **5** to have a restless desire (to do something): *they were itching to join the fight.*

itchy *adj* **itchier, itchiest 1** having an itch. **2 have itchy feet** to have a desire to travel. **itchiness** *n*

it'd it would *or* it had.

item *n* **1** a single thing in a list or collection. **2** a piece of information: *a news item.* **3** *Book-keeping* an entry in an account. **4** *Informal* a couple.

itemize *or* **-ise** *vb* **-izing, -ized** *or* **-ising, -ised** to put on a list or make a list of. **itemization** *or* **-isation** *n*

iterate *vb* **-ating, -ated** to say or do again. **iteration** *n* **iterative** *adj*

itinerant *adj* **1** working for a short time in various places. ~*n* **2** an itinerant worker or other person.

itinerary *n, pl* **-aries 1** a detailed plan of a journey. **2** a record of a journey. **3** a guidebook for travellers.

-itis *suffix forming nouns* indicating inflammation of a specified part: *tonsillitis.*

it'll it will *or* it shall.

its *adj* **1** of or belonging to it: *its left rear wheel; I can see its logical consequence.* ~*pron* **2** something belonging to it: *its is over there.*

it's it is *or* it has.

➤ Beware of mistaking the possessive *its* (no apostrophe) as in *The cat has hurt its paw,* for the abbreviation *it's* meaning *it is* or *it has: It's been a long time.*

itself *pron* **1 a** the reflexive form of *it: the cat scratched itself.* **b** used for emphasis: *even the money itself won't convince me.* **2** its normal or usual self: *my parrot doesn't seem itself these days.*

ITV (in Britain) Independent Television.

IUD intrauterine device: a coil-shaped contraceptive fitted into the womb.

I've I have.

IVF in vitro fertilization.

ivories *pl n Slang* **1** the keys of a piano. **2** the teeth. **3** dice.

ivory *n, pl* **-ries 1** a hard smooth creamy white type of bone that makes up a major part of the tusks of elephants. ~*adj* **2** yellowish-white. **ivory-like** *adj*

ivory tower *n* remoteness from the realities of everyday life. **ivory-towered** *adj*

IVR International Vehicle Registration.

ivy *n, pl* **ivies 1** a woody climbing or trailing plant with evergreen leaves and black berry-like fruits. **2** any of various other climbing or creeping plants, such as the poison ivy.

ixia *n* a southern African plant of the iris family with showy ornamental funnel-shaped flowers.

THESAURUS

moteness, retirement, seclusion, segregation, self-sufficiency, separation, solitude, withdrawal

issue *n.* **1.** affair, argument, concern, controversy, matter, matter of contention, point, point in question, problem, question, subject, topic **2.** copy, edition, impression, instalment, number, printing **3.** conclusion, consequence, culmination, effect, end, finale, outcome, pay-off (*informal*), result, termination, upshot **4.** children, descendants, heirs, offspring, progeny, scions, seed (*chiefly biblical*) **5.** circulation, delivery, dispersion, dissemination, distribution, granting, issuing, publication, sending out, supply, supplying **6. at issue** at variance, controversial, in disagreement, in dispute, to be decided, under discussion, unsettled **7. take issue** challenge, disagree, dispute, object, oppose, raise an objection, take exception ~*vb.* **8.** announce, broadcast, circulate, deliver, distribute, emit, give out, promulgate, publish, put in circulation, put out, release **9.** arise, be a consequence of, come forth, emanate, emerge, flow, originate, proceed, rise, spring, stem

itch *n.* **1.** irritation, itchiness, prickling, tingling **2.** craving, desire, hankering, hunger, longing, lust, passion, restlessness, yearning, yen (*informal*) ~*vb.* **3.** crawl, irritate, prickle, tickle, tingle **4.** ache, burn, crave, hanker, hunger, long, lust, pant, pine, yearn

itchy eager, edgy, fidgety, impatient, restive, restless, unsettled

item 1. article, aspect, component, consideration, detail, entry, matter, particular, point, thing **2.** account, article, bulletin, dispatch, feature, note, notice, paragraph, piece, report

itemize, -ise count, detail, document, enumerate, instance, inventory, list, number, particularize, record, set out, specify

itinerant *adj.* ambulatory, Gypsy, journeying, migratory, nomadic, peripatetic, roaming, roving, travelling, unsettled, vagabond, vagrant, wandering, wayfaring

itinerary 1. circuit, journey, line, programme, route, schedule, timetable, tour **2.** guide, guidebook

ivory tower cloister, refuge, remoteness, retreat, sanctum, seclusion, splendid isolation, unreality, world of one's own

J

J joule(s).

jab *vb* **jabbing, jabbed 1** to poke sharply. ~*n* **2** a quick short punch. **3** *Informal* an injection: *a flu jab.* **4** a sharp poke.

jabber *vb* **1** to speak very quickly and excitedly; chatter. ~*n* **2** quick excited chatter.

jacaranda *n* a tropical American tree with sweet-smelling wood and pale purple flowers.

jack *n* **1** a mechanical device used to raise a motor vehicle or other heavy object. **2** a playing card with a picture of a pageboy on it. **3** *Bowls* a small white bowl at which the players aim their bowls. **4** *Electrical engineering* a socket into which a plug can be inserted. **5** a flag flown at the bow of a ship, showing nationality. **6** one of the pieces used in the game of jacks. **7 every man jack** everyone without exception. ~See also **jack in, jacks, jack up.**

jackal *n* a doglike wild animal of Africa and Asia, which feeds on the decaying flesh of dead animals.

jackanapes *n* a mischievous child.

jackass *n* **1** a fool. **2** a male donkey. **3 laughing jackass** same as **kookaburra.**

jackboot *n* **1** a leather military boot reaching up to the knee. **2** brutal and authoritarian rule.

jackdaw *n* a large black-and-grey crowlike bird of Europe and Asia.

jacket *n* **1** a short coat with a front opening and long sleeves. **2** the skin of a potato. **3** same as **dust jacket.**

jacket potato *n* a potato baked in its skin.

Jack Frost *n* frost represented as a person.

jack in *vb Slang* to abandon (an attempt or enterprise).

jack-in-office *n* a self-important petty official.

jack-in-the-box *n* a toy consisting of a box containing a figure on a compressed spring, which jumps out when the lid is opened.

jackknife *vb* **-knifing, -knifed 1** (of an articulated lorry) to go out of control in such a way that the trailer swings round at a sharp angle to the cab. ~*n, pl* **-knives 2** a knife with a blade that can be folded into the handle. **3** a dive in which the diver bends at the waist in midair.

jack of all trades *n, pl* **jacks of all trades** a person who can do many different kinds of work; handyman.

jackpot *n* **1** the most valuable prize that can be won in a gambling game. **2 hit the jackpot** *Informal* to be very fortunate or very successful.

jack rabbit *n* a hare of W North America with very long hind legs and large ears.

jacks *n* a game in which metal, bone, or plastic pieces are thrown and then picked up between throws of a small ball.

Jack Tar *n Chiefly literary* a sailor.

jack up *vb* **1** to raise (a motor vehicle) with a jack. **2** to increase (prices or salaries).

Jacobean (jak-a-**bee**-an) *adj* of or in the reign of James I of England and Ireland (1603–25).

Jacobite *n History* a supporter of James II and his descendants.

Jacquard (**jak**-ard) *n* a fabric with an intricate design incorporated into the weave.

Jacuzzi (jak-**oo**-zee) *n Trademark* a large circular bath with a mechanism that swirls the water.

jade *n* **1** an ornamental semiprecious stone, usually green in colour. ~*adj* **2** bluish-green.

jaded *adj* tired or bored from overindulgence or overwork.

Jaffa *n* a large thick-skinned orange.

jag[1] *n Informal* same as **jab** (sense 3).

jag[2] *n Slang* a period of uncontrolled indulgence in an activity: *all-night crying jags.*

jagged (**jag**-gid) *adj* having an uneven edge with sharp points.

jaguar *n* a large wild cat of south and central America, with a spotted coat.

jail *or* **gaol** *n* **1** a prison. ~*vb* **2** to confine in prison.

jailbird *n Informal* a person who is or has often been in jail.

jailer *or* **gaoler** *n* a person in charge of a jail.

jake *adj* **she's jake** *Austral & NZ slang* it is all right.

jalopy (jal-**lop**-ee) *n, pl* **-lopies** *Informal* a dilapidated old car.

jam[1] *vb* **jamming, jammed 1** to wedge (an object) into a tight space or against another object: *the table was jammed against the wall.* **2** to fill (a place) with people or vehicles: *the surrounding roads were jammed for miles.* **3** to make or become stuck or locked: *the window was jammed open.* **4** *Radio* to prevent the clear reception of (radio communications) by transmitting other signals on the same wavelength. **5** *Slang* to play in a jam session. **6 jam on the brakes** to apply the brakes of a vehicle very suddenly. ~*n* **7** a situation where a large number of people or vehicles are crowded into a place: *a traffic jam.* **8** *Informal* a difficult situation: *you are in a bit of a jam.* **9** same as **jam session.**

jam[2] *n* a food made from fruit boiled with sugar until the mixture sets, used for spreading on bread.

THESAURUS

jab *vb./n.* dig, lunge, nudge, poke, prod, punch, stab, tap, thrust

jacket case, casing, coat, covering, envelope, folder, sheath, skin, wrapper, wrapping

jackpot award, bonanza, kitty, pool, pot, prize, reward, winnings

jack up 1. elevate, heave, hoist, lift, lift up, raise, rear **2.** accelerate, augment, boost, escalate, increase, inflate, put up, raise

jaded bored, clapped out (*informal*), dulled, exhausted, fagged (out) (*informal*), fatigued, spent, tired, tired-out, weary, zonked (*slang*)

jagged barbed, broken, cleft, craggy, indented, notched, pointed, ragged, ridged, rough, serrated, snaggy, spiked, toothed, uneven

jail, gaol 1. *n.* borstal, clink (*slang*), lockup, nick (*slang*), penitentiary (*U.S.*), prison, quod (*slang, chiefly Brit.*), reformatory, the slammer (*slang*), stir (*slang*) **2.** *vb.* confine, detain, immure, impound, imprison, incarcerate, lock up, send down

jailer, gaoler captor, guard, keeper, screw (*slang*), turnkey (*old-fashioned*), warden, warder

jam *vb.* **1.** cram, crowd, crush, force, pack, press, ram, squeeze, stuff, throng, wedge **2.** block, cease, clog, congest, halt, obstruct, stall, stick ~*n.* **3.** crowd, crush, horde, mass, mob, multitude, pack, press, swarm, throng **4.** *informal* bind, dilemma, fix (*informal*), hole

Jamaican *adj* **1** of Jamaica. ~*n* **2** a person from Jamaica.
jamb *n* a side post of a doorframe or window frame.
jamboree *n* a large gathering or celebration.
jammy *adj* **-mier, -miest 1** covered with or tasting like jam. **2** *Brit slang* lucky: *jammy so-and-sos!*
jam-packed *adj* filled to capacity.
jam session *n Slang* an improvised performance by jazz or rock musicians.
Jan. January.
jandal *n NZ* a rubber-soled sandal attached to the foot by a thong between the big toe and the next toe.
jangle *vb* **-gling, -gled 1** to make a harsh unpleasant ringing noise. **2** to produce an irritating or unpleasant effect on: *this may jangle a few nerves in Britain.*
janitor *n Chiefly Scot, US, & Canad* the caretaker of a school or other building.
January *n* the first month of the year.
japan *n* **1** a glossy black lacquer, originally from the Orient, which is used on wood or metal. ~*vb* **-panning, -panned 2** to varnish with japan.
Japanese *adj* **1** of Japan. ~*n* **2** (*pl* **-nese**) a person from Japan. **3** the language of Japan.
jape *n Old-fashioned* a joke or prank.
japonica *n* **1** a Japanese shrub with red flowers and yellowish fruit. **2** same as **camellia.**
jar[1] *n* **1** a wide-mouthed cylindrical glass container, used for storing food. **2** *Brit informal* a glass of beer.
jar[2] *vb* **jarring, jarred 1** to have an irritating or unpleasant effect: *sometimes a light remark jarred on her father.* **2** to be in disagreement or conflict: *their very different temperaments jarred.* **3** to jolt or bump. ~*n* **4** a jolt or shock. **jarring** *adj*
jardiniere *n* an ornamental pot or stand for plants.
jargon *n* **1** specialized language relating to a particular subject, profession, or group. **2** pretentious or unintelligible language.
jasmine *n* a shrub or climbing plant with sweet-smelling flowers.
jasper *n* a kind of quartz, usually red in colour, which is used as a gemstone and for ornamental decoration.
jaundice *n* yellowing of the skin and the whites of the eyes, caused by an excess of bile pigments in the blood.
jaundiced *adj* **1** bitter or cynical: *the financial markets are taking a jaundiced view of the Government's motives.* **2** having jaundice.
jaunt *n* **1** a pleasure trip or outing. ~*vb* **2** to go on a jaunt.
jaunty *adj* **-tier, -tiest 1** cheerful and energetic: *he was worried beneath the jaunty air.* **2** smart and attractive: *a jaunty little hat.* **jauntily** *adv*
Javanese *adj* **1** of the island of Java, in Indonesia. ~*n* **2** (*pl* **-nese**) a person from Java. **3** the language of Java.
javelin *n* a light spear thrown in a sports competition.
jaw *n* **1** either of the bones that hold the teeth and frame the mouth. **2** the lower part of the face below the mouth. **3** *Slang* a long chat. ~*vb* **4** *Slang* to have a long chat.
jawbone *n* the bone in the lower jaw of a person or animal.
jaws *pl n* **1** the mouth of a person or animal. **2** the parts of a machine or tool that grip an object. **3** the narrow opening of a gorge or valley. **4** a dangerous or threatening position: *to snatch victory from the jaws of defeat.*
jay *n* a bird of Europe and Asia with a pinkish-brown body and blue-and-black wings.
jaywalking *n* crossing the road in a dangerous or careless manner. **jaywalker** *n*
jazz *n* **1** a kind of popular music of African-American origin that has an exciting rhythm and often involves improvisation. **2 and all that jazz** *Slang* and other related things.
jazz up *vb Informal* **1** to play (a piece of music) in a jazzy style. **2** to make (something) appear more interesting or lively: *never seek to jazz up a plain story.*
jazzy *adj* **-zier, -ziest 1** colourful and modern: *jazzy shop fronts.* **2** of or like jazz.
JCB *n Trademark* a large machine used in building, that has a shovel on the front and a digger arm on the back.
jealous *adj* **1** suspicious or fearful of being displaced by a rival. **2** envious: *I was jealous of the girls who had boyfriends.* **3** resulting from jealousy: *my jealous tears.* **jealously** *adv*
jealousy *n, pl* **-ousies** the state of or an instance of feeling jealous.
Jean Baptiste (**zhon** bat-**east**) *n Canad slang* a French Canadian.
jeans *pl n* casual denim trousers.

THESAURUS

(*slang*), hot water, pickle (*informal*), plight, predicament, quandary, scrape (*informal*), spot (*informal*), strait, tight spot, trouble
jamboree beano (*Brit. slang*), carnival, carousal, carouse, celebration, festival, festivity, fête, frolic, jubilee, merriment, party, rave (*Brit. slang*), revelry, spree
jangle chime, clank, clash, clatter, jingle, rattle, vibrate
janitor *chiefly Scot., U.S., & Canad.* caretaker, concierge, custodian, doorkeeper, porter
jar[1] amphora, carafe, container, crock, flagon, jug, pitcher, pot, receptacle, urn, vase, vessel
jar[2] **1.** agitate, annoy, convulse, discompose, disturb, gall, get on one's nerves (*informal*), grate, grind, irk, irritate, nark (*slang*), nettle, offend, piss one off (*taboo slang*), rasp, rattle (*informal*) **2.** bicker, clash, contend, disagree, interfere, oppose, quarrel, wrangle **3.** jolt, rock, shake
jargon 1. argot, cant, dialect, idiom, lingo (*informal*), parlance, patois, slang, tongue, usage **2.** balderdash, bunkum *or* buncombe (*chiefly U.S.*), drivel, gabble, gibberish, gobbledegook, mumbo jumbo, nonsense, palaver, rigmarole, twaddle
jaundiced biased, bigoted, bitter, cynical, distorted, envious, hostile, jealous, partial, prejudiced, resentful, sceptical, spiteful, suspicious
jaunt airing, excursion, expedition, outing, promenade, ramble, stroll, tour, trip
jaunty airy, breezy, buoyant, carefree, dapper, gay, high-spirited, lively, perky, self-confident, showy, smart, sparky, sprightly, spruce, trim
jaw 1. *n.* chat, chinwag (*Brit. informal*), conversation, gossip, natter, talk **2.** *vb.* babble, chat, chatter, gossip, lecture, spout, talk
jaws abyss, aperture, entrance, gates, ingress, maw, mouth, opening, orifice
jazz up animate, enhance, enliven, heighten, improve
jealous 1. anxious, apprehensive, attentive, guarded, mistrustful, protective, rival, solicitous, suspicious, vigilant, wary, watchful, zealous **2.** covetous, desirous, envious, green, green-eyed, grudging, intolerant, invidious, resentful
jealousy covetousness, distrust, envy, heart-burning, ill-will, mistrust, possessiveness, resentment, spite, suspicion

Jeep *n Trademark* a small road vehicle with four-wheel drive.
jeer *vb* **1** to be derisive towards (someone). ~*n* **2** a cry of derision. **jeering** *adj, n*
Jehovah *n* God.
Jehovah's Witness *n* a member of a Christian Church whose followers believe that the end of the world is near.
jejune *adj* **1** simple and unsophisticated. **2** dull and uninteresting.
jejunum (jij-**june**-um) *n Anat* the part of the small intestine between the duodenum and the ileum.
Jekyll and Hyde *n* a person with two distinct personalities, one good and the other evil.
jell *vb* **1** to take on a definite form: *the changes have had little time to jell.* **2** same as **gel** (sense 2).
jellaba *n* a loose robe with a hood, worn by some Arab men.
jellied *adj* prepared in a jelly: *jellied eels.*
jelly *n, pl* **-lies 1** a fruit-flavoured dessert set with gelatine. **2** a food made from fruit juice boiled with sugar until the mixture sets, used for spreading on bread. **3** a savoury food preparation set with gelatine. **jelly-like** *adj*
jellyfish *n, pl* **-fish** a small sea creature with a jelly-like umbrella-shaped body and trailing tentacles.
jemmy *or US* **jimmy** *n, pl* **-mies** a short steel crowbar, used by burglars to prise open doors and windows.
jenny *n, pl* **-nies** a female donkey, ass, or wren.
jeopardize *or* **-ise** *vb* **-izing, -ized** *or* **-ising, -ised** to put (something) at risk: *the escalating violence that is jeopardizing current peace moves.*
jeopardy *n* danger of harm, loss, or death: *the survival of public hospitals is in jeopardy.*
jerboa *n* a small rodent of Asia and N Africa with long hind legs used for jumping.
jeremiad *n* a long mournful complaint.
jerepigo (jer-ree-**pee**-go) *n S African* a sweet fortified wine similar to port.
jerk *vb* **1** to move with an irregular or spasmodic motion. **2** to pull or push (something) abruptly or spasmodically. ~*n* **3** an abrupt or spasmodic movement. **4** an irregular jolting motion: *the irritating jerk that heralded a gear change.* **5** *Slang, chiefly US & Canad* a stupid or ignorant person.
jerkin *n* a short jacket.
jerky *adj* **jerkier, jerkiest** having an irregular jolting motion: *avoid any sudden or jerky movements.* **jerkily** *adv* **jerkiness** *n*
Jerry *n Old-fashioned, Brit slang* **1** (*pl* **-ries**) a German. **2** Germans collectively.
jerry-built *adj* (of houses) built badly with cheap materials.
jerry can *n* a flat-sided can used for carrying petrol or water.
jersey *n* **1** a knitted garment covering the upper part of the body. **2** a soft, slightly stretchy, machine-knitted fabric.
Jersey *n* a breed of reddish-brown dairy cattle that produces milk with a high butterfat content.
Jerusalem artichoke *n* a small yellowish-white vegetable that grows underground.
jest *n* **1** something done or said to amuse people. **2 in jest** as a joke: *many a true word is spoken in jest.* ~*vb* **3** to do or say something to amuse people.
jester *n* a professional clown employed by a king or nobleman during the Middle Ages.
Jesuit (**jezz**-yew-it) *n* a member of the Society of Jesus, a Roman Catholic religious order. **Jesuitical** *adj*
Jesus *interj Taboo slang* an oath expressing intense anger or shock.
jet[1] *n* **1** an aircraft driven by jet propulsion. **2** a thin stream of liquid or gas forced out of a small hole. **3** an outlet or nozzle through which a stream of liquid or gas is forced. ~*vb* **jetting, jetted 4** to travel by jet aircraft.
jet[2] *n* a hard black mineral that is polished and used in jewellery.
jet-black *adj* deep black.
jet engine *n* an aircraft engine that uses jet propulsion for forward motion.
jet lag *n* a feeling of fatigue and disorientation often experienced by air passengers who have crossed several time zones in a short space of time.
jet-propelled *adj* driven by jet propulsion.
jet propulsion *n* a method of propulsion by which an aircraft is moved forward by the force of the exhaust gases ejected from the rear.
jetsam *n* **1** goods thrown overboard to lighten a ship during a storm. **2 flotsam and jetsam** See **flotsam** (sense 2).
jet set *n* rich and fashionable people who travel widely for pleasure. **jet-setter** *n* **jet-setting** *adj*
jet ski *n* a small self-propelled vehicle resembling a scooter, which skims across water on a flat keel. **jet skiing** *n*
jettison *vb* **1** to abandon or give up: *jettisoning democracy in favour of fascism.* **2** to throw overboard.
jetty *n, pl* **-ties 1** a landing pier or dock. **2** a structure built from a shore out into the water to protect a harbour.
Jew *n* **1** a person whose religion is Judaism. **2** a descendant of the ancient Hebrews.

THESAURUS

jeer 1. *vb.* banter, barrack, cock a snook at (*Brit.*), contemn (*formal*), deride, flout, gibe, heckle, hector, knock (*informal*), mock, ridicule, scoff, sneer, taunt **2.** *n.* abuse, aspersion, boo, catcall, derision, gibe, hiss, hoot, obloquy, ridicule, scoff, sneer, taunt
jeopardize chance, endanger, expose, gamble, hazard, imperil, risk, stake, venture
jeopardy danger, endangerment, exposure, hazard, insecurity, liability, peril, pitfall, precariousness, risk, venture, vulnerability
jeremiad complaint, groan, keen, lament, lamentation, moan, plaint, wail
jerk jolt, lurch, pull, throw, thrust, tug, tweak, twitch, wrench, yank
jerky bouncy, bumpy, convulsive, fitful, jolting, jumpy, rough, shaky, spasmodic, tremulous, twitchy, uncontrolled
jerry-built cheap, defective, faulty, flimsy, ramshackle, rickety, shabby, slipshod, thrown together, unsubstantial
jest 1. *n.* banter, bon mot, crack (*slang*), fun, gag (*informal*), hoax, jape, joke, play, pleasantry, prank, quip, sally, sport, wisecrack (*informal*), witticism **2.** *vb.* banter, chaff, deride, gibe, jeer, joke, josh (*slang, chiefly U.S. & Canad.*), kid (*informal*), mock, quip, scoff, sneer, tease
jet *n.* **1.** flow, fountain, gush, spout, spray, spring, stream **2.** atomizer, nose, nozzle, rose, spout, sprayer, sprinkler ~*vb.* **3.** fly, soar, zoom
jettison abandon, discard, dump, eject, expel, heave, scrap, throw overboard, unload

jewel *n* **1** a precious or semiprecious stone. **2** a person or thing regarded as precious or special: *a fantastic little car, a real little jewel.* **3** a gemstone used as part of the machinery of a watch.

jewelled *or US* **jeweled** *adj* decorated with jewels.

jeweller *or US* **jeweler** *n* a person who buys, sells, and repairs jewellery.

jewellery *or US* **jewelry** *n* objects such as rings, necklaces, and bracelets, worn for decoration.

Jewess *n Now often offensive* a woman whose religion is Judaism.

Jewish *adj* of Jews or Judaism.

Jewry *n* Jews collectively.

jew's-harp *n* a small musical instrument held between the teeth and played by plucking a metal strip with the finger.

Jezebel *n* a wicked or shameless woman.

jib[1] *n* **1** *Naut* a triangular sail set in front of the foremast. **2 the cut of someone's jib** a person's manner or style.

jib[2] *vb* **jibbing, jibbed** *Chiefly Brit* **1** (of an animal) to stop short and refuse to go forwards: *my animal jibbed three times at wide leaps.* **2 jib at** to object to: *he jibs at any suggestion that his side are the underdogs.*

jib[3] *n* the projecting arm of a crane.

jibe[1] *n* **1** an insulting or taunting remark. ~*vb* **jibing, jibed 2** to make insulting or taunting remarks.

jibe[2] *vb* **jibing, jibed** *Informal* to be in accord or be consistent: *their apparent devotion hardly jibed with what he had heard about them.*

jibe[3] *vb* **jibing, jibed,** *n Naut* same as **gybe.**

jiffy *n, pl* **jiffies** *Informal* a very short time: *won't be a jiffy!*

Jiffy bag *n Trademark* a large padded envelope.

jig *n* **1** a lively folk dance. **2** music for this dance. **3** a mechanical device that holds and locates a part during machining. ~*vb* **jigging, jigged 4** to dance a jig. **5** to move with quick jerky movements.

jigger *n* a small whisky glass.

jiggered *adj Old-fashioned, informal* damned or blowed: *well, I'm jiggered, so that's where it went!*

jiggery-pokery *n Informal, chiefly Brit* dishonest behaviour; cheating.

jiggle *vb* **-gling, -gled** to move with quick jerky movements.

jigsaw *n* **1** Also called: **jigsaw puzzle** a puzzle in which the player has to put together a picture that has been cut into irregularly shaped interlocking pieces. **2** a mechanical saw with a fine steel blade for cutting along curved or irregular lines in sheets of material.

jihad *n* Islamic holy war against unbelievers.

jilt *vb* to leave or reject (a lover) abruptly or callously.

Jim Crow *n US* **1** the policy or practice of segregating Black people. **2** *Offensive* a Black person.

jingle *n* **1** a short catchy song used to advertise a product on radio or television. **2** a light ringing sound. ~*vb* **-gling, -gled 3** to make a light ringing sound.

jingoism *n* excessive and aggressive patriotism. **jingoistic** *or* **jingoist** *adj*

jink *vb* to move quickly or jerkily in order to dodge someone: *he jinked free and won a race to the line to level the scores.*

jinks *pl n* **high jinks** boisterous or mischievous behaviour.

jinni *or* **djinni** *n, pl* **jinn** *or* **djinn** a spirit in Muslim mythology that could take on human or animal form.

jinx *n* **1** someone or something believed to bring bad luck. ~*vb* **2** to bring bad luck to.

jitterbug *n* **1** a fast jerky American dance that was popular in the 1940s. ~*vb* **-bugging, -bugged 2** to dance the jitterbug.

jitters *pl n* **the** *Informal* a feeling of extreme nervousness experienced before an important event: *I had a case of the jitters during my first two speeches.*

jittery *adj* nervous.

jive *n* **1** a lively jerky dance that was popular in the 1940s and 1950s. ~*vb* **jiving, jived 2** to dance the jive. **jiver** *n*

Jnr Junior.

job *n* **1** a person's occupation or paid employment. **2** a piece of work; task. **3** the performance of a task: *he made a good job of the repair.* **4** *Informal* a difficult task: *they are having a job to fill his shoes.* **5** *Informal* a crime, esp. a robbery. **6 just the job** *Informal* exactly what is required. **7 make the best of a bad job** to cope as well as possible in unsatisfactory circumstances.

jobbing *adj* doing individual jobs for payment: *a jobbing gardener.*

Jobcentre *or* **job centre** *n Brit* a government office where advertisements of available jobs are displayed.

Jobclub *or* **Job Club** *n* a group of unemployed people which meets every weekday and is given advice on and help with job seeking.

jobless *adj* **1** unemployed. ~*pl n* **2** people who are unemployed: *the young jobless.*

job lot *n* a miscellaneous collection of articles sold together.

Job's comforter *n* a person who adds to someone else's distress while pretending to be sympathetic.

job sharing *n* an arrangement by which a job is shared by two part-time workers.

THESAURUS

jetty breakwater, dock, groyne, mole, pier, quay, wharf

jewel 1. brilliant, gemstone, ornament, precious stone, rock (*slang*), sparkler (*informal*), trinket **2.** charm, find, gem, humdinger (*slang*), masterpiece, paragon, pearl, prize, rarity, treasure, wonder

jewellery finery, gems, jewels, ornaments, precious stones, regalia, treasure, trinkets

Jezebel harlot, harridan, hussy, jade, virago, wanton, witch

jib *chiefly Brit.* balk, recoil, refuse, retreat, shrink, stop short

jig *vb.* bob, bounce, caper, jiggle, jounce, prance, shake, skip, twitch, wiggle, wobble

jingle *n.* **1.** chorus, ditty, doggerel, limerick, melody, song, tune **2.** clang, clangour, clink, rattle, reverberation, ringing, tinkle ~*vb.* **3.** chime, clatter, clink, jangle, rattle, ring, tinkle

jinx 1. *n.* black magic, curse, evil eye, hoodoo (*informal*), nemesis, plague, voodoo **2.** *vb.* bewitch, curse

jitters *informal* anxiety, fidgets, heebie-jeebies (*slang*), nerves, nervousness, tenseness, the shakes (*informal*), the willies (*informal*)

jittery agitated, anxious, fidgety, hyper (*informal*), jumpy, nervous, quivering, shaky, trembling, twitchy (*informal*), wired (*slang*)

job 1. activity, business, calling, capacity, career, craft, employment, function, livelihood, métier, occupation, office, position, post, profession, situation, trade, vocation **2.** affair, assignment, charge, chore, concern, contribution, duty, enterprise, errand, function, pursuit, responsibility, role, stint, task, undertaking, venture, work

jockey *n* **1** a person who rides horses in races as a profession. *~vb* **2 jockey for position** to try to obtain an advantage by skilful manoeuvring.

jockstrap *n* an elasticated belt with a pouch to support the genitals, worn by male athletes. Also called: **athletic support**

jocose (joke-**kohss**) *adj Old-fashioned* playful or humorous. **jocosely** *adv*

jocular *adj* **1** (of a person) often joking; good-humoured. **2** (of a remark) meant lightly or humorously. **jocularity** *n* **jocularly** *adv*

jocund (**jok**-kund) *adj Literary* cheerful or merry.

jodhpurs *pl n* trousers worn for riding, which are loose-fitting around the thighs and tight-fitting below the knees.

jog *vb* **jogging, jogged 1** to run at a gentle pace for exercise. **2** to nudge slightly. **3 jog along** to continue in a plodding way: *many people jog along in second gear for the whole of their lives* **4 jog someone's memory** to remind someone of something. *~n* **5** a slow run as a form of exercise. **jogger** *n* **jogging** *n*

joggle *vb* **-gling, -gled** to shake or move with a slightly jolting motion.

jog trot *n* an easy bouncy pace, midway between a walk and a trot.

john *n Slang, chiefly US & Canad* a toilet.

John Bull *n* England represented as a man.

johnny *n, pl* **-nies** *Brit old-fashioned, informal* a chap: *you legal johnnies.*

Johnny Canuck (kan-**nuk**) *n Canad informal* Canada represented as a man.

joie de vivre (**zhwah** de **veev**-ra) *n* enjoyment of life.

join *vb* **1** to become a member of (a club or organization). **2** to become part of (a queue or list). **3** to meet (someone) as a companion: *join me for a beer.* **4** to take part in (an activity): *join the war effort.* **5** (of two roads or rivers) to meet and come together. **6** to bring into contact: *join hands.* **7 join forces** to combine efforts with someone. *~n* **8** a place where two things are joined together. ~See also **join in, join up.**

joiner *n Chiefly Brit* a person whose job is making finished woodwork, such as window frames and stairs.

joinery *n* the skill or work of a joiner.

join in *vb* to take part in (an activity).

joint *adj* **1** shared by or belonging to two or more parties: *the two countries have issued a joint statement.* *~n* **2** *Anat* the junction between two or more bones: *a hip joint.* **3** a junction of two or more parts or objects: *a mortar joint.* **4** a piece of meat suitable for roasting. **5** *Slang* a building or place of entertainment: *strip joints.* **6** *Slang* a cannabis cigarette. **7 out of joint a** *Informal* out of order or out of keeping: *they find their routine lives out of joint with their training.* **b** (of a bone) knocked out of its normal position. **8 put someone's nose out of joint** See **nose** (sense 10). *~vb* **9** to provide a joint or joints. **10** to cut or divide (meat) into joints. **jointed** *adj* **jointly** *adv*

joint-stock company *n Brit* a business firm whose capital is owned jointly by shareholders.

join up *vb* to become a member of a military organization.

joist *n* a beam made of timber, steel, or concrete, used as a support in the construction of floors and roofs.

jojoba (hoe-**hoe**-ba) *n* a shrub whose seeds contain an oil used in cosmetics.

joke *n* **1** something that is said or done to amuse people. **2** someone or something that is ridiculous: *the country's inexperienced leaders are regarded as something of a joke.* **3 no joke** *Informal* a serious or difficult matter: *getting over mountain passes at ten thousand feet is no joke.* *~vb* **joking, joked 4** to say or do something to amuse people. **jokey** *adj* **jokingly** *adv*

joker *n* **1** a person who jokes a lot. **2** *Slang* a person regarded without respect: *waiting for the next jokers to sign up.* **3** an extra playing card in a pack, which can replace any other card in some games.

jol (**joll**) *S African slang ~n* **1** a party. *~vb* **jolling, jolled 2** to have a good time.

jollification *n* a merry festivity.

jollity *n* the condition of being jolly.

jolly *adj* **-lier, -liest 1** full of good humour. **2** involving a lot of fun: *big jolly birthday parties.* *~adv* **3** *Brit informal* very: *I'm going to have a jolly good try.* *~vb* **-lies, -lying, -lied 4 jolly along** *Informal* to try to keep (someone) cheerful by flattery or cheerful chat.

Jolly Roger *n* the traditional pirate flag, depicting a white skull and crossbones on a black background.

jolt *n* **1** a severe shock. **2** a sudden violent movement. *~vb* **3** to surprise or shock: *he was momentarily jolted by the news.* **4** to bump against (someone or something) with a sudden violent movement. **5** to move in a jerking manner.

THESAURUS

jobless idle, inactive, out-of-work, unemployed, unoccupied

jockey *vb.* **jockey for position** cajole, engineer, finagle (*informal*), ingratiate, insinuate, manage, manipulate, manoeuvre, negotiate, trim, wheedle

jocular amusing, comical, droll, facetious, frolicsome, funny, humorous, jesting, jocose, jocund, joking, jolly, jovial, playful, roguish, sportive, teasing, waggish, whimsical, witty

jog 1. canter, dogtrot, lope, run, trot **2.** bounce, jar, jerk, jiggle, joggle, jolt, jostle, jounce, rock, shake **3. jog along** lumber, plod, traipse (*informal*), tramp, trudge

joie de vivre ebullience, enjoyment, enthusiasm, gaiety, gusto, joy, joyfulness, pleasure, relish, zest

join 1. affiliate with, associate with, enlist, enrol, enter, sign up **2.** adjoin, conjoin, connect, meet **3.** combine, connect, fasten, link, tie, unite, yoke

joint *adj.* **1.** collective, combined, communal, concerted, consolidated, cooperative, joined, mutual, shared, united *~n.* **2.** articulation, connection, hinge, intersection, junction, juncture, knot, nexus, node, seam, union *~vb.* **3.** connect, couple, fasten, fit, join, unite **4.** carve, cut up, dismember, dissect, divide, segment, sever, sunder

jointly as one, collectively, in common, in conjunction, in league, in partnership, mutually, together, unitedly

joke *n.* **1.** frolic, fun, gag (*informal*), jape, jest, josh (*slang, chiefly U.S. & Canad.*), lark, play, prank, pun, quip, quirk, sally, sport, whimsy, wisecrack (*informal*), witticism, yarn **2.** buffoon, butt, clown, laughing stock, simpleton, target *~vb.* **3.** banter, chaff, deride, frolic, gambol, jest, kid (*informal*), mock, quip, ridicule, taunt, tease, wind up (*Brit. slang*)

joker buffoon, clown, comedian, comic, humorist, jester, prankster, trickster, wag, wit

jolly blithesome, carefree, cheerful, chirpy (*informal*), convivial, festive, frolicsome, funny, gay, genial, gladsome (*archaic*), hilarious, jocund, jovial, joyful, joyous, jubilant, merry, mirthful, playful, sportive, sprightly, upbeat (*informal*)

jolt *n.* **1.** blow, bolt from the blue, bombshell, reversal, setback, shock, surprise, thunderbolt **2.** bump, jar, jerk, jog, jump, lurch, quiver, shake, start *~vb.* **3.**

Jonah *n* a person believed to bring bad luck to those around him or her.

jonquil *n* a narcissus with sweet-smelling yellow or white flowers.

Jordanian *adj* 1 of Jordan. ~*n* 2 a person from Jordan.

josh *vb Slang, chiefly US & Canad* to joke or tease.

joss stick *n* a stick of incense, giving off a sweet smell when burnt.

jostle *vb* **-tling, -tled 1** to bump or push roughly: *television crews filming the scene were jostled by police.* 2 to compete with someone: *jostling for power.*

jot *vb* **jotting, jotted 1 jot down** to write a brief note of: *quickly jot down the answers to these questions.* ~*n* 2 the least bit: *it makes not one jot of difference.*

jotter *n* a small notebook.

jottings *pl n* notes jotted down.

joual (**zhwahl**) *n* nonstandard Canadian French dialect.

joule (**jool**) *n Physics* the SI unit of work or energy.

journal *n* 1 a newspaper or magazine. 2 a daily record of events.

journalese *n* a superficial style of writing regarded as typical of newspapers and magazines.

journalism *n* the profession of collecting, writing, and publishing news through newspapers and magazines or by radio and television.

journalist *n* a person who writes or edits news items for a newspaper or magazine or for radio or television. **journalistic** *adj*

journey *n* 1 the process of travelling from one place to another. 2 the time taken or distance travelled on a journey. ~*vb* 3 to make a journey.

journeyman *n, pl* **-men** a qualified craftsman who works for an employer.

joust *History* ~*n* 1 a combat with lances between two mounted knights. ~*vb* 2 to take part in such a tournament.

Jove *n* 1 Jupiter (the god). 2 **by Jove** *Old-fashioned* an exclamation of surprise or for emphasis.

jovial *adj* happy and cheerful. **joviality** *n* **jovially** *adv*

jowl[1] *n* 1 the lower jaw. 2 **cheek by jowl** See **cheek.** 3 **jowls** cheeks. **jowled** *adj*

jowl[2] *n* fatty flesh hanging from the lower jaw.

joy *n* 1 deep happiness and contentment. 2 something that brings deep happiness: *a thing of beauty is a joy for ever.* 3 *Brit informal* success or satisfaction: *we checked ports and airports without any joy.*

joyful *adj* feeling or bringing great joy: *joyful crowds; a joyful event.* **joyfully** *adv*

joyless *adj* feeling or bringing no joy.

joyous *adj* extremely happy and enthusiastic. **joyously** *adv*

joyride *n* a drive in a car one has stolen. **joyriding** *n* **joyrider** *n*

joystick *n* the control lever of an aircraft or a computer.

JP Justice of the Peace.

Jr Junior.

jube *n Austral & NZ informal* same as **jujube.**

jubilant *adj* feeling great joy. **jubilantly** *adv*

jubilation *n* a feeling of great joy and celebration.

jubilee *n* a special anniversary, esp. a 25th (**silver jubilee**) or 50th one (**golden jubilee**).

Judaic *adj* of Jews or Judaism.

Judaism *n* the religion of the Jews, based on the Old Testament and the Talmud.

Judas *n* a person who betrays a friend.

judder *vb Informal, chiefly Brit* to shake or vibrate violently: *the van juddered before it moved away.*

judge *n* 1 a public official with authority to hear cases and pass sentences in a court of law. 2 a person appointed to determine the result of a competition. 3 a person whose opinion on a particular subject is usually reliable: *a fine judge of men.* ~*vb* **judging, judged 4** to determine the result of (a competition). 5 to appraise critically: *she hopes people judge her on her work rather than her appearance.* 6 to decide (something) after inquiry: *we use a means test to judge the most needy cases.* 7 to believe or consider: *doctors judged that the benefits of such treatment outweighed the risk.*

judgment *or* **judgement** *n* 1 a decision formed after careful consideration: *the editorials reserve their judgment about the new political plan.* 2 the verdict pronounced by a court of law. 3 the ability to make critical distinctions and achieve a balanced viewpoint: *their judgment was unsound on foreign and defence*

THESAURUS

astonish, discompose, disturb, perturb, stagger, startle, stun, surprise, upset **4.** jar, jerk, jog, jostle, knock, push, shake, shove

jostle bump, butt, crowd, elbow, hustle, jog, joggle, jolt, press, push, scramble, shake, shove, squeeze, throng, thrust

journal 1. chronicle, daily, gazette, magazine, monthly, newspaper, paper, periodical, record, register, review, tabloid, weekly **2.** chronicle, commonplace book, daybook, diary, log, record

journalist broadcaster, columnist, commentator, contributor, correspondent, hack, newsman, newspaperman, pressman, reporter, scribe (*informal*), stringer

journey 1. *n.* excursion, expedition, jaunt, odyssey, outing, passage, peregrination, pilgrimage, progress, ramble, tour, travel, trek, trip, voyage **2.** *vb.* fare, fly, go, peregrinate, proceed, ramble, range, roam, rove, tour, travel, traverse, trek, voyage, wander, wend

jovial airy, animated, blithe, buoyant, cheery, convivial, cordial, gay, glad, happy, hilarious, jocose, jocund, jolly, jubilant, merry, mirthful

joy 1. bliss, delight, ecstasy, elation, exaltation, exultation, felicity, festivity, gaiety, gladness, glee, hilarity, pleasure, rapture, ravishment, satisfaction, transport **2.** charm, delight, gem, jewel, pride, prize, treasure, treat, wonder

joyful blithesome, cock-a-hoop, delighted, elated, enraptured, glad, gladsome (*archaic*), gratified, happy, jocund, jolly, jovial, jubilant, light-hearted, merry, over the moon (*informal*), pleased, rapt, satisfied

joyless cheerless, dejected, depressed, dismal, dispirited, downcast, dreary, gloomy, miserable, sad, unhappy

joyous cheerful, festive, heartening, joyful, merry, rapturous

jubilant cock-a-hoop, elated, enraptured, euphoric, excited, exuberant, exultant, glad, joyous, overjoyed, over the moon (*informal*), rejoicing, rhapsodic, thrilled, triumphal, triumphant

jubilation celebration, ecstasy, elation, excitement, exultation, festivity, jamboree, joy, jubilee, triumph

jubilee carnival, celebration, festival, festivity, fête, gala, holiday

judge *n.* **1.** beak (*Brit. slang*), justice, magistrate **2.** adjudicator, arbiter, arbitrator, moderator, referee, umpire **3.** appraiser, arbiter, assessor, authority, connoisseur, critic, evaluator, expert ~*vb.* **4.** adjudge, adjudicate, arbitrate, ascertain, conclude, decide, deter-

issues. **4** the formal decision of the judge of a competition. **5 against one's better judgment** contrary to what one thinks is sensible: *against my better judgment, I asked for another bourbon.* **6 pass judgment** to give one's opinion, usually a critical one, on a matter.
➤ The alternative spellings with or without an "e" between "g" and "m" are equally acceptable.

judgmental *or* **judgemental** *adj* making judgments, esp. critical ones, about other people's conduct.

Judgment Day *n Christianity* the occasion of the Last Judgment by God at the end of the world.

judicial *adj* **1** of judges or the administration of justice. **2** showing or using good judgment: *judicial self-restraint.* **judicially** *adv*

judiciary *n* the branch of the central authority in a country that administers justice.

judicious *adj* having or showing good judgment: *the judicious use of charge cards.* **judiciously** *adv*

judo *n* a sport derived from jujitsu, in which the two opponents try to throw or force each other on to the ground.

jug *n* a container with a handle and a small spout, used for holding and pouring liquids.

jugged hare *n* hare stewed in an earthenware pot.

juggernaut *n* **1** *Brit* a very large heavy lorry. **2** any terrible force that demands complete self-sacrifice.

juggle *vb* **-gling, -gled 1** to throw and catch several objects continuously so that most are in the air at the same time. **2** to keep (several activities) in progress at the same time: *women who are adept at juggling priorities.* **3** to manipulate (facts or figures) to suit one's purpose. **juggler** *n*

jugular *n* a large vein in the neck that carries blood to the heart from the head. Also called: **jugular vein**

juice *n* **1** a drink made from the liquid part of a fruit or vegetable: *grapefruit juice.* **2** *Informal* **a** petrol. **b** electricity. **3 juices a** the fluids in a person's or animal's body: *digestive juices.* **b** the liquid that comes out of meat when it is cooked.

juicy *adj* **juicier, juiciest 1** full of juice. **2** *Informal* interesting and exciting: *juicy details.*

jujitsu *n* the traditional Japanese system of unarmed self-defence.

juju *n* **1** a magic charm or fetish used by some tribes in W Africa. **2** the power associated with a juju.

jujube *n* a chewy sweet made of flavoured gelatine.

jukebox *n* an automatic coin-operated record player.

jukskei *n S African* a game in which a peg is thrown over a fixed distance at a stake fixed into the ground.

Jul. July.

julep *n* a sweet alcoholic drink, usually garnished with sprigs of mint.

Julian calendar *n* the calendar introduced by Julius Caesar, in which leap years occur every fourth year and in every centenary year.

julienne *adj* **1** (of vegetables or meat) cut into thin shreds. *~n* **2** a clear soup containing thinly shredded vegetables.

July *n, pl* **-lies** the seventh month of the year.

jumble *n* **1** a disordered mass or state. **2** articles donated for a jumble sale. *~vb* **-bling, -bled 3** to mix up.

jumble sale *n* a sale, usually of second-hand articles, in aid of charity.

jumbo *adj* **1** *Informal* very large: *jumbo prawns.* *~n, pl* **-bos 2** short for **jumbo jet**.

jumbo jet *n Informal* a very large jet-propelled airliner.

jump *vb* **1** to move suddenly up into the air by using the muscles in the legs and feet. **2** to move quickly: *he jumps on a No. 6 bus.* **3** to jerk with astonishment or shock: *he jumped when he heard a loud noise.* **4** (of prices) to rise suddenly or abruptly. **5** to change quickly from one subject to another: *any other comments before I jump on to the next section?* **6** *Informal* to attack without warning: *the officer was jumped by three prisoners who broke his jaw.* **7 jump down someone's throat** *Informal* to speak sharply to someone. **8 jump the gun** See **gun** (sense 3). **9 jump the queue a** to take a place in a queue ahead of people who are already queueing. **b** to have an unfair advantage over other people: *squatters should not be able to jump the queue for housing.* **10 jump to it** *Informal* to begin doing something immediately. *~n* **11** the act or an instance of jumping. **12** *Sport* any of several contests that involve jumping: *the long jump.* **13** a sudden rise: *a 78% jump in taxable profits.* **14** a sudden change from one subject to another: *stunning jumps from thought to thought.* **15** a step or degree: *one jump ahead of the competition.* **16 take a running jump** *Brit informal* a contemptuous expression of dismissal. *~See also* **jump at, jump on.**

jump at *vb* to accept eagerly: *I jumped at the chance to return to English county cricket.*

THESAURUS

mine, discern, distinguish, mediate, referee, umpire **5.** appraise, appreciate, assess, consider, criticize, esteem, estimate, evaluate, examine, rate, review, value

judgment *or* **judgement 1.** appraisal, assessment, conclusion, decision, deduction, determination, diagnosis, estimate, finding, opinion, valuation, view **2.** award (*Law*), decree, finding, order, ruling, sentence, verdict **3.** acumen, common sense, discernment, discrimination, intelligence, penetration, percipience, perspicacity, prudence, sagacity, sense, shrewdness, taste, understanding, wisdom **4.** conclusion, decision, result

judicial judiciary, juridical, legal, magisterial, official

judicious acute, astute, careful, cautious, circumspect, considered, diplomatic, discerning, discreet, discriminating, enlightened, expedient, informed, politic, prudent, rational, reasonable, sagacious, sage, sane, sapient, sensible, shrewd, skilful, sober, sound, thoughtful, well-advised, well-judged, wise

jug carafe, container, crock, ewer, jar, pitcher, urn, vessel

juggle alter, change, disguise, doctor (*informal*), falsify, fix (*informal*), manipulate, manoeuvre, misrepresent, modify, tamper with

juice extract, fluid, liquid, liquor, nectar, sap, secretion, serum

juicy 1. lush, moist, sappy, succulent, watery **2.** *informal* colourful, interesting, provocative, racy, risqué, sensational, spicy (*informal*), suggestive, vivid

jumble 1. *n.* chaos, clutter, confusion, disarrangement, disarray, disorder, farrago, gallimaufry, hodgepodge, hotchpotch (*U.S.*), litter, medley, *mélange,* mess, miscellany, mishmash, mixture, muddle, pig's breakfast (*informal*) **2.** *vb.* confound, confuse, disarrange, dishevel, disorder, disorganize, entangle, mistake, mix, muddle, ravel, shuffle, tangle

jumbo *informal* elephantine, giant, gigantic, ginormous (*informal*), huge, humongous (*U.S. slang*), immense, large, mega (*informal*), oversized

jump *vb.* **1.** bounce, bound, caper, clear, gambol, hop, hurdle, leap, skip, spring, vault **2.** flinch, jerk, recoil, start, wince **3.** advance, ascend, boost, escalate, gain, hike, increase, mount, rise, surge **4.** avoid, digress, evade, miss, omit, overshoot, skip, switch *~n.* **5.**

jumped-up *adj Informal* having suddenly risen in significance and appearing arrogant: *a jumped-up bunch of ex-student leaders.*

jumper[1] *n* **1** *Chiefly Brit* a knitted garment covering the upper part of the body. **2** *US & Canad* a pinafore dress.

jumper[2] *n* a person or animal that jumps.

jump jet *n Informal* a fixed-wing jet aircraft that can land and take off vertically.

jump leads *pl n* two heavy cables used to start a motor vehicle with a flat battery by connecting the flat battery to the battery of another vehicle.

jump on *vb Informal* to make a sudden physical or verbal attack on: *the press really jumped on him.*

jump-start *vb* **1** to start the engine of (a motor vehicle) by pushing or rolling it and then engaging the gears. *~n* **2** the act of starting a motor vehicle in this way.

jump suit *n* a one-piece garment combining trousers and top.

jumpy *adj* **jumpier, jumpiest** nervous or apprehensive.

Jun. **1** June. **2** Junior.

junction *n* a place where roads or railway lines meet, link, or cross each other.

juncture *n* a point in time, esp. a critical one: *the exact historical juncture when Britain decided to "peripheralize" India.*

June *n* the sixth month of the year.

jungle *n* **1** a forest area in a hot country with luxuriant vegetation. **2** a confused or confusing situation: *the administrative jungle.* **3** a situation where there is an intense struggle for survival: *the economic jungle.*

junior *adj* **1** lower in rank or position: *junior officers.* **2** younger: *world junior champion.* **3** *Brit* of school children between the ages of 7 and 11 approximately. **4** *US* of the third year of a four-year course at college or high school. *~n* **5** a person holding a low rank or position. **6** a person who is younger than another person: *the man she is to marry is twenty years her junior.* **7** *Brit* a junior school child. **8** *US* a junior student.

Junior *adj* the younger of two: usually used after a name to distinguish between two people of the same name: *Harry Connick Junior.*

juniper *n* an evergreen shrub with purple berries which are used to make gin.

junk[1] *n* **1** old or unwanted objects. **2** *Informal* rubbish: *the sheer junk written about astrology.* **3** *Slang* narcotic drugs, esp. heroin.

junk[2] *n* a Chinese sailing boat with a flat bottom and square sails.

junket *n* **1** an excursion made by a public official and paid for out of public funds. **2** a sweet dessert made of flavoured milk set with rennet. **3** a feast. **junketing** *n*

junk food *n* food with a low nutritional value.

junkie *n Informal* a drug addict.

junk mail *n* unsolicited mail advertising goods or services.

junta *n* a group of military officers holding the power in a country after a revolution.

Jupiter *n* **1** the king of the Roman gods. **2** the largest planet.

Jurassic *adj Geol* of the geological period about 180 million years ago, during which dinosaurs flourished.

juridical *adj* of law or the administration of justice.

jurisdiction *n* **1** the right or power to administer justice and to apply laws. **2** the exercise or extent of such right or power. **3** authority in general: *clubs under the FA's jurisdiction.*

jurisprudence *n* the science or philosophy of law.

jurist *n* a person who is an expert on law.

juror *n* a member of a jury.

jury *n, pl* **-ries** **1** a group of twelve people sworn to deliver a true verdict according to the evidence upon a case presented in a court of law. **2** a group of people appointed to judge a competition.

jury box *n* an enclosure where the jury sits in a court of law.

jury-rigged *adj Chiefly naut* set up in a makeshift manner.

just *adv* **1** very recently: *the results have just been published.* **2** at this very instant or in the very near future: *news is just coming in of a nuclear explosion.* **3** no more than; only: *nothing fancy, just solid German fare.* **4** exactly: *just the opposite.* **5** barely: *the swimmers arrived just in time for the opening ceremony.* **6** **just about** practically or virtually: *just about everyone.* **7** **just about to** very soon going to: *it was just about to explode.* **8** **just a moment, second,** *or* **minute** an expression requesting someone to wait for a short time. **9** **just now** **a** a short time ago: *as you said just now.* **b** at the present time: *he needs all the support he can get just now.* **c** *S African informal* in a little while. **10** **just so** arranged with precision: *a cottage with the gardens and rooms all just so.* *~adj* **11** fair and right: *a just war.* **justly** *adv* **justness** *n*

justice *n* **1** the quality of being just. **2** the administration of law according to prescribed and accepted principles. **3** a judge. **4** **bring to justice** to capture, try, and punish (a criminal). **5** **do justice to** to show to full advantage: *she wore white slacks and a sleeveless blouse that did full justice to her trim figure.*

THESAURUS

bound, buck, caper, hop, leap, skip, spring, vault **6.** jar, jerk, jolt, lurch, shock, start, swerve, twitch, wrench **7.** advance, augmentation, boost, increase, increment, rise, upsurge, upturn

jumper jersey, pullover, sweater, woolly

jumpy agitated, anxious, apprehensive, fidgety, hyper (*informal*), jittery (*informal*), nervous, on edge, restless, shaky, tense, timorous, twitchy (*informal*), wired (*slang*)

junction connection, coupling, joint, juncture, linking

juncture conjuncture, contingency, crisis, crux, emergency, exigency, moment, occasion, point, predicament, strait, time

junior inferior, lesser, lower, minor, secondary, subordinate, younger

junk clutter, debris, leavings, litter, oddments, odds and ends, refuse, rubbish, rummage, scrap, trash, waste

jurisdiction **1.** authority, command, control, dominion, influence, power, prerogative, rule, say, sway **2.** area, bounds, circuit, compass, district, dominion, field, orbit, province, range, scope, sphere, zone

just *adv.* **1.** hardly, lately, only now, recently, scarcely **2.** at most, but, merely, no more than, nothing but, only, simply, solely **3.** absolutely, completely, entirely, exactly, perfectly, precisely **4.** **just about** all but, almost, around, close to, nearly, not quite, practically, well-nigh *~adj.* **5.** appropriate, apt, blameless, conscientious, decent, deserved, due, equitable, fair, fairminded, fitting, good, honest, honourable, impartial, justified, lawful, legitimate, merited, proper, pure, reasonable, right, righteous, rightful, suitable, unbiased, upright, virtuous, well-deserved

justice **1.** equity, fairness, honesty, impartiality, integrity, justness, law, legality, legitimacy, reasonableness, rectitude, right **2.** judge, magistrate

justice of the peace *n* a magistrate who is authorized to act as a judge in a local court of law.

justifiable *adj* having a good cause or reason: *I reacted with justifiable indignation.* **justifiably** *adv*

justify *vb* **-fies, -fying, -fied 1** to prove (something) to be just or valid: *the idea of the ends justifying the means.* **2** to defend (an action) as being warranted: *an essay justifying his conversion to Catholicism.* **3** to arrange (text) when typing or printing so that both margins are straight. **justification** *n*

jute *n* a fibre that comes from the bark of an East Indian plant, used in making rope, sacks, and mats.

jut out *vb* **jutting, jutted** to stick out.

juvenile *adj* **1** young; not fully adult: *juvenile offenders.* **2** of or for young people: *juvenile court.* **3** immature in behaviour. ~*n* **4** a young person.

juvenile delinquent *n* a young person who is guilty of a crime. **juvenile delinquency** *n*

juvenilia *pl n* works produced in an artist's youth.

juxtapose *vb* **-posing, -posed** to place (two objects or ideas) close together or side by side. **juxtaposition** *n*

THESAURUS

justifiable acceptable, defensible, excusable, fit, lawful, legitimate, proper, reasonable, right, sound, tenable, understandable, valid, vindicable, warrantable, well-founded

justification 1. absolution, apology, approval, defence, exculpation, excuse, exoneration, explanation, extenuation, plea, rationalization, vindication **2.** basis, defence, grounds, plea, reason, warrant

justify absolve, acquit, approve, confirm, defend, establish, exculpate, excuse, exonerate, explain, legalize, legitimize, maintain, substantiate, support, sustain, uphold, validate, vindicate, warrant

justly accurately, correctly, equally, equitably, fairly, honestly, impartially, lawfully, properly

jut out bulge, extend, impend, overhang, poke, project, protrude, stick out

juvenile 1. *adj.* babyish, boyish, callow, childish, girlish, immature, inexperienced, infantile, jejune, puerile, undeveloped, unsophisticated, young, youthful **2.** *n.* adolescent, boy, child, girl, infant, minor, youth

juxtaposition adjacency, closeness, contact, contiguity, nearness, propinquity, proximity, vicinity

K

K 1 kelvin(s). 2 *Chess* king. 3 *Chem* potassium. 4 one thousand. 5 *Computers* a unit of 1024 words, bits, or bytes.

Kaffir (**kaf**-fer) *n S African offensive, obsolete* a Black African.

kaftan *or* **caftan** *n* 1 a long loose garment worn by men in eastern countries. 2 a woman's dress resembling this.

kahawai *n* a food and game fish of New Zealand.

kai *n NZ informal* food.

kail *n* same as **kale**.

kaiser (**kize**-er) *n History* a German or Austro-Hungarian emperor.

kak (**kuck**) *n S African taboo* 1 faeces. 2 rubbish.

kaka *n* a parrot of New Zealand.

kakapo *n, pl* **-pos** a ground-living nocturnal New Zealand parrot that resembles an owl.

kalashnikov *n* a Russian-made automatic rifle.

kale *n* a type of cabbage with crinkled leaves.

kaleidoscope *n* 1 a tube-shaped toy lined with angled mirrors and containing loose pieces of coloured paper that form intricate patterns when viewed through a hole in the end. 2 any complicated or rapidly changing set of colours, circumstances etc.: *a kaleidoscope of shifting political groups and alliances.* **kaleidoscopic** *adj*

kalends *pl n* same as **calends**.

kaleyard *n Scot* a vegetable garden.

Kamasutra (kah-ma-**soo**-tra) *n* **the** an ancient Hindu text on sex.

kamikaze (kam-mee-**kah**-zee) *n* 1 (in World War II) a Japanese pilot who performed a suicidal mission. *~adj* 2 (of an action) undertaken in the knowledge that it will result in the death or injury of the person performing it: *a kamikaze attack.*

Kamloops trout *n* a bright silvery rainbow trout common in British Columbia, Canada.

kangaroo *n, pl* **-roos** a large Australian marsupial with powerful hind legs used for leaping.

kangaroo court *n* an unofficial court set up by a group to discipline its members.

kaolin *n* a fine white clay used in making porcelain and in some medicines.

kapok *n* a fluffy fibre from a tropical tree, used for stuffing pillows and padding sleeping bags.

kaput (kap-**poot**) *adj Informal* ruined or broken: *the chronometer, incidentally, is kaput.*

karakul *n* 1 a sheep of central Asia, the lambs of which have soft curled dark hair. 2 the fur prepared from these lambs.

karaoke *n* a form of entertainment in which members of the public sing well-known songs over a prerecorded backing tape.

karate *n* a Japanese system of unarmed combat, in which punches, chops, and kicks are made with the hands, feet, elbows, and legs.

Karitane (kar-ree-**tah**-nee) *n NZ* a nurse for babies; nanny.

karma *n Hinduism, Buddhism* a person's actions affecting his or her fate in the next reincarnation.

karoo *or* **karroo** *n, pl* **-roos** *S African* an arid semidesert plateau of Southern Africa.

kaross (ka-**ross**) *n S African* a blanket made of animal skins sewn together.

kart *n* same as **go-kart**.

kasbah *n* same as **casbah**.

katydid *n* a large green grasshopper of North America.

kauri *n* a large New Zealand conifer grown for its valuable wood and resin.

kayak *n* 1 an Inuit canoe-like boat consisting of a frame covered with animal skins. 2 a fibreglass or canvas-covered canoe of similar design.

kazoo *n, pl* **-zoos** a cigar-shaped metal musical instrument that produces a buzzing sound when the player hums into it.

kbyte *Computers* kilobyte.

kcal kilocalorie.

kea *n* a large brown-green parrot of New Zealand.

kebab *n* a dish consisting of small pieces of meat and vegetables, usually threaded onto skewers and grilled.

kedge *Naut ~vb* **kedging, kedged** 1 to move (a ship) along by hauling in on the cable of a light anchor. *~n* 2 a light anchor used for kedging.

kedgeree *n Chiefly Brit* a dish consisting of rice, fish, and eggs.

keek *vb, n Scot* same as **peep**[1].

keel *n* 1 one of the main lengthways steel or timber pieces along the base of a ship, to which the frames are fastened. 2 **on an even keel** working or progressing smoothly without any sudden changes.

keelhaul *vb* 1 to reprimand (someone) harshly. 2 *History* to drag (someone) under the keel of a ship as a punishment.

keel over *vb* 1 (of an object) to turn upside down. 2 *Informal* (of a person) to collapse suddenly.

keelson *or* **kelson** *n* a lengthways beam fastened to the keel of a ship for strength.

keen[1] *adj* 1 eager or enthusiastic: *a keen gardener.* 2 **keen on** fond of; devoted to: *he is very keen on sport.* 3 intense or strong: *a keen interest in environmental issues.* 4 intelligent, quick, and perceptive: *a keen sense of humour.* 5 (of sight, smell, or hearing) capable of recognizing fine distinctions. 6 (of a knife or blade) having a sharp cutting edge. 7 very strong and cold: *a keen wind.* 8 very competitive: *keen prices.* **keenly** *adv* **keenness** *n*

keen[2] *vb* 1 to lament the dead. *~n* 2 a lament for the dead.

keep *vb* **keeping, kept** 1 to have or retain possession of (something). 2 to have temporary charge of: *he'd kept my broken beads in his pocket for me all evening.*

THESAURUS

kamikaze foolhardy, self-destructive, suicidal

keen 1. ardent, avid, devoted to, eager, ebullient, enthusiastic, fond of, into (*informal*) 2. earnest, fanatical, fervid, fierce, impassioned, intense, zealous 3. acid, acute, astute, biting, brilliant, canny, caustic, clever, cutting, discerning, discriminating, edged, finely honed, incisive, penetrating, perceptive, perspicacious, piercing, pointed, quick, razorlike, sagacious, sapient, sardonic, satirical, sensitive, sharp, shrewd, tart, trenchant, vitriolic, wise

keenness 1. ardour, avidity, avidness, diligence, eagerness, earnestness, ebullience, enthusiasm, fervour, impatience, intensity, passion, zeal, zest 2. acerbity, harshness, incisiveness, mordancy, penetration, pungency, rigour, severity, sharpness, sternness,

3 to store in a customary place: *I keep it at the back of the drawer with my journal.* 4 to remain or cause (someone or something) to remain in a specified state or condition: *keep still.* 5 to continue or cause (someone) to continue: *keep going straight on.* 6 to stay (in, on, or at a place or position): *keep to the paths.* 7 to have as part of normal stock: *they keep a small stock of first-class German wines.* 8 to support (someone) financially. 9 to detain (someone). 10 to be faithful to (something): *to keep a promise.* 11 (of food) to stay in good condition for a certain time: *fish doesn't keep very well.* 12 to observe (a religious festival) with rites or ceremonies. 13 to maintain by writing regular records in: *he keeps a nature diary in his spare time.* 14 to look after or maintain for use, pleasure, or profit: *an old man who kept goats and cows.* 15 to associate with: *she has started keeping bad company.* 16 **keep in with** to stay friendly with someone as they may be useful to you. 17 **how are you keeping?** are you well? ~*n* 18 the cost of food and other everyday expense: *I have to earn my keep.* 19 the main tower within the walls of a medieval castle or fortress. 20 **for keeps** *Informal* permanently. ~See also **keep at, keep away,** etc.

keep at *vb* 1 to persist in (an activity). 2 to compel (a person) to continue doing (a task).

keep away *vb* (often foll. by *from*) to prevent (someone) from going (somewhere).

keep back *vb* to refuse to reveal (something).

keep down *vb* 1 to hold (a group of people) under control. 2 to cause (numbers or costs) not to increase. 3 to lie low. 4 to cause (food) to stay in the stomach; not vomit.

keeper *n* 1 a person in charge of animals in a zoo. 2 a person in charge of a museum, collection, or section of a museum. 3 a person who supervises a person or thing: *the self-appointed keeper of the village conscience.* 4 short for **gamekeeper, goalkeeper** or **wicketkeeper.**

keep fit *n* exercises designed to promote physical fitness if performed regularly.

keep from *vb* 1 to restrain (oneself or someone else) from (doing something). 2 to preserve or protect (someone) from (something): *this will keep you from falling asleep.*

keeping *n* 1 **in keeping with** suitable or appropriate to or for. 2 **out of keeping with** unsuitable or inappropriate to or for.

keep off *vb* 1 to stay or cause (someone) to stay at a distance (from). 2 to avoid or cause to avoid (something): *to keep off alcohol; to keep babies off sugar.* 3 to avoid or cause (someone) to avoid (a topic).

keep on *vb* 1 to persist in (doing something): *petrol consumption keeps on rising.* 2 to continue to employ: *a skeleton staff of 20 is being kept on at the firm's offices in Croydon.* 3 **keep on about** to persist in talking about. 4 **keep on at** to nag (a person).

keep out *vb* 1 to remain or cause (someone) to remain outside. 2 **keep out of a** to cause (someone) to remain unexposed to (an unpleasant situation). **b** to avoid: *to keep out of trouble.*

keepsake *n* a gift kept in memory of the giver.

keep to *vb* 1 to do exactly what was expected of one: *he kept to his normal schedule.* 2 to be confined to: *she kept to her bed until her flu had cleared up.* 3 **keep oneself to oneself** to avoid the company of others. 4 **keep to oneself a** to avoid the company of others. **b** to avoid giving away (information).

keep up *vb* 1 to maintain (prices, standards, or one's morale) at the present level. 2 to maintain in good condition. 3 **keep up with a** to maintain a pace set by (someone). **b** to remain informed about: *he liked to think he kept up with current musical trends.* **c** to remain in contact with (someone). 4 **keep up with the Joneses** *Informal* to compete with one's friends or neighbours in material possessions.

keg *n* a small barrel in which beer is transported and stored.

kelp *n* a large brown seaweed rich in iodine and potash.

kelpie *n* (in Scottish folklore) a water spirit in the form of a horse.

kelson *n* same as **keelson.**

kelt *n* a salmon that has recently spawned.

Kelt *n* same as **Celt.**

kelvin *n Physics* the basic SI unit of thermodynamic temperature.

Kelvin scale *n Physics* a thermodynamic temperature scale starting at absolute zero.

ken *n* 1 **beyond one's ken** beyond one's range of knowledge. ~*vb* **kenning, kenned** *or* **kent** 2 *Scot & N English dialect* to know.

kendo *n* the Japanese sport of fencing using wooden staves.

kennel *n* 1 a hutlike shelter for a dog. 2 **kennels** a place where dogs are bred, trained, or boarded. ~*vb* **-nelling, -nelled** *or US* **-neling, -neled** to keep (a dog) in a kennel.

Kenyan *adj* 1 from Kenya. ~*n* 2 a person from Kenya.

THESAURUS

trenchancy, unkindness, virulence 3. astuteness, canniness, cleverness, discernment, insight, sagacity, sapience, sensitivity, shrewdness, wisdom

keep *vb.* 1. conserve, control, hold, maintain, possess, preserve, retain 2. accumulate, amass, carry, deal in, deposit, furnish, garner, heap, hold, pile, place, stack, stock, store, trade in 3. board, feed, foster, maintain, nourish, nurture, provide for, provision, subsidize, support, sustain, victual 4. arrest, block, check, constrain, control, curb, delay, detain, deter, hamper, hamstring, hinder, hold, hold back, impede, inhibit, keep back, limit, obstruct, prevent, restrain, retard, shackle, stall, withhold 5. adhere to, celebrate, commemorate, comply with, fulfil, hold, honour, obey, observe, perform, respect, solemnize 6. care for, defend, guard, look after, maintain, manage, mind, operate, protect, safeguard, shelter, shield, tend, watch over 7. accompany, associate with, consort with, fraternize with ~*n.* 8. board, food, livelihood, living, maintenance, means, nourishment, subsistence, support 9. castle, citadel, donjon, dungeon, fastness, stronghold, tower

keep at be steadfast, carry on, complete, continue, drudge, endure, finish, grind, labour, last, maintain, persevere, persist, remain, slave, stay, stick, toil

keep back censor, conceal, hide, reserve, suppress, withhold

keeper attendant, caretaker, curator, custodian, defender, gaoler, governor, guard, guardian, jailer, overseer, preserver, steward, superintendent, warden, warder

keeping accord, agreement, balance, compliance, conformity, congruity, consistency, correspondence, harmony, observance, proportion

keep on carry on, continue, endure, last, persevere, persist, prolong, remain

keepsake emblem, favour, memento, relic, remembrance, reminder, souvenir, symbol, token

keep up compete, contend, continue, emulate, keep

kepi *n* a French military cap with a flat top and a horizontal peak.

kept *vb* **1** the past of **keep. 2 kept woman** *or* **man** a person financially supported by someone in return for sexual favours.

keratin *n* a fibrous protein found in the hair and nails.

kerb *or US & Canad* **curb** *n* a line of stone or concrete forming an edge between a pavement and a roadway.

kerb crawling *n* the act of driving slowly beside a kerb to pick up a prostitute. **kerb crawler** *n*

kerbstone *or US & Canad* **curbstone** *n* one of a series of stones that form a kerb.

kerchief *n* a piece of cloth worn over the head or round the neck.

kerfuffle *n Informal, chiefly Brit* a noisy and disorderly incident.

kermes (**kur**-meez) *n* the dried bodies of female scale insects, used as a red dyestuff.

kernel *n* **1** the edible seed of a nut or fruit within the shell or stone. **2** the grain of a cereal, such as wheat, consisting of the seed in a hard husk. **3** the central or essential part of something: *there is a kernel of truth in these remarks.*

kerosene *n Chiefly US, Canad, Austral, & NZ* same as **paraffin** (sense 1).

kestrel *n* a small falcon that feeds on small animals such as mice.

ketch *n* a two-masted sailing ship.

ketchup *n* a thick cold sauce, usu. made of tomatoes.

ketone (**kee**-tone) *n Chem* any of a class of compounds with the general formula R′COR.

kettle *n* **1** a metal container with a handle and spout, for boiling water. **2 a different kettle of fish** a different matter entirely. **3 a fine kettle of fish** a difficult or awkward situation.

kettledrum *n* a large bowl-shaped metal drum that can be tuned to play specific notes.

key[1] *n* **1** a specially shaped metal instrument, for moving the bolt of a lock so as to lock or unlock a door, suitcase, etc. **2** an instrument that is turned to operate a valve, clock winding mechanism, etc. **3** any of a set of levers pressed to operate a typewriter, computer, or musical keyboard instrument. **4** a scale of musical notes that starts at one specific note. **5** something that is crucial in providing an explanation or interpretation. **6** a means of achieving a desired end: *education is the key to success in most walks of life today.* **7** a list of explanations of symbols, codes, or abbreviations. **8** pitch: *he spoke in a low key.* ~*adj* **9** of great importance: *five key players have withdrawn from the Scotland squad.* ~*vb* **10** to harmonize with: *training and educational programmes uniquely keyed for local needs.* **11** to adjust or fasten (something) with a key or some similar device. **12** same as **keyboard.** ~See also **key in.**

key[2] *n* same as **cay.**

keyboard *n* **1** a set of keys on a typewriter, computer, or piano. **2** a musical instrument played using a keyboard. ~*vb* **3** to enter (text) in type using a keyboard. **keyboarder** *n*

keyed up *adj* very excited or nervous.

key grip *n* the person in charge of moving and setting up camera tracks and scenery in a film or television studio.

keyhole *n* an opening for inserting a key into a lock.

keyhole surgery *n* surgery carried out using very small instruments, performed through a narrow hole cut in the body rather than through a major incision.

key in *vb* to enter (information or instructions) into a computer by means of a keyboard.

key money *n* a sum of money required from a new tenant of a house or flat before he or she moves in.

Keynesian (**cane**-zee-an) *adj* of the economic theories of JM Keynes, who argued that governments should fund public works to maintain full employment, accepting if necessary the consequence of inflation.

keynote *n* **1** a central or dominant idea in a speech or literary work. ~*adj* **2** central or dominating: *his keynote speech to the party conference.* ~*n* **3** the note on which a scale or key is based.

keypad *n* a small panel with a set of buttons for operating a teletext system, electronic calculator, etc.

keyring *n* a metal ring, often decorative, for keeping keys on.

key signature *n Music* a group of sharps or flats at the beginning of each stave line to indicate the key.

keystone *n* **1** the most important part of a process, organization, etc.: *the keystone of the government's economic policy.* **2** the central stone at the top of an arch.

keyword *n Computers* a word or phrase that a computer will search for in order to locate the information or file that the computer user has requested.

kg kilogram.

KG (in Britain) Knight of the Order of the Garter.

KGB (formerly) the Soviet secret police.

khaki *adj* **1** dull yellowish-brown. ~*n* **2** a hard-wearing fabric of this colour, used for military uniforms.

khan *n* a title of respect in Afghanistan and central Asia.

kHz kilohertz.

kia ora *interj NZ* good luck!

kibbutz *n, pl* **kibbutzim** a farm, factory, or other workplace in Israel, owned and run communally by its members.

kibosh *n* **put the kibosh on** *Slang* to put a stop to.

kick *vb* **1** to drive, push, or hit with the foot or feet. **2** to strike out with the feet, as in swimming. **3** to raise a leg high, as in dancing. **4** *Rugby* to score (a conversion, drop kick, or penalty) with a kick: *Hastings kicked two penalties for Scotland in the first half.* **5** (of a firearm) to recoil when fired. **6** *Informal* to object or resist: *school uniforms give children something to kick against.* **7** *Informal* to free oneself of (an addiction): *smokers who want to kick the habit.* **8 alive and kicking** *Informal* active and in good health. **9 kick someone upstairs** to promote someone to a higher but effectively powerless position. ~*n* **10** a thrust or blow with the foot. **11** any of certain rhythmic leg movements used in swimming. **12** the recoil of a firearm. **13** *Informal* an exciting effect: *we get a kick out of attacking opposing fans and overturning their*

THESAURUS

pace, maintain, match, persevere, preserve, rival, sustain, vie

keg barrel, cask, drum, firkin, hogshead, tun, vat

kernel core, essence, germ, gist, grain, marrow, nub, pith, seed, substance

key *n.* **1.** latchkey, opener **2.** *figurative* answer, clue, cue, explanation, guide, indicator, interpretation, lead, means, pointer, sign, solution, translation ~*adj.* **3.** basic, chief, crucial, decisive, essential, fundamental, important, leading, main, major, pivotal, principal

keynote centre, core, essence, gist, heart, kernel, marrow, pith, substance, theme

kick *vb.* **1.** boot, punt **2.** *figurative* complain, gripe (*informal*), grumble, object, oppose, protest, rebel, resist,

buses; a few small bets just for kicks. **14** *Informal* the intoxicating effect of an alcoholic drink: *a cocktail with a kick in it.* **15 kick in the teeth** *Slang* a humiliating rebuff. ~See also **kick about, kick off,** etc.

kick about *or* **around** *vb Informal* **1** to treat (someone) harshly. **2** to discuss (ideas) informally. **3** to lie neglected or forgotten: *there's a copy of that book kicking about somewhere.*

kickback *n* **1** part of an income paid to a person in return for an opportunity to make a profit, often by some illegal arrangement. **2** a strong reaction.

kick off *vb* **1** to start play in a game of football by kicking the ball from the centre of the field. **2** *Informal* to commence (a discussion, event, etc.). ~*n* **kickoff 3 a** the kick that officially starts a game of football. **b** the time when the first kick is due to take place. **4** *Informal* the time when an event is due to begin.

kick out *vb Informal* to dismiss (someone) or throw (someone) out forcefully.

kickstand *n* a short metal bar on a motorcycle, which when kicked into a vertical position holds the cycle upright when stationary.

kick-start *n also* **kick-starter 1** a pedal on a motorcycle that is kicked downwards to start the engine. ~*vb* **2** to start (a motorcycle) in this way. **3** to do something bold or drastic in order to begin or improve the performance of something: *to kick-start the economy.*

kick up *vb Informal* to cause (trouble).

kid[1] *n* **1** *Informal* a young person; child. **2** a young goat. **3** soft smooth leather made from the hide of a kid. ~*adj* **4** younger: *my kid sister.* ~*vb* **kidding, kidded 5** (of a goat) to give birth to (young).

kid[2] *vb* **kidding, kidded** *Informal* **1** to tease or deceive (someone) for fun. **2** to fool (oneself) into believing something: *don't kid yourself that no-one else knows.* **kidder** *n*

kiddie *n Informal* a child

kid gloves *pl n* **handle someone with kid gloves** to treat someone with great tact in order not to upset them.

kidnap *vb* **-napping, -napped** *or US* **-naping, -naped** to capture and hold (a person), usually for ransom. **kidnapper** *or US* **-naper** *n* **kidnapping** *or US* **-naping** *n*

kidney *n* **1** either of two bean-shaped organs at the back of the abdominal cavity. They filter waste products from the blood, which are excreted as urine. **2** the kidneys of certain animals used as food.

kidney bean *n* a reddish-brown kidney-shaped bean, edible when cooked.

kidney machine *n* a machine carrying out the functions of damaged human kidneys.

kidology *n Brit informal* the practice of bluffing or deception in order to gain a psychological advantage over someone.

kill *vb* **1** to cause the death of (a person or animal). **2** *Informal* to cause (someone) pain or discomfort: *my feet are killing me.* **3** to put an end to: *his infidelity had killed his marriage.* **4** *Informal* to quash or veto: *a Tory rebellion killed the Sunday Trading Bill.* **5** *Informal* to overwhelm (someone) completely with laughter, attraction, or surprise: *her jokes really kill me.* **6 kill oneself** *Informal* to overexert oneself. **7 kill time** to spend time on something unimportant or trivial while waiting for something: *I'm just killing time until I can talk to the other witnesses.* **8 kill two birds with one stone** to achieve two results with one action. ~*n* **9** the act of causing death at the end of a hunt or bullfight. **10** the animal or animals killed during a hunt. **11 in at the kill** present when something comes to a dramatic end with unpleasant results for someone else. **killer** *n*

killer whale *n* a black-and-white toothed whale, most common in cold seas.

killing *Informal* ~*adj* **1** very tiring: *a killing pace.* **2** extremely funny. **3** causing death; fatal. ~*n* **4** the act of causing death; slaying. **5 make a killing** to have a sudden financial success.

killjoy *n* a person who spoils other people's pleasure.

kiln *n* a large oven for burning, drying, or processing pottery, bricks, etc.

kilo *n, pl* **kilos** short for **kilogram** or **kilometre**.

kilo- *combining form* **1** denoting one thousand (10^3): *kilometre.* **2** (in computers) denoting 2^{10} (1024): *kilobyte.* In computer usage, *kilo-* is restricted to sizes of storage (e.g. *kilobit*) when it means 1024: in other computer contexts it retains its usual meaning of 1000.

kilobyte *n Computers* 1024 bytes.

kilocalorie *n* one thousand calories.

kilocycle *n* an old word for kilohertz.

kilogram *or* **kilogramme** *n* **1** one thousand grams. **2** the basic SI unit of mass.

kilohertz *n, pl* **kilohertz** one thousand hertz; one thousand cycles per second.

kilojoule *n* one thousand joules.

THESAURUS

spurn **3.** *informal* abandon, desist from, give up, leave off, quit, stop ~*n.* **4.** buzz (*slang*), enjoyment, excitement, fun, gratification, jollies (*slang*), pleasure, stimulation, thrill **5.** force, intensity, pep, power, punch, pungency, snap (*informal*), sparkle, strength, tang, verve, vitality, zest

kick off *vb.* begin, commence, get under way, initiate, kick-start, open, start

kickoff *n.* beginning, commencement, opening, outset, start

kick out discharge, dismiss, eject, evict, expel, get rid of, give the bum's rush (*slang*), kiss off (*slang, chiefly U.S. & Canad.*), oust, reject, remove, sack (*informal*), show one the door, throw out on one's ear (*informal*), toss out

kid[1] ankle-biter (*Austral. slang*), baby, bairn, boy, child, girl, infant, lad, lass, little one, rug rat (*slang*), sprog (*slang*), stripling, teenager, tot, youngster, youth

kid[2] bamboozle, beguile, cozen, delude, fool, gull (*archaic*), hoax, hoodwink, jest, joke, mock, plague, pretend, rag (*Brit.*), ridicule, tease, trick, wind up (*Brit. slang*)

kidnap abduct, capture, hijack, hold to ransom, remove, seize, steal

kill 1. assassinate, blow away (*slang, chiefly U.S.*), bump off (*slang*), butcher, destroy, dispatch, do away with, do in (*slang*), eradicate, execute, exterminate, extirpate, knock off (*slang*), liquidate, massacre, murder, neutralize, obliterate, slaughter, slay, take out (*slang*), take (someone's) life, waste (*informal*) **2.** *figurative* cancel, cease, deaden, defeat, extinguish, halt, quash, quell, ruin, scotch, smother, stifle, still, stop, suppress, veto

killer assassin, butcher, cutthroat, destroyer, executioner, exterminator, gunman, hit man (*slang*), liquidator, murderer, slaughterer, slayer

killing *adj.* **1.** *informal* debilitating, enervating, exhausting, fatiguing, punishing, tiring **2.** *informal* absurd, amusing, comical, hilarious, ludicrous, uproarious **3.** deadly, death-dealing, deathly, fatal, lethal, mortal, murderous ~*n.* **4.** bloodshed, carnage, execution, extermination, fatality, homicide, manslaughter, massacre, murder, slaughter, slaying **5.** *informal* bomb

kilolitre *or US* **kiloliter** *n* a measure of volume equivalent to one thousand litres.
kilometre *or US* **kilometer** *n* a unit of length equal to one thousand metres.
kiloton *n* **1** one thousand tons. **2** an explosive power, esp. of a nuclear weapon, equal to the power of 1000 tons of TNT.
kilovolt *n* one thousand volts.
kilowatt *n* one thousand watts.
kilowatt-hour *n* a unit of energy equal to the work done by a power of 1000 watts in one hour.
kilt *n* **1** a knee-length pleated tartan skirt, worn by men in Highland dress and by women and girls. *~vb* **2** to put pleats in (cloth). **kilted** *adj*
kimono (kim-**moan**-no) *n, pl* **-nos 1** a loose wide-sleeved Japanese robe, fastened with a sash. **2** a European dressing gown resembling this.
kin *n* **1** a person's relatives collectively. **2** See **next of kin.**
kind[1] *adj* **1** considerate, friendly, and helpful: *a good, kind, man; a few kind words.* **2** cordial; courteous: *reprinted by kind permission.*
kind[2] *n* **1** a class or group having characteristics in common: *what kind of music do you like?* **2** essential nature or character: *differences of degree rather than of kind.* **3 in kind a** (of payment) in goods or services rather than in money. **b** with something of the same sort: *the government threatened to retaliate in kind to any use of nuclear weapons.* **4 kind of** to a certain extent; loosely: *kind of hard; a kind of socialist.* **5 of a kind** of poorer quality or standard than is wanted or expected: *a few farmers wrest subsistence of a kind from the thin topsoil.*

➤ Note the singular/plural usage: *this* (or *that*) *kind of dog; these* (or *those*) *kinds of dog.* In the second, plural example, you can also say *these kinds of dogs.*

kindergarten *n* a school for young children, usually between the ages of 4 and 6.
kind-hearted *adj* considerate and sympathetic.
kindle *vb* **-dling, -dled 1** to set (a fire) alight or (of a fire) to start to burn. **2** to arouse or be aroused: *his passions were kindled as quickly as her own.*
kindling *n* material for starting a fire, such as dry wood or straw.
kindly *adj* **-lier, -liest 1** having a warm-hearted and caring nature. **2** pleasant or agreeable: *a kindly climate.* *~adv* **3** in a considerate or humane way. **4** please: *will you kindly stop prattling on about it!* **5 not take kindly to** to react unfavourably towards. **kindliness** *n*
kindness *n* **1** the quality of being kind. **2** a kind or helpful act.
kindred *adj* **1** having similar qualities. **2** related by blood or marriage. **3 kindred spirit** a person with whom one has something in common. *~n* **4** relationship by blood or marriage. **5** similarity in character. **6** a person's relatives collectively.
kine *pl n Archaic* cows or cattle.
kinematics (kin-nim-**mat**-iks) *n Physics* the study of the motion of bodies without reference to mass or force. **kinematic** *adj*
kinetic (kin-**net**-ik) *adj* relating to or caused by motion. **kinetically** *adv*
kinetic art *n* art, such as sculpture, that moves or has moving parts.
kinetic energy *n Physics* the energy of motion of a body equal to the work it would do if it were brought to rest.
kinetics *n Physics* the branch of mechanics concerned with the study of bodies in motion.
king *n* **1** a male ruler of a country who has inherited the throne from his parents. **2** a ruler or chief: *the king of the fairies.* **3** a person, animal, or thing considered as the best or most important of its kind: *the king of rock and roll.* **4** a playing card with a picture of a king on it. **5** a chessman, able to move one square in any direction: the object of the game is to checkmate one's opponent's king. **6** *Draughts* a piece which has moved entirely across the board and been crowned and which may therefore move backwards as well as forwards. **kingship** *n*
kingcup *n Brit* a yellow-flowered plant; marsh marigold.
kingdom *n* **1** a territory or state ruled by a king or queen. **2** any of the three groups into which natural objects may be divided: the animal, plant, and mineral kingdoms. **3** a place or area considered to be under the total power and control of a person, organization, or thing: *the kingdom of God.*
kingfisher *n* a fish-eating bird with a greenish-blue and orange plumage.

THESAURUS

(*slang*), bonanza, cleanup (*informal*), coup, gain, profit, success, windfall
killjoy dampener, damper, spoilsport, wet blanket (*informal*)
kin family, folk (*informal*), folks (*informal*), kindred, kinsfolk, kinsmen, kith, people, relations, relatives
kind[1] affectionate, amiable, amicable, beneficent, benevolent, benign, bounteous, charitable, clement, compassionate, congenial, considerate, cordial, courteous, friendly, generous, gentle, good, gracious, humane, indulgent, kind-hearted, kindly, lenient, loving, mild, neighbourly, obliging, philanthropic, propitious, sympathetic, tender-hearted, thoughtful, understanding
kind[2] **1.** brand, breed, class, family, genus, ilk, race, set, sort, species, stamp, variety **2.** character, description, essence, habit, manner, mould, nature, persuasion, sort, style, temperament, type
kind-hearted altruistic, amicable, compassionate, considerate, generous, good-natured, gracious, helpful, humane, kind, sympathetic, tender-hearted
kindle 1. fire, ignite, inflame, light, set fire to **2.** *figurative* agitate, animate, arouse, awaken, bestir, enkindle, exasperate, excite, foment, incite, induce, inflame, inspire, provoke, rouse, sharpen, stimulate, stir, thrill
kindliness amiability, beneficence, benevolence, benignity, charity, compassion, friendliness, gentleness, humanity, kind-heartedness, kindness, sympathy
kindly 1. *adj.* affable, beneficial, benevolent, benign, compassionate, cordial, favourable, genial, gentle, good-natured, hearty, helpful, kind, mild, pleasant, polite, sympathetic, warm **2.** *adv.* agreeably, cordially, graciously, politely, tenderly, thoughtfully
kindness 1. affection, amiability, beneficence, benevolence, charity, clemency, compassion, decency, fellow-feeling, generosity, gentleness, goodness, goodwill, grace, hospitality, humanity, indulgence, kindliness, magnanimity, patience, philanthropy, tenderness, tolerance, understanding **2.** aid, assistance, benefaction, bounty, favour, generosity, good deed, help, service
kindred *adj.* **1.** affiliated, akin, allied, cognate, congenial, corresponding, kin, like, matching, related, similar *~n.* **2.** affinity, consanguinity, relationship **3.** connections, family, flesh, kin, kinsfolk, kinsmen, lineage, relations, relatives
king crowned head, emperor, majesty, monarch, overlord, prince, ruler, sovereign

kingklip *n* an edible eel-like marine fish of S Africa.

king-of-arms *n, pl* **kings-of-arms** a person holding the highest rank of heraldic office.

kingpin *n* **1** the most important person in an organization. **2** a pivot pin that provides a steering joint in a motor vehicle.

king post *n Building* a vertical post connecting the apex of a triangular roof truss to the tie beam.

king-size *or* **king-sized** *adj* larger than a standard size.

kink *n* **1** a twist or bend in something such as a rope or hair. **2** *Informal* a flaw or quirk in someone's personality.

kinky *adj* **kinkier, kinkiest 1** *Slang* given to unusual sexual practices. **2** tightly looped or curled.

kinsfolk *pl n* one's family or relatives.

kinship *n* **1** blood relationship. **2** the state of having common characteristics.

kinsman *n, pl* **-men** a relation by blood or marriage. **kinswoman** *fem n*

kiosk *n* **1** a small booth from which cigarettes, newspapers, and sweets are sold. **2** *Chiefly Brit* a public telephone box.

kip *Brit slang* ~*n* **1** sleep: *a couple of hours' kip.* **2** a bed. ~*vb* **kipping, kipped 3** to sleep or take a nap. **4** **kip down** to sleep in a makeshift bed.

kipper *n* **1** a herring that has been cleaned, salted, and smoked. ~*vb* **2** to cure (a herring) by salting and smoking it.

kirk *n Scot* a church.

Kirsch *or* **Kirschwasser** *n* a brandy distilled from black cherries.

kismet *n* fate or destiny.

kiss *vb* **1** to touch with the lips as an expression of love, greeting, or respect. **2** to join lips with another person as an act of love or desire. **3** *Literary* to touch lightly: *a long, high free-kick that kissed the top of the crossbar.* ~*n* **4** a caress with the lips. **5** a light touch. **kissable** *adj*

kissagram *n* a greetings service in which a person is employed to present greetings by kissing the person celebrating.

kiss curl *n Brit* a circular curl of hair pressed flat against the cheek or forehead.

kisser *n Slang* the mouth or face.

kiss of life *n* **the** mouth-to-mouth resuscitation in which a person blows gently into the mouth of an unconscious person.

kit[1] *n* **1** a set of tools or supplies for use together or for a purpose: *a first-aid kit.* **2** the container for such a set. **3** a set of parts sold ready to be assembled: *a model aircraft kit.* **4** clothing and other personal effects, such as those of a soldier: *a complete set of school team kit.* ~See also **kit out.**

kit[2] *n NZ* a shopping bag made of string.

kitbag *n* a canvas or other bag for a serviceman's kit.

kitchen *n* a room equipped for preparing and cooking food.

kitchenette *n* a small kitchen or part of a room equipped for use as a kitchen.

kitchen garden *n* a garden for growing vegetables, herbs, etc.

kitchen tea *n Austral & NZ* a party held before a wedding to which guests bring kitchen equipment as presents.

kite *n* **1** a light frame covered with a thin material flown in the wind at the end of a length of string. **2** a bird of prey with a long forked tail and large wings. **3** a four-sided geometrical shape in which each side is equal in length to one of the sides joining it.

Kite mark *n Brit* the official mark in the form of a kite on articles approved by the British Standards Institution.

kith *n* **kith and kin** *Old-fashioned* one's friends and relations.

kit out *or* **up** *vb* **kitting, kitted** *Chiefly Brit* to provide with clothes or equipment needed for a particular activity.

kitsch *n* tawdry or sentimental art or literature. **kitschy** *adj*

kitten *n* **1** a young cat. **2** **have kittens** *Brit informal* to react with disapproval or anxiety: *she had kittens when she discovered the price.*

kittenish *adj* lively and flirtatious.

kittiwake *n* a type of seagull with pale grey black-tipped wings and a square-cut tail.

kitty[1] *n, pl* **-ties** a diminutive or affectionate name for a kitten or cat.

kitty[2] *n, pl* **-ties 1** any shared fund of money. **2** the pool in certain gambling games.

kiwi *n, pl* **kiwis 1** a flightless bird of New Zealand with a long beak, stout legs, and no tail. **2** *Informal except in NZ* a New Zealander. **3** *NZ informal* a lottery.

kiwi fruit *n* an edible fruit with a fuzzy brown skin and green flesh.

kJ kilojoule(s).

kl kilolitre(s).

klaxon *n* a type of loud horn used on fire engines and ambulances as a warning signal.

kleinhuisie (**klayn**-hay-see) *n S African* an outside toilet.

kleptomania *n Psychol* a strong impulse to steal. **kleptomaniac** *n*

klipspringer *n* a small agile antelope of rocky regions of Africa south of the Sahara.

kloof *n S African* a ravine or valley.

km kilometre(s).

THESAURUS

kingdom **1.** dominion, dynasty, empire, monarchy, realm, reign, sovereignty **2.** area, domain, field, province, sphere, territory

kink **1.** bend, coil, corkscrew, crimp, entanglement, frizz, knot, tangle, twist, wrinkle **2.** crotchet, eccentricity, fetish, foible, idiosyncrasy, quirk, singularity, vagary, whim

kinky **1.** bizarre, degenerate, depraved, deviant, licentious, outlandish, peculiar, perverted, pervy (*slang*), unconventional, unnatural, warped **2.** coiled, crimped, curled, curly, frizzled, frizzy, tangled, twisted

kinship **1.** blood relationship, consanguinity, kin, relation, ties of blood **2.** affinity, alliance, association, bearing, connection, correspondence, relationship, similarity

kinsman blood relative, fellow clansman, fellow tribesman, relation, relative

kiosk bookstall, booth, counter, newsstand, stall, stand

kiss *vb.* **1.** greet, peck (*informal*), salute **2.** canoodle (*slang*), neck (*informal*), osculate, smooch (*informal*), snog (*informal*) **3.** brush, caress, glance, graze, scrape, touch ~*n.* **4.** buss (*archaic*), osculation, peck (*informal*), smacker (*slang*)

kit **1.** accoutrements, apparatus, effects, equipment, gear, impedimenta, implements, instruments, outfit, paraphernalia, provisions, rig, supplies, tackle, tools, trappings, utensils **2.** clothes, gear

kitchen cookhouse, galley, kitchenette

knack ability, adroitness, aptitude, bent, capacity,

knack *n* **1** a skilful way of doing something. **2** an ability to do something difficult with apparent ease.

knacker *n Brit* a person who buys up old horses for slaughter.

knackered *adj Brit slang* **1** extremely tired: *they'd been marching for three hours and were absolutely knackered.* **2** broken or no longer functioning: *a knackered TV set.*

knapsack *n* a canvas or leather bag carried strapped on the back or shoulder.

knapweed *n* a plant with purplish thistle-like flowers.

knave *n* **1** *Cards* the jack. **2** *Archaic* a dishonest man. **knavish** *adj*

knavery *n, pl* **-eries** *Old-fashioned* dishonest behaviour.

knead *vb* **1** to work and press (a soft substance, such as dough) into a smooth mixture with the hands. **2** to squeeze or press with the hands. **kneader** *n*

knee *n* **1** the joint of the leg between the thigh and the lower leg. **2** the area around this joint. **3** the upper surface of a sitting person's thigh: *a little girl being cuddled on her father's knee.* **4** the part of a garment that covers the knee. **5 bring someone to his knees** to force someone into submission. *~vb* **kneeing, kneed 6** to strike, nudge, or push with the knee.

kneecap *n* **1** *Anat* a small flat triangular bone in front of and protecting the knee. *~vb* **-capping, -capped 2** (of terrorists) to shoot (a person) in the kneecap.

knee-deep *adj* **1** so deep as to reach or cover the knees. **2 a** sunk to the knees: *knee-deep in mud.* **b** deeply involved: *knee-deep in work.*

knee-high *adj* as high as the knee.

knee-jerk *n* **1** *Physiol* a sudden involuntary kick of the lower leg caused by a sharp tap on the tendon just below the kneecap. *~adj* **kneejerk 2** made or occurring as a predictable and automatic response: *a kneejerk reaction.*

kneel *vb* **kneeling, knelt** *or* **kneeled 1** to rest, fall, or support oneself on one's knees. *~n* **2** the act or position of kneeling.

knees-up *n Informal* a party.

knell *n* **1** the sound of a bell rung to announce a death or a funeral. **2** something that indicates death or destruction. *~vb* **3** to ring a knell. **4** to proclaim by a tolling bell.

knelt *vb* the past of **kneel.**

knew *vb* the past tense of **know.**

knickerbockers *pl n* loose-fitting short trousers gathered in at the knee.

knickers *pl n* a woman's or girl's undergarment covering the lower trunk and having separate legs or legholes.

knick-knack *n* a small ornament or trinket.

knife *n, pl* **knives 1** a cutting instrument or weapon consisting of a sharp-edged blade of metal fitted into a handle. *~vb* **knifing, knifed 2** to stab or kill with a knife. **knifelike** *adj*

knife edge *n* **1** the sharp cutting edge of a knife. **2** a critical point in the development of a situation: *the election result is still poised on a knife edge.*

knight *n* **1** a man who has been given a knighthood in recognition of his achievements. **2** (in medieval Europe) **a** a person who served his lord as a mounted and heavily armed soldier. **b** a devoted male admirer of a noblewoman, esp. her champion in a jousting tournament. **3** a chessman shaped like a horse's head, able to move either two squares horizontally and one square vertically or two squares vertically and one square horizontally. *~vb* **4** to make (a man) a knight.

knight errant *n, pl* **knights errant** (esp. in medieval romance) a knight who wanders in search of deeds of courage, chivalry, etc. **knight errantry** *n*

knighthood *n* an honorary title given to a man by the British sovereign in recognition of his achievements.

knightly *adj* of, resembling, or appropriate for a knight. **knightliness** *n*

knit *vb* **knitting, knitted** *or* **knit 1** to make (a garment) by looping (wool) using long eyeless needles or a knitting machine. **2** to join together closely. **3** to draw (one's eyebrows) together. *~n* **4** a fabric made by knitting. **knitter** *n*

knitting *n* knitted work or the process of producing it.

knitwear *n* knitted clothes, such as sweaters.

knives *n* the plural of **knife.**

knob *n* **1** a rounded projection from a surface, such as a rotating switch on a radio. **2** a rounded handle of a door or drawer. **3** a small amount of butter or margarine. **knoblike** *adj*

knobbly *adj* having or covered with small bumps: *a curious knobbly root vegetable.*

knobkerrie *n S African* a club or a stick with a rounded end.

knock *vb* **1** to give a blow or push to. **2** to rap sharply with the knuckles: *he knocked on the door of the guest room.* **3** to make by striking: *he knocked a hole in the wall.* **4** to collide (with). **5** to bring into a certain condition by hitting: *he was knocked unconscious in a collision.* **6** *Informal* to criticize adversely. **7** to emit a regular banging sound as a result of a fault: *the engine was knocking badly.* **8 knock on the head** to prevent the further development of (a plan). *~n* **9 a** a blow, push, or rap: *he gave the table a knock.* **b** the sound so

THESAURUS

dexterity, expertise, expertness, facility, flair, forte, genius, gift, handiness, ingenuity, propensity, quickness, skilfulness, skill, talent, trick

knave blackguard, bounder (*old-fashioned Brit. slang*), cheat, rapscallion, rascal, reprobate, rogue, rotter (*slang, chiefly Brit.*), scally (*Northwest English dialect*), scallywag (*informal*), scamp, scapegrace, scoundrel, scumbag (*slang*), swindler, varlet (*archaic*), villain

knavery chicanery, corruption, deceit, deception, dishonesty, double-dealing, duplicity, fraud, imposture, rascality, roguery, trickery, villainy

knead blend, form, manipulate, massage, mould, press, rub, shape, squeeze, stroke, work

kneel bow, bow down, curtsey, curtsy, genuflect, get down on one's knees, kowtow, make obeisance, stoop

knell 1. *vb.* announce, chime, herald, peal, resound, ring, sound, toll **2.** *n.* chime, peal, ringing, sound, toll

knickers bloomers, briefs, drawers, panties, smalls, underwear, undies

knick-knack bagatelle, bauble, bibelot, bric-a-brac, plaything, trifle, trinket

knife 1. *n.* blade, cutter, cutting tool **2.** *vb.* cut, impale, lacerate, pierce, slash, stab, wound

knit 1. affix, ally, bind, connect, contract, fasten, heal, interlace, intertwine, join, link, loop, mend, secure, tie, unite, weave **2.** crease, furrow, knot, pucker, wrinkle

knob boss, bump, bunch, hump, knot, knurl, lump, nub, projection, protrusion, protuberance, snag, stud

knock *vb.* **1.** belt (*informal*), buffet, chin (*slang*), clap, cuff, deck (*slang*), hit, lay one on (*slang*), punch, rap, slap, smack, smite (*archaic*), strike, thump, thwack **2.**

caused. **10** the sound of knocking in an engine or bearing. **11** *Informal* a misfortune, rejection, or setback. **12** *Informal* criticism. ~See also **knock about, knock back,** etc.

knock about *or* **around** *vb* **1** to wander or travel about: *I have knocked about the world through three continents.* **2** (foll. by *with*) to associate. **3** to treat brutally: *she looked knocked about, with bruises and cuts to her head.* **4** to consider or discuss informally. ~*adj* **knockabout 5** (of comedy) lively, boisterous, and physical.

knock back *vb Informal* **1** to drink quickly: *he fell over after knocking back eight pints of lager.* **2** to cost: *lunch for two here will knock you back fifty pounds.* **3** to reject or refuse: *I don't know any man who'd knock back an offer like that.* ~*n* **knockback 4** *Slang* a refusal or rejection.

knock down *vb* **1** to strike to the ground with a blow, such as in boxing. **2** (in auctions) to declare an article sold. **3** to demolish. **4** *Informal* to reduce (a price). ~*adj* **knockdown 5** powerful: *a knockdown argument.* **6** *Chiefly Brit* (of a price) very cheap. **7** easily dismantled: *knockdown furniture.*

knocker *n* **1** a metal object attached to a door by a hinge and used for knocking. **2 knockers** *Slang* a woman's breasts.

knock-knees *pl n* legs that are bent inwards at the knees. **knockkneed** *adj*

knock off *vb* **1** *Informal* to finish work: *around ten, the day shift knocked off.* **2** *Informal* to make or do hastily or easily: *she knocked off 600 books in all during her long life.* **3** *Informal* to take (an amount) off the price of (an article): *I'll knock off 10% if you pay cash.* **4** *Slang* to kill. **5** *Slang* to stop doing something; used as a command: *knock it off!*

knock-on *Rugby* ~*n* **1** the foul of playing the ball forward with the hand or arm. ~*vb* **knock on 2** to play (the ball) forward with the hand or arm.

knock-on effect *n* the indirect result of an action or decision.

knockout *n* **1** the act of rendering someone unconscious. **2** *Boxing* a blow that renders an opponent unable to continue after the referee has counted to ten. **3** a competition in which competitors are eliminated progressively. **4** *Informal* a person or thing that is very impressive or attractive: *at my youngest sister's wedding she was a knockout in navy and scarlet.* ~*vb* **knock out 5** to render (someone) unconscious. **6** *Boxing* to defeat (an opponent) by a knockout. **7** to destroy: *communications in many areas were knocked out by the earthquake.* **8** to eliminate from a knockout competition. **9** *Informal* to amaze: *the fantastic audience reaction knocked me out.*

knock up *vb* **1** Also: **knock together** *Informal* to make or assemble quickly: *my boyfriend can knock up a wonderful lasagne or chicken or steak.* **2** *Brit informal* to waken: *to knock someone up early.* **3** *Chiefly US slang* to make pregnant. **4** to practise before a game of tennis, squash, or badminton. ~*n* **knock-up 5** a practice session at tennis, squash, or badminton.

knoll *n* a small rounded hill.

knot *n* **1** a fastening formed by looping and tying pieces of rope, cord, or string. **2** a tangle, such as in hair. **3** a decorative bow, such as of ribbon. **4** a small cluster or huddled group: *a knot of passengers gathered on the platform.* **5** a bond: *to tie the knot of friendship.* **6 a** a hard mass of wood where a branch joins the trunk of a tree. **b** a cross section of this visible in timber. **7** a feeling of tightness, caused by tension or nervousness: *a dull knot of anxiety that sat in the pit of her stomach.* **8** a unit of speed used by ships and aircraft, equal to one nautical mile per hour. **9 at a rate of knots** very fast. **10 tie someone in knots** to confuse someone completely. ~*vb* **knotting, knotted 11** to tie or fasten in a knot. **12** to form into a knot. **13** to entangle or become entangled. **knotted** *adj* **knotless** *adj*

knothole *n* a hole in a piece of wood where a knot has been.

knotty *adj* **-tier, -tiest 1** full of knots. **2** extremely difficult or puzzling: *a knotty problem.*

know *vb* **knowing, knew, known 1** to be or feel certain of the truth or accuracy of (a fact, answer, or piece of information). **2** to be acquainted with: *I'd known him for many years, since I was seventeen.* **3** to have a grasp of or understand (a skill or language). **4** to understand or be aware of (something, or how to do or be something): *she knew how to get on with people.* **5** to experience: *you had to have known poverty before you could give money its true value, he claimed.* **6** to be intelligent, informed, or sensible enough (to do something): *how did he know to send the letter in the first place?* **7** to be able to distinguish: *I don't know one flower from another.* **8 know what's what** to know how one thing or things in general work. **9 you never know** things are uncertain. ~*n* **10 in the know** *Informal* aware or informed. **knowable** *adj*

know-all *n Informal, disparaging* a person who pretends or appears to know a lot more than other people.

know-how *n Informal* the ability to do something that is difficult or technical.

THESAURUS

informal abuse, asperse, belittle, carp, cavil, censure, condemn, criticize, deprecate, disparage, find fault, lambast(e), run down, slag (off) (*slang*), slam (*slang*) ~*n.* **3.** belt (*informal*), blow, box, clip, clout (*informal*), cuff, hammering, rap, slap, smack, thump **4.** blame, censure, condemnation, criticism, defeat, failure, heat (*slang, chiefly U.S. & Canad.*), rebuff, rejection, reversal, setback, slagging (off) (*slang*), stick (*slang*), stricture

knock about *or* **around 1.** ramble, range, roam, rove, traipse, travel, wander **2.** abuse, batter, beat up (*informal*), bruise, buffet, clobber (*slang*), damage, hit, hurt, lambast(e), maltreat, manhandle, maul, mistreat, strike, wound

knock down 1. batter, clout (*informal*), fell, floor, pound, smash, wallop (*informal*) **2.** demolish, destroy, level, raze, wreck

knock off 1. clock off, clock out, complete, conclude, finish, stop work, terminate **2.** assassinate, blow away (*slang, chiefly U.S.*), bump off (*slang*), do away with, do in (*slang*), kill, liquidate, murder, slay, take out (*slang*), waste (*informal*)

knockout 1. *coup de grâce*, kayo (*slang*), KO *or* K.O. (*slang*) **2.** hit, sensation, smash, smash-hit, stunner (*informal*), success, triumph, winner

knot *n.* **1.** bond, bow, braid, connection, joint, ligature, loop, rosette, tie **2.** assemblage, band, circle, clique, company, crew (*informal*), crowd, gang, group, mob, pack, set, squad ~*vb.* **3.** bind, complicate, entangle, knit, loop, secure, tether, tie, weave

know 1. apprehend, comprehend, experience, fathom, feel certain, ken (*Scot.*), learn, notice, perceive, realize, recognize, see, undergo, understand **2.** associate with, be acquainted with, be familiar with, fraternize with, have dealings with, have knowledge of, recognize **3.** differentiate, discern, distinguish, identify, make out, perceive, recognize, see, tell

know-how ability, adroitness, aptitude, capability, craft, dexterity, experience, expertise, faculty, flair,

knowing *adj* **1** suggesting secret knowledge: *Paul saw the knowing look that passed between them.* **2** cunning or shrewd. **3** deliberate. **knowingly** *adv* **knowingness** *n*

knowledge *n* **1** the facts or experiences known by a person or group of people. **2** the state of knowing. **3** specific information about a subject. **4 to my knowledge** as I understand it.

knowledgeable *or* **knowledgable** *adj* intelligent or well-informed. **knowledgeably** *or* **knowledgably** *adv*

known *vb* **1** the past participle of **know.** ~*adj* **2** identified: *consorting with known criminals.*

knuckle *n* **1** a joint of a finger. **2** the knee joint of a calf or pig. **3 near the knuckle** *Informal* likely to offend people because of frankness or rudeness. ~See also **knuckle down, knuckle under.**

knuckle down *vb* **-ling, -led** *Informal* to apply oneself conscientiously: *he's never been able to knuckle down and study anything for long.*

knuckle-duster *n* a metal appliance worn over the knuckles to add force to a blow.

knuckle under *vb* **-ling, -led** to give way under pressure or authority.

knurl *n* a small ridge, often one of a series.

KO *or* **k.o.** *vb* **KO'ing, KO'd; k.o.'ing, k.o.'d 1** to knock out. ~*n, pl* **KO's** *or* **k.o.'s 2** a knockout.

koala *or* **koala bear** *n* a tree-dwelling Australian marsupial with dense grey fur.

koeksister (**kook**-sist-er) *n S African* a plaited doughnut deep-fried and soaked in syrup.

kohl *n* a cosmetic powder used to darken the area around the eyes.

kohlrabi (kole-**rah**-bee) *n, pl* **-bies** a type of cabbage with an edible stem.

kokanee (coke-**can**-ee) *n* a freshwater salmon of lakes and rivers in W North America.

kola *n* same as **cola.**

kolkhoz (kol-**hawz**) *n* (formerly) a collective farm in the Soviet Union.

komatik (**koh**-ma-tik) *n Canad* a sledge with wooden runners and crossbars bound with animal hides.

kook *n US & Canad informal* an eccentric or foolish person. **kooky** *or* **kookie** *adj*

kookaburra *n* a large Australian kingfisher with a cackling cry.

kopeck *n* a Russian monetary unit worth one hundredth of a rouble.

koppie (**kop**-ee) *n S African* a small isolated hill.

Koran *n* the sacred book of Islam, believed by Muslims to be the infallible word of God dictated to Mohammed. **Koranic** *adj*

Korean *adj* **1** of Korea. ~*n* **2** a person from Korea. **3** the official language of North and South Korea.

kosher (**koh**-sher) *adj* **1** *Judaism* **a** conforming to religious law. **b** (of food) prepared in accordance with the dietary laws. **2** *Informal* legitimate, genuine, or proper. ~*n* **3** kosher food.

kowhai (**koh**-wye) *n* a small tree of New Zealand and Chile with clusters of yellow flowers.

kowtow *vb* **1** to be humble and very respectful (towards). **2** to touch the forehead to the ground in deference. ~*n* **3** the act of kowtowing.

kph kilometres per hour.

Kr *Chem* krypton.

kraal *n* **1** a Southern African hut village surrounded by a strong fence. **2** *S African* an enclosure for livestock.

krans (**krahnss**) *n S African* a sheer rock face.

kremlin *n* the citadel of any Russian city.

Kremlin *n* the central government of Russia and, formerly, the Soviet Union.

krill *n, pl* **krill** a small shrimplike crustacean.

krona *n, pl* **-nor** the standard monetary unit of Sweden.

krone (**kroh**-na) *n, pl* **-ner** (-ner) the standard monetary unit of Denmark or Norway.

krugerrand *n* a one-ounce gold coin minted in South Africa.

krypton *n Chem* an inert gaseous element occurring in trace amounts in air and used in fluorescent lights and lasers. Symbol: Kr

KS Kansas.

Kt Knight.

KT (in Britain) Knight of the Order of the Thistle.

kt. kiloton.

kudos (**kew**-doss) *n* personal fame or glory.

kudu *or* **koodoo** *n* a spiral-horned African antelope.

Ku Klux Klan *n* a secret organization of White Protestant Americans who use violence against Blacks and Jews. **Ku Klux Klanner** *n*

kukri *n* a heavy, curved knife used by Gurkhas.

kulak *n* (formerly) a property-owning Russian peasant.

kumera *or* **kumara** *n NZ* a sweet potato.

kümmel *n* a German liqueur flavoured with aniseed and cumin.

kumquat (**kumm**-kwott) *n* a citrus fruit resembling a tiny orange.

kung fu *n* a Chinese martial art combining techniques of karate and judo.

kuri *n NZ* a mongrel dog.

kV kilovolt.

kW kilowatt.

kwashiorkor *n* severe malnutrition of young children, caused by not eating enough protein.

kWh kilowatt-hour.

KWIC *Computers* keyword in context.

KWOC *Computers* keyword out of context.

KY Kentucky.

kyle *n Scot* a narrow strait or channel: *Kyle of Lochalsh.*

THESAURUS

ingenuity, knack, knowledge, proficiency, savoir-faire, skill, talent

knowing **1.** acute, cunning, eloquent, expressive, meaningful, perceptive, sagacious, shrewd, significant **2.** aware, conscious, deliberate, intended, intentional

knowingly consciously, deliberately, intentionally, on purpose, purposely, wilfully, wittingly

knowledge **1.** education, enlightenment, erudition, instruction, intelligence, learning, scholarship, schooling, science, tuition, wisdom **2.** acquaintance, cognizance, familiarity, information, intimacy, notice

knowledgeable acquainted, *au courant, au fait,* aware, clued-up (*informal*), cognizant, conscious, conversant, educated, erudite, experienced, familiar, intelligent, in the know (*informal*), learned, lettered, scholarly, understanding, well-informed

known acknowledged, admitted, avowed, celebrated, common, confessed, familiar, famous, manifest, noted, obvious, patent, plain, popular, published, recognized, well-known

knuckle under *vb.* accede, acquiesce, capitulate, give in, give way, submit, succumb, surrender, yield

L

l litre(s).
L **1** large. **2** Latin. **3** learner driver. **4** Usually written: £ pound. **5** the Roman numeral for 50.
L. *or* **l.** **1** lake. **2** left. **3** length. **4** (*pl* **LL** *or* **ll**) line.
la *n Music* same as **lah**.
La *Chem* lanthanum.
LA **1** Los Angeles. **2** Louisiana.
laager *n* (in Africa) a camp defended by a circular formation of wagons.
lab *n Informal* short for **laboratory**.
Lab *Politics* Labour.
label *n* **1** a piece of card or other material attached to an object to show its contents, ownership, use, or destination. **2** a brief descriptive term given to a person, group, or school of thought: *we would need a handy label to explain the new company.* ~*vb* **-belling, -belled** *or US* **-beling, -beled** **3** to attach a label to. **4** to describe or classify in a word or phrase.
labial (**lay**-bee-al) *adj* **1** of or near the lips. **2** *Phonetics* relating to a speech sound made using the lips. ~*n* **3** *Phonetics* a speech sound such as English *p* or *m*, that involves the lips.
labiate (**lay**-bee-ate) *n* **1** any of a family of plants with square stems, aromatic leaves, and a two-lipped flower, such as mint or thyme. ~*adj* **2** of this family.
labium (**lay**-bee-um) *n, pl* **-bia** (-bee-a) **1** a lip or liplike structure. **2** any one of the four lip-shaped folds of the vulva.
laboratory *n, pl* **-ries** a building or room equipped for conducting scientific research or for teaching practical science.
laborious *adj* involving great exertion or prolonged effort. **laboriously** *adv*
labour *or US & sometimes Canad* **labor** *n* **1** productive work, esp. physical work done for wages. **2** the people involved in this, as opposed to management. **3** the final stage of pregnancy, leading to childbirth. **4** difficult work or a difficult job. ~*vb* **5** to do physical work: *the girls were labouring madly on it.* **6** to work hard (for something). **7** to make one's way with difficulty: *she was now labouring down the return length.* **8** to emphasize too persistently: *I have laboured the point.* **9** (usually foll. by *under*) to be at a disadvantage because of a mistake or false belief: *she laboured under the illusion that I understood her.*
Labour Day *n* a public holiday in honour of work, held in Britain on May 1.
laboured *or US* **labored** *adj* undertaken with difficulty: *laboured breathing.*
labourer *or US* **laborer** *n* a person engaged in physical work.
labour exchange *n Brit* the former name for employment office.
Labour Party *n* **1** the major left-wing political party in Britain, which believes in democratic socialism and social equality. **2** any similar party in various other countries.
labour-saving *adj* (of a method or piece of equipment) reducing the amount of work or effort needed to carry out a task.
Labrador *or* **Labrador retriever** *n* a powerfully built dog with short dense black or golden hair.
laburnum *n* a small ornamental tree that has clusters of yellow drooping flowers. It is highly poisonous.
labyrinth (**lab**-er-inth) *n* **1** a mazelike network of tunnels or paths, either natural or man-made. **2** any complex or confusing system. **3** the interconnecting cavities of the internal ear. **labyrinthine** *adj*
lac *n* a resinous substance secreted by certain insects (**lac insects**), used in the manufacture of shellac.
lace *n* **1** a delicate decorative fabric made from threads woven in an open web of patterns. **2** a cord or string drawn through eyelets to fasten a shoe or garment. ~*vb* **lacing, laced** **3** to fasten (shoes) with a lace. **4** to draw (a cord or thread) through holes as when tying shoes. **5** to add a small amount of alcohol, a drug, or poison to (food or drink). **6** to intertwine; interlace.
lacerate (**lass**-er-rate) *vb* **-ating, -ated** **1** to tear (the flesh) jaggedly. **2** to hurt (the feelings): *would only lacerate an over-burdened conscience.* **laceration** *n*
lace up *vb* **1** to fasten (clothes or footwear) with laces. ~*adj* **lace-up** **2** (of footwear) to be fastened with laces. ~*n* **lace-up** **3** a shoe or boot which fastens with a lace.
lachrymal *adj* same as **lacrimal**.
lachrymose *adj* **1** given to weeping; tearful. **2** mournful; sad.
lacing *n Informal* a severe beating.
lack *n* **1** shortage or absence of something required or

THESAURUS

label *n.* **1.** docket (*chiefly Brit.*), flag, marker, sticker, tag, tally, ticket **2.** characterization, classification, description, epithet ~*vb.* **3.** docket (*chiefly Brit.*), flag, mark, stamp, sticker, tag, tally **4.** brand, call, characterize, class, classify, define, describe, designate, identify, name
labour *or U.S. & sometimes Canad.* **labor** *n.* **1.** industry, toil, work **2.** employees, hands, labourers, workers, work force, workmen **3.** childbirth, contractions, delivery, labour pains, pains, parturition, throes, travail **4.** donkey-work, drudgery, effort, exertion, grind (*informal*), industry, pains, painstaking, sweat (*informal*), toil, travail ~*vb.* **5.** drudge, endeavour, grind (*informal*), peg along *or* away (*chiefly Brit.*), plod, plug along *or* away (*informal*), slave, strive, struggle, sweat (*informal*), toil, travail, work **6.** dwell on, elaborate, make a federal case of (*U.S. informal*), make a production (out) of (*informal*), overdo, overemphasize, strain **7.** *usually with* **under** be a victim of, be burdened by, be disadvantaged, suffer
laboured awkward, difficult, forced, heavy, stiff, strained
labourer blue-collar worker, drudge, hand, manual worker, navvy (*Brit. informal*), unskilled worker, worker, working man, workman
labyrinth coil, complexity, complication, convolution, entanglement, intricacy, jungle, knotty problem, maze, perplexity, puzzle, riddle, snarl, tangle, windings
lace *n.* **1.** filigree, netting, openwork, tatting **2.** bootlace, cord, shoelace, string, thong, tie ~*vb.* **3.** attach, bind, close, do up, fasten, intertwine, interweave, thread, tie, twine **4.** add to, fortify, mix in, spike
lacerate **1.** claw, cut, gash, jag, maim, mangle, rend, rip, slash, tear, wound **2.** afflict, distress, harrow, rend, torment, torture, wound
lachrymose crying, dolorous, lugubrious, mournful, sad, tearful, weeping, weepy (*informal*), woeful
lack **1.** *n.* absence, dearth, deficiency, deprivation, destitution, insufficiency, need, privation, scantiness,

desired: *a lack of confidence.* ~*vb* **2** (often foll. by *in*) to be short (of) or have need (of): *lacking in sparkle.*

lackadaisical *adj* **1** lacking vitality and purpose. **2** lazy and careless in a dreamy way.

lackey *n* **1** a servile follower; hanger-on. **2** a liveried male servant or valet.

lacklustre *or US* **lackluster** *adj* lacking brilliance, force, or vitality.

laconic *adj* (of a person's speech) using few words. **laconically** *adv*

lacquer *n* **1** a hard glossy coating made by dissolving natural or synthetic resins in a solvent that evaporates quickly. **2** a black resin, obtained from certain trees, used to give a hard glossy finish to wooden furniture. **3** a clear sticky substance for spraying onto the hair to hold a style in place.

lacquered *adj* coated with lacquer.

lacrimal *or* **lachrymal** (**lack**-rim-al) *adj* of tears or the glands that secrete tears.

lacrosse *n* a sport in which two teams try to propel a ball into each other's goal using long-handled sticks with a pouched net at the end.

lactate[1] *vb* **-tating, -tated** (of mammals) to secrete milk.

lactate[2] *n* an ester or salt of lactic acid.

lactation *n* **1** the secretion of milk from the mammary glands. **2** the period during which milk is secreted.

lacteal *adj* **1** of or like milk. **2** (of lymphatic vessels) conveying or containing chyle. ~*n* **3** any of the lymphatic vessels that convey chyle from the small intestine to the blood.

lactic *adj* relating to or derived from milk.

lactic acid *n* a colourless syrupy acid found in sour milk and used as a preservative (**E270**) for foodstuffs.

lactose *n* a white crystalline sugar occurring in milk.

lacuna (lak-**kew**-na) *n, pl* **-nae** (-nee) a gap or space in a book or manuscript.

lacy *adj* **lacier, laciest** of or like lace.

lad *n* **1** a boy or young man. **2** *Informal* any male. **3 the lads** *Informal* a group of males.

ladder *n* **1** a portable frame consisting of two long parallel supports connected by steps, for climbing up or down. **2** any system thought of as having a series of ascending stages: *the career ladder.* **3** *Chiefly Brit* a line of connected stitches that have come undone in tights or stockings. ~*vb* **4** *Chiefly Brit* to have or cause to have a line of undone stitches.

ladder back *n* a chair in which the back is made of horizontal slats between two uprights.

lade *vb* **lading, laded, laden** *or* **laded 1** to put cargo on board (a ship) or (of a ship) to take on cargo. **2** (foll. by *with*) to burden or load.

laden *adj* **1** loaded. **2** burdened.

la-di-da *or* **lah-di-dah** *adj Informal* affected or pretentious in speech or manners.

ladies *or* **ladies' room** *n Informal* a women's public toilet.

lading *n* a load; cargo; freight.

ladle *n* **1** a long-handled spoon with a deep bowl for serving soup, stew, etc. ~*vb* **-dling, -dled 2** to serve out as with a ladle.

ladle out *vb Informal* to distribute (money, gifts, etc.) generously.

lady *n, pl* **-dies 1** a woman regarded as having the characteristics of a good family, such a dignified manners. **2** a polite name for a woman. ~*adj* **3** female: *a lady chef.*

Lady *n, pl* **-dies 1** (in Britain) a title borne by various classes of women of the peerage. **2 Our Lady** a title of the Virgin Mary.

ladybird *n* a small red beetle with black spots.

Lady Day *n* March 25, the feast of the Annunciation of the Virgin Mary: a quarter day in England, Wales, and Ireland.

lady-in-waiting *n, pl* **ladies-in-waiting** a lady who attends a queen or princess.

lady-killer *n Informal* a man who is or believes he is irresistible to women.

ladylike *adj* refined and fastidious.

Ladyship *n* (preceded by *Your* or *Her*) a title used to address or refer to any peeress except a duchess.

lady's-slipper *n* an orchid with reddish or purple flowers.

lag[1] *vb* **lagging, lagged 1** (often foll. by *behind*) to hang (back) or fall (behind) in movement, progress, or development. **2** to fall away in strength or intensity. ~*n* **3** a slowing down or falling behind. **4** the interval of time between two events, esp. between an action and its effect: *the time lag between mobilization and combat.*

lag[2] *vb* **lagging, lagged 1** to wrap (a pipe, cylinder, or boiler) with insulating material to prevent heat loss. ~*n* **2** the insulating casing of a steam cylinder or boiler.

lag[3] *n* **old lag** *Slang* a convict or ex-convict.

lager *n* a light-bodied beer.

laggard *n* a person who lags behind.

lagging *n* insulating material wrapped around pipes, boilers, or tanks to prevent loss of heat.

lagoon *n* a body of water cut off from the open sea by coral reefs or sand bars.

THESAURUS

scarcity, shortage, shortcoming, shortness, want **2.** *vb. often with* **in** be deficient in, be short of, be without, miss, need, require, want

lackadaisical 1. apathetic, dull, enervated, half-hearted, indifferent, languid, languorous, lethargic, limp, listless, spiritless **2.** abstracted, dreamy, idle, indolent, inert, lazy

lackey 1. brown-noser (*taboo slang*), creature, fawner, flatterer, flunky, hanger-on, instrument, menial, minion, parasite, pawn, sycophant, toady, tool, yes man **2.** attendant, flunky (*usually derogatory*), footman, manservant, valet, varlet (*old-fashioned*)

lacking defective, deficient, flawed, impaired, inadequate, minus (*informal*), missing, needing, wanting, without

lacklustre *or U.S.* **lackluster** boring, dim, drab, dry, dull, flat, leaden, lifeless, lustreless, muted, prosaic, sombre, unimaginative, uninspired, vapid

laconic brief, compact, concise, crisp, curt, pithy, sententious, short, succinct, terse, to the point

lad boy, chap (*informal*), fellow, guy (*informal*), juvenile, kid (*informal*), laddie (*Scot.*), schoolboy, shaver (*old-fashioned*), stripling, youngster, youth

laden burdened, charged, encumbered, fraught, full, hampered, loaded, oppressed, taxed, weighed down, weighted

lady-killer *informal* Casanova, Don Juan, heartbreaker, ladies' man, libertine, Lothario, philanderer, rake, roué, wolf (*old-fashioned informal*), womanizer

ladylike courtly, cultured, decorous, elegant, genteel, modest, polite, proper, refined, respectable, well-bred

lag 1. *often with* **behind** be behind, dawdle, delay, drag (behind), drag one's feet (*informal*), hang back, idle, linger, loiter, saunter, straggle, tarry, trail **2.** decrease, diminish, ebb, fail, fall off, flag, lose strength, slacken, wane

lah *n Music* (in tonic sol-fa) the sixth note of any ascending major scale.
laid *vb* the past of **lay**[1].
laid-back *adj* relaxed in style or character.
laid paper *n* paper with a regular pattern of lines impressed upon it.
lain *vb* the past participle of **lie**[2].
lair *n* **1** the resting place of a wild animal. **2** *Informal* a place of seclusion or hiding.
laird *n Scot* a landowner, esp. of a large estate.
laissez faire *or* **laisser faire** (**less**-ay **fair**) *n* the policy of nonintervention, esp. by a government in commerce.
laity (**lay**-it-ee) *n* **1** people who are not members of the clergy. **2** all the people who do not belong to a specific profession.
lake[1] *n* an expanse of water entirely surrounded by land.
lake[2] *n* **1** a bright pigment produced by combining organic colouring matter with an inorganic compound. **2** a red dye obtained by combining a metallic compound with cochineal.
Lake District *n* a region of lakes and mountains in NW England. Also called: **Lakeland, the Lakes**
lake trout *n* a yellow-spotted trout of the Great Lakes region of Canada.
lakh (**lahk**) *n* (in India) 100,000, esp. referring to this sum of rupees.
lam[1] *vb* **lamming, lammed** *Slang* to attack vigorously.
lam[2] *n* **on the lam** *US & Canad slang* making an escape.
lama *n* a Buddhist priest or monk in Mongolia or Tibet.
lamb *n* **1** the young of a sheep. **2** the meat of a young sheep eaten as food. **3** someone who is innocent, gentle, and good. *~vb* **4** (of a ewe) to give birth.
Lamb *n* **the Lamb** a title given to Christ.
lambast *or* **lambaste** *vb* **1** to beat severely. **2** to reprimand severely.
lambent *adj* **1** (of a flame or light) flickering softly over a surface. **2** (of wit or humour) light or brilliant. **lambency** *n*
lambing *n* **1** the birth of lambs at the end of winter. **2** the shepherd's work of tending the ewes and newborn lambs at this time.
lambskin *n* the skin of a lamb, usually with the wool still on, used to make coats, slippers, etc.
lame *adj* **1** disabled or crippled in the legs or feet. **2** weak; unconvincing: *lame arguments.* *~vb* **laming, lamed 3** to make lame. **lamely** *adv* **lameness** *n*
lamé (**lah**-may) *n* a fabric interwoven with gold or silver threads.
lame duck *n* a person who is unable to cope without the help of other people.
lament *vb* **1** to feel or express sorrow or regret (for or over). *~n* **2** an expression of sorrow. **3** a poem or song in which a death is lamented. **lamentation** *n*
lamentable *adj* very unfortunate or disappointing. **lamentably** *adv*
lamented *adj* grieved for: usually said of someone dead.
lamina *n, pl* **-nae** a thin plate, esp. of bone or mineral. **laminar** *adj*
laminate *vb* **-nating, -nated 1** to make (material in sheet form) by sticking together thin sheets. **2** to cover with a thin sheet of material. **3** to split or be split into thin sheets. *~n* **4** a material made by sticking sheets together. *~adj* **5** composed of lamina; laminated. **lamination** *n*
laminated *adj* **1** composed of many layers stuck together. **2** covered with a thin protective layer of plastic.
Lammas *n* August 1, formerly observed in England as a harvest festival: a quarter day in Scotland.
lamp *n* **1** a device that produces light: *an electric lamp; a gas lamp; an oil lamp.* **2** a device that produces radiation, esp. for therapeutic purposes: *an ultraviolet lamp.*
lampblack *n* a fine black soot used as a pigment in paint and ink.
lampoon *n* **1** a piece of writing ridiculing a person. *~vb* **2** to ridicule and criticize (someone) in a lampoon. **lampooner** *or* **lampoonist** *n*
lamppost *n* a metal or concrete pole supporting a lamp in a street.
lamprey *n* an eel-like fish with a round sucking mouth.
Lancastrian *n* **1** a person from Lancashire or Lancaster. **2** a supporter of the house of Lancaster in the Wars of the Roses (1455–85). *~adj* **3** of Lancashire or Lancaster. **4** of the house of Lancaster.
lance *n* **1** a long weapon with a pointed head used by horsemen. *~vb* **lancing, lanced 2** to pierce (an abscess or boil) with a lancet. **3** to pierce with or as with a lance.
lance corporal *n* a noncommissioned officer of the lowest rank.
lanceolate *adj* narrow and tapering to a point at each end, like some leaves.
lancer *n* (formerly) a cavalryman armed with a lance.
lancet *n* **1** a pointed surgical knife with two sharp edges. **2** short for **lancet arch or lancet window.**
lancet arch *n* a narrow acutely pointed arch.
lancet window *n* a narrow window with a lancet arch.
lancewood *n* a New Zealand tree with slender leaves.
Lancs Lancashire.

THESAURUS

laggard dawdler, idler, lingerer, loafer, loiterer, lounger, saunterer, skiver (*Brit. informal*), slowcoach (*Brit. informal*), sluggard (*old-fashioned*), snail, straggler
laid-back at ease, casual, easy-going, easy-oasy (*slang*), free and easy, relaxed, together (*slang*), unflappable (*informal*), unhurried
lair 1. burrow, den, earth, form, hole, nest, resting place **2.** *informal* den, hide-out, refuge, retreat, sanctuary
laissez faire, laisser faire free enterprise, free trade, individualism, live and let live, nonintervention
lame 1. crippled, defective, disabled, game, handicapped, hobbling, limping **2.** feeble, flimsy, inadequate, insufficient, pathetic, poor, thin, unconvincing, unsatisfactory, weak
lament *vb.* **1.** bemoan, bewail, complain, deplore, grieve, mourn, regret, sorrow, wail, weep *~n.* **2.** complaint, keening, lamentation, moan, moaning, plaint, ululation, wail, wailing **3.** dirge, elegy, monody, requiem, threnody
lamentable deplorable, distressing, grievous, harrowing, mournful, regrettable, sorrowful, tragic, unfortunate, woeful
lamentation dirge, grief, grieving, keening, lament, moan, mourning, plaint, sobbing, sorrow, ululation, wailing, weeping
lampoon 1. *n.* burlesque, caricature, parody, satire, send-up (*Brit. informal*), skit, takeoff (*informal*) **2.** *vb.*

land *n* **1** the solid part of the surface of the earth as distinct from seas and lakes. **2** ground, esp. with reference to its use or quality: *agricultural land.* **3** rural or agricultural areas: *he couldn't leave the land.* **4** *Law* ground owned as property. **5** a country, region, or area: *will bring peace and riches to your land.* ~*vb* **6** to come down or bring (something) down to earth after a flight or jump. **7** to transfer (something) or go from a ship to the shore: *sacks of malt were landed from barges.* **8** to come to or touch shore. **9** (in Canada) to be legally admitted to the country as an immigrant. **10** *Informal* to obtain: *he landed a handsomely paid job at Lloyd's.* **11** *Angling* to retrieve (a hooked fish) from the water. **12** *Informal* to deliver (a blow or punch). ~See also **land up. landless** *adj*

land agent *n* a person in charge of a landed estate.

landau (**lan**-daw) *n* a four-wheeled horse-drawn carriage with two folding hoods.

landed *adj* **1** owning land: *landed gentry.* **2** consisting of land: *landed property.*

landfall *n* the act of sighting or nearing land, esp. from the sea.

landfill *n* disposing of rubbish by covering it with earth.

land girl *n* a girl or woman who does farm work, esp. in wartime.

land-holder *n* a person who owns or occupies land. **land-holding** *adj, n*

landing *n* **1** the floor area at the top of a flight of stairs. **2** the act of coming to land, esp. after a flight or sea voyage. **3** a place of disembarkation.

landing field *n* an area of land on which aircraft land and from which they take off.

landing gear *n* the undercarriage of an aircraft.

landlady *n, pl* **-dies 1** a woman who owns and leases property. **2** a woman who owns or runs a lodging house or pub.

landlocked *adj* (of a country) completely surrounded by land.

landlord *n* **1** a man who owns and leases property. **2** a man who owns or runs a lodging house or pub.

landlubber *n Naut* any person without experience at sea.

landmark *n* **1** a prominent object in or feature of a particular landscape. **2** an important or unique event or development: *the Big Country score was a landmark in Hollywood music history.*

landmass *n* a large continuous area of land.

land mine *n Mil* an explosive device placed in the ground, usually detonated when someone steps on it or drives over it.

landowner *n* a person who owns land. **landowning** *n, adj*

landscape *n* **1** an extensive area of land regarded as being visually distinct. **2** a painting, drawing, or photograph depicting natural scenery. ~*vb* **-scaping, -scaped 3** to improve the natural features of (an area of land).

landscape gardening *n* the art of laying out grounds in imitation of natural scenery. **landscape gardener** *n*

landslide *n* **1** Also called: **landslip a** the sliding of a large mass of rocks and soil down the side of a mountain or cliff. **b** the material dislodged in this way. **2** an overwhelming electoral victory.

land up *vb* to arrive at a final point or condition.

landward *adj* **1** lying, facing, or moving towards land. **2** in the direction of the land. ~*adv also* **landwards 3** towards land.

lane *n* **1** a narrow road, esp. in the country. **2** one of the parallel strips into which the carriageway of a major road or motorway is divided. **3** any well-defined route or course, such as for ships or aircraft. **4** one of the parallel strips into which a running track or swimming bath is divided for races.

lang. language.

language *n* **1** a system of spoken sounds or conventional symbols for communicating thought. **2** the language of a particular nation or people. **3** the ability to use words to communicate. **4** any other means of communicating: *body language.* **5** the specialized vocabulary used by a particular group: *legal language.* **6** a particular style of verbal expression: *rough language.* **7** *Computers* See **programming language.**

language laboratory *n* a room in a school or college equipped with tape recorders, etc., for learning foreign languages.

languid *adj* lacking energy; dreamy and inactive. **languidly** *adv*

languish *vb Literary* **1** to suffer deprivation, hardship, or neglect: *she won't languish in jail for it.* **2** to lose or diminish in strength or energy: *the design languished into oblivion.* **3** (often foll. by *for*) to be listless with desire; pine. **languishing** *adj*

languor (**lang**-ger) *n Literary* a pleasant state of dreamy relaxation. **languorous** *adj*

THESAURUS

burlesque, caricature, make fun of, mock, parody, ridicule, satirize, send up (*Brit. informal*), take off (*informal*)

land *n.* **1.** dry land, earth, ground, terra firma **2.** dirt, ground, loam, soil **3.** countryside, farming, farmland, rural districts **4.** *Law* acres, estate, grounds, property, real property, realty **5.** country, district, fatherland, motherland, nation, province, region, territory, tract ~*vb.* **6.** alight, arrive, berth, come to rest, debark, disembark, dock, touch down **7.** *informal* acquire, gain, get, obtain, secure, win

landlord 1. freeholder, lessor, owner, proprietor **2.** host, hotelier, hotel-keeper, innkeeper

landmark 1. feature, monument **2.** crisis, milestone, turning point, watershed

landscape countryside, outlook, panorama, prospect, scene, scenery, view, vista

landslide avalanche, landslip, rockfall

land up arrive, end up, turn up, wind up

language 1. communication, conversation, discourse, expression, interchange, parlance, speech, talk, utterance, verbalization, vocalization **2.** argot, cant, dialect, idiom, jargon, lingo (*informal*), lingua franca, patois, speech, terminology, tongue, vernacular, vocabulary **3.** diction, expression, phraseology, phrasing, style, wording

languid drooping, dull, faint, feeble, heavy, inactive, indifferent, inert, lackadaisical, languorous, lazy, lethargic, limp, listless, pining, sickly, sluggish, spiritless, torpid, unenthusiastic, uninterested, weak, weary

languish *literary* **1.** be abandoned, be disregarded, be neglected, rot, suffer, waste away **2.** decline, droop, fade, fail, faint, flag, sicken, waste, weaken, wilt, wither **3.** *often with* **for** desire, eat one's heart out over, hanker, hunger, long, pine, sigh, want, yearn

languishing 1. declining, deteriorating, drooping, droopy, fading, failing, flagging, sickening, sinking, wasting away, weak, weakening, wilting, withering **2.** dreamy, longing, lovelorn, lovesick, melancholic, nostalgic, pensive, pining, soulful, tender, wistful, woebegone, yearning

lank 1. dull, lifeless, limp, long, lustreless, straggling

lank *adj* **1** (of hair) straight and limp. **2** thin or gaunt: *a lank bespectacled boy.*

lanky *adj* **lankier, lankiest** ungracefully tall and thin. **lankiness** *n*

lanolin *n* a yellowish sticky substance extracted from wool: used in some ointments.

lantern *n* **1** a light with a transparent protective case. **2** a raised part on top of a dome or roof which lets in light or air. **3** the upper part of a lighthouse that houses the light.

lantern jaw *n* a long hollow jaw that gives the face a drawn appearance. **lantern-jawed** *adj*

lanthanide series *n Chem* a class of 15 chemically related elements **(lanthanides)** with atomic numbers from 57 (lanthanum) to 71 (lutetium).

lanthanum *n Chem* a silvery-white metallic element of the lanthanide series: used in electronic devices and glass manufacture. Symbol: La

lanyard *n* **1** a cord worn round the neck to hold a whistle or knife. **2** *Naut* a line for extending or tightening rigging.

laodicean (lay-oh-**diss**-**see**-an) *adj* indifferent, esp. in religious matters.

lap[1] *n* **1** the area formed by the upper surface of the thighs of a seated person. **2** a protected place or environment: *in the lap of luxury.* **3** the part of a person's clothing that covers the lap. **4 drop in someone's lap** to give someone the responsibility of.

lap[2] *n* **1** one circuit of a racecourse or track. **2** a stage or part of a journey. **3 a** an overlapping part. **b** the extent of overlap. *~vb* **lapping, lapped 4** to overtake (an opponent) in a race so as to be one or more circuits ahead. **5** to enfold or wrap around. **6** to place or lie partly or completely over or project beyond: *deep-pile carpet that lapped against his ankles.* **7** to envelop or surround with comfort, love, or peace: *she was lapped by the luxury of Seymour House.*

lap[3] *vb* **lapping, lapped 1** (of small waves) to wash against (the shore or a boat) with light splashing sounds. **2** (often foll. by *up* esp. of animals) to scoop (a liquid) into the mouth with the tongue. *~n* **3** the act or sound of lapping. ~See also **lap up.**

lapdog *n* a small pet dog.

lapel (lap-**pel**) *n* the part on the front of a jacket or coat that folds back towards the shoulders.

lapidary *n, pl* **-daries 1** a person who cuts, polishes, sets, or deals in gemstones. *~adj* **2** of or relating to gemstones or the work of a lapidary.

lapis lazuli (**lap**-iss **lazz**-yew-lie) *n* a brilliant blue mineral used as a gemstone.

lap joint *n* a joint made by fastening together overlapping parts.

lap of honour *n* a ceremonial circuit of a racing track by the winner of a race.

Lapp *n* **1** Also: **Laplander** a member of a nomadic people living chiefly in N Scandinavia. **2** the language of this people. *~adj* **3** of this people or their language.

lappet *n* **1** a small hanging flap or piece of lace. **2** *Zool* a flap of flesh or membrane, such as the ear lobe or a bird's wattle.

lapse *n* **1** a temporary drop in standard as a result of forgetfulness or lack of concentration. **2** a moment or instance of bad behaviour, esp. by someone who is usually well-behaved. **3** a period of time sufficient for a change to take place: *the lapse between phone call and now.* **4** a gradual decline to a lower degree, condition, or state: *its lapse from the tradition of Disraeli.* **5** *Law* the loss of some right by neglecting to exercise or renew it. *~vb* **lapsing, lapsed 6** to drop in standard or fail to maintain a standard. **7** to decline gradually in status, condition, or degree. **8** to allow to end or become no longer valid, esp. through negligence: *a bid that lapsed last July.* **9** (usually foll. by *into*) to drift (into a condition): *she appeared to lapse into a brief reverie.* **10** (often foll. by *from*) to turn away (from beliefs or standards). **11** (of time) to slip away. **lapsed** *adj*

laptop *adj* (of a computer) small and light enough to be held on the user's lap.

lap up *vb* **1** to eat or drink. **2** to accept (information or attention) eagerly: *the public are lapping up the scandal.*

lapwing *n* a bird of the plover family with a crested head. Also called: **peewit**

larboard *n Naut* an old word for **port**[2] (sense 1).

larceny *n, pl* **-nies** *Law* theft. **larcenist** *n*

larch *n* **1** a coniferous tree with deciduous needle-like leaves and egg-shaped cones. **2** the wood of this tree.

lard *n* **1** the soft white fat obtained from pigs and prepared for use in cooking. *~vb* **2** to prepare (lean meat or poultry) by inserting small strips of bacon or fat before cooking. **3** to add unnecessary material to (speech or writing).

larder *n* a room or cupboard used for storing food.

lardy cake *n Brit* a sweet cake made of bread dough, lard, sugar, and dried fruit.

large *adj* **1** having a relatively great size, quantity, or extent; big. **2** of wide or broad scope, capacity, or range; comprehensive: *a large effect. ~n* **3 at large a** as a whole; in general: *both the Navy and the country at large.* **b** (of a dangerous criminal or wild animal) out of captivity; free. **c** in full detail. **largeness** *n*

large intestine *n* the part of the alimentary canal consisting of the caecum, colon, and rectum.

THESAURUS

2. attenuated, emaciated, gaunt, lanky, lean, rawboned, scraggy, scrawny, skinny, slender, slim, spare, thin

lanky angular, bony, gangling, gaunt, loose-jointed, rangy, rawboned, scraggy, scrawny, spare, tall, thin, weedy (*informal*)

lap[1] **1.** *n.* circle, circuit, course, distance, loop, orbit, round, tour **2.** *vb.* cover, enfold, envelop, fold, swaddle, swathe, turn, twist, wrap

lap[2] **1.** gurgle, plash, purl, ripple, slap, splash, swish, wash **2.** *often with* **up** drink, lick, sip, sup

lapse *n.* **1.** error, failing, fault, indiscretion, mistake, negligence, omission, oversight, slip **2.** break, gap, intermission, interruption, interval, lull, passage, pause **3.** backsliding, decline, descent, deterioration, drop, fall, relapse *~vb.* **4.** decline, degenerate, deteriorate, drop, fail, fall, sink, slide, slip **5.** become obsolete, become void, end, expire, run out, stop, terminate

lapsed 1. discontinued, ended, expired, finished, invalid, out-of-date, run out, unrenewed **2.** backsliding, lacking faith, nonpractising

large *adj.* **1.** big, bulky, colossal, considerable, elephantine, enormous, giant, gigantic, goodly, great, huge, humongous (*informal, chiefly U.S.*), immense, jumbo (*informal*), king-size, man-size, massive, mega (*slang*), monumental, sizable, substantial, tidy (*informal*), vast **2.** abundant, ample, broad, capacious, comprehensive, copious, extensive, full, generous, grand, grandiose, liberal, plentiful, roomy, spacious, sweeping, wide *~n.* **3. at large a.** as a whole, chiefly, generally, in general, in the main, mainly **b.** at liberty, free, on the loose, on the run, roaming, unconfined **c.** at length, considerably, exhaustively, greatly, in full detail

largely as a rule, by and large, chiefly, considerably,

largely *adv* principally; to a great extent.
large-scale *adj* 1 wide-ranging or extensive. 2 (of maps and models) constructed or drawn to a big scale.
largesse *or* **largess** (lar-**jess**) *n* the generous giving of gifts, favours, or money.
largish *adj* fairly large.
largo *Music ~adv* 1 in a slow and stately manner. *~n, pl* **-gos** 2 a piece or passage to be performed in a slow and stately manner.
lariat *n US & Canad* 1 a lasso. 2 a rope for tethering animals.
lark[1] *n* a small brown songbird, esp. the skylark.
lark[2] *Informal ~n* 1 a carefree adventure or frolic. 2 a harmless piece of mischief. 3 an activity or job viewed with disrespect. *~vb* 4 **lark about** to have a good time frolicking or playing pranks. **larky** *adj*
larkspur *n* a plant with blue, pink, or white flowers with slender spikes at the base.
larva *n, pl* **-vae** the immature form of many insects before it develops into its adult form. **larval** *adj*
laryngeal *adj* of or relating to the larynx.
laryngitis *n* inflammation of the larynx, causing huskiness or loss of voice.
larynx (**lar**-rinks) *n, pl* **larynges** (lar-**rin**-jeez) *or* **larynxes** a hollow organ forming part of the air passage to the lungs: it contains the vocal cords.
lasagne *or* **lasagna** (laz-**zan**-ya) *n* 1 a form of pasta in wide flat sheets. 2 a dish made from layers of lasagne, meat, and cheese.
lascar *n* an East Indian seaman.
lascivious (lass-**iv**-ee-uss) *adj* showing or producing sexual desire; lustful. **lasciviously** *adv*
laser (**lay**-zer) *n* a device that produces a very narrow intense beam of light, which is used for cutting very hard materials and in surgery etc.
laser printer *n* a computer printer that uses a laser beam to produce characters which are then transferred to paper.
lash[1] *n* 1 an eyelash. 2 a sharp cutting blow from a whip. 3 the flexible end of a whip. *~vb* 4 to hit (a person or thing) sharply with a whip, esp. formerly as punishment. 5 (of rain or waves) to beat forcefully against. 6 to attack (someone) with words of ridicule or scolding. 7 to flick or wave sharply to and fro: *his tail lashing in irritation.* 8 to urge as with a whip: *to lash the audience into a violent mood.* ~See also **lash out.**
lash[2] *vb* to bind or secure with rope, string, or cord.
lashing[1] *n* 1 a flogging. 2 a scolding.
lashing[2] *n* rope, string, or cord used for binding or securing.
lashings *pl n Brit old-fashioned, informal* large amounts; lots: *lashings of cream.*
lash out *vb* 1 to make a sudden verbal or physical attack. 2 *Informal* to spend extravagantly.
lass *n* a girl or young woman.
Lassa fever *n* a serious viral disease of Central West Africa, characterized by high fever and muscular pains.
lassie *n Scot & N English informal* a little lass; girl.
lassitude *n* physical or mental weariness.
lasso (lass-**oo**) *n, pl* **-sos** *or* **-soes** 1 a long rope with a noose at one end used for catching horses and cattle. *~vb* **-soing, -soed** 2 to catch as with a lasso. **lassoer** *n*
last[1] *adj* 1 being, happening, or coming at the end or after all others. 2 most recent: *last April.* 3 only remaining: *that's the last one.* 4 most extreme; utmost. 5 least suitable or likely: *China was the last place on earth he intended to go.* *~adv* 6 after all others. 7 most recently: *we last saw him on Thursday night.* 8 as the last or latest item. *~n* 9 **the last a** a person or thing that is last. **b** the final moment; end. 10 the final appearance, mention, or occurrence: *the last of this season's visitors.* 11 **at last** in the end; finally. 12 **at long last** finally, after difficulty or delay.
last[2] *vb* 1 to continue to exist for a length of time: *the soccer war lasted 100 hours.* 2 to be sufficient for the needs of (a person) for a length of time: *I shall make a couple of bottles to last me until next summer.* 3 to remain fresh, uninjured, or unaltered for a certain time: *the flowers haven't lasted well.* ~See also **last out.**
last[3] *n* the wooden or metal form on which a shoe or boot is made or repaired.
last-ditch *adj* done as a final resort: *a last-ditch attempt.*
lasting *adj* existing or remaining effective for a long time.
Last Judgment *n* **the Last Judgment** *Theol* God's verdict on the destinies of all human beings at the end of the world.
lastly *adv* 1 at the end or at the last point. 2 finally.
last-minute *adj* given or done at the latest possible time: *last-minute changes.*
last name *n* same as **surname.**
last out *vb* 1 to be sufficient for one's needs: *if the*

THESAURUS

extensively, generally, mainly, mostly, predominantly, primarily, principally, to a great extent, widely
large-scale broad, extensive, far-reaching, global, sweeping, vast, wholesale, wide, wide-ranging
largesse, largess alms-giving, benefaction, bounty, charity, generosity, liberality, munificence, open-handedness, philanthropy
lark *informal* 1. *n.* antic, caper, escapade, fling, frolic, fun, gambol, game, jape, mischief, prank, revel, rollick, romp, skylark, spree 2. *vb.* **lark about** caper, cavort, cut capers, frolic, gambol, have fun, make mischief, play, rollick, romp, sport
lash[1] *n.* 1. blow, hit, stripe, stroke, swipe (*informal*) *~vb.* 2. beat, birch, chastise, flagellate, flog, horsewhip, lambast(e), scourge, thrash, whip 3. beat, buffet, dash, drum, hammer, hit, knock, lambast(e), pound, punch, smack, strike 4. attack, belabour, berate, blast, castigate, censure, criticize, flay, lambast(e), lampoon, put down, ridicule, satirize, scold, tear into (*informal*), upbraid
lash[2] bind, fasten, join, make fast, rope, secure, strap, tie
lass bird (*slang, chiefly Brit.*), chick (*slang*), colleen (*Irish*), damsel, girl, lassie (*Scot & N English informal*), maid, maiden, miss, schoolgirl, wench (*facetious*), young woman
last[1] *adj.* 1. aftermost, at the end, hindmost, rearmost 2. latest, most recent 3. closing, concluding, extreme, final, furthest, remotest, terminal, ultimate, utmost *~adv.* 4. after, behind, bringing up the rear, in *or* at the end, in the rear *~n.* 5. **the last** close, completion, conclusion, end, ending, finale, finish, termination 6. **at last** at length, eventually, finally, in conclusion, in the end, ultimately
last[2] abide, carry on, continue, endure, hold out, keep, keep on, persist, remain, stand up, survive, wear
last-ditch all-out (*informal*), desperate, final, frantic, heroic, straining, struggling
lasting abiding, continuing, deep-rooted, durable, enduring, eternal, indelible, lifelong, long-standing, long-

energy supply lasts out. **2** to endure or survive: *I might not last out my hours of duty.*

last post *n Mil* **1** a bugle call used to signal the time to retire at night. **2** a similar call sounded at military funerals.

last rites *pl n Christianity* religious rites for those close to death.

last straw *n* a small incident, irritation, or setback that coming after others is too much to cope with.

Last Supper *n* **the** the meal eaten by Christ with his disciples on the night before his Crucifixion.

lat. latitude.

Lat. Latin.

latch *n* **1** a fastening for a gate or door that consists of a bar that may be slid or lowered into a groove, hole, or notch. **2** a spring-loaded door lock that can only be opened by a key from outside. *~vb* **3** to fasten, fit, or be fitted with a latch.

latchkey child *n* a child who has to let himself or herself in at home after school, as both parents are out at work.

latch on *vb Informal* **1** (often foll. by *to*) to attach oneself (to): *he should latch on to a man with a deal to do.* **2** to understand: *it took a while to latch on to what he was trying to say.*

late *adj* **1** occurring or arriving after the correct or expected time: *the plane will be late.* **2** towards or near the end: *the late afternoon.* **3** occurring or being at a relatively advanced time: *a late starter, his first novel was effectively his last.* **4** at an advanced time in the evening or at night: *it's late, I have to get back.* **5** having died recently: *the late Benny Hill.* **6** recent: *recollect the late defeats which your enemies have experienced.* **7** former: *the late manager of the team.* **8 of late** recently. *~adv* **9** after the correct or expected time: *Mark Wright arrived late.* **10** at a relatively advanced age: *coming late to motherhood.* **11** recently: *as late as in 1983, only 9 per cent of that labour force was unionized.* **12 late in the day a** at a late or advanced stage. **b** too late. **lateness** *n*

lateen *adj Naut* denoting a rig with a triangular sail bent to a yard hoisted to the head of a low mast.

Late Greek *n* the Greek language from about the 3rd to the 8th centuries AD.

Late Latin *n* the form of written Latin used from the 3rd to the 7th centuries AD.

lately *adv* in recent times; of late.

latent *adj* lying hidden and not yet developed within a person or thing. **latency** *n*

later *adj, adv* **1** the comparative of **late.** *~adv* **2** afterwards.

lateral (**lat**-ter-al) *adj* of or relating to the side or sides. **laterally** *adv*

lateral thinking *n* a way of solving problems by apparently illogical methods.

latest *adj, adv* **1** the superlative of **late.** *~adj* **2** most recent, modern, or new: *the latest fashions.* *~n* **3 at the latest** no later than the time specified.

latex *n* a milky fluid produced by many plants: latex from the rubber plant is used in the manufacture of rubber.

lath *n, pl* **laths** one of several thin narrow strips of wood used as a supporting framework for plaster or tiles.

lathe *n* a machine for shaping metal or wood by turning it against a fixed tool.

lather *n* **1** foam formed by soap or detergent in water. **2** foamy sweat, as produced by a horse. **3** *Informal* a state of agitation. *~vb* **4** to coat or become coated with lather. **5** to form a lather. **6** *Informal* to beat; flog. **lathery** *adj*

Latin *n* **1** the language of ancient Rome and the Roman Empire. **2** a member of any of those peoples whose languages are derived from Latin. *~adj* **3** of the Latin language. **4** of those peoples whose languages are derived from Latin. **5** of the Roman Catholic Church.

Latin America *n* those areas of South and Central America whose official languages are Spanish and Portuguese. **Latin American** *adj, n*

latish *adj, adv* rather late.

latitude *n* **1 a** an angular distance measured in degrees north or south of the equator. **b** (*often pl*) a region considered with regard to its distance from the equator. **2** scope for freedom of action and thought. **latitudinal** *adj*

latitudinarian *adj* **1** liberal, esp. in religious matters. *~n* **2** a person with latitudinarian views.

latrine *n* a toilet in a barracks or camp.

latter *n* **1 the latter** the second or second mentioned of two. *~adj* **2** near or nearer the end: *the latter half of the season.* **3** more advanced in time or sequence; later.

➤ *Latter* is used for the last mentioned of two items. When there are more, use *last-named.*

latter-day *adj* present-day; modern.

latterly *adv* recently; lately.

lattice (**lat**-iss) *n* **1** Also called: **latticework** a framework of strips of wood or metal interlaced in a diagonal pattern. **2** a gate, screen, or fence formed of such a framework. **3** an array of atoms, ions, or molecules in a crystal or an array of points indicating their

THESAURUS

term, perennial, permanent, perpetual, unceasing, undying, unending

lastly after all, all in all, at last, finally, in conclusion, in the end, to conclude, to sum up, ultimately

latch 1. *n.* bar, bolt, catch, clamp, fastening, hasp, hook, lock **2.** *vb.* bar, bolt, fasten, lock, make fast, secure

late *adj.* **1.** behind, behindhand, belated, delayed, last-minute, overdue, slow, tardy, unpunctual **2.** dead, deceased, departed **3.** advanced, fresh, modern, new, recent **4.** defunct, departed, ex-, former, old, past, preceding, previous *~adv.* **5.** at the last minute, behindhand, behind time, belatedly, dilatorily, slowly, tardily, unpunctually

lately in recent times, just now, latterly, not long ago, of late, recently

lateness advanced hour, belatedness, delay, late date, retardation, tardiness, unpunctuality

later *adv.* after, afterwards, by and by, in a while, in time, later on, next, subsequently, thereafter

lateral edgeways, flanking, side, sideward, sideways

latest current, fashionable, happening (*informal*), in, modern, most recent, newest, now, up-to-date, up-to-the-minute

lather *n.* **1.** bubbles, foam, froth, soap, soapsuds, suds **2.** *informal* dither (*chiefly Brit.*), fever, flap (*informal*), fluster, fuss, pother (*literary*), state (*informal*), stew (*informal*), sweat, tizzy (*informal*), twitter (*informal*) *~vb.* **3.** foam, froth, soap **4.** *informal* beat, cane, drub, flog, lambast(e), strike, thrash, whip

lathery bubbly, foamy, frothy, soapy, sudsy

latitude elbowroom, freedom, indulgence, laxity, leeway, liberty, licence, play, scope, unrestrictedness

latter closing, concluding, last, last-mentioned, later, latest, modern, recent, second

latterly hitherto, lately, of late, recently

positions in space. ~*vb* **-ticing, -ticed 4** to make, adorn, or supply with a lattice. **latticed** *adj*

Latvian *adj* **1** from Latvia. ~*n* **2** a person from Latvia. **3** the language of Latvia.

laud *Literary* ~*vb* **1** to praise or glorify. ~*n* **2** praise or glorification.

laudable *adj* deserving praise; commendable. **laudability** *n* **laudably** *adv*

laudanum (**lawd**-a-num) *n* a sedative extracted from opium.

laudatory *adj* (of speech or writing) expressing praise.

laugh *vb* **1** to express amusement or happiness by producing a series of inarticulate sounds. **2** to utter or express with laughter: *he laughed his derision at the play.* **3** to bring or force (oneself) into a certain condition by laughter: *laughing herself silly.* **4 laugh at** to make fun of; jeer at. **5 laugh up one's sleeve** to laugh secretly. ~*n* **6** the act or an instance of laughing. **7** *Informal* a person or thing that causes laughter: *he's a laugh, that one.* **8 the last laugh** final success after previous defeat. ~See also **laugh off. laughingly** *adv*

laughable *adj* ridiculous because so obviously inadequate or unsuccessful.

laughing gas *n* nitrous oxide used as an anaesthetic: it may cause laughter and exhilaration when inhaled.

laughing stock *n* a person or thing that is treated with ridicule.

laugh off *vb* to treat (something serious or difficult) lightly.

laughter *n* the action or noise of laughing.

launch[1] *vb* **1** to move (a vessel) into the water, esp. for the first time. **2 a** to start off or set in motion: *to launch an appeal.* **b** to put (a new product) on the market. **3** to set (a rocket, missile, or spacecraft) into motion. **4** to involve (oneself) totally and enthusiastically: *Francis launched himself into the transfer market with gusto.* **5 launch into** to start talking or writing (about). **6** (usually foll. by *out*) to start (out) on a new enterprise. ~*n* **7** an act or instance of launching. **launcher** *n*

launch[2] *n* an open motorboat.

launching pad *or* **launch pad** *n* a platform from which a spacecraft, rocket, or missile is launched.

launder *vb* **1** to wash and iron (clothes and linen). **2** to make (money illegally obtained) appear to be legally gained by passing it through foreign banks or legitimate enterprises.

Launderette *n Brit & NZ trademark* an establishment where clothes can be washed and dried, using coin-operated machines. Also called (US, Canad, and NZ): **Laundromat**

laundry *n, pl* **-dries 1** the clothes or linen to be laundered or that have been laundered. **2** a place where clothes and linen are washed and ironed.

laureate (**lor**-ee-at) *adj* **1** *Literary* crowned with laurel leaves as a sign of honour. ~*n* **2** short for **poet laureate. laureateship** *n*

laurel *n* **1** a small Mediterranean evergreen tree with glossy leaves. **2** (*pl*) a wreath of laurel, worn on the head as an emblem of victory or honour in classical times. **3** (*pl*) honour, distinction, or fame. **4 rest on one's laurels** to be satisfied with what one has already achieved and stop striving for further success. **5 look to one's laurels** to be on guard against one's rivals.

lav *n Brit informal* short for **lavatory.**

lava *n* **1** molten rock discharged by volcanoes. **2** any rock formed by the solidification of lava.

lavatorial *adj* characterized by frequent reference to excretion: *lavatorial humour.*

lavatory *n, pl* **-ries** same as **toilet.**

lavender *n* **1** a plant grown for its bluish-purple flowers and as the source of a sweet-smelling oil. **2** its dried flowers, used to perfume clothes. ~*adj* **3** pale bluish-purple.

lavender water *n* a light perfume made from lavender.

lavish *adj* **1** great in quantity or richness: *lavish banquets.* **2** very generous in giving. **3** extravagant; wasteful: *lavish spending habits.* ~*vb* **4** to give or to spend very generously or in great quantities. **lavishly** *adv*

law *n* **1** a rule or set of rules regulating what may or may not be done by members of a society or community. **2** a rule or body of rules made by the legislature or other authority. **3** the control enforced by such rules: *scant respect for the rule of law.* **4 the law a** the legal or judicial system. **b** the profession or practice of law. **c** *Informal* the police or a policeman. **5 law and order** the policy of strict enforcement of the law, esp. against crime and violence. **6** a rule of behaviour: *an unwritten law that Nanny knows best.* **7** Also called:

THESAURUS

lattice fretwork, grating, grid, grille, latticework, mesh, network, openwork, reticulation, tracery, trellis, web

laudable admirable, commendable, creditable, estimable, excellent, meritorious, of note, praiseworthy, worthy

laudatory acclamatory, adulatory, approbatory, approving, commendatory, complimentary, eulogistic, panegyrical

laugh *vb.* **1.** be convulsed (*informal*), be in stitches (*informal*), chortle, chuckle, crack up (*informal*), crease up (*informal*), giggle, guffaw, roar with laughter, snigger, split one's sides, titter **2. laugh at** belittle, deride, jeer, lampoon, make a mock of, make fun of, mock, ridicule, scoff at, take the mickey (out of) (*informal*), taunt ~*n.* **3.** belly laugh (*informal*), chortle, chuckle, giggle, guffaw, roar *or* shriek of laughter, snigger, titter **4.** *informal* card (*old-fashioned informal*), clown, comedian, comic, entertainer, hoot (*informal*), humorist, joke, lark, scream (*informal*), wag, wit

laughable absurd, derisive, derisory, farcical, ludicrous, nonsensical, preposterous, ridiculous, risible, worthy of scorn

laughing stock Aunt Sally (*Brit.*), butt, everybody's fool, fair game, figure of fun, target, victim

laugh off brush aside, dismiss, disregard, ignore, minimize, pooh-pooh, shrug off

laughter chortling, chuckling, giggling, guffawing, laughing, tittering

launch 1. cast, discharge, dispatch, fire, project, propel, send off, set afloat, set in motion, throw **2.** begin, commence, embark upon, inaugurate, initiate, instigate, introduce, open, start

laurel *plural* acclaim, awards, bays, Brownie points, commendation, credit, distinction, fame, glory, honour, kudos, praise, prestige, recognition, renown, reward

lavatory bathroom, bog (*slang*), cloakroom (*Brit. euphemistic*), Gents, john (*slang, chiefly U.S. & Canad.*), Ladies, latrine, loo (*Brit. informal*), powder room, (public) convenience, toilet, washroom, water closet, W.C.

lavish *adj.* **1.** abundant, copious, exuberant, lush, luxuriant, opulent, plentiful, profuse, prolific, sumptuous **2.** bountiful, effusive, free, generous, liberal, munificent, open-handed, unstinting **3.** exaggerated, ex-

law of nature a generalization based on a recurring fact or event. **8** the science or knowledge of law; jurisprudence. **9** a general principle, formula, or rule in mathematics, science, or philosophy: *the law of gravity.* **10 the Law** the laws contained in the first five books of the Old Testament. **11 go to law** to resort to legal proceedings on some matter. **12 lay down the law** to speak in an authoritative manner.

law-abiding *adj* obeying the laws: *a law-abiding citizen.*

lawbreaker *n* a person who breaks the law. **lawbreaking** *n, adj*

lawful *adj* allowed, recognized, or sanctioned by law; legal. **lawfully** *adv*

lawgiver *n* **1** the giver of a code of laws. **2** Also called: **lawmaker** a maker of laws. **lawgiving** *n, adj*

lawless *adj* **1** breaking the law, esp. in a wild or violent way: *lawless butchery.* **2** not having laws. **lawlessness** *n*

Law Lords *pl n* members of the House of Lords who sit as the highest court of appeal.

lawn[1] *n* an area of cultivated and mown grass.

lawn[2] *n* a fine linen or cotton fabric.

lawn mower *n* a hand-operated or power-operated machine for cutting grass.

lawn tennis *n* **1** tennis played on a grass court. **2** same as **tennis.**

lawrencium *n Chem* an element artificially produced from californium. Symbol: Lr

lawsuit *n* a case in a court of law brought by one person or group against another.

lawyer *n* a member of the legal profession who can advise clients about the law and represent them in court.

lax *adj* lacking firmness; not strict. **laxity** *n*

laxative *n* **1** a medicine that induces the emptying of the bowels. ~*adj* **2** easing the emptying of the bowels.

lay[1] *vb* **lays, laying, laid 1** to put in a low or horizontal position; cause to lie: *Mary laid a clean square of white towelling carefully on the grass.* **2** to establish as a basis: *ready to lay your new fashion foundations?* **3** to place or be in a particular state or position: *underneath lay a key.* **4** to regard as the responsibility of: *ridiculous attempts to lay the loss at the door of the Admiralty.* **5** to put forward: *ruses by which we lay claim on one another.* **6** to arrange or prepare: *she would lay her plans.* **7** to place in position: *he laid a wreath.* **8** (of birds, esp. the domestic hen) to produce (eggs). **9** to make (a bet) with (someone): *I'll lay money he's already gone home.* **10** to arrange (a table) for a meal. **11** to prepare (a fire) by arranging fuel in the grate. **12** *Taboo slang* to have sexual intercourse with. **13 lay bare** to reveal or explain: *a century of neurophysiology has now laid bare the structures of the brain.* **14 lay hold of** to seize or grasp. **15 lay oneself open** to make oneself vulnerable (to criticism or attack). **16 lay open** to reveal or disclose. **17 lay waste** to destroy completely. ~*n* **18** the manner or position in which something lies or is placed. **19** *Taboo, slang* **a** an act of sexual intercourse. **b** a sexual partner. ~See also **lay aside, lay down,** etc.

➤ *Lay* and *lie* are often confused. Lay takes an object: *He laid down his weapon; lie* does not take an object: *I'm going to lie down.*

lay[2] *vb* the past tense of **lie**[2].

lay[3] *adj* **1** of or involving people who are not members of the clergy. **2** nonprofessional or nonspecialist.

lay[4] *n* a short narrative poem intended to be sung.

layabout *n* a lazy person.

lay aside *vb* **1** to abandon or reject. **2** to put aside (one thing) in order to take up another. **3** to store or reserve for future use.

lay-by *n Brit* a place where drivers can stop by the side of a main road.

lay down *vb* **1** to place on the ground or a surface. **2** to sacrifice: *willing to lay down their lives for the truth.* **3** to formulate (a rule or principle). **4** to record (plans) on paper. **5** to store or stock: *the speed with which we lay down extra, unwanted fat.*

layer *n* **1** a single thickness of something, such as a cover or a coating on a surface. **2** a laying hen. **3** *Horticulture* a shoot that forms its own root while still attached to the parent plant. ~*vb* **4** to form or make a layer or layers.

layette *n* a complete set of clothing, bedclothes, and other accessories for a newborn baby.

lay figure *n* **1** an artist's jointed dummy, used esp. for

THESAURUS

cessive, extravagant, immoderate, improvident, intemperate, prodigal, thriftless, unreasonable, unrestrained, wasteful, wild ~*vb.* **4.** deluge, dissipate, expend, heap, pour, shower, spend, squander, waste

law 1. charter, code, constitution, jurisprudence **2.** act, canon, code, command, commandment, covenant, decree, demand, edict, enactment, order, ordinance, rule, statute **3.** axiom, canon, criterion, formula, precept, principle, regulation, standard **4. lay down the law** dictate, dogmatize, emphasize, pontificate

law-abiding compliant, dutiful, good, honest, honourable, lawful, obedient, orderly, peaceable, peaceful

lawbreaker convict, criminal, crook (*informal*), culprit, delinquent, felon (*Criminal law*), miscreant, offender, sinner, transgressor, trespasser, villain, violator, wrongdoer

lawful allowable, authorized, constitutional, just, legal, legalized, legitimate, licit, permissible, proper, rightful, valid, warranted

lawless anarchic, chaotic, disorderly, insubordinate, insurgent, mutinous, rebellious, reckless, riotous, seditious, ungoverned, unrestrained, unruly, wild

lawsuit action, argument, case, cause, contest, dispute, industrial tribunal, litigation, proceedings, prosecution, suit, trial

lawyer advocate, attorney, barrister, counsel, counsellor, legal adviser, solicitor

lax careless, casual, easy-going, lenient, neglectful, negligent, overindulgent, remiss, slack, slapdash, slipshod

lay[1] **1.** deposit, leave, place, put, set, settle, spread **2.** establish, plant, posit, set **3.** allocate, allot, ascribe, assign, attribute, charge, impute **4.** advance, bring forward, lodge, offer, present, put forward, submit **5.** arrange, concoct, contrive, design, devise, dispose, hatch, locate, organize, plan, plot, position, prepare, set out, work out **6.** bear, deposit, produce **7.** bet, gamble, give odds, hazard, risk, stake, wager **8. lay bare** disclose, divulge, explain, expose, reveal, show, unveil **9. lay hold of** get, get hold of, grab, grasp, grip, seize, snatch

lay[2] **1.** nonclerical, secular **2.** amateur, inexpert, nonprofessional, nonspecialist

layabout beachcomber, couch potato (*slang*), good-for-nothing, idler, laggard, loafer, lounger, ne'er-do-well, shirker, skiver (*Brit. slang*), vagrant, wastrel

lay aside abandon, cast aside, dismiss, postpone, put aside, put off, reject, shelve

lay down 1. discard, drop, give, give up, relinquish, surrender, yield **2.** affirm, assume, establish, formulate, ordain, postulate, prescribe, stipulate

studying effects of drapery. **2** a person considered to be subservient or unimportant.

lay in *vb* to accumulate and store: *they've already laid in five hundred bottles of great vintages.*

lay into *vb Informal* to attack or scold severely.

layman *or fem* **laywoman** *n, pl* **-men** *or* **-women** **1** a person who is not a member of the clergy. **2** a person who does not have specialized knowledge of a subject: *the layman's guide to nuclear power.*

lay off *vb* **1** to suspend (staff) during a slack period at work. **2** *Informal* to leave (a person, thing, or activity) alone: *"lay off the defence counsel bit!" he snapped.* ~*n* **lay-off** **3** a period of imposed unemployment.

lay on *vb* **1** to provide or supply: *they laid on a treat for the entourage.* **2** **lay it on thick** *Slang* to exaggerate, esp. when flattering.

lay out *vb* **1** to arrange or spread out. **2** to plan or design: *the main streets were laid out on a grid system.* **3** to prepare (a corpse) for burial. **4** *Informal* to spend (money), esp. lavishly. **5** *Informal* to knock (someone) unconscious. ~*n* **layout** **6** the arrangement or plan of something, such as a building. **7** the arrangement of printed material.

lay reader *n* **1** *Church of England* a person licensed to conduct religious services other than the Eucharist. **2** *RC Church* a layman chosen to read the epistle at Mass.

lay up *vb* **1** *Informal* to confine through illness: *laid up with a bad cold.* **2** to store for future use.

laze *vb* **lazing, lazed** **1** to be idle or lazy. **2** (often foll. by *away*) to spend (time) in idleness. ~*n* **3** time spent lazing.

lazy *adj* **lazier, laziest** **1** not inclined to work or exert oneself. **2** done in a relaxed manner with little effort. **3** moving in a sluggish manner: *the lazy drift of the bubbles.* **lazily** *adv* **laziness** *n*

lazybones *n Informal* a lazy person.

lb **1** pound (weight). **2** *Cricket* leg bye.

lbw *Cricket* leg before wicket.

lc **1** in the place cited. **2** *Printing* lower case.

LCD **1** liquid crystal display. **2** Also: **lcd** lowest common denominator.

lcm *or* **LCM** lowest common multiple.

lea *n* **1** *Poetic* a meadow or field. **2** grassland.

LEA Local Education Authority.

leach *vb* **1** to remove or be removed from a substance by a liquid passing through it. **2** to lose soluble substances by the action of a liquid passing through.

lead[1] *vb* **leading, led** **1** to show the way to (an individual or a group) by going with or ahead: *he led her into the house.* **2** to guide, control, or direct: *he dismounted and led his horse back.* **3** to influence someone to act, think, or behave in a certain way: *researching our family history has led her to correspond with relatives abroad.* **4** to have the principal part in (something): *planners led the development of policy.* **5** to go at the head of or have the top position in (something): *Prost now led the table with eighteen points.* **6** (of a road or way) to be the means of reaching a place: *the footbridge leads on to a fine promenade.* **7** to pass or spend: *I've led a happy life.* **8** to guide or be guided by physical means: *he took her firmly by the arm and led her home.* **9** to direct the course of (water, a rope, or wire) along or as if along a channel. **10** (foll. by *with*) to have as the most important item: *the Review leads with a critique of A Place of Greater Safety.* **11** *Brit music* to play first violin in (an orchestra). **12** to begin a round of cards by putting down the first card. ~*n* **13** the first or most prominent place. **14** example or leadership: *some of his children followed his lead.* **15** an advantage over others: *Essex have a lead of 24 points.* **16** an indication; clue: *we've got a lead on how the body got into the water.* **17** a length of leather, nylon, or chain used to walk or control a dog. **18** the principal role in a play, film, or other production, or the person playing such a role. **19** the most important news story in a newspaper: *the shooting makes the lead in the Times.* **20** the act of playing the first card in a round of cards or the card so played. **21** a wire, cable, or other conductor for making an electrical connection. ~*adj* **22** acting as a leader or lead: *lead singer.* ~See also **lead off, lead on,** etc.

lead[2] *n* **1** a heavy toxic bluish-white metallic element: used in alloys, cable sheaths, paints, and as a radiation shield. Symbol: Pb **2** **a** graphite used for drawing. **b** a thin stick of this as the core of a pencil. **3** a lead weight suspended on a line, used to take soundings of the depth of water. **4** lead weights or shot, as used in cartridges or fishing lines. **5** a thin strip of lead for holding small panes of glass or pieces of stained glass. **6** (*pl*) **a** thin sheets or strips of lead used as a roof covering. **b** a roof covered with such sheets. **7** Also called: **leading** *Printing* a thin strip of metal, formerly used for spacing between lines of type. ~*adj* **8** of, relat-

THESAURUS

layer bed, blanket, coat, coating, cover, covering, film, mantle, ply, row, seam, sheet, stratum, thickness, tier

lay in accumulate, amass, build up, collect, hoard, stockpile, stock up, store (up)

lay into *informal* assail, attack, belabour, hit out at, lambast(e), let fly at, pitch into (*informal*), set about

layman *or fem.* **laywoman** amateur, lay person, nonprofessional, outsider

lay off **1.** discharge, dismiss, drop, let go, make redundant, oust, pay off **2.** *informal* cease, desist, give it a rest (*informal*), give over (*informal*), give up, leave alone, leave off, let up, quit, stop

lay-off discharge, dismissal, unemployment

lay on **1.** cater (for), furnish, give, provide, purvey, supply **2.** **lay it on thick** *slang* butter up, exaggerate, flatter, overdo it, overpraise, soft-soap (*informal*)

lay out **1.** arrange, design, display, exhibit, plan, spread out **2.** *informal* disburse, expend, fork out (*slang*), invest, pay, shell out (*informal*), spend **3.** *informal* knock for six (*informal*), knock out, knock unconscious, KO *or* K.O. (*slang*)

layout arrangement, design, draft, formation, geography, outline, plan

laziness dilatoriness, do-nothingness, idleness, inactivity, indolence, slackness, sloth, slothfulness, slowness, sluggishness, tardiness

lazy **1.** idle, inactive, indolent, inert, remiss, shiftless, slack, slothful, slow, workshy **2.** drowsy, languid, languorous, lethargic, sleepy, slow-moving, sluggish, somnolent, torpid

leach drain, extract, filter, filtrate, percolate, seep, strain

lead *vb.* **1.** conduct, escort, guide, pilot, precede, show the way, steer, usher **2.** command, direct, govern, head, manage, preside over, supervise **3.** cause, dispose, draw, incline, induce, influence, persuade, prevail, prompt **4.** be ahead (of), blaze a trail, come first, exceed, excel, outdo, outstrip, surpass, transcend **5.** experience, have, live, pass, spend, undergo ~*n.* **6.** advance, advantage, cutting edge, edge, first place, margin, precedence, primacy, priority, start, supremacy, van, vanguard **7.** direction, example, guidance, leadership, model **8.** clue, guide, hint, indication, sug-

ing to, or containing lead. ~*vb* **9** to surround, cover, or secure with lead or leads.

leaded *adj* (of windows) made from many small panes of glass held together by lead strips.

leaden *adj* **1** heavy or sluggish: *my limbs felt leaden.* **2** of a dull greyish colour: *leaden November sky.* **3** made of lead. **4** gloomy, spiritless, or lifeless: *hollow characters and leaden dialogue.*

leader *n* **1** a person who rules, guides, or inspires others; head. **2** *Chiefly Brit* the leading editorial in a newspaper. Also: **leading article** **3** *Music* the principal first violinist of an orchestra who acts as the conductor's deputy. **4** the person or animal who is leading in a race. **5** the best or the most successful of its kind: *the company is a world leader in its field.* **6** the leading horse or dog in a team. **7** a strip of blank film or tape at the beginning of a reel. **8** *Bot* any of the long slender shoots that grow from the stem or branch of a tree. **leadership** *n*

lead-in *n* an introduction to a subject.

leading *adj* **1** principal or primary: *the leading designers.* **2** in the first position: *the leading driver.*

leading aircraftman *n* the rank above aircraftman in the British air force. **leading aircraftwoman** *fem n*

leading light *n* an important and influential person in an organization or campaign.

leading question *n* a question worded to suggest the desired answer, such as *What do you think of the horrible effects of pollution?*

leading rating *n* a rank in the Royal Navy comparable to a corporal in the army.

lead off *vb* to begin.

lead on *vb* to trick (someone) into believing or doing something wrong.

lead pencil *n* a pencil containing a thin stick of a graphite compound.

lead poisoning *n* acute or chronic poisoning by lead.

lead time *n Manufacturing* the time between the design of a product and its production.

lead up to *vb* **1** to act as a preliminary or introduction to. **2** to approach (a topic) gradually or cautiously.

leaf *n, pl* **leaves** **1** one of the flat usually green blades attached to the stem of a plant. **2** the foliage of a tree or plant: *shrubs have been planted for their leaf interest.* **3** **in leaf** (of shrubs or trees) with all its leaves fully opened. **4** a very thin sheet of metal. **5** one of the sheets of paper in a book. **6** a hinged, sliding, or detachable part, such as an extension to a table. **7** **take a leaf out of someone's book** to imitate someone in a particular course of action. **8** **turn over a new leaf** to begin a new and improved course of behaviour. ~*vb* **9** (usually foll. by *through*) to turn pages casually or hurriedly without reading them. **10** (of plants) to produce leaves. **leafless** *adj*

leafage *n* the leaves of plants.

leaflet *n* **1** a sheet of printed matter distributed, usually free, for advertising or information. **2** any small leaf. **3** one of the divisions of a compound leaf. ~*vb* **-leting, -leted** **4** to distribute leaflets (to).

leaf mould *n* a rich soil consisting of decayed leaves.

leafy *adj* **leafier, leafiest** **1** covered with leaves. **2** having many trees or shrubs: *a leafy suburb.*

league[1] *n* **1** an association of people or nations formed to promote the interests of its members. **2** an association of sporting clubs that organizes matches between member teams. **3** *Informal* a class or level: *the guy is not even in the same league.* **4** **in league (with)** working or planning together with. ~*vb* **leaguing, leagued** **5** to form or be formed into a league.

league[2] *n* an obsolete unit of distance of varying length: commonly equal to 3 miles (4.8 kilometres).

leak *n* **1** **a** a crack or hole that allows the accidental escape or entrance of liquid, gas, radiation, etc. **b** such escaping or entering liquid, etc. **2** a disclosure of secret information. **3** the loss of current from an electrical conductor because of faulty insulation. **4** the act or an instance of leaking. **5** *Slang* urination. ~*vb* **6** to enter or escape or allow to enter or escape through a crack or hole. **7** to make (secret information) public, esp. deliberately. **leaky** *adj*

leakage *n* the act or an instance or the result of leaking: *the leakage of 60 tonnes of oil.*

lean[1] *vb* **leaning; leant** *or* **leaned** **1** (foll. by *against, on* or *upon*) to rest or put (something) so that it rests against a support. **2** to bend or make (something) bend from an upright position. **3** (foll. by *to* or *towards*) to have or express a tendency or preference. ~*n* **4** the condition of bending from an upright position. ~See also **lean on.**

lean[2] *adj* **1** (esp. of a person) having a trim body with no surplus flesh. **2** (of meat) having little or no fat. **3**

THESAURUS

gestion, tip, trace **9.** leading role, principal, protagonist, star part, title role ~*adj.* **10.** chief, first, foremost, head, leading, main, most important, premier, primary, prime, principal

leader boss (*informal*), captain, chief, chieftain, commander, conductor, counsellor, director, guide, head, number one, principal, ringleader, ruler, superior

leadership **1.** administration, direction, directorship, domination, guidance, management, running, superintendency **2.** authority, command, control, influence, initiative, pre-eminence, supremacy, sway

leading chief, dominant, first, foremost, governing, greatest, highest, main, number one, outstanding, pre-eminent, primary, principal, ruling, superior

lead on beguile, deceive, draw on, entice, inveigle, lure, seduce, string along (*informal*), tempt

lead up to approach, intimate, introduce, make advances, make overtures, pave the way, prepare for, prepare the way, work round to

leaf *n.* **1.** blade, bract, flag, frond, needle, pad **2.** folio, page, sheet **3.** **turn over a new leaf** amend, begin anew, change, change one's ways, improve, reform ~*vb.* **4.** *usually with* **through** browse, flip, glance, riffle, skim, thumb (through) **5.** bud, green, put out leaves, turn green

leaflet advert (*Brit. informal*), bill, booklet, brochure, circular, handbill, mailshot, pamphlet

league *n.* **1.** alliance, association, band, coalition, combination, combine, compact, confederacy, confederation, consortium, federation, fellowship, fraternity, group, guild, order, partnership, union **2.** (*informal*), ability group, category, class, level **3.** **in league (with)** allied, collaborating, hand in glove, in cahoots (*informal*), leagued ~*vb.* **4.** ally, amalgamate, associate, band, collaborate, combine, confederate, join forces, unite

leak *n.* **1.** **a** aperture, chink, crack, crevice, fissure, hole, opening, puncture **b** drip, leakage, leaking, oozing, percolation, seepage **2.** disclosure, divulgence ~*vb.* **3.** discharge, drip, escape, exude, ooze, pass, percolate, seep, spill, trickle **4.** blow wide open (*slang*), disclose, divulge, give away, let slip, let the cat out of the bag, make known, make public, pass on, reveal, spill the beans (*informal*), tell

(of a period) sparse, difficult, or causing hardship: *these are lean days in Baghdad.* ~*n* **4** the part of meat that contains little or no fat. **leanness** *n*

leaning *n* a tendency or inclination.

lean on *vb* **1** *Informal* to try to influence (someone) by using threats. **2** to depend on (someone) for help and advice.

leant *vb* a past of **lean**[1].

lean-to *n, pl* **-tos** a building with a sloping roof attached to another building or a wall.

leap *vb* **leaping; leapt** *or* **leaped 1** to jump suddenly from one place to another. **2** (often foll. by *at*) to move or react quickly. **3** to jump over. ~*n* **4** the act of jumping. **5** an abrupt or important change or increase: *a leap to full European union.* **6 a leap in the dark** an action performed without knowledge of the consequences. **7 by leaps and bounds** with unexpectedly rapid progress.

leapfrog *n* **1** a children's game in which each player in turn leaps over the others' bent backs. ~*vb* **-frogging, -frogged 2 a** to play leapfrog. **b** to leap over (something). **3** to advance by jumps or stages.

leap year *n* a calendar year of 366 days, February 29 (**leap day**) being the additional day, that occurs every four years.

learn *vb* **learning; learnt** *or* **learned 1** to gain knowledge (of something) or acquire skill in (some art or practice). **2** to memorize (something). **3** to gain by experience, example, or practice: *I learned everything the hard way.* **4** (often foll. by *of* or *about*) to become informed; find out: *Captain Nelson learned of the disaster from his wireless.* **learnable** *adj* **learner** *n*

learned (**lurn**-id) *adj* **1** having great knowledge. **2** involving or characterized by scholarship: *your learned paper on the subject.*

learning *n* knowledge gained by studying.

lease *n* **1** a contract by which an owner rents buildings or land to another person for a specified period. **2 a new lease of life** a prospect of renewed energy, health, or happiness. ~*vb* **leasing, leased 3** to let or rent (land or buildings) by lease.

leasehold *n* **1** land or property held under a lease. **2** the holding of such property under lease. **leaseholder** *n*

leash *n* **1** a dog's lead. **2 straining at the leash** eagerly impatient to begin something. ~*vb* **3** to put a leash on.

least *adj, adv* **1 the least** the superlative of **little:** *without encountering the least sign of civilization; he is the least well-educated prime minister.* ~*adj* **2** of very little importance. **3** smallest. ~*adv* **4 at least** if nothing else: *at least I wrote.* **5 at the least** at the minimum: *at the very least you should have some self respect.* **6 not in the least** not at all: *you're not detaining me, not in the least.*

leastways *or US & Canad* **leastwise** *adv Informal* at least; anyway.

leather *n* **1** the skin of an animal made smooth and flexible by tanning and removing the hair. **2 leathers** leather clothes, esp. as worn by motorcyclists. ~*adj* **3** made of leather. ~*vb* **4** to whip as if with a leather strap. **5** to dress in leather.

leatherjacket *n* the tough-skinned larva of certain crane flies, which destroy the roots of grasses.

leathery *adj* looking or feeling like leather, esp. in toughness.

leave[1] *vb* **leaving, left 1** to go away (from a person or place). **2** to cause to remain behind, often by mistake, in a place: *I left the paper under the table.* **3** to cause to be or remain in a specified state: *the poll leaves the parties neck-and-neck.* **4** to stop attending or belonging to a particular organization or institution: *at seventeen she left the convent.* **5** to not eat something or not deal with something: *he left a half-eaten lunch.* **6** to result in; cause: *I have been terribly hurt by women, it leaves indelible marks.* **7** to allow (someone) to do something without interfering: *the governor left them to it for a further few hours.* **8** to be survived by (members of one's family): *he leaves a widow and one daughter.* **9** to bequeath: *her adored son left his millions to an unknown half-sister.* **10** to have as a remainder: *37 – 14 leaves 23.* **11 leave (someone) alone a** to stop annoying (someone). **b** to permit to stay or be alone. ~See also **leave off, leave out.**

leave[2] *n* **1** permission to be absent, for instance from work: *so I asked for leave.* **2** the length of such ab-

THESAURUS

leaky cracked, holey, leaking, not watertight, perforated, porous, punctured, split, waterlogged

lean[1] *vb.* **1.** *with* **against, on,** *or* **upon** be supported, prop, recline, repose, rest **2.** bend, heel, incline, slant, slope, tilt, tip **3.** *with* **to** *or* **towards** be disposed to, be prone to, favour, gravitate towards, have a propensity, prefer, tend

lean[2] *adj.* **1.** angular, bony, emaciated, gaunt, lank, rangy, scraggy, scrawny, skinny, slender, slim, spare, thin, unfatty, wiry **2.** bare, barren, inadequate, infertile, meagre, pitiful, poor, scanty, sparse, unfruitful, unproductive

leaning aptitude, bent, bias, disposition, inclination, liking, partiality, penchant, predilection, proclivity, proneness, propensity, taste, tendency

leap *vb.* **1.** bounce, bound, caper, cavort, frisk, gambol, hop, jump, skip, spring **2.** *often with* **at** arrive at, come to, form hastily, hasten, hurry, jump, reach, rush **3.** clear, jump (over), vault ~*n.* **4.** bound, caper, frisk, hop, jump, skip, spring, vault **5.** escalation, increase, rise, surge, upsurge, upswing

learn 1. acquire, attain, become able, grasp, imbibe, master, pick up **2.** commit to memory, get off pat, get (something) word-perfect, learn by heart, memorize **3.** *often with* **of** *or* **about** ascertain, detect, determine, discern, discover, find out, gain, gather, hear, suss (out) (*slang*), understand

learned academic, cultured, erudite, experienced, expert, highbrow, intellectual, lettered, literate, scholarly, skilled, versed, well-informed, well-read

learner 1. disciple, pupil, scholar, student, trainee **2.** apprentice, beginner, neophyte, novice, tyro

learning acquirements, attainments, culture, education, erudition, information, knowledge, letters, literature, lore, research, scholarship, schooling, study, tuition, wisdom

lease *vb.* charter, hire, let, loan, rent

leash 1. *n.* lead, rein, tether **2.** *vb.* fasten, secure, tether, tie up

least feeblest, fewest, last, lowest, meanest, minimum, minutest, poorest, slightest, smallest, tiniest

leathery durable, hard, hardened, leatherlike, rough, rugged, tough, wrinkled

leave[1] *vb.* **1.** abandon, abscond, decamp, depart, desert, disappear, do a bunk (*Brit. slang*), exit, flit (*informal*), forsake, go, go away, move, pull out, quit, relinquish, retire, set out, slope off, take off (*informal*), withdraw **2.** forget, lay down, leave behind, mislay **3.** cause, deposit, generate, produce, result in **4.** abandon, cease, desert, desist, drop, evacuate, forbear, give up, refrain, relinquish, renounce, stop, surrender **5.** allot, assign, cede, commit, consign, entrust, give over, refer **6.** bequeath, demise, hand down, transmit, will

leave[2] *n.* **1.** allowance, authorization, concession,

sence: *weekend leave.* **3** permission to do something: *refused leave to appeal.* **4 on leave** officially excused from work or duty. **5 take (one's) leave of** to say farewell to.

leaven (**lev**-ven) *n also* **leavening 1** any substance, such as yeast, that produces fermentation in dough and makes it rise. **2** an influence that produces a gradual change. *~vb* **3** to cause fermentation in (dough). **4** to spread through, causing a gradual change.

leave off *vb* **1** to stop; cease. **2** to stop wearing or using.

leave out *vb* to omit or exclude: *leave out everything not necessary to living.*

leaves *n* the plural of **leaf.**

leave-taking *n* a departing; a farewell.

leavings *pl n* things left behind unwanted, such as food on a plate.

Lebanese *adj* **1** from the Lebanon. *~n, pl* **-nese 2** a person from the Lebanon.

Lebensraum (**lay**-benz-rowm) *n* territory claimed by a nation or state because it is necessary for survival or growth.

lecherous (**letch**-er-uss) *adj* (of a man) having or showing strong and uncontrolled sexual desire. **lecher** *n* **lechery** *n*

lecithin (**less**-sith-in) *n Biochem* a yellow-brown compound found in plant and animal tissues, esp. egg yolk: used in making cosmetics and inks, and as an emulsifier and stabilizer (**E322**) in foods.

lectern *n* a sloping reading desk, esp. in a church.

lecture *n* **1** a talk on a particular subject delivered to an audience. **2** a lengthy scolding. *~vb* **-turing, -tured 3** to deliver a lecture (to an audience or class). **4** to scold (someone) at length. **lecturer** *n* **lectureship** *n*

led *vb* the past of **lead**[1].

LED *Electronics* light-emitting diode: a semiconductor that gives out light when an electric current is applied to it.

ledge *n* **1** a narrow horizontal surface that projects from a wall or window. **2** a narrow shelflike projection on a cliff or mountain.

ledger *n Book-keeping* the principal book in which the commercial transactions of a company are recorded.

ledger line *n Music* a short line above or below the staff used to indicate the pitch of notes higher or lower than the range of the staff.

lee *n* **1** a sheltered part or side; the side away from the direction from which the wind is blowing. *~adj* **2** *Naut* on, at, or towards the side away from the wind: *her lee rail was awash.*

leech *n* **1** a worm which has a sucker at each end of the body and feeds on the blood or tissues of other animals. **2** a person who lives off another person; parasite.

leek *n* a vegetable of the onion family with a slender white bulb and broad flat green overlapping leaves: the national emblem of Wales.

leer *vb* **1** to give a sneering or suggestive look or grin. *~n* **2** such a look.

leery *adj* **leerier, leeriest 1** *Slang* (foll. by *of*) suspicious or wary. **2** *Now chiefly dialect* knowing or sly.

lees *pl n* the sediment from an alcoholic drink.

leet *n Scot* a list of candidates for an office.

leeward *Chiefly naut ~adj* **1** of, in, or moving in the direction towards which the wind blows. *~n* **2** the side towards the lee. *~adv* **3** towards the lee.

leeway *n* **1** flexibility of action or expenditure: *he gave me a lot of leeway in the work I did.* **2** sideways drift of a boat or aircraft.

left[1] *adj* **1** denoting the side of something or someone that faces west when the front is turned towards the north. **2** on the left side of the body: *I grabbed it with my left hand.* **3** liberal, radical, or socialist. *~adv* **4** on or in the direction of the left. *~n* **5** a left side, direction, position, area, or part. **6 the left** the people in a political party or society who have more socialist or liberal views: *the biggest party of the French Left.* **7** *Boxing* **a** a blow with the left hand. **b** the left hand.

left[2] *vb* the past of **leave**[1].

left-hand *adj* **1** of, on, or towards the left. **2** for the left hand.

left-handed *adj* **1** better at using the left hand than the right. **2** done with the left hand. **3** designed for use by the left hand. **4** awkward or clumsy. **5** ambiguous or insincere: *a left-handed compliment.* **6** turning from right to left; anticlockwise. *~adv* **7** with the left hand. **left-hander** *n*

leftist *adj* **1** of or relating to the political left or its principles. *~n* **2** a person who supports the political left. **leftism** *n*

THESAURUS

consent, dispensation, freedom, liberty, permission, sanction **2.** furlough, holiday, leave of absence, sabbatical, time off, vacation

leaven *n.* **1.** barm, ferment, leavening, yeast **2.** catalyst, influence, inspiration *~vb.* **3.** ferment, lighten, raise, work **4.** elevate, imbue, inspire, permeate, pervade, quicken, stimulate, suffuse

leave off abstain, break off, cease, desist, discontinue, end, give over (*informal*), give up, halt, kick (*informal*), knock off (*informal*), refrain, stop

leave out bar, cast aside, count out, disregard, except, exclude, ignore, neglect, omit, overlook, reject

leavings bits, dregs, fragments, leftovers, pieces, refuse, remains, remnants, residue, scraps, spoil, sweepings, waste

lecherous carnal, concupiscent, lascivious, lewd, libidinous, licentious, lubricious (*formal or literary*), lustful, prurient, randy (*informal, chiefly Brit.*), raunchy (*slang*), ruttish, salacious, unchaste, wanton

lechery carnality, concupiscence, debauchery, lasciviousness, lecherousness, lewdness, libertinism, libidinousness, licentiousness, lust, lustfulness, profligacy, prurience, rakishness, randiness (*informal, chiefly Brit.*), salaciousness, sensuality, wantonness, womanizing

lecture *n.* **1.** address, discourse, disquisition, harangue, instruction, lesson, speech, talk **2.** castigation, censure, chiding, dressing-down (*informal*), going-over (*informal*), rebuke, reprimand, reproof, scolding, talking-to (*informal*), telling off (*informal*), wigging (*Brit. slang*) *~vb.* **3.** address, discourse, expound, give a talk, harangue, hold forth, speak, spout, talk, teach **4.** admonish, bawl out (*informal*), berate, carpet (*informal*), castigate, censure, chide, give a rocket (*Brit. & N.Z. informal*), rate, read the riot act, reprimand, reprove, scold, tear into (*informal*), tear (someone) off a strip (*Brit. informal*), tell off (*informal*)

ledge mantle, projection, ridge, shelf, sill, step

leer drool, eye, gloat, goggle, grin, ogle, smirk, squint, stare, wink

lees deposit, dregs, grounds, precipitate, refuse, sediment, settlings

leeway elbowroom, latitude, margin, play, room, scope, space

left *adj.* **1.** larboard (*Nautical*), left-hand, port, sinistral **2.** leftist, left-wing, liberal, progressive, radical, socialist

left-luggage office *n Brit* a place at a railway station or airport where luggage may be left for a small charge.

leftover *n* **1** (*often pl*) an unused portion, esp. of cooked food. *~adj* **2** left as an unused portion.

leftward *adj, adv also* **leftwards** on or towards the left.

left-wing *adj* **1** socialist or radical: *the party ditched many of its more left-wing policies.* **2** belonging to the more radical part of a political party: *a group of left-wing Conservatives.* *~n* **left wing 3** (*often cap*) the more radical or progressive section, esp. of a political party: *the Left Wing of the Labour Party.* **4** *Sports* **a** the left-hand side of the field of play. **b** a player positioned in this area in certain games. **left-winger** *n*

lefty *n, pl* **lefties** *Informal* **1** a left-winger. **2** *Chiefly US & Canad* a left-handed person.

leg *n* **1** either of the two lower limbs in humans, or any similar structure in animals that is used for movement or support. **2** the part of a garment that covers the leg. **3** a lower limb of an animal, esp. the thigh, used for food: *leg of lamb.* **4** something similar to a leg in appearance or function, such as one of the supports of a chair. **5** a section of a journey. **6** a single stage, lap, or length in a relay race. **7** one of a series of games, matches, or parts of games. **8** *Cricket* the side of the field to the left of and behind a right-handed batsman as he faces the bowler. **9 not have a leg to stand on** *Informal* to have no reasonable basis for an opinion or argument. **10 on one's last legs** worn out or exhausted. **11 to pull someone's leg** *Informal* to tease or make fun of someone. **12 shake a leg** *Informal* to hurry up. **13 stretch one's legs** to stand up or walk around, esp. after sitting for some time. *~vb* **legging, legged 14 leg it** *Informal* to walk, run, or hurry.

legacy *n, pl* **-cies 1** money or personal property left to someone by a will. **2** something handed down to a successor.

legal *adj* **1** established by or permitted by law; lawful. **2** of or relating to law. **3** relating to or characteristic of lawyers. **legally** *adv*

legal aid *n* financial assistance available to people who are unable to meet the full cost of legal proceedings.

legalese *n* the conventional language in which legal documents are written.

legalism *n* strict adherence to the letter of the law. **legalist** *n, adj* **legalistic** *adj*

legality *n, pl* **-ties** the state or quality of being legal or lawful.

legalize *or* **-ise** *vb* **-izing, -ized** *or* **-ising, -ised** to make lawful or legal. **legalization** *or* **-isation** *n*

legal tender *n* currency that a creditor must by law accept to pay a debt.

legate *n* a messenger, esp. one representing the Pope.

legatee *n* the recipient of a legacy.

legation *n* **1** a diplomatic mission headed by a minister. **2** the official residence and office of a diplomatic minister.

legato (leg-**ah**-toe) *Music ~adv* **1** smoothly and evenly. *~n, pl* **-tos 2** a style of playing with no gaps between notes.

leg before wicket *n Cricket* a dismissal on the grounds that a batsman has been struck on the leg by a bowled ball that otherwise would have hit the wicket. Abbrev.: **lbw**

leg break *n Cricket* a bowled ball that spins from leg to off on pitching.

leg bye *n Cricket* a run scored after the ball has hit the batsman's leg or some other part of his body, except his hand, without touching the bat. Abbrev.: **lb**

legend *n* **1** a popular story handed down from earlier times which may or may not be true. **2** such stories collectively. **3** a person whose fame makes him or her seem exceptional: *he is a living legend.* **4** modern stories about a famous person which may or may not be true: *no Garland fan could complain about sordid revelations tarnishing the legend.* **5** words written on something to explain it: *a pub mirror spelling out the legend "Saloon Bar".* **6** an explanation on a table, map, or chart, of the symbols used.

legendary *adj* **1** very famous: *the legendary beauty of the Alps.* **2** of or relating to legend. **3** described in legend: *the legendary birthplace of Aphrodite.*

legerdemain (lej-er-de-**main**) *n* **1** same as **sleight of hand. 2** cunning deception.

leger line *n* same as **ledger line.**

leggings *pl n* **1** an extra outer covering for the lower legs. **2** close-fitting trousers for women or children.

leggy *adj* **1** having unusually long legs. **2** (of a plant) having a long weak stem.

THESAURUS

left-handed 1. awkward, cack-handed (*informal*), careless, clumsy, fumbling, gauche, maladroit **2.** ambiguous, backhanded, double-edged, enigmatic, equivocal, indirect, ironic, sardonic

leftover 1. *n. often plural* leavings, oddments, odds and ends, remains, remnants, scraps **2.** *adj.* excess, extra, remaining, surplus, uneaten, unused, unwanted

leg *n.* **1.** limb, lower limb, member, pin (*informal*) **2.** brace, prop, support, upright **3.** lap, part, portion, section, segment, stage, stretch **4. not have a leg to stand on** *informal* be defenceless, be full of holes, be illogical, be invalid, be undermined, be vulnerable, lack support **5. on one's last legs** about to break down, about to collapse, at death's door, dying, exhausted, failing, giving up the ghost, worn out **6. pull someone's leg** *informal* chaff, deceive, fool, kid (*informal*), make fun of, tease, trick, wind up (*Brit. slang*) **7. shake a leg** *informal* get a move on (*informal*), get cracking (*informal*), hasten, hurry, look lively (*informal*), rush **8. stretch one's legs** exercise, go for a walk, move about, promenade, stroll, take a walk, take the air *~vb.* **9. leg it** *informal* go on foot, hurry, run, skedaddle (*informal*), walk

legacy 1. bequest, estate, gift, heirloom, inheritance **2.** birthright, endowment, heritage, inheritance, patrimony, throwback, tradition

legal 1. allowable, allowed, authorized, constitutional, lawful, legalized, legitimate, licit, permissible, proper, rightful, sanctioned, valid **2.** forensic, judicial, juridical

legality accordance with the law, admissibleness, lawfulness, legitimacy, permissibility, rightfulness, validity

legalize, legalise allow, approve, authorize, decriminalize, legitimate, legitimatize, license, permit, sanction, validate

legation consulate, delegation, diplomatic mission, embassy, envoys, ministry, representation

legend 1. fable, fiction, folk tale, myth, narrative, saga, story, tale, urban legend **2.** celebrity, luminary, marvel, megastar (*informal*), phenomenon, prodigy, spectacle, wonder **3.** caption, device, inscription, motto **4.** cipher, code, key, table of symbols

legendary 1. celebrated, famed, famous, illustrious, immortal, renowned, well-known **2.** apocryphal, fabled, fabulous, fanciful, fictitious, mythical, romantic, storied, traditional

leghorn *n* **1** a type of Italian wheat straw that is woven into hats. **2** any hat made from this straw.

Leghorn (leg-**gorn**) *n* a breed of domestic fowl.

legible *adj* (of handwriting) able to be read. **legibility** *n* **legibly** *adv*

legion *n* **1** any large military force: *the French Foreign Legion.* **2** (*often pl*) any very large number. **3** an infantry unit in the ancient Roman army of three to six thousand men. **4** an association of veterans. **legionary** *adj, n*

legionnaire *n* (*often cap*) a member of a legion.

Legionnaire's disease *n* a serious bacterial infection, with symptoms similar to pneumonia.

legislate *vb* **-lating, -lated 1** to make or pass laws. **2** to bring into effect by legislation. **legislator** *n*

legislation *n* **1** the act or process of making laws. **2** the laws so made.

legislative *adj* **1** of or relating to the process of making laws. **2** having the power or function of making laws: *a legislative assembly.*

legislature *n* a body of people authorized to make and repeal laws.

legitimate *adj* **1** authorized by or in accordance with law: *legitimate accounting practices.* **2** based on correct or acceptable principles of reasoning: *a legitimate argument.* **3** (of a child) born of parents legally married to each other. **4** of, relating to, or ruling by hereditary right: *under their legitimate ruling house.* **5** of or relating to serious drama as distinct from films, television, or vaudeville. *~vb* **-mating, -mated 6** to make, pronounce, or show to be legitimate. **legitimacy** *n* **legitimately** *adv*

legitimize *or* **-mise** *vb* **-mizing, -mized** *or* **-mising, -mised** to make legitimate; legalize. **legitimization** *or* **-misation** *n*

legless *adj* **1** without legs. **2** *Slang* very drunk.

Lego *n Trademark* a construction toy consisting of plastic bricks and other components that fit together.

leg-pull *n Brit informal* a practical joke.

legroom *n* space to move one's legs comfortably, as in a car.

leguaan *n* a large amphibious S African lizard.

legume *n* **1** the pod of a plant of the pea or bean family. **2** the seed from such pods, esp. beans or peas.

leguminous *adj* of or relating to any family of flowering plants having pods (or legumes) as fruits.

lei *n* (in Hawaii) a garland of flowers, worn around the neck.

Leics Leicestershire.

leisure *n* **1** time or opportunity for relaxation or hobbies. **2 at leisure a** having free time. **b** not occupied. **3 at one's leisure** when one has free time. **leisured** *adj*

leisure centre *n* a building providing facilities, such as a swimming pool, gym, and café, for a range of leisure pursuits.

leisurely *adj* **1** unhurried; relaxed. *~adv* **2** in a relaxed way. **leisureliness** *n*

leitmotif *or* **leitmotiv** (lite-mote-eef) *n* **1** *Music* a recurring melodic phrase used to suggest a character, thing, or idea. **2** an often repeated image in a literary work.

lekker *adj S African slang* pleasing, enjoyable, or tasty.

lemming *n* **1** a small rodent of northern and arctic regions, reputed to rush into the sea in large groups and drown. **2** a member of any group following an unthinking course towards destruction.

lemon *n* **1** a yellow oval edible fruit with juicy acidic flesh that grows on an evergreen tree in warm and tropical regions. **2** *Slang* a person or thing considered to be useless or defective. *~adj* **3** light yellow. **lemony** *adj*

lemonade *n* a drink made from lemon juice, sugar, and water or from carbonated water, citric acid, and sweetener.

lemon sole *n* an edible European flatfish.

lemon squash *n Brit* a drink made from a sweetened lemon concentrate and water.

lemur *n* a nocturnal animal, related to the monkey, with a foxy face and long tail, found on Madagascar.

lend *vb* **lending, lent 1** to permit the temporary use of. **2** to provide (money) temporarily, often at interest. **3** to contribute (some abstract quality): *painted trellis lends a classical air to any garden.* **4 lend an ear** to listen. **5 lend oneself** *or* **itself** to be appropriate for: *the building lends itself to loft conversion.* **lender** *n*

length *n* **1** the extent or measurement of something from end to end. **2** a specified distance, esp. between two positions: *the length of a cricket-pitch.* **3** a period of time, as between specified limits or moments. **4** the quality, state, or fact of being long rather than short. **5** a piece of something, usually longer than it is wide: *a length of twine.* **6** (*usually pl*) the amount of trouble

THESAURUS

legibility clarity, decipherability, ease of reading, legibleness, neatness, plainness, readability, readableness

legible clear, decipherable, distinct, easily read, easy to read, neat, plain, readable

legion *n.* **1.** army, brigade, company, division, force, troop **2.** *often plural* drove, horde, host, mass, multitude, myriad, number, throng

legislate codify, constitute, enact, establish, make laws, ordain, pass laws, prescribe, put in force

legislation 1. codification, enactment, lawmaking, prescription, regulation **2.** act, bill, charter, law, measure, regulation, ruling, statute

legislative congressional, judicial, juridical, jurisdictive, lawgiving, lawmaking, ordaining, parliamentary

legislator lawgiver, lawmaker, parliamentarian

legislature assembly, chamber, congress, house, lawmaking body, parliament, senate

legitimate *adj.* **1.** acknowledged, authentic, authorized, genuine, kosher (*informal*), lawful, legal, licit, proper, real, rightful, sanctioned, statutory, true **2.** admissible, correct, just, justifiable, logical, reasonable, sensible, valid, warranted, well-founded *~vb.* **3.** authorize, legalize, legitimatize, legitimize, permit, pronounce lawful, sanction

legitimatize *or* **legitimize** authorize, legalize, legitimate, permit, pronounce lawful, sanction

leisure 1. breathing space, ease, freedom, free time, holiday, liberty, opportunity, pause, quiet, recreation, relaxation, respite, rest, retirement, spare moments, spare time, time off, vacation **2. at leisure** available, free, not booked up, on holiday, unengaged, unoccupied **3. at one's leisure** at an unhurried pace, at one's convenience, deliberately, in one's own (good) time, unhurriedly, when it suits one, when one gets round to it (*informal*), without hurry

leisurely 1. *adj.* comfortable, easy, gentle, laid-back (*informal*), lazy, relaxed, restful, slow, unhurried **2.** *adv.* at one's convenience, at one's leisure, comfortably, deliberately, easily, indolently, lazily, lingeringly, slowly, unhurriedly, without haste

lend 1. accommodate one with, advance, loan **2.** add, afford, bestow, confer, contribute, furnish, give, grant, hand out, impart, present, provide, supply **3. lend an ear** give ear, hearken (*archaic*), heed, listen, take no-

taken in doing something: *to go to great lengths.* **7** *Prosody, phonetics* the duration of a vowel or syllable. **8 at length a** after a long interval or period of time. **b** in great detail.

lengthen *vb* to make or become longer.

lengthways *or* **lengthwise** *adv, adj* in, according to, or along the direction of length.

lengthy *adj* **lengthier, lengthiest** very long or tiresome. **lengthily** *adv* **lengthiness** *n*

lenient (lee-nee-ent) *adj* tolerant, not strict or severe. **leniency** *n* **leniently** *adv*

lenity *n, pl* **-ties** mercy or clemency.

lens *n* **1** a piece of glass or other transparent material with a curved surface or surfaces, used to bring together or spread rays of light passing through it: used in cameras, telescopes, and spectacles. **2** *Anat* a transparent structure in the eye, behind the iris, that focuses images on the retina.

lent *vb* the past of **lend.**

Lent *n Christianity* the period from Ash Wednesday to Easter Saturday, during which some Christians give up doing something they enjoy. **Lenten** *adj*

lentil *n* any of the small edible seeds of a leguminous Asian plant.

lento *Music ~adv* **1** slowly. *~n, pl* **-tos 2** a movement or passage performed slowly.

Leo *n Astrol* the fifth sign of the zodiac; the Lion.

leonine *adj* of or like a lion.

leopard *or fem* **leopardess** *n* a large African and Asian mammal of the cat family, which has a tawny yellow coat with black spots. Also called: **panther**

leotard *n* a tight-fitting garment covering the body from the shoulders to the thighs and worn by acrobats, ballet dancers, and people doing exercises.

leper *n* **1** a person who has leprosy. **2** a person who is avoided.

lepidopteran *n, pl* **-terans** *or* **-tera 1** an insect that has two pairs of fragile wings and develops from a caterpillar; a butterfly or moth. *~adj also* **lepidopterous 2** denoting such an insect.

lepidopterist *n* a person who studies or collects moths and butterflies.

leprechaun *n* (in Irish folklore) a mischievous elf.

leprosy *n Pathol* a chronic infectious disease, characterized by painful inflamed lumps beneath the skin and disfigurement and wasting away of affected parts. **leprous** *adj*

lepton *n Physics* any of a group of elementary particles with weak interactions.

lesbian *n* **1** a female homosexual. *~adj* **2** of or characteristic of lesbians. **lesbianism** *n*

lese-majesty (lezz-**maj**-ist-ee) *n* **1** an offence against the sovereign power in a state; treason. **2** an act of disrespect towards authority.

lesion *n* **1** any structural change in an organ or tissue resulting from injury or disease. **2** an injury or wound.

less *adj, adv* **1** the comparative of **little:** *less fibre; his sharpness will be blunted by playing less. ~adj* **2** *Not universally accepted* fewer. *~adv* **3 less of** to a smaller extent or degree: *it would become less of a problem.* **4 no less** *Sometimes ironic* used to indicate admiration or surprise: *sculpted by a famous Frenchman, Rodin no less. ~prep* **5** minus: *a two pounds-a-week rise (less tax).*

➤ Avoid confusion with *few(er). Less* is used with amounts that cannot be counted: *less time; less fuss. Few(er)* is used of things that can be counted.

lessee *n* a person to whom a lease is granted.

lessen *vb* to make or become less.

lesser *adj* not as great in quantity, size, or worth.

lesson *n* **1 a** a single period of instruction in a subject. **b** the content of such a period. **2** material assigned for individual study. **3** something from which useful knowledge or principles can be learned: *one could still learn an important lesson from these masters.* **4** an experience that serves as a warning or example: *the experience will prove a sobering lesson for the military.* **5** a passage of Scripture read during a church service.

lessor *n* a person who grants a lease of property.

lest *conj* **1** so as to prevent any possibility that: *one grabbed it lest a neighbour got there first.* **2** for fear that: *his anxiety lest anything mar the family event.*

let[1] *vb* **letting, let 1** to allow: *a child lets a friend play with his favourite toy.* **2** used as an auxiliary to express: **a** a request, proposal, or command, or to convey a warning or threat: *Well, let's try it; just let me catch you here again!* **b** an assumption or hypothesis: *let "a" equal "b".* **c** resigned acceptance of the inevitable: *let the worst happen.* **3** to allow someone to rent (property or accommodation). **4** to cause the movement of (something) in a specified direction: *this lets aluminium creep into the brain.* **5 let alone** not to mention: *I could hardly think, let alone find words to say.* **6 let alone** *or* **be** stop annoying or interfering with: *let the poor cat alone.* **7 let go** to relax one's hold (on). **8 let loose** to allow (a person or animal) to leave or escape. *~n* **9** *Brit* the act of letting property or accommodation. ~See also **let down, let off,** etc.

let[2] *n* **1** *Tennis, squash* etc. a minor infringement or

THESAURUS

tice **4. lend oneself** *or* **itself** be adaptable, be appropriate, be serviceable, fit, present opportunities of, suit

length 1. distance, extent, longitude, measure, reach, span **2.** duration, period, space, span, stretch, term **3.** elongation, extensiveness, lengthiness, protractedness **4.** measure, piece, portion, section, segment **5. at length a.** at last, at long last, eventually, finally, in the end **b.** completely, fully, in depth, in detail, thoroughly, to the full

lengthen continue, draw out, elongate, expand, extend, increase, make longer, prolong, protract, spin out, stretch

lengthy diffuse, drawn-out, extended, interminable, lengthened, long, long-drawn-out, long-winded, overlong, prolix, prolonged, protracted, tedious, verbose, very long

leniency clemency, compassion, forbearance, gentleness, indulgence, lenity, mercy, mildness, moderation, pity, quarter, tenderness, tolerance

lenient clement, compassionate, forbearing, forgiving, gentle, indulgent, kind, merciful, mild, sparing, tender, tolerant

lesbian 1. *n.* dyke (*slang*) **2.** *adj.* butch (*slang*), gay, homosexual

less 1. *adj.* shorter, slighter, smaller **2.** *adv.* **less of** to a smaller extent **3.** *prep.* excepting, lacking, minus, subtracting, without

lessen abate, abridge, contract, curtail, decrease, de-escalate, degrade, die down, diminish, dwindle, ease, erode, grow less, impair, lighten, lower, minimize, moderate, narrow, reduce, relax, shrink, slacken, slow down, weaken, wind down

lesser inferior, less important, lower, minor, secondary, slighter, subordinate, under-

lesson 1. class, coaching, instruction, period, schooling, teaching, tutoring **2.** assignment, drill, exercise, homework, lecture, practice, reading, recitation, task **3.** deterrent, example, exemplar, message, model, moral, precept

obstruction of the ball, requiring a point to be replayed. **2 without let or hindrance** without obstruction.

let down *vb* **1** to fail to satisfy the expectations of (someone); disappoint. **2** to lower. **3** to lengthen a garment by decreasing the hem. **4** to deflate: *to let down a tyre.* ~*n* **letdown 5** a disappointment.

lethal *adj* capable of causing death. **lethally** *adv*

lethargy *n, pl* **-gies 1** sluggishness or dullness. **2** an abnormal lack of energy. **lethargic** *adj* **lethargically** *adv*

let off *vb* **1** to excuse from (work or duties): *I'll let you off homework for a week.* **2** *Informal* to spare (someone) the expected punishment: *lots were let off because they couldn't be bothered to prosecute anybody.* **3** to explode or fire (a bomb, gun, or firework). **4** to release (liquid, air, or steam).

let on *vb Informal* **1** to reveal (a secret). **2** to pretend: *he let on that he was a pilgrim.*

let out *vb* **1** to emit: *he let out a scream.* **2** to allow to leave; release. **3** to make (property) available for people to rent. **4** to make (a garment) wider by reducing the seams. **5** to reveal (a secret). ~*n* **let-out 6** a chance to escape.

letter *n* **1** a written or printed message, usually enclosed in an envelope and sent by post. **2** any of a set of conventional symbols used in writing or printing a language: character of the alphabet. **3** the strict meaning of an agreement or document; exact wording: *the letter of the law.* **4 to the letter** precisely: *you have to follow treatment to the letter for it to be effective.* ~*vb* **5** to write or mark letters on (a sign). **lettering** *n*

letter bomb *n* an explosive device in an envelope or parcel that explodes when the envelope or parcel is opened.

letter box *n Chiefly Brit* **1** a slot in a door through which letters are delivered. **2** Also called: **pillar box, postbox** a public box into which letters and postcards are put for collection.

lettered *adj* **1** well educated. **2** printed or marked with letters.

letterhead *n* a printed heading on stationery giving the name and address of the sender.

letter of credit *n* a letter issued by a bank entitling the bearer to draw money from other banks.

letterpress *n* a method of printing in which ink is transferred from raised surfaces to paper by pressure.

letters *pl n* **1** literary knowledge or ability: *a man of letters.* **2** literary culture in general.

letters patent *pl n* See **patent** (senses 1, 3).

lettuce *n* a plant cultivated for its large edible leaves, which are used in salads.

let up *vb* **1** to diminish or stop. **2** (foll. by *on*) *Informal* to be less harsh (towards someone). ~*n* **let-up 3** *Informal* a lessening.

leucocyte (**loo**-koh-site) *n* any of the various large white cells in the blood of vertebrates.

leukaemia *or esp US* **leukemia** (loo-**kee**-mee-a) *n* an acute or chronic disease characterized by extreme overproduction of white blood cells.

levee[1] *n US* **1** a natural or artificial river embankment. **2** a quay.

levee[2] *n* a formal reception held by a sovereign just after rising from bed.

level *adj* **1** on a horizontal plane. **2** having an even surface. **3** being of the same height as something else: *the floor of the lean-to was level with the patio.* **4** equal to or even with (something or someone else): *Johnson was level with the overnight leader.* **5** not exceeding the upper edge of (a spoon etc.). **6** consistent or regular: *a level pulse.* **7 one's level best** the best one can do. ~*vb* **-elling, -elled** *or US* **-eling, -eled 8** (sometimes foll. by *off*) to make horizontal or even. **9** to make equal in position or status. **10** to direct (an accusation or criticism) emphatically at someone. **11** to focus (a look) directly at someone. **12** to aim (a weapon) horizontally. **13** to demolish completely. ~*n* **14** a horizontal line or plane. **15** a device, such as a spirit level, for determining whether a surface is horizontal. **16** position or status in a scale of values: *a high-level delegation.* **17** stage or degree of progress: *primary school level.* **18** a specified vertical position: *floor level.* **19** the topmost horizontal line or plane from which the height of something is calculated: *sea level.* **20** a flat even surface or area of land. **21** a degree or intensity reached on a measurable or notional

THESAURUS

let *vb.* **1.** allow, authorize, entitle, give leave, give permission, give the go-ahead (green light, O.K. *or* okay) (*informal*), grant, permit, sanction, tolerate, warrant **2.** hire, lease, rent

let down disappoint, disenchant, disillusion, dissatisfy, fail, fall short, leave in the lurch, leave stranded

letdown anticlimax, bitter pill, blow, comedown (*informal*), disappointment, disgruntlement, disillusionment, frustration, setback, washout (*informal*)

lethal baneful, dangerous, deadly, deathly, destructive, devastating, fatal, mortal, murderous, noxious, pernicious, poisonous, virulent

lethargic apathetic, comatose, debilitated, drowsy, dull, enervated, heavy, inactive, indifferent, inert, languid, lazy, listless, sleepy, slothful, slow, sluggish, somnolent, stupefied, torpid

lethargy apathy, drowsiness, dullness, inaction, indifference, inertia, languor, lassitude, listlessness, sleepiness, sloth, slowness, sluggishness, stupor, torpidity, torpor

let off 1. absolve, discharge, dispense, excuse, exempt, exonerate, forgive, pardon, release, spare **2.** detonate, discharge, emit, explode, exude, fire, give off, leak, release

let out 1. emit, give vent to, produce **2.** discharge, free, let go, liberate, release **3.** betray, blow wide open (*slang*), disclose, leak, let fall, let slip, make known, reveal

letter 1. acknowledgment, answer, communication, dispatch, epistle, line, message, missive, note, reply **2.** character, sign, symbol **3. to the letter** accurately, exactly, literally, precisely, strictly, word for word

letters belles-lettres, culture, erudition, humanities, learning, literature, scholarship

let up abate, decrease, diminish, ease (up), moderate, relax, slacken, stop, subside

let-up *informal* abatement, break, cessation, interval, lessening, lull, pause, recess, remission, respite, slackening

level *adj.* **1.** consistent, even, flat, horizontal, plain, plane, smooth, uniform **2.** aligned, balanced, commensurate, comparable, equal, equivalent, even, flush, in line, neck and neck, on a line, on a par, proportionate ~*vb.* **3.** *sometimes with* **off** even off *or* out, flatten, make flat, plane, smooth **4.** aim, beam, direct, focus, point, train **5.** bulldoze, demolish, destroy, devastate, equalize, flatten, knock down, lay low, pull down, raze, smooth, tear down, wreck ~*n.* **6.** horizontal, plane **7.** achievement, degree, grade, position, rank, stage, standard, standing, status **8.** altitude, elevation, height, vertical position **9.** flat surface, plain **10. on the level**

scale: *noise level.* **22 on the level** *Informal* sincere or genuine.

level crossing *n Brit, Austral, & NZ* a point at which a railway line and a road cross.

level-headed *adj* calm and sensible.

lever *n* **1** a handle used to operate machinery. **2** a bar used to move a heavy object or to prise something open. **3** a rigid bar that turns on a fixed support (fulcrum) to transfer effort and motion, for instance to move a load. **4** a means of exerting pressure in order to achieve an aim: *using the hostages as a lever to gain concessions from the West.* ~*vb* **5** to open or move with a lever.

leverage *n* **1** the mechanical advantage gained by using a lever. **2** the ability to influence people or events: *information gives leverage.*

leveraged buyout *n* a takeover bid in which a small company uses its assets, and those of the target company, to raise the loans required to finance the takeover.

leveret (**lev**-ver-it) *n* a young hare.

leviathan (lev-**vie**-ath-an) *n* any huge or powerful thing.

Levis *pl n Trademark* denim jeans.

levitate *vb* **-tating, -tated** to rise or cause to rise, suspended, in the air. **levitation** *n*

levity *n, pl* **-ties** a frivolous or too light-hearted attitude to serious matters.

levy (**lev**-vee) *vb* **levies, levying, levied 1** to impose and collect (a tax, tariff, or fine). **2** to conscript troops for service. ~*n, pl* **levies 3 a** the imposition and collection of taxes, tariffs, or fines. **b** the money so raised. **4** troops conscripted for service.

lewd *adj* indecently vulgar; obscene. **lewdly** *adv* **lewdness** *n*

lexical *adj* **1** relating to the vocabulary of a language. **2** relating to a lexicon. **lexically** *adv*

lexicography *n* the process or profession of compiling dictionaries. **lexicographer** *n*

lexicon *n* **1** a dictionary, esp. one of an ancient language such as Greek. **2** the vocabulary of a language or of an individual.

ley *n* land temporarily under grass.

Leyden jar (**lide**-en) *n Physics* an early type of capacitor consisting of a glass jar with the lower part of the inside and outside coated with tinfoil.

LGV (in Britain) large goods vehicle.

Li *Chem* lithium.

liability *n, pl* **-ties 1** someone or something that is a problem or embarrassment. **2** the state of being legally responsible. **3** (*often pl*) sums of money owed by an organization.

liable *adj* **1** *Not universally accepted* probable or likely: *weak and liable to give way.* **2** commonly suffering a condition: *he's liable to get colds in his chest.* **3** legally obliged or responsible; answerable.

➤ The use of *liable* to mean "likely" is informal. It generally means "responsible for": *He was liable for any damage.*

liaise *vb* **-aising, -aised** (usually foll. by *with*) to communicate and maintain contact with.

liaison *n* **1** communication and cooperative contact between groups. **2** a secretive or adulterous sexual relationship.

liana *n* a woody climbing and twining plant of tropical forests.

liar *n* a person who tells lies.

lib *n Informal* liberation: used in the name of certain movements: *women's lib; gay lib.*

Lib *Politics* Liberal.

libation (lie-**bay**-shun) *n* **a** the pouring-out of wine in honour of a deity. **b** the wine so poured out.

libel *n* **1** *Law* the publication of something false which damages a person's reputation. **2** any damaging or unflattering representation or statement. ~*vb* **-belling, -belled** *or US* **-beling, -beled 3** *Law* to make or publish a false damaging statement or representation about (a person). **libellous** *or* **libelous** *adj*

liberal *adj* **1** having social and political views that favour progress and reform. **2** generous in temperament or behaviour. **3** tolerant of other people. **4** using or existing in large quantities; lavish: *the world's finest gadgetry, in liberal quantities.* **5** not rigid; free: *a more liberal interpretation.* **6** (of an education) designed to

THESAURUS

informal above board, fair, genuine, honest, open, sincere, square, straight, straightforward, up front (*slang*)

level-headed balanced, calm, collected, composed, cool, dependable, even-tempered, reasonable, sane, self-possessed, sensible, steady, together (*slang*), unflappable (*informal*)

lever 1. *n.* bar, crowbar, handle, jemmy **2.** *vb.* force, jemmy, move, prise, purchase, raise

leverage ascendancy, authority, clout (*informal*), influence, pull (*informal*), purchasing power, rank, weight

levity buoyancy, facetiousness, fickleness, flightiness, flippancy, frivolity, giddiness, light-heartedness, light-mindedness, silliness, skittishness, triviality

levy *vb.* **1.** charge, collect, demand, exact, gather, impose, tax **2.** call, call up, conscript, mobilize, muster, press, raise, summon ~*n.* **3. a** assessment, collection, exaction, gathering, imposition **b** assessment, duty, excise, fee, imposition, impost, tariff, tax, toll

lewd bawdy, blue, dirty, impure, indecent, lascivious, libidinous, licentious, loose, lustful, obscene, pornographic, profligate, salacious, smutty, unchaste, vile, vulgar, wanton, wicked

lewdness bawdiness, carnality, crudity, debauchery, depravity, impurity, indecency, lasciviousness, lechery, licentiousness, obscenity, pornography, profligacy, salaciousness, smut, smuttiness, unchastity, vulgarity, wantonness

liability 1. burden, disadvantage, drag, drawback, encumbrance, handicap, hindrance, impediment, inconvenience, millstone, minus (*informal*), nuisance **2.** accountability, answerability, culpability, duty, obligation, onus, responsibility **3.** *often plural* arrear, debit, debt, indebtedness, obligation

liable 1. *not universally accepted* apt, disposed, inclined, likely, prone, tending **2.** exposed, open, subject, susceptible, vulnerable **3.** accountable, amenable, answerable, bound, chargeable, obligated, responsible

liaison 1. communication, connection, contact, go-between, hook-up, interchange, intermediary **2.** affair, amour, entanglement, illicit romance, intrigue, love affair, romance

liar fabricator, falsifier, fibber, perjurer, prevaricator, storyteller (*informal*)

libel 1. *n.* aspersion, calumny, defamation, denigration, obloquy, slander, smear, vituperation **2.** *vb. Law* blacken, calumniate, defame, derogate, drag (someone's) name through the mud, malign, revile, slander, slur, smear, traduce, vilify

libellous, libelous aspersive, calumniatory, calumnious, defamatory, derogatory, false, injurious, malicious, maligning, scurrilous, slanderous, traducing, untrue, vilifying, vituperative

develop general cultural interests and intellectual ability. **7 Liberal** of or relating to a Liberal Party. *~n* **8** a person who has liberal ideas or opinions. **liberalism** *n* **liberally** *adv*

Liberal Democrat *n* a member or supporter of the Liberal Democrats, a British centrist political party that advocates proportional representation.

liberality *n, pl* **-ties 1** generosity. **2** the quality of being broad-minded.

liberalize *or* **-ise** *vb* **-izing, -ized** *or* **-ising, -ised** to make (a law) less strict. **liberalization** *or* **-isation** *n*

Liberal Party *n* **1** *History* a British non-Socialist political party which advocated progress and reform. **2** any similar party in various other countries.

liberate *vb* **-ating, -ated 1** to free (someone) from social prejudices or injustices. **2** to give liberty to; make free. **3** to release (a country) from enemy occupation. **liberation** *n* **liberator** *n*

liberated *adj* **1** not bound by traditional sexual and social roles: *a liberated woman.* **2** given liberty. **3** released from enemy occupation.

libertarian *n* **1** a person who believes in freedom of thought and action. *~adj* **2** believing in freedom of thought and action.

libertine (lib-er-teen) *n* **1** a person who is promiscuous and unscrupulous. *~adj* **2** promiscuous and unscrupulous.

liberty *n, pl* **-ties 1** the freedom to choose, think, and act for oneself. **2** the right of unrestricted movement and access; freedom. **3** (*often pl*) a social action regarded as being forward or improper. **4 at liberty** free or unconfined. **5 at liberty to** unrestricted or authorized: *I am not at liberty to divulge his name.* **6 take liberties (with)** to be overfamiliar (towards someone).

libidinous *adj* characterized by excessive sexual desire. **libidinously** *adv*

libido (lib-ee-doe) *n, pl* **-dos 1** *Psychoanal* psychic energy from the id. **2** sexual urge or desire. **libidinal** *adj*

Libra *n Astrol* the seventh sign of the zodiac; the Scales.

librarian *n* a person in charge of or assisting in a library. **librarianship** *n*

library *n, pl* **-braries 1** a room or building where books and other literary materials are kept. **2** a collection of literary materials, films, tapes, or records, kept for borrowing or reference. **3** the building or institution that houses such a collection. **4** a set of books published as a series, often in a similar format. **5** *Computers* a collection of standard programs, usually stored on disk.

libretto *n, pl* **-tos** *or* **-ti** a text written for an opera. **librettist** *n*

Libyan *adj* **1** from Libya. *~n* **2** a person from Libya.

lice *n* the plural of **louse**.

licence *or US* **license** *n* **1** a document giving official permission to do, use, or own something. **2** formal permission or exemption. **3** intentional disregard of conventional rules to achieve a certain effect: *poetic licence.* **4** excessive freedom.

➤ Note the *-ce* ending for the noun *licence*, with *-se* for the verb *license*.

license *vb* **-censing, -censed 1** to grant a licence to or for. **2** to give permission to or for. **licensable** *adj*

licensee *n* a person who holds a licence, esp. one to sell alcoholic drink.

licentiate *n* a person who holds a certificate of competence to practise a certain profession.

licentious *adj* sexually unrestrained or promiscuous. **licentiousness** *n*

lichee *n* same as **lychee**.

lichen *n* any of various small mossy plants that grow in patches on tree trunks, bare ground, rocks, and stone walls.

lichgate *n* same as **lychgate**.

THESAURUS

liberal 1. advanced, humanistic, latitudinarian, libertarian, progressive, radical, reformist, right-on (*informal*) **2.** altruistic, beneficent, bounteous, bountiful, charitable, free-handed, generous, kind, open-handed, open-hearted, prodigal, unstinting **3.** advanced, broad-minded, catholic, enlightened, high-minded, humanitarian, indulgent, magnanimous, permissive, right-on (*informal*), tolerant, unbiased, unbigoted, unprejudiced **4.** abundant, ample, bountiful, copious, handsome, lavish, munificent, plentiful, profuse, rich **5.** broad, flexible, free, general, inexact, lenient, loose, not close, not literal, not strict

liberality 1. altruism, beneficence, benevolence, bounty, charity, free-handedness, generosity, kindness, largess *or* largesse, munificence, open-handedness, philanthropy **2.** breadth, broad-mindedness, candour, catholicity, impartiality, latitude, liberalism, libertarianism, magnanimity, permissiveness, progressivism, toleration

liberalize, liberalise ameliorate, broaden, ease, expand, extend, loosen, mitigate, moderate, modify, relax, slacken, soften, stretch

liberate deliver, discharge, emancipate, free, let loose, let out, manumit, redeem, release, rescue, set free

liberation deliverance, emancipation, enfranchisement, freedom, freeing, liberating, liberty, manumission, redemption, release, unfettering, unshackling

liberator deliverer, emancipator, freer, manumitter, redeemer, rescuer, saviour

libertine 1. *n.* debauchee, lecher, loose liver, profligate, rake, reprobate, roué, seducer, sensualist, voluptuary, womanizer **2.** *adj.* abandoned, corrupt, debauched, decadent, degenerate, depraved, dissolute, immoral, licentious, profligate, rakish, reprobate, voluptuous, wanton

liberty 1. autonomy, emancipation, freedom, immunity, independence, liberation, release, self-determination, sovereignty **2.** *often plural* disrespect, familiarity, forwardness, impertinence, impropriety, impudence, insolence, overfamiliarity, presumption, presumptuousness **3. at liberty** free, not confined, on the loose, unlimited, unoccupied, unrestricted

libidinous carnal, concupiscent, debauched, impure, incontinent, lascivious, lecherous, loose, lustful, prurient, randy (*informal, chiefly Brit.*), ruttish, salacious, sensual, unchaste, wanton, wicked

licence *n.* **1.** authority, authorization, carte blanche, certificate, charter, dispensation, entitlement, exemption, immunity, leave, liberty, permission, permit, privilege, right, warrant **2.** freedom, independence, latitude, liberty, self-determination **3.** abandon, anarchy, disorder, excess, immoderation, impropriety, indulgence, irresponsibility, lawlessness, laxity, profligacy, unruliness

license accredit, allow, authorize, certify, commission, empower, entitle, permit, sanction, warrant

licentious abandoned, debauched, disorderly, dissolute, immoral, impure, lascivious, lax, lewd, libertine, libidinous, lubricious (*formal or literary*), lustful, profligate, promiscuous, sensual, uncontrollable, uncontrolled, uncurbed, unruly, wanton

licentiousness abandon, debauchery, dissipation,

licit *adj Formal* lawful; permitted.

lick *vb* **1** to pass the tongue over in order to taste, wet, or clean. **2** to flicker over or round (something): *flames licked the gutters.* **3** *Informal* **a** to defeat. **b** to thrash. **4 lick into shape** to put into a satisfactory condition. **5 lick one's wounds** to retire after a defeat. ~*n* **6** an instance of passing the tongue over something. **7** a small amount: *a lick of paint.* **8** *Informal* a blow. **9** *Informal* a fast pace: *a pulsating rhythm taken at a lick.* **10 a lick and a promise** something hastily done, esp. a hurried wash.

licorice *n US & Canad* same as **liquorice.**

lid *n* **1** a removable or hinged cover: *a saucepan lid.* **2** short for **eyelid. 3 put the (tin) lid on** *Informal* to put an end to. **lidded** *adj*

lido (**lee**-doe) *n, pl* **-dos** *Brit* an open-air swimming pool or a part of a beach used by the public for swimming and sunbathing.

lie[1] *vb* **lying, lied 1** to speak untruthfully with the intention of deceiving. **2** to convey a false impression: *the camera cannot lie.* ~*n* **3** an untrue statement deliberately used to mislead. **4** something that is deliberately intended to deceive. **5 give the lie to a** to disprove. **b** to accuse of lying.

lie[2] *vb* **lying, lay, lain 1** (often foll. by *down*) to place oneself or be in a horizontal position. **2** to be situated: *I left the money lying on the table; Nepal became the only country lying between China and India.* **3** to be and remain (in a particular state or condition): *others of their species lie asleep.* **4** to stretch or extend: *an enormous task lies ahead.* **5** (usually foll. by *in*) to exist or comprise: *her charm lies in her inner beauty.* **6** (foll. by *with*) to rest (with): *the fault lies with the NHS.* ~*n* **7** the manner, place, or style in which something is situated. **8** an animal's lair. **9 lie of the land** the way in which a situation is developing. ~See also **lie down, lie in.**

➤ Note that the past of *lie* is *lay: She lay on the beach all day.* Do not confuse with the main verb *lay* meaning "put".

Liebfraumilch (**leeb**-frow-milk) *n* a sweet white wine from the German Rhine.

lied (**leed**) *n, pl* **lieder** *Music* a musical setting for solo voice and piano of a romantic or lyrical poem.

lie detector *n Informal* a device used to measure any increase in blood pressure, pulse rate, etc., of someone being questioned, which is thought to indicate that the person is lying.

lie down *vb* **1** to place oneself or be in a horizontal position in order to rest. **2** to yield to: *never take any attack on your candidate lying down.* ~*n* **lie-down 3** a rest.

liege (**leej**) *adj* **1** (of a lord) owed feudal allegiance: *their liege lord.* **2** (of a vassal or subject) owing feudal allegiance: *a liege subject.* **3** faithful; loyal. ~*n* **4** a liege lord. **5** a subject.

lie in *vb* **1** to remain in bed late into the morning. ~*n* **lie-in 2** a long stay in bed in the morning.

lien *n Law* a right to retain possession of someone else's property until a debt is paid.

lieu (**lyew**) *n* **in lieu of** instead of.

Lieut. lieutenant.

lieutenant (lef-**ten**-ant) *n* **1** a junior officer in the army, navy, or the US police force. **2** a person who acts as principal assistant. **lieutenancy** *n*

lieutenant colonel *n* an officer in an army, air force, or marine corps immediately junior to a colonel.

lieutenant commander *n* an officer in a navy immediately junior to a commander.

lieutenant general *n* a senior officer in an army, air force, or marine corps.

lieutenant governor *n* **1** a deputy governor. **2** (in Canada) the representative of the Crown in a province.

life *n, pl* **lives 1** the state or quality that identifies living beings, characterized chiefly by growth, reproduction, and response to stimuli. **2** the period between birth and death or between birth and the present time. **3** a living person or being: *riots which claimed 22 lives.* **4** the remainder or extent of one's life: *with that lady for the rest of her life.* **5** the process of living: *rituals gave his life stability.* **6** *Informal* a sentence of life imprisonment, usually approximating to fifteen years. **7** a characteristic state or mode of existence: *country life is best.* **8** the length of time that something is active or functioning: *the life of a battery.* **9** a present condition or mode of existence: *they are leading a joyous life.* **10** a biography. **11** the sum or course of human events and activities. **12** liveliness or high spirits: *full of life.* **13** a source of strength, animation, or vitality: *he was the life of the show.* **14** all living things collectively: *there is no life on Mars; marine life.* **15 a matter of life and death** a matter of extreme urgency. **16 as large as life** *Informal* real and living. **17 not on your life** *Informal* certainly not. **18 true to life** faithful to reality. **19 to the life** (of a copy of a painting or drawing) resembling the original exactly.

life assurance *n* insurance that provides for a sum of money to be paid to the insured person at a certain age or to the spouse or children on the death of the insured. Also called: **life insurance**

life belt *n* an inflatable ring used to keep a person afloat when in danger of drowning.

lifeblood *n* **1** the blood vital to life. **2** something that is essential for existence, development, or success.

THESAURUS

dissoluteness, lechery, lewdness, libertinism, libidinousness, lust, lustfulness, profligacy, promiscuity, prurience, salaciousness, salacity, wantonness

lick *vb.* **1.** brush, lap, taste, tongue, touch, wash **2.** dart, flick, flicker, ignite, kindle, play over, ripple, touch **3.** *informal* **a.** beat, blow out of the water (*slang*), clobber (*slang*), defeat, master, overcome, rout, run rings around (*informal*), tank (*slang*), trounce, undo, vanquish, wipe the floor with (*informal*) **b.** beat, clobber (*slang*), flog, lambast(e), slap, spank, strike, thrash, wallop (*informal*) ~*n.* **4.** bit, brush, dab, little, sample, speck, stroke, taste, touch **5.** *informal* clip (*informal*), pace, rate, speed

lie[1] **1.** *vb.* dissimulate, equivocate, fabricate, falsify, fib, forswear oneself, invent, misrepresent, perjure, prevaricate, tell a lie, tell untruths **2.** *n.* deceit, fabrication, falsehood, falsification, falsity, fib, fiction, invention, mendacity, prevarication, untruth, white lie

lie[2] *vb.* **1.** be prone, be prostrate, be recumbent, be supine, couch, loll, lounge, recline, repose, rest, sprawl, stretch out **2.** be, be buried, be found, be interred, be located, belong, be placed, be situated, exist, extend, remain **3.** *usually with* **in** be present, consist, dwell, exist, inhere, pertain

life 1. animation, being, breath, entity, growth, sentience, viability, vitality **2.** being, career, continuance, course, duration, existence, lifetime, span, time **3.** human, human being, individual, mortal, person, soul **4.** behaviour, conduct, life style, way of life **5.** autobiography, biography, career, confessions, history, life story, memoirs, story **6.** the human condition, the times, the world, this mortal coil, trials and tribulations, vicissitudes **7.** activity, animation, brio, energy, get-up-and-go (*informal*), go (*informal*), high spirits, liveliness, oomph (*informal*), pep, sparkle, spirit, verve, vigour, vitality, vivacity, zest **8.** animating spirit,

lifeboat *n* a boat used for rescuing people at sea.

life buoy *n* a buoyant device to keep people afloat in an emergency.

life cycle *n* the series of changes occurring in each generation of an animal or plant.

lifeguard *n* a person at a beach or pool whose job is to rescue people in danger of drowning.

life jacket *n* an inflatable sleeveless jacket worn to keep a person afloat when in danger of drowning.

lifeless *adj* **1** inanimate; dead. **2** lacking liveliness or animation. **3** unconscious.

lifelike *adj* closely resembling or representing life.

lifeline *n* **1** a single means of contact or support on which a person or an area relies. **2** a rope used for life-saving.

lifelong *adj* lasting for a lifetime.

life peer *n Brit* a peer whose title ceases at his or her death.

life preserver *n* **1** *Brit* a bludgeon kept for self-defence. **2** *US & Canad* a life belt or life jacket.

lifer *n Informal* a prisoner sentenced to life imprisonment.

life raft *n* a raft for emergency use at sea.

life-saver *n* **1** same as **lifeguard. 2** *Informal* a person or thing that gives help in time of need. **life-saving** *adj, n*

life science *n* any of the sciences concerned with the structure and behaviour of living organisms, such as biology, botany, or zoology.

life-size *or* **life-sized** *adj* representing actual size.

lifestyle *n* a set of attitudes, habits, and possessions regarded as typical of a particular group or an individual.

life-support *adj* (of equipment or treatment) necessary to sustain life.

lifetime *n* **1** the length of time a person is alive. **2 of a lifetime** (of an opportunity or experience) the most important or memorable.

lift *vb* **1** to rise or raise upwards to a higher place: *the breakdown truck was lifting the lorry.* **2** to move upwards: *he slowly lifted his hand.* **3** to raise in status or estimation: *lifted from poverty.* **4** to revoke or cancel: *the government lifted its restrictions on imported beef.* **5** to remove (plants or underground crops) from the ground for harvesting. **6** to disappear or disperse: *the tension lifted.* **7** *Informal* to plagiarize (music or writing). *~n* **8 a** *Brit* a compartment raised or lowered in a vertical shaft to transport people or goods to another floor in a building. **b** See **chair lift, ski lift. 9** a ride in a car or other vehicle as a passenger. **10** a rise in morale or feeling of cheerfulness. **11** the act of lifting. **12** the force that lifts airborne objects.

liftoff *n* the initial movement of a rocket as it leaves its launching pad.

ligament *n Anat* a band of tough tissue that connects various bones or cartilage.

ligature *n* **1** a link, bond, or tie. **2** *Printing* a character of two or more joined letters, such as fi, ffi. **3** *Music* a slur or the group of notes connected by it. *~vb* **-turing, -tured 4** to bind with a ligature.

light[1] *n* **1** the natural medium, electromagnetic radiation, that makes sight possible. **2** anything that illuminates, such as a lamp or candle. **3** See **traffic light. 4** a particular type of light: *dim yellow light.* **5 a** daylight. **b** daybreak; dawn. **6** anything that lets in light, such as a window. **7** an aspect or view: *we have seen the world in a new light.* **8** mental understanding or spiritual insight: *suddenly he saw the light.* **9** an outstanding person: *a leading light of the movement.* **10** brightness of countenance, esp. a sparkle in the eyes. **11 a** something that ignites, such as a spark or flame. **b** something used for igniting, such as a match. **12** See **lighthouse. 13 come to light** to become known or visible. **14 in (the) light of** taking into account. **15 see the light** to understand. **16 see the light (of day) a** to come into being. **b** to come to public notice. *~adj* **17** full of light. **18** (of a colour) pale: *light blue.* *~vb* **lighting, lighted** *or* **lit 19** to ignite. **20** (often foll. by *up*) to illuminate or cause to illuminate. **21** to guide by light. ~See also **light up. lightish** *adj*

light[2] *adj* **1** not heavy; weighing relatively little. **2** relatively low in density, strength, amount, degree, etc.: *light oil; light alloy.* **3** lacking sufficient weight. **4** not bulky or clumsy: *light bedclothes.* **5** not serious or difficult to understand; entertaining: *light music.* **6** graceful or agile: *light movements.* **7** without strong emphasis or serious meaning: *he gazed about with a light inattentive smile.* **8** easily digested: *a light lunch.* **9** relatively low in alcohol: *a light wine.* **10** without burdens, difficulties, or problems: *a light heart lives longest.* **11** dizzy or unclear: *a light head.* **12** (of bread or cake) spongy or well risen. **13** (of a vessel, lorry, or other transport) **a** designed to carry light loads. **b** not loaded. **14** carrying light arms or equipment: *light infantry.* **15** (of an industry) producing small consumer goods using light machinery. **16 make light of** to treat as insignificant or unimportant. *~adv* **17** with little equipment or luggage: *travelling light.* *~vb* **lighting, lighted**

THESAURUS

essence, heart, lifeblood, soul, spirit, vital spark **9.** creatures, living beings, living things, organisms, wildlife

lifeless 1. cold, dead, deceased, defunct, extinct, inanimate, inert **2.** cold, colourless, dull, flat, heavy, hollow, lacklustre, lethargic, listless, passive, pointless, slow, sluggish, spent, spiritless, static, stiff, torpid, wooden **3.** comatose, dead to the world (*informal*), in a faint, inert, insensate, insensible, out cold, out for six, unconscious

lifelike authentic, exact, faithful, graphic, natural, photographic, real, realistic, true-to-life, undistorted, vivid

lifelong constant, deep-rooted, enduring, for all one's life, for life, lasting, lifetime, long-lasting, long-standing, perennial, permanent, persistent

lifetime all one's born days, career, course, day(s), existence, life span, one's natural life, period, span, time

lift *vb.* **1.** ascend, bear aloft, buoy up, climb, draw up, elevate, hoist, mount, pick up, raise, raise high, rear, rise, upheave, uplift, upraise **2.** advance, ameliorate, boost, dignify, elevate, enhance, exalt, improve, promote, raise, upgrade **3.** annul, cancel, countermand, end, relax, remove, rescind, revoke, stop, terminate **4.** be dispelled, disappear, disperse, dissipate, vanish **5.** *informal* appropriate, copy, crib (*informal*), nick (*slang, chiefly Brit.*), pilfer, pinch (*informal*), pirate, plagiarize, pocket, purloin, steal, take, thieve *~n.* **6.** elevator (*U.S. & Canad.*) **7.** car ride, drive, ride, run, transport **8.** boost, encouragement, fillip, pick-me-up, reassurance, shot in the arm (*informal*), uplift

light[1] *n.* **1.** blaze, brightness, brilliance, effulgence, flash, glare, gleam, glint, glow, illumination, incandescence, lambency, luminescence, luminosity, lustre, phosphorescence, radiance, ray, refulgence, scintillation, shine, sparkle **2.** beacon, bulb, candle, flare, lamp, lantern, lighthouse, star, taper, torch, windowpane **3.** broad day, cockcrow, dawn, daybreak, daylight, daytime, morn (*poetic*), morning, sun, sunbeam, sunrise, sunshine **4.** angle, approach, aspect, attitude, context, interpretation, point of view, slant, vantage point, viewpoint **5.** awareness, comprehension, eluci-

or **lit 18** (esp. of birds) to settle or land after flight. **19** (foll. by *on* or *upon*) to discover by chance. ~See also **lights. lightish** *adj* **lightly** *adv* **lightness** *n*

light bulb *n* a hollow rounded glass fitting containing a gas and a thin metal filament that gives out light when an electric current is passed through it.

lighten[1] *vb* **1** to make less dark. **2** to shine; glow. **3** (of lightning) to flash.

lighten[2] *vb* **1** to make or become less heavy. **2** to make or become less burdensome. **3** to make or become more cheerful or lively.

lighter[1] *n* a small portable device for lighting cigarettes, etc.

lighter[2] *n* a flat-bottomed barge used in loading or unloading a ship.

light-fingered *adj* skilful at thieving, esp. by picking pockets.

light flyweight *n* an amateur boxer weighing up to 48 kg.

light-footed *adj* having a light tread.

light-headed *adj* giddy; feeling faint.

light-hearted *adj* cheerful or carefree in mood or disposition. **light-heartedly** *adv*

light heavyweight *n* a professional boxer weighing up to 175 pounds (79.5 kg) or an amateur weighing up to 81 kg. Also called: **cruiserweight**

lighthouse *n* a tower with a light to guide ships and warn of obstructions.

lighting *n* **1** the apparatus for and design of artificial light effects to a stage, film, or television set. **2** the act or quality of illumination.

lighting-up time *n* the time when vehicles are required by law to have their lights on.

light middleweight *n* an amateur boxer weighing up to 71 kg.

lightning *n* **1** a flash of light in the sky caused by a discharge of electricity. *~adj* **2** fast and sudden: *a lightning attack.*

lightning conductor *or* **rod** *n* a metal rod attached to the highest part of a building to divert lightning safely to earth.

light pen *n* a penlike photoelectric device that in conjunction with a computer can be used to draw lines or identify symbols on a VDU screen.

lights *pl n* the lungs of sheep, bullocks, and pigs, used for feeding pets.

lightship *n* a moored ship equipped as a lighthouse.

lights out *n* the time when residents of an institution are expected to retire to bed.

light up *vb* **1** to illuminate. **2** to make or become cheerful or animated: *their faces lit up and one dug the other in the ribs.* **3** to light a cigarette or pipe.

lightweight *adj* **1** not serious. **2** of relatively light weight. *~n* **3** *Informal* a person of little importance or influence. **4** a person or animal of relatively light weight. **5** a professional boxer weighing up to 135 pounds (61 kg) or an amateur weighing up to 60 kg.

light welterweight *n* an amateur boxer weighing up to 63.5 kg.

light year *n Astron* the distance travelled by light in one mean solar year, i.e. 9.4607×10^{15} metres.

ligneous *adj* of or like wood.

lignite (**lig**-nite) *n* a brown sedimentary rock with a woody texture: used as a fuel.

lignum vitae (**lig**-num **vite**-ee) *n* a tropical American tree with heavy resinous wood.

like[1] *adj* **1** resembling. *~prep* **2** in the manner of; similar to: *she was like a child; it looks like a traffic cone.* **3** such as: *a modern material, like carbon fibre.* **4** characteristic of. *~adv* **5** in the manner of: *cheering like mad.* **6** *Dialect* likely. *~conj* **7** *Not universally accepted* as though; as if: *I don't want to make it seem like I had this bad childhood.* **8** *Not universally accepted* in the same way as: *she doesn't dance like you do.* *~n* **9** the equal or counterpart of a person or thing. **10 the like** similar things: *magic, supernormal powers and the like.* **11 the likes** *or* **like of** people or things similar to (someone or something specified): *the theatre was not meant for the likes of him.*

like[2] *vb* **liking, liked 1** to find enjoyable. **2** to be fond

THESAURUS

dation, explanation, illustration, information, insight, knowledge, understanding **6.** example, exemplar, guiding light, model, paragon, shining example **7.** flame, lighter, match **8. come to light** appear, be disclosed, be discovered, be revealed, come out, transpire, turn up **9. in (the) light of** bearing in mind, because of, considering, in view of, taking into account, with knowledge of *~adj.* **10.** aglow, bright, brilliant, glowing, illuminated, luminous, lustrous, shining, sunny, well-lighted, well-lit **11.** bleached, blond, faded, fair, light-hued, light-toned, pale, pastel *~vb.* **12.** fire, ignite, inflame, kindle, set a match to **13.** *often with* **up** brighten, clarify, floodlight, flood with light, illuminate, illumine, irradiate, lighten, light up, put on, switch on, turn on

light[2] *adj.* **1.** airy, buoyant, delicate, lightweight, portable, slight **2.** faint, gentle, indistinct, mild, moderate, slight, soft, weak **3.** flimsy, insubstantial, scanty, underweight **4.** amusing, diverting, entertaining, frivolous, funny, gay, humorous, light-hearted, pleasing, superficial, trifling, trivial, witty **5.** agile, airy, graceful, light-footed, lithe, nimble, sprightly, sylphlike **6.** inconsequential, inconsiderable, insignificant, slight, trifling, trivial, unsubstantial **7.** digestible, frugal, modest, not heavy, not rich, restricted, small **8.** airy, animated, blithe, carefree, cheerful, cheery, fickle, frivolous, gay, lively, merry, sunny **9.** dizzy, giddy, light-headed, reeling, unsteady, volatile *~vb.* **10.** alight, land, perch, settle **11.** *with* **on** *or* **upon** chance, come across, discover, encounter, find, happen upon, hit upon, stumble on

lighten[1] become light, brighten, flash, gleam, illuminate, irradiate, light up, make bright, shine

lighten[2] **1.** disburden, ease, make lighter, reduce in weight, unload **2.** allay, alleviate, ameliorate, assuage, ease, facilitate, lessen, mitigate, reduce, relieve **3.** brighten, buoy up, cheer, elate, encourage, gladden, hearten, inspire, lift, perk up, revive

light-fingered crafty, crooked (*informal*), dishonest, furtive, pilfering, pinching (*informal*), shifty, sly, stealing, thieving, underhand

light-headed delirious, dizzy, faint, giddy, hazy, vertiginous, woozy (*informal*)

light-hearted blithe, blithesome (*literary*), bright, carefree, cheerful, chirpy (*informal*), effervescent, frolicsome, gay, genial, glad, gleeful, happy-go-lucky, insouciant, jocund, jolly, jovial, joyful, joyous, merry, playful, sunny, untroubled, upbeat (*informal*)

lightly 1. airily, delicately, faintly, gently, gingerly, slightly, softly, timidly **2.** moderately, sparingly, sparsely, thinly **3.** breezily, carelessly, flippantly, frivolously, heedlessly, indifferently, slightingly, thoughtlessly

lightweight *adj.* inconsequential, insignificant, of no account, paltry, petty, slight, trifling, trivial, unimportant, worthless

like[1] **1.** *adj.* akin, alike, allied, analogous, approximating, cognate, corresponding, equivalent, identical, par-

of. **3** to prefer or choose: *I'd like to go home.* **4** to feel disposed or inclined; choose; wish: *do as you like.* ~*n* **5** (*usually pl*) a favourable feeling, desire, or preference. **likeable** *or* **likable** *adj*

likelihood *n* chance; probability.

likely *adj* **1** tending or inclined: *likely to win.* **2** probable: *the likely effects of the tunnel.* **3** appropriate for a purpose or activity: *a likely candidate.* ~*adv* **4** probably or presumably. **5 not likely** *Informal* definitely not.

like-minded *adj* sharing similar opinions.

liken *vb* compare.

likeness *n* **1** resemblance. **2** portrait. **3** an imitative appearance; semblance: *in the likeness of a dragon.*

likewise *adv* **1** in addition; also. **2** similarly.

liking *n* **1** fondness. **2** what one likes or prefers: *if it's not to your liking, do let me know.*

lilac *n* **1** a small tree with large sprays of purple or white sweet-smelling flowers. ~*adj* **2** pale purple.

Lilliputian (lil-lip-**pew**-shun) *n* **1** a tiny person or being. ~*adj* **2** tiny; very small.

Lilo *n, pl* **-los** *Trademark* a type of inflatable plastic mattress.

lilt *n* **1** a pleasing musical quality in a speaking voice. **2** (in music) a jaunty rhythm. **3** a graceful rhythmic motion. ~*vb* **4** (of a voice, tune, or song) to rise and fall in a pleasant way. **5** to move gracefully and rhythmically. **lilting** *adj*

lily *n, pl* **lilies 1** a perennial plant, such as the tiger lily, with scaly bulbs and showy white or coloured flowers. **2** a water lily.

lily-livered *adj Old-fashioned* cowardly.

lily of the valley *n, pl* **lilies of the valley** a small plant with spikes of sweet-smelling white bell-shaped flowers.

limb[1] *n* **1** an arm, leg, or wing. **2** any of the main branches of a tree. **3 out on a limb a** in a precarious or questionable position. **b** *Brit* isolated, esp. because of unpopular opinions. **limbless** *adj*

limb[2] *n* the apparent outer edge of the sun, a moon, or a planet.

limber[1] *adj* **1** pliant; supple. **2** able to move or bend the body freely; agile.

limber[2] *n* **1** part of a gun carriage, consisting of an axle, pole, and two wheels. ~*vb* **2** to attach the limber (to a gun).

limber up *vb* to loosen stiff muscles by exercise.

limbo[1] *n, pl* **-bos 1** (*often cap*) *RC Church* (formerly) the supposed region intermediate between heaven and hell for the unbaptized. **2 in limbo** not knowing the result or next stage of something and powerless to influence it.

limbo[2] *n, pl* **-bos** a West Indian dance in which dancers lean backwards and pass under a horizontal bar which is gradually lowered.

lime[1] *n* **1** *Agriculture* calcium hydroxide spread as a dressing on acidic land. ~*vb* **liming, limed 2** to spread a calcium compound upon (land).

lime[2] *n* the green oval fruit of a small Asian citrus tree with acid fleshy pulp rich in vitamin C.

lime[3] *n* a European linden tree planted for ornament.

lime-green *adj* light yellowish-green.

limekiln *n* a kiln in which calcium carbonate is burned to produce quicklime.

limelight *n* **1** the glare of publicity: *this issue will remain in the limelight.* **2 a** a type of lamp, formerly used in stage lighting, in which lime is heated to white heat. **b** brilliant white light produced in this way.

limerick (**lim**-mer-ik) *n* a form of comic verse consisting of five lines.

limestone *n* rock consisting mainly of calcium carbonate: used as a building stone and in making cement.

limey *n US, Canad, & Austral slang* **1** a British person. **2** a British sailor or ship.

limit *n* **1** (*sometimes pl*) the ultimate extent amount of something: *each soloist was stretched to his or her limit by the demands of the vocal writing.* **2** (*often pl*) the boundary of a specific area: *beyond the city limits.* **3** the largest quantity or amount allowed. **4 the limit** *Informal* a person or thing that is intolerably exasperating. ~*vb* **-iting, -ited 5** to restrict. **limitable** *adj*

limitation *n* **1** a restriction or controlling of quantity, quality, or achievement. **2 limitations** the limit or extent of an ability to achieve something: *learn your own limitations.*

limited *adj* **1** having a limit; restricted. **2** without full-

THESAURUS

allel, relating, resembling, same, similar **2.** *n.* counterpart, equal, fellow, match, parallel, twin

like[2] *vb.* **1.** adore (*informal*), be fond of, be keen on, be partial to, delight in, dig (*slang*), enjoy, go for, love, relish, revel in **2.** admire, appreciate, approve, cherish, esteem, hold dear, prize, take a shine to (*informal*), take to **3.** care to, choose, choose to, desire, fancy, feel inclined, prefer, select, want, wish ~*n.* **4.** *usually plural* cup of tea (*informal*), favourite, liking, partiality, predilection, preference

likeable, likable agreeable, amiable, appealing, attractive, charming, engaging, friendly, genial, nice, pleasant, pleasing, sympathetic, winning, winsome

likelihood chance, good chance, liability, likeliness, possibility, probability, prospect, reasonableness, strong possibility

likely *adj.* **1.** anticipated, apt, disposed, expected, in a fair way, inclined, liable, on the cards, possible, probable, prone, tending, to be expected **2.** acceptable, agreeable, appropriate, befitting, fit, pleasing, proper, qualified, suitable ~*adv.* **3.** doubtlessly, in all probability, like as not (*informal*), like enough (*informal*), no doubt, presumably, probably

liken compare, equate, juxtapose, match, parallel, relate, set beside

likeness 1. affinity, correspondence, resemblance, similarity, similitude **2.** delineation, depiction, effigy, image, model, photograph, picture, portrait, representation, reproduction, study **3.** appearance, form, guise, semblance

liking affection, affinity, appreciation, attraction, bent, bias, desire, fondness, inclination, love, partiality, penchant, predilection, preference, proneness, propensity, soft spot, stomach, taste, tendency, thirst, weakness

limb 1. appendage, arm, extension, extremity, leg, member, part, wing **2.** bough, branch, offshoot, projection, spur

limelight attention, celebrity, fame, glare of publicity, prominence, public eye, publicity, public notice, recognition, stardom, the spotlight

limit *n.* **1.** *sometimes plural* bound, breaking point, cutoff point, deadline, end, end point, furthest bound, greatest extent, termination, the bitter end, ultimate, utmost **2.** *often plural* border, boundary, confines, edge, end, extent, frontier, pale, perimeter, periphery, precinct **3.** ceiling, check, curb, limitation, maximum, obstruction, restraint, restriction **4. the limit** *informal* enough, it (*informal*), the end, the last straw ~*vb.* **5.** bound, check, circumscribe, confine, curb, delimit, demarcate, fix, hem in, hinder, ration, restrain, restrict, specify, straiten

limitation block, check, condition, constraint, con-

ness or scope; narrow. **3** (of governing powers or sovereignty) restricted by a constitution, laws, or an assembly: *limited government.* **4** *Chiefly Brit* (of a business enterprise) owned by shareholders whose liability for the enterprise's debts is restricted.

limited edition *n* an edition of something, such as a book, which has been restricted to a particular number of copies.

limn *vb Old-fashioned* to represent in drawing or painting.

limousine *n* any large luxurious car.

limp[1] *vb* **1** to walk with an uneven step, esp. with a weak or injured leg. **2** to advance in a labouring or faltering manner. *~n* **3** an uneven walk or progress. **limping** *adj, n*

limp[2] *adj* **1** lacking firmness or stiffness. **2** not energetic or vital. **3** (of the binding of a book) paperback. **limply** *adv*

limpet *n* **1** a conical shellfish that clings tightly to rocks with its muscular foot. *~adj* **2** denoting certain weapons that are magnetically attached to their targets and resist removal: *limpet mines.*

limpid *adj* **1** clear or transparent. **2** (of speech or writing) clear and easy to understand. **limpidity** *n*

limy[1] *adj* **limier, limiest** of, like, or smeared with birdlime.

limy[2] *adj* **limier, limiest** of or tasting of lime (the fruit).

linage *n* **1** the number of lines in written or printed matter. **2** payment according to the number of lines.

linchpin *or* **lynchpin** *n* **1** a pin inserted through an axle to keep a wheel in position. **2** an essential person or thing: *she was the linchpin of the experiment.*

Lincs Lincolnshire.

linctus *n, pl* **-tuses** a soothing syrupy cough mixture.

linden *n* a large tree with heart-shaped leaves and fragrant yellowish flowers. See also **lime**[3].

line[1] *n* **1** a narrow continuous mark, such as one made by a pencil or brush. **2** a thin indented mark or wrinkle on skin. **3** a continuous length without breadth. **4** a boundary: *the United Nations established a provisional demarcation line.* **5** *Sport* **a** a white band indicating a division on a field or track. **b** a mark or imaginary mark at which a race begins or ends. **6** a boundary or limit: *the invidious dividing line between universities and polytechnics.* **7** the edge or contour of a shape: *the shoulder line.* **8** a wire or string with a particular function: *a long washing line.* **9** a telephone connection: *it was a very bad line.* **10** a conducting wire, cable, or circuit for electric-power transmission or telecommunications. **11** a system of travel or transportation: *a shipping line.* **12** a route between two points on a railway. **13** *Chiefly Brit* a railway track. **14** a course or direction of movement: *the birds' line of flight.* **15** a course of action or behaviour: *to adopt a more aggressive line.* **16** a policy or prescribed way of thinking: *city commentators supported the CBI line.* **17** a field of interest or activity: *heroin – that was their line.* **18** straight or orderly alignment: *stand in line.* **19** one kind of product or article: *a line of smart suits.* **20** a row of people or things. **21** a row of printed or written words. **22** a unit of verse consisting of words in a single row. **23** one of a number of narrow horizontal bands forming a television picture. **24** *Music* any of the five horizontal marks that make up the stave. **25** the most forward defensive position: *the front line.* **26** a formation of ships or soldiers abreast of each other. **27** the combatant forces of certain armies and navies. **28** *US & Canad* a queue. **29 all along the line** at every stage in a series. **30 draw the line (at)** to object (to) or set a limit (on): *I'm not a killer, I draw the line at that.* **31 drop someone a line** to send someone a short note. **32 get a line on** *Informal* to obtain information about. **33 in line for** likely to receive: *high achievers are in line for cash bonuses.* **34 in line with** conforming to. **35 lay** *or* **put on the line a** to speak frankly and directly. **b** to risk (one's career or reputation) on something. *~vb* **lining, lined 36** to mark with a line or lines. **37** to be or form a border: *the square was lined with stalls selling snacks.* **38** to place in or form a row, series, or alignment. ~See also **lines, line-up. lined** *adj*

line[2] *vb* **lining, lined 1** to attach an inside layer to. **2** to cover the inside of: *the works of Shakespeare lined his walls.* **3 line one's pockets** to make a lot of money, esp. dishonestly.

lineage (**lin**-ee-ij) *n* direct descent from an ancestor.

lineal *adj* **1** being in a direct line of descent from an ancestor. **2** of or derived from direct descent. **3** linear.

lineament *n* (*often pl*) a facial outline or feature.

linear (**lin**-ee-er) *adj* **1** of or in lines. **2** of or relating to length. **3** represented by a line or lines. **linearity** *n*

linear measure *n* a unit or system of units for the measurement of length.

lineation (lin-ee-**ay**-shun) *n* **1** the act of marking with lines. **2** an arrangement of lines.

line drawing *n* a drawing formed with lines only.

linen *n* **1** a hard-wearing fabric woven from the spun fibres of flax. **2** articles, such as sheets or tablecloths, made from linen cloth or from cotton.

line of fire *n* the flight path of a bullet discharged from a firearm.

line printer *n* an electromechanical device that

THESAURUS

trol, curb, disadvantage, drawback, impediment, obstruction, qualification, reservation, restraint, restriction, snag

limited 1. bounded, checked, circumscribed, confined, constrained, controlled, curbed, defined, finite, fixed, hampered, hemmed in, restricted **2.** cramped, diminished, inadequate, insufficient, minimal, narrow, reduced, restricted, scant, short, unsatisfactory

limp[1] **1.** *vb.* falter, hobble, hop, shamble, shuffle **2.** *n.* hobble, lameness

limp[2] *adj.* **1.** drooping, flabby, flaccid, flexible, floppy, lax, limber, loose, pliable, relaxed, slack, soft **2.** debilitated, enervated, exhausted, lethargic, spent, tired, weak, worn out

line[1] *n.* **1.** band, bar, channel, dash, groove, mark, rule, score, scratch, streak, stripe, stroke, underline **2.** crease, crow's foot, furrow, mark, wrinkle **3.** border, borderline, boundary, demarcation, edge, frontier, limit, mark **4.** configuration, contour, features, figure, outline, profile, silhouette **5.** cable, cord, filament, rope, strand, string, thread, wire, wisp **6.** axis, course, direction, path, route, track, trajectory **7.** approach, avenue, belief, course, course of action, ideology, method, policy, position, practice, procedure, scheme, system **8.** activity, area, business, calling, department, employment, field, forte, interest, job, occupation, profession, province, pursuit, specialization, trade, vocation **9.** column, crocodile (*Brit. informal*), file, procession, queue, rank, row, sequence, series **10.** disposition, firing line, formation, front, front line, position, trenches **11. draw the line (at)** lay down the law, object, prohibit, put one's foot down, restrict, set a limit **12. in line for** a candidate for, being considered for, due for, in the running for, next in succession to, on the short list for *~vb.* **13.** crease, cut, draw, furrow, inscribe, mark, rule, score, trace, underline **14.** border, bound, edge, fringe, rank, rim, skirt, verge

prints a line of characters at a time: used in printing and in computer systems.

liner[1] *n* 1 a passenger ship or aircraft, esp. one that is part of a commercial fleet. 2 Also called: **eyeliner** a cosmetic used to outline the eyes.

liner[2] *n* something used as a lining: *a plastic bin liner.*

lines *pl n* 1 the words of a theatrical role: *shaky sets, fluffed lines, and wooden plots.* 2 *Informal, chiefly Brit* a marriage certificate: *marriage lines.* 3 a school punishment of writing out the same sentence or phrase a specified number of times. 4 **read between the lines** to find an implicit meaning in addition to the obvious one.

linesman *n, pl* **-men** 1 an official who helps the referee or umpire in various sports, by indicating when the ball has gone out of play. 2 a person who maintains railway, electricity, or telephone lines.

line-up *n* 1 people or things assembled for a particular purpose: *Christmas TV line-up.* 2 the members of such an assembly. *~vb* **line up** 3 to form or organize a line-up.

ling[1] *n, pl* **ling** *or* **lings** a northern coastal food fish with a long slender body.

ling[2] *n* heather.

linger *vb* 1 to delay or prolong departure. 2 to survive in a weakened condition for some time before death. 3 to spend a long time doing or considering something. **lingering** *adj*

lingerie (**lan**-zher-ee) *n* women's underwear and nightwear.

lingo *n, pl* **-goes** *Informal* any foreign or unfamiliar language or jargon.

lingua franca *n, pl* **lingua francas** *or* **linguae francae** 1 a language used for communication among people of different mother tongues. 2 any system of communication providing mutual understanding.

lingual *adj* 1 *Anat* of the tongue. 2 articulated with the tongue. 3 *Rare* of language or languages. **lingually** *adv*

linguist *n* 1 a person who is skilled in foreign languages. 2 a person who studies linguistics.

linguistic *adj* 1 of language. 2 of linguistics. **linguistically** *adv*

linguistics *n* the scientific study of language.

liniment *n* a medicated oily liquid applied to the skin to relieve pain or stiffness.

lining *n* 1 material used to line a garment or curtain. 2 any interior covering: *the lining of the womb.*

link *n* 1 any of the separate rings that form a chain. 2 an emotional or logical relationship between people or things; association. 3 a connecting part or episode. 4 a type of communications connection: *a rail link; radio link.* *~vb* 5 (often foll. by *up*) to connect with or as if with links. 6 to connect by association.

linkage *n* 1 the act of linking or the state of being linked. 2 a system of links.

linkman *n, pl* **-men** a presenter of a television or radio programme consisting of a number of items broadcast from different locations.

links *pl n* a golf course.

link-up *n* a joining together of two systems or groups.

linnet *n* a brownish finch: the male has a red breast and forehead.

lino *n* short for **linoleum.**

linocut *n* 1 a design cut in relief in linoleum mounted on a block of wood. 2 a print made from such a block.

linoleum *n* a floor covering made of hessian or jute with a smooth decorative coating of powdered cork.

Linotype *n Trademark* a typesetting machine that casts an entire line of text on one piece of metal.

linseed *n* the seed of the flax plant.

linseed oil *n* a yellow oil extracted from flax seeds and used in making paints, inks, linoleum, and varnish.

lint *n* 1 an absorbent material with raised fibres on one side, used to dress wounds. 2 tiny shreds of yarn or cloth; fluff.

lintel *n* a horizontal beam over a door or window.

lion *n* 1 a large animal of the cat family found in Africa and India, with a tawny yellow coat and, in the male, a shaggy mane. 2 a courageous and strong person. 3 **the lion's share** the largest portion. **lioness** *fem n*

lion-hearted *adj* very brave; courageous.

lionize *or* **-ise** *vb* **-izing, -ized** *or* **-ising, -ised** to treat as a celebrity.

lip *n* 1 *Anat* either of the two fleshy folds surrounding the mouth. 2 any structure resembling a lip, such as the rim of a jug. 3 *Slang* impudent talk or backchat. 4 **bite one's lip** to avoid showing feelings of anger or distress. 5 **keep a stiff upper lip** to maintain one's composure during a time of trouble. 6 **lick** *or* **smack one's lips** to anticipate or recall something with glee or relish.

lipase *n Biochem* any of a group of enzymes that digest fat and are produced in the stomach and pancreas and occur in seeds.

lipid *n Biochem* any of a group of organic compounds including fats, oils, waxes, and sterols.

liposuction *n* a cosmetic surgical operation in which fat is removed from the body by suction.

lip-read *vb* **-reading, -read** to interpret speech by lip-reading.

lip-reading *n* a method used by the deaf to understand spoken words by interpreting movements of the speaker's lips. **lip-reader** *n*

lip service *n* **pay lip service to** to appear to support or obey something publicly while actually disregarding it.

lipstick *n* a cosmetic in the form of a stick, for colouring the lips.

liquefy *vb* **-fies, -fying, -fied** (esp. of a gas) to make or become liquid. **liquefaction** *n*

liqueur (lik-**cure**) *n* a highly flavoured sweetened alcoholic spirit, intended to be drunk after a meal.

THESAURUS

line[2] cover, face, fill, interline

lineament *often plural* configuration, countenance, face, feature, line, outline, physiognomy, trait, visage

lines part, script, words

line-up arrangement, array, row, selection, team

line up align, arrange, array, assemble, come up with, fall in, form ranks, lay on, marshal, obtain, order, organize, prepare, procure, produce, queue up, range, regiment, secure, straighten

linger 1. hang around, loiter, remain, stay, stop, tarry, wait 2. cling to life, die slowly, hang on, last, survive 3. dally, dawdle, delay, idle, lag, procrastinate, take one's time

lingering dragging, long-drawn-out, persistent, protracted, remaining, slow

link *n.* 1. component, constituent, division, element, member, part, piece 2. affiliation, affinity, association, attachment, bond, connection, joint, knot, liaison, relationship, tie, tie-up, vinculum *~vb.* 3. *often with* **up** attach, bind, connect, couple, fasten, join, tie, unite, yoke 4. associate, bracket, connect, identify, relate

lion brave man, champion, conqueror, fighter, hero, warrior

lip 1. brim, brink, edge, flange, margin, rim 2. *slang*

liquid *n* **1** a substance in a physical state which can change shape but not size. ~*adj* **2** of or being a liquid: *liquid medicines.* **3** shining and clear: *liquid sunlight days.* **4** flowing, fluent, or smooth. **5** (of assets) in the form of money or easily convertible into money.

liquidate *vb* **-dating, -dated 1** to settle or pay off (a debt or claim). **2** to dissolve a company and divide its assets among creditors. **3** to convert (assets) into cash. **4** to eliminate or kill.

liquidation *n* **1 a** the dissolving of a company by selling its assets to pay off its debts. **b go into liquidation** (of a business firm) to have its affairs so terminated. **2** destruction; elimination.

liquidator *n* an official appointed to liquidate a business.

liquid-crystal display *n* a display of numbers, characters, or images, esp. on a calculator, using cells containing a liquid with crystalline properties, that change their reflectivity when an electric field is applied to them.

liquidity *n* the state of being able to meet financial obligations.

liquidize *or* **-dise** *vb* **-izing, -ized** *or* **-ising, -ised 1** to make or become liquid; liquefy. **2** to process (food) in a liquidizer to make it liquid.

liquidizer *or* **-diser** *n* a kitchen appliance with blades for liquidizing food.

liquid measure *n* a unit or system of units for measuring volumes of liquids or their containers.

liquid oxygen *n* oxygen liquefied by cooling: used in rocket fuels.

liquid paraffin *n* an oily liquid obtained by petroleum distillation and used as a laxative.

liquor *n* **1** spirits or other alcoholic drinks. **2** any liquid in which food has been cooked.

liquorice *or US & Canad* **licorice** (**lik**-ker-iss) *n* **1** a chewy black sweet with a strong flavour. **2** the dried black root of a Mediterranean plant, used as a laxative and in confectionery.

lira *n, pl* **lire** *or* **liras 1** the standard monetary unit of Italy. **2** the standard monetary unit of Turkey.

lisle (rhymes with **mile**) *n* a strong fine cotton thread or fabric, formerly used to make stockings.

lisp *n* **1** a speech defect in which *s* and *z* are pronounced like the *th* sounds in English *thin* and *then* respectively. ~*vb* **2** to speak with a lisp.

LISP *n* a high-level computer programming language suitable for work in artificial intelligence.

lissom *or* **lissome** *adj* slim and graceful and agile in movement.

list[1] *n* **1** an item-by-item record of names or things, usually written one below the other. ~*vb* **2** to make a list of. **3** to include in a list.

list[2] *vb* **1** (esp. of ships) to lean to one side. ~*n* **2** a leaning to one side: *developed a list to starboard.*

listed building *n* (in Britain) a building protected from demolition or alteration because of its special historical or architectural interest.

listen *vb* **1** to concentrate on hearing something. **2** to take heed or pay attention: *listen, let me explain.* **listener** *n*

listen in *vb* (often foll. by *on* or *to*) to listen secretly to; eavesdrop.

listeriosis *n* a serious form of food poisoning, caused by bacteria of the genus *Listeria.*

listing *n* **1** a list or an entry in a list. **2 listings** lists of films, concerts, etc. printed in newspapers and magazines, and showing details such as times and venues.

listless *adj* lacking interest or energy. **listlessly** *adv*

list price *n* the selling price of merchandise as quoted in a catalogue or advertisement.

lists *pl n* **1** *History* the enclosed field of combat at a tournament. **2 enter the lists** to engage in a conflict or controversy.

lit *vb* a past of **light**[1] or **light**[2].

lit. 1 literal(ly). **2** literary. **3** literature.

litany *n, pl* **-nies 1** *Christianity* a prayer consisting of a series of invocations, each followed by the same response. **2** any tedious recital: *a litany of complaints.*

litchi *n* same as **lychee.**

liter *n US* same as **litre.**

literacy *n* **1** the ability to read and write. **2** the ability to use language effectively.

literal *adj* **1** in exact accordance with the explicit meaning of a word or text. **2** word for word: *a literal translation.* **3** dull or unimaginative: *she's very, very literal and flat in how she interprets what she sees.* **4** true; actual. ~*n* **5** a misprint or misspelling in a text. **literally** *adv*

➤ Note that *literally* means much the same as "actual-

THESAURUS

backchat (*informal*), cheek (*informal*), effrontery, impertinence, insolence, rudeness, sauce (*informal*) **3. lick** *or* **smack one's lips** anticipate, delight in, drool over, enjoy, gloat over, relish, savour, slaver over

liquid *n.* **1.** fluid, juice, liquor, solution ~*adj.* **2.** aqueous, flowing, fluid, liquefied, melted, molten, running, runny, thawed, wet **3.** bright, brilliant, clear, limpid, shining, translucent, transparent **4.** dulcet, fluent, mellifluent, mellifluous, melting, smooth, soft, sweet **5.** convertible, negotiable

liquidate 1. clear, discharge, honour, pay, pay off, settle, square **2.** abolish, annul, cancel, dissolve, terminate **3.** cash, convert to cash, realize, sell off, sell up **4.** annihilate, bump off (*slang*), destroy, dispatch, do away with, do in (*slang*), eliminate, exterminate, finish off, get rid of, kill, murder, remove, rub out (*U.S. slang*), silence, take out (*informal*), wipe out (*informal*)

liquor 1. alcohol, booze (*informal*), drink, grog, hooch (*informal*), intoxicant, juice (*informal*), spirits, strong drink **2.** broth, extract, gravy, infusion, juice, liquid, stock

list[1] **1.** *n.* catalogue, directory, file, index, inventory, invoice, leet (*Scot.*), listing, record, register, roll, schedule, series, syllabus, tabulation, tally **2.** *vb.* bill, book, catalogue, enrol, enter, enumerate, file, index, itemize, note, record, register, schedule, set down, tabulate, write down

list[2] **1.** *vb.* cant, careen, heel, heel over, incline, lean, tilt, tip **2.** *n.* cant, leaning, slant, tilt

listen 1. attend, be all ears, be attentive, give ear, hang on (someone's) words, hark, hear, hearken (*archaic*), keep one's ears open, lend an ear, pin back one's ears (*informal*), prick up one's ears **2.** concentrate, do as one is told, give heed to, heed, mind, obey, observe, pay attention, take notice

listless apathetic, enervated, heavy, impassive, inattentive, indifferent, indolent, inert, languid, languishing, lethargic, lifeless, limp, lymphatic, mopish, sluggish, spiritless, supine, torpid, vacant

literacy ability, articulacy, articulateness, cultivation, education, knowledge, learning, proficiency, scholarship

literal 1. accurate, close, exact, faithful, strict, verbatim, word for word **2.** boring, colourless, down-to-earth, dull, factual, matter-of-fact, prosaic, prosy, unimaginative, uninspired **3.** actual, bona fide, genuine,

ly". It is very loosely used to mean "just about" but this can be ambiguous.

literalism *n* the tendency to take words and statements in their literal sense. **literalist** *n*

literary *adj* **1** of or characteristic of literature: *literary criticism.* **2** knowledgeable about literature. **3** (of a word) used chiefly in written work; not colloquial. **literariness** *n*

literate *adj* **1** able to read and write. **2** educated. ~*n* **3** a literate person.

literati *pl n* literary or scholarly people.

literature *n* **1** written material such as poetry, novels, or essays. **2** the body of written work of a particular culture, people, or era: *Elizabethan literature.* **3** written or printed matter of a particular type or genre: *medical literature.* **4** the art or profession of a writer. **5** *Informal* printed matter on any subject.

lithe *adj* attractively graceful and supple in movement.

lithium *n Chem* a soft silvery element of the alkali metal series: the lightest known metal. Symbol: Li

litho *n, pl* **-thos,** *adj, adv* short for **lithography, lithograph, lithographic** or **lithographically.**

lithograph *n* **1** a print made by lithography. ~*vb* **2** to reproduce (pictures or text) by lithography. **lithographic** *adj* **lithographically** *adv*

lithography (lith-**og**-ra-fee) *n* a method of printing from a metal or stone surface on which the printing areas are made ink-receptive. **lithographer** *n*

Lithuanian *adj* **1** from Lithuania. ~*n* **2** a person from Lithuania. **3** the language of Lithuania.

litigant *n* a person involved in a lawsuit.

litigate *vb* **-gating, -gated 1** to bring or contest a lawsuit. **2** to engage in legal proceedings. **litigator** *n*

litigation *n* the process of bringing or contesting a lawsuit.

litigious (lit-**ij**-uss) *adj* frequently going to law.

litmus *n* a soluble powder obtained from lichens, which is turned red by acids and blue by alkalis. Paper treated with it (**litmus paper**) is used as an indicator in chemistry.

litmus test *n* something which is regarded as a simple and accurate test of a particular thing, for instance a person's attitude to an issue.

litotes *n, pl* **-tes** understatement used for effect, for example "She was not a little upset" meaning "She was extremely upset".

litre *or US* **liter** *n* a measure of volume equivalent to 1 cubic decimetre.

litter *n* **1** small items of rubbish carelessly dropped in public places. **2** a disordered or untidy collection of objects. **3** a group of animals produced at one birth. **4** straw or hay used as bedding for animals. **5** dry material used to line a receptacle in which a domestic cat can urinate and defecate. **6** (esp. formerly) a bed or seat held between parallel poles and used for carrying people. ~*vb* **7** to strew with litter. **8** to scatter or be scattered in an untidy fashion. **9** (of animals) to give birth to offspring. **10** to provide (an animal) with straw or hay for bedding.

litter lout *or US & Canad* **litterbug** *n Slang* a person who drops refuse in public places.

little *adj* **1** of small or less than average size. **2** young: *a little boy.* **3** endearingly familiar: *he was a sweet little man.* **4** contemptible, mean, or disagreeable: *some of my best friends were little squirts.* **5** a small quantity, extent, or duration of: *there was little money circulating; I could see little evidence of it.* ~*adv* **6** (usually preceded by *a*) to a small extent or degree; not a lot: *to sleep a little.* **7** not at all, or hardly: *army life varied little as the years passed.* **8** not much or often: *we go there very little now.* **9 little by little** by small degrees. ~*n* **10 make little of** to treat as insignificant. **11 think little of** to have a low opinion of. ~See also **less, lesser, least.**

little people *pl n Folklore* small supernatural beings, such as elves.

littoral *adj* **1** of or by the shore. ~*n* **2** a coastal region.

liturgy *n, pl* **-gies** the forms of public services officially prescribed by a Church. **liturgical** *adj*

livable *or* **liveable** *adj* (foll. by *with*) tolerable or pleasant to live (with).

live[1] *vb* **living, lived 1** to show the characteristics of life; be alive. **2** to remain alive or in existence. **3** to exist in a specified way: *to live at ease.* **4** to have one's home: *they live in London.* **5** to continue or last: *his childhood had always lived inside him.* **6** (foll. by *on, upon* or *by*) to support one's style of life: *forest dwellers who live by extracting rubber.* **7** (foll. by *with*) to endure the effects (of a crime or mistake); tolerate. **8** to pass or spend (one's life). **9** to enjoy life to the full: *he likes to live every day to the full.* **10** to put into practice in one's daily life: *the freedom to live his own life as he chooses.* **11 live and let live** to be tolerant. ~See also **live down, live in,** etc.

live[2] *adj* **1** alive; living. **2** *Radio, television* transmitted at the time of performance, rather than being prerecorded: *a live broadcast.* **3** actual: *I was able to speak to a real live Hurricane pilot.* **4** (of a record) recorded during a performance. **5** connected to a source of electric power: *a live cable.* **6** of current interest; controversial: *the document has become a live politi-*

THESAURUS

gospel, plain, real, simple, true, unexaggerated, unvarnished

literally actually, exactly, faithfully, plainly, precisely, really, simply, strictly, to the letter, truly, verbatim, word for word

literary bookish, erudite, formal, learned, lettered, literate, scholarly, well-read

literate cultivated, cultured, educated, erudite, informed, knowledgeable, learned, lettered, scholarly, well-informed, well-read

literature 1. belles-lettres, letters, lore, writings, written works **2.** *informal* brochure, information, leaflet, mailshot, pamphlet

lithe flexible, limber, lissom(e), loose-jointed, loose-limbed, pliable, pliant, supple

litigant claimant, contestant, disputant, litigator, party, plaintiff

litigate contest at law, file a suit, go to court, go to law, institute legal proceedings, press charges, prosecute, sue

litigation action, case, contending, disputing, lawsuit, process, prosecution

litter *n.* **1.** debris, detritus, fragments, garbage (*U.S.*), muck, refuse, rubbish, shreds **2.** clutter, confusion, disarray, disorder, jumble, mess, scatter, untidiness **3.** brood, family, offspring, progeny, young **4.** bedding, couch, floor cover, mulch, straw-bed **5.** palanquin, stretcher ~*vb.* **6.** clutter, derange, disarrange, disorder, mess up, scatter, strew

little *adj.* **1.** diminutive, dwarf, elfin, infinitesimal, Lilliputian, mini, miniature, minute, petite, pygmy *or* pigmy, short, slender, small, teensy-weensy, teeny-weeny, tiny, wee **2.** babyish, immature, infant, junior, undeveloped, young **3.** base, cheap, illiberal, mean, narrow-minded, petty, small-minded **4.** brief, fleeting, hardly any, hasty, inconsiderable, insignificant, insufficient, meagre, measly, negligible, paltry, passing, scant, short, short-lived, skimpy, small, sparse ~*adv.* **5.**

cal issue. **7** loaded or capable of exploding: *a live firing exercise with a 4.5in gun.* **8** (of a coal or ember) glowing or burning. *~adv* **9** during, at, or in the form of a live performance.

live down *vb* to withstand people's reactions to a crime or mistake until they forget it.

live in *vb* **1** to have one's home at the place where one works. *~adj* **live-in 2** resident: *a live-in nanny is a must; her live-in girlfriend.*

livelihood *n* one's job or other source of income.

livelong (liv-long) *adj Chiefly poetic* long or seemingly long: *all the livelong day.*

lively *adj* **-lier, -liest 1** full of life or vigour. **2** vivacious or animated. **3** vivid. **liveliness** *n*

liven *vb* (usually foll. by *up*) to make or become lively; enliven.

liver[1] *n* **1** a large glandular organ which secretes bile, balances nutrients, and removes certain poisons from the body. **2** the liver of certain animals used as food.

liver[2] *n* a person who lives in a specified way: *a fast liver.*

liveried *adj* wearing livery.

liverish *adj* **1** *Informal* having a disorder of the liver. **2** feeling disagreeable and slightly irritable.

Liverpudlian *adj* **1** of Liverpool, a city in NW England. *~n* **2** a person from Liverpool.

liver sausage *n* a sausage containing liver.

liverwort *n* a plant growing in wet places and resembling green seaweeds or leafy mosses.

livery *n, pl* **-eries 1** the identifying uniform of a servant. **2** distinctive dress or outward appearance. **3** the stabling, keeping, or hiring out of horses for money.

lives *n* the plural of **life.**

livestock *n* animals kept on a farm.

live together *vb* (of an unmarried couple) to live in the same house; cohabit.

live up to *vb* to fulfil (an expectation, obligation, or principle).

live wire *n* **1** *Informal* an energetic person. **2** a wire carrying an electric current.

livid *adj* **1** *Informal* extremely angry. **2** of a dark grey or purple colour: *livid bruises.*

living *adj* **1** possessing life; not dead or inanimate. **2** currently in use or valid: *a living alliance.* **3** seeming to be real: *a living doll.* **4** (of people or animals) existing in the present age. **5** very: *the living image.* **6** of or like everyday life: *living costs.* **7** of or involving those now alive: *one of our greatest living actors. ~n* **8** the condition of being alive. **9** the manner of one's life: *high living.* **10** one's financial means. **11** *Church of England* a benefice.

living room *n* a room in a private house or flat used for relaxation and entertainment.

living wage *n* a wage adequate for a worker to live on and support a family in reasonable comfort.

lizard *n* a reptile with an elongated body, four limbs, and a long tail.

ll. lines (of written matter).

llama *n* a South American mammal of the camel family, that is used as a beast of burden and is valued for its woolly fleece.

LLB Bachelor of Laws.

lo *interj Old-fashioned* look! see!: *lo and behold.*

loach *n* a freshwater fish with a long narrow body and barbels around the mouth.

load *n* **1** something to be borne or conveyed; weight. **2** the amount borne or conveyed. **3** something that weighs down or burdens: *I have enough of a load to carry right now.* **4** *Electronics* the power delivered by a machine, generator, or circuit. **5** an external force applied to a component or mechanism. **6 a load of** *Informal* a quantity of: *a load of half-truths.* **7 get a load of** *Informal* to pay attention to. *~vb* **8** to place cargo or goods upon (a ship or vehicle). **9** to burden or oppress. **10** to supply in abundance: *other treats are loaded with fat.* **11** to cause to be biased: *the dice are loaded.* **12** to put ammunition into (a firearm). **13** *Photog* to insert film in (a camera). **14** to weight or

THESAURUS

barely, hardly, not much, not quite, only just, scarcely **6.** hardly ever, not often, rarely, seldom **7. little by little** bit by bit, by degrees, gradually, imperceptibly, piecemeal, progressively, slowly, step by step

live[1] *vb.* **1.** be, be alive, breathe, draw breath, exist, have life **2.** be permanent, be remembered, last, persist, prevail, remain alive **3.** abide, dwell, hang out (*informal*), inhabit, lodge, occupy, reside, settle, stay (*chiefly Scot.*) **4.** abide, continue, earn a living, endure, fare, feed, get along, lead, make ends meet, pass, remain, subsist, support oneself, survive **5.** be happy, enjoy life, flourish, luxuriate, make the most of life, prosper, thrive

live[2] *adj.* **1.** alive, animate, breathing, existent, living, vital **2.** active, burning, controversial, current, hot, pertinent, pressing, prevalent, topical, unsettled, vital **3.** active, alight, blazing, burning, connected, glowing, hot, ignited, smouldering, switched on

livelihood employment, job, living, maintenance, means, (means of) support, occupation, (source of) income, subsistence, sustenance, work

liveliness activity, animation, boisterousness, brio, briskness, dynamism, energy, gaiety, quickness, smartness, spirit, sprightliness, vitality, vivacity

lively 1. active, agile, alert, brisk, chirpy (*informal*), energetic, full of pep (*informal*), keen, nimble, perky, quick, sprightly, spry, vigorous **2.** animated, blithe, blithesome, cheerful, chirpy (*informal*), frisky, frolicsome, gay, merry, sparkling, sparky, spirited, upbeat (*informal*), vivacious **3.** bright, colourful, exciting, forceful, invigorating, racy, refreshing, stimulating, vivid

liven *usually with* **up** animate, brighten, buck up (*informal*), enliven, hot up (*informal*), pep up, perk up, put life into, rouse, stir, vitalize, vivify

liverish crotchety (*informal*), crusty, disagreeable, grumpy, ill-humoured, irascible, irritable, peevish, ratty (*Brit. informal*), snappy, splenetic, tetchy

livery attire, clothing, costume, dress, garb, raiment (*archaic or poetic*), regalia, suit, uniform, vestments

live wire *informal* ball of fire (*informal*), dynamo, go-getter (*informal*), hustler (*U.S. informal*), life and soul of the party, self-starter

livid 1. *informal* angry, beside oneself, boiling, cross, enraged, exasperated, fuming, furious, incensed, indignant, infuriated, mad (*informal*), outraged **2.** angry, black-and-blue, bruised, contused, discoloured, purple

living *adj.* **1.** active, alive, animated, breathing, existing, in the land of the living (*informal*), lively, strong, vigorous, vital **2.** active, contemporary, continuing, current, developing, extant, in use, ongoing, operative, persisting *~n.* **3.** animation, being, existence, existing, life, subsistence **4.** life style, mode of living, way of life **5.** job, livelihood, maintenance, (means of) support, occupation, (source of) income, subsistence, sustenance, work **6.** *Church of England* benefice, incumbency, stipend

load *n.* **1.** bale, cargo, consignment, freight, lading, shipment **2.** affliction, burden, encumbrance, incubus, millstone, onus, oppression, pressure, trouble, weight,

bias (a roulette wheel or dice). **15** *Computers* to transfer (a program) to a memory. ~See also **loads. loader** *n*

loaded *adj* **1** carrying a load. **2** charged with ammunition. **3** (of a question or statement) containing a hidden trap or implication. **4** (of dice or a roulette wheel) weighted or otherwise biased. **5** *Slang* wealthy. **6** *Slang, chiefly US & Canad* drunk.

loads *pl n Informal* (often foll. by *of*) a lot.

loadstar *n* same as **lodestar.**

loadstone *n* same as **lodestone.**

loaf[1] *n, pl* **loaves 1** a shaped mass of baked bread. **2** any shaped or moulded mass of food, such as cooked meat. **3** *Slang* the head; common sense: *use your loaf!*

loaf[2] *vb* to loiter or lounge around in an idle way.

loafer *n* **1** a person who avoids work; idler. **2** *Chiefly US & Canad* a moccasin-like shoe.

loam *n* fertile soil consisting of sand, clay, and decaying organic material. **loamy** *adj*

loan *n* **1** money lent at interest for a fixed period of time. **2** the act of lending: *I am grateful to her for the loan of her book.* **3** property lent. **4 on loan** lent out; borrowed. ~*vb* **5** to lend (something, esp. money).

loan shark *n* a person who lends money at an extremely high interest rate, esp. illegally.

loath *or* **loth** (rhymes with **both**) *adj* (usually foll. by *to*) reluctant or unwilling.

➤ Distinguish between *loath* "reluctant" and *loathe* "be disgusted by".

loathe *vb* **loathing, loathed** to feel strong disgust for.

loathing *n* strong disgust.

loathsome *adj* causing loathing.

loaves *n* the plural of **loaf**[1].

lob *Sport* ~*n* **1** a ball struck or bowled in a high arc. ~*vb* **lobbing, lobbed 2** to hit or kick (a ball) in a high arc. **3** *Informal* to throw.

lobar (**loh**-ber) *adj* of or affecting a lobe.

lobate *adj* with or like lobes.

lobby *n, pl* **-bies 1** a room or corridor used as an entrance hall or vestibule. **2** a group which attempts to influence legislators on behalf of a particular interest. **3** *Chiefly Brit* a hall in a legislative building used for meetings between legislators and members of the public. **4** *Chiefly Brit* one of two corridors in a legislative building in which members vote. ~*vb* **-bies, -bying, -bied 5** to attempt to influence (legislators) in the formulation of policy.

lobbyist *n* a person who lobbies on behalf of a particular interest.

lobe *n* **1** any rounded projection. **2** the fleshy lower part of the external ear. **3** any subdivision of a bodily organ.

lobelia *n* a plant with blue, red, white, or yellow five-lobed flowers.

lobola *n* (in southern Africa) an African custom by which a bridegroom's family makes a payment in cattle or cash to the bride's family shortly before the marriage.

lobotomy *n, pl* **-mies** the surgical cutting of nerves in the frontal lobe of the brain to treat severe mental disorders.

lobscouse *n* a sailor's stew of meat, vegetables, and hardtack.

lobster *n, pl* **-sters** *or* **-ster 1** a large edible crustacean with large pincers and a long tail, which turns red when boiled. **2** its edible flesh.

lobster pot *n* a round basket made of open slats, used to catch lobsters.

local *adj* **1** of or concerning a particular area. **2** restricted to a particular place. **3** *Med* of, affecting, or confined to a limited area or part: *a local anaesthetic.* **4** (of a train or bus) stopping at all stations or stops. ~*n* **5** an inhabitant of a specified locality: *we swim, sunbathe, meet the locals, unwind.* **6** *Brit informal* a pub close to one's home. **locally** *adv*

local anaesthetic *n Med* See **anaesthesia.**

local authority *n Brit & NZ* the governing body of a county or district.

locale (loh-**kahl**) *n* the place where something happens or has happened.

local government *n* the government of the affairs of counties, towns, and districts by locally elected political bodies.

locality *n, pl* **-ties 1** a neighbourhood or area. **2** the site or scene of an event.

localize *or* **-ise** *vb* **-izing, -ized** *or* **-ising, -ised** to restrict (something) to a particular place.

locate *vb* **-cating, -cated 1** to discover the whereabouts of; find. **2** to situate or build: *located around the corner from the church.* **3** to become established or settled.

location *n* **1** a site or position; situation. **2** the act of

THESAURUS

worry ~*vb.* **3.** cram, fill, freight, heap, lade, pack, pile, stack, stuff **4.** burden, encumber, hamper, oppress, saddle with, trouble, weigh down, worry **5.** charge, make ready, prepare to fire, prime

loaded 1. burdened, charged, freighted, full, laden, weighted **2.** at the ready, charged, primed, ready to shoot *or* fire **3.** artful, insidious, manipulative, prejudicial, tricky **4.** biased, distorted, weighted **5.** *slang, chiefly U.S. & Canad.* affluent, flush (*informal*), moneyed, rich, rolling (*slang*), wealthy, well-heeled (*informal*), well off, well-to-do

loaf *n.* **1.** block, cake, cube, lump, slab **2.** *slang* block (*informal*), gumption (*Brit. informal*), head, noddle (*informal, chiefly Brit.*), nous (*old-fashioned, slang*), sense

loan 1. *n.* accommodation, advance, allowance, credit, mortgage, touch (*slang*) **2.** *vb.* accommodate, advance, allow, credit, lend, let out

loath, loth against, averse, backward, counter, disinclined, indisposed, opposed, reluctant, resisting, unwilling

loathing abhorrence, abomination, antipathy, aversion, detestation, disgust, execration, hatred, horror, odium, repugnance, repulsion, revulsion

loathsome abhorrent, abominable, detestable, disgusting, execrable, hateful, horrible, nasty, nauseating, obnoxious, obscene, odious, offensive, repugnant, repulsive, revolting, vile, yucky *or* yukky (*slang*)

lobby *n.* **1.** corridor, entrance hall, foyer, hall, hallway, passage, passageway, porch, vestibule **2.** pressure group ~*vb.* **3.** bring pressure to bear, campaign for, exert influence, influence, persuade, press for, pressure, promote, pull strings (*Brit. informal*), push for, solicit votes, urge

local *adj.* **1.** community, district, neighbourhood, parish, provincial, regional **2.** confined, limited, narrow, parochial, provincial, restricted, small-town ~*n.* **3.** inhabitant, native, resident

locality 1. area, district, neck of the woods (*informal*), neighbourhood, region, vicinity **2.** locale, location, place, position, scene, setting, site, spot

localize circumscribe, concentrate, confine, contain, delimit, delimitate, limit, restrain, restrict

locate 1. come across, detect, discover, find, lay

locating or the state of being located: *make their location and rescue a top priority.* **3** a place outside a studio where filming is done: *shot on location.* **4** (in South Africa) a Black African or Coloured township.

loc. cit. (in textual annotation) in the place cited.

loch *n Scot* **1** a lake. **2** a long narrow arm of the sea.

loci (**loh**-sigh) *n* the plural of **locus.**

lock[1] *n* **1** a device for fastening a door, drawer, lid, etc., and preventing unauthorized access. **2** a section of a canal or river closed off by gates between which the water level can be altered to aid boats moving from one level to the next. **3** *Brit* the extent to which a vehicle's front wheels will turn: *they adopted more steering lock.* **4** the interlocking of parts. **5** a mechanism that fires a gun. **6 lock, stock, and barrel** completely; entirely. **7** a wrestling hold. **8** Also called: **lock forward** *Rugby* a player in the second row of the scrum. *~vb* **9** to fasten or become fastened to prevent entry or exit. **10** to secure (a building) by locking all doors and windows. **11** to fix or become fixed together securely. **12** to become or cause to become immovable: *just before your knees lock.* **13** to clasp or entangle in a struggle or embrace. ~See also **lock out, lock up.**

lock[2] *n* **1** a strand or curl of hair. **2** (*pl*) *Chiefly literary* hair.

locker *n* a small compartment with a lock, used for temporarily storing clothes, valuables, or luggage.

locket *n* a small hinged ornamental pendant that holds a picture or keepsake.

lockjaw *n Pathol* a nontechnical name for **trismus** or **tetanus.**

lock out *vb* **1** to prevent from entering by locking a door. **2** to prevent (employees) from working during an industrial dispute, by shutting them out of the premises. *~n* **lockout 3** the closing of a place of employment by an employer, in order to force employees to accept terms.

locksmith *n* a person who makes or repairs locks.

lock up *vb* **1** to imprison. **2** to secure a building by locking all the doors and windows. *~n* **lockup 3** a jail. **4** *Brit* a garage or store separate from the main premises. **5** *Brit* a small shop with no attached quarters for the owner. *~adj* **lock-up 6** *Brit & NZ* (of premises) without living quarters: *a lock-up garage.*

loco[1] *n Informal* a locomotive.

loco[2] *adj Slang, chiefly US* insane.

locomotion *n* the act or power of moving.

locomotive *n* **1** a self-propelled engine for pulling trains. *~adj* **2** of locomotion.

locum *n Chiefly Brit* a person who stands in temporarily for a doctor or clergyman.

locus (**loh**-kuss) *n, pl* **loci 1** an area or place where something happens. **2** *Maths* a set of points or lines whose location satisfies or is determined by one or more specified conditions: *the locus of points equidistant from a given point is a circle.*

locust *n* **1** an African insect, related to the grasshopper, which travels in vast swarms, stripping large areas of vegetation. **2** a North American leguminous tree with prickly branches; the carob tree.

locution *n* **1** manner or style of speech. **2** a word, phrase, or expression.

lode *n* a vein of metallic ore.

lodestar *n* **1** a star, esp. the North Star, used in navigation or astronomy as a point of reference. **2** something that serves as a guide.

lodestone *n* **1 a** magnetic iron ore. **b** a piece of this, used as a magnet. **2** a person or thing regarded as a focus of attraction.

lodge *n* **1** *Chiefly Brit* the gatekeeper's house at the entrance to the grounds of a country mansion. **2** a house or cabin used occasionally by hunters, skiers, etc.: *a hunting lodge.* **3** a room used by porters in a university or college. **4** a local branch of certain societies. **5** a beaver's home. *~vb* **lodging, lodged 6** to provide or be provided with rented accommodation. **7** to live temporarily in rented accommodation. **8** to embed or be embedded: *the bullet lodged in his brain.* **9** to leave for safety or storage: *a report was lodged with the local police station.* **10** to bring (a charge or accusation) against someone: *the Brazilians lodged a complaint.* **11** (often foll. by *in* or *with*) to place (authority or power) in the control (of someone).

lodger *n* a person who pays rent in return for accommodation in someone else's home.

lodging *n* **1** a temporary residence: *where might I find a night's lodging?* **2** (*pl*) a rented room or rooms in another person's home.

loess (**loh**-iss) *n* a fine-grained soil, found mainly in river valleys, originally deposited by the wind.

loft *n* **1** the space inside a roof. **2** a gallery in a church. **3** a room over a stable used to store hay. **4** a raised house or coop in which pigeons are kept. **5** *Golf* **a** the angle of the face of the club used to elevate a ball. **b** the height reached by a struck ball. *~vb* **6** *Sport* to strike or kick (a ball) high in the air.

lofty *adj* **loftier, loftiest 1** of majestic or imposing height. **2** morally admirable: *lofty ideals.* **3** unpleasantly superior: *a lofty contempt.* **loftily** *adv* **loftiness** *n*

log[1] *n* **1** a section of a felled tree stripped of branches. **2 a** a detailed record of a voyage of a ship or aircraft. **b** a record of the hours flown by pilots and aircrews. **c** a book in which these records are made; logbook. **3** a device consisting of a float with an attached line, formerly used to measure the speed of a ship. **4 sleep like a log** to sleep without stirring. *~vb* **logging,**

THESAURUS

one's hands on, pin down, pinpoint, run to earth, track down, unearth **2.** establish, fix, place, put, seat, set, settle, situate

location bearings, locale, locus, place, point, position, site, situation, spot, venue, whereabouts

lock[1] *n.* **1.** bolt, clasp, fastening, padlock *~vb.* **2.** bolt, close, fasten, latch, seal, secure, shut **3.** clench, engage, entangle, entwine, join, link, mesh, unite **4.** clasp, clutch, embrace, encircle, enclose, grapple, grasp, hug, press

lock[2] curl, ringlet, strand, tress, tuft

lock out ban, bar, debar, exclude, keep out, refuse admittance to, shut out

lock up cage, confine, detain, imprison, incarcerate, jail, put behind bars, shut up

lockup cell, gaol, jail, police cell

lodge *n.* **1.** cabin, chalet, cottage, gatehouse, house, hunting lodge, hut, shelter **2.** assemblage, association, branch, chapter, club, group, society **3.** den, haunt, lair, retreat *~vb.* **4.** accommodate, billet, board, entertain, harbour, put up, quarter, room, shelter, sojourn, stay, stop **5.** become fixed, catch, come to rest, imbed, implant, stick **6.** deposit, file, lay, place, put, put on record, register, set, submit

lodger boarder, guest, paying guest, resident, roomer, tenant

lodging *plural* abode, accommodation, apartments, boarding, digs (*Brit. informal*), dwelling, habitation, quarters, residence, rooms, shelter

lofty 1. elevated, high, raised, sky-high, soaring, tall, towering **2.** dignified, distinguished, elevated, exalted, grand, illustrious, imposing, majestic, noble, renowned, stately, sublime, superior **3.** arrogant, conde-

logged **5** to saw logs from (trees). **6** to enter (a distance or event) in a logbook or log. ~See also **log in, log out.**

log² *n* short for **logarithm.**

loganberry *n, pl* **-ries** a purplish-red fruit, similar to a raspberry, that grows on a trailing prickly plant.

logarithm *n* the exponent indicating the power to which a fixed number, the base, must be raised to obtain a given number or variable. **logarithmic** *adj*

logbook *n* **1** a book containing the official record of trips made by a ship or aircraft. **2** *Brit informal* the registration document of a car.

loggerhead *n* **1** a large-headed turtle occurring in most seas. **2 at loggerheads** engaged in dispute or confrontation.

loggia (loj-ya) *n* a covered gallery on the side of a building.

logging *n* the work of felling, trimming, and transporting timber. **logger** *n*

logic *n* **1** the branch of philosophy that analyses the patterns of reasoning. **2** a particular system of reasoning. **3** reasoned thought or argument, as distinguished from irrationality. **4** the interdependence of a series of events or facts. **5** *Electronics, computers* the principles underlying the units in a computer system that produce results from data.

logical *adj* **1** relating to or characteristic of logic. **2** using or deduced from the principles of logic: *a logical conclusion.* **3** capable of or using clear and valid reasoning. **4** reasonable because of facts or events: *the logical choice.* **logically** *adv*

logician *n* a person who specializes in or is skilled at logic.

log in *vb* to gain entrance to a computer system by keying in a special command.

logistics *n* the detailed planning and organization of a large complex operation, such as a military campaign. **logistical** *or* **logistic** *adj* **logistically** *adv*

log jam *n Chiefly US & Canad* **1** a blockage caused by the crowding together of logs floating in a river. **2** a deadlock.

logo (loh-go) *n, pl* **-os** a special design that identifies a company or an organization and appears on all its products, printed material, etc.

log out *vb* to exit from a computer system by keying in a special command.

-logy *n combining form* **1** indicating the science or study of: *musicology.* **2** indicating writing or discourse: *trilogy; phraseology.* **-logical** *or* **-logic** *adj combining form* **-logist** *n combining form*

loin *n* **1** the part of the body between the pelvis and the ribs. **2** a cut of meat from this part of an animal. ~See also **loins.**

loincloth *n* a piece of cloth covering only the loins.

loins *pl n* **1** the hips and the inner surface of the legs where they join the body. **2** *Euphemistic* the genitals.

loiter *vb* to stand or wait aimlessly or idly.

loll *vb* **1** to lounge in a lazy manner. **2** to hang loosely: *a wet lolling tongue; his head lolled back and forth.*

lollipop *n* **1** a boiled sweet stuck on a small wooden stick. **2** *Brit* an ice lolly.

lollipop man *or* **lady** *n Brit informal* a person holding a circular sign on a pole who stops traffic to enable children to cross the road safely.

lollop *vb Chiefly Brit* to walk or run with a clumsy or relaxed bouncing movement.

lolly *n, pl* **-lies** **1** *Informal* a lollipop. **2** *Brit* short for **ice lolly.** **3** *Brit, Austral, & NZ slang* money. **4** *Austral & NZ informal* a sweet.

Londoner *n* a person from London.

London pride *n* a rock plant with a rosette of leaves and pink flowers.

lone *adj* **1** solitary: *a lone figure.* **2** isolated: *a lone isle guarded by the great Atlantic swell.* **3** unmarried or widowed: *a lone parent.*

lonely *adj* **-lier, -liest** **1** unhappy as a result of solitude. **2** resulting from the state of being alone: *command can be a lonely business.* **3** isolated and not much visited by people: *a lonely beach.* **loneliness** *n*

lonely hearts *adj* of or for people seeking a congenial companion or marriage partner: *lonely hearts ads.*

loner *n Informal* a person who prefers to be alone.

lonesome *adj* **1** *Chiefly US & Canad* lonely. **2** causing feelings of loneliness: *it was lonesome up here on the mountain.*

long¹ *adj* **1** having relatively great length in space or time. **2** having greater than the average or expected range, extent, or duration: *a long session of talks.* **3** seeming to occupy a greater time than is really so: *she was quiet a long moment.* **4** of a specified extent or duration: *trimmed to about two cms long.* **5** consisting of a large number of parts: *a long list.* **6** *Phonetics, prosody* (of a vowel) of relatively considerable duration. **7** from end to end; lengthwise. **8** *Finance* having large holdings of securities or commodities in anticipation of rising prices. **9 in the long run** ultimately; after or over a period of time. **10 long on** *Informal* plentifully supplied or endowed with: *long on show-biz gossip.* ~*adv* **11** for a certain time or period: *how long have we got?* **12** for or during an extensive period of time: *to talk long into the night.* **13** a considerable amount of time: *long after I met you; long ago.* **14 as** *or* **so long as a** for or during the same length of time

THESAURUS

scending, disdainful, haughty, high and mighty (*informal*), lordly, patronizing, proud, snooty (*informal*), supercilious, toffee-nosed (*slang, chiefly Brit.*)

log *n.* **1.** block, bole, chunk, piece of timber, stump, trunk **2.** account, chart, daybook, journal, listing, logbook, record, tally ~*vb.* **3.** chop, cut, fell, hew **4.** book, chart, make a note of, note, record, register, report, set down, tally

loggerhead **at loggerheads** at daggers drawn, at each other's throats, at enmity, at odds, estranged, feuding, in dispute, opposed, quarrelling

logic **1.** argumentation, deduction, dialectics, ratiocination, science of reasoning, syllogistic reasoning **2.** good reason, good sense, reason, sense, sound judgment **3.** chain of thought, coherence, connection, link, rationale, relationship

logical **1.** clear, cogent, coherent, consistent, deducible, pertinent, rational, reasonable, relevant, sound, valid, well-organized **2.** judicious, most likely, necessary, obvious, plausible, reasonable, sensible, wise

loiter dally, dawdle, delay, dilly dally (*informal*), hang about *or* around, idle, lag, linger, loaf, loll, saunter, skulk, stroll

loll **1.** flop, lean, loaf, lounge, recline, relax, slouch, slump, sprawl **2.** dangle, droop, drop, flap, flop, hang, hang loosely, sag

lone by oneself, deserted, isolated, lonesome, one, only, separate, separated, single, sole, solitary, unaccompanied

loneliness aloneness, desertedness, desolation, dreariness, forlornness, isolation, lonesomeness, seclusion, solitariness, solitude

lonely **1.** abandoned, destitute, estranged, forlorn, forsaken, friendless, lonesome, outcast **2.** alone, apart, by oneself, companionless, isolated, lone, single, solitary, withdrawn **3.** deserted, desolate, godforsaken,

that. **b** provided that; if. ~*n* **15** anything that is long. **16 before long** soon. **17 for long** for a long time. **18 the long and the short of it** the essential points or facts. **longish** *adj*

long[2] *vb* to have a strong desire for something or to do something: *the more I think of him the more I long to see him.*

long. longitude.

long- *adv* (*in combination*) for or lasting a long time: *long-established; long-lasting.*

longboat *n* **1** the largest boat carried aboard a commercial ship. **2** same as **longship.**

longbow *n* a large powerful hand-drawn bow.

long-distance *adj* **1** covering relatively long distances: *a long-distance race.* **2** (of telephone calls) connecting points relatively far apart.

longevity (lon-**jev**-it-ee) *n* long life.

long face *n* a glum expression.

longhand *n* ordinary handwriting, as opposed to typing or shorthand.

longing *n* **1** a strong feeling of wanting something one is unlikely ever to have. ~*adj* **2** having or showing desire: *longing glances.* **longingly** *adv*

longitude *n* distance in degrees east or west of the prime meridian at 0°.

longitudinal *adj* **1** of longitude or length. **2** placed or extended lengthways.

long johns *pl n Informal* long underpants.

long jump *n* an athletic contest of jumping the greatest length from a fixed mark.

long-life *adj* (of milk, batteries, etc.) lasting longer than the regular kind.

long-lived *adj* living or lasting for a long time.

long-playing *adj Old-fashioned* of or relating to an LP.

long-range *adj* **1** of or extending into the future: *a long-range economic forecast.* **2** (of vehicles, aircraft, or weapons) capable of covering great distances.

longship *n* a narrow open boat with oars and a square sail, used by the Vikings.

longshore drift *n* the movement of material along a beach, due to waves approaching the shore at an oblique angle.

longshoreman *n, pl* **-men** *US & Canad* a docker.

long shot *n* **1** an undertaking, guess, or possibility with little chance of success. **2** a bet against heavy odds. **3 not by a long shot** not by any means: *she wasn't beaten, not by a long shot.*

long-sighted *adj* **1** able to see only distant objects in focus. **2** far-sighted.

long-standing *adj* existing for a long time.

long-suffering *adj* enduring trouble or unhappiness without complaint.

long-term *adj* **1** lasting or extending over a long time: *a long-term commitment.* ~*n* **long term 2 in the long term** over a long period of time: *in the long term the cost of energy will have to go up.*

longtime *adj* of long standing: *his longtime colleague.*

long wave *n* a radio wave with a wavelength greater than 1000 metres.

longways *or US & Canad* **longwise** *adv* lengthways.

long-winded *adj* tiresomely long. **long-windedness** *n*

loo *n, pl* **loos** *Brit informal* a toilet.

loofah *n* a long rough-textured bath sponge made from the dried pod of a gourd.

look *vb* **1** (often foll. by *at*) to direct the eyes (towards): *he turned to look at her.* **2** (often foll. by *at*) to consider: *we shall now have a look at some problems.* **3** to give the impression of being; seem: *Luxembourg's timetable looks a winner.* **4** to face in a particular direction: *Morgan's Rock looks south.* **5** (foll. by *for*) to search or seek: *the department looks for reputable firms.* **6** (foll. by *into*) to carry out an investigation. **7** to direct a look at (someone) in a specified way: *she looks at Teresina suspiciously.* **8** to match in appearance with (something): *looking your best.* **9** to expect or hope (to do something): *we would look to derive a procedure that would account for most cases.* **10 look alive, lively, sharp,** *or* **smart** to hurry up; get busy. **11 look here** an expression used to attract someone's attention or add emphasis to a statement. ~*n* **12** an instance of looking: *a look of icy contempt.* **13** a view or sight (of something): *take a look at my view.* **14** (*often pl*) appearance to the eye or mind; aspect: *I'm not happy with the look of things here; better than you by the looks of it.* **15** style or fashion: *the look made famous by the great Russian.* ~*conj* **16** an expression demanding attention or showing annoyance: *look, I*

THESAURUS

isolated, off the beaten track (*informal*), out-of-the-way, remote, secluded, sequestered, solitary, unfrequented, uninhabited

long[1] *adj.* **1.** elongated, expanded, extended, extensive, far-reaching, lengthy, spread out, stretched **2.** dragging, interminable, late, lengthy, lingering, long-drawn-out, prolonged, protracted, slow, sustained, tardy

long[2] covet, crave, desire, dream of, eat one's heart out over, hanker, hunger, itch, lust, pine, want, wish, yearn

longing 1. *n.* ambition, aspiration, coveting, craving, desire, hankering, hope, hungering, itch, thirst, urge, wish, yearning, yen (*informal*) **2.** *adj.* anxious, ardent, avid, craving, desirous, eager, hungry, languishing, pining, wishful, wistful, yearning

long-lived enduring, full of years, long-lasting, old as Methuselah

long-standing abiding, enduring, established, fixed, hallowed by time, long-established, long-lasting, long-lived, time-honoured

long-suffering easygoing, forbearing, forgiving, patient, resigned, stoical, tolerant, uncomplaining

long-winded diffuse, discursive, garrulous, lengthy, long-drawn-out, overlong, prolix, prolonged, rambling, repetitious, tedious, verbose, wordy

look *vb.* **1.** *often with* **at** behold (*archaic or literary*), check, check out (*informal*), clock (*Brit. slang*), consider, contemplate, examine, eye, feast one's eyes upon, gape, gawk, gawp, gaze (*Brit. slang*), get a load of (*informal*), glance, glower, goggle, inspect, observe, ogle, peep, recce (*slang*), regard, rubberneck (*slang*), scan, scrutinize, see, stare, study, survey, take a dekko at (*Brit. slang*), take a gander at (*informal*), view, watch **2.** appear, display, evidence, exhibit, look like, make clear, manifest, present, seem, seem to be, show, strike one as **3.** face, front, front on, give onto, overlook **4.** *with* **for** forage, hunt, search, seek **5.** anticipate, await, expect, hope, reckon on ~*n.* **6.** examination, eyeful (*informal*), gander (*informal*), gaze, glance, glimpse, inspection, look-see (*slang*), observation, once-over (*informal*), peek, recce (*slang*), review, shufti (*Brit. slang*), sight, squint (*informal*), survey, view **7.** air, appearance, aspect, bearing, cast, complexion, countenance, demeanour, effect, expression, face, fashion, guise, manner, mien (*literary*), semblance

won't be coming back. ~See also **look after, look back**, etc. **looker** *n*

look after *vb* to take care of.

lookalike *n* a person or thing that is the double of another, often well-known, person or thing.

look back *vb* **1** to think about the past. **2 never looked back** was extremely successful: *he became the station's first major signing and never looked back.*

look down *vb* (foll. by *on* or *upon*) to treat as inferior or unimportant.

look forward to *vb* to anticipate with pleasure.

look-in *Informal* ~*n* **1** a chance to be chosen or participate: *before anyone else gets a look-in.* ~*vb* **look in 2** to pay a short visit.

looking glass *n* a mirror.

look on *vb* **1** to be a spectator. **2** to consider or regard: *I just looked on her as a friend.* **looker-on** *n*

lookout *n* **1** the act of watching for danger or for an opportunity: *on the lookout for attack.* **2** a person or people keeping such a watch. **3** a viewpoint from which a watch is kept. **4** *Informal* worry or concern: *that is my lookout rather than theirs.* **5** *Chiefly Brit* chances or prospect: *it's a bad lookout for Europe.* ~*vb* **look out 6** to be careful. **7** to watch out for: *look out particularly for oils that have been flavoured.* **8** to find and take out: *little time to look out clothes that she might need.* **9** (foll. by *on* or *over*) to face in a particular direction: *looking out over the courtyard.*

look over *vb* **1** to inspect or examine. ~*n* **look-over 2** an inspection.

look-see *n Slang* a brief inspection.

look up *vb* **1** to discover or confirm by checking in a reference book. **2** to improve: *things were looking up.* **3 look up to** to have respect for: *she looked up to him as a kind of father.* **4** to visit (a person): *I'll look you up when I'm in town.*

loom[1] *n* a machine for weaving yarn into cloth.

loom[2] *vb* **1** to appear indistinctly, esp. as a tall and threatening shape. **2** (of an event) to seem ominously close.

loon *n US & Canad* same as **diver** (sense 3).

loony *Slang* ~*adj* **loonier, looniest 1** insane. **2** foolish or ridiculous. ~*n, pl* **loonies 3** a foolish or insane person.

loop *n* **1** the rounded shape formed by a curved line that crosses itself: *a loop of the highway.* **2** any round or oval-shaped thing that is closed or nearly closed. **3** *Electronics* a closed circuit through which a signal can circulate. **4** a flight manoeuvre in which an aircraft flies vertically in a complete circle. **5** a continuous strip of film or tape. **6** *Computers* a series of instructions in a program, performed repeatedly until some specified condition is satisfied. ~*vb* **7** to make into a loop. **8** to fasten or encircle with a loop. **9** Also: **loop the loop** to fly or be flown vertically in a complete circle.

loophole *n* an ambiguity or omission in the law, which enables one to evade it.

loopy *adj* **loopier, loopiest** *Informal* slightly mad or crazy.

loose *adj* **1** (of clothing) not close-fitting: *the jacket loose and unbuttoned.* **2** free or released from confinement or restraint. **3** not tight, fastened, fixed, or tense. **4** not bundled, fastened, or put in a container: *loose tobacco.* **5** inexact or imprecise: *a loose translation.* **6** (of cash) accessible: *a lot of the loose money is floating around the city.* **7** *Old-fashioned* sexually promiscuous. **8** lacking a sense of propriety: *loose talk.* **9 at a loose end** bored because one has nothing to do. ~*n* **10 the loose** *Rugby* the part of play when the forwards close round the ball in a ruck or loose scrum. **11 on the loose** free from confinement or restraint. ~*adv* **12** in a loose manner; loosely. ~*vb* **loosing, loosed 13** to free or release from restraint or obligation: *he loosed the dogs.* **14** to unfasten or untie: *the guards loosed his arms.* **15** to make or become less strict, tight, firmly attached, or compact. **16** to let fly (a bullet, arrow, or other missile) **loosely** *adv* **looseness** *n*

➤ *Loose* and *lose* are often confused in spelling but rarely in meaning.

loosebox *n* an enclosed stall with a door in which an animal can be kept.

loose cannon *n* a person or thing, with the potential to cause considerable damage, that appears to be beyond customary control.

THESAURUS

look after attend to, care for, guard, keep an eye on, mind, nurse, protect, sit with, supervise, take care of, take charge of, tend, watch

look down *with* **on** *or* **upon** contemn, despise, disdain, hold in contempt, look down one's nose at (*informal*), misprize, scorn, sneer, spurn, treat with contempt, turn one's nose up (at) (*informal*)

look forward to anticipate, await, count on, count the days until, expect, hope for, long for, look for, wait for

lookout 1. guard, readiness, vigil, watch **2.** guard, sentinel, sentry, watchman **3.** beacon, citadel, observation post, observatory, post, tower, watchtower **4.** *informal* business, concern, pigeon (*Brit. informal*), worry **5.** *chiefly Brit.* chances, future, likelihood, outlook, prospect, view

look out be alert, be careful, be on guard, be vigilant, beware, keep an eye out, keep one's eyes open (peeled, skinned), pay attention, watch out

look over cast an eye over, check, check out (*informal*), examine, flick through, inspect, look through, monitor, peruse, scan, take a dekko at (*Brit. slang*), view, work over

look up 1. find, hunt for, research, search for, seek out, track down **2.** ameliorate, come along, get better, improve, perk up, pick up, progress, shape up (*informal*), show improvement **3. look up to** admire, defer to, esteem, have a high opinion of, honour, regard highly, respect, revere **4.** call (on), drop in on (*informal*), go to see, look in on, pay a visit to, visit

loom 1. appear, become visible, bulk large, dominate, emerge, hover, menace, overhang, overshadow, rise, soar, take shape, threaten, tower **2.** be imminent, hang over, impend, threaten

loop 1. *n.* bend, circle, coil, convolution, curl, curve, eyelet, hoop, kink, loophole, noose, ring, spiral, twirl, twist, whorl **2.** *vb.* bend, braid, circle, coil, connect, curl, curve round, encircle, fold, join, knot, roll, spiral, turn, twist, wind round

loophole avoidance, escape, evasion, excuse, let-out, means of escape, plea, pretence, pretext, subterfuge

loose *adj.* **1.** baggy, easy, hanging, loosened, not fitting, not tight, relaxed, slack, slackened, sloppy **2.** floating, free, insecure, movable, released, unattached, unbound, unconfined, unfastened, unfettered, unrestricted, unsecured, untied, wobbly **3.** diffuse, disconnected, disordered, ill-defined, imprecise, inaccurate, indefinite, indistinct, inexact, rambling, random, vague **4.** *old-fashioned* abandoned, debauched, disreputable, dissipated, dissolute, fast, immoral, lewd, libertine, licentious, profligate, promiscuous, unchaste, wanton **5.** careless, heedless, imprudent, lax, negligent, rash, thoughtless, unmindful ~*vb.* **6.** detach, disconnect,

loose-jointed *adj* supple and lithe.

loose-leaf *adj* (of a binder) allowing the removal and addition of pages.

loosen *vb* **1** to make or become less tight: *loosen and relax the ankle.* **2** (often foll. by *up*) to make or become less firm, compact, or rigid: *massage is used first to loosen up the muscles.* **3** to untie. **4** (often foll. by *up*) to make or become less strict: *the churches loosen up on sexual teachings.*

loot *n* **1** goods stolen in wartime or during riots; plunder. **2** *Informal* money. *~vb* **3** to plunder (a city) during war or riots. **4** to steal (money or goods) during war or riots. **looter** *n*

lop *vb* **lopping, lopped** (usually foll. by *off*) **1** to cut (parts) off a tree or body. **2** to cut out or eliminate any unnecessary parts: *some parts of the legislature were lopped off.*

lope *vb* **loping, loped 1** to move or run with a long easy stride. *~n* **2** a long steady gait or stride.

lop-eared *adj* (of animals) having ears that droop.

lopsided *adj* greater in weight, height, or size on one side.

loquacious *adj* talkative. **loquacity** *n*

lord *n* **1** a person with power or authority over others, such as a monarch or master. **2** a male member of the nobility. **3** (in medieval Europe) a feudal superior. **4 my lord** a respectful form of address used to a judge, bishop, or nobleman. *~vb* **5 lord it over someone** to act in a superior manner towards someone.

Lord *n* **1** *Christianity* a title given to God or Jesus Christ. **2** *Brit* a title given to certain male peers. **3** *Brit* a title given to certain high officials and judges. *~interj* **4** an exclamation of dismay or surprise: *Good Lord!*

Lord Chancellor *n Brit government* the cabinet minster who is head of the judiciary and Speaker of the House of Lords.

Lord Chief Justice *n* (in England and Wales) the judge who is second only to the Lord Chancellor and president of one division of the High Court of Justice.

Lord Lieutenant *n* **1** (in Britain) the representative of the Crown in a county. **2** (formerly) the British viceroy in Ireland.

lordly *adj* **-lier, -liest 1** haughty or arrogant. **2** of or suitable to a lord. **lordliness** *n*

Lord Mayor *n* the mayor in the City of London, in certain other English boroughs, and in some Australian cities.

Lord Privy Seal *n* (in Britain) the senior cabinet minister without official duties.

Lords *n* **the** short for **House of Lords.**

lordship *n* the position or authority of a lord.

Lordship *n* (preceded by *Your* or *His*) *Brit* a title used to address or refer to a bishop, a judge of the high court, or any peer except a duke.

Lord's Prayer *n* **the** the prayer taught by Jesus Christ to his disciples.

Lords Spiritual *pl n* (in Britain) the Anglican archbishops and senior bishops who are members of the House of Lords.

Lord's Supper *n* **the** same as **Holy Communion.**

Lords Temporal *pl n* (in Britain) the peers other than bishops in their capacity as members of the House of Lords.

lore *n* collective knowledge or wisdom on a particular subject.

lorgnette (lor-**nyet**) *n* a pair of spectacles or opera glasses mounted on a long handle.

lorry *n, pl* **-ries** a large motor vehicle for transporting heavy loads.

lose *vb* **losing, lost 1** to come to be without, through carelessness or by accident or theft. **2** to fail to keep or maintain: *to lose control.* **3** to suffer the loss of: *he will lose his redundancy money.* **4** to get rid of: *I've lost a stone this summer.* **5** to fail to get or make use of: *Lysenko never lost a chance to show his erudition.* **6** to be defeated in a fight or competition. **7** to fail to see, hear, or understand: *she lost sight of him.* **8** to waste: *so I'd lost a fortune.* **9** to go astray: *psychologists lose the trail.* **10** to allow to go astray or out of sight: *he lost, at the Gare de Lyon, a case with most of his early manuscripts.* **11** to cause the loss of: *I came in to have the gear attended to, which lost me a lap.* **12** to absorb or engross: *lost in thought.* **13** to die or cause the death of: *two lost as yacht sinks in storm.* **14** to outdistance or escape from: *there's some satisfaction in knowing that they've lost us.* **15** (of a timepiece) to run slow (by a specified amount).

➤ *Lose* and *loose* are often confused in spelling but rarely in meaning.

lose out *vb Informal* **1** to be defeated or unsuccessful. **2 lose out on** to fail to secure or make use of: *the yard has already lost out on a number of orders.*

THESAURUS

disengage, ease, free, let go, liberate, loosen, release, set free, slacken, unbind, unbridle, undo, unfasten, unleash, unloose, untie

loosen 1. detach, let out, separate, slacken, unbind, undo, unloose, unstick, untie, work free, work loose **2.** *often with* **up** ease up *or* off, go easy (*informal*), lessen, let up, lighten up (*slang*), mitigate, moderate, relax, soften, weaken

loot 1. *n.* booty, goods, haul, plunder, prize, spoils, swag (*slang*) **2.** *vb.* despoil, pillage, plunder, raid, ransack, ravage, rifle, rob, sack

lopsided askew, asymmetrical, awry, cockeyed, crooked, disproportionate, off balance, one-sided, out of shape, out of true, skewwhiff (*Brit. informal*), squint, tilting, unbalanced, unequal, uneven, warped

lord 1. commander, governor, king, leader, liege, master, monarch, overlord, potentate, prince, ruler, seigneur, sovereign, superior **2.** earl, noble, nobleman, peer, viscount **3. lord it over someone** act big (*slang*), be overbearing, boss around (*informal*), domineer, order around, play the lord, pull rank, put on airs, swagger

Lord *Christianity* Christ, God, Jehovah, Jesus Christ, the Almighty

lordly 1. arrogant, condescending, despotic, dictatorial, disdainful, domineering, haughty, high and mighty (*informal*), high-handed, hoity-toity (*informal*), imperious, lofty, overbearing, patronizing, proud, stuck-up (*informal*), supercilious, toffee-nosed (*slang, chiefly Brit.*), tyrannical **2.** aristocratic, dignified, exalted, gracious, grand, imperial, lofty, majestic, noble, princely, regal, stately

lore 1. beliefs, doctrine, experience, folk-wisdom, mythos, saws, sayings, teaching, traditional wisdom, traditions, wisdom **2.** erudition, knowhow (*informal*), knowledge, learning, letters, scholarship

lose 1. be deprived of, displace, drop, fail to keep, forget, mislay, misplace, miss, suffer loss **2.** capitulate, default, fail, fall short, forfeit, lose out on (*informal*), miss, pass up (*informal*), yield **3.** be defeated, be the loser, be worsted, come a cropper (*informal*), come to grief, get the worst of, lose out, suffer defeat, take a licking (*informal*) **4.** consume, deplete, dissipate, drain, exhaust, expend, lavish, misspend, squander, use up, waste **5.** confuse, miss, stray from, wander from **6.** dodge, duck, elude, escape, evade, give some-

loser *n* **1** a person or thing that loses. **2** *Informal* a person or thing that seems destined to fail: *he's a bit of a loser.*

losing *adj* unprofitable or failing: *a losing streak that cost him millions.*

loss *n* **1** the act or an instance of losing. **2** the person, thing, or amount lost: *a 34m pounds loss.* **3** the disadvantage or deprivation resulting from losing: *a loss of sovereignty.* **4 at a loss a** uncertain what to do; bewildered. **b** with income less than outlay: *they cannot afford to run branches at a loss.*

loss leader *n* an article offered at a low price to attract customers.

lost *vb* **1** the past of **lose.** *~adj* **2** unable to find one's way. **3** unable to be found or recovered. **4** confused or bewildered: *she seemed a bit lost.* **5** (sometimes foll. by *on*) not used, noticed, or understood by: *not that the propaganda value of the game was lost on the authorities.* **6** no longer possessed or existing: *lost credit.* **7** (foll. by *in*) engrossed (in): *he remained lost in his own thoughts.* **8** morally fallen: *a lost woman.* **9** damned: *a lost soul.*

lost cause *n Old-fashioned* something with no chance of success.

lot *pron* **1 a lot** a great number or quantity: *not that there was a lot to tell; a lot of people.* *~n* **2** a collection of things or people: *your lot have wasted enough time.* **3** destiny or fortune: *the refugees did not choose their lot.* **4** any object, such as a straw or slip of paper, drawn from others at random to make a selection or choice: *they could only be split by the drawing of lots; the casting by lots.* **5** the use of lots in making a choice: *chosen by lot.* **6** an item or set of items for sale in an auction. **7** *Chiefly US & Canad* an area of land: *to the parking lot.* **8 a bad lot** an unpleasant or disreputable person. **9 cast** *or* **throw in one's lot with someone** to join with voluntarily and share the fortunes of someone. **10 the lot** the entire amount or number. *~adv* **11** (preceded by *a*) *Informal* to a considerable extent, degree, or amount: *steroids are used a lot in weightlifting.* See also **lots.**

loth (rhymes with **both**) *adj* same as **loath.**

Lothario (loh-**thah**-ree-oh) *n, pl* **-os** a seducer.

lotion *n* a liquid preparation having a soothing, cleansing, or antiseptic action, applied to the skin.

lots *Informal ~pl n* **1** (often foll. by *of*) great numbers or quantities: *lots of friends; you can read lots into Nostradamus.* *~adv* **2** a great deal.

lottery *n, pl* **-teries 1** a method of raising money by selling tickets by which a winner is selected at random. **2** a venture whose outcome is a matter of luck.

lotto *n* a game of chance similar to bingo.

lotus *n* **1** (in Greek mythology) a fruit that induces dreamy forgetfulness in those who eat it. **2** any of several water lilies of tropical Africa and Asia, regarded as sacred. **3** a symbolic representation of such a plant.

lotus-eater *n* a person who lives in lazy forgetfulness.

lotus position *n* a seated cross-legged position with each foot on top of the opposite thigh, used in yoga and meditation.

loud *adj* **1** (of sound) relatively great in volume: *loud applause.* **2** making or able to make sounds of relatively great volume: *a loud voice.* **3** insistent and emphatic: *loud appeals.* **4** (of colours or patterns) harsh to look at. **5** noisy, vulgar, and offensive. *~adv* **6** in a loud manner. **7 out loud** audibly. **loudly** *adv* **loudness** *n*

loud-hailer *n* a portable loudspeaker with a built-in amplifier and microphone.

loudmouth *n* a person who talks too much, esp. in a boastful or indiscreet way. **loudmouthed** *adj*

loudspeaker *n* a device for converting electrical signals into sounds.

lough *n Irish* **1** a lake. **2** a long narrow arm of the sea.

lounge *n* **1** *Chiefly Brit* a living room in a private house. **2** same as **lounge bar. 3** a communal room in a hotel, ship, or airport, used for waiting or relaxing in. **4** the act of lounging. *~vb* **lounging, lounged 5** (often foll. by *about* or *around*) to sit or lie in a relaxed manner. **6** to pass time lazily or idly.

THESAURUS

one the slip, lap, leave behind, outdistance, outrun, outstrip, overtake, pass, shake off, slip away, throw off

loser also-ran, dud (*informal*), failure, flop (*informal*), lemon (*slang*), underdog, washout (*informal*)

loss 1. bereavement, deprivation, disappearance, drain, failure, forfeiture, losing, misfortune, mislaying, privation, squandering, waste **2.** casualties, cost, damage, dead, death toll, debit, debt, defeat, deficiency, deficit, depletion, destruction, detriment, disadvantage, fatalities, harm, hurt, impairment, injury, losings, number killed (captured, injured, missing, wounded), ruin, shrinkage **3. at a loss** at one's wits' end, baffled, bewildered, confused, helpless, nonplussed, perplexed, puzzled, stuck (*informal*), stumped

lost 1. adrift, astray, at sea, disoriented, off-course, off-track **2.** disappeared, forfeited, mislaid, misplaced, missed, missing, strayed, vanished, wayward **3.** baffled, bewildered, clueless (*slang*), confused, helpless, ignorant, mystified, perplexed, puzzled **4.** abolished, annihilated, bygone, consumed, dead, demolished, destroyed, devastated, dissipated, eradicated, exterminated, extinct, forgotten, gone, lapsed, misapplied, misdirected, misspent, misused, obliterated, obsolete, out-of-date, past, perished, ruined, squandered, unremembered, wasted, wiped out, wrecked **5.** *with* **in** absent, absorbed, abstracted, distracted, dreamy, engrossed, entranced, preoccupied, rapt, spellbound, taken up **6.** abandoned, corrupt, damned, depraved, dissolute, fallen, irreclaimable, licentious, profligate, unchaste, wanton

lot *pron.* **1. a lot** abundance, a great deal, heap(s), large amount, load(s) (*informal*), masses (*informal*), numbers, ocean(s), oodles (*informal*), piles (*informal*), plenty, quantities, reams (*informal*), scores, stack(s) *~n.* **2.** assortment, batch, bunch (*informal*), collection, consignment, crowd, group, quantity, set **3.** accident, chance, destiny, doom, fate, fortune, hazard, plight, portion **4. cast** *or* **throw in one's lot with someone** ally *or* align oneself with, join, join forces with, join fortunes with, make common cause with, support

lotion balm, cream, embrocation, liniment, salve, solution

lottery 1. draw, raffle, sweepstake **2.** chance, gamble, hazard, risk, toss-up (*informal*), venture

loud 1. blaring, blatant, boisterous, booming, clamorous, deafening, ear-piercing, ear-splitting, forte (*Music*), noisy, obstreperous, piercing, resounding, rowdy, sonorous, stentorian, strident, strong, thundering, tumultuous, turbulent, vehement, vociferous **2.** brash, brassy, flamboyant, flashy, garish, gaudy, glaring, lurid, naff (*Brit. slang*), ostentatious, showy, tacky (*informal*), tasteless, tawdry, vulgar **3.** brash, brazen, coarse, crass, crude, loud-mouthed (*informal*), offensive, raucous, vulgar

loudly at full volume, at the top of one's voice, clamorously, deafeningly, fortissimo (*Music*), lustily, noisily, shrilly, uproariously, vehemently, vigorously, vociferously

lounge *vb.* **1.** *often with* **about** *or* **around** laze, lie about, loaf, loiter, loll, recline, relax, saunter, sprawl,

lounge bar *n Brit* a more expensive and comfortable bar in a pub or hotel.

lounge suit *n* a man's suit for daytime wear.

lour *vb* same as **lower**[2].

lourie (rhymes with **dowry**) *or* **loerie** *n* a type of African bird with bright plumage.

louse *n* **1** (*pl* **lice**) a wingless blood-sucking insect which feeds off man and some animals. **2** (*pl* **louses**) *Slang* an unpleasant or dishonourable person.

louse up *vb* **lousing, loused** *Slang* to ruin or spoil.

lousy *adj* **lousier, lousiest 1** *Slang* very mean or unpleasant. **2** *Slang* inferior or bad. **3** *Slang* ill or unwell. **4** infested with lice.

lout *n* a crude or oafish person; boor. **loutish** *adj*

louvre *or US* **louver** (**loo**-ver) *n* **a** any of a set of horizontal slats in a door or window, slanted to admit air but not rain. **b** the slats and frame supporting them. **louvred** *or US* **louvered** *adj*

lovage *n* a European herb with greenish-white flowers.

love *vb* **loving, loved 1** to have a great affection for a person or thing. **2** to have passionate desire for someone. **3** to like (to do something) very much. *~n* **4** an intense emotion of affection towards a person or thing. **5** a deep feeling of sexual attraction. **6** wholehearted liking for or pleasure in something. **7** a beloved person: often used as an endearment. **8** *Brit informal* a commonplace term of address, not necessarily restricted to people one knows or has regard for. **9** (in tennis, squash, etc.) a score of zero. **10 fall in love** to become in love. **11 for love or money** in any circumstances. **12 in love** feeling a strong emotional and sexual attraction. **13 make love to a** to have sexual intercourse with. **b** *Now archaic* to court. **lovable** *or* **loveable** *adj*

love affair *n* a romantic or sexual relationship between two people who are not married to each other.

lovebird *n* any of several small African parrots often kept as cage birds.

lovebite *n* a temporary red mark left on a person's skin by a partner biting or sucking it during lovemaking.

love child *n Euphemistic* a child whose parents have not been married to each other.

loveless *adj* without love: *a loveless marriage.*

love-lies-bleeding *n* a plant with drooping spikes of small red flowers.

love life *n* a person's romantic or sexual relationships.

lovelorn *adj* miserable because of unreturned love or unhappiness in love.

lovely *adj* **-lier, -liest 1** very attractive or beautiful. **2** highly pleasing or enjoyable: *thanks for a lovely evening.* *~n, pl* **-lies 3** *Slang* an attractive woman: *curvaceous lovelies.* **loveliness** *n*

lovemaking *n* **1** sexual play and activity between lovers, including sexual intercourse. **2** *Archaic* courtship.

lover *n* **1** a person having a sexual relationship with another person outside marriage. **2** (*often pl*) either of the people involved in a love affair. **3** someone who loves a specified person or thing: *an animal-lover.*

lovesick *adj* pining or languishing because of love. **lovesickness** *n*

lovey-dovey *adj* making a sentimental or showy display of affection.

loving *adj* feeling or showing love and affection. **lovingly** *adv*

loving cup *n* a large two-handled cup out of which people drink in turn.

low[1] *adj* **1** having a relatively small distance from base to top: *a low wall.* **2** of less than usual amount, degree, quality, or cost: *low score; low inflation.* **3** situated at a relatively short distance above the ground, sea level, or the horizon: *heavy weather with low driving cloud.* **4** (of numbers) small. **5** involving or containing a relatively small amount of something: *low alcohol summer drinks.* **6** having little value or quality: *it sounds as if your self-confidence is low.* **7** coarse or vulgar: *that's a low blow, Jason.* **8** inferior in culture or status. **9** in a weakened physical or mental state. **10** with a hushed tone: *in a low, scared voice.* **11** low-necked: *a low neckline dress.* **12** *Music* of or having a relatively low pitch. **13** (of latitudes) situated not far north or south of the equator. **14** having little or no money. **15** unfavourable: *he has a low opinion of Ford.* **16** deep: *a low bow.* **17** (of a gear) providing a relatively low speed. *~adv* **18** in a low position, level, or degree: *the pilot flew low over the area.* **19** at a low pitch; deeply: *he's singing very low.* **20** cheaply: *the bank is having to buy high and sell low.* **21 lay low a** to make (someone) fall by a blow. **b** to overcome or destroy. **22 lie low** to keep or be concealed or quiet. *~n* **23** a low position, level, or degree: *shares hit new low.* **24** an area of low atmospheric pressure; depression. **lowness** *n*

THESAURUS

take it easy **2.** dawdle, fritter time away, hang out (*informal*), idle, kill time, pass time idly, potter, waste time

lour *see* LOWER

lout bear, boor, bumpkin, churl, clod, clumsy idiot, dolt, gawk, lubber, ned (*slang*), oaf, yahoo, yob *or* yobbo (*Brit. slang*)

lovable, loveable adorable, amiable, attractive, captivating, charming, cuddly, cute, delightful, enchanting, endearing, engaging, fetching (*informal*), likable *or* likeable, lovely, pleasing, sweet, winning, winsome

love *vb.* **1.** adore, adulate, be attached to, be in love with, cherish, dote on, have affection for, hold dear, idolize, prize, think the world of, treasure, worship **2.** appreciate, delight in, desire, enjoy, fancy, have a weakness for, like, relish, savour, take pleasure in *~n.* **3.** adoration, adulation, affection, amity, ardour, attachment, devotion, fondness, friendship, infatuation, liking, passion, rapture, regard, tenderness, warmth **4.** delight, devotion, enjoyment, fondness, inclination, liking, partiality, relish, soft spot, taste, weakness **5.** angel, beloved, darling, dear, dearest, dear one, inamorata, inamorato, loved one, lover, sweet, sweetheart, truelove **6. fall in love** bestow one's affections on, be taken with, fall for, lose one's heart (to), take a shine to (*informal*) **7. for love or money** by any means, ever, under any conditions **8. in love** besotted, charmed, enamoured, enraptured, infatuated, smitten

love affair affair, amour, intrigue, liaison, relationship, romance

lovely 1. admirable, adorable, amiable, attractive, beautiful, charming, comely, exquisite, graceful, handsome, pretty, sweet, winning **2.** agreeable, captivating, delightful, enchanting, engaging, enjoyable, gratifying, nice, pleasant, pleasing

lover admirer, beau, beloved, boyfriend, fancy man (*old-fashioned slang*), fancy woman (*old-fashioned slang*), fiancé, fiancée, flame (*informal*), girlfriend, inamorata, inamorato, paramour, suitor, swain (*archaic or poetic*), sweetheart, toy boy

loving affectionate, amorous, ardent, cordial, dear, demonstrative, devoted, doting, fond, friendly, kind, solicitous, tender, warm, warm-hearted

low *adj.* **1.** little, shallow, short, small, squat, stunted **2.** deficient, depleted, inadequate, inferior, insignifi-

low[2] *n also* **lowing 1** the sound uttered by cattle; moo. *~vb* **2** to make a mooing sound.

lowborn *adj Now rare* of ignoble or common parentage.

lowbrow *Disparaging ~n* **1** a person with uncultivated or nonintellectual tastes. *~adj* **2** of or for such a person.

Low Church *n* a section of the Church of England which stresses evangelical beliefs and practices. **Low-Church** *adj*

low comedy *n* comedy characterized by slapstick and physical action.

Low Countries *pl n* Belgium, Luxembourg, and the Netherlands.

low-down *Informal ~adj* **1** mean, underhand, and dishonest. *~n* **lowdown 2 the lowdown** information.

lower[1] *adj* **1** being below one or more other things: *the lower branches.* **2** reduced in amount or value: *lower rates.* **3 Lower** *Geol* denoting the early part of a period or formation. *~vb* **4** to cause or allow to move down: *she lowered her head.* **5** to behave in a way that damages one's respect: *she'd never lowered herself enough to make a call.* **6** to lessen or become less: *the cholesterol was lowered by medication.* **7** to make quieter or reduce the pitch of.

lower[2] *or* **lour** *vb* (of the sky or weather) to be overcast and menacing. **lowering** *or* **louring** *adj*

lower case *n* (in printing) small letters, as opposed to capital letters. **lower-case** *adj*

lower class *n* the class with the lowest position in society. **lower-class** *adj*

lower house *n* one of the houses of a parliament that has two chambers: usually the larger and more representative.

lowest common denominator *n Maths* the smallest integer or polynomial that is exactly divisible by each denominator of a set of fractions.

lowest common multiple *n Maths* the smallest number or quantity that is exactly divisible by each member of a set of numbers or quantities.

low frequency *n* any radio frequency lying between 300 and 30 kilohertz.

Low German *n* a language of N Germany, spoken in rural areas.

low-key *or* **low-keyed** *adj* **1** restrained or subdued. **2** having a low intensity or tone.

lowland *n* **1** relatively low ground. **2** (*often pl*) a low generally flat region. *~adj* **3** of a lowland or lowlands. **lowlander** *n*

Lowland *adj* of the Lowlands or the dialects of English spoken there. **Lowlander** *n*

Lowlands *n* a low generally flat region of S Central Scotland.

lowly *adj* **-lier, -liest 1** humble in position or status. **2** simple and unpretentious. **lowliness** *n*

Low Mass *n* a simplified form of Mass that is spoken rather than sung.

low-minded *adj* having a vulgar or crude mind. **low-mindedness** *n*

low-pitched *adj* **1** pitched low in tone. **2** (of a roof) with a shallow slope.

low profile *n* a deliberate shunning of publicity: *he kept a low profile.* **low-profile** *adj*

low-spirited *adj* depressed or dejected.

low-tech *adj* **1** of or using low technology. **2** in the style of interior design which uses items associated with low technology.

low technology *n* unsophisticated technology that is limited to the production of basic necessities.

low tide *n* the tide at its lowest level or the time at which it reaches this.

low water *n* **1** low tide. **2** the lowest level which a stretch of water reaches.

loyal *adj* **1** faithful to one's friends, country, or government. **2** of or expressing loyalty: *the loyal toast.* **loyally** *adv*

loyalist *n* a patriotic supporter of the sovereign or government. **loyalism** *n*

Loyalist *n* (in Northern Ireland) any of the Protestants wishing to retain Ulster's link with Britain.

loyalty *n, pl* **-ties 1** the quality of being loyal. **2** a feeling of friendship or duty towards someone or something.

lozenge *n* **1** *Med* a medicated tablet held in the mouth until it has dissolved. **2** *Geom* a rhombus.

LP *n* a gramophone record of 12 inches in diameter,

THESAURUS

cant, little, low-grade, meagre, measly, mediocre, paltry, pathetic, poor, puny, reduced, scant, second-rate, shoddy, small, sparse, substandard, trifling, worthless **3.** ground-level, low-lying **4.** coarse, common, crude, disgraceful, dishonourable, disreputable, gross, ill-bred, nasty, obscene, rough, rude, sordid, unbecoming, undignified, unrefined, vulgar **5.** abject, base, contemptible, degraded, humble, ignoble, lowborn, lowly, meek, menial, obscure, plain, plebeian, poor, servile, simple, unpretentious **6.** blue, debilitated, dejected, depressed, despondent, disheartened, dismal, down, downcast, down in the dumps (*informal*), dying, exhausted, fed up, feeble, forlorn, frail, gloomy, glum, ill, miserable, morose, prostrate, reduced, sad, sick as a parrot (*informal*), sinking, stricken, unhappy, weak **7.** gentle, hushed, muffled, muted, quiet, soft, subdued, whispered **8.** cheap, economical, inexpensive, moderate, modest, reasonable *~adv.* **9. lie low** conceal oneself, go to earth, go underground, hide, hide away, hide out, hole up, keep a low profile, keep out of sight, lurk, skulk, take cover

lowdown the lowdown *informal* dope (*informal*), gen (*Brit. informal*), info (*informal*), information, inside story, intelligence

lower[1] *adj.* **1.** inferior, junior, lesser, low-level, minor, secondary, second-class, smaller, subordinate, under **2.** curtailed, decreased, diminished, lessened, pared down, reduced *~vb.* **3.** depress, drop, fall, let down, make lower, sink, submerge, take down **4.** abase, belittle, condescend, debase, degrade, deign, demean, devalue, disgrace, downgrade, humble, humiliate, stoop **5.** abate, curtail, cut, decrease, diminish, lessen, minimize, moderate, prune, reduce, slash **6.** soften, tone down

lower[2], **lour** be brewing, blacken, cloud up *or* over, darken, loom, menace, threaten

low-key *or* **low-keyed** low-pitched, muffled, muted, played down, quiet, restrained, subdued, toned down, understated

lowly 1. humble, ignoble, inferior, lowborn, mean, obscure, plebeian, proletarian, subordinate **2.** average, common, homespun, modest, ordinary, plain, poor, simple, unpretentious

low-spirited apathetic, blue, dejected, depressed, despondent, dismal, down, down-hearted, down in the dumps (*informal*), fed up, gloomy, heavy-hearted, low, miserable, moody, sad, unhappy

loyal attached, constant, dependable, devoted, dutiful, faithful, immovable, patriotic, staunch, steadfast, tried and true, true, true-blue, true-hearted, trustworthy, trusty, unswerving, unwavering

loyalty allegiance, constancy, dependability, devo-

which holds about 20 or 25 minutes of sound on each side.

L-plate *n Brit* a red "L" on a white square attached to a motor vehicle to indicate a learner driver.

Lr *Chem* lawrencium.

LSD *n* lysergic acid diethylamide; an illegal hallucinogenic drug.

L.S.D., £.s.d., *or* **l.s.d.** pounds, shillings, pence.

Lt Lieutenant.

Ltd Limited (Liability).

Lu *Chem* lutetium.

lubber *n* **1** a big, awkward, or stupid person. **2** short for **landlubber. lubberly** *adj, adv* **lubberliness** *n*

lubricant *n* a lubricating substance, such as oil.

lubricate (**loo**-brik-ate) *vb* **-cating, -cated 1** to cover with an oily substance to lessen friction. **2** to make greasy, slippery, or smooth. **lubrication** *n*

lubricious (loo-**brish**-uss) *adj Formal or literary* lewd.

lucerne *n Brit* same as **alfalfa.**

lucid *adj* **1** clear and easily understood. **2** capable of clear thought, particularly between periods of insanity or delirium. **3** shining or glowing. **lucidity** *n* **lucidly** *adv*

Lucifer *n* Satan.

luck *n* **1** events that are subject to chance; fortune, good or bad. **2** success or good fortune. **3 down on one's luck** lacking good fortune to the extent of suffering hardship. **4 no such luck** *Informal* unfortunately not. **5 try one's luck** to attempt something that is uncertain.

luckless *adj* unfortunate or unlucky.

lucky *adj* **luckier, luckiest 1** having or bringing good fortune. **2** happening by chance, esp. as desired. **luckily** *adv*

lucky dip *n Brit, Austral, & NZ* a box filled with sawdust containing small prizes for which children search.

lucrative *adj* profitable.

lucre (**loo**-ker) *n Usually facetious* money or wealth: *filthy lucre.*

Luddite *n Brit history* **1** any of the textile workers opposed to mechanization, who organized machine-breaking between 1811 and 1816. **2** any opponent of industrial change or innovation. *~adj* **3** of the Luddites.

ludicrous *adj* absurd or ridiculous. **ludicrously** *adv*

ludo *n Brit* a simple board game in which players move counters forward by throwing dice.

luff *vb* **1** *Naut* to sail (a ship) into the wind. **2** to move the jib of a crane in order to shift a load.

lug[1] *vb* **lugging, lugged** to carry or drag with great effort.

lug[2] *n* **1** a projecting piece by which something is connected, supported, or lifted. **2** *Informal & Scot* an ear.

luggage *n* suitcases, trunks, and bags.

lugger *n Naut* a small working boat with an oblong sail.

lugubrious (loo-**goo**-bree-uss) *adj* mournful or gloomy.

lugworm *n* a large worm which lives in burrows on sandy shores and is often used as bait by fishermen.

lukewarm *adj* **1** (of a liquid) moderately warm; tepid. **2** lacking enthusiasm or conviction.

lull *vb* **1** to soothe (a person or animal) by soft sounds or motions. **2** to calm (fears or suspicions) by deception. *~n* **3** a short period of calm.

lullaby *n, pl* **-bies** a quiet song to lull a child to sleep.

lumbago (lum-**bay**-go) *n* pain in the lower back; low backache.

lumbar *adj* relating to the lower back.

lumbar puncture *n Med* insertion of a hollow needle into the lower spinal cord to withdraw fluid for diagnosis.

lumber[1] *n* **1** *Brit* unwanted disused household articles. **2** *Chiefly US & Canad* logs; sawn timber. *~vb* **3** *Brit informal* to burden with something unpleasant: *she was lumbered with a bill for about ninety pounds.* **4** to fill up with useless household articles. **5** *Chiefly US & Canad* to convert trees into marketable timber.

lumber[2] *vb* to move awkwardly and heavily. **lumbering** *adj*

THESAURUS

tion, faithfulness, fealty, fidelity, patriotism, reliability, staunchness, steadfastness, troth (*archaic*), true-heartedness, trueness, trustiness, trustworthiness

lubricate grease, make slippery, make smooth, oil, oil the wheels, smear, smooth the way

lucid 1. clear, clear-cut, comprehensible, crystal clear, distinct, evident, explicit, intelligible, limpid, obvious, pellucid, plain, transparent **2.** all there, clear-headed, *compos mentis,* in one's right mind, rational, reasonable, sane, sensible, sober, sound **3.** beaming, bright, brilliant, effulgent, gleaming, luminous, radiant, resplendent, shining

luck 1. accident, chance, destiny, fate, fortuity, fortune, hazard **2.** advantage, blessing, break (*informal*), fluke, godsend, good fortune, good luck, prosperity, serendipity, stroke, success, windfall

luckily 1. favourably, fortunately, happily, opportunely, propitiously, providentially **2.** as it chanced, as luck would have it, by chance, fortuitously

luckless calamitous, cursed, disastrous, doomed, hapless, hopeless, ill-fated, ill-starred, jinxed, star-crossed, unfortunate, unhappy, unlucky, unpropitious, unsuccessful

lucky 1. advantageous, blessed, charmed, favoured, fortunate, jammy (*Brit. slang*), prosperous, serendipitous, successful **2.** adventitious, auspicious, fortuitous, opportune, propitious, providential, timely

lucrative advantageous, fat, fruitful, gainful, high-income, money-making, paying, productive, profitable, remunerative, well-paid

lucre *usually facetious* gain, mammon, money, pelf (*contemptuous*), profit, riches, spoils, wealth

ludicrous absurd, burlesque, comic, comical, crazy, droll, farcical, funny, incongruous, laughable, nonsensical, odd, outlandish, preposterous, ridiculous, silly, zany

luggage baggage, bags, cases, gear, impedimenta, paraphernalia, suitcases, things, trunks

lugubrious dirgelike, dismal, doleful, dreary, funereal, gloomy, melancholy, morose, mournful, sad, serious, sombre, sorrowful, woebegone, woeful

lukewarm 1. blood-warm, tepid, warm **2.** apathetic, cold, cool, half-hearted, indifferent, laodicean, phlegmatic, unconcerned, unenthusiastic, uninterested, unresponsive

lull 1. *vb.* allay, calm, compose, hush, lullaby, pacify, quell, quiet, rock to sleep, soothe, still, subdue, tranquillize **2.** *n.* calm, calmness, hush, let-up (*informal*), pause, quiet, respite, silence, stillness, tranquillity

lullaby berceuse

lumber[1] *Brit.* **1.** *n.* castoffs, clutter, discards, jumble, junk, refuse, rubbish, trash, trumpery, white elephants **2.** *vb. informal* burden, encumber, impose upon, land, load, saddle

lumber[2] clump, lump along, plod, shamble, shuffle, stump, trudge, trundle, waddle

lumberjack *n* (esp. in North America) a person who fells trees and prepares the timber for transport.

luminary *n, pl* **-naries 1 a** a famous person. **b** an expert in a particular subject. **2** *Literary* something, such as the sun or moon, that gives off light.

luminescence *n Physics* the emission of light at low temperatures by any process other than burning. **luminescent** *adj*

luminous *adj* **1** reflecting or giving off light: *luminous colours.* **2** *Not in technical use* luminescent: *luminous sparklers.* **3** enlightening or wise. **luminosity** *n*

lump[1] *n* **1** a small solid mass without definite shape. **2** *Pathol* any small swelling or tumour. **3** *Informal* an awkward, heavy, or stupid person. **4 a lump in one's throat** a tight dry feeling in one's throat, usually caused by great emotion. **5 the lump** *Brit* self-employed workers in the building trade considered collectively. **6** *~adj* in the form of a lump or lumps: *lump sugar.* *~vb* **7** (often foll. by *together*) to consider as a single group, often without justification. **8** to grow into lumps or become lumpy.

lump[2] *vb* **lump it** *Informal* to accept something irrespective of personal preference: *if you don't like it, you can lump it.*

lumpectomy *n, pl* **-mies** surgical removal of a tumour in a breast.

lumpish *adj* stupid, clumsy, or heavy. **lumpishness** *n*

lump sum *n* a relatively large sum of money, paid at one time.

lumpy *adj* **lumpier, lumpiest** full of or having lumps. **lumpiness** *n*

lunacy *n, pl* **-cies 1** foolishness. **2** (formerly) any severe mental illness.

lunar *adj* relating to the moon: *lunar eclipse.*

lunatic *adj* **1** foolish; eccentric. **2** *Archaic* insane. *~n* **3** a foolish or annoying person. **4** *Archaic* a person who is insane.

lunatic asylum *n Offensive* a home or hospital for the mentally ill.

lunatic fringe *n* the members of a group who adopt views regarded as extreme.

lunch *n* **1** a meal eaten during the middle of the day. *~vb* **2** to eat lunch.

luncheon *n* a lunch, often a formal one.

luncheon meat *n* a ground mixture of meat (often pork) and cereal, usually tinned.

luncheon voucher *n* a voucher for a specified amount issued to employees and accepted by some restaurants as payment for food.

lunchroom *n US & Canad* a room where lunch is served or where students or employees may eat lunches they bring.

lung *n* the part of the body that allows an animal or bird to breathe air. Humans have two lungs, contained within the chest cavity.

lunge *n* **1** a sudden forward motion. **2** *Fencing* a thrust made by advancing the front foot and straightening the back leg. *~vb* **lunging, lunged 3** to move with a lunge. **4** *Fencing* to make a lunge.

lungfish *n, pl* **fish** or **-fishes** a freshwater fish with an air-breathing lung.

lupin *n* a garden plant with large spikes of brightly coloured flowers and flattened pods.

lupine *adj* of or like a wolf.

lupus *n* an ulcerous skin disease.

lurch[1] *vb* **1** to lean or tilt suddenly to one side. **2** to stagger. *~n* **3** a lurching movement.

lurch[2] *n* **leave someone in the lurch** to abandon someone in trouble.

lure *vb* **luring, lured 1** (sometimes foll. by *away* or *into*) to tempt or attract by the promise of reward. *~n* **2** a person or thing that lures. **3** *Angling* a brightly coloured artificial spinning bait. **4** *Falconry* a feathered decoy to which small pieces of meat can be attached.

lurid *adj* **1** vivid in shocking detail; sensational: *magazines whose lurid covers sickened him.* **2** glaring in colour. **3** horrible in savagery or violence: *reporting lurid crimes.* **luridly** *adv*

lurk *vb* **1** to move stealthily or be concealed, esp. for evil purposes. **2** to be present in an unobtrusive way; be latent.

lurking *adj* lingering but almost unacknowledged: *it confirms a lurking suspicion.*

THESAURUS

lumbering awkward, blundering, bovine, bumbling, clumsy, elephantine, heavy, heavy-footed, hulking, lubberly, overgrown, ponderous, ungainly, unwieldy

luminous bright, brilliant, glowing, illuminated, lighted, lit, luminescent, lustrous, radiant, resplendent, shining, vivid

lump[1] *n.* **1.** ball, bunch, cake, chunk, clod, cluster, dab, gob, gobbet, group, hunk, mass, nugget, piece, spot, wedge **2.** *Pathol.* bulge, bump, growth, hump, protrusion, protuberance, swelling, tumescence, tumour *~vb.* **3.** agglutinate, aggregate, batch, bunch, coalesce, collect, combine, conglomerate, consolidate, group, mass, pool, unite

lump[2] *vb.* **lump it** *informal* bear, brook, endure, put up with, stand, suffer, take, thole (*Scot. & Northern English*), tolerate

lunacy 1. aberration, absurdity, craziness, folly, foolhardiness, foolishness, idiocy, imbecility, madness, senselessness, stupidity, tomfoolery **2.** dementia, derangement, idiocy, insanity, madness, mania, psychosis

lunatic 1. *adj.* barmy (*slang*), bonkers (*slang, chiefly Brit.*), crackbrained, crackpot (*informal*), crazy, daft, demented, deranged, insane, irrational, loopy (*informal*), mad, maniacal, not the full shilling (*informal*), nuts (*slang*), off one's trolley (*slang*), out to lunch (*informal*), psychotic, unhinged, up the pole (*informal*) **2.** *n.* head-banger (*slang*), loony (*slang*), madman, maniac, nut (*slang*), nutcase (*slang*), nutter (*Brit. slang*), psychopath

lunge 1. *n.* charge, cut, jab, pass, pounce, spring, stab, swing, swipe (*informal*), thrust **2.** *vb.* bound, charge, cut, dash, dive, fall upon, hit at, jab, leap, pitch into (*informal*), plunge, poke, pounce, set upon, stab, strike at, thrust

lure 1. *vb. sometimes with* **away** *or* **into** allure, attract, beckon, decoy, draw, ensnare, entice, inveigle, invite, lead on, seduce, tempt **2.** *n.* allurement, attraction, bait, carrot (*informal*), come-on (*informal*), decoy, enticement, inducement, magnet, siren song, temptation

lurid 1. exaggerated, graphic, melodramatic, sensational, shocking, startling, unrestrained, vivid **2.** bloody, fiery, flaming, glaring, glowering, intense, livid, overbright, sanguine **3.** disgusting, ghastly, gory, grim, grisly, gruesome, macabre, revolting, savage, violent

lurk conceal oneself, crouch, go furtively, hide, lie in wait, move with stealth, prowl, skulk, slink, sneak, snoop

luscious appetizing, delectable, delicious, honeyed, juicy, mouth-watering, palatable, rich, savoury,

luscious (**lush**-uss) *adj* **1** extremely pleasurable to taste or smell. **2** very attractive.

lush[1] *adj* **1** (of vegetation) growing thickly and healthily. **2** luxurious, elaborate, or opulent.

lush[2] *n Slang* an alcoholic.

lust *n* **1** a strong sexual desire. **2** a strong desire or drive: *a lust for power.* ~*vb* **3** (often foll. by *after* or *for*) to have a passionate desire (for). **lustful** *adj* **lustfully** *adv*

lustre *or US* **luster** *n* **1** soft shining light reflected from a surface; sheen. **2** great splendour or glory. **3** a shiny metallic surface on some pottery and porcelain. **lustrous** *adj*

lusty *adj* **lustier, lustiest 1** healthy and full of strength and energy. **2** strong or invigorating. **lustily** *adv* **lustiness** *n*

lute *n* an ancient plucked stringed instrument with a long fingerboard and a body shaped like a half pear.

lutetium (loo-**tee**-shee-um) *n Chem* a silvery-white metallic element of the lanthanide series. Symbol: Lu

Lutheran *n* **1** a follower of Martin Luther (1483–1546), German leader of the Reformation, or a member of a Lutheran Church. ~*adj* **2** of or relating to Luther, his doctrines, or any of the Churches that follow these doctrines. **Lutheranism** *n*

luvvie *or* **luvvy** *n, pl* **-vies** *Facetious* a person who is involved in acting or the theatre.

lux *n, pl* **lux** the SI unit of illumination.

luxe *n* See **de luxe.**

Luxembourger *n* a person from Luxembourg.

luxuriant *adj* **1** rich and abundant; lush: *luxuriant foliage.* **2** very elaborate or ornate. **luxuriance** *n* **luxuriantly** *adv*

luxuriate *vb* **-ating, -ated 1 luxuriate in** to take self-indulgent pleasure in; revel in. **2** to flourish profusely.

luxurious *adj* **1** characterized by luxury. **2** enjoying or devoted to luxury. **luxuriously** *adv*

luxury *n, pl* **-ries 1** indulgence in rich and sumptuous living. **2** something considered an indulgence rather than a necessity. **3** ~*adj* relating to, indicating, or supplying luxury: *a luxury hotel.*

LV luncheon voucher.

lx lux.

lyceum *n* (now chiefly in the names of buildings) a public building for events such as concerts and lectures.

lychee (lie-**chee**) *n* a Chinese fruit with a whitish juicy pulp.

lychgate *or* **lichgate** *n* a roofed gate to a churchyard, formerly used as a temporary shelter for a coffin.

Lycra *n Trademark* a synthetic elastic fabric used for tight-fitting garments, such as swimsuits.

lye *n* **1** a caustic solution obtained from wood ash. **2** a concentrated solution of sodium hydroxide or potassium hydroxide.

lying *vb* the present participle of **lie**[1] or **lie**[2].

lying-in *n, pl* **lyings-in** *Old-fashioned* confinement in childbirth.

lymph *n* the almost colourless body fluid containing chiefly white blood cells. **lymphatic** *adj*

lymphatic system *n* a network of fine vessels by which lymph circulates throughout the body.

lymph node *n* any of many bean-shaped masses of tissue in the lymphatic system that help to protect against infection.

lymphocyte *n* a type of white blood cell.

lynch *vb* (of a mob) to kill (a person) for some supposed offence without a trial. **lynching** *n*

lynchpin *n* same as **linchpin.**

lynx *n, pl* **lynxes** *or* **lynx** a mammal of the cat family, with grey-brown mottled fur, tufted ears, and a short tail.

lynx-eyed *adj* having keen sight.

lyre *n* an ancient Greek U-shaped stringed instrument, similar to a harp but plucked with a plectrum.

lyrebird *n* an Australian bird, the male of which spreads its tail into the shape of a lyre during courtship.

lyric *adj* **1** (of poetry) **a** expressing the writer's personal feelings. **b** having the form and manner of a song. **2** of or relating to such poetry. **3** (of a singing voice) light and melodic. ~*n* **4** a short poem of songlike quality. **5 lyrics** the words of a popular song. **lyrically** *adv*

lyrical *adj* **1** same as **lyric** (senses 1, 2). **2** enthusiastic or effusive.

lyricism *n* **1** the quality or style of lyric poetry. **2** emotional outpouring.

lyricist *n* a person who writes the words for a song, opera, or musical.

THESAURUS

scrumptious (*informal*), succulent, sweet, toothsome, yummy (*slang*)

lush 1. abundant, dense, flourishing, green, lavish, overgrown, prolific, rank, teeming, verdant **2.** elaborate, extravagant, grand, lavish, luxurious, opulent, ornate, palatial, plush (*informal*), ritzy (*slang*), sumptuous

lust *n.* **1.** carnality, concupiscence, lasciviousness, lechery, lewdness, libido, licentiousness, pruriency, randiness (*informal, chiefly Brit.*), salaciousness, sensuality, the hots (*slang*), wantonness **2.** appetence *or* appetency, appetite, avidity, covetousness, craving, cupidity, desire, greed, longing, passion, thirst ~*vb.* **3.** *often with* **after** *or* **for** be consumed with desire for, covet, crave, desire, hunger for *or* after, need, slaver, want, yearn

lustre *or U.S.* **luster 1.** burnish, gleam, glint, glitter, gloss, glow, sheen, shimmer, shine, sparkle **2.** brightness, brilliance, dazzle, distinction, fame, glory, honour, illustriousness, lambency, luminousness, prestige, radiance, renown, resplendence

lusty brawny, energetic, hale, healthy, hearty, in fine fettle, powerful, red-blooded (*informal*), robust, rugged, stalwart, stout, strapping, strong, sturdy, vigorous, virile

luxurious 1. comfortable, costly, de luxe, expensive, lavish, magnificent, opulent, plush (*informal*), rich, ritzy (*slang*), splendid, sumptuous, well-appointed **2.** epicurean, pampered, pleasure-loving, self-indulgent, sensual, sybaritic, voluptuous

luxury 1. affluence, bliss, comfort, delight, enjoyment, gratification, hedonism, indulgence, opulence, pleasure, richness, satisfaction, splendour, sumptuousness, voluptuousness, wellbeing **2.** extra, extravagance, frill, indulgence, nonessential, treat

lyric *adj.* **1. a** expressive, lyrical **b** lyrical, melodic, musical, songlike **2.** clear, dulcet, flowing, graceful, light, silvery ~*n.* **3. lyrics** book, libretto, text, the words, words of a song

lyrical carried away, ecstatic, effusive, emotional, enthusiastic, expressive, impassioned, inspired, poetic, rapturous, rhapsodic

M

m 1 metre(s). 2 mile(s). 3 milli-. 4 million. 5 minute(s).
M 1 mach. 2 *Currency* mark(s). 3 medium. 4 mega-. 5 (in Britain) motorway. 6 the Roman numeral for 1000.
m. 1 male. 2 married. 3 masculine. 4 meridian. 5 month.
M. 1 Majesty. 2 Master. 3 (in titles) Member. 4 (*pl* **MM.** *or* **MM**) Monsieur.
ma *n* an informal word for mother.
MA 1 Massachusetts. 2 Master of Arts.
ma'am *n* short for **madam** (sense 1).
maas (**mahs**) *n S African* thick soured milk.
mac *or* **mack** *n Brit informal* a mackintosh.
Mac *n Chiefly US & Canad* an informal term of address to a man.
macabre (mak-**kahb**-ra) *adj* strange and horrible; gruesome.
macadam *n* a road surface made of compressed layers of small broken stones, esp. one bound together with tar or asphalt.
macadamize *or* **-ise** *vb* **-izing, -ized** *or* **-ising, -ised** to pave a road with macadam.
macaque (mak-**kahk**) *n* any of various Asian and African monkeys with cheek pouches and either a short tail or no tail.
macaroni *n, pl* **-nis** *or* **-nies** 1 pasta tubes made from wheat flour. 2 (in 18th-century Britain) a man who was excessively concerned with his clothes and appearance.
macaroon *n* a sweet biscuit made of ground almonds.
macaw *n* a large tropical American parrot with a long tail and brightly coloured feathers.
mace[1] *n* 1 a ceremonial staff carried by certain officials. 2 a club with a spiked metal head used in the Middle Ages.
mace[2] *n* a spice made from the dried outer casing of the nutmeg.
macebearer *n* a person who carries a mace in processions or ceremonies.
macerate (**mass**-er-ate) *vb* **-ating, -ated** to soften or be softened by soaking. **macerated** *adj* **maceration** *n*
Mach (**mak**) *n* a unit for expressing the speed of an aircraft as a multiple of the speed of sound: *an airliner capable of cruising at Mach 2.* See also **Mach number.**
machete (mash-**ett**-ee) *n* a broad heavy knife used for cutting or as a weapon.
Machiavellian (mak-ee-a-**vel**-yan) *adj* cleverly deceitful and unscrupulous. **Machiavellianism** *n*
machinations (mak-in-**nay**-shuns) *pl n* cunning schemes or plots to gain power or harm an opponent: *the machinations of a power-hungry institution.*
machine *n* 1 an assembly of components arranged so as to perform a particular task and usually powered by electricity. 2 a vehicle, such as a car or aircraft. 3 a system within an organization that controls activities and policies: *the party machine.* ~*vb* **-chining, -chined** 4 to shape, cut, or make something using a machine. **machinable** *adj*
machine gun *n* 1 a rapid-firing automatic gun, using small-arms ammunition. ~*vb* **machine-gun, -gunning, -gunned** 2 to shoot or fire at with a machine gun.
machine language *n* instructions for a computer in binary or hexadecimal code that require no conversion or translation by the computer.
machine-readable *adj* in a form suitable for processing by a computer.
machinery *n, pl* **-eries** 1 machines, machine parts, or machine systems collectively. 2 the mechanism of a machine. 3 the organization and procedures by which a system functions: *the machinery of international politics.*
machine shop *n* a workshop in which machine tools are operated.
machine tool *n* a power-driven machine, such as a lathe, for cutting and shaping metal, wood, or plastic.
machinist *n* 1 a person who operates machines to cut or process materials. 2 a maker or repairer of machines.
machismo (mak-**izz**-moh) *n* strong or exaggerated masculinity.
Mach number (**mak**) *n* the ratio of the speed of a body in a particular medium to the speed of sound in that medium.
macho (**match**-oh) *adj* 1 strongly or exaggeratedly masculine. ~*n* 2 strong or exaggerated masculinity.
mack *n Brit informal* same as **mac.**
mackerel *n, pl* **-rel** *or* **-rels** an edible sea fish with a greenish-blue body marked with wavy dark bands on the back.
mackintosh *or* **macintosh** *n* 1 a raincoat made of rubberized cloth. 2 any raincoat.
macramé (mak-**rah**-mee) *n* 1 the art of knotting and weaving coarse thread into patterns. 2 ornaments made in this way.
macro- *or before a vowel* **macr-** *combining form* large, long, or great: *macroscopic.*
macrobiotics *n* a dietary system which advocates whole grains and vegetables grown without chemical additives. **macrobiotic** *adj*
macrocarpa *n* a large Californian coniferous tree, used in New Zealand and elsewhere as a windbreak on farms and for rough timber.
macrocosm *n* a complex structure, such as the universe or society, regarded as a whole.
macroeconomics *n* the branch of economics concerned with the relationships between aggregates, such as consumption and investment, in a large economic system. **macroeconomic** *adj*
macromolecule *n* any very large molecule, such as a protein or synthetic polymer.
macron *n* a mark (¯) placed over a letter to represent a long vowel.
macroscopic *adj* 1 large enough to be visible to the naked eye. 2 concerned with large units.

THESAURUS

macabre cadaverous, deathlike, deathly, dreadful, eerie, frightening, frightful, ghastly, ghostly, ghoulish, grim, grisly, gruesome, hideous, horrid, morbid, unearthly, weird

machine 1. apparatus, appliance, contraption, contrivance, device, engine, instrument, mechanism, tool 2. agency, machinery, organization, party, setup (*informal*), structure, system

macula (**mak**-kew-la) *n, pl* **-ulae** (-yew-lee) *Anat* a small spot or area of distinct colour, such as a freckle.

mad *adj* **madder, maddest 1** mentally deranged; insane. **2** extremely foolish; senseless: *that was a mad thing to do!* **3** *Informal* angry or annoyed: *he's mad at her for the unjust accusation.* **4** extremely excited or confused: *a mad rush.* **5** (of animals) **a** unusually ferocious: *a mad bear.* **b** afflicted with rabies. **6 mad about, on** *or* **over** wildly enthusiastic about or fond of. **7 like mad** *Informal* with great energy, enthusiasm, or haste. **madness** *n*

madam *n, pl* **madams 1** (*pl* **mesdames**) a polite term of address for a woman. **2** a woman who runs a brothel. **3** *Brit informal* a spoilt or pert girl: *she is a thoroughly precocious little madam if ever there was one.*

madame (mad-**dam**) *n, pl* **mesdames** (may-**dam**) a French form of address equivalent to *Mrs.*

madcap *adj* **1** impulsive, reckless, or unlikely to succeed: *a madcap expansion of council bureaucracy.* ~*n* **2** an impulsive or reckless person.

mad cow disease *n Informal* same as **BSE.**

madden *vb* to make or become mad or angry. **maddening** *adj*

madder *n* **1** a plant with small yellow flowers and a red fleshy root. **2** a dark reddish-purple dye formerly obtained from its root. **3** an artificial pigment of this colour.

made *vb* **1** the past of **make.** ~*adj* **2** produced or shaped as specified: *handmade.* **3 get** *or* **have it made** *Informal* to be assured of success.

Madeira (mad-**deer**-a) *n* a fortified white wine from Madeira, an island in the N Atlantic.

Madeira cake *n* a type of rich sponge cake.

mademoiselle (mad-mwah-**zel**) *n, pl* **mesdemoiselles** (maid-mwah-**zel**) **1** a French form of address equivalent to *Miss.* **2** a French teacher or governess.

made-to-measure *adj* (of a piece of clothing) made specifically to fit the person who has ordered it.

made-up *adj* **1** invented or fictitious. **2** wearing make-up. **3** put together: *some made-up carpet shampoo.* **4** (of a road) surfaced with tarmac or concrete.

madhouse *n Informal* **1** a state of uproar or confusion. **2** *Old-fashioned* a mental hospital.

madly *adv* **1** in an insane or foolish manner. **2** with great speed and energy. **3** *Informal* extremely or excessively: *she was madly in love with him.*

madman *or fem* **madwoman** *n, pl* **-men** *or* **-women** a person who is insane.

Madonna *n* **1** *Chiefly RC Church* the Virgin Mary. **2** a picture or statue of the Virgin Mary.

madrigal *n* a type of 16th- or 17th-century part song for unaccompanied voices. **madrigalist** *n*

maelstrom (**male**-strom) *n* **1** a large powerful whirlpool. **2** any confused, violent, and destructive turmoil: *a maelstrom of adulterous passion.*

maenad (**mean**-ad) *n* **1** *Classical history* a female disciple of Dionysus, the Greek god of wine. **2** a frenzied woman.

maestro (**my**-stroh) *n, pl* **-tri** *or* **-tros 1** a distinguished musician or conductor. **2** any master of an art.

mae west *n Slang* an inflatable life jacket.

Mafia *n* **the** a secret criminal organization founded in Sicily, and carried to the US by Italian immigrants.

mafioso (maf-fee-**oh**-so) *n, pl* **-sos** *or* **-si** (-see) a member of the Mafia.

mag *n* short for **magazine** (sense 1).

magazine *n* **1** a periodic paperback publication containing written pieces and illustrations. **2** a television or radio programme made up of short nonfictional

THESAURUS

machinery 1. apparatus, equipment, gear, instruments, mechanism, tackle, tools, works **2.** agency, channels, machine, organization, procedure, structure, system

mad 1. aberrant, bananas (*slang*), barking (*slang*), barking mad (*slang*), barmy (*slang*), batty (*slang*), bonkers (*slang, chiefly Brit.*), crackers (*Brit. slang*), crackpot (*informal*), crazed, crazy (*informal*), cuckoo (*informal*), delirious, demented, deranged, distracted, flaky (*U.S. slang*), frantic, frenzied, insane, loony (*slang*), loopy (*informal*), lunatic, mental (*slang*), *non compos mentis*, not the full shilling (*informal*), nuts (*slang*), nutty (*slang*), off one's chump (*slang*), off one's head (*slang*), off one's nut (*slang*), off one's rocker (*slang*), off one's trolley (*slang*), of unsound mind, out of one's mind, out to lunch (*informal*), psychotic, rabid, raving, round the bend (*Brit. slang*), round the twist (*Brit. slang*), screwy (*informal*), unbalanced, unhinged, unstable **2.** absurd, asinine, daft (*informal*), foolhardy, foolish, imprudent, inane, irrational, ludicrous, nonsensical, preposterous, senseless, unreasonable, unsafe, unsound, wild **3.** *informal* angry, ape (*slang*), berserk, cross, enraged, exasperated, fuming, furious, incensed, infuriated, irate, irritated, livid (*informal*), raging, resentful, seeing red (*informal*), wild, wrathful **4.** abandoned, agitated, boisterous, ebullient, energetic, excited, frenetic, frenzied, gay, riotous, uncontrolled, unrestrained, wild **5.** ardent, avid, crazy, daft (*informal*), devoted, dotty (*slang, chiefly Brit.*), enamoured, enthusiastic, fanatical, fond, hooked, impassioned, infatuated, in love with, keen, nuts (*slang*), wild, zealous **6. like mad** *informal* energetically, enthusiastically, excitedly, furiously, madly, quickly, rapidly, speedily, unrestrainedly, violently, wildly, with might and main

madden annoy, craze, derange, drive one crazy (off one's head (*slang*), out of one's mind, round the bend (*Brit. slang*), round the twist (*Brit. slang*), to distraction), enrage, exasperate, gall, get one's hackles up, incense, inflame, infuriate, irritate, make one's blood boil, make one see red (*informal*), make one's hackles rise, nark (*Brit., Austral., & N.Z. slang*), piss one off (*taboo slang*), provoke, raise one's hackles, unhinge, upset, vex

made-up fabricated, false, fictional, imaginary, invented, make-believe, mythical, specious, trumped-up, unreal, untrue

madly 1. absurdly, crazily, deliriously, dementedly, distractedly, foolishly, frantically, frenziedly, hysterically, insanely, irrationally, ludicrously, nonsensically, rabidly, senselessly, unreasonably, wildly **2.** energetically, excitedly, furiously, hastily, hotfoot, hurriedly, like mad (*informal*), quickly, rapidly, recklessly, speedily, violently, wildly **3.** *informal* desperately, devotedly, exceedingly, excessively, extremely, intensely, passionately, to distraction

madman *or* **madwoman** headbanger (*informal*), headcase (*informal*), loony (*slang*), lunatic, maniac, mental case (*slang*), nut (*slang*), nutcase (*slang*), nutter (*Brit. slang*), psycho (*slang*), psychopath, psychotic

madness 1. craziness, delusion, dementia, derangement, distraction, insanity, lunacy, mania, mental illness, psychopathy, psychosis **2.** absurdity, daftness (*informal*), folly, foolhardiness, foolishness, idiocy, nonsense, preposterousness, wildness **3.** anger, exasperation, frenzy, fury, ire, rage, raving, wildness, wrath **4.** abandon, agitation, excitement, frenzy, furore, intoxication, riot, unrestraint, uproar **5.** ardour, craze, enthusiasm, fanaticism, fondness, infatuation, keenness, passion, rage, zeal

items. **3** a metal case holding several cartridges used in some firearms. **4** a rack for automatically feeding slides through a projector. **5** a place for storing weapons, explosives, or military equipment.

magenta (maj-**jen**-ta) *adj* deep purplish-red.

maggot *n* the limbless larva of various insects, esp. the housefly and blowfly. **maggoty** *adj*

magi (**maje**-eye) *pl n, sing* **magus** (**may**-guss) **1** See **magus. 2 the three Magi** *Christianity* the wise men from the East who came to worship the infant Jesus (Matthew 2:1–12).

magic *n* **1** the supposed power to make things happen by using supernatural means. **2** tricks done to entertain; conjuring. **3** any mysterious or extraordinary quality or power: *the magic of Placido Domingo.* **4 like magic** very quickly. *~adj also* **magical 5** of magic. **6** possessing or considered to possess mysterious powers. **7** unaccountably enchanting. **8** *Informal* wonderful or marvellous. *~vb* **-icking, -icked 9** to transform or produce as if by magic: *he had magicked up a gourmet meal at a moment's notice.* **magically** *adv*

magic away *vb* to cause to disappear as if by magic.

magic carpet *n* (in fairy stories) a carpet which can carry people through the air.

magician *n* **1** a conjuror. **2** a person with magic powers.

magic lantern *n* an early type of slide projector.

magisterial *adj* **1** commanding and authoritative. **2** of a magistrate. **magisterially** *adv*

magistracy *n, pl* **-cies 1** the office or function of a magistrate. **2** magistrates collectively.

magistrate *n* **1** a public officer concerned with the administration of law. **2** same as **justice of the peace.**

magistrates' court *n* (in England) a court that deals with minor crimes, certain civil actions, and preliminary hearings.

magma *n, pl* **-mas** *or* **-mata** hot molten rock within the earth's crust which sometimes finds its way to the surface where it solidifies to form igneous rock.

Magna Carta *n English history* the charter granted by King John at Runnymede in 1215, recognizing the rights and privileges of the barons, church, and freemen.

magnanimous *adj* generous and forgiving, esp. towards a defeated enemy. **magnanimity** *n* **magnanimously** *adv*

magnate *n* an influential or wealthy person, esp. in industry.

magnesia *n* a white tasteless substance used as an antacid and laxative; magnesium oxide.

magnesium *n Chem* a light silvery-white metallic element that burns with a very bright white flame. Symbol: Mg

magnet *n* **1** a piece of iron, steel, or lodestone that has the property of attracting iron to it. **2** a person or thing that exerts a great attraction: *these woods are a magnet for bird watchers.*

magnetic *adj* **1** of, producing, or operated by means of magnetism. **2** of or like a magnet. **3** capable of being made into a magnet. **4** exerting a powerful attraction: *political leaders of magnetic appeal.* **magnetically** *adv*

magnetic disk *n* a computer storage disk.

magnetic field *n* an area around a magnet in which its power of attraction is felt.

magnetic mine *n* a mine which detonates when a magnetic field such as that generated by the metal of a ship's hull is detected.

magnetic needle *n* a slender magnetized rod used in certain instruments, such as the magnetic compass, for indicating the direction of a magnetic field.

magnetic north *n* the direction in which a compass needle points, at an angle from the direction of true (geographic) north.

magnetic pole *n* either of two variable points on the earth's surface towards which a magnetic needle points.

magnetic storm *n* a sudden severe disturbance of the earth's magnetic field, caused by emission of charged particles from the sun.

magnetic tape *n* a long plastic strip coated with a magnetic substance, used to record sound or video signals or to store information in computers.

magnetism *n* **1** the property of attraction displayed by magnets. **2** powerful personal charm. **3** the branch of physics concerned with magnetic phenomena.

magnetite *n* a black magnetizable mineral that is an important source of iron.

magnetize *or* **-ise** *vb* **-izing, -ized** *or* **-ising, -ised 1** to make a substance or object magnetic. **2** to attract strongly: *he was magnetized by her smile.* **magnetizable** *or* **-isable** *adj* **magnetization** *or* **-isation** *n*

magneto (mag-**nee**-toe) *n, pl* **-tos** a small electric generator in which the magnetic field is produced by a permanent magnet, esp. one used to provide the spark in an internal-combustion engine.

magnetron *n* an electronic valve used with a mag-

THESAURUS

magazine 1. journal, pamphlet, paper, periodical **2.** ammunition dump, arsenal, depot, powder room (*obsolete*), store, storehouse, warehouse

magic *n.* **1.** black art, enchantment, necromancy, occultism, sorcery, spell, theurgy, witchcraft, wizardry **2.** conjuring, illusion, jugglery, legerdemain, prestidigitation, sleight of hand, trickery **3.** allurement, charm, enchantment, fascination, glamour, magnetism, power *~adj.* **4.** *Also* **magical** bewitching, charismatic, charming, enchanting, entrancing, fascinating, magnetic, marvellous, miraculous, spellbinding

magician 1. conjuror *or* conjurer, illusionist **2.** enchanter, enchantress, necromancer, sorcerer, thaumaturge (*rare*), theurgist, warlock, witch, wizard

magisterial arrogant, assertive, authoritative, bossy (*informal*), commanding, dictatorial, domineering, high-handed, imperious, lordly, masterful, overbearing, peremptory

magistrate J.P., judge, justice, justice of the peace, sheriff (*Scot.*)

magnanimity beneficence, big-heartedness, bountifulness, charitableness, generosity, high-mindedness, largess *or* largesse, munificence, nobility, open-handedness, selflessness, unselfishness

magnanimous beneficent, big, big-hearted, bountiful, charitable, free, generous, great-hearted, handsome, high-minded, kind, kindly, munificent, noble, open-handed, selfless, ungrudging, unselfish, unstinting

magnate baron, big cheese (*slang, old-fashioned*), big noise (*informal*), big shot (*informal*), big wheel (*slang*), bigwig (*informal*), captain of industry, chief, fat cat (*slang, chiefly U.S.*), leader, Mister Big (*slang, chiefly U.S.*), mogul, nabob (*informal*), notable, plutocrat, tycoon, V.I.P.

magnetic alluring, attractive, captivating, charismat-

netic field to generate microwave oscillations, used esp. in radar.

Magnificat *n Christianity* the hymn of the Virgin Mary (Luke 1:46 - 55), used as a canticle.

magnification *n* **1** the act of magnifying or the state of being magnified. **2** the degree to which something is magnified. **3** a magnified copy of something.

magnificent *adj* **1** splendid or impressive in appearance. **2** superb or very fine: *a magnificent performance.* **magnificence** *n* **magnificently** *adv*

magnify *vb* **-fies, -fying, -fied 1** to make something look bigger than it really is, for instance by using a lens or microscope. **2** to make something seem more important than it really is; exaggerate: *you are magnifying the problem out of all proportion.* **3** to make something sound louder than it really is: *the stethoscope magnifies internal body sounds.* **4** *Archaic* to glorify or praise. **magnified** *adj*

magnifying glass *or* **magnifier** *n* a convex lens used to produce an enlarged image of an object.

magniloquent *adj* (of speech) excessively grand, literary, and pompous. **magniloquence** *n*

magnitude *n* **1** relative importance: *an evil of the first magnitude.* **2** relative size or extent. **3** *Astron* the apparent brightness of a celestial body expressed on a numerical scale on which bright stars have a low value.

magnolia *n* an Asian and North American tree or shrub with white, pink, purple, or yellow showy flowers.

magnox *n* an alloy composed mainly of magnesium, used in fuel elements of some nuclear reactors (**magnox reactors**).

magnum *n, pl* **-nums** a wine bottle of twice the normal size, holding 1.5 litres.

magnum opus *n* a great work of art or literature, esp. the greatest single work of an artist.

magpie *n* **1** a bird of the crow family with black-and-white plumage, a long tail, and a chattering call. **2** *Brit* a person who hoards small objects.

magus (**may**-guss) *n, pl* **magi** (**maje**-eye) **1** a Zoroastrian priest. **2** an astrologer or magician of ancient times.

Magyar *n* **1** a member of the main ethnic group of Hungary. **2** the Hungarian language. *~adj* **3** of the Magyars.

maharaja *or* **maharajah** *n* the head of one of the royal families which formerly ruled parts of India.

maharani *or* **maharanee** *n* the wife of a maharaja.

maharishi *n Hinduism* a teacher of religious and mystical knowledge.

mahatma *n* a person revered for his holiness or wisdom: often used as a title or form of address: *Mahatma Gandhi.*

mah jong *or* **mah jongg** *n* a game of Chinese origin, played using tiles bearing various designs, in which the players try to obtain a winning combination of tiles.

mahogany *n, pl* **-nies 1** the hard reddish-brown wood of any of several tropical trees. *~adj* **2** reddish-brown.

mahout (ma-**howt**) *n* (in India and the East Indies) an elephant driver or keeper.

maid *n* **1** a female servant. **2** *Archaic or literary* a young unmarried girl; maiden.

maiden *n* **1** *Archaic or literary* a young unmarried girl, esp. a virgin. **2** *Horse racing* a horse that has never won a race. *~adj* **3** unmarried: *a maiden aunt.* **4** first or earliest: *maiden voyage.* **maidenhood** *n* **maidenly** *adj*

maidenhair fern *n* a fern with delicate hairlike fronds of small pale green leaflets.

maidenhead *n* **1** the hymen. **2** virginity or maidenhood.

maiden name *n* a woman's surname before marriage.

maiden over *n Cricket* an over in which no runs are scored.

maid of honour *n* **1** an unmarried lady attending a queen or princess. **2** *US & Canad* the principal unmarried attendant of a bride.

maidservant *n* a female servant.

mail[1] *n* **1** letters and packages transported and delivered by the post office. **2** the postal system. **3** a single collection or delivery of mail. **4** a train, ship, or aircraft that carries mail. **5** short for **electronic mail.** *~vb* **6** *Chiefly US & Canad* to send by mail.

mail[2] *n* flexible armour made of riveted metal rings or links. **mailed** *adj*

mailbag *n* a large bag for transporting or delivering mail.

mailbox *n US & Canad* a box outside a house into

THESAURUS

ic, charming, enchanting, entrancing, fascinating, hypnotic, irresistible, mesmerizing, seductive

magnetism allure, appeal, attraction, attractiveness, captivatingness, charisma, charm, draw, drawing power, enchantment, fascination, hypnotism, magic, mesmerism, power, pull, seductiveness, spell

magnification aggrandizement, amplification, augmentation, blow-up (*informal*), boost, build-up, deepening, dilation, enhancement, enlargement, exaggeration, expansion, heightening, increase, inflation, intensification

magnificence brilliance, éclat, glory, gorgeousness, grandeur, luxuriousness, luxury, majesty, nobility, opulence, pomp, resplendence, splendour, stateliness, sublimity, sumptuousness

magnificent august, brilliant, elegant, elevated, exalted, excellent, fine, glorious, gorgeous, grand, grandiose, imposing, impressive, lavish, luxurious, majestic, noble, opulent, outstanding, princely, regal, resplendent, rich, splendid, splendiferous (*facetious*), stately, striking, sublime, sumptuous, superb, superior, transcendent

magnify 1. aggrandize, amplify, augment, blow up (*informal*), boost, build up, deepen, dilate, enlarge, expand, heighten, increase, intensify **2.** blow up, blow up out of all proportion, dramatize, enhance, exaggerate, inflate, make a federal case of (*U.S. informal*), make a mountain out of a molehill, make a production (out) of (*informal*), overdo, overemphasize, overestimate, overplay, overrate, overstate

magnitude 1. consequence, eminence, grandeur, greatness, importance, mark, moment, note, significance, weight **2.** amount, amplitude, bigness, bulk, capacity, dimensions, enormity, expanse, extent, hugeness, immensity, intensity, largeness, mass, measure, proportions, quantity, size, space, strength, vastness, volume

maid 1. handmaiden (*archaic*), housemaid, maidservant, servant, serving-maid **2.** damsel, girl, lass, lassie (*informal*), maiden, miss, nymph (*poetic*), wench

maiden 1. *n.* damsel, girl, lass, lassie (*informal*), maid, miss, nymph (*poetic*), virgin, wench **2.** *adj.* first, inaugural, initial, initiatory, introductory

maidenly chaste, decent, decorous, demure, gentle, girlish, modest, pure, reserved, undefiled, unsullied, vestal, virginal, virtuous

which the postman puts letters for the occupiers of the house.

mail coach *n History* a fast stagecoach designed primarily for carrying mail.

mailing list *n* a register of names and addresses to which information or advertising matter is sent by post.

mailman *n, pl* **-men** *US & Canad* a postman.

mail order *n* a system of buying and selling goods by post.

mailshot *n* a posting of circulars, leaflets, or other advertising to a selected large number of people at once.

maim *vb* to injure badly or cruelly, with some permanent damage resulting.

main *adj* **1** chief or principal. *~n* **2** a principal pipe or line in a system used to distribute water, electricity, or gas. **3 mains** the main distribution network for water, gas, or electricity. **4** great strength or force: *with might and main.* **5** *Literary* the open ocean. **6 in the main** on the whole.

mainbrace *n Naut* **1** the rope that controls the movement of the spar of a ship's mainsail. **2 splice the mainbrace** See **splice.**

main clause *n Grammar* a clause that can stand alone as a sentence.

mainframe *n Computers* a high-speed general-purpose computer, with a large store capacity.

mainland *n* the main part of a land mass as opposed to an island.

main line *n* **1** *Railways* the chief route between two points, usually fed by branch lines. *~vb* **2** *Slang* to inject a drug into a vein.

mainly *adv* for the most part; principally.

mainmast *n Naut* the chief mast of a sailing vessel with two or more masts.

mainsail *n Naut* the largest and lowermost sail on the mainmast.

mainspring *n* **1** the chief cause or motive of something: *the mainspring of a dynamic economy.* **2** the chief spring of a watch or clock.

mainstay *n* **1** a chief support. **2** *Naut* a rope securing a mainmast.

mainstream *n* **1** the people or things representing the most common or generally accepted ideas and styles in a society, art form, etc.: *the mainstream of British political thought.* **2** the main current of a river. *~adj* **3** belonging to the social or cultural mainstream: *mainstream American movies.*

mainstreeting *n Canad* the practice of a politician walking about a town or city to try to gain votes.

maintain *vb* **1** to continue or keep in existence: *we must maintain good relations with them.* **2** to keep in proper or good condition: *an expensive car to maintain.* **3** to sustain or keep up a particular level or speed: *he set off at a high speed, but couldn't maintain it all the way.* **4** to enable a person to have the money, food and other things he or she needs to live: *the money maintained us for a month.* **5** to assert: *he had always maintained that he never wanted children.* **6** to defend against contradiction; uphold: *he maintained his innocence.*

maintenance *n* **1** the act of maintaining or the state of being maintained. **2** the process of keeping a car, building, etc. in good condition. **3** *Law* financial provision ordered to be made by way of periodical payments or a lump sum, usually for a separated or divorced spouse.

maisonette *n* a flat with more than one floor.

maitre d'hotel (**met**-ra dote-**tell**) *n, pl* **maitres d'hotel** a head waiter.

maize *n* a type of corn grown for its large yellow edible grains, which are used for food and as a source of oil. See also **sweet corn.**

Maj. Major.

majestic *adj* beautiful, dignified, and impressive. **majestically** *adv*

majesty *n* **1** great dignity and grandeur. **2** supreme power or authority.

Majesty *n, pl* **-ties** (preceded by *Your, His* or *Her*) a title used to address or refer to a sovereign or the wife or widow of a sovereign.

majolica *or* **maiolica** *n* a type of porous pottery glazed with bright metallic oxides. It was extensively made in Renaissance Italy.

major *adj* **1** greater in size, frequency, or importance than others of the same kind: *the major political parties.* **2** very serious or significant: *a major investigation.* **3** main or principal: *a major road.* **4** *Music* (of a scale) **a** having notes separated by a whole tone, except for the third and fourth notes, and seventh and eighth notes, which are separated by a semitone. **b** of or based on the major scale: *the key of D minor; a major third.* *~n* **5** a middle-ranking military officer. **6** *Music* a major key, chord, mode, or scale. **7** a person

THESAURUS

mail *n.* **1.** correspondence, letters, packages, parcels, post **2.** post, postal service, postal system *~vb.* **3.** dispatch, forward, post, send, send by mail *or* post

maim cripple, disable, hamstring, hurt, impair, incapacitate, injure, lame, mangle, mar, mutilate, put out of action, wound

main *adj.* **1.** capital, cardinal, central, chief, critical, crucial, essential, foremost, head, leading, necessary, outstanding, paramount, particular, predominant, pre-eminent, premier, primary, prime, principal, special, supreme, vital *~n.* **2.** cable, channel, conduit, duct, line, pipe **3.** effort, force, might, potency, power, strength **4. in the main** for the most part, generally, in general, mainly, mostly, on the whole

mainly above all, chiefly, first and foremost, for the most part, generally, in general, in the main, largely, mostly, most of all, on the whole, overall, predominantly, primarily, principally, substantially, to the greatest extent, usually

mainstay anchor, backbone, bulwark, buttress, chief support, linchpin, pillar, prop

maintain **1.** carry on, conserve, continue, finance, keep, keep up, look after, nurture, perpetuate, preserve, prolong, provide, retain, supply, support, sustain, uphold **2.** care for, keep in good repair, look after, take care of **3.** affirm, allege, assert, asseverate, aver, avow, claim, contend, declare, hold, insist, profess, state **4.** advocate, argue for, back, champion, defend, fight for, justify, plead for, stand by, take up the cudgels for, uphold, vindicate

maintenance **1.** care, carrying-on, conservation, continuance, continuation, keeping, nurture, perpetuation, preservation, prolongation, provision, repairs, retainment, supply, support, sustainment, sustention, upkeep **2.** aliment, alimony, allowance, food, keep, livelihood, living, subsistence, support, sustenance, upkeep

majestic august, awesome, dignified, elevated, exalted, grand, grandiose, imperial, imposing, impressive, kingly, lofty, magnificent, monumental, noble, pompous, princely, regal, royal, splendid, splendiferous (*facetious*), stately, sublime, superb

majesty augustness, awesomeness, dignity, exaltedness, glory, grandeur, imposingness, impressiveness,

who has reached the age of legal majority. **8** *US, Canad, Austral, & NZ* the principal field of study of a student. ~*vb* **9 major in** *US, Canad, Austral, & NZ* to study as one's principal subject: *he majored in economics.*

➤ *Major* strictly involves the comparison of one part with another: *He found the major part of the evidence.* Its use as a rough equivalent to "large" is very informal.

major-domo *n, pl* **-mos** the chief steward or butler of a great household.

majorette *n* one of a group of girls who practise formation marching and baton twirling.

major general *n* a senior military officer.

majority *n, pl* **-ties 1** the greater number or part of something. **2** (in an election) the number of votes or seats by which the strongest party or candidate beats the combined opposition or the runner-up. **3** the largest party or group that votes together in a meeting, council or parliament. **4** the age at which a person legally becomes an adult. **5 in the majority** forming or part of the group of people or things made up of more than half of a larger group.

make *vb* **making, made 1** to create, construct, establish, or draw up; bring into being: *houses made of stone; he will have to make a will.* **2** to cause to do or be; compel or induce: *please make her go away.* **3** to bring about or produce: *don't make a noise.* **4** to carry out or perform: *he made his first trip to China in 1987; she made an obscene gesture.* **5** to appoint: *they made him caretaker manager.* **6** to come into a specified state or condition: *to make merry.* **7** to become: *she will make a good diplomat.* **8** to cause or ensure the success of: *that news has made my day.* **9** to amount to: *5 and 5 make 10.* **10** to earn or be paid: *she's only making £100 a week.* **11** to have the qualities of or be suitable for: *what makes this book such a good read?* **12** to prepare for use: *she forgot to make her bed.* **13** to be the essential element in: *confidence makes a good salesman.* **14** to use for a specified purpose: *they will make this town their base.* **15** to deliver: *he made a very good speech.* **16** to consider to be: *what time do you make it?* **17** to cause to seem or represent as being: *her girlish pigtails made her look younger than she was; she made the experience sound most unpleasant.* **18** to acquire: *she doesn't make friends easily.* **19** to engage in: *they made war on the Turks.* **20** to travel a certain distance or to a certain place: *we can make at least three miles before it gets dark.* **21** to arrive in time for: *he didn't make the first act of the play.* **22** to win or score: *he made a break of 125.* **23** *Informal* to gain a place or position on or in: *to make the headlines.* **24 make a day** *or* **night of it** to cause an activity to last a day or night. **25 make eyes at** *Old-fashioned* to flirt with or ogle. **26 make it** *Informal* **a** to be able to attend: *I'm afraid I can't make it to your party.* **b** to be successful. **27 make like** *Slang, chiefly US & Canad* **a** to imitate. **b** to pretend. **28 make to, as if to** *or* **as though to** to act with the intention or with a show of doing something: *she made as if to hit him.* ~*n* **29** manufacturer; brand: *what make of car is that?* **30** the way in which something is made. **31 on the make** *Slang* out for profit or conquest. ~See also **make away, make for,** etc. **maker** *n*

make away *vb* **1** to depart in haste. **2 make away with a** to steal. **b** to kill or get rid of.

make believe *vb* **1** to pretend. ~*n* **make-believe 2** a fantasy or pretence.

make do *vb* to manage with an inferior alternative.

make for *vb* **1** to head towards. **2** to prepare to attack. **3** to help bring about: *this will make for a spectacular race.*

make of *vb* to interpret as the meaning of: *what did she make of it all?*

make off *vb* **1** to go or run away in haste. **2 make off with** to steal or abduct.

make out *vb* **1** to manage to see or hear. **2** to understand. **3** to write out: *I made out a cheque for £100.* **4**

THESAURUS

kingliness, loftiness, magnificence, nobility, pomp, queenliness, royalty, splendour, state, stateliness, sublimity

major 1. better, bigger, chief, elder, greater, head, higher, larger, lead, leading, main, most, senior, superior, supreme, uppermost **2.** critical, crucial, grave, great, important, notable, outstanding, pre-eminent, radical, serious, significant, vital, weighty

majority 1. best part, bulk, greater number, mass, more, most, plurality, preponderance, superiority **2.** adulthood, manhood, maturity, seniority, womanhood

make *vb.* **1.** assemble, build, compose, constitute, construct, create, draw up, enact, establish, fabricate, fashion, fix, forge, form, frame, manufacture, mould, originate, pass, produce, put together, shape, synthesize **2.** cause, coerce, compel, constrain, dragoon, drive, force, impel, induce, oblige, press, pressurize, prevail upon, railroad (*informal*), require **3.** accomplish, beget, bring about, cause, create, effect, engender, generate, give rise to, lead to, occasion, produce **4.** appoint, assign, create, designate, elect, install, invest, nominate, ordain **5.** add up to, amount to, compose, constitute, embody, form, represent **6.** acquire, clear, earn, gain, get, net, obtain, realize, secure, take in, win **7.** calculate, estimate, gauge, judge, reckon, suppose, think **8.** act, carry out, do, effect, engage in, execute, perform, practise, prosecute **9.** arrive at, arrive in time for, attain, catch, get to, meet, reach **10. make it** *informal* arrive (*informal*), be successful, come through, crack it (*informal*), cut it (*informal*), get on, get somewhere, prosper, pull through, succeed, survive ~*n.* **11.** brand, build, character, composition, constitution, construction, cut, designation, form, kind, make-up, mark, model, shape, sort, structure, style, type, variety

make away 1. abscond, beat a hasty retreat, clear out (*informal*), cut and run (*informal*), decamp, depart, do a runner (*slang*), flee, fly, fly the coop (*U.S. & Canad. informal*), make off, run away *or* off, run for it (*informal*), scoot, skedaddle (*informal*), slope off **2.** *with* **with** abduct, carry off, filch, kidnap, knock off (*slang*), make off with, nab (*informal*), nick (*slang, chiefly Brit.*), pilfer, pinch (*informal*), purloin, steal, swipe (*slang*) **3.** *with* **with** blow away (*slang, chiefly U.S.*), bump off (*slang*), destroy, dispose of, do away with, do in (*slang*), eliminate, get rid of, kill, murder, rub out (*U.S. slang*)

make-believe charade, dream, fantasy, imagination, play-acting, pretence, unreality

make believe act as if *or* though, dream, enact, fantasize, imagine, play, play-act, pretend

make do cope, get along *or* by, improvise, manage, muddle through, scrape along *or* by

make for 1. aim for, be bound for, head for *or* towards, proceed towards, steer (a course) for **2.** assail, assault, attack, fall on, fly at, go for, have a go at (*informal*), lunge at, set upon **3.** be conducive to, contribute to, facilitate, favour, promote

make off 1. abscond, beat a hasty retreat, bolt, clear out (*informal*), cut and run (*informal*), decamp, do a runner (*slang*), flee, fly, fly the coop (*U.S. & Canad. informal*), make away, run away *or* off, run for it (*informal*), skedaddle (*informal*), slope off, take to one's heels **2.** *with* **with** abduct, carry off, filch, kidnap,

to attempt to establish or prove: *she made me out to be a crook.* **5** to pretend: *he made out that he could play the piano.* **6** to manage or get on: *how did you make out in the exam?*

make over *vb* **1** to renovate or remodel: *she made over the dress to fit her sister.* ~*n* **makeover** **2** a complete remodelling. **3** a series of alterations, including beauty treatments and new clothes, intended to make an improvement to someone's appearance.

Maker *n* a title given to God.

makeshift *adj* serving as a temporary substitute.

make-up *n* **1** cosmetics, such as powder or lipstick. **2** the cosmetics used by an actor to adapt his or her appearance. **3** the arrangement of the parts of something. **4** mental or physical constitution. ~*vb* **make up** **5** to form or constitute: *these arguments make up the case for the defence.* **6** to devise or compose, sometimes with the intent to deceive: *she was well known for making up stories about herself.* **7** to supply what is lacking in; complete: *£3 billion is needed to make up the shortfall.* **8** Also: **make it up** to settle differences amicably. **9** **make up for** to compensate for: *one good year can make up for several bad ones.* **10** to apply cosmetics to the face. **11** **make up to** *Informal* **a** to make friendly overtures to. **b** to flirt with.

makeweight *n* an unimportant person or thing added to make up a lack.

making *n* **1** the act or process of producing something. **2** **be the making of** to cause the success of. **3** **in the making** in the process of becoming or being made.

makings *pl n* **have the makings of** to have the potentials, qualities, or materials necessary to make or become something: *it had the makings of a classic showdown.*

mako *n, pl* **makos** a powerful shark of the Atlantic and Pacific Oceans.

mal- *combining form* bad or badly; wrong or wrongly: *maladjusted; malfunction.*

malachite (**mal**-a-kite) *n* a green mineral used as a source of copper, and for making ornaments.

maladjustment *n Psychol* a failure to meet the demands of society, such as coping with problems and social relationships. **maladjusted** *adj*

maladminister *vb* to administer badly, inefficiently, or dishonestly. **maladministration** *n*

maladroit (mal-a-**droyt**) *adj* clumsy, awkward, or tactless. **maladroitly** *adv* **maladroitness** *n*

malady (**mal**-a-dee) *n, pl* **-dies** *Old-fashioned* any disease or illness.

malaise (mal-**laze**) *n* a vague feeling of unease, illness, or depression.

malapropism *n* the comic misuse of a word by confusion with one which sounds similar, for example *under the affluence of alcohol.*

malaria *n* a disease with recurring attacks of fever, caused by the bite of some types of mosquito. **malarial** *adj*

malarkey *n Slang* nonsense or rubbish.

Malay *n* **1** a member of a people living chiefly in Malaysia and Indonesia. **2** the language of this people. ~*adj* **3** of the Malays or their language.

Malayan *adj* **1** of Malaya. *n* **2** a person from Malaya.

Malaysian *adj* **1** of Malaysia. ~*n* **2** a person from Malaysia.

malcontent *n* a person who is discontented with the existing situation.

male *adj* **1** of the sex that can fertilize female reproductive cells. **2** of or characteristic of a man. **3** for or composed of men or boys: *a male choir.* **4** (of flowers) bearing stamens but lacking a pistil. **5** *Electronics, engineering* having a projecting part or parts that fit into a hollow counterpart: *a male plug.* ~*n* **6** a male person, animal, or plant. **maleness** *n*

male chauvinism *n* the belief, held by some men, that men are better and more important than women. **male chauvinist** *n, adj*

malediction (mal-lid-**dik**-shun) *n* the utterance of a curse against someone or something. **maledictory** *adj*

malefactor (**mal**-if-act-or) *n* a criminal or wrongdoer. **malefaction** *n*

THESAURUS

knock off (*slang*), make away with, nab (*informal*), nick (*slang, chiefly Brit.*), pilfer, pinch (*informal*), purloin, run away *or* off with, steal, swipe (*slang*)

make out **1.** descry, detect, discern, discover, distinguish, espy, perceive, recognize, see **2.** comprehend, decipher, fathom, follow, grasp, perceive, realize, see, suss (out) (*slang*), understand, work out **3.** complete, draw up, fill in *or* out, inscribe, write (out) **4.** demonstrate, describe, prove, represent, show **5.** assert, claim, let on, make as if *or* though, pretend **6.** fare, get on, manage, prosper, succeed, thrive

maker author, builder, constructor, director, fabricator, framer, manufacturer, producer

Maker Creator, God

makeshift jury (*chiefly nautical*), make-do, provisional, rough and ready, stopgap, substitute, temporary

make-up **1.** cosmetics, face (*informal*), greasepaint (*Theatre*), *maquillage,* paint (*informal*), powder, war paint (*informal, humorous*) **2.** arrangement, assembly, composition, configuration, constitution, construction, form, format, formation, organization, structure **3.** build, cast of mind, character, constitution, disposition, figure, frame of mind, make, nature, stamp, temper, temperament

make up **1.** compose, comprise, constitute, form **2.** coin, compose, concoct, construct, cook up (*informal*), create, devise, dream up, fabricate, formulate, frame, hatch, invent, manufacture, originate, trump up, write **3.** complete, fill, meet, supply **4.** bury the hatchet, call it quits, come to terms, compose, forgive and forget, make peace, mend, reconcile, settle, shake hands **5.** *with* **for** atone, balance, compensate, make amends, offset, recompense, redeem, redress, requite **6.** **make up to** *informal* chat up (*informal*), court, curry favour with, flirt with, make overtures to, woo

makings beginnings, capability, capacity, ingredients, materials, potentiality, potential(s), qualities

maladjusted alienated, disturbed, estranged, hung-up (*slang*), neurotic, unstable

maladministration blundering, bungling, corruption, dishonesty, incompetence, inefficiency, malfeasance (*Law*), malpractice, misgovernment, mismanagement, misrule

malady affliction, ailment, complaint, disease, disorder, ill, illness, indisposition, infirmity, sickness

malcontent agitator, complainer, fault-finder, grouch (*informal*), grouser, grumbler, mischief-maker, rebel, stirrer (*informal*), troublemaker

male manful, manlike, manly, masculine, virile

malefactor convict, criminal, crook (*informal*), culprit, delinquent, evildoer, felon, lawbreaker, miscreant, offender, outlaw, transgressor, villain, wrongdoer

malevolence hate, hatred, ill will, malice, maliciousness, malignity, rancour, spite, spitefulness, vengefulness, vindictiveness

malevolent baleful, evil-minded, hateful (*archaic*),

malevolent (mal-**lev**-a-lent) *adj* wishing evil to others; malicious. **malevolence** *n* **malevolently** *adv*

malfeasance (mal-**fee**-zanss) *n Law* wrongful or illegal behaviour, esp. by a public official.

malformation *n* **1** the condition of being faulty or abnormal in form or shape. **2** *Pathol* a deformity, esp. when congenital. **malformed** *adj*

malfunction *vb* **1** to fail to function properly or fail to function at all. ~*n* **2** failure to function properly or failure to function at all.

malice (**mal**-iss) *n* the desire to do harm or cause mischief to others. **malicious** *adj* **maliciously** *adv*

malice aforethought *n Law* a deliberate intention to do something unlawful.

malign (mal-**line**) *vb* **1** to say unpleasant and untrue things about someone; slander. ~*adj* **2** evil in influence or effect.

malignant (mal-**lig**-nant) *adj* **1** seeking to harm others. **2** tending to cause great harm; injurious. **3** *Pathol* (of a tumour) uncontrollable or resistant to therapy. **malignancy** *n*

malignity (mal-**lig**-nit-ee) *n* the condition of being malign or deadly.

malinger (mal-**ling**-ger) *vb* to pretend to be ill, or exaggerate how ill one is, to avoid work. **malingerer** *n*

mall (**mawl**) *n* **1** *US, Canad, Austral, & NZ* short for **shopping mall. 2** a shaded avenue, esp. one open to the public.

mallard *n, pl* **-lard** *or* **-lards** a common N hemisphere duck, the male of which has a dark green head.

malleable (**mal**-lee-a-bl) *adj* **1** (esp. of metal) capable of being hammered or pressed into shape without breaking. **2** able to be influenced. **malleability** *n* **malleably** *adv*

mallet *n* **1** a hammer with a large wooden head. **2** a long stick with a head like a hammer used to strike the ball in croquet or polo.

mallow *n* any of a group of European plants, with purple, pink, or white flowers.

malnourished *adj* physically weak due to lack of healthy food.

malnutrition *n* physical weakness resulting from insufficient food or an unbalanced diet.

malodorous (mal-**lode**-or-uss) *adj* having an unpleasant smell.

malpractice *n* illegal, unethical, or negligent professional conduct.

malt *n* **1** grain, such as barley, that is kiln-dried after it has been germinated by soaking in water. **2** See **malt whisky.** ~*vb* **3** to make into or become malt. **4** to make from malt or to add malt to. **malted** *adj* **malty** *adj*

Maltese *adj* **1** of Malta. ~*n* **2** (*pl* **-tese**) a person from Malta. **3** the language of Malta.

Maltese cross *n* a cross with triangular arms that taper towards the centre, sometimes with the outer sides curving in.

Malthusian (malth-**yew**-zee-an) *adj* of the theory stating that increases in population tend to exceed increases in the food supply and that therefore sexual restraint should be exercised.

maltose *n* a sugar formed by the action of enzymes on starch.

maltreat *vb* to treat badly, cruelly, or violently. **maltreatment** *n*

malt whisky *n* whisky made from malted barley.

malversation *n Rare* professional or public misconduct.

mam *n Informal or dialect* same as **mother.**

mama *or esp US* **mamma** (mam-**mah**) *n Old-fashioned, informal* same as **mother.**

mamba *n* a very poisonous tree snake found in tropical and Southern Africa.

mambo *n, pl* **-bos** a Latin American dance resembling the rumba.

mammal *n* a warm-blooded animal, such as a human being, dog or whale, the female of which produces milk to feed her babies. **mammalian** *adj, n*

mammary *adj* of the breasts or milk-producing glands.

mammary gland *n* any of the milk-producing glands in mammals, such as a woman's breast or a cow's udder.

mammon *n* wealth regarded as a source of evil and corruption, personified in the New Testament as a false god (**Mammon**).

mammoth *n* **1** a large extinct elephant with a hairy coat and long curved tusks. ~*adj* **2** gigantic.

mammy *n, pl* **-mies** *Informal or dialect* same as **mother.**

man *n, pl* **men 1** an adult male human being, as distinguished from a woman. **2** a human being of either sex; person: *all men are born equal.* **3** human beings collectively; mankind. **4** a human being regarded as representative of a particular period or category: *Neanderthal man.* **5** an adult male human being with qualities associated with the male, such as courage or virility: *take it like a man.* **6** an employee, servant, or representative. **7** a member of the armed forces who is not an officer. **8** a member of a group or team. **9** a husband, boyfriend, or male lover. **10** a movable piece

THESAURUS

hostile, ill-natured, maleficent, malicious, malign, malignant, pernicious, rancorous, spiteful, vengeful, vicious, vindictive

malformation crookedness, deformity, distortion, misshape, misshapenness

malfunction 1. *vb.* break down, develop a fault, fail, go wrong **2.** *n.* breakdown, defect, failure, fault, flaw, glitch, impairment

malice animosity, animus, bad blood, bitterness, enmity, evil intent, hate, hatred, ill will, malevolence, maliciousness, malignity, rancour, spite, spitefulness, spleen, vengefulness, venom, vindictiveness

malicious baleful, bitchy (*informal*), bitter, catty (*informal*), evil-minded, hateful, ill-disposed, ill-natured, injurious, malevolent, malignant, mischievous, pernicious, rancorous, resentful, shrewish, spiteful, vengeful, vicious

malign 1. *vb.* abuse, bad-mouth (*slang, chiefly U.S. & Canad.*), blacken (someone's name), calumniate, defame, denigrate, derogate, disparage, do a hatchet job on (*informal*), harm, injure, knock (*informal*), libel, revile, rubbish (*informal*), run down, slag (off) (*slang*), slander, smear, speak ill of, traduce, vilify **2.** *adj.* bad, baleful, baneful, deleterious, destructive, evil, harmful, hostile, hurtful, injurious, maleficent, malevolent, malignant, pernicious, vicious, wicked

malignant 1. baleful, bitter, destructive, harmful, hostile, hurtful, inimical, injurious, maleficent, malevolent, malicious, malign, of evil intent, pernicious, spiteful, vicious **2.** *Medical* cancerous, dangerous, deadly, fatal, irremediable, metastatic, uncontrollable, virulent

malpractice abuse, dereliction, misbehaviour, misconduct, mismanagement, negligence

maltreat abuse, bully, damage, handle roughly, harm, hurt, ill-treat, injure, mistreat

mammoth Brobdingnagian, colossal, elephantine, enormous, gargantuan, giant, gigantic, ginormous (*in-*

in various games, such as draughts. **11** *S African slang* any person: used as a term of address. **12 as one man** with unanimous action or response. **13 he's your man** he's the person needed. **14 man and boy** from childhood. **15 sort out the men from the boys** to discover who can cope with difficult or dangerous situations and who cannot. **16 to a man** without exception. *~vb* **manning, manned 17** to provide with sufficient people for operation or defence. **18** to take one's place at or near in readiness for action. **manhood** *n*

Man. Manitoba.

manacle (**man**-a-kl) *n* **1** a metal ring or chain put round the wrists or ankles, used to restrict the movements of a prisoner or convict. *~vb* **-cling, -cled 2** to put manacles on.

manage *vb* **-aging, -aged 1** to succeed in doing something: *we finally managed to sell our old house.* **2** to be in charge of; administer: *the company is badly managed.* **3** to have room or time for: *can you manage lunch tomorrow?* **4** to keep under control: *she disapproved of taking drugs to manage stress.* **5** to struggle on despite difficulties, esp. financial ones: *most people cannot manage on a cleaner's salary.* **manageable** *adj*

management *n* **1** the people responsible for running an organization or business. **2** managers or employers collectively. **3** the technique or practice of managing or controlling.

manager *n* **1** a person who manages an organization or business. **2** a person in charge of a sports team. **3** a person who controls the business affairs of an actor or entertainer. **manageress** *fem n*

➤ In professional life the title *manager* is used for either men or women. Elsewhere the term *manageress* is still in use.

managerial *adj* of a manager or management.

managing director *n* the senior director of a company, who has overall responsibility for the way it is run.

mañana (man-**yah**-na) *n, adv* **a** tomorrow. **b** some other and later time.

man-at-arms *n, pl* **men-at-arms** a soldier, esp. a medieval soldier.

manatee *n* a large plant-eating mammal occurring in tropical coastal waters of the Atlantic.

Manchu *n, pl* **-chus** *or* **-chu** a member of a Mongoloid people of Manchuria, a region of NE China, who conquered China in the 17th century, ruling until 1912.

Mancunian (man-**kew**-nee-an) *adj* **1** of Manchester, a city in NW England. *~n* **2** a person from Manchester.

mandala *n Hindu & Buddhist art* a circular design symbolizing the universe.

mandarin *n* **1** (in the Chinese Empire) a member of a senior grade of the bureaucracy. **2** a high-ranking official with extensive powers. **3** a person of standing and influence, esp. in literary or intellectual circles. **4** a small citrus fruit resembling the tangerine.

Mandarin Chinese *or* **Mandarin** *n* the official language of China since 1917.

mandate *n* **1** an official or authoritative command to carry out a particular task: *the UN force's mandate does not allow it to intervene.* **2** *Politics* the political authority given to a government or an elected representative through an electoral victory. **3** Also: **mandated territory** (formerly) a territory administered by one country on behalf of an international body. *~vb* **-dating, -dated 4** to delegate authority to. **5** to assign territory to a nation under a mandate.

mandatory *adj* **1** obligatory; compulsory. **2** having the nature or powers of a mandate. **mandatorily** *adv*

mandible *n* **1** the lower jawbone of a vertebrate. **2** either of the jawlike mouthparts of an insect. **3** either part of the bill of a bird, esp. the lower part.

mandolin *n* a musical instrument with four pairs of strings stretched over a small light body, usually played with a plectrum.

mandrake *n* a plant with a forked root. It was formerly thought to have magic powers and a narcotic was prepared from its root.

mandrel *or* **mandril** *n* **1** a spindle on which the object being worked on is supported in a lathe. **2** a shaft on which a machining tool is mounted.

mandrill *n* a monkey of W Africa. The male has red and blue markings on its face and buttocks.

mane *n* **1** the long hair that grows from the neck in such mammals as the lion and horse. **2** long thick human hair. **maned** *adj*

manege (man-**nayzh**) *n* **1** the art of training horses and riders. **2** a riding school.

maneuver *n, vb US* same as **manoeuvre.**

man Friday *n* **1** a loyal male servant or assistant. **2**

THESAURUS

formal), huge, immense, jumbo (*informal*), massive, mega (*slang*), mighty, monumental, mountainous, prodigious, stupendous, titanic, vast

man *n.* **1.** bloke (*Brit. informal*), chap (*informal*), gentleman, guy (*informal*), male **2.** adult, being, body, human, human being, individual, one, person, personage, somebody, soul **3.** Homo sapiens, humanity, humankind, human race, mankind, mortals, people **4.** attendant, employee, follower, hand, hireling, liegeman, manservant, retainer, servant, subject, subordinate, valet, vassal, worker, workman **5.** grunt (*U.S. slang*), serviceman, soldier, squaddie (*informal*) **6.** beau, boyfriend, husband, lover, partner, significant other (*U.S. informal*), spouse **7. to a man** bar none, every one, one and all, unanimously, without exception *~vb.* **8.** crew, fill, furnish with men, garrison, occupy, people, staff

manacle 1. *n.* bond, chain, fetter, handcuff, iron, shackle, tie **2.** *vb.* bind, chain, check, clap *or* put in irons, confine, constrain, curb, fetter, hamper, handcuff, inhibit, put in chains, restrain, shackle, tie one's hands

manage 1. accomplish, arrange, bring about *or* off, contrive, cope with, crack it (*informal*), cut it (*informal*), deal with, effect, engineer, succeed **2.** administer, be in charge (of), command, conduct, control, direct, govern, guide, handle, manipulate, oversee, preside over, rule, run, superintend, supervise **3.** carry on, cope, fare, get along, get by (*informal*), get on, make do, make out, muddle through, shift, survive

manageable amenable, compliant, controllable, convenient, docile, easy, governable, handy, submissive, tamable, tractable, user-friendly, wieldy

management 1. administration, board, bosses (*informal*), directorate, directors, employers, executive(s) **2.** administration, care, charge, command, conduct, control, direction, governance, government, guidance, handling, manipulation, operation, rule, running, superintendence, supervision

manager administrator, boss (*informal*), comptroller, conductor, controller, director, executive, gaffer (*informal, chiefly Brit.*), governor, head, organizer, overseer, proprietor, superintendent, supervisor

mandate authority, authorization, bidding, charge, command, commission, decree, directive, edict, fiat, injunction, instruction, order, precept, sanction, warrant

mandatory binding, compulsory, obligatory, required, requisite

Also: **girl Friday, person Friday** any person who does all the odd jobs that arise, esp. in an office.

manful *adj* determined and brave. **manfully** *adv*

manganese *n Chem* a brittle greyish-white metallic element used in making steel. Symbol: Mn

mange *n* a skin disease of domestic animals, characterized by itching and loss of hair.

mangelwurzel *n* a variety of beet with a large yellowish root.

manger *n* a trough in a stable or barn from which horses or cattle feed.

mangetout (**mawnzh**-too) *n* a variety of garden pea with an edible pod.

mangle[1] *vb* **-gling, -gled 1** to destroy or damage by crushing and twisting. **2** to spoil. **mangled** *adj*

mangle[2] *n* **1** a machine for pressing or squeezing water out of washed clothes, consisting of two heavy rollers between which the clothes are passed. *~vb* **-gling, -gled 2** to put through a mangle.

mango *n, pl* **-goes** *or* **-gos** the egg-shaped edible fruit of a tropical Asian tree, with a smooth rind and sweet juicy flesh.

mangrove *n* a tropical evergreen tree or shrub with intertwining aerial roots that forms dense thickets along coasts.

mangy *adj* **-gier, -giest 1** having mange. **2** scruffy or shabby. **mangily** *adv* **manginess** *n*

manhandle *vb* **-handling, -handled 1** to handle or push someone about roughly. **2** to move something by manpower rather than by machinery.

manhole *n* a hole with a detachable cover, through which a person can enter a sewer or pipe to inspect or repair it.

man-hour *n* a unit of work in industry, equal to the work done by one person in one hour.

manhunt *n* an organized search, usually by police, for a wanted man or fugitive.

mania *n* **1** an obsessional enthusiasm or liking. **2** a mental disorder characterized by great or violent excitement.

-mania *n combining form* indicating extreme or abnormal excitement aroused by something: *kleptomania.*

maniac *n* **1** a wild disorderly person. **2** a person who has a great craving or enthusiasm for something. **maniacal** (man-eye-ak-kl) *adj*

manic *adj* **1** extremely excited or energetic; frenzied: *manic, cavorting dancers.* **2** of, involving, or affected by mania: *deep depression broken by periods of manic excitement.*

manic-depressive *Psychiatry ~adj* **1** denoting a mental disorder characterized by an alternation between extreme euphoria and deep depression. *~n* **2** a person afflicted with this disorder.

manicure *n* **1** cosmetic care of the hands and fingernails. *~vb* **-curing, -cured 2** to care for the fingernails and hands. **manicurist** *n*

manifest *adj* **1** easily noticed, obvious. *~vb* **2** to reveal or display: *an additional symptom now manifested itself.* **3** to show by the way one behaves: *he manifested great personal bravery.* **4** (of a disembodied spirit) to appear in visible form. *~n* **5** a customs document containing particulars of a ship and its cargo. **6** a list of the cargo and passengers on an aeroplane. **manifestation** *n*

manifesto *n, pl* **-toes** *or* **-tos** a public declaration of intent or policy issued by a group of people, for instance by a political party.

manifold *adj Formal* **1** numerous and varied: *her talents are manifold.* *~n* **2** a pipe with a number of inlets or outlets, esp. one in a car engine.

manikin *n* **1** a little man; dwarf or child. **2** a model of the human body.

manila *or* **manilla** *n* a strong usually brown paper used to make envelopes.

man in the street *n* the average person.

manipulate *vb* **-lating, -lated 1** to handle or use skilfully. **2** to control something or someone cleverly or deviously. **manipulation** *n* **manipulator** *n* **manipulative** *adj*

mankind *n* **1** human beings collectively. **2** men collectively.

manly *adj* **-lier, -liest 1** possessing qualities, such as

THESAURUS

manful bold, brave, courageous, daring, determined, gallant, hardy, heroic, indomitable, intrepid, manly, noble, powerful, resolute, stalwart, stout, stout-hearted, strong, valiant, vigorous

manfully boldly, bravely, courageously, desperately, determinedly, gallantly, hard, heroically, intrepidly, like a Trojan, like one possessed, like the devil, nobly, powerfully, resolutely, stalwartly, stoutly, strongly, to the best of one's ability, valiantly, vigorously, with might and main

mangle butcher, cripple, crush, cut, deform, destroy, disfigure, distort, hack, lacerate, maim, mar, maul, mutilate, rend, ruin, spoil, tear, total (*slang*), trash (*slang*), wreck

mangy dirty, grungy (*slang, chiefly U.S.*), mean, moth-eaten, scabby (*informal*), scruffy, scuzzy (*slang, chiefly U.S.*), seedy, shabby, shoddy, squalid

manhandle 1. handle roughly, knock about *or* around, maul, paw (*informal*), pull, push, rough up **2.** carry, haul, heave, hump (*Brit. slang*), lift, manoeuvre, pull, push, shove, tug

manhood bravery, courage, determination, firmness, fortitude, hardihood, manfulness, manliness, masculinity, maturity, mettle, resolution, spirit, strength, valour, virility

mania 1. craving, craze, desire, enthusiasm, fad (*informal*), fetish, fixation, obsession, partiality, passion, preoccupation, rage, thing (*informal*) **2.** craziness, delirium, dementia, derangement, disorder, frenzy, insanity, lunacy, madness

maniac 1. headbanger (*informal*), headcase (*informal*), loony (*slang*), lunatic, madman, madwoman, nutcase (*slang*), nutter (*Brit. slang*), psycho (*slang*), psychopath **2.** enthusiast, fan, fanatic, fiend (*informal*), freak (*informal*)

manifest 1. *adj.* apparent, blatant, clear, conspicuous, distinct, evident, glaring, noticeable, obvious, open, palpable, patent, plain, unmistakable, visible **2.** *vb.* declare, demonstrate, display, establish, evince, exhibit, expose, express, make plain, prove, reveal, set forth, show

manifestation appearance, demonstration, disclosure, display, exhibition, exposure, expression, indication, instance, mark, materialization, revelation, show, sign, symptom, token

manifold abundant, assorted, copious, diverse, diversified, many, multifarious, multifold, multiple, multiplied, multitudinous, numerous, varied, various

manipulate 1. employ, handle, operate, ply, use, wield, work **2.** conduct, control, direct, engineer, guide, influence, manoeuvre, negotiate, steer

mankind Homo sapiens, humanity, humankind, human race, man, people

manliness boldness, bravery, courage, fearlessness, firmness, hardihood, heroism, independence, intrepidity, machismo, manfulness, manhood, masculinity,

vigour or courage, traditionally regarded as appropriate to a man; masculine. **2** characteristic of a man. **manliness** *n*

man-made *adj* made by humans; artificial.

manna *n* **1** *Bible* the miraculous food which sustained the Israelites in the wilderness (Exodus 16:14–3). **2** a windfall: *manna from heaven.*

manned *adj* having a human staff or crew: *one of the few remaining manned lighthouses in the UK.*

mannequin *n* **1** a woman who wears the clothes displayed at a fashion show; model. **2** a life-size dummy of the human body used to fit or display clothes.

manner *n* **1** the way a thing happens or is done. **2** a person's bearing and behaviour. **3** the style or customary way of doing something: *sculpture in the Greek manner.* **4** type or kind. **5 in a manner of speaking** in a way; so to speak. **6 to the manner born** naturally fitted to a specified role or activity.

mannered *adj* **1** (of speech or behaviour) unnaturally formal and put on to impress others. **2** having manners as specified: *ill-mannered.*

mannerism *n* **1** a distinctive and individual gesture way or way of speaking. **2** excessive use of a distinctive or affected manner, esp. in art or literature.

mannerly *adj* well-mannered and polite. **mannerliness** *n*

manners *pl n* **1** a person's social conduct viewed in the light of whether it is regarded as polite or acceptable or not: *his manners leave something to be desired; shockingly bad manners.* **2** a socially acceptable way of behaving: *it's not manners to point.*

mannish *adj* (of a woman) displaying qualities regarded as typical of a man.

manoeuvre *or US* **maneuver** (man-**noo**-ver) *vb* **-vring, -vred** *or* **-vering, -vered 1** to move or do something with dexterity and skill: *she manoeuvred the car into the parking space.* **2** to manipulate a situation in order to gain some advantage. **3** to perform a manoeuvre or manoeuvres. *~n* **4** a movement or action requiring dexterity and skill. **5** a contrived, complicated, and possibly deceptive plan or action. **6 manoeuvres** military or naval exercises, usually on a large scale. **7** a change in course of a ship or aircraft, esp. a complicated one. **8 room for manoeuvre** the possibility of changing one's plans or behaviour if it becomes necessary or desirable. **manoeuvrable** *or US* **maneuverable** *adj* **manoeuvrability** *or US* **maneuverability** *n*

manoeuvring *or US* **maneuvering** *n* the skilful manipulation of a situation to gain some advantage.

man-of-war *n, pl* **men-of-war 1** a warship. **2** short for **Portuguese man-of-war.**

manor *n* **1** (in medieval Europe) the lands and property controlled by a lord. **2** a large country house and its lands. **3** *Slang* a police district. **manorial** *adj*

manor house *n* a large country house, esp. one that was originally part of a medieval manor.

manpower *n* the number of people needed or available for a job.

manqué (**mong**-kay) *adj* unfulfilled; would-be: *an actor manqué.*

mansard *n* a roof with two slopes on both sides and both ends, the lower slopes being steeper than the upper.

manse *n* the house provided for a minister of some Christian denominations.

manservant *n, pl* **menservants** a male servant, esp. a valet.

mansion *n* **1** a large and imposing house. **2 Mansions** *Brit* a name given to some blocks of flats as part of their address: *18 Wilton Mansions.*

manslaughter *n Law* the unlawful but not deliberately planned killing of one human being by another.

mantel *n* a wooden, stone, or iron frame around a fireplace.

mantelpiece *n* a shelf above a fireplace often forming part of the mantel. Also: **mantel shelf, chimneypiece**

mantilla *n* a woman's lace or silk scarf covering the shoulders and head, worn esp. in Spain.

mantis *n, pl* **-tises** *or* **-tes** a carnivorous insect resembling a grasshopper, that rests with the first pair of legs raised as if in prayer. Also: **praying mantis**

mantissa *n* the part of a common logarithm consisting of the decimal point and the figures following it: *the mantissa of 2.4771 is .4771.*

mantle *n* **1** *Old-fashioned* a loose wrap or cloak. **2** anything that covers completely or envelops: *a mantle of snow covered the ground.* **3** the responsibilities and duties which go with a particular job or position: *he refuses to accept the mantle of leader.* **4** a small mesh dome used to increase illumination in a gas or oil lamp by becoming incandescent. **5** *Geol* the part of the earth between the crust and the core. *~vb* **-tling, -tled 6** to spread over or become spread over: *mountains mantled in lush vegetation.*

THESAURUS

mettle, resolution, stoutheartedness, valour, vigour, virility

manly bold, brave, butch (*slang*), courageous, daring, dauntless, fearless, gallant, hardy, heroic, macho, male, manful, masculine, muscular, noble, powerful, red-blooded (*informal*), resolute, robust, stouthearted, strapping, strong, valiant, valorous, vigorous, virile, well-built

man-made artificial, ersatz, manufactured, plastic (*slang*), synthetic

manner **1.** air, appearance, aspect, bearing, behaviour, comportment, conduct, demeanour, deportment, look, mien (*literary*), presence, tone **2.** approach, custom, fashion, form, genre, habit, line, means, method, mode, practice, procedure, process, routine, style, tack, tenor, usage, way, wont **3.** brand, breed, category, form, kind, nature, sort, type, variety

mannered affected, artificial, posed, pretentious, put-on, stilted

mannerism characteristic, foible, habit, idiosyncrasy, peculiarity, quirk, trait, trick

mannerly civil, civilized, courteous, decorous, genteel, gentlemanly, gracious, ladylike, polished, polite, refined, respectful, well-behaved, well-bred, well-mannered

manners **1.** bearing, behaviour, breeding, carriage, comportment, conduct, demeanour, deportment **2.** ceremony, courtesy, decorum, etiquette, formalities, good form, polish, politeness, politesse, proprieties, protocol, refinement, social graces, the done thing

manoeuvre *vb.* **1.** direct, drive, guide, handle, navigate, negotiate, pilot, steer **2.** contrive, devise, engineer, intrigue, machinate, manage, manipulate, plan, plot, pull strings, scheme, wangle (*informal*) *~n.* **3.** action, artifice, dodge, intrigue, machination, move, movement, plan, plot, ploy, ruse, scheme, stratagem, subterfuge, tactic, trick **4. manoeuvres** deployment, evolution, exercise, movement, operation

mansion abode, *chateau,* dwelling, habitation, hall, manor, residence, seat, villa

mantle *n.* **1.** *old-fashioned* cape, cloak, hood, shawl, wrap **2.** blanket, canopy, cloud, cover, covering, cur-

man-to-man *adj* characterized by frankness and sincerity: *a man-to-man discussion.*

mantra *n* **1** *Hinduism, Buddhism* any sacred word or syllable used as an object of concentration. **2** *Hinduism* a Vedic psalm of praise.

manual *adj* **1** of a hand or hands: *manual dexterity.* **2** physical as opposed to mental: *manual labour.* **3** operated or done by human labour rather than automatic or computer-aided means: *a manual gearbox.* ~*n* **4** a book of instructions or information. **5** *Music* one of the keyboards on an organ. **manually** *adv*

manufacture *vb* **-turing, -tured 1** to process or make goods on a large scale, esp. using machinery. **2** to invent or concoct evidence, an excuse, etc. ~*n* **3** the production of goods, esp. by industrial processes. **manufacturer** *n* **manufacturing** *n, adj*

manuka (**mah**-nook-a) *n* a New Zealand tree with strong elastic wood and aromatic leaves.

manumit (man-new-**mit**) *vb* **-mitting, -mitted** to free from slavery. **manumission** *n*

manure *n* **1** animal excrement used as a fertilizer. ~*vb* **-nuring, -nured 2** to spread manure upon fields or soil.

manuscript *n* **1** a book or other document written by hand. **2** the original handwritten or typed version of a book or article submitted by an author for publication.

Manx *adj* **1** of the Isle of Man. ~*n* **2** an almost extinct Celtic language of the Isle of Man. ~*pl n* **3 the Manx** the people of the Isle of Man. **Manxman** *n* **Manxwoman** *n*

Manx cat *n* a short-haired breed of cat without a tail.

many *adj* **1** a large number of; numerous: *many times; many people think the government is incompetent.* ~*pron* **2** a number of people or things, esp. a large one: *his many supporters; have as many as you want.* **3 many a** each of a considerable number of: *many a man.* ~*n* **4 the many** the majority of mankind, esp. the common people.

Maoism *n* Communism as interpreted in the theories and policies of Mao Tse-tung (1893–1976), Chinese statesman. **Maoist** *n, adj*

Maori *n* **1** (*pl* **-ris** *or* **-ri**) a member of the Polynesian people living in New Zealand since before the arrival of European settlers. **2** the language of this people. ~*adj* **3** of this people or their language.

map *n* **1** a diagrammatic representation of the earth's surface or part of it, showing the geographical distributions or positions of features such as roads, towns, relief, and rainfall. **2** a diagrammatic representation of the stars or of the surface of a celestial body. **3** *Maths* same as **function. 4 put on the map** to make (a town or company) well-known. ~*vb* **mapping, mapped 5** to make a map of. **6** *Maths* to represent or transform (a function, figure, or set). ~See also **map out.**

maple *n* **1** any of various trees or shrubs with five-pointed leaves and winged seeds borne in pairs. **2** the hard wood of any of these trees. ~See also **sugar maple.**

maple leaf *n* the leaf of the maple tree, the national emblem of Canada.

maple syrup *n* a very sweet syrup made from the sap of the sugar maple.

map out *vb* to plan or design.

mapping *n Maths* same as **function.**

maquis (mah-**kee**) *n, pl* **-quis** (**-kee**) **1** the French underground movement that fought against the German occupying forces in World War II. **2** a type of shrubby, mostly evergreen, vegetation found in coastal regions of the Mediterranean area.

mar *vb* **marring, marred** to spoil or be the one bad feature of: *Sicily's coastline is marred by high-rise hotels.*

Mar. March.

marabou *n* **1** a large black-and-white African stork. **2** the soft white down of this bird, used to trim hats etc.

maraca (mar-**rak**-a) *n* a shaken percussion instrument, usually one of a pair, consisting of a gourd or plastic shell filled with dried seeds or pebbles.

marae (mar-**rye**) *n NZ* a traditional Maori meeting place.

maraschino (mar-rass-**kee**-no) *n* a liqueur made from a type of sour cherry having a taste like bitter almonds.

maraschino cherry *n* a cherry preserved in maraschino.

marathon *n* **1** a race on foot of 26 miles 385 yards (42.195 kilometres). **2** any long or arduous task or event. ~*adj* **3** of or relating to a race on foot of 26 miles 385 yards (42.195 kilometres): *marathon runners.* **4** long and arduous: *a marathon nine hour meeting.*

maraud *vb* to wander or raid in search of plunder. **marauder** *n* **marauding** *adj*

marble *n* **1** a hard limestone rock, which usually has a mottled appearance and can be given a high polish. **2** a block of marble or work of art made of marble. **3** a small round glass ball used in playing marbles. ~*vb* **-bling, -bled 4** to mottle with variegated streaks in imitation of marble. **marbled** *adj*

marbles *n* a game in which marbles are rolled at one another.

marbling *n* **1** a mottled effect or pattern resembling marble. **2** the streaks of fat in lean meat.

marc *n* **1** the remains of grapes or other fruit that have been pressed for wine-making. **2** a brandy distilled from these.

THESAURUS

tain, envelope, pall, screen, shroud, veil ~*vb.* **3.** blanket, cloak, cloud, cover, disguise, envelop, hide, mask, overspread, screen, shroud, veil, wrap

manual 1. *adj.* done by hand, hand-operated, human, physical **2.** *n.* bible, guide, guidebook, handbook, instructions, workbook

manufacture *vb.* **1.** assemble, build, compose, construct, create, fabricate, forge, form, make, mass-produce, mould, process, produce, put together, shape, turn out **2.** concoct, cook up (*informal*), devise, fabricate, hatch, invent, make up, think up, trump up ~*n.* **3.** assembly, construction, creation, fabrication, making, mass-production, produce, production

manufacturer builder, constructor, creator, fabricator, factory-owner, industrialist, maker, producer

manure compost, droppings, dung, excrement, fertilizer, muck, ordure, slurry

many 1. *adj.* abundant, copious, countless, frequent, innumerable, manifold, multifarious, multifold, multitudinous, myriad, numerous, profuse, sundry, umpteen (*informal*), varied, various **2.** *pron.* a horde, a lot, a mass, a multitude, a thousand and one, heaps (*informal*), large numbers, lots (*informal*), piles (*informal*), plenty, scores, tons (*informal*), umpteen (*informal*) **3.** *n.* **the many** crowd, hoi polloi, majority, masses, multitude, people, rank and file

mar blemish, blight, blot, damage, deface, detract from, disfigure, harm, hurt, impair, injure, maim, mangle, mutilate, ruin, scar, spoil, stain, sully, taint, tarnish, vitiate

marcasite *n* **1** a pale yellow form of iron pyrites used in jewellery. **2** a cut and polished form of steel used for making jewellery.

march[1] *vb* **1** to walk with very regular steps, like a soldier. **2** to walk in a quick and determined manner, esp. when angry: *he marched into the kitchen without knocking.* **3** to make a person or group proceed: *he was marched back to his cell.* **4** (of an army, procession, etc.) to walk as an organized group: *the demonstrators marched down the main street.* **5** to advance or progress steadily: *time marches on.* ~*n* **6** a regular stride. **7** a long or exhausting walk. **8** the steady development or progress of something: *the continuous march of industrial development.* **9** a distance covered by marching. **10** an organized protest in which a large group of people walk somewhere together: *a march against racial violence.* **11** a piece of music suitable for marching to. **12 steal a march on** to gain an advantage over, esp. by a trick. **marcher** *n* **marching** *adj*

march[2] *n* **1** a border or boundary. **2** the land lying along a border or boundary, often of disputed ownership.

March *n* the third month of the year.

March hare *n* a hare during its breeding season in March, noted for its wild and excitable behaviour.

marching orders *pl n* **1** *Informal* dismissal, esp. from employment. **2** military orders, giving instructions about a march.

marchioness (marsh-on-**ness**) *n* **1** a woman who holds the rank of marquis or marquess. **2** the wife or widow of a marquis or marquess.

marchpane *n Archaic* marzipan.

Mardi Gras (**mar**-dee **grah**) *n* the festival of Shrove Tuesday, celebrated in some cities with great revelry.

mare[1] *n* the adult female of a horse or zebra.

mare[2] *n, pl* **maria** one of many huge dry plains on the surface of the moon or Mars, visible as dark markings.

mare's-nest *n* a discovery imagined to be important but proving to be worthless.

margarine *n* a butter substitute made from vegetable and animal fats.

marge *n Brit informal* margarine.

margin *n* **1** an edge, rim, or border: *we came to the margin of the wood; people on the margin of society.* **2** the blank space surrounding the text on a page. **3** an additional amount or one beyond the minimum necessary: *the margin of victory was seven lengths; a small margin of error.* **4** *Chiefly Austral* a payment made in addition to a basic wage, esp. for special skill or responsibility. **5** a limit beyond which something can no longer exist or function: *the margin of physical survival.* **6** *Econ* the minimum return below which an enterprise becomes unprofitable.

marginal *adj* **1** of, in, on, or forming a margin. **2** not important; insignificant: *he remained a rather marginal political figure.* **3** close to a limit, esp. a lower limit: *marginal legal ability.* **4** *Econ* relating to goods or services produced and sold at the margin of profitability: *marginal cost.* **5** *Politics chiefly Brit & NZ* of or designating a constituency in which elections tend to be won by small margins: *a marginal seat.* **6** designating agricultural land on the edge of fertile areas. ~*n* **7** *Politics chiefly Brit & NZ* a marginal constituency. **marginally** *adv*

marginalia *pl n* notes in the margin of a book, manuscript, or letter.

margrave *n* (formerly) a German nobleman ranking above a count.

marguerite *n* a garden plant with flowers resembling large daisies.

marigold *n* any of various plants cultivated for their yellow or orange flowers.

marijuana *or* **marihuana** (mar-ree-**wah**-na) *n* the dried leaves and flowers of the hemp plant, used as a drug, esp. in cigarettes.

marimba *n* a percussion instrument consisting of a set of hardwood plates placed over tuned metal resonators, played with soft-headed sticks.

marina *n* a harbour for yachts and other pleasure boats.

marinade *n* **1** a mixture of oil, wine, vinegar, etc., in which meat or fish is soaked before cooking. ~*vb* **-nading, -naded 2** same as **marinate.**

marinate *vb* **-nating, -nated** to soak in marinade. **marinated** *adj*

marine *adj* **1** of, found in, or relating to the sea. **2** of shipping or navigation. **3** used or adapted for use at sea. ~*n* **4** a soldier trained for land and sea combat. **5** a country's shipping or navy collectively: *the merchant marine.*

mariner (**mar**-in-er) *n* a sailor.

marionette *n* a puppet whose limbs are moved by strings.

marital *adj* of or relating to marriage. **maritally** *adv*

maritime *adj* **1** of or relating to shipping. **2** of, near, or living near the sea.

marjoram *n* a plant with sweet-scented leaves, used for seasoning food and in salads.

mark[1] *n* **1** a visible impression on a surface, such as a spot or scratch. **2** a sign, symbol, or other indication that distinguishes something. **3** a written or printed symbol, as used for punctuation. **4** a letter, number, or percentage used to grade academic work. **5** a thing that indicates position; marker. **6** an indication of some quality: *a mark of respect.* **7** a target or goal. **8** impression or influence: *this book displays the mark of its author's admiration of Kafka.* **9** (in trade names) a particular model or type of a vehicle, machine, etc.:

THESAURUS

maraud despoil, forage, foray, harry, loot, pillage, plunder, raid, ransack, ravage, reive (*dialect*), sack

marauder bandit, brigand, buccaneer, corsair, freebooter, mosstrooper, outlaw, pillager, pirate, plunderer, raider, ravager, reiver (*dialect*), robber

march[1] *vb.* **1.** file, footslog, pace, parade, stalk, stride, strut, tramp, tread, walk ~*n.* **2.** gait, pace, step, stride **3.** hike, routemarch, tramp, trek, walk **4.** advance, development, evolution, progress, progression **5.** demo (*informal*), demonstration, parade, procession

march[2] borderland, borders, boundaries, confines, frontiers, limits, marchlands

margin 1. border, bound, boundary, brim, brink, confine, edge, limit, perimeter, periphery, rim, side, verge **2.** allowance, compass, elbowroom, extra, latitude, leeway, play, room, scope, space, surplus

marginal 1. bordering, borderline, on the edge, peripheral **2.** insignificant, low, minimal, minor, negligible, slight, small

marijuana bhang, blow (*slang*), cannabis, charas, dope (*slang*), ganja, grass (*slang*), hash (*slang*), hashish, hemp, kif, mary jane (*U.S. slang*), pot (*slang*), sinsemilla, tea (*U.S. old-fashioned slang*), wacky baccy (*slang*), weed (*slang*)

marine maritime, nautical, naval, ocean-going, oceanic, pelagic, saltwater, sea, seafaring, seagoing, thalassic

mariner hand, Jack Tar, matelot (*slang, chiefly Brit.*), navigator, sailor, salt, sea dog, seafarer, seafaring man, seaman, tar

marital conjugal, connubial, married, matrimonial, nuptial, wedded

the Ford Escort Mark Two. **10** one of the temperature settings at which a gas oven can work: *bake at gas mark 5 for thirty minutes.* **11 make one's mark** to achieve recognition. **12 on your mark** *or* **marks** a command given to runners in a race to prepare themselves at the starting line. **13 up to the mark** meeting the desired standard. *~vb* **14** to make a visible impression, trace, or stain on. **15** to have a tendency to become dirty, scratched, or damaged: *this material marks easily.* **16** to characterize or distinguish: *the gritty determination that has marked his career.* **17** to designate someone as a particular type of person: *she would now be marked as a troublemaker.* **18** to label, esp. to indicate price. **19** to celebrate or commemorate an occasion or its anniversary: *a series of concerts to mark the 200th anniversary of Mozart's death.* **20** to pay attention to: *mark my words.* **21** to observe or notice. **22** to grade or evaluate academic work. **23** *Sport* to stay close to an opponent to hamper his or her play. **24 mark off** *or* **out** to set boundaries or limits on. **25 mark time a** to move the feet alternately as in marching but without advancing. **b** to wait for something more interesting to happen. ~See also **markdown, mark-up.**

mark[2] *n* See **Deutschmark.**

markdown *n* **1** a price reduction. *~vb* **mark down 2** to reduce in price. **3** to make a written note of: *she marked down the number of the getaway car.*

marked *adj* **1** obvious or noticeable: *a marked improvement.* **2** singled out, esp. as the target of attack: *a marked man.* **markedly** (**mark**-id-lee) *adv*

marker *n* **1** an object used to show the position of something. **2** Also called: **marker pen** a thick felt-tipped pen used for drawing and colouring.

market *n* **1** an occasion at which people meet to buy and sell merchandise. **2** a place at which a market is held. **3** the buying and selling of goods and services, esp. when unrestrained by political or social considerations: *the market has been brought into health care.* **4** the trading opportunities provided by a particular group of people: *the youth market.* **5** demand for a particular product. **6** short for **stock market. 7 be in the market for** to wish to buy. **8 on the market** available for purchase. **9 seller's** *or* **buyer's market** a market characterized by excess demand (or supply) and thus favourable to sellers (or buyers). *~adj* **10** of, relating to, or controlled by the buying and selling of goods and services, esp. when unrestrained by political or social considerations: *a market economy.* *~vb* **-keting, -keted 11** to offer or produce for sale. **marketable** *adj*

market garden *n Chiefly Brit* a place where fruit and vegetables are grown for sale. **market gardener** *n*

marketing *n* the part of a business which controls the way that goods or services are sold.

market maker *n Stock Exchange* a dealer in securities on the London Stock Exchange who can also deal with the public as a broker.

marketplace *n* **1** a place where a public market is held. **2** the commercial world of buying and selling.

market price *n* the prevailing price at which goods may be bought or sold.

market research *n* the study of customers' wants and purchases, and of the forces influencing them.

market town *n Chiefly Brit* the main town in an agricultural area, usually one where a market is regularly held.

marking *n* **1** the arrangement of colours on an animal or plant. **2** the assessment and correction of pupils' or students' written work by teachers.

marksman *n, pl* **-men** a person skilled in shooting. **marksmanship** *n*

mark-up *n* **1** an amount added to the cost of something to provide the seller with a profit. *~vb* **mark up 2** to increase the cost of something by an amount or percentage in order to make a profit.

marl *n* a fine-grained rock consisting of clay, limestone, and silt used as a fertilizer. **marly** *adj*

marlin *n, pl* **-lin** *or* **-lins** a large fish with a long spear-like upper jaw, found in warm and tropical seas.

marlinspike *or* **marlinespike** (**mar**-lin-spike) *n Naut* a pointed metal tool used in separating strands of rope.

marmalade *n* a jam made from citrus fruits, esp. oranges.

marmoreal (mar-**more**-ee-al) *adj* of or like marble.

marmoset *n* a small South American monkey with a long bushy tail.

marmot *n* any of various burrowing rodents of Europe, Asia, and North America. They are heavily built and have coarse fur.

maroon[1] *vb* **1** to abandon someone in a deserted area, esp. on an island. **2** to isolate in a helpless situation: *we're marooned here until the snow stops.* **marooned** *adj*

maroon[2] *adj* **1** dark purplish-red. *~n* **2** an exploding firework or flare used as a warning signal.

marque (**mark**) *n* a brand of product, esp. of a car.

marquee *n* a large tent used for a party, exhibition, etc.

marquess (**mar**-kwiss) *n* **1** (in the British Isles) a

THESAURUS

maritime 1. marine, nautical, naval, oceanic, sea, seafaring **2.** coastal, littoral, seaside

mark *n.* **1.** blemish, blot, blotch, bruise, dent, impression, line, nick, pock, scar, scratch, smirch, smudge, splotch, spot, stain, streak **2.** badge, blaze, brand, characteristic, device, earmark, emblem, evidence, feature, flag, hallmark, impression, incision, index, indication, label, note, print, proof, seal, sign, signet, stamp, symbol, symptom, token **3.** criterion, level, measure, norm, par, standard, yardstick **4.** aim, end, goal, object, objective, purpose, target **5. make one's mark** achieve recognition, be a success, find a place in the sun, get on in the world, make a success of oneself, make good, make it (*informal*), make something of oneself, prosper, succeed *~vb.* **6.** blemish, blot, blotch, brand, bruise, dent, impress, imprint, nick, scar, scratch, smirch, smudge, splotch, stain, streak **7.** brand, characterize, flag, identify, label, stamp **8.** betoken, denote, distinguish, evince, exemplify, illustrate, show **9.** attend, hearken (*archaic*), mind, note, notice, observe, pay attention, pay heed, regard, remark, watch **10.** appraise, assess, correct, evaluate, grade

marked apparent, blatant, clear, considerable, conspicuous, decided, distinct, evident, manifest, notable, noted, noticeable, obvious, outstanding, patent, prominent, pronounced, remarkable, salient, signal, striking

markedly clearly, considerably, conspicuously, decidedly, distinctly, evidently, greatly, manifestly, notably, noticeably, obviously, outstandingly, patently, remarkably, signally, strikingly, to a great extent

market 1. *n.* bazaar, fair, mart **2.** *vb.* offer for sale, retail, sell, vend

marketable in demand, merchantable, saleable, sought after, wanted

nobleman ranking between a duke and an earl. **2** See **marquis.**

marquetry *n, pl* **-quetries** a pattern of inlaid veneers of wood or metal used chiefly as ornamentation in furniture.

marquis *n, pl* **-quises** *or* **-quis** (in various countries) a nobleman ranking above a count, corresponding to a British marquess.

marquise (mar-**keez**) *n* **1** (in various countries) a marchioness. **2** a gemstone cut in a pointed oval shape.

marram grass *n* a grass that grows on sandy shores: often planted to stabilize sand dunes.

marriage *n* **1** the state or relationship of being husband and wife: *the institution of marriage.* **2** the contract made by a man and woman to live as husband and wife. **3** the ceremony formalizing this union; wedding. **4** a close union or relationship: *the marriage of scientific knowledge and industry.*

marriageable *adj* suitable for marriage, usually with reference to age.

marriage guidance *n* advice given by trained counsellors to couples who have problems in their married life.

married *adj* **1** having a husband or wife. **2** of marriage or married people: *married life.* ~*n* **3 marrieds** married people: *young marrieds.*

marrow *n* **1** the fatty tissue that fills the cavities of bones. **2** *Brit* short for **vegetable marrow.**

marrowfat *or* **marrow pea** *n* a variety of large pea.

marry[1] *vb* **-ries, -rying, -ried 1** to take (someone) as one's husband or wife. **2** to join or give in marriage. **3** Also: **marry up** to fit together or unite; join: *their playing marries Irish traditional music and rock.*

marry[2] *interj Archaic* an exclamation of surprise or anger.

Mars *n* **1** the Roman god of war. **2** the fourth planet from the sun.

Marseillaise (mar-say-**yaze**) *n* **the Marseillaise** the French national anthem.

marsh *n* low poorly drained land that is wet, muddy, and sometimes flooded. **marshy** *adj*

marshal *n* **1** (in some armies and air forces) an officer of the highest rank: *Field Marshall.* **2** an officer who organizes or controls ceremonies or public events. **3** *US* the chief police or fire officer in some states. **4** (formerly in England) an officer of the royal family or court. ~*vb* **-shalling, -shalled** *or US* **-shaling, -shaled 5** to arrange in order: *she marshalled her facts and came to a conclusion.* **6** to assemble and organize people or vehicles in readiness for onward movement. **7** to guide or lead, esp. in a ceremonious way: *she marshalled them towards the lecture theatre.* **marshalcy** *n*

marshalling yard *n Railways* a place where railway wagons are shunted and made up into trains.

Marshal of the Royal Air Force *n* the highest rank in the Royal Air Force.

marsh gas *n* a gas largely composed of methane formed when plants decay in the absence of air.

marshland *n* land consisting of marshes.

marshmallow *n* a spongy pink or white sweet.

marsh mallow *n* a plant that grows in salt marshes and has pale pink flowers. It was formerly used to make marshmallows.

marsupial (mar-**soop**-ee-al) *n* **1** a mammal, such as a kangaroo or an opossum, the female of which carries her babies in a pouch at the front of her body until they reach a mature state. ~*adj* **2** of or like a marsupial.

mart *n* a market or trading centre.

Martello tower *n* a round tower used for coastal defence.

marten *n, pl* **-tens** *or* **-ten 1** any of several agile weasel-like mammals with bushy tails and golden-brown to blackish fur. **2** the highly valued fur of these animals.

martial *adj* of or characteristic of war, soldiers, or the military life: *martial music.*

martial art *n* any of various philosophies and techniques of self-defence originating in the Far East, such as judo or karate.

martial law *n* rule of law maintained by military forces in the absence of civil law.

Martian (**marsh**-an) *adj* **1** of the planet Mars. ~*n* **2** an inhabitant of Mars, in science fiction.

martin *n* a bird of the swallow family with a square or slightly forked tail.

martinet *n* a person who maintains strict discipline.

martingale *n* a strap from the reins to the girth of a horse, preventing it from carrying its head too high.

martini *n* **1** (*often cap*) *Trademark* an Italian vermouth. **2** a cocktail of gin and vermouth.

Martinmas *n* the feast of St Martin on November 11: a quarter day in Scotland.

martyr *n* **1** a person who chooses to die rather than renounce his or her religious beliefs. **2** a person who suffers greatly or dies for a cause or belief. **3 a martyr to** suffering constantly from: *a martyr to arthritis.* ~*vb* **4** to make a martyr of. **martyrdom** *n*

marvel *vb* **-velling, -velled** *or US* **-veling, -veled 1** to be filled with surprise or wonder. ~*n* **2** something that causes wonder.

THESAURUS

marksman, -woman crack shot (*informal*), dead shot (*informal*), good shot, sharpshooter

maroon abandon, cast ashore, cast away, desert, leave, leave high and dry (*informal*), strand

marriage 1. espousal, match, matrimony, wedlock **2.** nuptial rites, nuptials, wedding, wedding ceremony **3.** alliance, amalgamation, association, confederation, coupling, link, merger, union

married 1. hitched (*slang*), joined, one, spliced (*informal*), united, wed, wedded **2.** conjugal, connubial, husbandly, marital, matrimonial, nuptial, spousal, wifely

marrow core, cream, essence, gist, heart, kernel, pith, quick, quintessence, soul, spirit, substance

marry 1. become man and wife, espouse, get hitched (*slang*), get spliced (*informal*), make an honest man *or* woman of, take the plunge (*informal*), take to wife, tie the knot (*informal*), walk down the aisle (*informal*), wed, wive (*archaic*) **2.** ally, bond, join, knit, link, match, merge, splice, tie, unify, unite, yoke

marsh bog, fen, morass, moss (*Scot. & northern English dialect*), quagmire, slough, swamp

marshal 1. align, arrange, array, assemble, collect, deploy, dispose, draw up, gather, group, line up, muster, order, organize, rank **2.** conduct, escort, guide, lead, shepherd, usher

marshy boggy, fenny, miry, quaggy, spongy, swampy, waterlogged, wet

martial bellicose, belligerent, brave, heroic, military, soldierly, warlike

martinet disciplinarian, drillmaster, stickler

martyrdom agony, anguish, ordeal, persecution, suffering, torment, torture

marvel 1. *vb.* be amazed, be awed, be filled with sur-

marvellous *or US* **marvelous** *adj* **1** excellent or splendid: *a marvellous idea.* **2** causing great wonder or surprise; extraordinary: *electricity is a marvellous thing.* **marvellously** *or US* **marvelously** *adv*

Marxism *n* the economic and political theories of Karl Marx (1818–83), German political philosopher, which argue that class struggle is the basic agency of historical change, and that capitalism will be superseded by communism. **Marxist** *n, adj*

marzipan *n* a mixture made from ground almonds, sugar, and egg whites that is put on top of cakes or used to make sweets.

masc. masculine.

mascara *n* a cosmetic for darkening the eyelashes.

mascot *n* a person, animal, or thing considered to bring good luck.

masculine *adj* **1** possessing qualities or characteristics considered typical of or appropriate to a man; manly. **2** unwomanly; not feminine. **3** *Grammar* denoting a gender of nouns that includes some male animate things. **4** *Prosody* denoting a rhyme between pairs of single final stressed syllables. **masculinity** *n*

maser *n* a device for amplifying microwaves, working on the same principle as a laser.

mash *n* **1** a soft pulpy mass. **2** *Agriculture* bran, meal, or malt mixed with warm water and used as food for horses, cattle, or poultry. **3** *Brit informal* mashed potatoes. *~vb* **4** to beat or crush into a mash. **mashed** *adj*

mask *n* **1** any covering for the whole or a part of the face worn for amusement, protection, or disguise. **2** behaviour that hides one's true feelings: *his mask of detachment.* **3** *Surgery* a sterile gauze covering for the nose and mouth worn to minimize the spread of germs. **4** a device placed over the nose and mouth to facilitate or prevent inhalation of a gas. **5** a moulded likeness of a face or head, such as a death mask. **6** the face or head of an animal such as a fox. *~vb* **7** to cover with or put on a mask. **8** to hide or disguise: *a high brick wall that masked the front of the building.* **9** to cover so as to protect. **masked** *adj*

masking tape *n* an adhesive tape used to protect surfaces surrounding an area to be painted.

masochism (**mass**-oh-kiz-zum) *n* **1** *Psychiatry* a condition in which pleasure, esp. sexual pleasure, is obtained from feeling pain or from being humiliated. **2** a tendency to take pleasure from one's own suffering. **masochist** *n, adj* **masochistic** *adj*

mason *n* a person skilled in building with stone.

Mason *n* a Freemason.

Masonic *adj* of Freemasons or Freemasonry.

masonry *n* **1** stonework or brickwork. **2** the craft of a mason.

Masonry *n* Freemasonry.

masque (**mask**) *n* a dramatic entertainment of the 16th to 17th centuries, consisting of dancing, dialogue, and song. **masquer** *n*

masquerade (mask-er-**aid**) *vb* **-ading, -aded 1** to pretend to be someone or something else. *~n* **2** an attempt to keep secret the real identity or nature of something: *he was unable to keep up his masquerade as the war's victor.* **3** a party at which the guests wear masks and costumes.

mass *n* **1** a large body of something without a definite shape. **2** a collection of the component parts of something: *a mass of fibres.* **3** a large amount or number, as of people. **4** the main part or majority. **5** the size of a body; bulk. **6** *Physics* a physical quantity expressing the amount of matter in a body. **7** (in painting or drawing) an area of unified colour, shade, or intensity. *~adj* **8** done or occurring on a large scale: *mass hysteria.* **9** consisting of a mass or large number, esp. of people: *a mass meeting.* *~vb* **10** to join together into a mass. ~See also **masses. massed** *adj*

Mass *n* **1** (in the Roman Catholic Church and certain other Christian churches) a service in which bread and wine are consecrated to represent the body and blood of Christ. **2** a musical setting of parts of this service.

massacre (**mass**-a-ker) *n* **1** the wanton or savage killing of large numbers of people. **2** *Informal* an overwhelming defeat. *~vb* **-cring, -cred 3** to kill people indiscriminately in large numbers. **4** *Informal* to defeat overwhelmingly.

massage (**mass**-ahzh) *n* **1** the kneading or rubbing of parts of the body to reduce pain or stiffness or help relaxation. *~vb* **-saging, -saged 2** to give a massage to. **3** to manipulate statistics or evidence to produce a desired result.

massage parlour *n* **1** a commercial establishment providing massages. **2** *Euphemistic* a place where men pay to have sex with prostitutes.

massasauga (mass-a-**saw**-ga) *n* a North American venomous snake with a horny rattle at the end of the tail.

masses *pl n* **1 the masses** ordinary people as a group. **2 masses of** *Informal, chiefly Brit* a great number or quantity of: *masses of food.*

masseur (mass-**ur**) *or fem* **masseuse** (mass-**uhz**) *n* a person who gives massages.

THESAURUS

prise, gape, gaze, goggle, wonder **2.** *n.* genius, miracle, phenomenon, portent, prodigy, whizz (*informal*), wonder

marvellous 1. *informal* brilliant, colossal, cracking (*Brit. informal*), excellent, fabulous (*informal*), fantastic (*informal*), glorious, great (*informal*), magnificent, mean (*slang*), sensational (*informal*), smashing (*informal*), sovereign, splendid, stupendous, super (*informal*), superb, terrific (*informal*), wonderful **2.** amazing, astonishing, astounding, breathtaking, brilliant, extraordinary, miraculous, phenomenal, prodigious, remarkable, sensational (*informal*), singular, spectacular, stupendous, wondrous (*archaic or literary*)

masculine bold, brave, butch (*slang*), gallant, hardy, macho, male, manful, manlike, manly, mannish, muscular, powerful, red-blooded (*informal*), resolute, robust, stout-hearted, strapping, strong, vigorous, virile, well-built

mask *n.* **1.** domino, false face, visor **2.** blind, camouflage, cloak, concealment, cover, cover-up, disguise, façade, front, guise, screen, semblance, show, veil, veneer *~vb.* **3.** camouflage, cloak, conceal, cover, disguise, hide, obscure, screen, veil

mass *n.* **1.** block, chunk, concretion, hunk, lump, piece **2.** accumulation, aggregation, assemblage, batch, bunch, collection, combination, conglomeration, heap, load, lot, pile, quantity, stack **3.** assemblage, band, body, bunch (*informal*), crowd, group, horde, host, lot, mob, number, throng, troop **4.** body, bulk, greater part, lion's share, majority, preponderance **5.** bulk, dimension, greatness, magnitude, size *~adj.* **6.** extensive, general, indiscriminate, large-scale, pandemic, popular, wholesale, widespread *~vb.* **7.** accumulate, amass, assemble, collect, congregate, forgather, gather, mob, muster, rally, swarm, throng

massacre 1. *n.* annihilation, blood bath, butchery, carnage, extermination, holocaust, killing, mass slaughter, murder, slaughter **2.** *vb.* annihilate, butcher, cut to pieces, exterminate, kill, liquidate, mow down, murder, slaughter, slay, wipe out

massage 1. *n.* acupressure, kneading, manipulation, reflexology, rubbing, rub-down, shiatsu **2.** *vb.* knead, manipulate, rub, rub down

massif (**mass**-seef) *n* a series of connected masses of rock forming a mountain range.

massive *adj* **1** (of objects) large, bulky, heavy, and usually solid. **2** impressive or imposing. **3** intensive or considerable: *a massive overdose.* **massively** *adv*

mass-market *adj* of, for, or appealing to a large number of people; popular: *mass-market newspapers.*

mass media *pl n* the means of communication that reach large numbers of people, such as television, newspapers, and radio.

mass noun *n* a noun that refers to an extended substance rather than to each of a set of objects, eg, *water* as opposed to *lake.*

mass number *n* the total number of protons and neutrons in the nucleus of an atom.

mass-produce *vb* **-producing, -produced** to manufacture standardized goods on a large scale by extensive use of machinery. **mass-produced** *adj* **mass-production** *n*

mass spectrometer *n* an instrument for analysing the composition of a sample of material, in which ions, produced from the sample, are separated by electric or magnetic fields according to their ratios of charge to mass.

mast[1] *n* **1** *Naut* a vertical pole for supporting sails, radar equipment, etc., above the deck of a ship. **2** a tall upright pole used as an aerial for radio or television broadcasting: *a television mast.* **3 before the mast** *Naut* as an apprentice seaman.

mast[2] *n* the fruit of forest trees, such as beech or oak, used as food for pigs.

mastaba *n* a mud-brick superstructure above tombs in ancient Egypt.

mastectomy (mass-**tek**-tom-ee) *n, pl* **-mies** surgical removal of a breast.

master *n* **1** the man who has authority over others, such as the head of a household, the employer of servants, or the owner of slaves or animals. **2** a person with exceptional skill at a certain thing: *B.B. King is a master of the blues.* **3** a person who has complete control of a situation: *the master of his portfolio.* **4** an original copy or tape from which duplicates are made. **5** a craftsman fully qualified to practise his trade and to train others: *a master builder.* **6** a player of a game, esp. chess or bridge, who has won a specified number of tournament games. **7** a highly regarded teacher or leader. **8** a graduate holding a master's degree. **9** the chief officer aboard a merchant ship. **10** *Chiefly Brit* a male teacher. **11** the superior person or side in a contest. **12** the heir apparent of a Scottish viscount or baron: *the Master of Ballantrae.* *~adj* **13** overall or controlling: *master plan.* **14** designating a mechanism that controls others: *master switch.* **15** main or principal: *master bedroom.* *~vb* **16** to become thoroughly proficient in. **17** to overcome or defeat.

Master *n* a title of address for a boy who is not old enough to be called *Mr.*

master aircrew *n* a rank in the Royal Air Force, equal to warrant officer.

masterful *adj* **1** showing great skill. **2** domineering or authoritarian. **masterfully** *adv*

master key *n* a key that opens all the locks of a set; passkey.

masterly *adj* showing great skill; expert.

mastermind *vb* **1** to plan and direct a complex task or project. *~n* **2** a person who plans and directs a complex task or project.

Master of Arts *n* a degree, usually postgraduate in a nonscientific subject, or a person holding this degree.

master of ceremonies *n* a person who presides over a public ceremony, formal dinner, or entertainment, introducing the events and performers.

Master of Science *n* a degree, usually postgraduate in a scientific subject, or a person holding this degree.

Master of the Rolls *n* (in England) the senior civil judge in the country and the head of the Public Record Office.

masterpiece *or* **masterwork** *n* **1** an outstanding work or performance. **2** the most outstanding piece of work of an artist or craftsman.

masterstroke *n* an outstanding piece of strategy, skill, or talent.

mastery *n, pl* **-teries** **1** outstanding skill or expertise. **2** complete power or control: *he had complete mastery over the country.*

masthead *n* **1** *Naut* the highest part of a mast. **2** the name of a newspaper or periodical printed at the top of the front page.

mastic *n* **1** an aromatic resin obtained from a Mediterranean tree and used to make varnishes and lacquers. **2** any of several putty-like substances used as a filler, adhesive, or seal.

THESAURUS

masses **the masses** common people, crowd, hoi polloi, multitude, the people, the punters (*informal*)

massive big, bulky, colossal, elephantine, enormous, extensive, gargantuan, gigantic, ginormous (*informal*), great, heavy, hefty, huge, hulking, immense, imposing, impressive, mammoth, monster, monumental, ponderous, solid, substantial, titanic, vast, weighty, whacking (*informal*), whopping (*informal*)

master *n.* **1.** boss (*informal*), captain, chief, commander, controller, director, employer, governor, head, lord, manager, overlord, overseer, owner, principal, ruler, skipper (*informal*), superintendent **2.** ace (*informal*), adept, dab hand (*Brit. informal*), doyen, expert, genius, grandmaster, maestro, past master, pro (*informal*), virtuoso, wizard **3.** guide, guru, instructor, pedagogue, preceptor, schoolmaster, spiritual leader, swami, teacher, tutor *~adj.* **4.** chief, controlling, foremost, grand, great, leading, main, predominant, prime, principal *~vb.* **5.** acquire, become proficient in, get the hang of (*informal*), grasp, learn **6.** bridle, check, conquer, curb, defeat, lick (*informal*), overcome, overpower, quash, quell, subdue, subjugate, suppress, tame, triumph over, vanquish

masterful **1.** adept, adroit, clever, consummate, crack (*informal*), deft, dexterous, excellent, expert, exquisite, fine, finished, first-rate, masterly, skilful, skilled, superior, superlative, supreme, world-class **2.** arrogant, bossy (*informal*), despotic, dictatorial, domineering, high-handed, imperious, magisterial, overbearing, overweening, peremptory, self-willed, tyrannical

masterly adept, adroit, clever, consummate, crack (*informal*), dexterous, excellent, expert, exquisite, fine, finished, first-rate, masterful, skilful, skilled, superior, superlative, supreme, world-class

mastermind **1.** *vb.* be the brains behind (*informal*), conceive, devise, direct, manage, organize, plan **2.** *n.* architect, authority, brain(s) (*informal*), director, engineer, genius, intellect, manager, organizer, planner, virtuoso

masterpiece *chef d'oeuvre,* classic, jewel, magnum opus, master work, *pièce de résistance, tour de force*

mastery **1.** ability, acquirement, attainment, cleverness, command, comprehension, deftness, dexterity, expertise, familiarity, finesse, grasp, know-how (*informal*), knowledge, proficiency, prowess, skill,

masticate *vb* **-cating, -cated** to chew food. **mastication** *n*
mastiff *n* a large powerful short-haired dog, usually fawn or brown with dark streaks.
mastitis *n* inflammation of the breast.
mastodon *n* an extinct elephant-like mammal.
mastoid *adj* **1** shaped like a nipple or breast. *~n* **2** a nipple-like projection of bone behind the ear. **3** *Informal* mastoiditis.
mastoiditis *n* inflammation of the mastoid.
masturbate *vb* **-bating, -bated** to fondle one's own genitals, or those of someone else, to cause sexual pleasure. **masturbation** *n*
mat[1] *n* **1** a thick flat piece of fabric used as a floor covering, a place to wipe one's shoes, etc. **2** a small pad of material used to protect a surface from heat or scratches from an object placed upon it. **3** a large piece of thick padded material put on the floor as a surface for wrestling, gymnastics, etc. *~vb* **matting, matted 4** to tangle or become tangled into a dense mass.
mat[2] *adj* same as **matt.**
matador *n* the bullfighter armed with a sword, who attempts to kill the bull.
matai *n* a New Zealand tree, the wood of which is used for timber for building.
match[1] *n* **1** a formal game or sports event in which people or teams compete. **2** a person or thing able to provide competition for another: *he has met his match.* **3** a person or thing that resembles, harmonizes with, or is equivalent to another: *the colours aren't a perfect match, but they're close enough; white wine is not a good match for steak.* **4** a person or thing that is an exact copy or equal of another. **5** a partnership between a man and a woman, as in marriage. **6** a person regarded as a possible partner in marriage: *for any number of men she would have been a good match.* *~vb* **7** to fit parts together. **8** to resemble, harmonize with, or equal one another or something else: *our bedroom curtains match the bedspread; she walked at a speed that he could barely match.* **9** to find a match for. **10 match with** *or* **against a** to compare in order to determine which is the superior. **b** to arrange a competition between. **matching** *adj*
match[2] *n* **1** a thin strip of wood or cardboard tipped with a chemical that ignites when scraped against a rough or specially treated surface. **2** a fuse used to fire cannons' explosives.
matchbox *n* a small box for holding matches.
match-fit *adj Sport* in good physical condition for competing in a match.
matchless *adj* unequalled.
matchmaker *n* a person who introduces people in the hope that they will form a couple. **matchmaking** *n, adj*
match play *n Golf* scoring according to the number of holes won and lost.
match point *n Sport* the final point needed to win a match.
matchstick *n* **1** the wooden part of a match. *~adj* **2** (esp. of drawn figures) thin and straight: *matchstick men.*
matchwood *n* **1** wood suitable for making matches. **2** splinters.
mate[1] *n* **1 a** *Informal, chiefly Brit, Austral, & NZ* a friend: often used as a term of address between males: *I spotted my mate Jimmy McCrae at the other end of the bar; that's all right, mate.* **b** an associate or colleague: *a classmate; the governor's running mate.* **2** the sexual partner of an animal. **3** a marriage partner. **4** *Naut* any officer below the master on a commercial ship. **5** (in some trades) an assistant: *a plumber's mate.* **6** one of a pair of matching items. *~vb* **mating, mated 7** to pair (a male and female animal) or (of animals) to pair for breeding. **8** to marry. **9** to join as a pair.
mate[2] *n, vb* **mating, mated** *Chess* same as **checkmate.**
mater *n Brit slang* mother: often used facetiously.
material *n* **1** the substance of which a thing is made. **2** cloth. **3** ideas or notes that a finished work may be based on: *the material of the story resembles an incident in his own life.* *~adj* **4** concerned with or composed of physical matter or substance; not relating to spiritual or abstract things: *the material universe.* **5** of or affecting economic or physical wellbeing: *material prosperity.* **6** relevant or pertinent: *material evidence.* ~See also **materials.**
materialism *n* **1** excessive interest in and desire for money or possessions. **2** the belief that only the material world exists. **materialist** *n, adj* **materialistic** *adj*
materialize *or* **-ise** *vb* **-izing, -ized** *or* **-ising, -ised 1** *Not universally accepted* to become fact; actually happen: *the promised pay rise never materialized.* **2** to appear after being invisible: *trees materialized out of the gloom.* **3** to take shape: *after hours of talks, a plan began to materialize.* **materialization** *or* **-isation** *n*

THESAURUS

understanding, virtuosity **2.** ascendancy, authority, command, conquest, control, domination, dominion, pre-eminence, rule, superiority, supremacy, sway, triumph, upper hand, victory, whip hand
match *n.* **1.** bout, competition, contest, game, head-to-head, test, trial **2.** competitor, counterpart, equal, equivalent, peer, rival **3.** companion, complement, counterpart, equal, equivalent, fellow, mate, tally **4.** copy, dead ringer (*slang*), double, duplicate, equal, lookalike, replica, ringer (*slang*), spit (*informal, chiefly Brit.*), spit and image (*informal*), spitting image (*informal*), twin **5.** affiliation, alliance, combination, couple, duet, item (*informal*), marriage, pair, pairing, partnership, union *~vb.* **6.** ally, combine, couple, join, link, marry, mate, pair, unite, yoke **7.** accompany, accord, adapt, agree, blend, coordinate, correspond, fit, go with, harmonize, suit, tally, tone with **8.** compare, compete, contend, emulate, equal, measure up to, oppose, pit against, rival, vie
matching analogous, comparable, coordinating, corresponding, double, duplicate, equal, equivalent, identical, like, paired, parallel, same, toning, twin
matchless consummate, exquisite, incomparable, inimitable, peerless, perfect, superlative, supreme, unequalled, unique, unmatched, unparalleled, unrivalled, unsurpassed
mate *n.* **1.** *informal* buddy (*informal*), china (*Brit. slang*), chum (*informal*), comrade, crony, friend, pal (*informal*) **2.** associate, colleague, companion, compeer, co-worker, fellow-worker **3.** better half (*humorous*), husband, partner, significant other (*U.S. informal*), spouse, wife **4.** assistant, helper, subordinate **5.** companion, double, fellow, match, twin *~vb.* **6.** breed, copulate, couple, pair **7.** marry, match, wed **8.** couple, join, match, pair, yoke
material *n.* **1.** body, constituents, element, matter, stuff, substance **2.** cloth, fabric, stuff **3.** data, evidence, facts, information, notes, work *~adj.* **4.** bodily, concrete, corporeal, fleshly, nonspiritual, palpable, physical, substantial, tangible, worldly **5.** applicable, apposite, apropos, germane, pertinent, relevant
materialize appear, come about, come into being,

materially *adv* to a significant extent: *we were not materially affected.*
materials *pl n* the equipment necessary for a particular activity: *building materials.*
materiel (mat-ear-ee-**ell**) *n* the materials and equipment of an organization, esp. of a military force.
maternal *adj* **1** of or characteristic of a mother. **2** related through the mother's side of the family: *his maternal uncle.* **maternally** *adv*
maternity *n* **1** motherhood. **2** motherliness. *~adj* **3** relating to women during pregnancy or childbirth: *maternity leave.*
mate's rates *pl n NZ informal* reduced charges offered to a friend or colleague: *a plumber friend did the job at mate's rates.*
matey *adj Brit informal* friendly or intimate.
math *n US & Canad informal* short for **mathematics.**
mathematical *adj* **1** using, used in, or relating to mathematics. **2** having the precision of mathematics. **mathematically** *adv*
mathematician *n* an expert or specialist in mathematics.
mathematics *n* **1** a group of related sciences, including algebra, geometry, and calculus, which use a specialized notation to study number, quantity, shape, and space. **2** numerical calculations involved in the solution of a problem.
maths *n Brit informal* short for **mathematics.**
matinee (**mat**-in-nay) *n* an afternoon performance of a play or film.
matinee coat *or* **jacket** *n* a short coat for a baby.
matins *n* an early morning service in various Christian Churches.
matriarch (**mate**-ree-ark) *n* the female head of a tribe or family. **matriarchal** *adj*
matriarchy *n, pl* **-chies** a form of social organization in which a female is head of the family or society, and descent and kinship are traced through the female line.
matrices (**may**-triss-seez) *n* a plural of **matrix.**
matricide *n* **1** the act of killing one's mother. **2** a person who kills his or her mother. **matricidal** *adj*
matriculate *vb* **-lating, -lated** to enrol or be enrolled in a college or university. **matriculation** *n*
matrilineal (mat-rill-**in**-ee-al) *adj* relating to descent through the female line.
matrimony *n* the state of being married. **matrimonial** *adj*
matrix (**may**-trix) *n, pl* **-trices** *or* **matrixes 1** the context or framework in which something is formed or develops: *a highly complex matrix of overlapping interests.* **2** the rock in which fossils or pebbles are embedded. **3** a mould, esp. one used in printing. **4** *Maths* a rectangular array of numbers elements set out in rows and columns.
matron *n* **1** a staid or dignified married woman. **2** a woman in charge of the domestic or medical arrangements in an institution. **3** *Brit* (formerly) the administrative head of the nursing staff in a hospital. **matronly** *adj*
matron of honour *n, pl* **matrons of honour** a married woman attending a bride.
matt *or* **matte** *adj* having a dull surface rather than a shiny one.
matted *adj* tangled into a thick mass.
matter *n* **1** the substance of which something, esp. a physical object, is made; material. **2** substance that occupies space and has mass, as distinguished from substance that is mental or spiritual. **3** substance of a specified type: *vegetable matter.* **4** an event, situation, or subject: *a matter of taste; the break-in is a matter for the police.* **5** a quantity or amount: *a matter of a few pounds.* **6** the content of written or verbal material as distinct from its style or form. **7** written material in general: *advertising matter.* **8** a secretion or discharge, such as pus. **9 for that matter** as regards that. **10 no matter a** regardless of; irrespective of: *you have to leave, no matter what she thinks.* **b** *~interj* it is unimportant. **11 the matter** wrong; the trouble: *there's nothing the matter.* *~vb* **12** to be of importance.
matter of fact *n* **1 as a matter of fact** actually; in fact. *~adj* **matter-of-fact 2** unimaginative or emotionless: *he conducted the executions in a completely matter-of-fact manner.*
matting *n* a coarsely woven fabric used as a floor covering.
mattock *n* a type of large pick that has one flat, horizontal end to its blade, used for loosening soil.
mattress *n* a large flat cushion with a strong cover, filled with cotton, foam rubber, etc., and often including coiled springs, used as a bed.
maturation *n* the process of becoming mature.
mature *adj* **1** fully developed physically or mentally; grown-up. **2** (of plans or theories) fully considered and thought-out. **3** sensible and balanced in personality and emotional behaviour. **4** due or payable: *a mature insurance policy.* **5** (of fruit, wine, or cheese) ripe or fully aged. *~vb* **-turing, -tured 6** to make or become mature. **7** (of bills or bonds) to become due for payment or repayment. **maturity** *n*
matzo *n, pl* **matzos** a large very thin biscuit of unleavened bread, traditionally eaten by Jews during Passover.

THESAURUS

come to pass, happen, occur, take place, take shape, turn up
materially considerably, essentially, gravely, greatly, much, seriously, significantly, substantially
maternal motherly
matrimonial conjugal, connubial, marital, married, nuptial, spousal, wedded, wedding
matrimony marital rites, marriage, nuptials, wedding ceremony, wedlock
matrix forge, mould, origin, source, womb
matted knotted, tangled, tousled, uncombed
matter *n.* **1.** body, material, stuff, substance **2.** affair, business, concern, episode, event, incident, issue, occurrence, proceeding, question, situation, subject, thing, topic, transaction **3.** amount, quantity, sum **4.** argument, context, purport, sense, subject, substance, text, thesis **5.** discharge, purulence, pus, secretion **6. the matter** complication, difficulty, distress, problem, trouble, upset, worry *~vb.* **7.** be important, be of consequence, carry weight, count, have influence, make a difference, mean something, signify
matter-of-fact deadpan, down-to-earth, dry, dull, emotionless, flat, lifeless, mundane, plain, prosaic, sober, unembellished, unimaginative, unsentimental, unvarnished
mature *adj.* **1.** adult, complete, full-grown, fully fledged, grown, grown-up, of age, seasoned **2.** perfect, prepared, ready **3.** matured, mellow, ripe, ripened *~vb.* **4.** age, become adult, bloom, blossom, come of age, develop, grow up, maturate, mellow, perfect, reach adulthood, ripen, season
maturity adulthood, completion, experience, full bloom, full growth, fullness, majority, manhood, maturation, matureness, perfection, ripeness, wisdom, womanhood

maudlin *adj* foolishly or tearfully sentimental, esp. as a result of drinking.
maul *vb* **1** to tear with the claws: *she was badly mauled by a lion.* **2** to criticize a play, performance, etc., severely: *the film was mauled by the critics.* **3** to handle roughly or clumsily. ~*n* **4** *Rugby* a loose scrum.
maunder *vb* to move, talk, or act aimlessly or idly.
mausoleum (maw-so-**lee**-um) *n* a large stately tomb.
mauve *adj* light purple.
maverick *n* **1** a person of independent or unorthodox views. **2** (in the U.S. and Canada) an unbranded stray calf. ~*adj* **3** (of a person or his or her views) independent and unorthodox.
maw *n* the mouth, throat, or stomach of an animal.
mawkish *adj* foolishly or embarrassingly sentimental. **mawkishness** *n*
max. maximum.
maxi *adj* **1** (of a garment) very long. **2** large or considerable.
maxilla *n, pl* **-lae** **1** the upper jawbone of a vertebrate. **2** any part of the mouth in insects and other arthropods. **maxillary** *adj*
maxim *n* a brief expression of a general truth, principle, or rule of conduct.
maximal *adj* of or being a maximum; the greatest possible.
maximize *or* **-ise** *vb* **-izing, -ized** *or* **-ising, -ised** to make as high or great as possible; increase to a maximum. **maximization** *or* **-isation** *n*
maximum *n, pl* **-mums** *or* **-ma** **1** the greatest possible amount or degree: *he gave the police the maximum of cooperation.* **2** the greatest amount recorded, allowed, or reached: *keep to a maximum of two drinks a day.* ~*adj* **3** of, being, or showing a maximum or maximums: *maximum speed.*
maxwell *n* the cgs unit of magnetic flux.
may[1] *vb, past* **might** used as an auxiliary to indicate or express: **1** that permission is requested by or granted to someone: *she may leave.* **2** the possibility that something could happen: *the lake may well dry up.* **3** ability or capacity, esp. in questions: *may I help you?* **4** a strong wish: *long may she reign.*
➤ In very careful usage *may* is used in preference to *can* for asking permission. *Might* is used to express a more tentative request: *May/might I ask a favour?*
may[2] *or* **may tree** *n Brit* same as **hawthorn.**
May *n* the fifth month of the year.
Maya *n* **1** (*pl* **-ya** *or* **-yas**) a member of an American Indian people of Central America, who once had an advanced civilization. **2** the language of this people. **Mayan** *n, adj*
maybe *adv* perhaps.
Mayday *n* the international radio distress signal.
May Day *n* the first day of May, traditionally a celebration of the coming of spring: in some countries now a holiday in honour of workers.
mayfly *n, pl* **-flies** a short-lived insect with large transparent wings.
mayhem *n* **1** any violent destruction or confusion. **2** *Law* the maiming of a person.
mayn't may not.
mayonnaise *n* a thick creamy sauce made from egg yolks, oil, and vinegar.
mayor *n* the civic head of a municipal council in many countries. **mayoral** *adj*
mayoralty *n, pl* **-ties** the office or term of office of a mayor.
mayoress *n* **1** *Chiefly Brit* the wife of a mayor. **2** a female mayor.
maypole *n* a tall pole around which people dance during May-Day celebrations.
May queen *n* a girl chosen to preside over May-Day celebrations.
maze *n* **1** a complex network of paths or passages designed to puzzle people who try and find their way through or out of it. **2** a puzzle in which the player must trace a path through a complex network of lines without touching or crossing any of them. **3** any confusing network or system: *a maze of regulations.*
mazurka *n* **1** a lively Polish dance in triple time. **2** music for this dance.
mb millibar.
Mb *Computers* megabyte.
MB **1** Bachelor of Medicine. **2** Manitoba.
MBE Member of the Order of the British Empire.
MC **1** Master of Ceremonies. **2** (in the U.S.) Member of Congress. **3** (in Britain) Military Cross.
MCC (in Britain) Marylebone Cricket Club.
MCh Master of Surgery.
Md *Chem* mendelevium.
MD **1** Doctor of Medicine. **2** Managing Director. **3** Maryland.
MDMA methylenedioxymethamphetamine: the chemical name for the drug ecstasy.
MDT (in the U.S. and Canada) Mountain Daylight Time.
me[1] *pron* (*objective*) **1** refers to the speaker or writer: *that hurts me.* ~*n* **2** *Informal* the personality of the speaker or writer or something that expresses it: *the real me.*
➤ The use of *it's me* in preference to *it's I* is accepted as quite standard.
me[2] *or* **mi** *n Music* (in tonic sol-fa) the third note of any ascending major scale.
ME **1** Maine. **2** Middle English. **3** myalgic encephalomyelitis: a condition characterized by painful muscles and general weakness sometimes persisting long after a viral illness.

THESAURUS

maudlin lachrymose, mawkish, mushy (*informal*), overemotional, sentimental, slushy (*informal*), soppy (*Brit. informal*), tearful, weepy (*informal*)
maul abuse, batter, beat, beat up (*informal*), claw, handle roughly, ill-treat, knock about *or* around, lacerate, lambast(e), mangle, manhandle, molest, paw, pummel, rough up, thrash
maunder babble, blather, blether, chatter, dawdle, dilly-dally (*informal*), drift, gabble, idle, loaf, meander, mooch (*slang*), potter, prattle, rabbit (on) (*Brit. informal*), ramble, rattle on, straggle, stray, traipse (*informal*)
mawkish emotional, feeble, gushy (*informal*), maudlin, mushy (*informal*), schmaltzy (*slang*), sentimental, slushy (*informal*), soppy (*Brit. informal*), twee
maxim adage, aphorism, apophthegm, axiom, byword, dictum, gnome, motto, proverb, rule, saw, saying
maximum **1.** *n.* apogee, ceiling, crest, extremity, height, most, peak, pinnacle, summit, top, upper limit, utmost, uttermost, zenith **2.** *adj.* greatest, highest, maximal, most, paramount, supreme, topmost, utmost
maybe it could be, mayhap (*archaic*), peradventure (*archaic*), perchance (*archaic*), perhaps, possibly
mayhem chaos, commotion, confusion, destruction, disorder, fracas, havoc, trouble, violence

mea culpa (**may**-ah **cool**-pah) an acknowledgment of guilt.

mead[1] *n* a wine-like alcoholic drink made from honey, often with spices added.

mead[2] *n Archaic or poetic* a meadow.

meadow *n* **1** a grassy field used for hay or for grazing animals. **2** a low-lying piece of grassland, often near a river.

meadowsweet *n* a plant with dense heads of small fragrant cream-coloured flowers.

meagre *or US* **meager** *adj* **1** not enough in amount or extent: *meagre wages.* **2** thin or emaciated.

meal[1] *n* **1** any of the regular occasions, such as breakfast or dinner, when food is served and eaten. **2** the food served and eaten. **3 make a meal of** *Informal* to perform a task with unnecessarily great effort.

meal[2] *n* **1** the edible part of a grain or bean pulse (excluding wheat) ground to a coarse powder. **2** *Scot* oatmeal. **3** *Chiefly US* maize flour. **mealy** *adj*

mealie *or* **mielie** *n (often pl) S African* same as **maize.**

meals-on-wheels *n* a service taking hot meals to the elderly or infirm in their own homes.

meal ticket *n Slang* a person or situation providing a source of livelihood or income.

mealy-mouthed *adj* unwilling or afraid to speak plainly.

mean[1] *vb* **meaning, meant 1** to intend to convey or express: *what do you mean by that?* **2** to denote, represent, or signify: *a red light means "stop!"; "gravid" is a technical term meaning "pregnant".* **3** to intend: *I meant to phone you earlier, but didn't have time.* **4** to say or do in all seriousness: *the boss means what she says.* **5** to have the importance specified: *music means everything to him.* **6** to destine or design for a certain person or purpose: *those sweets weren't meant for you.* **7** to produce, cause, or result in: *major road works will mean long traffic delays.* **8** to foretell: *those black clouds mean rain.* **9 mean well** to have good intentions.

mean[2] *adj* **1** *Chiefly Brit* not willing to give or use much of something, esp. money: *she was noticeably mean; don't be mean with the butter.* **2** unkind or spiteful: *a mean trick.* **3** *Informal* ashamed: *she felt mean about not letting the children stay out late.* **4** *Informal, chiefly US & Canad* bad-tempered or vicious. **5** shabby and poor: *a mean little room.* **6** *Slang* excellent or skilful: *he plays a mean trumpet.* **7 no mean a** of high quality: *no mean player.* **b** difficult: *no mean feat.* **meanly** *adv* **meanness** *n*

mean[3] *n* **1** the middle point, state, or course between limits or extremes. **2** *Maths* **a** the mid-point between the highest and lowest number in a set. **b** the average. *~adj* **3** intermediate in size or quantity. **4** occurring halfway between extremes or limits; average.

meander (mee-**and**-er) *vb* **1** (of a river, road, etc.) to follow a winding course. **2** to wander without definite aim or direction. *~n* **3** a curve or bend, as in a river. **4** a winding course or movement.

mean deviation *n Statistics* the difference between an observed value of a variable and its mean.

meanie *or* **meany** *n Informal* **1** *Chiefly Brit* a miserly person. **2** *Chiefly US* a nasty ill-tempered person.

meaning *n* **1** the sense or significance of a word, sentence, or symbol. **2** the inner, symbolic, or true interpretation or message: *the meaning of the New Testament.*

meaningful *adj* **1** serious and important: *a meaningful relationship.* **2** intended to express a feeling or opinion: *a meaningful pause.*

meaningless *adj* having no meaning or purpose; futile.

means *n* **1** the medium, method, or instrument used to obtain a result or achieve an end: *a means of trans-*

THESAURUS

maze 1. convolutions, intricacy, labyrinth, meander **2.** *figurative* bewilderment, confusion, imbroglio, mesh, perplexity, puzzle, snarl, tangle, uncertainty, web

meadow field, grassland, lea *(poetic)*, ley, pasture

meagre 1. deficient, exiguous *(formal)*, inadequate, insubstantial, little, measly, paltry, pathetic, poor, puny, scanty, scrimpy, short, skimpy, slender, slight, small, spare, sparse **2.** bony, emaciated, gaunt, hungry, lank, lean, scraggy, scrawny, skinny, starved, thin, underfed

mean[1] *vb.* **1.** betoken, connote, convey, denote, drive at, express, hint at, imply, indicate, purport, represent, say, signify, spell, stand for, suggest, symbolize **2.** aim, aspire, contemplate, design, desire, have in mind, intend, plan, propose, purpose, set out, want, wish **3.** design, destine, fate, fit, make, match, predestine, preordain, suit **4.** bring about, cause, engender, entail, give rise to, involve, lead to, necessitate, produce, result in **5.** adumbrate, augur, betoken, foreshadow, foretell, herald, portend, presage, promise

mean[2] *adj.* **1.** beggarly, close, mercenary, mingy *(Brit. informal)*, miserly, near *(informal)*, niggardly, parsimonious, penny-pinching, penurious, selfish, skimpy, stingy, tight, tight-fisted, ungenerous **2.** abject, base, callous, contemptible, degenerate, degraded, despicable, disgraceful, dishonourable, hard-hearted, ignoble, low-minded, narrow-minded, petty, scurvy, shabby, shameful, sordid, vile, wretched **3.** bad-tempered, cantankerous, churlish, disagreeable, hostile, ill-tempered, malicious, nasty, rude, sour, unfriendly, unpleasant **4.** beggarly, contemptible, down-at-heel, grungy *(slang, chiefly U.S.)*, insignificant, miserable, paltry, petty, poor, run-down, scruffy, scuzzy *(slang, chiefly U.S.)*, seedy, shabby, sordid, squalid, tawdry, wretched

mean[3] **1.** *n.* average, balance, compromise, happy medium, median, middle, middle course *or* way, mid-point, norm **2.** *adj.* average, intermediate, medial, median, medium, middle, middling, normal, standard

meander 1. *vb.* ramble, snake, stravaig *(Scot. & northern English dialect)*, stray, stroll, turn, wander, wind, zigzag **2.** *n.* bend, coil, curve, loop, turn, twist, zigzag

meaning connotation, denotation, drift, explanation, gist, implication, import, interpretation, message, purport, purpose, sense, significance, signification, substance, upshot, value

meaningful 1. important, material, purposeful, relevant, serious, significant, useful, valid, worthwhile **2.** eloquent, expressive, meaning, pointed, pregnant, speaking, suggestive

meaningless aimless, empty, futile, hollow, inane, inconsequential, insignificant, insubstantial, nonsensical, nugatory, pointless, purposeless, senseless, trifling, trivial, useless, vain, valueless, worthless

meanness 1. minginess *(Brit. informal)*, miserliness, niggardliness, parsimony, penuriousness, selfishness, stinginess, tight-fistedness **2.** abjectness, baseness, degeneracy, degradation, despicableness, disgracefulness, dishonourableness, low-mindedness, narrow-mindedness, pettiness, scurviness, shabbiness, shamefulness, sordidness, vileness, wretchedness **3.** bad temper, cantankerousness, churlishness, disagreeableness, hostility, ill temper, malice, maliciousness, nastiness, rudeness, sourness, unfriendliness, unpleasantness **4.** beggarliness, contemptibleness, insig-

port. ~*pl n* **2** income: *a man of means.* **3 by all means** without hesitation or doubt; certainly. **4 by means of** with the use or help of. **5 by no** *or* **not by any means** on no account; in no way.

means test *n* the checking of a person's income to determine whether he or she qualifies for financial aid. **means-tested** *adj*

meant *vb* the past of **mean**[1].

meantime *n* **1** the intervening period: *in the meantime.* ~*adv* **2** same as **meanwhile.**

mean time *or* **mean solar time** *n* the times, at a particular place, measured so as to give 24-hour days (mean solar days) throughout a year.

meanwhile *adv* **1** during the intervening period. **2** at the same time, esp. in another place.

meany *n, pl* **meanies** same as **meanie.**

measles *n* a highly contagious viral disease common in children, characterized by fever and a rash of small red spots. ~See also **German measles.**

measly *adj* **-slier, -sliest 1** *Informal* too small in quantity or value. **2** having or relating to measles.

measure *n* **1** the size, quantity, or degree of something, as discovered by measurement or calculation. **2** a device for measuring distance, volume, etc., such as a graduated scale or container. **3** a system or unit of measurement: *the joule is a measure of energy.* **4** an amount of alcoholic drink, esp. that served as standard in a bar. **5** degree or extent: *a measure of success.* **6** a particular action intended to achieve an effect: *radical measures are needed to cut unemployment.* **7** a legislative bill, act, or resolution. **8** *Music* same as **bar**[1] (sense 9). **9** *Prosody* poetic rhythm or metre. **10** *Prosody* a metrical foot. **11** *Old-fashioned* a dance. **12 for good measure** as an extra precaution or beyond requirements. ~*vb* **-uring, -ured 13** to determine the size, amount, etc., of by measurement: *he measured the room for a new carpet.* **14** to indicate or record the size, speed, force, etc., of: *this dial measures the pressure in the pipe.* **15** to have the size, quantity, etc., specified: *the room measures six feet.* **16** to estimate or assess: *you cannot measure intelligence purely by exam results.* **17** to function as a measurement of: *the ohm measures electrical resistance.* **18** to bring into competition or conflict with: *he measured his strength against that of his opponent.* ~See also **measure out, measures, measure up. measurable** *adj*

measured *adj* **1** slow or stately. **2** carefully considered; deliberate.

measurement *n* **1** the act or process of measuring. **2** an amount, extent, or size determined by measuring. **3** a system or unit used for measuring: *the kilometre is the standard measurement of distance in most countries.* **4 measurements** the size of a person's waist, chest, hips, etc., used when buying clothes.

measure out *vb* to carefully pour or put the required amount of (something) into a container: *she measured out a large whisky.*

measures *pl n* rock strata that contain a particular type of deposit: *coal measures.*

measure up *vb* **1** to take the measurement of (an area): *we went round and measured up for curtains.* **2 measure up to** to fulfil (expectations or standards).

measuring *adj* used to measure quantities, esp. in cooking: *a measuring jug.*

meat *n* **1** the flesh of animals used as food. **2** the essence or gist: *get to the meat of your lecture as quickly as possible.* **meatless** *adj*

meatball *n* minced beef, shaped into a ball before cooking.

meaty *adj* **meatier, meatiest 1** of, like, or full of meat. **2** heavily built; fleshy or brawny. **3** full of import or interest: *a meaty historical drama.*

Mecca *n* **1** the holy city of Islam. **2** a place that attracts many visitors.

mech. 1 mechanical. **2** mechanics.

mechanic *n* a person skilled in maintaining or operating machinery or motors.

mechanical *adj* **1** made, performed, or operated by machinery. **2** able to understand how machines work and how to repair or maintain them. **3 a** (of an action) done without thought or feeling. **b** (of a task) not requiring any thought; routine or repetitive. **4** of or involving the science of mechanics. **mechanically** *adv*

mechanical drawing *n* a drawing to scale of a machine or architectural plan from which dimensions can be taken.

mechanical engineering *n* the branch of engi-

THESAURUS

nificance, paltriness, pettiness, poorness, scruffiness, seediness, shabbiness, sordidness, squalor, tawdriness, wretchedness

means 1. agency, avenue, channel, course, expedient, instrument, measure, medium, method, mode, process, way **2.** affluence, capital, estate, fortune, funds, income, money, property, resources, riches, substance, wealth, wherewithal **3. by all means** absolutely, certainly, definitely, doubtlessly, of course, positively, surely **4. by means of** by dint of, by way of, through, using, utilizing, via, with the aid of **5. by no means** *or* **not by any means** absolutely not, definitely not, in no way, not at all, not in the least, not in the slightest, not the least bit, no way, on no account

meanwhile, meantime at the same time, concurrently, for now, for the duration, for the moment, for then, in the interim, in the interval, in the intervening time, in the meantime, in the meanwhile, simultaneously

measurable assessable, computable, determinable, gaugeable, material, perceptible, quantifiable, quantitative, significant

measure *n.* **1.** allotment, allowance, amount, amplitude, capacity, degree, extent, magnitude, portion, proportion, quantity, quota, range, ration, reach, scope, share, size **2.** gauge, metre, rule, scale, yardstick **3.** method, standard, system **4.** act, action, course, deed, expedient, manoeuvre, means, procedure, proceeding, step **5.** act, bill, enactment, law, resolution, statute **6.** beat, cadence, foot, metre, rhythm, verse **7. for good measure** as a bonus, besides, in addition, into the bargain, to boot ~*vb.* **8.** appraise, assess, calculate, calibrate, compute, determine, estimate, evaluate, gauge, judge, mark out, quantify, rate, size, sound, survey, value, weigh

measurement 1. appraisal, assessment, calculation, calibration, computation, estimation, evaluation, judgment, survey, valuation **2.** amount, amplitude, area, capacity, depth, dimension, extent, height, length, magnitude, size, volume, weight, width

measure out allot, apportion, assign, deal out, dispense, distribute, divide, dole out, issue, mete out, parcel out, pour out, share out

measure up to be adequate, be capable, be equal to, be fit, be suitable, be suited, come up to scratch (*informal*), come up to standard, compare, cut the mustard (*U.S. slang*), equal, fit *or* fill the bill, fulfil the expectations, make the grade (*informal*), match, meet, rival

meat core, essence, gist, heart, kernel, marrow, nub, nucleus, pith, point, substance

mechanical 1. automated, automatic, machine-driven **2.** automatic, cold, cursory, dead, emotionless, habitual, impersonal, instinctive, involuntary, lack-

neering concerned with the design, construction, and operation of machines.

mechanics *n* **1** the scientific study of motion and force. **2** the science of designing, constructing, and operating machines. *~pl n* **3** the technical aspects of something.

mechanism *n* **1** a system of moving parts that performs some function, esp. in a machine. **2** any mechanical device or part of such a device. **3** a process or technique: *the body's defence mechanisms.* **mechanistic** *adj*

mechanize *or* **-nise** *vb* **-nizing, -nized** *or* **-nising, -nised 1** to equip a factory or industry with machinery. **2** to make mechanical or automatic. **3** *Mil* to equip an army with armoured vehicles. **mechanization** *or* **-nisation** *n*

med. 1 medical. **2** medicine. **3** medieval. **4** medium.

MEd Master of Education.

medal *n* a small flat piece of metal bearing an inscription or image, given as an award or in commemoration of some outstanding event.

medallion *n* **1** a disc-shaped ornament worn on a chain round the neck. **2** a large medal. **3** a circular decorative device used in architecture.

medallist *or US* **medalist** *n Chiefly sport* a winner of a medal or medals.

meddle *vb* **-dling, -dled** to interfere annoyingly. **meddler** *n* **meddlesome** *adj*

media *n* **1** a plural of **medium. 2 the media** the mass media collectively. *~adj* **3** of or relating to the mass media: *media hype.*

➤ *Media* is a plural noun. There is an increasing tendency to use it also as a singular noun because of the ambiguous senses of *medium.*

mediaeval (med-ee-eve-al) *adj* same as **medieval.**

media event *n* an event that is staged for or exploited by the mass media.

medial (mee-dee-al) *adj* of or situated in the middle. **medially** *adv*

median *n* **1** a middle point, plane, or part. **2** *Geom* a straight line joining one corner of a triangle to the midpoint of the opposite side. **3** *Statistics* the middle value in a frequency distribution, below and above which lie values with equal total frequencies.

mediate (mee-dee-ate) *vb* **-ating, -ated 1** to intervene between people or in a dispute in order to bring about agreement. **2** to resolve differences by mediation. **3** to be changed slightly by (an experience or event): *clients' attitudes to social workers have often been mediated by their past experiences.* **mediation** *n* **mediator** *n*

medic *n Informal* a doctor, medical orderly, or medical student.

medical *adj* **1** of or relating to the science of medicine or to the treatment of patients without surgery. *~n* **2** *Informal* a medical examination. **medically** *adv*

medical certificate *n* **1** a doctor's certificate giving evidence of a person's unfitness for work. **2** a document stating the result of a satisfactory medical examination.

medicament (mid-**dik**-a-ment) *n* a medicine.

medicate *vb* **-cating, -cated 1** to treat a patient with a medicine. **2** to add a medication to a bandage, shampoo, etc. **medicative** *adj*

medication *n* **1** treatment with drugs or remedies. **2** a drug or remedy.

medicinal (mid-**diss**-in-al) *adj* relating to or having therapeutic properties. **medicinally** *adv*

medicine *n* **1** any substance used in treating or alleviating the symptoms of disease. **2** the science of preventing, diagnosing, or curing disease. **3** any nonsurgical branch of medical science. **4 take one's medicine** to accept a deserved punishment.

medicine man *n* (among certain peoples) a person believed to have supernatural powers of healing.

medico *n, pl* **-cos** *Informal* a doctor or medical student.

medieval *or* **mediaeval** (med-ee-eve-al) *adj* **1** of, relating to, or in the style of the Middle Ages. **2** *Informal* old-fashioned or primitive. **medievalist** *or* **mediaevalist** *n*

Medieval Greek *n* the Greek language from the 7th to 13th century AD.

Medieval Latin *n* the Latin language as used throughout Europe in the Middle Ages.

mediocre (mee-dee-**oak**-er) *adj* not very high quality; average or second rate. **mediocrity** (mee-dee-**ok**-rit-ee) *n*

meditate *vb* **-tating, -tated 1** to think about something deeply: *he meditated on the problem.* **2** to reflect deeply on spiritual matters. **3** to plan, consider, or think of doing something. **meditative** *adj* **meditator** *n*

meditation *n* **1** the act of meditating; reflection. **2**

THESAURUS

lustre, lifeless, machine-like, matter-of-fact, perfunctory, routine, spiritless, unconscious, unfeeling, unthinking

mechanism 1. action, components, gears, innards (*informal*), machinery, motor, workings, works **2.** apparatus, appliance, contrivance, device, instrument, machine, structure, system, tool **3.** agency, execution, functioning, means, medium, method, operation, performance, procedure, process, system, technique, workings

meddle butt in, interfere, intermeddle, interpose, intervene, intrude, pry, put one's oar in, put one's two cents in (*U.S. slang*), stick one's nose in (*informal*), tamper

mediate act as middleman, arbitrate, bring to an agreement, bring to terms, conciliate, intercede, interpose, intervene, make peace between, moderate, reconcile, referee, resolve, restore harmony, settle, step in (*informal*), umpire

mediator advocate, arbiter, arbitrator, go-between, honest broker, interceder, intermediary, judge, middleman, moderator, negotiator, peacemaker, referee, umpire

medicinal curative, healing, medical, remedial, restorative, therapeutic

medicine cure, drug, medicament, medication, physic (*rare*), remedy

medieval *or* **mediaeval 1.** Gothic **2.** *informal* antediluvian, antiquated, antique, archaic, old-fashioned, primitive, unenlightened

mediocre average, banal, commonplace, fair to middling (*informal*), indifferent, inferior, insignificant, mean, medium, middling, ordinary, passable, pedestrian, run-of-the-mill, second-rate, so-so (*informal*), tolerable, undistinguished, uninspired

mediocrity commonplaceness, indifference, inferiority, insignificance, ordinariness, poorness, unimportance

meditate 1. be in a brown study, cogitate, consider, contemplate, deliberate, muse, ponder, reflect, ruminate, study, think **2.** consider, contemplate, design, devise, have in mind, intend, mull over, plan, purpose, scheme, think over

contemplation of spiritual matters, esp. as a religious practice.

Mediterranean *adj* of the Mediterranean Sea, lying between S Europe, N Africa, and SW Asia, or the surrounding region.

medium *adj* **1** midway between extremes of size, amount, or degree: *fry over a medium heat; a man of medium height.* ~*n, pl* **-dia** *or* **-diums** **2** a middle state, degree, or condition: *the happy medium.* **3** a substance which has a particular effect or can be used for a particular purpose: *linseed oil is used as a thinning medium for oil paint.* **4** a means for communicating information or news to the public. **5** a person who can supposedly communicate with the dead. **6** the substance or surroundings in which an organism naturally lives or grows. **7** *Art* the category of a work of art, as determined by its materials: *his works in the photographic medium.*

medium wave *n* a radio wave with a wavelength between 100 and 1000 metres.

medlar *n* the apple-like fruit of a small Eurasian tree, which is not edible until it has begun to decay.

medley *n* **1** a mixture of various elements. **2** a musical composition consisting of various tunes arranged as a continuous whole. **3** *Swimming* a race in which a different stroke is used for each length.

medulla (mid-**dull**-la) *n, pl* **-las** *or* **-lae** (-lee) **1** *Anat* the innermost part of an organ or structure. **2** *Anat* the lower stalklike section of the brain. **3** *Bot* the central pith of a plant stem. **medullary** *adj*

medusa (mid-**dew**-za) *n, pl* **-sas** *or* **-sae** (-zee) jellyfish.

meek *adj* quiet, and ready to do what other people say. **meekly** *adv*

meerkat *n* a South African mongoose.

meerschaum (**meer**-shum) *n* **1** a white, heat-resistant, claylike mineral. **2** a tobacco pipe with a bowl made of this mineral.

meet[1] *vb* **meeting, met** **1** to be in or come to the same place at the same time as, either by arrangement or by accident: *I met him in town.* **2** to come into contact with something or each other: *his head met the ground with a crack; the town where the Rhine and the Moselle meet.* **3** to come to or be at the place of arrival of: *he met his train at noon.* **4** to make the acquaintance of or be introduced to someone or each other. **5** (of people) to gather together for a purpose: *the board meets once a week.* **6** to compete, play, or fight against. **7** to cope with effectively; satisfy: *they were unable to meet his demands.* **8** to pay for (something): *it is difficult to meet the cost of medical insurance.* **9** Also: **meet with** to experience or suffer: *he met his death at the Somme.* **10 more to this than meets the eye** there is more involved in this than appears. ~*n* **11** a sports meeting. **12** the assembly of hounds and huntsmen prior to a hunt.

➤ *Meet* is only followed by *with* in the context of misfortune: *I met his son; I met with an accident.*

meet[2] *adj Archaic* proper, fitting, or correct.

meeting *n* **1** an act of coming together: *a meeting was fixed for the following day.* **2** an assembly or gathering of people: *the meeting voted in favour.* **3** a sporting competition, as of athletes, or of horse racing.

mega *adj Slang* extremely good, great, or successful.

mega- *combining form* **1** denoting 10^6: *megawatt.* **2** (in computer technology) denoting 2^{20} (1 048 576): *megabyte.* **3** large or great: *megalith.* **4** *Informal* very great: *megastar.*

megabyte *n Computers* 2^{20} or 1 048 576 bytes.

megadeath *n* the death of a million people, esp. in a nuclear war or attack.

megahertz *n, pl* **megahertz** one million hertz; one million cycles per second.

megajoule *n* one million joules.

megalith *n* a very large stone, esp. one forming part of a prehistoric monument. **megalithic** *adj*

megalomania *n* **1** a mental illness characterized by delusions of power. **2** *Informal* a craving for power. **megalomaniac** *adj, n*

megaphone *n* a funnel-shaped instrument used to make someone's voice sound louder, esp. out of doors.

megapode *n* any of various ground-living birds of Australia, New Guinea, and adjacent islands. Their eggs incubate in mounds of sand or rotting vegetation.

megaton *n* **1** one million tons. **2** an explosive power, esp. of a nuclear weapon, equal to the power of one million tons of TNT.

megavolt *n* one million volts.

megawatt *n* one million watts.

meiosis (my-**oh**-siss) *n, pl* **-ses** (-seez) a type of cell division in which reproductive cells are produced, each containing half the chromosome number of the parent nucleus.

melamine *n* a colourless crystalline compound used in making synthetic resins.

melancholia (mel-an-**kole**-lee-a) *n* an old name for **depression** (sense 1).

melancholy (**mel**-an-kol-lee) *n, pl* **-cholies** **1** a ten-

THESAURUS

meditation brown study, cerebration, cogitation, concentration, contemplation, musing, pondering, reflection, reverie, ruminating, rumination, study, thought

medium *adj.* **1.** average, fair, intermediate, mean, medial, median, mediocre, middle, middling, midway ~*n.* **2.** average, centre, compromise, mean, middle, middle course (ground, path, way), midpoint **3.** agency, avenue, channel, form, instrument, instrumentality, means, mode, organ, vehicle, way **4.** channeller, spiritualist **5.** atmosphere, conditions, element, environment, habitat, influences, milieu, setting, surroundings

medley assortment, confusion, farrago, gallimaufry, hodgepodge, hotchpotch, jumble, *mélange,* miscellany, mishmash, mixed bag (*informal*), mixture, omnium-gatherum, pastiche, patchwork, potpourri

meek deferential, docile, forbearing, gentle, humble, long-suffering, mild, modest, patient, peaceful, soft, submissive, timid, unassuming, unpretentious, yielding

meet **1.** bump into, chance on, come across, confront, contact, encounter, find, happen on, run across, run into **2.** abut, adjoin, come together, connect, converge, cross, intersect, join, link up, touch, unite **3.** assemble, collect, come together, congregate, convene, forgather, gather, muster, rally **4.** answer, carry out, come up to, comply, cope with, discharge, equal, fulfil, gratify, handle, match, measure up, perform, satisfy **5.** bear, encounter, endure, experience, face, go through, suffer, undergo

meeting **1.** assignation, confrontation, encounter, engagement, introduction, rendezvous, tryst (*archaic*) **2.** assembly, audience, company, conclave, conference, congregation, congress, convention, convocation, gathering, get-together (*informal*), meet, powwow, rally, reunion, session

melancholy **1.** *n.* blues, dejection, depression, despondency, gloom, gloominess, low spirits, misery, pensiveness, sadness, sorrow, the hump (*Brit. informal*), unhappiness, woe **2.** *adj.* blue, dejected, depressed, despondent, disconsolate, dismal, dispirited, doleful, down, downcast, downhearted, down in the dumps (*informal*), down in the mouth, gloomy, glum,

dency to gloominess or depression. **2** a sad thoughtful state of mind. *~adj* **3** characterized by, causing, or expressing sadness. **melancholic** *adj, n*

melange (may-**lahnzh**) *n* a mixture or assortment: *a melange of historical facts and legends.*

melanin *n* a black pigment present in the hair, skin, and eyes of humans and animals.

melanoma *n, pl* **-mas** *or* **-mata** *Pathol* a tumour composed of dark-coloured cells, occurring in some skin cancers.

Melba toast *n* very thin crisp toast.

meld *vb* to merge or blend.

melee (**mel**-lay) *n* a noisy riotous fight or crowd.

mellifluous (mel-**lif**-flew-uss) *adj* (of sound) smooth and sweet.

mellow *adj* **1** (esp. of colours, light, or sounds) soft or rich: *the mellow stillness of a sunny Sunday morning.* **2** kind-hearted, esp. through maturity or old age. **3** genial and relaxed, for instance through the effects of alcohol or good food. **4** (esp. of fruits) sweet, ripe and full-flavoured. **5** (esp. of wine or cheese) have developed a full, smooth flavour as a result of maturing. **6** (of soil) soft and loamy. *~vb* **7** to make or become mellow.

melodeon *n* **1** a small accordion. **2** a keyboard instrument like a harmonium.

melodic (mel-**lod**-ik) *adj* **1** of or relating to melody. **2** tuneful and pleasant to the ear; melodious. **melodically** *adv*

melodious (mel-**lode**-ee-uss) *adj* **1** pleasant to the ear: *he gave a melodious chuckle.* **2** tuneful and melodic. **melodiousness** *n*

melodrama *n* **1** a play or film full of extravagant action and emotion. **2** overdramatic emotion or behaviour. **melodramatic** *adj* **melodramatics** *pl n*

melody *n, pl* **-dies** **1** *Music* a succession of notes forming a distinctive sequence; tune. **2** sounds that are pleasant because of their tone or arrangement, esp. words of poetry.

melon *n* any of various large edible fruits which have a hard rind and juicy flesh.

melt *vb* **1** to change from a solid into a liquid as a result of the action of heat. **2** to dissolve: *these sweets melt in the mouth.* **3** Also: **melt away** to diminish and finally disappear; fade away: *he felt his inner doubts melt away.* **4** to blend so that it is impossible to tell where one thing ends and another begins: *they melted into the trees until the gamekeeper had passed.* **5** to make or become emotional or sentimental; soften: *she melted into tears.* **meltingly** *adv*

meltdown *n* (in a nuclear reactor) the melting of the fuel rods, with the possible escape of radioactivity.

melting point *n* the temperature at which a solid turns into a liquid.

melting pot *n* a place or situation in which many races, ideas, etc., are mixed.

meltwater *n* melted snow or ice.

member *n* **1** a person who belongs to a group or organization such as a club or political party. **2** any part of a plant or animal, such as a limb or petal. **3** a Member of Parliament: *the member for Glasgow Central.* *~adj* **4** (of a country or group) belonging to an organization or alliance: *the member countries of the European Union.*

Member of Parliament *n* a person who has been elected to the House of Commons or the equivalent assembly in another country.

membership *n* **1** the members of an organization collectively. **2** the number of members. **3** the state of being a member.

membrane *n* a thin flexible tissue that covers, lines, or connects plant and animal organs or cells. **membranous** *adj*

memento *n, pl* **-tos** *or* **-toes** something that reminds one of past events; a souvenir.

memento mori *n, pl* **memento mori** an object intended to remind people of death.

memo *n, pl* **memos** short for **memorandum.**

memoir (**mem**-wahr) *n* a biography or historical account based on personal knowledge

memoirs *pl n* **1** a collection of reminiscences about a period or series of events, written from personal experience. **2** an autobiography.

memorabilia *pl n, sing* **-rabile** objects connected with famous people or events.

memorable *adj* worth remembering or easily remembered because it is very special or important. **memorably** *adv*

memorandum *n, pl* **-dums** *or* **-da** **1** a note sent by one person or department to another within a business organization. **2** a note of things to be remembered. **3** *Law* a short written summary of the terms of a transaction.

memorial *n* **1** something, such as a statue, built or displayed to preserve the memory of someone or something: *a war memorial.* *~adj* **2** in memory of someone or something: *a memorial service.*

memorize *or* **-rise** *vb* **-rizing, -rized** *or* **-rising, -rised** to commit to memory; learn by heart.

memory *n, pl* **-ries** **1** the ability of the mind to store

THESAURUS

heavy-hearted, joyless, low, low-spirited, lugubrious, melancholic, miserable, moody, mournful, pensive, sad, sombre, sorrowful, unhappy, woebegone, woeful

mellow *adj.* **1.** dulcet, euphonic, full, mellifluous, melodious, rich, rounded, smooth, sweet, tuneful, well-tuned **2.** cheerful, cordial, elevated, expansive, genial, half-tipsy, happy, jolly, jovial, merry (*Brit. informal*), relaxed **3.** delicate, full-flavoured, juicy, mature, perfect, rich, ripe, soft, sweet, well-matured *~vb.* **4.** develop, improve, mature, perfect, ripen, season, soften, sweeten

melodious concordant, dulcet, euphonious, harmonious, melodic, musical, silvery, sweet-sounding, sweet-toned, tuneful

melodramatic blood-and-thunder, extravagant, hammy (*informal*), histrionic, overdramatic, overemotional, sensational, stagy, theatrical

melody **1.** air, descant, music, refrain, song, strain, theme, tune **2.** euphony, harmony, melodiousness, music, musicality, tunefulness

melt **1.** deliquesce, diffuse, dissolve, flux, fuse, liquefy, soften, thaw **2.** *often with* **away** disappear, disperse, dissolve, evanesce, evaporate, fade, vanish

member **1.** associate, fellow, representative **2.** appendage, arm, component, constituent, element, extremity, leg, limb, organ, part, portion

membership **1.** associates, body, fellows, members **2.** belonging, enrolment, fellowship, participation

memoir account, biography, essay, journal, life, monograph, narrative, record, register

memoirs autobiography, diary, experiences, journals, life, life story, memories, recollections, reminiscences

memorable catchy, celebrated, distinguished, extraordinary, famous, historic, illustrious, important, impressive, momentous, notable, noteworthy, remarkable, signal, significant, striking, unforgettable

memorial **1.** *n.* cairn, memento, monument, plaque,

and recall past sensations, thoughts, and knowledge: *she can do it from memory.* **2** the sum of everything retained by the mind. **3** a particular recollection of an event or person: *I have a vivid memory of visiting Blackpool as a boy.* **4** the length of time one can remember: *my memory doesn't go that far back.* **5** commemoration: *in memory of our leader.* **6** a person's reputation after death: *a conductor of fond memory.* **7** a part of a computer in which information is stored.

memsahib *n* (formerly, in India) a term of respect used for a European married woman.

men *n* the plural of **man.**

menace *vb* **-acing, -aced 1** to threaten with violence or danger. *~n* **2** a threat; a source of danger. **3** *Informal* an annoying person or thing; nuisance. **menacing** *adj*

menage (may-**nahzh**) *n* a household.

ménage à trois (ah **trwah**) *n, pl* **ménages à trois** a sexual arrangement involving a married couple and the lover of one of them.

menagerie (min-**naj**-er-ee) *n* a collection of wild animals kept for exhibition.

mend *vb* **1** to repair something broken or not working. **2** to heal or recover: *a wound like that will take a while to mend.* **3** (esp. of behaviour) to improve; make or become better: *if you don't mend your ways you'll be in serious trouble.* *~n* **4** a mended area, esp. on a garment. **5 on the mend** regaining one's health.

mendacity *n* the tendency to be untruthful. **mendacious** *adj*

mendelevium *n Chem* an artificially produced radioactive element. Symbol: Md

Mendel's laws *pl n* the principles of heredity proposed by Gregor Mendel (1822–84), Austrian monk and botanist. **Mendelism** *n*

mendicant *adj* **1** begging. **2** (of a monk, nun, etc.) dependent on charity for food. *~n* **3** a mendicant friar. **4** a beggar.

meneer *n* a S African title of address equivalent to *sir* or *Mr.*

menfolk *pl n* men collectively, esp. the men of a particular family.

menhir (**men**-hear) *n* a single standing stone, dating from prehistoric times.

menial (**mean**-nee-al) *adj* **1** involving or doing boring work of low status. *~n* **2** a domestic servant.

meninges (min-**in**-jeez) *pl n, sing* **meninx** (**mean**-inks) the three membranes that surround the brain and spinal cord.

meningitis (men-in-**jite**-iss) *n* inflammation of the meninges, caused by infection and causing severe headache, fever, and rigidity of the neck muscles.

meniscus *n, pl* **-nisci** *or* **-niscuses 1** the curved upper surface of a liquid standing in a tube, produced by the surface tension. **2** a crescent-shaped lens.

menopause *n* the period during which a woman's menstrual cycle ceases, normally at an age of 45 to 50. **menopausal** *adj*

menorah (min-**or**-a) *n Judaism* a seven-branched candelabrum used as an emblem of Judaism.

menses (**men**-seez) *n* same as **menstruation.**

menstrual *adj* of or relating to menstruation: *the menstrual cycle.*

menstruate *vb* **-ating, -ated** to undergo menstruation.

menstruation *n* the approximately monthly discharge of blood from the womb in women of child-bearing age who are not pregnant.

mensuration *n* **1** the study of the measurement of geometric magnitudes such as length. **2** the act or process of measuring.

menswear *n* clothing for men.

mental *adj* **1** of, done by, or involving the mind: *mental alertness.* **2** done in the mind without using speech or writing: *mental arithmetic.* **3** affected by mental illness: *a mental patient.* **4** concerned with mental illness: *a mental hospital.* **5** *Slang* extremely foolish or eccentric. **mentally** *adv*

mental age *n* the age which a person is considered to have reached in thinking ability, judged by comparing his or her ability with the average for people of various ages: *a twenty-one-year-old woman with a mental age of only ten.*

mental handicap *n* any intellectual disability resulting from injury to or abnormal development of the brain. **mentally handicapped** *adj*

mental illness *n* any of various disorders in which a person's thoughts, emotions, or behaviour are so abnormal as to cause suffering to himself, herself, or other people.

mentality *n, pl* **-ties** a particular attitude or way of thinking: *the traditional civil service mentality.*

menthol *n* an organic compound found in peppermint oil and used as an antiseptic, decongestant, and painkiller. **mentholated** *adj*

mention *vb* **1** to refer to or speak about briefly or incidentally. **2** to include in a report, list etc., because of high standards or an outstanding achievement: *the*

THESAURUS

record, remembrance, souvenir **2.** *adj.* commemorative, monumental

memorize commit to memory, con (*archaic*), get by heart, learn, learn by heart, learn by rote, remember

memory 1. recall, recollection, remembrance, reminiscence, retention **2.** commemoration, honour, remembrance **3.** celebrity, fame, glory, name, renown, reputation, repute

menace *vb.* **1.** alarm, bode ill, browbeat, bully, frighten, impend, intimidate, loom, lower *or* lour, terrorize, threaten, utter threats to *~n.* **2.** danger, hazard, jeopardy, peril, threat **3.** *informal* annoyance, nuisance, pest, plague, troublemaker

menacing alarming, baleful, dangerous, forbidding, frightening, intimidating, intimidatory, looming, louring *or* lowering, minacious, minatory, ominous, threatening

mend *vb.* **1.** cure, darn, fix, heal, patch, rectify, refit, reform, remedy, renew, renovate, repair, restore, retouch **2.** convalesce, get better, heal, recover, recuperate **3.** amend, better, correct, emend, improve, rectify, reform, revise *~n.* **4.** darn, patch, repair, stitch **5. on the mend** convalescent, convalescing, getting better, improving, recovering, recuperating

mendacious deceitful, deceptive, dishonest, duplicitous, fallacious, false, fraudulent, insincere, lying, perfidious, perjured, untrue, untruthful

menial 1. *adj.* boring, dull, humdrum, low-status, routine, unskilled **2.** *n.* attendant, dogsbody (*informal*), domestic, drudge, flunky, labourer, lackey, serf, servant, skivvy (*chiefly Brit.*), slave, underling, varlet (*archaic*), vassal

menstruation flow (*informal*), menses, menstrual cycle, monthly (*informal*), period, that time of the month (*informal*), the curse (*informal*)

mental 1. cerebral, intellectual **2.** deranged, disturbed, insane, lunatic, mad, mentally ill, psychiatric, psychotic, unbalanced, unstable

mentality attitude, cast of mind, character, disposi-

hotel is mentioned in all the guidebooks; he was twice mentioned in dispatches during the war. **3 not to mention (something)** to say nothing of (something too obvious to mention). ~*n* **4** a slight reference or allusion. **5** a recognition or acknowledgment of high quality or an outstanding achievement.

mentor *n* an adviser or guide.

menu *n* **1** a list of dishes served at a meal or that can be ordered in a restaurant. **2** a list of options displayed on a visual display unit from which the operator can choose.

MEP (in Britain) Member of the European Parliament.

Mephistopheles (mef-iss-**stoff**-ill-eez) *n* a devil in medieval mythology to whom Faust sold his soul. **Mephistophelean** *adj*

mercantile *adj* of trade or traders; commercial.

Mercator projection (mer-**kate**-er) *n* a way of drawing maps in which latitude and longitude form a rectangular grid, scale being exaggerated with increasing distance from the equator.

mercenary *n, pl* **-naries 1** a soldier who fights for a foreign army for money. ~*adj* **2** motivated by greed or the desire for gain: *calculating and mercenary businessmen.* **3** of or relating to a mercenary or mercenaries.

mercerized *or* **-ised** *adj* (of cotton) treated with an alkali to make it strong and shiny.

merchandise *n* **1** goods for buying, selling, or trading with; commodities. ~*vb* **-dising, -dised 2** to engage in the commercial purchase and sale of goods or services; trade.

merchandising *n* **1** the selection and display of goods in a retail outlet. **2** commercial goods, esp. ones issued to exploit the popularity of a pop group, sporting event, etc.

merchant *n* **1** a person who buys and sells goods in large quantities and usually of one type: *a wine merchant.* **2** *Chiefly Scot, US, & Canad* a person engaged in retail trade; shopkeeper. **3** *Slang* a person dealing in something undesirable: *a gossip merchant.* ~*adj* **4** of ships involved in commercial trade or their crews: *a merchant sailor; the British merchant fleet.*

merchant bank *n Brit* a financial institution that deals primarily with foreign trade and business finance. **merchant banker** *n*

merchantman *n, pl* **-men** a merchant ship.

merchant navy *n* the ships or crew engaged in a nation's commercial shipping.

merciful *adj* **1** (of an act or event) giving relief from pain or suffering: *after months of illness, death came as a merciful release.* **2** showing or giving mercy; compassionate. **mercifully** *adv*

merciless *adj* without mercy; pitiless, cruel, or heartless. **mercilessly** *adv*

mercurial (mer-**cure**-ee-al) *adj* **1** lively and unpredictable: *a mercurial and temperamental chess player.* **2** of or containing mercury.

mercuric *adj* of or containing mercury in the divalent state.

mercurous *adj* of or containing mercury in the monovalent state.

mercury *n, pl* **-ries** *Chem* a silvery toxic metal, the only element liquid at normal temperatures, used in thermometers, barometers, lamps, and dental amalgams. Symbol: Hg

Mercury *n* **1** *Roman myth* the messenger of the gods. **2** the smallest planet and the one nearest the sun.

mercy *n, pl* **-cies 1** compassionate treatment of or attitude towards an offender or enemy who is in one's power. **2** the power to show mercy: *they threw themselves on the King's mercy.* **3** a relieving or welcome occurrence or act: *it was a mercy you turned up when you did.* **4 at the mercy of** in the power of. ~*adj* **5** done or undertaken in an attempt to relieve suffering or bring help: *a mercy mission.*

mercy killing *n* same as **euthanasia.**

mere[1] *adj* nothing more than: *a mere 100 yards from the station.* **merely** *adv*

mere[2] *n Dialect or archaic* a lake.

meretricious *adj* superficially or garishly attractive but of no real value.

merganser (mer-**gan**-ser) *n, pl* **-sers** *or* **-ser** a large crested marine diving duck.

merge *vb* **merging, merged 1** to combine, esp. so as to become part of a larger whole: *the two airlines merged in 1983.* **2** to blend gradually, without any sud-

THESAURUS

tion, frame of mind, make-up, outlook, personality, psychology, turn of mind, way of thinking

mentally in one's head, intellectually, in the mind, inwardly, psychologically, rationally, subjectively

mention *vb.* **1.** acknowledge, adduce, allude to, bring up, broach, call attention to, cite, communicate, declare, disclose, divulge, hint at, impart, intimate, make known, name, point out, recount, refer to, report, reveal, speak about *or* of, state, tell, touch upon **2. not to mention** as well as, besides, not counting, to say nothing of ~*n.* **3.** allusion, announcement, indication, notification, observation, reference, remark **4.** acknowledgment, citation, recognition, tribute

mentor adviser, coach, counsellor, guide, guru, instructor, teacher, tutor

menu bill of fare, carte du jour, tariff (*chiefly Brit.*)

mercantile commercial, marketable, trade, trading

mercenary *n.* **1.** freelance (*Hist.*), hireling, soldier of fortune ~*adj.* **2.** acquisitive, avaricious, bribable, covetous, grasping, greedy, money-grubbing (*informal*), sordid, venal **3.** bought, hired, paid, venal

merchandise 1. *n.* commodities, goods, produce, products, staples, stock, stock in trade, truck, wares **2.** *vb.* buy and sell, deal in, distribute, do business in, market, retail, sell, trade, traffic in, vend

merchant broker, dealer, purveyor, retailer, salesman, seller, shopkeeper, supplier, trader, tradesman, trafficker, vendor, wholesaler

merciful beneficent, benignant, clement, compassionate, forbearing, forgiving, generous, gracious, humane, kind, lenient, liberal, mild, pitying, soft, sparing, sympathetic, tender-hearted

merciless barbarous, callous, cruel, hard, hard-hearted, harsh, heartless, implacable, inexorable, inhumane, pitiless, relentless, ruthless, severe, unappeasable, unfeeling, unforgiving, unmerciful, unpitying, unsparing, unsympathetic

mercy 1. benevolence, charity, clemency, compassion, favour, forbearance, forgiveness, grace, kindness, leniency, pity, quarter **2.** blessing, boon, godsend, piece of luck, relief **3. at the mercy of** defenceless against, exposed to, in the clutches of, in the power of, naked before, open to, prey to, subject to, threatened by, unprotected against, vulnerable to

mere *adj.* absolute, bare, common, complete, entire, nothing more than, plain, pure, pure and simple, sheer, simple, stark, unadulterated, unmitigated, unmixed, utter

merge amalgamate, become lost in, be swallowed up by, blend, coalesce, combine, consolidate, converge,

den change being apparent: *late afternoon merged imperceptibly into early evening.*

merger *n* the act of merging, esp. the combination of two or more companies.

meridian *n* **1** one of the imaginary lines joining the north and south poles at right angles to the equator, designated by degrees of longitude from 0° at Greenwich to 180°. **2** (in acupuncture etc.) any of various channels through which vital energy is believed to circulate round the body.

meridional *adj* **1** of or along a meridian. **2** of or in the south, esp. the south of Europe.

meringue (mer-**rang**) *n* **1** stiffly beaten egg whites mixed with sugar and baked. **2** a small cake made from this mixture.

merino *n, pl* **-nos 1** a sheep with long fine wool, originally reared in Spain. **2** the yarn made from this wool.

merit *n* **1** worth or superior quality; excellence: *the film had two sequels, neither of much merit.* **2** an admirable or advantageous quality: *the relative merits of film and video as a medium of communication.* **3 have the merit of** to have a positive feature or advantage that the alternatives do not have: *the first version has the merit of being short.* **4 on its merits** on its intrinsic qualities or virtues. *~vb* **-iting, -ited 5** to be worthy of; deserve: *the issue merits much fuller discussion.*

meritocracy (mer-it-**tok**-rass-ee) *n, pl* **-cies** a social system in which power is held by the most talented or intelligent people. **meritocrat** *n* **meritocratic** *adj*

meritorious *adj* deserving praise for being good or worthwhile.

merlin *n* a small falcon with dark plumage.

mermaid *n* an imaginary sea creature with a woman's head and upper body and a fish's tail. **merman** *masc n*

merry *adj* **-rier, -riest 1** cheerful and jolly. **2** *Brit informal* slightly drunk. **3 make merry** to take part in noisy, cheerful celebrations or fun. **merrily** *adv* **merriment** *n*

merry-go-round *n* **1** a fairground roundabout. **2** a whirl of activity.

merrymaking *n* noisy, cheerful celebrations or fun. **merrymaker** *n*

mesalliance (mez-**zal**-ee-anss) *n* a marriage with a person of lower social status.

mescal (mess-**kal**) *n* **1** a globe-shaped cactus without spine found in Mexico and the southwestern US. **2** a Mexican alcoholic spirit similar to tequila.

mescaline *n* a hallucinogenic drug derived from the button-like top of the mescal cactus.

mesdames (may-**dam**) *n* the plural of **madame** or **madam** (sense 1).

mesdemoiselles (maid-mwah-**zel**) *n* the plural of **mademoiselle.**

mesembryanthemum *n* a low-growing plant with fleshy leaves and bright daisy-like flowers.

mesh *n* **1** a material resembling a net made from intersecting strands with a space between each strand. **2** an open space between the strands of a net or network: *the minimum permitted size of fishing net mesh.* **3** (*often pl*) the strands surrounding these spaces. **4** anything that ensnares or holds like a net. *~adj* **5** made from mesh: *a wire mesh fence.* *~vb* **6** to entangle or become entangled. **7** (of gear teeth) to engage or interlock. **8** to fit together closely or work in harmony: *Britain must mesh its policies with those of its neighbours.*

mesmerize *or* **-ise** *vb* **-izing, -ized** *or* **-ising, -ised 1** to fascinate and hold spellbound: *his voice had the entire audience mesmerized.* **2** *Archaic* to hypnotize. **mesmerism** *n* **mesmerizing** *adj*

Mesolithic (mess-oh-**lith**-ik) *adj* of the middle period of the Stone Age, in Europe from about 12 000 to 3000 BC.

meson (**mee**-zon) *n Physics* any of a group of elementary particles that has a mass between those of an electron and a proton.

mesosphere (**mess**-oh-sfeer) *n* the atmospheric layer above the stratosphere.

Mesozoic (mess-oh-**zoh**-ik) *adj Geol* of the geological era that began 225 million years ago and lasted about 155 million years, during which the dinosaurs emerged, flourished, then became extinct.

mess *n* **1** a state of untidiness or confusion, esp. a dirty or unpleasant one: *the house was in a mess.* **2** a confused and difficult situation; muddle: *the firm is in a terrible financial mess.* **3** *Informal* a dirty or untidy person or thing: *there was a nasty burnt mess in the saucepan.* **4** a building providing catering, and sometimes recreation, facilities for service personnel. **5** a group of service personnel who regularly eat together. **6** *Old-fashioned* a portion of soft or runny food: *a mess of pottage.* *~vb* **7** (of service personnel) to eat in a group. ~See also **mess about, mess up, mess with.**

mess about *or* **around** *vb* **1** to pass the time doing

THESAURUS

fuse, incorporate, intermix, join, meet, meld, melt into, mingle, mix, tone with, unite

merger amalgamation, coalition, combination, consolidation, fusion, incorporation, union

merit 1. *n.* advantage, asset, excellence, good, goodness, integrity, quality, strong point, talent, value, virtue, worth, worthiness **2.** *vb.* be entitled to, be worthy of, deserve, earn, have a claim to, have a right to, have coming to one, incur, rate, warrant

meritorious admirable, commendable, creditable, deserving, excellent, exemplary, good, honourable, laudable, praiseworthy, right, righteous, virtuous, worthy

merriment amusement, conviviality, festivity, frolic, fun, gaiety, glee, hilarity, jocularity, jollity, joviality, laughter, levity, liveliness, merrymaking, mirth, revelry, sport

merry 1. blithe, blithesome, carefree, cheerful, chirpy (*informal*), convivial, festive, frolicsome, fun-loving, gay, genial, glad, gleeful, happy, jocund, jolly, joyful, joyous, light-hearted, mirthful, rollicking, sportive, upbeat (*informal*), vivacious **2.** *Brit. informal* elevated (*informal*), happy, mellow, squiffy (*Brit. informal*), tiddly (*slang, chiefly Brit.*), tipsy **3. make merry** carouse, celebrate, enjoy oneself, feast, frolic, have a good time, have fun, make whoopee (*informal*), revel

mesh *n.* **1.** net, netting, network, plexus, reticulation, tracery, web **2.** entanglement, snare, tangle, toils, trap, web *~vb.* **3.** catch, enmesh, ensnare, entangle, net, snare, tangle, trap **4.** combine, come together, connect, coordinate, dovetail, engage, fit together, harmonize, interlock, knit

mesmerize absorb, captivate, enthral, entrance, fascinate, grip, hold spellbound, hypnotize, magnetize, spellbind

mess *n.* **1.** botch, chaos, clutter, cock-up (*Brit. slang*), confusion, dirtiness, disarray, disorder, disorganization, hash, hodgepodge (*U.S.*), hotchpotch, jumble, litter, mishmash, pig's breakfast (*informal*), shambles, state, turmoil, untidiness **2.** difficulty, dilemma, fine kettle of fish (*informal*), fix (*informal*), hot water (*informal*), imbroglio, jam (*informal*), mix-up, muddle,

trivial or silly things without any particular purpose or plan: *messing about in boats.* **2** to interfere or meddle: *you have no business messing around here.* **3** *Chiefly US* to engage in adultery.

message *n* **1** a communication from one person or group to another. **2** an implicit meaning or moral, as in a work of art. **3** a religious or political belief that someone attempts to communicate to others: *paintings with a fierce feminist message.* **4 get the message** *Informal* to understand.

messages *pl n Scot & NE English dialect* household shopping.

messenger *n* a person who takes messages from one person or group to another.

Messiah *n* **1** *Judaism* the awaited king of the Jews, who will be sent by God to free them. **2** *Christianity* Jesus Christ, when regarded in this role. **3** a liberator of a country or people.

Messianic *adj* **1** of or relating to a Messiah, or the arrival on Earth of a Messiah. **2 messianic** of or relating to the belief that someone or something will bring about a compete transformation of the existing social order: *a messianic zeal for the free market.*

messieurs (may-**syuh**) *n* the plural of **monsieur.**

mess jacket *n* a waist-length jacket, worn by officers in the mess for formal dinners.

mess kit *n* a soldier's eating utensils for use in the field.

Messrs (**mess**-erz) *n* the plural of **Mr.**

mess up *vb Informal* **1** to make untidy or dirty. **2** to spoil something, or do something badly: *he messed up his driving test.*

mess with *vb Informal, chiefly US* to interfere in, or become involved with, a dangerous person, thing, or situation: *he had started messing with drugs.*

messy *adj* **messier, messiest 1** dirty or untidy. **2** unpleasantly confused or complicated: *the messy, uncontrollable world of real life.* **messily** *adv* **messiness** *n*

met *vb* the past of **meet**[1].

Met *adj* **1** Meteorological: *the Met Office.* ~*n* **2 the Met** the Metropolitan Police, who operate in London.

metabolism (met-**tab**-ol-liz-zum) *n* the chemical processes that occur in living organisms, resulting in growth, production of energy, and elimination of waste. **metabolic** *adj*

metabolize *or* **-lise** *vb* **-lizing, -lized** *or* **-lising, -lised** to produce or be produced by metabolism.

metacarpus *n, pl* **-pi** the set of five long bones in the hand between the wrist and the fingers. **metacarpal** *adj, n*

metal *n* **1 a** *Chem* a chemical element, such as iron or copper, that reflects light and can be shaped, forms positive ions, and is a good conductor of heat and electricity. **b** an alloy, such as brass or steel, containing one or more of these elements. **2** short for **road metal. 3** *Informal* short for **heavy metal. 4 metals** the rails of a railway. ~*adj* **5** made of metal.

metalanguage *n* the language or system of symbols used to discuss another language or system.

metalled *or US* **metaled** *adj* (of a road) surfaced with crushed rock or small stones: *a metalled driveway.*

metallic *adj* **1** of or consisting of metal. **2** sounding like two pieces of metal hitting each other: *a metallic click.* **3** (of a voice) harsh, unpleasant, and unemotional. **4** shining like metal: *metallic paint.* **5** (of a taste) unpleasantly harsh and bitter.

metalliferous *adj* containing a metallic element.

metallography *n* the study of the composition and structure of metals.

metalloid *n Chem* a nonmetallic element, such as arsenic or silicon, that has some of the properties of a metal.

metallurgy *n* the scientific study of the structure, properties, extraction, and refining of metals. **metallurgical** *adj* **metallurgist** *n*

metalwork *n* **1** the craft of making articles from metal. **2** articles made from metal. **3** the metal part of something. **metalworker** *n*

metamorphic *adj* **1** (of rocks) altered considerably from the original structure and composition by pressure and heat. **2** of metamorphosis or metamorphism.

metamorphism *n* the process by which metamorphic rocks are formed.

metamorphose *vb* **-phosing, -phosed** to change from one state or thing into something different.

metamorphosis (met-a-**more**-foss-is) *n, pl* **-ses** (-seez) **1** a complete change of physical form or substance. **2** a complete change of character or appearance. **3** *Zool* the change of form that accompanies transformation into an adult in certain animals, for example the butterfly or frog.

metaphor *n* a figure of speech in which a word or phrase is applied to an object or action that it does not literally apply to in order to imply a resemblance, for example *he is a lion in battle.* **metaphorical** *adj* **metaphorically** *adv*

metaphysical *adj* **1** of metaphysics. **2** abstract, abstruse, or unduly theoretical.

Metaphysical *adj* denoting certain 17th-century poets who combined intense feeling with elaborate imagery.

metaphysics *n* **1** the philosophical study of the na-

THESAURUS

perplexity, pickle (*informal*), plight, predicament, spot (*informal*), stew (*informal*), tight spot

mess about *or* **around 1.** amuse oneself, dabble, fool (about *or* around), footle (*informal*), muck about (*informal*), piss about *or* around (*taboo slang*), play about *or* around, potter, trifle **2.** fiddle (*informal*), fool (about *or* around), interfere, meddle, piss about *or* around (*taboo slang*), play, tamper, tinker, toy

message 1. bulletin, communication, communiqué, dispatch, intimation, letter, memorandum, missive, note, notice, tidings, word **2.** idea, import, meaning, moral, point, purport, theme **3. get the message** catch on (*informal*), comprehend, get it, get the point, see, take the hint, twig (*Brit. informal*), understand

messenger agent, bearer, carrier, courier, delivery boy, emissary, envoy, errand-boy, go-between, harbinger, herald, runner

mess up 1. befoul, besmirch, clutter, dirty, disarrange, dishevel, foul, litter, pollute, scramble **2.** botch, bungle, cock up (*Brit. slang*), fuck up (*offensive taboo slang*), make a hash of (*informal*), muck up (*Brit. slang*), muddle, scramble

mess with fiddle (*informal*), interfere, meddle, play, tamper, tinker

messy chaotic, cluttered, confused, dirty, dishevelled, disordered, disorganized, grubby, littered, muddled, shambolic (*informal*), sloppy (*informal*), slovenly, unkempt, untidy

metaphor allegory, analogy, emblem, figure of speech, image, symbol, trope

metaphorical allegorical, emblematic, emblematical, figurative, symbolic

metaphysical 1. immaterial, impalpable, incorporeal, intangible, spiritual, supernatural, unreal, unsub-

ture of reality. **2** abstract or subtle discussion or reasoning.

metastasis (mit-**tass**-tiss-iss) *n, pl* **-ses** (-seez) *Pathol* the spreading of a disease, esp. cancer, from one part of the body to another.

metatarsus *n, pl* **-si** the set of five long bones in the foot between the toes and the ankle. **metatarsal** *adj, n*

metathesis (mit-**tath**-iss-iss) *n, pl* **-ses** (-seez) the transposition of two sounds or letters in a word.

metazoan (met-a-**zoh**-an) *n* **1** any animal having a body composed of many cells: includes all animals except sponges and protozoans. *~adj* **2** of the metazoans.

meteor *n* **1** a small piece of rock or metal that has entered the earth's atmosphere from space. **2** Also: **shooting star** the bright streak of light appearing in the sky due to a piece of rock or metal burning up because of friction as it falls through the atmosphere.

meteoric (meet-ee-**or**-rik) *adj* **1** of or relating to meteors. **2** brilliant and very rapid: *his meteoric rise to power.* **meteorically** *adv*

meteorite *n* the rocklike remains of a meteoroid that has collided with the earth.

meteoroid *n* any of the small celestial bodies that are thought to orbit the sun. When they enter the earth's atmosphere, they become visible as meteors.

meteorol. *or* **meteor.** **1** meteorological. **2** meteorology.

meteorology *n* the study of the earth's atmosphere and weather-forming processes, esp. for weather forecasting. **meteorological** *adj* **meteorologist** *n*

mete out *vb* **meting, meted** to impose or deal out something, usually something unpleasant: *the sentence meted out to him has proved controversial.*

meter[1] *n* **1** any device that measures and records the quantity or number of units of something that was used during a specified period or is being used at that moment: *a gas meter.* **2** short for **parking meter. 3** short for **taximeter.** *~vb* **4** to measure the amount of something used or a rate of flow with a meter.

meter[2] *n US* same as **metre**[1] or **metre**[2].

-meter *n combining form* **1** indicating an instrument for measuring: *barometer.* **2** *Prosody* indicating a verse having a specified number of feet: *pentameter.*

methadone *n* a drug similar to morphine, sometimes prescribed as a heroin substitute.

methanal *n* same as **formaldehyde.**

methane *n* a colourless odourless flammable gas, the main constituent of natural gas.

methane series *n* a series of saturated hydrocarbons with the general formula C_nH_{2n+2}.

methanol *n* a colourless poisonous liquid used as a solvent and fuel. Also: **methyl alcohol**

methinks *vb, past* **methought** *Archaic* it seems to me that.

method *n* **1** a way of doing something, esp. a systematic or regular one. **2** orderliness of thought or action. **3** the techniques of a particular field or subject.

Method *n* an acting technique in which the actor bases his or her role on the inner motivation of the character played.

methodical *adj* careful, well-organized, and systematic. **methodically** *adv*

Methodist *n* **1** a member of any of the Christian Nonconformist denominations that derive from the beliefs and practices of John Wesley and his followers. *~adj* **2** of or relating to Methodists or their Church. **Methodism** *n*

methodology *n, pl* **-gies 1** the system of methods and principles used in a particular discipline. **2** the philosophical study of method. **methodological** *adj*

methought *vb Archaic* the past tense of **methinks.**

meths *n Chiefly Brit, Austral, & NZ informal* methylated spirits.

methyl *adj* of or containing the monovalent saturated hydrocarbon group of atoms CH_3–: *methyl mercury.*

methyl alcohol *n* same as **methanol.**

methylate *vb* **-ating, -ated** to mix with methanol.

methylated spirits *n* alcohol that has been rendered undrinkable by the addition of methanol and a violet dye, used as a solvent or as a fuel for small lamps or heaters. Also: **methylated spirit**

methylene *adj* of, consisting of, or containing the divalent group of atoms –CH_2–: *a methylene group or radical.*

meticulous *adj* very precise about details; careful and thorough. **meticulously** *adv* **meticulousness** *n*

metier (**met**-ee-ay) *n* **1** a profession or trade. **2** a person's strong point or speciality.

Métis (met-**teess**) *n, pl* **-tis** (-**teess**, **-teez**) a person of mixed parentage, esp. the offspring of a North American Indian and a French Canadian. **Métisse** *fem n*

metonymy (mit-**on**-im-ee) *n, pl* **-mies** a figure of speech in which one thing is replaced by another associated with it, for instance the use of *Downing Street* to mean *the British government.*

metre[1] *or US* **meter** *n* the basic SI unit of length, equal to 100 centimetres (39.37 inches): *the majority of people are between one and a half and two metres tall.*

metre[2] *or US* **meter** *n* **1** *Prosody* the rhythmic arrangement of syllables in verse, usually according to the number and kind of feet in a line. **2** *Music chiefly US* the rhythmic arrangement of the beat in a piece of music.

metre-kilogram-second *n* See **mks units.**

metric *adj* of or relating to the metre or metric system: *use either all metric or all imperial measurements.*

metrical *or* **metric** *adj* **1** of or relating to measurement. **2** of or in poetic metre. **metrically** *adv*

metricate *vb* **-cating, -cated** to convert a measuring system or instrument to metric units. **metrication** *n*

metric system *n* any decimal system of units based on the metre. For scientific purposes SI units are used.

metric ton *n* (not in technical use) a tonne.

THESAURUS

stantial **2.** abstract, abstruse, deep, esoteric, high-flown, oversubtle, recondite, theoretical, transcendental

meteoric brief, brilliant, dazzling, ephemeral, fast, flashing, fleeting, momentary, overnight, rapid, spectacular, speedy, sudden, swift, transient

mete out administer, allot, apportion, assign, deal (out), dispense, distribute, divide, dole out, measure, parcel, portion, ration, share

method 1. approach, arrangement, course, fashion, form, manner, mode, modus operandi, plan, practice, procedure, process, programme, routine, rule, scheme, style, system, technique, way **2.** design, form, order, orderliness, organization, pattern, planning, purpose, regularity, structure, system

methodical businesslike, deliberate, disciplined, efficient, meticulous, neat, ordered, orderly, organized, painstaking, planned, precise, regular, structured, systematic, tidy, well-regulated

meticulous detailed, exact, fastidious, fussy, microscopic, painstaking, particular, perfectionist, precise, punctilious, scrupulous, strict, thorough

metro *n, pl* **-ros** an urban, usually underground, railway system in certain cities, such as Paris.

metronome *n* a device which indicates the speed music should be played at by producing a clicking sound from a pendulum with an adjustable period of swing.

metropolis (mit-**trop**-oh-liss) *n* the main city of a country or region.

metropolitan *adj* **1** of or characteristic of a metropolis. **2** of or consisting of a city and its suburbs: *the Tokyo metropolitan region.* **3** of or belonging to the home territories of a country, as opposed to overseas territories: *metropolitan France.* ~*n* **4** *Christianity* the senior clergyman, esp. an archbishop, in charge of an ecclesiastical province. **5** an inhabitant of a large city.

-metry *n combining form* indicating the process or science of measuring: *geometry.* **-metric** *adj combining form*

mettle *n* **1** courage or spirit: *the lack of mettle evident among British politicians.* **2** character or abilities: *the mettle saints are made of.* **3 on one's mettle** roused to making one's best efforts.

MeV million electronvolts (10^6 electronvolts).

mevrou (mef-**roe**) *n* a S African title of address equivalent to *madam* or *Mrs.*

mew[1] *n* **1** the characteristic high-pitched cry of a cat; miaow. ~*vb* **2** to make such a sound.

mew[2] *n* a seagull.

mewl *vb* **1** (esp. of a baby) to cry weakly; whimper. ~*n* **2** a weak or whimpering cry.

mews *n Chiefly Brit* **1** a yard or street lined by buildings originally used as stables but now often converted into dwellings. ~*adj* **2** (of a flat or house) located in a mews: *a mews cottage.*

Mex. **1** Mexican. **2** Mexico.

Mexican *adj* **1** of Mexico. ~*n* **2** a person from Mexico.

Mexican wave *n* the rippling effect produced when the spectators in successive sections of a sports stadium stand up while raising their arms and then sit down.

mezzanine (**mez**-zan-een) *n* an intermediate storey, esp. one between the ground and first floor.

mezzo (**met**-so) *adv* **1** *Music* moderately; quite: *mezzo-forte.* ~*n, pl* **-zos** **2** short for **mezzo-soprano.**

mezzo-soprano *n, pl* **-nos** **1** a female voice lower than soprano but higher than contralto. **2** a singer with such a voice.

mezzotint (**met**-so-tint) *n* **1** a method of engraving done by scraping and burnishing the roughened surface of a copper plate. **2** a print made from a plate so treated.

mg milligram.

Mg *Chem* magnesium.

M. Glam Mid Glamorgan.

Mgr **1** manager. **2** monseigneur. **3** monsignor.

MHz megahertz.

mi *n Music* same as **me**[2].

MI Michigan.

MI5 Military Intelligence, section five; the part of the British security services which combats spying and subversion in Britain.

MI6 Military Intelligence, section six; the part of the British security services which spies on other countries.

miaow (mee-**ow**) *n* **1** the characteristic high-pitched cry of a cat; mew. ~*vb* **2** to make such a sound.

miasma (mee-**azz**-ma) *n, pl* **-mata** *or* **-mas** an unwholesome or foreboding atmosphere.

mica (**my**-ka) *n* any of a group of minerals consisting of flakelike crystals of aluminium or potassium silicates. They have a high resistance to electricity and heat.

mice *n* the plural of **mouse.**

Michaelmas (**mik**-kl-mass) *n* Sept 29, the feast of St Michael the archangel; one of the four quarter days in England, Ireland, and Wales.

Michaelmas daisy *n Brit* a garden plant with small daisy-shaped purple, pink, or white flowers in autumn.

Mick *n Offensive slang* an Irishman.

mickey *n* **take the mickey (out of)** *Informal* to tease (someone).

Mickey Finn *n Slang* a drink containing a drug to make the drinker unconscious.

Mickey Mouse *adj Slang* trivial, insignificant, or amateurish: *a Mickey Mouse survey based on a tiny number of people.*

mickle *or* **muckle** *Archaic or Scot & N English dialect* ~*adj* **1** large or abundant. ~*adv* **2** much; greatly. ~*n* **3** a great amount.

micro *n, pl* **micros** short for **microcomputer** or **microprocessor.**

micro- *or* **micr-** *combining form* **1** small or minute: *microdot.* **2** involving the use of a microscope: *microscopy.* **3** denoting 10^{-6}: *microsecond.*

microbe *n* any microscopic organism, esp. a disease-causing bacterium. **microbial** *or* **microbic** *adj*

microbiology *n* the branch of biology involving the study of microorganisms.

microchemistry *n* chemical experimentation with minute quantities of material.

microchip *n* a tiny wafer of semiconductor material, such as silicon, containing an integrated circuit. Often shortened to: **chip**

microcircuit *n* a miniature electronic circuit in which a number of permanently connected components are contained in one small chip of semiconducting material.

microcomputer *n* a compact computer in which the central processing unit is contained in one or more silicon chips.

microcosm *n* **1** a miniature representation of something: *this area is a microcosm of France as a whole.* **2** man regarded as epitomizing the universe. **3 in microcosm** on a small scale. **microcosmic** *adj*

microdot *n* a greatly reduced photographic copy (about the size of a pinhead) of a document.

microeconomics *n* the branch of economics concerned with particular commodities, firms, or individuals and the relationships between them.

microelectronics *n* the branch of electronics concerned with microcircuits.

microfiche (**my**-kroh-feesh) *n* same as **fiche.**

microfilm *n* **1** a strip of film on which books or documents can be recorded in miniaturized form. ~*vb* **2** to photograph a page or document on microfilm.

microlight *or* **microlite** *n* a very small private aircraft with large wings.

micrometer (my-**krom**-it-er) *n* an instrument for the accurate measurement of small distances or angles.

microminiaturization *or* **-isation** *n* the production and use of very small electronic components.

THESAURUS

metier **1.** calling, craft, line, occupation, profession, pursuit, trade, vocation **2.** forte, speciality, specialty, strong point, strong suit

metropolis capital, city

micron (**my**-kron) *n* a unit of length equal to one millionth of a metre.
microorganism *n* any organism of microscopic size, such as a virus or bacterium.
microphone *n* a device for converting sound into electrical energy.
microprocessor *n Computers* a single integrated circuit which acts as the central processing unit in a small computer.
microscope *n* **1** an optical instrument that uses a lens or combination of lenses to produce a greatly magnified image of a small, close object. **2** any instrument, such as the electron microscope, for producing a greatly magnified visual image of a small object.
microscopic *adj* **1** too small to be seen except with a microscope. **2** very small; minute. **3** of or using a microscope. **microscopically** *adv*
microscopy *n* the use of microscopes.
microsecond *n* one millionth of a second.
microstructure *n* a structure on a microscopic scale, such as that of a metal or a cell.
microsurgery *n* intricate surgery performed using a special microscope and miniature precision instruments.
microwave *n* **1** an electromagnetic wave with a wavelength of between 0.3 and 0.001 metres: used in radar and cooking. **2** short for **microwave oven.** *~vb* **-waving, -waved 3** to cook in a microwave oven.
microwave detector *n* a device used by police for recording the speed of a motorist.
microwave oven *n* a type of cooker which uses microwaves to cook food quickly.
micturate *vb* **-rating, -rated** to urinate. **micturition** *n*
mid[1] *n Archaic* the middle.
mid[2] *or* **'mid** *prep Poetic* amid.
mid- *combining form* indicating a middle part, point, time, or position: *midday; mid-June; mid-Victorian.*
midair *n* some point above ground level, in the air.
midday *n* **1** twelve o'clock in the day; noon. **2** the middle part of the day, from late morning to early afternoon: *the midday sun.*
midden *n Archaic or dialect* a dunghill or pile of refuse.
middle *n* **1** an area or point equal in distance from the ends or edges of a place: *a hotel in the middle of town.* **2** the time between the first part and last part of an event or period of time: *the middle of June; the film got a bit boring in the middle.* **3** the part of the body around the stomach; waist. **4 in the middle of** busy doing something: *I'm in the middle of washing the dishes.* *~adj* **5** equally distant from the ends or outer edges of something; central: *the middle finger.* **6** having an equal number of elder and younger brothers and sisters: *he was the middle child of three.* **7** intermediate in status or situation: *middle management.* **8** avoiding extremes; moderate: *we must find a middle course between authoritarianism and anarchy.*
middle age *n* the period of life between youth and old age, usually considered to occur between the ages of 40 and 60. **middle-aged** *adj*
Middle Ages *n European history* **1** (broadly) the period from the fall of the W Roman Empire in 476 AD to the Italian Renaissance. **2** (narrowly) the period from about 1000 AD to the 15th century.
middle-age spread *or* **middle-aged spread** *n* the fat that appears round many people's waists when they become middle-aged.
Middle America *n* the US middle class, esp. those groups that are politically conservative.
middlebrow *Disparaging* *~n* **1** a person with conventional tastes and limited cultural appreciation. *~adj* **2** of or appealing to middlebrows.
middle C *n Music* the note written on the first ledger line below the treble staff or the first ledger line above the bass staff. On a piano it is near the middle of the keyboard.
middle class *n* **1** the social class between the working and upper classes. It consists of business and professional people. *~adj* **middle-class 2** of or characteristic of the middle class.
middle-distance *adj* **1** *Athletics* of or being a race of a length between the sprints and the distance events, esp. the 800 or 1500 metres: *a middle-distance runner.* *~n* **middle distance 2** the part of a painting between the foreground and the far distance.
middle ear *n* the sound-conducting part of the ear immediately inside the eardrum.
Middle East *n* the area around the E Mediterranean, esp. Israel and the Arab countries from Turkey to North Africa and eastwards to Iran. **Middle Eastern** *adj*
Middle English *n* the English language from about 1100 to about 1450.
Middle High German *n* High German from about 1200 to about 1500.
Middle Low German *n* Low German from about 1200 to about 1500.
middleman *n, pl* **-men 1** a trader who buys from the producer and sells to the consumer. **2** an intermediary or go-between.
middle name *n* **1** a name between a person's first name and surname. **2** a characteristic quality for which a person is known: *danger is my middle name.*
middle-of-the-road *adj* **1** not extreme, esp. in political views; moderate. **2** of or denoting popular music of wide general appeal.
middle school *n Brit* a school for children aged between 8 or 9 and 12 or 13.
middleweight *n* a professional boxer weighing up to 160 pounds (72.5 kg) or an amateur weighing up to 75 kg.
middling *adj* **1** neither very good nor very bad. **2** moderate in size. **3 fair to middling** neither good nor bad, esp. in health. *~adv* **4** *Informal* moderately: *middling well.*
Middx Middlesex.
midfield *n Soccer* the area between the two opposing defences.

THESAURUS

microbe bacillus, bacterium, bug (*informal*), germ, microorganism, virus
microscopic imperceptible, infinitesimal, invisible, minuscule, minute, negligible, teensy-weensy, teeny-weeny, tiny
midday noon, noonday, noontide, noontime, twelve noon, twelve o'clock
middle *n.* **1.** centre, focus, halfway point, heart, inside, mean, midpoint, midsection, midst, thick **2.** midriff, midsection, waist *~adj.* **3.** central, halfway, inner, inside, intermediate, intervening, mean, medial, median, medium, mid
middleman broker, distributor, entrepreneur, go-between, intermediary
middling adequate, all right, average, fair, indifferent,

midge *n* a small mosquito-like biting insect occurring in dancing swarms, esp. near water.

midget *n* **1** a dwarf whose skeleton and features are of normal proportions. *~adj* **2** much smaller than normal: *a midget submarine.*

midi- *combining form* of medium or middle size or length: *a midi-skirt.*

midi system *n* a complete set of compact hi-fi sound equipment designed as a single unit.

midland *n* the central or inland part of a country.

Midlands *n* **1 the Midlands** the central counties of England. *~adj* **2** of, in, or from the central counties of England: *a Midlands engineering firm.*

midmost *adj, adv* in the middle or midst.

midnight *n* **1** the middle of the night; 12 o'clock at night. *~adj* **2** happening or apparent at midnight or in the middle of the night: *midnight Mass.* **3 burn the midnight oil** to work or study late into the night.

midnight sun *n* the sun visible at midnight during the summer inside the Arctic and Antarctic circles.

mid-off *n Cricket* the fielding position on the off side closest to the bowler.

mid-on *n Cricket* the fielding position on the on side closest to the bowler.

midpoint *n* **1** the point on a line equally distant from either end. **2** a point in time halfway between the beginning and end of an event.

midriff *n* **1** the middle part of the human body between waist and chest. **2** *Anat* same as **diaphragm** (sense 1).

midshipman *n, pl* **-men** a naval officer of the lowest commissioned rank.

midships *adv, adj Naut* See **amidships.**

midst *n* **1 in our midst** among us. **2 in the midst of a** surrounded by. **b** at a point during.

midsummer *n* **1** the middle or height of summer. **2** same as **summer solstice.**

Midsummer Day *or* **Midsummer's Day** *n* June 24, the feast of St John the Baptist: one of the four quarter days in England, Ireland, and Wales.

midway *adj* **1** in or at the middle of the distance; halfway. *~adv* **2** to the middle of the distance.

midweek *n* the middle of the week.

Midwest *n* the N central part of the US. **Midwestern** *adj*

mid-wicket *n Cricket* the fielding position on the on side, roughly the same distance from both wickets, and halfway towards the boundary.

midwife *n, pl* **-wives** a person qualified to deliver babies and to care for women before, during, and after childbirth. **midwifery** (mid-**wiff**-fer-ree) *n*

midwinter *n* **1** the middle or depth of winter. **2** same as **winter solstice.**

mien (**mean**) *n Literary* a person's manner, bearing, or appearance.

miffed *adj Informal* offended or upset.

might[1] *vb* used as an auxiliary: **1** the past tense or subjunctive mood of **may**[1]: *he might have come.* **2** expressing possibility: *he might well have gone already.* See **may**[1] (sense 2).

➤ Both *might* and *may* can be used to express a tentative request: *Might/may I ask a favour?*

might[2] *n* **1** great power, strength, or vigour. **2 with all one's might** using all one's strength and energy. **3 (with) might and main** See **main.**

mighty *adj* **mightier, mightiest 1** powerful or strong. **2** very great in extent or importance. *~adv* **3** *Informal, chiefly US & Canad* very: *mighty hungry.* **mightily** *adv* **mightiness** *n*

mignonette (min-yon-**net**) *n* a plant with spikes of small fragrant greenish-white flowers.

migraine (**mee**-grain) *n* a throbbing headache usually affecting only one side of the head and commonly accompanied by nausea and visual disturbances.

migrant *n* **1** a person or animal that moves from one place to another. *~adj* **2** moving from one place to another: *migrant farm labourers.*

migrate *vb* **-grating, -grated 1** to go from one place to settle in another, esp. in a foreign country. **2** (of living creatures, esp. birds) to journey between different habitats at specific times of the year. **migration** *n* **migratory** *adj*

mikado *n, pl* **-dos** *Archaic* the Japanese emperor.

mike *n Informal* a microphone.

mil *n Photog* short for **millimetre:** *35-mil film.*

milady *n, pl* **-dies** (formerly) a continental title for an English gentlewoman.

milch (**miltch**) *adj* (esp. of cattle) kept for milk.

mild *adj* **1** (of a taste or sensation) not strong; bland. **2** gentle or temperate in character, climate, or behaviour. **3** not extreme; moderate: *mild criticism of senior officers.* **4** feeble; unassertive: *a mild protest.* *~n* **5** *Brit* a dark beer flavoured with fewer hops than bitter.

THESAURUS

mediocre, medium, moderate, modest, O.K. *or* okay (*informal*), ordinary, passable, run-of-the-mill, so-so (*informal*), tolerable, unexceptional, unremarkable

midget **1.** *n.* dwarf, homunculus, manikin, pygmy *or* pigmy, shrimp (*informal*), Tom Thumb **2.** *adj.* baby, dwarf, Lilliputian, little, miniature, pocket, pygmy *or* pigmy, small, teensy-weensy, teeny-weeny, tiny

midnight dead of night, middle of the night, the witching hour, twelve o'clock (at night)

midst **in the midst of** amidst, among, during, enveloped by, in the middle of, in the thick of, surrounded by

midway betwixt and between, halfway, in the middle

might **1.** ability, capability, capacity, clout (*informal*), efficacy, efficiency, energy, force, potency, power, prowess, puissance, strength, sway, valour, vigour **2.** **(with) might and main** as hard as one can, as hard as possible, forcefully, full blast, full force, lustily, manfully, mightily, vigorously, with all one's might *or* strength

mighty **1.** doughty, forceful, hardy, indomitable, lusty, manful, potent, powerful, puissant, Ramboesque, robust, stalwart, stout, strapping, strong, sturdy, vigorous **2.** bulky, colossal, elephantine, enormous, gigantic, ginormous (*informal*), grand, great, huge, immense, large, massive, monumental, prodigious, stupendous, titanic, towering, tremendous, vast

migrant **1.** *n.* drifter, emigrant, gypsy, immigrant, itinerant, nomad, rover, tinker, transient, traveller, vagrant, wanderer **2.** *adj.* drifting, gypsy, immigrant, itinerant, migratory, nomadic, roving, shifting, transient, travelling, vagrant, wandering

migrate drift, emigrate, journey, move, roam, rove, shift, travel, trek, voyage, wander

migration emigration, journey, movement, roving, shift, travel, trek, voyage, wandering

migratory itinerant, migrant, nomadic, peripatetic, roving, shifting, transient, travelling, unsettled, vagrant, wandering

mild **1.** amiable, balmy, bland, calm, clement, compassionate, docile, easy, easy-going, equable, forbearing, forgiving, gentle, indulgent, kind, meek, mellow, merciful, moderate, pacific, peaceable, placid, pleasant, serene, smooth, soft, temperate, tender, tranquil, warm **2.** emollient, lenitive, mollifying, soothing

mildew *n* **1** a disease of plants caused by a parasitic fungus. **2** same as **mould**². *~vb* **3** to affect or become affected with mildew. **mildewy** *adj*

mild steel *n* strong tough steel containing a small quantity of carbon.

mile *n* **1** Also: **statute mile** a unit of length used in the U.K., the U.S. and certain other countries, equal to 1760 yards. 1 mile is equivalent to 1.60934 kilometres. **2** See **nautical mile. 3** Also: **miles** *Informal* a great distance; great deal: *he missed by miles.* **4** a race extending over a mile. *~adv* **5 miles** very much: *it's miles better than their first album.*

mileage *n* **1** a distance expressed in miles. **2** the total number of miles that a motor vehicle has travelled. **3** the number of miles a motor vehicle will travel on one gallon of fuel. **4** *Informal* the usefulness or benefit of something: *the opposition is trying to make political mileage out of the issue.*

mileometer *or* **milometer** (mile-**om**-it-er) *n* a device that records the number of miles that a vehicle has travelled.

milepost *n Chiefly US & Canad* a signpost that shows the distance in miles to or from a place.

miler *n* an athlete, horse, etc., that specializes in races of one mile.

milestone *n* **1** a stone pillar that shows the distance in miles to or from a place. **2** a significant event in a life or history: *a milestone in Turkish-Bulgarian relations.*

milfoil *n* same as **yarrow.**

milieu (**meal**-yuh) *n, pl* **milieus** *or* **milieux** (**meal**-yuhz) the social and cultural environment in which a person or thing exists: *the film takes for its milieu an apparently wholesome small town.*

militant *adj* **1** very active or aggressive in the support of a cause. **2** *Formal* warring; engaged in warfare. *~n* **3** a militant person. **militancy** *n* **militantly** *adv*

militarism *n* the pursuit of policies intended to create and maintain aggressive and influential armed forces. **militarist** *n, adj* **militaristic** *adj*

militarized *or* **-ised** *adj* occupied by armed forces: *one of the most heavily militarized borders in the world.* **militarization** *or* **-isation** *n*

military *adj* **1** of or relating to the armed forces or war. **2** of or characteristic of soldiers. *~n* **3 the military** the armed services, esp. the army. **militarily** *adv*

military police *n* a corps within an army that performs police duties.

militate *vb* **-tating, -tated** (of facts or events) to have a strong influence or effect: *our position militated against counter-attacks.*

➤ Do not confuse *militate* with *mitigate* "make less severe".

militia (mill-**ish**-a) *n* a military force of trained civilians enlisted for use in emergency only. **militiaman** *n*

milk *n* **1 a** a whitish fluid secreted by the mammary glands of mature female mammals and used for feeding their young. **b** the milk of cows, goats, etc., used by humans as a food and to make cheese, butter and yogurt. **2** any similar fluid, such as the juice of a coconut. *~vb* **3** to draw milk from the udder of a cow or other animal. **4** to extract as much money, help, or value as possible from: *he was accused of milking the situation for his own ends.* **milker** *n* **milkiness** *n* **milky** *adj*

milk-and-water *adj* weak, feeble, or insipid.

milk bar *n Brit* (formerly) a snack bar at which milk drinks and light refreshments are served.

milk chocolate *n* chocolate that has been made with milk, having a creamy taste.

milk float *n Brit* a small electrically powered vehicle used to deliver milk to houses.

milkmaid *n* a girl or woman who milks cows.

milkman *n, pl* **-men** a man who delivers milk to people's houses.

milk of magnesia *n* a suspension of magnesium hydroxide in water, used as an antacid and laxative.

milk pudding *n Chiefly Brit* a pudding made by cooking milk with a grain, esp. rice.

milk round *n Brit* **1** a route along which a milkman regularly delivers milk. **2** a regular series of visits made by recruitment officers from industry to colleges.

milk shake *n* a cold frothy drink made of milk, flavouring, and sometimes ice cream, whisked together.

milksop *n* a feeble or ineffectual man or youth.

milk tooth *n* any of the first set of teeth in young children.

Milky Way *n* **1** the diffuse band of light stretching across the night sky that consists of millions of distant stars in our galaxy. **2** the galaxy in which the Earth is situated.

mill *n* **1** a building where grain is crushed and ground to make flour. **2** a factory, esp. one which processes raw materials: *a steel mill.* **3** any of various processing or manufacturing machines, esp. one that grinds, presses, or rolls. **4** a small device for grinding solids: *a pepper mill.* **5 go** *or* **be put through the mill** to have an unpleasant experience or ordeal. *~vb* **6** to grind, press, or process in or as if in a mill. **7** to groove or flute the edge of a coin. **8** to move about in a confused manner: *the corridor was full of people milling about.*

milled *adj* **1** crushed or ground in a mill: *freshly milled black pepper.* **2** (of a coin) having a grooved and often raised edge.

millennium (mill-**en**-nee-um) *n, pl* **-niums** *or* **-nia** (-nee-a) **1** a period of one thousand years. **2 the Millennium** *Christianity* the period of a thousand years of Christ's awaited reign upon earth. **3** a future period of peace and happiness. **millennial** *adj*

millepede *n* same as **millipede.**

miller *n History* a person who owns or operates a mill, esp. a corn mill.

miller's thumb *n* a small freshwater European fish with a flattened body.

THESAURUS

mildness blandness, calmness, clemency, docility, forbearance, gentleness, indulgence, kindness, leniency, lenity, meekness, mellowness, moderation, placidity, smoothness, softness, temperateness, tenderness, tranquillity, warmth

milieu background, element, environment, locale, location, *mise en scène,* scene, setting, sphere, surroundings

militant *adj.* **1.** active, aggressive, assertive, combative, vigorous **2.** belligerent, combating, contending, embattled, fighting, in arms, warring *~n.* **3.** activist, belligerent, combatant, fighter, gladiator, partisan, warrior

military 1. *adj.* armed, martial, soldierlike, soldierly, warlike **2.** *n.* armed forces, army, forces, services

militia fencibles (*History*), National Guard (*U.S.*), reserve(s), Territorial Army (*Brit.*), yeomanry (*History*)

milk *vb.* **1.** drain, draw off, express, extract, let out, press, siphon, tap **2.** bleed, drain, exploit, extract, impose on, pump, take advantage of, use, wring

milk-and-water feeble, innocuous, insipid, jejune, nerdy (*slang*), vapid, weak, weedy (*informal*), wimpish *or* wimpy (*informal*), wishy-washy (*informal*)

millesimal (mill-**less**-im-al) *adj* **1** denoting or consisting of a thousandth. *~n* **2** a thousandth part of something.

millet *n* a cereal grass cultivated for its edible grain and as animal fodder.

milli- *combining form* denoting 10^{-3}: *millimetre.*

milliard *n Brit* (no longer in technical use) a thousand million.

millibar *n* a unit of atmospheric pressure equal to 100 newtons per square metre.

milligram *or* **milligramme** *n* one thousandth of a gram.

millilitre *or US* **milliliter** *n* a measure of volume equivalent to one thousandth of a litre.

millimetre *or US* **millimeter** *n* a unit of length equal to one thousandth of a metre.

milliner *n* a person who makes or sells women's hats. **millinery** *n*

million *n, pl* **-lions** *or* **-lion** **1** the number equal to one thousand thousands: 1 000 000 or 10^6. **2** (*often pl*) *Informal* an extremely large but unspecified number: *I've got a million things to do today.* **millionth** *n, adj*

millionaire *n* a person who has money or property worth at least a million pounds, dollars, etc. **millionairess** *fem n*

millipede *or* **millepede** *n* a small crawling animal with a cylindrical many-segmented body, each segment of which bears two pairs of legs.

millisecond *n* one thousandth of a second.

millpond *n* a pool which provides water to turn a millwheel.

millrace *n* the current of water that turns a millwheel.

millstone *n* **1** one of a pair of heavy flat stones that are rotated one against the other to grind grain. **2** a heavy burden of responsibility or obligation: *the debt had become a millstone round his neck.*

millstream *n* a stream of water used to turn a millwheel.

millwheel *n* a water wheel that drives a mill.

milometer (mile-**om**-it-er) *n* same as **mileometer.**

milord *n* (formerly) a continental title used for an English gentleman.

milt *n* the male reproductive gland, sperm, or semen of a fish.

mime *n* **1** an style of acting using only gesture and bodily movement and not words. **2** a performer specializing in this. **3** a performance in this style. *~vb* **miming, mimed** **4** to express or describe something in actions or gestures without using speech. **5** (of musicians) to pretend to be singing or playing music that is actually prerecorded. **mimer** *n*

Mimeograph (**mim**-ee-oh-grahf) *n* **1** *Trademark* an office machine for printing multiple copies from a stencil. *~vb* **2** to print copies using this machine.

mimetic (mim-**met**-ik) *adj* **1** imitating or representing something: *most photographs are mimetic representations of the real world.* **2** *Biol* of or showing mimicry.

mimic *vb* **-icking, -icked** **1** to imitate a person or a way of acting or speaking, esp. to entertain or make fun of. **2** to take on the appearance of: *certain flies mimic wasps.* **3** to copy closely or in a servile manner: *social climbers in the colonies began to mimic their conquerors.* *~n* **4** a person or an animal, such as a parrot, that is clever at mimicking.

mimicry *n, pl* **-ries** **1** the act or art of copying or imitating closely. **2** *Biol* the resemblance shown by one animal species to another dangerous or inedible one, which protects it from predators.

mimosa *n* a tropical shrub with ball-like clusters of yellow flowers and leaves sensitive to touch and light.

min. **1** minimum. **2** minute *or* minutes.

Min. **1** Minister. **2** Ministry.

mina *n* same as **myna.**

minaret *n* a slender tower of a mosque with one or more balconies.

minatory *adj* threatening or menacing.

mince *vb* **mincing, minced** **1** to chop, grind, or cut into very small pieces. **2** to walk or speak in an affected dainty manner. **3 not mince one's words** be direct and to the point rather than making an effort to avoid upsetting people. *~n* **4** *Chiefly Brit* minced meat. **minced** *adj* **mincer** *n*

mincemeat *n* **1** a mixture of dried fruit and spices used for filling pies. **2 make mincemeat of** *Informal* to defeat completely.

mince pie *n* a small round pastry tart filled with mincemeat.

mincing *adj* (of a person or their style of walking or speaking) affectedly elegant.

mind *n* **1** the part of a person responsible for thought, feelings, and intention. **2** intelligence as opposed to feelings or wishes. **3** memory or recollection: *his name didn't spring to mind immediately.* **4** a person considered as an intellectual being: *one of Europe's greatest minds.* **5** the condition or state of a person's feelings or thoughts: *a confused state of mind.* **6** an intention or desire: *I have a mind to go.* **7** attention or thoughts: *keep your mind on the job.* **8** a sound mental state; sanity: *he's out of his mind.* **9 change one's mind** to alter one's decision or opinion. **10 give someone a piece of one's mind** scold someone severely. **11 in two minds** undecided or wavering. **12 make up one's mind** reach a decision. **13 on one's mind** in one's thoughts. **14 to my mind** in my opinion. *~vb* **15** to take offence at: *do you mind if I open a window?* **16** to pay attention to: *to mind one's own business.* **17** to

THESAURUS

mill *n.* **1.** factory, foundry, plant, shop, works **2.** crusher, grinder *~vb.* **3.** comminute, crush, granulate, grate, grind, pound, powder, press, pulverize **4.** crowd, seethe, swarm, throng

millstone **1.** grindstone, quernstone **2.** affliction, burden, dead weight, drag, encumbrance, load, weight

mime **1.** *n.* dumb show, gesture, mummery, pantomime **2.** *vb.* act out, gesture, represent, simulate

mimic *vb.* **1.** ape, caricature, do (*informal*), imitate, impersonate, parody, take off (*informal*) **2.** echo, look like, mirror, resemble, simulate, take on the appearance of *~n.* **3.** caricaturist, copycat (*informal*), imitator, impersonator, impressionist, parodist

mince **1.** chop, crumble, cut, grind, hash **2.** attitudinize, give oneself airs, ponce (*slang*), pose, posture **3.** *as in* **not mince one's words** diminish, euphemize, extenuate, hold back, moderate, palliate, soften, spare, tone down, weaken

mincing affected, camp (*informal*), dainty, effeminate, foppish, lah-di-dah (*informal*), nice, niminy-piminy, poncy (*slang*), precious, pretentious, sissy

mind *n.* **1.** brain(s) (*informal*), grey matter (*informal*), intellect, intelligence, mentality, ratiocination, reason, sense, spirit, understanding, wits **2.** brain, head, imagination, psyche **3.** memory, recollection, remembrance **4.** brain (*informal*), genius, intellect, intellectual, thinker **5.** bent, desire, disposition, fancy, inclination, intention, leaning, notion, purpose, tendency, urge, will, wish **6.** attention, concentration, thinking, thoughts **7.** judgment, marbles (*informal*), mental balance, rationality, reason, sanity, senses, wits **8. in two**

make certain; ensure: *mind you tell him.* **18** to take care of: *mind the shop.* **19** to be cautious or careful about: *mind how you go.* **20** *Dialect* to remember. ~See also **mind out.**

mind-boggling *adj* so large, complicated, or surprising that it causes surprise and shock: *mind-boggling wealth.*

minded *adj* having a mind or inclination as specified: *commercially minded.*

minder *n* **1** *Slang* an aide or assistant, esp. one employed as a bodyguard or public relations officer for someone. **2** short for **child minder.**

mindful *adj* **mindful of** being aware of and taking into account: *the company is ever mindful of the need to find new markets.*

mindless *adj* **1** stupid or careless. **2** requiring little or no intellectual effort. **3** heedless: *mindless of the risks involved.* **mindlessly** *adv* **mindlessness** *n*

mind out *vb Brit* to be careful or pay attention.

mind-reader *n* a person seemingly able to make out the thoughts of another.

mind's eye *n* **in one's mind's eye** in one's imagination.

mine[1] *pron* **1** something or someone belonging to or associated with me: *it's a great favourite of mine.* **2 of mine** belonging to or associated with me. *~adj* **3** *Archaic* same as **my:** *mine eyes; mine host.*

mine[2] *n* **1** a place where minerals, esp. coal, ores, or precious stones, are dug from the ground. **2** a type of bomb placed in water or under the ground, and designed to destroy ships, vehicles, or people passing over or near it. **3** a profitable source or abundant supply: *a mine of information.* *~vb* **mining, mined 4** to dig minerals from the ground: *lead has been mined here for over three centuries.* **5** to dig a hole or tunnel, esp. in order to obtain minerals. **6** to place explosive mines in or on: *the retreating troops had mined the bridge.*

mine dump *n S African* a large mound of waste material from gold-mining operations.

minefield *n* **1** an area of ground or water containing explosive mines. **2** a subject or situation full of hidden problems.

minelayer *n* a warship or aircraft for carrying and laying mines.

miner *n* a person who works in a mine, esp. a coal mine.

mineral *n* **1** a naturally occurring solid inorganic substance with a characteristic chemical composition and structure. **2** any inorganic matter. **3** any substance obtained by mining, esp. a metal ore. **4** *Brit* a soft drink containing carbonated water and flavourings. *~adj* **5** of, containing, or resembling minerals.

mineral acid *n* any acid which can be produced from a mineral.

mineralogy (min-er-**al**-a-jee) *n* the scientific study of minerals. **mineralogical** *adj* **mineralogist** *n*

mineral water *n* water containing dissolved mineral salts or gases.

minestrone (min-ness-**strone**-ee) *n* a soup made from a variety of vegetables and pasta.

minesweeper *n* a naval vessel equipped to clear mines.

Ming *adj* of or relating to Chinese porcelain from the time of the Ming dynasty, which ruled China from 1368 to 1644.

mingle *vb* **-gling, -gled 1** to mix or blend. **2** to associate or mix with a group of people: *the performers mingled with the audience after the show.*

mingy *adj* **-gier, -giest** *Brit informal* mean or miserly.

mini *adj* **1** small; miniature. **2** (of a skirt or dress) very short. *~n, pl* **minis 3** something very small of its kind, esp. a miniskirt.

mini- *combining form* smaller or shorter than the standard size: *minibus; miniseries.*

miniature *n* **1** a model or representation on a very small scale. **2** a very small painting, esp. a portrait. **3** a very small bottle of whisky or other spirits, which can hold 50 millilitres. **4 in miniature** on a small scale. *~adj* **5** much smaller than usual; small-scale. **miniaturist** *n*

miniaturize *or* **-ise** *vb* **-izing, -ized** *or* **-ising, -ised** to make a very small version of something, esp. electronic components. **miniaturization** *or* **-isation** *n*

minibus *n* a small bus.

minicab *n Brit* an ordinary car used as a taxi.

minicomputer *n* a small digital computer which is more powerful than a microcomputer.

minim *n* **1** a unit of fluid measure equal to one sixtieth of a drachm. **2** *Music* a note with the time value of half a semibreve.

minimal *adj* of the least possible quantity or degree.

minimalism *n* **1** a type of music based on the repetition of simple elements. **2** a design or style using the simplest and fewest elements to create the maximum effect. **minimalist** *adj, n*

THESAURUS

minds dithering (*chiefly Brit.*), hesitant, shillyshallying (*informal*), swithering (*Scot.*), uncertain, undecided, unsure, vacillating, wavering **9. make up one's mind** choose, come to a decision, decide, determine, reach a decision, resolve, settle **10.** *as in* **to my mind** attitude, belief, feeling, judgment, opinion, outlook, point of view, sentiment, thoughts, view, way of thinking *~vb.* **11.** be affronted, be bothered, care, disapprove, dislike, look askance at, object, resent, take offence **12.** adhere to, attend, comply with, follow, heed, listen to, mark, note, notice, obey, observe, pay attention, pay heed to, regard, respect, take heed, watch **13.** be sure, ensure, make certain **14.** attend to, guard, have charge of, keep an eye on, look after, take care of, tend, watch **15.** be careful, be cautious, be on (one's) guard, be wary, take care, watch

mindful alert, alive to, attentive, aware, careful, chary, cognizant, conscious, heedful, regardful, respectful, sensible, thoughtful, wary, watchful

mindless 1. asinine, braindead (*informal*), brutish, careless, foolish, forgetful, gratuitous, heedless, idiotic, imbecilic, inane, inattentive, moronic, neglectful, negligent, oblivious, obtuse, stupid, thoughtless, unintelligent, unmindful, unthinking, witless **2.** automatic, brainless, mechanical

mind out be careful, be on one's guard, beware, keep one's eyes open, look out, pay attention, take care, watch

mine *n.* **1.** coalfield, colliery, deposit, excavation, lode, pit, shaft, vein **2.** abundance, fund, hoard, reserve, source, stock, store, supply, treasury, wealth *~vb.* **3.** delve, dig for, dig up, excavate, extract, hew, quarry, unearth **4.** burrow, dig, excavate, tunnel **5.** lay mines in *or* under, sow with mines

miner coalminer, collier (*Brit.*), mineworker, pitman (*Brit.*)

mingle 1. alloy, blend, coalesce, combine, commingle, compound, intermingle, intermix, interweave, join, marry, meld, merge, mix, unite **2.** associate, circulate, consort, fraternize, hang about *or* around, hang out (*informal*), hobnob, rub shoulders (*informal*), socialize

miniature *adj.* baby, diminutive, dwarf, Lilliputian, little, midget, mini, minuscule, minute, pocket, pygmy

minimize *or* **-mise** *vb* **-mizing, -mized** *or* **-mising, -mised 1** to reduce to the lowest possible degree or amount: *these measures should help minimize our costs.* **2** to regard or treat as less important than it really is; belittle: *I don't want to minimize the importance of her contribution.*

minimum *n, pl* **-mums** *or* **-ma 1** the least possible amount, degree, or quantity: *fry the burgers in the minimum of oil.* **2** the least amount recorded, allowed, or reached: *soak the beans for a minimum of eight hours.* ~*adj* **3** of, being, or showing a minimum or minimums: *the minimum age.*

minimum lending rate *n* (formerly) the minimum rate at which the Bank of England would lend money: replaced in 1981 by the base rate.

minimum wage *n* the lowest wage that an employer is permitted to pay by law or union contract.

mining *n* **1** the act, process, or industry of extracting coal or ores from the earth. **2** *Mil* the process of laying mines.

minion *n* a servile assistant.

miniseries *n, pl* **-series** a television programme in several parts that is shown on consecutive days over a short period.

miniskirt *n* a very short skirt.

minister *n* **1** (esp. in Presbyterian and some Nonconformist Churches) a member of the clergy. **2** a head of a government department. **3** a diplomat with a lower rank than an ambassador. ~*vb* **4 minister to** to attend to the needs of. **ministerial** *adj*

minister of state *n* (in the British Parliament) a minister, usually below cabinet rank, appointed to assist a senior minister.

Minister of the Crown *n Brit* any Government minister of cabinet rank.

ministrations *pl n* the giving of help or service: *the ministrations of the chaplain.*

ministry *n, pl* **-tries 1** the profession or duties of a minister of religion. **2** ministers considered as a group. **3 a** a government department headed by a minister. **b** the buildings of such a department.

mink *n, pl* **mink** *or* **minks 1** a mammal of Europe, Asia, and North America, resembling a large stoat. **2** its highly valued fur. **3** a garment made of this, esp. a woman's coat or stole.

minneola *n* a juicy citrus fruit that is a cross between a tangerine and a grapefruit.

minnow *n, pl* **-nows** *or* **-now** a small slender European freshwater fish.

Minoan (min-**no**-an) *adj* of or denoting the Bronze Age culture of Crete from about 3000 BC to about 1100 BC.

minor *adj* **1** lesser or secondary in size, frequency, or importance than others of the same kind: *a minor poet.* **2** not very serious or significant: *minor injuries.* **3** *Music* **a** (of a scale) having a semitone between the second and third and fifth and sixth notes (**natural minor**). **b** of or based on the minor scale: *his quintet in C minor; a minor third.* ~*n* **4** a person below the age of legal majority. **5** *US & Canad education* a subsidiary subject. **6** *Music* a minor key, chord, mode, or scale. ~*vb* **7 minor in** *US education* to study as a subsidiary subject: *to minor in politics.*

minority *n, pl* **-ties 1** the smaller of two parts, factions, or groups. **2** a group that is different, esp. racially or politically, from a larger group of which it is a part. **3 in the minority** forming or part of the group of people or things made up of less than half of a larger group. ~*adj* **4** relating to or being a minority: *a minority sport.*

minster *n Brit* any of certain cathedrals and large churches, usually originally connected to a monastery.

minstrel *n* **1** a medieval singer and musician. **2** a performer in a minstrel show.

minstrel show *n* a theatrical entertainment consisting of songs and dances performed by actors wearing black face make-up.

mint[1] *n* **1** any of various plants with aromatic leaves used for seasoning and flavouring. **2** a sweet flavoured with mint. **minty** *adj*

mint[2] *n* **1** a factory where the official coins of a country are made. **2** a very large amount of money. ~*adj* **3 in mint condition** in perfect condition; as if new. ~*vb* **4** to make coins by stamping metal. **5** to invent or create: *no-one knows who first minted the term "yuppie".*

minuet (min-new-**wet**) *n* **1** a stately court dance of the 17th and 18th centuries in triple time. **2** music for this dance.

minus *prep* **1** reduced by the subtraction of: *six minus two equals four.* **2** *Informal* without or lacking: *he returned minus his jacket.* ~*adj* **3** indicating or involving subtraction: *a minus sign.* **4** Also: **negative** less than zero: *it's minus eight degrees in Montreal today.* **5** *Education* slightly below the standard of a particular grade: *a C minus for maths.* ~*n* **6** short for **minus sign. 7** a negative quantity. **8** *Informal* something detrimental or negative.

minuscule (**min**-niss-skyool) *adj* very small.

minus sign *n* the symbol –, indicating subtraction, a negative quantity, or a negative electrical charge.

minute[1] *n* **1** 60 seconds; one sixtieth of an hour. **2** any

THESAURUS

or pigmy, reduced, scaled-down, small, teensy-weensy, teeny-weeny, tiny, toy, wee

minimal least, least possible, littlest, minimum, nominal, slightest, smallest, token

minimize 1. abbreviate, attenuate, curtail, decrease, diminish, miniaturize, prune, reduce, shrink **2.** belittle, decry, deprecate, depreciate, discount, disparage, make light *or* little of, play down, underestimate, underrate

minimum 1. *n.* bottom, depth, least, lowest, nadir, slightest **2.** *adj.* least, least possible, littlest, lowest, minimal, slightest, smallest

minion bootlicker (*informal*), creature, darling, dependant, favourite, flatterer, flunky, follower, hanger-on, henchman, hireling, lackey, lickspittle, myrmidon, parasite, pet, sycophant, toady, underling, yes man

minister *n.* **1.** chaplain, churchman, clergyman, cleric, divine, ecclesiastic, padre (*informal*), parson, pastor, preacher, priest, rector, vicar **2.** Cabinet minister *or* member, front-bencher (*Brit.*), front bench spokesman *or* spokesperson (*Brit.*), secretary of state (*Brit.*) ~*vb.* **3.** accommodate, administer, answer, attend, be solicitous of, cater to, pander to, serve, take care of, tend

ministry 1. holy orders, the church, the priesthood, the pulpit **2.** administration, bureau, cabinet, council, department, government, office

minor inconsequential, inconsiderable, inferior, insignificant, junior, lesser, light, negligible, paltry, petty, secondary, slight, small, smaller, subordinate, trifling, trivial, unimportant, younger

minstrel bard, harper, jongleur, musician, singer, songstress, troubadour

mint *n.* **1.** bomb (*Brit. slang*), bundle (*slang*), fortune, heap (*informal*), King's ransom, million, packet (*slang*), pile (*informal*) ~*adj.* **2.** *as in* **in mint condition** brand-new, excellent, first-class, fresh, perfect, unblemished, undamaged, untarnished ~*vb.* **3.** cast,

very short period of time; moment: *I'll be with you in a minute.* **3** the distance that can be travelled in a minute: *it's about ten minutes away.* **4** a measure of angle equal to one sixtieth of a degree. **5 up to the minute** the very latest or newest. ~*vb* **-uting, -uted 6** to record in minutes: *the decision was minuted in 1990.* ~See also **minutes.**

minute^2 *adj* **1** very small; tiny. **2** precise or detailed: *a minute examination.* **minutely** *adv*

minutes *pl n* an official record of the proceedings of a meeting or conference.

minute steak *n* a small piece of steak that can be cooked quickly.

minutiae (my-**new**-shee-eye) *pl n, sing* **-tia** trifling or precise details.

minx *n* a bold or flirtatious girl.

Miocene (**my**-oh-seen) *adj Geol* of the epoch of geological time about 25 million years ago.

miracle *n* **1** an event contrary to the laws of nature and attributed to a supernatural cause. **2** any amazing and fortunate event: *it's a miracle that no-one was killed in the accident.* **3** a marvellous example of something: *a miracle of organization.*

miracle play *n* a medieval play based on a biblical story or the life of a saint.

miraculous *adj* **1** like a miracle. **2** surprising or remarkable.

mirage (mir-**rahzh**) *n* **1** an image of a distant object or sheet of water, often inverted or distorted, caused by atmospheric refraction by hot air. **2** something illusory: *the mirage of economic recovery.*

mire *n* **1** a boggy or marshy area. **2** mud, muck, or dirt. **3** an unpleasant or difficult situation that is difficult to get out of: *the country sank deeper into the economic mire.* ~*vb* **miring, mired 4** to sink or be stuck in a mire: *the company has been mired in financial scandal.*

mirror *n* **1** a sheet of glass with a metal coating on its back, that reflects an image of an object placed in front of it. **2** a thing that reflects or depicts something else. ~*vb* **3** to reflect or represent faithfully: *the book inevitably mirrors my own interests.*

mirror ball *n* a large revolving ball covered with small pieces of mirror glass so that it reflects light in changing patterns: used in discos and ballrooms.

mirror image *n* an image or object that has left and right reversed as if seen in a mirror.

mirth *n* laughter, gaiety, or merriment. **mirthful** *adj* **mirthless** *adj*

MIRV multiple independently targeted re-entry vehicle: a missile that has several warheads, each one being aimed at a different target.

mis- *prefix* **1** wrong or bad; wrongly or badly: *misunderstanding; mislead.* **2** lack of; not: *mistrust.*

misadventure *n* **1** an unlucky event; misfortune. **2** *Law* accidental death not due to crime or negligence.

misaligned *adj* not properly aligned; out of true. **misalignment** *n*

misalliance *n* an unsuitable alliance or marriage.

misanthrope (**miz**-zan-thrope) *or* **misanthropist** (miz-**zan**-throp-ist) *n* a person who dislikes or distrusts people in general. **misanthropic** (miz-zan-**throp**-ik) *adj* **misanthropy** (miz-**zan**-throp-ee) *n*

misapply *vb* **-plies, -plying, -plied** to use something for a purpose for which it is not intended or is not suited. **misapplication** *n*

misapprehend *vb* to misunderstand. **misapprehension** *n*

misappropriate *vb* **-ating, -ated** to take and use money dishonestly. **misappropriation** *n*

misbegotten *adj* **1** planned or designed badly or

THESAURUS

coin, make, produce, punch, stamp, strike **4.** coin, construct, devise, fabricate, fashion, forge, invent, make up, produce, think up

minute^1 *n.* **1.** sixtieth of an hour, sixty seconds **2.** flash, instant, jiffy (*informal*), moment, second, shake (*informal*), tick (*Brit. informal*), trice **3. up to the minute** all the rage, in, latest, modish, (most) fashionable, newest, now (*informal*), smart, stylish, trendiest, trendy (*Brit. informal*), up to date, vogue, with it (*informal*)

minute^2 *adj.* **1.** diminutive, fine, inconsiderable, infinitesimal, Lilliputian, little, microscopic, miniature, minuscule, negligible, paltry, petty, picayune (*U.S.*), piddling (*informal*), slender, slight, small, teensy-weensy, teeny-weeny, tiny, trifling, trivial, unimportant **2.** close, critical, detailed, exact, exhaustive, meticulous, painstaking, precise, punctilious

minutely closely, critically, exactly, exhaustively, in detail, meticulously, painstakingly, precisely, with a fine-tooth comb

minutes memorandum, notes, proceedings, record(s), transactions, transcript

minutiae details, finer points, niceties, particulars, subtleties, trifles, trivia

minx baggage (*informal, old-fashioned*), coquette, flirt, hoyden, hussy, jade, tomboy, wanton (*old-fashioned*)

miracle marvel, phenomenon, prodigy, wonder

miraculous amazing, astonishing, astounding, extraordinary, incredible, inexplicable, magical, marvellous, phenomenal, preternatural, prodigious, superhuman, supernatural, unaccountable, unbelievable, wonderful, wondrous (*archaic or literary*)

mirage hallucination, illusion, optical illusion, phantasm

mire *n.* **1.** bog, marsh, morass, quagmire, swamp **2.** dirt, muck, mud, ooze, slime ~*vb.* **3.** bog down, catch up, enmesh, entangle, involve

mirror *n.* **1.** glass, looking-glass, reflector, speculum **2.** copy, double, image, likeness, reflection, replica, representation, twin ~*vb.* **3.** copy, depict, echo, emulate, follow, reflect, represent, show

mirth amusement, cheerfulness, festivity, frolic, fun, gaiety, gladness, glee, hilarity, jocularity, jollity, joviality, joyousness, laughter, levity, merriment, merrymaking, pleasure, rejoicing, revelry, sport

mirthful amused, amusing, blithe, cheerful, cheery, festive, frolicsome, funny, gay, glad, gladsome (*archaic*), happy, hilarious, jocund, jolly, jovial, laughable, light-hearted, merry, playful, sportive, uproarious, vivacious

misadventure accident, bad break (*informal*), bad luck, bummer (*slang*), calamity, catastrophe, debacle, disaster, failure, ill fortune, ill luck, mischance, misfortune, mishap, reverse, setback

misanthrope cynic, egoist, egotist, mankind-hater, misanthropist

misapprehend get hold of the wrong end of the stick, get the wrong idea *or* impression, misconceive, misconstrue, misinterpret, misread, mistake, misunderstand

misapprehension delusion, error, fallacy, false belief, false impression, misconception, misconstruction, misinterpretation, misreading, mistake, misunderstanding, wrong idea *or* impression

with dishonourable motives or aims. **2** *Literary or dialect* illegitimate; bastard.
misbehave *vb* **-having, -haved** to behave badly. **misbehaviour** *or US* **misbehavior** *n*
miscalculate *vb* **-lating, -lated** to calculate or judge wrongly: *we miscalculated the strength of the opposition.* **miscalculation** *n*
miscall *vb* to call by the wrong name.
miscarriage *n* **1** spontaneous premature expulsion of a fetus from the womb, esp. before the 20th week of pregnancy. **2** an act of mismanagement or failure: *a miscarriage of justice.*
miscarry *vb* **-ries, -rying, -ried 1** to expel a fetus prematurely from the womb. **2** to fail.
miscast *vb* **-casting, -cast** to cast a role or an actor in a play or film inappropriately: *the role of the avaricious boss was miscast; she was miscast as Cassandra.*
miscegenation (miss-ij-in-**nay**-shun) *n* interbreeding of races, esp. where differences of colour are involved.
miscellaneous (miss-sel-**lane**-ee-uss) *adj* composed of or containing a variety of things; mixed or assorted.
miscellany (miss-**sell**-a-nee) *n, pl* **-nies** a mixed assortment of items.
mischance *n* **1** bad luck. **2** an unlucky event or accident.
mischief *n* **1** annoying but not malicious behaviour that causes trouble or irritation. **2** an inclination to tease. **3** injury or harm caused by a person or thing.
mischief-maker *n* someone who deliberately causes trouble. **mischief-making** *n*
mischievous (**miss**-chiv-uss) *adj* **1** full of mischief. **2** teasing; slightly malicious. **3** intended to cause harm: *a purveyor of mischievous disinformation.* **mischievously** *adv*
miscible (**miss**-sib-bl) *adj* able to be mixed: *miscible with water.* **miscibility** *n*
misconceived *adj* false, mistaken, or badly thought-out: *a misconceived conception of loyalty.*
misconception *n* a false or mistaken view, idea, or belief.
misconduct *n* behaviour, such as adultery or professional negligence, that is regarded as immoral or unethical.
misconstrue *vb* **-struing, -strued** to interpret mistakenly. **misconstruction** *n*
miscreant (**miss**-kree-ant) *n* a wrongdoer or villain.
misdeal *vb* **-dealing, -dealt 1** to deal out cards incorrectly. ~*n* **2** a faulty deal.
misdeed *n* an evil or illegal action.
misdemeanour *or US* **misdemeanor** *n* **1** a minor wrongdoing. **2** *Criminal law* (formerly) an offence less serious than a felony.
misdirect *vb* to give someone wrong directions or instructions. **misdirection** *n*
mise en scène (**meez** on **sane**) *n* **1** the stage setting and scenery in a play. **2** the environment of an event.
miser *n* a person who hoards money and hates spending it. **miserly** *adj*
miserable *adj* **1** unhappy or depressed; wretched. **2** causing misery or discomfort: *a miserable existence.* **3** sordid or squalid: *miserable living conditions.* **4** mean or ungenerous: *a miserable pension.* **miserableness** *n* **miserably** *adv*

THESAURUS

misappropriate defalcate (*Law*), embezzle, misapply, misspend, misuse, peculate, pocket, steal, swindle
misbehave act up (*informal*), be bad, be insubordinate, be naughty, carry on (*informal*), get up to mischief (*informal*), muck about (*Brit. slang*)
misbehaviour acting up (*informal*), bad behaviour, impropriety, incivility, indiscipline, insubordination, mischief, misconduct, misdeeds, misdemeanour, monkey business (*informal*), naughtiness, rudeness, shenanigans (*informal*)
miscalculate blunder, calculate wrongly, err, get (it) wrong, go wrong, make a mistake, misjudge, overestimate, overrate, slip up, underestimate, underrate
miscarriage 1. spontaneous abortion **2.** botch (*informal*), breakdown, error, failure, misadventure, mischance, misfire, mishap, mismanagement, nonsuccess, perversion, thwarting, undoing
miscarry 1. abort **2.** come to grief, come to nothing, fail, fall through, gang agley (*Scot.*), go amiss, go astray, go awry, go wrong, misfire
miscellaneous assorted, confused, diverse, diversified, heterogeneous, indiscriminate, jumbled, manifold, many, mingled, mixed, motley, multifarious, multiform, promiscuous, sundry, varied, various
miscellany anthology, assortment, collection, diversity, farrago, gallimaufry, hotchpotch, jumble, medley, *mélange*, mixed bag, mixture, potpourri, variety
mischance accident, bad break (*informal*), bad luck, bummer (*slang*), calamity, contretemps, disaster, ill chance, ill fortune, ill luck, infelicity, misadventure, misfortune, mishap
mischief 1. devilment, impishness, misbehaviour, monkey business (*informal*), naughtiness, pranks, roguery, roguishness, shenanigans (*informal*), trouble, waywardness **2.** damage, detriment, disadvantage, disruption, evil, harm, hurt, injury, misfortune, trouble
mischievous 1. arch, bad, badly behaved, exasperating, frolicsome, impish, naughty, playful, puckish, rascally, roguish, sportive, teasing, troublesome, vexatious, wayward **2.** bad, damaging, deleterious, destructive, detrimental, evil, harmful, hurtful, injurious, malicious, malignant, pernicious, sinful, spiteful, troublesome, vicious, wicked
misconception delusion, error, fallacy, misapprehension, misconstruction, mistaken belief, misunderstanding, wrong end of the stick, wrong idea
misconduct delinquency, dereliction, immorality, impropriety, malfeasance (*Law*), malpractice, malversation (*rare*), misbehaviour, misdemeanour, mismanagement, naughtiness, rudeness, transgression, unethical behaviour, wrongdoing
misdemeanour fault, infringement, misbehaviour, misconduct, misdeed, offence, peccadillo, transgression, trespass
miser cheapskate (*informal*), niggard, penny-pincher (*informal*), Scrooge, skinflint, tightwad (*U.S. & Canad. slang*)
miserable 1. afflicted, broken-hearted, crestfallen, dejected, depressed, desolate, despondent, disconsolate, dismal, distressed, doleful, down, downcast, down in the mouth (*informal*), forlorn, gloomy, heartbroken, melancholy, mournful, sorrowful, unhappy, woebegone, wretched **2.** destitute, dirt-poor (*informal*), down and out, flat broke (*informal*), impoverished, indigent, meagre, needy, penniless, poor, poverty-stricken, scanty, short, without two pennies to rub together (*informal*) **3.** abject, bad, contemptible, deplorable, despicable, detestable, disgraceful, lamentable, low, mean, pathetic, piteous, pitiable, scurvy, shabby, shameful, sordid, sorry, squalid, vile, worthless, wretched
miserly avaricious, beggarly, close, close-fisted, covetous, grasping, illiberal, mean, mingy (*Brit. informal*),

misericord *n* a ledge projecting from the underside of the hinged seat of a choir stall in a church, which the occupant can rest against while standing.

misery *n, pl* **-eries** **1** intense unhappiness or suffering. **2** something which causes such unhappiness. **3** squalid or poverty-stricken conditions. **4** *Brit informal* a person who is habitually depressed: *he is such a misery.*

misfire *vb* **-firing, -fired** **1** (of a firearm) to fail to fire as expected. **2** (of a motor engine or vehicle) to fail to fire at the appropriate time. **3** to fail to have the intended result; go wrong: *he was injured when a practical joke misfired.* ~*n* **4** the act or an instance of misfiring.

misfit *n* a person who is not suited to the role, social group, etc., he or she finds himself or herself in.

misfortune *n* **1** bad luck. **2** an unfortunate event.

misgivings *pl n* feelings of uncertainty, fear, or doubt.

misgovern *vb* to govern badly. **misgovernment** *n*

misguided *adj* mistaken or unwise.

mishandle *vb* **-dling, -dled** to handle or treat badly or inefficiently.

mishap *n* a minor accident.

mishear *vb* **-hearing, -heard** to fail to hear what someone says correctly.

mishit *Sport* ~*n* **1** a faulty shot, kick, or stroke. ~*vb* **-hitting, -hit** **2** to hit or kick a ball with a faulty stroke.

mishmash *n* a confused collection or mixture.

misinform *vb* to give incorrect information to. **misinformation** *n*

misinterpret *vb* to understand or represent something wrongly: *the press misinterpreted the President's remarks.* **misinterpretation** *n*

misjudge *vb* **-judging, -judged** to judge wrongly or unfairly. **misjudgment** *or* **misjudgement** *n*

mislay *vb* **-lays, -laying, -laid** to lose something temporarily, esp. by forgetting where it is.

mislead *vb* **-leading, -led** to give false or confusing information to.

misleading *adj* giving a false or confusing impression: *misleading use of statistical data.*

mismanage *vb* **-aging, -aged** to organize or run something badly. **mismanagement** *n*

mismatch *vb* **1** to form an unsuitable partner, opponent, or set. ~*n* **2** an unsuitable match. **mismatched** *adj*

misnamed *adj* having an inappropriate or misleading name: *the grotesquely misnamed Freedom Party.*

misnomer (miss-**no**-mer) *n* **1** an incorrect or unsuitable name for a person or thing. **2** the use of the wrong name.

misogyny (miss-**oj**-in-ee) *n* hatred of women. **misogynist** *n* **misogynous** *adj*

misplace *vb* **-placing, -placed** **1** to lose something temporarily by forgetting where it was placed. **2** to put something in the wrong place.

misplaced *adj* **1** (of an emotion or action) directed towards a person or thing that does not deserve it: *misplaced optimism.* **2** put in the wrong place: *a scrappy game dominated by misplaced kicking.*

misprint *n* **1** an error in printing. ~*vb* **2** to print a letter incorrectly.

misprision *n Law* the concealment of the commission of a felony or an act of treason.

mispronounce *vb* **-nouncing, -nounced** to pro-

THESAURUS

miserable (*Scot.*), near, niggardly, parsimonious, penny-pinching (*informal*), penurious, sordid, stingy, tightfisted, ungenerous

misery **1.** agony, anguish, depression, desolation, despair, discomfort, distress, gloom, grief, hardship, melancholy, sadness, sorrow, suffering, torment, torture, unhappiness, woe, wretchedness **2.** affliction, bitter pill (*informal*), burden, calamity, catastrophe, curse, disaster, hardship, load, misfortune, ordeal, sorrow, trial, tribulation, trouble, woe **3.** destitution, indigence, need, penury, poverty, privation, sordidness, squalor, want, wretchedness **4.** *Brit. informal* grouch (*informal*), killjoy, moaner, pessimist, prophet of doom, sourpuss (*informal*), spoilsport, wet blanket (*informal*)

misfire fail, fail to go off, fall through, go phut (*informal*), go wrong, miscarry

misfit eccentric, fish out of water (*informal*), nonconformist, oddball (*informal*), square peg (in a round hole) (*informal*)

misfortune **1.** bad luck, evil fortune, hard luck, ill luck, infelicity **2.** accident, adversity, affliction, blow, bummer (*slang*), calamity, disaster, evil chance, failure, hardship, harm, loss, misadventure, mischance, misery, mishap, reverse, setback, stroke of bad luck, tragedy, trial, tribulation, trouble

misgiving anxiety, apprehension, distrust, doubt, dubiety, hesitation, qualm, reservation, scruple, suspicion, trepidation, uncertainty, unease, worry

misguided deluded, erroneous, foolish, ill-advised, imprudent, injudicious, labouring under a delusion *or* misapprehension, misled, misplaced, mistaken, uncalled-for, unreasonable, unwarranted, unwise

mishandle bodge (*informal*), botch, bungle, make a hash of (*informal*), make a mess of, mess up (*informal*), mismanage, muff, screw (up) (*informal*)

mishap accident, adversity, bad luck, calamity, contretemps, disaster, evil chance, evil fortune, hard luck, ill fortune, ill luck, infelicity, misadventure, mischance, misfortune

misinform deceive, give (someone) a bum steer (*informal, chiefly U.S.*), give (someone) duff gen (*Brit. informal*), misdirect, misguide, mislead

misinterpret distort, falsify, get wrong, misapprehend, misconceive, misconstrue, misjudge, misread, misrepresent, mistake, misunderstand, pervert

misjudge be wrong about, get the wrong idea about, miscalculate, overestimate, overrate, underestimate, underrate

mislay be unable to find, be unable to put *or* lay one's hand on, forget the whereabouts of, lose, lose track of, misplace, miss

mislead beguile, bluff, deceive, delude, fool, give (someone) a bum steer (*informal, chiefly U.S.*), hoodwink, lead astray, misdirect, misguide, misinform, pull the wool over (someone's) eyes (*informal*), take in (*informal*)

misleading ambiguous, casuistical, confusing, deceitful, deceptive, delusive, delusory, disingenuous, evasive, false, sophistical, specious, spurious, tricky (*informal*), unstraightforward

mismanage be incompetent, be inefficient, bodge (*informal*), botch, bungle, make a hash of (*informal*), make a mess of, maladminister, mess up, misconduct, misdirect, misgovern, mishandle

misplace **1.** be unable to find, be unable to put *or* lay one's hand on, forget the whereabouts of, lose, lose track of, misfile, mislay, miss, put in the wrong place **2.** place unwisely, place wrongly

misprint corrigendum, erratum, literal, mistake, printing error, typo (*informal*), typographical error

nounce a word or name wrongly. **mispronunciation** *n*

misquote *vb* **-quoting, -quoted** to quote inaccurately. **misquotation** *n*

misread *vb* **-reading, -read 1** to misinterpret or misunderstand: *he misread her politeness as approval.* **2** to read incorrectly.

misrepresent *vb* to represent wrongly or inaccurately. **misrepresentation** *n*

misrule *vb* **-ruling, -ruled 1** to govern inefficiently or without justice. *~n* **2** inefficient or unjust government. **3** disorder or lawlessness.

miss[1] *vb* **1** to fail to notice, see, or hear: *it's right at the top of the hill, so you can't miss it; I missed what he said because I was talking at the time.* **2** to fail to hit something aimed at: *he threw a stone at the dog but missed.* **3** to fail to achieve or reach: *they narrowly missed promotion last season.* **4** to fail to take advantage of: *he never missed a chance to make money.* **5** to fail or be unable to be present: *he had missed the last three meetings.* **6** to be too late for: *we missed the bus and had to walk.* **7** to fail to take advantage of: *he never missed a chance to make money.* **8** to discover or regret the loss or absence of: *the boys miss their father when he's away on business.* **9** to escape or avoid narrowly: *it missed the helicopters rotors by inches.* *~n* **10** a failure to hit, reach, etc.: *an easy miss in the second frame gave his opponent the advantage.* **11 give something a miss** to decide not to do, go to, or take part in something: *I'll give the pub a miss and have a quiet night in.* ~See also **miss out.**

miss[2] *n Informal* an unmarried woman or girl.

Miss *n* a title of a girl or unmarried woman, usually used before the surname: *Miss Brown to you.*

missal *n RC Church* a book containing the prayers and rites of the Masses for a complete year.

misshapen *adj* badly shaped; deformed.

missile *n* **1** a rocket with an exploding warhead, used as a weapon. **2** an object or weapon that is thrown, launched, or fired at a target.

missing *adj* **1** not in its proper or usual place and unable to be found. **2** not able to be traced and not known to be dead: *seven men were reported missing after the raid.* **3** not included in something although it perhaps should have been: *two things are missing from the report.*

missing link *n* **1** any missing section or part in a series. **2 the missing link** a hypothetical extinct animal, formerly thought to be intermediate between the apes and man.

mission *n* **1** a specific task or duty assigned to a person or group of people. **2** a task or duty that a person believes he or she must achieve; vocation: *he felt it was his mission to pass on his knowledge to other people.* **3** a group of people representing or working for a particular country or organization in a foreign country: *the UN peacekeeping mission.* **4** a group of people sent by a church to a foreign country to do religious and social work. **5** the building in which a church or government mission is based. **6** the dispatch of aircraft or spacecraft to achieve a particular task. **7** a charitable centre that offers shelter or aid to the poor or needy.

missionary *n, pl* **-aries 1** a person sent abroad by a church to do religious and social work. *~adj* **2** of or relating to missionaries: *missionary work.* **3** resulting from a desire to convert people to one's own beliefs: *missionary zeal.*

mission statement *n* an official statement of the aims and objectives of a business or other organization.

missive *n* a formal or official letter.

miss out *vb* **1** to leave out or overlook. **2 miss out on** to fail to take part in (something enjoyable or beneficial): *she'd missed out on going to university.*

misspell *vb* **-spelling, -spelt** *or* **-spelled** to spell a word wrongly. **misspelling** *n*

misspend *vb* **-spending, -spent** to waste or spend unwisely. **misspent** *adj*

missus *or* **missis** *n* **1** *Informal* one's wife or the wife of the person addressed or referred to: *the missus is a fabulous cook.* **2** an informal term of address for a woman.

missy *n, pl* **missies** *Informal* an affectionate or disparaging form of address to a girl.

mist *n* **1** a thin fog. **2** a fine spray of liquid, such as that produced by an aerosol container. **3** condensed water vapour on a surface. **4** something that causes haziness or lack of clarity, such as a film of tears. *~vb* **5** to cover or be covered with mist: *the windscreen has misted up again; his eyes misted over and he shook with rage.* **misty** *adj* **mistiness** *n*

mistake *n* **1** an error or blunder. **2** a misconception or misunderstanding. *~vb* **-taking, -took, -taken 3** to misunderstand or misinterpret: *the chaplain quite mistook her meaning.* **4** to confuse a person or thing with

THESAURUS

misquote distort, falsify, garble, mangle, misreport, misrepresent, misstate, muddle, pervert, quote *or* take out of context, twist

misrepresent belie, disguise, distort, falsify, garble, misinterpret, misstate, pervert, twist

misrule 1. bad government, maladministration, misgovernment, mismanagement **2.** anarchy, chaos, confusion, disorder, lawlessness, tumult, turmoil

miss[1] *vb.* **1.** avoid, be late for, blunder, err, escape, evade, fail, fail to grasp, fail to notice, forego, lack, leave out, let go, let slip, lose, miscarry, mistake, omit, overlook, pass over, pass up, skip, slip, trip **2.** feel the loss of, hunger for, long for, need, pine for, want, wish, yearn for *~n.* **3.** blunder, error, failure, fault, loss, mistake, omission, oversight, want

miss[2] damsel, girl, lass, lassie (*informal*), maid, maiden, schoolgirl, spinster, young lady

misshapen contorted, crippled, crooked, deformed, distorted, grotesque, ill-made, ill-proportioned, malformed, twisted, ugly, ungainly, unshapely, unsightly, warped, wry

missile projectile, rocket, weapon

missing absent, astray, gone, lacking, left behind, left out, lost, mislaid, misplaced, not present, nowhere to be found, unaccounted-for, wanting

mission 1. aim, assignment, business, calling, charge, commission, duty, errand, goal, job, office, operation, purpose, pursuit, quest, task, trust, undertaking, vocation, work **2.** commission, delegation, deputation, embassy, legation, ministry, task force

missionary apostle, converter, evangelist, preacher, propagandist, proselytizer

missive communication, dispatch, epistle, letter, memorandum, message, note, report

misspent dissipated, idle, imprudent, misapplied, prodigal, profitless, squandered, thrown away, wasted

mist 1. *n.* cloud, condensation, dew, drizzle, film, fog, haar (*Eastern Brit.*), haze, smog, spray, steam, vapour **2.** *vb.* becloud, befog, blur, cloud, film, fog, obscure, steam (up)

mistake *n.* **1.** bloomer (*Brit. informal*), blunder, boob (*Brit. slang*), boo-boo (*informal*), clanger (*informal*), erratum, error, error of judgment, false move, fault, faux pas, gaffe, goof (*informal*), howler (*informal*), in-

another: *they saw the HMS Sheffield and mistook her for the Bismarck.* **5** to choose badly or incorrectly: *he mistook his path.*

mistaken *adj* **1** wrong in opinion or judgment. **2** arising from error in opinion or judgment: *a mistaken viewpoint.*

mister *n* an informal form of address for a man.

Mister *n* the full form of **Mr.**

mistime *vb* **-timing, -timed** to do or say at the wrong time.

mistle thrush *or* **missel thrush** *n* a large European thrush with a brown back and spotted breast.

mistletoe *n* a Eurasian evergreen shrub with waxy white berries, which grows as a parasite on various trees.

mistook *vb* the past tense of **mistake.**

mistral *n* a strong cold dry northerly wind of S France.

mistreat *vb* to treat badly. **mistreatment** *n*

mistress *n* **1** a woman who has a continuing sexual relationship with a man who is usually married to somebody else. **2** a woman in a position of authority, ownership, or control. **3** a woman having control over something specified: *she is a mistress of disguise.* **4** *Chiefly Brit* a female teacher.

mistrial *n Law* a trial which is invalid because of some error.

mistrust *vb* **1** to have doubts or suspicions about. *~n* **2** lack of trust. **mistrustful** *adj* **mistrustfully** *adv*

misunderstand *vb* **-standing, -stood** to fail to understand properly.

misunderstanding *n* **1** a failure to understand properly. **2** a disagreement.

misunderstood *adj* not properly or sympathetically understood: *a misunderstood adolescent.*

misuse *n* **1** incorrect, improper, or careless use: *misuse of drugs.* **2** cruel or inhumane treatment. *~vb* **-using, -used 3** to use wrongly. **4** to treat badly or harshly.

mite[1] *n* any of numerous very small creatures of the spider family some of which live as parasites.

mite[2] *n* **1** a very small creature or thing. **2** a very small sum of money. **3 a mite** *Informal* somewhat: *the main course was a mite bland.*

mitigate *vb* **-gating, -gated** to make less severe or harsh. **mitigating** *adj* **mitigation** *n*

➤ *Mitigate* is often confused with *militate* "have an influence on".

mitosis *n* a type of cell division in which the nucleus divides into two nuclei each containing the same number of chromosomes as the parent nucleus.

mitre *or US* **miter** (**my**-ter) *n* **1** *Christianity* the headdress of a bishop or abbot, consisting of a tall pointed cleft cap. **2** Also: **mitre joint** a corner joint formed by cutting bevels of equal angles at the ends of each piece of material. *~vb* **-tring, -tred** *or* **-tering, -tered 3** to join with a mitre joint.

mitt *n* **1** a glovelike hand covering that does not cover the fingers. **2** short for **mitten. 3** *Slang* a hand. **4** a baseball glove.

mitten *n* a glove with one section for the thumb and a single section for the fingers.

mix *vb* **1** to combine or blend into one mass or substance: *mix the water, yeast, and flour into a smooth dough.* **2** to be able to combine into one substance: *oil and water do not mix.* **3** to form by combining different substances: *to mix cement.* **4** to do at the same time: *to mix business and pleasure.* **5** to be outgoing in social situations: *he mixed well.* **6** *Music* to balance and adjust individual performers' parts to make an overall sound by electronic means. *~n* **7** something

THESAURUS

accuracy, miscalculation, misconception, misstep, misunderstanding, oversight, slip, slip-up (*informal*), solecism *~vb.* **2.** get wrong, misapprehend, misconceive, misconstrue, misinterpret, misjudge, misread, misunderstand **3.** accept as, confound, confuse with, misinterpret as, mix up with, take for

mistaken barking up the wrong tree (*informal*), erroneous, fallacious, false, faulty, inaccurate, inappropriate, incorrect, in the wrong, labouring under a misapprehension, misguided, misinformed, misled, off target, off the mark, unfounded, unsound, wide of the mark, wrong

mistakenly by mistake, erroneously, fallaciously, falsely, inaccurately, inappropriately, incorrectly, in error, misguidedly, wrongly

mistimed badly timed, ill-timed, inconvenient, inopportune, unseasonable, unsynchronized, untimely

mistreat abuse, brutalize, handle roughly, harm, ill-treat, ill-use, injure, knock about *or* around, maltreat, manhandle, maul, misuse, molest, rough up, wrong

mistress concubine, doxy (*archaic*), fancy woman (*slang*), floozy (*slang*), girlfriend, inamorata, kept woman, ladylove (*rare*), lover, paramour

mistrust 1. *vb.* apprehend, beware, be wary of, distrust, doubt, fear, have doubts about, suspect **2.** *n.* apprehension, distrust, doubt, dubiety, fear, misgiving, scepticism, suspicion, uncertainty, wariness

mistrustful apprehensive, cautious, chary, cynical, distrustful, doubtful, dubious, fearful, hesitant, leery (*slang*), nervous, sceptical, suspicious, uncertain, wary

misty bleary, blurred, cloudy, dark, dim, foggy, fuzzy, hazy, indistinct, murky, nebulous, obscure, opaque, overcast, unclear, vague

misunderstand get (it) wrong, get the wrong end of the stick, get the wrong idea (about), misapprehend, misconceive, misconstrue, mishear, misinterpret, misjudge, misread, miss the point (of), mistake

misunderstanding 1. error, false impression, misapprehension, misconception, misconstruction, misinterpretation, misjudgment, misreading, mistake, mix-up, wrong idea **2.** argument, breach, conflict, difference, difficulty, disagreement, discord, dissension, falling-out (*informal*), quarrel, rift, rupture, squabble, variance

misunderstood misconstrued, misheard, misinterpreted, misjudged, misread, unappreciated, unrecognized

misuse *n.* **1.** abuse, corruption, desecration, dissipation, misapplication, misemployment, misusage, perversion, profanation, solecism, squandering, waste **2.** abuse, cruel treatment, exploitation, harm, ill-treatment, ill-usage, inhumane treatment, injury, maltreatment, manhandling, mistreatment, rough handling *~vb.* **3.** abuse, corrupt, desecrate, dissipate, misapply, misemploy, pervert, profane, prostitute, squander, waste **4.** abuse, brutalize, exploit, handle roughly, harm, ill-treat, ill-use, injure, maltreat, manhandle, maul, mistreat, molest, wrong

mitigate abate, allay, appease, assuage, blunt, calm, check, diminish, dull, ease, extenuate, lessen, lighten, moderate, modify, mollify, pacify, palliate, placate, quiet, reduce the force of, remit, soften, soothe, subdue, take the edge off, temper, tone down, tranquillize, weaken

mitigation abatement, allaying, alleviation, assuagement, diminution, easement, extenuation, moderation, mollification, palliation, relief, remission

mix *vb.* **1.** alloy, amalgamate, associate, blend, coa-

produced by mixing; mixture. **8** a mixture of ingredients, esp. one commercially prepared for making a cake. **9** *Music* the sound produced by mixing. ~See also **mix-up. mixed** *adj*

mixed bag *n Informal* something made up of different elements, characteristics, or people.

mixed blessing *n* an event or situation with both advantages and disadvantages.

mixed doubles *pl n Tennis, badminton* a doubles game with a man and a woman as partners on each side.

mixed economy *n* an economy in which some companies are privately owned and others are owned by the government.

mixed farming *n* farming involving both the growing of crops and the keeping of livestock. **mixed farm** *n*

mixed grill *n* a dish of several kinds of grilled meat, tomatoes, and mushrooms.

mixed marriage *n* a marriage between people of different races or religions.

mixed metaphor *n* a combination of incongruous metaphors, such as *when the Nazi jackboots sing their swan song.*

mixed-up *adj* in a state of mental confusion.

mixer *n* **1** a kitchen appliance, usually electrical, used for mixing foods. **2** any of various other devices or machines used for mixing things: *a cement mixer.* **3** a nonalcoholic drink such as tonic water or ginger ale that is mixed with an alcoholic drink. **4** *Informal* a person considered in relation to his or her ability to mix socially: *he's not a good mixer.*

mixture *n* **1** something produced by blending or combining other things: *top with the cheese and breadcrumb mixture.* **2** a combination of different things, such as feelings: *he speaks of her with a mixture of loyalty and regret.* **3** *Chem* a substance consisting of two or more substances mixed together without any chemical bonding between them.

mix-up *n* **1** a confused condition or situation. ~*vb* **mix up 2** to make into a mixture. **3** to confuse: *he mixes Ryan up with Lee.* **4 mixed up in** involved in (an activity or group, esp. one that is illegal): *she's mixed up in a drugs racket.*

mizzenmast *n Naut* (on a vessel with three or more masts) the third mast from the bow.

MJ megajoule.

Mk (in trade names) mark.

mks units *pl n* a metric system of units based on the metre, kilogram, and second: it forms the basis of the SI units.

ml 1 millilitre(s). **2** mile(s).

ML Medieval Latin.

MLitt Master of Letters.

Mlle *or* **Mlle.** *pl* **Mlles** *or* **Mlles.** the French equivalent of *Miss.*

MLR minimum lending rate.

mm millimetre(s).

Mme *pl* **Mmes** the French equivalent of *Mrs.*

MMR a combined vaccine against measles, mumps, and rubella, given to very young children.

MMus Master of Music.

Mn *Chem* manganese.

MN Minnesota.

mnemonic (nim-**on**-ik) *n* **1** something, for instance a verse, intended to help the memory. ~*adj* **2** aiding or meant to aid one's memory. **mnemonically** *adv*

mo *n Informal, chiefly Brit* short for **moment** (sense 1).

Mo *Chem* molybdenum.

MO 1 Medical Officer. **2** Missouri.

m.o. *or* **MO 1** mail order. **2** money order.

moa *n* a recently extinct large flightless bird of New Zealand that resembled the ostrich.

moan *n* **1** a low prolonged cry of pain or suffering. **2** any similar sound, esp. that made by the wind. **3** *Informal* a grumble or complaint. ~*vb* **4** to make a low cry of, or talk in a way suggesting, pain or suffering: *he moaned in pain.* **5** to make a sound like a moan: *the wind moaned through the trees.* **6** *Informal* to grumble or complain. **moaner** *n*

moat *n* a wide ditch, originally filled with water, surrounding a fortified place such as a castle.

mob *n* **1** a riotous or disorderly crowd of people. **2** *Informal* any group of people. **3** the masses. **4** *Slang* a gang of criminals. ~*vb* **mobbing, mobbed 5** to attack in a group resembling a mob. **6** to surround in a crowd to acclaim or attack: *she was mobbed by her fans when she left the theatre.*

mobcap *n* a woman's 18th-century cotton cap with a pouched crown.

mobile *adj* **1** able to move or be moved: *mobile toilets.* **2** changing quickly in expression: *a mobile face.* **3** *Sociol* (of individuals or social groups) moving within and between classes, occupations, and local-

THESAURUS

lesce, combine, commingle, commix, compound, cross, fuse, incorporate, intermingle, interweave, join, jumble, meld, merge, mingle, put together, unite **2.** associate, come together, consort, fraternize, hang out (*informal*), hobnob, join, mingle, socialize ~*n.* **3.** alloy, amalgam, assortment, blend, combination, compound, fusion, medley, meld, mixture

mixed 1. alloyed, amalgamated, blended, combined, composite, compound, fused, incorporated, joint, mingled, united **2.** assorted, cosmopolitan, diverse, diversified, heterogeneous, manifold, miscellaneous, motley, varied **3.** crossbred, hybrid, interbred, interdenominational, mongrel **4.** ambivalent, equivocal, indecisive, uncertain

mixed-up at sea, bewildered, confused, distraught, disturbed, maladjusted, muddled, perplexed, puzzled, upset

mixture admixture, alloy, amalgam, amalgamation, association, assortment, blend, brew, combine, composite, compound, concoction, conglomeration, cross, fusion, hotchpotch, jumble, medley, *mélange,* meld, miscellany, mix, potpourri, union, variety

mix-up confusion, disorder, jumble, mess, mistake, misunderstanding, muddle, snarl-up (*informal, chiefly Brit.*), tangle

mix up 1. blend, combine, commix, mix **2.** bewilder, confound, confuse, disturb, fluster, muddle, perplex, puzzle, throw into confusion, unnerve, upset **3.** embroil, entangle, implicate, involve, rope in

moan *n.* **1.** groan, lament, lamentation, sigh, sob, sough, wail, whine **2.** *informal* beef (*slang*), bitch (*slang*), complaint, gripe (*informal*), grouch (*informal*), grouse, grumble, protest, whine ~*vb.* **3.** bemoan, bewail, deplore, grieve, groan, keen, lament, mourn, sigh, sob, sough, whine **4.** *informal* beef (*slang*), bitch (*slang*), bleat, carp, complain, gripe (*informal*), groan, grouch (*informal*), grouse, grumble, moan and groan, whine, whinge (*informal*)

mob *n.* **1.** assemblage, body, collection, company, crew (*informal*), crowd, drove, flock, gang, gathering, group, herd, horde, host, lot, mass, multitude, pack, press, set, swarm, throng, troop **2.** great unwashed (*informal & derogatory*), hoi polloi, masses, rabble, riff-

ities. ~*n* **4** a light structure suspended in midair with delicately balanced parts that are set in motion by air currents. **5** short for **mobile phone. mobility** *n*

mobile home *n* a large caravan, usually staying in one place, which people live in permanently.

mobile phone *n* a portable telephone powered by batteries.

mobilize *or* **-lise** *vb* **-lizing, -lized** *or* **-lising, -lised** **1** to prepare for war or another emergency by organizing resources and the armed services. **2** to organize for a purpose: *we must mobilize local residents behind our campaign.* **mobilization** *or* **-lisation** *n*

mobster *n US* a member of a criminal organization; gangster.

moccasin *n* **1** a type of soft leather shoe traditionally worn by some Native American peoples. **2** a soft leather shoe with a raised seam at the front above the toe.

mocha (**mock**-a) *n* **1** a dark brown coffee originally imported from the port of Mocha in Arabia. **2** a flavouring made from coffee and chocolate.

mock *vb* **1** to behave with scorn or contempt towards a person or thing: *her husband mocked her attempts to educate herself.* **2** to imitate or mimic, esp. in fun. **3** to defy or frustrate: *the team mocked the visitors' attempts to score.* ~*n* **4 mocks** *Informal* (in England and Wales) school examinations taken as practice before public exams. ~*adj* **5** sham or imitation: *mock Georgian windows.* **6** serving as an imitation or substitute, esp. for practice purposes: *a mock battle.* ~See also **mock-up. mocking** *n, adj*

mockers *pl n* **put the mockers on** *Informal* to ruin the chances of success of.

mockery *n, pl* **-eries** **1** ridicule, contempt, or derision. **2** a person, thing, or action that is so worthless that it seems like a parody: *the interview was a mockery from start to finish.* **3 make a mockery of something** to make something appear worthless or foolish: *the judge's decision makes a mockery of the law.*

mock-heroic *adj* (of a literary work, esp. a poem) imitating the style of heroic poetry in order to satirize an unheroic subject.

mockingbird *n* an American songbird which can mimic the song of other birds.

mock orange *n* a shrub with white fragrant flowers like those of the orange.

mock turtle soup *n* an imitation turtle soup made from a calf's head.

mock-up *n* a working full-scale model of a machine or apparatus for test or research purposes.

mod[1] *n Brit* a member of a group of teenagers, originally in the mid-1960s, who were very clothes-conscious and rode motor scooters.

mod[2] *n* an annual Highland Gaelic meeting with musical and literary competitions.

MOD (in Britain) Ministry of Defence.

mod. **1** moderate. **2** modern.

modal (**mode**-al) *adj* **1** of or relating to mode or manner. **2** *Grammar* (of a verb form or auxiliary verb) expressing possibility, intention, or necessity rather than actuality: "can", "might" and "will" are examples of modal verbs in English. **3** *Music* of or relating to a mode. **modality** *n*

mod cons *pl n Informal* modern conveniences, such as hot water and heating.

mode *n* **1** a manner or way of doing, acting, or existing. **2** a particular fashion or style. **3** *Music* any of the various scales of notes within one octave. **4** *Maths* the most frequently occurring of a range of values.

model *n* **1** a three-dimensional representation, usually on a smaller scale, of a device or structure: *an architect's model of the proposed new housing estate.* **2** an example or pattern that people might want to follow: *her success makes her an excellent role model for other young Black women.* **3** an outstanding example of its kind: *the report is a model of clarity.* **4** a person who poses for a sculptor, painter, or photographer. **5** a person who wears clothes to display them to prospective buyers; mannequin. **6** a design or style of a particular product: *the cheapest model of this car has a 1300cc engine.* **7** a theoretical description of the way a system or process works: *a computer model of the British economy.* ~*adj* **8** excellent or perfect: *a model husband.* **9** being a small-scale representation of: *a model aeroplane.* ~*vb* **-elling, -elled** *or US* **-eling, -eled** **10** to make a model of: *he modelled a plane out of balsa wood.* **11** to plan or create according to a model or models: *it had a constitution modelled on that of the United States.* **12** to display (clothing and accessories) as a mannequin. **13** to pose for a sculptor, painter, or photographer.

modem (**mode**-em) *n Computers* a device for transmitting information between two computers by a telephone line, consisting of a modulator that converts computer signals into audio signals and a corresponding demodulator.

moderate *adj* **1** not extreme or excessive: *a man of moderate views; moderate consumption of alcohol.* **2** (of a size, rate, intensity, etc.) towards the middle of the range of possible values: *a moderate-sized garden; a moderate breeze.* **3** of average quality or extent: *moderate success.* ~*n* **4** a person who holds moderate

THESAURUS

raff, scum ~*vb.* **3.** crowd around, jostle, overrun, set upon, surround, swarm around

mobile **1.** ambulatory, itinerant, locomotive, migrant, motile, movable, moving, peripatetic, portable, travelling, wandering **2.** animated, changeable, ever-changing, expressive

mobilize activate, animate, call to arms, call up, get *or* make ready, marshal, muster, organize, prepare, put in motion, rally, ready

mock *vb.* **1.** chaff, deride, flout, insult, jeer, laugh at, laugh to scorn, make fun of, poke fun at, ridicule, scoff, scorn, show contempt for, sneer, take the mickey (out of) (*informal*), take the piss (out of) (*taboo slang*), taunt, tease, wind up (*Brit. slang*) **2.** ape, burlesque, caricature, counterfeit, do (*informal*), imitate, lampoon, mimic, parody, satirize, send up (*Brit. informal*), take off (*informal*), travesty **3.** defeat, defy, disappoint, foil, frustrate, thwart ~*adj.* **4.** artificial, bogus, counterfeit, dummy, ersatz, fake, faked, false, feigned, forged, fraudulent, imitation, phoney *or* phony (*informal*), pretended, pseudo (*informal*), sham, spurious

mockery **1.** contempt, contumely, derision, disdain, disrespect, gibes, insults, jeering, ridicule, scoffing, scorn **2.** apology, disappointment, farce, joke, letdown, travesty

mocking contemptuous, derisive, derisory, disdainful, disrespectful, insulting, irreverent, sarcastic, sardonic, satiric, satirical, scoffing, scornful, taunting

model *n.* **1.** copy, dummy, facsimile, image, imitation, miniature, mock-up, replica, representation **2.** archetype, design, epitome, example, exemplar, gauge, ideal, lodestar, mould, norm, original, par, paradigm, paragon, pattern, prototype, standard, type **3.** poser, sitter, subject **4.** mannequin, supermodel **5.** configuration, design, form, kind, mark, mode, stamp, style, type, variety, version ~*adj.* **6.** copy, dummy, facsimile, imitation, miniature **7.** archetypal, exemplary, ideal, illustrative, paradigmatic, perfect, standard, typical ~*vb.*

views, esp. in politics. ~*vb* **-ating, -ated 5** to make or become less extreme or violent: *he has moderated his opinions since then.* **6** to preside over a meeting, discussion, etc. **moderately** *adv*

moderation *n* **1** the quality of being moderate. **2** the act of moderating. **3 in moderation** within moderate or reasonable limits.

moderato (mod-er-**ah**-toe) *adv Music* **1** at a moderate speed. **2** with restraint: *allegro moderato.*

moderator *n* **1** *Presbyterian Church* a minister appointed to preside over a Church court, synod, or general assembly. **2** a person who presides over at a public or legislative assembly. **3** a material, such as heavy water, used for slowing down neutrons in nuclear reactors.

modern *adj* **1** of the present or a recent time; contemporary: *there have been very few outbreaks of the disease in modern times.* **2** using the latest techniques, equipment, etc.; up-to-date: *modern and efficient railways.* **3** of contemporary styles or schools of art, literature, and music, esp. those of an experimental kind. ~*n* **4** a contemporary person. **modernity** *n*

Modern English *n* the English language since about 1450.

modernism *n* a early- and mid-twentieth century movement in art, literature and music that rejected traditional styles and techniques. **modernist** *n, adj*

modernize *or* **-ise** *vb* **-izing, -ized** *or* **-ising, -ised 1** to make modern in style, methods, or equipment: *a commitment to modernizing industry.* **2** to adopt modern ways or ideas. **modernization** *or* **-isation** *n*

modern languages *n* the languages spoken in present-day Europe, with the exception of English.

modern pentathlon *n* an athletic contest consisting of five different events: horse riding with jumps, fencing with electric épée, freestyle swimming, pistol shooting, and cross-country running.

modest *adj* **1** having a humble opinion of oneself or one's accomplishments. **2** not extreme or excessive: *a modest increase in inflation.* **3** not ostentatious or pretentious: *a modest flat in the suburbs.* **4** shy or easily embarrassed. **5** *Old-fashioned* (esp. of clothes) not revealing much of the body: *a modest dress.* **modestly** *adv* **modesty** *n*

modicum *n* a small amount.

modifier *n Grammar* a word or phrase that makes the sense of another word more specific: for example, the noun *garage* is a modifier of *door* in *garage door.*

modify *vb* **-fies, -fying, -fied 1** to change or alter slightly. **2** to make less extreme or uncompromising. **3** *Grammar* (of a word or phrase) to act as a modifier to another word or phrase. **modification** *n*

modish (**mode**-ish) *adj* in the current fashion or style. **modishly** *adv*

modiste (mode-**east**) *n* a fashionable dressmaker or milliner.

modulate *vb* **-lating, -lated 1** to change the tone, pitch, or volume of (one's voice). **2** to adjust or regulate the degree of: *the hormone which modulates the development of the sexual organs.* **3** *Music* to change from one key to another. **4** *Physics, electronics* to superimpose the amplitude, frequency, or phase of a wave or signal onto another wave or signal. **modulation** *n* **modulator** *n*

module *n* **1** a standard self-contained unit, such as an assembly of electronic components or a standardized piece of furniture, that can be used in combination with other units. **2** *Astronautics* a self-contained separable unit making up a spacecraft. **3** *Education* a short course of study that together with other such courses counts towards a qualification. **modular** *adj*

modulus *n, pl* **-li** *Physics* a coefficient expressing a specified property, for instance elasticity, of a specified substance.

modus operandi (**mode**-uss op-er-**an**-die) *n, pl* **modi operandi** (**mode**-eye) method of operating.

modus vivendi (**mode**-uss viv-**venn**-die) *n, pl* **modi vivendi** (**mode**-eye) a working arrangement between conflicting interests.

moggy *or* **mog** *n, pl* **moggies** *or* **mogs** *Brit slang* a cat.

mogul (**moh**-gl) *n* an important or powerful person.

Mogul *adj* of or relating to a Muslim dynasty of Indian emperors established in 1526.

MOH (in Britain) Medical Officer of Health.

mohair *n* **1** the long soft silky hair of the Angora goat. **2** a fabric made from yarn of this hair and cotton or wool.

THESAURUS

8. carve, cast, design, fashion, form, mould, sculpt, shape, stamp **9.** base, be imitative of, fashion, imitate, pattern, plan **10.** display, show off, sport (*informal*), wear

moderate *adj.* **1.** calm, controlled, cool, deliberate, equable, gentle, judicious, limited, middle-of-the-road, mild, modest, peaceable, reasonable, restrained, sober, steady, temperate **2.** average, fair, fairish, fair to middling (*informal*), indifferent, mediocre, medium, middling, ordinary, passable, so-so (*informal*), unexceptional ~*vb.* **3.** abate, allay, appease, assuage, calm, control, curb, decrease, diminish, ease, lessen, mitigate, modulate, pacify, play down, quiet, regulate, relax, repress, restrain, soften, soft-pedal (*informal*), subdue, tame, temper, tone down **4.** arbitrate, chair, judge, mediate, preside, referee, take the chair

moderately fairly, gently, in moderation, passably, quite, rather, reasonably, slightly, somewhat, to a degree, tolerably, to some extent, within limits, within reason

moderation **1.** calmness, composure, coolness, equanimity, fairness, judiciousness, justice, justness, mildness, moderateness, reasonableness, restraint, sedateness, temperance **2. in moderation** moderately, within limits, within reason

modern contemporary, current, fresh, late, latest, new, newfangled, novel, present, present-day, recent, twentieth-century, up-to-date, up-to-the-minute, with it (*informal*)

modernize bring into the twentieth century, bring up to date, face-lift, make over, rejuvenate, remake, remodel, renew, renovate, revamp, update

modest **1.** bashful, blushing, coy, demure, diffident, discreet, humble, meek, quiet, reserved, reticent, retiring, self-conscious, self-effacing, shy, simple, unassuming, unpretentious **2.** fair, limited, middling, moderate, ordinary, small, unexceptional

modesty bashfulness, coyness, decency, demureness, diffidence, discreetness, humbleness, humility, lack of pretension, meekness, propriety, quietness, reserve, reticence, self-effacement, shyness, simplicity, timidity, unobtrusiveness, unpretentiousness

modification adjustment, alteration, change, modulation, mutation, qualification, refinement, reformation, restriction, revision, variation

modify **1.** adapt, adjust, alter, change, convert, recast, redo, refashion, reform, remodel, reorganize, reshape, revise, rework, transform, vary **2.** abate, ease, lessen, limit, lower, moderate, qualify, reduce, relax, restrain, restrict, soften, temper, tone down

mogul baron, bashaw, big cheese (*slang, old-fashioned*), big gun (*informal*), big noise (*informal*),

Mohawk *n* **1** a member of a N American Indian people formerly living along the Mohawk river. **2** the language of this people.

mohican *n* a punk hairstyle in which the head is shaved at the sides and the remaining strip of hair is worn stiffly erect and often brightly coloured.

moiety (**moy**-it-ee) *n, pl* **-ties 1** a half. **2** one of two parts or divisions of something.

moire (**mwahr**) *n* a fabric, usually silk, with a watered effect.

moiré (**mwahr**-ray) *adj* **1** having a watered or wavelike pattern. ~*n* **2** such a pattern, impressed on fabrics. **3** a fabric, usually silk, with such a pattern. **4** Also: **moiré pattern** a pattern seen when two geometrical patterns, such as grids, are visually superimposed.

moist *adj* slightly damp or wet.

moisten *vb* to make or become moist.

moisture *n* water diffused as vapour or condensed on or in objects.

moisturize *or* **-ise** *vb* **-izing, -ized** *or* **-ising, -ised** to add moisture to the air or the skin. **moisturizer** *or* **-iser** *n*

moke *n Brit slang* a donkey.

mol *Chem* mole.

mol. 1 molecular. **2** molecule.

molar *n* **1** a large back tooth specialized for crushing and chewing food. ~*adj* **2** of any of these teeth.

molasses *n* **1** the thick brown bitter syrup obtained from sugar during refining. **2** *US & Canad* same as **treacle.**

mold *n, vb US* same as **mould.**

mole[1] *n* a small dark raised spot on the skin.

mole[2] *n* **1** a small burrowing mammal with velvety dark fur and forelimbs specialized for digging. **2** *Informal* a spy who has infiltrated an organization and become a trusted member of it.

mole[3] *n Chem* the basic SI unit of amount of substance: the amount that contains as many elementary entities as there are atoms in 0.012 kilogram of carbon-12.

mole[4] *n* **1** a breakwater. **2** a harbour protected by a breakwater.

molecular (mol-**lek**-yew-lar) *adj* of or relating to molecules.

molecular compound *n Chem* a compound in which the atoms are linked by covalent bonds to form molecules.

molecular formula *n Chem* a chemical formula indicating the number and type of atoms in a molecule, but not its structure: *NH_3 is the molecular formula of ammonia.*

molecular weight *n Chem* the sum of all the atomic weights of the atoms in a molecule.

molecule (**mol**-lik-kyool) *n* **1** the simplest unit of a chemical compound that can exist, consisting of two or more atoms held together by chemical bonds. **2** a very small particle.

molehill *n* **1** the small mound of earth thrown up by a burrowing mole. **2 make a mountain out of a molehill** to exaggerate an unimportant matter out of all proportion.

molest *vb* **1** to accost or attack someone, esp. a woman or child with the intention of assaulting her or him sexually. **2** to disturb or injure, esp. by using or threatening violence: *killing, capturing, or molesting the local wildlife was strictly forbidden.* **molestation** *n* **molester** *n*

moll *n Slang* a gangster's female accomplice or girlfriend.

mollify *vb* **-fies, -fying, -fied** to make someone less angry or upset; soothe: *he sought to mollify his critics.* **mollification** *n*

mollusc *or US* **mollusk** *n* an invertebrate with a soft unsegmented body and often a shell, such as a snail, mussel, or octopus.

mollycoddle *vb* **-coddling, -coddled** to give an excessive amount of care and protection to.

Molotov cocktail *n* an simple bomb made from a bottle filled with petrol and a cloth wick; petrol bomb.

molt *vb, n US* same as **moult.**

molten *adj* so hot that it has melted and formed a liquid: *molten metal.*

molto *adv Music* very: *allegro molto; molto adagio.*

molybdenum (mol-**lib**-din-um) *n Chem* a very hard silvery-white metallic element used in alloys, esp. to harden and strengthen steels. Symbol: Mo

mom *n Informal, chiefly US & Canad* same as **mother.**

moment *n* **1** a short period of time. **2** a specific instant or point in time: *at that moment the phone rang.* **3 the moment** the present point of time: *for the moment he is out of prison.* **4** importance, significance, or value: *a matter of greatest moment.* **5** *Physics* **a** a tendency to produce motion, esp. rotation about a point or axis. **b** the product of a physical quantity, such as force or mass, and its distance from a fixed reference point.

momentary *adj* lasting for only a moment; temporary. **momentarily** *adv*

➤ Note that some American speakers use *momentarily* to mean "soon" rather than "for a moment".

moment of truth *n* a moment when a person or thing is put to the test.

momentous (moh-**men**-tuss) *adj* of great significance. **momentousness** *n*

momentum (moh-**men**-tum) *n* **1** the impetus to go forward, develop, or get stronger: *the campaign steadily gathered support and momentum.* **2** the impetus of

THESAURUS

big shot (*informal*), big wheel (*slang*), lord, magnate, nabob (*informal*), notable, personage, potentate, tycoon, V.I.P.

moist clammy, damp, dampish, dank, dewy, dripping, drizzly, humid, not dry, rainy, soggy, wet, wettish

moisten bedew, damp, dampen, humidify, lick, moisturize, soak, water, wet

moisture damp, dampness, dankness, dew, humidity, liquid, perspiration, sweat, water, wateriness, wetness

molecule atom, iota, jot, mite, mote, particle, speck

molest 1. abuse, accost, assail, attack, harm, hurt, ill-treat, injure, interfere with, maltreat, manhandle **2.** abuse, afflict, annoy, badger, beset, bother, bug (*informal*), disturb, harass, harry, hector, irritate, persecute, pester, plague, tease, torment, upset, vex, worry

moment 1. flash, instant, jiffy (*informal*), minute, no time, second, shake (*informal*), split second, tick (*Brit. informal*), trice, twinkling, two shakes (*informal*), two shakes of a lamb's tail (*informal*) **2.** hour, instant, juncture, point, point in time, stage, time **3.** concern, consequence, gravity, import, importance, seriousness, significance, substance, value, weight, weightiness, worth

momentarily briefly, for a moment (little while, minute, second, short time, short while), for an instant, for the nonce, temporarily

momentary brief, ephemeral, evanescent, fleeting, flying, fugitive, hasty, passing, quick, short, short-lived, temporary, transitory

a moving body: *the sledge gathered momentum as it slid ever faster down the slope.* **3** *Physics* the product of a body's mass and its velocity.

momma *n Chiefly US* an informal or childish word for **mother.**

Mon. Monday.

mon- *combining form* See **mono-.**

monad *n* **1** *Philosophy* any fundamental singular metaphysical entity. **2** a single-celled organism. **3** an atom, ion, or radical with a valency of one.

monandrous *adj* **1** *Biol* having only one stamen in each flower. **2** having only one male sexual partner over a period of time.

monarch *n* a sovereign head of state, esp. a king, queen, or emperor, who rules by hereditary right. **monarchical** *or* **monarchic** *adj*

monarchism *n* the belief that a country should have a hereditary ruler, such as a king, rather than an elected one. **monarchist** *n, adj*

monarchy *n, pl* **-chies 1** a form of government in which supreme authority is held by a single hereditary ruler, such as a king. **2** a country reigned over by a monarch.

monastery *n, pl* **-teries** the building or group of buildings where a community of monks lives.

monastic *adj* **1** of or relating to monasteries, monks, or nuns. **2** (of a way of life) simple and austere; ascetic. **monasticism** *n*

monatomic *adj Chem* **1** (of an element) consisting of single atoms. **2** (of a compound or molecule) having only one atom or group that can be replaced in a reaction.

Monday *n* the second day of the week, and the first day of the working week.

monetarism *n* **1** the theory that inflation is caused by an excess quantity of money in an economy. **2** an economic policy based on this theory and a belief in the efficiency of free market forces. **monetarist** *n, adj*

monetary *adj* of money or currency.

money *n* **1** a means of payment and measure of value: *some cultures used to use shells as money.* **2** the official currency, in the form of banknotes or coins, issued by a government. **3 moneys** *or* **monies** *Law old-fashioned* a financial sum or income. **4** an unspecified amount of wealth: *money to lend.* **5** *Informal* a rich person or rich people: *he married money.* **6 for one's money** in one's opinion. **7 one's money's worth** full value for the money one has paid for something. **8 put money on** to place a bet on.

moneybags *n Informal* a very rich person.

moneychanger *n* a person engaged in the business of exchanging currencies or money.

moneyed *or* **monied** *adj* having a great deal of money; rich.

money-grubbing *adj Informal* seeking greedily to obtain money. **money-grubber** *n*

moneylender *n* a person who lends money at interest as a living.

moneymaker *n* **1** a person whose chief concern is to make money. **2** a person or thing that is or might be profitable. **moneymaking** *adj, n*

money-spinner *n Informal* an enterprise, idea, or thing that is a source of wealth.

-monger *n combining form* **1** indicating a trader or dealer: *an ironmonger.* **2** indicating a promoter of something: *a warmonger.*

mongol *n* (not in technical use) a person affected by Down's syndrome. **mongoloid** *n, adj*

Mongolian *adj* **1** of Mongolia. ~*n* **2** a person from Mongolia. **3** the language of Mongolia.

mongolism *n Pathol* a former name (not in technical use) for **Down's syndrome.**

Mongoloid *adj* of a major racial group of mankind, characterized by yellowish skin, straight black hair, and slanting eyes: includes most of the people of Asia, the American Indians, and the Eskimos.

mongoose *n, pl* **-gooses** a small long-tailed predatory mammal of Asia and Africa that kills snakes.

mongrel *n* **1** a dog of mixed breeding. **2** something made up of things from a variety of sources: *despite using components from three other cars, this new model is no mongrel.* ~*adj* **3** of mixed breeding or origin.

monied *adj* same as **moneyed.**

monies *n Law old-fashioned* a plural of **money.**

monism *n Philosophy* the doctrine that reality consists of only one basic substance or element, such as mind or matter. **monist** *n, adj*

monition *n* a warning or caution.

monitor *n* **1** a person or device that warns, checks, controls, or keeps a continuous record of something. **2** *Education* a pupil assisting a teacher with various duties. **3** a television set or loudspeaker used in a studio for checking what is being transmitted or recorded. **4** a large predatory lizard inhabiting warm regions of Africa, Asia, and Australia. ~*vb* **5** to act as a monitor of. **6** to observe or record the condition or performance of a person or thing. **7** to check a broadcast for acceptable quality or content. **monitorial** *adj*

monitory *adj* acting as or giving a warning.

monk *n* a male member of a religious community

THESAURUS

momentous consequential, critical, crucial, decisive, earth-shaking (*informal*), fateful, grave, historic, important, of moment, pivotal, serious, significant, vital, weighty

momentum drive, energy, force, impetus, power, propulsion, push, strength, thrust

monarch crowned head, emperor, empress, king, potentate, prince, princess, queen, ruler, sovereign

monarchy **1.** absolutism, autocracy, despotism, kingship, royalism, sovereignty **2.** empire, kingdom, principality, realm

monastery abbey, cloister, convent, friary, house, nunnery, priory, religious community

monastic ascetic, austere, celibate, cloistered, contemplative, eremitic, hermit-like, monkish, reclusive, secluded, sequestered, withdrawn

monetary budgetary, capital, cash, financial, fiscal, pecuniary

money ackers (*slang*), banknotes, brass (*Northern English dialect*), bread (*slang*), capital, cash, coin, currency, dosh (*Brit. & Austral. slang*), dough (*slang*), filthy lucre (*facetious*), funds, hard cash, legal tender, lolly (*Brit. slang*), loot (*informal*), megabucks (*U.S. & Canad. slang*), moolah (*slang*), necessary (*informal*), needful (*informal*), pelf (*contemptuous*), readies (*informal*), riches, shekels (*informal*), silver, specie, spondulicks (*slang*), the ready (*informal*), the wherewithal, wealth

moneymaking *adj.* gainful, going, lucrative, paying, profitable, remunerative, successful, thriving

mongrel **1.** *n.* cross, crossbreed, half-breed, hybrid, mixed breed **2.** *adj.* bastard, crossbred, half-breed, hybrid, of mixed breed

monitor **1.** *n.* guide, invigilator, overseer, prefect

bound by vows of poverty, chastity, and obedience. **monkish** *adj*

monkey *n* **1** any long-tailed primate that is not a lemur or tarsier. **2** (loosely) any primate that is not a human. **3** a naughty or mischievous child. **4** *Slang* £500 or $500. *~vb* **5 monkey around** *or* **about with** to meddle or tinker with.

monkey business *n Informal* mischievous or dishonest behaviour or acts.

monkey nut *n Brit* a peanut.

monkey puzzle *n* a South American coniferous tree with branches shaped like a candelabrum and stiff sharp leaves.

monkey tricks *or US* **monkey shines** *pl n Informal* mischievous behaviour or acts.

monkey wrench *n* a wrench with adjustable jaws.

monkshood *n* a poisonous plant with hooded blue-purple flowers.

mono *adj* **1** short for **monophonic.** *~n* **2** monophonic sound.

mono- *or before a vowel* **mon-** *combining form* **1** one; single: *monorail; monolingual.* **2** *Chem* indicating that a chemical compound contains a single specified atom or group: *monoxide.*

monobasic *adj Chem* (of an acid, such as hydrogen chloride) having only one replaceable hydrogen atom per molecule.

monochromatic *adj* (of light or other electromagnetic radiation) having only one wavelength.

monochrome *adj* **1** *Photog, television* black-and-white. *~n* **2** a painting or drawing done in a range of tones of a single colour.

monocle (**mon**-a-kl) *n* (formerly) a lens worn for correcting defective sight in one eye only, held in position by the facial muscles. **monocled** *adj*

monocline *n* a fold in stratified rocks in which the strata are inclined in the same direction from the horizontal. **monoclinal** *adj, n*

monoclinic *adj Crystallog* of the crystal system characterized by three unequal axes, one pair of which are not at right angles to each other.

monoclonal antibody *n* an antibody produced from a single clone of cells grown in a culture.

monocotyledon (mon-no-kot-ill-**leed**-on) *n* any flowering plant with a single embryonic seed leaf, such as the grasses, lilies, palms, and orchids.

monocular *adj* having or intended for the use of only one eye.

monody *n, pl* **-dies 1** (in Greek tragedy) an ode sung by a single actor. **2** *Music* a style of composition consisting of a single vocal part, usually with accompaniment. **monodist** *n*

monoecious (mon-**ee**-shuss) *adj* **1** (of some flowering plants) having the male and female reproductive organs in separate flowers on the same plant. **2** (of some animals and lower plants) hermaphrodite.

monogamy *n* the state or practice of having only one husband or wife at a time. **monogamous** *adj*

monogram *n* a design of one or more letters, esp. initials, on clothing, stationery, etc.

monograph *n* a paper, book, or other work concerned with a single subject or aspect of a subject.

monolingual *adj* knowing or expressed in only one language.

monolith *n* **1** a large block of stone. **2** a statue, obelisk, or column cut from one block of stone. **3** something which can be regarded as forming one large, single, whole: *the Christian religion should not be thought of as a monolith.* **monolithic** *adj*

monologue *n* **1** a long speech made by one actor in a play or film; soliloquy. **2** a dramatic piece for a single performer. **3** any long speech by one person, esp. one which prevents other people talking or expressing their views.

monomania *n* an obsession with one thing or idea. **monomaniac** *n, adj*

monomer *n Chem* a compound whose molecules can join together to form a polymer.

monomial *n Maths* an expression consisting of a single term, such as *5ax.*

mononucleosis (mon-oh-new-klee-**oh**-siss) *n* **infectious mononucleosis** same as **glandular fever.**

monophonic *adj* (of a system of broadcasting, recording, or reproducing sound) using only one channel between source and loudspeaker. Short form: **mono**

monoplane *n* an aeroplane with only one pair of wings.

monopolize *or* **-lise** *vb* **-lizing, -lized** *or* **-lising, -lised 1** to have full control or use of, to the exclusion of others. **2** to hold exclusive control of a market or supply.

monopoly *n, pl* **-lies 1** exclusive control of the market supply of a product or service. **2 a** an enterprise exercising this control. **b** the product or service so controlled. **3** *Law* the exclusive right granted to a person or company by the state to trade in a specified commodity or area. **4** exclusive control, possession, or use of something. **monopolist** *n* **monopolistic** *adj*

Monopoly *n Trademark* a board game for two to six players who deal in "property" as they move tokens around the board.

monorail *n* a single-rail railway.

monosaccharide *n* a simple sugar, such as glucose, that cannot be broken down into other sugars.

monosodium glutamate *n* a substance which enhances protein flavours: used as a food additive.

monosyllable *n* a word of one syllable. **monosyllabic** *adj*

monotheism *n* the belief or doctrine that there is only one God. **monotheist** *n, adj* **monotheistic** *adj*

monotone *n* **1** a single unvaried pitch level in speech or sound. **2** a way of speaking which lacks variety of pitch or expression: *he rambled on in a dull monotone.* **3** lack of variety in style or expression. *~adj* **4** unvarying.

THESAURUS

(*Brit.*), supervisor, watchdog **2.** *vb.* check, follow, keep an eye on, keep track of, observe, oversee, record, scan, supervise, survey, watch

monk brother, friar (*loosely*), monastic, religious

monkey *n.* **1.** primate, simian **2.** devil, imp, mischief maker, rascal, rogue, scamp *~vb.* **3.** fiddle (*informal*), fool, interfere, meddle, mess, play, tamper, tinker, trifle

monkey business carry-on (*informal, chiefly Brit.*), chicanery, clowning, funny business, hanky-panky (*informal*), mischief, monkey tricks, pranks, shenanigans (*informal*), skulduggery (*informal*), skylarking (*informal*), tomfoolery, trickery

monolithic colossal, giant, gigantic, huge, immovable, impenetrable, imposing, intractable, massive, monumental, solid, substantial, undifferentiated, undivided, unitary

monologue harangue, lecture, sermon, soliloquy, speech

monopolize control, corner, corner the market in, dominate, engross, exercise *or* have a monopoly of, hog (*slang*), keep to oneself, take over, take up

monotonous all the same, boring, colourless, dron-

monotonous *adj* tedious because of lack of variety. **monotonously** *adv*

monotony *n, pl* **-nies 1** wearisome routine; dullness. **2** lack of variety in pitch or tone.

monounsaturated *adj* of a group of vegetable oils, such as olive oil, that have a neutral effect on cholesterol in the body.

monovalent *adj Chem* **1** having a valency of one. **2** having only one valency. **monovalence** *or* **monovalency** *n*

monoxide *n* an oxide that contains one oxygen atom per molecule.

Monseigneur (mon-sen-**nyur**) *n, pl* **Messeigneurs** (may-sen-**nyur**) a title given to French prelates and princes.

monsieur (muss-**syuh**) *n, pl* **messieurs** (may-**syuh**) a French form of address equivalent to *sir* or *Mr.*

Monsignor *n, pl* **Monsignors** *or* **Monsignori** *RC Church* a title given to certain senior clergymen.

monsoon *n* **1** a seasonal wind of S Asia which blows from the southwest in summer and from the northeast in winter. **2** the rainy season when the SW monsoon blows, from about April to October.

mons pubis (monz **pew**-biss) *n, pl* **montes pubis** (**mon**-teez) the fatty flesh in human males over the junction of the pubic bones.

monster *n* **1** an imaginary beast, usually frightening in appearance. **2** a very large person, animal, or thing. **3** an exceptionally cruel or wicked person. **4** a person, animal, or plant with a marked deformity.

monstrance *n RC Church* a vessel in which the consecrated Host is exposed for adoration.

monstrosity *n, pl* **-ties 1** an outrageous or ugly person or thing. **2** the state or quality of being monstrous.

monstrous *adj* **1** hideous or unnatural in size or character. **2** atrocious, unjust, or shocking: *the President described the invasion as monstrous.* **3** huge. **4** of or like a monster. **5** (of plants and animals) abnormal in structure. **monstrously** *adv*

mons veneris (monz **ven**-er-iss) *n, pl* **montes veneris** (**mon**-teez) the fatty flesh in human females over the junction of the pubic bones.

montage (**mon**-tahzh) *n* **1** a picture made by combining material from various sources, such as other pictures or photographs. **2** the technique of producing pictures in this way. **3** a method of film editing by juxtaposition or partial superimposition of several shots to form a single image. **4** a film sequence of this kind.

month *n* **1** one of the twelve divisions (**calendar months**) of the calendar year. **2** a period of time extending from one date to a corresponding date in the next calendar month. **3** a period of four weeks or of 30 days.

monthly *adj* **1** happening or payable once every month: *a monthly magazine.* **2** lasting or valid for a month: *a monthly travel pass.* ~*adv* **3** once a month. ~*n, pl* **-lies 4** a magazine published once a month.

monument *n* **1** something, such as a statue or building, erected in commemoration of a person or event. **2** an ancient building which is regarded as an important part of a country's history. **3** an exceptional example of the results of something: *the whole town is a monument to bad sixties' architecture.*

monumental *adj* **1** large, impressive, or likely to last or be remembered for a long time: *a monumental three-volume biography.* **2** of or being a monument. **3** *Informal* extreme: *a monumental gamble.*

moo *n* **1** the characteristic deep long sound made by a cow. ~*vb* **2** to make this sound; low.

mooch *vb Slang* **1** to loiter or walk aimlessly. **2** to cadge or scrounge.

mood[1] *n* **1** a temporary state of mind or temper: *a happy mood.* **2** a sullen or gloomy state of mind, esp. when temporary: *she's in a mood.* **3** a prevailing atmosphere or feeling: *the current mood of disenchantment with politics.* **4 in the mood** inclined to do or have (something).

mood[2] *n Grammar* a form of a verb indicating whether the verb expresses a fact (indicative mood), a wish or supposition (subjunctive mood), or a command (imperative mood).

THESAURUS

ing, dull, flat, ho-hum (*informal*), humdrum, mind-numbing, plodding, repetitious, repetitive, samey (*informal*), soporific, tedious, tiresome, toneless, unchanging, uniform, uninflected, unvaried, wearisome

monotony boredom, colourlessness, dullness, flatness, humdrumness, monotonousness, repetitiousness, repetitiveness, routine, sameness, tediousness, tedium, tiresomeness, uniformity, wearisomeness

monster 1. behemoth, Brobdingnagian, colossus, giant, leviathan, mammoth, titan **2.** barbarian, beast, bogeyman, brute, demon, devil, fiend, ghoul, ogre, savage, villain **3.** freak, monstrosity, mutant

monstrosity 1. eyesore, freak, horror, monster, mutant, ogre **2.** abnormality, atrocity, dreadfulness, evil, frightfulness, heinousness, hellishness, hideousness, horror, loathsomeness, obscenity

monstrous 1. abnormal, dreadful, enormous, fiendish, freakish, frightful, grotesque, gruesome, hellish, hideous, horrendous, horrible, obscene, terrible, unnatural **2.** atrocious, cruel, devilish, diabolical, disgraceful, egregious, evil, fiendish, foul, heinous, horrifying, infamous, inhuman, intolerable, loathsome, odious, outrageous, satanic, scandalous, shocking, vicious, villainous **3.** colossal, elephantine, enormous, gargantuan, giant, gigantic, ginormous (*informal*), great, huge, immense, mammoth, massive, prodigious, stupendous, titanic, towering, tremendous, vast

month four weeks, moon, thirty days

monument 1. cairn, cenotaph, commemoration, gravestone, headstone, marker, mausoleum, memorial, obelisk, pillar, shrine, statue, tombstone **2.** memento, record, remembrance, reminder, testament, token, witness

monumental 1. awe-inspiring, awesome, classic, enduring, enormous, epoch-making, historic, immortal, important, lasting, majestic, memorable, outstanding, prodigious, significant, stupendous, unforgettable **2.** commemorative, funerary, memorial, monolithic **3.** *informal* catastrophic, colossal, egregious, gigantic, great, horrible, immense, indefensible, massive, staggering, terrible, tremendous, unforgivable, whopping (*informal*)

mood 1. disposition, frame of mind, humour, spirit, state of mind, temper, tenor, vein **2.** bad temper, blues, depression, doldrums, dumps (*informal*), fit of pique, grumps (*informal*), low spirits, melancholy, sulk, the hump (*Brit. informal*), the sulks **3. in the mood** disposed (towards), eager, favourable, inclined, interested, in the (right) frame of mind, keen, minded, willing

moody 1. angry, broody, cantankerous, crabbed, crabby, crestfallen, cross, crotchety (*informal*), crusty, curt, dismal, doleful, dour, downcast, down in the dumps (*informal*), down in the mouth (*informal*), frowning, gloomy, glum, huffy, ill-humoured, ill-tempered, in a huff, in the doldrums, introspective, irascible, irritable, lugubrious, melancholy, miserable, mopish, mopy, morose, offended, out of sorts (*informal*), pensive, petulant, piqued, sad, saturnine, short-tempered, splenetic, sulky, sullen, temperamental, testy, tetchy, touchy, waspish, wounded **2.** capricious,

moody *adj* **moodier, moodiest 1** sullen, sulky, or gloomy. **2** temperamental or changeable. **moodily** *adv* **moodiness** *n*

Moog *n Music trademark* a type of synthesizer.

mooi *adj S African slang* pleasing or nice.

mooli *n* a type of large white radish.

moon *n* **1** the natural satellite of the earth. **2** this satellite as it is seen during its revolution around the earth, esp. at one of its phases: *new moon; full moon.* **3** any natural satellite of a planet. **4** a month. **5 over the moon** *Informal* extremely happy; ecstatic. ~*vb* **6 moon about** *or* **around** to be idle in a listless or dreamy way. **moonless** *adj*

moonbeam *n* a ray of moonlight.

moon-faced *adj* having a round face.

moonlight *n* **1** light from the sun received on earth after reflection by the moon. ~*adj* **2** illuminated by the moon: *a moonlight walk.* ~*vb* **-lighting, -lighted 3** *Informal* to work at a secondary job, esp. illegally. **moonlighter** *n*

moonlight flit *n Brit informal* a hurried departure at night to avoid paying rent.

moonlit *adj* illuminated by the moon.

moonscape *n* the surface of the moon or a picture or model of it.

moonshine *n* **1** *US & Canad* illegally distilled or smuggled whisky. **2** foolish or nonsensical talk or thought.

moonshot *n* the launching of a spacecraft to the moon.

moonstone *n* a white translucent form of feldspar, used as a gem.

moonstruck *adj* slightly mad or odd, as if affected by the moon.

moony *adj* **moonier, mooniest** *Informal* dreamy or listless.

moor[1] *n* an expanse of open uncultivated ground covered with heather, coarse grass, and bracken.

moor[2] *vb* to secure a ship or boat with cables, ropes, or anchors so that it remains in one place. **moorage** *n*

Moor *n* a member of a Muslim people of North Africa who ruled Spain between the 8th and 15th centuries. **Moorish** *adj*

moorhen *n* a waterfowl with black plumage and a red bill.

mooring *n* a place where a ship or boat can be tied up or anchored.

moorings *pl n Naut* the ropes and anchors used in mooring a vessel.

moorland *n Brit* an area of moor.

moose *n, pl* **moose** a large North American deer with large flattened antlers; the American elk.

moot *adj* **1** subject or open to debate: *a moot point.* ~*vb* **2** to suggest or bring up for debate: *a compromise proposal, involving building fewer flats, was mooted.* ~*n* **3** (in Anglo-Saxon England) a local administrative assembly.

mop *n* **1** a tool with a head made of twists of cotton or sponge and a long handle used for washing or polishing floors. **2** a similar tool, except smaller and without a long handle, used to wash dishes. **3** a thick untidy mass of hair. ~*vb* **mopping, mopped 4** to clean or soak up with or as if with a mop: *she mopped her brow with a handkerchief.* ~See also **mop up.**

mope *vb* **moping, moped 1** to be gloomy or apathetic. **2** to walk around in a gloomy and aimless manner.

moped *n* a light motorcycle not over 50cc.

mopes *pl n* **the** the low spirits.

mopoke *n* **1** a small spotted owl of Australia and New Zealand. **2** *Austral & NZ slang* a slow or lugubrious person.

moppet *n* same as **poppet.**

mop up *vb* **1** to clean with a mop. **2** *Informal* to complete the last remaining stages of a job. **3** *Mil* to clear remaining enemy forces after a battle, by killing them or taking them prisoner.

moquette *n* a thick velvety fabric used for carpets and upholstery.

moraine *n* a ridge or mound formed from debris deposited by a glacier.

moral *adj* **1** concerned with or relating to the distinction between good and bad or right and wrong behaviour: *moral sense.* **2** based on a sense of right and wrong: *moral duty.* **3** (of support or a victory) psychological rather than practical. ~*n* **4** a lesson about right or wrong behaviour that is shown in a fable or event. **5 morals** principles of behaviour in accordance with standards of right and wrong. **morally** *adv*

morale (mor-**rahl**) *n* the degree of confidence or optimism of a person or group.

moralist *n* **1** a person who has a strong sense of right and wrong. **2** someone who criticizes other people for not doing what he or she thinks is morally correct. **moralistic** *adj*

morality *n, pl* **-ties 1** good moral conduct. **2** the degree to which something is morally acceptable: *we discussed the morality of fox-hunting.* **3** a system of moral principles.

morality play *n* a medieval type of drama concerned with the conflict between personified virtues and vices.

moralize *or* **-ise** *vb* **-izing, -ized** *or* **-ising, -ised 1** to discuss or consider something in the light of one's own moral beliefs, esp. with disapproval. **2** to interpret or explain in a moral sense. **3** to improve the morals of.

THESAURUS

changeable, erratic, faddish, fickle, fitful, flighty, impulsive, inconstant, mercurial, temperamental, unpredictable, unstable, unsteady, volatile

moon 1. *n.* satellite **2.** *vb.* daydream, idle, languish, mooch (*slang*), mope, waste time

moor[1] fell (*Brit.*), heath, moorland, muir (*Scot.*)

moor[2] anchor, berth, dock, fasten, fix, lash, make fast, secure, tie up

moot 1. *adj.* arguable, at issue, contestable, controversial, debatable, disputable, doubtful, open, open to debate, undecided, unresolved, unsettled **2.** *vb.* bring up, broach, introduce, propose, put forward, suggest, ventilate

mop *n.* **1.** sponge, squeegee, swab **2.** mane, shock, tangle, thatch ~*vb.* **3.** clean, soak up, sponge, swab, wash, wipe

mop up 1. clean up, mop, soak up, sponge, swab, wash, wipe **2.** *Military* account for, clean out, clear, eliminate, finish off, neutralize, pacify, round up, secure

moral *adj.* **1.** blameless, chaste, decent, ethical, good, high-minded, honest, honourable, incorruptible, innocent, just, meritorious, noble, principled, proper, pure, right, righteous, upright, upstanding, virtuous **2.** ethical ~*n.* **3.** lesson, meaning, message, point, significance **4. morals** behaviour, conduct, ethics, habits, integrity, manners, morality, mores, principles, scruples, standards

morale confidence, esprit de corps, heart, mettle, self-esteem, spirit, temper

morality 1. chastity, decency, ethicality, ethicalness, goodness, honesty, integrity, justice, principle, recti-

moral philosophy *n* the branch of philosophy dealing with ethics.
morass *n* **1** a tract of swampy low-lying land. **2** a disordered, confusing, or muddled state of affairs.
moratorium *n, pl* **-ria** *or* **-riums 1** a legally authorized postponement of the payment of a debt. **2** an agreed suspension of activity.
moray *n* a large marine eel marked with brilliant colours.
morbid *adj* **1** having an unusual interest in death or unpleasant events. **2** *Med* relating to or characterized by disease. **morbidity** *n* **morbidly** *adv*
mordant *adj* **1** sarcastic or caustic: *mordant wit.* ~*n* **2** a substance used in dyeing to fix colours. **3** an acid or other corrosive fluid used to etch lines on a printing plate.
more *adj* **1** the comparative of **much** or **many:** *more joy than you know; even more are leaving the country.* **2** additional or further: *no more apples.* **3 more of** to a greater extent or degree: *more of a nuisance.* ~*adv* **4** used to form the comparative of some adjectives and adverbs: *more quickly.* **5** the comparative of **much:** *people listen to the radio more now.* **6 more or less a** as an estimate; approximately. **b** to an unspecified extent or degree: *the film was a disaster, more or less.*
moreish *or* **morish** *adj Informal* (of food) causing a desire for more.
morel *n* an edible mushroom with a pitted cap.
morello *n, pl* **-los** a variety of small dark sour cherry.
moreover *adv* in addition to what has already been said.
morepork *n Chiefly NZ* same as **mopoke.**
mores (**more**-rayz) *pl n* the customs and conventions embodying the fundamental values of a community.
morganatic *adj* of or designating a marriage between a person of high rank and a person of low rank, by which the latter is not elevated to the higher rank and any children have no rights to inherit the higher party's titles or property.
morgue *n* **1** a mortuary. **2** *Informal* a store of clippings and back numbers used for reference in a newspaper.
moribund *adj* **1** near death. **2** no longer performing effectively or usefully: *Romania's moribund economy.*
morish *adj* same as **moreish.**
Mormon *n* **1** a member of the Church of Jesus Christ of Latter-day Saints, founded in 1830 in New York by Joseph Smith. ~*adj* **2** of the Mormons, their Church, or their beliefs. **Mormonism** *n*
morn *n Poetic* morning.
mornay *adj* served with a cheese sauce: *haddock mornay.*
morning *n* **1** the first part of the day, ending at noon. **2** daybreak; dawn. **3 the morning after** *Informal* the after effects of excess, esp. a hangover. ~*adj* **4** of or in the morning: *morning coffee.*
morning dress *n* formal daytime dress for men, consisting of a frock coat with the front cut away (**morning coat**), usually with grey trousers and top hat.
morning-glory *n, pl* **-ries** a tropical climbing plant with trumpet-shaped blue, pink, or white flowers, which close in late afternoon.
mornings *adv Informal* in the morning, esp. regularly, or during every morning.
morning sickness *n* nausea occurring shortly after rising in early pregnancy.
morning star *n* a planet, usually Venus, seen just before sunrise.
Moroccan *adj* **1** of Morocco. ~*n* **2** a person from Morocco.
morocco *n* a fine soft leather made from goatskins.
moron *n* **1** *Informal, derogatory* a foolish or stupid person. **2** (formerly) a person having an intelligence quotient of between 50 and 70. **moronic** *adj*
morose (mor-**rohss**) *adj* ill-tempered, sullen, and unwilling to talk very much. **morosely** *adv*
morpheme *n Linguistics* a speech element having a meaning or grammatical function that cannot be subdivided into further such elements.
morphine *or* **morphia** *n* a drug extracted from opium: used in medicine as an anaesthetic and sedative.
morphology *n* the science of forms and structures of organisms or words. **morphological** *adj*
morris dance *n* an old English folk dance performed by men (**morris men**) who wear a traditional costume decorated with bells.
morrow *n* **the morrow** *Old-fashioned or poetic* **1** the next day. **2** the morning.
Morse code *n* a code used internationally for transmitting messages, in which letters and numbers are represented by groups of dots and dashes, or by shorter and longer sounds.

THESAURUS

tude, righteousness, rightness, uprightness, virtue **2.** conduct, ethics, habits, ideals, manners, moral code, morals, mores, philosophy, principles, standards
moratorium freeze, halt, postponement, respite, standstill, stay, suspension
morbid 1. brooding, funereal, ghoulish, gloomy, grim, melancholy, pessimistic, sick, sombre, unhealthy, unwholesome **2.** ailing, deadly, diseased, infected, malignant, pathological, sick, sickly, unhealthy, unsound
more 1. *adj.* added, additional, extra, fresh, further, new, other, spare, supplementary **2.** *adv.* better, further, longer, to a greater extent
moreover additionally, also, as well, besides, further, furthermore, in addition, into the bargain, likewise, to boot, too, what is more, withal (*literary*)
morgue mortuary
moribund 1. at death's door, breathing one's last, doomed, dying, fading fast, failing, (having) one foot in the grave, *in extremis,* near death, near the end, on one's deathbed, on one's last legs **2.** at a standstill, declining, forceless, obsolescent, on its last legs, on the way out, stagnant, stagnating, standing still, waning, weak
morning a.m., break of day, dawn, daybreak, forenoon, morn (*poetic*), morrow (*archaic*), sunrise
moron airhead (*slang*), ass, berk (*Brit. slang*), blockhead, bonehead (*slang*), charlie (*Brit. informal*), cretin, dickhead (*slang*), dimwit (*informal*), dipstick (*Brit. slang*), divvy (*Brit. slang*), dolt, dope (*informal*), dork (*slang*), dummy (*slang*), dunce, dunderhead, fool, halfwit, idiot, imbecile, jerk (*slang, chiefly U.S. & Canad.*), lamebrain (*informal*), mental defective, muttonhead (*slang*), nerd *or* nurd (*slang*), nitwit (*informal*), numbskull *or* numskull, oaf, pillock (*Brit. slang*), plank (*Brit. slang*), plonker (*slang*), prat (*slang*), prick (*derogatory slang*), schmuck (*U.S. slang*), simpleton, thickhead, twit (*informal, chiefly Brit.*), wally (*slang*)
morose blue, churlish, crabbed, crabby, cross, crusty, depressed, dour, down, down in the dumps (*informal*), gloomy, glum, grouchy (*informal*), gruff, ill-humoured, ill-natured, ill-tempered, in a bad mood, low, melancholy, miserable, moody, mournful, perverse, pessimistic, saturnine, sour, sulky, sullen, surly, taciturn
morsel bit, bite, crumb, fraction, fragment, grain,

morsel *n* a small piece of something, esp. of food.
mortal *adj* **1** (of living beings, esp. humans) destined to die sometime rather than living forever. **2** causing death; fatal: *a mortal wound.* **3** deadly or unrelenting: *he is my mortal enemy.* **4** of or resulting from the fear of death: *mortal terror.* **5** of or involving life or the world: *the hangman's noose ended his mortal existence.* **6** great or very intense: *mortal pain.* **7** *Informal* conceivable or possible: *there was no mortal reason to leave.* **8** *Slang* long and tedious: *for three mortal hours.* ~*n* **9** a human being. **mortally** *adv*
mortality *n, pl* **-ties 1** the condition of being mortal. **2** great loss of life, as in war or disaster. **3** the number of deaths in a given period.
mortal sin *n Christianity* a sin that will lead to damnation unless repented of.
mortar *n* **1** a small cannon that fires shells in high arcs. **2** a mixture of cement or lime or both with sand and water, used to hold bricks or stones together. **3** a vessel, usually bowl-shaped, in which substances are crushed with a pestle. ~*vb* **4** to fire on with mortars. **5** to join bricks or stones with mortar.
mortarboard *n* **1** a black tasselled academic cap with a flat square top. **2** a small square board with a handle on the underside for carrying mortar.
mortgage *n* **1** an agreement under which a person borrows money to buy property, esp. a house, and the lender can take possession of the property if the borrower fails to repay the money. **2** a loan obtained under such an agreement: *a mortgage of £35 000.* **3** a regular repayment of money borrowed under such an agreement: *a mortgage of £247 per month.* ~*vb* **-gaging, -gaged 4** to pledge a house or other property as security for the repayment of a loan. ~*adj* **5** of or relating to a mortgage: *a mortgage payment.*
mortgagee *n* the person or organization who lends money in a mortgage agreement.
mortgagor *or* **-ger** *n* the person who borrows money in a mortgage agreement.
mortice *or* **mortise** (**more**-tiss) *n* **1** a slot or recess cut into a piece of wood or stone to receive a matching projection (tenon) on another piece, or a mortice lock. ~*vb* **-ticing, -ticed** *or* **-tising, -tised 2** to cut a slot or recess in a piece of wood or stone. **3** to join two pieces of wood or stone by means of a mortice and tenon.
mortice lock *n* a lock set into the edge of a door so that the mechanism of the lock is enclosed by the door.
mortician *n Chiefly US* same as **undertaker.**
mortify *vb* **-fies, -fying, -fied 1** to make someone feel ashamed or embarrassed. **2** *Christianity* to subdue one's emotions, the body, etc., by self-denial. **3** (of flesh) to become gangrenous. **mortification** *n* **mortifying** *adj*
mortuary *n, pl* **-aries** a building or room where dead bodies are kept before cremation or burial.
mosaic (moh-**zay**-ik) *n* a design or decoration made up of small pieces of coloured glass or stone.
Mosaic *adj* of or relating to Moses or the laws and traditions ascribed to him.
moselle *n* a German white wine from the valley of the river Moselle.
mosey *vb* **mosey along** *or* **on** *Informal* to walk slowly and casually; amble.
Moslem *n, pl* **-lems** *or* **-lem,** *adj* same as **Muslim.**
mosque *n* a Muslim place of worship.
mosquito *n, pl* **-toes** *or* **-tos** a two-winged insect, the females of which pierce the skin of humans and animals to suck their blood.
mosquito net *n* a fine curtain or net to keep mosquitoes away, esp. hung over a bed.
moss *n* **1** a very small flowerless plant typically growing in dense mats on trees, rocks, or moist ground. **2** *Scot & N English* a peat bog or marsh. **mossy** *adj*
mossie *n S African* the common sparrow.
moss rose *n* a variety of rose that has a mossy stem and fragrant pink flowers.
most *n* **1** the greatest number or degree: *twenty pounds is the most I can afford.* **2** the majority: *most of his records are dreadful.* **3 at (the) most** at the maximum: *she is fifteen at the most.* **4 make the most of** to use to the best advantage: *they made the most of their chances.* ~*adj* **5** of or being the majority of a group of things or people or the largest part of something: *most people don't share your views.* **6 the most** the superlative of **many** or **much:** *he has the most talent.* ~*adv* **7 the most** used to form the superlative of some adjectives and adverbs: *the most beautiful women in the world.* **8** the superlative of **much:** *what do you like most about your job?* **9** very; exceedingly: *a most unfortunate accident.*
mostly *adv* **1** almost entirely; generally: *the men at the party were mostly young.* **2** on many or most occasions; usually: *rattlesnakes mostly hunt at night.*
Most Reverend *n* (in Britain) a courtesy title applied to archbishops.
mot (moh) *n* short for **bon mot.**
MOT 1 *Brit* short for **MOT test. 2** *Brit* the certificate

THESAURUS

mouthful, nibble, part, piece, scrap, segment, slice, snack, soupçon, tad (*informal, chiefly U.S.*), taste, titbit
mortal *adj.* **1.** ephemeral, impermanent, passing, transient **2.** deadly, death-dealing, destructive, fatal, killing, lethal, murderous, terminal **3.** bitter, deadly, implacable, irreconcilable, out-and-out, remorseless, sworn, to the death, unrelenting **4.** corporeal, earthly, human, sublunary, temporal, worldly **5.** agonizing, awful, dire, enormous, extreme, grave, great, intense, severe, terrible ~*n.* **6.** being, body, earthling, human, human being, individual, man, person, woman
mortality 1. ephemerality, humanity, impermanence, temporality, transience **2.** bloodshed, carnage, death, destruction, fatality, killing, loss of life
mortification 1. abasement, annoyance, chagrin, discomfiture, dissatisfaction, embarrassment, humiliation, loss of face, shame, vexation **2.** abasement, chastening, control, denial, discipline, subjugation **3.** *Medical* corruption, festering, gangrene, necrosis, putrescence
mortified 1. abashed, affronted, annoyed, ashamed, chagrined, chastened, confounded, crushed, deflated, discomfited, displeased, embarrassed, given a showing-up (*informal*), humbled, humiliated, made to eat humble pie (*informal*), put down, put out (*informal*), put to shame, rendered speechless, shamed, vexed **2.** abased, chastened, conquered, controlled, crushed, disciplined, subdued **3.** *of flesh* decayed, gangrenous, necrotic, rotted
mortify 1. abase, abash, affront, annoy, chasten, confound, crush, deflate, disappoint, discomfit, displease, embarrass, humble, humiliate, make (someone) eat humble pie (*informal*), put down, put to shame, shame, take (someone) down a peg (*informal*), vex **2.** abase, chasten, control, deny, discipline, subdue **3.** *of flesh* become gangrenous, corrupt, deaden, die, fester, gangrene, necrose, putrefy
mortuary funeral home (*U.S.*), funeral parlour, morgue
mostly above all, almost entirely, as a rule, chiefly,

showing that a vehicle has passed its MOT test. **3** *NZ* Ministry of Transport.

mote *n* a tiny speck.

motel *n* a roadside hotel for motorists.

motet (moh-**tet**) *n* a religious song for a choir in which several voices, usually unaccompanied, sing contrasting parts simultaneously.

moth *n* any of numerous chiefly nocturnal insects resembling butterflies, that typically have stout bodies and do not have club-shaped antennae.

mothball *n* **1** a small ball of camphor or naphthalene placed in stored clothing to repel clothes moths. **2 put in mothballs** to postpone work on. *~vb* **3** to take something out of operation but maintain it for future use. **4** to postpone work on.

moth-eaten *adj* **1** decayed or scruffy. **2** eaten away by or as if by moths.

mother *n* **1** a female who has given birth to offspring. **2** a person's own mother. **3** a title given to certain members of female religious orders. **4** motherly qualities, such as maternal affection: *it appealed to the mother in her.* **5 the mother of** a female or thing that creates, founds, or protects something: *the mother of modern feminism; necessity is the mother of invention.* *~adj* **6** of or relating to a female or thing that creates, founds, or protects something: *our mother company is in New York.* **7** native or innate: *mother wit.* *~vb* **8** to give birth to or produce. **9** to nurture or protect. **motherless** *adj* **motherly** *adj*

Mother Carey's chicken *n* same as **stormy petrel.**

mother country *n* **1** the original country of colonists or settlers. **2** a person's native country.

motherhood *n* the state of being a mother.

Mothering Sunday *n Brit* the fourth Sunday in Lent, when mothers traditionally receive presents from their children. Also called: **Mother's Day**

mother-in-law *n, pl* **mothers-in-law** the mother of one's wife or husband.

motherland *n* a person's native country.

mother-of-pearl *n* a hard iridescent substance that forms the inner layer of the shells of certain molluscs, such as the oyster.

Mother's Day *n* **1** See **Mothering Sunday. 2** *US & Canad* the second Sunday in May, observed as a day in honour of mothers.

mother superior *n, pl* **mother superiors** *or* **mothers superior** the head of a community of nuns.

mother tongue *n* the language first learned by a child.

mothproof *adj* **1** (esp. of clothes) chemically treated so as to repel clothes moths. *~vb* **2** to make mothproof.

motif (moh-**teef**) *n* **1** a distinctive idea, esp. a theme elaborated on in a piece of music or literature. **2** a recurring shape in a design. **3** a single decoration, such as a symbol or name on a piece of clothing.

motion *n* **1** the process of continual change in the position of an object; movement: *the motion of the earth round the sun.* **2** a movement or gesture: *he made stabbing motions with the spear.* **3** a way or style of moving: *massage the back with steady circular motions.* **4** a formal proposal to be discussed and voted on in a debate or meeting. **5** *Brit* **a** the evacuation of the bowels. **b** excrement. **6 go through the motions** to do something mechanically or without sincerity. **7 set in motion** to make operational or start functioning. *~vb* **8** to signal or direct a person by a movement or gesture: *she motioned to me to sit down.* **motionless** *adj*

motion picture *n US & Canad* a film; movie.

motivate *vb* **-vating, -vated 1** to give a reason or inspiration for a course of action to someone: *he was motivated purely by greed.* **2** to inspire and encourage someone to do something: *a good teacher must motivate her pupils.* **motivation** *n*

motive *n* **1** the reason, whether conscious or unconscious, for a certain course of action. **2** same as **motif** (sense 2). *~adj* **3** of or causing motion: *a motive force.*

motive power *n* **1** any source of energy used to produce motion. **2** the means of supplying power to an engine or vehicle.

mot juste (moh **zhoost**) *n, pl* **mots justes** the appropriate word or expression.

motley *adj* **1** made up of people or things of different types: *a motley assortment of mules, donkeys, and camels.* **2** multicoloured. *~n* **3** *History* the costume of a jester.

motocross *n* the sport of motorcycle racing across rough ground.

motor *n* **1** the engine, esp. an internal-combustion engine, of a vehicle. **2** a machine that converts energy, esp. electrical energy, into mechanical energy. **3** *Chiefly Brit informal* a car. *~adj* **4** *Chiefly Brit* of or relating

THESAURUS

customarily, for the most part, generally, largely, mainly, most often, on the whole, particularly, predominantly, primarily, principally, usually

moth-eaten antiquated, decayed, decrepit, dilapidated, grungy (*slang, chiefly U.S.*), obsolete, outdated, outworn, ragged, scuzzy (*slang, chiefly U.S.*), seedy, shabby, stale, tattered, threadbare, worn-out

mother *n.* **1.** dam, ma (*informal*), mater, mom (*U.S. informal*), mum (*Brit. informal*), mummy (*Brit. informal*), old lady (*informal*), old woman (*informal*) *~adj.* **2.** connate, inborn, innate, native, natural *~vb.* **3.** bear, bring forth, drop, give birth to, produce **4.** care for, cherish, nurse, nurture, protect, raise, rear, tend

motherly affectionate, caring, comforting, fond, gentle, kind, loving, maternal, protective, sheltering, tender, warm

motion *n.* **1.** action, change, flow, locomotion, mobility, motility, move, movement, passage, passing, progress, travel **2.** gesticulation, gesture, sign, signal, wave **3.** proposal, proposition, recommendation, submission, suggestion **4. in motion** afoot, functioning, going, in progress, moving, on the go (*informal*), on the move (*informal*), operational, travelling, under way, working *~vb.* **5.** beckon, direct, gesticulate, gesture, nod, signal, wave

motionless at a standstill, at rest, calm, fixed, frozen, halted, immobile, inanimate, inert, lifeless, paralysed, standing, static, stationary, still, stock-still, transfixed, unmoved, unmoving

motivate actuate, arouse, bring, cause, draw, drive, get going, give incentive to, impel, induce, inspire, inspirit, instigate, lead, move, persuade, prod, prompt, provoke, set off, set on, stimulate, stir, trigger

motivation 1. ambition, desire, drive, hunger, inspiration, interest, wish **2.** impulse, incentive, incitement, inducement, inspiration, instigation, motive, persuasion, reason, spur, stimulus

motive 1. *n.* cause, design, ground(s), incentive, incitement, inducement, influence, inspiration, intention, mainspring, motivation, object, occasion, purpose, rationale, reason, spur, stimulus, thinking **2.** *adj.* activating, driving, impelling, motivating, moving, operative, prompting

motley 1. assorted, disparate, dissimilar, diversified, heterogeneous, mingled, miscellaneous, mixed, unlike,

to cars and other vehicles powered by petrol or diesel engines: *the motor industry.* **5** powered by or relating to a motor: *a new synthetic motor oil.* **6** *Physiol* producing or causing motion. *~vb* **7** to travel by car. **8** *Informal* to move fast. **motorized** *or* **-ised** *adj*

motorbicycle *n* **1** a motorcycle. **2** a moped.

motorbike *n Informal* a motorcycle.

motorboat *n* any boat powered by a motor.

motorcade *n* a procession of cars carrying an important person or people.

motorcar *n* a more formal word for **car.**

motorcycle *n* a two-wheeled vehicle driven by an engine. **motorcyclist** *n*

motorist *n* a driver of a car.

motorman *n, pl* **-men** the driver of an electric train.

motor scooter *n* a light motorcycle with small wheels and an enclosed engine.

motor vehicle *n* a road vehicle driven by an engine.

motorway *n Brit, Austral, & NZ* a dual carriageway for fast-moving traffic, with no stopping permitted and no crossroads.

Motown *n Trademark* music combining rhythm and blues and pop.

motte *n History* a mound on which a castle was built.

MOT test *n* (in Britain) a compulsory annual test of the roadworthiness of motor vehicles over 3 years old.

mottled *adj* coloured with streaks or blotches of different shades. **mottling** *n*

motto *n, pl* **-toes** *or* **-tos 1** a short saying expressing the guiding maxim or ideal of a family or organization, esp. when part of a coat of arms. **2** a verse or maxim contained in a paper cracker. **3** a quotation prefacing a book or chapter of a book.

mould[1] *or US* **mold** *n* **1** a shaped hollow container into which a liquid material is poured so that it can set in a particular shape: *pour the mixture into a buttered mould, cover, and steam for two hours.* **2** a shape, nature, or type: *an orthodox Communist in the Stalinist mould.* **3** a framework around which something is constructed or shaped: *the heated glass is shaped round a mould inside a kiln.* **4** something, esp. a food, made in or on a mould: *salmon mould. ~vb* **5** to make in a mould. **6** to shape or form: *a figure moulded out of clay.* **7** to influence or direct: *cultural factors moulding our everyday life.*

mould[2] *or US* **mold** *n* a coating or discoloration caused by various fungi that develop in a damp atmosphere on food, fabrics, and walls.

mould[3] *or US* **mold** *n* loose soil, esp. when rich in organic matter: *leaf mould.*

mouldboard *or US* **moldboard** *n* the curved blade of a plough, which turns over the furrow.

moulder *or US* **molder** *vb* to crumble or cause to crumble, as through decay: *John Brown's body lies mouldering in the grave.*

moulding *or US* **molding** *n* a shaped ornamental edging.

mouldy *or US* **moldy** *adj* **-dier, -diest 1** covered with mould. **2** stale or musty, esp. from age or lack of use. **3** *Slang* dull or boring.

moult *or US* **molt** *vb* **1** (of birds and animals) to shed feathers, hair, or skin so that they can be replaced by a new growth. *~n* **2** the periodic process of moulting.

mound *n* **1** a heap of earth, debris, etc. **2** any heap or pile. **3** a small natural hill.

mount[1] *vb* **1** to climb or ascend: *he mounted the stairs to his flat.* **2** to get up on a horse, a platform, etc. **3** Also: **mount up** to increase or accumulate: *costs do mount up; the tension mounted.* **4** to fix onto a backing, setting, or support: *sensors mounted on motorway bridges.* **5** to organize and stage a campaign, a play, etc.: *the Allies mounted a counter attack on the eastern front. ~n* **6** a backing, setting, or support onto which something is fixed: *a diamond set in a gold mount.* **7** a horse for riding: *none of his mounts at yesterday's race meeting finished better than third.*

mount[2] *n* a mountain or hill: used in literature and (when cap.) in proper names: *Mount Etna.*

mountain *n* **1** a very large, high, and steep hill: *the highest mountain in the Alps.* **2** a huge heap or mass: *a mountain of papers.* **3** a surplus of a commodity, esp. in the European Union: *a butter mountain. ~adj* **4** of, found on, or for use on a mountain or mountains: *a mountain village.*

mountain ash *n* a tree with clusters of small white flowers and bright red berries; rowan.

mountain bike *n* a type of bicycle with straight handlebars and heavy-duty tyres, originally designed for use over rough hilly ground.

mountain cat *n* any of various wild animals of the cat family, such as the bobcat, lynx, or puma.

mountaineer *n* **1** a person who climbs mountains. *~vb* **2** to climb mountains. **mountaineering** *n*

mountain goat *n* a wild goat inhabiting mountainous regions.

mountain lion *n* a puma.

mountainous *adj* **1** having many mountains: *a mountainous region.* **2** like a mountain or mountains, esp. in size: *mountainous waves.*

mountain sickness *n* nausea, headache, and

THESAURUS

varied **2.** chequered, multicoloured, particoloured, polychromatic, polychrome, polychromous, rainbow, variegated

mottled blotchy, brindled, chequered, dappled, flecked, freckled, marbled, piebald, pied, speckled, spotted, stippled, streaked, tabby, variegated

motto adage, byword, cry, dictum, formula, gnome, maxim, precept, proverb, rule, saw, saying, slogan, watchword

mould[1] *n.* **1.** cast, die, form, matrix, pattern, shape, stamp **2.** brand, build, calibre, character, configuration, construction, cut, design, fashion, form, format, frame, ilk, kidney, kind, line, make, nature, pattern, quality, shape, stamp, structure, style, type *~vb.* **3.** carve, cast, construct, create, fashion, forge, form, make, model, sculpt, shape, stamp, work **4.** affect, control, direct, form, influence, make, shape

mould[2] blight, fungus, mildew, mouldiness, mustiness

mouldy bad, blighted, decaying, fusty, mildewed, musty, rotten, rotting, spoiled, stale

mound 1. drift, heap, pile, stack **2.** bank, dune, embankment, hill, hillock, knoll, rise

mount *vb.* **1.** ascend, clamber up, climb, escalade, go up, make one's way up, scale **2.** bestride, climb onto, climb up on, get astride, get (up) on, jump on **3.** accumulate, build, escalate, grow, increase, intensify, multiply, pile up, swell **4.** emplace, fit, install, place, position, put in place, set up **5.** deliver, exhibit, get up (*informal*), launch, prepare, produce, put on stage, ready, set in motion, stage *~n.* **6.** backing, base, fixture, foil, frame, mounting, setting, stand, support **7.** horse, steed (*literary*)

mountain 1. alp, ben (*Scot.*), elevation, eminence, fell (*Brit.*), height, mount, Munro, peak **2.** abundance, heap, mass, mound, pile, stack, ton

mountainous 1. alpine, high, highland, rocky, soar-

shortness of breath caused by climbing to high altitudes.

mountebank *n* **1** (formerly) a person who sold quack medicines in public places. **2** a charlatan or fake.

mounted *adj* riding horses: *mounted police.*

Mountie *or* **Mounty** *n, pl* **Mounties** *Informal* a member of the Royal Canadian Mounted Police.

mounting *n* same as **mount**[1] (sense 6).

mourn *vb* to feel or express sadness for the death or loss of someone or something. **mourner** *n*

mournful *adj* **1** feeling or expressing grief and sadness: *he stood by, a mournful expression on his face.* **2** (of a sound) suggestive or reminiscent of grief or sadness: *the locomotive gave a mournful bellow.* **mournfully** *adv*

mourning *n* **1** sorrow or grief, esp. over a death. **2** the conventional symbols of grief for a death, such as the wearing of black. **3** the period of time during which a death is officially mourned. *~adj* **4** of or relating to mourning.

mouse *n, pl* **mice** **1** a small long-tailed rodent similar to but smaller than a rat. **2** a quiet, timid, or cowardly person. **3** *Computers* a hand-held device used to control cursor movements and computing functions without keying. *~vb* **mousing, moused** **4** *Rare* to stalk and catch mice.

mouser *n* a cat or other animal that is used to catch mice.

mousetrap *n* **1** a spring-loaded trap for killing mice. **2** *Brit informal* cheese of mediocre quality.

moussaka *n* a dish originating in the Balkan States, consisting of meat, aubergines, and tomatoes, topped with cheese sauce.

mousse *n* **1** a light creamy dessert made with eggs, cream, and fruit set with gelatine. **2** a similar dish made from fish or meat. **3** short for **styling mousse.**

moustache *or US* **mustache** *n* unshaved hair growing on the upper lip.

mousy *or* **mousey** *adj* **mousier, mousiest** **1** (of hair) dull light brown in colour. **2** shy or ineffectual. **mousiness** *n*

mouth *n, pl* **mouths** **1** the opening through which many animals take in food and issue sounds. **2** the visible part of the mouth; lips. **3** a person regarded as a consumer of food: *three mouths to feed.* **4** a particular manner of speaking: *a foul mouth.* **5** *Informal* boastful, rude, or excessive talk: *she is all mouth.* **6** the point where a river issues into a sea or lake. **7** an opening, such as that of a bottle, tunnel, or gun. **8** **down in the mouth** in low spirits. *~vb* **9** to form words with movements of the lips but without speaking. **10** to speak or say something insincerely, esp. in public: *ministers mouthing platitudes.*

mouthful *n, pl* **-fuls** **1** the amount of food or drink put into the mouth at any one time when eating or drinking. **2** a long word, phrase, or name that is difficult to say. **3** *Brit informal* an abusive response: *I asked him to move and he just gave me a mouthful.*

mouth organ *n* same as **harmonica.**

mouthpiece *n* **1** the part of a wind instrument into which the player blows. **2** the part of a telephone receiver into which a person speaks. **3** a person or publication expressing the views of an organization.

mouthwash *n* a medicated solution for gargling and cleansing the mouth.

mouthwatering *adj* (of food) making one want to eat it, because it looks or smells delicious.

movable *or* **moveable** *adj* **1** able to be moved; not fixed. **2** (of a festival, esp. Easter) varying in date from year to year. *~n* **3** **movables** movable articles, esp. furniture.

move *vb* **moving, moved** **1** to go or take from one place to another; change in position: *I moved your books off the table.* **2** to start to live or work in a different place: *I moved to Brighton from Bristol last year.* **3** to be or cause to be in motion: *the trees were moving in the wind; the car moved slowly down the road.* **4** to act or begin to act: *the government plans to move to reduce crime.* **5** to cause or prompt to do something: *public opinion moved the President to act.* **6** to change the time when something is scheduled to happen: *can I move the appointment to Friday afternoon, please?* **7** to arouse affection, pity, or compassion in; touch: *her story moved me to tears.* **8** to change, progress, or develop in a specified way: *the conversation moved to more personal matters.* **9** to suggest a proposal formally, as in a debate: *to move a motion.* **10** to spend most of one's time with a specified social group: *they both move in theatrical, arty circles.* **11** (in board games) to change the position of a piece. **12** (of machines) to work or operate. **13** **a** (of the bowels) to excrete waste. **b** to cause the bowels to excrete waste. **14** (of merchandise) to be disposed of by being bought. **15** to travel quickly: *this car can really move.* **16** **move heaven and earth** do everything possible to achieve a result. *~n* **17** the act of moving; movement. **18** one of a sequence of actions, usually part of a plan: *the first real move towards disarmament.* **19** the act of moving one's home or place of business. **20** (in board games) **a** a player's turn to move his piece. **b** a manoeuvre of a piece. **21** **get a move on** *Informal* to hurry up. **22** **make a move** *Informal* **a** to prepare or begin to leave a place to go somewhere else: *we'd better make a move if we want to be home before dark.* **b** to do something which will

THESAURUS

ing, steep, towering, upland **2.** daunting, enormous, gigantic, great, huge, hulking, immense, mammoth, mighty, monumental, ponderous, prodigious

mourn bemoan, bewail, deplore, grieve, keen, lament, miss, rue, sorrow, wail, wear black, weep

mournful brokenhearted, cheerless, desolate, disconsolate, dismal, downcast, funereal, gloomy, grief-stricken, grieving, heartbroken, heavy, heavy-hearted, joyless, lugubrious, melancholy, miserable, plaintive, rueful, sad, sombre, tragic, unhappy, woeful

mourning **1.** bereavement, grief, grieving, keening, lamentation, weeping, woe **2.** black, sackcloth and ashes, weeds, widow's weeds

mouth *n.* **1.** chops (*slang*), gob (*slang, esp. Brit.*), jaws, lips, maw, trap (*slang*), yap (*slang*) **2.** *informal* backchat (*informal*), boasting, braggadocio, bragging, cheek (*informal*), empty talk, gas (*informal*), hot air (*slang*), idle talk, impudence, insolence, lip (*slang*), rudeness, sauce (*informal*) **3.** aperture, cavity, crevice, door, entrance, gateway, inlet, lips, opening, orifice, rim **4.** **down in the mouth** blue, crestfallen, dejected, depressed, disheartened, dispirited, down, downcast, down in the dumps (*informal*), in low spirits, melancholy, miserable, sad, unhappy

mouthful bit, bite, drop, forkful, little, morsel, sample, sip, spoonful, sup, swallow, taste

mouthpiece agent, delegate, journal, organ, periodical, publication, representative, spokesman, spokeswoman

movable detachable, mobile, not fixed, portable, transferable, transportable

move *vb.* **1.** advance, budge, carry, change, change position, drift, go, march, proceed, progress, shift, stir, switch, transfer, transport, transpose, walk **2.** change

produce a response: *neither of us wanted to make the first move.* **23 on the move** travelling from place to place.

move in *vb* **1** Also: **move into** to start to live in a different house or flat. **2** to start to live in the same house or flat as: *he moved in with his girlfriend.* **3** to attack a person or place, or try to gain influence or control over a person or activity: *the police moved in to break up the demonstration.*

movement *n* **1** the act, process, or an instance of moving. **2** the manner of moving: *their movement is jerky.* **3 a** a group of people with a common ideology. **b** the organized action and campaigning of such a group: *a successful movement to abolish child labour.* **4** a trend or tendency: *a movement towards shorter working hours.* **5** *Finance* a change in the price or value of shares, a currency, etc.: *adverse currency movements.* **6** *Music* a principal self-contained section of a large-scale work, such as a symphony. **7 movements** a person's location and activities during a specific time: *police were trying to piece together the recent movements of the two men.* **8 a** the evacuation of the bowels. **b** the matter evacuated. **9** the mechanism which drives and regulates a watch or clock.

move on *vb* **1** to leave one place in order to go elsewhere: *we spent three days in Perth before moving on towards Inverness.* **2** to order (someone) to leave and go elsewhere: *we were moved on by the police.* **3** to finish one thing and turn one's attention to something else: *can we move on to the next question?*

move over *vb* **1** to change one's position in order to make room for someone else: *if you moved over there'd be room for us both on the couch.* **2** to leave one's job so that someone else can have it: *she decided to move over to let someone younger onto the board.*

mover *n* **1** a person or animal that moves in a particular way: *a slow mover.* **2** the person who first puts forward a proposal. **3** *US & Canad* a removal firm or a person who works for one.

movie *n* **1** *Chiefly US informal* a cinema film. **2 the movies** the cinema: *I want to go to the movies tonight.*

moving *adj* **1** arousing or touching the emotions: *a moving account of her son's death.* **2** changing or capable of changing position: *a moving target.* **movingly** *adv*

moving staircase *or* **stairway** *n* an escalator.

mow *vb* **mowing, mowed, mowed** *or* **mown 1** to cut down grass or crops: *a tractor chugged along, mowing hay.* **2** to cut the growing vegetation of a field or lawn: *to mow a meadow.* **mower** *n*

mow down *vb* to kill in large numbers, esp. by gunfire.

mown *vb* the past participle of **mow.**

mozzarella (mot-sa-rel-la) *n* a moist white curd cheese originally made in Italy from buffalo milk.

MP 1 Member of Parliament. **2** Military Police. **3** Mounted Police.

mpg miles per gallon.

mph miles per hour.

MPhil Master of Philosophy.

Mr *n, pl* **Messrs** a title used before a man's name or before some office that he holds: *Mr Pickwick; Mr President.*

Mrs *n, pl* **Mrs** *or* **Mesdames** a title used before the name of a married woman.

ms millisecond(s).

Ms (**mizz**) *n* a title used before the name of a woman to avoid indicating whether she is married or not.

MS 1 Mississippi. **2** multiple sclerosis.

MS. *or* **ms.** *pl* **MSS** *or* **mss** manuscript.

MSc Master of Science.

MSF Manufacturing, Science, and Finance (Union).

MSG monosodium glutamate.

MST Mountain Standard Time.

mt megaton.

Mt Mount: *Mt Everest.*

MT Montana.

mt. megaton.

MTech (in the U.S. and Canada) Master of Technology.

much *adj* **more, most 1** a large amount or degree of: *there isn't much wine left.* ~*n* **2** a large amount or degree. **3 a bit much** *Informal* rather excessive. **4 make much of a** to make sense of: *he couldn't make much of her letter.* **b** to give importance to: *the press made much of the story.* **5 not much of** not to any appreciable degree or extent: *he's not much of a cook.* **6 not up to much** *Informal* of a low standard: *this beer is not up to much.* ~*adv* **7** considerably: *I'm much better now.* **8** practically or nearly: *it's much the same.* **9** often or a great deal: *that doesn't happen much these days.* **10 (as) much as** even though; although: *much as I'd like to, I can't come.* ~See also **more, most.**

muchness *n* **much of a muchness** *Brit* very similar.

mucilage (**mew-sill-ij**) *n* **1** a sticky substance used as an adhesive, such as gum or glue. **2** a glutinous substance secreted by certain plants. **mucilaginous** *adj*

muck *n* **1** dirt or filth. **2** farmyard dung or decaying vegetable matter. **3** *Slang, chiefly Brit* something of

THESAURUS

residence, flit (*Scot. & northern English dialect*), go away, leave, migrate, move house, quit, relocate, remove **3.** activate, drive, impel, motivate, operate, prod, propel, push, set going, shift, shove, start, turn **4.** actuate, affect, agitate, cause, excite, give rise to, impel, impress, incite, induce, influence, inspire, instigate, lead, make an impression on, motivate, persuade, prompt, rouse, stimulate, touch, urge **5.** advocate, propose, put forward, recommend, suggest, urge ~*n.* **6.** act, action, deed, manoeuvre, measure, motion, movement, ploy, shift, step, stratagem, stroke, turn **7.** change of address, flit (*Scot. & northern English dialect*), flitting (*Scot. & northern English dialect*), migration, relocation, removal, shift, transfer **8. get a move on** get cracking (*informal*), get going, hurry (up), make haste, shake a leg (*informal*), speed up, step on it (*informal*), stir oneself **9. on the move** in transit, journeying, moving, on the road (*informal*), on the run, on the wing, travelling, under way, voyaging

movement 1. act, action, activity, advance, agitation, change, development, displacement, exercise, flow, gesture, manoeuvre, motion, move, moving, operation, progress, progression, shift, steps, stir, stirring, transfer **2.** camp, campaign, crusade, drive, faction, front, group, grouping, organization, party **3.** current, drift, flow, swing, tendency, trend **4.** *Music* division, part, passage, section **5.** action, innards (*informal*), machinery, mechanism, workings, works

moving 1. affecting, arousing, emotional, emotive, exciting, impelling, impressive, inspiring, pathetic, persuasive, poignant, stirring, touching **2.** mobile, motile, movable, portable, running, unfixed

mow crop, cut, scythe, shear, trim

mow down blow away (*slang, chiefly U.S.*), butcher, cut down, cut to pieces, massacre, shoot down, slaughter

much 1. *adj.* abundant, a lot of, ample, considerable, copious, great, plenteous, plenty of, sizeable, substantial **2.** *n.* a good deal, a great deal, a lot, an appreciable amount, heaps (*informal*), loads (*informal*), lots (*in-*

poor quality; rubbish: *I don't want to eat this muck.* **4 make a muck of** *Slang, chiefly Brit* to ruin or spoil. ~*vb* **5** to spread manure upon. ~See **also muck about, muck in,** etc.

muck about *or* **around** *vb Brit slang* **1** to waste time by misbehaving or being silly. **2 muck about with** to interfere with, annoy, or waste the time of.

muck in *vb Brit slang* to share duties or work with other people.

muck out *vb* to clean (a barn, stable, etc.).

muckraking *n* seeking out and exposing scandal relating to well-known people. **muckraker** *n*

mucksweat *n Brit informal* profuse sweat.

muck up *vb Informal* to ruin, spoil, or do very badly: *I mucked up my driving test.*

mucky *adj* **1** dirty or muddy: *don't come in here with your mucky boots on!* **2** sexually explicit; obscene: *a mucky book.*

mucous membrane *n* a mucus-secreting tissue that lines body cavities or passages.

mucus (**mew**-kuss) *n* the slimy protective secretion of the mucous membranes. **mucosity** *n* **mucous** *adj*

mud *n* **1** soft wet earth, as found on the ground after rain or at the bottom of ponds. **2 (someone's) name is mud** *Informal* (someone) is disgraced. **3 throw mud at** *Informal* slander or vilify. ~*adj* **4** made from mud or dried mud: *a mud hut.*

mud bath *n* **1** a medicinal bath in heated mud. **2** a dirty or muddy place, occasion, or state: *heavy rain turned the pitch into a mud bath.*

muddle *n* **1** a state of untidiness or confusion: *the files are in a terrible muddle.* **2** a state of mental confusion or uncertainty: *the government are in a muddle over the economy.* ~*vb* **-dling, -dled 3** Also: **muddle up** to mix up or confuse (objects or items): *you've got your books all muddled up with mine.* **4** to make (someone) confused: *don't muddle her with too many suggestions.* **muddled** *adj*

muddleheaded *adj* mentally confused or vague.

muddle through *vb Chiefly Brit* to succeed in spite of lack of organization.

muddy *adj* **-dier, -diest 1** covered or filled with mud. **2** not clear or bright: *muddy colours.* **3** cloudy: *a muddy liquid.* **4** (esp. of thoughts) confused or vague. ~*vb* **-dies, -dying, -died 5** to make muddy. **6** to make a situation or issue less clear: *the allegations of sexual misconduct only serve to muddy the issue.* **muddily** *adv*

mud flat *n* an area of low muddy land that is covered at high tide but not at low tide.

mud flow *n* the rapid downhill movement of a mass of mud, typically in the shape of a tongue.

mudguard *n* a curved part of a bicycle or other vehicle attached above the wheels to reduce the amount of water or mud thrown up by them.

mudpack *n* a cosmetic paste applied to the face to improve the complexion.

mudpie *n* a mass of mud moulded into a pielike shape by a child.

mudslinging *n* the making of malicious personal attacks on an opponent, esp. in politics. **mudslinger** *n*

muesli (**mewz**-lee) *n* a mixture of rolled oats, nuts, and dried fruit, usually eaten with milk.

muezzin (moo-**ezz**-in) *n Islam* the official of a mosque who calls the faithful to prayer from the minaret.

muff[1] *n* a tube of fur or cloth into which the hands are placed for warmth.

muff[2] *vb* **1** to do (something) badly: *I muffed my chance to make a good impression.* **2** to bungle (a shot or catch).

muffin *n* **1** *Brit* a thick round baked yeast roll, usually toasted and served with butter. **2** *Chiefly US & Canad* a small cup-shaped sweet bread roll, usually eaten hot with butter.

muffle *vb* **-fling, -fled 1** to deaden (a sound or noise), esp. by wrapping the source of it in something: *the sound was muffled by the double glazing.* **2** to wrap up in a scarf or coat for warmth. **3** to censor or restrict: *an attempt to muffle criticism.* **muffled** *adj*

muffler *n* **1** a thick scarf worn for warmth. **2** *US & Canad* a device to deaden sound, esp. one on a car exhaust; silencer.

mufti *n* civilian clothes worn by a person who normally wears a military uniform.

mug[1] *n* **1** a large drinking cup with a handle. **2** the quantity held by a mug or its contents: *a mug of coffee.*

mug[2] *n* **1** *Slang* a person's face or mouth: *keep your ugly mug out of this.* **2** *Slang* a gullible person, esp.

THESAURUS

formal), plenty **3.** *adv.* a great deal, a lot, considerably, decidedly, exceedingly, frequently, greatly, indeed, often, regularly

muck 1. crud (*slang*), dirt, filth, gunge (*informal*), gunk (*informal*), mire, mud, ooze, scum, sewage, slime, sludge **2.** crap (*taboo slang*), dung, manure, ordure, shit (*taboo*) **3. make a muck of** *slang* blow (*slang*), botch, bungle, cock up (*Brit. slang*), fuck up (*offensive taboo slang*), make a mess *or* hash of, mar, mess up, muff, ruin, screw up (*informal*), spoil

muck up blow (*slang*), bodge (*informal*), botch, bungle, cock up (*Brit. slang*), fuck up (*offensive taboo slang*), make a hash of, make a mess of, make a muck of (*slang*), mar, mess up, muff, ruin, screw up (*informal*), spoil

mud clay, dirt, mire, ooze, silt, slime, sludge

muddle *n.* **1.** chaos, clutter, confusion, daze, disarray, disorder, disorganization, fankle (*Scot.*), hodgepodge (*U.S.*), hotchpotch, jumble, mess, mix-up, perplexity, pig's breakfast (*informal*), plight, predicament, ravel, tangle ~*vb.* **2.** confuse, disarrange, disorder, disorganize, jumble, make a mess of, mess, mix up, ravel, scramble, spoil, tangle **3.** befuddle, bewilder, confound, confuse, daze, disorient, perplex, stupefy

muddled 1. chaotic, confused, disarrayed, disordered, disorganized, higgledy-piggledy (*informal*), jumbled, messy, mixed-up, scrambled, tangled **2.** at sea, befuddled, bewildered, confused, dazed, disoriented, perplexed, stupefied, vague **3.** confused, incoherent, loose, muddleheaded, unclear, woolly

muddy *adj.* **1.** bespattered, boggy, clarty (*Scot., & northern English dialect*), dirty, grimy, marshy, miry, mucky, mud-caked, quaggy, soiled, swampy **2.** blurred, dingy, dull, flat, lustreless, smoky, unclear, washed-out **3.** cloudy, dirty, foul, impure, opaque, turbid **4.** confused, fuzzy, hazy, indistinct, muddled, unclear, vague, woolly ~*vb.* **5.** begrime, bespatter, cloud, dirty, smear, smirch, soil

muffle 1. deaden, dull, gag, hush, muzzle, quieten, silence, soften, stifle, suppress **2.** cloak, conceal, cover, disguise, envelop, hood, mask, shroud, swaddle, swathe, wrap up

muffled dim, dull, faint, indistinct, muted, stifled, strangled, subdued, suppressed

mug[1] beaker, cup, flagon, jug, pot, tankard, toby jug

mug[2] charlie (*Brit. informal*), chump (*informal*) (*archaic*), easy *or* soft touch (*slang*), fool, innocent, mark (*slang*), muggins (*Brit. slang*), simpleton, sucker (*slang*)

one who is swindled easily. **3 a mug's game** a worthless activity.

mug[3] *vb* **mugging, mugged** to attack someone in order to rob them. **mugger** *n* **mugging** *n*

muggins *n Brit slang* **a** a stupid or gullible person. **b** a title used humorously to refer to oneself.

muggy *adj* **-gier, -giest** (of weather or air) unpleasantly warm and humid. **mugginess** *n*

mug shot *n Informal* a photograph of a person's face, esp. one resembling a police-file picture.

mug up *vb Brit slang* to study a subject hard, esp. for an exam.

mujaheddin *or* **mujahedeen** (moo-ja-hed-**deen**) *pl n* fundamentalist Muslim guerrillas.

mukluk *n* a soft boot, usually of sealskin, worn by Inuits.

mulatto (mew-**lat**-toe) *n, pl* **-tos** *or* **-toes** a person with one Black and one White parent.

mulberry *n, pl* **-ries 1** a tree with edible blackberry-like fruit, the leaves of which are used to feed silkworms. **2** the fruit of any of these trees. *~adj* **3** dark purple.

mulch *n* **1** a mixture of half-rotten vegetable matter and peat used to protect the roots of plants or enrich the soil. *~vb* **2** to cover soil with mulch.

mule[1] *n* **1** the sterile offspring of a male donkey and a female horse. **2** a machine that spins cotton into yarn.

mule[2] *n* a backless shoe or slipper.

muleteer *n* a person who drives mules.

mulish *adj* stubborn; obstinate.

mull *n Scot* a promontory or headland: *the Mull of Galloway.*

mullah *n* (formerly) a Muslim scholar, teacher, or religious leader.

mulled *adj* (of wine or ale) flavoured with sugar and spices and served hot.

mullet *n, pl* **mullets** *or* **mullet** any of various marine food fishes such as the red mullet.

mulligatawny *n* a curry-flavoured soup of Anglo-Indian origin.

mullion *n* a slender vertical bar between the casements or panes of a window. **mullioned** *adj*

mull over *vb* to study or ponder: *he mulled over the arrangements.*

multi- *combining form* **1** many or much: *multimillion.* **2** more than one: *multistorey.*

multicoloured *adj* having many colours.

multicultural *adj* of or for the cultures of several different races.

multifarious (mull-tee-**fare**-ee-uss) *adj* many and varied: *multifarious religious movements and political divisions sprang up around this time.*

multiflora rose *n* a climbing rose with clusters of small fragrant flowers.

multiform *adj* having many shapes or forms.

multilateral *adj* of or involving more than two nations or parties: *multilateral trade negotiations.*

multilingual *adj* **1** able to speak more than two languages. **2** written or expressed in more than two languages: *a multilingual leaflet.*

multimedia *pl n* **1** the combined use of media such as television and slides. **2** *Computers* of or relating to systems that can manipulate data in a variety of forms, such as sound, graphics, or text.

multimillionaire *n* a person who has money or property worth several million pounds, dollars, etc.

multinational *adj* **1** (of a large business company) operating in several countries. **2** involving people from several countries: *a multinational peacekeeping force.* *~n* **3** a large company operating in several countries.

multiparous (mull-**tip**-a-russ) *adj* producing many offspring at one birth.

multiple *adj* **1** having or involving more than one part, individual, or element. *~n* **2** a number or polynomial which can be divided by another specified one an exact number of times: *6 is a multiple of 2.* **multiply** *adv*

multiple-choice *adj* (of a test or question) giving a number of possible answers out of which the correct one must be chosen.

multiple sclerosis *n* a chronic progressive disease of the central nervous system, resulting in speech and visual disorders, tremor, muscular incoordination, and partial paralysis.

multiplex *n, pl* **-plexes 1** a purpose-built complex containing several cinemas and usually restaurants and bars. *~adj* **2** having many elements; complex.

multiplicand *n* a number to be multiplied by another number (the **multiplier**).

multiplication *n* **1** a mathematical operation, equivalent to adding a number to itself a specified number of times. For instance, 4 multiplied by 3 equals 12 (i.e. 4+4+4). **2** the act of multiplying or state of being multiplied.

multiplication sign *n* the symbol ×, placed between numbers to be multiplied.

multiplication table *n* a table giving the results of multiplying two numbers together.

multiplicity *n, pl* **-ties 1** a large number or great variety. **2** the state of being multiple.

multiplier *n* a number by which another number (the **multiplicand**) is multiplied.

multiply *vb* **-plies, -plying, -plied 1** to increase or cause to increase in number, quantity, or degree. **2** to combine numbers or quantities by multiplication. **3** to increase in number by reproduction.

multipurpose *adj* having many uses: *a giant multipurpose enterprise.*

multiracial *adj* consisting of or involving people of many races: *a multiracial society.* **multiracialism** *n*

multistage *adj* (of a rocket or missile) having several stages, each of which can be jettisoned after it has burnt out.

multistorey *adj* (of a building) having many storeys.

multitrack *adj* (in sound recording) using tape containing two or more tracks.

THESAURUS

mug[3] assail, assault, attack, beat up, do over (*Brit., Austral., & N.Z. slang*), duff up (*Brit. slang*), hold up, lay into (*informal*), put the boot in (*slang*), rob, set about *or* upon, steam (*informal*)

muggy clammy, close, damp, humid, moist, oppressive, sticky, stuffy, sultry

mug up bone up on (*informal*), burn the midnight oil (*informal*), cram (*informal*), get up (*informal*), study, swot (*Brit. informal*)

mull over consider, contemplate, deliberate, examine, meditate, muse on, ponder, reflect on, review, ruminate, study, think about, think over, turn over in one's mind, weigh

multifarious different, diverse, diversified, legion, manifold, many, miscellaneous, multiform, multiple, multitudinous, numerous, sundry, varied, variegated

multiple collective, manifold, many, multitudinous, numerous, several, sundry, various

multiply accumulate, augment, breed, build up, expand, extend, increase, proliferate, propagate, reproduce, spread

multitude *n* **1** a large number of people or things: *a multitude of different pressure groups.* **2 the multitude** the common people. **multitudinous** *adj*

multi-user *adj* (of a computer) capable of being used by several people at once.

mum[1] *n Informal, chiefly Brit* same as **mother.**

mum[2] *adj* **1 keep mum** remain silent. **2 mum's the word** keep quiet (about something).

mumble *vb* **-bling, -bled 1** to speak or say something indistinctly, with the mouth partly closed: *I could hear him mumbling under his breath.* ~*n* **2** an indistinct or low utterance or sound.

mumbo jumbo *n* **1** meaningless language; nonsense or gibberish. **2** foolish religious ritual or incantation.

mummer *n* one of a group of masked performers in a folk play or mime.

mummery *n, pl* **-meries 1** a performance by mummers. **2** hypocritical or ostentatious ceremony.

mummified *adj* (of a body) preserved as a mummy. **mummification** *n*

mummy[1] *n, pl* **-mies** an embalmed body as prepared for burial in ancient Egypt.

mummy[2] *n, pl* **-mies** *Chiefly Brit* a child's word for **mother.**

mumps *n* an infectious viral disease in which the glands below the ear become swollen and painful.

munch *vb* to chew noisily and steadily.

mundane *adj* **1** everyday, ordinary, and therefore not very interesting. **2** relating to the world or worldly matters.

mung bean *n* an E Asian bean plant grown for its edible seeds which are used as a source of bean sprouts.

municipal *adj* of or relating to a town or city or its local government.

municipality *n, pl* **-ties 1** a city, town, or district enjoying local self-government. **2** the governing body of such a unit.

munificent (mew-**niff**-fiss-sent) *adj* very generous. **munificence** *n*

muniments (**mew**-nim-ments) *pl n Law* the title deeds and other documentary evidence relating to the title to land.

munitions (mew-**nish**-unz) *pl n* military equipment and stores, esp. ammunition.

muon (**mew**-on) *n* a positive or negative elementary particle with a mass 207 times that of an electron.

mural (**myoor**-al) *n* **1** a large painting on a wall. ~*adj* **2** of or relating to a wall. **muralist** *n*

murder *n* **1** the unlawful intentional killing of one human being by another. **2** *Informal* something dangerous, difficult, or unpleasant: *shopping on Christmas Eve is murder.* **3 cry blue murder** *Informal* to make an outcry. **4 get away with murder** *Informal* to do as one pleases without ever being punished. ~*vb* **5** to kill someone intentionally and unlawfully. **6** *Informal* to ruin a piece of music or drama by performing it very badly: *he absolutely murdered that song.* **7** *Informal* to beat decisively: *they'll murder them in the home tie.* **murderer** *n* **murderess** *fem n* **murderous** *adj*

murk *n* thick gloomy darkness.

murky *adj* **murkier, murkiest 1** gloomy or dark. **2** cloudy or hard to see through: *a murky stagnant pond.* **3** obscure and suspicious; shady: *murky goings-on; his murky past.* **murkily** *adv* **murkiness** *n*

murmur *vb* **1** to speak or say in a quiet indistinct way. **2** to complain. ~*n* **3** a continuous low indistinct sound, such as that of a distant conversation. **4** an indistinct utterance: *a murmur of protest.* **5** a complaint or grumble: *he left without a murmur.* **6** *Med* any abnormal soft blowing sound heard usually over the chest: *a heart murmur.* **murmuring** *n, adj* **murmurous** *adj*

Murphy's Law *n* same as **Sod's Law.**

murrain (**murr**-rin) *n* any plaguelike disease in cattle.

mus. 1 museum. **2** music. **3** musical.

MusB *or* **MusBac** Bachelor of Music.

muscle *n* **1** a tissue in the body composed of bundles of elongated cells which produce movement in an organ or part by contracting or relaxing. **2** an organ composed of muscle tissue: *the heart is essentially just another muscle.* **3** strength or force: *we do not have the political muscle to force through these reforms.*

THESAURUS

multitude 1. army, assemblage, assembly, collection, concourse, congregation, crowd, great number, horde, host, legion, lot, lots (*informal*), mass, mob, myriad, sea, swarm, throng **2. the multitude** common people, herd, hoi polloi, mob, populace, proletariat, public, rabble

munch champ, chew, chomp, crunch, masticate, scrunch

mundane 1. banal, commonplace, day-to-day, everyday, humdrum, ordinary, prosaic, quotidian (*literary*), routine, workaday **2.** earthly, fleshly, human, material, mortal, sublunary, temporal, terrestrial, worldly

municipal borough, city, civic, community, public, town, urban

municipality borough, burgh (*Scot.*), city, district, town, township, urban community

munificence beneficence, benevolence, big-heartedness, bounteousness, bounty, generosity, generousness, largess *or* largesse, liberality, magnanimousness, open-handedness, philanthropy

munificent beneficent, benevolent, big-hearted, bounteous, bountiful, free-handed, generous, lavish, liberal, magnanimous, open-handed, philanthropical, princely, rich, unstinting

murder *n.* **1.** assassination, bloodshed, butchery, carnage, homicide, killing, manslaughter, massacre, slaying **2.** *informal* agony, an ordeal, a trial, danger, difficulty, hell (*informal*), misery, trouble ~*vb.* **3.** assassinate, blow away (*slang, chiefly U.S.*), bump off (*slang*), butcher, destroy, dispatch, do in (*informal*), do to death, eliminate (*slang*), hit (*slang*), kill, massacre, rub out (*U.S. slang*), slaughter, slay, take out (*slang*), take the life of, waste (*informal*) **4.** abuse, butcher, destroy, mangle, mar, misuse, ruin, spoil **5.** *informal* beat decisively, blow out of the water (*slang*), cream (*slang, chiefly U.S.*), defeat utterly, drub, hammer (*informal*), lick (*informal*), make mincemeat of (*informal*), slaughter, tank (*slang*), thrash, wipe the floor with (*informal*)

murderer assassin, butcher, cutthroat, hit man (*slang*), homicide, killer, slaughterer, slayer

murderous 1. barbarous, bloodthirsty, bloody, brutal, cruel, deadly, death-dealing, destructive, devastating, fatal, fell (*archaic*), ferocious, internecine, lethal, sanguinary, savage, slaughterous, withering **2.** *informal* arduous, dangerous, difficult, exhausting, harrowing, hellish (*informal*), killing (*informal*), sapping, strenuous, unpleasant

murky cheerless, cloudy, dark, dim, dismal, dreary, dull, dusky, foggy, gloomy, grey, impenetrable, misty, nebulous, obscure, overcast

murmur *vb.* **1.** babble, buzz, drone, hum, mumble, mutter, purr, rumble, speak in an undertone, whisper **2.** beef (*slang*), carp, cavil, complain, gripe (*informal*), grouse, grumble, moan (*informal*), whinge ~*n.* **3.** babble, buzzing, drone, humming, mumble, muttering,

~*vb* **-cling, -cled 4 muscle in** to force one's way into a situation; intrude: *I don't like the way he's trying to muscle in here.*

muscle-bound *adj* having overdeveloped and inelastic muscles.

muscleman *n, pl* **-men 1** a man with highly developed muscles. **2** a henchman employed to intimidate or use violence upon victims.

Muscovite *adj* **1** of Moscow, a city in Russia. ~*n* **2** a person from Moscow.

muscular *adj* **1** having well-developed muscles; brawny. **2** of or consisting of muscle: *great muscular effort is needed.* **3** forceful or powerful: *a muscular account of Schumann's Fourth Symphony.* **muscularity** *n*

muscular dystrophy *n* a hereditary disease in which the muscles gradually weaken and waste away.

musculature *n* the arrangement of muscles in an organ, part, or organism.

MusD *or* **MusDoc** Doctor of Music.

muse[1] *vb* **musing, mused** to think deeply and at length about: *she mused unhappily on how right her sister had been.*

muse[2] *n* **the muse** a force or person, esp. a woman, that inspires a creative artist.

Muses *pl n Greek myth* the nine sister goddesses, each of whom was the protector of a different art or science.

museum *n* a building where objects of historical, artistic, or scientific interest are exhibited and preserved.

museum piece *n Informal* a very old or old-fashioned object or building.

mush[1] *n* **1** a soft pulpy mass. **2** *Informal* cloying sentimentality.

mush[2] *Canad* ~*interj* **1** an order to dogs in a sled team to start up or go faster. ~*vb* **2** to travel by or drive a dogsled.

mushroom *n* **1** an edible fungus consisting of a cap at the end of a stem. **2** something resembling a mushroom in shape or rapid growth. ~*vb* **3** to grow rapidly: *consumer debt mushroomed rapidly in 1989.*

mushroom cloud *n* the large mushroom-shaped cloud produced by a nuclear explosion.

mushy *adj* **mushier, mushiest 1** soft and pulpy. **2** *Informal* excessively sentimental.

music *n* **1** an art form consisting of sequences of sounds organized melodically, harmonically, and rhythmically. **2** such sounds, esp. when produced by singing or musical instruments. **3** any written or printed representation of musical sounds: *I can't read music.* **4** any sequence of sounds perceived as pleasing or harmonious. **5 face the music** *Informal* to confront the consequences of one's actions. **6 music to one's ears** something, such as a piece of news, that one is pleased to hear.

musical *adj* **1** of or used in music. **2** talented in or fond of music. **3** pleasant-sounding; harmonious: *musical laughter.* **4** involving or set to music: *a musical biography of Judy Garland.* ~*n* **5** a play or film that has dialogue interspersed with songs and dances. **musicality** *n* **musically** *adv*

musical box *n* a box containing a mechanical instrument that plays tunes when the box is opened.

musical chairs *n* **1** a game in which the players run round a row of chairs while music plays. There is one more player than there are chairs, and when the music stops the player who cannot find a chair to sit on is out. **2** any situation involving a number of people in a series of interrelated changes: *the dismissal of the Chancellor started a game of musical chairs in the Cabinet.*

music centre *n* a single hi-fi unit containing a turntable, radio, and cassette player.

music hall *n Chiefly Brit* (formerly) **1** a variety entertainment consisting of songs and comic turns. **2** a theatre at which such entertainments were staged.

musician *n* a person who plays or composes music, esp. as a profession.

musicianship *n* the technical and interpretive skills involved in singing or playing music: *the piano part is simple but performed with great musicianship.*

musicology *n* the scholarly study of music. **musicologist** *n*

musk *n* **1** a strong-smelling glandular secretion of the male musk deer, used in perfumery. **2** any similar substance produced by animals or plants, or manufactured synthetically.

musk deer *n* a small central Asian mountain deer.

muskeg *n Chiefly Canad* an area of undrained boggy land.

musket *n* a long-barrelled muzzle-loading gun fired from the shoulder, a forerunner of the rifle. **musketeer** *n*

muskmelon *n* any of several varieties of melon, such as the cantaloupe and honeydew.

musk ox *n* a large ox, which has a dark shaggy coat, downward-curving horns, and emits a musky smell.

muskrat *n, pl* **-rats** *or* **-rat 1** a North American beaver-like amphibious rodent. **2** the brown fur of this animal.

musk rose *n* a Mediterranean rose, cultivated for its white musk-scented flowers.

musky *adj* **muskier, muskiest** having a heady sweet smell. **muskiness** *n*

Muslim *or* **Moslem** *n, pl* **-lims** *or* **-lim 1** a follower of the religion of Islam. ~*adj* **2** of or relating to Islam.

muslin *n* a very fine plain-weave cotton fabric.

musquash *n* muskrat fur.

muss *vb US & Canad informal* to make untidy; rumple: *watch you don't muss up my hair!*

mussel *n* an edible shellfish, with a dark slightly elongated hinged shell, which lives attached to rocks.

must[1] *vb* used as an auxiliary to express or indicate: **1** the need or necessity to do something: *I must go to the shops.* **2** obligation or requirement: *you must not smoke in here.* **3** the probable correctness of a statement: *he must be finished by now.* **4** inevitability: *all good things must come to an end.* **5** determination: *I must try and finish this.* **6** conviction or certainty on

THESAURUS

purr, rumble, susurrus (*literary*), undertone, whisper, whispering **4.** beef (*slang*), complaint, gripe (*informal*), grouse, grumble, moan (*informal*), whinge

muscle *n.* **1.** muscle tissue, sinew, tendon, thew **2.** brawn, clout (*informal*), force, forcefulness, might, potency, power, stamina, strength, sturdiness, weight ~*vb.* **3. muscle in** *informal* butt in, elbow one's way in, force one's way in, impose oneself

muscular athletic, beefy (*informal*), brawny, husky (*informal*), lusty, powerful, powerfully built, robust, sinewy, stalwart, strapping, strong, sturdy, thickset, vigorous, well-knit

muse be in a brown study, be lost in thought, brood, cogitate, consider, contemplate, deliberate, dream, meditate, mull over, ponder, reflect, ruminate, speculate, think, think over, weigh

mushroom boom, burgeon, expand, flourish, grow rapidly, increase, luxuriate, proliferate, shoot up, spread, spring up, sprout

the part of the speaker: *you must be kidding!* ~*n* **7** an essential or necessary thing: *strong boots are a must for hill walking.*

must[2] *n* the pressed juice of grapes or other fruit ready for fermentation.

mustache *n US* same as **moustache.**

mustachio *n, pl* **-chios** *Often humorous* a moustache, esp. a bushy or elaborate one. **mustachioed** *adj*

mustang *n* a small breed of horse, often wild or half wild, found in the southwestern US.

mustard *n* **1** a hot, spicy paste made from the powdered seeds of any of a family of plants. **2** any of these plants, which have yellow flowers and slender pods. ~*adj* **3** brownish-yellow.

mustard and cress *n* seedlings of white mustard and garden cress, used in salads and as a garnish.

mustard gas *n* an oily liquid with poisonous vapour used in chemical warfare, esp. in World War I, which can cause blindness, burns, and sometimes death.

mustard plaster *n Med* a mixture of powdered black mustard seeds applied to the skin for its counterirritant effects.

muster *vb* **1** to summon or gather: *I put as much disbelief in my expression as I could muster.* **2** to call or be called together for duty or inspection: *the battalion mustered on the bank of the river.* ~*n* **3** an assembly of military personnel for duty or inspection. **4** a collection, assembly, or gathering. **5 pass muster** to be acceptable.

musty *adj* **-tier, -tiest 1** smelling or tasting old, stale, or mouldy. **2** old-fashioned, dull, or hackneyed: *musty ideas.* **mustily** *adv* **mustiness** *n*

mutable (**mew**-tab-bl) *adj* able to or tending to change. **mutability** *n*

mutant (**mew**-tant) *n* **1** an animal, organism, or gene that has undergone mutation. ~*adj* **2** of or resulting from mutation.

mutate (mew-**tate**) *vb* **-tating, -tated** to undergo or cause to undergo mutation.

mutation (mew-**tay**-shun) *n* **1** a change or alteration. **2** a change in the chromosomes or genes of a cell which may affect the structure and development of the resultant offspring. **3** a physical characteristic in an organism resulting from this type of chromosomal change.

mute *adj* **1** not giving out sound or speech; silent. **2** unable to speak; dumb. **3** unspoken or unexpressed: *she shot him a look of mute entreaty.* **4** (of a letter in a word) silent: *the "k" in "know" is mute.* ~*n* **5** a person who is unable to speak. **6** any of various devices used to soften the tone of stringed or brass instruments. ~*vb* **muting, muted 7** to reduce the volume or soften the tone of a musical instrument by means of a mute or soft pedal. **8** to reduce the volume of a sound: *the double glazing muted the noise of the traffic.* **mutely** *adv* **muteness** *n*

muted *adj* **1** (of a sound or colour) softened: *a muted pink shirt.* **2** (of an emotion or action) subdued or restrained: *his response was muted.* **3** (of a musical instrument) being played while fitted with a mute: *muted trumpet.*

mute swan *n* the swan most commonly seen in Britain, which has a pure white plumage and an orange-red bill.

muti (**moo**-tee) *n S African* medicine, esp. herbal.

mutilate (**mew**-till-ate) *vb* **-lating, -lated 1** to injure by tearing or cutting off a limb or essential part; maim. **2** to damage a book or text so as to render it unintelligible. **3** to spoil or damage severely: *why did he mutilate his favourite tapes and leave ours alone?* **mutilated** *adj* **mutilation** *n* **mutilator** *n*

mutineer *n* a person who mutinies.

mutinous *adj* **1** openly rebellious. **2** characteristic or indicative of mutiny.

mutiny (**mew**-tin-ee) *n, pl* **-nies 1** open rebellion against authority, esp. by sailors or soldiers against their officers. ~*vb* **-nies, -nying, -nied 2** to engage in mutiny.

mutt *n Slang* **1** a foolish or stupid person. **2** a mongrel dog.

mutter *vb* **1** to say something or speak in a low and indistinct tone: *he muttered an excuse.* **2** to grumble. ~*n* **3** a muttered sound or complaint. **muttering** *n, adj*

mutton *n* **1** the flesh of mature sheep, used as food. **2 mutton dressed as lamb** an older person dressed up to look young.

muttonchops *pl n* side whiskers trimmed in the shape of chops.

muttonhead *n Slang* a stupid or ignorant person.

mutual (**mew**-chew-al) *adj* **1** experienced or expressed by each of two or more people about the other; reciprocal. *mutual support.* **2** common to or shared by two or more people: *a mutual friend.* **3** denoting an organization, such as an insurance company, in which

THESAURUS

musical dulcet, euphonic, euphonious, harmonious, lilting, lyrical, melodic, melodious, sweet-sounding, tuneful

must duty, essential, fundamental, imperative, necessary thing, necessity, obligation, prerequisite, requirement, requisite, *sine qua non*

muster *vb.* **1.** assemble, call together, call up, collect, come together, congregate, convene, convoke, enrol, gather, group, marshal, meet, mobilize, rally, round up, summon ~*n.* **2.** assemblage, assembly, collection, concourse, congregation, convention, convocation, gathering, meeting, mobilization, rally, roundup **3. pass muster** be acceptable, be *or* come up to scratch, fill the bill (*informal*), make the grade, measure up, qualify

musty 1. airless, dank, decayed, frowsty, fusty, mildewed, mildewy, mouldy, old, smelly, stale, stuffy **2.** ancient, antediluvian, antiquated, banal, clichéd, dull, hackneyed, hoary, moth-eaten, obsolete, old-fashioned, stale, threadbare, trite, worn-out

mutability alteration, change, evolution, metamorphosis, transition, variation, vicissitude

mutable adaptable, alterable, changeable, changing, fickle, flexible, immutable, inconsistent, inconstant, irresolute, uncertain, undependable, unreliable, unsettled, unstable, unsteady, vacillating, variable, volatile, wavering

mute 1. *adj.* aphasic, dumb, mum, silent, speechless, unexpressed, unspeaking, unspoken, voiceless, wordless **2.** *vb.* dampen, deaden, lower, moderate, muffle, soften, soft-pedal, subdue, tone down, turn down

mutilate 1. amputate, butcher, cripple, cut to pieces, cut up, damage, disable, disfigure, dismember, hack, injure, lacerate, lame, maim, mangle **2.** adulterate, bowdlerize, butcher, censor, cut, damage, distort, expurgate, hack, mar, spoil

mutinous bolshie (*Brit. informal*), contumacious, disobedient, insubordinate, insurgent, rebellious, refractory, revolutionary, riotous, seditious, subversive, turbulent, ungovernable, unmanageable, unruly

mutiny 1. *n.* defiance, disobedience, insubordination, insurrection, rebellion, refusal to obey orders, resistance, revolt, revolution, riot, rising, strike, uprising **2.**

the policyholders or investors share the profits and expenses and there are no shareholders. **mutuality** *n* **mutually** *adv*

➤ The objection that something *mutual* holds between two people only is outdated; nowadays *mutual* is equivalent to "shared, in common".

Muzak *n Trademark* recorded light music played in places such as restaurants and shops.

muzzle *n* **1** the projecting part of an animal's face, usually the jaws and nose. **2** a guard, made of plastic or strap of strong material, fitted over an animal's nose and jaws to prevent it biting or eating. **3** the front end of a gun barrel. *~vb* **-zling, -zled 4** to prevent from being heard or noticed: *an attempt to muzzle the press.* **5** to put a muzzle on an animal.

muzzy *adj* **-zier, -ziest 1** confused and groggy: *he felt muzzy and hung over.* **2** blurred or hazy: *the picture was muzzy and out of focus.* **muzzily** *adv* **muzziness** *n*

MV megavolt.

MW 1 megawatt. **2** *Radio* medium wave.

Mx *Physics* maxwell.

my *adj* **1** of, belonging to, or associated with the speaker or writer (me): *my own way of doing things.* **2** used in various forms of address: *my lord.* *~interj* **3** an exclamation of surprise or awe: *my, how you've grown!*

mycelium (mice-**eel**-lee-um) *n, pl* **-lia** (-lee-a) the mass forming the body of a fungus.

Mycenaean (mice-in-**ee**-an) *adj* of or relating to the Aegean civilization of Mycenae, a city in S Greece (1400–1100 BC).

mycology *n* the study of fungi.

myelin (**my**-ill-in) *n* a white tissue forming an insulating sheath around certain nerve fibres.

myeloma (my-ill-**oh**-ma) *n, pl* **-mas** *or* **-mata** (-ma-ta) a tumour of the bone marrow.

myna, mynah, *or* **mina** *n* a tropical Asian starling which can mimic human speech.

Mynheer (min-**near**) *n* a Dutch title of address equivalent to *Sir* or *Mr.*

myocardium *n, pl* **-dia** the muscular tissue of the heart. **myocardial** *adj*

myopia (my-**oh**-pee-a) *n* inability to see distant objects clearly because the images are focused in front of the retina; short-sightedness. **myopic** (my-**op**-ik) *adj*

myriad (**mir**-ree-ad) *adj* **1** innumerable: *the myriad demands of the modern world.* *~n* **2** a large indefinite number: *myriads of tiny yellow flowers.*

myriapod *n* an invertebrate with a long segmented body and many legs, such as a centipede.

myrmidon *n* a follower or henchman.

myrrh (**mur**) *n* the aromatic resin of an African or Asian shrub or tree, used in perfume, incense, and medicine.

myrtle (**mur**-tl) *n* an evergreen shrub with pink or white flowers and aromatic blue-black berries.

myself *pron* **1** the reflexive form of *I* or *me*: *I really enjoyed myself at the party.* **2** I or me in person, as distinct from anyone else: *I myself know of no answer.* **3** my usual self: *I'm not myself today.*

mysterious *adj* **1** of unknown cause or nature: *a mysterious illness.* **2** creating a feeling of strangeness, curiosity, or wonder: *a fascinating and mysterious old woman.* **mysteriously** *adv*

mystery *n, pl* **-teries 1** an unexplained or inexplicable event or phenomenon. **2** a person or thing that arouses curiosity or suspense because of an unknown, obscure, or enigmatic quality. **3** a story or film which arouses suspense and curiosity because of facts concealed. **4** a religious rite, such as the Eucharist in Christianity.

mystery play *n* (in the Middle Ages) a type of drama based on the life of Christ.

mystery tour *n* an excursion to an unspecified destination.

mystic *n* **1** a person who achieves mystical experience. *~adj* **2** same as **mystical.**

mystical *adj* **1** relating to or characteristic of mysticism. **2** *Christianity* having a sacred significance that is beyond human understanding. **3** having occult or metaphysical significance. **mystically** *adv*

mysticism *n* **1** belief in or experience of a reality beyond normal human understanding or experience. **2** the use of prayer and meditation in an attempt to achieve direct intuitive experience of the divine.

mystify *vb* **-fies, -fying, -fied 1** to confuse, bewilder, or puzzle: *his success mystifies many in the fashion industry.* **2** to make obscure: *it is important for us not to mystify the function of the scientist.* **mystification** *n* **mystifying** *adj*

mystique (miss-**steek**) *n* an aura of mystery, power, and awe that surrounds a person or thing.

myth *n* **1 a** a story about superhuman beings of an earlier age, usually of how natural phenomena or social customs came into existence. **b** same as **mythology** (senses 1, 3). **2 a** an idea or explanation which is widely held but untrue or unproven: *the myth that the USA is a classless society.* **b** a person or thing whose

THESAURUS

vb. be insubordinate, defy authority, disobey, rebel, refuse to obey orders, resist, revolt, rise up, strike

mutter complain, grouch (*informal*), grouse, grumble, mumble, murmur, rumble

mutual common, communal, correlative, interactive, interchangeable, interchanged, joint, reciprocal, reciprocated, requited, returned, shared

muzzle *n.* **1.** jaws, mouth, nose, snout **2.** gag, guard *~vb.* **3.** censor, choke, curb, gag, restrain, silence, stifle, suppress

myopic near-sighted, short-sighted

myriad 1. *adj.* a thousand and one, countless, immeasurable, incalculable, innumerable, multitudinous, untold **2.** *n.* a million, army, a thousand, flood, horde, host, millions, mountain, multitude, scores, sea, swarm, thousands

mysterious abstruse, arcane, baffling, concealed, covert, cryptic, curious, dark, Delphic, enigmatic, furtive, hidden, impenetrable, incomprehensible, inexplicable, inscrutable, insoluble, mystical, mystifying, obscure, perplexing, puzzling, recondite, secret, secretive, sphinxlike, strange, uncanny, unfathomable, unknown, veiled, weird

mystery conundrum, enigma, problem, puzzle, question, riddle, secrecy, secret, teaser

mystic, mystical abstruse, arcane, cabalistic, cryptic, enigmatical, esoteric, hidden, inscrutable, metaphysical, mysterious, nonrational, occult, otherworldly, paranormal, preternatural, supernatural, transcendental

mystify baffle, bamboozle (*informal*), beat (*slang*), befog, bewilder, confound, confuse, elude, escape, flummox, nonplus, perplex, puzzle, stump

myth 1. allegory, fable, fairy story, fiction, folk tale, legend, parable, saga, story, tradition, urban legend **2.** delusion, fancy, fantasy, figment, illusion, imagination, superstition, tall story

existence is fictional or unproven: *the Loch Ness Monster is a myth.*

myth. 1 mythological. 2 mythology.

mythical *or* **mythic** *adj* 1 of or relating to myth. 2 imaginary or fictitious. **mythically** *adv*

mythology *n, pl* **-gies** 1 myths collectively, esp. those associated with a particular culture or person. 2 a body of stories about a person, institution, etc. 3 the study of myths. **mythological** *adj*

myxoedema *or US* **myxedema** (mix-id-**deem**-a) *n* a disease caused by an underactive thyroid gland, characterized by puffy eyes, face, and hands, and mental sluggishness.

myxomatosis (mix-a-mat-**oh**-siss) *n* an infectious and usually fatal viral disease of rabbits causing swellings and tumours.

THESAURUS

mythical 1. allegorical, chimerical, fabled, fabulous, fairy-tale, legendary, mythological, storied 2. fabricated, fanciful, fantasy, fictitious, imaginary, invented, made-up, make-believe, nonexistent, pretended, unreal, untrue

mythology folklore, folk tales, legend, lore, mythos, myths, stories, tradition

N

n[1] 1 nano-. 2 neutron.

n[2] *n* 1 *Maths* a number whose value is not stated: *two to the power n.* ~*adj* 2 an indefinite number of: *there are n objects in the box.* **nth** *adj*

N 1 *Chess* knight. 2 *Chem* nitrogen. 3 *Physics* newton(s). 4 North(ern). 5 nuclear: *N plant.*

n. 1 neuter. 2 noun. 3 number.

N. 1 National(ist). 2 Navy. 3 New. 4 Norse.

Na *Chem* sodium.

NA North America.

n/a not applicable: used to indicate that a question on a form is not relevant to the person filling it in.

Naafi *n* 1 Navy, Army, and Air Force Institutes. 2 a canteen or shop run by this organization for military personnel.

naan *n* same as **nan bread.**

naartjie (**nahr**-chee) *n S African* a tangerine.

nab *vb* **nabbing, nabbed** *Informal* 1 to arrest (someone). 2 to catch (someone) doing something wrong.

nabob (**nay**-bob) *n Informal* a rich or important person.

nacelle (nah-**sell**) *n* a streamlined enclosure on an aircraft, esp. one housing an engine.

nacre (**nay**-ker) *n* mother-of-pearl. **nacreous** *adj*

nadir *n* 1 the point in the sky directly below an observer and opposite the zenith. 2 the lowest or worst point of anything: *I had touched the very nadir of despair.*

naevus *or US* **nevus** (**nee**-vuss) *n, pl* **-vi** a birthmark or mole.

naff *adj Brit slang* in poor taste: *naff frocks and trouser suits.* **naffness** *n*

nag[1] *vb* **nagging, nagged** 1 to scold or find fault constantly. 2 **nag at** to be a constant source of discomfort or worry to. ~*n* 3 a person who nags. **nagging** *adj, n*

nag[2] *n* 1 *Often disparaging* an old horse. 2 a small riding horse.

naiad (**nye**-ad) *n, pl* **naiads** *or* **naiades** (**nye**-ad-deez) *Greek myth* a water nymph.

nail *n* 1 a piece of metal with a point at one end and a head at the other, hit with a hammer to join two objects together. 2 the hard covering of the upper tips of the fingers and toes. 3 **hit the nail on the head** to say something exactly correct or accurate. 4 **on the nail** at once: *he paid always in cash, always on the nail.* ~*vb* 5 to attach (something) with nails. 6 *Informal* to arrest or catch (someone).

nail down *vb* 1 to secure or fasten down with nails or as if with nails. 2 to force an agreement from. 3 to settle in a definite way: *a compromise was agreed in principle but has not yet been nailed down.*

nailfile *n* a small metal file used to shape and smooth the nails.

nail varnish *or* **polish** *n* a thick liquid applied to the nails as a cosmetic.

naive (nye-**eev**) *adj* 1 innocent and gullible. 2 simple and lacking sophistication: *naive art.* **naively** *adv*

naivety (nye-**eev**-tee) *or* **naïveté** *n* the state or quality of being naive.

naked *adj* 1 without clothes. 2 not concealed: *naked aggression.* 3 without any covering: *it was dimly lit by naked bulbs.* 4 **the naked eye** the eye unassisted by any optical instrument: *difficult to spot with the naked eye.* **nakedly** *adv* **nakedness** *n*

namby-pamby *adj* excessively sentimental or prim.

name *n* 1 a word or term by which a person or thing is known. 2 reputation, esp. a good one: *he was making a name for himself.* 3 a famous person: *she's a big name now.* 4 **call someone names** *or* **a name** to insult someone by using rude words to describe him or her. 5 **in name only** not possessing the powers or status implied by one's title: *a leadership in name only.* 6 **in the name of a** for the sake of: *in the name of decency.* **b** by the authority of: *in the name of the law.* 7 **name of the game** the most significant or important aspect of something: *survival is the name of the game in wartime.* 8 **to one's name** in one's possession: *she hasn't a penny to her name.* ~*vb* **naming, named** 9 to give a name to. 10 to refer to by name: *he refused to name his source.* 11 to fix or specify: *he named a time for the meeting.* 12 to appoint: *she was named Journalist of the Year.* 13 to ban (an MP) from the House of Commons by mentioning him or her formally by name as being guilty of disorderly conduct. 14 **name**

THESAURUS

nadir bottom, depths, lowest point, minimum, rock bottom, zero

nag[1] **1.** *vb.* annoy, badger, bend someone's ear (*informal*), be on one's back (*slang*), berate, chivvy, goad, harass, harry, hassle (*informal*), henpeck, irritate, nark (*Brit., Austral., & N.Z. slang*), pester, plague, provoke, scold, torment, upbraid, vex, worry **2.** *n.* harpy, scold, shrew, tartar, termagant, virago

nag[2] hack, horse, jade

nagging continuous, critical, distressing, irritating, painful, persistent, scolding, shrewish, worrying

nail *vb.* attach, beat, fasten, fix, hammer, join, pin, secure, tack

naive artless, callow, candid, childlike, confiding, credulous, frank, green, guileless, gullible, ingenuous, innocent, jejune, natural, open, simple, trusting, unaffected, unpretentious, unsophisticated, unsuspicious, unworldly

naiveté artlessness, callowness, candour, credulity, frankness, guilelessness, gullibility, inexperience, ingenuousness, innocence, naturalness, openness, simplicity

naked 1. bare, buck naked (*slang*), denuded, disrobed, divested, exposed, in one's birthday suit (*informal*), in the altogether (*informal*), in the buff (*informal*), in the raw (*informal*), naked as the day one was born (*informal*), nude, starkers (*informal*), stripped, unclothed, unconcealed, uncovered, undraped, undressed, without a stitch on (*informal*) **2.** blatant, evident, manifest, open, overt, patent, plain, simple, stark, unadorned, undisguised, unexaggerated, unmistakable, unqualified, unvarnished

nakedness 1. baldness, bareness, nudity, undress **2.** openness, plainness, simplicity, starkness

namby-pamby anaemic, colourless, feeble, insipid, mawkish, prim, prissy (*informal*), sentimental, spineless, vapid, weak, weedy (*informal*), wimpish *or* wimpy (*informal*), wishy-washy (*informal*)

name *n.* **1.** appellation, cognomen, denomination, designation, epithet, handle (*slang*), moniker *or* monicker (*slang*), nickname, sobriquet, term, title **2.** character, credit, distinction, eminence, esteem, fame, honour, note, praise, renown, reputation, repute ~*vb.* **3.** baptize, call, christen, denominate, dub, entitle,

names to cite people in order to blame or accuse them.

name day *n RC Church* the feast day of a saint whose name one bears.

name-dropping *n Informal* the practice of referring to famous people as though they were friends, in order to impress others.

nameless *adj* **1** without a name. **2** unspecified: *the individual concerned had better remain nameless.* **3** too horrible to speak about: *the nameless dread.*

namely *adv* that is to say.

nameplate *n* a small sign on or next to a door giving the occupant's name and, sometimes, profession.

namesake *n* a person or thing with the same name as another.

nan bread *or* **naan** *n* a slightly leavened Indian bread in a large flat leaf shape.

nancy *n, pl* **-cies** *Brit offensive slang* an effeminate or homosexual boy or man. Also called: **nancy boy**

nanny *n, pl* **-nies 1** a woman whose job is looking after young children. *~vb* **nannies, nannying, nannied 2** to nurse or look after someone else's children. **3** to be too protective towards (someone).

nanny goat *n* a female goat.

nano- *combining form* denoting one thousand millionth (10^{-9}): *nanosecond.*

nap[1] *n* **1** a short sleep. *~vb* **napping, napped 2** to have a short sleep. **3 catch someone napping** to catch someone unprepared: *they don't want to be caught napping when the army moves again.*

nap[2] *n* the raised fibres of velvet or similar cloth.

nap[3] *n* **1** a card game similar to whist. **2** *Horse racing* a tipster's choice for a certain winner. *~vb* **napping, napped 3** *Horse racing* to name (a horse) as a likely winner.

napalm *n* **1** a highly inflammable jellied petrol, used in firebombs and flame-throwers. *~vb* **2** to attack (people or places) with napalm.

nape *n* the back of the neck.

naphtha *n Chem* a liquid mixture distilled from coal tar or petroleum: used as a solvent and in petrol.

naphthalene *n Chem* a white crystalline substance distilled from coal tar or petroleum, used in mothballs, dyes, and explosives.

napkin *n* **1** a piece of cloth or paper for wiping the mouth or protecting the clothes while eating. **2** same as **sanitary towel.**

nappy *n, pl* **-pies** *Brit* a piece of soft absorbent material, usually disposable, wrapped around the waist and between the legs of a baby to absorb its urine and excrement.

narcissism *n* an exceptional interest in or admiration for oneself. **narcissistic** *adj*

narcissus (nahr-**siss**-uss) *n, pl* **-cissi** (-**siss**-eye) a yellow, orange, or white flower related to the daffodil.

narcosis *n* unconsciousness caused by a narcotic or general anaesthetic.

narcotic *n* **1** a drug, such as opium or morphine, that produces numbness and drowsiness, used medicinally but addictive. *~adj* **2** of narcotics or narcosis.

nark *Slang ~vb* **1** to annoy. *~n* **2** an informer or spy: *copper's nark.* **3** someone who complains in an irritating or whining manner.

narky *adj* **narkier, narkiest** *Slang* irritable, complaining, or sarcastic.

narrate *vb* **-rating, -rated 1** to tell (a story); relate. **2** to speak the words accompanying and telling what is happening in a film or TV programme. **narrator** *n*

narration *n* **1** a narrating. **2** a narrated account or story.

narrative *n* **1** an account of events. **2** the part of a literary work that relates events. *~adj* **3** telling a story: *a narrative account of the main events.* **4** of narration: *narrative clarity.*

narrow *adj* **1** small in breadth in comparison to length. **2** limited in range, extent, or outlook: *a narrow circle of academics.* **3** with little margin: *a narrow advantage.* *~vb* **4** to make or become narrow. **5 narrow down** to restrict or limit: *the search can be narrowed down to a single room.* -See also **narrows. narrowly** *adv* **narrowness** *n*

narrowboat *n* a long bargelike canal boat.

narrow gauge *n* **1** a railway track with less than 56½. *~adj* **narrow-gauge 2** denoting a railway with a narrow gauge.

narrow-minded *adj* bigoted, intolerant, or prejudiced. **narrow-mindedness** *n*

narrows *pl n* a narrow part of a strait, river, or current.

narwhal *n* an arctic whale with a long spiral tusk.

NASA (in the US) National Aeronautics and Space Administration.

nasal *adj* **1** of the nose. **2** (of a sound) pronounced with air passing through the nose. **3** (of a voice) characterized by nasal sounds. **nasally** *adv*

THESAURUS

label, style, term **4.** appoint, choose, cite, classify, commission, designate, flag, identify, mention, nominate, select, specify

nameless 1. anonymous, innominate, undesignated, unnamed, untitled **2.** abominable, horrible, indescribable, ineffable, inexpressible, unmentionable, unspeakable, unutterable

namely i.e., specifically, that is to say, to wit, viz.

nap[1] **1.** *n.* catnap, forty winks (*informal*), kip (*Brit. slang*), rest, shuteye (*slang*), siesta, sleep, zizz (*Brit. informal*) **2.** *vb.* catnap, doze, drop off (*informal*), drowse, kip (*Brit. slang*), nod, nod off (*informal*), rest, sleep, snooze (*informal*), zizz (*Brit. informal*)

nap[2] down, fibre, grain, pile, shag, weave

narcissism egotism, self-admiration, self-love, vanity

narcotic 1. *n.* anaesthetic, analgesic, anodyne, drug, opiate, painkiller, sedative, tranquillizer **2.** *adj.* analgesic, calming, dulling, hypnotic, numbing, painkilling, sedative, somnolent, soporific, stupefacient, stupefactive, stupefying

narrate chronicle, describe, detail, recite, recount, rehearse, relate, repeat, report, set forth, tell, unfold

narration description, explanation, reading, recital, rehearsal, relation, storytelling, telling, voice-over (*in film*)

narrative account, chronicle, detail, history, report, statement, story, tale

narrator annalist, author, bard, chronicler, commentator, raconteur, reciter, relater, reporter, storyteller, writer

narrow *adj.* **1.** attenuated, fine, slender, slim, spare, tapering, thin **2.** circumscribed, close, confined, constricted, contracted, cramped, incapacious, limited, meagre, near, pinched, restricted, scanty, straitened, tight *~vb.* **3.** circumscribe, constrict, diminish, limit, reduce, simplify, straiten, tighten

narrowly barely, by a whisker *or* hair's-breadth, just, only just, scarcely

narrow-minded biased, bigoted, conservative, hidebound, illiberal, insular, intolerant, opinionated, parochial, petty, prejudiced, provincial, reactionary, short-sighted, small-minded, strait-laced

narrows channel, gulf, passage, sound, straits

nasalize *or* **-ise** *vb* **-izing, -ized** *or* **-ising, -ised** to pronounce or speak nasally.
nascent *adj Formal* starting to grow or develop.
nasturtium *n* a plant with yellow, red, or orange trumpet-shaped flowers.
nasty *adj* **-tier, -tiest 1** unpleasant: *a nasty odour.* **2** dangerous or painful: *a nasty burn.* **3** (of a person) spiteful or ill-natured. ~*n, pl* **-ties 4** something unpleasant: *video nasties.* **nastily** *adv* **nastiness** *n*
nat. 1 national. 2 nationalist.
natal (**nay**-tl) *adj* of or relating to birth.
nation *n* a large body of people of one or more cultures or races, organized into a single state: *a major industrialised nation.*
national *adj* **1** of or serving a nation as a whole. **2** characteristic of a particular nation: *the national character.* ~*n* **3** a citizen of a particular country: *Belgian nationals.* **4** a national newspaper. **nationally** *adv*
national anthem *n* a patriotic song adopted by a nation for use on public occasions.
National Curriculum *n* (in England and Wales) the curriculum of subjects taught in state schools since 1989.
national debt *n* the total outstanding borrowings of a nation's central government.
national grid *n Brit* **1** a network of high-voltage power lines linking major electric power stations. **2** the arrangement of vertical and horizontal lines on an ordnance survey map.
National Health Service *n* (in Britain) the system of national medical services financed mainly by taxation.
national insurance *n* (in Britain) state insurance based on contributions from employees and employers, providing payments to the unemployed, the sick, and the retired.
nationalism *n* **1** a policy of national independence. **2** patriotism, sometimes to an excessive degree. **nationalist** *n, adj* **nationalistic** *adj*
nationality *n, pl* **-ties 1** the fact of being a citizen of a particular nation. **2** a group of people of the same race: *young men of all nationalities.*
nationalize *or* **-ise** *vb* **-izing, -ized** *or* **-ising, -ised** to put (an industry or a company) under state control. **nationalization** *or* **-isation** *n*
national park *n* an area of countryside protected by a national government for its scenic or environmental importance and visited by the public.
national service *n Chiefly Brit* compulsory military service.
National Socialism *n German history* the doctrines and practices of the Nazis, involving the supremacy of Hitler, anti-Semitism, state control of the economy, and national expansion. **National Socialist** *n, adj*
national superannuation *n NZ* a government pension paid to people of 65 years and over; retirement pension.
National Trust *n* (in Britain) an organization concerned with the preservation of historic buildings and areas of natural beauty.
nationwide *adj* covering or available to the whole of a nation.
native *adj* **1** relating to a place where a person was born: *native land.* **2** born in a specified place: *a native New Yorker.* **3 native to** originating in: *a plant native to alpine regions.* **4** natural or inborn: *native genius.* **5** relating to the original inhabitants of a country: *archaeology may uncover magnificent native artefacts.* **6 go native** (of a settler) to adopt the lifestyle of the local population. ~*n* **7** a person born in a specified place: *a native of Palermo.* **8** an indigenous animal or plant: *the saffron crocus is a native of Asia Minor.* **9** a member of the original race of a country, as opposed to colonial immigrants.
Native American *n* same as **American Indian.**
nativity *n, pl* **-ties** birth or origin.
Nativity *n Christianity* **1** the birth of Jesus Christ. **2** the feast of Christmas celebrating this.
NATO *or* **Nato** North Atlantic Treaty Organization: an international organization established for purposes of collective security.
natter *Informal, chiefly Brit* ~*vb* **1** to talk idly and at length. ~*n* **2** a long idle chat.
natterjack *n* a greyish-brown toad with reddish warty lumps.
natty *adj* **-tier, -tiest** *Informal* smart and spruce. **nattily** *adv*
natural *adj* **1** as is normal or to be expected: *the natural consequence.* **2** genuine or spontaneous: *talking in a relaxed, natural manner.* **3** of, according to, existing in, or produced by nature: *natural disasters.* **4** not acquired; inborn: *their natural enthusiasm.* **5** not created by human beings. **6** not synthetic: *natural fibres such as wool.* **7** (of a parent) not adoptive. **8** (of a child) illegitimate. **9** *Music* not sharp or flat: *F natural.* ~*n* **10**

THESAURUS

nastiness 1. defilement, dirtiness, filth, filthiness, foulness, impurity, pollution, squalor, uncleanliness **2.** disagreeableness, malice, meanness, offensiveness, spitefulness, unpleasantness
nasty 1. dirty, disagreeable, disgusting, filthy, foul, grotty (*slang*), horrible, loathsome, malodorous, mephitic, nauseating, noisome, objectionable, obnoxious, odious, offensive, polluted, repellent, repugnant, sickening, unappetizing, unpleasant, vile, yucky *or* yukky (*slang*) **2.** bad, critical, dangerous, painful, serious, severe **3.** abusive, annoying, bad-tempered, despicable, disagreeable, distasteful, malicious, mean, spiteful, unpleasant, vicious, vile
nation commonwealth, community, country, people, population, race, realm, society, state, tribe
national 1. *adj.* civil, countrywide, governmental, nationwide, public, state, widespread **2.** *n.* citizen, inhabitant, native, resident, subject
nationalism allegiance, chauvinism, fealty, jingoism, loyalty, nationality, patriotism
nationality birth, ethnic group, nation, race
nationwide countrywide, general, national, overall, widespread
native *adj.* **1.** domestic, home, home-grown, home-made, indigenous, local, mother, vernacular **2.** built-in, congenital, endemic, genuine, hereditary, inborn, inbred, indigenous, ingrained, inherent, inherited, innate, instinctive, intrinsic, inveterate, natal, natural, original, real **3.** aboriginal, autochthonous ~*n.* **4.** aborigine, autochthon, citizen, countryman, dweller, inhabitant, national, resident
natter 1. *vb.* blather, blether, chatter, gabble, gossip, jabber, jaw (*slang*), palaver, prate, prattle, rabbit (on) (*Brit. informal*), talk, talk idly, witter (*informal*) **2.** *n.* blather, blether, chat, chinwag (*Brit. informal*), chitchat, confabulation, conversation, gab (*informal*), gabble, gabfest (*informal, chiefly U.S. & Canad.*), gossip, jabber, jaw (*slang*), palaver, prattle, talk
natty chic, crucial (*slang*), dapper, elegant, fashionable, neat, smart, snazzy (*informal*), spruce, stylish, trendy (*Brit. informal*), trim, well-dressed, well-turned-out
natural 1. common, everyday, legitimate, logical,

Informal a person with an inborn talent or skill: *she's a natural at bridge.* **11** *Music* a note that is neither sharp nor flat. **naturalness** *n*

natural gas *n* a gaseous mixture, consisting mainly of methane, found below ground; used widely as a fuel.

natural history *n* the study of animals and plants in the wild.

naturalism *n* a movement in art and literature advocating detailed realism. **naturalistic** *adj*

naturalist *n* **1** a student of natural history. **2** a person who advocates or practises naturalism.

naturalize *or* **-ise** *vb* **-izing, -ized** *or* **-ising, -ised 1** to give citizenship to (a person born in another country). **2** to introduce (a plant or animal) into another region. **3** to cause (a foreign word or custom) to be adopted. **naturalization** *or* **-isation** *n*

natural logarithm *n* a logarithm which has the irrational number e as a base.

naturally *adv* **1** of course; surely. **2** in a natural or normal way. **3** instinctively.

natural number *n* a positive integer, such as 1, 2, 3, 4 etc.

natural philosophy *n Old-fashioned* physics.

natural resources *pl n* naturally occurring materials such as coal, oil, and minerals.

natural science *n* any of the sciences dealing with the study of the physical world, such as biology, physics, chemistry, and geology.

natural selection *n* a process by which only those creatures and plants well adapted to their environment survive.

natural wastage *n* a reduction in the number of employees through not replacing those who leave, rather than by dismissing employees or making them redundant.

nature *n* **1** the whole system of the existence, forces, and events of the physical world that are not controlled by human beings. **2** fundamental or essential qualities: *the theory and nature of science.* **3** kind or sort: *problems of a financial nature.* **4** temperament or personality: *an amiable and pleasant nature.* **5 by nature** essentially: *he was by nature a cautious man.* **6 in the nature of** essentially; by way of: *it was in the nature of a debate rather than an argument.*

nature reserve *n* an area of land that is preserved and managed in order to protect its animal and plant life.

nature study *n* the study of animals and plants by direct observation.

nature trail *n* a path through countryside, signposted to draw attention to natural features of interest.

naturism *n* same as **nudism. naturist** *n, adj*

naught *n* **1** *Archaic or literary* nothing. **2** *Chiefly US* the figure 0. *~adv* **3** *Archaic or literary* not at all: *signifying naught.*

naughty *adj* **-tier, -tiest 1** (of children) mischievous or disobedient. **2** mildly indecent: *naughty lingerie.* **naughtily** *adv* **naughtiness** *n*

nausea (**naw**-zee-a) *n* **1** the feeling of being about to vomit. **2** disgust.

nauseate *vb* **-ating, -ated 1** to cause (someone) to feel sick. **2** to arouse feelings of disgust in (someone). **nauseating** *adj*

nauseous *adj* **1** as if about to be sick: *He felt nauseous.* **2** sickening.

nautical *adj* of the sea, ships, or navigation.

nautical mile *n* a unit of length, used in navigation, equal to 1852 metres (6076·103 feet).

nautilus *n, pl* **-luses** *or* **-li** a sea creature with a shell and tentacles.

naval *adj* of or relating to a navy or ships.

nave[1] *n* the long central part of a church.

nave[2] *n* the hub of a wheel.

navel *n* the slight hollow in the centre of the abdomen, where the umbilical cord was attached.

navel orange *n* a sweet orange that has a navel-like hollow at the top.

navigable *adj* **1** wide, deep, or safe enough to be sailed through: *the navigable portion of the Nile.* **2** able to be steered: *the boat has to be watertight and navigable.*

navigate *vb* **-gating, -gated 1** to direct or plot the course or position of a ship or aircraft. **2** to travel over or through safely: *your cousin, who's just navigated the Amazon.* **3** *Informal* to direct (oneself) carefully or safely: *he navigated his unsteady way to the bar.* **4** (of a passenger in a vehicle) to read the map and give directions to the driver. **navigation** *n* **navigational** *adj* **navigator** *n*

navvy *n, pl* **-vies** *Brit informal* a labourer on a building site or road.

THESAURUS

normal, ordinary, regular, typical, usual **2.** artless, candid, frank, genuine, ingenuous, open, real, simple, spontaneous, unaffected, unpretentious, unsophisticated, unstudied **3.** characteristic, congenital, essential, inborn, indigenous, inherent, innate, instinctive, intuitive, natal, native **4.** organic, plain, pure, unbleached, unmixed, unpolished, unrefined, whole

naturalism factualism, realism, verisimilitude

naturalist 1. biologist, botanist, ecologist, zoologist **2.** factualist, realist

naturalize acclimate, acclimatize, acculturate, accustom, adapt, adopt, domesticate, enfranchise, familiarize, grant citizenship, habituate

naturally *adv.* as anticipated, customarily, genuinely, informally, normally, simply, spontaneously, typically, unaffectedly, unpretentiously

nature 1. cosmos, creation, earth, environment, universe, world **2.** attributes, character, complexion, constitution, essence, features, make-up, quality, traits **3.** category, description, kind, sort, species, style, type, variety **4.** disposition, humour, mood, outlook, temper, temperament

naughty 1. annoying, bad, disobedient, exasperating, fractious, impish, misbehaved, mischievous, perverse, playful, refractory, roguish, sinful, teasing, wayward, wicked, worthless **2.** bawdy, blue, improper, lewd, obscene, off-colour, ribald, risqué, smutty, vulgar

nausea 1. biliousness, queasiness, retching, sickness, squeamishness, vomiting **2.** abhorrence, aversion, disgust, loathing, odium, repugnance, revulsion

nauseate disgust, gross out (*U.S. slang*), horrify, offend, repel, repulse, revolt, sicken, turn one's stomach

nautical marine, maritime, naval, oceanic, seafaring, seagoing, yachting

naval marine, maritime, nautical, oceanic

navel bellybutton (*informal*), omphalos (*literary*), umbilicus

navigable 1. clear, negotiable, passable, traversable, unobstructed **2.** controllable, dirigible, sailable, steerable

navigate con (*Nautical*), cross, cruise, direct, drive, guide, handle, journey, manoeuvre, pilot, plan, plot, sail, skipper, steer, voyage

navigation cruising, helmsmanship, pilotage, sailing, seamanship, steering, voyaging

navy *n, pl* **-vies 1** the branch of a country's armed services comprising warships with their crews, and all their supporting services. **2** the warships of a nation. *~adj* **3** short for **navy-blue.**

navy-blue *adj* very dark blue.

nawab (na-**wahb**) *n* (formerly) a Muslim ruler or powerful landowner in India.

nay *interj* **1** *Old-fashioned* no. *~n* **2** a person who votes against a motion. *~adv* **3** used for emphasis: *I want, nay, need to know.*

Nazarene *n* **1 the Nazarene** Jesus Christ. **2** *Old-fashioned* a Christian. **3** a person from Nazareth, a town in N Israel. *~adj* **4** of Nazareth.

Nazi *n, pl* **-zis 1** a member of the fascist National Socialist German Workers' Party, which came to power in Germany in 1933 under Adolf Hitler. *~adj* **2** of or relating to the Nazis. **Nazism** *n*

nb *Cricket* no-ball.

Nb *Chem* niobium.

NB 1 New Brunswick. **2** note well.

NC 1 North Carolina. **2** *Brit education* National Curriculum.

NCO noncommissioned officer.

Nd *Chem* neodymium.

ND North Dakota.

NDT Newfoundland Daylight Time.

Ne *Chem* neon.

NE 1 Nebraska. **2** northeast(ern).

ne- *combining form* same as **neo-:** *Nearctic.*

Neanderthal (nee-**ann**-der-tahl) *adj* **1** of a type of primitive man that lived in Europe before 12 000 BC. **2** *Informal* with excessively conservative views: *his notoriously Neanderthal attitude to women.*

neap *n* short for **neap tide.**

Neapolitan *adj* **1** of Naples, a city in SW Italy. *~n* **2** a person from Naples.

neap tide *n* a tide that occurs at the first and last quarter of the moon when there is the smallest rise and fall in tidal level.

near *prep* **1** at or to a place or time not far away from. *~adv* **2** at or to a place or time not far away. **3** short for **nearly:** *the pain damn near crippled him.* *~adj* **4** at or in a place or time not far away: *in the near future.* **5** closely connected or intimate: *a near relation.* **6** almost being the thing specified: *a mood of near rebellion.* *~vb* **7** to draw close (to): *the participants are nearing agreement.* *~n* **8** the left side of a horse or vehicle. **nearness** *n*

nearby *adj, adv* not far away.

Near East *n* same as **Middle East.**

nearly *adv* **1** almost. **2 not nearly** nowhere near: *it's not nearly as easy as it looks.*

near miss *n* **1** any attempt that just fails to succeed. **2** an incident in which two aircraft or vehicles narrowly avoid collision. **3** a bomb or shot that does not quite hit the target.

nearside *n* **1** *Chiefly Brit* the side of a vehicle that is nearer the kerb. **2** the left side of an animal.

near-sighted *adj* same as **short-sighted.**

near thing *n Informal* an event whose outcome is nearly a failure or a disaster, or only just a success.

neat *adj* **1** clean and tidy. **2** smoothly or competently done: *a neat answer.* **3** (of alcoholic drinks) undiluted. **4** *Slang, chiefly US & Canad* admirable; excellent. **neatly** *adv* **neatness** *n*

neaten *vb* to make neat.

neath *prep Archaic* short for **beneath.**

neb *n Archaic or dialect* the beak of a bird or the nose of an animal.

nebula (**neb**-yew-la) *n, pl* **-lae** (-lee) *Astron* a hazy cloud of particles and gases. **nebular** *adj*

nebulous *adj* vague and unclear: *a nebulous concept.*

NEC National Executive Committee.

necessaries *pl n* essential items: *the necessaries and comforts of life.*

necessarily *adv* **1** as a certainty: *the factors were not necessarily connected with one another.* **2** inevitably: *our summary of this arrangement is necessarily brief.*

necessary *adj* **1** needed in order to obtain the desired result: *the necessary skills.* **2** certain or unavoidable: *the necessary consequences.* *~n* **3 the necessary** *Informal* the money required for a particular pur-

THESAURUS

navigator mariner, pilot, seaman

navvy ganger, labourer, worker, workman

navy argosy (*archaic*), armada, fleet, flotilla, warships

near *adj.* **1.** adjacent, adjoining, alongside, approaching, at close quarters, beside, bordering, close, close by, contiguous, forthcoming, imminent, impending, in the offing, looming, near-at-hand, nearby, neighbouring, next, nigh, on the cards (*informal*), proximate, touching, upcoming, within sniffing distance (*informal*) **2.** akin, allied, attached, connected, dear, familiar, intimate, related

nearby 1. *adj.* adjacent, adjoining, convenient, handy, neighbouring **2.** *adv.* at close quarters, close at hand, not far away, proximate, within reach, within sniffing distance (*informal*)

nearly *adv.* about, all but, almost, approaching, approximately, as good as, closely, just about, not quite, practically, roughly, virtually, well-nigh

nearness 1. accessibility, availability, closeness, contiguity, handiness, immediacy, imminence, juxtaposition, propinquity, proximity, vicinity **2.** dearness, familiarity, intimacy

near-sighted myopic, short-sighted

near thing close shave (*informal*), narrow escape, near miss

neat 1. accurate, dainty, fastidious, methodical, nice, orderly, shipshape, smart, spick-and-span, spruce, straight, systematic, tidy, trim, uncluttered **2.** adept, adroit, agile, apt, clever, deft, dexterous, efficient, effortless, elegant, expert, graceful, handy, nimble, practised, precise, skilful, stylish, well-judged **3.** *of alcoholic drinks* pure, straight, undiluted, unmixed

neatly 1. accurately, daintily, fastidiously, methodically, nicely, smartly, sprucely, systematically, tidily **2.** adeptly, adroitly, agilely, aptly, cleverly, deftly, dexterously, efficiently, effortlessly, elegantly, expertly, gracefully, handily, nimbly, precisely, skilfully, stylishly

neatness 1. accuracy, daintiness, fastidiousness, methodicalness, niceness, nicety, orderliness, smartness, spruceness, straightness, tidiness, trimness **2.** adeptness, adroitness, agility, aptness, cleverness, deftness, dexterity, efficiency, effortlessness, elegance, expertness, grace, gracefulness, handiness, nimbleness, preciseness, precision, skilfulness, skill, style, stylishness

nebulous ambiguous, amorphous, cloudy, confused, dim, hazy, imprecise, indefinite, indeterminate, indistinct, misty, murky, obscure, shadowy, shapeless, uncertain, unclear, unformed, vague

necessarily accordingly, automatically, axiomatically, by definition, certainly, compulsorily, consequently, incontrovertibly, ineluctably, inevitably, inexorably, irresistibly, naturally, of course, of necessity, perforce, undoubtedly, willy-nilly

pose. **4 do the necessary** *Informal* to do something that is necessary in a particular situation. ~See also **necessaries.**

necessitate *vb* **-tating, -tated** to compel or require.

necessitous *adj Literary* very needy.

necessity *n, pl* **-ties 1** a set of circumstances that inevitably requires a certain result: *the necessity to maintain safety standards.* **2** something needed: *the daily necessities.* **3** great poverty. **4 of necessity** inevitably.

neck *n* **1** the part of the body connecting the head with the rest of the body. **2** the part of a garment around the neck. **3** the long narrow part of a bottle or violin. **4** the length of a horse's head and neck taken as the distance by which one horse beats another in a race: *to win by a neck.* **5** *Informal* impudence. **6 by a neck** by a very small margin: *she held on to win by a neck.* **7 get it in the neck** *Informal* to be reprimanded or punished severely. **8 neck and neck** absolutely level in a race or competition. **9 neck of the woods** *Informal* a particular area: *how did they get to this neck of the woods?* **10 stick one's neck out** *Informal* to risk criticism or ridicule by speaking one's mind. **11 up to one's neck in** to be deeply involved in: *he was up to his neck in the scandal.* ~*vb* **12** *Informal* (of two people) to kiss each other passionately.

neckband *n* a band around the neck of a garment.

neckerchief *n* a piece of cloth worn tied round the neck.

necklace *n* **1** a decorative piece of jewellery worn round the neck. **2** (in South Africa) a tyre soaked in petrol, placed round a person's neck, and set on fire in order to burn the person to death.

neckline *n* the shape or position of the upper edge of a dress or top.

necktie *n US* same as **tie** (sense 5).

necromancy (**neck**-rome-man-see) *n* **1** communication with the dead. **2** sorcery. **necromancer** *n*

necrophilia *n* sexual attraction for or sexual intercourse with dead bodies.

necropolis (neck-**rop**-pol-liss) *n* a cemetery.

necrosis *n* **1** *Biol, med* the death of cells in the body, as from an interruption of the blood supply. **2** *Bot* death of plant tissue due to disease or frost. **necrotic** *adj*

nectar *n* **1** a sugary fluid produced by flowers and collected by bees. **2** *Classical myth* the drink of the gods. **3** any delicious drink.

nectarine *n* a smooth-skinned variety of peach.

ned *n Scot Slang* a hooligan.

NEDC (formerly) National Economic Development Council. Also (informal): **Neddy**

née *prep* indicating the maiden name of a married woman: *Jane Gray (née Blandish).*

need *vb* **1** to require or be in want of: *they desperately need success.* **2** to be obliged: *the government may need to impose a statutory levy.* **3** used to express necessity or obligation and does not add -s when used with singular nouns or pronouns: *need he go?* ~*n* **4** the condition of lacking something: *he has need of a new coat.* **5** a requirement: *the need for closer economic co-operation.* **6** necessity: *there was no need for an explanation.* **7** poverty or destitution: *the money will go to those areas where need is greatest.* **8** distress: *help has been given to those in need.* ~See also **needs.**

needful *adj* **1** necessary or required. ~*n* **2 the needful** *Informal* what is necessary, usually money.

needle *n* **1** a pointed slender piece of metal with a hole in it through which thread is passed for sewing. **2** a long pointed rod used in knitting. **3** same as **stylus. 4** *Med* the long hollow pointed part of a hypodermic syringe, which is inserted into the body. **5** a pointer on the scale of a measuring instrument. **6** a long narrow stiff leaf: *pine needles.* **7** *Informal* intense rivalry or ill-feeling in a sports match. **8** short for **magnetic needle. 9 have** *or* **get the needle** *Brit informal* to be annoyed. ~*vb* **-dling, -dled 10** *Informal* to goad or provoke.

needlecord *n* a fine-ribbed corduroy fabric.

needlepoint *n* **1** embroidery done on canvas. **2** lace made by needles on a paper pattern.

needless *adj* not required; unnecessary. **needlessly** *adv*

needlewoman *n, pl* **-women** a woman who does needlework.

needlework *n* sewing and embroidery.

needs *adv* **1** necessarily: *they must needs be admired.* ~*pl n* **2** what is required: *he provides them with their needs.*

needy *adj* **needier, neediest** in need of financial support.

ne'er *adv Poetic* never.

ne'er-do-well *n* **1** an irresponsible or lazy person. ~*adj* **2** useless; worthless: *his ne'er-do-well brother.*

nefarious (nif-**fair**-ee-uss) *adj Literary* evil; wicked.

neg. negative.

THESAURUS

necessary 1. compulsory, *de rigueur,* essential, imperative, indispensable, mandatory, needed, needful, obligatory, required, requisite, vital **2.** certain, fated, inescapable, inevitable, inexorable, unavoidable

necessitate call for, coerce, compel, constrain, demand, entail, force, impel, make necessary, oblige, require

necessity 1. desideratum, essential, fundamental, necessary, need, prerequisite, requirement, requisite, *sine qua non,* want **2.** destitution, extremity, indigence, need, penury, poverty, privation

need *vb.* **1.** call for, demand, entail, have occasion to *or* for, lack, miss, necessitate, require, want ~*n.* **2.** longing, requisite, want, wish **3.** demand, desideratum, essential, requirement, requisite **4.** emergency, exigency, necessity, obligation, urgency, want **5.** deprivation, destitution, distress, extremity, impecuniousness, inadequacy, indigence, insufficiency, lack, neediness, paucity, penury, poverty, privation, shortage

needful essential, indispensable, necessary, needed, required, requisite, stipulated, vital

needle *vb. informal* aggravate (*informal*), annoy, bait, be on one's back (*slang*), gall, get in one's hair (*informal*), get on one's nerves (*informal*), goad, harass, hassle (*informal*), irk, irritate, nag, nark (*Brit., Austral., & N.Z. slang*), nettle, pester, piss one off (*taboo slang*), prick, prod, provoke, rile, ruffle, spur, sting, taunt

needless causeless, dispensable, excessive, expendable, gratuitous, groundless, nonessential, pointless, redundant, superfluous, uncalled-for, undesired, unnecessary, unwanted, useless

needlework embroidery, fancywork, needlecraft, sewing, stitching, tailoring

needy deprived, destitute, dirt-poor (*informal*), disadvantaged, impecunious, impoverished, indigent, on the breadline (*informal*), penniless, poor, poverty-stricken, underprivileged

nefarious abominable, atrocious, base, criminal, depraved, detestable, dreadful, evil, execrable, foul, heinous, horrible, infamous, infernal, iniquitous, monstrous, odious, opprobrious, shameful, sinful, vicious, vile, villainous, wicked

negate *vb* **-gating, -gated 1** to cause to have no value or effect: *his prejudices largely negate his accomplishments.* **2** to deny the existence of.

negation *n* **1** the opposite or absence of something. **2** a negative thing or condition. **3** a negating.

negative *adj* **1** expressing a refusal or denial: *a negative response.* **2** lacking positive qualities, such as enthusiasm or optimism. **3** *Med* indicating absence of the condition for which a test was made. **4** *Physics* **a** (of an electric charge) having the same electrical charge as an electron. **b** (of a body or system) having a negative electric charge; having an excess of electrons. **5** same as **minus** (sense 4). **6** measured in a direction opposite to that regarded as positive. **7** short for **electronegative. 8** of a photographic negative. *~n* **9** a statement or act of denial or refusal. **10** *Photog* a piece of photographic film, exposed and developed, bearing an image with a reversal of tones or colours, from which positive prints are made. **11** a word or expression with a negative meaning, such as *not.* **12** a quantity less than zero. **13 in the negative** indicating denial or refusal. **negatively** *adv*

negativism *n* a tendency to be unconstructively critical. **negativist** *n, adj*

neglect *vb* **1** to fail to give due care or attention to: *she had neglected her child.* **2** to fail (to do something) through carelessness: *he neglected to greet his guests.* **3** to disregard: *he neglected his duty.* *~n* **4** lack of due care or attention: *the city had a look of shabbiness and neglect.* **5** the state of being neglected.

neglectful *adj* not paying enough care or attention: *abusive and neglectful parents.*

negligee (**neg**-lee-zhay) *n* a woman's light, usually lace-trimmed dressing gown.

negligence *n* neglect or carelessness. **negligent** *adj* **negligently** *adv*

negligible *adj* so small or unimportant as to be not worth considering.

negotiable *adj* **1** able to be changed or agreed by discussion: *the prices were negotiable.* **2** (of a bill of exchange or promissory note) legally transferable.

negotiate *vb* **-ating, -ated 1** to talk with others in order to reach (an agreement). **2** to succeed in passing round or over (a place or a problem). **negotiation** *n* **negotiator** *n*

Negro *Old-fashioned ~n, pl* **-groes 1** a member of any of the Black peoples originating in Africa. *~adj* **2** of Negroes.

Negroid *adj* of or relating to the Negro race.

neigh *n* **1** the high-pitched sound made by a horse. *~vb* **2** to make this sound.

neighbour *or US* **neighbor** *n* **1** a person who lives near or next to another. **2** a person, thing, or country near or next to another.

neighbourhood *or US* **neighborhood** *n* **1** a district where people live. **2** the immediate environment; surroundings. **3** the people in a district. **4 in the neighbourhood of** approximately. *~adj* **5** in and for a district: *our neighbourhood cinema.*

neighbouring *or US* **neighboring** *adj* situated nearby: *the neighbouring island.*

neighbourly *or US* **neighborly** *adj* kind, friendly, and helpful.

neither *adj* **1** not one nor the other (of two): *neither enterprise went well.* *~pron* **2** not one nor the other (of two): *neither completed the full term.* *~conj* **3 a** (used preceding alternatives joined by *nor*) not: *sparing neither strength nor courage.* **b** same as **nor** (sense 2). *~adv* **4** *Not standard* same as **either** (sense 4).

➤ When *neither* is followed by a plural noun it is acceptable to make the verb plural too: *Neither of these books are useful.*

nelson *n* a wrestling hold in which a wrestler places his arm or arms under his opponent's arm or arms from behind and exerts pressure with his palms on the back of his opponent's neck.

nematode *n* a slender unsegmented cylindrical worm.

nemesis (**nem**-miss-iss) *n, pl* **-ses** (-seez) a means of retribution or vengeance.

neo- *combining form* new, recent, or a modern form of: *neoclassicism; neo-Nazi.*

neoclassicism *n* a late 18th- and early 19th-century style of art and architecture, based on ancient Roman and Greek models. **neoclassical** *adj*

neocolonialism *n* political control wielded by one country over another through control of its economy. **neocolonial** *adj*

neodymium *n Chem* a toxic silvery-white metallic element of the lanthanide series. Symbol: Nd

THESAURUS

negate 1. abrogate, annul, cancel, countermand, invalidate, neutralize, nullify, obviate, repeal, rescind, retract, reverse, revoke, void, wipe out **2.** contradict, deny, disallow, disprove, gainsay (*archaic or literary*), oppose, rebut, refute

negation 1. antithesis, antonym, contradiction, contrary, converse, counterpart, denial, disavowal, disclaimer, inverse, opposite, rejection, renunciation, reverse **2.** cancellation, neutralization, nullification, opposition, proscription, refusal, repudiation, veto

negative *adj.* **1.** contradictory, contrary, denying, dissenting, opposing, recusant, refusing, rejecting, resisting **2.** antagonistic, colourless, contrary, cynical, gloomy, jaundiced, neutral, pessimistic, uncooperative, unenthusiastic, uninterested, unwilling, weak *~n.* **3.** contradiction, denial, refusal

neglect *vb.* **1.** be remiss, evade, forget, let slide, omit, pass over, procrastinate, shirk, skimp **2.** contemn, discount, disdain, disregard, ignore, leave alone, overlook, pass by, rebuff, scorn, slight, spurn *~n.* **3.** carelessness, default, dereliction, disdain, disregard, disrespect, failure, forgetfulness, heedlessness, inattention, indifference, laxity, laxness, neglectfulness, negligence, oversight, remissness, slackness, slight, slovenliness, unconcern

negligence carelessness, default, dereliction, disregard, failure, forgetfulness, heedlessness, inadvertence, inattention, inattentiveness, indifference, laxity, laxness, neglect, omission, oversight, remissness, shortcoming, slackness, thoughtlessness

negligent careless, cursory, disregardful, forgetful, heedless, inadvertent, inattentive, indifferent, neglectful, nonchalant, offhand, regardless, remiss, slack, slapdash, slipshod, thoughtless, unmindful, unthinking

negligible imperceptible, inconsequential, insignificant, minor, minute, nickel-and-dime (*U.S. slang*), petty, small, trifling, trivial, unimportant

negotiable debatable, discussable *or* discussible, transactional, transferable, variable

negotiate 1. adjudicate, arbitrate, arrange, bargain, conciliate, confer, consult, contract, deal, debate, discuss, handle, manage, mediate, parley, settle, transact, work out **2.** clear, cross, get over, get past, get round, pass, pass through, surmount

negotiation arbitration, bargaining, debate, diplomacy, discussion, mediation, transaction, wheeling and dealing (*informal*)

neighbourhood community, confines, district, environs, locale, locality, precincts, proximity, purlieus, quarter, region, surroundings, vicinity

Neolithic *adj* of the period that lasted in Europe from about 4000 to 2400 BC, characterized by primitive farming and the use of polished stone and flint tools and weapons.

neologism (nee-**ol**-a-jiz-zum) *n* a newly coined word, or an established word used in a new sense.

neon *n* **1** *Chem* a colourless odourless rare gas, used in illuminated signs and lights. Symbol: Ne ~*adj* **2** of or illuminated by neon: *a flashing neon sign.*

neonatal *adj* relating to the first few weeks of a baby's life. **neonate** *n*

neon light *n* a glass tube containing neon, which gives a pink or red glow when a voltage is applied.

neophyte *n Formal* **1** a beginner. **2** a person newly converted to a religious faith. **3** a novice in a religious order.

Nepali (nip-**paw**-lee) *or* **Nepalese** (nep-pal-**leez**) *adj* **1** of Nepal. ~*n* **2** (*pl* **-pali, -palis,** *or* **-palese**) a person from Nepal. **3** the language of Nepal.

nephew *n* a son of one's sister or brother.

nephritis (nif-**frite**-tiss) *n* inflammation of the kidney.

nepotism (**nep**-a-tiz-zum) *n* favouritism shown to relatives and friends by those with power.

Neptune *n* **1** the Roman god of the sea. **2** the eighth planet from the sun.

neptunium *n Chem* a silvery metallic element synthesized in the production of plutonium. Symbol: Np

nerd *n Slang* **1** a boring or unpopular person, esp. one who is obsessed with a particular subject: *a computer nerd.* **2** a stupid and feeble person. **nerdish** *or* **nurdish** *adj*

nervate *adj* (of leaves) with veins.

nerve *n* **1** a cordlike bundle of fibres that conducts impulses between the brain and other parts of the body. **2** bravery and determination. **3** *Informal* impudence: *you've got a nerve!* **4 lose one's nerve** to lose self-confidence and become afraid about what one is doing. **5 strain every nerve** to make every effort (to do something). ~*vb* **nerving, nerved 6 nerve oneself** to prepare oneself (to do something difficult or unpleasant). ~See also **nerves.**

nerve cell *n* same as **neuron.**

nerve centre *n* **1** a place from which a system or organization is controlled: *an underground nerve centre of intelligence.* **2** a group of nerve cells associated with a specific function.

nerve gas *n* a poisonous gas which effects the nervous system.

nerveless *adj* **1** (of fingers or hands) without feeling; numb. **2** (of a person) fearless.

nerve-racking *or* **nerve-wracking** *adj* very distressing or harrowing.

nerves *pl n Informal* **1** anxiety or tension: *nerves can often be the cause of wedding-day hitches.* **2** the ability or inability to remain calm in a difficult situation: *his nerves are in a shocking state.* **3 get on someone's nerves** to irritate someone.

nervous *adj* **1** apprehensive or worried. **2** excitable; highly strung. **3** of or relating to the nerves: *the nervous system.* **nervously** *adv* **nervousness** *n*

nervous breakdown *n* a mental illness in which the sufferer ceases to function properly, and experiences symptoms including tiredness, anxiety, and deep depression.

nervous system *n* the brain, spinal column, and nerves, which together control thought, feeling, and movement. See **neuron.**

nervy *adj* **nervier, nerviest** *Brit informal* excitable or nervous.

ness *n* a headland or cape.

-ness *n suffix* indicating state, condition, or quality: *greatness; selfishness.*

nest *n* **1** a place or structure in which birds or other animals lay eggs or give birth to young. **2** a cosy or secluded place. **3** a set of things of graduated sizes designed to fit together: *a nest of tables.* ~*vb* **4** to make or inhabit a nest. **5** (of a set of objects) to fit one inside another. **6** *Computers* to position (data) within other data at different ranks or levels.

nest egg *n* a fund of money kept in reserve.

nestle *vb* **-tling, -tled 1** to snuggle or cuddle closely. **2** to be in a sheltered position: *honey-coloured stone villages nestling in wooded valleys.*

nestling *n* a young bird not yet able to fly.

net[1] *n* **1** a very fine fabric made from intersecting strands of material with a space between each strand. **2** a piece of net, used to protect or hold things or to trap animals. **3** (in certain sports) a strip of net over which the ball or shuttlecock must be hit. **4** the goal in soccer or hockey. **5** a strategy intended to trap people: *innocent fans were caught in the police net.* ~*vb* **netting, netted 6** to catch (a fish or other animal) in a net.

net[2] *or* **nett** *adj* **1** remaining after all deductions, as

THESAURUS

neighbouring abutting, adjacent, adjoining, bordering, connecting, contiguous, near, nearby, nearest, next, surrounding

nerve *n.* **1.** balls (*taboo slang*), ballsiness (*taboo slang*), bottle (*Brit. slang*), bravery, coolness, courage, daring, determination, endurance, energy, fearlessness, firmness, force, fortitude, gameness, grit, guts (*informal*), hardihood, intrepidity, mettle, might, pluck, resolution, spirit, spunk (*informal*), steadfastness, vigour, will **2.** *informal* audacity, boldness, brass (*informal*), brass neck (*Brit. informal*), brazenness, cheek (*informal*), chutzpah (*U.S. & Canad. informal*), effrontery, front, gall, impertinence, impudence, insolence, neck (*informal*), sauce (*informal*), temerity ~*vb.* **3.** brace, embolden, encourage, fortify, hearten, invigorate, steel, strengthen

nerve-racking annoying, difficult, distressing, frightening, harassing, harrowing, maddening, stressful, tense, trying, worrying

nerves anxiety, fretfulness, heebie-jeebies (*slang*), nervousness, strain, stress, tension, worry

nervous agitated, anxious, apprehensive, edgy, excitable, fearful, fidgety, flustered, hesitant, highly strung, hyper (*informal*), hysterical, jittery (*informal*), jumpy, nervy (*Brit. informal*), neurotic, on edge, ruffled, shaky, tense, timid, timorous, twitchy (*informal*), uneasy, uptight (*informal*), weak, wired (*slang*), worried

nervous breakdown breakdown, collapse, crack-up (*informal*), nervous disorder, neurasthenia (*obsolete*)

nervousness agitation, anxiety, disquiet, excitability, fluster, perturbation, tension, timidity, touchiness, tremulousness, worry

nest den, haunt, hideaway, refuge, resort, retreat, snuggery

nest egg cache, deposit, fall-back, fund(s), reserve, savings, store

nestle cuddle, curl up, huddle, nuzzle, snuggle

nestling chick, fledgling

net[1] **1.** *n.* lacework, lattice, mesh, netting, network, openwork, tracery, web **2.** *vb.* bag, capture, catch, enmesh, ensnare, entangle, nab (*informal*), trap

for taxes and expenses: *net income.* **2** (of weight) excluding the weight of wrapping or container. **3** final or conclusive: *the net effect.* ~*vb* **netting, netted 4** to yield or earn as a clear profit.

netball *n* a team game, usually played by women, in which a ball has to be thrown through a net hanging from a ring at the top of a pole.

nether *adj Old-fashioned* lower or under: *nether regions.*

nethermost *adj* lowest.

nether world *n* **1** the underworld. **2** hell. Also called: **nether regions**

net profit *n* gross profit minus all operating expenses such as wages and overheads.

nett *adj, vb* same as **net**[2].

netting *n* a fabric or structure made of net.

nettle *n* **1** a plant with stinging hairs on the leaves. **2 grasp the nettle** to attempt something unpleasant with boldness and courage.

nettled *adj* irritated or annoyed.

nettle rash *n* a skin condition, usually caused by an allergy, in which itchy red or white raised patches appear.

network *n* **1** a system of intersecting lines, roads, veins, etc. **2** an interconnecting group or system: *a network of sympathizers and safe-houses.* **3** *Radio, television* a group of broadcasting stations that all transmit the same programme at the same time. **4** *Electronics, computers* a system of interconnected components or circuits. ~*vb* **5** *Radio, television* to broadcast (a programme) over a network.

neural *adj* of a nerve or the nervous system.

neuralgia *n* severe pain along a nerve. **neuralgic** *adj*

neuritis (nyoor-**rite**-tiss) *n* inflammation of a nerve or nerves, often causing pain and loss of function in the affected part.

neurology *n Med* the scientific study of the nervous system. **neurological** *adj* **neurologist** *n*

neuron *or* **neurone** *n* a cell specialized to conduct nerve impulses.

neurosis (nyoor-**oh**-siss) *n, pl* **-ses** (-seez) a mental disorder producing hysteria, anxiety, depression, or obsessive behaviour.

neurosurgery *n Med* the branch of surgery concerned with the nervous system. **neurosurgeon** *n* **neurosurgical** *adj*

neurotic *adj* **1** tending to be emotionally unstable. **2** afflicted by neurosis. ~*n* **3** a person afflicted with a neurosis or tending to be emotionally unstable.

neuter *adj* **1** *Grammar* denoting a gender of nouns which are neither male nor female. **2** (of animals and plants) sexually underdeveloped. ~*n* **3** *Grammar* **a** the neuter gender. **b** a neuter noun. **4** a sexually underdeveloped female insect, such as a worker bee. **5** a castrated animal. ~*vb* **6** to castrate (an animal).

neutral *adj* **1** not taking any side in a war or dispute. **2** of or belonging to a neutral party or country. **3** not displaying any emotions or opinions. **4** (of a colour) not definite or striking. **5** *Chem* neither acidic nor alkaline. **6** *Physics* having zero charge or potential. ~*n* **7** a neutral person or nation. **8** the position of the controls of a gearbox that leaves the gears unconnected to the engine. **neutrality** *n*

neutralize *or* **-ise** *vb* **-izing, -ized** *or* **-ising, -ised 1** to make electrically or chemically neutral. **2** to make ineffective by counteracting. **3** to make (a country) neutral by international agreement: *the great powers neutralized Belgium in the 19th century.* **neutralization** *or* **-isation** *n*

neutrino (new-**tree**-no) *n, pl* **-nos** *Physics* an elementary particle with no mass or electrical charge.

neutron *n Physics* a neutral elementary particle of about the same mass as a proton.

neutron bomb *n* a nuclear weapon designed to kill people and animals while leaving buildings virtually undamaged.

never *adv* **1** at no time; not ever. **2** certainly not; not at all. **3** Also: **well I never!** surely not!

➤ Avoid the use of *never* with the past tense to mean *not: I didn't see her* (not *I never saw her*).

never-ending *adj* long and boring.

nevermore *adv Literary* never again.

never-never *n* **the never-never** *Informal* hire-purchase: *they are buying it on the never-never.*

never-never land *n* an imaginary idyllic place.

nevertheless *adv* in spite of that.

new *adj* **1** recently made, brought into being, or acquired: *a new car.* **2** of a kind never before existing; novel: *a new approach to monetary policy.* **3** recently discovered: *testing new drugs.* **4** recently introduced to or inexperienced in a place or situation: *new to this game.* **5** fresh; additional: *you can acquire new skills.* **6** unknown: *this is new to me.* **7** (of a cycle) beginning again: *a new era.* **8** (of crops) harvested early: *new po-*

THESAURUS

net[2], **nett** *adj.* **1.** after taxes, clear, final, take-home **2.** closing, conclusive, final ~*vb.* **3.** accumulate, bring in, clear, earn, gain, make, realize, reap, yield

nether *old-fashioned* basal, below, beneath, bottom, inferior, lower, Stygian, under, underground

nether world Avernus, Hades, hell, infernal regions, nether regions, underworld

nettled aggrieved, angry, annoyed, chafed, cross, exasperated, galled, goaded, hacked (off) (*U.S. slang*), harassed, huffy, incensed, irritable, irritated, peeved, peevish, piqued, pissed off (*taboo slang*), provoked, put out, ratty (*Brit. & N.Z. informal*), riled, ruffled, stung, teased, tetchy, touchy, vexed

network arrangement, channels, circuitry, complex, convolution, grid, grill, interconnections, labyrinth, maze, mesh, net, nexus, organization, plexus, structure, system, tracks, web

neurosis abnormality, affliction, derangement, deviation, instability, maladjustment, mental disturbance, mental illness, obsession, phobia, psychological *or* emotional disorder

neurotic abnormal, anxious, compulsive, deviant, disordered, distraught, disturbed, hyper (*informal*), maladjusted, manic, nervous, obsessive, overwrought, twitchy (*informal*), unhealthy, unstable

neuter *vb.* castrate, doctor (*informal*), dress, emasculate, fix (*informal*), geld, spay

neutral 1. disinterested, dispassionate, even-handed, impartial, indifferent, nonaligned, nonbelligerent, noncombatant, noncommittal, nonpartisan, sitting on the fence, unaligned, unbiased, uncommitted, undecided, uninvolved, unprejudiced **2.** achromatic, colourless, dull, expressionless, indeterminate, indistinct, indistinguishable, intermediate, toneless, undefined

neutrality detachment, disinterestedness, impartiality, nonalignment, noninterference, noninterventionism, noninvolvement, nonpartisanship

neutralize cancel, compensate for, counteract, counterbalance, frustrate, invalidate, negate, nullify, offset, undo

nevertheless but, even so, (even) though, however, nonetheless, notwithstanding, regardless, still, yet

new 1. advanced, all-singing, all-dancing, contemporary, current, different, fresh, happening (*informal*), latest, modern, modernistic, modish, newfangled,

tatoes. **9** changed for the better: *she returned a new woman.* ~*adv* **10** recently, newly: *new-laid eggs.* ~See also **news. newish** *adj* **newness** *n*

New Age *n* **1** a late 1980s philosophy characterized by a belief in alternative medicine, astrology, and spiritualism. ~*adj* **2** of the New Age: *New Age therapies.* **New Ager** *n*

New Age Music *n* a type of gentle melodic largely instrumental popular music originating in the USA in the late 1980s.

newborn *adj* recently or just born.

New Canadian *n Canad* a recent immigrant to Canada.

new chum *n Austral & NZ informal* a recent British immigrant.

newcomer *n* a recent arrival or participant.

newel *n* **1** Also called: **newel post** the post at the top or bottom of a flight of stairs that supports the handrail. **2** the central pillar of a winding staircase.

newfangled *adj* objectionably or unnecessarily modern.

New Jerusalem *n Christianity* heaven.

New Latin *n* the form of Latin used since the Renaissance, mainly for scientific names.

newly *adv* **1** recently. **2** again; anew: *newly interpreted.*

newlyweds *pl n* a recently married couple.

New Man *n* **the New Man** a type of modern man who allows the caring side of his nature to show by being supportive and by sharing child care and housework.

new maths *n Brit* an approach to mathematics in which basic set theory is introduced at an elementary level.

new moon *n* the moon when it appears as a narrow crescent at the beginning of its cycle.

news *n* **1** important or interesting new happenings. **2** information about such events, reported in the mass media. **3 the news** a television or radio programme presenting such information. **4** interesting or important new information: *it's news to me.* **5** a person or thing widely reported in the mass media: *reggae is suddenly big news again.*

news agency *n* an organisation that collects news reports and sells them to newspapers, magazines, and TV and radio stations.

newsagent *n* a shopkeeper who sells newspapers and magazines.

newscast *n* a radio or television broadcast of the news. **newscaster** *n*

news conference *n* same as **press conference.**

newsflash *n* a brief item of important news, which interrupts a radio or television programme.

newsletter *n* a periodical bulletin issued to members of a group.

newspaper *n* a weekly or daily publication consisting of folded sheets and containing news, features, and advertisements.

newspeak *n* the language of politicians and officials regarded as deliberately ambiguous and misleading.

newsprint *n* an inexpensive wood-pulp paper used for newspapers.

newsreader *n* a news announcer on radio or television.

newsreel *n* a short film with a commentary which presents current events.

newsroom *n* a room in a newspaper office or broadcasting station where news is received and prepared for publication or broadcasting.

newsstand *n* a portable stand from which newspapers are sold.

New Style *n* the present method of reckoning dates using the Gregorian calendar.

newsworthy *adj* sufficiently interesting to be reported as news.

newsy *adj* **newsier, newsiest** (of a letter) full of news.

newt *n* a small amphibious creature with a long slender body and tail and short legs.

New Testament *n* the second part of the Christian Bible, dealing with the life and teachings of Christ and his followers.

newton *n* the SI unit of force that gives an acceleration of 1 metre per second per second to a mass of 1 kilogram.

new town *n* (in Britain) a town planned as a complete unit and built with government sponsorship.

new wave *n* a movement in politics, the arts, or music that consciously breaks with traditional values.

New World *n* **the New World** the western hemisphere of the world, esp. the Americas.

New Year *n* the first day or days of the year in various calendars, usually a holiday.

New Year's Day *n* January 1, celebrated as a holiday in many countries.

New Year's Eve *n* December 31.

New Zealander *n* a person from New Zealand.

next *adj* **1** immediately following: *the next generation.* **2** immediately adjoining: *in the next room.* **3** closest to in degree: *the next-best thing.* ~*adv* **4** at a time immediately to follow: *the patient to be examined next.* **5 next to a** adjacent to: *the house next to ours.* **b** following in degree: *next to my wife, I love you most.* **c** almost: *the evidence is next to totally useless.*

next door *adj, adv* in, at, or to the adjacent house or flat: *the Cabinet retired next door; the people next door.*

next of kin *n* a person's closest relative.

nexus *n, pl* **nexus 1** a connection or link. **2** a connected group or series.

NF Newfoundland.

Nfld. Newfoundland.

ngati (**nah**-tee) *n, pl* **ngati** *NZ* a tribe or clan.

NH New Hampshire.

NHS (in Britain) National Health Service.

Ni *Chem* nickel.

NI **1** (in Britain) National Insurance. **2** Northern Ireland.

nib *n* the writing point of a pen.

THESAURUS

novel, original, recent, state-of-the-art, topical, ultramodern, unfamiliar, unknown, unused, unusual, up-to-date, virgin **2.** added, additional, extra, more, supplementary **3.** altered, changed, improved, modernized, redesigned, renewed, restored

newcomer alien, arrival, beginner, foreigner, immigrant, incomer, Johnny-come-lately (*informal*), novice, outsider, parvenu, settler, stranger

newfangled all-singing, all-dancing, contemporary, fashionable, gimmicky, modern, new, new-fashioned, novel, recent, state-of-the-art

newly anew, freshly, just, lately, latterly, recently

news account, advice, bulletin, communiqué, dirt (*U.S. slang*), disclosure, dispatch, exposé, gen (*Brit. informal*), gossip, hearsay, information, intelligence, latest (*informal*), leak, news flash, release, report, revelation, rumour, scandal, statement, story, tidings, word

next *adj.* **1.** consequent, ensuing, following, later, sub-

nibble *vb* **-bling, -bled 1** to take little bites (of). **2** to bite gently: *she nibbled at her lower lip.* ~*n* **3** a little bite. **4** a light hurried meal.

nibs *n* **his** *or* **her nibs** *Slang* a mock title used of an important or self-important person.

NICAM near-instantaneous companding system: a technique for coding audio signals into digital form.

nice *adj* **1** pleasant. **2** kind: *it's nice of you to worry about me.* **3** good or satisfactory: *a nice clean operation.* **4** subtle: *a nice distinction.* **nicely** *adv* **niceness** *n*

➤ It is mistaken to suggest that the adjective *nice* should never be used, but, since it has been overused, it should be used sparingly.

nicety *n, pl* **-ties 1** a subtle point: *the niceties of our arguments.* **2** a refinement or delicacy: *social niceties.* **3 to a nicety** precisely.

niche (**neesh**) *n* **1** a recess in a wall for a statue or ornament. **2** a position exactly suitable for the person occupying it: *perhaps I will find my niche in a desk job.*

nick *vb* **1** to make a small cut in. **2** *Slang* to steal. **3** *Slang* to arrest. ~*n* **4** a small notch or cut. **5** *Slang* a prison or police station. **6** *Informal* condition: *in good nick.* **7 in the nick of time** just in time.

nickel *n* **1** *Chem* a silvery-white metallic element that is often used in alloys. Symbol: Ni **2** a US or Canadian coin worth five cents.

nickelodeon *n US* an early type of jukebox.

nickel silver *n* an alloy containing copper, zinc, and nickel.

nicker *n, pl* **nicker** *Brit slang* a pound sterling.

nick-nack *n* same as **knick-knack.**

nickname *n* **1** a familiar, pet, or derisory name given to a person or place. ~*vb* **-naming, -named 2** to call (a person or place) by a nickname: *Gaius Caesar Augustus Germanicus, nicknamed Caligula.*

nicotine *n* a poisonous alkaloid found in tobacco. **nicotinic** *adj*

nictitating membrane *n* (in reptiles, birds, and some mammals) a thin fold of skin under the eyelid that can be drawn across the eye.

niece *n* a daughter of one's sister or brother.

niff *Brit slang* ~*n* **1** a stink. ~*vb* **2** to stink. **niffy** *adj*

nifty *adj* **-tier, -tiest** *Informal* neat or smart.

Nigerian *adj* **1** of Nigeria. ~*n* **2** a person from Nigeria.

niggard *n* a stingy person.

niggardly *adj* not generous: *it pays its staff on a niggardly scale.* **niggardliness** *n*

nigger *n Offensive* a Black person.

niggle *vb* **-gling, -gled 1** to worry slightly. **2** to find fault continually. ~*n* **3** a small worry or doubt. **4** a trivial objection or complaint. **niggling** *adj*

nigh *adj, adv, prep Archaic, poetic* near.

night *n* **1** the period of darkness that occurs each 24 hours, between sunset and sunrise. **2** the period between sunset and bedtime; evening. **3** the time between bedtime and morning. **4** nightfall or dusk. **5** an evening designated for a specific activity: *opening night.* **6 make a night of it** to celebrate the whole evening. ~*adj* **7** of, occurring, or working at night: *the night sky.* ~See also **nights.**

nightcap *n* **1** a drink taken just before bedtime. **2** a soft cap formerly worn in bed.

nightclub *n* a place of entertainment open until late at night, usually offering drink, a floor show, and dancing.

THESAURUS

sequent, succeeding **2.** adjacent, adjoining, closest, nearest, neighbouring ~*adv.* **3.** afterwards, closely, following, later, subsequently, thereafter

nibble 1. *vb.* bite, eat, gnaw, munch, nip, peck, pick at **2.** *n.* bite, crumb, morsel, peck, snack, *soupçon*, taste, titbit

nice 1. agreeable, amiable, attractive, charming, commendable, courteous, delightful, friendly, good, kind, likable *or* likeable, pleasant, pleasurable, polite, prepossessing, refined, well-mannered **2.** accurate, careful, critical, delicate, discriminating, exact, exacting, fastidious, fine, meticulous, precise, rigorous, scrupulous, strict, subtle

nicely 1. acceptably, agreeably, amiably, attractively, charmingly, commendably, courteously, delightfully, kindly, likably *or* likeably, pleasantly, pleasingly, pleasurably, politely, prepossessingly, well **2.** accurately, carefully, critically, delicately, exactingly, exactly, fastidiously, finely, meticulously, precisely, rigorously, scrupulously, strictly, subtly

niceness 1. agreeableness, amiability, attractiveness, charm, courtesy, delightfulness, friendliness, good manners, goodness, kindness, likableness *or* likeableness, pleasantness, pleasurableness, politeness, refinement **2.** accuracy, care, carefulness, criticalness, delicacy, discrimination, exactingness, exactitude, exactness, fastidiousness, fineness, meticulosity, meticulousness, preciseness, precision, rigorousness, rigour, scrupulosity, scrupulousness, strictness, subtleness, subtlety

nicety 1. accuracy, exactness, fastidiousness, finesse, meticulousness, minuteness, precision **2.** daintiness, delicacy, discrimination, distinction, nuance, refinement

niche 1. alcove, corner, hollow, nook, opening, recess **2.** calling, pigeonhole (*informal*), place, position, slot (*informal*), vocation

nick chip, cut, damage, dent, mark, notch, scar, score, scratch, snick

nickname diminutive, epithet, familiar name, handle (*slang*), label, moniker *or* monicker (*slang*), pet name, sobriquet

niggard cheapskate (*informal*), cheeseparer, meanie *or* meany (*informal, chiefly Brit.*), miser, penny-pincher (*informal*), Scrooge, skinflint, tight-arse (*taboo slang*), tight-ass (*U.S. taboo slang*)

niggardliness avarice, avariciousness, beggarliness, closeness, covetousness, frugality, grudgingness, inadequacy, insufficiency, meagreness, meanness, mercenariness, miserableness, miserliness, paltriness, parsimony, penuriousness, scantiness, skimpiness, smallness, sordidness, sparingness, stinginess, thrift, tightfistedness, ungenerousness, wretchedness

niggardly avaricious, beggarly, close, covetous, frugal, grudging, inadequate, insufficient, meagre, mean, measly, mercenary, miserable, miserly, paltry, parsimonious, penurious, scant, scanty, Scroogelike, skimpy, small, sordid, sparing, stinging, stingy, tight-arse (*taboo slang*), tight-arsed (*taboo slang*), tight as a duck's arse (*taboo slang*), tight-ass (*U.S. taboo slang*), tight-assed (*U.S. taboo slang*), tightfisted, ungenerous, wretched

niggle 1. annoy, irritate, rankle, worry **2.** carp, cavil, criticize, find fault, fuss

niggling 1. gnawing, irritating, persistent, troubling, worrying **2.** cavilling, finicky, fussy, insignificant, minor, nit-picking (*informal*), pettifogging, petty, picky (*informal*), piddling (*informal*), quibbling, trifling, unimportant

nightdress *n* a loose dress worn in bed by women or girls.
nightfall *n* the approach of darkness; dusk.
nightgown *n* same as **nightdress.**
nightie *n Informal* short for **nightdress.**
nightingale *n* a small bird with a musical song, usually heard at night.
nightjar *n* a nocturnal bird with a harsh cry.
nightlife *n* the entertainment and social activities available at night in a town or city: *New York nightlife.*
night-light *n* a dim light left on overnight.
nightlong *adj, adv* throughout the night.
nightly *adj* **1** happening each night. *~adv* **2** each night.
nightmare *n* **1** a terrifying or deeply distressing dream. **2** a terrifying or unpleasant experience. **3** a thing that is feared: *wheels and loose straps are a baggage handler's nightmare.* **nightmarish** *adj*
nights *adv Informal* at night or on most nights: *he works nights.*
night safe *n* a safe built into the outside wall of a bank, in which customers can deposit money when the bank is closed.
night school *n* an educational institution that holds classes in the evening.
nightshade *n* a plant which produces poisonous berries with bell-shaped flowers.
nightshirt *n* a long loose shirtlike garment worn in bed.
night soil *n Archaic* human excrement collected at night from cesspools or privies.
nightspot *n Informal* a nightclub.
night-time *n* the time from sunset to sunrise.
night watch *n* **1** a watch or guard kept at night for security. **2** the period of time this watch is kept.
night watchman *n* a person who keeps guard at night on a factory or other building.
nihilism **(nye-ill-liz-zum)** *n* a total rejection of all established authority and institutions. **nihilist** *n, adj* **nihilistic** *adj*
-nik *suffix forming nouns* indicating a person associated with a particular state or quality: *refusenik.*
nil *n* nothing: used esp. as a score in games.
nimble *adj* **1** agile and quick in movement. **2** mentally alert or acute. **nimbly** *adv*
nimbus *n, pl* **-bi** *or* **-buses 1** a dark grey rain cloud. **2** a halo.
NIMBY not in my back yard: used of people who are opposed to any building or changes that will affect them directly.
nincompoop *n Informal* a stupid person.
nine *n* **1** the cardinal number that is the sum of one and eight. **2** a numeral, 9 or IX, representing this number. **3** something representing or consisting of nine units. **4 dressed up to the nines** *Informal* elaborately dressed. **5 999** (in Britain) the telephone number of the emergency services. *~adj* **6** amounting to nine: *nine men.* **ninth** *adj, n*
nine-days wonder *n* something that arouses great interest, but only for a short period.
ninefold *adj* **1** having nine times as many or as much. **2** having nine parts. *~adv* **3** by nine times as much or as much.
ninepins *n* the game of skittles.
nineteen *n* **1** the cardinal number that is the sum of ten and nine. **2** a numeral, 19 or XIX, representing this number. **3** something representing or consisting of nineteen units. **4 talk nineteen to the dozen** to talk very fast. *~adj* **5** amounting to nineteen: *nineteen years.* **nineteenth** *adj, n*
nineteenth hole *n Golf slang* the bar in a golf clubhouse.
ninety *n, pl* **-ties 1** the cardinal number that is the product of ten and nine. **2** a numeral, 90 or XC, representing this number. **3** something representing or consisting of ninety units. **4 nineties** the numbers 90 to 99, esp. when used to refer to a year of someone's life or of a century. *~adj* **5** amounting to ninety: *ninety degrees.* **ninetieth** *adj, n*
ninja *n, pl* **-ja** *or* **-jas** a person skilled in **ninjutsu**, a Japanese martial art characterized by stealthy movement and camouflage.
ninny *n, pl* **-nies** a stupid person.
niobium *n Chem* a white superconductive metallic element. Symbol: Nb
nip[1] *vb* **nipping, nipped 1** *Informal* to hurry. **2** to pinch or squeeze. **3** to bite lightly. **4** (of the cold) to affect (someone) with a stinging sensation. **5** to check the growth of (something): *a trite script nips all hope in the bud.* *~n* **6** a pinch or light bite. **7** sharp coldness: *a nip in the air.*
nip[2] *n* a small drink of spirits.
nipper *n Informal* a small child.
nipple *n* **1** the small projection in the centre of each breast, which in females contains the outlet of the milk ducts. **2** a small projection through which oil or grease can be put into a machine or component.

THESAURUS

night dark, darkness, dead of night, hours of darkness, night-time, night watches
nightfall dusk, eve (*archaic*), evening, eventide, gloaming (*Scot. or poetic*), sundown, sunset, twilight, vespers
nightly *adj./adv.* each night, every night, night after night, nights (*informal*)
nightmare 1. bad dream, hallucination, incubus, succubus **2.** horror, ordeal, torment, trial, tribulation
nil duck, love, naught, *nihil,* none, nothing, zero, zilch (*slang*)
nimble active, agile, alert, brisk, deft, dexterous, lively, nippy (*Brit. informal*), proficient, prompt, quick, quick-witted, ready, smart, sprightly, spry, swift
nimbly actively, acutely, agilely, alertly, briskly, deftly, dexterously, easily, fast, fleetly, hotfoot, posthaste, proficiently, promptly, pronto (*informal*), quickly, quick-wittedly, readily, sharply, smartly, speedily, spryly, swiftly
nimbus ambience, atmosphere, aura, aureole, cloud, corona, glow, halo
nincompoop berk (*Brit. slang*), blockhead, charlie (*Brit. informal*), coot, dickhead (*slang*), dimwit (*informal*), dipstick (*Brit. slang*), divvy (*slang*), dolt, dork (*slang*), dunce, dweeb (*U.S. slang*), fool, fuckwit (*taboo slang*), geek (*slang*), gonzo (*slang*), idiot, jerk (*slang, chiefly U.S. & Canad.*), lamebrain (*informal*), nerd *or* nurd (*slang*), ninny, nitwit (*informal*), noodle, numskull *or* numbskull, oaf, pillock (*Brit. slang*), plank (*Brit. slang*), plonker (*slang*), prat (*slang*), prick (*derogatory slang*), schmuck (*U.S. slang*), simpleton, twit (*informal, chiefly Brit.*), wally (*slang*)
nip[1] *vb.* **1.** bite, catch, clip, compress, grip, nibble, pinch, snag, snap, snip, squeeze, tweak, twitch **2.** check, frustrate, thwart
nip[2] *n.* dram, draught, drop, finger, mouthful, portion, shot (*informal*), sip, snifter (*informal*), *soupçon,* sup, swallow, taste
nipper *informal* ankle-biter (*Austral. slang*), baby,

nippy *adj* **-pier, -piest 1** (of weather) frosty or chilly. **2** *Informal* quick or nimble. **3** (of a motor vehicle) small and relatively powerful.

nirvana (near-**vah**-na) *n Buddhism, Hinduism* the ultimate state of spiritual enlightenment and bliss attained by extinction of all desires and individual existence.

nisi (**nye**-sigh) *adj* See **decree nisi.**

Nissen hut *n* a tunnel-shaped military shelter made of corrugated steel.

nit[1] *n* the egg or larva of a louse.

nit[2] *n Informal* short for **nitwit.**

nit-picking *Informal ~n* **1** a concern with insignificant details, usually with the intention of finding fault. *~adj* **2** showing such concern.

nitrate *Chem ~n* **1** a salt or ester of nitric acid. **2** a fertilizer containing nitrate salts. *~vb* **-trating, -trated 3** to treat with nitric acid or a nitrate. **4** to convert or be converted into a nitrate. **nitration** *n*

nitre *or US* **niter** *n Chem* same as **potassium nitrate.**

nitric *adj Chem* of or containing nitrogen.

nitric acid *n Chem* a colourless corrosive liquid widely used in industry.

nitride *n Chem* a compound of nitrogen with a more electropositive element.

nitrify *vb* **-fies, -fying, -fied** *Chem* **1** to treat (a substance) or cause (a substance) to react with nitrogen. **2** to treat (soil) with nitrates. **3** to convert (ammonium compounds) into nitrates by oxidation. **nitrification** *n*

nitrite *n Chem* a salt or ester of nitrous acid.

nitro- *or before a vowel* **nitr-** *combining form* indicating that: **1** a chemical compound contains the univalent group, $-NO_2$: *nitrobenzene.* **2** a chemical compound which is a nitrate ester: *nitrocellulose.*

nitrogen (**nite**-roj-jen) *n Chem* a colourless odourless gas that forms four-fifths of the air and is an essential part of all animal and plant life. Symbol: N **nitrogenous** *adj*

nitrogen cycle *n* the natural cycle by which nitrates in the soil, derived from dead organic matter, are absorbed by plants and reduced to nitrates again when the plants and the animals feeding on them die and decay.

nitrogen fixation *n* the conversion of atmospheric nitrogen into nitrogen compounds by soil bacteria.

nitroglycerine *or* **nitroglycerin** *n Chem* a thick pale yellow explosive liquid made from glycerol and nitric and sulphuric acids.

nitrous *adj Chem* derived from or containing nitrogen in a low valency state.

nitrous acid *n Chem* a weak acid known only in solution and in the form of nitrite salts.

nitrous oxide *n Chem* a colourless gas used as an anaesthetic.

nitty-gritty *n* **the nitty-gritty** *Informal* the basic facts of a matter or situation.

nitwit *n Informal* a stupid person.

NJ New Jersey.

nkosi (ing-**koss**-ee) *n S African* a term of address to a superior; master; chief.

NM New Mexico.

no[1] *interj* **1** used to express denial, disagreement, or refusal. *~n, pl* **noes** *or* **nos 2** an answer or vote of *no.* **3** a person who answers or votes *no.*

no[2] *adj* **1** not any, not a, or not one: *I have no money; no comment.* **2** not at all: *he's no exception.* **3** not: *no taller than a child.* **4 no way!** an expression of emphatic refusal or denial.

No[1] *or* **Noh** *n, pl* **No** *or* **Noh** the stylized classical drama of Japan, using music and dancing.

No[2] *Chem* nobelium.

No. *or* **no.** *pl* **Nos.** *or* **nos.** number.

n.o. *Cricket* not out.

nob *n Slang, chiefly Brit* a person of wealth or social distinction.

no-ball *n Cricket* an improperly bowled ball, for which the batting side scores a run. Abbrev.: **nb**

nobble *vb* **-bling, -bled** *Brit slang* **1** to attract the attention of (someone) in order to talk to him or her. **2** to bribe or threaten. **3** to disable (a racehorse) to stop it from winning. **4** to steal.

nobelium *n Chem* a radioactive element produced artificially from curium. Symbol: No

Nobel prize (no-**bell**) *n* a prize for outstanding contributions to chemistry, physics, physiology and medicine, literature, economics, and peace that may be awarded annually.

nobility *n* **1** the quality of being noble; dignity. **2** the class of people who hold titles and high social rank.

noble *adj* **1** having or showing high moral qualities: *a noble cause.* **2** belonging to a class of people who hold titles and high social rank. **3** impressive and magnificent: *a noble beast.* **4** *Chem* (of certain metals) resisting oxidation. *~n* **5** a person who holds a title and high social rank. **nobly** *adv*

noble gas *n* any of the unreactive gases helium, neon, argon, krypton, xenon, and radon.

nobleman *or fem* **noblewoman** *n, pl* **-men** *or* **-women** a person of noble rank.

noblesse oblige (no-**bless** oh-**bleezh**) *n Often ironic* the supposed obligation of the nobility to be honourable and generous.

THESAURUS

boy, child, girl, infant, kid (*informal*), little one, rug rat (*slang*), sprog (*slang*), tot

nipple boob (*slang*), breast, dug, mamilla, pap, papilla, teat, tit, udder

nippy 1. biting, chilly, nipping, sharp, stinging **2.** *informal* active, agile, fast, nimble, quick, spry

nit-picking captious, carping, cavilling, finicky, fussy, hairsplitting, pedantic, pettifogging, quibbling

nitty-gritty basics, brass tacks (*informal*), core, crux, essence, essentials, facts, fundamentals, gist, heart of the matter, reality, substance

nitwit *informal* dickhead (*slang*), dimwit (*informal*), dipstick (*Brit. slang*), divvy (*slang*), dork (*slang*), dummy (*slang*), fool, fuckwit (*taboo slang*), geek (*slang*), halfwit, lamebrain (*informal*), nincompoop, ninny, oaf, plank (*Brit. slang*), simpleton

nob aristo (*informal*), aristocrat, big shot (*informal*), bigwig (*informal*), celeb (*informal*), fat cat (*slang, chiefly U.S.*), nabob (*informal*), toff (*Brit. slang*), V.I.P.

nobble *Brit. slang* **1.** bribe, get at, influence, intimidate, outwit, threaten, win over **2.** disable, handicap, incapacitate, weaken **3.** filch, knock off (*slang*), nick (*slang, chiefly Brit.*), pilfer, pinch (*informal*), purloin, snitch (*slang*), steal, swipe (*slang*)

nobility 1. dignity, eminence, excellence, grandeur, greatness, illustriousness, loftiness, magnificence, majesty, nobleness, stateliness, sublimity, superiority, worthiness **2.** aristocracy, elite, high society, lords, nobles, patricians, peerage, ruling class, upper class

noble *adj.* **1.** generous, honourable, magnanimous, upright, virtuous, worthy **2.** aristocratic, blue-blooded, gentle (*archaic*), highborn, lordly, patrician, titled **3.** august, dignified, distinguished, elevated, eminent, excellent, grand, great, imposing, impressive, lofty,

nobody *pron* **1** no person; no-one. *~n, pl* **-bodies 2** a person of no importance.
➤ *Nobody* is equivalent in its uses to *no-one.*

nock *n* **1** a notch on an arrow that fits on the bowstring. **2** a groove at either end of a bow that holds the bowstring.

no-claims bonus *or* **no-claim bonus** *n* a reduction in the cost of an insurance policy made if no claims have been made in a specified period.

nocturnal *adj* **1** of the night. **2** (of animals) active at night.

nocturne *n* a short dreamy piece of music.

nod *vb* **nodding, nodded 1** to lower and raise (one's head) briefly, to express agreement or greeting. **2** to express by nodding: *he nodded his approval.* **3** to sway or bend forwards and back. **4** to let one's head fall forward with sleep. **5 nodding acquaintance** a slight knowledge (of a subject or person). *~n* **6** a quick down-and-up movement of the head, in agreement. **7 land of Nod** an imaginary land of sleep.

noddle *n Informal, chiefly Brit* the head or brains.

noddy *n, pl* **-dies 1** a tropical tern with a dark plumage. **2** a fool.

node *n* **1** *Bot* the point on a plant stem from which the leaves grow. **2** *Maths* a point at which a curve crosses itself. **3** a knot or knob. **4** *Physics* a point in a vibrating body at which there is practically no vibration. **5** *Anat* any natural bulge or swelling: *lymph node.* **6** *Astron* either of the two points at which the orbit of a body intersects the path of the sun or the orbit of another body. **nodal** *adj*

nod off *vb Informal* to fall asleep.

nodule *n* **1** a small rounded lump, knot, or node. **2** a rounded mineral growth on the root of a plant such as clover. **nodular** *adj*

Noel *n* same as **Christmas.**

nog *n* an alcoholic drink containing beaten egg.

noggin *n* **1** *Informal* the head. **2** a small quantity of spirits.

no-go area *n* a district that is barricaded off so that the police or army can enter only by force.

noise *n* **1** a sound, usually a loud or disturbing one. **2** loud shouting; din. **3** an undesired electrical disturbance in a signal. **4 noises** conventional utterances conveying a reaction: *he made the appropriate noises.* *~vb* **noising, noised 5 be noised abroad** (of news or gossip) to be spread.

noiseless *adj* making little or no sound. **noiselessly** *adv*

noisette (nwah-**zett**) *n* a hazelnut chocolate.

noisome *adj Formal* **1** (of smells) offensive. **2** extremely unpleasant.

noisy *adj* **noisier, noisiest 1** making a lot of noise. **2** (of a place) full of noise. **noisily** *adv*

nomad *n* **1** a member of a tribe who move from place to place to find pasture and food. **2** a wanderer. **nomadic** *adj*

no-man's-land *n* land between boundaries, esp. an unoccupied zone between opposing forces.

nom de plume *n, pl* **noms de plume** same as **pen name.**

nomenclature (no-**men**-klatch-er) *n Formal* the system of names used in a particular subject.

nominal *adj* **1** in name only: *nominal independence.* **2** very small in comparison with real worth: *a nominal amount of aid.* **nominally** *adv*

nominalism *n* the philosophical theory that a general word, such as *dog,* is merely a name and does not denote a real object. **nominalist** *n*

nominal value *n* same as **par value.**

nominate *vb* **-nating, -nated 1** to propose (someone) as a candidate. **2** to appoint (someone) to an office or position. **nomination** *n*

nominative *n Grammar* a grammatical case in some languages that identifies the subject of a verb.

nominee *n* a person who is nominated to an office or as a candidate.

non- *prefix* indicating: **1** negation: *nonexistent.* **2** refusal or failure: *noncooperation.* **3** exclusion from a specified class: *nonfiction.* **4** lack or absence: *nonevent.*

nonaddictive *adj* not causing addiction.

nonage *n* **1** *Law* the state of being under full legal age for various actions. **2** a period of immaturity.

nonagenarian *n* a person who is from 90 to 99 years old.

nonaggression *n* the policy of not attacking other countries.

nonagon *n Geom* a figure with nine sides. **nonagonal** *adj*

nonalcoholic *adj* containing no alcohol.

nonaligned *adj* (of a country) not part of a major alliance or power bloc. **nonalignment** *n*

nonbeliever *n* a person who does not follow a particular religious movement.

nonbelligerent *adj* (of a country) not taking part in a war.

THESAURUS

splendid, stately, superb *~n.* **4.** aristo (*informal*), aristocrat, lord, nobleman, peer

nobody 1. *pron.* no-one **2.** *n.* cipher, lightweight (*informal*), menial, nonentity, nothing (*informal*)

nocturnal night, nightly, night-time, of the night

nod *vb.* **1.** acknowledge, bob, bow, dip, duck, gesture, indicate, nutate (*rare*), salute, signal **2.** agree, assent, concur, show agreement **3.** be sleepy, doze, droop, drowse, kip (*Brit. slang*), nap, sleep, slump, zizz (*Brit. informal*) *~n.* **4.** acknowledgment, beck, gesture, greeting, indication, salute, sign, signal

noise 1. *n.* babble, blare, clamour, clatter, commotion, cry, din, fracas, hubbub, outcry, pandemonium, racket, row, sound, talk, tumult, uproar **2.** *vb.* advertise, bruit, circulate, gossip, publicize, repeat, report, rumour, spread

noiseless hushed, inaudible, mute, muted, quiet, silent, soundless, still

noisy boisterous, cacophonous, chattering, clamorous, deafening, ear-splitting, loud, obstreperous, piercing, riotous, strident, tumultuous, turbulent, uproarious, vociferous

nomad drifter, itinerant, migrant, rambler, rover, vagabond, wanderer

nomadic itinerant, migrant, migratory, pastoral, peripatetic, roaming, roving, travelling, vagrant, wandering

nom de plume alias, assumed name, nom de guerre, pen name, pseudonym

nomenclature classification, codification, phraseology, taxonomy, terminology, vocabulary

nominal 1. formal, ostensible, pretended, professed, puppet, purported, self-styled, so-called, supposed, theoretical, titular **2.** inconsiderable, insignificant, minimal, small, symbolic, token, trifling, trivial

nominate appoint, assign, choose, commission, designate, elect, elevate, empower, name, present, propose, recommend, select, submit, suggest, term

nomination appointment, choice, designation, election, proposal, recommendation, selection, suggestion

nonce *n* **for the nonce** for the present.
nonce word *n* a word coined for a single occasion.
nonchalant (**non**-shall-ant) *adj* casually unconcerned or indifferent. **nonchalance** *n* **nonchalantly** *adv*
non-com *n* short for **noncommissioned officer.**
noncombatant *n* a member of the armed forces whose duties do not include fighting, such as a chaplain or surgeon.
noncombustible *adj* not capable of igniting and burning.
noncommissioned officer *n* (in the armed forces) a person who is appointed as a subordinate officer, from the lower ranks, rather than by a commission.
noncommittal *adj* not committing oneself to any particular opinion.
noncompliance *n* failure or refusal to do as requested.
non compos mentis *adj* of unsound mind.
nonconductor *n* a substance that is a poor conductor of heat, electricity, or sound.
nonconformist *n* **1** a person who does not conform to generally accepted patterns of behaviour or thought. ~*adj* **2** (of behaviour or ideas) not conforming to accepted patterns. **nonconformity** *n*
Nonconformist *n* **1** a member of a Protestant group separated from the Church of England. ~*adj* **2** of or relating to Nonconformists.
noncontributory *adj* denoting a pension scheme for employees, the premiums of which are paid entirely by the employer.
non-cooperation *n* the refusal to do more than is legally or contractually required of one.
noncustodial *adj* not involving imprisonment: *a noncustodial sentence.*
nondescript *adj* lacking outstanding features.
nondrinker *n* a person who does not drink alcohol.
none *pron* **1** not any: *none of the men was represented by a lawyer; none of it meant anything to him.* **2** noone; nobody: *none could deny it.* **3 none the** in no degree: *her parents were none the wiser.*
➤ Although *none* means "not one", and can take a singular verb, it more often takes a plural: *None of them are mine.*
nonentity (non-**enn**-tit-tee) *n, pl* **-ties** an insignificant person or thing.
nonessential *adj* not absolutely necessary.
nonetheless *adv* despite that; however.
nonevent *n* a disappointing or insignificant occurrence which was expected to be important.
nonexistent *adj* not existing in a particular place. **nonexistence** *n*
nonferrous *adj* **1** denoting a metal other than iron. **2** not containing iron.
nonfiction *n* writing that deals with facts or real events.
nonflammable *adj* not easily set on fire.
nonfunctional *adj* having no practical function.
nonintervention *n* refusal to intervene in the affairs of others.
noniron *adj* not requiring ironing.
nonmember *n* a person who is not a member of a particular club or organization.
nonmetal *n Chem* a chemical element that forms acidic oxides and is a poor conductor of heat and electricity. **nonmetallic** *adj*
nonmoral *adj* not involving morality; neither moral nor immoral.
non-native *adj* not originating in a particular place.
non-nuclear *adj* not involving or using nuclear power or weapons.
no-nonsense *adj* sensible, practical, and straightforward: *a no-nonsense approach to crime.*
nonpareil (non-par-**rail**) *n* a person or thing that is unsurpassed.
nonpartisan *adj* not supporting any single political party.
nonpayment *n* failure to pay money owed.
nonplussed *or US* **nonplused** *adj* perplexed.
nonprofessional *adj* not earning a living at a specified occupation: *nonprofessional investors.*
non-profit-making *adj* not intended to make a profit.
nonproliferation *n* limitation of the production or spread of something such as nuclear or chemical weapons.
nonrepresentational *adj Art* same as **abstract.**
nonresident *n* a person who does not live in a particular country or place.

THESAURUS

nominee aspirant, candidate, contestant, entrant, favourite, protégé, runner
nonaligned impartial, neutral, uncommitted, undecided
nonchalance calm, composure, cool (*slang*), equanimity, imperturbability, indifference, sang-froid, self-possession, unconcern
nonchalant airy, apathetic, blasé, calm, careless, casual, collected, cool, detached, dispassionate, indifferent, insouciant, laid-back (*informal*), offhand, unconcerned, unemotional, unfazed (*informal*), unperturbed
noncombatant civilian, neutral, nonbelligerent
noncommittal ambiguous, careful, cautious, circumspect, discreet, equivocal, evasive, guarded, indefinite, neutral, politic, reserved, tactful, temporizing, tentative, unrevealing, vague, wary
non compos mentis crazy, deranged, insane, mentally ill, of unsound mind, unbalanced, unhinged
nonconformist dissenter, dissentient, eccentric, heretic, iconoclast, individualist, maverick, protester, radical, rebel
nondescript characterless, common or garden (*informal*), commonplace, dull, featureless, indeterminate, mousy, ordinary, unclassifiable, unclassified, undistinguished, unexceptional, uninspiring, uninteresting, unmemorable, unremarkable, vague
none bugger all (*slang*), f.a. (*Brit. slang*), fuck all (*taboo slang*), nil, nobody, no-one, no part, not a bit, not any, nothing, not one, sod all (*Brit. slang*), sweet F.A. (*Brit. slang*), sweet Fanny Adams (*Brit. slang*), zero
nonentity cipher, lightweight (*informal*), mediocrity, nobody, small fry, unimportant person
nonessential dispensable, excessive, expendable, extraneous, inessential, peripheral, superfluous, unimportant, unnecessary
nonetheless despite that, even so, however, in spite of that, nevertheless, yet
nonsense absurdity, balderdash, balls (*taboo slang*), bilge (*informal*), blather, bombast, bosh (*informal*), bull (*slang*), bullshit (*taboo slang*), bunk (*informal*), bunkum *or* buncombe (*chiefly U.S.*), claptrap (*informal*), cobblers (*Brit. taboo slang*), crap (*slang*), double Dutch (*Brit. informal*), drivel, eyewash (*informal*), fa-

nonsectarian *adj* not confined to any specific subdivision of a religious group.
nonsense *n* **1** something that has or makes no sense. **2** unintelligible language. **3** foolish behaviour: *she'll stand no nonsense.* **nonsensical** *adj*
non sequitur (**sek**-wit-tur) *n* a statement having little or no relation to what preceded it.
nonslip *adj* designed to prevent slipping: *a nonslip mat.*
nonsmoker *n* **1** a person who does not smoke. **2** a train carriage or compartment in which smoking is forbidden.
nonsmoking *or* **no-smoking** *adj* denoting an area in which smoking is forbidden.
nonstandard *adj* denoting words, expressions, or pronunciations that are not regarded as correct by educated native speakers of a language.
nonstarter *n* a person or an idea that has little chance of success.
nonstick *adj* (of cooking utensils) coated with a substance that food will not stick to when cooked.
nonstop *adj, adv* without a stop: *two weeks of nonstop rain; most days his phone rings nonstop.*
nontoxic *adj* not poisonous.
non-U *adj Brit informal* (of language or behaviour) not characteristic of the upper classes.
nonunion *adj* **1** (of a company) not employing trade union members: *a nonunion shop.* **2** (of a person) not belonging to a trade union.
nonverbal *adj* not involving the use of language.
nonviolent *adj* using peaceful methods to bring about change. **nonviolence** *n*
nonvoter *n* **1** a person who does not vote. **2** a person not eligible to vote.
nonvoting *adj Finance* (of shares in a company) not entitling the holder to vote at company meetings.
non-White *adj* **1** belonging to a race of people not European in origin. *~n* **2** a member of one of these races.
noodle *n* a simpleton.
noodles *pl n* ribbon-like strips of pasta.
nook *n* **1** a corner or recess. **2** a secluded or sheltered place.
noon *n* the middle of the day; 12 o'clock.
noonday *n* noon.
no-one *or* **no one** *pron* no person; nobody.
➤ When *no-one* refers to "people in general" it may be followed by a plural: *No-one finished their drink.*
noose *n* a loop in the end of a rope, tied with a slipknot, such as one used to hang people.
nope *interj Informal* no.
nor *conj* **1** (used to join alternatives, the first of which is preceded by *neither*) and not: *neither willing nor able.* **2** and not .... either: *he had not arrived yet, nor had any of the models.*
nordic *adj Skiing* of competitions in cross-country racing and ski-jumping.
Nordic *adj* of Scandinavia or its typically tall, blond, and blue-eyed people.
norm *n* a standard that is required, desired, or regarded as normal.
normal *adj* **1** usual, regular, or typical: *the study of normal behaviour.* **2** free from mental or physical disorder. **3** *Geom* same as **perpendicular** (sense 1). *~n* **4** the usual, regular, or typical state, degree, or form. **5** *Geom* a perpendicular line or plane. **normality** *or esp US* **normalcy** *n*
normalize *or* **-ise** *vb* **-izing, -ized** *or* **-ising, -ised 1** to make or become normal. **2** to bring into conformity with a standard. **normalization** *or* **-isation** *n*
normally *adv* **1** as a rule; usually. **2** in a normal manner.
Norman *n* **1** a person from Normandy in N France, esp. one of the people who conquered England in 1066. **2** same as **Norman French.** *~adj* **3** of the Normans or their dialect of French. **4** of Normandy. **5** of a style of architecture used in Britain from the Norman Conquest until the 12th century, with rounded arches and massive masonry walls.
Norman French *n* the medieval Norman and English dialect of Old French.
normative *adj* of or establishing a norm or standard: *a normative model.*
Norn *n Norse myth* any of the three virgin goddesses of fate.
Norse *adj* **1** of ancient and medieval Scandinavia. **2** of Norway. *~n* **3 a** the N group of Germanic languages spoken in Scandinavia. **b** any one of these languages, esp. in their ancient or medieval forms.
Norseman *n, pl* **-men** same as **Viking.**
north *n* **1** one of the four cardinal points of the compass, at 0° or 360°. **2** the direction along a meridian towards the North Pole. **3** the direction in which a compass needle points; magnetic north. **4 the north** any area lying in or towards the north. *~adj* **5** in or towards the north. **6** (esp. of the wind) from the north. *~adv* **7** in, to, or towards the north.
North *n* **1 the North a** the northern part of England, generally regarded as reaching the southern boundaries of Yorkshire, Derbyshire, and Cheshire. **b** (in the US) the states north of the Mason-Dixon Line that were known as the Free States during the Civil War. **c** the economically and technically advanced countries

THESAURUS

tuity, folly, foolishness, garbage (*informal*), gibberish, guff (*slang*), hogwash, hokum (*slang, chiefly U.S. & Canad.*), horsefeathers (*U.S. slang*), hot air (*informal*), idiocy, inanity, jest, ludicrousness, moonshine, pap, piffle (*informal*), poppycock (*informal*), ridiculousness, rot, rubbish, senselessness, shit (*taboo slang*), silliness, stuff, stupidity, tommyrot, tosh (*slang, chiefly Brit.*), trash, tripe (*informal*), twaddle, waffle (*informal, chiefly Brit.*)
nonstop 1. *adj.* ceaseless, constant, continuous, direct, endless, incessant, interminable, relentless, steady, unbroken, unending, unfaltering, uninterrupted, unremitting **2.** *adv.* ceaselessly, constantly, continuously, directly, endlessly, incessantly, interminably, relentlessly, steadily, unbrokenly, unendingly, unfalteringly, uninterruptedly, unremittingly, without stopping
nook alcove, cavity, corner, cranny, crevice, cubbyhole, hide-out, inglenook (*Brit.*), niche, opening, recess, retreat
noon high noon, midday, noonday, noontide, noontime, twelve noon
norm average, benchmark, criterion, mean, measure, model, par, pattern, rule, standard, type, yardstick
normal 1. accustomed, acknowledged, average, common, conventional, habitual, natural, ordinary, popular, regular, routine, run-of-the-mill, standard, typical, usual **2.** rational, reasonable, sane, well-adjusted
normality 1. accustomedness, averageness, commonness, commonplaceness, conventionality, habitualness, naturalness, ordinariness, popularity, regularity, routineness, typicality, usualness **2.** adjustment, balance, rationality, reason, sanity

of the world. *~adj* **2** of or denoting the northern part of a country or area.
Northants Northamptonshire.
northbound *adj* going towards the north.
North Country *n* **the North Country** same as **North** (sense 1a).
northeast *n* **1** the direction midway between north and east. **2 the northeast** any area lying in or towards the northeast. *~adj also* **northeastern 3** (*sometimes cap*) of or denoting that part of a country or area which lies in the northeast. **4** situated in, moving towards, or facing the northeast. **5** (esp. of the wind) from the northeast. *~adv* **6** in, to, or towards the northeast. **northeasterly** *adj, adv, n*
Northeast *n* **the Northeast** the northeastern part of England, esp. Northumberland and Durham.
northeaster *n* a strong wind or storm from the northeast.
northerly *adj* **1** of or in the north. *~adv, adj* **2** towards the north. **3** from the north: *a cold northerly wind.*
northern *adj* **1** situated in or towards the north. **2** facing or moving towards the north. **3** (*sometimes cap*) of or characteristic of the north or North. **northernmost** *adj*
Northerner *n* a person from the north of a country or area, esp. England.
northern hemisphere *n* that half of the globe lying north of the equator.
northern lights *pl n* same as **aurora borealis.**
Northman *n, pl* **-men** same as **Viking.**
North Pole *n* the northernmost point on the earth's axis, at a latitude of 90°N, which has very low temperatures.
North Star *n* **the North Star** same as **Pole Star.**
Northumb. Northumberland.
northward *adj, adv also* **northwards 1** towards the north. *~n* **2** the northward part or direction.
northwest *n* **1** the direction midway between north and west. **2 the northwest** any area lying in or towards the northwest. *~adj also* **northwestern 3** (*sometimes cap*) of or denoting that part of a country or area which lies in the northwest. **4** situated in, moving towards, or facing the northwest. **5** (esp. of the wind) from the northwest. *~adv* **6** in, to, or towards the northwest. **northwesterly** *adj, adv, n*
Northwest *n* **the Northwest** the northwestern part of England, esp. Lancashire and the Lake District.
northwester *n* a strong wind or storm from the northwest.
Norwegian *adj* **1** of Norway. *~n* **2** a person from Norway. **3** the language of Norway.
Nos. *or* **nos.** numbers.
nose *n* **1** the organ situated above the mouth, used for smelling and breathing. **2** the sense of smell. **3** the front part of a vehicle. **4** the distinctive smell of a wine or perfume. **5** instinctive skill in finding something: *he had a nose for media events.* **6 get up someone's nose** *Informal* to annoy someone. **7 keep one's nose clean** to stay out of trouble. **8 look down one's nose at** *Informal* to be haughty towards. **9 pay through the nose** *Informal* to pay a high price. **10 put someone's nose out of joint** *Informal* to make someone envious by doing what he would have liked to do or had expected to do. **11 rub someone's nose in it** *Informal* to remind someone unkindly of a failing or error. **12 turn up one's nose at** *Informal* to show contempt for. **13 win by a nose** to win by a narrow margin. *~vb* **nosing, nosed 14** to move forward slowly and carefully: *a motorboat nosed out of the mist.* **15** to pry or snoop. **16 nose out** to discover by searching or prying.
nosebag *n* a bag containing feed, fastened around the head of a horse.
noseband *n* the part of a horse's bridle that goes around the nose.
nosebleed *n* bleeding from the nose.
nose cone *n* the cone-shaped front section of a missile or spacecraft.
nose dive *n* **1** (of an aircraft) a sudden plunge with the nose pointing downwards. **2** *Informal* a sudden drop: *when we fail our self-confidence takes a nose dive.* *~vb* **nose-dive, -diving, -dived 3** to take a nose dive.
nosegay *n* a small bunch of flowers.
nosey *or* **nosy** *adj* **nosier, nosiest** *Informal* prying or inquisitive. **nosiness** *n*
nosey parker *n Informal, chiefly Brit* a prying person.
nosh *Slang ~n* **1** food. *~vb* **2** to eat.
nosh-up *n Brit slang* a large meal.
nostalgia *n* **1** a sentimental yearning for the past. **2** homesickness. **nostalgic** *adj* **nostalgically** *adv*
nostril *n* either of the two openings at the end of the nose.
nostrum *n* **1** a quack medicine. **2** a favourite remedy.
nosy *adj* **nosier, nosiest** same as **nosey.**
not *adv* **1** used to negate the sentence, phrase, or word that it modifies: *I will not stand for it.* **2 not that** which is not to say that: *not that I've ever heard him complain.*
nota bene (**note-a ben-nay**) note well; take note.
notable (**note-a-bl**) *adj* **1** worthy of being noted; remarkable. *~n* **2** a person of distinction. **notability** *n* **notably** *adv*
notary *or* **notary public** (**note-a-ree**) *n, pl* **nota-**

THESAURUS

normally as a rule, commonly, habitually, ordinarily, regularly, typically, usually
north 1. *adj.* Arctic, boreal, northerly, northern, polar **2.** *adv.* northerly, northward(s)
nose *n.* **1.** beak, bill, conk (*slang*), hooter (*slang*), neb (*archaic or dialect*), proboscis, schnozzle (*slang, chiefly U.S.*), snitch (*slang*), snout (*slang*) *~vb.* **2.** ease forward, nudge, nuzzle, push, shove **3.** meddle, pry, snoop (*informal*)
nose dive dive, drop, plummet, plunge
nosegay bouquet, posy
nosey, nosy curious, eavesdropping, inquisitive, interfering, intrusive, meddlesome, prying, snooping (*informal*)
nostalgia homesickness, longing, pining, regret, regretfulness, remembrance, reminiscence, wistfulness, yearning
nostalgic emotional, homesick, longing, maudlin, regretful, sentimental, wistful
nostrum cure, cure-all, drug, elixir, medicine, panacea, patent medicine, potion, quack medicine, remedy, sovereign cure, specific, treatment
notability celebrity, distinction, eminence, esteem, fame, renown
notable 1. *adj.* celebrated, conspicuous, distinguished, eminent, evident, extraordinary, famous, manifest, marked, memorable, noteworthy, noticeable, notorious, outstanding, pre-eminent, pronounced, rare, remarkable, renowned, striking, uncommon, unusual, well-known **2.** *n.* celeb (*informal*), celebrity,

ries *or* **notaries public** a public official, usually a solicitor, who is legally authorized to attest and certify documents.

notation (no-**tay**-shun) *n* **1** representation of numbers or quantities in a system by a series of symbols. **2** a set of such symbols.

notch *n* **1** a V-shaped cut. **2** *Informal* a step or level: *the economy moved up another notch.* ~*vb* **3** to cut a notch in. **4 notch up** *Informal* to score or achieve: *he notched up a hat trick of wins.*

note *n* **1** a brief informal letter. **2** a brief record in writing for future reference. **3** a critical comment or explanation in a book. **4** an official written communication, as from a government or from a doctor. **5** short for **banknote. 6** *Chiefly Brit* a musical sound of a particular pitch. **7** a written symbol representing the pitch and duration of a musical sound. **8** *Chiefly Brit* a key on a piano, organ, or other keyboard instrument. **9** a particular feeling or atmosphere: *an optimistic note.* **10** a distinctive vocal sound, as of a type of animal. **11** a sound used as a signal or warning: *the note to retreat was sounded.* **12** short for **promissory note. 13 of note a** distinguished or famous. **b** important: *nothing of note.* **14 strike the right note** to behave appropriately. **15 take note of** to pay attention to. ~*vb* **noting, noted 16** to notice; pay attention to: *such criticism should be noted.* **17** to make a written note of: *he noted it in his diary.* **18** to remark upon: *I note that you do not wear shoes.*

notebook *n* a book for writing in.

notecase *n* same as **wallet.**

noted *adj* well-known: *a noted scholar.*

notelet *n* a folded card with a printed design on the front, for writing informal letters.

notepad *n* a number of sheets of paper fastened together along one edge, used for writing notes or letters on.

notepaper *n* paper used for writing letters.

noteworthy *adj* worth noting; remarkable.

nothing *pron* **1** not anything: *I felt nothing.* **2** a matter of no importance: *don't worry, it's nothing.* **3** absence of meaning, value, or worth: *the industry shrank to almost nothing.* **4** the figure 0. **5 have** *or* **be nothing to do with** to have no connection with. **6 nothing but** not something other than; only. **7 nothing doing** *Informal* an expression of dismissal or refusal. **8 nothing less than** downright: *nothing less than complete withdrawal.* **9 think nothing of something** to regard something as easy or natural. ~*adv* **10** not at all: *he looked nothing like his brother.* ~*n* **11** *Informal* a person or thing of no importance or significance.

➤ *Nothing* is usually followed by a singular verb but, if it comes before a plural noun, this can sound odd: *Nothing but books was/were on the shelf.* A solution is to rephrase the sentence: *Only books were....*

nothingness *n* **1** nonexistence. **2** total insignificance.

notice *n* **1** observation or attention: *to attract notice.* **2** a displayed placard or announcement giving information. **3** advance notification of something such as intention to end a contract of employment: *she handed in her notice.* **4** a theatrical or literary review: *the film reaped ecstatic notices.* **5 take notice** to pay attention. **6 take no notice of** to ignore or disregard. **7 at short notice** with very little notification. ~*vb* **-ticing, -ticed 8** to become aware (of). **9** to point out or remark upon.

noticeable *adj* easily seen or detected. **noticeably** *adv*

notice board *n* a board on which notices are displayed.

notifiable *adj* having to be reported to the authorities: *a notifiable disease.*

notification *n* **1** the act of notifying someone of something. **2** a formal announcement.

notify *vb* **-fies, -fying, -fied** to inform: *notify gas and electricity companies of your moving date.*

notion *n* **1** an idea or opinion. **2** a whim.

notional *adj* hypothetical, imaginary, or unreal: *a notional dividend payment.*

notorious *adj* well known for some bad reason. **notoriety** *n* **notoriously** *adv*

not proven *adj* a verdict in Scottish courts, given

THESAURUS

dignitary, megastar (*informal*), notability, personage, superstar, V.I.P., worthy

notably conspicuously, distinctly, especially, markedly, noticeably, outstandingly, particularly, remarkably, signally, strikingly, uncommonly

notation characters, code, script, signs, symbols, system

notch *n.* **1.** cleft, cut, incision, indentation, mark, nick, score **2.** *informal* cut (*informal*), degree, grade, level, step ~*vb.* **3.** cut, indent, mark, nick, score, scratch **4. notch up** achieve, gain, make, register, score

note 1. *n.* annotation, comment, communication, epistle, gloss, jotting, letter, memo, memorandum, message, minute, record, remark, reminder **2.** *vb.* denote, designate, indicate, mark, mention, notice, observe, perceive, record, register, remark, see

notebook diary, exercise book, Filofax (*Trademark*), jotter, journal, memorandum book, notepad, record book

noted acclaimed, celebrated, conspicuous, distinguished, eminent, famous, illustrious, notable, prominent, recognized, renowned, well-known

noteworthy exceptional, extraordinary, important, notable, outstanding, remarkable, significant, unusual

nothing bagatelle, cipher, emptiness, naught, nobody, nonentity, nonexistence, nothingness, nought, nullity, trifle, void, zero

nothingness 1. nihility, nonbeing, nonexistence, nullity, oblivion **2.** insignificance, unimportance, worthlessness

notice *n.* **1.** cognizance, consideration, heed, interest, note, observation, regard **2.** advertisement, comment, criticism, poster, review, sign **3.** advice, announcement, communication, instruction, intelligence, intimation, news, notification, order, warning ~*vb.* **4.** detect, discern, distinguish, heed, mark, mind, note, observe, perceive, remark, see, spot

noticeable appreciable, blatant, clear, conspicuous, distinct, evident, manifest, observable, obvious, perceptible, plain, striking, unmistakable

notification advice, announcement, declaration, information, intelligence, message, notice, notifying, publication, statement, telling, warning

notify acquaint, advise, alert, announce, apprise, declare, inform, publish, tell, warn

notion 1. apprehension, belief, concept, conception, idea, impression, inkling, judgment, knowledge, opinion, sentiment, understanding, view **2.** caprice, desire, fancy, impulse, inclination, whim, wish

notional abstract, conceptual, fanciful, hypothetical, ideal, imaginary, speculative, theoretical, unreal, visionary

notoriety dishonour, disrepute, infamy, obloquy, opprobrium, scandal

when there is insufficient evidence to convict the accused.

no-trump *Cards* ~*n* **1** a bid or hand without trumps. ~*adj* **2** (of a hand) suitable for playing without trumps.

Notts Nottinghamshire.

notwithstanding *prep* **1** in spite of. ~*adv* **2** nevertheless.

nougat *n* a hard chewy pink or white sweet containing chopped nuts.

nought *n* **1** the figure 0. ~*n, adv* **2** same as **naught**.

noughts and crosses *n Brit* a game in which two players, one using a nought, the other a cross, alternately mark squares formed by two pairs of crossed lines, the winner being the first to get three of his or her symbols in a row.

noun *n* a word that refers to a person, place, or thing.

nourish *vb* **1** to provide with the food necessary for life and growth. **2** to encourage or foster (an idea or feeling). **nourishing** *adj*

nourishment *n* the food needed to nourish the body.

nous *n Old-fashioned, slang* common sense.

nouveau riche (**noo**-voh **reesh**) *n, pl* **nouveaux riches** (**noo**-voh **reesh**) a person who has become wealthy recently and is regarded as vulgar.

nouvelle cuisine (**noo**-vell kwee-**zeen**) *n* a style of preparing and presenting food with light sauces and unusual combinations of flavours.

Nov. November.

nova *n, pl* **-vae** *or* **-vas** a star that undergoes an explosion and fast increase of brightness, then gradually decreases to its original brightness.

novel[1] *n* a long fictional story in book form.

novel[2] *adj* fresh, new, or original: *a novel approach.*

novelette *n* a short novel, usually one regarded as trivial or sentimental.

novelist *n* a writer of novels.

novella *n, pl* **-las** a short narrative tale or short novel.

novelty *n, pl* **-ties** **1** the quality of being new and interesting. **2** a new or unusual experience or thing. **3** a small cheap toy or trinket.

November *n* the eleventh month of the year.

novena (no-vee-na) *n, pl* **-nae** (-nee) *or* **-nas** *RC Church* a set of prayers or services on nine consecutive days.

novice (**nov**-viss) *n* **1** a beginner. **2** a person who has entered a religious order but has not yet taken vows.

novitiate *or* **noviciate** *n* **1** the period of being a novice. **2** the part of a monastery or convent where the novices live.

now *adv* **1** at or for the present time. **2** immediately: *bring it now.* **3** in these times; nowadays. **4** given the present circumstances: *now do you understand why?* **5 a** used as a hesitation word: *now, I can't really say.* **b** used for emphasis: *now listen to this.* **c** used at the end of a command: *run along now.* **6 just now a** very recently: *he left just now.* **b** very soon: *I'm going just now.* **7 now and again** *or* **then** occasionally. **8 now now!** an exclamation used to tell someone off or to calm someone. ~*conj* **9** Also: **now that** seeing that: *now you're here, you can help me.* ~*n* **10** the present time: *now is the time to go.*

nowadays *adv* in these times: *nowadays his work is regarded as out-of-date.*

Nowell *n* same as **Noel**.

nowhere *adv* **1** in, at, or to no place. **2 getting nowhere** *Informal* making no progress. **3 nowhere near** far from: *the stadium is nowhere near completion.* ~*n* **4 in the middle of nowhere** (of a place) completely isolated.

nowt *n N English dialect* nothing.

noxious *adj* **1** poisonous or harmful. **2** extremely unpleasant.

nozzle *n* a projecting spout from which fluid is discharged.

Np *Chem* neptunium.

nr near.

NS **1** New Style (method of reckoning dates). **2** Nova Scotia.

NSPCC (in Britain) National Society for the Prevention of Cruelty to Children.

NST Newfoundland Standard Time.

NSW New South Wales.

NT **1** (in Britain) National Trust. **2** New Testament.

-n't not: added to *be* or *have,* or auxiliary verbs: *can't; don't; isn't.*

nth *adj* See **n**[2].

nuance (**new**-ahnss) *n* a subtle difference, as in colour, meaning, or tone.

nub *n* the point or gist: *this is the nub of his theory.*

nubble *n* a small lump. **nubbly** *adj*

nubile (**new**-bile) *adj* (of a young woman) **1** sexually attractive. **2** old enough or mature enough for marriage.

nuclear *adj* **1** of nuclear weapons or energy. **2** of an atomic nucleus: *nuclear fission.*

nuclear bomb *n* a bomb whose force is due to uncontrolled nuclear fusion or fission.

nuclear energy *n* energy released during a nuclear reaction as a result of fission or fusion.

nuclear family *n Sociol, anthropol* a family consisting only of parents and their offspring.

nuclear fission *n Nuclear physics* the splitting of an atomic nucleus, either spontaneously or by bombard-

THESAURUS

notorious dishonourable, disreputable, infamous, opprobrious, scandalous

notoriously dishonourably, disreputably, infamously, opprobriously, scandalously

notwithstanding although, despite, (even) though, however, nevertheless, nonetheless, though, yet

nought naught, nil, nothing, nothingness, zero

nourish **1.** attend, feed, furnish, nurse, nurture, supply, sustain, tend **2.** comfort, cultivate, encourage, foster, maintain, promote, support

nourishing alimentative, beneficial, healthful, health-giving, nutritious, nutritive, wholesome

nourishment aliment, diet, food, nutriment, nutrition, sustenance, tack (*informal*), viands, victuals, vittles (*obsolete or dialect*)

nouveau riche arriviste, new-rich, parvenu, upstart

novel[1] *n.* fiction, narrative, romance, story, tale

novel[2] *adj.* different, fresh, ground-breaking, innovative, new, original, rare, singular, strange, uncommon, unfamiliar, unusual

novelty **1.** freshness, innovation, newness, oddity, originality, strangeness, surprise, unfamiliarity, uniqueness **2.** bagatelle, bauble, curiosity, gadget, gewgaw, gimcrack, gimmick, knick-knack, memento, souvenir, trifle, trinket

novice amateur, apprentice, beginner, convert, learner, neophyte, newcomer, novitiate, probationer, pupil, trainee, tyro

now **1.** at once, immediately, instanter (*Law*), instantly, presently (*Scot. & U.S.*), promptly, straightaway **2.** any more, at the moment, nowadays, these days **3.** **now and again** *or* **then** at times, from time to time,

ment by a neutron: used in atomic bombs and nuclear power plants.

nuclear-free *adj* (of an area) barred, esp. by local authorities, from being supplied with nuclear-generated electricity and from storing nuclear waste or weapons.

nuclear fusion *n Nuclear physics* the combination of two nuclei to form a heavier nucleus with the release of energy: used in hydrogen bombs.

nuclear physics *n* the branch of physics concerned with the structure of the nucleus and the behaviour of its particles.

nuclear power *n* power produced by a nuclear reactor.

nuclear reaction *n Physics* a process in which the structure and energy content of an atomic nucleus is changed by interaction with another nucleus or particle.

nuclear reactor *n Nuclear physics* a device in which a nuclear reaction is maintained and controlled to produce nuclear energy.

nuclear winter *n* a theoretical period of low temperatures and little light that has been suggested would occur after a nuclear war.

nucleate *adj* 1 having a nucleus. *~vb* **-ating, -ated** 2 to form a nucleus.

nuclei (**new**-klee-eye) *n* the plural of **nucleus.**

nucleic acid *n Biochem* a complex compound, such as DNA or RNA, found in all living cells.

nucleon *n Physics* a proton or neutron.

nucleonics *n* the branch of physics concerned with the applications of nuclear energy. **nucleonic** *adj*

nucleus *n, pl* **-clei** 1 *Physics* the positively charged centre of an atom, made of protons and neutrons, about which electrons orbit. 2 a central thing around which others are grouped. 3 a centre of growth or development: *the nucleus of a new relationship.* 4 *Biol* the part of a cell that contains the chromosomes and associated molecules that control the characteristics and growth of the cell. 5 *Chem* a fundamental group of atoms in a molecule serving as the base structure for related compounds.

nude *adj* 1 completely undressed. *~n* 2 a naked figure in painting, sculpture, or photography. 3 **in the nude** naked. **nudity** *n*

nudge *vb* **nudging, nudged** 1 to push (someone) gently with the elbow to get attention. 2 to push (something or someone) lightly: *the dog nudged the stick with its nose.* 3 to persuade (someone) gently. *~n* 4 a gentle poke or push.

nudism *n* the practice of not wearing clothes, for reasons of health. **nudist** *n, adj*

nugatory (**new**-gat-tree) *adj Formal* 1 of little value. 2 not valid: *their rejection rendered the treaty nugatory.*

nugget *n* 1 a small lump of gold in its natural state. 2 something small but valuable: *a nugget of useful knowledge.*

nuisance *n* 1 a person or thing that causes annoyance or bother. *~adj* 2 causing annoyance or bother: *nuisance calls.*

nuke *Slang ~vb* **nuking, nuked** 1 to attack with nuclear weapons. *~n* 2 a nuclear bomb.

null *adj* 1 **null and void** not legally valid. 2 **null set** *Maths* a set with no members. **nullity** *n*

nullify *vb* **-fies, -fying, -fied** 1 to make (something) ineffective. 2 to make (something) legally void. **nullification** *n*

NUM National Union of Mineworkers.

numb *adj* 1 deprived of feeling through cold, shock, or fear. 2 unable to move; paralysed. *~vb* 3 to make numb. **numbly** *adv* **numbness** *n*

number *n* 1 a concept of quantity that is or can be derived from a single unit, a sum of units, or zero. 2 the word or symbol used to represent a number. 3 a numeral or string of numerals used to identify a person or thing: *an account number.* 4 the person or thing so identified: *he was seeded number two.* 5 sum or quantity: *a very large number of people have telephoned.* 6 one of a series, as of a magazine. 7 a self-contained piece of pop or jazz music. 8 a group of people: *one of their number might be willing.* 9 *Informal* an admired article: *that little number is by Dior.* 10 *Grammar* classification of words depending on how many people or things are referred to. 11 **any number of** many. 12 **beyond** *or* **without number** innumerable. 13 **have someone's number** *Informal* to have discovered someone's true character or intentions. 14 **one's number is up** *Brit informal* one is about to die. *~vb* 15 to count. 16 to assign a number to: *numbered seats.* 17 to add up to: *the illustrations numbered well over fifty.* 18 to include in a group: *he numbered several Americans among his friends.* 19 **one's days are numbered** something unpleasant, such as death, is likely to happen to one soon.

number crunching *n Computers* the large-scale processing of numerical data.

numberless *adj* too many to be counted.

number one *n* 1 *Informal* oneself: *he looks after number one.* 2 *Informal* the best-selling pop record in any one week. *~adj* 3 first in importance, urgency, or quality: *he's their number one suspect.*

THESAURUS

infrequently, intermittently, occasionally, on and off, once in a while, on occasion, sometimes, sporadically

nowadays any more, at the moment, in this day and age, now, these days, today

nucleus basis, centre, core, focus, heart, kernel, nub, pivot

nude *au naturel,* bare, buck naked (*slang*), disrobed, exposed, in one's birthday suit (*informal*), in the altogether (*informal*), in the buff (*informal*), in the raw (*informal*), naked, naked as the day one was born (*informal*), starkers (*informal*), stark naked, stripped, unclad, unclothed, uncovered, undraped, undressed, without a stitch on (*informal*)

nudge *vb.* bump, dig, elbow, jog, poke, prod, push, shove, touch

nudity bareness, dishabille, nakedness, nudism, undress

nugget chunk, clump, hunk, lump, mass, piece

nuisance annoyance, bore, bother, drag (*informal*), gall, hassle (*informal*), inconvenience, infliction, irritation, offence, pain in the arse (*taboo informal*), pest, plague, problem, trouble, vexation

nullify abolish, abrogate, annul, bring to naught, cancel, counteract, countervail, invalidate, negate, neutralize, obviate, quash, rebut, render null and void, repeal, rescind, revoke, veto, void

numb **1.** *adj.* benumbed, dead, deadened, frozen, immobilized, insensible, insensitive, paralysed, stupefied, torpid, unfeeling **2.** *vb.* benumb, deaden, dull, freeze, immobilize, paralyse, stun, stupefy

number *n.* **1.** character, count, digit, figure, integer, numeral, sum, total, unit **2.** aggregate, amount, collection, company, crowd, horde, many, multitude, quantity, throng **3.** copy, edition, imprint, issue, printing *~vb.* **4.** account, add, calculate, compute, count, enumerate, include, reckon, tell, total

numberplate *n* a plate on the front or back of a motor vehicle showing the registration number.
Number Ten *n* 10 Downing Street, the British prime minister's official London residence.
numbskull *or* **numskull** *n* a stupid person.
numeral *n* a word or symbol used to express a sum or quantity.
numerate *adj* able to do basic arithmetic. **numeracy** *n*
numeration *n* **1** the act or process of numbering or counting. **2** a system of numbering.
numerator *n Maths* the number above the line in a fraction.
numerical *adj* measured or expressed in numbers: *record the severity of your symptoms in numerical form.* **numerically** *adv*
numerology *n* the study of numbers and of their supposed influence on human affairs.
numerous *adj* **1** many: *they carried out numerous bombings.* **2** consisting of a large number of people or things: *the cast is not as numerous as one might suppose.*
numinous *adj Formal* **1** arousing spiritual or religious emotions. **2** mysterious or awe-inspiring.
numismatics *n* the study or collection of coins or medals. **numismatist** *n*
numskull *n* same as **numbskull.**
nun *n* a female member of a religious order.
nuncio *n, pl* **-cios** *RC Church* a papal ambassador.
nunnery *n, pl* **-neries** a convent.
nunny bag *n Canad* (in Newfoundland) a small sealskin haversack.
nuptial *adj* relating to marriage: *a nuptial blessing.*
nuptials *pl n* a wedding.
nurd *n Slang* same as **nerd.**
nurse *n* **1** a person trained to look after sick people, usu. in a hospital. **2** short for **nursemaid.** ~*vb* **nursing, nursed 3** to look after (a sick person). **4** to breast-feed (a baby). **5** (of a baby) to feed at its mother's breast. **6** to try to cure (an ailment). **7** to harbour or foster (a feeling). **8** to clasp fondly: *she nursed her drink.* **nursing** *n, adj*
nursemaid *or* **nurserymaid** *n* a woman employed to look after children.
nursery *n, pl* **-ries 1** a room in a house where children sleep or play. **2** a place where children are taken care of when their parents are at work. **3** a place where plants and young trees are grown for sale.
nurseryman *n, pl* **-men** a person who raises plants and trees for sale.
nursery nurse *n* a person trained to look after children of pre-school age.
nursery rhyme *n* a short traditional verse or song for children.
nursery school *n* a school for young children from three to five years old.
nursery slopes *pl n* gentle slopes used by beginners in skiing.
nursery stakes *pl n* a race for two-year-old horses.
nursing home *n* a private hospital or home for people who are old or ill.
nursing officer *n* the administrative head of the nursing staff of a hospital.
nurture *n* **1** the act or process of promoting the development of a child or young plant. ~*vb* **-turing, -tured 2** to promote or encourage the development of.
nut *n* **1** a dry one-seeded fruit that grows inside a hard shell. **2** the edible inner part of such a fruit. **3** a small piece of metal with a hole in it, that screws on to a bolt. **4** *Slang* an eccentric or insane person. **5** *Slang* the head. **6** *Slang* an enthusiast: *a health nut.* **7** *Brit* a small piece of coal. **8 do one's nut** *Brit slang* to be very angry. **9 a hard** *or* **tough nut to crack** a person or thing that presents difficulties. ~See also **nuts.**
NUT National Union of Teachers.
nutcase *n Slang* an insane person.
nutcracker *n* a device for cracking the shells of nuts. Also: **nutcrackers**
nuthatch *n* a songbird that feeds on insects, seeds, and nuts.
nutmeg *n* a spice made from the seed of a tropical tree.
nutria (**new**-tree-a) *n* the fur of the coypu.
nutrient (**new**-tree-ent) *n* **1** a substance that provides nourishment. ~*adj* **2** providing nourishment.
nutriment (**new**-tree-ment) *n* the food or nourishment required by all living things to grow and stay healthy.
nutrition (new-**trish**-un) *n* **1** the process of taking in and absorbing nutrients. **2** the process of being nourished. **3** the study of nutrition. **nutritional** *adj* **nutritionist** *n*
nutritious *adj* providing nourishment.
nutritive *adj* of nutrition; nutritious.
nuts *adj Slang* **1** insane. **2 nuts about** very fond of or enthusiastic about.
nuts and bolts *pl n Informal* the essential or practical details.
nutshell *n* **in a nutshell** in essence; briefly.
nutter *n Brit slang* an insane person.
nutty *adj* **-tier, -tiest 1** containing or resembling nuts. **2** *Slang* insane or eccentric. **nuttiness** *n*
nux vomica *n* the seed of a tree, which contains strychnine.

THESAURUS

numberless countless, endless, infinite, innumerable, multitudinous, myriad, unnumbered, untold
numbness deadness, dullness, insensibility, insensitivity, paralysis, stupefaction, torpor, unfeelingness
numeral character, cipher, digit, figure, integer, number, symbol
numerous abundant, copious, many, plentiful, profuse, several
nunnery abbey, cloister, convent, house, monastery
nuptials espousal (*archaic*), marriage, matrimony, wedding
nurse *vb.* **1.** care for, look after, minister to, tend, treat **2.** breast-feed, feed, nourish, nurture, suckle, wet-nurse **3.** cherish, cultivate, encourage, foster, harbour, keep alive, preserve, promote, succour, support
nurture 1. *n.* development, discipline, education, instruction, rearing, training, upbringing **2.** *vb.* bring up, cultivate, develop, discipline, educate, instruct, rear, school, support, sustain, tend, train
nut 1. kernel, pip, seed, stone **2.** *slang* crackpot (*informal*), crank (*informal*), eccentric, headbanger (*informal*), headcase (*informal*), loony (*slang*), lunatic, madman, maniac, nutcase (*slang*), nutter (*Brit. slang*), oddball (*informal*), psycho (*slang*), wacko (*slang*) **3.** *slang* brain, head, mind, reason, senses
nutrition food, nourishment, nutriment, sustenance
nutritious beneficial, healthful, health-giving, invigorating, nourishing, nutritive, strengthening, wholesome
nuts bananas (*slang*), barking (*slang*), barking mad (*slang*), batty (*slang*), crazy (*informal*), demented, deranged, eccentric, insane, irrational, loony (*slang*), loopy (*informal*), mad, not the full shilling (*informal*),

nuzzle *vb* **-zling, -zled** to push or rub gently with the nose or snout.
NV Nevada.
NW northwest(ern).
NWT Northwest Territories (of Canada).
NY New York.
NYC New York City.
nylon *n* a synthetic material used for clothing and many other products.
nylons *pl n* stockings made of nylon.
nymph *n* **1** *Myth* a spirit of nature, represented as a beautiful young woman. **2** the larva of certain insects, resembling the adult form. **3** *Chiefly poetic* a beautiful young woman.
nymphet *n* a girl who is sexually precocious and desirable.
nympho *n, pl* **-phos** *Informal* short for **nymphomaniac.**
nymphomaniac *n* a woman with an abnormally intense sexual desire. **nymphomania** *n*
NZ, N.Z., *or* **N. Zeal.** New Zealand.

THESAURUS

nutty (*slang*), off one's trolley (*slang*), out to lunch (*informal*), psycho (*slang*), psychopathic, up the pole (*informal*)

O

O[1] **1** *Chem* oxygen. **2** Old. **3** same as **nought.**

O[2] *interj* same as **oh.**

o. *or* **O.** old.

o' *prep Informal or old-fashioned* of: *a cup o' tea.*

oaf *n* a stupid or clumsy person. **oafish** *adj*

oak *n* **1** a large forest tree with hard wood, acorns as fruits, and leaves with rounded projections. **2** the wood of this tree, used as building timber and for making furniture. **oaken** *adj*

oak apple *or* **gall** *n* a brownish round lump or ball produced on oak trees by certain wasps.

Oaks *n* **the Oaks** an annual horse race for three-year-old fillies, run at Epsom.

oakum *n* loose fibre obtained by unravelling old rope, used for filling cracks in wooden ships.

OAP (in Britain) old age pensioner.

oar *n* **1** a long pole with a broad blade, used for rowing a boat. **2 put** *or* **stick one's oar in** to interfere or interrupt.

oarsman *or fem* **oarswoman** *n, pl* **-men** *or* **-women** a person who rows. **oarsmanship** *n*

oasis *n, pl* **-ses 1** a fertile patch in a desert. **2** a place or situation offering relief in the midst of difficulty.

oast *n Chiefly Brit* an oven for drying hops.

oast house *n Chiefly Brit* a building containing ovens for drying hops.

oat *n* **1** a hard cereal grown as food. **2 oats** the edible grain of this cereal. **3 sow one's wild oats** to have casual sexual relationships while young. **oaten** *adj*

oatcake *n* a thin unsweetened biscuit made of oatmeal.

oath *n, pl* **oaths 1** a solemn promise, esp. to tell the truth in a court of law. **2** an offensive or blasphemous expression; a swearword. **3 on** *or* **under oath** having made a solemn promise to tell the truth, esp. in a court of law.

oatmeal *n* **1** a coarse flour made by grinding oats. *~adj* **2** greyish-yellow.

ob. (on tombstones) he *or* she died.

obbligato (ob-lig-**gah**-toe) *Music ~adj* **1** not to be omitted in performance. *~n, pl* **-tos 2** an essential part or accompaniment: *with oboe obbligato.*

obdurate *adj* not to be persuaded; hardhearted or obstinate. **obduracy** *n*

OBE Officer of the Order of the British Empire.

obedient *adj* obeying or willing to obey. **obedience** *n* **obediently** *adv*

obeisance (oh-**bay**-sanss) *n Formal* **1** an attitude of respect or humble obedience. **2** a bow or curtsy showing this attitude. **obeisant** *adj*

obelisk (**ob**-bill-isk) *n* **1** a four-sided stone pillar that tapers to a pyramid at the top. **2** *Printing* same as **dagger** (sense 2).

obese (oh-**beess**) *adj* very fat. **obesity** *n*

obey *vb* **1** to carry out instructions or orders; be obedient. **2** to act in accordance with one's feelings, an impulse, etc.: *I had obeyed the impulse to open the gate and had walked up the drive.*

obfuscate *vb* **-cating, -cated** *Formal* to make something unnecessarily difficult to understand. **obfuscation** *n* **obfuscatory** *adj*

obituary *n, pl* **-aries** a published announcement of a death, usually with a short biography of the dead person. **obituarist** *n*

obj. **1** objection. **2** *Grammar* object(ive).

object[1] *n* **1** a thing that can be touched or seen. **2** a person or thing seen as a focus for feelings, actions, or thought: *she had become for him an object of compassion.* **3** an aim or purpose: *the main object of the exercise.* **4** *Philosophy* that which can be perceived by the mind, as contrasted with the thinking subject. **5** *Grammar* a noun, pronoun, or noun phrase that receives the action of a verb or is governed by a preposition, such as *the bottle* in *she threw the bottle.* **6 no object** not a hindrance or obstacle: *money's no object.*

object[2] *vb* **1** to express disapproval or opposition: *my colleagues objected strongly to further delays.* **2** to

THESAURUS

oaf airhead (*slang*), berk (*Brit. slang*), blockhead, bonehead (*slang*), booby, brute, charlie (*Brit. informal*), clod, coot, dickhead (*slang*), dipstick (*Brit. slang*), divvy (*Brit. slang*), dolt, dork (*slang*), dullard, dummy (*slang*), dunce, dweeb (*U.S. slang*), fool, fuckwit (*taboo slang*), galoot (*slang, chiefly U.S.*), gawk, geek (*slang*), gonzo (*slang*), goon, gorilla (*informal*), halfwit, idiot, imbecile, jerk (*slang, chiefly U.S. & Canad.*), lout, lummox (*informal*), moron, nerd *or* nurd (*slang*), nincompoop, nitwit (*informal*), numskull *or* numbskull, pillock (*Brit. slang*), plank (*Brit. slang*), plonker (*slang*), prat (*slang*), sap (*slang*), schmuck (*U.S. slang*), simpleton, twit (*informal, chiefly Brit.*), wally (*slang*)

oafish blockish, boneheaded (*slang*), bovine, brutish, dense, dim, dim-witted (*informal*), doltish, dozy (*Brit. informal*), dull, dumb (*informal*), heavy, loutish, lubberly, lumbering, moronic, obtuse, slow on the uptake (*informal*), stupid, thick

oasis *figurative* haven, island, refuge, resting place, retreat, sanctuary, sanctum

oath 1. affirmation, avowal, bond, pledge, promise, sworn statement, vow, word **2.** blasphemy, curse, cuss (*informal*), expletive, imprecation, malediction, profanity, strong language, swearword

obdurate adamant, callous, dogged, firm, fixed, hard, hard-hearted, harsh, immovable, implacable, inexorable, inflexible, mulish, obstinate, perverse, pig-headed, relentless, stiff-necked, stubborn, unbending, unfeeling, unimpressible, unrelenting, unshakable, unyielding

obedience accordance, acquiescence, agreement, compliance, conformability, deference, docility, dutifulness, duty, observance, respect, reverence, submission, submissiveness, subservience, tractability

obedient acquiescent, amenable, biddable, compliant, deferential, docile, duteous, dutiful, law-abiding, observant, regardful, respectful, submissive, subservient, tractable, under control, well-trained, yielding

obelisk column, monolith, monument, needle, pillar, shaft

obese corpulent, fat, fleshy, gross, heavy, outsize, overweight, paunchy, plump, podgy, portly, roly-poly, rotund, stout, tubby, well-upholstered (*informal*)

obesity beef (*informal*), bulk, corpulence, *embonpoint,* fatness, fleshiness, grossness, overweight, portliness, stoutness, tubbiness, weight problem

obey abide by, act upon, adhere to, be ruled by, bow to, carry out, come to heel, comply, conform, discharge, do what is expected, do what one is told, embrace, execute, follow, fulfil, get into line, give in, give way, heed, keep, knuckle under (*informal*), mind, ob-

state as one's reason for opposing: *he objected that his small staff would be unable to handle the added work.* **objector** *n*

objection *n* **1** an expression or feeling of opposition or disapproval. **2** a reason for opposing something: *the planning officer had raised no objection.*

objectionable *adj* offensive or unacceptable.

objective *n* **1** an aim or purpose: *the objective is to highlight the environmental threat to the planet.* **2** *Grammar* a grammatical case in some languages that identifies the direct object of a verb or preposition. **3** *Optics* the lens nearest to the object observed in an optical instrument. ~*adj* **4** not distorted by personal feelings or bias: *I have tried to be as objective as possible in my presentation.* **5** of or relating to actual facts as opposed to thoughts or feelings: *stand back and try to take a more objective view of your life as a whole.* **6** existing independently of the mind; real. **objectival** *adj* **objectively** *adv* **objectivity** *n*

object lesson *n* a practical demonstration of some principle or ideal.

objet d'art (ob-zhay **dahr**) *n, pl* **objets d'art** (ob-zhay **dahr**) a small object considered to be of artistic worth.

oblate *adj Geom* (of a sphere) flattened at the poles: *the oblate spheroid of the earth.*

oblation *n* **1** *Christianity* the offering of bread and wine to God at Communion. **2** any offering made for religious purposes. **oblational** *adj*

obligated *adj* being morally or legally bound to do something: *they are obligated to provide temporary accommodation.* **obligative** *adj*

obligation *n* **1** a moral or legal duty. **2** the binding power of such a duty: *I feel under some obligation to help you with your education.* **3** a sense of being in debt because of a service or favour: *I don't want him marrying me out of obligation.*

obligatory *adj* required or compulsory because of custom or law.

oblige *vb* **obliging, obliged 1** to compel someone by legal, moral, or physical means to do something. **2** to make (someone) indebted or grateful for a favour: *I am obliged to you for your help.* **3** to do a favour to someone: *she obliged the guests with a song.*

obliging *adj* willing to be helpful. **obligingly** *adv*

oblique (oh-**bleak**) *adj* **1** at an angle; slanting. **2** *Geom* (of lines or planes) neither perpendicular nor parallel to one another. **3** indirect or evasive: *only oblique references have been made to the anti-government unrest.* ~*n* **4** same as **solidus. obliquely** *adv* **obliqueness** *n*

oblique angle *n* an angle that is not a right angle or any multiple of a right angle.

obliterate *vb* **-rating, -rated** to destroy every trace of; wipe out completely. **obliteration** *n*

oblivion *n* **1** the condition of being forgotten or disregarded: *the Marxist-Leninist wing of the party looks set to sink into oblivion.* **2** the state of being unaware or unconscious: *guests seemed to feel a social obligation to drink themselves into oblivion.*

oblivious *adj* unaware or unconscious: *oblivious of her soaking clothes; I was oblivious to the beauty.* **obliviousness** *n*

oblong *adj* **1** having an elongated, rectangular shape. ~*n* **2** a figure or object having this shape.

obloquy (**ob**-lock-wee) *n, pl* **-quies** *Formal* **1** abusive statements or blame: *the British press was held up to moral obloquy.* **2** disgrace brought about by this: *the punishment of lifelong public obloquy and private embarrassment.*

THESAURUS

serve, perform, respond, serve, submit, succumb, surrender (to), take orders from, toe the line, yield

object[1] *n.* **1.** article, body, entity, fact, item, phenomenon, reality, thing **2.** aim, butt, focus, recipient, target, victim **3.** design, end, end in view, end purpose, goal, idea, intent, intention, motive, objective, point, purpose, reason

object[2] *vb.* argue against, demur, expostulate, oppose, protest, raise objections, take exception

objection cavil, censure, counter-argument, demur, doubt, exception, niggle (*informal*), opposition, protest, remonstrance, scruple

objectionable abhorrent, deplorable, disagreeable, dislikable *or* dislikeable, displeasing, distasteful, exceptionable, indecorous, insufferable, intolerable, noxious, obnoxious, offensive, regrettable, repugnant, unacceptable, undesirable, unpleasant, unseemly, unsociable

objective 1. *n.* aim, ambition, aspiration, design, end, end in view, goal, intention, mark, object, purpose, target **2.** *adj.* detached, disinterested, dispassionate, equitable, even-handed, fair, impartial, impersonal, judicial, just, open-minded, unbiased, uncoloured, unemotional, uninvolved, unprejudiced

objectively disinterestedly, dispassionately, even-handedly, impartially, with an open mind, with objectivity *or* impartiality, without fear or favour

objectivity detachment, disinterest, disinterestedness, dispassion, equitableness, impartiality, impersonality

obligation 1. agreement, bond, commitment, contract, debt, engagement, promise, understanding **2.** accountability, accountableness, burden, charge, compulsion, duty, liability, must, onus, requirement, responsibility, trust

obligatory binding, coercive, compulsory, *de rigueur,* enforced, essential, imperative, mandatory, necessary, required, requisite, unavoidable

oblige 1. bind, coerce, compel, constrain, dragoon, force, impel, make, necessitate, obligate, railroad (*informal*), require **2.** accommodate, benefit, do (someone) a favour *or* a kindness, favour, gratify, indulge, please, put oneself out for, serve

obliging accommodating, agreeable, amiable, civil, complaisant, considerate, cooperative, courteous, eager to please, friendly, good-natured, helpful, kind, polite, willing

oblique 1. angled, aslant, at an angle, inclined, slanted, slanting, sloped, sloping, tilted **2.** backhanded, circuitous, circumlocutory, evasive, implied, indirect, roundabout, sidelong

obliquely 1. aslant, aslope, at an angle, diagonally, slantwise **2.** circuitously, evasively, in a roundabout manner *or* way, indirectly, not in so many words

obliterate annihilate, blot out, cancel, delete, destroy, efface, eradicate, erase, expunge, extirpate, root out, wipe off the face of the earth, wipe out

obliteration annihilation, deletion, effacement, elimination, eradication, erasure, expunction, extirpation, wiping (blotting, rooting) out

oblivion 1. eclipse, extinction, limbo, nothingness, obscurity, void **2.** forgetfulness, insensibility, obliviousness, unawareness, unconsciousness

oblivious blind, careless, deaf, disregardful, forgetful, heedless, ignorant, inattentive, insensible, neglectful, negligent, regardless, unaware, unconcerned, unconscious, unmindful, unobservant

obnoxious abhorrent, abominable, detestable, disagreeable, disgusting, dislikable *or* dislikeable, foul, hateable, hateful, horrid, insufferable, loathsome,

obnoxious *adj* extremely unpleasant. **obnoxiousness** *n*
oboe *n* a double-reeded woodwind instrument with a penetrating nasal tone. **oboist** *n*
obs. obsolete.
obscene *adj* **1** offensive to accepted standards of decency or modesty. **2** *Law* tending to deprave or corrupt: *an obscene publication.* **3** disgusting: *a great dark obscene pool of blood.* **obscenity** *n*
obscure *adj* **1** not well-known: *the concerts feature several obscure artists.* **2** not easily understood: *the contracts are written in obscure language.* **3** unclear or indistinct. *~vb* **-scuring, -scured 4** to make unclear or vague; hide: *no amount of bluster could obscure the fact that the prime minister had run out of excuses.* **5** to cover or cloud over. **obscuration** *n* **obscurity** *n*
obsequies (**ob**-sick-weez) *pl n, sing* **-quy** *Formal* funeral rites.
obsequious (ob-**seek**-wee-uss) *adj* being overattentive in order to gain favour. **obsequiousness** *n*
observance *n* **1** the observing of a law or custom. **2** a ritual, ceremony, or practice, esp. of a religion.
observant *adj* quick to notice details around one; sharp-eyed.
observation *n* **1** the act of watching or the state of being watched. **2** a comment or remark. **3** detailed examination of something before analysis, diagnosis, or interpretation: *you may be admitted to hospital for observation and rest.* **4** the facts learned from observing. **5** the ability to notice things: *she has good powers of observation.* **observational** *adj*
observatory *n, pl* **-ries** a building specially designed and equipped for studying the weather and the stars.
observe *vb* **-serving, -served 1** to see or notice: *it is worth observing that old Chinese maps and charts usually show south at the top.* **2** to watch (something) carefully. **3** to make scientific examinations of. **4** to remark: *the speaker observed that times had changed.* **5** to keep (a law or custom). **observable** *adj* **observer** *n*
obsessed *adj* thinking about someone or something all the time: *he had become obsessed with her.* **obsessive** *adj*
obsession *n* **1** something that preoccupies a person to the exclusion of other things: *his principal obsession was with trying to economize.* **2** *Psychiatry* a persistent idea or impulse, often associated with anxiety and mental illness. **obsessional** *adj*
obsidian *n* a dark glassy volcanic rock.
obsolescent *adj* becoming obsolete or out of date. **obsolescence** *n*
obsolete *adj* no longer used; out of date.
obstacle *n* **1** a situation or event that prevents something being done: *there are obstacles which could slow the development of a vaccine.* **2** a person or thing that hinders movement.

THESAURUS

nasty, nauseating, objectionable, obscene, odious, offensive, repellent, reprehensible, repugnant, repulsive, revolting, sickening, unpleasant
obscene bawdy, blue, coarse, dirty, disgusting, filthy, foul, gross, immodest, immoral, improper, impure, indecent, lewd, licentious, loose, offensive, pornographic, prurient, ribald, salacious, scabrous, shameless, smutty, suggestive, unchaste, unwholesome
obscenity bawdiness, blueness, coarseness, dirtiness, filthiness, foulness, grossness, immodesty, impurity, lewdness, licentiousness, pornography, prurience, salacity, smuttiness, suggestiveness, vileness
obscure *adj.* **1.** humble, inconspicuous, inglorious, little-known, lowly, minor, nameless, out-of-the-way, remote, undistinguished, unheard-of, unhonoured, unimportant, unknown, unnoted, unseen, unsung **2.** abstruse, ambiguous, arcane, concealed, confusing, cryptic, deep, Delphic, doubtful, enigmatic, esoteric, hazy, hidden, incomprehensible, indefinite, intricate, involved, mysterious, occult, opaque, recondite, unclear, vague *~vb.* **3.** conceal, cover, disguise, hide, muddy, obfuscate, screen, throw a veil over, veil **4.** adumbrate, bedim, befog, block, block out, blur, cloak, cloud, darken, dim, dull, eclipse, mask, overshadow, shade, shroud
obscurity 1. inconspicuousness, ingloriousness, insignificance, lowliness, namelessness, nonrecognition, unimportance **2.** abstruseness, ambiguity, complexity, impenetrableness, incomprehensibility, intricacy, reconditeness, vagueness
observable apparent, appreciable, blatant, clear, detectable, discernible, evident, noticeable, obvious, open, patent, perceivable, perceptible, recognizable, visible
observance 1. adherence to, attention, carrying out, celebration, compliance, discharge, fulfilment, heeding, honouring, notice, observation, performance **2.** ceremonial, ceremony, custom, fashion, form, formality, practice, rite, ritual, service, tradition
observant alert, attentive, eagle-eyed, heedful, mindful, perceptive, quick, sharp-eyed, vigilant, watchful, wide-awake
observation 1. attention, cognition, consideration, examination, experience, information, inspection, knowledge, monitoring, notice, review, scrutiny, study, surveillance, watching **2.** annotation, comment, finding, note, opinion, pronouncement, reflection, remark, thought, utterance
observe 1. detect, discern, discover, espy, note, notice, perceive, see, spot, witness **2.** check, check out (*informal*), clock (*Brit. slang*), contemplate, eyeball (*U.S. slang*), get a load of (*informal*), keep an eye on (*informal*), keep under observation, look at, monitor, pay attention to, recce (*slang*), regard, scrutinize, study, survey, take a dekko at (*Brit. slang*), view, watch **3.** animadvert, comment, declare, mention, note, opine, remark, say, state **4.** abide by, adhere to, celebrate, commemorate, comply, conform to, follow, fulfil, heed, honour, keep, mind, obey, perform, remember, respect, solemnize
observer beholder, bystander, commentator, eyewitness, looker-on, onlooker, spectator, spotter, viewer, watcher, witness
obsessed beset, dominated, gripped, hag-ridden, haunted, hung up on (*slang*), immersed in, infatuated, in the grip of, preoccupied, troubled
obsession bee in one's bonnet (*informal*), complex, enthusiasm, fetish, fixation, hang-up (*informal*), *idée fixe,* infatuation, mania, phobia, preoccupation, ruling passion, thing (*informal*)
obsessive besetting, compulsive, consuming, fixed, gripping, haunting, tormenting, unforgettable
obsolescent ageing, declining, dying out, not with it (*informal*), on the decline, on the wane, on the way out, past its prime, waning
obsolete anachronistic, ancient, antediluvian, antiquated, antique, archaic, bygone, dated, *démodé,* discarded, disused, extinct, musty, old, old-fashioned, old hat, out, outmoded, out-of-date, out of fashion, out of the ark (*informal*), outworn, passé, superannuated
obstacle bar, barrier, block, check, difficulty, hin-

obstetrician *n* a doctor who specializes in obstetrics.

obstetrics *n* the branch of medicine concerned with pregnancy and childbirth. **obstetric** *adj*

obstinate *adj* **1** keeping stubbornly to a particular opinion or course of action. **2** difficult to treat or deal with: *obstinate weeds.* **obstinacy** *n* **obstinately** *adv*

obstreperous *adj* noisy and difficult to control: *her obstreperous teenage son.*

obstruct *vb* **1** to block a way with an obstacle. **2** to make progress or activity difficult: *this government will never obstruct the course of justice.* **3** to block a clear view of.

obstruction *n* **1** a person or thing that obstructs. **2** the act of obstructing or being obstructed. **3** *Sport* the act of unfairly impeding an opposing player.

obstructionist *n* a person who deliberately obstructs legal or parliamentary business. **obstructionism** *n*

obstructive *adj* deliberately causing difficulties or delays. **obstructively** *adv* **obstructiveness** *n*

obtain *vb* **1** to gain possession of; get. **2** *Formal* to be customary or accepted: *silence obtains from eight in the evening.* **obtainable** *adj*

obtrude *vb* **-truding, -truded 1** to push oneself or one's opinions on others in an unwelcome way. **2** to be or make unpleasantly noticeable. **obtrusion** *n*

obtrusive *adj* unpleasantly noticeable: *the music should fit your mood, it shouldn't be too obtrusive.* **obtrusiveness** *n*

obtuse *adj* **1** mentally slow or emotionally insensitive. **2** *Maths* (of an angle) between 90° and 180°. **3** not sharp or pointed; blunt. **obtuseness** *n*

obverse *n* **1** a counterpart or opposite: *his true personality being the obverse of his outer image.* **2** the side of a coin that bears the main design. **3** the front, top, or main surface of anything.

obviate *vb* **-ating, -ated** *Formal* to avoid or prevent (a need or difficulty): *a mediator will obviate the need for independent legal advice.*

obvious *adj* **1** easy to see or understand. ~*n* **2 state the obvious** to say something that is unnecessary or already known: *he is prone to stating the obvious.* **obviously** *adv* **obviousness** *n*

ocarina *n* a small egg-shaped wind instrument with a mouthpiece and finger holes.

occasion *n* **1** a particular event or the time at which it happens. **2** a need or reason to do or be something: *we barely knew him and never had occasion to speak of him.* **3** a suitable time or opportunity to do something. **4** a special event, time, or celebration: *a wedding day is a truly special occasion.* **5 on occasion** every so often. **6 rise to the occasion** to meet the special demands of a situation. ~*vb* **7** *Formal* to cause, esp. incidentally.

occasional *adj* happening from time to time; not frequent or regular. **occasionally** *adv*

occasional table *n* a small table with no regular use.

Occident *n* the western hemisphere, esp. Europe and America. **Occidental** *adj*

occiput (**ox**-sip-putt) *n* *Anat* the back of the head or skull. **occipital** *adj*

occlude *vb* **-cluding, -cluded** *Formal* **1** to block or stop up a passage or opening: *the arteries are occluded by deposits of plaque.* **2** to shut in or out: *slowly occluding him from Nash's vision.* **3** *Chem* (of a solid) to absorb and retain a gas or other substance. **occlusion** *n*

occluded front *n* *Meteorol* the front formed when the cold front of a depression overtakes a warm front, raising the warm air from ground level.

occult *adj* **1** involving mystical or supernatural phenomena or powers. **2** beyond ordinary human understanding. **3** secret or mysterious. ~*n* **4 the occult** the

THESAURUS

drance, hitch, hurdle, impediment, interference, interruption, obstruction, snag, stumbling block

obstinacy doggedness, firmness, inflexibility, intransigence, mulishness, obduracy, perseverance, persistence, pertinacity, pig-headedness, resoluteness, stubbornness, tenacity, wilfulness

obstinate contumacious, determined, dogged, firm, headstrong, immovable, inflexible, intractable, intransigent, mulish, opinionated, persistent, pertinacious, perverse, pig-headed, recalcitrant, refractory, self-willed, steadfast, stiff-necked, strong-minded, stubborn, tenacious, unyielding, wilful

obstreperous boisterous, clamorous, disorderly, loud, noisy, out of control, out of hand, rackety, rambunctious (*informal*), rampaging, raucous, restive, riotous, rip-roaring (*informal*), roistering, roisterous, rough, rowdy, stroppy (*Brit. slang*), tempestuous, tumultuous, turbulent, uncontrolled, undisciplined, unmanageable, unruly, uproarious, vociferous, wild

obstruct arrest, bar, barricade, block, bring to a standstill, bung, check, choke, clog, cumber, curb, cut off, frustrate, get in the way of, hamper, hamstring, hide, hinder, hold up, impede, inhibit, interfere with, interrupt, mask, obscure, prevent, restrict, retard, shield, shut off, slow down, stop, thwart, trammel

obstruction bar, barricade, barrier, block, blockage, check, difficulty, hindrance, impediment, obstacle, occlusion, snag, stop, stoppage, trammel

obstructive awkward, blocking, delaying, hindering, inhibiting, preventative, restrictive, stalling, unco-operative, unhelpful

obtain 1. achieve, acquire, attain, come by, earn, gain, get, get hold of, get one's hands on, procure, score (*slang*), secure **2.** *formal* be in force, be prevalent, be the case, exist, hold, prevail, stand

obtainable achievable, at hand, attainable, available, on tap (*informal*), procurable, ready, realizable, to be had

obtrusive blatant, noticeable, obvious, prominent, protruding, protuberant, sticking out

obvious apparent, blatant, clear, clear as a bell, conspicuous, distinct, evident, indisputable, manifest, much in evidence, noticeable, open, overt, palpable, patent, perceptible, plain, plain as the nose on your face (*informal*), pronounced, recognizable, right under one's nose (*informal*), self-evident, self-explanatory, staring one in the face (*informal*), sticking out a mile (*informal*), straightforward, transparent, unconcealed, undeniable, undisguised, unmistakable, unsubtle, visible

obviously certainly, clearly, distinctly, manifestly, of course, palpably, patently, plainly, undeniably, unmistakably, unquestionably, without doubt

occasion *n.* **1.** call, cause, excuse, ground(s), inducement, influence, justification, motive, prompting, provocation, reason **2.** chance, convenience, incident, moment, occurrence, opening, opportunity, time, window **3.** affair, celebration, event, experience, happening, occurrence ~*vb.* **4.** *formal* bring about, cause, create, effect, elicit, engender, evoke, generate, give rise to, induce, influence, inspire, lead to, move, originate, persuade, produce, prompt, provoke

occasional casual, desultory, incidental, infrequent, intermittent, irregular, odd, rare, sporadic, uncommon

knowledge and study of occult phenomena and powers.

occupancy *n, pl* **-cies** 1 the act of occupying a property. 2 the period of time during which one is an occupant of a property.

occupant *n* a person occupying a property, position, or place.

occupation *n* 1 a person's job or profession. 2 any activity on which someone's time is spent: *a pleasant and rewarding occupation.* 3 the control of a country by a foreign military power. 4 the act of occupying or the state of being occupied: *the occupation of Kuwait.* **occupational** *adj*

occupational hazard *n* something unpleasant that occurs due to your job: *frequent colds are an occupational hazard in teaching.*

occupational therapy *n* treatment of people with physical, emotional, or social problems using purposeful activity to help them overcome or learn to accept their problems.

occupier *n Brit* the person who lives in a particular house, whether as owner or tenant.

occupy *vb* **-pies, -pying, -pied** 1 to live, stay, or work in (a house, flat, or office). 2 to keep (someone or someone's mind) busy. 3 to take up (time or space). 4 to move in and take control of (a country or other place): *soldiers have occupied the country's television station.* 5 to fill or hold (a position or office).

occur *vb* **-curring, -curred** 1 to happen. 2 to be found or be present; exist. 3 **occur to** to come into the mind of.

➤ Avoid the use of *occur* (or *happen*) for events that are planned. Compare *An accident occurred* with *A wedding took place.*

occurrence *n* 1 something that happens. 2 the fact of occurring: *the likelihood of its occurrence increases with age.*

ocean *n* 1 the vast area of salt water covering about 70 per cent of the earth's surface. 2 one of the five principal divisions of this, the Atlantic, Pacific, Indian, Arctic, and Antarctic. 3 *Informal* a huge quantity or expanse: *oceans of replies.* 4 *Literary* the sea. **oceanic** *adj*

ocean-going *adj* (of a ship or boat) suited for travel on the open ocean.

oceanography *n* the study of oceans and their environment. **oceanographer** *n* **oceanographic** *adj*

ocelot (**oss**-ill-lot) *n* a large cat of Central and South America with a dark-spotted yellow-grey coat.

och *interj Scot & Irish* an expression of surprise, annoyance, or disagreement.

oche (**ok**-kee) *n Darts* a mark on the floor behind which a player must stand when throwing a dart.

ochre *or US* **ocher** (**oak**-er) *n* 1 a yellow or reddish-brown earth used in paints or dyes. *~adj* 2 moderate yellow-orange to orange.

o'clock *adv* used after a number between one and twelve to specify an hour: *five o'clock in the morning.*

OCR optical character reader *or* recognition.

Oct. October.

octagon *n* a geometric figure with eight sides. **octagonal** *adj*

octahedron (ok-ta-**heed**-ron) *n, pl* **-drons** *or* **-dra** a solid figure with eight plane faces.

octane *n* a liquid hydrocarbon found in petroleum.

octane number *or* **rating** *n* a number indicating the quality of a petrol.

octave *n* 1 **a** the musical interval between the first note and the eighth note of a major or minor scale. **b** the higher of these two notes. **c** the series of notes filling this interval. 2 *Prosody* a rhythmic group of eight lines of verse.

octavo *n, pl* **-vos** 1 a book size resulting from folding a sheet of paper of a standard size to form eight leaves. 2 a book or sheet of this size.

octet *n* 1 a group of eight instrumentalists or singers. 2 a piece of music for eight performers.

October *n* the tenth month of the year.

octogenarian *n* 1 a person between 80 and 89 years old. *~adj* 2 between 80 and 89 years old.

octopus *n, pl* **-puses** a sea creature with a soft oval body and eight long tentacles with suckers.

ocular *adj* of or relating to the eyes or sight.

oculist *n Old-fashioned* an ophthalmologist.

OD *Informal ~n* 1 an overdose of a drug. *~vb* **OD'ing, OD'd** 2 to take an overdose of a drug.

odalisque (**ode**-a-lisk) *n* a female slave in a harem.

odd *adj* 1 unusual or peculiar: *odd behaviour.* 2 occasional or incidental: *the odd letter from a friend abroad, the occasional postcard from a chum.* 3 leftover or additional: *we use up odd pieces of fabric to make up jerseys in wild designs.* 4 (of a number) not divisible by two. 5 being part of a pair or set when the other or others are missing: *the drawer was full of odd socks.* 6 somewhat more than the round numbers specified: *for the past twenty-odd years.* 7 **odd man** *or*

THESAURUS

occasionally at intervals, at times, (every) now and then, every so often, from time to time, irregularly, now and again, off and on, on and off, once in a while, on occasion, periodically, sometimes

occupant addressee, denizen, holder, incumbent, indweller, inhabitant, inmate, lessee, occupier, resident, tenant, user

occupation 1. activity, business, calling, craft, employment, job, line (of work), post, profession, pursuit, trade, vocation, walk of life, work 2. conquest, foreign rule, invasion, seizure, subjugation 3. control, holding, occupancy, possession, residence, tenancy, tenure, use

occupy 1. be established in, be in residence in, dwell in, ensconce oneself in, establish oneself in, inhabit, live in, own, possess, reside in, stay in (*Scot.*), tenant 2. *often passive* absorb, amuse, busy, divert, employ, engage, engross, entertain, hold the attention of, immerse, interest, involve, keep busy *or* occupied, monopolize, preoccupy, take up, tie up 3. cover, fill, hold, permeate, pervade, take up, use, utilize 4. capture, garrison, hold, invade, keep, overrun, seize, take over, take possession of

occur 1. arise, befall, betide, chance, come about, come off (*informal*), come to pass (*archaic*), crop up (*informal*), eventuate, happen, materialize, result, take place, turn up (*informal*) 2. appear, be found, be met with, be present, develop, exist, manifest itself, obtain, show itself 3. *with* **to** come to mind, come to one, cross one's mind, dawn on, enter one's head, spring to mind, strike one, suggest (offer, present) itself

occurrence 1. adventure, affair, circumstance, episode, event, happening, incident, instance, proceeding, transaction 2. appearance, development, existence, manifestation, materialization

odd 1. abnormal, atypical, bizarre, curious, deviant, different, eccentric, exceptional, extraordinary, fantastic, freak, freakish, freaky (*slang*), funny, irregular, kinky (*informal*), oddball (*informal*), off-the-wall (*slang*), outlandish, out of the ordinary, outré, peculiar, quaint, queer, rare, remarkable, rum (*Brit. slang*), singular, strange, uncanny, uncommon, unconventional, unusual, wacko (*slang*), weird, whimsical 2. casual,

one out a person or thing excluded from others forming a group or unit. ~See also **odds. oddly** *adv* **oddness** *n*

oddball *n Informal* a strange or eccentric person.

oddity *n, pl* **-ties 1** an odd person or thing. **2** a peculiar characteristic. **3** the quality of being or appearing unusual or strange.

oddments *pl n* odd pieces or things; leftovers: *oddments of wool.*

odds *pl n* **1** the probability, expressed as a ratio, that something will or will not happen: *the odds against an acquittal had stabilized at six to four.* **2** the difference, expressed as a ratio, between the money placed on a bet and the amount that would be received as winning payment: *the current odds are ten to one.* **3** the likelihood that a certain state of affairs will be so: *the odds are that you are going to fail.* **4** the advantage that one contender is judged to have over another: *the odds are in his favour.* **5 it makes no odds** *Brit* it does not matter. **6 at odds** in conflict or at variance. **7 over the odds** more than is expected or necessary.

odds and ends *pl n* small, usually unimportant, objects, jobs to be done, etc.: *I have brought a few odds and ends with me.*

odds-on *adj* having a better than even chance of winning.

ode *n* a lyric poem, usually addressed to a particular subject, with lines of varying lengths and metres.

odious *adj* offensive or hateful: *I steeled myself for the odious task.* **odiousness** *n*

odium (**oh**-dee-um) *n Formal* widespread dislike or disapproval of a person or action.

odometer (odd-**om**-it-er) *n US & Canad* same as **mileometer.**

odoriferous *adj Formal* having or giving off a pleasant smell.

odour *or US* **odor** *n* a particular and distinctive scent or smell. **odorous** *adj* **odourless** *adj*

odyssey (**odd**-iss-ee) *n* a long eventful journey.

OECD Organization for Economic Cooperation and Development.

oedema *or* **edema** (id-**deem**-a) *n, pl* **-mata** *Pathol* an abnormal accumulation of fluid in the tissues of the body, causing swelling.

Oedipus complex (ee-dip-puss) *n Psychoanal* the usually unconscious sexual desire of a child, esp. a male child, for the parent of the opposite sex. **oedipal** *adj*

o'er *prep, adv Poetic* over.

oesophagus (ee-**soff**-a-guss) *n, pl* **-gi** (-guy) the tube through which food travels from the throat to the stomach; gullet. **oesophageal** *adj*

oestrogen (ee-stra-jen) *n* a female sex hormone that controls the reproductive cycle, and prepares the body for pregnancy.

oestrus (ee-struss) *n* a regularly occurring period of fertility and sexual receptivity in the reproductive cycle of most female mammals, except humans; heat.

of *prep* **1** belonging to; situated in or coming from; because of: *the inhabitants of former East Germany; I saw five people die of chronic hepatitis.* **2** used after words or phrases expressing quantities: *a pint of milk.* **3** specifying an amount or value: *we had to release the bombs at a height of 400 metres.* **4** made up of, containing, or characterized by: *a length of rope; she is a woman of enviable beauty.* **5** used to link a verbal noun with a following noun or noun phrase that is either the subject or the object of the verb: *the sudden slipping of the plates of the Earth's crust; the bombing of civilian targets.* **6** at a given distance or space of time from: *you can still find wood within a mile of the village; he had been within hours of leaving for Romania.* **7** used to specify or give more information about: *the city of Glasgow; a meeting on the subject of regional security.* **8** about or concerning: *speaking of boycotts.* **9** *US* before the hour of: *about quarter of eight in the evening.*

➤ Only when *of* means 'belonging to' can an apostrophe be used: *Bill's dog* (*the dog of Bill*).

off *prep* **1** so as to be no longer in contact with: *take the wok off the heat.* **2** so as to be no longer attached to or associated with: *making use of benefit disqualification to terrorize the unemployed off the register.* **3** away from: *he was driven off the road.* **4** situated near to or leading away from: *they were laying out a bombing range off the coast.* **5** no longer having a liking for: *she's gone off you lately.* **6** no longer using: *he was helped to stay off heroin for a year.* ~*adv* **7** so as to deactivate or disengage: *turn off the gas supply.* **8 a** so as to get rid of: *he was flying at midnight so he had to sleep off his hangover.* **b** as a reduction in price: *she took twenty per cent off.* **9** spent away from work or other duties: *it was the assistant manager's day off.* **10** away; at a distance: *the men dashed back to their car and sped off.* **11** away in the future: *the date was six weeks off.* **12** so as to be no longer taking place: *the investigation was hastily called off.* **13** removed from contact with something: *he took the jacket off.* **14 off and on** occasionally; not regularly or continuously: *we lived together off and on.* ~*adj* **15** not on; no longer operating: *her bedroom light was off.* **16** cancelled or postponed: *the deal is off and your deposit will be returned in full.* **17** in a specified condition, esp. regarding money or provisions: *a married man with four children is better off on the dole; how are you off for money?* **18** not up to the usual standard: *an off year for good wine.* **19** no longer on the menu: *haddock is off.* **20** (of food or drink) having gone bad or sour: *this milk is off.* ~*n* **21** *Cricket* the side of the field to the right of a right-handed batsman when he is facing the

THESAURUS

fragmentary, incidental, irregular, miscellaneous, occasional, periodic, random, seasonal, sundry, varied, various **3.** leftover, lone, remaining, single, solitary, spare, surplus, unconsumed, uneven, unmatched, unpaired

oddity 1. card (*informal*), crank (*informal*), fish out of water, maverick, misfit, nut (*slang*), oddball (*informal*), screwball (*slang, chiefly U.S. & Canad.*), wacko (*slang*), weirdo *or* weirdie (*informal*) **2.** abnormality, anomaly, eccentricity, freak, idiosyncrasy, irregularity, kink, peculiarity, phenomenon, quirk, rarity **3.** abnormality, bizarreness, eccentricity, extraordinariness, freakishness, incongruity, oddness, outlandishness, peculiarity, queerness, singularity, strangeness, unconventionality, unnaturalness

odds 1. balance, chances, likelihood, probability **2.** advantage, allowance, edge, lead, superiority **3. at odds** at daggers drawn, at loggerheads, at sixes and sevens, at variance, in conflict, in disagreement, in opposition to, not in keeping, on bad terms, out of line

odds and ends bits, bits and pieces, debris, leavings, litter, oddments, remnants, rubbish, scraps, sundry *or* miscellaneous items

odious abhorrent, abominable, detestable, disgusting, execrable, foul, hateful, horrible, horrid, loathsome, obnoxious, obscene, offensive, repellent, repugnant, repulsive, revolting, unpleasant, vile, yucky *or* yukky (*slang*)

odour aroma, bouquet, essence, fragrance, niff (*Brit. slang*), perfume, redolence, scent, smell, stench, stink

bowler.

➤ Avoid using *of* after *off*: *He got off the bus* (not *off of*). The use of *off* to mean *from* is very informal: *They brought milk from* (rather than *off*) *a farmer.*

offal *n* the edible internal parts of an animal, such as the heart or liver.

offbeat *adj* unusual, unconventional, or eccentric.

off colour *adj* **1** *Chiefly Brit* slightly ill; unwell. **2** slightly indecent: *an off colour joke.*

offcut *n* a piece of paper, wood, or fabric remaining after the main pieces have been cut; remnant.

offence *or US* **offense** *n* **1** a breaking of a law or rule; crime. **2** annoyance or anger. **3** a cause of annoyance or anger. **4 give offence** to cause to feel upset or angry. **5 take offence** to feel hurt or offended.

offend *vb* **1** to hurt the feelings of (a person); insult. **2** to be disagreeable to; disgust: *the lady was offended by what she saw.* **3** to commit a crime. **offender** *n* **offending** *adj*

offensive *adj* **1** unpleasant or disgusting to the senses: *there was an offensive smell of beer.* **2** causing annoyance or anger; insulting. **3** for the purpose of attack rather than defence. *~n* **4** an attitude or position of aggression: *to go on the offensive.* **5** an attack or hostile action: *troops had launched a major offensive against the rebel forces.* **offensively** *adv*

offer *vb* **1** to present for acceptance or rejection: *I offered her a lift.* **2** to provide: *this department offers a wide range of courses.* **3** to present itself: *if an opportunity should offer.* **4** to be willing (to do something): *his father offered to pay his tuition.* **5** to put forward (a proposal, information, or opinion) for consideration: *may I offer a different view?* **6** to present for sale. **7** to propose as payment; bid. **8** to present (a prayer or sacrifice) as an act of worship. **9** to show readiness for: *to offer resistance.* *~n* **10** something that is offered. **11** the act of offering.

offering *n* **1** something that is offered. **2** a contribution to the funds of a religious organization. **3** a sacrifice to a god.

offertory *n, pl* **-tories** *Christianity* **1** the part of a church service when the bread and wine for communion are offered for consecration. **2** the collection of money at this service. **3** the prayers said or sung while the worshippers' offerings are being brought to the altar.

offhand *adj also* **offhanded 1** curt or casual in manner: *I felt calm enough to adopt a casual offhand manner.* *~adv* **2** without preparation: *I don't know offhand why that should be so.* **offhandedly** *adv* **offhandedness** *n*

office *n* **1** a room, set of rooms, or building in which business, professional duties, or clerical work are carried out. **2** a department of an organization dealing with particular business: *cheque books were sent from the printer to the bank's sorting office.* **3** the group of people working in an office: *she assured him that the office was running smoothly.* **4** a government department or agency: *Office of Fair Trading.* **5** a position of trust or authority, as in a government: *he would not seek a second term of office.* **6** a place where tickets, information, or some service can be obtained: *give the ticket office a ring.* **7** *Christianity* a religious ceremony or service. **8 good offices** the help given by someone

THESAURUS

off *adv.* **1.** apart, aside, away, elsewhere, out *~adj.* **2.** absent, cancelled, finished, gone, inoperative, postponed, unavailable **3.** bad, below par, disappointing, disheartening, displeasing, low-quality, mortifying, poor, quiet, slack, substandard, unrewarding, unsatisfactory **4.** bad, decomposed, high, mouldy, rancid, rotten, sour, turned

off and on (every) now and again, every once in a while, from time to time, intermittently, now and then, occasionally, on and off, sometimes, sporadically

offbeat bizarre, Bohemian, eccentric, far-out (*slang*), freaky (*slang*), idiosyncratic, kinky (*informal*), novel, oddball (*informal*), off-the-wall (*slang*), outré, rum (*Brit. slang*), strange, uncommon, unconventional, unorthodox, unusual, wacko (*slang*), way-out (*informal*), weird

off colour ill, not up to par, off form, out of sorts, peaky, peely-wally (*Scot.*), poorly (*informal*), queasy, run down, sick, under par, under the weather (*informal*), unwell, washed out

offence 1. breach of conduct, crime, delinquency, fault, lapse, misdeed, misdemeanour, peccadillo, sin, transgression, trespass, wrong, wrongdoing **2.** anger, annoyance, displeasure, hard feelings, huff, indignation, ire (*literary*), needle (*informal*), pique, resentment, umbrage, wounded feelings, wrath **3.** affront, displeasure, harm, hurt, indignity, injury, injustice, insult, outrage, put-down (*slang*), slight, snub **4. take offence** be disgruntled, be offended, get riled, go into a huff, resent, take the huff, take the needle (*informal*), take umbrage

offend 1. affront, aggravate (*informal*), annoy, disgruntle, displease, fret, gall, give offence, hurt (someone's) feelings, insult, irritate, miff (*informal*), nark (*Brit., Austral., & N.Z. slang*), outrage, pain, pique, piss one off (*taboo slang*), provoke, put down, put (someone's) back up, rile, slight, snub, tread on (someone's) toes (*informal*), upset, vex, wound **2.** be disagreeable to, disgust, gross out (*U.S. slang*), make (someone) sick, nauseate, repel, repulse, sicken, turn (someone) off (*informal*)

offended affronted, disgruntled, displeased, huffy, in a huff, miffed (*informal*), outraged, pained, piqued, put out (*informal*), resentful, smarting, stung, upset

offender criminal, crook, culprit, delinquent, lawbreaker, malefactor, miscreant, sinner, transgressor, villain, wrongdoer

offensive *adj.* **1.** abominable, detestable, disagreeable, disgusting, grisly, loathsome, nasty, nauseating, noisome, obnoxious, odious, repellent, revolting, sickening, unpalatable, unpleasant, unsavoury, vile, yucky *or* yukky (*slang*) **2.** abusive, annoying, detestable, discourteous, displeasing, disrespectful, embarrassing, impertinent, insolent, insulting, irritating, objectionable, rude, uncivil, unmannerly **3.** aggressive, attacking, invading *~n.* **4. on the offensive** advancing, aggressive, attacking, invading, invasive, on the warpath (*informal*) **5.** attack, drive, onslaught, push (*informal*)

offer *vb.* **1.** afford, furnish, make available, place at (someone's) disposal, present, provide, purvey, show **2.** be at (someone's) service, come forward, offer one's services, volunteer **3.** advance, extend, move, propose, put forth, put forward, submit, suggest **4.** bid, extend, give, hold out, proffer, put on the market, put under the hammer, put up for sale, tender *~n.* **5.** attempt, bid, endeavour, essay, overture, proposal, proposition, submission, suggestion, tender

offering contribution, donation, gift, hand-out, oblation (*in religious contexts*), present, sacrifice, subscription

offhand 1. *adj.* abrupt, aloof, brusque, careless, casual, cavalier, couldn't-care-less, curt, glib, informal, offhanded, perfunctory, take-it-or-leave-it (*informal*), unceremonious, unconcerned, uninterested **2.** *adv.* ad lib, extempore, impromptu, just like that (*informal*), off the cuff (*informal*), off the top of one's head (*informal*), without preparation

office 1. appointment, business, capacity, charge,

to someone else: *Syria's good offices led to the release of two western hostages.* 9 **in** *or* **out of office** (of a government) in *or* out of power.

officer *n* 1 a person in the armed services, or on a non-naval ship, who holds a position of authority. 2 a policeman or policewoman. 3 a person holding a position of authority in a government or organization.

official *adj* 1 of an office or position of authority: *I'm not here in any official capacity.* 2 approved by or derived from authority: *there has been no official announcement.* 3 formal or ceremonial: *he was speaking at an official dinner in Warsaw.* ~*n* 4 a person holding a position of authority. **officially** *adv*

officialdom *n* officials or bureaucrats collectively.

officialese *n* language typical of official documents, esp. when wordy or pompous.

Official Receiver *n* an officer appointed by the government to deal with the affairs of a bankrupt person or company.

officiate *vb* **-ating, -ated** 1 to perform the duties of an office; act in an official capacity: *the referee will officiate at the match.* 2 to conduct a religious or other ceremony: *the priest officiated at the wedding.* **officiation** *n* **officiator** *n*

officious *adj* offering unwanted advice or services; interfering. **officiousness** *n*

offing *n* 1 the part of the sea that can be seen from the shore. 2 **in the offing** not far off; likely to occur soon.

off key *adj, adv Music* out of tune.

off-licence *n Brit* a shop or a counter in a shop where alcoholic drink is sold for drinking elsewhere.

off-line *adj* (of computer equipment) not directly connected to or controlled by the central processing unit of a computer.

off-load *vb* to get rid of (something unpleasant), usually by giving it to someone else: *you take all the credit and off-load all the blame.*

off-peak *adj* (of services) used at times other than those of greatest demand.

off-putting *adj Brit informal* rather unpleasant or disturbing: *it can be very off-putting when you first visit a social security office.*

offset *vb* **-setting, -set** 1 to cancel out or compensate for. 2 to print (something) using the offset process. ~*n* 3 a printing method in which the impression is made onto a surface, such as a rubber roller, which transfers it to the paper. 4 *Bot* a short runner in certain plants that produces roots and shoots at the tip.

offshoot *n* 1 a shoot growing from the main stem of a plant. 2 something that has developed from something else.

offshore *adj, adv* 1 away from or at some distance from the shore. ~*adj* 2 sited or conducted at sea: *he reversed his position on offshore drilling.*

offside *adj, adv* 1 *Sport* (of a player) in a position illegally ahead of the ball when it is played. ~*n* 2 *Chiefly Brit* the side of a vehicle nearest the centre of the road.

offspring *n* 1 the immediate descendant or descendants of a person or animal. 2 a product, outcome, or result: *the women's liberation movement was the offspring of the 1960s.*

off-the-peg *adj* (of clothing) ready to wear; not produced especially for the person buying.

oft *adv Old-fashioned or poetic* short for **often.**

often *adv* 1 frequently; much of the time. 2 **as often as not** quite frequently. 3 **every so often** occasionally. 4 **more often than not** in more than half the instances.

ogee arch (oh-jee) *n* a pointed arch made with an S-shaped curve on each side.

ogle *vb* **ogling, ogled** to stare at (someone) lustfully.

O grade *n* (formerly) 1 the basic level of the Scottish Certificate of Education. 2 a pass in a particular subject at O grade: *she has eight O grades.*

ogre *n* 1 (in folklore) a man-eating giant. 2 any monstrous or cruel person. **ogreish** *adj* **ogress** *fem n*

oh *interj* an exclamation of surprise, pain, pleasure, fear, or annoyance.

OH Ohio.

ohm *n* the SI unit of electric resistance.

OHMS (in Britain and the Commonwealth) On Her (*or* His) Majesty's Service.

oil *n* 1 any of a number of viscous liquids with a smooth sticky feel, which are usually flammable, insoluble in water, and are obtained from plants, animals, or mineral deposits by synthesis. 2 same as **petroleum.** 3 a substance derived from petroleum and used for lubrication. 4 *Brit* paraffin as a domestic fuel. 5 oil colour or paint. 6 an oil painting. ~*vb* 7 to lubricate with oil or apply oil to. 8 **oil the wheels** to make things run smoothly.

oilcloth *n* a cotton fabric treated with oil or a synthet-

THESAURUS

commission, duty, employment, function, obligation, occupation, place, post, responsibility, role, service, situation, station, trust, work 2. **good offices** advocacy, aegis, aid, auspices, backing, favour, help, intercession, intervention, mediation, patronage, recommendation, referral, support, word

officer agent, appointee, bureaucrat, dignitary, executive, functionary, office-holder, official, public servant, representative

official 1. *adj.* accredited, authentic, authoritative, authorized, bona fide, certified, endorsed, ex officio, formal, legitimate, licensed, proper, sanctioned, straight from the horse's mouth (*informal*) 2. *n.* agent, bureaucrat, executive, functionary, office bearer, officer, representative

officiate chair, conduct, emcee (*informal*), manage, oversee, preside, serve, superintend

officious bustling, dictatorial, forward, impertinent, inquisitive, interfering, intrusive, meddlesome, meddling, mischievous, obtrusive, opinionated, overbusy, overzealous, pushy (*informal*), self-important

offing in the offing close at hand, coming up, hovering, imminent, in prospect, in the immediate future, in the wings, on the horizon, on the way, upcoming

off-load disburden, discharge, dump, get rid of, jettison, lighten, shift, take off, transfer, unburden, unload, unship

off-putting daunting, discomfiting, disconcerting, discouraging, dismaying, dispiriting, disturbing, formidable, frustrating, intimidating, unnerving, unsettling, upsetting

offset balance out, cancel out, compensate for, counteract, counterbalance, counterpoise, make up for, neutralize

offshoot 1. branch, limb, outgrowth, sprout 2. adjunct, appendage, by-product, development, spin-off

offspring brood, child, children, descendant, descendants, family, fry, heir, heirs, issue, kids (*informal*), progeny, scion, seed (*chiefly biblical*), spawn, successor, successors, young

often again and again, frequently, generally, many a time, much, oft (*archaic or poetic*), oftentimes (*archaic*), ofttimes (*archaic*), over and over again, repeatedly, time after time, time and again

ic resin to make it waterproof, formerly used esp. for tablecloths.

oilfield *n* an area containing reserves of oil.

oilfired *adj* using oil as fuel.

oil paint *n* a thick paint made of pigment ground in linseed oil.

oil painting *n* **1** a picture painted with oil paints. **2** the art of painting with oil paints.

oil rig *n* a structure used as a base when drilling an oil well.

oilskin *n* **1** a thick cotton fabric treated with oil to make it waterproof. **2** a protective outer garment made of this fabric.

oil slick *n* a mass of floating oil covering an area of water.

oil well *n* a well bored into the earth or sea bed to a supply of oil.

oily *adj* **oilier, oiliest 1** soaked or covered with oil. **2** of, containing, or like oil. **3** attempting to gain favour by insincere behaviour and flattery. **oiliness** *n*

oink *interj* the grunt of a pig or an imitation of this.

ointment *n* a smooth greasy substance applied to the skin to heal or protect, or as a cosmetic.

OK Oklahoma.

O.K. *Informal ~interj* **1** an expression of approval or agreement. *~adj, adv* **2** in good or satisfactory condition. *~vb* **O.K.ing, O.K.ed 3** to approve or endorse. *~n, pl* **O.K.s 4** approval or agreement.

okapi (oh-**kah**-pee) *n, pl* **-pis** *or* **-pi** an African mammal related to the giraffe, but with a shorter neck, a reddish coat, and white stripes on the legs.

okay *interj, adj, adv, vb, n* same as **O.K.**.

okra *n* a tall plant with long green pods that are used as food.

old *adj* **1** having lived or existed for a long time: *the old woman; burning witches is one old custom I've no desire to see revived.* **2** of or relating to advanced years or a long life: *I twisted my knee as I tried to squat and cursed old age.* **3** worn with age or use: *the old bathroom fittings.* **4** having lived or existed for a specified period: *he is 60 years old.* **5** the earlier or earliest of two or more things with the same name: *the old edition; the Old Testament.* **6** designating the form of a language in which the earliest known records are written: *Old English.* **7** familiar through long acquaintance or repetition: *an old acquaintance; the legalization argument is an old and familiar one.* **8** dear: used as a term of affection or familiarity: *always rely on old Tom to turn out.* **9** out of date; unfashionable. **10** former or previous: *my old housekeeper lent me some money.* **11** of long standing: *he's an old and respected member of staff.* **12 good old days** an earlier period of time regarded as better than the present. *~n* **13** an earlier or past time: *in days of old.* **oldish** *adj*

old age pension *n* a former name for **retirement pension. old age pensioner** *n*

Old Bailey *n* the Central Criminal Court of England.

old boy *n* **1** *Brit* a male ex-pupil of a school. **2** *Informal, chiefly Brit* **a** a familiar form of address used to refer to a man. **b** an old man.

old country *n* the country of origin of an immigrant or an immigrant's ancestors.

olde *adj Facetious* quaint.

olden *adj Archaic or poetic* old: *in the olden days the girls were married young.*

Old English *n* the English language of the Anglo-Saxons, spoken from the fifth century AD to about 1100. Also called: **Anglo-Saxon**

Old English sheepdog *n* a large sheepdog with thick shaggy hair.

old-fashioned *adj* **1** in the style of a previous period; outdated: *she wore her hair in a strangely old-fashioned tight hairdo.* **2** favouring or denoting the styles or ideas of a former time: *old-fashioned values.*

old flame *n Informal, old-fashioned* a person with whom one once had a romantic relationship.

Old French *n* the French language in its earliest forms, from about the 9th century up to about 1400.

old girl *n* **1** *Brit* a female ex-pupil of a school. **2** *Informal, chiefly Brit* **a** a familiar form of address used to refer to a woman. **b** an old woman.

old guard *n* a group of people in an organization who have traditional values: *the company's old guard is making way for a new, more youthful team.*

old hand *n* a skilled or experienced person.

old hat *adj* old-fashioned or dull.

Old High German *n* a group of West Germanic dialects that developed into modern German; High German up to about 1200.

oldie *n Informal* an old song, film, or person.

old lady *n Informal* one's mother or wife.

old maid *n* **1** a woman regarded as unlikely ever to marry; spinster. **2** *Informal* a prim, fussy, or excessively cautious person.

old man *n* **1** *Informal* one's father or husband. **2** an affectionate form of address used to a man.

old master *n* **1** one of the great European painters of the period 1500 to 1800. **2** a painting by one of these.

old moon *n* a phase of the moon between last quarter and new moon, when it appears as a waning crescent.

Old Nick *n Informal* Satan.

THESAURUS

ogre bogey, bogeyman, bugbear, demon, devil, giant, monster, spectre

oil *vb.* grease, lubricate

ointment balm, cerate, cream, embrocation, emollient, liniment, lotion, salve, unguent

O.K., okay 1. *interj.* agreed, all right, right, roger, very good, very well, yes **2.** *adj.* acceptable, accurate, adequate, all right, approved, convenient, correct, fair, fine, good, in order, middling, not bad (*informal*), passable, permitted, satisfactory, so-so (*informal*), tolerable **3.** *vb.* agree to, approve, authorize, consent to, endorse, entitle, give one's consent to, give the go-ahead (green light, thumbs up (*informal*)) to, pass, rubber-stamp (*informal*), sanction, say yes to **4.** *n.* agreement, approbation, approval, assent, authorization, consent, endorsement, go-ahead (*informal*), green light, permission, sanction, say-so (*informal*), seal of approval

old 1. advanced in years, aged, ancient, decrepit, elderly, full of years, getting on, grey, grey-haired, grizzled, hoary, mature, over the hill (*informal*), past one's prime, patriarchal, senescent, senile, venerable **2.** antediluvian, antiquated, antique, cast-off, crumbling, dated, decayed, done, hackneyed, obsolete, old-fashioned, outdated, outmoded, out-of-date, passé, stale, superannuated, timeworn, unfashionable, unoriginal, worn-out **3.** age-old, experienced, familiar, hardened, long-established, of long standing, practised, skilled, time-honoured, traditional, versed, veteran, vintage **4.** earlier, erstwhile, ex-, former, one-time, previous, quondam

old-fashioned ancient, antiquated, archaic, behind the times, dated, dead, *démodé,* fusty, musty, not with

old school *n* a group of people favouring traditional or conservative ideas or practices.

old school tie *n* the system of mutual help supposed to operate among the former pupils of public schools.

Old Style *n* the former method of reckoning dates using the Julian calendar.

Old Testament *n* the first part of the Christian Bible, containing the sacred Scriptures of the Hebrews.

old-time *adj* of or relating to a former time; old-fashioned: *an old-time waltz.*

old wives' tale *n* a belief, usually superstitious or foolish, passed on by word of mouth as a piece of traditional wisdom.

old woman *n* **1** *Informal* one's mother or wife. **2** a timid, fussy, or cautious person. **old-womanish** *adj*

Old World *n* that part of the world that was known to Europeans before the discovery of the Americas; the eastern hemisphere.

old-world *adj* of or characteristic of former times; quaint or traditional.

oleaginous (oh-lee-**aj**-in-uss) *adj* like or producing oil; oily.

oleander (oh-lee-**ann**-der) *n* an evergreen Mediterranean shrub with fragrant white, pink, or purple flowers.

O level *n* (formerly) **1** the basic level of the General Certificate of Education. **2** a pass in a particular subject at O level: *a very intelligent young woman with ten O levels.*

olfactory *adj* of the sense of smell.

oligarchy (**ol**-lee-gark-ee) *n, pl* **-chies 1** government by a small group of people. **2** a state governed this way. **3** a small group of people governing such a state. **oligarchic** *or* **oligarchical** *adj*

Oligocene (**ol**-lig-go-seen) *adj Geol* of the epoch of geological time about 35 million years ago.

oligopoly *n, pl* **-lies** *Econ* a market situation in which control over the supply of a commodity is held by a small number of producers.

olive *n* **1** an evergreen Mediterranean tree. **2** the small green or black bitter-tasting fruit of this tree. *~adj* **3** short for **olive-green.**

olive branch *n* a peace offering: *I should offer some kind of olive branch and get in touch with them.*

olive-green *adj* deep yellowish-green.

olive oil *n* a yellowish-green oil pressed from ripe olives and used in cooking and medicines.

Olympiad *n* **1** a staging of the modern Olympic Games. **2** an international contest in chess or other games.

Olympian *adj* **1** of Mount Olympus or the classical Greek gods. **2** majestic or godlike. *~n* **3** a competitor in the Olympic Games. **4** a god of Mount Olympus.

Olympic *adj* of the Olympic Games.

Olympic Games *n* **1** an ancient Greek festival, held every fourth year in honour of Zeus, consisting of games and festivities. **2** Also called: **the Olympics** the modern revival of these games, consisting of international athletic and sporting contests held every four years in a selected country.

OM Order of Merit (a Brit. title).

ombudsman *n, pl* **-men** an official who investigates citizens' complaints against the government or its servants.

omega *n* **1** the 24th and last letter of the Greek alphabet (Ω, ω). **2** the ending or last of a series.

omelette *or esp US* **omelet** *n* a dish of beaten eggs cooked in a flat pan and often folded round a savoury filling.

omen *n* **1** a thing or occurrence regarded as a sign of future happiness or disaster. **2** prophetic significance: *birds of ill omen.*

ominous *adj* warning of evil. **ominously** *adv*

omission *n* **1** something that has been left out or passed over. **2** an act of missing out or failing to do something: *we regret the omission of these and the names of the other fine artists.*

omit *vb* **omitting, omitted 1** to fail to include; leave out. **2** to fail (to do something).

omnibus *n, pl* **-buses 1** a collection of works by one author or several works on a similar topic, reprinted in one volume. **2** Also called: **omnibus edition** a television or radio programme consisting of two or more episodes of a serial broadcast earlier in the week. **3** *Old-fashioned* a bus. *~adj* **4** consisting of or dealing with several different things at once: *the BBC intends to increase the number of omnibus programmes.*

omnipotent (om-**nip**-a-tent) *adj* having very great or unlimited power. **omnipotence** *n*

omnipresent *adj* (esp. of a god) present in all places at the same time. **omnipresence** *n*

omniscient (om-**niss**-ee-ent) *adj Formal* knowing or seeming to know everything. **omniscience** *n*

omnivore (**om**-niv-vore) *n* an animal that eats any type of food.

omnivorous (om-**niv**-or-uss) *adj* **1** eating any type of food. **2** taking in everything indiscriminately: *his omnivorous sociability has meant constant hard work for his wife.*

on *prep* **1** in contact with or at the surface of: *let the cakes stand in the tins on a wire rack; she had dirt on her dress.* **2** attached to: *a piece of paper on a clipboard.* **3** carried with: *the message found on her.* **4** near to or along the side of: *the hotel is on the coast.* **5** within the time limits of (a day or date): *they returned to Moscow on 22nd September.* **6** being performed upon or relayed through the medium of: *a construction of refined sounds played on special musical instruments; what's on television?* **7** at the occasion of: *she had received numerous letters congratulating her on her election.* **8** immediately after or at the same time as: *check with the tourist office on arrival.* **9** through the use of: *an extraordinarily vigorous man who thrives on physical activity; the program runs on the Unix operating system.* **10** regularly taking (a

THESAURUS

it (*informal*), obsolescent, obsolete, (old-)fogyish, old hat, old-time, outdated, outmoded, out-of-date, out of style, out of the ark (*informal*), passé, past, square (*informal*), superannuated, unfashionable

old-time ancient, antique, bygone, former, old-fashioned, past, vintage

old-world archaic, ceremonious, chivalrous, courtly, gallant, old-fashioned, picturesque, quaint, traditional

omen augury, foreboding, foretoken, indication, portent, premonition, presage, prognostication, sign, warning, writing on the wall

ominous baleful, dark, fateful, forbidding, foreboding, inauspicious, menacing, minatory, portentous, premonitory, sinister, threatening, unpromising, unpropitious

omission default, exclusion, failure, forgetfulness, gap, lack, leaving out, neglect, noninclusion, oversight

omit disregard, drop, eliminate, exclude, fail, forget, give (something) a miss (*informal*), leave out, leave (something) undone, let (something) slide, miss (out), neglect, overlook, pass over, skip

omnipotence divine right, invincibility, mastery,

drug): *she's on the pill.* **11** by means of (a mode of transport): *his only way up the hill had to be on foot; they get around on bicycles.* **12** in the process or course of: *he is away on a climbing expedition; coal miners have been on strike for six weeks.* **13** concerned with or relating to: *ten million viewers watched the recent series on homelessness.* **14** (of a statement or action) having as basis or grounds: *I have it on good authority.* **15** charged to: *all drinks are on the house for the rest of the evening.* **16** staked as a bet: *I'll have $50 on the favourite.* ~*adv* **17** in operation; functioning: *the lights had been left on all night.* **18** attached to, surrounding, or placed in contact with something: *they escaped with nothing on except sleeveless shirts and shorts.* **19** taking place: *what do you have on tonight?* **20** continuously or persistently: *the crisis must not be allowed to drag on indefinitely.* **21** forwards or further: *they trudged on.* **22 on and off** occasionally; not regularly or continuously. **23 on and on** without ceasing; continually. ~*adj* **24** *Informal* performing: *who's on next?* **25** *Informal* definitely taking place: *is the party still on?* **26** *Informal* tolerable, practicable, or acceptable: *I'm not going, that's just not on.* **27 on at** *Informal* nagging: *he was always on at her to stop smoking.* ~*n* **28** *Cricket* the side of the field to the left of a right-handed batsman when he is facing the bowler.

ON Ontario.

onager *n, pl* **-gri** *or* **-gers** a wild ass of Persia.

onanism *n* **1** withdrawal in sexual intercourse before ejaculation. **2** masturbation.

ONC (in Britain) Ordinary National Certificate.

once *adv* **1** one time; on one occasion only. **2** at some past time, but no longer: *I was in love once.* **3** by one degree (of relationship): *he was Deirdre's cousin once removed.* **4 once and for all** conclusively; for the last time. **5 once in a while** occasionally; now and then. **6 once or twice** a few times. **7 once upon a time** used to begin fairy tales and children's stories. ~*conj* **8** as soon as: *once you have learned good grammar you can leave it to nature and forget it.* ~*n* **9** one occasion or case: *once is enough.* **10 all at once a** suddenly. **b** simultaneously. **11 at once a** immediately. **b** simultaneously. **12 for once** this time, even if at no other time.

once-over *n Informal* a quick examination or appraisal.

oncogene (**ong**-koh-jean) *n* a gene present in all cells, that when abnormally activated can cause cancer.

oncoming *adj* coming nearer in space or time; approaching: *oncoming traffic.*

OND (in Britain) Ordinary National Diploma.

one *adj, n* **1** single or lone (person or thing); not two or more: *one civilian has died and thirty-three have been injured.* **2** only or unique (person or thing): *he is the one to make correct judgments and influence the public; she was unique, inimitable, one of a kind.* **3** a specified (person or thing) as distinct from another or others of its kind: *place one hand under the knee and the other under the ankle; which one is correct?* **4 one or two** a few. ~*adj* **5** a certain, indefinite, or unspecified (time): *one day he would learn the truth about her.* **6** *Informal, emphatic* a: *we're on to one hell of a story.* ~*pron* **7** an indefinite person regarded as typical of every person: *one can always hope that there won't be an accident.* **8** any indefinite person: *one can catch fine trout in this stream.* **9** I or me: *one only wonders what he has against the dogs.* ~*n* **10** the smallest natural number and first cardinal number. **11** a numeral, 1 or I, representing this number. **12** something representing or consisting of one unit. **13** *Informal* a joke or story: *have you heard the one about the actress and the bishop?* **14 (all) in one** combined or united. **15 all one** of no consequence: *leave if you want to, it's all one to me.* **16 at one with** in agreement or harmony with. **17 one and all** everyone, without exception. **18 one by one** one at a time; individually.

➤ Avoid overuse of the pronoun *one* as a substitute for *I.* Many listeners find it affected. The pronouns *I* and *one* should not be mixed within the same group of sentences. Choose one of them and continue with it.

one another *pron* each other: *they seem to genuinely care for one another.*

one-armed bandit *n Informal* a fruit machine operated by pulling down a lever at one side.

one-dimensional *adj* **1** having one dimension. **2** completely lacking in depth or complexity: *the production staging is one-dimensional and the direction rigid.*

one-horse *adj Informal* small or insignificant: *they are eighty miles from the nearest one-horse town.*

one-liner *n Informal* a short joke or witty remark.

oneness *n* **1** agreement. **2** uniqueness. **3** sameness.

one-night stand *n* **1** *Informal* a sexual encounter lasting only one evening or night. **2** a performance given only once at any one place.

one-off *n Brit* something that happens or is made only once.

onerous (**own**-er-uss) *adj* (of a task) difficult to carry out. **onerousness** *n*

oneself *pron* **1** the reflexive form of *one.* **2** one's normal or usual self: *one doesn't feel oneself after such an experience.*

one-sided *adj* **1** considering or favouring only one side of a matter: *it is a one-sided debate.* **2** having all the advantage on one side: *it was a one-sided match with Brazil missing a succession of chances.*

one-stop *adj* having or providing a range of services or goods in one place: *one-stop shopping.*

One Thousand Guineas *n* **the One Thousand**

THESAURUS

sovereignty, supremacy, supreme power, undisputed sway

omnipotent all-powerful, almighty, supreme

on and off discontinuously, (every) now and again, fitfully, from time to time, intermittently, now and then, off and on, on occasion, sometimes, spasmodically

once *adv.* **1.** at one time, formerly, in the old days, in the past, in times gone by, in times past, long ago, once upon a time, previously **2. once and for all** conclusively, decisively, finally, for all time, for good, for the last time, permanently, positively, with finality **3. once in a while** at intervals, at times, every now and then, from time to time, now and again, occasionally, once in a blue moon (*informal*), on occasion, sometimes ~*n.* **4. at once a.** directly, forthwith, immediately, instantly, now, right away, straight away, straightway (*archaic*), this (very) minute, without delay, without hesitation **b.** at *or* in one go (*informal*), at the same time, simultaneously, together

one-horse backwoods, inferior, minor, obscure, petty, quiet, sleepy, slow, small, small-time (*informal*), tinpot (*Brit. informal*), unimportant

onerous backbreaking, burdensome, crushing, demanding, difficult, exacting, exhausting, exigent, formidable, grave, hard, heavy, laborious, oppressive, responsible, taxing, weighty

one-sided biased, coloured, discriminatory, inequitable, lopsided, partial, partisan, prejudiced, unequal, unfair, unjust

Guineas an annual horse race for three-year-old fillies, run at Newmarket.

one-time *adj* at some time in the past; former.

one-to-one *adj* **1** (of two or more things) corresponding exactly. **2** denoting a relationship or encounter in which someone is involved with only one other person: *one-to-one meetings.* **3** *Maths* involving the pairing of each member of one set with only one member of another set, without remainder.

one-track *adj Informal* obsessed with one idea or subject: *she's got a one-track mind.*

one-up *adj Informal* having an advantage or lead over someone else. **one-upmanship** *n*

one-way *adj* **1** moving or allowing travel in one direction only: *the town centre has a baffling one-way system.* **2** involving no reciprocal obligation or action: *he does not get anything back out of the one-way relationship.*

ongoing *adj* in progress; continuing: *there are still ongoing discussions about the future role of NATO.*

onion *n* **1** a vegetable with an edible bulb with a strong smell and taste. **2 know one's onions** *Brit slang* to be fully acquainted with a subject. **oniony** *adj*

on-line *adj* (of computer equipment) directly connected to and controlled by the central processing unit of a computer.

onlooker *n* a person who observes without taking part. **onlooking** *adj*

only *adj* **1** alone of its or their kind: *I will be talking to the only journalist to have been inside the prison.* **2** (of a child) having no brothers or sisters. **3** unique by virtue of superiority; best: *first class is the only way to travel.* **4 one and only** incomparable: *the one and only Diana Ross.* ~*adv* **5** without anyone or anything else being included; alone: *only you can decide if you can abide by this compromise.* **6** merely or just: *it's only Henry.* **7** no more or no greater than: *I was talking to a priest only a minute ago.* **8** merely: *they had only to turn up to win the competition.* **9** not earlier than; not until: *I've only found out today why you wouldn't come.* **10 if only** *or* **if ... only** used to introduce a wish or hope. **11 only too** extremely: *they were only too willing to do anything to help.* ~*conj* **12** but or however: *those countries are going through the same cycle, only a little later than us.*
➤ The use of *only* to connect sentences is rather informal: *I would come only I'm busy.* In formal use *only* is placed directly before the words it modifies: *The club opens only on Thursdays* but in everyday use this becomes: *The club only opens on Thursdays.*

o.n.o. or near(est) offer.

onomatopoeia (on-a-mat-a-**pee**-a) *n* use of a word which imitates the sound it represents, such as *hiss.* **onomatopoeic** *or* **onomatopoetic** *adj*

onrush *n* a forceful forward rush or flow; surge.

onset *n* a start; beginning.

onshore *adj, adv* **1** towards the land: *a stiff onshore wind.* **2** on land; not at sea.

onside *adj, adv Sport* (of a player) in a legal position, for example, behind the ball or with a required number of opponents between oneself and the opposing team's goal line.

onslaught *n* a violent attack.

Ont. Ontario.

onto *or* **on to** *prep* **1** to a position that is on: *step onto the train.* **2** having discovered or become aware of: *the police are onto us.* **3** into contact with: *get onto the factory.*

ontology *n Philosophy* the study of the nature of being. **ontological** *adj*

onus (**own**-uss) *n, pl* **onuses** a responsibility, task, or burden: *the courts put the onus on parents.*

onward *adj* **1** directed or moving forward. ~*adv also* **onwards 2** continuing; progressing.

onyx *n* a kind of quartz with alternating coloured layers, used as a gemstone.

oodles *pl n Informal* great quantities: *he has shown he can raise oodles of cash.*

Ookpik *n Canad trademark* a sealskin doll resembling an owl, used abroad as a symbol of Canadian handicrafts.

oolite (**oh**-a-lite) *n* a limestone made up of tiny grains of calcium carbonate. **oolitic** *adj*

oom *n S African* a title of respect used to refer to an elderly man.

oomiak *or* **oomiac** *n* same as **umiak.**

oompah *n* a representation of the sound made by a deep brass instrument, esp. in brass band music.

oomph *n Informal* enthusiasm, vigour, or energy.

oops *interj* an exclamation of surprise or of apology when someone has a slight accident or makes a mistake.

ooze[1] *vb* **oozing, oozed 1** to flow or leak out slowly; seep. **2** (of a substance) to discharge moisture. **3** to overflow with (a feeling or quality): *he oozes confidence.* ~*n* **4** a slow flowing or leaking. **oozy** *adj*

ooze[2] *n* a soft thin mud, such as that found at the bottom of a lake, river, or sea.

op. opus.

opacity (ohp-**ass**-it-tee) *n, pl* **-ties 1** the state or quality of being opaque. **2** the quality of being difficult to understand; unintelligibility.

opal *n* a precious stone, usually milky or bluish in colour, with shimmering changing reflections.

opalescent *adj* having shimmering changing reflections, like opal. **opalescence** *n*

opaque *adj* **1** not able to be seen through; not transparent or translucent. **2** hard to understand; unintelligible.

op. cit. (op **sit**) (in textual annotations) in the work cited.

OPEC Organization of Petroleum-Exporting Countries.

open *adj* **1** not closed, fastened, or blocked up: *the doctor's office was open.* **2** not enclosed, covered, or wrapped: *the parcel was open.* **3** extended, expanded, or unfolded: *an open flower.* **4** ready for business: *some of the crafts rooms and photography shops are open all night.* **5** (of a job) available: *all the positions on the council should be open to females.* **6** unob-

THESAURUS

one-time erstwhile, ex-, former, late, previous, quondam, sometime

onlooker bystander, eyewitness, looker-on, observer, spectator, viewer, watcher, witness

only 1. *adj.* exclusive, individual, lone, one and only, single, sole, solitary, unique **2.** *adv.* at most, barely, exclusively, just, merely, purely, simply

onomatopoeic echoic, imitative, onomatopoetic

onslaught assault, attack, blitz, charge, offensive, onrush, onset

onus burden, liability, load, obligation, responsibility, task

ooze[1] bleed, discharge, drain, dribble, drip, drop, emit, escape, exude, filter, leach, leak, overflow with, percolate, seep, strain, sweat, weep

ooze[2] alluvium, mire, muck, mud, silt, slime, sludge

opaque 1. clouded, cloudy, dim, dull, filmy, hazy,

structed by buildings or trees: *we lived in a small market town surrounded by open countryside.* **7** free to all to join in, enter, or use: *there was an open competition and I was appointed.* **8** (of a season or period) not restricted for purposes of hunting game of various kinds. **9** not decided or finalized: *the legality of these sales is still an open question.* **10** ready to consider new ideas: *I was able to approach their problem with an open mind.* **11** honest and frank. **12** generous: *she has given me love and the open hand.* **13** exposed to view; blatant: *there has never been such sustained and open criticism of the President.* **14** unprotected; susceptible: *a change of policy which would leave vulnerable youths open to exploitation.* **15** having spaces or gaps: *open ranks; an open texture.* **16** *Music* **a** (of a string) not stopped with the finger. **b** (of a note) played on such a string. **17** *Sport* (of a goal or court) unguarded or relatively unprotected. **18** (of a wound) exposed to the air. ~*vb* **19** to make or become open: *it was easy to open the back door and to slip noiselessly outside; she knelt and tried to open the drawer.* **20** to set or be set in action; start: *the US will have to open talks on Palestinian rights; I want to open a dress shop.* **21** to arrange for (a bank account), usually by making an initial deposit. **22** to declare open ceremonially or officially. ~*n* **23 the open** any wide or unobstructed area. **24** *Sport* a competition which all may enter. **opener** *n* **openly** *adv* **openness** *n*

open air *n* the place or space where the air is unenclosed; outdoors.

open-and-shut *adj* easily decided or solved; obvious: *an open-and-shut case.*

opencast mining *n Brit* mining by excavating from the surface.

open day *n* a special occasion on which a school, university, or other institution is open for the public to visit.

open-ended *adj* **1** without definite limits; unrestricted: *the schedule is open-ended.* **2** (of an activity) done without the aim of attaining a particular result or decision: *the dangers of open-ended military involvement.*

open-eyed *adj* **1** with the eyes wide open, as in amazement. **2** watchful; alert.

open-handed *adj* generous.

open-hearted *adj* **1** kind or generous. **2** willing to speak one's mind; candid.

open-heart surgery *n* surgical repair of the heart during which the heart is exposed and the blood circulation is maintained mechanically.

open house *n* a situation in which people allow friends or visitors to come to their house whenever they want to.

opening *n* **1** the beginning or first part of something. **2** the first performance of a theatrical production. **3** an opportunity or chance: *an opening into show business.* **4** a hole or gap.

opening time *n Brit* the time at which public houses can legally open for business.

open letter *n* a letter, esp. one of protest, addressed to an individual but published in a newspaper or magazine for all to read.

open market *n* a process by which prices are decided by supply and demand and goods are sold anywhere.

open-minded *adj* willing to consider new ideas; unprejudiced.

open-mouthed *adj* gaping in surprise.

open-plan *adj* having no or few dividing walls between areas: *the house includes an open-plan living room and dining area.*

open prison *n* a prison in which the prisoners are not locked up, thus extending the range of work they can do.

open secret *n* something that is supposed to be secret but is widely known.

Open University *n* (in Britain) a university teaching by means of television and radio lectures, correspondence courses, and summer schools.

open up *vb* **1** to make or become accessible: *the Berlin Wall came down and opened up new territory for dramatists.* **2** to speak freely or without self-restraint. **3** to start firing a gun or guns. **4** *Informal* to increase the speed of (a vehicle).

open verdict *n* a finding by a coroner's jury of death without stating the cause.

opera[1] *n* **1** a dramatic work in which most or all of the text is sung to orchestral accompaniment. **2** the branch of music or drama relating to operas. **3** a group

THESAURUS

impenetrable, lustreless, muddied, muddy, murky, obfuscated, turbid **2.** abstruse, baffling, cryptic, difficult, enigmatic, incomprehensible, obscure, unclear, unfathomable, unintelligible

open *adj.* **1.** agape, ajar, expanded, extended, gaping, revealed, spread out, unbarred, unclosed, uncovered, unfastened, unfolded, unfurled, unlocked, unobstructed, unsealed, yawning **2.** airy, bare, clear, exposed, extensive, free, navigable, not built-up, passable, rolling, spacious, sweeping, uncluttered, uncrowded, unenclosed, unfenced, unsheltered, wide, wide-open **3.** accessible, available, free, general, nondiscriminatory, public, unconditional, unengaged, unoccupied, unqualified, unrestricted, vacant **4.** arguable, debatable, moot, undecided, unresolved, unsettled, up in the air, yet to be decided **5.** disinterested, free, impartial, objective, receptive, unbiased, uncommitted, unprejudiced **6.** artless, candid, fair, frank, guileless, honest, ingenuous, innocent, natural, sincere, transparent, unreserved **7.** bounteous, bountiful, generous, liberal, munificent, prodigal **8.** apparent, avowed, barefaced, blatant, clear, conspicuous, downright, evident, flagrant, frank, manifest, noticeable, obvious, overt, plain, unconcealed, undisguised, visible **9.** defenceless, disposed, exposed, liable, susceptible, undefended, unfortified, unprotected, vulnerable **10.** fretted, holey, honeycombed, lacy, loose, openwork, porous, spongy ~*vb.* **11.** clear, crack, expand, spread (out), throw wide, unbar, unblock, unclose, uncork, uncover, undo, unfasten, unfold, unfurl, unlock, unroll, unseal, untie, unwrap **12.** begin, begin business, commence, get *or* start the ball rolling, inaugurate, initiate, kick off (*informal*), launch, set in motion, set up shop, start

open-handed bountiful, free, generous, lavish, liberal, munificent, prodigal, unstinting

opening 1. beginning, birth, commencement, dawn, inauguration, inception, initiation, kickoff (*informal*), launch, launching, onset, opening move, outset, overture, start **2.** break (*informal*), chance, look-in (*informal*), occasion, opportunity, place, vacancy, window **3.** aperture, breach, break, chink, cleft, crack, fissure, gap, hole, interstice, orifice, perforation, rent, rupture, slot, space, split, vent

openly 1. candidly, face to face, forthrightly, frankly, overtly, plainly, straight from the shoulder (*informal*), unhesitatingly, unreservedly **2.** blatantly, brazenly, flagrantly, in full view, in public, publicly, shamelessly, unabashedly, unashamedly, wantonly, without pretence

open-minded broad, broad-minded, catholic, dis-

that produces or performs operas. **4** a theatre where opera is performed.

opera[2] *n* a plural of **opus.**

operable *adj* **1** capable of being treated by a surgical operation. **2** capable of being operated or put into practice. **operability** *n*

opera glasses *pl n* small low-powered binoculars used by audiences in theatres.

opera house *n* a theatre specially designed for the performance of operas.

operand *n Maths* a quantity, variable, or function upon which an operation is performed.

operate *vb* **-ating, -ated 1** to work. **2** to control the working of (a machine). **3** to manage, direct, or run (a business or system). **4** to perform a surgical operation (upon a person or animal). **5** to conduct military or naval operations.

operatic *adj* **1** of or relating to opera. **2** overdramatic or exaggerated: *he was about to go out with his operatic strut.*

operating system *n* the software controlling a computer.

operating theatre *or US* **room** *n* a room in which surgical operations are performed.

operation *n* **1** the act or method of operating. **2** the condition of being in action: *there are twenty teleworking centres in operation around the country.* **3** an action or series of actions done to produce a particular result: *a large-scale police operation has been in place to manage the heavy traffic.* **4** *Surgery* a surgical procedure carried out to remove, replace, or repair a diseased or damaged part of the body. **5** a military or naval manoeuvre. **6** *Maths* any procedure, such as addition, in which a number is derived from another number or numbers by applying specific rules.

operational *adj* **1** in working order and ready for use. **2** of or relating to an action done to produce a particular result.

operations research *n* the analysis of problems in business and industry. Also called: **operational research**

operative (**op**-rat-tiv) *adj* **1** in force, effect, or operation: *the Youth Training Scheme was operative by the end of 1983.* **2** (of a word) particularly relevant or significant: *"if" is the operative word.* **3** of or relating to a surgical operation. ~*n* **4** a worker with a special skill.

operator *n* **1** a person who operates a machine or instrument, esp. a telephone switchboard. **2** a person who runs a business: *your tour operator will arrange a visa for you.* **3** *Informal* a person who manipulates affairs and other people: *she considered him a shrewd operator who only liked to appear to be simple.* **4** *Maths* any symbol, term, or letter used to indicate or express a specific operation or process.

operculum (oh-**perk**-yew-lum) *n, pl* **-la** (-la) *or* **-lums** a covering flap or lidlike structure in animals or plants.

operetta *n* a type of comic or light-hearted opera.

ophthalmia *n* inflammation of the eyeball or conjunctiva.

ophthalmic *adj* of or relating to the eye.

ophthalmic optician *n* See **optician** (sense 1).

ophthalmology *n* the branch of medicine concerned with the eye and its diseases. **ophthalmologist** *n*

ophthalmoscope *n* an instrument for examining the interior of the eye

opiate (**oh**-pee-ate) *n* **1** a narcotic or sedative drug containing opium. **2** something that causes mental dullness or inactivity.

opine *vb* **opining, opined** *Formal* to hold or express an opinion: *he opined that the navy would have to start again from the beginning.*

opinion *n* **1** belief not founded on certainty or proof but on what seems probable. **2** evaluation or estimation of a person or thing: *they seemed to share my high opinion of her.* **3** a judgment given by an expert: *medical opinion.* **4 a matter of opinion** a point open to question.

opinionated *adj* holding very strong opinions which one is convinced are right.

opinion poll *n* same as **poll** (sense 1).

opium (**oh**-pee-um) *n* an addictive narcotic drug made from the seed capsules of the opium poppy and used in medicine as a painkiller and sedative.

opossum *n, pl* **-sums** *or* **-sum 1** a thick-furred American marsupial, with a long snout and a hairless prehensile tail. **2** *Austral & NZ* a similar Australian animal, such as a phalanger.

opponent *n* a person who opposes another in a contest, battle, or argument.

opportune *adj Formal* **1** happening at a time that is suitable or advantageous: *there was an opportune*

THESAURUS

passionate, enlightened, free, impartial, liberal, reasonable, receptive, tolerant, unbiased, undogmatic, unprejudiced

operate 1. act, be in action, function, go, perform, run, work **2.** be in charge of, handle, manage, manoeuvre, use, work **3.** perform surgery

operation 1. action, affair, course, exercise, motion, movement, performance, procedure, process, use, working **2. in operation** effective, functioning, going, in action, in force, operative **3.** affair, business, deal, enterprise, proceeding, transaction, undertaking **4.** surgery **5.** assault, campaign, exercise, manoeuvre

operational functional, going, in working order, operative, prepared, ready, usable, viable, workable, working

operative *adj.* **1.** active, current, effective, efficient, functional, functioning, in force, in operation, operational, serviceable, standing, workable **2.** crucial, important, indicative, influential, key, relevant, significant ~*n.* **3.** artisan, employee, hand, labourer, machinist, mechanic, worker

operator 1. conductor, driver, handler, mechanic, operative, practitioner, skilled employee, technician, worker **2.** administrator, contractor, dealer, director, manager, speculator, trader **3.** *informal* Machiavellian, machinator, manipulator, mover, shyster (*slang, chiefly U.S.*), smart aleck (*informal*), wheeler-dealer (*informal*), worker

opinion 1. assessment, belief, conception, conjecture, estimation, feeling, idea, impression, judgment, mind, notion, persuasion, point of view, sentiment, theory, view **2. matter of opinion** debatable point, matter of judgment, moot point, open question, open to debate, up to the individual

opinionated adamant, biased, bigoted, bull-headed, cocksure, dictatorial, doctrinaire, dogmatic, inflexible, obdurate, obstinate, overbearing, pig-headed, prejudiced, self-assertive, single-minded, stubborn, uncompromising

opponent adversary, antagonist, challenger, competitor, contestant, disputant, dissentient, enemy, foe, opposer, rival, the opposition

opportune advantageous, appropriate, apt, auspicious, convenient, favourable, felicitous, fit, fitting, fortunate, happy, lucky, proper, propitious, seasonable, suitable, timely, well-timed

knock at the door. **2** (of time) suitable for a particular purpose: *I have arrived at a very opportune moment.*

opportunist *n* **1** a person who adapts his or her actions to take advantage of opportunities and circumstances without regard for principles. *~adj* **2** taking advantage of opportunities and circumstances in this way. **opportunism** *n* **opportunistic** *adj*

opportunity *n, pl* **-ties 1** a favourable combination of circumstances. **2** a good chance or prospect.

opposable *adj Zool* (of the thumb) capable of touching the tip of all the other fingers.

oppose *vb* **-posing, -posed 1** Also: **be opposed to** to be against (something or someone) in speech or action. **2 as opposed to** in strong contrast with: *I'm a realist as opposed to a theorist.* **opposing** *adj*

opposite *adj* **1** situated on the other or further side. **2** facing or going in contrary directions: *he saw another small craft heading the opposite way.* **3** completely different: *I have a different, in fact, opposite view on this subject.* **4** *Maths* (of a side in a triangle) facing a specified angle. *~n* **5** a person or thing that is opposite; antithesis. *~prep* **6** facing; across from. *~adv* **7** in an opposite position: *fragments smashed through the windows of the house opposite.*

opposite number *n* a person holding an equivalent position in another group or organization.

opposition *n* **1** the act of opposing or being opposed. **2** hostility, resistance, or disagreement. **3** a person or group antagonistic or opposed to another. **4** a political party or group opposed to the ruling party or government. **5** *Astrol* a diametrically opposite position of two heavenly bodies.

oppress *vb* **1** to put down or control by cruelty or force. **2** to make anxious or uncomfortable. **oppression** *n* **oppressor** *n*

oppressive *adj* **1** cruel, harsh, or tyrannical. **2** uncomfortable or depressing: *a small flat can become rather oppressive.* **3** (of weather) hot and humid. **oppressiveness** *n*

opprobrium (op-**probe**-ree-um) *n Formal* **1** the state of being abused or scornfully criticized. **2** a cause of disgrace or shame. **opprobrious** *adj*

oppugn (op-**pewn**) *vb Formal* to call into question; dispute.

opt *vb* to show preference (for) or choose (to do something).

optic *adj* of the eye or vision.

optical *adj* **1** of or involving light or optics. **2** of the eye or the sense of sight; optic. **3** (of a lens) helping vision.

optical character reader *n* a computer device enabling letters and numbers to be optically scanned and input to a storage device.

optical fibre *n* a thin flexible glass fibre used in fibre optics to transmit information.

optician *n* **1** Also called: **ophthalmic optician** a person who is qualified to examine the eyes and prescribe and supply spectacles and contact lenses. **2** Also called: **dispensing optician** a person who supplies and fits spectacle frames and lenses, but is not qualified to prescribe lenses.

optic nerve *n* a cranial nerve of vertebrates that conducts nerve impulses from the retina of the eye to the brain.

optics *n* the science dealing with light and vision.

optimal *adj* best or most favourable.

optimism *n* **1** the tendency to take the most hopeful view in all matters. **2** *Philosophy* the doctrine of the ultimate triumph of good over evil. **optimist** *n* **optimistic** *adj* **optimistically** *adv*

optimize *or* **-mise** *vb* **-mizing, -mized** *or* **-mising, -mised** to make the most of.

optimum *n, pl* **-ma** *or* **-mums 1** the most favourable conditions or best compromise possible. *~adj* **2** most favourable or advantageous; best: *balance is a critical part of an optimum diet.*

option *n* **1** the power or liberty to choose: *we have no option other than to fully comply.* **2** something that is or may be chosen: *the menu includes a vegetarian option.* **3** an exclusive right, usually for a limited period,

THESAURUS

opportunism expediency, exploitation, Machiavellianism, making hay while the sun shines (*informal*), pragmatism, realism, *Realpolitik,* striking while the iron is hot (*informal*), unscrupulousness

opportunity break (*informal*), chance, convenience, hour, look-in (*informal*), moment, occasion, opening, scope, time, window

oppose bar, block, check, combat, confront, contradict, counter, counterattack, defy, face, fight, fly in the face of, hinder, obstruct, prevent, resist, speak against, stand up to, take a stand against, take issue with, take on, thwart, withstand

opposed against, antagonistic, anti (*informal*), antipathetic, antithetical, averse, clashing, conflicting, contra (*informal*), contrary, dissentient, hostile, incompatible, inimical, in opposition, opposing, opposite

opposing antagonistic, antipathetic, clashing, combatant, conflicting, contrary, enemy, hostile, incompatible, irreconcilable, opposed, opposite, rival, warring

opposite *adj.* **1.** corresponding, facing, fronting **2.** adverse, antagonistic, antithetical, conflicting, contradictory, contrary, contrasted, different, differing, diverse, hostile, inconsistent, inimical, irreconcilable, opposed, reverse, unlike *~n.* **3.** antithesis, contradiction, contrary, converse, inverse, reverse, the other extreme, the other side of the coin (*informal*)

opposition 1. antagonism, competition, contrariety, counteraction, disapproval, hostility, obstruction, obstructiveness, prevention, resistance, unfriendliness **2.** antagonist, competition, foe, opponent, other side, rival

oppress 1. abuse, crush, harry, maltreat, overpower, overwhelm, persecute, rule with an iron hand, subdue, subjugate, suppress, trample underfoot, tyrannize over, wrong **2.** afflict, burden, depress, dispirit, harass, lie *or* weigh heavy upon, sadden, take the heart out of, torment, vex

oppression abuse, brutality, calamity, cruelty, hardship, harshness, injury, injustice, iron hand, maltreatment, misery, persecution, severity, subjection, suffering, tyranny

oppressive 1. brutal, burdensome, cruel, despotic, grinding, harsh, heavy, inhuman, onerous, overbearing, overwhelming, repressive, severe, tyrannical, unjust **2.** airless, close, heavy, humid, muggy, overpowering, stifling, stuffy, suffocating, sultry, torrid

oppressor autocrat, bully, despot, harrier, intimidator, iron hand, persecutor, scourge, slave-driver, taskmaster, tormentor, tyrant

opt (for) choose, decide (on), elect, exercise one's discretion (in favour of), go for, make a selection, plump for, prefer

optimistic assured, bright, buoyant, buoyed up, cheerful, confident, disposed to take a favourable view, encouraged, expectant, hopeful, idealistic, positive, sanguine, seen through rose-coloured spectacles, Utopian

optimum *adj.* A1 *or* A-one (*informal*), best, choicest,

to buy or sell something at a future date: *a producer could extend his option on the material for another six months.* **4 keep** *or* **leave one's options open** not to commit oneself. **5 soft option** an easy alternative.

optional *adj* possible but not compulsory; open to choice.

optometrist (op-**tom**-met-trist) *n* a person qualified to examine the eyes and prescribe and supply spectacles and contact lenses. **optometry** *n*

opt out *vb* **1** (often foll. by *of*) to choose not to be involved (in) or part (of), used esp. of schools and hospitals that leave the public sector. *~n* **opt-out 2** the act of opting out, esp. of a local authority administration.

opulent (**op**-pew-lent) *adj* **1** having or indicating wealth. **2** abundant or plentiful. **opulence** *n*

opus (**oh**-puss) *n, pl* **opuses** *or* **opera** an artistic creation, esp. a musical work by a particular composer, numbered in order of publication: *Beethoven's opus 61.*

or *conj* used to join: **1** alternatives: *do you want to go out or stay at home?* **2** rephrasings of the same thing: *twelve, or a dozen.*

OR Oregon.

oracle *n* **1** a shrine in ancient Greece or Rome at which gods were consulted through the medium of a priest or priestess for advice or prophecy. **2** a prophecy or statement made by an oracle. **3** any person believed to indicate future action with infallible authority.

Oracle *n Trademark* Optional Reception of Announcements by Coded Line Electronics: the teletext service of Independent Television.

oracular *adj* **1** of or like an oracle. **2** wise and prophetic. **3** mysterious or ambiguous.

oral *adj* **1** spoken or verbal; using spoken words. **2** of or for use in the mouth: *an oral thermometer.* **3** (of a drug) to be taken by mouth: *an oral contraceptive.* *~n* **4** an examination in which the questions and answers are spoken rather than written. **orally** *adv*

orange *n* **1** a round reddish-yellow juicy citrus fruit. **2** the evergreen tree on which it grows. **3** a colour between red and yellow; the colour of an orange. *~adj* **4** of a colour between red and yellow.

orangeade *n* a usually fizzy orange-flavoured drink.

orange blossom *n* the flowers of the orange tree, traditionally worn by brides.

Orangeman *n, pl* **-men** a member of a political society founded in Ireland in 1795 to uphold Protestantism.

orangery *n, pl* **-eries** a conservatory or greenhouse in which orange trees are grown in cooler climates.

orangey *adj* slightly orange.

orang-utan *or* **orang-outang** *n* a large ape of the forests of Sumatra and Borneo, with shaggy reddish-brown hair and long arms.

oration *n* a formal or ceremonial public speech.

orator (**or**-rat-tor) *n* a person who gives an oration, esp. one skilled in persuasive public speaking.

oratorio (or-rat-**tor**-ee-oh) *n, pl* **-rios** a musical composition for soloists, chorus, and orchestra, based on a religious theme.

oratory[1] (**or**-rat-tree) *n* the art or skill of public speaking.

oratory[2] *n, pl* **-ries** a small room or building set apart for private prayer.

orb *n* **1** an ornamental sphere with a cross on top, carried by a king or queen in important ceremonies. **2** a sphere; globe. **3** *Poetic* the eye. **4** *Obsolete or poetic* a heavenly body, such as the sun.

orbit *n* **1** the curved path followed by something, such as a heavenly body or spacecraft, in its motion around another body. **2** a range or sphere of action or influence. **3** the eye socket. *~vb* **-biting, -bited 4** to move around (a heavenly body) in an orbit. **5** to send (a satellite or spacecraft) into orbit. **orbital** *adj*

Orcadian *n* **1** a person from the Orkneys. *~adj* **2** of the Orkneys.

orchard *n* an area of land on which fruit trees are grown.

orchestra *n* **1** a large group of musicians whose members play a variety of different instruments. **2** Also called: **orchestra pit** the space, in front of or under the stage, reserved for musicians in a theatre. **orchestral** *adj*

orchestrate *vb* **-trating, -trated 1** to score or arrange (a piece of music) for orchestra. **2** to arrange (something) in order to produce a particular result: *he had orchestrated today's meeting.* **orchestration** *n*

orchid *n* a plant having flowers of unusual shapes and beautiful colours, usually with one lip-shaped petal which is larger than the other two.

ordain *vb* **1** to make (someone) a member of the clergy. **2** *Formal* to decree or order with authority. **ordainment** *n*

THESAURUS

flawless, highest, ideal, most favourable *or* advantageous, optimal, peak, perfect, superlative

option alternative, choice, election, preference, selection

optional discretionary, elective, extra, noncompulsory, open, possible, up to the individual, voluntary

opulence 1. affluence, big bucks (*informal, chiefly U.S.*), big money, Easy Street (*informal*), fortune, lavishness, luxuriance, luxury, megabucks (*U.S. & Canad. slang*), plenty, pretty penny (*informal*), prosperity, riches, richness, sumptuousness, tidy sum (*informal*), wad (*U.S. & Canad. slang*), wealth **2.** abundance, copiousness, cornucopia, fullness, profusion, richness, superabundance

opulent 1. affluent, lavish, luxurious, moneyed, prosperous, rich, sumptuous, wealthy, well-heeled (*informal*), well-off, well-to-do **2.** abundant, copious, lavish, luxuriant, plentiful, profuse, prolific

oracle 1. answer, augury, divination, divine utterance, prediction, prognostication, prophecy, revelation, vision **2.** adviser, augur, authority, Cassandra, guru, high priest, horse's mouth, mastermind, mentor, prophet, pundit, seer, sibyl, soothsayer, source, wizard

oral spoken, verbal, viva voce, vocal

oration address, declamation, discourse, harangue, homily, lecture, speech, spiel (*informal*)

orator declaimer, lecturer, public speaker, rhetorician, speaker

oratory declamation, elocution, eloquence, grandiloquence, public speaking, rhetoric, speechifying, speech-making, spieling (*informal*)

orb ball, circle, globe, ring, round, sphere

orbit *n.* **1.** circle, course, cycle, ellipse, path, revolution, rotation, track, trajectory **2.** ambit, compass, course, domain, influence, range, reach, scope, sphere, sphere of influence, sweep *~vb.* **3.** circle, circumnavigate, encircle, revolve around

orchestrate 1. arrange, score **2.** arrange, concert, coordinate, integrate, organize, present, put together, set up, stage-manage

ordain 1. anoint, appoint, call, consecrate, destine, elect, frock, invest, nominate **2.** decree, demand, dic-

ordeal *n* **1** a severe or trying experience. **2** *History* a method of trial in which the accused person was subjected to physical danger.

order *n* **1** an instruction that must be obeyed; command. **2** a state in which everything is arranged logically, comprehensibly, or naturally: *she strove to keep more order in the house.* **3** an arrangement of things in succession; sequence: *group them by letter and then put them in numerical order.* **4** an established or customary system of society: *there is an opportunity here for a new world order.* **5** a peaceful or harmonious condition of society: *riot police were called in to restore order.* **6 a** an instruction to supply something in return for payment: *the waitress came to take their order.* **b** the thing or things supplied. **7** a written instruction to pay money: *post the coupon below with a cheque or postal order.* **8** a social class: *the result will be harmful to society as a whole and to the lower orders in particular.* **9** *Biol* one of the groups into which a class is divided, containing one or more families. **10** kind or sort: *the orchestra played superbly and the singing was of the highest order.* **11** Also called: **religious order** a religious community of monks or nuns. **12** a group of people who have been awarded a particular honour: *the Order of the Garter.* **13** the office or rank of a Christian minister: *he studied for the priesthood as a young man, but never took Holy Orders.* **14** the procedure and rules followed by an assembly or meeting: *a point of order.* **15** one of the five major classical styles of architecture, classified by the type of columns used. **16 a tall order** something difficult or demanding. **17 in order a** in sequence. **b** properly arranged: *everything is in order for your trip.* **c** appropriate or fitting. **18 in order that** so that. **19 in order to** so that it is possible to: *a healthy diet is necessary in order to keep fit.* **20 in** *or* **of the order of** amounting approximately to: *summer temperatures are usually in the order of thirty-five degrees.* **21 keep order** to ensure that people obey the law or behave in an acceptable manner. **22 on order** having been ordered but not yet delivered. **23 out of order a** not in sequence. **b** not working: *the lift was out of order, so we had to use the stairs.* **c** not following the rules or customary procedure: *the chairperson ruled the motion out of order.* **24 to order** according to a buyer's specifications. *~vb* **25** to command or instruct (to do something): *she ordered her son to wash the dishes; the police ordered her into the house.* **26** to request (something) to be supplied in return for payment: *I ordered a new car three weeks ago, but it hasn't been delivered yet.* **27** to arrange (things) methodically or in their proper places. *~interj* **28** an exclamation demanding that orderly behaviour be restored.

order around *or* **about** *vb* to repeatedly tell (someone) what to do in a bossy or unsympathetic way: *it was intolerable that those two fat slobs could order her around.*

orderly *adj* **1** tidy or well-organized: *they evacuated the building in an orderly manner.* **2** well-behaved; law-abiding. *~n, pl* **-lies 3** *Med* a male hospital attendant. **4** *Mil* a soldier whose duty is to carry orders or perform minor tasks for a more senior officer. **orderliness** *n*

Order of Merit *n Brit* an order awarded for outstanding achievement in any field.

order paper *n* a list indicating the order of business, esp. in Parliament.

ordinal number *n* a number indicating position in a sequence, such as *first, second, third.*

ordinance *n* an official rule or order.

ordinarily *adv* in ordinary circumstances; usually; normally.

ordinary *adj* **1** usual or normal: *it was an ordinary working day for them.* **2** not special or different in any way: *what do ordinary Germans feel about reunification?* **3** dull or unexciting: *the restaurant charged very high prices for very ordinary cooking.* *~n, pl* **-naries 4** *RC Church* the parts of the Mass that do not vary from day to day. **5 out of the ordinary** unusual.

THESAURUS

tate, enact, enjoin, establish, fix, lay down, legislate, order, prescribe, pronounce, rule, set, will

ordeal affliction, agony, anguish, hardship, nightmare, suffering, test, torture, trial, tribulation(s), trouble(s)

order *n.* **1.** behest, canon, command, decree, dictate, direction, directive, injunction, instruction, law, mandate, ordinance, precept, regulation, rule, say-so (*informal*), stipulation **2.** arrangement, harmony, method, neatness, orderliness, organization, pattern, plan, propriety, regularity, symmetry, system, tidiness **3.** arrangement, array, categorization, classification, codification, disposal, disposition, grouping, layout, line, line-up, ordering, placement, progression, sequence, series, setup (*informal*), structure, succession **4.** caste, class, degree, grade, hierarchy, pecking order (*informal*), position, rank, status **5.** calm, control, discipline, law, law and order, peace, quiet, tranquillity **6.** application, booking, commission, request, requisition, reservation **7.** breed, cast, class, family, genre, genus, ilk, kind, sort, species, subclass, taxonomic group, tribe, type **8.** association, brotherhood, community, company, fraternity, guild, league, lodge, organization, sect, sisterhood, society, union **9. in order a.** arranged, in sequence, neat, orderly, shipshape, tidy **b.** acceptable, appropriate, called for, correct, fitting, O.K. *or* okay (*informal*), right, suitable **10. out of order a.** broken, broken-down, bust (*informal*), gone haywire (*informal*), gone phut (*informal*), in disrepair, inoperative, kaput (*informal*), nonfunctional, not working, on the blink (*slang*), on the fritz (*U.S. slang*), out of commission, U/S (*informal*), wonky (*Brit. slang*) **b.** improper, indecorous, not cricket (*informal*), not done, not on (*informal*), out of place, out of turn, uncalled-for, wrong *~vb.* **11.** adjure, bid, charge, command, decree, demand, direct, enact, enjoin, instruct, ordain, prescribe, require **12.** apply for, authorize, book, call for, contract for, engage, prescribe, request, reserve, send away for **13.** adjust, align, arrange, catalogue, class, classify, conduct, control, dispose, group, lay out, manage, marshal, neaten, organize, put to rights, regulate, set in order, sort out, systematize, tabulate, tidy

orderly *adj.* **1.** businesslike, in apple-pie order (*informal*), in order, methodical, neat, regular, scientific, shipshape, systematic, systematized, tidy, trim, well-organized, well-regulated **2.** controlled, decorous, disciplined, law-abiding, nonviolent, peaceable, quiet, restrained, well-behaved

ordinarily as a rule, commonly, customarily, generally, habitually, in general, in the general run (of things), in the usual way, normally, usually

ordinary 1. accustomed, banal, common, customary, established, everyday, habitual, humdrum, mundane, normal, prevailing, quotidian, regular, routine, settled, standard, stock, typical, usual, wonted **2.** common or garden (*informal*), conventional, familiar, homespun, household, humble, modest, plain, prosaic, run-of-the-mill, simple, unmemorable, unpretentious, unremarkable, workaday **3.** average, commonplace, fair, indifferent, inferior, mean, mediocre, pedestrian, second-rate, stereotyped, undistinguished, unexceptional, uninspired, unremarkable **4. out of the ordinary** atypical, distinguished, exceptional, exciting, extraordinary, high-calibre, imaginative, important, impressive,

Ordinary level *n* the formal name for **O level.**

ordinary rating *n* a rank in the Royal Navy equivalent to that of a private in the army.

ordinary seaman *n* a seaman of the lowest rank.

ordinary shares *pl n Brit* shares issued by a company entitling their holders to a dividend according to the profits of the company and to a claim on net assets.

ordinate *n Maths* the vertical coordinate of a point in a two-dimensional system of coordinates.

ordination *n* the act or ceremony of making someone a member of the clergy.

ordnance *n* **1** weapons and other military supplies. **2 the ordnance** a government department dealing with military supplies.

Ordnance Survey *n* the British government organization that produces detailed maps of Britain and Ireland.

Ordovician (or-doe-**vish**-ee-an) *adj Geol* of the period of geological time about 500 million years ago

ordure *n* excrement; dung.

ore *n* rock or mineral from which valuable substances such as metals can be extracted.

oregano (or-rig-**gah**-no) *n* a sweet-smelling herb used as seasoning.

organ *n* **1** a part in animals and plants that is adapted to perform a particular function, for example the heart or lungs. **2 a** a musical keyboard instrument which produces sound by forcing air through pipes of a variety of lengths. **b** Also called: **electric organ** a keyboard instrument which produces similar sounds electronically. **3** a means of communication, such as a newspaper issued by a specialist group or party. **4** *Euphemistic* a penis.

organdie *n* a fine, slightly stiff cotton fabric.

organ-grinder *n* (formerly) an entertainer who played a barrel organ in the streets.

organic *adj* **1** of, produced by, or found in plants or animals: *the rocks were carefully searched for organic remains.* **2** not using, or grown without, artificial fertilizers or pesticides: *organic vegetables; an organic farm.* **3** *Chem* of or belonging to the class of chemical compounds that are formed from carbon. **4** (of change or development) gradual and natural rather than sudden or forced. **5** made up of many different parts which contribute to the way in which the whole society or structure works: *an organic whole.* **organically** *adv*

organic chemistry *n Chem* the branch of chemistry dealing with carbon compounds.

organism *n* **1** an animal or plant. **2** anything resembling a living creature in structure, behaviour, or complexity: *cities are more complicated organisms than farming villages.*

organist *n* a person who plays the organ.

organization *or* **-isation** *n* **1** an organized group of people, such as a club, society, union, or business. **2** the act of organizing: *setting up the European tour took a lot of organization.* **3** the structure and arrangement of the different parts of something: *the report recommended radical changes in the organization of the social services department.* **4** the state of being organized: *the material in this essay lacks any sort of organization.* **organizational** *or* **-isational** *adj*

organize *or* **-ise** *vb* **-izing, -ized** *or* **-ising, -ised 1** to plan and arrange (something): *we organized a protest meeting in the village hall.* **2** to arrange systematically: *the files are organized in alphabetical order and by date.* **3** to form, join, or recruit (people) into a trade union: *the seasonal nature of tourism makes it difficult for hotel workers to organize.* **organizer** *or* **-iser** *n*

organized *or* **-ised** *adj* **1** planned and controlled on a large scale and involving many people: *organized crime.* **2** orderly and efficient: *a highly organized campaign.* **3** (of the workers in a factory or office) belonging to a trade union: *socialism is especially popular among organized labour.*

organza *n* a thin stiff fabric of silk, cotton, or synthetic fibre.

orgasm *n* the most intense point of pleasure and excitement during sexual activity. **orgasmic** *adj*

orgy *n, pl* **-gies 1** a wild party involving promiscuous sexual activity and excessive drinking. **2** an act of immoderate or frenzied indulgence: *the rioters were engaged in an orgy of destruction.* **orgiastic** *adj*

oriel window *or* **oriel** *n* a window built out from the wall of a house at an upper level.

orient *vb* **1** to adjust or align (oneself or one's ideas) according to surroundings or circumstances: *new employees can take some time to orient themselves to the company's procedures.* **2** to position or set (a map or chart) with relation to the points of the compass or other specific directions. **3 be oriented to** *or* **towards** to work or act with a particular aim, idea, or person in mind: *many people feel that Britain is too much oriented to the Americans.* ~*n* **4** *Poetic* the east.

Orient *n* **the Orient** East Asia.

oriental *adj* eastern.

Oriental *adj* **1** of the Orient. ~*n* **2** a person from the Orient.

orientate *vb* **-tating, -tated** same as **orient.**

-orientated *or* **-oriented** *adj combining form* interested in or directed towards the thing specified: *career-orientated women.*

orientation *n* **1** the activities and aims that a person or organization is interested in: *the course has a practical rather than theoretical orientation.* **2** the position of an object with relation to the points of the compass or other specific directions: *the room's southerly orientation means that it receives a lot of light.* ~*adj* **3** of

THESAURUS

inspired, noteworthy, outstanding, rare, remarkable, significant, special, striking, superior, uncommon, unusual

organ agency, channel, forum, journal, means, medium, mouthpiece, newspaper, paper, periodical, publication, vehicle, voice

organism animal, being, body, creature, entity, living thing, structure

organization 1. association, body, combine, company, concern, confederation, consortium, corporation, federation, group, institution, league, outfit (*informal*), syndicate **2.** assembling, assembly, construction, coordination, direction, disposal, formation, forming, formulation, making, management, methodology, organizing, planning, regulation, running, standardization, structuring **3.** arrangement, chemistry, composition, configuration, conformation, constitution, design, format, framework, grouping, make-up, method, organism, pattern, plan, structure, system, unity, whole

organize arrange, be responsible for, catalogue, classify, codify, constitute, construct, coordinate, dispose, establish, form, frame, get going, get together, group, lay the foundations of, lick into shape, look after, marshal, pigeonhole, put in order, put together, run, see to (*informal*), set up, shape, straighten out, systematize, tabulate, take care of

orgy 1. bacchanal, bacchanalia, carousal, debauch, revel, revelry, Saturnalia **2.** binge (*informal*), bout, ex-

or providing information or training needed to understand a new situation or environment: *nearly every college has an orientation programme.*

orienteering *n* a sport in which contestants race on foot over a cross-country course consisting of checkpoints found with the aid of a map and compass.

orifice (**or**-rif-fiss) *n* an opening or hole through which something can pass, esp. one in the body such as the mouth or anus.

orig. 1 origin. 2 original(ly).

origami (or-rig-**gah**-mee) *n* the art, originally Japanese, of folding paper intricately into decorative shapes.

origin *n* **1** the point, source, or event from which something develops: *the origin of the term "jazz" is obscure; the war had its origin in the clash between rival nationalists.* **2** the country, race, or social class of a person's parents or ancestors: *an Australian of Greek origin; he was proud of his working-class origins.* **3** *Maths* the point at which the horizontal and vertical axes intersect.

original *adj* **1** first or earliest: *the dining room also has attractive original beams.* **2** fresh and unusual; not copied from or based on something else: *the composer's work has created some original and attractive choreography.* **3** able to think of or carry out new ideas or concepts: *he is an excitingly original writer.* **4** being the first and genuine form of something, from which a copy or translation is made: *all French recipes were translated from the original abridged versions.* ~*n* **5** the first and genuine form of something, from which others are copied or translated: *the original is in the British Museum.* **6** a person or thing used as a model in art or literature: *she claimed to be the original on whom Lawrence based Lady Chatterley.* **originality** *n* **originally** *adv*

original sin *n* a state of sin believed by some Christians to be inborn in all human beings as a result of Adam's disobedience.

originate *vb* **-nating, -nated** to come or bring (something) into existence: *humans probably originated in East Africa.* **origination** *n* **originator** *n*

oriole *n* a songbird with a long pointed bill and a mostly yellow-and-black plumage.

ormolu *n* a gold-coloured alloy of copper, tin, or zinc, used to decorate furniture and other articles.

ornament *n* **1** anything that adorns someone or something; decoration: *the room's only ornament was a dim, oily picture of the Holy Family.* **2** decorations collectively: *he had no watch, nor ornament of any kind.* **3** a small decorative object: *I hit a garden ornament while parking.* **4** a person whose character or talent makes them an asset to society or the group to which they belong: *an ornament of the firm.* **5** *Music* a note or group of notes which embellishes the melody but is not an integral part of it, for instance a trill. ~*vb* **6** to decorate or adorn: *the hall had a high ceiling, ornamented with plaster fruits and flowers.* **ornamental** *adj* **ornamentation** *n* **ornamented** *adj*

ornate *adj* **1** heavily or elaborately decorated: *an ornate ceiling painted with allegorical figures.* **2** (of style in writing) overelaborate; using many literary expressions. **ornately** *adv*

ornithology *n* the study of birds. **ornithological** *adj* **ornithologist** *n*

orotund *adj* **1** (of the voice) resonant and booming. **2** (of speech or writing) pompous; containing many long or formal words.

orphan *n* **1** a child whose parents are dead. ~*vb* **2** to cause (someone) to become an orphan: *she was orphaned at 16 when her parents died in a car crash.*

orphanage *n* a children's home for orphans and abandoned children.

orphaned *adj* having no living parents.

orrery *n, pl* **-ries** a mechanical model of the solar system in which the planets can be moved around the sun.

orris *n* **1** a kind of iris that has fragrant roots. **2** Also: **orrisroot** the root of this plant prepared and used as perfume.

orthodontics *n* the branch of dentistry concerned with correcting irregularities of the teeth. **orthodontic** *adj* **orthodontist** *n*

orthodox *adj* conforming to traditional or established standards in religion, behaviour, or attitudes:

THESAURUS

cess, indulgence, overindulgence, splurge, spree, surfeit

orientation bearings, coordination, direction, location, position, sense of direction

orifice aperture, cleft, hole, mouth, opening, perforation, pore, rent, vent

origin **1.** base, basis, beginning, birth, cause, commencement, creation, dawning, derivation, early stages, emergence, font (*poetic*), foundation, fount, fountain, fountainhead, genesis, inauguration, inception, launch, origination, outset, provenance, root, roots, source, spring, start, wellspring **2.** ancestry, beginnings, birth, descent, extraction, family, heritage, lineage, parentage, pedigree, stock

original *adj.* **1.** aboriginal, autochthonous, commencing, earliest, early, embryonic, first, infant, initial, introductory, opening, primary, primitive, primordial, pristine, rudimentary, starting **2.** creative, fertile, fresh, ground-breaking, imaginative, ingenious, innovative, innovatory, inventive, new, novel, resourceful, seminal, unconventional, unprecedented, untried, unusual **3.** archetypal, authentic, first, first-hand, genuine, master, primary, prototypical ~*n.* **4.** archetype, master, model, paradigm, pattern, precedent, prototype, standard, type

originality boldness, break with tradition, cleverness, creativeness, creative spirit, creativity, daring, freshness, imagination, imaginativeness, individuality, ingenuity, innovation, innovativeness, inventiveness, new ideas, newness, novelty, resourcefulness, unconventionality, unorthodoxy

originally at first, at the outset, at the start, by origin (birth, derivation), first, initially, in the beginning, in the first place, to begin with

originate arise, be born, begin, bring about, come, conceive, create, derive, develop, discover, emanate, emerge, evolve, flow, form, formulate, generate, give birth to, inaugurate, initiate, institute, introduce, invent, issue, launch, pioneer, proceed, produce, result, rise, set in motion, set up, spring, start, stem

originator architect, author, creator, father, founder, generator, innovator, inventor, maker, mother, pioneer, prime mover

ornament *n.* **1.** accessory, adornment, bauble, decoration, embellishment, festoon, frill, furbelow, garnish, gewgaw, knick-knack, trimming, trinket **2.** flower, honour, jewel, leading light, pride, treasure ~*vb.* **3.** adorn, beautify, brighten, deck, decorate, dress up, embellish, festoon, garnish, gild, grace, prettify, prink, trim

ornamental attractive, beautifying, decorative, embellishing, for show, showy

ornamentation adornment, decoration, elaboration, embellishment, embroidery, frills, ornateness

ornate aureate, baroque, beautiful, bedecked, busy,

orthodox medicine; the concerto has a more orthodox structure than is usual for this composer. **orthodoxy** *n*

Orthodox *adj* **1** of the Orthodox Church of Eastern Europe. **2** of or being the form of Judaism characterized by traditional interpretation of and strict adherence to Mosaic Law: *an Orthodox Jew.*

Orthodox Church *n* the Christian Church dominant in Eastern Europe, which has the Greek Patriarch of Constantinople as its head.

orthography *n* **1** spelling considered to be correct: *British and American orthography is different in many cases.* **2** the study of spelling. **orthographic** *adj*

orthopaedics *or US* **orthopedics** *n* the branch of surgery concerned with disorders of the bones and joints. **orthopaedic** *or US* **orthopedic** *adj* **orthopaedist** *or US* **orthopedist** *n*

ortolan *n* a small European songbird eaten as a delicacy.

oryx *n* any of various large straight-horned African antelopes.

Os *Chem* osmium.

OS **1** Ordnance Survey. **2** outsize(d).

Oscar *n* an award in the form of a small gold statuette awarded annually in the US for outstanding achievements in various aspects of the film industry: *he won an Oscar for Best Supporting Actor in 1974.*

oscillate (**oss**-ill-late) *vb* **-lating, -lated 1** to swing repeatedly back and forth: *its wings oscillate up and down many times a second.* **2** to waver between two extremes of opinion, attitude, or behaviour: *the government oscillates between a desire for reform and a desire to keep its powers intact.* **3** *Physics* (of an electric current) to vary between minimum and maximum values. **oscillation** *n* **oscillator** *n*

oscilloscope (oss-**sill**-oh-scope) *n* an instrument that produces a visual representation of an oscillating electric current on the screen of a cathode-ray tube.

osier (**oh**-zee-er) *n* **1** a willow tree whose flexible branches or twigs are used for making baskets and furniture. **2** a twig or branch from this tree.

osmium *n Chem* a very hard brittle bluish-white metal, the heaviest known element. Symbol: Os

osmoregulation *n Zool* the adjustment of the osmotic pressure of a cell or organism in relation to the surrounding fluid.

osmosis *n* **1** the diffusion of liquids through a membrane until they are mixed. **2** the process by which people or ideas influence each other gradually and subtly. **osmotic** *adj*

osprey *n* a large fish-eating bird of prey, with a dark back and whitish head and underparts.

osseous *adj* consisting of or like bone.

ossify *vb* **-fies, -fying, -fied 1** to change into bone; harden. **2** to become rigid, inflexible, or unprogressive: *ossified traditions.* **ossification** *n*

ostensible *adj* apparent or seeming; alleged: *our ostensible common interest is boats.* **ostensibly** *adv*

ostensive *adj* directly showing or pointing out: *he gave ostensive definitions to things.*

ostentation *n* pretentious, showy, or vulgar display: *she felt the gold taps in the bathroom were tasteless ostentation.* **ostentatious** *adj* **ostentatiously** *adv*

osteoarthritis (ost-ee-oh-arth-**rite**-iss) *n* chronic inflammation of the joints, causing pain and stiffness.

osteopathy *n* a system of healing based on the manipulation of bones or muscle. **osteopath** *n*

osteoporosis (ost-ee-oh-pore-**oh**-siss) *n* brittleness of the bones, caused by lack of calcium.

ostinato *n, pl* **-tos** *Music* a persistently repeated phrase or rhythm.

ostler *n* (formerly) a stableman at an inn.

ostracize *or* **-cise** *vb* **-cizing, -cized** *or* **-cising, -cised** to exclude or banish (a person) from a particular group or from society: *he was ostracized from his family when his affair became known.* **ostracism** *n*

ostrich *n* **1** a large African bird which runs fast but cannot fly, and has a long neck, long legs, and soft dark feathers. **2** a person who refuses to recognize an unpleasant truth: *he accused the Minister of being "an ostrich with its head stuck in the sand, while all around him unemployment soars".*

OT Old Testament.

OTC (in Britain) Officers' Training Corps.

OTE (esp. in job adverts) on target earnings: the minimum amount of money a salesman is expected to make.

other *adj* **1** remaining (one or ones) in a group of which one or some have been specified: *she wasn't getting on with the other children.* **2** being a different one or ones from the one or ones already specified or understood: *other people might not be so tolerant of your behaviour; are you sure it's not in your other pocket?* **3** refers to a place or time which is not the one the speaker or writer is in: *results in other countries have been most encouraging.* **4** additional; further: *there is one other thing for the government to do.* **5 every other** every alternate: *the doctor sees me every other week.* **6 other than a** apart from: *he knew little of the country other than it was Muslim.* **b** different from: *treatment other than a hearing aid will be possible for those with inner ear deafness.* **7 or other** used to add vagueness to the preceding word or phrase: *he could take some evening course or other which could lead to an extra qualification; he was called away from the house on some pretext or other.* **8 the other day** a few days ago. ~*n* **9** an additional

THESAURUS

convoluted, decorated, elaborate, elegant, fancy, florid, flowery, fussy, high-wrought, ornamented, overelaborate, rococo

orthodox accepted, approved, conformist, conventional, correct, customary, doctrinal, established, kosher (*informal*), official, received, sound, traditional, true, well-established

orthodoxy authenticity, authoritativeness, authority, conformism, conformity, conventionality, devotion, devoutness, faithfulness, inflexibility, received wisdom, soundness, traditionalism

oscillate fluctuate, seesaw, sway, swing, vacillate, vary, vibrate, waver

oscillation fluctuation, instability, seesawing, swing, vacillation, variation, wavering

ossify fossilize, freeze, harden, petrify, solidify, stiffen

ostensible alleged, apparent, avowed, exhibited, manifest, outward, plausible, pretended, professed, purported, seeming, so-called, specious, superficial, supposed

ostensibly apparently, for the ostensible purpose of, on the face of it, on the surface, professedly, seemingly, supposedly, to all intents and purposes

ostentation affectation, boasting, display, exhibitionism, flamboyance, flashiness, flaunting, flourish, pageantry, parade, pomp, pretension, pretentiousness, show, showiness, showing off (*informal*), swank (*informal*), vaunting, window-dressing

ostentatious boastful, brash, conspicuous, crass, dashing, extravagant, flamboyant, flash (*informal*), flashy, flaunted, gaudy, loud, obtrusive, pompous, pretentious, showy, swanky (*informal*), vain, vulgar

person or thing: *show me one other.* **10 others** people apart from the person who is being spoken or written about: *she devoted her entire life to helping others.* **11 the others** the people or things remaining in a group of which one or some have been specified: *I can't speak for the others.* ~*adv* **12** otherwise; differently: *they couldn't behave other than they do.* **otherness** *n*

other ranks *pl n Chiefly Brit* (in the armed forces) all those who do not hold a commissioned rank.

otherwise *conj* **1** or else; if not, then: *I was fifty but said I was forty, otherwise I'd never have got a job.* ~*adv* **2** differently: *it was fruitless to pretend or to hope otherwise.* **3** in other respects: *shrewd psychological twists perk up an otherwise predictable story line.* ~*adj* **4** different: *circumstances beyond our control dictated that it should be otherwise.* ~*pron* **5 or otherwise** or not; or the opposite: *he didn't want company, talkative or otherwise.*

otherworldly *adj* **1** concerned with spiritual rather than practical matters: *his otherworldly manner concealed a ruthless business mind.* **2** mystical or supernatural: *this part of Italy has an otherworldly beauty.*

otiose (**oh**-tee-oze) *adj* serving no useful purpose: *such a strike is almost otiose.*

OTT *Brit slang* over the top.

otter *n* a small freshwater fish-eating animal with smooth brown fur, a streamlined body, and webbed feet.

ottoman *n, pl* **-mans** a storage chest with a padded lid for use as a seat.

Ottoman *adj* **1** *History* of the Ottomans or the Ottoman Empire, the Turkish empire which lasted from the late 13th century until the end of World War I, and at its height included the Balkans and much of N Africa. ~*n, pl* **-mans 2** a member of a Turkish people who formed the basis of this empire.

ou (**oh**) *n S African slang* a man, bloke, or chap.

OU 1 the Open University. **2** Oxford University.

oubaas (**oh**-bahss) *n S African* a man in authority.

oubliette (oo-blee-**ett**) *n History* a dungeon, the only entrance to which is a trap door in the ceiling.

ouch *interj* an exclamation of sharp sudden pain.

ought *vb* used to express: **1** duty or obligation: *she ought to tell this to the police.* **2** advisability: *we ought to get the roof repaired before the attics get any damper.* **3** probability or expectation: *a good lawyer ought to be able to fix it for you.* **4** a desire on the part of the speaker: *you ought to have a good breakfast before you hit the road.*

➤ In standard English *did* and *had* are not used with *ought*: *ought not to* (not *didn't/hadn't ought to*).

oughtn't ought not.

Ouija board *or* **Ouija** (**weej**-a) *n Trademark* a board on which are marked the letters of the alphabet. Answers to questions are spelt out by a pointer, which is supposedly guided by spirits.

ouma (**oh**-mah) *n S African* **1** grandmother, often as a title with a surname. **2** *Slang* any elderly woman.

ounce *n* **1** a unit of weight equal to one sixteenth of a pound or 28.4 grams. **2** short for **fluid ounce. 3** a small amount: *you haven't got one ounce of control over her.*

OUP (in Northern Ireland) Official Unionist Party.

oupa (**oh**-pah) *n S African* **1** grandfather, often as a title with a surname. **2** *Slang* any elderly man.

our *adj* **1** of, belonging to, or associated with us: *our daughter.* **2** a formal word for *my* used by monarchs.

Our Father *n* same as the **Lord's Prayer.**

ours *pron* **1** something belonging to us: *ours are smaller guns than those; the money is ours.* **2 of ours** belonging to or associated with us: *my wife and a friend of ours had both deserted me.*

ourself *pron Archaic* a formal word for *myself* used by monarchs.

ourselves *pron* **1 a** the reflexive form of *we* or *us*: *we humiliated ourselves.* **b** used for emphasis: *we ourselves will finish it.* **2** our usual selves: *we've not been feeling quite ourselves since the accident.* **3** *Nonstandard* used instead of *we* or *us* in compound noun phrases: *other people and ourselves.*

ousel *n* same as **ouzel.**

oust *vb* to force (someone) out of a position; expel: *the coup which ousted the President.*

ouster *n US* an act or instance of forcing someone out of a position: *the demonstrators called for the ouster of the police chief.*

out *adv, adj* **1** away from the inside of a place: *she took her purse out; inspection of the eggs should be done when the hen is out of the nest.* **2** away from one's home or place of work for a short time: *I called earlier but you were out; a search party is out looking for survivors.* **3** no longer burning, shining, or functioning: *he switched the light out; the living-room fire went out while we were next door eating.* **4** used up; not having any more of: *their supplies ran out after two weeks; we're out of milk.* **5** public; revealed: *our dirty little secret is out.* **6** available to the public: *her biography will be out in December.* **7** (of the sun, stars, or moon) visible. **8** in bloom: *the roses are out early this year.* **9** not in fashion or current usage: *trying to be trendy is out.* **10** excluded from consideration: *cost cutting is out of the question.* **11** not allowed: *smoking on duty is out.* **12 out for** *or* **to** wanting or intent on (something or doing something): *the young soldiers were out for revenge; they're out to get me.* **13** *Sport* (of a player in a sport like cricket or baseball) no longer batting because he or she has been dismissed by being caught, bowled, etc. **14** on strike. **15** in or into a state of unconsciousness: *he went outside and passed out in an alley.* **16** used to indicate a burst of activity as indicated by a verb: *war broke out in the Gulf.* **17** out of existence: *the mistakes were scored out.* **18** to the fullest extent: *spread out.* **19** loudly; clearly: *he cried out in shock and pain.* **20** to a conclusion; completely: *she'd worked it out for herself.* **21** existing: *the friendliest dog out.* **22** inaccurate or incorrect: *the estimate was out by sixty pounds.* **23** not in office or authority: *she was finally voted out as party leader.* **24** (of a period of time) completed: *before the year is out.* **25** openly homosexual: *I came out as a lesbian when I was still in my teens.* **26** *Old-fashioned* (of a young woman) in or into upper-class society life: *Lucinda had a large party when she came out.* **27 out of a** at or to a point outside: *the train pulled out of the station.* **b** away from; not in: *they're out of touch with reality; out of focus.* **c** because of; motivated by: *out of jealousy.* **d** from (a material or source): *made out of plastic.* **e** no longer in a specified state or condition: *out of work; out of practice.* ~*adj* **28** directed or indicating direction outwards: *the out tray.* **29** *Informal* not concealing one's homosexuality. ~*prep* **30** *US or nonstandard* out of; out through: *he*

THESAURUS

ostracize avoid, banish, blackball, blacklist, boycott, cast out, cold-shoulder, exclude, excommunicate, exile, expatriate, expel, give (someone) the cold shoulder, reject, send to Coventry, shun, snub

other *adj.* **1.** contrasting, different, dissimilar, distinct, diverse, remaining, separate, unrelated, variant **2.** added, additional, alternative, auxiliary, extra, further, more, spare, supplementary

ran out the door. ~*interj* **31 a** an exclamation of dismissal. **b** (in signalling and radio) an expression used to signal that the speaker is signing off: *over and out!* ~*vb* **32** *Informal* (of homosexuals) to expose (a public figure) as being a fellow homosexual.

out- *prefix* **1** excelling or surpassing in a particular action: *outlast; outlive.* **2** at or from a point away, outside: *outpost; outpatient.* **3** going away, outward: *outcrop; outgrowth.*

outage *n* a period of power failure.

out and about *adj* regularly going out of the house to work, take part in social activity, etc., esp. after an illness.

out-and-out *adj* absolute; thorough: *it's an out-and-out lie.*

outback *n* the remote bush country of Australia.

outbid *vb* **-bidding, -bidded** *or* **-bid** to offer a higher price than (another person).

outboard motor *n* a portable petrol engine that can be attached externally to the stern of a boat to propel it.

outbreak *n* a sudden occurrence of disease or war.

outbuilding *n* same as **outhouse.**

outburst *n* **1** a sudden strong expression of emotion, esp. of anger: *such emotional outbursts do nothing to help calm discussion of the matter.* **2** a sudden period of violent activity: *this sudden outburst of violence has come as a shock.*

outcast *n* a person who is rejected or excluded from a particular group or from society.

outclass *vb* to surpass (someone) in performance or quality.

outcome *n* the result or consequence of something.

outcrop *n* part of a rock formation that sticks out of the earth.

outcry *n, pl* **-cries** a widespread or vehement protest: *there was great popular outcry against the plan for a dual-carriageway.*

outdated *adj* old-fashioned or obsolete.

outdistance *vb* **-tancing, -tanced 1** to surpass (someone) in a particular activity. **2** to leave (other competitors) behind in a race.

outdo *vb* **-doing, -did, -done** to be more successful or better than (someone or something) in performance: *this car easily outdoes its rivals when it comes to comfort.*

outdoor *adj* **1** taking place, existing, or intended for use in the open air: *have a swim at the beach or outdoor pool; she was just taking off her outdoor clothing.* **2** fond of the outdoors: *Paul was a butch outdoor type.*

outdoors *adv* **1** in the open air; outside: *he hardly ever went outdoors.* ~*n* **2** the world outside or far away from buildings; the open air: *he'd forgotten his fear of the outdoors.*

outer *adj* **1** on the outside; external: *the building's outer walls were painted pale pink.* **2** further from the middle: *the outer suburbs.* ~*n* **3** *Archery* **a** the white outermost ring on a target. **b** a shot that hits this ring.

outermost *adj* furthest from the centre or middle.

outer space *n* space beyond the atmosphere of the earth.

outface *vb* **-facing, -faced** to subdue or disconcert (someone) by staring.

outfall *n* the mouth of a river, drain, or pipe: *the survey measured pollution levels near sewer outfalls.*

outfield *n* **1** *Cricket* the area of the field far from the pitch. **2** *Baseball* the area of the playing field beyond the lines connecting first, second, and third bases. **outfielder** *n*

outfit *n* **1** a set of clothes worn together. **2** *Informal* a group of people working together as a unit. **3** a set of equipment for a particular task; kit: *a complete anti-snakebite outfit.*

outfitter *n* *Old-fashioned* a shop or person that sells men's clothes.

outflank *vb* **1** to go around and beyond the side of (an enemy army). **2** to get the better of (someone).

outflow *n* **1** anything that flows out, such as liquid or money. **2** the amount that flows out.

THESAURUS

otherwise 1. *conj.* if not, or else, or then 2. *adv.* any other way, contrarily, differently

ounce atom, crumb, drop, grain, iota, particle, scrap, shred, speck, trace, whit

out *adj.* 1. abroad, absent, away, elsewhere, gone, not at home, outside 2. at an end, cold, dead, doused, ended, exhausted, expired, extinguished, finished, used up 3. antiquated, behind the times, dated, dead, *démodé,* old-fashioned, old hat, passé, square (*informal*), unfashionable 4. impossible, not allowed, not on (*informal*), ruled out, unacceptable

out-and-out absolute, arrant, complete, consummate, deep-dyed (*usually derogatory*), downright, dyed-in-the-wool, outright, perfect, thoroughgoing, total, unmitigated, unqualified, utter

outbreak burst, epidemic, eruption, explosion, flare-up, flash, outburst, rash, spasm, upsurge

outburst access, attack, discharge, eruption, explosion, fit of temper, flare-up, gush, outbreak, outpouring, paroxysm, spasm, storm, surge

outcast *n.* castaway, derelict, displaced person, exile, leper, pariah, *persona non grata,* refugee, reprobate, untouchable, vagabond, wretch

outclass be a cut above (*informal*), beat, eclipse, exceed, excel, leave *or* put in the shade, leave standing (*informal*), outdistance, outdo, outrank, outshine, outstrip, overshadow, run rings around (*informal*), surpass

outcome aftereffect, aftermath, conclusion, consequence, end, end result, issue, payoff (*informal*), result, sequel, upshot

outcry clamour, commotion, complaint, cry, exclamation, howl, hue and cry, hullaballoo, noise, outburst, protest, scream, screech, uproar, yell

outdated antiquated, antique, archaic, behind the times, *démodé,* obsolete, old-fashioned, outmoded, out-of-date, out of style, passé, unfashionable

outdistance leave behind, leave standing (*informal*), lose, outrun, outstrip, shake off

outdo beat, be one up on, best, eclipse, exceed, excel, get the better of, go one better than (*informal*), outclass, outdistance, outfox, outmanoeuvre, outshine, outsmart (*informal*), overcome, run rings around (*informal*), surpass, top, transcend

outdoor alfresco, open-air, out-of-door(s), outside

outer exposed, exterior, external, outlying, outside, outward, peripheral, remote, superficial, surface

outfit 1. accoutrements, clothes, costume, ensemble, garb, gear (*informal*), get-up (*informal*), kit, rigout (*informal*), suit, togs (*informal*), trappings 2. *informal* clique, company, corps, coterie, crew, firm, group, organization, set, setup (*informal*), squad, team, unit

outfitter clothier, costumier, couturier, dressmaker, haberdasher (*U.S.*), modiste, tailor

outflow discharge, drainage, ebb, effluence, efflux,

outfox *vb* to defeat or foil (someone) by being more cunning; outsmart.

outgoing *adj* **1** leaving: *some members of the outgoing government continued to attend the peace talks.* **2** friendly and sociable.

outgoings *pl n* expenses.

outgrow *vb* **-growing, -grew, -grown 1** to grow too large for (clothes or shoes): *it's amazing how quickly children outgrow their clothes.* **2** to lose (a way of behaving or thinking) in the course of becoming more mature: *most teenagers outgrow their moodiness as they near adulthood.* **3** to grow larger or faster than (someone or something): *the weeds threatened to outgrow and choke the rice plants.*

outgrowth *n* **1** a natural development or consequence: *he argued that religion was an outgrowth of magic.* **2** a thing growing out of a main body; offshoot.

outhouse *n* a building near to, but separate from, a main building.

outing *n* **1** a trip or excursion. **2** *Informal* the naming by homosexuals of other prominent homosexuals, often against their will.

outlandish *adj* extremely unconventional; bizarre.

outlast *vb* to last longer than.

outlaw *n* **1** *History* a criminal who has been deprived of legal protection and rights. *~vb* **2** to make (something) illegal: *the European Court has outlawed sex discrimination in pensions.* **3** *History* to make (someone) an outlaw. **outlawed** *adj*

outlay *n* the money, effort, or time spent on something.

outlet *n* **1** a means of expressing one's feelings: *the shock would give her an outlet for her own grief.* **2 a** a market for a product: *there is a huge sales outlet for personal computers.* **b** a shop or organization selling the goods of a particular producer or wholesaler or manufacturer: *the company now has outlets in 31 British towns.* **3** an opening permitting escape or release: *make sure the exhaust outlet is not blocked.*

outline *n* **1** a general explanation or description of something, which does not give all the details: *the course gave a brief outline of twentieth-century music.* **2 outlines** the important features of something: *the outlines of his theory are correct, we just need to fill in the details.* **3** the general shape of something, esp. when only the profile and not the details are visible: *it was still light enough to see the outline of the distant mountains.* **4** a drawing showing only the external lines of an object. *~vb* **-lining, -lined 5** to give the main features or general idea of (something): *I outlined what we had done and what we had still to do.* **6** to show the general shape of an object but not its details, as light does coming from behind an object: *we could see the towers of the city outlined against the night sky.*

outlive *vb* **-living, -lived 1** to live longer than (someone): *she only outlived her husband by a few months.* **2** to live beyond (a date or period): *the sparrow outlived the winter.* **3 outlive its usefulness** to be no longer useful or necessary: *some argued that the organization had outlived its usefulness.*

outlook *n* **1** a general attitude to life: *my whole outlook on life had changed.* **2** the probable condition or outcome of something: *the economic outlook is not good.* **3** the weather forecast for the next few days: *the outlook for the weekend.* **4** the view from a place: *a dreary outlook of chimneys and smoke.*

outlying *adj* far away from the main area.

outmanoeuvre *or US* **outmaneuver** *vb* **-vring, -vred** *or* **-vering, -vered** to gain an advantage over (someone) by skilful dealing: *the management outmanoeuvred us into accepting redundancies.*

outmatch *vb* to surpass or outdo (someone).

outmoded *adj* no longer fashionable or accepted.

outnumber *vb* to exceed in number: *they were outnumbered by fifty to one.*

out of bounds *adj, adv* **1 out of bounds to** not to be entered by: *the area has been out of bounds to foreign journalists and closed to tourists.* **2** (in a sport such as golf) outside the boundaries of the course or playing area.

out-of-date *adj, adv* old-fashioned; outmoded.

out of doors *adv* in the open air; outside.

out of pocket *adj* having lost or spent money: *I was ten pounds out of pocket after paying for their drinks.*

out-of-the-way *adj* remote and isolated: *an out-of-the-way village in the Bavarian Forest.*

THESAURUS

effusion, emanation, emergence, gush, issue, jet, outfall, outpouring, rush, spout

outgoing **1.** departing, ex-, former, last, leaving, past, retiring, withdrawing **2.** approachable, communicative, cordial, demonstrative, easy, expansive, extrovert, friendly, genial, gregarious, informal, open, sociable, sympathetic, unreserved, warm

outgoings costs, expenditure, expenses, outlay, overheads

outing excursion, expedition, jaunt, pleasure trip, spin (*informal*), trip

outlandish alien, barbarous, bizarre, eccentric, exotic, fantastic, far-out (*slang*), foreign, freakish, grotesque, *outré*, preposterous, queer, strange, unheard-of, weird

outlaw **1.** *n.* bandit, brigand, desperado, fugitive, highwayman, marauder, outcast, pariah, robber **2.** *vb.* ban, banish, bar, condemn, disallow, embargo, exclude, forbid, interdict, make illegal, prohibit, proscribe

outlay *n.* cost, disbursement, expenditure, expenses, investment, outgoings, spending

outlet **1.** avenue, channel, duct, egress, exit, means of expression, opening, orifice, release, safety valve, vent, way out **2.** market, shop, store

outline *n.* **1.** bare facts, main features, recapitulation, résumé, rough idea, rundown, summary, synopsis, thumbnail sketch **2.** configuration, contour, delineation, figure, form, profile, shape, silhouette **3.** draft, drawing, frame, framework, layout, lineament(s), plan, rough, skeleton, sketch, tracing *~vb.* **4.** delineate, draft, plan, rough out, sketch (in), summarize, trace

outlive come through, endure beyond, live through, outlast, survive

outlook **1.** angle, attitude, frame of mind, perspective, point of view, slant, standpoint, viewpoint, views **2.** expectations, forecast, future, prospect **3.** aspect, panorama, prospect, scene, view, vista

outlying backwoods, distant, far-flung, in the middle of nowhere, outer, out-of-the-way, peripheral, provincial, remote

outmoded anachronistic, antediluvian, antiquated, antique, archaic, behind the times, bygone, dated, *démodé*, fossilized, obsolescent, obsolete, olden (*archaic*), oldfangled, old-fashioned, old-time, out, out-of-date, out of style, outworn, passé, square (*informal*), superannuated, superseded, unfashionable, unusable

out-of-date antiquated, archaic, dated, discarded, elapsed, expired, extinct, invalid, lapsed, obsolete, old, old-fashioned, outmoded, outworn, passé, stale, superannuated, superseded, unfashionable

out-of-the-way distant, far-flung, inaccessible, iso-

out-of-work *adj* unemployed: *an out-of-work engineer.*

outpace *vb* **-pacing, -paced 1** to go faster than (someone). **2** to surpass or outdo (someone or something) in growth, development, etc.: *the increase in the number of households is outpacing the number of houses being built.*

outpatient *n* a patient who visits a hospital for treatment but does not stay there overnight.

outpost *n* a small settlement in a distant part of the country or in a foreign country, which is used for military or trading purposes.

outpouring *n* **1** a great amount of something that is produced very rapidly: *a prolific outpouring of ideas and energy.* **2** a passionate outburst: *the hysterical outpourings of fanatics.*

output *n* **1** the amount of something that is made or produced: *our weekly output has increased by 240 tonnes.* **2** *Electronics* the power, voltage, or current delivered by a circuit or component. **3** *Computers* the information produced by a computer. *~vb* **-putting, -putted** *or* **-put 4** *Computers* to produce (data) at the end of a process.

outrage *n* **1** deep indignation, anger, or resentment: *she felt a sense of outrage that he should abandon her like that.* **2** an extremely vicious or cruel act; gross violation of decency, morality, or honour: *there have been reports of another bombing outrage in the capital.* *~vb* **-raging, -raged 3** to cause deep indignation, anger, or resentment in (someone): *they were outraged by the news of the assassination.*

outrageous *adj* **1** unusual and shocking: *his sense of humour made him say and do the most outrageous things.* **2** shocking and socially or morally unacceptable: *I will fight these outrageous accusations of corruption in the courts if necessary.* **outrageously** *adv*

outrank *vb* to be of higher rank than (someone).

outré (**oo**-tray) *adj* eccentric and rather shocking.

outrider *n* a person who rides a motorcycle or horse in front of or beside an official vehicle as an attendant or guard.

outrigger *n* **1** a stabilizing framework projecting from the side of a boat or canoe. **2** a boat or canoe equipped with such a framework.

outright *adj* **1** complete; total: *he is close to an outright victory.* **2** straightforward and direct: *outright hostility.* *~adv* **3** completely: *the film was banned outright.* **4** instantly: *my driver was killed outright.* **5** openly: *ask her outright why she treated you as she did.*

outrun *vb* **-running, -ran, -run 1** to run faster or further than (someone). **2** to develop faster than (something): *the population of the city is in danger of outrunning the supply of houses.*

outsell *vb* **-selling, -sold** to be sold in greater quantities than: *CDs are now outselling cassettes.*

outset *n* a start; beginning: *we never really hit it off from the outset.*

outshine *vb* **-shining, -shone** to be better than (someone) at something: *she has begun to outshine me in sports.*

outside *prep* **1** on or to the exterior of: *a crowd gathered outside the court.* **2** beyond the limits of: *it was outside my experience and beyond my ability.* **3** apart from; other than: *no one knows outside us.* *~adj* **4** on or of the outside: *an outside light is also a good idea.* **5** remote; unlikely: *I still had an outside chance of the title.* **6** coming from outside a particular group or organization: *the patient had been subjected to outside influences.* **7** of or being the lane in a road which is further from the side than other lanes going in the same direction: *he was doing 120 in the outside lane.* *~adv* **8** outside a specified thing or place; out of doors: *we went outside to get some fresh air.* **9** *Slang* not in prison. *~n* **10** the external side or surface of something. **11 at the outside** *Informal* at the very most: *I'll be away four days at the outside.*

➤ *Outside* is not followed by *of* in standard English.

outside broadcast *n Radio, television* a broadcast not made from a studio.

outsider *n* **1** a person excluded from a group. **2** a contestant thought unlikely to win.

outsize *adj also* **outsized 1** very large or larger than normal. *~n* **2** an outsize garment.

outskirts *pl n* the parts of a town or city that are furthest from the centre: *an office in the northernmost outskirts of Glasgow.*

outsmart *vb Informal* same as **outwit.**

outspan *S African ~n* **1** an area on a farm kept available for travellers to rest and refresh their animals.

THESAURUS

lated, lonely, obscure, off the beaten track, outlying, remote, secluded, unfrequented

out-of-work idle, jobless, laid off, on the dole (*Brit.*), out of a job, redundant, unemployed

outpouring cascade, deluge, effluence, efflux, effusion, emanation, flow, flux, issue, outflow, spate, spurt, stream, torrent

output achievement, manufacture, product, production, productivity, yield

outrage *n.* **1.** anger, fury, hurt, indignation, resentment, shock, wrath **2.** abuse, affront, atrocity, barbarism, desecration, enormity, evil, indignity, inhumanity, injury, insult, offence, profanation, rape, ravishing, shock, violation, violence *~vb.* **3.** affront, incense, infuriate, madden, make one's blood boil, offend, scandalize, shock

outrageous 1. disgraceful, excessive, exorbitant, extravagant, immoderate, offensive, OTT (*slang*), over the top (*slang*), preposterous, scandalous, shocking, steep (*informal*), unreasonable **2.** abominable, atrocious, barbaric, beastly, egregious, flagrant, heinous, horrible, infamous, inhuman, iniquitous, nefarious, scandalous, shocking, unspeakable, villainous, violent, wicked

outright *adj.* **1.** absolute, arrant, complete, consummate, deep-dyed (*usually derogatory*), downright, out-and-out, perfect, pure, thorough, thoroughgoing, total, unconditional, undeniable, unmitigated, unqualified, utter, wholesale **2.** definite, direct, flat, straightforward, unequivocal, unqualified *~adv.* **3.** absolutely, completely, explicitly, openly, overtly, straightforwardly, thoroughly, to the full, without hesitation, without restraint **4.** at once, cleanly, immediately, instantaneously, instantly, on the spot, straight away, there and then, without more ado

outset beginning, commencement, early days, inauguration, inception, kickoff (*informal*), onset, opening, start, starting point

outshine be head and shoulders above, be superior to, better, eclipse, leave *or* put in the shade, outclass, outdo, outstrip, overshadow, surpass, top, transcend, upstage

outside *adj.* **1.** exterior, external, extramural, extraneous, extreme, out, outdoor, outer, outermost, outward, surface **2.** distant, faint, marginal, negligible, remote, slight, slim, small, unlikely *~n.* **3.** exterior, façade, face, front, skin, surface, topside

outsider alien, foreigner, incomer, interloper, intrud-

~vb **-spanning, -spanned 2** to unharness or unyoke (animals).

outspoken *adj* **1** saying exactly what one thinks: *an outspoken critic of human rights abuses.* **2** spoken candidly: *she is known for her outspoken views.* **outspokenness** *n*

outspread *adj* spread or stretched out as far as possible: *a gull glided by with outspread wings.*

outstanding *adj* **1** very good; excellent: *an outstanding performance.* **2** still to be dealt with or paid: *outstanding bills; a few outstanding problems have to be put right.* **3** very obvious or important: *there are significant exceptions, of which oil is the outstanding example.* **outstandingly** *adv*

outstation *n* a station or post in a remote region.

outstay *vb* same as **overstay.**

outstretched *adj* extended or stretched out as far as possible: *he pushed a wad of drachma notes into the young man's outstretched hand.*

outstrip *vb* **-stripping, -stripped 1** to surpass (someone) in a particular activity: *his newspapers outstrip all others in vulgarity.* **2** to go faster than (someone).

outtake *n* an unreleased take from a recording session, film, or television programme.

out tray *n* a shallow basket in an office for collecting letters and documents that are to be sent out.

outvote *vb* **-voting, -voted** to defeat (someone) by getting more votes than him or her.

outward *adj* **1** apparent or superficial: *to outward appearances the house is largely unchanged today.* **2** of or relating to the outside: *outward shape.* **3** (of a journey) away from a place to which one intends to return. *~adv also* **outwards 4** in an outward direction; towards the outside. **outwardly** *adv*

outweigh *vb* **1** to be more important, significant, or influential than: *these niggles are outweighed by the excellent cooking and service.* **2** to be heavier than.

outwit *vb* **-witting, -witted** to gain an advantage over (someone) by cunning or ingenuity.

outworks *pl n Mil* defences which lie outside the main fortifications of a fort etc.

outworn *adj* (of a belief or custom) old-fashioned and no longer of any use or relevance: *there is no point in pandering to outworn superstition.*

ouzel *or* **ousel** (**ooze**-el) *n* same as **dipper** (sense 2).

ouzo (**ooze**-oh) *n, pl* **ouzos** a strong aniseed-flavoured alcoholic drink from Greece.

ova *n* the plural of **ovum.**

oval *adj* **1** egg-shaped. *~n* **2** anything that is oval in shape, such as a sports ground.

ovary *n, pl* **-ries 1** a reproductive organ in women and female animals in which eggs are produced. **2** *Bot* the lower part of a pistil, containing the ovules. **ovarian** *adj*

ovate *adj* shaped like an egg: *the tree has bluish-green, ovate leaves.*

ovation *n* an enthusiastic round of applause.

oven *n* an enclosed heated compartment or container for baking or roasting food, or for drying or firing ceramics.

ovenable *adj* suitable for cooking in or using in an oven.

over *prep* **1** directly above; across the top or upper surface of: *set the frying pan over a low heat.* **2** on or to the other side of: *the pilot flew over the blue waters.* **3** during or throughout (a period of time): *over the next few months it became clear what was happening.* **4** throughout the whole extent of: *It will be heard all over Britain as midnight strikes.* **5** by means of (an instrument of telecommunication): *there was an announcement over the Tannoy system.* **6** more than: *she had met him over a year ago.* **7** concerning; about: *there has been much argument over these figures.* **8** while occupied in: *I'll tell you over dinner tonight.* **9** having recovered from the effects of: *he appeared to be over his niggling injury problems.* **10 all over someone** *Informal* extremely affectionate or attentive towards someone. **11 over and above** added to; in addition to. *~adv* **12** in a state, condition, or position over something: *to climb over.* **13** onto its side: *the jug toppled over.* **14** at or to a point across an intervening space: *she carried him over to the other side of the river.* **15** covering the whole area: *there's poverty the world over.* **16** from beginning to end: *to read a document over.* **17 all over a** finished. **b** over one's entire body. **c** typically: *that's him all over.* **18 over again** once more. **19 over and over (again)** repeatedly. *~interj* **20** (in signalling and radio) it is now your turn to speak. *~adj* **21** finished; no longer in progress: *the second round of voting is over. ~adv, adj* **22** remaining; surplus: *there wasn't any money left over. ~n* **23** *Cricket* **a** a series of six balls bowled by a bowler from the same end of the pitch. **b** the play during this.

THESAURUS

er, newcomer, nonmember, odd man out, outlander, stranger

outskirts borders, boundary, edge, environs, periphery, suburbia, suburbs, vicinity

outspoken abrupt, blunt, candid, direct, downright, explicit, forthright, frank, free, free-spoken, open, plain-spoken, round, unceremonious, undissembling, unequivocal, unreserved

outstanding 1. celebrated, distinguished, eminent, excellent, exceptional, great, important, impressive, meritorious, pre-eminent, special, superior, superlative, well-known **2.** due, ongoing, open, owing, payable, pending, remaining, uncollected, unpaid, unresolved, unsettled **3.** arresting, conspicuous, eye-catching, marked, memorable, notable, noteworthy, prominent, salient, signal, striking

outward *adj.* apparent, evident, exterior, external, noticeable, observable, obvious, ostensible, outer, outside, perceptible, superficial, surface, visible

outwardly apparently, as far as one can see, externally, officially, on the face of it, on the surface, ostensibly, professedly, seemingly, superficially, to all appearances, to all intents and purposes, to the eye

outweigh cancel (out), compensate for, eclipse, make up for, outbalance, overcome, override, predominate, preponderate, prevail over, take precedence over, tip the scales

outwit cheat, circumvent, deceive, defraud, dupe, get the better of, gull (*archaic*), make a fool *or* monkey of, outfox, outmanoeuvre, outsmart (*informal*), outthink, put one over on (*informal*), run rings round (*informal*), swindle, take in (*informal*)

outworn abandoned, antiquated, behind the times, defunct, discredited, disused, exhausted, hackneyed, obsolete, outdated, outmoded, out-of-date, overused, rejected, stale, superannuated, threadbare, tired, worn-out

oval *adj.* egg-shaped, ellipsoidal, elliptical, ovate, oviform, ovoid

ovation acclaim, acclamation, applause, cheering, cheers, clapping, laudation, plaudits, tribute

over *prep.* **1.** above, on, on top of, superior to, upon **2.** above, exceeding, in excess of, more than **3. over and above** added to, as well as, besides, in addition to, let alone, not to mention, on top of, plus *~adv.* **4.** above,

over- *prefix* **1** excessive or excessively: *overcharge; overdue.* **2** superior in rank: *overlord.* **3** indicating location or movement above: *overhang.* **4** downwards from above: *overthrow.*

overabundance *n* more than is really needed; excess.

overact *vb* to act in an exaggerated way.

overactive *adj* more active than is normal or desirable: *an overactive thyroid gland.*

overall *adj* **1** from one end to the other: *the overall length.* **2** including everything; total: *the overall cost.* ~*adv* **3** in general; on the whole: *overall, I think this is the better car.* ~*n* **4** *Brit* a coat-shaped work garment worn over ordinary clothes as a protection against dirt. **5 overalls** work trousers with a bib and braces or jacket attached, worn over ordinary clothes as a protection against dirt and wear.

overambitious *adj* attempting more than one has the ability to do well: *good plain cookery marred by overambitious sauces*

overarm *Sport, esp cricket* ~*adj* **1** bowled, thrown, or performed with the arm raised above the shoulder. ~*adv* **2** with the arm raised above the shoulder.

overawe *vb* **-awing, -awed** to affect (someone) with an overpowering sense of awe: *he was overawed by the prospect of meeting the Prime Minister.*

overbalance *vb* **-ancing, -anced** to lose one's balance.

overbearing *adj* **1** imposing one's views in an unpleasant or forceful manner. **2** of particular or overriding importance: *an overbearing need.*

overblown *adj* inflated or excessive: *humiliation comes from having overblown expectations for yourself.*

overboard *adv* **1** from a boat or ship into the water: *he is believed to have fallen overboard and drowned.* **2 go overboard** *Informal* **a** to be extremely enthusiastic. **b** to go to extremes. **3 throw overboard** to reject or abandon (an idea or a plan).

overburden *vb* to have more of something than it is possible to cope with: *the city's streets are already overburdened by rush-hour motorists.*

overcast *adj* (of the sky or weather) cloudy.

overcharge *vb* **-charging, -charged** to charge too high a price.

overcoat *n* a warm heavy coat worn in cold weather.

overcome *vb* **-coming, -came, -come 1** to deal successfully with or control (a problem or feeling): *once I'd overcome my initial nerves I discovered hang-gliding was great fun.* **2** (of an emotion or a feeling) to affect (someone) strongly or make (someone) powerless: *he was overcome by a sudden surge of jealousy.* **3** to defeat (someone) in a conflict.

overcompensate *vb* **-sating, -sated** to attempt to make up for or cancel out (something) to an unnecessary degree: *when bookings dropped slightly, the company overcompensated by slashing the price of its holidays by 50%.*

overconfident *adj* having more belief in one's abilities than is justified.

overcook *vb* to spoil food by cooking it for too long.

overcrowded *adj* containing more people or things than is desirable: *overcrowded commuter trains.*

overcrowding *n* the cramming of too many people into too small a space: *prison overcrowding and poor conditions.*

overdo *vb* **-doing, -did, -done 1** to do (something) to excess. **2** to exaggerate (something). **3** to cook (something) too long. **4 overdo it** *or* **things** to something to a greater degree than is advisable or healthy.

overdose *n* **1** a larger dose of a drug than is safe: *she tried to kill herself with an overdose of alcohol and drugs.* ~*vb* **-dosing, -dosed 2** to take more of a drug than is safe, either accidentally or deliberately: *this drug is rarely prescribed because it is easy to overdose fatally on it.*

overdraft *n* **1** the withdrawal of more money from a bank account than there is in it. **2** the amount of money withdrawn thus.

overdraw *vb* **-drawing, -drew, -drawn** to withdraw more money from a bank account than is in it.

overdrawn *adj* **1** having overdrawn one's bank account. **2** (of an account) in debit.

overdressed *adj* wearing clothes which are too elaborate or formal for the occasion.

overdrive *n* **1** a very high gear in a motor vehicle,

THESAURUS

aloft, on high, overhead **5. over and over (again)** ad nauseam, again and again, frequently, often, repeatedly, time and again ~*adj.* **6.** accomplished, ancient history (*informal*), at an end, by, bygone, closed, completed, concluded, done (with), ended, finished, gone, past, settled, up (*informal*) ~*adj./adv.* **7.** beyond, extra, in addition, in excess, left over, remaining, superfluous, surplus, unused

overact exaggerate, ham *or* ham up (*informal*), overdo, overplay

overall 1. *adj.* all-embracing, blanket, complete, comprehensive, general, global, inclusive, long-range, long-term, total, umbrella **2.** *adv.* generally speaking, in general, in (the) large, in the long term, on the whole

overawe abash, alarm, browbeat, cow, daunt, frighten, intimidate, scare, terrify

overbalance capsize, keel over, lose one's balance, lose one's footing, overset, overturn, slip, take a tumble, tip over, topple over, tumble, turn turtle, upset

overbearing arrogant, autocratic, bossy (*informal*), cavalier, despotic, dictatorial, dogmatic, domineering, haughty, high-handed, imperious, lordly, magisterial, officious, oppressive, overweening, peremptory, supercilious, superior, tyrannical

overcast clouded, clouded over, cloudy, darkened, dismal, dreary, dull, grey, hazy, leaden, louring *or* lowering, murky, sombre, sunless, threatening

overcharge cheat, clip (*slang*), diddle (*informal*), do (*slang*), fleece, rip off (*slang*), rook (*slang*), short-change, skin (*slang*), sting (*informal*), surcharge

overcome *vb.* beat, best, be victorious, blow out of the water (*slang*), clobber (*slang*), come out on top (*informal*), conquer, crush, defeat, get the better of, lick (*informal*), master, overpower, overthrow, overwhelm, prevail, render incapable (helpless, powerless), rise above, subdue, subjugate, surmount, survive, tank (*slang*), triumph over, undo, vanquish, weather, wipe the floor with (*informal*), worst

overconfident brash, cocksure, foolhardy, hubristic, overweening, presumptuous, riding for a fall (*informal*), uppish (*Brit. informal*)

overcrowded choked, congested, crammed full, hoatching (*Scot.*), jam-packed, like the Black Hole of Calcutta, overloaded, overpopulated, packed (out), swarming

overdo 1. be intemperate, belabour, carry too far, do to death (*informal*), exaggerate, gild the lily, go overboard (*informal*), go to extremes, lay it on thick (*informal*), not know when to stop, overindulge, overplay, overreach, overstate, overuse, overwork, run riot **2. overdo it** *or* **things** bite off more than one can chew, burn the candle at both ends (*informal*), drive

used at high speeds to reduce wear. **2** a state of great activity or excitement: *the government propaganda machine went into overdrive to try to play down the Minister's comments.*

overdub *vb* **-dubbing, -dubbed 1** to add (new sounds) to a tape in such a way that the old and the new sounds can be heard. *~n* **2** a sound or series of sounds added by this method.

overdue *adj* **1** not having arrived or happened by the time expected or desired: *a reassessment of policy on this issue is long overdue.* **2** (of money) not having been paid by the required date: *his rent was three weeks overdue.* **3** (of a library book) not having been returned to the library by the required date.

overeat *vb* **-eating, -ate, -eaten** to eat more than is necessary or healthy.

overemphasize *or* **-sise** *vb* **-sizing, -sized** *or* **-sising, -sised** to give (something) more importance than is necessary or appropriate.

overestimate *vb* **-mating, -mated** to believe something or someone to be bigger, more important, or better than is the case. **overestimation** *n*

overexcited *adj* excessively enthusiastic or agitated.

overexert *vb* to exhaust or injure oneself by doing too much. **overexertion** *n*

overexposed *adj* (of a photograph) too light in colour because the film has been exposed to light for too long.

overfeed *vb* **-feeding, -fed** to give (a person, plant, or animal) more food than is necessary or healthy.

overfill *vb* to put more into (something) than there is room for.

overflow *vb* **-flowing, -flowed, -flown 1** to flow over (a brim). **2** to be filled beyond capacity so as to spill over. **3 overflow with** to be filled with (an emotion): *a letter overflowing with passion and ardour.* *~n* **4** something that overflows, usually a liquid. **5** an outlet that enables surplus liquid to be drained off. **6** the amount by which a limit or capacity is exceeded. *~adj* **7** of or being a subsidiary thing for use when there is no room left in the main one: *an overflow car park.*

overgraze *vb* **-grazing, -grazed** to graze (land) too intensively so that it is damaged and no longer provides nourishment.

overgrown *adj* covered over with plants or weeds: *they headed up the overgrown and winding trail.*

overhang *vb* **-hanging, -hung 1** to project or hang over beyond (something). *~n* **2** an overhanging part or object.

overhaul *vb* **1** to examine (a system or an idea) carefully for faults. **2** to make repairs or adjustments to (a vehicle or machine). **3** to overtake (a vehicle or person). *~n* **4** a thorough examination and repair.

overhead *adj, adv* above head height.

overhead projector *n* a projector that throws an enlarged image of a transparency onto a surface above and behind the person using it.

overheads *pl n* the general costs of running a business, such as rent, electricity, and stationery.

overhear *vb* **-hearing, -heard** to hear (a speaker or remark) unintentionally or without the knowledge of the speaker.

overheat *vb* **1** to make or become too hot. **2** to cause (an economy) to tend towards inflation. **3 become overheated** (of a person, discussion, etc.) to become angry or agitated: *the Colonel becomes overheated if he sees the term "Ms" in the newspaper.*

overindulge *vb* **-dulging, -dulged** to do too much of something pleasant, such as eating or drinking: *nobody ever wants a hangover, but we all overindulge occasionally.* **overindulgence** *n*

overjoyed *adj* extremely pleased.

overkill *n* any treatment that is greater than that required: *the overkill in negative propaganda resulted in this upsurge.*

overlap *vb* **-lapping, -lapped 1** (of two things) to share part of the same space as or lie partly over (each other): *slice the meat and lay it in overlapping slices in a serving dish.* **2** to coincide partly in time or subject: *their careers have overlapped for the last ten years.* *~n* **3** a part that overlaps. **4** the amount or length of something overlapping.

overlay *vb* **-laying, -laid 1** to cover (a surface) with an applied decoration: *a woollen cloth overlaid with gold and silver embroidery.* *~n* **2** something that is laid over something else; a covering. **3** an applied decoration or layer, for example of gold leaf.

overleaf *adv* on the other side of the page.

overlie *vb* **-lying, -lay, -lain** to lie on or cover (something or someone): *a thin layer of black dust overlay everything.*

overload *vb* **1** to put too large a load on or in (some-

THESAURUS

oneself, fatigue, go too far, have too many irons in the fire, overburden, overload, overtax one's strength, overtire, overwork, strain *or* overstrain oneself, wear oneself out

overdue behindhand, behind schedule, behind time, belated, late, long delayed, not before time (*informal*), owing, tardy, unpunctual

overeat binge (*informal*), gorge, gormandize, guzzle, make a pig of oneself (*informal*), overindulge, pack away (*slang*), pig away (*slang*), pig out (*slang*), stuff, stuff oneself

overemphasize belabour, blow up out of all proportion, lay too much stress on, make a big thing of (*informal*), make a federal case of (*U.S. informal*), make a mountain out of a molehill (*informal*), make a production (out) of (*informal*), make something out of nothing, make too much of, overdramatize, overstress

overflow 1. *vb.* bubble (brim, fall, pour, run, slop, well) over, discharge, pour out, run with, shower, spill, spray, surge **2.** *n.* discharge, flash flood, flood, flooding, inundation, overabundance, spill, spilling over, surplus

overhang *vb.* beetle, bulge, cast a shadow, extend, impend, jut, loom, project, protrude, stick out, threaten

overhaul *vb.* **1.** check, do up (*informal*), examine, inspect, recondition, re-examine, repair, restore, service, survey **2.** catch up with, draw level with, get ahead of, overtake, pass *~n.* **3.** check, checkup, examination, going-over (*informal*), inspection, reconditioning, service

overhead 1. *adv.* above, aloft, atop, in the sky, on high, skyward, up above, upward **2.** *adj.* aerial, overhanging, roof, upper

overheads burden, oncosts, operating cost(s), running cost(s)

overindulge be immoderate *or* intemperate, drink *or* eat too much, have a binge (*informal*), live it up (*informal*), make a pig of oneself (*informal*), overdo it, pig out (*slang*)

overindulgence excess, immoderation, intemperance, overeating, surfeit

overjoyed cock-a-hoop, delighted, deliriously happy, elated, euphoric, happy as a lark, in raptures, joyful, jubilant, on cloud nine (*informal*), only too happy, over the moon (*informal*), rapt, rapturous, thrilled, tickled pink (*informal*), transported

thing): *the aircraft was dangerously overloaded.* **2** to cause (a transport system) to be unable to function properly because too many people or vehicles are using it: *Heathrow Airport was already overloaded by 1972.* **3** to try to put more electricity through a system than the system can cope with. *~n* **4** an excessive load.

overlook *vb* **1** to fail to notice (something). **2** to disregard or ignore (misbehaviour or a fault): *I'm prepared to overlook your failure, but don't do it again.* **3** to give a view of (something) from above: *my flat in Battersea overlooks the river.*

overlord *n* a supreme lord or master.

overly *adv* too; excessively.

overman *vb* **-manning, -manned** to provide with too many staff: *the company is not overmanned overall, but it has too many managers and not enough productive workers.* **overmanned** *adj* **overmanning** *n*

overmuch *adv, adj* too much; very much.

overnight *adv* **1** during the night. **2** in or as if in the course of one night; suddenly: *we are not saying that a change like this would happen overnight.* *~adj* **3** done in, occurring in, or lasting the night: *the army has ordered an overnight curfew.* **4** staying for one night: *overnight guests.* **5** for use during a single night: *should I pack an overnight case?* **6** happening very quickly; sudden: *he doesn't expect the programme to be an overnight success.*

overpaid *adj* earning more money than one deserves.

overpass *n* same as **flyover.**

overplay *vb* **1** to overemphasize (something). **2 overplay one's hand** to overestimate the worth or strength of one's position.

overpopulated *adj* (of a town or country) having more people living in it than it can support.

overpopulation *n* the state of being overpopulated.

overpower *vb* **1** to conquer or subdue (someone) by superior force. **2** to have such a strong effect on (someone) as to make him or her helpless or ineffective: *I was so appalled, so overpowered by my guilt and my shame that I was unable to speak.* **overpowering** *adj*

overpriced *adj* costing more than it is thought to be worth.

overprint *vb* **1** to print (additional matter or another colour) onto (something already printed). *~n* **2** additional matter or another colour printed onto something already printed.

overqualified *adj* having more professional or academic qualifications than are required for a job.

overrate *vb* to have too high an opinion of: *the director's role was seriously overrated.*

overreach *vb* **overreach oneself** to fail by trying to be too clever or achieve too much: *he built up a successful media empire before he overreached himself and lost much of his fortune.*

overreact *vb* to react more strongly or forcefully than is necessary: *allergies happen when the body overreacts to a harmless substance.* **overreaction** *n*

override *vb* **-riding, -rode, -ridden 1** to set aside or disregard (a person or a person's decisions) by having superior authority or power: *the managing director can override any decision he doesn't like.* **2** to be more important than or replace (something): *the day-to-day struggle for survival overrode all moral considerations.* **overriding** *adj*

overripe *adj* (of a fruit or vegetable) so ripe that it has started to decay or go soft.

overrule *vb* **-ruling, -ruled 1** to reverse the decision of (a person or organization with less power): *the President overruled the hardliners in the party who wanted to use force.* **2** to rule or decide against (an argument or decision): *the initial judgment was overruled by the Supreme Court.*

overrun *vb* **-running, -ran, -run 1** to conquer (territory) rapidly by force of number. **2** to spread over (a place) rapidly: *dirty tenements, overrun by lice, rats and roaches.* **3** to extend or run beyond a set limit: *Tuesday's lunch overran by three-quarters of an hour.*

overseas *adv* **1** across the sea; abroad. *~adj* **2** of, to, from, or in a distant country or countries. *~n* **3** *Informal* a foreign country or foreign countries collectively.

oversee *vb* **-seeing, -saw, -seen** to watch over and direct (someone or something); supervise. **overseer** *n*

oversell *vb* **-selling, -sold** to exaggerate the merits or abilities of.

oversew *vb* **-sewing, -sewed; -sewn** *or* **-sewed** to sew (two edges) with stitches that pass over them both.

oversexed *adj* more interested in sex than is thought decent.

THESAURUS

overlay 1. *vb.* adorn, blanket, cover, inlay, laminate, ornament, overspread, superimpose, veneer **2.** *n.* adornment, appliqué, covering, decoration, ornamentation, veneer

overload burden, encumber, oppress, overburden, overcharge, overtax, saddle (with), strain, weigh down

overlook 1. disregard, fail to notice, forget, ignore, leave out of consideration, leave undone, miss, neglect, omit, pass, slight, slip up on **2.** blink at, condone, disregard, excuse, forgive, let bygones be bygones, let one off with, let pass, let ride, make allowances for, pardon, turn a blind eye to, wink at **3.** afford a view of, command a view of, front on to, give upon, have a view of, look over *or* out on

overly exceedingly, excessively, immoderately, inordinately, over, too, unduly, very much

overpower beat, clobber (*slang*), conquer, crush, defeat, get the upper hand over, immobilize, knock out, lick (*informal*), master, overcome, overthrow, overwhelm, quell, subdue, subjugate, vanquish

overpowering compelling, extreme, forceful, invincible, irrefutable, irresistible, nauseating, overwhelming, powerful, sickening, strong, suffocating, telling, unbearable, uncontrollable

overrate assess too highly, exaggerate, make too much of, overestimate, overpraise, overprize, oversell, overvalue, rate too highly, think *or* expect too much of, think too highly of

override annul, cancel, countermand, discount, disregard, ignore, nullify, outweigh, overrule, quash, reverse, ride roughshod over, set aside, supersede, take no account of, trample underfoot, upset, vanquish

overriding cardinal, compelling, determining, dominant, final, major, number one, overruling, paramount, pivotal, predominant, prevailing, primary, prime, ruling, supreme, ultimate

overrule alter, annul, cancel, countermand, disallow, invalidate, make null and void, outvote, override, overturn, recall, repeal, rescind, reverse, revoke, rule against, set aside, veto

overrun 1. conquer, invade, occupy, overcome, overpower, overwhelm, put to flight, rout, swamp **2.** choke, infest, inundate, overflow, overgrow, permeate, ravage, spread like wildfire, spread over, surge over, swarm over **3.** exceed, go beyond, overshoot, run over *or* on

overseer boss (*informal*), chief, foreman, gaffer (*in-*

overshadow *vb* **1** to make (someone or something) seem insignificant or less important by comparison. **2** to sadden the atmosphere of: *news of their teammate's injury overshadowed the victory celebrations.*
overshoe *n* a protective shoe worn over an ordinary shoe.
overshoot *vb* **-shooting, -shot** to go beyond (a mark or target): *the plane overshot the main runway.*
overshot *adj* (of a water wheel) driven by a flow of water that passes over the wheel.
oversight *n* a mistake caused by not noticing something.
oversimplify *vb* **-fies, -fying, -fied** to make something seem simpler than it really is: *the Nationalist's analysis oversimplifies the problems facing the country today.*
oversized *adj* much larger than the usual size.
oversleep *vb* **-sleeping, -slept** to sleep beyond the intended time for getting up.
overspend *vb* **-spending, -spent** to spend more than one can afford.
overspill *n* the rehousing of people from crowded cities in smaller towns.
overstate *vb* **-stating, -stated** to state (something) too strongly; overemphasize. **overstatement** *n*
overstay *vb* **overstay one's welcome** to stay as a guest longer than one's host or hostess would like.
overstep *vb* **-stepping, -stepped 1** to go beyond the limits of what is thought acceptable: *he had overstepped his authority by acting without consulting his superiors.* **2 overstep the mark** to go too far and behave in an unacceptable way.
overstretch *vb* **1** to attempt to do more than there is time or capability for: *for the first time in her career she may have overstretched her talents.* **2** to damage (something) by stretching it further than it can safely go: *he overstretched his Achilles tendon.* **overstretched** *adj*
overstrung *adj* too highly strung; tense.
oversubscribe *vb* **-scribing, -scribed** to apply for or try to buy more of something than is available: *the company's new share offer was heavily oversubscribed.*
overt *adj* done or shown in an open and obvious way: *jurors were now looking at the defendant with overt hostility.* **overtly** *adv*
overtake *vb* **-taking, -took, -taken 1** *Chiefly Brit* to move past (another vehicle or person) travelling in the same direction. **2** to do better than (someone) after catching up with him or her. **3** to come upon (someone) suddenly or unexpectedly: *a mortal tiredness overtook him.*
overtax *vb* **1** to impose too great a strain on: *a singer who had overtaxed her voice.* **2** to tax (people) too heavily.
over-the-top *adj Brit slang* excessive; beyond the usual or acceptable bounds of behaviour.
overthrow *vb* **-throwing, -threw, -thrown 1** to defeat and replace (a ruler or government) by force. **2** to replace (standards or values). ~*n* **3** downfall or destruction: *the overthrow of the US-backed dictatorship.*
overtime *n* **1** work at a regular job done in addition to regular working hours. **2** pay for such work. ~*adv* **3** in addition to one's regular working hours: *she had been working overtime and she fell asleep at the wheel.*
overtone *n* **1** an additional meaning or hint: *I don't want to deny that from time to time there are political overtones.* **2** *Music, acoustics* any of the tones, with the exception of the principal or lowest one, that make up a musical sound.
overture *n* **1** *Music* **a** a piece of orchestral music played at the beginning of an opera, oratorio, or ballet, musical comedy, or film, often containing the main musical themes of the work. **b** a one-movement orchestral piece, usu. having a descriptive or evocative title: *the 1812 Overture.* **2 overtures** opening moves towards a new relationship or agreement: *the German government made a variety of friendly overtures towards the French.*
overturn *vb* **1** to turn over or upside down. **2** to overrule or reverse (a legal decision). **3** to overthrow or destroy (a government).
overvalue *vb* **-valuing, -valued** to regard (someone or something) as much more important or valuable than is the case: *his approach overvalues hard work and undervalues true skill.* **overvalued** *adj*
overview *n* a general survey.
overweening *adj* (of opinions or qualities) exces-

THESAURUS

formal, chiefly Brit.), manager, master, super (*informal*), superintendent, superior, supervisor
overshadow 1. dominate, dwarf, eclipse, excel, leave *or* put in the shade, outshine, outweigh, render insignificant by comparison, rise above, steal the limelight from, surpass, take precedence over, throw into the shade, tower above **2.** blight, cast a gloom upon, mar, ruin, sadden, spoil, take the edge off, take the pleasure *or* enjoyment out of, temper
oversight blunder, carelessness, delinquency, error, fault, inattention, lapse, laxity, mistake, neglect, omission, slip
overt apparent, blatant, manifest, observable, obvious, open, patent, plain, public, unconcealed, undisguised, visible
overtake 1. catch up with, do better than, draw level with, get past, leave behind, outdistance, outdo, outstrip, overhaul, pass **2.** befall, catch unprepared, come upon, engulf, happen, hit, overwhelm, strike, take by surprise
overthrow *vb.* **1.** abolish, beat, bring down, conquer, crush, defeat, depose, dethrone, do away with, master, oust, overcome, overpower, overwhelm, subdue, subjugate, topple, unseat, vanquish **2.** bring to ruin, demolish, destroy, knock down, level, overturn, put an end to ~*n.* **3.** defeat, deposition, destruction, dethronement, discomfiture, disestablishment, displacement, dispossession, downfall, end, fall, ousting, prostration, rout, ruin, subjugation, subversion, suppression, undoing, unseating
overtone association, connotation, flavour, hint, implication, innuendo, intimation, nuance, sense, suggestion, undercurrent
overture 1. *Music* introduction, opening, prelude **2. overtures** advances, approaches, conciliatory moves, invitations, offers, opening moves, proposals, propositions, signals, tenders
overturn 1. capsize, keel over, knock over *or* down, overbalance, reverse, spill, tip over, topple, tumble, upend, upset, upturn **2.** abolish, annul, bring down, countermand, depose, destroy, invalidate, obviate, overthrow, repeal, rescind, reverse, set aside, unseat
overweening arrogant, cavalier, cocksure, cocky, conceited, egotistical, haughty, high and mighty (*informal*), high-handed, insolent, lordly, opinionated, pompous, presumptuous, proud, self-confident, supercilious, uppish (*Brit. informal*), vain, vainglorious
overweight *adj.* ample, bulky, buxom, chubby,

sive or immoderate: *your modesty is a cover for your overweening conceit.*

overweight *adj* **1** (of a person) weighing more than is healthy. **2** weighing more than is usual or permitted.

overwhelm *vb* **1** to overpower the thoughts, emotions, or senses of (someone): *we were overwhelmed with grief.* **2** to overcome (people) with irresistible force: *gang violence has overwhelmed an ailing police force.* **overwhelming** *adj* **overwhelmingly** *adv*

overwork *vb* **1** to work too hard or too long. **2** to use (something) too much: *anti-communism was already being overworked by others.* ~*n* **3** excessive work.

overwrought *adj* tense, nervous, and agitated.

oviduct *n Anat* the tube through which eggs are conveyed from an ovary.

oviform *adj Biol* shaped like an egg.

ovine *adj* of or like a sheep.

oviparous (oh-**vip**-par-uss) *adj Zool* producing eggs that hatch outside the body of the mother.

ovoid (**oh**-void) *adj* egg-shaped.

ovulate (ov-yew-late) *vb* **-lating, -lated** *Biol* to produce or release eggs from an ovary. **ovulation** *n*

ovule *n* **1** *Bot* the part of a plant that contains the egg cell and develops into the seed after fertilization. **2** *Zool* an immature ovum.

ovum (**oh**-vum) *n, pl* **ova** an unfertilized female egg cell.

owe *vb* **owing, owed 1** to be under an obligation to pay an amount of money to (someone): *you owe me ten pounds.* **2** to feel an obligation to do or give: *I think I owe you an apology.* **3 owe something to** to have something as a result of: *many serving officers owe their present position to the former president.*

owing *adj* **1** not yet paid; due: *the bailiffs seized goods worth far more than the amount owing.* **2 owing to** because of; as a result of: *the flight was delayed owing to fog.*

owl *n* a bird of prey which has a flat face, large eyes, and a small hooked beak, and which is active at night. **owlish** *adj*

own *adj (preceded by a possessive)* **1** used to emphasize that something belongs to a particular person: *rely on your own instincts.* ~*pron (preceded by a possessive)* **2** the one or ones belonging to a particular person: *I had one of my own.* **3** the people that someone feels loyalty to, esp. relations: *we all look after our own around here.* **4 come into one's own** to fulfil one's potential. **5 hold one's own** to have the necessary ability to deal successfully with a situation: *he chose a partner who could hold her own with the best.* **6 on one's own a** without help: *you'll never manage to lift that on your own.* **b** by oneself; alone: *he lives on his own in a flat in town.* ~*vb* **7** to have (something) as one's possession. **8** Also: **own up to** to confess or admit: *I must own to a great horror of war.* **owner** *n* **ownership** *n*

owner-occupier *n* someone who owns the house in which he or she lives.

own goal *n* **1** *Soccer* a goal scored by a player accidentally playing the ball into his own team's net. **2** *Informal* any action that results in disadvantage to the person who took it or to his or her associates: *the minister's admission was the latest in a series of own goals by the government.*

ox *n, pl* **oxen** a castrated bull used for pulling heavy loads and for meat.

oxalic acid *n* a colourless poisonous acid found in many plants.

oxbow lake *n* a crescent-shaped lake on the flood plain of a river and constituting remnant of a former meander.

Oxbridge *n* the British universities of Oxford and Cambridge considered together.

oxen *n* the plural of **ox.**

Oxfam Oxford Committee for Famine Relief.

oxidation *n* the act or process of oxidizing.

oxide *n Chem* a compound of oxygen with another element.

oxidize *or* **-dise** *vb* **-dizing, -dized** *or* **-dising, -dised** to react chemically with oxygen, as in burning or rusting. **oxidization** *or* **-disation** *n*

Oxon Oxfordshire.

Oxon. (in degree titles) of Oxford University.

oxtail *n* the tail of an ox, used in soups and stews.

oxyacetylene *n* a mixture of oxygen and acetylene, used in blowlamps for cutting or welding metals at high temperatures.

oxygen *n Chem* a colourless odourless gaseous element essential to life processes and to combustion. Symbol: O

oxygenate *vb* **-ating, -ated** to add oxygen to: *to oxygenate blood.*

oxygen mask *n* a small bowl-shaped object which is connected via a pipe to an cylinder of oxygen and can be placed over a person's nose and mouth to help him or her breathe.

THESAURUS

chunky, corpulent, fat, fleshy, gross, heavy, hefty, huge, massive, obese, on the plump side, outsize, plump, podgy, portly, stout, tubby (*informal*), well-padded (*informal*), well-upholstered (*informal*)

overwhelm 1. bowl over (*informal*), confuse, devastate, knock (someone) for six (*informal*), overcome, overpower, prostrate, render speechless, stagger **2.** crush, cut to pieces, destroy, massacre, overpower, overrun, rout

overwhelming breathtaking, crushing, devastating, invincible, irresistible, overpowering, shattering, stunning, towering, uncontrollable, vast, vastly superior

overwork be a slave-driver *or* hard taskmaster to, burden, burn the midnight oil, drive into the ground, exhaust, exploit, fatigue, oppress, overstrain, overtax, overuse, prostrate, strain, sweat (*informal*), wear out, weary, work one's fingers to the bone

overwrought agitated, beside oneself, distracted, excited, frantic, in a state (tizzy (*informal*), twitter (*informal*)) (*informal*), keyed up, on edge, overexcited, overworked, stirred, strung up (*informal*), tense, uptight (*informal*), wired (*slang*), worked up (*informal*), wound up (*informal*)

owe be beholden to, be in arrears, be in debt, be obligated *or* indebted, be under an obligation to

owing *adj.* due, outstanding, overdue, owed, payable, unpaid, unsettled

owing to *prep.* as a result of, because of, on account of

own *adj.* **1.** individual, particular, personal, private **2. hold one's own** compete, keep going, keep one's end up, keep one's head above water, maintain one's position **3. on one's own** alone, by oneself, by one's own efforts, independently, isolated, left to one's own devices, off one's own bat, on one's tod (*Brit. slang*), singly, (standing) on one's own two feet, unaided, unassisted ~*vb.* **4.** be in possession of, be responsible for, enjoy, have, hold, keep, possess, retain **5. own up to** acknowledge, admit, allow, allow to be valid, avow, come clean about (*informal*), concede, confess, disclose, go along with, grant, make a clean breast of, recognize, tell the truth about

oxygen tent *n Med* a transparent enclosure covering a bedridden patient, into which oxygen is released to aid breathing.

oxymoron (ox-see-**more**-on) *n* a figure of speech that combines two apparently contradictory terms, for example *cruel kindness*.

oyez *or* **oyes** *interj* a cry usually uttered three times by a public crier or court official calling for silence and attention.

oyster *n* **1** an edible shellfish, some types of which produce pearls. **2 the world is your oyster** you are in a position where there is every possible chance of personal advancement and satisfaction. *~adj* **3** greyish-white.

oystercatcher *n* a wading bird with black-and-white plumage and a long stout red bill.

oz *or* **oz.** ounce.

ozone *n* **1** a form of oxygen with a strong odour, formed by an electric discharge in the atmosphere. **2** *Informal* clean bracing air, as found at the seaside.

ozone layer *n* a layer of ozone in the upper atmosphere that absorbs harmful ultraviolet rays from the sun.

THESAURUS

owner holder, landlord, lord, master, mistress, possessor, proprietor, proprietress, proprietrix

ownership dominion, possession, proprietary rights, proprietorship, right of possession, title

P

p *or* **P** *n, pl* **p's, P's,** *or* **Ps 1** the 16th letter of the English alphabet. **2 mind one's p's and q's** to be careful to behave correctly and use polite language.

p (in Britain) penny *or* pence.

P 1 *Chem* phosphorus. **2** (on road signs) parking. **3** *Chess* pawn.

p. 1 (*pl* **pp.**) page. **2** per.

pa *n Informal* father.

Pa 1 *Chem* protactinium. **2** *Physics* pascal.

PA 1 Pennsylvania. **2** personal assistant. **3** public-address system.

p.a. yearly.

pace[1] *n* **1 a** a single step in walking. **b** the length of a step. **2** speed of walking or running. **3** speed of doing some other activity: *efforts to accelerate the pace of change are unlikely to succeed.* **4** manner of walking. **5 keep pace with** to advance at the same speed as. **6 put someone through his** *or* **her paces** to test someone's ability. **7 set the pace** to determine the speed at which a group advances. ~*vb* **pacing, paced 8** to walk with regular steps, often in anxiety or impatience: *he paced up and down the foyer impatiently.* **9** to set the speed for (the competitors) in a race. **10 pace out** to measure by paces.

pace[2] *prep* with due respect to: used to express polite disagreement.

pacemaker *n* **1** an electronic device positioned in the body, next to the heart, to regulate the heartbeat. **2** a competitor who, by leading a race, causes it to be run at a particular speed.

pachyderm (**pak**-ee-durm) *n* a large thick-skinned mammal, such as an elephant or rhinoceros.

pacific *adj Formal* tending to bring peace; peaceful.

Pacific *adj* of the Pacific Ocean, the world's largest and deepest ocean, lying between Asia and Australia and America, or its islands.

pacifier *n US & Canad* a baby's dummy.

pacifist *n* a person who is totally opposed to violence and refuses to take part in war. **pacifism** *n*

pacify *vb* **-fies, -fying, -fied** to soothe or calm. **pacification** *n*

pack[1] *n* **1** a bundle or load carried on the back. **2** *Chiefly Brit* a complete set of playing cards. **3** a group of animals that hunt together: *a pack of hounds.* **4** *Rugby* the forwards of a team. **5** any collection of people or things: *a pack of lies.* **6** *Chiefly US & Canad* same as **packet** (sense 1). **7** an organized group of Cub Scouts or Brownie Guides. **8** same as **rucksack** or **backpack. 9** Also called: **face pack** a cream treatment that cleanses and tones the skin. ~*vb* **10** to put (articles) in a case or container for moving. **11** to roll (articles) up into a bundle. **12** to press tightly together; cram: *thousands of people packed into the city's main square.* **13** (foll. by *off*) to send away hastily: *their young son came in to say good night and was packed off to bed.* **14** *Slang* to be able to deliver a specified amount of unexpected or violent force or power: *the film's unexpected ending packs quite a punch.* **15** *US informal* to carry (a gun) habitually. **16 send someone packing** *Informal* to dismiss someone abruptly. ~See also **pack in, pack up.**

pack[2] *vb* to fill (a committee, jury, or audience) with one's own supporters.

package *n* **1** a small parcel. **2** Also: **package deal** a deal in which separate items are presented together as a unit. **3** *US & Canad* same as **packet** (sense 1). ~*vb* **-aging, -aged 4** to put (something) into a package. **packaging** *n*

package holiday *n* a holiday in which everything is arranged by one company for a fixed price.

packet *n* **1** a container, together with its contents: *a packet of crisps.* **2** a small parcel. **3** Also: **packet boat** a boat that transports mail, passengers, or goods on a fixed short route. **4** *Slang* a large sum of money: *the manager was paid a packet to keep his mouth shut.*

packhorse *n* a horse used to carry goods.

pack ice *n* a large area of floating ice, consisting of pieces that have become massed together.

pack in *vb Informal* to stop doing (something): *I'm going to pack it in and resign.*

packing *n* material, such as paper or plastic, used to protect packed goods.

packthread *n* a strong thread for sewing or tying up packages.

pack up *vb* **1** to put (articles) in a bag or case before leaving. **2** *Informal* to stop doing (something). **3** (of a machine) break down.

pact *n* a formal agreement between two or more parties.

pad[1] *n* **1** a thick piece of soft material used for comfort, shape, protection, or absorption. **2** a number of sheets of paper fastened together along one edge. **3**

THESAURUS

pace *n.* **1.** gait, measure, step, stride, tread, walk **2.** clip (*informal*), lick (*informal*), momentum, motion, movement, progress, rate, speed, tempo, time, velocity ~*vb.* **3.** march, patrol, pound, stride, walk back and forth, walk up and down **4. pace out** count, determine, mark out, measure, step

pacific *formal* appeasing, conciliatory, diplomatic, dovelike, friendly, gentle, mild, nonbelligerent, nonviolent, pacificatory, pacifist, peaceable, peace-loving, peacemaking, placatory, propitiatory

pacifist conscientious objector, dove, passive resister, peace lover

pack *n.* **1.** back pack, bale, bundle, burden, fardel (*archaic*), kit, kitbag, knapsack, load, package, packet, parcel, rucksack, truss **2.** assemblage, band, bunch, collection, company, crew, crowd, deck, drove, flock, gang, group, herd, lot, mob, set, troop ~*vb.* **3.** batch, bundle, burden, load, package, packet, store, stow **4.** charge, compact, compress, cram, crowd, fill, jam, mob, press, ram, stuff, tamp, throng, wedge **5.** *with* **off** bundle out, dismiss, hustle out, send away, send packing (*informal*), send someone about his business

package *n.* **1.** box, carton, container, packet, parcel **2.** amalgamation, combination, entity, unit, whole ~*vb.* **3.** batch, box, pack, packet, parcel (up), wrap, wrap up

packet 1. bag, carton, container, package, parcel, poke (*dialect*), wrapper, wrapping **2.** *slang* big money, bomb (*Brit. slang*), bundle (*slang*), fortune, king's ransom (*informal*), lot(s), mint, pile (*informal*), pot(s) (*informal*), pretty penny (*informal*), tidy sum (*informal*)

pack in *informal* cease, chuck (*informal*), desist, give up *or* over, jack in, kick (*informal*), leave off, stop

pack up 1. put away, store, tidy up **2.** *informal* call it a day (*informal*), finish, give up, pack in (*informal*) **3.** break down, conk out (*informal*), fail, give out, stall, stop

the fleshy cushioned underpart of an animal's paw. **4** a level area or flat-topped structure, from which rockets are launched or helicopters take off. **5** the floating leaf of the water lily. **6** *Slang* a person's residence. ~*vb* **padding, padded 7** to fill (something) out with soft material for comfort, shape, or protection. **8 pad out** to lengthen (a speech or piece of writing) with unnecessary words or pieces of information.

pad[2] *vb* **padding, padded 1** to walk with a soft or muffled step. **2** to travel (a route) on foot: *men padding the streets in cheap sneakers.*

padded cell *n* a room with padded walls in a psychiatric hospital, in which patients who are likely to injure themselves are placed.

padding *n* **1** any soft material used to pad something. **2** unnecessary information put into a speech or written work to make it longer.

paddle[1] *n* **1** a short light oar with a flat blade at one or both ends. **2** a paddle wheel used to move a boat. **3** a blade of a water wheel or paddle wheel. ~*vb* **-dling, -dled 4** to move (a boat) with a paddle. **5** to swim with short rapid strokes, like a dog. **6** *US & Canad informal* to spank.

paddle[2] *vb* **-dling, -dled 1** to walk barefoot in shallow water. **2** to dabble (one's fingers, hands, or feet) in water. ~*n* **3** the act of paddling in water.

paddle steamer *n* a ship propelled by paddle wheels turned by a steam engine.

paddle wheel *n* a large wheel fitted with paddles, turned by an engine to propel a ship.

paddock *n* **1** a small enclosed field for horses. **2** (in horse racing) the enclosure in which horses are paraded and mounted before a race.

paddy[1] *n, pl* **-dies 1** Also: **paddy field** a field planted with rice. **2** rice as a growing crop or when harvested but not yet milled.

paddy[2] *n, pl* **-dies** *Brit informal* a fit of temper.

padkos (**pudd**-koss) *n S African* snacks and provisions for a journey.

padlock *n* **1** a detachable lock with a hinged hoop fastened through a ring on the object to be secured. ~*vb* **2** to fasten (something) with a padlock.

padre (**pah**-dray) *n Informal* a chaplain to the armed forces.

paean (**pee**-an) *n Literary* an expression of praise or joy.

paediatrician *or US* **pediatrician** *n* a doctor who specializes in children's diseases.

paediatrics *or US* **pediatrics** *n* the branch of medicine concerned with children and their diseases. **paediatric** *or US* **pediatric** *adj*

paedophile *or US* **pedophile** *n* a person who is sexually attracted to children.

paedophilia *or US* **pedophilia** *n* the condition of being sexually attracted to children.

paella (pie-**ell**-a) *n* a Spanish dish made from rice, shellfish, chicken, and vegetables.

pagan *adj* **1** having, being, or relating to religious beliefs, esp. ancient ones, which are not part of any of the world's major religions: *this was the site of a pagan temple to the sun.* **2** irreligious. ~*n* **3** a person who does not belong to any of the world's major religions. **4** a person without any religion. **paganism** *n*

page[1] *n* **1** one side of one of the leaves of a book, newspaper, or magazine. **2** one of the leaves of a book, newspaper, or magazine. **3** *Literary* a period or event: *a new page in the country's political history.*

page[2] *n* **1** a small boy who attends a bride at her wedding. **2** a youth employed to run errands for the guests in a hotel or club. **3** *Medieval history* a boy in training for knighthood. ~*vb* **paging, paged 4** to summon (a person), by bleeper or loudspeaker, in order to pass on a message.

pageant *n* **1** an outdoor show portraying scenes from history. **2** any magnificent display or procession.

pageantry *n* spectacular display or ceremony.

pageboy *n* **1** a hairstyle in which the hair is smooth and the same medium length with the ends curled under. **2** same as **page**[2] (sense 2).

pagination *n* the numbering in sequence of the pages of a book or manuscript. **paginate** *vb*

pagoda *n* a pyramid-shaped Asian temple or tower.

paid *vb* **1** past of **pay. 2 put paid to** to end or destroy: *a knee injury put paid to his promising sporting career.*

pail *n* **1** a bucket. **2** Also called: **pailful** the amount contained in a pail: *a pail of water.*

pain *n* **1** physical hurt or discomfort caused by injury or illness. **2** emotional suffering. **3 on pain of** subject to the penalty of: *orders which their soldiers were bound to follow on pain of death.* **4** Also called: **pain in the neck** *Informal* a person or thing that is annoying or irritating. ~*vb* **5** to cause (a person) physical or

THESAURUS

pact agreement, alliance, arrangement, bargain, bond, compact, concord, concordat, contract, convention, covenant, deal, league, protocol, treaty, understanding

pad *n.* **1.** buffer, cushion, protection, stiffening, stuffing, wad **2.** block, jotter, notepad, tablet, writing pad **3.** foot, paw, sole **4.** *slang* apartment, flat, hang-out (*informal*), home, place, quarters, room ~*vb.* **5.** cushion, fill, line, pack, protect, shape, stuff **6. pad out** amplify, augment, eke, elaborate, fill out, flesh out, inflate, lengthen, protract, spin out, stretch

padding 1. filling, packing, stuffing, wadding **2.** hot air (*informal*), prolixity, verbiage, verbosity, waffle (*informal, chiefly Brit.*), wordiness

paddle[1] **1.** *n.* oar, scull, sweep **2.** *vb.* oar, propel, pull, row, scull

paddle[2] dabble, plash, slop, splash (about), stir, wade

pagan 1. *adj.* Gentile, heathen, heathenish, idolatrous, infidel, irreligious, polytheistic **2.** *n.* Gentile, heathen, idolater, infidel, polytheist, unbeliever

page[1] **1.** folio, leaf, sheet, side **2.** *literary* chapter, episode, epoch, era, event, incident, period, phase, point, stage, time

page[2] **1.** *n.* attendant, bellboy (*U.S.*), footboy, pageboy, servant, squire **2.** *vb.* announce, call, call out, preconize, seek, send for, summon

pageant display, extravaganza, parade, procession, ritual, show, spectacle, tableau

pageantry display, drama, extravagance, glamour, glitter, grandeur, magnificence, parade, pomp, show, showiness, spectacle, splash (*informal*), splendour, state, theatricality

pain *n.* **1.** ache, cramp, discomfort, hurt, irritation, pang, smarting, soreness, spasm, suffering, tenderness, throb, throe (*rare*), trouble, twinge **2.** affliction, agony, anguish, bitterness, distress, grief, hardship, heartache, misery, suffering, torment, torture, tribulation, woe, wretchedness **3.** *informal* aggravation, annoyance, bore, bother, drag (*informal*), gall, headache (*informal*), irritation, nuisance, pain in the arse (*taboo informal*), pain in the neck (*informal*), pest, vexation ~*vb.* **4.** ail, chafe, discomfort, harm, hurt, inflame, injure, smart, sting, throb **5.** afflict, aggrieve, agonize, cut to the quick, disquiet, distress, grieve, hurt, sadden, torment, torture, vex, worry, wound **6.** *informal*

mental suffering. **6** *Informal* to annoy; irritate. ~See also **pains. painless** *adj*

pained *adj* having or suggesting pain or distress: *a pained look.*

painful *adj* **1** causing pain or distress: *painful inflammation of the joints; he began the painful task of making funeral arrangements.* **2** affected with pain: *the symptoms include fever and painful joints.* **3** tedious or difficult: *the hours passed with painful slowness.* **4** *Informal* extremely bad: *a painful so-called comedy.* **painfully** *adv*

painkiller *n* a drug that relieves pain.

pains *pl n* care or trouble: *they are at great pains to appear realistic and responsible.*

painstaking *adj* extremely careful and thorough. **painstakingly** *adv*

paint *n* **1** a coloured substance, spread on a surface with a brush or a roller, that forms a hard coating. **2** a dry film of paint on a surface. **3** *Informal* face make-up. ~*vb* **4** to apply paint to paper or canvas to make (a picture) of. **5** to coat (a surface) with paint. **6** to describe vividly in words: *the survey paints a dismal picture of growing hunger and disease.* **7** to apply make-up to (the face). **8** to apply (liquid) to (a surface): *paint the varnish on and leave it dry for at least four hours.* **9 paint the town red** *Informal* to celebrate in a lively way.

paintbrush *n* a brush used to apply paint.

painted lady *n* a butterfly with pale brownish-red mottled wings.

painter[1] *n* **1** an artist who paints pictures. **2** a person who paints surfaces of buildings as a trade.

painter[2] *n* a rope attached to the bow of a boat for tying it up.

painting *n* **1** a picture produced by using paint. **2** the art of producing pictures by applying paints to paper or canvas. **3** the act of applying paint to a surface.

paintwork *n* the covering of paint on parts of a vehicle, building, etc.: *someone had damaged the Porsche by scraping a key along its paintwork.*

pair *n* **1** two identical or similar things matched for use together: *a pair of shoes.* **2** two people, animals, or things used or grouped together: *a pair of tickets.* **3** an object consisting of two identical or similar parts joined together: *a pair of jeans.* **4** a male and a female animal of the same species kept for breeding purposes. **5** *Parliament* two opposed members who both agree not to vote on a specified motion. **6** two playing cards of the same denomination. **7** one member of a matching pair: *I can't find the pair to this glove.* ~*vb* **8** to group (people or things) in twos. **9 pair off** to separate into groups of two.

➤ *Pair* is followed by a singular verb if it refers to a unit: *A pair of shoes was on the floor,* and by a plural verb if it refers to two individuals: *That pair are good friends.*

paisley pattern *or* **paisley** *n* a detailed pattern of small curving shapes, used in fabric.

pajamas *pl n US* pyjamas.

pakeha (**pah**-kee-hah) *n, pl* **pakeha** *or* **pakehas** *NZ* a person of European descent, as distinct from a Maori.

Paki *Brit slang, offensive* ~*n* **1** a Pakistani or person of Pakistani descent. ~*adj* **2** Pakistani or of Pakistani descent.

Pakistani *adj* **1** of Pakistan. ~*n* **2** a person from Pakistan.

pal *Informal* ~*n* **1** a close friend. ~*vb* **palling, palled 2 pal up with** to become friends with.

palace *n* **1** the official residence of a king, queen, president, or archbishop. **2** a large and richly furnished building.

paladin *n* **1** one of the legendary twelve peers of Charlemagne's court. **2** (formerly) a knight who did battle for a king or queen.

palaeo- *or US* **paleo-** *combining form* old, ancient, or prehistoric: *palaeobotany.*

Palaeocene *or US* **Paleocene** (**pal**-ee oh seen) *adj Geol* of the epoch of geological time about 65 million years ago.

palaeography *or US* **paleography** (pal-ee-**og**-ra-fee) *n* the study of ancient handwriting.

Palaeolithic *or US* **Paleolithic** (pal-ee-oh-**lith**-ik) *adj* of the period from about 2.5 to 3 million years ago until about 12 000 BC during which primitive man emerged and unpolished chipped stone tools were made.

palaeontology *or US* **paleontology** (pal-ee-on-**tol**-a-jee) *n* the study of past geological periods and fossils. **palaeontologist** *or US* **paleontologist** *n*

Palaeozoic *or US* **Paleozoic** (pal-ee-oh-**zoh**-ik) *adj Geol* of the geological era that lasted from about 600 million years ago to 230 million years ago.

palanquin (pal-an-**keen**) *n* (formerly, in the Orient) a covered bed in which someone could be carried on the shoulders of four men.

THESAURUS

annoy, exasperate, gall, harass, irritate, nark (*slang*), rile, vex

pained aggrieved, anguished, distressed, hurt, injured, miffed (*informal*), offended, reproachful, stung, unhappy, upset, worried, wounded

painful 1. afflictive, disagreeable, distasteful, distressing, grievous, saddening, unpleasant **2.** aching, agonizing, excruciating, harrowing, hurting, inflamed, raw, smarting, sore, tender, throbbing **3.** arduous, difficult, hard, laborious, severe, tedious, troublesome, trying, vexatious **4.** *informal* abysmal, awful, dire, dreadful, excruciating, extremely bad, godawful, terrible

painfully alarmingly, clearly, deplorably, distressingly, dreadfully, excessively, markedly, sadly, unfortunately, woefully

painkiller anaesthetic, analgesic, anodyne, drug, palliative, remedy, sedative

painless easy, effortless, fast, no trouble, pain-free, quick, simple, trouble-free

pains assiduousness, bother, care, diligence, effort, industry, labour, special attention, trouble

painstaking assiduous, careful, conscientious, diligent, earnest, exacting, hard-working, industrious, meticulous, persevering, punctilious, scrupulous, sedulous, strenuous, thorough, thoroughgoing

paint *n.* **1.** colour, colouring, dye, emulsion, pigment, stain, tint **2.** *informal* cosmetics, face (*informal*), greasepaint, make-up, *maquillage,* war paint (*informal*) ~*vb.* **3.** catch a likeness, delineate, depict, draw, figure, picture, portray, represent, sketch **4.** apply, coat, colour, cover, daub, decorate, slap on (*informal*) **5.** bring to life, capture, conjure up a vision, depict, describe, evoke, make one see, portray, put graphically, recount, tell vividly **6. paint the town red** *informal* carouse, celebrate, go on a binge (*informal*), go on a spree, go on the town, live it up (*informal*), make merry, make whoopee (*informal*), revel

pair 1. *n.* brace, combination, couple, doublet, duo, match, matched set, span, twins, two of a kind, twosome, yoke **2.** *vb.* bracket, couple, join, marry, match, match up, mate, pair off, put together, team, twin, wed, yoke

palatable 1. appetizing, delectable, delicious, luscious, mouthwatering, savoury, tasty, toothsome **2.**

palatable *adj* **1** (of food or drink) pleasant to taste. **2** (of an experience or idea) acceptable or satisfactory.

palate *n* **1** the roof of the mouth. **2** the sense of taste: *a range of dishes to tempt every palate.*

palatial *adj* like a palace; magnificent.

palatinate *n* a territory ruled by a palatine prince or noble or a count palatine.

palatine *adj* possessing royal prerogatives: *a count palatine.*

palaver (pal-**lah**-ver) *n* time-consuming fuss: *all the palaver involved in obtaining a visa.*

pale[1] *adj* **1** (of a colour) whitish and not very strong: *pale yellow.* **2** (of a complexion) having a whitish appearance, usually because of illness, shock, or fear. **3** lacking brightness or colour: *the pale, chill light of an October afternoon.* ~*vb* **paling, paled 4** to become pale or paler. **paleness** *n*

pale[2] *n* **1** a wooden post used in fences. **2 a** a fence made of pales. **b** a boundary. **3 beyond the pale** outside the limits of social convention: *the destruction of forests is beyond the pale.*

paleface *n* an offensive term for a White person, said to have been used by North American Indians.

Palestinian *adj* **1** of Palestine, an area in the Middle East between the Jordan River and the Mediterranean. ~*n* **2** an Arab from this area, esp. one living in Israel or Israeli-occupied territory or as a refugee.

palette *n* **1** a flat board used by artists to mix paints. **2** the range of colours characteristic of a particular artist or school of painting: *he uses a cool palette with no strong red.*

palette knife *n* a spatula with a thin flexible blade used in painting or cookery.

palindrome *n* a word or phrase that reads the same backwards or forwards, such as *able was I ere I saw Elba.*

paling *n* **1** a fence made of pales. **2** pales collectively. **3** a single pale.

palisade *n* **1** a fence made of stakes driven into the ground. **2** one of the stakes used in such a fence.

pall[1] *n* **1** a cloth spread over a coffin. **2** a coffin at a funeral ceremony. **3** a dark heavy covering: *a pall of smoke and dust hung in the air.* **4** a depressing atmosphere: *a pall hung on them all after his death.*

pall[2] *vb* to become boring or uninteresting, esp. by continuing for too long: *any pleasure had palled long before the two-hour programme was over.*

Palladian *adj* of a style of architecture characterized by symmetry and the revival and development of ancient Roman styles.

palladium *n Chem* a rare silvery-white element of the platinum metal group, used in jewellery. Symbol: Pd

pallbearer *n* a person who helps to carry or who escorts the coffin at a funeral.

pallet[1] *n* a straw-filled mattress or bed.

pallet[2] *n* **1** a tool with a flat, sometimes flexible, blade used for shaping pottery. **2** a portable platform for storing and moving goods.

palliasse *n* a straw-filled mattress; pallet.

palliate *vb* **-ating, -ated 1** to lessen the severity of (pain or disease) without curing it. **2** to cause (an offence) to seem less serious.

palliative *adj* **1** relieving without curing. ~*n* **2** something that palliates, such as a sedative drug. **3** something that alleviates or lessens a problem: *equal pay was a palliative for the growing unrest among women.*

pallid *adj* **1** lacking colour, brightness, or vigour: *a pallid autumn sun.* **2** lacking energy or vitality; insipid: *many militants find the party's socialism too pallid.*

pallor *n* paleness of complexion, usually because of illness, shock, or fear.

pally *adj* **-lier, -liest** *Informal* on friendly terms.

palm[1] *n* **1** the inner surface of the hand from the wrist to the base of the fingers. **2** the part of a glove that covers the palm. **3 in the palm of one's hand** at one's mercy or command: *he had the jury in the palm of his hand.* ~*vb* **4** to hide (something) in the hand: *he palmed the key.* ~See also **palm off.**

palm[2] *or* **palm tree** *n* a tropical or subtropical tree with a straight unbranched trunk crowned with long pointed leaves.

palmate *adj* shaped like an open hand: *palmate leaves.*

palmetto *n, pl* **-tos** a small palm tree with fan-shaped leaves.

palmistry *n* fortune-telling by examining the lines and bumps of the hand. **palmist** *n*

palm off *vb* **1** to get rid or (someone or something) by passing it on to another: *the risk has to be shared with subcontractors, not simply palmed off on them.* **2** to divert (someone) by a lie or excuse: *Mark was palmed off with a series of excuses.*

palm oil *n* an oil obtained from the fruit of certain palm trees, used as an edible fat and in soap.

Palm Sunday *n* the Sunday before Easter.

palmy *adj* **palmier, palmiest 1** successful, prosperous and happy: *the palmy days of youth.* **2** covered with palm trees: *palmy beaches.*

palomino *n, pl* **-nos** a golden or cream horse with a white mane and tail.

palpable *adj* **1** obvious: *palpable nonsense.* **2** (of a feeling or an atmosphere) so intense that it seems capable of being touched: *an air of palpable gloom hung over him.* **palpably** *adv*

palpate *vb* **-pating, -pated** *Med* to examine (an area of the body) by touching. **palpation** *n*

THESAURUS

acceptable, agreeable, attractive, enjoyable, fair, pleasant, satisfactory

palate appetite, heart, stomach, taste

palatial de luxe, gorgeous, grand, grandiose, illustrious, imposing, luxurious, magnificent, majestic, opulent, plush (*informal*), regal, spacious, splendid, splendiferous (*facetious, old-fashioned*), stately, sumptuous

pale *adj.* **1.** dim, faint, feeble, inadequate, poor, thin, weak **2.** anaemic, ashen, ashy, bleached, bloodless, colourless, faded, light, pallid, pasty, sallow, wan, washed-out, white, whitish ~*vb.* **3.** become pale, blanch, go white, lose colour, whiten **4.** decrease, dim, diminish, dull, fade, grow dull, lessen, lose lustre

pall *vb.* become dull *or* tedious, bore, cloy, glut, jade, satiate, sicken, surfeit, tire, weary

palm 1. hand, hook, mitt (*slang*), paw (*informal*) **2. in the palm of one's hand** at one's mercy, in one's clutches (control, power)

palm off 1. foist on, force upon, impose upon, take advantage of, thrust upon, unload upon **2.** fob off, foist off, pass off

palmy flourishing, fortunate, glorious, golden, halcyon, happy, joyous, luxurious, prosperous, thriving, triumphant

palpable 1. apparent, blatant, clear, conspicuous, evident, manifest, obvious, open, patent, plain, unmistakable, visible **2.** concrete, material, real, solid, substantial, tangible, touchable

palpitate beat, flutter, pitapat, pitter-patter, pound, pulsate, pulse, quiver, shiver, throb, tremble, vibrate

palpitate *vb* **-tating, -tated 1** (of the heart) to beat rapidly. **2** to flutter or tremble. **palpitation** *n*

palsy (**pawl**-zee) *n Pathol* paralysis of a specified type: *cerebral palsy.* **palsied** *adj*

paltry *adj* **-trier, -triest** insignificant.

pampas *n* the extensive grassy plains of South America.

pampas grass *n* a South American grass with large feathery silver-coloured flower branches.

pamper *vb* to treat (someone) with excessive indulgence or care; spoil.

pamphlet *n* a thin paper-covered booklet, often on a subject of current interest.

pamphleteer *n* a person who writes or issues pamphlets.

pan[1] *n* **1** a wide long-handled metal container used in cooking. **2** any of various similar containers used in industry, etc. **3** either of the two dishes on a set of scales. **4** *Brit* the bowl of a lavatory. **5** a natural or artificial hollow in the ground: *a saltpan.* ~*vb* **panning, panned 6** to sift gold from (a river) in a shallow pan. **7** *Informal* to criticize harshly: *his first film was panned by the critics.* ~See also **pan out.**

pan[2] *vb* **panning, panned 1** to move (a film camera) to follow a moving object or to take in a whole scene. ~*n* **2** the act of panning.

pan- *combining form* including or relating to all parts or members: *Pan-American.*

panacea (pan-a-**see**-a) *n* a remedy for all diseases or problems.

panache (pan-**ash**) *n* a confident and stylish manner: *the orchestra played with great panache.*

panama hat *or* **panama** *n* a straw hat with a rounded crown and a wide brim.

Pan-American *adj* of North, South, and Central America collectively.

panatella *n* a long slender cigar.

pancake *n* **1** a thin flat circle of fried batter. **2** Also called: **pancake landing** an aircraft landing made by levelling out a few feet from the ground and then dropping onto it.

Pancake Day *n* Shrove Tuesday, when people traditionally eat pancakes.

panchromatic *adj Photog* (of an emulsion or film) sensitive to light of all colours.

pancreas (**pang**-kree-ass) *n* a large gland behind the stomach, that produces insulin and aids digestion. **pancreatic** *adj*

panda *n* **1** Also called: **giant panda** a large black-and-white bearlike animal from the bamboo forests of China. **2** Also called: **lesser** *or* **red panda** a raccoon-like animal of the mountain forests of S Asia, with a reddish-brown coat and ringed tail.

panda car *n Brit* a police patrol car.

pandemic *adj* (of a disease) occurring over a wide geographical area.

pandemonium *n* wild confusion; uproar.

pander *vb* **1** (foll. by *to*) to indulge (a person or his or her desires): *he pandered to popular fears.* ~*n* **2** *Chiefly archaic* a person who procures a sexual partner for someone.

pandit *n Hinduism* same as **pundit** (sense 2).

Pandora's box *n* a source of many unforeseen difficulties.

pane *n* a sheet of glass in a window or door.

panegyric (pan-ee-**jirr**-rik) *n* a formal speech or piece of writing that praises a person or event.

panel *n* **1** a distinct section of a larger surface area, such as that in a door. **2** any distinct section of something formed from a sheet of material, such as part of a car body. **3** a piece of material inserted in a garment. **4** a group of people acting as a team, such as in a quiz or a discussion before an audience. **5** *Law* **a** a list of jurors. **b** the people on a jury. **6** short for **instrument panel.** ~*adj* **7** of a group acting as a panel: *a panel game.* ~*vb* **-elling, -elled** *or US* **-eling, -eled 8** to cover or decorate with panels.

panel beater *n* a person who repairs damage to car bodies.

panelling *or US* **paneling** *n* panels collectively, such as on a wall or ceiling.

panellist *or US* **panelist** *n* a member of a panel, usually on radio or television.

panel van *n Austral & NZ* a small van.

pang *n* a sudden sharp feeling of pain or sadness.

pangolin *n* an animal of tropical countries with a scaly body and a long snout for feeding on ants and termites. Also called: **scaly anteater**

panic *n* **1** a sudden overwhelming feeling of terror or anxiety, sometimes affecting a whole group of people. ~*adj* **2** of or resulting from such terror: *panic measures.* ~*vb* **-icking, -icked 3** to feel or cause to feel panic. **panicky** *adj*

THESAURUS

palsied *Pathol.* arthritic, crippled, debilitated, disabled, helpless, paralysed, paralytic, rheumatic, sclerotic, shaking, shaky, spastic, trembling

paltry base, beggarly, contemptible, crappy (*slang*), derisory, despicable, inconsiderable, insignificant, low, meagre, mean, measly, Mickey Mouse (*slang*), minor, miserable, petty, picayune (*U.S. and Canad. informal*), piddling (*informal*), pitiful, poor, puny, slight, small, sorry, trifling, trivial, unimportant, worthless, wretched

pamper baby, cater to one's every whim, coddle, cosset, fondle, gratify, humour, indulge, mollycoddle, pander to, pet, spoil

pamphlet booklet, brochure, circular, folder, leaflet, tract

pan[1] *n.* **1.** container, pot, saucepan, vessel ~*vb.* **2.** look for, search for, separate, sift out, wash **3.** *informal* blast, censure, criticize, flay, hammer (*Brit. informal*), knock (*informal*), lambast(e), put down, roast (*informal*), rubbish (*informal*), slag (off) (*slang*), slam (*slang*), slate (*informal*), tear into (*informal*), throw brickbats at (*informal*)

pan[2] *vb.* follow, move, scan, sweep, swing, track, traverse

panacea cure-all, elixir, nostrum

panache brio, dash, élan, flair, flamboyance, flourish, spirit, style, swagger, verve

pandemonium babel, bedlam, chaos, clamour, commotion, confusion, din, hubbub, hue and cry, hullabaloo, racket, ruckus (*informal*), ruction (*informal*), rumpus, tumult, turmoil, uproar

pang ache, agony, anguish, discomfort, distress, gripe, pain, prick, spasm, stab, sting, stitch, throe (*rare*), twinge, wrench

panic *n.* **1.** agitation, alarm, consternation, dismay, fear, fright, horror, hysteria, scare, terror ~*vb.* **2.** become hysterical, be terror-stricken, go to pieces, lose one's bottle (*Brit. slang*), lose one's nerve, overreact **3.** alarm, put the wind up (someone) (*informal*), scare, startle, terrify, unnerve

panicky afraid, agitated, distressed, fearful, frantic, frenzied, frightened, hysterical, in a flap (*informal*), in a tizzy (*informal*), jittery (*informal*), nervous, windy (*slang*), worked up, worried

panicle *n Bot* a loose, irregularly branched cluster of flowers, such as in the oat.

panic-stricken *adj* affected by panic.

panjandrum *n* a pompous self-important official.

pannier *n* **1** one of a pair of bags fixed on either side of the back wheel of a bicycle or motorcycle. **2** one of a pair of large baskets slung over a beast of burden.

panoply (**pan**-a-plee) *n* a magnificent array: *ambassadors equipped with the full panoply of diplomatic bags, codes and cyphers.*

panorama *n* **1** a wide unbroken view in all directions: *the beautiful panorama of the Cornish coast.* **2** a wide or comprehensive survey of a subject: *the panorama of American life.* **3** a picture of a scene unrolled before spectators a part at a time so as to appear continuous. **panoramic** *adj*

pan out *vb* **1** *Informal* to work out; result: *Parker's research did not pan out too well.* **2** (of gravel) to yield gold by panning.

panpipes *pl n* a musical wind instrument made of tubes of decreasing lengths joined together.

pansy *n, pl* **-sies 1** a garden plant whose flowers have rounded white, yellow, or purple velvety petals. **2** *Offensive slang* an effeminate or homosexual man or boy.

pant *vb* **1** to breathe with noisy gasps after exertion. **2** to say (something) while breathing in this way. **3** (foll. by *for*) to have a frantic desire for. *~n* **4** the act of panting.

pantaloons *pl n* baggy trousers gathered at the ankles.

pantechnicon *n Brit* a large van used for furniture removals.

pantheism *n* **1** the belief that God is present in everything. **2** readiness to worship all gods. **pantheist** *n* **pantheistic** *adj*

pantheon *n* **1** (in ancient Greece or Rome) a temple built to honour all the gods. **2** all the gods of a particular creed: *the Celtic pantheon of horse gods.* **3** a group of very important people: *he deserves a place in the pantheon of social reformers.*

panther *n* a leopard, usually a black one.

panties *pl n* women's or children's underpants.

pantihose *pl n US & Austral* women's tights.

pantile *n* a roofing tile, with an S-shaped cross section.

panto *n, pl* **-tos** *Brit informal* short for **pantomime** (sense 1).

pantograph *n* **1** an instrument for copying drawings or maps to any scale. **2** a device on the roof of an electric train to carry the current from an overhead wire.

pantomime *n* **1** (in Britain) a play based on a fairy tale and performed at Christmas time. **2** a theatrical entertainment in which words are replaced by gestures and bodily actions. **3** *Informal, chiefly Brit* a confused or farcical situation.

pantry *n, pl* **-tries** a small room or large cupboard in which food is kept.

pants *pl n* **1** *Brit* an undergarment with two leg holes, covering the body from the waist or hips to the thighs. **2** *US & Canad* trousers. **3 bore** *or* **scare the pants off someone** *Informal* to bore or scare someone very much.

pantyhose *pl n NZ* women's tights.

pap[1] *n* **1** a soft food for babies or invalids. **2** worthless or oversimplified entertainment or information. **3** *S African* maize porridge.

pap[2] *n Old-fashioned, Scot & N English dialect* a nipple or teat.

papa (pap-**pah**) *n Old-fashioned, informal* father.

papacy (**pay**-pa-see) *n, pl* **-cies 1** the office or term of office of a pope. **2** the system of government in the Roman Catholic Church that has the pope as its head.

papal *adj* of the pope or the papacy.

paparazzo (pap-a-**rat**-so) *n, pl* **-razzi** (-**rat**-see) a freelance photographer who specializes in taking shots of famous people without their knowledge or consent.

papaya (pap-**pie**-a) *n* a large green fruit with a sweet yellow flesh, that grows in the West Indies.

paper *n* **1** a flexible material made in sheets from wood pulp or other fibres and used for writing on, decorating walls, or wrapping parcels. **2** short for **newspaper** or **wallpaper. 3** (*pl*) documents, such as a passport, which can identify the bearer. **4** a set of examination questions. **5** (*pl*) the collected diaries or letters of someone's private or public life. **6** a lecture or an essay on a specific subject. **7 on paper** in theory, as opposed to fact: *countless ideas which look good on paper just don't work in practice.* *~adj* **8** made of paper: *paper towels; a paper bag.* **9** recorded on paper but not yet existing in practice: *a paper profit of more than $50 million.* *~vb* **10** to cover (walls) with wallpaper. ~See also **paper over. papery** *adj*

paperback *n* **1** a book with covers made of flexible card. *~adj* **2** of a paperback or publication of paperbacks: *a paperback novel.*

paperboy *or* **papergirl** *n* a boy or girl employed to deliver newspapers to people's homes.

paper chase *n* a cross-country run in which a runner lays a trail of paper for others to follow.

paperclip *n* a bent wire clip for holding sheets of paper together.

paperhanger *n* a person who hangs wallpaper as an occupation.

paperknife *n, pl* **-knives** a knife-shaped object with a blunt blade for opening sealed envelopes.

THESAURUS

panic-stricken aghast, agitated, alarmed, appalled, fearful, frenzied, frightened, frightened out of one's wits, frightened to death, horrified, horror-stricken, hysterical, in a cold sweat (*informal*), panicky, petrified, scared, scared stiff, startled, terrified, terror-stricken, unnerved

panoply array, attire, dress, garb, get-up (*informal*), insignia, raiment (*archaic or poetic*), regalia, show, trappings, turnout

panorama 1. bird's-eye view, prospect, scenery, scenic view, view, vista **2.** overall picture, overview, perspective, survey

panoramic all-embracing, bird's-eye, comprehensive, extensive, far-reaching, general, inclusive, overall, scenic, sweeping, wide

pant *vb.* **1.** blow, breathe, gasp, heave, huff, palpitate, puff, throb, wheeze **2.** *with* **for** ache, covet, crave, desire, eat one's heart out over, hanker after, hunger, long, pine, set one's heart on, sigh, thirst, want, yearn *~n.* **3.** gasp, huff, puff, wheeze

pants 1. *Brit.* boxer shorts, briefs, drawers, knickers, panties, underpants, Y-fronts (*Trademark*) **2.** *U.S. & Canad.* slacks, trousers

pap 1. baby food, mash, mush, pulp **2.** drivel, rubbish, trash, trivia

paper *n.* **1.** daily, gazette, journal, news, newspaper, organ, rag (*informal*) **2.** *plural* certificate, deed, documents, instrument, record **3.** *plural* archive, diaries, documents, dossier, file, letters, records **4.** analysis, article, assignment, composition, critique, dissertation, essay, examination, monograph, report, script, study, thesis, treatise **5. on paper** ideally, in the abstract, in

paper money *n* banknotes, rather than coins.

paper over *vb* to conceal (something unpleasant or difficult).

paperweight *n* a small heavy object placed on top of loose papers to prevent them from scattering.

paperwork *n* clerical work, such as the writing of reports or letters.

papier-mâché (**pap**-yay **mash**-ay) *n* **1** a hard substance made of layers of paper mixed with paste and moulded when moist. *~adj* **2** made of papier-mâché.

papilla (pap-**pill**-a) *n, pl* **-lae** (-lee) *Biol* a small projection of tissue at the base of a hair, tooth, or feather. **papillary** *adj*

papist *n, adj Usually offensive* same as **Roman Catholic.**

papoose *n* an American Indian baby.

paprika *n* a mild powdered seasoning made from red peppers.

Pap test *or* **smear** *n Med* same as **cervical smear.**

papyrus (pap-**ire**-uss) *n, pl* **-ri** (-rye) *or* **-ruses 1** a tall water plant of Africa. **2** a kind of paper made from the stem of this plant, used by the ancient Egyptians, Greeks, and Romans. **3** an ancient document written on this paper.

par *n* **1** the usual or average condition: *I feel slightly below par most of the time.* **2 on a par with** equal or equivalent to: *an environmental disaster on a par with Chernobyl.* **3** *Golf* a standard score for a hole or course that a good player should make: *she was four under par with two holes to play.* **4** *Finance* the established value of the unit of one national currency in terms of the unit of another. **5** *Commerce* short for **par value. 6 par for the course** to be expected: *random acts of violence were par for the course in the capital.*

par. **1** paragraph. **2** parenthesis.

para *n Informal* **1** a paratrooper. **2** a paragraph.

para- *or before a vowel* **par-** *prefix* **1** beside or near: *parameter.* **2** beyond: *parapsychology.* **3** resembling: *paratyphoid fever.*

parable *n* a short story that uses familiar situations to illustrate a religious or moral point.

parabola (par-**ab**-bol-a) *n Geom* an open plane curve formed by the intersection of a cone by a plane parallel to its side. **parabolic** *adj*

paracetamol *n* a mild pain-relieving drug.

parachute *n* **1** a large fabric canopy connected by a harness, that slows the descent of a person or package from an aircraft. *~vb* **-chuting, -chuted 2** to land or to drop (supplies or troops) by parachute from an aircraft. **parachutist** *n*

parade *n* **1** an ordered march or procession. **2** a public promenade or street of shops. **3** a blatant but sometimes insincere display: *a man who made a parade of liking his own company best.* *~vb* **-rading, -raded 4** to exhibit or flaunt: *he neither paraded nor disguised his devout faith.* **5** to walk or march, esp. in a procession.

parade ground *n* a place where soldiers assemble regularly for inspection or display.

paradigm (**par**-a-dime) *n* a model or example: *his experience is a paradigm for the young artist.*

paradise *n* **1** heaven; where the good go after death. **2** the Garden of Eden. **3** any place or condition that fulfils a person's desires.

paradise duck *n* a New Zealand duck with bright feathers.

paradox *n* **1** a statement that seems self-contradictory but may be true: *it's a strange paradox that a musician must practise improvising to become a good improviser.* **2** a self-contradictory proposition, such as *I always tell lies.* **3** a person or thing that is made up of contradictory elements. **paradoxical** *adj* **paradoxically** *adv*

paraffin *n* **1** a liquid mixture distilled from petroleum or shale and used as a fuel or solvent. **2** *Chem* the former name for **alkane.**

paraffin wax *n* a white waxlike substance distilled from petroleum and used to make candles and as a sealing agent.

paragon *n* a model of perfection: *a paragon of female integrity and determination.*

paragraph *n* **1** section of a piece of writing, usually devoted to one idea, which begins on a new line and is often indented. **2** *Printing* the character ¶, used to indicate the beginning of a new paragraph. *~vb* **3** to put (a piece of writing) into paragraphs.

parakeet *n* a small colourful parrot with a long tail.

parallax *n* an apparent change in an object's position due to a change in the observer's position.

parallel *adj* **1** separated by an equal distance at every point: *parallel lines; a path parallel to the main road.* **2** precisely corresponding: *we decide our salaries by comparison with parallel jobs in other charities.* **3** *Computers* operating on several items of information or instructions at the same time. *~n* **4** *Maths* one of a set of parallel lines or planes. **5** something with similar features to another. **6** a comparison; similarity between two things: *she attempted to excuse herself by drawing a parallel between her behaviour and ours.* **7** Also called: **parallel of latitude** any of the imaginary lines around the earth parallel to the equator, marking

THESAURUS

theory, theoretically *~adj.* **6.** cardboard, disposable, flimsy, insubstantial, paper-thin, papery, thin *~vb.* **7.** cover with paper, hang, line, paste up, wallpaper

papery flimsy, fragile, frail, insubstantial, light, lightweight, paperlike, paper-thin, thin

par *n.* **1.** average, level, mean, median, norm, standard, usual **2. on a par with** equal to, much the same as, the same as **3. par for the course** average, expected, ordinary, predictable, standard, typical, usual

parable allegory, exemplum, fable, lesson, moral tale, story

parade *n.* **1.** array, cavalcade, ceremony, column, march, pageant, procession, review, spectacle, train **2.** array, display, exhibition, flaunting, ostentation, pomp, show, spectacle, vaunting *~vb.* **3.** air, brandish, display, exhibit, flaunt, make a show of, show, show off (*informal*), strut, swagger, vaunt **4.** defile, march, process

paradise **1.** City of God, divine abode, Elysium, heaven, heavenly kingdom, Promised Land, Zion (*Christianity*) **2.** Eden, Garden of Eden **3.** bliss, delight, felicity, heaven, seventh heaven, utopia

paradox absurdity, ambiguity, anomaly, contradiction, enigma, inconsistency, mystery, oddity, puzzle

paradoxical absurd, ambiguous, baffling, confounding, contradictory, enigmatic, equivocal, illogical, impossible, improbable, inconsistent, oracular, puzzling, riddling

paragon apotheosis, archetype, criterion, cynosure, epitome, exemplar, ideal, jewel, masterpiece, model, nonpareil, norm, paradigm, pattern, prototype, quintessence, standard

paragraph clause, item, notice, part, passage, portion, section, subdivision

parallel *adj.* **1.** aligned, alongside, coextensive, equidistant, side by side **2.** akin, analogous, complementary, correspondent, corresponding, like, matching, resembling, similar, uniform *~n.* **3.** analogue, comple-

degrees of latitude. 8 *Printing* the character ||, used as a reference mark. ~*vb* 9 to correspond to: *the increase in smoking is paralleled by a increase in lung cancer.*

parallel bars *pl n Gymnastics* a pair of wooden bars on upright posts used for various exercises.

parallelepiped (par-a-lel-ee-**pipe**-ed) *n Geom* a solid shape whose six faces are parallelograms.

parallelism *n* 1 the state of being parallel. 2 a close likeness.

parallelogram *n Geom* a plane figure whose opposite sides are parallel and equal in length.

paralyse *or US* **-lyze** *vb* **-lysing, -lysed** *or* **-lyzing, -lyzed** 1 *Pathol* to affect with paralysis. 2 to make immobile: *he was paralysed by fear.*

paralysis *n* 1 *Pathol* inability to move all or part of the body due to damage to the nervous system. 2 a state of inactivity: *the economic chaos and political paralysis into which the country has sunk.*

paralytic *adj* 1 of or relating to paralysis. 2 *Brit informal* very drunk. ~*n* 3 a person who is paralysed.

paramecium (par-a-**mee**-see-um) *n, pl* **-cia** (-see-a) a single-celled animal which lives in ponds, puddles, and sewage filters and swims by means of cilia.

paramedic *n* a person, such as a member of an ambulance crew, whose work supplements that of the medical profession. **paramedical** *adj*

parameter (par-**am**-it-er) *n* 1 *Maths* an arbitrary constant that determines the specific form of a mathematical expression, such as *a* and *b* in $y = ax^2 + b$. 2 *Informal* any limiting factor: *exchange rates are allowed to fluctuate only within designated parameters.*

paramilitary *adj* denoting a group of people organized on military lines.

paramount *adj* of the greatest importance.

paramour *n Old-fashioned* an adulterous lover.

paranoia *n* 1 a mental disorder which causes delusions of grandeur or of persecution. 2 *Informal* intense fear or suspicion, usually unfounded. **paranoid** *or* **paranoiac** *adj, n*

paranormal *adj* 1 beyond normal scientific explanation. ~*n* 2 **the paranormal** paranormal happenings or matters generally.

parapet *n* 1 a low wall or railing along the edge of a balcony or roof. 2 *Mil* a mound of sandbags in front of a trench to conceal and protect troops from fire.

paraphernalia *n* various articles or bits of equipment.

paraphrase *n* 1 an expression of a statement or text in other words. ~*vb* **-phrasing, -phrased** 2 to put (a statement or text) into other words.

paraplegia (par-a-**pleej**-ya) *n Pathol* paralysis of the lower half of the body. **paraplegic** *adj, n*

parapsychology *n* the study of mental phenomena such as telepathy.

Paraquat *n Trademark* an extremely poisonous weedkiller.

parasite *n* 1 an animal or plant that lives in or on another from which it obtains nourishment. 2 a person who habitually lives at the expense of others; sponger. **parasitic** *adj*

parasol *n* an umbrella-like sunshade.

paratrooper *n* a member of the paratroops.

paratroops *pl n* troops trained to be dropped by parachute into a battle area.

paratyphoid fever *n* a disease resembling but less severe than typhoid fever.

parboil *vb* to boil (food) until partially cooked.

parcel *n* 1 something wrapped up; a package. 2 a group of people or things sharing something in common: *a parcel of fools.* 3 a distinct portion of land: *he was the recipient of a substantial parcel of land.* ~*vb* **-celling, -celled** *or US* **-celing, -celed** 4 (often foll. by *up*) to wrap (something) up into a parcel. 5 (foll. by *out*) to divide (something) into portions: *the children were parcelled out to relatives.*

parch *vb* 1 to deprive (something) of water; dry up: *the summer sun parched the hills.* 2 to make (someone) very thirsty: *I'm parched. Have we got any lemonade?*

parchment *n* 1 a thick smooth material made from animal skin and used for writing on. 2 a manuscript made of this material. 3 a stiff yellowish paper resembling parchment.

pardon *vb* 1 to forgive or excuse: *I hope you'll par-*

THESAURUS

ment, corollary, counterpart, duplicate, equal, equivalent, likeness, match, twin **4.** analogy, comparison, correlation, correspondence, likeness, parallelism, resemblance, similarity ~*vb.* **5.** agree, be alike, chime with, compare, complement, conform, correlate, correspond, equal, keep pace (with), match

paralyse 1. *Pathol.* cripple, debilitate, disable, incapacitate, lame **2.** anaesthetize, arrest, benumb, freeze, halt, immobilize, numb, petrify, stop dead, stun, stupefy, transfix

paralysis 1. *Pathol.* immobility, palsy **2.** arrest, breakdown, halt, shutdown, stagnation, standstill, stoppage

paralytic *adj.* **1.** crippled, disabled, immobile, immobilized, incapacitated, lame, numb, palsied, paralysed **2.** *Brit. informal* blotto (*slang*), drunk, inebriated, intoxicated, legless (*slang*), pie-eyed (*slang*), pissed (*Brit. taboo slang*), plastered (*slang*), sloshed (*slang, chiefly Brit.*), stewed (*slang*), stoned (*slang*), zonked (*slang*)

parameter *informal* constant, criterion, framework, guideline, limit, limitation, restriction, specification

paramount capital, cardinal, chief, dominant, eminent, first, foremost, main, outstanding, predominant, pre-eminent, primary, prime, principal, superior, supreme

paraphernalia accoutrements, apparatus, appurtenances, baggage, belongings, clobber (*Brit. slang*), effects, equipage, equipment, gear, impedimenta, material, stuff, tackle, things, trappings

paraphrase 1. *n.* interpretation, rehash, rendering, rendition, rephrasing, restatement, rewording, translation, version **2.** *vb.* express in other words *or* one's own words, interpret, rehash, render, rephrase, restate, reword

parasite bloodsucker (*informal*), cadger, drone (*Brit.*), hanger-on, leech, scrounger (*informal*), sponge (*informal*), sponger (*informal*)

parasitic bloodsucking (*informal*), cadging, leechlike, scrounging (*informal*), sponging (*informal*)

parcel *n.* **1.** bundle, carton, pack, package, packet **2.** band, batch, bunch, collection, company, crew, crowd, gang, group, lot, pack **3.** piece of land, plot, property, tract ~*vb.* **4.** *often with* **up** do up, pack, package, tie up, wrap **5.** *with* **out** allocate, allot, apportion, carve up, deal out, dispense, distribute, divide, dole out, mete out, portion, share out, split up

parch blister, burn, dehydrate, desiccate, dry up, evaporate, make thirsty, scorch, sear, shrivel, wither

pardon 1. *vb.* absolve, acquit, amnesty, condone, exculpate, excuse, exonerate, forgive, let off (*informal*), overlook, remit, reprieve **2.** *n.* absolution, acquittal, allowance, amnesty, condonation, discharge, excuse,

don the wait. ~*n* **2** forgiveness. **3** official release from punishment for a crime. ~*interj* **4** Also: **pardon me, I beg your pardon a** sorry; excuse me. **b** what did you say? **pardonable** *adj*

pare *vb* **paring, pared 1** to peel (the outer layer) from (something): *thinly pare the rind from the grapefruit.* **2** to trim or cut the edge of. **3** to decrease bit by bit: *the government is prepared to pare down the armed forces.*

parent *n* **1** a father or mother. **2** a person acting as a father or mother; guardian. **3** a plant or animal that has produced one or more plants or animals. **parental** *adj* **parenthood** *n*

parentage *n* ancestry or family.

parent company *n* a company that owns a number of smaller companies.

parenthesis (par-**en**-thiss-iss) *n, pl* **-ses** (-seez) **1** a word or phrase inserted into a passage, and marked off by brackets or dashes. **2** Also called: **bracket** either of a pair of characters ( ), used to enclose such a phrase. **parenthetical** *adj* **parenthetically** *adv*

parenting *n* the activity of bringing up children.

parent-teacher association *n* an organization consisting of the parents and teachers of school pupils formed in order to discuss the children's progress.

par excellence *adv* beyond comparison: *this book justifies its claim to be a reference work par excellence.*

parfait (par-**fay**) *n* a dessert consisting of layers of ice cream, fruit, and sauce, topped with whipped cream, and served in a tall glass.

pariah (par-**rye**-a) *n* a social outcast.

parietal (par-**rye**-it-al) *adj Anat, biol* of or forming the walls of a body cavity: *the parietal bones of the skull.*

paring *n* something that has been cut off something.

parish *n* **1** an area that has its own church and clergyman. **2** the people who live in a parish. **3** (in England and, formerly, Wales) the smallest unit of local government.

parish clerk *n* a person who assists in various church duties.

parish council *n* (in England and, formerly, Wales) the administrative body of a parish. See **parish** (sense 3).

parishioner *n* a person who lives in a particular parish.

parish register *n* a book in which the births, baptisms, marriages, and deaths in a parish are recorded.

parity *n* **1** equality, for example of rank or pay. **2** close or exact equivalence: *the company maintained parity with the competition.* **3** *Finance* equivalence between the units of currency of two countries.

park *n* **1** a large area of open land for recreational use by the public. **2** a piece of open land for public recreation in a town. **3** a large area of private land surrounding a country house. **4** an area designed to accommodate a number of related enterprises: *a science park.* **5** *US & Canad* a playing field or sports stadium. **6 the park** *Brit informal* the pitch in soccer. ~*vb* **7** to stop and leave (a vehicle) temporarily: *I parked between the two cars already outside; police vans were parked on every street corner.* **8** *Informal* to leave or put (someone or something) somewhere: *she parked herself on the sofa and stayed there all evening.* **parking** *n*

parka *n* a long jacket with a quilted lining and a fur-trimmed hood.

parkin *n Brit* a moist spicy ginger cake usually containing oatmeal.

parking meter *n* a coin-operated device beside a parking space that indicates how long a vehicle may be left parked.

parking ticket *n* the notice of a fine served on a motorist for a parking offence.

Parkinson's disease *or* **Parkinsonism** *n* a progressive disorder of the central nervous system which causes tremor, rigidity, and impaired muscular coordination.

Parkinson's law *n* the notion that work expands to fill the time available for its completion.

parkland *n* grassland with scattered trees.

parky *adj* **parkier, parkiest** *Brit informal* (of the weather) chilly.

parlance *n* the manner of speaking associated with a particular group or subject: *he had, in Marxist parlance, a "petit bourgeois" mentality.*

parley *Old-fashioned* ~*n* **1** a discussion between members of opposing sides to decide terms of agreement. ~*vb* **2** to have a parley.

parliament *n* a law-making assembly of a country.

Parliament *n* **1** the highest law-making authority in Britain, consisting of the House of Commons, the House of Lords, and the sovereign. **2** the equivalent law-making authority in another country.

parliamentarian *n* an expert in parliamentary procedures.

parliamentary *adj* **1** of or from a parliament: *parliamentary elections.* **2** conforming to the procedures of a parliament: *parliamentary language.*

parlour *or US* **parlor** *n* **1** *Old-fashioned* a living

THESAURUS

exoneration, forgiveness, grace, indulgence, mercy, release, remission, reprieve

pardonable allowable, condonable, excusable, forgivable, minor, not serious, permissible, understandable, venial

parent begetter, father, guardian, mother, procreator, progenitor, sire

parentage ancestry, birth, derivation, descent, extraction, family, line, lineage, origin, paternity, pedigree, race, stirps, stock

pariah exile, leper, outcast, outlaw, undesirable, unperson, untouchable

parish church, churchgoers, community, congregation, flock, fold, parishioners

parity 1. consistency, equality, equal terms, equivalence, par, parallelism, quits (*informal*), uniformity, unity **2.** affinity, agreement, analogy, conformity, congruity, correspondence, likeness, resemblance, sameness, similarity, similitude

park 1. *n.* estate, garden, grounds, parkland, pleasure garden, recreation ground, woodland **2.** *vb.* leave, manoeuvre, position, station

parley *old-fashioned* **1.** *n.* colloquy, confab (*informal*), conference, congress, council, dialogue, discussion, meeting, palaver, powwow, seminar, talk(s) **2.** *vb.* confabulate, confer, deliberate, discuss, negotiate, palaver, powwow, speak, talk

parliament assembly, congress, convocation, council, diet, legislature, senate, talking shop (*informal*)

Parliament Houses of Parliament, Mother of Parliaments, the House, the House of Commons and the House of Lords, Westminster

parliamentary congressional, deliberative, governmental, lawgiving, lawmaking, legislative

parlour *or U.S.* **parlor** *old-fashioned* best room, drawing room, front room, lounge, reception room, sitting room

room for receiving visitors. **2** a room or shop equipped as a place of business: *an ice-cream parlour.*

parlous *adj Archaic or humorous* dangerously bad; dire: *the parlous state of the economy.*

Parmesan (**par**-miz-zan) *n* a hard strong-flavoured cheese used grated on pasta dishes and soups.

parochial *adj* **1** narrow in outlook; provincial. **2** of or relating to a parish. **parochialism** *n*

parody *n, pl* **-dies 1** a piece of music or literature that mimics the style of another composer or author in a humorous way. **2** something done so badly that it seems like an intentional mockery. *~vb* **-dies, -dying, -died 3** to make a parody of. **parodist** *n*

parole *n* **1** the freeing of a prisoner before his or her sentence has run out, on condition that he or she behaves well. **2** a promise given by a prisoner to behave well if granted liberty or partial liberty. **3 on parole** conditionally released from prison. *~vb* **-roling, -roled 4** to place (a person) on parole.

parotid gland *n Anat* either of a pair of salivary glands in front of and below the ears.

paroxysm *n* **1** an uncontrollable outburst of emotion: *a paroxysm of grief.* **2** *Pathol* **a** a sudden attack or recurrence of a disease. **b** a fit or convulsion. **paroxysmal** *adj*

parquet (**par**-kay) *n* **1** a floor covering made of blocks of wood. *~vb* **2** to cover (a floor) with parquetry.

parquetry (**par**-kit-tree) *n* pieces of wood arranged in a geometric pattern, used to cover floors.

parr *n* a salmon up to two years of age.

parricide *n* **1** a person who kills one of his or her parents. **2** the act of killing either of one's parents. **parricidal** *adj*

parrot *n* **1** a tropical bird with a short hooked beak, bright plumage, and an ability to mimic human speech. **2** a person who repeats or imitates someone else's words. **3 sick as a parrot** *Usually facetious* extremely disappointed. *~vb* **-roting, -roted 4** to repeat or imitate (someone else's words) without understanding them.

parrot fever *n* same as **psittacosis.**

parry *vb* **-ries, -rying, -ried 1** to ward off (an attack). **2** to avoid answering (questions) in a clever way. *~n, pl* **-ries 3** an instance of parrying. **4** a skilful evasion of a question.

parse (**parz**) *vb* **parsing, parsed** to analyse (a sentence or the words in a sentence) grammatically.

parsec *n* a unit of astronomical distance equivalent to 3.0857×10^{16} metres or 3.262 light years.

parsimony *n Formal* extreme caution in spending. **parsimonious** *adj*

parsley *n* a herb with curled pleasant-smelling leaves, used for seasoning and decorating food.

parsnip *n* a long tapering cream-coloured root vegetable.

parson *n* **1** a parish priest in the Church of England. **2** any clergyman.

parsonage *n* the residence of a parson, provided by the parish.

parson's nose *n* the rump of a fowl when cooked.

part *n* **1** a piece or portion. **2** one of several equal divisions: *a salad dressing made with two parts oil to one part vinegar.* **3** an actor's role in a play. **4** a person's duty: *his ancestors had done their part nobly and well at Bannockburn.* **5** an involvement in or contribution to something: *he was jailed for his part in the fraud.* **6** a region or area: *he's well known in these parts; the weather in this part of the country is extreme.* **7** *Anat* an area of the body. **8** a component that can be replaced in a vehicle or machine. **9** *US & Canad* same as **parting** (sense 2). **10** *Music* a melodic line assigned to one or more instrumentalists or singers. **11 for my part** as far as I am concerned. **12 for the most part** generally. **13 in part** to some degree; partly. **14 on the part of** on behalf of. **15 part and parcel of** an essential ingredient of. **16 play a part a** to pretend to be what one is not. **b** (foll. by *in*) to have something to do with: *examinations play a large part in education and in schools.* **17 take part in** to participate in. **18 take someone's part** to support someone, for example in an argument. **19 take something in good part** to respond to (teasing or criticism) with good humour. *~vb* **20** to divide or separate from one another: *her lips parted in laughter; the cord parted with a pop.* **21** to go away from one another: *we parted with handshakes all round.* **22 part with** to give up: *check carefully before you part with your cash.* **23 part from** to cause (someone) to give up: *I was astonished at the way Henry parted his audience*

THESAURUS

parlous *archaic or humorous* chancy (*informal*), dangerous, desperate, difficult, dire, hairy (*slang*), hazardous, perilous, risky

parochial insular, inward-looking, limited, narrow, narrow-minded, parish-pump, petty, provincial, restricted, small-minded

parody *n.* **1.** burlesque, caricature, imitation, lampoon, satire, send-up (*Brit. informal*), skit, spoof (*informal*), takeoff (*informal*) **2.** apology, caricature, farce, mockery, travesty *~vb.* **3.** burlesque, caricature, do a takeoff of (*informal*), lampoon, mimic, poke fun at, satirize, send up (*Brit. informal*), take off (*informal*), take the piss out of (*taboo slang*), travesty

paroxysm attack, convulsion, eruption, fit, flare-up (*informal*), outburst, seizure, spasm

parrot 1. *n.* copycat (*informal*), imitator, (little) echo, mimic **2.** *vb.* copy, echo, imitate, mimic, reiterate, repeat

parry 1. block, deflect, fend off, hold at bay, rebuff, repel, repulse, stave off, ward off **2.** avoid, circumvent, dodge, duck (*informal*), evade, fence, fight shy of, shun, sidestep

parsimonious cheeseparing, frugal, grasping, mean, mingy (*Brit. informal*), miserable, miserly, near (*informal*), niggardly, penny-pinching (*informal*), penurious, saving, scrimpy, sparing, stingy, stinting, tight-fisted

parsimony *formal* frugality, meanness, minginess (*Brit. informal*), miserliness, nearness (*informal*), niggardliness, penny-pinching (*informal*), stinginess, tightness

parson churchman, clergyman, cleric, divine, ecclesiastic, incumbent, man of God, man of the cloth, minister, pastor, preacher, priest, rector, reverend (*informal*), vicar

part *n.* **1.** bit, fraction, fragment, lot, particle, piece, portion, scrap, section, sector, segment, share, slice **2.** character, lines, role **3.** bit, business, capacity, charge, duty, function, involvement, office, place, responsibility, role, say, share, task, work **4.** area, district, neck of the woods (*informal*), neighbourhood, quarter, region, territory, vicinity **5.** limb, member, organ **6.** component, constituent **7. for the most part** chiefly, generally, in the main, largely, mainly, mostly, on the whole, principally **8. in part** a little, in some measure, partially, partly, slightly, somewhat, to a certain extent, to some degree **9. on the part of** for the sake of, in support of, in the name of, on behalf of **10. take part in** associate oneself with, be instrumental in, be involved in, have a hand in, join in, partake in, participate in,

from their money. **24** to split: *the path parts here.* **25** to arrange (the hair) in such a way that a line of scalp is left showing. ~*adv* **26** to some extent; partly: *this book is part history, part travelogue.* ~See also **parts.**

partake *vb* **-taking, -took, -taken 1 partake of** to take (food or drink). **2 partake in** to take part in.

parterre *n* **1** a formally patterned flower garden. **2** the pit of a theatre.

Parthian shot *n* a hostile remark or gesture delivered while departing.

partial *adj* **1** relating to only a part; not complete: *partial deafness.* **2** biased: *religious programmes can be as partial as they like.* **3 partial to** having a particular liking for. **partiality** *n* **partially** *adv*

participate *vb* **-pating, -pated participate in** to become actively involved in. **participant** *n* **participation** *n* **participatory** *adj*

participle *n Grammar* a form of a verb that is used in compound tenses or as an adjective. See also **present participle, past participle. participial** *adj*

particle *n* **1** an extremely small piece or amount: *clean thoroughly to remove all particles of dirt.* **2** *Grammar* an uninflected part of speech, such as an interjection or preposition. **3** *Physics* a minute piece of matter, such as an electron or proton.

parti-coloured *or US* **particolored** *adj* having different colours in different parts.

particular *adj* **1** of, belonging to, or being one person or thing; specific: *the particular type of tuition on offer.* **2** exceptional or special: *the report voices particular concern over the state of the country's manufacturing industry.* **3** providing specific details or circumstances: *a particular account.* **4** difficult to please; fussy. ~*n* **5** a separate distinct item as opposed to a generalization: *moving from the general to the particular.* **6** an item of information; detail: *she refused to go into particulars.* **7 in particular** especially or exactly: *three painters in particular were responsible for these developments.* **particularly** *adv*

particularity *n, pl* **-ties 1** great attentiveness to detail. **2** the state of being particular as opposed to general; individuality.

particularize *or* **-ise** *vb* **-izing, -ized** *or* **-ising, -ised** to give details about (something). **particularization** *or* **-isation** *n*

parting *n* **1** a departure or leave-taking. **2** *Brit* the line of scalp showing when sections of hair are combed in opposite directions. **3** the act of dividing (something): *the parting of the Red Sea.*

partisan *n* **1** a person who supports a particular cause or party. **2** a member of an armed resistance group within occupied territory. ~*adj* **3** prejudiced or one-sided. **partisanship** *n*

partition *n* **1** a large screen or thin wall that divides a room. **2** the division of a country into two or more independent countries. ~*vb* **3** to separate (a room) into sections: *the shower is partitioned off from the rest of the bathroom.* **4** to divide (a country) into separate self-governing parts: *the subcontinent was partitioned into India and Pakistan.*

partitive *Grammar* ~*adj* **1** (of a noun) referring to part of something. The phrase *some of the butter* is a partitive construction. ~*n* **2** a partitive word, such as *some* or *any.*

partly *adv* not completely.

partner *n* **1** either member of a couple in a relationship. **2** a member of a business partnership. **3** one of a pair of dancers or of players on the same side in a game: *her bridge partner.* **4** an ally or companion: *the country's main European trading partner.* ~*vb* **5** to be the partner of (someone).

THESAURUS

play a part in, put one's twopence-worth in, take a hand in ~*vb.* **11.** break, cleave, come apart, detach, disconnect, disjoin, dismantle, disunite, divide, rend, separate, sever, split, tear **12.** break up, depart, go, go away, go (their) separate ways, leave, part company, quit, say goodbye, separate, split up, take one's leave, withdraw **13. part with** abandon, discard, forgo, give up, let go of, relinquish, renounce, sacrifice, surrender, yield

partake 1. partake of consume, eat, receive, share, take **2. partake in** engage, enter into, participate, share, take part

partial 1. fragmentary, imperfect, incomplete, limited, uncompleted, unfinished **2.** biased, discriminatory, influenced, interested, one-sided, partisan, predisposed, prejudiced, tendentious, unfair, unjust **3. partial to** fond of, having a liking (soft spot, weakness) for, keen on, taken with

partiality 1. bias, favouritism, partisanship, predisposition, preference, prejudice **2.** affinity, cup of tea (*informal*), fondness, inclination, liking, love, penchant, predilection, predisposition, preference, proclivity, taste, weakness

partially fractionally, halfway, incompletely, in part, moderately, not wholly, partly, piecemeal, somewhat, to a certain extent *or* degree

participant associate, contributor, member, partaker, participator, party, shareholder

participate be a participant, be a party to, engage in, enter into, get in on the act, have a hand in, join in, partake, perform, share, take part

participation assistance, contribution, involvement, joining in, partaking, partnership, sharing in, taking part

particle atom, bit, crumb, grain, iota, jot, mite, molecule, mote, piece, scrap, shred, speck, tittle, whit

particular *adj.* **1.** distinct, exact, express, peculiar, precise, specific **2.** especial, exceptional, marked, notable, noteworthy, remarkable, singular, special, uncommon, unusual **3.** blow-by-blow, circumstantial, detailed, itemized, minute, painstaking, precise, selective, thorough **4.** choosy (*informal*), critical, dainty, demanding, discriminating, exacting, fastidious, finicky, fussy, meticulous, pernickety (*informal*), picky (*informal*) ~*n.* **5.** circumstance, detail, fact, feature, item, specification **6. in particular** distinctly, especially, exactly, expressly, particularly, specifically

particularly 1. distinctly, especially, explicitly, expressly, in particular, specifically **2.** decidedly, especially, exceptionally, markedly, notably, outstandingly, peculiarly, singularly, surprisingly, uncommonly, unusually

parting 1. adieu, departure, farewell, going, goodbye, leave-taking, valediction **2.** breaking, detachment, divergence, division, partition, rift, rupture, separation, split

partisan *n.* **1.** adherent, backer, champion, devotee, disciple, follower, stalwart, supporter, upholder, votary **2.** guerrilla, irregular, resistance fighter, underground fighter ~*adj.* **3.** biased, factional, interested, one-sided, partial, prejudiced, sectarian, tendentious

partition *n.* **1.** barrier, divider, room divider, screen, wall **2.** dividing, division, segregation, separation, severance, splitting ~*vb.* **3.** divide, portion, section, segment, separate, split up, subdivide

partly halfway, incompletely, in part, in some measure, not fully, partially, relatively, slightly, somewhat, to a certain degree *or* extent, up to a certain point

partner 1. bedfellow, consort, helpmate, husband,

partnership *n* **1** a relationship in which two or more people or organizations work together in a business venture. **2** the condition of being a partner.

part of speech *n Grammar* a class of words, such as a noun, verb, or adjective, sharing important syntactic or semantic features.

partook *vb* the past tense of **partake**.

partridge *n, pl* **-tridges** *or* **-tridge** a game bird with an orange-brown head, greyish neck, and a short rust-coloured tail.

parts *pl n Literary* abilities or talents: *a man of many parts.*

part song *n* a song composed in harmonized parts.

part-time *adj* **1** for less than the normal full working time: *a part-time job.* ~*adv* **part time 2** on a part-time basis: *he works part time.* **part-timer** *n*

parturient *adj Formal* giving birth.

parturition *n* the process of giving birth.

party *n, pl* **-ties 1** a social gathering for pleasure. **2** a group of people involved in the same activity: *a search party.* **3** a group of people sharing a common political aim. **4** the person or people who take part in or are involved in something, esp. a legal action or dispute: *a judge in a wig and gown who will decide who the guilty party is.* **5** *Informal, humorous* a person: *he's an odd old party.* ~*vb* **-ties, -tying, -tied 6** *Informal* to celebrate; have a good time.

party line *n* **1** the policies of a political party. **2** a telephone line shared by two or more subscribers.

party wall *n Property law* a common wall separating two properties.

par value *n* the value printed on a share certificate or bond at the time of its issue.

parvenu *or fem* **parvenue** (**par**-ven-new) *n* a person newly risen to a position of power or wealth who is considered to lack culture or education.

pascal *n* the SI unit of pressure; the pressure exerted on an area of 1 square metre by a force of 1 newton.

Pascal *n* a high-level computer programming language developed as a teaching language.

paschal (**pask**-l) *adj* **1** of or relating to the Passover. **2** of or relating to Easter.

pas de deux (pah de **duh**) *n, pl* **pas de deux** *Ballet* a dance for two people.

pasha *n* (formerly) a high official of the Ottoman Empire: placed after a name when used as a title.

paso doble (**pass**-so **dobe**-lay) *n* **1** a modern ballroom dance in fast duple time. **2** music for this dance.

pas op (**pass** op) *interj S African* beware.

pasqueflower *n* a small purple-flowered plant of Europe and Asia.

pass *vb* **1** to go by or past (a person or thing). **2** to continue or extend in a particular direction: *the road to Camerino passes through some fine scenery.* **3** to go through or cause (something) to go through (an obstacle or barrier): *the bullet passed through his head.* **4** to be successful in (a test or examination). **5** to spend (time) or (of time) go by: *the time passed surprisingly quickly.* **6** to hand over or be handed over: *she passed me her glass.* **7** to be inherited by: *his mother's small estate had passed to him after her death.* **8** *Sport* to hit, kick, or throw (the ball) to another player. **9** (of a law-making body) to agree to (a law or proposal): *the bill was passed by parliament last week.* **10** to pronounce (judgment): *the court is expected to pass sentence later today.* **11** to move onwards or over: *a flicker of amusement passed over his face.* **12** to exceed: *Australia's population has just passed the seventeen million mark.* **13** to go without comment: *the insult passed unnoticed.* **14** to choose not to answer a question or not to make a bid or a play in card games. **15** to discharge (urine etc.) from the body. **16** to come to an end or disappear: *the madness will soon pass.* **17** (foll. by *for* or *as*) to be likely to be mistaken for (someone or something else): *the few sunny days that pass for summer in this country.* **18** *Old-fashioned* to take place: *what passed at the meeting?* **19 pass away** *or* **on** *Euphemistic* to die. ~*n* **20** a successful result in an examination or test. **21** *Sport* the transfer of a ball from one player to another. **22** a route through a range of mountains where there is a gap between peaks. **23** a permit or licence. **24** *Mil* a document authorizing leave of absence. **25** *Bridge etc* an instance of choosing not to answer a question or not to make a bid or a play in card games. **26 make a pass at** *Informal* to try to persuade (someone) to have sex: *he made a pass at his secretary.* **27 a pretty pass** a bad state of affairs. ~See also **pass off, pass out,** etc.

pass. passive.

passable *adj* **1** adequate or acceptable: *passable if*

THESAURUS

mate, spouse, wife **2.** accomplice, ally, associate, bedfellow, collaborator, colleague, companion, comrade, confederate, copartner, helper, mate, participant, team-mate

partnership 1. alliance, association, combine, company, conglomerate, cooperative, corporation, firm, house, society, union **2.** companionship, connection, cooperation, copartnership, fellowship, interest, participation, sharing

parts *literary* ability, accomplishments, attributes, calibre, capabilities, endowments, faculties, genius, gifts, intellect, intelligence, talents

party 1. at-home, bash (*informal*), beano (*Brit. old-fashioned, slang*), celebration, do (*informal*), festivity, function, gathering, get-together (*informal*), knees-up (*informal*), rave (*Brit. slang*), reception, shindig (*informal*), social, social gathering, soirée **2.** band, body, bunch (*informal*), company, crew, detachment (*Military*), gang, gathering, group, squad, team, unit **3.** alliance, association, cabal, camp, clique, coalition, combination, confederacy, coterie, faction, grouping, league, schism, set, side **4.** contractor (*Law*), defendant, litigant, participant, plaintiff **5.** *informal, humorous* individual, person, somebody, someone

pass *vb.* **1.** depart, elapse, flow, go, go by *or* past, lapse, leave, move, move onwards, proceed, roll, run **2.** answer, come up to scratch (*informal*), do, get through, graduate, pass muster, qualify, succeed, suffice, suit **3.** beguile, devote, employ, experience, fill, occupy, spend, suffer, undergo, while away **4.** convey, deliver, exchange, give, hand, kick, let have, reach, send, throw, transfer, transmit **5.** accept, adopt, approve, authorize, decree, enact, establish, legislate, ordain, ratify, sanction, validate **6.** declare, deliver, express, pronounce, utter **7.** beat, exceed, excel, go beyond, outdistance, outdo, outstrip, surmount, surpass, transcend **8.** disregard, ignore, miss, neglect, not heed, omit, overlook, skip (*informal*) **9.** crap (*taboo slang*), defecate, discharge, eliminate, empty, evacuate, excrete, expel, shit (*taboo slang*), void **10.** blow over, cease, die, disappear, dissolve, dwindle, ebb, end, evaporate, expire, fade, go, melt away, terminate, vanish, wane **11.** *with* **for** *or* **as** be accepted as, be mistaken for, be regarded as, be taken for, impersonate, serve as **12.** *old-fashioned* befall, come up, develop, fall out, happen, occur, take place **13. pass away** *or* **on** *euphemistic* croak (*slang*), decease, depart (this life), die, expire, kick the bucket (*slang*), pass on, pass over, peg out (*informal*), snuff it (*informal*) ~*n.* **14.** canyon, col, defile, gap, gorge, ravine **15.** authoriza-

hardly faultless German. **2** (of a road, path, etc.) capable of being travelled along: *most main roads are passable with care despite the snow.* **passably** *adv*

passage *n* **1** a channel or opening providing a way through. **2** a hall or corridor. **3** a section of a written work, speech, or piece of music. **4** a journey by ship. **5** the act of passing from one place or condition to another: *Ireland faced a tough passage to qualify for the World Cup finals.* **6** the right or freedom to pass: *the aid convoys were guaranteed safe passage through rebel-held areas.* **7** the establishing of a law by a law-making body.

passageway *n* corridor or passage.

passbook *n* **1** a book issued by a bank or building society for recording deposits and withdrawals. **2** *S African* an official identity document.

passé (**pas**-say) *adj* out-of-date: *smoking is a bit passé these days.*

passenger *n* **1** a person travelling in a vehicle driven by someone else. **2** *Chiefly Brit* a member of a team who does not take an equal share of the work: *you'll have to pull your weight – we can't afford passengers.*

passer-by *n, pl* **passers-by** a person who is walking past someone or something.

passerine *adj* **1** belonging to an order of perching birds that includes the larks, finches, and starlings. ~*n* **2** any bird of this order.

passim *adv* throughout: used to indicate that what is referred to occurs frequently in a particular piece of writing.

passing *adj* **1** momentary or short-lived: *a passing fad.* **2** casual or superficial: *a passing resemblance.* ~*n* **3** *Euphemistic* death. **4** the ending of something: *the passing of the old order in Eastern Europe.* **5 in passing** briefly and without going into detail; incidentally: *this fact is only noted in passing.*

passion *n* **1** intense sexual love. **2** any strongly felt emotion. **3** a strong enthusiasm for something: *a passion for football.* **4** the object of an intense desire or enthusiasm: *flying is his abiding passion.* **passionless** *adj*

Passion *n* the sufferings of Christ from the Last Supper to his death on the cross.

passionate *adj* **1** showing intense sexual desire. **2** capable of or revealing intense emotion: *a passionate speech.* **passionately** *adv*

passionflower *n* a tropical plant with brightly coloured showy flowers.

passion fruit *n* the edible egg-shaped fruit of the passionflower.

Passion play *n* a play about the Passion of Christ.

passive *adj* **1** not taking an active part. **2** submissive and receptive to outside forces. **3** *Grammar* denoting a form of verbs used to indicate that the subject is the recipient of the action, as *was broken* in *The glass was broken by a boy.* **4** *Chem* (of a substance) chemically unreactive. ~*n* **5** *Grammar* the passive form of a verb. **passively** *adv* **passivity** *n*

passive resistance *n* resistance to a government or the law by nonviolent acts such as fasting, peaceful demonstrations, or refusing to cooperate.

passive smoking *n* the unwilling inhalation of smoke from other people's cigarettes by a nonsmoker.

passkey *n* **1** a private key. **2** same as **master key** or **skeleton key.**

pass law *n* (in South Africa) a law restricting the movement of Black Africans.

pass off *vb* **1** to present (something or oneself) under false pretences: *women who passed themselves off effectively as men.* **2** to come to a gradual end: *the effects of the gas passed off relatively peacefully.* **3** to take place: *the main demonstration passed off peacefully.*

pass out *vb* **1** *Informal* to become unconscious; faint. **2** *Brit* (of an officer cadet) to qualify for a military commission.

pass over *vb* **1** to take no notice of; disregard: *she claims she had been passed over for promotion because she is a woman.* **2** to ignore or not discuss: *this disaster can not be passed over lightly.*

Passover *n* an eight-day Jewish festival commemorating the sparing of the Israelites in Egypt.

passport *n* **1** an official document issued by a government, which identifies the holder and grants him or her permission to travel abroad. **2** an asset that gains a

THESAURUS

tion, identification, identity card, licence, passport, permission, permit, safe-conduct, ticket, warrant

passable 1. acceptable, adequate, admissible, allowable, all right, average, fair, fair enough, mediocre, middling, moderate, not too bad, ordinary, presentable, so-so (*informal*), tolerable, unexceptional **2.** clear, crossable, navigable, open, traversable, unobstructed

passage 1. alley, avenue, channel, course, lane, opening, path, road, route, thoroughfare, way **2.** corridor, doorway, entrance, entrance hall, exit, hall, hallway, lobby, passageway, vestibule **3.** clause, excerpt, extract, paragraph, piece, quotation, reading, section, sentence, text, verse **4.** crossing, journey, tour, trek, trip, voyage **5.** advance, change, conversion, flow, motion, movement, passing, progress, progression, transit, transition **6.** allowance, authorization, freedom, permission, right, safe-conduct, visa, warrant **7.** acceptance, enactment, establishment, legalization, legislation, passing, ratification

passenger fare, hitchhiker, pillion rider, rider, traveller

passer-by bystander, onlooker, witness

passing *adj.* **1.** brief, ephemeral, fleeting, momentary, short, short-lived, temporary, transient, transitory **2.** casual, cursory, glancing, hasty, quick, shallow, short, slight, superficial ~*n.* **3.** *euphemistic* death, decease, demise, end, finish, loss, termination **4. in passing** accidentally, by the bye, by the way, en passant, incidentally, on the way

passion 1. adoration, affection, ardour, attachment, concupiscence, desire, fondness, infatuation, itch, keenness, love, lust, the hots (*slang*) **2.** animation, ardour, eagerness, emotion, excitement, feeling, fervour, fire, heat, intensity, joy, rapture, spirit, transport, warmth, zeal, zest **3.** bug (*informal*), craving, craze, enthusiasm, fancy, fascination, idol, infatuation, mania, obsession

passionate 1. amorous, ardent, aroused, desirous, erotic, hot, loving, lustful, sensual, sexy (*informal*), steamy (*informal*), wanton **2.** animated, ardent, eager, emotional, enthusiastic, excited, fervent, fervid, fierce, flaming, frenzied, heartfelt, impassioned, impetuous, impulsive, intense, strong, vehement, warm, wild, zealous

passive acquiescent, compliant, docile, enduring, inactive, inert, lifeless, long-suffering, nonviolent, patient, quiescent, receptive, resigned, submissive, unassertive, uninvolved, unresisting

pass off 1. counterfeit, fake, feign, make a pretence of, palm off **2.** come to an end, die away, disappear, fade out, vanish **3.** be completed, go off, happen, occur, take place, turn out

pass out *informal* become unconscious, black out (*informal*), drop, faint, flake out (*informal*), keel over (*informal*), lose consciousness, swoon (*literary*)

person admission or acceptance: *good qualifications are no automatic passport to a job.*

pass up *vb Informal* to let (something) go by; disregard: *am I passing up my one chance to be really happy?*

password *n* a secret word or phrase that ensures admission by proving identity or membership.

past *adj* **1** of the time before the present: *the average temperature has increased in the fairly recent past.* **2** no longer in existence: *past happiness.* **3** immediately previous: *the past year.* **4** former: *a past president.* **5** *Grammar* indicating a tense of verbs used to describe actions that have been begun or completed at the time of speaking. ~*n* **6 the past** the period of time before the present: *a familiar face from the past.* **7** the history of a person or nation. **8** an earlier disreputable period of someone's life: *a woman with a bit of a past.* **9** *Grammar* **a** the past tense. **b** a verb in the past tense. ~*adv* **10** at a time before the present; ago: *three years past.* ~*prep* **11** beyond in time: *it's past midnight.* **12** beyond in place: *a procession of mourners filed past the coffin.* **13** beyond the limit of: *riches past his wildest dreams.* **14 not put it past someone** to consider someone capable of (a particular action): *I wouldn't put it past him to double-cross us.* **15 past it** *Informal* unable to do the things one could do when younger.

pasta *n* a type of food, such as spaghetti, that is made from a dough of flour and water and formed into different shapes.

paste *n* **1** a soft moist mixture, such as toothpaste. **2** an adhesive made from water and flour or starch, for use with paper. **3** a smooth creamy preparation of fish, meat, or vegetables for spreading on bread: *sausage paste.* **4** dough for making pastry. **5** a hard shiny glass used to make imitation gems. ~*vb* **pasting, pasted 6** to attach by paste: *she bought a scrapbook and carefully pasted in it all her clippings.* **7** *Slang* to beat or defeat (someone).

pasteboard *n* a stiff board made by pasting layers of paper together.

pastel *n* **1 a** a crayon made of ground pigment bound with gum. **b** a picture drawn with such crayons. **2** a pale delicate colour. ~*adj* **3** (of a colour) pale and delicate: *pastel pink.*

pastern *n* the part of a horse's foot between the fetlock and the hoof.

paste-up *n Printing* a sheet of paper or board with artwork and proofs pasted on it, which is photographed prior to making a plate.

pasteurize *or* **-ise** *vb* **-izing, -ized** *or* **-ising, -ised** to destroy bacteria (in beverages or solid foods) by a special heating process. **pasteurization** *or* **-isation** *n*

pastiche (past-**eesh**) *n* a work of art that mixes styles or copies the style of another artist.

pastille *n* a small fruit-flavoured and sometimes medicated sweet.

pastime *n* an activity which makes time pass pleasantly.

pasting *n* **1** *Slang* a thrashing or heavy defeat. **2** *Informal* strong criticism.

past master *n* a person with a talent for or experience in a particular activity: *he was a past-master at manipulating the media for his own ends.*

pastor *n* a clergyman in charge of a congregation.

pastoral *adj* **1** of or depicting country life or scenery. **2** (of land) used for pasture. **3** of or relating to a clergyman or his duties. **4** of or relating to shepherds or their work. ~*n* **5** a literary work, picture, or piece of music portraying country life. **6** a letter from a bishop to the clergy or people of his diocese.

pastorale (past-or-**ahl**) *n, pl* **-rales** a musical composition that suggests country life.

pastoralism *n* a system of agriculture in dry grassland regions based on raising stock such as cattle, sheep, or goats. **pastoralist** *n*

past participle *n Grammar* a form of verb used to form compound past tenses and passive forms of the verb and to modify nouns: *spoken is the past participle of spoke.*

pastrami *n* highly seasoned smoked beef.

pastry *n* **1** a dough of flour, water, and fat. **2** (*pl* **-tries**) an individual cake or pie. **3** baked foods, such as tarts, made with this dough.

pasturage *n* **1** the business of grazing cattle. **2** same as **pasture.**

pasture *n* **1** land covered with grass, suitable for grazing by farm animals. **2** the grass growing on this land.

pasty[1] (**pay**-stee) *adj* **pastier, pastiest** (of the complexion) pale and unhealthy-looking.

pasty[2] (**past**-ee) *n, pl* **pasties** a round of pastry folded over a filling of meat and vegetables.

pat[1] *vb* **patting, patted 1** to tap (someone or something) lightly with the hand. **2** to shape (something) with a flat instrument or the palm of the hand. **3 pat someone on the back** *Informal* to congratulate someone. ~*n* **4** a gentle tap or stroke. **5** a small shaped lump of something soft, such as butter. **6 pat on the back** *Informal* an indication of approval.

pat[2] *adv* **1** Also: **off pat** thoroughly learned: *he had all his answers off pat.* **2 stand pat** *Chiefly US & Canad* to stick firmly to a belief or decision. ~*adj* **3** quick, ready, or glib: *a pat generalization.*

patch *n* **1** a piece of material used to cover a hole in a

THESAURUS

pass over discount, disregard, forget, ignore, not dwell on, omit, overlook, pass by, take no notice of

pass up *informal* abstain, decline, forgo, give (something) a miss (*informal*), ignore, let go, let slip, miss, neglect, refuse, reject

password countersign, key word, open sesame, signal, watchword

past *adj.* **1.** ancient, bygone, early, erstwhile, foregoing, former, late, long-ago, olden, preceding, previous, prior, quondam, recent **2.** accomplished, completed, done, elapsed, ended, extinct, finished, forgotten, gone, over, over and done with, spent ~*n.* **3. the past** antiquity, days gone by, days of yore, former times, good old days, history, long ago, olden days, old times, times past, yesteryear (*literary*) **4.** background, experience, history, life, past life ~*prep.* **5.** after, beyond, farther than, later than, outside, over, subsequent to

paste 1. *n.* adhesive, cement, glue, gum, mucilage **2.** *vb.* cement, fasten, fix, glue, gum, stick

pastel *adj.* delicate, light, muted, pale, soft, soft-hued

pastiche blend, farrago, hotchpotch, medley, *mélange,* miscellany, mixture, motley

pastime activity, amusement, distraction, diversion, entertainment, game, hobby, leisure, play, recreation, relaxation, sport

past master ace (*informal*), artist, dab hand (*Brit. informal*), expert, old hand, virtuoso, wizard

pastor churchman, clergyman, divine, ecclesiastic, minister, parson, priest, rector, vicar

pastoral *adj.* **1.** Arcadian (*literary*), bucolic, country, idyllic, rural, rustic, simple **2.** clerical, ecclesiastical, ministerial, priestly

pasture grass, grassland, grazing, grazing land, lea (*poetic*), meadow, pasturage

garment. **2** a small contrasting section: *there was a bald patch on the top of his head.* **3** a small plot of land. **4** *Med* a protective covering for an injured eye. **5** a scrap or remnant. **6** the area under someone's supervision, such as a policeman or social worker. **7 a bad patch** a difficult time. **8 not a patch on** not nearly as good as. *~vb* **9** to mend (a garment) with a patch. **10 patch up a** to mend (something) hurriedly or carelessly. **b** to make up (a quarrel). **11 patch together** to produce (something) by piecing parts together hurriedly or carelessly.

patchwork *n* **1** needlework done by sewing together pieces of different materials. **2** something made up of various parts.

patchy *adj* **patchier, patchiest 1** of uneven quality or intensity: *since then her career has been patchy.* **2** having or forming patches.

pate *n Old-fashioned or humorous* the head or the crown of the head.

pâté (**pat**-ay) *n* a spread of finely minced meat, fish, or vegetables often served as a starter.

pâté de foie gras (de fwah **grah**) *n* a smooth rich paste made from the liver of specially fattened geese.

patella (pat-**tell**-a) *n, pl* **-lae** (-lee) *Anat* kneecap. **patellar** *adj*

paten (**pat**-in) *n* a plate, usually made of silver or gold, used for the bread at Communion.

patent *n* **1 a** an official document granting the exclusive right to make, use, and sell an invention for a limited period. **b** the right granted by such a document. **2** an invention protected by a patent. *~adj* **3** open or available for inspection: *letters patent.* **4** obvious: *their scorn was patent to everyone.* **5** concerning protection of or appointment by a patent. **6** (of food, drugs, etc.) made or held under a patent. *~vb* **7** to obtain a patent for (an invention).

patent leather *n* leather processed with lacquer to give a hard glossy surface.

patently *adv* clearly and obviously: *a patently absurd explanation.*

patent medicine *n* a medicine with a patent, available without a prescription.

Patent Office *n* a government department that issues patents.

pater *n Brit humorous* father.

paternal *adj* **1** fatherly: *paternal authority.* **2** related through one's father: *his paternal grandmother.* **paternally** *adv*

paternalism *n* authority exercised in a way that limits individual responsibility. **paternalistic** *adj*

paternity *n* **1** the fact or state of being a father. **2** descent or derivation from a father.

paternity suit *n* legal proceedings, usually brought by an unmarried mother, in order to gain legal recognition that a particular man is the father of her child.

Paternoster *n RC Church* the Lord's Prayer.

path *n, pl* **paths 1** a road or way, often a narrow trodden track. **2** a surfaced walk, such as through a garden. **3** the course or direction in which something moves: *his car skidded into the path of an oncoming lorry.* **4** a course of conduct: *the path of reconciliation and forgiveness.*

pathetic *adj* **1** arousing pity or sympathy. **2** distressingly inadequate: *his pathetic attempt to maintain a stiff upper lip failed.* **pathetically** *adv*

pathetic fallacy *n* (in literature) the presentation of inanimate objects in nature as possessing human feelings.

pathogen *n* any agent, such as a bacterium, that can cause disease. **pathogenic** *adj*

pathological *adj* **1** of or relating to pathology. **2** *Informal* compulsively motivated: *pathological jealousy.*

pathology *n* the branch of medicine that studies diseases. **pathologist** *n*

pathos *n* the power, for example in literature, of arousing feelings of pity or sorrow.

pathway *n* a path.

patience *n* **1** the capacity for calmly enduring difficult situations: *the endless patience of the nurses.* **2** the ability to wait calmly for something to happen without complaining or giving up: *he urged the international community to have patience to allow sanctions to work.* **3** *Brit* a card game for one player only.

patient *adj* **1** enduring difficult situations with an even temper. **2** persevering or diligent: *his years of patient work may finally pay off.* *~n* **3** a person who is receiving medical care. **patiently** *adv*

patina *n* **1** a film formed on the surface of a metal. **2** the sheen on the surface of an old object, caused by age and much handling.

patio *n, pl* **-tios 1** a paved area adjoining a house. **2** an open inner courtyard in a Spanish or Spanish-American house.

THESAURUS

pat *vb.* **1.** caress, dab, fondle, pet, slap, stroke, tap, touch *~n.* **2.** clap, dab, light blow, slap, stroke, tap **3.** cake, dab, lump, portion, small piece

patch *n.* **1.** piece of material, reinforcement **2.** bit, scrap, shred, small piece, spot, stretch **3.** area, ground, land, plot, tract *~vb.* **4.** cover, fix, mend, reinforce, repair, sew up **5. patch up** bury the hatchet, conciliate, make friends, placate, restore, settle, settle differences, smooth

patchwork confusion, hash, hotchpotch, jumble, medley, mishmash, mixture, pastiche

patchy bitty, erratic, fitful, inconstant, irregular, random, sketchy, spotty, uneven, variable, varying

patent **1.** *n.* copyright, invention, licence **2.** *adj.* apparent, blatant, clear, conspicuous, downright, evident, flagrant, glaring, indisputable, manifest, obvious, open, palpable, transparent, unconcealed, unequivocal, unmistakable

paternal **1.** benevolent, concerned, fatherlike, fatherly, protective, solicitous, vigilant **2.** patrilineal, patrimonial

paternity **1.** fatherhood, fathership **2.** descent, extraction, family, lineage, parentage

path **1.** footpath, footway, pathway, towpath, track, trail, walkway **2.** avenue, course, direction, passage, procedure, road, route, track, walk, way

pathetic **1.** affecting, distressing, harrowing, heartbreaking, heart-rending, melting, moving, pitiable, plaintive, poignant, sad, tender, touching **2.** deplorable, feeble, inadequate, lamentable, meagre, measly, miserable, paltry, petty, pitiful, poor, puny, sorry, wet (*Brit. informal*), woeful

pathos pitiableness, pitifulness, plaintiveness, poignancy, sadness

patience **1.** calmness, composure, cool (*slang*), equanimity, even temper, forbearance, imperturbability, restraint, serenity, sufferance, tolerance, toleration **2.** constancy, diligence, endurance, fortitude, long-suffering, perseverance, persistence, resignation, stoicism, submission

patient *adj.* **1.** accommodating, even-tempered, forbearing, forgiving, indulgent, lenient, mild, tolerant, understanding **2.** calm, composed, enduring, long-

patisserie (pat-**eess**-er-ee) *n* **1** a shop where fancy pastries are sold. **2** such pastries.

patois (**pat**-wah) *n, pl* **patois** (**pat**-wahz) **1** a regional dialect of a language. **2** the jargon of a particular group.

patrial *n* (in Britain, formerly) a person with a right by statute to live in the United Kingdom, and so not subject to immigration control.

patriarch *n* **1** the male head of a tribe or family. **2** *Bible* any of the men regarded as the fathers of the human race or of the Hebrew people. **3 a** *RC Church* the pope. **b** *Eastern Orthodox Church* a highest-ranking bishop. **4** an old man who is respected. **patriarchal** *adj*

patriarchate *n* the office, jurisdiction or residence of a patriarch.

patriarchy *n* **1** a form of social organization in which males hold most of the power. **2** (*pl* **-chies**) a society governed by such a system.

patrician *n* **1** a member of the nobility of ancient Rome. **2** an aristocrat. **3** a person of refined conduct and tastes. *~adj* **4** (in ancient Rome) of or relating to patricians. **5** aristocratic.

patricide *n* **1** the act of killing one's father. **2** a person who kills his or her father. **patricidal** *adj*

patrimony *n, pl* **-nies** an inheritance from one's father or other ancestor.

patriot *n* a person who loves his or her country and passionately supports its interests. **patriotic** *adj* **patriotically** *adv* **patriotism** *n*

patrol *n* **1** the action of going round an area or building at regular intervals for purposes of security or observation. **2** a person or group that carries out such an action. **3** a group of soldiers or ships involved in patrolling a particular area. **4** a division of a troop of Scouts or Guides. *~vb* **-trolling, -trolled 5** to engage in a patrol of (a place).

patrol car *n* a police car used for patrolling streets.

patron *n* **1** a person who financially supports artists, writers, musicians, or charities. **2** a regular customer of a shop, hotel, etc.

patronage *n* **1** the support or custom given by a patron. **2** (in politics) the ability or power to appoint people to jobs. **3** a condescending manner.

patronize *or* **-ise** *vb* **-izing, -ized** *or* **-ising, -ised 1** to treat (someone) in a condescending way. **2** to be a patron of. **patronizing** *or* **-ising** *adj* **patronizingly** *or* **-isingly** *adv*

patron saint *n* a saint regarded as the particular guardian of a country or a group of people.

patronymic *n* a name derived from one's father's or a male ancestor.

patter[1] *vb* **1** to make repeated light tapping sound. **2** to walk with quick soft steps. *~n* **3** a quick succession of light tapping sounds, such as by feet: *the steady patter of rain against the window.*

patter[2] *n* **1** the glib rapid speech of comedians or salesmen. **2** chatter. **3** the jargon of a particular group. *~vb* **4** to speak glibly and rapidly.

pattern *n* **1** an arrangement of repeated parts or decorative designs. **2** a regular recognizable way that something is done: *I followed a normal eating pattern.* **3** a plan or diagram used as a guide to making something: *a knitting pattern.* **4** a model worthy of imitation: *a pattern of kindness.* **5** a representative sample. *~vb* **6** (foll. by *after* or *on*) to model: *an orchestra patterned after Count Basie's.*

patterned *n* having a decorative pattern on it: *a selection of plain and patterned fabrics.*

patty *n, pl* **-ties** a small round meat pie.

paua (**poh**-a) *n* an edible shellfish of New Zealand, which has a pearly shell used for jewellery.

paucity *n Formal* **1** scarcity. **2** smallness of amount or number.

paunch *n* a protruding belly or abdomen. **paunchy** *adj*

pauper *n Old-fashioned* **1** a person who is extremely poor. **2** (formerly) a person supported by public charity.

THESAURUS

suffering, persevering, persistent, philosophical, quiet, resigned, self-possessed, serene, stoical, submissive, uncomplaining, untiring *~n.* **3.** case, invalid, sick person, sufferer

patriot chauvinist, flag-waver (*informal*), jingo, lover of one's country, loyalist, nationalist

patriotic chauvinistic, flag-waving (*informal*), jingoistic, loyal, nationalistic

patriotism flag-waving (*informal*), jingoism, love of one's country, loyalty, nationalism

patrol *n.* **1.** guarding, policing, protecting, rounds, safeguarding, vigilance, watching **2.** garrison, guard, patrolman, sentinel, watch, watchman *~vb.* **3.** cruise, guard, inspect, keep guard, keep watch, make the rounds, police, pound, range, safeguard, walk the beat

patron 1. advocate, angel (*informal*), backer, benefactor, champion, defender, friend, guardian, helper, philanthropist, protagonist, protector, sponsor, supporter **2.** buyer, client, customer, frequenter, habitué, shopper

patronage 1. aid, assistance, backing, benefaction, championship, encouragement, espousal, help, promotion, sponsorship, support **2.** condescension, deigning, disdain, patronizing, stooping

patronize, patronise 1. be lofty with, look down on, talk down to, treat as inferior, treat condescendingly, treat like a child **2.** assist, back, befriend, foster, fund, help, maintain, promote, sponsor, subscribe to, support **3.** be a customer *or* client of, buy from, deal with, do business with, frequent, shop at, trade with

patronizing, patronising condescending, contemptuous, disdainful, gracious, haughty, lofty, snobbish, stooping, supercilious, superior, toffee-nosed (*slang, chiefly Brit.*)

patter[1] *vb.* **1.** beat, pat, pelt, pitapat, pitter-patter, rat-a-tat, spatter, tap **2.** scurry, scuttle, skip, tiptoe, trip, walk lightly *~n.* **3.** pattering, pitapat, pitter-patter, tapping

patter[2] *n.* **1.** line, monologue, pitch, spiel (*informal*) **2.** chatter, gabble, jabber, nattering, prattle, yak (*slang*) **3.** argot, cant, jargon, lingo (*informal*), patois, slang, vernacular *~vb.* **4.** babble, blab, chatter, hold forth, jabber, prate, rattle off, rattle on, spiel (*informal*), spout (*informal*), tattle

pattern *n.* **1.** arrangement, decoration, decorative design, design, device, figure, motif, ornament **2.** arrangement, method, order, orderliness, plan, sequence, system **3.** design, diagram, guide, instructions, original, plan, stencil, template **4.** archetype, criterion, example, exemplar, guide, model, norm, original, par, paradigm, paragon, prototype, sample, specimen, standard *~vb.* **5.** copy, emulate, follow, form, imitate, model, mould, order, shape, style

paucity *formal* dearth, deficiency, fewness, insufficiency, lack, meagreness, paltriness, poverty, rarity, scantiness, scarcity, shortage, slenderness, slightness, smallness, sparseness, sparsity

paunch abdomen, beer-belly (*informal*), belly, corporation (*informal*), pot, potbelly, spare tyre (*Brit. slang*), spread (*informal*)

pause *vb* **pausing, paused 1** to stop doing (something) for a short time. **2** to hesitate: *she answered him without pausing.* ~*n* **3** a temporary stop or rest in speech or action. **4** *Music* a continuation of a note or rest beyond its normal length. **5 give someone pause** to cause someone to hesitate: *it gave him pause for reflection.*

pavane (pav-**van**) *n* **1** a slow and stately dance of the 16th and 17th centuries. **2** music for this dance.

pave *vb* **paving, paved 1** to cover (a road or area of ground) with a firm surface to make it suitable for walking or travelling on. **2 pave the way for** to prepare or make easier: *the arrests paved the way for the biggest-ever Mafia trial.*

pavement *n* **1** a hard-surfaced path for pedestrians, alongside and a little higher than a road. **2** the material used in paving. **3** *US* the surface of a road.

pavilion *n* **1** *Brit* a building at a sports ground, esp. a cricket pitch, in which players can wash and change. **2** an open building or temporary structure used for exhibitions. **3** a summerhouse or other decorative shelter. **4** a large ornate tent.

paving *n* **1** a paved surface. **2** material used for a pavement.

pavlova *n* a meringue cake topped with whipped cream and fruit.

paw *n* **1** a four-legged mammal's foot with claws and pads. **2** *Informal* a hand. ~*vb* **3** to scrape or hit with the paws. **4** *Informal* to touch or caress (someone) in a rough or overfamiliar manner.

pawl *n* a pivoted lever shaped to engage with a ratchet to prevent motion in a particular direction.

pawn[1] *vb* **1** to deposit (an article) as security for money borrowed. **2** to stake or risk: *I will pawn my honour on this matter.* ~*n* **3** an article deposited as security. **4** the condition of being so deposited: *in pawn.*

pawn[2] *n* **1** a chessman of the lowest value, usually able to move only one square forward at a time. **2** a person manipulated by someone else: *our city is just a pawn in the power games of others.*

pawnbroker *n* a person licensed to lend money on goods deposited. **pawnbroking** *n*

Pawnee *n, pl* **Pawnees** *or* **Pawnee 1** a member of a group of N American Indian peoples, formerly living in Nebraska and Kansas, now chiefly in Oklahoma. **2** the language of these peoples.

pawnshop *n* the premises of a pawnbroker.

pawpaw (**paw**-paw) *n* same as **papaya.**

pax *n* **1** *Chiefly RC Church* the kiss of peace. ~*interj* **2** *Brit school slang* a call signalling a desire to end hostilities.

pay *vb* **pays, paying, paid 1** to give (money) in return for goods or services: *Willie paid for the drinks; nurses are not very well paid.* **2** to settle (a debt or obligation) by giving or doing something: *he has paid his debt to society.* **3** to suffer: *she paid dearly for her mistake.* **4** to give (a compliment, regards, attention, etc.). **5** to profit or benefit (someone): *it doesn't always pay to be honest.* **6** to make (a visit or call). **7** to yield a return of: *the account pays 5% interest.* **8 pay one's way a** to contribute one's share of expenses. **b** to remain solvent without outside help. ~*n* **9** money given in return for work or services; a salary or wage. **10 in the pay of** employed by. ~See also **pay back, pay for,** etc.

payable *adj* **1** (often foll. by *on*) due to be paid: *the instalments are payable on the third of each month.* **2** that is capable of being paid: *pensions are payable to those disabled during the wars.*

pay back *vb* **1** to repay (a loan). **2** to make (someone) suffer for a wrong he or she has done you: *I want to pay him back for all the suffering he's caused me.*

pay bed *n* a bed in a hospital used by a patient who is paying for treatment.

PAYE (in Britain and New Zealand) pay as you earn; a system by which income tax is deducted by employers and paid directly to the government.

payee *n* the person to whom a cheque or money order is made out.

pay for *vb* **1** to make payment for. **2** to suffer or be punished for (a mistake).

paying guest *n Euphemistic* a lodger.

payload *n* **1** the amount of passengers, cargo, or bombs which an aircraft can carry. **2** the part of a cargo which earns revenue. **3** the explosive power of a warhead or bomb carried by a missile or aircraft.

paymaster *n* an official responsible for the payment of wages and salaries.

payment *n* **1** the act of paying. **2** a sum of money paid. **3** something given in return; punishment or reward.

pay off *vb* **1** to pay the complete amount of (a debt). **2** to pay (someone) all that is due in wages and dismiss him or her from employment. **3** to turn out successfully: *her persistence finally paid off.* **4** *Informal* to give a bribe to. ~*n* **payoff 5** *Informal* the climax or outcome of events. **6** *Informal* a bribe. **7** the final

THESAURUS

pauper *old-fashioned* bankrupt, beggar, down-and-out, have-not, indigent, insolvent, mendicant, poor person

pause 1. *vb.* break, cease, delay, deliberate, desist, discontinue, halt, have a breather (*informal*), hesitate, interrupt, rest, stop briefly, take a break, wait, waver **2.** *n.* break, breather (*informal*), caesura, cessation, delay, discontinuance, gap, halt, hesitation, interlude, intermission, interruption, interval, let-up (*informal*), lull, respite, rest, stay, stoppage, wait

pave asphalt, concrete, cover, flag, floor, macadamize, surface, tar, tile

paw *vb. informal* grab, handle roughly, manhandle, maul, molest

pawn[1] **1.** *vb.* deposit, hazard, hock (*informal*), mortgage, pledge, pop (*informal*), stake, wager **2.** *n.* assurance, bond, collateral, gage, guarantee, guaranty, pledge, security

pawn[2] *n.* cat's-paw, creature, dupe, instrument, plaything, puppet, stooge (*slang*), tool, toy

pay *vb.* **1.** clear, compensate, cough up (*informal*), discharge, foot, give, honour, liquidate, meet, offer, recompense, reimburse, remit, remunerate, render, requite, reward, settle, square up **2.** answer for, atone, be punished, compensate, get one's deserts, make amends, suffer, suffer the consequences **3.** bestow, extend, give, grant, hand out, present, proffer, render **4.** be advantageous, benefit, be profitable, be remunerative, be worthwhile, make a return, make money, provide a living, repay, serve **5.** bring in, produce, profit, return, yield ~*n.* **6.** allowance, compensation, earnings, emoluments, fee, hand-out, hire, income, payment, recompense, reimbursement, remuneration, reward, salary, stipend, takings, wages

payable due, mature, obligatory, outstanding, owed, owing, receivable, to be paid

pay back 1. refund, reimburse, repay, return, settle up, square **2.** get even with (*informal*), get one's own back, hit back, reciprocate, recompense, retaliate, settle a score

payment 1. defrayal, discharge, outlay, paying, remittance, settlement **2.** advance, deposit, instalment, portion, premium, remittance **3.** fee, hire, remuneration, reward, wage

payment of a debt. **8** the final settlement, esp. in retribution: *the payoff came when the gang besieged the squealer's house.*

payola *n Informal* a bribe to secure special treatment, esp. to promote a commercial product.

pay out *vb* **1** to spend (money) on a particular thing. **2** to release (a rope) gradually, bit by bit. *~n* **payout 3** a sum of money paid out.

payphone *n* a coin-operated telephone.

payroll *n* a list of employees, giving the salary or wage of each.

payslip *n* a note given to an employee stating his or her salary or wage and detailing the deductions.

pay up *vb* to pay (money) promptly or in full.

Pb *Chem* lead.

pc **1** per cent. **2** postcard.

PC **1** personal computer. **2** (in Britain) Police Constable. **3** *Informal* short for **politically correct. 4** (in Britain) Privy Council *or* Counsellor. **5** (in Canada) Progressive Conservative.

pd paid.

Pd *Chem* palladium.

PDSA (in Britain) People's Dispensary for Sick Animals.

PDT Pacific Daylight Time.

PE **1** physical education. **2** Prince Edward Island.

pea *n* **1** an annual climbing plant with green pods containing green seeds. **2** the seed of this plant, eaten as a vegetable.

peace *n* **1** stillness or silence. **2** absence of mental anxiety: *peace of mind.* **3** absence of war. **4** harmony between people or groups. **5** a treaty marking the end of a war. **6** law and order within a state: *a breach of the peace.* **7 at peace a** dead: *the old lady is at peace now.* **b** in a state of harmony or serenity. **8 hold** *or* **keep one's peace** to keep silent. **9 keep the peace** to maintain law and order.

peaceable *adj* **1** inclined towards peace. **2** tranquil or calm.

peaceful *adj* **1** not in a state of war or disagreement. **2** calm or tranquil. **peacefully** *adv*

peacemaker *n* a person who brings about peace, esp. between others.

peace offering *n* something given or said in order to restore peace: *I bought Mum some flowers as a peace offering.*

peace pipe *n* a long decorated pipe smoked by North American Indians, esp. as a token of peace.

peacetime *n* a period without war.

peach *n* **1** a soft juicy fruit with a downy skin, yellowish-orange sweet flesh, and a single stone. **2** *Informal* a person or thing that is especially pleasing: *a peach of a goal.* *~adj* **3** pale pinkish-orange.

peach melba *n* a dessert made of halved peaches, vanilla ice cream, and raspberries.

peachy *adj* **peachier, peachiest** of or like a peach, esp. in colour or texture.

peacock *n, pl* **-cocks** *or* **-cock 1** a large male bird of the pheasant family with a crested head and a very large fanlike tail with blue and green eyelike spots. **2** a vain strutting person. **peahen** *fem n*

peafowl *n* peacock or peahen.

peak *n* **1** a pointed tip or projection: *the peak of the roof.* **2 a** the pointed summit of a mountain. **b** a mountain with a pointed summit. **3** the point of greatest success or achievement: *the peak of his career.* **4** a projecting piece on the front of some caps. *~vb* **5** to form or reach a peak. *~adj* **6** of or relating to a period of greatest demand: *hotels are generally dearer in peak season.*

peaked *adj* having a peak.

peak load *n* the maximum load on an electrical power-supply system.

peaky *adj* **peakier, peakiest** pale and sickly.

peal *n* **1** a long loud echoing sound, such as of bells or thunder. *~vb* **2** to sound with a peal or peals.

peanut *n* a plant with edible nutlike seeds which ripen underground. See also **peanuts.**

peanut butter *n* a brownish oily paste made from peanuts.

peanuts *n Slang* a trifling amount of money.

pear *n* a sweet juicy fruit with a narrow top and a rounded base.

pearl *n* **1** a hard smooth greyish-white rounded object found inside the shell of a clam or oyster and much valued as a gem. **2** See **mother-of-pearl. 3** a person or thing that is like a pearl in beauty or value. *~adj* **4** of, made of, or set with pearl or mother-of-pearl. *~vb* **5** to set with or as if with pearls. **6** to shape into or assume a pearl-like form or colour. **7** to dive for pearls.

pearl barley *n* barley ground into small round grains, used in soups and stews.

pearly *adj* **pearlier, pearliest 1** resembling a pearl, esp. in lustre. **2** decorated with pearls or mother-of-pearl.

Pearly Gates *pl n Informal* the entrance to heaven.

pearly king *or fem* **pearly queen** *n* the London barrow vendor whose ceremonial clothes display the most lavish collection of pearl buttons.

peasant *n* **1** a member of a low social class em-

THESAURUS

pay off 1. clear, discharge, liquidate, pay in full, settle, square **2.** discharge, dismiss, fire, lay off, let go, sack (*informal*) **3.** be effective (profitable, successful), succeed, work **4.** *informal* bribe, buy off, corrupt, get at, grease the palm of (*slang*), oil (*informal*), suborn

pay out cough up (*informal*), disburse, expend, fork out *or* over *or* up (*slang*), lay out (*informal*), shell out (*informal*), spend

peace 1. calm, calmness, hush, peacefulness, quiet, quietude, repose, rest, silence, stillness, tranquillity **2.** calm, composure, contentment, placidity, relaxation, repose, serenity **3.** accord, agreement, amity, concord, harmony **4.** armistice, cessation of hostilities, conciliation, pacification, treaty, truce

peaceable 1. amiable, amicable, conciliatory, dovish, friendly, gentle, inoffensive, mild, nonbelligerent, pacific, peaceful, peace-loving, placid, unwarlike **2.** balmy, calm, peaceful, quiet, restful, serene, still, tranquil, undisturbed

peaceful 1. amicable, at peace, free from strife, friendly, harmonious, nonviolent, on friendly *or* good terms, without hostility **2.** calm, gentle, placid, quiet, restful, serene, still, tranquil, undisturbed, unruffled, untroubled

peacemaker appeaser, arbitrator, conciliator, mediator, pacifier, peacemonger

peak *n.* **1.** apex, brow, crest, pinnacle, point, summit, tip, top **2.** acme, apogee, climax, crown, culmination, high point, maximum point, zenith *~vb.* **3.** be at its height, climax, come to a head, culminate, reach its highest point, reach the zenith

peal 1. *n.* blast, carillon, chime, clamour, clang, clap, crash, resounding, reverberation, ring, ringing, roar, rumble, sound, tintinnabulation **2.** *vb.* chime, crack, crash, resonate, resound, reverberate, ring, roar, roll, rumble, sound, toll

peasant 1. churl (*archaic*), countryman, rustic, son

ployed in agricultural labour. **2** *Informal* an uncouth or uncultured person.

peasantry *n* peasants as a class.

pease *n, pl* **pease** *Archaic or dialect* same as **pea.**

pease pudding *n* (esp. in Britain) a dish of split peas that have been soaked and boiled.

peasouper *n* **1** *Informal, chiefly Brit* thick dirty yellowish fog. **2** *Canad slang* a French Canadian.

peat *n* decaying vegetable matter found in uplands and bogs and used as a fuel (when dried) and as a fertilizer.

pebble *n* **1** a small smooth rounded stone, esp. one worn by the action of water. *~vb* **-bling, -bled 2** to cover with pebbles. **pebbly** *adj*

pebble dash *n Brit* a finish for external walls consisting of small stones set in plaster.

pec *n Informal* a pectoral muscle: *a gigolo with flowing blond locks and rippling pecs.*

pecan (**pee**-kan) *n* a smooth oval nut with a sweet oily kernel that grows on hickory trees in the Southern US.

peccadillo *n, pl* **-los** *or* **-loes** a trivial misdeed.

peccary *n, pl* **-ries** *or* **-ry** a piglike animal of American forests.

peck[1] *vb* **1** to strike or pick up with the beak. **2** *Informal* to kiss (a person) quickly and lightly. **3 peck at** to eat slowly and reluctantly: *pecking away at your lunch.* *~n* **4** a quick light blow from a bird's beak. **5** a mark made by such a blow. **6** *Informal* a quick light kiss.

peck[2] *n* an obsolete unit of liquid measure equal to one quarter of a bushel or 2 gallons (9.1 litres).

pecker *n* **keep one's pecker up** *Brit slang* to remain cheerful.

pecking order *n* the order of seniority or power in a group: *she came from a family low in the social pecking order.*

peckish *adj Informal, chiefly Brit* feeling slightly hungry.

pectin *n Biochem* a water-soluble carbohydrate that occurs in ripe fruit: used in the manufacture of jams because of its ability to gel.

pectoral *adj* **1** of or relating to the chest, breast, or thorax: *pectoral fins.* **2** worn on the breast or chest: *a pectoral cross.* *~n* **3** a pectoral organ or part, esp. a muscle or fin.

pectoral fin *n* a fin, just behind the head in fishes, that helps to control the direction of movement.

peculate *vb* **-lating, -lated** *Literary* to embezzle (public money). **peculation** *n*

peculiar *adj* **1** strange or odd: *a peculiar idea.* **2** distinct or special. **3** (foll. by *to*) belonging exclusively (to): *a fish peculiar to these waters.*

peculiarity *n, pl* **-ties 1** a strange or unusual habit; eccentricity. **2** a distinguishing trait. **3** the state or quality of being peculiar.

pecuniary *adj* **1** of or relating to money. **2** *Law* (of an offence) involving a monetary penalty.

pedagogue *or US sometimes* **pedagog** *n* a teacher, esp. a pedantic one. **pedagogic** *adj*

pedagogy (**ped**-a-goj-ee) *n* the principles, practice, or profession of teaching.

pedal[1] *n* **1** a foot-operated lever used to control a vehicle or machine, or to modify the tone of a musical instrument. *~vb* **-alling, -alled** *or US* **-aling, -aled 2** to propel (a bicycle) by operating the pedals. **3** to operate the pedals of an organ or piano.

pedal[2] *adj* of the foot or feet.

pedant *n* a person who is concerned chiefly with insignificant detail or who relies too much on academic learning. **pedantic** *adj* **pedantically** *adv*

pedantry *n, pl* **-ries** the practice of being a pedant, esp. in the minute observance of petty rules or details.

peddle *vb* **-dling, -dled 1** to sell (goods) from place to place. **2** to sell illegal drugs. **3** to advocate (an idea or information) persistently: *the version of events being peddled by his opponents.*

pederast *or* **paederast** *n* a man who has homosexual relations with boys. **pederasty** *or* **paederasty** *n*

pedestal *n* **1** a base that supports something, such as a statue. **2 put someone on a pedestal** to admire someone very much.

pedestrian *n* **1** a person who travels on foot. *~adj* **2** dull or commonplace: *a pedestrian performance.*

pedestrian crossing *n Brit* a path across a road marked as a crossing for pedestrians.

pedestrianize *or* **-ise** *vb* **-izing, -ized** *or* **-ising, -ised** to convert (a street or shopping area) into an area for pedestrians only.

pedestrian precinct *n* an area of a town for pedestrians only, esp. an area of shops.

pedicure *n* medical or cosmetic treatment of the feet.

pedigree *n* **1** the line of descent of a purebred ani-

THESAURUS

of the soil, swain (*archaic or poetic*) **2.** *informal* boor, churl, country bumpkin, hick (*informal, chiefly U.S. & Canad.*), lout, provincial, yokel

peccadillo error, indiscretion, infraction, lapse, misdeed, misdemeanour, petty offence, slip, trifling fault

peck *vb./n.* bite, dig, hit, jab, kiss, nibble, pick, poke, prick, strike, tap

peculiar **1.** abnormal, bizarre, curious, eccentric, exceptional, extraordinary, far-out (*slang*), freakish, funny, odd, offbeat, off-the-wall (*slang*), outlandish, out-of-the-way, outré, quaint, queer, singular, strange, uncommon, unconventional, unusual, wacko (*slang*), weird **2.** appropriate, characteristic, distinct, distinctive, distinguishing, endemic, idiosyncratic, individual, local, particular, personal, private, restricted, special, specific, unique

peculiarity **1.** abnormality, bizarreness, eccentricity, foible, freakishness, idiosyncrasy, mannerism, oddity, odd trait, queerness, quirk **2.** attribute, characteristic, distinctiveness, feature, mark, particularity, property, quality, singularity, speciality, trait

pedagogue *or U.S. sometimes* **pedagog** dogmatist, educator, instructor, master, mistress, pedant, schoolmaster, schoolmistress, teacher

pedantic abstruse, academic, bookish, didactic, donnish, erudite, formal, fussy, hairsplitting, nitpicking (*informal*), particular, pedagogic, picky (*informal*), pompous, precise, priggish, punctilious, scholastic, schoolmasterly, sententious, stilted

pedantry bookishness, finicality, hairsplitting, overnicety, pedagogism, pettifoggery, pomposity, punctiliousness, quibbling, sophistry, stuffiness

peddle flog (*slang*), hawk, market, push (*informal*), sell, sell door to door, trade, vend

pedestal **1.** base, dado (*Architect.*), foot, foundation, mounting, pier, plinth, socle, stand, support **2. put someone on a pedestal** apotheosize, deify, dignify, ennoble, exalt, glorify, idealize, worship

pedestrian **1.** *n.* footslogger, foot-traveller, walker **2.** *adj.* banal, boring, commonplace, dull, flat, ho-hum (*informal*), humdrum, mediocre, mundane, ordinary, plodding, prosaic, run-of-the-mill, unimaginative, uninspired, uninteresting

mal. **2** a document recording this. **3** a genealogical table, esp. one indicating pure ancestry.

pediment *n* a triangular part over a door, as used in classical architecture.

pedlar *or esp US* **peddler** *n* a person who peddles.

pedometer (pid-**dom**-it-er) *n* a device that measures the distance walked by recording the number of steps taken.

peduncle *n* **1** *Bot* a plant stalk bearing a flower cluster or solitary flower. **2** *Anat, pathol* any stalklike structure. **peduncular** *adj*

pee *Informal* ~*vb* **peeing, peed 1** to urinate. ~*n* **2** urine. **3** the act of urinating.

peek *vb* **1** to glance quickly or secretly. ~*n* **2** such a glance.

peel *vb* **1** to remove the skin or rind of (a fruit or vegetable). **2** to come off in flakes. **3** (of a person or part of the body) to shed skin in flakes as a result of sunburn. ~*n* **4** the skin or rind of a fruit, etc.

peelings *pl n* strips of skin or rind that have been peeled off: *potato peelings.*

peel off *vb* **1** to remove or be removed by peeling: *this softens the paint, which can then be peeled off.* **2** *Slang* to take off one's clothes or a piece of clothing. **3** to leave a group of moving people, vehicles etc. by taking a course that curves away to one side: *a couple of aircraft peeled off to attack the enemy bombers.*

peen *n* the end of a hammer head opposite the striking face, often rounded or wedge-shaped.

peep[1] *vb* **1** to look slyly or quickly, such as through a small opening or from a hidden place. **2** to appear partially or briefly: *the sun peeped through the clouds.* ~*n* **3** a quick or sly look. **4** the first appearance: *the peep of dawn.*

peep[2] *vb* **1** (esp. of young birds) to make small shrill noises. ~*n* **2** a peeping sound.

Peeping Tom *n* a man who furtively observes women undressing.

peepshow *n* a box containing a series of pictures that can be seen through a small hole.

peer[1] *n* **1** a member of a nobility. **2** a person who holds any of the five grades of the British nobility: duke, marquess, earl, viscount, and baron. **3** a person of equal social standing, rank, age, etc.: *he is greatly respected by his peers in the arts world.*

peer[2] *vb* **1** to look intently or as if with difficulty: *Walter peered anxiously at his father's face.* **2** to appear dimly: *the sun peered through the fog.*

peerage *n* **1** the whole body of peers; aristocracy. **2** the position, rank, or title of a peer.

peeress *n* **1** a woman holding the rank of a peer. **2** the wife or widow of a peer.

peer group *n* a social group composed of people of similar age and status.

peerless *adj* having no equals; unsurpassed.

peeve *Informal* ~*vb* **peeving, peeved 1** to irritate or annoy: *the way he looked at her peeved her.* ~*n* **2** something that irritates: *my pet peeve.* **peeved** *adj*

peevish *adj* fretful or irritable. **peevishly** *adv*

peewit *or* **pewit** *n* same as **lapwing.**

peg *n* **1** a small pin or bolt used to join two parts together, to fasten, or to mark. **2** a hook or knob for hanging things on. **3** *Music* a pin on a stringed instrument which can be turned to tune the string wound around it. **4** Also called: **clothes peg** a split or hinged pin for fastening wet clothes to a line to dry. **5** *Brit* a small drink of spirits. **6** an opportunity or pretext for doing something: *the play's subject matter provides a perfect peg for a discussion of issues like morality and faith.* **7 bring** *or* **take (someone) down a peg** to lower the pride of (someone). **8 off the peg** *Chiefly Brit* (of clothes) ready-to-wear, as opposed to tailor-made. ~*vb* **pegging, pegged 9** to insert a peg into. **10** to secure with pegs: *the balloon was pegged down to stop it drifting away.* **11** to mark (a score) with pegs, as in some card games. **12** *Chiefly Brit* to work steadily: *he pegged away at his job for years.* **13** to fix or maintain something, such as prices, at a particular level or value: *a fixed rate mortgage, pegged at 9.6 per cent.*

pegboard *n* **1** a board with holes into which small pegs can be fitted, used for playing certain games or keeping a score. **2** hardboard with rows of holes from which articles may be hung for display.

peg leg *n Informal* **1** an artificial leg. **2** a person with an artificial leg.

peg out *vb* **1** *Informal* to collapse or die. **2** to mark or secure with pegs: *the scientists pegged out a hectare of land in order to study every plant in it.*

PEI Prince Edward Island.

peignoir (**pay**-nwahr) *n* a woman's light dressing gown.

pejorative (pij-**jor**-a-tiv) *adj* **1** (of a word or expression) having an insulting or critical sense. ~*n* **2** a pejorative word or expression.

peke *n Informal* a Pekingese dog.

Pekingese *or* **Pekinese** *n* **1** (*pl* **-ese**) a small dog with a long straight coat, curled plumed tail, and short wrinkled muzzle. **2** (*pl* **-ese**) a person from Peking, in NE China. **3** the dialect of Mandarin Chinese spoken in Peking. ~*adj* **4** of Peking.

THESAURUS

pedigree ancestry, blood, breed, derivation, descent, extraction, family, family tree, genealogy, heritage, line, lineage, race, stemma, stock

peek 1. *vb.* glance, keek (*Scot.*), look, peep, peer, snatch a glimpse, sneak a look, spy, take *or* have a gander (*informal*), take a look **2.** *n.* blink, gander (*informal*), glance, glimpse, keek (*Scot.*), look, look-see (*slang*), peep, shufti (*Brit. slang*)

peel 1. *vb.* flake off, pare, scale, skin, strip off **2.** *n.* peeling, rind, skin

peep *vb.* **1.** keek (*Scot.*), look from hiding, look surreptitiously, peek, peer, sneak a look, spy, steal a look **2.** appear briefly, emerge, peer out, show partially ~*n.* **3.** gander (*informal*), glimpse, keek (*Scot.*), look, look-see (*slang*), peek, shufti (*Brit. slang*)

peer[1] *n.* **1.** aristo (*informal*), aristocrat, baron, count, duke, earl, lord, marquess, marquis, noble, nobleman, viscount **2.** coequal, compeer, equal, fellow, like, match

peer[2] *vb.* **1.** gaze, inspect, peep, scan, scrutinize, snoop, spy, squinny, squint **2.** appear, become visible, emerge, peep out

peerage aristocracy, lords and ladies, nobility, peers, titled classes

peerless beyond compare, excellent, incomparable, matchless, nonpareil, outstanding, second to none, superlative, unequalled, unique, unmatched, unparalleled, unrivalled, unsurpassed

peevish acrimonious, cantankerous, captious, childish, churlish, crabbed, cross, crotchety (*informal*), crusty, fractious, fretful, grumpy, huffy, ill-natured, ill-tempered, irritable, liverish, pettish, petulant, querulous, ratty (*Brit. informal*), short-tempered, shrewish, snappy, splenetic, sulky, sullen, surly, testy, tetchy, touchy, waspish, whingeing (*informal*)

pelargonium *n* a plant with circular leaves and red, pink, or white flowers: includes many cultivated geraniums.

pelf *n Contemptuous* money or wealth.

pelican *n* a large water bird with a pouch beneath its long bill for holding fish.

pelican crossing *n* a type of road crossing with a pedestrian-operated traffic-light system.

pelisse (pel-**leess**) *n* a cloak or loose coat which is usually fur-trimmed.

pellagra *n Pathol* a disease caused by a diet lacking in vitamin B, which results in scaling of the skin, diarrhoea and mental disorder.

pellet *n* **1** a small round ball, esp. of compressed matter. **2 a** an imitation bullet used in toy guns. **b** a piece of small shot. **3** a small pill.

pell-mell *adv* **1** in a confused headlong rush: *the hounds ran pell-mell into the yard.* **2** in a disorderly manner: *the things were piled pell-mell in the room.*

pellucid *adj Literary* **1** transparent or translucent. **2** extremely clear in style and meaning.

pelmet *n* a board or piece of fabric used to conceal the curtain rail.

pelota *n* a game played by two players who use a basket strapped to their wrists or a wooden racket to propel a ball against a specially marked wall.

pelt[1] *vb* **1** to throw (missiles) at. **2** (foll. by *along*, etc.) to hurry. **3** to rain heavily. ~*n* **4** a blow. **5 at full pelt** very quickly: *she ran down the street at full pelt.*

pelt[2] *n* the skin or fur of an animal, esp. as material for clothing or rugs: *the lucrative international trade in beaver pelts.*

pelvis *n* **1** the framework of bones at the base of the spine, to which the hips are attached. **2** the bones that form this structure. **pelvic** *adj*

pen[1] *n* **1** an instrument for writing or drawing using ink. See also **ballpoint, fountain pen. 2 the pen** writing as an occupation. ~*vb* **penning, penned 3** to write or compose.

pen[2] *n* **1** an enclosure in which domestic animals are kept. **2** any place of confinement. ~*vb* **penning, penned** *or* **pent 3** to enclose (animals) in a pen. **4 penned in** to be or feel trapped or confined: *she stood penned in by bodies at the front of the crowd.*

pen[3] *n US & Canad informal* short for **penitentiary** (sense 1).

pen[4] *n* a female swan.

Pen. Peninsula.

penal (**pee**-nal) *adj* **1** of or relating to punishment. **2** used as a place of punishment: *a penal colony.* **penally** *adv*

penal code *n* the body of laws relating to crime and punishment.

penalize *or* **-ise** *vb* **-izing, -ized** *or* **-ising, -ised 1** to impose a penalty on (someone) for breaking a law or rule. **2** to inflict a disadvantage on: *why should I be penalized just because I'm a woman?* **penalization** *or* **-isation** *n*

penalty *n, pl* **-ties 1** a legal punishment for a crime or offence. **2** loss or suffering as a result of one's own action: *we are now paying the penalty for neglecting to keep our equipment up to date.* **3** *Sport, games, etc* a handicap awarded against a player or team for illegal play, such as a free shot at goal by the opposing team.

penalty box *n* **1** Also called: **penalty area** *Soccer* a rectangular area in front of the goal, within which a penalty is awarded for a serious foul by the defending team. **2** *Ice hockey* a bench for players serving time penalties.

penance *n* **1** voluntary self-punishment to make amends for a sin. **2** *RC Church* a sacrament in which repentant sinners are forgiven provided they confess their sins to a priest and perform a penance.

pence *n* a plural of **penny.**

penchant (**pon**-shon) *n* strong inclination or liking: *a stylish woman with a penchant for dark glasses.*

pencil *n* **1** a rod of graphite encased in wood which is used for writing or drawing. ~*vb* **-cilling, -cilled** *or US* **-ciling, -ciled 2** to draw, colour, write, or mark with a pencil. **3 pencil in** to note, arrange, or include provisionally or tentatively.

pendant *n* **a** an ornament worn on a chain round the neck. **b** an ornament that hangs from a piece of jewellery.

pendent *adj Literary* **1** dangling. **2** jutting.

pending *prep* **1** while waiting for. ~*adj* **2** not yet decided or settled. **3** imminent: *these developments have been pending for some time.*

pendulous *adj Literary* hanging downwards and swinging freely.

pendulum *n* **1** a weight suspended so it swings freely under the influence of gravity. **2** such a device used to regulate a clock mechanism. **3** a movement from one attitude or belief towards its opposite: *the pendulum has swung back to more punitive measures.*

penetrate *vb* **-trating, -trated 1** to find or force a way into or through. **2** to diffuse through; permeate: *the smell of cooking penetrated through to the sitting room.* **3** to see through: *the sunlight did not penetrate the thick canopy of leaves.* **4** (of a man) to insert the penis into the vagina of (a woman). **5** to grasp the

THESAURUS

peg *vb.* **1.** attach, fasten, fix, join, make fast, secure **2.** *chiefly Brit.* apply oneself to, beaver away (*Brit. informal*), keep at it, keep going, keep on, persist, plod along, plug away at (*informal*), stick to it, work at, work away **3.** control, fix, freeze, limit, set

pelt *vb.* **1.** assail, batter, beat, belabour, bombard, cast, hurl, pepper, pummel, shower, sling, strike, thrash, throw, wallop (*informal*) **2.** *with* **along** *etc.* belt (*slang*), burn rubber (*informal*), career, charge, dash, hurry, run fast, rush, shoot, speed, tear, whiz (*informal*) **3.** bucket down (*informal*), pour, rain cats and dogs (*informal*), rain hard, teem

pen[1] *vb.* commit to paper, compose, draft, draw up, jot down, write

pen[2] **1.** *n.* cage, coop, enclosure, fold, hutch, pound, sty **2.** *vb.* cage, confine, coop up, enclose, fence in, hedge, hem in, hurdle, impound, mew (up), pound, shut up *or* in

penal corrective, disciplinary, penalizing, punitive, retributive

penalize award a penalty against (*Sport*), correct, discipline, handicap, impose a penalty on, inflict a handicap on, punish, put at a disadvantage

penalty disadvantage, fine, forfeit, forfeiture, handicap, mulct, price, punishment, retribution

penance atonement, mortification, penalty, punishment, reparation, sackcloth and ashes

penchant affinity, bent, bias, disposition, fondness, inclination, leaning, liking, partiality, predilection, predisposition, proclivity, proneness, propensity, taste, tendency, turn

pending awaiting, forthcoming, hanging fire, imminent, impending, in the balance, in the offing, undecided, undetermined, unsettled, up in the air

penetrate 1. bore, enter, go through, impale, perforate, pierce, prick, probe, stab **2.** diffuse, enter, get in,

meaning of (a principle, etc.). **penetrable** *adj* **penetrative** *adj*

penetrating *adj* tending to or able to penetrate: *a penetrating mind; a penetrating voice.*

penetration *n* **1** the act or an instance of penetrating. **2** the ability or power to penetrate. **3** keen insight or perception.

pen friend *n* a person with whom one exchanges letters, often a person in another country whom one has not met.

penguin *n* a flightless black-and-white Antarctic sea bird with webbed feet and wings modified as flippers for swimming.

penicillin *n* an antibiotic used to treat diseases caused by bacteria.

peninsula *n* a narrow strip of land projecting from the mainland into a sea or lake. **peninsular** *adj*

penis *n, pl* **-nises** *or* **-nes** the organ of copulation in higher vertebrates, also used for urinating in many mammals. **penile** *adj*

penitent *adj* **1** feeling regret for one's sins; repentant. *~n* **2** a person who is penitent. **penitence** *n*

penitential *adj* of, showing, or as a penance.

penitentiary *n, pl* **-ries 1** (in the US and Canada) a state or federal prison. *~adj* **2** of or for penance. **3** used for punishment and reformation: *the penitentiary system.*

penknife *n, pl* **-knives** a small knife with one or more blades that fold into the handle.

penmanship *n Formal* style or technique of writing by hand.

pen name *n* a name used by a writer instead of his or her real name; nom de plume.

pennant *n* **1** a long narrow flag, esp. one used by ships as identification or for signalling. **2** *Chiefly US, Canad, & Austral* a flag indicating the winning of a championship in certain sports.

penniless *adj* very poor.

pennon *n* **1** a long flag, often tapering and divided at the end, originally a knight's personal flag. **2** a small tapering or triangular flag flown by a ship or boat.

penny *n, pl* **pennies** *or* **pence 1** *Brit* **a** a monetary unit worth one hundredth of a pound. **b** (before 1971) a bronze or copper coin worth one twelfth of a shilling. **2** (*pl* **pennies**) *US & Canad* a cent. **3** *Informal, chiefly Brit* the least amount of money: *I don't have a penny.* **4 a pretty penny** *Informal* a considerable sum of money. **5 spend a penny** *Brit informal* to urinate. **6 the penny dropped** *Informal, chiefly Brit* the explanation of something was finally understood.

Penny Black *n* the first adhesive postage stamp, issued in Britain in 1840.

penny-dreadful *n, pl* **-fuls** *Brit informal* a cheap, often lurid book or magazine.

penny-farthing *n Brit* an early type of bicycle with a large front wheel and a small rear wheel.

penny-pinching *adj* **1** excessively careful with money; miserly. *~n* **2** miserliness. **penny-pincher** *n*

pennyroyal *n* a Eurasian plant with hairy leaves and small mauve flowers, which provides an aromatic oil used in medicine.

penny-wise *adj* **penny-wise and pound-foolish** careful or thrifty in small matters but wasteful in large ventures.

pennywort *n* a Eurasian rock plant with whitish-green tubular flowers and rounded leaves.

pennyworth *n* **1** the amount that can be bought for a penny. **2** a small or insignificant amount of something: *they'd thrown in their pennyworth of opinion.*

penology (pee-**nol**-a-jee) *n* the study of the punishment of criminals and of prison management.

pen pal *n Informal* same as **pen friend.**

penpusher *n* a person whose work involves a lot of boring paperwork. **penpushing** *adj, n*

pension[1] *n* **1** a regular payment made by the state or a former employer to a person who has retired or to a widowed or disabled person. *~vb* **2** to grant a pension to. **pensionable** *adj* **pensioner** *n*

pension[2] (**pon**-syon) *n* (in France and some other countries) a relatively cheap boarding house.

pension off *vb* to cause (someone) to retire from a job and pay him or her a pension.

pensive *adj* deeply thoughtful, often with a tinge of sadness. **pensively** *adv*

pent *vb* a past of **pen**[2].

penta- *combining form* five: *pentagon; pentameter.*

pentacle *n* same as **pentagram.**

pentagon *n Geom* a figure with five sides. **pentagonal** *adj*

Pentagon *n* a five-sided building that houses the headquarters of the US Department of Defense.

pentagram *n* a star-shaped figure with five points.

pentameter (pen-**tam**-it-er) *n* a line of poetry consisting of five metrical feet.

Pentateuch (**pent**-a-tyuke) *n* the first five books of the Old Testament. **Pentateuchal** *adj*

pentathlon *n* an athletic contest consisting of five different events. See also **modern pentathlon.**

pentatonic scale *n Music* a scale consisting of five notes.

pentavalent *adj Chem* having a valency of five.

Pentecost *n* a Christian festival occurring on Whit

THESAURUS

infiltrate, permeate, pervade, seep, suffuse **3.** comprehend, decipher, discern, fathom, figure out (*informal*), get to the bottom of, grasp, suss (out) (*slang*), understand, unravel, work out

penetrating 1. biting, carrying, harsh, intrusive, pervasive, piercing, pungent, sharp, shrill, stinging, strong **2.** acute, astute, critical, discerning, discriminating, incisive, intelligent, keen, perceptive, perspicacious, profound, quick, sagacious, searching, sharp, sharp-witted, shrewd

penetration 1. entrance, entry, incision, inroad, invasion, perforation, piercing, puncturing **2.** acuteness, astuteness, discernment, insight, keenness, perception, perspicacity, sharpness, shrewdness, wit

penitence compunction, contrition, regret, remorse, repentance, ruefulness, self-reproach, shame, sorrow

penitent *adj.* abject, apologetic, atoning, conscience-stricken, contrite, regretful, remorseful, repentant, rueful, sorrowful, sorry

penmanship *formal* calligraphy, fist (*informal*), hand, handwriting, longhand, script, writing

pen name allonym, nom de plume, pseudonym

pennant banderole, banner, ensign, flag, jack, pennon, streamer

penniless bankrupt, broke (*informal*), cleaned out (*slang*), destitute, dirt-poor (*informal*), down and out, flat broke (*informal*), impecunious, impoverished, indigent, moneyless, necessitous, needy, on one's uppers, penurious, poor, poverty-stricken, ruined, short, skint (*Brit. slang*), stony-broke (*Brit. slang*), strapped (*slang*), without a penny to one's name, without two pennies to rub together (*informal*)

pension allowance, annuity, benefit, superannuation

pensioner O.A.P., retired person, senior citizen

Sunday celebrating the descent of the Holy Ghost to the apostles.

Pentecostal *adj* relating to any of the Christian groups that have a charismatic and fundamentalist approach to Christianity.

penthouse *n* a luxurious flat built on the top floor or roof of a building.

pent-up *adj* not released; repressed: *pent-up frustration.*

penultimate *adj* second last.

penumbra *n, pl* **-brae** *or* **-bras 1** the partially shadowed region which surrounds the full shadow in an eclipse. **2** *Literary* a partial shadow. **penumbral** *adj*

penurious *adj Formal* **1** niggardly with money. **2** lacking money or means.

penury *n Formal* **1** extreme poverty. **2** extreme scarcity.

peon *n* a Spanish-American farm labourer or unskilled worker.

peony *n, pl* **-nies** a garden plant with showy pink, red, white, or yellow flowers.

people *pl n* **1** persons collectively or in general. **2 a** group of persons considered together: *old people suffer from anaemia more often than younger people do.* **3** (*pl* **-ples**) the persons living in a particular country: *the American people.* **4** one's family or ancestors: *her people originally came from Skye.* **5 the people a** the mass of ordinary persons without rank or privileges. **b** the body of persons in a country who are entitled to vote. *~vb* **-pling, -pled 6** to provide with inhabitants: *the centre of the continent is sparsely peopled.*

pep *n* **1** high spirits, energy, or vitality. *~vb* **pepping, pepped 2 pep up** to make more lively or interesting: *the company has spent thousands trying to pep up its image.*

peplum *n, pl* **-lums** *or* **-la** a flared ruffle attached to the waist of a garment.

pepper *n* **1** a sharp hot condiment obtained from the fruit of an East Indian climbing plant. **2** Also called: **capsicum** a colourful tropical fruit used as a vegetable and a condiment. *~vb* **3** to season with pepper. **4** to sprinkle liberally: *his speech is heavily peppered with Americanisms.* **5** to pelt with small missiles.

pepper-and-salt *adj* **1** (of a fabric) marked with a fine mixture of black and white. **2** (of hair) streaked with grey.

peppercorn *n* the small dried berry of the pepper plant.

peppercorn rent *n* a rent that is very low or nominal.

pepper mill *n* a small hand mill used to grind peppercorns.

peppermint *n* **1** a mint plant which produces a pungent oil, used as a flavouring. **2** a sweet flavoured with peppermint.

peppery *adj* **1** tasting of pepper. **2** irritable.

pep pill *n Informal* a tablet containing a stimulant drug.

pepsin *n* an enzyme produced in the stomach, which, when activated by acid, breaks down proteins.

pep talk *n Informal* a talk designed to increase confidence and enthusiasm.

peptic *adj* **1** of or relating to digestion. **2** of or caused by pepsin or the action of the digestive juices: *a peptic ulcer.*

peptic ulcer *n* ulcer in the stomach or duodenum.

peptide *n Chem* a compound consisting of two or more amino acids linked by chemical bonding between the amino group of one and the carboxyl group of another.

per *prep* **1** for every: *three pence per pound; 30 pounds per week.* **2** by; through. **3 as per** according to: *proceed as per the instructions.* **4 as per usual** *or* **as per normal** *Informal* as usual.

peradventure *Archaic ~adv* **1** by chance; perhaps. *~n* **2** chance or doubt.

perambulate *vb* **-lating, -lated** *Formal* to walk about (a place). **perambulation** *n*

perambulator *n Formal* same as **pram.**

per annum *adv* in each year.

per capita *adj, adv* of or for each person: *the average per capita wage has increased.*

perceive *vb* **-ceiving, -ceived 1** to become aware of (something) through the senses. **2** to understand or grasp. **perceivable** *adj*

per cent *adv* **1** in each hundred. Symbol: % *~n also* **percent 2** a percentage or proportion.

percentage *n* **1** proportion or rate per hundred parts. **2** any proportion in relation to the whole: *a small percentage of the population.* **3** *Informal* profit or advantage.

percentile *n* one of 99 actual or notional values of a variable dividing its distribution into 100 groups with equal frequencies.

perceptible *adj* able to be perceived; recognizable. **perceptibly** *adv*

perception *n* **1** the act of perceiving. **2** insight or intuition: *his acute perception of other people's emotions.* **3** the ability to perceive. **4** way of viewing: *ad-*

THESAURUS

pensive blue (*informal*), cogitative, contemplative, dreamy, grave, meditative, melancholy, mournful, musing, preoccupied, reflective, ruminative, sad, serious, sober, solemn, sorrowful, thoughtful, wistful

pent-up bottled up, bridled, checked, constrained, curbed, held back, inhibited, repressed, smothered, stifled, suppressed

penury *formal* **1.** beggary, destitution, indigence, need, pauperism, poverty, privation, straitened circumstances, want **2.** dearth, deficiency, lack, paucity, scantiness, scarcity, shortage, sparseness

people *n.* **1.** human beings, humanity, humans, mankind, men and women, mortals, persons **2.** citizens, clan, community, family, folk, inhabitants, nation, population, public, race, tribe **3. the people** commonalty, crowd, general public, grass roots, hoi polloi, masses, mob, multitude, plebs, populace, rabble, rank and file, the herd *~vb.* **4.** colonize, inhabit, occupy, populate, settle

pepper *vb.* **1.** flavour, season, spice **2.** bespeckle, dot, fleck, spatter, speck, sprinkle, stipple, stud **3.** bombard, pelt, riddle, scatter, shower

peppery 1. fiery, highly seasoned, hot, piquant, pungent, spicy **2.** choleric, hot-tempered, irascible, irritable, quick-tempered, snappish, testy, touchy, vitriolic, waspish

perceive 1. be aware of, behold, descry, discern, discover, distinguish, espy, make out, note, notice, observe, recognize, remark, see, spot **2.** appreciate, apprehend, comprehend, conclude, deduce, feel, gather, get (*informal*), grasp, know, learn, realize, see, sense, suss (out) (*slang*), understand

perceptible apparent, appreciable, blatant, clear, conspicuous, detectable, discernible, distinct, evident, noticeable, observable, obvious, palpable, perceivable, recognizable, tangible, visible

perception apprehension, awareness, conception, consciousness, discernment, feeling, grasp, idea, im-

vertising affects the customer's perception of a product. **perceptual** *adj*

perceptive *adj* **1** observant. **2** able to perceive. **perceptively** *adv* **perceptiveness** *n*

perch[1] *n* **1** a branch or other resting place above ground for a bird. **2** any raised resting place: *from his perch on the bar stool.* ~*vb* **3** (of birds) to alight or rest on a perch: *it fluttered to the branch and perched there for a moment.* **4** to place or position precariously: *he was perched uneasily on the edge of his chair.*

perch[2] *n, pl* **perch** *or* **perches** a spiny-finned edible freshwater fish of Europe and North America.

perchance *adv Archaic or poetic* **1** perhaps. **2** by chance.

percipient *adj Formal* quick at perceiving; observant. **percipience** *n*

percolate *vb* **-lating, -lated 1** to pass or filter through very small holes: *the light percolating through the stained-glass windows cast coloured patterns on the floor.* **2** to spread gradually: *his theories percolated through the academic community.* **3** to make (coffee) or (of coffee) to be made in a percolator. **percolation** *n*

percolator *n* a coffeepot in which boiling water is forced up through a tube and filters down through the coffee grounds into a container.

percussion *n* **1** the striking of one thing against another. **2** *Music* percussion instruments collectively. **percussive** *adj*

percussion cap *n* a detonator which contains material that explodes when struck.

percussion instrument *n* a musical instrument, such as the drums, that produces a sound when struck directly.

percussionist *n Music* a person who plays percussion instruments.

perdition *n* **1** *Christianity* final and unalterable spiritual ruin; damnation. **2** same as **hell.**

peregrinate *vb* **-nating, -nated** *Formal* to travel or wander about from place to place. **peregrination** *n*

peregrine falcon *n* a European falcon with dark plumage on the back and wings and lighter underparts.

peremptory *adj* **1** urgent or commanding: *a peremptory knock on the door.* **2** expecting immediate obedience without any discussion: *he gave peremptory instructions to his son.* **3** dogmatic. **peremptorily** *adv*

perennial *adj* **1** lasting throughout the year or through many years. ~*n* **2** a plant that continues its growth for at least three years.

perestroika *n* (in the late 1980s) the policy of restructuring the Soviet economy and political system.

perfect *adj* **1** having all essential elements. **2** faultless: *a perfect circle.* **3** correct or precise: *perfect timing.* **4** utter or absolute: *a perfect stranger.* **5** excellent in all respects: *a perfect day.* **6** *Maths* exactly divisible into equal integral or polynomial roots: *36 is a perfect square.* **7** *Grammar* denoting a tense of verbs used to describe a completed action. ~*n* **8** *Grammar* the perfect tense. ~*vb* **9** to improve to one's satisfaction: *he is in Paris to perfect his French.* **10** to make fully accomplished: *he perfected the system.* **perfectly** *adv*

perfectible *adj* capable of becoming or being made perfect. **perfectibility** *n*

perfection *n* the state or quality of being perfect.

perfectionism *n* the demand for the highest standard of excellence. **perfectionist** *n, adj*

perfect pitch *n* same as **absolute pitch.**

perfidious *adj Literary* treacherous or deceitful. **perfidy** *n*

perforate *vb* **-rating, -rated 1** to make a hole or holes in. **2** to punch rows of holes between (stamps) for ease of separation. **perforable** *adj* **perforator** *n*

perforation *n* **1** a hole or holes made in something. **2** a series of punched holes, such as that between individual stamps.

perforce *adv Formal* of necessity.

perform *vb* **1** to carry out (an action): *the hospital performs more than a hundred such operations each year.* **2** to present (a play or concert): *he performed a*

THESAURUS

pression, insight, notion, observation, recognition, sensation, sense, taste, understanding

perceptive acute, alert, astute, aware, discerning, insightful, intuitive, observant, penetrating, percipient, perspicacious, quick, responsive, sensitive, sharp

perch 1. *n.* branch, pole, post, resting place, roost **2.** *vb.* alight, balance, land, rest, roost, settle, sit on

perchance *archaic or poetic* by chance, for all one knows, maybe, peradventure (*archaic*), perhaps, possibly, probably

percipient *formal* alert, alive, astute, aware, discerning, discriminating, intelligent, penetrating, perceptive, perspicacious, quick-witted, sharp, wide-awake

percolate drain, drip, exude, filter, filtrate, leach, ooze, penetrate, permeate, pervade, seep, strain, transfuse

percussion blow, brunt, bump, clash, collision, concussion, crash, impact, jolt, knock, shock, smash, thump

peremptory 1. absolute, binding, categorical, commanding, compelling, decisive, final, imperative, incontrovertible, irrefutable, obligatory, undeniable **2.** arbitrary, assertive, authoritative, autocratic, bossy (*informal*), dictatorial, dogmatic, domineering, high-handed, imperious, intolerant, overbearing

perennial abiding, chronic, constant, continual, continuing, enduring, incessant, inveterate, lasting, lifelong, persistent, recurrent, unchanging

perfect *adj.* **1.** absolute, complete, completed, consummate, entire, finished, full, out-and-out, sheer, unadulterated, unalloyed, unmitigated, utter, whole **2.** blameless, clean, excellent, faultless, flawless, ideal, immaculate, impeccable, pure, splendid, spotless, sublime, superb, superlative, supreme, unblemished, unmarred, untarnished **3.** accurate, close, correct, exact, faithful, precise, right, spot-on (*Brit. informal*), strict, true, unerring ~*vb.* **4.** ameliorate, cultivate, develop, elaborate, hone, improve, polish, refine **5.** accomplish, achieve, carry out, complete, consummate, effect, finish, fulfil, perform, realize

perfection 1. completeness, exactness, excellence, exquisiteness, faultlessness, integrity, maturity, perfectness, precision, purity, sublimity, superiority, wholeness **2.** acme, crown, ideal, paragon **3.** accomplishment, achievement, achieving, completion, consummation, evolution, fulfilment, realization

perfectionist formalist, precisian, precisionist, purist, stickler

perfectly 1. absolutely, altogether, completely, consummately, entirely, fully, quite, thoroughly, totally, utterly, wholly **2.** admirably, exquisitely, faultlessly, flawlessly, ideally, impeccably, superbly, superlatively, supremely, to perfection, wonderfully

perfidious *literary* corrupt, deceitful, dishonest, disloyal, double-dealing, double-faced, faithless, false, traitorous, treacherous, treasonous, two-faced, unfaithful, untrustworthy

perfidy *literary* betrayal, deceit, disloyalty, double-dealing, duplicity, faithlessness, falsity, infidelity, perfidiousness, treachery, treason

couple of songs from his new album. **3** to fulfil: *you have performed the first of two conditions.* **performable** *adj* **performer** *n*

performance *n* **1** the act or process of performing. **2** an artistic or dramatic production: *the concert includes the first performance of a new trumpet concerto.* **3** manner or quality of functioning: *the car's overall performance is excellent.* **4** *Informal* conduct or behaviour, esp. when distasteful: *what did you mean by that performance at the restaurant?*

perfume *n* **1** a liquid cosmetic worn for its pleasant smell. **2** a fragrant smell. *~vb* **-fuming, -fumed 3** to impart a perfume to. **perfumed** *adj*

perfumer *n* a person who makes or sells perfume. **perfumery** *n*

perfunctory *adj Formal* done only as a matter of routine: *he gave his wife a perfunctory kiss.* **perfunctorily** *adv* **perfunctoriness** *n*

pergola *n* an arched trellis or framework that supports climbing plants.

perhaps *adv* **1** possibly; maybe. **2** approximately; roughly: *it would have taken perhaps three or four minutes.*

perianth *n Bot* the outer part of a flower.

pericardium *n, pl* **-dia** the membranous sac enclosing the heart. **pericardial** *adj*

pericarp *n Bot* the part of a fruit enclosing the seed that develops from the wall of the ovary.

perigee *n Astron* the point in its orbit around the earth when the moon or a satellite is nearest the earth.

perihelion *n, pl* **-lia** *Astron* the point in its orbit around the sun when a planet or comet is nearest the sun.

peril *n* great danger or jeopardy. **perilous** *adj*

perimeter (per-**rim**-it-er) *n* **1** *Maths* **a** the curve or line enclosing a plane area. **b** the length of this curve or line. **2** any boundary around something.

perinatal *adj* of or occurring in the period from about three months before to one month after birth.

perineum (per-rin-**nee**-um) *n, pl* **-nea** (-**nee**-a) *Anat* the region of the body between the anus and the genitals. **perineal** *adj*

period *n* **1** a portion of time: *six inches of rain fell in a 24-hour period.* **2** a portion of time specified in some way: *the President's first period of office.* **3** an occurrence of menstruation. **4** *Geol* a unit of geological time during which a system of rocks is formed: *the Jurassic period.* **5** a division of time at school, college, or university when a particular subject is taught. **6** *Physics, maths* the time taken to complete one cycle of a regularly recurring phenomenon. **7** *Chem* one of the horizontal rows of elements in the periodic table. **8** *Chiefly US & Canad* same as **full stop.** *~adj* **9** dating from or in the style of an earlier time: *a performance on period instruments.*

periodic *adj* recurring at intervals. **periodically** *adv* **periodicity** *n*

periodical *n* **1** a publication issued at regular intervals, usually monthly or weekly. *~adj* **2** of or relating to such publications. **3** periodic or occasional.

periodic law *n Chem* the principle that the chemical properties of the elements are periodic functions of their atomic numbers.

periodic table *n Chem* a table of the elements, arranged in order of increasing atomic number, based on the periodic law.

peripatetic (per-rip-a-**tet**-ik) *adj* **1** travelling from place to place. **2** *Brit* employed in two or more educational establishments and travelling from one to another: *a peripatetic violin teacher.* *~n* **3** a peripatetic person.

peripheral (per-**if**-er-al) *adj* **1** not relating to the most important part of something; incidental. **2** of or relating to a periphery. *~n* **3** *Computers* any device, such as a disk drive, concerned with input/output or storage.

periphery (per-**if**-er-ee) *n, pl* **-eries 1** the boundary or edge of an area or group: *slums sprouted up on the periphery of the city.* **2** fringes of a field of activity: *less developed countries on the periphery of the capitalist system.*

periphrasis (per-**if**-ra-siss) *n, pl* **-rases** (-ra-seez) a roundabout way of expressing something; circumlocution.

periscope *n* an optical instrument used, esp. in submarines, to give a view of objects on a different level.

perish *vb* **1** to be destroyed or die. **2** to cause to suffer: *we were perished with cold.* **3** to rot or cause to rot: *to prevent your swimsuit from perishing, rinse it in clean water before it dries.*

perishable *adj* **1** liable to rot. *~n* **2** (*often pl*) a perishable article, esp. food.

THESAURUS

perforate bore, drill, hole, honeycomb, penetrate, pierce, punch, puncture

perform 1. accomplish, achieve, act, bring about, carry out, complete, comply with, discharge, do, effect, execute, fulfil, function, observe, pull off, satisfy, transact, work **2.** act, appear as, depict, enact, play, present, produce, put on, render, represent, stage

performance 1. accomplishment, achievement, act, carrying out, completion, conduct, consummation, discharge, execution, exploit, feat, fulfilment, work **2.** acting, appearance, exhibition, gig (*informal*), interpretation, play, portrayal, presentation, production, representation, show **3.** action, conduct, efficiency, functioning, operation, practice, running, working **4.** *informal* act, behaviour, bother, business, carry-on (*informal, chiefly Brit.*), fuss, pother, rigmarole, to-do

performer actor, actress, artiste, play-actor, player, Thespian, trouper

perfume aroma, attar, balminess, bouquet, cologne, essence, fragrance, incense, niff (*Brit. slang*), odour, redolence, scent, smell, sweetness

perfunctory *formal* automatic, careless, cursory, heedless, inattentive, indifferent, mechanical, negligent, offhand, routine, sketchy, slipshod, slovenly, stereotyped, superficial, unconcerned, unthinking, wooden

perhaps as the case may be, conceivably, feasibly, for all one knows, it may be, maybe, perchance (*archaic or poetic*), possibly

peril danger, exposure, hazard, insecurity, jeopardy, menace, pitfall, risk, uncertainty, vulnerability

perilous chancy (*informal*), dangerous, exposed, fraught with danger, hairy (*slang*), hazardous, parlous (*archaic or humorous*), precarious, risky, threatening, unsafe, unsure, vulnerable

perimeter ambit, border, borderline, boundary, bounds, circumference, confines, edge, limit, margin, periphery

period 1. aeon, age, course, cycle, date, days, epoch, era, generation, season, stage, term, time, years **2.** interval, season, space, span, spell, stretch, term, time, while

periodical *n.* journal, magazine, monthly, organ, paper, publication, quarterly, review, serial, weekly

perish 1. be destroyed, be killed, be lost, collapse, decease, decline, die, disappear, expire, fall, go under,

perishing *adj* **1** (of weather) *Informal* extremely cold. **2** *Slang* confounded or blasted: *get rid of the perishing lot!*

peristalsis (per-riss-**tal**-siss) *n, pl* **-ses** (-seez) *Physiol* the wavelike involuntary muscular contractions of the walls of the digestive tract. **peristaltic** *adj*

peritoneum (per-rit-toe-**nee**-um) *n, pl* **-nea** (-**nee**-a) *or* **-neums** a serous sac that lines the walls of the abdominal cavity and covers the abdominal organs. **peritoneal** *adj*

peritonitis (per-rit-tone-**ite**-iss) *n* inflammation of the peritoneum, causing severe abdominal pain.

periwig *n Historical* a wig formerly worn by men.

periwinkle[1] *n* same as **winkle** (sense 1).

periwinkle[2] *n* a Eurasian evergreen plant with trailing stems and blue flowers.

perjure *vb* **-juring, -jured perjure oneself** *Criminal law* to deliberately give false evidence while under oath. **perjurer** *n*

perjury (**per**-jer-ee) *n, pl* **-juries** *Criminal law* the act of deliberately giving false evidence while under oath.

perk[1] *n Brit informal* an incidental benefit gained from a job, such as a company car.

perk[2] *vb Informal* short for **percolate** (sense 3).

perk up *vb* **1** to make or become more cheerful. **2** to rise or cause to rise briskly: *the dog's ears perked up suddenly.*

perky *adj* **perkier, perkiest 1** jaunty or lively. **2** confident or spirited.

perlemoen (**per**-la-moon) *n S African* same as **abalone.**

perm[1] *n* **1** a hairstyle with long-lasting waves or curls produced by treating the hair with chemicals. *~vb* **2** to give a perm to (hair).

perm[2] *n Informal* short for **permutation** (sense 4).

permafrost *n* ground that is permanently frozen.

permanent *adj* **1** existing or intended to exist forever: *a permanent solution.* **2** not expected to change: *a permanent condition.* **permanence** *n* **permanently** *adv*

permanent wave *n* same as **perm**[1] (sense 1).

permanent way *n Chiefly Brit* the track of a railway, including the sleepers and rails.

permanganate *n* a salt of an acid containing manganese, used as a disinfectant.

permeable *adj* capable of being permeated, esp. by liquids. **permeability** *n*

permeate *vb* **-ating, -ated 1** to penetrate or spread throughout (something): *his mystical philosophy permeates everything he creates.* **2** to pass through or cause to pass through by osmosis or diffusion: *the rain permeated her anorak.* **permeation** *n*

Permian *adj Geol* of the period of geological time about 280 million years ago.

permissible *adj* permitted or allowable. **permissibility** *n*

permission *n* authorization to do something.

permissive *adj* tolerant or lenient, esp. in sexual matters: *the so-called permissive society.* **permissiveness** *n*

permit *vb* **-mitting, -mitted 1** to allow (something) to be done or to happen: *smoking is not permitted in the office.* **2** to allow (someone) to do something: *her father does not permit her to eat sweets.* **3** to allow the possibility (of): *they saw each other as often as time and circumstances permitted.* *~n* **4** an official document granting permission to do something.

permutate *vb* **-tating, -tated** to alter the sequence or arrangement (of): *endlessly permutating three basic designs.*

permutation *n* **1** *Maths* an ordered arrangement of the numbers or terms of a set into specified groups: *the permutations of a, b, and c, taken two at a time, are ab, ba, ac, ca, bc, cb.* **2** a combination of items made by reordering. **3** a transformation. **4** a fixed combination for selections of results on football pools.

pernicious *adj Formal* **1** wicked or malicious: *pernicious lies.* **2** causing grave harm; deadly.

pernicious anaemia *n* a severe form of anaemia resulting in a reduction of the red blood cells, weakness, and a sore tongue.

THESAURUS

lose one's life, pass away, vanish **2.** decay, decompose, disintegrate, moulder, rot, waste, wither

perishable decaying, decomposable, destructible, easily spoilt, liable to rot, short-lived, unstable

perjure oneself *Criminal law* bear false witness, commit perjury, forswear, give false testimony, lie under oath, swear falsely

perjury *Criminal law* bearing false witness, false oath, false statement, false swearing, forswearing, giving false testimony, lying under oath, oath breaking, violation of an oath, wilful falsehood

perk *Brit. informal* benefit, bonus, dividend, extra, fringe benefit, icing on the cake, perquisite (*formal*), plus

permanence constancy, continuance, continuity, dependability, durability, duration, endurance, finality, fixedness, fixity, immortality, indestructibility, lastingness, perdurability (*rare*), permanency, perpetuity, stability, survival

permanent abiding, constant, durable, enduring, eternal, everlasting, fixed, immovable, immutable, imperishable, indestructible, invariable, lasting, long-lasting, perennial, perpetual, persistent, stable, steadfast, unchanging, unfading

permeate charge, diffuse throughout, fill, filter through, imbue, impregnate, infiltrate, pass through, penetrate, percolate, pervade, saturate, seep through, soak through, spread throughout

permissible acceptable, admissible, allowable, all right, authorized, kosher (*informal*), lawful, legal, legitimate, licit (*formal*), O.K. *or* okay (*informal*), permitted, proper, sanctioned

permission allowance, approval, assent, authorization, consent, dispensation, freedom, go-ahead (*informal*), green light, leave, liberty, licence, permit, sanction, sufferance, tolerance

permissive acquiescent, easy-going, forbearing, free, indulgent, latitudinarian, lax, lenient, liberal, open-minded, tolerant

permit 1. *vb.* admit, agree, allow, authorize, consent, empower, enable, endorse, endure, entitle, give leave *or* permission, grant, let, license, own, sanction, suffer, tolerate, warrant **2.** *n.* authorization, liberty, licence, pass, passport, permission, sanction, warrant

permutation alteration, change, shift, transformation, transmutation, transposition

pernicious *formal* bad, baleful, baneful (*archaic*), damaging, dangerous, deadly, deleterious, destructive, detrimental, evil, fatal, harmful, hurtful, injurious, maleficent, malevolent, malicious, malign, malignant, noisome, noxious, offensive, pestilent, poisonous, ruinous, venomous, wicked

pernickety *informal* **1.** careful, carping, difficult to please, exacting, fastidious, finicky, fussy, hair-splitting, nit-picking (*informal*), overprecise, pains-

pernickety *adj Informal* **1** excessively fussy about details. **2** (of a task) requiring close attention.

peroration *n Formal* the concluding part of a speech which sums up the points made previously.

peroxide *n* **1** hydrogen peroxide used as a hair bleach. **2** any of a class of metallic oxides, such as sodium peroxide, Na_2O_2. *~adj* **3** bleached with or resembling peroxide: *a peroxide blonde.* *~vb* **-iding, -ided 4** to bleach (the hair) with peroxide.

perpendicular *adj* **1** at right angles to a given line or surface. **2** upright; vertical. **3** denoting a style of English Gothic architecture characterized by vertical lines. *~n* **4** *Geom* a line or plane perpendicular to another. **perpendicularity** *n*

perpetrate *vb* **-trating, -trated** to perform or be responsible for (a deception or crime). **perpetration** *n* **perpetrator** *n*

perpetual *adj* **1** never ending or never changing: *Mexico's colourful scenery and nearly perpetual sunshine.* **2** continually repeated: *his mother's perpetual worries about his health.* **perpetually** *adv*

perpetual motion *n* motion of a hypothetical mechanism that continues indefinitely without any external source of energy.

perpetuate *vb* **-ating, -ated** to cause to continue: *images that perpetuate stereotypes of Blacks as illiterate, happy-go-lucky entertainers.* **perpetuation** *n*

perpetuity *n, pl* **-ties 1** eternity. **2** the state of being perpetual. **3** something perpetual, such as a pension that is payable indefinitely. **4 in perpetuity** forever.

perplex *vb* **1** to puzzle or bewilder. **2** to complicate: *this merely perplexes the issue.* **perplexing** *adj*

perplexity *n, pl* **-ties 1** the state of being perplexed. **2** something that perplexes.

perquisite *n Formal* same as **perk**[1].

perry *n, pl* **-ries** an alcoholic drink made from fermented pear juice.

per se (per **say**) *adv* in itself.

persecute *vb* **-cuting, -cuted 1** to oppress or maltreat (someone), because of race or religion. **2** to harass (someone) persistently. **persecution** *n* **persecutor** *n*

perseverance *n* continued steady belief or efforts; persistence.

persevere *vb* **-severing, -severed** (often foll. by *with* or *in*) to continue to make an effort despite difficulties.

Persian *adj* **1** of ancient Persia or modern Iran. *~n* **2** a person from Persia (now Iran). **3** the language of Iran or of Persia.

Persian carpet *n* a hand-made carpet or rug with flowing or geometric designs in rich colours.

Persian cat *n* a long-haired variety of domestic cat.

Persian lamb *n* **1** a black loosely curled fur from the karakul lamb. **2** a karakul lamb.

persiflage (**per**-sif-flahzh) *n Literary* light frivolous conversation or writing.

persimmon *n* a sweet red tropical fruit.

persist *vb* **1** to continue without interruption: *if the symptoms persist, see your doctor.* **2** (often foll. by *in* or *with*) to continue obstinately despite opposition: *she persisted in using these controversial methods.*

persistent *adj* **1** unrelenting: *persistent rain.* **2** showing persistence: *she was a persistent woman.* **persistence** *n* **persistently** *adv*

person *n, pl* **people** *or* **persons 1** an individual human being. **2** the body of a human being: *he was found to have a knife concealed about his person.* **3** *Grammar* a category into which pronouns and forms of verbs are subdivided to show whether they refer to the speaker, the person addressed, or some other individual or thing. **4 in person** actually doing something or being somewhere oneself: *I had the chance to hear her speak in person.*

➤ *Person* is generally used in the singular and *people* is used to indicate more than one. The plural *persons* is

THESAURUS

taking, particular, picky (*informal*), punctilious **2.** detailed, exacting, fiddly, fine, tricky

peroration *formal* closing remarks, conclusion, recapitulation, recapping (*informal*), reiteration, summing-up

perpendicular at right angles to, on end, plumb, straight, upright, vertical

perpetrate be responsible for, bring about, carry out, commit, do, effect, enact, execute, inflict, perform, wreak

perpetual 1. abiding, endless, enduring, eternal, everlasting, immortal, infinite, lasting, never-ending, perennial, permanent, unchanging, undying, unending **2.** ceaseless, constant, continual, continuous, endless, incessant, interminable, never-ending, perennial, persistent, recurrent, repeated, unceasing, unfailing, uninterrupted, unremitting

perpetuate continue, eternalize, immortalize, keep alive, keep going, keep up, maintain, preserve, sustain

perplex 1. baffle, befuddle, beset, bewilder, confound, confuse, dumbfound, flummox, mix up, muddle, mystify, nonplus, puzzle, stump **2.** complicate, encumber, entangle, involve, jumble, mix up, snarl up, tangle, thicken

perplexing baffling, bewildering, complex, complicated, confusing, difficult, enigmatic, hard, inexplicable, intricate, involved, knotty, labyrinthine, mysterious, mystifying, paradoxical, puzzling, strange, taxing, thorny, unaccountable, weird

perplexity 1. bafflement, bewilderment, confusion, incomprehension, mystification, puzzlement, stupefaction **2.** complexity, difficulty, inextricability, intricacy, involvement, obscurity **3.** difficulty, dilemma, enigma, fix (*informal*), knotty problem, mystery, paradox, puzzle, snarl

perquisite *formal see* PERK

persecute 1. afflict, be on one's back (*slang*), distress, dragoon, harass, hassle (*informal*), hound, hunt, ill-treat, injure, maltreat, martyr, molest, oppress, pursue, torment, torture, victimize **2.** annoy, badger, bait, bother, pester, tease, vex, worry

perseverance constancy, dedication, determination, diligence, doggedness, endurance, indefatigability, persistence, pertinacity, purposefulness, resolution, sedulity, stamina, steadfastness, tenacity

persevere be determined *or* resolved, carry on, continue, endure, go on, hang on, hold fast, hold on (*informal*), keep going, keep on *or* at, maintain, persist, plug away (*informal*), pursue, remain, stand firm, stick to

persist 1. abide, carry on, continue, endure, keep up, last, linger, remain **2.** *with* **in** *or* **with** be resolute, continue, hold on (*informal*), insist, persevere, stand firm

persistence constancy, determination, diligence, doggedness, endurance, grit, indefatigability, perseverance, pertinacity, pluck, resolution, stamina, steadfastness, tenacity, tirelessness

persistent 1. constant, continual, continuous, endless, incessant, interminable, never-ending, perpetual, relentless, repeated, unrelenting, unremitting **2.** assiduous, determined, dogged, enduring, fixed, immovable, indefatigable, obdurate, obstinate, persevering,

restricted to formal notices.

-person *n combining form* sometimes used instead of *man* and *woman* or *lady*: *chairperson.*

persona (per-**soh**-na) *n, pl* **-nae** (-nee) the personality that a person adopts and presents to other people.

personable *adj* pleasant in appearance and personality.

personage *n* **1** an important or distinguished person. **2** any person.

personal *adj* **1** of the private aspects of a person's life: *redundancy can put an enormous strain on personal relationships.* **2** of a person's body: *personal hygiene.* **3** belonging to, or for the sole use of, a particular individual: *he disappeared, leaving his passport, diary and other personal belongings in his flat.* **4** undertaken by an individual: *the sponsorship deal requires him to make a number of personal appearances for publicity purposes.* **5** offensive in respect of an individual's personality or intimate affairs: *he has suffered a lifetime of personal remarks about his weight.* **6** having the attributes of an individual conscious being: *a personal God.* **7** *Grammar* of person. **8** *Law* of movable property, such as money.

personal assistant *n* a person who is employed to help someone with his or her work, esp. the secretarial and administrative aspects of it.

personal column *n* a newspaper column containing personal messages and advertisements.

personal computer *n* a small computer used for word processing or computer games.

personality *n, pl* **-ties 1** *Psychol* the distinctive characteristics which make an individual unique. **2** the distinctive character of a person which makes him or her socially attractive: *some people find him lacking in personality and a bit colourless.* **3** a well-known person in a certain field; celebrity. **4** a remarkable person: *she is a personality to be reckoned with.* **5** (*often pl*) an offensive personal remark: *the argument never degenerated into personalities.*

personalize *or* **-ise** *vb* **-izing, -ized** *or* **-ising, -ised 1** to base (an argument or discussion) around people's characters rather than on abstract arguments. **2** to mark (stationery or clothing) with a person's initials or name. **3** same as **personify.**

personally *adv* **1** without the help of others: *she had seen to it personally that permission was granted.* **2** in one's own opinion: *personally, I think it's overrated.* **3** as if referring to oneself: *yes, he was rather rude but it's not worth taking it personally.* **4** as a person: *I don't like him personally, but he's fine to work with.*

personal organizer *n* **1** a diary for storing personal records, appointments, etc. **2** a pocket-sized electronic device that performs the same functions.

personal pronoun *n* a pronoun such as *I, you, he, she, it, we,* and *they* that represents a definite person or thing.

personal stereo *n* a small portable audio cassette player used with lightweight headphones.

persona non grata (non **grah**-ta) *n, pl* **personae non gratae** (**grah**-tee) an unacceptable person.

personate *vb* **-ating, -ated** *Criminal law* to assume the identity of (another person) with intent to deceive. **personation** *n*

personify *vb* **-fies, -fying, -fied 1** to give human characteristics to (a thing or abstraction). **2** to represent (an abstract quality) in human or animal form. **3** (of a person or thing) to represent (an abstract quality), as in art. **4** to be the embodiment of: *she can be charm personified.* **personification** *n*

personnel *n* **1** the people employed in an organization or for a service. **2** the department in an organization that appoints or keeps records of employees. **3** (in the armed forces) people, as opposed to machinery or equipment.

perspective *n* **1** a way of regarding situations or facts and judging their relative importance: *the female perspective on sex and love.* **2** objectivity: *Kay's problems helped me put my minor worries into perspective.* **3** a method of drawing that gives the effect of solidity and relative distances and sizes. **4** the appearance of objects or buildings relative to each other, determined by their distance from the viewer.

Perspex *n Trademark* a clear acrylic resin used as a substitute for glass.

perspicacious *adj Formal* acutely perceptive or discerning. **perspicacity** *n*

perspicuous *adj Literary* (of speech or writing) easily understood; lucid. **perspicuity** *n*

THESAURUS

pertinacious, resolute, steadfast, steady, stiff-necked, stubborn, tenacious, tireless, unflagging

person 1. being, body, human, human being, individual, living soul, soul **2. in person** bodily, in the flesh, oneself, personally

personable affable, agreeable, amiable, attractive, charming, good-looking, handsome, likeable *or* likable, nice, pleasant, pleasing, presentable, winning

personage big noise (*informal*), big shot (*informal*), celebrity, dignitary, luminary, megastar (*informal*), notable, personality, public figure, somebody, V.I.P., well-known person, worthy

personal 1. exclusive, individual, intimate, own, particular, peculiar, private, privy, special **2.** bodily, corporal, corporeal, exterior, material, physical **3.** derogatory, disparaging, insulting, nasty, offensive, pejorative, slighting

personality 1. *Psychol.* character, disposition, identity, individuality, make-up, nature, psyche, temper, temperament, traits **2.** attraction, attractiveness, character, charisma, charm, dynamism, likableness *or* likeableness, magnetism, pleasantness **3.** celebrity, famous name, household name, megastar (*informal*), notable, personage, star, well-known face, well-known person

personally 1. alone, by oneself, independently, in person, in the flesh, on one's own, solely **2.** for oneself, for one's part, from one's own viewpoint, in one's own view **3.** individualistically, individually, privately, specially, subjectively

personate *Criminal law* act, depict, enact, feign, imitate, impersonate, play-act, portray, represent

personification embodiment, epitome, image, incarnation, likeness, portrayal, recreation, representation, semblance

personify body forth, embody, epitomize, exemplify, express, incarnate, mirror, represent, symbolize, typify

personnel employees, helpers, human resources, members, men and women, people, staff, workers, work force

perspective angle, attitude, broad view, context, frame of reference, objectivity, outlook, overview, proportion, relation, relative importance, relativity, way of looking

perspicacious *formal* acute, alert, astute, aware, clear-sighted, clever, discerning, keen, observant, penetrating, perceptive, percipient, sagacious, sharp, sharp-witted, shrewd

perspicacity acumen, acuteness, discernment, discrimination, insight, keenness, penetration, perceptiveness, percipience, perspicuity (*literary*), saga-

perspiration *n* **1** the salty fluid secreted by the sweat glands of the skin; sweat. **2** the act of sweating.
perspire *vb* **-spiring, -spired** to sweat.
persuade *vb* **-suading, -suaded 1** to make (someone) do something by reason or charm: *we tried to persuade him not to come up the mountain with us.* **2** to cause to believe; convince: *persuading people of the need for enforced environmental protection may be difficult.* **persuadable** *adj*
persuasion *n* **1** the act of persuading. **2** the power to persuade. **3** a set of beliefs; creed: *the Roman Catholic persuasion; literary intellectuals of the modernist persuasion.*
persuasive *adj* able to persuade: *a persuasive argument.* **persuasively** *adv*
pert *adj* **1** saucy or impudent. **2** attractive in a neat way: *pert buttocks.*
pertain *vb* (often foll. by *to*) **1** to have reference or relevance: *the notes pertaining to the case.* **2** to be appropriate. **3** to belong (*to*) or be a part (*of*).
pertinacious *adj* **1** doggedly resolute in purpose or belief. **2** stubbornly persistent. **pertinacity** *n*
pertinent *adj* relating to the matter at hand; relevant. **pertinence** *n*
perturb *vb* **1** to disturb the composure of. **2** to throw into disorder.
perturbation *n Literary* anxiety or worry.
peruke *n Historical* a wig for men worn in the 17th and 18th centuries.
peruse *vb* **-rusing, -rused 1** to read or examine with care. **2** to browse or read in a leisurely way. **perusal** *n*
pervade *vb* **-vading, -vaded** to spread through or throughout (something). **pervasion** *n* **pervasive** *adj*
perverse *adj* **1** deliberately acting in a way different from what is regarded as normal or proper. **2** wayward or contrary; obstinate. **perversely** *adv* **perversity** *n*
perversion *n* **1** any abnormal means of obtaining sexual satisfaction. **2** the act of perverting.
pervert *vb* **1** to use wrongly or badly. **2** to interpret wrongly or badly; distort. **3** to lead (someone) into abnormal behaviour, esp. sexually; corrupt. **4** to debase. *~n* **5** a person who practises sexual perversion. **perverted** *adj*
pervious *adj* **1** able to be penetrated; permeable: *the thin walls were pervious to the slightest sound.* **2** receptive to new ideas; open-minded.
Pesach *or* **Pesah** (**pay**-sahk) *n* same as **Passover.**
peseta (pess-**say**-ta) *n* the standard monetary unit of Spain.
pesky *adj* **peskier, peskiest** *US & Canad informal* troublesome.
peso (**pay**-so) *n, pl* **-sos** the standard monetary unit of Chile, Colombia, Cuba, the Dominican Republic, Mexico, the Philippines, and Uruguay.
pessary *n, pl* **-ries** *Med* **1** a device worn in the vagina, either as a support for the uterus or as a contraceptive. **2** a vaginal suppository.

THESAURUS

ciousness, sagacity, sharpness, shrewdness, suss (*slang*), wit
perspiration exudation, moisture, sweat, wetness
perspire be damp, be wet, drip, exude, glow, pour with sweat, secrete, sweat, swelter
persuade 1. actuate, advise, allure, bring round (*informal*), coax, counsel, entice, impel, incite, induce, influence, inveigle, prevail upon, prompt, sway, talk into, urge, win over **2.** cause to believe, convert, convince, satisfy
persuasion 1. blandishment, cajolery, conversion, enticement, exhortation, inducement, influencing, inveiglement, wheedling **2.** cogency, force, persuasiveness, potency, power, pull (*informal*) **3.** belief, certitude, conviction, credo, creed, faith, firm belief, fixed opinion, opinion, tenet, views
persuasive cogent, compelling, convincing, credible, effective, eloquent, forceful, impelling, impressive, inducing, influential, logical, moving, plausible, sound, telling, touching, valid, weighty, winning
pertain *often with* **to** appertain, apply, be appropriate, bear on, befit, belong, be part of, be relevant, concern, refer, regard, relate
pertinacious bull-headed, determined, dogged, headstrong, inflexible, intractable, mulish, obdurate, obstinate, persevering, persistent, perverse, pig-headed, relentless, resolute, self-willed, stiff-necked, strong-willed, stubborn, tenacious, unyielding, wilful
pertinent admissible, applicable, apposite, appropriate, apropos, apt, fit, fitting, germane, material, pat, proper, relevant, suitable, to the point, to the purpose
pertness audacity, brashness, brass (*informal*), bumptiousness, cheek (*informal*), cheekiness, chutzpah (*U.S. & Canad. informal*), cockiness, effrontery, forwardness, front, impertinence, impudence, insolence, presumption, rudeness, sauciness
perturb 1. agitate, alarm, bother, discompose, disconcert, discountenance, disquiet, disturb, faze, fluster, ruffle, trouble, unnerve, unsettle, upset, vex, worry **2.** confuse, disarrange, disorder, muddle, unsettle
perusal browse, check, examination, inspection, look through, read, scrutiny, study
peruse browse, check, examine, inspect, look through, read, run one's eye over, scan, scrutinize, study, work over
pervade affect, charge, diffuse, extend, fill, imbue, infuse, overspread, penetrate, percolate, permeate, spread through, suffuse
pervasive common, extensive, general, inescapable, omnipresent, permeating, pervading, prevalent, rife, ubiquitous, universal, widespread
perverse 1. abnormal, contradictory, contrary, delinquent, depraved, deviant, disobedient, froward, improper, incorrect, miscreant, rebellious, refractory, troublesome, unhealthy, unmanageable, unreasonable **2.** contrary, contumacious, cross-grained, dogged, headstrong, intractable, intransigent, mulish, obdurate, obstinate, pig-headed, stiff-necked, stubborn, unyielding, wayward, wilful, wrong-headed
perversion 1. aberration, abnormality, debauchery, depravity, deviation, immorality, kinkiness (*slang*), unnaturalness, vice, vitiation, wickedness **2.** corruption, distortion, falsification, misinterpretation, misrepresentation, misuse, twisting
perversity contradictiveness, contradictoriness, contrariness, contumacy, frowardness, intransigence, obduracy, refractoriness, waywardness, wrong-headedness
pervert *vb.* **1.** abuse, distort, falsify, garble, misconstrue, misinterpret, misrepresent, misuse, twist, warp **2.** corrupt, debase, debauch, degrade, deprave, desecrate, initiate, lead astray, subvert *~n.* **3.** debauchee, degenerate, deviant, weirdo (*informal*)
perverted aberrant, abnormal, corrupt, debased, debauched, depraved, deviant, distorted, evil, immoral, impaired, kinky (*slang*), misguided, pervy (*slang*), sick, twisted, unhealthy, unnatural, vicious, vitiated, warped, wicked
pessimism cynicism, dejection, depression, despair, despondency, distrust, gloom, gloominess, gloomy

pessimism *n* **1** the tendency to expect the worst in all things. **2** the doctrine of the ultimate triumph of evil over good. **pessimist** *n* **pessimistic** *adj* **pessimistically** *adv*

pest *n* **1** an annoying person or thing; nuisance. **2** any organism that damages crops, or injures or irritates livestock or man.

pester *vb* to annoy or nag continually.

pesticide *n* a chemical used to destroy pests, esp. insects.

pestilence *n Literary* any deadly epidemic disease, such as the plague.

pestilent *adj* **1** annoying or irritating. **2** highly destructive morally or physically. **3** likely to cause infectious disease. **pestilential** *adj*

pestle *n* a club-shaped instrument for grinding or pounding substances in a mortar.

pet[1] *n* **1** a tame animal kept for companionship or pleasure. **2** a person who is favoured or indulged: *teacher's pet.* ~*adj* **3** kept as a pet: *a pet hamster.* **4** of or for pet animals: *pet food.* **5** strongly felt or particularly cherished: *a pet hatred; he would not stand by and let his pet project be abandoned.* ~*vb* **petting, petted 6** to treat as a pet; pamper. **7** to pat or stroke affectionately. **8** *Informal* (of two people) to caress each other in an erotic manner.

pet[2] *n* a fit of sulkiness.

petal *n* any of the brightly coloured leaflike parts which form the head of a flower. **petalled** *adj*

petard *n* **1** (formerly) a device containing explosives used to break through a wall or door. **2 hoist with one's own petard** being the victim of one's own schemes.

peter out *vb* to come gradually to an end: *the road petered out into a rutted track.*

Peter Pan *n* a youthful or immature man.

pethidine (**peth**-id-een) *n* a white crystalline water-soluble drug used to relieve pain.

petiole *n Bot* the stalk which attaches a leaf to a plant.

petit bourgeois (pet-ee **boor**-zhwah) *n, pl* **petits bourgeois** (pet-ee **boor**-zhwahz) the lower middle class.

petite (pit-**eat**) *adj* (of a woman) small and dainty.

petit four (pet-ee **four**) *n, pl* **petits fours** (pet-ee **fours**) a very small fancy cake or biscuit.

petition *n* **1** a written document signed by a large number of people demanding some form of action from a government or other authority. **2** any formal request to a higher authority. **3** *Law* a formal application in writing made to a court asking for some specific judicial action: *she filed a petition for divorce.* ~*vb* **4** to address or present a petition to (a government or to someone in authority): *he petitioned the Crown for mercy.* **5** (foll. by *for*) to seek by petition: *the firm's creditors petitioned for liquidation.* **petitioner** *n*

petit mal (pet-ee **mal**) *n* a mild form of epilepsy in which there are periods of loss of consciousness for up to 30 seconds.

petit point (pet-ee **point**) *n* **1** a small diagonal needlepoint stitch used for fine detail. **2** work done with such stitches.

pet name *n* an affectionate nickname for a close friend or family member.

petrel *n* a sea bird with a hooked bill and tubular nostrils, such as the albatross, storm petrel, or shearwater.

Petri dish (**peat**-ree) *n* a shallow dish used in laboratories, esp. for producing cultures of bacteria.

petrify *vb* **-fies, -fying, -fied 1** to stun or daze with fear: *he was petrified of going to jail.* **2** (of organic material) to turn to stone. **3** to make or become unable to change or develop: *a society petrified by outmoded conventions.* **petrification** *n*

petrochemical *n* a substance, such as acetone, obtained from petroleum. **petrochemistry** *n*

petrodollar *n* money earned by a country by exporting petroleum.

petrol *n* a volatile flammable liquid obtained from petroleum and used as a fuel for internal-combustion engines.

petrolatum (pet-rol-**late**-um) *n* a translucent jellylike substance obtained from petroleum: used as a lubricant and in medicine as an ointment base.

petrol bomb *n* a simple grenade consisting of a bottle filled with petrol. A piece of cloth is put in the neck

THESAURUS

outlook, glumness, hopelessness, melancholy, the hump (*Brit. informal*)

pessimist cynic, defeatist, doomster, gloom merchant (*informal*), kill-joy, melancholic, misanthrope, prophet of doom, wet blanket (*informal*), worrier

pessimistic bleak, cynical, dark, dejected, depressed, despairing, despondent, distrustful, downhearted, fatalistic, foreboding, gloomy, glum, hopeless, melancholy, misanthropic, morose, resigned, sad

pest 1. annoyance, bane, bore, bother, drag (*informal*), gall, irritation, nuisance, pain (*informal*), pain in the arse (*taboo informal*), thorn in one's side *or* flesh, trial, vexation **2.** bane, blight, bug, curse, epidemic, infection, pestilence, plague, scourge

pester aggravate (*informal*), annoy, badger, bedevil, bend someone's ear (*informal*), be on one's back (*slang*), bother, bug (*informal*), chivvy (*Brit.*), disturb, drive one up the wall (*slang*), fret, get at, get in one's hair (*informal*), get on one's nerves (*informal*), harass, harry, hassle (*informal*), irk, nag, pick on, plague, torment, worry

pestilence *literary* affliction, bane, Black Death, blight, cancer, canker, curse, epidemic, pandemic, plague, scourge, visitation

pestilential 1. annoying, dangerous, deleterious, destructive, detrimental, evil, foul, harmful, hazardous, injurious, pernicious, ruinous, troublesome **2.** catching, contagious, contaminated, deadly, disease-ridden, infectious, malignant, noxious, pestiferous, poisonous, venomous

pet[1] *n.* **1.** apple of one's eye, blue-eyed boy (*informal*), darling, favourite, idol, jewel, treasure ~*adj.* **2.** domesticated, house, house-broken, house-trained (*Brit.*), tame, trained **3.** cherished, dearest, dear to one's heart, favoured, favourite, particular, preferred, special ~*vb.* **4.** baby, coddle, cosset, mollycoddle, pamper, spoil **5.** caress, fondle, pat, stroke **6.** *informal* canoodle (*slang*), cuddle, kiss, neck (*informal*), smooch (*informal*), snog (*Brit. slang*)

pet[2] bad mood, huff, ill temper, paddy (*Brit. informal*), pique, pout, sulk, sulks, tantrum, temper

peter out come to nothing, die out, dwindle, ebb, evaporate, fade, fail, give out, run dry, run out, stop, taper off, wane

petition 1. *n.* address, appeal, application, entreaty, invocation, memorial, plea, prayer, request, round robin, solicitation, suit, supplication **2.** *vb.* adjure, appeal, ask, beg, beseech, call upon, crave, entreat, plead, pray, press, solicit, sue, supplicate, urge

petrified 1. aghast, appalled, dazed, dumbfounded, frozen, horrified, numb, scared stiff, shocked, speechless, stunned, stupefied, terrified, terror-stricken **2.** fossilized, ossified, rocklike

petrify 1. amaze, appal, astonish, astound, confound,

of the bottle and set alight just before the bomb is thrown.

petroleum *n* a dark-coloured thick flammable crude oil occurring in sedimentary rocks, consisting mainly of hydrocarbons: the source of petrol and paraffin.

petroleum jelly *n* same as **petrolatum.**

petrol station *n Brit* same as **filling station.**

petticoat *n* a woman's underskirt.

pettifogging *adj* excessively concerned with unimportant detail. **pettifogger** *n*

pettish *adj* peevish or fretful. **pettishness** *n*

petty *adj* **-tier, -tiest 1** trivial or unimportant: *petty details.* **2** small-minded: *petty spite.* **3** low in importance: *petty criminals.* **pettily** *adv* **pettiness** *n*

petty cash *n* a small cash fund for minor incidental expenses.

petty officer *n* a noncommissioned officer in the navy.

petulant *adj* unreasonably irritable or peevish. **petulance** *n* **petulantly** *adv*

petunia *n* a tropical American plant with pink, white, or purple funnel-shaped flowers.

pew *n* **1** (in a church) **a** a long benchlike seat with a back, used by the congregation. **b** an enclosed compartment reserved for the use of a family or group. **2 take a pew** *Brit* take a seat.

pewter *n* **1** an alloy containing tin, lead, and sometimes copper and antimony. **2** dishes or kitchen utensils made from pewter.

pfennig (**fen**-ig) *n* a German monetary unit worth one hundredth of a mark.

PG indicating a film certified for viewing by anyone, but which contains scenes that may be unsuitable for children, for whom parental guidance is necessary.

pH *n* potential of hydrogen; a measure of the acidity or alkalinity of a solution.

phaeton (**fate**-on) *n* a light four-wheeled horse-drawn carriage with or without a top.

phagocyte (**fag**-go-site) *n* a cell or protozoan that engulfs particles, such as microorganisms.

phalanger *n* an Australian marsupial with dense fur and a long tail.

phalanx (**fal**-lanks) *n, pl* **phalanxes** *or* **phalanges** (fal-**lan**-jeez) **1** any closely grouped mass of people: *a solid phalanx of reporters and photographers.* **2** a number of people united for a common purpose. **3** an ancient Greek battle formation of infantry in close ranks.

phallic *adj* of or resembling a phallus: *a phallic symbol.*

phallus (**fal**-luss) *n, pl* **-li** (-lie) *or* **-luses 1** same as **penis. 2** an image of the penis as a symbol of reproductive power.

phantasm *n* **1** a phantom. **2** an unreal vision; illusion. **phantasmal** *adj*

phantasmagoria *n* a shifting medley of dreamlike figures. **phantasmagoric** *adj*

phantasy *n, pl* **-sies** *Archaic* same as **fantasy.**

phantom *n* **1** an apparition or spectre. **2** the visible representation of something abstract, such as in a dream or hallucination: *the phantom of liberty.* ~*adj* **3** deceptive or unreal: *she regularly took days off for what her bosses considered phantom illnesses.*

Pharaoh (**fare**-oh) *n* the title of the ancient Egyptian kings.

Pharisee *n* **1** a member of an ancient Jewish sect teaching strict observance of Jewish traditions. **2** (*often not cap*) a self-righteous or hypocritical person. **Pharisaic** *adj*

pharmaceutical *adj* of or relating to drugs or pharmacy.

pharmaceutics *n* same as **pharmacy** (sense 1).

pharmacist *n* a person qualified to prepare and dispense drugs.

pharmacology *n* the science or study of drugs **pharmacological** *adj* **pharmacologist** *n*

pharmacopoeia (far-ma-koh-**pee**-a) *n* an authoritative book containing a list of medicinal drugs along with their uses, preparation and dosages.

pharmacy *n* **1** the preparation and dispensing of drugs. **2** (*pl* **-cies**) a dispensary.

pharyngitis (far-rin-**jite**-iss) *n* inflammation of the pharynx, causing a sore throat.

pharynx (**far**-rinks) *n, pl* **pharynges** (far-**rin**-jeez) *or* **pharynxes** the part of the alimentary canal between the mouth and the oesophagus. **pharyngeal** *adj*

phase *n* **1** any distinct or characteristic stage in a sequence of events: *these two CDs sum up two distinct phases in the singer's career.* **2** *Astron* one of the recurring shapes of the portion of the moon, Mercury, or Venus illuminated by the sun. **3** *Physics* a particular stage in a periodic process or phenomenon. **4** *Physics* **in** *or* **out of phase** (of two waves or signals) reaching or not reaching corresponding phases at the same time. ~*vb* **phasing, phased 5** to do or introduce gradually: *the redundancies will be phased over two years.*

phase in *vb* to introduce in a gradual or cautious manner: *the scheme was phased in over seven years.*

phase out *vb* to discontinue gradually: *rent subsidies are being phased out.*

PhD Doctor of Philosophy.

pheasant *n* a long-tailed bird with a brightly coloured plumage in the male: native to Asia but introduced elsewhere.

phenobarbitone *or* **phenobarbital** *n* a sedative used to treat insomnia and epilepsy.

phenol *n* a white crystalline derivative of benzene, used as an antiseptic and disinfectant and in the

THESAURUS

dumbfound, horrify, immobilize, paralyse, stun, stupefy, terrify, transfix **2.** calcify, fossilize, harden, set, solidify, turn to stone

petty 1. contemptible, inconsiderable, inessential, inferior, insignificant, little, measly (*informal*), negligible, paltry, piddling (*informal*), slight, small, trifling, trivial, unimportant **2.** cheap, grudging, mean, mean-minded, shabby, small-minded, spiteful, stingy, ungenerous **3.** inferior, junior, lesser, lower, minor, secondary, subordinate

petulance bad temper, crabbiness, ill humour, irritability, peevishness, pettishness, pique, pouts, querulousness, spleen, sulkiness, sullenness, waspishness

petulant bad-tempered, captious, cavilling, crabbed, cross, crusty, fault-finding, fretful, huffy, ill-humoured, impatient, irritable, moody, peevish, perverse, pouting, querulous, ratty (*Brit. informal*), snappish, sour, sulky, sullen, ungracious, waspish

phantom 1. apparition, ghost, phantasm, shade (*literary*), spectre, spirit, spook (*informal*), wraith **2.** chimera, figment, figment of the imagination, hallucination, illusion, vision

pharisee canter, dissembler, dissimulator, fraud, humbug, hypocrite, phoney *or esp. U.S.* phony (*informal*), pietist

phase aspect, chapter, condition, development, juncture, period, point, position, stage, state, step, time

phase out axe (*informal*), close, deactivate, dispose

manufacture of resins, explosives, and pharmaceutical substances.

phenomena *n* a plural of **phenomenon.**

phenomenal *adj* **1** extraordinary or outstanding: *a phenomenal success.* **2** of or relating to a phenomenon. **phenomenally** *adv*

phenomenalism *n Philosophy* the doctrine that all knowledge comes from sense perception. **phenomenalist** *n, adj*

phenomenon *n, pl* **-ena** *or* **-enons 1** anything that can be perceived as an occurrence or fact. **2** any remarkable occurrence or person.

➤ Avoid using *phenomena* as a singular.

phenotype *n* the physical form of an organism as determined by the interaction of its genetic make-up and its environment.

phenyl (**fee**-nile) *adj* of, containing, or consisting of the monovalent group C_6H_5, derived from benzene: *a phenyl group.*

phew *interj* an exclamation of relief, surprise, disbelief, or weariness.

phial *n* a small bottle for liquid medicine.

phil. **1** philharmonic. **2** philosophy.

philadelphus *n* a shrub grown for its strongly scented showy flowers.

philander *vb* (of a man) to flirt or have many casual love affairs with women. **philanderer** *n* **philandering** *adj, n*

philanthropy *n, pl* **-pies 1** the practice of helping people less well-off than oneself. **2** love of mankind in general. **philanthropic** *adj* **philanthropist** *n*

philately (fill-**lat**-a-lee) *n* the collection and study of postage stamps. **philatelist** *n*

philharmonic *adj* **1** fond of music. *~n* **2** a specific choir, orchestra, or musical society: *the Vienna Philharmonic.*

philippic *n* a bitter verbal attack.

Philippine *adj, n* same as **Filipino.**

philistine *n* **1** a person who is hostile towards culture and the arts. *~adj* **2** boorishly uncultured. **philistinism** *n*

Philistine *n* a member of the non-Semitic people who inhabited ancient Palestine.

philology *n* (no longer in scholarly use) the science of the structure and development of languages. **philological** *adj* **philologist** *n*

philosopher *n* **1** a person who studies philosophy. **2** a person who remains calm and stoical in the face of difficulties or disappointments.

philosopher's stone *n* a substance thought by alchemists to be capable of changing base metals into gold.

philosophical *or* **philosophic** *adj* **1** of or relating to philosophy or philosophers. **2** calm and stoical in the face of difficulties or disappointments. **philosophically** *adv*

philosophize *or* **-phise** *vb* **-phizing, -phized** *or* **-phising, -phised** to discuss in a philosophical manner. **philosophizer** *or* **-phiser** *n*

philosophy *n, pl* **-phies 1** the academic study of knowledge, thought, and the meaning of life. **2** the particular doctrines of a specific individual or school relating to these issues: *the philosophy of John Locke.* **3** any system of beliefs or values. **4** a personal outlook or viewpoint.

philtre *or US* **philter** *n* a drink supposed to arouse desire.

phlebitis (fleb-**bite**-iss) *n* inflammation of a vein, usually in the legs. **phlebitic** *adj*

phlegm (**flem**) *n* **1** the thick yellowish substance secreted by the walls of the respiratory tract. **2** apathy or stolidity. **3** calmness. **phlegmy** *adj*

phlegmatic (fleg-**mat**-ik) *adj* having an unemotional disposition.

phloem (**flow**-em) *n Bot* the plant tissue that acts as a path for the distribution of food substances to all parts of the plant.

phlox *n, pl* **phlox** *or* **phloxes** a plant with clusters of white, red, or purple flowers.

phobia *n Psychiatry* an intense and irrational fear of a given situation or thing. **phobic** *adj, n*

Phoenician (fon-**nish**-un) *adj* **1** of Phoenicia, an ancient E Mediterranean country. *~n* **2** a person from Phoenicia.

THESAURUS

of gradually, ease off, eliminate, pull out, remove, replace, run down, taper off, terminate, wind down, wind up, withdraw

phenomenal exceptional, extraordinary, fantastic, marvellous, miraculous, notable, outstanding, prodigious, remarkable, sensational, singular, uncommon, unique, unparalleled, unusual, wondrous (*old-fashioned or literary*)

phenomenon **1.** circumstance, episode, event, fact, happening, incident, occurrence **2.** exception, marvel, miracle, nonpareil, prodigy, rarity, sensation, sight, spectacle, wonder

philander coquet, court, dally, flirt, fool around (*informal*), toy, trifle, womanize (*informal*)

philanderer Casanova, dallier, Don Juan, flirt, gallant, gay dog, ladies' man, lady-killer (*informal*), Lothario, playboy, stud (*slang*), trifler, wolf (*informal*), womanizer (*informal*)

philanthropic alms-giving, altruistic, beneficent, benevolent, benignant, charitable, gracious, humane, humanitarian, kind, kind-hearted, munificent, public-spirited

philanthropist alms-giver, altruist, benefactor, contributor, donor, giver, humanitarian, patron

philanthropy alms-giving, altruism, beneficence, benevolence, benignity, bounty, brotherly love, charitableness, charity, generosity, humanitarianism, kind-heartedness, largesse *or* largess, liberality, munificence, open-handedness, patronage, public-spiritedness

philistine **1.** *n.* barbarian, boor, bourgeois, ignoramus, lout, lowbrow, vulgarian, yahoo **2.** *adj.* anti-intellectual, boorish, bourgeois, crass, ignorant, lowbrow, tasteless, uncultivated, uncultured, uneducated, unrefined

philosopher dialectician, logician, mahatma, metaphysician, sage, seeker after truth, theorist, thinker, wise man

philosophical, philosophic **1.** abstract, erudite, learned, logical, rational, sagacious, theoretical, thoughtful, wise **2.** calm, collected, composed, cool, impassive, imperturbable, patient, resigned, sedate, serene, stoical, tranquil, unruffled

philosophy **1.** aesthetics, knowledge, logic, metaphysics, rationalism, reason, reasoning, thinking, thought, wisdom **2.** attitude to life, basic idea, beliefs, convictions, doctrine, ideology, principle, tenets, thinking, values, viewpoint, world-view

phlegmatic apathetic, bovine, cold, dull, frigid, heavy, impassive, indifferent, lethargic, listless, lymphatic, matter-of-fact, placid, sluggish, stoical, stolid, undemonstrative, unemotional, unfeeling

phobia *Psychiatry* aversion, detestation, dislike, distaste, dread, fear, hatred, horror, irrational fear, loath-

phoenix *n* a legendary Arabian bird said to set fire to itself and rise anew from the ashes every 500 years.

phone *n, vb* **phoning, phoned** short for **telephone.**

phonecard *n* a card used instead of coins to operate certain public telephones.

phone-in *n* a radio or television programme in which telephone questions or comments from the public are broadcast live as part of a discussion.

phoneme *n Linguistics* one of the set of speech sounds in any given language that serve to distinguish one word from another. **phonemic** *adj*

phonemics *n* the classification and analysis of the phonemes of a language.

phonetic *adj* **1** of phonetics. **2** denoting any perceptible distinction between one speech sound and another. **3** conforming to pronunciation: *phonetic spelling.* **phonetically** *adv*

phonetics *n* the study of speech processes, including the production, perception, and analysis of speech sounds.

phoney *or esp US* **phony** *Informal ~adj* **-nier, -niest 1** not genuine: *a phoney Belgian 50-franc coin.* **2** (of a person) insincere or pretentious. *~n, pl* **-neys** *or esp US* **-nies 3** an insincere or pretentious person. **4** something that is not genuine.

phonograph *n* **1** an early form of record player capable of recording and reproducing sound on wax cylinders. **2** *US & Canad* a record player.

phonology *n, pl* **-gies 1** the study of the sound system in a language. **2** such a sound system. **phonological** *adj*

phooey *interj Informal* an exclamation of scorn or contempt.

phosgene (**foz**-jean) *n* a poisonous gas used in warfare.

phosphate *n* **1** any salt or ester of any phosphoric acid. **2** (*often pl*) chemical fertilizer containing phosphorous compounds. **phosphatic** *adj*

phosphor *n* a substance capable of emitting light when irradiated with particles of electromagnetic radiation.

phosphoresce *vb* **-rescing, -resced** to exhibit phosphorescence.

phosphorescence *n* **1** *Physics* a fluorescence that persists after the bombarding radiation producing it has stopped. **2** the light emitted in phosphorescence. **phosphorescent** *adj*

phosphoric *adj* of or containing phosphorus in the pentavalent state.

phosphorous *adj* of or containing phosphorus in the trivalent state.

phosphorus *n Chem* a toxic flammable nonmetallic element which appears luminous in the dark. It exists in two forms, white and red. Symbol: P

photo *n, pl* **-tos** short for **photograph.**

photo- *combining form* **1** of or produced by light: *photosynthesis.* **2** indicating a photographic process: *photolithography.*

photocell *n* a cell which produces a current or voltage when exposed to light or other electromagnetic radiation.

photocopier *n* a machine using light-sensitive photographic materials to reproduce written, printed, or graphic work.

photocopy *n, pl* **-copies 1** a photographic reproduction of written, printed, or graphic work. *~vb* **-copies, -copying, -copied 2** to reproduce on photographic material.

photoelectric *adj* of or concerned with electric or electronic effects caused by light or other electromagnetic radiation. **photoelectricity** *n*

photoengraving *n* **1** a photomechanical process for producing letterpress printing plates. **2** a print made from such a plate. **photoengrave** *vb*

photo finish *n* a finish of a race in which contestants are so close that a photograph is needed to decide the result.

Photofit *n Trademark* a picture of someone wanted by the police which has been made by combining photographs of different facial features resembling those of the wanted person.

photoflash *n* same as **flashbulb.**

photoflood *n* a highly incandescent electric lamp used for indoor photography and television.

photogenic *adj* **1** (esp. of a person) always looking attractive in photographs. **2** *Biol* producing or emitting light.

photograph *n* **1** a picture made by the chemical action of light on sensitive film. *~vb* **2** to take a photograph of.

photographic *adj* **1** of or like photography or a photograph. **2** (of a person's memory) able to retain facts or appearances in precise detail. **photographically** *adv*

photography *n* **1** the process of recording images on sensitized material by the action of light. **2** the practice of taking photographs. **photographer** *n*

photogravure *n* a process in which an etched metal plate for printing is produced by photography.

photolithography *n* a lithographic printing process using photographically made plates. **photolithographer** *n*

photometer (foe-**tom**-it-er) *n* an instrument used to measure the intensity of light.

photometry (foe-**tom**-it-tree) *n* the branch of physics concerned with the measurement of the intensity of light. **photometrist** *n*

photomontage (foe-toe-mon-**tahzh**) *n* **1** the combination of several photographs to produce one picture. **2** a picture produced in this way.

photon *n Physics* a quantum of electromagnetic radiation energy, such as light, having both particle and wave behaviour.

photosensitive *adj* sensitive to electromagnetic radiation, esp. light.

Photostat *n* **1** *Trademark* a type of photocopying machine or process. **2** any copy made by such a machine. *~vb* **-statting** *or* **-stating, -statted** *or* **-stated 3** to make a Photostat copy (of).

photosynthesis *n* (in plants) the process by which a green plant uses sunlight to build up carbohydrate reserves. **photosynthesize** *or* **-sise** *vb* **photosynthetic** *adj*

phototropism (foe-toe-**trope**-iz-zum) *n* the growth of plants towards a source of light. **phototropic** *adj*

THESAURUS

ing, obsession, overwhelming anxiety, repulsion, revulsion, terror, thing (*informal*)

phone *see* TELEPHONE

phoney *or esp. U.S.* **phony** *informal* **1.** *adj.* affected, assumed, bogus, counterfeit, ersatz, fake, false, forged, imitation, pseudo (*informal*), put-on, sham, spurious, trick **2.** *n.* counterfeit, fake, faker, forgery, fraud, humbug, impostor, pretender, pseud (*informal*), sham

photograph 1. *n.* image, likeness, photo (*informal*), picture, print, shot, slide, snap (*informal*), snapshot, transparency **2.** *vb.* capture on film, film, get a shot of, record, shoot, snap (*informal*), take, take a picture of, take (someone's) picture

phrasal verb *n* a phrase that consists of a verb plus an adverb or preposition, esp. one whose meaning cannot be deduced from its parts, such as *take in* meaning *deceive*.

phrase *n* **1** a group of words forming a unit of meaning in a sentence. **2** an idiomatic or original expression. **3** *Music* a small group of notes forming a coherent unit of melody. *~vb* **phrasing, phrased 4** to express orally or in a phrase. **5** *Music* to divide (a melodic line or part) into musical phrases, esp. in performance. **phrasal** *adj*

phrase book *n* a book containing frequently used expressions and their equivalent in a foreign language.

phraseology *n, pl* **-gies** the manner in which words or phrases are used.

phrasing *n* **1** the exact words used to say or write something. **2** the way in which someone who is performing a piece of music or reading aloud divides up the work being performed by pausing slightly in appropriate places.

phrenology *n* (formerly) the study of the shape and size of the skull as a means of finding out a person's character and mental ability. **phrenological** *adj* **phrenologist** *n*

phut *Informal ~n* **1** a representation of a muffled explosive sound. *~adv* **2 go phut** to break down or collapse.

phylactery *n, pl* **-teries** *Judaism* either of the pair of square cases containing biblical passages, worn by Jewish men on the left arm and head during weekday morning prayers.

phylum *n, pl* **-la** *Biol* one of the major groups into which the animal and plant kingdoms are divided, containing one or more classes.

physical *adj* **1** of the body, as distinguished from the mind or spirit. **2** of material things or nature: *the physical world.* **3** of or concerned with matter and energy. **4** of or relating to physics. **physically** *adv*

physical education *n* training and practice in sports and gymnastics.

physical geography *n* the branch of geography that deals with the natural features of the earth's surface.

physical jerks *pl n Brit informal* repetitive keep-fit exercises.

physical science *n* any of the sciences concerned with nonliving matter, such as physics, chemistry, astronomy, and geology.

physician *n* **1** a medical doctor. **2** *Archaic* a healer.

physicist *n* a person versed in or studying physics.

physics *n* **1** the branch of science concerned with the properties of matter and energy and the relationships between them. **2** physical properties of behaviour: *the physics of the electron.*

physio *n* **1** short for **physiotherapy. 2** (*pl* **physios**) short for **physiotherapist.**

physiognomy (fiz-ee-**on**-om-ee) *n* **1** a person's face considered as an indication of personality. **2** the outward appearance of something: *the changed physiognomy of the forests.*

physiography *n* same as **physical geography.**

physiology *n* **1** the branch of science concerned with the functioning of organisms. **2** the processes and functions of all or part of an organism. **physiologist** *n* **physiological** *adj*

physiotherapy *n* the treatment of disease or injury by physical means, such as massage or exercises, rather than by drugs. **physiotherapist** *n*

physique *n* person's bodily build and muscular development.

pi *n, pl* **pis 1** the 16th letter in the Greek alphabet (Π, π). **2** *Maths* a number that is the ratio of the circumference of a circle to its diameter; approximate value: 3.141 592... Symbol: π

pia mater (**pie**-a **mate**-er) *n* the innermost of the three membranes that cover the brain and spinal cord.

pianissimo *adj, adv Music* to be performed very quietly.

pianist *n* a person who plays the piano.

piano[1] *n, pl* **-anos** a musical instrument played by depressing keys that cause hammers to strike strings and produce audible vibrations.

piano[2] *adj, adv Music* to be performed softly.

piano accordion *n* an accordion in which the right hand plays a piano-like keyboard. **piano accordionist** *n*

pianoforte (pee-ann-oh-**for**-tee) *n* the full name for **piano**[1].

Pianola (pee-an-**oh**-la) *n Trademark* a type of mechanical piano, the music for which is encoded in perforations in a paper roll.

piazza *n* **1** a large open square in an Italian town. **2** *Chiefly Brit* a covered passageway or gallery.

pibroch (**pee**-brok) *n* a form of music for Scottish bagpipes, consisting of a theme and variations.

pic *n, pl* **pics** *or* **pix** *Informal* a photograph or illustration.

pica (**pie**-ka) *n* **1** a size of printer's type giving 6 lines to the inch. **2** a size of typewriter type that has 10 characters to the inch.

picador *n Bullfighting* a horseman who wounds the bull with a lance to weaken it.

picaresque *adj* of or relating to a type of fiction in which the hero, a rogue, goes through a series of episodic adventures.

picayune (pick-a-**yoon**) *US & Canad informal ~adj* **1** of small value or importance. **2** mean or petty. *~n* **3** any coin of little value, such as a five-cent piece. **4** an unimportant person or thing.

piccalilli *n* a pickle of mixed vegetables in a mustard sauce.

piccanin *n S African informal* a Black African child.

piccaninny *or esp US* **pickaninny** *n, pl* **-nies** *Offensive* a small Black or Aboriginal child.

piccolo *n, pl* **-los** a woodwind instrument an octave higher than the flute.

pick[1] *vb* **1** to choose or select. **2** to gather (fruit, berries, or crops) from (a tree, bush, or field). **3** to remove loose particles from: *she picked some bits of fluff off her sleeve.* **4** to pierce or break up (a hard surface) with a pick. **5** (foll. by *at*) to nibble (at) without

THESAURUS

photographic accurate, cinematic, detailed, exact, faithful, filmic, graphic, lifelike, minute, natural, pictorial, precise, realistic, retentive, visual, vivid

phrase 1. *n.* expression, group of words, idiom, locution, motto, remark, saying, tag, utterance, way of speaking **2.** *vb.* couch, express, formulate, frame, present, put, put into words, say, term, utter, voice, word

phraseology choice of words, diction, expression, idiom, language, parlance, phrase, phrasing, speech, style, syntax, wording

physical 1. bodily, carnal, corporal, corporeal, earthly, fleshly, incarnate, mortal, somatic, unspiritual **2.** material, natural, palpable, real, sensible, solid, substantial, tangible, visible

physician doc (*informal*), doctor, doctor of medicine, general practitioner, G.P., healer, M.D., medic

appetite. 6 to provoke (an argument or fight) deliberately. 7 to separate (strands or fibres), as in weaving. 8 to steal from (someone's pocket). 9 to open (a lock) with an instrument other than a key. 10 to make (one's way) carefully on foot: *they picked their way through the rubble.* 11 **pick and choose** to select fastidiously or fussily. *~n* 12 choice: *take your pick.* 13 the best: *the pick of the country's young cricketers.* ~See also **pick off, pick on,** etc.

pick[2] *n* 1 a tool with a handle and a long curved steel head, used for loosening soil or breaking rocks. 2 any tool used for picking, such as an ice pick or toothpick. 3 a plectrum.

pickaback *n, adv* same as **piggyback.**

pickaxe *or US* **pickax** *n* a large pick.

picket *n* 1 a person or group standing outside a workplace to dissuade strikebreakers from entering. 2 a small unit of troops posted to give early warning of attack. 3 a pointed stake that is driven into the ground to support a fence. *~vb* **-eting, -eted** 4 to act as pickets outside (a workplace).

picket fence *n* a fence consisting of pickets driven into the ground.

picket line *n* a line of people acting as pickets.

pickings *pl n* money or profits acquired easily.

pickle *n* 1 (*often pl*) food, esp. vegetables preserved in vinegar or brine. 2 a liquid or marinade, such as spiced vinegar, for preserving vegetables, meat, or fish. 3 *Informal* an awkward or difficult situation: *to be in a pickle; he got into a bit of a pickle with the Inland Revenue.* *~vb* **-ling, -led** 4 to preserve or treat in a pickling liquid.

pickled *adj* 1 (of food) preserved in a pickling liquid. 2 *Informal* drunk.

pick-me-up *n Informal* a tonic, esp. a special drink taken as a stimulant.

pick off *vb* to aim at and shoot (people or things) one by one.

pick on *vb* to continually treat someone unfairly.

pick out *vb* 1 to select for use or special consideration: *she picked out a wide gold wedding ring.* 2 to distinguish (an object from its surroundings), such as in painting: *the wall panels are light brown, with their edges picked out in gold.* 3 to recognize (a person or thing): *the culprit was picked out at a police identification parade.* 4 to play (a tune) tentatively, as by ear.

pickpocket *n* a person who steals from the pockets of others in public places.

pick up *vb* 1 to lift or raise: *he picked up his glass.* 2 to obtain or purchase: *a couple of pictures she had picked up in a flea market in Paris.* 3 to improve in health or condition: *the tourist trade has picked up after the slump caused by the Gulf War.* 4 to learn as one goes along: *she had a good car and picked up languages quickly.* 5 to raise (oneself) after a fall or setback: *she picked herself up and got on with her life.* 6 to resume; return to. 7 to accept the responsibility for paying (a bill). 8 to collect or give a lift to (passengers or goods). 9 *Informal* to become acquainted with for a sexual purpose. 10 *Informal* to arrest. 11 to receive (sounds or signals).

pick-up *n* 1 a small truck with an open body used for light deliveries. 2 *Informal* a casual acquaintance made for a sexual purpose. 3 *Informal* **a** a stop to collect passengers or goods **b** the people or things collected. 4 a device which converts vibrations into electrical signals, such as that to which a record player stylus is attached.

picky *adj* **pickier, pickiest** *Informal* fussy; finicky.

picnic *n* 1 an excursion on which people bring food to be eaten in the open air. 2 an informal meal eaten out-of-doors. 3 *Informal* an easy or agreeable task: *the press had a picnic.* *~vb* **-nicking, -nicked** 4 to eat or take part in a picnic. **picnicker** *n*

pico- *combining form* denoting 10^{-12}: *picofarad.*

picot (**peek**-oh) *n* any of a pattern of small loops, for example on lace.

Pict *n* a member of any of the peoples who lived in N Britain in the first to the fourth centuries AD. **Pictish** *adj*

pictograph *n* 1 a picture or symbol standing for a word or group of words, as in written Chinese. 2 Also called: **pictogram** a chart on which symbols are used to represent values. **pictographic** *adj*

pictorial *adj* 1 relating to or expressed by pictures. *~n* 2 a periodical containing many pictures.

picture *n* 1 a visual representation produced on a surface, such as in a photograph or painting. 2 a mental image: *neither had any clear picture of whom they were looking for.* 3 a description or account of a situa-

THESAURUS

(*informal*), medical practitioner, medico (*informal*), specialist

physique body, build, constitution, figure, form, frame, make-up, shape, structure

pick *vb.* **1.** choose, decide upon, elect, fix upon, hand-pick, mark out, opt for, select, settle upon, sift out, single out, sort out **2.** collect, cull, cut, gather, harvest, pluck, pull **3.** *with* **at** have no appetite, nibble, peck at, play *or* toy with, push the food round the plate **4.** foment, incite, instigate, provoke, start **5.** break into, break open, crack, force, jemmy, open, prise open **6.** be tentative, find *or* make one's way, move cautiously, tread carefully, work through *~n.* **7.** choice, choosing, decision, option, preference, selection **8.** choicest, *crème de la crème,* elect, elite, flower, pride, prize, the best, the cream, the tops (*slang*)

picket *n.* **1.** demonstrator, flying picket, picketer, protester **2.** guard, lookout, patrol, scout, sentinel, sentry, spotter, vedette (*Military*), watch **3.** pale, paling, palisade, peg, post, stake, stanchion, upright *~vb.* **4.** blockade, boycott, demonstrate

pickle 1. *n. informal* bind (*informal*), difficulty, dilemma, fix (*informal*), hot water (*informal*), jam (*informal*), predicament, quandary, scrape (*informal*), spot (*informal*), tight spot **2.** *vb.* cure, keep, marinade, preserve, steep

pick-me-up *informal* bracer (*informal*), drink, pick-up (*slang*), refreshment, restorative, shot in the arm (*informal*), stimulant, tonic

pick on badger, bait, blame, bully, goad, hector, tease, torment

pick out 1. choose, cull, hand-pick, select, separate the sheep from the goats, single out, sort out **2.** discriminate, distinguish, make distinct, make out, notice, perceive, recognize, tell apart

pick up *vb.* **1.** gather, grasp, hoist, lift, raise, take up, uplift **2.** buy, come across, find, garner, happen upon, obtain, purchase, score (*slang*) **3.** gain, gain ground, get better, improve, make a comeback (*informal*), mend, perk up, rally, recover, take a turn for the better **4.** acquire, get the hang of (*informal*), learn, master **5.** call for, collect, get, give someone a lift, go to get, uplift (*Scot.*) **6.** *slang* apprehend, arrest, bust (*informal*), collar (*informal*), do (*slang*), lift (*slang*), nab (*informal*), nail (*informal*), nick (*slang, chiefly Brit.*), pinch (*informal*), pull in (*Brit. slang*), run in (*slang*), take into custody

picnic 1. excursion, outdoor meal, outing **2.** *informal* breeze (*U.S. & Canad. informal*), child's play (*infor-*

tion considered as an observable scene: *the reports do not provide an accurate picture of the spread of AIDS.* **4** a person or thing resembling another: *he is the picture of a perfect host.* **5** a person or scene typifying a particular state: *his face was a picture of dejection.* **6** the image on a television screen. **7** a cinema film. **8 the pictures** *Chiefly Brit* a cinema or film show. **9 in the picture** informed about a situation. *~vb* **-turing, -tured 10** to visualize or imagine. **11** to describe or depict vividly: *a documentary that had pictured the police as good-natured dolts.* **12** to put in a picture or make a picture of: *the women pictured above are all the same age.*

picture rail *n* the rail near the top of a wall from which pictures are hung.

picturesque *adj* **1** visually pleasing, as in being striking or quaint: *a small picturesque harbour.* **2** (of language) graphic or vivid.

picture window *n* a large window with a single pane of glass, usually facing a view.

piddle *vb* **-dling, -dled 1** *Informal* to urinate. **2 piddle about, around** *or* **away** to spend (one's time) aimlessly: *we have been piddling around for seven months.*

piddling *adj Informal* petty or trivial.

pidgin *n* a language made up of elements of two or more languages and used between the speakers of the languages involved.

pidgin English *n* a pidgin in which one of the languages involved is English.

pie *n* **1** a sweet or savoury filling baked in pastry. **2 pie in the sky** illusory hope or promise of some future good.

piebald *adj* **1** marked in two colours, esp. black and white. *~n* **2** a black-and-white horse.

piece *n* **1** a separate bit or part. **2** an instance or occurrence: *a piece of luck.* **3** an example or specimen of a style or type: *each piece of furniture is crafted from native red pine by traditional methods.* **4** a literary, musical, or artistic composition. **5** a coin: *a fifty-pence piece.* **6** a firearm or cannon. **7** a small object used in playing various games: *a chess piece.* **8 go to pieces** (of a person) to lose control of oneself; have a breakdown. *~vb* **piecing, pieced 9** (often foll. by *together*) to fit or assemble bit by bit. **10** (often foll. by *up*) to patch or make up (a garment) by adding pieces.

pièce de résistance (**pyess** de ray-**zeest**-onss) *n* the most outstanding item in a series.

piece goods *pl n* goods, esp. fabrics, made in standard widths and lengths.

piecemeal *adv* **1** bit by bit; gradually. *~adj* **2** fragmentary or unsystematic: *a piecemeal approach.*

piece of eight *n, pl* **pieces of eight** a former Spanish coin worth eight reals.

piecework *n* work paid for according to the quantity produced.

pie chart *n* a circular graph divided into sectors proportional to the sizes of the quantities represented.

pied *adj* having markings of two or more colours.

pied-à-terre (**pyay**-da-**tair**) *n, pl* **pieds-à-terre** (**pyay**-da-**tair**) a flat or other lodging for occasional use.

pie-eyed *adj Slang* drunk.

pier *n* **1** a structure with a deck that is built out over water and used as a landing place or promenade. **2** a pillar or support that bears heavy loads. **3** the part of a wall between two adjacent openings.

pierce *vb* **piercing, pierced 1** to make a hole in (something) with a sharp point. **2** to force (a way) through (something). **3** (of light) to shine through (darkness). **4** (of sounds or cries) to sound sharply through (the silence). **5** to penetrate: *the cold pierced the air.* **piercing** *adj*

pier glass *n* a tall narrow mirror, designed to hang on the wall between windows.

Pierrot (**pier**-roe) *n* a male character from French pantomime with a whitened face, white costume, and pointed hat.

pietism *n* exaggerated piety.

piety *n, pl* **-ties 1** dutiful devotion to God and observance of religious principles. **2** the quality of being pious. **3** a pious action or saying.

piezoelectric effect (pie-eez-oh-ill-**ek**-trik) *or* **piezoelectricity** *n Physics* **a** the production of electricity by applying a mechanical stress to certain crystals. **b** the converse effect in which stress is produced in a crystal as a result of an applied voltage.

piffle *n Informal* nonsense.

THESAURUS

mal), cinch (*informal*), piece of cake (*informal*), pushover (*informal*), walkover (*informal*)

pictorial expressive, graphic, illustrated, picturesque, representational, scenic, striking, vivid

picture *n.* **1.** delineation, drawing, effigy, engraving, illustration, image, likeness, painting, photograph, portrait, portrayal, print, representation, similitude, sketch **2.** account, depiction, description, image, impression, re-creation, report **3.** carbon copy, copy, dead ringer (*slang*), double, duplicate, image, likeness, living image, lookalike, replica, ringer (*slang*), spit (*informal, chiefly Brit.*), spit and image (*informal*), spitting image (*informal*), twin **4.** archetype, embodiment, epitome, essence, living example, perfect example, personification **5.** film, flick (*slang*), motion picture, movie (*U.S. informal*) *~vb.* **6.** conceive of, envision, imagine, see, see in the mind's eye, visualize **7.** delineate, depict, describe, draw, illustrate, paint, photograph, portray, render, represent, show, sketch

picturesque attractive, beautiful, charming, colourful, graphic, pretty, quaint, scenic, striking, vivid

piddling *informal* crappy (*slang*), derisory, fiddling, insignificant, little, measly (*informal*), Mickey Mouse (*slang*), paltry, petty, piffling (*informal*), poxy (*slang*), puny, trifling, trivial, unimportant, useless, worthless

piebald black and white, brindled, dappled, flecked, mottled, pied, speckled, spotted

piece *n.* **1.** allotment, bit, chunk, division, fraction, fragment, length, morsel, mouthful, part, portion, quantity, scrap, section, segment, share, shred, slice **2.** case, example, instance, occurrence, sample, specimen, stroke **3.** article, bit (*informal*), composition, creation, item, production, study, work, work of art **4. go to pieces** break down, crack up (*informal*), crumple, disintegrate, fall apart, lose control, lose one's head *~vb.* **5.** *often with* **together** assemble, compose, fix, join, mend, patch, repair, restore, unite

pièce de résistance chef-d'oeuvre, jewel, masterpiece, masterwork, showpiece

piecemeal 1. *adv.* at intervals, bit by bit, by degrees, by fits and starts, fitfully, intermittently, little by little, partially, slowly **2.** *adj.* fragmentary, intermittent, interrupted, partial, patchy, spotty, unsystematic

pier *n.* **1.** jetty, landing place, promenade, quay, wharf **2.** buttress, column, pile, piling, pillar, post, support, upright

pierce bore, drill, enter, impale, penetrate, perforate, prick, probe, puncture, run through, spike, stab, stick into, transfix

piffling *adj Informal* worthless; trivial.
pig *n* **1** a mammal with a long head, a snout, and bristle-covered skin, which is kept and killed for pork, ham, and bacon. **2** *Informal* a dirty, greedy, or bad-mannered person. **3** *Offensive slang* a policeman. **4** a mass of metal cast into a simple shape. **5** *Brit informal* something that is difficult or unpleasant: *the coast is a pig for little boats.* **6 a pig in a poke** something bought or received without previous sight or knowledge. **7 make a pig of oneself** *Informal* to overeat. *~vb* **pigging, pigged 8** (of a sow) to give birth. **9** (often foll. by *out*) *Informal* to eat greedily or to excess: *she had pigged out on pizza before the show.*
pigeon[1] *n* **1** a bird which has a heavy body, small head, and short legs, and is usually grey in colour. **2** *Slang* a victim or dupe.
pigeon[2] *n Brit informal* concern or responsibility: *this is our pigeon – there's nothing to keep you.*
pigeonhole *n* **1** a small compartment, such as in a bureau, for filing papers. *~vb* **-holing, -holed 2** to classify or categorize. **3** to put aside.
pigeon-toed *adj* with the toes or feet turned inwards.
piggery *n, pl* **-geries** a place where pigs are kept.
piggish *adj* **1** like a pig in appetite or manners. **2** stubborn. **piggishness** *n*
piggy *n, pl* **-gies 1** a child's word for a **pig**. *~adj* **-gier, -giest 2** same as **piggish.**
piggyback *or* **pickaback** *n* **1** a ride on the back and shoulders of another person. *~adv, adj* **2** on the back and shoulders of another person.
piggy bank *n* a child's bank shaped like a pig with a slot for coins.
pig-headed *adj* stupidly stubborn.
pig iron *n* crude iron produced in a blast furnace and poured into moulds.
Pig Islander *n NZ informal* a New Zealander.
piglet *n* a young pig.
pigment *n* **1** any substance which gives colour to paint or dye. **2** a substance which occurs in plant or animal tissue and produces a characteristic colour. **pigmentary** *adj*
pigmentation *n* colouring in plants, animals, or humans, caused by the presence of pigments.
Pigmy *n, pl* **-mies** same as **Pygmy.**
pigskin *n* **1** the skin of the domestic pig. **2** leather made of this skin. **3** *US & Canad informal* a football.
pigsty *or US & Canad* **pigpen** *n, pl* **-sties 1** a pen for pigs. **2** *Brit* an untidy place.
pigswill *n* waste food or other edible matter fed to pigs.
pigtail *n* a plait of hair or one of two plaits on either side of the face.
pike[1] *n, pl* **pike** *or* **pikes** a large predatory freshwater fish with a broad flat snout, strong teeth, and a long body covered with small scales.
pike[2] *n* a medieval weapon consisting of a metal spearhead on a long pole. **pikeman** *n*
pikestaff *n* **1** the wooden handle of a pike. **2 plain as a pikestaff** very obvious or noticeable.
pilaster *n* a shallow rectangular column attached to the face of a wall. **pilastered** *adj*
pilau *or* **pilaf** *n* a Middle Eastern dish, consisting of rice flavoured with spices and cooked in stock, to which meat, poultry, or fish may be added.
pilchard *n* a small edible sea fish of the herring family, with a rounded body covered with large scales.
pile[1] *n* **1** a collection of objects laid on top of one another. **2** *Informal* a large amount: *boxing has made him a pile of money; I've got piles of work to do.* **3** same as **pyre. 4** a large building or group of buildings. **5** *Physics* a nuclear reactor. *~vb* **piling, piled 6** (often foll. by *up*) to collect or be collected into a pile: *snow piled up in the drive.* **7** (foll. by *in, into, off, out,* etc.) to move in a group, often in a hurried manner: *the crew piled into the van.* **8 pile it on** *Informal* to exaggerate. ~See also **pile up.**
pile[2] *n* a long heavy beam driven into the ground as a foundation for a structure.
pile[3] *n* the fibres in a fabric that stand up or out from the weave, such as in carpeting or velvet.
pile-driver *n* a machine that drives piles into the ground.
piles *pl n* swollen veins in the rectum; haemorrhoids.
pile up *vb* **1** to gather or be gathered in a pile. *~n* **pile-up 2** *Informal* a traffic accident involving several vehicles.
pilfer *vb* to steal (minor items) in small quantities.
pilgrim *n* **1** a person who journeys to a holy place. **2** any wayfarer.
pilgrimage *n* **1** a journey to a shrine or other holy place. **2** a journey or long search made for sentimental reasons: *a sentimental pilgrimage to the poet's birthplace.*

THESAURUS

piercing ear-splitting, high-pitched, loud, penetrating, sharp, shattering, shrill
piety devotion, devoutness, dutifulness, duty, faith, godliness, grace, holiness, piousness, religion, reverence, sanctity, veneration
pig 1. boar, grunter, hog, piggy, piglet, porker, shoat, sow, swine **2.** *informal* animal, beast, boor, brute, glutton, guzzler, hog (*informal*), slob (*slang*), sloven, swine
pigeon[1] **1.** bird, dove, squab **2.** *slang* dupe, fall guy (*informal*), mug (*Brit. slang*), sucker (*slang*), victim
pigeon[2] *Brit. informal* baby (*slang*), business, concern, lookout (*informal*), responsibility, worry
pigeonhole *n.* **1.** compartment, cubbyhole, cubicle, locker, niche, place, section *~vb.* **2.** catalogue, characterize, classify, codify, compartmentalize, label, slot (*informal*), sort **3.** defer, file, postpone, put off, shelve
pig-headed bull-headed, contrary, cross-grained, dense, froward, inflexible, mulish, obstinate, perverse, self-willed, stiff-necked, stubborn, stupid, unyielding, wilful, wrong-headed
pigment colorant, colour, colouring, colouring matter, dye, dyestuff, paint, stain, tincture, tint
pile[1] *n.* **1.** accumulation, assemblage, assortment, collection, heap, hoard, mass, mound, mountain, stack, stockpile **2.** *informal* a lot, great deal, ocean, oodles (*informal*), quantity, stacks **3.** building, edifice, erection, structure *~vb.* **4.** *often with* **up** accumulate, amass, assemble, collect, gather, heap, hoard, load up, mass, stack, store **5.** *often with* **in, into, off, out,** *etc.* charge, crowd, crush, flock, flood, jam, pack, rush, stream
pile[2] beam, column, foundation, pier, piling, pillar, post, support, upright
pile[3] down, fibre, filament, fur, hair, nap, plush, shag, surface
piles haemorrhoids
pile-up *informal* accident, collision, crash, multiple collision, smash, smash-up (*informal*)
pilfer appropriate, embezzle, filch, knock off (*slang*), lift (*informal*), nick (*slang, chiefly Brit.*), pinch (*informal*), purloin, rifle, rob, snaffle (*Brit. informal*), snitch (*slang*), steal, swipe (*slang*), take, thieve, walk off with

Pilgrim Fathers *pl n* the English Puritans who founded Plymouth Colony in SE Massachusetts (1620).

pill *n* **1** a small mass of medicine intended to be swallowed whole. **2 the pill** *Informal* an oral contraceptive taken by a woman. **3** something unpleasant that must be endured: *her reinstatement was a bitter pill to swallow; the pill was sweetened by a reduction in interest.*

pillage *vb* **-laging, -laged 1** to steal property violently, often in war. *~n* **2** the act of pillaging. **3** something obtained by pillaging; booty.

pillar *n* **1** an upright support of stone, brick, or metal; column. **2** something resembling this: *a pillar of smoke.* **3** a prominent supporter or member: *a pillar of society.* **4 from pillar to post** from one place to another.

pillar box *n* (in Britain) a red pillar-shaped public letter box situated in the street.

pillbox *n* **1** a box for pills. **2** a small enclosed fort of reinforced concrete. **3** a small round hat.

pillion *n* **1** a seat for a passenger behind the rider of a motorcycle or horse. *~adv* **2** on a pillion: *the motorbike on which he was riding pillion.*

pillock *n Slang* a stupid or annoying person.

pillory *n, pl* **-ries 1** *Historical* a wooden frame in which offenders were locked by the neck and wrists and exposed to public abuse and ridicule. *~vb* **-ries, -rying, -ried 2** to expose to public ridicule. **3** to punish by putting in a pillory.

pillow *n* **1** a cloth bag stuffed with feathers, polyester fibre, or pieces of foam rubber used to support the head in bed. *~vb* **2** to rest (one's head) on or as if on a pillow: *he pillowed his head in her lap.*

pillowcase *or* **pillowslip** *n* a removable washable cover for a pillow.

pilot *n* **1** a person who is qualified to fly an aircraft or spacecraft. **2** a person employed to steer a ship into or out of a port. **3** a person who acts as a guide. *~adj* **4** serving as a test or trial: *a pilot scheme.* **5** serving as a guide: *a pilot beacon.* *~vb* **-loting, -loted 6** to act as pilot of. **7** to guide or lead (a project or people): *the bill was piloted through the Commons by Disraeli.*

pilot light *n* a small flame that lights the main burner of a gas appliance.

pilot officer *n* the most junior commissioned rank in certain air forces.

pimento *n, pl* **-tos** same as **allspice** or **pimiento.**

pimiento (pim-**yen**-toe) *n, pl* **-tos** a Spanish pepper with a red fruit used as a vegetable.

pimp *n* **1** a man who obtains customers for a prostitute, in return for a share of his or her earnings. *~vb* **2** to act as a pimp.

pimpernel *n* a plant, such as the scarlet pimpernel, typically having small star-shaped flowers.

pimple *n* a small swollen infected spot on the skin. **pimpled** *adj* **pimply** *adj*

pin *n* **1** a short stiff straight piece of wire with a pointed end and a rounded head: used mainly for fastening. **2** short for **cotter pin, hairpin, rolling pin** or **safety pin. 3** a wooden or metal peg. **4** a pin-shaped brooch. **5** (in various bowling games) a club-shaped wooden object set up in groups as a target. **6** a clip that prevents a hand grenade from exploding until it is removed or released. **7** *Golf* the flagpole marking the hole on a green. **8** *Informal* a leg. *~vb* **pinning, pinned 9** to fasten with a pin or pins. **10** to seize and hold fast: *they pinned his arms behind his back.* **11 pin something on someone** *Informal* to place the blame for something on someone: *corruption charges are the easiest to pin on former dictators.* ~See also **pin down.**

PIN Personal Identity Number: a code number used in conjunction with a bank card to enable an account holder to use certain computerized systems, such as cash dispensers.

pinafore *n* **1** *Chiefly Brit* an apron with a bib. **2** a dress with a sleeveless bodice or bib top, worn over a jumper or blouse.

pinball *n* an electrically operated table game in which the player shoots a small ball through several hazards.

pince-nez (panss-**nay**) *n, pl* **pince-nez** glasses that are held in place only by means of a clip over the bridge of the nose.

pincers *pl n* **1** a gripping tool consisting of two hinged arms and curved jaws. **2** the jointed grasping arms of crabs and lobsters.

pinch *vb* **1** to squeeze (something, esp. flesh) between a finger and thumb. **2** to squeeze by being too tight: *shoes that pinch.* **3** to cause stinging pain to: *the cold pinched his face.* **4** to make thin or drawn-looking, such as from grief or cold. **5** *Informal* to steal. **6** *Informal* to arrest. **7** (usually foll. by *out* or *back*) to remove the tips of (a plant shoot) to correct or encourage growth. *~n* **8** a squeeze or sustained nip. **9** the quantity that can be taken up between a thumb and finger: *a pinch of ground ginger.* **10** extreme stress or need: *most companies are feeling the pinch of recession.* **11 at a pinch** if absolutely necessary. **12 feel the pinch** to be forced to economize.

pinchbeck *n* **1** an alloy of copper and zinc, used as imitation gold. *~adj* **2** sham or cheap.

THESAURUS

pilgrim crusader, hajji *or* hadji, palmer, traveller, wanderer, wayfarer

pilgrimage crusade, excursion, expedition, hajj *or* hadj, journey, mission, tour, trip

pill 1. bolus, capsule, pellet, pilule, tablet **2. the pill** oral contraceptive **3.** *slang* bore, drag (*informal*), nuisance, pain (*informal*), pain in the neck (*informal*), pest, trial

pillage *vb.* **1.** despoil, freeboot, loot, maraud, plunder, raid, ransack, ravage, rifle, rob, sack, strip *~n.* **2.** depredation, devastation, marauding, plunder, rapine, robbery, sack, spoliation **3.** booty, loot, plunder, spoils

pillar 1. column, pier, pilaster, piling, post, prop, shaft, stanchion, support, upright **2.** leader, leading light (*informal*), mainstay, rock, supporter, tower of strength, upholder, worthy

pillory *vb.* brand, cast a slur on, denounce, expose to ridicule, heap *or* pour scorn on, hold up to shame, lash, show up, stigmatize

pilot 1. *n.* airman, aviator, captain, conductor, coxswain, director, flier, guide, helmsman, leader, navigator, steersman **2.** *adj.* experimental, model, test, trial **3.** *vb.* conduct, control, direct, drive, fly, guide, handle, lead, manage, navigate, operate, shepherd, steer

pimple boil, pustule, spot, swelling, zit (*slang*)

pin *vb.* **1.** affix, attach, fasten, fix, join, secure **2.** fix, hold down, hold fast, immobilize, pinion, press, restrain

pinch *vb.* **1.** compress, grasp, nip, press, squeeze, tweak **2.** chafe, confine, cramp, crush, hurt, pain **3.** *informal* filch, knock off (*slang*), lift (*informal*), nick (*slang, chiefly Brit.*), pilfer, purloin, rob, snaffle (*Brit. informal*), snatch, snitch (*slang*), steal, swipe (*slang*) **4.** *informal* apprehend, arrest, bust (*informal*), collar (*informal*), do (*slang*), lift (*slang*), nab (*informal*), nail (*informal*), nick (*slang, chiefly Brit.*), pick up (*slang*), pull in (*Brit. slang*), run in (*slang*), take into custody *~n.* **5.** nip, squeeze, tweak **6.** bit, dash, jot, mite, small

pincushion *n* a small cushion in which pins are stuck ready for use.

pin down *vb* **1** to force (someone) to make a decision or carry out a promise. **2** to define clearly: *the courts have found it difficult to pin down what exactly obscenity is.*

pine[1] *n* **1** an evergreen tree with long needle-shaped leaves and brown cones. **2** the light-coloured wood of this tree.

pine[2] *vb* **pining, pined 1** (often foll. by *for*) to feel great longing (for). **2** (often foll. by *away*) to become ill or thin through grief or longing.

pineal gland *or* **body** (**pin**-ee-al) *n* a small cone-shaped gland at the base of the brain.

pineapple *n* an large tropical fruit with juicy flesh and a thick hard skin.

pine cone *n* the woody seed case of a pine tree.

pine marten *n* a mammal of N European and Asian coniferous woods, with dark brown fur and a creamy-yellow patch on the throat.

ping *n* **1** a short high-pitched sound, such as of a bullet striking metal. *~vb* **2** to make such a noise.

pinger *n* a device that makes a pinging sound, esp. a timer.

Ping-Pong *n Trademark* same as **table tennis.**

pinhead *n* **1** the head of a pin. **2** *Informal* a stupid person. **pinheaded** *adj*

pinhole *n* a small hole made with or as if with a pin.

pinion[1] *n* **1** *Chiefly poetic* a bird's wing. **2** the outer part of a bird's wing including the flight feathers. *~vb* **3** to immobilize (someone) by holding or tying his or her arms. **4** to confine.

pinion[2] *n* a cogwheel that engages with a larger wheel or rack.

pink[1] *n* **1** a colour between red and white. **2** anything pink, such as pink paint or pink clothing: *packaged in pink.* **3** a garden plant with pink, red, or white fragrant flowers. **4 in the pink** in good health. *~adj* **5** of a colour between red and white. **6** *Brit informal* having mild left-wing sympathies. *~vb* **7** same as **knock** (sense 7). **pinkish** *or* **pinky** *adj*

pink[2] *vb* to cut with pinking shears.

pinkie *or* **pinky** *n, pl* **-ies** *Scot, US, & Canad* the little finger.

pinking shears *pl n* scissors with a serrated edge that give a wavy edge to material cut and so prevent fraying.

pin money *n* a small amount of extra money earned to buy small luxuries.

pinna *n Anat* the external part of the ear.

pinnace *n* a ship's boat.

pinnacle *n* **1** the highest point of fame or success. **2** a towering peak of a mountain. **3** a slender spire.

pinnate *adj Bot* (of compound leaves) having leaflets growing opposite each other in pairs.

pinny *n, pl* **-nies** an informal or child's name for **pinafore** (sense 1).

pinotage (**pin**-oh-tazh) *n S African* a red wine blended from the Pinot Noir and Hermitage grapes that is unique to South Africa.

pinpoint *vb* **1** to locate or identify exactly: *we've pinpointed the fault.* *~adj* **2** exact: *pinpoint accuracy.*

pinprick *n* a small irritation or annoyance.

pins and needles *n Informal* a tingling sensation in a part of the body.

pinstripe *n* (in textiles) a very narrow stripe in fabric or the fabric itself.

pint *n* **1** *Brit* a unit of liquid measure equal to one eighth of an Imperial gallon (0.568 litre). **2** *US* a unit of liquid measure equal to one eighth of a US gallon (0.473 litre). **3** *Brit informal* a pint of beer.

pinta *n Informal* a pint of milk.

pintail *n, pl* **-tails** *or* **-tail** a greyish-brown duck with a pointed tail.

pintle *n* a pin or bolt forming the pivot of a hinge.

pinto *US & Canad ~adj* **1** marked with patches of white; piebald. *~n, pl* **-tos 2** a pinto horse.

pint-size *or* **pint-sized** *adj Informal* very small.

pin tuck *n* a narrow, ornamental fold used on shirt fronts and dress bodices.

pin-up *n* **1** *Informal* a picture of a sexually attractive person, often partially or totally undressed. **2** *Slang* a person who has appeared in such a picture. **3** a photograph of a famous personality.

pinwheel *n* same as **Catherine wheel.**

Pinyin *n* a system of spelling used to represent Chinese in Roman letters.

pion *or* **pi meson** *n Physics* any of three subatomic particles which are classified as mesons.

pioneer *n* **1** an explorer or settler of a new land or region. **2** an originator or developer of something new. *~vb* **3** to be a pioneer (in or of). **4** to initiate or develop: *the new technique was pioneered in France.*

pious *adj* **1** religious or devout. **2** insincerely reverent; sanctimonious. **piousness** *n*

pip[1] *n* the seed of a fleshy fruit, such as an apple or pear.

pip[2] *n* **1** a short high-pitched sound used as a time signal on radio. **2** any of the spots on a playing card, dice, or domino. **3** *Informal* the emblem worn on the shoulder by junior officers in the British Army, indicating their rank.

pip[3] *n* **1** a contagious disease of poultry. **2** *Facetious slang* a minor human ailment. **3 give someone the pip** *Brit slang* to annoy someone: *it really gives me the pip.*

THESAURUS

quantity, *soupçon,* speck, taste **7.** crisis, difficulty, emergency, exigency, hardship, necessity, oppression, pass, plight, predicament, pressure, strait, stress

pin down 1. compel, constrain, force, make, press, pressurize **2.** designate, determine, home in on, identify, locate, name, pinpoint, specify

pine 1. *often with* **for** ache, carry a torch for, covet, crave, desire, eat one's heart out over, hanker, hunger for, long, lust after, sigh, thirst for, wish, yearn **2.** *often with* **away** decay, decline, droop, dwindle, fade, flag, languish, peak, sicken, sink, waste, weaken, wilt, wither

pinion *vb.* bind, chain, confine, fasten, fetter, immobilize, manacle, pin down, shackle, tie

pink *adj.* flesh, flushed, reddish, rose, roseate, rosy, salmon

pinnacle 1. acme, apex, apogee, crest, crown, eminence, height, meridian, peak, summit, top, vertex, zenith **2.** belfry, cone, needle, obelisk, pyramid, spire, steeple

pinpoint define, distinguish, get a fix on, home in on, identify, locate, spot

pint *Brit. informal* ale, beer, jar (*Brit. informal*), jug (*Brit. informal*)

pioneer *n.* **1.** colonist, colonizer, explorer, frontiersman, settler **2.** developer, founder, founding father, innovator, leader, trailblazer *~vb.* **3.** create, develop, discover, establish, initiate, instigate, institute, invent, launch, lay the groundwork, map out, open up, originate, prepare, show the way, start, take the lead

pious 1. dedicated, devoted, devout, God-fearing, godly, holy, religious, reverent, righteous, saintly,

pip[4] *vb* **pipping, pipped pip someone at the post** *Brit slang* to defeat someone whose success seems certain.

pipe *n* **1** a long tube for conveying water, oil, or gas. **2 a** a tube with a small bowl at the end for smoking tobacco. **b** the amount of tobacco that fills the bowl of a pipe. **3 put that in your pipe and smoke it** *Informal* accept that fact if you can. **4** *Zool, bot* any of various hollow organs, such as the respiratory passage of certain animals. **5 a** a tubular instrument in which air vibrates and produces a musical sound. **b** any of the tubular devices on an organ. **6 the pipes** See **bagpipes. 7** a boatswain's whistle. *~vb* **piping, piped 8** to play (music) on a pipe. **9** to summon or lead by a pipe: *to pipe in the haggis.* **10 a** to signal orders to (the crew) by a boatswain's pipe. **b** to signal the arrival or departure of: *he piped his entire ship's company on deck.* **11** to utter in a shrill tone. **12** to convey (water, oil, or gas) by pipe. **13** to force cream or icing through a shaped nozzle to decorate food. ~See also **pipe down, pipe up.**

pipeclay *n* a fine white pure clay, used in tobacco pipes and pottery and to whiten leather and similar materials.

pipe cleaner *n* a short length of wire covered with tiny tufts of yarn: used to clean the stem of a tobacco pipe.

piped music *n* light music played as background music in public places.

pipe down *vb Informal* to stop talking or making noise.

pipe dream *n* a fanciful or impossible plan or hope.

pipeline *n* **1** a long pipe for transporting oil, water, or gas. **2** a means of communication. **3 in the pipeline** in preparation.

pipe organ *n* same as **organ** (sense 2a).

piper *n* a person who plays a pipe or bagpipes.

pipette *n* a slender glass tube for transferring or measuring out liquids.

pipe up *vb* to speak up unexpectedly.

pipi *n, pl* **pipi** *or* **pipis 1** an Australian mollusc of sandy beaches widely used as bait. **2** an edible shellfish of New Zealand.

piping *n* **1** a system of pipes. **2** a string of icing or cream used to decorate cakes and desserts. **3** a thin strip of covered cord or material, used to edge hems or cushions. **4** the sound of a pipe or bagpipes. **5** a shrill voice or whistling sound: *a dove's cool piping.* *~adj* **6** making a shrill sound. *~adv* **7 piping hot** extremely hot.

pipistrelle *n* a type of small brownish bat found throughout the world.

pipit *n* a small songbird with a brownish speckled plumage and a long tail.

pippin *n* a type of eating apple.

pipsqueak *n Informal* an insignificant or contemptible person.

piquant (**pee**-kant) *adj* **1** having a spicy taste. **2** stimulating to the mind: *love was a forbidden piquant secret.* **piquancy** *n*

pique (**peek**) *n* **1** a feeling of resentment or irritation, such as from hurt pride. *~vb* **piquing, piqued 2** to hurt (someone's) pride. **3** to excite (curiosity or interest).

piqué (**pee**-kay) *n* a stiff ribbed fabric of cotton, silk, or spun rayon.

piquet (pik-**ket**) *n* a card game for two people played with a reduced pack.

piracy *n, pl* **-cies 1** *Brit* robbery on the seas. **2** a crime, such as hijacking, committed aboard a ship or aircraft. **3** the unauthorized use of patented or copyrighted material.

piranha *n* a small fierce freshwater fish of tropical America, with strong jaws and sharp teeth.

pirate *n* **1** a person who commits piracy. **2** a vessel used by pirates. **3** a person who illegally sells or publishes someone else's literary or artistic work. **4** a person or group of people who broadcast illegally. *~vb* **-rating, -rated 5** to sell or reproduce (artistic work, ideas, etc.) illegally. **piratical** *adj*

pirouette *n* **1** a body spin performed on the toes or the ball of the foot. *~vb* **-etting, -etted 2** to perform a pirouette.

piscatorial *adj Formal* of or relating to fish, fishing, or fishermen.

Pisces *n Astrol* the twelfth sign of the zodiac; the Fishes.

pisciculture (**piss**-ee-cult-cher) *n Formal* the rearing and breeding of fish under controlled conditions.

piscine (**piss**-sign) *adj* of or resembling a fish.

piss *Taboo ~vb* **1** to urinate. **2** to discharge as or in one's urine: *to piss blood.* *~n* **3** an act of urinating. **4** urine. **5 take the piss** to make fun of or mock someone.

piss down *vb Taboo slang* to rain heavily.

pissed *adj Brit taboo slang* drunk.

piss off *vb Taboo slang* **1** to annoy or disappoint. **2** *Chiefly Brit* to go away: often used to dismiss a person.

pistachio *n, pl* **-chios** a Mediterranean nut with a hard shell and an edible green kernel.

piste (**peest**) *n* a slope or course for skiing.

pistil *n* the seed-bearing part of a flower.

THESAURUS

spiritual **2.** goody-goody, holier-than-thou, hypocritical, pietistic, religiose, sanctimonious, self-righteous, unctuous

pipe *n.* **1.** conduit, conveyor, duct, hose, line, main, passage, pipeline, tube **2.** briar, clay, meerschaum **3.** fife, horn, tooter, whistle, wind instrument *~vb.* **4.** cheep, peep, play, sing, sound, tootle, trill, tweet, twitter, warble, whistle **5.** bring in, channel, conduct, convey, siphon, supply, transmit

pipe down *informal* belt up (*slang*), be quiet, button it (*slang*), button one's lip (*slang*), hold one's tongue, hush, put a sock in it (*Brit. slang*), quieten down, shush, shut one's mouth, shut up (*informal*), silence

pipeline 1. conduit, conveyor, duct, line, passage, pipe, tube **2. in the pipeline** brewing, coming, getting ready, in process, in production, on the way, under way

piquant 1. acerbic, biting, highly-seasoned, peppery, pungent, savoury, sharp, spicy, stinging, tangy, tart, with a kick (*informal*), zesty **2.** interesting, lively, provocative, racy, salty, scintillating, sparkling, spirited, stimulating

pique *n.* **1.** annoyance, displeasure, grudge, huff, hurt feelings, irritation, miff (*informal*), offence, resentment, umbrage, vexation, wounded pride *~vb.* **2.** affront, annoy, displease, gall, get (*informal*), incense, irk, irritate, miff (*informal*), mortify, nark (*slang*), nettle, offend, peeve (*informal*), provoke, put out, put someone's nose out of joint (*informal*), rile, sting, vex, wound **3.** arouse, excite, galvanize, goad, kindle, provoke, rouse, spur, stimulate, stir, whet

piracy buccaneering, freebooting, hijacking, infringement, plagiarism, rapine, robbery at sea, stealing, theft

pirate *n.* **1.** buccaneer, corsair, filibuster, freebooter, marauder, raider, rover, sea robber, sea rover, sea

pistillate *adj Bot* (of plants) having pistils.
pistol *n* a short-barrelled handgun.
pistol-whip *vb* **-whipping, -whipped** *US* to beat or strike with a pistol barrel.
piston *n* a cylindrical part that slides to and fro in a hollow cylinder: in an engine it is attached by a rod to other parts, thus its movement causes the other parts to move.
pit[1] *n* **1** a large deep opening in the ground. **2** a coal mine. **3** *Anat* **a** a small natural depression on the surface of a body or organ. **b** the floor of any natural bodily cavity: *the pit of the stomach.* **4** *Pathol* a pockmark. **5** a concealed danger or difficulty. **6** an area at the side of a motor-racing track for servicing or refuelling vehicles. **7 the pit** hell. **8** the area occupied by the orchestra in a theatre. **9** an enclosure for fighting animals or birds. **10** the back of the ground floor of a theatre. **11** same as **pitfall** (sense 2). *~vb* **pitting, pitted 12** (often foll. by *against*) to match in opposition, esp. as antagonists: *sister pitted against sister.* **13** to mark with small dents or scars. **14** to place or bury in a pit. **15 pit one's wits against** to compete against in a test or contest. ~See also **pits.**
pit[2] *Chiefly US & Canad ~n* **1** the stone of various fruits. *~vb* **pitting, pitted 2** to remove the stone from (a fruit).
pitapat *adv* **1** with quick light taps. *~n* **2** such taps.
pit bull terrier *n* a strong muscular terrier with a short coat.
pitch[1] *vb* **1** to hurl or throw. **2** to set up (a tent or camp). **3** to slope or fall forwards or downwards: *she pitched forwards like a diver.* **4** (of a ship or plane) to dip and raise its back and front alternately. **5** to set the level or tone of: *his ambitions were pitched too high.* **6** to aim to sell (a product) to a specified market or on a specified basis. **7** *Music* to sing or play (a note or interval) accurately. *~n* **8** *Chiefly Brit* (in many sports) the field of play. **9** a level of emotion: *children can wind their parents up to a pitch of anger and guilt.* **10** the degree or angle of slope. **11** the distance between corresponding points or adjacent threads on a screw thread. **12** the pitching motion of a ship or plane. **13** *Music* the highness or lowness of a note in relation to other notes: *low pitch.* **14** the act or manner of pitching a ball. **15** *Chiefly Brit* the place where a street or market trader regularly sells. **16** *Slang* a persuasive sales talk, esp. one routinely repeated. ~See also **pitch in, pitch into.**
pitch[2] *n* **1** a thick sticky substance formed from coal tar and used for paving or waterproofing. **2** any similar substance, such as asphalt, occurring as a natural deposit. *~vb* **3** to apply pitch to.
pitch-black *adj* extremely dark; unlit: *it was a wild night, pitch-black, with howling gales.*
pitchblende *n* a blackish mineral which is the principal source of uranium and radium.
pitch-dark *adj* extremely or completely dark.
pitched battle *n* a fierce fight.
pitcher[1] *n* a large jug, usually rounded with a narrow neck.
pitcher[2] *n Baseball* the player on the fielding team who throws the ball to the batter.
pitcher plant *n* a plant with pitcher-like leaves that attract and trap insects, which are then digested.
pitchfork *n* **1** a long-handled fork with two or three long curved prongs for tossing hay. *~vb* **2** to use a pitchfork on (something).
pitch in *vb* to cooperate or contribute.
pitch into *vb Informal* to attack (someone) physically or verbally.
pitch pine *n* a pine tree of North America: a source of turpentine and pitch.
pitch pipe *n* a small pipe that sounds a note to establish the correct starting note for unaccompanied singing.
piteous *adj* arousing or deserving pity: *the piteous mewing of an injured kitten.* **piteousness** *n*
pitfall *n* **1** an unsuspected difficulty or danger. **2** a trap in the form of a concealed pit, designed to catch men or wild animals.
pith *n* **1** the soft white lining inside the rind of fruits such as the orange. **2** the essential part: *religion was formerly the very pith of Scottish life.* **3** the soft spongy tissue in the centre of the stem of certain plants.
pithead *n* the top of a mine shaft and the buildings and hoisting gear around it.
pith helmet *n* a lightweight hat made of the pith of the sola, an E Indian swamp plant, that is worn for protection from the sun.
pithy *adj* **pithier, pithiest 1** terse and full of meaning. **2** of, resembling, or full of pith. **pithiness** *n*
pitiable *adj* arousing or deserving pity or contempt. **pitiableness** *n*
pitiful *adj* arousing or deserving great pity or contempt. **pitifully** *adv* **pitifulness** *n*

THESAURUS

wolf **2.** cribber (*informal*), infringer, plagiarist, plagiarizer *~vb.* **3.** appropriate, borrow, copy, crib (*informal*), lift (*informal*), plagiarize, poach, reproduce, steal
pit *n.* **1.** abyss, cavity, chasm, coal mine, crater, dent, depression, dimple, excavation, gulf, hole, hollow, indentation, mine, pockmark, pothole, trench *~vb.* **2.** *often with* **against** match, oppose, put in opposition, set against **3.** dent, dint, gouge, hole, indent, mark, nick, notch, pockmark, scar
pitch *vb.* **1.** bung (*Brit. slang*), cast, chuck (*informal*), fling, heave, hurl, launch, lob (*informal*), sling, throw, toss **2.** erect, fix, locate, place, plant, put up, raise, settle, set up, station **3.** dive, drop, fall headlong, stagger, topple, tumble **4.** flounder, lurch, make heavy weather, plunge, roll, toss, wallow, welter *~n.* **5.** *chiefly Brit.* field of play, ground, park (*U.S. & Canad.*), sports field **6.** degree, height, level, point **7.** angle, cant, dip, gradient, incline, slope, steepness, tilt **8.** *Music* harmonic, modulation, sound, timbre, tone **9.** *slang* line, patter, sales talk, spiel (*informal*)
pitch-black dark, ebony, inky, jet, jet-black, pitch-dark, raven, sable, unlit
pitch in chip in (*informal*), contribute, cooperate, do one's bit, help, join in, lend a hand, participate
piteous affecting, deplorable, dismal, distressing, doleful, grievous, harrowing, heartbreaking, heart-rending, lamentable, miserable, mournful, moving, pathetic, pitiable, pitiful, plaintive, poignant, sad, sorrowful, woeful, wretched
pitfall **1.** banana skin (*informal*), catch, danger, difficulty, drawback, hazard, peril, snag, trap **2.** deadfall, downfall, pit, snare, trap
pith core, crux, essence, gist, heart, heart of the matter, kernel, marrow, meat, nub, point, quintessence, salient point, the long and the short of it
pithy brief, cogent, compact, concise, epigrammatic, expressive, finely honed, forceful, laconic, meaningful, pointed, short, succinct, terse, to the point, trenchant
pitiful **1.** deplorable, distressing, grievous, harrowing, heartbreaking, heart-rending, lamentable, miserable, pathetic, piteous, pitiable, sad, woeful, wretched **2.** abject, base, beggarly, contemptible, despicable, dismal, inadequate, insignificant, low, mean, measly, miserable, paltry, scurvy, shabby, sorry, vile, worthless

pitiless *adj* feeling no pity or mercy. **pitilessly** *adv*

piton (**peet**-on) *n Mountaineering* a metal spike that may be driven into a crack and used to secure a rope.

pits *pl n* **the pits** *Slang* the worst possible person, place, or thing.

pitta bread *or* **pitta** *n* a flat rounded slightly leavened bread, orig. from the Middle East.

pittance *n* a very small amount of money.

pitter-patter *n* **1** the sound of light rapid taps or pats, such as of rain drops. *~vb* **2** to make such a sound.

pituitary *or* **pituitary gland** *n* the gland at the base of the brain which secretes hormones that affect skeletal growth, development of the sex glands, and other functions of the body.

pity *n, pl* **pities 1** sorrow felt for the sufferings of others. **2 have** *or* **take pity on** to have sympathy or show mercy for. **3** a cause of regret: *it's a great pity he did not live longer.* *~vb* **pities, pitying, pitied 4** to feel pity for. **pitying** *adj*

pivot *n* **1** a central shaft around which something turns. **2** the central person or thing necessary for progress or success. *~vb* **-oting, -oted 3** to turn on or provide with a pivot.

pivotal *adj* **1** of crucial importance. **2** of or acting as a pivot.

pix *n Informal* a plural of **pic.**

pixie *or* **pixy** *n, pl* **pixies** (in folklore) a fairy or elf.

pizza *n* a dish of Italian origin consisting of a baked disc of dough covered with a wide variety of savoury toppings.

pizzazz *or* **pizazz** *n Informal* an attractive combination of energy and style.

pizzicato (pit-see-**kah**-toe) *adj, adv Music* (in music for the violin family) to be plucked with the finger.

Pl. (in street names) Place.

plaas *n S African* a farm.

placard *n* **1** a notice that is paraded in public. *~vb* **2** to attach placards to.

placate *vb* **-cating, -cated** to calm (someone) to stop him or her feeling angry or upset. **placatory** *adj*

place *n* **1** a particular part of a space or of a surface. **2** a geographical point, such as a town or city. **3** a position or rank in a sequence or order. **4** an open square lined with houses in a city or town. **5** space or room. **6** a house or living quarters: *he's buying his own place.* **7** any building or area set aside for a specific purpose. **8** the point reached in reading or speaking: *her finger was pressed to the page as if marking her place.* **9** right or duty: *it's not my place to do their job for them.* **10** appointment, position, or job: *there is intense competition for places at Britain's medical schools.* **11** position, condition, or state: *Britain's place in the world.* **12** a space or seat, as at a dining table. **13** *Maths* the relative position of a digit in a number. **14 all over the place** in disorder or disarray. **15 go places** *Informal* to become successful. **16 in** *or* **out of place** in or out of the proper or customary position. **17 in place of a** instead of: *leeks can be used in place of the broccoli.* **b** in exchange for: *he gave her it in place of her ring.* **18 know one's place** to be aware of one's inferior position. **19 put someone in his** *or* **her place** to humble someone who is arrogant, conceited, etc. **20 take place** to happen or occur. **21 take the place of** to be a substitute for. *~vb* **placing, placed 22** to put in a particular or appropriate place: *Dave placed his glass on the table beside him.* **23** to find or indicate the place of: *I bet you the media couldn't have placed Neath on the map before the by-election.* **24** to identify or classify by linking with an appropriate context: *I felt I should know him, but could not quite place him.* **25** to make (an order or bet). **26** to find a home or job for (someone). **27** (often foll. by *with*) to put under the care (of). **28** *Brit* (of a racehorse, greyhound, athlete, etc.) to arrive in first, second, third, or sometimes fourth place.

placebo (plas-**see**-bo) *n, pl* **-bos** *or* **-boes** *Med* an inactive substance given to a patient usually to compare its effects with those of a real drug but sometimes for the psychological benefit gained by the patient through believing that he or she is receiving treatment.

place kick *n Rugby, American football, etc* a kick in which the ball is placed in position before it is kicked.

placement *n* **1** arrangement or position. **2** a temporary job which someone is given as part of a training course: *many pupils have been on work placements with local businesses.* **3** the act or an instance of finding someone a job or a home: *the main task of the adoption agency is to find the best family placement for each child.*

placenta (plass-**ent**-a) *n, pl* **-tas** *or* **-tae** the organ formed in the womb of most mammals during preg-

THESAURUS

pitiless brutal, callous, cold-blooded, cold-hearted, cruel, hardhearted, harsh, heartless, implacable, inexorable, inhuman, merciless, relentless, ruthless, uncaring, unfeeling, unmerciful, unsympathetic

pittance allowance, chicken feed (*slang*), drop, mite, modicum, peanuts (*slang*), portion, ration, slave wages, trifle

pity *n.* **1.** charity, clemency, commiseration, compassion, condolence, fellow feeling, forbearance, kindness, mercy, quarter, sympathy, tenderness, understanding **2. have** *or* **take pity on** feel compassion for, forgive, have mercy on, melt, pardon, put out of one's misery, relent, reprieve, show mercy, spare **3.** crime (*informal*), crying shame, misfortune, regret, sad thing, shame, sin *~vb.* **4.** bleed for, commiserate with, condole with, feel for, feel sorry for, grieve for, have compassion for, sympathize with, weep for

pivot *n.* **1.** axis, axle, fulcrum, spindle, swivel **2.** centre, focal point, heart, hinge, hub, kingpin *~vb.* **3.** revolve, rotate, spin, swivel, turn, twirl **4.** be contingent, depend, hang, hinge, rely, revolve round, turn

pixie *or* **pixy** brownie, elf, fairy, peri, sprite

placard advertisement, bill, poster, public notice, sticker

placate appease, assuage, calm, conciliate, humour, mollify, pacify, propitiate, satisfy, soothe, win over

place *n.* **1.** area, location, locus, point, position, site, situation, spot, station, venue, whereabouts **2.** city, district, hamlet, locale, locality, neighbourhood, quarter, region, town, vicinity, village **3.** grade, position, rank, station, status **4.** accommodation, room, space, stead **5.** abode, apartment, domicile, dwelling, flat, home, house, manor, mansion, pad (*slang*), property, residence, seat **6.** affair, charge, concern, duty, function, prerogative, responsibility, right, role **7.** appointment, berth (*informal*), billet (*informal*), employment, job, position, post **8. in place of** as an alternative to, as a substitute for, in exchange for, in lieu of, instead of, taking the place of **9. put (someone) in his** *or* **her place** bring down, cut down to size, humble, humiliate, make (someone) eat humble pie, make (someone) swallow his pride, mortify, take down a peg (*informal*) **10. take place** befall, betide, come about, come to pass (*archaic*), go on, happen, occur, transpire (*informal*) *~vb.* **11.** bung (*Brit. slang*), deposit, dispose, establish, fix, install, lay, locate, plant, position, put, rest, set, settle, situate, stand, station, stick (*informal*) **12.** associate, identify, know, put one's fin-

nancy, providing oxygen and nutrients for the fetus. **placental** *adj*

place setting *n* the cutlery, crockery, and glassware laid for one person at a dining table.

placid *adj* having a calm appearance or nature: *placid waters; a placid temperament.* **placidity** *or* **placidness** *n* **placidly** *adv*

placket *n Dressmaking* an opening at the waist of a dress or skirt for buttons or zips or for access to a pocket.

plagiarize *or* **-rise** (**play**-jer-ize) *vb* **-rizing, -rized** *or* **-rising, -rised** to steal ideas or passages from (another's work) and present them as one's own. **plagiarism** *n* **plagiarizer** *or* **-riser** *n*

plague *n* **1** any widespread and usually highly contagious disease with a high fatality rate. **2** an infectious disease of rodents transmitted to man by the bite of the rat flea; bubonic plague. **3** something that afflicts or harasses: *a plague of locusts.* **4** *Informal* a nuisance. *~vb* **plaguing, plagued 5** to afflict or harass: *a playing career plagued by injury.* **6** *Informal* to annoy or pester.

plaice *n, pl* **plaice** *or* **plaices** an edible European flatfish with a brown body marked with red or orange spots.

plaid *n* **1** a long piece of tartan cloth worn over the shoulder as part of Highland costume. **2** a crisscross weave or cloth.

Plaid Cymru (plide **kumm**-ree) *n* the Welsh nationalist party.

plain *adj* **1** flat or smooth. **2** easily understood: *he made it plain what he wanted from me.* **3** honest or blunt: *the plain fact is that my mother has no time for me.* **4** without adornment: *a plain brown envelope.* **5** not good-looking. **6** (of fabric) without pattern or of simple weave. **7** lowly, esp. in social rank or education: *the plain people of Ireland.* **8** *Knitting* of or done in plain stitch. *~n* **9** a level stretch of country. **10** a simple stitch in knitting made by passing the wool round the front of the needle. *~adv* **11** clearly or simply: *that's just plain stupid!* **plainly** *adv* **plainness** *n*

plainchant *n* same as **plainsong.**

plain chocolate *n* chocolate with a slightly bitter flavour and dark colour.

plain clothes *pl n* ordinary clothes, as opposed to uniform, worn by a detective on duty.

plain flour *n* flour to which no raising agent has been added.

plain sailing *n* **1** *Informal* smooth or easy progress. **2** *Naut* sailing in a body of water that is unobstructed; clear sailing.

plainsong *n* the style of unaccompanied choral music used in the medieval Church, esp. in Gregorian chant.

plain speaking *n* saying exactly what one thinks. **plain-spoken** *adj*

plaint *n* **1** *Archaic* a complaint or lamentation. **2** *Law* a statement in writing of grounds of complaint made to a court of law.

plaintiff *n* a person who sues in a court of law.

plaintive *adj* sad and mournful. **plaintively** *adv*

plait (**platt**) *n* **1** a length of hair that has been plaited. *~vb* **2** to intertwine (strands or strips) in a pattern.

plan *n* **1** a method thought out for doing or achieving something. **2** a detailed drawing to scale of a horizontal section through a building. **3** an outline or sketch. *~vb* **planning, planned 4** to form a plan (for). **5** to make a plan of (a building). **6** to intend. **planner** *n*

planchette *n* a device that writes messages under supposed spirit guidance.

plane[1] *n* **1** an aeroplane. **2** *Maths* a flat surface in which a straight line joining any two of its points lies entirely on that surface. **3** a level surface: *an inclined plane.* **4** a level of existence or attainment: *her ambition was set on a higher plane than pulling pints in a pub.* *~adj* **5** level or flat. **6** *Maths* lying entirely in one plane. *~vb* **planing, planed 7** to glide or skim: *they planed over the ice.*

plane[2] *n* **1** a tool with a steel blade for smoothing timber. *~vb* **planing, planed 2** to smooth (timber) using a plane. **3** (often foll. by *away* or *off*) to remove using a plane.

planet *n* any of the nine celestial bodies, Mercury, Venus, Earth, Mars, Jupiter, Saturn, Uranus, Neptune,

THESAURUS

ger on, recognize, remember, set in context **13.** *often with* **with** allocate, appoint, assign, charge, commission, entrust, give

placid calm, collected, composed, cool, equable, even, even-tempered, gentle, halcyon, imperturbable, mild, peaceful, quiet, self-possessed, serene, still, tranquil, undisturbed, unexcitable, unmoved, unruffled, untroubled

plagiarize, plagiarise appropriate, borrow, crib (*informal*), infringe, lift (*informal*), pirate, steal, thieve

plague *n.* **1.** contagion, disease, epidemic, infection, pandemic, pestilence **2.** affliction, bane, blight, calamity, cancer, curse, evil, scourge, torment, trial **3.** *informal* aggravation (*informal*), annoyance, bother, hassle (*informal*), irritant, nuisance, pain (*informal*), pest, problem, thorn in one's flesh, vexation *~vb.* **4.** *informal* afflict, annoy, badger, bedevil, be on one's back (*slang*), bother, disturb, fret, get in one's hair (*informal*), get on one's nerves (*informal*), harass, harry, hassle (*informal*), haunt, molest, pain, persecute, pester, tease, torment, torture, trouble, vex

plain *adj.* **1.** even, flat, level, plane, smooth **2.** apparent, clear, comprehensible, distinct, evident, legible, lucid, manifest, obvious, patent, transparent, unambiguous, understandable, unmistakable, visible **3.** artless, blunt, candid, direct, downright, forthright, frank, guileless, honest, ingenuous, open, outspoken, sincere, straightforward, upfront (*informal*) **4.** austere, bare, basic, discreet, modest, muted, pure, restrained, severe, simple, Spartan, stark, unadorned, unembellished, unornamented, unpatterned, unvarnished **5.** ill-favoured, no oil painting (*informal*), not beautiful, not striking, ordinary, ugly, unalluring, unattractive, unlovely, unprepossessing **6.** common, commonplace, everyday, frugal, homely, lowly, modest, ordinary, simple, unaffected, unpretentious, workaday *~n.* **7.** flatland, grassland, llano, lowland, mesa, open country, plateau, prairie, steppe, tableland

plain-spoken blunt, candid, direct, downright, explicit, forthright, frank, open, outright, outspoken, straightforward, unequivocal, upfront (*informal*)

plaintive disconsolate, doleful, grief-stricken, grievous, heart-rending, melancholy, mournful, pathetic, piteous, pitiful, rueful, sad, sorrowful, wistful, woebegone, woeful

plan *n.* **1.** contrivance, design, device, idea, method, plot, procedure, programme, project, proposal, proposition, scenario, scheme, strategy, suggestion, system **2.** blueprint, chart, delineation, diagram, drawing, illustration, layout, map, representation, scale drawing, sketch *~vb.* **3.** arrange, concoct, contrive, design, devise, draft, formulate, frame, invent, organize, outline, plot, prepare, represent, scheme, think out **4.** aim, contemplate, envisage, foresee, intend, mean, propose, purpose

plane *n.* **1.** aeroplane, aircraft, jet **2.** flat surface, level

or Pluto, that revolve around the sun in oval-shaped orbits. **planetary** *adj*

planetarium *n, pl* **-iums** *or* **-ia 1** an instrument for projecting images of the sun, moon, stars, and planets onto a domed ceiling. **2** a building in which such an instrument is housed.

planetoid (**plan**-it-oid) *n* See **asteroid.**

plane tree *or* **plane** *n* a tree with rounded heads of fruit and leaves with pointed lobes.

plangent (**plan**-jent) *adj* (of sounds) mournful and resounding.

plank *n* **1** a long flat piece of sawn timber. **2** one of the policies in a political party's programme. **3 walk the plank** to be forced by sailors to walk to one's death off the end of a plank jutting out from the side of a ship.

planking *n* a number of planks.

plankton *n* the small drifting plants and animals on the surface layer of a sea or lake.

planning permission *n* formal permission granted by a local authority for the construction, alteration, or change of use of a building.

plant *n* **1** a living organism that grows in the ground and lacks the power of movement. **2** the land, building, and equipment used in an industry or business. **3** a factory or workshop. **4** mobile mechanical equipment for construction or road-making. **5** *Informal* a thing positioned secretly for discovery by someone else, often in order to incriminate an innocent person. *~vb* **6** to set (seeds or crops) into the ground to grow: *it's the wrong time of year for planting roses.* **7** to place firmly in position: *I planted my chair beside hers.* **8** to introduce into someone's mind: *once Wendy had planted the idea in the minds of the owners, they quite fancied selling.* **9** *Slang* to deliver (a blow or kiss). **10** *Informal* to position or hide (someone) in order to deceive or observe. **11** *Informal* to hide or secrete (something), usually for some illegal purpose or in order to incriminate someone.

plantain[1] *n* a plant with a rosette of broad leaves and a slender spike of small greenish flowers.

plantain[2] *n* **1** a large tropical fruit like a green-skinned banana. **2** the tree on which this fruit grows.

plantation *n* **1** an estate, esp. in tropical countries, where cash crops such as rubber or coffee are grown on a large scale. **2** a group of cultivated trees or plants. **3** (formerly) a colony of settlers.

planter *n* **1** the owner or manager of a plantation. **2** a decorative pot for house plants.

plantigrade *adj* walking on the entire sole of the foot, as humans and bears do.

plaque *n* **1** a commemorative inscribed stone or metal plate. **2** Also called: **dental plaque** a filmy deposit on teeth consisting of mucus, bacteria, and food, that causes decay.

plasma *n* **1** the clear yellowish fluid portion of blood which contains the corpuscles and cells. **2** a sterilized preparation of such fluid, taken from the blood, for use in transfusions. **3** a former name for **protoplasm.** **4** *Physics* a hot ionized gas containing positive ions and free electrons.

plaster *n* **1** a mixture of lime, sand, and water that is applied to a wall or ceiling as a soft paste and dries as a hard coating. **2** *Brit* an adhesive strip of material for dressing a cut or wound. **3** short for **mustard plaster** or **plaster of Paris.** *~vb* **4** to coat (a wall or ceiling) with plaster. **5** to apply like plaster: *he plastered his face with shaving cream.* **6** to cause to lie flat or to adhere: *his hair was plastered to his forehead.* **plasterer** *n*

plasterboard *n* a thin rigid board, made of plaster compressed between two layers of fibreboard, used to form or cover interior walls.

plastered *adj Slang* drunk.

plaster of Paris *n* a white powder that sets to a hard solid when mixed with water, used for making sculptures and casts for setting broken limbs.

plastic *n* **1** any of a large number of synthetic materials that can be moulded when soft and then set. **2** *Informal* Also called: **plastic money** credit cards etc. as opposed to cash. *~adj* **3** made of plastic. **4** easily influenced. **5** capable of being moulded or formed. **6** of moulding or modelling: *the plastic arts.* **7** *Slang* superficially attractive yet artificial or false: *glamorous models with plastic smiles.* **plasticity** *n*

plastic bomb *n* a bomb consisting of plastic explosive fitted around a detonator.

plastic bullet *n* a solid PVC cylinder fired by the police in riot control.

plastic explosive *n* an adhesive jelly-like explosive substance.

Plasticine *n Trademark* a soft coloured material used, esp. by children, for modelling.

plasticize *or* **-cise** *vb* **-cizing, -cized** *or* **-cising, -cised** to make or become plastic.

plasticizer *or* **-ciser** *n* a substance added to a plastic material to soften it and improve flexibility.

plastic surgery *n* the branch of surgery concerned with the repair or reconstruction of missing, injured, or malformed tissues or parts. **plastic surgeon** *n*

plate *n* **1** a shallow dish made of porcelain, earthenware, glass, etc., on which food is served. **2** Also called: **plateful** the contents of a plate. **3** a shallow dish for receiving a collection in church. **4** flat metal of even thickness obtained by rolling. **5** a thin coating of metal usually on another metal. **6** dishes or cutlery made of gold or silver. **7** a sheet of metal, plastic, or rubber having a printing surface produced by a process such as stereotyping. **8** a print taken from such a sheet or from a woodcut. **9** a thin flat sheet of a substance, such as glass. **10** a small piece of metal or plastic with an inscription, fixed to another surface: *a brass name plate.* **11** *Photog* a sheet of glass coated with photographic emulsion on which an image can be formed by exposure to light. **12** *Informal* same as **denture.** **13** *Anat* any flat platelike structure. **14** a cup awarded to the winner of a sporting contest, esp. a horse race. **15** any of the rigid layers of the earth's crust. **16 have a lot on one's plate** to have many pressing things to deal with. **17 on a plate** acquired

THESAURUS

surface **3.** condition, degree, footing, level, position, stratum *~adj.* **4.** even, flat, flush, horizontal, level, plain, regular, smooth, uniform *~vb.* **5.** glide, sail, skate, skim

plant *n.* **1.** bush, flower, herb, shrub, vegetable, weed **2.** apparatus, equipment, gear, machinery **3.** factory, foundry, mill, shop, works, yard *~vb.* **4.** implant, put in the ground, scatter, seed, set out, sow, transplant **5.** establish, fix, found, imbed, insert, institute, lodge, root, set, settle

plaque badge, brooch, cartouch(e), medal, medallion, panel, plate, slab, tablet

plaster *n.* **1.** gypsum, mortar, plaster of Paris, stucco **2.** *Brit.* adhesive plaster, bandage, dressing, Elastoplast (*Trademark*), sticking plaster *~vb.* **3.** bedaub, besmear, coat, cover, daub, overlay, smear, spread

plastic *adj.* **1.** compliant, docile, easily influenced, impressionable, malleable, manageable, pliable, receptive, responsive, tractable **2.** ductile, fictile, flexible, mouldable, pliable, pliant, soft, supple, tensile **3.** *slang*

without trouble: *he got the job handed to him on a plate.* ~*vb* **plating, plated 18** to coat (a metal surface) with a thin layer of another metal. **19** to cover with metal plates, usually for protection. **20** to form (metal) into plate, usually by rolling.

plateau (**plat**-oh) *n, pl* **-eaus** *or* **-eaux** (-ohs) **1** a wide level area of high land. **2** a relatively long period of stability: *the body temperature rises to a plateau that it keeps until shortly before bedtime.*

plated *adj* coated with a layer of metal.

plate glass *n* glass produced in thin sheets, used for windows and mirrors.

platelayer *n Brit* a workman who lays and maintains railway track.

platelet *n* a minute particle occurring in the blood of vertebrates and involved in the clotting of the blood.

platen *n* **1** the roller on a typewriter, against which the keys strike. **2** a flat plate in a printing press that presses the paper against the type.

platform *n* **1** a raised floor. **2** a raised area at a railway station where passengers get on or off the trains. **3** See **drilling platform**. **4** the declared aims of a political party. **5** the thick raised sole of some shoes.

platform ticket *n* a ticket for admission to railway platforms but not for travel.

plating *n* **1** a coating of metal. **2** a layer or covering of metal plates.

platinum *n* a silvery-white metallic element, very resistant to heat and chemicals: used in jewellery, laboratory apparatus, electrical contacts, dentistry, electroplating, and as a catalyst. Symbol: Pt

platinum blonde *n* a girl or woman with silvery-blonde hair.

platitude *n* a trite or unoriginal remark: *it's a platitude, but people need people.* **platitudinous** *adj*

platonic *adj* friendly or affectionate but without physical desire: *platonic love.*

Platonic *adj* of the philosopher Plato or his teachings.

Platonism (**plate**-on-iz-zum) *n* the teachings of Plato (?427–?347 BC), Greek philosopher, and his followers. **Platonist** *n*

platoon *n Mil* a subunit of a company, usually comprising three sections of ten to twelve men.

platteland *n* **the platteland** (in South Africa) the country districts or rural areas.

platter *n* a large shallow, usually oval, dish.

platypus *or* **duck-billed platypus** *n, pl* **-puses** an Australian egg-laying amphibious mammal, with dense fur, webbed feet, and a ducklike bill.

plaudit *n* (*usually pl*) an expression of enthusiastic approval.

plausible *adj* **1** apparently reasonable or true: *a plausible excuse.* **2** apparently trustworthy or believable: *he is an extraordinarily plausible liar.* **plausibility** *n* **plausibly** *adv*

play *vb* **1** to occupy oneself in (a sport or recreation). **2** to compete against (someone) in a sport or game: *Scotland play Wales in Cardiff next week.* **3** to fulfil (a particular role) in a team game: *he usually plays in midfield.* **4** (often foll. by *about* or *around*) to behave carelessly: *he's only playing with your affections, you know.* **5** to act the part (of) in a dramatic piece: *he has played Hamlet to packed Broadway houses.* **6** to perform (a dramatic piece). **7 a** to perform (music) on an instrument. **b** to be able to perform on (a musical instrument): *she plays the bassoon.* **8** to send out (water) or cause to send out water: *they played a hose across the wrecked building.* **9** to cause (a radio etc.) to emit sound. **10** to move freely or quickly: *the light played across the water.* **11** *Stock Exchange* to speculate for gain in (a market). **12** *Angling* to tire (a hooked fish) by alternately letting out and reeling in the line. **13** to put (a card) into play. **14** to gamble. **15 play fair** *or* **false with** to act fairly *or* unfairly with. **16 play for time** to gain time to one's advantage by the use of delaying tactics. **17 play into the hands of** to act unwittingly to the advantage of (an opponent). ~*n* **18 a** a dramatic piece written for performance by actors. **b** the performance of such a piece. **19** games or other activity undertaken for pleasure. **20** the playing of a game or the time during which a game is in progress: *rain stopped play.* **21** conduct: *fair play.* **22** gambling. **23** activity or operation: *radio allows full play to your imagination.* **24** scope for freedom of movement: *there was a lot of play in the rope.* **25** free or rapidly shifting motion: *the play of light on the water.* **26** fun or jest: *I used to throw cushions at her in play.* **27 in** *or* **out of play** (of a ball in a game) in *or* not in a position for continuing play according to the rules. **28 make a play for** *Informal* to make an obvious attempt to gain (something). ~See also **play along, playback,** etc. **playable** *adj*

play along *vb* to cooperate (with) temporarily: *I'll play along with them for the moment.*

playback *n* **1** the playing of a recording on magnetic

THESAURUS

artificial, false, meretricious, phoney *or* phony (*informal*), pseudo (*informal*), sham, specious, spurious, superficial, synthetic

plate *n.* **1.** dish, platter, trencher (*History*) **2.** course, dish, helping, portion, serving **3.** layer, panel, sheet, slab **4.** illustration, lithograph, print ~*vb.* **5.** anodize, coat, cover, electroplate, face, gild, laminate, nickel, overlay, platinize, silver

plateau 1. highland, table, tableland, upland **2.** level, levelling off, stability, stage

platform 1. dais, podium, rostrum, stage, stand **2.** manifesto, objective(s), party line, policy, principle, programme, tenet(s)

platitude banality, bromide, cliché, commonplace, hackneyed saying, inanity, stereotype, trite remark, truism

platitudinous banal, clichéd, commonplace, corny (*slang*), hack, hackneyed, overworked, set, stale, stereotyped, stock, tired, trite, truistic, vapid, well-worn

platoon *Military* company, group, outfit (*informal*), patrol, squad, squadron, team

platter charger, dish, plate, salver, tray, trencher (*History*)

plausible believable, colourable, conceivable, credible, likely, persuasive, possible, probable, reasonable, specious, tenable, verisimilar

play *vb.* **1.** amuse oneself, caper, engage in games, entertain oneself, fool, frisk, frolic, gambol, have fun, revel, romp, sport, trifle **2.** be in a team, challenge, compete, contend against, participate, rival, take on, take part, vie with **3.** act, act the part of, execute, impersonate, perform, personate, portray, represent, take the part of **4.** bet, chance, gamble, hazard, punt (*chiefly Brit.*), risk, speculate, take, wager **5. play for time** delay, drag one's feet (*informal*), filibuster, hang fire, procrastinate, stall, temporize ~*n.* **6.** comedy, drama, dramatic piece, entertainment, farce, masque, performance, piece, radio play, show, soap opera, stage show, television drama, tragedy **7.** amusement, caper, diversion, entertainment, frolic, fun, gambol, game, jest, pastime, prank, recreation, romp, sport **8.** gambling, gaming **9.** action, activity, employment, function, operation, transaction, working **10.** action, activity, elbowroom, exercise, give (*informal*), lati-

tape. *~vb* **play back 2** to listen to or watch (something recorded).

playbill *n* a poster or bill advertising a play.

playboy *n* a rich man who devotes himself to such pleasures as nightclubs and female company.

play down *vb* to minimize the importance of: *she played down the problems of the company.*

player *n* **1** a person who takes part in a game or sport. **2** a person who plays a musical instrument. **3** *Informal* a leading participant in a particular field or activity: *one of the key players in Chinese politics.* **4** an actor.

player piano *n* a mechanical piano; Pianola.

playful *adj* **1** good-natured and humorous: *a playful remark.* **2** full of high spirits and fun: *a playful child.* **playfully** *adv*

playgoer *n* a person who goes often to the theatre.

playground *n* **1** an outdoor area for children's play, either with swings and slides, or adjoining a school. **2** a place or activity enjoyed by a specified person or group: *they oppose turning the island into a tourist playground.*

playgroup *n* a regular meeting of infants for supervised creative play.

playhouse *n* a theatre.

playing field *n* (*sometimes pl*) *Chiefly Brit* a field or open space used for sport.

playlist *n* a list of records chosen for playing, such as on a radio station.

playmate *n* a companion in play.

play off *vb* **1** to set (two people) against each other for one's own ends: *she delighted in playing one parent off against the other.* **2** to take part in a play-off. *~n* **play-off 3** *Sport* an extra contest to decide the winner when there is a tie. **4** *Chiefly US & Canad* a contest or series of games to determine a championship.

play on *vb* to exploit (the feelings or weakness of another): *he played on my sympathy.*

play on words *n* same as **pun**.

playpen *n* a small portable enclosure in which a young child can safely be left to play.

playschool *n* a nursery group for preschool children.

plaything *n* **1** a toy. **2** a person regarded or treated as a toy.

playtime *n* a time for play or recreation, such as a school break.

play up *vb* **1** to highlight: *the temptation is to play up the sensational aspects of the story.* **2** *Brit informal* to behave in an unruly way. **3** to give (one) trouble or not be working properly: *my back's playing me up again; the photocopier's started to play up.* **4 play up to** to try to please by flattery.

playwright *n* a person who writes plays.

plaza *n* **1** an open public square, usually in Spain. **2** *Chiefly US & Canad* a modern shopping complex.

PLC *or* **plc** Public Limited Company.

plea *n* **1** an emotional appeal. **2** *Law* a statement by or on behalf of a defendant. **3** an excuse: *his plea of poverty rings a little hollow.*

plead *vb* **pleading, pleaded, plead** *or esp Scot & US* **pled 1** (sometimes foll. by *with*) to ask with deep feeling. **2** to give as an excuse: *whenever she invites him to dinner, he pleads a prior engagement.* **3** *Law* to declare oneself to be (guilty or not guilty) of the charge made against one. **4** *Law* to present (a case) in a court of law.

pleadings *pl n Law* the formal written statements presented by the plaintiff and defendant in a lawsuit.

pleasant *adj* **1** pleasing or enjoyable: *what a pleasant surprise.* **2** having pleasing manners or appearance: *he was a pleasant boy.* **pleasantly** *adv*

pleasantry *n, pl* **-ries 1** (*often pl*) a polite or jocular remark: *we exchanged pleasantries about the weather.* **2** agreeable jocularity.

please *vb* **pleasing, pleased 1** to give pleasure or satisfaction to (a person). **2** to regard as suitable or satisfying: *he can get almost anyone he pleases to work with him.* **3 if you please** if you wish, sometimes used in ironic exclamation. **4 pleased with**

THESAURUS

tude, leeway, margin, motion, movement, operation, range, room, scope, space, sweep, swing **11.** foolery, fun, humour, jest, joking, lark (*informal*), prank, sport, teasing

playboy gay dog, ladies' man, lady-killer (*informal*), lover boy (*slang*), man about town, philanderer, pleasure seeker, rake, roué, socialite, womanizer

play down gloss over, make light of, make little of, minimize, set no store by, soft-pedal (*informal*), underplay, underrate

player 1. competitor, contestant, participant, sportsman, sportswoman, team member **2.** artist, instrumentalist, musician, music maker, performer, virtuoso **3.** actor, actress, entertainer, performer, Thespian, trouper

playful 1. arch, coy, flirtatious, good-natured, humorous, jesting, jokey, joking, roguish, teasing, tongue-in-cheek, waggish **2.** cheerful, coltish, frisky, frolicsome, gay, impish, joyous, kittenish, larkish (*informal*), lively, merry, mischievous, puckish, rollicking, spirited, sportive, sprightly, vivacious

playmate chum (*informal*), companion, comrade, friend, neighbour, pal (*informal*), playfellow

play on *or* **upon** abuse, capitalize on, exploit, impose on, milk, profit by, take advantage of, trade on, turn to account, utilize

plaything amusement, bauble, game, gewgaw, gimcrack, pastime, toy, trifle, trinket

play up 1. accentuate, bring to the fore, call attention to, emphasize, highlight, magnify, point up, stress, turn the spotlight on, underline **2.** *Brit. informal* be awkward, be bolshie (*Brit. informal*), be cussed (*informal*), be disobedient, be stroppy (*Brit. slang*), give trouble, misbehave **3.** *Brit. informal* be painful, be sore, bother, give one gyp (*Brit. & N.Z. slang*), give one trouble, hurt, pain, trouble **4.** *Brit. informal* be on the blink (*slang*), be wonky (*Brit. slang*), malfunction, not work properly **5. play up to** *informal* bootlick (*informal*), brown-nose (*taboo slang*), butter up, curry favour, fawn, flatter, get in with, ingratiate oneself, pander to, suck up to (*informal*), toady

playwright dramatist, dramaturge, dramaturgist

plea 1. appeal, begging, entreaty, intercession, overture, petition, prayer, request, suit, supplication **2.** *Law* action, allegation, cause, suit **3.** apology, claim, defence, excuse, explanation, extenuation, justification, pretext, vindication

plead 1. *sometimes with* **with** appeal (to), ask, beg, beseech, crave, entreat, implore, importune, petition, request, solicit, supplicate **2.** adduce, allege, argue, assert, maintain, put forward, use as an excuse

pleasant 1. acceptable, agreeable, amusing, delectable, delightful, enjoyable, fine, gratifying, lovely, nice, pleasing, pleasurable, refreshing, satisfying, welcome **2.** affable, agreeable, amiable, charming, cheerful, cheery, congenial, engaging, friendly, genial, good-humoured, likeable *or* likable, nice

pleasantry badinage, banter, bon mot, good-natured

happy because of. **5 please oneself** to do as one likes. ~*adv* **6** used in making polite requests or pleading: *please sit down.* **7 yes please** a polite phrase used to accept an offer or invitation. **pleased** *adj*

pleasing *adj* giving pleasure.

pleasurable *adj* enjoyable or agreeable. **pleasurably** *adv*

pleasure *n* **1** a feeling of happiness and contentment: *the pleasure of hearing good music.* **2** something that gives enjoyment: *his garden was his only pleasure.* **3** the activity of enjoying oneself: *business before pleasure.* **4** *Euphemistic* sexual gratification: *he took his pleasure of her.* **5** a person's preference.

pleat *n* **1** a fold formed by doubling back fabric and pressing or stitching into place. ~*vb* **2** to arrange (material) in pleats.

pleb *n Brit informal, often offensive* a common vulgar person.

plebeian (pleb-**ee**-an) *adj* **1** of the lower social classes. **2** unrefined: *plebeian tastes.* ~*n* **3** one of the common people, usually of ancient Rome. **4** a coarse or unrefined person.

plebiscite (**pleb**-iss-ite) *n* a direct vote by all the electorate on an issue of national importance.

plectrum *n, pl* **-tra** *or* **-trums** an implement for plucking the strings of a guitar or similar instrument.

pled *vb US or (esp in legal usage) Scot* a past of **plead.**

pledge *n* **1** a solemn promise. **2 a** something valuable given as a guarantee that a promise will be kept or a debt paid. **b** the condition of being used as security: *in pledge.* **3** a token: *a pledge of good faith.* **4** an assurance of support or goodwill, given by drinking a toast: *we drank a pledge to their success.* **5 take** *or* **sign the pledge** to vow not to drink alcohol. ~*vb* **pledging, pledged 6** to promise solemnly. **7** to bind by or as if by a pledge: *I was pledged to secrecy.* **8** to give (one's word or property) as a guarantee. **9** to drink a toast to (a person or cause).

Pleiocene *adj, n* same as **Pliocene.**

Pleistocene (**ply**-stow-seen) *adj Geol* of the epoch of geological time about 600 000 years ago.

plenary *adj* **1** (of an assembly) attended by all the members. **2** full or complete: *plenary powers.*

plenipotentiary *adj* **1** (usually of a diplomat) invested with full authority. ~*n, pl* **-aries 2** a diplomat or representative who has full authority to transact business.

plenitude *n Literary* **1** abundance. **2** fullness or completeness.

plenteous *adj Literary* **1** abundant: *a plenteous supply.* **2** producing abundantly: *a plenteous harvest.*

plentiful *adj* existing in large amounts or numbers. **plentifully** *adv*

plenty *n, pl* **-ties 1** (often foll. by *of*) a great number or amount: *plenty of time.* **2** abundance: *an age of plenty.* ~*adj* **3** very many: *there's plenty more fish in the sea.* ~*adv* **4** *Informal* more than adequately: *that's plenty fast enough for me.*

pleonasm *n Rhetoric* **1** the use of more words than necessary, such as *a tiny little child.* **2** an unnecessary word or phrase. **pleonastic** *adj*

plethora *n* an excess.

pleura (**ploor**-a) *n, pl* **pleurae** (**ploor**-ee) *Anat* the thin transparent membrane enveloping the lungs. **pleural** *adj*

pleurisy *n* inflammation of the pleura, making breathing painful. **pleuritic** *adj, n*

plexus *n, pl* **-uses** *or* **-us** a complex network of nerves or blood vessels.

pliable *adj* **1** easily bent: *pliable branches.* **2** easily influenced: *his easy and pliable nature.* **pliability** *n*

pliant *adj* **1** easily bent; supple: *pliant young willow and hazel twigs.* **2** easily influenced: *he was a far more pliant subordinate than his predecessor.* **pliancy** *n*

pliers *pl n* a gripping tool consisting of two hinged arms usually with serrated jaws.

plight[1] *n* a dangerous or difficult situation.

plight[2] *vb* **plight one's troth** *Old-fashioned* to make a promise to marry.

THESAURUS

remark, jest, joke, josh (*slang, chiefly U.S. & Canad.*), quip, sally, witticism

please 1. amuse, charm, cheer, content, delight, entertain, give pleasure to, gladden, gratify, humour, indulge, rejoice, satisfy, suit, tickle, tickle pink (*informal*) **2.** be inclined, choose, desire, like, opt, prefer, see fit, want, will, wish

pleased chuffed (*Brit. slang*), contented, delighted, euphoric, glad, gratified, happy, in high spirits, over the moon (*informal*), pleased as punch (*informal*), rapt, satisfied, thrilled, tickled, tickled pink (*informal*)

pleasing agreeable, amiable, amusing, attractive, charming, delightful, engaging, enjoyable, entertaining, gratifying, likable *or* likeable, pleasurable, polite, satisfying, winning

pleasure 1. amusement, bliss, comfort, contentment, delectation, delight, diversion, ease, enjoyment, gladness, gratification, happiness, jollies (*slang*), joy, recreation, satisfaction, solace **2.** choice, command, desire, inclination, mind, option, preference, purpose, will, wish

plebeian 1. *adj.* base, coarse, common, ignoble, low, lowborn, lower-class, mean, non-U (*Brit. informal*), proletarian, uncultivated, unrefined, vulgar, working-class **2.** *n.* commoner, common man, man in the street, peasant, pleb, prole (*derogatory slang, chiefly Brit.*), proletarian

pledge *n.* **1.** assurance, covenant, oath, promise, undertaking, vow, warrant, word, word of honour **2.** bail, bond, collateral, deposit, earnest, gage, guarantee, pawn, security, surety **3.** health, toast ~*vb.* **4.** contract, engage, give one's oath (word, word of honour), promise, swear, undertake, vouch, vow **5.** bind, engage, guarantee, mortgage, plight **6.** drink the health of, drink to, toast

plentiful abundant, ample, bountiful *or* bounteous (*literary*), complete, copious, generous, inexhaustible, infinite, lavish, liberal, overflowing, plenteous, profuse

plenty 1. *often with* **of** abundance, enough, fund, good deal, great deal, heap(s) (*informal*), lots (*informal*), mass, masses, mine, mountain(s), oodles (*informal*), pile(s) (*informal*), plethora, quantities, quantity, stack(s), store, sufficiency, volume **2.** abundance, affluence, copiousness, fertility, fruitfulness, luxury, opulence, plenitude, plenteousness, plentifulness, profusion, prosperity, wealth

plethora excess, glut, overabundance, profusion, superabundance, superfluity, surfeit, surplus

pliable 1. bendable, bendy, ductile, flexible, limber, lithe, malleable, plastic, pliant, supple, tensile **2.** adaptable, compliant, docile, easily led, impressionable, influenceable, manageable, persuadable, pliant, receptive, responsive, susceptible, tractable, yielding

pliant 1. bendable, bendy, ductile, flexible, lithe, plastic, pliable, supple, tensile **2.** adaptable, biddable, compliant, easily led, impressionable, influenceable, manageable, persuadable, pliable, susceptible, tractable, yielding

plight *n.* case, circumstances, condition, difficulty, dilemma, extremity, hole (*slang*), hot water (*informal*),

Plimsoll line *n* a line on the hull of a ship showing the level that the water should reach if the ship is properly loaded.

plimsolls *pl n Brit* light rubber-soled canvas sports shoes.

plinth *n* **1** a base on which a statue stands. **2** the slab that forms the base of a column or pedestal.

Pliocene *or* **Pleiocene** (**ply**-oh-seen) *adj Geol* of the epoch of geological time about 10 million years ago.

PLO Palestine Liberation Organization.

plod *vb* **plodding, plodded 1** to walk with heavy slow steps. **2** to work slowly and steadily. *~n* **3** the act of plodding. **plodder** *n*

plonk[1] *vb* **1** to put down heavily and carelessly: *he plonked himself down on the sofa.* *~n* **2** the act or sound of plonking.

plonk[2] *n Informal* cheap inferior wine.

plonker *n Slang* a stupid person.

plop *n* **1** the sound made by an object dropping into water without a splash. *~vb* **plopping, plopped 2** to drop with such a sound: *a tear rolled down his cheek and plopped into his soup.* **3** to fall or be placed heavily or carelessly: *we plopped down on the bed and went straight to sleep.*

plosive *Phonetics ~adj* **1** pronounced with a sudden release of breath. *~n* **2** a plosive consonant.

plot[1] *n* **1** a secret plan for an illegal purpose. **2** the story of a play, novel, or film. *~vb* **plotting, plotted 3** to plan secretly; conspire. **4** to mark (a course) on a map. **5** to make a plan or map of. **6 a** to locate (points) on a graph by means of coordinates. **b** to draw (a curve) through these points. **7** to construct the plot of (a play, novel, or film). **plotter** *n*

plot[2] *n* a small piece of land: *there was a small vegetable plot at the foot of the garden.*

plough *or esp US* **plow** *n* **1** an agricultural tool for cutting or turning over the earth. **2** a similar tool used for clearing snow. *~vb* **3** to turn over (the soil) with a plough. **4** to make (furrows or grooves) in (something) with or as if with a plough. **5** (sometimes foll. by *through*) to move (through something) in the manner of a plough: *the ship ploughed through the water.* **6** (foll. by *through*) to work at slowly or perseveringly. **7** to invest (money): *he ploughed the profits back into the business.* **8 plough into** (of a vehicle, plane, etc.) to run uncontrollably into (something): *the aircraft ploughed into a motorway embankment.*

Plough *n* **the Plough** the group of the seven brightest stars in the constellation Ursa Major.

ploughman *or esp US* **plowman** *n, pl* **-men** a man who ploughs.

ploughman's lunch *n* a snack lunch consisting of bread and cheese with pickle.

ploughshare *or esp US* **plowshare** *n* the cutting blade of a plough.

plover *n* a shore bird with a round head, straight bill, and long pointed wings.

plow *n, vb US* same as **plough.**

ploy *n* a manoeuvre designed to gain an advantage in a situation: *a cheap political ploy.*

pluck *vb* **1** to pull or pick off. **2** to pull out the feathers of (a bird for cooking). **3** (foll. by *off, away,* etc.) *Archaic* to pull (something) forcibly or violently (from something or someone). **4** to sound the strings of (a musical instrument) with the fingers or a plectrum. **5** *Slang* to swindle. *~n* **6** courage. **7** a pull or tug. **8** the heart, liver, and lungs of an animal used for food.

pluck up *vb* to summon up (courage).

plucky *adj* **pluckier, pluckiest** courageous. **pluckily** *adv* **pluckiness** *n*

plug *n* **1** an object used to block up holes or waste pipes. **2** a device with one or more pins which connects an appliance to an electricity supply. **3** *Informal* a favourable mention of a product etc., for example on television, to encourage people to buy it. **4** See **spark plug. 5** a piece of tobacco for chewing. *~vb* **plugging, plugged 6** to block or seal (a hole or gap) with a plug. **7** *Informal* to make frequent favourable mentions of (a product etc.), for example on television. **8** *Slang* to shoot: *he lifted the rifle and plugged the deer.* **9** *Slang* to punch. **10** (foll. by *along, away,* etc.) *Informal* to work steadily.

plug in *vb* to connect (an electrical appliance) to a power source by pushing a plug into a socket.

plum *n* **1** an oval dark red or yellow fruit with a stone in the middle, that grows on a small tree. **2** a raisin, as used in a cake or pudding. **3** *Informal* something of a superior or desirable kind. *~adj* **4** made from plums: *plum cake.* **5** dark reddish-purple. **6** very desirable: *plum targets for attack.*

plumage *n* the feathers of a bird.

plumb *vb* **1** to understand (something obscure): *to plumb a mystery.* **2 plumb the depths** to experience the worst extremes of: *to plumb the depths of despair.* **3** to test the alignment of or make vertical with a

THESAURUS

jam (*informal*), perplexity, pickle (*informal*), predicament, scrape (*informal*), situation, spot (*informal*), state, straits, tight spot, trouble

plod 1. clump, drag, lumber, slog, stomp (*informal*), tramp, tread, trudge **2.** drudge, grind (*informal*), grub, labour, peg away, persevere, plough through, plug away (*informal*), slog, soldier on, toil

plot[1] *n.* **1.** cabal, conspiracy, intrigue, machination, plan, scheme, stratagem **2.** action, narrative, outline, scenario, story, story line, subject, theme, thread *~vb.* **3.** cabal, collude, conspire, contrive, hatch, intrigue, machinate, manoeuvre, plan, scheme **4.** calculate, chart, compute, draft, draw, locate, map, mark, outline **5.** brew, conceive, concoct, contrive, cook up (*informal*), design, devise, frame, hatch, imagine, lay, project

plot[2] *n.* allotment, area, ground, lot, parcel, patch, tract

plough *vb.* **1.** break ground, cultivate, dig, furrow, ridge, till, turn over **2.** *sometimes with* **through** cut, drive, flounder, forge, plod, plunge, press, push, stagger, surge, wade **3. plough into** bulldoze, career, crash, hurtle, plunge, shove, smash

pluck *vb.* **1.** draw, pick, pull out *or* off **2.** *with* **off, away,** *etc. archaic* catch, clutch, jerk, pull at, snatch, tug, tweak, yank **3.** finger, pick, plunk, strum, thrum, twang *~n.* **4.** backbone, balls (*taboo slang*), boldness, bottle (*Brit. slang*), bravery, courage, determination, grit, guts (*informal*), hardihood, heart, intrepidity, mettle, nerve, resolution, spirit, spunk (*informal*)

plucky bold, brave, courageous, daring, doughty, feisty (*informal, chiefly U.S. & Canad.*), game, gritty, gutsy (*slang*), hardy, have-a-go (*informal*), heroic, intrepid, mettlesome, spirited, spunky (*informal*), undaunted, unflinching, valiant

plug *n.* **1.** bung, cork, spigot, stopper, stopple **2.** *informal* advert (*Brit. informal*), advertisement, good word, hype, mention, publicity, puff, push *~vb.* **3.** block, bung, choke, close, cork, cover, fill, pack, seal, stop, stopper, stopple, stop up, stuff **4.** *informal* advertise, build up, hype, mention, promote, publicize, puff, push, write up **5.** *slang* blow away (*slang, chiefly U.S.*), gun down, pick off, pop, pot, put a bullet in, shoot **6.**

plumb line. **4** (foll. by *in* or *into*) to connect (an appliance or fixture) to a water pipe or drainage system: *the shower should be plumbed in professionally.* ~*n* **5** a lead weight hanging at the end of a string and used to test the depth of water or to test whether something is vertical. **6 out of plumb** not vertical. ~*adv* **7** vertical or perpendicular. **8** *Informal, chiefly US* utterly: *plumb stupid.* **9** *Informal* exactly: *plumb in the centre.*

plumber *n* a person who fits and repairs pipes and fixtures for water, drainage, or gas systems.

plumbing *n* **1** the pipes and fixtures used in a water, drainage, or gas system. **2** the trade or work of a plumber.

plumb line *n* a string with a metal weight at one end, used to test the depth of water or to test whether something is vertical.

plume *n* **1** a large ornamental feather. **2** a group of feathers worn as a badge or ornament on a hat. **3** something like a plume: *a plume of smoke.* ~*vb* **pluming, plumed 4** to adorn with plumes. **5** (of a bird) to preen (its feathers). **6** (foll. by *on* or *upon*) to be proud of oneself or one's achievements, esp. unjustifiably: *she was pluming herself on her figure.*

plummet *vb* **-meting, -meted 1** to plunge downward. ~*n* **2** the weight on a plumb line or fishing line.

plummy *adj* **-mier, -miest 1** of, full of, or like plums: *a red wine full of ripe plummy fruit.* **2** *Brit informal* (of a voice) deep, rich, and usually upper-class in manner: *his plummy condescending voice.* **3** *Brit informal* desirable: *they lived plummy lives in the hills of Tuscany.*

plump[1] *adj* **1** full or rounded: *until puberty I was really quite plump.* ~*vb* **2** (often foll. by *up* or *out*) to make (something) fuller or rounded: *she plumped up the cushions on the couch.* **plumpness** *n*

plump[2] *vb* **1** (often foll. by *down, into,* etc.) to drop or sit suddenly and heavily: *he plumped down on the seat.* **2 plump for** to choose one from a selection. ~*n* **3** a heavy abrupt fall or the sound of this. ~*adv* **4** suddenly or heavily. **5** directly: *the plane landed plump in the middle of the field.* **6** in a blunt, direct, or decisive manner.

plum pudding *n Brit* a boiled or steamed pudding made with flour, suet, and dried fruit.

plumy *adj* **plumier, plumiest 1** like a feather. **2** covered or adorned with feathers.

plunder *vb* **1** to seize (valuables or goods) from (a place) by force, usually in wartime; loot. ~*n* **2** anything plundered; booty. **3** the act of plundering; pillage.

plunge *vb* **plunging, plunged 1** (usually foll. by *into*) to thrust or throw (something or oneself) forcibly or suddenly: *they plunged into the sea; he plunged the knife in to the hilt.* **2** to throw or be thrown into a certain condition: *the room was plunged into darkness.* **3** (usually foll. by *into*) to involve or become involved deeply (in). **4** to move swiftly or impetuously. **5** to descend very suddenly or steeply: *temperatures were plunging.* **6** *Informal* to gamble recklessly. ~*n* **7** a leap or dive. **8** *Informal* a swim. **9** a pitching motion. **10 take the plunge** *Informal* to make a risky decision which cannot be reversed later.

plunger *n* **1** a rubber suction cup used to clear blocked drains. **2** a device with a plunging motion; piston.

plunk *vb* **1** to pluck the strings of (an instrument) to produce a twanging sound. **2** (often foll. by *down*) to drop or be dropped heavily. ~*n* **3** the act or sound of plunking.

pluperfect *Grammar* ~*adj* **1** denoting a tense of verbs used to describe an action completed before a past time. In English this is a compound tense formed with *had* plus the past participle. ~*n* **2** the pluperfect tense.

plural *adj* **1** of or consisting of more than one. **2** *Grammar* denoting a word indicating more than one. ~*n* **3** *Grammar* **a** the plural number. **b** a plural form.

pluralism *n* **1** the existence and toleration in a society of a variety of groups of different ethnic origins, cultures, or religions. **2** the holding of more than one office by a person. **pluralist** *n, adj* **pluralistic** *adj*

plurality *n, pl* **-ties 1** the state of being plural. **2** *Maths* a number greater than one. **3** a large number. **4** a majority.

pluralize *or* **-ise** *vb* **-izing, -ized** *or* **-ising, -ised** to make or become plural.

plus *prep* **1** increased by the addition of: *four plus two.* **2** with the addition of: *a good salary, plus a company car.* ~*adj* **3** indicating addition: *a plus sign.* **4** *Maths* same as **positive** (sense 7). **5** on the positive part of a scale. **6** indicating the positive side of an electrical circuit. **7** involving advantage: *a plus factor.* **8** *Informal* having a value above the value stated: *it must be worth a thousand pounds plus.* **9** slightly above a specified standard: *he received a B plus for his essay.* ~*n* **10** a plus sign (+), indicating addition. **11** a positive quantity. **12** *Informal* something positive or an advantage. **13** a gain, surplus, or advantage.

➤ Avoid using *plus* to mean "additionally" except in very informal contexts.

plus fours *pl n* men's baggy knickerbockers gathered in at the knee, now only worn for hunting or golf.

plush *n* **1** a velvety fabric with a long soft pile, used for furniture coverings. ~*adj* **2** Also: **plushy** *Informal* luxurious.

Pluto *n* **1** *Greek myth* the god of the underworld. **2** the second smallest planet and the farthest from the sun.

plutocracy *n, pl* **-cies 1** government by the wealthy. **2** a state ruled by the wealthy. **3** a group that exercises power on account of its wealth. **plutocratic** *adj*

plutocrat *n* a person who is powerful because of being very rich.

plutonic *adj* (of igneous rocks) formed from molten

THESAURUS

with **along, away,** *etc. informal* drudge, grind (*informal*), labour, peg away, plod, slog, toil

plum 1. *n. informal* bonus, cream, find, pick, prize, treasure **2.** *adj.* best, choice, first-class, prize

plumb *vb.* **1.** delve, explore, fathom, gauge, go into, measure, penetrate, probe, search, sound, unravel ~*n.* **2.** lead, plumb bob, plummet, weight ~*adv.* **3.** perpendicularly, up and down, vertically **4.** *informal* bang, exactly, precisely, slap, spot-on (*Brit. informal*)

plume 1. *n.* aigrette, crest, feather, pinion, quill **2.** *vb. with* **on** *or* **upon** congratulate oneself, pat oneself on the back, pique oneself, preen oneself, pride oneself

plump *adj.* beefy (*informal*), burly, buxom, chubby, corpulent, dumpy, fat, fleshy, full, obese, podgy, portly, roly-poly, rotund, round, stout, tubby, well-covered

plunder 1. *vb.* despoil, devastate, loot, pillage, raid, ransack, ravage, rifle, rob, sack, spoil, steal, strip **2.** *n.* booty, ill-gotten gains, loot, pillage, prey, prize, rapine, spoils, swag (*slang*)

plunge *vb.* **1.** *usually with* **into** cast, descend, dip, dive, douse, drop, fall, go down, immerse, jump, nosedive, pitch, plummet, sink, submerge, swoop, throw, tumble **2.** career, charge, dash, hurtle, lurch, rush, tear ~*n.* **3.** descent, dive, drop, fall, immersion, jump, submersion, swoop

plus 1. *prep.* added to, and, coupled with, with, with the addition of **2.** *adj.* added, additional, add-on, extra, positive, supplementary **3.** *n. informal* advantage,

rock that has cooled and solidified below the earth's surface.

plutonium *n Chem* a toxic radioactive metallic element, used in nuclear reactors and weapons. Symbol: Pu

pluvial *adj Geog, geol* of or due to the action of rain.

ply[1] *vb* **plies, plying, plied 1** to work at (a job or trade). **2** to use (a tool). **3** (usually foll. by *with*) to provide (with) or subject (to) persistently: *he plied us with drink; he plied me with questions.* **4** to work steadily. **5** (of a ship) to travel regularly along (a route): *to ply the trade routes.*

ply[2] *n, pl* **plies 1** a layer or thickness, such as of fabric or wood. **2** one of the strands twisted together to make rope or yarn.

Plymouth Brethren *pl n* a Puritanical religious sect with no organized ministry.

plywood *n* a board made of thin layers of wood glued together under pressure, with the grain of one layer at right angles to the grain of the next.

Pm *Chem* promethium.

PM 1 Prime Minister. **2** Postmaster. **3** Paymaster.

p.m. 1 after noon. **2** postmortem (examination).

PMG 1 Postmaster General. **2** Paymaster General.

PMS premenstrual syndrome.

PMT premenstrual tension.

pneumatic *adj* **1** operated by compressed air: *pneumatic drill.* **2** containing compressed air: *a pneumatic tyre.* **3** of or concerned with air, gases, or wind.

pneumatics *n* the branch of physics concerned with the mechanical properties of air and other gases.

pneumonia *n* inflammation of one or both lungs.

po *n, pl* **pos** *Brit old-fashioned, informal* a chamber pot.

Po *Chem* polonium.

PO 1 Also: **p.o.** postal order. **2** Post Office. **3** petty officer. **4** Pilot Officer.

poach[1] *vb* **1** to catch (game or fish) illegally on someone else's land. **2 a** to encroach on (someone's rights or duties). **b** to steal (an idea, employee, or player). **poacher** *n*

poach[2] *vb* to simmer (food) very gently in liquid.

pock *n* **1** a pus-filled blister resulting from smallpox. **2** a pockmark.

pocket *n* **1** a small pouch sewn into clothing for carrying small articles. **2** any pouchlike container, esp. for catching balls at the edge of a snooker table. **3** a small isolated area or group: *a pocket of resistance.* **4** a cavity in the earth, such as one containing ore. **5 in one's pocket** under one's control. **6 out of pocket** having made a loss. *~vb* **-eting, -eted 7** to put into one's pocket. **8** to take secretly or dishonestly. **9** *Billiards* to drive (a ball) into a pocket. **10** to conceal or suppress: *he pocketed his pride and asked for help.* *~adj* **11** small: *a pocket edition.*

pocketbook *n Chiefly US* a small case for money and papers.

pocket borough *n* (before the Reform Act of 1832) an English borough constituency controlled by one person or family.

pocketful *n, pl* **-fuls** as much as a pocket will hold.

pocketknife *n, pl* **-knives** a small knife with one or more blades that fold into the handle; penknife.

pocket money *n* **1** *Brit* a small weekly sum of money given to children by parents. **2** money for small personal expenses.

pockmarked *adj* **1** (of the skin) marked with pitted scars after the healing of smallpox. **2** (of a surface) covered in many small hollows: *the building is pockmarked with bullet holes.* **pockmark** *n*

pod *n* **1 a** a long narrow seedcase containing peas, beans, etc. **b** the seedcase as distinct from the seeds. *~vb* **podding, podded 2** to remove the pod from.

podgy *adj* **podgier, podgiest** short and fat. **podginess** *n*

podium *n, pl* **-diums** *or* **-dia 1** a small raised platform used by conductors or speakers. **2** a plinth that supports a colonnade or wall.

poem *n* **1** a literary work, often in verse, usually dealing with emotional or descriptive themes in a rhythmic form. **2** a literary work that is not in verse but deals with emotional or descriptive themes in a rhythmic form: *a prose poem.* **3** anything like a poem in beauty or effect: *his painting is a poem on creation.*

poep (**poop**) *n S African taboo* **1** an emission of intestinal gas from the anus. **2** a mean or despicable person.

poesy *n Archaic* poetry.

poet *n* **1** a writer of poetry. **2** a person with great imagination and creativity.

poetaster *n* a writer of inferior verse.

poetic *or* **poetical** *adj* **1** like poetry, by being expressive or imaginative. **2** of poetry or poets. **3** recounted in verse.

poetic justice *n* an appropriate punishment or reward for previous actions.

poetic licence *n* freedom from the normal rules of language or truth, as in poetry.

poet laureate *n, pl* **poets laureate** *Brit* the poet selected by the British sovereign to write poems on important occasions.

poetry *n* **1** poems in general. **2** the art or craft of writing poems. **3** a poetic quality that prompts an emotional response: *her acting was full of poetry.*

po-faced *adj* wearing a disapproving stern expression.

pogey *or* **pogy** (**pohg**-ee) *n, pl* **pogeys** *or* **pogies** *Canad slang* **1** financial or other relief given to the unemployed by the government; dole. **2** unemployment insurance. **3** the office that gives out relief to the unemployed.

pogo stick *n* a pole with steps for the feet and a spring at the bottom, so that the user can bounce up, down, and along on it.

THESAURUS

asset, benefit, bonus, extra, gain, good point, icing on the cake, perk (*Brit. informal*), surplus

plutocrat capitalist, magnate, millionaire, moneybags (*informal*), rich man, tycoon

ply 1. carry on, exercise, follow, practise, pursue, work at **2.** employ, handle, manipulate, swing, utilize, wield

poach appropriate, encroach, hunt *or* fish illegally, infringe, intrude, plunder, rob, steal, steal game, trespass

pocket 1. *n.* bag, compartment, hollow, pouch, receptacle, sack **2.** *vb.* appropriate, filch, help oneself to, lift (*informal*), pilfer, purloin, snaffle (*Brit. informal*), steal, take **3.** *adj.* abridged, compact, concise, little, miniature, pint-size(d) (*informal*), portable, potted (*informal*), small

pod *n./vb.* hull, husk, shell

podgy chubby, chunky, dumpy, fat, fleshy, plump, roly-poly, rotund, short and fat, squat, stout, stubby, stumpy, tubby

podium dais, platform, rostrum, stage

poem lyric, ode, rhyme, song, sonnet, verse

poet bard, lyricist, rhymer, versifier

pogrom *n* an organized persecution and massacre.

poi *n NZ* a ball of woven flax swung rhythmically by Maori women during poi dances.

poi dance *n NZ* a women's formation dance that involves singing and twirling a poi.

poignant *adj* **1** sharply painful to the feelings: *a poignant reminder.* **2** cutting: *poignant wit.* **3** pertinent in mental appeal: *a poignant subject.* **poignancy** *n*

poinsettia *n* a shrub of Mexico and Central America, widely grown for its showy scarlet bracts, which resemble petals.

point *n* **1** the essential idea in an argument or discussion: *I agreed with the point he made.* **2** a reason or aim: *what is the point of this exercise?* **3** a detail or item. **4** a characteristic: *he has his good points.* **5** a location or position. **6** a dot or tiny mark. **7** a dot used as a decimal point or a full stop. **8** the sharp tip of anything: *the point of the spear.* **9** a headland: *the soaring cliffs at Dwerja Point in the southwest of the island.* **10** *Maths* a geometric element having a position located by coordinates, but no magnitude. **11** a specific condition or degree: *freezing point.* **12** a moment: *at that point he left.* **13** (*often pl*) any of the extremities, such as the tail, ears, or feet, of a domestic animal. **14** (*often pl*) *Ballet* the tip of the toes. **15** a single unit for measuring something such as value, or of scoring in a game. **16** *Printing* a unit of measurement equal to one twelfth of a pica. **17** *Navigation* one of the 32 direction marks on the compass. **18** *Cricket* a fielding position at right angles to the batsman on the off side. **19** either of the two electrical contacts that make or break the circuit in the distributor of a motor vehicle. **20** *Brit, Austral, & NZ* (*often pl*) a movable section of railway track used to direct a train from one line to another. **21** *Brit* short for **power point. 22** *Boxing* a mark awarded for a scoring blow or knockdown. **23 at** *or* **on the point of** about to; on the verge of: *on the point of leaving.* **24 beside the point** irrelevant. **25 make a point of a** to make a habit of (something). **b** to do (something) because one thinks it important. **26 to the point** relevant. **27 up to a point** not completely. ~*vb* **28** (usually foll. by *at* or *to*) to show the position or direction of something by extending a finger or other pointed object towards it. **29** (usually foll. by *at* or *to*) to single out one person or thing from among several: *all the symptoms pointed to epilepsy.* **30** to direct or face in a specific direction: *point me in the right direction.* **31** to finish or repair the joints in brickwork with mortar or cement. **32** (of gun dogs) to show where game is lying by standing rigidly with the muzzle turned towards it. ~See also **point out.**

point-blank *adj* **1** fired at a very close target. **2** plain or blunt: *a point-blank refusal to discuss the matter.* ~*adv* **3** directly or bluntly: *the Minister was asked point-blank if he intended to resign.*

point duty *n* the control of traffic by a policeman at a road junction.

pointed *adj* **1** having a sharp tip. **2** cutting or incisive: *pointed wit.* **3** obviously directed at a particular person: *a pointed remark.* **4** emphasized or obvious: *pointed ignorance.* **pointedly** *adv*

pointer *n* **1** something that is a helpful indicator of how a situation has arisen or may turn out: *a significant pointer to the likely resumption of talks.* **2** an indicator on a measuring instrument. **3** a long stick used by teachers, to point out particular features on a map, chart, etc. **4** a large smooth-coated gun dog.

pointillism (**pwan**-till-iz-zum) *n* a technique used by some impressionist painters, in which dots of colour are placed side by side so that they merge when seen from a distance. **pointillist** *n, adj*

pointing *n* the insertion of mortar between the joints in brickwork.

pointless *adj* without meaning or purpose.

point of no return *n* a point at which one is committed to continuing with an action.

point of order *n, pl* **points of order** an objection in a meeting to the departure from the proper procedure.

point of view *n, pl* **points of view 1** a mental viewpoint or attitude: *she refuses to see the other person's point of view.* **2** a way of considering something: *a scientific point of view.*

point out *vb* to draw someone's attention to.

point-to-point *n Brit* a steeplechase organized by a hunt.

poise *n* **1** dignified manner. **2** physical balance: *the poise of a natural model.* **3** mental balance: *he recov-*

THESAURUS

poetic *or* **poetical** elegiac, lyric, lyrical, metrical, rhythmical, songlike

poetry metrical composition, poems, poesy (*archaic*), rhyme, rhyming, verse

poignancy 1. emotion, emotionalism, evocativeness, feeling, pathos, piteousness, plaintiveness, sadness, sentiment, tenderness **2.** intensity, keenness, piquancy, sharpness

poignant 1. affecting, agonizing, bitter, distressing, harrowing, heartbreaking, heart-rending, intense, moving, painful, pathetic, sad, touching, upsetting **2.** acute, biting, caustic, keen, penetrating, piercing, pointed, sarcastic, severe

point *n.* **1.** burden, core, crux, drift, essence, gist, heart, import, main idea, marrow, matter, meaning, nub, pith, proposition, question, subject, text, theme, thrust **2.** aim, design, end, goal, intent, intention, motive, object, objective, purpose, reason, use, usefulness, utility **3.** aspect, detail, facet, feature, instance, item, nicety, particular **4.** aspect, attribute, characteristic, peculiarity, property, quality, respect, side, trait **5.** location, place, position, site, spot, stage, station **6.** dot, full stop, mark, period, speck, stop **7.** apex, end, nib, prong, sharp end, spike, spur, summit, tine, tip, top **8.** bill, cape, foreland, head, headland, ness (*archaic*), promontory **9.** circumstance, condition, degree, extent, position, stage **10.** instant, juncture, moment, time, very minute **11.** score, tally, unit **12. beside the point** immaterial, incidental, inconsequential, irrelevant, not to the purpose, off the subject, out of the way, pointless, unimportant, without connection **13. to the point** applicable, apposite, appropriate, apropos, apt, brief, fitting, germane, pertinent, pithy, pointed, relevant, short, suitable, terse ~*vb.* **14.** *usually with* **at** *or* **to** bespeak, call attention to, denote, designate, direct, indicate, show, signify **15.** aim, bring to bear, direct, level, train

point-blank 1. *adj.* abrupt, blunt, categorical, direct, downright, explicit, express, plain, straight-from-the-shoulder, unreserved **2.** *adv.* bluntly, brusquely, candidly, directly, explicitly, forthrightly, frankly, openly, overtly, plainly, straight, straightforwardly

pointed 1. acute, barbed, edged, sharp **2.** accurate, acute, biting, cutting, incisive, keen, penetrating, pertinent, sharp, telling, trenchant

pointer 1. advice, caution, hint, information, recommendation, suggestion, tip, warning **2.** guide, hand, indicator, needle

pointless absurd, aimless, fruitless, futile, inane, ineffectual, irrelevant, meaningless, nonsensical, senseless, silly, stupid, unavailing, unproductive, unprofitable, useless, vague, vain, worthless

point out allude to, bring up, call attention to, identify, indicate, mention, remind, reveal, show, specify

ered his poise. ~*vb* **poising, poised 4** to be balanced or suspended. **5** to be held in readiness: *the cats were poised to spring on her.*

poised *adj* **1** absolutely ready. **2** behaving with or showing poise.

poison *n* **1** a substance that causes death or injury when swallowed or absorbed. **2** something that destroys or corrupts: *the poison of Nazism.* ~*vb* **3** to give poison to someone. **4** to add poison to something. **5** to have a harmful or evil effect on. **6** (foll. by *against*) to turn (a person's mind) against: *he poisoned her mind against me.* **poisoner** *n*

poison ivy *n* a North American climbing plant that causes an itching rash if it touches the skin.

poisonous *adj* **1** of or like a poison. **2** malicious.

poison-pen letter *n* a malicious anonymous letter.

poke[1] *vb* **poking, poked 1** to jab or prod with an elbow, finger, etc. **2** to make a hole by poking. **3** (sometimes foll. by *at*) to thrust (at): *she poked at the food with her fork.* **4** (usually foll. by *in, through,* etc.) to thrust forward or out: *yellow hair poked from beneath his cap.* **5** to stir (a fire) by poking. **6** (often foll. by *about* or *around*) to search or pry. **7 poke one's nose into** to meddle in. ~*n* **8** a jab or prod.

poke[2] *n* **1** *Dialect* a pocket or bag. **2 a pig in a poke** See **pig.**

poker[1] *n* a metal rod with a handle for stirring a fire.

poker[2] *n* a card game of bluff and skill in which players bet on the hands dealt.

poker face *n Informal* an expressionless face, such as that of a poker player trying to hide the value of his or her cards. **poker-faced** *adj*

pokerwork *n* the art of producing pictures or designs on wood by burning it with a heated metal point.

poky *adj* **pokier, pokiest** (of a room) small and cramped. **pokiness** *n*

pol. 1 political. **2** politics.

polar *adj* **1** of or near either of the earth's poles or the area inside the Arctic or Antarctic Circles. **2** of or having a pole or polarity. **3** directly opposite in tendency or nature: *polar opposites.*

polar bear *n* a white bear of coastal regions of the North Pole.

polar circle *n* the Arctic or Antarctic Circle.

polarity *n, pl* **-ties 1** the state of having two directly opposite tendencies or opinions. **2** the condition of a body which has opposing physical properties, usually magnetic poles or electric charge. **3** the particular state of a part with polarity: *an electrode with positive polarity.*

polarization *or* **-isation** *n* **1** the condition of having or giving polarity. **2** *Physics* the condition in which waves of light or other radiation are restricted to certain directions of vibration.

polarize *or* **-ise** *vb* **-izing, -ized** *or* **-ising, -ised 1** to cause people to adopt directly opposite opinions: *political opinion had polarized since the restoration of democracy.* **2** to have or give polarity or polarization.

Polaroid *n Trademark* **1** a type of plastic that polarizes light: used in sunglasses to eliminate glare. **2 Polaroid camera** a camera that produces a finished print by developing and processing it inside the camera within a few seconds.

polder *n* a stretch of land reclaimed from the sea.

pole[1] *n* **1** a long slender rounded piece of wood, metal, or other material. **2 up the pole** *Brit, Austral, & NZ informal* **a** slightly mad. **b** in a predicament.

pole[2] *n* **1** either end of the earth's axis of rotation. See also **North Pole, South Pole. 2** *Physics* **a** either of the opposite forces of a magnet. **b** either of two points at which there are opposite electric charges. **3** either of two directly opposite tendencies or opinions. **4 poles apart** having widely divergent opinions or tastes.

Pole *n* a person from Poland.

poleaxe *or US* **poleax** *vb* **-axing, -axed 1** to hit or stun with a heavy blow. ~*n* **2** an axe formerly used in battle or used by a butcher.

polecat *n, pl* **-cats** *or* **-cat 1** a dark brown mammal like a weasel that gives off a foul smell. **2** *US* a skunk.

polemic (pol-em-ik) *n* **1** a fierce attack on or defence of a particular opinion, belief, etc.: *anti-capitalist polemic.* ~*adj also* **polemical 2** of or involving dispute or controversy. **polemicist** *n*

polemics *n* the art of dispute.

pole position *n* **1** (in motor racing) the starting position on the inside of the front row, generally considered the best one. **2** an advantageous starting position.

pole star *n* a guiding principle or rule.

Pole Star *n* **the Pole Star** the star closest to the N celestial pole.

pole vault *n* **1 the pole vault** a field event in which competitors try to clear a high bar with the aid of a very flexible long pole. ~*vb* **pole-vault 2** to perform or compete in the pole vault. **pole-vaulter** *n*

police *n* **1** (often preceded by *the*) the organized civil force in a state which keeps law and order. **2** the men and women who are members of such a force. **3** an

THESAURUS

poise 1. *n.* aplomb, assurance, calmness, composure, cool (*slang*), coolness, dignity, elegance, equanimity, equilibrium, grace, presence, presence of mind, sangfroid, savoir-faire, self-possession, serenity **2.** *vb.* balance, float, hang, hang in midair, hang suspended, hold, hover, position, support, suspend

poised 1. all set, in the wings, on the brink, prepared, ready, standing by, waiting **2.** calm, collected, composed, debonair, dignified, graceful, nonchalant, self-confident, self-possessed, serene, suave, together (*informal*), unfazed (*informal*), unruffled, urbane

poison *n.* **1.** bane, toxin, venom **2.** bane, blight, cancer, canker, contagion, contamination, corruption, malignancy, miasma, virus ~*vb.* **3.** adulterate, contaminate, envenom, give (someone) poison, infect, kill, murder, pollute **4.** corrupt, defile, deprave, pervert, subvert, taint, undermine, vitiate, warp

poisonous 1. deadly, fatal, lethal, mortal, noxious, toxic, venomous, virulent **2.** baleful, baneful, corruptive, evil, malicious, noxious, pernicious, pestiferous, pestilential, vicious

poke *vb.* **1.** butt, dig, elbow, hit, jab, nudge, prod, punch, push, shove, stab, stick, thrust **2.** *often with* **about** *or* **around** butt in, interfere, intrude, meddle, nose, peek, poke one's nose into (*informal*), pry, snoop (*informal*), tamper ~*n.* **3.** butt, dig, hit, jab, nudge, prod, punch, thrust

poky confined, cramped, incommodious, narrow, small, tiny

polar 1. Antarctic, Arctic, cold, extreme, freezing, frozen, furthest, glacial, icy, terminal **2.** antagonistic, antipodal, antithetical, contradictory, contrary, diametric, opposed, opposite

pole[1] bar, mast, post, rod, shaft, spar, staff, standard, stick

pole[2] **1.** antipode, extremity, limit, terminus **2. poles apart** at opposite ends of the earth, at opposite extremes, incompatible, irreconcilable, miles apart, widely separated, worlds apart

organized body with a similar function: *security police.* ~*vb* **-licing, -liced 4** to maintain order or control by means of a police force or similar body.

police dog *n* a dog trained to help the police.

policeman *or fem* **policewoman** *n, pl* **-men** *or* **-women** a member of a police force.

police state *n* a state in which a government controls people's freedom through the police.

police station *n* the office of the police force of a district.

policy[1] *n, pl* **-cies 1** a plan of action adopted by a person, group, or government. **2** *Archaic* wisdom or prudence.

policy[2] *n, pl* **-cies** a document containing an insurance contract. **policyholder** *n*

polio *n* short for **poliomyelitis.**

poliomyelitis (pole-ee-oh-my-el-**lite**-iss) *n* a viral disease which affects the brain and spinal cord, often causing paralysis.

polish *vb* **1** to make smooth and shiny by rubbing. **2** to perfect or complete: *media experts he had hired to polish his image.* **3** to make or become elegant or refined: *not having polished his south London accent didn't help his career.* ~*n* **4** a substance used for polishing. **5** a shine or gloss. **6** elegance or refinement.

Polish *adj* **1** of Poland. ~*n* **2** the language of Poland.

polished *adj* **1** accomplished: *a polished actor.* **2** done or performed well or professionally: *a polished performance.*

polish off *vb Informal* **1** to finish completely. **2** to dispose of or kill.

polish up *vb* **1** to make smooth and shiny by polishing. **2** to improve (a skill or ability) by working at it: *I'm going to evening classes to polish up my German.*

Politburo *n* the chief decision-making committee of a Communist country.

polite *adj* **1** having good manners; courteous. **2** cultivated or refined: *polite society.* **3** socially correct but insincere: *he smiled a polite response and stifled an urge to scream.* **politely** *adv* **politeness** *n*

politic *adj* **1** wise or possibly advantageous: *I didn't feel it was politic to mention it.* **2** artful or shrewd: *a politic manager.* **3** crafty; cunning: *a politic old scoundrel.* **4** *Archaic* political. See also **body politic.**

political *adj* **1** of the state, government, or public administration. **2** relating to or interested in politics: *she was always a very political person.* **3** of the parties and the partisan aspects of politics: *the government blames political opponents for fanning the unrest.* **politically** *adv*

politically correct *adj* displaying liberal attitudes, esp. in using vocabulary which is intended to avoid any implied prejudice.

political prisoner *n* a person imprisoned for holding particular political beliefs.

political science *n* the study of the state, government, and politics. **political scientist** *n*

politician *n* a person actively engaged in politics, esp. a member of parliament.

politicize *or* **-cise** *vb* **-cizing, -cized** *or* **-cising, -cised 1** to make political or politically aware. **2** to take part in political discussion or activity. **politicization** *or* **-cisation** *n*

politics *n* **1** (*functioning as sing*) the art and science of government. **2** (*functioning as pl*) political opinions or sympathies: *his conservative politics.* **3** (*functioning as pl*) political activities or affairs: *party politics.* **4** (*functioning as sing*) the business or profession of politics. **5** (*functioning as sing or pl*) any activity concerned with the acquisition of power: *company politics are often vicious.*

polity *n, pl* **-ties** *Formal* **1** a politically organized state, church, or society. **2** a form of government of a state, church, or society.

polka *n* **1** a lively 19th-century dance. **2** music for this dance. ~*vb* **-kaing, -kaed 3** to dance a polka.

polka dots *pl n* a regular pattern of small bold spots on a fabric.

poll *n* **1** Also called: **opinion poll** the questioning of a random sample of people to find out the general opinion. **2** the casting, recording, or counting of votes in an election. **3** the result of such a voting: *a marginal poll.* **4** the head. ~*vb* **5** to receive (a certain number of votes). **6** to record the votes of: *he polled the whole town.* **7** to question (a person, etc.) as part of an opinion poll. **8** to vote in an election. **9** to clip or shear. **10** to remove or cut short the horns of (cattle).

pollack *or* **pollock** *n, pl* **-lacks, -lack, -locks,** *or* **-lock** a food fish related to the cod, found in northern seas.

pollard *n* **1** an animal that has shed its horns or has had them removed. **2** a tree with its branches cut back to encourage a more bushy growth. ~*vb* **3** to cut back the top branches of (a tree) to make it grow bushy. **pollarded** *adj*

pollen *n* a fine powder produced by flowers to fertilize other flowers of the same species.

THESAURUS

police *n.* **1.** constabulary, fuzz (*slang*), law enforcement agency, police force, the law (*informal*) ~*vb.* **2.** control, guard, keep in order, keep the peace, patrol, protect, regulate, watch

policeman bobby (*informal*), constable, cop (*slang*), copper (*slang*), fuzz (*slang*), officer, peeler (*obsolete Brit. slang*), pig (*slang*)

policy 1. action, approach, code, course, custom, guideline, line, plan, practice, procedure, programme, protocol, rule, scheme, stratagem, theory **2.** *archaic* discretion, good sense, prudence, sagacity, shrewdness, wisdom

polish *vb.* **1.** brighten, buff, burnish, clean, furbish, rub, shine, smooth, wax **2.** brush up, correct, cultivate, emend, enhance, finish, improve, perfect, refine, touch up ~*n.* **3.** varnish, wax **4.** brightness, brilliance, finish, glaze, gloss, lustre, sheen, smoothness, sparkle, veneer **5.** breeding, class (*informal*), elegance, finesse, finish, grace, politesse, refinement, style, suavity, urbanity

polished accomplished, adept, expert, faultless, fine, flawless, impeccable, masterly, outstanding, professional, skilful, superlative

polish off 1. consume, down, eat up, finish, put away, shift (*informal*), swill, wolf **2.** blow away (*slang, chiefly U.S.*), bump off (*informal*), dispose of, do away with, do in (*slang*), eliminate, get rid of, kill, liquidate, murder, take out (*slang*)

polite 1. affable, civil, complaisant, courteous, deferential, gracious, mannerly, obliging, respectful, well-behaved, well-mannered **2.** civilized, courtly, cultured, elegant, genteel, polished, refined, urbane, well-bred

politic 1. advisable, diplomatic, discreet, expedient, in one's best interests, judicious, prudent, sagacious, sensible, tactful, wise **2.** artful, astute, canny, crafty, cunning, designing, ingenious, intriguing, Machiavellian, scheming, shrewd, sly, subtle, unscrupulous

politician legislator, Member of Parliament, M.P., office bearer, public servant, statesman

politics 1. affairs of state, civics, government, government policy, political science, polity, statecraft, statesmanship **2.** Machiavellianism, machination, power struggle

poll *n.* **1.** ballot, canvass, census, count, Gallup Poll,

pollen count *n* a measure of the amount of pollen in the air over a 24-hour period, often published as a warning to hay fever sufferers.

pollinate *vb* **-nating, -nated** to fertilize by the transfer of pollen. **pollination** *n*

polling booth *n* a compartment in which a voter can mark his or her ballot paper in private during an election.

polling station *n* a building where voters go during an election to cast their votes.

pollock *n* same as **pollack.**

pollster *n* a person who conducts opinion polls.

poll tax *n* any tax levied per head of adult population, esp. the tax which replaced domestic rates (in Scotland from 1989 and England and Wales from 1990, until 1993).

pollutant *n* a substance that pollutes, usually the chemical waste of an industrial process.

pollute *vb* **-luting, -luted 1** to contaminate with poisonous or harmful substances. **2** to corrupt morally. **pollution** *n*

polo *n* **1** a game like hockey played on horseback with long-handled mallets and a wooden ball. **2** short for **water polo.**

polonaise *n* **1** a stately Polish dance. **2** music for this dance.

polo neck *n* a sweater with a high tight turned-over collar.

polonium *n Chem* a rare radioactive element found in trace amounts in uranium ores. Symbol: Po

polo shirt *n* a cotton short-sleeved shirt with a collar and three-button opening at the neck.

poltergeist *n* a spirit believed to be responsible for noises and acts of mischief, such as throwing objects about.

poltroon *n Obsolete* a complete coward.

poly *n, pl* **polys** *Informal* short for **polytechnic.**

poly- *combining form* many or much: *polyhedron; polysyllabic.*

polyandry *n* the practice of having more than one husband at the same time. **polyandrous** *adj*

polyanthus *n, pl* **-thuses** a hybrid garden primrose with brightly coloured flowers.

polychromatic *adj* **1** having many colours. **2** (of radiation) containing more than one wavelength.

polyester *n* a synthetic material used to make plastics and textile fibres.

polyethylene *n* same as **polythene.**

polygamy (pol-**ig**-a-mee) *n* the practice of having more than one wife or husband at the same time. **polygamist** *n* **polygamous** *adj*

polyglot *adj* **1** able to speak many languages. **2** written in or using many languages. *~n* **3** a person who can speak many languages.

polygon *n* a geometrical figure with three or more sides and angles. **polygonal** *adj*

polygraph *n* an instrument for recording pulse rate and perspiration, often used as a lie detector.

polygyny *n* the practice of having more than one wife at the same time. **polygynous** *adj*

polyhedron *n, pl* **-drons** *or* **-dra** a solid figure with four or more sides. **polyhedral** *adj*

polymath *n* a person of great and varied learning.

polymer *n* a natural or synthetic compound with large molecules made up of simple molecules of the same kind.

polymeric *adj* of or being a polymer: *polymeric materials such as PVC.*

polymerization *or* **-isation** *n* the process of forming a polymer. **polymerize** *or* **-ise** *vb*

polymorphous *or* **polymorphic** *adj* having, or passing through many different forms or stages.

Polynesian *adj* **1** of Polynesia. *~n* **2** a person from Polynesia. **3** any of the languages of Polynesia.

polynomial *Maths ~adj* **1** consisting of two or more terms. *~n* **2** an algebraic expression consisting of the sum of a number of terms.

polyp *n* **1** *Zool* a small sea creature that has a hollow cylindrical body with a ring of tentacles around the mouth. **2** *Pathol* a small growth on the surface of a mucous membrane.

polyphonic *adj Music* consisting of several melodies played together.

polyphony (pol-**if**-on-ee) *n, pl* **-nies** polyphonic style of composition or a piece of music using it.

polysaccharide *n* a carbohydrate which consists of a number of linked sugar molecules, such as starch or cellulose.

polystyrene *n* a synthetic material used esp. as white rigid foam for insulating and packing.

polysyllable *n* a word having more than two syllables. **polysyllabic** *adj*

polytechnic *n* **1** *Brit* (formerly) a college offering advanced courses in many subjects at and below degree level. *~adj* **2** of or relating to technical instruction.

polytheism *n* belief in more than one god. **polytheistic** *adj* **polytheist** *n*

polythene *n* a light plastic material made from ethylene, usually made into thin sheets or bags.

polyunsaturated *adj* of a group of fats that are less likely to contribute to the build-up of cholesterol in the body.

polyurethane *n* a synthetic material used esp. in paints.

polyvinyl chloride *n* See **PVC.**

pomace (**pumm**-iss) *n* apple pulp left after pressing for juice.

pomade *n* a perfumed oil put on the hair to make it smooth and shiny, esp. formerly.

pomander *n* **1** a mixture of sweet-smelling substances in a container, used to perfume drawers or cupboards. **2** a container for such a mixture.

pomegranate *n* a round tropical fruit with a tough reddish rind containing many seeds in a juicy red pulp.

pomelo (**pom**-ill-oh) *n, pl* **-los** the edible yellow fruit, like a grapefruit, of a tropical tree.

Pomeranian *n* a toy dog with a long straight silky coat.

pomfret (**pum**-frit) *or* **pomfret-cake** *n* a small black rounded liquorice sweet.

pommel *n* **1** the raised part on the front of a saddle. **2** a knob at the top of a sword handle. *~vb* **-melling, -melled** *or US* **-meling, -meled 3** same as **pummel.**

pommy *n, pl* **-mies** (*sometimes cap*) *Slang* a word

THESAURUS

(public) opinion poll, sampling, survey **2.** figures, returns, tally, vote, voting *~vb.* **3.** register, tally **4.** ballot, canvass, interview, question, sample, survey

pollute 1. adulterate, befoul, contaminate, dirty, foul, infect, make filthy, mar, poison, smirch, soil, spoil, stain, taint **2.** besmirch, corrupt, debase, debauch, defile, deprave, desecrate, dishonour, profane, sully, violate

pollution adulteration, contamination, corruption, defilement, dirtying, foulness, impurity, taint, uncleanness, vitiation

used by Australians and New Zealanders for a British person. Sometimes shortened to: **pom**

pomp *n* **1** stately display or ceremony. **2** ostentatious display.

pompom *n* **1** a decorative ball of tufted silk or wool. **2** the small round flower head of some dahlias and chrysanthemums.

pom-pom *n* an automatic rapid-firing gun.

pompous *adj* **1** foolishly dignified or self-important. **2** foolishly grand in style: *a pompous speech.* **pomposity** *n* **pompously** *adv*

ponce *Offensive slang, chiefly Brit* ~*n* **1** an effeminate man. **2** same as **pimp.** ~*vb* **poncing, ponced 3** (often foll. by *around* or *about*) to act stupidly or waste time.

poncho *n, pl* **-chos** a type of cloak made of a piece of cloth with a hole in the middle for the head.

pond *n* a pool of still water.

ponder *vb* (sometimes foll. by *on* or *over*) to consider thoroughly or deeply. **ponderable** *adj*

ponderous *adj* **1** serious and dull: *much of the film is ponderous and pretentious.* **2** heavy or huge. **3** (of movement) slow and clumsy.

pondok *or* **pondokkie** *n* (in southern Africa) a crudely made house or shack.

pondweed *n* a plant which grows in ponds and slow streams.

pong *Brit informal* ~*n* **1** a strong unpleasant smell. ~*vb* **2** to give off a strong unpleasant smell. **pongy** *adj*

ponga (**pong**-a) *n* a tall New Zealand tree fern with large leathery leaves.

poniard (**pon**-yerd) *n* a small slender dagger.

pontiff *n* the Pope.

pontifical *adj* **1** of a pontiff. **2** pompous or dogmatic in manner.

pontificate *vb* **-cating, -cated 1** to speak in a dogmatic manner. **2** to officiate as a pontiff. ~*n* **3** the term of office of a Pope.

pontoon[1] *n* a floating platform used to support a bridge.

pontoon[2] *n* a card game in which players try to obtain sets of cards worth less than 21 points.

pony *n, pl* **-nies** a breed of small horse.

ponytail *n* a hairstyle in which the hair is tied in a bunch at the back of the head and hangs down like a tail.

pony trekking *n* the pastime of riding ponies cross-country.

poodle *n* a dog with curly hair, which is sometimes clipped.

poof *n Brit & Austral offensive slang* a male homosexual.

pooh *interj* an exclamation of disdain, scorn, or disgust.

pooh-pooh *vb* to express disdain or scorn for.

pool[1] *n* **1** a small body of still water. **2** a small body of spilt liquid: *a pool of blood.* **3** See **swimming pool. 4** a deep part of a stream or river.

pool[2] *n* **1** a shared fund of resources or workers: *a typing pool.* **2** a billiard game in which all the balls are potted with the cue ball. **3** the combined stakes of those betting in many gambling games. **4** *Commerce* a group of producers who agree to maintain output levels and high prices. ~*vb* **5** to put into a common fund.

pools *pl n* **the pools** *Brit* a nationwide mainly postal form of gambling which bets on the results of football matches.

poop *n Naut* a raised part at the back of a sailing ship.

pooped *adj US & Canad slang* exhausted or tired: *if I wasn't so pooped I'd run over and have a look at it.*

poor *adj* **1** having little money and few possessions. **2** less than is necessary or expected: *it was a poor reward for all his effort.* **3** (sometimes foll. by *in*) lacking in (something): *a food which is rich in energy but poor in vitamins.* **4** inferior: *poor quality.* **5** disappointing or disagreeable: *a poor play.* **6** pitiable; unlucky: *poor John is ill.* **7 poor man's (something)** a cheaper substitute for (something): *pewter, sometimes known as poor man's silver.*

poorhouse *n* same as **workhouse.**

poor law *n English history* a law providing for support of the poor from parish funds.

poorly *adv* **1** badly. ~*adj* **2** *Informal* rather ill.

poor White *n Often offensive* a poverty-stricken

THESAURUS

pomp 1. ceremony, éclat, flourish, grandeur, magnificence, pageant, pageantry, parade, solemnity, splendour, state **2.** display, grandiosity, ostentation, pomposity, show, vainglory

pompous 1. affected, arrogant, bloated, grandiose, imperious, magisterial, ostentatious, overbearing, pontifical, portentous, pretentious, puffed up, self-important, showy, supercilious, vainglorious **2.** boastful, bombastic, flatulent, fustian, grandiloquent, high-flown, inflated, magniloquent, orotund, overblown, turgid, windy

pond dew pond, duck pond, fish pond, millpond, pool, small lake, tarn

ponder *sometimes with* **on** *or* **over** brood, cerebrate, cogitate, consider, contemplate, deliberate, examine, excogitate, give thought to, meditate, mull over, muse, puzzle over, reflect, ruminate, study, think, weigh

ponderous 1. dreary, dull, heavy, laboured, lifeless, long-winded, pedantic, pedestrian, plodding, prolix, stilted, stodgy, tedious, verbose **2.** bulky, cumbersome, cumbrous, heavy, hefty, huge, massive, unwieldy, weighty **3.** awkward, clumsy, elephantine, graceless, heavy-footed, laborious, lumbering

pontificate declaim, dogmatize, expound, hold forth, lay down the law, preach, pronounce, sound off

pooh-pooh belittle, brush aside, deride, disdain, dismiss, disregard, make little of, play down, scoff, scorn, slight, sneer, sniff at, spurn, turn up one's nose at (*informal*)

pool[1] **1.** lake, mere, pond, puddle, splash, tarn **2.** swimming bath, swimming pool

pool[2] *n.* **1.** collective, combine, consortium, group, syndicate, team, trust **2.** bank, funds, jackpot, kitty, pot, stakes ~*vb.* **3.** amalgamate, combine, join forces, league, merge, put together, share

poor 1. badly off, broke (*informal*), destitute, dirt-poor (*informal*), down and out, flat broke (*informal*), hard up (*informal*), impecunious, impoverished, indigent, in need, in want, necessitous, needy, on one's beam-ends, on one's uppers, on the rocks, penniless, penurious, poverty-stricken, short, skint (*Brit. slang*), stony-broke (*Brit. slang*), without two pennies to rub together (*informal*) **2.** deficient, exiguous, inadequate, incomplete, insufficient, lacking, meagre, measly, miserable, niggardly, pitiable, reduced, scant, scanty, skimpy, slight, sparse, straitened **3.** below par, crappy (*slang*), faulty, feeble, inferior, low-grade, mediocre, piss-poor (*taboo slang*), rotten (*informal*), rubbishy, second-rate, shabby, shoddy, sorry, substandard, unsatisfactory, valueless, weak, worthless **4.** hapless, ill-fated, luckless, miserable, pathetic, pitiable, unfortunate, unhappy, unlucky, wretched

poorly 1. *adv.* badly, crudely, inadequately, incompetently, inexpertly, inferiorly, insufficiently, meanly, shabbily, unsatisfactorily, unsuccessfully **2.** *adj.* in-

White person, usually in the southern US or South Africa.

pop[1] *vb* **popping, popped 1** to make or cause to make a small explosive sound. **2** (often foll. by *in, out,* etc.) *Informal* to enter or leave briefly or suddenly. **3** to place suddenly or unexpectedly: *Benny popped a sweet into his mouth.* **4** to burst with a small explosive sound. **5** (of the eyes) to protrude. **6** *Informal* to pawn. **7 pop the question** *Informal* to propose marriage. *~n* **8** a light sharp explosive sound. **9** *Informal* a nonalcoholic fizzy drink. *~adv* **10** with a pop. ~See also **pop off.**

pop[2] *n* **1** music of general appeal, esp. to young people, that usually has a strong rhythm and uses electrical amplification. *~adj* **2** relating to pop music: *a pop concert.* **3** *Informal* short for **popular.**

pop[3] *n Informal* **1** father. **2** an old man.

pop. 1 population. **2** popular(ly).

pop art *n* a movement in modern art that uses the methods, styles, and themes of popular culture and mass media.

popcorn *n* grains of maize heated until they puff up and burst.

Pope *n* the bishop of Rome as head of the Roman Catholic Church.

popery (**pope**-er-ee) *n Offensive* Roman Catholicism.

popeyed *adj* **1** staring in astonishment. **2** having bulging eyes.

popgun *n* a toy gun that fires a pellet or cork by means of compressed air.

popinjay *n* a conceited or talkative person.

popish (**pope**-ish) *adj Offensive* relating to Roman Catholicism.

poplar *n* a tall slender tree with light soft wood, triangular leaves, and catkins.

poplin *n* a strong plain-woven fabric, usually of cotton, with fine ribbing.

pop off *vb Informal* **1** to depart suddenly. **2** to die suddenly.

poppadom *or* **poppadum** *n* a thin round crisp fried Indian bread.

popper *n Brit informal* a press stud.

poppet *n* a term of affection for a small child or sweetheart.

popping crease *n Cricket* a line in front of and parallel with the wicket where the batsman stands.

poppy *n, pl* **-pies 1** a plant with showy red, orange, or white flowers. **2** a drug, such as opium, obtained from these plants. **3** an artificial red poppy worn to mark Remembrance Sunday. *~adj* **4** reddish-orange.

poppycock *n Informal* nonsense.

Poppy Day *n Informal* Remembrance Sunday.

populace *n* the common people; masses.

popular *adj* **1** widely liked or admired. **2** (often foll. by *with*) liked by a particular person or group: *the bay is popular with windsurfers and water-skiers.* **3** common among the general public: *the groundswell of popular feeling.* **4** designed to appeal to a mass audience: *an attack on him in the popular press.* **popularity** *n* **popularly** *adv*

popular front *n* a left-wing group or party opposed to fascism.

popularize *or* **-ise** *vb* **-izing, -ized** *or* **-ising, -ised 1** to make popular. **2** to make easily understandable. **popularization** *or* **-isation** *n*

populate *vb* **-lating, -lated 1** (*often passive*) to live in: *a mountainous region populated mainly by Armenians.* **2** to provide with inhabitants. **populated** *adj*

population *n* **1** all the inhabitants of a place. **2** the number of such inhabitants. **3** all the people of a particular class in a place: *the bulk of the rural population lives in poverty.* **4** *Ecology* a group of individuals of the same species inhabiting a given area: *a population of grey seals.*

populism *n* a political strategy based on a calculated appeal to the interests or prejudices of ordinary people: *the Islamic radicals preach a heady message of populism and religion.* **populist** *adj, n*

populous *adj* containing many inhabitants.

porangi (**pore**-ang-ee) *adj NZ informal* crazy; mad.

porbeagle *n* a kind of shark.

porcelain *n* **1** a delicate type of china. **2** an object or objects made of this.

porch *n* a covered approach to the entrance of a building.

porcine *adj* of or like a pig.

porcupine *n* a large rodent covered with long pointed quills.

pore[1] *vb* **poring, pored pore over** to examine or study intently: *a wife who pored over account books and ledgers all day.*

pore[2] *n* **1** a small opening in the skin or surface of an animal or plant. **2** any small hole, such as a tiny gap in a rock.

poriferan (por-**riff**-er-an) *n Biol* a sponge.

pork *n* the flesh of pigs used as food.

porker *n* a pig fattened for food.

pork pie *n* a pie with a minced pork filling.

THESAURUS

formal ailing, below par, ill, indisposed, off colour, out of sorts, rotten (*informal*), seedy (*informal*), sick, under the weather (*informal*), unwell

pop *vb.* **1.** bang, burst, crack, explode, go off, report, snap **2.** *informal often with* **in, out,** *etc.* appear, call, come *or* go suddenly, drop in (*informal*), leave quickly, nip in (*Brit. informal*), nip out (*Brit. informal*), visit **3.** *esp. of eyes* bulge, protrude, stick out *~n.* **4.** bang, burst, crack, explosion, noise, report **5.** *informal* fizzy drink, lemonade, soda water, soft drink

Pope Bishop of Rome, Holy Father, pontiff, Vicar of Christ

populace commonalty, crowd, general public, hoi polloi, inhabitants, masses, mob, multitude, people, rabble, throng

popular 1. accepted, approved, celebrated, famous, fashionable, favoured, favourite, in, in demand, in favour, liked, sought-after, well-liked **2.** common, conventional, current, general, prevailing, prevalent, public, standard, stock, ubiquitous, universal, widespread

popularity acceptance, acclaim, adoration, approval, celebrity, currency, esteem, fame, favour, idolization, lionization, recognition, regard, renown, reputation, repute, vogue

popularize disseminate, familiarize, give currency to, give mass appeal, make available to all, simplify, spread, universalize

popularly commonly, conventionally, customarily, generally, ordinarily, regularly, traditionally, universally, usually, widely

populate colonize, inhabit, live in, occupy, people, settle

population citizenry, community, denizens, folk, inhabitants, natives, people, populace, residents, society

populous crowded, heavily populated, overpopulated, packed, populated, swarming, teeming, thronged

pore[1] *vb.* **pore over** brood, contemplate, dwell on,

porky *adj* **porkier, porkiest 1** of or like pork. **2** *Informal* fat or obese.

porn *or* **porno** *n, adj Informal* short for **pornography** or **pornographic.**

pornography *n* writings, pictures, or films designed to be sexually exciting. **pornographer** *n* **pornographic** *adj*

porous *adj* **1** allowing air and liquids to be absorbed. **2** *Biol, geol* having pores. **porosity** *n*

porphyry (**por**-fir-ee) *n, pl* **-ries** a reddish-purple rock with large crystals of feldspar in it. **porphyritic** *adj*

porpoise *n, pl* **-poise** *or* **-poises** a small mammal of the whale family with a blunt snout.

porridge *n* **1** a dish made of oatmeal or other cereal, cooked in water or milk. **2** *Slang* a term of imprisonment.

porringer *n* a small dish, often with a handle, used esp. formerly for soup or porridge.

port[1] *n* a town with a harbour where ships can load and unload.

port[2] *n* **1** the left side of an aircraft or ship when facing the front of it. *~vb* **2** to turn or be turned towards the port.

port[3] *n* a strong sweet fortified wine, usually dark red.

port[4] *n Naut* **a** an opening with a watertight door in the side of a ship, used for loading, etc. **b** See **porthole.**

portable *adj* **1** easily carried. *~n* **2** an article designed to be easily carried, such as a television or typewriter. **portability** *n*

portage *n* **1** the transporting of boats and supplies overland between navigable waterways. **2** the route used for such transport. *~vb* **-taging, -taged 3** to transport (boats and supplies) in this way.

portal *n Literary* a large and impressive gateway or doorway.

portcullis *n* an iron grating suspended in a castle gateway, that can be lowered to bar the entrance.

portend *vb* to be an omen of: *the changes in the Cabinet do not portend any significant shift in policy.*

portent *n* **1** a sign of a future event. **2** great or ominous significance: *matters of great portent.* **3** a marvel.

portentous *adj* **1** of great or ominous significance. **2** self-important or pompous: *there was nothing portentous or solemn about him.*

porter[1] *n* **1** a man employed to carry luggage at a railway station or hotel. **2** a hospital worker who transfers patients between rooms. **porterage** *n*

porter[2] *n Chiefly Brit* a doorman or gatekeeper of a building.

porter[3] *n Brit* a dark sweet ale brewed from black malt.

porterhouse *n* a thick choice beef steak. Also called: **porterhouse steak**

portfolio *n, pl* **-os 1** a flat case for carrying maps, drawings, or papers. **2** selected examples, such as drawings or photographs, that show an artist's recent work. **3** the area of responsibility of the head of a government department: *the defence portfolio.* **4 Minister without portfolio** a cabinet minister without responsibility for a government department. **5** a list of investments held by an investor.

porthole *n* a small round window in a ship or aircraft.

portico *n, pl* **-coes** *or* **-cos** a porch or covered walkway with columns supporting the roof.

portion *n* **1** a part of a whole. **2** a part belonging to a person or group. **3** a helping of food served to one person. **4** *Law* a dowry. **5** *Literary* someone's fate or destiny: *utter disaster was my portion.* *~vb* **6** to divide (something) into shares.

portion out *vb* to distribute or share (something) among a group of people: *the British portioned out the oil-rich lands to various sheikhs.*

portly *adj* **-lier, -liest** stout or rather fat.

portmanteau *n, pl* **-teaus** *or* **-teaux** *Old-fashioned* a large suitcase made of stiff leather that opens out into two compartments.

portmanteau word *n* a word made by joining together the beginning and end of two other words, such as *brunch.* Also called: **blend**

portrait *n* **1** a painting, drawing, or photograph of a person, often only of the face. **2** a description. **portraitist** *n*

portraiture *n* **1** the art of making portraits. **2** a description. **3 a** a portrait. **b** portraits collectively.

portray *vb* to describe or represent (someone) by artistic means, such as in writing or on film. **portrayal** *n*

Portuguese *adj* **1** of Portugal. *~n* **2** (*pl* **-guese**) a person from Portugal. **3** the language of Portugal and Brazil.

THESAURUS

examine, go over, peruse, ponder, read, scrutinize, study, work over

pore[2] *n.* hole, opening, orifice, outlet, stoma

pornographic blue, dirty, filthy, indecent, lewd, obscene, offensive, prurient, salacious, smutty

pornography dirt, erotica, filth, indecency, obscenity, porn (*informal*), porno (*informal*), smut

porous absorbent, absorptive, penetrable, permeable, pervious, spongy

port anchorage, harbour, haven, roads, roadstead, seaport

portable compact, convenient, easily carried, handy, light, lightweight, manageable, movable, portative

portend augur, bespeak, betoken, bode, foreshadow, foretell, foretoken, forewarn, harbinger, herald, indicate, omen, point to, predict, presage, prognosticate, promise, threaten, warn of

portent augury, foreboding, foreshadowing, forewarning, harbinger, indication, omen, premonition, presage, presentiment, prognostic, prognostication, sign, threat, warning

portentous 1. alarming, crucial, fateful, forbidding, important, menacing, minatory, momentous, ominous, significant, sinister, threatening **2.** pompous, ponderous, pontifical, self-important, solemn

porter[1] baggage attendant, bearer, carrier

porter[2] caretaker, concierge, doorman, gatekeeper, janitor

portion *n.* **1.** bit, fraction, fragment, morsel, part, piece, scrap, section, segment **2.** allocation, allotment, allowance, division, lot, measure, parcel, quantity, quota, ration, share **3.** helping, piece, serving **4.** *Literary* cup, destiny, fate, fortune, lot, luck *~vb.* **5.** allocate, allot, apportion, assign, deal, distribute, divide, divvy up (*informal*), dole out, parcel out, partition, share out

portrait 1. image, likeness, painting, photograph, picture, portraiture, representation, sketch **2.** account, characterization, depiction, description, portrayal, profile, thumbnail sketch, vignette

portray act the part of, characterize, delineate, depict, describe, draw, figure, illustrate, limn, paint, paint a mental picture of, picture, play, put in words, render, represent, sketch

Portuguese man-of-war *n* a large sea creature like a jellyfish, with long stinging tentacles.

pose *vb* **posing, posed 1** to take up a particular position to be photographed or drawn. **2** to behave in an affected way in order to impress others. **3** (often foll. by *as*) to pretend to be (someone one is not). **4** to create or be (a problem, threat, etc.): *dressing complicated wounds has always posed a problem for doctors.* **5** to put forward or ask: *the question you posed earlier.* ~*n* **6** a position taken up for an artist or photographer. **7** behaviour adopted for effect.

poser[1] *n* **1** *Informal* a person who likes to be seen in trendy clothes in fashionable places. **2** a person who poses.

poser[2] *n* a baffling question.

poseur *n* a person who behaves in an affected way in order to impress others.

posh *adj Informal, chiefly Brit* **1** smart or elegant. **2** upper-class.

posit (**pozz**-it) *vb* **-iting, -ited** to lay down as a basis for argument: *the archetypes posited by modern psychology.*

position *n* **1** place or location: *the hotel is in an elevated position above the River Wye.* **2** the proper or usual place. **3** the way in which a person or thing is placed or arranged: *an upright position.* **4** point of view; attitude: *the Catholic Church's position on contraception.* **5** social status, esp. high social standing. **6** a job; appointment. **7** *Sport* a player's allotted role or place in the playing area. **8 in a position to** able to: *you were not in a position to repay the money.* **9** *Mil* a place occupied for tactical reasons. ~*vb* **10** to put in the proper or usual place; locate. **positional** *adj*

positive *adj* **1** expressing certainty: *a positive answer.* **2** definite or certain: *are you absolutely positive about the date?* **3** tending to emphasize what is good; constructive: *positive thinking.* **4** tending towards progress or improvement: *investment that could have a positive impact on the company's fortunes.* **5** *Philosophy* constructive rather than sceptical. **6** *Informal* complete; downright: *a positive delight.* **7** *Maths* having a value greater than zero: *a positive number.* **8** *Grammar* denoting the unmodified form of an adjective as opposed to its comparative or superlative form. **9** *Physics* (of an electric charge) having an opposite charge to that of an electron. **10** *Physics* short for **electropositive. 11** *Med* (of the result of an examination or test) indicating the presence of a suspected condition or organism. ~*n* **12** something positive. **13** *Maths* a quantity greater than zero. **14** *Photog* a print showing an image whose colours and tones correspond to those of the original subject. **15** *Grammar* the positive degree of an adjective or adverb. **16** a positive object, such as a terminal in a cell. **positively** *adv* **positiveness** *n*

positive discrimination *n* the provision of special opportunities for a disadvantaged group.

positive vetting *n* the thorough checking of all aspects of a person's life to ensure his or her suitability for a position that may involve national security.

positivism *n* a system of philosophy that accepts only things that can be seen or proved. **positivist** *n, adj*

positron *n Physics* the antiparticle of the electron, having the same mass but an equal and opposite charge.

poss. 1 possible. **2** possession. **3** possessive. **4** possibly.

posse (**poss**-ee) *n* **1** *US* a selected group of men on whom the sheriff may call for assistance. **2** *Informal* a group of friends or associates: *a posse of reporters.* **3** (in W Canada) a troop of horses and riders who perform at rodeos.

possess *vb* **1** to have as one's property; own. **2** to have as a quality or attribute: *he possessed an innate elegance, authority, and wit on screen.* **3** to gain control over or dominate: *absolute terror possessed her.* **possessor** *n*

possessed *adj* **1** (foll. by *of*) owning or having: *he is possessed of a calm maturity far beyond his years.* **2** under the influence of a powerful force, such as a spirit or strong emotion: *possessed by the devil; she was possessed by a frenzied urge to get out of Moscow.*

possession *n* **1** the state of possessing; ownership: *how had this compromising picture come into the possession of the press?* **2** anything that is possessed. **3 possessions** wealth or property. **4** the state of being controlled by or as if by evil spirits. **5** the occupancy of land or property: *troops had taken possession of the airport.* **6** a territory subject to a foreign state. **7** the criminal offence of having something illegal on one's

THESAURUS

portrayal characterization, delineation, depiction, description, impersonation, interpretation, performance, picture, rendering, representation

pose *vb.* **1.** arrange, model, position, sit, sit for **2.** affect, attitudinize, posture, put on airs, show off (*informal*), strike an attitude **3.** *often with* **as** feign, impersonate, masquerade as, pass oneself off as, pretend to be, profess to be, sham **4.** advance, posit, present, propound, put, put forward, set, state, submit ~*n.* **5.** attitude, bearing, mien (*literary*), position, posture, stance **6.** act, affectation, air, attitudinizing, façade, front, mannerism, masquerade, posturing, pretence, role

poser brain-teaser (*informal*), conundrum, enigma, knotty point, problem, puzzle, question, riddle, teaser, tough one, vexed question

position *n.* **1.** area, bearings, locale, locality, location, place, point, post, reference, site, situation, spot, station, whereabouts **2.** arrangement, attitude, disposition, pose, posture, stance **3.** angle, attitude, belief, opinion, outlook, point of view, slant, stance, stand, standpoint, view, viewpoint **4.** caste, class, consequence, eminence, importance, place, prestige, rank, reputation, standing, station, stature, status **5.** capacity, duty, employment, function, job, occupation, office, place, post, role, situation ~*vb.* **6.** arrange, array, dispose, fix, lay out, locate, place, put, set, settle, stand, stick (*informal*)

positive 1. absolute, actual, affirmative, categorical, certain, clear, clear-cut, conclusive, concrete, decisive, definite, direct, explicit, express, firm, incontrovertible, indisputable, real, unequivocal, unmistakable **2.** assured, certain, confident, convinced, sure **3.** beneficial, constructive, effective, efficacious, forward-looking, helpful, practical, productive, progressive, useful **4.** *informal* absolute, complete, consummate, out-and-out, perfect, rank, thorough, thoroughgoing, unmitigated, utter

positively absolutely, assuredly, categorically, certainly, definitely, emphatically, firmly, surely, undeniably, unequivocally, unmistakably, unquestionably, with certainty, without qualification

possess 1. be blessed with, be born with, be endowed with, enjoy, have, have to one's name, hold, own **2.** acquire, control, dominate, hold, occupy, seize, take over, take possession of

possessed bedevilled, berserk, bewitched, consumed, crazed, cursed, demented, enchanted, frenetic, frenzied, hag-ridden, haunted, maddened, obsessed, raving, under a spell

person: *arrested for drug dealing and possession.* **8** *Sport* control of the ball by a player: *County had most of the possession, but couldn't score.*

possessive *adj* **1** of possession. **2** desiring excessively to possess or dominate: *a possessive husband.* **3** *Grammar* denoting a form of a noun or pronoun used to convey possession, as *my* or *Harry's*: *a possessive pronoun.* ~*n* **4** *Grammar* **a** the possessive case. **b** a word in the possessive case. **possessiveness** *n*

possibility *n, pl* **-ties 1** the state of being possible. **2** anything that is possible. **3** a competitor or candidate with a chance of success. **4** a future prospect or potential: *all sorts of possibilities began to open up.*

possible *adj* **1** capable of existing, happening, or proving true: *the earliest possible moment.* **2** capable of being done: *I am grateful to the library staff for making this work possible.* **3** having potential: *a possible buyer.* **4** feasible but less than probable: *it's possible that's what he meant, but I doubt it.* ~*n* **5** same as **possibility** (sense 3).

possibly *adv* **1** perhaps or maybe. **2** by any means; at all: *he can't possibly come.*

possum *n* **1** *Informal* an opossum. **2** *Austral & NZ* a phalanger. **3 play possum** to pretend to be dead, ignorant, or asleep in order to deceive an opponent.

post[1] *n* **1** *Brit* an official system of mail delivery. **2** *Chiefly Brit* letters or packages that are transported and delivered by the Post Office; mail. **3** *Chiefly Brit* a single collection or delivery of mail. **4** *Brit* a postbox or post office: *take this to the post.* ~*vb* **5** *Chiefly Brit* to send by post. **6** *Book-keeping* **a** to enter (an item) in a ledger. **b** (often foll. by *up*) to enter all paper items in (a ledger). **7 keep someone posted** to inform someone regularly of the latest news.

post[2] *n* **1** a length of wood, metal, or concrete fixed upright to support or mark something. **2** *Horse racing* **a** either of two upright poles marking the beginning and end of a racecourse. **b** the finish of a horse race. ~*vb* **3** (sometimes foll. by *up*) to put up (a notice) in a public place. **4** to publish (a name) on a list.

post[3] *n* **1** a position to which a person is appointed; job. **2** a position to which a soldier or guard is assigned for duty. **3** a permanent military establishment. **4** *Brit* either of two military bugle calls (**first post** and **last post**) giving notice of the time to retire for the night. ~*vb* **5** *Chiefly Brit* to send (someone) to a new place to work. **6** to assign to or station at a particular place or position: *guards were posted at the doors.*

post- *prefix* **1** after in time: *postgraduate.* **2** behind: *postdated.*

postage *n* the charge for sending a piece of mail by post.

postage stamp *n* same as **stamp** (sense 1).

postal *adj* of a Post Office or the mail-delivery service.

postal order *n* a written money order sent by post and cashed at a post office by the person who receives it.

postbag *n* **1** *Chiefly Brit* a mailbag. **2** the mail received by a magazine, radio programme, or public figure.

postbox *n* same as **letter box** (sense 2).

postcard *n* a card, often with a picture on one side, for sending a message by post without an envelope.

post chaise (**shaze**) *n Old-fashioned* a four-wheeled horse-drawn coach formerly used as a rapid means of carrying mail and passengers.

postcode *n* a system of letters and numbers used to aid the sorting of mail.

postdate *vb* **-dating, -dated 1** to write a future date on (a cheque or document). **2** to occur at a later date than. **3** to assign a date to (an event or period) that is later than its previously assigned date.

poster *n* **1** a large notice displayed in a public place as an advertisement. **2** a large printed picture.

poste restante *n* a post-office department where mail is kept until it is called for.

posterior *n* **1** *Formal or humorous* the buttocks. ~*adj* **2** at the back of or behind something: *posterior leg muscles.* **3** coming after in a series or time.

posterity *n* **1** future generations. **2** all of one's descendants.

postern *n* a small back door or gate.

post-free *adv, adj* **1** *Brit* with the postage prepaid. **2** free of postal charge.

postgraduate *n* **1** a person who is studying for a more advanced qualification after obtaining a degree. ~*adj* **2** of or for postgraduates.

posthaste *adv* with great speed.

posthumous (**poss**-tume-uss) *adj* **1** happening after one's death. **2** born after the death of one's father. **3** (of a book) published after the author's death. **posthumously** *adv*

postilion *or* **postillion** *n* (esp. formerly) a person who rides one of a pair of horses drawing a coach.

postimpressionism *n* a movement in painting in France at the end of the 19th century which rejected Impressionism but adapted its use of pure colour to paint with greater subjective emotion. **postimpressionist** *n, adj*

posting *n* a job to which someone is assigned by his or her employer which involves moving to a particular town or country: *Bonn was his third posting overseas.*

THESAURUS

possession **1.** control, custody, hold, occupancy, occupation, ownership, proprietorship, tenure, title **2. possessions** assets, belongings, chattels, effects, estate, goods and chattels, property, things, wealth **3.** colony, dominion, protectorate, province, territory

possessive acquisitive, controlling, covetous, dominating, domineering, grasping, jealous, overprotective, selfish

possibility **1.** feasibility, likelihood, plausibility, potentiality, practicability, workableness **2.** chance, hazard, hope, liability, likelihood, odds, probability, prospect, risk **3.** capabilities, potential, potentiality, promise, prospects, talent

possible **1.** conceivable, credible, hypothetical, imaginable, likely, potential **2.** attainable, feasible, on (*informal*), practicable, realizable, viable, within reach, workable **3.** hopeful, likely, potential, probable, promising

possibly **1.** maybe, peradventure (*archaic*), perchance (*archaic or poetic*), perhaps **2.** at all, by any chance, by any means, in any way

post[1] *n.* **1.** *chiefly Brit.* collection, delivery, mail, postal service ~*vb.* **2.** *chiefly Brit.* dispatch, mail, send, transmit **3. keep someone posted** advise, brief, fill in on (*informal*), inform, notify, report to

post[2] **1.** *n.* column, newel, pale, palisade, picket, pillar, pole, shaft, stake, standard, stock, support, upright **2.** *vb. sometimes with* **up** advertise, affix, announce, display, make known, pin up, proclaim, promulgate, publicize, publish, put up, stick up

post[3] *n.* **1.** appointment, assignment, employment, job, office, place, position, situation **2.** beat, place, position, station ~*vb.* **3.** assign, establish, locate, place, position, put, situate, station

poster advertisement, announcement, bill, notice, placard, public notice, sticker

postman *or fem* **postwoman** *n, pl* **-men** *or* **-women** a person who collects and delivers mail.

postmark *n* **1** an official mark stamped on mail, showing the place and date of posting. *~vb* **2** to put such a mark on (mail).

postmaster *or fem* **postmistress** *n* an official in charge of a post office.

postmaster general *n, pl* **postmasters general** the executive head of the postal service.

postmeridian *adj* occurring after noon.

postmortem *n* **1** In full: **postmortem examination** medical examination of a dead body to discover the cause of death. **2** analysis of a recent event: *a postmortem on the party's recent appalling by-election results.* *~adj* **3** occurring after death.

postnatal *adj* occurring after childbirth: *postnatal depression.*

post office *n* a building where stamps are sold and postal business is conducted.

Post Office *n* a government department responsible for postal services.

postoperative *adj* of or occurring in the period after a surgical operation.

postpaid *adv, adj* with the postage prepaid.

postpone *vb* **-poning, -poned** to put off until a future time. **postponement** *n*

postpositive *adj Grammar* (of an adjective) placed after the word it modifies.

postprandial *adj Formal* after dinner.

postscript *n* a message added at the end of a letter, after the signature.

postulant *n* an applicant for admission to a religious order.

postulate *Formal ~vb* **-lating, -lated 1** to assume to be true as the basis of an argument or theory. **2** to ask, demand, or claim. *~n* **3** something postulated. **postulation** *n*

posture *n* **1** a position or way in which a person stands, walks, etc.: *good posture.* **2** a mental attitude: *a cooperative posture.* **3** an affected attitude: *an intellectual posture.* *~vb* **-turing, -tured 4** to behave in an exaggerated way to attract attention. **5** to assume an affected attitude. **postural** *adj*

postviral fatigue syndrome *or* **postviral syndrome** *n* same as **ME** (sense 3).

postwar *adj* occurring or existing after a war.

posy *n, pl* **-sies** a small bunch of flowers.

pot[1] *n* **1** a round deep container, often with a handle and lid, used for cooking. **2** the amount that a pot will hold. **3** short for **flowerpot** or **teapot. 4** a handmade piece of pottery. **5** *Billiards etc* a shot by which a ball is pocketed. **6** a chamber pot. **7** the money in the pool in gambling games. **8** (*often pl*) *Informal* a large sum of money. **9** *Informal* a cup or other trophy. **10** See **potbelly. 11 go to pot** to go to ruin. *~vb* **potting, potted 12** to put (a plant) in soil in a flowerpot. **13** *Billiards etc* to pocket (a ball). **14** to preserve (food) in a pot. **15** to shoot (game) for food rather than for sport. **16** to shoot casually or without careful aim. **17** *Informal* to capture or win.

pot[2] *n Slang* cannabis.

potable (**pote**-a-bl) *adj Formal* drinkable.

potage (po-**tahzh**) *n* thick soup.

potash *n* **1** potassium carbonate, used as fertilizer. **2** a compound containing potassium: *permanganate of potash.*

potassium *n Chem* a light silvery element of the alkali metal group. Symbol: K

potassium nitrate *n* a crystalline compound used in gunpowders, fertilizers, and as a preservative for foods (**E252**).

potation *n Formal* **1** the act of drinking. **2** a drink, usually alcoholic.

potato *n, pl* **-toes 1** a starchy vegetable that grows underground. **2** the plant from which this vegetable is obtained.

potato beetle *n* same as **Colorado beetle.**

potato crisp *n* same as **crisp** (sense 7).

potbelly *n, pl* **-lies 1** a bulging belly. **2** a person with such a belly.

potboiler *n Informal* an inferior work of art produced quickly to make money.

pot-bound *adj* (of a pot plant) having roots too big for its pot, so that it is unable to grow further.

poteen *or* **poitín** *n* (in Ireland) illegally made alcoholic drink.

potent *adj* **1** having great power or influence. **2** (of arguments) persuasive or forceful. **3** highly effective: *a potent poison.* **4** (of a male) capable of having sexual intercourse. **potency** *n*

potentate *n* a ruler or monarch.

potential *adj* **1 a** possible but not yet actual: *potential buyers.* **b** capable of being or becoming; latent: *potential danger.* *~n* **2** ability or talent not yet in full use: *she has great potential as a painter.* **3** In full: **electric potential** the work required to transfer a unit positive electric charge from an infinite distance to a given point. **potentially** *adv*

potential difference *n* the difference in electric potential between two points in an electric field, measured in volts.

potential energy *n* the energy which an object has stored up because of its position.

potentiality *n, pl* **-ties** latent capacity for becoming or developing.

pother (rhymes with **bother**) *n Literary* a fuss or commotion.

potherb *n* a plant whose leaves, flowers, or stems are used in cooking.

THESAURUS

posterity 1. future, future generations, succeeding generations **2.** children, descendants, family, heirs, issue, offspring, progeny, scions, seed (*chiefly Bible*)

postmortem *n.* analysis, autopsy, dissection, examination, necropsy

postpone adjourn, defer, delay, hold over, put back, put off, shelve, suspend, table, take a rain check on (*informal*)

postponement adjournment, deferment, deferral, delay, moratorium, respite, stay, suspension

postscript addition, afterthought, afterword, appendix, P.S., supplement

postulate advance, assume, hypothesize, posit, predicate, presuppose, propose, put forward, suppose, take for granted, theorize

posture *n.* **1.** attitude, bearing, carriage, disposition, mien (*literary*), pose, position, set, stance **2.** attitude, disposition, feeling, frame of mind, inclination, mood, outlook, point of view, stance, standpoint *~vb.* **3.** affect, attitudinize, do for effect, make a show, pose, put on airs, show off (*informal*), try to attract attention

potent 1. authoritative, commanding, dominant, dynamic, influential, powerful **2.** cogent, compelling, convincing, effective, forceful, impressive, persuasive, telling **3.** efficacious, forceful, mighty, powerful, puissant, strong, vigorous

potential 1. *adj.* budding, dormant, embryonic, fu-

pothole *n* **1** a hole in the surface of a road. **2** a deep hole in a limestone area.

potholing *n Brit* the sport of exploring underground caves. **potholer** *n*

pothook *n* **1** an S-shaped hook for suspending a pot over a fire. **2** an S-shaped mark in handwriting.

pothunter *n* **1** a hunter who disregards the rules of sport. **2** *Informal* a person who enters competitions solely to win prizes.

potion *n* a drink of medicine, poison, or some supposedly magic liquid.

potluck *n* **take potluck** *Informal* to accept whatever happens to be available: *we'll take potluck at whatever restaurant might still be open.*

potpourri (po-**poor**-ee) *n, pl* **-ris 1** a fragrant mixture of dried flower petals. **2** an assortment or medley.

pot roast *n* meat cooked slowly in a covered pot with very little liquid.

potsherd *n* a broken piece of pottery.

pot shot *n* **1** a shot taken without careful aim. **2** a shot fired at an animal within easy range.

pottage *n* a thick soup or stew.

potted *adj* **1** grown in a pot: *potted plant.* **2** cooked or preserved in a pot: *potted shrimps.* **3** *Informal* shortened or abridged: *a potted history.*

potter[1] *n* a person who makes pottery.

potter[2] *or esp US & Canad* **putter** *vb* **1 potter about, around** *or* **away** to be busy in a pleasant but aimless way: *he potters away doing God knows what all day.* **2** to move with little energy or direction: *I saw him pottering off to see to his canaries.*

Potteries *n* **the Potteries** a region of W central England, in Staffordshire, where many china industries are situated.

potter's wheel *n* a flat spinning disc on which clay is shaped by hand.

pottery *n, pl* **-teries 1** articles made from baked clay. **2** a place where such articles are made. **3** the craft of making such articles.

potting shed *n* a garden hut in which plants are put in flowerpots and potting materials are stored.

potty[1] *adj* **-tier, -tiest** *Brit informal* **1** slightly crazy. **2** trivial or insignificant. **3** (foll. by *about*) very keen (on). **pottiness** *n*

potty[2] *n, pl* **-ties** a bowl used as a toilet by a small child.

pouch *n* **1** a small bag. **2** a baglike pocket in various animals, such as the cheek fold in hamsters. ~*vb* **3** to place in or as if in a pouch. **4** to make or be made into a pouch.

pouf *or* **pouffe** (**poof**) *n* a large solid cushion used as a seat.

poulterer *n* a person who sells poultry.

poultice (**pole**-tiss) *n Med* a moist dressing, often heated, applied to painful and swollen parts of the body.

poultry *n* domestic fowls.

pounce *vb* **pouncing, pounced 1** (often foll. by *on* or *upon*) to spring upon suddenly to attack or capture. ~*n* **2** the act of pouncing; a spring or swoop.

pound[1] *n* **1** the standard monetary unit of the United Kingdom, made up of 100 pence. Official name: **pound sterling 2** the standard monetary unit of various other countries, such as Cyprus and Malta. **3** a unit of weight made up of 16 ounces and equal to 0.454 kilograms.

pound[2] *vb* **1** (sometimes foll. by *on* or *at*) to hit heavily and repeatedly. **2** to crush to pieces or to powder. **3** (foll. by *out*) to produce, by typing heavily. **4** (of the heart) to throb heavily. **5** to run with heavy steps.

pound[3] *n* an enclosure for stray dogs or officially removed vehicles.

poundage *n* **1** a charge of so much per pound of weight. **2** a charge of so much per pound sterling.

-pounder *n combining form* **1** something weighing a specified number of pounds: *a 200-pounder.* **2** something worth a specified number of pounds: *a ten-pounder.* **3** a gun that discharges a shell weighing a specified number of pounds: *a two-pounder.*

pour *vb* **1** to flow or cause to flow out in a stream. **2** to rain heavily. **3** to be given or obtained in large amounts: *foreign aid is pouring into Iran.* **4** to move together in large numbers: *the fans poured onto the pitch.*

pourboire (**poor**-bwahr) *n* a tip or gratuity.

pout *vb* **1** to thrust out (the lips) sullenly or provocatively. **2** to swell out; protrude. ~*n* **3** a pouting.

pouter *n* a breed of domestic pigeon that can puff out its crop.

poverty *n* **1** the state of lacking adequate food or money. **2** lack or scarcity: *a poverty of information.* **3** inferior quality or inadequacy: *the poverty of political debate in this country.*

poverty-stricken *adj* extremely poor.

poverty trap *n* the situation of being unable to raise one's living standard because any extra income would result in state benefits being reduced or withdrawn.

THESAURUS

ture, hidden, inherent, latent, likely, possible, promising, undeveloped, unrealized **2.** *n.* ability, aptitude, capability, capacity, possibility, potentiality, power, the makings, what it takes (*informal*), wherewithal

potion brew, concoction, cup, dose, draught, elixir, mixture, philtre, tonic

potter dabble, fiddle (*informal*), footle (*informal*), fritter, mess about, tinker

pottery ceramics, earthenware, stoneware, terra cotta

pouch bag, container, pocket, purse, sack

pounce 1. *vb. often with* **on** *or* **upon** ambush, attack, bound onto, dash at, drop, fall upon, jump, leap at, snatch, spring, strike, swoop, take by surprise, take unawares **2.** *n.* assault, attack, bound, jump, leap, spring, swoop

pound[1] **1.** *sometimes with* **on** *or* **at** batter, beat, belabour, clobber (*slang*), hammer, pelt, pummel, strike, thrash, thump **2.** crush, powder, pulverize **3.** *with* **out** bang, beat, hammer, thump **4.** beat, palpitate, pitapat, pulsate, pulse, throb **5.** clomp, march, stomp (*informal*), thunder, tramp

pound[2] *n.* compound, enclosure, pen, yard

pour 1. course, decant, emit, flow, gush, let flow, run, rush, spew, spill, splash, spout, stream **2.** bucket down (*informal*), come down in torrents, pelt (down), rain, rain cats and dogs (*informal*), rain hard *or* heavily, sheet, teem **3.** crowd, stream, swarm, teem, throng

pout 1. *vb.* glower, look petulant, look sullen, lour *or* lower, mope, pull a long face, purse one's lips, sulk, turn down the corners of one's mouth **2.** *n.* glower, long face, sullen look

poverty 1. beggary, destitution, distress, hand-to-mouth existence, hardship, indigence, insolvency, necessitousness, necessity, need, pauperism, pennilessness, penury, privation, want **2.** dearth, deficiency, insufficiency, lack, paucity, scarcity, shortage

poverty-stricken bankrupt, broke (*informal*), destitute, dirt-poor (*informal*), distressed, down and out, flat broke (*informal*), impecunious, impoverished, indigent, needy, on one's beam-ends, on one's uppers,

pow *interj* an exclamation to indicate that a collision or explosion has taken place.

POW prisoner of war.

powder *n* **1** a substance in the form of tiny loose particles. **2** a medicine or cosmetic in this form. *~vb* **3** to cover or sprinkle with powder. **powdery** *adj*

powdered *adj* **1** sold in the form of a powder, esp. one which has been formed by grinding or drying the original material: *powdered milk.* **2** covered or made up with a cosmetic in the form of a powder: *liveried footmen in powdered wigs.*

powder keg *n* **1** a potential source of violence or disaster: *a political powder keg.* **2** a small barrel for holding gunpowder.

powder puff *n* a soft pad used to apply cosmetic powder to the skin.

powder room *n* a ladies' cloakroom or toilet.

power *n* **1** ability to do something. **2** (*often pl*) a specific ability or faculty. **3** political, financial, or social force or authority: *men's use of power over women in a subordinate position in the workforce; economic power is the bedrock of political power.* **4** a position of control, esp. over the running of a country: *he seized power in a coup in 1966.* **5** a state with political, industrial, or military strength. **6** a person or group having authority. **7** a prerogative or privilege: *the power of veto.* **8** official or legal authority. **9** *Maths* the value of a number or quantity raised to some exponent. **10** *Physics, engineering* a measure of the rate of doing work expressed as the work done per unit time. **11** the rate at which electrical energy is fed into or taken from a device or system, measured in watts. **12** mechanical energy as opposed to manual labour. **13** a particular form of energy: *nuclear power.* **14** the magnifying capacity of a lens or optical system. **15** *Informal* a great deal: *a power of good.* **16 the powers that be** established authority. *~vb* **17** to supply with power. *~adj* **18** producing or using electrical energy: *a power tool.*

powerboat *n* a fast powerful motorboat.

power cut *n* a temporary interruption in the supply of electricity.

powerful *adj* **1** having great power. **2** extremely effective: *a powerful drug.* **powerfully** *adv* **powerfulness** *n*

powerhouse *n* **1** *Informal* a forceful person or thing. **2** an electrical generating station.

powerless *adj* without control or authority. **powerlessness** *n*

power of attorney *n* **1** legal authority to act for another person. **2** the document conferring such authority.

power point *n* an electrical socket fitted into a wall for plugging in electrical appliances.

power-sharing *n* a political arrangement in which all the groups in a society take part in the running of the country: *one of the main obstacles to peace has been the question of power-sharing among the various factions.*

power station *n* an installation for generating and distributing electricity.

power steering *n* a type of steering in vehicles in which the turning of the steering wheel is assisted by power from the engine.

powwow *n* **1** a talk or meeting. **2** a meeting of North American Indians. *~vb* **3** to hold a powwow.

pox *n* **1** a disease in which pus-filled blisters or pimples form on the skin. **2 the pox** *Informal* syphilis.

p & p *Brit* postage and packing.

pp **1** past participle. **2** (in signing documents on behalf of someone else) by delegation to.

➤ The original meaning of *pp* (Latin *per procurationem*) is "by delegation to", so traditionally *pp* is written before the name of the typist to show that she or he has signed the letter on behalf of someone else. Nowadays the meaning has been overtaken by the sense of "on behalf of" and *pp* is often written before the name of the person who composed the letter.

pp. pages.

PPS **1** parliamentary private secretary. **2** additional postscript.

PQ **1** Province of Quebec. **2** (in Canada) Parti Québecois.

pr *pl* **prs** pair.

Pr *Chem* praseodymium.

PR **1** proportional representation. **2** public relations.

pr. **1** price. **2** pronoun.

practicable *adj* **1** capable of being done. **2** usable. **practicability** *n*

practical *adj* **1** involving experience or actual use rather than theory. **2** concerned with everyday matters: *the kind of practical and emotional upheaval that divorce can bring.* **3** sensible, useful, and effective rather than fashionable or attractive: *it's a marvellous design, because it's comfortable, it's practical, and it actually looks good.* **4** involving the simple basics: *practical skills.* **5** being very close to (a state); virtual: *it's a practical certainty.* *~n* **6** an examination or lesson in which something has to be made or done. **practicality** *n* **practically** *adv*

THESAURUS

penniless, penurious, poor, short, skint (*Brit. slang*), stony-broke (*Brit. slang*), without two pennies to rub together (*informal*)

powder **1.** *n.* dust, fine grains, loose particles, pounce, talc **2.** *vb.* cover, crush, dredge, dust, scatter, sprinkle, strew

power **1.** ability, capability, capacity, competence, competency, faculty, potential **2.** ascendancy, authority, bottom, command, control, dominance, domination, dominion, influence, mastery, rule, sovereignty, supremacy, sway **3.** authority, authorization, licence, prerogative, privilege, right, warrant

powerful **1.** authoritative, commanding, controlling, dominant, influential, prevailing, puissant, sovereign, supreme **2.** cogent, compelling, convincing, effective, effectual, forceful, forcible, impressive, persuasive, striking, telling, weighty

powerfully forcefully, forcibly, hard, mightily, strongly, vigorously, with might and main

powerless debilitated, defenceless, dependent, disabled, disenfranchised, disfranchised, etiolated, feeble, frail, helpless, impotent, incapable, incapacitated, ineffective, ineffectual, infirm, paralysed, prostrate, subject, tied, unarmed, vulnerable, weak

practicability advantage, feasibility, operability, possibility, practicality, use, usefulness, value, viability, workability

practicable achievable, attainable, feasible, performable, possible, viable, within the realm of possibility, workable

practical **1.** applied, efficient, empirical, experimental, factual, functional, pragmatic, realistic, utilitarian **2.** businesslike, down-to-earth, everyday, hard-headed, matter-of-fact, mundane, ordinary, realistic, sensible, workaday **3.** serviceable, sound, useful, workable

practically **1.** clearly, matter-of-factly, rationally, realistically, reasonably, sensibly, unsentimentally, with common sense **2.** all but, almost, basically, close to,

practical joke *n* a trick intended to make someone look foolish. **practical joker** *n*

practice *n* **1** something done regularly or repeatedly. **2** repetition of an activity in order to gain skill: *regular practice is essential if you want to play an instrument well.* **3** the business or surgery of a doctor or lawyer. **4** the act of doing something: *I'm not sure how effective these methods will be when put into practice.* **5 in practice a** what actually happens as distinct from what is supposed to happen: *many ideas which look good on paper just don't work in practice.* **b** skilled in something through having had a lot of regular recent experience at it: *I still go shooting, just to keep in practice.* **6 out of practice** not having had much regular recent experience at an activity: *although out of practice, I still love playing my violin.*
➤ Note the *-ice* ending for the noun, with *-ise* for the verb (*practise*).

practise *or US* **practice** *vb* **-tising, -tised** *or* **-ticing, -ticed 1** to do repeatedly in order to gain skill. **2** to take part in or follow (a religion etc.): *none of them practise Islam.* **3** to work at (a profession): *he originally intended to practise medicine.* **4** to do regularly: *they practise meditation.*
➤ Note the *-ise* ending for the verb, with *-ice* for the noun (*practice*).

practised *adj* expert or skilled because of long experience in a skill or field: *the doctor answered with a practised smoothness.*

practising *adj* taking part in an activity or career on a regular basis: *a practising barrister.*

practitioner *n* a person who practises a profession.

praetor (**pree**-tor) *n* (in ancient Rome) a senior magistrate ranking just below the consuls. **praetorian** *adj, n*

pragmatic *adj* **1** concerned with practical consequences rather than theory. **2** *Philosophy* of pragmatism. **pragmatically** *adv*

pragmatism *n* **1** policy dictated by practical consequences rather than by theory. **2** *Philosophy* the doctrine that the content of a concept consists only in its practical applicability. **pragmatist** *n, adj*

prairie *n* (*often pl*) a large treeless area of grassland of the central US and S Canada.

prairie dog *n* a rodent that lives in burrows in the N American prairies.

praise *vb* **praising, praised 1** to express admiration or approval for. **2** to express thanks and worship to (one's God). ~*n* **3** the expression of admiration or approval. **4 sing someone's praises** to praise someone highly.

praiseworthy *adj* deserving praise; commendable.

praline (**prah**-leen) *n* a sweet made of nuts with caramelized sugar.

pram *n Brit* a four-wheeled carriage for a baby, pushed by a person on foot.

prance *vb* **prancing, pranced 1** to walk with exaggerated movements. **2** (of an animal) to move with high springing steps. ~*n* **3** the act of prancing.

prang *Old-fashioned slang* ~*n* **1** a crash in an aircraft or car. ~*vb* **2** to crash or damage (an aircraft or car).

prank *n* a mischievous trick. **prankster** *n*

praseodymium (pray-zee-oh-**dim**-ee-um) *n Chem* a silvery-white element of the lanthanide series of metals. Symbol: Pr

prat *n Offensive* an incompetent or ineffectual person.

prate *vb* **prating, prated 1** to talk idly and at length. ~*n* **2** chatter.

prattle *vb* **-tling, -tled 1** to chatter in a foolish or childish way. ~*n* **2** foolish or childish talk.

prawn *n* a small edible shellfish.

praxis *n* **1** practice as opposed to the theory. **2** accepted practice or custom.

pray *vb* **1** to say prayers (to one's God). **2** to ask earnestly; beg. ~*adv* **3** *Archaic* I beg you; please: *pray, leave us alone.*

prayer[1] *n* **1** a thanksgiving or an appeal spoken to one's God. **2** a set form of words used in praying: *the Lord's Prayer.* **3** an earnest request. **4** the practice of praying: *call the faithful to prayer.* **5** (*often pl*) a form of devotion spent mainly praying: *morning prayers.* **6** something prayed for.

prayer[2] *n* a person who prays.

prayer book *n* a book of prayers used in church or at home.

prayer mat *or* **prayer rug** *n* the small carpet on which a Muslim performs his or her daily prayers.

prayer wheel *n Buddhism* (in Tibet) a cylinder inscribed with prayers, each turning of which is counted as an uttered prayer.

THESAURUS

essentially, fundamentally, in effect, just about, nearly, to all intents and purposes, very nearly, virtually, well-nigh

practice 1. custom, habit, method, mode, praxis, routine, rule, system, tradition, usage, use, usual procedure, way, wont **2.** discipline, drill, exercise, preparation, rehearsal, repetition, study, training, work-out **3.** business, career, profession, vocation, work **4.** action, application, effect, exercise, experience, operation, use

practise 1. discipline, drill, exercise, go over, go through, polish, prepare, rehearse, repeat, study, train, warm up, work out **2.** apply, carry out, do, follow, live up to, observe, perform, put into practice **3.** carry on, engage in, ply, pursue, specialize in, undertake, work at

practised able, accomplished, experienced, expert, proficient, qualified, seasoned, skilled, trained, versed

pragmatic businesslike, down-to-earth, efficient, hard-headed, matter-of-fact, practical, realistic, sensible, utilitarian

praise *vb.* **1.** acclaim, admire, applaud, approve, cheer, compliment, congratulate, crack up (*informal*), cry up, eulogize, extol, honour, laud, pay tribute to, sing the praises of **2.** adore, bless, exalt, give thanks to, glorify, magnify (*archaic*), pay homage to, worship ~*n.* **3.** acclaim, acclamation, accolade, adoration, applause, approbation, approval, cheering, commendation, compliment, congratulation, devotion, encomium, eulogy, glory, good word, homage, kudos, laudation, ovation, panegyric, plaudit, thanks, tribute, worship

praiseworthy admirable, commendable, creditable, estimable, excellent, exemplary, fine, honourable, laudable, meritorious, worthy

prance 1. parade, show off (*informal*), stalk, strut, swagger, swank (*informal*) **2.** bound, caper, cavort, dance, frisk, gambol, jump, leap, romp, skip, spring, trip

prank antic, caper, escapade, frolic, jape, lark (*informal*), practical joke, skylarking (*informal*), trick

prattle babble, blather, blether, chatter, clack, drivel, gabble, jabber, patter, rabbit (on) (*Brit. informal*), rattle on, run on, twitter, waffle (*informal, chiefly Brit.*), witter (*informal*)

pray 1. offer a prayer, recite the rosary, say one's prayers **2.** adjure, ask, beg, beseech, call upon, crave, cry for, entreat, implore, importune, invoke, petition, plead, request, solicit, sue, supplicate, urge

praying mantis *n* same as **mantis.**

pre- *prefix* before in time or position: *predate; preeminent.*

preach *vb* **1** to talk on a religious theme as part of a church service. **2** to speak in support of (something) in a moralizing way.

preacher *n* a person who preaches.

preamble *n* an introduction that comes before something spoken or written.

prearranged *adj* arranged beforehand. **prearrangement** *n*

prebend *n* **1** the allowance paid by a cathedral or collegiate church to a canon or member of the chapter. **2** the land or tithe from which this is paid. **prebendal** *adj*

prebendary *n, pl* **-daries** a clergyman who is a member of the chapter of a cathedral.

Precambrian *or* **Pre-Cambrian** *adj Geol* of the earliest geological era, lasting from about 4500 million years ago to 600 million years ago.

precancerous *adj* relating to cells that show signs that they may develop cancer.

precarious *adj* (of a position or situation) dangerous or insecure. **precariously** *adv*

precaution *n* an action taken in advance to prevent an undesirable event. **precautionary** *adj*

precede *vb* **-ceding, -ceded** to go or be before (someone or something) in time, place, or rank.

precedence (**press**-ee-denss) *n* formal order of rank or position.

precedent *n* **1** a previous occurrence used to justify taking the same action in later similar situations. **2** *Law* a judicial decision that serves as an authority for deciding a later case. *~adj* **3** preceding.

precentor *n* a person who leads the singing in church services.

precept *n* **1** a rule of conduct. **2** a rule for morals. **3** *Law* a writ or warrant. **preceptive** *adj*

preceptor *n Rare* an instructor. **preceptorial** *adj*

precession *n* **1** the act of preceding. **2** the motion of a spinning body, in which the axis of rotation sweeps out a cone. **3 precession of the equinoxes** the slightly earlier occurrence of the equinoxes each year.

precinct *n* **1** an area in a town closed to traffic: *a shopping precinct.* **2** an enclosed area around a building. **3** *US* an administrative area of a city.

precincts *pl n* the surrounding region.

preciosity (presh-ee-**oss**-it-ee) *n, pl* **-ties** affectation.

precious *adj* **1** very costly or valuable. **2** loved and treasured. **3** very affected in speech, manners, or behaviour. **4** *Informal* worthless: *nothing is too good for his precious dog.* *~adv* **5** *Informal* very: *there's precious little to do in this town.*

precious metal *n* gold, silver, or platinum.

precious stone *n* a rare mineral, such as diamond, ruby, or opal, that is highly valued as a gem.

precipice *n* the very steep face of a cliff.

precipitant *adj* **1** hasty or rash. **2** rushing or falling rapidly. *~n* **3** something which helps bring about an event or condition: *stressful events are often the precipitant for a manic attack.*

precipitate *vb* **-tating, -tated 1** to cause to happen earlier than expected: *the scandal could bring the government down, precipitating a general election.* **2** to condense or cause to condense and fall as snow or rain. **3** *Chem* to cause to be deposited in solid form from a solution. **4** to throw from a height: *the encircled soldiers chose to precipitate themselves into the ocean.* *~adj* **5** done rashly or hastily. **6** rushing ahead. *~n* **7** *Chem* a precipitated solid.

precipitation *n* **1** the formation of a chemical precipitate. **2** *Meteorol* **a** rain, hail, snow, or sleet formed by condensation of water vapour in the atmosphere. **b** the falling of these. **3** rash haste: *they decamped with the utmost precipitation.*

precipitous *adj* **1** very steep: *precipitous cliffs.* **2** very quick and severe: *a precipitous decline.* **3** rapid and unplanned; hasty: *European governments urged the Americans not to make a precipitous decision.*

précis (**pray**-see) *n, pl* **précis 1** a short summary of a longer text. *~vb* **2** to make a précis of.

precise *adj* **1** particular or exact: *this precise moment.* **2** strictly correct in amount or value: *precise*

THESAURUS

prayer 1. communion, devotion, invocation, litany, orison, supplication **2.** appeal, entreaty, petition, plea, request, suit, supplication

preach 1. address, deliver a sermon, evangelize, exhort, orate **2.** admonish, advocate, exhort, harangue, lecture, moralize, sermonize, urge

preacher clergyman, evangelist, minister, missionary, parson, revivalist

preamble exordium, foreword, introduction, opening move, opening statement *or* remarks, overture, preface, prelude, proem, prolegomenon

precarious chancy (*informal*), dangerous, dicey (*informal, chiefly Brit.*), dodgy (*Brit., Austral., & N.Z. informal*), doubtful, dubious, hairy (*slang*), hazardous, insecure, perilous, risky, shaky, slippery, touch and go, tricky, uncertain, unreliable, unsafe, unsettled, unstable, unsteady, unsure

precaution insurance, preventative measure, protection, provision, safeguard, safety measure

precede antecede, antedate, come first, forerun, go ahead of, go before, head, herald, introduce, lead, pave the way, preface, take precedence, usher

precedence antecedence, lead, pre-eminence, preference, primacy, priority, rank, seniority, superiority, supremacy

precedent *n.* antecedent, authority, criterion, example, exemplar, instance, model, paradigm, pattern, previous example, prototype, standard

precept 1. behest, canon, command, commandment, decree, dictum, direction, instruction, law, mandate, order, ordinance, principle, regulation, rule, statute **2.** axiom, byword, dictum, guideline, maxim, motto, principle, rule, saying

precinct 1. area, district, quarter, section, sector, zone **2.** bound, boundary, confine, enclosure, limit

precincts borders, bounds, confines, district, environs, limits, milieu, neighbourhood, purlieus, region, surrounding area

precious 1. choice, costly, dear, expensive, exquisite, fine, high-priced, inestimable, invaluable, priceless, prized, rare, recherché, valuable **2.** adored, beloved, cherished, darling, dear, dearest, favourite, idolized, loved, prized, treasured, valued **3.** affected, artificial, fastidious, twee (*Brit. informal*)

precipice bluff, brink, cliff, cliff face, crag, height, rock face, sheer drop, steep

precipitate *vb.* **1.** accelerate, advance, bring on, dispatch, expedite, further, hasten, hurry, press, push forward, quicken, speed up, trigger **2.** cast, discharge, fling, hurl, launch, let fly, send forth, throw *~adj.* **3.** frantic, harum-scarum, hasty, heedless, hurried, ill-advised, impetuous, impulsive, indiscreet, madcap, precipitous, rash, reckless **4.** breakneck, headlong, plunging, rapid, rushing, swift, violent

precipitous 1. abrupt, dizzy, falling sharply, high, perpendicular, sheer, steep **2.** abrupt, careless, harum-

measurements. **3** working with total accuracy: *precise instruments.* **4** strict in observing rules or standards. **precisely** *adv*

precision *n* **1** the quality of being precise. *~adj* **2** accurate: *precision engineering.*

preclude *vb* **-cluding, -cluded** *Formal* to make impossible to happen.

precocious *adj* having developed or matured early or too soon. **precocity** *n*

precognition *n Psychol* the alleged ability to foresee future events.

preconceived *adj* (of ideas etc.) formed without real experience or reliable information. **preconception** *n*

precondition *n* something that is necessary before something else can come about.

precursor *n* **1** something that comes before and signals something to follow; a forerunner. **2** a predecessor.

pred. predicate.

predacious *adj* (of animals) habitually hunting and killing other animals for food.

predate *vb* **-dating, -dated** **1** to occur at an earlier date than. **2** to write a date on (a document) that is earlier than the actual date.

predator *n* an animal that kills and eats other animals.

predatory (**pred**-a-tree) *adj* **1** (of animals) habitually hunting and killing other animals for food. **2** eager to gain at the expense of others.

predecease *vb* **-ceasing, -ceased** to die before (someone else).

predecessor *n* **1** a person who precedes another in an office or position. **2** an ancestor. **3** something that precedes something else: *the library will be more extravagant than its predecessors.*

predestination *n Christian theol* the belief that future events have already been decided by God.

predestined *adj Christian theol* determined in advance by God.

predetermine *vb* **-mining, -mined** **1** to determine beforehand. **2** to influence or bias. **predetermined** *adj*

predicable *adj* capable of being predicated.

predicament *n* an embarrassing or difficult situation.

predicant (**pred**-ik-ant) *adj* **1** of preaching. *~n* **2** a member of a religious order founded for preaching, usually a Dominican.

predicate *n* **1** *Grammar* the part of a sentence in which something is said about the subject. **2** *Logic* something that is asserted about the subject of a proposition. *~vb* **-cating, -cated** **3** to depend or be based: *political aims which are predicated upon a feminist view of women's oppression.* **4** to declare or assert: *it has been predicated that if we continue with our current sexual behaviour every family will have an AIDS victim.* **5** *Logic* to assert (something) about the subject of a proposition. **predication** *n* **predicative** *adj*

predict *vb* to tell about in advance; prophesy. **predictable** *adj* **predictably** *adv* **predictor** *n*

prediction *n* **1** the act of forecasting in advance. **2** something that is forecast in advance.

predikant (prod ik **ant**) *n* a minister in the Dutch Reformed Church in South Africa.

predilection *n Formal* a preference or liking.

predispose *vb* **-posing, -posed** (often foll. by *to*) **1** to influence (someone) in favour of something: *some scientists' social class background predisposes them*

THESAURUS

scarum, hasty, heedless, hurried, ill-advised, precipitate, rash, reckless, sudden

precise **1.** absolute, accurate, actual, clear-cut, correct, definite, exact, explicit, express, fixed, literal, particular, specific, strict, unequivocal **2.** careful, ceremonious, exact, fastidious, finicky, formal, inflexible, meticulous, nice, particular, prim, punctilious, puritanical, rigid, scrupulous, stiff, strict

precisely absolutely, accurately, bang, correctly, exactly, just, just so, literally, neither more nor less, plumb (*informal*), slap (*informal*), smack (*informal*), square, squarely, strictly

precision accuracy, care, correctness, definiteness, exactitude, exactness, fidelity, meticulousness, nicety, particularity, preciseness, rigour

preclude *formal* check, debar, exclude, forestall, hinder, inhibit, make impossible, make impracticable, obviate, prevent, prohibit, put a stop to, restrain, rule out, stop

precocious advanced, ahead, bright, developed, forward, quick, smart

preconception bias, notion, preconceived idea *or* notion, predisposition, prejudice, prepossession, presumption, presupposition

precondition essential, must, necessity, prerequisite, requirement, sine qua non

precursor **1.** forerunner, harbinger, herald, messenger, usher, vanguard **2.** antecedent, forebear, forerunner, originator, pioneer, predecessor

predatory **1.** carnivorous, hunting, predacious, rapacious, raptorial, ravening **2.** despoiling, greedy, marauding, pillaging, plundering, rapacious, ravaging, thieving, voracious

predecessor **1.** antecedent, forerunner, precursor, previous (former, prior) job holder **2.** ancestor, antecedent, forebear, forefather

predestination *Christian theol.* destiny, doom, fate, foreordainment, foreordination, lot, necessity, predetermination

predetermined agreed, arranged in advance, cut and dried (*informal*), decided beforehand, fixed, prearranged, preplanned, set, settled, set up

predicament corner, dilemma, emergency, fix (*informal*), hole (*slang*), hot water (*informal*), jam (*informal*), mess, pickle (*informal*), pinch, plight, quandary, scrape (*informal*), situation, spot (*informal*), state, tight spot

predicate **1.** base, build, establish, found, ground, postulate, rest **2.** affirm, assert, aver, avouch, avow, contend, declare, maintain, proclaim, state

predict augur, divine, forebode, forecast, foresee, foretell, portend, presage, prognosticate, prophesy, soothsay

predictable anticipated, calculable, certain, expected, foreseeable, foreseen, likely, reliable, sure, surefire (*informal*)

prediction augury, divination, forecast, prognosis, prognostication, prophecy, soothsaying, sortilege

predilection *formal* bias, cup of tea (*informal*), fancy, fondness, inclination, leaning, liking, love, partiality, penchant, predisposition, preference, proclivity, proneness, propensity, taste, tendency, weakness

predispose affect, bias, dispose, incline, induce, influence, lead, make (one) of a mind to, prejudice, prepare, prime, prompt, sway

predisposition bent, bias, disposition, inclination, likelihood, penchant, potentiality, predilection, pro-

to view the natural world in a certain way. **2** to make (someone) susceptible to something: *a high-fat diet appears to predispose men towards heart disease.* **predisposition** *n*

predominant *adj* being more important or noticeable than others: *improved living conditions probably played the predominant role in reducing disease in the nineteenth century.* **predominance** *n* **predominantly** *adv*

predominate *vb* **-nating, -nated 1** to be the most important or controlling aspect or part: *the image of brutal repression that has tended to predominate since the protests were crushed.* **2** to form the greatest part or be most common: *women and children predominate in this gathering.*

pre-eminent *adj* outstanding. **pre-eminence** *n*

pre-empt *vb* to prevent an action by doing something which makes it pointless or impossible: *he pre-empted his expulsion from the party by resigning.*

pre-emption *n Law* the purchase of or right to buy property in advance of others.

pre-emptive *adj Mil* designed to damage or destroy an enemy's attacking strength before it can be used: *a pre-emptive strike.*

preen *vb* **1** (of birds) to clean or trim (feathers) with the beak. **2** to smarten (oneself) carefully. **3** (often foll. by *on*) to be self-satisfied.

pref. 1 preface. **2** prefatory. **3** preference. **4** preferred. **5** prefix.

prefab *n* a prefabricated house.

prefabricated *adj* (of a building) made in shaped sections for quick assembly.

preface (**pref**-iss) *n* **1** an introduction to a book, usually explaining its intention or content. **2** anything introductory. *~vb* **-acing, -aced 3** to say or do something before proceeding to the main part. **4** to act as a preface to.

prefatory *adj* concerning a preface.

prefect *n* **1** *Brit, Austral, & NZ* a senior pupil in a school with limited power over the behaviour of other pupils. **2** (in some countries) the chief administrative officer in a department.

prefecture *n* the office or area of authority of a prefect.

prefer *vb* **-ferring, -ferred 1** to like better: *most people prefer television to reading books.* **2** *Law* to put (charges) before a court for judgment. **3** (*often passive*) to promote over another or others.

preferable *adj* more desirable or suitable. **preferably** *adv*

preference *n* **1** a liking for one thing above the rest. **2** a person or thing preferred.

preference shares *pl n Brit* shares issued by a company which give their holders a priority over ordinary shareholders to payment of dividend.

preferential *adj* **1** showing preference: *preferential treatment.* **2** indicating a special favourable status in business affairs: *the President is to renew China's preferential trading status.* **3** indicating a voting system which allows voters to rank candidates in order of preference: *a multi-option referendum with preferential voting.*

preferment *n* promotion to a higher position.

prefigure *vb* **-uring, -ured 1** to represent or suggest in advance. **2** to imagine beforehand.

prefix *n* **1** *Grammar* a letter or group of letters put at the beginning of a word to make a new word, such as *un-* in *unhappy.* **2** a title put before a name, such as *Mr.* *~vb* **3** *Grammar* to add (a letter or group of letters) as a prefix to the beginning of a word. **4** to put before.

pregnant *adj* **1** carrying a fetus or fetuses within the womb. **2** full of meaning or significance: *a pregnant pause.* **pregnancy** *n*

prehensile *adj* capable of curling round objects and grasping them: *a prehensile tail.*

prehistoric *adj* of man's development before the appearance of the written word. **prehistory** *n*

preindustrial *adj* of a time before the mechanization of industry.

THESAURUS

clivity, proneness, propensity, susceptibility, tendency, willingness

predominance ascendancy, control, dominance, dominion, edge, greater number, hold, leadership, mastery, paramountcy, preponderance, supremacy, sway, upper hand, weight

predominant ascendant, capital, chief, controlling, dominant, important, leading, main, notable, paramount, preponderant, prevailing, prevalent, primary, prime, principal, prominent, ruling, sovereign, superior, supreme, top-priority

predominate be most noticeable, carry weight, get the upper hand, hold sway, outweigh, overrule, overshadow, preponderate, prevail, reign, rule, tell

pre-eminence distinction, excellence, paramountcy, predominance, prestige, prominence, renown, superiority, supremacy, transcendence

pre-eminent chief, consummate, distinguished, excellent, foremost, incomparable, matchless, outstanding, paramount, peerless, predominant, renowned, superior, supreme, transcendent, unequalled, unrivalled, unsurpassed

pre-empt acquire, anticipate, appropriate, arrogate, assume, seize, take over, usurp

preen 1. clean, plume **2.** array, deck out, doll up (*slang*), dress up, prettify, primp, prink, spruce up, titivate, trim **3.** *often with* **on** congratulate oneself, pique oneself, plume oneself, pride oneself

preface 1. *n.* foreword, introduction, preamble, preliminary, prelude, proem (*formal*), prologue **2.** *vb.* begin, introduce, launch, lead up to, open, precede, prefix

prefer 1. adopt, be partial to, choose, desire, elect, fancy, favour, go for, incline towards, like better, opt for, pick, plump for, select, single out, wish, would rather, would sooner **2.** *Law* file, lodge, place, present, press, put forward **3.** *often passive* advance, aggrandize, elevate, move up, promote, raise, upgrade

preferable best, better, choice, chosen, favoured, more desirable, more eligible, superior, worthier

preferably as a matter of choice, by choice, first, in *or* for preference, much rather, much sooner, rather, sooner, willingly

preference choice, cup of tea (*informal*), desire, election, favourite, first choice, option, partiality, pick, predilection, selection, top of the list

preferential advantageous, better, favoured, partial, partisan, privileged, special, superior

preferment advancement, dignity, elevation, exaltation, promotion, rise, upgrading

pregnancy gestation, gravidity

pregnant 1. big *or* heavy with child, expectant, expecting (*informal*), gravid, in the club (*Brit. slang*), in the family way (*informal*), in the pudding club (*slang*), with child **2.** charged, eloquent, expressive, loaded, meaningful, pointed, significant, suggestive, telling, weighty

prejudge *vb* **-judging, -judged** to judge before knowing all the facts.

prejudice *n* **1** an unreasonable or unfair dislike or preference. **2** intolerance of or dislike for people because they belong to a specific race, religion, or group: *class prejudice.* **3** the act or condition of holding such opinions. **4** harm or detriment: *conduct to the prejudice of good order and military discipline.* **5 without prejudice** *Law* without harm to an existing right or claim. ~*vb* **-dicing, -diced 6** to cause (someone) to have a prejudice. **7** to harm: *the incident prejudiced his campaign.*

prejudicial *adj* harmful; damaging.

prelacy *n, pl* **-cies 1 a** the office or status of a prelate. **b** prelates collectively. **2** *Often offensive* government of the Church by prelates.

prelate (prel-it) *n* a clergyman of high rank, such as a bishop.

preliminaries *pl n* same as **prelims.**

preliminary *adj* **1** occurring before or in preparation; introductory. ~*n, pl* **-naries 2** an action or event occurring before or in preparation for an activity: *the discussions are a preliminary to the main negotiations.* **3** a qualifying contest held before a main competition.

prelims *pl n* **1** the pages of a book, such as the title page and contents, which come before the main text. **2** the first public examinations in some universities.

prelude (prel-yewd) *n* **1 a** an introductory movement in music. **b** a short piece of music for piano or organ. **2** an event introducing or preceding the main event. ~*vb* **-uding, -uded 3** to act as a prelude to (something). **4** to introduce by a prelude.

premarital *adj* occurring before marriage: *premarital sex.*

premature *adj* **1** happening or done before the normal or expected time: *premature ageing.* **2** impulsive or hasty: *a premature judgment.* **3** (of a baby) born weeks before the date when it was due to be born. **prematurely** *adv*

premedication *n Surgery* any drugs given to prepare a patient for a general anaesthetic.

premeditated *adj* planned in advance. **premeditation** *n*

premenstrual *adj* occurring or experienced before a menstrual period.

premenstrual tension *or* **syndrome** *n* symptoms, such as nervous tension, that may be experienced because of hormonal changes in the days before a menstrual period starts.

premier *n* **1** a prime minister. **2** a head of government of a Canadian province or Australian state. ~*adj* **3** first in importance or rank: *Torbay, Devon's premier resort.* **4** first in occurrence. **premiership** *n*

premiere *n* **1** the first public performance of a film, play, or opera. ~*vb* **-ering, -ered 2** to give a premiere of: *the play was premiered last year in Johannesburg.*

premise *or* **premiss** *n Logic* a statement that is assumed to be true and is used as a basis for an argument.

premises *pl n* **1** a piece of land together with its buildings. **2** *Law* (in a deed) the matters referred to previously.

premium *n* **1** an extra sum of money added to a standard rate, price, or wage: *the superior taste persuades me to pay the premium for bottled water.* **2** the (regular) amount paid for an insurance policy. **3** the amount above the usual value at which something sells: *some even pay a premium of up to 15 per cent for the privilege.* **4** great value or regard: *we do put a very high premium on common sense.* **5 at a premium a** in great demand, usually because of scarcity. **b** at a higher price than usual.

Premium Savings Bonds *pl n* (in Britain) savings certificates issued by the government, on which no interest is paid, but there is a monthly draw for cash prizes. Also called: **premium bonds**

premolar *n* a tooth between the canine and first molar in adult humans.

THESAURUS

prehistoric earliest, early, primeval, primitive, primordial

prejudge anticipate, forejudge, jump to conclusions, make a hasty assessment, presume, presuppose

prejudice *n.* **1.** bias, jaundiced eye, partiality, preconceived notion, preconception, prejudgment, warp **2.** bigotry, chauvinism, discrimination, injustice, intolerance, narrow-mindedness, racism, sexism, unfairness **3.** damage, detriment, disadvantage, harm, hurt, impairment, loss, mischief ~*vb.* **4.** bias, colour, distort, influence, jaundice, poison, predispose, prepossess, slant, sway, warp **5.** damage, harm, hinder, hurt, impair, injure, mar, spoil, undermine

prejudicial counterproductive, damaging, deleterious, detrimental, disadvantageous, harmful, hurtful, inimical, injurious, undermining, unfavourable

preliminary 1. *adj.* exploratory, first, initial, initiatory, introductory, opening, pilot, precursory, prefatory, preparatory, prior, qualifying, test, trial **2.** *n.* beginning, first round, foundation, groundwork, initiation, introduction, opening, overture, preamble, preface, prelims, prelude, preparation, start

prelude beginning, commencement, curtain-raiser, foreword, intro (*informal*), introduction, overture, preamble, preface, preliminary, preparation, proem, prologue, start

premature 1. abortive, early, embryonic, forward, green, immature, incomplete, predeveloped, raw, undeveloped, unfledged, unripe, unseasonable, untimely **2.** hasty, ill-considered, ill-timed, impulsive, inopportune, overhasty, precipitate, previous (*informal*), rash, too soon, untimely

prematurely 1. before one's time, too early, too soon, untimely **2.** at half-cock, half-cocked, overhastily, precipitately, rashly, too hastily, too soon

premeditated aforethought, calculated, conscious, considered, contrived, deliberate, intended, intentional, planned, prepense, studied, wilful

premeditation deliberation, design, determination, forethought, intention, malice aforethought, planning, plotting, prearrangement, predetermination, purpose

premier *n.* **1.** chancellor, head of government, P.M., prime minister ~*adj.* **2.** arch, chief, first, foremost, head, highest, leading, main, primary, prime, principal, top **3.** earliest, first, inaugural, initial, original

premiere debut, first night, first performance, first showing, opening

premise, premiss argument, assertion, assumption, ground, hypothesis, postulate, postulation, presupposition, proposition, supposition, thesis

premises building, establishment, place, property, site

premium 1. bonus, boon, bounty, fee, percentage (*informal*), perk (*Brit. informal*), perquisite, prize, recompense, remuneration, reward **2.** appreciation, regard, stock, store, value **3. at a premium** beyond one's means, costly, expensive, hard to come by, in great demand, in short supply, like gold dust, not to be had for love or money, rare, scarce, valuable

premonition apprehension, feeling, feeling in one's bones, foreboding, forewarning, funny feeling (*infor-*

premonition *n* a feeling that something unpleasant is going to happen; foreboding. **premonitory** *adj*

prenatal *adj* before birth; during pregnancy.

preoccupy *vb* **-pies, -pying, -pied** to fill the thoughts or mind of (someone) to the exclusion of other things. **preoccupation** *n*

preordained *adj* decreed or determined in advance.

prep *n Informal* short for **preparation** (sense 4).

prep. 1 preparation. 2 preparatory. 3 preposition.

prepacked *adj* (of goods) sold already wrapped.

prepaid *adj* paid for in advance.

preparation *n* **1** the act of preparing or being prepared. **2** (*often pl*) something done in order to prepare for something else: *to make preparations for a wedding.* **3** something that is prepared, such as a medicine. **4** *Old-fashioned* **a** homework. **b** the period reserved for this.

preparatory (prip-**par**-a-tree) *adj* **1** preparing for: *a preparatory meeting to organize the negotiations.* **2** introductory. **3 preparatory to** before: *Jack cleared his throat preparatory to speaking.*

preparatory school *n* **1** (in Britain) a private school for children between the ages of 6 and 13, generally preparing pupils for public school. **2** (in the U.S.) a private secondary school preparing pupils for college.

prepare *vb* **-paring, -pared 1** to make or get ready: *the army prepared for battle.* **2** to put together using parts or ingredients: *he had spent most of the afternoon preparing the meal.* **3** to equip or outfit, as for an expedition. **4 be prepared to** to be willing and able to: *I'm not prepared to say.*

prepay *vb* **-paying, -paid** to pay for in advance. **prepayment** *n*

preponderant *adj* greater in amount, force, or influence. **preponderance** *n*

preponderate *vb* **-ating, -ated** (often foll. by *over*) to be more powerful, important, or numerous (than).

preposition *n* a word used before a noun or pronoun to relate it to the other words, for example *in* in *he is in the car.* **prepositional** *adj*

prepossess *vb* **1** to make a favourable impression in advance. **2** to preoccupy or engross mentally. **prepossession** *n*

prepossessing *adj* making a favourable impression; attractive.

preposterous *adj* utterly absurd.

prep school *n Informal* See **preparatory school.**

prepuce (**pree**-pyewss) *n* **1** the retractable fold of skin covering the tip of the penis; foreskin. **2** the retractable fold of skin covering the tip of the clitoris.

Pre-Raphaelite (pree-**raff**-a-lite) *n* **1** a member of a group of painters in the nineteenth century who revived the style considered typical of Italian painting before Raphael. *~adj* **2** of or in the manner of Pre-Raphaelite painting and painters.

prerecord *vb* to record (music or a programme) in advance so that it can be played or broadcast later. **prerecorded** *adj*

prerequisite *n* **1** something that is required before something else is possible. *~adj* **2** required before something else is possible.

prerogative *n* a special privilege or right.

pres. 1 present (time). 2 presidential.

Pres. President.

presage (**press**-ij) *vb* **-aging, -aged 1** to be a warning or sign of something about to happen: *the windless air presaged disaster.* *~n* **2** an omen. **3** a misgiving.

presbyopia *n Med* a gradual inability of the eye to focus on nearby objects.

presbyter *n* **1** (in some episcopal Churches) an official with administrative and priestly duties. **2** (in the Presbyterian Church) an elder. **presbyterial** *adj*

presbyterian *adj* **1** of or designating Church government by lay elders. *~n* **2** someone who supports this type of Church government. **presbyterianism** *n*

Presbyterian *adj* **1** of any of the Protestant Churches governed by lay elders. *~n* **2** a member of a Presbyterian Church. **Presbyterianism** *n*

presbytery *n, pl* **-teries 1** *Presbyterian Church* a local Church court. **2** *RC Church* the residence of a parish priest. **3** elders collectively. **4** the part of a church east of the choir; a sanctuary.

preschool *adj* of or for children below the age of five: *a preschool playgroup.*

THESAURUS

mal), hunch, idea, intuition, misgiving, omen, portent, presage, presentiment, sign, suspicion, warning

preoccupation **1.** absence of mind, absent-mindedness, absorption, abstraction, brown study, daydreaming, engrossment, immersion, inattentiveness, musing, oblivion, pensiveness, prepossession, reverie, woolgathering **2.** bee in one's bonnet, concern, fixation, hang-up (*informal*), hobbyhorse, *idée fixe*, obsession, pet subject

preparation **1.** anticipation, development, getting ready, groundwork, precaution, preparedness, preparing, provision, putting in order, readiness **2.** *often plural* arrangement, measure, plan, provision **3.** composition, compound, concoction, medicine, mixture, tincture **4.** *old-fashioned* homework, prep (*informal*), revision, schoolwork, study, swotting (*Brit. informal*)

preparatory **1.** basic, elementary, introductory, opening, prefatory, preliminary, preparative, primary **2. preparatory to** before, in advance of, in anticipation of, in preparation for, prior to

prepare **1.** adapt, adjust, anticipate, arrange, brace, coach, dispose, form, fortify, gird, groom, make provision, make ready, plan, practise, prime, put in order, ready, steel, strengthen, train, warm up **2.** assemble, concoct, construct, contrive, draw up, fashion, fix up, get up (*informal*), make, produce, put together, turn out **3.** accoutre, equip, fit, fit out, furnish, outfit, provide, supply

preponderance ascendancy, bulk, dominance, domination, dominion, extensiveness, greater numbers, greater part, lion's share, mass, power, predominance, prevalence, superiority, supremacy, sway, weight

preponderant ascendant, dominant, extensive, foremost, greater, important, larger, paramount, predominant, prevailing, prevalent, significant

prepossessing alluring, amiable, appealing, attractive, beautiful, bewitching, captivating, charming, engaging, fair, fascinating, fetching, glamorous, good-looking, handsome, inviting, likable *or* likeable, lovable, magnetic, pleasing, striking, taking, winning

preposterous absurd, asinine, bizarre, crazy, excessive, exorbitant, extravagant, extreme, foolish, impossible, incredible, insane, irrational, laughable, ludicrous, monstrous, nonsensical, out of the question, outrageous, ridiculous, senseless, shocking, unreasonable, unthinkable

prerequisite **1.** *n.* condition, essential, imperative, must, necessity, precondition, qualification, requirement, requisite, sine qua non **2.** *adj.* called for, essential, imperative, indispensable, mandatory, necessary,

prescience (**press**-ee-enss) *n Formal* knowledge of events before they happen. **prescient** *adj*

prescribe *vb* **-scribing, -scribed 1** *Med* to recommend the use of (a medicine or other remedy). **2** to lay down as a rule.

prescript *n* something laid down or prescribed.

prescription *n* **1 a** written instructions from a doctor for the preparation and use of a medicine. **b** the medicine prescribed. **2** written instructions from an optician specifying the lenses needed to correct bad eyesight. **3** a prescribing.

prescriptive *adj* **1** laying down rules. **2** based on tradition.

presence *n* **1** the fact of being in a specified place: *the test detects the presence of sugar in the urine.* **2** impressive personal appearance or bearing: *a person of dignified and commanding presence.* **3** the company or nearness of a person: *she seemed completely unaware of my presence.* **4** *Mil* a force stationed in another country: *the American-led military presence in the Gulf.* **5** an invisible spirit felt to be nearby: *I felt a presence in the room.*

presence of mind *n* the ability to stay calm and act sensibly in a crisis.

present[1] *adj* **1** being in a specified place: *he had been present at the birth of his son.* **2** existing or happening now. **3** current: *the present exchange rate.* **4** *Grammar* of a verb tense used when the action described is happening now. *~n* **5** *Grammar* the present tense. **6 at present** now. **7 for the present** for now; temporarily. **8 the present** the time being; now. ~See also **presents.**

present[2] *n* **1** a gift. *~vb* **2** to introduce (a person) formally to another. **3** to introduce to the public: *the Museum of Modern Art is presenting a retrospective of his work.* **4** to introduce and compere (a radio or television show). **5** to show or exhibit: *they took advantage of every tax dodge that presented itself.* **6** to bring about: *the case presented a large number of legal difficulties.* **7** to put forward or submit: *they presented a petition to the Prime Minister.* **8** to give or offer formally: *he was presented with a watch to celebrate his twenty-five years with the company.* **9** to hand over for action or payment: *to present a bill.* **10** to portray in a particular way: *her lawyer presented her as a naive woman who had got into bad company.* **11** to aim (a weapon). **12 present arms** to salute with one's weapon.

presentable *adj* **1** fit to be seen by or introduced to other people. **2** acceptable: *the team reached a presentable total.* **presentability** *n*

presentation *n* **1** the act of presenting or being presented. **2** the manner of presenting. **3** a formal ceremony in which an award is made. **4** a public performance, such as a play or a ballet.

present-day *adj* of the modern day; current: *even by present-day standards these were large aircraft.*

presenter *n* a person who introduces a radio or television show and links the items in it.

presentiment (priz-**zen**-tim-ent) *n* a sense that something unpleasant is about to happen; premonition.

presently *adv* **1** soon: *you will understand presently.* **2** *Chiefly Scot, US, & Canad* at the moment: *those methods are presently being developed.*

present participle *n Grammar* a form of verb, ending in *-ing,* which is used to describe action that is happening at the same time as that of the main verb.

present perfect *adj, n Grammar* same as **perfect** (senses 7, 8).

presents *pl n Law* used in a deed or document to refer to itself: *know all men by these presents.*

preservative *n* **1** a chemical added to foods to prevent decay. *~adj* **2** preventing decay.

preserve *vb* **-serving, -served 1** to keep safe from change or extinction; protect: *we are interested in preserving world peace.* **2** to protect from decay or damage: *the carefully preserved village of Cregneish.* **3** to treat (food) in order to prevent it from decaying. **4** to maintain; keep up: *the 1.2% increase in earnings needed to preserve living standards.* *~n* **5** an area of inter-

THESAURUS

needful, obligatory, of the essence, required, requisite, vital

prerogative advantage, authority, birthright, choice, claim, droit, due, exemption, immunity, liberty, perquisite, privilege, right, sanction, title

prescribe appoint, assign, command, decree, define, dictate, direct, enjoin, establish, fix, impose, lay down, ordain, order, require, rule, set, specify, stipulate

prescription a direction, formula, instruction, recipe **b** drug, medicine, mixture, preparation, remedy

presence 1. attendance, being, companionship, company, existence, habitation, inhabitance, occupancy, residence **2.** air, appearance, aspect, aura, bearing, carriage, comportment, demeanour, ease, mien (*literary*), personality, poise, self-assurance **3.** closeness, immediate circle, nearness, neighbourhood, propinquity, proximity, vicinity **4.** apparition, ghost, manifestation, shade (*literary*), spectre, spirit, supernatural being

presence of mind alertness, aplomb, calmness, composure, cool (*slang*), coolness, imperturbability, level-headedness, phlegm, quickness, sang-froid, self-assurance, self-command, self-possession, wits

present[1] *adj.* **1.** accounted for, at hand, available, here, in attendance, near, nearby, ready, there, to hand **2.** contemporary, current, existent, existing, extant, immediate, instant, present-day *~n.* **3. at present** at the moment, just now, now, nowadays, right now **4. for the present** for a while, for the moment, for the nonce, for the time being, in the meantime, not for long, provisionally, temporarily **5. the present** here and now, now, present moment, the time being, this day and age, today

present[2] *n.* **1.** benefaction, boon, bounty, donation, endowment, favour, gift, grant, gratuity, hand-out, largess *or* largesse, offering, prezzie (*informal*) *~vb.* **2.** acquaint with, introduce, make known **3.** demonstrate, display, exhibit, give, mount, put before the public, put on, show, stage **4.** adduce, advance, declare, expound, extend, hold out, introduce, offer, pose, produce, proffer, put forward, raise, recount, relate, state, submit, suggest, tender **5.** award, bestow, confer, donate, entrust, furnish, give, grant, hand out, hand over, offer, proffer, put at (someone's) disposal

presentable acceptable, becoming, decent, fit to be seen, good enough, not bad (*informal*), O.K. *or* okay (*informal*), passable, proper, respectable, satisfactory, suitable, tolerable

presentation 1. award, bestowal, conferral, donation, giving, investiture, offering **2.** appearance, arrangement, delivery, exposition, production, rendition, staging, submission **3.** demonstration, display, exhibition, performance, production, representation, show

presentiment anticipation, apprehension, expectation, fear, feeling, foreboding, forecast, forethought, hunch, intuition, misgiving, premonition, presage

presently anon (*old-fashioned or informal*), before long, by and by, in a minute, in a moment, in a short while, pretty soon (*informal*), shortly, soon

preservation conservation, defence, keeping, main-

est restricted to a particular person or group: *working-class preserves such as pigeon racing.* **6** (*usually pl*) fruit preserved by cooking in sugar. **7** an area where game is kept for private hunting or fishing. **preservation** *n*

preset *vb* **-setting, -set 1** to set the timer on a piece of equipment so that it starts to work at a specific time. *~adj* **2** (of equipment) with the controls set in advance.

preshrunk *adj* (of fabric or a garment) having been shrunk during manufacture so that further shrinkage will not occur when washed.

preside *vb* **-siding, -sided 1** to chair a meeting. **2** to exercise authority: *he presided over the burning of the books.*

presidency *n, pl* **-cies** the office or term of a president.

president *n* **1** the head of state of a republic, esp. of the US. **2** the head of a company, society, or institution. **3** a person who presides over a meeting. **4** the head of certain establishments of higher education. **presidential** *adj*

presidium *n* (in Communist countries) a permanent administrative committee.

press[1] *vb* **1** to apply weight or force to: *he pressed the button on the camera.* **2** to squeeze: *she pressed his hand.* **3** to compress to alter in shape. **4** to smooth out creases by applying pressure or heat. **5** to make (objects) from soft material by pressing with a mould. **6** to crush to force out (juice). **7** to urge (someone) insistently: *they pressed for an answer.* **8** to force or compel: *I was pressed into playing rugby at school.* **9** to plead or put forward strongly: *they intend to press their claim for damages in the courts.* **10** to be urgent: *time presses.* **11** (sometimes foll. by *on* or *forward*) to continue in a determined way: *they pressed on with their journey.* **12** to crowd; push: *shoppers press along the pavements.* **13 pressed for** short of: *pressed for time.* *~n* **14** any machine that exerts pressure to form or cut materials or to extract liquids or compress solids. **15** See **printing press. 16** the art or process of printing. **17 go to press** to go to be printed: *when is this book going to press?* **18 the press a** news media collectively, esp. newspapers. **b** journalists collectively. **19** the opinions and reviews in the newspapers: *the government is not receiving a good press at the moment.* **20** the act of pressing or state of being pressed: *at the press of a button.* **21** a crowd: *a press of people at the exit.* **22** a cupboard for storing clothes or linen.

press[2] *vb* **1** to recruit (men) forcibly for military service. **2** to use for a purpose other than intended: *press into service.*

press agent *n* a person employed to obtain favourable publicity for an individual or organization.

press box *n* a room at a sports ground reserved for reporters.

press conference *n* an interview for reporters given by a famous person.

press gallery *n* an area for newspaper reporters, esp. in a parliament.

press gang *n* **1** (formerly) a group of men used to capture men and boys and forced them to join the navy. *~vb* **press-gang 2** to force (a person) to join the navy by a press gang. **3** to persuade (someone) to do something that he or she does not want to do: *he was press-ganged into joining the family business.*

pressing *adj* **1** demanding immediate attention. *~n* **2** a large number of gramophone records produced at one time.

press stud *n* a fastener in which one part with a projecting knob snaps into a hole on another part.

press-up *n* an exercise in which the body is raised from and lowered to the floor by straightening and bending the arms.

pressure *n* **1** the state of pressing or being pressed. **2** the application of force by one body on the surface of another. **3** urgent claims or demands: *to work under pressure.* **4** a condition that is hard to bear: *the pressure of grief.* **5** *Physics* the force applied to a unit area of a surface. **6 bring pressure to bear on** to use influence or authority to persuade. *~vb* **-suring, -sured 7** to persuade forcefully: *he was pressured into resignation.*

pressure cooker *n* an airtight pot which cooks food quickly by steam under pressure. **pressure-cook** *vb*

pressure group *n* a group that tries to influence policies or public opinion.

pressurize *or* **-ise** *vb* **-izing, -ized** *or* **-ising, -ised 1** to increase the pressure in (an aircraft cabin, etc.) in order to maintain approximately atmospheric pressure when the external pressure is low. **2** to make insistent demands of (someone): *do not be pressurized into making a decision.* **pressurization** *or* **-isation** *n*

Prestel *n Trademark* (in Britain) the Post Office public viewdata service.

prestidigitation *n Formal* same as **sleight of hand. prestidigitator** *n*

prestige *n* **1** high status or respect resulting from success or achievements: *a symbol of French power and prestige.* **2** the power to impress: *a humdrum family car with no prestige.* **prestigious** *adj*

presto *Music ~adv* **1** very fast. *~n, pl* **-tos 2** a passage to be played very quickly.

THESAURUS

tenance, perpetuation, protection, safeguarding, safekeeping, safety, salvation, security, storage, support, upholding

preserve *vb.* **1.** care for, conserve, defend, guard, keep, protect, safeguard, save, secure, shelter, shield **2.** continue, keep, keep up, maintain, perpetuate, retain, sustain, uphold *~n.* **3.** area, domain, field, realm, specialism, sphere **4.** *usually plural* confection, confiture, conserve, jam, jelly, marmalade, sweetmeat **5.** game reserve, reservation, reserve, sanctuary

preside administer, be at the head of, be in authority, chair, conduct, control, direct, govern, head, lead, manage, officiate, run, supervise

press *vb.* **1.** bear down on, compress, condense, crush, depress, force down, jam, mash, push, reduce, squeeze, stuff **2.** calender, finish, flatten, iron, mangle, smooth, steam **3.** beg, entreat, exhort, implore, importune, petition, plead, pressurize, sue, supplicate, urge **4.** compel, constrain, demand, enforce, enjoin, force, insist on **5.** cluster, crowd, flock, gather, hasten, herd, hurry, mill, push, rush, seethe, surge, swarm, throng *~n.* **6. the press a.** Fleet Street, fourth estate, journalism, news media, newspapers, the papers **b.** columnists, correspondents, gentlemen of the press, journalists, journos (*slang*), newsmen, photographers, pressmen, reporters **7.** bunch, crowd, crush, flock, herd, horde, host, mob, multitude, pack, push (*informal*), swarm, throng

pressing burning, constraining, crucial, exigent, high-priority, imperative, important, importunate, serious, urgent, vital

pressure 1. compressing, compression, crushing, force, heaviness, squeezing, weight **2.** adversity, affliction, burden, demands, difficulty, distress, exigency, hassle (*informal*), heat, hurry, load, press, strain, stress, urgency

prestressed concrete *n* concrete that contains stretched steel wires.
presumably *adv* one supposes or guesses; probably: *he emerged from what was presumably the kitchen carrying a tray.*
presume *vb* **-suming, -sumed 1** to take (something) for granted: *I presume he's dead.* **2** to dare (to): *I would not presume to lecture you on medical matters, Dr Jacobs.* **3** (foll. by *on* or *upon*) to rely or depend: *don't presume on his agreement.* **4** (foll. by *on* or *upon*) to take advantage (of): *I'm afraid I presumed on Aunt Ginny's generosity.* **presumedly** *adv* **presuming** *adj*
presumption *n* **1** the act of presuming. **2** a basis on which an assumption is made. **3** bold insolent behaviour. **4** a belief or assumption based on reasonable evidence. **presumptive** *adj*
presumptuous *adj* bold and insolent.
presuppose *vb* **-posing, -posed 1** to require as a previous condition in order to be true: *the idea of integration presupposes a disintegrated state.* **2** to take for granted. **presupposition** *n*
pretence *or US* **pretense** *n* **1** an action or claim that could mislead people into believing something which is not true: *Daniel made a pretence of carefully reading it; the pretence that many of the unemployed are on "training schemes".* **2** a false display; affectation: *she abandoned all pretence of work and watched me.* **3** a claim, esp. a false one, to a right, title, or distinction. **4** make-believe. **5** a pretext: *they were placed in a ghetto on the pretence that they would be safe there.*
pretend *vb* **1** to claim or give the appearance of (something untrue): *he pretended to be asleep.* **2** to make believe: *one of the actresses pretended to urinate into a bucket.* **3** (foll. by *to*) to present a claim, esp. a doubtful one: *to pretend to the throne.*
pretender *n* a person who makes a false or disputed claim to a throne or title.
pretension *n* (*often pl*) a false claim to merit or importance.
pretentious *adj* **1** making (unjustified) claims to special merit or importance: *many critics thought her work and ideas pretentious and empty.* **2** vulgarly showy; ostentatious: *a family restaurant with no pretentious furnishing.*
preterite *or esp US* **preterit** (**pret**-er-it) *Grammar ~n* **1** a past tense of verbs, such as *jumped, swam.* **2** a verb in this tense. *~adj* **3** expressing such a past tense.
preternatural *adj* beyond what is natural; supernatural.
pretext *n* a false reason given to hide the real one: *delivering the book had been a good pretext for seeing her again.*
prettify *vb* **-fies, -fying, -fied** to make pretty.
pretty *adj* **-tier, -tiest 1** attractive in a delicate or graceful way. **2** pleasant to look at. **3** *Informal, often ironical* excellent or fine: *well, this is a pretty state of affairs to have got into.* *~adv* **4** *Informal* fairly: *I think he and Nicholas got on pretty well.* **5 sitting pretty** *Informal* in a favourable state. **prettily** *adv* **prettiness** *n*
pretty-pretty *adj Informal* excessively pretty.
pretzel *n* a brittle salted biscuit in the shape of a knot.
prevail *vb* **1** (often foll. by *over* or *against*) to prove superior; gain mastery: *moderate nationalists have until now prevailed over the radicals.* **2** to be the most important feature: *a casual good-natured mood prevailed.* **3** to be generally established: *this attitude*

THESAURUS

prestige authority, bottom, Brownie points, cachet, celebrity, credit, distinction, eminence, esteem, fame, honour, importance, influence, kudos, regard, renown, reputation, standing, stature, status, weight
presumably apparently, doubtless, doubtlessly, in all likelihood, in all probability, it would seem, likely, most likely, on the face of it, probably, seemingly
presume 1. assume, believe, conjecture, guess (*informal, chiefly U.S. & Canad.*), infer, posit, postulate, presuppose, suppose, surmise, take for granted, take it, think **2.** dare, go so far, have the audacity, make bold, make so bold, take the liberty, undertake, venture **3.** *with* **on** *or* **upon** bank on, count on, depend, rely, trust
presumption 1. basis, chance, grounds, likelihood, plausibility, probability, reason **2.** assurance, audacity, boldness, brass (*informal*), brass neck (*Brit. informal*), cheek (*informal*), chutzpah (*U.S. & Canad. informal*), effrontery, forwardness, front, gall (*informal*), impudence, insolence, neck (*informal*), nerve (*informal*), presumptuousness, temerity **3.** anticipation, assumption, belief, conjecture, guess, hypothesis, opinion, premiss, presupposition, supposition, surmise
presumptuous arrogant, audacious, bigheaded (*informal*), bold, conceited, foolhardy, forward, insolent, overconfident, overfamiliar, overweening, presuming, pushy (*informal*), rash, too big for one's boots, uppish (*Brit. informal*)
presuppose accept, assume, consider, imply, posit, postulate, presume, suppose, take as read, take for granted, take it
presupposition assumption, belief, hypothesis, preconceived idea, preconception, premiss, presumption, supposition, theory
pretence *or U.S.* **pretense 1.** acting, charade, deceit, deception, fabrication, fakery, faking, falsehood, feigning, invention, make-believe, sham, simulation, subterfuge, trickery **2.** affectation, appearance, artifice, display, façade, hokum (*slang, chiefly U.S. & Canad.*), posing, posturing, pretentiousness, show, veneer **3.** claim, cloak, colour, cover, excuse, façade, garb, guise, mask, masquerade, pretext, ruse, semblance, show, veil, wile
pretend 1. affect, allege, assume, counterfeit, dissemble, dissimulate, fake, falsify, feign, impersonate, make out, pass oneself off as, profess, put on, sham, simulate **2.** act, imagine, make believe, make up, play, play the part of, suppose **3.** *with* **to** allege, aspire, claim, lay claim, profess, purport
pretender aspirant, claimant, claimer
pretension *often plural* aspiration, assertion, assumption, claim, demand, pretence, profession
pretentious affected, assuming, bombastic, conceited, exaggerated, extravagant, flaunting, grandiloquent, grandiose, highfalutin (*informal*), high-flown, high-sounding, hollow, inflated, magniloquent, mannered, ostentatious, overambitious, pompous, puffed up, showy, snobbish, specious, vainglorious
pretext affectation, alleged reason, appearance, cloak, cover, device, excuse, guise, mask, ploy, pretence, red herring, ruse, semblance, show, simulation, veil
pretty *adj.* **1.** bijou, dainty, delicate, elegant, fine, graceful, neat, nice, pleasing, tasteful, trim **2.** appealing, attractive, beautiful, bonny, charming, comely, cute, fair, good-looking, lovely, personable *~adv.* **3.** *informal* fairly, kind of (*informal*), moderately, quite, rather, reasonably, somewhat
prevail 1. *often with* **over** *or* **against** be victorious, carry the day, gain mastery, overcome, overrule, prove superior, succeed, triumph, win **2.** abound, be current

has prevailed in Britain for many years. **4 prevail on** *or* **upon** to succeed in persuading: *she prevailed upon her parents to let her go to London.*

prevailing *adj* **1** widespread: *the prevailing mood.* **2** most usual: *the prevailing wind is from the west.*

prevalent *adj* widespread or common. **prevalence** *n*

prevaricate *vb* **-cating, -cated** to avoid giving a direct or truthful answer. **prevarication** *n* **prevaricator** *n*

prevent *vb* **1** to keep from happening: *vitamin C prevented scurvy.* **2** (often foll. by *from*) to keep (someone from doing something): *circumstances prevented her from coming.* **preventable** *adj* **prevention** *n*

preventive *adj* **1** intended to prevent or hinder. **2** *Med* tending to prevent disease. *~n* **3** something that serves to prevent. **4** *Med* any drug or agent that tends to prevent disease. Also: **preventative**

preview *n* **1** an opportunity to see a film, exhibition, or play before it is shown to the public. *~vb* **2** to view in advance.

previous *adj* **1** coming or happening before. **2** *Informal* happening too soon; premature: *such criticism is a bit previous because no definite decision has yet been taken.* **3 previous to** before. **previously** *adv*

prewar *adj* relating to the period before a war, esp. before World War I or II.

prey *n* **1** an animal hunted and killed for food by another animal. **2** the victim of a hostile person, influence, emotion, or illness.: *children are falling prey to the disease.* **3 bird** *or* **beast of prey** a bird or animal that kills and eats other birds or animals. *~vb* (often foll. by *on* or *upon*) **4** to hunt and kill for food. **5** to worry or obsess: *it preyed on his conscience.* **6** to make a victim (of others), by profiting at their expense.

price *n* **1** the amount of money for which a thing is bought or sold. **2** the cost at which something is obtained: *the price of making the wrong decision.* **3 at any price** whatever the price or cost. **4 at a price** at a high price. **5** *Gambling* odds. **6 what price (something)?** what are the chances of (something) happening now? *~vb* **pricing, priced 7** to fix the price of. **8** to discover the price of.

price-fixing *n* the setting of prices by agreement among producers and distributors.

priceless *adj* **1** extremely valuable. **2** *Informal* extremely amusing.

pricey *adj* **pricier, priciest** *Informal* expensive.

prick *vb* **1** to pierce lightly with a sharp point. **2** to cause a piercing sensation (in): *a needle pricked her finger.* **3** to cause a sharp emotional pain (in): *the film pricked our consciences about the plight of the American Indians.* **4 prick up one's ears a** (of a dog) to make the ears stand erect. **b** (of a person) to listen attentively. *~n* **5** a sudden sharp pain caused by pricking. **6** a mark made by a sharp point. **7** a sharp emotional pain: *a prick of conscience.* **8** *Slang taboo* a penis. **9** *Slang offensive* a man who provokes contempt.

prickle *n* **1** *Bot* a thorn or spike on a plant. **2** a pricking or stinging sensation. *~vb* **-ling, -led 3** to feel a stinging sensation.

prickly *adj* **-lier, -liest 1** having prickles. **2** tingling or

THESAURUS

(prevalent, widespread), exist generally, obtain, predominate, preponderate **3. prevail on** *or* **upon** bring round, convince, dispose, incline, induce, influence, persuade, prompt, sway, talk into, win over

prevailing common, current, customary, established, fashionable, general, in style, in vogue, ordinary, popular, prevalent, set, usual, widespread

prevalence acceptance, commonness, common occurrence, currency, frequency, pervasiveness, popularity, profusion, regularity, ubiquity, universality

prevalent accepted, common, commonplace, current, customary, established, everyday, extensive, frequent, general, habitual, popular, rampant, rife, ubiquitous, universal, usual, widespread

prevaricate beat about the bush, beg the question, cavil, deceive, dodge, equivocate, evade, flannel (*Brit. informal*), hedge, lie, palter, quibble, shift, shuffle, stretch the truth, tergiversate (*formal*)

prevarication cavilling, deceit, deception, equivocation, evasion, falsehood, falsification, lie, misrepresentation, pretence, quibbling, tergiversation (*formal*), untruth

prevent anticipate, avert, avoid, balk, bar, block, check, counteract, defend against, foil, forestall, frustrate, hamper, head off, hinder, impede, inhibit, intercept, nip in the bud, obstruct, obviate, preclude, restrain, stave off, stop, thwart, ward off

prevention 1. anticipation, avoidance, deterrence, elimination, forestalling, precaution, preclusion, safeguard, thwarting **2.** bar, check, deterrence, frustration, hindrance, impediment, interruption, obstacle, obstruction, stoppage

preventive *adj.* **1.** hampering, hindering, impeding, obstructive **2.** counteractive, deterrent, inhibitory, precautionary, prophylactic, protective, shielding *~n.* **3.** block, hindrance, impediment, obstacle, obstruction **4.** deterrent, neutralizer, prevention, prophylactic, protection, protective, remedy, safeguard, shield

previous 1. antecedent, anterior, earlier, erstwhile, ex-, foregoing, former, one-time, past, preceding, prior, quondam, sometime **2.** *informal* ahead of oneself, precipitate, premature, too early, too soon, untimely

previously at one time, a while ago, before, beforehand, earlier, formerly, heretofore, hitherto, in advance, in anticipation, in days *or* years gone by, in the past, once, then, until now

prey *n.* **1.** game, kill, quarry **2.** dupe, fall guy (*informal*), mark, mug (*slang*), target, victim *~vb.* **3.** devour, eat, feed upon, hunt, live off, seize **4.** burden, distress, hang over, haunt, oppress, trouble, weigh down, weigh heavily, worry **5.** blackmail, bleed (*informal*), bully, exploit, intimidate, take advantage of, terrorize, victimize

price *n.* **1.** amount, asking price, assessment, bill, charge, cost, damage (*informal*), estimate, expenditure, expense, face value, fee, figure, outlay, payment, rate, valuation, value, worth **2.** consequences, cost, penalty, sacrifice, toll **3. at any price** anyhow, cost what it may, expense no object, no matter what the cost, regardless, whatever the cost *~vb.* **4.** assess, cost, estimate, evaluate, put a price on, rate, value

priceless 1. beyond price, cherished, costly, dear, expensive, incalculable, incomparable, inestimable, invaluable, irreplaceable, precious, prized, rare, rich, treasured, worth a king's ransom **2.** *informal* absurd, amusing, comic, droll, funny, hilarious, killing (*informal*), rib-tickling, ridiculous, riotous, side-splitting

prick *vb.* **1.** bore, impale, jab, lance, perforate, pierce, pink, punch, puncture, stab **2.** bite, itch, prickle, smart, sting, tingle **3.** cut, distress, grieve, move, pain, stab, touch, trouble, wound *~n.* **4.** cut, gash, hole, perforation, pinhole, puncture, wound **5.** gnawing, pang, prickle, smart, spasm, sting, twinge

prickle *n.* **1.** barb, needle, point, spike, spine, spur, thorn **2.** chill, goose flesh, pins and needles (*informal*),

stinging: *he had a prickly feeling down his back.* **3** touchy or irritable: *Canadians are notoriously prickly about being taken for Americans.*

prickly heat *n* an itchy rash that occurs in very hot moist weather.

prickly pear *n* **1** a tropical cactus with edible oval fruit. **2** the fruit of this plant.

pride *n* **1** a feeling of satisfaction about one's achievements. **2** an excessively high opinion of oneself. **3** satisfaction in one's own or another's success or achievements: *his obvious pride in his son's achievements.* **4** a sense of dignity and self-respect: *he must swallow his pride and ally himself with his political enemies.* **5** one of the better or most admirable parts of something: *the National Health Service has long been the pride of Britain.* **6** a group of lions. **7 pride and joy** the main source of pride: *the car was his pride and joy.* **8 pride of place** the most important position. *~vb* **priding, prided 9** (foll. by *on* or *upon*) to take pride in (oneself) for.

prie dieu (**pree-dyuh**) *n* an upright frame with a ledge for kneeling upon, for use when praying.

priest *n* **1** (in the Christian Church) a person ordained to administer the sacraments and preach. **2** a minister of any religion. **3** an official who performs religious ceremonies. **priestess** *fem n* **priesthood** *n* **priestly** *adj*

prig *n* a person who is smugly self-righteous and narrow-minded. **priggish** *adj* **priggishness** *n*

prim *adj* **primmer, primmest** affectedly proper, or formal, and rather prudish. **primly** *adv*

prima ballerina *n* a leading female ballet dancer.

primacy *n, pl* **-cies 1** the state of being first in rank, grade, or order. **2** *Christianity* the office of an archbishop.

prima donna *n, pl* **prima donnas 1** a leading female opera singer. **2** *Informal* a temperamental person.

primaeval *adj* same as **primeval.**

prima facie (**prime**-a **fay**-shee) *adv* as it seems at first.

primal *adj* **1** of basic causes or origins. **2** chief or most important.

primarily *adv* **1** chiefly or mainly. **2** originally.

primary *adj* **1** first in importance. **2** first in position or time, as in a series: *he argued that the country was only in the primary stage of socialism.* **3** fundamental or basic: *the new policy will put the emphasis on primary health care rather than hospital care.* **4** being the first stage; elementary: *all new recruits participated in the same primary training courses.* **5** relating to the education of children up to the age of 11 or 12. **6** (of an industry) involving the obtaining of raw materials. **7** (of the flight feathers of a bird's wing) outer and longest. **8** being the part of an electric circuit in which a changing current causes a current in a neighbouring circuit: *a primary coil.* *~n, pl* **-ries 9** a person or thing that is first in position, time, or importance. **10** (in the US) an election in which the voters of a state choose a candidate for office. Full name: **primary election 11** a primary school. **12** a primary colour. **13** any of the outer and longest flight feathers of a bird's wing. **14** a primary part of an electric circuit.

primary accent *or* **stress** *n Linguistics* the strongest accent in a word.

primary colours *pl n* **1** *Physics* the colours red, green, and blue from which all other colours can be obtained by mixing. **2** *Art* the colours red, yellow, and blue from which all other colours can be obtained by mixing.

primary school *n* **1** (in England and Wales) a school for children between the ages of 5 and 11. **2** (in Scotland) a school for children between the ages of 5 and 12. **3** (in the US and Canada) a school equivalent to the first three or four grades of elementary school.

primate[1] *n* a mammal with flexible hands and feet and a highly developed brain, such as a monkey, an ape, or a human being.

primate[2] *n* an archbishop.

prime *adj* **1** first in importance: *the prime aim.* **2** of the highest quality: *prime beef.* **3** typical: *a prime example.* *~n* **4** the time when a thing is at its best. **5** a period of power, vigour, and activity: *he was in the prime of life.* **6** *Maths* short for **prime number.** *~vb* **priming, primed 7** to give (someone) information in advance to prepare him or her. **8** to prepare (a surface) for painting. **9** to prepare (a gun or mine) before deto-

THESAURUS

smart, tickle, tingle, tingling *~vb.* **3.** itch, smart, sting, tingle, twitch **4.** jab, nick, prick, stick

prickly 1. barbed, brambly, briery, bristly, spiny, thorny **2.** crawling, itchy, pricking, prickling, scratchy, sharp, smarting, stinging, tingling **3.** bad-tempered, cantankerous, edgy, fractious, grumpy, irritable, liverish, peevish, pettish, petulant, ratty (*Brit. & N.Z. informal*), shirty (*slang, chiefly Brit.*), snappish, stroppy (*Brit. slang*), tetchy, touchy, waspish

pride *n.* **1.** amour-propre, dignity, honour, self-esteem, self-respect, self-worth **2.** arrogance, bigheadedness (*informal*), conceit, egotism, haughtiness, hauteur, hubris, loftiness, presumption, pretension, pretentiousness, self-importance, self-love, smugness, snobbery, superciliousness, vainglory, vanity **3.** delight, gratification, joy, pleasure, satisfaction **4.** best, boast, choice, cream, elite, flower, gem, glory, jewel, pick, pride and joy, prize, treasure *~vb.* **5.** *with* **on** *or* **upon** be proud of, boast, brag, congratulate oneself, crow, exult, flatter oneself, glory in, pique, plume, preen, revel in, take pride, vaunt

priest churchman, clergyman, cleric, curate, divine, ecclesiastic, father, father confessor, holy man, man of God, man of the cloth, minister, padre (*informal*), pastor, vicar

priestly canonical, clerical, ecclesiastic, hieratic, pastoral, priestlike, sacerdotal

prig goody-goody (*informal*), old maid (*informal*), pedant, prude, puritan, stuffed shirt (*informal*)

priggish goody-goody (*informal*), holier-than-thou, narrow-minded, pedantic, prim, prudish, puritanical, self-righteous, self-satisfied, smug, starchy (*informal*), stiff, stuffy

prim demure, fastidious, formal, fussy, old-maidish (*informal*), particular, precise, priggish, prissy (*informal*), proper, prudish, puritanical, schoolmarmish (*Brit. informal*), starchy (*informal*), stiff, strait-laced

prima donna diva, leading lady, star

primarily 1. above all, basically, chiefly, especially, essentially, for the most part, fundamentally, generally, largely, mainly, mostly, on the whole, principally **2.** at first, at *or* from the start, first and foremost, initially, in the beginning, in the first place, originally

primary 1. best, capital, cardinal, chief, dominant, first, greatest, highest, leading, main, paramount, prime, principal, top **2.** aboriginal, earliest, initial, original, primal, primeval, primitive, primordial, pristine **3.** basic, beginning, bog-standard (*informal*), elemental, essential, fundamental, radical, ultimate, underlying **4.** elementary, introductory, rudimentary, simple

prime *adj.* **1.** chief, leading, main, predominant, pre-eminent, primary, principal, ruling, senior **2.** best, capital, choice, excellent, first-class, first-rate, grade A,

nating or firing. **10** to fill (a pump) with its working fluid, to expel air from it before starting. **11** to prepare (something).

prime meridian *n* the 0° meridian from which the other meridians are worked out, usually taken to pass through Greenwich.

Prime Minister *n* the leader of a government.

prime mover *n* a person or thing which was important in helping create an idea, situation, etc.: *he was the prime mover behind the coup.*

prime number *n* an integer that cannot be divided into other integers but is only divisible by itself or 1, such as 2, 3, 7, and 11.

primer[1] *n* **1** a substance applied to a surface as a base coat or sealer. **2** a device for detonating the main charge in a gun or mine.

primer[2] *n* an introductory text, such as a school textbook.

primeval (prime-**ee**-val) *adj* of the earliest age of the world.

primitive *adj* **1** of or belonging to the beginning. **2** *Biol* of an early stage in development: *primitive amphibians.* **3** characteristic of an early simple state, esp. in being crude or basic: *a primitive dwelling.* ~*n* **4** a primitive person or thing. **5** a painter of any era whose work appears childlike or untrained. **6** a work by such an artist.

primogeniture *n* **1** *Formal* the state of being the first-born child. **2** *Law* the right of an eldest son to inherit all the property of his parents.

primordial *adj Formal* existing at or from the beginning.

primp *vb* to tidy (one's hair or clothes) fussily.

primrose *n* **1** a wild plant which has pale yellow flowers in spring. ~*adj* **2** Also: **primrose yellow** pale yellow. **3** of primroses.

primrose path *n* (often preceded by *the*) a pleasurable way of life.

primula *n* a type of primrose with brightly coloured funnel-shaped flowers.

Primus *n Trademark* a portable paraffin cooking stove, used esp. by campers.

prince *n* **1** a male member of a royal family, esp. the son of the king or queen. **2** the male ruler of a small country. **3** an outstanding member of a specified group: *Dryden, that prince of poets.*

prince consort *n* the husband of a queen, who is himself a prince.

princely *adj* **-lier, -liest 1** of or characteristic of a prince. **2** generous or lavish.

Prince of Wales *n* the eldest son of the British sovereign.

princess *n* **1** a female member of a royal family, esp. the daughter of the king or queen. **2** the wife of a prince.

Princess Royal *n* title sometimes given to the eldest daughter of the British sovereign.

principal *adj* **1** first in importance, rank, or value: *salt is the principal source of sodium in our diets; the Republic's two principal parties.* ~*n* **2** the head of a school or other educational institution. **3** a person who holds one of the most important positions in an organization: *she became a principal in the home finance department.* **4** the leading actor in a play. **5** *Law* **a** a person who engages another to act as his or her agent. **b** a person who takes an active part in a crime. **c** the person held responsible for fulfilling an obligation. **6** *Finance* **a** capital or property, as contrasted with income. **b** the original amount of a debt on which interest is calculated. **principally** *adv*

➤ Distinguish the spellings of *principal* and *principle.* These are different words but often confused.

principal boy *n* the leading male role in a pantomime, traditionally played by a woman.

principality *n, pl* **-ties** a territory ruled by a prince.

principal parts *pl n Grammar* the main verb forms, from which all other verb forms may be deduced.

principle *n* **1** a moral rule guiding personal conduct: *he'd stoop to anything – he has no principles.* **2** a set of such moral rules: *a man of principle.* **3** a basic or general truth: *the principle of freedom of expression.* **4** a basic law or rule underlying a particular theory or philosophy: *the government has been deceitful and has violated basic principles of democracy.* **5** a general law in science: *the principle of the conservation of mass.* **6** *Chem* a constituent of a substance that determines its characteristics. **7 in principle** in theory though not always in practice. **8 on principle** because of one's beliefs.

➤ Distinguish the spellings of *principle* and *principal.* These are different words but often confused.

principled *adj* (of a person or action) guided by moral rules: *principled opposition to the war.*

prink *vb* **1** to dress (oneself) finely. **2** to preen oneself.

print *vb* **1** to reproduce (a newspaper, book, etc.) in large quantities by mechanical or electronic means. **2** to reproduce (text or pictures) by applying ink to paper. **3** to write in letters that are not joined up. **4** to stamp (fabric) with a design. **5** to produce (a photograph) from a negative. **6** to fix in the mind or memory. ~*n* **7** printed content, such as newsprint. **8** a printed publication, such as a book. **9 in print a** in printed or published form. **b** (of a book) available from a publisher. **10 out of print** no longer available from a pub-

THESAURUS

highest, quality, select, selected, superior, top ~*n.* **3.** best days, bloom, flower, full flowering, height, heyday, maturity, peak, perfection, zenith **4.** beginning, morning, opening, spring, start ~*vb.* **5.** brief, clue in (*informal*), clue up (*informal*), fill in (*informal*), gen up (*Brit. informal*), give someone the lowdown (*informal*), inform, notify, tell **6.** break in, coach, fit, get ready, groom, make ready, prepare, train

primeval ancient, earliest, early, first, old, original, prehistoric, primal, primitive, primordial, pristine

primitive 1. earliest, early, elementary, first, original, primary, primeval, primordial, pristine **2.** barbarian, barbaric, crude, rough, rude, rudimentary, savage, simple, uncivilized, uncultivated, undeveloped, unrefined

prince lord, monarch, potentate, ruler, sovereign

princely 1. august, dignified, grand, high-born, imperial, imposing, lofty, magnificent, majestic, noble, regal, royal, sovereign, stately **2.** bounteous, bountiful, generous, gracious, lavish, liberal, magnanimous, munificent, open-handed, rich

principal *adj.* **1.** capital, cardinal, chief, controlling, dominant, essential, first, foremost, highest, key, leading, main, most important, paramount, pre-eminent, primary, prime, strongest ~*n.* **2.** dean, director, head (*informal*), headmaster, headmistress, head teacher, master, rector **3.** boss (*informal*), chief, director, head, leader, master, ruler, superintendent **4.** lead, leader, star **5.** *Finance* assets, capital, capital funds, money

principally above all, chiefly, especially, first and foremost, for the most part, in the main, largely, mainly, mostly, particularly, predominantly, primarily

principle 1. assumption, axiom, canon, criterion, dictum, doctrine, dogma, ethic, formula, fundamental, golden rule, law, maxim, moral law, precept, proposi-

lisher. **11** a picture printed from an engraved plate or wood block. **12** printed text, with regard to the typeface: *italic print.* **13** a photograph produced from a negative. **14** a fabric with a printed design. **15** a mark made by pressing something onto a surface. **16** See **fingerprint.** ~See also **print out.**

printed circuit *n* an electronic circuit in which the wiring is a metallic coating printed on a thin insulating board.

printer *n* **1** a person or business engaged in printing. **2** a machine that prints. **3** *Computers* a machine that prints out results on paper.

printing *n* **1** the process of producing printed matter. **2** printed text. **3** all the copies of a book printed at one time. **4** a form of writing in which the letters are not joined together.

printing press *n* a machine used for printing.

print out *vb* **1** *Computers* to produce (printed information). ~*n* **print-out** *or* **printout 2** printed information from a computer.

prior[1] *adj* **1** previous: *prior knowledge.* **2 prior to** before.

prior[2] *n* **1** the head monk in a priory. **2** the abbot's deputy in a monastery. **prioress** *fem n*

priority *n, pl* **-ties 1** the most important thing that must be dealt with first. **2** the right to be or go before others.

priory *n, pl* **-ories** a religious house where certain orders of monks or nuns live.

prise *or* **prize** *vb* **prising, prised** *or* **prizing, prized** to force open or out by levering.

prism *n* **1** a transparent block, often with triangular ends and rectangular sides, used to disperse light into a spectrum or refract it in optical instruments. **2** *Maths* a polyhedron possessing a uniform cross section.

prismatic *adj* **1** of or shaped like a prism. **2** exhibiting bright spectral colours; rainbow-like: *prismatic light.*

prison *n* **1** a public building used to hold convicted criminals and accused people awaiting trial. **2** any place of confinement.

prisoner *n* **1** a person kept in prison as a punishment for a crime, or while awaiting trial. **2** a person confined by any restraints: *he's a prisoner of his own past.* **3 take (someone) prisoner** to capture and hold (someone) as a prisoner.

prisoner of war *n* a serviceman captured by an enemy in wartime.

prissy *adj* **-sier, -siest** prim and prudish. **prissily** *adv*

pristine *adj* **1** completely new, clean, and pure: *pristine white plates.* **2** of or involving the original, unchanged, and unspoilt period or state: *the viewing of wild game in its pristine natural state.*

privacy *n* **1** the condition of being private. **2** secrecy.

private *adj* **1** not for general or public use: *a private bathroom.* **2** confidential or secret: *a private conversation.* **3** involving someone's domestic and personal life rather than his or her work or business: *what I do in my private life is none of your business.* **4** owned or paid for by individuals rather than by the government: *private enterprise.* **5** not publicly known: *they had private reasons for the decision.* **6** having no public office, rank, or position: *the Red Cross received donations from private citizens.* **7** (of a place) quiet and secluded: *the garden is completely private.* **8** (of a person) quiet and retiring: *she was private – her life was her own.* ~*n* **9** a soldier of the lowest rank in the army. **10 in private** in secret. **privately** *adv*

private bill *n* a bill presented to Parliament on behalf of a private individual or corporation.

private company *n* a limited company that does not issue shares for public subscription.

private detective *n* a person hired by a client to do detective work.

privateer *n* **1** a privately owned armed vessel authorized by the government to take part in a war. **2** a captain of such a ship.

private eye *n Informal* a private detective.

private income *n* income from sources other than employment, such as investment.

private member *n* a Member of Parliament who is not a government minister.

private member's bill *n* a law proposed by a Member of Parliament who is not a government minister.

private parts *or* **privates** *pl n Euphemistic* the genitals.

private school *n* a school controlled by a private body, accepting mostly fee-paying pupils.

private sector *n* the part of a country's economy that consists of privately owned enterprises.

privation *n Formal* loss or lack of the necessities of life.

privative (**priv**-a-tiv) *adj* **1** causing privation. **2** *Grammar* expressing lack or absence, for example *-less* and *un-*.

privatize *or* **-ise** *vb* **-izing, -ized** *or* **-ising, -ised** to sell (a state-owned company) to individuals or a private company. **privatization** *or* **-isation** *n*

privet *n* a bushy evergreen shrub used for hedges.

THESAURUS

tion, rule, standard, truth, verity **2.** attitude, belief, code, credo, ethic, morality, opinion, tenet **3. in principle** ideally, in essence, in theory, theoretically

print *vb.* **1.** engrave, go to press, impress, imprint, issue, mark, publish, put to bed (*informal*), run off, stamp ~*n.* **2.** book, magazine, newspaper, newsprint, periodical, printed matter, publication, typescript **3. in print a.** in black and white, on paper, on the streets, out, printed, published **b.** available, current, in the shops, obtainable, on the market, on the shelves **4. out of print** no longer published, o.p., unavailable, unobtainable **5.** copy, engraving, picture, reproduction **6.** characters, face, font (*chiefly U.S.*), fount, lettering, letters, type, typeface **7.** photo (*informal*), photograph, picture

priority first concern, greater importance, precedence, pre-eminence, preference, prerogative, rank, right of way, seniority, superiority, supremacy, the lead

priory abbey, cloister, convent, monastery, nunnery, religious house

prison clink (*slang*), confinement, dungeon, gaol, jail, lockup, nick (*Brit. slang*), penal institution, penitentiary (*U.S.*), pound, quod (*slang, chiefly Brit.*), slammer (*slang*), stir (*slang*)

prisoner 1. con (*slang*), convict, jailbird, old lag (*slang*) **2.** captive, detainee, hostage, internee

privacy 1. isolation, privateness, retirement, retreat, seclusion, separateness, sequestration, solitude **2.** clandestineness, concealment, confidentiality, secrecy

private *adj.* **1.** exclusive, individual, intimate, own, particular, personal, reserved, special **2.** clandestine, closet, confidential, covert, hush-hush (*informal*), in camera, inside, off the record, privy (*archaic*), secret, unofficial **3.** independent, nonpublic **4.** concealed, isolated, not overlooked, retired, secluded, secret, separate, sequestered, solitary, withdrawn ~*n.* **5.** enlisted man (*U.S.*), private soldier, squaddie *or* squaddy (*Brit.*

privilege *n* **1** a benefit or advantage granted only to certain people: *a privilege of rank.* **2** the opportunity to do something which gives you great satisfaction and which most people never have the chance to do: *I had the privilege of meeting the Queen when she visited our school.* **3** the power and advantages that come with great wealth or high social class: *the use of violence to protect class privilege and thwart popular democracy.*

privileged *adj* enjoying a special right or immunity.

privy *adj* **privier, priviest 1 privy to** sharing in the knowledge of something secret. **2** *Archaic* secret. *~n, pl* **privies 3** *Obsolete* a toilet, esp. an outside one.

Privy Council *n* **1** the private council of the British king or queen. **2** (in Canada) a formal body of advisers of the governor general. **Privy Counsellor** *n*

privy purse *n* an allowance voted by Parliament for the private expenses of the king or queen.

privy seal *n* (in Britain) a seal affixed to certain documents of state.

prize[1] *n* **1** something of value, such as a trophy, given to the winner of a contest or game. **2** something given to the winner of any game of chance, lottery, etc. **3** something striven for. *~adj* **4** winning or likely to win a prize: *a prize bull.*

prize[2] *vb* **prizing, prized** to value highly.

prizefight *n* a boxing match for a prize or purse. **prizefighter** *n*

pro[1] *adv* **1** in favour of a motion etc. *~prep* **2** in favour of. *~n, pl* **pros 3** (*usually pl*) an argument or vote in favour of a proposal or motion. ~See also **pros and cons.**

pro[2] *n, pl* **pros,** *adj Informal* **1** short for **professional. 2** a prostitute.

PRO public relations officer.

pro-[1] *prefix* **1** in favour of; supporting: *pro-Chinese.* **2** acting as a substitute for: *pronoun.*

pro-[2] *prefix* before in time or position: *proboscis.*

probability *n, pl* **-ties 1** the condition of being probable. **2** an event or other thing that is likely to happen or be true. **3** *Statistics* a measure of the likelihood of an event happening.

probable *adj* **1** likely to happen or be true. **2** most likely: *the probable cause of the accident. ~n* **3** a person who is likely to be chosen for a team, event, etc.

probably *adv* in all likelihood or probability: *the wedding's probably going to be in late August.*

probate *n* **1** the process of officially proving the validity of a will. **2** the official certificate stating that a will is genuine.

probation *n* **1** a system of dealing with offenders, esp. juvenile ones, by placing them under supervision. **2 on probation a** under the supervision of a probation officer. **b** undergoing a test or trial period, such as at the start of a new job. **probationary** *adj*

probationer *n* a person on probation.

probation officer *n* an officer of a court who supervises offenders placed on probation.

probe *vb* **probing, probed 1** to search into closely. **2** to poke or examine (something) with or as if with a probe: *he probed carefully with his fingertips. ~n* **3** *Surgery* a slender instrument for exploring a wound etc. **4** a thorough inquiry, such as one into corrupt practices. **5** See **space probe.**

probity *n Formal* honesty; integrity.

problem *n* **1** something or someone that is difficult to deal with. **2** a puzzle or question set for solving. **3** *Maths* a statement requiring a solution usually by means of several operations. *~adj* **4** of a literary work that deals with difficult moral questions: *a problem play.* **5** difficult to deal with or creating difficulties for others: *a problem child.*

problematic *or* **problematical** *adj* difficult to solve or deal with.

proboscis (pro-**boss**-iss) *n* **1** a long flexible trunk or snout, such as an elephant's. **2** the elongated mouth part of certain insects.

procedure *n* **1** a way of doing something, esp. an established method. **2** the established form of conducting the business of a legislature. **procedural** *adj*

proceed *vb* **1** to advance or carry on, esp. after stopping. **2** (often foll. by *with*) to start or continue doing: *he proceeded to pour himself a large whisky.* **3** *Formal* to walk or go. **4** (often foll. by *against*) to start a legal action. **5** *Formal* to arise from: *their mutual dislike proceeded from differences of political opinion.*

proceeding *n* **1** an act or course of action. **2** (*pl*) the

THESAURUS

slang), tommy (*Brit. old-fashioned, informal*) **6. in private** behind closed doors, confidentially, in camera, in secret, personally, privately

privilege advantage, benefit, birthright, claim, concession, due, entitlement, franchise, freedom, immunity, liberty, prerogative, right, sanction

privileged advantaged, allowed, elite, empowered, entitled, exempt, favoured, free, granted, honoured, indulged, licensed, powerful, ruling, sanctioned, special, vested

prize[1] *n.* **1.** accolade, award, honour, premium, reward, trophy **2.** haul, jackpot, purse, stakes, windfall, winnings **3.** aim, ambition, conquest, desire, gain, goal, hope *~adj.* **4.** award-winning, best, champion, first-rate, outstanding, top, topnotch (*informal*), winning

prize[2] *vb.* appreciate, cherish, esteem, hold dear, regard highly, set store by, treasure, value

probability chance(s), expectation, liability, likelihood, likeliness, odds, presumption, prospect

probable apparent, credible, feasible, likely, most likely, odds-on, on the cards, ostensible, plausible, possible, presumable, presumed, reasonable, seeming, verisimilar

probably as likely as not, doubtless, in all likelihood, in all probability, likely, maybe, most likely, perchance (*archaic or poetic*), perhaps, possibly, presumably

probation apprenticeship, examination, initiation, novitiate, test, trial, trial period

probe *vb.* **1.** examine, explore, go into, investigate, look into, query, research, scrutinize, search, sift, sound, test, verify, work over **2.** explore, feel around, poke, prod *~n.* **3.** detection, examination, exploration, inquest, inquiry, investigation, research, scrutiny, study

problem *n.* **1.** can of worms (*informal*), complication, difficulty, dilemma, disagreement, dispute, disputed point, doubt, hard nut to crack (*informal*), point at issue, predicament, quandary, trouble **2.** brain-teaser (*informal*), conundrum, enigma, poser, puzzle, question, riddle, teaser *~adj.* **3.** delinquent, difficult, intractable, uncontrollable, unmanageable, unruly

problematic *or* **problematical** chancy (*informal*), debatable, doubtful, dubious, enigmatic, moot, open to doubt, problematical, puzzling, questionable, tricky, uncertain, unsettled

procedure action, conduct, course, custom, form, formula, method, modus operandi, operation, performance, plan of action, policy, practice, process, routine, scheme, step, strategy, system, transaction

proceed 1. advance, carry on, continue, get going, get on with, get under way with, go ahead, go on, make a start, move on, press on, progress, set in mo-

events of an occasion: *millions watched the proceedings on television.* **3** (*pl*) the minutes of the meetings of a society. **4** (*pl*) legal action.

proceeds *pl n* the amount of money obtained from an event or activity.

process[1] *n* **1** a series of actions or changes: *a process of genuine national reconciliation.* **2** a series of natural developments which result in an overall change: *the ageing process.* **3** a method of doing or producing something: *an effort to bring advanced technology and new processes into British industry.* **4 in the process of** during or in the course of. **5 a** a summons to appear in court. **b** an action at law. **6** a natural outgrowth or projection of a part or organism. *~vb* **7** to handle or prepare by a special method of manufacture. **8** *Computers* to perform operations on (data) in order to obtain the required information.

process[2] *vb* to move in an orderly or ceremonial group: *the cult members processed through the streets to the music of tambourines.*

processed *adj* (of food) treated by adding colouring, preservatives, etc., to improve its appearance or the period it will stay edible: *processed cheese.*

procession *n* **1** a line of people or vehicles moving forwards in an orderly or ceremonial manner. **2** the act of proceeding in a regular formation.

processional *adj* **1** of or suitable for a procession: *the processional route.* *~n* **2** *Christianity* a hymn sung as the clergy enter church.

processor *n* **1** *Computers* same as **central processing unit.** **2** a person or thing that carries out a process.

proclaim *vb* **1** to announce publicly; declare: *Greece was proclaimed an independent kingdom in 1832.* **2** to indicate plainly: *the sharp hard glint in the eye proclaimed her determination.* **proclamation** *n*

proclivity *n, pl* **-ties** *Formal* a tendency or inclination.

procrastinate *vb* **-nating, -nated** to put off (an action) until later; delay. **procrastination** *n* **procrastinator** *n*

procreate *vb* **-ating, -ated** *Formal* to produce (offspring). **procreative** *adj* **procreation** *n*

Procrustean *adj* ruthlessly enforcing uniformity.

proctor *n* a member of the staff of certain universities having duties including the enforcement of discipline. **proctorial** *adj*

procurator fiscal *n* (in Scotland) a legal officer who acts as public prosecutor and coroner.

procure *vb* **-curing, -cured 1** to get or provide: *it remained very difficult to procure food and fuel.* **2** to obtain (people) to act as prostitutes. **procurement** *n*

procurer *n* a person who obtains people to act as prostitutes.

prod *vb* **prodding, prodded 1** to poke with a pointed object. **2** to rouse (someone) to action. *~n* **3** the act of prodding. **4** a reminder.

prodigal *adj* **1** recklessly wasteful or extravagant. **2 prodigal of** lavish with: *you are prodigal of both your toil and your talent.* *~n* **3** a person who squanders money. **prodigality** *n*

prodigious *adj* **1** very large or immense. **2** wonderful or amazing.

prodigy *n, pl* **-gies 1** a person, esp. a child, with marvellous talent. **2** anything that is a cause of wonder.

produce *vb* **-ducing, -duced 1** to bring (something) into existence. **2** to present to view: *he produced his passport.* **3** to make: *this area produces much of Spain's best wine.* **4** to give birth to. **5** to present on stage, film, or television: *the girls and boys write and produce their own plays.* **6** to act as producer of. *~n* **7**

THESAURUS

tion **2.** *formal* arise, come, derive, emanate, ensue, flow, follow, issue, originate, result, spring, stem

proceeding 1. act, action, course of action, deed, measure, move, occurrence, procedure, process, step, undertaking, venture **2.** *plural* account, affairs, annals, archives, business, dealings, doings, matters, minutes, records, report, transactions

proceeds earnings, gain, income, produce, products, profit, receipts, returns, revenue, takings, yield

process *n.* **1.** action, course, course of action, manner, means, measure, method, mode, operation, performance, practice, procedure, proceeding, system, transaction **2.** advance, course, development, evolution, formation, growth, movement, progress, progression, stage, step, unfolding **3.** action, case, suit, trial *~vb.* **4.** deal with, dispose of, fulfil, handle, take care of **5.** alter, convert, prepare, refine, transform, treat

procession cavalcade, column, cortege, file, march, motorcade, parade, train

proclaim advertise, affirm, announce, blaze (abroad), blazon (abroad), circulate, declare, enunciate, give out, herald, indicate, make known, profess, promulgate, publish, shout *or* proclaim from the housetops (*informal*), show, trumpet

proclamation announcement, declaration, decree, edict, manifesto, notice, notification, promulgation, pronouncement, pronunciamento, publication

procrastinate adjourn, be dilatory, dally, defer, delay, drag one's feet (*informal*), gain time, play a waiting game, play for time, postpone, prolong, protract, put off, retard, stall, temporize

procure acquire, appropriate, buy, come by, earn, effect, find, gain, get, get hold of, lay hands on, manage to get, obtain, pick up, purchase, secure, win

prod *vb.* **1.** dig, drive, elbow, jab, nudge, poke, prick, propel, push, shove **2.** egg on, goad, impel, incite, motivate, move, prompt, rouse, spur, stimulate, stir up, urge *~n.* **3.** boost, dig, elbow, jab, nudge, poke, push, shove **4.** boost, cue, prompt, reminder, signal, stimulus

prodigal *adj.* **1.** excessive, extravagant, immoderate, improvident, intemperate, profligate, reckless, spendthrift, squandering, wanton, wasteful *~n.* **2.** big spender, profligate, spendthrift, squanderer, wastrel

prodigality abandon, dissipation, excess, extravagance, immoderation, intemperance, profligacy, recklessness, squandering, wantonness, waste, wastefulness

prodigious 1. colossal, enormous, giant, gigantic, huge, immeasurable, immense, inordinate, mammoth, massive, monstrous, monumental, stupendous, tremendous, vast **2.** abnormal, amazing, astounding, exceptional, extraordinary, fabulous, fantastic (*informal*), flabbergasting (*informal*), impressive, marvellous, miraculous, phenomenal, remarkable, staggering, startling, striking, stupendous, unusual, wonderful

prodigy 1. brainbox, child genius, genius, mastermind, talent, whiz (*informal*), whiz kid (*informal*), wizard, wonder child **2.** marvel, miracle, one in a million, phenomenon, rare bird (*informal*), sensation, wonder

produce *vb.* **1.** beget, breed, bring about, cause, effect, engender, generate, give rise to, make for, occasion, provoke, set off **2.** advance, bring forward, bring to light, demonstrate, exhibit, offer, present, put forward, set forth, show **3.** compose, construct, create, develop, fabricate, invent, make, manufacture, origi-

food grown for sale: *farm produce.* **8** something produced. **producible** *adj*

producer *n* **1** a person with the financial and administrative responsibility for a film or television programme. **2** *Brit* a person responsible for the artistic direction of a play. **3** a person who supervises the arrangement, performance, and mixing of a recording. **4** a person or thing that produces.

product *n* **1** something produced. **2** a consequence: *their skill was the product of hours of training.* **3** *Maths* the result achieved by multiplication.

production *n* **1** the act of producing. **2** anything that is produced. **3** the amount produced or the rate at which it is produced. **4** *Econ* the creation or manufacture of goods and services. **5** any work created as a result of literary or artistic effort. **6** the presentation of a play, opera, etc. **7** *Brit* the artistic direction of a play. **8** the overall sound of a recording.

production line *n* a system in a factory in which an item being manufactured is moved from machine to machine by conveyor belt, and each machine carries out one step in the manufacture of the item.

productive *adj* **1** producing or having the power to produce. **2** yielding favourable results. **3** *Econ* producing goods and services that have exchange value: *the country's productive capacity.* **4** (foll. by *of*) resulting in: *a period highly productive of books and ideas.* **productivity** *n*

proem (**pro**-em) *n Formal* an introduction or preface.

Prof. Professor.

profane *adj* **1** showing disrespect for religion or something sacred. **2** secular. **3** coarse or blasphemous: *profane language.* ~*vb* **-faning, -faned 4** to treat (something sacred) with irreverence. **5** to put to an unworthy use. **profanation** *n*

profanity *n, pl* **-ties 1** the quality of being profane. **2** coarse or blasphemous action or speech.

profess *vb* **1** to claim (something as true), often falsely: *he professes not to want the job of prime minister.* **2** to acknowledge openly: *he professed great relief at getting some rest.* **3** to have as one's belief or religion: *most Indonesians profess the Islamic faith.* **professed** *adj*

profession *n* **1** a type of work that requires special training, such as in law or medicine. **2** the people employed in such an occupation. **3** a declaration of a belief or feeling.

professional *adj* **1** of a profession. **2** taking part in an activity, such as sport or music, as a means of livelihood. **3** displaying a high level of competence or skill: *a professional and polished performance.* **4** undertaken or performed by people who are paid: *professional golf.* ~*n* **5** a professional person. **professionalism** *n* **professionally** *adv*

professor *n* **1** the highest rank of teacher in a university. **2** *Chiefly US & Canad* any teacher in a university or college. **3** *Rare* a person who professes his or her opinions or beliefs. **professorial** *adj* **professorship** *n*

proffer *vb Formal* to offer for acceptance.

proficient *adj* skilled; expert. **proficiency** *n*

profile *n* **1** an outline, esp. of the human face, as seen from the side. **2** a short biographical sketch.

profit *n* **1** (*often pl*) money gained in business or trade. **2** a benefit or advantage. ~*vb* **-iting, -ited 3** to

THESAURUS

nate, put together, turn out **4.** bear, bring forth, deliver **5.** direct, do, exhibit, mount, present, put before the public, put on, show, stage ~*n.* **6.** crop, fruit and vegetables, greengrocery, harvest, product, yield

producer 1. director, impresario **2.** farmer, grower, maker, manufacturer

product 1. artefact, commodity, concoction, creation, goods, invention, merchandise, produce, production, work **2.** consequence, effect, fruit, issue, legacy, offshoot, outcome, result, returns, spin-off, upshot, yield

production 1. assembly, construction, creation, fabrication, formation, making, manufacture, manufacturing, origination, preparation, producing **2.** direction, management, presentation, staging

productive 1. creative, dynamic, energetic, fecund, fertile, fruitful, generative, inventive, plentiful, producing, prolific, rich, teeming, vigorous **2.** advantageous, beneficial, constructive, effective, fruitful, gainful, gratifying, profitable, rewarding, useful, valuable, worthwhile

productivity abundance, mass production, output, production, productive capacity, productiveness, work rate, yield

profane *adj.* **1.** disrespectful, godless, heathen, idolatrous, impious, impure, irreligious, irreverent, pagan, sacrilegious, sinful, ungodly, wicked **2.** lay, secular, temporal, unconsecrated, unhallowed, unholy, unsanctified, worldly **3.** abusive, blasphemous, coarse, crude, filthy, foul, obscene, vulgar ~*vb.* **4.** abuse, commit sacrilege, contaminate, debase, defile, desecrate, misuse, pervert, pollute, prostitute, violate, vitiate

profanity abuse, blasphemy, curse, cursing, execration, foul language, four-letter word, impiety, imprecation, irreverence, malediction, obscenity, profaneness, sacrilege, swearing, swearword

profess acknowledge, admit, affirm, announce, assert, asseverate, aver, avow, certify, confess, confirm, declare, maintain, own, proclaim, state, vouch

professed 1. alleged, apparent, ostensible, pretended, purported, self-styled, so-called, *soi-disant,* supposed, would-be **2.** avowed, certified, confirmed, declared, proclaimed, self-acknowledged, self-confessed

profession 1. business, calling, career, employment, line, line of work, métier, occupation, office, position, sphere, vocation, walk of life **2.** acknowledgment, affirmation, assertion, attestation, avowal, claim, confession, declaration, statement, testimony, vow

professional 1. *adj.* ace (*informal*), adept, competent, crack (*slang*), efficient, experienced, expert, finished, masterly, polished, practised, proficient, qualified, skilled, slick, trained **2.** *n.* adept, authority, buff (*informal*), dab hand (*Brit. informal*), expert, hotshot (*informal*), maestro, master, past master, pro (*informal*), specialist, virtuoso, whizz (*informal*), wizard

professor don (*Brit.*), fellow (*Brit.*), head of faculty, prof (*informal*)

proficiency ability, accomplishment, aptitude, competence, craft, dexterity, expertise, expertness, facility, knack, know-how (*informal*), mastery, skilfulness, skill, talent

proficient able, accomplished, adept, apt, capable, clever, competent, conversant, efficient, experienced, expert, gifted, masterly, qualified, skilful, skilled, talented, trained, versed

profile *n.* **1.** contour, drawing, figure, form, outline, portrait, shape, side view, silhouette, sketch **2.** biography, characterization, character sketch, sketch, thumbnail sketch, vignette

profit *n.* **1.** *often plural* bottom line, earnings, emoluments, gain, percentage (*informal*), proceeds, receipts, return, revenue, surplus, takings, winnings, yield **2.** advancement, advantage, avail, benefit, gain, good, interest, use, value ~*vb.* **3.** capitalize on, cash in on (*informal*), clean up (*informal*), earn, exploit, gain, learn

gain a profit or advantage: *we do not want to profit from someone else's problems.*

profitable *adj* making profit. **profitability** *n* **profitably** *adv*

profit and loss *n Book-keeping* an account showing the year's income and expense items and indicating gross and net profit or loss.

profiteer *n* **1** a person who makes excessive profits at the expense of the public. *~vb* **2** to make excessive profits. **profiteering** *n*

profit-sharing *n* a system in which a portion of the net profit of a business is shared among its employees.

profligate *adj* **1** recklessly extravagant. **2** shamelessly immoral. *~n* **3** a profligate person. **profligacy** *n*

pro forma *adj* **1** laying down a set form. *~adv* **2** performed in a set manner.

profound *adj* **1** showing or needing great knowledge: *a profound knowledge of Greek literature.* **2** strongly felt; intense: *profound relief.* **3** extensive: *profound changes.* **4** situated at or having a great depth. **profoundly** *adv* **profundity** *n*

profuse *adj* **1** plentiful or abundant: *he broke out in a profuse sweat.* **2** (often foll. by *in*) generous in the giving (of): *he was profuse in his apologies.* **profusely** *adv* **profusion** *n*

progenitor (pro-**jen**-it-er) *n* **1** a direct ancestor. **2** an originator or founder.

progeny (**proj**-in-ee) *n, pl* **-nies** **1** offspring; descendants. **2** an outcome.

progesterone *n* a hormone, produced in the ovary, that prepares the womb for pregnancy and prevents further ovulation.

prognathous *adj* having a projecting lower jaw.

prognosis *n, pl* **-noses** **1** *Med* a forecast about the course or outcome of an illness. **2** any forecast.

prognosticate *vb* **-cating, -cated** **1** to foretell (future events). **2** to indicate or suggest beforehand. **prognostication** *n* **prognosticator** *n*

program *n* **1** a sequence of coded instructions which enables a computer to perform various tasks. *~vb* **-gramming, -grammed** **2** to arrange (data) so that it can be processed by a computer. **3** to feed a program into (a computer). **programmer** *n*

programmable *or* **programable** *adj* capable of being programmed for computer processing.

programme *or US* **program** *n* **1** a planned series of events. **2** a broadcast on radio or television. **3** a printed list of items or performers in an entertainment. *~vb* **-gramming, -grammed** *or US* **-graming, -gramed** **4** to schedule (something) as a programme. **programmatic** *adj*

programming language *n* a language system by which instructions to a computer are coded, that is understood by both user and computer.

progress *n* **1** improvement or development. **2** movement forward or advance. **3 in progress** taking place. *~vb* **4** to become more advanced or skilful. **5** to move forward.

progression *n* **1** the act of progressing; advancement. **2** the act or an instance of moving from one thing in a sequence to the next. **3** *Maths* a sequence of numbers in which each term differs from the succeeding term by a fixed ratio.

progressive *adj* **1** favouring political or social reform. **2** happening gradually: *a progressive illness.* **3**

THESAURUS

from, make a killing (*informal*), make capital of, make good use of, make money, make the most of, put to good use, rake in (*informal*), reap the benefit of, take advantage of, turn to advantage *or* account, use, utilize

profitable **1.** commercial, cost-effective, fruitful, gainful, lucrative, money-making, paying, remunerative, rewarding, worthwhile **2.** advantageous, beneficial, economic, expedient, fruitful, productive, rewarding, serviceable, useful, valuable, worthwhile

profiteer **1.** *n.* exploiter, racketeer **2.** *vb.* exploit, fleece, make someone pay through the nose, overcharge, racketeer, skin (*slang*), sting (*informal*)

profligate *adj.* **1.** extravagant, immoderate, improvident, prodigal, reckless, spendthrift, squandering, wasteful **2.** abandoned, corrupt, debauched, degenerate, depraved, dissipated, dissolute, immoral, iniquitous, libertine, licentious, loose, promiscuous, shameless, unprincipled, vicious, vitiated, wanton, wicked, wild *~n.* **3.** prodigal, spendthrift, squanderer, waster, wastrel **4.** debauchee, degenerate, dissipater, libertine, rake, reprobate, roué

profound **1.** abstruse, deep, discerning, erudite, learned, penetrating, philosophical, recondite, sagacious, sage, serious, skilled, subtle, thoughtful, weighty, wise **2.** abject, acute, deeply felt, extreme, great, heartfelt, heartrending, hearty, intense, keen, sincere **3.** absolute, complete, consummate, exhaustive, extensive, extreme, far-reaching, intense, out-and-out, pronounced, thoroughgoing, total, unqualified, utter **4.** abysmal, bottomless, cavernous, deep, fathomless, yawning

profoundly abjectly, acutely, deeply, extremely, from the bottom of one's heart, greatly, heartily, intensely, keenly, seriously, sincerely, thoroughly, very

profuse **1.** abundant, ample, bountiful, copious, luxuriant, overflowing, plentiful, prolific, teeming **2.** *often with* **in** excessive, extravagant, exuberant, fulsome, generous, immoderate, lavish, liberal, open-handed, prodigal, unstinting

profusion abundance, bounty, copiousness, cornucopia, excess, extravagance, exuberance, glut, lavishness, luxuriance, multitude, oversupply, plenitude, plethora, prodigality, quantity, riot, superabundance, superfluity, surplus, wealth

progeny breed, children, descendants, family, issue, lineage, offspring, posterity, race, scions, seed (*chiefly Bible*), stock, young

programme *or U.S.* **program** *n.* **1.** design, order of the day, plan, plan of action, procedure, project, scheme **2.** broadcast, performance, presentation, production, show **3.** agenda, curriculum, line-up, list, listing, list of players, order of events, order of the day, plan, schedule, syllabus, timetable *~vb.* **4.** arrange, bill, book, design, engage, formulate, itemize, lay on, line up, list, map out, plan, prearrange, schedule, work out

progress *n.* **1.** advance, advancement, amelioration, betterment, breakthrough, development, gain, gaining ground, growth, headway, improvement, increase, progression, promotion, step forward **2.** advance, course, movement, onward course, passage, progression, way **3. in progress** being done, going on, happening, occurring, proceeding, taking place, under way *~vb.* **4.** advance, ameliorate, better, blossom, develop, gain, grow, improve, increase, mature **5.** advance, come on, continue, cover ground, forge ahead, gain ground, gather way, get on, go forward, make headway, make one's way, make strides, move on, proceed, travel

progression **1.** advance, advancement, furtherance, gain, headway, movement forward, progress **2.** chain, course, cycle, order, sequence, series, string, succession

progressive **1.** advanced, avant-garde, dynamic, enlightened, enterprising, forward-looking, go-ahead, lib-

(of a dance, card game, etc.) involving a regular change of partners. *~n* **4** a person who favours political or social reform. **progressively** *adv*

prohibit *vb* **-iting, -ited 1** to forbid by law or other authority. **2** to hinder or prevent: *the paucity of information prohibits us from drawing reliable conclusions.* **prohibitor** *n*

➤ The idiom is *prohibit* someone *from* doing something.

prohibition *n* **1** the act of forbidding. **2** a legal ban on the sale or drinking of alcohol. **3** an order or decree that forbids. **prohibitionist** *n*

Prohibition *n* the period (1920–33) when making, selling, and transporting alcohol was banned in the US. **Prohibitionist** *n*

prohibitive *adj* **1** (esp. of prices) too high to be affordable. **2** prohibiting or tending to prohibit: *a prohibitive distance.*

project *n* **1** a proposal or plan. **2** a detailed study of a particular subject. *~vb* **3** to make a prediction based on known data and observations. **4** to cause (an image) to appear on a surface. **5** to communicate (an impression): *he wants to project an image of a deep-thinking articulate gentleman.* **6** to jut out. **7** to cause (one's voice) to be heard clearly at a distance. **8** to transport in the imagination: *it's hard to project oneself into his situation.*

projectile *n* **1** an object thrown as a weapon or fired from a gun. *~adj* **2** designed to be thrown forwards. **3** projecting forwards.

projection *n* **1** a part that juts out. **2** a forecast based on known data. **3** the process of showing film on a screen. **4** the representation on a flat surface of a three-dimensional figure or curved line.

projectionist *n* a person who operates a film projector.

projector *n* an apparatus for projecting photographic images, film, or slides onto a screen.

prolapse *Pathol ~n* **1** Also: **prolapsus** the slipping down of an internal organ of the body from its normal position. *~vb* **-lapsing, -lapsed 2** (of an internal organ) to slip from its normal position.

prolapsed *adj Pathol* (of an internal organ) having slipped from its normal position.

prolate *adj Geom* having a polar diameter which is longer than the equatorial diameter.

prole *n Offensive slang, chiefly Brit* a proletarian.

proletarian (pro-lit-**air**-ee-an) *adj* **1** of the proletariat. *~n* **2** a member of the proletariat.

proletariat (pro-lit-**air**-ee-at) *n* the working class.

proliferate *vb* **-ating, -ated 1** to increase rapidly in numbers. **2** to grow or reproduce (new parts, such as cells) rapidly. **proliferation** *n*

prolific *adj* **1** producing a constant creative output: *a prolific author.* **2** producing fruit or offspring in abundance. **3** (often foll. by *in* or *of*) rich or fruitful. **prolifically** *adv*

prolix *adj* (of a speech or piece of writing) overlong and boring. **prolixity** *n*

prologue *or US often* **prolog** *n* **1** an introduction to a play or book. **2** an event that comes before another: *this success was a happy prologue to their transatlantic tour.*

prolong *vb* to make (something) last longer. **prolongation** *n*

prom *n* **1** *Brit* short for **promenade** (sense 1). or **promenade concert. 2** *US & Canad informal* a formal dance held at a high school or college.

PROM *n Computers* Programmable Read Only Memory.

promenade *n* **1** *Chiefly Brit* a paved walkway along the seafront at a holiday resort. **2** *Old-fashioned* a leisurely walk for pleasure or display. *~vb* **-nading, -naded 3** *Old-fashioned* to take a leisurely walk.

promenade concert *n* a concert at which some of the audience stand rather than sit.

promethium (pro-**meeth**-ee-um) *n Chem* an artificial radioactive element of the lanthanide series. Symbol: Pm

prominent *adj* **1** standing out from the surroundings;

THESAURUS

eral, modern, radical, reformist, revolutionary, up-and-coming **2.** accelerating, advancing, continuing, continuous, developing, escalating, growing, increasing, intensifying, ongoing

prohibit 1. ban, debar, disallow, forbid, interdict, outlaw, proscribe, veto **2.** constrain, hamper, hinder, impede, make impossible, obstruct, preclude, prevent, restrict, rule out, stop

prohibition 1. constraint, exclusion, forbiddance, interdiction, negation, obstruction, prevention, restriction **2.** ban, bar, boycott, disallowance, embargo, injunction, interdict, proscription, veto

prohibitive 1. beyond one's means, excessive, exorbitant, extortionate, high-priced, preposterous, sky-high, steep (*informal*) **2.** forbidding, prohibiting, proscriptive, repressive, restraining, restrictive, suppressive

project *n.* **1.** activity, assignment, design, enterprise, job, occupation, plan, programme, proposal, scheme, task, undertaking, venture, work *~vb.* **2.** calculate, estimate, extrapolate, forecast, gauge, predetermine, predict, reckon **3.** beetle, bulge, extend, jut, overhang, protrude, stand out, stick out

projectile bullet, missile, rocket, shell

projection 1. bulge, eaves, jut, ledge, overhang, protrusion, protuberance, ridge, shelf, sill **2.** calculation, computation, estimate, estimation, extrapolation, forecast, prediction, reckoning **3.** blueprint, diagram, map, outline, plan, representation

proletarian 1. *adj.* cloth-cap (*informal*), common, plebeian, working-class **2.** *n.* commoner, man of the people, pleb (*Brit. informal, often offensive*), plebeian, prole (*offensive slang, chiefly Brit.*), worker

proletariat commonalty, commoners, hoi polloi, labouring classes, lower classes, lower orders, plebs (*Brit. informal, often offensive*), proles (*offensive slang, chiefly Brit.*), the common people, the herd, the masses, the rabble (*contemptuous*), wage-earners, working class

prolific abundant, bountiful, copious, fecund, fertile, fruitful, generative, luxuriant, productive, profuse, rank, rich, teeming

prologue *or U.S. often* **prolog** foreword, introduction, preamble, preface, preliminary, prelude, proem

prolong carry on, continue, delay, drag out, draw out, extend, lengthen, make longer, perpetuate, protract, spin out, stretch

promenade *n.* **1.** *chiefly Brit.* boulevard, esplanade, parade, prom, public walk, walkway **2.** *old-fashioned* airing, constitutional, saunter, stroll, turn, walk *~vb.* **3.** *old-fashioned* perambulate, saunter, stretch one's legs, stroll, take a walk, walk

prominence 1. conspicuousness, markedness, outstandingness, precedence, salience, specialness, top billing, weight **2.** celebrity, distinction, eminence, fame, greatness, importance, name, notability, pre-eminence, prestige, rank, reputation, standing **3.** bulge, jutting, projection, protrusion, protuberance, swelling

prominent 1. blatant, conspicuous, easily seen, eye-

noticeable. **2** widely known; famous. **3** jutting or projecting outwards: *prominent eyes.* **prominence** *n* **prominently** *adv*

promiscuous *adj* **1** taking part in many casual sexual relationships. **2** *Formal* consisting of different elements mingled indiscriminately. **promiscuity** *n*

promise *vb* **-ising, -ised 1** to say that one will definitely do or not do something: *I promise I'll have it finished by the end of the week.* **2** to undertake to give (something to someone): *he promised me a car for my birthday.* **3** to show signs of; seem likely: *she promises to be a fine singer.* **4** to assure (someone) of the certainty of something: *everything's fine, I promise you.* ~*n* **5** an undertaking to do or not do something. **6** indication of future success: *a young player who shows great promise.*

Promised Land *n* **1** *Bible* the land of Canaan. **2** any longed-for place where one expects to find greater happiness.

promising *adj* likely to succeed or turn out well.

promissory note *n Commerce chiefly US* a written promise to pay a stated sum of money to a particular person on a certain date or on demand.

promo *n, pl* **-mos** *Informal* an item produced to promote a product, esp. a video used to promote a pop record.

promontory *n, pl* **-ries** a point of high land that juts out into the sea.

promote *vb* **-moting, -moted 1** to encourage the progress or success of: *all attempts to promote a lasting ceasefire have failed.* **2** to raise to a higher rank or position. **3** to encourage the sale of (a product) by advertising. **4** to work for: *he actively promoted reform.* **promotion** *n* **promotional** *adj*

promoter *n* **1** a person who helps to organize and finance an event, esp. a sports one. **2** a person or thing that encourages the progress or success of: *a promoter of terrorism.*

prompt *vb* **1** to cause (an action); bring about: *the killings prompted an anti-Mafia crackdown.* **2** to motivate or cause someone to do something: *I still don't know what prompted me to go.* **3** to remind (an actor) of lines forgotten during a performance. **4** to refresh the memory of. ~*adj* **5** done without delay. **6** quick to act. ~*adv* **7** *Informal* punctually: *the concert starts at 8 o'clock prompt.* ~*n* **8** anything that serves to remind. **promptly** *adv* **promptness** *n*

prompter *n* a person offstage who reminds the actors of forgotten lines.

promulgate *vb* **-gating, -gated 1** to put (a law or decree) into effect by announcing it officially. **2** to make widely known. **promulgation** *n* **promulgator** *n*

pron. **1** pronoun. **2** pronunciation.

prone *adj* **1** having a tendency to be affected by or do something: *I am prone to indigestion.* **2** lying face downwards; prostrate.

prong *n* a long pointed projection from an instrument or tool such as a fork.

pronominal *adj Grammar* relating to or playing the part of a pronoun.

pronoun *n* a word, such as *she* or *it*, that replaces a noun or noun phrase that has already been or is about to be mentioned.

pronounce *vb* **-nouncing, -nounced 1** to speak (a sound or sounds), esp. clearly or in a certain way. **2** to announce or declare officially: *I now pronounce you man and wife.* **3** to declare as one's judgment: *he pro-*

THESAURUS

catching, in the foreground, noticeable, obtrusive, obvious, outstanding, pronounced, remarkable, salient, striking, to the fore, unmistakable **2.** big-time (*informal*), celebrated, chief, distinguished, eminent, famous, foremost, important, leading, main, major league (*informal*), notable, noted, outstanding, popular, pre-eminent, renowned, respected, top, well-known, well-thought-of **3.** bulging, hanging over, jutting, projecting, protruding, protrusive, protuberant, standing out

promiscuous **1.** abandoned, debauched, dissipated, dissolute, fast, immoral, lax, libertine, licentious, loose, of easy virtue, profligate, unbridled, unchaste, wanton, wild **2.** *formal* chaotic, confused, disordered, diverse, heterogeneous, ill-assorted, indiscriminate, intermingled, intermixed, jumbled, mingled, miscellaneous, mixed, motley

promise *vb.* **1.** assure, contract, cross one's heart, engage, give an undertaking, give one's word, guarantee, pledge, plight, stipulate, swear, take an oath, undertake, vouch, vow, warrant **2.** augur, bespeak, betoken, bid fair, denote, give hope of, hint at, hold a probability, hold out hopes of, indicate, lead one to expect, look like, seem likely to, show signs of, suggest ~*n.* **3.** assurance, bond, commitment, compact, covenant, engagement, guarantee, oath, pledge, undertaking, vow, word, word of honour **4.** ability, aptitude, capability, capacity, flair, potential, talent

promising **1.** able, gifted, likely, rising, talented, up-and-coming **2.** auspicious, bright, encouraging, favourable, full of promise, hopeful, likely, propitious, reassuring, rosy

promote **1.** advance, aid, assist, back, boost, contribute to, develop, encourage, forward, foster, further, help, nurture, stimulate, support **2.** aggrandize, dignify, elevate, exalt, honour, kick upstairs (*informal*), prefer, raise, upgrade **3.** advertise, beat the drum for (*informal*), hype, plug (*informal*), publicize, puff, push, sell **4.** advocate, call attention to, champion, endorse, espouse, popularize, prescribe, push for, recommend, speak for, sponsor, support, urge, work for

promotion **1.** advancement, advocacy, backing, boosting, cultivation, development, encouragement, espousal, furtherance, progress, support **2.** advancement, aggrandizement, elevation, ennoblement, exaltation, honour, move up, preferment, rise, upgrading **3.** advertising, advertising campaign, ballyhoo (*informal*), hard sell, hype, media hype, plugging (*informal*), propaganda, publicity, puffery (*informal*), pushing

prompt *vb.* **1.** call forth, cause, elicit, evoke, give rise to, occasion, provoke **2.** cause, impel, incite, induce, inspire, instigate, motivate, move, provoke, spur, stimulate, urge **3.** assist, cue, help out, jog the memory, prod, refresh the memory, remind ~*adj.* **4.** early, immediate, instant, instantaneous, on time, punctual, quick, rapid, speedy, swift, timely, unhesitating **5.** alert, brisk, eager, efficient, expeditious, quick, ready, responsive, smart, willing ~*adv.* **6.** *informal* exactly, on the dot, promptly, punctually, sharp ~*n.* **7.** cue, help, hint, jog, jolt, prod, reminder, spur, stimulus

promptly at once, by return, directly, hotfoot, immediately, instantly, on the dot, on time, posthaste, pronto (*informal*), punctually, quickly, speedily, swiftly, unhesitatingly

promptness alacrity, alertness, briskness, dispatch, eagerness, haste, promptitude, punctuality, quickness, readiness, speed, swiftness, willingness

promulgate advertise, announce, broadcast, circulate, communicate, declare, decree, disseminate, issue, make known, make public, notify, proclaim, promote, publish, spread

prone **1.** apt, bent, disposed, given, inclined, liable, likely, predisposed, subject, susceptible, tending **2.**

nounced the wine drinkable. **pronounceable** *adj*
➤ Note the difference in spelling between *pronounce* and *pronunciation.* The pronunciation also changes from "nown" to "nun".

pronounced *adj* very noticeable: *a pronounced London accent.*

pronouncement *n* a formal announcement.

pronto *adv Informal* at once.

pronunciation *n* **1** the recognized way to pronounce sounds in a given language. **2** the way in which someone pronounces words.
➤ Note the difference in spelling between *pronounce* and *pronunciation.* The pronunciation also changes from "nown" to "nun".

proof *n* **1** any evidence that confirms that something is true or exists. **2** *Law* the total evidence upon which a court bases its verdict. **3** *Maths, logic* a sequence of steps or statements that establishes the truth of a proposition. **4** the act of testing the truth of something. **5** an early copy of printed matter for checking before final production. **6** *Photog* a trial print from a negative. **7** (esp. formerly) a defined level of alcoholic content used as a standard measure for comparing the alcoholic strength of other liquids: *Moldavian ruby port, seventeen degrees proof.* ~*adj* **8** (foll. by *against*) able to withstand: *proof against tears.* **9** (esp. formerly) having a level of alcoholic content used as a standard measure for comparing the alcoholic strength of other liquids. ~*vb* **10** to take a proof from (type matter). **11** to render (something) proof, esp. to waterproof.

proofread *vb* **-reading, -read** to read and correct (printer's proofs). **proofreader** *n*

proof spirit *n* (in Britain) an alcoholic beverage that contains a standard percentage of alcohol.

prop[1] *vb* **propping, propped** (often foll. by *up*) **1** to support (something or someone) in an upright position: *she was propped up by pillows.* **2** to sustain or support: *the type of measures necessary to prop up the sagging US economy.* **3** (often foll. by *against*) to place or lean. ~*n* **4** something that gives rigid support, such as a pole. **5** a person or thing giving moral support.

prop[2] *n* a movable object used on the set of a film or play.

prop[3] *n Informal* a propeller.

prop. **1** proper(ly). **2** property. **3** proposition. **4** proprietor.

propaganda *n* **1** the organized promotion of information to assist or damage the cause of a government or movement. **2** such information. **propagandist** *n, adj*

propagate *vb* **-gating, -gated** **1** to spread (information or ideas). **2** *Biol* to reproduce or breed. **3** *Horticulture* to produce (plants). **4** *Physics* to transmit, esp. in the form of a wave: *the electrical signal is propagated through a specialized group of conducting fibres.* **propagation** *n* **propagator** *n*

propane *n* a flammable gas found in petroleum and used as a fuel.

propel *vb* **-pelling, -pelled** to cause to move forwards. **propellant** *n, adj*

propeller *n* a revolving shaft with blades to drive a ship or aircraft.

propensity *n, pl* **-ties** *Formal* a natural tendency: *his problem had always been a propensity to live beyond his means.*

proper *adj* **1** real or genuine: *a proper home.* **2** appropriate or usual: *good wine must have the proper balance of sugar and acid.* **3** suited to a particular purpose: *they set out without any proper climbing gear.* **4** correct in behaviour: *in many societies it is not considered proper for a woman to show her legs.* **5** excessively moral: *she was very strait-laced and proper.* **6** being or forming the main or central part of something: *a suburb some miles west of the city proper.* **7** *Brit informal* complete: *you made him look a proper fool.* **properly** *adv*

proper fraction *n* a fraction in which the numerator has a lower absolute value than the denominator, for example $\frac{1}{2}$.

proper noun *or* **name** *n* the name of a person or place, for example *Iceland* or *Patrick.*

property *n, pl* **-ties** **1** something owned. **2** *Law* the right to possess, use, and dispose of anything. **3** pos-

THESAURUS

face down, flat, horizontal, lying down, procumbent, prostrate, recumbent, supine

prong point, projection, spike, tine, tip

pronounce **1.** accent, articulate, enunciate, say, sound, speak, stress, utter, vocalize, voice **2.** affirm, announce, assert, declare, decree, deliver, judge, proclaim

pronounced broad, clear, conspicuous, decided, definite, distinct, evident, marked, noticeable, obvious, striking, strong, unmistakable

pronouncement announcement, declaration, decree, dictum, edict, judgment, manifesto, notification, proclamation, promulgation, pronunciamento, statement

pronunciation accent, accentuation, articulation, diction, elocution, enunciation, inflection, intonation, speech, stress

proof *n.* **1.** attestation, authentication, certification, confirmation, corroboration, demonstration, evidence, substantiation, testimony, verification **2.** page proof, pull (*Printing*), trial impression, trial print

prop *vb.* **1.** *often with* **up** bolster, brace, buttress, hold up, maintain, shore, stay, support, sustain, truss, uphold **2.** *often with* **against** lean, rest, set, stand ~*n.* **3.** brace, buttress, mainstay, stanchion, stay, support, truss

propaganda advertising, agitprop, ballyhoo (*informal*), brainwashing, disinformation, hype, information, newspeak, promotion, publicity

propagate **1.** broadcast, circulate, diffuse, disseminate, make known, proclaim, promote, promulgate, publicize, publish, spread, transmit **2.** *Biol.* beget, breed, engender, generate, increase, multiply, procreate, produce, proliferate, reproduce

propagation **1.** circulation, communication, diffusion, dissemination, distribution, promotion, promulgation, spread, spreading, transmission **2.** breeding, generation, increase, multiplication, procreation, proliferation, reproduction

propel drive, force, impel, launch, push, send, set in motion, shoot, shove, start, thrust

propensity *formal* aptness, bent, bias, disposition, inclination, leaning, liability, penchant, predisposition, proclivity, proneness, susceptibility, tendency, weakness

proper **1.** appropriate, apt, becoming, befitting, fit, fitting, legitimate, meet (*archaic*), right, suitable, suited **2.** accepted, conventional, correct, decent, decorous, de rigueur, established, formal, genteel, gentlemanly, kosher, ladylike (*informal*), mannerly, orthodox, polite, punctilious, refined, respectable, right, seemly

property **1.** assets, belongings, building(s), capital, chattels, effects, estate, goods, holdings, house(s), means, possessions, resources, riches, wealth **2.** acres,

sessions collectively. **4** land or buildings owned by someone. **5** a quality or attribute: *the oils have healing properties.* **6** same as **prop**[2].

prophecy *n, pl* **-cies 1** a prediction. **2 a** a message revealing God's will. **b** the act of uttering such a message. **3** the function or activity of a prophet.

➤ Note the difference in spelling between the noun (*prophecy*) and the verb (*prophesy*).

prophesy *vb* **-sies, -sying, -sied** to foretell.

prophet *n* **1** a person supposedly chosen by God to pass on His message. **2** a person who predicts the future: *a prophet of doom.* **3** a spokesman for, or advocate of, some cause: *a prophet of revolution.* **prophetess** *fem n*

Prophet *n* **the** the main name used of Mohammed, the founder of Islam.

prophetic *adj* **1** foretelling what will happen. **2** of the nature of a prophecy. **prophetically** *adv*

prophylactic *adj* **1** preventing disease. *~n* **2** a drug or device that prevents disease. **3** *Chiefly US* a condom.

propinquity *n Formal* nearness in time, place, or relationship.

propitiate *vb* **-ating, -ated** to appease (someone, esp. a god or spirit); make well disposed. **propitiable** *adj* **propitiation** *n* **propitiator** *n* **propitiatory** *adj*

propitious *adj* **1** favourable or auspicious: *a propitious moment.* **2** likely to prove favourable; advantageous: *his origins were not propitious for a literary career.*

proponent *n* a person who argues in favour of something.

proportion *n* **1** relative size or extent: *a large proportion of our revenue comes from advertisements.* **2** correct relationship between parts. **3** a part considered with respect to the whole: *the proportion of women in the total workforce.* **4 proportions** dimensions or size: *a building of vast proportions.* **5** *Maths* a relationship between four numbers in which the ratio of the first pair equals the ratio of the second pair. **6 in proportion a** comparable in size, rate of increase, etc. **b** without exaggerating. *~vb* **7** to adjust in relative amount or size: *the size of the crops are very rarely proportioned to the wants of the inhabitants.* **8** to cause to be harmonious in relationship of parts.

proportional *adj* **1** being in proportion. *~n* **2** *Maths* an unknown term in a proportion, for example in *a/b = c/x, x is the fourth proportional.* **proportionally** *adv*

proportional representation *n* the representation of political parties in parliament in proportion to the votes they win.

proportionate *adj* being in proper proportion. **proportionately** *adv*

proposal *n* **1** the act of proposing. **2** a suggestion put forward for consideration. **3** an offer of marriage.

propose *vb* **-posing, -posed 1** to put forward (a plan) for consideration. **2** to nominate (someone) for a position. **3** to intend (to do something): *I don't propose to waste any more time discussing it.* **4** to ask people to drink a toast. **5** (often foll. by *to*) to make an offer of marriage.

proposition *n* **1** a proposal or offer. **2** *Logic* a statement that affirms or denies something and is capable of being true or false. **3** *Maths* a statement or theorem, usually containing its proof. **4** *Informal* a person or matter to be dealt with: *even among experienced climbers the mountain is considered a tough proposition.* **5** *Informal* an invitation to engage in sexual intercourse. *~vb* **6** to invite (someone) to engage in sexual intercourse.

propound *vb* to put forward for consideration.

proprietary *adj* **1** denoting a product manufactured and distributed under a trade name. **2** possessive: *she watched them with a proprietary eye.* **3** privately owned and controlled.

proprietor *n* an owner of a business establishment. **proprietress** *fem n* **proprietorial** *adj*

propriety *n, pl* **-ties 1** the quality or state of being appropriate or fitting. **2** correct conduct. **3 the proprieties** the standards of behaviour considered correct by polite society.

propulsion *n* **1** a force that moves (something) forward. **2** the act of propelling or the state of being propelled. **propulsive** *adj*

THESAURUS

estate, freehold, holding, land, real estate, real property, realty, title **3.** ability, attribute, characteristic, feature, hallmark, idiosyncrasy, mark, peculiarity, quality, trait, virtue

prophecy augury, divination, forecast, foretelling, prediction, prognosis, prognostication, revelation, second sight, soothsaying, sortilege

prophesy augur, divine, forecast, foresee, foretell, forewarn, predict, presage, prognosticate, soothsay

prophet augur, clairvoyant, diviner, forecaster, oracle, prognosticator, prophesier, seer, sibyl, soothsayer

prophetic augural, divinatory, foreshadowing, mantic, oracular, predictive, presaging, prescient, prognostic, sibylline

propitious advantageous, auspicious, bright, encouraging, favourable, fortunate, full of promise, happy, lucky, opportune, promising, prosperous, rosy, timely

proportion 1. distribution, ratio, relationship, relative amount **2.** agreement, balance, congruity, correspondence, harmony, symmetry **3.** amount, cut (*informal*), division, fraction, measure, part, percentage, quota, segment, share **4. proportions** amplitude, breadth, bulk, capacity, dimensions, expanse, extent, magnitude, measurements, range, scope, size, volume

proportional balanced, commensurate, comparable, compatible, consistent, correspondent, corresponding, equitable, equivalent, even, in proportion, just

proposal bid, design, motion, offer, overture, plan, presentation, proffer, programme, project, proposition, recommendation, scheme, suggestion, tender, terms

propose 1. advance, come up with, present, proffer, propound, put forward, submit, suggest, tender **2.** introduce, invite, name, nominate, present, put up, recommend **3.** aim, design, have every intention, have in mind, intend, mean, plan, purpose, scheme **4.** *often with* **to** ask for someone's hand (in marriage), offer marriage, pay suit, pop the question (*informal*)

proposition 1. *n.* motion, plan, programme, project, proposal, recommendation, scheme, suggestion **2.** *vb.* accost, make an improper suggestion, make an indecent proposal, solicit

propound advance, advocate, contend, lay down, postulate, present, propose, put forward, set forth, submit, suggest

proprietor deed holder, freeholder, landlady, landlord, landowner, owner, possessor, titleholder

propriety 1. appropriateness, aptness, becomingness, correctness, fitness, rightness, seemliness, suitableness **2.** breeding, courtesy, decency, decorum, delicacy, etiquette, good form, good manners, manners, modesty, politeness, protocol, punctilio, rectitude, refinement, respectability, seemliness **3. the proprieties** accepted conduct, amenities, civilities, etiquette, niceties, rules of conduct, social code, social conventions, social graces, the done thing

pro rata *adv, adj* in proportion.

prorogue *vb* **-roguing, -rogued** to suspend (parliament) without dissolving it. **prorogation** *n*

prosaic (pro-**zay**-ik) *adj* **1** lacking imagination; dull. **2** having the characteristics of prose. **prosaically** *adv*

pros and cons *pl n* the advantages and disadvantages of a situation.

proscenium *n, pl* **-nia** *or* **-niums** the arch in a theatre separating the stage from the auditorium.

proscribe *vb* **-scribing, -scribed 1** to condemn or prohibit (something). **2** to outlaw or banish. **proscription** *n* **proscriptive** *adj*

prose *n* **1** ordinary spoken or written language in contrast to poetry. **2** a passage set for translation into a foreign language. **3** commonplace or dull talk. *~vb* **prosing, prosed 4** to speak or write in a tedious style.

prosecute *vb* **-cuting, -cuted 1** to bring a criminal charge against (someone). **2** to continue to do (something): *the business of prosecuting a cold war through propaganda.* **3 a** to seek redress by legal proceedings. **b** to institute or conduct a prosecution. **prosecutor** *n*

prosecution *n* **1** the bringing of criminal charges against (someone). **2** the institution and conduct of legal proceedings against a person. **3** the lawyers acting for the Crown to put the case against a person. **4** the carrying out of something begun.

proselyte (**pross**-ill-ite) *n* a recent convert. **proselytism** *n*

proselytize *or* **-ise** (**pross**-ill-it-ize) *vb* **-izing, -ized** *or* **-ising, -ised** to attempt to convert (someone).

prosody (**pross**-a-dee) *n* **1** the study of poetic metre and techniques. **2** the vocal patterns in a language. **prosodic** *adj* **prosodist** *n*

prospect *n* **1** (*usually pl*) a probability of future success: *a job with impossible workloads and poor career prospects.* **2** expectation, or something anticipated: *she was terrified at the prospect of bringing up two babies on her own.* **3** *Old-fashioned* a view or scene: *a prospect of spires, domes, and tower.* *~vb* **4** (sometimes foll. by *for*) to search for gold or other valuable minerals.

prospective *adj* **1** future: *prospective customers.* **2** expected or likely: *the prospective loss.* **prospectively** *adv*

prospector *n* a person who searches for gold or other valuable minerals.

prospectus *n, pl* **-tuses** a booklet produced by a university, company, etc., giving details about it and its activities.

prosper *vb* to be successful.

prosperity *n* success and wealth.

prosperous *adj* wealthy and successful.

prostate *n* a gland in male mammals that surrounds the neck of the bladder. Also called: **prostate gland**

prosthesis (pross-**theess**-iss) *n, pl* **-ses** (-seez) *Surgery* **a** the replacement of a missing body part with an artificial substitute. **b** an artificial body part such as a limb, eye, or tooth. **prosthetic** *adj*

prostitute *n* **1** a person who offers sexual intercourse in return for payment. *~vb* **-tuting, -tuted 2** to offer (oneself or another) in sexual intercourse for money. **3** to offer (oneself or one's talent) for unworthy purposes. **prostitution** *n*

prostrate *adj* **1** lying face downwards. **2** physically or emotionally exhausted. *~vb* **-trating, -trated 3** to lie face downwards. **4** to exhaust physically or emotionally. **prostration** *n*

prosy *adj* **prosier, prosiest** dull and long-winded. **prosily** *adv*

Prot. **1** Protectorate. **2** Protestant.

protactinium *n Chem* a toxic radioactive metallic element. Symbol: Pa

protagonist *n* **1** a supporter of a cause: *one of the most active protagonists of British membership of the EC.* **2** the leading character in a play or story.

protea (**pro**-tee-a) *n* an African shrub with showy heads of flowers.

protean (pro-**tee**-an) *adj* capable of constantly changing shape or form: *he is a protean stylist who*

THESAURUS

propulsion drive, impetus, impulse, impulsion, momentum, motive power, power, pressure, propelling force, push, thrust

prosaic banal, boring, commonplace, dry, dull, everyday, flat, hackneyed, humdrum, matter-of-fact, mundane, ordinary, pedestrian, routine, stale, tame, trite, unimaginative, uninspiring, vapid, workaday

proscribe 1. ban, boycott, censure, condemn, damn, denounce, doom, embargo, forbid, interdict, prohibit, reject **2.** banish, blackball, deport, exclude, excommunicate, exile, expatriate, expel, ostracize, outlaw

prosecute 1. arraign, bring action against, bring suit against, bring to trial, do (*slang*), indict, litigate, prefer charges, put in the dock, put on trial, seek redress, sue, summon, take to court, try **2.** carry through, continue, follow through, persevere, persist, pursue, see through

prospect *n.* **1.** *usually plural* chance, likelihood, possibility **2.** anticipation, calculation, contemplation, expectation, future, hope, odds, opening, outlook, plan, presumption, probability, promise, proposal, thought **3.** *old-fashioned* landscape, outlook, panorama, perspective, scene, sight, spectacle, view, vision, vista *~vb.* **4.** explore, go after, look for, search, seek, survey

prospective about to be, anticipated, approaching, awaited, coming, destined, eventual, expected, forthcoming, future, hoped-for, imminent, intended, likely, looked-for, possible, potential, soon-to-be, -to-be, to come, upcoming

prospectus announcement, catalogue, conspectus, list, outline, plan, programme, scheme, syllabus, synopsis

prosper advance, be fortunate, bloom, do well, fare well, flourish, flower, get on, grow rich, make good, make it (*informal*), progress, succeed, thrive

prosperity affluence, boom, ease, fortune, good fortune, good times, life of luxury, life of Riley (*informal*), luxury, plenty, prosperousness, riches, success, the good life, wealth, well-being

prosperous affluent, blooming, booming, doing well, flourishing, fortunate, in clover (*informal*), in the money (*informal*), lucky, moneyed, on the up and up (*Brit.*), opulent, prospering, rich, successful, thriving, wealthy, well-heeled (*informal*), well-off, well-to-do

prostitute 1. *n.* call girl, courtesan (*History*), fallen woman, harlot, hooker (*slang*), pro (*slang*), *streetwalker,* tart (*informal*), *whore, working girl* (*facetious slang*) **2.** *vb.* cheapen, debase, degrade, demean, devalue, misapply, pervert, profane

prostrate *adj.* **1.** flat, horizontal, procumbent, prone **2.** at a low ebb, dejected, depressed, desolate, drained, exhausted, fagged out (*informal*), fallen, inconsolable, overcome, spent, worn out *~vb.* **3.** drain, exhaust, fag out (*informal*), fatigue, sap, tire, wear out, weary

protagonist 1. advocate, champion, exponent, leader, mainstay, moving spirit, prime mover, standard-bearer, supporter **2.** central character, hero, heroine, lead, leading character, principal

protean changeable, ever-changing, many-sided,

can move from blues to ballads with consummate ease.

protect *vb* **1** to defend from trouble, harm, or loss. **2** *Econ* to assist (domestic industries) by taxing imports.

protection *n* **1** the act of protecting or the condition of being protected. **2** something that keeps (one) safe. **3 a** the charging of taxes on imports, to protect domestic industries. **b** Also called: **protectionism** the policy of such taxation. **4** *Informal* Also called: **protection money** money paid to gangsters to avoid attack or damage. **protectionism** *n* **protectionist** *n, adj*

protective *adj* **1** giving protection: *protective clothing.* **2** tending or wishing to protect someone. **protectively** *adv* **protectiveness** *n*

protector *n* **1** a person or thing that protects. **2** *History* a person who acts for the king or queen during his or her childhood, absence, or incapacity. **protectress** *fem n*

protectorate *n* **1** a territory largely controlled by a stronger state. **2** the office or term of office of a protector.

protégé *or fem* **protégée** (**pro**-tizh-ay) *n* a person who is protected and helped by another.

protein *n* any of a large group of nitrogenous compounds that are essential for life.

pro tempore *adv, adj* for the time being. Often shortened to: **pro tem**

protest *n* **1** public, often organized, demonstration of objection. **2** a strong objection. **3** a formal statement declaring that a debtor has dishonoured a bill. **4** the act of protesting. *~vb* **5** to take part in a public demonstration to express one's support for or disapproval of an action, proposal, etc.: *the workers marched through the city to protest against the closure of their factory.* **6** to disagree or object: *"I'm OK," she protested.* **7** to assert in a formal or solemn manner: *all three repeatedly protested their innocence.* **8** *Chiefly US* to object forcefully to: *students and teachers have protested the budget reductions.* **protestant** *adj, n* **protester** *n*

➤ The verb *protest* is followed by *against* and then the noun. In American English it can be directly followed by a noun.

Protestant *n* **1** a follower of any of the Christian Churches that separated from the Roman Catholic Church in the sixteenth century. *~adj* **2** of or relating to any of these Churches or their followers. **Protestantism** *n*

protestation *n Formal* a strong declaration.

protium *n* the most common isotope of hydrogen, with a mass number of 1.

proto- *or sometimes before a vowel* **prot-** *combining form* **1** first: *protomartyr.* **2** original: *prototype.*

protocol *n* **1** the rules of behaviour for formal occasions. **2** a record of an agreement in international negotiations.

proton *n* a positively charged elementary particle, found in the nucleus of an atom.

protoplasm *n Biol* a complex colourless substance forming the living contents of a cell. **protoplasmic** *adj*

prototype *n* **1** an early model of a product, which is tested so that the design can be changed if necessary. **2** a person or thing that serves as an example of a type.

protozoan (pro-toe-**zoe**-an) *n, pl* **-zoa** a very tiny single-celled invertebrate, such as an amoeba. Also: **protozoon**

protract *vb* to lengthen or extend (a situation etc.). **protracted** *adj* **protraction** *n*

protractor *n* an instrument for measuring angles, usually a flat semicircular piece of plastic.

protrude *vb* **-truding, -truded** to stick out or project. **protrusion** *n* **protrusive** *adj*

protuberant *adj* swelling out; bulging. **protuberance** *n*

proud *adj* **1** feeling pleasure or satisfaction: *she was proud of her daughter's success.* **2** feeling honoured. **3** haughty or arrogant. **4** causing pride: *the city's proud history.* **5** dignified: *too proud to accept charity.* **6** (of a surface or edge) projecting or protruding. *~adv* **7 do**

THESAURUS

mercurial, multiform, mutable, polymorphous, temperamental, variable, versatile, volatile

protect care for, chaperon, cover, cover up for, defend, foster, give sanctuary, guard, harbour, keep, keep safe, look after, mount *or* stand guard over, preserve, safeguard, save, screen, secure, shelter, shield, stick up for (*informal*), support, take under one's wing, watch over

protection 1. aegis, care, charge, custody, defence, guardianship, guarding, preservation, protecting, safeguard, safekeeping, safety, security **2.** armour, barrier, buffer, bulwark, cover, guard, refuge, safeguard, screen, shelter, shield

protective careful, covering, defensive, fatherly, insulating, jealous, maternal, motherly, paternal, possessive, protecting, safeguarding, sheltering, shielding, vigilant, warm, watchful

protector advocate, benefactor, bodyguard, champion, counsel, defender, guard, guardian, guardian angel, knight in shining armour, patron, safeguard, tower of strength

protégé, protégée charge, dependant, discovery, pupil, student, ward

protest *n.* **1.** complaint, declaration, demur, demurral, disapproval, dissent, formal complaint, objection, outcry, protestation, remonstrance *~vb.* **2.** complain, cry out, demonstrate, demur, disagree, disapprove, expostulate, express disapproval, kick (against) (*informal*), object, oppose, remonstrate, say no to, take exception **3.** affirm, argue, assert, asseverate, attest, avow, contend, declare, insist, maintain, profess, testify, vow

protestation *formal* **1.** complaint, disagreement, dissent, expostulation, objection, outcry, protest, remonstrance, remonstration **2.** affirmation, asseveration, avowal, declaration, oath, pledge, profession, vow

protester agitator, demonstrator, dissenter, dissident, protest marcher, rebel

protocol 1. code of behaviour, conventions, courtesies, customs, decorum, etiquette, formalities, good form, manners, politesse, propriety, rules of conduct **2.** agreement, compact, concordat, contract, convention, covenant, pact, treaty

prototype archetype, example, first, mock-up, model, norm, original, paradigm, pattern, precedent, standard, type

protract continue, drag on *or* out, draw out, extend, keep going, lengthen, prolong, spin out, stretch out

protracted dragged out, drawn-out, extended, interminable, lengthy, long, long-drawn-out, never-ending, overlong, prolonged, spun out, time-consuming

protrude bulge, come through, extend, jut, obtrude, point, pop (*of eyes*), project, shoot out, stand out, start (from), stick out

protrusion bulge, bump, hump, jut, lump, outgrowth, projection, protuberance, swelling

protuberance bulge, bump, excrescence, hump,

someone proud to entertain someone on a grand scale: *Mum did us all proud last Christmas.* **proudly** *adv*

proud flesh *n* a mass of tissue formed around a healing wound.

prove *vb* **proving, proved; proved** *or* **proven 1** to establish the validity of: *such a claim is difficult to prove scientifically.* **2** to demonstrate or test: *the autopsy proved that she had drowned.* **3** *Law* to establish the genuineness of (a will). **4** to show (oneself) to be: *he proved equal to the task.* **5** to be found to be: *it proved to be a trap.* **6** (of dough) to rise in a warm place before baking. **provable** *adj*

proven *vb* **1** a past participle of **prove. 2** See **not proven.** ~*adj* **3** known from experience to work: *a proven ability to make money.*

provenance (**prov**-in-anss) *n* a place of origin.

Provençal (prov-on-**sahl**) *adj* **1** of Provence, in SE France. ~*n* **2** a language of Provence. **3** a person from Provence.

provender *n Old-fashioned* fodder for livestock.

proverb *n* a short memorable saying that expresses a truth or gives a warning, for example is *half a loaf is better than no bread.*

proverbial *adj* **1** well-known because commonly or traditionally referred to. **2** of a proverb. **proverbially** *adv*

provide *vb* **-viding, -vided 1** to make available. **2** to afford; yield: *social activities providing the opportunity to meet new people.* **3** (often foll. by *for* or *against*) to take careful precautions: *we provide for the possibility of illness in the examination regulations.* **4** (foll. by *for*) to support financially: *both parents should be expected to provide for their children.* **5** *Formal* **provide for** (of a law, treaty, etc.) to make possible: *a bill providing for stiffer penalties for racial discrimination.* **provider** *n*

providence *n* **1** God or nature seen as a protective force that oversees people's lives. **2** the foresight shown by a person in the management of his or her affairs.

Providence *n Christianity* God, esp. as showing foreseeing care of his creatures.

provident *adj* **1** thrifty. **2** showing foresight.

providential *adj* fortunate, as if through divine involvement.

provident society *n* same as **friendly society.**

providing *or* **provided** *conj* on condition (that): *the deal is on, providing he passes his medical.*

➤ The usage is either *providing* on its own or *provided that* (not *providing that*).

province *n* **1** a territory governed as a unit of a country or empire. **2** an area of learning, activity, etc. **3 the provinces** those parts of a country lying outside the capital.

provincewide *Canad* ~*adj* **1** relating to the whole of a province: *a provincewide referendum.* ~*adv* **2** throughout a province: *an advertising campaign to go provincewide.*

provincial *adj* **1** of a province. **2** unsophisticated or narrow-minded. **3** *NZ* denoting a football team representing a province. ~*n* **4** an unsophisticated person. **5** a person from a province or the provinces. **provincialism** *n*

provision *n* **1** the act of supplying something. **2** something supplied. **3** (*pl*) food and other necessities. **4** a condition incorporated in a document. **5 make provision for** to make arrangements for beforehand: *many restaurants still make no provision for nonsmokers.* ~*vb* **6** to supply with provisions.

THESAURUS

knob, lump, outgrowth, process, projection, prominence, protrusion, swelling, tumour

proud 1. appreciative, content, contented, glad, gratified, honoured, pleased, satisfied, self-respecting, well-pleased **2.** arrogant, boastful, conceited, disdainful, egotistical, haughty, high and mighty (*informal*), imperious, lordly, narcissistic, overbearing, presumptuous, self-important, self-satisfied, snobbish, snooty (*informal*), stuck-up (*informal*), supercilious, toffee-nosed (*slang, chiefly Brit.*), vain **3.** exalted, glorious, gratifying, illustrious, memorable, pleasing, red-letter, rewarding, satisfying **4.** august, distinguished, eminent, grand, great, illustrious, imposing, magnificent, majestic, noble, splendid, stately

prove 1. ascertain, attest, authenticate, bear out, confirm, corroborate, demonstrate, determine, establish, evidence, evince, justify, show, show clearly, substantiate, verify **2.** analyse, assay, check, examine, experiment, put to the test, put to trial, test, try **3.** be found to be, come out, end up, result, turn out

proverb adage, aphorism, apophthegm, byword, dictum, maxim, saw (*old-fashioned*), saying

proverbial accepted, acknowledged, archetypal, axiomatic, conventional, current, customary, famed, famous, legendary, notorious, self-evident, time-honoured, traditional, typical, unquestioned, well-known

provide 1. accommodate, cater, contribute, equip, furnish, outfit, provision, purvey, stock up, supply **2.** add, afford, bring, give, impart, lend, present, produce, render, serve, yield **3.** *often with* **for** *or* **against** anticipate, arrange for, forearm, get ready, make arrangements, make plans, plan ahead, plan for, prepare for, take measures, take precautions **4.** *with* **for** care for, keep, look after, maintain, support, sustain, take care of

providence 1. destiny, divine intervention, fate, fortune, God's will, predestination **2.** care, caution, discretion, far-sightedness, foresight, forethought, perspicacity, presence of mind, prudence

provident canny, careful, cautious, discreet, economical, equipped, far-seeing, far-sighted, forearmed, foresighted, frugal, prudent, sagacious, shrewd, thrifty, vigilant, well-prepared, wise

providential fortuitous, fortunate, happy, heaven-sent, lucky, opportune, timely, welcome

provider 1. benefactor, donor, giver, source, supplier **2.** breadwinner, earner, mainstay, supporter, wage earner

providing *or* **provided** *conj.* as long as, contingent upon, given, if and only if, in case, in the event, on condition, on the assumption, subject to, upon these terms, with the proviso, with the understanding

province 1. colony, county, department, dependency, district, division, domain, patch, region, section, territory, tract, zone **2.** area, business, capacity, charge, concern, duty, employment, field, function, line, orbit, part, pigeon (*Brit. informal*), post, responsibility, role, sphere, turf (*informal*)

provincial *adj.* **1.** country, home-grown, homespun, local, rural, rustic **2.** insular, inward-looking, limited, narrow, narrow-minded, parish-pump, parochial, small-minded, uninformed, unsophisticated, upcountry ~*n.* **3.** hick (*informal, chiefly U.S. & Canad.*), rustic, yokel

provision 1. accoutrement, catering, equipping, fitting out, furnishing, providing, supplying, victualling **2.** **provisions** comestibles, eatables, eats (*slang*), edibles, fare, feed, food, foodstuff, groceries, grub

provisional *adj* temporary or conditional: *a provisional diagnosis.* **provisionally** *adv*

Provisional *n* a member of the Provisional IRA or Sinn Féin.

proviso (pro-**vize**-oh) *n, pl* **-sos** *or* **-soes** a condition or stipulation. **provisory** *adj*

provocation *n* **1** the act of provoking or inciting. **2** something that causes indignation or anger.

provocative *adj* provoking or inciting, esp. to anger or sexual desire: *a provocative remark.* **provocatively** *adv*

provoke *vb* **-voking, -voked 1** to deliberately act in a way intended to anger someone: *waving a red cape, Delgado provoked the animal into charging.* **2** to incite or stimulate: *the army seems to have provoked this latest confrontation.* **3** (often foll. by *into*) to cause a person to react in a particular, often angry, way: *keeping your true motives hidden may provoke others into being just as two-faced with you.* **4** to bring about: *the case has provoked furious public debate.* **provoking** *adj*

provost *n* **1** the head of certain university colleges or schools. **2** the chief councillor of a Scottish town.

provost marshal *n* the officer in charge of military police in a camp or city.

prow *n* the bow of a vessel.

prowess *n* **1** superior skill or ability. **2** bravery or fearlessness.

prowl *vb* **1** (sometimes foll. by *around* or *about*) to move stealthily around (a place) as if in search of prey or plunder. *~n* **2** the act of prowling. **3 on the prowl** moving around stealthily. **prowler** *n*

prox. proximo (next month).

proximate *adj* **1** next or nearest in space or time. **2** very near. **3** immediately coming before or following in a series. **4** approximate.

proximity *n* **1** nearness in space or time. **2** nearness or closeness in a series.

proxy *n, pl* **proxies 1** a person authorized to act on behalf of someone else: *the firm's creditors can vote either in person or by proxy.* **2** the authority to act on behalf of someone else.

prude *n* a person who is excessively modest or prim, esp. regarding sex. **prudery** *n* **prudish** *adj*

prudent *adj* **1** sensible and careful. **2** discreet or cautious. **3** exercising good judgment. **prudence** *n* **prudently** *adv*

prudential *adj Old-fashioned* showing prudence: *prudential reasons.* **prudentially** *adv*

prune[1] *n* a purplish-black partially dried plum.

prune[2] *vb* **pruning, pruned 1** to cut off dead or surplus branches of (a tree or shrub). **2** to shorten or reduce.

prurient *adj* **1** excessively interested in sexual matters. **2** exciting lustfulness. **prurience** *n*

Prussian *adj* **1** of Prussia, a former German state. *~n* **2** a person from Prussia.

prussic acid *n* the extremely poisonous solution of hydrogen cyanide.

pry *vb* **pries, prying, pried** (often foll. by *into*) to make an impertinent or uninvited inquiry (about a private matter).

PS 1 Also: **ps** postscript. **2** private secretary.

psalm *n* (*often cap*) any of the sacred songs that make up a book (Psalms) of the Old Testament.

psalmist *n* a writer of psalms.

psalmody *n, pl* **-dies** the singing of sacred music.

Psalter *n* **1** the Book of Psalms. **2** a book containing a version of Psalms.

psaltery *n, pl* **-teries** an ancient musical instrument played by plucking strings.

THESAURUS

(*slang*), nosebag (*slang*), provender (*old-fashioned*), rations, stores, supplies, sustenance, viands, victuals **3.** agreement, clause, condition, demand, proviso, requirement, rider, specification, stipulation, term

provisional conditional, contingent, interim, limited, pro tem, provisory, qualified, stopgap, temporary, tentative, transitional

proviso clause, condition, limitation, provision, qualification, requirement, reservation, restriction, rider, stipulation, strings

provocation 1. cause, grounds, incitement, inducement, instigation, justification, motivation, reason, stimulus **2.** affront, annoyance, challenge, dare, grievance, indignity, injury, insult, offence, red rag, taunt, vexation

provocative 1. aggravating (*informal*), annoying, challenging, disturbing, galling, goading, incensing, insulting, offensive, outrageous, provoking, stimulating **2.** alluring, arousing, erotic, exciting, inviting, seductive, sexy (*informal*), stimulating, suggestive, tantalizing, tempting

provoke 1. affront, aggravate (*informal*), anger, annoy, chafe, enrage, exasperate, gall, get in one's hair (*informal*), get on one's nerves (*informal*), hassle (*informal*), incense, infuriate, insult, irk, irritate, madden, make one's blood boil, nark (*slang*), offend, pique, piss one off (*taboo slang*), put out, rile, try one's patience, vex **2.** bring about, bring on *or* down, call forth, cause, draw forth, elicit, evoke, excite, fire, generate, give rise to, incite, induce, inflame, inspire, instigate, kindle, lead to, motivate, move, occasion, precipitate, produce, promote, prompt, rouse, stimulate, stir

prow bow(s), fore, forepart, front, head, nose, stem

prowess 1. ability, accomplishment, adeptness, adroitness, aptitude, attainment, command, dexterity, excellence, expertise, expertness, facility, genius, mastery, skill, talent **2.** boldness, bravery, courage, daring, dauntlessness, doughtiness, fearlessness, gallantry, hardihood, heroism, intrepidity, mettle, valiance, valour

prowl *sometimes with* **around** *or* **about** cruise, hunt, lurk, move stealthily, nose around, patrol, range, roam, rove, scavenge, skulk, slink, sneak, stalk, steal

proximity adjacency, closeness, contiguity, juxtaposition, nearness, neighbourhood, propinquity, vicinity

proxy agent, attorney, delegate, deputy, factor, representative, substitute, surrogate

prude old maid (*informal*), prig, puritan, schoolmarm (*Brit. informal*)

prudence canniness, care, caution, circumspection, common sense, discretion, good sense, heedfulness, judgment, judiciousness, sagacity, vigilance, wariness, wisdom

prudent canny, careful, cautious, circumspect, discerning, discreet, judicious, politic, sagacious, sage, sensible, shrewd, vigilant, wary, wise

prudery old-maidishness (*informal*), overmodesty, priggishness, primness, prudishness, puritanicalness, squeamishness, starchiness (*informal*), strictness, stuffiness

prudish demure, narrow-minded, old-maidish (*informal*), overmodest, overnice, priggish, prim, prissy (*informal*), proper, puritanical, schoolmarmish (*Brit. informal*), squeamish, starchy (*informal*), strait-laced, stuffy, Victorian

prune clip, cut, cut back, dock, lop, pare down, reduce, shape, shorten, snip, trim

pry *often with* **into** be a busybody, be inquisitive, be

PSBR (in Britain) public sector borrowing requirement: the money needed by the public sector of the economy for items not paid for by income.

psephology (sef-**fol**-a-jee) *n* the statistical and sociological study of elections. **psephologist** *n*

pseud *n Informal* a pretentious person.

pseudo *adj Informal* not genuine.

pseudo- *or sometimes before a vowel* **pseud-** *combining form* false, pretending, or unauthentic: *pseudo-intellectual.*

pseudonym *n* a fictitious name adopted, esp. by an author. **pseudonymity** *n* **pseudonymous** *adj*

psittacosis *n* a viral disease of parrots that can be passed on to humans.

psoriasis (so-**rye**-a-siss) *n* a skin disease with reddish spots and patches covered with silvery scales.

psst *interj* a sound made to attract someone's attention, esp. without others noticing.

PST Pacific Standard Time.

PSV public service vehicle.

psyche *n* the human mind or soul.

psychedelic *adj* **1** denoting a drug that causes hallucinations. **2** *Informal* having vivid colours and complex patterns similar to those experienced during hallucinations.

psychiatry *n* the branch of medicine concerned with the study and treatment of mental disorders. **psychiatric** *adj* **psychiatrist** *n*

psychic *adj* **1** having mental powers which cannot be explained by natural laws. **2** relating to the mind. ~*n* **3** a person who has psychic powers. **psychical** *adj*

psycho *Informal* ~*n, pl* **-chos** **1** same as **psychopath.** ~*adj* **2** same as **psychopathic.**

psycho- *or sometimes before a vowel* **psych-** *combining form* indicating the mind or mental processes: *psychology; psychosomatic.*

psychoanalyse *or esp US* **-lyze** *vb* **-lysing, -lysed** *or* **-lyzing, -lyzed** to examine or treat (a person) by psychoanalysis.

psychoanalysis *n* a method of treating mental and emotional disorders by discussion and analysis of the patient's thoughts and feelings. **psychoanalyst** *n* **psychoanalytical** *or* **psychoanalytic** *adj*

psychogenic *adj Psychol* (esp. of disorders or symptoms) of mental, rather than organic, origin.

psychological *adj* **1** relating to the mind or mental activity. **2** relating to psychology. **3** having its origin in the mind: *his backaches are purely psychological.* **psychologically** *adv*

psychological moment *n* the best time for achieving the desired response or effect.

psychological warfare *n* the military application of psychology, esp. to influence morale in time of war.

psychology *n, pl* **-gies** **1** the scientific study of all forms of human and animal behaviour. **2** *Informal* the mental make-up of a person. **psychologist** *n*

psychopath *n* a person afflicted with a personality disorder which causes him or her to commit antisocial and sometimes violent acts. **psychopathic** *adj*

psychopathology *n* the scientific study of mental disorders.

psychopathy (sike-**op**-ath-ee) *n* any mental disorder or disease.

psychosis (sike-**oh**-siss) *n, pl* **-ses** (-seez) a severe mental disorder in which the sufferer's contact with reality becomes highly distorted. **psychotic** *adj*

psychosomatic *adj* (of a physical disorder) thought to have psychological causes, such as stress.

psychotherapy *n* the treatment of nervous disorders by psychological methods. **psychotherapeutic** *adj* **psychotherapist** *n*

psych up *vb* to prepare (oneself or another) mentally for a contest or task.

pt **1** part. **2** past tense. **3** point. **4** port. **5** pro tempore.

Pt *Chem* platinum.

PT *Old-fashioned* physical training.

pt. pint.

PTA Parent-Teacher Association.

ptarmigan (**tar**-mig-an) *n* a bird of the grouse family that turns white in winter.

Pte. *Mil* private.

pterodactyl (terr-roe-**dak**-til) *n* an extinct flying reptile with batlike wings.

PTO *or* **pto** please turn over.

Ptolemaic (tol-lim-**may**-ik) *adj* relating to Ptolemy, the 2nd-century AD Greek astronomer, or to his belief that the earth was in the centre of the universe.

ptomaine *or* **ptomain** (**toe**-main) *n* any of a group of poisonous alkaloids found in decaying matter.

Pu *Chem* plutonium.

pub *n* **1** *Chiefly Brit* a building with a licensed bar where alcoholic drinks may be bought and drunk. **2** *Austral & NZ* a hotel.

pub. **1** public. **2** publication. **3** published. **4** publisher. **5** publishing.

pub-crawl *n Informal, chiefly Brit* a drinking tour of a number of pubs.

puberty (**pew**-ber-tee) *n* the beginning of sexual maturity. **pubertal** *adj*

pubes (**pew**-beez) *n, pl* **pubes** **1** the region above the genitals. **2** pubic hair. **3** the plural of **pubis.**

THESAURUS

nosy (*informal*), ferret about, interfere, intrude, meddle, nose into, peep, peer, poke, poke one's nose in *or* into (*informal*), snoop (*informal*)

pseudo *adj.* artificial, bogus, counterfeit, ersatz, fake, false, imitation, mock, not genuine, phoney *or* phony (*informal*), pretended, quasi-, sham, spurious

pseudonym alias, assumed name, false name, incognito, nom de guerre, nom de plume, pen name, professional name, stage name

psyche essential nature, individuality, inner man, innermost self, mind, personality, self, soul, spirit, subconscious, true being

psychiatrist analyst, headshrinker (*slang*), psychoanalyser, psychoanalyst, psychologist, psychotherapist, shrink (*slang*), therapist

psychic **1.** clairvoyant, extrasensory, mystic, occult, preternatural, supernatural, telekinetic, telepathic **2.** mental, psychogenic, psychological, spiritual

psychological **1.** cerebral, cognitive, intellectual, mental **2.** all in the mind, emotional, imaginary, irrational, psychosomatic, subconscious, subjective, unconscious, unreal

psychology **1.** behaviourism, science of mind, study of personality **2.** *informal* attitude, mental make-up, mental processes, thought processes, way of thinking, what makes one tick

psychopath head-banger (*informal*), insane person, lunatic, madman, maniac, mental case (*slang*), nutcase (*slang*), nutter (*Brit. slang*), psychotic, sociopath

psychotic *adj.* certifiable, demented, deranged, insane, lunatic, mad, mental (*slang*), *non compos mentis,* off one's chump (head (*slang*), rocker (*slang*), trolley (*slang*)) (*slang*), psychopathic, unbalanced

pub *or* **public house** bar, boozer (*Brit., Austral., & N.Z. informal*), inn, local (*Brit. informal*), roadhouse,

pubescent *adj* **1** arriving or arrived at puberty. **2** covered with down, as some plants and animals. **pubescence** *n*

pubic (**pew**-bik) *adj* of or relating to the pubes or pubis: *pubic hair.*

pubis *n, pl* **-bes** one of the three sections of the hipbone that forms part of the pelvis.

public *adj* **1** relating to the people as a whole. **2** open to all: *public gardens.* **3** well-known: *a public figure.* **4** performed or made openly: *public proclamation.* **5** maintained by and for the community: *a public library.* **6** open, acknowledged, or notorious: *a public scandal.* **7 go public a** (of a private company) to offer shares for sale to the public: *few German firms have gone public in recent years.* **b** to make information, plans, etc., known: *the group would not have gone public with its suspicions unless it was fully convinced of them.* ~*n* **8** the community or people in general. **9** a particular section of the community: *the racing public.* **publicly** *adv*

public-address system *n* a system of microphones, amplifiers, and loudspeakers for increasing the sound level of speech or music at public gatherings.

publican *n* (in Britain) a person who owns or runs a public house.

publication *n* **1** the publishing of a printed work. **2** any printed work offered for sale. **3** the act of making information known to the public.

public bar *n* a bar in a hotel or pub which is cheaper and more basically furnished than the lounge or saloon bar.

public company *or* **public limited company** *n* a limited company whose shares may be purchased by the public.

public convenience *n* a public toilet.

public enemy *n* a notorious person who is considered a danger to the public.

public house *n* **1** *Brit* a pub. **2** *US & Canad* an inn or small hotel.

publicist *n* a person, such as a press agent or journalist, who publicizes something.

publicity *n* **1** the process or information used to arouse public attention. **2** the public interest so aroused.

publicize *or* **-cise** *vb* **-cizing, -cized** *or* **-cising, -cised** to bring to public attention.

public lending right *n* the right of authors to receive payment when their books are borrowed from public libraries.

public prosecutor *n Law* an official in charge of prosecuting important cases.

public relations *n* the practice of gaining the public's goodwill and approval for an organization.

public school *n* **1** (in England and Wales) a private independent fee-paying secondary school. **2** (in certain Canadian provinces) a public elementary school as distinguished from a separate school. **3** any school that is part of a free local educational system.

public sector *n* the part of a country's economy that consists of state-owned industries and services.

public servant *n* **1** an elected or appointed holder of a public office. **2** *Austral & NZ* a civil servant.

public service *n Austral & NZ* the civil service.

public-spirited *adj* having or showing an active interest in the good of the community.

public utility *n* an organization that supplies water, gas, or electricity to the public.

publish *vb* **1** to produce and issue (printed matter) for sale. **2** to have one's written work issued for publication. **3** to announce formally or in public. **publishing** *n*

publisher *n* **1** a company or person that publishes books, periodicals, music, etc. **2** *US & Canad* the proprietor of a newspaper.

puce *adj* dark brownish-purple: *his face suddenly puce with futile rage.*

puck[1] *n* a small disc of hard rubber used in ice hockey.

puck[2] *n* a mischievous or evil spirit. **puckish** *adj*

pucker *vb* **1** to gather into wrinkles. ~*n* **2** a wrinkle or crease.

pudding *n* **1** a dessert, esp. a cooked one served hot. **2** a savoury dish with pastry or batter: *steak-and-kidney pudding.* **3** a sausage-like mass of meat: *black pudding.*

puddle *n* **1** a small pool of water, esp. of rain. **2** a worked mixture of wet clay and sand that is impervious to water. ~*vb* **-dling, -dled 3** to make (clay etc.) into puddle. **4** to subject (iron) to puddling. **puddly** *adj*

pudenda *pl n* the human genitals, esp. of a female.

pudgy *adj* **pudgier, pudgiest** *Chiefly US* podgy. **pudginess** *n*

puerile *adj* silly and childish. **puerility** *n*

puerperal (pew-**er**-per-al) *adj* concerning the period following childbirth.

puerperal fever *n* a serious, formerly widespread, form of blood poisoning caused by infection during childbirth.

THESAURUS

taproom (*old-fashioned*), tavern, watering hole (*facetious slang*)

puberty adolescence, awkward age, juvenescence, pubescence, teenage, teens, young adulthood

public *adj.* **1.** civic, civil, common, general, national, popular, social, state, universal, widespread **2.** accessible, communal, community, free to all, not private, open, open to the public, unrestricted **3.** important, prominent, respected, well-known **4.** acknowledged, exposed, in circulation, known, notorious, obvious, open, overt, patent, plain, published, recognized ~*n.* **5.** citizens, commonalty, community, country, electorate, everyone, hoi polloi, masses, multitude, nation, people, populace, population, society, voters **6.** audience, buyers, clientele, followers, following, patrons, supporters, those interested, trade

publication 1. advertisement, airing, announcement, appearance, broadcasting, declaration, disclosure, dissemination, notification, proclamation, promulgation, publishing, reporting **2.** book, booklet, brochure, handbill, hardback, issue, leaflet, magazine, newspaper, pamphlet, paperback, periodical, title

publicity advertising, attention, ballyhoo (*informal*), boost, build-up, hype, plug (*informal*), press, promotion, public notice, puff

publicize, publicise advertise, beat the drum for (*informal*), bring to public notice, broadcast, give publicity to, hype, make known, play up, plug (*informal*), promote, puff, push, spotlight, spread about, write up

public-spirited altruistic, charitable, community-minded, generous, humanitarian, philanthropic, unselfish

publish 1. bring out, issue, print, produce, put out **2.** advertise, announce, blow wide open (*slang*), broadcast, circulate, communicate, declare, disclose, distribute, divulge, impart, leak, proclaim, promulgate, publicize, reveal, spread

pudding afters (*Brit. informal*), dessert, last course, second course, sweet

puerperium (pure-**peer**-ee-um) *n* the period after childbirth.

puff *n* **1** a short quick blast of breath, wind, or smoke. **2** the amount of wind or smoke released in a puff. **3** the sound made by a puff. **4 out of puff** out of breath: *by the third flight of stairs she was out of puff.* **5** an act of inhaling and expelling cigarette smoke. **6** a light pastry usually filled with cream and jam. ~*vb* **7** to blow or breathe in short quick blasts. **8** (often foll. by *out*) to cause to be out of breath. **9** to take draws at (a cigarette). **10** to move with or by the emission of puffs: *the steam train puffed up the incline.* **11** (often foll. by *up* or *out*) to swell. **puffy** *adj*

puff adder *n* a large venomous African viper whose body swells when alarmed.

puffball *n* a ball-shaped fungus that sends out a cloud of brown spores when mature.

puffin *n* a black-and-white sea bird with a brightly coloured beak.

puff pastry *or US* **puff paste** *n* a light flaky pastry.

pug *n* a small dog with a smooth coat, lightly curled tail, and a short wrinkled nose.

pugilist (**pew**-jil-ist) *n* a boxer. **pugilism** *n* **pugilistic** *adj*

pugnacious *adj* ready and eager to fight. **pugnacity** *n*

pug nose *n* a short stubby upturned nose. **pug-nosed** *adj*

puissance *n* a showjumping competition that tests a horse's ability to jump large obstacles.

puissant (**pew**-iss-sant) *adj Archaic or poetic* powerful.

puke *Slang* ~*vb* **puking, puked 1** to vomit. ~*n* **2** the act of vomiting. **3** the matter vomited.

pukeko (**puck**-a-koh) *n, pl* **-kos** a brightly coloured New Zealand wading bird.

pukka *adj Anglo-Indian* **1** properly done, constructed, etc. **2** genuine or real.

pulchritude *n Formal or literary* physical beauty. **pulchritudinous** *adj*

pule *vb* **puling, puled** *Literary* to whine or whimper.

pull *vb* **1** to exert force on (an object) to draw it towards the source of the force. **2** to strain or stretch. **3** to remove or extract: *he pulled a crumpled tenner from his pocket.* **4** *Informal* to draw out (a weapon) for use: *he pulled a knife on his attacker.* **5** *Informal* to attract: *the game is expected to pull a large crowd.* **6** (usually foll. by *on* or *at*) to drink or inhale deeply: *he pulled on his pipe.* **7** to possess or exercise the power to move: *this car doesn't pull well on hills.* **8** *Printing* to take (a proof) from type. **9** *Golf, baseball, etc* to hit (a ball) away from the direction in which the player intended to hit it. **10** *Cricket* to hit (a ball) to the leg side. **11** to row (a boat) or take a stroke of (an oar) in rowing. **12 pull a face** to make a grimace. **13 pull a fast one** *Slang* to play a sly trick. **14 pull apart** *or* **to pieces** to criticize harshly. **15 pull (one's) punches** to limit the force of one's criticisms or blows. ~*n* **16** the act of pulling. **17** the force used in pulling: *the pull of the moon affects the tides.* **18** the act of taking in drink or smoke. **19** *Printing* a proof taken from type. **20** something used for pulling, such as a handle. **21** *Informal* power or influence: *his uncle is chairman of the company, so he has quite a lot of pull.* **22** *Informal* the power to attract attention or support. **23** a single stroke of an oar in rowing. **24** the act of pulling the ball in golf, cricket, etc. ~See also **pull down, pull in,** etc.

pull down *vb* to destroy or demolish: *the old houses were pulled down.*

pullet *n* a hen less than one year old.

pulley *n* a wheel with a grooved rim in which a belt, chain, or piece of rope runs in order to lift weights by a downward pull.

pull in *vb* **1** Also: **pull over** (of a motor vehicle) to draw in to the side of the road. **2** (often foll. by *to*) to reach a destination: *the train pulled in to the station.* **3** to attract: *his appearance will pull in the crowds.* **4** *Brit slang* to arrest. **5** to earn (money): *he pulls in at least thirty thousand a year.*

Pullman *n, pl* **-mans** a luxurious railway coach.

pull off *vb Informal* to succeed in accomplishing (something difficult): *to pull off a million-pound deal.*

pull out *vb* **1** (of a motor vehicle) **a** to draw away from the side of the road. **b** to move out from behind another vehicle to overtake. **2** to depart: *the train pulled out of the station.* **3** to withdraw: *several companies have pulled out of the student market.* **4** to remove by pulling. **5** to abandon a situation.

pullover *n* a sweater that is pulled on over the head.

pull through *vb* to survive or recover, esp. after a serious illness.

pull together *vb* **1** to cooperate or work in harmony. **2 pull oneself together** *Informal* to regain one's self-control.

THESAURUS

puerile babyish, childish, foolish, immature, inane, infantile, irresponsible, jejune, juvenile, naive, petty, ridiculous, silly, trivial, weak

puff *n.* **1.** blast, breath, draught, emanation, flurry, gust, whiff **2.** drag (*slang*), pull, smoke ~*vb.* **3.** blow, breathe, exhale, gasp, gulp, pant, wheeze **4.** drag (*slang*), draw, inhale, pull at *or* on, smoke, suck **5.** *often with* **up** *or* **out** bloat, dilate, distend, expand, inflate, swell

puffy bloated, distended, enlarged, inflamed, inflated, puffed up, swollen

pugilist boxer, bruiser (*informal*), fighter, prizefighter

pugnacious aggressive, antagonistic, argumentative, bellicose, belligerent, choleric, combative, contentious, disputatious, hot-tempered, irascible, irritable, petulant, quarrelsome

pull *vb.* **1.** drag, draw, haul, jerk, tow, trail, tug, yank **2.** dislocate, rend, rip, sprain, strain, stretch, tear, wrench **3.** cull, draw out, extract, gather, pick, pluck, remove, take out, uproot, weed **4.** *informal* attract, draw, entice, lure, magnetize **5. pull apart** *or* **to pieces** attack, blast, criticize, find fault, flay, lambast(e), lay into (*informal*), pan (*informal*), pick holes in, put down, run down, slam (*slang*), slate (*informal*), tear into (*informal*) ~*n.* **6.** jerk, tug, twitch, yank **7.** effort, exertion, force, forcefulness, influence **8.** drag (*slang*), inhalation, puff **9.** *informal* advantage, bottom, clout (*informal*), influence, leverage, muscle, power, weight

pull down bulldoze, demolish, destroy, raze, remove

pull off *informal* accomplish, bring off, carry out, crack it (*informal*), cut it (*informal*), manage, score a success, secure one's object, succeed

pull out abandon, depart, evacuate, leave, quit, rat on, retreat, stop participating, withdraw

pull through come through, get better, get over, pull round, rally, recover, survive, weather

pull together **pull oneself together** *informal* buck up (*informal*), get a grip on oneself, get over it, regain composure, snap out of it (*informal*)

pull up **1.** brake, come to a halt, halt, reach a standstill, stop **2.** dig out, lift, raise, uproot **3.** admonish, bawl out (*informal*), carpet (*informal*), castigate, dress down (*informal*), give a rocket (*Brit. & N.Z. informal*),

pull up *vb* **1** (of a motor vehicle) to stop. **2** to remove by the roots. **3** to rebuke.

pulmonary *adj* **1** of or affecting the lungs. **2** having lungs or lunglike organs.

pulp *n* **1** a soft wet substance made from matter which has been crushed or beaten: *mash the strawberries to a pulp.* **2** the soft fleshy part of a fruit or vegetable: *halve the tomatoes then scoop the seeds and pulp into a bowl.* **3** printed or recorded material with little depth or designed to shock: *pulp fiction; a tape player churned out disco pulp.* ~*vb* **4** to reduce a material to pulp: *he began to pulp the orange in his fingers.* **pulpy** *adj*

pulpit *n* **1** a raised platform in churches used for preaching. **2** (usually preceded by *the*) preaching or the clergy.

pulpwood *n* pine, spruce, or any other soft wood used to make paper.

pulsar *n* a very small star which emits regular pulses of radio waves.

pulsate *vb* **-sating, -sated 1** to expand and contract rhythmically, like a heartbeat. **2** to quiver or vibrate: *the images pulsate with energy and light.* **3** *Physics* to vary in intensity or magnitude. **pulsation** *n*

pulse¹ *n* **1** *Physiol* **a** the regular beating of blood through the arteries at each heartbeat. **b** a single such beat. **2** *Physics, electronics* a sudden change in a quantity, such as a voltage, that is normally constant in a system. **3** a regular beat or vibration. **4** bustle or excitement: *the lively pulse of a city.* **5** the feelings or thoughts of a group as they can be measured: *the political pulse of the capital.* ~*vb* **pulsing, pulsed 6** to beat, throb, or vibrate.

pulse² *n* the edible seeds of pod-bearing plants, such as peas, beans, and lentils.

pulverize *or* **-ise** *vb* **-izing, -ized** *or* **ising, -ised 1** to reduce to fine particles by crushing or grinding. **2** to destroy completely. **pulverization** *or* **-isation** *n*

puma *n* a large American wild cat with a plain greyish-brown coat and a long tail.

pumice (**pumm**-iss) *n* a light porous stone used for scouring and for removing hard skin. Also called: **pumice stone**

pummel *vb* **-melling, -melled** *or US* **-meling, -meled** to strike repeatedly with the fists.

pump¹ *n* **1** a device to force a gas or liquid to move in a particular direction. ~*vb* **2** (sometimes foll. by *from, out,* etc.) to raise or drive (air, liquid, etc.) with a pump, esp. into or from something. **3** (usually foll. by *in* or *into*) to supply in large amounts: *pumping money into the economy.* **4** to operate (a handle etc.) in the manner of a pump: *he was warmly applauded, and his hand was pumped by well-wishers.* **5** to obtain information from (someone) by persistent questioning. **6 pump iron** *Slang* to exercise with weights; do bodybuilding exercises.

pump² *n* **1** a shoe with a rubber sole, used in games such as tennis; plimsoll. **2** a low-cut low-heeled shoe, worn for dancing.

pumpernickel *n* a slightly sour black bread made of coarse rye flour.

pumpkin *n* **1** a large round fruit with a thick orange rind, pulpy flesh, and many seeds. **2** the creeping plant that bears this fruit.

pun *n* **1** the use of words to exploit double meanings for humorous effect, for example *my dog's a champion boxer.* ~*vb* **punning, punned 2** to make puns.

punch¹ *vb* **1** to strike at with a clenched fist. ~*n* **2** a blow with the fist. **3** *Informal* point or vigour: *the jokes are mildly amusing but lack any real punch.*

punch² *n* **1** a tool or machine for shaping, piercing, or engraving. **2** *Computers* a device for making holes in a card or paper tape. ~*vb* **3** to pierce, cut, stamp, shape, or drive with a punch.

punch³ *n* a mixed drink containing fruit juice and, usually, alcoholic liquor, generally hot and spiced.

Punch *n* the main character in the children's puppet show, Punch and Judy.

punchbag *n* a stuffed or inflated bag suspended by a flexible rod, that is punched for exercise, esp. boxing training.

punchball *n* a stuffed or inflated ball supported by a flexible rod, that is punched for exercise, esp. boxing training.

punchbowl *n* a large bowl for serving punch.

punch-drunk *adj* dazed and confused through suffering repeated blows to the head.

punched card *or esp US* **punch card** *n Computers* a card on which data can be coded in the form of punched holes.

Punchinello *n, pl* **-los** *or* **-loes** a clown from Italian puppet shows, the origin of Punch.

punch line *n* the last line of a joke or funny story that gives it its point.

punch-up *n Brit informal* a fight or brawl.

punchy *adj* **punchier, punchiest** *Informal* effective or forceful: *learn to compose short concise punchy letters*

punctilious *adj Formal* **1** paying careful attention to correct social behaviour. **2** attentive to detail. **punctiliously** *adv*

punctual *adj* **1** arriving or taking place at an arranged time. **2** (of a person) always keeping exactly to arranged times. **punctuality** *n* **punctually** *adv*

THESAURUS

read the riot act, rebuke, reprimand, reprove, take to task, tear into (*informal*), tear (someone) off a strip (*Brit. informal*), tell off (*informal*), tick off (*informal*)

pulp *n.* **1.** mash, mush, pap, paste, pomace, semiliquid, semisolid **2.** flesh, marrow, soft part ~*vb.* **3.** crush, mash, pulverize, squash, triturate

pulse **1.** *n.* beat, beating, oscillation, pulsation, rhythm, stroke, throb, throbbing, vibration **2.** *vb.* beat, pulsate, throb, tick, vibrate

pump *vb.* **1.** *sometimes with* **from** *or* **out** bail out, drain, draw off, drive out, empty, force out, siphon **2.** *usually with* **in** *or* **into** drive, force, inject, pour, push, send, supply **3.** cross-examine, give (someone) the third degree, grill (*informal*), interrogate, probe, question closely, quiz, worm out of

pun double entendre, play on words, quip, witticism

punch¹ *vb.* **1.** bash (*informal*), belt (*informal*), biff (*slang*), bop (*informal*), box, clout (*informal*), hit, plug (*slang*), pummel, slam, slug, smash, sock (*slang*), strike, wallop (*informal*) ~*n.* **2.** bash (*informal*), biff (*slang*), blow, bop (*informal*), clout (*informal*), hit, jab, knock, plug (*slang*), sock (*slang*), thump, wallop (*informal*) **3.** *informal* bite, drive, effectiveness, force, forcefulness, impact, point, verve, vigour

punch² *vb.* bore, cut, drill, perforate, pierce, pink, prick, puncture, stamp

punch-drunk befuddled, confused, dazed, groggy (*informal*), in a daze, knocked silly, punchy (*informal*), reeling, slaphappy (*informal*), staggering, stupefied, unsteady, woozy (*informal*)

punctilious *formal* careful, ceremonious, conscientious, exact, finicky, formal, fussy, meticulous, nice, particular, precise, proper, scrupulous, strict

punctual early, exact, in good time, on the dot, on

punctuate *vb* **-ating, -ated 1** to insert punctuation marks into (a written text). **2** to interrupt at frequent intervals: *the meeting was punctuated by heckling.* **3** to emphasize: *he punctuated the question by pressing the muzzle into the pilot's neck.*

punctuation *n* **1** the use of symbols, such as commas, to indicate speech patterns and meaning not otherwise shown by the written language. **2** the symbols used for this purpose.

punctuation mark *n* any of the signs used in punctuation, such as a comma.

puncture *n* **1** a small hole made by a sharp object. **2** a tear and loss of pressure in a tyre. **3** the act of puncturing or perforating. *~vb* **-turing, -tured 4** to pierce a hole in (something) with a sharp object. **5** to cause (a tyre etc.) to lose pressure by piercing.

pundit *n* **1** an expert on a subject who often speaks or writes about it for a non-specialist audience: *Spain's leading sports pundit, who hosts two TV programmes.* **2** a Hindu scholar learned in Sanskrit, religion, philosophy, or law.

pungent *adj* **1** having a strong sharp bitter smell or taste. **2** (of speech or writing) biting; critical. **pungency** *n*

punish *vb* **1** to force (someone) to undergo a penalty for some crime or misbehaviour. **2** to inflict punishment for (some crime or misbehaviour). **3** to treat harshly, esp. by overexertion: *he continued to punish himself in the gym.* **punishable** *adj* **punishing** *adj*

punishment *n* **1** a penalty for a crime or offence. **2** the act of punishing or state of being punished. **3** *Informal* rough physical treatment: *the boxer's face could not withstand further punishment.*

punitive (**pew**-nit-tiv) *adj* relating to punishment: *punitive measures.*

punk *n* **1** a worthless person. **2** a youth movement of the late 1970s, characterized by anti-Establishment slogans, short spiky hair, and the wearing of worthless articles such as safety pins for decoration. **3** short for **punk rock. 4** a follower of the punk movement or of punk rock. *~adj* **5** relating to the punk youth movement of the late 1970s: *a punk band.* **6** worthless or insignificant.

punkah *or* **punka** *n* (in India) a ceiling fan made of a cloth stretched over a rectangular frame.

punk rock *n* rock music of the punk youth movement of the late 1970s, characterized by energy and aggressive lyrics and performance. **punk rocker** *n*

punnet *n Chiefly Brit* a small basket for fruit.

punster *n* a person who is fond of making puns.

punt[1] *n* **1** an open flat-bottomed boat, propelled by a pole. *~vb* **2** to propel (a punt) by pushing with a pole on the bottom of a river.

punt[2] *n* **1** a kick in certain sports, such as rugby, in which the ball is dropped and kicked before it hits the ground. *~vb* **2** to kick (a ball) using a punt.

punt[3] *Chiefly Brit ~vb* **1** to gamble or bet. *~n* **2** a gamble or bet, esp. against the bank, such as in roulette.

punt[4] *n* the standard monetary unit of the Republic of Ireland.

punter *n* **1** a person who places a bet. **2** *Informal* any member of the public, esp. when a customer: *the punters are flocking into the sales.*

puny *adj* **-nier, -niest** small and weakly.

pup *n* **1 a** a young dog; puppy. **b** the young of various other animals, such as the seal. *~vb* **pupping, pupped 2** (of dogs, seals, etc.) to give birth to pups.

pupa (**pew**-pa) *n, pl* **-pae** (-pee) *or* **-pas** an insect at the stage of development between larva and adult. **pupal** *adj*

pupil[1] *n* a student who is taught by a teacher.

pupil[2] *n* the dark circular opening at the centre of the iris of the eye.

puppet *n* **1** a small doll or figure moved by strings attached to its limbs or by the hand inserted in its cloth body. **2** a person or state that appears independent but is controlled by another: *the former cabinet ministers have denied that they are puppets of a foreign government.*

puppeteer *n* a person who operates puppets.

puppy *n, pl* **-pies 1** a young dog. **2** *Informal, contemptuous* a brash or conceited young man. **puppyish** *adj*

puppy fat *n* fatty tissue that develops in childhood or adolescence and usually disappears with maturity.

purblind *adj* **1** partly or nearly blind. **2** lacking in understanding.

purchase *vb* **-chasing, -chased 1** to obtain (goods)

THESAURUS

time, precise, prompt, punctilious, seasonable, strict, timely

punctuality promptitude, promptness, readiness, regularity

punctuate 1. break, interject, interrupt, intersperse, pepper, sprinkle **2.** accentuate, emphasize, lay stress on, mark, point up, stress, underline

puncture *n.* **1.** break, cut, damage, hole, leak, nick, opening, perforation, rupture, slit **2.** flat, flat tyre *~vb.* **3.** bore, cut, impale, nick, penetrate, perforate, pierce, prick, rupture **4.** deflate, flatten

pundit buff (*informal*), maestro, one of the cognoscenti, (self-appointed) authority *or* expert

pungent 1. acerbic, acid, acrid, aromatic, bitter, highly flavoured, hot, peppery, piquant, seasoned, sharp, sour, spicy, stinging, strong, tangy, tart **2.** acrimonious, acute, barbed, biting, caustic, cutting, incisive, keen, mordacious, mordant, penetrating, piercing, poignant, pointed, sarcastic, scathing, sharp, stinging, stringent, telling, trenchant, vitriolic

punish beat, castigate, chasten, chastise, correct, discipline, flog, give a lesson to, lash, penalize, rap someone's knuckles, scourge, sentence, slap someone's wrist, whip

punishable blameworthy, chargeable, convictable, criminal, culpable, indictable

punishing arduous, backbreaking, burdensome, demanding, exhausting, grinding, gruelling, hard, strenuous, taxing, tiring, uphill, wearing

punishment 1. chastening, chastisement, comeuppance (*slang*), correction, discipline, just deserts, penalty, penance, punitive measures, retribution, sanction, what for (*informal*) **2.** *informal* abuse, beating, hard work, maltreatment, manhandling, pain, rough treatment, slave labour, torture, victimization

punitive in reprisal, in retaliation, punitory, retaliative, retaliatory, revengeful, vindictive

punt *chiefly Brit. vb.* **1.** back, bet, gamble, lay, stake, wager *~n.* **2.** bet, gamble, stake, wager

punter *n.* **1.** backer, better, gambler, punt (*chiefly Brit.*) **2.** *informal* bloke (*Brit. informal*), fellow, guy (*informal*), man in the street, person **3.** *informal* client, customer

puny diminutive, dwarfish, feeble, frail, inconsequential, inferior, insignificant, little, minor, paltry, petty, piddling (*informal*), pint-sized (*informal*), pygmy, sickly, stunted, tiny, trifling, trivial, underfed, undersized, undeveloped, weak, weakly, worthless

pupil beginner, catechumen, disciple, learner, neophyte, novice, scholar, schoolboy, schoolgirl, student, trainee, tyro

by payment. **2** to obtain by effort or sacrifice: *he had purchased his freedom at the expense of his principles.* ~*n* **3** something that is bought. **4** the act of buying. **5** the mechanical advantage achieved by a lever. **6** a firm leverage or grip. **purchaser** *n*

purdah *n* the custom in some Muslim and Hindu communities of keeping women in seclusion, with clothing that conceals them completely when they go out.

pure *adj* **1** not mixed with any other materials or elements: *pure wool.* **2** free from tainting or polluting matter: *pure water.* **3** innocent: *pure love.* **4** complete: *Pamela's presence on that particular flight was pure chance.* **5** (of a subject) studied in its theoretical aspects rather than for its practical applications: *pure mathematics.* **6** of unmixed descent. **purely** *adv* **pureness** *n*

purebred *adj* denoting a pure strain obtained through many generations of controlled breeding.

puree (**pure**-ray) *n* **1** a smooth thick pulp of sieved fruit, vegetables, meat, or fish. ~*vb* **-reeing, -reed 2** to make (foods) into a puree.

purgative *Med* ~*n* **1** a medicine for emptying the bowels. ~*adj* **2** causing emptying of the bowels.

purgatory *n* **1** *Chiefly RC Church* a place in which the souls of those who have died undergo limited suffering for their sins on earth before they go to heaven. **2** a situation of temporary suffering or torment: *it was purgatory living in the same house as him.* **purgatorial** *adj*

purge *vb* **purging, purged 1** to rid (something) of undesirable qualities. **2** to rid (an organization etc.) of undesirable people. **3 a** to empty (the bowels). **b** to cause (a person) to empty his or her bowels. **4 a** *Law* to clear (a person) of a charge. **b** to free (oneself) of guilt by showing repentance. **5** to be purified. ~*n* **6** the act or process of purging. **7** the removal of undesirables from a state, organization, or political party. **8** a medicine that empties the bowels.

purify *vb* **-fies, -fying, -fied 1** to free (something) of harmful or inferior matter. **2** to free (a person) from sin or guilt. **3** to make clean, for example in a religious ceremony. **purification** *n*

purism *n* strict insistence on the correct usage or style, such as in grammar or art. **purist** *adj, n* **puristic** *adj*

puritan *n* **1** a person who follows strict moral or religious principles. ~*adj* **2** of or like a puritan: *he maintained a streak of puritan self-denial.* **puritanism** *n*

Puritan *History* ~*n* **1** a member of the extreme English Protestants who wished to strip the Church of England of most of its rituals. ~*adj* **2** of or relating to the Puritans. **Puritanism** *n*

puritanical *adj* **1** *Usually disparaging* strict in moral or religious outlook. **2** (*sometimes cap*) of or relating to a puritan or the Puritans. **puritanically** *adv*

purity *n* the state or quality of being pure.

purl[1] *n* **1** a knitting stitch made by doing a plain stitch backwards. **2** a decorative border, such as of lace. ~*vb* **3** to knit in purl stitch.

purl[2] *vb Literary* (of a stream) to flow with a gentle movement and a murmuring sound.

purlieu (**per**-lyoo) *n* **1** *English history* land on the edge of a royal forest. **2** (*usually pl*) *Literary* a neighbouring area; outskirts. **3** (*often pl*) *Literary* a place one frequents: *the committee was the purlieu of civil servants.*

purlin *or* **purline** *n* a horizontal beam that supports the rafters of a roof.

purloin *vb Formal* to steal.

purple *n* **1** a colour between red and blue. **2** cloth of this colour, often used to symbolize royalty or nobility. **3** the official robe of a cardinal. **4** anything purple, such as purple paint or purple clothing: *a large lady, unwisely dressed in purple.* ~*adj* **5** of a colour between red and blue. **6** (of writing) excessively elaborate: *purple prose.* **purplish** *adj*

purple heart *n Informal, chiefly Brit* a heart-shaped purple tablet consisting mainly of amphetamine.

Purple Heart *n* a decoration awarded to members of the US Armed Forces wounded in action.

purport *vb* **1** to claim to be or do something, esp. falsely: *painkillers may actually cause the headaches they purport to cure.* **2** (of speech or writing) to signify or imply. ~*n* **3** meaning or significance.

purpose *n* **1** the reason for which anything is done, created, or exists. **2** a fixed design or idea that is the object of an action. **3** determination: *his easy manner only lightly conceals a clear sense of purpose.* **4** prac-

THESAURUS

puppet 1. doll, marionette **2.** cat's-paw, creature, dupe, figurehead, instrument, mouthpiece, pawn, stooge, tool

purchase *vb.* **1.** acquire, buy, come by, gain, get, get hold of, invest in, make a purchase, obtain, pay for, pick up, procure, secure, shop for **2.** achieve, attain, earn, gain, realize, win ~*n.* **3.** acquisition, asset, buy, gain, investment, possession, property **4.** foothold, footing, grasp, grip, hold, lever, leverage, toehold

pure 1. authentic, clear, flawless, genuine, natural, neat, perfect, real, simple, straight, true, unalloyed, unmixed **2.** clean, disinfected, germ-free, immaculate, pasteurized, sanitary, spotless, squeaky-clean, sterile, sterilized, unadulterated, unblemished, uncontaminated, unpolluted, untainted, wholesome **3.** blameless, chaste, guileless, honest, immaculate, impeccable, innocent, maidenly, modest, true, uncorrupted, undefiled, unspotted, unstained, unsullied, upright, virgin, virginal, virtuous **4.** absolute, complete, mere, outright, sheer, thorough, unmitigated, unqualified, utter **5.** abstract, academic, philosophical, speculative, theoretical

purely absolutely, completely, entirely, exclusively, just, merely, only, plainly, simply, solely, totally, wholly

purge *vb.* **1.** axe (*informal*), clean out, dismiss, do away with, eject, eradicate, expel, exterminate, get rid of, kill, liquidate, oust, remove, rid of, rout out, sweep out, wipe out **2.** absolve, clear, exonerate, expiate, forgive, pardon **3.** cleanse, purify, wash ~*n.* **4.** cleanup, crushing, ejection, elimination, eradication, expulsion, liquidation, reign of terror, removal, suppression, witch hunt **5.** aperient (*Medical*), cathartic, dose of salts, emetic, enema, laxative, purgative (*Medical*)

purify 1. clarify, clean, cleanse, decontaminate, disinfect, filter, fumigate, refine, sanitize, wash **2.** absolve, cleanse, exculpate, exonerate, lustrate, redeem, sanctify, shrive

purist classicist, formalist, pedant, precisian, stickler

puritan 1. *n.* fanatic, moralist, pietist, prude, rigorist, zealot **2.** *adj.* ascetic, austere, hidebound, intolerant, moralistic, narrow, narrow-minded, prudish, puritanical, severe, strait-laced, strict

puritanical *usually disparaging* ascetic, austere, bigoted, disapproving, fanatical, forbidding, narrow, narrow-minded, prim, proper, prudish, puritan, rigid, severe, stiff, strait-laced, strict, stuffy

purpose *n.* **1.** aim, design, function, idea, intention, object, point, principle, reason **2.** aim, ambition, aspiration, design, desire, end, goal, hope, intention, ob-

tical advantage or use: *we debated senseless points of dogma for hours to no fruitful purpose.* **5 on purpose** intentionally. ~*vb* **-posing, -posed 6** to intend or determine to do (something).

purpose-built *adj* made to serve a specific purpose.

purposeful *adj* with a fixed and definite purpose; determined. **purposefully** *adv*

purposely *adv* on purpose.

purposive *adj Formal* **1** having or showing a definite intention: *the establishment of the camps lacks a purposive trend towards a solution.* **2** useful.

purr *vb* **1** (esp. of cats) to make a low vibrant sound, usually considered as expressing pleasure. **2** to express (pleasure) by this sound or by a sound suggestive of purring. ~*n* **3** a purring sound.

purse *n* **1** a small pouch for carrying money. **2** *US & Canad* a woman's handbag. **3** wealth or resources: *the public purse appeared bottomless.* **4** a sum of money that is offered as a prize. ~*vb* **pursing, pursed 5** to pull (the lips) into a small rounded shape.

purser *n* an officer aboard a ship who keeps the accounts.

purse strings *pl n* **hold the purse strings** to control the spending of a particular family, group, etc.

pursuance *n Formal* the carrying out of an action or plan: *the pursuance of duty had taken him abroad.*

pursue *vb* **-suing, -sued 1** to follow (a person, vehicle, or animal) in order to capture or overtake. **2** to try hard to achieve (some desire or aim). **3** to follow the guidelines of (a plan or policy). **4** to apply oneself to (studies or interests). **5** to follow persistently or seek to become acquainted with: *was his desire to pursue and marry Carol based purely on her looks?* **6** to continue to discuss or argue (a point or subject). **pursuer** *n*

pursuit *n* **1** the act of pursuing. **2** an occupation or pastime.

pursuivant (**purse**-iv-ant) *n* the lowest rank of heraldic officer.

purulent (**pure**-yew-lent) *adj* of, relating to, or containing pus. **purulence** *n*

purvey *vb* **1** to sell or provide (foodstuffs). **2** to provide or make available: *the foreign ministry used him to purvey sensitive items of diplomatic news.* **purveyor** *n*

purview *n* **1** scope of operation: *each designation falls under the purview of a different ministry.* **2** breadth or range of outlook: *he hopes that the purview of science will be widened.*

pus *n* the yellowish fluid that comes from inflamed or infected tissue.

push *vb* **1** (sometimes foll. by *off, away,* etc.) to apply steady force to in order to move. **2** to thrust (one's way) through something, such as a crowd. **3** (sometimes foll. by *for*) to be an advocate or promoter (of): *there are many groups you can join to push for change.* **4** to spur or drive (oneself or another person) in order to achieve more effort or better results: *you must be careful not to push your children too hard.* **5** *Informal* to sell (narcotic drugs) illegally. ~*n* **6** the act of pushing; thrust. **7** *Informal* drive or determination: *everything depends on him having the push to obtain the money.* **8** *Informal* a special effort to achieve something: *when this push spent itself it was obvious the bid had failed.* **9 the push** *Informal, chiefly Brit* dismissal from employment. ~See also **push about, push off,** etc.

push about *or* **around** *vb Informal* to bully: *don't let them push you around.*

push-bike *n Brit informal* a bicycle.

push button *n* **1** an electrical switch operated by pressing a button. ~*adj* **push-button 2** operated by a push button: *a push-button radio.*

pushchair *n Brit* a small folding chair on wheels in which a small child can be wheeled around: *escalators are difficult with pushchairs.*

pushed *adj* (often foll. by *for*) *Informal* short of: *pushed for time.*

pusher *n Informal* a person who sells illegal drugs.

THESAURUS

ject, objective, plan, project, scheme, target, view, wish **3.** constancy, determination, firmness, persistence, resolution, resolve, single-mindedness, steadfastness, tenacity, will **4.** advantage, avail, benefit, effect, gain, good, outcome, profit, result, return, use, utility **5. on purpose** by design, deliberately, designedly, intentionally, knowingly, purposely, wilfully, wittingly ~*vb.* **6.** aim, aspire, commit oneself, contemplate, decide, design, determine, have a mind to, intend, make up one's mind, mean, meditate, plan, propose, resolve, set one's sights on, think to, work towards

purposely by design, calculatedly, consciously, deliberately, designedly, expressly, intentionally, knowingly, on purpose, wilfully, with intent

purse *n.* **1.** money-bag, pouch, wallet **2.** coffers, exchequer, funds, means, money, resources, treasury, wealth, wherewithal **3.** award, gift, present, prize, reward ~*vb.* **4.** close, contract, knit, pout, press together, pucker, tighten, wrinkle

pursue 1. accompany, attend, chase, dog, follow, give chase to, go after, harass, harry, haunt, hound, hunt, hunt down, plague, run after, shadow, stalk, tail (*informal*), track **2.** aim for, aspire to, desire, have as one's goal, purpose, seek, strive for, try for, work towards **3.** adhere to, carry on, continue, cultivate, hold to, keep on, maintain, persevere in, persist in, proceed, see through **4.** apply oneself, carry on, conduct, engage in, perform, ply, practise, prosecute, tackle, wage, work at **5.** chase after, court, make up to (*informal*), pay attention to, pay court to, set one's cap at, woo

pursuit 1. chase, hunt, hunting, inquiry, quest, search, seeking, tracking, trail, trailing **2.** activity, hobby, interest, line, occupation, pastime, pleasure, vocation

purview 1. ambit, compass, confine(s), extent, field, limit, orbit, province, range, reach, scope, sphere **2.** comprehension, ken, overview, perspective, range of view, understanding

push *vb.* **1.** depress, drive, poke, press, propel, ram, shove, thrust **2.** elbow, jostle, make *or* force one's way, move, shoulder, shove, squeeze, thrust **3.** *sometimes with* **for** advertise, boost, cry up, hype, make known, plug (*informal*), promote, propagandize, publicize **4.** browbeat, coerce, constrain, dragoon, egg on, encourage, exert influence on, expedite, hurry, impel, incite, influence, oblige, persuade, press, prod, speed (up), spur, urge ~*n.* **5.** butt, jolt, nudge, poke, prod, shove, thrust **6.** *informal* ambition, determination, drive, dynamism, energy, enterprise, get-up-and-go (*informal*), go (*informal*), gumption (*informal*), initiative, pep, vigour, vitality **7.** *informal* advance, assault, attack, charge, effort, offensive, onset, thrust **8. the push** *informal, chiefly Brit.* discharge, dismissal, marching orders (*informal*), one's books (*informal*), one's cards, the boot (*slang*), the (old) heave-ho (*informal*), the order of the boot (*slang*), the sack (*informal*)

pushed *often with* **for** hurried, in difficulty, pressed,

pushing *prep* **1** almost or nearly (a certain age, speed, etc.): *pushing fifty.* ~*adj* **2** aggressively ambitious.

push off *vb Informal* to go away; leave.

pushover *n Informal* **1** something that is easily achieved. **2** a person, team, etc., that is easily taken advantage of or defeated.

push-start *vb* **1** to start (a motor vehicle) by pushing it, thus turning the engine. ~*n* **2** this process.

push through *vb* to force to accept: *the President needs their votes to push through his economic package.*

pushy *adj* **pushier, pushiest** *Informal* offensively assertive or ambitious.

pusillanimous *adj Formal* timid and cowardly: *the authorities have been too pusillanimous in condemning the violence.* **pusillanimity** *n*

puss *n* **1** *Informal* a cat. **2** *Slang* a girl or woman.

pussy[1] *n, pl* **pussies 1** Also called: **pussycat** *Informal* a cat. **2** *Taboo slang* the female genitals.

pussy[2] *adj* **-sier, -siest** containing or full of pus.

pussyfoot *vb Informal* **1** to move about stealthily. **2** to avoid committing oneself: *don't let's pussyfoot about naming the hit man.*

pussy willow *n* a willow tree with silvery silky catkins.

pustulate *vb* **-lating, -lated** to form into pustules.

pustule *n* a small inflamed raised area of skin containing pus. **pustular** *adj*

put *vb* **putting, put 1** to cause to be (in a position or place): *he put the book on the table.* **2** to cause to be (in a state or condition): *what can be done to put things right?* **3** to lay (blame, emphasis, etc.) on a person or thing: *don't try to put the blame on someone else!* **4** to set or commit (to an action, task, or duty), esp. by force: *she put him to work weeding the garden.* **5** to estimate or judge: *I wouldn't put him in the same class as Verdi as a composer.* **6** (foll. by *to*) to utilize: *he put his culinary skills to good use when he opened a restaurant.* **7** to express: *he didn't put it quite as crudely as that.* **8** to make (an end or limit): *opponents claim the scheme will put an end to much of the sailing and boating in the area.* **9** to present for consideration; propose: *he put the question to the committee.* **10** to invest (money) in or expend (time or energy) on: *he put five thousand pounds into the project.* **11** to throw or cast: *put the shot.* ~*n* **12** a throw, esp. in putting the shot. ~See also **put about, put across,** etc.

put about *vb* **1** to make widely known: *a rumour was put about that he had been drunk.* **2** *Naut* to change course.

put across *vb* to communicate successfully: *he's not very good at putting his ideas across.*

put aside *vb* **1** to save: *try to put some money aside in case of emergencies.* **2** to disregard: *put aside adolescent fantasies of romance.*

putative (**pew**-tat-iv) *adj Formal* **1** commonly regarded as being: *the desire of the putative father to establish his possible paternity.* **2** considered to exist or have existed; inferred: *a putative earlier form.*

put away *vb* **1** to save: *it takes a lot of discipline to put away for your old age.* **2** *Informal* to lock up in a prison, mental institution, etc.: *we have enough evidence to put him away for life.* **3** *Informal* to eat or drink in large amounts: *he put away three beers and three huge shots of brandy.*

put back *vb* **1** to return to its former place. **2** to move to a later time: *the UK release of her new album has been put back until January.*

put down *vb* **1** to make a written record of. **2** to repress: *the rising was put down with revolting cruelty.* **3** to consider: *I'd put him down as a complete fool.* **4** to attribute: *the government's defeat in the election can be put down to a general desire for change.* **5** to put (an animal) to death. **6** *Slang* to belittle or humiliate. ~*n* **put-down 7** *Informal* a cruelly crushing remark.

put forward *vb* **1** to propose or suggest. **2** to offer the name of; nominate.

put in *vb* **1** to devote (time or effort): *the competitors who did best were the ones who had put in some practice.* **2** (often foll. by *for*) to apply (for a job). **3** to submit: *they have put in an official complaint.* **4** *Naut* to bring a vessel into port.

put off *vb* **1** to postpone: *ministers have put off making a final decision until next month.* **2** to evade (a person) by delay: *they tried to put him off, but he came anyway.* **3** to cause extreme dislike in: *he was*

THESAURUS

rushed, short of, tight, under pressure, up against it (*informal*)

pushing ambitious, determined, driving, dynamic, enterprising, go-ahead, on the go, purposeful, resourceful

pushover *informal* **1.** breeze (*U.S. & Canad. informal*), cakewalk (*informal*), child's play (*informal*), cinch (*slang*), doddle (*Brit. slang*), picnic (*informal*), piece of cake (*Brit. informal*), walkover (*informal*) **2.** chump (*informal*), easy game (*informal*), easy *or* soft mark (*informal*), mug (*Brit. slang*), soft touch (*slang*), stooge (*slang*), sucker (*slang*), walkover (*informal*)

pussyfoot *informal* **1.** creep, prowl, slink, steal, tiptoe, tread warily **2.** beat about the bush, be noncommittal, equivocate, flannel (*Brit. informal*), hedge, hum and haw, prevaricate, sit on the fence, tergiversate (*formal*)

pustule abscess, blister, boil, fester, gathering, pimple, ulcer, zit (*slang*)

put 1. bring, deposit, establish, fix, lay, place, position, rest, set, settle, situate **2.** commit, condemn, consign, doom, enjoin, impose, inflict, levy, subject **3.** assign, constrain, employ, force, induce, make, oblige, require, set, subject to **4.** express, phrase, pose, set, state, utter, word **5.** advance, bring forward, forward, offer, posit, present, propose, set before, submit, tender **6.** cast, fling, heave, hurl, lob, pitch, throw, toss

put across communicate, convey, explain, get across, get through, make clear, make oneself understood, spell out

put aside 1. cache, deposit, keep in reserve, lay by, salt away, save, squirrel away, stockpile, store, stow away **2.** bury, discount, disregard, forget, ignore

putative *formal* alleged, assumed, commonly believed, imputed, presumed, presumptive, reported, reputed, supposed

put away 1. deposit, keep, lay in, put by, save, set aside, store away **2.** *informal* certify, commit, confine, institutionalize, lock up **3.** *informal* consume, devour, eat up, gobble, gulp down, wolf down

put down 1. enter, inscribe, log, record, set down, take down, transcribe, write down **2.** crush, quash, quell, repress, silence, stamp out, suppress **3.** ascribe, attribute, impute, set down **4.** destroy, do away with, put away, put out of its misery, put to sleep **5.** *slang* condemn, crush, deflate, dismiss, disparage, humiliate, mortify, reject, shame, slight, snub

put forward advance, introduce, move, nominate, prescribe, present, press, proffer, propose, recommend, submit, suggest, tender

put off by her appearance. **4** to cause to lose interest in: *the accident put him off driving.*

put on *vb* **1** to dress oneself in. **2** to adopt (an attitude or feeling) insincerely: *I don't see why you have to put on that fake American accent.* **3** to present (a play or show). **4** to add: *I've put on nearly a stone since September.* **5** to cause (an electrical device) to function: *she put on the light.* **6** to bet (money) on a horse race or game. **7** to impose: *the government has put a tax on gas and electricity.*

put out *vb* **1 a** to annoy or anger. **b** to disturb or confuse. **2** to extinguish (a fire, light, etc.). **3** to inconvenience (someone): *I hope I'm not putting you out.* **4** to select or lay out for use: *she put out two clean cloths in the kitchen.* **5** to publish or broadcast: *she put out a statement denying the rumours.* **6** to dislocate: *he put his back out digging the garden.*

put over *vb Informal* to communicate (facts or information).

putrefy *vb* **-fies, -fying, -fied** *Formal* (of organic matter) to rot and produce an offensive smell. **putrefaction** *n*

putrescent *adj Formal* becoming putrid; rotting. **putrescence** *n*

putrid *adj* **1** (of organic matter) rotting: *putrid meat.* **2** sickening or foul: *a putrid stench.* **3** *Informal* deficient in quality or value: *a penchant for putrid puns.* **4** morally corrupt. **putridity** *n*

putsch *n* a violent and sudden political revolt: *an attempted putsch against the general.*

putt *Golf ~n* **1** a stroke on the green with a putter to roll the ball into or near the hole. *~vb* **2** to strike (the ball) in this way.

puttee *n* (*usually pl*) (esp. as part of a military uniform) a strip of cloth worn wound around the leg from the ankle to the knee.

putter *n Golf* a club with a short shaft for putting.

put through *vb* **1** to connect by telephone: *I'm sorry, you've been put through to the wrong extension.* **2** to carry out to a conclusion: *he put through his plan.*

putting green *n* (on a golf course) the area of closely mown grass around the hole.

putty *n, pl* **-ties 1** a stiff paste used to fix glass into frames and fill cracks in woodwork. *~vb* **-ties, -tying, -tied 2** to fix or fill with putty.

put up *vb* **1** to build or erect: *I want to put up some shelves in the living room.* **2** to accommodate or be accommodated at: *can you put me up for tonight?* **3** to increase (prices). **4** to submit (a plan, case, etc.). **5** to offer: *the factory is being put up for sale.* **6** to give: *they put up a good fight.* **7** to provide (money) for: *they put up 35 per cent of the film's budget.* **8** to nominate or be nominated as a candidate: *the party have yet to decide whether to put up a candidate.* **9 put up to** to incite to: *I wonder who put them up to it?* **10 put up with** *Informal* to endure or tolerate. *~adj* **put-up 11** *Informal* dishonestly or craftily prearranged: *a put-up job.*

put upon *vb* to take advantage of (someone): *he's always being put upon.*

puzzle *vb* **-zling, -zled 1** to baffle or bewilder. **2 puzzle out** to solve (a problem) by mental effort. **3 puzzle over** to think deeply about in an attempt to understand: *he puzzled over the squiggles and curves on the paper. ~n* **4** a problem that cannot be easily solved. **5** a toy, game, or question presenting a problem that requires skill or ingenuity for its solution. **puzzlement** *n* **puzzled** *adj* **puzzler** *n* **puzzling** *adj*

PVC polyvinyl chloride.

PW policewoman.

PWR pressurized-water reactor.

pyaemia *or* **pyemia** *n Med* blood poisoning with pus-forming microorganisms in the blood.

pye-dog *or* **pi-dog** *n* a half-wild Asian dog with no owner.

pygmy *n, pl* **-mies 1** something that is a very small example of its type. **2** an abnormally undersized per-

THESAURUS

put off 1. defer, delay, hold over, postpone, put back, put on the back burner (*informal*), reschedule, take a rain check on (*informal*) **2.** discourage, dishearten, dissuade

put on 1. change into, don, dress, get dressed in, slip into **2.** affect, assume, fake, feign, make believe, play-act, pretend, sham, simulate **3.** do, mount, present, produce, show, stage **4.** add, gain, increase by **5.** back, bet, lay, place, wager

put out 1. anger, annoy, confound, disturb, exasperate, harass, irk, irritate, nettle, perturb, provoke, vex **2.** blow out, douse, extinguish, quench, smother, snuff out, stamp out **3.** bother, discomfit, discommode, discompose, disconcert, discountenance, disturb, embarrass, impose upon, incommode, inconvenience, put on the spot, trouble, upset **4.** bring out, broadcast, circulate, issue, make known, make public, publish, release

putrefy *formal* corrupt, decay, decompose, deteriorate, go bad, rot, spoil, stink, taint

putrescent *formal* decaying, decomposing, going bad, rotting, stinking

putrid bad, contaminated, corrupt, decayed, decomposed, fetid, foul, off, putrefied, rancid, rank, reeking, rotten, rotting, spoiled, stinking, tainted

put through accomplish, achieve, bring off, carry through, conclude, do, effect, execute, manage, pull off, realize

put up 1. build, construct, erect, fabricate, raise **2.** accommodate, board, entertain, give one lodging, house, lodge, take in **3.** float, nominate, offer, present, propose, put forward, recommend, submit **4.** advance, give, invest, pay, pledge, provide, supply **5. put up to** egg on, encourage, goad, incite, instigate, prompt, put the idea into one's head, urge **6. put up with** *informal* abide, bear, brook, endure, lump (*informal*), pocket, stand, stand for, stomach, suffer, swallow, take, tolerate

puzzle *vb.* **1.** baffle, beat (*slang*), bewilder, confound, confuse, flummox, mystify, nonplus, perplex, stump **2. puzzle out** clear up, crack, crack the code, decipher, figure out, find the key, get it, get the answer, resolve, see, solve, sort out, suss (out) (*slang*), think through, unravel, work out **3. puzzle over** ask oneself, brood, cudgel *or* rack one's brains, mull over, muse, ponder, study, think about, think hard, wonder *~n.* **4.** brainteaser (*informal*), conundrum, enigma, labyrinth, maze, mystery, paradox, poser, problem, question, question mark, riddle, teaser

puzzled at a loss, at sea, baffled, beaten, bewildered, clueless, confused, doubtful, flummoxed, in a fog, lost, mixed up, mystified, nonplussed, perplexed, stuck, stumped, without a clue

puzzlement bafflement, bewilderment, confusion, disorientation, doubt, doubtfulness, mystification, perplexity, questioning, surprise, uncertainty, wonder

puzzling abstruse, ambiguous, baffling, bewildering, beyond one, enigmatic, full of surprises, hard, incomprehensible, inexplicable, involved, knotty, labyrinthine, misleading, mystifying, oracular, perplexing, unaccountable, unclear, unfathomable

pygmy *n.* **1.** dwarf, Lilliputian, manikin, midget, shrimp (*informal*), Tom Thumb **2.** cipher, lightweight

son. **3** a person of little importance or significance. *~adj* **4** very small: *the pygmy anteater.*

Pygmy *n, pl* **-mies** a member of one of the very short peoples of Equatorial Africa.

pyjamas *or US* **pajamas** *pl n* a loose-fitting jacket or top and trousers worn to sleep in.

pylon *n* a large vertical steel tower-like structure supporting high-tension electrical cables.

pyorrhoea *or esp US* **pyorrhea** (pire-**ree**-a) *n Med* a discharge of pus, esp. in disease of the gums or tooth sockets.

pyramid *n* **1** a huge stone building with a square base and four sloping triangular sides meeting in a point, such as the royal tombs built by the ancient Egyptians. **2** *Maths* a solid figure with a polygonal base and triangular sides that meet in a common vertex. **pyramidal** *adj*

pyramid selling *n* the practice of selling distributors batches of goods which they then subdivide and sell to other distributors, this process continuing until the final distributors are left with a stock that is unsaleable except at a loss.

pyre *n* a pile of wood for cremating a corpse.

pyrethrum (pie-**reeth**-rum) *n* **1** a Eurasian chrysanthemum with white, pink, red, or purple flowers. **2** an insecticide prepared from dried pyrethrum flowers.

pyretic (pie-**ret**-ik) *adj Pathol* of, relating to, or characterized by fever.

Pyrex *n Trademark* a variety of heat-resistant glassware used in cookery and chemical apparatus.

pyrite (**pie**-rite) *n* a yellow mineral consisting of iron sulphide in cubic crystalline form. Formula: FeS_2.

pyrites (pie-**rite**-eez) *n, pl* **-tes 1** same as **pyrite. 2** a disulphide of a metal, esp. of copper and tin.

pyromania *n Psychiatry* the uncontrollable impulse and practice of setting things on fire. **pyromaniac** *n, adj*

pyrotechnics *n* **1** the art of making fireworks. **2** a firework display. **3** a brilliant display of skill: *all those courtroom pyrotechnics.* **pyrotechnic** *adj*

Pyrrhic victory (**pir**-ik) *n* a victory in which the victor's losses are as great as those of the defeated.

Pythagoras' theorem (pie-**thag**-or-ass) *n* the theorem that in a right-angled triangle the square of the length of the hypotenuse equals the sum of the squares of the other two sides.

python *n* a large nonpoisonous snake of Australia, Africa, and S Asia, which kills its prey by crushing it with its body.

pyx *n Christianity* any receptacle in which the bread used in Holy Communion is kept.

THESAURUS

(*informal*), mediocrity, nobody, nonentity, pipsqueak (*informal*), small fry *~adj.* **3.** baby, diminutive, dwarf, dwarfish, elfin, Lilliputian, midget, miniature, minuscule, pocket, small, stunted, teensy-weensy, teeny-weeny, tiny, undersized, wee

Q

Q 1 *Chess* queen. 2 question.
q. 1 quart. 2 quarter. 3 question. 4 quire.
Q. 1 Quebec. 2 Queen. 3 question.
QC Queen's Counsel.
QED which was to be shown or proved.
QLD Queensland.
QM Quartermaster.
qr. *pl* **qrs** 1 quarter. 2 quire.
qt *pl* **qt** *or* **qts** quart.
q.t. *n* **on the q.t.** *Informal* secretly.
qua (**kwah**) *prep* in the capacity of; by virtue of being.
quack[1] *vb* 1 (of a duck) to utter a harsh guttural sound. 2 to make a noise like a duck. ~*n* 3 the sound made by a duck.
quack[2] *n* 1 an unqualified person who claims medical knowledge. 2 *Brit, Austral, & NZ informal* a doctor. **quackery** *n*
quad[1] *n* short for **quadrangle** (sense 1).
quad[2] *n Informal* a quadruplet.
quad[3] *n* 1 quadraphonics. ~*adj* 2 quadraphonic.
quadrangle *n* 1 a rectangular courtyard with buildings on all four sides. 2 *Geom* a figure consisting of four points connected by four lines. **quadrangular** *adj*
quadrant *n* 1 *Geom* **a** a quarter of the circumference of a circle. **b** the area enclosed by two perpendicular radii of a circle. 2 a piece of a mechanism in the form of a quarter circle. 3 an instrument formerly used in astronomy and navigation for measuring the altitudes of stars.
quadraphonic *adj* using four independent channels to reproduce or record sound. **quadraphonics** *n*
quadrate *n* 1 a cube or square, or a square or cubelike object. ~*vb* **-rating, -rated** 2 to make square or rectangular.
quadratic *Maths* ~*n* 1 Also called: **quadratic equation** an equation in which the variable is raised to the power of two, but nowhere raised to a higher power: *solve the quadratic equation* $2x^2-3x-6=3$. ~*adj* 2 of or relating to the second power.
quadrennial *adj* 1 occurring every four years. 2 lasting four years.
quadri- *or before a vowel* **quadr-** *combining form* four: *quadrilateral.*
quadrilateral *adj* 1 having four sides. ~*n* 2 a polygon with four sides.
quadrille *n* 1 a square dance for four couples. 2 music for this dance.
quadrillion *n, pl* **-lions** *or* **-lion** 1 (in Britain, France, and Germany) the number represented as one followed by 24 zeros (10^{24}). 2 (in the US and Canada) the number represented as one followed by 15 zeros (10^{15}).
quadriplegia *n* paralysis of all four limbs. **quadriplegic** *adj, n*
quadruped (**kwod**-roo-ped) *n* an animal, esp. a mammal, that has four legs.
quadruple *vb* **-pling, -pled** 1 to multiply by four. ~*adj* 2 four times as much or as many. 3 consisting of four parts. 4 *Music* having four beats in each bar. ~*n* 5 a quantity or number four times as great as another.
quadruplet *n* one of four children born at one birth.
quadruplicate *adj* 1 fourfold or quadruple. ~*vb* **-cating, -cated** 2 to multiply or be multiplied by four.
quaff (**kwoff**) *vb Old-fashioned* to drink heartily or in one draught.
quagga *n, pl* **-gas** *or* **-ga** a recently extinct zebra, striped only on the head and shoulders.
quagmire (**kwog**-mire) *n* a soft wet area of land that gives way under the feet; bog.
quail[1] *n, pl* **quails** *or* **quail** a small game bird of the partridge family.
quail[2] *vb* to shrink back with fear; cower.
quaint *adj* attractively unusual, esp. in an old-fashioned style.
quake *vb* **quaking, quaked** 1 to shake or tremble with or as if with fear. 2 to shudder because of instability. ~*n* 3 *Informal* an earthquake.
Quaker *n* a member of a Christian sect, the Society of Friends. **Quakerism** *n*
qualification *n* 1 an official record of achievement awarded on the successful completion of a course of training or passing of an examination. 2 an ability, quality, or attribute, esp. one that fits a person to perform a particular job or task. 3 a condition that modifies or limits; restriction. 4 the act of qualifying or being qualified.
qualified *adj* 1 having successfully completed a training course or passed the exams necessary in order to be entitled to work in a particular profession: *a qualified lawyer.* 2 having the abilities, qualities, or attributes necessary to perform a particular job or task. 3 having completed a training or degree course and gained the relevant certificates. 4 limited or restricted; not wholehearted: *the mission was only a qualified success.*
qualify *vb* **-fies, -fying, -fied** 1 to have the abilities or attributes required in order to do or have something, such as a job: *he qualified as a teacher; she did not qualify for a State pension at that time.* 2 to moderate or restrict (a statement one has made). 3 to describe or be described as having a particular quality: *it was neither witty nor subtle enough to qualify as a spoof.* 4 to be successful in one stage of a competition

THESAURUS

quack charlatan, fake, fraud, humbug, impostor, mountebank, phoney *or* phony (*informal*), pretender
quagmire bog, fen, marsh, mire, morass, quicksand, slough, swamp
quail blanch, blench, cower, cringe, droop, faint, falter, flinch, have cold feet (*informal*), quake, recoil, shake, shrink, shudder, tremble
quaint antiquated, antique, artful, charming, gothic, ingenious, old-fashioned, old-world, picturesque
quake convulse, move, pulsate, quail, quiver, rock, shake, shiver, shudder, throb, totter, tremble, vibrate, waver, wobble
qualification **1.** ability, accomplishment, aptitude, attribute, capability, capacity, eligibility, endowment(s), fitness, quality, skill, suitability, suitableness **2.** allowance, caveat, condition, criterion, exception, exemption, limitation, modification, objection, prerequisite, proviso, requirement, reservation, restriction, rider, stipulation
qualified **1.** able, accomplished, adept, capable, certificated, competent, efficient, equipped, experienced, expert, fit, knowledgeable, licensed, practised, proficient, skilful, talented, trained **2.** bounded, circumscribed, conditional, confined, contingent, equivocal,

and as a result progress to the next stage: *Lewis failed to qualify for the 100 metres.* **5** *Grammar* to modify the sense of (a word). **qualifier** *n*

qualitative *adj* involving or relating to distinctions based on quality.

qualitative analysis *n Chem* analysis of a substance to determine its constituents.

quality *n, pl* **-ties 1** degree or standard of excellence. **2** a distinguishing characteristic or attribute. **3** the basic character or nature of something. **4** a feature of personality. **5** (formerly) high social status. *~adj* **6** excellent or superior: *a quality product.*

quality control *n* checking of the relative quality of a manufactured product, usually by testing samples.

qualm (**kwahm**) *n* **1** a pang of conscience; scruple. **2** a sudden sensation of misgiving. **3** a sudden feeling of sickness or nausea.

quandary *n, pl* **-ries** a situation in which it is difficult to decide what to do; predicament; dilemma.

quango *n, pl* **-gos** a semipublic government financed administrative body whose members are appointed by the government.

quantify *vb* **-fies, -fying, -fied** to discover or express the quantity of. **quantifiable** *adj* **quantification** *n*

quantitative *adj* **1** involving considerations of amount or size. **2** capable of being measured.

quantitative analysis *n Chem* analysis of a substance to determine the proportions of its constituents.

quantity *n, pl* **-ties 1** a specified or definite amount or number. **2** the aspect of anything that can be measured, weighed, or counted. **3** a large amount. **4** *Maths* an entity having a magnitude that may be denoted by a numerical expression.

quantity surveyor *n* a person who estimates the cost of the materials and labour necessary for a construction job.

quantum *n, pl* **-ta 1** an amount or quantity, esp. a specific amount. **2** *Physics* the smallest quantity of some physical property that a system can possess. *~adj* **3** of or designating a major breakthrough or sudden advance: *a quantum leap in business computing.*

quantum theory *n* a theory concerning the behaviour of physical systems based on the idea that they can only possess certain properties, such as energy and angular momentum, in discrete amounts (quanta).

quarantine *n* **1** a period of isolation, esp. of people or animals arriving from abroad, to prevent the spread of disease. *~vb* **-tining, -tined 2** to isolate in or as if in quarantine.

quark *n Physics* the hypothetical elementary particle supposed to be a fundamental unit of all baryons and mesons.

quarrel *n* **1** an angry disagreement; argument. **2** a cause of dispute; grievance. *~vb* **-relling, -relled** *or US* **-reling, -reled** (often foll. by *with*) **3** to engage in a disagreement or dispute; argue. **4** to find fault; complain.

quarrelsome *adj* inclined to quarrel or disagree.

quarry[1] *n, pl* **-ries 1** a place where stone is dug from the surface of the earth. *~vb* **-ries, -rying, -ried 2** to extract (stone) from a quarry.

quarry[2] *n, pl* **-ries 1** an animal that is being hunted; prey. **2** anything pursued.

quarry tile *n* an unglazed floor tile.

quart *n* a unit of liquid measure equal to one quarter of a gallon or two pints (1.136 litres).

quarter *n* **1** one of four equal parts of something such as an object or quantity. **2** the fraction equal to one divided by four ($\frac{1}{4}$). **3** a fourth part of a year; three months. **4** *Informal* a unit of weight equal to four ounces (113.4 grams). **5** a region or district of a town or city: *the French quarter of New Orleans.* **6** a region, direction, or point of the compass. **7** *US & Canad* a coin worth 25 cents. **8** short for **quarter-hour. 9** *Astron* **a** one fourth of the moon's period of revolution around the earth. **b** either of two phases of the moon when half of the lighted surface is visible. **10** (*sometimes pl*) an unspecified person or group of people: *it met stiff opposition in some quarters.* **11** mercy or pity shown to a defeated opponent: *no quarter was asked or given.* **12** any of the four limbs of a quadruped. *~vb* **13** to divide into four equal parts. **14** (formerly) to dismember (a human body). **15** to billet or be billeted in lodgings. **16** *Heraldry* to divide (a shield) into four separate bearings. *~adj* **17** being or consisting of one of four equal parts. *~See also* **quarters.**

quarterback *n* a player in American football who directs attacking play.

THESAURUS

guarded, limited, modified, provisional, reserved, restricted

qualify 1. capacitate, certify, commission, condition, empower, endow, equip, fit, ground, permit, prepare, ready, sanction, train **2.** abate, adapt, assuage, circumscribe, diminish, ease, lessen, limit, mitigate, moderate, modify, modulate, reduce, regulate, restrain, restrict, soften, temper, vary **3.** characterize, describe, designate, distinguish, modify, name

quality 1. calibre, distinction, excellence, grade, merit, position, pre-eminence, rank, standing, status, superiority, value, worth **2.** aspect, attribute, characteristic, condition, feature, mark, peculiarity, property, trait **3.** character, constitution, description, essence, kind, make, nature, sort **4.** *formerly* aristocracy, gentry, nobility, ruling class, upper class

qualm 1. anxiety, apprehension, compunction, disquiet, doubt, hesitation, misgiving, regret, reluctance, remorse, scruple, twinge *or* pang of conscience, uncertainty, uneasiness **2.** agony, attack, nausea, pang, queasiness, sickness, spasm, twinge

quandary bewilderment, cleft stick, delicate situation, difficulty, dilemma, doubt, embarrassment, impasse, perplexity, plight, predicament, puzzle, strait, uncertainty

quantity 1. aggregate, allotment, amount, lot, number, part, portion, quota, sum, total **2.** bulk, capacity, expanse, extent, greatness, length, magnitude, mass, measure, size, volume

quarrel *n.* **1.** affray, altercation, argument, brawl, breach, broil, commotion, contention, controversy, difference (of opinion), disagreement, discord, disputation, dispute, dissension, dissidence, disturbance, feud, fight, fracas, fray, misunderstanding, row, scrap (*informal*), shindig (*informal*), shindy (*informal*), skirmish, spat, squabble, strife, tiff, tumult, vendetta, wrangle *~vb.* **2.** altercate, argue, bicker, brawl, clash, differ, disagree, dispute, fall out (*informal*), fight, row, spar, squabble, wrangle **3.** carp, cavil, complain, decry, disapprove, find fault, object to, take exception to

quarrelsome argumentative, belligerent, cat-and-dog (*informal*), choleric, combative, contentious, cross, disputatious, fractious, ill-tempered, irascible, irritable, peevish, petulant, pugnacious, querulous

quarry aim, game, goal, objective, prey, prize, victim

quarter *n.* **1.** area, direction, district, locality, location, neighbourhood, part, place, point, position, prov-

quarter day *n* any of four days in the year when certain payments become due.

quarterdeck *n Naut* the rear part of the upper deck of a ship, traditionally for official or ceremonial use.

quarterfinal *n* the round before the semifinal in a competition.

quarter-hour *n* **1** a period of 15 minutes. **2** either of the points of time 15 minutes before or after the hour.

quarterlight *n Brit* a small pivoted window in the door of a car.

quarterly *adj* **1** occurring, done, due, or issued at intervals of three months. *~n, pl* **-lies 2** a periodical issued every three months. *~adv* **3** once every three months.

quartermaster *n* **1** a military officer responsible for accommodation, food, and equipment. **2** a naval officer responsible for navigation.

quarters *pl n* accommodation, esp. as provided for military personnel.

quarter sessions *n* (formerly) a court with limited jurisdiction, held four times a year.

quarterstaff *n, pl* **-staves** a stout iron-tipped wooden staff about 6ft long, formerly used as a weapon.

quartet *n* **1** a group of four singers or instrumentalists. **2** a piece of music for four performers. **3** any group of four.

quartile *n* **1** one of three values of a variable dividing its distribution into four groups with equal frequencies. *~adj* **2** of a quartile.

quarto *n, pl* **-tos** a book size resulting from folding a sheet of paper into four leaves or eight pages.

quartz *n* a hard glossy mineral consisting of crystalline silicon dioxide.

quartz clock *or* **watch** *n* a very accurate clock or watch that is operated by a vibrating quartz crystal.

quartz crystal *n* a thin plate or rod cut from a piece of quartz and ground so that it vibrates at a particular frequency.

quasar (**kway**-zar) *n* any of a class of extremely distant starlike objects that are powerful sources of radio waves and other forms of energy.

quash *vb* **1** to officially reject (something, such as a judgment or decision) as invalid. **2** to defeat or suppress forcefully and completely.

quasi- (**kway**-zie) *combining form* **1** almost but not really; seemingly: *a quasi-religious cult.* **2** resembling but not actually being; so-called: *a quasi-scholar.*

quassia (**kwosh**-a) *n* **1** a tropical American tree with bitter bark and wood. **2** the wood of this tree or a bitter compound extracted from it, used in insecticides.

quaternary *adj* consisting of four parts.

Quaternary *adj Geol* of the most recent period of geological time, which started about one million years ago.

quatrain *n* a stanza or poem of four lines.

quatrefoil *n* **1** a leaf composed of four leaflets. **2** *Archit* a carved ornament of four arcs about a common centre.

quattrocento (kwat-roe-**chen**-toe) *n* the 15th century, esp. in reference to Renaissance Italian art.

quaver *vb* **1** (esp. of the voice) to quiver or tremble. **2** to say or sing (something) with a trembling voice. *~n* **3** *Music* a note having the time value of an eighth of a semibreve. **4** a tremulous sound or note. **quavering** *adj*

quay (**kee**) *n* a wharf built parallel to the shoreline.

Que. Quebec.

queasy *adj* **-sier, -siest 1** having the feeling that one is about to vomit; nauseous. **2** feeling or causing uneasiness. **queasily** *adv* **queasiness** *n*

queen *n* **1** a female sovereign who is the official ruler or head of state. **2** the wife of a king. **3** a woman, thing, or place considered the best or most important of her or its kind: *the rose is considered the queen of garden flowers.* **4** *Slang* an effeminate male homosexual. **5** the only fertile female in a colony of bees, wasps, or ants. **6** a playing card with a picture of a queen on it. **7** a chessman, able to move in a straight line in any direction. *~vb* **8** *Chess* to promote (a pawn) to a queen when it reaches the eighth rank. **9 queen it** *Informal* to behave in an overbearing manner: *she is more beautiful than ever and still queening it over everybody.* **queenly** *adj*

Queen Anne *adj* **1** of or in an 18th-century style of furniture characterized by the use of curves. **2** of or in an early 18th-century English architectural style characterized by the use of red bricks and classical ornamentation.

queen consort *n* the wife of a reigning king.

queen mother *n* the widow of a former king who is also the mother of the reigning sovereign.

queen post *n Building* one of a pair of vertical posts that connect the tie beam of a truss to the principal rafters of a roof.

Queen's Bench *n* one of the divisions of the High Court of Justice.

Queensberry rules *pl n* **1** the code of rules followed in modern boxing. **2** *Informal* gentlemanly conduct, esp. in a dispute.

Queen's Counsel *n* **1** (in Britain) a barrister or advocate appointed Counsel to the Crown. **2** (in Canada) an honorary title bestowed on lawyers with long experience.

Queen's English *n* correctly spoken and written British English.

queen's evidence *n English law* evidence given for the Crown against former associates in crime by an accomplice.

Queen's Guide *or* **Scout** *n* a Guide or Scout who has passed the highest tests of proficiency.

queen's highway *n* **1** (in Britain) any public road or right of way. **2** (in Canada) a main road maintained by the provincial government.

queer *adj* **1** not normal or usual; odd or strange. **2** dubious; shady. **3** faint, giddy, or queasy. **4** *Informal, usually offensive* homosexual. **5** *Informal* eccentric or

THESAURUS

ince, region, side, spot, station, territory, zone **2.** clemency, compassion, favour, forgiveness, leniency, mercy, pity *~vb.* **3.** accommodate, billet, board, house, install, lodge, place, post, put up, station

quarters abode, accommodation, barracks, billet, cantonment (*Military*), chambers, digs (*Brit. informal*), domicile, dwelling, habitation, lodging, lodgings, post, residence, rooms, shelter, station

quash 1. annul, cancel, declare null and void, invalidate, nullify, overrule, overthrow, rescind, reverse, revoke, set aside, void **2.** beat, crush, destroy, extinguish, extirpate, overthrow, put down, quell, quench, repress, squash, subdue, suppress

quasi- 1. almost, apparently, partly, seemingly, supposedly **2.** apparent, fake, mock, near, nominal, pretended, pseudo-, seeming, semi-, sham, so-called, synthetic, virtual, would-be

quaver 1. *vb.* flicker, flutter, oscillate, pulsate, quake, quiver, shake, shudder, thrill, tremble, trill, twitter, vibrate, waver **2.** *n.* break, quiver, shake, sob, throb, tremble, trembling, tremor, trill, vibration, warble

queen 1. consort, monarch, ruler, sovereign **2.** diva,

slightly mad. ~*n* **6** *Informal, usually offensive* a homosexual. ~*vb* **7 queer someone's pitch** *Informal* to spoil or thwart someone's chances of something.

queer street *n* **in queer street** *Informal* in a difficult financial situation, esp. debt or bankruptcy.

quell *vb* **1** to suppress (rebellion or unrest); subdue. **2** to overcome or allay.

quench *vb* **1** to satisfy (one's thirst). **2** to put out; extinguish. **3** to suppress or subdue. **4** *Metallurgy* to cool (hot metal) by plunging it into cold water.

quern *n* a stone hand mill for grinding corn.

querulous (**kwer**-yew-luss) *adj* complaining; whining or peevish. **querulously** *adv*

query *n, pl* **-ries 1** a question, esp. one expressing doubt. **2** a question mark. ~*vb* **-ries, -rying, -ried 3** to express uncertainty, doubt, or an objection concerning (something). **4** to express as a query; ask.

quest *n* **1** a looking for or seeking; search. **2** the object of a search; a goal or target. ~*vb* **3 quest for** to go in search of. **4** (of dogs) to search for game.

question *n* **1** a form of words addressed to a person in order to obtain an answer; interrogative sentence. **2** a point at issue: *they were silent on the question of social justice.* **3** a difficulty or uncertainty. **4 a** an act of asking. **b** an investigation into some problem. **5** a motion presented for debate. **6 beyond (all) question** beyond (any) doubt. **7 call something into question a** to make something the subject of disagreement. **b** to cast doubt upon the validity or truth of something. **8 in question** under discussion: *the area in question was not contaminated.* **9 out of the question** beyond consideration; impossible. ~*vb* **10** to put a question or questions to (a person); interrogate. **11** to make (something) the subject of dispute. **12** to express uncertainty; doubt.

questionable *adj* **1** (esp. of a person's morality or honesty) doubtful. **2** of disputable value or authority. **questionably** *adv*

questioner *n* a person who asks a question.

questioning *adj* **1** proceeding from or characterized by doubt or uncertainty. **2** intellectually inquisitive: *a questioning mind.* ~*n* **3** interrogation.

question mark *n* **1** the punctuation mark (?), used at the end of questions. **2** a doubt or uncertainty: *a question mark still hangs over their success.*

question master *n Brit* the person chairing a radio or television quiz or panel game.

questionnaire *n* a set of questions on a form, used to collect statistical information or opinions from people.

question time *n* (in parliamentary bodies of the British type) the time set aside each day for questions to government ministers.

queue *Chiefly Brit* ~*n* **1** a line of people or vehicles waiting for something. ~*vb* **queueing** *or* **queuing, queued 2** (often foll. by *up*) to form or remain in a line while waiting.

quibble *vb* **-bling, -bled 1** to make trivial objections. ~*n* **2** a trivial objection or equivocation, esp. one used to avoid an issue. **3** *Archaic* a pun.

quiche (**keesh**) *n* a savoury flan with an egg custard filling to which cheese, bacon, or vegetables are added.

quick *adj* **1** characterized by rapidity of movement or action; fast. **2** lasting or taking a short time. **3** immediate or prompt: *her quick action minimized the damage.* **4** eager or ready to perform (an action): *quick to condemn.* **5** responsive to stimulation; alert; lively: *they were impressed by his quick mind.* **6** easily excited or aroused: *he is impulsive and has a quick temper.* **7** nimble in one's movements or actions; deft: *she has quick hands.* ~*n* **8** any area of sensitive flesh, esp. that under a nail. **9 cut someone to the quick** to hurt someone's feelings deeply. **10 the quick** *Archaic* living people. ~*adv* **11** in a rapid manner; swiftly. **quickly** *adv* **quickness** *n*

quick-change artist *n* an actor or entertainer who undertakes several rapid changes of costume during a performance.

THESAURUS

doyenne, ideal, idol, mistress, model, perfection, prima donna, star

queer 1. abnormal, anomalous, atypical, curious, disquieting, droll, eerie, erratic, extraordinary, funny, odd, outlandish, *outré*, peculiar, remarkable, rum (*Brit. slang*), singular, strange, uncanny, uncommon, unconventional, unnatural, unorthodox, unusual, weird **2.** doubtful, dubious, fishy (*informal*), irregular, mysterious, puzzling, questionable, shady (*informal*), suspicious **3.** dizzy, faint, giddy, light-headed, queasy, reeling, uneasy **4.** crazy, demented, eccentric, idiosyncratic, irrational, mad, odd, touched, unbalanced, unhinged

quell 1. conquer, crush, defeat, extinguish, overcome, overpower, put down, quash, squelch, stamp out, stifle, subdue, suppress, vanquish **2.** allay, alleviate, appease, assuage, calm, compose, deaden, dull, mitigate, moderate, mollify, pacify, quiet, silence, soothe

quench 1. allay, appease, cool, sate, satiate, satisfy, slake **2.** check, crush, destroy, douse, end, extinguish, put out, smother, snuff out, squelch, stifle, suppress

querulous cantankerous, captious, carping, censorious, complaining, critical, cross, discontented, dissatisfied, fault-finding, fretful, grouchy (*informal*), grumbling, hard to please, irascible, irritable, murmuring, peevish, petulant, plaintive, ratty (*Brit. & N.Z. informal*), sour, testy, tetchy, touchy, waspish, whining

query *n.* **1.** demand, doubt, hesitation, inquiry, objection, problem, question, reservation, scepticism, suspicion ~*vb.* **2.** ask, enquire, question **3.** challenge, disbelieve, dispute, distrust, doubt, mistrust, suspect

quest *n.* adventure, crusade, enterprise, expedition, exploration, hunt, journey, mission, pilgrimage, pursuit, search, voyage

question *n.* **1.** issue, motion, point, point at issue, proposal, proposition, subject, theme, topic **2.** argument, confusion, contention, controversy, debate, difficulty, dispute, doubt, dubiety, misgiving, problem, query, uncertainty **3.** examination, inquiry, interrogation, investigation **4. in question** at issue, in doubt, open to debate, under discussion **5. out of the question** impossible, inconceivable, not to be thought of, unthinkable ~*vb.* **6.** ask, catechize, cross-examine, enquire, examine, grill (*informal*), interrogate, interview, investigate, probe, pump (*informal*), quiz, sound out

questionable arguable, controversial, controvertible, debatable, disputable, dodgy (*Brit., Austral., & N.Z. informal*), doubtful, dubious, dubitable, equivocal, fishy (*informal*), iffy (*informal*), moot, paradoxical, problematical, shady (*informal*), suspect, suspicious, uncertain, unproven, unreliable

queue chain, concatenation, file, line, order, progression, sequence, series, string, succession, train

quibble 1. *vb.* carp, cavil, equivocate, evade, pretend, prevaricate, shift, split hairs **2.** *n.* artifice, cavil, complaint, criticism, duplicity, equivocation, evasion, nicety, niggle, objection, pretence, prevarication, protest, quirk, shift, sophism, subterfuge, subtlety

quick 1. active, brief, brisk, cursory, expeditious, express, fast, fleet, hasty, headlong, hurried, perfunctory, prompt, quickie (*informal*), rapid, speedy, sudden, swift **2.** agile, alert, animated, energetic, flying, keen,

quicken *vb* **1** to make or become faster; accelerate. **2** to impart to or receive vigour or enthusiasm: *science quickens the imagination.* **3 a** (of a fetus) to begin to show signs of life. **b** (of a pregnant woman) to reach the stage of pregnancy at which movements of the fetus can be felt.

quick-freeze *vb* **-freezing, -froze, -frozen** to preserve (food) by subjecting it to rapid refrigeration.

quickie *Informal ~n* **1** anything made or done rapidly. *~adj* **2** made or done rapidly: *a quickie divorce.*

quicklime *n* a white caustic solid, mainly composed of calcium oxide, used in the manufacture of glass and steel.

quicksand *n* a deep mass of loose wet sand that sucks anything on top of it inextricably into it.

quickset *Chiefly Brit ~adj* **1** (of plants or cuttings) planted so as to form a hedge. *~n* **2** a hedge composed of such plants.

quicksilver *n* the metal mercury.

quickstep *n* **1** a modern ballroom dance in rapid quadruple time. **2** music for this dance.

quick-tempered *adj* easy to anger.

quick-witted *adj* having a keenly alert mind. **quick-wittedness** *n*

quid[1] *n, pl* **quid** *Brit slang* **1** a pound (sterling). **2 be quids in** to be in a very favourable or advantageous position.

quid[2] *n* a piece of tobacco for chewing.

quiddity *n, pl* **-ties 1** the essential nature of something. **2** a petty or trifling distinction.

quid pro quo *n, pl* **quid pro quos** one thing, esp. an advantage or object, given in exchange for another.

quiescent (kwee-**ess**-ent) *adj Formal* quiet, inactive, or dormant. **quiescence** *n*

quiet *adj* **1** characterized by an absence of noise. **2** calm or tranquil: *the sea is quiet today.* **3** untroubled: *a quiet life.* **4** not busy: *business is quiet this morning.* **5** private or secret: *I had a quiet word with her.* **6** free from anger, impatience, or other extreme emotion. **7** not showy: *quiet colours; a quiet wedding.* **8** modest or reserved: *quiet humour.* *~n* **9** the state of being silent, peaceful, or untroubled. **10 on the quiet** without other people knowing. *~vb* **11** to make or become calm or silent. **quietly** *adv* **quietness** *n*

quieten *vb Chiefly Brit* **1** (often foll. by *down*) to make or become calm or silent. **2** to allay (fear or doubts).

quietism *n Formal* passivity and calmness of mind towards external events. **quietist** *n, adj*

quietude *n Formal* quietness, peace, or tranquillity.

quietus *n, pl* **-tuses 1** *Literary* a release from life; death. **2** the discharge or settlement of debts or duties.

quiff *n Brit* a tuft of hair brushed up above the forehead.

quill *n* **1** Also called: **quill pen** a feather made into a pen. **2 a** any of the large stiff feathers of the wing or tail of a bird. **b** the hollow stem of a feather. **3** any of the stiff hollow spines of a porcupine or hedgehog.

quilt *n* **1** a cover for a bed, consisting of a soft filling sewn between two layers of material, usually with crisscross seams. **2** a continental quilt; duvet. *~vb* **3** to stitch together two layers of (fabric) with padding between them. **quilted** *adj*

quin *n* a quintuplet.

quince *n* the acid-tasting pear-shaped fruit of an Asian tree, used in preserves.

quincunx *n* a group of five objects arranged in the shape of a rectangle with one at each corner and the fifth in the centre.

quinine *n* a bitter drug extracted from cinchona bark, used as a tonic and formerly in malaria therapy.

quinquennial *adj* occurring once every five years or over a period of five years.

quinquereme *n* an ancient Roman galley with five banks of oars.

quinsy *n* inflammation of the tonsils and throat, with abscesses.

quint *n US & Canad* a quintuplet.

quintal *n* **1** a unit of weight equal to (esp. in Britain) 112 pounds (50.85 kg) or (esp. in US) 100 pounds (45.36 kg). **2** a unit of weight equal to 100 kilograms.

quintessence *n* **1** the most perfect representation of a quality or state. **2** an extract of a substance containing its central nature in its most concentrated form. **quintessential** *adj*

quintet *n* **1** a group of five singers or instrumen-

THESAURUS

lively, nimble, spirited, sprightly, spry, vivacious, -winged **3.** abrupt, curt, excitable, hasty, impatient, irascible, irritable, passionate, petulant, testy, touchy

quicken 1. accelerate, dispatch, expedite, hasten, hurry, impel, precipitate, speed **2.** activate, animate, arouse, energize, excite, galvanize, incite, inspire, invigorate, kindle, refresh, reinvigorate, resuscitate, revitalize, revive, rouse, stimulate, strengthen, vitalize, vivify

quickly abruptly, apace, at a rate of knots (*informal*), at *or* on the double, at speed, briskly, expeditiously, fast, hastily, hell for leather (*informal*), hotfoot, hurriedly, immediately, instantly, posthaste, promptly, pronto (*informal*), quick, rapidly, soon, speedily, swiftly, with all speed

quick-tempered choleric, excitable, fiery, hot-tempered, impatient, impulsive, irascible, irritable, petulant, quarrelsome, ratty (*Brit. informal*), shrewish, splenetic, testy, tetchy, waspish

quick-witted alert, astute, clever, keen, perceptive, sharp, shrewd, smart

quiescent calm, dormant, in abeyance, inactive, latent, motionless, peaceful, placid, quiet, resting, serene, silent, smooth, still, tranquil, unagitated, undisturbed, unmoving, unruffled

quiet *adj.* **1.** dumb, hushed, inaudible, low, low-pitched, noiseless, peaceful, silent, soft, soundless **2.** calm, contented, gentle, mild, motionless, pacific, peaceful, placid, restful, serene, smooth, tranquil, untroubled **3.** isolated, private, retired, secluded, secret, sequestered, undisturbed, unfrequented **4.** collected, docile, even-tempered, gentle, imperturbable, meek, mild, phlegmatic, reserved, retiring, sedate, shy, unexcitable **5.** conservative, modest, plain, restrained, simple, sober, subdued, unassuming, unobtrusive, unpretentious *~n.* **6.** calmness, ease, peace, quietness, repose, rest, serenity, silence, stillness, tranquillity

quieten *vb.* allay, alleviate, appease, assuage, blunt, calm, compose, deaden, dull, hush, lull, mitigate, mollify, muffle, mute, palliate, quell, quiet, shush (*informal*), silence, soothe, stifle, still, stop, subdue, tranquillize

quietly 1. confidentially, dumbly, in a low voice *or* whisper, in an undertone, inaudibly, in hushed tones, in silence, mutely, noiselessly, privately, secretly, silently, softly, without talking **2.** calmly, contentedly, dispassionately, meekly, mildly, patiently, placidly, serenely, undemonstratively **3.** coyly, demurely, diffidently, humbly, modestly, unassumingly, unobtrusively, unostentatiously, unpretentiously

quietness calm, calmness, hush, peace, placidity,

talists. **2** a piece of music for five performers **3** any group of five.

quintillion *n, pl* **-lions** *or* **-lion 1** (in Britain, France, and Germany) the number represented as one followed by 30 zeros (10^{30}). **2** (in the US and Canada) the number represented as one followed by 18 zeros (10^{18}).

quintuple *vb* **-pling, -pled 1** to multiply by five. *~adj* **2** five times as much or as many. **3** consisting of five parts. *~n* **4** a quantity or number five times as great as another.

quintuplet *n* one of five children born at one birth.

quip *n* **1** a witty saying. *~vb* **quipping, quipped 2** to make a quip.

quire *n* a set of 24 or 25 sheets of paper.

quirk *n* **1** a peculiarity of character; mannerism or foible. **2** an unexpected twist or turn: *a strange quirk of fate.* **quirky** *adj*

quisling *n* a traitor who aids an occupying enemy force; collaborator.

quit *vb* **quitting, quit 1** to stop (doing something). **2** to resign (from): *the Prime Minister's decision to quit; he quit his job as a salesman.* **3** to leave (a place). **quitter** *n*

quitch *or* **quitch grass** *n* same as **couch grass.**

quite *adv* **1** (*not used with a negative*) to a greater than average extent; somewhat: *he found her quite attractive.* **2** absolutely: *you're quite right.* **3** in actuality; truly. **4 quite a** *or* **an** of an exceptional kind: *she is quite a girl.* **5 quite something** a remarkable thing or person. *~interj* **6** an expression used to indicate agreement.

➤ Note that because *quite* can mean "extremely": *quite amazing;* or can express a reservation: *quite friendly,* it should be used carefully.

quits *adj Informal* **1** on an equal footing. **2 call it quits** to end a dispute or contest, agreeing that honours are even.

quittance *n* **1** release from debt or other obligation. **2** a document certifying this.

quiver[1] *vb* **1** to shake with a tremulous movement; tremble. *~n* **2** a shaking or trembling. **quivering** *adj*

quiver[2] *n* a case for holding or carrying arrows.

quixotic (kwik-**sot**-ik) *adj* unrealistically optimistic or chivalrous. **quixotically** *adv*

quiz *n, pl* **quizzes 1** an entertainment in which the knowledge of the players is tested by a series of questions. **2** any set of quick questions designed to test knowledge. **3** an investigation by close questioning. *~vb* **quizzing, quizzed 4** to investigate by close questioning; interrogate.

quizzical *adj* questioning and mocking or supercilious. **quizzically** *adv*

quod *n Slang, chiefly Brit* a jail.

quoin *n* **1** an external corner of a wall. **2** the stone forming the outer corner of a wall; a cornerstone. **3** a wedge.

quoit *n* a large ring used in the game of quoits.

quoits *n* a game in which quoits are tossed at a stake in the ground in attempts to encircle it.

quondam *adj Formal* of an earlier time; former: *her quondam employers.*

quorate *adj* having or being a quorum: *the meeting is now quorate.*

quorum *n* the minimum number of members required to be present in a meeting or assembly before any business can be transacted.

quota *n* **1** the share that is due from, due to, or allocated to a person or group. **2** the prescribed number or quantity allowed, required, or admitted.

quotation *n* **1** a written or spoken passage repeated exactly in a later work, speech, or conversation, usually with an acknowledgment of its source. **2** the act of quoting. **3** an estimate of costs submitted by a contractor to a prospective client.

quotation marks *pl n* the punctuation marks used to begin and end a quotation, either " and " or ' and '.

quote *vb* **quoting, quoted 1** to repeat (words) exactly from (an earlier work, speech, or conversation), usually with an acknowledgment of their source. **2** to state a price for goods or a job of work. **3** to put quotation marks round (words). *~n* **4** *Informal* a quotation. **5 quotes** *Informal* quotation marks. *~interj* **6** an expression used to indicate that the words that follow are a quotation. **quotable** *adj*

quoth *vb Archaic* (used before *I, he* or *she*) said.

quotidian *adj* **1** daily. **2** *Literary* commonplace. **3** (esp. of fever) recurring daily.

quotient *n* the result of the division of one number or quantity by another.

Quran (koo-**rahn**) *n* same as **Koran.**

q.v. (denoting a cross-reference) which (word, item, etc.) see.

qwerty *or* **QWERTY keyboard** *n* the standard English language typewriter or computer keyboard with the characters q, w, e, r, t, and y at the top left of the keyboard.

THESAURUS

quiescence, quiet, quietude, repose, rest, serenity, silence, still, stillness, tranquillity

quilt bedspread, counterpane, coverlet, duvet, eiderdown

quip *n.* badinage, *bon mot,* counterattack, gibe, jest, joke, pleasantry, repartee, retort, riposte, sally, wisecrack (*informal*), witticism

quirk aberration, caprice, characteristic, eccentricity, fancy, fetish, foible, habit, *idée fixe,* idiosyncrasy, kink, mannerism, oddity, peculiarity, singularity, trait, vagary, whim

quisling betrayer, collaborator, fifth columnist, Judas, renegade, traitor, turncoat

quit *vb.* **1.** abandon, cease, conclude, discontinue, drop, end, give up, halt, stop, suspend **2.** abandon, abdicate, decamp, depart, desert, exit, forsake, go, leave, pull out, relinquish, renounce, resign, retire, step down (*informal*), surrender, take off (*informal*), withdraw

quite 1. fairly, moderately, rather, reasonably, relatively, somewhat, to a certain extent, to some degree **2.** absolutely, completely, considerably, entirely, fully, in all respects, largely, perfectly, precisely, totally, wholly, without reservation **3.** in fact, in reality, in truth, really, truly

quiver 1. *vb.* agitate, convulse, oscillate, palpitate, pulsate, quake, quaver, shake, shiver, shudder, tremble, vibrate **2.** *n.* convulsion, oscillation, palpitation, pulsation, shake, shiver, shudder, spasm, throb, tic, tremble, tremor, vibration

quiz 1. *n.* examination, investigation, questioning, test **2.** *vb.* ask, catechize, examine, grill (*informal*), interrogate, investigate, pump (*informal*), question

quota allocation, allowance, assignment, cut (*informal*), part, portion, proportion, ration, share, slice, whack (*informal*)

quotation 1. citation, cutting, excerpt, extract, passage, quote (*informal*), reference, selection **2.** bid price, charge, cost, estimate, figure, price, quote (*informal*), rate, tender

quote adduce, attest, cite, detail, extract, instance, name, paraphrase, proclaim, recall, recite, recollect, refer to, repeat, retell

R

r 1 radius. 2 ratio. 3 right. 4 *Cricket* run(s).

R 1 *Chem* radical. 2 Regina. 3 Registered Trademark. 4 *Physics, electronics* resistance. 5 Rex. 6 River. 7 *Chess* rook.

Ra *Chem* radium.

RA 1 rear admiral. 2 Royal Academy. 3 Royal Artillery.

rabbi (**rab**-bye) *n, pl* **-bis** 1 the spiritual leader of a Jewish congregation. 2 an expert in or teacher of Jewish Law. **rabbinical** *adj*

rabbit *n, pl* **-bits** *or* **-bit** 1 a common burrowing mammal with long ears and a short fluffy tail. ~*vb* **-biting, -bited** 2 *Brit informal* to talk too much: *he keeps rabbiting on about interrogation.*

rabbiting *n* **go rabbiting** to hunt rabbits.

rabbit punch *n* a short sharp blow to the back of the neck.

rabble *n* 1 a disorderly crowd of noisy people. 2 **the rabble** *Contemptuous* the common people.

rabble-rouser *n* a person who stirs up the feelings of the mob. **rabble-rousing** *adj, n*

Rabelaisian *adj* characterized by broad, often bawdy humour and sharp satire.

rabid *adj* 1 fanatical: *a rabid separatist.* 2 having rabies. **rabidity** *n*

rabies (**ray**-beez) *n Pathol* a fatal infectious viral disease of the nervous system transmitted by dogs and certain other animals.

RAC Royal Automobile Club.

raccoon *or* **racoon** *n, pl* **-coons** *or* **-coon** a small American mammal with a long striped tail.

race[1] *n* 1 a contest of speed. 2 any competition or rivalry: *the arms race.* 3 a rapid current of water. 4 a channel of a stream: *a mill race.* 5 *Austral & NZ* a narrow passage through which sheep pass individually, as to a sheep dip. ~*vb* **racing, raced** 6 to take part in a contest of speed with (someone). 7 to enter (an animal or vehicle) in a race: *to race greyhounds.* 8 to travel as fast as possible. 9 (of an engine) to run faster than normal. 10 (of the heart) to beat faster than normal. ~See also **races. racer** *n* **racing** *adj, n*

race[2] *n* 1 a group of people of common ancestry with distinguishing physical features, such as skin colour or build. 2 **the human race** human beings collectively. 3 a group of animals or plants having common characteristics that distinguish them from other members of the same species.

racecourse *n* a long broad track on which horses are raced.

racehorse *n* a horse specially bred for racing.

raceme (rass-**eem**) *n Bot* a cluster of flowers along a central stem, as in the foxglove.

race meeting *n* a series of horse or greyhound races held at the same place.

race relations *pl n* the relations between members of two or more races within a single community.

race riot *n* a riot involving violence between people of different races.

races *pl n* **the races** a series of contests of speed between horses or greyhounds over a fixed course.

racetrack *n* 1 a circuit used for races between cars, bicycles, or runners. 2 *US & Canad* a racecourse.

racial *adj* 1 relating to the division of the human species into races. 2 typically associated with any such group. **racially** *adv*

racism *or* **racialism** *n* 1 hostile or oppressive behaviour towards people because they belong to a different race. 2 the belief that some races are innately superior to others because of hereditary characteristics. **racist** *or* **racialist** *n, adj*

rack[1] *n* 1 a framework for holding particular articles, such as coats or luggage. 2 a straight bar with teeth on its edge, to work with a cogwheel. 3 **the rack** *History* an instrument of torture that stretched the body of the victim. ~*vb* 4 to cause great suffering to: *Germany was racked by food riots.* 5 **rack one's brains** to try very hard to think of something.

rack[2] *n* **go to rack and ruin** to be destroyed through neglect.

rack[3] *vb* to clear (wine or beer) by siphoning it off from the dregs.

rack[4] *n* the neck or rib part of a joint of meat.

rack-and-pinion *n* a device for converting rotary into linear motion and vice versa, in which a gearwheel (the pinion) engages with a flat toothed bar (the rack).

racket[1] *n* 1 a noisy disturbance. 2 an illegal activity done to make money. 3 *Slang* a business or occupation: *I've been in the racket since I was sixteen.* ~*vb* **-eting, -eted** 4 to make a commotion. **rackety** *adj*

racket[2] *or* **racquet** *n* a bat consisting of an oval frame surrounding a mesh of strings, with a handle, used in tennis, badminton, and squash. ~See also **rackets.**

racketeer *n* a person who makes money from illegal activities. **racketeering** *n*

rackets *n* a game similar to squash, played by two or four people.

rack-rent *n* an extortionate rent.

raconteur (rak-on-**tur**) *n* a person skilled in telling stories.

THESAURUS

rabble 1. canaille, crowd, herd, horde, mob, swarm, throng 2. *contemptuous* canaille, commonalty, commoners, common people, crowd, dregs, hoi polloi, lower classes, lumpenproletariat, masses, peasantry, populace, proletariat, riffraff, scum, the great unwashed (*informal & derogatory*), trash (*chiefly U.S. & Canad.*)

rabid 1. bigoted, extreme, fanatical, fervent, intemperate, intolerant, irrational, narrow-minded, zealous 2. hydrophobic, mad

race[1] 1. *n.* chase, competition, contention, contest, dash, pursuit, rivalry 2. *vb.* barrel (along) (*informal, chiefly U.S. & Canad.*), burn rubber (*informal*), career, compete, contest, dart, dash, fly, gallop, hare (*Brit. informal*), hasten, hurry, run, run like mad (*informal*), speed, tear, zoom

race[2] blood, breed, clan, ethnic group, family, folk, house, issue, kin, kindred, line, lineage, nation, offspring, people, progeny, seed (*chiefly biblical*), stock, tribe, type

racial ethnic, ethnological, folk, genealogical, genetic, national, tribal

rack 1. *n.* frame, framework, stand, structure 2. *vb.* afflict, agonize, crucify, distress, excruciate, harass, harrow, oppress, pain, torment, torture

racket 1. babel, ballyhoo (*informal*), clamour, commotion, din, disturbance, fuss, hubbub, hullabaloo,

racoon *n, pl* **-coons** *or* **-coon** same as **raccoon.**

racquet *n* same as **racket**[2].

racy *adj* **racier, raciest 1** slightly shocking. **2** spirited or lively. **racily** *adv* **raciness** *n*

rad radian.

RADA (in Britain) Royal Academy of Dramatic Art.

radar *n* **1** a method of detecting the position and velocity of a distant object by bouncing a narrow beam of extremely high-frequency radio pulses off it. **2** the equipment used in this.

radar trap *n* a device which uses radar to detect motorists who break the speed limit.

raddled *adj* (of a person) untidy or run-down in appearance.

radial *adj* **1** spreading out from a common central point. **2** of a radius or ray. **3** short for **radial-ply.** *~n* **4** a radial-ply tyre. **radially** *adv*

radial-ply *adj* (of a tyre) having the fabric cords in the outer casing running radially to enable the sidewalls to be flexible.

radian *n* an SI unit of plane angle; the angle between two radii of a circle that cut off on the circumference an arc equal in length to the radius.

radiant *adj* **1** characterized by health and happiness: *radiant good looks.* **2** shining. **3** emitted as radiation: *radiant heat.* **4** sending out heat by radiation: *radiant heaters.* **radiance** *n* **radiantly** *adv*

radiant energy *n* energy that is emitted or propagated in the form of particles or electromagnetic radiation.

radiate *vb* **-ating, -ated 1** to spread out from a central point. **2** to show (an emotion or quality) to a great degree: *she radiated competence and composure.* **3** to emit or be emitted as radiation. *~adj* **4** having rays or a radial structure.

radiation *n* **1** *Physics* **a** the emission of energy as particles, electromagnetic waves or sound. **b** the particles or waves emitted. **2** the process of radiating.

radiation sickness *n* illness caused by overexposure to radioactive material or x-rays.

radiator *n* **1** a device for heating a room or building, consisting of a series of pipes containing hot water. **2** a device for cooling an internal-combustion engine, consisting of thin-walled tubes containing water.

radical *adj* **1** favouring fundamental change in political or social conditions: *a radical student movement.* **2** of the essential nature of a person or thing; fundamental: *a radical fault.* **3** searching or thorough: *a radical interpretation.* **4** *Maths* of or containing roots of numbers or quantities. *~n* **5** a person who favours fundamental change in existing institutions or in political, social, or economic conditions. **6** *Maths* a root of a number or quantity, such as $\sqrt[3]{5}$, $\sqrt{x}$. **7** *Chem* an atom or group of atoms which acts as a unit during chemical reactions. **radicalism** *n* **radically** *adv*

radicalize *or* **-ise** *vb* **-izing, -ized** *or* **-ising, -ised** to make (a person, group, or situation) radical or more radical.

radical sign *n* the symbol √ placed before a number or quantity to indicate the extraction of a root, esp. a square root. The value of a higher root is indicated by a raised digit in front of the symbol, as in $\sqrt[3]{}$.

radicchio (rad-**deek**-ee-oh) *n, pl* **-chios** an Italian variety of chicory, with purple leaves streaked with white that are eaten raw in salads.

radicle *n Bot* **a** the part of the embryo of seed-bearing plants that develops into the main root. **b** a very small root or rootlike part.

radii *n* a plural of **radius.**

radio *n, pl* **-dios 1** the use of electromagnetic waves for broadcasting or two-way communication without the use of linking wires. **2** an electronic device for converting radio signals into sounds. **3** a communications device for sending and receiving messages using radio waves. **4** sound broadcasting. *~vb* **5** to transmit (a message) by radio. *~adj* **6** of, relating to, or using radio broadcasting or radio signals: *a radio interview.* **7** using or producing electromagnetic waves in the range used for radio signals: *radio astronomy.*

radio- *combining form* denoting: **1** radio. **2** radioactivity or radiation: *radiocarbon.*

radioactive *adj* showing or using radioactivity.

radioactivity *n* the spontaneous emission of radiation from atomic nuclei. The radiation can consist of alpha or beta particles, or gamma rays.

radio astronomy *n* astronomy using a radio telescope to analyse signals received from radio sources in space.

radiocarbon *n* a radioactive isotope of carbon, esp. carbon-14.

radiocarbon dating *n* same as **carbon dating.**

radiochemistry *n* the chemistry of radioactive substances.

radio-controlled *adj* controlled by signals sent by radio.

radio frequency *n* any electromagnetic frequency that lies in the range 10 kilohertz to 300 000 megahertz and can be used for broadcasting.

radiogram *n Brit* an old-fashioned combined radio and record player.

radiograph *n* an image produced on a special photographic film or plate by radiation, usually by x-rays.

radiography (ray-dee-**og**-ra-fee) *n* the production of radiographs for use in medicine or industry. **radiographer** *n*

radioisotope *n* a radioactive isotope.

radiology (ray-dee-**ol**-a-jee) *n* the use of x-rays and radioactive substances in the diagnosis and treatment of disease. **radiologist** *n*

radioscopy (ray-dee-**oss**-kop-ee) *n* examination of a person or object by means of a fluorescent screen and an x-ray source.

THESAURUS

noise, outcry, pandemonium, row, shouting, tumult, uproar **2.** criminal activity, fraud, illegal enterprise, scheme **3.** *slang* business, game (*informal*), line, occupation

racy 1. bawdy, blue, broad, immodest, indecent, indelicate, naughty, near the knuckle (*informal*), off colour, risqué, smutty, spicy (*informal*), suggestive **2.** animated, buoyant, dramatic, energetic, entertaining, exciting, exhilarating, heady, lively, sexy (*informal*), sparkling, spirited, stimulating, vigorous, zestful

radiance 1. delight, gaiety, happiness, joy, pleasure, rapture, warmth **2.** brightness, brilliance, effulgence, glare, gleam, glitter, glow, incandescence, light, luminosity, lustre, resplendence, shine

radiant 1. beaming, beatific, blissful, delighted, ecstatic, gay, glowing, happy, joyful, joyous, rapt, rapturous **2.** beaming, bright, brilliant, effulgent, gleaming, glittering, glorious, glowing, incandescent, luminous, lustrous, resplendent, shining, sparkling, sunny

radiate branch out, diffuse, disseminate, diverge, emanate, emit, give off *or* out, gleam, glitter, issue, pour, scatter, send out, shed, shine, spread, spread out

radiation emanation, emission, rays

radical *adj.* **1.** complete, drastic, entire, excessive, extreme, extremist, fanatical, revolutionary, severe,

radiosonde *n* an airborne instrument to send meteorological information back to earth by radio.

radiotelegraphy *n* telegraphy in which messages are transmitted by radio waves.

radiotelephone *n* a telephone which sends and receives messages using radio waves rather than wires. **radiotelephony** *n*

radio telescope *n* an instrument used in radio astronomy to pick up and analyse radio waves from space.

radiotherapy *n* the treatment of disease, esp. cancer, by radiation.

radish *n* a small hot-flavoured red root vegetable eaten raw in salads.

radium *n Chem* a highly radioactive luminescent metallic element, found in pitchblende. Symbol: Ra

radius (**ray**-dee-uss) *n, pl* **-dii** (-dee-eye) *or* **-diuses** **1** a straight line joining the centre of a circle to any point on the circumference. **2** the length of this line. **3** *Anat* the outer, slightly shorter of the two bones of the forearm. **4** a circular area of a specified size round a central point: *within a seven mile radius of the club.*

radon (**ray**-don) *n Chem* a colourless radioactive element of the noble gas group. Symbol: Rn

RAF Royal Air Force.

Rafferty *or* **Rafferty's rules** *pl n Austral & NZ slang* no rules at all.

raffia *n* a fibre obtained from the leaves of a palm tree, used for weaving.

raffish *adj* unconventional or slightly disreputable.

raffle *n* **1** a lottery, often to raise money for charity, in which the prizes are goods rather than money. *~vb* **-fling, -fled** **2** to offer as a prize in a raffle.

raft *n* a floating platform of logs or planks tied together.

rafter *n* any of the parallel sloping beams that form the framework of a roof.

rag[1] *n* **1** a small piece of cloth. **2** *Informal* a newspaper. **3** **rags** old tattered clothing. **4** **from rags to riches** from being extremely poor to being extremely wealthy.

rag[2] *vb* **ragging, ragged** **1** to tease. **2** *Brit* to play rough practical jokes on. *~n* **3** *Brit* a boisterous practical jokes. *~adj* **4** (in British universities and colleges) of various events organized to raise money for charity: *a rag week.*

rag[3] *n* a piece of ragtime music.

ragamuffin *n* a ragged dirty child.

rag-and-bone man *n Brit* a man who goes from street to street buying old clothes and furniture.

ragbag *n* a confused mixture: *the traditional ragbag of art traders.*

rage *n* **1** intense anger or passion. **2** a fashion or craze: *the dance was the rage of Europe.* **3** **all the rage** *Informal* very popular. **4** *Austral & NZ informal* a dance or party. *~vb* **raging, raged** **5** to feel or show intense anger. **6** to proceed violently and without restraint: *the argument was still raging.*

ragged (**rag**-gid) *adj* **1** dressed in shabby or torn clothes. **2** (of clothes) tattered and torn. **3** having a rough or uneven surface or edge. **4** neglected or untidy: *the ragged stone-built village.*

ragged robin *n* a plant that has pink or white flowers with ragged petals.

raglan *adj* **1** (of a sleeve) joined to the garment by diagonal seams from the collar to the underarm. **2** (of a garment) with this style of sleeve.

ragout (rag-**goo**) *n* a richly seasoned stew of meat and vegetables.

ragtag *n* **ragtag and bobtail** the common people.

ragtime *n* a style of jazz piano music with a syncopated melody.

rag trade *n Informal* the clothing business.

ragwort *n* a plant with ragged leaves and yellow flowers.

raid *n* **1** a sudden surprise attack: *a bombing raid.* **2** a surprise visit by police searching for people or goods: *a drugs raid.* *~vb* **3** to make a raid on. **4** to sneak into (a place) in order to steal. **raider** *n*

rail[1] *n* **1** a horizontal bar supported by vertical posts, used as a fence or barrier. **2** a horizontal bar on which to hang things: *a curtain rail.* **3** one of a pair of parallel bars that serve as a running surface for the wheels of a train. **4** railway: *by car or by rail.* **5** **go off the rails** to start behaving improperly or eccentrically. *~vb* **6** to fence (an area) with rails.

rail[2] *vb* **rail against** *or* **at** to complain bitterly or loudly about.

rail[3] *n* a small wading marsh bird.

railcard *n Brit* an identity card, which pensioners or young people can buy, entitling them to cheaper rail travel.

railhead *n* **1** a terminal of a railway. **2** the farthest point reached by completed track on an unfinished railway.

railing *n* a fence made of rails supported by posts.

raillery *n, pl* **-leries** good-natured teasing.

railroad *n* **1** *US* a railway. *~vb* **2** *Informal* to force (a person) into an action with haste or by unfair means.

railway *n* **1** a track composed of a line of parallel metal rails fixed to sleepers, for trains to run on. **2** any track for the wheels of a vehicle to run on: *a cable railway.* **3** the rolling stock, buildings, and tracks used in such a transport system. **4** the organization responsible for operating a railway network.

raiment *n Archaic or poetic* clothing.

THESAURUS

sweeping, thorough, violent **2.** basic, constitutional, deep-seated, essential, fundamental, innate, native, natural, organic, profound, thoroughgoing *~n.* **3.** extremist, fanatic, militant, revolutionary

raffle draw, lottery, sweep, sweepstake

ragbag confusion, hotchpotch, jumble, medley, miscellany, mixture, omnium-gatherum, potpourri

rage *n.* **1.** agitation, anger, frenzy, fury, high dudgeon, ire, madness, mania, obsession, passion, rampage, raving, vehemence, violence, wrath **2.** craze, enthusiasm, fad (*informal*), fashion, latest thing, mode, style, vogue *~vb.* **3.** be beside oneself, be furious, blow a fuse (*slang, chiefly U.S.*), blow one's top, blow up (*informal*), chafe, crack up (*informal*), fly off the handle (*informal*), foam at the mouth, fret, fume, go off the deep end (*informal*), go up the wall (*slang*), rant and rave, rave, see red (*informal*), seethe, storm, throw a fit (*informal*) **4.** be at its height, be uncontrollable, rampage, storm, surge

ragged **1.** contemptible, down at heel, frayed, in holes, in rags, in tatters, mean, poor, rent, scraggy, shabby, shaggy, tattered, tatty, threadbare, torn, unkempt, worn-out **2.** crude, jagged, notched, poor, rough, rugged, serrated, uneven, unfinished **3.** broken, desultory, disorganized, fragmented, irregular, uneven

rags castoffs, old clothes, tattered clothing, tatters

raid **1.** *n.* attack, break-in, descent, foray, hit-and-run attack, incursion, inroad, invasion, irruption, onset, sally, seizure, sortie, surprise attack **2.** *vb.* assault, attack, break into, descend on, fall upon, forage (*Military*), foray, invade, pillage, plunder, rifle, sack, sally forth, swoop down upon

rain *n* **1 a** water falling from the sky in drops formed by the condensation of water vapour in the atmosphere. **b** a fall of rain. **2** a large quantity of anything falling rapidly: *a rain of stones descended on the police.* **3 (come) rain or (come) shine** regardless of circumstances. **4 right as rain** *Informal* perfectly all right. *~vb* **5** to fall as rain: *it's raining back home.* **6** to fall rapidly and in large quantities: *steel rungs and sawdust raining down.* **7 rained off** cancelled or postponed because of rain. US and Canad. term: **rained out** ~See also **rains. rainy** *adj*

rainbird *n S African* a common name for **Burchell's coucal**, a bird whose call is believed to be a sign of impending rain.

rainbow *n* an arched display in the sky of the colours of the spectrum, caused by the refraction and reflection of the sun's rays through rain.

rainbow trout *n* a freshwater trout with black spots and two red stripes.

rain check *n* **take a rain check** *Informal* to request or accept the postponement of an offer.

raincoat *n* a coat made of a waterproof material.

rainfall *n* the amount of rain, hail, or snow in a specified place and time.

rainforest *n* dense forest found in tropical areas of heavy rainfall.

rains *pl n* **the rains** the season in the tropics when there is a lot of rain.

rainstorm *n* a storm with heavy rain.

rainwater *n* pure water from rain.

rainy day *n* a future time of need, esp. financial need.

raise *vb* **raising, raised 1** to lift to a higher position or level. **2** to place in an upright position. **3** to increase in amount, quality, or intensity: *to raise interest rates.* **4** to collect or gather together: *to raise additional capital; to raise an army.* **5** to cause to be expressed: *to raise a smile.* **6** to stir up. **7** to bring up: *to raise a family.* **8** to grow: *to raise a crop.* **9** to put forward for consideration: *they raised controversial issues.* **10** to arouse from sleep or death. **11** to build: *to raise a barn.* **12** to bring to an end: *to raise a siege.* **13** to establish radio communications with: *we raised Moscow last night.* **14** to advance in rank; promote. **15** *Maths* to multiply (a number) by itself a specified number of times: *8 is 2 raised to the power 3.* **16** to cause (dough) to rise, as by the addition of yeast. **17** *Cards* to bet more than the previous player. **18 raise Cain a** to create a disturbance. **b** to protest vehemently. *~n* **19** *US & Canad* an increase in pay.

raised *adj* higher than the surrounding area: *a small raised platform.*

raisin *n* a dried grape.

raison d'être (**ray**-zon **det**-ra) *n, pl* **raisons d'être** (**ray**-zon **det**-ra) reason or justification for existence.

raita (**rye**-ta) *n* an Indian dish of chopped cucumber, mint, etc., in yogurt, served with curry.

Raj *n* **the Raj** the British government in India before 1947.

raja *or* **rajah** *n History* an Indian prince or ruler.

rake[1] *n* **1** a farm or garden tool consisting of a row of teeth set in a headpiece attached to a long shaft and used for gathering leaves or straw, or for smoothing loose earth. **2** any of various implements similar in shape or function. *~vb* **raking, raked 3** to scrape or gather with a rake. **4** to smooth (a surface) with a rake. **5** Also: **rake out** to clear (ashes) from (a fire). **6 rake together** *or* **up** to gather (items or people) with difficulty, as from a limited supply. **7** to search or examine carefully: *raking over the past is not always popular.* **8** to direct (gunfire) along the length of (a target): *the machine guns raked up and down their line.* **9** to scrape or graze: *he raked the tip of his shoe across the pavement.* ~See also **rake in, rake-off,** etc.

rake[2] *n* an immoral man.

rake[3] *n* **1** the degree to which an object slopes. *~vb* **raking, raked 2** to slope from the vertical, esp. (of a ship's mast) towards the stern. **3** to construct with a backward slope.

raked *adj* (of a surface) sloping so that it is higher at the back than at the front.

rake in *vb Informal* to acquire (money) in large amounts.

rake-off *n Slang* a share of profits, esp. an illegal one.

rake up *vb* to bring back memories of (a forgotten unpleasant event): *she doesn't want to rake up the past.*

rakish[1] (**ray**-kish) *adj* dashing or jaunty: *a hat which he wore at a rakish angle.*

rakish[2] *adj* immoral: *a rakish life of drinking and womanizing.* **rakishly** *adv*

rallentando *Music ~adj, adv* **1** becoming slower. *~n* **2** a passage in which the music becomes slower.

rally[1] *n, pl* **-lies 1** a large gathering of people for a meeting. **2** a marked recovery of strength, as during illness. **3** *Stock Exchange* a sharp increase in price or trading activity after a decline. **4** *Tennis, squash, etc* an exchange of several shots before one player wins the point. **5** a car-driving competition on public roads. *~vb* **-lies, -lying, -lied 6** to bring or come together after being dispersed. **7** to bring or come together for a common cause. **8** to summon up (one's strength or

THESAURUS

raider attacker, forager (*Military*), invader, marauder, plunderer, reiver (*dialect*), robber, thief

railing balustrade, barrier, fence, paling, rails

rain *n.* **1.** cloudburst, deluge, downpour, drizzle, fall, precipitation, raindrops, rainfall, showers **2.** deluge, flood, hail, shower, spate, stream, torrent, volley *~vb.* **3.** bucket down (*informal*), come down in buckets (*informal*), drizzle, fall, pelt (down), pour, rain cats and dogs (*informal*), shower, teem **4.** deposit, drop, fall, shower, sprinkle

rainy damp, drizzly, showery, wet

raise 1. advance, amplify, augment, boost, elevate, enhance, enlarge, escalate, exaggerate, heighten, hike (up) (*informal*), increase, inflate, intensify, jack up, magnify, promote, put up, reinforce, strengthen, upgrade **2.** elevate, erect, exalt, heave, hoist, lift, put up, set upright, uplift **3.** assemble, collect, form, gather, get, levy, mass, mobilize, muster, obtain, rally, recruit **4.** bring about, cause, create, engender, give rise to, occasion, originate, produce, provoke, start **5.** activate, arouse, awaken, cause, evoke, excite, foment, foster, incite, instigate, kindle, motivate, provoke, rouse, set on foot, stir up, summon up, whip up **6.** breed, bring up, cultivate, develop, grow, nurture, produce, propagate, rear **7.** advance, bring up, broach, introduce, moot, put forward, suggest **8.** assemble, build, construct, erect, fabricate, form, make, put up, raise **9.** abandon, end, give up, lift, relieve, relinquish, remove, terminate **10.** aggrandize, dignify, elevate, exalt, honour, kick upstairs (*informal*), prefer, promote, raise, upgrade

rake[1] *vb.* **1.** collect, gather, remove, scrape up **2.** break up, harrow, hoe, scour, scrape, scratch **3.** *with* **together** *or* **up** assemble, collect, dig up, dredge up, gather, scrape together **4.** comb, examine, hunt, ransack, scan, scour, scrutinize, search **5.** enfilade (*Military*), pepper, sweep **6.** graze, scrape, scratch

rake[2] *n.* debauchee, dissolute man, lecher, libertine, playboy, profligate, roué, sensualist, voluptuary

spirits). **9** to recover (sometimes only temporarily) from an illness. **10** *Stock Exchange* to increase sharply after a decline.

rally[2] *vb* **-lies, -lying, -lied** to mock or tease (someone) in a good-natured way.

rally round *vb* to group together to help someone.

ram *n* **1** an uncastrated adult male sheep. **2** a hydraulically or pneumatically driven piston. **3** the falling weight of a pile driver. **4** short for **battering ram.** *~vb* **ramming, rammed 5** to strike against with force. **6** to force or drive: *he rammed his sword into the man's belly.* **7** to stuff or cram. **8 ram something home** to make something clear or obvious: *to ram home the message.* **9 ram something down someone's throat** to put forward or emphasize an argument or idea with excessive force.

RAM *Computers* random access memory: a temporary storage space which loses its contents when the computer is switched off.

Ramadan *n* **1** the ninth month of the Muslim year, 30 days long, during which strict fasting is observed from sunrise to sunset. **2** the fast itself.

ramble *vb* **-bling, -bled 1** to walk for relaxation, sometimes with no particular direction. **2** to speak or write in a confused style. **3** to grow or develop in a random fashion. *~n* **4** a walk, esp. in the countryside.

rambler *n* **1** a person who takes country walks. **2** a climbing rose.

rambling *adj* **1** long and irregularly shaped: *a rambling fourteenth-century church.* **2** (of speech or writing) confused and long-winded. *~n* **3** the activity of going for long walks in the country.

RAMC Royal Army Medical Corps.

ramekin (**ram**-ik-in) *n* a small container for baking and serving one portion of food.

ramification *n* **1 ramifications** the consequences or complications resulting from an action. **2** a structure of branching parts.

ramify *vb* **-fies, -fying, -fied 1** to become complex. **2** to spread in branches; subdivide.

ramp *n* **1** a slope that joins two surfaces at different levels. **2** a place where the level of a road surface changes because of road works. **3** a movable stairway by which passengers enter and leave an aircraft. **4** a small hump on a road to make traffic slow down.

rampage *vb* **-paging, -paged 1** to rush about violently. *~n* **2 on the rampage** behaving violently or destructively.

rampant *adj* **1** growing or spreading uncontrollably. **2** *Heraldry* (of a beast) standing on the hind legs, the right foreleg raised above the left: *a lion rampant.*

rampart *n* a mound of earth or wall built to protect a fort or city.

rampike *n Canad* a tall tree that has been burned bare of branches.

ram raid *n Informal* a raid on a shop in which a stolen car is driven into the window. **ram raider** *n*

ramrod *n* **1** a long thin rod for cleaning the barrel of a gun or forcing gunpowder into an old-fashioned gun. *~adj* **2** (of someone's posture) very straight and upright.

ramshackle *adj* badly made or cared for: *a curious ramshackle building.*

ran *vb* the past tense of **run.**

ranch *n* **1** a large cattle farm in the American West. **2** *Chiefly US & Canad* a large farm for the rearing of a particular kind of livestock or crop: *he owned a yak ranch in Tibet.* *~vb* **3** to run a ranch. **rancher** *n*

rancherie *n* (in British Columbia, Canada) a settlement of North American Indians.

rancid *adj* (of fatty foods) stale and having an offensive smell. **rancidity** *n*

rancour *or US* **rancor** *n* deep bitter hate. **rancorous** *adj*

rand *n* the standard monetary unit of the Republic of South Africa.

THESAURUS

rakish breezy, dapper, dashing, debonair, devil-may-care, flashy, jaunty, natty (*informal*), raffish, smart, snazzy (*informal*), sporty

rally *n.* **1.** assembly, conference, congregation, congress, convention, convocation, gathering, mass meeting, meeting, muster **2.** comeback (*informal*), improvement, recovery, recuperation, renewal, resurgence, revival, turn for the better *~vb.* **3.** bring *or* come to order, reassemble, re-form, regroup, reorganize, unite **4.** assemble, bond together, bring *or* come together, collect, convene, gather, get together, marshal, mobilize, muster, organize, round up, summon, unite **5.** come round, get better, get one's second wind, improve, perk up, pick up, pull through, recover, recuperate, regain one's strength, revive, take a turn for the better

ram *vb.* **1.** butt, collide with, crash, dash, drive, force, hit, impact, run into, slam, smash, strike **2.** beat, cram, crowd, drum, force, hammer, jam, pack, pound, stuff, tamp, thrust

ramble *vb.* **1.** amble, drift, perambulate, peregrinate, range, roam, rove, saunter, straggle, stravaig (*Scot. & northern English dialect*), stray, stroll, traipse (*informal*), walk, wander **2.** babble, chatter, digress, expatiate, maunder, rabbit (on) (*Brit. informal*), rattle on, run off at the mouth (*slang*), waffle (*informal, chiefly Brit.*), wander, witter on (*informal*) **3.** meander, snake, twist and turn, wind, zigzag *~n.* **4.** excursion, hike, perambulation, peregrination, roaming, roving, saunter, stroll, tour, traipse (*informal*), trip, walk

rambler drifter, hiker, roamer, rover, stroller, walker, wanderer, wayfarer

rambling 1. irregular, sprawling, spreading, straggling, trailing **2.** circuitous, desultory, diffuse, digressive, disconnected, discursive, disjointed, incoherent, irregular, long-winded, periphrastic, prolix, wordy

ramification 1. *plural* complications, consequences, developments, outcome, upshot **2.** branch, development, divarication, division, excrescence, extension, forking, offshoot, outgrowth, subdivision

ramp grade, gradient, incline, inclined plane, rise, slope

rampage 1. *vb.* go ape (*slang*), go apeshit (*slang*), go berserk, rage, run amuck, run riot, run wild, storm, tear **2.** *n.* **on the rampage** amuck, berserk, destructive, out of control, raging, rampant, riotous, violent, wild

rampant 1. epidemic, exuberant, luxuriant, prevalent, profuse, rank, rife, spreading like wildfire, unchecked, uncontrolled, unrestrained, widespread **2.** *Heraldry* erect, rearing, standing, upright

rampart barricade, bastion, breastwork, bulwark, defence, earthwork, embankment, fence, fort, fortification, guard, parapet, security, stronghold, wall

ramshackle broken-down, crumbling, decrepit, derelict, dilapidated, flimsy, jerry-built, rickety, shaky, tottering, tumbledown, unsafe, unsteady

rancid bad, fetid, foul, frowsty, fusty, musty, off, putrid, rank, rotten, sour, stale, strong-smelling, tainted

random 1. *adj.* accidental, adventitious, aimless, arbitrary, casual, chance, desultory, fortuitous, haphazard, hit or miss, incidental, indiscriminate, purposeless, spot, stray, unplanned, unpremeditated **2.** *n.* **at**

random *adj* **1** lacking any definite plan or prearranged order: *a random sample.* ~*n* **2 at random** not following any prearranged order. **randomly** *adv* **randomness** *n*

random access *n* a method of reading data from a computer file without having to read through the file from the beginning.

randy *adj* **randier, randiest** *Informal* sexually aroused. **randily** *adv* **randiness** *n*

ranee *n* same as **rani.**

rang *vb* the past tense of **ring**[1].

rangatira (rung-a-teer-a) *n NZ* a Maori chief of either sex.

range *n* **1** the limits within which a person or thing can function effectively: *academic ability range.* **2 a** the maximum effective distance of a projectile fired from a weapon. **b** the distance between a target and a weapon. **3** the total distance which a ship, aircraft, or vehicle can travel without taking on fresh fuel. **4** the difference in pitch between the highest and lowest note of a voice or musical instrument. **5** a whole set of related things: *a range of treatments was available.* **6** the total products of a manufacturer, designer, or stockist: *the latest skin-care range.* **7** the limits within which something can lie: *a range of prices.* **8** *US & Canad* an extensive tract of open land on which livestock can graze. **9** a chain of mountains. **10** an area set aside for shooting practice or rocket testing. **11** a large cooking stove with one or more ovens. **12** *Maths* the set of values that a function or variable can take. ~*vb* **ranging, ranged 13** to vary between one point and another. **14** to cover a specified period or specified things: *attitudes ranged from sympathy to indifference.* **15** to roam (over). **16** to establish or be situated in a line or series. **17** to put into a specific category: *they ranged themselves with the opposition.*

rangefinder *n* an instrument for finding how far away an object is.

ranger *n* **1** an official in charge of a park or nature reserve. **2** *US* an armed trooper employed to police a State or district: *a Texas ranger.*

Ranger *or* **Ranger Guide** *n Brit* a member of the senior branch of the Guides.

rangy (rain-jee) *adj* **rangier, rangiest** having long slender limbs.

rani *or* **ranee** *n* the wife or widow of a raja.

rank[1] *n* **1** a position within a social organization: *the rank of superintendent.* **2** high social or other standing: *accusations were made against people of high rank.* **3** a person's social class: *it was too grand for someone of his lowly rank.* **4** the position of an item in any ordering or sequence. **5** a line or row of people or things. **6** *Brit* a place where taxis wait to be hired. **7** a line of people, esp. soldiers, positioned one beside the other. **8** any of the eight horizontal rows of squares on a chessboard. **9 close ranks** to maintain solidarity. **10 pull rank** to get one's own way by virtue of one's superior position. **11 rank and file** the ordinary people or members of a group. **12 the ranks** the common soldiers. ~*vb* **13** to give or hold a specific position in an organization or group. **14** to arrange in rows or lines. **15** to arrange in sequence: *it ranks a lowly nineteenth worldwide.* **16** to be important: *the legendary coronation stone ranks high in the hearts of patriots.*

rank[2] *adj* **1** complete or absolute: *rank incompetence.* **2** smelling offensively strong. **3** growing too quickly: *rank weeds.*

rankle *vb* **-kling, -kled** to continue to cause resentment or bitterness.

ransack *vb* **1** to search through every part of (a place or thing). **2** to plunder or pillage.

ransom *n* **1** the money demanded in return for the release of someone who has been kidnapped. **2 hold to ransom a** to keep (a prisoner) in confinement until payment is received. **b** to attempt to force (a person) to do something. ~*vb* **3** to pay money to obtain the release of (a prisoner). **4** to set free (a prisoner) in return for money. **ransomer** *n*

rant *vb* **1** to talk in a loud and excited way. ~*n* **2** loud excited speech. **ranting** *adj, n*

ranunculus *n, pl* **-luses** *or* **-li** a genus of plants including the buttercup.

RAOC Royal Army Ordnance Corps.

rap[1] *vb* **rapping, rapped 1** to hit with a sharp quick blow. **2** to knock loudly and sharply. **3 rap out** to utter in sharp rapid speech: *he rapped out his address.* **4** to perform a rhythmic monologue with musical backing. **5** *Slang* to talk in a relaxed and friendly way. **6** to rebuke or criticize sharply. **7 rap over the knuckles** to reprimand. ~*n* **8** a sharp quick blow or the sound produced by it. **9** a fast rhythmic monologue over a musical backing. **10** a sharp rebuke or criti-

THESAURUS

random accidentally, adventitiously, aimlessly, arbitrarily, by chance, casually, haphazardly, indiscriminately, irregularly, purposelessly, randomly, unsystematically, willy-nilly

range *n.* **1.** ambit, amplitude, area, bounds, compass, confines, distance, domain, extent, field, latitude, limits, orbit, pale, parameters (*informal*), province, purview, radius, reach, scope, span, sphere, sweep **2.** assortment, class, collection, gamut, kind, lot, order, selection, series, sort, variety **3.** chain, file, line, rank, row, sequence, series, string, tier ~*vb.* **4.** extend, fluctuate, go, reach, run, stretch, vary between **5.** cruise, explore, ramble, roam, rove, straggle, stray, stroll, sweep, traverse, wander **6.** arrange, bracket, catalogue, categorize, class, classify, file, grade, group, pigeonhole, rank **7.** align, arrange, array, dispose, draw up, line up, order

rank[1] *n.* **1.** caste, class, classification, degree, dignity, division, echelon, grade, level, nobility, order, position, quality, sort, standing, station, status, stratum, type **2.** column, file, formation, group, line, range, row, series, tier ~*vb.* **3.** align, arrange, array, class, classify, dispose, grade, line up, locate, marshal, order, position, range, sort

rank[2] **1.** absolute, arrant, blatant, complete, downright, egregious, excessive, extravagant, flagrant, glaring, gross, rampant, sheer, thorough, total, undisguised, unmitigated, utter **2.** bad, disagreeable, disgusting, fetid, foul, fusty, gamy, musty, noisome, noxious, off, offensive, olid, pungent, putrid, rancid, revolting, stale, stinking, strong-smelling, yucky *or* yukky (*slang*) **3.** abundant, dense, exuberant, flourishing, lush, luxuriant, productive, profuse, strong-growing, vigorous

rank and file 1. lower ranks, men, other ranks, private soldiers, soldiers, troops **2.** body, general public, Joe Public (*slang*), Joe Six-Pack (*U.S. slang*), majority, mass, masses

rankle anger, annoy, chafe, embitter, fester, gall, get one's goat (*slang*), get on one's nerves (*informal*), irk, irritate, piss one off (*taboo slang*), rile

ransack 1. comb, explore, go through, rake, rummage, scour, search, turn inside out **2.** despoil, gut, loot, pillage, plunder, raid, ravage, rifle, sack, strip

ransom 1. *n.* money, payment, payoff, price **2.** *vb.* buy (someone) out (*informal*), buy the freedom of, deliver, liberate, obtain *or* pay for the release of, redeem, release, rescue, set free

rant 1. *vb.* bellow, bluster, cry, declaim, rave, roar,

cism. **11** *Slang* a legal charge: *a murder rap.* **12 take the rap** *Slang* to suffer the punishment for a crime, whether guilty or not. **rapper** *n*

rap[2] *n* **not care a rap** to not care in the least: *she didn't care a rap for us.*

rapacious *adj* **1** greedy or grasping. **2** (of animals or birds) living by catching prey. **rapacity** *n*

rape[1] *vb* **raping, raped 1** to force (someone) to submit to sexual intercourse. *~n* **2** the act of raping. **3** any violation or abuse: *the rape of the country's natural resources.* **rapist** *n*

rape[2] *n* a yellow-flowered plant cultivated for its seeds, **rapeseed,** which yield a useful oil, **rape oil,** and as a fodder plant.

rapid *adj* **1** (of an action) taking or lasting a short time. **2** acting or moving quickly: *a rapid advance.* **rapidly** *adv* **rapidity** *n*

rapid eye movement *n* the movement of the eyeballs while a person is dreaming.

rapids *pl n* part of a river where the water is very fast and turbulent.

rapier (**ray**-pyer) *n* a long narrow two-edged sword.

rapine (**rap**-pine) *n* pillage or plundering.

rapport (rap-**pore**) *n* a sympathetic relationship or understanding.

rapprochement (rap-**prosh**-mong) *n* a re-establishment of friendly relations: *the policy of rapprochement with Eastern Europe.*

rapscallion *n Old-fashioned* a rascal or rogue.

rapt *adj* **1** totally engrossed: *rapt attention.* **2** arising from or showing rapture: *with a rapt look on his face.*

raptor *n* any bird of prey. **raptorial** *adj*

rapture *n* **1** extreme happiness or delight. **2 raptures** ecstatic joy: *they will be in raptures over the rugged scenery.* **rapturous** *adj*

rare[1] *adj* **1** uncommon or unusual: *a rare plant.* **2** not happening or done very often: *a rare appearance in London.* **3** of uncommonly high quality: *a rare beauty.* **4** (of air at high altitudes) having low density; thin.

rare[2] *adj* (of meat) very lightly cooked.

rarebit *n* short for **Welsh rarebit.**

rare earth *n Chem* **1** any oxide of a lanthanide. **2** Also called: **rare-earth element** any element of the lanthanide series.

rarefied (**rare**-if-ide) *adj* **1** highly specialized: *the rarefied world of classical ballet.* **2** (of air) thin. **3** exalted in character: *the rarefied heights of academic excellence.*

rarely *adv* **1** hardly ever. **2** to an unusual degree; exceptionally.

raring *adj* **raring to do something** keen and willing to do something.

rarity *n, pl* **-ties 1** something that is valuable because it is unusual. **2** the state of being rare.

rascal *n* **1** a scoundrel or rogue. **2** a mischievous child. **rascally** *adj*

rase *vb* **rasing, rased** same as **raze.**

rash[1] *adj* acting or done without proper thought or consideration; hasty: *rash actions.* **rashly** *adv* **rashness** *n*

rash[2] *n* **1** an outbreak of spots or patches on the skin, caused by illness or allergy. **2** an outbreak of occurrences: *a rash of censorship trials.*

rasher *n* a thin slice of bacon.

rasp *n* **1** a harsh grating noise. **2** a coarse file with rows of raised teeth. *~vb* **3** to say or speak in a grating voice. **4** to make a harsh grating noise. **5** to scrape or rub (something) roughly. **6** to irritate (one's nerves).

raspberry *n, pl* **-ries 1** the red fruit of a prickly shrub of Europe and North America. **2** *Informal* a

THESAURUS

shout, spout (*informal*), vociferate, yell **2.** *n.* bluster, bombast, diatribe, harangue, philippic, rhetoric, tirade, vociferation

rapacious avaricious, extortionate, grasping, greedy, insatiable, marauding, plundering, predatory, preying, ravenous, usurious, voracious, wolfish

rapacity avarice, avidity, cupidity, graspingness, greed, greediness, insatiableness, predatoriness, rapaciousness, ravenousness, usury, voraciousness, voracity, wolfishness

rape *vb.* **1.** outrage, ravish, sexually assault, violate *~n.* **2.** outrage, ravishment, sexual assault, violation **3.** depredation, despoilment, despoliation, pillage, plundering, rapine, sack, spoliation

rapid brisk, expeditious, express, fast, fleet, flying, hasty, hurried, precipitate, prompt, quick, quickie (*informal*), speedy, swift

rapidity alacrity, briskness, celerity, dispatch, expedition, fleetness, haste, hurry, precipitateness, promptitude, promptness, quickness, rush, speed, speediness, swiftness, velocity

rapidly apace, at speed, briskly, expeditiously, fast, hastily, hotfoot, hurriedly, in a hurry, in a rush, in haste, like a shot, posthaste, precipitately, promptly, pronto (*informal*), quickly, speedily, swiftly, with dispatch

rapport affinity, bond, empathy, harmony, interrelationship, link, relationship, sympathy, tie, understanding

rapt absorbed, carried away, engrossed, enthralled, entranced, fascinated, gripped, held, intent, preoccupied, spellbound

rapture beatitude, bliss, cloud nine (*informal*), delectation, delight, ecstasy, enthusiasm, euphoria, exaltation, felicity, happiness, joy, ravishment, rhapsody, seventh heaven, spell, transport

rapturous blissful, delighted, ecstatic, enthusiastic, euphoric, exalted, happy, in seventh heaven, joyful, joyous, on cloud nine (*informal*), overjoyed, over the moon (*informal*), rapt, ravished, rhapsodic, transported

rare **1.** exceptional, few, infrequent, out of the ordinary, recherché, scarce, singular, sparse, sporadic, strange, thin on the ground, uncommon, unusual **2.** admirable, choice, excellent, exquisite, extreme, fine, great, incomparable, peerless, superb, superlative

rarely **1.** almost never, hardly, hardly ever, infrequently, little, once in a blue moon, once in a while, only now and then, on rare occasions, scarcely ever, seldom **2.** exceptionally, extraordinarily, finely, notably, remarkably, singularly, uncommonly, unusually

rarity **1.** curio, curiosity, find, gem, one-off, pearl, treasure **2.** infrequency, scarcity, shortage, singularity, sparseness, strangeness, uncommonness, unusualness

rascal blackguard, devil, disgrace, good-for-nothing, imp, knave (*archaic*), miscreant, ne'er-do-well, rake, rapscallion, reprobate, rogue, scally (*Northwest English dialect*), scallywag (*informal*), scamp, scoundrel, varmint (*informal*), villain, wastrel, wretch

rash[1] adventurous, audacious, brash, careless, foolhardy, harebrained, harum-scarum, hasty, headlong, headstrong, heedless, helter-skelter, hot-headed, ill-advised, ill-considered, impetuous, imprudent, impulsive, incautious, indiscreet, injudicious, madcap, precipitate, premature, reckless, thoughtless, unguarded, unthinking, unwary, venturesome

rash[2] **1.** eruption, outbreak **2.** epidemic, flood, outbreak, plague, series, spate, succession, wave

rashness adventurousness, audacity, brashness,

sputtering noise made with the tongue and lips to express contempt: *she blew a loud raspberry.*

Rastafarian *or* **Rasta** *n* **1** a believer in a religion of Jamaican origin that regards Ras Tafari, the former emperor of Ethiopia, Haile Selassie, as God. *~adj* **2** of Rastafarians.

rat *n* **1** a long-tailed rodent, similar to but larger than a mouse. **2** *Informal* someone who is disloyal or treacherous. **3 smell a rat** to detect something suspicious. *~vb* **ratting, ratted 4 rat on a** to betray (someone): *good friends don't rat on each other.* **b** to go back on (an agreement): *his ex-wife claims he ratted on their divorce settlement.* **5** to hunt and kill rats.

ratafia (rat-a-**fee**-a) *n* **1** a liqueur made from fruit. **2** an almond-flavoured biscuit.

rat-a-tat *or* **rat-a-tat-tat** *n* a repeated knocking or tapping sound.

ratatouille (rat-a-**twee**) *n* a vegetable casserole made of stewed tomatoes, aubergines, etc.

ratbag *n Slang* a despicable person.

ratchet *n* **1** a device in which a toothed rack or wheel is engaged by a pivoted lever which permits motion in one direction only. **2** the toothed rack or wheel in such a device.

rate[1] *n* **1** a quantity or amount considered in relation to or measured against another quantity or amount: *a rate of 70 miles an hour.* **2** a price or charge with reference to a standard or scale: *an exchange rate.* **3** the speed of progress or change: *crime is increasing at an alarming rate.* **4** a charge made per unit for a commodity or service. **5** See **rates. 6** relative quality: *a third-rate power.* **7 at any rate** in any case. *~vb* **rating, rated 8** to assign a position on a scale of relative values: *he is rated as one of the top caterers in the country.* **9** to estimate the value of: *we rate your services highly.* **10** to consider or regard: *it could hardly be rated a success.* **11** to be worthy of: *it barely rates a mention.* **12** *Informal* to have a high opinion of: *the cognoscenti have always rated his political skills.*

rate[2] *vb* **rating, rated** to scold or criticize severely.

rateable *adj* **1** able to be rated or evaluated. **2** *Brit* (of property) liable to payment of rates.

rateable value *n Brit* (formerly) a fixed value assigned to a property, used to assess the rates due on it.

rate-cap *vb* **-capping, -capped** (formerly, in Britain) to put an upper limit on the rates charged by a local council. **rate-capping** *n*

ratepayer *n Brit* (formerly) a person who pays local rates on a building.

rates *pl n Brit* (formerly) a tax on property levied by a local authority.

rather *adv* **1** fairly: *that was a rather narrow escape.* **2** to a limited extent: *I rather thought that was the case.* **3** more truly or appropriately: *they tend to be cat rather than dog people.* **4** more willingly: *I would rather go straight home. ~interj* **5** an expression of strong affirmation: *Is it worth seeing? Rather!*

ratify *vb* **-fies, -fying, -fied** to give formal approval to. **ratification** *n*

rating *n* **1** a valuation or assessment. **2** a classification according to order or grade. **3** a noncommissioned sailor. **4 ratings** the size of the audience for a TV or radio programme.

ratio *n, pl* **-tios 1** the relationship between two numbers or amounts expressed as a proportion: *a ratio of one instructor to every five pupils.* **2** *Maths* a quotient of two numbers or quantities.

ration *n* **1** a fixed allowance of something that is scarce, such as food or petrol in wartime. **2 rations** a fixed daily allowance of food, such as that given to a soldier. *~vb* **3** to restrict the distribution of (something): *the government has rationed petrol.* **4** to distribute a fixed amount of something to each person in a group. **rationing** *n*

rational *adj* **1** reasonable or sensible. **2** using reason or logic in thinking out a problem. **3** capable of reasoning: *man is a rational being.* **4** sane: *rational behaviour.* **5** *Maths* able to be expressed as a ratio of two integers: *a rational number.* **rationality** *n* **rationally** *adv*

rationale (rash-a-**nahl**) *n* the reason for an action or belief.

rationalism *n* the philosophy that regards reason as the only basis for beliefs or actions. **rationalist** *n* **rationalistic** *adj*

rationalize *or* **-ise** *vb* **-izing, -ized** *or* **-ising, -ised 1** to find reasons to justify or explain (one's actions). **2** to apply logic or reason to (something). **3** to get rid of unnecessary equipment or staff to make (a business) more efficient. **rationalization** *or* **-isation** *n*

rational number *n* any real number that can be expressed in the form *a/b,* where *a* and *b* are integers and *b* is not zero, as 7 or $\frac{7}{3}$.

rat race *n* a continual routine of hectic competitive activity: *get out of the rat race for a while.*

THESAURUS

carelessness, foolhardiness, hastiness, heedlessness, indiscretion, precipitation, recklessness, temerity, thoughtlessness

rate *n.* **1.** degree, percentage, proportion, ratio, relation, scale, standard **2.** charge, cost, dues, duty, fee, figure, hire, price, tariff, tax, toll **3.** gait, measure, pace, speed, tempo, time, velocity **4.** class, classification, degree, grade, position, quality, rank, rating, status, value, worth **5. at any rate** anyhow, anyway, at all events, in any case, nevertheless *~vb.* **6.** adjudge, appraise, assess, class, classify, consider, count, esteem, estimate, evaluate, grade, measure, rank, reckon, regard, value, weigh **7.** be entitled to, be worthy of, deserve, merit **8.** *informal* admire, esteem, respect, think highly of, value

rather 1. a bit, a little, fairly, kind of (*informal*), moderately, pretty (*informal*), quite, relatively, slightly, somewhat, sort of (*informal*), to some degree, to some extent **2.** instead, more readily, more willingly, preferably, sooner

ratify affirm, approve, authenticate, authorize, bear out, bind, certify, confirm, consent to, corroborate, endorse, establish, sanction, sign, uphold, validate

rating class, classification, degree, designation, estimate, evaluation, grade, order, placing, position, rank, rate, standing, status

ratio arrangement, correlation, correspondence, equation, fraction, percentage, proportion, rate, relation, relationship

ration *n.* **1.** allotment, allowance, dole, helping, measure, part, portion, provision, quota, share **2.** *plural* commons (*Brit.*), food, provender, provisions, stores, supplies *~vb.* **3.** budget, conserve, control, limit, restrict, save **4.** allocate, allot, apportion, deal, distribute, dole, give out, issue, measure out, mete, parcel out

rational 1. enlightened, intelligent, judicious, logical, lucid, realistic, reasonable, sagacious, sane, sensible, sound, wise **2.** cerebral, cognitive, ratiocinative, reasoning, thinking **3.** all there (*informal*), balanced, *compos mentis,* in one's right mind, lucid, normal, of sound mind, sane

rationale exposition, grounds, logic, motivation, philosophy, principle, *raison d'être,* reasons, theory

rationalize 1. account for, excuse, explain away, extenuate, justify, make allowance for, make excuses

rattan *n* a climbing palm with tough stems used for wickerwork and canes.

ratter *n* a dog or cat that catches and kills rats.

rattle *vb* **-tling, -tled 1** to make a rapid succession of short sharp sounds, such as when loose pellets are shaken in a container. **2** to send, move, or drive with such a sound: *rain rattled against the window.* **3** to shake briskly causing sharp sounds. **4** *Informal* to frighten or confuse. **5 rattle off** *or* **out** to recite perfunctorily or rapidly. **6 rattle on** *or* **away** to talk quickly and at length about something unimportant. **7 rattle through** to do (something) very quickly: *she rattled through a translation.* ~*n* **8** a rapid succession of short sharp sounds. **9** a baby's toy filled with small pellets that rattle when shaken. **rattly** *adj*

rattlesnake *n* a poisonous snake with loose horny segments on the tail that make a rattling sound.

rattletrap *n Informal* a broken-down old vehicle.

rattling *adv Informal, old-fashioned* very: *a rattling good yarn.*

ratty *adj* **-tier, -tiest 1** *Brit informal* cross and irritable. **2** *Informal* (of the hair) straggly and greasy. **rattily** *adv* **rattiness** *n*

raucous *adj* loud and harsh.

raunchy *adj* **-chier, -chiest** *Slang* sexy or earthy.

ravage *vb* **-aging, -aged 1** to cause extensive damage to. ~*n* **2 ravages** the damaging effects: *the ravages of weather and pollution.*

rave *vb* **raving, raved 1** to talk in a wild or incoherent manner. **2** *Informal* to write or speak (about) with great enthusiasm. ~*n* **3** *Informal* an enthusiastically favourable review. **4** *Slang* a professionally organized large-scale party with electronic dance music. **5** a name given to various types of dance music, such as techno, that feature fast electronic rhythm.

ravel *vb* **-elling, -elled** *or US* **-eling, -eled 1** to tangle or become entangled. **2** (of a fabric) to fray out in loose ends; unravel.

raven *n* **1** a large bird of the crow family with shiny black feathers. ~*adj* **2** (of hair) shiny black.

ravening *adj* (of animals) hungrily searching for prey.

ravenous *adj* **1** very hungry. **2** ravening. **ravenously** *adv*

raver *n Brit slang* a person who leads a wild or uninhibited social life.

ravine (rav-**veen**) *n* a deep narrow steep-sided valley worn by a stream.

raving *adj* **1** delirious. **2** *Informal* great or exceptional: *a raving beauty.* ~*adv* **3** to an excessive degree: *raving mad.* ~*n* **4 ravings** frenzied or wildly extravagant talk.

ravioli *pl n* small squares of pasta with a savoury filling, such as meat or cheese.

ravish *vb* **1** to enrapture or delight: *tourists ravished by our brilliant costumes.* **2** *Literary* to rape. **ravishment** *n*

ravishing *adj* lovely or delightful. **ravishingly** *adv*

raw *adj* **1** (of food) not cooked. **2** in an unfinished or unrefined state: *raw sewage.* **3** not selected or modified: *raw data.* **4** (of the skin or a wound) painful, with the surface scraped away. **5** untrained or inexperienced: *a raw recruit.* **6** (of the weather) harshly cold and damp. **7** frank or realistic: *a raw reality.* **8 raw deal** *Informal* unfair or dishonest treatment. ~*n* **9 in the raw a** *Informal* naked. **b** in a natural and uncivilized state: *to see life in the raw.* **10 on the raw** *Brit informal* sensitive to upset: *my nerves are on the raw today.*

rawboned *adj* having a lean bony physique.

rawhide *n* **1** untanned hide. **2** a whip or rope made of strips of this.

Rawlplug *n Trademark* a short fibre or plastic tube used to provide a fixing in a wall for a screw.

ray[1] *n* **1** a narrow beam of light. **2** any of a set of lines spreading from a central point. **3** a slight indication: *a ray of hope.* **4** *Maths* a straight line extending from a point. **5** a thin beam of electromagnetic radiation or particles. **6** any of the spines that support the fin of a fish.

ray[2] *n* a sea fish related to the sharks, with a flattened body and a long whiplike tail.

ray[3] *n Music* (in tonic sol-fa) the second note of any ascending major scale.

rayon *n* a textile fibre or fabric made from cellulose.

raze *or* **rase** *vb* **razing, razed** *or* **rasing, rased** to destroy (buildings or a town) completely.

razoo *n, pl* **-zoos** *Austral & NZ informal* an imaginary coin: *we haven't got a brass razoo.*

THESAURUS

for, vindicate **2.** apply logic to, elucidate, reason out, resolve, think through **3.** make cuts, make more efficient, streamline, trim

rattle *vb.* **1.** bang, clatter, jangle **2.** bounce, jar, jiggle, jolt, jounce, shake, vibrate **3.** *informal* discomfit, discompose, disconcert, discountenance, disturb, faze, frighten, perturb, put (someone) off his stride, put (someone) out of countenance, scare, shake, upset **4.** *with* **off** *or* **out** list, recite, reel off, rehearse, run through, spiel off (*informal*) **5.** *with* **on** blether, cackle, chatter, gabble, gibber, jabber, prate, prattle, rabbit (on) (*Brit. informal*), run on, witter (*informal*), yak (away) (*slang*)

raucous grating, harsh, hoarse, husky, loud, noisy, rasping, rough, strident

ravage 1. *vb.* demolish, desolate, despoil, destroy, devastate, gut, lay waste, leave in ruins, loot, pillage, plunder, ransack, raze, ruin, sack, shatter, spoil, wreak havoc on, wreck **2.** *n. plural* damage, demolition, depredation, desolation, destruction, devastation, havoc, pillage, plunder, rapine, ruin, ruination, spoliation, waste

rave *vb.* **1.** babble, be delirious, fume, go mad (*informal*), rage, rant, roar, run amuck, splutter, storm, talk wildly, thunder **2.** *informal* be delighted by, be mad about (*informal*), be wild about (*informal*), cry up, enthuse, gush, praise, rhapsodize ~*n.* **3.** *informal* acclaim, applause, encomium, praise

ravenous 1. famished, starved, starving, very hungry **2.** avaricious, covetous, devouring, ferocious, gluttonous, grasping, greedy, insatiable, insatiate, predatory, rapacious, ravening, voracious, wolfish

ravine canyon, clough (*dialect*), defile, gap (*U.S.*), gorge, gulch (*U.S.*), gully, linn (*Scot.*), pass

raving berserk, crazed, crazy, delirious, frantic, frenzied, furious, hysterical, insane, irrational, mad, out of one's mind, rabid, raging, wild

raw 1. bloody (*of meat*), fresh, natural, uncooked, undressed, unprepared **2.** basic, coarse, crude, green, natural, organic, rough, unfinished, unprocessed, unrefined, unripe, untreated **3.** abraded, chafed, grazed, open, scratched, sensitive, skinned, sore, tender **4.** callow, green, ignorant, immature, inexperienced, new, undisciplined, unpractised, unseasoned, unskilled, untrained, untried **5.** biting, bitter, bleak, chill, chilly, cold, damp, freezing, harsh, parky (*Brit. informal*), piercing, unpleasant, wet **6.** bare, blunt, brutal, candid, frank, naked, plain, realistic, unembellished, unvarnished

razor *n* an implement with a sharp blade, used for shaving.
razorbill *n* a black-and-white sea bird with a stout sideways flattened bill.
razor shell *n* **1** a burrowing shellfish with a long narrow shell. **2** this shell.
razor wire *n* strong wire with pieces of sharp metal set across it at intervals.
razzle-dazzle *or* **razzmatazz** *n Slang* **1** noisy or showy fuss or activity. **2** a spree or frolic.
R & B rhythm and blues.
Rb *Chem* rubidium.
RC 1 Red Cross. 2 Roman Catholic.
R & D research and development.
Rd road.
re[1] *prep* with reference to.
➤ In commercial correspondence the use of *re* is becoming less frequent in favour of *with reference to* or *about*.
re[2] *n Music* same as **ray**[3].
Re *Chem* rhenium.
RE 1 Religious Education. 2 Royal Engineers.
re- *prefix* used with many main words to mean: **1** repetition of an action: *remarry*. **2** return to a previous condition: *renew*.
reach *vb* **1** to arrive at or get to (a place). **2** to make a movement (towards), as if to grasp or touch: *she reached for her bag.* **3** to succeed in touching: *I can't reach that shelf unless I stand on a chair.* **4** to make contact or communication with: *to reach a wider audience.* **5** to extend as far as (a point or place): *to reach the ceiling.* **6** to come to (a certain condition or situation): *to reach a compromise.* **7** to arrive at or amount to (an amount or value): *temperatures in Greece reached 35° yesterday.* **8** *Informal* to give (something to a person) with the outstretched hand. *~n* **9** the extent or distance of reaching: *within easy reach.* **10** the range of influence or power: *it symbolized America's global reach.* **11 reaches** a section of river, land, or sky: *the quieter reaches of the upper Thames.* **reachable** *adj*
reach-me-down *adj* cheap and ready-made or second-hand: *a reach-me-down suit.*
reacquaint *vb* **reacquaint oneself with** *or* **become reacquainted with** to get to know (someone) again.
react *vb* **1** (of a person or thing) to act in response to another person, a stimulus, or a situation. **2 react against** to act in an opposing or contrary manner. **3** *Chem* to undergo a chemical reaction. **4** *Physics* to exert an equal force in the opposite direction to an acting force.
reactance *n Electricity* the resistance to the flow of an alternating current caused by the inductance or capacitance of the circuit.
reactant *n* a substance that participates in a chemical reaction.
reaction *n* **1** a physical or emotional response to a stimulus. **2** any action resisting another. **3** opposition to change. **4** *Med* any effect produced by a drug or by a substance (allergen) to which a person is allergic. **5** *Chem* a process that involves changes in the structure and energy content of atoms, molecules, or ions. **6** the equal and opposite force that acts on a body whenever it exerts a force on another body. **7 reactions** someone's ability to act in response to something that happens.
reactionary *adj* **1** opposed to political or social change. *~n, pl* **-aries 2** a person opposed to radical change.
reactivate *vb* **-vating, -vated** to make (something) active again. **reactivation** *n*
reactive *adj* **1** readily taking part in chemical reactions: *ozone is a highly reactive form of oxygen gas.* **2** of or having a reactance. **3** responsive to stimulus **reactively** *adv* **reactivity** *n*
reactor *n* short for **nuclear reactor.**
read *vb* **reading, read 1** to look at and understand or take in (written or printed matter). **2** to look at and say aloud. **3** to have a certain wording: *the memorandum read as follows.* **4** to interpret in a specified way: *it can be read as satire.* **5** to interpret the significance or meaning of: *an astrologer who reads Tarot.* **6** to register or show: *the meter reads 100.* **7** to make out the true nature or mood of: *she had read his thoughts.* **8** to interpret (signs, characters, etc.) other than by visual means: *to read Braille.* **9** to have sufficient knowledge of (a language) to understand the written word. **10** to undertake a course of study in (a subject): *to read economics.* **11** to gain knowledge by reading: *he read about the war.* **12** to hear and understand, esp. when using a two-way radio: *we are reading you loud and clear.* **13** *Computers* to obtain (data) from a storage device, such as magnetic tape. *~n* **14** matter suitable for reading: *this book is a very good read.* **15** a spell of reading. ~See also **read into, read out,** etc.
readable *adj* **1** enjoyable to read. **2** (of handwriting or print) legible.
reader *n* **1** a person who reads. **2** a person who reads aloud in public. **3** a person who reads and judges manuscripts sent to a publisher. **4** a book of texts for those learning a foreign language. **5** *Brit* a member of staff below a professor but above a senior lecturer at a university. **6** a proofreader. **7** short for **lay reader.**

THESAURUS

ray 1. bar, beam, flash, gleam, shaft **2.** flicker, glimmer, hint, indication, scintilla, spark, trace
raze bulldoze, demolish, destroy, flatten, knock down, level, pull down, remove, ruin, tear down, throw down
reach *vb.* **1.** arrive at, attain, get as far as, get to, land at, make **2.** contact, extend to, get (a) hold of, go as far as, grasp, stretch to, touch **3.** communicate with, contact, establish contact with, find, get, get hold of, get in touch with, get through to, make contact with **4.** amount to, arrive at, attain, climb to, come to, drop, fall, move, rise, sink **5.** *informal* hand, hold out, pass, stretch *~n.* **6.** ambit, capacity, command, compass, distance, extension, extent, grasp, influence, jurisdiction, mastery, power, range, scope, spread, stretch, sweep
react acknowledge, answer, reply, respond
reaction 1. acknowledgment, answer, feedback, reply, response **2.** compensation, counteraction, counterbalance, counterpoise, recoil **3.** conservatism, counter-revolution, obscurantism, the right
reactionary 1. *adj.* blimpish, conservative, counter-revolutionary, obscurantist, rightist **2.** *n.* Colonel Blimp, conservative, counter-revolutionary, die-hard, obscurantist, rightist, right-winger
read 1. glance at, look at, peruse, pore over, refer to, run one's eye over, scan, study **2.** announce, declaim, deliver, recite, speak, utter **3.** comprehend, construe, decipher, discover, interpret, perceive the meaning of, see, understand **4.** display, indicate, record, register, show
readily 1. cheerfully, eagerly, freely, gladly, promptly, quickly, voluntarily, willingly, with good grace, with pleasure **2.** at once, easily, effortlessly, hotfoot, in no time, quickly, right away, smoothly, speedily, straight away, unhesitatingly, without delay, without demur, without difficulty, without hesitation
readiness 1. fitness, maturity, preparation, prepar-

readership *n* all the readers collectively of a publication or author: *a new format would alienate its readership.*

reading *n* **1** the act of reading. **2** ability to read: *disputes over methods of teaching reading.* **3** material for reading. **4** a public recital of a literary work. **5** a measurement indicated by a gauge or dial. **6** *Parliamentary procedure* one of the three stages in the passage of a bill through a legislative assembly. **7** the form of a particular word or passage in a given text. **8** an interpretation of a situation or something said. *~adj* **9** of or for reading: *reading glasses.*

read into *vb* to discover in a statement (meanings not intended by the speaker or writer): *one of the implications we must read into the work.*

readjust *vb* to adapt to a new situation. **readjustment** *n*

readmit *vb* **-mitting, -mitted** to let (a person or country) back into a place or organization. **readmission** *n*

read out *vb* **1** to read (something) aloud. **2** to retrieve information from a computer memory. *~n* **readout 3** the information retrieved from a computer memory.

read up *vb* to read intensively about (a subject) in order to get information: *he had read up on the cases.*

read-write head *n Computers* an electromagnet that can both read and write information on a magnetic tape or disk.

ready *adj* **readier, readiest 1** prepared for use or action. **2** prompt or eager: *the ready use of corporal punishment.* **3** quick or intelligent: *a ready wit.* **4 ready to** on the point of or liable to: *ready to pounce.* **5** easily available: *his ready tears.* *~n* **6** *Informal* same as **ready money. 7 at the ready** poised for use: *with pen at the ready.* *~vb* **readies, readying, readied 8** to make ready; prepare. **readily** *adv* **readiness** *n*

ready-made *adj* **1** for immediate use by any customer. **2** extremely convenient or ideally suited: *fame affords a ready-made soapbox.*

ready money *n* cash for immediate use. Also: **the ready, the readies**

reaffirm *vb* to state again. **reaffirmation** *n*

reafforest *vb* to plant new trees in (an area that was formerly forested). **reafforestation** *n*

reagent (ree-**age**-ent) *n* a chemical substance that reacts with another, used to detect the presence of the other.

real[1] *adj* **1** existing or occurring in the physical world. **2** actual: *the real agenda.* **3** important or serious: *the real challenge.* **4** rightly so called: *a real friend.* **5** genuine: *the council has no real authority.* **6** (of food or drink) made in a traditional way to ensure the best flavour. **7** *Maths* involving or containing real numbers alone. **8** relating to immovable property such as land or buildings: *real estate.* **9** *Econ* (of prices or incomes) considered in terms of purchasing power rather than nominal currency value. **10 the real thing** the genuine article, not a substitute or imitation.

➤ To intensify an adjective, use the adverb form *really,* not *real: He's really strong.*

real[2] *n* a former small Spanish or Spanish-American silver coin.

real ale *n* beer that has fermented in the barrel.

real estate *n Chiefly US & Canad* immovable property, esp. land and houses.

realignment (ree-a-**line**-ment) *n* a new arrangement or organization: *a realignment of British politics.*

realism *n* **1** awareness or acceptance of things as they are, as opposed to the abstract or ideal. **2** a style in art or literature that attempts to show the world as it really is. **3** *Philosophy* the theory that physical objects continue to exist whether they are perceived or not. **realist** *n* **realistic** *adj* **realistically** *adv*

reality *n, pl* **-ties 1** the state of things as they are or appear to be, rather than as one might wish them to be. **2** something that is real. **3** the state of being real. **4 in reality** in fact.

realize *or* **-ise** *vb* **-izing, -ized** *or* **-ising, -ised 1** to be aware of or grasp the significance of. **2** to achieve (a plan or ambition). **3** to convert (property or goods) into cash. **4** (of goods or property) to sell for (a certain sum): *this table realized £800 at auction.* **5** to produce

THESAURUS

edness, ripeness **2.** aptness, eagerness, gameness (*informal*), inclination, keenness, willingness **3.** adroitness, dexterity, ease, facility, handiness, promptitude, promptness, quickness, rapidity, skill **4. in readiness** all set, at *or* on hand, at the ready, fit, prepared, primed, ready, set, waiting, waiting in the wings

reading 1. examination, inspection, perusal, review, scrutiny, study **2.** book-learning, edification, education, erudition, knowledge, learning, scholarship **3.** homily, lecture, lesson, performance, recital, rendering, rendition, sermon **4.** conception, construction, grasp, impression, interpretation, treatment, understanding, version

ready *adj.* **1.** all set, arranged, completed, fit, in readiness, organized, prepared, primed, ripe, set **2.** agreeable, apt, disposed, eager, game (*informal*), glad, happy, have-a-go (*informal*), inclined, keen, minded, predisposed, prone, willing **3.** acute, adroit, alert, apt, astute, bright, clever, deft, dexterous, expert, handy, intelligent, keen, perceptive, prompt, quick, quick-witted, rapid, resourceful, sharp, skilful, smart **4.** *as in* **ready to** about, close, in danger of, liable, likely, on the brink of, on the point of, on the verge of **5.** accessible, at *or* on hand, at one's fingertips, at the ready, available, close to hand, convenient, handy, near, on call, on tap (*informal*), present *~n.* **6. at the ready** in readiness, poised, prepared, ready for action, waiting *~vb.* **7.** arrange, equip, fit out, get ready, make ready, order, organize, prepare, set

real absolute, actual, authentic, bona fide, certain, essential, existent, factual, genuine, heartfelt, honest, intrinsic, legitimate, positive, right, rightful, sincere, true, unaffected, unfeigned, valid, veritable

realistic 1. businesslike, common-sense, down-to-earth, hard-headed, level-headed, matter-of-fact, practical, pragmatic, rational, real, sensible, sober, unromantic, unsentimental **2.** authentic, faithful, genuine, graphic, lifelike, natural, naturalistic, representational, true, true to life, truthful

reality 1. actuality, authenticity, certainty, corporeality, fact, genuineness, materiality, realism, truth, validity, verisimilitude, verity **2. in reality** actually, as a matter of fact, in actuality, in fact, in point of fact, in truth, really

realization 1. appreciation, apprehension, awareness, cognizance, comprehension, conception, consciousness, grasp, imagination, perception, recognition, understanding **2.** accomplishment, achievement, carrying-out, completion, consummation, effectuation, fulfilment

realize 1. appreciate, apprehend, be cognizant of, become aware of, become conscious of, catch on (*informal*), comprehend, conceive, grasp, imagine, recognize, take in, twig (*Brit. informal*), understand **2.** accomplish, actualize, bring about, bring off, bring to fruition, carry out *or* through, complete, consummate, do, effect, effectuate, fulfil, incarnate, make concrete,

a complete work of art from an idea or draft. **realizable** *or* **-isable** *adj* **realization** *or* **-isation** *n*

really *adv* **1** truly: *really boring.* **2** in reality: *it's really quite harmless.* ~*interj* **3** an exclamation of dismay, doubt, or surprise.

➤ To intensify an adjective, use the adverb form *really,* not *real: He's really strong.*

realm *n* **1** a kingdom. **2** a field of interest or study: *the realm of science.*

real number *n* any rational or irrational number.

real tennis *n* an ancient form of tennis played in a four-walled indoor court.

real-time *adj* (of a computer system) processing data as it is received.

realtor *n US & Canad* an estate agent.

realty *n* same as **real estate.**

ream *n* **1** a number of sheets of paper, now equal to 500 or 516 sheets (20 quires). **2 reams** *Informal* a large quantity (of written material): *reams of verse.*

reap *vb* **1** to cut and gather (a harvest). **2** to receive as the result of a previous activity: *reap the benefits of our efforts.*

reaper *n* **1** a person who reaps or a machine for reaping. **2 the grim reaper** death.

reappear *vb* to come back into view. **reappearance** *n*

reappraise *vb* **-praising, -praised** to consider or review (something) to see if changes are needed. **reappraisal** *n*

rear[1] *n* **1** the back part. **2** the area or position that lies at the back. **3** *Informal* the buttocks. **4 bring up the rear** to come last. ~*adj* **5** of or in the rear: *the rear carriage.*

rear[2] *vb* **1** to care for and educate (children) until maturity. **2** to breed (animals) or grow (plants). **3** (of a horse) to lift the front legs in the air and stand nearly upright. **4** to place or lift (something) upright.

rear admiral *n* a high-ranking naval officer.

rearguard *n* **1** the troops who protect the rear of a military formation. **2 rearguard action** an effort to prevent or postpone something that is unavoidable.

rearm *vb* **1** to arm again. **2** to equip with better weapons. **rearmament** *n*

rearmost *adj* nearest the back.

rearrange *vb* **-ranging, -ranged** to organize differently. **rearrangement** *n*

rear-view mirror *n* a mirror on a motor vehicle enabling the driver to see the traffic behind.

rearward *adj* **1** in the rear. ~*adv also* **rearwards 2** towards the rear.

reason *n* **1** a cause or motive for a belief or action: *he had two reasons for his dark mood.* **2** the ability to think or argue rationally. **3** an argument in favour of or a justification for something: *there is every reason to encourage people to keep fit.* **4** sanity. **5 by reason of** because of. **6 within reason** within moderate or justifiable bounds. **7 it stands to reason** it is logical or obvious. ~*vb* **8** to think logically in forming conclusions. **9 reason with** to persuade by logical arguments into doing something. **10 reason out** to work out (a problem) by reasoning.

reasonable *adj* **1** sensible. **2** not making unfair demands. **3** logical: *a reasonable explanation.* **4** moderate in price. **5** average: *a reasonable amount of luck.* **reasonably** *adv* **reasonableness** *n*

reasoned *adj* well thought out or well presented: *a reasoned explanation.*

reasoning *n* **1** the process of drawing conclusions from facts or evidence. **2** the conclusions reached in this way.

reassemble *vb* **-bling, -bled** to put back together again.

reassert *vb* **1** to state or declare again. **2 reassert oneself** to become significant or noticeable again: *reality had reasserted itself.*

reassess *vb* to reconsider the value or importance of. **reassessment** *n*

reassure *vb* **-assuring, -assured** to relieve (someone) of anxieties. **reassurance** *n* **reassuring** *adj*

rebate[1] *n* a refund or discount.

rebate[2] *or* **rabbet** *n* **1** a groove cut into a piece of timber into which another piece fits. ~*vb* **-beting, -beted 2** to cut a rabbet in. **3** to join (pieces of timber) with a rabbet.

rebel *vb* **-belling, -belled 1** to fight against the ruling power. **2** to reject accepted conventions of behaviour.

THESAURUS

make happen, perform, reify **3.** acquire, bring *or* take in, clear, earn, gain, get, go for, make, net, obtain, produce, sell for

really absolutely, actually, assuredly, categorically, certainly, genuinely, in actuality, indeed, in fact, in reality, positively, surely, truly, undoubtedly, verily (*literary*), without a doubt

reap acquire, bring in, collect, cut, derive, gain, garner, gather, get, harvest, obtain, win

rear[1] **1.** *n.* back, back end, end, rearguard, stern, tail, tail end **2.** *adj.* aft, after (*Nautical*), back, following, hind, hindmost, last, trailing

rear[2] *vb.* **1.** breed, bring up, care for, cultivate, educate, foster, grow, nurse, nurture, raise, train **2.** elevate, hoist, hold up, lift, raise, set upright

reason *n.* **1.** aim, basis, cause, design, end, goal, grounds, impetus, incentive, inducement, intention, motive, object, occasion, purpose, target, warrant, why and wherefore (*informal*) **2.** apprehension, brains, comprehension, intellect, judgment, logic, mind, ratiocination, rationality, reasoning, understanding **3.** apologia, apology, argument, case, defence, excuse, explanation, exposition, ground, justification, rationale, vindication **4.** mind, moderation, sanity, sense(s), sensibleness, sound mind, wisdom **5. within reason** in moderation, proper, reasonable, sensible, warrantable, within bounds, within limits

~*vb.* **6.** conclude, deduce, draw conclusions, infer, make out, resolve, solve, syllogize, think, work out **7.** *with* **with** argue, bring round (*informal*), debate, dispute, dissuade, expostulate, move, persuade, prevail upon, remonstrate, show (someone) the error of his ways, talk into *or* out of, urge, win over

reasonable **1.** advisable, arguable, believable, credible, intelligent, judicious, justifiable, logical, plausible, practical, rational, reasoned, sane, sensible, sober, sound, tenable, well-advised, well thought-out, wise **2.** acceptable, average, equitable, fair, fit, honest, inexpensive, just, moderate, modest, O.K. *or* okay (*informal*), proper, right, tolerable, within reason

reasoned clear, logical, sensible, systematic, well expressed, well presented, well thought-out

reasoning **1.** analysis, cogitation, deduction, logic, ratiocination, reason, thinking, thought **2.** argument, case, exposition, hypothesis, interpretation, proof, train of thought

reassure bolster, buoy up, cheer up, comfort, encourage, hearten, inspirit, put *or* set one's mind at rest, relieve (someone) of anxiety, restore confidence to

rebel *vb.* **1.** defy, disobey, dissent, man the barricades, mutiny, refuse to obey, resist, revolt, rise up, take to the streets, take up arms ~*n.* **2.** insurgent, insurrectionary, mutineer, resistance fighter, revolutionary, revolutionist, secessionist **3.** apostate, dissenter,

~*n* **3** a person who rebels. **4** a person who rejects accepted conventions of behaviour. ~*adj* **5** rebelling: *rebel councillors.*

rebellion *n* **1** organized opposition to a government or other authority involving the use of violence. **2** nonviolent opposition to a government or other authority: *a Tory backbenchers' rebellion.* **3** rejection of accepted conventions of behaviour.

rebellious *adj* rebelling or showing a tendency towards rebellion. **rebelliously** *adv*

rebirth *n* a revival or renaissance: *the rebirth of their nation.*

reboot *vb* to shut down and then restart (a computer system).

rebore *or* **reboring** *n* the boring of a cylinder to restore its true shape.

reborn *adj* active again after a period of inactivity.

rebound *vb* **1** to spring back from a sudden impact. **2** (of a plan or action) to misfire so as to hurt the person responsible. ~*n* **3** the act of rebounding. **4 on the rebound** *Informal* while recovering from rejection: *she married him on the rebound.*

rebuff *vb* **1** to snub and reject an offer or suggestion. ~*n* **2** a blunt refusal; snub.

rebuild *vb* **-building, -built 1** to build (a building or town) again, after severe damage. **2** to develop (something such as a business or relationship) again after destruction or damage.

rebuke *vb* **-buking, -buked 1** to scold sternly. ~*n* **2** a stern scolding.

rebus (ree-buss) *n, pl* **-buses** a puzzle consisting of pictures and symbols representing syllables and words.

rebut *vb* **-butting, -butted** to prove that (a claim) is untrue. **rebuttal** *n*

recalcitrant *adj* wilfully disobedient. **recalcitrance** *n*

recall *vb* **1** to bring back to mind. **2** to order to return. **3** to annul or cancel. ~*n* **4** the ability to remember things. **5** an order to return.

recant *vb* to take back (a former belief or statement) publicly. **recantation** *n*

recap *Informal* ~*vb* **-capping, -capped 1** to recapitulate. ~*n* **2** a recapitulation.

recapitulate *vb* **-lating, -lated** to restate the main points of (an argument or speech).

recapitulation *n* **1** the act of recapitulating. **2** *Music* the repeating of earlier themes, esp. in the final section of a movement.

recapture *vb* **-turing, -tured 1** to relive vividly (a former experience or sensation): *recaptured some of those first feelings.* **2** to capture again. ~*n* **3** the act of recapturing.

recast *vb* **-casting, -cast 1** to give a new form or shape to: *he found the organization wholly recast.* **2** to change the actors or singers in (a play, musical, or opera). **3** to rework (a piece of writing or music): *she has recast most of my book.*

recce *Slang* ~*vb* **-ceing, -ced** *or* **-ceed 1** to reconnoitre. ~*n* **2** reconnaissance.

recede *vb* **-ceding, -ceded 1** to withdraw from a point or limit: *the tide had receded.* **2** to become more distant: *the threat of intervention had receded.* **3** (of a man's hair) to stop growing at the temples and above the forehead. **4** to slope backwards: *a receding chin.*

receipt *n* **1** a written acknowledgment that money or goods have been received. **2** the act of receiving. **3 receipts** money taken in over a particular period by a shop or business.

receive *vb* **-ceiving, -ceived 1** to get (something offered or sent to one). **2** to experience: *he received a knife wound.* **3** to greet (guests). **4** to have (an honour) bestowed: *he received the Order of the Garter.* **5** to admit (a person) to a society or condition: *he was received into the Church.* **6** to convert (incoming radio or television signals) into sounds or pictures. **7** to be informed of (news). **8** to react to: *the article was well*

THESAURUS

heretic, nonconformist, schismatic ~*adj.* **4.** insubordinate, insurgent, insurrectionary, mutinous, rebellious, revolutionary

rebellion 1. insurgence, insurgency, insurrection, mutiny, resistance, revolt, revolution, rising, uprising **2.** apostasy, defiance, disobedience, dissent, heresy, insubordination, nonconformity, schism

rebellious defiant, disaffected, disloyal, disobedient, disorderly, insubordinate, insurgent, insurrectionary, intractable, mutinous, rebel, recalcitrant, refractory, revolutionary, seditious, turbulent, ungovernable, unruly

rebirth new beginning, regeneration, reincarnation, renaissance, renascence, renewal, restoration, resurgence, resurrection, revitalization, revival

rebound *vb.* **1.** bounce, recoil, return, ricochet, spring back **2.** backfire, boomerang, misfire, recoil ~*n.* **3.** bounce, comeback, kickback, repercussion, return, ricochet

rebuff 1. *vb.* brush off (*slang*), check, cold-shoulder, cut, decline, deny, discourage, put off, refuse, reject, repulse, resist, slight, snub, spurn, turn down **2.** *n.* brushoff (*slang*), check, cold shoulder, defeat, denial, discouragement, knock-back (*slang*), opposition, refusal, rejection, repulse, slight, snub, the (old) heave-ho (*informal*), thumbs down

rebuke 1. *vb.* admonish, bawl out (*informal*), berate, blame, carpet (*informal*), castigate, censure, chide, dress down (*informal*), give a rocket (*Brit. & N.Z. informal*), haul (someone) over the coals (*informal*), lecture, read the riot act, reprehend, reprimand, reproach, reprove, scold, take to task, tear into (*informal*), tear (someone) off a strip (*informal*), tell off (*informal*), tick off (*informal*), upbraid **2.** *n.* admonition, blame, castigation, censure, dressing down (*informal*), lecture, reprimand, reproach, reproof, reproval, row, telling-off (*informal*), ticking-off (*informal*), tongue-lashing, wigging (*Brit. slang*)

recalcitrant contrary, contumacious, defiant, disobedient, insubordinate, intractable, obstinate, refractory, stubborn, uncontrollable, ungovernable, unmanageable, unruly, unwilling, wayward, wilful

recall *vb.* **1.** bring *or* call to mind, call *or* summon up, evoke, look *or* think back to, mind (*dialect*), recollect, remember, reminisce about **2.** call back, call in, take back, withdraw **3.** abjure, annul, cancel, countermand, nullify, repeal, rescind, retract, revoke, withdraw ~*n.* **4.** memory, recollection, remembrance

recant abjure, apostatize, deny, disavow, disclaim, disown, forswear, recall, renege, renounce, repudiate, retract, revoke, take back, unsay, withdraw

recapitulate go over again, outline, recap (*informal*), recount, reiterate, repeat, restate, review, run over, run through again, sum up

recede 1. abate, draw back, ebb, fall back, go back, regress, retire, retreat, retrocede, retrogress, return, subside, withdraw **2.** abate, decline, diminish, dwindle, fade, lessen, shrink, sink, wane

receipt 1. acknowledgment, counterfoil, proof of purchase, sales slip, stub, voucher **2.** acceptance, delivery, receiving, reception, recipience **3. receipts** gains, gate, income, proceeds, profits, return, takings

receive 1. accept, accept delivery of, acquire, be

received. **9** to support or sustain (the weight of something). **10** *Tennis etc* to play at the other end from the server. **11** *Brit* to buy and sell stolen goods.

received *adj* generally accepted or believed: *contrary to received wisdom.*

Received Pronunciation *n* the accent of standard Southern British English.

receiver *n* **1** the detachable part of a telephone that is held to the ear. **2** the equipment in a telephone, radio, or television that converts the incoming signals into sound or pictures. **3** a person appointed by a court to manage property of a bankrupt. **4** a person who receives stolen goods knowing they have been stolen.

receivership *n Law* the state of being administered by a receiver: *the company went into receivership.*

recent *adj* **1** having happened lately. **2** new. **recently** *adv*

Recent *adj* same as **Holocene.**

receptacle *n* **1** an object used to contain something. **2** *Bot* the enlarged or modified tip of the flower stalk that bears the flower.

reception *n* **1** an area in an office, hotel, etc., where visitors are received or reservations dealt with. **2** a formal party for guests, esp. after a wedding. **3** the manner in which something is received: *an enthusiastic reception.* **4** the act of formally welcoming. **5** *Radio, television* the quality of a received broadcast: *the reception was poor.*

receptionist *n* a person employed to receive guests or clients and deal with reservations and appointments.

reception room *n* a room in a private house suitable for entertaining guests.

receptive *adj* willing to consider and accept new ideas or suggestions. **receptivity** *or* **receptiveness** *n*

receptor *n Physiol* a sensory nerve ending that changes specific stimuli into nerve impulses.

recess *n* **1** a space, such as an alcove, set back in a wall. **2** a holiday between sessions of work. **3** **recesses** secret hidden places: *the recesses of her brain.* **4** *US & Canad* a break between classes at a school.

recessed *adj* hidden or placed in a recess.

recession *n* **1** a period of economic difficulty when little is being bought or sold. **2** the act of receding.

recessional *n* a hymn sung as the clergy and choir withdraw after a church service.

recessive *adj* **1** tending to recede. **2** *Genetics* (in a pair of genes) designating a gene that has a characteristic which will only be passed on if the other gene has the same characteristic.

recharge *vb* **-charging, -charged** to cause (a battery) to take in and store electricity again. **rechargeable** *adj*

recherché (rish-**air**-shay) *adj* **1** studiedly refined or elegant. **2** known only to connoisseurs.

recidivism *n* habitual relapse into crime. **recidivist** *n, adj*

recipe *n* **1** a list of ingredients and directions for making a particular dish. **2** a method for achieving something: *a recipe for industrial chaos.*

recipient *n* a person who receives something.

reciprocal (ris-**sip**-pro-kl) *adj* **1** done or felt by each of two people or groups to or about the other: *a reciprocal agreement.* **2** given or done in return: *a reciprocal invitation.* **3** *Grammar* (of a pronoun) indicating that action is given and received by each subject, for example, *each other* in *they started to shout at each other.* ~*n* **4** Also called: **inverse** *Maths* a number or quantity that when multiplied by a given number or quantity gives a product of one: *the reciprocal of 2 is 0.5.* **reciprocally** *adv*

reciprocate *vb* **-cating, -cated 1** to give or feel in return: *not everyone reciprocated his enthusiasm.* **2** (of a machine part) to move backwards and forwards. **reciprocation** *n*

reciprocity *n* **1** reciprocal action or relation. **2** a mutual exchange of commercial or other privileges.

recital (ris-**site**-al) *n* **1** a musical performance by a soloist or soloists. **2** the act of reciting something learned or prepared. **3** a narration or description: *she plagued her with the recital of constant ailments and illnesses.*

recitation *n* **1** the act of reciting poetry or prose from memory. **2** something recited.

recitative (ress-it-a-**teev**) *n* a narrative passage in an opera or oratorio, reflecting the natural rhythms of speech.

recite *vb* **-citing, -cited 1** to repeat (a poem or pas-

THESAURUS

given, be in receipt of, collect, derive, get, obtain, pick up, take **2.** bear, be subjected to, encounter, experience, go through, meet with, suffer, sustain, undergo **3.** accommodate, admit, be at home to, entertain, greet, meet, take in, welcome **4.** apprehend, be informed of, be told, gather, hear, perceive

recent contemporary, current, fresh, happening (*informal*), late, latter, latter-day, modern, new, novel, present-day, up-to-date, young

recently currently, freshly, lately, latterly, newly, not long ago, of late

receptacle container, holder, repository

reception 1. do (*informal*), entertainment, function, levee, party, soirée **2.** acceptance, admission, receipt, receiving **3.** acknowledgment, greeting, reaction, recognition, response, treatment, welcome

receptive amenable, interested, open, open-minded, open to suggestions, responsive, sensitive, susceptible, sympathetic

recess 1. alcove, bay, cavity, corner, depression, hollow, indentation, niche, nook, oriel **2.** break, cessation of business, closure, holiday, intermission, interval, respite, rest, vacation **3. recesses** bowels, depths, heart, innards (*informal*), innermost parts, reaches, retreats, secret places

recession decline, depression, downturn, drop, slump

recipe 1. directions, ingredients, instructions, receipt (*obsolete*) **2.** formula, method, modus operandi, prescription, procedure, process, programme, technique

reciprocal alternate, complementary, corresponding, equivalent, exchanged, give-and-take, interchangeable, interdependent, mutual

reciprocate feel in return, interchange, reply, respond, return, return the compliment, swap

recital 1. concert, performance, show **2.** narration, performance, reading, recitation, rendering, repetition, version **3.** account, description, detailing, enumeration, narration, recapitulation, recitation, rehearsal, relation, statement, story, tale, telling

recitation lecture, narration, passage, performance, piece, reading, recital, rendering, telling

recite declaim, deliver, describe, detail, do one's party piece (*informal*), enumerate, itemize, narrate, perform, recapitulate, recount, rehearse, relate, repeat, speak, tell

sage) aloud from memory before an audience. **2** to give a detailed account of.

reckless *adj* having no regard for danger or consequences: *reckless driving.*

reckon *vb* **1** *Informal* to be of the opinion: *she reckoned she could find them.* **2** to consider: *he reckoned himself a failure.* **3** to calculate or compute. **4** to expect. **5 reckon with** *or* **without** to take into account or fail to take into account: *there is this ancestral hatred to reckon with.* **6 reckon on** *or* **upon** to rely on or expect: *they can't reckon on your automatic support.*

reckoning *n* **1** counting or calculating: *by his reckoning, he owed him nearly £50.* **2** retribution for one's actions: *the moment of reckoning came.* **3** settlement of an account or bill.

reclaim *vb* **1** to get back possession of: *the club is now trying to reclaim the money from the blockaders.* **2** to convert (unusable or submerged land) into land suitable for farming or building on. **3** to recover (useful substances) from waste products. **reclamation** *n*

recline *vb* **-clining, -clined** to rest in a leaning position.

reclining *adj* (of a seat) with a back that can be adjusted to slope at various angles.

recluse *n* a person who lives alone and avoids people. **reclusive** *adj*

recognition *n* **1** the act of recognizing. **2** acceptance or acknowledgment. **3** formal acknowledgment of a government or of the independence of a country. **4 in recognition of** as a token of thanks for.

recognizance *or* **recognisance** (rik-**og**-nizz-anss) *n Law* **a** an undertaking made before a court or magistrate to do something specified, such as to appear in court on a stated day. **b** a sum of money promised as a guarantee of this undertaking.

recognize *or* **-nise** *vb* **-nizing, -nized** *or* **-nising, -nised 1** to identify (a person or thing) as someone or something already known. **2** to accept or be aware of (a fact or problem): *to recognize change.* **3** to acknowledge formally the status or legality of (something or someone): *an organization recognized by the UN.* **4** to show approval or appreciation of (something). **5** to make formal acknowledgment of (a claim or duty): *I must ask for her to be recognized as a hostile witness.* **recognizable** *or* **-isable** *adj*

recoil *vb* **1** to jerk or spring back. **2** to draw back in fear or horror. **3** (of an action) to go wrong so as to hurt the person responsible. *~n* **4** the backward movement of a gun when fired. **5** the act of recoiling.

recollect *vb* to remember. **recollection** *n*

recommend *vb* **1** to advise as the best course or choice. **2** to praise or commend: *I would wholeheartedly recommend his books.* **3** to make attractive or advisable: *she has everything to recommend her.* **recommendation** *n*

recompense *vb* **-pensing, -pensed 1** to pay or reward for work or help. **2** to compensate or make up for loss or injury. *~n* **3** compensation for loss or injury. **4** reward or repayment.

reconcile *vb* **-ciling, -ciled 1** to make (two apparently conflicting things) compatible or consistent with each other: *in many cases science and religion are reconciled.* **2** to re-establish friendly relations with (a person or people) or between (people). **3** to accept or cause to accept (an unpleasant situation): *we reconciled ourselves to a change.* **reconciliation** *n*

THESAURUS

reckless careless, daredevil, devil-may-care, foolhardy, harebrained, harum-scarum, hasty, headlong, heedless, ill-advised, imprudent, inattentive, incautious, indiscreet, irresponsible, madcap, mindless, negligent, precipitate, rash, regardless, thoughtless, wild

reckon 1. *informal* assume, believe, be of the opinion, conjecture, expect, fancy, guess (*informal, chiefly U.S. & Canad.*), imagine, suppose, surmise, think **2.** account, appraise, consider, count, deem, esteem, estimate, evaluate, gauge, hold, judge, look upon, rate, regard, think of **3.** add up, calculate, compute, count, enumerate, figure, number, tally, total **4.** *with* **with** anticipate, bargain for, bear in mind, be prepared for, expect, foresee, plan for, take cognizance of, take into account **5.** *with* **on** *or* **upon** bank, calculate, count, depend, hope for, rely, take for granted, trust in

reckoning 1. adding, addition, calculation, computation, count, counting, estimate, summation, working **2.** doom, judgment, last judgment, retribution **3.** account, bill, charge, due, score, settlement

reclaim get *or* take back, recapture, recover, redeem, reform, regain, regenerate, reinstate, rescue, restore, retrieve, salvage

recline be recumbent, lay (something) down, lean, lie (down), loll, lounge, repose, rest, sprawl, stretch out

recluse anchoress, anchorite, ascetic, eremite, hermit, monk, solitary

recognition 1. detection, discovery, identification, recall, recollection, remembrance **2.** acceptance, acknowledgment, admission, allowance, appreciation, avowal, awareness, cognizance, concession, confession, notice, perception, realization, respect, understanding **3.** *as in* **in recognition of** acknowledgment, appreciation, approval, gratitude, greeting, honour, salute

recognize 1. identify, know, know again, make out, notice, place, recall, recollect, remember, spot **2.** accept, acknowledge, admit, allow, appreciate, avow, be aware of, concede, confess, grant, own, perceive, realize, respect, see, understand **3.** acknowledge, appreciate, approve, greet, honour, salute

recoil *vb.* **1.** jerk back, kick, react, rebound, resile, spring back **2.** balk at, draw back, falter, flinch, quail, shrink, shy away **3.** backfire, boomerang, go wrong, misfire, rebound *~n.* **4.** backlash, kick, reaction, rebound, repercussion

recollect call to mind, mind (*dialect*), place, recall, remember, reminisce, summon up

recollection impression, memory, mental image, recall, remembrance, reminiscence

recommend 1. advise, advocate, counsel, enjoin, exhort, prescribe, propose, put forward, suggest, urge **2.** approve, commend, endorse, praise, put in a good word for, speak well of, vouch for **3.** make attractive (acceptable, appealing, interesting)

recommendation 1. advice, counsel, proposal, suggestion, urging **2.** advocacy, approbation, approval, blessing, commendation, endorsement, favourable mention, good word, plug (*informal*), praise, reference, sanction, testimonial

reconcile 1. appease, bring to terms, conciliate, make peace between, pacify, placate, propitiate, re-establish friendly relations between, restore harmony between, reunite **2.** accept, accommodate, get used, make the best of, put up with (*informal*), resign, submit, yield

reconciliation 1. appeasement, conciliation, détente, pacification, propitiation, *rapprochement,* reconcilement, reunion, understanding **2.** accommodation, adjustment, compromise, harmony, rectification, settlement

recondite abstruse, arcane, cabbalistic, concealed, dark, deep, difficult, esoteric, hidden, involved, mysterious, mystical, obscure, occult, profound, secret

recondite *adj Formal* **1** requiring special knowledge. **2** dealing with abstruse or profound subjects.

recondition *vb* to restore to good condition or working order: *a reconditioned engine.* **reconditioned** *adj*

reconnaissance (rik-**kon**-iss-anss) *n* **1** the process of obtaining information about the position and movements of an enemy. **2** a preliminary inspection.

reconnoitre *or US* **reconnoiter** (rek-a-**noy**-ter) *vb* to make a reconnaissance of.

reconsider *vb* to think about again, with a view to changing one's policy or course of action. **reconsideration** *n*

reconstitute *vb* **-tuting, -tuted 1** to reorganize in a slightly different form. **2** to restore (dried food) to its former state by adding water. **reconstitution** *n*

reconstruct *vb* **1** to build again. **2** to reorganize: *three works proved useful in reconstructing the training routine.* **3** to form a picture of (a past event, esp. a crime) by piecing together evidence. **reconstruction** *n*

reconvene *vb* to gather together again after an interval.

record *n* (**rek**-ord) **1** a document or other thing that preserves information. **2 records** information or data on a subject collected over a long period: *dental records.* **3** a thin disc of a plastic material upon which sound has been recorded in a continuous spiral groove on each side. **4** the best recorded achievement in some field: *her score set a Games record.* **5** the known facts about a person's achievements. **6** a list of crimes of which an accused person has previously been convicted. **7** anything serving as evidence or as a memorial: *the First World War is a record of human folly.* **8** *Computers* a group of data or piece of information preserved as a unit in machine-readable form. **9 for the record** for the sake of strict factual accuracy. **10 go on record** to state one's views publicly. **11 have a record** to have previous criminal convictions. **12 off the record** not for publication. **13 on record a** stated in a public document. **b** publicly known. *~adj* **14** the highest or lowest, or best or worst ever achieved: *record losses.* *~vb* (rik-**kord**) **15** to put in writing to preserve the true facts: *to record the minutes of a meeting.* **16** to preserve (sound, TV programmes, etc.) on plastic disc, magnetic tape, etc., for reproduction on a playback device. **17** to show or register.

recorded delivery *n* a postal service by which an official receipt is obtained for the posting and delivery of a letter or parcel.

recorder *n* **1** a person or machine that records, esp. a video, cassette, or tape recorder. **2** *Music* a wind instrument, blown through the end with finger-holes and a reedlike tone. **3** (in England and Wales) a barrister or solicitor appointed to sit as a part-time judge in the crown court.

recording *n* **1** something that has been recorded. **2** the process of storing sounds or visual signals for later use.

record player *n* a device for reproducing the sounds stored on a record.

recount *vb* to tell the story or details of.

re-count *vb* **1** to count again. *~n* **2** a second or further count, esp. of votes in an election.

recoup (rik-**koop**) *vb* **1** to regain or make good (a loss). **2** to reimburse or compensate (someone) for a loss. **recoupment** *n*

recourse *n* **1 have recourse to** to turn to a source of help or course of action. **2** a source of help or course of action that is turned to when in difficulty.

recover *vb* **1** (of a person) to regain health, spirits, or composure. **2** to regain a former and better condition: *real wages have recovered from the recession.* **3** to find again or obtain the return of (something lost). **4** to get back or make good (expense or loss). **5** to obtain (useful substances) from waste. **6** *Law* to gain (something) by the judgment of a court: *it should be possible to recover damages.* **recoverable** *adj*

recovery *n, pl* **-eries 1** the act of recovering from sickness, a shock, or a setback. **2** restoration to a former and better condition. **3** the regaining of something lost. **4** the extraction of useful substances from waste.

recreant *n Archaic* a disloyal or cowardly person.

THESAURUS

recondition do up (*informal*), fix up (*informal, chiefly U.S. & Canad.*), overhaul, remodel, renew, renovate, repair, restore, revamp

reconnaissance exploration, inspection, investigation, observation, patrol, recce (*slang*), reconnoitring, scan, scouting, scrutiny, survey

reconnoitre case (*slang*), explore, get the lie of the land, inspect, investigate, make a reconnaissance (of), observe, patrol, recce (*slang*), scan, scout, scrutinize, see how the land lies, spy out, survey

reconsider change one's mind, have second thoughts, reassess, re-evaluate, re-examine, rethink, review, revise, take another look at, think again, think better of, think over, think twice

reconstruct 1. reassemble, rebuild, recreate, re-establish, reform, regenerate, remake, remodel, renovate, reorganize, restore **2.** build up, build up a picture of, deduce, piece together

record *n.* **1.** account, annals, archives, chronicle, diary, document, entry, file, journal, log, memoir, memorandum, memorial, minute, register, report **2.** album, black disc, disc, EP, forty-five, gramophone record, LP, platter (*U.S. slang*), recording, release, seventy-eight, single, twelve inch, vinyl **3.** background, career, curriculum vitae, history, performance, track record (*informal*) **4.** documentation, evidence, memorial, remembrance, testimony, trace, witness **5. off the record** confidential, confidentially, in confidence, in private, not for publication, private, sub rosa, under the rose, unofficial, unofficially *~vb.* **6.** chalk up (*informal*), chronicle, document, enrol, enter, inscribe, log, minute, note, preserve, put down, put on file, put on record, register, report, set down, take down, transcribe, write down **7.** cut, lay down (*slang*), make a recording of, put on wax (*informal*), tape, tape-record, video, video-tape, wax (*informal*) **8.** contain, give evidence of, indicate, read, register, say, show

recorder annalist, archivist, chronicler, clerk, diarist, historian, registrar, scorekeeper, scorer, scribe

recording CD, compact disc, disc, gramophone record, record, tape, video

recount depict, describe, detail, enumerate, give an account of, narrate, portray, recite, rehearse, relate, repeat, report, tell, tell the story of

recourse alternative, appeal, choice, expedient, option, refuge, remedy, resort, resource, way out

recover 1. bounce back, come round, convalesce, feel oneself again, get back on one's feet, get better, get well, heal, improve, mend, pick up, pull through, rally, recuperate, regain one's health *or* strength, revive, take a turn for the better **2.** find again, get back, make good, recapture, reclaim, recoup, redeem, regain, repair, repossess, restore, retake, retrieve, take back, win back

recovery 1. convalescence, healing, improvement, mending, rally, recuperation, return to health, revival,

re-create *vb* **-creating, -created** to make happen or exist again. **re-creation** *n*

recreation *n* an activity done for pleasure or relaxation. **recreational** *adj*

recreation ground *n* an area of publicly owned land where sports and games may be played.

recrimination *n* accusations made by two people or groups about each other: *bitter recrimination.* **recriminatory** *adj*

recrudescence *n Literary* an outbreak of trouble or a disease after a period of quiet.

recruit *vb* **1** to enlist (people) for military service. **2** to enrol or obtain (members or support). *~n* **3** a newly joined member of a military service. **4** a new member or supporter. **recruitment** *n*

rectal *adj* of the rectum.

rectangle *n* an oblong shape with four straight sides and four right angles. **rectangular** *adj*

rectify *vb* **-fies, -fying, -fied 1** to put right; correct. **2** *Chem* to separate (a substance) from a mixture by distillation. **3** *Electricity* to convert (alternating current) into direct current. **rectification** *n* **rectifier** *n*

rectilinear (rek-tee-**lin**-ee-er) *adj Formal* **1** in a straight line. **2** bounded by or formed of straight lines.

rectitude *n* moral or religious correctness: *a model of rectitude.*

recto *n, pl* **-tos 1** the right-hand page of a book. **2** the front of a sheet of printed paper.

rector *n* **1** *Church of England* a clergyman in charge of a parish. **2** *RC Church* a cleric in charge of a college or congregation. **3** *Chiefly Brit* the head of certain academic institutions. **4** (in Scotland) a high-ranking official in a university, elected by the students. **rectorship** *n*

rectory *n, pl* **-ries** the house of a rector.

rectum *n, pl* **-tums** *or* **-ta** the lower part of the alimentary canal, ending in the anus.

recumbent *adj* lying down.

recuperate *vb* **-ating, -ated** to recover from illness or exhaustion. **recuperation** *n* **recuperative** *adj*

recur *vb* **-curring, -curred 1** to happen or occur again. **2** (of a thought or feeling) to come back to the mind. **recurrence** *n* **recurrent** *adj* **recurring** *adj*

recurring decimal *n* a rational number that contains a pattern of digits repeated indefinitely after the decimal point: *1 divided by 11 gives the recurring decimal 0.09090909...*

recusant (**rek**-yew-zant) *n* **1** *History* a Roman Catholic who did not attend the services of the Church of England. **2** a person who refuses to obey authority. **recusancy** *n*

recycle *vb* **-cling, -cled 1** to reprocess (something already used) for further use: *public demand for recycled paper.* **2** to pass (a substance) through a system again for further use. **recyclable** *adj*

red *adj* **redder, reddest 1** of a colour varying from crimson to orange; of the colour of blood. **2** reddish in colour or having parts or marks that are reddish: *red deer.* **3** flushed in the face from anger or shame. **4** (of the eyes) bloodshot. **5** (of wine) made from black grapes and coloured by their skins. *~n* **6** the colour red; the colour of blood. **7** anything red, such as red clothing or red paint: *she had dressed in red.* **8 in the red** *Informal* in debt. **9 see red** *Informal* to become very angry. **redness** *n* **reddish** *adj*

Red *Informal ~n* **1** a Communist or socialist. *~adj* **2** Communist or socialist.

red admiral *n* a butterfly with black wings with red and white markings.

red blood cell *n* same as **erythrocyte.**

red-blooded *adj Informal* vigorous or virile.

redbreast *n* a robin.

redbrick *adj* (of a university) founded in the late 19th or early 20th century.

red card *n Soccer* a piece of red pasteboard raised by a referee to indicate that a player has been sent off.

red carpet *n* very special treatment given to an important guest.

redcoat *n* **1** *History* a British soldier. **2** *Canad informal* a Mountie.

Red Crescent *n* the name and symbol used by the Red Cross in Muslim countries.

Red Cross *n* an international organization (**Red Cross Society**) which helps victims of war or natural disaster.

redcurrant *n* a very small red edible fruit that grows in bunches on a bush.

red deer *n* a large deer of Europe and Asia, which has a reddish-brown coat and a short tail.

THESAURUS

turn for the better **2.** amelioration, betterment, improvement, rally, rehabilitation, restoration, revival, upturn **3.** recapture, reclamation, redemption, repair, repossession, restoration, retrieval

recreation amusement, distraction, diversion, enjoyment, entertainment, exercise, fun, hobby, leisure activity, pastime, play, pleasure, refreshment, relaxation, relief, sport

recrimination bickering, counterattack, countercharge, mutual accusation, name-calling, quarrel, retaliation, retort, squabbling

recruit *vb.* **1.** draft, enlist, enrol **2.** engage, enrol, gather, obtain, procure, take on, win (over) *~n.* **3.** apprentice, beginner, convert, greenhorn (*informal*), helper, initiate, learner, neophyte, novice, proselyte, rookie (*informal*), trainee, tyro

rectify 1. adjust, amend, correct, emend, fix, improve, make good, mend, put right, redress, reform, remedy, repair, right, square **2.** *Chem.* distil, purify, refine, separate

rectitude correctness, decency, equity, goodness, honesty, honour, incorruptibility, integrity, justice, morality, principle, probity, righteousness, scrupulousness, uprightness, virtue

recuperate convalesce, get back on one's feet, get better, improve, mend, pick up, recover, regain one's health

recur 1. come again, come and go, come back, happen again, persist, reappear, repeat, return, revert **2.** be remembered, come back, haunt one's thoughts, return to mind, run through one's mind

recurrent continued, cyclical, frequent, habitual, periodic, recurring, regular, repeated, repetitive

recycle reclaim, reprocess, reuse, salvage, save

red *adj.* **1.** carmine, cherry, coral, crimson, gules (*Heraldry*), maroon, pink, rose, ruby, scarlet, vermilion, wine **2.** bay, carroty, chestnut, flame-coloured, flaming, foxy, reddish, sandy, titian **3.** blushing, embarrassed, florid, flushed, rubicund, shamefaced, suffused **4.** bloodshot, inflamed, red-rimmed *~n.* **5. in the red** *informal* bankrupt, in arrears, in debit, in debt, in deficit, insolvent, on the rocks, overdrawn, owing money, showing a loss **6. see red** *informal* be beside oneself with rage, become enraged, be *or* get very angry, blow a fuse (*slang, chiefly U.S.*), blow one's top, boil, crack up (*informal*), fly off the handle (*informal*), go mad (*informal*), go off one's head (*slang*), go off the deep end (*informal*), go up the wall

redden *vb* **1** to make or become red or redder. **2** to blush.

redecorate *vb* to paint or wallpaper (a room) again. **redecoration** *n*

redeem *vb* **1** to make up for. **2** to reinstate (oneself) in someone's good opinion: *he missed a penalty but redeemed himself by setting up the winning goal.* **3** *Christianity* (of Christ as Saviour) to free (humanity) from sin by death on the Cross. **4** to buy back: *she didn't have the money to redeem it.* **5** to pay off (a loan or debt). **6** to convert (bonds or shares) into cash. **7** to exchange (coupons) for goods. **8** to fulfil (a promise): *I vowed to abide by the bill and have redeemed my pledge.* **redeemable** *adj* **redeemer** *n*

Redeemer *n* **the Redeemer** *Christianity* Jesus Christ.

redeeming *adj* making up for faults or deficiencies: *the soundtrack is the film's only redeeming feature.*

redemption *n* **1** the act of redeeming. **2** the state of being redeemed. **3** *Christianity* deliverance from sin through the incarnation and death of Christ. **redemptive** *adj*

redeploy *vb* to assign (people) to new positions or tasks. **redeployment** *n*

redevelop *vb* to rebuild or renovate (an area or building). **redeveloper** *n* **redevelopment** *n*

redfish *n, pl* **-fish** *or* **-fishes** *Canad* same as **kokanee.**

red flag *n* **1** a symbol of revolution. **2** a warning of danger.

red-handed *adj* **catch someone red-handed** to catch someone in the act of doing something wrong or illegal.

red hat *n* the broad-brimmed crimson hat given to cardinals as the symbol of their rank.

redhead *n* a person with reddish hair. **redheaded** *adj*

red herring *n* something which diverts attention from the main issue.

red-hot *adj* **1** (of metal) glowing hot. **2** extremely hot. **3** very keen or excited. **4** furious: *one of those red-hot blazes of temper.* **5** very recent or topical: *red-hot information.*

red-hot poker *n* a garden plant with spikes of red or yellow flowers.

Red Indian *n, adj Offensive* American Indian.

redirect *vb* **1** to send in a new direction or course. **2** to send (mail) to a different address.

redistribute *vb* **-uting, -uted** to share out in a different way: *to redistribute the world's wealth.*

redistribution *n* **1** the act of redistributing. **2** a revision of the number of seats that each province has in the Canadian House of Commons, made every ten years.

red lead *n* a bright-red poisonous insoluble oxide of lead.

red-letter day *n* a memorably important or happy occasion.

red light *n* **1** a traffic signal to stop. **2** a danger signal.

red-light district *n* an area where many prostitutes work.

red meat *n* meat, such as beef or lamb, that is dark brown when cooked.

redo *vb* **-doing, -did, -done 1** to do over again in order to improve. **2** *Informal* to redecorate: *we should consider redoing some of the rooms.*

redolent *adj* **redolent of** *or* **with 1** reminiscent or suggestive of: *a castle redolent of historical novels.* **2** smelling of: *the warm heavy air was redolent of sea and flowers.* **redolence** *n*

redouble *vb* **-bling, -bled 1** to make or become much greater: *the party will have to redouble its efforts.* **2** *Bridge* to double (an opponent's double).

redoubt *n* **1** a small fort defending a hill top or pass. **2** a stronghold.

redoubtable *adj* to be feared and respected: *the redoubtable Mr Brooks.* **redoubtably** *adv*

redound *vb* **1 redound to** to have an advantageous or disadvantageous effect on: *individual rights redound to the common good.* **2 redound on** *or* **upon** to recoil or rebound.

redox *n* a chemical reaction between two substances, in which one is oxidized and the other reduced.

red pepper *n* **1** the red ripe fruit of the sweet pepper, eaten as a vegetable. **2** same as **cayenne pepper.**

redraft *vb* to write a second copy of (a letter, proposal, essay, etc.).

red rag *n* something that infuriates or provokes: *it's a red rag to Britain.*

redress *vb* **1** to make amends for. **2** to adjust in order to make fair or equal: *to redress the balance.* *~n* **3** compensation or reparation. **4** the setting right of a wrong.

red salmon *n* a salmon with reddish flesh.

redshank *n* a large common European sandpiper with red legs.

red shift *n* the appearance of lines in the spectrum of distant stars nearer the red end of the spectrum than on earth: used to calculate the velocity of objects in relation to the earth.

redskin *n Informal, offensive* an American Indian.

red squirrel *n* a reddish-brown squirrel of Europe and Asia.

redstart *n* **1** a European songbird of the thrush family, the male of which has an orange-brown tail and breast. **2** a North American warbler.

red tape *n* time-consuming official rules or procedure.

reduce *vb* **-ducing, -duced 1** to bring down or lower: *monitoring could reduce the number of perinatal deaths.* **2** to weaken or lessen: *vegetarian diets reduce cancer risk.* **3** to bring by force or necessity to some state or action: *it reduced her to helpless laughter.* **4** to slim. **5** to set out systematically as an aid to understanding: *reducing the problem to three main issues.* **6** *Cookery* to thicken (a sauce) by boiling away some of its liquid. **7** to impoverish: *to be in reduced circumstances.* **8** *Chem* **a** to undergo a chemical reaction with hydrogen. **b** to lose oxygen atoms. **c** to increase

THESAURUS

(*slang*), lose one's rag (*slang*), lose one's temper, seethe

redden blush, colour (up), crimson, flush, go red, suffuse

redeem 1. atone for, compensate for, defray, make amends for, make good, make up for, offset, outweigh, redress, save **2.** absolve, rehabilitate, reinstate, restore to favour **3.** buy back, reclaim, recover, recover possession of, regain, repossess, repurchase, retrieve, win back **4.** cash (in), change, exchange, trade in

redemption 1. amends, atonement, compensation, expiation, reparation **2.** deliverance, emancipation, liberation, ransom, release, rescue, salvation **3.** reclamation, recovery, repossession, repurchase, retrieval

redress *vb.* **1.** compensate for, make amends (reparation, restitution) for, make up for, pay for, put right, recompense for **2.** adjust, amend, balance, correct, ease, even up, mend, put right, rectify, reform, regulate, relieve, remedy, repair, restore the balance, square *~n.* **3.** amends, atonement, compensation,

the number of electrons. **9** *Maths* to simplify the form of (an expression or equation), esp. by substitution of one term by another. **reducible** *adj*

reduction *n* **1** the act of reducing. **2** the amount by which something is reduced. **3** a reduced form of an original, such as a copy of a document on a smaller scale. **reductive** *adj*

redundant *adj* **1** deprived of one's job because it is no longer necessary or sufficiently profitable. **2** surplus to requirements. **redundancy** *n*

reduplicate *vb* **-cating, -cated** to make double; repeat.

redwood *n* a giant Californian conifer with reddish bark.

re-echo *vb* **-oing, -oed** to echo over and over again.

reed *n* **1** a tall grass that grows in swamps and shallow water. **2** a straight hollow stem of this plant. **3** *Music* **a** a thin piece of cane or metal in certain wind instruments, which vibrates producing a musical note when the instrument is blown. **b** a wind instrument or organ pipe that sounds by means of a reed.

reedy *adj* **reedier, reediest 1** harsh or thin in tone: *his reedy, hesitant voice.* **2** (of a place) full of reeds. **reedily** *adv* **reediness** *n*

reef[1] *n* **1** a ridge of rock, sand, or coral, lying just beneath the surface of the sea. **2** a vein of ore.

reef[2] *Naut* ~*n* **1** the part of a sail which can be rolled up to reduce its area. ~*vb* **2** to reduce the area of (sail) by taking in a reef.

reefer *n* **1** Also called: **reefer jacket** a man's short heavy double-breasted woollen jacket. **2** *Old-fashioned, slang* a hand-rolled cigarette containing cannabis.

reef knot *n* a knot consisting of two overhand knots turned opposite ways.

reek *vb* **1** to give off a strong unpleasant smell. **2 reek of** to give a strong suggestion of: *the scene had reeked of insincerity.* **3** *Dialect* to give off smoke or fumes. ~*n* **4** a strong unpleasant smell. **5** *Dialect* smoke or steam.

reel[1] *n* **1** a cylindrical object or frame that turns on an axis and onto which film, tape, wire, or thread is wound. **2** a winding device attached to a fishing rod, used for casting and winding in the line. **3** a roll of film for projection. ~*vb* **4 reel in** to wind or draw in on a reel.

reel[2] *vb* **1** to move unsteadily or spin round, as if about to fall. **2** to be in a state of confusion or stress: *my mind was still reeling.*

reel[3] *n* **1** a lively Scottish dance. **2** music for this dance.

re-elect *vb* to vote for (someone) to retain his or her position, for example as a Member of Parliament. **re-election** *n*

reel off *vb* to recite or write fluently or quickly.

re-enact *vb* to act out (a previous event) again. **re-enactment** *n*

re-enter *vb* **1** to come back into (a place, esp. a country). **2** (of a spacecraft) to return into (the earth's atmosphere). **re-entry** *n*

re-equip *vb* **-equipping, -equipped** to provide with fresh supplies, components, etc.

re-establish *vb* to create or set up (an organization, link, etc.) again. **re-establishment** *n*

reeve *n* **1** *English history* the local representative of the king in a shire until the early 11th century. **2** (in medieval England) a steward who supervised the daily affairs of a manor. **3** *Canad government* (in some provinces) a president of a local council.

re-examine *vb* **-examining, -examined** to inspect or investigate again. **re-examination** *n*

ref *n Informal* the referee in a sport.

refectory *n, pl* **-ries** a dining hall in a religious or academic institution.

refectory table *n* a long narrow dining table supported by two trestles.

refer *vb* **-ferring, -ferred refer to 1** to mention or allude to. **2** to be relevant or relate (to): *the word cancer refers to many quite specific different diseases.* **3** to seek information (from): *he referred to his notes.* **4** to direct the attention of (someone) for information: *the reader is referred to the introduction.* **5** to direct (a patient or client) to another doctor or agency: *her GP referred her to a specialist.* **6** to hand over for consideration or decision: *to refer a complaint to another department.* **referable** *or* **referrable** *adj* **referral** *n*

➤ *Refer* includes the sense "back" in its meaning. Avoid using *refer back* unless the context involves sending papers back to a committee for further consideration.

referee *n* **1** the umpire in various sports, such as football and boxing. **2** a person who is willing to provide a reference for someone for a job. **3** a person referred to for a decision or opinion in a dispute. ~*vb* **-eeing, -eed 4** to act as a referee.

reference *n* **1** the act of referring. **2** a mention: *this book contains several references to the Civil War.* **3** direction to a passage elsewhere in a book or to another book. **4** a book or passage referred to. **5** a written testimonial regarding one's character or capabilities. **6** a person referred to for such a testimonial. **7** relation or restriction, esp. to or by membership of a specific group: *without reference to sex or age.* **8 with**

THESAURUS

paymente, recompense, reparation, requital, restitution **4.** assistance, correction, cure, ease, help, justice, rectification, relief, remedy, satisfaction

reduce 1. abate, abridge, bring down the price of, cheapen, contract, curtail, cut, cut down, debase, decrease, depress, dilute, diminish, discount, impair, lessen, lower, mark down, moderate, shorten, slash, slow down, tone down, truncate, turn down, weaken, wind down **2.** bring, bring to the point of, conquer, drive, force, master, overpower, subdue, vanquish **3.** be *or* go on a diet, diet, lose weight, shed weight, slenderize (*chiefly U.S.*), slim, trim **4.** bankrupt, break, impoverish, pauperize, ruin

redundant *de trop,* excessive, extra, inessential, inordinate, superfluous, supernumerary, surplus, unnecessary, unwanted

reek *vb.* **1.** hum (*slang*), pong (*Brit. informal*), smell, smell to high heaven, stink **2.** be characterized by, be permeated by, be redolent of **3.** *dialect* fume, give off smoke *or* fumes, smoke, steam ~*n.* **4.** effluvium, odour, pong (*Brit. informal*), smell, stench, stink **5.** *dialect* exhalation, fumes, smoke, steam, vapour

reel go round and round, lurch, pitch, revolve, rock, roll, spin, stagger, stumble, sway, swim, swirl, totter, twirl, waver, whirl, wobble

refer 1. allude, bring up, cite, hint, invoke, make mention of, make reference, mention, speak of, touch on **2.** apply, be directed to, belong, be relevant to, concern, pertain, relate **3.** apply, consult, go, have recourse to, look up, seek information from, turn to **4.** direct, guide, point, recommend, send **5.** commit, consign, deliver, hand over, pass on, submit, transfer, turn over

referee 1. *n.* adjudicator, arbiter, arbitrator, judge, ref (*informal*), umpire **2.** *vb.* adjudicate, arbitrate, judge, mediate, umpire

reference 1. allusion, citation, mention, note, quotation, remark **2.** certification, character, credentials,

reference to concerning. *~adj* **9** containing information or facts: *reference books.* **referential** *adj*

referendum *n, pl* **-dums** *or* **-da** a direct vote of the electorate on a question of importance.

refill *vb* **1** to fill (something) again. *~n* **2** a second or subsequent filling: *I held out my glass for a refill.* **3** a replacement supply of something in a permanent container. **refillable** *adj*

refine *vb* **-fining, -fined 1** to make free from impurities; purify. **2** to improve: *surgical techniques are constantly being refined.* **3** to separate (a mixture) into pure constituents: *molasses is a residual syrup obtained during sugar refining.*

refined *adj* **1** cultured or polite. **2** freed from impurities. **3** highly developed and effective: *refined intelligence tests.*

refinement *n* **1** an improvement to something, such as a piece of equipment. **2** fineness of taste or manners. **3** a subtle point or distinction. **4** the act of refining.

refinery *n, pl* **-eries** a factory for purifying a raw material, such as sugar or oil.

refit *vb* **-fitting, -fitted 1** to make (a ship) ready for use again by repairing or re-equipping. *~n* **2** a repair or re-equipping for further use.

reflation *n* an increase in the supply of money and credit designed to encourage economic activity. **reflate** *vb* **reflationary** *adj*

reflect *vb* **1** (of a surface or object) to throw back (light, heat, or sound). **2** (of a mirror) to form an image of (something) by reflection. **3** to show: *many of her books reflect her obsession with fine art.* **4** to consider carefully. **5 reflect on** *or* **upon** to cause to be regarded in a specified way: *the incident reflects very badly on me.* **6** to bring as a consequence: *the programme reflected great credit on the technicians.*

reflecting telescope *n* a telescope in which the initial image is formed by a concave mirror.

reflection *n* **1** the act of reflecting. **2** the return of rays of light, heat, or sound. **3** an image of a an object given back in a mirror. **4** careful or long consideration. **5 on reflection** after careful consideration or reconsideration. **6** discredit or blame: *it's a sad reflection on modern morality.* **7** *Maths* a transformation of a shape in which right and left, or top and bottom, are reversed.

reflective *adj* **1** characterized by quiet thought or contemplation. **2** capable of reflecting: *a reflective coating.*

reflector *n* **1** a polished surface for reflecting light. **2** a reflecting telescope.

reflex *n* **1** an immediate involuntary response to a given stimulus. **2** a mechanical response to a particular situation, involving no conscious decision. **3** an image produced by reflection. *~adj* **4** of or caused by a reflex: *a reflex action.* **5** reflected. **6** *Maths* (of an angle) between 180° and 360°.

reflex camera *n* a camera which uses a mirror to channel light from a lens to the viewfinder, so that the image seen is the same as the image photographed.

reflexive *adj* **1** *Grammar* denoting a pronoun that refers back to the subject of a sentence or clause. Thus, in *that man thinks a great deal of himself,* the pronoun *himself* is reflexive. **2** *Grammar* denoting a verb used with a reflexive pronoun as its direct object, as in *to dress oneself.* **3** *Physiol* of or relating to a reflex. *~n* **4** a reflexive pronoun or verb.

reflexology *n* foot massage as a therapy in alternative medicine. **reflexologist** *n*

reform *n* **1** correction of abuses or malpractices: *a programme of economic reforms.* **2** improvement of morals or behaviour. *~vb* **3** to improve (a law or institution) by correcting abuses. **4** to give up or cause to give up a bad habit or way of life. **reformative** *adj* **reformer** *n*

reformation (ref-fer-**may**-shun) *n* **1** a reforming. **2 the Reformation** a religious movement in 16th-century Europe that began as an attempt to reform the Roman Catholic Church and resulted in the establishment of the Protestant Churches.

reformatory *n, pl* **-ries** (formerly) a place where young offenders were sent to be reformed.

Reformed *adj* of a Protestant Church, esp. a Calvinist one.

reformist *adj* **1** advocating reform rather than abolition, esp. of a religion or a political movement. *~n* **2** a person advocating reform.

refract *vb* to cause light, heat, or sound to undergo refraction. **refractive** *adj* **refractor** *n*

refracting telescope *n* a type of telescope in which the image is formed by a set of lenses. Also called: **refractor**

refraction *n Physics* **1** the change in direction of a wave, such as light or sound, in passing from one medium to another in which it has a different velocity. **2** the amount by which a wave is refracted.

refractory *adj* **1** *Formal* stubborn or rebellious. **2** *Med* not responding to treatment. **3** (of a material)

THESAURUS

endorsement, good word, recommendation, testimonial **3.** applicability, bearing, concern, connection, consideration, regard, relation, respect

referendum plebiscite, popular vote, public vote

refine 1. clarify, cleanse, distil, filter, process, purify, rarefy **2.** civilize, cultivate, elevate, hone, improve, perfect, polish, temper

refined 1. civil, civilized, courtly, cultivated, cultured, elegant, genteel, gentlemanly, gracious, ladylike, polished, polite, sophisticated, urbane, well-bred, well-mannered **2.** clarified, clean, distilled, filtered, processed, pure, purified **3.** cultured, delicate, discerning, discriminating, exact, fastidious, fine, nice, precise, punctilious, sensitive, sublime, subtle

refinement 1. breeding, civility, civilization, courtesy, courtliness, cultivation, culture, delicacy, discrimination, elegance, fastidiousness, fineness, finesse, finish, gentility, good breeding, good manners, grace, graciousness, polish, politeness, politesse, precision, sophistication, style, taste, urbanity **2.** fine point, fine tuning, nicety, nuance, subtlety **3.** clarification, cleansing, distillation, filtering, processing, purification, rarefaction, rectification

reflect 1. echo, give back, imitate, mirror, reproduce, return, throw back **2.** bear out, bespeak, communicate, demonstrate, display, evince, exhibit, express, indicate, manifest, reveal, show **3.** cogitate, consider, contemplate, deliberate, meditate, mull over, muse, ponder, ruminate, think, wonder

reflection 1. counterpart, echo, image, mirror image **2.** cerebration, cogitation, consideration, contemplation, deliberation, idea, impression, meditation, musing, observation, opinion, perusal, pondering, rumination, study, thinking, thought, view **3.** aspersion, censure, criticism, derogation, imputation, reproach, slur

reform *n.* **1.** amelioration, amendment, betterment, correction, improvement, rectification, rehabilitation, renovation *~vb.* **2.** ameliorate, amend, better, correct, emend, improve, mend, rebuild, reclaim, reconstitute, reconstruct, rectify, regenerate, rehabilitate, remodel, renovate, reorganize, repair, restore, revolutionize **3.** clean up one's act (*informal*), get back on the straight and narrow (*informal*), get it together (*informal*), get

able to withstand high temperatures without fusion or decomposition.

refrain[1] *vb* **refrain from** to keep oneself from doing.

refrain[2] *n* **1** a frequently repeated part of a song. **2** a much repeated saying or idea.

refrangible *adj* capable of being refracted.

refresh *vb* **1** to revive or reinvigorate, for example through rest, drink, or food. **2** to stimulate (the memory). **refresher** *n*

refresher course *n* a course designed to improve or update a person's knowledge of a subject.

refreshing *adj* **1** having a reviving effect. **2** pleasantly different or new: *refreshing candour.*

refreshment *n* **1** the act of refreshing. **2 refreshments** snacks and drinks served as a light meal.

refrigerant *n* **1** a fluid capable of vaporizing at low temperatures, used in refrigerators. *~adj* **2** causing cooling or freezing.

refrigerate *vb* **-ating, -ated** to chill or freeze in order to preserve. **refrigeration** *n*

refrigerator *n* the full name for **fridge.**

refuel *vb* **-elling, -elled** *or US* **-eling, -eled** to supply or be supplied with fresh fuel.

refuge *n* **1** shelter or protection from danger or hardship. **2** a place, person, or thing that offers protection or help.

refugee *n* a person who has fled from some danger, such as war or political persecution.

refulgent *adj Literary* shining brightly. **refulgence** *n*

refund *vb* **1** to give back (money). **2** to pay back (a person). *~n* **3** return of money to a purchaser or the amount returned. **refundable** *adj*

refurbish *vb* to renovate and brighten up. **refurbishment** *n*

refusal *n* **1** the act of refusing. **2** the opportunity to reject or accept: *he was given first refusal on all three scripts.*

refuse[1] *vb* **-fusing, -fused 1** to be determined not (to do something): *he refuses to consider it.* **2** to decline to give or allow (something) to (someone): *if the judge refuses bail, he'll appeal.* **3** to decline to accept (something offered): *he refused the captaincy.* **4** (of a horse) to be unwilling to jump a fence.

refuse[2] *n* anything thrown away; rubbish.

refusenik *n* **1** (formerly) a Jew in the USSR who was refused permission to emigrate. **2** a person who refuses to obey a law or cooperate with the government because of strong beliefs.

refute *vb* **-futing, -futed** to prove (a statement or theory) to be false or incorrect. **refutation** *n*

➤ *Refute* is not the same as *deny.* It means "show evidence to disprove something", while *deny* means only "say something is not true".

regain *vb* **1** to get back or recover. **2** to reach again: *to regain the shore.*

regal *adj* **1** of or fit for a king or queen. **2** splendid and dignified; magnificent: *a luxury cruise liner on her serene and regal way around the better ports.* **regality** *n* **regally** *adv*

regale *vb* **-galing, -galed 1** to give delight or amusement to: *she would regale her friends with stories.* **2** to provide with abundant food or drink.

regalia *n* the ceremonial emblems or robes of royalty or high office.

regard *vb* **1** to look upon or think of in a specified way: *angina can therefore be regarded as heart cramp.* **2** to look closely or attentively at (something or someone). **3** to take notice of: *he has never regarded the conventions.* **4 as regards** on the subject of. *~n* **5** respect or affection: *you haven't a high regard for her opinion.* **6** attention: *he eats what he wants with no regard to health.* **7** a gaze or look. **8** reference or connection: *with regard to my complaint.* **9 regards** an expression of goodwill: *give her my regards.*

regardful *adj* **regardful of** paying attention to.

regarding *prep* on the subject of; relating to.

regardless *adj* **1 regardless of** taking no notice of:

THESAURUS

one's act together (*informal*), go straight (*informal*), mend one's ways, pull one's socks up (*Brit. informal*), shape up (*informal*), turn over a new leaf

refrain *vb.* abstain, avoid, cease, desist, do without, eschew, forbear, give up, kick (*informal*), leave off, renounce, stop

refresh 1. brace, breathe new life into, cheer, cool, enliven, freshen, inspirit, reanimate, reinvigorate, rejuvenate, restore, revitalize, revive, revivify, stimulate **2.** brush up (*informal*), jog, prod, prompt, renew, stimulate

refreshing bracing, cooling, different, fresh, inspiriting, invigorating, new, novel, original, revivifying, stimulating, thirst-quenching

refreshment 1. enlivenment, freshening, reanimation, renewal, renovation, repair, restoration, revival, stimulation **2. refreshments** drinks, food and drink, snacks, titbits

refrigerate chill, cool, freeze, keep cold

refuge asylum, bolt hole, harbour, haven, hide-out, protection, resort, retreat, sanctuary, security, shelter

refugee displaced person, émigré, escapee, exile, fugitive, runaway

refund 1. *vb.* give back, make good, pay back, reimburse, repay, restore, return **2.** *n.* reimbursement, repayment, return

refurbish clean up, do up (*informal*), mend, overhaul, re-equip, refit, remodel, renovate, repair, restore, revamp, set to rights, spruce up

refusal 1. defiance, denial, knockback (*slang*), negation, no, rebuff, rejection, repudiation, thumbs down **2.** choice, consideration, opportunity, option

refuse[1] *vb.* abstain, decline, deny, reject, repel, repudiate, say no, spurn, turn down, withhold

refuse[2] *n.* dregs, dross, garbage, junk (*informal*), leavings, lees, litter, offscourings, rubbish, scum, sediment, sweepings, trash, waste

refute confute, counter, discredit, disprove, give the lie to, negate, overthrow, prove false, rebut, silence

regain 1. get back, recapture, recoup, recover, redeem, repossess, retake, retrieve, take back, win back **2.** get back to, reach again, reattain, return to

regard *vb.* **1.** account, adjudge, believe, consider, deem, esteem, estimate, hold, imagine, judge, look upon, rate, see, suppose, think, treat, value, view **2.** behold, check, check out (*informal*), eye, gaze at, look closely at, mark, notice, observe, remark, scrutinize, take a dekko at (*Brit. slang*), view, watch **3.** attend, heed, listen to, mind, note, pay attention to, respect, take into consideration, take notice of **4.** *as in* **as regards** apply to, be relevant to, concern, have a bearing on, have to do with, interest, pertain to, relate to *~n.* **5.** account, affection, attachment, care, concern, consideration, deference, esteem, honour, love, note, reputation, repute, respect, store, sympathy, thought **6.** attention, heed, interest, mind, notice **7.** gaze, glance, look, scrutiny, stare **8. regards** best wishes, compliments, good wishes, greetings, respects, salutations

regarding about, apropos, as regards, as to, concerning, in *or* with regard to, in re, in respect of, in the mat-

the illness can affect anyone regardless of their social class. ~*adv* **2** in spite of everything: *I carried on regardless.*

regatta *n* a series of races of boats or yachts.

regency *n, pl* **-cies 1** government by a regent. **2** the status of a regent. **3** a period when a regent is in power.

Regency *adj* of the regency (1811-20) of the Prince of Wales (later George IV) or the styles of architecture or furniture produced during it.

regenerate *vb* (ri-**jen**-er-ate) **-ating, -ated 1** to undergo or cause to undergo physical, economic, or spiritual renewal. **2** to come or bring into existence once again. **3** to replace (lost or damaged tissues or organs) by new growth. ~*adj* (ri-**jen**-er-it) **4** physically, economically, or spiritually renewed. **regeneration** *n* **regenerative** *adj*

regent *n* **1** the ruler of a country during the childhood, absence, or illness of its monarch. **2** *US & Canad* a member of the governing board of certain schools and colleges. ~*adj* **3** acting as a regent: *the Prince Regent.*

reggae *n* a type of popular music of Jamaican origin with a strong beat.

regicide *n* **1** the killing of a king. **2** a person who kills a king.

regime (ray-**zheem**) *n* **1** a system of government. **2** a particular administration: *the corrupt regime.* **3** *Med* a regimen.

regimen *n* a prescribed system of diet and exercise.

regiment *n* **1** an organized body of troops as a unit in the army. **2** a large number or group. **regimental** *adj*

regimentals *pl n* **1** the uniform and insignia of a regiment. **2** military uniform.

regimental sergeant major *n Mil* the senior warrant officer in a regiment or battalion.

regimented *adj* very strictly controlled: *the regimented confines of the school.* **regimentation** *n*

Regina *n* queen: now used chiefly in documents and inscriptions.

region *n* **1** an administrative division of a country. **2** an area considered as a unit for geographical or social reasons. **3** a sphere of activity or interest. **4** a part of the body: *the lumbar region.* **5 in the region of** approximately: *in the region of 100 000 troops.* **6 the regions** the parts of a country away from the capital: *discord between Moscow and the regions.* **regional** *adj*

regionalism *n* **1** the division of a country or organization into geographical regions each having some autonomy. **2** loyalty to one's home region.

register *n* **1** an official list recording names, events, or transactions. **2** the book in which such a list is written. **3** a device that records data, totals sums of money, etc.: *a cash register.* **4** a style of speaking or writing, such as slang, used in particular circumstances or social situations. **5** *Music* **a** the timbre characteristic of a certain manner of voice production. **b** any of the stops on an organ in respect of its tonal quality: *the flute register.* ~*vb* **6** to enter (an event, person's name, ownership, etc.) in a register. **7** to show on a scale or other measuring instrument. **8** to show in a person's face or bearing: *his face registered surprise.* **9** *Informal* to have an effect or make an impression: *the news did not register at first.* **10** to have a letter or parcel insured against loss by the Post Office: *registered mail.* **registration** *n*

register office *n Brit* a government office where civil marriages are performed and births, marriages, and deaths are recorded.

registrar *n* **1** a person who keeps official records. **2** an official responsible for student records and enrolment in a college. **3** *Brit & NZ* a hospital doctor senior to a houseman but junior to a consultant.

registration document *n Brit* a document giving identification details of a vehicle, including its owner's name.

registration number *n* a sequence of letters and numbers given to a motor vehicle when it is registered, displayed on numberplates at the front and rear.

registry *n, pl* **-tries 1** a place where official records are kept. **2** the registration of a ship's country of origin: *a ship of Liberian registry.*

registry office *n Brit* same as **register office.**

Regius professor (**reej**-yuss) *n Brit* a person appointed by the Crown to a university chair founded by a royal patron.

regress *vb* **1** to return to a former and worse condition. ~*n* **2** return to a former and worse condition. **regressive** *adj*

regression *n* **1** the act of regressing. **2** *Psychol* the use by an adult of behaviour more appropriate to a child.

regret *vb* **-gretting, -gretted 1** to feel sorry or upset about. **2** to express apology or distress: *we regret any misunderstanding caused.* ~*n* **3** a feeling of repentance, guilt, or sorrow. **4 regrets** a polite expression of

THESAURUS

ter of, on the subject of, re, respecting, with reference to

regardless 1. *adj.* disregarding, heedless, inattentive, inconsiderate, indifferent, neglectful, negligent, rash, reckless, remiss, unconcerned, unmindful **2.** *adv.* anyway, come what may, despite everything, for all that, in any case, in spite of everything, nevertheless, no matter what, nonetheless

regenerate breathe new life into, change, inspirit, invigorate, reawaken, reconstruct, re-establish, reinvigorate, rejuvenate, renew, renovate, reproduce, restore, revive, revivify, uplift

regime administration, establishment, government, leadership, management, reign, rule, system

regiment *vb.* bully, control, discipline, order, organize, regulate, systematize

region 1. area, country, district, division, expanse, land, locality, part, patch, place, province, quarter, section, sector, territory, tract, turf (*U.S. slang*), zone **2.** area, locality, neighbourhood, range, scope, vicinity **3.** domain, field, province, realm, sphere, world

regional district, local, parochial, provincial, sectional, zonal

register *n.* **1.** annals, archives, catalogue, chronicle, diary, file, ledger, list, log, memorandum, record, roll, roster, schedule ~*vb.* **2.** catalogue, check in, chronicle, enlist, enrol, enter, inscribe, list, note, record, set down, sign on *or* up, take down **3.** be shown, bespeak, betray, display, exhibit, express, indicate, manifest, mark, read, record, reflect, reveal, say, show **4.** *informal* come home, dawn on, get through, have an effect, impress, make an impression, sink in, tell

regress backslide, degenerate, deteriorate, ebb, fall away *or* off, fall back, go back, lapse, lose ground, recede, relapse, retreat, retrocede, retrogress, return, revert, wane

regret 1. *vb.* bemoan, be upset, bewail, deplore, feel remorse for, feel sorry for, grieve, lament, miss, mourn, repent, rue, weep over **2.** *n.* bitterness, compunction, contrition, disappointment, grief, lamentation, pang of conscience, penitence, remorse, repentance, ruefulness, self-reproach, sorrow

refusal: *she had sent her regrets.* **regretful** *adj* **regretfully** *adv* **regrettable** *adj* **regrettably** *adv*

regroup *vb* **1** to reorganize (military forces) after an attack or a defeat. **2** to rearrange into a new grouping.

regular *adj* **1** normal, customary, or usual. **2** symmetrical or even: *regular features.* **3** according to a uniform principle, arrangement, or order. **4** occurring at fixed or prearranged intervals: *we run regular advertisements in the press.* **5** following a set rule or normal practice. **6** *Grammar* following the usual pattern of formation in a language: *regular verbs.* **7** of or serving in the permanent military services: *the regular armed forces.* **8** *Maths* (of a polygon) having all its sides and angles the same. **9** officially qualified or recognized: *he's not a regular doctor.* **10** *Informal* not constipated: *eating fresh vegetables helps keep you regular.* **11** *US & Canad informal* likeable: *a regular guy.* **12** complete or utter: *a regular fool.* **13** subject to the rule of an established religious community: *canons regular.* ~*n* **14** a professional long-term serviceman in a military unit. **15** *Informal* a frequent customer or visitor. **regularity** *n* **regularize** *or* **-ise** *vb* **regularly** *adv*

regulate *vb* **-lating, -lated 1** to control by means of rules: *a code of practice to regulate advertising by schools.* **2** to adjust slightly: *he had to take drugs to regulate his heartbeat.* **regulatory** *adj*

regulation *n* **1** a rule that governs procedure or behaviour. **2** the act of regulating. ~*adj* **3** in accordance with rules or conventions: *dressed in the orchestra's regulation black tie.*

regulator *n* **1** a mechanism that automatically controls pressure, temperature, etc. **2** the mechanism by which the speed of a clock is regulated.

regurgitate *vb* **-tating, -tated 1** to vomit. **2** (of some birds and animals) to bring back (partly digested food) to the mouth to feed the young. **3** to reproduce (ideas or facts) without understanding them. **regurgitation** *n*

rehabilitate *vb* **-tating, -tated 1** to help (a person) to readapt to society after illness or imprisonment. **2** to restore to a former position or rank. **3** to restore the good reputation of. **rehabilitation** *n*

rehash *vb* **1** to use (old or already used ideas) in a slightly different form without real improvement. ~*n* **2** old ideas presented in a new form.

rehearse *vb* **-hearsing, -hearsed 1** to practise (a play, concert, etc.) for public performance. **2** to repeat aloud: *he rehearsed his familiar views on the press.* **3** to train (a person) for public performance. **rehearsal** *n* **rehearser** *n*

rehouse *vb* **-housing, -housed** to provide with a new and better home.

Reich (**rike**) *n* the former German state, esp. the Nazi dictatorship in Germany from 1933–45 (**Third Reich**).

reign *n* **1** the period during which a monarch is the official ruler of a country. **2** a period during which a person or thing is dominant: *a reign of terror.* ~*vb* **3** to rule (a country). **4** to be supreme: *a sense of confusion reigns in the capital.*

reigning *adj* currently holding a title or championship: *the reigning world champion.*

reimburse *vb* **-bursing, -bursed** to repay (someone) for (expenses or losses). **reimbursement** *n*

rein *n* **1 reins a** long narrow straps attached to a bit to control a horse. **b** narrow straps attached to a harness to control a young child. **c** means of control: *to take up the reins of government.* **2 give (a) free rein** to allow a considerable amount of freedom. **3 keep a tight rein on** to control carefully: *we have to keep a tight rein on expenditure.* ~*vb* **4** to restrain or halt with reins. **5** to control or limit: *public spending was reined in.* ~See also **rein in.**

reincarnate *vb* **-nating, -nated** to be born again in a different body: *souls may be reincarnated in human forms.*

reincarnation *n* **1** the belief that after death the soul is reborn in another body. **2** an instance of rebirth in another body. **3** reappearance in a new form of a principle or idea: *he was the reincarnation of the old Republican Party isolationist.*

reindeer *n, pl* **-deer** *or* **-deers** a deer with large branched antlers that lives in the arctic regions.

reinforce *vb* **-inforcing, -inforced 1** to give added emphasis to (an idea or feeling): *his tired face reinforced his own weariness.* **2** to make physically stronger or harder: *the plastic panels were reinforced with carbon fibre.* **3** to give added support to (a mili-

THESAURUS

regrettable deplorable, disappointing, distressing, ill-advised, lamentable, pitiable, sad, shameful, unfortunate, unhappy, woeful, wrong

regular 1. common, commonplace, customary, daily, everyday, habitual, normal, ordinary, routine, typical, unvarying, usual **2.** balanced, even, flat, level, smooth, straight, symmetrical, uniform **3.** consistent, constant, established, even, fixed, ordered, periodic, rhythmic, set, stated, steady, systematic, uniform **4.** dependable, efficient, formal, methodical, orderly, standardized, steady, systematic

regulate adjust, administer, arrange, balance, conduct, control, direct, fit, govern, guide, handle, manage, moderate, modulate, monitor, order, organize, oversee, rule, run, settle, superintend, supervise, systematize, tune

regulation *n.* **1.** commandment, decree, dictate, direction, edict, law, order, ordinance, precept, procedure, requirement, rule, standing order, statute **2.** adjustment, administration, arrangement, control, direction, governance, government, management, modulation, supervision, tuning ~*adj.* **3.** customary, mandatory, normal, official, prescribed, required, standard, usual

rehabilitate 1. adjust, redeem, reform, reintegrate, save **2.** clear, convert, make good, mend, rebuild, recondition, reconstitute, reconstruct, re-establish, reinstate, reinvigorate, renew, renovate, restore

rehearsal 1. drill, going-over (*informal*), practice, practice session, preparation, reading, rehearsing, run-through **2.** account, catalogue, description, enumeration, list, narration, recital, recounting, relation, telling

rehearse 1. act, drill, go over, practise, prepare, ready, recite, repeat, run through, study, train, try out **2.** delineate, depict, describe, detail, enumerate, go over, list, narrate, recite, recount, relate, review, run through, spell out, tell, trot out (*informal*)

reign *n.* **1.** ascendancy, command, control, dominion, empire, hegemony, influence, monarchy, power, rule, sovereignty, supremacy, sway ~*vb.* **2.** administer, be in power, command, govern, hold sway, influence, occupy *or* sit on the throne, rule, wear the crown, wield the sceptre **3.** be rampant, be rife, be supreme, hold sway, obtain, predominate, prevail

rein *n.* **1. give (a) free rein (to)** free, give a blank cheque (to), give a free hand, give carte blanche, give (someone) his head, give way to, indulge, let go, remove restraints **2. keep a tight rein on** brake, bridle, check, control, curb, harness, hold, restraint, restriction ~*vb.* **3.** bridle, check, control, curb, halt, hold, hold back, limit, restrain, restrict, slow down

reincarnation metempsychosis, rebirth, transmigration of souls

tary force) by providing more men or equipment: *the army garrison had been reinforced with helicopters.* **reinforcement** *n*

reinforced concrete *n* concrete with steel bars or mesh embedded in it to strengthen it.

rein in *vb* **1** to stop (a horse) by pulling on the reins. **2** to restrict or stop: *either prices or wage packets had to be reined in.*

reinstate *vb* **-stating, -stated 1** to restore to a former rank or status. **2** to cause to exist or be important again: *reinstate some semblance of order.* **reinstatement** *n*

reinvigorate *vb* to give renewed energy to; refresh.

reissue *n* **1** a book, record, etc., that is published or released again after being unavailable for a time. ~*vb* **2** to publish or release (a book, record, etc.) again after a period of unavailability.

reiterate *vb* **-ating, -ated** *Formal* to repeat again and again. **reiteration** *n*

reject *vb* **1** to refuse to accept, use, or believe. **2** to deny to (a person) the feelings hoped for: *the boy had been rejected by his mother.* **3** to pass over or throw out as useless. **4** (of an organism) to fail to accept (a tissue graft or organ transplant). ~*n* **5** a person or thing rejected as not up to standard. **rejection** *n*

rejig *vb* **-jigging, -jigged 1** to re-equip (a factory or plant). **2** *Informal* to rearrange or manipulate, sometimes in an unscrupulous way: *the promoter hastily rejigged the running order.*

rejoice *vb* **-joicing, -joiced** to feel or express great happiness. **rejoicing** *n*

rejoin[1] *vb* to come together with (someone or something) again.

rejoin[2] *vb* to reply in a sharp or witty way.

rejoinder *n* a sharp or witty reply.

rejuvenate *vb* **-nating, -nated** to give back youth or vitality to. **rejuvenation** *n*

rekindle *vb* **-dling, -dled** to arouse (former emotions or interests).

relapse *vb* **-lapsing, -lapsed 1** to fall back into bad habits or illness. ~*n* **2** the act of relapsing. **3** the return of ill health after an apparent or partial recovery.

relate *vb* **-lating, -lated 1** to establish a relation between. **2** to have reference or relation to. **3** to have an understanding (of people or ideas): *the inability to relate to others.* **4** to tell (a story) or describe (an event).

related *adj* **1** linked by kinship or marriage. **2** connected or associated: *salts and related compounds.*

relation *n* **1** the connection between things or people. **2** a person who is connected by blood or marriage. **3** connection by blood or marriage. **4** an account or narrative. **5 in** *or* **with relation to** with reference to.

relations *pl n* **1** social or political dealings between individuals or groups. **2** family or relatives. **3** *Euphemistic* sexual intercourse.

relationship *n* **1** the dealings and feelings that exist between people or groups. **2** an emotional or sexual affair. **3** the connection between two things: *the relationship between exercise and mental health.* **4** association by blood or marriage.

relative *adj* **1** true to a certain degree or extent: *a zone of relative affluence.* **2** having significance only in relation to something else: *time is relative.* **3 relative to** in proportion to: *it will benefit from high growth in earnings relative to prices.* **4** respective: *the relative qualities of speed and accuracy.* **5** relevant: *the facts relative to the enquiry.* **6** *Grammar* of a clause (**relative clause**) that modifies a noun or pronoun occurring earlier in the sentence. **7** *Grammar* of or belonging to a class of words, such as *who, which,* or *that,* which function as conjunctions introducing relative clauses. ~*n* **8** a person who is related by blood or marriage. **relatively** *adv*

relative atomic mass *n* same as **atomic weight.**

relativity *n* **1** either of two theories developed by Al-

THESAURUS

reinforce augment, bolster, buttress, emphasize, fortify, harden, increase, prop, shore up, stiffen, strengthen, stress, supplement, support, toughen, underline

reinforcement 1. addition, amplification, augmentation, enlargement, fortification, increase, strengthening, supplement **2.** brace, buttress, prop, shore, stay, support **3.** *plural* additional *or* fresh troops, auxiliaries, reserves, support

reinstate bring back, recall, re-establish, rehabilitate, replace, restore, return

reject *vb.* **1.** cast aside, decline, deny, despise, disallow, discard, eliminate, exclude, jettison, jilt, rebuff, refuse, renounce, repel, repudiate, repulse, say no to, scrap, spurn, turn down, veto **2.** bin, discard, throw away *or* out ~*n.* **3.** castoff, failure, flotsam, second

rejection brushoff, denial, dismissal, elimination, exclusion, knock-back (*slang*), rebuff, refusal, renunciation, repudiation, the (old) heave-ho (*informal*), thumbs down, veto

rejoice be glad (happy, overjoyed), celebrate, delight, exult, glory, joy, jump for joy, make merry, revel, triumph

rejoicing celebration, cheer, delight, elation, exultation, festivity, gaiety, gladness, happiness, joy, jubilation, merrymaking, revelry, triumph

relapse *vb.* **1.** backslide, degenerate, deteriorate, fade, fail, fall back, lapse, regress, retrogress, revert, sicken, sink, slip back, weaken, worsen ~*n.* **2.** backsliding, fall from grace, lapse, recidivism, regression, retrogression, reversion **3.** deterioration, recurrence, setback, turn for the worse, weakening, worsening

relate 1. ally, associate, connect, coordinate, correlate, couple, join, link **2.** appertain, apply, bear upon, be relevant to, concern, have reference to, have to do with, pertain, refer **3.** chronicle, describe, detail, give an account of, impart, narrate, present, recite, recount, rehearse, report, set forth, tell

related 1. akin, cognate, consanguineous, kin, kindred **2.** accompanying, affiliated, akin, allied, associated, cognate, concomitant, connected, correlated, interconnected, joint, linked

relation 1. application, bearing, bond, comparison, connection, correlation, interdependence, link, pertinence, reference, regard, similarity, tie-in **2.** kin, kinsman, kinswoman, relative **3.** affiliation, affinity, consanguinity, kindred, kinship, propinquity, relationship **4.** account, description, narration, narrative, recital, recountal, report, story, tale

relations 1. affairs, associations, communications, connections, contact, dealings, interaction, intercourse, liaison, meetings, rapport, relationship, terms **2.** clan, family, kin, kindred, kinsfolk, kinsmen, relatives, tribe

relationship affair, affinity, association, bond, communications, conjunction, connection, correlation, exchange, kinship, liaison, link, parallel, proportion, rapport, ratio, similarity, tie-up

relative *adj.* **1.** allied, associated, comparative, connected, contingent, corresponding, dependent, proportionate, reciprocal, related, respective **2.** *with* **to** corresponding to, in proportion to, proportional to **3.** applicable, apposite, appropriate, appurtenant, apropos, germane, pertinent, relevant ~*n.* **4.** connection, kins-

bert Einstein, the **special theory of relativity**, which requires that the laws of physics shall be the same as seen by any two different observers in uniform relative motion, and the **general theory of relativity**, which considers observers with relative acceleration and leads to a theory of gravitation. **2** the state of being relative.

relax *vb* **1** to make or become less tense, looser, or less rigid. **2** to ease up from effort or attention. **3** to make (rules or discipline) less strict. **4** to become more friendly. **5** to lessen the intensity of: *he relaxed his vigilance in the lulls between terrorist attacks.* **relaxed** *adj*

relaxation *n* **1** rest after work or effort. **2** a form of recreation: *his favoured form of relaxation was walking on the local moors.* **3** the act of relaxing.

relay *n* **1** a fresh set of people or animals relieving others. **2** short for **relay race. 3** an automatic device that controls a valve or switch, esp. one in which a small change in current or voltage controls the switching on or off of circuits. **4** *Radio* a combination of a receiver and transmitter designed to receive radio signals and retransmit them. *~vb* **5** to pass on (a message). **6** to retransmit (a signal) by means of a relay. **7** *Brit* to broadcast (a performance or event) as it happens.

relay race *n* a race between teams in which each contestant covers a specified portion of the distance.

release *vb* **-leasing, -leased 1** to free (a person or animal) from captivity or imprisonment. **2** to free (someone) from obligation or duty. **3** to free (something) from (one's grip). **4** to allow news or information to be made public or available. **5** to allow (something) to move freely: *she released the handbrake.* **6** to issue (a record, film, or book) for sale or public showing. **7** to give out heat, energy, radiation, etc.: *the explosion released a cloud of toxic gas. ~n* **8** the act of freeing or state of being freed. **9** a statement to the press. **10** the act of issuing for sale or publication. **11** something issued for sale or public showing: *the record was originally released six years ago.*

relegate *vb* **-gating, -gated 1** to put in a less important position. **2** to demote (a sports team) to a lower division: *four clubs were relegated from the first division.* **relegation** *n*

relent *vb* **1** to change one's mind about some decision. **2** to become milder or less severe: *the weather relented.*

relentless *adj* **1** never stopping or reducing in severity: *relentless deterioration in standards.* **2** (of a person) determined and pitiless.

relevant *adj* to do with the matter in hand. **relevance** *n*

reliable *adj* able to be trusted. **reliability** *n* **reliably** *adv*

reliance *n* the state of relying on or trusting (a person or thing). **reliant** *adj*

relic *n* **1** an object or custom that has survived from the past. **2** something valued for its past associations. **3 relics** remaining parts or traces. **4** *RC Church, Eastern Church* a body part or possession of a saint, venerated as holy.

relict *n Archaic* **1** a relic. **2** a widow.

relief *n* **1** a feeling of cheerfulness that follows the removal of anxiety, pain, or distress. **2** a temporary pause in anxiety, pain, or distress. **3** money, food, or clothing given to people in special need: *disaster relief.* **4** the act of freeing a besieged town or fortress: *the relief of Mafeking.* **5** a person who replaces another at some task or duty. **6** a bus, plane, etc., that carries additional passengers when a scheduled service is full. **7** Also called: **relievo** *Sculpture, archit* the projection of a carved design from the surface. **8** any vivid effect resulting from contrast: *a welcome relief.* **9** the difference between the highest and lowest level: *study the map of relief and the rainfall map.* **10 on relief** *US & Canad* (of people) in receipt of government aid because of personal need.

relief map *n* a map showing the shape and height of the land surface by contours and shading.

relieve *vb* **-lieving, -lieved 1** to lessen (pain, distress, boredom, etc.). **2** to bring assistance to (someone in need): *a plan to relieve those facing hunger.* **3** to free (someone) from an obligation: *a further attempt to relieve the taxpayers of their burdens.* **4** to take over the duties of (someone): *the night nurse came in to relieve her.* **5** to free (a besieged town or fort). **6 relieve oneself** to urinate or defecate. **7** to set off by contrast: *painted walls are marginally re-*

THESAURUS

man, kinswoman, member of one's *or* the family, relation

relatively comparatively, in *or* by comparison, rather, somewhat, to some extent

relax 1. be *or* feel at ease, calm, laze, let oneself go (*informal*), let one's hair down (*informal*), lighten up (*slang*), loosen up, put one's feet up, rest, soften, take it easy, take one's ease, unbend, unwind **2.** abate, diminish, ease, ebb, lessen, let up, loosen, lower, mitigate, moderate, reduce, relieve, slacken, weaken

relaxation 1. amusement, enjoyment, entertainment, fun, leisure, pleasure, recreation, refreshment, rest **2.** abatement, diminution, easing, lessening, let-up (*informal*), moderation, reduction, slackening, weakening

relay *n.* **1.** relief, shift, turn **2.** *vb.* broadcast, carry, communicate, hand on, pass on, send, spread, transmit

release *vb.* **1.** deliver, discharge, disengage, drop, emancipate, extricate, free, let go, let out, liberate, loose, manumit, set free, turn loose, unbridle, unchain, undo, unfasten, unfetter, unloose, unshackle, untie **2.** absolve, acquit, dispense, excuse, exempt, exonerate, let go, let off **3.** break, circulate, disseminate, distribute, issue, launch, make known, make public, present, publish, put out, unveil *~n.* **4.** acquittal, deliverance, delivery, discharge, emancipation, freedom, liberation, liberty, manumission, relief **5.** announcement, issue, offering, proclamation, publication

relent 1. acquiesce, be merciful, capitulate, change one's mind, come round, forbear, give in, give quarter, give way, have pity, melt, show mercy, soften, unbend, yield **2.** die down, drop, ease, fall, let up, relax, slacken, slow, weaken

relentless 1. incessant, nonstop, persistent, punishing, sustained, unabated, unbroken, unfaltering, unflagging, unrelenting, unrelieved, unremitting, unstoppable **2.** cruel, fierce, grim, hard, harsh, implacable, inexorable, inflexible, merciless, pitiless, remorseless, ruthless, uncompromising, undeviating, unforgiving, unrelenting, unstoppable, unyielding

relevant admissible, applicable, apposite, appropriate, apt, fitting, germane, material, pertinent, proper, related, relative, significant, suited, to the point, to the purpose

reliable certain, dependable, faithful, honest, predictable, regular, reputable, responsible, safe, sound, stable, staunch, sure, tried and true, true, trustworthy, trusty, unfailing, upright

relic fragment, keepsake, memento, remembrance, remnant, scrap, souvenir, survival, token, trace, vestige

relief 1. abatement, alleviation, assuagement, balm, comfort, cure, deliverance, ease, easement, mitigation, palliation, release, remedy, solace **2.** break, breather

lieved by some abstract prints. **8** *Informal* to take from: *the prince had relieved him of his duties.* **relieved** *adj*

religion *n* **1** belief in or worship of a supernatural power or powers considered to be divine or to have control of human destiny. **2** any formal expression of such belief: *the Christian religion.* **3** *Chiefly RC Church* the way of life entered upon by monks and nuns: *to enter religion.*

religious *adj* **1** of religion. **2** pious or devout. **3** scrupulous or conscientious: *religious attention to detail.* **4** *Christianity* relating to the way of life of monks and nuns. *~n* **5** *Christianity* a monk or nun. **religiously** *adv*

relinquish *vb Formal* **1** to give up: *that hope has to be relinquished.* **2** to renounce (a claim or right). **3** to release one's hold on. **relinquishment** *n*

reliquary (**rel**-lik-wer-ee) *n, pl* **-quaries** a container for relics of saints.

relish *vb* **1** to savour or enjoy (an experience) to the full. **2** to anticipate eagerly. *~n* **3** liking or enjoyment: *he has an enormous relish for life.* **4** pleasurable anticipation: *his early relish for a new challenge.* **5** an appetizing or spicy food, such as a pickle, added to a main dish to improve its flavour. **6** a zestful quality: *he tells stories with great relish.*

relive *vb* **-living, -lived** to experience (a sensation or event) again, esp. in the imagination.

reload *vb* to put fresh ammunition into (a firearm).

relocate *vb* **-cating, -cated** to move or be moved to a new place of work. **relocation** *n*

reluctance *n* **1** unwillingness to do something. **2** *Physics* a measure of the resistance of a closed magnetic circuit to a magnetic flux.

reluctant *adj* unwilling or disinclined. **reluctantly** *adv*

rely *vb* **-lies, -lying, -lied rely on** *or* **upon a** to be dependent on: *the organization relies on voluntary contributions.* **b** to have trust or confidence in: *you can rely on his judgment.*

REM rapid eye movement.

remain *vb* **1** to continue to be: *the situation remains alarming.* **2** to stay behind or in the same place: *to remain at home.* **3** to be left after use or the passage of time. **4** to be left to be done, said, etc.: *whether this will be a long-term trend remains to be seen.*

remainder *n* **1** a part or portion that is left after use or the passage of time: *we ate some biscuits and the remainder of the jam.* **2** *Maths* **a** the amount left over when one quantity cannot be exactly divided by another: *for 10 ÷ 3, the remainder is 1.* **b** the amount left over when one quantity is subtracted from another. **3** a number of copies of a book sold cheaply because it has been impossible to sell them at full price. *~vb* **4** to sell (copies of a book) as a remainder.

remains *pl n* **1** parts left over from something after use or the passage of time: *the remains of the old Roman fortress.* **2** a corpse.

remake *vb* **-making, -made 1** to make again in a different way. *~n* **2** a new version of an old film.

remand *vb* **1** *Law* to send (a prisoner or accused person) back into custody or put on bail before trial. *~n* **2** the sending of a person back into custody or putting on bail before trial. **3 on remand** in custody or on bail awaiting trial.

remand centre *n* (in Britain) a place where accused people are detained while awaiting trial.

remark *vb* **1** to pass a casual comment (about). **2** to say. **3** to observe or notice. *~n* **4** a brief casually expressed thought or opinion.

remarkable *adj* **1** worthy of note or attention: *a remarkable career.* **2** striking or extraordinary: *a thing of remarkable beauty.* **remarkably** *adv*

remarry *vb* **-ries, -rying, -ried** to marry again following a divorce or the death of one's previous spouse. **remarriage** *n*

REME Royal Electrical and Mechanical Engineers.

remedial *adj* **1** providing or intended as a remedy. **2** of special teaching for slow learners: *remedial classes.* **remedially** *adv*

remedy *n, pl* **-edies 1** a drug or treatment for curing pain or disease. **2** a way of solving a problem: *every*

THESAURUS

(*informal*), diversion, let-up (*informal*), refreshment, relaxation, remission, respite, rest **3.** aid, assistance, help, succour, support, sustenance

relieve 1. abate, allay, alleviate, appease, assuage, calm, comfort, console, cure, diminish, dull, ease, mitigate, mollify, palliate, relax, salve, soften, solace, soothe **2.** aid, assist, bring aid to, help, succour, support, sustain **3.** deliver, discharge, disembarrass, disencumber, exempt, free, release, unburden **4.** give (someone) a break *or* rest, stand in for, substitute for, take over from, take the place of

religious 1. churchgoing, devotional, devout, divine, doctrinal, faithful, god-fearing, godly, holy, pious, pure, reverent, righteous, sacred, scriptural, sectarian, spiritual, theological **2.** conscientious, exact, faithful, fastidious, meticulous, punctilious, rigid, rigorous, scrupulous, unerring, unswerving

relish *vb.* **1.** appreciate, delight in, enjoy, fancy, like, luxuriate in, prefer, revel in, savour, taste *~n.* **2.** appetite, appreciation, enjoyment, fancy, fondness, gusto, liking, love, partiality, penchant, predilection, stomach, taste, zest **3.** appetizer, condiment, sauce, seasoning

reluctance aversion, backwardness, disinclination, dislike, disrelish, distaste, hesitancy, indisposition, loathing, repugnance, unwillingness

reluctant averse, backward, disinclined, grudging, hesitant, indisposed, loath, recalcitrant, slow, unenthusiastic, unwilling

rely bank, be confident of, be sure of, bet, count, depend, have confidence in, lean, reckon, repose trust in, swear by, trust

remain abide, be left, cling, continue, delay, dwell, endure, go on, last, linger, persist, prevail, rest, stand, stay, stay behind, stay put (*informal*), survive, tarry, wait

remainder balance, butt, dregs, excess, leavings, oddment, relic, remains, remnant, residue, residuum, rest, stub, surplus, tail end, trace, vestige(s)

remains 1. balance, crumbs, debris, detritus, dregs, fragments, leavings, leftovers, oddments, odds and ends, pieces, relics, remainder, remnants, residue, rest, scraps, traces, vestiges **2.** body, cadaver, carcass, corpse

remark *vb.* **1.** comment, declare, mention, observe, pass comment, reflect, say, state **2.** espy, heed, make out, mark, note, notice, observe, perceive, regard, see, take note *or* notice of *~n.* **3.** assertion, comment, declaration, observation, opinion, reflection, statement, thought, utterance, word

remarkable conspicuous, distinguished, extraordinary, famous, impressive, miraculous, notable, noteworthy, odd, outstanding, phenomenal, pre-eminent, prominent, rare, signal, singular, strange, striking, surprising, uncommon, unusual, wonderful

remedy *n.* **1.** antidote, counteractive, cure, medicament, medicine, nostrum, panacea, physic (*rare*), relief, restorative, specific, therapy, treatment **2.** anti-

statesman promised a remedy for unemployment. ~*vb* **-edies, -edying, -edied 3** to put right or improve. **remediable** *adj*

remember *vb* **1** to become aware of (something forgotten) again. **2** to keep (an idea, intention, etc.) in one's mind: *remember to write.* **3** to give money to (someone), as in a will or in tipping. **4 remember to** to mention (a person's name) to another person, by way of greeting: *remember me to her.* **5** to commemorate: *we are here to remember the dead.*

remembrance *n* **1** a memory. **2** a memento or keepsake. **3** the act of honouring some past event or person.

Remembrance Day *n* **1** (in Britain) Remembrance Sunday. **2** (in Canada) a statutory holiday observed on November 11 in memory of the dead of both World Wars.

Remembrance Sunday *n* (in Britain) the Sunday closest to November 11th, on which the dead of both World Wars are commemorated.

remind *vb* **1** to cause to remember: *remind her that she was on duty.* **2** to put in mind (of someone or something): *you remind me of Alice in Wonderland.*

reminder *n* **1** something that recalls the past. **2** a note to remind a person of something not done.

reminisce *vb* **-niscing, -nisced** to talk or write about old times or past experiences.

reminiscence *n* **1** the act of recalling or narrating past experiences. **2** something remembered from the past. **3 reminiscences** stories about a person's life, often presented in a book.

reminiscent *adj* **1 reminiscent of** reminding or suggestive of. **2** characterized by reminiscence.

remiss *adj Formal* careless in attention to duty or responsibility.

remission *n* **1** a reduction in the length of a prison term. **2** forgiveness for sin. **3** easing of intensity of the symptoms of a disease. **4** a release from an obligation.

remit *vb* (rim-**mitt**) **-mitting, -mitted 1** to send (money) for goods or services. **2** to cancel (a punishment or debt). **3** *Law* to send back (a case) to a lower court for further consideration. **4** to slacken or ease off. **5** *Archaic* to forgive (crime or sins). ~*n* (**ree**-mitt) **6** area of authority: *within the review body's remit.*

remittance *n* money sent as payment.

remittent *adj* (of a disease) periodically less severe.

remix *vb* **1** to change the relative prominence of each performer's part of (a recording). ~*n* **2** a remixed version of a recording.

remnant *n* **1** a part left over. **2** a piece of material from the end of a roll. **3** a surviving trace or vestige: *the authorities drafted in the military to crush any remnant of protest.*

remodel *vb* **-elling, -elled** to give a different shape or form to: *a renaissance of boutiques and remodelled apartments; the country is planning to remodel its armed forces.*

remonstrance *n Formal* a strong protest about something.

remonstrate *vb* **-strating, -strated** *Formal* to argue in protest or objection: *the player remonstrated loudly with the official.* **remonstration** *n*

remorse *n* a sense of deep regret and guilt for something one did. **remorseful** *adj*

remorseless *adj* **1** constantly unkind and lacking pity: *remorseless fate.* **2** continually intense: *the superintendent's remorseless gaze.*

remote *adj* **1** far away. **2** far from civilization. **3** distant in time. **4** not relevant: *the issues seem remote from the general population.* **5** (of a person's manner) aloof or abstracted. **6** slight or faint: *a remote possibility.* **7** operated from a distance; remote-controlled: *a remote manipulator arm.* **remotely** *adv*

remote control *n* control of an apparatus from a

THESAURUS

dote, corrective, countermeasure, nostrum, panacea, redress, relief, solution ~*vb.* **3.** ameliorate, correct, cure, ease, fix, put right, rectify, redress, reform, relieve, repair, set to rights, solve, treat

remember bear in mind, call to mind, call up, commemorate, keep in mind, look back (on), mind (*dialect*), recall, recognize, recollect, reminisce, retain, summon up, think back

remind awaken memories of, bring back to, bring to mind, call to mind, call up, jog one's memory, make (someone) remember, prompt, put in mind, refresh one's memory

reminiscence anecdote, memoir, memory, recall, recollection, reflection, remembrance, retrospection, review

reminiscent evocative, redolent, remindful, similar, suggestive

remiss careless, culpable, delinquent, derelict, dilatory, forgetful, heedless, inattentive, indifferent, lackadaisical, lax, neglectful, negligent, regardless, slack, slapdash, slipshod, sloppy (*informal*), slothful, slow, tardy, thoughtless, unmindful

remission 1. absolution, acquittal, amnesty, discharge, pardon, release, reprieve **2.** absolution, excuse, exemption, exoneration, forgiveness, indulgence **3.** abatement, abeyance, alleviation, amelioration, decrease, diminution, ebb, lessening, let-up (*informal*), lull, moderation, reduction, relaxation, respite, suspension

remit *vb.* **1.** dispatch, forward, mail, post, send, transmit **2.** cancel, desist, forbear, halt, repeal, rescind, stop **3.** abate, alleviate, decrease, diminish, dwindle, ease up, fall away, mitigate, moderate, reduce, relax, sink, slacken, soften, wane, weaken ~*n.* **4.** authorization, brief, guidelines, instructions, orders, terms of reference

remittance allowance, consideration, fee, payment

remnant balance, bit, butt, end, fragment, hangover, leftovers, oddment, piece, remainder, remains, residue, residuum, rest, rump, scrap, shred, stub, survival, tail end, trace, vestige

remonstrate argue, challenge, complain, dispute, dissent, object, protest, take exception, take issue

remorse anguish, bad *or* guilty conscience, compassion, compunction, contrition, grief, guilt, pangs of conscience, penitence, pity, regret, repentance, ruefulness, self-reproach, shame, sorrow

remorseful apologetic, ashamed, chastened, conscience-stricken, contrite, guilt-ridden, guilty, penitent, regretful, repentant, rueful, sad, self-reproachful, sorrowful, sorry

remorseless 1. callous, cruel, hard, hardhearted, harsh, implacable, inhumane, merciless, pitiless, ruthless, savage, uncompassionate, unforgiving, unmerciful **2.** inexorable, relentless, unrelenting, unremitting, unstoppable

remote 1. distant, far, faraway, far-off **2.** backwoods, godforsaken, inaccessible, in the back of beyond, in the middle of nowhere, isolated, lonely, off the beaten track, outlying, out-of-the-way, secluded **3.** alien, extraneous, extrinsic, foreign, immaterial, irrelevant, outside, removed, unconnected, unrelated **4.** abstracted, aloof, cold, detached, distant, faraway, indifferent, introspective, introverted, removed, reserved, stand-

distance by radio or electrical signals. **remote-controlled** *adj*

remould *vb* **1** to change completely: *to remould the country.* **2** to bond a new tread onto the casing of (a worn pneumatic tyre). ~*n* **3** a tyre made by this process.

removable *adj* capable of being removed from a place or released from another object: *a farmer's truck with removable wooden sides.*

removal *n* **1** the act of removing or state of being removed. **2** the process of moving one's possessions from a previous address to a new one.

remove *vb* **-moving, -moved 1** to take away and place elsewhere. **2** to take (clothing) off. **3** get rid of. **4** to dismiss (someone) from office. **5** *Formal* to change the location of one's home or place of business. ~*n* **6** the degree of difference: *one remove away from complete rebuttal.* **7** *Brit* (in certain schools) a class or form.

removed *adj* **1** very different or distant: *madness seemed far removed from the sunny order of things.* **2** separated by a degree of descent: *the child of a person's first cousin is their first cousin once removed.*

remunerate *vb* **-ating, -ated** *Formal* to reward or pay for work or service. **remuneration** *n* **remunerative** *adj*

renaissance *n* a renewal of interest or creativity in an area: *the English musical renaissance.*

Renaissance *n* **1 the Renaissance** the great revival of art, literature, and learning in Europe in the 14th, 15th, and 16th centuries. ~*adj* **2** of or from the Renaissance.

renal (ree-nal) *adj* of the kidneys.

renascent *adj Literary* becoming active or vigorous again: *renascent nationalism.* **renascence** *n*

rend *vb* **rending, rent** *Literary* **1** to tear violently. **2** (of a sound) to break (the silence) with a shrill or piercing tone.

render *vb* **1** to cause to become: *he was rendered unconscious by his wound.* **2** to give or provide (aid, a service, etc.). **3** *Formal* to present or submit (a bill). **4** to translate. **5** to represent in painting, music, or acting. **6** to yield or give: *he rendered up his soul to God.* **7** to cover with plaster. **8** to melt down (fat). **rendering** *n*

rendezvous (**ron**-day-voo) *n, pl* **-vous** (-vooz) **1** an appointment to meet at a specified time and place. **2** a place where people meet. ~*vb* **3** to meet at a specified time or place.

rendition *n Formal* **1** a performance of a piece of music or a dramatic role. **2** a translation.

renegade *n* a person who deserts a cause for another.

renege (rin-**nayg**) *vb* **-neging, -neged** to go back (on an agreement or promise): *the politicians reneged on every promise.*

renew *vb* **1** to begin again. **2** to take up again after a break: *they wanted to renew diplomatic ties.* **3** to make valid again: *we didn't renew the lease.* **4** to grow again. **5** to restore to a new or fresh condition. **6** to replace (an old or worn-out part or piece). **7** to restate or reaffirm (a promise). **renewable** *adj* **renewal** *n*

rennet *n* a substance prepared from the stomachs of calves and used for curdling milk to make cheese.

renounce *vb* **-nouncing, -nounced 1** to give up (a belief or habit) voluntarily. **2** to give up formally (a claim or right): *he would renounce his rights to the throne.*

renovate *vb* **-vating, -vated** to restore to good condition. **renovation** *n* **renovator** *n*

renown *n* widespread good reputation.

renowned *adj* famous.

rent[1] *vb* **1** to give or have use of (land, a building, a machine, etc.) in return for periodic payments. ~*n* **2** a payment made periodically for the use of land, a building, a machine, etc.

rent[2] *n* **1** a slit made by tearing. ~*vb* **2** the past of **rend.**

rental *n* **1** the amount paid or received as rent. ~*adj* **2** of or relating to rent.

THESAURUS

offish, unapproachable, uncommunicative, uninterested, uninvolved, withdrawn **5.** doubtful, dubious, faint, implausible, inconsiderable, meagre, negligible, outside, poor, slender, slight, slim, small, unlikely

removal 1. abstraction, dislodgment, dismissal, displacement, dispossession, ejection, elimination, eradication, erasure, expulsion, expunction, extraction, purging, stripping, subtraction, taking off, uprooting, withdrawal **2.** departure, flitting (*Scot. & northern English dialect*), move, relocation, transfer

remove 1. abstract, dislodge, move, transfer, transport, wipe out, withdraw **2.** doff, shed, take off **3.** abolish, amputate, carry off *or* away, delete, depose, detach, dethrone, discharge, dismiss, displace, do away with, efface, eject, eliminate, erase, excise, expel, expunge, extract, get rid of, give the bum's rush (*slang*), move, oust, purge, relegate, show one the door, strike out, take away, take out, throw out, throw out on one's ear (*informal*), unseat, wipe out, withdraw **4.** depart, flit (*Scot. & northern English dialect*), move, move away, quit, relocate, shift, transfer, transport, vacate

remuneration compensation, earnings, emolument, fee, income, indemnity, pay, payment, profit, recompense, reimbursement, reparation, repayment, retainer, return, reward, salary, stipend, wages

remunerative economic, gainful, lucrative, moneymaking, paying, profitable, recompensing, rewarding, rich, worthwhile

renaissance, renascence awakening, new birth, new dawn, reappearance, reawakening, rebirth, reemergence, regeneration, renewal, restoration, resurgence, resurrection, revival

render 1. cause to become, leave, make **2.** contribute, deliver, furnish, give, hand out, make available, pay, present, provide, show, submit, supply, tender, turn over, yield **3.** interpret, put, restate, transcribe, translate **4.** act, depict, do, give, interpret, perform, play, portray, present, represent **5.** cede, deliver, give, give up, hand over, relinquish, surrender, turn over, yield

renew begin again, breathe new life into, bring up to date, continue, extend, mend, modernize, overhaul, prolong, reaffirm, recommence, recreate, re-establish, refit, refresh, refurbish, regenerate, rejuvenate, renovate, reopen, repair, repeat, replace, replenish, restate, restock, restore, resume, revitalize, transform

renounce abandon, abdicate, abjure, abnegate, abstain from, cast off, decline, deny, discard, disclaim, disown, eschew, forgo, forsake, forswear, give up, leave off, quit, recant, reject, relinquish, renege, repudiate, resign, retract, spurn, swear off, throw off, waive, wash one's hands of

renovate do up (*informal*), modernize, overhaul, recondition, reconstitute, recreate, refit, reform, refurbish, rehabilitate, remodel, renew, repair, restore, revamp

renowned acclaimed, celebrated, distinguished, eminent, esteemed, famed, famous, illustrious, notable, noted, well-known

rent boy *n* a young male prostitute.
rentier (**ron**-tee-ay) *n* a person who lives off unearned income such as rents or interest.
renunciation *n* **1** the act or an instance of renouncing. **2** a formal declaration renouncing something.
reopen *vb* to open again after a period of being closed or suspended: *the Supreme Court has agreed to reopen the case.*
reorder *vb* to change the order of; organize differently.
reorganize *or* **-ise** *vb* **-izing, -ized** *or* **-ising, -ised** to organize in a new and more efficient way. **reorganization** *or* **-isation** *n*
rep[1] *n Theatre* short for **repertory company.**
rep[2] *n* **1** a sales representative. **2** someone elected to represent a group of people: *the union rep.* **3** *NZ informal* a rugby player selected to represent his district.
repair[1] *vb* **1** to restore (something damaged or broken) to good condition or working order. **2** to make up for (a mistake or injury). **3** to heal (a breach or division) in (something): *he is attempting to repair his country's relations with America.* ~*n* **4** the act, task, or process of repairing. **5** a part that has been repaired. **6** state or condition: *many museums may have to close because they are in such bad repair.* **repairable** *adj*
repair[2] *vb* **repair to** to go to (a place).
reparable (**rep**-rab-bl) *adj* able to be repaired or remedied.
reparation *n* **1** the act of making up for loss or injury. **2 reparations** compensation paid by a defeated nation after a war for the damage and injuries it caused.
repartee *n* **1** conversation consisting of witty remarks. **2** a sharp witty remark made as a reply.
repast *n Literary* a meal.
repatriate *vb* **-ating, -ated 1** to send back (a person) to the country of his or her birth or citizenship. ~*n* **2** a person who has been repatriated. **repatriation** *n*
repay *vb* **-paying, -paid 1** to refund or reimburse. **2** to make a return for (something): *to repay hospitality.* **repayable** *adj* **repayment** *n*
repeal *vb* **1** to cancel (a law) officially. ~*n* **2** the act of repealing: *the repeal of the Corn Laws.* **repealable** *adj*
repeat *vb* **1** to say, write, or do again. **2** to tell to another person (the secrets told to one by someone else). **3** to recite (a poem, etc.) from memory. **4** to occur more than once: *this pattern repeats itself many times.* **5** (of food) to be tasted again after eating as the result of belching. **6** to say (the words or sounds) uttered by someone else; echo. ~*n* **7** the act or an instance of repeating. **8** a word, action, pattern, etc., that is repeated. **9** *Radio, television* a broadcast of a programme which has been broadcast before. **10** *Music* a passage that is an exact restatement of the passage preceding it. **repeated** *adj* **repeatedly** *adv* **repeatable** *adj*
repeater *n* **1** a gun capable of firing several shots without reloading. **2** a clock or watch which strikes the hour or quarter-hour just past, when a spring is pressed.
repel *vb* **-pelling, -pelled 1** to cause (someone) to feel disgusted. **2** to force or drive back (someone or something). **3** to be effective in keeping away or controlling: *these buzzers are claimed to repel female mosquitoes.* **4** to fail to mix with or absorb: *water and oil repel each other.* **5** to reject or spurn: *she repelled his advances.*
repellent *adj* **1** disgusting or distasteful. **2** resisting water etc. ~*n* **3** a chemical used to keep insects or other creatures away.
repent *vb* to feel regret for (something bad one has done). **repentance** *n* **repentant** *adj*

THESAURUS

rent[1] **1.** *vb.* charter, hire, lease, let **2.** *n.* fee, hire, lease, payment, rental, tariff
rent[2] breach, break, chink, crack, flaw, gash, hole, opening, perforation, rip, slash, slit, split, tear
renunciation abandonment, abdication, abjuration, abnegation, abstention, denial, disavowal, disclaimer, eschewal, forswearing, giving up, rejection, relinquishment, repudiation, resignation, spurning, surrender, waiver
repair[1] *vb.* **1.** compensate for, fix, heal, make good, make up for, mend, patch, patch up, put back together, put right, recover, rectify, redress, renew, renovate, restore, restore to working order, retrieve, square ~*n.* **2.** adjustment, darn, mend, overhaul, patch, restoration **3.** condition, fettle, form, nick (*informal*), shape (*informal*), state
repair[2] betake oneself, go, head for, leave for, move, remove, retire, set off for, withdraw
reparation amends, atonement, compensation, damages, indemnity, propitiation, recompense, redress, renewal, repair, requital, restitution, satisfaction
repartee badinage, banter, bon mot, persiflage, pleasantry, raillery, riposte, sally, wit, witticism, wittiness, wordplay
repay 1. compensate, make restitution, pay back, recompense, refund, reimburse, remunerate, requite, restore, return, reward, settle up with, square **2.** avenge, even *or* settle the score with, get back at, get even with (*informal*), get one's own back on (*informal*), hit back, make reprisal, reciprocate, retaliate, return the compliment, revenge
repeal 1. *vb.* abolish, abrogate, annul, cancel, countermand, declare null and void, invalidate, nullify, recall, rescind, reverse, revoke, set aside, withdraw **2.** *n.* abolition, abrogation, annulment, cancellation, invalidation, nullification, rescinding, rescindment, revocation, withdrawal
repeat *vb.* **1.** duplicate, echo, iterate, redo, reiterate, relate, renew, replay, reproduce, rerun, reshow **2.** quote, recapitulate, recite, rehearse, relate, restate, retell ~*n.* **3.** duplicate, echo, recapitulation, reiteration, repetition, replay, reproduction **4.** rerun, reshowing
repeatedly again and again, frequently, many a time and oft (*archaic or poetic*), many times, often, over and over, time after time, time and (time) again
repel 1. disgust, give one the creeps (*informal*), gross out (*U.S. slang*), make one shudder, make one sick, nauseate, offend, put one off, revolt, sicken, turn one off (*informal*), turn one's stomach **2.** beat off, check, confront, decline, drive off, fight, hold off, keep at arm's length, oppose, parry, put to flight, rebuff, refuse, reject, repulse, resist, ward off
repellent 1. abhorrent, abominable, cringe-making (*Brit. informal*), discouraging, disgusting, distasteful, hateful, horrid, loathsome, nauseating, noxious, obnoxious, obscene, odious, offensive, off-putting (*Brit. informal*), repugnant, repulsive, revolting, sickening, yucky *or* yukky (*slang*) **2.** impermeable, proof, repelling, resistant
repent atone, be ashamed, be contrite, be sorry, deplore, feel remorse, lament, regret, relent, reproach oneself, rue, see the error of one's ways, show penitence, sorrow
repentance compunction, contrition, grief, guilt, penitence, regret, remorse, sackcloth and ashes, self-reproach, sorriness, sorrow

repercussion *n* **1 repercussions** results or consequences of an action or event. **2** an echo or reverberation.
repertoire *n* **1** all the works that a company or performer can perform. **2** the entire stock of skills or techniques that someone or something, such as a computer, is capable of.
repertory *n, pl* **-ries 1** same as **repertoire** (sense 2). **2** short for **repertory company.**
repertory company *n* a permanent theatre company producing a succession of plays.
repetition *n* **1** the act of repeating. **2** a thing that is repeated. **3** a replica or copy. **repetitious** *adj* **repetitive** *adj*
rephrase *vb* **-phrasing, -phrased** to express in different words. **rephrasing** *n*
repine *vb* **-pining, -pined** *Literary* to be worried or discontented.
replace *vb* **-placing, -placed 1** to take the place of. **2** to substitute a person or thing for (another): *we need to replace that chair.* **3** to put (something) back in its rightful place.
replacement *n* **1** the act or process of replacing. **2** a person or thing that replaces another.
replay *n* **1** a showing again of a sequence of action immediately after it happens. **2** a second sports match played because an earlier game was drawn. *~vb* **3** to play (a recording, match, etc.) again.
replenish *vb* to make full or complete again by supplying what has been used up. **replenishment** *n*
replete *adj* **1** pleasantly full of food and drink. **2** well supplied: *a world replete with true horror.* **repletion** *n*
replica *n* an exact copy.
replicate *vb* **-cating, -cated** to make or be an exact copy of; reproduce. **replication** *n*
reply *vb* **-plies, -plying, -plied 1** to make answer (to) in words or writing or by an action. **2** to say (something) in answer: *she replied that she did not believe him.* *~n, pl* **-plies 3** an answer or response.
report *vb* **1** to give an account (of). **2** to give an account of the results of an investigation (into): *the commission is to report on global warming.* **3** to make a formal report on (a subject). **4** to make a formal complaint about. **5** to present (oneself) at an appointed place or for a specific purpose: *report to the manager's office.* **6 report to** to be responsible to and under the authority of. **7** to act as a reporter. *~n* **8** an account prepared after investigation and published or broadcast. **9** an account of the discussions of a committee or other group of people: *I have the report of the mining union.* **10** a story for which there is no absolute proof: *according to report, he is not dead.* **11** *Brit* a statement on the progress of a school child. **12** a loud bang made by a gun or explosion. **13** comment on a person's character or actions: *he is of good report here.* **reportedly** *adv*
reported speech *n* a report of what someone said that gives the content of the speech without repeating the exact words.
reporter *n* a person who gathers news for a newspaper or broadcasting organization.
repose[1] *n* **1** a state of quiet restfulness. **2** calmness or composure. **3** sleep. *~vb* **-posing, -posed 4** to lie or lay down at rest. **5** to lie when dead.
repose[2] *vb* **-posing, -posed** to put (trust) in a person or thing.
reposition *vb* to place in a different position.
repository *n, pl* **-ries 1** a place or container in which things can be stored for safety. **2** a person to whom a secret is entrusted.
repossess *vb* (of a lender) to take back (property) from a customer who is behind with payments, for example mortgage repayments. **repossession** *n*
reprehend *vb* to find fault with.
reprehensible *adj* deserving criticism: *Willie's reprehensible behaviour.*

THESAURUS

repentant apologetic, ashamed, chastened, contrite, penitent, regretful, remorseful, rueful, self-reproachful, sorry
repercussion 1. repercussions backlash, consequence, result, sequel, side effect **2.** echo, rebound, recoil, reverberation
repetition duplication, echo, iteration, reappearance, recapitulation, recital, recurrence, redundancy, rehearsal, reiteration, relation, renewal, repeat, repetitiousness, replication, restatement, return, tautology
repetitive boring, dull, mechanical, monotonous, recurrent, samey (*informal*), tedious, unchanging, unvaried
repine brood, complain, eat one's heart out, fret, grieve, grumble, lament, languish, moan, mope, murmur, sulk
replace 1. follow, oust, stand in lieu of, substitute, succeed, supersede, supplant, take over from, take the place of **2.** put back, re-establish, reinstate, restore
replacement double, fill-in, proxy, stand-in, substitute, successor, surrogate, understudy
replenish fill, furnish, make up, provide, refill, reload, renew, replace, restock, restore, stock, supply, top up
replete abounding, brimful, brimming, charged, chock-full, crammed, filled, full, full to bursting, full up, glutted, gorged, jammed, jam-packed, sated, satiated, stuffed, teeming, well-provided, well-stocked
reply 1. *vb.* acknowledge, answer, come back, counter, echo, make answer, react, reciprocate, rejoin, respond, retaliate, retort, return, riposte, write back **2.** *n.* acknowledgment, answer, comeback (*informal*), counter, counterattack, echo, reaction, reciprocation, rejoinder, response, retaliation, retort, return, riposte
report *vb.* **1.** air, announce, bring word, broadcast, circulate, communicate, cover, declare, describe, detail, document, give an account of, inform of, mention, narrate, note, notify, pass on, proclaim, publish, recite, record, recount, relate, relay, state, tell, write up **2.** appear, arrive, be present, clock in *or* on, come, present oneself, show up (*informal*), turn up *~n.* **3.** account, announcement, article, communication, communiqué, declaration, description, detail, dispatch, information, message, narrative, news, note, paper, piece, recital, record, relation, statement, story, summary, tale, tidings, version, word, write-up **4.** gossip, hearsay, rumour, talk **5.** bang, blast, boom, crack, crash, detonation, discharge, explosion, noise, reverberation, sound **6.** character, eminence, esteem, fame, regard, reputation, repute
reporter announcer, correspondent, hack (*derogatory*), journalist, journo (*slang*), newscaster, newshound (*informal*), newspaperman, newspaperwoman, pressman, writer
repose *n.* **1.** ease, inactivity, peace, quiet, quietness, quietude, relaxation, respite, rest, restfulness, sleep, slumber, stillness, tranquillity **2.** aplomb, calmness, composure, dignity, equanimity, peace of mind, poise, self-possession, serenity, tranquillity *~vb.* **3.** drowse, lay down, lie, lie down, lie upon, recline, relax, rest, rest upon, sleep, slumber, take it easy, take one's ease
reprehensible bad, blameworthy, censurable, con-

represent *vb* **1** to act as the authorized delegate for (a person, country, etc.): *she represented her country at the Olympic Games.* **2** to act as a substitute (for). **3** to stand as an equivalent of. **4** to be a means of expressing: *the lights are relit to represent resurrection.* **5** to display the characteristics of: *romanticism in music is represented by Liszt.* **6** to describe as having a specified character or quality: *the magical bird was often represented as having two heads.* **7** to state or explain. **8** to present an image of through a picture or sculpture. **9** to bring clearly before the mind.

representation *n* **1** the state of being represented. **2** anything that represents, such as a pictorial portrait. **3 representations** formal statements made to an official body by a person making a complaint. **representational** *adj*

representative *n* **1** a person chosen to act for or represent a group. **2** a person who tries to sell the products or services of a firm. **3** a typical example. *~adj* **4** typical of a class or kind. **5** representing. **6** including examples of all the interests or types in a group. **7** acting as deputy for another. **8** of a political system in which people choose a person to make decisions on their behalf.

repress *vb* **1** to keep (feelings) under control. **2** to restrict the freedom of: *he continued to repress his people.* **3** *Psychol* to banish (unpleasant thoughts) from one's conscious mind. **repression** *n* **repressive** *adj*

reprieve *vb* **-prieving, -prieved 1** to postpone the execution of (a condemned person). **2** to give temporary relief to. *~n* **3** a postponement or cancellation of a punishment. **4** a warrant granting a postponement or cancellation. **5** a temporary relief from pain or harm.

reprimand *vb* **1** to blame (someone) officially for a fault. *~n* **2** an instance of blaming someone officially.

reprint *vb* **1** to print further copies of (a book). *~n* **2** a reprinted copy.

reprisal *n* an act of taking revenge: *brutal reprisals against civilians.*

reproach *n* **1** blame or rebuke. **2** a scolding. **3 beyond reproach** beyond criticism. *~vb* **4** to express disapproval (of someone's actions). **reproachful** *adj*

reprobate (rep-roh-bate) *n* **1** an unprincipled bad person. *~adj* **2** morally unprincipled.

reprobation *n Literary* disapproval or blame.

reproduce *vb* **-ducing, -duced 1** to make a copy or representation of. **2** *Biol* to produce offspring. **3** to recreate. **reproducible** *adj*

reproduction *n* **1** *Biol* a process by which an animal or plant produces one or more individuals similar to itself. **2** a copy of a work of art. **3** the quality of sound from an audio system. **4** the act or process of repro-

THESAURUS

demnable, culpable, delinquent, discreditable, disgraceful, errant, erring, ignoble, objectionable, opprobrious, remiss, shameful, unworthy

represent 1. describe as, make out to be, pass off as, pose as, pretend to be **2.** act for, be, betoken, correspond to, equal, equate with, express, mean, serve as, speak for, stand for, substitute for, symbolize **3.** embody, epitomize, exemplify, personify, symbolize, typify **4.** delineate, denote, depict, describe, designate, evoke, express, illustrate, outline, picture, portray, render, reproduce, show, sketch

representation 1. account, delineation, depiction, description, illustration, image, likeness, model, narration, narrative, picture, portrait, portrayal, relation, resemblance, sketch **2.** *plural* account, argument, explanation, exposition, expostulation, remonstrance, statement

representative *n.* **1.** agent, commissioner, councillor, delegate, deputy, member, member of parliament, M.P., proxy, spokesman, spokeswoman **2.** agent, commercial traveller, rep, salesman, traveller **3.** archetype, embodiment, epitome, exemplar, personification, type, typical example *~adj.* **4.** archetypal, characteristic, emblematic, evocative, exemplary, illustrative, symbolic, typical **5.** chosen, delegated, elected, elective

repress 1. bottle up, hold back, hold in, inhibit, keep in check, master, muffle, overcome, restrain, smother, stifle, suppress, swallow **2.** chasten, check, control, crush, curb, keep in check, master, overpower, quash, quell, restrain, silence, subdue, subjugate, suppress

repression authoritarianism, censorship, coercion, constraint, control, despotism, domination, restraint, subjugation, suppression, tyranny

repressive absolute, authoritarian, coercive, despotic, dictatorial, harsh, oppressive, severe, tough, tyrannical

reprieve *vb.* **1.** grant a stay of execution to, let off the hook (*slang*), pardon, postpone *or* remit the punishment of **2.** abate, allay, alleviate, mitigate, palliate, relieve, respite *~n.* **3.** abeyance, amnesty, deferment, pardon, postponement, remission, stay of execution, suspension **4.** abatement, alleviation, let-up (*informal*), mitigation, palliation, relief, respite

reprimand 1. *vb.* admonish, bawl out (*informal*), blame, carpet (*informal*), castigate, censure, check, chide, dress down (*informal*), give a rocket (*Brit. & N.Z. informal*), give (someone) a row (*informal*), haul over the coals (*informal*), lecture, rap over the knuckles, read the riot act, rebuke, reprehend, reproach, reprove, scold, send one away with a flea in one's ear (*informal*), take to task, tear into (*informal*), tear (someone) off a strip (*Brit. informal*), tell off (*informal*), tick off (*informal*), tongue-lash, upbraid **2.** *n.* admonition, blame, castigation, censure, dressing-down (*informal*), flea in one's ear (*informal*), lecture, rebuke, reprehension, reproach, reproof, row, talking-to (*informal*), telling-off (*informal*), ticking-off (*informal*), tongue-lashing, wigging (*Brit. slang*)

reprisal an eye for an eye, counterstroke, requital, retaliation, retribution, revenge, vengeance

reproach 1. *n.* abuse, blame, blemish, censure, condemnation, contempt, disapproval, discredit, disgrace, dishonour, disrepute, ignominy, indignity, obloquy, odium, opprobrium, scorn, shame, slight, slur, stain, stigma **2.** *vb.* abuse, bawl out (*informal*), blame, blast, carpet (*informal*), censure, chide, condemn, criticize, defame, discredit, disparage, find fault with, give a rocket (*Brit. & N.Z. informal*), lambast(e), read the riot act, rebuke, reprehend, reprimand, reprove, scold, take to task, tear into (*informal*), tear (someone) off a strip (*Brit. informal*), upbraid

reproachful abusive, admonitory, castigatory, censorious, condemnatory, contemptuous, critical, disappointed, disapproving, fault-finding, reproving, scolding, upbraiding

reproduce 1. copy, duplicate, echo, emulate, imitate, match, mirror, parallel, print, recreate, repeat, replicate, represent, transcribe **2.** *Biol.* breed, generate, multiply, procreate, produce young, proliferate, propagate, spawn

reproduction 1. *Biol.* breeding, generation, increase, multiplication, procreation, proliferation, propagation **2.** copy, duplicate, facsimile, imitation, picture, print, replica

ducing. *~adj* **5** made in imitation of an earlier style: *reproduction furniture.* **reproductive** *adj*

reproof *n* a severe blaming of someone for a fault.

reprove *vb* **-proving, -proved** to speak severely to (someone) about a fault. **reprovingly** *adv*

reptile *n* **1** a cold-blooded animal, such as a tortoise, snake, or crocodile, that has an outer covering of horny scales or plates and lays eggs. **2** a contemptible grovelling person. **reptilian** *adj*

republic *n* **1** a form of government in which the people or their elected representatives possess the supreme power. **2** a country in which the head of state is an elected or nominated president.

republican *adj* **1** of or supporting a republic. *~n* **2** a person who supports or advocates a republic. **republicanism** *n*

Republican *adj* **1** belonging to the Republican Party, the more conservative of the two main political parties in the US. **2** belonging to the Irish Republican Army. *~n* **3** a member or supporter of the Republican Party in the US. **4** a member or supporter of the Irish Republican Army. **Republicanism** *n*

repudiate (rip-**pew**-dee-ate) *vb* **-ating, -ated 1** to reject the authority or validity of. **2** to disown (a person). **3** to refuse to acknowledge or pay (a debt). **repudiation** *n*

repugnant *adj* offensive or disgusting. **repugnance** *n*

repulse *vb* **-pulsing, -pulsed 1** to be disgusting to: *this act of feminist rage repulsed as many as it delighted.* **2** to drive (an army) back. **3** to reject with coldness or discourtesy: *she repulsed his advances.* *~n* **4** a driving back. **5** a cold discourteous rejection or refusal.

repulsion *n* **1** a feeling of disgust or aversion. **2** *Physics* a force separating two objects, such as the force between two like electric charges.

repulsive *adj* **1** disgusting or distasteful. **2** *Physics* of repulsion. **repulsively** *adv*

reputable (**rep**-pew-tab-bl) *adj* trustworthy or respectable. **reputably** *adv*

reputation *n* **1** the opinion generally held of a person or thing. **2** a high opinion generally held about a person or thing. **3** notoriety or fame, esp. for some specified characteristic.

repute *n* good reputation: *a sculptor of international repute.*

reputed *adj* supposed or rumoured: *the island was reputed to have held a Roman temple; the reputed murderess.* **reputedly** *adv*

request *vb* **1** to ask for or politely demand: *we requested a formal meeting with the committee.* *~n* **2** the act or an instance of asking for something. **3** something asked for. **4 on request** if asked for: *most companies will send samples on request.*

request stop *n* a point on a route at which a bus stops only if signalled to do so.

Requiem (**rek**-wee-em) *n* **1** *RC Church* a Mass celebrated for the dead. **2** a musical setting of this Mass.

require *vb* **-quiring, -quired 1** to need. **2** to be a necessary condition: *the decision requires a logical common-sense approach.* **3** to insist upon. **4** to order or command: *family doctors are required to produce annual reports.*

➤ *Require* suggests a demand imposed by some regulation. *Need* is usually something that comes from a person.

requirement *n* **1** something demanded or imposed as an obligation. **2** a specific need or want.

requisite (**rek**-wizz-it) *adj* **1** absolutely essential. *~n* **2** something essential.

requisition *vb* **1** to demand and take for use, esp. for military or public use. *~n* **2** a formal request or demand for the use of something. **3** the act of taking something over, esp. for military or public use. **4** a formal written demand.

requite *vb* **-quiting, -quited** to return to someone

THESAURUS

reproof admonition, blame, castigation, censure, chiding, condemnation, criticism, dressing-down (*informal*), rebuke, reprehension, reprimand, reproach, reproval, scolding, ticking-off (*informal*), tongue-lashing, upbraiding

reprove abuse, admonish, bawl out (*informal*), berate, blame, carpet (*informal*), censure, check, chide, condemn, give a rocket (*Brit. & N.Z. informal*), read the riot act, rebuke, reprehend, reprimand, scold, take to task, tear into (*informal*), tear (someone) off a strip (*Brit. informal*), tell off (*informal*), tick off (*informal*), upbraid

repudiate abandon, abjure, cast off, cut off, deny, desert, disavow, discard, disclaim, disown, forsake, reject, renounce, rescind, retract, reverse, revoke, turn one's back on, wash one's hands of

repugnant abhorrent, abominable, disgusting, distasteful, foul, hateful, horrid, loathsome, nauseating, objectionable, obnoxious, odious, offensive, repellent, revolting, sickening, vile

repulsive abhorrent, abominable, disagreeable, disgusting, distasteful, forbidding, foul, hateful, hideous, horrid, loathsome, nauseating, objectionable, obnoxious, obscene, odious, offensive, repellent, revolting, sickening, ugly, unpleasant, vile

reputable creditable, estimable, excellent, good, honourable, honoured, legitimate, of good repute, reliable, respectable, trustworthy, upright, well-thought-of, worthy

reputation character, credit, distinction, eminence, esteem, estimation, fame, honour, name, opinion, renown, repute, standing, stature

repute celebrity, distinction, eminence, esteem, estimation, fame, name, renown, reputation, standing, stature

reputed accounted, alleged, believed, considered, deemed, estimated, held, ostensible, putative, reckoned, regarded, rumoured, said, seeming, supposed, thought

reputedly allegedly, apparently, ostensibly, seemingly, supposedly

request 1. *vb.* appeal for, apply for, ask (for), beg, beseech, call for, demand, desire, entreat, petition, pray, put in for, requisition, seek, solicit, sue for, supplicate **2.** *n.* appeal, application, asking, begging, call, demand, desire, entreaty, petition, prayer, requisition, solicitation, suit, supplication

require 1. crave, depend upon, desire, have need of, lack, miss, need, stand in need of, want, wish **2.** call for, demand, entail, involve, necessitate, take **3.** ask, beg, beseech, bid, call upon, command, compel, constrain, demand, direct, enjoin, exact, insist upon, instruct, oblige, order, request

requirement demand, desideratum, essential, lack, must, necessity, need, precondition, prerequisite, qualification, requisite, *sine qua non,* specification, stipulation, want

requisite 1. *adj.* called for, essential, indispensable, mandatory, necessary, needed, needful, obligatory, prerequisite, required, vital **2.** *n.* condition, desideratum, essential, must, necessity, need, precondition, prerequisite, requirement, *sine qua non*

requisition *vb.* **1.** appropriate, commandeer, occupy,

(the same treatment or feeling as received): *an Australian who requites her love.* **requital** *n*

reredos (**rear**-doss) *n* a screen or wall decoration at the back of an altar.

reroute *vb* **-routing, -routed** to send or direct by a different route.

rerun *n* **1** a film or programme that is broadcast again. **2** a race that is run again. ~*vb* **-running, -ran, -run 3** to put on (a film or programme) again. **4** to run (a race) again.

resale *n* the selling again of something purchased.

reschedule *vb* **-uling, -uled** to change the time, date, or schedule of: *the show has been rescheduled for August.*

rescind *vb* to annul or repeal. **rescission** *n*

rescue *vb* **-cuing, -cued 1** to bring (someone or something) out of danger or trouble. ~*n* **2** the act or an instance of rescuing. **rescuer** *n*

reseal *vb* to close or secure tightly again.

research *n* **1** systematic investigation to establish facts or collect information on a subject. ~*vb* **2** to carry out investigations into (a subject). **researcher** *n*

resemble *vb* **-bling, -bled** to be or look like. **resemblance** *n*

resent *vb* to feel bitter or indignant about. **resentful** *adj* **resentment** *n*

reservation *n* **1** a doubt: *his only reservation was, did he have the stamina?* **2** an exception or limitation that prevents one's wholehearted acceptance: *work I admire without reservation.* **3** a seat, room, etc. that has been reserved. **4** an area of land set aside for use by a particular group: *the Cherokee reservation.* **5** short for **central reservation.**

reserve *vb* **-serving, -served 1** to keep back or set aside for future use. **2** to obtain by arranging beforehand: *I phoned to reserve two tickets.* **3** to keep for oneself: *the association reserves the right to charge a fee.* **4** to delay announcing (a legal judgment). ~*n* **5** something kept back or set aside for future use. **6** the state or condition of being reserved: *we're keeping these two in reserve.* **7** *Sport* a substitute. **8** an area of publicly owned land used for sport, etc.: *a wildlife reserve.* **9** the hiding of one's feelings and personality. **10** the part of a nation's armed services not in active service. **11 reserves** *Finance* money or assets held by a bank or business to meet future expenses. **12** *Canad* an Indian reservation.

reserved *adj* **1** not showing one's feelings. **2** set aside for use by a particular person.

reserve price *n Brit* the minimum price acceptable to the owner of property being auctioned or sold.

reservist *n* a member of a nation's military reserve.

reservoir *n* **1** a natural or artificial lake for storing water for community use. **2** a large supply of something: *a vast reservoir of youthful enthusiasm.*

resettle *vb* **-tling, -tled** to settle to live in a different place. **resettlement** *n*

reshuffle *n* **1** a reorganization of jobs in a government or company. ~*vb* **-fling, -fled 2** to reorganize jobs or duties in a government or company.

reside *vb* **-siding, -sided** *Formal* **1** to live permanently (in a place): *my daughter resides in Europe.* **2** to be present (in): *desire resides in the unconscious.*

residence *n* **1** a person's home or house. **2** a large imposing house. **3** the fact of residing in a place. **4** a period of residing in a place. **5 in residence a** living in a particular place: *the Monarch was not in residence.* **b** (of an artist) working for a set period at a college, gallery, etc.: *composer in residence.*

resident *n* **1** a person who lives in a place. **2** a bird or animal that does not migrate. ~*adj* **3** living in a place. **4** living at a place in order to carry out a job: *a resident custodian.* **5** employed for one's specialized abilities:

THESAURUS

seize, take over, take possession of ~*n.* **2.** application, call, demand, request, summons **3.** appropriation, commandeering, occupation, seizure, takeover

rescue 1. *vb.* deliver, extricate, free, get out, liberate, recover, redeem, release, salvage, save, save the life of, set free **2.** *n.* deliverance, extrication, liberation, recovery, redemption, release, relief, salvage, salvation, saving

research 1. *n.* analysis, delving, examination, experimentation, exploration, fact-finding, groundwork, inquiry, investigation, probe, scrutiny, study **2.** *vb.* analyse, consult the archives, do tests, examine, experiment, explore, investigate, look into, make inquiries, probe, scrutinize, study

resemblance affinity, analogy, closeness, comparability, comparison, conformity, correspondence, counterpart, facsimile, image, kinship, likeness, parallel, parity, sameness, semblance, similarity, similitude

resemble bear a resemblance to, be like, be similar to, duplicate, echo, favour (*informal*), look like, mirror, parallel, put one in mind of, remind one of, take after

resent be angry about, bear a grudge about, begrudge, be in a huff about, be offended by, dislike, feel bitter about, grudge, harbour a grudge against, have hard feelings about, object to, take amiss, take as an insult, take exception to, take offence at, take umbrage at

resentful aggrieved, angry, bitter, embittered, exasperated, grudging, huffish, huffy, hurt, in a huff, incensed, indignant, in high dudgeon, irate, jealous, miffed (*informal*), offended, peeved (*informal*), piqued, put out, revengeful, unforgiving, wounded

resentment anger, animosity, bitterness, displeasure, fury, grudge, huff, hurt, ill feeling, ill will, indignation, ire, irritation, malice, pique, rage, rancour, umbrage, vexation, wrath

reservation 1. condition, demur, doubt, hesitancy, proviso, qualification, rider, scepticism, scruple, stipulation **2.** enclave, homeland, preserve, reserve, sanctuary, territory, tract

reserve *vb.* **1.** conserve, hang on to, hoard, hold, husband, keep, keep back, lay up, preserve, put by, retain, save, set aside, stockpile, store, withhold **2.** book, engage, prearrange, retain, secure **3.** defer, delay, keep back, postpone, put off, withhold ~*n.* **4.** backlog, cache, capital, fall-back, fund, hoard, reservoir, savings, stock, stockpile, store, supply **5.** park, preserve, reservation, sanctuary, tract **6.** aloofness, constraint, coolness, formality, modesty, reluctance, reservation, restraint, reticence, secretiveness, shyness, silence, taciturnity

reserved 1. aloof, cautious, close-mouthed, cold, cool, demure, formal, modest, prim, restrained, reticent, retiring, secretive, shy, silent, standoffish, taciturn, unapproachable, uncommunicative, undemonstrative, unforthcoming, unresponsive, unsociable **2.** booked, engaged, held, kept, restricted, retained, set aside, spoken for, taken

reservoir 1. basin, lake, pond, tank **2.** accumulation, fund, pool, reserves, source, stock, stockpile, store, supply

reside *formal* **1.** abide, dwell, hang out (*informal*), have one's home, inhabit, live, lodge, remain, settle, sojourn, stay **2.** abide, be intrinsic to, be vested, consist, dwell, exist, inhere, lie, rest with

the Museum's resident expert on seventeenth-century Dutch art. **6** (of birds and animals) not in the habit of migrating.

residential *adj* **1** (of a part of a town) consisting mainly of houses. **2** providing living accommodation: *residential clubs for homeless boys.*

residential school *n* a government boarding school in N Canada for Indian and Inuit students.

residual *adj* **1** of or being a remainder. ~*n* **2** something left over as a residue.

residue *n* **1** what is left over after something has been removed. **2** *Law* what is left of an estate after the discharge of debts and distribution of specific gifts.

residuum *n, pl* **-ua** same as **residue.**

resign *vb* **1** to give up office or a job. **2** to accept (an unpleasant fact): *he resigned himself to the inevitable.* **3** to give up (a right or claim).

resignation *n* **1** the act of resigning. **2** a formal document stating one's intention to resign. **3** passive endurance of difficulties: *full of quiet resignation*

resigned *adj* content to endure something unpleasant. **resignedly** *adv*

resilient *adj* **1** (of a person) recovering easily and quickly from misfortune or illness. **2** (of an object) capable of regaining its original shape or position after bending or stretching. **resilience** *n*

resin (**rezz**-in) *n* **1** a solid or semisolid substance obtained from certain plants: *cannabis resin.* **2** a similar substance produced synthetically. **resinous** *adj*

resist *vb* **1** to stand firm against or oppose: *the party's old guard continue to resist economic reform.* **2** to refrain from in spite of temptation: *I couldn't resist a huge portion of almond cake.* **3** to refuse to comply with: *to resist arrest.* **4** to be proof against: *airport design should be strengthened to help resist explosion.* **resistible** *adj*

resistance *n* **1** the act of resisting. **2** the capacity to withstand something, esp. the body's natural capacity to withstand disease. **3** *Electricity* the opposition to a flow of electric current through a circuit, component, or substance. **4** any force that slows or hampers movement: *wind resistance.* **5 line of least resistance** the easiest, but not necessarily the best, course of action. **resistant** *adj, n*

Resistance *n* **the Resistance** an illegal organization fighting for national liberty in a country under enemy occupation.

resistor *n* an electrical component designed to introduce a known value of resistance into a circuit.

resit *vb* **-sitting, -sat 1** to sit (an examination) again. ~*n* **2** an examination which one must sit again.

resolute *adj* firm in purpose or belief. **resolutely** *adv*

resolution *n* **1** firmness or determination. **2** a decision to do something. **3** a formal expression of opinion by a meeting. **4** the act of resolving. **5** *Music* the process in harmony whereby a dissonant note or chord is followed by a consonant one. **6** the ability of a television to reproduce fine detail. **7** *Physics* Also called: **resolving power** the ability of a telescope or microscope to produce separate images of closely placed objects.

resolvable *or* **resoluble** *adj* able to be resolved or analysed.

resolve *vb* **-solving, -solved 1** to decide or determine firmly. **2** to express (an opinion) formally by a vote. **3** to separate or cause to separate into (constituent parts). **4** to find the answer or solution to. **5** to explain away or dispel: *to resolve the controversy.* **6** *Music* to follow (a dissonant note or chord) by one producing a consonance. **7** *Physics* to distinguish between (separate parts) of (an image) as in a microscope, telescope, or other optical instrument. ~*n* **8** absolute determination: *he spoke of his resolve to deal with the problem of terrorism.*

THESAURUS

residence 1. abode, domicile, dwelling, flat, habitation, home, house, household, lodging, pad (*slang*), place, quarters **2.** hall, manor, mansion, palace, seat, villa **3.** occupancy, occupation, sojourn, stay, tenancy

resident 1. *n.* citizen, denizen, indweller, inhabitant, local, lodger, occupant, tenant **2.** *adj.* dwelling, inhabiting, living, local, neighbourhood, settled

residue balance, dregs, excess, extra, leftovers, remainder, remains, remnant, residuum, rest, surplus

resign 1. abandon, abdicate, cede, forgo, forsake, give in one's notice, give up, hand over, leave, quit, relinquish, renounce, step down (*informal*), surrender, turn over, vacate, yield **2.** *as in* **resign oneself** accept, acquiesce, bow, give in, give up, reconcile, submit, succumb, yield

resignation 1. abandonment, abdication, departure, leaving, notice, relinquishment, renunciation, retirement, surrender **2.** acceptance, acquiescence, compliance, endurance, forbearing, fortitude, nonresistance, passivity, patience, submission, sufferance

resigned acquiescent, compliant, long-suffering, patient, stoical, subdued, submissive, unprotesting, unresisting

resilient 1. bouncy, buoyant, feisty (*informal, chiefly U.S. & Canad.*), hardy, irrepressible, quick to recover, strong, tough **2.** bouncy, elastic, flexible, plastic, pliable, rubbery, springy, supple, whippy

resist 1. battle, be proof against, check, combat, confront, contend with, counteract, countervail, curb, defy, dispute, fight back, hinder, hold out against, oppose, put up a fight (against), refuse, repel, stand up to, struggle against, thwart, weather, withstand **2.** abstain from, avoid, forbear, forgo, keep from, leave alone, prevent oneself from, refrain from, refuse, turn down

resistance battle, combat, contention, counteraction, defiance, fight, fighting, hindrance, impediment, intransigence, obstruction, opposition, refusal, struggle

resistant 1. hard, impervious, insusceptible, proof against, strong, tough, unaffected by, unyielding **2.** antagonistic, combative, defiant, dissident, hostile, intractable, intransigent, opposed, recalcitrant, unwilling

resolute bold, constant, determined, dogged, firm, fixed, immovable, inflexible, obstinate, persevering, purposeful, relentless, set, stalwart, staunch, steadfast, strong-willed, stubborn, tenacious, unbending, undaunted, unflinching, unshakable, unshaken, unwavering

resolution 1. boldness, constancy, courage, dedication, determination, doggedness, earnestness, energy, firmness, fortitude, obstinacy, perseverance, purpose, relentlessness, resoluteness, resolve, sincerity, staunchness, staying power, steadfastness, stubbornness, tenacity, willpower **2.** aim, decision, declaration, determination, intent, intention, judgment, motion, purpose, resolve, verdict **3.** answer, end, finding, outcome, settlement, solution, solving, sorting out, unravelling, upshot, working out

resolve *vb.* **1.** agree, conclude, decide, design, determine, fix, intend, make up one's mind, purpose, settle, undertake **2.** analyse, break down, clear, disentangle, disintegrate, dissect, reduce, separate, solve, split up, unravel **3.** answer, clear up, crack, elucidate, explain, fathom, find the solution to, suss (out) (*slang*), work out **4.** banish, clear up, dispel, remove, sort out ~*n.* **5.**

resolved *adj* determined.
resonance *n* **1** the condition or quality of being resonant. **2** sound produced by a body vibrating in sympathy with a neighbouring source of sound.
resonant *adj* **1** resounding or re-echoing. **2** producing resonance: *the resonant cavities of the mouth.* **3** full of resonance: *his voice is a resonant baritone.*
resonate *vb* **-nating, -nated** to resound or cause to resound. **resonator** *n*
resort *vb* **1 resort to** to have recourse (to) for help, use, etc.: *some people have resorted to begging for food.* **2** to go, esp. often or habitually: *to resort to the beach.* ~*n* **3** a place to which many people go for holidays. **4** the use of something as a means or aid. **5 last resort** the last possible course of action open to a person.
resound (riz-**zownd**) *vb* **1** to ring or echo with sound. **2** (of sounds) to echo or ring. **3** to be widely known: *his fame resounded throughout India.*
resounding *adj* **1** echoing. **2** clear and emphatic: *he won a resounding victory.* **resoundingly** *adv*
resource *n* **1 resources** sources of economic wealth, esp. of a country or business enterprise: *mineral resources.* **2 resources** money available for use. **3** something resorted to for aid or support: *he saw the university as a resource for the community.* **4** the ability to deal with problems: *a man of resource.* **5** a means of doing something: *resistance was their only resource.*
resourceful *adj* capable and full of initiative. **resourcefulness** *n*
respect *n* **1** consideration: *respect for my feelings.* **2** an attitude of deference or esteem. **3** the state of being honoured or esteemed. **4** a detail or characteristic: *in virtually all respects boys develop more slowly than girls.* **5 in respect of** *or* **with respect to** in reference or relation to. **6 respects** polite greetings: *he paid his respects to her and left.* ~*vb* **7** to have an attitude of esteem towards: *she is the person I most respect and wish to emulate.* **8** to pay proper attention or consideration to: *he called on rebel groups to respect a cease-fire.* **respecter** *n*
respectable *adj* **1** worthy of respect. **2** having good social standing or reputation. **3** relatively or fairly good: *they obtained respectable results.* **4** fit to be seen by other people. **respectability** *n* **respectably** *adv*
respectful *adj* full of or showing respect. **respectfully** *adv*
respecting *prep* on the subject of.
respective *adj* relating separately to each of several people or things: *the culprits will be repatriated to their respective countries.*
respectively *adv* (in listing things that refer to another list) separately in the order given: *Patrese and Mansell were second and third fastest respectively.*
respiration (ress-per-**ray**-shun) *n* **1** breathing. **2** the process in living organisms of taking in oxygen and giving out carbon dioxide. **3** the breakdown of complex organic substances that takes place in the cells of animals and plants, producing energy and carbon dioxide. **respiratory** *adj*
respirator *n* **1** a device worn over the mouth and nose to prevent the breathing in of poisonous fumes. **2** an apparatus for providing artificial respiration.
respire *vb* **-spiring, -spired 1** to breathe. **2** to undergo respiration.
respite *n* **1** a interval of rest: *I allowed myself a six months respite to enjoy my family.* **2** a temporary delay.
resplendent *adj* **1** brilliant or splendid in appearance. **2** shining. **resplendence** *n*
respond *vb* **1** to state or utter (something) in reply. **2** to act in reply: *the government must respond accordingly to our recommendations.* **3** to react favourably: *most headaches will respond to the use of relaxants.*
respondent *n Law* a person against whom a petition is brought.
response *n* **1** the act of responding. **2** a reply or reaction. **3** a reaction to stimulation of the nervous sys-

THESAURUS

boldness, courage, determination, earnestness, firmness, resoluteness, resolution, steadfastness, willpower
resort *vb.* **1. resort to** avail oneself of, bring into play, employ, exercise, fall back on, have recourse to, look to, make use of, turn to, use, utilize **2.** frequent, go, haunt, head for, repair, visit ~*n.* **3.** haunt, holiday centre, refuge, retreat, spot, tourist centre **4.** alternative, chance, course, expedient, hope, possibility, recourse, reference
resound echo, fill the air, re-echo, resonate, reverberate, ring
resounding 1. booming, echoing, full, powerful, resonant, reverberating, rich, ringing, sonorous, sounding, vibrant **2.** clear, clear-cut, comfortable, emphatic, overwhelming, unequivocal
resource 1. resources assets, holdings, materials, means, property, reserves, supplies **2. resources** assets, capital, funds, means, money, riches, wealth, wherewithal **3.** ability, capability, cleverness, ingenuity, initiative, inventiveness, quick-wittedness, resourcefulness, talent **4.** course, expedient, means, resort
resourceful able, bright, capable, clever, creative, imaginative, ingenious, inventive, quick-witted, sharp, talented
respect *n.* **1.** admiration, appreciation, approbation, consideration, deference, esteem, estimation, honour, recognition, regard, reverence, veneration **2.** aspect, characteristic, detail, facet, feature, matter, particular, point, sense, way **3. in respect of** *also* **with respect to** bearing, connection, reference, regard, relation **4. respects** compliments, good wishes, greetings, regards, salutations ~*vb.* **5.** admire, adore, appreciate, defer to, esteem, have a good *or* high opinion of, honour, look up to, recognize, regard, revere, reverence, set store by, show consideration for, think highly of, value, venerate **6.** abide by, adhere to, attend, comply with, follow, heed, honour, notice, obey, observe, pay attention to, regard, show consideration for
respectable 1. admirable, decent, decorous, dignified, estimable, good, honest, honourable, proper, reputable, respected, upright, venerable, worthy **2.** ample, appreciable, considerable, decent, fair, fairly good, goodly, presentable, reasonable, sizable, substantial, tidy (*informal*), tolerable
respective corresponding, individual, own, particular, personal, relevant, separate, several, specific, various
respite 1. break, breather (*informal*), breathing space, cessation, halt, hiatus, intermission, interruption, interval, let-up (*informal*), lull, pause, recess, relaxation, relief, rest **2.** adjournment, delay, moratorium, postponement, reprieve, stay, suspension
respond acknowledge, act in response, answer, come back, counter, react, reciprocate, rejoin, reply, retort, return
response acknowledgment, answer, comeback (*in-*

tem. **4 responses** *Christianity* the words recited or sung in reply to the priest at a church service.

responsibility *n, pl* **-ties 1** the state of being responsible. **2** a person or thing for which one is responsible.

responsible *adj* **1 responsible for** having control or authority over. **2** being the agent or cause (of some action): *only a small number of students were responsible for the disturbances.* **3 responsible to** being accountable for one's actions and decisions to: *management should be made more responsible to shareholders.* **4** rational and accountable for one's own actions. **5** (of a position or duty) involving decision and accountability. **responsibly** *adv*

responsive *adj* reacting quickly or favourably to something. **responsiveness** *n*

respray *n* a new coat of paint applied to a vehicle.

rest[1] *n* **1** relaxation from exertion or labour. **2** a period of inactivity. **3** relief or refreshment. **4** calm. **5** death regarded as repose: *now he has gone to his eternal rest.* **6 at rest a** not moving. **b** calm. **c** dead. **d** asleep. **7** a pause or interval. **8** a mark in a musical score indicating a pause lasting a specific time. **9** a thing or place on which to put something for support or to steady it. **10 lay to rest** to bury (a dead person). *~vb* **11** to become or make refreshed. **12** to position (oneself, etc.) for rest or relaxation. **13** to place for support or steadying: *he slumped forward to rest his head on his forearms.* **14** to depend or rely: *his presidency rested on the outcome of the crisis.* **15** to direct (one's eyes) or (of one's eyes) to be directed: *she rested her gaze on the face of the statue.* **16** to be at ease. **17** to cease or cause to cease from motion or exertion. **18** to remain without further attention or action: *she refused to let the matter rest.* **19** *Law* to finish the introduction of evidence in (a case). **20** to put pastry in a cool place to allow the gluten to contract.

rest[2] *n* **1 the rest a** something left; remainder. **b** the others: *the rest of the world. ~vb* **2** to continue to be (as specified): *your conscience can rest easy.*

rest area *n Austral & NZ* a motorist's stopping place off a highway, equipped with tables and seats.

restart *vb* to commence (something) or set (something) in motion again.

restate *vb* to state or affirm (something) again or in a different way. **restatement** *n*

restaurant *n* a place where meals are prepared and served to customers.

restaurant car *n Brit* a railway coach in which meals are served.

restaurateur (rest-er-a-**tur**) *n* a person who owns or runs a restaurant.

rest-cure *n* a rest taken as part of a course of medical treatment.

restful *adj* relaxing or soothing.

restitution *n* **1** the act of giving back something that has been lost or stolen. **2** *Law* compensation for loss or injury.

restive *adj* **1** restless or uneasy. **2** impatient of control or authority.

restless *adj* **1** bored or dissatisfied. **2** unable to stay still or quiet. **3** not restful: *a restless sleep.* **restlessly** *adv* **restlessness** *n*

restoration *n* **1** the act of restoring to a former or original condition, place, etc. **2** the giving back of something lost or stolen. **3** something restored, replaced, or reconstructed. **4** a model or representation of a ruin or extinct animal. **5 the Restoration** *Brit* the

THESAURUS

formal), counterattack, counterblast, feedback, reaction, rejoinder, reply, retort, return, riposte

responsibility **1.** accountability, amenability, answerability, care, charge, duty, liability, obligation, onus, trust **2.** blame, burden, culpability, fault, guilt **3.** conscientiousness, dependability, level-headedness, maturity, rationality, reliability, sensibleness, soberness, stability, trustworthiness **4.** authority, importance, power

responsible **1. responsible for** at the helm, carrying the can (*informal*), in authority, in charge, in control **2.** at fault, culpable, guilty, to blame **3. responsible to** accountable, answerable, bound, duty-bound, subject, under obligation **4.** adult, conscientious, dependable, level-headed, mature, rational, reliable, sensible, sober, sound, stable, trustworthy **5.** authoritative, decision-making, executive, high, important

responsive alive, awake, aware, forthcoming, impressionable, open, perceptive, quick to react, reactive, receptive, sensitive, sharp, susceptible, sympathetic

rest[1] *n.* **1.** calm, doze, forty winks (*informal*), idleness, inactivity, leisure, lie-down, motionlessness, nap, refreshment, relaxation, relief, repose, siesta, sleep, slumber, snooze (*informal*), somnolence, standstill, stillness, tranquillity **2.** break, breather (*informal*), breathing space, cessation, halt, holiday, interlude, intermission, interval, lull, pause, respite, stop, time off, vacation **3. at rest** asleep, at a standstill, at peace, calm, dead, motionless, peaceful, resting, sleeping, still, stopped, tranquil, unmoving **4.** base, holder, prop, shelf, stand, support, trestle *~vb.* **5.** be at ease, be calm, doze, drowse, have a snooze (*informal*), have forty winks (*informal*), idle, kip (*Brit. slang*), laze, lie down, lie still, nap, put one's feet up, refresh oneself, relax, sit down, sleep, slumber, snooze (*informal*), take a nap, take it easy, take one's ease **6.** be supported, lay, lean, lie, prop, recline, repose, sit, stand, stretch out **7.** base, be based, be founded, depend, found, hang, hinge, lie, rely, reside, turn **8.** break off, cease, come to a standstill, desist, discontinue, halt, have a break, knock off (*informal*), stay, stop, take a breather (*informal*)

rest[2] **1.** *n.* **the rest** balance, excess, leftovers, others, remainder, remains, remnants, residue, residuum, rump, surplus **2.** *vb.* be left, continue being, go on being, keep, remain, stay

restful calm, calming, comfortable, languid, pacific, peaceful, placid, quiet, relaxed, relaxing, serene, sleepy, soothing, tranquil, tranquillizing, undisturbed, unhurried

restive agitated, edgy, fidgety, fractious, fretful, ill at ease, impatient, jittery (*informal*), jumpy, nervous, on edge, recalcitrant, refractory, restless, uneasy, unquiet, unruly

restless **1.** agitated, anxious, disturbed, edgy, fidgeting, fidgety, fitful, fretful, ill at ease, jumpy, nervous, on edge, restive, sleepless, tossing and turning, troubled, uneasy, unquiet, unruly, unsettled, worried **2.** active, bustling, changeable, footloose, hurried, inconstant, irresolute, moving, nomadic, roving, transient, turbulent, unsettled, unstable, unsteady, wandering

restlessness **1.** agitation, ants in one's pants (*slang*), anxiety, disquiet, disturbance, edginess, fitfulness, fretfulness, heebie-jeebies (*slang*), inquietude, insomnia, jitters (*informal*), jumpiness, nervousness, restiveness, uneasiness, worriedness **2.** activity, bustle, hurry, hurry-scurry, inconstancy, instability, movement, transience, turbulence, turmoil, unrest, unsettledness

restoration **1.** reconstruction, recovery, refreshment, refurbishing, rehabilitation, rejuvenation, re-

re-establishment of the monarchy in 1660 or the reign of Charles II (1660–85).

restorative (rist-**or**-a-tiv) *adj* **1** giving back health or good spirits. ~*n* **2** a food or medicine that gives back health or good spirits.

restore *vb* **-storing, -stored 1** to return (something) to its original or former condition. **2** to bring back to health or good spirits. **3** to return (something lost or stolen) to its owner. **4** to re-enforce or re-establish: *he must restore confidence in himself and his government; they worked to restore the monarchy.* **5** to reconstruct (a ruin, extinct animal, etc.). **restorer** *n*

restrain *vb* **1** to hold (someone) back from some action. **2** to limit or restrict: *restrain any tendency to impulse-buy.* **3** to deprive (someone) of liberty.

restrained *adj* not displaying emotion.

restraint *n* **1** something that restrains. **2** the ability to control one's impulses or passions. **3** a restraining or being restrained.

restrict *vb* to confine or keep within certain limits. **restrictive** *adj*

restriction *n* a rule or situation that limits or controls something or someone: *severe financial restrictions.*

restrictive practice *n Brit* **1** a trading agreement against the public interest. **2** a practice of a union or other group tending to limit the freedom of other workers or employers.

rest room *n US & Canad* a toilet in a public building.

restructure *vb* **-turing, -tured** to organize in a different way: *to restructure the world economy.*

result *n* **1** the outcome or consequence of an action, policy, etc. **2** the final score of a sporting contest. **3** a number or value obtained by solving a mathematical problem. **4** a favourable result, esp. a victory or success: *the best chance of a result is at Cheltenham.* **5 results** the marks or grades obtained in an examination. ~*vb* **6 result from** to be the outcome or consequence of: *poverty resulting from high unemployment.* **7 result in** to end in (a specified way): *negotiations which resulted in the Treaty of Paris.*

resultant *adj* **1** arising as a result: *the resultant publicity.* ~*n* **2** *Maths, physics* a single vector that is the vector sum of two or more other vectors, such as a force which results from two other forces acting on a single point.

resume *vb* **-suming, -sumed 1** to begin again or go on with (something interrupted). **2** to occupy again or recover: *he will resume his party posts today.*

résumé (**rezz**-yew-may) *n* **1** a short descriptive summary. **2** *US & Canad* a curriculum vitae.

resumption *n* the act of resuming or beginning again.

resurgence *n* a rising again to vigour: *worldwide religious resurgence.* **resurgent** *adj*

resurrect *vb* **1** to bring or be brought back to life from death. **2** to bring back into use or activity.

resurrection *n* **1** a return to life by a dead person. **2** revival or renewal. **3 the Resurrection a** *Christian theol* the rising again of Christ from the tomb three days after his death. **b** the rising again from the dead of all people at the Last Judgment.

resuscitate (ris-**suss**-it-tate) *vb* **-tating, -tated** to restore to consciousness. **resuscitation** *n*

retail *n* **1** the sale of goods individually or in small quantities to the public. ~*adj* **2** of or engaged in such selling: *auctioneers have been successful in cornering the retail market.* ~*adv* **3** in small amounts or at a retail price. ~*vb* **4** to sell or be sold in small quantities to the public. **5** to relate (gossip or scandal) in detail. **retailer** *n*

retain *vb* **1** to keep in one's possession. **2** to be able to hold or contain: *with this method the salmon retains its flavour and texture.* **3** *Law* to engage the services of (a barrister) by payment of a preliminary fee. **4** (of a person) to be able to remember (something) without difficulty. **5** to hold in position.

THESAURUS

newal, renovation, repair, revitalization, revival **2.** recovery, re-establishment, reinstallation, reinstatement, replacement, restitution, return

restore 1. fix, mend, rebuild, recondition, reconstruct, recover, refurbish, rehabilitate, renew, renovate, repair, retouch, set to rights, touch up **2.** bring back to health, build up, reanimate, refresh, rejuvenate, revitalize, revive, revivify, strengthen **3.** bring back, give back, hand back, recover, re-establish, reinstate, replace, retrocede, return, send back **4.** reconstitute, re-enforce, reimpose, reinstate, reintroduce

restrain 1. bridle, check, confine, constrain, contain, control, curb, curtail, debar, govern, hamper, handicap, harness, hinder, hold, hold back, inhibit, keep, keep under control, limit, muzzle, prevent, rein, repress, restrict, straiten, subdue, suppress **2.** arrest, bind, chain, confine, detain, fetter, hold, imprison, jail, lock up, manacle, pinion, tie up

restrained calm, controlled, mild, moderate, muted, reasonable, reticent, self-controlled, soft, steady, temperate, undemonstrative

restraint 1. coercion, command, compulsion, confines, constraint, control, curtailment, grip, hindrance, hold, inhibition, limitation, moderation, prevention, restriction, self-control, self-discipline, self-possession, self-restraint, suppression **2.** ban, boycott, bridle, check, curb, embargo, interdict, limit, limitation, rein, taboo

restrict bound, circumscribe, confine, contain, cramp, demarcate, hamper, handicap, hem in, impede, inhibit, keep within bounds *or* limits, limit, regulate, restrain, straiten

restriction check, condition, confinement, constraint, containment, control, curb, demarcation, handicap, inhibition, limitation, regulation, restraint, rule, stipulation

result *n.* **1.** conclusion, consequence, decision, development, effect, end, event, fruit, issue, outcome, product, reaction, sequel, termination, upshot ~*vb.* **2.** *with* **from** appear, arise, derive, develop, emanate, ensue, eventuate, flow, follow, happen, issue, spring, stem, turn out **3.** *with* **in** culminate, end, finish, pan out (*informal*), terminate, wind up

resume 1. begin again, carry on, continue, go on, proceed, recommence, reinstitute, reopen, restart, take up *or* pick up where one left off **2.** assume again, occupy again, reoccupy, take back, take up again

resumption carrying on, continuation, fresh outbreak, new beginning, re-establishment, renewal, reopening, restart, resurgence

resurrect 1. raise from the dead, restore to life, revive **2.** breathe new life into, bring back, reintroduce, renew, revive

resurrection comeback (*informal*), raising *or* rising from the dead, reappearance, rebirth, renaissance, renascence, renewal, restoration, resurgence, resuscitation, return, return from the dead, revival

resuscitate breathe new life into, bring round, bring to life, give artificial respiration to, give the kiss of life, quicken, reanimate, renew, rescue, restore, resurrect, revitalize, revive, revivify, save

retain 1. contain, detain, grasp, grip, hang *or* hold onto, hold, hold back, hold fast, keep, keep possession of, maintain, preserve, reserve, restrain, save **2.** com-

retainer *n* **1** a fee paid in advance to engage someone's services. **2** a reduced rent paid for a room or flat to reserve it for future use. **3** a servant who has been with a family for a long time.

retaining wall *n* a wall constructed to hold back earth, loose rock, etc.

retake *vb* **-taking, -took, -taken 1** to recapture: *to retake Jerusalem.* **2** to take something, such as an examination or vote, again. ~*n* **3** *Films* a rephotographed scene.

retaliate *vb* **-ating, -ated 1** to repay some injury or wrong in kind. **2** to cast (accusations) back upon a person. **retaliation** *n* **retaliatory** *adj*

retard *vb* to delay or slow down (the progress or development). **retardant** *n, adj* **retardation** *n*

retarded *adj* underdeveloped mentally.

retch *vb* **1** to undergo spasms of the stomach as if one is vomiting. ~*n* **2** an involuntary spasm of the stomach.

retention *n* **1** the act of retaining or state of being retained. **2** the capacity to remember. **3** *Pathol* the abnormal holding of something within the body, esp. fluid. **retentive** *adj*

rethink *vb* **-thinking, -thought 1** to think about (something) again with a view to changing one's tactics. ~*n* **2** the act or an instance of thinking again.

reticent *adj* not willing to say or tell much. **reticence** *n*

reticulate *adj* in the form of a network or having a network of parts: *a reticulate leaf.* **reticulation** *n*

retina *n, pl* **-nas** *or* **-nae** the light-sensitive inner lining of the back of the eyeball. **retinal** *adj*

retinue *n* a band of attendants accompanying an important person.

retire *vb* **-tiring, -tired 1** to give up or to cause (a person) to give up work, esp. on reaching pensionable age. **2** to go away into seclusion. **3** to go to bed. **4** to withdraw from a sporting contest, esp. because of injury. **5** to pull back (troops) from battle or (of troops) to fall back. **retired** *adj* **retirement** *n*

retirement pension *n* a regular payment made by the state or a former employee to a retired person over a specified age.

retiring *adj* very shy.

retort[1] *vb* **1** to reply quickly, wittily, or angrily. **2** to use (an argument) against its originator. ~*n* **3** a sharp, angry, or witty reply. **4** an argument used against its originator.

retort[2] *n* **1** a glass vessel with a long tapering neck that is bent down, used for distillation. **2** a vessel used for heating ores in the production of metals or heating coal to produce gas.

retouch *vb* to restore or improve (a painting or photograph) with new touches.

retrace *vb* **-tracing, -traced 1** to go back over (one's steps or a route). **2** to go over (a story) from the beginning.

retract *vb* **1** to withdraw (a statement, charge, etc.) as invalid or unjustified. **2** to go back on (a promise or agreement). **3** to draw in (a part or appendage): *the rear wheels are retracted for tight spaces.* **retraction** *n*

retractile *adj* capable of being drawn in: *the retractile claws of a cat.*

retrain *vb* to train to do a new or different job. **retraining** *n*

retread *vb* **-treading, -treaded 1** to bond a new tread onto (a worn tyre). ~*n* **2** a remoulded tyre.

retreat *vb* **1** *Mil* to withdraw or retire in the face of or from action with an enemy. **2** to retire or withdraw to seclusion or shelter. **3** to alter one's opinion about something. ~*n* **4** the act of retreating or withdrawing. **5** *Mil* **a** a withdrawal or retirement in the face of the enemy. **b** a bugle call signifying withdrawal or retirement. **6** a place to which one may retire, esp. for religious contemplation. **7** a period of seclusion, esp. for religious contemplation. **8** the act of altering one's opinion about something.

retrench *vb* to reduce expenditure. **retrenchment** *n*

retrial *n* a second trial of a defendant in a court of law.

retribution *n* punishment or vengeance for evil deeds. **retributive** *adj*

THESAURUS

mission, employ, engage, hire, pay, reserve **3.** bear in mind, impress on the memory, keep in mind, memorize, recall, recollect, remember

retainer 1. advance, deposit, fee **2.** attendant, dependant, domestic, flunky, footman, henchman, lackey, servant, supporter, valet, vassal

retaliate even the score, exact retribution, get back at, get even with (*informal*), get one's own back (*informal*), give as good as one gets (*informal*), give one a taste of one's own medicine, give tit for tat, hit back, make reprisal, pay one back in one's own coin, reciprocate, return like for like, strike back, take an eye for an eye, take revenge, wreak vengeance

retaliation an eye for an eye, a taste of one's own medicine, repayment, reprisal, requital, retribution, revenge, tit for tat, vengeance

retard arrest, brake, check, clog, decelerate, defer, delay, detain, encumber, handicap, hinder, hold back *or* up, impede, obstruct, set back, slow down, stall

reticence quietness, reserve, restraint, secretiveness, silence, taciturnity, uncommunicativeness, unforthcomingness

reticent close-mouthed, mum, quiet, reserved, restrained, secretive, silent, taciturn, tight-lipped, uncommunicative, unforthcoming, unspeaking

retire 1. be pensioned off, (be) put out to grass (*informal*), give up work, stop working **2.** absent oneself, betake oneself, depart, exit, go away, leave, remove, withdraw **3.** go to bed, go to one's room, go to sleep, hit the sack (*slang*), turn in (*informal*) **4.** fall back, give ground, give way, pull back, pull out, recede, retreat, withdraw

retirement loneliness, obscurity, privacy, retreat, seclusion, solitude, withdrawal

retiring bashful, coy, demure, diffident, humble, meek, modest, quiet, reclusive, reserved, reticent, self-effacing, shrinking, shy, timid, timorous, unassertive, unassuming

retract 1. cancel, deny, disavow, disclaim, disown, recall, recant, renege, renounce, repeal, repudiate, rescind, reverse, revoke, take back, unsay, withdraw **2.** back out of, go back on, renege on **3.** draw in, pull back, pull in, reel in, sheathe

retreat *vb.* **1.** back away, depart, draw back, ebb, fall back, give ground, go back, leave, pull back, recede, recoil, retire, shrink, turn tail, withdraw ~*n.* **2.** departure, ebb, evacuation, flight, retirement, withdrawal **3.** asylum, den, haunt, haven, hideaway, privacy, refuge, resort, sanctuary, seclusion, shelter

retrench curtail, cut, cut back, decrease, diminish, economize, husband, lessen, limit, make economies, pare, prune, reduce, save, tighten one's belt, trim

retrenchment contraction, cost-cutting, curtailment, cut, cutback, economy, pruning, reduction, rundown, tightening one's belt

retribution an eye for an eye, compensation, justice,

retrieve *vb* **-trieving, -trieved 1** to get or fetch back again. **2** to bring back to a more satisfactory state: *his attempt to retrieve the situation.* **3** to rescue or save. **4** to recover (stored information) from a computer system. **5** (of dogs) to find and fetch (shot birds and animals). **6** to remember. *~n* **7** the chance of being retrieved: *beyond retrieve.* **retrievable** *adj* **retrieval** *n*

retriever *n* a dog trained to retrieve shot birds and animals.

retro *adj* associated with or revived from the past: *swap sandals for heeled mules to complete the retro look.*

retro- *prefix* **1** back or backwards: *retroactive.* **2** located behind: *retrochoir.*

retroactive *adj* effective from a date in the past: *justice through retroactive legislation is never justice.*

retrograde *adj* **1** tending towards an earlier worse condition. **2** moving or bending backwards. **3** (esp. of order) reverse or inverse. *~vb* **-grading, -graded 4** to go backwards or deteriorate.

retrogress *vb* to go back to an earlier worse condition. **retrogression** *n* **retrogressive** *adj*

retrorocket *n* a small rocket on a larger rocket or a spacecraft, that produces thrust in the opposite direction to the direction of flight in order to slow down.

retrospect *n* **in retrospect** when looking back on the past.

retrospective *adj* **1** looking back in time. **2** applying from a date in the past: *retrospective legislation.* *~n* **3** an exhibition of an artist's life's work.

retroussé (rit-**troo**-say) *adj* (of a nose) turned upwards.

retsina *n* a Greek wine flavoured with resin.

return *vb* **1** to come back to a former place or state. **2** to give, put, or send back. **3** to repay with something of equivalent value: *she returned the compliment.* **4** *Sport* to hit, throw, or play (a ball) back. **5** to recur or reappear: *as he relaxed his appetite returned.* **6** to come back or revert in thought or speech: *let's return to what he said.* **7** to earn or yield (profit or interest). **8** to answer or reply. **9** to vote into office. **10** *Law* (of a jury) to deliver (a verdict). *~n* **11** the act or an instance of coming back. **12** the act of being returned. **13** replacement or restoration: *the return of law and order.* **14** something that is given or sent back. **15** *Sport* the act of playing or throwing a ball back. **16** a recurrence or reappearance: *the return of tuberculosis.* **17** the yield or profit from an investment or venture. **18** a statement of one's taxable income (a **tax return**). **19** an answer or reply. **20** *Brit, Austral, & NZ* short for **return ticket. 21 in return** in exchange. **22 returns** statement of the votes counted at an election. **23 by return (of post)** *Brit* by the next post back to the sender. **24 many happy returns (of the day)** a conventional birthday greeting. *~adj* **25** of or being a return: *the team is keen on a return match.* **returnable** *adj*

returned man *n Canad* a soldier who has served abroad. Also (Austral. and NZ): **returned soldier**

returning officer *n* an official in charge of conducting an election in a constituency.

return ticket *n Brit, Austral, & NZ* a ticket allowing a passenger to travel to a place and back.

reunify *vb* **-fies, -fying, -fied** to bring together again something previously divided. **reunification** *n*

reunion *n* **1** a gathering of people who have been apart. **2** the act of coming together again.

reunite *vb* **-niting, -nited** to bring or come together again after a separation.

reuse *n* **1** the act of using something again. *~vb* **-using, -used 2** to use again. **reusable** *adj*

rev *Informal ~n* **1** revolution per minute (of an engine). *~vb* **revving, revved 2** to increase the speed of revolution of (an engine).

rev. 1 revise(d). 2 revision.

Rev. Reverend.

revalue *vb* **-valuing, -valued** to adjust the exchange value of (a currency) upwards. **revaluation** *n*

revamp *vb* to patch up or renovate.

Revd. Reverend.

reveal *vb* **1** to disclose or divulge (a secret). **2** to expose to view or show (something concealed). **3** (of God) to disclose (divine truths).

revealing *adj* **1** disclosing information that one did not know: *she made several revealing remarks during the interview.* **2** (of clothes) showing more of the body than is usual.

reveille (riv-**val**-ee) *n* a signal given by a bugle or drum to awaken soldiers or sailors in the morning.

revel *vb* **-elling, -elled** *or US* **-eling, -eled 1 revel in** to take pleasure or wallow in: *he would revel in his victory.* **2** to take part in noisy festivities. *~n* **3 revels** noisy merrymaking. **reveller** *n*

revelation *n* **1** the act of making known a truth which was previously secret. **2** a fact newly made known. **3** a person or experience that proves to be different from expectations: *New York State could prove*

THESAURUS

Nemesis, punishment, reckoning, recompense, redress, repayment, reprisal, requital, retaliation, revenge, reward, satisfaction, vengeance

retrieve fetch back, get back, recall, recapture, recoup, recover, redeem, regain, repair, repossess, rescue, restore, salvage, save, win back

retrospect afterthought, hindsight, recollection, reexamination, remembrance, reminiscence, review, survey

return *vb.* **1.** come back, come round again, go back, reappear, rebound, recoil, recur, repair, retreat, revert, turn back **2.** carry back, convey, give back, put back, re-establish, reinstate, remit, render, replace, restore, send, send back, take back, transmit **3.** give back, pay back, reciprocate, recompense, refund, reimburse, repay, requite **4.** bring in, earn, make, net, repay, yield **5.** answer, come back (with), communicate, rejoin, reply, respond, retort **6.** choose, elect, pick, vote in **7.** announce, arrive at, bring in, come to, deliver, render, report, submit *~n.* **8.** homecoming, reappearance **9.** reestablishment, reinstatement, replacement, restoration **10.** reappearance, recrudescence, recurrence **11.** advantage, benefit, gain, income, interest, proceeds, profit, revenue, takings, yield **12.** compensation, earnings, income, profit, receipts, revenue, reward **13.** account, form, list, report, statement, summary **14.** answer, comeback (*informal*), rejoinder, reply, response, retort, riposte

reveal 1. announce, betray, blow wide open (*slang*), broadcast, communicate, disclose, divulge, give away, give out, impart, leak, let on, let out, let slip, make known, make public, proclaim, publish, tell **2.** bare, bring to light, display, exhibit, expose to view, lay bare, manifest, open, show, uncover, unearth, unmask, unveil

revel *vb.* **1.** *with* **in** bask, crow, delight, drool, gloat, indulge, joy, lap up, luxuriate, rejoice, relish, savour, take pleasure, thrive on, wallow **2.** carouse, celebrate, go on a spree, live it up (*informal*), make merry, paint the town red (*informal*), push the boat out (*Brit. informal*), rave (*Brit. slang*), roister, whoop it up (*informal*) *~n.* **3.** *often plural* beano (*Brit. slang*), carousal,

a *revelation to first-time visitors.* **4** *Christianity* God's disclosure of his own nature and his purpose for mankind.

Revelation *or* **Revelations** *n Informal* the last book of the New Testament, containing visionary descriptions of heaven, and of the end of the world.

revelry *n, pl* **-ries** noisy or unrestrained merrymaking.

revenge *n* **1** vengeance for wrongs or injury received. **2** something done as a means of vengeance. *~vb* **-venging, -venged 3** to inflict equivalent injury or damage for (injury received). **4** to take vengeance for (oneself or another). **revengeful** *adj*

revenue *n* **1** income, esp. that obtained by a government from taxation. **2** a government department responsible for collecting taxes.

reverberate *vb* **-ating, -ated 1** to resound or re-echo. **2** to reflect or be reflected many times. **reverberation** *n*

revere *vb* **-vering, -vered** to be in awe of and respect deeply.

reverence *n* profound respect. **reverential** *adj*

Reverence *n* **Your** *or* **His Reverence** a title sometimes used for a Roman Catholic priest.

reverend *adj* **1** worthy of reverence. **2** relating to or designating a clergyman. *~n* **3** *Informal* a clergyman.

Reverend *adj* a title of respect for a clergyman.

reverent *adj* feeling or expressing reverence.

reverie *n* absent-minded daydream.

revers (riv-**veer**) *n, pl* **-vers** the turned-back lining of part of a garment, such as the lapel or cuff.

reverse *vb* **-versing, -versed 1** to turn or set in an opposite direction, order, or position. **2** to change into something different or contrary: *the cabinet intends to reverse the trend of recent polls.* **3** to move backwards or in an opposite direction: *as he started to reverse the car, the bomb exploded.* **4** to run (machinery) in the opposite direction to normal. **5** to turn inside out. **6** *Law* to revoke or set aside (a judgment or decree). **7** **reverse the charges** to make a telephone call at the recipient's expense. *~n* **8** the opposite or contrary of something. **9** the back or rear side of something. **10** a change to an opposite position, state, or direction. **11** a change for the worse. **12** the gear by which a motor vehicle can be made to go backwards. **13** the side of a coin bearing a secondary design. **14** **in reverse** in an opposite or backward direction. **15** **the reverse of** not at all: *the result was the reverse of his expectations.* *~adj* **16** opposite or contrary in direction, position, etc. **17** denoting the gear by which a motor vehicle can be made to go backwards. **reversal** *n*

reversible *adj* **1** capable of being reversed: *the effect of the operation may not be reversible.* **2** (of a garment) made so that either side may be used as the outer side.

reversing lights *pl n* a pair of lights on the rear of a motor vehicle that go on when the vehicle is moving backwards.

reversion *n* **1** a return to an earlier condition, practice, or belief. **2** *Biol* the return of individuals or organs to a more primitive condition or type. **3** the rightful passing of property to the owner or designated heir.

revert *vb* **1** to go back to a former state. **2** *Biol* (of individuals or organs) to return to a more primitive, earlier, or simpler condition or type. **3** to come back to a subject. **4** *Property law* (of an estate) to return to its former owner.

review *n* **1** a critical assessment of a book, film, etc. **2** a publication containing such articles. **3** a general survey or report: *the new curriculum is to be set up a year after the conclusions of the review are due.* **4** a formal or official inspection. **5** the act or an instance of reviewing. **6** a second consideration; re-examination. **7** a retrospective survey. **8** *Law* a re-examination of a case. *~vb* **9** to hold or write a review of. **10** to examine again: *the committee will review the ban in the summer.* **11** to look back upon (a period of time or sequence of events): *he reviewed his achievements with pride.* **12** to inspect formally or officially: *when he*

THESAURUS

celebration, debauch, festivity, gala, jollification, merrymaking, party, rave-up (*Brit. slang*), saturnalia, spree

revelation announcement, betrayal, broadcasting, communication, disclosure, discovery, display, exhibition, exposé, exposition, exposure, giveaway, leak, manifestation, news, proclamation, publication, telling, uncovering, unearthing, unveiling

reveller carouser, celebrator, merrymaker, partygoer, pleasure-seeker, roisterer

revelry beano (*Brit. slang*), carousal, carousing, celebration, debauch, debauchery, festivity, fun, jollification, jollity, merrymaking, party, rave-up (*Brit. slang*), roistering, saturnalia, spree

revenge **1.** *n.* an eye for an eye, reprisal, requital, retaliation, retribution, satisfaction, vengeance, vindictiveness **2.** *vb.* avenge, even the score for, get one's own back for (*informal*), hit back, make reprisal for, repay, requite, retaliate, take an eye for an eye for, take revenge for, vindicate

revenue gain, income, interest, proceeds, profits, receipts, returns, rewards, takings, yield

reverberate echo, rebound, recoil, re-echo, resound, ring, vibrate

revere adore, be in awe of, defer to, exalt, have a high opinion of, honour, look up to, put on a pedestal, respect, reverence, think highly of, venerate, worship

reverence admiration, adoration, awe, deference, devotion, high esteem, homage, honour, respect, veneration, worship

reverent adoring, awed, decorous, deferential, devout, humble, loving, meek, pious, respectful, reverential, solemn, submissive

reverse *vb.* **1.** invert, transpose, turn back, turn over, turn round, turn upside down, upend **2.** alter, annul, cancel, change, countermand, declare null and void, invalidate, negate, overrule, overset, overthrow, overturn, quash, repeal, rescind, retract, revoke, set aside, undo, upset **3.** back, backtrack, back up, go backwards, move backwards, retreat *~n.* **4.** antithesis, contradiction, contrary, converse, inverse, opposite **5.** back, flip side, other side, rear, underside, verso, wrong side **6.** adversity, affliction, blow, check, defeat, disappointment, failure, hardship, misadventure, misfortune, mishap, repulse, reversal, setback, trial, vicissitude *~adj.* **7.** back to front, backward, contrary, converse, inverse, inverted, opposite

revert backslide, come back, go back, hark back, lapse, recur, regress, relapse, resume, return, take up where one left off

review *n.* **1.** commentary, critical assessment, criticism, critique, evaluation, judgment, notice, study **2.** journal, magazine, periodical **3.** analysis, examination, perusal, report, scrutiny, study, survey **4.** another look, fresh look, reassessment, recapitulation, reconsideration, re-evaluation, re-examination, rethink, retrospect, revision, second look *~vb.* **5.** assess, criticize, discuss, evaluate, examine, give one's opinion of, inspect, judge, read through, scrutinize, study, weigh, write a critique of **6.** go over again, look at again, reassess, recapitulate, reconsider, re-evaluate, re-examine,

reviewed the troops they cheered him. **13** *Law* to re-examine (a decision) judicially.

reviewer *n* a person who writes reviews of books, films, etc.

revile *vb* **-viling, -viled** to be abusively scornful of: *his works were reviled and admired in equal measure.*

revise *vb* **-vising, -vised 1** to change or alter: *he grudgingly revised his opinion.* **2** to prepare a new edition of (a previously printed work). **3** to read (something) several times in order to learn it in preparation for an examination.

Revised Version *n* a revision of the Authorized Version of the Bible published between 1881 and 1885.

revision *n* **1** the act or process of revising. **2** a corrected or new version of a book, article, etc.

revisionism *n* **1** (in Marxist ideology) any dangerous departure from the true interpretation of Marx's teachings. **2** the advocacy of revision of some political theory. **revisionist** *n, adj*

revisory *adj* of or having the power of revision.

revitalize *or* **-ise** *vb* **-izing, -ized** *or* **-ising, -ised** to make more lively or active.

revival *n* **1** a reviving or being revived. **2** a reawakening of religious faith. **3** a new production of a play that has not been recently performed. **4** a renewed use or interest in: *there has been an Art Deco revival.*

revivalism *n* a movement that seeks to revive religious faith. **revivalist** *n, adj*

revive *vb* **-viving, -vived 1** to make or become lively or active again. **2** to bring or be brought back to life, consciousness, or strength: *revived by a drop of whisky.* **3** *Theatre* to put on a new production of (an old play).

revivify *vb* **-fies, -fying, -fied** to give new life to. **revivification** *n*

revoke *vb* **-voking, -voked 1** to take back or cancel (an agreement, will, etc.). **2** *Cards* to break a rule by failing to follow suit when able to do so. *~n* **3** *Cards* the act of revoking. **revocation** *n*

revolt *n* **1** a rebellion or uprising against authority. **2 in revolt** in the state of rebelling. *~vb* **3** to rise up in rebellion against authority. **4** to cause to feel disgust.

revolting *adj* horrible and disgusting.

revolution *n* **1** the overthrow of a regime or political system by the governed. **2** (in Marxist theory) the transition from one system of production in a society to the next. **3** a far-reaching and drastic change. **4 a** movement in or as if in a circle. **b** one complete turn in a circle: *33 revolutions per minute.*

revolutionary *adj* **1** of or like a revolution. **2** advocating or engaged in revolution. **3** radically new or different: *they have designed revolutionary new materials to build power stations.* *~n, pl* **-aries 4** a person who advocates or engages in revolution.

revolutionize *or* **-ise** *vb* **-izing, -ized** *or* **-ising, -ised** to bring about a radical change in.

revolve *vb* **-volving, -volved 1** to move or cause to move around a centre. **2 revolve around** to be centred or focused upon: *the campaign revolves around one man.* **3** to occur periodically or in cycles. **4** to consider or be considered. **revolvable** *adj*

revolver *n* a pistol with a revolving cylinder that allows several shots to be fired without reloading.

revolving door *n* a door with four leaves at right angles to each other, revolving about a vertical axis.

revue *n* a theatrical entertainment with topical sketches and songs.

revulsion *n* a violent feeling of disgust.

reward *n* **1** something given in return for a service. **2** a sum of money offered for finding a criminal or missing property. **3** something received in return for good or evil: *sacrifice provided its own reward.* *~vb* **4** to give something to (someone) for a service rendered.

THESAURUS

rethink, revise, run over, take another look at, think over **7.** call to mind, look back on, recall, recollect, reflect on, remember, summon up

reviewer commentator, critic, essayist, judge

revise 1. alter, amend, change, correct, edit, emend, modify, reconsider, redo, re-examine, revamp, review, rework, rewrite, update **2.** go over, memorize, reread, run through, study, swot up (*Brit. informal*)

revision 1. homework, memorizing, rereading, studying, swotting (*Brit. informal*) **2.** alteration, amendment, change, correction, editing, emendation, modification, re-examination, review, rewriting, updating

revival awakening, quickening, reanimation, reawakening, rebirth, recrudescence, refreshment, renaissance, renascence, renewal, restoration, resurgence, resurrection, resuscitation, revitalization, revivification

revive animate, awaken, breathe new life into, bring back to life, bring round, cheer, come round, comfort, invigorate, quicken, rally, reanimate, recover, refresh, rekindle, renew, renovate, restore, resuscitate, revitalize, rouse, spring up again

revoke abolish, abrogate, annul, call back, cancel, countermand, declare null and void, disclaim, invalidate, negate, nullify, quash, recall, recant, renege, renounce, repeal, repudiate, rescind, retract, reverse, set aside, take back, withdraw

revolt *n.* **1.** defection, insurgency, insurrection, mutiny, putsch, rebellion, revolution, rising, sedition, uprising *~vb.* **2.** defect, mutiny, rebel, resist, rise, take to the streets, take up arms (against) **3.** disgust, give one the creeps (*informal*), make one's flesh creep, nauseate, offend, repel, repulse, shock, sicken, turn off (*informal*), turn one's stomach

revolting abhorrent, abominable, appalling, disgusting, distasteful, foul, horrible, horrid, loathsome, nasty, nauseating, nauseous, noisome, obnoxious, obscene, offensive, repellent, repugnant, repulsive, shocking, sickening

revolution *n.* **1.** insurgency, mutiny, rebellion, revolt, rising, uprising **2.** drastic *or* radical change, innovation, metamorphosis, reformation, sea change, shift, transformation, upheaval **3.** circle, circuit, cycle, gyration, lap, orbit, rotation, round, spin, turn, wheel, whirl

revolutionary *adj.* **1.** extremist, insurgent, insurrectionary, mutinous, radical, rebel, seditious, subversive **2.** avant-garde, different, drastic, experimental, fundamental, ground-breaking, innovative, new, novel, progressive, radical, thoroughgoing *~n.* **3.** insurgent, insurrectionary, insurrectionist, mutineer, rebel, revolutionist

revolve 1. circle, go round, gyrate, orbit, rotate, spin, turn, twist, wheel, whirl **2.** consider, deliberate, meditate, mull over, ponder, reflect, ruminate, study, think about, think over, turn over (in one's mind)

revulsion abhorrence, abomination, aversion, detestation, disgust, distaste, loathing, odium, recoil, repugnance, repulsion

reward *n.* **1.** benefit, bonus, bounty, compensation, gain, honour, merit, payment, premium, prize, profit, recompense, remuneration, repayment, requital, return, wages **2.** comeuppance (*slang*), desert, just deserts, punishment, requital, retribution *~vb.* **3.** compensate, honour, make it worth one's while, pay, recompense, remunerate, repay, requite

rewarding *adj* giving personal satisfaction: *my most professionally rewarding experience.*

rewarewa (ray-wa-**ray**-wa) *n* a tall New Zealand tree with reddish wood.

rewind *vb* **-winding, -wound** to run (a tape or film) back to an earlier point in order to replay.

rewire *vb* **-wiring, -wired** to provide (a house, engine, etc.) with new wiring.

reword *vb* to alter the wording of.

rework *vb* to improve or bring up to date: *they need to rework the system.* **reworking** *n*

rewrite *vb* **-writing, -wrote, -written 1** to write again in a different way. *~n* **2** something rewritten.

Rex *n* king: now used chiefly in documents and inscriptions.

Rf *US chem* rutherfordium.

RFC Rugby Football Club.

RGN Registered General Nurse.

Rh 1 *Chem* rhodium. **2** See **Rh factor.**

rhapsodize *or* **-dise** *vb* **-dizing, -dized** *or* **-dising, -dised** to speak or write with extravagant enthusiasm.

rhapsody *n, pl* **-dies 1** *Music* a freely structured and emotional piece of music. **2** an expression of ecstatic enthusiasm. **rhapsodic** *adj*

rhea (**ree**-a) *n* a large fast-running flightless bird of South America, similar to the ostrich.

rhenium *n Chem* a silvery-white metallic element with a high melting point. Symbol: Re

rheostat *n* a variable resistor in an electrical circuit, such as one used to dim lights. **rheostatic** *adj*

rhesus factor (**ree**-suss) *n* See **Rh factor.**

rhesus monkey *n* a small long-tailed monkey of S Asia.

rhetoric (**ret**-a-rik) *n* **1** the art of using speech or writing to persuade or influence. **2** artificial or exaggerated language: *there's been no shortage of soaring rhetoric at this summit.* **rhetorical** (rit-**tor**-ik-kl) *adj*

rhetorical question *n* a question to which no answer is required, used for dramatic effect, for example *who knows?*

rheum (**room**) *n* a watery discharge from the eyes or nose. **rheumy** *adj*

rheumatic *adj* **1** caused by or affected by rheumatism. *~n* **2** a person suffering from rheumatism. **rheumatically** *adv*

rheumatic fever *n* a disease with inflammation and pain in the joints.

rheumatics *n Informal* rheumatism.

rheumatism *n* any painful disorder of joints, muscles, or connective tissue.

rheumatoid *adj* (of symptoms) resembling rheumatism.

rheumatoid arthritis *n* a chronic disease causing painful swelling of the joints.

Rh factor *n* an antigen commonly found in human blood: the terms **Rh positive** and **Rh negative** are used to indicate its presence or absence.

rhinestone *n* an imitation diamond made of glass.

rhino *n, pl* **-nos** *or* **-no** a rhinoceros.

rhinoceros *n, pl* **-oses** *or* **-os** a large plant-eating mammal of SE Asia and Africa with one or two horns on the nose and a very thick skin.

rhizome *n* a thick horizontal underground stem whose buds develop into new plants.

rhodium *n Chem* a hard silvery-white metallic element, used to harden platinum and palladium. Symbol: Rh

rhododendron *n* an evergreen shrub with clusters of showy flowers.

rhombohedron (rom-boh-**heed**-ron) *n, pl* **-drons** *or* **-dra** (-dra) a six-sided prism whose sides are parallelograms.

rhomboid *n* **1** a parallelogram with adjacent sides of unequal length. It resembles a rectangle but does not have 90° angles. *~adj also* **rhomboidal 2** having such a shape.

rhombus (**rom**-buss) *n, pl* **-buses** *or* **-bi** (-bye) a parallelogram with sides of equal length but no right angles. **rhombic** *adj*

rhubarb *n* **1** a large-leaved plant with long green and red stalks which can be cooked and eaten. **2** a related plant of central Asia, whose root can be dried and used as a laxative or astringent. *~interj, n* **3** the noise made by actors to simulate conversation, esp. by repeating the word *rhubarb.*

rhyme *n* **1** sameness of the final sounds in lines of verse or in words. **2** a word that is identical to another in its final sound: "*while*" *is a rhyme for* "*mile*". **3** a piece of poetry with corresponding sounds at the ends of the lines. **4 rhyme or reason** sense or meaning. *~vb* **rhyming, rhymed 5** (of a word) to form a rhyme with another word. **6** to compose (verse) in a metrical structure.

rhymester *n* a mediocre poet.

rhyming slang *n* slang in which a word is replaced by another word or phrase that rhymes with it, e.g. *apples and pears* meaning *stairs.*

rhythm *n* **1** any regular movement or beat: *the side-effects can cause changes in the rhythm of the heart beat.* **2** any regular pattern that occurs over a period of time: *the seasonal rhythm of the agricultural year.* **3 a** the arrangement of the durations of and stress on the notes of a piece of music, usually laid out in regular groups (**bars**) of beats. **b** any specific arrangement of such groupings: *waltz rhythm.* **4** (in poetry) the arrangement of words to form a regular pattern of stresses. **rhythmical** *or* **rhythmic** *adj* **rhythmically** *adv*

rhythm and blues *n* a kind of popular music of Black American origin, derived from and influenced by the blues.

rhythm method *n* a method of contraception in which intercourse is avoided at times when conception is most likely.

RI Rhode Island.

rialto *n, pl* **-tos** a market or exchange.

rib[1] *n* **1** one of the curved bones forming the framework of the upper part of the body and attached to the spinal column. **2** a cut of meat including one or more ribs. **3** a curved supporting part, such as in the hull of

THESAURUS

rewarding advantageous, beneficial, economic, edifying, enriching, fruitful, fulfilling, gainful, gratifying, pleasing, productive, profitable, remunerative, satisfying, valuable, worthwhile

rhetoric 1. eloquence, oratory **2.** bombast, fustian, grandiloquence, hot air (*informal*), hyperbole, magniloquence, pomposity, rant, verbosity, wordiness

rhetorical 1. linguistic, oratorical, stylistic, verbal **2.** bombastic, declamatory, flamboyant, flashy, florid, flowery, grandiloquent, high-flown, high-sounding, hyperbolic, magniloquent, oratorical, pompous, pretentious, showy, silver-tongued, verbose, windy

rhyme *n.* **1.** ode, poem, poetry, song, verse **2. rhyme or reason** logic, meaning, method, plan, sense *~vb.* **3.** chime, harmonize, sound like

rhythm accent, beat, cadence, flow, lilt, measure (*Prosody*), metre, movement, pattern, periodicity, pulse, swing, tempo, time

a boat. **4** one of a series of raised rows in knitted fabric. *~vb* **ribbing, ribbed 5** to provide or support with ribs. **6** to knit to form a rib pattern. **ribbed** *adj*

rib[2] *vb* **ribbing, ribbed** *Informal* to tease or ridicule. **ribbing** *n*

RIBA Royal Institute of British Architects.

ribald *adj* coarse or obscene in a humorous or mocking way. **ribaldry** *n*

riband *or* **ribband** *n* a ribbon awarded for some achievement.

ribbing *n* **1** a pattern of ribs in knitted material. **2** a framework or structure of ribs.

ribbon *n* **1** a narrow strip of fine material used for trimming, tying, etc. **2** a long narrow strip of inked cloth or plastic used to produce print in a typewriter. **3** a small strip of coloured cloth worn as a badge or as a symbol of an award. **4** a long thin strip: *a ribbon of white water.* **5 ribbons** ragged strips or shreds: *his clothes were torn to ribbons; his credibility was shot to ribbons.*

ribbon development *n Brit* the building of houses along a main road.

ribbonwood *n* a small evergreen tree of New Zealand.

ribcage *n* the bony structure formed by the ribs that encloses the lungs.

riboflavin (rye-boe-**flay**-vin) *n* a vitamin of the B complex that occurs in green vegetables, milk, fish, eggs, liver, and kidney: used as a yellow or orange food colouring (**E101**). Also called: **vitamin** $\mathbf{B_2}$

ribonucleic acid *n* the full name of **RNA.**

rice *n* **1** the edible grain of an erect grass that grows on wet ground in warm climates. *~vb* **ricing, riced 2** *US & Canad* to sieve (potatoes or other vegetables) to a coarse mashed consistency.

rice paper *n* **1** a thin edible paper made from rice straw. **2** a thin Chinese paper made from the rice-paper plant, the pith of which is flattened into sheets.

rich *adj* **1** owning a lot of money or property. **2** well supplied (with a desirable substance or quality): *a country rich with cultural interest.* **3** having an abundance of natural resources, minerals, etc.: *a land rich in unexploited minerals.* **4** producing abundantly: *the island is a blend of hilly moorland and rich farmland.* **5** luxuriant or prolific: *the meadows rich with corn.* **6** (of food) containing much fat or sugar. **7** having a full-bodied flavour: *a gloriously rich Cabernet-dominated wine.* **8** (of colour) intense or vivid: *her hair had a rich auburn tint.* **9** (of sound or a voice) full or resonant. **10** very amusing or ridiculous: *a rich joke.* **11** (of a fuel-air mixture) containing a relatively high proportion of fuel. **richness** *n*

riches *pl n* valuable possessions or desirable substances: *the unexpected riches of Georgian culture.*

richly *adv* **1** in a rich or elaborate manner: *the rooms are richly decorated with a variety of classical motifs.* **2** fully and appropriately: *he left the field to a richly deserved standing ovation.*

Richter scale *n* a scale for expressing the intensity of an earthquake, ranging from 0 to over 8.

rick[1] *n* a large stack of hay or straw.

rick[2] *vb* **1** to wrench or sprain (a joint). *~n* **2** a wrench or sprain of a joint.

rickets *n* a disease of children, caused by a deficiency of vitamin D and characterized by softening of developing bone, and hence bow legs.

rickety *adj* **1** likely to collapse or break: *a rickety wooden table.* **2** resembling or afflicted with rickets. **ricketiness** *n*

rickrack *or* **ricrac** *n* a zigzag braid used for trimming.

rickshaw *or* **ricksha** *n* **1** a small two-wheeled passenger vehicle pulled by one or two people, used in parts of Asia. **2** a similar vehicle with three wheels, propelled by a person pedalling.

ricochet (**rik**-osh-ay) *vb* **-cheting, -cheted** *or* **-chetting, -chetted 1** (of a bullet) to rebound from a surface. *~n* **2** the motion or sound of a rebounding bullet.

ricotta *n* a soft white unsalted Italian cheese made from sheep's milk.

rid *vb* **ridding, rid** *or* **ridded 1 rid of** to relieve (oneself) or make a place free of (something undesirable). **2 get rid of** to relieve or free oneself of (something undesirable).

riddance *n* **good riddance** relief at getting rid of someone or something.

ridden *vb* **1** the past participle of **ride.** *~adj* **2** afflicted or affected by the thing specified: *the police found three bullet-ridden bodies.*

riddle[1] *n* **1** a question, puzzle, or verse phrased so that ingenuity is required to find the answer or meaning. **2** a puzzling person or thing. *~vb* **-dling, -dled 3** to speak in riddles.

riddle[2] *vb* **-dling, -dled 1** to pierce with many holes. **2** to put through a sieve. *~n* **3** a coarse sieve.

riddled *adj* **riddled with** full of (something undesirable): *riddled with mistakes.*

ride *vb* **riding, rode, ridden 1** to sit on and control the movements of (a horse or other animal). **2** to sit on and propel (a bicycle or motorcycle). **3** to travel on or in a vehicle: *he rides around in a chauffeur-driven Rolls-Royce.* **4** to travel over: *they rode the country-*

THESAURUS

rhythmic, rhythmical cadenced, flowing, harmonious, lilting, melodious, metrical, musical, periodic, pulsating, throbbing

ribald bawdy, blue, broad, coarse, earthy, filthy, gross, indecent, licentious, naughty, near the knuckle (*informal*), obscene, off colour, Rabelaisian, racy, raunchy (*slang*), risqué, rude, scurrilous, smutty, vulgar

rich 1. affluent, filthy rich, flush (*informal*), loaded (*slang*), made of money (*informal*), moneyed, opulent, propertied, prosperous, rolling (*slang*), stinking rich (*informal*), wealthy, well-heeled (*informal*), well-off, well-to-do **2.** abounding, full, productive, well-endowed, well-provided, well-stocked, well-supplied **3.** abounding, abundant, ample, copious, exuberant, fecund, fertile, fruitful, full, lush, luxurious, plenteous, plentiful, productive, prolific **4.** creamy, delicious, fatty, flavoursome, full-bodied, heavy, highly-flavoured, juicy, luscious, savoury, spicy, succulent, sweet, tasty **5.** bright, deep, gay, intense, strong, vibrant, vivid, warm **6.** deep, dulcet, full, mellifluous, mellow, resonant **7.** amusing, comical, funny, hilarious, humorous, laughable, ludicrous, ridiculous, risible, side-splitting

riches abundance, affluence, assets, fortune, gold, money, opulence, plenty, property, resources, richness, substance, treasure, wealth

richly 1. elaborately, elegantly, expensively, exquisitely, gorgeously, lavishly, luxuriously, opulently, palatially, splendidly, sumptuously **2.** amply, appropriately, fully, in full measure, properly, suitably, thoroughly, well

rid 1. clear, deliver, disabuse, disburden, disembarrass, disencumber, free, lighten, make free, purge, relieve, unburden **2. get rid of** dispense with, dispose of, do away with, dump, eject, eliminate, expel, give the bum's rush (*slang*), jettison, remove, shake off, throw away *or* out, unload, weed out

side in search of shelter. **5** to travel through or be carried across (sea, sky, etc.): *the moon was riding high.* **6** *US & Canad* to cause to be carried: *to ride someone out of town.* **7** (of a vessel) to lie at anchor. **8** to tyrannize over or dominate: *politicians must stop riding roughshod over voters' wishes.* **9 be riding on** to be dependent on (something) for success: *a lot is riding on the profits of the film.* **10** *Informal* to continue undisturbed: *let it ride.* **11 riding high** popular and successful. ~*n* **12** a journey on a bicycle, on horseback, or in a vehicle. **13** transport in a vehicle: *most of us have been told not to accept rides from strangers.* **14** the type of movement experienced in a vehicle: *a bumpy ride.* **15** a path for riding on horseback. **16 take for a ride** *Informal* to cheat or deceive.

ride out *vb* to survive (a period of difficulty or danger) successfully.

rider *n* **1** a person who rides. **2** an extra clause or condition added to a document.

ride up *vb* (of a garment) to move up from the proper position.

ridge *n* **1** a long narrow raised land formation with sloping sides. **2** a long narrow raised strip on a flat surface. **3** the top of a roof where the two sloping sides meet. **4** *Meteorol* an elongated area of high pressure. **ridged** *adj* **ridgy** *adj*

ridgepole *n* **1** a timber along the ridge of a roof, to which the rafters are attached. **2** the horizontal pole at the apex of a tent.

ridicule *n* **1** language or behaviour intended to humiliate or mock. ~*vb* **-culing, -culed 2** to make fun of or mock.

ridiculous *adj* worthy of or causing ridicule.

riding[1] *n* the art or practice of horsemanship.

riding[2] *n* **1 Riding** any of the three former administrative divisions of Yorkshire: North Riding, East Riding, and West Riding. **2** *Canad* an electoral constituency.

riding crop *n* a short whip with a handle at one end for opening gates.

riesling *n* a medium-dry white wine.

rife *adj* **1** widespread or common. **2 rife with** full of: *the media is rife with speculation.*

riff *n Jazz, rock* a short repeated melodic figure used as an introduction or accompaniment.

riffle *vb* **-fling, -fled 1** to flick through (papers or pages) quickly: *I riffled through the rest of the memos.* ~*n* **2** *US & Canad* **a** a rapid in a stream. **b** a rocky shoal causing a rapid. **c** a ripple on water. **3** a riffling.

riffraff *n* worthless or disreputable people.

rifle[1] *n* **1** a firearm having a long barrel with a spirally grooved interior, which gives the bullet a spinning motion and thus greater accuracy over a longer range. **2 Rifles** a unit of soldiers equipped with rifles: *the Burma Rifles.* ~*vb* **-fling, -fled 3** to cut spiral grooves inside the barrel of (a gun). **rifled** *adj*

rifle[2] *vb* **-fling, -fled 1** to search (a house or safe) and steal from it. **2** to steal and carry off: *he rifled whatever valuables he could lay his hands on.*

rift *n* **1** a break in friendly relations between people or groups of people. **2** a gap or space made by splitting.

rift valley *n* a long narrow valley resulting from the subsidence of land between two faults.

rig *vb* **rigging, rigged 1** to arrange in a dishonest way, for profit or advantage: *he claimed that the poll was rigged.* **2** to set up or prepare (something) hastily ready for use. **3** *Naut* to equip (a vessel or mast) with (sails or rigging). ~*n* **4** an apparatus for drilling for oil and gas. **5** *Naut* the arrangement of the sails and masts of a vessel. **6** apparatus or equipment. **7** *Informal* an outfit of clothes. **8** *US & Canad* an articulated lorry. ~See also **rig out, rig up.**

-rigged *adj* (of a sailing vessel) having a rig of a certain kind: *a square-rigged ship.*

rigging *n* the ropes and cables supporting a ship's masts and sails.

right *adj* **1** morally or legally acceptable or correct: *his conduct seemed reasonable, even right.* **2** correct or true: *the customer is always right.* **3** appropriate, suitable, or proper: *there were problems involved in finding the right candidate.* **4** most favourable or convenient: *she waited until the right moment to broach the subject.* **5** in a satisfactory condition: *things are right again now.* **6** accurate: *is that clock right?* **7** correct in opinion or judgment. **8** sound in mind or body. **9** of or on the side of something or someone that faces east when the front is turned towards the north. **10** conservative or reactionary: *it was alleged he was an agent of the right wing.* **11** *Geom* formed by or containing a line or plane perpendicular to another line or plane: *a right angle.* **12** of or on the side of cloth worn or facing outwards. **13 in one's right mind** sane. **14 she'll be right** *Austral & NZ informal* that's all right; not to worry. **15 the right side of a** in favour with: *you'd better stay on the right side of him.* **b** younger than: *he's still on the right side of fifty.* **16 too right** *Informal* an exclamation of agreement. ~*adv* **17** correctly: *if we change the structure of local government we must do it right.* **18** in the appropriate manner: *do it right next time!* **19** straight or directly: *let's go right to bed.* **20** in the direction of the east from the point of view of a person or thing facing north. **21** all the way: *he drove right up to the gate.* **22** without delay: *I'll be right over.* **23** exactly or precisely: *right here.* **24** fittingly: *it serves him right.* **25** to good or favourable advantage: *it all came out right in the end.* ~*n* **26** a freedom or power that is morally or legally due to a person: *the defendant had an absolute right to a fair trial.* **27** anything that accords with the principles of legal or moral justice. **28 in the right** the state of being in accordance with reason or truth. **29** the right side, direction, or part: *the right of the army.* **30 the Right** the supporters or advocates of conservatism or reaction:

THESAURUS

riddle brain-teaser (*informal*), conundrum, enigma, mystery, poser, problem, puzzle, teaser

ride *vb.* **1.** control, handle, manage, sit on **2.** be borne (carried, supported), float, go, journey, move, progress, sit, travel **3.** dominate, enslave, grip, haunt, oppress, tyrannize over ~*n.* **4.** drive, jaunt, journey, lift, outing, spin (*informal*), trip, whirl (*informal*)

ridicule 1. *n.* banter, chaff, derision, gibe, irony, jeer, laughter, mockery, raillery, sarcasm, satire, scorn, sneer, taunting **2.** *vb.* banter, caricature, chaff, deride, humiliate, jeer, lampoon, laugh at, laugh out of court, laugh to scorn, make a fool of, make fun of, make one a laughing stock, mock, parody, poke fun at, pooh-pooh, satirize, scoff, send up (*Brit. informal*), sneer, take the mickey out of (*informal*), take the piss (out of) (*taboo slang*), taunt

ridiculous absurd, comical, contemptible, derisory, farcical, foolish, funny, hilarious, inane, incredible, laughable, ludicrous, nonsensical, outrageous, preposterous, risible, silly, stupid, unbelievable

rifle *vb.* burgle, despoil, go through, gut, loot, pillage, plunder, ransack, rob, rummage, sack, strip

rift 1. alienation, breach, difference, disagreement, division, estrangement, falling out (*informal*), quarrel, schism, separation, split **2.** breach, break, chink, cleavage, cleft, crack, cranny, crevice, fault, fissure, flaw, fracture, gap, opening, space, split

rig *vb.* **1.** arrange, doctor, engineer, fake, falsify, fiddle

the rise of the far Right in France. **31** *Boxing* a punch with the right hand. **32 rights** *Finance* the privilege of a company's shareholders to subscribe for new issues of the company's shares on advantageous terms. **33 by right** *or* **rights** properly: *by rights he should have won.* **34 in one's own right** having a claim or title oneself rather than through marriage or other connection. **35 to rights** consistent with justice or orderly arrangement: *he put the matter to rights.* ~*vb* **36** to bring or come back to a normal or correct state. **37** to bring or come back to a vertical position: *he slipped and righted himself at once.* **38** to compensate for or redress: *there is a wrong to be righted.* **39** to make (something) accord with truth or facts. ~*interj* **40** an expression of agreement or compliance.

right angle *n* **1** an angle of 90° or $\pi/2$ radians. **2 at right angles** perpendicular or perpendicularly. **right-angled** *adj*

right-angled triangle *n* a triangle with one angle which is a right angle.

right away *adv* without delay.

righteous (**rye**-chuss) *adj* **1** moral, just, or virtuous: *the lieutenant was a righteous cop.* **2** morally justifiable or right: *her eyes were blazing with righteous indignation.* **righteousness** *n*

rightful *adj* **1** in accordance with what is right. **2** having a legally or morally just claim: *he is the rightful heir to her fortune.* **3** held by virtue of a legal or just claim: *these moves will restore them to their rightful homes.* **rightfully** *adv*

right-hand *adj* **1** of, on, or towards the right: *in the top right-hand corner.* **2** for the right hand. **3 right-hand man** a person's most valuable assistant.

right-handed *adj* **1** more adept with the right hand than with the left. **2** made for or by the right hand. **3** turning from left to right.

rightist *adj* **1** of the political right or its principles. ~*n* **2** a supporter of the political right. **rightism** *n*

rightly *adv* **1** in accordance with the true facts or justice. **2** with good reason: *he was rightly praised for his constancy.*

right-minded *or* **right-thinking** *adj* holding opinions or principles considered acceptable by the speaker.

right of way *n, pl* **rights of way 1** the right of one vehicle or ship to go before another. **2 a** the legal right of someone to pass over someone else's land. **b** the path used by this right.

Right Reverend *adj* (in Britain) a title of respect for a bishop.

rightward *adj* **1** situated on or directed towards the right. ~*adv also* **rightwards 2** on or towards the right.

right whale *n* a large grey or black whalebone whale with a large head.

right-wing *adj* **1** conservative or reactionary: *the right-wing bias of much of the British press.* **2** belonging to the more conservative part of a political party: *a group of right-wing Labour MPs.* ~*n* **right wing 3** (*often cap*) the more conservative or reactionary section, esp. of a political party: *the Right Wing of the Conservative Party.* **4** *Sports* **a** the right-hand side of the field of play. **b** a player positioned in this area in certain games. **right-winger** *n*

rigid *adj* **1** inflexible or strict: *the talks will be general without a rigid agenda.* **2** physically unyielding or stiff: *use only rigid plastic containers.* **rigidity** *n* **rigidly** *adv*

rigmarole *n* **1** a long complicated procedure. **2** a set of incoherent or pointless statements.

rigor mortis *n* the stiffness of joints and muscles of a dead body.

rigorous *adj* **1** harsh, strict, or severe: *rigorous enforcement of the libel laws.* **2** severely accurate: *rigorous scientific testing.*

rigour *or US* **rigor** *n* **1** a severe or cruel circumstance: *the rigours of forced labour.* **2** strictness in judgment or conduct. **3** harsh but just treatment.

rig out *vb* **1** to dress: *I was rigged out in my usual*

THESAURUS

with (*informal*), fix (*informal*), gerrymander, juggle, manipulate, tamper with, trump up ~*n.* **2.** accoutrements, apparatus, equipage, equipment, fitments, fittings, fixtures, gear, machinery, outfit, tackle

right *adj.* **1.** equitable, ethical, fair, good, honest, honourable, just, lawful, moral, proper, righteous, true, upright, virtuous **2.** accurate, admissible, authentic, correct, exact, factual, genuine, precise, satisfactory, sound, spot-on (*Brit. informal*), true, unerring, valid, veracious **3.** advantageous, appropriate, becoming, *comme il faut*, convenient, deserved, desirable, done, due, favourable, fit, fitting, ideal, opportune, proper, propitious, rightful, seemly, suitable **4.** all there (*informal*), balanced, *compos mentis*, fine, fit, healthy, in good health, in the pink, lucid, normal, rational, reasonable, sane, sound, unimpaired, up to par, well **5.** conservative, reactionary, Tory ~*adv.* **6.** accurately, aright, correctly, exactly, factually, genuinely, precisely, truly **7.** appropriately, aptly, befittingly, fittingly, properly, satisfactorily, suitably **8.** absolutely, all the way, altogether, completely, entirely, perfectly, quite, thoroughly, totally, utterly, wholly **9.** directly, immediately, instantly, promptly, quickly, straight, straightaway, without delay **10.** advantageously, beneficially, favourably, for the better, fortunately, to advantage, well ~*n.* **11.** authority, business, claim, due, freedom, interest, liberty, licence, permission, power, prerogative, privilege, title **12.** good, goodness, honour, integrity, justice, lawfulness, legality, morality, propriety, reason, rectitude, righteousness, truth, uprightness, virtue **13. by right** *or* **rights** equitably, in fairness, justly, properly **14. to rights** arranged, in order, straight, tidy ~*vb.* **15.** compensate for, correct, fix, put right, rectify, redress, repair, settle, set upright, sort out, straighten, vindicate

right away at once, directly, forthwith, immediately, instantly, now, posthaste, promptly, pronto (*informal*), right off, straightaway, straight off (*informal*), this instant, without delay, without hesitation

righteous blameless, equitable, ethical, fair, good, honest, honourable, just, law-abiding, moral, pure, squeaky-clean, upright, virtuous

righteousness blamelessness, equity, ethicalness, faithfulness, goodness, honesty, honour, integrity, justice, morality, probity, purity, rectitude, uprightness, virtue

rigid adamant, austere, exact, fixed, harsh, inflexible, intransigent, invariable, rigorous, set, severe, stern, stiff, strict, stringent, unalterable, unbending, uncompromising, undeviating, unrelenting, unyielding

rigorous 1. hard, harsh, inflexible, rigid, severe, stern, strict, stringent, tough **2.** accurate, conscientious, exact, meticulous, nice, painstaking, precise, punctilious, scrupulous, thorough

rigour 1. asperity, austerity, firmness, hardness, hardship, harshness, inflexibility, ordeal, privation, rigidity, sternness, strictness, stringency, suffering, trial **2.** accuracy, conscientiousness, exactitude, exactness, meticulousness, preciseness, precision, punctiliousness, thoroughness

rig out *vb.* **1.** array, attire, clothe, costume, dress, kit out **2.** equip, fit, furnish, kit out, outfit, set up ~*n.*

green shell suit. **2** to equip: *his car is rigged out with gadgets.* ~*n* **rigout 3** *Informal* a person's clothing or costume.

rig up *vb* to set up or build temporarily: *they rigged up a loudspeaker system.*

rile *vb* **riling, riled 1** to annoy or anger. **2** *US & Canad* to stir up (a liquid).

rill *n* a small stream.

rim *n* **1** the raised edge of an object. **2** the outer part of a wheel to which the tyre is attached. **rimless** *adj*

rime[1] *Literary* ~*n* **1** frost formed by the freezing of water droplets in fog onto solid objects. ~*vb* **riming, rimed 2** to cover with rime or something resembling it. **rimy** *adj*

rime[2] *n, vb* **riming, rimed** *Archaic* same as **rhyme.**

rind *n* a hard outer layer on fruits, bacon, or cheese.

ring[1] *vb* **ringing, rang, rung 1** to give out a clear resonant sound, like that of a bell. **2** to cause (a bell) to give out a ringing sound or (of a bell) to give out such a sound. **3** *Chiefly Brit* to call (a person) by telephone. **4 ring for** to call by means of a bell: *ring for the maid.* **5** (of a building or place) to be filled with sound: *the church rang with singing.* **6** (of the ears) to have the sensation of humming or ringing. **7 ring a bell** to bring something to the mind or memory: *the name doesn't ring a bell.* **8 ring down the curtain a** to lower the curtain at the end of a theatrical performance. **b ring down the curtain on** to put an end to. **9 ring true** *or* **false** to give the impression of being true *or* false. ~*n* **10** the act of or a sound made by ringing. **11** a sound produced by or sounding like a bell. **12** *Informal, chiefly Brit* a telephone call. **13** an inherent quality: *it has the ring of possibility to it.* ~See also **ring in, ring off,** etc.

➤ The simple past is *rang: He rang the bell.* Avoid the use of the past participle *rung* for the simple past.

ring[2] *n* **1** a circular band of a precious metal worn on the finger. **2** any object or mark that is circular in shape. **3** a group of people or things standing or arranged in a circle: *a ring of standing stones.* **4** a circular path or course: *crowds of people walking round in a ring.* **5** a circular enclosure where circus acts perform or livestock is sold at a market. **6** a square raised platform, marked off by ropes, in which contestants box or wrestle. **7** a group of people, usually illegal, who control a specified market: *a drugs ring.* **8** *Chem* a closed loop of atoms in a molecule. **9** one of the systems of circular bands orbiting the planets Saturn, Uranus, and Jupiter. **10 the ring** the sport of boxing. **11 throw one's hat in the ring** to announce one's intention to be a candidate or contestant. **12 run rings around** *Informal* to outclass completely. ~*vb* **ringing, ringed 13** to put a ring round. **14** to mark (a bird) with a ring or clip for subsequent identification. **15** to kill (a tree) by cutting the bark round the trunk. **16** to fit a ring in the nose of (a bull, etc.) so that it can be led easily. **ringed** *adj*

ring binder *n* a loose-leaf binder with metal rings that can be opened to insert perforated paper.

ringdove *n* a wood pigeon.

ringer *n* a person or thing that is almost identical to another. Also called: **dead ringer**

ring finger *n* the third finger, esp. of the left hand, on which a wedding ring is worn.

ring in *vb* to report to someone by telephone.

ringleader *n* a person who leads others in illegal or mischievous actions.

ringlet *n* a lock of hair hanging down in a spiral curl. **ringleted** *adj*

ring main *n* a domestic electrical supply in which outlet sockets are connected to the mains supply through a continuous closed circuit (**ring circuit**).

ringmaster *n* the master of ceremonies in a circus.

ring off *vb Chiefly Brit* to end a telephone conversation by replacing the receiver.

ring out *vb* to send out a loud resounding noise: *I heard those shots ring out.*

ring road *n* a main road that bypasses a town or town centre.

ringside *n* **1** the row of seats nearest a boxing or wrestling ring. ~*adj* **2** providing a close uninterrupted view: *a ringside seat for the election.*

ring up *vb* **1** *Chiefly Brit* to make a telephone call to. **2** to record on a cash register. **3 ring up the curtain a** to begin a theatrical performance. **b ring up the curtain on** to make a start on.

ringworm *n* a fungal infection of the skin producing itchy patches.

rink *n* **1** a sheet of ice for skating on, usually indoors. **2** an area for roller-skating on. **3** a building for ice skating or roller-skating. **4** (in bowls or curling) **a** a strip of grass or ice on which a game is played. **b** the players on one side in a game.

rinkhals (**rink**-hals) *n, pl* **-hals** *or* **-halses** a highly venomous snake of Southern Africa capable of spitting its venom accurately at its victim's eyes.

rink rat *n Canad slang* a youth who helps with odd chores at an ice-hockey rink in return for free admission to games.

rinse *vb* **rinsing, rinsed 1** to remove soap or shampoo from (clothes, dishes, or hair) by washing it out with clean water. **2** to wash lightly, esp. without using soap. **3** to cleanse the mouth by swirling water or mouthwash in it and then spitting the liquid out. **4** to give a light tint to (hair). ~*n* **5** the act or an instance of rinsing. **6** *Hairdressing* a liquid to tint hair: *a blue rinse.*

riot *n* **1** a disturbance made by an unruly mob. **2** an occasion of lively enjoyment. **3** a dazzling display: *the pansies provided the essential riot of colour.* **4** *Slang* a

THESAURUS

3. rig-out apparel, clobber (*Brit. slang*), clothing, costume, dress, garb, gear (*informal*), get-up (*informal*), habit, outfit, raiment (*archaic or poetic*), togs

rig up arrange, assemble, build, cobble together, construct, erect, fix up, improvise, put together, put up, set up, throw together

rim border, brim, brink, circumference, edge, flange, lip, margin, verge

rind crust, husk, integument, outer layer, peel, skin

ring[1] *vb.* **1.** chime, clang, peal, resonate, resound, reverberate, sound, toll **2.** call, phone, telephone ~*n.* **3.** chime, knell, peal **4.** *informal* bell (*Brit. slang*), buzz (*informal*), call, phone call

ring[2] *n.* **1.** band, circle, circuit, halo, hoop, loop, round **2.** arena, circus, enclosure, rink **3.** association, band, cabal, cartel, cell, circle, clique, combine, coterie, crew (*informal*), gang, group, junta, knot, mob, organization, syndicate ~*vb.* **4.** circumscribe, encircle, enclose, encompass, gird, girdle, hem in, seal off, surround

rinse 1. *vb.* bathe, clean, cleanse, dip, splash, wash, wash out, wet **2.** *n.* bath, dip, splash, wash, wetting

riot *n.* **1.** anarchy, commotion, confusion, disorder, disturbance, donnybrook, fray, lawlessness, mob violence, quarrel, row, street fighting, strife, tumult, turbulence, turmoil, upheaval, uproar **2.** binge, carousal, excess, festivity, frolic, high jinks, jollification, merrymaking, revelry, romp **3.** display, extravaganza, flourish, show, splash **4. run riot a.** be out of control, break *or* cut loose, go wild, let oneself go, raise hell,

very amusing person or thing. **5 read the riot act** to reprimand severely. **6 run riot a** to behave without restraint. **b** (of plants) to grow profusely. ~*vb* **7** to take part in a riot. **rioter** *n* **rioting** *n*

riotous *adj* **1** unrestrained and excessive: *riotous decadence.* **2** unruly or rebellious. **3** characterized by unrestrained merriment: *riotous celebration.*

riot shield *n* a large shield used by police controlling crowds.

rip *vb* **ripping, ripped 1** to tear or be torn violently or roughly. **2** to remove hastily or roughly. **3** *Informal* to move violently or hurriedly. **4 let rip** to act or speak without restraint. ~*n* **5** a tear or split. ~See also **rip off.**

RIP may he, she, *or* they rest in peace.

riparian (rip-**pair**-ee-an) *adj Formal* of or on the bank of a river.

ripcord *n* a cord pulled to open a parachute from its pack.

ripe *adj* **1** mature enough to be eaten or used: *a round ripe apple.* **2** fully developed in mind or body. **3** suitable: *wait until the time is ripe.* **4 ripe for** ready or eager to (undertake or undergo an action): *China was ripe for revolution.* **5 ripe old age** an elderly but healthy age.

ripen *vb* **1** to make or become ripe. **2** to mature.

rip off *Slang* ~*vb* **1** to cheat by overcharging. **2** to steal (something). ~*n* **rip-off 3** a grossly overpriced article. **4** the act of stealing or cheating.

riposte (rip-**posst**) *n* **1** a swift clever reply. **2** *Fencing* a counterattack made immediately after a successful parry. ~*vb* **-posting, -posted 3** to make a riposte.

ripple *n* **1** a slight wave on the surface of water. **2** a slight ruffling of a surface. **3** a sound like water flowing gently in ripples: *a ripple of applause.* **4** vanilla ice cream with stripes of another ice cream through it: *raspberry ripple.* ~*vb* **-pling, -pled 5** to form ripples or flow with a waving motion. **6** (of sounds) to rise and fall gently. **rippling** *adj*

rip-roaring *adj Informal* boisterous and exciting.

ripsaw *n* a handsaw for cutting along the grain of timber.

rise *vb* **rising, rose, risen 1** to get up from a lying, sitting, or kneeling position. **2** to get out of bed, esp. to begin one's day: *she rises at 5 a.m. every day to look after her horse.* **3** to move from a lower to a higher position or place. **4** to appear above the horizon: *as the sun rises higher the mist disappears.* **5** to slope upwards: *the road crossed the valley then rose to a low ridge.* **6** to increase in height or level: *the tide rose.* **7** to swell up: *dough rises.* **8** to increase in strength or degree: *frustration is rising amongst sections of the population.* **9** to increase in amount or value: *living costs are rising at an annual rate of nine per cent.* **10** *Informal* to respond (to a challenge or remark). **11** to revolt: *the people rose against their oppressors.* **12** (of a court or parliament) to adjourn. **13** to be resurrected. **14** to become erect or rigid: *the hairs on his neck rose in fear.* **15** to originate: *that river rises in the mountains.* **16** *Angling* (of fish) to come to the surface of the water. ~*n* **17** the act or an instance of rising. **18** a piece of rising ground. **19** an increase in wages. **20** an increase in amount, cost, or quantity. **21** an increase in height. **22** an increase in status or position. **23** an increase in degree or intensity. **24** the vertical height of a step or of a flight of stairs. **25 get** *or* **take a rise out of** *Slang* to provoke an angry reaction from. **26 give rise to** to cause the development of.

riser *n* **1** a person who rises from bed: *an early riser.* **2** the vertical part of a step.

risible (**riz**-zib-bl) *adj Formal* ridiculous.

rising *n* **1** a rebellion. ~*adj* **2** increasing in rank or maturity.

rising damp *n* seepage of moisture from the ground into the walls of buildings.

risk *n* **1** the possibility of bringing about misfortune or loss. **2** a person or thing considered as a potential hazard: *in parts of the world transfusions carry the risk of infection.* **3 at risk** in a dangerous situation. **4 take** *or* **run a risk** to act without regard to the danger involved. ~*vb* **5** to act in spite of the possibility of (injury or loss): *if they clamp down they risk a revolution.* **6** to expose to danger or loss. **risky** *adj*

risotto *n, pl* **-tos** a dish of rice cooked in stock with vegetables, meat, etc.

risqué (**risk**-ay) *adj* making slightly rude references to sex: *risqué humour.*

rissole *n* a mixture of minced cooked meat coated in egg and breadcrumbs and fried.

ritardando *adj, adv* same as **rallentando.**

rite *n* **1** a formal act which forms part of a religious ceremony: *the rite of burial.* **2** a custom that is carried out within a particular group: *the barbaric rites of public execution.* **3** a particular body of such acts, esp. of

THESAURUS

rampage, throw off all restraint **b.** grow like weeds, grow profusely, luxuriate, spread like wildfire ~*vb.* **5.** fight in the streets, go on the rampage, raise an uproar, rampage, run riot, take to the streets

riotous 1. anarchic, disorderly, insubordinate, lawless, mutinous, rampageous, rebellious, refractory, rowdy, tumultuous, ungovernable, unruly, uproarious, violent **2.** boisterous, loud, luxurious, noisy, orgiastic, roisterous, rollicking, saturnalian, side-splitting, unrestrained, uproarious, wanton, wild

ripe 1. accomplished, complete, finished, fully developed, fully grown, mature, mellow, perfect, prepared, ready, ripened, seasoned **2.** auspicious, favourable, ideal, opportune, right, suitable, timely

ripen burgeon, come of age, come to fruition, develop, get ready, grow ripe, make ripe, mature, prepare, season

riposte 1. *n.* answer, comeback (*informal*), counterattack, rejoinder, repartee, reply, response, retort, return, sally **2.** *vb.* answer, come back, reciprocate, rejoin, reply, respond, retort, return

rise *vb.* **1.** arise, get out of bed, get to one's feet, get up, rise and shine, stand up, surface **2.** arise, ascend, climb, enlarge, go up, grow, improve, increase, intensify, levitate, lift, mount, move up, soar, swell, wax **3.** ascend, climb, get steeper, go uphill, mount, slope upwards **4.** mount the barricades, mutiny, rebel, resist, revolt, take up arms **5.** appear, become apparent, crop up, emanate, emerge, eventuate, flow, happen, issue, occur, originate, spring, turn up ~*n.* **6.** advance, ascent, climb, improvement, increase, upsurge, upswing, upturn, upward turn **7.** acclivity, ascent, elevation, hillock, incline, rising ground, upward slope **8.** increment, pay increase, raise (*U.S.*) **9.** advancement, aggrandizement, climb, progress, promotion **10. give rise to** bring about, bring on, cause, effect, produce, provoke, result in

risk 1. *n.* chance, danger, gamble, hazard, jeopardy, peril, pitfall, possibility, speculation, uncertainty **2.** *vb.* chance, dare, endanger, expose to danger, gamble, hazard, imperil, jeopardize, put in jeopardy, take a chance on, venture

risky chancy (*informal*), dangerous, dicey (*informal, chiefly Brit.*), dodgy (*Brit., Austral., & N.Z. informal*), fraught with danger, hazardous, perilous, precarious, touch-and-go, tricky, uncertain, unsafe

rite act, ceremonial, ceremony, communion, custom,

a particular Christian Church: *the traditional Anglican rite.*

rite of passage *n* a ceremony or event that marks an important change in a person's life.

ritual *n* **1** a religious or other ceremony involving a series of fixed actions performed in a certain order. **2** these ceremonies collectively: *people need ritual.* **3** regular repeated action or behaviour. **4** stereotyped activity or behaviour. *~adj* **5** of or like rituals. **ritually** *adv*

ritualism *n* exaggerated emphasis on the importance of rites and ceremonies. **ritualistic** *adj* **ritualistically** *adv*

ritzy *adj* **ritzier, ritziest** *Slang* luxurious or elegant.

rival *n* **1** a person or group that competes with another for the same object or in the same field. **2** a person or thing that is considered the equal of another: *she is without rival in the field of physics.* *~adj* **3** in the position of a rival. *~vb* **-valling, -valled** *or US* **-valing, -valed 4** to be the equal or near equal of: *his inactive lateness was rivalled only by that of his brother.* **5** to try to equal or surpass.

rivalry *n, pl* **-ries** active competition between people or groups.

riven *adj Old-fashioned* **1** split apart: *the party is riven by factions.* **2** torn to shreds.

river *n* **1** a large natural stream of fresh water flowing along a definite course into the sea, a lake, or a larger river. **2** an abundant stream or flow: *rivers of blood.*

rivet (**riv** vit) *n* **1** a short metal pin for fastening metal plates, with a head at one end, the other end being hammered flat after being put through holes in the plates. *~vb* **-eting, -eted 2** to join by riveting. **3** to cause a person's attention to be fixed in fascination or horror: *their eyes riveted on the protesters.* **riveter** *n*

riveting *adj* very interesting or exciting.

rivulet *n* a small stream.

RM 1 Royal Mail. **2** Royal Marines. **3** (in Canada) Rural Municipality.

RMT (National Union of) Rail, Maritime and Transport (Workers).

Rn *Chem* radon.

RN 1 (in Canada) Registered Nurse. **2** Royal Navy.

RNA *n Biochem* ribonucleic acid: any of a group of nucleic acids, present in all living cells, that play an essential role in the synthesis of proteins.

RNLI Royal National Lifeboat Institution.

roach[1] *n, pl* **roaches** *or* **roach** a European freshwater food fish.

roach[2] *n Chiefly US & Canad* a cockroach.

road *n* **1** a route, usually surfaced, used by travellers and vehicles to get from one place to another. **2** a street. **3** a way or course: *on the road to recovery.* **4** *Naut* same as **roadstead. 5 one for the road** *Informal* a last alcoholic drink before leaving. **6 on the road** travelling about.

roadblock *n* a barrier set up across a road by the police or military, in order to stop and check vehicles.

road hog *n Informal* a selfish or aggressive driver.

roadholding *n* the extent to which a vehicle is stable and does not skid on bends or wet roads.

roadhouse *n* a pub or restaurant at the side of a road.

roadie *n Informal* a person who transports and sets up equipment for a band.

road metal *n* crushed rock or broken stone used in building roads.

road show *n* **1** *Radio* a live broadcast from a radio van taking a particular programme on a tour of the country. **2** a group of entertainers on tour.

roadside *n* **1** the edge of a road. *~adj* **2** by the edge or side of a road: *a roadside café.*

roadstead *n Naut* a partly sheltered anchorage.

roadster *n Old-fashioned* an open car with only two seats.

road tax *n* a tax paid on vehicles used on the roads.

road test *n* **1** a test of something, such as a vehicle in actual use. *~vb* **road-test 2** to test (a vehicle etc.) in actual use.

roadway *n* the part of a road that is used by vehicles.

roadworks *pl n* repairs to a road or cable under a road, esp. when they block part of the road.

roadworthy *adj* (of a motor vehicle) mechanically sound. **roadworthiness** *n*

roam *vb* to walk about with no fixed purpose or direction.

roan *adj* **1** (of a horse) having a brown or black coat sprinkled with white hairs. *~n* **2** a horse with such a coat.

roar *vb* **1** (of lions and other animals) to make loud growling cries. **2** to shout (something) with a loud deep cry: *"Don't do that!" he roared at me.* **3** to make a very loud noise: *the engine roared.* **4** to laugh in a loud hearty manner. **5** (of a fire) to burn fiercely with a roaring sound. *~n* **6** a roaring noise: *there was a roar as the train came in.* **7** a loud deep cry, uttered by a person or crowd, esp. in anger or triumph: *a roar of approval came from the crowd.*

roaring *adj* **1 a roaring trade** a brisk and profitable business. *~adv* **2 roaring drunk** noisily or boisterously drunk.

roast *vb* **1** to cook (food) by dry heat in an oven or over a fire. **2** to brown or dry (coffee or nuts) by exposure to heat. **3** to make or be extremely hot. **4** *Informal* to criticize severely. *~n* **5** a roasted joint of meat. *~adj* **6** cooked by roasting: *roast beef.* **roaster** *n*

roasting *Informal ~adj* **1** extremely hot. *~n* **2** severe criticism or scolding.

THESAURUS

form, formality, liturgy, mystery, observance, ordinance, practice, procedure, ritual, sacrament, service, solemnity, usage

ritual *n.* **1.** ceremonial, ceremony, communion, liturgy, mystery, observance, rite, sacrament, service *~adj.* **2.** ceremonial, ceremonious, conventional, customary, formal, habitual, prescribed, procedural, routine, stereotyped

rival *n.* **1.** adversary, antagonist, challenger, competitor, contender, contestant, opponent **2.** compeer, equal, equivalent, fellow, match, peer *~adj.* **3.** competing, competitive, conflicting, emulating, opposed, opposing *~vb.* **4.** be a match for, bear comparison with, come up to, compare with, compete, contend, emulate, equal, match, measure up to, oppose, seek to displace, vie with

rivalry antagonism, competition, competitiveness, conflict, contention, contest, duel, opposition, struggle, vying

road 1. avenue, course, direction, highway, lane, motorway, path, pathway, roadway, route, street, thoroughfare, track, way **2.** *Nautical* anchorage, roadstead

roam drift, meander, peregrinate (*formal*), prowl, ramble, range, rove, stray, stroll, travel, walk, wander

roar *vb.* **1.** bay, bellow, cry, howl **2.** bawl, cry, howl, shout, thunder, vociferate, yell **3.** clamour, crash, howl, rumble, thunder **4.** crack up (*informal*), guffaw, hoot, laugh heartily, split one's sides (*informal*) *~n.* **5.**

rob *vb* **robbing, robbed 1** to take something from (a person or place) illegally. **2** to deprive, esp. of something deserved: *I can't forgive him for robbing me of an Olympic gold.* **robber** *n*

robbery *n, pl* **-beries 1** *Criminal law* the stealing of property from a person by using or threatening to use force. **2** the act or an instance of robbing.

robe *n* **1** a long loose flowing garment. **2** a dressing gown or bathrobe. ~*vb* **robing, robed 3** to put a robe on.

robin *n* **1** Also called: **robin redbreast** a small Old World songbird with a brown back and an orange-red breast and face. **2** a North American thrush similar to but larger than the Old World robin.

robot *n* **1** a machine programmed to perform specific tasks in a human manner, esp. one with a human shape. **2** a person of machine-like efficiency. **3** *S African* a set of traffic lights. **robotic** *adj*

robotics *n* the science of designing, building, and using robots.

robust *adj* **1** very strong and healthy. **2** sturdily built: *the new generation of robust lasers.* **3** requiring or displaying physical strength: *robust tackles.*

roc *n* (in Arabian legend) a bird of enormous size and power.

rock[1] *n* **1** *Geol* the mass of mineral matter that makes up part of the earth's crust; stone. **2** a large rugged mass of stone. **3** *US, Canad, & Austral* a stone. **4** *Brit* a hard peppermint-flavoured sweet, usually in the shape of a long stick. **5** a person or thing on which one can always depend: *your loyalty is a rock.* **6** *Slang* a precious jewel. **7 on the rocks a** (of a marriage) about to end. **b** (of an alcoholic drink) served with ice.

rock[2] *vb* **1** to move from side to side or backwards and forwards. **2** to shake or move (something) violently. **3** to feel or cause to feel shock: *the case had rocked the British Establishment.* **4** to dance to or play rock music. ~*n* **5** Also called: **rock music** a style of pop music with a heavy beat. **6** a rocking motion. ~*adj* **7** of or relating to rock music.

rockabilly *n* a fast style of White rock music which originated in the mid-1950s in the US South.

rock and roll *or* **rock'n'roll** *n* a type of pop music originating in the 1950s as a blend of rhythm and blues and country and western.

rock bottom *n* the lowest possible level.

rock cake *n* a small fruit cake with a rough surface.

rock crystal *n* a pure transparent colourless quartz.

rock dove *n* a common dove from which domestic and wild pigeons are descended.

rocker *n* **1** a rocking chair. **2** either of two curved supports on which a rocking chair stands. **3** a rock music performer or fan. **4 off one's rocker** *Slang* crazy.

rockery *n, pl* **-eries** a garden built of rocks and soil, for growing rock plants.

rocket *n* **1** a self-propelling device, usually cylindrical, which produces thrust by expelling through a nozzle the gases produced by burning fuel, such as one used as a firework or distress signal. **2** any vehicle propelled by a rocket engine, as a weapon or carrying a spacecraft. **3** *Informal* a severe reprimand: *my sister gave me a rocket for writing such dangerous nonsense.* ~*vb* **-eting, -eted 4** to increase rapidly: *within six years their turnover had rocketed to £450 000.* **5** to attack with rockets.

rocketry *n* the science and technology of the design and operation of rockets.

rock garden *n* a garden featuring rocks or rockeries.

rocking chair *n* a chair set on curving supports so that the sitter may rock backwards and forwards.

rocking horse *n* a toy horse mounted on a pair of rocking supports on which a child can rock to and fro.

rock melon *n US, Austral, & NZ* same as **cantaloupe.**

rock plant *n* a plant that grows on rocks or in rocky ground.

rock pool *n* a small pool between rocks on the seashore.

rock salmon *n Brit* a former term for dogfish when used as a food.

rock salt *n* common salt as a naturally occurring solid mineral.

rock tripe *n Canad* any edible lichen that grows on rocks.

rocky[1] *adj* **rockier, rockiest** covered with rocks: *rocky and sandy shores.* **rockiness** *n*

rocky[2] *adj* **rockier, rockiest** shaky or unstable: *a rocky relationship.* **rockiness** *n*

rococo (rok-**koe**-koe) *adj* **1** relating to an 18th-century style of architecture, decoration, and music characterized by elaborate ornamentation. **2** excessively elaborate in style.

rod *n* **1** a thin straight pole made of wood or metal. **2** a cane used to beat people as a punishment. **3** short for **fishing rod. 4** a type of cell in the retina, sensitive to dim light. **rodlike** *adj*

rode *vb* the past tense of **ride.**

rodent *n* a small mammal with teeth specialized for gnawing, such as a rat, mouse, or squirrel. **rodentlike** *adj*

rodeo *n, pl* **-deos** a display of the skills of cowboys, including bareback riding.

rodomontade *n Literary* boastful words or behaviour.

THESAURUS

bellow, belly laugh (*informal*), cry, guffaw, hoot, howl, outcry, shout, yell **6.** clamour, crash, cry, howl, rumble, thunder

rob 1. burgle, cheat, con (*informal*), defraud, dispossess, hold up, loot, mug (*informal*), pillage, plunder, raid, ransack, rifle, rip off (*slang*), sack, strip, swindle **2.** cheat, deprive, do out of (*informal*)

robber bandit, brigand, burglar, cheat, con man (*informal*), fraud, highwayman, looter, mugger (*informal*), pirate, plunderer, raider, stealer, swindler, thief

robbery burglary, depredation, embezzlement, filching, fraud, hold-up, larceny, mugging (*informal*), pillage, plunder, raid, rip-off (*slang*), stealing, stick-up (*slang, chiefly U.S.*), swindle, theft, thievery

robe *n.* **1.** costume, gown, habit, vestment **2.** bathrobe, dressing gown, housecoat, negligee, peignoir, wrapper ~*vb.* **3.** apparel (*archaic*), attire, clothe, drape, dress, garb

robot android, automaton, machine, mechanical man

robust able-bodied, athletic, brawny, fit, hale, hardy, healthy, hearty, husky (*informal*), in fine fettle, in good health, lusty, muscular, powerful, rude, rugged, sinewy, sound, staunch, stout, strapping, strong, sturdy, thickset, tough, vigorous, well

rock[1] **1.** boulder, stone **2.** anchor, bulwark, cornerstone, foundation, mainstay, protection, support, tower of strength

rock[2] **1.** lurch, pitch, reel, roll, sway, swing, toss, wobble **2.** astonish, astound, daze, dumbfound, jar, set one back on one's heels (*informal*), shake, shock, stagger, stun, surprise

roe[1] *n* the ovary and eggs of a female fish, sometimes eaten as food.

roe[2] *or* **roe deer** *n* a small graceful deer with short antlers.

roentgen (**ront**-gan) *n* a unit measuring a radiation dose.

roger *interj* **1** (used in signalling) message received and understood. **2** an expression of agreement.

rogue *n* **1** a dishonest or unprincipled person. **2** a mischievous person. **3** any inferior or defective specimen, esp. of a plant. *~adj* **4** (of a wild animal) having a savage temper and living apart from the herd: *a rogue elephant.* **roguish** *adj*

roguery *n, pl* **-gueries** dishonest or immoral behaviour.

rogues' gallery *n* a collection of photographs of known criminals kept by the police for identification purposes.

roister *vb Old-fashioned* to enjoy oneself noisily and boisterously. **roisterer** *n*

role *n* **1** a task or function: *their role in international relations.* **2** an actor's part in a production.

role model *n* a person regarded by others, esp. younger people, as a good example to follow.

roll *vb* **1** to move along by turning over and over. **2** to move along on wheels or rollers. **3** to curl or make by curling into a ball or tube. **4** to move along in an undulating movement. **5** to rotate wholly or partially: *he would snort in derision, roll his eyes, and heave a deep sigh.* **6** to spread out flat or smooth with a roller or rolling pin: *roll the pastry out thinly.* **7** (of a ship or aircraft) to turn from side to side around the longitudinal axis. **8** to operate or begin to operate: *the cameras continued to roll as she pulled up to the nightclub.* **9** to make a continuous deep reverberating sound: *the thunder rolled.* **10** to walk in a swaying manner: *the drunks came rolling home.* **11** to appear like a series of waves: *mountain ranges rolling away in every direction.* **12** to pass or elapse: *watching the time roll away.* **13** (of animals) to turn onto the back and kick. **14** to trill or cause to be trilled: *she rolled her r's.* **15** to throw (dice). *~n* **16** the act or an instance of rolling. **17** anything rolled up into a tube: *a roll of paper towels.* **18** a small cake of bread for one person. **19** a flat pastry or cake rolled up with a meat, jam, or other filling. **20** an official list or register of names: *the electoral roll.* **21** a complete rotation about its longitudinal axis by an aircraft. **22** a continuous deep reverberating sound: *the roll of musketry.* **23** a swaying or unsteady movement or gait. **24** a rounded mass: *rolls of fat.* **25** a very rapid beating of the sticks on a drum. **26 strike off the roll** to expel from membership of a professional association. ~See also **roll in, roll on,** etc.

roll call *n* the reading aloud of an official list of names, to check who is present.

rolled gold *n* a metal, such as brass, coated with a thin layer of gold.

roller *n* **1** a rotating cylinder used for smoothing, supporting a thing to be moved, spreading paint, etc. **2** a small tube around which hair may be wound in order to make it curly. **3** a long heavy wave of the sea. **4** a cylinder fitted on pivots, used to enable heavy objects to be easily moved.

rollerblade *n* a type of roller skate in which the wheels are set in a single straight line under the boot.

roller coaster *n* (at a funfair) a narrow railway with open carriages, sharp curves and steep slopes.

roller skate *n* **1** a shoe with four small wheels that enable the wearer to glide swiftly over a floor. *~vb* **roller-skate, -skating, -skated 2** to move on roller skates. **roller skater** *n*

roller towel *n* **1** a towel with the two ends sewn together, hung on a roller. **2** a towel wound inside a roller enabling a clean section to be pulled out when needed.

rollicking *adj* boisterously carefree: *the fourth volume is a rollicking read.*

roll in *vb* **1** to arrive in large numbers. **2 be rolling in** *Slang* to have plenty of (money etc.).

rolling *adj* **1** having gentle rising and falling slopes: *rolling hills.* **2** (of a walk) slow and swaying. **3** subject to regular review and updating: *a 10-year rolling programme.* **4** progressing by stages or in succession: *a rolling campaign.*

rolling mill *n* **1** a factory where metal ingots are passed between rollers to produce sheets or bars of the required shape. **2** a machine with rollers for doing this.

rolling pin *n* a cylinder with handles at both ends used for rolling pastry.

rolling stock *n* the locomotives and coaches of a railway.

rolling stone *n* a restless or wandering person.

rollmop *n* a herring fillet rolled around onion slices and pickled.

rollneck *adj* (of a garment) having a high neck that is worn rolled over.

roll of honour *n* a list of those who have died in war for their country.

roll on *interj* **1** *Brit* used to express the wish that an eagerly anticipated event will come quickly: *roll on the next light-hearted romp.* *~adj* **roll-on 2** (of a deodorant) applied by means of a revolving ball fitted into the neck of the container.

roll-on/roll-off *adj* denoting a ship designed so that vehicles can be driven straight on and straight off.

roll-top *adj* (of a desk) having a slatted wooden panel that can be pulled down over the writing surface when not in use.

THESAURUS

rocky boulder-strewn, craggy, pebbly, rough, rugged, stony

rod **1.** bar, baton, crook, dowel, mace, pole, sceptre, shaft, staff, stick, wand **2.** birch, cane, switch

rogue blackguard, charlatan, cheat, con man (*informal*), crook (*informal*), deceiver, devil, fraud, knave (*archaic*), mountebank, ne'er-do-well, rascal, reprobate, scoundrel, scumbag (*slang*), sharper, swindler, villain

role **1.** capacity, duty, function, job, part, position, post, task **2.** character, impersonation, part, portrayal, representation

roll *vb.* **1.** elapse, flow, go past, go round, gyrate, pass, pivot, reel, revolve, rock, rotate, run, spin, swivel, trundle, turn, twirl, undulate, wheel, whirl **2.** bind, coil, curl, enfold, entwine, envelop, furl, swathe, twist, wind, wrap **3.** even, flatten, level, press, smooth, spread **4.** billow, lurch, reel, rock, sway, swing, toss, tumble, wallow, welter **5.** boom, drum, echo, grumble, resound, reverberate, roar, rumble, thunder **6.** lumber, lurch, reel, stagger, swagger, sway, waddle *~n.* **7.** cycle, gyration, reel, revolution, rotation, run, spin, turn, twirl, undulation, wheel, whirl **8.** ball, bobbin, cylinder, reel, scroll, spool **9.** annals, catalogue, census, chronicle, directory, index, inventory, list, record, register, roster, schedule, scroll, table **10.** boom, drumming, growl, grumble, resonance, reverberation, roar, rumble, thunder

rollicking *adj.* boisterous, carefree, cavorting, devil-may-care, exuberant, frisky, frolicsome, hearty, jaunty,

roll up *vb* **1** to form into a cylindrical shape: *roll up a length of black material.* **2** *Informal* to arrive. *~n* **roll-up 3** *Informal* a cigarette made by the smoker from loose tobacco and cigarette papers.

roly-poly *adj* **1** plump or chubby. *~n, pl* **-lies 2** *Brit* a strip of suet pastry spread with jam, rolled up, and baked or steamed.

ROM *n Computers* read only memory: a storage device that holds data permanently and cannot be altered by the programmer.

roman *adj* **1** in or relating to the vertical style of printing type used for most printed matter. *~n* **2** roman type.

Roman *adj* **1** of Rome, a city in Italy, or its inhabitants in ancient or modern times. **2** of Roman Catholicism or the Roman Catholic Church. *~n* **3** a person from ancient or modern Rome.

Roman alphabet *n* the alphabet evolved by the ancient Romans for writing Latin, used for writing most of the languages of W Europe, including English.

Roman candle *n* a firework that produces a steady stream of coloured sparks.

Roman Catholic *adj* **1** of the Roman Catholic Church. *~n* **2** a member of this Church. **Roman Catholicism** *n*

Roman Catholic Church *n* the Christian Church over which the pope presides.

romance *n* **1** a love affair. **2** love, esp. romantic love idealized for its purity or beauty. **3** a spirit of or inclination for adventure or mystery. **4** a mysterious or sentimental quality. **5** a story or film dealing with love, usually in an idealized way. **6** a story or film dealing with events and characters remote from ordinary life. **7** an extravagant, absurd, or fantastic account. **8** a medieval narrative dealing with adventures of chivalrous heroes. *~vb* **-mancing, -manced 9** to tell extravagant or improbable lies.

Romance *adj* of the languages derived from Latin, such as French, Spanish, and Italian.

Romanesque *adj* of or in the style of architecture used in Europe from the 9th to the 12th century, characterized by rounded arches and massive walls.

Romanian *adj* **1** of Romania. *~n* **2** a person from Romania. **3** the language of Romania.

Roman nose *n* a nose with a high prominent bridge.

Roman numerals *pl n* the letters used as numerals by the Romans, used occasionally today: I (= 1), V (= 5), X (= 10), L (= 50), C (= 100), D (= 500), and M (= 1000). VI = 6(V + I) but IV = 4(V – I).

romantic *adj* **1** of or dealing with love. **2** idealistic but impractical: *a romantic notion.* **3** evoking or given to thoughts and feelings of love: *romantic images.* **4** **Romantic** relating to a movement in European art, music, and literature in the late 18th and early 19th centuries, characterized by an emphasis on feeling and content rather than order and form. *~n* **5** a person who is idealistic or amorous. **6** a person who likes or produces artistic works in the style of Romanticism. **romantically** *adv*

romanticism *n* **1** idealistic but unrealistic thoughts and feelings. **2** **Romanticism** the spirit and style of the Romantic art, music, and literature of the late 18th and early 19th centuries. **romanticist** *n*

romanticize *or* **-cise** *vb* **-cizing, -cized** *or* **-cising, -cised** to describe or regard (something or someone) in an unrealistic and idealized way: *the Victorian legacy of romanticizing family life.*

Romany *n* **1** (*pl* **-nies**) a Gypsy. **2** the language of the Gypsies.

Romeo *n, pl* **Romeos** an ardent male lover.

romp *vb* **1** to play or run about wildly or joyfully. **2** **romp home** *or* **in** to win a race or other competition easily. **3** **romp through** to do (something) quickly and easily. *~n* **4** a noisy or boisterous game or prank.

rompers *pl n* **1** Also called: **romper suit** a one-piece baby garment combining trousers and a top. **2** *NZ* a type of costume worn by schoolgirls for games and gymnastics.

rondavel *n S African* a small circular building with a cone-shaped roof.

rondeau (**ron**-doe) *n, pl* **-deaux** (-doe) a poem consisting of 13 or 10 lines with the opening words of the first line used as a refrain.

rondo *n, pl* **-dos** a piece of music with a leading theme continually returned to: often forms the last movement of a sonata or concerto.

roo *n, pl* **roos** *Austral informal* a kangaroo.

rood *n* **1** *Christianity* the Cross. **2** a crucifix.

rood screen *n* (in a church) a screen separating the nave from the choir.

roof *n, pl* **roofs 1** a structure that covers or forms the top of a building. **2** the top covering of a vehicle, oven, or other structure. **3** the highest part of the mouth or a cave. **4** **hit** *or* **go through the roof** *Informal* to get extremely angry. **5** **raise the roof** *Informal* to be very noisy. *~vb* **6** to put a roof on.

roof garden *n* a garden on a flat roof of a building.

roofing *n* material used to build a roof.

roof rack *n* a rack for carrying luggage attached to the roof of a car.

rooftree *n* same as **ridgepole.**

rooibos (**roy**-boss) *n S African* a kind of tea made from the leaves of a South African wild shrub. Also called: **rooibos tea, bush tea**

rooinek (**roy**-neck) *n S African facetious* an Englishman.

rook[1] *n* **1** a large black bird of the crow family. *~vb* **2** *Old-fashioned, slang* to cheat or swindle.

rook[2] *n* a chessman that may move any number of unoccupied squares in a straight line, horizontally or vertically; castle.

rookery *n, pl* **-eries 1** a group of nesting rooks. **2** a colony of penguins or seals.

rookie *n Informal* a newcomer without much experience.

room *n* **1** an area within a building enclosed by a

THESAURUS

jovial, joyous, lively, merry, playful, rip-roaring (*informal*), romping, spirited, sportive, sprightly, swashbuckling

roly-poly buxom, chubby, fat, overweight, plump, podgy, pudgy, rotund, rounded, tubby

romance *n.* **1.** affair, *affaire (du coeur)*, affair of the heart, amour, attachment, intrigue, liaison, love affair, passion, relationship **2.** adventure, charm, colour, excitement, exoticness, fascination, glamour, mystery, nostalgia, sentiment **3.** love story, melodrama, tear-jerker (*informal*) **4.** fairy tale, fantasy, idyll, legend **5.** absurdity, exaggeration, fabrication, fairy tale, fiction, flight of fancy, invention, tall story (*informal*), trumped-up story *~vb.* **6.** exaggerate, fantasize, let one's imagination run away with one, make up stories, stretch the truth, tell stories

romantic *adj.* **1.** amorous, fond, lovey-dovey, loving, mushy (*informal*), passionate, sentimental, sloppy (*informal*), soppy (*Brit. informal*), tender **2.** dreamy, high-flown, idealistic, impractical, quixotic, starry-eyed, unrealistic, utopian, visionary, whimsical *~n.* **3.** Don Quixote, dreamer, idealist, romancer, sentimentalist, utopian, visionary

floor, a ceiling, and walls. **2** the people present in a room: *the whole room was laughing.* **3** unoccupied or unobstructed space: *there wasn't enough room.* **4 room for** opportunity or scope for: *there was no room for acts of heroism.* **5 rooms** lodgings. ~*vb* **6** *US* to occupy or share a rented room: *I roomed with him for five years.*

rooming house *n US* a house with self-contained furnished rooms or flats for renting.

roommate *n* a person with whom one shares a room or apartment.

room service *n* service in a hotel providing food and drinks in guests' rooms.

roomy *adj* **roomier, roomiest** with plenty of space inside: *a roomy entrance hall.* **roominess** *n*

roost *n* **1** a place where birds rest or sleep. ~*vb* **2** to rest or sleep on a roost. **3 come home to roost** to have unfavourable repercussions. **4 rule the roost** to have authority over people in a particular place.

rooster *n Chiefly US & Canad* the male of the domestic fowl; a cock.

root[1] *n* **1** the part of a plant that anchors the rest of the plant in the ground and absorbs water and mineral salts from the soil. **2** a plant with an edible root, such as a carrot. **3** *Anat* the part of a tooth, hair, or nail that is below the skin. **4 roots** a person's sense of belonging in a place, esp. the one in which he or she was brought up. **5** source or origin. **6** the essential part or nature of something: *the root of a problem.* **7** *Linguistics* the form of a word from which other words and forms are derived. **8** *Maths* a quantity that when multiplied by itself a certain number of times equals a given quantity: *what is the cube root of a thousand?* **9** Also called: **solution** *Maths* a number that when substituted for the variable satisfies a given equation. **10** *Austral & NZ slang* sexual intercourse. **11 root and branch** entirely or utterly. ~*vb* **12** Also: **take root** to establish a root and begin to grow. **13** Also: **take root** to become established or embedded. **14** *Austral & NZ slang* to have sexual intercourse (with). ~See also **root out, roots.**

root[2] *vb* **1** to dig up the earth in search of food, using the snout: *dogs were rooting in the rushes for bones.* **2** *Informal* to search vigorously but unsystematically: *she was rooting around in her large untidy purse.*

root canal *n* the passage in the root of a tooth through which its nerves and blood vessels enter.

root crop *n* a crop, such as potato or turnip, cultivated for its roots.

root for *vb Informal* to give support to (a team or contestant).

rootle *vb* **-ling, -led** *Brit* same as **root**[2].

rootless *adj* having no sense of belonging: *a rootless city dweller.*

root mean square *n* the square root of the average of the squares of a set of numbers or quantities, for example *the root mean square of* 1, 2, *and* 4 *is* $\sqrt{((1^2 + 2^2 + 4^2)/3)} = \sqrt{7}$.

root out *vb* to get rid of completely: *a major drive to root out corruption.*

roots *adj* (of popular music) going back to the origins of a style, esp. in being unpretentious: *roots reggae.*

rootstock *n* same as **rhizome.**

rope *n* **1** a fairly thick cord made of intertwined fibres or wire. **2** a row of objects fastened to form a line: *a twenty-inch rope of pearls.* **3 know the ropes** to have a thorough understanding of a particular activity. **4 the rope a** a rope noose used for hanging someone. **b** death by hanging. ~*vb* **roping, roped 5** to tie with a rope. **6 rope off** to enclose or divide with a rope.

rope in *vb Brit* to persuade to take part in some activity.

ropey *or* **ropy** *adj* **ropier, ropiest** *Informal* **1** poor or unsatisfactory in quality: *a ropey performance.* **2** slightly unwell. **ropiness** *n*

Roquefort *n* a strong blue-veined cheese made from ewes' and goats' milk.

ro-ro *adj* (of a ferry) roll-on/roll-off.

rorqual *n* a whalebone whale with a fin on the back.

Rorschach test (**ror**-shahk) *n Psychol* a personality test consisting of a number of unstructured inkblots for interpretation.

rosaceous *adj* of or belonging to a family of plants typically having five-petalled flowers, which includes the rose, strawberry, and many fruit trees.

rosary *n, pl* **-saries** *RC Church* **1** a series of prayers counted on a string of beads. **2** a string of beads used to count these prayers as they are recited.

rose[1] *n* **1** a shrub or climbing plant with prickly stems and fragrant flowers. **2** the flower of any of these plants. **3** a plant similar to this, such as the Christmas rose. **4** a perforated cap fitted to a watering can or hose, causing the water to come out in a spray. **5 bed of roses** a situation of comfort or ease. ~*adj* **6** reddish-pink.

rose[2] *vb* the past tense of **rise.**

rosé (**roe**-zay) *n* a pink wine.

roseate (**roe**-zee-ate) *adj* **1** of the colour rose or pink. **2** excessively optimistic.

rosebay willowherb *n* a widespread perennial plant that has spikes of deep pink flowers.

rosebud *n* a rose which has not yet fully opened.

rose-coloured *adj* **1** reddish-pink. **2 see through rose-coloured** *or* **rose-tinted glasses** *or* **spectacles** to view in an unrealistically optimistic light.

rosehip *n* the berry-like fruit of a rose plant.

rosemary *n, pl* **-maries** an aromatic European shrub widely cultivated for its grey-green evergreen leaves, which are used in cookery and perfumes.

THESAURUS

rook *vb.* bilk, cheat, clip (*slang*), defraud, diddle (*informal*), do (*slang*), fleece, overcharge, rip off (*slang*), sting (*informal*), swindle

room 1. apartment, chamber, hall, office **2.** allowance, area, capacity, compass, elbowroom, expanse, extent, latitude, leeway, margin, play, range, scope, space, territory, volume **3.** *as in* **room for** chance, occasion, opportunity, scope

roomy ample, broad, capacious, commodious, extensive, generous, large, sizable, spacious, wide

root *n.* **1.** radicle, rhizome, stem, tuber **2. roots** birthplace, cradle, family, heritage, home, origins, sense of belonging **3.** base, beginnings, bottom, cause, core, crux, derivation, essence, foundation, fountainhead, fundamental, germ, heart, mainspring, nub, nucleus, occasion, origin, seat, seed, source, starting point **4. root and branch** completely, entirely, finally, radically, thoroughly, totally, to the last man, utterly, wholly, without exception ~*vb.* **5.** anchor, become established, become settled, embed, entrench, establish, fasten, fix, ground, implant, moor, set, stick, take root

root out abolish, cut out, destroy, do away with, efface, eliminate, eradicate, erase, exterminate, extirpate, get rid of, remove, tear out by the roots, uproot, weed out

rope *n.* **1.** cable, cord, hawser, line, strand **2. know the ropes** be an old hand, be experienced, be knowledgeable, know all the ins and outs, know one's way around, know the score (*informal*), know what's what, know where it's at (*slang*) **3. the rope** capital pun-

rosette *n* a rose-shaped decoration, esp. a circular bunch of ribbons.

rose-water *n* scented water made by the distillation of rose petals.

rose window *n* a circular window with spokes branching out from the centre to form a symmetrical roselike pattern.

rosewood *n* a fragrant dark wood used to make furniture.

rosin (**rozz**-in) *n* **1** a translucent brittle substance produced from turpentine and used for treating the bows of stringed instruments. *~vb* **2** to apply rosin to.

ROSPA (in Britain) Royal Society for the Prevention of Accidents.

roster *n* **1** a list showing the order in which people are to perform a duty. *~vb* **2** to place on a roster.

rostrum *n, pl* **-trums** *or* **-tra** a platform or stage.

rosy *adj* **rosier, rosiest 1** of the colour rose or pink: *rosy cheeks.* **2** hopeful or promising: *the analysis revealed a far from rosy picture.* **rosiness** *n*

rot *vb* **rotting, rotted 1** to decay or cause to decay. **2** to deteriorate slowly, mentally and physically: *I thought he was either dead or rotting in a Chinese jail.* *~n* **3** the process of rotting or the state of being rotten. **4** something decomposed. **5** short for **dry rot. 6** a plant or animal disease which causes decay of the tissues. **7** nonsense.

rota *n* a list of people who take it in turn to do a particular task.

rotary *adj* **1** revolving. **2** operating by rotation. *~n, pl* **-ries 3** *US & Canad* a traffic roundabout.

Rotary Club *n* a club that is part of **Rotary International**, an international association of professional and businessmen who raise money for charity. **Rotarian** *n, adj*

rotate *vb* **-tating, -tated 1** to turn around a centre or pivot. **2** to follow or cause to follow a set sequence. **3** to regularly change the type of crop grown on a piece of land in order to preserve the fertility of the soil. **rotation** *n* **rotational** *adj*

rote *adj* **1** done by routine repetition: *rote learning.* *~n* **2 by rote** by repetition: *we learned by rote.*

rotgut *n Facetious slang* alcoholic drink of inferior quality.

rotisserie *n* a rotating spit on which meat and poultry can be cooked.

rotor *n* **1** the rotating part of a machine or device, such as the revolving arm of the distributor of an internal-combustion engine. **2** a rotating device with blades projecting from a hub which produces thrust to lift a helicopter.

Rotovator *n Trademark* a mechanical cultivator with rotary blades.

rotten *adj* **1** decomposing or decaying. **2** breaking up through age or hard use: *the window frames are rotten.* **3** *Informal* very bad: *what rotten luck!* **4** morally corrupt: *this country's politics are rotten and out of date.* **5** *Informal* miserably unwell: *I had glandular fever and spent that year feeling rotten.* **6** *Informal* distressed and embarrassed: *I'm feeling rotten as a matter of fact, rotten and guilty.*

rotter *n Old-fashioned slang* a despicable person.

Rottweiler (**rot**-vile-er) *n* a large sturdy dog with a smooth black-and-tan coat and a docked tail.

rotund (roe-**tund**) *adj* **1** round and plump. **2** (of speech) pompous or grand. **rotundity** *n* **rotundly** *adv*

rotunda *n* a circular building or room, esp. with a dome.

rouble *or* **ruble** (**roo**-bl) *n* the standard monetary unit of the former Soviet republics.

roué (**roo**-ay) *n* a man who leads a sensual and immoral life.

rouge *n* **1** a red cosmetic for adding colour to the cheeks. *~vb* **rouging, rouged 2** to apply rouge to.

rough *adj* **1** not smooth; uneven or irregular. **2** not using enough care or gentleness. **3** difficult or unpleasant: *tomorrow will be a rough day.* **4** approximate: *a rough guess.* **5** violent or stormy. **6** troubled by violence or crime: *he lived in a rough area.* **7** incomplete or basic: *a rough draft.* **8** lacking refinement: *a*

THESAURUS

ishment, hanging, noose *~vb.* **4.** bind, fasten, hitch, lash, lasso, moor, pinion, tether, tie

rope in drag in, engage, enlist, inveigle, involve, persuade, talk into

roster agenda, catalogue, inventory, list, listing, register, roll, rota, schedule, scroll, table

rostrum dais, platform, podium, stage

rosy 1. pink, red, roseate, rose-coloured, ruddy **2.** auspicious, bright, cheerful, encouraging, favourable, hopeful, optimistic, promising, reassuring, roseate, rose-coloured, sunny

rot *vb.* **1.** corrode, corrupt, crumble, decay, decompose, degenerate, deteriorate, disintegrate, fester, go bad, moulder, perish, putrefy, spoil, taint **2.** decline, degenerate, deteriorate, languish, waste away, wither away *~n.* **3.** blight, canker, corrosion, corruption, decay, decomposition, deterioration, disintegration, mould, putrefaction, putrescence **4.** balderdash, balls (*taboo slang*), bilge (*informal*), bosh (*informal*), bull (*slang*), bullshit (*taboo slang*), bunk (*informal*), bunkum *or* buncombe (*chiefly U.S.*), claptrap (*informal*), cobblers (*Brit. taboo slang*), codswallop (*Brit. slang*), crap (*slang*), drivel, eyewash (*informal*), garbage (*chiefly U.S.*), guff (*slang*), hogwash, hokum (*slang, chiefly U.S. & Canad.*), hot air (*informal*), moonshine, nonsense, pap, piffle (*informal*), poppycock (*informal*), rubbish, shit (*taboo slang*), stuff and nonsense, tommyrot, tosh (*slang, chiefly Brit.*), tripe (*informal*), twaddle

rotary gyratory, revolving, rotating, rotational, spinning, turning

rotate 1. go round, gyrate, pirouette, pivot, reel, revolve, spin, swivel, turn, wheel **2.** alternate, follow in sequence, interchange, switch, take turns

rotation 1. gyration, orbit, pirouette, reel, revolution, spin, spinning, turn, turning, wheel **2.** alternation, cycle, interchanging, sequence, succession, switching

rotten 1. bad, corroded, corrupt, crumbling, decayed, decaying, decomposed, decomposing, disintegrating, festering, fetid, foul, mouldering, mouldy, perished, putrescent, putrid, rank, sour, stinking, tainted, unsound **2.** *informal* bad, crummy (*slang*), deplorable, disappointing, inferior, lousy (*slang*), poor, regrettable, ropey *or* ropy (*Brit. informal*), sorry, substandard, unacceptable, unfortunate, unsatisfactory **3.** bent (*slang*), corrupt, crooked (*informal*), deceitful, degenerate, dishonest, dishonourable, disloyal, faithless, immoral, mercenary, perfidious, treacherous, untrustworthy, venal, vicious **4.** *informal* bad, below par, ill, off colour, poorly (*informal*), ropey *or* ropy (*Brit. informal*), rough (*informal*), sick, under the weather (*informal*), unwell

rotter bad lot, blackguard, blighter (*Brit. informal*), bounder (*old-fashioned Brit. slang*), cad (*Brit. informal*), cur, louse (*slang*), rat (*informal*), stinker (*slang*), swine

rotund 1. chubby, corpulent, fat, fleshy, heavy, obese,

rough shelter. **9** (of ground) covered with scrub or rubble. **10** harsh or grating to the ear. **11** harsh or sharp: *the rough interrogation of my father.* **12** unfair: *rough luck.* **13** *Informal* ill: *Feeling rough? A good stiff drink will soon fix that!* **14** shaggy or hairy: *the rough wool of her sweater.* **15** (of work etc.) requiring physical rather than mental effort: *wear gloves for any rough work.* ~*vb* **16** to make rough. **17 rough it** *Informal* to live without the usual comforts of life. ~*n* **18** rough ground. **19** a sketch or preliminary piece of artwork. **20** *Informal* a violent person. **21 in rough** in an unfinished or crude state. **22 the rough** *Golf* the part of the course beside the fairways where the grass is untrimmed. **23** the unpleasant side of something: *you have to take the rough with the smooth.* ~*adv* **24** roughly. **25 sleep rough** to spend the night in the open without shelter. ~See also **rough out, rough up.**
roughly *adv*

roughage *n* the coarse indigestible constituents of food, which help digestion.

rough-and-ready *adj* **1** hastily prepared but adequate for the purpose. **2** (of a person) without formality or refinement.

rough-and-tumble *n* **1** a playful fight. **2** a disorderly situation.

roughcast *n* **1** a mixture of plaster and small stones for outside walls. ~*vb* **-casting, -cast 2** to put roughcast on (a wall).

rough diamond *n* **1** an unpolished diamond. **2** a kind or trustworthy person whose manners are not good.

roughen *vb* to make or become rough.

rough-hewn *adj* roughly shaped or cut without being properly finished.

roughhouse *n Slang* rough or noisy behaviour.

roughneck *n Slang* **1** a violent person. **2** a worker on an oil rig.

rough out *vb* to prepare (a sketch or report) in preliminary form: *he offered to rough out some designs for the sets.*

roughshod *adv* **ride roughshod over** to act with complete disregard for.

rough up *vb Informal* to beat up.

roulette *n* a gambling game in which a ball is dropped onto a revolving wheel with numbered slots.

round *adj* **1** having a flat circular shape, like a hoop. **2** having the shape of a ball. **3** curved; not angular. **4** involving or using circular motion. **5** complete. **6** *Maths* **a** forming or expressed by a whole number, with no fraction. **b** expressed to the nearest ten, hundred, or thousand: *in round figures.* ~*adv* **7** on all or most sides. **8** on or outside the circumference or perimeter: *ponds which are steeply sided all round.* **9** in rotation or revolution: *she swung round on me.* **10** by a circuitous route: *the old shoreline from Gravesend round to Rye.* **11** to all members of a group: *handing cigarettes round.* **12** to a specific place: *the boys invited him round.* **13 all year round** throughout the year. ~*prep* **14** surrounding or encircling: *wrap your sash round the wound.* **15** on all or most sides of: *the man turned in a circle, looking all round him.* **16** on or outside the circumference or perimeter of. **17** from place to place in: *a trip round the island in an ancient bus.* **18** reached by making a partial circuit about: *just round the corner.* **19** revolving about: *if you have two bodies in orbit, they orbit round their common centre of gravity.* ~*vb* **20** to move round: *as he rounded the last corner, he raised a fist.* ~*n* **21** a round shape or object. **22** a session: *a round of talks.* **23** a series: *the petty round of domestic matters.* **24** a series of calls: *a paper round.* **25 the daily round** the usual activities of a person's day. **26** a playing of all the holes on a golf course. **27** a stage of a competition: *the first round of the Portuguese Open.* **28** one of a number of periods in a boxing or wrestling match. **29** a single turn of play by each player in a card game. **30** a number of drinks bought at one time for a group of people. **31** a bullet or shell for a gun. **32** a single discharge by a gun. **33** *Music* a part song in which the voices follow each other at equal intervals. **34** circular movement. **35 a** a single slice of bread. **b** a serving of sandwiches made from two complete slices of bread. **36** a general outburst: *a round of applause.* **37 in the round a** in full detail. **b** *Theatre* with the audience all round the stage. **38 go the rounds** (of information or infection) to be passed around from person to person. ~See also **round down, round off.**

roundabout *n* **1** a road junction in which traffic moves in one direction around a central island. **2** a revolving circular platform, often with seats, on which people ride for amusement. ~*adj* **3** not straightforward: *the roundabout sea route; she thought of asking about it in a roundabout way.* ~*adv, prep* **round about 4** approximately: *round about 1900.*

round dance *n* **1** a dance in which the dancers form

THESAURUS

plump, podgy, portly, roly-poly, rounded, stout, tubby **2.** full, grandiloquent, magniloquent, orotund, resonant, rich, round, sonorous

rough *adj.* **1.** arduous, austere, hard, rugged, spartan, tough, uncomfortable, unpleasant, unrefined **2.** approximate, estimated, foggy, general, hazy, imprecise, inexact, sketchy, vague **3.** agitated, boisterous, choppy, inclement, squally, stormy, tempestuous, turbulent, wild **4.** hard, harsh, nasty, rowdy, tough, unpleasant, violent **5.** basic, crude, cursory, formless, hasty, imperfect, incomplete, quick, raw, rough-and-ready, rough-hewn, rudimentary, shapeless, sketchy, unfinished, unpolished, unrefined **6.** crude, raw, rough-hewn, uncut, undressed, unhewn, unpolished, unprocessed, unwrought **7.** broken, bumpy, craggy, irregular, jagged, rocky, rugged, stony, uneven **8.** cacophonous, discordant, grating, gruff, harsh, inharmonious, jarring, rasping, raucous, unmusical **9.** bearish, bluff, blunt, brusque, churlish, coarse, curt, discourteous, ill-bred, ill-mannered, impolite, inconsiderate, indelicate, loutish, rude, unceremonious, uncivil, uncouth, uncultured, ungracious, unmannerly, unpolished, unrefined, untutored **10.** *informal* below par, ill, not a hundred per cent (*informal*), off colour, poorly (*informal*), ropey *or* ropy (*Brit. informal*), rotten (*informal*), sick, under the weather (*informal*), unwell, upset **11.** bristly, bushy, coarse, dishevelled, disordered, fuzzy, hairy, shaggy, tangled, tousled, uncut, unshaven, unshorn ~*n.* **12.** draft, mock-up, outline, preliminary sketch, suggestion **13.** *informal* bruiser, bully boy, lager lout, rowdy, ruffian, thug, tough, yob

rough up bash up (*informal*), batter, beat the living daylights out of (*informal*), beat up, do over (*Brit., Austral., & N.Z. slang*), give a (good) kicking, knock about *or* around, maltreat, manhandle, mistreat, thrash

round *adj.* **1.** annular, circular, disc-shaped, ring-shaped **2.** ball-shaped, globe-shaped, globular, rotund, spherical **3.** bowed, bulbous, curved, curvilinear, cylindrical, rounded **4.** complete, entire, full, solid, unbroken, undivided, whole ~*vb.* **5.** bypass, circle, circumnavigate, flank, go round, skirt, turn ~*n.* **6.** ball, band, circle, disc, globe, orb, ring, sphere **7.** bout, cycle, sequence, series, session, succession **8.** beat, circuit, compass, course, routine, schedule, series, tour, turn **9.** division, lap, level, period, session, stage, turn **10.** bullet, cartridge, discharge, shell, shot

roundabout **1.** *n.* carousel, merry-go-round **2.** *adj.*

a circle. **2** a ballroom dance, such as the waltz, in which couples revolve.

round down *vb* to lower (a number) to the nearest whole number or ten, hundred, or thousand below it.

roundel *n* **1** a circular identifying mark on military aircraft. **2** a small circular object.

roundelay *n* a song in which a line or phrase is repeated as a refrain.

rounders *n Brit* a bat and ball game in which players run between posts after hitting the ball.

Roundhead *n English history* a supporter of Parliament against Charles I during the Civil War.

roundhouse *n US & Canad* a circular building in which railway locomotives are serviced.

roundly *adv* bluntly or thoroughly: *the Church roundly criticized the bill.*

round off *vb* to complete agreeably or successfully: *our afternoon was rounded off with coffee and biscuits.*

round on *vb* to attack or reply to (someone) with sudden irritation or anger.

round robin *n* **1** a petition with the signatures in a circle to disguise the order of signing. **2** a tournament in which each player plays against every other player.

round-shouldered *adj* denoting poor posture with drooping shoulders and a slight forward bending of the back.

round table *n* a meeting of people on equal terms for discussion.

Round Table *n* **1** (in Arthurian legend) the table of King Arthur, shaped so that his knights could sit around as equals. **2** one of an organization of clubs of young business and professional men who meet in order to further charitable work.

round-the-clock *adj* throughout the day and night.

round trip *n* a journey to a place and back again.

round up *vb* **1** to gather together: *the police had rounded up a circle of drug users.* **2** to raise (a number) to the nearest whole number or ten, hundred, or thousand above it. *~n* **roundup 3** a summary or discussion of news and information. **4** the act of gathering together livestock or people.

roundworm *n* a worm that is a common intestinal parasite of man.

rouse *vb* **rousing, roused 1** to wake up. **2** to provoke or excite: *his temper was roused and he had a gun.* **3 rouse oneself** to become energetic.

rousing *adj* lively or vigorous: *a rousing speech.*

roustabout *n* an unskilled labourer on an oil rig.

rout[1] *n* **1** an overwhelming defeat. **2** a disorderly retreat. **3** a noisy rabble. *~vb* **4** to defeat and put to flight.

rout[2] *vb* **1** to find by searching. **2** to drive out: *the dissidents had been routed out.* **3** to dig (something) up.

route *n* **1** the choice of roads taken to get to a place. **2** a fixed path followed by buses, trains, etc. between two places. **3** a chosen way or method: *the route to prosperity. ~vb* **routeing, routed 4** to send by a particular route.

routemarch *n Mil* a long training march.

routine *n* **1** a usual or regular method of procedure. **2** the boring repetition of tasks: *mindless routine.* **3** a set sequence of dance steps. **4** *Computers* a program or part of a program performing a specific function: *an input routine. ~adj* **5** relating to or characteristic of routine.

roux (**roo**) *n* a cooked mixture of fat and flour used as a basis for sauces.

rove *vb* **roving, roved 1** to wander about (a place). **2** (of the eyes) to look around. **rover** *n*

row[1] *n* **1** an arrangement of people or things in a line: *a row of shops.* **2** a line of seats in a cinema or theatre. **3** *Brit* a street lined with identical houses. **4** *Maths* a horizontal line of numbers. **5 in a row** in succession: *five championships in a row.*

row[2] *vb* **1** to propel (a boat) by using oars. **2** to carry (people or goods) in a rowing boat. **3** to take part in the racing of rowing boats as a sport. *~n* **4** an act or spell of rowing. **5** an excursion in a rowing boat. **rowing** *n*

row[3] *Informal ~n* **1** a noisy quarrel. **2** a controversy or dispute: *the row over Europe.* **3** a noisy disturbance: *go to the insurance offices and kick up a row about your money.* **4** a reprimand. *~vb* **5** to quarrel noisily.

rowan *n* a European tree with white flowers and red berries; mountain ash.

rowdy *adj* **-dier, -diest 1** rough, noisy, or disorderly. *~n, pl* **-dies 2** a person like this. **rowdily** *adv*

THESAURUS

circuitous, circumlocutory, devious, discursive, evasive, indirect, meandering, oblique, periphrastic, tortuous

round off bring to a close, cap, close, complete, conclude, crown, finish off, put the finishing touch to, settle

round up assemble, bring together, collect, drive, gather, group, herd, marshal, muster, rally

rouse 1. arouse, awaken, call, get up, rise, wake, wake up **2.** agitate, anger, animate, arouse, bestir, disturb, excite, exhilarate, galvanize, get going, incite, inflame, instigate, move, prod, provoke, startle, stimulate, stir, whip up

rousing brisk, electrifying, exciting, exhilarating, inflammatory, inspiring, lively, moving, spirited, stimulating, stirring, vigorous

rout 1. *n.* beating, debacle, defeat, disorderly retreat, drubbing, headlong flight, hiding (*informal*), licking (*informal*), overthrow, overwhelming defeat, pasting (*slang*), ruin, shambles, thrashing **2.** *vb.* beat, chase, clobber (*slang*), conquer, crush, cut to pieces, defeat, destroy, dispel, drive off, drub, lick (*informal*), overpower, overthrow, put to flight, put to rout, scatter, tank (*slang*), thrash, throw back in confusion, wipe the floor with (*informal*), worst

route 1. *n.* avenue, beat, circuit, course, direction, itinerary, journey, passage, path, road, round, run, way **2.** *vb.* convey, direct, dispatch, forward, send, steer

routine *n.* **1.** custom, formula, grind (*informal*), groove, method, order, pattern, practice, procedure, programme, usage, way, wont **2.** *adj.* conventional, customary, everyday, familiar, habitual, normal, ordinary, standard, typical, usual, wonted, workaday

row[1] bank, column, file, line, queue, range, rank, sequence, series, string, tier

row[2] *informal n.* **1.** altercation, brawl, commotion, controversy, dispute, disturbance, falling-out (*informal*), fracas, fray, fuss, noise, quarrel, racket, ruckus (*informal*), ruction (*informal*), rumpus, scrap (*informal*), shindig (*informal*), shindy (*informal*), shouting match (*informal*), slanging match (*Brit.*), squabble, tiff, trouble, tumult, uproar **2.** castigation, dressing-down (*informal*), flea in one's ear (*informal*), lecture, reprimand, reproof, rollicking (*Brit. informal*), talking-to (*informal*), telling-off (*informal*), ticking-off (*informal*), tongue-lashing *~vb.* **3.** argue, brawl, dispute, fight, scrap (*informal*), spar, squabble, wrangle

rowel (rhymes with **towel**) *n* a small spiked wheel at the end of a spur.

rowing boat *n Chiefly Brit* a small pleasure boat propelled by oars. Usual US and Canad. word: **rowboat**

rowlock *n* a swivelling device attached to the top of the side of a boat that holds an oar in place.

royal *adj* 1 of or relating to a king or queen or a member of his or her family: *the royal yacht.* 2 **Royal** supported by or in the service of royalty: *the Royal Society of Medicine.* 3 very grand: *royal treatment.* ~*n* 4 *Informal* a king or queen or a member of his or her family. **royally** *adv*

Royal Air Force *n* the air force of Great Britain.

royal-blue *adj* deep blue.

royalist *n* 1 a supporter of a monarch or monarchy. ~*adj* 2 of or relating to royalists. **royalism** *n*

royal jelly *n* a substance secreted by worker bees and fed to all larvae when very young and to larvae destined to become queens throughout their growth.

Royal Marines *pl n Brit* a corps of soldiers specially trained in amphibious warfare.

Royal Navy *n* the navy of Great Britain.

royalty *n, pl* **-ties** 1 royal people. 2 the rank or power of a king or queen. 3 a percentage of the revenue from the sale of a book, performance of a work, use of a patented invention or of land, paid to the author, inventor, or owner.

royal warrant *n* an authorization to a tradesman to supply goods to a royal household.

RPI (in Britain) retail price index: a measure of the changes in the average level of retail prices of selected goods.

rpm revolutions per minute.

RR 1 Right Reverend. 2 *US & Canad* rural route.

RSA 1 Republic of South Africa. 2 (in New Zealand) Returned Services Association. 3 Royal Scottish Academy. 4 Royal Society of Arts.

RSI repetitive strain injury: pain in the arm caused by repeated awkward movements, such as in typing.

RSM regimental sergeant major.

RSPCA (in Britain) Royal Society for the Prevention of Cruelty to Animals.

RSVP please reply.

Rt Hon. Right Honourable: a title of respect for a Privy Councillor, certain peers, and the Lord Mayor or Lord Provost of certain cities.

Ru *Chem* ruthenium.

rub *vb* **rubbing, rubbed** 1 to apply pressure and friction to (something) with a circular or backwards-and-forwards movement. 2 to move (something) with pressure along or against (a surface). 3 to clean, polish, or dry by rubbing. 4 to spread with pressure, esp. so that it can be absorbed: *rub beeswax into all polishable surfaces.* 5 to chafe or fray through rubbing. 6 to mix (fat) into flour with the fingertips, as in making pastry. 7 **rub it in** to emphasize an unpleasant fact. 8 **rub up the wrong way** to annoy. ~*n* 9 the act of rubbing. 10 **the rub** the obstacle or difficulty: *there's the rub.* ~See also **rub along, rub down,** etc.

rub along *vb Brit* 1 to have a friendly relationship. 2 to continue in spite of difficulties.

rubato *Music* ~*n, pl* **-tos** 1 flexibility of tempo in performance: *his playing brought much beautifully felt but never sentimental rubato to the music.* ~*adj, adv* 2 to be played with a flexible tempo.

rubber[1] *n* 1 an elastic material obtained from the latex of certain plants, such as the rubber tree. 2 a similar substance produced synthetically. 3 *Chiefly Brit* a piece of rubber used for erasing something written. 4 *US slang* a condom. 5 **rubbers** *US* rubber-coated waterproof overshoes. ~*adj* 6 made of or producing rubber. **rubbery** *adj*

rubber[2] *n* 1 *Bridge, whist* a match of three games. 2 a series of matches or games in various sports.

rubber band *n* a continuous loop of thin rubber, used to hold papers together.

rubberize *or* **-ise** *vb* **-izing, -ized** *or* **-ising, -ised** to coat or treat with rubber.

rubberneck *US slang* ~*vb* 1 to stare in a naive or foolish manner. ~*n* 2 a person who stares inquisitively. 3 a sightseer or tourist.

rubber plant *n* 1 a large house plant with glossy leathery leaves. 2 same as **rubber tree.**

rubber stamp *n* 1 a device used for imprinting dates or signatures on forms or invoices. 2 automatic authorization of something. 3 a person or body that gives official approval to decisions taken elsewhere but has no real power. ~*vb* **rubber-stamp** 4 *Informal* to approve automatically.

rubber tree *n* a tropical tree cultivated for its latex, which is the major source of commercial rubber.

rubbing *n* an impression taken of an engraved or raised design by laying paper over it and rubbing with wax or charcoal.

rubbish *n* 1 discarded or waste matter. 2 anything worthless or of poor quality: *the rubbish on television.* 3 foolish words or speech. ~*vb* 4 *Informal* to criticize. **rubbishy** *adj*

rubble *n* 1 debris from ruined buildings. 2 pieces of broken stones or bricks.

rub down *vb* 1 to prepare (a surface) for painting by rubbing it with sandpaper. 2 to dry or clean (an animal or person) vigorously, esp. after exercise.

rubella (roo-**bell**-a) *n* a mild contagious viral disease characterized by cough, sore throat, and skin rash. Also called: **German measles**

Rubicon (**roo**-bik-on) *n* **cross the Rubicon** to commit oneself to a course of action which cannot be altered.

rubicund (**roo**-bik-kund) *adj Old-fashioned* of a reddish colour.

rubidium (roo-**bid**-ee-um) *n Chem* a soft highly reactive radioactive metallic element used in electronic valves, photocells, and special glass. Symbol: Rb

ruble *n* same as **rouble.**

THESAURUS

rowdy 1. *adj.* boisterous, disorderly, loud, loutish, noisy, obstreperous, rough, unruly, uproarious, wild 2. *n.* brawler, casual, hooligan, lager lout, lout, ned (*Scot.*), rough (*informal*), ruffian, tearaway (*Brit.*), tough, troublemaker, yahoo, yob *or* yobbo (*Brit. slang*)

royal 1. imperial, kinglike, kingly, monarchical, princely, queenly, regal, sovereign 2. august, grand, impressive, magnificent, majestic, splendid, stately, superb, superior

rub *vb.* 1. abrade, caress, chafe, clean, fray, grate, knead, massage, polish, scour, scrape, shine, smooth, stroke, wipe 2. apply, put, smear, spread 3. **rub up the wrong way** aggravate (*informal*), anger, annoy, bug (*informal*), get in one's hair (*informal*), get one's goat (*slang*), get on one's nerves (*informal*), get under one's skin (*informal*), irk, irritate, nark (*Brit., Austral., & N.Z. slang*), peeve (*informal*), piss one off (*taboo slang*), vex ~*n.* 4. caress, kneading, massage, polish, shine, stroke, wipe 5. catch, difficulty, drawback, hindrance, hitch, impediment, obstacle, problem, snag, trouble

rubbish 1. debris, dregs, dross, flotsam and jetsam, garbage (*chiefly U.S.*), junk (*informal*), litter, lumber,

rub off *vb* **1** to remove or be removed by rubbing: *rub the skins off the hazelnuts.* **2** to have an effect through close association: *glamour can rub off on you by association.*

rub out *vb* **1** to remove or be removed with a rubber. **2** *US slang* to murder.

rubric (**roo**-brik) *n* **1** a set of rules of conduct or procedure, esp. one for the conduct of Christian church services. **2** a title or heading in a book.

ruby *n, pl* **-bies 1** a deep red transparent precious gemstone. *~adj* **2** deep red. **3** denoting a fortieth anniversary: *a ruby wedding.*

RUC Royal Ulster Constabulary.

ruche *n* a strip of pleated or frilled lace or ribbon used to decorate clothes.

ruck[1] *n* **1 the ruck** ordinary people, often in a crowd. **2** *Rugby* a loose scrum that forms around the ball when it is on the ground.

ruck[2] *n* **1** a wrinkle or crease. *~vb* **2** to wrinkle or crease: *his shoe had rucked up one corner of the rug.*

rucksack *n* a large bag, with two straps, carried on the back.

ruction *n Informal* **1** an uproar. **2 ructions** an unpleasant row.

rudder *n* **1** *Naut* a vertical hinged piece that projects into the water at the stern, used to steer a boat. **2** a vertical control surface attached to the rear of the fin used to steer an aircraft. **rudderless** *adj*

ruddy *adj* **-dier, -diest 1** (of the complexion) having a healthy reddish colour. **2** red or pink: *a ruddy glow.* *~adv, adj* **3** *Informal* bloody: *too ruddy slow; I just went through the ruddy ceiling.*

rude *adj* **1** insulting or impolite. **2** vulgar or obscene: *rude words.* **3** unexpected and unpleasant: *we received a rude awakening.* **4** roughly or crudely made: *the rude hovels.* **5** robust or sturdy: *the very picture of rude health.* **6** lacking refinement. **rudely** *adv* **rudeness** *n*

rudiment *n* **1 rudiments a** the simplest and most basic stages of a subject. **b** a partially developed version of something: *the rudiments of a democratic society.* **2** *Biol* an organ or part that is incompletely developed or no longer functions. **rudimentary** *adj*

rue[1] *vb* **ruing, rued** *Literary* to feel regret for.

rue[2] *n* an aromatic shrub with bitter evergreen leaves formerly used in medicine.

rueful *adj* feeling or expressing sorrow or regret: *a rueful smile.* **ruefully** *adv*

ruff[1] *n* **1** a circular pleated or fluted cloth collar. **2** a natural growth of long or coloured hair or feathers around the necks of certain animals or birds. **3** a bird of the sandpiper family.

ruff[2] *n, vb Cards* same as **trump**[1] (senses 1, 2).

ruffian *n* a violent lawless person.

ruffle *vb* **-fling, -fled 1** to disturb the smoothness of: *the wind was ruffling Dad's hair.* **2** to annoy or irritate. **3** (of a bird) to erect its feathers in anger or display. **4** to flick cards or pages rapidly. *~n* **5** a strip of pleated material used as a trim.

rufous *adj* (of birds or animals) reddish-brown.

rug *n* **1** a small carpet. **2** a thick woollen blanket. **3** *Slang* a wig. **4 pull the rug out from under** to betray or leave defenceless.

rugby *or* **rugby football** *n* a form of football played with an oval ball in which the handling and carrying of the ball is permitted.

rugby league *n* a form of rugby played between teams of 13 players, in which professionalism is allowed.

rugby union *n* a form of rugby played only by amateurs, in teams of 15.

rugged (**rug**-gid) *adj* **1** rocky or steep: *the rugged mountains of Sicily's interior.* **2** with an uneven or jagged surface. **3** (of the face) strong-featured. **4** rough, sturdy, or determined in character. **5** (of equipment or machines) designed to withstand rough treatment or use in rough conditions.

rugger *n Informal, chiefly Brit* rugby.

ruin *vb* **1** to destroy or spoil completely. **2** to cause (someone) to lose money: *the first war ruined him.* *~n* **3** the state of being destroyed or decayed. **4** loss of

THESAURUS

offal, refuse, scrap, trash, waste **2.** balderdash, balls (*taboo slang*), bilge (*informal*), bosh (*informal*), bull (*slang*), bunkum *or* buncombe (*chiefly U.S.*), claptrap (*informal*), cobblers (*Brit. taboo slang*), codswallop (*Brit. slang*), crap (*slang*), drivel, garbage (*chiefly U.S.*), gibberish, guff (*slang*), hot air (*informal*), nonsense, pap, piffle (*informal*), poppycock (*informal*), rot, shit (*taboo slang*), stuff and nonsense, trash, tripe (*informal*), twaddle

rub out 1. cancel, delete, efface, erase, excise, expunge, obliterate, remove, wipe out **2.** *U.S. slang* assassinate, blow away (*slang, chiefly U.S.*), bump off (*slang*), butcher, dispatch, do in (*informal*), eliminate (*slang*), hit (*slang*), kill, knock off (*slang*), murder, slaughter, slay, take out (*slang*), waste (*informal*)

ruddy 1. blooming, blushing, florid, flushed, glowing, healthy, radiant, red, rosy, rubicund, sunburnt **2.** crimson, pink, red, reddish, roseate, ruby, scarlet

rude 1. abrupt, abusive, blunt, brusque, cheeky, churlish, curt, discourteous, disrespectful, ill-mannered, impertinent, impolite, impudent, inconsiderate, insolent, insulting, offhand, peremptory, short, uncivil, unmannerly **2.** barbarous, boorish, brutish, coarse, crude, graceless, gross, ignorant, illiterate, loutish, low, oafish, obscene, rough, savage, scurrilous, uncivilized, uncouth, uncultured, uneducated, ungracious, unpolished, unrefined, untutored, vulgar **3.** abrupt, harsh, sharp, startling, sudden, unpleasant, violent **4.** artless, crude, inartistic, inelegant, makeshift, primitive, raw, rough, rough-hewn, roughly-made, simple

rudimentary basic, early, elementary, embryonic, fundamental, immature, initial, introductory, primary, primitive, undeveloped, vestigial

rudiments basics, beginnings, elements, essentials, first principles, foundation, fundamentals

rueful conscience-stricken, contrite, dismal, doleful, lugubrious, melancholy, mournful, penitent, pitiable, pitiful, plaintive, regretful, remorseful, repentant, sad, sorrowful, sorry, woebegone, woeful

ruffian brute, bully boy, heavy (*slang*), hoodlum, hooligan, lager lout, rowdy, thug, tough, villain

ruffle 1. derange, disarrange, discompose, dishevel, disorder, mess up, rumple, tousle, wrinkle **2.** agitate, annoy, confuse, disconcert, disquiet, disturb, faze, fluster, harass, hassle (*informal*), irritate, nettle, peeve (*informal*), perturb, put out, rattle (*informal*), shake up (*informal*), stir, torment, trouble, unnerve, unsettle, upset, vex, worry

rugged 1. broken, bumpy, craggy, difficult, irregular, jagged, ragged, rocky, rough, stark, uneven **2.** furrowed, leathery, lined, rough-hewn, strong-featured, weather-beaten, weathered, worn, wrinkled **3.** dour, gruff, hard, harsh, rough, severe, sour, stern, surly

ruin *vb.* **1.** botch, bring down, bring to nothing, bring to ruin, crush, defeat, demolish, destroy, devastate, lay in ruins, lay waste, make a mess of, mess up, overthrow, overturn, overwhelm, raze, shatter, smash, spoil, wreak havoc upon, wreck **2.** bankrupt, break, impoverish, pauperize *~n.* **3.** breakdown, collapse,

wealth or position. **5** a destroyed or decayed building or town. **6** something that is severely damaged: *my heart was an aching ruin.*

ruination *n* **1** the act of ruining or the state of being ruined. **2** something that causes ruin.

ruinous *adj* **1** causing ruin or destruction. **2** more expensive than can reasonably be afforded: *ruinous rates of exchange.* **ruinously** *adv*

rule *n* **1** a statement of what is allowed, for example in a game or procedure. **2** a customary form or procedure: *he has his own rule: be firm, be clear, but never be rude.* **3 the rule** the common order of things: *humanitarian gestures were more the exception than the rule.* **4** the exercise of governmental authority or control: *the rule of President Marcos.* **5** the period of time in which a monarch or government has power: *four decades of Communist rule.* **6** a device with a straight edge for guiding or measuring: *a slide rule.* **7** *Printing* a long thin line or dash. **8** *Christianity* a systematic body of laws and customs followed by members of a religious order. **9** *Law* an order by a court or judge. **10 as a rule** usually. *~vb* **ruling, ruled 11** to govern (people or a political unit). **12** to be pre-eminent or superior. **13** to be customary or prevalent: *chaos ruled as the scene turned into one of total confusion.* **14** to decide authoritatively: *the judges ruled that men could be prosecuted for rape offences against their wives.* **15** to mark with straight parallel lines or one straight line. **16** to restrain or control.

rule of thumb *n* a rough and practical approach, based on experience, rather than theory.

rule out *vb* **1** to dismiss from consideration. **2** to make impossible.

ruler *n* **1** a person who rules or commands. **2** a strip of wood, metal, or plastic, with straight edges, used for measuring and drawing straight lines.

ruling *adj* **1** controlling or exercising authority. **2** predominant. *~n* **3** a decision of someone in authority.

rum[1] *n* alcoholic drink made from sugar cane.

rum[2] *adj* **rummer, rummest** *Brit slang* strange or unusual.

Rumanian *adj, n* same as **Romanian.**

rumba *n* **1** a rhythmic and syncopated dance of Cuban origin. **2** music for this dance.

rumble *vb* **-bling, -bled 1** to make or cause to make a deep echoing sound: *thunder rumbled overhead.* **2** to move with such a sound: *a slow freight train rumbled past.* **3** *Brit slang* to find out about (someone or something): *his real identity was rumbled.* *~n* **4** a deep resonant sound. **5** *US & NZ slang* a gang fight. **rumbling** *adj, n*

rumbustious *adj* boisterous or unruly.

ruminant *n* **1** a mammal that chews the cud, such as cattle, deer, goats, and camels. *~adj* **2** of ruminants. **3** meditating or contemplating in a slow quiet way.

ruminate *vb* **-nating, -nated 1** (of ruminants) to chew (the cud). **2** to meditate or ponder. **rumination** *n* **ruminative** *adj*

rummage *vb* **-maging, -maged 1** to search untidily. *~n* **2** an untidy search through a collection of things.

rummage sale *n* *US & Canad* a jumble sale.

rummy *n* a card game based on collecting sets and sequences.

rumour *or US* **rumor** *n* **1** information, often a mixture of truth and untruth, told by one person to another. **2** gossip or common talk. *~vb* **3 be rumoured** to be circulated as a rumour: *he is rumoured to have at least 53 yachts.*

rump *n* **1** a person's buttocks. **2** the rear part of an animal's or bird's body. **3** Also called: **rump steak** a cut of beef from the rump. **4** a small core of members within a group who remain loyal to it: *the rump of the once-influential communist party.*

rumple *vb* **-pling, -pled** to make or become crumpled or dishevelled.

rumpus *n, pl* **-puses** a noisy or confused commotion.

run *vb* **running, ran, run 1** to move on foot at a rapid pace. **2** to pass over (a distance or route) in running: *being a man isn't about running the fastest mile.* **3** to take part in (a race): *I ran a decent race.* **4** to carry out as if by running: *he is running errands for his big brother.* **5** to flee. **6** to travel somewhere in a vehicle. **7** to give a lift to (someone) in a vehicle: *one wet day I ran her down to the service.* **8** to drive or maintain and operate (a vehicle). **9** to travel regularly between aces on a route: *trains running through the night.* **10** to move or pass quickly: *he ran his hand across his forehead.* **11** to function or cause to function: *run the video tape backwards.* **12** to manage: *he ran a small hotel.* **13** to continue in a particular direction or for a particular time or distance: *a road running alongside the Nile; a performing arts festival running in the city*

THESAURUS

crackup (*informal*), damage, decay, defeat, destruction, devastation, disintegration, disrepair, dissolution, downfall, failure, fall, havoc, nemesis, overthrow, ruination, subversion, the end, undoing, Waterloo, wreck, wreckage **4.** bankruptcy, collapse, crash, destitution, failure, fall, insolvency

ruinous baleful, baneful (*archaic*), calamitous, catastrophic, crippling, deadly, deleterious, destructive, devastating, dire, disastrous, extravagant, fatal, immoderate, injurious, murderous, noxious, pernicious, shattering, wasteful

rule *n.* **1.** axiom, canon, criterion, decree, dictum, direction, guide, guideline, law, maxim, order, ordinance, precept, principle, regulation, ruling, standard, tenet **2.** course, formula, method, policy, procedure, way **3.** condition, convention, custom, form, habit, order *or* way of things, practice, procedure, routine, tradition, wont **4.** administration, ascendancy, authority, command, control, direction, domination, dominion, empire, government, influence, jurisdiction, leadership, mastery, power, regime, reign, supremacy, sway **5. as a rule** customarily, for the most part, generally, mainly, normally, on the whole, ordinarily, usually *~vb.* **6.** administer, be in authority, be in power, be number one (*informal*), command, control, direct, dominate, govern, guide, hold sway, lead, manage, preside over, regulate, reign, wear the crown **7.** be customary (pre-eminent, prevalent, superior), hold sway, obtain, predominate, preponderate, prevail **8.** adjudge, adjudicate, decide, decree, determine, establish, find, judge, lay down, pronounce, resolve, settle

rule out ban, debar, dismiss, disqualify, eliminate, exclude, forbid, leave out, obviate, preclude, prevent, prohibit, proscribe, reject

ruler 1. commander, controller, crowned head, emperor, empress, governor, head of state, king, leader, lord, monarch, potentate, prince, princess, queen, sovereign **2.** measure, rule, straight edge, yardstick

ruling *adj.* **1.** commanding, controlling, dominant, governing, leading, regnant, reigning, upper **2.** chief, current, dominant, main, predominant, pre-eminent, preponderant, prevailing, prevalent, principal, supreme *~n.* **3.** adjudication, decision, decree, finding, judgment, pronouncement, resolution, verdict

ruminate brood, chew over, cogitate, consider, contemplate, deliberate, meditate, mull over, muse, ponder, reflect, revolve, think, turn over in one's mind, weigh

rumour 1. *n.* buzz, canard, dirt (*informal*), gossip,

for six weeks. **14** *Law* to have legal force or effect: *the club's lease runs out next May.* **15** to be subjected to or affected by: *she ran a high risk of losing her hair.* **16** to tend or incline: *he was of medium height and running to fat.* **17** to recur persistently or be inherent: *the capacity for infidelity ran in the genes.* **18** to flow or cause (liquids) to flow: *sweat ran down her face.* **19** to dissolve and spread: *the soles of the shoes peeled off and the colours ran.* **20** (of stitches) to unravel. **21** to spread or circulate: *rumours ran around quickly.* **22** to publish or be published in a newspaper or magazine: *Today ran a jubilant front-page headline.* **23** *Chiefly US & Canad* to stand as a candidate for political or other office: *he has formally announced his decision to run for the office of President.* **24** to get past or through: *the oil tanker was hit as it tried to run the blockade.* **25** to smuggle (goods, esp. arms). **26** (of fish) to migrate upstream from the sea, esp. in order to spawn. **27** *Cricket* to score (a run or number of runs) by hitting the ball and running between the wickets. *~n* **28** the act or an instance of running: *he broke into a run.* **29** a distance covered by running or a period of running: *many of the men fell down from the long run of five miles.* **30** a trip in a vehicle, esp. for pleasure: *our only treat is a run in the car to Dartmoor.* **31** free and unrestricted access: *he had the run of the house.* **32 a** a period of time during which a machine or computer operates. **b** the amount of work performed in such a period. **33** a continuous or sustained period: *a run of seven defeats.* **34** a continuous sequence of performances: *"The Rape of the Belt" had a good run at the Piccadilly.* **35** *Cards* a sequence of winning cards in one suit: *a run of spades.* **36** type, class, or category: *he had nothing in common with the usual run of terrorists.* **37** a continuous and urgent demand: *a run on the pound.* **38** a series of unravelled stitches, esp. in tights. **39** a steeply inclined course, esp. a snow-covered one used for skiing. **40** an enclosure for domestic fowls or other animals: *the chicken run.* **41** (esp. in Australia and New Zealand) a tract of land for grazing livestock. **42** the migration of fish upstream in order to spawn. **43** *Music* a rapid scalelike passage of notes. **44** *Cricket* a score of one, normally achieved by both batsmen running from one end of the wicket to the other after one of them has hit the ball. **45** *Baseball* an instance of a batter touching all four bases safely, thereby scoring. **46 a run for one's money** *Informal* **a** a close competition. **b** pleasure or success from an activity. **47 in the long run** as an eventual outcome. **48 on the run** escaping from arrest. **49 the runs** *Slang* diarrhoea. ~See also **runabout.**

runabout *n* **1** a small car used for short journeys. *~vb* **run about 2** to move busily from place to place.

run across *vb* to meet unexpectedly by chance.

run along *vb* to go away.

run away *vb* **1** to go away. **2** to escape. **3** (of a horse) to gallop away uncontrollably: *the horse ran away with him.* **4 run away with a** to abscond or elope with: *I ran away with David.* **b** to escape from the control of: *he let his imagination run away with him.* **c** to win easily or be certain of victory in (a competition): *the Spaniards at one stage seemed to be running away with the match.* *~n* **runaway 5** a person or animal that runs away. *~adj* **runaway 6** no longer under control: *a runaway train.* **7** (of a race or victory) easily won.

run down *vb* **1** to be rude about: *he is busy running us down and insulting other Europeans.* **2** to reduce in number or size: *it should be possible to run down the existing hospitals almost entirely.* **3** (of a device such as a clock or battery) to lose power gradually and cease to function. **4** to hit and knock to the ground with a moving vehicle. **5** to pursue and find or capture: *while I was there, Moscow ran me down, convinced I was ready to defect.* *~adj* **run-down 6** tired or ill. **7** shabby or dilapidated. *~n* **rundown 8** a reduction in number or size. **9** a brief review or summary.

THESAURUS

hearsay, news, report, story, talk, tidings, whisper, word **2.** *vb.* circulate, gossip, noise abroad, pass around, publish, put about, report, say, tell, whisper

run *vb.* **1.** bolt, career, dart, dash, gallop, hare (*Brit. informal*), hasten, hotfoot, hurry, jog, leg it (*informal*), lope, race, rush, scamper, scramble, scud, scurry, speed, sprint **2.** abscond, beat a retreat, beat it (*slang*), bolt, clear out, cut and run (*informal*), decamp, depart, do a runner (*slang*), escape, flee, fly the coop (*U.S. & Canad. informal*), leg it (*informal*), make a run for it, make off, scarper (*Brit. slang*), show a clean pair of heels, skedaddle (*informal*), take flight, take off (*informal*), take to one's heels **3.** bear, carry, convey, drive, give a lift to, manoeuvre, operate, propel, transport **4.** go, operate, ply **5.** course, glide, go, move, pass, roll, skim, slide **6.** function, go, operate, perform, tick, work **7.** administer, be in charge of, boss (*informal*), carry on, conduct, control, coordinate, direct, handle, head, lead, look after, manage, mastermind, operate, oversee, own, regulate, superintend, supervise, take care of **8.** continue, extend, go, last, lie, proceed, range, reach, stretch **9.** cascade, discharge, flow, go, gush, issue, leak, move, pour, proceed, spill, spout, stream **10.** be diffused, bleed, lose colour, mix, spread **11.** come apart, come undone, ladder, tear, unravel **12.** be current, circulate, climb, go round, spread, trail **13.** display, feature, print, publish **14.** be a candidate, challenge, compete, contend, put oneself up for, stand, take part **15.** deal in, ship, smuggle, sneak, traffic in *~n.* **16.** dash, gallop, jog, race, rush, sprint, spurt **17.** drive, excursion, jaunt, journey, joy ride (*informal*), lift, outing, ride, round, spin (*informal*), trip **18.** chain, course, cycle, passage, period, round, season, sequence, series, spell, streak, stretch, string **19.** category, class, kind, order, sort, type, variety **20.** application, demand, pressure, rush **21.** ladder, rip, snag, tear **22.** coop, enclosure, pen **23. in the long run** at the end of the day, eventually, in the end, in the final analysis, in time, ultimately, when all is said and done **24. on the run** at liberty, escaping, fugitive, in flight, on the lam (*U.S. slang*), on the loose

run across bump into, chance upon, come across, come upon, encounter, meet, meet with, run into

run away *~vb* **1.** abscond, beat it (*slang*), bolt, clear out, cut and run (*informal*), decamp, do a bunk (*Brit. slang*), do a runner (*slang*), escape, flee, fly the coop (*U.S. & Canad. informal*), hook it (*slang*), make a run for it, run off, scarper (*Brit. slang*), scram (*informal*), show a clean pair of heels, skedaddle (*informal*), take flight, take off, take to one's heels **2.** *with* **with a.** abduct, abscond, elope **b.** romp home, walk it (*informal*), win by a mile (*informal*), win easily, win hands down *~n.* **3. runaway** absconder, deserter, escapee, escaper, fugitive, refugee, truant *~adj.* **4. runaway** escaped, fleeing, fugitive, loose, out of control, uncontrolled, wild **5. runaway** easily won, easy, effortless

run down *~vb* **1.** bad-mouth (*slang, chiefly U.S. & Canad.*), belittle, criticize adversely, decry, defame, denigrate, disparage, knock (*informal*), put down, revile, rubbish (*informal*), slag (off) (*slang*), speak ill of, vilify **2.** curtail, cut, cut back, decrease, drop, pare down, reduce, trim **3.** hit, knock down, knock over, run into, run over, strike *~adj* **4. run-down** below par, debilitated, drained, enervated, exhausted, fatigued, out of condition, peaky, tired, under the weather (*informal*), unhealthy, weak, weary, worn-out **5. run-down** broken-down, decrepit, dilapidated, dingy, ramshackle, seedy, shabby, tumble-down, worn-out *~n.* **6.**

rune *n* **1** any of the characters of the earliest Germanic alphabet. **2** an obscure piece of writing using mysterious symbols. **runic** *adj*

rung[1] *n* **1** one of the bars forming the steps of a ladder. **2** a crosspiece between the legs of a chair.

rung[2] *vb* the past participle of **ring**[1].

run in *vb* **1** to run (an engine) gently, usually when it is new. **2** *Informal* to arrest. *~n* **run-in 3** *Informal* an argument or quarrel.

run into *vb* **1** to be beset by: *the mission has run into difficulty.* **2** to meet unexpectedly. **3** to extend to: *the cost of the scheme runs into millions of pounds.* **4** to collide with.

runnel *n Literary* a small stream.

runner *n* **1** a competitor in a race. **2** a messenger for a firm. **3** a person involved in smuggling. **4 a** either of the strips of metal or wood on which a sledge runs. **b** the blade of an ice skate. **5** *Bot* a slender horizontal stem of a plant, such as the strawberry, that grows along the surface of the soil and produces new roots and shoots. **6** a long strip of cloth used to decorate a table or as a rug. **7** a roller or guide for a sliding component.

runner bean *n* the edible pod and seeds of a type of climbing bean plant.

runner-up *n, pl* **runners-up** a person who comes second in a competition.

running *adj* **1** maintained continuously: *a running battle.* **2** without interruption: *for the third day running.* **3 a** flowing: *rinse them under cold running water.* **b** supplied through a tap: *there is no electricity, no running water, and no telephone.* **4** operating: *running costs.* **5** discharging pus: *a running sore.* **6** accomplished at a run: *a running jump.* **7** moving or slipping easily, as a rope or a knot. *~n* **8** the act of moving or flowing quickly. **9** management or organization: *the running of the farm.* **10** the operation or maintenance of a machine. **11 in** *or* **out of the running** having *or* not having a good chance in a competition. **12 make the running** to set the pace in a competition or race.

running board *n* a board along the side of a vehicle, for help in stepping into it.

running head *n Printing* a heading printed at the top of every page of a book.

running mate *n* **1** *US* a candidate for the lesser of two linked positions, esp. a candidate for the vice-presidency. **2** a horse that pairs another in a team.

running repairs *pl n* repairs that are done without greatly disrupting operations.

runny *adj* **-nier, -niest 1** tending to flow: *a runny egg.* **2** producing moisture: *a runny nose.*

run off *vb* **1** to leave quickly. **2 run off with a** to run away with in order to marry or live with. **b** to steal. **3** to produce (copies of a document) on a machine. **4** to drain (liquid) or (of liquid) to be drained. *~n* **run-off 5** an extra race or contest to decide the winner after a tie. **6** *NZ* grazing land for cattle.

run-of-the-mill *adj* ordinary or average.

run on *vb* to continue without interruption.

run out *vb* **1** to use up or (of a supply) to be used up: *we soon ran out of gas.* **2** to become invalid: *my passport has run out.* **3 run out on** *Informal* to desert or abandon. **4** *Cricket* to dismiss (a running batsman) by breaking the wicket with the ball while he is running between the wickets. *~n* **run-out 5** *Cricket* dismissal of a batsman by running him out.

run over *vb* **1** to knock down (a person) with a moving vehicle. **2** to overflow. **3** to examine hastily.

runt *n* **1** the smallest and weakest young animal in a litter. **2** an undersized or inferior person.

run through *vb* **1** to practise or rehearse. **2** to pierce with a sword or other weapon. *~n* **run-through 3** a practice or rehearsal.

run to *vb* **1** to reach an amount or size: *the testimony ran to a million words.* **2** to be or have enough money for: *we do not run to these luxuries, I am afraid.*

run up *vb* **1** to amass: *running up massive debts.* **2** to make by sewing together quickly. **3 run up against** to experience (difficulties). *~n* **run-up 4** the time just before an event: *the run-up to the elections.*

runway *n* a hard level roadway where aircraft take off and land.

rupee *n* the standard monetary unit of a number of countries including India and Pakistan.

rupture *n* **1** the act of breaking or the state of being

THESAURUS

rundown briefing, outline, précis, recap (*informal*), résumé, review, run-through, sketch, summary, synopsis

run in 1. break in gently, run gently **2.** *informal* apprehend, arrest, bust (*informal*), collar (*informal*), feel one's collar (*slang*), jail, lift (*slang*), nab (*informal*), nail (*informal*), pick up, pinch (*informal*), pull in (*Brit. slang*), take into custody, take to jail, throw in jail

run into 1. be beset by, be confronted by, encounter, meet with **2.** bump into, chance upon, come across, come upon, encounter, meet, run across **3.** bump into, collide with, crash into, dash against, hit, ram, strike

runner 1. athlete, harrier, jogger, miler, sprinter **2.** courier, dispatch bearer, errand boy, messenger **3.** *Bot.* offshoot, shoot, sprig, sprout, stem, tendril

running *adj.* **1.** constant, continuous, incessant, in succession, on the trot (*informal*), perpetual, together, unbroken, unceasing, uninterrupted **2.** flowing, moving, streaming *~n.* **3.** administration, charge, conduct, control, coordination, direction, leadership, management, organization, regulation, superintendency, supervision **4.** functioning, maintenance, operation, performance, working **5.** *as in* **in** *or* **out of the running** competition, contention, contest

run off 1. bolt, clear out, cut and run (*informal*), decamp, do a runner (*slang*), escape, flee, fly the coop (*U.S. & Canad. informal*), make off, run away, scarper (*Brit. slang*), show a clean pair of heels, skedaddle (*informal*), take flight, take to one's heels **2.** *with* **with a.** abscond, elope, run away **b.** lift (*informal*), make off, pinch (*informal*), purloin, run away, steal, swipe (*slang*) **3.** churn out (*informal*), duplicate, print, produce **4.** bleed, drain, flow away, siphon, tap

run-of-the-mill average, banal, common, commonplace, fair, mediocre, middling, modest, ordinary, passable, tolerable, undistinguished, unexceptional, unexciting, unimpressive

run out 1. be cleaned out, be exhausted, be out of, cease, close, come to a close, dry up, end, exhaust one's supply of, expire, fail, finish, give out, have no more of, have none left, have no remaining, peter out, terminate **2.** *with* **on** *informal* abandon, desert, forsake, leave high and dry, leave holding the baby, leave in the lurch, rat (*informal*), run away from

run over 1. hit, knock down, knock over, run down, strike **2.** brim over, overflow, spill, spill over **3.** check, examine, go over, go through, review, run through, survey

run through 1. go over, practise, read, rehearse, run over **2.** impale, pierce, spit, stab, stick, transfix

rupture *n.* **1.** breach, break, burst, cleavage, cleft, crack, fissure, fracture, rent, split, tear **2.** altercation, breach, break, bust-up (*informal*), contention, disagreement, disruption, estrangement, falling-out (*in-*

broken. **2** a breach of peaceful or friendly relations. **3** *Pathol* a hernia. *~vb* **-turing, -tured 4** to break or burst. **5** to cause a breach in relations or friendship. **6** to affect or be affected with a hernia.

rural *adj* in or of the countryside.

rural dean *n Chiefly Brit* a clergyman with authority over a group of parishes.

rural route *n US & Canad* a mail service or route in a rural area.

ruse (**rooz**) *n* an action or plan intended to mislead someone.

rush[1] *vb* **1** to move or do very quickly. **2** to force (someone) to act hastily. **3** to make a sudden attack upon (a person or place). **4** to proceed or approach in a reckless manner. **5** to come or flow quickly or suddenly: *the water rushed in, and the next instant the boat was swamped.* *~n* **6** a sudden quick or violent movement. **7** a sudden demand or need. **8** a sudden surge towards someone or something: *the gold rush.* **9** a sudden surge of sensation. **10** a sudden flow of air or liquid. **11 rushes** (in film-making) the initial prints of a scene before editing. *~adj* **12** done with speed or urgency: *a rush job.*

rush[2] *n* a plant which grows in wet places and has a slender pithy stem. **rushy** *adj*

rush hour *n* a period at the beginning and end of the working day when large numbers of people are travelling to or from work.

rush light *n* an old-fashioned candle made of rushes.

rusk *n* a hard brown crisp biscuit, often used for feeding babies.

russet *adj* **1** *Literary* reddish-brown. *~n* **2** an apple with a rough reddish-brown skin.

Russian *adj* **1** of Russia. *~n* **2** a person from Russia. **3** the official language of Russia and, formerly, of the Soviet Union.

Russian roulette *n* an act of bravado in which a person spins the cylinder of a revolver loaded with only one cartridge and presses the trigger with the barrel against his or her own head.

rust *n* **1** a reddish-brown oxide coating formed on iron or steel by the action of oxygen and moisture. **2** a fungal disease of plants which produces a reddish-brown discolouration. *~adj* **3** reddish-brown. *~vb* **4** to become coated with a layer of rust. **5** to deteriorate through lack of use: *my brain had rusted up.*

rustic *adj* **1** of or resembling country people. **2** of or living in the country. **3** crude, awkward, or uncouth. **4** made of untrimmed branches: *rustic furniture.* *~n* **5** a person from the country. **rusticity** *n*

rusticate *vb* **-cating, -cated 1** *Brit* to send (a student) down from university for a specified time as a punishment. **2** to retire to the country. **3** to make or become rustic.

rustle[1] *vb* **-tling, -tled 1** to make a low crisp whispering sound: *the leaves rustled in the breeze.* *~n* **2** this sound.

rustle[2] *vb* **-tling, -tled** *Chiefly US & Canad* to steal (livestock). **rustler** *n*

rustle up *vb Informal* to prepare or find at short notice.

rusty *adj* **rustier, rustiest 1** affected by rust: *a rusty old freighter.* **2** reddish-brown. **3** out of practice in a skill or subject: *your skills may be a little rusty, but your past experience will more than make up for that.* **rustily** *adv* **rustiness** *n*

rut[1] *n* **1** a groove or furrow in a soft road, caused by wheels. **2** dull settled habits or way of living: *his career was in a rut.*

rut[2] *n* **1** a recurrent period of sexual excitement in certain male ruminants. *~vb* **rutting, rutted 2** (of male ruminants) to be in a period of sexual excitement.

ruthenium *n Chem* a rare hard brittle white metallic element. Symbol: Ru

rutherfordium *n US chem* an artificially produced radioactive element. Symbol: Rf

ruthless *adj* **1** feeling or showing no mercy. **2** thorough and forceful, regardless of effect: *the ruthless pursuit of cost-effectiveness.* **ruthlessly** *adv* **ruthlessness** *n*

rutted *adj* (of a road) very uneven because of ruts.

RV Revised Version (of the Bible).

rye *n* **1** a tall grasslike cereal grown for its light brown grain. **2** the grain of this plant. **3** Also called: **rye whiskey** whisky distilled from rye. **4** *US* short for **rye bread.**

rye bread *n* bread made entirely or partly from rye flour.

rye-grass *n* any of several grasses grown for fodder.

THESAURUS

formal), feud, hostility, quarrel, rift, schism, split **3.** *Pathol.* hernia *~vb.* **4.** break, burst, cleave, crack, fracture, puncture, rend, separate, sever, split, tear **5.** break off, cause a breach, come between, disrupt, divide, split

rural agrarian, agricultural, Arcadian, bucolic, countrified, country, hick (*informal, chiefly U.S. & Canad.*), pastoral, rustic, sylvan, upcountry

ruse artifice, blind, deception, device, dodge, hoax, imposture, manoeuvre, ploy, sham, stratagem, subterfuge, trick, wile

rush *vb.* **1.** accelerate, barrel (along) (*informal, chiefly U.S. & Canad.*), bolt, career, dart, dash, dispatch, expedite, fly, hasten, hotfoot, hurry, hustle, lose no time, make haste, make short work of, press, push, quicken, race, run, scramble, scurry, shoot, speed, speed up, sprint, stampede, tear **2.** attack, capture, charge, overcome, storm, take by storm *~n.* **3.** charge, dash, dispatch, expedition, haste, hurry, race, scramble, speed, stampede, surge, swiftness, urgency **4.** assault, charge, onslaught, push, storm, surge *~adj.* **5.** brisk, cursory, emergency, expeditious, fast, hasty, hurried, prompt, quick, rapid, swift, urgent

rust *n.* **1.** corrosion, oxidation **2.** blight, mildew, mould, must, rot *~vb.* **3.** corrode, oxidize **4.** atrophy, decay, decline, deteriorate, go stale, stagnate, tarnish

rustic *adj.* **1.** Arcadian, bucolic, countrified, country, pastoral, rural, sylvan, upcountry **2.** awkward, boorish, churlish, coarse, crude, graceless, hick (*informal, chiefly U.S. & Canad.*), homely, homespun, loutish, maladroit, plain, rough, simple, unaffected, uncouth, uncultured, unmannerly, unpolished, unrefined, unsophisticated *~n.* **3.** bumpkin, country boy, country cousin, countryman, countrywoman, hayseed (*U.S. & Canad. informal*), hick (*informal, chiefly U.S. & Canad.*), hillbilly, peasant, son of the soil, yokel

rustle 1. *vb.* crackle, crinkle, susurrate (*literary*), swish, whish, whisper **2.** *n.* crackle, crinkling, rustling, susurration (*literary*), whisper

rusty 1. corroded, oxidized, rust-covered, rusted **2.** chestnut, coppery, reddish, reddish-brown, russet, rust-coloured **3.** deficient, deteriorated, impaired, not what it was, out of practice, sluggish, stale

rut *n.* **1.** furrow, gouge, groove, indentation, pothole, track, trough, wheelmark **2.** dead end, groove, habit, humdrum existence, pattern, routine, system

ruthless adamant, barbarous, brutal, callous, cruel, ferocious, fierce, hard, hard-hearted, harsh, heartless, inexorable, inhuman, merciless, pitiless, relentless, remorseless, savage, severe, stern, unfeeling, unmerciful, unpitying, unrelenting, without pity

S

s second (of time).
S **1** South(ern). **2** *Chem* sulphur. **3** *Physics* siemens.
-'s *suffix* **1** forming the possessive singular of nouns and some pronouns: *woman's; one's.* **2** forming the possessive plural of nouns whose plurals do not end in *-s*: *children's.* **3** forming the plural of numbers, letters, or symbols: *20's.* **4** *Informal* contraction of *is* or *has*: *it's over.* **5** *Informal* contraction of *us* with *let*: *let's go.*
SA **1** Salvation Army. **2** South Africa. **3** South America. **4** South Australia.
Sabbath *n* **1** Saturday, observed by Jews as the day of worship and rest. **2** Sunday, observed by Christians as the day of worship and rest.
sabbatical *adj* **1** denoting a period of leave granted at intervals to university teachers for rest, study, or travel: *a sabbatical year.* *~n* **2** a sabbatical period.
SABC South African Broadcasting Corporation.
sable *n, pl* **-bles** *or* **-ble** **1** a marten of N Asia, N Europe, and America, with dark brown luxuriant fur. **2** the highly valued fur of this animal, used to make coats and hats. *~adj* **3** dark brown-to-black.
sable antelope *n* a large black African antelope with stout backward-curving horns.
sabot (**sab**-oh) *n* a heavy wooden or wooden-soled shoe; clog.
sabotage *n* **1** the deliberate destruction or damage of equipment, for example by enemy agents or dissatisfied employees. **2** deliberate obstruction of or damage to a cause or effort. *~vb* **-taging, -taged** **3** to destroy or disrupt by sabotage.
saboteur *n* a person who commits sabotage.
sabre *or US* **saber** *n* **1** a heavy single-edged cavalry sword with a curved blade. **2** a light sword used in fencing, with a narrow V-shaped blade.
sac *n* a pouch or pouchlike part in an animal or plant.
saccharin *n* an artificial sweetener.
saccharine *adj* **1** excessively sweet or sentimental: *saccharine ballads.* **2** like or containing sugar or saccharin.
sacerdotal *adj Formal* of priests or the priesthood.
sachet *n* **1** a small sealed usually plastic envelope containing a small portion of a substance such as shampoo. **2** a small soft bag of perfumed powder, placed in drawers to scent clothing.
sack[1] *n* **1** a large bag made of coarse cloth or thick paper and used for carrying or storing goods. **2** the amount contained in a sack. **3 the sack** *Informal* dismissal from employment. **4** *Slang* bed. **5 hit the sack** *Slang* to go to bed. *~vb* **6** *Informal* to dismiss from employment. **sacklike** *adj*
sack[2] *n* **1** the plundering of a captured town or city by an army or mob. *~vb* **2** to plunder and partially destroy (a town or city).
sackbut *n* a medieval form of trombone.
sackcloth *n* **1** same as **sacking. 2** garments made of such cloth, worn formerly to indicate mourning. **3 sackcloth and ashes** an exaggerated attempt to apologize or compensate for a mistake or wrongdoing.
sacking *n* coarse cloth woven from flax, hemp, or jute, and used to make sacks.
sacrament *n* **1** a symbolic religious ceremony in the Christian Church, such as baptism or communion. **2** Holy Communion. **3** something regarded as sacred. **sacramental** *adj*
sacred *adj* **1** exclusively devoted to a god or gods; holy. **2** connected with religion or intended for religious use: *sacred music.* **3** regarded as too important to be changed or interfered with: *sacred principles of free speech.* **4 sacred to** dedicated to: *the site is sacred to Vishnu.*
sacred cow *n Informal* a person, custom, belief, or institution regarded as being beyond criticism.
sacrifice *n* **1** a surrender of something of value in order to gain something more desirable or prevent some evil. **2** a ritual killing of a person or animal as an offering to a god. **3** a symbolic offering of something to a god. **4** the person or animal killed or offered. *~vb* **-ficing, -ficed** **5** to make a sacrifice (of). **6** *Chess* to permit or force one's opponent to capture (a piece) as a tactical move. **sacrificial** *adj*
sacrifice paddock *n NZ* a grassed field which is allowed to be grazed completely so that it can be cultivated and sown again later.
sacrilege *n* **1** the misuse of or disrespect shown to something sacred. **2** disrespect for a person who is widely admired or a belief that is widely accepted: *it is a sacrilege to offend democracy.* **sacrilegious** *adj*
sacristan *n* a person in charge of the contents of a church; sexton.
sacristy *n, pl* **-ties** a room attached to a church or chapel where the sacred objects are kept.
sacrosanct *adj* regarded as too important to be criticized or changed: *weekend rest days were considered sacrosanct by staff.* **sacrosanctity** *n*
sacrum (**say**-krum) *n, pl* **-cra** *Anat* the large wedge-shaped bone in the lower part of the back.
sad *adj* **sadder, saddest** **1** feeling sorrow; unhappy. **2**

THESAURUS

sabotage **1.** *n.* damage, destruction, disruption, subversion, treachery, treason, wrecking **2.** *vb.* cripple, damage, destroy, disable, disrupt, incapacitate, sap the foundations of, subvert, throw a spanner in the works (*Brit. informal*), undermine, vandalize, wreck
sack[1] *informal* **1.** *n.* **the sack** discharge, dismissal, termination of employment, the axe (*informal*), the boot (*slang*), the chop (*Brit. slang*), the (old) heave-ho (*informal*), the order of the boot (*slang*), the push (*slang*) **2.** *vb.* axe (*informal*), discharge, dismiss, fire (*informal*), give (someone) his books (*informal*), give (someone) his cards, give (someone) his marching orders, give (someone) the boot (*slang*), give (someone) the elbow, kick out (*informal*), kiss off (*slang, chiefly U.S. & Canad.*)
sack[2] **1.** *n.* depredation, despoliation, destruction, devastation, looting, pillage, plunder, plundering, rape, rapine, ravage, ruin, waste **2.** *vb.* demolish, depredate (*rare*), despoil, destroy, devastate, lay waste, loot, maraud, pillage, plunder, raid, ravage, rifle, rob, ruin, spoil, strip
sackcloth and ashes compunction, contrition, grief, hair shirt, mortification, mourning, penitence, remorse, repentance
sacred **1.** blessed, consecrated, divine, hallowed, holy, revered, sanctified, venerable **2.** ecclesiastical, holy, religious, solemn **3.** inviolable, inviolate, invulnerable, protected, sacrosanct, secure
sacrifice **1.** *n.* burnt offering, destruction, holocaust, immolation, loss, oblation, renunciation, surrender, votive offering **2.** *vb.* forego, forfeit, give up, immolate, let go, lose, offer, offer up, surrender

causing, suggesting, or expressing sorrow: *a sad story.* **3** deplorably bad: *the garden was in a sad state.* **4** regrettable: *it's rather sad he can't be with us.* **sadly** *adv* **sadness** *n*

sadden *vb* to make (someone) sad.

saddle *n* **1** a seat for a rider, usually made of leather, placed on a horse's back and secured under belly. **2** a similar seat on a bicycle, motorcycle, or tractor. **3** a cut of meat, esp. mutton, consisting of both loins. **4 in the saddle** in a position of control. *~vb* **-dling, -dled 5** to put a saddle on (a horse): *we saddled up at dawn.* **6 saddle with** to burden with (a responsibility): *he was also saddled with debt.*

saddleback *n* **1** an animal with a marking resembling a saddle on its back. **2** a hill with a concave outline at the top. **saddle-backed** *adj*

saddlebag *n* a pouch or small bag attached to the saddle of a horse, bicycle, or motorcycle.

saddle horse *n* a horse trained for riding only.

saddler *n* a person who makes, deals in, or repairs saddles and other leather equipment for horses.

saddlery *n, pl* **-dleries 1** saddles and harness for horses collectively. **2** the work or place of work of a saddler.

saddle soap *n* a soft soap used to preserve and clean leather.

saddletree *n* the frame of a saddle.

Sadducee (**sad**-yew-see) *n Judaism* a member of an ancient Jewish sect that denied the resurrection of the dead and accepted only the traditional written law.

sadhu (**sah**-doo) *n* a Hindu wandering holy man.

sadism (**say**-diz-zum) *n* the gaining of pleasure, esp. sexual pleasure, from infliction of suffering on another person. **sadist** *n* **sadistic** *adj* **sadistically** *adv*

sadomasochism *n* **1** the combination of sadistic and masochistic elements in one person, characterized by both submissive and aggressive periods in relationships with others. **2** a sexual practice in which one partner adopts a masochistic role and the other a sadistic one. **sadomasochist** *n* **sadomasochistic** *adj*

s.a.e. stamped addressed envelope.

safari *n, pl* **-ris** an overland expedition for hunting or observing animals, esp. in Africa.

safari park *n* an enclosed park in which wild animals are kept uncaged in the open and can be viewed by the public from cars or buses.

safe *adj* **1** giving security or protection from harm: *a safe environment.* **2** free from danger: *she doesn't feel safe.* **3** taking or involving no risks: *a safe bet.* **4** not dangerous: *the beef is safe to eat.* **5 on the safe side** as a precaution. *~n* **6** a strong metal container with a secure lock, for storing money or valuables. **safely** *adv*

safe-conduct *n* **1** a document giving official permission to travel through a dangerous region, esp. in time of war. **2** the protection given by such a document.

safe-deposit *or* **safety-deposit** *n* a place with facilities for the safe storage of money and valuables.

safeguard *vb* **1** to protect (something) from being harmed or destroyed. *~n* **2** a person or thing that ensures protection against danger or harm: *safeguards to prevent air collisions.*

safekeeping *n* protection from theft or damage: *gold given to Britain for safekeeping.*

safe sex *n* nonpenetrative sex, or intercourse using a condom, intended to prevent the spread of AIDS.

safety *n, pl* **-ties 1** the quality or state of being free from danger. **2** shelter: *they swam to safety.*

safety belt *n* same as **seat belt.**

safety catch *n* a mechanism on a gun that prevents it from being fired accidentally.

safety curtain *n* a fireproof curtain that can be lowered to separate the auditorium from the stage in a theatre to prevent the spread of a fire.

safety lamp *n* a miner's oil lamp designed to prevent it from igniting combustible gas.

safety match *n* a match that will light only when struck against a specially prepared surface.

safety net *n* **1** a large net under a trapeze or high wire to catch performers if they fall. **2** something that can be relied on for help in the event of difficulties: *the social security safety net.*

safety pin *n* a pin bent back on itself so that it forms a spring, with the point shielded by a guard when closed.

safety razor *n* a razor with a guard over the blade or blades to protect the skin from deep cuts.

safety valve *n* **1** a valve in a boiler or machine that allows fluid or gases to escape at excess pressure. **2** an outlet that allows one to express strong feelings without harming or offending other people: *sport acted as a safety valve for his pent-up frustrations.*

safflower *n* a thistle-like plant with orange-yellow flowers, which yields a dye and an oil used in paints, medicines, and cooking.

THESAURUS

sacrilege blasphemy, desecration, heresy, impiety, irreverence, mockery, profanation, profaneness, profanity, violation

sad 1. blue, cheerless, dejected, depressed, disconsolate, dismal, doleful, down, downcast, down in the dumps (*informal*), down in the mouth (*informal*), gloomy, glum, grief-stricken, grieved, heavy-hearted, low, low-spirited, lugubrious, melancholy, mournful, pensive, sick at heart, sombre, triste (*old-fashioned*), unhappy, wistful, woebegone **2.** calamitous, dark, depressing, disastrous, dismal, grievous, harrowing, heart-rending, lachrymose, moving, pathetic, pitiable, pitiful, poignant, sorry, tearful, tragic, upsetting **3.** bad, deplorable, dismal, distressing, grave, lamentable, miserable, regrettable, serious, shabby, sorry, to be deplored, unfortunate, unhappy, unsatisfactory, wretched

sadden aggrieve, bring tears to one's eyes, cast a gloom upon, cast down, dash, deject, depress, desolate, dispirit, distress, grieve, make blue, make one's heart bleed, upset

sadistic barbarous, beastly, brutal, cruel, fiendish, inhuman, perverse, perverted, ruthless, savage, vicious

sadness bleakness, cheerlessness, dejection, depression, despondency, dolefulness, gloominess, grief, heavy heart, melancholy, misery, mournfulness, poignancy, sorrow, sorrowfulness, the blues, the dumps (*informal*), the hump (*Brit. informal*), tragedy, unhappiness, wretchedness

safe *adj.* **1.** all right, free from harm, impregnable, in safety, intact, O.K. *or* okay (*informal*), out of danger, out of harm's way, protected, safe and sound, secure, undamaged, unharmed, unhurt, unscathed **2.** certain, impregnable, risk-free, riskless, secure, sound **3.** harmless, innocuous, nonpoisonous, nontoxic, pure, tame, unpolluted, wholesome *~n.* **4.** coffer, deposit box, repository, safe-deposit box, strongbox, vault

safeguard 1. *vb.* defend, guard, look after, preserve, protect, screen, shield, watch over **2.** *n.* aegis, armour, bulwark, convoy, defence, escort, guard, protection, security, shield, surety

saffron *n* **1** a type of crocus with purple or white flowers with orange stigmas. **2** the dried orange-coloured stigmas of this plant, used for colouring or flavouring. *~adj* **3** orange-yellow.

sag *vb* **sagging, sagged 1** to sink in the middle, under weight or pressure: *the bed sagged nearly to the floor.* **2** (of courage or spirits) to weaken or tire. **3** (of clothes) to hang loosely or unevenly. **4** to fall in value: *the stock market sagged.* *~n* **5** the act or state of sagging. **saggy** *adj*

saga (**sah**-ga) *n* **1** a medieval Scandinavian legend telling the adventures of a hero or a family. **2** *Informal* a long story or series of events: *the long-running saga of the hostage issue.*

sagacious *adj Formal* wise or sensible. **sagaciously** *adv* **sagacity** *n*

sage[1] *n* **1** a person, esp. an old man, regarded as being very wise. *~adj* **2** very wise or knowledgeable, esp. as the result of age or experience.

sage[2] *n* **1** a Mediterranean plant with grey-green leaves which are used in cooking for flavouring. **2** short for **sagebrush.**

sagebrush *n* an aromatic plant of W North America, with silver-green leaves and large clusters of small white flowers.

Sagittarius *n Astrol* the ninth sign of the zodiac; the Archer.

sago *n* an edible starch from the powdered pith of the sago palm tree, used for puddings and as a thickening agent.

sahib *n* an Indian term of address equivalent to *sir,* formerly used as a mark of respect to a European man.

said *adj* **1** named or mentioned already: *she had heard that the said lady was also a medium.* *~vb* **2** the past of **say.**

sail *n* **1** a sheet of canvas or other fabric, spread on rigging to catch the wind and move a ship over water. **2** a voyage on such a ship: *a six-mile sail.* **3** a ship or ships with sails: *to travel by sail.* **4** one of the revolving arms of a windmill. **5 set sail** to begin a voyage by water. **6 under sail a** under way. **b** with sail hoisted. *~vb* **7** to travel in a boat or ship: *to sail around the world.* **8** to begin a voyage: *he hoped to sail at eleven.* **9** (of a ship) to move over the water. **10** to navigate (a ship): *she sailed the schooner up the channel.* **11** to sail over: *he had already sailed the Pacific.* **12** to move along smoothly. **13 sail into** *Informal* to make a violent attack on. **14 sail through** to progress quickly or effortlessly: *the top seed sailed through to the second round.*

sailboard *n* a board with a mast and a single sail, used for windsurfing.

sailcloth *n* **1** the fabric used for making sails. **2** a canvas-like cloth used for clothing.

sailfish *n, pl* **-fish** *or* **-fishes** a large tropical game fish, with a long sail-like fin on its back.

sailor *n* **1** any member of a ship's crew, esp. one below the rank of officer. **2** a person considered as liable or not liable to seasickness: *a good sailor.*

sainfoin (**san**-foin) *n* a Eurasian plant with pink flowers, widely grown as feed for grazing farm animals.

saint *n* **1** a person who after death is formally recognized by a Christian Church as deserving special honour because of having lived a very holy life. **2** an exceptionally good person. **sainthood** *n* **saintlike** *adj*

Saint Bernard *n* a very large dog with a dense red-and-white coat, formerly used as a mountain-rescue dog.

sainted *adj* **1** formally recognized by a Christian Church as a saint. **2** having the qualities, such as patience and kindness, of a saint. **3** hallowed or holy.

Saint John's wort *n* a plant with yellow flowers.

Saint Leger *n* an annual horse race for three-year-old horses, run at Doncaster.

saintly *adj* behaving in a very good, patient, or holy way. **saintliness** *n*

Saint Vitus's dance *n Pathol* a nontechnical name for **chorea.**

saithe *n Brit* a dark-coloured food fish found in northern seas.

sake[1] *n* **1 for someone's** *or* **one's own sake** for the benefit or interest of someone *or* oneself. **2 for the sake of something** for the purpose of obtaining or achieving something. **3 for its own sake** for the enjoyment obtained by doing something. **4** used in various exclamations of annoyance, impatience, or urgency: *for God's sake.*

sake[2] *or* **saki** (**sah**-kee) *n* a Japanese alcoholic drink made from fermented rice.

salaam (sal-**ahm**) *n* **1** a Muslim greeting consisting of a deep bow with the right palm on the forehead. **2** a greeting signifying peace. *~vb* **3** to make a salaam (to).

salacious *adj* **1** having an excessive interest in sex. **2** (of books, films, or jokes) concerned with sex in an unnecessarily detailed way. **salaciousness** *n*

salad *n* a dish of raw vegetables, often served with a dressing, eaten as a separate course or as part of a main course.

salad days *pl n* a period of youth and inexperience.

salad dressing *n* a sauce for salad, such as oil and vinegar or mayonnaise.

salamander *n* a tailed amphibian which looks like a lizard.

salami *n* a highly spiced sausage, usually flavoured with garlic.

salaried *adj* earning or providing a salary: *a salaried employee; a salaried position.*

salary *n, pl* **-ries** a fixed regular payment made by an employer, usually monthly, for professional or office work.

sale *n* **1** the exchange of goods or property for an agreed sum of money. **2** the amount sold. **3** an event at

THESAURUS

safely in one piece, in safety, safe and sound, securely, with impunity, without risk, with safety

safety assurance, cover, immunity, impregnability, protection, refuge, sanctuary, security, shelter

sage 1. *n.* authority, elder, expert, guru, mahatma, man of learning, master, philosopher, pundit, savant, Solomon, wise man **2.** *adj.* acute, canny, discerning, intelligent, judicious, learned, perspicacious, politic, prudent, sagacious, sapient, sensible, wise

sail *vb.* **1.** cast *or* weigh anchor, embark, get under way, hoist the blue peter, put to sea, set sail **2.** captain, cruise, go by water, navigate, pilot, ride the waves, skipper, steer, voyage **3.** drift, float, fly, glide, scud, shoot, skim, skirr, soar, sweep, wing **4.** *with* **into** *informal* assault, attack, begin, belabour, fall upon, get going, get to work on, lambast(e), set about, tear into (*informal*)

sailor Jack Tar (*chiefly literary*), lascar, leatherneck (*slang*), marine, mariner, navigator, salt, sea dog, seafarer, seafaring man, seaman, tar (*informal*)

saintly angelic, beatific, blameless, blessed, devout, full of good works, god-fearing, godly, holy, pious, religious, righteous, sainted, saintlike, sinless, virtuous, worthy

which goods are sold at reduced prices. **4** an auction. **5 sales** the department dealing with selling its company's products.

saleable *or US* **salable** *adj* fit for selling or capable of being sold. **saleability** *or US* **salability** *n*

sale of work *n* a sale of articles, often handmade, the proceeds of which go to a charity.

saleroom *n Chiefly Brit* a room where objects are displayed for sale by auction.

salesgirl *n* a young woman who sells goods in a shop.

salesman *n, pl* **-men 1** a man who sells goods in a shop. **2** short for **travelling salesman.**

salesmanship *n* the technique of or skill in selling.

salesperson *n, pl* **-people** *or* **-persons** a person who sells goods in a shop.

sales pitch *or* **talk** *n* persuasive talk used by a salesperson in persuading a customer to buy something.

saleswoman *n, pl* **-women** a woman who sells goods in a shop.

salicylic acid (sal-liss-**ill**-ik) *n* a white crystalline substance used to make aspirin and as a fungicide.

salient (**say**-lee-ent) *adj* **1** (of points or facts) most important: *the salient points of his speech.* ~*n* **2** *Mil* a projection of the forward line of an army into enemy-held territory.

saline (**say**-line) *adj* **1** of or containing salt: *a saline flavour.* **2** *Med* of or relating to a saline: *a saline drip.* ~*n* **3** *Med* a solution of sodium chloride and water. **salinity** *n*

salinization *or* **-isation** *n* the process by which salts accumulate in undrained land, damaging its potential for plant growth.

saliva (sal-**lie**-va) *n* the watery fluid secreted by glands in the mouth, which aids digestion. **salivary** *adj*

salivate *vb* **-vating, -vated** to produce saliva, esp. an excessive amount. **salivation** *n*

sallow *adj* (of human skin) of an unhealthy pale or yellowish colour. **sallowness** *n*

sally *n, pl* **-lies 1** a witty remark. **2** a sudden brief attack by troops. **3** an excursion. ~*vb* **-lies, -lying, -lied 4 sally forth a** to set out on a journey. **b** to set out in an energetic manner.

salmon *n, pl* **-ons** *or* **-on** a large pink-fleshed fish which is highly valued for food and sport: salmon live in the sea but return to fresh water to spawn.

salmonella (sal-mon-**ell**-a) *n* a kind of bacteria that can cause food poisoning.

salmon ladder *n* a series of steps designed to enable salmon to move upstream to their breeding grounds.

salon *n* **1** a commercial establishment in which hairdressers or fashion designers carry on their business. **2** an elegant room in a large house in which guests are received. **3** an informal gathering, esp. in the 18th, 19th, and early 20th centuries, of major literary, artistic, and political figures in a fashionable household. **4** an art exhibition.

saloon *n* **1** a two-door or four-door car with a fixed roof. **2** *Brit* a comfortable but more expensive bar in a pub or hotel. **3** a large public room on a passenger ship. **4** *Chiefly US & Canad* a place where alcoholic drink is sold and consumed.

salsa *n* **1** a lively Puerto Rican dance. **2** big-band music accompanying this dance.

salsify *n, pl* **-fies** a Mediterranean plant with a long white edible root.

salt *n* **1** sodium chloride, a white crystalline substance, used for seasoning and preserving food. **2** *Chem* a crystalline solid compound formed from an acid by replacing its hydrogen with a metal. **3** lively wit: *his humour added salt to the discussion.* **4 old salt** an experienced sailor. **5 rub salt into someone's wounds** to make an unpleasant situation even worse for someone. **6 salt of the earth** a person or people regarded as the finest of their kind. **7 take something with a pinch of salt** to refuse to believe something is completely true or accurate. **8 worth one's salt** worthy of one's pay; efficient. ~*vb* **9** to season or preserve with salt. **10** to scatter salt over (an iced road or path) to melt the ice. ~*adj* **11** preserved in or tasting of salt: *salt beef.* ~See also **salt away, salts. salted** *adj*

SALT Strategic Arms Limitation Talks *or* Treaty.

salt away *vb* to hoard or save (money) for the future.

saltcellar *n* a small container for salt used at the table.

salt lick *n* **1** a place where wild animals go to lick salt deposits. **2** a block of salt given to domestic animals to lick.

saltpetre *or US* **saltpeter** *n* same as **potassium nitrate.**

salts *pl n* **1** *Med* mineral salts used as a medicine. **2 like a dose of salts** *Informal* very quickly.

saltwater *adj* of or inhabiting salt water, esp. the sea: *saltwater fish.*

salty *adj* **saltier, saltiest 1** of, tasting of, or containing salt. **2** (esp. of humour) sharp and witty. **saltiness** *n*

salubrious *adj* favourable to health. **salubrity** *n*

Saluki *n* a tall hound with a smooth coat and long fringes on the ears and tail.

salutary *adj* **1** (of an experience) producing a beneficial result despite being unpleasant: *a salutary reminder.* **2** promoting health.

salutation *n Formal* a greeting by words or actions.

salute *vb* **-luting, -luted 1** to greet with friendly

THESAURUS

salary earnings, emolument, income, pay, remuneration, stipend, wage, wages

sale auction, deal, disposal, marketing, selling, transaction, vending

salient arresting, conspicuous, important, jutting, marked, noticeable, outstanding, projecting, prominent, pronounced, protruding, remarkable, signal, striking

sallow anaemic, bilious, jaundiced-looking, pale, pallid, pasty, sickly, unhealthy, wan, yellowish

sally *n.* **1.** bon mot, crack (*informal*), jest, joke, quip, retort, riposte, smart remark, wisecrack (*informal*), witticism **2.** *Military* foray, incursion, offensive, raid, sortie, thrust **3.** escapade, excursion, frolic, jaunt, trip ~*vb.* **4.** erupt, go forth, issue, rush, set out, surge

salt *n.* **1.** flavour, relish, savour, seasoning, taste **2.** Attic wit, bite, dry humour, liveliness, piquancy, punch, pungency, sarcasm, sharpness, wit, zest, zip (*informal*) **3. old salt** mariner, sailor, sea dog, seaman, tar (*informal*) **4. with a pinch of salt** cynically, disbelievingly, doubtfully, sceptically, suspiciously, with reservations ~*adj.* **5.** brackish, briny, saline, salted, salty

salty 1. brackish, briny, over-salted, saline, salt, salted **2.** colourful, humorous, lively, piquant, pungent, racy, sharp, snappy (*informal*), spicy, tangy, tart, witty, zestful

salubrious beneficial, good for one, healthful, health-giving, healthy, invigorating, salutary, wholesome

words or gestures of respect, such as bowing. **2** to acknowledge with praise: *the statement salutes the changes of the past year.* **3** *Mil* to pay formal respect to (someone) by raising the right hand to the forehead. *~n* **4** the act of saluting as a formal military gesture of respect. **5** the act of firing guns as a military greeting of honour.

salvage *n* **1** the rescue of a ship or its cargo from loss at sea. **2** the saving of any goods or property from destruction or waste. **3** the goods or property so saved. **4** compensation paid for the salvage of a ship or its cargo. *~vb* **-vaging, -vaged 5** to save (goods or property) from shipwreck, destruction, or waste. **6** to gain (something beneficial) from a failure: *it's too late to salvage anything from the whole dismal display.* **salvageable** *adj*

salvation *n* **1** the act of preserving someone or something from harm. **2** a person or thing that preserves from harm. **3** *Christianity* the fact or state of being saved from the influence or consequences of sin.

Salvation Army *n* a Christian body organized on military lines for working among the poor and spreading the Christian faith.

salve *n* **1** an ointment for wounds. **2** anything that heals or soothes. *~vb* **salving, salved 3 salve one's conscience** to do something in order to feel less guilty.

salver *n* a tray, usually a silver one, on which something is presented.

salvia *n* any small plant or shrub of the sage genus.

salvo *n, pl* **-vos** *or* **-voes 1** a simultaneous discharge of guns in battle or on a ceremonial occasion. **2** an outburst of applause or questions.

sal volatile (**sal** vol-**at**-ill-ee) *n* a solution of ammonium carbonate, used as smelling salts.

SAM surface-to-air missile.

Samaritan *n* **1** short for **Good Samaritan. 2** a member of a voluntary organization (**the Samaritans**) whose aim is to help people in distress or despair.

samarium *n Chem* a silvery metallic element of the rare-earth series. Symbol: Sm

samba *n, pl* **-bas 1** a lively Brazilian dance. **2** music for this dance.

same *adj* (usually preceded by *the*) **1** being the very one: *she is wearing the same hat.* **2** being the one previously referred to: *it causes problems for the same reason.* **3** alike in kind or quantity: *the same age.* **4** unchanged in character or nature: *his attitude is the same as ever.* **5 all the same** *or* **just the same** nevertheless; even so. **6 be all the same** to be a matter of indifference: *it was all the same to me.* *~adv* **7** in the same way; similarly: *I felt much the same.* *~n* **8 the same** something that is like something else in kind or quantity: *this is basically much more of the same.* **sameness** *n*

samizdat *n* (in the former Soviet Union) a system of secret printing and distribution of banned literature.

samosa *n* (in Indian cookery) a small fried triangular spiced meat or vegetable pasty. Also (in S Africa): **samoosa**

samovar *n* a Russian metal tea urn in which the water is heated by an inner container.

Samoyed *n* a dog with a thick white coat and a tightly curled tail.

sampan *n* a small flat-bottomed boat with oars, used esp. in China.

samphire *n* a plant found on rocks by the seashore.

sample *n* **1** a small part of anything, taken as being representative of a whole. *~vb* **-pling, -pled 2** to take a sample or samples of. **3** *Music* **a** to take a short extract from (one record) and mix it into a different backing track. **b** to record (a sound) and feed it into a computerized synthesizer so that it can be reproduced at any pitch. **sampling** *n*

sampler *n* **1** a piece of embroidery done to show the embroiderer's skill in using many different stitches. **2** *Music* a piece of electronic equipment used for sampling.

Samson *n* a man of outstanding physical strength.

samurai *n, pl* **-rai** a member of the aristocratic warrior caste of feudal Japan.

sanatorium *or US* **sanitarium** *n, pl* **-riums** *or* **-ria 1** an institution providing medical treatment and rest for invalids or convalescents. **2** *Brit* a room in a boarding school where sick pupils may be treated.

sanctify *vb* **-fies, -fying, -fied 1** to make holy. **2** to free from sin. **3** to approve (an action or practice) as religiously binding: *she is trying to make amends for her marriage not being sanctified.* **sanctification** *n*

sanctimonious *adj* pretending to be very religious and virtuous.

sanction *n* **1** permission granted by authority: *official sanction.* **2** support or approval: *they could not exist without his sanction.* **3** something that gives binding force to a law, such as a penalty for breaking it or a reward for obeying it. **4 sanctions** coercive measures, such as boycotts and trade embargoes, taken by one or more states against another guilty of violating international law. *~vb* **5** to officially approve

THESAURUS

salutary advantageous, beneficial, good, good for one, healthful, healthy, salubrious

salutation address, greeting, obeisance, salute, welcome

salute *vb.* **1.** accost, acknowledge, address, doff one's cap to, greet, hail, kiss, pay one's respects to, salaam, welcome **2.** acknowledge, honour, pay tribute *or* homage to, present arms, recognize, take one's hat off to (*informal*) *~n.* **3.** address, greeting, kiss, obeisance, recognition, salaam, salutation, tribute

salvage *vb.* glean, recover, redeem, rescue, restore, retrieve, save

salvation deliverance, escape, lifeline, preservation, redemption, rescue, restoration, saving

same *adj.* **1.** aforementioned, aforesaid, selfsame, very **2.** alike, corresponding, duplicate, equal, equivalent, identical, indistinguishable, interchangeable, synonymous, twin **3.** changeless, consistent, constant, invariable, unaltered, unchanged, unfailing, uniform, unvarying **4. all the same** *or* **just the same** after all, anyhow, be that as it may, in any event, just the same, nevertheless, nonetheless, still

sameness consistency, identicalness, identity, indistinguishability, lack of variety, likeness, monotony, oneness, predictability, repetition, resemblance, similarity, standardization, tedium, uniformity

sample 1. *n.* cross section, example, exemplification, illustration, indication, instance, model, pattern, representative, sign, specimen **2.** *vb.* experience, inspect, partake of, taste, test, try

sanctify absolve, anoint, bless, cleanse, consecrate, hallow, purify, set apart

sanctimonious canting, false, goody-goody (*informal*), holier-than-thou, hypocritical, pharisaical, pious, priggish, self-righteous, self-satisfied, smug, too good to be true, unctuous

sanction *n.* **1.** allowance, approbation, approval, authority, authorization, backing, confirmation, countenance, endorsement, O.K. *or* okay (*informal*), ratification, stamp *or* seal of approval, support **2.** *often plural* ban, boycott, coercive measures, embargo, penalty

of or allow: *they do not want to sanction direct payments.* **6** to confirm or ratify.

sanctity *n* the quality of something considered so holy or important it must be respected totally: *the sanctity of the Sabbath; the sanctity of marriage.*

sanctuary *n, pl* **-aries 1** a holy place, such as a consecrated building or shrine. **2** the part of a church nearest the main altar. **3** a place of refuge or protection for someone who is being chased or hunted. **4** refuge or safety: *the sanctuary of your own home.* **5** a place, protected by law, where animals can live and breed without interference.

sanctum *n, pl* **-tums** *or* **-ta 1** a sacred or holy place. **2** a room or place of total privacy.

sand *n* **1** a powdery substance consisting of very small rock or mineral grains, found on the seashore and in deserts. **2 sands** a large sandy area, esp. on the seashore or in a desert. *~vb* **3** to smooth or polish the surface of (something) with sandpaper or a sander. **4** to fill with sand: *the channel sanded up.*

sandal *n* a light shoe consisting of a sole held on the foot by thongs or straps. **sandalled** *or US* **sandaled** *adj*

sandalwood *n* **1** the hard light-coloured wood of a S Asian or Australian tree, which is used for carving and for incense, and which yields an aromatic oil used in perfumes. **2** a tree yielding this wood.

sandbag *n* **1** a sack filled with sand used to make a temporary defence against gunfire or flood water. *~vb* **-bagging, -bagged 2** to protect or strengthen with sandbags.

sandbank *or* **sand bar** *n* a bank of sand in a sea or river, that may be exposed at low tide.

sandblast *n* **1** a jet of sand blown from a nozzle under air or steam pressure. *~vb* **2** to clean or decorate (a surface) with a sandblast. **sandblaster** *n*

sandboy *n* **happy as a sandboy** very happy.

sand castle *n* a model of a castle made from sand.

sander *n* a power-driven tool for smoothing surfaces, removing layers of paint from walls, etc.

sandman *n, pl* **-men** (in folklore) a magical person supposed to put children to sleep by sprinkling sand in their eyes.

sand martin *n* a small brown European songbird which nests in tunnels bored in sand or river banks.

sandpaper *n* **1** a strong paper coated with sand or other abrasive material for smoothing or polishing a surface. *~vb* **2** to smooth or polish (a surface) with sandpaper.

sandpiper *n* a wading shore bird with a long bill and slender legs.

sandpit *n* a shallow pit or container holding sand for children to play in.

sandshoes *pl n* light canvas shoes with rubber soles.

sandstone *n* a sedimentary rock consisting mainly of sand grains, much used in building.

sandstorm *n* a strong wind that whips up clouds of sand, esp. in a desert.

sandwich *n* **1** two or more slices of bread, usually buttered, with a layer of food between them. *~vb* **2** to place between two other things: *shops sandwiched between flats.*

sandwich board *n* one of two connected boards that are hung over the shoulders in front of and behind a person to display advertisements.

sandwich course *n* an educational course consisting of alternate periods of study and industrial work.

sandy *adj* **sandier, sandiest 1** resembling, containing, or covered with sand. **2** (of hair) reddish-yellow. **sandiness** *n*

sane *adj* **1** having a normal healthy mind. **2** sensible or well-judged: *sane advice.*

sang *vb* the past tense of **sing.**

sang-froid (sahng-**frwah**) *n* composure and calmness in a difficult situation.

sangoma (sang-**go**-ma) *n S African* a witch doctor.

sangria *n* a Spanish drink of red wine, sugar, and orange or lemon juice.

sanguinary *adj Formal* **1** (of a battle or fight) involving much violence and bloodshed. **2** (of a person) eager to see violence and bloodshed. **3** of or stained with blood.

sanguine *adj* **1** cheerful and confident. **2** (of the complexion) ruddy.

Sanhedrin (**san**-id-rin) *n Judaism* the highest court and supreme council of the ancient Jewish nation.

sanitary *adj* **1** promoting health by getting rid of dirt and germs. **2** free from dirt or germs; hygienic.

sanitary towel *or esp US* **napkin** *n* a pad worn externally by women during menstruation to absorb the flow of blood.

sanitation *n* **1** the use of sanitary measures to maintain public health. **2** drainage and disposal of sewage.

sanity *n* **1** the state of having a normal healthy mind. **2** good sense or soundness of judgment.

sank *vb* a past tense of **sink.**

sans-culotte (sanz-kew-**lot**) *n* a revolutionary extremist.

Sanskrit *n* the classical literary language of India, used since ancient times for religious purposes. **Sanskritic** *adj*

Santa Claus *n* the legendary patron saint of children, who brings presents to children on Christmas Eve, commonly identified with Saint Nicholas.

sap[1] *n* **1** a thin liquid that circulates in a plant, carrying food and water. **2** *Slang* a gullible person. *~vb* **sapping, sapped 3** to drain of sap.

sap[2] *vb* **sapping, sapped 1** to weaken or exhaust the strength or confidence of. **2** to undermine (an enemy

THESAURUS

~vb. **3.** allow, approve, authorize, back, countenance, endorse, entitle, lend one's name to, permit, support, vouch for

sanctity devotion, godliness, goodness, grace, holiness, inviolability, piety, purity, religiousness, righteousness, sacredness, sanctitude, solemnity, spirituality

sanctuary 1. altar, church, Holy of Holies, sanctum, shrine, temple **2.** asylum, haven, protection, refuge, retreat, shelter **3.** conservation area, national park, nature reserve, reserve

sane 1. all there (*informal*), *compos mentis*, in one's right mind, in possession of all one's faculties, lucid, mentally sound, normal, of sound mind, rational **2.** balanced, judicious, level-headed, moderate, reasonable, sensible, sober, sound

sanguine 1. animated, assured, buoyant, cheerful, confident, hopeful, in good heart, lively, optimistic, spirited **2.** florid, red, rubicund, ruddy

sanitary clean, germ-free, healthy, hygienic, salubrious, unpolluted, wholesome

sanity 1. mental health, normality, rationality, reason, right mind (*informal*), saneness, stability **2.** common sense, good sense, judiciousness, level-headedness, rationality, sense, soundness of judgment

sap[1] *n.* **1.** animating force, essence, lifeblood, vital fluid **2.** *slang* charlie (*Brit. old-fashioned informal*), chump (*informal*), drip (*informal*), fool, idiot, jerk

position) by digging saps. ~*n* **3** a deep and narrow trench used to approach or undermine an enemy position.

sapient (**say**-pee-ent) *adj Often used ironically* having great wisdom or sound judgment. **sapience** *n*

sapling *n* a young tree.

saponify *vb* **-fies, -fying, -fied** *Chem* to convert (a fat) into a soap by treatment with alkali. **saponification** *n*

sapper *n* **1** a soldier who digs trenches. **2** (in the British Army) a private of the Royal Engineers.

sapphire *n* **1** a transparent blue precious stone. ~*adj* **2** deep blue.

sappy *adj* **-pier, -piest** (of plants) full of sap.

saprophyte *n Biol* any plant, such as a fungus, that lives and feeds on dead organic matter.

sarabande *or* **saraband** *n* **1** a stately slow Spanish dance. **2** music for this dance.

Saracen *n* **1** an Arab or Muslim who opposed the Crusades. ~*adj* **2** of the Saracens.

sarcasm *n* **1** mocking or ironic language intended to insult someone. **2** the use or tone of such language.

sarcastic *adj* **1** full of or showing sarcasm. **2** tending to use sarcasm: *a sarcastic critic.* **sarcastically** *adv*

sarcoma *n Pathol* a malignant tumour beginning in connective tissue.

sarcophagus (sahr-**koff**-a-guss) *n, pl* **-gi** (-guy) *or* **-guses** a stone or marble coffin or tomb, esp. one bearing sculpture or inscriptions.

sardine *n, pl* **-dine** *or* **-dines 1** a small fish of the herring family, often preserved in tightly packed tins. **2 like sardines** very closely crowded together.

sardonic *adj* (of behaviour) mocking or scornful. **sardonically** *adv*

sardonyx *n* a type of gemstone with alternating reddish-brown and white parallel bands.

sargassum *n* a floating brown seaweed with long stringy fronds containing air sacs.

sarge *n Informal* sergeant.

sari *or* **saree** *n, pl* **-ris** *or* **-rees** the traditional dress of Hindu women, consisting of a very long piece of cloth swathed around the body with one end over the shoulder.

sarking *n Scot, N English, & NZ* flat planking supporting the roof cladding of a building.

sarky *adj* **-kier, -kiest** *Brit informal* sarcastic.

sarmie *n S African children's slang* a sandwich.

sarnie *n S English informal* a sandwich.

sarong *n* a garment worn by Malaysian men and women, consisting of a long piece of cloth tucked around the waist or under the armpits.

sarsaparilla *n* a nonalcoholic drink prepared from the roots of a tropical American climbing plant.

sartorial *adj Formal* of men's clothes or tailoring: *sartorial elegance.*

SAS Special Air Service.

sash[1] *n* a long piece of cloth worn around the waist or over one shoulder, usu. as a symbol of rank.

sash[2] *n* **1** a frame that contains the panes of a window or door. **2** a complete frame together with panes of glass.

sashay *vb Informal* to move or walk in a casual or a showy manner: *the models sashayed down the catwalk.*

sash cord *n* a strong cord connecting a weight to the sliding half of a sash window.

sashimi (sah-**shee**-mee) *n* a Japanese dish of thin fillets of raw fish.

sash window *n* a window consisting of two sashes placed one above the other so that the window can be opened by sliding one frame over the front of the other.

Sask. Saskatchewan.

sassafras *n* a tree of North America, with aromatic bark used medicinally and as a flavouring.

Sassenach *n Scot & occasionally Irish* an English person.

sat *vb* the past of **sit**.

Sat. Saturday.

Satan *n* the Devil.

satanic *adj* **1** of Satan. **2** supremely evil or wicked.

Satanism *n* the worship of Satan. **Satanist** *n, adj*

satchel *n* a small bag, usually with a shoulder strap, used for carrying school books.

sate *vb* **sating, sated** to satisfy (a desire or appetite) fully.

satellite *n* **1** a man-made device orbiting the earth or another planet, used in communications or to collect scientific information. **2** a heavenly body orbiting a planet or star: *the earth is a satellite of the sun.* **3** a country controlled by or dependent on a more powerful one. ~*adj* **4** of, used in, or relating to the transmission of television signals from a satellite to the home: *satellite TV; a satellite dish.*

satiate (**say**-she-ate) *vb* **-ating, -ated** to provide with more than enough, so as to disgust or weary: *enough cakes to satiate several children.* **satiable** *adj* **satiation** *n*

satiety (sat-**tie**-a-tee) *n Formal* the feeling of having had too much.

satin *n* **1** a fabric, usually made from silk or rayon, closely woven to give a smooth glossy surface on one side. ~*adj* **2** like satin in texture: *satin polyurethane varnish.* **satiny** *adj*

satinwood *n* **1** a hard wood with a satiny texture, used in fine furniture. **2** the East Indian tree yielding this wood.

THESAURUS

(*slang, chiefly U.S. & Canad.*), muggins (*Brit. slang*), nerd *or* nurd (*slang*), nincompoop, ninny, nitwit (*informal*), noddy, numskull *or* numbskull, oaf, plonker (*slang*), prat (*slang*), simpleton, twit (*informal*), wally (*slang*), weakling, wet (*Brit. informal*)

sap[2] *vb.* bleed, deplete, devitalize, drain, enervate, erode, exhaust, rob, undermine, weaken, wear down

sarcasm bitterness, causticness, contempt, cynicism, derision, irony, mockery, mordancy, satire, scorn, sneering, venom, vitriol

sarcastic acerbic, acid, acrimonious, backhanded, bitchy (*informal*), biting, caustic, contemptuous, cutting, cynical, derisive, disparaging, ironical, mocking, mordacious, mordant, sardonic, sarky (*Brit. informal*), satirical, sharp, sneering, taunting, vitriolic

sardonic bitter, cynical, derisive, dry, ironical, jeering, malevolent, malicious, malignant, mocking, mordacious, mordant, sarcastic, sneering, wry

Satan Apollyon, Beelzebub, Lord of the Flies, Lucifer, Mephistopheles, Old Nick (*informal*), Old Scratch (*informal*), Prince of Darkness, The Devil, The Evil One

satanic accursed, black, demoniac, demoniacal, demonic, devilish, diabolic, evil, fiendish, hellish, infernal, inhuman, iniquitous, malevolent, malignant, wicked

satellite *n.* communications satellite, moon, sputnik

satiate cloy, glut, gorge, jade, nauseate, overfill, stuff

satire burlesque, caricature, irony, lampoon, parody, pasquinade, raillery, ridicule, sarcasm, send-up (*Brit.*

satire *n* **1** the use of ridicule to expose incompetence, evil, or corruption. **2** a play, novel, or poem containing satire. **satirical** *adj*

satirist *n* **1** a writer of satire. **2** a person who uses satire.

satirize *or* **-rise** *vb* **-rizing, -rized** *or* **-rising, -rised** to ridicule (a person or thing) by means of satire. **satirization** *or* **-risation** *n*

satisfaction *n* **1** the pleasure obtained from the fulfilment of a desire. **2** something that brings fulfilment: *craft workers get satisfaction from their work.* **3** compensation or an apology for a wrong done: *consumers unable to get satisfaction from the gas board.*

satisfactory *adj* **1** adequate or acceptable. **2** giving satisfaction. **satisfactorily** *adv*

satisfy *vb* **-fies, -fying, -fied 1** to fulfil the desires or needs of (a person): *his answer didn't satisfy me.* **2** to provide sufficiently for (a need or desire): *to satisfy public demand.* **3** to convince: *that trip did seem to satisfy her that he was dead.* **4** to fulfil the requirements of: *unable to satisfy the conditions set by the commission.* **satisfiable** *adj* **satisfying** *adj*

satrap *n* (in ancient Persia) a provincial governor or subordinate ruler.

SATs standard assessment tasks.

satsuma *n* a small loose-skinned variety of orange with easily separable segments.

saturate *vb* **-rating, -rated 1** to soak completely. **2** to fill so completely that no more can be added: *saturating the area with their men.* **3** *Chem* to combine (a substance) or (of a substance) to be combined with the greatest possible amount of another substance.

saturation *n* **1** the process or state that occurs when one substance is filled so full of another substance that no more can be added. **2** *Mil* the use of very heavy force, esp. bombing, against an area.

saturation point *n* **1** the point at which the maximum amount of a substance has been absorbed. **2** the point at which some capacity is at its fullest; limit: *the market is close to saturation point.*

Saturday *n* the seventh day of the week.

Saturn *n* **1** the Roman god of agriculture. **2** the sixth planet from the sun, second largest in the solar system, around which revolve concentric rings.

Saturnalia *n, pl* **-lia** *or* **-lias 1** the ancient Roman festival of Saturn, renowned for its unrestrained revelry. **2 saturnalia** a wild party or orgy.

saturnine *adj* having a gloomy temperament or appearance.

satyr *n* **1** *Greek myth* a woodland god represented as having a man's body with the ears, horns, tail, and legs of a goat. **2** a man who has strong sexual desires.

sauce *n* **1** a liquid added to food to enhance its flavour. **2** anything that adds interest or zest. **3** *Informal* impudent language or behaviour.

sauce boat *n* a boat-shaped container for serving sauce.

saucepan *n* a metal pan with a long handle and often a lid, used for cooking food.

saucer *n* **1** a small round dish on which a cup is set. **2** something shaped like a saucer. **saucerful** *n*

saucy *adj* **saucier, sauciest 1** cheeky or slightly rude in an amusing and light-hearted way. **2** jaunty and boldly smart: *a saucy hat.* **sauciness** *n*

sauerkraut *n* a German dish of finely shredded pickled cabbage.

sault (**soo**) *n Canad* a waterfall or rapids.

sauna *n* **1** a Finnish-style hot steam bath, usually followed by a cold plunge. **2** the place in which such a bath is taken.

saunter *vb* **1** to walk in a leisurely manner; stroll. *~n* **2** a leisurely pace or stroll.

saurian *adj* of or resembling a lizard.

sausage *n* **1** finely minced meat mixed with fat, cereal, and seasonings, in a tube-shaped casing. **2** an object shaped like a sausage. **3 not a sausage** *Informal* nothing at all.

sausage dog *n Informal* same as **dachshund.**

sausage roll *n Brit* a roll of sausage meat in pastry.

sauté (**so**-tay) *vb* **-téing** *or* **-téeing, -téed 1** to fry

THESAURUS

informal), skit, spoof (*informal*), takeoff (*informal*), travesty, wit

satirical biting, bitter, burlesque, caustic, censorious, cutting, cynical, incisive, ironical, mocking, mordacious, mordant, pungent, Rabelaisian, sarcastic, sardonic, taunting, vitriolic

satirize, -rise abuse, burlesque, censure, criticize, deride, hold up to ridicule, lampoon, lash, parody, pillory, ridicule, send up (*Brit. informal*), take off (*informal*), travesty

satisfaction 1. comfort, complacency, content, contentedness, contentment, ease, enjoyment, gratification, happiness, peace of mind, pleasure, pride, repletion, satiety, well-being **2.** achievement, appeasing, assuaging, fulfilment, gratification, resolution, settlement **3.** amends, atonement, compensation, damages, indemnification, justice, recompense, redress, reimbursement, remuneration, reparation, requital, restitution, settlement, vindication

satisfactory acceptable, adequate, all right, average, competent, fair, good enough, passable, sufficient, suitable, up to standard, up to the mark

satisfied at ease, complacent, content, contented, convinced, easy in one's mind, happy, like the cat that swallowed the canary (*informal*), pacified, positive, smug, sure

satisfy 1. appease, assuage, content, feed, fill, gratify, indulge, mollify, pacify, pander to, please, quench, sate, satiate, slake, surfeit **2.** answer, be enough (adequate, sufficient), come up to expectations, do, fill the bill (*informal*), fulfil, meet, qualify, serve, serve the purpose, suffice **3.** assure, convince, dispel (someone's) doubts, persuade, put (someone's) mind at rest, quiet, reassure **4.** answer, comply with, discharge, fulfil, meet, pay (off), settle, square up

satisfying cheering, convincing, filling, gratifying, pleasing, pleasurable, satisfactory

saturate douse, drench, imbue, impregnate, ret (*used of flax, etc.*), seep, soak, souse, steep, suffuse, waterlog, wet through

saturated drenched, dripping, soaked, soaked to the skin, soaking (wet), sodden, sopping (wet), waterlogged, wet through, wringing wet

sauce *informal* audacity, backchat (*informal*), brass (*informal*), brass neck (*Brit. informal*), cheek (*informal*), cheekiness, disrespectfulness, front, impertinence, impudence, insolence, lip (*slang*), neck (*informal*), nerve (*informal*), rudeness

sauciness backchat (*informal*), brass (*informal*), brazenness, cheek (*informal*), flippancy, impertinence, impudence, insolence, lip (*slang*), pertness, rudeness, sauce (*informal*)

saucy 1. cheeky (*informal*), disrespectful, flip (*informal*), flippant, forward, fresh (*informal*), impertinent, impudent, insolent, pert, presumptuous, rude, smart-alecky (*informal*) **2.** dashing, gay, jaunty, natty (*informal*), perky, rakish, sporty

saunter 1. *vb.* amble, dally, linger, loiter, meander, mosey (*informal*), ramble, roam, rove, stroll, take a

(food) quickly in a little fat. ~*n* **2** a dish of sautéed food. ~*adj* **3** sautéed until lightly brown: *sauté potatoes.*

Sauternes (so-**turn**) *n* a sweet white wine produced in the southern Bordeaux district of France.

savage *adj* **1** wild and untamed: *savage tigers.* **2** fierce and cruel: *savage cries.* **3** (of peoples) uncivilized or primitive: *savage tribes.* **4** rude, crude, and violent: *savage behaviour on the terraces.* **5** (of terrain) wild and uncultivated. ~*n* **6** a member of an uncivilized or primitive society. **7** a fierce or vicious person. ~*vb* **-aging, -aged 8** to attack ferociously and wound: *savaged by a wild dog.* **9** to criticize extremely severely: *savaged by the press for incompetence.* **savagely** *adv*

savagery *n, pl* **-ries** viciousness and cruelty.

savannah *or* **savanna** *n* open grasslands, usually with scattered bushes or trees, in Africa.

savant *n* a very wise and knowledgeable man. **savante** *fem n*

save[1] *vb* **saving, saved 1** to rescue or preserve (a person or thing) from danger or harm. **2** to avoid the spending, waste, or loss of (something): *an appeal on television for the public to save energy.* **3** to set aside or reserve (money or goods) for future use: *I'm saving for a vintage Mercedes.* **4** to treat with care so as to preserve. **5** to prevent the necessity for: *a chance saved him from having to make up his mind.* **6** *Sport* to prevent (a goal) by stopping (a ball or puck). **7** *Christianity* to free (someone) from the influence or consequences of sin. ~*n* **8** *Sport* the act of saving a goal. **9** *Computers* an instruction to write information from the memory onto a tape or disk. **savable** *or* **saveable** *adj* **saver** *n*

save[2] *Old-fashioned* ~*prep* **1** (often foll. by *for*) with the exception of: *the stage was empty save for a single chair.* ~*conj* **2** but.

save as you earn *n* (in Britain) a savings scheme operated by the government, in which regular deposits are made into a savings account from a salary.

saveloy *n* a highly seasoned smoked sausage made from salted pork.

saving *n* **1** preservation from destruction or danger. **2** a reduction in the amount of time or money used. **3 savings** money saved for future use. ~*adj* **4** tending to rescue or preserve. ~*prep* **5** with the exception of.

saving grace *n* a good quality in a person that prevents him or her from being entirely bad or worthless.

saviour *or US* **savior** *n* a person who rescues another person or a thing from danger or harm.

Saviour *or US* **Savior** *n Christianity* Jesus Christ, regarded as the saviour of people from sin.

savoir-faire (**sav**-wahr-**fair**) *n* the ability to say and do the right thing in any situation.

savory *n, pl* **-vories** an aromatic plant whose leaves are used in cooking.

savour *or US* **savor** *vb* **1** to enjoy and appreciate (food or drink) slowly. **2** to enjoy (a pleasure) for as long as possible: *an experience to be savoured.* **3 savour of a** to have a suggestion of: *that could savour of ostentation.* **b** to possess the taste or smell of: *the vegetables savoured of coriander.* ~*n* **4** the taste or smell of something. **5** a slight but distinctive quality or trace.

savoury *or US* **savory** *adj* **1** salty or spicy: *savoury foods.* **2** attractive to the sense of taste or smell. **3** pleasant or acceptable: *one of the book's less savoury characters.* ~*n, pl* **-ries 4** *Chiefly Brit* a savoury dish served before or after a meal. **savouriness** *or US* **savoriness** *n*

savoy *n* a cabbage with a compact head and wrinkled leaves.

savvy *Slang* ~*vb* **-vies, -vying, -vied 1** to understand. ~*n* **2** understanding or common sense.

saw[1] *n* **1** a cutting tool with a toothed metal blade or edge, either operated by hand or powered by electricity. ~*vb* **sawing, sawed; sawed** *or* **sawn 2** to cut with or as if with a saw. **3** to form by sawing. **4** to move (an object) from side to side as if moving a saw.

saw[2] *vb* the past tense of **see**[1].

saw[3] *n Old-fashioned* a wise saying or proverb.

sawdust *n* particles of wood formed by sawing.

sawfish *n, pl* **-fish** *or* **-fishes** a sharklike ray with a long toothed snout resembling a saw.

sawmill *n* a factory where timber is sawn into planks.

sawn *vb* a past participle of **saw**[1].

sawn-off *or esp US* **sawed-off** *adj* (of a shotgun) having the barrel cut short to make concealment of the weapon easier.

sawyer *n* a person who saws timber for a living.

sax *n Informal* short for **saxophone**.

THESAURUS

stroll, tarry, wander **2.** *n.* airing, amble, breather, constitutional, perambulation, promenade, ramble, stroll, turn, walk

savage *adj.* **1.** feral, rough, rugged, uncivilized, uncultivated, undomesticated, untamed, wild **2.** barbarous, beastly, bestial, bloodthirsty, bloody, brutal, brutish, cruel, devilish, diabolical, ferocious, fierce, harsh, inhuman, merciless, murderous, pitiless, ravening, ruthless, sadistic, vicious **3.** in a state of nature, nonliterate, primitive, rude, unspoilt ~*n.* **4.** autochthon, barbarian, heathen, indigene, native, primitive **5.** beast, brute, fiend, monster ~*vb.* **6.** attack, lacerate, mangle, maul, tear into (*informal*)

savagery barbarity, bestiality, bloodthirstiness, brutality, cruelty, ferocity, fierceness, inhumanity, ruthlessness, sadism, viciousness

save 1. bail (someone) out, come to (someone's) rescue, deliver, free, liberate, recover, redeem, rescue, salvage, set free **2.** be frugal, be thrifty, collect, economize, gather, hide away, hoard, hold, husband, keep, keep up one's sleeve (*informal*), lay by, put aside for a rainy day, put by, reserve, retrench, salt away, set aside, store, tighten one's belt (*informal*), treasure up **3.** conserve, guard, keep safe, look after, preserve, protect, safeguard, screen, shield, take care of **4.** hinder, obviate, prevent, rule out, spare

saving *n.* **1.** bargain, discount, economy, reduction **2.** *Plural* fall-back, fund, nest egg, provision for a rainy day, reserves, resources, store ~*adj.* **3.** compensatory, extenuating, qualifying, redeeming

saviour defender, deliverer, friend in need, Good Samaritan, guardian, knight in shining armour, liberator, preserver, protector, redeemer, rescuer, salvation

Saviour Christ, Jesus, Messiah, Redeemer

savoir-faire accomplishment, address, diplomacy, discretion, finesse, poise, social graces, social know-how (*informal*), tact, urbanity

savour *vb.* **1.** appreciate, delight in, drool, enjoy, enjoy to the full, gloat over, like, luxuriate in, partake, relish, revel in, smack one's lips over **2.** *often with* **of** bear the hallmarks, be indicative, be suggestive, partake, show signs, smack, suggest, verge on ~*n.* **3.** flavour, piquancy, relish, smack, smell, tang, taste, zest **4.** distinctive quality, excitement, flavour, interest, salt, spice, zest

savoury 1. agreeable, appetizing, dainty, delectable, delicious, full-flavoured, good, luscious, mouthwatering, palatable, piquant, rich, scrumptious (*informal*),

saxifrage *n* an alpine rock plant with small white, yellow, purple, or pink flowers.

Saxon *n* **1** a member of a West Germanic people who raided and settled parts of Britain in the fifth and sixth centuries AD. **2** any of the West Germanic dialects spoken by the ancient Saxons. *~adj* **3** of the ancient Saxons or their language.

saxophone *n* a brass wind instrument with keys and a curved metal body. **saxophonist** *n*

say *vb* **saying, said 1** to speak or utter. **2** to express (an idea) in words: *I can't say what I feel.* **3** to state (an opinion or fact) positively: *I say you are wrong.* **4** to indicate or show: *the clock says ten to nine.* **5** to recite: *to say grace.* **6** to report or allege: *they say we shall have rain today.* **7** to suppose as an example or possibility: *let us say that he is lying.* **8** to convey by means of artistic expression: *what does the artist have to say in this picture?* **9** to make a case for: *there is much to be said for it.* **10 go without saying** to be so obvious as to need no explanation. **11 to say the least** at the very least. *~adv* **12** approximately: *there were, say, 20 people present.* **13** for example: *choose a number, say, four.* *~n* **14** the right or chance to speak: *the opposition has hardly had a say in these affairs.* **15** authority, esp. to influence a decision: *he has a lot of say.*

SAYE (in Britain) save as you earn.

saying *n* a well-known phrase or sentence expressing a belief or a truth.

Sb *Chem* antimony.

Sc *Chem* scandium.

SC 1 South Carolina. **2** *Austral & NZ* School Certificate; a certificate awarded to secondary school pupils who have passed public exams.

scab *n* **1** the dried crusty surface of a healing skin wound or sore. **2** *Disparaging* a person who refuses to support a trade union's actions, and continues to work during a strike. **3** a contagious disease of sheep, caused by a mite. **4** a fungal disease of plants. *~vb* **scabbing, scabbed 5** to become covered with a scab. **6** *Disparaging* to work as a scab.

scabbard *n* a holder for a sword or dagger.

scabby *adj* **-bier, -biest 1** *Pathol* covered with scabs. **2** *Informal* mean or despicable. **scabbiness** *n*

scabies (**skay**-beez) *n* a contagious skin infection caused by a mite, characterized by intense itching.

scabious (**skay**-bee-uss) *n* a plant with showy blue, red, or whitish dome-shaped flower heads.

scabrous (**skay**-bruss) *adj* **1** rough and scaly. **2** indecent or crude: *scabrous stand-up comedy.*

scaffold *n* **1** a temporary framework used to support workmen and materials during the construction or repair of a building. **2** a raised wooden platform on which criminals are hanged; gallows.

scaffolding *n* **1** a scaffold or scaffolds. **2** the building materials used to make scaffolds.

scalar *Maths ~n* **1** a quantity, such as time or temperature, that has magnitude but not direction. *~adj* **2** having magnitude but not direction.

scald *vb* **1** to burn with hot liquid or steam. **2** to sterilize with boiling water. **3** to heat (a liquid) almost to boiling point. *~n* **4** a burn caused by scalding.

scale[1] *n* **1** one of the thin flat overlapping plates covering the bodies of fishes and reptiles. **2** a thin flat piece or flake. **3** a coating which sometimes forms in kettles and hot-water pipes in areas where the water is hard. **4** tartar formed on the teeth. *~vb* **scaling, scaled 5** to remove the scales or coating from. **6** to peel off in flakes or scales. **7** to cover or become covered with scales. **scaly** *adj*

scale[2] *n* **1** (*often pl*) a machine or device for weighing. **2** one of the pans of a balance. **3 tip the scales** to have a decisive influence. **4 tip the scales at** to amount in weight to.

scale[3] *n* **1** a sequence of marks at regular intervals, used as a reference in making measurements. **2** a measuring instrument with such a scale. **3** the ratio between the size of something real and that of a representation of it: *the map has a scale of 1:10 000.* **4** a series of degrees or graded system of things: *the Western wage scale for the same work.* **5** a relative degree or extent: *growing flowers on a very small scale.* **6** *Music* a sequence of notes taken in ascending or descending order, esp. within one octave. **7** *Maths* the notation of a given number system: *the decimal scale.* *~vb* **scaling, scaled 8** to climb to the top of (an object or height): *the men scaled a wall.* **9 scale up** *or* **down** to increase *or* reduce proportionately in size: *the wing resembled that of a DC-3 scaled up to a span exceeding 138 ft; the search was scaled down.*

scalene *adj Maths* (of a triangle) having all sides of unequal length.

scallion *n* a spring onion.

scallop *n* **1** an edible marine mollusc with two fluted fan-shaped shells. **2** a single shell of this mollusc. **3** one of a series of small curves along an edge. **scalloping** *n*

scalloped *adj* decorated with small curves along the edge.

scallywag *n Informal* a badly behaved but likeable person; rascal.

scalp *n* **1** *Anat* the skin and hair covering the top of the head. **2** (formerly among North American Indians) a part of this removed as a trophy from a slain enemy. *~vb* **3** to cut the scalp from. **4** *Informal, chiefly US* to buy and resell so as to make a high or quick profit.

THESAURUS

spicy, tangy, tasty, toothsome **2.** decent, edifying, honest, reputable, respectable, wholesome

saw adage, aphorism, apophthegm, axiom, byword, dictum, gnome, maxim, proverb, saying

say *vb.* **1.** add, affirm, announce, assert, asseverate, come out with (*informal*), declare, give voice *or* utterance to, maintain, mention, pronounce, put into words, remark, speak, state, utter, voice **2.** answer, disclose, divulge, give as one's opinion, make known, reply, respond, reveal, tell **3.** deliver, do, orate, perform, read, recite, rehearse, render, repeat **4.** allege, bruit, claim, noise abroad, put about, report, rumour, suggest **5.** assume, conjecture, dare say, estimate, guess, hazard a guess, imagine, judge, presume, suppose, surmise **6.** communicate, convey, express, give the impression that, imply **7. go without saying** be accepted, be a matter of course, be obvious, be self-evident, be taken as read, be taken for granted, be understood **8. to say the least** at the very least, to put it mildly, without any exaggeration *~n.* **9.** crack (*informal*), turn (chance, opportunity) to speak, voice, vote **10.** authority, clout (*informal*), influence, power, sway, weight

saying adage, aphorism, apophthegm, axiom, byword, dictum, gnome, maxim, proverb, saw, slogan

scale[1] *n.* flake, lamina, layer, plate, squama (*Biol.*)

scale[2] *n.* **1.** calibration, degrees, gamut, gradation, graduated system, graduation, hierarchy, ladder, pecking order (*informal*), progression, ranking, register, seniority system, sequence, series, spectrum, spread, steps **2.** proportion, ratio **3.** degree, extent, range, reach, scope, way *~vb.* **4.** ascend, clamber, climb, escalade, mount, surmount **5. scale up** *or* **down** adjust, proportion, regulate

scalpel *n* a small surgical knife with a very sharp thin blade.
scam *n Slang* a stratagem for gain; a swindle
scamp *n* a mischievous person, esp. a child.
scamper *vb* **1** to run about hurriedly or quickly. *~n* **2** the act of scampering.
scampi *n* large prawns, usually eaten fried in breadcrumbs.
scan *vb* **scanning, scanned 1** to scrutinize carefully. **2** to glance over quickly. **3** *Prosody* to analyse (verse) by examining its rhythmical structure. **4** *Prosody* (of a line or verse) to be metrically correct. **5** to examine or search (an area) by systematically moving a beam of light or electrons, or a radar or sonar beam over it. **6** *Med* to obtain an image of (a part of the body) by means of ultrasound or a scanner. *~n* **7** an instance of scanning.
scandal *n* **1** a disgraceful action or event: *the chairman resigned after a loans scandal.* **2** shame or outrage arising from a disgraceful action or event: *the figures were a national scandal.* **3** malicious gossip. **scandalous** *adj* **scandalously** *adv*
scandalize *or* **-ise** *vb* **-izing, -ized** *or* **-ising, -ised** to shock or be shocked by improper behaviour.
scandalmonger *n* a person who spreads or enjoys scandal or gossip.
Scandinavian *adj* **1** of Scandinavia (Norway, Sweden, Denmark, and often Finland, Iceland, and the Faeroe Islands). *~n* **2** a person from Scandinavia. **3** the northern group of Germanic languages, consisting of Swedish, Danish, Norwegian, Icelandic, and Faeroese.
scandium *n Chem* a rare silvery-white metallic element. Symbol: Sc
scanner *n* **1** an aerial or similar device designed to transmit or receive signals, esp. radar signals. **2** a device used in medical diagnosis to obtain an image of an internal organ or part.
scansion *n* the metrical scanning of verse.
scant *adj* scarcely sufficient: *some issues will get scant attention.*
scanty *adj* **scantier, scantiest** barely sufficient or not sufficient. **scantily** *adv* **scantiness** *n*
scapegoat *n* a person made to bear the blame for others.
scapula (**skap**-pew-la) *n, pl* **-lae** (-lee) the technical name for **shoulder blade.**
scapular *adj* **1** *Anat* of the scapula. *~n* **2** a loose sleeveless garment worn by monks over their habits.
scar[1] *n* **1** a mark left on the skin following the healing of a wound. **2** a permanent effect on a person's character resulting from emotional distress. **3** a mark on a plant where a leaf was formerly attached. **4** a mark of damage. *~vb* **scarring, scarred 5** to mark or become marked with a scar.
scar[2] *n* a bare craggy rock formation.
scarab *n* **1** the black dung-beetle, regarded by the ancient Egyptians as divine. **2** an image or carving of this beetle.
scarce *adj* **1** insufficient to meet the demand: *scarce water resources.* **2** not common; rarely found. **3 make oneself scarce** *Informal* to go away. *~adv* **4** *Archaic or literary* scarcely.
scarcely *adv* **1** hardly at all. **2** *Often used ironically* probably or definitely not: *that is scarcely justification for your actions.*
➤ **As** ***scarcely*** **has a negative sense it is followed by** *ever* or *any* (not *never* or *no*).
scarcity *n, pl* **-ties** an inadequate supply.
scare *vb* **scaring, scared 1** to frighten or be frightened. **2 scare away** *or* **off** to drive away by frightening. *~n* **3** a sudden attack of fear or alarm: *you gave me a scare.* **4** a period of general fear or alarm: *the latest AIDS scare.*
scarecrow *n* **1** an object, usually in the shape of a man, made out of sticks and old clothes, to scare birds away from crops. **2** *Informal* a raggedly dressed person.
scaremonger *n* a person who starts or spreads rumours of disaster to frighten people. **scaremongering** *n*
scarf[1] *n, pl* **scarves** *or* **scarfs** a piece of material worn around the head, neck, or shoulders.
scarf[2] *n, pl* **scarfs 1** a joint between two pieces of timber made by notching the ends and strapping or gluing the two pieces together. *~vb* **2** to join (two pieces of timber) by means of a scarf.
scarify *vb* **-fies, -fying, -fied 1** *Surgery* to make slight incisions in (the skin). **2** *Agriculture* to break up

THESAURUS

scaly flaky, scabrous, scurfy
scamp devil, imp, knave (*archaic*), mischief-maker, monkey, pickle (*Brit. informal*), prankster, rascal, rogue, scallywag (*informal*), toerag (*slang*), tyke (*informal*), whippersnapper (*old-fashioned*), wretch
scamper beetle, dart, dash, fly, hasten, hie (*archaic*), hurry, romp, run, scoot, scurry, scuttle, sprint
scan *vb.* **1.** check, check out (*informal*), examine, investigate, recce (*slang*), scour, scrutinize, search **2.** get a load of (*informal*), glance over, look one up and down, look through, run one's eye over, run over, size up (*informal*), skim, survey, sweep, take a dekko at (*Brit. slang*), take stock of
scandal **1.** crime, crying shame (*informal*), disgrace, embarrassment, offence, sin, wrongdoing **2.** calumny, defamation, detraction, discredit, disgrace, dishonour, ignominy, infamy, obloquy, offence, opprobrium, reproach, shame, stigma **3.** abuse, aspersion, backbiting, dirt, dirty linen (*informal*), gossip, rumours, skeleton in the cupboard, slander, talk, tattle
scandalize, -ise affront, appal, cause a few raised eyebrows (*informal*), disgust, horrify, offend, outrage, shock
scandalous **1.** atrocious, disgraceful, disreputable, highly improper, infamous, monstrous, odious, opprobrious, outrageous, shameful, shocking, unseemly **2.** defamatory, gossiping, libellous, scurrilous, slanderous, untrue
scant bare, barely sufficient, deficient, inadequate, insufficient, limited, little, minimal, sparse
scanty bare, deficient, exiguous, inadequate, insufficient, meagre, narrow, poor, restricted, scant, short, skimpy, slender, sparing, sparse, thin
scapegoat fall guy (*informal*), whipping boy
scar **1.** *n.* blemish, cicatrix, injury, mark, wound **2.** *vb.* brand, damage, disfigure, mark, traumatize
scarce at a premium, deficient, few, few and far between, infrequent, in short supply, insufficient, rare, seldom met with, uncommon, unusual, wanting
scarcely **1.** barely, hardly, only just, scarce (*archaic*) **2.** (*often used ironically*), by no means, definitely not, hardly, not at all, on no account, under no circumstances
scarcity dearth, deficiency, infrequency, insufficiency, lack, paucity, poverty, rareness, shortage, undersupply, want
scare **1.** *vb.* alarm, daunt, dismay, frighten, give (someone) a fright, give (someone) a turn (*informal*), intimidate, panic, put the wind up (someone) (*informal*), shock, startle, terrify, terrorize **2.** *n.* alarm, alert, fright, panic, shock, start, terror

and loosen (topsoil). **3** to criticize without mercy. **scarification** *n*

scarlatina *n* the technical name for **scarlet fever.**

scarlet *adj* bright red.

scarlet fever *n* an acute contagious disease characterized by fever, a sore throat, and a red rash on the body.

scarp *n* **1** a steep slope or ridge of rock. **2** *Fortifications* the side of a ditch cut nearest to a rampart.

scarper *vb Brit slang* to run away or escape.

scarves *n* a plural of **scarf**[1].

scary *adj* **scarier, scariest** *Informal* quite frightening.

scat[1] *vb* **scatting, scatted** *Informal* to go away in haste.

scat[2] *n* **1** a type of jazz singing using improvised vocal sounds instead of words. ~*vb* **scatting, scatted 2** to sing jazz in this way.

scathing *adj* harshly critical: *a scathing review of the play.* **scathingly** *adv*

scatology *n* preoccupation with obscenity, esp. with references to excrement. **scatological** *adj*

scatter *vb* **1** to throw about in various directions: *scatter some oatmeal on top of the cake.* **2** to separate and move in various directions; disperse: *the infantry were scattering.* ~*n* **3** the act of scattering. **4** a number of objects scattered about.

scatterbrain *n* a person who is incapable of serious thought or concentration. **scatterbrained** *adj*

scatty *adj* **-tier, -tiest** *Brit informal* rather absent-minded. **scattiness** *n*

scavenge *vb* **-enging, -enged** to search for (anything usable) among discarded material.

scavenger *n* **1** a person who collects things discarded by others. **2** any animal that feeds on discarded or decaying matter.

SCE (in Scotland) Scottish Certificate of Education.

scenario *n, pl* **-narios 1** a summary of the plot and characters of a play or film. **2** an imagined sequence of future events: *the likeliest scenario is another general election.*

scene *n* **1** the place where an action or event, real or imaginary, occurs. **2** an incident or situation, real or imaginary, esp. as described or represented. **3** a division of an act of a play, in which the setting is fixed and the action is continuous. **4** *Films* a shot or series of shots that constitutes a unit of the action. **5** the backcloths or screens used to represent a location in a play or film set. **6** the view of a place or landscape. **7** a display of emotion or loss of temper in public: *you do not want to cause a scene.* **8** *Informal* a particular activity or aspect of life, and all the things associated with it: *the club scene.* **9 behind the scenes a** backstage. **b** in secret or in private.

scenery *n, pl* **-eries 1** the natural features of a landscape. **2** *Theatre* the painted backcloths or screens used to represent a location in a theatre or studio.

scenic *adj* **1** of or having beautiful natural scenery: *untouched scenic areas.* **2** of the stage or stage scenery: *scenic artists.*

scent *n* **1** a distinctive smell, esp. a pleasant one. **2** a smell left in passing, by which a person or animal may be traced. **3** a trail or series of clues by which something is followed: *he must have got on to the scent of the story through you.* **4** perfume. ~*vb* **5** to become aware of by smelling. **6** to suspect: *he scented the beginnings of irritation in the car.* **7** to fill with odour or fragrance. **scented** *adj*

sceptic *or US* **skeptic** (**skep**-tik) *n* **1** a person who habitually doubts generally accepted beliefs. **2** a person who doubts the truth of a religion. **sceptical** *or US* **skeptical** *adj* **sceptically** *or US* **skeptically** *adv* **scepticism** *or US* **skepticism** *n*

sceptre *or US* **scepter** *n* an ornamental rod symbolizing royal power. **sceptred** *or US* **sceptered** *adj*

Schadenfreude (**shah**-den-froy-da) *n* one person's delight in another's misfortune.

schedule *n* **1** a timed plan of procedure for a project. **2** a list of details or items: *the schedule of priorities.* **3** a timetable. ~*vb* **-uling, -uled 4** to plan and arrange (something) to happen at a certain time. **5** to make a schedule or include in a schedule.

schema *n, pl* **-mata** an outline of a plan or theory.

schematic *adj* presented as a diagram or plan. **schematically** *adv*

schematize *or* **-tise** *vb* **-tizing, -tized** *or* **-tising, -tised** to form into or arrange in a systematic arrangement or plan.

scheme *n* **1** a systematic plan for a course of action. **2** a systematic arrangement of parts or features: *colour scheme.* **3** a secret plot. **4** a chart, diagram, or outline. **5** *Chiefly Brit* a plan formally adopted by a gov-

THESAURUS

scared fearful, frightened, panicky, panic-stricken, petrified, scared shitless (*taboo slang*), shaken, shit-scared (*taboo slang*), startled, terrified

scathing belittling, biting, brutal, caustic, critical, cutting, harsh, mordacious, mordant, sarcastic, savage, scornful, searing, trenchant, vitriolic, withering

scatter 1. broadcast, diffuse, disseminate, fling, litter, shower, sow, spread, sprinkle, strew **2.** disband, dispel, disperse, dissipate, disunite, put to flight, separate

scatterbrain bird-brain (*informal*), butterfly, featherbrain, flibbertigibbet (*old-fashioned*), grasshopper mind, madcap

scenario master plan, outline, résumé, rundown, scheme, sequence of events, sketch, story line, summary, synopsis

scene 1. area, locality, place, position, setting, site, situation, spot, whereabouts **2.** display, drama, exhibition, pageant, picture, representation, show, sight, spectacle, tableau **3.** act, division, episode, incident, part, stage **4.** backdrop, background, location, *mise en scène*, set, setting **5.** landscape, panorama, prospect, view, vista **6.** carry-on (*informal, chiefly Brit.*), commotion, confrontation, display of emotion, drama, exhibition, fuss, performance, row, tantrum, to-do, upset **7.** *informal* arena, business, environment, field of interest, milieu, world

scenery 1. landscape, surroundings, terrain, view, vista **2.** *Theatre* backdrop, decor, flats, *mise en scène*, set, setting, stage set

scent *n.* **1.** aroma, bouquet, fragrance, niff (*Brit. slang*), odour, perfume, redolence, smell **2.** spoor, track, trail ~*vb.* **3.** be on the track *or* trail of, detect, discern, get wind of (*informal*), nose out, recognize, sense, smell, sniff, sniff out

scented aromatic, fragrant, odoriferous, perfumed, redolent, sweet-smelling

sceptic agnostic, cynic, disbeliever, doubter, doubting Thomas, scoffer, unbeliever

sceptical cynical, disbelieving, doubtful, doubting, dubious, hesitating, incredulous, mistrustful, questioning, quizzical, scoffing, unbelieving, unconvinced

scepticism agnosticism, cynicism, disbelief, doubt, incredulity, suspicion, unbelief

schedule 1. *n.* agenda, calendar, catalogue, inventory, itinerary, list, list of appointments, plan, programme, timetable **2.** *vb.* appoint, arrange, be due, book, organize, plan, programme, slot (*informal*), time

ernment or organization: *a pension scheme.* ~*vb* **scheming, schemed 6** to plan in an underhand manner. **schemer** *n* **scheming** *adj, n*

scherzo (**skairt**-so) *n, pl* **-zos** a quick lively piece of music, often the second or third movement in a sonata or symphony.

schilling *n* the standard monetary unit of Austria.

schism (**skizz**-um) *n* the division of a group, esp. a religious group, into opposing factions, due to differences in doctrine. **schismatic** *adj*

schist (**skist**) *n* a crystalline rock which splits into thin layers.

schizo (**skit**-so) *Offensive* ~*adj* 1 schizophrenic. ~*n, pl* **-os** 2 a schizophrenic person.

schizoid *adj* 1 *Psychol* having a personality disorder characterized by extreme shyness and extreme sensitivity. 2 *Informal* characterized by conflicting or contradictory ideas or attitudes. ~*n* 3 a person who has a schizoid personality.

schizophrenia *n* 1 a psychotic disorder characterized by withdrawal from reality, hallucinations, or emotional instability. 2 *Informal* behaviour that seems to be motivated by contradictory or conflicting principles. **schizophrenic** *adj, n*

schmaltz *n* excessive sentimentality, esp. in music. **schmaltzy** *adj*

schnapps *n* a strong dry alcoholic drink distilled from potatoes.

schnitzel *n* a thin slice of meat, esp. veal.

scholar *n* 1 a person who studies an academic subject. 2 a student who has a scholarship. 3 a pupil. **scholarly** *adj*

scholarship *n* 1 academic achievement; learning gained by serious study. 2 financial aid provided for a scholar because of academic merit.

scholastic *adj* 1 of schools, scholars, or education. 2 of or relating to scholasticism. ~*n* 3 a scholarly person. 4 a disciple or adherent of scholasticism.

scholasticism *n* the system of philosophy, theology, and teaching that dominated medieval Europe and was based on the writings of Aristotle.

school[1] *n* 1 a place where children are educated. 2 the staff and pupils of a school. 3 a regular session of instruction in a school: *we stayed behind after school.* 4 a faculty or department specializing in a particular subject: *the dental school.* 5 a place or sphere of activity that instructs: *the school of hard knocks.* 6 a group of artists, writers, or thinkers, linked by the same style, teachers, or methods. 7 *Informal* a group assembled for a common purpose, such as gambling: *a card school.* ~*vb* 8 to educate or train: *she schooled herself to be as ambitious as her sister.*

school[2] *n* a group of sea-living animals that swim together, such as fish, whales, or dolphins.

schoolboy *n* a boy attending school.

schooled *adj* **schooled in** trained or educated in: *well schooled in history.*

schoolgirl *n* a girl attending school.

schoolhouse *n* 1 a building used as a school. 2 a house attached to a school.

schooling *n* the education a person receives at school.

schoolmarm *n Informal* 1 a woman schoolteacher. 2 a woman who is old-fashioned and easily shocked by bad language or references to sex.

schoolmaster *or fem* **schoolmistress** *n* a person who teaches in or runs a school.

schoolteacher *n* a person who teaches in a school.

school year *n* 1 a twelve-month period, usually of three terms, during which pupils remain in the same class. 2 the time during this period when the school is open.

schooner *n* 1 a sailing ship with at least two masts, one at the back and one at the front. 2 *Brit* a large glass for sherry. 3 *US, Canad, Austral, & NZ* a large glass for beer.

schottische *n* 1 a 19th-century German dance resembling a slow polka. 2 music for this dance.

schuss (**shooss**) *n Skiing* a straight high-speed downhill run.

sciatic *adj* 1 *Anat* of the hip or the hipbone. 2 of or afflicted with sciatica.

sciatica *n* severe pain in the large nerve in the back of the leg.

science *n* 1 the study of the nature and behaviour of the physical universe, based on observation, experiment, and measurement. 2 the knowledge obtained by these methods. 3 any particular branch of this knowledge: *medical science.* 4 any body of knowledge organized in a way resembling that of the physical sciences but concerned with other subjects: *political science.*

science fiction *n* stories and films that make imaginative use of scientific knowledge or theories.

science park *n* an area where scientific research and commercial development are carried on in cooperation.

scientific *adj* 1 relating to science or a particular science: *scientific discovery.* 2 done in a systematic way, using experiments or tests. **scientifically** *adv*

scientist *n* a person who studies or practises a science.

sci-fi *n* short for **science fiction.**

THESAURUS

scheme *n.* **1.** contrivance, course of action, design, device, plan, programme, project, proposal, strategy, system, tactics, theory **2.** conspiracy, dodge, game (*informal*), intrigue, machinations, manoeuvre, plot, ploy, ruse, shift, stratagem, subterfuge **3.** arrangement, blueprint, chart, codification, diagram, disposition, draft, layout, outline, pattern, schedule, schema, system ~*vb.* **4.** collude, conspire, intrigue, machinate, manoeuvre, plot, wheel and deal (*informal*)

scheming artful, calculating, conniving, cunning, deceitful, designing, duplicitous, foxy, Machiavellian, slippery, sly, tricky, underhand, wily

schism breach, break, discord, disunion, division, rift, rupture, separation, splintering, split

scholar 1. academic, bookworm, egghead (*informal*), intellectual, man of letters, savant **2.** disciple, learner, pupil, schoolboy, schoolgirl, student

scholarly academic, bookish, erudite, intellectual, learned, lettered, scholastic, studious, well-read

scholarship 1. accomplishments, attainments, book-learning, education, erudition, knowledge, learning, lore **2.** bursary, exhibition, fellowship

scholastic academic, bookish, learned, lettered, literary, scholarly

school *n.* **1.** academy, alma mater, college, department, discipline, faculty, institute, institution, seminary **2.** adherents, circle, class, clique, denomination, devotees, disciples, faction, followers, following, group, pupils, schism, sect, set ~*vb.* **3.** coach, discipline, drill, educate, indoctrinate, instruct, prepare, prime, train, tutor, verse

schooling book-learning, education, formal education, teaching, tuition

schoolteacher instructor, pedagogue, schoolmarm (*informal*), schoolmaster, schoolmistress

scimitar *n* a curved oriental sword.
scintilla (sin-**till**-a) *n* a very small amount; hint or trace.
scintillate *vb* **-lating, -lated** to give off (sparks); sparkle. **scintillation** *n*
scintillating *adj* (of conversation or humour) very lively and amusing.
scion (**sy**-on) *n* **1** a descendant or young member of a family. **2** a shoot of a plant for grafting onto another plant.
scissors *pl n* a cutting instrument held in one hand, with two crossed blades pivoted so that they close together on what is to be cut.
sclera (**skleer**-a) *n Biol* the tough white substance that forms the outer covering of the eyeball.
sclerosis (skleer-**oh**-siss) *n, pl* **-ses** (-seez) *Pathol* an abnormal hardening or thickening of body tissues, esp. of the nervous system or the inner wall of arteries.
sclerotic (skleer-**rot**-ik) *adj* **1** of or relating to the sclera. **2** of, relating to, or having sclerosis.
scoff[1] *vb* **1** (often foll. by *at*) to speak in a scornful and mocking way about (something). *~n* **2** a mocking expression; jeer. **scoffing** *adj, n*
scoff[2] *vb Informal, chiefly Brit* to eat (food) fast and greedily.
scold *vb* **1** to find fault with or rebuke (a person) harshly. **2** *Old-fashioned* to use harsh or abusive language. *~n* **3** a person, esp. a woman, who constantly scolds. **scolding** *n*
scollop *n, vb* same as **scallop.**
sconce *n* a bracket fixed to a wall for holding candles or lights.
scone *n* a small plain cake baked in an oven or on a griddle.
scoop *n* **1** a spoonlike tool with a deep bowl, used for handling loose or soft materials such as flour or ice cream. **2** the deep shovel of a mechanical digger. **3** the amount taken up by a scoop. **4** the act of scooping or dredging. **5** a news story reported in one newspaper before all the others. *~vb* **6** (often foll. by *up*) to take up and remove (something) with or as if with a scoop. **7 scoop out** to hollow out with or as if with a scoop. **8** to beat (rival newspapers) in reporting a news item.
scoot *vb* to leave or move quickly.
scooter *n* **1** a child's small cycle which is ridden by pushing the ground with one foot. **2** a light motorcycle with a small engine.
scope *n* **1** opportunity for using abilities: *ample scope for creative work.* **2** range of view or grasp: *that is outside my scope.* **3** the area covered by an activity or topic: *the scope of his essay was vast.*
scorbutic (score-**byewt**-ik) *adj* of or having scurvy.
scorch *vb* **1** to burn or become burnt slightly on the surface. **2** to parch or shrivel from heat. **3** *Informal* to criticize harshly. *~n* **4** a slight burn. **5** a mark caused by the application of excessive heat. **scorching** *adj*
scorcher *n Informal* a very hot day.
score *n* **1** the total number of points made by a side or individual in a game. **2** the act of scoring a point or points: *there was no score and three minutes remained.* **3 the score** *Informal* the actual situation: *what's the score on this business?* **4** *Old-fashioned* a group or set of twenty: *three score years and ten.* **5 scores of** lots of: *we received scores of letters.* **6** *Music* a written version of a piece of music showing parts for each musician. **7 a** the incidental music for a film or play. **b** the songs and music for a stage or film musical. **8** a mark or scratch. **9** a record of money due: *what's the score for the drinks?* **10** an amount recorded as due. **11** a reason: *some objections were made on the score of sentiment.* **12** a grievance: *a score to settle.* **13 over the score** *Informal* excessive or unfair. *~vb* **scoring, scored 14** to gain (a point or points) in a game or contest. **15** to make a total score of. **16** to keep a record of the score (of). **17** to be worth (a certain number of points) in a game: *red aces score twenty.* **18** to make cuts or lines in or on. **19** *Slang* to purchase an illegal drug. **20** *Slang* to succeed in finding a sexual partner. **21** to arrange (a piece of music) for specific instruments or voices. **22** to write the music

THESAURUS

science body of knowledge, branch of knowledge, discipline
scientific accurate, controlled, exact, mathematical, precise, systematic
scintillate blaze, coruscate, flash, give off sparks, gleam, glint, glisten, glitter, sparkle, twinkle
scintillating animated, bright, brilliant, dazzling, ebullient, exciting, glittering, lively, sparkling, stimulating, witty
scoff belittle, deride, despise, flout, jeer, jibe, knock (*informal*), laugh at, make light of, make sport of, mock, poke fun at, pooh-pooh, revile, ridicule, scorn, slag (off) (*slang*), sneer, take the piss (out of) (*taboo slang*), taunt, twit
scold 1. *vb.* bawl out (*informal*), berate, blame, bring (someone) to book, carpet (*informal*), castigate, censure, chide, find fault with, give a rocket (*Brit. & N.Z. informal*), give (someone) a dressing-down (row, talking-to (*informal*)) (*informal*), go on at, haul (someone) over the coals (*informal*), have (someone) on the carpet (*informal*), lecture, nag, rate, read the riot act, rebuke, remonstrate with, reprimand, reproach, reprove, take (someone) to task, tear into (*informal*), tear (someone) off a strip (*Brit. informal*), tell off (*informal*), tick off (*informal*), upbraid, vituperate **2.** *n.* nag, shrew, termagant (*literary*)
scolding dressing-down (*informal*), (good) talking-to (*informal*), lecture, piece of one's mind, rebuke, row, telling-off (*informal*), ticking-off (*informal*), tongue-lashing, wigging (*Brit. slang*)
scoop *n.* **1.** dipper, ladle, spoon **2.** coup, exclusive, exposé, inside story, revelation, sensation *~vb.* **3.** *often with* **up** clear away, gather up, lift, pick up, remove, sweep up *or* away, take up **4.** *with* **out** bail, dig, dip, empty, excavate, gouge, hollow, ladle, scrape, shovel
scope ambit, area, capacity, compass, confines, elbowroom, extent, field of reference, freedom, latitude, liberty, opportunity, orbit, outlook, purview, range, reach, room, space, span, sphere
scorch blacken, blister, burn, char, parch, roast, sear, shrivel, singe, wither
scorching baking, boiling, broiling, burning, fiery, flaming, red-hot, roasting, searing, sizzling, sweltering, torrid, tropical, unbearably hot
score *n.* **1.** grade, mark, outcome, points, record, result, total **2. the score** *informal* the facts, the reality, the setup (*informal*), the situation, the truth **3.** *plural* a flock, a great number, an army, a throng, crowds, droves, hosts, hundreds, legions, lots, masses, millions, multitudes, myriads, swarms, very many **4.** account, amount due, bill, charge, debt, obligation, reckoning, tab (*U.S. informal*), tally, total **5.** account, basis, cause, ground, grounds, reason **6.** a bone to pick, grievance, grudge, injury, injustice, wrong *~vb.* **7.** achieve, amass, chalk up (*informal*), gain, make, notch up (*informal*), win **8.** count, keep a tally of, keep count, record, register, tally **9.** crosshatch, cut, deface, gouge, graze, indent, mar, mark, nick, notch, scrape, scratch, slash **10.** *Music* adapt, arrange, orchestrate, set **11.** gain an advantage, go down well with (some-

for (a film or play). **23** to achieve (success or an advantage): *your idea scored with the boss.*

scoreboard *n Sport* a board for displaying the score of a game or match.

scorecard *n* **1** a card on which scores are recorded in games such as golf. **2** a card identifying the players in a sports match, esp. cricket.

score off *vb* to make a clever or insulting reply to what someone has just said: *they spent the evening scoring off each other.*

scorer *n* **1** a player of a sport who scores a goal, run, or point: *Gooch was the top scorer for Essex yet again.* **2** a person who keeps note of the score of a match or competition as it is being played.

scoria (**score**-ee-a) *n* **1** *Geol* a mass of solidified lava containing many cavities. **2** refuse left after ore has been smelted.

scorn *n* **1** open contempt for a person or thing. *~vb* **2** to treat with contempt: *she attacked the government for scorning her profession.* **3** to refuse to have or do (something) because it is felt to be undesirable or wrong: *youths who scorn traditional morals.* **scornful** *adj* **scornfully** *adv*

Scorpio *n Astrol* the eighth sign of the zodiac; the Scorpion.

scorpion *n* a small lobster-shaped animal with a sting at the end of a jointed tail.

Scot *n* a person from Scotland.

Scot. **1** Scotland. **2** Scottish.

scotch *vb* **1** to put an end to: *she had scotched the idea of bingo in the church.* **2** to wound without killing.

Scotch[1] *Not universally accepted ~adj* **1** same as **Scottish.** *~pl n* **2 the Scotch** the Scots.

➤ Scotch is used only in certain fixed expressions like *Scotch egg.*

Scotch[2] *n* whisky distilled in Scotland from fermented malted barley.

Scotch broth *n Brit* a thick soup made from mutton or beef stock, vegetables, and pearl barley.

Scotch egg *n Brit* a hard-boiled egg encased in sausage meat and bread crumbs, and fried.

Scotch mist *n* a heavy wet mist or drizzle.

scot-free *adv, adj* without harm or punishment: *the real crooks got off scot-free.*

Scotland Yard *n* the headquarters of the police force of metropolitan London.

Scots *adj* **1** of Scotland. *~n* **2** any of the English dialects spoken or written in Scotland.

Scotsman *or fem* **Scotswoman** *n, pl* **-men** *or* **-women** a person from Scotland.

Scots pine *n* **1** a coniferous tree found in Europe and Asia, with needle-like leaves and brown cones. **2** the wood of this tree.

Scotticism *n* a Scottish expression or word.

Scottish *adj* of Scotland.

scoundrel *n Old-fashioned* a person who cheats and deceives.

scour[1] *vb* **1** to clean or polish (a surface) by rubbing with something rough. **2** to clear (a channel) by the force of water. *~n* **3** the act of scouring. **scourer** *n*

scour[2] *vb* **1** to search thoroughly and energetically: *he had scoured auction salerooms.* **2** to move quickly over (land) in search or pursuit.

scourge *n* **1** a person who or thing that causes affliction or suffering. **2** a whip formerly used for punishing people. *~vb* **scourging, scourged 3** to cause severe suffering to. **4** to whip.

Scouse *Brit informal ~n* **1** a person from Liverpool. **2** the Liverpool dialect. *~adj* **3** of Liverpool, its people, or their dialect.

scout *n* **1** *Mil* a person sent to find out the position of the enemy. **2** same as **talent scout. 3** the act or an instance of scouting. *~vb* **4** to examine or observe (something) in order to obtain information. **5 scout about** *or* **around** to go in search of.

Scout *or* **scout** *n* a member of the Scout Association, an organization for boys which aims to develop character and promote outdoor activities. **Scouting** *n*

scow *n* an unpowered barge used for carrying freight.

scowl *vb* **1** to have an angry or bad-tempered facial expression. *~n* **2** an angry or bad-tempered facial expression.

scrabble *vb* **-bling, -bled 1** to scrape at or grope for something with hands, feet, or claws: *scrabbling with his feet to find a foothold.* **2** to move one's hands about in order to find something one cannot see: *scrabbling in her handbag for a comb.*

Scrabble *n Trademark* a board game in which words are formed by placing letter tiles in a pattern similar to a crossword puzzle.

THESAURUS

one), impress, make a hit (*informal*), make an impact *or* impression, make a point, put oneself across, triumph

score off be one up on (*informal*), get the better of, have the laugh on, humiliate, make a fool of, make (someone) look silly, worst

scorn 1. *n.* contempt, contemptuousness, contumely, derision, despite, disdain, disparagement, mockery, sarcasm, scornfulness, slight, sneer **2.** *vb.* be above, consider beneath one, contemn, curl one's lip at, deride, disdain, flout, hold in contempt, look down on, make fun of, reject, scoff at, slight, sneer at, spurn, turn up one's nose at (*informal*)

scornful contemptuous, contumelious, defiant, derisive, disdainful, haughty, insolent, insulting, jeering, mocking, sarcastic, sardonic, scathing, scoffing, slighting, sneering, supercilious, withering

scornfully contemptuously, disdainfully, dismissively, scathingly, slightingly, with a sneer, with contempt, with disdain, witheringly, with lip curled

Scots Caledonian, Scottish

scoundrel bastard (*offensive*), blackguard, bugger (*taboo slang*), cheat, good-for-nothing, heel (*slang*), incorrigible, knave (*archaic*), miscreant, ne'er-do-well, rascal, reprobate, rogue, rotter (*old-fashioned slang*), scamp, scumbag (*slang*), shit (*slang*), swine, turd (*slang*), vagabond, villain, wretch

scour[1] abrade, buff, burnish, clean, cleanse, flush, furbish, polish, purge, rub, scrub, wash, whiten

scour[2] beat, comb, forage, go over with a fine-tooth comb, hunt, look high and low, rake, ransack, search

scourge *n.* **1.** affliction, bane, curse, infliction, misfortune, penalty, pest, plague, punishment, terror, torment, visitation **2.** cat, cat-o'-nine-tails, lash, strap, switch, thong, whip *~vb.* **3.** afflict, curse, excoriate, harass, plague, terrorize, torment **4.** beat, belt (*informal*), cane, castigate, chastise, discipline, flog, horsewhip, lash, lather (*informal*), leather, punish, take a strap to, tan (someone's) hide (*slang*), thrash, trounce, wallop (*informal*), whale, whip

scout *n.* **1.** *Mil.* advance guard, escort, lookout, outrider, precursor, reconnoitrer, vanguard *~vb.* **2.** case (*slang*), check out, investigate, make a reconnaissance, observe, probe, recce (*slang*), reconnoitre, see how the land lies, spy, spy out, survey, watch **3. scout about** *or* **around** cast around for, ferret out, hunt for, look for, search for, search out, seek, track down

scrag *n* **1** the thin end of a neck of veal or mutton. **2** a thin or scrawny person or animal.

scraggy *adj* **-gier, -giest** unpleasantly thin and bony. **scragginess** *n*

scram[1] *vb* **scramming, scrammed** *Informal* to leave very quickly.

scram[2] *n* **1** an emergency shutdown of a nuclear reactor. *~vb* **scramming, scrammed 2** (of a nuclear reactor) to shut down or be shut down in an emergency.

scramble *vb* **-bling, -bled 1** to climb or crawl hurriedly by using the hands to aid movement. **2** to go hurriedly or in a disorderly manner. **3** to compete with others in a rough and undignified way: *spectators scrambled for the best seats.* **4** to jumble together in a haphazard manner. **5** to cook (eggs that have been whisked up with milk) in a pan. **6** *Mil* (of a crew or aircraft) to take off quickly in an emergency. **7** to make (transmitted speech) unintelligible by the use of an electronic scrambler. *~n* **8** the act of scrambling. **9** a climb or trek over difficult ground. **10** a rough and undignified struggle to gain possession of something. **11** *Mil* an immediate takeoff of crew or aircraft in an emergency. **12** *Brit* a motorcycle race across rough open ground.

scrambler *n* an electronic device that makes broadcast or telephone messages unintelligible without a special receiver.

scrap[1] *n* **1** a small piece of something larger; fragment. **2** waste material or used articles, often collected and reprocessed. **3 scraps** pieces of leftover food. *~vb* **scrapping, scrapped 4** to discard as useless.

scrap[2] *Informal ~n* **1** a fight or quarrel. *~vb* **scrapping, scrapped 2** to quarrel or fight.

scrapbook *n* a book of blank pages in which newspaper cuttings or pictures are stuck.

scrape *vb* **scraping, scraped 1** to move (a rough or sharp object) across (a surface). **2** (often foll. by *away* or *off*) to remove (a layer) by rubbing. **3** to produce a grating sound by rubbing against (something else). **4** to injure or damage by scraping: *he had scraped his knees.* **5 scrimp and scrape** See **scrimp** (sense 2). *~n* **6** the act or sound of scraping. **7** a scraped place: *a scrape on the car door.* **8** *Informal* an awkward or embarrassing situation. **9** *Informal* a conflict or struggle. **scraper** *n*

scrape through *vb* to succeed in or survive with difficulty: *both teams had scraped through their semifinals.*

scrape together *or* **up** *vb* to collect with difficulty: *he scraped together enough money to travel.*

scrapheap *n* **on the scrapheap** (of people or things) no longer required: *I was tossed on the scrapheap at a very early age.*

scrappy *adj* **-pier, -piest** badly organized or done: *a scrappy draft of a chapter of my thesis.*

scratch *vb* **1** to mark or cut (the surface of something) with a rough or sharp instrument. **2** (often foll. by *at, out,* etc.) to tear or dig with the nails or claws. **3** to scrape (the surface of the skin) with the nails to relieve itching. **4** to rub against (the skin) causing a slight cut. **5** to make or cause to make a grating sound. **6** (sometimes foll. by *out*) to erase or cross out. **7** to withdraw from a race or (in the US) an election. *~n* **8** the act of scratching. **9** a slight cut on a person's or an animal's body. **10** a mark made by scratching. **11** a slight grating sound. **12 from scratch** *Informal* from the very beginning. **13 not up to scratch** *Informal* not up to standard. *~adj* **14** put together at short notice: *a scratch team.* **15** *Sport* with no handicap allowed: *a scratch golfer.* **scratchy** *adj*

scratchcard *n* a ticket that reveals whether or not the holder is eligible for a prize when the surface is removed by scratching.

scratching *n Music* a sound produced when the record groove in contact with the stylus of a record player is moved back and forth by hand.

scrawl *vb* **1** to write carelessly or hastily. *~n* **2** careless or scribbled writing. **scrawly** *adj*

scrawny *adj* **scrawnier, scrawniest** very thin and bony. **scrawniness** *n*

scream *vb* **1** to make a sharp piercing cry or sound because of fear or pain. **2** (of a machine) to make a high-pitched noise. **3** to laugh wildly. **4** to utter with a scream: *he screamed abuse up into the sky.* **5** to be unpleasantly conspicuous: *bad news screaming out from the headlines.* *~n* **6** a sharp piercing cry or sound,

THESAURUS

scowl 1. *vb.* frown, glower, grimace, look daggers at, lour *or* lower **2.** *n.* black look, dirty look, frown, glower, grimace

scramble *vb.* **1.** clamber, climb, crawl, move with difficulty, push, scrabble, struggle, swarm **2.** contend, hasten, jockey for position, jostle, look lively *or* snappy (*informal*), make haste, push, run, rush, strive, vie *~n.* **3.** climb, trek **4.** commotion, competition, confusion, free-for-all (*informal*), hassle (*informal*), hustle, melee, muddle, race, rat race, rush, struggle, tussle

scrap[1] *n.* **1.** atom, bit, bite, crumb, fragment, grain, iota, mite, modicum, morsel, mouthful, part, particle, piece, portion, remnant, sliver, snatch, snippet, trace **2.** junk, off cuts, waste **3.** *plural* bits, leavings, leftovers, remains, scrapings *~vb.* **4.** abandon, break up, chuck (*informal*), demolish, discard, dispense with, ditch (*slang*), drop, get rid of, jettison, junk (*informal*), shed, throw away *or* out, throw on the scrapheap, toss out, trash (*slang*), write off

scrap[2] **1.** *n.* argument, battle, brawl, disagreement, dispute, dust-up (*informal*), fight, quarrel, row, scrimmage, scuffle, set-to (*informal*), shindig (*informal*), shindy (*informal*), squabble, tiff, wrangle **2.** *vb.* argue, barney (*informal*), bicker, come to blows, fall out (*informal*), fight, have a shouting match (*informal*), have words, row, spar, squabble, wrangle

scrape *vb.* **1.** clean, erase, file, remove, rub, scour **2.** grate, grind, rasp, scratch, screech, set one's teeth on edge, squeak **3.** abrade, bark, graze, rub, scratch, scuff, skin *~n.* **4.** *informal* awkward *or* embarrassing situation, difficulty, dilemma, distress, fix (*informal*), mess, plight, predicament, pretty pickle (*informal*), spot (*informal*), tight spot, trouble

scrape through barely make it, cut it fine (*informal*), get by (*informal*), have a close shave (*informal*), struggle

scrappy bitty, disjointed, fragmentary, incomplete, perfunctory, piecemeal, sketchy, thrown together

scratch *vb.* **1.** claw, cut, damage, etch, grate, graze, incise, lacerate, make a mark on, mark, rub, score, scrape **2.** annul, cancel, delete, eliminate, erase, pull out, stand down, strike off, withdraw *~n.* **3.** blemish, claw mark, gash, graze, laceration, mark, scrape **4. not up to scratch** *informal* inadequate, incapable, incompetent, insufficient, not up to snuff (*informal*), not up to standard, unacceptable, unsatisfactory *~adj.* **5.** haphazard, hastily prepared, impromptu, improvised, rough, rough-and-ready

scrawl doodle, scrabble, scratch, scribble, squiggle, writing

scream *vb.* **1.** bawl, cry, holler (*informal*), screech, shriek, shrill, sing out, squeal, yell **2.** be conspicuous, clash, jar, shriek *~n.* **3.** howl, outcry, screech, shriek, wail, yell, yelp **4.** *informal* card (*informal*), caution (*in-*

esp. of fear or pain. **7** *Informal* a very funny person or thing.

scree *n* a pile of rock fragments at the foot of a cliff or hill, often forming a sloping heap.

screech[1] *n* **1** a shrill or high-pitched sound or cry. ~*vb* **2** to utter a shrill cry. **screechy** *adj*

screech[2] *n Canad slang* **1** a dark rum. **2** any strong cheap drink.

screech owl *n* **1** *Brit* same as **barn owl. 2** a small North American barn owl.

screed *n* a long tiresome speech or piece of writing.

screen *n* **1** the blank surface of a television set, VDU, or radar receiver, on which a visible image is formed. **2** the white surface on which films or slides are projected. **3 the screen** the film industry or films collectively. **4** a light movable frame, panel, or partition used to shelter, divide, or conceal. **5** anything that shelters, protects, or conceals: *a screen of leaves blocking out the sun.* **6** a frame containing a mesh that is used to keep out insects. ~*vb* **7** (sometimes foll. by *off*) to shelter, protect, or conceal with or as if with a screen. **8** to test or check (an individual or group) so as to assess suitability for a task or to detect the presence of a disease or weapons: *women screened for breast cancer.* **9** to show (a film) in the cinema or show (a programme) on television.

screenplay *n* the script for a film, including instructions for sets and camera work.

screen process *n* a method of printing by forcing ink through a fine mesh of silk or nylon, some parts of which have been treated so as not to let the ink pass.

screenwriter *n* a person who writes screenplays.

screw *n* **1** a metal pin with a spiral ridge along its length, twisted into materials to fasten them together. **2** a threaded cylindrical rod that engages with a similarly threaded cylindrical hole. **3** a thread in a cylindrical hole corresponding with the one on the screw with which it is designed to engage. **4** anything resembling a screw in shape. **5** *Slang* a prison guard. **6** *Taboo slang* an act of or partner in sexual intercourse. **7 have a screw loose** *Informal* to be insane. **8 put the screws on** *Slang* to use force on or threatening behaviour against. ~*vb* **9** to rotate (a screw or bolt) so as to drive it into or draw it out of a material. **10** to twist or turn: *she screwed up the sheet of paper.* **11** to attach or fasten with or as if with a screw or screws. **12** *Informal* to take advantage of, esp. illegally: *screwed by big business.* **13** *Informal* to distort or contort: *his face was screwed up in pain.* **14** (often foll. by *out of*) *Informal* to force out of; extort. **15** *Taboo slang* to have sexual intercourse (with). **16 have one's head screwed on the right way** *Informal* to be sensible. ~See also **screw up.**

screwball *Slang, chiefly US & Canad* ~*n* **1** an odd or eccentric person. ~*adj* **2** crazy or eccentric: *a screwball comedy.*

screwdriver *n* **1** a tool used for turning screws, consisting of a long thin metal rod with a flattened tip that fits into a slot in the head of the screw. **2** a drink consisting of orange juice and vodka.

screw top *n* **1** a bottle top that screws onto the bottle, allowing the bottle to be resealed after use. **2** a bottle with such a top.

screw up *vb* **1** *Informal* to mishandle or spoil (something): *that screws up all my arrangements.* **2** to twist out of shape or distort. **3 screw up one's courage** to force oneself to be brave. **screwed-up** *adj*

screwy *adj* **screwier, screwiest** *Informal* crazy or eccentric.

scribble *vb* **-bling, -bled 1** to write or draw quickly and roughly. **2** to make meaningless or illegible marks (on). ~*n* **3** something written or drawn quickly or roughly. **4** meaningless or illegible marks. **scribbler** *n* **scribbly** *adj*

scribe *n* **1** a person who made handwritten copies of manuscripts or documents before the invention of printing. **2** *Bible* a recognized scholar and teacher of the Jewish Law.

scrimmage *n* **1** a rough or disorderly struggle. ~*vb* **-maging, -maged 2** to take part in a scrimmage.

scrimp *vb* **1** to be very sparing in the use of something: *they were scrimping by on the last of the potatoes.* **2 scrimp and save** *or* **scrape** to spend as little money as possible.

scrip *n Finance* a certificate representing a claim to shares or stocks.

script *n* **1** the text of a play, TV programme, or film for the use of performers. **2** an alphabet or system of writing: *Cyrillic script.* **3** a candidate's answer paper in an examination. **4** handwriting. **5** a typeface which looks like handwriting. ~*vb* **6** to write a script for.

scripture *n* the sacred writings of a religion. **scriptural** *adj*

Scripture *n Christianity* the Old and New Testaments.

scriptwriter *n* a person who writes scripts, esp. for a film or TV programme. **scriptwriting** *n*

scrofula *n No longer in technical use* tuberculosis of the lymphatic glands. **scrofulous** *adj*

scroll *n* **1** a roll of parchment or paper, usually inscribed with writing. **2** an ancient book in the form of a roll of parchment, papyrus, or paper. **3** a decorative carving or moulding resembling a scroll. ~*vb* **4** *Computers* to move (text) on a screen in order to view a section that cannot be fitted into a single display.

Scrooge *n* a mean or miserly person.

scrotum *n* the pouch of skin containing the testicles in most male mammals.

THESAURUS

formal), character (*informal*), comedian, comic, entertainer, hoot (*informal*), joker, laugh, riot (*slang*), sensation, wag, wit

screen *n.* **1.** mesh, net, partition, room divider **2.** awning, canopy, cloak, concealment, cover, guard, hedge, mantle, shade, shelter, shield, shroud ~*vb.* **3.** cloak, conceal, cover, defend, guard, hide, mask, protect, safeguard, shade, shelter, shield, shroud, shut out, veil **4.** cull, evaluate, examine, filter, gauge, grade, process, riddle, scan, sieve, sift, sort, vet **5.** broadcast, present, put on, show

screw *vb.* **1.** tighten, turn, twist, work in **2.** *informal* bring pressure to bear on, coerce, constrain, force, hold a knife to (someone's) throat, oppress, pressurize, put the screws on (*informal*), squeeze **3.** contort, contract, crumple, distort, pucker, wrinkle **4.** *often with* **out of** *informal* bleed, extort, extract, wrest, wring

scribble *vb.* dash off, doodle, jot, pen, scratch, scrawl, write

scribe amanuensis, clerk, copyist, notary (*archaic*), secretary, writer

script 1. book, copy, dialogue, libretto, lines, manuscript, text, words **2.** calligraphy, hand, handwriting, letters, longhand, penmanship, writing

Scripture Holy Bible, Holy Scripture, Holy Writ, The Bible, The Book of Books, The Good Book, The Gospels, The Scriptures, The Word, The Word of God

scroll inventory, list, parchment, roll

Scrooge cheapskate (*informal*), meanie *or* meany (*informal, chiefly Brit.*), miser, money-grubber (*informal*), niggard, penny-pincher (*informal*), skinflint

scrounge *vb* **scrounging, scrounged** *Informal* to get (something) by asking for it rather than buying it or working for it. **scrounger** *n*

scrub[1] *vb* **scrubbing, scrubbed 1** to rub (something) hard in order to clean it. **2** to remove (dirt) by rubbing with a brush and water. **3 scrub up** (of a surgeon) to wash the hands and arms thoroughly before operating. **4** *Informal* to delete or cancel (an idea or plan). *~n* **5** the act of scrubbing.

scrub[2] *n* **1** vegetation consisting of stunted trees or bushes growing in a dry area. **2** an area of dry land covered with such vegetation. *~adj* **3** stunted or inferior: *scrub pines.*

scrubber *n* **1** *Offensive slang* a woman who has many sexual partners. **2** a device that removes pollutants from the gases that are produced when coal is burned industrially.

scrubby *adj* **-bier, -biest 1** (of land) rough, dry, and covered with scrub. **2** (of plants) stunted. **3** *Brit informal* shabby or untidy.

scruff[1] *n* the nape of the neck: *the sergeant had him by the scruff of the neck.*

scruff[2] *n Informal* a very untidy person.

scruffy *adj* **scruffier, scruffiest** dirty and untidy in appearance.

scrum *n* **1** *Rugby* a formation in which players from each side form a tight pack and push against each other in an attempt to get the ball which is thrown on the ground between them. **2** *Informal* a disorderly struggle. *~vb* **scrumming, scrummed 3** (usually foll. by *down*) *Rugby* to form a scrum.

scrum half *n Rugby* a player who puts in the ball at scrums and tries to regain its possession in order to pass it to his team's backs.

scrummage *n, vb* **-maging, -maged 1** *Rugby* same as **scrum. 2** same as **scrimmage.**

scrump *vb Dialect* to steal (apples) from an orchard or garden.

scrumptious *adj Informal* delicious or very attractive.

scrumpy *n* a rough dry cider brewed in the West Country of England.

scrunch *vb* **1** to press or crush noisily or be pressed or crushed noisily. *~n* **2** the act or sound of scrunching: *the scrunch of tyres on gravel.*

scrunchie *n* a loop of elastic covered loosely with fabric, used to hold the hair in a ponytail.

scruple *n* **1** a doubt or hesitation as to what is morally right in a certain situation: *he had no scruples about the drug trade. ~vb* **-pling, -pled 2** to have doubts (about), esp. on moral grounds.

scrupulous *adj* **1** taking great care to do what is fair, honest, or morally right. **2** very careful or precise: *scrupulous attention to detail.* **scrupulously** *adv*

scrutinize *or* **-nise** *vb* **-nizing, -nized** *or* **-nising, -nised** to examine carefully or in minute detail.

scrutiny *n, pl* **-nies 1** very careful study or observation. **2** a searching look.

scuba (**skew**-ba) *n* an apparatus used in skin diving, consisting of cylinders containing compressed air attached to a breathing apparatus.

scud *vb* **scudding, scudded 1** (esp. of clouds) to move along quickly. **2** *Naut* to run before a gale. *~n* **3** the act of scudding. **4** spray, rain, or clouds driven by the wind.

scuff *vb* **1** to drag (the feet) while walking. **2** to scrape (one's shoes) by doing so. *~n* **3** a mark caused by scuffing. **4** the act or sound of scuffing.

scuffle *vb* **-fling, -fled 1** to fight in a disorderly manner. *~n* **2** a short disorganized fight. **3** a scuffling sound.

scull *n* **1** a single oar moved from side to side over the back of a boat. **2** one of a pair of small oars, both of which are pulled by one oarsman. **3** a racing boat rowed by one oarsman pulling two oars. *~vb* **4** to row (a boat) with a scull. **sculler** *n*

scullery *n, pl* **-leries** *Chiefly Brit* a small room where washing-up and other kitchen work is done.

scullion *n Archaic* a servant employed to do the hard work in a kitchen.

sculpt *vb* same as **sculpture.**

sculptor *or fem* **sculptress** *n* a person who makes sculptures.

sculpture *n* **1** the art of making figures or designs in wood, plaster, stone, or metal. **2** works or a work made in this way. *~vb* **-turing, -tured 3** to carve (a material) into figures or designs. **4** to represent (a person or thing) in sculpture. **5** to form or be formed in the manner of sculpture: *limestone sculptured by fast-flowing streams.* **sculptural** *adj*

scum *n* **1** a layer of impure or waste matter that forms on the surface of a liquid: *the build-up of soap scum.* **2** a person or people regarded as worthless or criminal. *~vb* **scumming, scummed 3** to remove scum from. **4** *Rare* to form a layer of or become covered with scum. **scummy** *adj*

scumbag *n Slang* an offensive or despicable person.

scungy (**skun**-jee) *adj* **scungier, scungiest** *Austral & NZ slang* miserable or sordid.

scunner *Dialect, chiefly Scot ~vb* **1** to produce a feeling of dislike in. *~n* **2 take a scunner to** to take a strong dislike to. **3** a person or thing that is disliked.

scupper[1] *n Naut* a drain or spout in a ship's side allowing water on the deck to flow overboard.

scupper[2] *vb* **1** *Brit slang* to defeat or ruin: *a deliber-*

THESAURUS

scrounge beg, blag (*slang*), bum (*informal*), cadge, forage for, freeload (*slang*), hunt around (for), mooch (*slang*), sponge (*informal*), touch (someone) for (*slang*), wheedle

scrounger bum (*informal*), cadger, freeloader (*slang*), parasite, sponger (*informal*)

scrub *vb.* **1.** clean, cleanse, rub, scour **2.** *informal* abandon, abolish, call off, cancel, delete, discontinue, do away with, drop, forget about, give up

scruffy disreputable, frowzy, ill-groomed, mangy, messy, ragged, run-down, scrubby (*Brit. informal*), seedy, shabby, slatternly, sloppy (*informal*), slovenly, sluttish, squalid, tattered, tatty, ungroomed, unkempt, untidy

scrupulous careful, conscientious, exact, fastidious, honourable, meticulous, minute, moral, nice, painstaking, precise, principled, punctilious, rigorous, strict, upright

scrutinize analyse, dissect, examine, explore, inquire into, inspect, investigate, peruse, pore over, probe, research, scan, search, sift, study, work over

scrutiny analysis, close study, examination, exploration, inquiry, inspection, investigation, perusal, search, sifting, study

scuffle 1. *vb.* clash, come to blows, contend, exchange blows, fight, grapple, jostle, struggle, tussle **2.** *n.* affray (*Law*), barney (*informal*), brawl, commotion, disturbance, fight, fray, ruction(s) (*informal*), rumpus, scrap (*informal*), scrimmage, set-to (*informal*), shindig (*informal*), shindy (*informal*), skirmish, tussle

sculpture *vb.* carve, chisel, cut, fashion, form, hew, model, mould, sculpt, shape

ate attempt to scupper the peace talks. **2** to sink (one's ship) deliberately.

scurf *n* **1** same as **dandruff. 2** any flaky or scaly matter sticking to or peeling off a surface. **scurfy** *adj*

scurrilous *adj* untrue or unfair, insulting, and designed to damage a person's reputation: *scurrilous allegations.* **scurrility** *n*

scurry *vb* **-ries, -rying, -ried 1** to run quickly with short steps. *~n, pl* **-ries 2** a quick hurrying movement or the sound of this movement. **3** a short shower of rain or snow.

scurvy *n* **1** a disease caused by a lack of vitamin C, resulting in weakness, spongy gums, and bleeding beneath the skin. *~adj* **-vier, -viest 2** *Old-fashioned* deserving contempt. **scurviness** *n*

scut *n* the short tail of animals such as the deer and rabbit.

scuttle[1] *n* same as **coal scuttle.**

scuttle[2] *vb* **-tling, -tled 1** to run with short quick steps. *~n* **2** a hurried pace or run.

scuttle[3] *vb* **-tling, -tled 1** *Naut* to cause (a ship) to sink by making holes in the sides or bottom. **2** to ruin (hopes or plans) or have them ruined: *a policy scuttled by popular resistance.* *~n* **3** *Naut* a small hatch in a ship's deck or side.

Scylla (sill-a) *n* **1** (in classical mythology) a sea monster believed to drown sailors navigating the Straits of Messina. **2 between Scylla and Charybdis** in an awkward situation in which avoidance of either of two dangers means exposure to the other.

scythe *n* **1** a long-handled tool for cutting grass or grain, with a curved sharpened blade that is swung parallel to the ground. *~vb* **scything, scythed 2** to cut (grass or grain) with a scythe.

SD South Dakota.

SDI Strategic Defense Initiative.

SDLP (in Northern Ireland) Social Democratic and Labour Party.

Se *Chem* selenium.

SE southeast(ern).

sea *n* **1 the sea** the mass of salt water that covers three-quarters of the earth's surface. **2 a** one of the smaller areas of this: *the Irish Sea.* **b** a large inland area of water: *the Caspian Sea.* **3** the area on or close to the edge of the sea, esp. as a place where holidays are taken: *a day by the sea.* **4** strong and uneven swirling movement of waves: *rough seas.* **5** anything resembling the sea in size or movement: *a sea of red and yellow flags.* **6 at sea a** on the ocean. **b** in a state of confusion or uncertainty. **7 go to sea** to become a sailor. **8 put out to sea** to start a sea voyage.

sea anchor *n Naut* a canvas-covered frame, dragged in the water behind a ship to slow it down or reduce drifting.

sea anemone *n* a marine animal with a round body and rings of tentacles which trap food from the water.

sea bird *n* a bird that lives on or near the sea.

seaboard *n* land bordering on the sea.

seaborne *adj* **1** carried on or by the sea. **2** transported by ship: *seaborne reinforcements.*

sea breeze *n* a breeze blowing inland from the sea.

sea cow *n* **1** a whalelike mammal such as a dugong or manatee. **2** *Archaic* a walrus.

sea dog *n* an experienced or old sailor.

seafarer *n* **1** a traveller who goes by sea. **2** a sailor.

seafaring *adj* **1** travelling by sea. **2** working as a sailor. *~n* **3** the act of travelling by sea. **4** the work of a sailor.

seafood *n* edible saltwater fish or shellfish.

seafront *n* a built-up area facing the sea.

seagoing *adj* built for travelling on the sea.

sea-green *adj* bluish-green.

seagull *n* same as **gull.**

sea horse *n* a small marine fish with a horselike head, which swims upright.

sea kale *n* a European coastal plant with broad fleshy leaves and asparagus-like shoots that can be eaten.

seal[1] *n* **1** a special design impressed on a piece of wax, lead, or paper, fixed to a letter or document as a mark of authentication. **2** a stamp or signet ring engraved with a design to form such an impression. **3** a substance placed over an envelope or container, so that it cannot be opened without the seal being broken. **4** something that serves as an official confirmation of approval: *seal of approval.* **5** any substance or device used to close an opening tightly. **6 set the seal on** to confirm something: *the experience set the seal on their friendship.* *~vb* **7** to close or secure with or as if with a seal: *once the manuscripts were sealed up, they were forgotten about.* **8 seal off** to enclose or isolate (a place) completely. **9** to close tightly so as to make airtight or watertight. **10** to inject a compound around the edges of something to make it airtight or watertight. **11** to attach a seal to or stamp with a seal. **12** to finalize or authorize. **13 seal one's fate** to make sure one dies or fails. **14 seal one's lips** to promise not to reveal a secret. **sealable** *adj*

seal[2] *n* **1** a fish-eating mammal with four flippers, which lives in the sea but comes ashore to breed. **2** sealskin. *~vb* **3** to hunt seals.

sealant *n* any substance, such as wax, used for sealing, esp. to make airtight or watertight.

sea legs *pl n Informal* the ability to maintain one's balance on board ship and to avoid being seasick.

sea level *n* the average level of the sea's surface in relation to the land.

sealing wax *n* a hard material made of shellac and turpentine, which softens when heated and which is used to make a seal.

sea lion *n* a type of large seal found in the Pacific Ocean.

THESAURUS

scum 1. algae, crust, dross, film, froth, impurities, scruff **2.** *canaille,* dregs of society, dross, lowest of the low, rabble, ragtag and bobtail, riffraff, rubbish, trash (*chiefly U.S. & Canad.*)

scurrilous abusive, coarse, defamatory, foul, foul-mouthed, gross, indecent, infamous, insulting, low, obscene, offensive, Rabelaisian, ribald, salacious, scabrous, scandalous, slanderous, vituperative, vulgar

scurry 1. *vb.* beetle, dart, dash, fly, hurry, race, scamper, scoot, scud, scuttle, skim, sprint, whisk **2.** *n.* bustle, flurry, scampering, whirl

scuttle beetle, bustle, hare (*Brit. informal*), hasten, hurry, run, rush, scamper, scoot, scramble, scud, scurry

sea 1. main (*literary*), ocean, the briny (*informal*), the deep, the waves **2.** abundance, expanse, mass, multitude, plethora, profusion, sheet, vast number **3. at sea** adrift, astray, at a loss, at sixes and sevens, baffled, bewildered, confused, disoriented, lost, mystified, puzzled, upset

seafaring marine, maritime, nautical, naval, oceanic

seal *n.* **1.** assurance, attestation, authentication, confirmation, imprimatur, insignia, notification, ratification, stamp *~vb.* **2.** bung, close, cork, enclose, fasten, make airtight, plug, secure, shut, stop, stopper, stop up, waterproof **3.** *with* **off** board up, fence off, isolate,

Sea Lord *n* (in Britain) a naval officer on the admiralty board of the Ministry of Defence.

sealskin *n* the skin or prepared fur of a seal, used to make coats.

seam *n* **1** the line along which pieces of fabric are joined by stitching. **2** a ridge or line made by joining two edges: *the seam between the old and the new buildings.* **3** a long narrow layer of coal, marble, or ore formed between layers of other rocks. **4** a mark or line like a seam, such as a wrinkle or scar. *~adj* **5** *Cricket* of a style of bowling in which the bowler uses the stitched seam round the ball in order to make it swing in flight and after touching the ground: *a seam bowler.* *~vb* **6** to join together by or as if by a seam. **7** to mark with furrows or wrinkles. **seamless** *adj*

seaman *n, pl* **-men 1** a man ranking below an officer in a navy. **2** a sailor.

seamanship *n* skill in navigating and operating a ship.

seamer *or* **seam bowler** *n Cricket* a fast bowler who makes the ball bounce on its seam so that it will change direction.

seamstress *n* a woman who sews, esp. professionally.

seamy *adj* **seamier, seamiest** involving the sordid and unpleasant aspects of life, such as crime, prostitution, poverty, and violence. **seaminess** *n*

seance *or* **séance** (**say**-onss) *n* a meeting at which a spiritualist attempts to communicate with the spirits of the dead.

seaplane *n* an aircraft that is designed to land on and take off from water.

seaport *n* a town or city with a harbour for boats and ships.

sear *vb* **1** to scorch or burn the surface of. **2** to cause to wither.

search *vb* **1** to look through (a place) thoroughly in order to find someone or something. **2** to examine (a person) for hidden objects. **3** to look at or examine (something) closely: *I searched my heart for one good thing she had done.* **4 search out** to find by searching. **5** to make a search. **6 search me** *Informal* I don't know. *~n* **7** an attempt to find something by looking somewhere.

searching *adj* keen or thorough: *a searching analysis.* **searchingly** *adv*

searchlight *n* **1** a light with a powerful beam that can be shone in any direction. **2** the beam of light produced by this device.

search warrant *n* a legal document allowing a policeman to enter and search premises.

seascape *n* a drawing, painting, or photograph of a scene at sea.

Sea Scout *n* a member of the branch of the Scouts which gives training in seamanship.

seashell *n* the empty shell of a marine mollusc.

seashore *n* land bordering on the sea.

seasick *adj* suffering from nausea and dizziness caused by the movement of a ship at sea. **seasickness** *n*

seaside *n* an area, esp. a holiday resort, bordering on the sea.

season *n* **1** one of the four divisions of the year (spring, summer, autumn, and winter), each of which has characteristic weather conditions. **2** a period of the year characterized by particular conditions or activities: *the typhoon season; the football season.* **3** the period during which any particular species of animal, bird, or fish is legally permitted to be caught or killed: *the deer season.* **4** any definite or indefinite period: *the busy season.* **5** any period during which a show or play is performed at one venue: *the show ran for three seasons.* **6 in season a** (of game) permitted to be killed. **b** (of fresh food) readily available. **c** (of animals) ready to mate. *~vb* **7** to add herbs, salt, pepper, or spice to (food) in order to enhance the flavour. **8** (in the preparation of timber) to dry and harden. **9** to make experienced: *old men seasoned by living.* **seasoned** *adj*

seasonable *adj* **1** suitable for the season: *a seasonable Christmas snow scene.* **2** coming or happening just at the right time: *seasonable advice.*

seasonal *adj* of or depending on a certain season or seasons of the year: *seasonal employment.* **seasonally** *adv*

seasoning *n* something that is added to food to enhance the flavour.

season ticket *n* a ticket for a series of events or number of journeys, usually bought at a reduced rate.

seat *n* **1** a piece of furniture designed for sitting on, such as a chair. **2** the part of a chair or other piece of furniture on which one sits. **3** a place to sit in a theatre, esp. one that requires a ticket: *front-row seats for Starlight Express.* **4** the buttocks. **5** the part of a garment covering the buttocks. **6** the part or surface on which an object rests. **7** the place or centre in which something is based: *the seat of government.* **8** a country mansion. **9** a membership or the right to membership of a legislative or administrative body: *a seat on the council.* **10** *Chiefly Brit* a parliamentary constituency. **11** the manner in which a rider sits on a horse. *~vb* **12** to bring to or place on a seat. **13** to provide seats for: *the dining hall seats 150 people.* **14** to set firmly in place.

THESAURUS

put out of bounds, quarantine, segregate **4.** assure, attest, authenticate, confirm, establish, ratify, stamp, validate **5.** clinch, conclude, consummate, finalize, settle, shake hands on (*informal*)

seam *n.* **1.** closure, joint, suture (*Surgery*) **2.** layer, lode, stratum, vein **3.** furrow, line, ridge, scar, wrinkle

search *vb.* **1.** cast around, check, comb, examine, explore, ferret, go over with a fine-tooth comb, inquire, inspect, investigate, leave no stone unturned, look, look high and low, probe, pry, ransack, rifle through, rummage through, scour, scrutinize, seek, sift, turn inside out, turn upside down **2.** check, examine, frisk (*informal*) *~n.* **3.** examination, exploration, going-over (*informal*), hunt, inquiry, inspection, investigation, pursuit, quest, researches, rummage, scrutiny

searching *adj.* close, intent, keen, minute, penetrating, piercing, probing, quizzical, severe, sharp, thorough

season *n.* **1.** division, interval, juncture, occasion, opportunity, period, spell, term, time, time of year *~vb.* **2.** colour, enliven, flavour, lace, leaven, pep up, salt, salt and pepper, spice **3.** acclimatize, accustom, anneal, discipline, habituate, harden, inure, mature, prepare, toughen, train

seasonable appropriate, convenient, fit, opportune, providential, suitable, timely, welcome, well-timed

seasoned battle-scarred, experienced, hardened, long-serving, mature, old, practised, time-served, veteran, weathered, well-versed

seasoning condiment, dressing, flavouring, relish, salt and pepper, sauce, spice

seat *n.* **1.** bench, chair, pew, settle, stall, stool, throne **2.** base, bed, bottom, cause, footing, foundation, ground, groundwork **3.** axis, capital, centre, cradle, headquarters, heart, hub, location, place, site, situation, source, station **4.** abode, ancestral hall, house,

seat belt *n* a strap attached to a car or aircraft seat, worn across the body to prevent a person being thrown forward in the event of a collision.

seating *n* **1** seats which are provided somewhere, esp. in a public place: *the grandstand has seating for 10 000; hard plastic seating.* ~*adj* **2** of or relating to the provision of places to sit: *the delegation leader complained about the seating arrangements.*

sea urchin *n* a small sea animal with a round body enclosed in a spiny shell.

seaward *adv also* **seawards 1** towards the sea. ~*adj* **2** directed or moving towards the sea.

seaweed *n* any plant growing in the sea or on the seashore.

seaworthy *adj* (of a ship) in a fit condition for a sea voyage. **seaworthiness** *n*

sebaceous *adj* of, like, or secreting fat.

sebaceous glands *pl n* the small glands in the skin that secrete oil into hair follicles and onto most of the body surface.

sebum (**see**-bum) *n* the oily substance secreted by the sebaceous glands.

sec[1] *adj* (of wines) dry.

sec[2] *n Informal* a second (of time): *hang on a sec.*

sec[3] secant.

sec. 1 second (of time). **2** secondary. **3** secretary.

secant (**seek**-ant) *n* **1** (in trigonometry) the ratio of the length of the hypotenuse to the length of the adjacent side in a right-angled triangle; the reciprocal of cosine. **2** a straight line that intersects a curve.

secateurs *pl n Chiefly Brit* a small pair of gardening shears for pruning.

secede *vb* **-ceding, -ceded** to make a formal withdrawal of membership from a political alliance, federation, or group: *it will secede from the federation within six months.*

secession *n* the act of seceding. **secessionism** *n* **secessionist** *n, adj*

seclude *vb* **-cluding, -cluded 1** to remove from contact with others. **2** to shut off or screen from view.

secluded *adj* **1** kept apart from the company of others: *a secluded private life.* **2** private and sheltered: *a secluded cottage.*

seclusion *n* the state of being secluded; privacy.

second[1] *adj* **1** coming directly after the first in order. **2** rated, graded, or ranked between the first and third levels. **3** alternate: *every second Saturday.* **4** another of the same kind; additional: *a second chance.* **5** resembling or comparable to a person or event from the past: *a second Virgin Mary.* **6** of lesser importance or position; inferior. **7** denoting the second lowest forward gear in a motor vehicle. **8** *Music* denoting a musical part, voice, or instrument subordinate to or lower in pitch than another (the first): *the second tenors.* **9 at second hand** by hearsay. ~*n* **10** a person or thing that is second. **11** *Brit education* an honours degree of the second class. **12** the second lowest forward gear in a motor vehicle. **13** (in boxing or duelling) an attendant who looks after a boxer or duellist. **14 seconds a** *Informal* a second helping of food or the second course of a meal. **b** goods that are sold cheaply because they are slightly faulty. ~*vb* **15** to give aid or backing to. **16** (in boxing or duelling) to act as second to (a boxer or duellist). **17** to express formal support for (a motion proposed in a meeting). ~*adv* **18** Also: **secondly** in the second place.

second[2] *n* **1** the basic SI unit of time, equal to $\frac{1}{60}$ of a minute. **2** $\frac{1}{60}$ of a minute of angle. **3** a very short period of time.

second[3] (sik-**kond**) *vb Brit* to transfer (a person) temporarily to another job. **secondment** *n*

secondary *adj* **1** below the first in rank or importance: *a secondary consideration.* **2** coming next after the first: *secondary cancers.* **3** derived from or depending on what is primary or first: *a secondary source.* **4** of or relating to the education of young people between the ages of 11 and 18: *secondary education.* **5** (of an industry) involving the manufacture of goods from raw materials. ~*n, pl* **-aries 6** a person or thing that is secondary.

secondary colour *n* a colour formed by mixing two primary colours.

secondary picketing *n* the picketing by striking workers of the premises of a firm that supplies or distributes goods to or from their employer.

second-best *adj* **1** next to the best. ~*adv* **second best 2 come off second best** *Informal* to fail to win against someone. ~*n* **second best 3** an inferior alternative.

second chamber *n* the upper house of a two-chamber system of government.

second childhood *n* the time in an old person's life when he or she starts to suffer from memory loss and confusion; senility.

second class *n* **1** the class or grade next in value, rank, or quality to the first. ~*adj* **second-class 2** of the class or grade next to the best in value, rank, or quality. **3** shoddy or inferior. **4** denoting the class of accommodation in a hotel or on a train, aircraft, or ship, lower in quality and price than first class. **5** (of mail) sent by a cheaper type of postage and taking slightly longer to arrive than first-class mail. ~*adv* **6** by second-class mail, transport, etc.

Second Coming *n* the prophesied return of Christ to earth at the Last Judgment.

second cousin *n* the child of one's parent's first cousin.

second-degree burn *n* a burn in which blisters appear on the skin.

second fiddle *n Informal* a person who has a secondary status.

second floor *n Brit* the storey of a building immedi-

THESAURUS

mansion, residence **5.** chair, constituency, incumbency, membership, place ~*vb.* **6.** accommodate, cater for, contain, have room *or* capacity for, hold, sit, take **7.** deposit, fix, install, locate, place, set, settle, sit

seating accommodation, chairs, places, room, seats

secede break with, disaffiliate, leave, pull out, quit, resign, retire, separate, split from, withdraw

secluded cloistered, cut off, isolated, lonely, off the beaten track, out-of-the-way, private, reclusive, remote, retired, sequestered, sheltered, solitary, tucked away, unfrequented

seclusion concealment, hiding, isolation, privacy, purdah, remoteness, retirement, retreat, shelter, solitude

second[1] *adj.* **1.** following, next, subsequent, succeeding **2.** additional, alternative, extra, further, other, repeated **3.** double, duplicate, reproduction, twin **4.** inferior, lesser, lower, secondary, subordinate, supporting ~*vb.* **5.** advance, aid, approve, assist, back, encourage, endorse, forward, further, give moral support to, go along with, help, promote, support

second[2] *n.* flash, instant, jiffy (*informal*), minute, moment, sec (*informal*), split second, tick (*Brit. informal*), trice, twinkling, twinkling of an eye, two shakes of a lamb's tail (*informal*)

ately above the first and two floors up from the ground.

second hand *n* a pointer on the face of a watch or clock that indicates the seconds.

second-hand *adj* **1** previously owned or used. **2** not from an original source or one's own experience: *second-hand opinions.* **3** dealing in or selling goods that are not new: *second-hand furniture shops.* ~*adv* **4** from a source of previously owned or used goods: *they preferred to buy second-hand.* **5** not directly or from one's own experience: *his knowledge had been gleaned second-hand.*

second lieutenant *n* an officer holding the lowest commissioned rank in an army or navy.

secondly *adv* same as **second**[1] (sense 18).

second nature *n* a habit or characteristic practised for so long that it seems to be part of one's character.

second person *n* the form of a pronoun or verb used to refer to the person or people being addressed.

second-rate *adj* **1** not of the highest quality; mediocre. **2** second in importance or rank: *a second-rate citizen.*

second sight *n* the supposed ability to foresee the future or see actions taking place elsewhere.

second thoughts *pl n* a revised opinion or idea on a matter already considered.

second wind *n* **1** the return of normal breathing following difficult or strenuous exercise. **2** renewed ability to continue in an effort.

secrecy *n, pl* **-cies 1** the state of being secret. **2** the ability or tendency to keep things secret.

secret *adj* **1** kept hidden or separate from the knowledge of all or all but a few others. **2** secretive: *she had become a secret drinker.* **3** operating without the knowledge of outsiders: *secret organizations.* ~*n* **4** something kept or to be kept hidden. **5** something unrevealed; a mystery: *the secrets of nature.* **6** an underlying explanation or reason: *the secret of great-looking hair.* **7 in secret** without the knowledge of others. **secretly** *adv*

secret agent *n* a person employed by a government to find out the military and political secrets of other governments.

secretaire (sek-rit-**air**) *n* same as **escritoire.**

secretariat *n* **1 a** an office responsible for the secretarial, clerical, and administrative affairs of a legislative body or international organization. **b** the staff of such an office or department. **2** the premises of a secretariat.

secretary *n, pl* **-taries 1** a person who handles correspondence, keeps records, and does general clerical work for an individual or organization. **2** the official manager of the day-to-day business of a society, club, or committee. **3** (in Britain) a senior civil servant who assists a government minister. **4** (in the U.S.) the head of a government administrative department. **secretarial** *adj*

secretary bird *n* a large long-legged African bird of prey.

secretary-general *n, pl* **secretaries-general** the chief administrative official of a legislative body or international organization.

secretary of state *n* **1** (in Britain) the head of a major government department. **2** (in the U.S.) the head of the government department in charge of foreign affairs.

secrete[1] *vb* **-creting, -creted** (of a cell, organ, or gland) to produce and release (a substance). **secretory** (sik-**reet**-or-ee) *adj*

secrete[2] *vb* **-creting, -creted** to put in a hiding place.

secretion *n* **1** a substance that is released from a cell, organ, or gland. **2** the process involved in producing and releasing such a substance.

secretive *adj* hiding feelings and intentions. **secretively** *adv*

secret police *n* a police force that operates secretly to suppress opposition to the government.

secret service *n* a government agency or department that conducts intelligence or counterintelligence operations.

sect *n* **1** a subdivision of a larger religious or political group, esp. one regarded as extreme in its beliefs or practices. **2** a group of people with a common interest or philosophy.

sectarian *adj* **1** of or belonging to a sect. **2** narrow-minded as a result of supporting a particular sect. ~*n* **3** a member of a sect. **sectarianism** *n*

section *n* **1** a part cut off or separated from the main body of something: *a non-smoking section.* **2** a part or subdivision of a piece of writing or a book: *the business section.* **3** a distinct part of a country or community: *the Arabic section.* **4** *Surgery* the act or process of cutting or separating by cutting. **5** *Geom* a plane

THESAURUS

secondary derivative, derived, indirect, resultant, resulting, second-hand

second-class *adj.* indifferent, inferior, mediocre, outclassed, second-best, second-rate, undistinguished, uninspiring

second-hand 1. *adj.* handed down, hand-me-down (*informal*), nearly new, reach-me-down (*informal*), used **2.** *adv.* at second-hand, indirectly, on the grapevine (*informal*)

second-rate cheap, cheap and nasty (*informal*), commonplace, inferior, low-grade, low-quality, mediocre, poor, rubbishy, shoddy, substandard, tacky (*informal*), tawdry

secrecy 1. concealment, confidentiality, huggermugger (*archaic*), mystery, privacy, retirement, seclusion, silence, solitude, surreptitiousness **2.** clandestineness, covertness, furtiveness, secretiveness, stealth

secret *adj.* **1.** backstairs, camouflaged, cloak-and-dagger, close, closet (*informal*), concealed, conspiratorial, covered, covert, disguised, furtive, hidden, hole-and-corner (*informal*), hush-hush (*informal*), reticent, shrouded, undercover, underground, under wraps, undisclosed, unknown, unpublished, unrevealed, unseen **2.** close, deep, discreet, reticent, secretive, sly, stealthy, underhand **3.** abstruse, arcane, cabbalistic, clandestine, classified, cryptic, esoteric, mysterious, occult, recondite ~*n.* **4.** code, confidence, enigma, formula, key, mystery, recipe, skeleton in the cupboard **5. in secret** behind closed doors, by stealth, huggermugger (*archaic*), in camera, incognito, secretly, slyly, surreptitiously

secretive cagey (*informal*), clamlike, close, cryptic, deep, enigmatic, playing one's cards close to one's chest, reserved, reticent, tight-lipped, uncommunicative, unforthcoming, withdrawn

secretly behind closed doors, behind (someone's) back, clandestinely, confidentially, covertly, furtively, in camera, in confidence, in one's heart, in one's inmost thoughts, in secret, on the q.t. (*informal*), on the sly, privately, quietly, stealthily, surreptitiously, unobserved

sect camp, denomination, division, faction, group, party, schism, school, school of thought, splinter group, wing

sectarian 1. *adj.* bigoted, clannish, cliquish, doctrinaire, dogmatic, exclusive, factional, fanatic, fanatical,

surface formed by cutting through a solid. **6** short for **Caesarean section.** *~vb* **7** to cut or divide into sections. **8** to commit (a mentally disturbed person) to a mental hospital.

sectional *adj* **1** concerned with a particular area or group within a country or community, esp. to the exclusion of others: *narrow sectional interests.* **2** made of sections. **3** of a section.

sector *n* **1** a part or subdivision, esp. of a society or an economy: *the public sector.* **2** *Geom* either portion of a circle bounded by two radii and the arc cut off by them. **3** a portion into which an area is divided for military operations.

secular *adj* **1** relating to worldly as opposed to sacred things. **2** not connected with religion or the church. **3** (of clerics) not bound by religious vows to a monastic or other order.

secularism *n* the belief that religion should have no place in civil affairs. **secularist** *n, adj*

secularize *or* **-ise** *vb* **-izing, -ized** *or* **-ising, -ised** to change (something, such as education) so that it is no longer connected with religion or the Church. **secularization** *or* **-isation** *n*

secure *adj* **1** free from danger or damage. **2** free from fear, doubt, or care. **3** tightly locked or well protected. **4** fixed or tied firmly in position. **5** able to be relied on: *secure profits.* *~vb* **-curing, -cured 6** to obtain: *to secure a change in German policy.* **7** to make or become free from danger or fear. **8** to make safe from loss, theft, or attack. **9** to guarantee (payment of a loan) by giving something as security. **securely** *adv*

security *n, pl* **-ties 1** precautions taken to ensure against theft, espionage, or other danger. **2** the state of being free from danger, damage, or worry. **3** assured freedom from poverty: *the security of a weekly pay cheque.* **4** a certificate of ownership, such as a share, stock, or bond. **5** something given or pledged to guarantee payment of a loan.

security risk *n* someone or something thought to be a threat to state security.

sedan *n US, Canad, & NZ* a saloon car.

sedan chair *n* an enclosed chair for one passenger, carried on poles by two bearers, commonly used in the 17th and 18th centuries.

sedate[1] *adj* **1** quiet, calm, and dignified. **2** slow or unhurried: *a sedate walk to the beach.* **sedately** *adv*

sedate[2] *vb* **-dating, -dated** to calm down or make sleepy by giving a sedative drug to.

sedation *n* **1** a state of calm, esp. when brought about by sedatives. **2** the administration of a sedative.

sedative *adj* **1** having a soothing or calming effect. *~n* **2** *Med* a sedative drug or agent that makes people sleep or calm down.

sedentary (**sed**-en-tree) *adj* **1** done sitting down and involving very little exercise: *a sedentary job.* **2** tending to sit about without taking much exercise.

sedge *n* a coarse grasslike plant growing on wet ground. **sedgy** *adj*

sedge warbler *n* a European songbird living in marshy areas.

sediment *n* **1** matter that settles to the bottom of a liquid. **2** material that has been deposited by water, ice, or wind. **sedimentary** *adj*

sedition *n* speech, writing, or behaviour intended to encourage rebellion or resistance against the government. **seditionary** *n, adj* **seditious** *adj*

seduce *vb* **-ducing, -duced 1** to persuade to have sexual intercourse. **2** to tempt into wrongdoing. **seduction** *n*

seductive *adj* **1** (of a woman) sexually attractive. **2** very attractive or tempting: *a seductive argument.* **seductively** *adv* **seductiveness** *n*

sedulous *adj* diligent or painstaking. **sedulously** *adv*

sedum *n* a rock plant with thick clusters of white, yellow, or pink flowers.

see[1] *vb* **seeing, saw, seen 1** to look at or recognize with the eyes. **2** to understand: *I explained the problem but he could not see it.* **3** to perceive or be aware of: *she had never seen him so angry.* **4** to view, watch, or attend: *we had barely seen a dozen movies in our lives.* **5** to foresee: *they could see what their fate was to be.* **6** to find out (a fact): *I was ringing to see whether you'd got it.* **7** to make sure (of something) or

THESAURUS

hidebound, insular, limited, narrow-minded, parochial, partisan, rigid **2.** *n.* adherent, bigot, disciple, dogmatist, extremist, fanatic, partisan, true believer, zealot

section *n.* **1.** component, cross section, division, fraction, fragment, instalment, part, passage, piece, portion, sample, segment, slice, subdivision **2.** area, department, district, region, sector, zone

sector area, category, district, division, part, quarter, region, stratum, subdivision, zone

secular civil, earthly, laic, lay, nonspiritual, profane, state, temporal, worldly

secure *adj.* **1.** immune, impregnable, out of harm's way, protected, safe, sheltered, shielded, unassailable, undamaged, unharmed **2.** assured, certain, confident, easy, reassured, sure **3.** dependable, fast, fastened, firm, fixed, fortified, immovable, stable, steady, tight **4.** absolute, conclusive, definite, in the bag (*informal*), reliable, solid, steadfast, tried and true, well-founded *~vb.* **5.** acquire, come by, gain, get, get hold of, land (*informal*), make sure of, obtain, pick up, procure, score (*slang*), win possession of **6.** attach, batten down, bolt, chain, fasten, fix, lash, lock, lock up, make fast, moor, padlock, rivet, tie up **7.** assure, ensure, guarantee, insure

security 1. defence, guards, precautions, protection, safeguards, safety measures, surveillance **2.** assurance, certainty, confidence, conviction, ease of mind, freedom from doubt, positiveness, reliance, sureness **3.** collateral, gage, guarantee, hostage, insurance, pawn, pledge, surety

sedate calm, collected, composed, cool, decorous, deliberate, demure, dignified, earnest, grave, imperturbable, middle-aged, placid, proper, quiet, seemly, serene, serious, slow-moving, sober, solemn, staid, tranquil, unflappable (*informal*), unruffled

sedative 1. *adj.* allaying, anodyne, calmative, calming, relaxing, sleep-inducing, soothing, soporific, tranquillizing **2.** *n. Med.* anodyne, calmative, narcotic, opiate, sleeping pill, tranquillizer

sedentary desk, desk-bound, inactive, motionless, seated, sitting, torpid

sediment deposit, dregs, grounds, lees, precipitate, residuum, settlings

sedition agitation, disloyalty, incitement to riot, rabble-rousing, subversion, treason

seditious disloyal, dissident, insubordinate, mutinous, rebellious, refractory, revolutionary, subversive, treasonable

seduce 1. betray, corrupt, debauch, deflower, deprave, dishonour **2.** allure, attract, beguile, deceive, decoy, ensnare, entice, inveigle, lead astray, lure, mislead, tempt

seduction 1. corruption, defloration **2.** allure, enticement, lure, snare, temptation

seductive alluring, attractive, beguiling, bewitching, captivating, come-hither (*informal*), come-to-bed (*in-

take care (of something): *see that he is never in a position to do these things again; you must see to it.* **8** to consider or decide: *see if you can come next week.* **9** to have experience of: *he had seen active service in the revolution.* **10** to meet or pay a visit to: *I see my specialist every three months.* **11** to receive: *the Prime Minister will see the deputation now.* **12** to frequent the company of: *we've been seeing each other since then.* **13** to accompany: *she saw him to the door.* **14** to refer to or look up: *see page 35.* **15** (in gambling, esp. in poker) to match (another player's bet) or match the bet of (another player) by staking an equal sum. **16 see fit** to consider it proper (to do something): *I did not see fit to send them home.* **17 see you, see you later** *or* **be seeing you** an expression of farewell. ~See also **see about, see into,** etc.

see[2] *n* the diocese of a bishop or the place within it where his cathedral is situated.

see about *vb* **1** to take care of: *I'll see about some coffee.* **2** to investigate: *to see about a new car.*

seed *n* **1** *Bot* the mature fertilized grain of a plant, containing an embryo ready for germination. **2** such seeds used for sowing. **3** the source, beginning, or origin of anything: *the seeds of dissent.* **4** *Chiefly Bible* descendants; offspring: *the seed of David.* **5** *Sport* a player ranked according to his or her ability. **6 go** *or* **run to seed a** (of plants) to produce and shed seeds after flowering. **b** to lose strength or usefulness. ~*vb* **7** to plant (seeds) in (soil). **8** (of plants) to produce or shed seeds. **9** to remove the seeds from (fruit or plants). **10** to scatter silver iodide in (clouds) in order to cause rain. **11** to arrange (the draw of a tournament) so that outstanding teams or players will not meet in the early rounds. **seedless** *adj*

seedbed *n* **1** an area of soil prepared for the growing of seedlings before they are transplanted. **2** the place where something develops: *a seedbed of immorality.*

seedling *n* a plant produced from a seed, esp. a very young plant.

seed pearl *n* a very small pearl.

seed pod *n Bot* a carpel or pistil enclosing the seeds of a plant, esp. a flowering plant.

seedy *adj* **seedier, seediest 1** shabby in appearance: *a seedy cinema.* **2** *Informal* physically unwell. **3** (of a plant) at the stage of producing seeds. **seediness** *n*

seeing *n* **1** the sense or faculty of sight. ~*conj* **2** (often foll. by *that*) in light of the fact (that).

see into *vb* to discover the true nature of: *he could see into my intentions.*

seek *vb* **seeking, sought 1** to try to find by searching: *to seek employment.* **2** to try to obtain: *to seek a diplomatic solution.* **3** to try (to do something): *we seek to establish a stable relationship.*

seek out *vb* to search hard for and find (a specific person or thing): *you should seek out healthy role models.*

seem *vb* **1** to appear to the mind or eye; give the impression of: *the car seems to be running well.* **2** to appear to be: *there seems no need for all this nonsense.* **3** to have the impression: *I seem to remember you were there too.*

seeming *adj* apparent but not real: *his seeming willingness to participate.* **seemingly** *adv*

seemly *adj* **-lier, -liest** *Formal* proper or fitting.

seen *vb* the past participle of **see**[1].

see off *vb* **1** to be present at the departure of (a person going on a journey): *your sisters came to see you off.* **2** *Informal* to cause to leave or depart, esp. by force.

seep *vb* to leak through slowly; ooze. **seepage** *n*

seer *n* a person who can supposedly see into the future.

seersucker *n* a light cotton fabric with a slightly crinkled surface.

seesaw *n* **1** a plank balanced in the middle so that two people seated on the ends can ride up and down by pushing on the ground with their feet. **2** an up-and-down or back-and-forth movement. ~*vb* **3** to move up and down or back and forth alternately.

seethe *vb* **seething, seethed 1** to be in a state of extreme anger or indignation without publicly showing these feelings. **2** (of a liquid) to boil or foam. **seething** *adj*

THESAURUS

formal), enticing, flirtatious, inviting, irresistible, provocative, ravishing, sexy (*informal*), siren, specious, tempting

see *vb.* **1.** behold, catch a glimpse of, catch sight of, check, check out (*informal*), clock (*Brit. slang*), descry, discern, distinguish, espy, get a load of (*informal*), glimpse, heed, identify, lay *or* clap eyes on (*informal*), look, make out, mark, note, notice, observe, perceive, recognize, regard, sight, spot, take a dekko at (*Brit. slang*), view, witness **2.** appreciate, catch on (*informal*), comprehend, fathom, feel, follow, get, get the drift of, get the hang of (*informal*), grasp, know, make out, realize, take in, understand **3.** anticipate, divine, envisage, foresee, foretell, imagine, picture, visualize **4.** ascertain, determine, discover, find out, investigate, learn, make inquiries, refer to **5.** ensure, guarantee, make certain, make sure, mind, see to it, take care **6.** consider, decide, deliberate, give some thought to, judge, make up one's mind, mull over, reflect, think over **7.** confer with, consult, encounter, interview, meet, receive, run into, speak to, visit **8.** consort *or* associate with, court, date (*informal, chiefly U.S.*), go out with, go steady with (*informal*), keep company with, walk out with (*obsolete*) **9.** accompany, attend, escort, lead, show, usher, walk

see about 1. attend to, consider, deal with, give some thought to, look after, see to, take care of **2.** investigate, look into, make inquiries, research

seed 1. *Bot.* egg, egg cell, embryo, germ, grain, kernel, ovule, ovum, pip, spore **2.** beginning, germ, inkling, nucleus, source, start, suspicion **3.** *chiefly Bible* children, descendants, heirs, issue, offspring, progeny, race, scions, spawn, successors **4. go** *or* **run to seed** decay, decline, degenerate, deteriorate, go downhill (*informal*), go to pieces, go to pot, go to rack and ruin, go to waste, let oneself go, retrogress

seedy 1. crummy (*slang*), decaying, dilapidated, down at heel, faded, grotty (*slang*), grubby, mangy, old, run-down, scruffy, shabby, sleazy, slovenly, squalid, tatty, unkempt, worn **2.** *informal* ailing, ill, off colour, out of sorts, poorly (*informal*), sickly, under the weather (*informal*), unwell

seeing *conj.* as, inasmuch as, in view of the fact that, since

seek 1. be after, follow, go gunning for, go in pursuit (quest, search) of, hunt, inquire, look for, pursue, search for **2.** aim, aspire to, attempt, endeavour, essay, have a go (*informal*), strive, try

seem appear, assume, give the impression, have the *or* every appearance of, look, look as if, look like, look to be, pretend, sound like, strike one as being

seemly appropriate, becoming, befitting, decent, decorous, fit, fitting, in good taste, nice, proper, suitable, suited, the done thing

seer augur, predictor, prophet, sibyl, soothsayer

seesaw *vb.* alternate, fluctuate, go from one extreme to the other, oscillate, pitch, swing, teeter

seethe 1. be in a state (*informal*), be livid (furious, incensed), breathe fire and slaughter, foam at the

see through *vb* **1** to perceive the true nature of: *it was difficult to see through people.* **2** to remain with until the end or completion: *not all of them saw it through.* **3** to help out in a time of need or trouble: *he helped see her through her divorce.* ~*adj* **see-through** **4** (of clothing) made of thin cloth so that the wearer's body or underclothes are visible.

segment *n* **1** one of several parts or sections into which an object is divided. **2** *Maths* **a** a part of a circle cut off by an intersecting line. **b** a part of a sphere cut off by an intersecting plane or planes. ~*vb* **3** to cut or divide into segments. **segmental** *adj* **segmentation** *n*

segregate *vb* **-gating, -gated** **1** to set apart from others or from the main group. **2** to impose segregation on (a racial or minority group).

segregation *n* **1** the practice or policy of creating separate facilities within the same society for the use of a racial or minority group. **2** the act of segregating. **segregational** *adj* **segregationist** *n*

seigneur *n* a feudal lord, esp. in France. **seigneurial** *adj*

seine (**sane**) *n* **1** a large fishing net that hangs vertically in the water by means of floats at the top and weights at the bottom. ~*vb* **seining, seined** **2** to catch (fish) using this net.

seismic *adj* relating to or caused by earthquakes.

seismograph *n* an instrument that records the intensity and duration of earthquakes. **seismographer** *n* **seismography** *n*

seismology *n* the branch of geology concerned with the study of earthquakes. **seismologist** *n*

seismometer *n* same as **seismograph.**

seize *vb* **seizing, seized** **1** to take hold of forcibly or quickly; grab. **2** to take immediate advantage of: *real journalists would have seized the opportunity.* **3** to take legal possession of. **4** (sometimes foll. by *on* or *upon*) to understand quickly: *she immediately seized his idea.* **5** to affect or fill the mind of suddenly: *a wild frenzy seized her.* **6** to take by force or capture: *the rebels seized a tank factory.* **7** (often foll. by *up* of mechanical parts) to become jammed through overheating.

seizure *n* **1** *Pathol* a sudden violent attack of an illness, such as an epileptic convulsion. **2** the act of seizing: *a seizure of drug traffickers' assets.*

seldom *adv* rarely; not often.

select *vb* **1** to choose (someone or something) in preference to another or others. ~*adj* **2** chosen in preference to others. **3** restricted to a particular group; exclusive: *a select audience.* **selector** *n*

select committee *n* (in Britain) a small committee of members of parliament, set up to investigate and report on a specified matter.

selection *n* **1** a selecting or being selected. **2** a thing or number of things that have been selected. **3** a range from which something may be selected: *a good selection of reasonably priced wines.* **4** *Biol* the process by which certain organisms or individuals are reproduced and survive in preference to others.

selective *adj* **1** tending to choose carefully or characterized by careful choice: *they were very selective in their television watching.* **2** of or characterized by selection. **selectively** *adv* **selectivity** *n*

selenium *n Chem* a nonmetallic element used in photocells, solar cells, and in xerography. Symbol: Se

self *n, pl* **selves** **1** the distinct individuality or identity of a person or thing. **2** a person's typical bodily make-up or personal characteristics: *back to my old self after the scare.* **3** one's own welfare or interests: *he only thinks of self.* **4** an individual's consciousness of his or her own identity or being. ~*pron* **5** *Not standard* myself, yourself, himself, or herself: *setting goals for self and others.*

self- *combining form* used with many main words to mean: **1** of oneself or itself: *self-defence.* **2** by, to, in, due to, for, or from the self: *self-employed; self-respect.* **3** automatic or automatically: *self-propelled.*

self-abnegation *n* the denial of one's own interests in favour of the interests of others.

self-absorption *n* preoccupation with oneself to the exclusion of others. **self-absorbed** *adj*

self-abuse *n* masturbation.

self-addressed *adj* addressed for return to the sender.

self-aggrandizement *or* **self-aggrandisement** *n* the act of increasing one's own power, wealth, or importance.

self-appointed *adj* having assumed authority without the agreement of others: *self-appointed moralists.*

self-assertion *n* the act of putting forward one's own opinions or demanding one's rights, esp. in an aggressive or confident manner. **self-assertive** *adj*

self-assurance *n* confidence in oneself, one's abilities, or one's judgment. **self-assured** *adj*

self-catering *adj* (of accommodation) for tenants providing and preparing their own food.

THESAURUS

mouth, fume, get hot under the collar (*informal*), rage, see red (*informal*), simmer, storm **2.** boil, bubble, churn, ferment, fizz, foam, froth

see through *vb.* **1.** be undeceived by, be wise to (*informal*), fathom, get to the bottom of, have (someone's) number (*informal*), not fall for, penetrate **2. see (something *or* someone) through** help out, keep at, persevere (with), persist, see out, stay to the bitter end, stick by, stick out (*informal*), support

segment bit, compartment, division, part, piece, portion, section, slice, wedge

segregate discriminate against, dissociate, isolate, separate, set apart, single out

segregation apartheid (*formerly in South Africa*), discrimination, isolation, separation

seize **1.** catch up, clutch, collar (*informal*), fasten, grab, grasp, grip, lay hands on, snatch, take **2.** abduct, annex, appropriate, arrest, capture, commandeer, confiscate, hijack, impound, take by storm, take captive, take possession of

seizure **1.** *Pathol.* attack, convulsion, fit, paroxysm, spasm **2.** abduction, annexation, apprehension, arrest, capture, commandeering, confiscation, grabbing, taking

seldom hardly ever, infrequently, not often, occasionally, once in a blue moon (*informal*), rarely, scarcely ever

select *vb.* **1.** choose, opt for, pick, prefer, single out, sort out ~*adj.* **2.** choice, excellent, first-class, first-rate, hand-picked, picked, posh (*informal, chiefly Brit.*), preferable, prime, rare, recherché, selected, special, superior, topnotch (*informal*) **3.** cliquish, elite, exclusive, limited, privileged

selection **1.** choice, choosing, option, pick, preference **2.** anthology, assortment, choice, collection, line-up, medley, miscellany, potpourri, range, variety

selective careful, discerning, discriminating, discriminatory, eclectic, particular

self-assurance assertiveness, confidence, positiveness, self-confidence, self-possession

self-centred *or US* **self-centered** *adj* totally preoccupied with one's own concerns.
self-certification *n* (in Britain) the completion of a form by a worker stating that his or her absence was due to sickness.
self-coloured *or US* **self-colored** *adj* **1** having only a single and uniform colour: *a self-coloured tie.* **2** (of cloth or wool) having the natural or original colour.
self-confessed *adj* according to one's own admission: *a self-confessed addict.*
self-confidence *n* confidence in oneself, one's abilities, or one's judgment. **self-confident** *adj*
self-conscious *adj* embarrassed or ill at ease through being unduly aware of oneself as the object of the attention of others. **self-consciously** *adv* **self-consciousness** *n*
self-contained *adj* **1** containing within itself all parts necessary for completeness. **2** (of a flat) having its own kitchen, bathroom, and toilet not shared by others.
self-control *n* the ability to control one's feelings, emotions, or reactions. **self-controlled** *adj*
self-deception *or* **self-deceit** *n* the act or an instance of deceiving oneself.
self-defence *or US* **self-defense** *n* **1** the act or skill of defending oneself against physical attack. **2** the act of defending one's actions, ideas, or rights.
self-denial *n* the repression or sacrifice of one's own desires. **self-denying** *adj*
self-determination *n* **1** the ability to make a decision for oneself without influence from outside. **2** the right of a nation or people to determine its own form of government. **self-determined** *adj*
self-discipline *n* the act of controlling or power to control one's own feelings, desires, or behaviour. **self-disciplined** *adj*
self-drive *adj* relating to a hired vehicle that is driven by the hirer.
self-educated *adj* educated through one's own efforts without formal instruction.
self-effacement *n* the act of making oneself or one's actions seem less important than they are because of modesty or timidity. **self-effacing** *adj*
self-employed *adj* earning one's living in one's own business, rather than as the employee of another.
self-esteem *n* respect for or a favourable opinion of oneself.
self-evident *adj* so obvious that no proof or explanation is needed. **self-evidently** *adv*
self-explanatory *adj* understandable without explanation.
self-expression *n* the expression of one's own personality or feelings, esp. in the creative arts. **self-expressive** *adj*
self-government *n* the government of a country, nation, or community by its own people. **self-governing** *adj*
self-help *n* **1** the use of one's own abilities and resources to help oneself without relying on the assistance of others. **2** the practice of solving one's problems within a group of people with similar problems.
self-image *n* one's own idea of oneself or sense of one's worth.
self-important *adj* having an unduly high opinion of one's own importance. **self-importance** *n*
self-improvement *n* the improvement of one's position, skills, or education by one's own efforts.
self-indulgent *adj* tending to allow oneself to have or do things that one enjoys. **self-indulgence** *n*
self-interest *n* **1** one's personal interest or advantage. **2** the pursuit of one's own interest. **self-interested** *adj*
selfish *adj* **1** caring too much about oneself and not enough about others. **2** (of behaviour or attitude) motivated by self-interest. **selfishly** *adv* **selfishness** *n*
selfless *adj* putting other people's interests before one's own. **selflessly** *adv* **selflessness** *n*
self-made *adj* having achieved wealth or status by one's own efforts.
self-opinionated *adj* clinging stubbornly to one's own opinions.
self-pity *n* pity for oneself, esp. when greatly exaggerated. **self-pitying** *adj*
self-pollination *n Bot* the transfer of pollen from the anthers to the stigma of the same flower.
self-possessed *adj* having control of one's emotions or behaviour, esp. in difficult situations. **self-possession** *n*
self-preservation *n* the instinctive behaviour that protects one from danger or injury.
self-propelled *adj* **1** (of a vehicle) driven by its own engine rather than drawn by a locomotive, horse, etc. **2** (of a rocket launcher or artillery piece) mounted on a motor vehicle. **self-propelling** *adj*
self-raising *adj* (of flour) having a raising agent, such as baking powder, already added.
self-realization *or* **-isation** *n* the fulfilment of one's own potential or abilities.

THESAURUS

self-centred egoistical, egotistical, inward looking, narcissistic, self-absorbed, selfish, self-seeking, wrapped up in oneself
self-confidence aplomb, confidence, high morale, nerve, poise, self-assurance, self-reliance, self-respect
self-confident assured, confident, fearless, poised, secure, self-assured, self-reliant, sure of oneself
self-conscious affected, awkward, bashful, diffident, embarrassed, ill at ease, insecure, nervous, out of countenance, shamefaced, sheepish, uncomfortable
self-control calmness, cool, coolness, restraint, self-discipline, self-mastery, self-restraint, strength of mind *or* will, willpower
self-esteem *amour-propre,* confidence, faith in oneself, pride, self-assurance, self-regard, self-respect, vanity
self-evident axiomatic, clear, incontrovertible, inescapable, manifestly *or* patently true, obvious, undeniable, written all over (something)
self-government autonomy, democracy, home rule, independence, self-determination, self-rule, sovereignty
self-important arrogant, big-headed, bumptious, cocky, conceited, overbearing, pompous, presumptuous, pushy (*informal*), strutting, swaggering, swollen-headed
self-indulgence dissipation, excess, extravagance, incontinence, intemperance, self-gratification, sensualism
selfish egoistical, egotistical, greedy, looking out for number one (*informal*), mean, mercenary, narrow, self-centred, self-interested, self-seeking, ungenerous
selfless altruistic, generous, magnanimous, self-denying, self-sacrificing, ungrudging, unselfish
self-possessed collected, confident, cool, cool as

self-regard *n* **1** concern for one's own interest. **2** proper esteem for oneself.

self-reliance *n* reliance on oneself or one's own abilities. **self-reliant** *adj*

self-reproach *n* the act of finding fault with or blaming oneself.

self-respect *n* a feeling of confidence and pride in one's own abilities and worth. **self-respecting** *adj*

self-restraint *n* control imposed by oneself on one's own feelings, desires, or actions.

self-righteous *adj* thinking oneself more virtuous than others. **self-righteousness** *n*

self-sacrifice *n* the giving up of one's own interests for the wellbeing of others. **self-sacrificing** *adj*

selfsame *adj* the very same: *this was the selfsame woman I'd met on the train.*

self-satisfied *adj* smug and complacently satisfied with oneself or one's own actions. **self-satisfaction** *n*

self-sealing *adj* **1** (of an envelope) sealable by pressure alone. **2** (of a tyre) automatically sealing small punctures.

self-seeking *n* **1** the act or an instance of seeking one's own profit or interests. *~adj* **2** inclined to promote only one's own profit or interests: *self-seeking politicians.* **self-seeker** *n*

self-service *adj* **1** of or denoting a shop or restaurant where the customers serve themselves and then pay a cashier. *~n* **2** the practice of serving oneself and then paying a cashier.

self-serving *adj* continually seeking one's own advantage, esp. at the expense of others.

self-starter *n* **1** an electric motor used to start an internal-combustion engine. **2** a person who is strongly motivated and shows initiative at work.

self-styled *adj* using a title or name that one has given oneself, esp. without right or justification; so-called: *the self-styled leader of the rebellion.*

self-sufficient *adj* able to provide for or support oneself without the help of others. **self-sufficiency** *n*

self-supporting *adj* **1** able to support or maintain oneself without the help of others. **2** able to stand up or hold firm without support, props, or attachments.

self-willed *adj* stubbornly determined to have one's own way, esp. at the expense of others.

self-winding *adj* (of a wristwatch) having a mechanism which winds itself automatically.

sell *vb* **selling, sold 1** to exchange (something) for money. **2** to deal in (objects or property): *he sells used cars.* **3** to give up or surrender for a price or reward: *to sell one's honour.* **4 sell for** to have a specified price: *they sell for 10 pence each.* **5** to promote the sale of (objects or property): *sex sells cigarettes.* **6** to gain acceptance of: *he'll sell an idea to a producer.* **7** to be in demand on the market: *his books did not sell well enough.* **8 sell down the river** *Informal* to betray. **9 sell oneself a** to convince someone else of one's potential or worth. **b** to give up one's moral standards for a price or reward. **10 sell someone short** *Informal* to undervalue someone. *~n* **11** the act or an instance of selling: *the hard sell.* ~See also **sell off, sell out, sell up. seller** *n*

sell-by date *n* **1** the date printed on packaged food specifying the date after which the food should not be sold. **2 past one's sell-by date** beyond one's prime.

sell off *vb* to sell (remaining items) at reduced prices.

Sellotape *n* **1** *Trademark* a type of transparent adhesive tape. *~vb* **-taping, -taped 2** to seal or stick using adhesive tape.

sell out *vb* **1** to dispose of (something) completely by selling. **2** *Informal* to betray in order to gain an advantage or benefit. *~n* **sellout 3** *Informal* a performance of a show etc. for which all tickets are sold. **4** a commercial success. **5** *Informal* a betrayal.

sell up *vb Chiefly Brit* to sell all one's goods or property.

selvage *or* **selvedge** *n* a specially woven edge on a length of fabric to prevent it from unravelling. **selvaged** *adj*

selves *n* the plural of **self.**

semantic *adj* **1** of or relating to the meanings of words. **2** of or relating to semantics.

semantics *n* the branch of linguistics that deals with the study of meaning.

semaphore *n* **1** a system of signalling by holding two flags in different positions to represent letters of the alphabet. *~vb* **-phoring, -phored 2** to signal (information) by semaphore.

semblance *n* outward or superficial appearance: *some semblance of order had been established.*

semen *n* the thick whitish fluid containing spermatozoa that is produced by the male reproductive organs and ejaculated from the penis.

semester *n Chiefly US & Canad* either of two divisions of the academic year.

semi *n Brit informal* short for **semidetached** (sense 2).

semi- *prefix* used with many main words to mean: **1** half: *semicircle.* **2** partly or almost: *semiprofessional.* **3** occurring twice in a specified period: *semiweekly.*

semiannual *adj* **1** occurring every half-year. **2** lasting for half a year.

semiarid *adj* denoting land that lies on the edges of a

THESAURUS

a cucumber (*informal*), poised, self-assured, sure of oneself, together (*slang*), unruffled

self-reliant able to stand on one's own two feet (*informal*), capable, independent, self-sufficient, self-supporting

self-respect *amour-propre,* dignity, faith in oneself, morale, one's own image, pride, self-esteem

self-righteous complacent, goody-goody (*informal*), holier-than-thou, hypocritical, pharisaic, pi (*Brit. slang*), pietistic, pious, priggish, sanctimonious, self-satisfied, smug, superior, too good to be true

self-sacrifice altruism, generosity, self-abnegation, self-denial, selflessness

self-satisfaction complacency, contentment, ease of mind, flush of success, glow of achievement, pride, self-approbation, self-approval, smugness

self-satisfied complacent, flushed with success, like a cat that has swallowed the cream *or* the canary, pleased with oneself, proud of oneself, puffed up, self-congratulatory, smug, well-pleased

self-seeking *adj.* acquisitive, calculating, careerist, fortune-hunting, gold-digging, looking out for number one (*informal*), mercenary, on the make (*slang*), opportunistic, out for what one can get, self-interested, selfish, self-serving

sell 1. barter, dispose of, exchange, put up for sale, trade **2.** be in the business of, deal in, handle, hawk, market, merchandise, peddle, retail, stock, trade in, traffic in, vend **3.** gain acceptance for, promote, put across

seller agent, dealer, merchant, purveyor, rep, representative, retailer, salesman, saleswoman, shopkeeper, supplier, tradesman, traveller, vendor

sell out 1. be out of stock of, dispose of, get rid of, run out of, sell up **2.** *informal* betray, break faith with,

desert but has a slightly higher rainfall (above 300 mm) so that some farming is possible.

semiautomatic *adj* **1** (of a firearm) self-loading but firing only one shot at each pull of the trigger. ~*n* **2** a semiautomatic firearm.

semibreve *n Music* a note, now the longest in common use, with a time value that may be divided by any power of 2 to give all other notes.

semicircle *n* **1** one half of a circle. **2** anything having the shape or form of half a circle. **semicircular** *adj*

semicolon *n* the punctuation mark (;) used to separate clauses or items in a list, or to indicate a pause longer than that of a comma and shorter than that of a full stop.

semiconductor *n Physics* a substance, such as silicon, which has an electrical conductivity that increases with temperature.

semiconscious *adj* not fully conscious. **semiconsciousness** *n*

semidetached *adj* **1** (of a house) joined to another house on one side by a common wall. ~*n* **2** a semidetached house: *the mock Georgian semidetached.*

semifinal *n* the round before the final in a competition. **semifinalist** *n*

seminal *adj* **1** highly original and influential: *seminal thinkers.* **2** potentially capable of development. **3** of semen: *seminal fluid.* **4** *Biol* of seed.

seminar *n* **1** a small group of students meeting regularly under the guidance of a tutor for study and discussion. **2** one such meeting.

seminary *n, pl* **-naries** a college for the training of priests. **seminarian** *n*

semiotics *n* the study of human communication, esp. communication using signs and symbols. **semiotic** *adj*

semipermeable *adj* (of a cell membrane) allowing small molecules to pass through but not large ones.

semiprecious *adj* (of certain stones) having less value than a precious stone.

semiprofessional *adj* **1** (of a person) engaged in an activity or sport part time for pay. **2** (of an activity or sport) engaged in by semiprofessional people. ~*n* **3** a semiprofessional person.

semiquaver *n Music* a note having the time value of one-sixteenth of a semibreve.

semirigid *adj* (of an airship) maintaining shape by means of a main supporting keel and internal gas pressure.

semiskilled *adj* partly skilled or trained but not sufficiently so to perform specialized work.

Semite *n* a member of the group of peoples who speak a Semitic language, such as the Jews and Arabs.

Semitic *n* **1** a group of languages that includes Arabic, Hebrew, and Aramaic. ~*adj* **2** of this group of languages. **3** of any of the peoples speaking a Semitic language, esp. the Jews or the Arabs. **4** same as **Jewish.**

semitone *n* the smallest interval between two notes in Western music represented on a piano by the difference in pitch between any two adjacent keys. **semitonic** *adj*

semitropical *adj* bordering on the tropics; nearly tropical. **semitropics** *pl n*

semivowel *n Phonetics* a vowel-like sound that acts like a consonant, such as the sound *w* in *well.*

semolina *n* the large hard grains of wheat left after flour has been milled, used for making puddings and pasta.

Semtex *n Trademark* a pliable plastic explosive.

SEN (in Britain) State Enrolled Nurse.

Sen. *or* **sen.** **1** senate. **2** senator. **3** senior.

senate *n* the main governing body at some universities.

Senate *n* the upper chamber of the legislatures of Australia, the US, Canada, and many other countries.

senator *n* a member of a Senate. **senatorial** *adj*

send *vb* **sending, sent 1** to cause (a person or thing) to go or be taken or transmitted to another place: *send a cheque or postal order.* **2 send for** to dispatch a request or command for (someone or something): *she had sent for me.* **3** to cause to go to a place or point: *the bullet sent him flying into the air.* **4** to bring to a state or condition: *his schemes to send her mad.* **5** to cause to happen or come: *the thunderstorm sent by the gods.* **6** *Old-fashioned, slang* to move to excitement or rapture: *this music really sends me.* **sender** *n*

send down *vb* **1** *Brit* to expel from a university. **2** *Informal* to send to prison.

sendoff *n* **1** *Informal* a show of good wishes to a person about to set off on a journey or start a new career. ~*vb* **send off 2** to dispatch (something, such as a letter). **3** *Sport* (of a referee) to dismiss (a player) from the field of play for some offence.

send up *Brit informal* ~*vb* **1** to make fun of by doing an imitation or parody. ~*n* **send-up 2** a parody or imitation.

senescent *adj Formal* growing old. **senescence** *n*

seneschal (**sen**-ish-al) *n History* a steward of the household of a medieval prince or nobleman.

senile *adj* mentally or physically weak or infirm on account of old age. **senility** *n*

senior *adj* **1** higher in rank or length of service. **2** older in years: *senior citizens.* **3** *Education* of or designating more advanced or older pupils or students. ~*n* **4** a senior person.

Senior *adj Chiefly US* being older than someone of the same name: *Joe Yule Senior.*

senior aircraftman *n* an ordinary rank in the Royal Air Force.

senior citizen *n* an old person, esp. a pensioner.

seniority *n, pl* **-ties 1** the state of being senior. **2** degree of power or importance in an organization from length of continuous service.

senior service *n Brit* the Royal Navy.

senna *n* **1** a tropical plant with yellow flowers and long pods. **2** the dried leaves and pods of this plant, used as a laxative.

señor (sen-**nyor**) *n* a Spanish form of address equivalent to *sir* or *Mr.*

señora (sen-**nyor**-a) *n* a Spanish form of address equivalent to *madam* or *Mrs.*

THESAURUS

double-cross (*informal*), fail, give away, play false, rat on (*informal*), sell down the river (*informal*), stab in the back

send 1. communicate, consign, convey, direct, dispatch, forward, remit, transmit **2. send for** call for, demand, order, request, summon **3.** cast, deliver, fire, fling, hurl, let fly, propel, shoot **4.** *old-fashioned slang* charm, delight, electrify, enrapture, enthral, excite, intoxicate, move, please, ravish, stir, thrill, titillate, turn (someone) on (*slang*)

sendoff departure, farewell, going-away party, leave-taking, start, valediction

senile decrepit, doddering, doting, failing, imbecile, in one's dotage, in one's second childhood

señorita (sen-nyor-ee-ta) *n* a Spanish form of address equivalent to *madam* or *Miss*.

sensation *n* **1** the power of feeling things physically: *I lose all sensation in my hands.* **2** a physical feeling: *a burning sensation in the throat.* **3** a general feeling or awareness: *a sensation of vague resentment.* **4** a state of excitement: *imagine the sensation in Washington!* **5** an exciting person or thing: *you'll be a sensation.*

sensational *adj* **1** causing intense feelings of shock, anger, or excitement: *sensational allegations.* **2** *Informal* extremely good: *the views are sensational.* **3** of the senses or sensation. **sensationally** *adv*

sensationalism *n* the deliberate use of sensational language or subject matter to arouse feelings of shock, anger, or excitement. **sensationalist** *adj, n*

sense *n* **1** any of the faculties (sight, hearing, touch, taste, and smell) by which the mind receives information about the external world or the state of the body. **2** the ability to perceive. **3** a feeling perceived through one of the senses: *a sense of warmth.* **4** a mental perception or awareness: *a sense of security.* **5** ability to make moral judgments: *a sense of honour.* **6** (*usually pl*) sound practical judgment or intelligence: *a man lost his senses and killed his wife.* **7** reason or purpose: *no sense in continuing.* **8** general meaning: *he couldn't understand every word but he got the sense of what they were saying.* **9** specific meaning; definition: *the three senses of the word.* **10 make sense** to be understandable or practical. ~*vb* **sensing, sensed** **11** to perceive without the evidence of the senses: *he sensed that she was impressed.* **12** to perceive through the senses.

senseless *adj* **1** having no meaning or purpose: *a senseless act of violence.* **2** unconscious. **senselessly** *adv* **senselessness** *n*

sense organ *n* a part of the body that receives stimuli and transmits them as sensations to the brain.

sensibility *n, pl* **-ties** **1** (*often pl*) the ability to experience deep feelings. **2** (*usually pl*) the tendency to be influenced or offended: *its sheer callousness offended her sensibilities.* **3** the ability to perceive or feel.

sensible *adj* **1** having or showing good sense or judgment. **2** (of clothing and footwear) practical and hard-wearing. **3** capable of receiving sensation. **4** capable of being perceived by the senses. **5** perceptible to the mind. **6** *Literary* aware: *sensible of your kindness.* **sensibly** *adv*

sensitive *adj* **1** easily hurt; tender. **2** responsive to external stimuli or impressions. **3** easily offended or shocked. **4** (of a subject or issue) liable to arouse controversy or strong feelings. **5** (of an instrument) capable of registering small differences or changes in amounts. **6** *Photog* responding readily to light: *a sensitive emulsion.* **7** *Chiefly US* connected with matters affecting national security. **sensitively** *adv* **sensitivity** *n*

sensitize *or* **-tise** *vb* **-tizing, -tized** *or* **-tising, -tised** to make sensitive. **sensitization** *or* **-tisation** *n*

sensor *n* a device that detects or measures a physical property, such as radiation.

sensory *adj* relating to the physical senses.

sensual *adj* **1** giving pleasure to the body and senses rather than the mind: *soft sensual music.* **2** having a strong liking for physical, esp. sexual, pleasures. **3** of

THESAURUS

senior *adj.* elder, higher ranking, major (*Brit.*), older, superior

seniority eldership, longer service, precedence, priority, rank, superiority

sensation **1.** awareness, consciousness, feeling, impression, perception, sense, tingle **2.** agitation, commotion, crowd puller (*informal*), excitement, furore, hit (*informal*), scandal, stir, surprise, thrill, vibes (*slang*)

sensational **1.** amazing, astounding, breathtaking, dramatic, electrifying, exciting, hair-raising, horrifying, lurid, melodramatic, revealing, scandalous, sensationalistic, shock-horror (*facetious*), shocking, spectacular, staggering, startling, thrilling **2.** *informal* brilliant, cracking (*Brit. informal*), crucial (*slang*), def (*slang*), excellent, exceptional, fabulous (*informal*), first class, impressive, marvellous, mean (*slang*), mega (*slang*), mind-blowing (*informal*), out of this world (*informal*), smashing (*informal*), sovereign, superb

sense *n.* **1.** faculty, feeling, sensation, sensibility **2.** appreciation, atmosphere, aura, awareness, consciousness, feel, impression, intuition, perception, premonition, presentiment, sentiment **3.** *usually plural* brains (*informal*), clear-headedness, cleverness, common sense, discernment, discrimination, gumption (*Brit. informal*), intelligence, judgment, mother wit, nous (*Brit. slang*), quickness, reason, sagacity, sanity, sharpness, smarts (*slang, chiefly U.S.*), tact, understanding, wisdom, wit(s) **4.** advantage, good, logic, point, purpose, reason, use, value, worth **5.** definition, denotation, drift, gist, implication, import, interpretation, meaning, message, nuance, purport, significance, signification, substance ~*vb.* **6.** appreciate, apprehend, be aware of, discern, divine, feel, get the impression, grasp, have a feeling in one's bones (*informal*), have a funny feeling (*informal*), have a hunch, just know, notice, observe, perceive, pick up, realize, suspect, understand

senseless **1.** absurd, asinine, crazy, daft (*informal*), fatuous, foolish, goofy (*informal*), halfwitted, idiotic, illogical, imbecilic, inane, incongruous, inconsistent, irrational, ludicrous, mad, meaningless, mindless, moronic, nonsensical, pointless, ridiculous, silly, simple, stupid, unintelligent, unreasonable, unwise **2.** anaesthetized, cold, deadened, insensate, insensible, numb, numbed, out, out cold, stunned, unconscious, unfeeling

sensibility **1.** *often plural* responsiveness, sensitiveness, sensitivity, susceptibility **2.** *usually plural* emotions, feelings, moral sense, sentiments, susceptibilities **3.** appreciation, awareness, delicacy, discernment, insight, intuition, perceptiveness, taste

sensible **1.** canny, discreet, discriminating, down-to-earth, far-sighted, intelligent, judicious, matter-of-fact, practical, prudent, rational, realistic, reasonable, sagacious, sage, sane, shrewd, sober, sound, well-reasoned, well-thought-out, wise **2.** appreciable, considerable, discernable, noticeable, palpable, perceptible, significant, tangible, visible **3.** *usually with* **of** *literary* acquainted with, alive to, aware, conscious, convinced, mindful, observant, sensitive to, understanding

sensitive **1.** acute, delicate, easily affected, fine, impressionable, keen, perceptive, precise, reactive, responsive, sentient, susceptible **2.** delicate, easily upset (hurt, offended), irritable, temperamental, tender, thin-skinned, touchy

sensitivity delicacy, reactiveness, reactivity, receptiveness, responsiveness, sensitiveness, susceptibility

sensual **1.** erotic, lascivious, lecherous, lewd, libidinous, licentious, lustful, randy (*informal, chiefly Brit.*), raunchy (*slang*), sexual, sexy (*informal*), steamy (*informal*), unchaste **2.** animal, bodily, carnal, epicurean, fleshly, luxurious, physical, unspiritual, voluptuous

the body and senses rather than the mind or soul. **sensualist** *n*

sensuality *n* **1** the quality or state of being sensual. **2** enjoyment of physical, esp. sexual, pleasures.

sensuous *adj* **1** pleasing to the senses of the mind or body: *the sensuous rhythms of the drums.* **2** (of a person) appreciating qualities perceived by the senses. **sensuously** *adv*

sent *vb* the past of **send.**

sentence *n* **1** a sequence of words constituting a statement, question, or a command that begins with a capital letter and ends with a full stop when written down. **2 a** the decision of a law court as to what punishment is passed on a convicted person. **b** the punishment passed on a convicted person. *~vb* **-tencing, -tenced 3** to pronounce sentence on (a convicted person) in a lawcourt. **sentential** *adj*

sententious *adj Formal* **1** trying to sound wise. **2** making pompous remarks about morality. **sententiously** *adv*

sentient (**sen**-tee-ent, **sen**-shent) *adj* capable of perception and feeling. **sentience** *n*

sentiment *n* **1** a mental attitude based on a mixture of thoughts and feelings: *anti-American sentiment.* **2** (*often pl*) a thought, opinion, or attitude expressed in words: *his sentiments were echoed by subsequent speakers.* **3** feelings such as tenderness, romance, and sadness, esp. when exaggerated: *a man without the softness of sentiment.*

sentimental *adj* **1** feeling or expressing tenderness, romance, or sadness to an exaggerated extent. **2** appealing to the emotions, esp. to romantic feelings: *she kept the ring for sentimental reasons.* **sentimentalism** *n* **sentimentalist** *n* **sentimentality** *n* **sentimentally** *adv*

sentimentalize *or* **-ise** *vb* **-izing, -ized** *or* **-ising, -ised** to make sentimental or behave sentimentally.

sentimental value *n* the value of an article to a particular person because of the emotions it arouses.

sentinel *n Old-fashioned* a sentry.

sentry *n, pl* **-tries** a soldier who keeps watch and guards a camp or building.

sentry box *n* a small shelter with an open front in which a sentry stands during bad weather.

sepal *n Bot* a leaflike division of the calyx of a flower.

separable *adj* able to be separated.

separate *vb* **-rating, -rated 1** to act as a barrier between: *the narrow stretch of water which separates Europe from Asia.* **2** to part or be parted from a mass or group. **3** to distinguish: *it's what separates the women from the boys.* **4** to divide or be divided into component parts. **5** to sever or be severed. **6** (of a couple) to stop living together. *~adj* **7** existing or considered independently: *a separate issue.* **8** set apart from the main body or mass. **9** distinct or individual. **separately** *adv* **separateness** *n* **separator** *n*

separates *pl n* clothes, such as skirts, blouses, and trousers, that only cover part of the body and are designed to be worn together or separately.

separate school *n* (in certain Canadian provinces) a school for a large religious minority financed by provincial grants in addition to the education tax.

separation *n* **1** the act of separating: *the separation of child from mother.* **2** *Family law* the living apart of a married couple without divorce. **3** a mark, line, or object that separates one thing from another.

separatist *n* a person who advocates the separation of his or her own group from an organization or country. **separatism** *n*

sepia *adj* dark reddish-brown, like the colour of very old photographs.

sepoy *n* (formerly) an Indian soldier in the service of the British.

sepsis *n* poisoning caused by the presence of pus-forming bacteria in the body.

sept *n* a clan, esp. in Ireland or Scotland.

Sept. September.

September *n* the ninth month of the year.

septennial *adj* **1** occurring every seven years. **2** lasting seven years.

septet *n* **1** a group of seven performers. **2** a piece of music for seven performers.

septic *adj* of or caused by harmful bacteria. **septicity** *n*

THESAURUS

sensuality animalism, carnality, eroticism, lasciviousness, lecherousness, lewdness, libidinousness, licentiousness, prurience, salaciousness, sexiness (*informal*), voluptuousness

sensuous epicurean, gratifying, hedonistic, lush, pleasurable, rich, sensory, sumptuous, sybaritic

sentence 1. *n.* condemnation, decision, decree, doom, judgment, order, pronouncement, ruling, verdict **2.** *vb.* condemn, doom, mete out justice to, pass judgment on, penalize

sententious *formal* **1.** aphoristic, axiomatic, brief, compact, concise, epigrammatic, gnomic, laconic, pithy, pointed, short, succinct, terse **2.** canting, judgmental, moralistic, pompous, ponderous, preachifying (*informal*), sanctimonious

sentiment 1. emotion, sensibility, soft-heartedness, tender feeling, tenderness **2.** *often plural* attitude, belief, feeling, idea, judgment, opinion, persuasion, saying, thought, view, way of thinking **3.** emotionalism, mawkishness, overemotionalism, romanticism, sentimentality, slush (*informal*)

sentimental corny (*slang*), dewy-eyed, emotional, gushy (*informal*), impressionable, maudlin, mawkish, mushy (*informal*), nostalgic, overemotional, pathetic, romantic, schmaltzy (*slang*), simpering, sloppy (*informal*), slushy (*informal*), soft-hearted, tearful, tear-jerking (*informal*), tender, touching, weepy (*informal*)

sentimentality bathos, corniness (*slang*), emotionalism, gush (*informal*), mawkishness, mush (*informal*), nostalgia, play on the emotions, romanticism, schmaltz (*slang*), sloppiness (*informal*), slush (*informal*), sob stuff (*informal*), tenderness

separable detachable, distinguishable, divisible, scissile, severable

separate *vb.* **1.** discriminate between, isolate, put on one side, segregate, single out, sort out **2.** break off, cleave, come apart, come away, come between, detach, disconnect, disentangle, disjoin, divide, keep apart, remove, sever, split, sunder, uncouple **3.** bifurcate, break up, disunite, diverge, divorce, estrange, go different ways, part, part company, set at variance *or* at odds, split up *~adj.* **4.** detached, disconnected, discrete, disjointed, divided, divorced, isolated, unattached, unconnected **5.** alone, apart, autonomous, distinct, independent, individual, particular, single, solitary

separated apart, broken up, disassociated, disconnected, disunited, divided, living apart, parted, put asunder, separate, split up, sundered

separately alone, apart, independently, individually, one at a time, one by one, personally, severally, singly

separation 1. break, detachment, disconnection, disengagement, disjunction, dissociation, disunion, division, gap, segregation, severance **2.** break-up, di-

septicaemia *or* **septicemia** (sep-tis-**see**-mee-a) *n* an infection of the blood which develops in a wound.

septic tank *n* a tank in which sewage is decomposed by the action of bacteria.

septuagenarian *n* **1** a person who is between 70 and 79 years old. ~*adj* **2** between 70 and 79 years old.

Septuagint (**sept**-yew-a-jint) *n* the ancient Greek version of the Old Testament, including the Apocrypha.

septum *n, pl* **-ta** *Biol, anat* a dividing partition between two tissues or cavities, such as in the nose.

septuple *vb* **-pling, -pled 1** to multiply by seven. ~*adj* **2** seven times as much or as many. **3** consisting of seven parts. ~*n* **4** a quantity or number seven times as great as another.

sepulchral (sip-**pulk**-ral) *adj* **1** gloomy and solemn, like a tomb or grave. **2** of a sepulchre.

sepulchre *or US* **sepulcher** (**sep**-pulk-er) *n* **1** a burial vault, tomb, or grave. ~*vb* **-chring, -chred** *or* **-chering, -chered 2** to bury in a sepulchre.

sepulture (**sep**-pult-cher) *n* the act of placing in a sepulchre.

sequel *n* **1** a novel, play, or film that continues the story of an earlier one. **2** anything that happens after or as a result of something else: *there was an amusing sequel to this incident.*

sequence *n* **1** an arrangement of two or more things in a successive order. **2** the successive order of two or more things: *chronological sequence.* **3** an action or event that follows another or others. **4** *Maths* an ordered set of numbers or other quantities in one-to-one correspondence with the integers 1 to *n*. **5** a section of a film forming a single uninterrupted episode.

sequential *adj* happening in a fixed order or sequence.

sequester *vb* **1** to seclude: *he could sequester himself in his own home.* **2** *Law* same as **sequestrate.**

sequestrate *vb* **-trating, -trated** *Law* to confiscate (property) temporarily until creditors are satisfied or a court order is complied with. **sequestration** *n* **sequestrator** *n*

sequin *n* a small piece of shiny metal foil used to decorate clothes. **sequined** *adj*

sequoia *n* a giant Californian coniferous tree.

seraglio (sir-**ah**-lee-oh) *n, pl* **-raglios 1** the part of a Muslim house or palace where the owner's wives live. **2** a Turkish sultan's palace.

seraph *n, pl* **-aphim** *Theol* a member of the highest order of angels. **seraphic** *adj*

Serb *adj, n* same as **Serbian.**

Serbian *adj* **1** of Serbia. ~*n* **2** a person from Serbia. **3** the dialect of Serbo-Croatian spoken in Serbia.

Serbo-Croatian *or* **Serbo-Croat** *n* **1** the chief official language of Serbia and Croatia. ~*adj* **2** of this language.

serenade *n* **1** a piece of music played or sung to a woman by a lover. **2** a piece of music suitable for this. **3** an orchestral suite for a small ensemble. ~*vb* **-nading, -naded 4** to sing or play a serenade to (someone).

serendipity *n* the gift of making fortunate discoveries by accident.

serene *adj* **1** peaceful or calm. **2** (of the sky) clear or bright. **serenely** *adv* **serenity** *n*

serf *n* (esp. in medieval Europe) a labourer who could not leave the land on which he worked. **serfdom** *n*

serge *n* a strong fabric made of wool, cotton, silk, or rayon, used for clothing.

sergeant *n* **1** a noncommissioned officer in the armed forces. **2** (in Britain) a police officer ranking between constable and inspector.

sergeant at arms *n* a parliamentary or court officer responsible for keeping order.

sergeant major *n* a noncommissioned officer of the highest rank in the army.

serial *n* **1** a story published or broadcast in instalments at regular intervals. **2** a publication that is regularly issued and consecutively numbered. ~*adj* **3** of, in, or forming a series. **4** published or presented as a serial.

serialize *or* **-ise** *vb* **-izing, -ized** *or* **-ising, -ised** to publish or present in the form of a serial. **serialization** *or* **-isation** *n*

serial killer *n* a person who commits a number of murders.

serial number *n* any of the consecutive numbers given to objects in a series for identification.

series *n, pl* **-ries 1** a group or succession of related things. **2** a set of radio or television programmes dealing with the same subject, esp. one having the same characters but different stories. **3** *Maths* the sum of a finite or infinite sequence of numbers or quantities. **4** *Electronics* an arrangement of two or more components connected in a circuit so that the same current flows in turn through each of them: *a number of resistors in series.* **5** *Geol* a set of layers that represent the rocks formed during an epoch.

seriocomic (seer-ee-oh-**kom**-ik) *adj* mixing serious and comic elements.

serious *adj* **1** giving cause for concern: *the situation is serious.* **2** concerned with important matters: *there are some serious questions that need to be answered.* **3** not cheerful; grave: *I am a serious person.* **4** in earnest; sincere: *he believes we are serious.* **5** requiring

THESAURUS

vorce, estrangement, farewell, leave-taking, parting, rift, split, split-up

septic festering, infected, poisoned, pussy, putrefactive, putrefying, putrid, suppurating, toxic

sepulchre burial place, grave, mausoleum, sarcophagus, tomb, vault

sequel conclusion, consequence, continuation, development, end, follow-up, issue, outcome, payoff (*informal*), result, upshot

sequence arrangement, chain, course, cycle, order, procession, progression, series, succession

seraphic angelic, beatific, blissful, celestial, divine, heavenly, holy, pure, sublime

serene 1. calm, composed, imperturbable, peaceful, placid, sedate, tranquil, undisturbed, unruffled, untroubled **2.** bright, clear, cloudless, fair, halcyon, unclouded

serenity 1. calm, calmness, composure, peace, peacefulness, peace of mind, placidity, quietness, quietude, stillness, tranquillity **2.** brightness, clearness, fairness

series arrangement, chain, course, line, order, progression, run, sequence, set, string, succession, train

serious 1. acute, alarming, critical, dangerous, grave, severe **2.** crucial, deep, difficult, far-reaching, fateful, grim, important, momentous, no laughing matter, of moment *or* consequence, pressing, significant, urgent, weighty, worrying **3.** grave, humourless, long-faced, pensive, sedate, sober, solemn, stern, thoughtful, unsmiling **4.** deliberate, determined, earnest, genuine, honest, in earnest, resolute, resolved, sincere

seriously 1. acutely, badly, critically, dangerously, distressingly, gravely, grievously, severely, sorely **2.** all joking aside, earnestly, gravely, in all conscience, in

concentration: *a serious book.* **6** *Informal* impressive because of its substantial quantity or quality: *serious money.* **seriously** *adv* **seriousness** *n*

serjeant *n* same as **sergeant.**

sermon *n* **1** a speech on a religious or moral subject given by a clergyman as part of a church service. **2** *Disparaging* a serious talk on behaviour, morals, or duty, esp. a long and tedious one.

seropositive (seer-oh-**poz**-zit-iv) *adj* (of a person whose blood has been tested for a specific disease, such as AIDS) showing a significant level of serum antibodies, indicating the presence of the disease.

serous (**seer**-uss) *adj* of, containing, or like serum.

serpent *n* **1** *Literary* a snake. **2** a devious person.

serpentine[1] *adj* twisting like a snake.

serpentine[2] *n* a soft green or brownish-red mineral.

serrated *adj* having a notched or sawlike edge. **serration** *n*

serried *adj Literary* in close formation: *the serried ranks of fans.*

serum (**seer**-um) *n* **1** the yellowish watery fluid left after blood has clotted. **2** this fluid from the blood of immunized animals used for inoculation or vaccination. **3** *Physiol, zool* any clear watery animal fluid.

serval *n* a slender African wild cat with black-spotted tawny fur.

servant *n* **1** a person employed to do household work for another person. **2** a person or thing that is useful or provides a service: *a distinguished servant of this country.*

serve *vb* **serving, served 1** to be of service to (a person, community, or cause); help. **2** to perform an official duty or duties: *he served on several university committees.* **3** to attend to (customers) in a shop. **4** to provide (guests) with food or drink: *he served dinner guests German wine.* **5** to provide (food or drink) for customers: *breakfast is served from 7 a.m.* **6** to provide with something needed by the public: *the community served by the school.* **7** to work as a servant for (a person). **8** to go through (a period of police or military service, apprenticeship, or imprisonment). **9** to meet the needs of: *they serve a purpose.* **10** to perform a function: *the attacks only served to strengthen their resolve.* **11** (of a male animal) to mate with (a female animal). **12** *Tennis, squash, etc* to put (the ball) into play. **13** to deliver (a legal document) to (a person). **14 serve someone right** *Informal* to be what someone deserves, esp. for doing something stupid or wrong. *~n* **15** *Tennis, squash, etc* short for **service** (sense 12). **server** *n*

service *n* **1** an act of help or assistance. **2** an organization or system that provides something needed by the public: *a consumer information service.* **3** a department of public employment and its employees: *the diplomatic service.* **4** the installation or maintenance of goods provided by a dealer after a sale. **5** availability for use by the public: *the new plane could be in service within fifteen years.* **6** a regular check made on a machine or vehicle in which parts are tested, cleaned, or replaced if worn. **7** the serving of guests or customers: *service is included on the wine list.* **8** one of the branches of the armed forces. **9** the serving of food: *silver service.* **10** a set of dishes, cups, and plates for use at table. **11** a formal religious ceremony. **12** *Tennis, squash, etc* **a** the act, manner, or right of serving the ball. **b** the game in which a particular player serves: *she dropped only one point on her service.* *~adj* **13** of or for the use of servants or employees: *a service elevator.* **14** serving the public rather than producing goods: *service industries.* *~vb* **-vicing, -viced 15** to provide service or services to. **16** to check and repair (a vehicle or machine). **17** (of a male animal) to mate with (a female animal). ~See also **services.**

serviceable *adj* **1** performing effectively: *serviceable boots.* **2** able or ready to be used: *five remaining serviceable aircraft.* **serviceability** *n*

service area *n* a place on a motorway with a garage, restaurants, and toilets.

service car *n NZ* a bus operating on a long-distance route.

service charge *n* a percentage added to a bill in a hotel or restaurant to pay for service.

service flat *n* a flat where domestic services are provided by the management.

serviceman *n, pl* **-men 1** a person in the armed services. **2** a man employed to service and maintain equipment. **servicewoman** *fem n*

service road *n Brit* a narrow road running parallel to a main road that provides access to houses and shops situated along its length.

services *pl n* **1** work performed in a job: *the OBE for her services to the community.* **2 the services** the armed forces. **3** a system of providing the public with something it needs, such as gas or water.

service station *n* **1** a place that sells fuel, oil, and spare parts for motor vehicles. **2** same as **service area.**

serviette *n Chiefly Brit* a table napkin.

servile *adj* **1** too eager to obey people; fawning. **2** of or suitable for a slave. **servility** *n*

serving *n* a portion of food.

servitor *n Archaic* a servant or attendant.

servitude *n Formal* **1** slavery or bondage. **2** the state or condition of being completely dominated.

servomechanism *n* a device which converts a small force into a larger force, used esp. in steering mechanisms.

sesame (**sess**-am-ee) *n* a plant of the East Indies, grown for its seeds and oil, which are used in cooking.

THESAURUS

earnest, no joking (*informal*), sincerely, solemnly, thoughtfully, with a straight face

seriousness 1. danger, gravity, importance, moment, significance, urgency, weight **2.** earnestness, gravitas, gravity, humourlessness, sedateness, sobriety, solemnity, staidness, sternness

sermon 1. address, exhortation, homily **2.** *disparaging* dressing-down (*informal*), harangue, lecture, talking-to (*informal*)

servant attendant, domestic, drudge, help, helper, lackey, maid, menial, retainer, servitor (*archaic*), skivvy (*chiefly Brit.*), slave, varlet (*old-fashioned*), vassal

serve 1. aid, assist, attend to, be in the service of, be of assistance, be of use, help, minister to, oblige, succour, wait on, work for **2.** act, attend, complete, discharge, do, fulfil, go through, observe, officiate, pass, perform **3.** arrange, deal, deliver, dish up, distribute, handle, present, provide, purvey, set out, supply **4.** answer, answer the purpose, be acceptable, be adequate, be good enough, content, do, do duty as, do the work of, fill the bill (*informal*), function as, satisfy, suffice, suit

service *n.* **1.** advantage, assistance, avail, benefit, help, ministrations, supply, use, usefulness, utility **2.** business, duty, employ, employment, labour, office, work **3.** check, maintenance, overhaul, servicing **4.** ceremony, function, observance, rite, worship *~vb.* **5.** check, fine-tune, go over, maintain, overhaul, recondition, repair, tune (up)

serviceable advantageous, beneficial, convenient,

sessile *adj* **1** (of flowers or leaves) having no stalk. **2** (of animals such as the barnacle) fixed in one position.

session *n* **1** any period devoted to a particular activity. **2** a meeting of a court, parliament, or council. **3** a series or period of such meetings. **4** a school or university term or year. **sessional** *adj*

sestet *n* **1** *Prosody* the last six lines of a sonnet. **2** same as **sextet** (sense 1).

set[1] *vb* **setting, set 1** to put in a specified position or state: *I set him free.* **2 set to** *or* **on** to bring (something) into contact with (something else): *three prisoners set fire to their cells.* **3** to put into order or make ready: *set the table.* **4** to make or become firm or rigid: *before the eggs begin to set.* **5** to put (a broken bone) or (of a broken bone) to be put into a normal position for healing. **6** to adjust (a clock or other instrument) to a particular position. **7** to arrange or establish: *to set a date for diplomatic talks; it set the standards of performance.* **8** to prescribe or assign (a task or material for study): *the examiners have set 'Paradise Lost'.* **9** to arrange (hair) while wet, so that it dries in position. **10** to place a jewel in (a setting): *a ring set with diamonds.* **11** to provide music for (a poem or other text to be sung). **12** *Printing* **a** to arrange (type) for printing. **b** to put (text) into type. **13** to arrange (a stage or television studio) with scenery and props. **14 set to** *or* **on** to value (something) at a specified price or worth: *he set a high price on his services.* **15** (of the sun or moon) to disappear beneath the horizon. **16** (of plants) to produce (fruits or seeds) or (of fruits or seeds) to develop. **17** to place (a hen) on (eggs) to incubate them. **18** (of a gun dog) to turn in the direction of game birds. *~n* **19** the act of setting. **20** a condition of firmness or hardness. **21** manner of standing; posture: *the set of his shoulders.* **22** the scenery and other props used in a play or film. **23** same as **sett**. *~adj* **24** fixed or established by authority or agreement: *set hours of work.* **25** rigid or inflexible: *she is set in her ways.* **26** unmoving; fixed: *a set expression on his face.* **27** conventional or stereotyped: *she made her apology in set phrases.* **28 set in** (of a scene or story) represented as happening at a certain time or place: *a European film set in Africa.* **29 set on** *or* **upon** determined to (do or achieve something): *why are you so set upon avoiding me?* **30** ready: *all set to go.* **31** (of material for study) prescribed for students' preparation for an examination. ~See also **set about, set against**, etc.

set[2] *n* **1** a number of objects or people grouped or belonging together: *a set of slides.* **2** a group of people who associate with each other or have similar interests: *the tennis set.* **3** *Maths* a collection of numbers or objects that satisfy a given condition or share a property. **4** a television or piece of radio equipment. **5** *Sport* a group of games or points in a match, of which the winner must win a certain number. **6** a series of songs or tunes performed by a musician or group on a given occasion: *the front row spent the rest of the set craning their necks.*

set about *vb* **1** to start or begin. **2** to attack.

set against *vb* **1** to balance or compare. **2** to cause to be unfriendly to: *the war set brother against brother.*

set aside *vb* **1** to reserve for a special purpose. **2** to discard or reject.

set back *vb* **1** to delay or hinder. **2** *Informal* to cost (a person) a specified amount. *~n* **setback 3** anything that delays progress.

set down *vb* **1** to record in writing. **2** *Brit* to allow (passengers) to get off a bus etc.

set forth *vb Formal or archaic* **1** to state or present (an argument or facts). **2** to start out on a journey.

set in *vb* **1** to begin and continue for some time: *decadence has set in.* **2** to insert.

set off *vb* **1** to start a journey. **2** to cause (a person) to act or do something, such as laugh. **3** to cause to explode. **4** to act as a contrast to: *blue suits you, sets off the colour of your hair.*

set on *or* **upon** *vb* to attack or cause to attack: *they set the dogs on him.*

set out *vb* **1** to present, arrange, or display. **2** to give a full account of: *the policy was set out in an interview*

THESAURUS

dependable, durable, efficient, functional, hardwearing, helpful, operative, practical, profitable, usable, useful, utilitarian

session assembly, conference, congress, discussion, get-together (*informal*), hearing, meeting, period, seminar, sitting, term

set[1] *vb.* **1.** aim, apply, deposit, direct, embed, fasten, fix, install, lay, locate, lodge, mount, park (*informal*), place, plant, plonk, plump, position, put, rest, seat, situate, station, stick, turn **2.** arrange, lay, make ready, prepare, spread **3.** cake, condense, congeal, crystallize, gel, gelatinize, harden, solidify, stiffen, thicken **4.** adjust, coordinate, rectify, regulate, synchronize **5.** agree upon, allocate, appoint, arrange, assign, conclude, decide (upon), designate, determine, establish, fix, fix up, name, ordain, regulate, resolve, schedule, settle, specify **6.** decline, dip, disappear, go down, sink, subside, vanish *~n.* **7.** attitude, bearing, carriage, fit, hang, position, posture, turn **8.** *mise en scène*, scene, scenery, setting, stage set, stage setting *~adj.* **9.** agreed, appointed, arranged, customary, decided, definite, established, firm, fixed, prearranged, predetermined, prescribed, regular, scheduled, settled, usual **10.** entrenched, firm, hard and fast, hardened, hidebound, immovable, inflexible, rigid, strict, stubborn **11.** artificial, conventional, formal, hackneyed, rehearsed, routine, standard, stereotyped, stock, traditional, unspontaneous **12.** *with* **on** *or* **upon** bent, determined, intent, resolute

set[2] *n.* **1.** assemblage, assortment, batch, collection, compendium, coordinated group, kit, outfit, series **2.** band, circle, class, clique, company, coterie, crew (*informal*), crowd, faction, gang, group, outfit, posse (*informal*), schism, sect

set about 1. address oneself to, attack, begin, get cracking (*informal*), get down to, get to work, get weaving (*informal*), make a start on, put one's shoulder to the wheel (*informal*), roll up one's sleeves, sail into (*informal*), set to, start, tackle, take the first step, wade into **2.** assail, assault, attack, belabour, lambast(e), mug (*informal*), sail into (*informal*)

set aside 1. keep, keep back, put on one side, reserve, save, select, separate, set apart, single out **2.** abrogate, annul, cancel, discard, dismiss, nullify, overrule, overturn, quash, reject, render null and void, repudiate, reverse

setback bit of trouble, blow, check, defeat, disappointment, hitch, hold-up, misfortune, rebuff, reverse, upset

set off 1. depart, embark, leave, sally forth, set out, start out **2.** detonate, explode, ignite, kick-start, light, set in motion, touch off, trigger off **3.** bring out the highlights in, enhance, show off

set on *or* **upon** assail, assault, attack, fall upon, fly at, go for, incite, instigate, let fly at, pitch into (*informal*), pounce on, sail into (*informal*), set about, sic, spur on, urge

set out 1. arrange, array, describe, detail, display, dispose, elaborate, elucidate, exhibit, explain, expose

with the BBC. **3** to begin or embark on an undertaking, esp. a journey.

set piece *n* **1** a work of literature, music, or art, intended to create an impressive effect. **2** *Football, hockey, etc* an attacking move from a corner or free kick.

set square *n* a thin flat piece of plastic or metal in the shape of a right-angled triangle, used in technical drawing.

sett *or* **set** *n* **1** a badger's burrow. **2** a small rectangular paving block made of stone.

settee *n* a seat, for two or more people, with a back and usually with arms; couch.

setter *n* a large long-haired dog originally bred for hunting.

set theory *n Maths* the branch of mathematics concerned with the properties and interrelationships of sets.

setting *n* **1** the surroundings in which something is set. **2** the scenery, properties, or background used to create the location for a stage play or film. **3** a piece of music written for the words of a text. **4** the decorative metalwork in which a gem is set. **5** the plates and cutlery for a single place at a table. **6** one of the positions or levels to which the controls of a machine can be adjusted.

settle[1] *vb* **-tling, -tled 1** to put in order: *he settled his affairs before he died.* **2** to arrange or be arranged firmly or comfortably: *he settled into his own chair by the fire.* **3** to come down to rest: *a bird settled on top of the hedge.* **4** to establish or become established as a resident: *they eventually settled in Glasgow.* **5** to establish or become established in a way of life or a job. **6** to migrate to (a country) and form a community; colonize. **7** to make or become quiet, calm, or stable. **8** to cause (sediment) to sink to the bottom in a liquid or (of sediment) to sink thus. **9** to subside: *the dust settled.* **10** (sometimes foll. by *up*) to pay off (a bill or debt). **11** to decide or dispose of: *to settle an argument.* **12** (often foll. by *on* or *upon*) to agree or fix: *they settled on an elementary code.* **13** (usually foll. by *on* or *upon*) to give (a title or property) to a person by gift or legal deed: *he settled his property on his wife.* **14** to decide (a legal dispute) by agreement without court action: *they settled out of court.*

settle[2] *n* a long wooden bench with a high back and arms, sometimes having a storage space under the seat.

settle down *vb* **1** to make or become quiet and orderly. **2 settle down to** to remove all distractions and concentrate on: *we settled down to a favourite movie.* **3** to adopt an orderly and routine way of life, esp. after marriage.

settle for *vb* to accept or agree to in spite of dissatisfaction.

settlement *n* **1** an act of settling. **2** a place newly settled; colony. **3** subsidence of all or part of a building. **4** an official agreement ending a dispute. **5** *Law* **a** an arrangement by which property is transferred to a person's possession. **b** the deed transferring such property.

settler *n* a person who settles in a new country or a colony.

set to *vb* **1** to begin working. **2** to start fighting. *~n* **set-to 3** *Informal* a brief disagreement or fight.

set up *vb* **1** to build or construct: *the soldiers had actually set up a munitions factory.* **2** to put into a position of power or wealth. **3** to begin or enable (someone) to begin (a new venture): *he set up a small shop.* **4** to begin or produce: *to set up a nuclear chain reaction.* **5** to establish: *Broad set up a world record.* **6** *Informal* to cause (a person) to be blamed or accused. **7** to restore the health of: *a pub lunch set me up nicely.* *~n* **setup 8** *Informal* the way in which anything is organized or arranged. **9** *Slang* an event the result of which is prearranged.

seven *n* **1** the cardinal number that is the sum of one and six. **2** a numeral, 7 or VII, representing this number. **3** something representing or consisting of seven units. *~adj* **4** amounting to seven: *seven weeks.* **seventh** *adj, n*

sevenfold *adj* **1** having seven times as many or as much. **2** composed of seven parts. *~adv* **3** by seven times as many or as much.

seven seas *pl n Old-fashioned* all the oceans of the world.

seventeen *n* **1** the cardinal number that is the sum of ten and seven. **2** a numeral, 17 or XVII, representing this number. **3** something representing or consisting of seventeen units. *~adj* **4** amounting to seventeen: *seventeen children.* **seventeenth** *adj, n*

seventh heaven *n* a state of supreme happiness.

seventy *n, pl* **-ties 1** the cardinal number that is the product of ten and seven. **2** a numeral, 70 or LXX, representing this number. **3** something representing or consisting of seventy units. *~adj* **4** amounting to seventy: *seventy countries.* **seventieth** *adj, n*

sever *vb* **1** to cut right through or cut off (something): *it accidentally severed the electrical cable.* **2** to break off (a tie or relationship). **severable** *adj* **severance** *n*

several *adj* **1** more than a few: *I spoke to several doc-*

THESAURUS

to view, lay out, present, set forth **2.** begin, embark, get under way, hit the road (*slang*), sally forth, set off, start out, take to the road

setting backdrop, background, context, frame, locale, location, *mise en scène,* mounting, perspective, scene, scenery, set, site, surround, surroundings

settle 1. adjust, dispose, order, put into order, regulate, set to rights, straighten out, work out **2.** alight, bed down, come to rest, descend, land, light, make oneself comfortable **3.** dwell, inhabit, live, make one's home, move to, put down roots, reside, set up home, take up residence **4.** colonize, found, people, pioneer, plant, populate **5.** allay, calm, compose, lull, pacify, quell, quiet, quieten, reassure, relax, relieve, sedate, soothe, tranquillize **6.** decline, fall, sink, subside **7.** choose, clear up, complete, conclude, decide, dispose of, put an end to, reconcile, resolve **8.** acquit oneself of, clear, discharge, liquidate, pay, quit, square (up) **9.** *often with* **on** *or* **upon** agree, appoint, arrange, choose, come to an agreement, confirm, decide, determine, establish, fix

settlement 1. adjustment, agreement, arrangement, completion, conclusion, confirmation, disposition, establishment, resolution, termination, working out **2.** colonization, colony, community, encampment, hamlet, outpost, peopling **3.** clearance, clearing, defrayal, discharge, liquidation, payment, satisfaction

settler colonist, colonizer, frontiersman, immigrant, pioneer, planter

set-to *informal* argument, argy-bargy (*Brit. informal*), barney (*informal*), brush, disagreement, dust-up (*informal*), fight, fracas, quarrel, row, scrap (*informal*), slanging match (*Brit.*), spat, squabble, wrangle

set up 1. assemble, build, construct, elevate, erect, put together, put up, raise **2.** back, build up, establish, finance, promote, put some beef into (*informal*), strengthen, subsidize **3.** arrange, begin, compose, establish, found, initiate, install, institute, make provision for, organize, prearrange, prepare

tors. **2** *Formal* various or separate: *the members with their several occupations.* **3** *Formal* distinct or different: *misfortune visited her three several times.*

severally *adv Formal* individually or separately: *the Western nations severally rather than jointly decided that they would have to act without Russia.*

severance pay *n* compensation paid by a firm to an employee who has to leave because the job he or she was appointed to do no longer exists.

severe *adj* **1** strict or harsh in the treatment of others: *a severe parent.* **2** serious in appearance or manner: *a severe look; a severe hairdo.* **3** very intense or unpleasant: *severe chest pains; the punishments are severe.* **4** causing discomfort by its harshness: *severe frost.* **5** hard to perform or accomplish: *a severe challenge.* **severely** *adv* **severity** *n*

Seville orange *n* a bitter orange used to make marmalade.

Sèvres (sev-ra) *n* a kind of fine French porcelain.

sew *vb* **sewing, sewed; sewn** *or* **sewed 1** to join with thread repeatedly passed through with a needle. **2** to attach, fasten, or close by sewing. ~See also **sew up.**

sewage *n* waste matter or excrement carried away in sewers or drains.

sewage farm *n* a place where sewage is treated so that it can be used as manure or disposed of safely.

sewer *n* a drain or pipe, usually underground, used to carry away surface water or sewage.

sewerage *n* **1** a system of sewers. **2** the removal of surface water or sewage by means of sewers.

sewing *n* a piece of fabric or an article, that is sewn or to be sewn.

sewing machine *n* a machine that sews material with a needle driven by an electric motor.

sewn *vb* a past participle of **sew.**

sew up *vb* **1** to fasten or mend completely by sewing. **2** *Informal* to complete or negotiate successfully: *the deal was sewn up just before the deadline.*

sex *n* **1** the state of being either male or female. **2** either of the two categories, male or female, into which organisms are divided. **3** sexual intercourse. **4** feelings or behaviour connected with having sex or the desire to have sex. **5** sexual matters in general. ~*adj* **6** of sexual matters: *sex education.* **7** based on or resulting from the difference between the sexes: *sex discrimination.* ~*vb* **8** to find out the sex of (an animal).

sexagenarian *n* **1** a person who is between 60 and 69 years old. ~*adj* **2** between 60 and 69 years old.

sex appeal *n* sexual attractiveness.

sex chromosome *n* either of the chromosomes that determine the sex of an animal.

sexism *n* discrimination against the members of one sex, usually women. **sexist** *n, adj*

sexless *adj* **1** neither male nor female. **2** having no sexual desires. **3** sexually unattractive.

sex object *n* someone, esp. a woman, regarded only in terms of physical attractiveness and not as a person.

sexology *n* the study of sexual behaviour in human beings. **sexologist** *n*

sextant *n* an instrument used in navigation for measuring angular distance, for example between the sun and the horizon, to calculate the position of a ship or aircraft.

sextet *n* **1** a group of six performers. **2** a piece of music for six performers. **3** a group of six people or things.

sexton *n* a man employed to look after a church and its churchyard.

sextuple *vb* **-pling, -pled 1** to multiply by six. ~*adj* **2** six times as much or as many. **3** consisting of six parts. ~*n* **4** a quantity or number six times as great as another.

sextuplet *n* one of six children born at one birth.

sexual *adj* **1** of or characterized by sex. **2** (of reproduction) characterized by the union of male and female reproductive cells. **3** of or relating to the differences between males and females. **sexuality** *n* **sexually** *adv*

sexual harassment *n* the unwelcome directing of sexual remarks, looks, or advances, usually at a woman in the workplace.

sexual intercourse *n* the sexual act in which the male's erect penis is inserted into the female's vagina, usually followed by the ejaculation of semen.

sexy *adj* **sexier, sexiest** *Informal* **1** sexually exciting or attractive: *a sexy voice.* **2** interesting, exciting, or trendy: *a sexy project; a sexy new car.* **sexiness** *n*

SF *or* **sf** science fiction.

SFA Scottish Football Association.

S. Glam South Glamorgan.

Sgt. Sergeant.

sh *interj* be quiet!

THESAURUS

setup arrangement, circumstances, conditions, organization, regime, structure, system

several *adj.* assorted, different, disparate, distinct, diverse, indefinite, individual, manifold, many, particular, respective, single, some, sundry, various

severe 1. austere, cruel, Draconian, drastic, hard, harsh, inexorable, iron-handed, oppressive, pitiless, relentless, rigid, strict, unbending, unrelenting **2.** cold, disapproving, dour, flinty, forbidding, grave, grim, serious, sober, stern, strait-laced, tight-lipped, unsmiling **3.** acute, bitter, critical, dangerous, distressing, extreme, fierce, grinding, inclement, intense, violent **4.** arduous, demanding, difficult, exacting, fierce, hard, punishing, rigorous, stringent, taxing, tough, unrelenting

severely 1. harshly, rigorously, sharply, sternly, strictly, with an iron hand, with a rod of iron **2.** acutely, badly, critically, dangerously, extremely, gravely, hard, sorely

severity austerity, gravity, hardness, harshness, plainness, rigour, seriousness, severeness, sternness, strictness, stringency, toughness

sex 1. gender **2.** coition, coitus, copulation, fornication, going to bed (with someone), intimacy, lovemaking, (sexual) intercourse, sexual relations **3.** desire, facts of life, libido, reproduction, sexuality, the birds and the bees (*informal*)

sexual 1. carnal, coital, erotic, intimate, of the flesh, sensual, sexy (*informal*) **2.** genital, procreative, reproductive, sex, venereal

sexual intercourse bonking (*informal*), carnal knowledge, coition, coitus, congress, consummation, copulation, coupling, fucking (*taboo*), mating, penetration, screwing (*taboo*), shagging (*taboo*), union

sexuality bodily appetites, carnality, desire, eroticism, lust, sensuality, sexiness (*informal*), virility, voluptuousness

sexy *informal* arousing, bedroom, cuddly, erotic, flirtatious, inviting, kissable, naughty, provocative, provoking, seductive, sensual, sensuous, slinky, suggestive, titillating, voluptuous

shabby 1. dilapidated, down at heel, faded, frayed, having seen better days, mean, neglected, poor, ragged, run-down, scruffy, seedy, tattered, tatty, the worse for wear, threadbare, worn, worn-out **2.** cheap, contemptible, despicable, dirty, dishonourable, igno-

shabby *adj* **-bier, -biest 1** old and worn in appearance. **2** wearing worn and dirty clothes. **3** behaving in a mean or unfair way: *shabby manoeuvres.* **shabbily** *adv* **shabbiness** *n*

shack *n* **1** a roughly built hut. *~vb* **2 shack up with** *Slang* to live with (a lover).

shackle *n* **1** one of a pair of metal rings joined by a chain for securing someone's wrists or ankles. **2 shackles** anything that confines or restricts freedom: *free from the shackles of its feudal past.* **3** a metal loop or link closed by a bolt, used for securing ropes or chains. *~vb* **-ling, -led 4** to fasten with shackles. **5** to restrict or hamper: *an economy shackled by central control.*

shad *n, pl* **shad** *or* **shads** a herring-like food fish.

shade *n* **1** relative darkness produced by blocking out sunlight. **2** a place sheltered from the sun by trees, buildings, etc. **3** something used to provide a shield or protection from a direct source of light, such as a lamp shade. **4** a shaded area in a painting or drawing. **5** any of the different hues of a colour: *a much darker shade of grey.* **6** a slight amount: *a shade of reluctance.* **7 put someone** *or* **something in the shade** to be so impressive as to make another person or thing seem unimportant by comparison. **8** *Literary* a ghost. *~vb* **shading, shaded 9** to screen or protect from heat or light. **10** to make darker or dimmer. **11** to represent (a darker area) in (a painting or drawing), by graded areas of tone, lines, or dots. **12** to change slightly or by degrees.

shades *pl n* **1** *Slang* sunglasses. **2 shades of** a reminder of: *shades of Margaret Thatcher.*

shading *n* the graded areas of tone, lines, or dots, indicating light and dark in a painting or drawing.

shadow *n* **1** a dark image or shape cast on a surface when something stands between a light and the surface. **2** a patch of shade. **3** the dark portions of a picture. **4** a hint or faint trace: *a shadow of a doubt.* **5** a person less powerful or vigorous than his or her former self. **6** a threatening influence: *news of the murder cast a shadow over the village.* **7** a person who always accompanies another. **8** a person who trails another in secret, such as a detective. *~adj* **9** *Brit* designating a member or members of the main opposition party in Parliament who would hold ministerial office if their party were in power: *the shadow chancellor.* *~vb* **10** to cast a shade or shadow over. **11** to make dark or gloomy. **12** to follow or trail secretly.

shadow-box *vb Boxing* to box against an imaginary opponent for practice. **shadow-boxing** *n*

shadowy *adj* **1** (of a place) full of shadows; shady. **2** faint or dark like a shadow: *a shadowy figure.* **3** mysterious or not well known: *the shadowy world of espionage.*

shady *adj* **shadier, shadiest 1** full of shade; shaded. **2** giving or casting shade. **3** *Informal* of doubtful honesty or legality: *shady business dealings.* **shadiness** *n*

shaft *n* **1 a** a spear or arrow. **b** its long narrow stem. **2 shaft of wit** *or* **humour** a clever or amusing remark. **3** a ray or streak of light. **4** the long straight narrow handle of a tool or golf club. **5** a revolving rod in a machine that transmits motion or power. **6** one of the bars between which an animal is harnessed to a vehicle. **7** *Archit* the middle part of a column or pier, between the base and the capital. **8** a vertical passageway through a building for a lift. **9** a vertical passageway into a mine.

shag[1] *n* **1** coarse shredded tobacco. **2** a matted tangle of hair or wool. *~adj* **3** (of a carpet) having long thick woollen threads.

shag[2] *n* a kind of cormorant.

shag[3] *vb* **shagging, shagged** *Brit slang* **1** *Taboo* to have sexual intercourse with (a person). **2 shagged out** exhausted.

shaggy *adj* **-gier, -giest 1** having or covered with rough unkempt fur, hair, or wool: *shaggy cattle.* **2** rough and untidy. **shagginess** *n*

shagreen *n* **1** the skin of a shark, used as an abrasive. **2** a rough grainy leather made from certain animal hides.

shah *n* a ruler of certain Middle Eastern countries, esp. (formerly) Iran.

shake *vb* **shaking, shook, shaken 1** to move up and down or back and forth with short quick movements. **2** to be or make unsteady. **3** (of a voice) to tremble because of anger or nervousness. **4** to clasp or grasp (the hand) of (a person) in greeting or agreement: *they shook hands.* **5 shake on it** *Informal* to shake hands in agreement or reconciliation. **6** to wave vigorously and angrily: *he shook his fist.* **7** (often foll. by *up*) to frighten or unsettle. **8** to shock, disturb, or upset: *he was badly shaken but unharmed.* **9** to undermine or weaken: *a team whose morale had been badly shaken.* **10** *US & Canad informal* to get rid of. **11** *Music* to perform a trill on (a note). **12 shake one's head** to indicate disagreement or disapproval by moving the head from side to side. *~n* **13** the act or an instance of shaking. **14** a tremor or vibration. **15 the shakes** *Informal* a state of uncontrollable trembling. **16** *Informal* a very

THESAURUS

ble, low, low-down (*informal*), mean, rotten (*informal*), scurvy, shameful, shoddy, ungentlemanly, unworthy

shade *n.* **1.** coolness, dimness, dusk, gloom, gloominess, obscurity, screen, semidarkness, shadiness, shadow, shadows **2.** blind, canopy, cover, covering, curtain, screen, shield, veil **3.** colour, hue, stain, tinge, tint, tone **4.** amount, dash, degree, difference, gradation, hint, nuance, semblance, suggestion, suspicion, trace, variety **5. put someone** *or* **something in the shade** eclipse, make pale by comparison, outclass, outshine, overshadow **6.** *literary* apparition, eidolon, ghost, manes, phantom, shadow, spectre, spirit *~vb.* **7.** cast a shadow over, cloud, conceal, cover, darken, dim, hide, mute, obscure, protect, screen, shadow, shield, shut out the light, veil

shadow *n.* **1.** cover, darkness, dimness, dusk, gathering darkness, gloaming (*Scot. or poetic*), gloom, obscurity, protection, shade, shelter **2.** hint, suggestion, suspicion, trace *~vb.* **3.** cast a shadow over, darken, overhang, screen, shade, shield **4.** dog, follow, spy on, stalk, tail (*informal*), trail

shadowy 1. crepuscular, dark, dim, dusky, funereal, gloomy, indistinct, murky, obscure, shaded, shady **2.** dim, dreamlike, faint, ghostly, illusory, imaginary, impalpable, intangible, nebulous, obscure, phantom, spectral, undefined, unreal, unsubstantial, vague, wraithlike

shady 1. cool, dim, leafy, shaded, shadowy **2.** *informal* crooked, disreputable, dodgy (*Brit., Austral., & N.Z. informal*), dubious, fishy (*informal*), questionable, shifty, slippery, suspect, suspicious, unethical, unscrupulous, untrustworthy

shaft 1. beam, gleam, ray, streak **2.** handle, pole, rod, shank, stem, upright

shaggy hairy, hirsute, long-haired, rough, tousled, unkempt, unshorn

shake *vb.* **1.** bump, fluctuate, jar, joggle, jolt, jounce, oscillate, quake, quiver, rock, shiver, shudder, sway, totter, tremble, vibrate, waver, wobble **2.** brandish, flourish, wave **3.** discompose, distress, disturb, frighten, intimidate, move, rattle (*informal*), shock, unnerve, upset **4.** impair, pull the rug out from under (*infor-*

short period of time: *in half a shake.* **17** *Music* same as **trill** (sense 1). **18** short for **milk shake.** ~See also **shake down, shake off, shake up.**

shake down *vb* **1** to go to bed, esp. in a makeshift bed. ~*n* **shakedown 2** a makeshift bed.

shake off *vb* **1** to remove or get rid of: *I have been trying to shake off the stigma for some time.* **2** to escape from; get away from: *they switched to a blue car in a bid to shake off reporters.*

shaker *n* **1** a container used for shaking a powdered substance onto something: *a flour shaker.* **2** a container in which the ingredients of alcoholic drinks are shaken together.

Shakespearean *or* **Shakespearian** *adj* **1** of William Shakespeare, English dramatist and poet, or his works. ~*n* **2** a student of or specialist in Shakespeare's works.

shake up *vb* **1** to mix by shaking. **2** to reorganize drastically. **3** *Informal* to shock mentally or physically: *the thunderstorm really shook me up.* ~*n* **shake-up 4** *Informal* a radical reorganization, such as the reorganization of employees in a company.

shako (**shack**-oh) *n, pl* **shakos** a tall cylindrical peaked military hat with a plume.

shaky *adj* **shakier, shakiest 1** weak and unsteady, esp. due to illness or shock. **2** uncertain or doubtful: *their prospects are shaky.* **3** tending to shake or tremble. **shakily** *adv*

shale *n* a flaky sedimentary rock formed by compression of successive layers of clay.

shall *vb, past* **should** used as an auxiliary: **1** (esp. with *I* or *we* as subject) to make the future tense: *we shall see you tomorrow.* **2** (with *you, he, she, it, they,* or a noun as subject) **a** to indicate determination on the part of the speaker: *you shall pay for this!* **b** to indicate compulsion or obligation, now esp. in official documents. **3** (with *I* or *we* as subject) in questions asking for advice or agreement: *what shall we do now?; shall I shut the door?*

➤ The use of *shall* with *I* and *we* is a matter of preference, not rule. *Shall* is commonly used for questions in southern England but less often in the north and Scotland.

shallot (shal-**lot**) *n* a small, onion-like plant used in cooking for flavouring.

shallow *adj* **1** having little depth. **2** not involving sincere feelings or serious thought. **3** (of breathing) consisting of short breaths. ~*n* **4** (*often pl*) a shallow place in a body of water. **shallowness** *n*

sham *n* **1** anything that is not genuine or is not what it appears to be. **2** a person who pretends to be something other than he or she is. ~*adj* **3** not real or genuine. ~*vb* **shamming, shammed 4** to fake or feign (something); pretend: *he made a point of shamming nervousness.*

shaman (**sham**-man) *n* **1** a priest of shamanism. **2** a medicine man or witch doctor of a similar religion.

shamanism (**sham**-man-iz-zum) *n* a religion of northern Asia, based on a belief in good and evil spirits who can be influenced or controlled only by the shamans. **shamanist** *n, adj*

shamble *vb* **-bling, -bled 1** to walk or move along in an awkward shuffling way. ~*n* **2** an awkward or shuffling walk. **shambling** *adj, n*

shambles *n* **1** a disorderly or badly organized event or place: *the bathroom was a shambles.* **2** a butcher's slaughterhouse. **3** *Old-fashioned* any scene of great slaughter.

shambolic *adj Informal* completely disorganized.

shame *n* **1** a painful emotion resulting from an awareness of having done something wrong or foolish. **2** capacity to feel such an emotion: *have they no shame?* **3** loss of respect; disgrace. **4** a person or thing that causes this. **5** a cause for regret or disappointment: *it's a shame to rush back.* **6 put to shame** to show up as being inferior by comparison: *his essay put mine to shame.* ~*interj* **7** *S African informal* **a** an expression of sympathy. **b** an expression of pleasure or endearment. ~*vb* **shaming, shamed 8** to cause to feel shame. **9** to bring shame on. **10** (often foll. by *into*) to force someone to do something by making him or her feel ashamed not to: *he was finally shamed into paying the bill.*

shamefaced *adj* embarrassed or guilty. **shamefacedly** *adv*

shameful *adj* causing or deserving shame: *a shameful lack of concern.* **shamefully** *adv*

shameless *adj* **1** having no sense of shame: *a shameless manipulator.* **2** without decency or modesty: *a shameless attempt to stifle democracy.* **shamelessly** *adv*

shammy *n, pl* **-mies** *Informal* a piece of chamois leather.

shampoo *n* **1** a soapy liquid used to wash the hair. **2**

THESAURUS

mal), undermine, weaken ~*n.* **5.** agitation, convulsion, disturbance, jar, jerk, jolt, jounce, pulsation, quaking, shiver, shock, shudder, trembling, tremor, vibration **6.** *informal* instant, jiffy (*informal*), moment, second, tick (*Brit. informal*), trice

shake off dislodge, elude, get away from, get rid of, get shot of (*slang*), give the slip, leave behind, lose, rid oneself of, throw off

shake up agitate, churn (up), disturb, mix, overturn, reorganize, shock, stir (up), turn upside down, unsettle, upset

shaky 1. all of a quiver (*informal*), faltering, insecure, precarious, quivery, rickety, tottering, trembling, tremulous, unstable, unsteady, weak, wobbly **2.** dubious, iffy (*informal*), questionable, suspect, uncertain, undependable, unreliable, unsound, unsupported

shallow 1. *adj.* empty, flimsy, foolish, frivolous, idle, ignorant, meaningless, puerile, simple, skin-deep, slight, superficial, surface, trivial, unintelligent **2.** *n. often plural* bank, flat, sandbank, sand bar, shelf, shoal

sham 1. *n.* counterfeit, feint, forgery, fraud, hoax, humbug, imitation, impostor, imposture, phoney (*informal*), pretence, pretender, pseud (*informal*), wolf in sheep's clothing **2.** *adj.* artificial, bogus, counterfeit, ersatz, false, feigned, imitation, mock, phoney (*informal*), pretended, pseud (*informal*), pseudo (*informal*), simulated, spurious, synthetic **3.** *vb.* affect, assume, counterfeit, fake, feign, imitate, play possum, pretend, put on, simulate

shame *n.* **1.** abashment, chagrin, compunction, embarrassment, humiliation, ignominy, loss of face, mortification, shamefacedness **2.** blot, contempt, degradation, derision, discredit, disgrace, dishonour, disrepute, ill repute, infamy, obloquy, odium, opprobrium, reproach, scandal, skeleton in the cupboard, smear **3. put to shame** disgrace, eclipse, outclass, outdo, outstrip, show up, surpass ~*vb.* **4.** abash, confound, disconcert, disgrace, embarrass, humble, humiliate, mortify, reproach, ridicule, take (someone) down a peg (*informal*) **5.** blot, debase, defile, degrade, discredit, dishonour, smear, stain

shameful atrocious, base, dastardly, degrading, disgraceful, dishonourable, ignominious, indecent, infamous, low, mean, outrageous, reprehensible, scandalous, unbecoming, unworthy, vile, wicked

shameless abandoned, audacious, barefaced, brash, brazen, corrupt, depraved, dissolute, flagrant, har-

a similar liquid for washing carpets or upholstery. **3** the process of shampooing. *~vb* **-pooing, -pooed 4** to wash (the hair, carpets, or upholstery) with shampoo.

shamrock *n* a small clover-like plant with three round leaves on each stem: the national emblem of Ireland.

shandy *n, pl* **-dies** a drink made of beer and lemonade.

shanghai *Slang ~vb* **-haiing, -haied 1** to force or trick (someone) into doing something. **2** *History* to kidnap (a man) and force him to serve at sea. **3** *Austral & NZ* to shoot with a catapult. *~n* **4** *Austral & NZ* a catapult.

shank *n* **1** the part of the leg between the knee and the ankle. **2** a cut of meat from the top part of an animal's shank. **3** the long narrow part of a tool, key, spoon, etc.

shanks's pony *or US* **shanks's mare** *n Informal* one's own legs as a means of transport.

shan't shall not.

shantung *n* a heavy Chinese silk with a knobbly surface.

shanty[1] *n, pl* **-ties** a small rough hut; crude dwelling.

shanty[2] *or* **chanty** *n, pl* **-ties** a rhythmical song originally sung by sailors when working.

shantytown *n* a town of poor people living in shanties.

shape *n* **1** the outward form of an object, produced by its outline. **2** the figure or outline of the body of a person. **3** organized or definite form: *to preserve the union in its present shape.* **4** the specific form that anything takes on: *a gold locket in the shape of a heart.* **5** pattern or mould. **6** condition or state of efficiency: *in poor shape.* **7 take shape** to assume a definite form. *~vb* **shaping, shaped 8** (often foll. by *into* or *up*) to receive or cause to receive shape or form: *spinach shaped into a ball.* **9** to mould into a particular pattern or form. **10** to devise or develop: *to shape a system of free trade.* ~See also **shape up.**

shapeless *adj* **1** (of a person or object) lacking a pleasing shape: *a shapeless dress.* **2** having no definite shape or form: *a shapeless mound.* **shapelessness** *n*

shapely *adj* **-lier, -liest** (esp. of a woman's body or legs) pleasing or attractive in shape. **shapeliness** *n*

shape up *vb Informal* **1** to progress or develop satisfactorily. **2** to develop a definite or proper form. **3** to start working efficiently or behaving properly: *shape up or face the sack.*

shard *n* a broken piece or fragment of pottery, glass, or metal.

share[1] *n* **1** a part or portion of something that belongs to or is contributed by a person or group. **2** (*often pl*) any of the equal parts into which the capital stock of a company is divided. *~vb* **sharing, shared 3** (often foll. by *out*) to divide and distribute. **4** to receive or contribute a portion of: *we shared a bottle of mineral water.* **5** to join with another or others in the use of (something): *the four women share a house.* **6** to go through (a similar experience) as others: *we all shared the nightmare of toothache.* **7** to tell others about (something). **8** to have the same (beliefs or opinions) as others: *universal values shared by both east and west.*

share[2] *n* short for **ploughshare.**

shareholder *n* the owner of one or more shares in a company.

shark *n* **1** a large, usually predatory fish with a long body, two dorsal fins, and rows of sharp teeth. **2** *Disparaging* a person who swindles or extorts money from other people.

sharkskin *n* a smooth glossy fabric used for sportswear.

sharp *adj* **1** having a keen cutting edge. **2** tapering to an edge or point. **3** involving a sudden change in direction: *a sharp bend on a road; a sharp rise in prices.* **4** moving, acting, or reacting quickly: *sharp reflexes.* **5** clearly defined: *a sharp contrast.* **6** quick to notice or understand things; keen-witted. **7** clever in an underhand way: *sharp practices.* **8** bitter or harsh: *a sharp response.* **9** shrill or penetrating: *a sharp cry of horror.* **10** having a bitter or sour taste. **11** (of pain or cold) acute or biting: *a sharp gust of wind.* **12** *Music* **a** (of a note) raised in pitch by one semitone: *F sharp.* **b** (of an instrument or voice) out of tune by being too high in pitch. **13** *Informal* neat and stylish: *a sharp dresser.* *~adv* **14** promptly. **15** exactly: *at ten o'clock sharp.* **16** *Music* **a** higher than a standard pitch. **b** out of tune by being too high in pitch: *she sings sharp.* *~n* **17** *Music* **a** an accidental that raises the pitch of a note by one semitone. Symbol: ♯ **b** a note affected by this accidental. **18** *Informal* a cheat; a cardsharp. **sharpish** *adj* **sharply** *adv* **sharpness** *n*

sharpen *vb* to make or become sharp or sharper. **sharpener** *n*

sharper *n* a person who cheats or swindles; fraud.

sharpshooter *n* a skilled marksman.

sharp-tongued *adj* very critical or sarcastic.

sharp-witted *adj* very intelligent and perceptive.

THESAURUS

dened, immodest, improper, impudent, incorrigible, indecent, insolent, profligate, reprobate, unabashed, unashamed, unblushing, unprincipled, wanton

shape *n.* **1.** build, configuration, contours, cut, figure, form, lines, make, outline, profile, silhouette **2.** frame, model, mould, pattern **3.** condition, fettle, health, kilter, state, trim *~vb.* **4.** create, fashion, form, make, model, mould, produce **5.** accommodate, adapt, convert, define, develop, devise, frame, guide, modify, plan, prepare, regulate, remodel

shapeless amorphous, asymmetrical, battered, embryonic, formless, indeterminate, irregular, misshapen, nebulous, undeveloped, unstructured

share 1. *n.* allotment, allowance, contribution, cut (*informal*), division, due, lot, part, portion, proportion, quota, ration, whack (*informal*) **2.** *vb.* apportion, assign, distribute, divide, go Dutch (*informal*), go fifty-fifty (*informal*), go halves, parcel out, partake, participate, receive, split, use in common

sharp *adj.* **1.** acute, cutting, honed, jagged, keen, knife-edged, knifelike, pointed, razor-sharp, serrated, sharpened, spiky **2.** abrupt, distinct, extreme, marked, sudden **3.** clear, clear-cut, crisp, distinct, well-defined **4.** alert, apt, astute, bright, clever, discerning, knowing, long-headed, observant, penetrating, perceptive, quick, quick-witted, ready, subtle **5.** artful, crafty, cunning, dishonest, fly (*slang*), shrewd, sly, smart, unscrupulous, wily **6.** acerbic, acrimonious, barbed, biting, bitter, caustic, cutting, harsh, hurtful, mordacious, mordant, sarcastic, sardonic, scathing, severe, trenchant, vitriolic **7.** acerbic, acetic, acid, acrid, burning, hot, piquant, pungent, sour, tart, vinegary **8.** *informal* chic, classy (*slang*), dressy, fashionable, natty (*informal*), smart, snappy, stylish, trendy (*informal*) *~adv.* **9.** exactly, on the dot, on time, precisely, promptly, punctually

sharpen edge, grind, hone, put an edge on, strop, whet

shatter 1. break, burst, crack, crush, crush to smithereens, demolish, explode, implode, pulverize, shiver, smash, split **2.** blast, blight, bring to nought, demolish, destroy, disable, exhaust, impair, overturn, ruin, tor-

shatter *vb* **1** to break suddenly into many small pieces. **2** to damage badly or destroy: *to shatter American confidence.* **3** to upset (someone) greatly: *the whole experience shattered me.* **shattering** *adj*

shattered *adj Informal* **1** completely exhausted. **2** badly upset: *he was shattered by the separation.*

shave *vb* **shaving, shaved; shaved** *or* **shaven 1** to remove (the beard or hair) from (the face, head, or body) by using a razor or shaver. **2** to remove thin slices from (wood or other material) with a sharp cutting tool. **3** to touch (someone or something) lightly in passing. ~*n* **4** the act or an instance of shaving. **5** the removal of hair from a man's face by a razor. **6** a tool for cutting off thin slices. **7 close shave** *Informal* a narrow escape.

shaver *n* **1** an electrically powered razor. **2** *Old-fashioned* a young boy.

Shavian (**shave**-ee-an) *adj* **1** of or like George Bernard Shaw, Irish dramatist noted for his sharp wit, or his works. ~*n* **2** an admirer of Shaw or his works.

shaving *n* **1** a thin slice of something such as wood, which has been shaved off. *adj* **2** used when shaving: *shaving foam.*

shawl *n* a piece of woollen cloth worn over the head or shoulders by a woman or wrapped around a baby.

she *pron* refers to: **1** the female person or animal previously mentioned or in question: *she is my sister.* **2** something regarded as female, such as a car, ship, or nation. ~*n* **3** a female person or animal.

sheaf *n, pl* **sheaves 1** a bundle of papers tied together. **2** a bundle of reaped corn tied together. ~*vb* **3** to bind or tie into a sheaf.

shear *vb* **shearing, sheared** *or Austral & NZ sometimes* **shore; sheared** *or* **shorn 1** to remove (the fleece) of (a sheep) by cutting or clipping. **2** to cut or cut through (something) with shears or a sharp instrument. **3** *Engineering* to cause (a part) to break or (of a part) to break through strain or twisting. ~*n* **4** breakage caused through strain or twisting. ~See also **shears. shearer** *n*

shears *pl n* **a** large scissors, used for sheep shearing. **b** a large scissor-like cutting tool with flat blades, used for cutting hedges.

sheath *n, pl* **sheaths 1** a case or covering for the blade of a knife or sword. **2** *Biol* a structure that encloses or protects. **3** same as **condom. 4** a close-fitting dress.

sheathe *vb* **sheathing, sheathed 1** to insert (a knife or sword) into a sheath. **2** to cover with a sheathe or sheathing.

sheathing *n* any material used as an outer layer.

sheaves *n* the plural of **sheaf.**

shebeen *or* **shebean** *n Scot, Irish, & S African* a place where alcoholic drink is sold illegally.

shed[1] *n* **1** a small, roughly made building used for storing garden tools, etc. **2** a large barnlike building used for various purposes at factories, train stations, etc.: *a locomotive shed.*

shed[2] *vb* **shedding, shed 1** to get rid of: *250 workers shed by the company.* **2 shed tears** to cry. **3 shed light on** to make (a problem or situation) easier to understand. **4** to cast off (skin, hair, or leaves): *the trees were already beginning to shed their leaves.* **5** to cause to flow off: *this coat sheds water.* **6** to separate or divide (a group of sheep).

sheen *n* a glistening brightness on the surface of something: *grass with a sheen of dew on it.*

sheep *n, pl* **sheep 1** a cud-chewing mammal with a thick woolly coat, kept for its wool or meat. **2** a timid person. **3 like sheep** (of a group of people) allowing a single person to dictate their actions or beliefs. **4 separate the sheep from the goats** to pick out the members of a group who are superior in some respects. **sheeplike** *adj*

sheep-dip *n* **1** a liquid disinfectant and insecticide in which sheep are immersed. **2** a deep trough containing such a liquid.

sheepdog *n* **1** a dog used for herding sheep. **2** a breed of dog reared originally for herding sheep.

sheepfold *n* a pen or enclosure for sheep.

sheepish *adj* embarrassed because of feeling foolish. **sheepishly** *adv*

sheepshank *n* a knot made in a rope to shorten it temporarily.

sheepskin *n* the skin of a sheep with the wool still attached, used to make clothing and rugs.

sheer[1] *adj* **1** absolute; complete: *sheer amazement.* **2** perpendicular; very steep: *the sheer rock face.* **3** (of textiles) light, delicate, and see-through. ~*adv* **4** steeply: *the cliff drops sheer to the sea.*

sheer[2] *vb* **sheer off** *or* **away (from) a** to change course suddenly. **b** to avoid an unpleasant person, thing, or topic.

sheet[1] *n* **1** a large rectangular piece of cloth used as an inner bed cover. **2** a thin piece of material such as paper or glass, usually rectangular. **3** a broad continuous surface or layer: *a sheet of ice.* **4** a newspaper. ~*vb* **5** to provide with, cover, or wrap in a sheet. **6** (often foll. by *down*) to rain very heavily.

sheet[2] *n Naut* a line or rope for controlling the position of a sail.

sheet anchor *n* **1** *Naut* a large strong anchor for use in an emergency. **2** a person or thing that can always be relied on.

sheeting *n* any material from which sheets are made.

sheet metal *n* metal formed into a thin sheet by rolling or hammering.

sheet music *n* music printed on individual sheets of paper.

sheikh *or* **sheik** (**shake**) *n* (in Muslim countries) **a** the head of an Arab tribe, village, or family. **b** a religious leader. **sheikhdom** *or* **sheikdom** *n*

sheila *n Austral & NZ informal* a girl or woman.

shekel *n* **1** the monetary unit of Israel. **2 shekels** *Informal* money.

shelduck *or masc* **sheldrake** *n, pl* **-ducks, -duck,** *or* **-drakes -drake** a large brightly coloured wild duck of Europe and Asia.

shelf *n, pl* **shelves 1** a board fixed horizontally against a wall or in a cupboard, for holding things. **2** a projecting layer of ice or rock on land or in the sea. **3**

THESAURUS

pedo, wreck **3.** break (someone's) heart, crush, devastate, dumbfound, knock the stuffing out of (someone) (*informal*), upset

shave *vb.* **1.** crop, pare, plane, shear, trim **2.** brush, graze, touch

shed *vb.* **1.** afford, cast, diffuse, drop, emit, give, give forth, pour forth, radiate, scatter, shower, spill, throw **2.** cast off, discard, exuviate, moult, slough

sheepish abashed, ashamed, chagrined, embarrassed, foolish, mortified, self-conscious, shamefaced, silly, uncomfortable

sheer 1. absolute, arrant, complete, downright, out-and-out, pure, rank, thoroughgoing, total, unadulterated, unalloyed, unmitigated, unqualified, utter **2.** abrupt, perpendicular, precipitous, steep **3.** *of textiles* diaphanous, fine, gauzy, gossamer, see-through, thin, transparent

sheet 1. area, blanket, covering, expanse, stretch,

off the shelf (of products in shops) sold as standard. **4 on the shelf** put aside or abandoned; used esp. of unmarried women considered to be past the age of marriage.

shelf life *n* the length of time a packaged product will remain fresh or usable.

shell *n* **1** the protective outer layer of an egg, fruit, or nut. **2** the hard outer covering of an animal such as a crab or tortoise. **3** any hard outer case. **4** the external structure of a building, car, or ship, esp. one that is unfinished or gutted by fire. **5** an explosive artillery projectile that can be fired from a large gun. **6** a small-arms cartridge. **7** *Rowing* a very light narrow racing boat. **8 come** *or* **bring out of one's shell** to become *or* help to become less shy and reserved. *~vb* **9** to remove the shell or husk from. **10** to attack with artillery shells. ~See also **shell out. shell-like** *adj*

she'll she will *or* she shall.

shellac *n* **1** a yellowish resin used in varnishes and polishes. **2** a varnish made by dissolving shellac in alcohol. *~vb* **-lacking, -lacked 3** to coat with shellac.

shellfish *n, pl* **-fish** *or* **-fishes** a sea-living animal, esp. one that can be eaten, having a shell.

shell out *vb Informal* to pay out or hand over (money).

shell shock *n* a nervous disorder characterized by anxiety and depression that occurs as a result of lengthy exposure to battle conditions. **shell-shocked** *adj*

shell suit *n* a lightweight tracksuit made of a waterproof nylon layer over a cotton layer.

Shelta *n* a secret language based on Gaelic, used by some travelling people in Ireland and Britain.

shelter *n* **1** something that provides cover or protection from weather or danger. **2** the protection given by such a cover. *~vb* **3** to take cover from bad weather. **4** to provide with a place to live or a hiding place: *dissidents sheltering in foreign embassies.*

sheltered *adj* **1** protected from wind and rain. **2** protected from unpleasant or upsetting experiences: *a sheltered childhood.* **3** specially designed to provide a safe environment for the elderly, handicapped, or disabled: *sheltered housing.*

shelve[1] *vb* **shelving, shelved 1** to put aside or postpone: *to shelve a project.* **2** to place (something, such as a book) on a shelf. **3** to provide with shelves: *to shelve a cupboard.* **4** to dismiss (someone) from active service.

shelve[2] *vb* **shelving, shelved** to slope away gradually.

shelves *n* the plural of **shelf.**

shelving *n* **1** material for shelves. **2** shelves collectively.

shenanigans *pl n Informal* **1** mischief or nonsense. **2** trickery or deception.

shepherd *n* **1** a person employed to tend sheep. **2** *Christianity* a clergyman when considered as the moral and spiritual guide of the people in the parish. *~vb* **3** to guide or watch over (people). **shepherdess** *fem n*

shepherd's pie *n Chiefly Brit* a baked dish of minced meat covered with mashed potato.

Sheraton *adj* denoting light and elegant furniture made by or in the style of Thomas Sheraton, English furniture maker.

sherbet *n* **1** a fruit-flavoured slightly fizzy powder, eaten as a sweet or used to make a drink. **2** *US & Canad* same as **sorbet.**

sheriff *n* **1** (in the U.S.) the chief elected law-enforcement officer in a county. **2** (in Canada) a municipal officer who enforces court orders and escorts convicted criminals to prison. **3** (in England and Wales) the chief executive officer of the Crown in a county, having chiefly ceremonial duties. **4** (in Scotland) a judge in a sheriff court.

sheriff court *n* (in Scotland) a court having powers to try all but the most serious crimes and to deal with most civil actions.

Sherpa *n, pl* **-pas** *or* **-pa** a member of a Tibetan people living on the southern slopes of the Himalayas.

sherry *n, pl* **-ries** a pale or dark brown fortified wine, originally from southern Spain.

Shetland pony *n* a very small sturdy breed of pony with a long shaggy mane and tail.

shibboleth *n* **1** a slogan or catch phrase, usually considered outworn, that characterizes a particular party or sect: *the shibboleth of Western strategy.* **2** a custom, phrase, or use of language that reliably distinguishes a member of one group or class from another.

shickered *adj Austral & NZ slang* drunk.

shied *vb* the past of **shy**[1], **shy**[2].

shield *n* **1** a piece of defensive armour carried in the hand or on the arm to protect the body from blows or missiles. **2** any person or thing that protects, hides, or defends: *a wind shield.* **3** *Heraldry* a representation of a shield used for displaying a coat of arms. **4** anything that resembles a shield in shape, such as a trophy in a sports competition. *~vb* **5** to protect, hide, or defend (someone or something) from danger or harm: *an industry shielded from competition.*

shift *vb* **1** to move from one place or position to another. **2** to pass (blame or responsibility) onto someone else: *he was trying to shift the blame to me.* **3** to change (gear) in a motor vehicle. **4** to remove or be removed: *no detergent can shift these stains.* **5** *US* to change for another or others. **6** *Slang* to move quickly. *~n* **7** the act or an instance of shifting. **8 a** a group of

THESAURUS

sweep **2.** coat, film, folio, lamina, layer, leaf, membrane, overlay, pane, panel, piece, plate, slab, stratum, surface, veneer

shell *n.* **1.** carapace, case, husk, pod **2.** chassis, frame, framework, hull, skeleton, structure *~vb.* **3.** attack, barrage, blitz, bomb, bombard, strafe, strike

shelter 1. *n.* asylum, cover, covert, defence, guard, haven, protection, refuge, retreat, roof over one's head, safety, sanctuary, screen, security, shiel (*Scot.*), umbrella **2.** *vb.* cover, defend, guard, harbour, hide, protect, safeguard, seek refuge, shield, take in, take shelter

sheltered cloistered, conventual, ensconced, hermitic, isolated, protected, quiet, reclusive, retired, screened, secluded, shaded, shielded, withdrawn

shelve defer, dismiss, freeze, hold in abeyance, hold over, lay aside, mothball, pigeonhole, postpone, put aside, put off, put on ice, put on the back burner (*informal*), suspend, table (*U.S.*), take a rain check on (*informal*)

shepherd *vb.* conduct, convoy, guide, herd, marshal, steer, usher

shield *n.* **1.** buckler, escutcheon (*Heraldry*) **2.** aegis, bulwark, cover, defence, guard, protection, rampart, safeguard, screen, shelter, ward (*archaic*) *~vb.* **3.** cover, defend, guard, protect, safeguard, screen, shelter, ward off

shift 1. *vb.* alter, budge, change, displace, fluctuate, move, move around, rearrange, relocate, remove, reposition, swerve, switch, transfer, transpose, vary,

workers who work during a specific period. **b** the period of time worked by such a group. **9** a method or scheme. **10** a loose-fitting straight underskirt or dress.

shiftless *adj* lacking in ambition or initiative.

shifty *adj* **shiftier, shiftiest** looking deceitful and not to be trusted. **shiftiness** *n*

shillelagh (shil-**lay**-lee) *n* (in Ireland) a heavy club.

shilling *n* **1** a former British coin worth one twentieth of a pound, replaced by the 5p piece in 1970. **2** the standard monetary unit in several E African countries.

shillyshally *vb* **-shallies, -shallying, -shallied** *Informal* to be indecisive.

shim *n* **1** a thin strip of material placed between two close surfaces to fill a gap. *~vb* **shimming, shimmed** **2** to fit or fill up with a shim.

shimmer *vb* **1** to shine with a faint unsteady light. *~n* **2** a faint unsteady light. **shimmering** *or* **shimmery** *adj*

shin *n* **1** the front part of the lower leg. **2** *Chiefly Brit* a cut of beef including the lower foreleg. *~vb* **shinning, shinned 3 shin up** to climb (something, such as a rope or pole) by gripping with the hands or arms and the legs and hauling oneself up.

shinbone *n* the nontechnical name for **tibia.**

shindig *or* **shindy** *n, pl* **-digs** *or* **-dies** *Slang* **1** a noisy party or dance. **2** a quarrel or brawl.

shine *vb* **shining, shone 1** to give off or reflect light. **2** to direct the light of (a lamp or torch): *I shone a torch at the ceiling.* **3** (*pt & pp* **shined**) to make clean and bright by polishing: *they earned money by shining shoes.* **4** to be very good at something: *she shone in most subjects; she shone at school.* **5** to appear very bright and clear: *her hair shone like gold. ~n* **6** brightness or lustre. **7 take a shine to someone** *Informal* to take a liking to someone.

shiner *n Informal* a black eye.

shingle[1] *n* **1** a thin rectangular tile laid with others in overlapping rows to cover a roof or a wall. **2** a woman's short-cropped hairstyle. *~vb* **-gling, -gled 3** to cover (a roof or a wall) with shingles. **4** to cut (the hair) in a short-cropped style.

shingle[2] *n* coarse gravel found on beaches.

shingles *n* a disease causing a rash of small blisters along a nerve.

Shinto *n* a Japanese religion in which ancestors and nature spirits are worshipped. **Shintoism** *n* **Shintoist** *n, adj*

shinty *n* **1** a game like hockey but with taller goals. **2** (*pl* **-ties**) the stick used in this game.

shiny *adj* **shinier, shiniest 1** bright and polished. **2** (of clothes or material) worn to a smooth and glossy state by continual wear or rubbing.

ship *n* **1** a large seagoing vessel with engines or sails. **2** short for **airship** or **spaceship. 3 when one's ship comes in** when one has become successful. *~vb* **shipping, shipped 4** to send or transport by any carrier, esp. a ship. **5** *Naut* to take in (water) over the side. **6** to bring or go aboard a vessel: *to ship oars.* **7** (often foll. by *off*) *Informal* to send away: *they were shipped off to foreign countries.* **8** to be hired to serve aboard a ship: *I shipped aboard a Liverpool liner.*

shipboard *adj* taking place or used aboard a ship: *a shipboard romance.*

shipbuilder *n* a person or company that builds ships. **shipbuilding** *n*

shipmate *n* a sailor who serves on the same ship as another.

shipment *n* **1** goods shipped together as part of the same lot: *a shipment of arms.* **2** the act of shipping cargo.

shipper *n* a person or company that ships.

shipping *n* **1** the business of transporting freight, esp. by ship. **2** ships collectively: *all shipping should stay clear of the harbour.*

shipshape *adj* **1** neat or orderly. *~adv* **2** in a neat and orderly manner.

shipwreck *n* **1** the destruction of a ship at sea. **2** the remains of a wrecked ship. **3** ruin or destruction: *the shipwreck of the old science. ~vb* **4** to wreck or destroy (a ship). **5** to bring to ruin or destruction.

shipwright *n* someone, esp. a carpenter, who builds or repairs ships.

shipyard *n* a place where ships are built and repaired.

shire *n* **1** a county. **2 the Shires** the Midland counties of England.

shire horse *n* a large powerful breed of working horse.

shirk *vb* to avoid doing (work or a duty). **shirker** *n*

shirt *n* **1** an item of clothing worn on the upper part of the body, usually with a collar and sleeves and buttoning up the front. **2 keep your shirt on** *Informal* keep your temper. **3 put one's shirt on something** *Informal* to bet all one has on something.

shirtsleeve *n* **1** the sleeve of a shirt. **2 in one's shirtsleeves** not wearing a jacket.

shirt-tail *n* the part of a shirt that extends below the waist.

shirtwaister *or US* **shirtwaist** *n* a woman's dress with a tailored bodice resembling a shirt.

shirty *adj* **shirtier, shirtiest** *Slang, chiefly Brit* bad-tempered or annoyed.

shish kebab *n* a dish of small pieces of meat and vegetables grilled on a skewer.

shit *Taboo ~vb* **shitting, shitted, shit** *or* **shat 1** to defecate. *~n* **2** faeces; excrement. **3** *Slang* rubbish; nonsense. **4** *Slang* a worthless person. *~interj* **5** *Slang* an exclamation of anger or disgust. **shitty** *adj*

shiver[1] *vb* **1** to tremble from cold or fear. *~n* **2** a tremble caused by cold or fear. **3 the shivers** a fit of shivering through fear or illness. **shivering** *n, adj* **shivery** *adj*

THESAURUS

veer **2.** *n.* about-turn, alteration, change, displacement, fluctuation, modification, move, permutation, rearrangement, removal, shifting, switch, transfer, veering

shifty contriving, crafty, deceitful, devious, duplicitous, evasive, fly-by-night (*informal*), furtive, scheming, slippery, sly, tricky, underhand, unprincipled, untrustworthy, wily

shimmer 1. *vb.* dance, gleam, glisten, phosphoresce, scintillate, twinkle **2.** *n.* diffused light, gleam, glimmer, glow, incandescence, iridescence, lustre, phosphorescence, unsteady light

shine *vb.* **1.** beam, emit light, flash, give off light, glare, gleam, glimmer, glisten, glitter, glow, radiate, scintillate, shimmer, sparkle, twinkle **2.** brush, buff, burnish, polish, rub up **3.** be conspicuous (distinguished, outstanding, pre-eminent), excel, stand out, stand out in a crowd, star *~n.* **4.** brightness, glare, glaze, gleam, gloss, lambency, light, luminosity, lustre, patina, polish, radiance, sheen, shimmer, sparkle

shiny agleam, bright, burnished, gleaming, glistening, glossy, lustrous, nitid (*poetic*), polished, sheeny

shirk avoid, dodge, duck (out of) (*informal*), evade, get out of, shun, sidestep, skive (*Brit. slang*), slack

shirker clock-watcher, dodger, idler, malingerer, quitter, shirk, skiver (*Brit. slang*), slacker

shiver[2] *vb* **1** to break into fragments. *~n* **2** a splintered piece.

shoal[1] *n* **1** a large group of fish swimming together. **2** a large group of people or things.

shoal[2] *n* **1** a stretch of shallow water. **2** a sandbank or rocky area, esp. one that can be seen at low water. *~vb* **3** to make or become shallow.

shock[1] *vb* **1** to cause (someone) to experience extreme horror, disgust, or astonishment: *the similarity shocked me.* **2** to cause a state of shock in (a person). *~n* **3** a sudden and violent blow or impact. **4 a** a sudden and violent emotional disturbance. **b** something causing this. **5** *Pathol* a condition in which a person's blood cannot flow properly because of severe injury, burns, or fright. **6** pain and muscular spasm caused by an electric current passing through a person's body. **shocker** *n*

shock[2] *n* **1** a number of grain sheaves set on end in a field to dry. *~vb* **2** to set up (sheaves) in shocks.

shock[3] *n* a thick bushy mass of hair.

shock absorber *n* any device designed to absorb mechanical shock, esp. one fitted to a motor vehicle to reduce the effects of travelling over bumpy surfaces.

shocking *adj* **1** *Informal* very bad or terrible: *a shocking match at Leicester.* **2** causing dismay or disgust: *a shocking lack of concern.* **3 shocking pink** (of) a very bright shade of pink.

shockproof *adj* capable of absorbing shock without damage.

shock tactics *pl n* the use of unexpected or unexpectedly forceful methods to carry out a plan.

shock therapy *or* **treatment** *n* the treatment of certain mental conditions by passing an electric current through the patient's brain.

shod *vb* a past of **shoe.**

shoddy *adj* **-dier, -diest 1** made or done badly or carelessly: *shoddy goods.* **2** of poor quality; shabby. **shoddily** *adv* **shoddiness** *n*

shoe *n* **1** one of a matching pair of coverings shaped to fit the foot, made of leather or other strong material and ending below the ankle. **2** anything resembling a shoe in shape, function, or position. **3** short for **horseshoe. 4 be in a person's shoes** *Informal* to be in another person's situation. *~vb* **shoeing, shod 5** to fit (a horse) with horseshoes.

shoehorn *n* a smooth curved piece of metal or plastic inserted at the heel of a shoe to ease the foot into it.

shoelace *n* a cord for fastening shoes.

shoemaker *n* a person who makes or repairs shoes or boots. **shoemaking** *n*

shoestring *n* **1** same as **shoelace. 2** *Informal* a very small amount of money: *the theatre will be run on a shoestring.*

shoetree *n* a long piece of metal, plastic, or wood, put into a shoe or boot to keep its shape.

shone *vb* a past of **shine.**

shoo *interj* **1** go away!: used to drive away unwanted or annoying animals or people. *~vb* **shooing, shooed 2** to drive away by crying "shoo".

shook *vb* the past tense of **shake.**

shoot *vb* **shooting, shot 1** to hit, wound, or kill with a missile fired from a weapon. **2** to fire (a missile or missiles) from a weapon. **3** to fire (a weapon). **4** to hunt game with a gun for sport. **5** to send out or be sent out quickly and aggressively: *he shot questions at her.* **6** to move very rapidly: *the car shot forward.* **7** to go or pass quickly over or through: *he was trying to shoot the white water.* **8** to slide or push into or out of a fastening: *she shot the bolt quickly.* **9** (of a plant) to sprout (a new growth). **10** to photograph or film. **11** *Sport* to hit or kick the ball at goal. *~n* **12** the act of shooting. **13** a new growth or sprout of a plant. **14** *Chiefly Brit* a meeting or party organized for hunting game with guns. **15** an area where game can be hunted with guns. **16** *Informal* a photographic assignment. **shooter** *n*

shooting gallery *n* a long narrow room where people practise shooting.

shooting star *n Informal* a meteor.

shooting stick *n* a walking stick with a spike at one end and a folding seat at the other.

shoot up *vb* **1** to grow or increase rapidly: *crime rates have shot up; as my peers started to shoot up, I stopped growing.* **2** *Slang* to inject oneself with heroin or another strong drug.

shop *n* **1** a place for the sale of goods and services. **2** a place where a specified type of work is done; workshop: *a repair shop.* **3 all over the shop** *Informal* scattered everywhere: *his papers were all over the shop.* **4 shut up shop** to close business at the end of the day or permanently. **5 talk shop** *Informal* to discuss one's business or work, esp. on a social occasion. *~vb* **shopping, shopped 6** (often foll. by *for*) to visit a shop or shops in order to buy (goods). **7** *Slang, chiefly Brit* to inform on (someone), esp. to the police. **shopper** *n*

shop around *vb Informal* **1** to visit a number of shops or stores to compare goods and prices. **2** to consider a number of possibilities before making a choice.

shop assistant *n* a person who serves in a shop.

shop floor *n* **1** the production area of a factory. **2** workers, esp. factory workers, as opposed to management.

shopkeeper *n* a person who owns or manages a shop. **shopkeeping** *n*

shoplifter *n* a customer who steals goods from a shop. **shoplifting** *n*

THESAURUS

shiver *vb.* break, crack, fragment, shatter, smash, smash to smithereens, splinter

shivery chilled, chilly, cold, quaking, quivery, shaking, shuddery, trembly

shock *vb.* **1.** agitate, appal, astound, disgust, disquiet, give (someone) a turn (*informal*), horrify, jar, jolt, nauseate, numb, offend, outrage, paralyse, revolt, scandalize, shake, shake out of one's complacency, shake up (*informal*), sicken, stagger, stun, stupefy, traumatize, unsettle *~n.* **2.** blow, clash, collision, encounter, impact, jarring, jolt **3.** blow, bolt from the blue, bombshell, breakdown, collapse, consternation, distress, disturbance, prostration, state of shock, stupefaction, stupor, trauma, turn (*informal*), upset

shocking abominable, appalling, atrocious, detestable, disgraceful, disgusting, disquieting, distressing, dreadful, foul, frightful, ghastly, hellacious (*U.S. slang*), hideous, horrible, horrifying, loathsome, monstrous, nauseating, obscene, odious, offensive, outrageous, repulsive, revolting, scandalous, sickening, stupefying, unspeakable

shoddy cheap-jack (*informal*), cheapo (*informal*), inferior, junky (*informal*), poor, rubbishy, second-rate, slipshod, tacky (*informal*), tatty, tawdry, trashy

shoemaker bootmaker, cobbler

shoot *vb.* **1.** bag, blast (*slang*), blow away (*slang, chiefly U.S.*), bring down, hit, kill, open fire, pick off, plug (*slang*), pump full of lead (*slang*), zap (*slang*) **2.** discharge, emit, fire, fling, hurl, launch, let fly, project, propel **3.** bolt, burn rubber (*informal*), charge, dart, dash, flash, fly, hurtle, race, rush, scoot, speed, spring,

shopping *n* **1** the act of going to shops and buying things. **2** things that have been bought in shops.
shopping centre *n* **1** a complex of stores, restaurants, and sometimes banks, usually under the same roof. **2** the area of a town where most of the shops are situated.
shopping list *n* **1** a written list of things to be bought when out shopping. **2** any list of things desired or demanded: *a long shopping list of amendments to the treaty.*
shopping mall *n* a large enclosed shopping centre.
shopping plaza *n Chiefly US & Canad* a shopping centre, usually a small group of stores built as a strip.
shopsoiled *adj* slightly dirty or faded, from being displayed in a shop.
shop steward *n* a trade-union official elected by his or her fellow workers to be their representative in dealing with their employer.
shoptalk *n* conversation about one's work, carried on outside working hours.
shopwalker *n Brit* (esp. formerly) a person employed by a department store to assist sales personnel and help customers.
shore[1] *n* **1** the land along the edge of a sea, lake, or wide river. **2** land, as opposed to water: *150 yards from shore.* **3 shores** a country: *foreign shores.*
shore[2] *n* **1** a prop placed under or against something as a support. *~vb* **shoring, shored 2 shore up a** to prop up (an unsteady building or wall) with a strong support. **b** to strengthen or support (something weak): *lower interest rates to shore up the economy.*
shoreline *n* the edge of a sea, lake, or wide river.
shorn *vb* a past participle of **shear.**
short *adj* **1** of little length; not long. **2** of little height; not tall. **3** not lasting long. **4** not enough: *the number of places laid at the table was short by four.* **5 short of** *or* **on** lacking in: *short of cash; short on detail.* **6** concise: *a short book.* **7** (of drinks) consisting chiefly of a spirit, such as whisky. **8** (of someone's memory) lacking the ability to retain a lot of facts. **9** (of a person's manner) abrupt and rather rude: *Kemp was short with her.* **10** (of betting odds) almost even. **11** *Finance* **a** not possessing at the time of sale the stocks or commodities one sells. **b** relating to such sales, which depend on falling prices for profit. **12** *Phonetics* (of a vowel) of relatively brief duration. **13** (of pastry) crumbly in texture. **14 in short supply** scarce. **15 short and sweet** brief and to the point. **16 short for** a shortened form of. *~adv* **17** abruptly: *to stop short.* **18 be caught short** to have a sudden need to go to the toilet. **19 go short** not to have enough. **20 short of** except: *nothing short of a single currency will do.* *~n* **21** a drink of spirits. **22** a short film shown before the main feature in a cinema. **23** same as **short circuit. 24 for short** *Informal* as a shortened form: *cystic fibrosis, CF for short.* **25 in short** briefly. *~vb* **26** to short-circuit. ~See also **shorts. shortness** *n*
shortage *n* not enough of something needed.
shortbread *n* a rich crumbly biscuit made with butter.
shortcake *n* **1** shortbread. **2** a dessert made of layers of biscuit or cake filled with fruit and cream.
short-change *vb* **-changing, -changed 1** to give (someone) less than the correct change. **2** *Slang* to cheat or swindle (someone).
short circuit *n* **1** a faulty or accidental connection in an electric circuit, which deflects current through a path of low resistance, usually causing the failure of the circuit. *~vb* **short-circuit 2** to develop a short circuit. **3** to bypass (a procedure): *she wrote to them direct and short-circuited the job agency.* **4** to hinder or frustrate (a plan).
shortcoming *n* a fault or weakness.
shortcrust pastry *n* a type of pastry with a crisp but crumbly texture.
short cut *n* **1** a route that is shorter than the usual one. **2** a way of saving time or effort.
shorten *vb* to make or become short or shorter.
shortening *n* butter or other fat, used in pastry to make it crumbly.
shortfall *n* **1** failure to meet a requirement. **2** the amount of such a failure; deficit.
shorthand *n* a system of rapid writing using simple strokes and other symbols to represent words or phrases.
short-handed *adj* (of a company or organization) lacking enough staff to do the required work.
shorthand typist *n Brit* a person skilled in the use of shorthand and in typing.
shorthorn *n* a member of a breed of cattle with short horns.
short list *Chiefly Brit ~n* **1** Also called (Scot.): **short leet** a list of suitable candidates for a job or prize, from which the successful candidate will be selected. *~vb* **short-list 2** to put (someone) on a short list.
short-lived *adj* lasting only for a short time: *his authority was short-lived.*
shortly *adv* **1** in a short time; soon. **2** spoken in a cross and impatient manner.
shorts *pl n* **1** trousers reaching the top of the thigh or partway to the knee. **2** *Chiefly US & Canad* men's underpants.
short shrift *n* brief and unsympathetic treatment.
short-sighted *adj* **1** unable to see faraway things clearly. **2** not taking likely future developments into account: *a short-sighted approach to the problem.* **short-sightedness** *n*

THESAURUS

streak, tear, whisk, whiz (*informal*) **4.** bud, burgeon, germinate, put forth new growth, sprout *~n.* **5.** branch, bud, offshoot, scion, slip, sprig, sprout, twig
shore beach, coast, foreshore, lakeside, sands, seaboard (*chiefly U.S.*), seashore, strand (*poetic*), waterside
short *adj.* **1.** abridged, brief, compendious, compressed, concise, curtailed, laconic, pithy, sententious, succinct, summary, terse **2.** diminutive, dumpy, little, low, petite, small, squat, wee **3.** brief, fleeting, momentary, short-lived, short-term **4. short of** *or* **on** deficient, inadequate, insufficient, lacking, limited, low (on), meagre, poor, scant, scanty, scarce, short-handed, slender, slim, sparse, tight, wanting **5.** abrupt, blunt, brusque, crusty, curt, discourteous, gruff, impolite, offhand, sharp, terse, testy, uncivil **6.** *of pastry* brittle, crisp, crumbly, friable *~adv.* **7.** abruptly, by surprise, suddenly, unaware, without warning *~n.* **8. in short** briefly, in a nutshell, in a word, in essence, to come to the point, to cut a long story short, to put it briefly
shortage dearth, deficiency, deficit, failure, inadequacy, insufficiency, lack, leanness, paucity, poverty, scarcity, shortfall, want
shortcoming defect, drawback, failing, fault, flaw, foible, frailty, imperfection, weakness, weak point
shorten abbreviate, abridge, curtail, cut, cut back, cut down, decrease, diminish, dock, lessen, prune, reduce, trim, truncate, turn up
short-sighted 1. myopic, near-sighted **2.** careless, ill-advised, ill-considered, impolitic, impractical, improvident, imprudent, injudicious, unthinking

short-tempered *adj* easily angered.
short-term *adj* of, for, or lasting a short time.
short wave *n* a radio wave with a wavelength in the range 10–100 metres.
short-winded *adj* tending to run out of breath easily.
shot[1] *n* **1** the act or an instance of firing a gun or rifle. **2** *Sport* the act or an instance of hitting, kicking, or throwing the ball. **3** small round lead pellets used in shotguns. **4** a person with specified skill in shooting: *my father was quite a good shot.* **5** *Informal* an attempt: *a second shot at writing a better treaty.* **6** *Informal* a guess. **7 a** a single photograph. **b** an uninterrupted sequence of film taken by a single camera. **8** *Informal* an injection of a vaccine or narcotic drug. **9** *Informal* a drink of spirits. **10** the launching of a rocket or spacecraft to a specified destination: *a moon shot.* **11** *Sport* a heavy metal ball used in the shot put. **12 like a shot** without hesitating. **13 shot in the arm** *Informal* something that brings back energy or confidence. **14 shot in the dark** a wild guess.
shot[2] *vb* **1** the past of **shoot.** *~adj* **2** (of textiles) woven to give a changing colour effect. **3** streaked with colour: *dark hair shot with streaks of grey.*
shotgun *n* a gun for firing a charge of shot at short range.
shot put *n* an athletic event in which contestants hurl a heavy metal ball called a shot as far as possible. **shot-putter** *n*
should *vb* the past tense of **shall:** used to indicate that an action is considered by the speaker to be obligatory (*you should go*) or to form the subjunctive mood (*I should like to see you; if I should die; should I be late, start without me.*).
shoulder *n* **1** the part of the body where the arm, wing, or foreleg joins the trunk. **2** a cut of meat including the upper part of the foreleg. **3** the part of an item of clothing that covers the shoulder. **4** the strip of unpaved land that borders a road. **5 a shoulder to cry on** a person one turns to for sympathy with one's troubles. **6 put one's shoulder to the wheel** *Informal* to work very hard. **7 rub shoulders with someone** *Informal* to mix with someone socially. **8 shoulder to shoulder a** side by side. **b** working together. *~vb* **9** to accept (blame or responsibility). **10** to push with one's shoulder: *he shouldered his way through the crowd.* **11** to lift or carry on one's shoulders. **12 shoulder arms** *Mil* to bring one's rifle vertically close to one's right side.
shoulder blade *n* either of two large flat triangular bones one on each side of the back part of the shoulder.
shoulder strap *n* a strap worn over the shoulder to hold up an item of clothing or to support a bag.
shouldn't should not.
shout *n* **1** a loud call or cry. **2** *Informal* one's turn to buy a round of drinks. *~vb* **3** to cry out loudly. **4** *Austral & NZ informal* to treat (someone) to (something, such as a round of drinks).
shout down *vb* to silence (someone) by talking loudly.
shove *vb* **shoving, shoved 1** to give a violent push to. **2** to push (one's way) roughly. **3** *Informal* to put (something) somewhere quickly and carelessly: *shove it into the boot.* *~n* **4** a rough push.
shovel *n* **1** a tool for lifting or moving loose material, consisting of a broad blade attached to a large handle. **2** a machine or part of a machine resembling a shovel in function. *~vb* **-elling, -elled** *or US* **-eling, -eled 3** to lift or move (loose material) with a shovel. **4** to put away large quantities of (something) quickly: *shovelling food into their mouths.*
shove off *vb Informal* to go away; depart.
show *vb* **showing, showed; shown** *or* **showed 1** to make, be, or become visible or noticeable: *to show an interest; excitement showed on everyone's face.* **2** to present for inspection: *someone showed me the plans.* **3** to demonstrate or prove: *evidence showed that this was the most economical way.* **4** to instruct by demonstration: *she showed me how to feed the pullets.* **5** to indicate: *the device shows changes in the pressure.* **6** to behave towards (someone) in a particular way: *to show mercy.* **7** to exhibit or display (works of art): *three artists are showing at the gallery.* **8** to present (a film or play) or (of a film or play) to be presented. **9** to guide or escort: *he offered to show me around.* **10** *Informal* to arrive. *~n* **11** a theatrical or other entertainment: *a magic show.* **12** a display or exhibition: *a show of paintings.* **13** something done to create an impression: *a show of indignation.* **14** vain and conspicuous display: *it was nothing but mere show.* **15** *Slang, chiefly Brit* a thing or affair: *jolly good show.* ~See also **show off, show up.**
show business *n* the entertainment industry. Also (informal): **show biz**
showcase *n* **1** a setting in which something is displayed to best advantage: *a showcase for young opera*

THESAURUS

short-tempered choleric, fiery, hot-tempered, impatient, irascible, peppery, quick-tempered, ratty (*Brit. informal*), testy, touchy
shot *n.* **1.** discharge, lob, pot shot, throw **2.** ball, bullet, lead, pellet, projectile, slug **3.** marksman, shooter **4.** *informal* attempt, chance, conjecture, crack (*informal*), effort, endeavour, essay, go (*informal*), guess, opportunity, stab (*informal*), surmise, try, turn **5. like a shot** at once, eagerly, immediately, like a flash, quickly, unhesitatingly **6. shot in the arm** *informal* boost, encouragement, fillip, impetus, lift, stimulus
shoulder *n.* **1. put one's shoulder to the wheel** *informal* apply oneself, buckle down to (*informal*), exert oneself, get down to, make every effort, set to work, strive **2. rub shoulders with** *informal* associate with, consort with, fraternize with, hobnob with, mix with, socialize with **3. shoulder to shoulder** as one, in cooperation, in partnership, in unity, jointly, side by side, together, united *~vb.* **4.** accept, assume, bear, be responsible for, carry, take on, take upon oneself **5.** elbow, jostle, press, push, shove, thrust
shout 1. *n.* bellow, call, cry, roar, scream, yell **2.** *vb.* bawl, bay, bellow, call (out), cry (out), holler (*informal*), raise one's voice, roar, scream, yell
shout down drown, drown out, overwhelm, silence
shove *vb.* crowd, drive, elbow, impel, jostle, press, propel, push, shoulder, thrust
shovel *vb.* convey, dredge, heap, ladle, load, move, scoop, shift, spoon, toss
show *vb.* **1.** appear, be visible, blow wide open (*slang*), disclose, display, divulge, evidence, evince, exhibit, indicate, make known, manifest, present, register, reveal, testify to **2.** assert, clarify, demonstrate, elucidate, evince, explain, instruct, point out, present, prove, teach **3.** accord, act with, bestow, confer, grant **4.** accompany, attend, conduct, escort, guide, lead *~n.* **5.** entertainment, presentation, production **6.** array, demonstration, display, exhibition, expo (*informal*), exposition, fair, manifestation, pageant, pageantry, parade, representation, sight, spectacle, view **7.** affectation, air, appearance, display, illusion, likeness, ostentation, parade, pose, pretence, pretext, profession, semblance

singers. **2** a glass case used to display objects in a museum or shop.

showdown *n Informal* a major confrontation that settles a dispute.

shower *n* **1 a** a kind of bathing in which a person stands upright and is sprayed with water from a nozzle. **b** a device, room, or booth for such bathing. **2** a brief period of rain, hail, sleet, or snow. **3** a sudden fall of many small light objects: *a shower of loose gravel.* **4** *Brit slang* a worthless or contemptible group of people. **5** *US, Canad, Austral & NZ* a party held to honour and present gifts to a prospective bride or prospective mother. ~*vb* **6** to take a shower. **7** to sprinkle with or as if with a shower: *the walkers were showered by volcanic ash.* **8** to present (someone) with things liberally: *he showered her with presents.* **showery** *adj*

showing *n* **1** a presentation, exhibition, or display. **2** manner of presentation.

showjumping *n* the sport of riding horses in competitions to demonstrate skill in jumping. **showjumper** *n*

showman *n, pl* **-men 1** a person skilled at presenting anything in an effective manner. **2** a person who presents or produces a show. **showmanship** *n*

shown *vb* a past participle of **show.**

show off *vb* **1** to exhibit or display (something) so as to invite admiration: *he was eager to show off his new car.* **2** *Informal* to flaunt skills, knowledge, or looks in order to attract attention or impress people. ~*n* **show-off 3** *Informal* a person who flaunts his or her skills, knowledge, or looks in order to attract attention or impress people.

showpiece *n* **1** anything displayed or exhibited. **2** something admired as a fine example of its type: *an orchestral showpiece.*

showplace *n* a place visited for its beauty or interest.

showroom *n* a room in which goods for sale, esp. cars or electrical or gas appliances, are on display.

show up *vb* **1** to reveal or be revealed clearly. **2** to expose the faults or defects of (someone or something) by comparison. **3** *Informal* to put (someone) to shame; embarrass. **4** *Informal* to arrive.

showy *adj* **showier, showiest 1** colourful, bright in appearance, and very noticeable, and perhaps rather vulgar: *showy jewellery.* **2** making an imposing display. **showily** *adv* **showiness** *n*

shrank *vb* a past tense of **shrink.**

shrapnel *n* **1** an artillery shell containing a number of small pellets or bullets which it is designed to scatter on explosion. **2** fragments from this type of shell.

shred *n* **1** a long narrow piece torn off something. **2** a very small amount: *not a shred of truth.* ~*vb* **shredding, shredded** *or* **shred 3** to tear into shreds. **shredder** *n*

shrew *n* **1** a small mouselike animal with a long snout. **2** a bad-tempered nagging woman. **shrewish** *adj*

shrewd *adj* intelligent and making good judgments. **shrewdly** *adv* **shrewdness** *n*

shriek *n* **1** a high-pitched scream. ~*vb* **2** to utter (words or sounds) in a high-pitched tone.

shrift *n* See **short shrift.**

shrike *n* a bird with a heavy hooked bill, which kills small animals by dashing them on thorns.

shrill *adj* **1** (of a sound) sharp and high-pitched. ~*vb* **2** to utter (words or sounds) in a shrill tone. **shrillness** *n* **shrilly** *adv*

shrimp *n* **1** a small edible shellfish with a long tail and a pair of pincers. **2** *Informal* a small person. ~*vb* **3** to fish for shrimps.

shrine *n* **1** a place of worship associated with a sacred person or object. **2** a container for sacred relics. **3** the tomb of a saint or other holy person. **4** a place that is visited and honoured because of its association with a famous person or event: *he'd come to worship at the shrine of Mozart.*

shrink *vb* **shrinking, shrank** *or* **shrunk; shrunk** *or* **shrunken 1** to become or cause to become smaller, sometimes because of wetness, heat, or cold. **2 shrink from a** to withdraw or move away through fear: *they didn't shrink from danger.* **b** to feel great reluctance (to perform a task or duty). ~*n* **3** *Slang* a psychiatrist.

shrinkage *n* **1** the fact of shrinking. **2** the amount by which anything decreases in size, value, or weight.

shrink-wrap *vb* **-wrapping, -wrapped** to package (a product) in a flexible plastic wrapping which shrinks about its contours to seal it.

shrivel *vb* **-elling, -elled** *or US* **-eling, -eled** to become dry and withered.

THESAURUS

showdown *informal* breaking point, clash, climax, confrontation, crisis, culmination, denouement, exposé, face-off (*slang*), moment of truth

shower *n.* **1.** barrage, deluge, fusillade, plethora, rain, stream, torrent, volley **2.** *Brit. slang* bunch of layabouts, crew, rabble ~*vb.* **3.** deluge, heap, inundate, lavish, load, pour, rain, spray, sprinkle

showing *n.* **1.** demonstration, display, exhibition, presentation, staging **2.** account of oneself, appearance, demonstration, impression, performance, show, track record

showman entertainer, impresario, performer, publicist, stage manager

show off 1. advertise, demonstrate, display, exhibit, flaunt, parade, spread out **2.** *informal* boast, brag, make a spectacle of oneself, shoot a line (*informal*), swagger

show up 1. expose, highlight, lay bare, pinpoint, put the spotlight on, reveal, unmask **2.** *informal* embarrass, let down, mortify, put to shame, shame, show in a bad light **3.** *informal* appear, arrive, come, make an appearance, put in an appearance, turn up

shred *n.* **1.** bit, fragment, piece, rag, ribbon, scrap, sliver, snippet, tatter **2.** atom, grain, iota, jot, particle, scrap, trace, whit

shrewd acute, artful, astute, calculated, calculating, canny, clever, crafty, cunning, discerning, discriminating, far-seeing, far-sighted, fly (*slang*), intelligent, keen, knowing, long-headed, perceptive, perspicacious, sagacious, sharp, sly, smart, wily

shrewdly artfully, astutely, cannily, cleverly, far-sightedly, knowingly, perceptively, perspicaciously, sagaciously, with all one's wits about one, with consummate skill

shrewdness acumen, acuteness, astuteness, canniness, discernment, grasp, judgment, penetration, perspicacity, quick wits, sagacity, sharpness, smartness, suss (*slang*)

shriek *vb./n.* cry, holler, howl, scream, screech, squeal, wail, whoop, yell

shrill acute, ear-piercing, ear-splitting, high, high-pitched, penetrating, piercing, piping, screeching, sharp

shrink 1. contract, decrease, deflate, diminish, drop off, dwindle, fall off, grow smaller, lessen, narrow, shorten, shrivel, wither, wrinkle **2. shrink from** cower, cringe, draw back, flinch, hang back, quail, recoil, retire, shy away, wince, withdraw

shrivel dehydrate, desiccate, dwindle, shrink, wilt, wither, wizen, wrinkle

shroud *n* **1** a piece of cloth used to wrap a dead body. **2** anything that hides things: *a shroud of smoke.* ~*vb* **3** to hide or obscure (something): *shrouded in uncertainty; shrouded by smog.*

Shrove Tuesday *n* the day before Ash Wednesday.

shrub *n* a woody plant, smaller than a tree, with several stems instead of a trunk. **shrubby** *adj*

shrubbery *n, pl* **-beries 1** an area planted with shrubs. **2** shrubs collectively.

shrug *vb* **shrugging, shrugged 1** to draw up and drop (the shoulders) as a sign of indifference or doubt. ~*n* **2** the action of shrugging.

shrug off *vb* **1** to treat (a matter) as unimportant. **2** to get rid of (someone).

shrunk *vb* a past tense and past participle of **shrink.**

shrunken *vb* **1** a past participle of **shrink.** ~*adj* **2** reduced in size.

shudder *vb* **1** to shake or tremble suddenly and violently from horror or fear. **2** (of a machine) to shake violently. ~*n* **3** a shiver of fear or horror.

shuffle *vb* **-fling, -fled 1** to walk or move (the feet) with a slow dragging motion. **2** to mix together in a jumbled mass: *the chairman shuffled his papers.* **3** to mix up (playing cards) so as to change their order. ~*n* **4** an instance of shuffling. **5** a rearrangement: *a shuffle of top management.* **6** a dance with short dragging movements of the feet.

shufti *n Brit slang* a look; peep.

shun *vb* **shunning, shunned** to avoid deliberately.

shunt *vb* **1** to move (objects or people) to a different position. **2** *Railways* to transfer (engines or carriages) from track to track. ~*n* **3** the act of shunting. **4** a railway point. **5** *Electronics* a conductor connected in parallel across a part of a circuit to divert a known fraction of the current. **6** *Informal* a collision where one vehicle runs into the back of another.

shush *interj* **1** be quiet! hush! ~*vb* **2** to quiet (someone) by saying "shush".

shut *vb* **shutting, shut 1** to move (something) so as to cover an opening: *shut the door.* **2** to close (something) by bringing together the parts: *Ridley shut the folder.* **3 shut up** to close or lock the doors of: *let's shut up the shop.* **4 shut in** to confine or enclose. **5 shut out** to prevent from entering. **6** (of a shop or other establishment) to stop operating for the day: *the late-night rush after the pubs shut.* ~*adj* **7** closed or fastened. ~See also **shutdown, shut off,** etc.

shutdown *n* **1** the closing of a factory, shop, or other business. ~*vb* **shut down 2** to discontinue operations permanently.

shuteye *n Slang* sleep.

shut off *vb* **1** to cut off the flow or supply of. **2** to turn off and stop working: *I shut off the car engine.* **3** to isolate or separate: *ghettoes shut off from the rest of society.*

shut out *vb* **1** to keep out or exclude. **2** to conceal from sight: *blinds were drawn to shut out the sun.*

shutter *n* **1** a hinged doorlike cover, usually one of a pair, for closing off a window. **2 put up the shutters** to close business at the end of the day or permanently. **3** *Photog* a device in a camera that opens to allow light through the lens so as to expose the film when a photograph is taken. ~*vb* **4** to close or equip with a shutter or shutters.

shuttle *n* **1** a bus, train, or aircraft that makes frequent journeys between two places which are fairly near to each other. **2** a bobbin-like device used in weaving to pass the weft thread between the warp threads. **3** a small bobbin-like device used to hold the thread in a sewing machine. ~*vb* **-tling, -tled 4** to travel back and forth.

shuttlecock *n* a rounded piece of cork or plastic with feathers stuck in one end, struck to and fro in badminton.

shut up *vb* **1** *Informal* to stop talking or cause (someone) to stop talking: often used in commands. **2** to confine or imprison (someone).

shy[1] *adj* **1** not at ease in the company of others. **2** easily frightened; timid. **3 shy of** cautious or wary of. **4** reluctant or unwilling: *camera-shy; workshy.* ~*vb* **shies, shying, shied 5** to move back or aside suddenly from fear: *with a terrified whinny the horse shied.* **6 shy away from** to draw back from (doing something), through lack of confidence. ~*n, pl* **shies 7** a sudden movement back or aside from fear. **shyly** *adv* **shyness** *n*

shy[2] *vb* **shies, shying, shied 1** to throw (something). ~*n, pl* **shies 2** a quick throw.

Shylock *n* an unsympathetic and demanding person to whom one owes money.

si *n Music* same as **te.**

Si *Chem* silicon.

SI See **SI unit.**

Siamese *n, pl* **-mese 1** same as **Siamese cat.** ~*adj, n, pl* **-mese 2** (formerly) same as **Thai.**

Siamese cat *n* a breed of cat with cream fur, dark ears and face, and blue eyes.

Siamese twins *pl n* twins born joined together at some part of the body.

sibilant *adj* **1** having a hissing sound. ~*n* **2** *Phonetics* a consonant, such as *s* or *z,* that is pronounced with a hissing sound.

THESAURUS

shrivelled desiccated, dried up, dry, sere (*archaic*), shrunken, withered, wizened, wrinkled

shroud *n.* **1.** cerecloth, cerement, covering, grave clothes, winding sheet **2.** cloud, mantle, pall, screen, veil ~*vb.* **3.** blanket, cloak, conceal, cover, envelop, hide, screen, swathe, veil

shudder 1. *vb.* convulse, quake, quiver, shake, shiver, tremble **2.** *n.* convulsion, quiver, spasm, trembling, tremor

shuffle *vb.* **1.** drag, scrape, scuff, scuffle, shamble **2.** confuse, disarrange, disorder, intermix, jumble, mix, rearrange, shift

shun avoid, cold-shoulder, elude, eschew, evade, fight shy of, give (someone *or* something) a wide berth, have no part in, keep away from, shy away from, steer clear of

shut 1. bar, close, draw to, fasten, push to, seal, secure, slam **2.** *with* **in** cage, confine, enclose, exclude, impound, imprison, pound, wall off *or* up

shut down cease, cease operating, close, discontinue, halt, shut up, stop, switch off

shut out bar, black, blackball, debar, exclude, keep out, lock out, ostracize

shuttle *vb.* alternate, commute, go back and forth, go to and fro, ply, seesaw, shunt

shut up 1. *informal* be quiet, button it (*slang*), button one's lip (*slang*), fall silent, gag, hold one's tongue, hush, keep one's trap shut (*slang*), muzzle, pipe down (*slang*), put a sock in it (*Brit. slang*), silence **2.** box in, cage, confine, coop up, immure, imprison, incarcerate, intern, keep in

shy 1. *adj.* backward, bashful, cautious, chary, coy, diffident, distrustful, hesitant, modest, mousy, nervous, reserved, reticent, retiring, self-conscious, self-effacing, shrinking, suspicious, timid, wary **2.** *vb.* balk,

sibling *n* a brother or sister.

sibyl *n* (in ancient Greece and Rome) a prophetess. **sibylline** *adj*

sic[1] *adv* thus: inserted in brackets in a text to indicate that an odd spelling or reading is in fact what was written, even though it is or appears to be wrong.

sic[2] *vb* **sicking, sicked 1** to attack: used only in commands to a dog. **2** to urge (a dog) to attack (someone).

sick *adj* **1** vomiting or likely to vomit. **2** physically or mentally unwell. **3** of or for ill people: *sick pay.* **4** deeply affected with mental or spiritual distress: *sick at heart.* **5** mentally disturbed. **6** *Informal* making fun of death, illness, or misfortune: *a sick joke.* **7 sick of** *or* **sick and tired of** *Informal* disgusted by or weary of: *I'm sick of this town.* ~*n, vb* **8** *Informal* same as **vomit.**

sickbay *n* a room for the treatment of sick people, for example on a ship.

sicken *vb* **1** to make (someone) feel nauseated or disgusted. **2 sicken for** to show symptoms of (an illness).

sickening *adj* **1** causing horror or disgust: *sickening scenes of violence.* **2** *Informal* extremely annoying. **sickeningly** *adv*

sickie *n Austral & NZ informal* a day of sick leave from work.

sickle *n* a tool for cutting grass and grain crops, with a curved blade and a short handle.

sick leave *n* leave of absence from work through illness.

sickly *adj* **-lier, -liest 1** weak and unhealthy. **2** (of a person) looking pale and unwell: *sickly pallor.* **3** unpleasant to smell, taste, or look at. **4** showing excessive emotion in a weak and rather pathetic way: *a sickly tune.* ~*adv* **5** suggesting sickness: *sickly pale.* **sickliness** *n*

sickness *n* **1** a particular illness or disease: *sleeping sickness.* **2** the state of being ill or unhealthy: *absent from work due to sickness.* **3** a feeling of queasiness in the stomach followed by vomiting.

side *n* **1** a line or surface that borders anything. **2** *Geom* a line forming part of the perimeter of a plane figure: *a square has four sides.* **3** either of two parts into which an object, surface, or area can be divided: *the right side and the left side.* **4** either of the two surfaces of a flat object: *write on both sides of the page.* **5** the sloping part of a hill or bank. **6** either the left or the right half of the body, esp. the area around the waist: *he took a nine millimetre bullet in the side.* **7** the area immediately next to a person or thing: *at the side of my bed.* **8** a place within an area identified by reference to a central point: *the south side of the island.* **9** the area at the edge of something, as opposed to the centre: *the far side of the square.* **10** aspect or part: *there is a positive side to truancy.* **11** one of two or more contesting groups or teams: *the two sides will meet in the final.* **12** a position held in opposition to another in a dispute. **13** a line of descent through one parent: *a relative on his father's side.* **14** *Informal* a television channel. **15** *Brit slang* conceit or cheek: *to put on side.* **16 on one side** apart from the rest. **17 on the side** in addition to a person's main work: *she did a little public speaking on the side.* **18 side by side** close together. **19 side by side with** beside or near to. **20 take sides** to support one party in a dispute against another. ~*adj* **21** situated at the side: *the side entrance.* **22** less important: *a side issue.* ~*vb* **siding, sided 23 side with** to support (one party in a dispute).

sideboard *n* a piece of furniture for a dining room, with drawers, cupboards, and shelves to hold tableware.

sideboards *or esp US & Canad* **sideburns** *pl n* a man's whiskers grown down either side of the face in front of the ears.

sidecar *n* a small passenger car attached to the side of a motorcycle.

side effect *n* **1** a usually unwanted effect caused by a drug in addition to its intended one. **2** any additional effect, usually an undesirable one: *the unforeseen side effects of the end of the Cold War.*

sidekick *n Informal* a close friend or associate.

sidelight *n* **1** *Brit* either of two small lights at the front of a motor vehicle. **2** either of the two navigational lights used by ships at night.

sideline *n* an extra job in addition to one's main job.

sidelines *pl n* **1** *Sport* **a** the lines that mark the side boundaries of a playing area. **b** the area just outside the playing area, where substitute players sit. **2 on the sidelines a** only passively involved: *on the sidelines of the EU.* **b** waiting to join in an activity.

sidelong *adj* **1** directed to the side; oblique. ~*adv* **2** from the side; obliquely.

sidereal (side-eer-ee-al) *adj* of or determined with reference to the stars: *the sidereal time.*

side-saddle *n* **1** a riding saddle originally designed for women in skirts, allowing the rider to sit with both legs on the same side of the horse. ~*adv* **2** on a side-saddle.

sideshow *n* **1** an event or incident considered less

THESAURUS

buck, draw back, flinch, quail, rear, recoil, start, swerve, take fright, wince

shyness bashfulness, diffidence, lack of confidence, modesty, mousiness, nervousness, reticence, self-consciousness, timidity, timidness, timorousness

sick 1. green around the gills (*informal*), ill, nauseated, nauseous, puking (*slang*), qualmish, queasy **2.** ailing, diseased, feeble, indisposed, laid up (*informal*), on the sick list (*informal*), poorly (*informal*), under par (*informal*), under the weather, unwell, weak **3.** *informal* black, ghoulish, macabre, morbid, sadistic **4.** *with* **of** *informal* blasé, bored, disgusted, displeased, fed up, jaded, revolted, satiated, tired, weary

sicken 1. disgust, gross out (*U.S. slang*), make one's gorge rise, nauseate, repel, revolt, turn one's stomach **2. sicken for** ail, be stricken by, contract, fall ill, go down with, show symptoms of, take sick

sickening cringe-making (*Brit. informal*), disgusting, distasteful, foul, loathsome, nauseating, nauseous, noisome, offensive, putrid, repulsive, revolting, stomach-turning (*informal*), vile, yucky *or* yukky (*slang*)

sickly 1. ailing, bilious, bloodless, delicate, faint, feeble, indisposed, infirm, in poor health, lacklustre, languid, pallid, peaky, pining, unhealthy, wan, weak **2.** bilious (*informal*), cloying, mawkish, nauseating, revolting (*informal*), syrupy (*informal*)

sickness 1. affliction, ailment, bug (*informal*), complaint, disease, disorder, illness, indisposition, infirmity, malady **2.** (the) collywobbles (*slang*), nausea, puking (*slang*), queasiness, vomiting

side *n.* **1.** border, boundary, division, edge, limit, margin, part, perimeter, periphery, rim, sector, verge **2.** aspect, face, facet, flank, hand, part, surface, view **3.** camp, cause, faction, party, sect, team **4.** *Brit. slang* airs, arrogance, insolence, pretentiousness ~*adj.* **5.** flanking, lateral **6.** ancillary, incidental, indirect, lesser, marginal, minor, oblique, roundabout, secondary, subordinate, subsidiary ~*vb.* **7. side with** ally with, associate oneself with, befriend, favour, go along with,

important than another: *a mere sideshow compared to the war on the Russian front.* **2** a small show or entertainment offered along with the main show at a circus or fair.

side-splitting *adj* causing a great deal of laughter.

sidestep *vb* **-stepping, -stepped 1** to step out of the way of (something). **2** to dodge (an issue). *~n* **side step 3** a movement to one side, such as in dancing or boxing.

sideswipe *n* **1** an unexpected criticism of someone or something while discussing another subject. **2** a glancing blow along or from the side. *~vb* **-swiping, -swiped 3** to make a sideswipe.

sidetrack *vb* to distract (someone) from a main subject.

sidewalk *n US & Canad* a pavement.

sideways *adv* **1** moving, facing, or inclining towards one side. **2** from one side; obliquely. **3** with one side forward. *~adj* **4** moving or directed to or from one side.

side whiskers *pl n* same as **sideboards.**

siding *n* a short stretch of railway track connected to a main line, used for loading and unloading freight and storing engines and carriages.

sidle *vb* **-dling, -dled** to walk slowly and carefully, not wanting to be noticed.

SIDS sudden infant death syndrome; cot death.

siege *n* **1** a military operation carried out to capture a place by surrounding and blockading it. **2** a similar operation carried out by police, for example to force people out of a place. **3 lay siege to** to subject (a place) to a siege.

siemens *n, pl* **siemens** the SI unit of electrical conductance.

sienna *n* **1** a natural earth used as a reddish-brown or yellowish-brown pigment. *~adj* **2 burnt sienna** reddish-brown. **3 raw sienna** yellowish-brown.

sierra *n* a range of mountains with jagged peaks in Spain or America.

sies (**siss**) *interj S African informal* same as **sis**[2].

siesta *n* an afternoon nap, taken in hot countries.

sieve (**siv**) *n* **1** a utensil with a mesh through which a substance is sifted or strained. *~vb* **sieving, sieved 2** to sift or strain through a sieve.

sift *vb* **1** to sieve (a powdery substance) in order to remove the coarser particles. **2** to examine (information or evidence) carefully to select what is important.

sigh *vb* **1** to draw in and audibly let out a deep breath as an expression of sadness, tiredness, longing, or relief. **2** to make a sound resembling this. **3 sigh for** to long for. **4** to say (something) with a sigh. *~n* **5** the act or sound of sighing.

sight *n* **1** the ability to see; vision. **2** an instance of seeing. **3** the range of vision: *the cemetery was out of sight.* **4** anything that is seen. **5** point of view; judgment: *nothing has changed in my sight.* **6** *Informal* anything unpleasant to see: *she looked a sight in the streetlamps.* **7** a device for guiding the eye in aiming a gun or making an observation with an optical instrument. **8** an aim or observation made with such a device. **9 sights** anything worth seeing: *the great sights of Barcelona.* **10 a sight** *Informal* a great deal: *it's a sight warmer than in the hall.* **11 a sight for sore eyes** a welcome sight. **12 catch sight of** to glimpse. **13 know someone by sight** to be able to recognize someone without having ever been introduced. **14 lose sight of a** to be unable to see (something) any longer. **b** to forget: *we lose sight of priorities.* **15 on sight** as soon as someone or something is seen. **16 set one's sights on** to have (a specified goal) in mind. **17 sight unseen** without having seen the object concerned: *he would have taken it sight unseen.* *~vb* **18** to see (someone or something) briefly or suddenly: *the wanted men were sighted in Manchester.* **19** to aim (a firearm) using the sight.

sighted *adj* not blind.

sightless *adj* blind.

sight-read *vb* **-reading, -read** to sing or play (music in a printed form) without previous preparation. **sight-reading** *n*

sightscreen *n Cricket* a large white screen placed near the boundary behind the bowler, which helps the batsman see the ball.

sightseeing *n Informal* visiting famous or interesting sights in a place. **sightseer** *n*

sigma *n* **1** the 18th letter in the Greek alphabet (Σ, σ). **2** *Maths* the symbol Σ, indicating summation.

sign *n* **1** something that indicates a fact or condition that is not immediately or outwardly observable: *a sign of tension.* **2** a gesture, mark, or symbol intended to convey an idea or information. **3** a board or placard displayed in public and intended to advertise, inform, or warn. **4** a conventional mark or symbol that has a specific meaning, for example £ for pounds. **5** *Maths* **a** any symbol used to indicate an operation: *a minus sign.* **b** a symbol used to indicate whether a number or expression is positive or negative. **6** a visible indication: *no sign of the enemy.* **7** an omen. **8** *Med* any evidence of the presence of a disease or disorder. **9** *Astrol* short for **sign of the zodiac.** *~vb* **10** to write (one's name) on (a document or letter) to show its authenticity or one's agreement. **11** to communicate using sign language. **12** to make a sign to someone so

THESAURUS

join with, second, support, take the part of, team up with (*informal*)

sidelong *adj.* covert, indirect, oblique, sideways

sidestep avoid, bypass, circumvent, dodge, duck (*informal*), elude, evade, find a way round, skip, skirt

sidetrack deflect, distract, divert, lead off the subject

sideways 1. *adv.* crabwise, edgeways, laterally, obliquely, sidelong, sidewards, to the side **2.** *adj.* oblique, side, sidelong, slanted

siesta catnap, doze, forty winks (*informal*), kip (*Brit. slang*), nap, rest, sleep, snooze (*informal*)

sieve 1. *n.* colander, riddle, screen, sifter, strainer **2.** *vb.* bolt, remove, riddle, separate, sift, strain

sift 1. bolt, filter, pan, part, riddle, separate, sieve **2.** analyse, examine, fathom, go through, investigate, pore over, probe, research, screen, scrutinize, work over

sigh *vb.* **1.** breathe, complain, grieve, lament, moan, sorrow, sough, suspire (*archaic*) **2.** *often with* **for** eat one's heart out over, languish, long, mourn, pine, yearn

sight *n.* **1.** eye, eyes, eyesight, seeing, vision **2.** appearance, apprehension, eyeshot, field of vision, ken, perception, range of vision, view, viewing, visibility **3.** *informal* blot on the landscape (*informal*), eyesore, fright (*informal*), mess, monstrosity, spectacle **4.** **catch sight of** descry, espy, glimpse, recognize, spot, view *~vb.* **5.** behold, discern, distinguish, make out, observe, perceive, see, spot

sign *n.* **1.** clue, evidence, gesture, giveaway, hint, indication, manifestation, mark, note, proof, signal, spoor, suggestion, symptom, token, trace, vestige **2.** board, notice, placard, warning **3.** badge, character, cipher, device, emblem, ensign, figure, logo, mark, representation, symbol **4.** augury, auspice, foreboding, forewarning, omen, portent, presage, warning, writing on the

as to convey an idea or information. **13** to engage or be engaged by signing a contract: *I dreamed of signing for Liverpool when I was young.* ~See also **sign away, sign in,** etc.

signal *n* **1** any sign, gesture, sound, or action used to communicate information. **2** anything that causes immediate action: *this is the signal for a detailed examination of the risk.* **3 a** a variable voltage, current, or electromagnetic wave, by which information is conveyed through an electronic circuit. **b** the information so conveyed. *~adj* **4** *Formal* very important: *a signal triumph for the government.* *~vb* **-nalling, -nalled** *or US* **-naling, -naled 5** to communicate (information) by signal. **signally** *adv*

signal box *n* a building from which railway signals are operated.

signalman *n, pl* **-men** a railwayman in charge of the signals and points within a section.

signatory (**sig**-na-tree) *n, pl* **-ries 1** a person, organization, or state that has signed a document such as a treaty. *~adj* **2** having signed a document or treaty.

signature *n* **1** a person's name written by himself or herself, used in signing something. **2** a distinctive characteristic that identifies a person or animal. **3** *Music* a sign at the beginning of a piece to show key or time. **4** *Printing* a sheet of paper printed with several pages, which when folded becomes a section of a book.

signature tune *n Brit* a piece of music used to introduce a particular television or radio programme.

sign away *vb* to give up one's right to (something): *she was determined not to sign away Britain's sovereignty.*

signboard *n* a board carrying a sign or notice, often to advertise a business or product.

signet *n* a small seal used to make documents official.

signet ring *n* a finger ring engraved with an initial or other emblem.

significance *n* **1** the effect something is likely to have on other things: *an event of important significance in British history.* **2** meaning: *the occult significance of the symbol.*

significant *adj* **1** very important. **2** having or expressing a meaning. **significantly** *adv*

significant figures *pl n Maths* **1** the figures of a number that express a magnitude to a specified degree of accuracy: *3.141 59 to four significant figures is 3.142.* **2** the number of such figures: *3.142 has four significant figures.*

signify *vb* **-fies, -fying, -fied 1** to indicate or suggest. **2** to stand as a symbol or sign for: *a blue line on the map signified a river.* **3** to be important.

sign in *vb* **1** to sign a register on arrival at a place. **2** to admit (a nonmember) to a club or institution as a guest by signing a register on his or her behalf.

sign language *n* a system of communication using hand and arm movements, such as one used by deaf people.

sign off *vb* to announce the end of a radio or television programme.

sign of the zodiac *n Astrol* any of the 12 areas into which the zodiac is divided.

sign on *vb* **1** *Brit* to register and report regularly at an unemployment-benefit office. **2** to commit oneself to a job or activity by signing a form or contract.

signor (see-**nyor**) *n* an Italian form of address equivalent to *sir* or *Mr.*

signora (see-**nyor**-a) *n* an Italian form of address equivalent to *madam* or *Mrs.*

signorina (see-nyor-**ee**-na) *n* an Italian form of address equivalent to *madam* or *Miss.*

sign out *vb* to sign a register to indicate that one is leaving a place.

signpost *n* **1** a road sign displaying information, such as the distance to the next town. **2** an indication as to how an event is likely to develop or advice on what course of action should be taken. *~vb* **3** to mark (the way) with signposts.

sign up *vb* **1** to agree to do a job or course by signing a document. **2** to enlist for military service.

Sikh (**seek**) *n* **1** a member of an Indian religion that teaches that there is only one God. *~adj* **2** of the Sikhs or their religious beliefs or customs. **Sikhism** *n*

silage (**sile**-ij) *n* a fodder crop harvested while green and partially fermented in a silo.

silence *n* **1** the state or quality of being silent. **2** the absence of sound. **3** refusal or failure to speak or communicate when expected: *he's broken his silence on the issue.* *~vb* **-lencing, -lenced 4** to cause (someone or something) to become silent. **5** to put a stop to: *a way of silencing criticism.*

silencer *n* any device designed to reduce noise, for example one fitted to the exhaust system of a motor vehicle or one fitted to the muzzle of a gun.

silent *adj* **1** tending to speak very little. **2** failing to speak or communicate when expected: *they remained silent as minutes passed.* **3** producing no noise: *the silent room.* **4** not spoken: *silent reproach.* **5** (of a letter) used in the spelling of a word but not pronounced, such as the *k* in *know.* **6** (of a film) having no soundtrack. **silently** *adv*

THESAURUS

wall *~vb.* **5.** autograph, endorse, initial, inscribe, set one's hand to, subscribe **6.** beckon, gesticulate, gesture, indicate, signal, use sign language, wave

signal 1. *n.* beacon, cue, flare, gesture, go-ahead (*informal*), green light, indication, indicator, mark, sign, token **2.** *adj. formal* conspicuous, distinguished, eminent, exceptional, extraordinary, famous, memorable, momentous, notable, noteworthy, outstanding, remarkable, significant, striking **3.** *vb.* beckon, communicate, gesticulate, gesture, give a sign to, indicate, motion, nod, sign, wave

significance 1. consequence, consideration, importance, impressiveness, matter, moment, relevance, weight **2.** force, implication(s), import, meaning, message, point, purport, sense, signification

significant 1. critical, important, material, momentous, noteworthy, serious, vital, weighty **2.** denoting, eloquent, expressing, expressive, indicative, knowing, meaning, meaningful, pregnant, suggestive

signify 1. announce, be a sign of, betoken, communicate, connote, convey, denote, evidence, exhibit, express, imply, indicate, intimate, matter, mean, portend, proclaim, represent, show, stand for, suggest, symbolize **2.** be of importance *or* significance, carry weight, count, matter

silence *n.* **1.** calm, hush, lull, noiselessness, peace, quiescence, quiet, stillness **2.** dumbness, muteness, reticence, speechlessness, taciturnity, uncommunicativeness *~vb.* **3.** cut off, cut short, deaden, extinguish, gag, muffle, quell, quiet, quieten, stifle, still, strike dumb, subdue, suppress

silent 1. dumb, mum, mute, nonvocal, not talkative, speechless, struck dumb, taciturn, tongue-tied, uncommunicative, unspeaking, voiceless, wordless **2.** hushed, muted, noiseless, quiet, soundless, still, stilly (*poetic*) **3.** aphonic (*Phonetics*), implicit, implied, tacit, understood, unexpressed, unpronounced, unspoken

silhouette *n* **1** the outline of a dark shape seen against a light background. **2** an outline drawing, often a profile portrait, filled in with black. *~vb* **-etting, -etted 3** to show (something) in silhouette.

silica *n* a hard glossy mineral, silicon dioxide, which occurs naturally as quartz and is used in the manufacture of glass.

silicate *n Mineral* a compound of silicon, oxygen, and a metal.

silicon *n* **1** *Chem* a brittle non-metallic element: used in transistors, solar cells, and alloys. Symbol: Si *~adj* **2** denoting an area of a country that contains much high-technology industry: *the Silicon Glen.*

silicon chip *n* same as **chip** (sense 3).

silicone *n Chem* a tough synthetic material made from silicon and used in lubricants, paints, and resins.

silicosis *n Pathol* a lung disease caused by breathing in silica dust.

silk *n* **1** the fine soft fibre produced by a silkworm. **2** thread or fabric made from this fibre. **3 silks** clothing made of this. **4** *Brit* **a** the gown worn by a Queen's (or King's) Counsel. **b** *Informal* a Queen's (or King's) Counsel. **c take silk** to become a Queen's (or King's) Counsel.

silken *adj* **1** made of silk. **2** *Literary* smooth and soft: *her silken hair.*

silk-screen printing *n* same as **screen process.**

silkworm *n* a caterpillar that spins a cocoon of silk.

silky *adj* **silkier, silkiest 1** soft, smooth, and shiny. **2** (of a voice or manner) smooth and elegant. **silkiness** *n*

sill *n* **1** a shelf at the bottom of a window, either inside or outside a room. **2** the lower horizontal part of a window or door frame.

silly *adj* **-lier, -liest 1** behaving in a foolish or childish way. **2** *Old-fashioned* unable to think sensibly, as if from a blow. **3** *Cricket* (of a fielding position) near the batsman's wicket: *silly mid-off. ~n, pl* **-lies 4** *Informal* a foolish person. **silliness** *n*

silo *n, pl* **-los 1** an airtight pit or tower in which silage is made and stored. **2** an underground structure in which missile systems are sited for protection.

silt *n* **1** a fine sediment of mud or clay deposited by moving water. *~vb* **2 silt up** to fill or choke up with silt: *the channels have been silted up.*

Silurian (sile-**yoor**-ee-an) *adj Geol* of the period of geological time about 425 million years ago, during which fishes first appeared.

silvan *adj* same as **sylvan.**

silver *n* **1** a precious greyish-white metallic element: used in jewellery, tableware, and coins. Symbol: Ag **2** a coin or coins made of silver. **3** any household articles made of silver. **4** short for **silver medal.** *~adj* **5** greyish-white: *silver hair.* **6** (of anniversaries) the 25th in a series: *Silver Jubilee; silver wedding. ~vb* **7** to coat with silver or a silvery substance: *a company that silvers their own mirrors.* **8** to cause (something) to become silvery in colour: *the sun silvered the tarmac.*

silver beet *n* a beet of Australia and New Zealand with edible spinach-like leaves.

silver birch *n* a tree with silvery-white peeling bark.

silverfish *n, pl* **-fish** *or* **-fishes 1** a small wingless silver-coloured insect. **2** a silver-coloured fish.

silver lining *n* a hopeful side of an otherwise desperate or unhappy situation.

silver medal *n* a medal of silver awarded to a competitor who comes second in a contest or race.

silver plate *n* **1** a thin layer of silver deposited on a base metal. **2** articles, such as tableware, made of silver plate. **silver-plate** *vb*

silver screen *n Informal* films collectively or the film industry.

silverside *n Brit & NZ* a cut of beef from below the rump and above the leg.

silversmith *n* a craftsman who makes or repairs items made of silver.

silver thaw *n Canad* **1** a freezing rainstorm. **2** same as **glitter. 3**

silverware *n* items, such as tableware, made of or plated with silver.

silvery *adj* **1** having the appearance or colour of silver: *her silvery eyes.* **2** having a clear ringing sound: *a cascade of silvery notes.*

silviculture *n* the cultivation of forest trees.

simian *adj* **1** of or resembling a monkey or ape. *~n* **2** a monkey or ape.

similar *adj* **1** alike but not identical. **2** *Geom* (of two or more figures) different in size or position, but with exactly the same shape. **similarity** *n* **similarly** *adv*

➤ Do not confuse *similar* and *same. Similar* is "alike but not identical"; *same* means "identical".

simile (**sim**-ill-ee) *n* a figure of speech that likens one thing to another of a different category, introduced by *as* or *like.*

similitude *n Formal* likeness; similarity.

simmer *vb* **1** to cook (food) gently at just below boiling point. **2** (of violence or conflict) to threaten to break out: *revolt simmering among rural MPs. ~n* **3** the state of simmering.

simmer down *vb Informal* to calm down after being angry.

simnel cake *n Brit* a fruit cake covered with marzipan, traditionally eaten during Lent or at Easter.

simony (**sime**-on-ee) *n Christianity* the practice of buying or selling Church benefits such as pardons.

THESAURUS

silently as quietly as a mouse (*informal*), dumbly, inaudibly, in silence, mutely, noiselessly, quietly, soundlessly, speechlessly, without a sound, wordlessly

silhouette 1. *n.* delineation, form, outline, profile, shape **2.** *vb.* delineate, etch, outline, stand out

silky silken, sleek, smooth, velvety

silly *adj.* **1.** absurd, asinine, brainless, childish, dopey (*slang*), dozy (*Brit. informal*), fatuous, foolhardy, foolish, frivolous, giddy, goofy (*informal*), idiotic, immature, imprudent, inane, inappropriate, irresponsible, meaningless, pointless, preposterous, puerile, ridiculous, senseless, stupid, unwise, witless **2.** *old-fashioned* benumbed, dazed, groggy (*informal*), in a daze, muzzy, stunned, stupefied *~n.* **3.** *informal* clot (*Brit. informal*), duffer (*informal*), goose (*informal*), ignoramus, nerd *or* nurd (*slang*), ninny, nitwit (*informal*), plonker (*slang*), prat (*offensive*), simpleton, twit (*informal, chiefly Brit.*), wally (*slang*)

silver 1. *n.* silver plate, silverware **2.** *adj.* pearly, silvered, silvery

similar alike, analogous, close, comparable, congruous, corresponding, homogenous, in agreement, much the same, resembling, uniform

similarity affinity, agreement, analogy, closeness, comparability, concordance, congruence, correspondence, likeness, point of comparison, relation, resemblance, sameness, similitude

similarly by the same token, correspondingly, in like manner, likewise

simmer *vb.* be angry (agitated, tense, uptight (*informal*)), boil, burn, fume, rage, see red (*informal*), seethe, smart, smoulder

simoom *n* a hot suffocating sand-laden desert wind.
simper *vb* **1** to smile in a silly and mannered way. **2** to say (something) with a simper. *~n* **3** a simpering smile. **simpering** *adj*
simple *adj* **1** easy to understand or do: *in simple English; simple exercises.* **2** plain and not elaborate: *a simple red skirt; a simple answer.* **3** not combined or complex: *simple diagnostic equipment.* **4** leading an uncomplicated life: *I am a simple man myself.* **5** sincere or frank: *a simple apology.* **6** of humble background: *the simple country girl.* **7** *Informal* mentally retarded. **8** straightforward: *a simple matter of choice.* **9** *Music* denoting a time where the number of beats per bar may be two, three, or four. **simplicity** *n*
simple fraction *n Maths* a fraction in which the numerator and denominator are both whole numbers.
simple fracture *n* a fracture in which the broken bone does not pierce the skin.
simple interest *n Finance* interest paid only on the original amount of a debt.
simple-minded *adj* **1** (of people) naive and unsophisticated. **2** (of opinions or explanations) not taking the complexity of an issue or subject into account. **simple-mindedness** *n*
simple sentence *n* a sentence consisting of a single main clause.
simpleton *n* a foolish or stupid person.
simplify *vb* **-fies, -fying, -fied 1** to make (something) less complicated. **2** *Maths* to reduce (an equation or fraction) to its simplest form. **simplification** *n*
simplistic *adj* (of an opinion or interpretation) too simple or naive.
simply *adv* **1** in a simple manner: *an interesting book, simply written.* **2** merely; just: *he's simply too slow.* **3** absolutely: *a simply enormous success.*
simulate *vb* **-lating, -lated 1** to pretend to feel or perform (an emotion or action); imitate: *I tried to simulate anger.* **2** to imitate the conditions of (a situation), as in carrying out an experiment: *we can then simulate global warming.* **3** to have the appearance of: *the wood had been painted to simulate stone.* **simulated** *adj* **simulation** *n*
simulator *n* a device that simulates specific conditions for the purposes of research or training: *a flight simulator.*
simultaneous *adj* occurring or existing at the same time. **simultaneously** *adv* **simultaneity** *n*
simultaneous equations *pl n Maths* a set of equations that are all satisfied by the same values of the variables, the number of variables being equal to the number of equations.
sin[1] *n* **1** the breaking of a religious or moral law. **2** any offence against a principle or standard. **3 live in sin** *Old-fashioned, informal* (of an unmarried couple) to live together. *~vb* **sinning, sinned 4** to commit a sin. **sinner** *n*
sin[2] *Maths* sine.
SIN (in Canada) Social Insurance Number.
sin bin *n Slang* the area in which ice hockey players must sit for a specified period after committing a serious foul.
since *prep* **1** during the period of time after: *one of their worst winters since 1945.* *~conj* **2** continuously from the time given: *they've been standing in line ever since she arrived.* **3** for the reason that; because. *~adv* **4** from that time: *I have often been asked since.*
➤ Avoid the use of *ago* with *since*. It is redundant: *It is ten years since he wrote his book* (not *ten years ago since*).
sincere *adj* genuine and honest: *sincere concern.* **sincerely** *adv* **sincerity** *n*
sine *n* (in trigonometry) the ratio of the length of the opposite side to that of the hypotenuse in a right-angled triangle.
sinecure (**sin**-ee-cure) *n* a paid job that involves very little work or responsibility.
sine die (**sin**-ay **dee**-ay) *adv* without fixing a day for future action or meeting.
sine qua non (**sin**-ay kwah **non**) *n* an essential requirement.

THESAURUS

simmer down *informal* calm down, collect oneself, contain oneself, control oneself, cool off *or* down, get down off one's high horse (*informal*), grow quieter, unwind (*informal*)
simple 1. clear, easy, elementary, intelligible, lucid, manageable, plain, straightforward, uncomplicated, understandable, uninvolved **2.** classic, clean, natural, plain, Spartan, unadorned, uncluttered, unembellished, unfussy **3.** elementary, pure, single, unalloyed, unblended, uncombined, undivided, unmixed **4.** bald, basic, direct, frank, honest, naked, plain, sincere, stark, undeniable, unvarnished **5.** homely, humble, lowly, modest, rustic, unpretentious **6.** *informal* brainless, credulous, dense, dumb (*informal*), feeble, feeble-minded, foolish, half-witted, moronic, obtuse, shallow, silly, slow, stupid, thick
simple-minded artless, natural, unsophisticated
simpleton berk (*Brit. slang*), blockhead, booby, charlie (*Brit. old-fashioned informal*), coot (*old-fashioned*), dolt, dope (*informal*), dullard, dunce, fool, goose (*informal*), greenhorn (*informal*), idiot, imbecile (*informal*), jerk (*slang, chiefly U.S. & Canad.*), moron, nerd *or* nurd (*slang*), nincompoop, ninny, nitwit (*informal*), numskull, oaf, stupid (*informal*), twerp (*informal*), twit (*informal, chiefly Brit.*), wally (*slang*)
simplicity 1. absence of complications, clarity, clearness, ease, easiness, elementariness, obviousness, straightforwardness **2.** clean lines, lack of adornment, modesty, naturalness, plainness, purity, restraint
simplify abridge, decipher, disentangle, facilitate, make intelligible, reduce to essentials, streamline
simply 1. clearly, directly, easily, intelligibly, modestly, naturally, plainly, straightforwardly, unaffectedly, unpretentiously, without any elaboration **2.** just, merely, only, purely, solely **3.** absolutely, altogether, completely, really, totally, unreservedly, utterly, wholly
simultaneous at the same time, coincident, coinciding, concurrent, contemporaneous, synchronous
simultaneously all together, at the same time, concurrently, in chorus, in concert, in the same breath, in unison, together
sin 1. *n.* crime, damnation, error, evil, guilt, iniquity, misdeed, offence, sinfulness, transgression (*formal*), trespass (*archaic*), ungodliness, unrighteousness, wickedness, wrong, wrongdoing **2.** *vb.* err, fall, fall from grace, go astray, lapse, offend, transgress (*formal*), trespass (*archaic*)
sincere artless, bona fide, candid, earnest, frank, genuine, guileless, heartfelt, honest, natural, no-nonsense, open, real, serious, straightforward, true, unaffected, unfeigned, upfront (*informal*), wholehearted
sincerely earnestly, genuinely, honestly, in all sincerity, in earnest, in good faith, really, seriously, truly, wholeheartedly
sincerity artlessness, bona fides, candour, frankness, genuineness, good faith, guilelessness, honesty, pro-

sinew *n* **1** *Anat* a tough fibrous cord connecting muscle to bone. **2** *Literary* physical strength.

sinewy *adj* lean and muscular.

sinful *adj* **1** having committed or tending to commit sin: *I am a sinful man.* **2** being a sin; wicked: *sinful acts.*

sing *vb* **singing, sang, sung 1** to produce musical sounds with the voice. **2** to perform (a song). **3** (of certain birds and insects) to make musical calls. **4 sing of** to tell a story in song about: *the minstrels sang of courtly love.* **5** to make a humming, ringing, or whistling sound: *the arrow sang past his ear.* **6** (of one's ears) to be filled with a continuous ringing sound. **7** to bring (someone) to a given state by singing: *I sang him to sleep.* **8** *Slang, chiefly US* to act as an informer. ~See also **sing out. singer** *n* **singing** *adj, n*

➤ The simple past of *sing* is *sang: He sang the chorus.* Avoid the use of the past participle *sung* for the simple past.

sing. singular.

singe *vb* **singeing, singed 1** to burn slightly without setting alight; scorch: *it singed his sheepskin.* ~*n* **2** a slight burn.

Singhalese *n, pl* **-lese,** *adj* same as **Sinhalese.**

singing telegram *n* **1** a service by which a person is employed to present greetings to someone on a special occasion by singing. **2** the greetings presented in this way. **3** the person who presents the greetings.

single *adj* **1** existing alone; solitary: *the cottage's single chimney.* **2** distinct from others of the same kind: *every single housing society.* **3** designed for one user: *a single room.* **4** unmarried. **5** even one: *there was not a single bathroom.* **6** (of a flower) having only one circle of petals. **7 single combat** a duel or fight involving two individuals. ~*n* **8** a hotel bedroom for one person. **9** a gramophone record that is 7 inches in diameter and has one short song or tune on each side. **10** *Cricket* a hit from which one run is scored. **11 a** *Brit* a pound note or coin. **b** *US & Canad* a dollar bill. **12** a ticket valid for a one-way journey only. ~*vb* **-gling, -gled 13 single out** to select from a group of people or things: *the judge had singled him out for praise.* ~See also **singles.**

single-breasted *adj* (of a jacket or coat) having the fronts overlapping only slightly and with one row of buttons.

single cream *n* cream which has a relatively low fat content and does not thicken when beaten.

single-decker *n Brit informal* a bus with only one passenger deck.

single entry *n* a book-keeping system in which all transactions are entered in one account only.

single file *n* a line of people, one behind the other.

single-handed *adj, adv* unaided or working alone: *the first single-handed sail in my boat; she had to take on the world single-handed.* **single-handedly** *adv*

single-minded *adj* having one purpose or aim only; dedicated. **single-mindedly** *adv* **single-mindedness** *n*

single-parent family *n* a family consisting of one parent and his or her child or children living together, the other parent being dead or permanently absent.

singles *pl n Sport* a match played with one person on each side.

singles bar *n* a bar that is a social meeting place for single people.

singlet *n Chiefly Brit* a man's sleeveless vest.

single ticket *n Brit* same as **single** (sense 12).

singleton *n Cards* the only card of a particular suit held by a player.

singly *adv* one at a time; one by one.

sing out *vb* to call out loudly.

singsong *n* **1** *Brit* an informal group singing session. ~*adj* **2** (of a voice) having a repetitive rise and fall in tone.

singular *adj* **1** *Grammar* (of a word or form) denoting only one person or thing: *a singular noun.* **2** remarkable; extraordinary: *one of the singular achievements.* **3** unusual; odd: *a lovable but very singular old woman.* ~*n* **4** *Grammar* the singular form of a word. **singularity** *n* **singularly** *adv*

Sinhalese *or* **Singhalese** *n* **1** (*pl* **-lese**) a member of a people living mainly in Sri Lanka. **2** the language of this people. ~*adj* **3** of this people. ~See also **Sri Lankan.**

sinister *adj* **1** threatening or suggesting evil or harm: *a sinister conspiracy.* **2** *Heraldry* of, on, or starting from the bearer's left side.

sink *vb* **sinking, sank, sunk** *or* **sunken 1** to submerge (in liquid). **2** to cause (a ship) to submerge by attacking it with bombs, torpedoes, etc. **3** to appear to descend towards or below the horizon. **4** to make or become lower in amount or value: *sterling sank to a record low against the Deutschmark.* **5** to move or fall into a lower position, esp. due to tiredness or weakness: *she sank back in her chair.* **6 sink into** to pass into a lower state or condition, esp. an unpleasant one: *to sink into debt.* **7** (of a voice) to become quieter. **8** to become weaker in health. **9** to dig (something sharp) into a solid object: *she sank her teeth into the steak.* **10** *Informal* to drink (a number of alcoholic drinks). **11** to dig, drill, or excavate (a hole or shaft). **12** to drive (a stake) into the ground. **13 sink in** *or* **into** to invest (money) in (a venture). **14** *Golf, snooker* to hit

THESAURUS

bity, seriousness, straightforwardness, truth, wholeheartedness

sinecure cushy number (*informal*), gravy train (*slang*), money for jam *or* old rope (*informal*), soft job (*informal*), soft option

sinful bad, corrupt, criminal, depraved, erring, guilty, immoral, iniquitous, irreligious, morally wrong, ungodly, unholy, unrighteous, wicked

sing 1. carol, chant, chirp, croon, make melody, pipe, trill, vocalize, warble, yodel **2.** buzz, hum, purr, whine, whistle **3.** *slang, chiefly U.S.* betray, blow the whistle (on) (*informal*), grass (*Brit. slang*), inform (on), peach (*slang*), rat (on) (*informal*), shop (*slang, chiefly Brit.*), spill one's guts (*slang*), spill the beans (*informal*), squeal (*slang*), tell all, turn in (*informal*)

singe burn, char, scorch, sear

singer cantor, chorister, crooner, minstrel, soloist, songster, songstress, troubadour, vocalist

single *adj.* **1.** distinct, individual, lone, one, only, particular, separate, singular, sole, solitary, unique **2.** free, unattached, unmarried, unwed ~*vb.* **3.** *usually with* **out** choose, cull, distinguish, fix on, pick, pick on *or* out, put on one side, select, separate, set apart, winnow

single-minded dedicated, determined, dogged, fixed, hellbent (*informal*), monomaniacal, steadfast, stubborn, tireless, undeviating, unswerving, unwavering

singly individually, one at a time, one by one, separately

singular 1. conspicuous, eminent, exceptional, notable, noteworthy, outstanding, prodigious, rare, remarkable, uncommon, unique, unparalleled **2.** atypical, curious, eccentric, extraordinary, odd, oddball (*informal*), out-of-the-way, outré, peculiar, puzzling, queer, strange, unusual, wacko (*slang*)

(the ball) into the hole or pocket: *Azinger sank a nine-foot putt.* ~*n* **15** a fixed basin in a kitchen or bathroom, with a water supply and drainpipe.

sinker *n* a weight attached to a fishing line or net to cause it to sink in water.

sink in *vb* (of a fact) to become fully understood: *the euphoria wore off as the implications sank in.*

sinking fund *n* a fund set aside to repay a long-term debt.

Sinn Féin (shin **fane**) *n* an Irish Republican political movement linked to the IRA.

Sino- *combining form* Chinese: *Sino-European; Sinology.*

Sinology (sine-**ol**-a-jee) *n* the study of Chinese history, language, and culture. **Sinologist** *n*

sinuous *adj Literary* **1** full of curves. **2** having smooth twisting movements: *sinuous dances.* **sinuosity** *n*

sinus (**sine**-uss) *n Anat* a hollow space in bone, such as one in the skull opening into a nasal cavity.

sinusitis *n* inflammation of the membrane lining a sinus, esp. a nasal sinus.

Sioux (**soo**) *n* **1** (*pl* **Sioux**) a member of a group of N American Indian peoples, formerly living over a wide area from Lake Michigan to the Rocky Mountains. **2** any of the languages of these peoples.

sip *vb* **sipping, sipped 1** to drink (a liquid) in small mouthfuls. ~*n* **2** an amount sipped. **3** an instance of sipping.

siphon *or* **syphon** *n* **1** a tube which uses air pressure to draw liquid from a container. **2** same as **soda siphon.** ~*vb* **3 siphon off a** to draw (liquid) off through a siphon. **b** to redirect (resources or money), esp. dishonestly, into other projects or bank accounts.

sir *n* a polite term of address for a man.

Sir *n* a title placed before the name of a knight or baronet: *Sir David Attenborough.*

sire *n* **1** a male parent of a horse or other domestic animal. **2** *Archaic* a respectful form of address used to a king. ~*vb* **siring, sired 3** to father.

siren *n* **1** a device that gives out a loud wailing sound as a warning or signal. **2 Siren** *Greek myth* a sea nymph whose singing lured sailors to destruction on the rocks. **3** a woman who is attractive but dangerous to men.

sirloin *n* a prime cut of beef from the upper part of the loin.

sirocco *n, pl* **-cos** a hot stifling wind blowing from N Africa into S Europe.

sis[1] *n Informal* short for **sister.**

sis[2] *or* **sies** (**siss**) *interj S African informal* an exclamation of disgust.

sisal (**size**-al) *n* a stiff fibre obtained from a Mexican plant and used for making rope.

siskin *n* a yellow-and-black finch.

sissy *or* **cissy** *n, pl* **-sies 1** an effeminate, weak, or cowardly person. ~*adj* **2** effeminate, weak, or cowardly.

sister *n* **1** a woman or girl having the same parents as another person. **2** a female fellow member of a group, race, or profession. **3** a female nurse in charge of a ward. **4** *Chiefly RC Church* a nun. ~*adj* **5** of the same class, origin, or design, as another: *its sister paper.*

sisterhood *n* **1** the state of being sisters or like sisters. **2** a religious group of women. **3** a group of women united by a common interest or belief.

sister-in-law *n, pl* **sisters-in-law 1** the sister of one's husband or wife. **2** one's brother's wife.

sisterly *adj* of or like a sister; affectionate.

sit *vb* **sitting, sat 1** to rest one's body upright on the buttocks: *she had to sit on the ground.* **2** to cause (someone) to rest in such a position: *they sat their grandfather in the shade.* **3** (of an animal) to rest with the rear part of its body lowered to the ground. **4** (of a bird) to perch or roost. **5 sit on** (of a bird) to cover its eggs so as to hatch them. **6** to be located: *the bank sits in the middle of the village.* **7** to pose for a painting or photograph. **8** to occupy a seat in some official capacity: *no police representatives will sit on the committee* **9** (of a parliament or court) to be in session. **10** to remain unused: *his car sat in the garage.* **11** (of clothes) to fit or hang in a certain way: *that dress sits well on you.* **12** *Chiefly Brit* to take (an examination): *he's sitting his finals.* **13 sit for** *Chiefly Brit* to be a candidate for (a qualification): *he sat for a degree in medicine.* **14 sit tight** *Informal* **a** to wait patiently. **b** to maintain one's position firmly. ~See also **sit back, sit down,** etc.

sitar *n* an Indian stringed musical instrument with a long neck and a rounded body.

sit back *vb* to relax or be passive when action should be taken: *we can't just sit back and let this continue.*

sitcom *n Informal* (on television or radio) a comedy series involving the same characters in various everyday situations: *yet another unfunny sitcom set in Perth.*

sit down *vb* **1** to adopt or cause (someone) to adopt a sitting position. **2 sit down under** to suffer (insults or humiliations) without resistance. ~*n* **sit-down 3** a short rest sitting down. ~*adj* **sit-down 4** (of a meal) eaten while sitting down at a table.

sit-down strike *n* a strike in which workers refuse to leave their place of employment until a settlement is reached.

site *n* **1** the piece of ground where something was, is, or is intended to be located: *a building site; a car park built on the site of a Roman fort.* ~*vb* **siting, sited 2** to locate (something) on a specific site.

sit-in *n* **1** a protest in which the demonstrators sit in a public place and refuse to move. ~*vb* **sit in 2 sit in for** to stand in as a substitute for (someone). **3 sit in on** to be present at (a meeting) as an observer.

sitkamer (**sit**-kahm-er) *n S African* a sitting room.

sitka spruce *n* a tall North American spruce tree, now often grown in Britain.

sit on *vb Informal* to delay action on: *they are sitting on their information.*

sit out *vb* **1** to endure to the end: *just sit it out, and it*

THESAURUS

sinister baleful, dire, disquieting, evil, forbidding, injurious, malevolent, malign, malignant, menacing, ominous, threatening

sink *vb.* **1.** cave in, decline, descend, dip, disappear, droop, drop, drown, ebb, engulf, fall, founder, go down, go under, lower, merge, plummet, plunge, sag, slope, submerge, subside **2.** abate, collapse, drop, fall, lapse, relapse, retrogress, slip, slump, subside **3.** decay, decline, decrease, degenerate, depreciate, deteriorate, die, diminish, dwindle, fade, fail, flag, go downhill (*informal*), lessen, weaken, worsen **4.** bore, dig, drill, drive, excavate, lay, put down

sinner evildoer, malefactor, miscreant, offender, reprobate, transgressor (*formal*), wrongdoer

sip 1. *vb.* sample, sup, taste **2.** *n.* drop, swallow, taste, thimbleful

siren charmer, *femme fatale,* seductress, temptress, vamp (*informal*), witch

sit 1. be seated, perch, rest, settle, take a seat, take the

will pass eventually. **2** to take no part in (a dance or game).

sitter *n* **1** a person posing for his or her portrait or photograph. **2** same as **baby-sitter.**

sitting *n* **1** a continuous period of being seated at some activity: *you may not be able to complete it in one sitting.* **2** one of the times when a meal is served, when there is not enough space for everyone to eat at the same time: *the second sitting.* **3** a period of posing for a painting or photograph. **4** a meeting of an official body to conduct business. *~adj* **5** current: *a sitting member of Congress.* **6** seated: *a sitting position.*

sitting duck *n Informal* a person or thing in a defenceless or vulnerable position.

sitting room *n* a room in a house or flat where people sit and relax.

sitting tenant *n* a tenant occupying a house or flat.

situate *vb* **-ating, -ated** *Formal* to place.

situation *n* **1 a** a state of affairs. **b** a complex or critical state of affairs. **2** location and surroundings. **3** social or financial circumstances. **4** a position of employment.

situation comedy *n* same as **sitcom.**

sit up *vb* **1** to raise oneself from a lying position into a sitting one. **2** to remain out of bed until a late hour. **3** *Informal* to become suddenly interested: *make the world sit up and take notice.* *~n* **sit-up 4** a physical exercise in which the body is brought into a sitting position from one of lying on the back.

SI unit *n* any of the units (metre, kilogram, second, ampere, kelvin, candela, mole, and those derived from them) adopted for international use under the Système International d'Unités, now employed for all scientific and most technical purposes.

six *n* **1** the cardinal number that is the sum of one and five. **2** a numeral, 6 or VI, representing this number. **3** something representing or consisting of six units. **4** *Cricket* a score of six runs, obtained by hitting the ball so that it crosses the boundary without bouncing. **5 at sixes and sevens** in a state of confusion. **6 knock someone for six** *Informal* to upset or overwhelm someone completely. **7 six of one and half a dozen of the other** a situation in which there is no real difference between the alternatives. *~adj* **8** amounting to six: *six days.* **sixth** *adj, n*

sixfold *adj* **1** having six times as many or as much. **2** composed of six parts. *~adv* **3** by six times as many or as much.

sixpence *n* (formerly) a small British coin worth six old pennies, or 2½.

six-shooter *n US informal* a revolver that fires six shots without reloading.

sixteen *n* **1** the cardinal number that is the sum of ten and six. **2** a numeral, 16 or XVI, representing this number. **3** something representing or consisting of sixteen units. *~adj* **4** amounting to sixteen: *sixteen years.* **sixteenth** *adj, n*

sixth form *n* (in England and Wales) the most senior form in a secondary school, in which pupils over sixteen may take A levels or retake GCSEs. **sixth-former** *n*

sixth sense *n* the supposed ability of knowing something instinctively without having any evidence for it.

sixty *n, pl* **-ties 1** the cardinal number that is the product of ten and six. **2** a numeral, 60 or LX, representing this number. **3** something representing or consisting of sixty units. *~adj* **4** amounting to sixty: *sixty seconds.* **sixtieth** *adj, n*

sizable *or* **sizeable** *adj* quite large.

size[1] *n* **1** the dimensions, amount, or extent of something. **2** large dimensions, amount, or extent: *I was overwhelmed by the sheer size of the city.* **3** one of a series of standard measurements for goods: *he takes size 11 shoes.* **4** *Informal* state of affairs as summarized: *that's about the size of it.* *~vb* **sizing, sized 5** to sort (things) according to size.

size[2] *n* **1** a thin gluey substance that is used as a sealer. *~vb* **sizing, sized 2** to treat (a surface) with size.

sized *adj* of a specified size: *average-sized.*

size up *vb Informal* to make an assessment of (a person or situation).

sizzle *vb* **-zling, -zled 1** to make a hissing sound like the sound of frying fat. **2** *Informal* to be very hot: *the city was sizzling in a hot summer spell.* **3** *Informal* to be very angry. *~n* **4** a hissing sound. **sizzling** *adj*

sjambok (**sham**-bock) *S African ~n* **1** a whip or riding crop made of hide. *~vb* **-bokking, -bokked 2** to beat with a sjambok.

SK Saskatchewan.

skate[1] *n* **1** same as **ice skate** or **roller skate. 2 get one's skates on** *Informal* to hurry. *~vb* **skating, skated 3** to glide on or as if on skates. **4 skate on thin ice** to place oneself in a dangerous situation. **skater** *n* **skating** *n*

skate[2] *n, pl* **skate** *or* **skates** a large edible marine fish with a broad flat body.

skateboard *n* **1** a narrow board mounted on roller-skate wheels, usually ridden while standing up. *~vb* **2** to ride on a skateboard. **skateboarding** *n*

skate round *or* **over** *vb* to avoid discussing or dealing with (a matter) fully.

skean-dhu (**skee-an-doo**) *n* a dagger worn in the sock as part of Highland dress.

skedaddle *vb* **-dling, -dled** *Informal* to run off hastily.

skein *n* **1** a length of yarn or thread wound in a loose coil. **2** a flock of geese in flight.

skeleton *n* **1** the hard framework of bones that supports and protects the organs and muscles of the body. **2** the essential framework of any structure: *a metal skeleton supporting the roof and floors.* **3** *Informal* an extremely thin person or animal. **4** an outline consisting of bare essentials: *the mere skeleton of a script.* **5 skeleton in the cupboard** *or* **closet** an embarrassing or scandalous fact from the past that is kept secret. *~adj* **6** reduced to a minimum: *a skeleton staff.* **skeletal** *adj*

THESAURUS

weight off one's feet **2.** assemble, be in session, convene, deliberate, meet, officiate, preside

site 1. *n.* ground, location, place, plot, position, setting, spot **2.** *vb.* install, locate, place, position, set, situate

sitting *n.* congress, consultation, get-together (*informal*), hearing, meeting, period, session

situation 1. ball game (*informal*), case, circumstances, condition, kettle of fish (*informal*), plight, scenario, state, state of affairs, status quo, the picture (*informal*) **2.** locale, locality, location, place, position, seat, setting, site, spot **3.** berth (*informal*), employment, job, office, place, position, post

size amount, bigness, bulk, dimensions, extent, greatness, hugeness, immensity, largeness, magnitude, mass, measurement(s), proportions, range, vastness, volume

size up *informal* appraise, assess, evaluate, eye up, get (something) taped (*Brit. informal*), get the measure of, take stock of

skeleton key *n* a key designed so that it can open many different locks.
skelm *n S African informal* a villain or crook.
skeptic *n US & archaic* same as **sceptic.**
skerry *n, pl* **-ries** a rocky island or reef.
sketch *n* **1** a quick rough drawing. **2** a brief descriptive piece of writing. **3** a short funny piece of acting forming part of a show. **4** any brief outline. *~vb* **5** to make a quick rough drawing (of). **6 sketch out** to make a brief description of: *they sketched out plans for the invasion.*
sketchbook *n* a book of blank pages for sketching on.
sketchy *adj* **sketchier, sketchiest** giving only a rough or incomplete description. **sketchily** *adv*
skew *adj* **1** having a slanting position. *~n* **2** a slanting position. *~vb* **3** to take or cause to take a slanting position: *our boat skewed off course.*
skewbald *adj* **1** marked with patches of white and another colour. *~n* **2** a horse with this marking.
skewed *adj* distorted or biased because of prejudice or lack of information: *a skewed conception of religion.*
skewer *n* **1** a long pin for holding meat together during cooking. *~vb* **2** to fasten or pierce with or as if with a skewer.
skewwhiff *adj Brit informal* crooked or slanting.
ski *n, pl* **skis** *or* **ski 1** one of a pair of long runners that are used, fastened to boots, for gliding over snow. *~vb* **skiing, skied** *or* **ski'd 2** to travel on skis. **skier** *n* **skiing** *n*
skid *vb* **skidding, skidded 1** (of a vehicle or person) to slide sideways while in motion. *~n* **2** an instance of skidding.
skidoo *Canad ~n, pl* **-doos 1** a type of snowmobile. *~vb* **-dooing, -dooed 2** to travel using a snowmobile.
skid row *n Slang, chiefly US & Canad* a poor and neglected area of a city, inhabited by down-and-outs.
skiff *n* a small narrow boat for one person.
ski jump *n* a steep snow-covered slope ending in a horizontal ramp from which skiers compete to make the longest jump.
skilful *or US* **skillful** *adj* having or showing skill. **skilfully** *or US* **skillfully** *adv*
ski lift *n* a series of chairs hanging from a power-driven cable for carrying skiers up a slope.
skill *n* **1** special ability or expertise enabling one to perform an activity very well. **2** something, such as a trade, requiring special training or expertise. **skilled** *adj*
skillet *n* **1** a small frying pan. **2** *Chiefly Brit* a long-handled cooking pot.
skim *vb* **skimming, skimmed 1** to remove floating material from the surface of (a liquid): *skim any impurities off the surface.* **2** to glide smoothly over (a surface). **3** to throw (a flat stone) across a surface, so that it bounces: *two men skimmed stones on the surface of the sea.* **4** (often foll. by *through*) to read (a piece of writing) quickly and without taking in the details.
skimmed *or* **skim milk** *n* milk from which the cream has been removed.
skimp *vb* **1** to be extremely sparing or supply (someone) sparingly. **2** to do (something) carelessly or with inadequate materials.
skimpy *adj* **skimpier, skimpiest** inadequate in amount or size; scant.
skin *n* **1** the tissue forming the outer covering of the body. **2** a person's complexion: *sallow skin.* **3** any outer layer or covering: *potato skin.* **4** a thin solid layer on the surface of a liquid: *custard with a thick skin on it.* **5** the outer covering of a furry animal, removed and prepared for use. **6** a container for liquids, made from animal skin. **7 by the skin of one's teeth** by a narrow margin. **8 get under one's skin** *Informal* to annoy one. **9 no skin off one's nose** *Informal* not a matter that concerns one. **10 save one's skin** to save one from death or harm. **11 skin and bone** extremely thin. **12 thick** *or* **thin skin** an insensitive *or* sensitive nature. *~vb* **skinning, skinned 13** to remove the outer covering from (a dead animal). **14** to injure (a part of the body) by scraping some of the skin off: *I had skinned my knuckles.* **15** *Slang* to swindle. **skinless** *adj*
skin-deep *adj* not of real importance; superficial: *beauty is only skin-deep.*
skin diving *n* underwater swimming using only light breathing apparatus and without a special diving suit. **skin-diver** *n*
skin flick *n Slang* a pornographic film.
skinflint *n* a very mean person.
skin graft *n* a piece of skin removed from one part of the body and surgically grafted at the site of a severe burn or other injury.
skinhead *n Brit* a White youth who has closely cropped hair and wears heavy boots and braces.
skinny *adj* **-nier, -niest** extremely thin.
skint *adj Brit slang* without money, esp. only temporarily.
skintight *adj* (of garments) fitting tightly over the body; clinging.
skip[1] *vb* **skipping, skipped 1** to move lightly by hop-

THESAURUS

sizzle crackle, frizzle, fry, hiss, spit, sputter
skeleton bare bones, bones, draft, frame, framework, outline, sketch, structure
sketch 1. *n.* delineation, design, draft, drawing, outline, plan, skeleton **2.** *vb.* block out, delineate, depict, draft, draw, outline, paint, plot, portray, represent, rough out
sketchy bitty, cobbled together, crude, cursory, inadequate, incomplete, outline, perfunctory, rough, scrappy, skimpy, slight, superficial, unfinished, vague
skilful able, accomplished, adept, adroit, apt, clever, competent, dexterous, experienced, expert, handy, masterly, practised, professional, proficient, quick, ready, skilled, trained
skill ability, accomplishment, adroitness, aptitude, art, cleverness, competence, craft, dexterity, experience, expertise, expertness, facility, finesse, handiness, ingenuity, intelligence, knack, proficiency, quickness, readiness, skilfulness, talent, technique
skilled able, accomplished, a dab hand at (*Brit. informal*), experienced, expert, masterly, practised, professional, proficient, skilful, trained
skim 1. cream, separate **2.** brush, coast, dart, float, fly, glide, sail, soar **3.** *often with* **through** glance, run one's eye over, scan, skip (*informal*), thumb *or* leaf through
skimp be mean with, be niggardly, be sparing with, cut corners, pinch, scamp, scant, scrimp, stint, withhold
skin *n.* **1.** casing, coating, crust, film, husk, membrane, outside, peel, rind **2.** fell, hide, integument, pelt, tegument **3. by the skin of one's teeth** by a hair's-breadth, by a narrow margin, by a whisker (*informal*), narrowly, only just **4. get under one's skin** *informal* aggravate (*informal*), annoy, get in one's hair (*informal*), get on one's nerves (*informal*), grate on, irk, irritate, needle (*informal*), nettle, piss one off (*taboo*

ping from one foot to the other. **2** to jump over a skipping-rope. **3** to cause (a stone) to skim over a surface or (of a stone) to move in this way. **4** to pass over or miss out; omit: *I skipped a few paragraphs.* **5 skip through** *Informal* to read or deal with (something) quickly or without great effort or concentration. **6 skip it!** *Informal* it doesn't matter! **7** *Informal* to miss deliberately: *she skipped the class.* **8** *Informal, chiefly US & Canad* to leave (a place) in a hurry: *he skipped town three years later.* ~*n* **9** a skipping movement or action.

skip[2] *n* **1** a large open container for transporting building materials or rubbish. **2** a cage used as a lift in mines.

ski pants *pl n* stretch trousers, worn for skiing or leisure, which are kept taut by straps under the feet.

skipper *n* **1** the captain of a ship or aircraft. **2** the captain of a sporting team. ~*vb* **3** to be the captain of.

skipping *n* the act of jumping over a rope held either by the person jumping or by two other people, as a game or for exercise.

skipping-rope *n Brit* a rope that is held in the hands and swung round and down so that the holder or others can jump over it.

skirl *Scot & N English dialect* ~*n* **1** the sound of bagpipes. ~*vb* **2** (of bagpipes) to give out a shrill sound.

skirmish *n* **1** a brief or minor fight or argument. ~*vb* **2** to take part in a skirmish.

skirt *n* **1** a woman's or girl's garment hanging from the waist. **2** the part of a dress or coat below the waist. **3** a circular hanging flap, for example round the base of a hovercraft. **4** *Brit* a cut of beef from the flank. **5 bit of skirt** *Offensive slang* a girl or woman. ~*vb* **6** to lie along or form the edge of (something): *a track skirting the foot of the mountain.* **7** to go around the outer edge of (something): *we skirted the township.* **8** to avoid dealing with (an issue): *I was skirting around the real issues.*

skirting board *n* a narrow board round the bottom of an interior wall where it joins the floor.

ski stick *or* **pole** *n* one of a pair of sharp pointed sticks used by skiers to gain speed and maintain balance.

skit *n* a short funny or satirical sketch.

ski tow *n* a device for pulling skiers uphill, usually a motor-driven rope grasped by the skier while riding on his or her skis.

skittish *adj* **1** playful or lively. **2** (of a horse) excitable and easily frightened.

skittle *n* **1** a bottle-shaped object used as a target in a game of skittles. **2 skittles** a bowling game in which players knock over as many skittles as possible by rolling a wooden ball at them.

skive *vb* **skiving, skived** (often foll. by *off*) *Brit informal* to avoid work or responsibility. **skiver** *n*

skivvy *Chiefly Brit often disparaging* ~*n, pl* **-vies 1** a female servant who does menial work; drudge. ~*vb* **-vies, -vying, -vied 2** to work as a skivvy.

skookum *adj W Canad* large.

skua *n* a large predatory gull living in cold marine regions.

skulduggery *or US* **skullduggery** *n Informal* underhand dealing to achieve an aim.

skulk *vb* **1** to move stealthily, so as to avoid notice. **2** to lie in hiding; lurk.

skull *n* **1** the bony framework of the head. **2** *Informal* the head or mind: *that would have penetrated even your thick skull.*

skull and crossbones *n* a picture of the human skull above two crossed bones, formerly on the pirate flag, now used as a warning of danger or death.

skullcap *n* a closely fitting brimless cap.

skunk *n, pl* **skunk** *or* **skunks 1** a mammal with a black-and-white coat and bushy tail, which gives out a foul-smelling fluid when attacked. **2** *Informal* an unpleasant or unfair person.

sky *n, pl* **skies 1** the upper atmosphere as seen from earth. **2 praise to the skies** praise rather excessively. ~*vb* **skies, skying, skied 3** *Informal* to hit (a ball) high in the air: *Payton skied his shot over the bar.*

sky-blue *adj* bright clear blue.

skydiving *n* the sport of jumping from an aircraft and falling freely or performing manoeuvres before opening the parachute. **skydiver** *n*

sky-high *adj, adv* **1** very high: *inflation was sky-high after the war.* **2 blow sky-high** to destroy completely.

skyjack *vb* to hijack (an aircraft).

skylark *n* **1** a lark that sings while soaring at a great height. ~*vb* **2** *Old-fashioned* to play or frolic.

skylight *n* a window placed in a roof or ceiling to let in daylight.

skyline *n* **1** the line at which the earth and sky appear to meet. **2** the outline of buildings, trees, or hills, seen against the sky.

skyrocket *n* **1** same as **rocket** (sense 1). ~*vb* **2** *Informal* to rise very quickly.

skyscraper *n* a very tall building.

skyward *adj* **1** towards the sky. ~*adv also* **skywards 2** towards the sky.

slab *n* a broad flat thick piece of wood, stone, or other material.

slack[1] *adj* **1** not tight, tense, or taut: *the slack jaw hung open.* **2** careless in one's work. **3** (esp. of water) moving slowly. **4** (of trade) not busy. ~*n* **5** a part that is slack or hangs loose: *take up the slack.* **6** a period of less busy activity. ~*vb* **7** to neglect (one's work or

THESAURUS

slang), rub up the wrong way ~*vb.* **5.** abrade, bark, excoriate, flay, graze, peel, scrape

skinny emaciated, lean, scraggy, skeletal, skin-and-bone (*informal*), thin, twiggy, undernourished

skip *vb.* **1.** bob, bounce, caper, cavort, dance, flit, frisk, gambol, hop, prance, trip **2.** eschew, give (something) a miss, leave out, miss out, omit, pass over, skim over **3.** *informal* cut (*informal*), dog it *or* dog off (*dialect*), miss, play truant from

skirmish 1. *n.* affair, affray (*Law*), battle, brush, clash, combat, conflict, contest, dust-up (*informal*), encounter, engagement, fracas, incident, scrap (*informal*), scrimmage, set-to (*informal*), spat, tussle **2.** *vb.* clash, collide, come to blows, scrap (*informal*), tussle

skirt *vb.* **1.** border, edge, flank, lie alongside **2.** *often with* **around** *or* **round** avoid, body-swerve (*Scot.*), bypass, circumvent, detour, evade, steer clear of

skit burlesque, parody, sketch, spoof (*informal*), take-off (*informal*), travesty, turn

skulk creep, lie in wait, loiter, lurk, pad, prowl, slink, sneak

sky *n.* **1.** azure (*poetic*), empyrean (*poetic*), firmament, heavens, upper atmosphere, vault of heaven **2. to the skies** excessively, extravagantly, fulsomely, highly, immoderately, inordinately, profusely

slab chunk, hunk, lump, piece, portion, slice, wedge, wodge (*Brit. informal*)

slack *adj.* **1.** baggy, easy, flaccid, flexible, lax, limp, loose, not taut, relaxed **2.** asleep on the job (*informal*), easy-going, idle, inactive, inattentive, lax, lazy, neglectful, negligent, permissive, remiss, slapdash, slipshod,

duty). **8** (often foll. by *off*) to loosen or slacken. ~See also **slacks. slackness** *n*

slack[2] *n* small pieces of coal with a high ash content.

slacken *vb* (often foll. by *off*) **1** to make or become looser. **2** to make or become slower or less intense: *plans to slacken the pace of economic reform.*

slacker *n* a person who evades work or duty; shirker.

slacks *pl n Old-fashioned* casual trousers.

slag *n* **1** the waste material left after metal has been smelted. ~*vb* **slagging, slagged 2** *Slang* to criticize in an unpleasant way: *I don't think anyone can slag it off.* **slagging** *n* **slaggy** *adj*

slag heap *n* a pile of waste matter from metal smelting or coal mining.

slain *vb* the past participle of **slay.**

slake *vb* **slaking, slaked 1** *Literary* to satisfy (thirst or desire). **2** to add water to (lime) to produce calcium hydroxide.

slalom *n Skiing, canoeing* a race over a winding course marked by artificial obstacles.

slam[1] *vb* **slamming, slammed 1** to close violently and noisily. **2** to throw (something) down violently. **3** *Slang* to criticize harshly: *his new proposals were slammed by the opposition.* **4** to strike with violent force: *he slammed the ball into the back of the net.* ~*n* **5** the act or noise of slamming.

slam[2] *n* the winning of all (**grand slam**) or all but one (**little slam**) of the 13 tricks at bridge.

slammer *n* **the slammer** *Slang* prison.

slander *n* **1** *Law* a false and damaging statement about a person. **2** the crime of making such a statement. ~*vb* **3** to utter slander (about). **slanderous** *adj*

slang *n* **1** informal language not used in formal speech or writing and often restricted to a particular social group or profession. ~*vb* **2** to use insulting language to (someone). **slangy** *adj*

slanging match *n* an angry quarrel in which people trade insults.

slant *vb* **1** to lean at an angle; slope. **2** to write or present (information) in a biased way. ~*n* **3** a sloping line or position. **4** a point of view, esp. a biased one: *a right-wing slant on the story.* **5 on a** *or* **the slant** sloping. ~*adj* **6** oblique; sloping. **slanting** *adj* **slantwise** *adv*

slap *n* **1** a sharp blow or smack with something flat, such as the open hand. **2** the sound made by or as if by such a blow. **3 slap and tickle** *Brit old-fashioned informal* sexual play. **4 a slap in the face** an unexpected rejection or insult. **5 a slap on the back** congratulations. ~*vb* **slapping, slapped 6** to strike sharply with something flat, such as the open hand. **7** to bring (something) down forcefully: *he slapped down a fiver.* **8** (usually foll. by *against*) to strike (something) with a slapping sound. **9** *Informal, chiefly Brit* to cover with quickly or carelessly: *she slapped on some make-up.* **10 slap on the back** to congratulate. ~*adv Informal* **11** exactly: *slap in the middle.* **12 slap into** forcibly or abruptly into: *he ran slap into the guard.*

slap-bang *adv Informal, chiefly Brit* **1** directly or exactly: *he's on holiday in LA and has run slap-bang into a famous face.* **2** forcefully and abruptly: *he'd gone and run slap-bang into the watchman.*

slapdash *adv* **1** carelessly or hastily. ~*adj* **2** careless or hasty.

slaphappy *adj* **pier, piest** *Informal* cheerfully careless.

slapstick *n* rough and high-spirited comedy in which the characters behave childishly.

slap-up *adj Brit informal* (esp. of meals) large and expensive.

slash *vb* **1** to cut (a person or thing) with sharp sweeping strokes. **2** to make large gashes in: *I slashed the tyres of his van.* **3** to reduce drastically: *to slash costs.* **4** to criticize harshly. ~*n* **5** a sharp sweeping stroke. **6** a cut made by such a stroke. **7** same as **solidus. 8** *Brit slang* the act of urinating.

slasher *n NZ* a tool used for cutting scrub or undergrowth in the bush.

slat *n* a narrow thin strip of wood or metal, such as used in a Venetian blind.

slate[1] *n* **1** a dark grey rock that can be easily split into thin layers and is used as a roofing material. **2** a roofing tile of slate. **3** (formerly) a writing tablet of slate. **4** *Chiefly US & Canad* a list of candidates in an election. **5 wipe the slate clean** forget about past mistakes or failures and start afresh. **6 on the slate** *Brit informal* on credit. ~*vb* **slating, slated 7** to cover (a roof) with slates. **8** *Chiefly US* to plan or schedule: *another exercise is slated for tomorrow.* **slaty** *adj*

THESAURUS

tardy **3.** dull, inactive, quiet, slow, slow-moving, sluggish ~*n.* **4.** excess, give (*informal*), leeway, looseness, play, room ~*vb.* **5.** bob off (*Brit. slang*), dodge, flag, idle, neglect, relax, shirk, skive (*Brit. slang*), slacken

slacken *often with* **off** abate, decrease, diminish, drop off, ease (off), lessen, let up, loosen, moderate, reduce, relax, release, slack off, slow down, tire

slacker dodger, do-nothing, good-for-nothing, idler, layabout, loafer, passenger, shirker, skiver (*Brit. slang*)

slam 1. bang, crash, dash, fling, hurl, smash, throw, thump **2.** *slang* attack, blast, castigate, criticize, damn, excoriate, lambast(e), pan (*informal*), pillory, shoot down (*informal*), slate (*informal*), tear into (*informal*), vilify

slander 1. *n.* aspersion, backbiting, calumny, defamation, detraction, libel, misrepresentation, muckraking, obloquy, scandal, smear **2.** *vb.* backbite, blacken (someone's) name, calumniate, decry, defame, detract, disparage, libel, malign, slur, smear, traduce, vilify

slanderous abusive, calumnious, damaging, defamatory, libellous, malicious

slang *vb.* abuse, berate, call names, hurl insults at, insult, inveigh against, malign, rail against, revile, vilify, vituperate

slant *vb.* **1.** angle off, bend, bevel, cant, heel, incline, lean, list, shelve, skew, slope, tilt **2.** angle, bias, colour, distort, twist, weight ~*n.* **3.** camber, declination, diagonal, gradient, incline, pitch, rake, ramp, slope, tilt **4.** angle, attitude, bias, emphasis, leaning, one-sidedness, point of view, prejudice, viewpoint

slanting angled, aslant, asymmetrical, at an angle, bent, canted, diagonal, inclined, oblique, on the bias, sideways, slanted, slantwise, sloping, tilted, tilting

slap *n.* **1.** bang, blow, clout (*informal*), cuff, smack, spank, wallop (*informal*), whack **2. a slap in the face** affront, blow, humiliation, insult, put-down, rebuff, rebuke, rejection, repulse, snub ~*vb.* **3.** bang, clap, clout (*informal*), cuff, hit, spank, strike, whack **4.** *informal, chiefly Brit.* daub, plaster, plonk, spread ~*adv.* **5.** *informal* bang, directly, exactly, plumb (*informal*), precisely, slap-bang (*informal*), smack (*informal*)

slapdash careless, clumsy, disorderly, haphazard, hasty, hurried, last-minute, messy, negligent, perfunctory, slipshod, sloppy (*informal*), slovenly, thoughtless, thrown-together, untidy

slash *vb.* **1.** cut, gash, hack, lacerate, rend, rip, score, slit **2.** cut, drop, lower, reduce ~*n.* **3.** cut, gash, incision, laceration, rent, rip, slit

slate *vb. informal, chiefly Brit.* berate, blame, blast,

slate[2] *vb* **slating, slated** *Informal, chiefly Brit* to criticize harshly: *the new series was slated by the critics.* **slating** *n*

slattern *n Old-fashioned* a dirty and untidy woman. **slatternliness** *n* **slatternly** *adj*

slaughter *n* **1** the indiscriminate or brutal killing of large numbers of people. **2** the savage killing of a person. **3** the killing of animals for food. ~*vb* **4** to kill indiscriminately or in large numbers. **5** to kill brutally. **6** to kill (animals) for food. **7** *Informal* (in sport) to defeat easily.

slaughterhouse *n* a place where animals are killed for food.

Slav *n* a member of any of the peoples of E Europe or the former Soviet Union who speak a Slavonic language.

slave *n* **1** a person legally owned by another for whom he or she has to work without freedom, pay, or rights. **2** a person under the domination of another or of some habit or influence: *a slave to party doctrine.* **3** *Informal* a badly-paid person doing menial tasks. ~*vb* **slaving, slaved 4** (often foll. by *away* or *over*) to work very hard for little or no money.

slave-driver *n* **1** a person who makes people work very hard. **2** (esp. formerly) a person forcing slaves to work.

slaver[1] *n* **1** (esp. formerly) a dealer in slaves. **2** *History* a ship used in the slave trade.

slaver[2] *vb* **1** to dribble saliva. **2** (often foll. by *over*) to drool (over someone), making flattering remarks. ~*n* **3** saliva dribbling from the mouth. **4** *Informal* nonsense.

slavery *n* **1** the state or condition of being a slave. **2** the practise of owning slaves. **3** hard work with little reward.

slave trade *n* the buying and selling of slaves, esp. the transportation of Black Africans to America and the Caribbean from the 16th to the 19th centuries.

slavish *adj* **1** of or like a slave. **2** imitating or copying exactly without any originality: *a slavish adherence to the conventions of Italian opera.* **slavishly** *adv*

Slavonic *or esp US* **Slavic** *n* **1** a group of languages including Bulgarian, Russian, Polish, and Czech. ~*adj* **2** of this group of languages. **3** of the people who speak these languages.

slay *vb* **slaying, slew, slain** *Archaic or literary* to kill, esp. violently. **slayer** *n*

sleazy *adj* **-zier, -ziest** dirty, run-down, and not respectable: *a sleazy hotel.* **sleaziness** *n*

sledge[1] *or esp US & Canad* **sled** *n* **1** a vehicle mounted on runners, drawn by horses or dogs, for transporting people or goods over snow. **2** a light wooden frame used, esp. by children, for sliding over snow. ~*vb* **sledging, sledged 3** to travel by sledge.

sledge[2] *n* short for **sledgehammer.**

sledgehammer *n* **1** a large heavy hammer with a long handle, used for breaking rocks and concrete. ~*adj* **2** crushingly powerful: *the sledgehammer approach.*

sleek *adj* **1** smooth, shiny, and glossy: *sleek blond hair.* **2** (of a person) elegantly dressed.

sleep *n* **1** a state of rest during which the eyes are closed, the muscles and nerves are relaxed, and the mind is unconscious. **2** a period spent sleeping. **3** the substance sometimes found in the corner of the eyes after sleep. **4** a state of inactivity, like sleep. **5** *Poetic* death. ~*vb* **sleeping, slept 6** to be in or as in the state of sleep. **7** to be inactive or unaware: *their defence slept as we scored another try.* **8** to have sleeping accommodation for (a certain number): *the villa sleeps ten.* **9** *Poetic* to be dead. **10 sleep on it** to delay making a decision about (something) until the next day, in order to think about it. ~See also **sleep around, sleep in,** etc.

sleep around *vb Informal* to have many sexual partners.

sleeper *n* **1** a railway sleeping car or compartment. **2** *Brit* one of the blocks supporting the rails on a railway track. **3** *Chiefly Brit* a small plain gold ring worn in a pierced ear lobe to prevent the hole from closing up. **4** *Informal* a person or thing that achieves success after an initial period of obscurity.

sleep in *vb Brit* to sleep longer than usual.

sleeping bag *n* a large well-padded bag for sleeping in, esp. outdoors.

sleeping car *n* a railway carriage with small rooms containing beds for passengers to sleep in.

sleeping partner *n* a partner in a business who shares in the financing but does not take part in its management.

sleeping pill *n* a pill containing a drug that induces sleep.

sleeping policeman *n* a bump built across a road to prevent motorists from driving too fast.

sleeping sickness *n* an infectious, usually fatal, African disease transmitted by the bite of the tsetse fly, causing fever and sluggishness.

THESAURUS

castigate, censure, criticize, excoriate, haul over the coals (*informal*), lambast(e), lay into (*informal*), pan (*informal*), pitch into (*informal*), rail against, rap (someone's) knuckles, rebuke, roast (*informal*), scold, slam (*slang*), slang, take to task, tear into (*informal*), tear (someone) off a strip (*informal*)

slaughter *n.* **1.** blood bath, bloodshed, butchery, carnage, extermination, holocaust, killing, liquidation, massacre, murder, slaying (*archaic or literary*) ~*vb.* **2.** butcher, destroy, do to death, exterminate, kill, liquidate, massacre, murder, put to the sword, slay (*archaic or literary*), take out (*slang*) **3.** *informal* blow out of the water (*slang*), crush, defeat, hammer (*informal*), lick (*informal*), overwhelm, rout, tank (*slang*), thrash, trounce, undo, vanquish, wipe the floor with (*informal*)

slaughterhouse abattoir, butchery, shambles

slave 1. *n.* bondservant, drudge, scullion (*archaic*), serf, servant, skivvy (*chiefly Brit.*), varlet (*old-fashioned*), vassal, villein **2.** *vb. often with* **away** *or* **over** drudge, grind (*informal*), skivvy (*Brit.*), slog, sweat, toil, work one's fingers to the bone

slavery bondage, captivity, enslavement, serfdom, servitude, subjugation, thrall, vassalage

slavish 1. abject, base, cringing, despicable, fawning, grovelling, low, mean, menial, obsequious, servile, submissive, sycophantic **2.** conventional, imitative, second-hand, unimaginative, uninspired, unoriginal

slay *archaic or literary* annihilate, assassinate, butcher, destroy, dispatch, do away with, do in (*slang*), eliminate, exterminate, kill, massacre, mow down, murder, rub out (*U.S. slang*), slaughter

sleek glossy, lustrous, shiny, smooth, well-fed, well-groomed

sleep 1. *n.* beauty sleep (*informal*), dormancy, doze, forty winks (*informal*), hibernation, kip (*Brit. slang*), nap, repose, rest, shuteye (*slang*), siesta, slumber(s), snooze (*informal*), zizz (*Brit. informal*) **2.** *vb.* be in the land of Nod, catnap, doze, drop off (*informal*), drowse, hibernate, kip (*Brit. slang*), nod off (*informal*), rest in the arms of Morpheus, slumber, snooze (*informal*), snore, take a nap, take forty winks (*informal*), zizz (*Brit. informal*)

sleepless 1. disturbed, insomniac, restless, unsleep-

sleepless *adj* **1** (of a night) one during which one does not sleep. **2** unable to sleep. **3** *Chiefly poetic* always active. **sleeplessness** *n*

sleep off *vb Informal* to get rid of by sleeping: *go home and sleep it off.*

sleep out *vb* to sleep in the open air.

sleep together *vb* to have sexual intercourse and, usually, spend the night together.

sleepwalk *vb* to walk while asleep. **sleepwalker** *n* **sleepwalking** *n*

sleep with *vb* to have sexual intercourse and, usually, spend the night with.

sleepy *adj* **sleepier, sleepiest 1** tired and ready for sleep. **2** (of a place) without activity or excitement: *a sleepy little town.* **sleepily** *adv*

sleet *n* **1** partly melted falling snow or hail or (esp. U.S.) partly frozen rain. *~vb* **2** to fall as sleet.

sleeve *n* **1** the part of a garment covering the arm. **2** a tubelike part which fits over or completely encloses another part. **3** a flat cardboard container to protect a gramophone record. **4 up one's sleeve** secretly ready: *he has a few more surprises up his sleeve.* **sleeveless** *adj*

sleigh *n* **1** same as **sledge**[1] (sense 1). *~vb* **2** to travel by sleigh.

sleight (**slite**) *n Old-fashioned* skill or cunning.

sleight of hand *n* **1** the skilful use of the hands when performing magic tricks. **2** the performance of such tricks.

slender *adj* **1** (esp. of a person's figure) slim and graceful. **2** of small width relative to length or height. **3** small or inadequate in amount or size: *a slender advantage.*

slept *vb* the past of **sleep.**

sleuth (rhymes with **tooth**) *n Informal* a detective.

slew[1] *vb* the past tense of **slay.**

slew[2] *or esp US* **slue** *vb* **1** to slide or skid sideways: *the bus slewed across the road.* *~n* **2** the act of slewing.

slice *n* **1** a thin flat piece or wedge cut from something: *a slice of tomato.* **2** a share or portion: *the biggest slice of their income.* **3** a kitchen tool having a broad flat blade: *a fish slice.* **4** *Sport* a shot that causes the ball to go to one side, rather than straight ahead. *~vb* **slicing, sliced 5** to cut (something) into slices. **6** (usually foll. by *through*) to cut through cleanly and effortlessly, with or as if with a knife. **7** (usually foll. by *off, from, away*) to cut or be cut (from) a larger piece. **8** *Sport* to play (a ball) with a slice.

slick *adj* **1** (esp. of speech) easy and persuasive: *a slick answer.* **2** skilfully devised or executed: *a slick marketing effort.* **3** *Informal, chiefly US & Canad* shrewd; sly. **4** *Informal* well-made and attractive, but superficial: *a slick publication.* **5** *Chiefly US & Canad* slippery. *~n* **6** a slippery area, esp. a patch of oil floating on water. *~vb* **7** to make smooth or shiny: *long hair slicked back with gel.*

slide *vb* **sliding, slid, slid 1** to move smoothly along a surface in continual contact with it: *doors that slide open.* **2** to slip: *he slid on his back.* **3** (usually foll. by *into, out of, away from*) to pass or move smoothly and quietly: *she slid out of her seat.* **4** (usually foll. by *into*) to go (into a specified condition) gradually: *the rest of Europe slid into depression.* **5** (of a currency) to lose value gradually. **6 let slide** to allow to change to a worse state by neglect: *past chairmen have undoubtedly let things slide.* *~n* **7** the act or an instance of sliding. **8** a small glass plate on which specimens are placed for study under a microscope. **9** a photograph on a transparent base, mounted in a frame, that can be viewed by means of a projector. **10** a smooth surface, such as ice, for sliding on. **11** a structure with a steep smooth slope for sliding down in playgrounds. **12** *Chiefly Brit* an ornamental clip to hold hair in place. **13** the sliding curved tube of a trombone that is moved in and out to allow different notes to be played.

slide rule *n* a device formerly used to make mathematical calculations consisting of two strips, one sliding along a central groove in the other, each strip graduated in two or more logarithmic scales of numbers.

sliding scale *n* a variable scale according to which things such as wages or prices alter in response to changes in other factors.

slight *adj* **1** small in quantity or extent: *a slight improvement.* **2** not very important or lacking in substance: *her political career was honourable but relatively slight.* **3** slim and delicate. *~vb* **4** to insult (someone) by behaving rudely; snub. *~n* **5** an act of snubbing (someone). **slightly** *adv*

slim *adj* **slimmer, slimmest 1** (of a person) attractively thin. **2** small in width relative to height or length: *a slim book.* **3** poor; meagre: *a slim chance of progress.* *~vb* **4** to make or become slim by diets and exercise. **5** to reduce in size: *that would slim the overheads.* **slimmer** *n* **slimming** *n*

Slim *n* the E African name for **AIDS.**

slime *n* **1** soft runny mud or any sticky substance esp. when disgusting or unpleasant. **2** a thick, sticky substance produced by some fish, slugs, and fungi.

THESAURUS

ing, wakeful **2.** alert, unsleeping, vigilant, watchful, wide awake

sleeplessness insomnia, wakefulness

sleepwalker noctambulist, somnambulist

sleepwalking noctambulation, noctambulism, somnambulation, somnambulism

sleepy 1. drowsy, dull, heavy, inactive, lethargic, sluggish, slumbersome, somnolent, torpid **2.** dull, hypnotic, inactive, quiet, sleep-inducing, slow, slumberous, somnolent, soporific

slender 1. lean, narrow, slight, slim, svelte, sylphlike, willowy **2.** inadequate, inconsiderable, insufficient, little, meagre, scant, scanty, small, spare

sleuth *informal* detective, private eye (*informal*), (private) investigator, tail (*informal*)

slice 1. *n.* cut, helping, piece, portion, segment, share, sliver, wedge **2.** *vb.* carve, cut, divide, sever

slick *adj.* **1.** glib, meretricious, plausible, polished, smooth, sophistical, specious **2.** adroit, deft, dexterous, dextrous, polished, professional, sharp, skilful *~vb.* **3.** make glossy, plaster down, sleek, smarm down (*Brit. informal*), smooth

slide *vb.* **1.** coast, glide, glissade, skim, slip, slither, toboggan, veer **2. let slide** forget, gloss over, ignore, let ride, neglect, pass over, push to the back of one's mind, turn a blind eye to

slight *adj.* **1.** feeble, inconsiderable, insignificant, insubstantial, meagre, measly, minor, modest, negligible, paltry, scanty, small, superficial, trifling, trivial, unimportant, weak **2.** delicate, feeble, fragile, lightly-built, slim, small, spare *~vb.* **3.** affront, cold-shoulder, despise, disdain, disparage, give offence *or* umbrage to, ignore, insult, neglect, put down, scorn, show disrespect for, snub, treat with contempt *~n.* **4.** affront, contempt, discourtesy, disdain, disregard, disrespect, inattention, indifference, insult, neglect, rebuff, slap in the face (*informal*), snub, (the) cold shoulder

slightly a little, marginally, on a small scale, somewhat, to some extent *or* degree

slim *adj.* **1.** lean, narrow, slender, slight, svelte, sylph-

slimy *adj* **slimier, slimiest 1** of, like, or covered with slime. **2** *Chiefly Brit* pleasant and friendly in an insincere way.

sling[1] *n* **1** *Med* a wide piece of cloth suspended from the neck for supporting an injured hand or arm. **2** a rope or strap by which something may be lifted. **3** a simple weapon consisting of a strap tied to cords, in which a stone is whirled and then released. *~vb* **slinging, slung 4** *Informal* to throw. **5** to carry or hang loosely from or as if from a sling: *her shoulder bag was slung across her chest.* **6** to hurl with or as if with a sling.

sling[2] *n* a sweetened mixed drink with a spirit base: *gin sling.*

slingback *n* a shoe with a strap instead of a complete covering for the heel.

sling off at *vb Austral & NZ informal* to mock and jeer.

slink *vb* **slinking, slunk** to move or act in a quiet and secretive way from fear or guilt.

slinky *adj* **slinkier, slinkiest** *Informal* **1** (of clothes) figure-hugging. **2** moving in an alluring way.

slip[1] *vb* **slipping, slipped 1** to lose balance and slide unexpectedly: *he slipped on some leaves.* **2** to let loose or be let loose: *the rope slipped from his fingers.* **3** to move smoothly and easily: *small enough to slip into a pocket.* **4** to place quickly or stealthily: *he slipped the pistol back into his holster.* **5** to put on or take off easily or quickly: *we had slipped off our sandals.* **6** to pass out of (the mind or memory). **7** to move or pass quickly and without being noticed: *we slipped out of the ballroom.* **8** to make a mistake. **9** to decline in health or mental ability. **10** to become worse or lower: *sales had slipped below the level for June of last year.* **11** to dislocate (a disc in the spine). **12** to pass (a stitch) from one needle to another without knitting it. **13 let slip a** to allow to escape. **b** to say unintentionally. *~n* **14** a slipping. **15** a mistake or oversight: *a slip in the British defence.* **16** a woman's sleeveless undergarment, worn under a dress. **17** same as **slipway. 18** *Cricket* a fielding position a little behind and to the offside of the wicketkeeper. **19 give someone the slip** to escape from someone. ~See also **slip up.**

slip[2] *n* **1** a small piece of paper: *the registration slip.* **2** a cutting taken from a plant. **3** a young slim person: *a slip of a girl.*

slip[3] *n* clay mixed with water to a thin paste, used for decorating or patching a ceramic piece.

slipe *n NZ* wool removed from the pelt of a slaughtered sheep by immersion in a chemical bath.

slipknot *n* a nooselike knot tied so that it will slip along the rope round which it is made.

slip-on *adj* **1** (of a garment or shoe) without laces or buttons so as to be easily and quickly put on. *~n* **2** a slip-on garment or shoe.

slipped disc *n Pathol* a painful condition in which one of the discs which connects the bones of the spine becomes displaced and presses on a nerve.

slipper *n* a light soft shoe for indoor wear. **slippered** *adj*

slippery *adj* **1** liable or tending to cause objects to slip: *the road was slippery.* **2** liable to slip from one's grasp: *a bar of slippery soap.* **3** not to be trusted: *slippery politicians.* **slipperiness** *n*

slippy *adj* **-pier, -piest** *Informal or dialect* same as **slippery** (senses 1, 2). **slippiness** *n*

slip road *n Brit* a short road connecting a motorway to another road.

slipshod *adj* **1** (of an action) done in a careless way without attention to detail: *a slipshod piece of research.* **2** (of a person's appearance) untidy and slovenly.

slip-slop *n S African* same as **flip-flop.**

slipstream *n* the stream of air forced backwards by an aircraft or car.

slip up *Informal ~vb* **1** to make a mistake. *~n* **slip-up 2** a mistake.

slipway *n* a large ramp that slopes down from the shore into the water, on which a ship is built or repaired and from which it is launched.

slit *n* **1** a long narrow cut or opening. *~vb* **slitting, slit 2** to make a straight long cut in (something).

slither *vb* **1** to move or slide unsteadily, such as on a slippery surface. **2** to move along the ground in a twisting way: *a snake slithered towards the tree. ~n* **3** a slithering movement. **slithery** *adj*

sliver (sliv-ver) *n* **1** a small thin piece that is cut or broken off lengthwise. *~vb* **2** to cut into slivers.

Sloane Ranger *n Informal* (in Britain) a young upper-class woman having a home in London and in the country, characterized as wearing expensive informal clothes.

slob *n Informal* a lazy and untidy person. **slobbish** *adj*

slobber *vb* **1** to dribble (liquid or saliva) from the mouth. **2 slobber over** to behave in an excessively sentimental way towards (someone). *~n* **3** liquid or saliva spilt from the mouth. **slobbery** *adj*

slob ice *n Canad* sludgy masses of floating ice.

sloe *n* **1** the small sour blue-black fruit of the blackthorn. **2** same as **blackthorn.**

sloe-eyed *adj* having dark almond-shaped eyes.

slog *vb* **slogging, slogged 1** to work hard and steadily. **2** to make one's way with difficulty: *we slogged our*

THESAURUS

like, thin, trim **2.** faint, poor, remote, slender, slight *~vb.* **3.** diet, lose weight, reduce

slimy 1. clammy, glutinous, miry, mucous, muddy, oozy, viscous **2.** *chiefly Brit.* creeping, grovelling, obsequious, oily, servile, smarmy (*Brit. informal*), soapy (*slang*), sycophantic, toadying, unctuous

sling *vb.* **1.** *informal* cast, chuck (*informal*), fling, heave, hurl, lob (*informal*), shy, throw, toss **2.** dangle, hang, suspend, swing

slink creep, prowl, pussyfoot (*informal*), skulk, slip, sneak, steal

slip *vb.* **1.** fall, lose one's balance, miss *or* lose one's footing, skid, trip (over) **2.** glide, skate, slide, slither **3.** conceal, creep, hide, insinuate oneself, sneak, steal **4.** blunder, boob (*Brit. slang*), err, go wrong, make a mistake, miscalculate, misjudge, mistake **5. let slip** blurt out, come out with (*informal*), disclose, divulge, give away, leak, let out (*informal*), let the cat out of the bag, reveal *~n.* **6.** bloomer (*Brit. informal*), blunder, boob (*Brit. slang*), error, failure, fault, faux pas, imprudence, indiscretion, mistake, omission, oversight, slip of the tongue, slip-up (*informal*) **7. give someone the slip** dodge, elude, escape from, evade, get away from, lose (someone), outwit, shake (someone) off

slippery 1. glassy, greasy, icy, lubricious (*formal or literary*), perilous, skiddy (*informal*), slippy (*informal or dialect*), smooth, unsafe, unstable, unsteady **2.** crafty, cunning, devious, dishonest, duplicitous, evasive, false, foxy, shifty, sneaky, treacherous, tricky, two-faced, unpredictable, unreliable, untrustworthy

slipshod careless, casual, loose, slapdash, sloppy (*informal*), slovenly, unsystematic, untidy

slit 1. *n.* cut, fissure, gash, incision, opening, rent, split, tear **2.** *vb.* cut (open), gash, impale, knife, lance, pierce, rip, slash, split open

way through the snow. **3** to hit hard. *~n* **4** long exhausting work. **5** a long and difficult walk. **6** a heavy blow.

slogan *n* a catchword or phrase used in politics or advertising.

sloop *n* a small sailing ship with a single mast.

slop *vb* **slopping, slopped 1** (often foll. by *about*) to splash or spill (liquid). **2 slop over** *Informal, chiefly US & Canad* to be excessively sentimental. *~n* **3** a puddle of spilt liquid. **4 slops** liquid refuse and waste food used to feed animals, esp. pigs. **5** (*often pl*) *Informal* liquid food.

slope *n* **1** a stretch of ground where one end is higher than the other. **2 slopes** hills or foothills. **3** any slanting surface. **4** the angle of such a slant. *~vb* **sloping, sloped 5** to slant or cause to slant. **6** (esp. of natural features) to have one end or part higher than another: *the bank sloped sharply down to the river.* **7 slope off** *or* **away** *Informal* to go quietly and quickly in order to avoid something or someone. **8 slope arms** *Mil* (formerly) to hold (a rifle) in a sloping position against the shoulder.

slop out *vb* (of prisoners) to empty chamber pots and collect water.

sloppy *adj* **-pier, -piest 1** *Informal* careless or untidy: *sloppy workmanship.* **2** *Informal* excessively sentimental and romantic. **3** wet; slushy. **sloppily** *adv* **sloppiness** *n*

slosh *n, vb* **1** *Informal* to throw or pour (liquid) carelessly. **2** (often foll. by *about* or *around*) *Informal* **a** to shake or stir (something) in a liquid. **b** (of a person) to splash (around) in water or mud. **3** (usually foll. by *about* or *around*) *Informal* to shake (a container of liquid) or (of liquid in a container) to be shaken. **4** *Brit slang* to deal a heavy blow to. *~n* **5** the sound of splashing liquid. **6** slush. **7** *Brit slang* a heavy blow. **sloshy** *adj*

sloshed *adj Slang, chiefly Brit* drunk.

slot *n* **1** a narrow opening or groove, such as one in a vending machine for inserting a coin. **2** *Informal* a place in a series or scheme: *the late-night slot when people stop watching TV.* *~vb* **slotting, slotted 3** to make a slot or slots in. **4** (usually foll. by *in* or *into*) to fit or be fitted into a slot: *I could fit you into the 9am slot.*

sloth (rhymes with **both**) *n* **1** a slow-moving shaggy-coated animal of Central and South America, which hangs upside down in trees by its long arms and feeds on vegetation. **2** *Formal* laziness, esp. regarding work.

slothful *adj* lazy and unwilling to work.

slot machine *n* a machine, esp. for vending food and cigarettes or featuring an electronic game on which to gamble, worked by placing a coin in a slot.

slouch *vb* **1** to sit, stand, or move with a drooping posture. *~n* **2** a drooping posture. **3 be no slouch** *Informal* be very good or talented: *he was no slouch himself as a negotiator.*

slouch hat *n* a soft hat with a brim that can be pulled down over the ears.

slough[1] (rhymes with **now**) *n* **1** a swamp or marshy area. **2** (rhymes with **blue**) *US & Canad* a large hole where water collects. **3** despair or hopeless depression.

slough[2] **(sluff)** *n* **1** any outer covering that is shed, such as the dead outer layer of the skin of a snake. *~vb* **slough off 2** to shed (an outer covering) or (of an outer covering) to be shed: *the dead cells would slough off.* **3** to get rid of (something unwanted or unnecessary): *she tried hard to slough off her old personality.*

Slovak *adj* **1** of Slovakia. *~n* **2** a person from Slovakia. **3** the language of Slovakia.

sloven *n* a person who is always untidy or careless in appearance or behaviour.

Slovene *adj also* **Slovenian 1** of Slovenia. *~n* **2** Also: **Slovenian** a person from Slovenia. **3** the language of Slovenia.

slovenly *adj* **1** always unclean or untidy. **2** negligent and careless: *to write in such a slovenly style.* *~adv* **3** in a slovenly manner. **slovenliness** *n*

slow *adj* **1** taking a longer time than is usual or expected. **2** lacking speed: *slow movements.* **3** adapted to or producing slow movement: *the slow lane.* **4** (of a clock or watch) showing a time earlier than the correct time. **5** not quick to understand: *slow on the uptake.* **6** dull or uninteresting: *the play was very slow.* **7** not easily aroused: *he is slow to anger.* **8** (of business) not busy; slack. **9** (of a fire or oven) giving off low heat. **10** *Photog* requiring a relatively long time of exposure: *a slow film.* *~adv* **11** in a slow manner. *~vb* **12**

THESAURUS

slither *vb.* glide, skitter, slide, slink, slip, snake, undulate

slog *vb.* **1.** apply oneself to, labour, peg away at, persevere, plod, plough through, slave, toil, tramp, trek, trudge, work **2.** hit, hit for six, punch, slosh (*Brit. slang*), slug, sock (*slang*), strike, thump, wallop (*informal*) *~n.* **3.** effort, exertion, hike, labour, struggle, tramp, trek, trudge

slogan catch phrase, catchword, jingle, motto

slope *n.* **1.** brae (*Scot.*), declination, declivity, descent, gradient, inclination, incline, ramp, rise, scarp, slant, tilt *~vb.* **2.** drop away, fall, incline, lean, pitch, rise, slant, tilt **3.** *with* **off** *or* **away** *informal* creep, make oneself scarce, skulk, slink, slip, steal

sloping bevelled, cant, inclined, inclining, leaning, oblique, slanting

sloppy 1. *informal* amateurish, careless, clumsy, hit-or-miss (*informal*), inattentive, messy, slipshod, slovenly, unkempt, untidy, weak **2.** *informal* banal, gushing, mawkish, mushy (*informal*), overemotional, sentimental, slushy (*informal*), soppy (*Brit. informal*), trite, wet (*Brit. informal*) **3.** sludgy, slushy, splashy, watery, wet

slot *n.* **1.** aperture, channel, groove, hole, slit, vent **2.** *informal* niche, opening, place, position, space, time, vacancy *~vb.* **3.** adjust, assign, fit, fit in, insert, pigeonhole

sloth faineance, idleness, inactivity, indolence, inertia, laziness, slackness, slothfulness, sluggishness, torpor

slothful do-nothing (*informal*), idle, inactive, indolent, inert, lazy, skiving (*Brit. slang*), slack, sluggish, torpid, workshy

slouch *vb.* droop, loll, slump, stoop

slovenly careless, disorderly, heedless, loose, negligent, slack, slapdash, slatternly, slipshod, sloppy (*informal*), unkempt, untidy

slow *adj.* **1.** gradual, lingering, long-drawn-out, prolonged, protracted, time-consuming **2.** creeping, dawdling, deliberate, easy, lackadaisical, laggard, lagging, lazy, leaden, leisurely, loitering, measured, plodding, ponderous, slow-moving, sluggardly, sluggish, tortoise-like, unhurried **3.** blockish, bovine, braindead (*informal*), dense, dim, dozy (*Brit. informal*), dull, dull-witted, dumb (*informal*), obtuse, retarded, slow on the uptake (*informal*), slow-witted, stupid, thick, unresponsive **4.** boring, conservative, dead, dead-and-alive (*Brit.*), dull, inactive, sluggish, stagnant, tame, tedious, uneventful, uninteresting, unproductive, unprogressive, wearisome *~vb.* **5.** *often with* **up** *or* **down** brake, check, curb, decelerate, delay, detain, handicap, hold

(often foll. by *up* or *down*) to decrease or cause to decrease in speed or activity. **slowly** *adv*

slowcoach *n Brit informal* a person who moves or works slowly.

slow motion *n* **1** *Films, television* action that is made to appear slower than normal by filming at a faster rate or by replaying a video recording more slowly. *~adj* **slow-motion 2** of or relating to such action. **3** moving at considerably less than usual speed.

slow virus *n* a type of virus that is present in the body for a long time before it becomes active or infectious.

slowworm *n* a legless lizard with a brownish-grey snakelike body.

sludge *n* **1** soft mud or snow. **2** any muddy or slushy sediment. **3** sewage. **sludgy** *adj*

slug[1] *n* a mollusc like a snail but without a shell.

slug[2] *n* **1** a bullet. **2** *Printing* a line of type produced by a Linotype machine. **3** *Informal* a mouthful of alcoholic drink, esp. spirits: *he poured out a large slug of Scotch.*

slug[3] *vb* **slugging, slugged 1** *Chiefly US & Canad* to hit very hard. *~n* **2** *US & Canad* a heavy blow.

sluggard *n Old-fashioned* a very lazy person.

sluggish *adj* **1** lacking energy. **2** moving or working at slower than the normal rate: *the sluggish waters of the canal.*

sluice *n* **1** a channel that carries a rapid current of water, with a sluicegate to control the flow. **2** the water controlled by a sluicegate. **3** same as **sluicegate. 4** *Mining* a sloping trough for washing ore. *~vb* **sluicing, sluiced 5** to draw off or drain with a sluice. **6** to wash with a stream of water. **7** (often foll. by *away* or *out*) (of water) to run or flow from or as if from a sluice.

sluicegate *n* a valve or gate fitted to a sluice to control the rate of flow of water.

slum *n* **1** an overcrowded and badly maintained house. **2** (*often pl*) a poor rundown overpopulated section of a city. *~vb* **slumming, slummed 3** to visit slums, esp. for curiosity. **4 slum it** to temporarily and deliberately experience poorer places or conditions. **slummy** *adj*

slumber *Literary ~vb* **1** to sleep. *~n* **2** sleep. **slumbering** *adj*

slump *vb* **1** (of commercial activity or prices) to decline suddenly. **2** to sink or fall heavily and suddenly: *she slumped back with exhaustion. ~n* **3** a severe decline in commercial activity or prices; depression. **4** a sudden or marked decline or failure: *a slump in demand for oil.*

slung *vb* the past of **sling**[1].

slunk *vb* the past of **slink.**

slur *vb* **slurring, slurred 1** to pronounce or say (words) unclearly. **2** to make insulting remarks about. **3** *Music* to sing or play (successive notes) smoothly by moving from one to the other without a break. **4** (often foll. by *over*) to treat hastily or carelessly. *~n* **5** a insulting remark intended to damage someone's reputation. **6** a slurring of words. **7** *Music* **a** a slurring of successive notes. **b** the curved line (⌒ or ‿) indicating this.

slurp *Informal ~vb* **1** to eat or drink (something) noisily. *~n* **2** a slurping sound.

slurry *n, pl* **-ries** a thin watery mixture of something such as cement or mud.

slush *n* **1** any watery muddy substance, esp. melting snow. **2** *Informal* sloppily sentimental language or writing. **slushy** *adj*

slush fund *n* a fund for financing political or commercial corruption.

slut *n Offensive* a promiscuous woman. **sluttish** *adj*

sly *adj* **slyer, slyest** *or* **slier, sliest 1** (of a person's remarks or gestures) indicating that he or she knows something of which other people may be unaware: *she had the feeling they were poking sly fun at her.* **2** secretive and skilled at deception: *a sly trickster.* **3** roguish: *sly comedy.* **4 on the sly** secretively: *they were smoking on the sly behind the shed.* **slyly** *adv*

Sm *Chem* samarium.

smack[1] *vb* **1** to slap sharply. **2** to strike loudly or to be struck loudly. **3** to open and close (the lips) loudly to show pleasure or anticipation. *~n* **4** a sharp loud slap, or the sound of such a slap. **5** a loud kiss. **6** a sharp sound made by the lips in enjoyment. **7 smack in the eye** *Informal, chiefly Brit* a snub or rejection. *~adv Informal* **8** directly; squarely: *smack in the middle.* **9** sharply and unexpectedly: *he ran smack into one of the men.*

smack[2] *n* **1** a slight flavour or suggestion (of something): *the smack of loss of self-control.* **2** *Slang* heroin. *~vb* **smack of a** to have a slight smell or flavour (of something). **b** to have a suggestion (of something): *it smacks of discrimination.*

smack[3] *n* a small single-masted fishing vessel.

smacker *n Slang* **1** a loud kiss. **2** a pound note or dollar bill.

small *adj* **1** not large in size or amount. **2** of little importance or on a minor scale: *a small detail.* **3** mean, ungenerous, or petty: *a small mind.* **4** modest or humble: *small beginnings.* **5 feel small** to be humiliated. **6** (of a child or animal) young; not mature. **7** unimportant or trivial: *a small matter.* **8** (of a letter) written or printed in lower case rather as a capital. *~adv* **9** into

THESAURUS

up, lag, reduce speed, rein in, relax, restrict, retard, slacken (off), spin out

slowly at a snail's pace, at one's leisure, by degrees, gradually, in one's own (good) time, leisurely, ploddingly, steadily, taking one's time, unhurriedly, with leaden steps

sluggish dull, heavy, inactive, indolent, inert, lethargic, lifeless, listless, phlegmatic, slothful, slow, slow-moving, torpid, unresponsive

slumber *literary vb.* be inactive, doze, drowse, kip (*Brit. slang*), lie dormant, nap, repose, sleep, snooze (*informal*), zizz (*Brit. informal*)

slump 1. *vb.* collapse, crash, decline, deteriorate, fall, fall off, go downhill (*informal*), plummet, plunge, reach a new low, sink, slip **2.** *n.* collapse, crash, decline, depreciation, depression, downturn, drop, failure, fall, falling-off, low, recession, reverse, stagnation, trough

slur *n.* affront, aspersion, blot, brand, calumny, discredit, disgrace, innuendo, insinuation, insult, reproach, smear, stain, stigma

slut *offensive* scrubber (*offensive slang*), slattern (*old-fashioned*), sloven, tart (*informal*), trollop (*derogatory*)

sly *adj.* **1.** arch, impish, knowing, mischievous, roguish **2.** artful, astute, clever, conniving, covert, crafty, cunning, devious, foxy, furtive, guileful, insidious, scheming, secret, shifty, stealthy, subtle, underhand, wily *~n.* **3. on the sly** behind (someone's) back, covertly, like a thief in the night, on the quiet, privately, secretly, surreptitiously, underhandedly, under the counter (*informal*)

smack *vb.* **1.** box, clap, cuff, hit, pat, slap, sock (*slang*), spank, strike, tap *~n.* **2.** blow, crack, slap **3. smack in the eye** *informal, chiefly Brit.* blow, rebuff, repulse, setback, slap in the face, snub *~adv.* **4.** *infor-*

small pieces: *cut it small.* ~*n* **10** the small narrow part of the back. **11 smalls** *Informal, chiefly Brit* underwear. **smallish** *adj* **smallness** *n*

small beer *n Informal, chiefly Brit* people or things of no importance.

small change *n* coins of low value.

small fry *pl n* **1** people regarded as unimportant. **2** young children.

small goods *pl n Austral & NZ* meats bought from a delicatessen, such as sausages.

smallholding *n* a piece of agricultural land smaller than a farm. **smallholder** *n*

small hours *pl n* the early hours of the morning, after midnight and before dawn.

small intestine *n Anat* the narrow, longer part of the alimentary canal, in which digestion is completed.

small-minded *adj* having narrow selfish attitudes; petty.

smallpox *n* a contagious disease causing fever, a rash, and blisters which usually leave permanent scars.

small print *n* details in a contract or document printed in small type, esp. when considered as containing important information that people may regret not reading.

small-scale *adj* of limited size or scope.

small screen *n* **the small screen** television, esp. in contrast to cinema: *despite his film success, he has achieved little on the small screen.*

small talk *n* light conversation for social occasions.

small-time *adj Informal* operating on a limited scale; minor: *a small-time smuggler.*

smarm *vb Brit informal* **1** to bring (oneself) into favour (with). **2** *Old-fashioned* (often foll. by *down*) to flatten (the hair) with oil.

smarmy *adj* **smarmier, smarmiest** unpleasantly flattering or polite.

smart *adj* **1** clean and neatly dressed. **2** intelligent and shrewd. **3** quick and witty in speech: *a smart talker.* **4** (of places or events) fashionable; chic: *smart restaurants.* **5** vigorous or brisk: *a smart pace.* **6** causing a sharp stinging pain. **7** (of a weapon) containing an electronic device which enables it to be guided to its target: *a smart bomb.* ~*vb* **8** to feel or cause a sharp stinging physical or mental pain: *I was still smarting from the insult.* ~*n* **9** a stinging pain or feeling. ~*adv* **10** in a smart manner. ~See also **smarts. smartly** *adv* **smartness** *n*

smart aleck *n Informal* a person who thinks he or she is an expert on every subject; know-all.

smart card *n* a plastic card with integrated circuits used for storing and processing computer data.

smarten *vb* (usually foll. by *up*) to make or become smart.

smarts *pl n Slang, chiefly US* know-how, intelligence, or wits: *the street smarts of the old crooks.*

smash *vb* **1** to break into pieces violently and noisily. **2** (often foll. by *against, through* or *into*) to throw or crash (against) violently, causing shattering: *his head smashed against a window.* **3** to hit or collide forcefully and suddenly. **4** *Racket sports* to hit (the ball) fast and powerfully with an overhead stroke. **5** to defeat or destroy: *the police had smashed a major drug ring.* ~*n* **6** an act or sound of smashing. **7** a violent collision of vehicles. **8** *Racket sports* a fast and powerful overhead stroke. **9** *Informal* a show, record or film which is very popular with the public. ~*adv* **10** with a smash.

smash-and-grab *adj Informal* of a robbery in which a shop window is broken and the contents removed.

smasher *n Informal, chiefly Brit* a person or thing that is very attractive or outstanding.

smashing *adj Informal, chiefly Brit* excellent or first-rate.

smash-up *Informal* ~*n* **1** a bad collision or crash involving motor vehicles. ~*vb* **smash up 2** to damage to the point of complete destruction: *two men smashed up a bar.*

smattering *n* a slight or superficial knowledge: *I knew a smattering of Russian.*

smear *vb* **1** to spread with a greasy or sticky substance. **2** to apply (a greasy or sticky substance) thickly. **3** to rub so as to produce a smudge. **4** to spread false and damaging rumours (about). ~*n* **5** a dirty mark or smudge. **6** a false but damaging rumour spread by a rival or enemy. **7** *Med* a small amount of a substance smeared onto a glass slide for examination under a microscope. **smeary** *adj*

smear test *n Med* same as **Pap test.**

smell *vb* **smelling, smelt** *or* **smelled 1** to perceive the scent of (a substance) with the nose. **2** to have a specified kind of smell: *it smells fruity; your supper smells good.* **3** (often foll. by *of*) to emit an odour (of): *the place smells of milk and babies.* **4** to give off an

THESAURUS

mal directly, exactly, plumb, point-blank, precisely, right, slap (*informal*), squarely, straight

small 1. diminutive, immature, Lilliputian, little, mini, miniature, minute, petite, pint-size, pint-sized (*informal*), pocket-sized, puny, pygmy, slight, teeny, tiny, undersized, wee, young **2.** inadequate, inconsiderable, insufficient, limited, meagre, measly, scant, scanty **3.** base, grudging, illiberal, mean, narrow, petty, selfish **4.** humble, modest, small-scale, unpretentious **5.** insignificant, lesser, minor, negligible, paltry, petty, trifling, trivial, unimportant

small-minded bigoted, envious, grudging, hidebound, intolerant, mean, narrow-minded, petty, rigid, ungenerous

smart *adj.* **1.** chic, elegant, fashionable, fine, modish, natty (*informal*), neat, snappy, spruce, stylish, trendy (*Brit. informal*), trim, well turned out **2.** acute, adept, agile, apt, astute, bright, brisk, canny, clever, ingenious, intelligent, keen, nimble, quick, quick-witted, ready, sharp, shrewd **3.** effective, impertinent, nimble-witted, pointed, ready, saucy, witty **4.** hard, painful, piercing, sharp, stinging ~*vb.* **5.** burn, hurt, pain, sting, throb, tingle ~*n.* **6.** burning sensation, pain, pang, smarting, soreness, sting

smash *vb.* **1.** break, collide, crash, crush, demolish, disintegrate, pulverize, shatter, shiver **2.** defeat, destroy, lay waste, overthrow, ruin, total (*slang*), trash (*slang*), wreck ~*n.* **3.** accident, collision, crash, pile-up (*informal*), smash-up (*informal*)

smashing *informal, chiefly Brit.* brilliant (*informal*), cracking (*Brit. informal*), crucial (*slang*), def (*slang*), excellent, exhilarating, fabulous (*informal*), fantastic (*informal*), first-class, first-rate, great (*informal*), magnificent, marvellous, mean (*slang*), mega (*slang*), out of this world (*informal*), sensational (*informal*), sovereign (*old-fashioned*), stupendous, super (*informal*), superb, superlative, terrific (*informal*), topping (*Brit. slang*), wonderful, world-class

smattering bit, dash, elements, modicum, rudiments, smatter, sprinkling

smear *vb.* **1.** bedaub, blur, coat, cover, daub, dirty, patch, plaster, rub on, smirch, smudge, soil, spread over, stain, sully **2.** asperse, besmirch, blacken, calumniate, drag (someone's) name through the mud,

unpleasant odour. **5** (often foll. by *out*) to detect through instinct: *I smell trouble.* **6** to use the sense of smell; sniff. **7 smell of** to indicate or suggest: *anything that smells of devaluation.* ~*n* **8** the sense by which scents or odours are perceived. **9** an odour or scent. **10** the act of smelling.

smelling salts *pl n* a preparation containing crystals of ammonium carbonate, used to revive a person feeling faint.

smelly *adj* **smellier, smelliest** having a nasty smell. **smelliness** *n*

smelt[1] *vb* to extract (a metal) from (an ore) by heating.

smelt[2] *n, pl* **smelt** *or* **smelts** a small silvery food fish.

smelt[3] *vb* a past tense and past participle of **smell.**

smelter *n* an industrial plant in which smelting is carried out.

smile *n* **1** a facial expression in which the corners of the mouth are turned up, showing amusement or friendliness. ~*vb* **smiling, smiled 2** to give a smile. **3 smile at a** to look at with a kindly expression. **b** to look with amusement at. **4 smile on** *or* **upon** to regard favourably: *fortune smiled on us today.* **5** to express by a smile: *he smiled a comrade's greeting.*

smirch *vb* **1** to disgrace. **2** to dirty or soil. ~*n* **3** a disgrace. **4** a smear or stain.

smirk *n* **1** a smug smile. ~*vb* **2** to give such a smile.

smite *vb* **smiting, smote; smitten** *or* **smit** *Archaic, Biblical* **1** to strike with a heavy blow. **2** to affect severely: *hunger smites him again.* **3** to burden with an affliction in order to punish: *God smote the enemies of the righteous.* **4 smite on** to strike abruptly and with force: *the sun smote down on him.*

smith *n* **1** a person who works in metal: *goldsmith.* **2** See **blacksmith.**

smithereens *pl n* shattered fragments.

smithy *n, pl* **smithies** the workshop of a blacksmith; forge.

smitten *vb* **1** a past participle of **smite.** ~*adj* **2** deeply affected by love (for).

smock *n* **1** a loose overall worn to protect the clothes. **2** a loose blouselike garment worn by women. **3** a loose protective overgarment decorated with smocking, worn formerly by farm workers. ~*vb* **4** to gather (material) by sewing in a honeycomb pattern.

smocking *n* ornamental needlework used to gather material.

smog *n* a mixture of smoke and fog that occurs in some industrial areas. **smoggy** *adj*

smoke *n* **1** the cloudy mass that rises from something burning. **2** the act of smoking tobacco. **3** *Informal* a cigarette or cigar. **4 go up in smoke a** to come to nothing. **b** to burn up vigorously. ~*vb* **smoking, smoked 5** to give off smoke: *a smoking fireplace.* **6 a** to draw the smoke of (burning tobacco) into the mouth and exhale it again. **b** to do this habitually. **7** to cure (meat, cheese, or fish) by treating with smoke.

Smoke *n* **the Smoke** *Informal* short for **Big Smoke.**

smokeless *adj* having or producing little or no smoke: *smokeless fuel.*

smokeless zone *n* an area where only smokeless fuels may be used.

smoke out *vb* **1** to drive (a person or animal) out of a hiding place by filling it with smoke. **2** to bring (someone) out of secrecy and into the open: *they smoked out the plotters.*

smoker *n* **1** a person who habitually smokes tobacco. **2** a train compartment where smoking is permitted.

smoke screen *n* **1** something said or done to hide the truth. **2** *Mil* a cloud of smoke used to provide cover for manoeuvres.

smokestack *n* a tall chimney that carries smoke away from a factory.

smoko *or* **smokeho** (**smoke**-oh) *n, pl* **-kos** *or* **-hos** *Austral & NZ informal* **1** a short break from work for tea or a cigarette. **2** refreshment taken during this break.

smoky *adj* **smokier, smokiest 1** filled with or giving off smoke, sometimes excessively: *smoky coal or wood fires.* **2** having the colour of smoke. **3** having the taste or smell of smoke. **4** made dirty or hazy by smoke. **smokiness** *n*

smolt *n* a young salmon at the stage when it migrates from fresh water to the sea.

smooch *Slang* ~*vb* **1** (of two people) to kiss and cuddle. **2** *Brit* to dance very slowly with one's arms around another person or (of two people) to dance together in such a way. ~*n* **3** the act of smooching.

smoodge *or* **smooge** *vb* **smoodging, smoodged** *or* **smooging, smooged** *Austral & NZ* **1** same as **smooch** (sense 1). **2** to attempt to gain favour through flattery.

smooth *adj* **1** having an even surface with no roughness, bumps, or holes. **2** without obstructions or difficulties: *smooth progress towards an agreement.* **3** without lumps: *a smooth paste.* **4** free from jolts and bumps: *a smooth landing.* **5** not harsh in taste; mellow: *an excellent smooth wine.* **6** charming or persuasive but possibly insincere. ~*adv* **7** in a smooth manner. ~*vb* **8** (often foll. by *down*) to make or become even or without roughness. **9** (often foll. by *out* or *away*) to remove in order to make smooth: *smoothing out the creases.* **10** to make calm; soothe. **11** to make easier: *Moscow smoothed the path to democracy.* ~*n* **12** the smooth part of something. **13** the act of smoothing. **smoothly** *adv*

smoothie *n Slang* a man who is so confident, well-dressed, and charming that one is suspicious of his motives and doubts his honesty.

smooth over *vb* to ease or gloss over: *their fears are now being smoothed over.*

smooth-talking *adj* confident and persuasive but not necessarily honest or sincere.

smorgasbord *n* a variety of savoury dishes served as hors d'oeuvres or as a buffet meal.

smote *vb* the past tense of **smite.**

THESAURUS

malign, sully, tarnish, traduce, vilify ~*n.* **3.** blot, blotch, daub, smirch, smudge, splotch, streak **4.** calumny, defamation, libel, mudslinging, slander, vilification, whispering campaign

smell *vb.* **1.** get a whiff of, nose, scent, sniff **2.** be malodorous, hum (*slang*), niff (*Brit. slang*), pong (*Brit. informal*), reek, stink, stink to high heaven (*informal*), whiff (*Brit. slang*) ~*n.* **3.** aroma, bouquet, fetor, fragrance, niff (*Brit. slang*), odour, perfume, pong (*Brit. informal*), redolence, scent, stench, stink, whiff

smirk *n.* grin, leer, simper, smug look, sneer

smitten beguiled, bewitched, bowled over (*informal*), captivated, charmed, enamoured, infatuated, swept off one's feet

smoky black, grey, grimy, hazy, murky, reeky, smoke-darkened, sooty, thick

smooth *adj.* **1.** even, flat, flush, horizontal, level, plain, plane, unwrinkled **2.** easy, effortless, flowing, fluent, frictionless, regular, rhythmic, steady, unbroken, uneventful, uniform, uninterrupted, untroubled, well-ordered **3.** agreeable, bland, mellow, mild, pleasant, soothing **4.** debonair, facile, glib, ingratiating, persuasive, silky, slick, smarmy (*Brit. informal*), suave, unctuous, urbane ~*vb.* **5.** flatten, iron, level, plane, pol-

smother *vb* **1** to extinguish (a fire) by covering so as to cut it off from the air. **2** to suffocate. **3** to surround or overwhelm (with): *she smothered him with her idea of affection.* **4** to suppress or stifle: *he smothered an ironic chuckle.* **5** to cover over thickly: *ice cream smothered with sauce.*

smoulder *or US* **smolder** *vb* **1** to burn slowly without flames, usually giving off smoke. **2** (of emotions) to exist in a suppressed state without being released.

smudge *vb* **smudging, smudged 1** to make or become smeared or soiled. *~n* **2** a smear or dirty mark. **3** a blurred form or area: *the dull smudge of a ship.* **smudgy** *adj*

smug *adj* **smugger, smuggest** very pleased with oneself; self-satisfied. **smugly** *adv* **smugness** *n*

smuggle *vb* **-gling, -gled 1** to import or export (goods that are prohibited or subject to taxation) secretly. **2** (often foll. by *into* or *out of*) to bring or take secretly: *he was smuggled out of the country unnoticed.* **smuggler** *n* **smuggling** *n*

smut *n* **1** stories, pictures, or jokes relating to sex or nudity. **2** a speck of soot or a dark mark left by soot. **3** a disease of cereals, in which black sooty masses cover the affected parts. **smutty** *adj*

Sn *Chem* tin.

snack *n* a light quick meal eaten between or in place of main meals.

snack bar *n* a place where light meals or snacks are sold.

snaffle *n* **1** a mouthpiece for controlling a horse. *~vb* **-fling, -fled 2** *Brit informal* to steal or take. **3** to fit or control (a horse) with a snaffle.

snafu (snaf-**foo**) *Slang chiefly mil ~n* **1** confusion or chaos regarded as the normal state. *~adj* **2** confused or muddled up, as usual.

snag *n* **1** a small problem or difficulty: *one possible snag in his plans.* **2** a sharp projecting point that may catch on things. **3** a small hole in a fabric caused by a sharp object. **4** a tree stump in a river bed that is a danger to navigation. *~vb* **snagging, snagged 5** to tear or catch on a snag.

snail *n* a slow-moving mollusc with a spiral shell.

snail's pace *n* a very slow speed.

snake *n* **1** a long scaly limbless reptile. **2** Also: **snake in the grass** a person, esp. a colleague or friend, who secretly acts against one. *~vb* **snaking, snaked 3** to glide or move in a winding course, like a snake.

snakebite *n* **1** the bite of a snake. **2** a drink of cider and lager.

snake charmer *n* an entertainer who appears to hypnotize snakes by playing music.

snakes and ladders *n* a board game in which players move counters along a series of squares by means of dice, going up the ladders to squares nearer the finish and down the snakes to squares nearer the start.

snaky *adj* **snakier, snakiest 1** twisting or winding. **2** treacherous.

snap *vb* **snapping, snapped 1** to break suddenly, esp. with a sharp sound. **2** to make or cause to make a sudden sharp cracking sound: *he snapped his fingers.* **3** to move or close with a sudden sharp sound: *I snapped the lid shut.* **4** to move in a sudden or abrupt way. **5** to give way or collapse suddenly under strain: *one day someone's temper will snap.* **6** to panic when a situation becomes too difficult to cope with: *he could snap at any moment.* **7** (often foll. by *at* or *up*) to seize suddenly or quickly. **8** (often foll. by *at* of animals) to bite at suddenly. **9** to speak (words) sharply and angrily. **10** to take a photograph of. **11 snap one's fingers at** *Informal* to defy or dismiss contemptuously. **12 snap out of it** *Informal* to recover quickly, esp. from depression or anger. *~n* **13** the act of breaking suddenly or the sound of a sudden breakage. **14** a sudden sharp sound. **15** a clasp or fastener that closes with a snapping sound. **16** a sudden grab or bite. **17** a thin crisp biscuit: *brandy snaps.* **18** *Informal* an informal photograph taken with a simple camera. **19** See **cold snap. 20** *Brit* a card game in which the word *snap* is called when two similar cards are turned up. *~adj* **21** done on the spur of the moment: *snap judgments.* *~adv* **22** with a snap. *~interj* **23 a** *Cards* the word called while playing snap. **b** a cry used to draw attention to the similarity of two things. ~See also **snap up.**

snapdragon *n* a plant with spikes of colourful flowers that can open and shut like a mouth; antirrhinum.

snap fastener *n* same as **press stud.**

snappy *adj* **-pier, -piest 1** smart and fashionable: *snappy designs.* **2** Also: **snappish** (of someone's behaviour) irritable, unfriendly, and cross. **3** brisk or lively: *short snappy movements.* **4 make it snappy** *Slang* hurry up! **snappiness** *n*

snapshot *n* same as **snap** (sense 18).

snap up *vb* to take advantage of eagerly and quickly: *the tickets have been snapped up.*

snare[1] *n* **1** a trap for birds or small animals, usually a flexible loop that is drawn tight around the prey. **2** anything that traps someone or something unawares. *~vb* **snaring, snared 3** to catch in or as if in a snare.

THESAURUS

ish, press **6.** allay, alleviate, appease, assuage, calm, ease, extenuate, facilitate, iron out the difficulties of, mitigate, mollify, palliate, pave the way, soften

smother 1. choke, extinguish, snuff, stifle, strangle, suffocate **2.** cocoon, envelop, heap, inundate, overwhelm, shower, shroud, surround **3.** conceal, hide, keep back, muffle, repress, stifle, suppress

smoulder be resentful, boil, burn, fester, fume, rage, seethe, simmer, smart under

smug complacent, conceited, holier-than-thou, priggish, self-opinionated, self-righteous, self-satisfied, superior

snack bite, bite to eat, break, elevenses (*Brit. informal*), light meal, nibble, refreshment(s), titbit

snag 1. *n.* catch, complication, difficulty, disadvantage, downside, drawback, hitch, inconvenience, obstacle, problem, stumbling block, the rub **2.** *vb.* catch, hole, rip, tear

snap *vb.* **1.** break, come apart, crack, give way, separate **2.** click, crackle, pop **3.** bite, bite at, catch, grip, nip, seize, snatch **4.** bark, flare out, flash, fly off the handle at (*informal*), growl, jump down (someone's) throat (*informal*), lash out at, retort, snarl, speak sharply **5. snap one's fingers at** *informal* cock a snook at (*Brit.*), defy, flout, pay no attention to, scorn, set at naught, wave two fingers at (*slang*) **6. snap out of it** *informal* cheer up, get a grip on oneself, get over, liven up, perk up, pull oneself together (*informal*), recover *~n.* **7.** crackle, fillip, flick, pop **8.** bite, grab, nip *~adj.* **9.** abrupt, immediate, instant, on-the-spot, sudden, unpremeditated

snappy 1. chic, dapper, fashionable, modish, natty (*informal*), smart, stylish, trendy (*Brit. informal*), up-to-the-minute, voguish **2.** apt to fly off the handle (*informal*), cross, edgy, hasty, impatient, irritable, like a bear with a sore head (*informal*), quick-tempered, ratty (*Brit. informal*), snappish, tart, testy, tetchy, touchy, waspish **3. make it snappy** *slang* be quick, buck up (*informal*), get a move on (*informal*), get one's skates on, hurry (up), look lively, make haste

snare[2] *n Music* a set of strings fitted against the lower head of a snare drum, which produces a rattling sound when the drum is beaten.

snare drum *n Music* a small drum fitted with a snare.

snarl[1] *vb* **1** (of an animal) to growl fiercely with bared teeth. **2** to speak or say (something) fiercely: *he snarled out a command to a subordinate.* ~*n* **3** a fierce growl or facial expression. **4** the act of snarling.

snarl[2] *n* **1** a complicated or confused state. **2** a tangled mass. ~*vb* **3 snarl up** to become, be, or make confused or complicated: *the postal service was snarled up at Christmas.*

snarl-up *n Informal, chiefly Brit* a confused, disorganized situation such as a traffic jam.

snatch *vb* **1** to seize or grasp (something) suddenly: *she snatched the paper.* **2** (usually foll. by *at*) to attempt to seize suddenly. **3** to take hurriedly: *these players had snatched a few hours sleep.* **4** to remove suddenly: *she snatched her hand away.* ~*n* **5** an act of snatching. **6** a small piece or incomplete part: *snatches of song.* **7** a brief spell: *snatches of sleep.* **8** *Slang, chiefly US* an act of kidnapping. **9** *Brit slang* a robbery: *a wages snatch.*

snazzy *adj* **-zier, -ziest** *Informal* (esp. of clothes) stylish and flashy.

sneak *vb* **1** to move quietly, trying not be noticed. **2** to behave in a cowardly or underhand manner. **3** to bring, take, or put secretly: *we sneaked him over the border.* **4** *Informal, chiefly Brit* (esp. in schools) to tell tales. ~*n* **5** a person who acts in an underhand or cowardly manner. ~*adj* **6** without warning: *a sneak attack.* **sneaky** *adj*

sneakers *pl n Chiefly US & Canad* canvas shoes with rubber soles.

sneaking *adj* **1** slight but nagging: *a sneaking suspicion.* **2** secret: *a sneaking admiration.* **3** acting in a cowardly and furtive way.

sneak thief *n* a burglar who sneaks into houses through open doors and windows.

sneer *n* **1** a facial expression showing distaste or contempt, typically with a curled upper lip. **2** a remark showing distaste or contempt. ~*vb* **3** to make a facial expression of scorn or contempt. **4** to say (something) in a scornful manner. **sneering** *adj, n*

sneeze *vb* **sneezing, sneezed 1** to expel air from the nose suddenly and without control, esp. as the result of irritation in the nostrils. ~*n* **2** the act or sound of sneezing.

sneeze at *vb Informal* to ignore or dismiss lightly: *the money's not to be sneezed at.*

snick *n* **1** a small cut in something; notch. **2** *Cricket* a glancing blow off the edge of the bat. ~*vb* **3** to make a small cut or notch in (something). **4** *Cricket* to hit (the ball) with a snick.

snicker *n, vb Chiefly US & Canad* same as **snigger.**

snide *adj* (of comments) critical in an unfair and nasty way.

sniff *vb* **1** to inhale through the nose in short audible breaths. **2** (often foll. by *at*) to smell by sniffing. ~*n* **3** the act or sound of sniffing. **sniffer** *n*

sniff at *vb* to express contempt or dislike for.

sniffer dog *n* a police dog trained to locate drugs or explosives by smell.

sniffle *vb* **-fling, -fled 1** to sniff repeatedly when the nasal passages are blocked up. ~*n* **2** the act or sound of sniffling.

sniffles *or* **snuffles** *pl n* **the sniffles** *Informal* a cold in the head.

sniff out *vb* to discover after some searching: *they eventually sniffed out a suitable Parliamentary seat for him.*

sniffy *adj* **-fier, -fiest** *Informal* contemptuous or scornful.

snifter *n* **1** *Informal* a small quantity of alcoholic drink. **2** a pear-shaped brandy glass.

snig *vb* **snigging, snigged** *NZ* to drag (a felled log) by a chain or cable.

snigger *n* **1** a quiet and disrespectful laugh kept to oneself. ~*vb* **2** to utter such a laugh.

snip *vb* **snipping, snipped 1** to cut with small quick strokes with scissors or shears. ~*n* **2** *Informal, chiefly Brit* a bargain. **3** the act or sound of snipping. **4** a small piece snipped off. **5** a small cut made by snipping.

snipe *n, pl* **snipe** *or* **snipes 1** a wading bird with a long straight bill. ~*vb* **sniping, sniped 2** (often foll. by *at*) to shoot (someone) from a place of hiding. **3** (often foll. by *at*) to make critical remarks about. **sniper** *n*

snippet *n* a small scrap or fragment: *the odd snippet of knowledge.*

snitch *Slang* ~*vb* **1** to act as an informer. **2** to steal small amounts. ~*n* **3** an informer.

snitchy *adj* **snitchier, snitchiest** *NZ informal* bad-tempered or irritable.

snivel *vb* **-elling, -elled** *or US* **-eling, -eled 1** to cry and sniff in a self-pitying way. **2** to say (something) tearfully; whine. **3** to have a runny nose. ~*n* **4** the act of snivelling.

THESAURUS

snap up avail oneself of, grab, grasp, nab (*informal*), pounce upon, seize, swoop down on, take advantage of

snare 1. *n.* catch, gin, net, noose, pitfall, springe, trap, wire **2.** *vb.* catch, entrap, net, seize, springe, trap, wire

snarl[1] *vb.* growl, grumble, mumble, murmur, show its teeth (*of an animal*)

snarl[2] *vb. often with* **up** complicate, confuse, embroil, enmesh, entangle, entwine, muddle, ravel, tangle

snarl-up *informal, chiefly Brit.* confusion, entanglement, muddle, tangle, (traffic) jam

snatch 1. *vb.* catch up, clutch, gain, grab, grasp, grip, make off with, pluck, pull, rescue, seize, take, win, wrench, wrest **2.** *n.* bit, fragment, part, piece, smattering, snippet, spell

sneak *vb.* **1.** cower, lurk, pad, sidle, skulk, slink, slip, smuggle, steal **2.** *informal, chiefly Brit.* grass on (*Brit. slang*), inform on, shop (*slang, chiefly Brit.*), sing (*slang, chiefly U.S.*), spill one's guts (*slang*), tell on (*informal*), tell tales ~*n.* **3.** informer, snake in the grass, telltale ~*adj.* **4.** clandestine, furtive, quick, secret, stealthy, surprise

sneaking 1. intuitive, nagging, niggling, persistent, uncomfortable, worrying **2.** hidden, private, secret, suppressed, unavowed, unconfessed, undivulged, unexpressed, unvoiced **3.** contemptible, furtive, mean, sly, sneaky, surreptitious, two-faced, underhand

sneer 1. *n.* derision, disdain, jeer, jibe, mockery, ridicule, scorn, snigger **2.** *vb.* curl one's lip, deride, disdain, hold in contempt, hold up to ridicule, jeer, jibe, laugh, look down on, mock, ridicule, scoff, scorn, sniff at, snigger, turn up one's nose (*informal*)

sniff *vb.* breathe, inhale, smell, snuff, snuffle

snigger giggle, laugh, smirk, sneer, snicker (*chiefly U.S. & Canad.*), titter

snip *vb.* **1.** clip, crop, cut, dock, nick, nip off, notch, shave, trim ~*n.* **2.** *informal, chiefly Brit.* bargain, giveaway, good buy, steal (*informal*) **3.** bit, clipping, fragment, piece, scrap, shred, snippet

snob *n* **1** a person who tries to associate with those of higher social status and who hates those of a lower social status. **2** a person who feels smugly superior with regard to his or her tastes or interests: *a cultural snob.* **snobbery** *n* **snobbish** *adj*

snoek (**snook**) *n* a South African edible marine fish.

snoep (**snoop**) *adj S African informal* mean or tight-fisted.

snog *Brit slang* ~*vb* **snogging, snogged 1** to kiss and cuddle. ~*n* **2** the act of kissing and cuddling.

snood *n* a pouchlike hat loosely holding a woman's hair at the back.

snook *n* **cock a snook at** *Brit* **a** to make a rude gesture at (someone) by putting one thumb to the nose with the fingers of the hand outstretched. **b** to show contempt for (someone in authority) without fear of punishment.

snooker *n* **1** a game played on a billiard table with 15 red balls, six balls of other colours, and a white cue ball. **2** a shot in which the cue ball is left in a position such that another ball blocks the target ball. ~*vb* **3** to leave (an opponent) in an unfavourable position by playing a snooker. **4** to put someone in a position where he or she can do nothing.

snoop *Informal* ~*vb* **1** (often foll. by *about* or *around*) to pry into the private business of others. ~*n* **2** the act of snooping. **snooper** *n* **snoopy** *adj*

snooty *adj* **snootier, snootiest** *Informal* behaving as if superior to other people; snobbish.

snooze *Informal* ~*vb* **snoozing, snoozed 1** to take a brief light sleep. ~*n* **2** a nap.

snore *vb* **snoring, snored 1** to breathe with snorting sounds while asleep. ~*n* **2** the act or sound of snoring.

snorkel *n* **1** a tube allowing a swimmer to breathe while face down on the surface of the water. **2** a device supplying air to a submarine when under water. ~*vb* **-kelling, -kelled** *or US* **-keling, -keled 3** to swim with a snorkel.

snort *vb* **1** to exhale air noisily through the nostrils. **2** to express contempt or annoyance by snorting. **3** to say with a snort. ~*n* **4** a loud exhalation of air through the nostrils to express contempt or annoyance: *Clare gave a snort of disgust.*

snot *n Usually considered vulgar* **1** mucus from the nose. **2** *Slang* an annoying or disgusting person.

snotty *adj* **-tier, -tiest** *Considered vulgar* **1** dirty with nasal discharge. **2** having a proud and superior attitude. **3** *Slang* contemptible; nasty. **snottiness** *n*

snout *n* **1** the projecting nose and jaws of an animal. **2** anything projecting like a snout: *the snout of a gun.* **3** *Slang* a person's nose.

snow *n* **1** frozen vapour falling from the sky in flakes. **2** a layer of snow on the ground. **3** a falling of snow. **4** *Slang* cocaine. ~*vb* **5** (with *it* as subject) to be the case that snow is falling: *it's snowing today.* **6** (usually passive, foll. by *over, under, in* or *up*) to cover or confine with a heavy fall of snow. **7** to fall as or like snow. **8** **be snowed under** to be overwhelmed, esp. with paperwork. **snowy** *adj*

snowball *n* **1** snow pressed into a ball for throwing. ~*vb* **2** to increase rapidly in size or importance: *production snowballed between 1950 and 1970.* **3** to throw snowballs at.

snowberry *n, pl* **-ries** a shrub grown for its white berries.

snow-blind *adj* blinded for a short time by the intense reflection of sunlight from snow. **snow blindness** *n*

snowbound *adj* shut in or blocked off by snow.

snowcap *n* a cap of snow on top of a mountain. **snowcapped** *adj*

snowdrift *n* a bank of deep snow driven together by the wind.

snowdrop *n* a plant with small drooping white bell-shaped flowers.

snowfall *n* **1** a fall of snow. **2** *Meteorol* the amount of snow that falls in a specified place and time.

snowflake *n* a single crystal of snow.

snow goose *n* a North American goose with white feathers and black wing tips.

snow line *n* (on a mountain) the altitude above which there is permanent snow.

snowman *n, pl* **-men** a figure like a person, made of packed snow.

snowmobile *n* a motor vehicle for travelling on snow, esp. one with caterpillar tracks and front skis.

snowplough *or esp US* **snowplow** *n* a vehicle for clearing away snow.

snowshoe *n* a racket-shaped frame with a network of thongs stretched across it, worn on the feet to make walking on snow less difficult.

snowstorm *n* a storm with heavy snow.

SNP Scottish National Party.

Snr *or* **snr** senior.

snub *vb* **snubbing, snubbed 1** to insult (someone) deliberately. ~*n* **2** a deliberately insulting act or remark. ~*adj* **3** (of a nose) short and turned up.

snub-nosed *adj* having a short turned-up nose.

snuff[1] *vb* **1** to inhale through the nose. **2** (esp. of an animal) to examine by sniffing. ~*n* **3** a sniff.

snuff[2] *n* finely powdered tobacco for sniffing up the nostrils.

snuff[3] *vb* **1** (often foll. by *out*) to put out (a candle). **2** to cut off the charred part of (a candle wick). **3** (usually foll. by *out*) *Informal* to put an end to. **4** **snuff it** *Brit informal* to die. ~*n* **5** the burned portion of the wick of a candle.

snuffbox *n* a small container for holding snuff.

snuffle *vb* **-fling, -fled 1** to breathe noisily or with difficulty. **2** to say or speak through the nose. **3** to cry and sniff in a self-pitying way. ~*n* **4** an act or the sound of snuffling. **snuffly** *adj*

snug *adj* **snugger, snuggest 1** comfortably warm

THESAURUS

snivel blubber, cry, gripe (*informal*), grizzle (*informal, chiefly Brit.*), mewl, moan, sniffle, snuffle, weep, whimper, whine, whinge (*informal*)

snobbery airs, arrogance, condescension, pretension, pride, side (*Brit. slang*), snobbishness, snootiness (*informal*), uppishness (*Brit. informal*)

snobbish arrogant, condescending, high and mighty (*informal*), hoity-toity (*informal*), patronizing, pretentious, snooty (*informal*), stuck-up (*informal*), superior, toffee-nosed (*slang, chiefly Brit.*), uppish (*Brit. informal*), uppity

snoop *often with* **about** *or* **around** *informal* interfere, poke one's nose in (*informal*), pry, spy

snooper *informal* busybody, meddler, nosy parker (*informal*), pry, snoop (*informal*)

snooze *informal* **1.** *vb.* catnap, doze, drop off (*informal*), drowse, kip (*Brit. slang*), nap, nod off (*informal*), take forty winks (*informal*) **2.** *n.* catnap, doze, forty winks (*informal*), kip (*Brit. slang*), nap, siesta

snub 1. *vb.* cold-shoulder, cut (*informal*), cut dead (*informal*), give (someone) the brushoff (*slang*), give (someone) the cold shoulder, humble, humiliate, mortify, put down, rebuff, shame, slight **2.** *n.* affront,

and well protected; cosy: *safe and snug in their living rooms.* **2** small but comfortable: *a snug office.* **3** fitting closely and comfortably. *~n* **4** (in Britain and Ireland) a small room in a pub. **snugly** *adv*

snuggery *n, pl* **-geries** a cosy and comfortable place or room.

snuggle *vb* **-gling, -gled** to nestle into (a person or thing) for warmth or from affection.

so[1] *adv* **1** to such an extent: *the river is so dirty that it smells.* **2** to the same extent as: *she is not so old as you.* **3** extremely: *it's so lovely.* **4** also: *I can speak Spanish and so can you.* **5** thereupon: *and so we ended up in France.* **6** in the state or manner expressed or implied: *they're happy and will remain so.* **7 and so on** *or* **forth** and continuing similarly. **8 or so** approximately: *fifty or so people came to see me.* **9 so be it** an expression of agreement or resignation. **10 so much a** a certain degree or amount (of). **b** a lot (of): *it's just so much nonsense.* **11 so much for a** no more need be said about. **b** used to express contempt for something that has failed: *so much for all our plans.* *~conj* (often foll. by *that*) **12** in order (that): *to die so that you might live.* **13** with the consequence (that): *he was late home, so that there was trouble.* **14 so as** in order (to): *to diet so as to lose weight.* **15** *Not universally accepted* in consequence: *she wasn't needed, so she left.* **16 so what!** *Informal* that is unimportant. *~pron* **17** used to substitute for a clause or sentence, which may be understood: *you'll stop because I said so.* *~adj* **18** true: *it can't be so.* *~interj* **19** an exclamation of surprise or triumph.

so[2] *n Music* same as **soh.**

soak *vb* **1** to put or lie in a liquid so as to become thoroughly wet. **2** (usually foll. by *in* or *into*) (of a liquid) to penetrate or permeate. **3** (usually foll. by *in* or *up*) to take in; absorb: *white clay soaks up excess oil.* *~n* **4** a soaking or being soaked. **5** *Slang* a person who drinks very heavily. **soaking** *n, adj*

so-and-so *n, pl* **so-and-sos** *Informal* **1** a person whose name is not specified. **2** *Euphemistic* a person regarded as unpleasant; a name used in place of a swear word: *you're a dirty so-and-so.*

soap *n* **1** a compound of alkali and fat, used with water as a cleaning agent. **2** *Informal* short for **soap opera.** *~vb* **3** to apply soap to.

soapbox *n* a crate used as a platform for making speeches.

soap opera *n* an on-going television or radio serial about the daily lives of a group of people.

soapstone *n* a soft mineral used for making table tops and ornaments.

soapsuds *pl n* foam or lather produced when soap is mixed with water.

soapy *adj* **soapier, soapiest 1** containing or covered with soap: *a soapy liquid.* **2** like soap in texture, smell, or taste: *the cheese had a soapy taste.* **3** *Slang* flattering or persuasive. **soapiness** *n*

soar *vb* **1** to rise or fly upwards into the air. **2** (of a bird or aircraft) to glide while maintaining altitude. **3** to rise or increase suddenly above the usual level: *television ratings soared.*

sob *vb* **sobbing, sobbed 1** to cry noisily, breathing in short gasps. **2** to speak with sobs. *~n* **3** the act or sound of sobbing.

sober *adj* **1** not drunk. **2** tending to drink only moderate quantities of alcohol. **3** serious and thoughtful: *a sober and serious fellow.* **4** (of colours) plain and dull. **5** free from exaggeration: *a fairly sober version of what happened.* *~vb* **6** (usually foll. by *up*) to make or become less drunk. **sobering** *adj*

sobriety *n* the state of being sober.

sobriquet *or* **soubriquet** (**so**-brik-ay) *n* a nickname.

sob story *n* a tale of personal misfortune or bad luck intended to arouse sympathy.

Soc. *or* **soc. 1** socialist. **2** society.

soca (**soak**-a) *n* a mixture of soul and calypso music popular in the E Caribbean.

so-called *adj* called (in the speaker's opinion, wrongly) by that name: *so-called military experts.*

soccer *n* a game in which two teams of eleven players try to kick or head a ball into their opponents' goal, only the goalkeeper on either side being allowed to touch the ball with his hands.

sociable *adj* **1** friendly and enjoying other people's company. **2** (of an occasion) providing the opportunity for relaxed and friendly companionship. **sociability** *n* **sociably** *adv*

social *adj* **1** living or preferring to live in a community rather than alone. **2** of or relating to human society or organization. **3** of the way people live and work together in groups: *social organization.* **4** of or for companionship or communal activities: *social clubs.* **5** of or engaged in social services: *a social worker.* **6** relating to a certain class of society: *social misfits.* **7** (of certain species of insects) living together in organized colonies: *social bees.* *~n* **8** an informal gathering. **socially** *adv*

THESAURUS

brushoff (*slang*), humiliation, insult, put-down, slap in the face

snug 1. comfortable, comfy (*informal*), cosy, homely, intimate, sheltered, warm **2.** close, compact, neat, trim

snuggle cuddle, nestle, nuzzle

soak *vb.* **1.** bathe, damp, drench, immerse, infuse, marinate (*Cookery*), moisten, penetrate, permeate, saturate, seep, steep, wet **2.** *usually with* **in** *or* **up** absorb, assimilate, drink in, take up *or* in

soaking *adj.* drenched, dripping, saturated, soaked, soaked to the skin, sodden, sopping, streaming, waterlogged, wet through, wringing wet

soar 1. ascend, fly, mount, rise, tower, wing **2.** climb, escalate, rise, rocket, shoot up

sob *vb.* bawl, blubber, boohoo, cry, greet (*Scot. or archaic*), howl, shed tears, snivel, weep

sober *adj.* **1.** abstemious, abstinent, moderate, on the wagon (*informal*), temperate **2.** calm, clear-headed, cold, composed, cool, dispassionate, grave, level-headed, lucid, peaceful, practical, rational, realistic, reasonable, sedate, serene, serious, solemn, sound, staid, steady, unexcited, unruffled **3.** dark, drab, plain, quiet, severe, sombre, subdued *~vb.* **4.** *usually with* **up** bring (someone) back to earth, calm down, clear one's head, come *or* bring to one's senses, give (someone) pause for thought, make (someone) stop and think

sobriety abstemiousness, abstinence, calmness, composure, coolness, gravity, level-headedness, moderation, nonindulgence, reasonableness, restraint, sedateness, self-restraint, seriousness, soberness, solemnity, staidness, steadiness, temperance

so-called alleged, ostensible, pretended, professed, self-styled, supposed

sociability affability, companionability, congeniality, conviviality, cordiality, friendliness, gregariousness, neighbourliness

sociable accessible, affable, approachable, companionable, conversable, convivial, cordial, familiar, friendly, genial, gregarious, neighbourly, outgoing, social, warm

social *adj.* **1.** companionable, friendly, gregarious, neighbourly, sociable **2.** collective, common, commu-

Social Charter *n* a proposed declaration of the rights, minimum wages, etc. of workers in the European Union.

social climber *n* a person who tries to associate with people from a higher social class in the hope that he or she will be thought also to be upper-class.

social contract *or* **compact** *n* an agreement among individuals to cooperate for greater security, which results in the loss of some personal liberties.

social democrat *n* **1** a person who is in favour of a market or mixed economy but believes the State must play an active role in ensuring social justice and equality of opportunity. **2** (formerly) a person who believed in the gradual transformation of capitalism into democratic socialism. **social democracy** *n*

social fund *n* (in Britain) a social security fund from which loans or payments may be made to people in cases of extreme need.

socialism *n* a political and economic theory or system in which the means of production, distribution, and exchange are owned by the community collectively, usually through the state. **socialist** *n, adj*

socialite *n* a person who goes to many events attended by the rich, famous, and fashionable.

socialize *or* **-ise** *vb* **-izing, -ized** *or* **-ising, -ised 1** to meet others socially. **2** to prepare for life in society. **3** *Chiefly US* to organize along socialist principles. **socialization** *or* **-isation** *n*

social science *n* the systematic study of society and of human relationships within society. **social scientist** *n*

social security *n* state provision for the welfare of the elderly, unemployed, or sick, through pensions and other financial aid.

social services *pl n* welfare services provided by local authorities for people with particular social needs.

social studies *n* (in British schools) the study of how people live and organize themselves in society.

social welfare *n* **1** social services provided by a state for the benefit of its citizens. **2** (in New Zealand) a government department concerned with pensions and benefits for the elderly, the sick, etc.

social work *n* social services that give help and advice to the poor, the elderly, and families with problems. **social worker** *n*

society *n, pl* **-ties 1** human beings considered as a group. **2** a group of people forming a single community with its own distinctive culture and institutions. **3** the structure, culture, and institutions of such a group. **4** an organized group of people sharing a common aim or interest: *a dramatic society.* **5** the rich and fashionable class of society collectively. **6** *Old-fashioned* companionship: *I enjoy her society.*

Society of Friends *n* the Quakers.

Society of Jesus *n* the religious order of the Jesuits.

socioeconomic *adj* of or involving economic and social factors.

sociology *n* the study of the development, organization, functioning, and classification of human societies. **sociological** *adj* **sociologist** *n*

sociopolitical *adj* of or involving political and social factors.

sock[1] *n* **1** a cloth covering for the foot, reaching to between the ankle and knee and worn inside a shoe. **2 pull one's socks up** *Brit informal* to make a determined effort to improve. **3 put a sock in it** *Brit slang* be quiet!

sock[2] *Slang* ~*vb* **1** to hit hard. ~*n* **2** a hard blow.

socket *n* **1** a device into which an electric plug can be inserted in order to make a connection in a circuit. **2** *Anat* a bony hollow into which a part or structure fits: *the hip socket.*

Socratic *adj* of the Greek philosopher Socrates, or his teachings.

Socratic method *n Philosophy* the method of instruction used by Socrates, in which a series of questions and answers lead to a logical conclusion.

sod[1] *n* **1** a piece of grass-covered surface soil; turf. **2** *Poetic* the ground.

sod[2] *Slang, chiefly Brit* ~*n* **1** an unpleasant person. **2** *Jocular* a person, esp. an unlucky one: *the poor sod hasn't been out for weeks.* **3 sod all** *Slang* nothing. ~*interj* **4 sod it** an exclamation of annoyance. **sodding** *adj*

soda *n* **1** a simple compound of sodium, such as sodium carbonate or sodium bicarbonate. **2** same as **soda water. 3** *US & Canad* a sweet fizzy drink.

soda bread *n* a type of bread raised with sodium bicarbonate.

soda fountain *n US & Canad* **1** a counter that serves soft drinks and snacks. **2** a device dispensing soda water.

soda siphon *n* a sealed bottle containing soda water under pressure, which is forced up a tube when a lever is pressed.

soda water *n* a fizzy drink made by charging water with carbon dioxide under pressure.

sodden *adj* **1** soaking wet. **2** (of someone's senses) dulled, esp. by excessive drinking.

sodium *n Chem* a very reactive soft silvery white metallic element. Symbol: Na

sodium bicarbonate *n* a white soluble crystalline compound used in fizzy drinks, baking powder, and in medicine as an antacid.

sodium carbonate *n* a colourless or white soluble crystalline compound used in the manufacture of glass, ceramics, soap, and paper, and as a cleansing agent.

sodium chlorate *n* a colourless crystalline compound used as a bleaching agent, antiseptic, and weedkiller.

sodium chloride *n* common table salt; a soluble colourless crystalline compound widely used as a seasoning and preservative for food and in the manufacture of chemicals, glass, and soap.

sodium hydroxide *n* a white strongly alkaline solid used in making rayon, paper, and soap.

sodomite *n* a person who practises sodomy.

sodomy *n* anal intercourse committed by a man with another man or a woman.

Sod's Law *n Informal* a humorous saying stating

THESAURUS

nal, community, general, group, organized, public ~*n.* **3.** do (*informal*), gathering, get-together (*informal*), party

socialize be a good mixer, entertain, fraternize, get about *or* around, get together, go out, mix

society 1. civilization, culture, humanity, mankind, people, population, social order, the community, the general public, the public, the world at large **2.** association, brotherhood, circle, club, corporation, fellowship, fraternity, group, guild, institute, league, order, organization, sisterhood, union **3.** elite, gentry, high society, polite society, the country set, the nobs (*slang*), the smart set, the swells (*informal*), the toffs (*Brit. slang*), the top drawer, upper classes, upper

that if something can go wrong or turn out inconveniently it will.

sofa *n* a long comfortable seat with back and arms for two or more people.

soft *adj* **1** easy to dent, shape, or cut: *soft material.* **2** not hard; giving way easily under pressure: *a soft bed.* **3** fine, smooth, or fluffy to the touch: *soft fur.* **4** (of music or sounds) quiet and pleasing. **5** (of light or colour) not excessively bright or harsh. **6** (of a breeze or climate) temperate, mild, or pleasant. **7** with smooth curves rather than sharp edges: *soft focus.* **8** kind or lenient, often to excess. **9** easy to influence or make demands on: *he's a soft touch.* **10** *Informal* feeble or silly; simple: *soft in the head.* **11** not strong or able to endure hardship. **12** (of a drug) nonaddictive. **13** *Informal* requiring little effort; easy: *a soft option.* **14** *Chem* (of water) relatively free of mineral salts and therefore easily able to make soap lather. **15** loving and tender: *soft words.* **16** *Phonetics* denoting the consonants *c* and *g* when they are pronounced sibilantly, as in *cent* and *germ.* **17 soft on a** lenient towards: *he was accused of being soft on criminals.* **b** experiencing romantic love for. *~adv* **18** softly: *to speak soft. ~interj* **19** *Archaic* quiet! **softly** *adv*

softball *n* a game similar to baseball, played using a larger softer ball.

soft-boiled *adj* (of an egg) boiled for a short time so that the yolk is still soft.

soft coal *n* same as **bituminous coal.**

soft drink *n* a nonalcoholic drink.

soften *vb* **1** to make or become soft or softer. **2** to make or become more sympathetic and less critical: *the farmers softened their opposition to the legislation.* **3** to lessen the severity or difficulty of: *foreign relief softened the hardship of a terrible winter.* **softener** *n*

soft furnishings *pl n Brit* curtains, hangings, rugs, and covers.

softhearted *adj* kind and sympathetic.

soft option *n* the easiest of a number of choices.

soft palate *n* the fleshy part at the back of the roof of the mouth.

soft-pedal *vb* **-alling, -alled** *or US* **-aling, -aled 1** to deliberately avoid emphasizing (something): *he was soft-pedalling the question of tax increases. ~n* **soft pedal 2** a pedal on a piano that softens the tone.

soft sell *n* a method of selling based on subtle suggestion and gentle persuasion.

soft-soap *vb Informal* to flatter (a person).

soft-spoken *adj* speaking or said with a soft gentle voice.

soft touch *n Informal* a person who is easily persuaded to perform favours for, or lend money to, other people.

software *n Computers* the programs used with a computer.

softwood *n* the wood of coniferous trees.

softy *or* **softie** *n, pl* **softies** *Informal* a person who is easily hurt or upset.

soggy *adj* **-gier, -giest 1** soaked with liquid: *a soggy running track.* **2** moist and heavy: *a soggy sandwich.* **sogginess** *n*

soh *n Music* the fifth note of any ascending major scale.

soigné *or fem* **soignée** (**swah**-nyay) *adj* neat, elegant, and well-dressed.

soil[1] *n* **1** the top layer of the land surface of the earth. **2** a specific type of this material: *sandy soil.* **3** land, country, or region: *back on British soil.*

soil[2] *vb* **1** to make or become dirty or stained. **2** to bring disgrace upon: *he's soiled our reputation. ~n* **3** a soiled spot. **4** refuse, manure, or excrement.

soiree (**swah**-ray) *n* an evening social gathering.

sojourn (**soj**-urn) *Literary ~n* **1** a short stay in a place. *~vb* **2** to stay temporarily: *he sojourned in Basle during a short illness.* –

sol[1] *n Music* same as **soh.**

sol[2] *n Chem* a liquid colloidal solution.

solace (**sol**-iss) *n* **1** comfort in misery or disappointment: *it drove him to seek increasing solace in alcohol.* **2** something that gives comfort or consolation: *his music was a solace to me during my illness. ~vb* **-acing, -aced 3** to give comfort or cheer to (a person) in time of sorrow or distress.

solar *adj* **1** of the sun: *a solar eclipse.* **2** operating by or using the energy of the sun: *solar cell.*

solarium *n, pl* **-lariums** *or* **-laria** a place with beds equipped with ultraviolet lights used for giving people an artificial suntan.

solar plexus *n* **1** *Anat* a network of nerves behind the stomach. **2** *Not in technical use* the vulnerable part of the stomach beneath the diaphragm.

solar system *n* the system containing the sun and the planets, comets, and asteroids that go round it.

sold *vb* **1** the past of **sell.** *~adj* **2 sold on** *Slang* enthusiastic and uncritical about.

solder *n* **1** an alloy used for joining two metal surfaces by melting the alloy so that it forms a thin layer between the surfaces. *~vb* **2** to join or mend or be joined or mended with solder.

soldering iron *n* a hand tool with an iron or copper tip that is heated and used to melt and apply solder.

THESAURUS

crust (*informal*) **4.** *old-fashioned* camaraderie, companionship, company, fellowship, friendship

sodden boggy, drenched, marshy, miry, saturated, soaked, soggy, sopping, waterlogged

soft 1. bendable, ductile (*of metals*), elastic, flexible, impressible, malleable, mouldable, plastic, pliable, supple, tensile **2.** creamy, cushioned, cushiony, doughy, elastic, gelatinous, pulpy, quaggy, spongy, squashy, swampy, yielding **3.** downy, feathery, fleecy, flowing, fluid, furry, like a baby's bottom (*informal*), rounded, silky, smooth, velvety **4.** balmy, bland, caressing, delicate, diffuse, dim, dimmed, dulcet, faint, gentle, light, low, mellifluous, mellow, melodious, mild, murmured, muted, pale, pastel, pleasing, quiet, restful, shaded, soft-toned, soothing, subdued, sweet, temperate, twilight, understated, whispered **5.** compassionate, gentle, kind, pitying, sensitive, sentimental, sympathetic, tender, tenderhearted **6.** easy-going, indulgent, lax, lenient, liberal, overindulgent, permissive, spineless, weak **7.** *informal* a bit lacking (*informal*), daft (*informal*), feeble-minded, foolish, silly, simple, soft in the head (*informal*), soppy (*Brit. informal*) **8.** *informal* comfortable, cushy (*informal*), easy, undemanding

soften abate, allay, alleviate, appease, assuage, calm, cushion, diminish, ease, lessen, lighten, lower, melt, mitigate, moderate, modify, mollify, muffle, palliate, quell, relax, soothe, still, subdue, temper, tone down, turn down

softhearted charitable, compassionate, generous, indulgent, kind, sentimental, sympathetic, tender, tenderhearted, warm-hearted

soil[1] *n.* clay, dirt, dust, earth, ground, loam

soil[2] *vb.* besmirch, defile, dirty, foul, muddy, pollute, smear, smirch, spatter, spot, stain, sully, tarnish

solace 1. *n.* alleviation, assuagement, comfort, conso-

soldier *n* **1 a** a person who serves or has served in an army. **b** a person who is not an officer in an army. ~*vb* **2** to serve as a soldier. **soldierly** *adj*

soldier of fortune *n* a man who seeks money or adventure as a soldier; mercenary.

soldier on *vb* to continue one's efforts despite difficulties or pressure.

sole[1] *adj* **1** being the only one; only. **2** not shared; exclusive: *sole ownership.*

sole[2] *n* **1** the underside of the foot. **2** the underside of a shoe. **3** the lower surface of an object. ~*vb* **soling, soled 4** to provide (a shoe) with a sole.

sole[3] *n, pl* **sole** *or* **soles** an edible marine flatfish.

solecism (sol-iss-iz-zum) *n Formal* **1** a minor grammatical mistake in speech or writing. **2** an action considered not to be good manners. **solecistic** *adj*

solely *adv* **1** only; completely: *an action intended solely to line his own pockets.* **2** without others.

solemn *adj* **1** very serious; deeply sincere: *my solemn promise.* **2** marked by ceremony or formality: *a solemn ritual.* **3** serious or glum: *a solemn look on her face.* **solemnly** *adv*

solemnity *n, pl* **-ties 1** the state or quality of being solemn. **2** a solemn ceremony or ritual.

solemnize *or* **-nise** *vb* **-nizing, -nized** *or* **-nising, -nised 1** to celebrate or perform (a ceremony, esp. of marriage). **2** to make solemn or serious. **solemnization** *or* **-nisation** *n*

solenoid (sole-in-oid) *n* a coil of wire, usually cylindrical, in which a magnetic field is set up by passing a current through it. **solenoidal** *adj*

sol-fa *n* short for **tonic sol-fa.**

solicit *vb* **1** *Formal* to seek or request, esp. formally: *she was brushed aside when soliciting his support for the vote.* **2** to approach (a person) with an offer of sex in return for money. **solicitation** *n*

solicitor *n* (in Britain) a lawyer who advises clients on matters of law, draws up legal documents, and prepares cases for barristers.

Solicitor General *n, pl* **Solicitors General** (in Britain) the law officer of the Crown ranking next to the Attorney General (in Scotland to the Lord Advocate) and acting as his assistant.

solicitous *adj Formal* **1** anxious about someone's welfare. **2** eager. **solicitousness** *n*

solicitude *n Formal* anxiety or concern for someone's welfare.

solid *adj* **1** (of a substance) in a physical state in which it resists changes in size and shape; not liquid or gaseous. **2** consisting of matter all through; not hollow. **3** of the same substance all through: *solid gold.* **4** firm, strong, or substantial: *the solid door of a farmhouse.* **5** proved or provable: *solid evidence.* **6** law-abiding and respectable: *solid family men.* **7** (of a meal or food) substantial. **8** without interruption; continuous or unbroken: *solid bombardment.* **9** financially sound: *a solid institution.* **10** strongly united or established: *a solid marriage.* **11** *Geom* having or relating to three dimensions. **12** adequate; sound, but not brilliant: *a solid career.* **13** of a single uniform colour or tone. ~*n* **14** *Geom* a three-dimensional shape. **15** a solid substance. **solidity** *n* **solidly** *adv*

solidarity *n, pl* **-ties** agreement in interests or aims among members of a group; total unity.

solid geometry *n* the branch of geometry concerned with three-dimensional figures.

solidify *vb* **-fies, -fying, -fied 1** to make or become solid or hard. **2** to make or become strong or unlikely to change: *a move that solidified the allegiance of our followers.* **solidification** *n*

solid-state *adj* (of an electronic device) using a semiconductor component, such as a transistor or silicon chip, in which current flow is through solid material, rather than a valve or mechanical part, in which current flow is through a vacuum.

solidus *n, pl* **-di** a short oblique stroke used in text to separate items, such as *and/or.*

soliloquize *or* **-quise** *vb* **-quizing, -quized** *or* **-quising, -quised** to say a soliloquy.

soliloquy *n, pl* **-quies** a speech made by a person while alone, esp. in a play.

solipsism *n Philosophy* the doctrine that the self is the only thing known to exist. **solipsist** *n*

solitaire *n* **1** a game played by one person, involving moving and taking pegs in a pegboard with the object of being left with only one. **2** a gem, esp. a diamond, set alone in a ring. **3** *US* patience (the card game).

solitary *adj* **1** experienced or performed alone: *a solitary dinner.* **2** living a life of solitude: *a solitary child.* **3** single; alone: *the solitary cigarette in the ashtray.* **4** having few friends; lonely. **5** (of a place) without people; empty. ~*n, pl* **-taries 6** a person who lives on his or her own; hermit. **7** *Informal* short for **solitary confinement:** *I can't put him back in solitary.* **solitariness** *n*

THESAURUS

lation, relief **2.** *vb.* allay, alleviate, comfort, console, mitigate, soften, soothe

soldier enlisted man (*U.S.*), fighter, GI (*U.S. informal*), man-at-arms, military man, redcoat (*history*), serviceman, Tommy (*Brit. old-fashioned*), trooper, warrior

sole alone, exclusive, individual, one, one and only, only, single, singular, solitary

solecism bloomer (*Brit. informal*), blunder, breach of etiquette, faux pas, gaffe, gaucherie, impropriety, incongruity, indecorum, lapse, mistake

solely alone, completely, entirely, exclusively, merely, only, single-handedly, singly

solemn 1. august, awe-inspiring, ceremonial, ceremonious, dignified, formal, grand, grave, imposing, impressive, majestic, momentous, stately **2.** earnest, glum, grave, portentous, sedate, serious, sober, staid, thoughtful

solemnize celebrate, commemorate, honour, keep, observe

solicit ask, beg, beseech, canvass, crave, entreat, implore, importune, petition, plead for, pray, seek, supplicate

solicitous anxious, apprehensive, attentive, careful, caring, concerned, eager, earnest, troubled, uneasy, worried, zealous

solicitude anxiety, attentiveness, care, concern, considerateness, consideration, regard, worry

solid *adj.* **1.** compact, concrete, dense, firm, hard, massed, stable, strong, sturdy, substantial, unshakable **2.** genuine, pure, real **3.** constant, decent, dependable, estimable, law-abiding, level-headed, reliable, sensible, serious, sober, trusty, upright, upstanding, worthy **4.** agreed, complete, continuous, unalloyed, unanimous, unbroken, undivided, uninterrupted, united, unmixed

solidarity accord, camaraderie, cohesion, community of interest, concordance, esprit de corps, harmony, like-mindedness, singleness of purpose, soundness, stability, team spirit, unanimity, unification, unity

solidify cake, coagulate, cohere, congeal, gel, harden, set

solitary *adj.* **1.** alone, lone, single, sole **2.** cloistered, companionless, friendless, hermitical, lonely, lone-

solitary confinement *n* isolation of a prisoner in a special cell.
solitude *n* the state of being alone.
solo *n, pl* **-los 1** a piece of music or section of a piece of music for one performer: *a trumpet solo.* **2** any performance by an individual without assistance. *~adj* **3** performed by an individual without assistance: *a solo dance.* **4** Also: **solo whist** a card game in which each person plays on his or her own. *~adv* **5** by oneself; alone: *to fly solo across the Atlantic.* **soloist** *n*
Solomon *n* any person considered to be very wise.
Solomon's seal *n* a plant with greenish flowers and long waxy leaves.
so long *interj* **1** *Informal* farewell; goodbye. *~adv* **2** *S African slang* for the time being; meanwhile.
solstice *n* either the shortest day of the year (**winter solstice**) or the longest day of the year (**summer solstice**).
soluble *adj* **1** (of a substance) capable of being dissolved. **2** (of a mystery or problem) capable of being solved. **solubility** *n*
solute *n Chem* the substance in a solution that is dissolved.
solution *n* **1** a specific answer to or way of answering a problem. **2** the act or process of solving a problem. **3** *Chem* a mixture of two or more substances in which the molecules or atoms of the substances are completely dispersed. **4** the act or process of forming a solution. **5** the state of being dissolved: *the sugar is held in solution.*
solve *vb* **solving, solved** to find the explanation for or solution to (a mystery or problem). **solvable** *adj*
solvent *adj* **1** having enough money to pay off one's debts. **2** (of a liquid) capable of dissolving other substances. *~n* **3** a liquid capable of dissolving other substances. **solvency** *n*
solvent abuse *n* the deliberate inhaling of intoxicating fumes from certain solvents.
somatic *adj* of or relating to the body as distinct from the mind: *somatic symptoms.*
sombre *or US* **somber** *adj* **1** serious, sad, or gloomy: *a sombre message.* **2** (of a place) dim or gloomy. **3** (of colour or clothes) dull or dark. **sombrely** *or US* **somberly** *adv*
sombrero *n, pl* **-ros** a wide-brimmed Mexican hat.
some *adj* **1** unknown or unspecified: *some man called for you.* **2** an unknown or unspecified quantity or number of: *I've got some money.* **3 a** a considerable number or amount of: *he lived some years afterwards.* **b** a little: *show some respect.* **4** *Informal* an impressive or remarkable: *that was some game!* *~pron* **5** certain unknown or unspecified people or things: *some can teach and others can't.* **6** an unknown or unspecified quantity of something or number of people or things: *he will sell some in his pub.* *~adv* **7** approximately: *some thirty pounds.*
somebody *pron* **1** some person; someone. *~n, pl* **-bodies 2** a person of great importance: *he was a somebody.*
➤ *Somebody* is singular and in formal usage is followed by a singular verb or pronoun. Informal usage favours the use of the plural *they* to avoid the use of the clumsy *he or she: If I annoy somebody, they* (rather than *he or she*) *will take it out on me.*
someday *adv* at some unspecified time in the future.
somehow *adv* **1** in some unspecified way. **2** for some unknown reason: *somehow I can't do it.*
someone *pron* some person; somebody.
➤ *Someone* is singular and in formal usage is followed by a singular verb or pronoun. Informal usage favours the use of the plural *they* to avoid the use of the clumsy *he or she: If I annoy someone, they* (rather than *he or she*) *will take it out on me.*
someplace *adv US & Canad informal* same as **somewhere.**
somersault *n* **1** a leap or roll in which the head is placed on the ground and the trunk and legs are turned over it. *~vb* **2** to perform a somersault.
something *pron* **1** an unspecified or unknown thing; some thing: *there was something wrong.* **2** an unspecified or unknown amount: *something less than a hundred.* **3** an impressive or important person, thing, or event: *isn't that something?* **4 something else** *Slang, chiefly US* a remarkable person or thing. *~adv* **5** to some degree; somewhat: *he looks something like me.*
sometime *adv* **1** at some unspecified point of time. *~adj* **2** former: *a sometime actress.*
sometimes *adv* now and then; from time to time.
someway *adv* in some unspecified manner.
somewhat *adv* rather; a bit: *somewhat surprising.*
somewhere *adv* **1** in, to, or at some unknown or unspecified place, point, or amount: *somewhere down south; somewhere between 35 and 45 per cent.* **2 getting somewhere** *Informal* making progress.
somnambulism *n Formal* the condition of walking in one's sleep. **somnambulist** *n*
somnolent *adj Formal* drowsy; sleepy. **somnolence** *n*
son *n* **1** a male offspring. **2** a form of address for a man or boy who is younger than the speaker. **3** a male who comes from a certain place or one closely connected with a certain thing: *a good son of the church.*
Son *n Christianity* the second member of the Trinity, Jesus Christ.
sonar *n* a device that locates objects by the reflection

THESAURUS

some, reclusive, unsociable, unsocial **3.** desolate, hidden, isolated, lonely, out-of-the-way, remote, retired, secluded, sequestered, unfrequented, unvisited *~n.* **4.** hermit, introvert, loner (*informal*), lone wolf, recluse
solitude isolation, loneliness, privacy, reclusiveness, retirement, seclusion
solution 1. answer, clarification, elucidation, explanation, explication, key, resolution, result, solving, unfolding, unravelling **2.** blend, compound, emulsion, mix, mixture, solvent, suspension (*Chem.*) **3.** disconnection, dissolution, liquefaction, melting
solve answer, clarify, clear up, crack, decipher, disentangle, elucidate, explain, expound, get to the bottom of, interpret, resolve, suss (out) (*slang*), unfold, unravel, work out
sombre 1. doleful, gloomy, grave, joyless, lugubrious, melancholy, mournful, sad, sober **2.** dark, dim, dismal, drab, dull, dusky, funereal, gloomy, obscure, sepulchral, shadowy, shady, sober
somebody *n.* big noise (*informal*), big shot (*informal*), big wheel (*slang*), bigwig (*informal*), celeb (*informal*), celebrity, dignitary, heavyweight (*informal*), household name, luminary, megastar (*informal*), name, notable, personage, person of note, public figure, star, superstar, VIP
someday eventually, one day, one of these (fine) days, sooner or later, ultimately
somehow by fair means or foul, by hook or (by) crook, by some means or other, come hell or high water (*informal*), come what may, one way or another
sometimes at times, every now and then, every so often, from time to time, now and again, now and then, occasionally, off and on, once in a while, on occasion

of sound waves: used in underwater navigation and target detection.

sonata *n* a piece of classical music, usually in three or more movements, for piano or for another instrument with or without piano.

son et lumière (**sonn** ay **loom**-yair) *n* an entertainment staged at night at a famous building or historical site, at which its history is described by a speaker accompanied by lighting effects and music.

song *n* **1** a piece of music with words, composed for the voice. **2** the tuneful call made by certain birds or insects. **3** the act or process of singing: *he broke into song.* **4 for a song** at a bargain price. **5 make a song and dance** *Brit informal* to make an unnecessary fuss.

songbird *n* any bird that has a musical call.

songololo (song-gol-**loll**-o) *n, pl* **-los** *S African* a kind of millipede.

songstress *n* a female singer of popular songs.

song thrush *n* a common thrush that repeats each note of its song.

sonic *adj* of, involving, or producing sound.

sonic barrier *n* same as **sound barrier.**

sonic boom *n* a loud explosive sound caused by the shock wave of an aircraft travelling at supersonic speed.

son-in-law *n, pl* **sons-in-law** the husband of one's daughter.

sonnet *n Prosody* a verse form consisting of 14 lines with a fixed rhyme scheme and rhythm pattern.

sonny *n Often patronizing* a familiar term of address to a boy or man.

sonorous *adj* **1** (of a sound) deep or rich. **2** (of speech) using language that is unnecessarily complicated and difficult to understand; pompous. **sonority** *n*

soon *adv* **1** in or after a short time; before long. **2 as soon as** at the very moment that: *as soon as he had closed the door.* **3 as soon ... as** used to indicate that the first alternative is slightly preferable to the second: *they'd just as soon die for him as live.*

sooner *adv* **1** the comparative of **soon:** *I only wish I'd been back sooner.* **2** rather; in preference: *he would sooner leave the party than break with me.* **3 no sooner ... than** immediately after or when: *no sooner had he spoken than the stench drifted up.* **4 sooner or later** eventually.

soot *n* a black powder formed by the incomplete burning of organic substances such as coal. **sooty** *adj*

sooth *n* **in sooth** *Archaic or poetic* in truth.

soothe *vb* **soothing, soothed 1** to make (a worried or angry person) calm and relaxed. **2** (of an ointment or cream) to relieve (pain). **soothing** *adj*

soothsayer *n* a person who makes predictions about the future; prophet.

sop *n* **1** a small bribe or concession given or made to someone to keep them from causing trouble: *a sop to her conscience.* **2** *Informal* a stupid or weak person. **3 sops** food soaked in a liquid before being eaten. *~vb* **sopping, sopped 4 sop up** to soak up or absorb (liquid).

sophism *n* an argument that seems reasonable but is actually false and misleading.

sophist *n* a person who uses clever but false arguments. **sophistic** *adj*

sophisticate *vb* **-cating, -cated 1** to make (someone) less natural or innocent, such as by education. **2** to make (a machine or method) more complex or refined. *~n* **3** a sophisticated person. **sophistication** *n*

sophisticated *adj* **1** having or appealing to fashionable and refined tastes and habits: *a sophisticated restaurant.* **2** intelligent, knowledgeable, or able to appreciate culture and the arts: *a sophisticated concert audience.* **3** (of machines or methods) complex and using advanced technology.

sophistry *n* **1** the practice of using arguments which seem clever but are actually false and misleading. **2** (*pl* **-ries**) an instance of this.

sophomore *n Chiefly US & Canad* a second-year student at a secondary (high) school or college.

soporific *adj* **1** causing sleep. *~n* **2** a drug that causes sleep.

sopping *adj* completely soaked; wet through. Also: **sopping wet**

soppy *adj* **-pier, -piest** *Brit informal* foolishly sentimental: *a soppy love song.* **soppily** *adv*

soprano *n, pl* **-pranos 1** the highest adult female voice. **2** the voice of a young boy before puberty. **3** a singer with such a voice. **4** the highest or second highest instrument in a family of instruments. *~adj* **5** denoting a musical instrument that is the highest or second highest pitched in its family: *the soprano saxophone.* **6** of or relating to the highest female voice, or the voice of a young boy: *the part is quite possibly the most demanding soprano role Wagner ever wrote.*

sorbet *n* a flavoured water ice.

sorcerer *or fem* **sorceress** *n* a person who uses magic powers; a wizard.

sorcery *n, pl* **-ceries** witchcraft or magic.

sordid *adj* **1** dirty, depressing, and squalid: *a sordid backstreet in a slum area.* **2** relating to sex in a crude

THESAURUS

somnolent *formal* comatose, dozy, drowsy, half-awake, heavy-eyed, nodding off (*informal*), sleepy, soporific, torpid

song air, anthem, ballad, canticle, canzonet, carol, chant, chorus, ditty, hymn, lay, lyric, melody, number, pop song, psalm, shanty, strain, tune

soon anon (*old-fashioned or informal*), any minute now, before long, in a little while, in a minute, in a short time, in the near future, shortly

soothe allay, alleviate, appease, assuage, calm, calm down, compose, ease, hush, lull, mitigate, mollify, pacify, quiet, relieve, settle, smooth down, soften, still, tranquillize

soothing balsamic, calming, demulcent, easeful, emollient, lenitive, palliative, relaxing, restful

soothsayer augur, diviner, foreteller, prophet, seer, sibyl

sophisticated 1. blasé, citified, cosmopolitan, cultivated, cultured, jet-set, refined, seasoned, urbane, worldly, worldly-wise, world-weary **2.** advanced, complex, complicated, delicate, elaborate, highly-developed, intricate, multifaceted, refined, subtle

sophistication finesse, poise, savoir-faire, *savoir-vivre,* urbanity, worldliness, worldly wisdom

sophistry casuistry, fallacy, quibble, sophism

soporific 1. *adj.* hypnotic, sedative, sleep-inducing, sleepy, somnolent (*formal*), tranquillizing **2.** *n.* anaesthetic, hypnotic, narcotic, opiate, sedative, tranquillizer

soppy *Brit. informal* corny (*slang*), daft (*informal*), drippy (*informal*), gushy (*informal*), lovey-dovey, mawkish, overemotional, schmaltzy (*slang*), sentimental, silly, slushy (*informal*), soft (*informal*), weepy (*informal*)

sorcerer *or* **sorceress** enchanter *or* enchantress, magician, magus, necromancer, warlock, witch, wizard

sorcery black art, black magic, charm, divination,

or unpleasant way: *the sordid details of his affair.* **3** involving immoral and selfish behaviour: *the sordid history of the slave trade.*

sore *adj* **1** (of a wound, injury, etc.) painfully sensitive; tender. **2** causing annoyance and resentment: *a sore point.* **3** upset and angered: *she's still sore about last night.* **4** *Literary* urgent; pressing: *in sore need of firm government.* ~*n* **5** a painful or sensitive wound or injury. ~*adv* **6 sore afraid** *Archaic* greatly frightened.

sorely *adv* greatly: *sorely disappointed.*

sorghum *n* a grass grown for grain and as a source of syrup.

sorority *n, pl* **-ties** *Chiefly US* a society of female students.

sorrel *n* a plant with bitter-tasting leaves which are used in salads and sauces.

sorrow *n* **1** deep sadness or regret, associated with death or sympathy for another's misfortune. **2** a particular cause of this. ~*vb* **3** *Literary* to feel deep sadness about (death or another's misfortunes); mourn. **sorrowful** *adj* **sorrowfully** *adv*

sorry *adj* **-rier, -riest 1** (often foll. by *for, about*) feeling or expressing pity, sympathy, grief, or regret: *I'm sorry about this.* **2** in bad mental or physical condition: *a sorry state.* **3** poor: *a sorry performance.* ~*interj* **4** an exclamation expressing apology or asking someone to repeat what he or she has said.

sort *n* **1** a class, group, or kind sharing certain characteristics or qualities. **2** *Informal* a type of character: *she was a good sort.* **3** a more or less adequate example: *a sort of dream machine.* **4 of sorts** *or* **of a sort a** of a poorer quality: *she was wearing a uniform of sorts.* **b** of a kind not quite as intended or desired: *it was a reward, of sorts, for my efforts.* **5 out of sorts** not in normal good health or temper. **6 sort of** as it were; rather: *I sort of quit; sort of insensitive.* ~*vb* **7** to arrange (things or people) according to class or type. **8** to put (something) into working order; fix. **9** to arrange (computer information) by machine in an order the user finds convenient.

➤ Note the singular/plural usage: *this* (or *that*) *sort of thing; these* (or *those*) *sorts of thing.* In the second, plural example you can also say *these sorts of things.*

sortie *n* **1** a short or relatively short return trip. **2** (of troops) a raid into enemy territory. **3** an operational flight made by a military aircraft. ~*vb* **-tieing, -tied 4** to make a sortie.

sort out *vb* **1** to find a solution to (a problem): *did they sort out the mess?* **2** to take or separate (things or people) from a larger group: *to sort out the wheat from the chaff.* **3** to organize (things or people) into an orderly and disciplined group. **4** *Informal* to punish or tell off (someone).

SOS *n* **1** an international code signal of distress in which the letters SOS are repeatedly spelt out in Morse code. **2** *Informal* any call for help.

so-so *Informal* ~*adj* **1** neither good nor bad. ~*adv* **2** in an average or indifferent way.

sot *n* a person who is frequently drunk. **sottish** *adj*

sotto voce (**sot**-toe **voe**-chay) *adv* with a soft voice.

sou *n* **1** a former French coin of low value. **2** *Old-fashioned* a very small amount of money: *the tax man never saw a sou from this income.*

soubrette (soo-**brett**) *n* a minor female role in comedy, often that of a pert maid.

soubriquet *n* same as **sobriquet.**

soufflé (**soo**-flay) *n* a light fluffy dish made with beaten egg whites and other ingredients such as cheese or chocolate.

sough (rhymes with **now**) *vb Literary* (of the wind) to make a sighing sound.

sought (**sawt**) *vb* the past of **seek.**

souk (**sook**) *n* an open-air marketplace in Muslim countries.

soul *n* **1** the spiritual part of a person, regarded as the centre of personality, intellect, will, and emotions: believed by many to survive the body after death. **2** the essential part or fundamental nature of anything: *the soul of contemporary America.* **3** deep and sincere feelings: *you've got no soul.* **4** Also called: **soul music** a type of Black music using blues and elements of jazz, gospel, and pop. **5** a person regarded as a good exam-

THESAURUS

enchantment, incantation, magic, necromancy, spell, witchcraft, witchery, wizardry

sordid 1. dirty, filthy, foul, mean, seamy, seedy, sleazy, slovenly, slummy, squalid, unclean, wretched **2.** base, debauched, degenerate, degraded, despicable, disreputable, low, shabby, shameful, vicious, vile **3.** avaricious, corrupt, covetous, grasping, mercenary, miserly, niggardly, selfish, self-seeking, ungenerous, venal

sore *adj.* **1.** angry, burning, chafed, inflamed, irritated, painful, raw, reddened, sensitive, smarting, tender **2.** annoying, distressing, grievous, harrowing, severe, sharp, troublesome **3.** afflicted, aggrieved, angry, annoyed, cross, grieved, hurt, irked, irritated, pained, peeved (*informal*), resentful, stung, upset, vexed **4.** *literary* acute, critical, desperate, dire, extreme, pressing, urgent ~*n.* **5.** abscess, boil, chafe, gathering, inflammation, ulcer

sorrow *n.* **1.** affliction, anguish, distress, grief, heartache, heartbreak, misery, mourning, regret, sadness, unhappiness, woe **2.** affliction, blow, bummer (*slang*), hardship, misfortune, trial, tribulation, trouble, woe, worry ~*vb.* **3.** *literary* agonize, bemoan, be sad, bewail, eat one's heart out, grieve, lament, moan, mourn, weep

sorrowful affecting, afflicted, dejected, depressed, disconsolate, dismal, distressing, doleful, grievous, harrowing, heartbroken, heart-rending, heavy-hearted, lamentable, lugubrious, melancholy, miserable, mournful, painful, piteous, rueful, sad, sick at heart, sorry, tearful, unhappy, woebegone, woeful, wretched

sorry 1. apologetic, conscience-stricken, contrite, guilt-ridden, in sackcloth and ashes, penitent, regretful, remorseful, repentant, self-reproachful, shamefaced **2.** disconsolate, distressed, grieved, melancholy, mournful, sad, sorrowful, unhappy **3.** abject, base, deplorable, dismal, distressing, mean, miserable, paltry, pathetic, piteous, pitiable, pitiful, poor, sad, shabby, vile, wretched

sort *n.* **1.** brand, breed, category, character, class, denomination, description, family, genus, group, ilk, kind, make, nature, order, quality, race, species, stamp, style, type, variety **2. out of sorts** crotchety, down in the dumps (*informal*), down in the mouth (*informal*), grouchy (*informal*), in low spirits, mopy, not up to par, not up to snuff (*informal*), off colour, poorly (*informal*), under the weather (*informal*) **3. sort of** as it were, in part, moderately, rather, reasonably, slightly, somewhat, to some extent ~*vb.* **4.** arrange, assort, catalogue, categorize, choose, class, classify, distribute, divide, file, grade, group, order, put in order, rank, select, separate, systematize, tabulate

sort out 1. clarify, clear up, organize, put *or* get straight, resolve, tidy up **2.** pick out, put on one side, segregate, select, separate, sift

soul 1. animating principle, essence, intellect, life, mind, psyche, reason, spirit, vital force **2.** embodiment, epitome, essence, incarnation, personification,

ple of some quality: *the soul of prudence.* **6** a person: *there was hardly a soul there.* **7 the life and soul** *Informal* a person who is lively, entertaining, and fun to be with: *the life and soul of the campus.*

soul-destroying *adj* (of an occupation or situation) very boring and repetitive.

soul food *n Informal* food, such as chitterlings and yams, which is traditionally eaten by U.S. Blacks.

soulful *adj* expressing deep feelings: *a soulful performance of one of Tchaikovsky's songs.*

soulless *adj* **1** lacking human qualities; mechanical: *soulless materialism.* **2** (of a person) lacking in sensitivity or emotion.

soul mate *n* a person with whom one gets along well because of having shared interests and experiences.

soul-searching *n* deep examination of one's actions and feelings.

sound[1] *n* **1** anything that can be heard; noise. **2** *Physics* mechanical vibrations that travel in waves through the air, water, etc. **3** the sensation produced by such vibrations in the organs of hearing. **4** the impression one has of something: *I didn't really like the sound of it.* **5 sounds** *Slang* music, esp. rock, jazz, or pop. ~*vb* **6** to make or cause (an instrument, etc.) to make a sound. **7** to announce (something) by a sound: *guns sound the end of the two minutes silence.* **8** to make a noise with a certain quality: *her voice sounded shrill.* **9** to suggest (a particular idea or quality): *his argument sounded false.* **10** to pronounce (something) clearly: *to sound one's r's.* ~See also **sound off.**

sound[2] *adj* **1** free from damage, injury, or decay; in good condition. **2** firm or substantial: *sound documentary evidence.* **3** financially safe or stable: *a sound investment.* **4** showing good judgment or reasoning; wise: *sound advice.* **5** morally correct; honest. **6** (of sleep) deep and uninterrupted. **7** thorough: *a sound defeat.* ~*adv* **8 sound asleep** in a deep sleep. **soundly** *adv*

sound[3] *vb* **1** to measure the depth of (a well, the sea, etc.). **2** *Med* to examine (a part of the body) by tapping or with a stethoscope. ~See also **sound out.**

sound[4] *n* a channel between two larger areas of sea or between an island and the mainland.

sound barrier *n* a sudden increase in the force of air against an aircraft flying at or above the speed of sound.

sound bite *n* a short pithy sentence or phrase extracted from a longer speech for use on television or radio: *complicated political messages cannot be properly reduced to fifteen-second sound bites.*

sound effects *pl n* sounds artificially produced to make a play, esp. a radio play, more realistic.

sounding board *n* a person or group used to test a new idea or policy.

soundings *pl n* **1** measurements of the depth of a river, lake, or sea. **2** questions asked of someone in order to find out his or her opinion: *soundings among colleagues had revealed enthusiasm for the plan.*

sound off *vb* to speak angrily or loudly: *he is forever sounding off on issues of the day.*

sound out *vb* to question (someone) in order to discover his or her opinion: *you might try sounding him out about his family.*

soundproof *adj* **1** (of a room) built so that no sound can get in or out. ~*vb* **2** to make (a room) soundproof.

soundtrack *n* the recorded sound accompaniment to a film.

sound wave *n* a wave that carries sound.

soup *n* **1** a food made by cooking meat, fish, or vegetables in a stock. **2 in the soup** *Slang* in trouble or difficulties. **soupy** *adj*

soupçon (**soop**-sonn) *n* a slight amount; dash.

souped-up *adj Slang* (of a car, motorbike, or engine) adjusted so as to be faster or more powerful than normal.

soup kitchen *n* a place where food and drink is served to needy people.

sour *adj* **1** having a sharp biting taste like the taste of lemon juice or vinegar. **2** made acid or bad, such as when milk ferments. **3** (of a person's mood) bad-tempered and unfriendly. **4 go** *or* **turn sour** to become less enjoyable or happy: *the dream has turned sour.* ~*vb* **5** to make or become less enjoyable or friendly: *relations soured shortly after the war.* **sourly** *adv*

source *n* **1** the origin or starting point: *the source of discontent among fishermen.* **2** any person, book, or organization that provides information for a news report or for research. **3** the area or spring where a river or stream begins.

sour cream *n* cream soured by bacteria for use in cooking.

sour grapes *n* the attitude of pretending to hate something because one cannot have it oneself.

sourpuss *n Informal* a person who is always gloomy, pessimistic, or bitter.

souse *vb* **sousing, soused 1** to plunge (something) into water or other liquid. **2** to drench. **3** to steep or cook (food) in a marinade. ~*n* **4** the liquid used in pickling. **5** the act or process of sousing.

soused *adj Slang* drunk.

soutane (soo-**tan**) *n RC Church* a priest's robe.

south *n* **1** one of the four cardinal points of the com-

THESAURUS

quintessence, type **3.** animation, ardour, courage, energy, feeling, fervour, force, inspiration, nobility, vitality, vivacity **4.** being, body, creature, individual, man, mortal, person, woman

sound[1] *n.* **1.** din, noise, report, resonance, reverberation, tone, voice **2.** drift, idea, implication(s), impression, look, tenor ~*vb.* **3.** echo, resonate, resound, reverberate **4.** announce, articulate, declare, enunciate, express, pronounce, signal, utter **5.** appear, give the impression of, look, seem, strike one as being

sound[2] *adj.* **1.** complete, entire, firm, fit, hale, hale and hearty, healthy, intact, perfect, robust, solid, sturdy, substantial, undamaged, unhurt, unimpaired, uninjured, vigorous, well-constructed, whole **2.** established, orthodox, proven, recognized, reliable, reputable, safe, secure, solid, solvent, stable, tried-and-true **3.** correct, fair, just, level-headed, logical, orthodox, proper, prudent, rational, reasonable, reliable, responsible, right, right-thinking, sensible, true, trustworthy, valid, well-founded, well-grounded, wise **4.** deep, peaceful, unbroken, undisturbed, untroubled

sound[3] *vb.* **1.** fathom, plumb, probe **2.** *Med.* examine, inspect, investigate, test

sound out canvass, examine, probe, pump, question, see how the land lies

sour *adj.* **1.** acerbic, acetic, acid, acidulated, bitter, pungent, sharp, tart, unpleasant **2.** bad, curdled, fermented, gone off, rancid, turned, unsavoury, unwholesome **3.** acrid, acrimonious, churlish, crabbed, cynical, disagreeable, discontented, embittered, grouchy (*informal*), grudging, ill-natured, ill-tempered, jaundiced, peevish, tart, ungenerous, waspish ~*vb.* **4.** alienate, disenchant, embitter, exacerbate, exasperate, turn off (*informal*)

source 1. author, begetter, beginning, cause, commencement, derivation, fount, fountainhead, origin,

pass, at 180° from north. **2** the direction along a line of latitude towards the South Pole. **3 the south** any area lying in or towards the south. *~adj* **4** situated in, moving towards, or facing the south. **5** (esp. of the wind) from the south. *~adv* **6** in, to, or towards the south.

South *n* **1 the South a** the southern part of England. **b** (in the U.S.) the Southern states that formed the Confederacy during the Civil War. **c** the countries of the world that are not technically and economically advanced. *~adj* **2** of or denoting the southern part of a country, area, etc.

South African *adj* **1** of the Republic of South Africa. *~n* **2** a person from the Republic of South Africa.

southbound *adj* going towards the south.

southeast *n* **1** the direction midway between south and east. **2 the southeast** any area lying in or towards the southeast. *~adj also* **southeastern 3** of or denoting that part of a country or area which lies in the southeast. **4** situated in, moving towards, or facing the southeast. **5** (esp. of the wind) from the southeast. *~adv* **6** in, to, or towards the southeast. **southeasterly** *adj, adv, n*

Southeast *n* the southeast of Britain, esp. the London area.

southeaster *n* a strong wind or storm from the southeast.

southerly *adj* **1** of or in the south. *~adv, adj* **2** towards the south. **3** from the south: *light southerly winds.*

southern *adj* **1** situated in or towards the south. **2** facing or moving towards the south. **3** (*sometimes cap*) of or characteristic of the south or South. **southernmost** *adj*

Southerner *n* a person from the south of a country or area, esp. England or the US.

southern hemisphere *n* that half of the globe lying south of the equator.

southern lights *pl n* same as **aurora australis.**

southpaw *Informal ~n* **1** any left-handed person, esp. a boxer. *~adj* **2** left-handed.

South Pole *n* the southernmost point on the earth's axis, at a latitude of 90°S, which has very low temperatures.

South Seas *pl n* the seas south of the equator.

southward *adj, adv also* **southwards 1** towards the south. *~n* **2** the southward part or direction.

southwest *n* **1** the direction midway between west and south. **2 the southwest** any area lying in or towards the southwest. *~adj also* **southwestern 3** of or denoting that part of a country or area which lies in the southwest. **4** situated in, moving towards, or facing the southwest. **5** (esp. of the wind) from the southwest. *~adv* **6** in, to, or towards the southwest. **southwesterly** *adj, adv, n*

Southwest *n* the southwestern part of Britain, esp. Cornwall, Devon, and Somerset.

southwester *n* a strong wind or storm from the southwest.

souvenir *n* an object that reminds one of a certain place, occasion, or person; memento.

sou'wester *n* a seaman's hat with a broad brim that covers the back of the neck.

sovereign *n* **1** the Royal ruler of a country. **2** a former British gold coin worth one pound sterling. *~adj* **3** independent of outside authority; not governed by another country: *a sovereign nation.* **4** supreme in rank or authority: *a sovereign queen.* **5** *Old-fashioned* excellent or outstanding: *a sovereign remedy for epilepsy.*

sovereignty *n, pl* **-ties 1** the political power a nation has to govern itself. **2** the position or authority of a sovereign.

soviet *n* (in the former Soviet Union) an elected government council at the local, regional, and national levels.

Soviet *adj* **1** of the former Soviet Union. *~n* **2** a person from the former Soviet Union.

sow[1] *vb* **sowing, sowed; sown** *or* **sowed 1** to scatter or plant (seed) in or on (the ground) so that it may grow: *sow sweet peas in pots; farmers sow their fields with fewer varieties.* **2** to implant or introduce: *to sow confusion among the other members.*

sow[2] *n* a female adult pig.

soya bean *or US & Canad* **soybean** *n* a plant whose bean is used for food and as a source of oil.

soy sauce *n* a salty dark brown sauce made from fermented soya beans, used in Chinese cookery.

sozzled *adj Informal* drunk.

spa *n* a mineral-water spring or a resort where such a spring is found.

space *n* **1** the unlimited three-dimensional expanse in which all objects exist. **2** an interval of distance or time between two points, objects, or events. **3** a blank portion or area. **4** unoccupied area or room: *barely enough space to walk around.* **5** the region beyond the earth's atmosphere containing other planets, stars, and galaxies; the universe. *~vb* **spacing, spaced 6** to place or arrange (things) at intervals or with spaces between them.

space age *n* **1** the period in which the exploration of space has become possible. *~adj* **space-age 2** very modern, futuristic, or using the latest technology: *a space-age helmet.*

space-bar *n* a bar on a typewriter that is pressed in order to leave a space between words or letters.

space capsule *n* the part of a spacecraft in which the crew live and work.

spacecraft *n* a vehicle that can be used for travel in space.

spaced-out *adj Informal* vague and dreamy, as if influenced by drugs.

Space Invaders *n Trademark* a video game in which players try to defend themselves against attacking enemy spacecraft.

spaceman *or fem* **spacewoman** *n, pl* **-men** *or fem* **-women** a person who travels in space.

space probe *n* a small vehicle equipped to gather scientific information, normally transmitted back to earth by radio, about a planet or conditions in space.

spaceship *n* (in science fiction) a spacecraft used for travel between planets and galaxies.

THESAURUS

originator, rise, spring, wellspring **2.** authority, informant

souse drench, immerse, marinate (*Cookery*), pickle, soak, steep

souvenir keepsake, memento, relic, reminder, token

sovereign *n.* **1.** chief, emperor, empress, king, monarch, potentate, prince, queen, ruler, shah, supreme ruler, tsar *~adj.* **2.** absolute, chief, dominant, imperial, kingly, monarchal, paramount, predominant, principal, queenly, regal, royal, ruling, supreme, unlimited **3.** *old-fashioned* effectual, efficacious, efficient, excellent

sovereignty ascendancy, domination, kingship, primacy, supremacy, supreme power, suzerainty, sway

sow disseminate, implant, inseminate, lodge, plant, scatter, seed

space 1. amplitude, capacity, elbow room, expanse, extension, extent, leeway, margin, play, room, scope, spaciousness, volume **2.** duration, interval, period,

space shuttle *n* a manned reusable spacecraft designed for making regular flights.

space station *n* a large manned artificial satellite used as a base for scientific research in space and for people travelling in space.

spacesuit *n* a sealed protective suit worn by astronauts.

space-time *or* **space-time continuum** *n Physics* the four-dimensional continuum having three space coordinates and one time coordinate that together completely specify the location of an object or an event.

spacious *adj* having or providing a lot of space; roomy. **spaciousness** *n*

spade[1] *n* **1** a tool for digging, with a flat steel blade and a long wooden handle. **2 call a spade a spade** to speak plainly and frankly.

spade[2] *n* **1 a spades** the suit of playing cards marked with a black leaf-shaped symbol. **b** a card with one or more of these symbols on it. **2** *Offensive* a Black person. **3 in spades** *Informal* in plenty: *all you need is talent in spades.*

spadework *n* dull or routine work done as preparation for a project or activity.

spadix (**spade**-ix) *n, pl* **spadices** (spade-**ice**-eez) *Bot* a spike of small flowers on a fleshy stem.

spaghetti *n* pasta in the form of long strings.

spaghetti junction *n* a junction between motorways with a large number of intersecting roads.

spaghetti western *n* a cowboy film made in Europe by an Italian director.

spake *vb Archaic* a past tense of **speak**.

Spam *n Trademark* a cold meat made from pork and spices.

span *n* **1** the interval or distance between two points, such as the ends of a bridge. **2** the complete extent: *that span of time.* **3** short for **wingspan. 4** a unit of length based on the width of a stretched hand, usually taken as nine inches (23 cms). *~vb* **spanning, spanned 5** to stretch or extend across, over, or around: *her career spanned fifty years; to span the Danube.*

spangle *n* **1** a small piece of shiny material used as a decoration on clothes or hair; sequin. *~vb* **-gling, -gled 2** to cover or decorate (something) with spangles.

Spaniard *n* a person from Spain.

spaniel *n* a dog with long drooping ears and a silky coat.

Spanish *adj* **1** of Spain. *~n* **2** the official language of Spain, Mexico, and most countries of South and Central America. *~pl n* **3 the Spanish** the people of Spain.

Spanish fly *n* a beetle, the dried body of which is used in medicine.

Spanish Main *n* **1** the N coast of South America. **2** the Caribbean Sea, the S part of which was frequented by pirates.

spank *vb* **1** to slap (someone) with the open hand, on the buttocks or legs. *~n* **2** such a slap.

spanking[1] *n* a series of spanks, usually as a punishment for children.

spanking[2] *adj* **1** *Informal* outstandingly fine or smart: *spanking new uniforms.* **2** very fast: *a spanking pace.*

spanner *n* **1** a tool for gripping and turning a nut or bolt. **2 throw a spanner in the works** *Brit informal* to cause a problem that prevents things from running smoothly.

spanspek *n S African* a cantaloupe melon.

spar[1] *n* a pole used as a ship's mast, boom, or yard.

spar[2] *vb* **sparring, sparred 1** *Boxing, martial arts* to fight using light punches for practice. **2** to argue with someone. *~n* **3** an argument.

spar[3] *n* a light-coloured, crystalline, easily split mineral.

spare *adj* **1** extra to what is needed: *there are some spare chairs at the back.* **2** able to be used when needed: *a spare parking space.* **3** (of a person) tall and thin. **4** (of a style) plain and without unnecessary decoration or details; austere: *a spare but beautiful novel.* **5** *Brit slang* frantic with anger or worry: *the boss went spare. ~n* **6** an extra thing kept in case it is needed. *~vb* **sparing, spared 7** to stop from killing, punishing, or injuring (someone). **8** to protect (someone) from (something) unpleasant: *spare me the sermon.* **9** to be able to afford or give: *can you spare me a moment to talk.* **10 not spare oneself** to try one's hardest. **11 to spare** more than is required: *a few hours to spare.*

spare part *n* a replacement piece of mechanical or electrical equipment kept in case the original component becomes damaged or worn.

spareribs *pl n* a cut of pork ribs with most of the meat trimmed off.

spare tyre *n* **1** an additional tyre kept in a motor vehicle in case of puncture. **2** *Brit slang* a roll of fat just above the waist.

sparing *adj* (sometimes foll. by *of*) economical (with): *she was mercifully sparing in her use of jargon.* **sparingly** *adv*

spark *n* **1** a fiery particle thrown out from a fire or caused by friction. **2** a short flash of light followed by a sharp crackling noise, produced by a sudden electrical discharge through the air. **3** a trace or hint: *a spark of goodwill.* **4** liveliness, enthusiasm, or humour: *that spark in her eye. ~vb* **5** to give off sparks. **6** to cause to

THESAURUS

span, time, while **3.** blank, distance, gap, interval, lacuna, omission

spaceman *or* **spacewoman** astronaut, cosmonaut

spacious ample, broad, capacious, comfortable, commodious, expansive, extensive, huge, large, roomy, sizable, uncrowded, vast

spadework donkey-work, groundwork, labour, preparation

span *n.* **1.** amount, distance, extent, length, reach, spread, stretch **2.** duration, period, spell, term *~vb.* **3.** arch across, bridge, cover, cross, extend across, link, range over, traverse, vault

spank *vb.* belt (*informal*), cuff, give (someone) a hiding (*informal*), put (someone) over one's knee, slap, smack, tan (*slang*), wallop (*informal*), whack

spar *vb.* **1.** *Boxing, martial arts* exchange blows, scrap (*informal*), skirmish, wrestle **2.** argue, bicker, dispute, fall out (*informal*), have a tiff, lead a cat-and-dog life, row, skirmish, spat, squabble, wrangle

spare *adj.* **1.** additional, emergency, extra, free, going begging, in excess, in reserve, leftover, odd, over, superfluous, supernumerary, surplus, unoccupied, unused, unwanted **2.** gaunt, lank, lean, meagre, slender, slight, slim, wiry *~vb.* **3.** be merciful to, deal leniently with, go easy on (*informal*), have mercy on, leave, let off (*informal*), pardon, refrain from, release, relieve from, save from **4.** afford, allow, bestow, dispense with, do without, give, grant, let (someone) have, manage without, part with, relinquish

sparing careful, chary, cost-conscious, economical, frugal, money-conscious, prudent, saving, thrifty

spark *n.* **1.** flare, flash, flicker, gleam, glint, scintillation, spit **2.** atom, hint, jot, scintilla, scrap, trace, ves-

start; trigger: *the incident sparked off an angry exchange.*

sparkle *vb* **-kling, -kled 1** to glitter with many bright points of light. **2** (of wine or mineral water) to be slightly fizzy. **3** to be lively, witty, and intelligent. *~n* **4** a small bright point of light. **5** liveliness and wit.

sparkler *n* **1** a type of hand-held firework that throws out sparks. **2** *Informal* a sparkling gem; esp. a diamond.

spark plug *n* a device in an internal-combustion engine that ignites the fuel by producing an electric spark.

sparring partner *n* **1** a person who practises with a boxer during training. **2** a person with whom one has friendly arguments.

sparrow *n* a very common small brown or grey bird which feeds on seeds and insects.

sparrowhawk *n* a small hawk which preys on smaller birds.

sparse *adj* small in amount and spread out widely: *a sparse population.* **sparsely** *adv*

Spartan *adj* **1** of or relating to the ancient Greek city of Sparta. **2** (of a way of life) strict or simple and with no luxuries: *Spartan accommodation.* *~n* **3** a citizen of Sparta. **4** a person who leads a strict or simple life without luxuries.

spasm *n* **1** a sudden tightening of the muscles, over which one has no control. **2** a sudden burst of activity or feeling: *a spasm of applause; sudden spasms of anger.*

spasmodic *adj* taking place in sudden short spells: *spasmodic bouts of illness.* **spasmodically** *adv*

spastic *n* **1** a person who has cerebral palsy, and therefore has difficulty controlling his or her muscles. *~adj* **2** affected by involuntary muscle contractions: *a spastic colon.* **3** suffering from cerebral palsy.

spat[1] *n* a slight quarrel.

spat[2] *vb* a past of **spit**[1].

spate *n* **1** a large number of things happening within a period of time: *a spate of bombings.* **2** a fast flow or outpouring: *an incomprehensible spate of words.* **3 in spate** *Chiefly Brit* (of a river) flooded.

spathe *n Bot* a large leaf that surrounds the base of a flower cluster.

spatial *adj* of or relating to size, area, or position: *spatial dimensions.* **spatially** *adv*

spats *pl n* cloth or leather coverings formerly worn by men over the ankle and instep.

spatter *vb* **1** to scatter or splash (a substance, esp. a liquid) in scattered drops: *spattering mud in all directions.* **2** to sprinkle (an object or a surface) with a liquid. *~n* **3** the sound of spattering. **4** something spattered, such as a spot or splash.

spatula *n* a utensil with a broad flat blade, used in cooking and by doctors.

spawn *n* **1** the jelly-like mass of eggs laid by fish, amphibians, or molluscs. *~vb* **2** (of fish, amphibians, or molluscs) to lay eggs. **3** to cause (something) to be created: *the depressed economy spawned the riots.*

spay *vb* to remove the ovaries from (a female animal).

speak *vb* **speaking, spoke, spoken 1** to say words; talk. **2** to communicate or express (something) in words. **3** to give a speech or lecture. **4** to know how to talk in (a specified language): *I don't speak French.* **5 on speaking terms** on good terms; friendly. **6 so to speak** as it were. **7 speak one's mind** to express one's opinions honestly and plainly. **8 to speak of** of a significant nature: *no licensing laws to speak of.*

speakeasy *n, pl* **-easies** *US* a place where alcoholic drink was sold illegally during Prohibition.

speaker *n* **1** a person who speaks, esp. someone making a speech. **2** a person who speaks a particular language: *a fluent Tibetan and English speaker.* **3** same as **loudspeaker.**

Speaker *n* the official chairman of a law-making body.

speak for *vb* **1** to speak on behalf of (other people). **2 speak for itself** to be so obvious that no further comment is necessary: *his work on the convention speaks for itself.* **3 speak for yourself!** *Informal* do not presume that other people agree with you!

speak up *or* **out** *vb* **1** to state one's beliefs bravely and firmly. **2** to speak more loudly and clearly.

spear[1] *n* **1** a weapon consisting of a long pole with a sharp point. *~vb* **2** to pierce (someone or something) with a spear or other pointed object: *she took her fork and speared an oyster from its shell.*

spear[2] *n* **1** a slender shoot, such as of grass. **2** a single stalk of broccoli or asparagus.

spearhead *vb* **1** to lead (an attack or a campaign). *~n* **2** the leading force in an attack or campaign.

spearmint *n* a minty flavouring used for sweets and toothpaste, which comes from a purple-flowered plant.

spec *n* **on spec** *Informal* as a risk or gamble: *I still tend to buy on spec.*

special *adj* **1** distinguished from or better than others of its kind: *a special occasion.* **2** designed or reserved for a specific purpose: *special equipment.* **3** not usual; different from normal: *a special case.* **4** particular or primary: *a special interest in gifted children.* **5** relating to the education of children with disabilities: *a special school.* *~n* **6** a product, TV programme, etc., which is

THESAURUS

tige *~vb.* **3.** animate, excite, inspire, kick-start, kindle, precipitate, prod, provoke, rouse, set in motion, set off, start, stimulate, stir, touch off, trigger (off)

sparkle *vb.* **1.** beam, coruscate (*formal*), dance, flash, gleam, glint, glisten, glitter, glow, scintillate, shimmer, shine, spark, twinkle, wink **2.** bubble, effervesce, fizz, fizzle *~n.* **3.** brilliance, coruscation (*formal*), dazzle, flash, flicker, gleam, glint, radiance, spark, twinkle **4.** animation, brio, dash, élan, gaiety, life, panache, spirit, vim (*slang*), vitality, vivacity, zip (*informal*)

Spartan *adj.* abstemious, ascetic, austere, bleak, disciplined, extreme, frugal, plain, rigorous, self-denying, severe, stern, strict, stringent

spasm 1. contraction, convulsion, paroxysm, throe (*rare*), twitch **2.** access, burst, eruption, fit, frenzy, outburst, seizure

spasmodic convulsive, erratic, fitful, intermittent, irregular, jerky, sporadic

spate deluge, flood, flow, outpouring, rush, torrent

speak 1. articulate, communicate, converse, discourse, enunciate, express, make known, pronounce, say, state, talk, tell, utter, voice **2.** address, argue, declaim, deliver an address, descant, discourse, harangue, hold forth, lecture, plead, speechify, spiel (*informal*), spout

speaker lecturer, mouthpiece, orator, public speaker, spokesman, spokesperson, spokeswoman

speak for act for *or* on behalf of, appear for, hold a brief for, hold a mandate for, represent

speak up *or* **out 1.** have one's say, make one's position plain, sound off, speak one's mind, stand up and be counted **2.** make oneself heard, say it loud and clear, speak loudly

spearhead *vb.* be in the van, blaze the trail, head,

only available or shown at a certain time: *a two-hour Christmas special live from Hollywood.* 7 a meal, usually at a low price, in a bar or restaurant. 8 short for **special constable. specially** *adv*

Special Branch *n* (in Britain) the department of the police force that is concerned with political security.

special constable *n* a person recruited for occasional police duties, such as in an emergency.

special delivery *n* the delivery of a piece of mail outside the time of a scheduled delivery, for an extra fee.

special effects *pl n Films* techniques used in the production of scenes that cannot be achieved by normal methods: *the special effects and make-up are totally convincing.*

specialist *n* 1 a person who is an expert in a particular activity or subject. 2 a doctor who concentrates on treating one particular category of diseases or the diseases of one particular part of the body: *an eye specialist.* ~*adj* 3 particular to or concentrating on one subject or activity: *a specialist comic shop.*

speciality *or esp US & Canad* **specialty** *n, pl* **-ties** 1 a special interest or skill. 2 a service, product, or type of food specialized in.

specialize *or* **-ise** *vb* **-izing, -ized** *or* **-ising, -ised** 1 to concentrate all one's efforts on studying a particular subject, occupation, or activity: *an expert who specializes in transport.* 2 to modify (something) for a special use or purpose: *plants have evolved and specialized in every type of habitat.* **specialization** *or* **-isation** *n*

special licence *n Brit* a licence allowing a marriage to take place without following all the usual legal procedures.

specialty *n, pl* **-ties** *Chiefly US & Canad* same as **speciality.**

specie *n* coins as distinct from paper money.

species *n, pl* **-cies** *Biol* one of the groups into which a genus is divided, the members of which are able to interbreed.

specific *adj* 1 particular or definite: *a specific area of economic policy.* 2 precise and exact: *try and be more specific.* ~*n* 3 **specifics** particular qualities or aspects of something: *the specifics of the situation.* 4 *Med* any drug used to treat a particular disease. **specifically** *adv* **specificity** *n*

specification *n* 1 a detailed description of features in the design of something: *engines built to racing specification.* 2 a requirement or detail which is clearly stated: *the main specification was that a good degree was required.* 3 the specifying of something.

specific gravity *n Physics* the ratio of the density of a substance to the density of water.

specific heat capacity *n Physics* the quantity of heat required to raise the temperature of unit mass of a substance by one degree centigrade.

specify *vb* **-fies, -fying, -fied** 1 to state or describe (something) clearly. 2 to state (something) as a condition: *the rules specify the number of prisoners to be kept in each cell.*

specimen *n* 1 an individual or part regarded as typical of its group or class. 2 *Med* a sample of tissue, blood, or urine taken for analysis. 3 *Informal* a person: *I'm quite a healthy specimen.*

specious (**spee**-shuss) *adj* apparently correct or true, but actually wrong or false.

speck *n* 1 a very small mark or spot. 2 a small or tiny piece of something: *a speck of fluff.*

speckle *vb* **-ling, -led** 1 to mark (something) with speckles. ~*n* 2 a small mark or spot, such as on the skin or on an egg. **speckled** *adj*

specs *pl n Informal* short for **spectacles.**

spectacle *n* 1 a strange, interesting, or ridiculous scene. 2 an impressive public show: *the opening ceremony of the Olympics was an impressive spectacle.* 3 **make a spectacle of oneself** to draw attention to oneself by behaving foolishly.

spectacles *pl n* a pair of glasses for correcting faulty vision.

spectacular *adj* 1 impressive, grand, or dramatic. ~*n* 2 a spectacular show. **spectacularly** *adv*

spectate *vb* **-tating, -tated** to be a spectator, watch.

spectator *n* a person viewing anything; onlooker.

spectator ion *n Chem* an ion which is present in a mixture but plays no part in a reaction.

spectre *or US* **specter** *n* 1 a ghost. 2 an unpleasant or menacing vision in one's imagination: *the spectre of famine.* **spectral** *adj*

spectrometer (speck-**trom**-it-er) *n Physics* an instrument for producing a spectrum, usually one in which wavelength, energy, or intensity can be measured.

spectroscope *n Physics* an instrument for forming or recording a spectrum by passing a light ray through a prism or grating.

spectrum *n, pl* **-tra** 1 *Physics* the distribution of colours produced when white light is dispersed by a

THESAURUS

initiate, launch, lay the first stone, lead, lead the way, pioneer, set in motion, set off

special 1. distinguished, especial, exceptional, extraordinary, festive, gala, important, memorable, momentous, out of the ordinary, red-letter, significant, uncommon, unique, unusual 2. appropriate, certain, characteristic, distinctive, especial, individual, particular, peculiar, precise, specialized, specific 3. chief, main, major, particular, primary

specialist *n.* authority, buff (*informal*), connoisseur, consultant, expert, hotshot (*informal*), master, professional, whizz (*informal*)

speciality bag, claim to fame, distinctive *or* distinguishing feature, forte, métier, *pièce de résistance,* special, specialty

species breed, category, class, collection, description, genus, group, kind, sort, type, variety

specific *adj.* clear-cut, definite, exact, explicit, express, limited, particular, precise, unambiguous, unequivocal

specification condition, detail, item, particular, qualification, requirement, stipulation

specify be specific about, cite, define, designate, detail, enumerate, indicate, individualize, itemize, mention, name, particularize, spell out, stipulate

specimen copy, embodiment, example, exemplar, exemplification, exhibit, individual, instance, model, pattern, proof, representative, sample, type

specious casuistic, deceptive, fallacious, misleading, plausible, sophistic, unsound

speck blemish, blot, defect, dot, fault, flaw, fleck, mark, mote, speckle, spot, stain

speckled brindled, dappled, dotted, flecked, freckled, mottled, speckledy, spotted, spotty, sprinkled, stippled

spectacle 1. curiosity, laughing stock, marvel, phenomenon, scene, sight, wonder 2. display, event, exhibition, extravaganza, pageant, parade, performance, show, sight

spectacular 1. *adj.* breathtaking, daring, dazzling, dramatic, eye-catching, fantastic (*informal*), grand, impressive, magnificent, marked, remarkable, sensa-

prism or grating: violet, indigo, blue, green, yellow, orange, and red. **2** *Physics* the whole range of electromagnetic radiation with respect to its wavelength or frequency. **3** a range or scale of anything such as opinions or emotions.

speculate *vb* **-lating, -lated 1** to form opinions about something, esp. its future consequences, based on the information available; conjecture. **2** to buy securities or property in the hope of selling them at a profit. **speculation** *n* **speculative** *adj* **speculator** *n*

sped *vb* a past of **speed.**

speech *n* **1** the ability to speak: *the loss of speech.* **2** spoken language: *Doran's lack of coherent speech.* **3** a talk given to an audience: *a speech to parliament.* **4** a person's manner of speaking: *her speech was extremely slow.* **5** a national or regional language or dialect: *Canadian speech.*

speech day *n Brit* (in schools) an annual day on which prizes are presented and speeches are made by guest speakers.

speechify *vb* **-fies, -fying, -fied** to make a dull or pompous speech.

speechless *adj* **1** unable to speak for a short time because of great emotion or shock. **2** unable to be expressed in words: *speechless disbelief.*

speech therapy *n* the treatment of people with speech problems.

speed *n* **1** the quality of acting or moving fast; swiftness. **2** the rate at which something moves or happens. **3** a gear ratio in a motor vehicle or bicycle: *five-speed gearbox.* **4** *Photog* a measure of the sensitivity to light of a particular type of film. **5** *Slang* amphetamine. **6 at speed** quickly. ~*vb* **speeding, sped** *or* **speeded 7** to move or go somewhere quickly. **8** to drive a motor vehicle faster than the legal limit. ~See also **speed up.**

speedboat *n* a high-speed motorboat.

speed limit *n* the maximum speed at which a vehicle may legally travel on a particular road.

speedo *n, pl* **speedos** *Informal* a speedometer.

speedometer *n* a dial in a vehicle which shows the speed of travel.

speed trap *n* a place on a road where the police check that passing vehicles are not being driven at an illegally high speed.

speed up *vb* to accelerate.

speedway *n* **1** the sport of racing on light powerful motorcycles round cinder tracks. **2** the track or stadium where such races are held.

speedwell *n* a small blue or pinkish-white flower.

speedy *adj* **speedier, speediest 1** done without delay. **2** (of a vehicle) able to travel fast. **speedily** *adv*

speleology *n* the scientific study of caves.

spell[1] *vb* **spelling, spelt** *or* **spelled 1** to write or name in correct order the letters that make up (a word): *how do you spell that name?* **2** (of letters) to make up (a word): *c-a-t spells cat.* **3** to indicate (a particular result): *share price slump spells disaster.* ~See also **spell out.**

spell[2] *n* **1** a sequence of words used to perform magic. **2** the effect of a spell: *the wizard's spell was broken.* **3 under someone's spell** fascinated by someone.

spell[3] *n* **1** a period of time of weather or activity: *the dry spell; a short spell in prison.* **2** a period of duty after which one person or group relieves another. **3** *Scot, Austral & NZ* a period of rest.

spellbinding *adj* so fascinating that nothing else can be thought of: *his spellbinding speeches.*

spellbound *adj* completely fascinated; as if in a trance.

spelling *n* **1** the way a word is spelt: *the British spelling of "theatre".* **2** a person's ability to spell: *my spelling used to be excellent.*

spell out *vb* **1** to make (something) as easy to understand as possible: *to spell out the implications.* **2** to read with difficulty, working out each word letter by letter.

spelt *vb* a past of **spell**[1].

spend *vb* **spending, spent 1** to pay out (money). **2** to pass (time) in a specific way or place: *I spent a year*

THESAURUS

tional, splendid, staggering, striking, stunning (*informal*) **2.** *n.* display, extravaganza, show, spectacle

spectator beholder, bystander, eyewitness, looker-on, observer, onlooker, viewer, watcher, witness

speculate 1. cogitate, conjecture, consider, contemplate, deliberate, hypothesize, meditate, muse, scheme, suppose, surmise, theorize, wonder **2.** gamble, have a flutter (*informal*), hazard, play the market, risk, take a chance with, venture

speculation 1. conjecture, consideration, contemplation, deliberation, guess, guesswork, hypothesis, opinion, supposition, surmise, theory **2.** gamble, gambling, hazard, risk

speculative 1. abstract, academic, conjectural, hypothetical, notional, suppositional, tentative, theoretical **2.** chancy (*informal*), dicey (*informal, chiefly Brit.*), hazardous, risky, uncertain, unpredictable

speech 1. communication, conversation, dialogue, discussion, intercourse, talk **2.** address, discourse, disquisition, harangue, homily, lecture, oration, spiel (*informal*) **3.** articulation, dialect, diction, enunciation, idiom, jargon, language, lingo (*informal*), parlance, tongue, utterance, voice

speechless 1. aghast, amazed, astounded, dazed, dumbfounded, dumbstruck, shocked, thunderstruck **2.** dumb, inarticulate, mum, mute, silent, tongue-tied, unable to get a word out (*informal*), wordless

speed 1. *n.* acceleration, celerity, expedition, fleetness, haste, hurry, momentum, pace, precipitation, quickness, rapidity, rush, swiftness, velocity **2.** *vb.* belt (along) (*slang*), bomb (along), bowl along, burn rubber (*informal*), career, dispatch, exceed the speed limit, expedite, flash, gallop, get a move on (*informal*), go hell for leather (*informal*), go like a bat out of hell (*slang*), go like the wind, hasten, hurry, lose no time, make haste, press on, put one's foot down (*informal*), quicken, race, rush, sprint, step on it (*informal*), tear, urge, zoom

speed up accelerate, gather momentum, get moving, get under way, increase, increase the tempo, open up the throttle, put one's foot down (*informal*), put on speed

speedy expeditious, express, fast, fleet, fleet of foot, hasty, headlong, hurried, immediate, nimble, precipitate, prompt, quick, quickie (*informal*), rapid, summary, swift, winged

spell[1] *vb.* amount to, augur, herald, imply, indicate, mean, point to, portend, presage, promise, signify, suggest

spell[2] *n.* **1.** abracadabra, charm, conjuration, exorcism, incantation, sorcery, witchery **2.** allure, bewitchment, enchantment, fascination, glamour, magic, trance

spell[3] *n.* bout, course, interval, patch, period, season, stint, stretch, term, time, tour of duty, turn

spellbound bemused, bewitched, captivated, charmed, enthralled, entranced, fascinated, gripped, hooked, mesmerized, possessed, rapt, transfixed, transported, under a spell

spelling orthography

in Budapest. **3** to concentrate (effort) on an activity: *a lot of energy was spent organizing the holiday.* **4** to use up completely: *the hurricane spent its force.* **spending** *n*

spendthrift *n* **1** a person who spends money wastefully. *~adj* **2** of or like a spendthrift: *a spendthrift policy.*

spent *vb* **1** the past of **spend.** *~adj* **2** used up or exhausted.

sperm *n* **1** (*pl* **sperm** *or* **sperms**) one of the male reproductive cells released in the semen during ejaculation. **2** same as **semen.**

spermaceti (sper-ma-**set**-ee) *n* a white waxy substance obtained from the sperm whale.

spermatozoon (sper-ma-toe-**zoe**-on) *n, pl* **-zoa** same as **sperm** (sense 1).

spermicide *n* a substance, esp. a cream or jelly, that kills sperm, used as a means of contraception. **spermicidal** *adj*

sperm oil *n* an oil obtained from the head of the sperm whale, used as a lubricant.

sperm whale *n* a large whale which is hunted for spermaceti and ambergris.

spew *vb* **1** to vomit. **2** to send or be sent out in a stream: *the hydrant spewed a tidal wave of water.*

sphagnum *n* a moss which is found in bogs and which decays to form peat.

sphere *n* **1** *Geom* a round solid figure in which every point on the surface is equally distant from the centre. **2** an object having this shape, such as a planet. **3** a particular field of activity. **4** people of the same rank or with shared interests: *a humbler social sphere.*

spherical *adj* shaped like a sphere.

spheroid *n Geom* a solid figure that is almost but not exactly a sphere.

sphincter *n Anat* a ring of muscle surrounding the opening of a hollow organ and contracting to close it.

sphinx *n* **1** one of the huge statues built by the ancient Egyptians, with the body of a lion and the head of a man. **2** a mysterious person.

Sphinx *n* **1** the huge statue of a sphinx near the pyramids at El Gîza in Egypt. **2** *Greek myth* a monster with a woman's head and a lion's body, who set a riddle for travellers, killing them when they failed to answer it. Oedipus answered the riddle and the Sphinx then killed herself.

spice *n* **1 a** an aromatic substance, such as ginger or cinnamon, used as flavouring. **b** such substances collectively. **2** something that makes life or an activity more exciting. *~vb* **spicing, spiced 3** to flavour (food) with spices. **4** to add excitement or interest to (something): *they spiced their letters with pointed demands.*

spick-and-span *adj* very neat and clean.

spicy *adj* **spicier, spiciest 1** strongly flavoured with spices. **2** *Informal* slightly scandalous: *spicy new story lines.*

spider *n* a small eight-legged creature, many species of which weave webs in which to trap insects for food. **spidery** *adj*

spider monkey *n* a tree-living monkey with very long legs, a long tail, and a small head.

spiel *n* a prepared speech made to persuade someone to buy or do something.

spigot *n* **1** a stopper for the vent hole of a cask. **2** a wooden tap fitted to a cask.

spike[1] *n* **1** a sharp-pointed metal object: *a high fence with iron spikes.* **2** anything long and pointed: *a hedgehog bristling with spikes.* **3** a long metal nail. **4 spikes** sports shoes with metal spikes on the soles for greater grip. *~vb* **spiking, spiked 5** to secure or supply (something) with spikes: *spiked shoes.* **6** to drive a spike or spikes into. **7** to add alcohol to (a drink). **spiky** *adj*

spike[2] *n Bot* **1** an arrangement of flowers attached at the base to a long stem. **2** an ear of grain.

spikenard *n* **1** a fragrant Indian plant with rose-purple flowers. **2** an ointment obtained from this plant.

spill[1] *vb* **spilling, spilt** *or* **spilled 1** to pour from or as from a container by accident. **2** (of large numbers of people) to come out of a place: *rival groups spilled out from the station.* **3** to shed (blood). **4 spill the beans** *Informal* to give away a secret. *~n* **5** *Informal* a fall from a motorbike, bike, or horse, esp. in a competition. **6** an amount of liquid spilt. **spillage** *n*

spill[2] *n* a splinter of wood or strip of paper for lighting pipes or fires.

spillikin *n* a thin strip of wood, cardboard, or plastic used in spillikins.

spillikins *n Brit* a game in which players try to pick each spillikin from a heap without moving the others.

spin *vb* **spinning, spun 1** to revolve or cause to revolve quickly. **2** to draw out and twist (fibres, such as silk or cotton) into thread. **3** (of a spider or silkworm) to form (a web or cocoon) from a silky fibre that comes out of the body. **4 spin a yarn** to tell an unlikely story. **5** *Sport* to throw, hit, or kick (a ball) so that it spins and changes direction or changes speed on bouncing. **6** same as **spin-dry. 7** to grow dizzy: *her head was spinning.* *~n* **8** a fast rotating motion. **9** a

THESAURUS

spell out 1. clarify, elucidate, explicate, make clear *or* plain, make explicit, specify **2.** discern, make out, puzzle out

spend 1. disburse, expend, fork out (*slang*), lay out, pay out, shell out (*informal*), splash out (*Brit. informal*) **2.** apply, bestow, concentrate, devote, employ, exert, invest, lavish, put in, use **3.** blow (*slang*), consume, deplete, dispense, dissipate, drain, empty, exhaust, fritter away, run through, squander, use up, waste

spendthrift 1. *n.* big spender, prodigal, profligate, spender, squanderer, waster, wastrel **2.** *adj.* extravagant, improvident, prodigal, profligate, wasteful

spent *adj.* all in (*slang*), burnt out, bushed (*informal*), clapped out (*Austral. & N.Z.*), consumed, dead beat (*informal*), debilitated, dog-tired (*informal*), done in *or* up (*informal*), drained, exhausted, expended, fagged (out) (*informal*), finished, gone, knackered (*slang*), played out (*informal*), prostrate, ready to drop (*informal*), shattered (*informal*), tired out, used up, weakened, wearied, weary, whacked (*Brit. informal*), worn out, zonked (*informal*)

sphere 1. ball, circle, globe, globule, orb **2.** capacity, compass, department, domain, employment, field, function, pale, patch, province, range, rank, realm, scope, station, stratum, territory, turf (*U.S. slang*), walk of life

spherical globe-shaped, globular, orbicular, rotund, round

spice *n.* **1.** relish, savour, seasoning **2.** colour, excitement, gusto, kick (*informal*), pep, piquancy, tang, zap (*slang*), zest, zip (*informal*)

spike 1. *n.* barb, point, prong, spine **2.** *vb.* impale, spear, spit, stick

spill *vb.* **1.** discharge, disgorge, overflow, overturn, scatter, shed, slop over, spill *or* run over, throw off, upset **2. spill the beans** *informal* betray a secret, blab, blow the gaff (*Brit. slang*), give the game away, grass (*Brit. slang*), inform, let the cat out of the bag, shop (*slang, chiefly Brit.*), sing (*slang, chiefly U.S.*),

flight manoeuvre in which an aircraft flies in a downward spiral. **10** *Sport* a spinning motion given to a ball. **11** *Informal* a short car drive taken for pleasure. ~See also **spin out. spinning** *n*

spina bifida *n* a condition in which part of the spinal cord protrudes through a gap in the backbone, sometimes causing paralysis.

spinach *n* a dark green leafy vegetable.

spinal column *n* same as **spine** (sense 1).

spinal cord *n* the thick cord of nerve tissue within the spine, which connects the brain to the nerves of the body.

spin bowler *n Cricket* same as **spinner** (sense 1a).

spindle *n* **1** a rotating rod that acts as an axle. **2** a rod with a notch in the top for drawing out, twisting and winding the thread in spinning.

spindly *adj* **-dlier, -dliest** tall, thin, and frail.

spindrift *n* spray blown up from the sea.

spin-dry *vb* **-dries, -drying, -dried** to dry (clothes) in a spin-dryer.

spin-dryer *n* a device that removes water from washed clothes by spinning them in a perforated drum.

spine *n* **1** the row of bony segments that surround and protect the spinal cord. **2** the back of a book, record sleeve, or video-tape box. **3** a sharp point on the body of an animal or on a plant. **spinal** *adj*

spine-chiller *n* a frightening film or story. **spine-chilling** *adj*

spineless *adj* **1** behaving in a cowardly way. **2** (of an animal) having no spine.

spinet *n* a small harpsichord.

spinnaker *n* a large triangular sail on a racing yacht.

spinner *n* **1** *Cricket* **a** a bowler who specializes in spinning the ball with his or her fingers to make it change direction when it bounces or strikes the batsman's bat. **b** a ball that is bowled with a spinning motion. **2** a small round object used in angling to attract fish to the bait by spinning in the water. **3** a person who makes thread by spinning.

spinneret *n* an organ through which silk threads come out of the body of a spider or insect.

spinney *n Chiefly Brit* a small wood.

spinning jenny *n* an early type of spinning frame with several spindles.

spinning wheel *n* a wheel-like machine for spinning at home, having one hand- or foot-operated spindle.

spin-off *n* **1** a product or development that unexpectedly results from activities designed to achieve something else: *new energy sources could occur as a spin-off from the space effort.* **2** a television series involving some of the characters from an earlier successful series.

spin out *vb* **1** to take longer than necessary to do (something). **2** to make (money) last as long as possible.

spinster *n* an unmarried woman. **spinsterish** *adj*

spiny *adj* **spinier, spiniest** (of animals or plants) covered with spines.

spiracle (**spire**-a-kl) *n Zool* a small blowhole for breathing through, such as that of a whale.

spiraea *or esp US* **spirea** (spire-**ee**-a) *n* a plant with small white or pink flowers.

spiral *n* **1** *Geom* a plane curve formed by a point winding about a fixed point at an ever-increasing distance from it. **2** something that follows a winding course or that has a twisting form. **3** *Econ* a continuous upward or downward movement in economic activity or prices. ~*adj* **4** having the shape of a spiral: *a spiral staircase.* ~*vb* **-ralling, -ralled** *or US* **-raling, -raled 5** to follow a spiral course or be in the shape of a spiral. **6** to increase or decrease with steady acceleration: *oil prices continue to spiral.* **spirally** *adv*

spire *n* the tall cone-shaped structure on the top of a church.

spirit[1] *n* **1** the nonphysical aspect of a person concerned with profound thoughts and emotions. **2** the nonphysical part of a person believed to live on after death. **3** a shared feeling: *a spirit of fun and adventure.* **4** mood or attitude: *fighting spirit.* **5** a person's character or temperament: *the indomitable spirit of the Polish people.* **6** liveliness shown in what a person does: *it has been undertaken with spirit.* **7** the feelings that motivate someone to survive in difficult times or live according to his or her beliefs: *someone had broken his spirit.* **8 spirits** an emotional state: *in good spirits.* **9** the way in which something, such as a law or an agreement, was intended to be interpreted: *they acted against the spirit of the treaty.* **10** a supernatural being, such as a ghost. ~*vb* **-iting, -ited 11 spirit away** *or* **off** to carry (someone or something) off mysteriously or secretly.

spirit[2] *n* **1** (*usually pl*) distilled alcoholic liquor, such as whisky or gin. **2** *Chem* **a** a solution of ethanol obtained by distillation. **b** the essence of a substance, extracted as a liquid by distillation. **3** *Pharmacol* a solution of a volatile oil in alcohol.

spirited *adj* **1** showing liveliness or courage: *a spirit-*

THESAURUS

spill one's guts (*slang*), split (*slang*), squeal (*slang*), talk out of turn, tattle, tell all ~*n.* **3.** *informal* accident, cropper (*informal*), fall, tumble

spin *vb.* **1.** gyrate, pirouette, reel, revolve, rotate, turn, twirl, twist, wheel, whirl **2.** be giddy, be in a whirl, grow dizzy, reel, swim, whirl ~*n.* **3.** gyration, revolution, roll, twist, whirl **4.** *informal* drive, hurl (*Scot.*), joyride (*informal*), ride, turn, whirl

spine 1. backbone, spinal column, vertebrae, vertebral column **2.** barb, needle, quill, rachis, ray, spike, spur

spine-chilling bloodcurdling, eerie, frightening, hair-raising, horrifying, scary (*informal*), spooky (*informal*), terrifying

spineless cowardly, faint-hearted, feeble, gutless (*informal*), inadequate, ineffective, irresolute, lily-livered, soft, spiritless, squeamish, submissive, vacillating, weak, weak-kneed (*informal*), weak-willed, without a will of one's own, yellow (*informal*)

spin out amplify, delay, drag out, draw out, extend, lengthen, pad out, prolong, prolongate, protract

spiral 1. *n.* coil, corkscrew, curlicue, gyre (*literary*), helix, screw, volute, whorl **2.** *adj.* circular, coiled, corkscrew, helical, scrolled, voluted, whorled, winding

spirit *n.* **1.** air, breath, life, life force, psyche, soul, vital spark **2.** attitude, character, complexion, disposition, essence, humour, outlook, quality, temper, temperament **3.** animation, ardour, backbone, balls (*taboo slang*), courage, dauntlessness, earnestness, energy, enterprise, enthusiasm, fire, force, gameness, grit, guts (*informal*), life, liveliness, mettle, resolution, sparkle, spunk (*informal*), stoutheartedness, vigour, warmth, zest **4.** motivation, resolution, resolve, will, willpower **5.** *plural* feelings, frame of mind, humour, mood, morale **6.** essence, intent, intention, meaning, purport, purpose, sense, substance **7.** apparition, eidolon, ghost, phantom, shade (*literary*), shadow, spectre, spook (*informal*), sprite, vision ~*vb.* **8.** *with* **away** *or* **off** abduct, abstract, carry, convey, make away with,

ed rendition of Schubert's ninth symphony; a spirited defence of the government's policy. **2** characterized by the mood as specified: *high-spirited; mean-spirited.*

spirit gum *n* a solution of gum in ether, used to stick on false hair.

spirit lamp *n* a lamp that burns methylated or other spirits instead of oil.

spirit level *n* a device for checking whether a surface is level, consisting of a block of wood or metal containing a tube partially filled with liquid set so that the air bubble in it rests between two marks on the tube when the block is level.

spiritual *adj* **1** relating to a person's beliefs as opposed to his or her physical or material needs. **2** relating to religious beliefs. **3 one's spiritual home** the place where one feels one belongs. *~n* **4** Also called: **Negro spiritual** a type of religious folk song originally sung by Black slaves in the American South. **spirituality** *n* **spiritually** *adv*

spiritualism *n* the belief that the spirits of the dead can communicate with the living. **spiritualist** *n*

spirituous *adj* containing alcohol.

spirogyra (spire-oh-**jire**-a) *n* a green freshwater plant that floats on the surface of ponds and ditches.

spit[1] *vb* **spitting, spat** *or* **spit 1** to force saliva out of one's mouth. **2** to force (something) out of one's mouth: *he spat tobacco into an old coffee can.* **3** (of a fire or hot fat) to throw out sparks or particles violently and explosively. **4** to rain very lightly. **5** (often foll. by *out*) to say (words) in a violent angry way. **6** to show contempt or hatred by spitting. **7 spit it out!** *Brit informal* a command given to someone to say what is on his or her mind. *~n* **8** same as **spittle. 9** *Informal, chiefly Brit* same as **spitting image.**

spit[2] *n* **1** a pointed rod for skewering and roasting meat over a fire or in an oven. **2** a long narrow strip of land jutting out into the sea.

spit and polish *n Informal* thorough cleaning and polishing.

spite *n* **1** deliberate nastiness. **2 in spite of** regardless of: *he loved them in spite of their shortcomings. ~vb* **spiting, spited 3** to annoy (someone) deliberately, out of spite: *it was to spite his father.* **spiteful** *adj* **spitefully** *adv*

spitfire *n* a woman or girl who is easily angered.

spitting image *n Informal* a person who looks very like someone else.

spittle *n* the fluid that is produced in the mouth; saliva.

spittoon *n* a bowl for people to spit into.

spitz *n* a stockily built dog with a pointed face, erect ears, and a tightly curled tail.

spiv *n Brit slang* a smartly dressed man who makes a living by underhand dealings; black marketeer.

splash *vb* **1** to scatter (liquid) on (something). **2** to cause (liquid) to fall or (of liquid) to be scattered in drops. **3** to display (a photograph or story) prominently in a newspaper. *~n* **4** a splashing sound. **5** an amount splashed. **6** a patch (of colour or light). **7 make a splash** *Informal* to attract a lot of attention. **8** a small amount of liquid added to a drink.

splashdown *n* **1** the landing of a spacecraft on water at the end of a flight. *~vb* **splash down 2** (of a spacecraft) to make a splashdown.

splash out *n* to spend a lot of money on a treat or luxury: *she planned to splash out on a good holiday.*

splatter *vb* **1** to splash (something or someone) with small blobs. *~n* **2** a splash of liquid.

splay *vb* to spread out, with ends spreading out in different directions: *her hair splayed over the pillow.*

splayfooted *adj* same as **flat-footed.**

spleen *n* **1** a spongy organ near the stomach, which filters bacteria from the blood. **2** spitefulness or bad temper: *we vent our spleen on drug barons.*

spleenwort *n* a kind of fern that grows on walls.

splendid *adj* **1** very good: *a splendid match.* **2** beautiful or impressive: *a splendid Roman temple.* **splendidly** *adv*

splendiferous *adj Facetious, old-fashioned* grand in appearance.

splendour *or US* **splendor** *n* **1** beauty or impressiveness. **2 splendours** the impressive or beautiful features of something: *the splendours of the Emperor's Palace.*

splenetic *adj Literary* irritable or bad-tempered.

splice *vb* **splicing, spliced 1** to join up the trimmed ends of (two pieces of wire, film, or tape) with an ad-

---

THESAURUS

purloin, remove, seize, snaffle (*Brit. informal*), steal, whisk

spirited active, animated, ardent, bold, courageous, energetic, feisty (*informal, chiefly U.S. & Canad.*), game, have-a-go (*informal*), high-spirited, lively, mettlesome, plucky, sparkling, sprightly, spunky (*informal*), vigorous, vivacious

spiritual devotional, divine, ethereal, ghostly, holy, immaterial, incorporeal, nonmaterial, otherworldly, pure, religious, sacred

spit *vb.* discharge, eject, expectorate, hiss, spew, splutter, sputter, throw out

spite *n.* **1.** animosity, bitchiness (*slang*), gall, grudge, hate, hatred, ill will, malevolence, malice, malignity, pique, rancour, spitefulness, spleen, venom **2. in spite of** despite, (even) though, in defiance of, notwithstanding, regardless of *~vb.* **3.** annoy, discomfit, gall, harm, hurt, injure, needle (*informal*), nettle, offend, pique, provoke, put out, put (someone's) nose out of joint (*informal*), vex

spiteful barbed, bitchy (*informal*), catty (*informal*), cruel, ill-disposed, ill-natured, malevolent, malicious, malignant, nasty, rancorous, shrewish, snide, splenetic, venomous, vindictive

splash *vb.* **1.** bespatter, shower, slop, slosh (*informal*), spatter, splodge, spray, spread, sprinkle, squirt, strew, wet **2.** blazon, broadcast, flaunt, headline, plaster, publicize, tout, trumpet *~n.* **3.** burst, dash, patch, spattering, splodge, touch **4. make a splash** *informal* be ostentatious, cause a stir, cut a dash, go overboard (*informal*), go to town, splurge

splash out be extravagant, lash out (*informal*), push the boat out (*Brit. informal*), spare no expense, spend, splurge

spleen acrimony, anger, animosity, animus, bad temper, bile, bitterness, gall, hatred, hostility, ill humour, ill will, malevolence, malice, malignity, peevishness, pique, rancour, resentment, spite, spitefulness, venom, vindictiveness, wrath

splendid 1. cracking (*Brit. informal*), crucial (*slang*), def (*slang*), excellent, fantastic (*informal*), fine, first-class, glorious, great (*informal*), marvellous, mean (*slang*), mega (*slang*), sovereign, topping (*Brit. slang*), wonderful **2.** admirable, brilliant, dazzling, exceptional, glorious, gorgeous, grand, illustrious, imposing, impressive, lavish, luxurious, magnificent, ornate, outstanding, rare, remarkable, resplendent, rich, splendiferous (*facetious*), sumptuous, superb

splendour brightness, brilliance, ceremony, dazzle, display, éclat, effulgence, glory, gorgeousness, grandeur, lustre, magnificence, majesty, pomp, radiance, refulgence, renown, resplendence, richness, show, solemnity, spectacle, stateliness, sumptuousness

hesive material. **2** to join (two ropes) by interweaving the ends. **3 get spliced** *Informal* to get married.

splint *n* a piece of wood used to support a broken bone.

splinter *n* **1** a small thin sharp piece broken off, esp. from wood. *~vb* **2** to break or be broken into small sharp fragments.

splinter group *n* a number of members of an organization, who split from the main body and form an independent group of their own.

split *vb* **splitting, split 1** to break or cause (something) to break into separate pieces. **2** to separate (a piece) or (of a piece) to be separated from (something). **3** (of a group) to separate into smaller groups, through disagreement: *the council is split over rent increases.* **4** (often foll. by *up*) to divide (something) among two or more people. **5** *Slang* to leave a place. **6 split on** *Slang* to betray; inform: *he didn't tell tales or split on him.* **7 split one's sides** to laugh a great deal. *~n* **8** a gap or rift caused by splitting. **9** a division in a group or the smaller group resulting from such a division. **10** a dessert of sliced fruit and ice cream, covered with whipped cream and nuts: *banana split.* *~adj* **11** having a split or splits: *split ends.* ~See also **splits, split up.**

split infinitive *n* (in English grammar) an infinitive used with another word between *to* and the verb, as in *to really finish it.* This is often thought to be incorrect.

split-level *adj* (of a house or room) having the floor level of one part about half a storey above that of the other.

split pea *n* a pea dried and split and used in soups or as a vegetable.

split personality *n* **1** the tendency to change mood very quickly. **2** a disorder in which a person's mind appears to have separated into two or more personalities.

splits *n* (in gymnastics and dancing) the act of sitting with both legs outstretched, pointing in opposite directions, and at right angles to the body.

split second *n* **1** an extremely short period of time; instant. *~adj* **split-second 2** made in an extremely short time: *split-second timing.*

splitting *adj* (of a headache) extremely painful.

split up *vb* **1** to separate (something) into parts; divide. **2** (of a couple) to end a relationship or marriage. **3** (of a group of people) to go off in different directions. *~n* **split-up 4** the act of separating.

splodge *or US* **splotch** *n* **1** a large uneven spot or stain. *~vb* **splodging, splodged 2** to mark (something) with a splodge or splodges.

splurge *n* **1** a bout of spending money extravagantly. *~vb* **splurging, splurged 2** (foll. by *on*) to spend (money) extravagantly: *they rushed out to splurge their pocket money on chocolate.*

splutter *vb* **1** to spit out (something) from the mouth when choking or laughing. **2** to say (words) with spitting sounds when choking or in a rage. **3** to throw out or to be thrown out explosively: *sparks spluttered from the fire.* *~n* **4** the act or noise of spluttering.

Spode *n* china or porcelain manufactured by the English potter Josiah Spode or his company.

spoil *vb* **spoiling, spoilt** *or* **spoiled 1** to make (something) less valuable, beautiful, or useful. **2** to weaken the character of (a child) by giving it all it wants. **3** (of yourself) to indulge one's desires: *go ahead and spoil yourself.* **4** (of food) to become unfit for consumption. **5 be spoiling for** to have an aggressive urge for: *he is spoiling for a fight.* ~See also **spoils.**

spoilage *n* an amount of material that has been spoilt.

spoiler *n* **1** a device fitted to an aircraft wing to increase drag and reduce lift. **2** a similar device fitted to a car.

spoils *pl n* **1** valuables seized during war. **2** the rewards and benefits of having political power.

spoilsport *n Informal* a person who spoils the enjoyment of other people.

spoke[1] *vb* the past tense of **speak.**

spoke[2] *n* **1** a bar joining the centre of a wheel to the rim. **2 put a spoke in someone's wheel** *Brit* to create a difficulty for someone.

spoken *vb* **1** the past participle of **speak.** *~adj* **2** said in speech: *spoken commands.* **3** having speech as specified: *quiet-spoken.* **4 spoken for** engaged or reserved.

spokesman, spokesperson, *or* **spokeswoman** *n, pl* **-men, -people,** *or* **-women** a person chosen to speak on behalf of another person or group.

spoliation *n* the act or an instance of plundering: *the spoliation of the countryside.*

spondee *n Prosody* a metrical foot of two long syllables. **spondaic** *adj*

sponge *n* **1** a sea animal with a porous absorbent elastic skeleton. **2** the skeleton of a sponge, or a piece of artificial sponge, used for bathing or cleaning. **3** a soft absorbent material like a sponge. **4** Also called: **sponge cake** a light cake made of eggs, sugar, and flour. **5** Also called: **sponge pudding** *Brit* a light steamed or baked spongy pudding. **6** a rub with a wet sponge. *~vb* **sponging, sponged 7** (often foll. by

THESAURUS

splice *vb.* braid, entwine, graft, interlace, intertwine, intertwist, interweave, join, knit, marry, mesh, plait, unite, wed, yoke

splinter 1. *n.* chip, flake, fragment, needle, paring, shaving, sliver **2.** *vb.* break into smithereens, disintegrate, fracture, shatter, shiver, split

split *vb.* **1.** bifurcate, branch, break, break up, burst, cleave, come apart, come undone, crack, disband, disunite, diverge, fork, gape, give way, go separate ways, open, part, pull apart, rend, rip, separate, slash, slit, snap, splinter **2.** *often with* **up** allocate, allot, apportion, carve up, distribute, divide, divvy up (*informal*), dole out, halve, parcel out, partition, share out, slice up **3.** *with* **on** *slang* betray, give away, grass (*Brit. slang*), inform on, peach (*slang*), shop (*slang, chiefly Brit.*), sing (*slang, chiefly U.S.*), spill one's guts (*slang*), squeal (*slang*) *~n.* **4.** breach, crack, damage, division, fissure, gap, rent, rip, separation, slash, slit, tear **5.** breach, break, break-up, difference, discord, disruption, dissension, disunion, divergence, division, estrangement, partition, rift, rupture, schism *~adj.* **6.** ambivalent, bisected, broken, cleft, cracked, divided, dual, fractured, ruptured, twofold

split up break up, disband, divorce, go separate ways, part, part company, separate

spoil *vb.* **1.** blemish, blow (*slang*), damage, debase, deface, destroy, disfigure, harm, impair, injure, mar, mess up, ruin, scar, total (*slang*), trash (*slang*), undo, upset, wreck **2.** baby, coddle, cosset, indulge, kill with kindness, mollycoddle, overindulge, pamper, spoon-feed **3.** addle, become tainted, curdle, decay, decompose, go bad, go off (*Brit. informal*), mildew, putrefy, rot, turn **4. spoiling for** bent upon, desirous of, eager for, enthusiastic about, keen to, looking for, out to get (*informal*), raring to

spoilsport damper, dog in the manger, killjoy, misery (*Brit. informal*), party pooper (*informal*), wet blanket (*informal*)

down) to clean (something) by rubbing it with a wet sponge. **8** to remove (marks) by rubbing them with a wet sponge. **9** (usually foll. by *off* or *on*) to get (something) from someone by taking advantage of his or her generosity: *stop sponging off the rest of us!* **spongy** *adj*

sponge bag *n* a small waterproof bag for holding toiletries when travelling.

sponger *n Informal* a person who lives off other people by continually taking advantage of their generosity.

sponsor *n* **1** a person or group that promotes another person or group in an activity or the activity itself, either for profit or for charity. **2** *Chiefly US & Canad* a person or firm that pays the costs of a radio or television programme in return for advertising time. **3** a person who presents and supports a proposal or suggestion. **4** a person who makes certain promises on behalf of a person being baptized and takes responsibility for his or her Christian upbringing. *~vb* **5** to act as a sponsor for (someone or something). **sponsored** *adj* **sponsorship** *n*

spontaneous *adj* **1** not planned or arranged; impulsive: *a spontaneous celebration.* **2** occurring through natural processes without outside influence: *a spontaneous explosion.* **spontaneously** *adv* **spontaneity** *n*

spontaneous combustion *n Chem* the bursting into flame of a substance as a result of internal oxidation processes, without heat from an outside source.

spoof *Informal ~n* **1** an imitation of a film, TV programme, etc., that exaggerates in an amusing way the most memorable features of the original. **2** a good-humoured trick or deception. *~vb* **3** to fool (a person) with a trick or deception.

spook *Informal ~n* **1** a ghost. **2** a strange and frightening person. *~vb US & Canad* **3** to frighten: *it was the wind that spooked her.* **spooky** *adj*

spool *n* a cylinder around which film, thread, or tape can be wound.

spoon *n* **1** a small shallow bowl attached to a handle, used for eating, stirring, or serving food. **2 be born with a silver spoon in one's mouth** to be born into a very rich and respected family. *~vb* **3** to scoop up (food or liquid) with a spoon. **4** *Old-fashioned slang* to kiss and cuddle.

spoonbill *n* a wading bird with a long flat bill.

spoonerism *n* the accidental changing over of the first sounds of a pair of words, often with an amusing result, such as *hush my brat* for *brush my hat.*

spoon-feed *vb* **-feeding, -fed 1** to feed (someone, usually a baby) using a spoon. **2** to give (someone) too much help.

spoor *n* the trail of an animal.

sporadic *adj* happening at irregular intervals; intermittent: *sporadic bursts of gunfire.* **sporadically** *adv*

spore *n* a reproductive body, produced by nonflowering plants and bacteria, that develops into a new individual.

sporran *n* a large pouch worn hanging from a belt in front of the kilt in Scottish Highland dress.

sport *n* **1** an activity for exercise, pleasure, or competition: *your favourite sport.* **2** such activities collectively: *the minister for sport.* **3** the enjoyment gained from a pastime: *just for the sport of it.* **4** playful or good-humoured joking: *I only did it in sport.* **5** *Informal* a person who accepts defeat or teasing cheerfully. **6 make sport of someone** to make fun of someone. **7** an animal or plant that is very different from others of the same species, usually because of a mutation. **8** *Austral & NZ informal* a term of address between males. *~vb* **9** *Informal* to wear proudly: *sporting a pair of bright yellow shorts.* ~See also **sports.**

sporting *adj* **1** of sport. **2** behaving in a fair and decent way. **3 a sporting chance** reasonable likelihood of happening: *a sporting chance of winning.*

sportive *adj* playful or high-spirited.

sports *adj* **1** of or used in sports: *a sports arena.* *~n* **2** Also called: **sports day** *Brit* a meeting held at a school or college for competitions in athletic events.

sports car *n* a fast car with a low body and usually seating only two people.

sportscast *n US* a programme of sports news. **sportscaster** *n*

sports jacket *n* a man's casual jacket, usually made of tweed. Also called: *US, Austral, & NZ* **sports coat**

sportsman *n, pl* **-men 1** a man who plays sports. **2** a person who plays by the rules, is fair, and accepts defeat with good humour. **sportsman-like** *adj* **sportsmanship** *n*

sportsperson *n* a person who plays sports.

sportswear *n* clothes worn for sport or outdoor leisure wear.

sportswoman *n, pl* **-women** a woman who plays sports.

sporty *adj* **sportier, sportiest 1** (of a person) interested in sport. **2** (of clothes) suitable for sport. **3** (of a car) small and fast. **sportily** *adv* **sportiness** *n*

spot *n* **1** a small mark on a surface, which has a different colour or texture from its surroundings. **2** a location: *a spot where they could sit.* **3** a small mark or pimple on the skin. **4** a feature of something that has the attribute mentioned: *the one bright spot in his whole day; the high spot of our trip.* **5** *Informal, chiefly Brit* a small amount: *a spot of bother.* **6** *Informal* an awkward situation: *I'm sometimes in a spot.* **7** a part of a show, TV programme, etc., reserved for a specific performer or type of entertainment. **8** short for **spotlight** (sense 1). **9 in a tight spot** in a difficult situation. **10 knock spots off someone** to be much better than someone. **11 on the spot a** immediately: *he decided on the spot to fly down.* **b** at the place in question: *the expert weapons man on the spot.* **c** in an awkward situation: *the British government will be put on the spot.* **12 soft spot** a special affection for someone: *a soft spot for older men.* *~vb* **spotting, spotted 13** to see (something or someone) suddenly.

THESAURUS

spoken by word of mouth, expressed, oral, phonetic, put into words, said, told, unwritten, uttered, verbal, viva voce, voiced

spongy absorbent, cushioned, cushiony, elastic, light, porous, springy

sponsor 1. *n.* angel (*informal*), backer, godparent, guarantor, patron, promoter **2.** *vb.* back, finance, fund, guarantee, lend one's name to, patronize, promote, put up the money for, subsidize

spontaneous extempore, free, impromptu, impulsive, instinctive, natural, unbidden, uncompelled, unconstrained, unforced, unpremeditated, unprompted, voluntary, willing

spontaneously extempore, freely, impromptu, impulsively, instinctively, off one's own bat, off the cuff (*informal*), of one's own accord, on impulse, quite unprompted, voluntarily

sporadic infrequent, intermittent, irregular, isolated, occasional, on and off, random, scattered, spasmodic

sport *n.* **1.** amusement, diversion, entertainment, exercise, game, pastime, physical activity, play, recreation **2.** badinage, banter, frolic, fun, jest, joking, josh (*slang, chiefly U.S. & Canad.*), kidding (*informal*), mer-

14 to put stains or spots on (something). 15 (of some fabrics) to be prone to marking by liquids: *silk spots easily.* 16 to take note of (the numbers of trains or planes observed). 17 (of scouts, agents, etc.) to look out for (talented but unknown actors, sportspersons, etc.). 18 to rain lightly.

spot check *n* a quick unplanned inspection.

spotless *adj* 1 perfectly clean. 2 free from moral flaws: *a spotless reputation.* **spotlessly** *adv*

spotlight *n* 1 a powerful light focused so as to light up a small area. 2 **the spotlight** the centre of attention: *the spotlight moved to the president.* ~*vb* **-lighting, -lit** *or* **-lighted** 3 to direct a spotlight on (something). 4 to focus attention on (something).

spot-on *adj Brit informal* absolutely correct; very accurate: *they're spot-on in terms of style.*

spotted *adj* 1 having a pattern of spots. 2 marked with stains.

spotted dick *n Brit* suet pudding containing dried fruit.

spotter *n* a person whose hobby is watching for and noting numbers or types of trains or planes.

spotty *adj* **-tier, -tiest** 1 covered with spots or pimples. 2 not consistent; irregular in quality: *a rather spotty performance.* **spottiness** *n*

spouse *n* a person's partner in marriage.

spout *vb* 1 (of a liquid or flames) to pour out in a stream or jet. 2 *Informal* to talk about (something) in a boring way or without much thought. ~*n* 3 a projecting tube or lip for pouring liquids. 4 a stream or jet of liquid. 5 **up the spout** *Slang* **a** ruined or lost: *the motor industry is up the spout.* **b** pregnant.

spouting *n NZ* **a** a rainwater downpipe on the outside of a building. **b** such pipes collectively.

sprain *vb* 1 to injure (a joint) by a sudden twist. ~*n* 2 this injury, which causes swelling and temporary disability.

sprang *vb* a past tense of **spring.**

sprat *n* a small edible fish like a herring.

sprawl *vb* 1 to sit or lie with one's arms and legs spread out. 2 to spread out untidily over a large area: *the pulp mill sprawled over the narrow flats.* ~*n* 3 the part of a city or town that has not been planned and spreads out untidily over a large area: *the huge Los Angeles sprawl.* **sprawling** *adj*

spray[1] *n* 1 fine drops of a liquid. 2 **a** a liquid under pressure designed to be discharged in fine drops from an aerosol or atomizer: *hair spray.* **b** the aerosol or atomizer itself. 3 a number of small objects flying through the air: *a spray of bullets.* ~*vb* 4 to scatter in fine drops. 5 to squirt (a liquid) from an aerosol or atomizer. 6 to cover with a spray: *spray the crops.*

spray[2] *n* 1 a sprig or branch with buds, leaves, flowers, or berries. 2 an ornament or design like this.

spray gun *n* a device for spraying fine drops of paint, etc.

spread *vb* **spreading, spread** 1 to open out or unfold to the fullest width: *spread the material out.* 2 to extend over a larger expanse: *the subsequent unrest spread countrywide.* 3 to apply as a coating: *spread the paste evenly over your skin.* 4 to be displayed to its fullest extent: *the shining bay spread out below.* 5 to send or be sent out in all directions or to many people: *the news spread quickly; the sandflies that spread the disease.* 6 to distribute or be distributed evenly: *we were advised to spread the workload over the whole year.* ~*n* 7 a spreading; distribution, dispersion, or expansion: *the spread of higher education.* 8 *Informal* a large meal. 9 *Informal* the wingspan of an aircraft or bird. 10 *Informal, chiefly US & Canad* a ranch or other large area of land. 11 a soft food which can be spread: *cheese spread.* 12 two facing pages in a book or magazine. 13 a widening of the hips and waist: *middle-age spread.*

spread-eagled *adj* with arms and legs outstretched.

spree *n* a session of overindulgence, usually in drinking or spending money.

sprig *n* 1 a shoot, twig, or sprout. 2 an ornamental device like this. **sprigged** *adj*

sprightly *adj* **-lier, -liest** lively and active. **sprightliness** *n*

THESAURUS

riment, mirth, raillery, teasing ~*vb.* 3. *informal* display, exhibit, show off, wear

sporting fair, game (*informal*), gentlemanly, sportsman-like

spot *n.* 1. blemish, blot, blotch, daub, discoloration, flaw, mark, pimple, plook (*Scot.*), pustule, scar, smudge, speck, speckle, stain, taint, zit (*slang*) 2. locality, location, place, point, position, scene, site, situation 3. *informal, chiefly Brit.* bit, little, morsel, splash 4. *informal* difficulty, hot water (*informal*), mess, plight, predicament, quandary, tight spot, trouble ~*vb.* 5. catch sight of, descry, detect, discern, espy, identify, make out, observe, pick out, recognize, see, sight 6. besmirch, blot, dirty, dot, fleck, mark, mottle, scar, smirch, soil, spatter, speckle, splodge, splotch, stain, sully, taint, tarnish

spotless above reproach, blameless, chaste, clean, faultless, flawless, gleaming, immaculate, impeccable, innocent, irreproachable, pure, shining, snowy, unblemished, unimpeachable, unstained, unsullied, untarnished, virgin, virginal, white

spotlight 1. *n.* attention, fame, interest, limelight, notoriety, public attention, public eye 2. *vb.* accentuate, draw attention to, feature, focus attention on, give prominence to, highlight, illuminate, point up, throw into relief

spotted dappled, dotted, flecked, mottled, pied, polka-dot, specked, speckled

spouse better half (*humorous*), companion, consort, helpmate, husband, mate, partner, wife

spout *vb.* 1. discharge, emit, erupt, gush, jet, shoot, spray, spurt, squirt, stream, surge 2. *informal* declaim, expatiate, go on (*informal*), hold forth, orate, pontificate, rabbit (on) (*Brit. informal*), ramble (on), rant, speechify, spiel (*informal*), talk

sprawl *vb.* flop, loll, lounge, ramble, slouch, slump, spread, straggle, trail

spray[1] *n.* 1. drizzle, droplets, fine mist, moisture, spindrift, spoondrift 2. aerosol, atomizer, sprinkler ~*vb.* 3. atomize, diffuse, scatter, shower, sprinkle

spray[2] *n.* bough, branch, corsage, floral arrangement, shoot, sprig

spread *vb.* 1. be displayed, bloat, broaden, dilate, expand, extend, fan out, open, open out, sprawl, stretch, swell, unfold, unfurl, unroll, widen 2. escalate, multiply, mushroom, proliferate 3. advertise, blazon, broadcast, bruit, cast, circulate, cover, diffuse, disseminate, distribute, make known, make public, proclaim, promulgate, propagate, publicize, publish, radiate, scatter, shed, strew, transmit ~*n.* 4. advance, advancement, development, diffusion, dispersion, dissemination, escalation, expansion, increase, proliferation, spreading, suffusion, transmission 5. *informal* array, banquet, blowout (*slang*), feast, repast

spree beano (*Brit. slang*), bender (*informal*), binge (*informal*), carousal, debauch, fling, jag (*slang*), junketing, orgy, revel, splurge

spring *vb* **springing, sprang** *or* **sprung; sprung 1** to jump suddenly upwards or forwards. **2** to return or be returned into natural shape from a forced position by elasticity: *the coil sprang back.* **3** to cause (something) to happen unexpectedly: *the national coach sprang a surprise.* **4** (usually foll. by *from*) to originate; be descended: *this motivation springs from their inborn curiosity; Truman sprang from ordinary people.* **5** (often foll. by *up*) to come into being or appear suddenly: *new courses will spring up.* **6** to provide (something, such as a mattress) with springs. **7** *Informal* to arrange the escape of (someone) from prison. *~n* **8** the season between winter and summer. **9** a leap or jump. **10** a coil which can be compressed, stretched, or bent and then return to its original shape when released. **11** a natural pool forming the source of a stream. **12** elasticity. **springlike** *adj*

spring balance *or esp US* **spring scale** *n* a device that indicates the weight of an object by the extension of a spring to which the object is attached.

springboard *n* **1** a flexible board used to gain height or momentum in diving or gymnastics. **2** anything that makes it possible for an activity to begin: *the meeting acted as a springboard for future negotiations.*

springbok *n, pl* **-bok** *or* **-boks 1** a S African antelope which moves in leaps. **2** a person who has represented S Africa in a national sports team.

spring chicken *n* **1** *Chiefly US* a young chicken, which is tender for cooking. **2 he** *or* **she is no spring chicken** *Informal* he *or* she is no longer young.

spring-clean *vb* **1** to clean (a house) thoroughly, traditionally at the end of winter. *~n* **2** an instance of this. **spring-cleaning** *n*

spring onion *n* a small onion with a tiny bulb and long green leaves, eaten in salads.

spring roll *n* an Oriental dish consisting of a savoury mixture rolled in a thin pancake and fried.

spring tide *n* either of the two tides at or just after new moon and full moon: the greatest rise and fall in tidal level.

springtime *n* the season of spring.

springy *adj* **springier, springiest** (of an object) having the quality of returning to its original shape after being pressed or pulled. **springiness** *n*

sprinkle *vb* **-kling, -kled 1** to scatter (liquid or powder) in tiny drops over (something). **2** to distribute over (something): *a dozen mud huts sprinkled around it.* **sprinkler** *n*

sprinkling *n* a small quantity or amount: *a sprinkling of diamonds.*

sprint *n* **1** *Athletics* **a** a short race run at top speed. **b** a fast run at the end of a longer race. **2** any quick run. *~vb* **3** to run or cycle a short distance at top speed. **sprinter** *n*

sprit *n Naut* a light pole set diagonally across a sail to extend it.

sprite *n* (in folklore) a fairy or elf.

spritsail *n Naut* a sail mounted on a sprit.

spritzer *n* a tall drink of wine and soda water.

sprocket *n* **1** Also called: **sprocket wheel** a wheel with teeth on the rim, that drives or is driven by a chain. **2** a cylindrical wheel with teeth on one or both rims for pulling film through a camera or projector.

sprout *vb* **1** (of a plant or seed) to produce (new leaves or shoots). **2** (often foll. by *up*) to begin to grow or develop. *~n* **3** a new shoot or bud. **4** same as **Brussels sprout.**

spruce[1] *n* **1** an evergreen pyramid-shaped tree with needle-like leaves. **2** the light-coloured wood of this tree.

spruce[2] *adj* neat and smart.

spruce up *vb* **sprucing, spruced** to make neat and smart.

sprung *vb* a past tense and the past participle of **spring.**

spry *adj* **spryer, spryest** *or* **sprier, spriest** active and lively; nimble.

spud *n Informal* a potato.

spume *n Literary* **1** foam or froth on the sea. *~vb* **spuming, spumed 2** (of the sea) to foam or froth.

spun *vb* **1** the past of **spin.** *~adj* **2** made by spinning: *spun sugar; spun silk.*

spunk *n Old-fashioned, informal* courage or spirit. **spunky** *adj*

spur *n* **1** an incentive to get something done. **2** a sharp spiked wheel on the heel of a rider's boot used to urge the horse on. **3** a sharp horny part sticking out from a cock's leg. **4** a ridge sticking out from a mountain side. **5 on the spur of the moment** suddenly and without planning; on impulse. **6 win one's spurs** to prove one's ability. *~vb* **spurring, spurred 7** (often foll. by *on*) to encourage (someone).

spurge *n* a plant with milky sap and small flowers.

spurious *adj* not genuine or real.

spurn *vb* to reject (a person or thing) with contempt.

THESAURUS

sprightly active, agile, airy, alert, animated, blithe, brisk, cheerful, energetic, frolicsome, gay, jaunty, joyous, lively, nimble, perky, playful, spirited, sportive, spry, vivacious

spring *vb.* **1.** bounce, bound, hop, jump, leap, rebound, recoil, vault **2.** *usually with* **from** arise, be derived, be descended, come, derive, descend, emanate, emerge, grow, issue, originate, proceed, start, stem **3.** *with* **up** appear, burgeon, come into existence *or* being, develop, mushroom, shoot up *~n.* **4.** bound, buck, hop, jump, leap, saltation, vault **5.** bounce, bounciness, buoyancy, elasticity, flexibility, give (*informal*), recoil, resilience, springiness

sprinkle *vb.* dredge, dust, pepper, powder, scatter, shower, spray, strew

sprinkling admixture, dash, dusting, few, handful, scatter, scattering, smattering, sprinkle

sprint *vb.* dart, dash, go at top speed, hare (*Brit. informal*), hotfoot, put on a burst of speed, race, scamper, shoot, tear, whizz (*informal*)

sprite apparition, brownie, dryad, elf, fairy, goblin, imp, leprechaun, naiad, nymph, Oceanid (*Greek myth.*), peri, pixie, spirit, sylph

sprout *vb.* bud, develop, germinate, grow, push, shoot, spring, vegetate

spruce as if one had just stepped out of a bandbox, dainty, dapper, elegant, natty (*informal*), neat, smart, soigné *or fem.* soignée, trim, well-groomed, well turned out

spry active, agile, alert, brisk, nimble, nippy (*Brit. informal*), quick, ready, sprightly, supple

spur *n.* **1.** impetus, impulse, incentive, incitement, inducement, motive, stimulus **2.** goad, prick, rowel **3. on the spur of the moment** impetuously, impromptu, impulsively, on impulse, on the spot, unpremeditatedly, unthinkingly, without planning, without thinking *~vb.* **4.** animate, drive, goad, impel, incite, press, prick, prod, prompt, stimulate, urge

spurious artificial, bogus, contrived, counterfeit, deceitful, ersatz, fake, false, feigned, forged, imitation, mock, phoney (*informal*), pretended, pseudo (*informal*), sham, simulated, specious, unauthentic

spurn cold-shoulder, contemn, despise, disdain, dis-

spurt *vb* **1** to gush or cause (something) to gush out in a sudden powerful stream or jet. **2** to make a sudden effort. ~*n* **3** a short burst of activity, speed, or energy. **4** a sudden powerful stream or jet.

sputnik *n* a Russian artificial satellite.

sputter *vb, n* same as **splutter.**

sputum *n, pl* **-ta** saliva, usually mixed with mucus.

spy *n, pl* **spies 1** a person employed to find out secret information about other countries or organizations. **2** a person who secretly keeps watch on others. ~*vb* **spies, spying, spied 3** (foll. by *on*) to keep a secret watch on someone. **4** to work as a spy. **5** to catch sight of (someone or something); notice.

spyglass *n* a small telescope.

spy out *vb* to discover (something) secretly.

sq. square.

Sqn. Ldr. squadron leader.

squab *n, pl* **squabs** *or* **squab** a young bird yet to leave the nest.

squabble *vb* **-bling, -bled 1** to quarrel over a small matter. ~*n* **2** a petty quarrel.

squad *n* **1** the smallest military formation, usually a dozen soldiers. **2** any small group of people working together: *the fraud squad.* **3** *Sport* a number of players from which a team is to be selected.

squadron *n* the basic unit of an air force.

squadron leader *n* a fairly senior commissioned officer in the air force; the rank above flight lieutenant.

squalid *adj* **1** dirty, untidy, and in bad condition. **2** unpleasant, selfish, and often dishonest: *this squalid affair.*

squall[1] *n* a sudden strong wind or short violent storm.

squall[2] *vb* **1** to cry noisily; yell. ~*n* **2** a noisy cry or yell.

squalor *n* **1** dirty, poor, and untidy physical conditions. **2** the condition of being squalid.

squander *vb* to waste (money or resources).

square *n* **1** a geometric figure with four equal sides and four right angles. **2** anything of this shape. **3** an open area in a town bordered by buildings or streets. **4** *Maths* the number produced when a number is multiplied by itself: *9 is the square of 3, written* 3^2. **5** *Informal* any person who is dull or unfashionable. **6 go back to square one** to return to the start because of failure or lack of progress. ~*adj* **7** being a square in shape. **8 a** having the same area as that of a square with sides of a specified length: *a circle of four square feet.* **b** denoting a square having a specified length on each side: *a box four feet square.* **9** straight or level: *I don't think that painting is square.* **10** fair and honest: *a square deal.* **11** *Informal* dull or unfashionable. **12** having all debts or accounts settled: *if I give you 50 pence, then we'll be square.* **13 all square** on equal terms; even in score. **14 square peg in a round hole** *Informal* a misfit. ~*vb* **squaring, squared 15** *Maths* to multiply (a number or quantity) by itself. **16** to position so as to be straight or level: *bravely he squared his shoulders.* **17** to settle (a debt or account). **18** to level the score in (a game). **19** to be or cause to be consistent: *it would not have squared with her image.* ~*adv* **20** *Informal* same as **squarely.** ~See also **square off, square up.**

square-bashing *n Brit mil slang* marching and other drill on a parade ground.

square bracket *n* either of a pair of characters [ ], used to separate a section of writing or printing from the main text.

square dance *n* a country dance in which the couples are arranged in squares.

square leg *n Cricket* a fielding position on the on side, at right angles to the batsman.

squarely *adv* **1** directly; straight: *he looked her squarely in the eye.* **2** in an honest and frank way: *you should face squarely anything that worries you.*

square meal *n* a meal which is large enough to leave the eater feeling full: *we gave him his first square meal in days.*

square off *vb* to stand up as if ready to start boxing or fighting.

square-rigged *adj Naut* having sails set at right angles to the keel.

square root *n* a number that when multiplied by itself gives a given number: *the square roots of 4 are 2 and −2.*

square up *vb* **1** to settle bills or debts. **2 square up to** to prepare to confront (a problem or a person).

squash[1] *vb* **1** to press or squeeze (something) so as to flatten it. **2** to overcome (a difficult situation), often with force. **3 squash in** *or* **into** to push or force (oneself or a thing) into a confined space. **4** to humiliate (someone) with a sarcastic reply. ~*n* **5** *Brit* a drink made from fruit juice or fruit syrup diluted with water. **6** a crowd of people in a confined space. **7** Also called: **squash rackets** a game for two players played in an

THESAURUS

regard, put down, rebuff, reject, repulse, scorn, slight, snub, turn one's nose up at (*informal*)

spurt 1. *vb.* burst, erupt, gush, jet, shoot, spew, squirt, surge **2.** *n.* access, burst, fit, rush, spate, surge

spy *n.* **1.** double agent, fifth columnist, foreign agent, mole, nark (*slang*), secret agent, secret service agent, undercover agent ~*vb.* **2.** *with* **on** follow, keep under surveillance, keep watch on, shadow, tail (*informal*), trail, watch **3.** catch sight of, descry, espy, glimpse, notice, observe, set eyes on, spot

squabble 1. *vb.* argue, bicker, brawl, clash, dispute, fall out (*informal*), fight, have words, quarrel, row, scrap (*informal*), spar, wrangle **2.** *n.* argument, barney (*informal*), difference of opinion, disagreement, dispute, fight, row, scrap (*informal*), set-to (*informal*), spat, tiff

squad band, company, crew, force, gang, group, team, troop

squalid broken-down, decayed, dirty, disgusting, fetid, filthy, foul, low, nasty, poverty-stricken, repulsive, run-down, seedy, sleazy, slovenly, slummy, sordid, unclean, yucky *or* yukky (*slang*)

squalor decay, filth, foulness, meanness, sleaziness, slumminess, squalidness, wretchedness

squander be prodigal with, blow (*slang*), consume, dissipate, expend, fritter away, frivol away, lavish, misspend, misuse, run through, scatter, spend, spend like water, throw away, waste

square *n.* **1.** *informal* antediluvian, back number (*informal*), conservative, die-hard, dinosaur, fuddy-duddy (*informal*), old buffer (*Brit. informal*), (old) fogey, stick-in-the-mud (*informal*), traditionalist ~*adj.* **2.** above board, decent, equitable, ethical, fair, fair and square, genuine, honest, just, kosher (*informal*), on the level (*informal*), on the up and up, straight, straightforward, upfront (*informal*), upright **3.** *informal* behind the times, bourgeois, conservative, conventional, old-fashioned, out-of-date, straight (*slang*), strait-laced, stuffy ~*vb.* **4.** accommodate, adapt, adjust, align, even up, level, regulate, suit, tailor, true (up) **5.** *often with* **with** accord, agree, conform, correspond, fit, harmonize, match, reconcile, tally

square up balance, clear (up), discharge, liquidate, make even, pay off, quit, satisfy, settle

enclosed court with a small rubber ball and long-handled rackets.

squash[2] *n, pl* **squashes** *or* **squash** *US & Canad* a marrow-like vegetable.

squashy *adj* **squashier, squashiest** soft and easily squashed.

squat *vb* **squatting, squatted 1** to crouch with the knees bent and the weight on the feet. **2** *Law* to occupy an unused building to which one has no legal right. *~adj* **3** short and thick. *~n* **4** a building occupied by squatters.

squatter *n* an illegal occupier of an unused building.

squaw *n Offensive* a North American Indian woman.

squawk *n* **1** a loud harsh cry, esp. one made by a bird. **2** *Informal* a loud complaint. *~vb* **3** to make a squawk.

squeak *n* **1** a short high-pitched cry or sound. **2 a narrow squeak** *Informal* a narrow escape or success. *~vb* **3** to make a squeak. **4 squeak through** *or* **by** to pass (an examination), but only just. **squeaky** *adj* **squeakiness** *n*

squeal *n* **1** a long high-pitched yelp. *~vb* **2** to make a squeal. **3** *Slang* to inform on someone to the police. **4** *Informal, chiefly Brit* to complain loudly. **squealer** *n*

squeamish *adj* easily shocked or upset by unpleasant sights or events.

squeegee *n* a tool with a rubber blade used for wiping away excess water from a surface.

squeeze *vb* **squeezing, squeezed 1** to grip or press (something) firmly. **2** to crush or press (something) so as to extract (a liquid): *squeeze the tomato and strain the juice; freshly squeezed lemon juice.* **3** to push (oneself or a thing) into a confined space. **4** to hug (someone) closely. **5** to obtain (something) by great effort or force: *to squeeze the last dollar out of every deal.* *~n* **6** a squeezing. **7** a hug. **8** a crush of people in a confined space. **9** *Chiefly Brit* a restriction on borrowing made by a government to control price inflation. **10** an amount extracted by squeezing: *a squeeze of lime.* **11 put the squeeze on someone** *Informal* to put pressure on someone in order to obtain something.

squelch *vb* **1** to make a wet sucking noise, such as by walking through mud. **2** *Informal* to silence (someone) with a sarcastic or wounding reply. *~n* **3** a squelching sound. **squelchy** *adj*

squib *n* **1** a firework that burns with a hissing noise before exploding. **2 damp squib** something expected to be exciting or successful but turning out to be a disappointment.

squid *n, pl* **squid** *or* **squids** a sea creature with ten tentacles and a long soft body.

squiffy *adj* **-fier, -fiest** *Brit informal* slightly drunk.

squiggle *n* a wavy line. **squiggly** *adj*

squill *n* a Mediterranean plant of the lily family.

squint *vb* **1** to have eyes which face in different directions. **2** to glance sideways. *~n* **3** an eye disorder in which one or both eyes turn inwards or outwards from the nose. **4** *Informal* a quick look; glance: *take a squint at the map.* *~adj* **5** *Informal* not straight; crooked.

squire *n* **1** a country gentleman in England, usually the main landowner in a country community. **2** *Informal, chiefly Brit* a term of address used by one man to another. **3** *History* a knight's young attendant. *~vb* **squiring, squired 4** *Old-fashioned* (of a man) to escort (a woman).

squirm *vb* **1** to wriggle. **2** to feel embarrassed or guilty. *~n* **3** a wriggling movement.

squirrel *n* a small bushy-tailed animal that lives in trees.

squirt *vb* **1** to force (a liquid) or (of a liquid) to be forced out of a narrow opening. **2** to cover or spatter (a person or thing) with liquid in this way. *~n* **3** a jet of liquid. **4** a squirting. **5** *Informal* a small or insignificant person.

squish *vb* **1** to crush (something) with a soft squelching sound. **2** to make a squelching sound. *~n* **3** a soft squelching sound. **squishy** *adj*

Sr 1 (after a name) senior. **2** Señor. **3** *Chem* strontium.

Sri Lankan *adj* **1** of Sri Lanka. *~n* **2** a person from Sri Lanka.

SRN (formerly in Britain) State Registered Nurse.

SS 1 an organization in the Nazi party that provided Hitler's bodyguard, security forces, and concentration-camp guards. **2** steamship.

St 1 Saint. **2** Street.

st. stone.

stab *vb* **stabbing, stabbed 1** to pierce with a sharp pointed instrument. **2** (often foll. by *at*) to make a thrust (at); jab. **3 stab someone in the back** to do harm to someone by betraying him or her. *~n* **4** a stabbing. **5** a sudden, usually unpleasant, sensation: *a stab of jealousy.* **6** *Informal* an attempt: *you've got to have a stab at it.* **7 stab in the back** an act of betrayal that harms a person. **stabbing** *n*

THESAURUS

squash *vb.* **1.** compress, crush, distort, flatten, mash, pound, press, pulp, smash, stamp on, trample down **2.** annihilate, crush, humiliate, put down (*slang*), put (someone) in his *or* her place, quash, quell, silence, sit on (*informal*), suppress

squawk *vb.* **1.** cackle, crow, cry, hoot, screech, yelp **2.** *informal* complain, kick up a fuss (*informal*), protest, raise Cain (*slang*), squeal (*informal, chiefly Brit.*)

squeak *vb.* peep, pipe, shrill, squeal, whine, yelp

squeal *n.* **1.** scream, screech, shriek, wail, yell, yelp, yowl *~vb.* **2.** scream, screech, shout, shriek, shrill, wail, yelp **3.** *slang* betray, blab, grass (*Brit. slang*), inform on, rat on (*informal*), sell (someone) down the river (*informal*), shop (*slang, chiefly Brit.*), sing (*slang, chiefly U.S.*), snitch (*slang*), spill one's guts (*slang*), tell all **4.** *informal,chiefly Brit.* complain, kick up a fuss (*informal*), moan, protest, squawk (*informal*)

squeamish delicate, fastidious, finicky, nice (*rare*), particular, prissy (*informal*), prudish, punctilious, scrupulous, strait-laced

squeeze *vb.* **1.** clutch, compress, crush, grip, nip, pinch, press, squash, wring **2.** cram, crowd, force, jam, jostle, pack, press, ram, stuff, thrust, wedge **3.** clasp, cuddle, embrace, enfold, hold tight, hug **4.** bleed (*informal*), bring pressure to bear on, extort, lean on (*informal*), milk, oppress, pressurize, put the screws on (*informal*), put the squeeze on (*informal*), wrest *~n.* **5.** clasp, embrace, handclasp, hold, hug **6.** congestion, crowd, crush, jam, press, squash

squire *vb. old-fashioned* accompany, attend, companion, escort

squirm agonize, fidget, flounder, shift, twist, wiggle, wriggle, writhe

stab *vb.* **1.** bayonet, cut, gore, impale, injure, jab, knife, pierce, puncture, run through, spear, stick, thrust, transfix, wound **2. stab someone in the back** betray, break faith with, deceive, do the dirty on (*Brit. slang*), double-cross (*informal*), give the Judas kiss to, inform on, let down, play false, sell, sell out (*informal*), slander *~n.* **3.** gash, incision, jab, puncture, rent, thrust, wound **4.** ache, pang, prick, twinge **5.** *informal* attempt, endeavour, essay, give it one's best shot (*informal*), have a go (crack (*informal*), shot (*informal*),

stability *n* the quality of being stable: *the security and stability of married life.*

stabilize *or* **-lise** *vb* **-lizing, -lized** *or* **-lising, -lised** to make or become stable or more stable. **stabilization** *or* **-lisation** *n*

stabilizer *or* **-liser** *n* **1** a device for stabilizing a child's bicycle, an aircraft, or a ship. **2** a substance added to food to preserve its texture.

stable[1] *n* **1** a building where horses are kept. **2** an organization that breeds and trains racehorses. **3** an organization that manages or trains several entertainers or athletes. *~vb* **-bling, -bled 4** to put or keep (a horse) in a stable.

stable[2] *adj* **1** steady in position or balance; firm. **2** lasting and not likely to experience any sudden changes: *a stable environment.* **3** having a calm personality; not moody. **4** *Physics* (of an elementary particle) not subject to decay. **5** *Chem* (of a chemical compound) not easily decomposed.

staccato (stak-**ah**-toe) *adj* **1** *Music* (of notes) short and separate. **2** consisting of short abrupt sounds: *the staccato sound of high-heels on the stairs.* *~adv* **3** in a staccato manner.

stack *n* **1** a pile of things, one on top of the other. **2** a large neat pile of hay or straw. **3 stacks** a large amount: *there's still stacks for us to do.* **4** same as **chimney stack** or **smokestack. 5** an area in a computer memory for temporary storage. *~vb* **6** to place (things) in a stack. **7** to load or fill (something) up with piles of objects: *Henry was watching her stack the dishwasher.* **8** to control (a number of aircraft) waiting to land at an airport so that each flies at a different altitude.

stack up *vb* to compare with someone or something else: *how does this stack up against what you have?*

stadium *n, pl* **-diums** *or* **-dia** a large sports arena with tiered rows of seats for spectators.

staff *n, pl for senses 1 & 2* **staffs;** *for senses 3 & 4* **staffs** *or* **staves 1** the people employed in a company, school, or organization. **2** *Mil* the officers appointed to assist a commander. **3** a stick with some special use, such as a walking stick or an emblem of authority. **4** *Music* a set of five horizontal lines on which music is written and which, along with a clef, indicates pitch. *~vb* **5** to provide (a company, school, or organization) with a staff.

staff nurse *n* a qualified nurse ranking just below a sister or charge nurse.

Staffs Staffordshire.

staff sergeant *n Mil* a noncommissioned officer in an army or in the US Air Force or Marine Corps.

stag *n* the adult male of a deer.

stag beetle *n* a beetle with large branched jaws.

stage *n* **1** a step or period of development, growth, or progress. **2** the platform in a theatre where actors perform. **3 the stage** the theatre as a profession. **4** the scene of an event or action. **5** a part of a journey: *the last stage of his tour around France.* **6** short for **stagecoach. 7** *Brit* a division of a bus route for which there is a fixed fare. *~vb* **staging, staged 8** to present (a dramatic production) on stage: *to stage "Hamlet".* **9** to organize and carry out (an event).

stagecoach *n* a large four-wheeled horse-drawn vehicle formerly used to carry passengers and mail on a regular route.

stage direction *n* an instruction to an actor, written into the script of a play.

stage door *n* a door at a theatre leading backstage.

stage fright *n* feelings of fear and nervousness felt by a person about to appear in front of an audience.

stagehand *n* a person who sets the stage and moves props in a theatre.

stage-manage *vb* **-managing, -managed** to arrange (an event) from behind the scenes.

stage manager *n* a person who supervises the stage arrangements of a production at a theatre.

stage-struck *adj* having a great desire to act.

stage whisper *n* **1** a loud whisper from an actor, intended to be heard by the audience. **2** any loud whisper that is intended to be overheard.

stagflation *n* inflation combined with stagnant or falling output and employment.

stagger *vb* **1** to walk unsteadily. **2** to amaze or shock (someone): *it staggered her that there was any liaison between them.* **3** to arrange (events) so as not to happen at the same time: *staggered elections.* *~n* **4** a staggering. **staggering** *adj* **staggeringly** *adv*

staggers *n* a disease of horses and other domestic animals that causes staggering.

staging *n* a temporary support used in building.

stagnant *adj* **1** (of water) stale from not moving. **2** unsuccessful or dull from lack of change or development.

stagnate *vb* **-nating, -nated** to become inactive or unchanging: *people in old age only stagnate when they have no interests.* **stagnation** *n*

stag night *or* **party** *n* a party for men only, held for a man who is about to get married.

stagy *or US* **stagey** *adj* **stagier, stagiest** too theatrical or dramatic.

staid *adj* serious, rather dull, and old-fashioned in behaviour or appearance.

stain *vb* **1** to discolour (something) with marks that are not easily removed. **2** to dye (something) with a lasting pigment. *~n* **3** a mark or discoloration that is not easily removed. **4** an incident in someone's life

THESAURUS

stab (*informal*)) (*informal*), try, try one's hand at, venture

stability constancy, durability, firmness, permanence, solidity, soundness, steadfastness, steadiness, strength

stable abiding, constant, deep-rooted, durable, enduring, established, fast, firm, fixed, immovable, immutable, invariable, lasting, permanent, reliable, secure, sound, staunch, steadfast, steady, strong, sturdy, sure, unalterable, unchangeable, unwavering, well-founded

stack 1. *n.* clamp (*Brit. agriculture*), cock, heap, hoard, load, mass, mound, mountain, pile **2.** *vb.* accumulate, amass, assemble, bank up, heap up, load, pile, stockpile

staff *n.* **1.** employees, lecturers, officers, organization, personnel, teachers, team, workers, workforce **2.** cane, crook, pole, prop, rod, sceptre, stave, wand

stage 1. *n.* division, juncture, lap, leg, length, level, period, phase, point, step **2.** *vb.* arrange, do, engineer, give, lay on, mount, orchestrate, organize, perform, play, present, produce, put on

stagger *vb.* **1.** falter, hesitate, lurch, reel, sway, teeter, totter, vacillate, waver, wobble **2.** amaze, astonish, astound, bowl over (*informal*), confound, dumbfound, flabbergast, give (someone) a shock, nonplus, overwhelm, shake, shock, strike (someone) dumb, stun, stupefy, surprise, take (someone) aback, take (someone's) breath away, throw off balance **3.** alternate, overlap, step, zigzag

stagnant brackish, motionless, quiet, sluggish, stale, standing, still

stagnate decay, decline, deteriorate, fester, go to seed, idle, languish, lie fallow, rot, rust, stand still, vegetate

that has damaged his or her reputation: *a stain on his character.* **5** a liquid used to penetrate the surface of a material, such as wood, and colour it without covering up the surface or grain.

stained glass *n* glass that has been coloured for artistic purposes.

stainless steel *n* a type of steel that does not rust, as it contains large amounts of chromium.

stair *n* **1** one step in a flight of stairs. **2** a series of steps: *he fled down the back stair.* See also **stairs.**

staircase *n* a flight of stairs, usually with a handrail or banisters.

stairs *pl n* a flight of steps going from one level to another, usually indoors.

stairway *n* a staircase.

stairwell *n* a vertical shaft in a building that contains a staircase.

stake[1] *n* **1** a stick or metal bar driven into the ground as part of a fence or as a support or marker. **2 be burned at the stake** to be executed by being tied to a stake in the centre of a pile of wood that is then set on fire. *~vb* **staking, staked 3** to lay (a claim) to land or rights. **4** to support (something, such as a plant) with a stake.

stake[2] *n* **1** the money that a player must risk in order to take part in a gambling game or make a bet. **2** an interest, usually financial, held in something: *a 50% stake in a new consortium.* **3 at stake** at risk. **4 stakes a** the money that a player has available for gambling. **b** a prize in a race or contest. **c** a horse race in which all owners of competing horses contribute to the prize. *~vb* **staking, staked 5** to risk (something, such as money) on a result. **6** to give financial support to (a business).

stakeout *n* **1** *Slang, chiefly US & Canad* a police surveillance of an area or house. *~vb* **stake out 2** *Slang, chiefly US & Canad* to keep an area or house under surveillance. **3** to surround (a piece of land) with stakes.

stalactite *n* an icicle-shaped mass of calcium carbonate hanging from the roof of a cave: formed by continually dripping water.

stalagmite *n* a large pointed mass of calcium carbonate sticking up from the floor of a cave: formed by continually dripping water from a stalactite.

stale *adj* **1** (esp. of food) no longer fresh, having being kept too long. **2** (of air) stagnant and having an unpleasant smell. **3** lacking in enthusiasm or ideas through overwork or lack of variety. **4** uninteresting from having been done or seen too many times: *such achievements now seem stale today.* **5** no longer new: *her war had become stale news.* **staleness** *n*

stalemate *n* **1** a chess position in which any of a player's moves would place his king in check: in this position the game ends in a draw. **2** a situation in which further action by two opposing forces is impossible or will not achieve anything; deadlock.

Stalinism *n* the policies associated with Joseph Stalin, general secretary of the Communist Party of the Soviet Union 1922–53, which resulted in rapid industrialization, state terror as a means of political control, and the abolition of collective leadership. **Stalinist** *n, adj*

stalk[1] *n* **1** the main stem of a plant. **2** a stem that joins a leaf or flower to the main stem of a plant.

stalk[2] *vb* **1** to follow (an animal or person) quietly and secretly in order to catch or kill them. **2** to pursue persistently and, sometimes, attack (a person with whom one is obsessed, often a celebrity). **3** to spread over (a place) in a menacing way: *danger stalked the streets.* **4** to walk in an angry, arrogant, or stiff way.

stalking-horse *n* something or someone used to hide a true purpose; pretext.

stall[1] *n* **1** a small stand for the display and sale of goods. **2** a compartment in a stable or shed for a single animal. **3** any small room or compartment: *a shower stall.* *~vb* **4** to stop (a motor vehicle or its engine) or (of a motor vehicle or its engine) to stop, by incorrect use of the clutch or incorrect adjustment of the fuel mixture.

stall[2] *vb* to employ delaying tactics towards (someone); be evasive.

stallion *n* an uncastrated male horse, usually used for breeding.

stalls *n* **1** *Brit* the seats on the ground floor of a theatre or cinema. **2** (in a church) a row of seats, divided by armrests or a small screen, for the choir or clergy.

stalwart (**stawl**-wart) *adj* **1** strong and sturdy. **2** loyal and reliable. *~n* **3** a hard-working and loyal supporter.

stamen *n* the part of a flower that produces pollen.

stamina *n* energy and strength sustained while performing an activity over a long time.

stammer *vb* **1** to speak or say (something) with involuntary pauses or repetition, as a result of a speech disorder or through fear or nervousness. *~n* **2** a speech disorder characterized by involuntary repetitions and pauses.

stamp *n* **1** a printed paper label attached to a piece of mail to show that the required postage has been paid. **2** a token issued by a shop or business after a purchase that can be saved and exchanged for other goods sold by that shop or business. **3** the action or an act of stamping. **4** an instrument for stamping a design or words. **5** a design, device, or mark that has been stamped. **6** a characteristic feature: *the stamp of inevitability.* **7** *Brit informal* a national insurance contribution, formerly recorded by a stamp on an official card.

THESAURUS

staid calm, composed, decorous, demure, grave, quiet, sedate, self-restrained, serious, sober, solemn, steady

stain *vb.* **1.** blemish, blot, colour, dirty, discolour, dye, mark, smirch, soil, spot, tarnish, tinge *~n.* **2.** blemish, blot, discoloration, dye, smirch, spot, tint **3.** blemish, blot on the escutcheon, disgrace, dishonour, infamy, reproach, shame, slur, stigma

stake[1] *n.* **1.** pale, paling, palisade, picket, pole, post, spike, stave, stick *~vb.* **2.** define, delimit, demarcate, lay claim to, mark out, outline, reserve **3.** brace, prop, secure, support, tether, tie up

stake[2] *n.* **1.** ante, bet, chance, hazard, peril, pledge, risk, venture, wager **2.** claim, concern, interest, investment, involvement, share *~vb.* **3.** bet, chance, gamble, hazard, imperil, jeopardize, pledge, put on, risk, venture, wager

stale 1. decayed, dry, faded, fetid, flat, fusty, hard, insipid, musty, old, sour, stagnant, tasteless **2.** antiquated, banal, cliché-ridden, common, commonplace, drab, effete, flat, hackneyed, insipid, old hat, overused, platitudinous, repetitious, stereotyped, threadbare, trite, unoriginal, worn-out

stalk *vb.* **1.** creep up on, follow, haunt, hunt, pursue, shadow, tail (*informal*), track **2.** flounce, march, pace, stride, strut

stalwart athletic, beefy (*informal*), brawny, daring, dependable, hefty (*informal*), husky (*informal*), indomitable, intrepid, lusty, manly, muscular, redoubtable, robust, rugged, sinewy, staunch, stout, strapping, strong, sturdy, valiant, vigorous

stamina energy, force, grit, indefatigability, lustiness, power, power of endurance, resilience, resistance, staying power, strength, vigour

8 type or class: *men of his stamp.* ~*vb* **9** (often foll. by *on*) to bring (one's foot) down heavily. **10** to walk with heavy or noisy footsteps. **11** to characterize: *a performance that stamped him as a star.* **12** **stamp on** to subdue or restrain: *all of which have stamped on dissent.* **13** to impress or mark (a pattern or sign) on. **14** to mark (something) with an official seal or device. **15** to have a strong effect on: *a picture vividly stamped on memory.* **16** to stick a stamp on (an envelope or parcel).

stampede *n* **1** a sudden rush of frightened animals or of a crowd. ~*vb* **-peding, -peded 2** to run away in a stampede.

stamping ground *n* a favourite meeting place.

stamp out *vb* **1** to put an end to (something) by force; suppress: *an attempt to stamp out democracy.* **2** to put out by stamping: *I stamped out my cigarette.*

stance *n* **1** an attitude towards a particular matter: *a tough stance in the trade talks.* **2** the manner and position in which a person stands. **3** *Sport* the position taken when about to play the ball.

stanch (**stahnch**) *vb* same as **staunch**².

stanchion *n* a vertical pole or bar used as a support.

stand *vb* **standing, stood 1** to be upright. **2** to rise to an upright position. **3** to place (something) upright. **4** to be situated: *the property stands in a prime position.* **5** to have a specified height when standing: *the structure stands sixty feet above the river.* **6** to be in a specified position: *Turkey stands to gain handsomely.* **7** to be in a specified state or condition: *how he stands in comparison to others.* **8** to remain unchanged or valid: *the Conservatives were forced to let much of the legislation stand.* **9** **stand at** (of a score or an account) to be in the specified position: *now the total stands at nine.* **10** to tolerate or bear: *Christopher can't stand him.* **11** to survive: *stand the test of time.* **12** (often foll. by *for*) *Chiefly Brit* to be a candidate: *to stand for president.* **13** *Informal* to buy: *to stand someone a drink.* **14** **stand a chance** to have a chance of succeeding. **15** **stand one's ground** to face a difficult situation bravely. **16** **stand trial** to be tried in a law court. ~*n* **17** a stall or counter selling goods: *the hot dog stand.* **18** a structure at a sports ground where people can sit or stand. **19** the act or an instance of standing. **20** a firmly held opinion: *its firm stand on sanctions.* **21** *US* a place in a law court where a witness stands. **22** a rack on which coats and hats may be hung. **23** a small table or piece of furniture where articles may be placed or stored: *an umbrella stand.* **24** an effort to defend oneself or one's beliefs against attack or criticism: *a last stand against superior forces.* **25** *Cricket* a long period at the wicket by two batsmen. **26** See **one-night stand.** ~See also **stand by, stand down,** etc.

standard *n* **1** a level of quality: *cuisine of a high standard.* **2** an accepted example of something against which others are judged or measured: *the work was good by any standard.* **3** a moral principle of behaviour. **4** a flag of a nation or cause. **5** an upright pole or beam used as a support: *a lamp standard.* **6** a song that has remained popular for many years. ~*adj* **7** of a usual, medium, or accepted kind: *a standard cost.* **8** of recognized authority: *a standard reference book.* **9** denoting pronunciations or grammar regarded as correct and acceptable by educated native speakers.

standard assessment tasks *pl n* national standardized tests for assessing school pupils.

standard-bearer *n* **1** a leader of a movement or party. **2** a person who carries a flag in battle or in a march.

standard gauge *n* **1** a railway track with a distance of 56½ inches (1.435m) between the lines: used on most railways. ~*adj* **standard-gauge 2** denoting a railway with a standard gauge.

Standard Grade *n* (in Scotland) **1** an examination designed to test skills and knowledge, replacing the O Grade. **2** a pass in an examination at this level.

standardize *or* **-ise** *vb* **-izing, -ized** *or* **-ising, -ised** to make (things) standard: *to standardize the preparation process.* **standardization** *or* **-isation** *n*

standard lamp *n* a tall electric lamp that has a shade and stands on a base.

standard of living *n* the level of comfort and wealth of a person, group, or country.

standard time *n* the official local time of a region or country determined by the distance from Greenwich of a line of longitude passing through the area.

stand by *vb* **1** to be available and ready to act if needed: *stand by for firing.* **2** to be present as an onlooker or without taking any action: *the military police stood by watching idly.* **3** to be faithful to: *his wife will stand by him.* ~*n* **stand-by 4** a person or thing that is ready for use or can be relied on in an emergency. **5** **on stand-by** ready for action or use. ~*adj* **stand-by 6** not booked in advance but subject to availability: *stand-by planes.*

stand down *vb* to resign or withdraw, often in favour of another.

stand for *vb* **1** to represent: *AIDS stands for Acquired Immune Deficiency Syndrome.* **2** to support

THESAURUS

stammer *vb.* falter, hesitate, hum and haw, pause, splutter, stumble, stutter

stamp *n.* **1.** brand, cast, earmark, hallmark, imprint, mark, mould, signature **2.** breed, cast, character, cut, description, fashion, form, kind, sort, type ~*vb.* **3.** beat, crush, trample **4.** betray, brand, categorize, exhibit, identify, label, mark, pronounce, reveal, show to be, typecast **5.** engrave, fix, impress, imprint, inscribe, mark, mould, print

stampede *n.* charge, flight, rout, rush, scattering

stamp out crush, destroy, eliminate, eradicate, extinguish, extirpate, put down, put out, quell, quench, scotch, suppress

stance 1. attitude, position, stand, standpoint, viewpoint **2.** bearing, carriage, deportment, posture

stand *vb.* **1.** be upright, be vertical, erect, mount, place, position, put, rank, rise, set **2.** be in force, belong, be situated *or* located, be valid, continue, exist, halt, hold, obtain, pause, prevail, remain, rest, stay, stop **3.** abide, allow, bear, brook, cope with, countenance, endure, experience, handle, put up with (*informal*), stomach, submit to, suffer, support, sustain, take, thole (*Scot. & N English*), tolerate, undergo, wear (*Brit. slang*), weather, withstand ~*n.* **4.** base, booth, bracket, dais, frame, grandstand, place, platform, rack, rank, stage, staging, stall, stance (*chiefly Scot.*), support, table **5.** attitude, determination, firm stand, opinion, position, stance, standpoint

standard *n.* **1.** average, benchmark, canon, criterion, example, gauge, grade, guide, guideline, measure, model, norm, par, pattern, principle, requirement, rule, sample, specification, touchstone, type, yardstick **2.** *often plural* code of honour, ethics, ideals, moral principles, morals, principles **3.** banner, colours, ensign, flag, pennant, pennon, streamer ~*adj.* **4.** accepted, average, basic, customary, normal, orthodox, popular, prevailing, regular, set, staple, stock, typical, usual **5.** approved, authoritative, classic, definitive, established, official, recognized

standardize assimilate, bring into line, institutionalize, mass-produce, regiment, stereotype

and represent (an idea or a belief): *to stand for liberty and truth.* **3** *Informal* to tolerate or bear: *I won't stand for this!*

stand in *vb* **1** to act as a substitute: *she stood in for her father.* ~*n* **stand-in 2** a person who acts as a substitute for another.

standing *adj* **1** permanent, fixed, or lasting: *it was a standing joke.* **2** used to stand in or on: *standing room only.* **3** *Athletics* (of a jump or the start of a race) begun from a standing position. ~*n* **4** social or financial status or reputation: *her international standing.* **5** duration: *a friendship of at least ten years' standing.*

standing order *n* **1** an instruction to a bank to pay a fixed amount to a person or organization at regular intervals. **2** a rule or order governing the procedure of an organization.

standoff *n* **1** *US & Canad* the act or an instance of standing off or apart. **2** a deadlock or stalemate. ~*vb* **stand off 3** to stay at a distance.

standoffish *adj* behaving in a formal and unfriendly way.

stand out *vb* **1** to be more impressive or important than others of the same kind: *his passing ability stood out in this game.* **2** to be noticeable because of looking different: *her long fair hair made her stand out from the rest.* **3** to refuse to agree or comply: *a hero who stood out against foreign domination.*

standpipe *n* a temporary vertical pipe installed in a street and supplying water when household water supplies are cut off.

standpoint *n* a point of view from which a matter is considered.

standstill *n* a complete stoppage or halt: *all traffic came to a standstill.*

stand to *vb* **1** *Mil* to take up positions in order to defend against attack. **2 stand to reason** to be obvious or logical: *it stands to reason you will play better.*

stand up *vb* **1** to rise to one's feet. **2** *Informal* to fail to keep a date with (a boyfriend or girlfriend): *sometimes he would stand me up.* **3** to be accepted as satisfactory or true: *the decision would not stand up in court.* **4 stand up for** to support or defend. **5 stand up to a** to confront or resist (someone) bravely. **b** to withstand and endure (something, such as criticism). ~*adj* **stand-up 6** (of a comedian) telling jokes alone to an audience. **7** done while standing: *a stand-up breakfast.* **8** (of a fight or row) angry and unrestrained.

stank *vb* a past tense of **stink.**

stanza *n Prosody* a verse of a poem.

staple[1] *n* **1** a short length of wire bent into a square U-shape, used to fasten papers or secure things. ~*vb* **-pling, -pled 2** to secure (things) with staples.

staple[2] *adj* **1** of prime importance; principal: *the staple diet of a country.* ~*n* **2** something that forms a main part of the product, consumption, or trade of a region. **3** a main constituent of anything: *the personal reflections which make up the staple of the book.*

stapler *n* a device used to fasten things together with a staple.

star *n* **1** a planet or meteor visible in the clear night sky as a point of light. **2** a hot gaseous mass, such as the sun, that radiates energy as heat and light, or in some cases as radio waves and x-rays. **3 stars** same as **horoscope** (sense 1). **4** an emblem with five or more radiating points, often used as a symbol of rank or an award: *the RAC awarded the hotel three stars.* **5** same as **asterisk. 6** a famous person from the sports, acting, or music professions. **7 see stars** to see flashes of light after a blow on the head. ~*vb* **starring, starred 8** to feature (an actor or actress) or (of an actor or actress) to be featured as a star: *Olivier starred in "Hamlet".* **9** to mark (something) with a star or stars.

starboard *n* **1** the right side of an aeroplane or ship when facing forwards. ~*adj* **2** of or on the starboard.

starch *n* **1** a carbohydrate forming the main food element in bread, potatoes, and rice: in solution with water it is used to stiffen fabric. **2** food containing a large amount of starch. ~*vb* **3** to stiffen (cloth) with starch.

starchy *adj* **starchier, starchiest 1** of or containing starch. **2** (of a person's behaviour) very formal and humourless.

star-crossed *adj* (of lovers) destined to misfortune.

stardom *n* the status of a star in the entertainment or sport world.

stare *vb* **staring, stared 1** (often foll. by *at*) to look at for a long time. **2 stare one in the face** to be glaringly obvious. ~*n* **3** a long fixed look.

starfish *n, pl* **-fish** *or* **-fishes** a star-shaped sea creature with a flat body and five limbs.

star fruit *n* same as **carambola.**

stargazer *n Informal* an astrologer. **stargazing** *n*

stark *adj* **1** harsh, unpleasant, and plain: *a stark choice.* **2** grim, desolate, and lacking any beautiful features: *the stark landscapes.* **3** utter; absolute: *in stark contrast.* ~*adv* **4** completely: *stark staring bonkers.* **starkly** *adv* **starkness** *n*

stark-naked *adj* completely naked. Also (informal): **starkers**

starlet *n* a young actress who has the potential to become a star.

THESAURUS

stand by 1. be prepared, wait, wait in the wings **2.** back, befriend, be loyal to, champion, defend, stick up for (*informal*), support, take (someone's) part, uphold

stand for 1. betoken, denote, exemplify, indicate, mean, represent, signify, symbolize **2.** *informal* bear, brook, endure, lie down under (*informal*), put up with, suffer, tolerate, wear (*Brit. informal*)

standing *adj.* **1.** fixed, lasting, permanent, perpetual, regular, repeated ~*n.* **2.** condition, credit, eminence, estimation, footing, position, rank, reputation, repute, station, status **3.** continuance, duration, existence, experience

stand out attract attention, be highlighted, be prominent (conspicuous, distinct, obvious, striking), be thrown into relief, bulk large, catch the eye, leap to the eye, project, stare one in the face (*informal*), stick out a mile (*informal*)

standpoint angle, point of view, position, post, stance, station, vantage point, viewpoint

stand up for champion, come to the defence of, defend, side with, stick up for (*informal*), support, uphold

star celeb (*informal*), celebrity, draw, idol, lead, leading man *or* lady, luminary, main attraction, megastar (*informal*), name

stare *vb.* gape, gawk, gawp (*Brit. slang*), gaze, goggle, look, ogle, rubberneck (*U.S. slang*), watch

stark *adj.* **1.** austere, bare, barren, bleak, cold, depressing, desolate, drear (*literary*), dreary, forsaken, godforsaken, grim, hard, harsh, plain, severe, solitary, unadorned **2.** absolute, arrant, bald, bare, blunt, consummate, downright, entire, flagrant, out-and-out, palpable, patent, pure, sheer, simple, unalloyed, unmitigated, utter ~*adv.* **3.** absolutely, altogether, clean (*not standard*), completely, entirely, quite, utterly, wholly

stark-naked buck naked (*slang*), in a state of nature, in one's birthday suit (*informal*), in the altogether (*informal*), in the buff (*informal*), in the raw (*infor-

starlight *n* the light that comes from the stars.

starling *n* a common songbird with shiny blackish feathers and a short tail.

starlit *adj* lit by starlight.

Star of David *n* a symbol of Judaism, consisting of a star formed by two interlaced equilateral triangles.

starry *adj* **-rier, -riest 1** (of a sky or night) full of or lit by stars. **2** of or like a star or stars: *a starry cast.*

starry-eyed *adj* full of unrealistic hopes and dreams; naive.

Stars and Stripes *n* the national flag of the United States of America.

star sign *n Astrol* the sign of the zodiac under which a person was born.

Star-Spangled Banner *n* **1** the national anthem of the United States of America. **2** same as **Stars and Stripes.**

star-studded *adj* featuring many well-known performers: *a star-studded premiere.*

start *vb* **1** to begin (something or to do something): *to start a war; we've already started building.* **2** to set or be set in motion: *he started the van.* **3** to make a sudden involuntary movement from fright or surprise; jump. **4** to establish; set up: *to start a state lottery.* **5** to support (someone) in the first part of a career or activity. **6** *Brit informal* to begin quarrelling or causing a disturbance: *don't start with me.* **7 to start with** in the first place. ~*n* **8** the first part of something. **9** the place or time at which something begins. **10** a signal to begin, such as in a race. **11** a lead or advantage, either in time or distance, in a competitive activity: *he had an hour's start on me.* **12** a slight involuntary movement from fright or surprise: *I awoke with a start.* **13** an opportunity to enter a career or begin a project. **14 for a start** in the first place. ~See also **start off, start on,** etc.

starter *n* **1** *Chiefly Brit* the first course of a meal. **2 for starters** *Slang* in the first place. **3** a device for starting an internal-combustion engine. **4** a person who signals the start of a race. **5** a competitor in a race or contest. **6 under starter's orders** (of competitors in a race) waiting for the signal to start.

startle *vb* **-tling, -tled** to slightly surprise or frighten someone. **startling** *adj*

start off *vb* **1** to set out on a journey. **2** to be or make the first step in (an activity): *beginners should start off with a walking programme.* **3** to cause (a person) to do something, such as laugh.

start on *vb Brit informal* to pick a quarrel with: *they started on me.*

start out *vb* **1** to set out on a journey. **2** to take the first steps in a career or on a course of action: *I started out as a beautician; it started out as a joke.*

start up *vb* **1** to come or cause (something, such as a business) to come into being; found. **2** to set (something) in motion: *she started up the car.*

starve *vb* **starving, starved 1** to die from lack of food. **2** to deliberately prevent (a person or animal) from having any food. **3** *Informal* to be very hungry: *we're both starving.* **4 starve of** to deprive (someone) of something needed: *the heart is starved of oxygen.* **5 starve into** to force someone into a specified state by starving: *an attempt to starve him into submission.* **starvation** *n*

Star Wars *n* (in the US) a proposed system of artificial satellites armed with lasers to destroy enemy missiles in space.

stash *vb* **1** (often foll. by *away*) *Informal* to store (money or valuables) in a secret place for safekeeping. ~*n* **2** *Informal, chiefly US & Canad* a secret store, usually of illegal drugs, or the place where this is hidden.

state *n* **1** the condition or circumstances of a person or thing. **2** a sovereign political power or community. **3** the territory of such a community. **4** the sphere of power in such a community: *matters of state.* **5** (*often cap*) one of a number of areas or communities having their own governments and forming a federation under a sovereign government, such as in the US. **6** (*often cap*) the government, civil service, and armed forces. **7 in a state** *Informal* in an emotional or very worried condition. **8 lie in state** (of a body) to be placed on public view before burial. **9 state of affairs** circumstances or condition: *this wonderful state of affairs.* **10** grand and luxurious lifestyle, as enjoyed by royalty, aristocrats, or the wealthy: *living in state.* ~*adj* **11** controlled or financed by a state: *state ownership.* **12** of or concerning the State: *state secrets.* **13** involving ceremony: *a state visit.* ~*vb* **stating, stated 14** to express (something) in words.

State Enrolled Nurse *n* a nurse who has completed a two-year training course.

state house *n NZ* a rented house built by the government.

stateless *adj* not belonging to any country: *stateless refugees.*

stately *adj* **-lier, -liest** having a dignified, impressive,

THESAURUS

mal), naked, naked as the day one was born (*informal*), nude, stark, starkers (*informal*), stripped, unclad, undressed, without a stitch on (*informal*)

start *vb.* **1.** appear, arise, begin, come into being, come into existence, commence, depart, first see the light of day, get on the road, get under way, go ahead, hit the road (*informal*), issue, leave, originate, pitch in (*informal*), sally forth, set off, set out **2.** activate, embark upon, engender, enter upon, get going, initiate, instigate, kick off (*informal*), kick-start, make a beginning, open, originate, put one's hand to the plough (*informal*), set about, set in motion, start the ball rolling, take the first step, take the plunge (*informal*), trigger, turn on **3.** blench, flinch, jerk, jump, recoil, shy, twitch **4.** begin, create, establish, father, found, inaugurate, initiate, institute, introduce, launch, lay the foundations of, pioneer, set up ~*n.* **5.** beginning, birth, commencement, dawn, first step(s), foundation, inauguration, inception, initiation, kickoff (*informal*), onset, opening, opening move, outset **6.** advantage, edge, head start, lead **7.** convulsion, jar, jump, spasm, twitch **8.** backing, break (*informal*), chance, helping hand, introduction, opening, opportunity, sponsorship

startle agitate, alarm, amaze, astonish, astound, frighten, give (someone) a turn (*informal*), make (someone) jump, scare, shock, surprise, take (someone) aback

startling alarming, astonishing, astounding, extraordinary, shocking, staggering, sudden, surprising, unexpected, unforeseen

starving *informal* faint from lack of food, famished, hungering, hungry, ravenous, ready to eat a horse (*informal*), sharp-set, starved

state *n.* **1.** case, category, circumstances, condition, mode, pass, plight, position, predicament, shape, situation, state of affairs **2.** body politic, commonwealth, country, federation, government, kingdom, land, nation, republic, territory **3. in a state** *informal* agitated, all steamed up (*slang*), anxious, distressed, disturbed, flustered, het up, panic-stricken, ruffled, upset, uptight (*informal*) ~*vb.* **4.** affirm, articulate, assert, asseverate, aver, declare, enumerate, explain, expound, express,

and graceful appearance or manner: *the Rolls-Royce approached him at a stately speed.* **stateliness** *n*

stately home *n Brit* a large old mansion, usually one open to the public.

statement *n* **1** something stated, usually a formal prepared announcement or reply. **2** an account prepared by a bank at regular intervals for a client to show all credits and debits and the balance at the end of the period. **3** an account containing a summary of bills or invoices and showing the total amount due. **4** the act of stating.

state of the art *n* **1** the current level of knowledge and development achieved in a technology, science, or art. *~adj* **state-of-the-art 2** the most recent and therefore considered the best; up-to-the-minute: *state-of-the-art computers.*

State Registered Nurse *n* (formerly in Britain) a nurse who has completed an extensive three-year training course.

stateroom *n* **1** a private room on a ship. **2** *Chiefly Brit* a large room in a palace, etc., used on ceremonial occasions.

States *pl n* **the States** *Informal* the United States of America.

state school *n* a school funded by the state, in which education is free.

statesman *n, pl* **-men** an experienced and respected political leader. **statesmanship** *n*

static *adj* **1** not active, changing, or moving; stationary. **2** *Physics* (of a weight, force, or pressure) acting but causing no movement. **3** *Physics* of forces that do not produce movement. *~n* **4** hissing or crackling or a speckled picture caused by interference in the reception of radio or television transmissions. **5** electric sparks or crackling produced by friction.

static electricity *n* same as **static** (sense 5).

statics *n* the branch of mechanics concerned with the forces producing a state of equilibrium.

station *n* **1** a place along a route or line at which a bus or train stops to pick up passengers or goods. **2** the headquarters of an organization such as the police or fire service. **3** a building with special equipment for some particular purpose: *power station; a filling station.* **4** a television or radio channel. **5** *Mil* a place of duty. **6** position in society: *he had ideas above his station.* **7** *Austral & NZ* a large sheep or cattle farm. **8** the place or position where a person is assigned to stand: *every man stood at this station.* *~vb* **9** to assign (someone) to a station.

stationary *adj* not moving: *a line of stationary traffic.*

stationer *n* a person or shop selling stationery.

stationery *n* writing materials, such as paper, envelopes, and pens.

stationmaster *n* the senior official in charge of a railway station.

Stations of the Cross *pl n RC Church* **1** a series of 14 crosses with pictures or carvings, arranged around the walls of a church, to commemorate 14 stages in Christ's journey to Calvary. **2** a series of 14 prayers relating to each of these stages.

station wagon *n US* an estate car.

statistic *n* a numerical fact collected and classified systematically. **statistical** *adj* **statistically** *adv* **statistician** *n*

statistics *n* **1** the science dealing with the collection, classification, and interpretation of numerical information. *~pl n* **2** numerical information which has been collected, classified, and interpreted.

statuary *n* statues collectively.

statue *n* a sculpture of a human or animal figure, usually life-size or larger.

statuesque (stat-yoo-**esk**) *adj* (of a woman) tall and well-proportioned; like a classical statue.

statuette *n* a small statue.

stature *n* **1** height and size of a person. **2** the reputation of a person or their achievements: *a batsman of international stature.* **3** moral or intellectual distinction.

status *n* **1** a person's position in society. **2** the esteem in which people hold a person: *priests feel they have lost some of their status in society.* **3** the legal or official standing or classification of a person or country: *the status of refugees; Ireland's non-aligned status.* **4** degree of importance.

status quo *n* the existing state of affairs.

status symbol *n* a possession regarded as a mark of social position or wealth.

statute *n* **1** a law made by a government and expressed in a formal document. **2** a permanent rule made by a company or other institution.

statute law *n* **1** a law made by a government. **2** such laws collectively.

statutory *adj* **1** required or authorized by law. **2** (of an offence) declared by law to be punishable.

staunch[1] *adj* strong and loyal: *a staunch supporter.* **staunchly** *adv*

staunch[2] *or* **stanch** *vb* to stop the flow of (blood) from someone's body.

stave *n* **1** one of the long strips of wood joined together to form a barrel or bucket. **2** a stick carried as a symbol of office. **3** a verse of a poem. **4** *Music* same as **staff.** *~vb* **staving, stove 5 stave in** to burst a hole in something.

stave off *vb* **staving, staved** to delay (something) for a short time: *to stave off political rebellion.*

staves *n* a plural of **staff** or **stave.**

stay[1] *vb* **1** to continue or remain in a place, position, or condition: *to stay away; to stay inside.* **2** to lodge as a guest or visitor temporarily: *we stay with friends.* **3** *Scot & S African* to reside permanently; live. **4** to endure (something testing or difficult): *you have stayed the course this long.* *~n* **5** the period spent in one place. **6** the postponement of an order of a court of law: *a stay of execution.*

THESAURUS

present, propound, put, report, say, specify, utter, voice

stately august, ceremonious, deliberate, dignified, elegant, grand, imperial, imposing, impressive, lofty, majestic, measured, noble, pompous, regal, royal, solemn

statement account, announcement, communication, communiqué, declaration, explanation, proclamation, recital, relation, report, testimony, utterance

static changeless, constant, fixed, immobile, inert, motionless, stagnant, stationary, still, unmoving, unvarying

station *n.* **1.** base, depot, headquarters, location, place, position, post, seat, situation **2.** appointment, business, calling, employment, grade, occupation, position, post, rank, situation, sphere, standing, status *~vb.* **3.** assign, establish, fix, garrison, install, locate, post, set

stationary at a standstill, fixed, inert, moored, motionless, parked, standing, static, stock-still, unmoving

status condition, consequence, degree, distinction, eminence, grade, position, prestige, rank, standing

stay *vb.* **1.** abide, continue, delay, establish oneself, halt, hang around (*informal*), hover, linger, loiter, pause, put down roots, remain, reside, settle, sojourn,

stay[2] *n* something that supports or steadies something, such as a prop or buttress.
stay[3] *n* a rope or chain supporting a ship's mast or funnel.
stay-at-home *adj* **1** (of a person) enjoying a quiet, settled, and unadventurous life. ~*n* **2** a stay-at-home person.
staying power *n* endurance to complete something undertaken; stamina.
stays *pl n* old-fashioned corsets with bones in them.
staysail *n* a sail fastened on a stay.
STD sexually transmitted disease.
STD code *n Brit* a code preceding a local telephone number, allowing a caller to dial direct without the operator's help.
stead *n* **1 stand someone in good stead** to be useful to someone in the future. **2** *Rare* the function or position that should be taken by another: *I cannot let you rule in my stead.*
steadfast *adj* dedicated and unwavering. **steadfastly** *adv* **steadfastness** *n*
steady *adj* **steadier, steadiest 1** firm and not shaking. **2** without much change or variation: *we're on a steady course.* **3** continuous: *a steady decline.* **4** not easily excited; sober. **5** regular; habitual: *the steady drinking of alcohol.* ~*vb* **steadies, steadying, steadied 6** to make or become steady. ~*adv* **7** in a steady manner. **8 go steady** *Informal* to date one person regularly. ~*n, pl* **steadies 9** *Informal* one's regular boyfriend or girlfriend. ~*interj* **10** a warning to keep calm or be careful. **steadily** *adv* **steadiness** *n*
steady state *n Physics* the condition of a system when all or most changes or disturbances have been eliminated from it.
steak *n* **1** a lean piece of beef for grilling or frying. **2** a cut of beef for braising or stewing. **3** a thick slice of pork, veal, or fish.
steakhouse *n* a restaurant that specializes in steaks.
steal *vb* **stealing, stole, stolen 1** to take (something) from someone without permission or unlawfully. **2** to use (someone else's ideas or work) without acknowledgment. **3** to move quietly and carefully, not wanting to be noticed: *my father stole up behind her.* **4 steal the show** (of a performer) to draw the audience's attention to oneself and away from the other performers. **5** to obtain or do (something) stealthily: *I stole a glance behind.* ~*n* **6** *US & Canad informal* something acquired easily or at little cost.
stealth *n* **1** moving carefully and quietly, so as to avoid being seen. **2** cunning or underhand behaviour. **stealthy** *adj* **stealthily** *adv*
steam *n* **1** the vapour into which water changes when boiled. **2** the mist formed when such vapour condenses in the atmosphere. **3** *Informal* power, energy, or speed. **4 let off steam** *Informal* to release pent-up energy or feelings. **5 pick up steam** *Informal* to gather momentum. ~*adj* **6** operated, heated, or powered by steam: *a steam train.* ~*vb* **7** to give off steam. **8** (of a vehicle) to move by steam power. **9** *Informal* to proceed quickly and often forcefully. **10** to cook (food) in steam. **11** to treat (something) with steam, such as in cleaning or pressing clothes. **12 steam open** *or* **off** to use steam in order to open or remove (something): *let me steam open this letter.* ~See also **steam up.**
steam engine *n* an engine worked by steam.
steamer *n* **1** a boat or ship driven by steam engines. **2** a container with holes in the bottom, used to cook food by steam.
steam iron *n* an electric iron that uses steam to take creases out of clothes.
steamroller *n* **1** a steam-powered vehicle with heavy rollers used for flattening road surfaces during road-making. ~*vb* **2** to make (someone) do what one wants by overpowering force.
steamship *n* a ship powered by steam engines.
steam up *vb* **1** to cover (windows or glasses) or (of windows or glasses) to become covered with steam. **2 steamed up** *Slang* excited or angry.
steamy *adj* **steamier, steamiest 1** full of steam. **2** *Informal* (of books, films, etc.) erotic.
steatite (**stee**-a-tite) *n* same as **soapstone.**
steed *n Archaic or literary* a horse.
steel *n* **1** an alloy of iron and carbon, often with small quantities of other elements. **2** a steel rod used for sharpening knives. **3** courage and mental toughness. ~*vb* **4** to prepare (oneself) for coping with something unpleasant: *he had steeled himself to accept the fact.* **steely** *adj*
steel band *n Music* a band of people playing on metal drums, popular in the West Indies.
steel-grey *adj* dark bluish-grey.
steel wool *n* a mass of fine steel fibres, used for cleaning metal surfaces.
steelworks *n* a factory where steel is made. **steelworker** *n*
steep[1] *adj* **1** having a sharp slope. **2** *Informal* (of a fee, price, or demand) unreasonably high; excessive. **steeply** *adv* **steepness** *n*
steep[2] *vb* **1** to soak or be soaked in a liquid in order to soften or cleanse. **2 steeped in** filled with: *an industry steeped in tradition.*
steepen *vb* to become or cause (something) to become steep or steeper.

THESAURUS

stand, stay put, stop, tarry, wait ~*n.* **2.** holiday, sojourn, stop, stopover, visit **3.** deferment, delay, halt, pause, postponement, remission, reprieve, stopping, suspension
steadfast constant, dedicated, dependable, established, faithful, fast, firm, fixed, immovable, intent, loyal, persevering, reliable, resolute, single-minded, stable, stalwart, staunch, steady, unfaltering, unflinching, unswerving, unwavering
steady *adj.* **1.** firm, fixed, immovable, safe, stable, substantial, unchangeable, uniform **2.** balanced, calm, dependable, equable, having both feet on the ground, imperturbable, level-headed, reliable, sedate, sensible, serene, serious-minded, settled, sober, staid, staunch, steadfast **3.** ceaseless, confirmed, consistent, constant, continuous, even, faithful, habitual, incessant, nonstop, persistent, regular, rhythmic, unbroken, unfaltering, unfluctuating, uninterrupted, unremitting, unvarying, unwavering ~*vb.* **4.** balance, brace, secure, stabilize, support **5.** compose *or* calm oneself, cool down, get a grip on oneself, sober (up)
steal 1. appropriate, be light-fingered, embezzle, filch, lift (*informal*), misappropriate, nick (*slang, chiefly Brit.*), peculate (*literary*), pilfer, pinch (*informal*), pirate, plagiarize, poach, purloin, shoplift, snitch (*slang*), swipe (*slang*), take, thieve, walk *or* make off with **2.** creep, flit, insinuate oneself, slink, slip, sneak, tiptoe
stealing embezzlement, larceny, misappropriation, pilferage, pilfering, plagiarism, robbery, shoplifting, theft, thievery, thieving
stealth furtiveness, secrecy, slyness, sneakiness, stealthiness, surreptitiousness, unobtrusiveness
stealthy clandestine, covert, furtive, secret, secretive, skulking, sly, sneaking, sneaky, surreptitious, underhand

steeple *n* a tall ornamental tower on a church roof.

steeplechase *n* **1** a horse race over a course with fences to be jumped. **2** a track race in which the runners have to leap hurdles and a water jump. *~vb* **-chasing, -chased 3** to race in a steeplechase.

steeplejack *n* a person who repairs steeples and chimneys.

steer[1] *vb* **1** to direct the course of (a vehicle or vessel) with a steering wheel or rudder. **2** to direct the movements or course of (a person, conversation, or activity). **3** to follow (a specified course): *the Dutch government steered a middle course.* **4 steer clear of** to avoid.

steer[2] *n* a castrated male ox or bull.

steerage *n* **1** the cheapest accommodation on a passenger ship. **2** steering.

steering committee *n* a committee set up to prepare and arrange topics to be discussed, and the order of business, for a government, etc.

steering wheel *n* a wheel turned by the driver of a vehicle in order to change direction.

steersman *n, pl* **-men** the person who steers a vessel.

stein (**stine**) *n* an earthenware beer mug.

stela (**steal-a**) *or* **stele** (**steal-ee**) *n, pl* **stelae** (**steal-ee**) *or* **steles** an upright stone slab or column decorated with figures or inscriptions, common in prehistoric times.

stellar *adj* relating to the stars.

stem[1] *n* **1** the long thin central part of a plant. **2** a stalk that bears a flower, fruit, or leaf. **3** the long slender part of anything, such as a wineglass. **4** *Linguistics* the form of a word that remains after removal of all inflectional endings. *~vb* **stemming, stemmed 5 stem from** originate from: *this tradition stems from pre-Christian times.*

stem[2] *vb* **stemming, stemmed** to stop or hinder the spread of (something): *to stem the flow of firearms.*

stemmed *adj* having a stem: *long-stemmed roses.*

stench *n* a strong and very unpleasant smell.

stencil *n* **1** a thin sheet with a cut-out pattern through which ink or paint passes to form the pattern on the surface below. **2** a design or letters made in this way. *~vb* **-cilling, -cilled** *or US* **-ciling, -ciled 3** to make (a design or letters) with a stencil.

Sten gun *n* a light sub-machine-gun.

stenographer *n US & Canad* a shorthand typist.

stentorian *adj* (of the voice) very loud: *a stentorian tone.*

step *n* **1** the act of moving and setting down one's foot, such as when walking. **2** the distance covered by such a movement. **3** the sound made by such a movement. **4** one of a sequence of foot movements that make up a dance. **5** one of a sequence of actions taken in order to achieve a goal. **6** a degree or rank in a series or scale. **7** a flat surface for placing the foot on when going up or down. **8** manner of walking: *he moved with a purposeful step.* **9 steps a** a flight of stairs, usually out of doors. **b** same as **stepladder. 10** a short easily travelled distance: *Mexico and Brazil were only a step away.* **11 break step** to stop marching in step. **12 in step a** marching or dancing in time or at the same pace as other people. **b** *Informal* in agreement: *in step with the West on this issue.* **13 out of step a** not marching or dancing in time or at the same pace as other people. **b** *Informal* not in agreement: *out of step with the political mood.* **14 step by step** gradually. **15 take steps** to do what is necessary (to achieve something). **16 watch one's step a** *Informal* to behave with caution. **b** to walk carefully. *~vb* **stepping, stepped 17** to move by taking a step, such as in walking. **18** to walk a short distance: *please step this way.* **19 step into** to enter (a situation) apparently without difficulty: *she stepped into a life of luxury.* ~See also **step down, step in,** etc.

stepbrother *n* a son of one's stepmother or stepfather.

stepchild *n, pl* **-children** a stepson or stepdaughter.

stepdaughter *n* a daughter of one's husband or wife by an earlier relationship.

step down *vb Informal* to resign from a position.

stepfather *n* a man who has married one's mother after the death or divorce of one's father.

stephanotis (**stef-fan-note-iss**) *n* a tropical climbing shrub with sweet-smelling white flowers.

step in *vb Informal* to intervene (in a quarrel or difficult situation).

stepladder *n* a small folding portable ladder with a supporting frame.

stepmother *n* a woman who has married one's father after the death or divorce of one's mother.

step on *vb* **1** to place or press one's foot on (something): *he stepped on the brakes.* **2** *Informal* to behave badly towards (a person in a less powerful position). **3 step on it** *Informal* to go more quickly; hurry up.

step out *vb* **1** to leave a room briefly. **2** to walk quickly, taking long strides.

step-parent *n* a stepfather or stepmother.

steppes *pl n* wide grassy plains without trees.

stepping stone *n* **1** one of a series of stones acting as footrests for crossing a stream. **2** a stage in a person's progress towards a goal: *it was a big stepping stone in his career.*

stepsister *n* a daughter of one's stepmother or stepfather.

stepson *n* a son of one's husband or wife by an earlier relationship.

step up *vb Informal* to increase (something) by stages; accelerate.

THESAURUS

steep *adj.* **1.** abrupt, headlong, precipitous, sheer **2.** *informal* excessive, exorbitant, extortionate, extreme, high, overpriced, stiff, uncalled-for, unreasonable

steer 1. administer, be in the driver's seat, conduct, control, direct, govern, guide, handle, pilot **2. steer clear of** avoid, circumvent, eschew, evade, give a wide berth to, sheer off, shun

stem[1] **1.** *n.* axis, branch, peduncle, shoot, stalk, stock, trunk **2.** *vb. with* **from** arise, be caused (bred, brought about, generated) by, derive, develop, emanate, flow, issue, originate

stem[2] *vb.* bring to a standstill, check, contain, curb, dam, hold back, oppose, resist, restrain, staunch, stay (*archaic*), stop, withstand

step *n.* **1.** footfall, footprint, footstep, gait, impression, pace, print, stride, trace, track, walk **2.** act, action, deed, expedient, manoeuvre, means, measure, move, procedure, proceeding **3.** degree, level, rank, remove **4. in step** *informal* coinciding, conforming, in harmony (agreement, conformity, unison), in line **5. out of step** *informal* erratic, incongruous, in disagreement, out of harmony, out of line, out of phase, pulling different ways **6. take steps** act, intervene, move in, prepare, take action, take measures, take the initiative **7. watch one's step** *informal* be discreet (canny, careful, cautious), be on one's guard, have one's wits about one, look out, mind how one goes, mind one's p's and q's, take care, take heed, tread carefully ~*vb.* **8.** move, pace, tread, walk

stereo *adj* **1** (of a sound system) using two or more separate microphones to feed two or more loudspeakers through separate channels. ~*n, pl* **stereos 2** a music system in which sound is directed through two speakers. **3** sound broadcast or played in stereo.

stereophonic *adj* same as **stereo** (sense 1).

stereoscopic *adj* having a three-dimensional effect.

stereotype *n* **1** a set of characteristics or a fixed idea considered to represent a particular kind of person. **2** an idea or convention that has grown stale through fixed usage. ~*vb* **-typing, -typed 3** to form a standard image or idea of (a type of person).

sterile *adj* **1** free from germs. **2** unable to produce offspring. **3** (of plants) not producing or bearing seeds. **4** lacking inspiration or energy; unproductive. **sterility** *n*

sterilize *or* **-lise** *vb* **-lizing, -lized** *or* **-lising, -lised** to make sterile. **sterilization** *or* **-lisation** *n*

sterling *n* **1** British money: *sterling fell by almost a pfennig.* ~*adj* **2;** genuine and reliable: first-class: *he has a reputation for sterling honesty.*

sterling silver *n* **1** an alloy containing at least 92.5 per cent of silver. **2** articles made of sterling silver.

stern[1] *adj* **1** strict and serious: *he's a very stern taskmaster.* **2** difficult and often unpleasant: *the stern demands of the day.* **3** (of a facial expression) severe and disapproving. **sternly** *adv*

stern[2] *n* the rear part of a boat or ship.

sternum *n, pl* **-na** *or* **-nums** a long flat bone in the front of the body, to which the collarbone and most of the ribs are attached.

steroid *n Biochem* an organic compound containing a carbon ring system, such as sterols and many hormones.

sterol *n Biochem* a natural insoluble alcohol such as cholesterol and ergosterol.

stertorous *adj* (of breathing) laboured and noisy.

stet *vb* **stetting, stetted 1** used as an instruction to indicate to a printer that certain deleted matter is to be kept. **2** to mark (matter) in this way.

stethoscope *n Med* an instrument for listening to the sounds made inside the body, consisting of a hollow disc that transmits the sound through hollow tubes to earpieces.

stetson *n* a felt hat with a broad brim and high crown, worn mainly by cowboys.

stevedore *n Chiefly US* a person employed to load or unload ships.

stew *n* **1** a dish of meat, fish, or other food, cooked slowly in a closed pot. **2 in a stew** *Informal* in a troubled or worried state. ~*vb* **3** to cook by long slow simmering in a closed pot. **4** *Informal* (of a person) to be too hot. **5** to cause (tea) to become bitter or (of tea) to become bitter through infusing for too long. **6 stew in one's own juice** to suffer, without help, the results of one's actions.

steward *n* **1** a person who looks after passengers and serves meals on a ship or aircraft. **2** an official who helps to supervise a public event, such as a race. **3** a person who administers someone else's property. **4** a person who manages the eating arrangements, staff, or service at a club or hotel. **5** See **shop steward.** ~*vb* **6** to act as a steward (of).

stewardess *n* a female steward on an aircraft or ship.

stewed *adj* **1** (of food) cooked by stewing. **2** *Brit* (of tea) bitter through having been left to infuse for too long. **3** *Slang* drunk.

stick[1] *n* **1** a small thin branch of a tree. **2 a** a long thin piece of wood. **b** such a piece of wood shaped for a special purpose: *a walking stick; a hockey stick.* **3** a piece of something shaped like a stick: *a stick of cinnamon.* **4** *Slang* verbal abuse, criticism: *they gave me a lot of stick.* **5 the sticks** a country area considered backward or unsophisticated: *places out in the sticks.* **6 sticks** pieces of furniture: *these few sticks are all I have.* **7** *Informal* a person: *not a bad old stick.* **8 get hold of the wrong end of the stick** to misunderstand a situation or an explanation completely.

stick[2] *vb* **sticking, stuck 1** to push (a pointed object) or (of a pointed object) to be pushed into another object. **2** to fasten (something) in position by pins, nails, or glue: *she just stuck the label on.* **3** to extend beyond something else; protrude: *he stuck his head out of the door.* **4** *Informal* to place (something) in a specified position: *stick it in the oven.* **5** to fasten or be fastened by or as if by an adhesive. **6** to come or be brought to a standstill: *stuck in a rut; two army lorries stuck behind us.* **7** to remain for a long time: *the room that sticks in my mind the most.* **8** *Slang, chiefly Brit* to tolerate; abide: *you couldn't stick it for more than two days.* **9 be stuck** *Informal* to be at a loss for; to be baffled or puzzled: *I'm stuck; stuck for words.* ~See also **stick around, stick by,** etc.

stick around *vb Informal* to remain in a place, often when waiting for something.

stick by *vb* to remain faithful to: *she's stuck by me for sixty years.*

sticker *n* a small piece of paper with a picture or writing on it that can be stuck to a surface.

sticking plaster *n* a piece of adhesive material used for covering slight wounds.

stick insect *n* a tropical insect with a long thin body and legs, which looks like a twig.

stick-in-the-mud *n Informal* a person who is unwilling to try anything new or do anything exciting.

THESAURUS

step in *informal* become involved, chip in (*informal*), intercede, intervene, take action, take a hand

step up *informal* accelerate, augment, boost, escalate, increase, intensify, raise, speed up, up

stereotype 1. *n.* formula, mould, pattern, received idea **2.** *vb.* categorize, conventionalize, dub, pigeonhole, standardize, take to be, typecast

sterile 1. antiseptic, aseptic, disinfected, germ-free, sterilized **2.** abortive, bare, barren, dry, empty, fruitless, infecund, unfruitful, unproductive, unprofitable, unprolific

sterilize disinfect, fumigate, purify

sterling authentic, excellent, fine, first-class, genuine, pure, real, sound, standard, substantial, superlative, true

stern austere, authoritarian, bitter, cruel, drastic, flinty, forbidding, frowning, grim, hard, harsh, inflexible, relentless, rigid, rigorous, serious, severe, steely, strict, unrelenting, unsparing, unyielding

stick[1] *n.* **1.** baton, birch, cane, crook, pole, rod, sceptre, staff, stake, switch, twig, wand **2.** *Brit. slang* abuse, blame, criticism, flak (*informal*), hostility, punishment **3.** *informal* dinosaur, fuddy-duddy (*informal*), (old) fogey, pain (*informal*), prig, stick-in-the-mud (*informal*)

stick[2] *vb.* **1.** dig, gore, insert, jab, penetrate, pierce, pin, poke, prod, puncture, spear, stab, thrust, transfix **2.** adhere, affix, attach, bind, bond, cement, cleave, cling, fasten, fix, fuse, glue, hold, hold on, join, paste, weld **3.** bulge, extend, jut, obtrude, poke, project, protrude, show **4.** *informal* deposit, drop, fix, install, lay, place, plant, plonk, position, put, set, store, stuff **5.** be bogged down, become immobilized, be embedded, catch, clog, come to a standstill, jam, lodge, snag, stop

stickleback *n* a small fish with sharp spines along its back.

stickler *n* a person who insists on something: *a stickler for punctuality.*

stick out *vb* **1** to (cause to) project from something else: *she stuck her tongue out at me.* **2** *Informal* to endure (something unpleasant): *she would stick it out for a year.* **3 stick out a mile** *or* **like a sore thumb** *Informal* to be very obvious. **4 stick out for** to continue to demand (something), refusing to accept anything less.

stick to *vb* **1** to adhere or cause (something) to adhere to: *the soil sticks to the blade.* **2** to remain faithful to (a person, promise, or rule). **3** not to move away from: *stick to the agreement.*

stick-up *n Slang, chiefly US* a robbery at gunpoint; hold-up.

stick up for *vb Informal* to support or defend (oneself, another person, or a principle).

sticky *adj* **stickier, stickiest 1** covered with a substance that sticks to other things: *sticky little fingers.* **2** intended to stick to a surface: *sticky labels.* **3** *Informal* difficult or painful: *a sticky meeting.* **4** (of weather) unpleasantly warm and humid. **stickiness** *n*

sticky wicket *n* **on a sticky wicket** *Informal* in a difficult situation.

stiff *adj* **1** firm and not easily bent. **2** moving with pain or difficulty: *stiff and aching joints.* **3** not moving easily: *the door is stiff.* **4** difficult or severe: *a stiff challenge; stiff penalties.* **5** formal and not relaxed. **6** fairly firm in consistency; thick. **7** powerful: *a stiff breeze.* **8** (of a drink) containing a lot of alcohol. *~n* **9** *Slang* a corpse. *~adv* **10** completely or utterly: *I was bored stiff.* **stiffly** *adv* **stiffness** *n*

stiffen *vb* to make or become stiff or stiffer.

stiff-necked *adj* proud and stubborn.

stifle *vb* **-fling, -fled 1** to stop oneself from expressing (a yawn or cry). **2** to stop (something) from continuing: *the new leadership stifled all internal debate.* **3** to feel discomfort and difficulty in breathing. **4** to kill (someone) by preventing him or her from breathing.

stifling *adj* uncomfortably hot and stuffy.

stigma *n, pl* **stigmas** *or* **stigmata 1** a mark of social disgrace: *a stigma attached to being redundant.* **2** *Bot* the part of a flower that receives pollen. **3 stigmata** *Christianity* marks resembling the wounds of the crucified Christ, believed to appear on the bodies of certain people.

stigmatize *or* **-tise** *vb* **-tizing, -tized** *or* **-tising, -tised** to regard as being shameful.

stile *n* a set of steps in a wall or fence to allow people, but not animals, to pass over.

stiletto *n, pl* **-tos 1** Also called: **spike heel, stiletto heel** a high narrow heel on a woman's shoe or a shoe with such a heel. **2** a small dagger with a slender tapered blade.

still[1] *adv* **1** continuing now or in the future as in the past: *she still loved the theatre.* **2** up to this or that time; yet. **3** even or yet: *still more pressure on the government.* **4** even then; nevertheless: *the baby has been fed and still cries.* **5** quietly or without movement: *keep still.* *~adj* **6** motionless; stationary. **7** undisturbed; silent and calm. **8** (of a soft drink) not fizzy. *~n* **9** *Poetic* silence or tranquillity: *the still of night.* **10** a still photograph from a film. *~vb* **11** to make or become quiet or calm. **12** to relieve or end: *Fowler stilled his conscience.* **stillness** *n*

still[2] *n* an apparatus for distilling spirits.

stillborn *adj* **1** (of a baby) dead at birth. **2** (of an idea or plan) completely unsuccessful. **stillbirth** *n*

still life *n, pl* **still lifes 1** a painting or drawing of objects such as fruit or flowers. **2** this kind of painting or drawing.

still room *n Brit* **1** a room in which distilling is carried out. **2** a room for storing food in a large house.

stilt *n* **1** either of a pair of long poles with footrests for walking raised from the ground. **2** a long post or column used with others to support a building above ground level.

stilted *adj* (of speech, writing, or behaviour) formal or pompous; not flowing continuously or naturally.

Stilton *n Trademark* a strong-flavoured blue-veined cheese.

stimulant *n* **1** a drug, food, or drink that makes the body work faster, increases heart rate, and makes sleeping difficult. **2** any stimulating thing. *~adj* **3** stimulating.

stimulate *vb* **-lating, -lated 1** to encourage to start or progress further: *a cut in interest rates should help stimulate economic recovery.* **2** to fill (a person) with ideas or enthusiasm: *books satisfy a part of the intel-*

THESAURUS

6. linger, persist, remain, stay **7.** *slang, chiefly Brit.* abide, bear up under, endure, get on with, stand, stomach, take, tolerate

stick to adhere to, cleave to, continue in, honour, keep, persevere in, remain loyal (faithful, true), stick at

sticky 1. adhesive, clinging, gluey, glutinous, gooey (*informal*), gummy, syrupy, tacky, tenacious, viscid, viscous **2.** *informal* awkward, delicate, difficult, discomforting, embarrassing, hairy (*slang*), nasty, painful, thorny, tricky, unpleasant **3.** clammy, close, humid, muggy, oppressive, sultry, sweltering

stiff 1. brittle, firm, hard, hardened, inelastic, inflexible, rigid, solid, solidified, taut, tense, tight, unbending, unyielding **2.** arthritic, awkward, clumsy, creaky (*informal*), crude, graceless, inelegant, jerky, rheumaticky (*informal*), ungainly, ungraceful, unsupple **3.** arduous, austere, cruel, difficult, drastic, exacting, extreme, fatiguing, formidable, great, hard, harsh, heavy, inexorable, laborious, oppressive, pitiless, rigorous, severe, sharp, strict, stringent, tough, trying, uphill **4.** artificial, austere, ceremonious, chilly, cold, constrained, forced, formal, laboured, mannered, pompous, priggish, prim, punctilious, standoffish, starchy (*informal*), stilted, uneasy, unnatural, unrelaxed, wooden **5.** brisk, fresh, powerful, strong, vigorous

stiffen brace, coagulate, congeal, crystallize, harden, jell, reinforce, set, solidify, starch, tauten, tense, thicken

stifle 1. check, choke back, cover up, curb, extinguish, hush, muffle, prevent, repress, restrain, silence, smother, stop, suppress **2.** asphyxiate, choke, smother, strangle, suffocate

still 1. *adj.* at rest, calm, hushed, inert, lifeless, motionless, noiseless, pacific, peaceful, placid, quiet, restful, serene, silent, smooth, stationary, stilly (*poetic*), tranquil, undisturbed, unruffled, unstirring **2.** *n. poetic* hush, peace, quiet, silence, stillness, tranquillity **3.** *vb.* allay, alleviate, appease, calm, hush, lull, pacify, quiet, quieten, settle, silence, smooth, smooth over, soothe, subdue, tranquillize

stilted artificial, bombastic, constrained, forced, grandiloquent, high-flown, high-sounding, inflated, laboured, pedantic, pompous, pretentious, stiff, unnatural, wooden

stimulant energizer, pep pill (*informal*), pick-me-up (*informal*), restorative, reviver, tonic, upper (*slang*)

stimulate animate, arouse, encourage, fan, fire, fo-

lect that needs to be stimulated. **3** *Physiol* to excite (a nerve or organ) with a stimulus. **stimulation** *n*

stimulating *adj* **1** inspiring new ideas or enthusiasm. **2** (of a physical activity) making one feel refreshed and energetic; invigorating.

stimulus (**stim**-myew-luss) *n, pl* **-li** (-lie) **1** something that acts as an incentive to (someone). **2** something, such as a drug or electrical impulse, that is capable of causing a response in a person or an animal.

sting *vb* **stinging, stung 1** (of certain animals and plants) to inflict a wound on (someone) by the injection of poison. **2** to cause (someone) to feel a sharp physical pain: *her hand was stinging.* **3** to offend or upset (someone) with a critical remark: *I was stung by what he said.* **4** to provoke (a response) by angering: *the consulate would be stung into convulsive action.* **5** *Informal* to cheat (someone) by overcharging. *~n* **6** a skin wound caused by stinging. **7** pain caused by or as if by a sting. **8** a mental pain: *the sting of memory.* **9** the sharp pointed organ of certain animals or plants used to inject poison. **10** *Slang* a deceptive trick. **11** *Slang* a trap set up by the police to entice a person to commit a crime, thereby producing evidence. **stinging** *adj*

stinging nettle *n* same as **nettle** (sense 1).

stingray *n* a flat fish with a jagged whiplike tail capable of inflicting painful wounds.

stingy *adj* **-gier, -giest** very mean. **stinginess** *n*

stink *n* **1** a strong unpleasant smell. **2 make, create** *or* **kick up a stink** *Slang* to make a fuss. *~vb* **stinking, stank** *or* **stunk; stunk 3** to give off a strong unpleasant smell. **4** *Slang* to be thoroughly bad or unpleasant: *the script stinks, the casting stinks.*

stink bomb *n* a small glass globe used by practical jokers: it releases a liquid with a strong unpleasant smell when broken.

stinker *n Slang* a difficult or very unpleasant person or thing.

stinking *adj* **1** having a strong unpleasant smell. **2** *Informal* unpleasant or disgusting. *~adv* **3 stinking rich** *Informal* very wealthy.

stink out *vb* **1** to drive (people) away by a foul smell. **2** *Brit* to cause (a place) to stink: *I won't have it stinking the car out!*

stint *vb* **1** to be miserly with (something): *don't stint on paper napkins.* *~n* **2** a given amount of work.

stipend (**sty**-pend) *n* a regular salary or allowance, esp. that paid to a clergyman. **stipendiary** *adj*

stipple *vb* **-pling, -pled** to draw, engrave, or paint (something) using dots or flecks.

stipulate *vb* **-lating, -lated** to specify (something) as a condition of an agreement. **stipulation** *n*

stir[1] *vb* **stirring, stirred 1** to mix up (a liquid) by moving a spoon or stick around in it. **2** to move slightly. **3 stir from** to depart (from one's usual or preferred place). **4** to get up after sleeping. **5** to excite or move (someone) emotionally. **6** to move (oneself) quickly or vigorously; exert (oneself). **7** to wake up: *to stir someone from sleep.* *~n* **8** a stirring. **9** a strong reaction, usually of excitement: *she created a stir wherever she went.* ~See also **stir up.**

stir[2] *n Slang* prison: *in stir.*

stir-crazy *adj Slang, chiefly US & Canad* mentally disturbed as a result of being in prison.

stir-fry *vb* **-fries, -frying, -fried 1** to cook (food) quickly by stirring it in a wok or frying pan over a high heat. *~n, pl* **-fries 2** a dish cooked in this way.

stirrer *n Informal* a person who deliberately causes trouble.

stirring *adj* causing emotion, excitement, and enthusiasm.

stirrup *n* a metal loop attached to a saddle for supporting a rider's foot.

stirrup cup *n* a cup containing an alcoholic drink offered to riders before a fox hunt.

stirrup pump *n* a hand-operated pump, the base of which is placed in a bucket of water: used in fighting fires.

stir up *vb* **1** to cause (leaves or dust) to rise up and swirl around. **2** to set (something) in motion: *that fact has stirred up resentment.*

stitch *n* **1** a link made by drawing a thread through material with a needle. **2** a loop of yarn formed around a needle or hook in knitting or crocheting. **3** a particular kind of stitch. **4** *Informal* a link of thread joining the edges of a wound together. **5** a sharp pain in the side caused by running or exercising. **6 in stitches** *Informal* laughing uncontrollably. **7 not a stitch** *Informal* no clothes at all. *~vb* **8** to sew or fasten (something) with stitches. **stitching** *n*

stoat *n* a small brown N European mammal related to the weasels: in winter it has a white coat and is then known as an ermine.

stock *n* **1** the total amount of goods kept on the premises of a shop or business. **2** a supply of something stored for future use. **3** *Finance* **a** the money raised by a company through selling shares entitling their holders to dividends, partial ownership, and usually voting rights. **b** the proportion of this money held by an individual shareholder. **c** the shares of a specified

THESAURUS

ment, goad, impel, incite, inflame, instigate, prod, prompt, provoke, quicken, rouse, spur, turn on (*slang*), urge, whet

stimulating exciting, exhilarating, galvanic, inspiring, intriguing, provocative, provoking, rousing, stirring, thought-provoking

stimulus encouragement, fillip, goad, incentive, incitement, inducement, provocation, shot in the arm (*informal*), spur

sting *vb.* **1.** burn, hurt, pain, smart, tingle, wound **2.** anger, gall, incense, inflame, infuriate, nettle, pique, provoke, rile **3.** *informal* cheat, defraud, do (*slang*), fleece, overcharge, rip off (*slang*), skin (*slang*), stiff (*slang*), swindle, take for a ride (*informal*)

stint 1. *vb.* begrudge, be sparing (frugal, mean, mingy (*Brit. informal*), parsimonious), economize, hold back, save, scrimp, skimp on, spoil the ship for a ha'p'orth of tar, withhold **2.** *n.* assignment, bit, period, quota, share, shift, spell, stretch, term, time, tour, turn

stipulate agree, contract, covenant, engage, guarantee, insist upon, lay down, lay down *or* impose conditions, make a point of, pledge, postulate, promise, require, settle, specify

stipulation agreement, clause, condition, contract, engagement, precondition, prerequisite, provision, proviso, qualification, requirement, restriction, rider, settlement, *sine qua non,* specification, term

stir *vb.* **1.** agitate, beat, disturb, flutter, mix, move, quiver, rustle, shake, tremble **2.** affect, animate, arouse, awaken, electrify, excite, fire, incite, inflame, inspire, instigate, kindle, move, prod, prompt, provoke, quicken, raise, rouse, spur, stimulate, thrill, touch, urge **3.** bestir, be up and about (*informal*), budge, exert oneself, get a move on (*informal*), get moving *informal* hasten, look lively (*informal*), make an effort, mill about, move, shake a leg (*informal*) *~n.* **4.** activity, ado, agitation, bustle, commotion, disorder, disturbance, excitement, ferment, flurry, fuss, movement, to-do, tumult, uproar

company or industry. **4** farm animals bred and kept for their meat, skins, etc. **5** the original type from which a particular race, family, or group is descended. **6** the handle of a rifle, held by the firer against the shoulder. **7** a liquid produced by simmering meat, fish, bones, or vegetables, and used to make soups and sauces. **8** a kind of plant grown for its brightly coloured flowers. **9** *Old-fashioned* the degree of status a person has. **10** See **laughing stock. 11 in stock** stored on the premises or available for sale or use. **12 out of stock** not immediately available for sale or use. **13 take stock** to think carefully about a situation before making a decision. *~adj* **14** staple; standard: *stock sizes in clothes.* **15** being a cliché; hackneyed: *the stock answer.* *~vb* **16** to keep (goods) for sale. **17** to obtain a store of (something) for future use or sale: *to stock up on food.* **18** to supply (a farm) with animals or (a lake or stream) with fish. ~See also **stocks.**

stockade *n* an enclosure or barrier of large wooden posts.

stockbreeder *n* a person who breeds or rears farm animals.

stockbroker *n* a person who buys and sells stocks and shares for customers and receives a percentage of their profits. **stockbroking** *n*

stock car *n* a car that has been strengthened and modified for a form of racing in which the cars often collide.

stock cube *n* a small solid cube made from dried meat or vegetables, used to add flavouring to stew, soup, etc.

stock exchange *n* **1 a** a highly organized market for the purchase and sale of stocks and shares, operated by professional stockbrokers and market makers according to fixed rules. **b** a place where stocks and shares are traded. **2** the prices or trading activity of a stock exchange: *the stock exchange has been rising.*

stockholder *n* an owner of some of a company's stock.

stockinette *n* a machine-knitted elastic fabric.

stocking *n* a long piece of close-fitting nylon or knitted yarn covering the foot and part or all of a woman's leg.

stockinged *adj* **in one's stockinged feet** wearing stockings, tights, or socks but no shoes.

stocking stitch *n* alternate rows of plain and purl in knitting.

stock in trade *n* a person's typical behaviour or usual work: *practicality is the farmer's stock in trade.*

stockist *n Commerce Brit* a dealer who stocks a particular product.

stock market *n* same as **stock exchange.**

stockpile *vb* **-piling, -piled 1** to store a large quantity of (something) for future use. *~n* **2** a large store gathered for future use.

stockpot *n Chiefly Brit* a pot in which stock for soup is made.

stockroom *n* a room in which a stock of goods is kept in a shop or factory.

stock route *n Austral & NZ* a route designated for droving farm animals, so as to avoid traffic.

stocks *pl n History* an instrument of punishment consisting of a heavy wooden frame with holes in which the feet, hands, or head of an offender were locked.

stock-still *adv* absolutely still; motionlessly.

stocktaking *n* **1** the counting and valuing of goods in a shop or business. **2** a reassessment of a person's current situation and prospects.

stocky *adj* **stockier, stockiest** (of a person) short but well-built. **stockily** *adv* **stockiness** *n*

stockyard *n* a large yard with pens or covered buildings where farm animals are sold.

stodge *n Informal* heavy and filling starchy food.

stodgy *adj* **stodgier, stodgiest 1** (of food) full of starch and very filling. **2** (of a person) dull, serious, or excessively formal. **stodginess** *n*

stoep (**stoop**) *n* (in South Africa) a verandah.

stoic (**stow**-ik) *n* **1** a person who suffers great difficulties without showing his or her emotions. *~adj* **2** same as **stoical.**

Stoic *n* **1** a member of the ancient Greek school of philosophy which believed that virtue and happiness could be achieved only by calmly accepting Fate. *~adj* **2** of or relating to the Stoics. **Stoicism** *n*

stoical *adj* suffering great difficulties without showing one's feelings. **stoically** *adv* **stoicism** (**stow**-iss-iz-zum) *n*

stoke *vb* **stoking, stoked 1** to feed and tend (a fire or furnace). **2** to excite or encourage (a strong emotion) in oneself or someone else.

stokehold *n Naut* the hold for a ship's boilers; fire room.

stokehole *n* a hole in a furnace through which it is stoked.

stoker *n* a person employed to tend a furnace on a ship or train powered by steam.

stole[1] *vb* the past tense of **steal.**

stole[2] *n* a long scarf or shawl, worn by women.

stolen *vb* the past participle of **steal.**

stolid *adj* showing little or no emotion or interest in anything. **stolidity** *n* **stolidly** *adv*

stoma (**stow**-ma) *n, pl* **stomata** (**stow**-ma-ta) **1** *Bot* a

THESAURUS

stirring animating, dramatic, emotive, exciting, exhilarating, heady, impassioned, inspiring, intoxicating, lively, moving, rousing, spirited, stimulating, thrilling

stock *n.* **1.** array, assets, assortment, cache, choice, commodities, fund, goods, hoard, inventory, merchandise, range, reserve, reservoir, selection, stockpile, store, supply, variety, wares **2.** *Finance* capital, funds, investment, property **3.** beasts, cattle, domestic animals, flocks, herds, horses, livestock, sheep **4.** ancestry, background, breed, descent, extraction, family, forebears, house, line, lineage, line of descent, parentage, pedigree, race, strain, type, variety **5. take stock** appraise, estimate, review the situation, see how the land lies, size up (*informal*), weigh up *~adj.* **6.** banal, basic, commonplace, conventional, customary, formal, hackneyed, ordinary, overused, regular, routine, run-of-the-mill, set, standard, staple, stereotyped, traditional, trite, usual, worn-out *~vb.* **7.** deal in, handle, keep, sell, supply, trade in **8.** *with* **up** accumulate, amass, buy up, gather, hoard, lay in, put away, replenish, save, store (up), supply **9.** equip, fill, fit out, furnish, kit out, provide with, provision, supply

stocky chunky, dumpy, mesomorphic, solid, stubby, stumpy, sturdy, thickset

stodgy 1. filling, heavy, leaden, starchy, substantial **2.** boring, dull, dull as ditchwater, formal, fuddy-duddy (*informal*), heavy going, ho-hum (*informal*), laboured, staid, stuffy, tedious, turgid, unexciting, unimaginative, uninspired

stoical calm, cool, dispassionate, impassive, imperturbable, indifferent, long-suffering, philosophical, phlegmatic, resigned, stoic, stolid

stoicism acceptance, calmness, dispassion, fatalism, forbearance, fortitude, impassivity, imperturbability, indifference, long-suffering, patience, resignation, stolidity

pore in a plant leaf that controls the passage of gases into and out of the plant. **2** *Zool* a mouth or mouthlike part.

stomach *n* **1** an organ inside the body in which food is stored until it has been partially digested. **2** the front of the body around the waist. **3** desire or appetite: *he still has the stomach for a fight.* ~*vb* **4** to put up with: *liberals could not stomach the rest of the package.*

stomachache *n* pain in the stomach, such as from indigestion. Also called: **stomach upset, upset stomach**

stomacher *n History* a decorative V-shaped panel of stiff material worn over the chest and stomach mainly by women.

stomach pump *n Med* a pump with a long tube used for removing the contents of a person's stomach, for instance after he or she has swallowed poison.

stomp *vb* to tread or stamp heavily.

stompie *n S African slang* **1** a cigarette butt. **2** a short man.

stone *n* **1** the hard nonmetallic material of which rocks are made. **2** a small lump of rock. **3** Also called: **gemstone** a precious or semiprecious stone that has been cut and polished. **4** a piece of rock used for some particular purpose: *gravestone; millstone.* **5** the hard central part of fruits such as the peach or date. **6** (*pl* **stone**) *Brit* a unit of weight equal to 14 pounds or 6.350 kilograms. **7** *Pathol* a hard deposit formed in the kidney or bladder. **8 heart of stone** a hard or unemotional personality. **9 leave no stone unturned** to do everything possible to achieve something. ~*adj* **10** made of stoneware: *the polished stone planter.* ~*vb* **stoning, stoned 11** to throw stones at (someone), for example as a punishment. **12** to remove the stones from (a fruit).

Stone Age *n* a phase of human culture identified by the use of tools made of stone.

stonechat *n* a songbird that has black feathers and a reddish-brown breast.

stone-cold *adj* **1** completely cold. ~*adv* **2 stone-cold sober** completely sober.

stoned *adj Slang* under the influence of drugs or alcohol.

stone-deaf *adj* completely deaf.

stone fruit *n* same as **drupe.**

stoneground *adj* **1** (of flour) made by crushing grain between two large stones. **2** made with stoneground flour: *stoneground wholemeal bread.*

stonemason *n* a person who is skilled in preparing stone for building.

stone's throw *n* a short distance.

stonewall *vb* **1** to deliberately prolong a discussion by being long-winded or evasive. **2** *Cricket* (of a batsman) to play defensively.

stoneware *n* a hard type of pottery, fired at a very high temperature.

stonewashed *adj* (of clothes or fabric) given a worn faded look by being washed with many small pieces of stone.

stonework *n* any structure or part of a building made of stone.

stony *or* **stoney** *adj* **stonier, stoniest 1** (of ground) rough and covered with stones: *the stony path.* **2** (of a face, voice, or attitude) unfriendly and unsympathetic. **stonily** *adv*

stony-broke *adj Brit slang* completely without money.

stood *vb* the past of **stand.**

stooge *n* **1** an actor who feeds lines to a comedian or acts as the butt of his jokes. **2** *Slang* someone who is taken advantage of by someone in a superior position.

stool *n* **1** a seat with legs but no back. **2** waste matter from the bowels.

stool pigeon *n* an informer for the police.

stoop[1] *vb* **1** to bend (the body) forward and downward. **2** to stand or walk with head and shoulders habitually bent forward. **3 stoop to** to lower one's normal standards of behaviour; degrade oneself: *no real journalist would stoop to faking.* ~*n* **4** the act, position, or habit of stooping. **stooping** *adj*

stoop[2] *n US* an open porch or small platform with steps leading up to it at the entrance to a building.

stop *vb* **stopping, stopped 1** to cease from doing (something); discontinue. **2** to cause (something moving) to halt or (of something moving) to come to a halt. **3** to prevent the continuance or completion of (something). **4** (often foll. by *from*) to prevent or restrain: *I stopped her from going on any further.* **5** to keep back: *no agreement to stop arms supplies.* **6 stop up** to block or plug: *to stop up a pipe.* **7** to stay or rest: *we stopped at a camp site for a change.* **8** to instruct a bank not to honour (a cheque). **9** to deduct (money) from pay. **10** *Informal* to receive (a blow or hit). **11** *Music* to alter the vibrating length of (a string on a violin, guitar, etc.) by pressing down on it at some point with the finger. **12 stop at nothing** to be prepared to do anything; be ruthless. ~*n* **13** prevention of movement or progress: *you can put a stop to it quite easily.* **14** the act of stopping or the state of being stopped: *the car lurched to a stop.* **15** a place where something halts or pauses: *a bus stop.* **16** the act or an instance of blocking or obstructing. **17** a device that prevents, limits, or ends the motion of a mechanism or moving part. **18** *Brit* a full stop. **19** *Music* a knob on an organ that is operated to allow sets of pipes to sound. **20 pull out all the stops** to make a great effort.

THESAURUS

stolid apathetic, bovine, doltish, dozy (*Brit. informal*), dull, heavy, lumpish, obtuse, slow, stupid, unemotional, wooden

stomach *n.* **1.** abdomen, belly, gut (*informal*), inside(s) (*informal*), paunch, pot, potbelly, spare tyre (*informal*), tummy (*informal*) **2.** appetite, desire, inclination, mind, relish, taste ~*vb.* **3.** abide, bear, endure, put up with (*informal*), reconcile *or* resign oneself to, submit to, suffer, swallow, take, tolerate

stony adamant, blank, callous, chilly, expressionless, frigid, hard, harsh, heartless, hostile, icy, indifferent, inexorable, merciless, obdurate, pitiless, unfeeling, unforgiving, unresponsive

stoop *vb.* **1.** be bowed *or* round-shouldered, bend, bow, crouch, descend, duck, hunch, incline, kneel, lean, squat **2.** *often with* **to** condescend, deign, demean oneself, descend, lower oneself, resort, sink, vouchsafe ~*n.* **3.** bad posture, droop, round-shoulderedness, sag, slouch, slump

stop *vb.* **1.** axe (*informal*), be over, break off, bring *or* come to a halt, bring *or* come to a standstill, call it a day (*informal*), cease, come to an end, conclude, cut out (*informal*), cut short, desist, discontinue, draw up, end, finish, halt, leave off, pack in (*Brit. informal*), pause, peter out, pull up, put an end to, quit, refrain, run down, run its course, shut down, stall, terminate **2.** arrest, bar, block, break, bung (*informal*), check, close, forestall, frustrate, hinder, hold back, impede, intercept, interrupt, obstruct, plug, prevent, rein in, repress, restrain, seal, silence, staunch, stem, suspend **3.** break one's journey, lodge, put up, rest, sojourn (*literary*), stay, tarry (*old-fashioned*) ~*n.* **4.** bar, block, break, check, control, hindrance, impediment, plug,

stopbank *n NZ* an embankment to prevent flooding.

stopcock *n* a valve used to control or stop the flow of a fluid in a pipe.

stopgap *n* a thing that serves as a substitute for a short time until replaced by something more suitable.

stop off *vb* (often foll. by *at*) to halt and call somewhere on the way to another place.

stopover *n* **1** a break in a journey. *~vb* **stop over 2** to make a stopover.

stoppage *n* **1** the act of stopping something or the state of being stopped: *a heart stoppage.* **2** a deduction of money, such as taxation, from pay. **3** an organized stopping of work during industrial action.

stoppage time *n* same as **injury time.**

stopper *n* a plug for closing a bottle, pipe, etc.

stop press *n Brit* news items inserted into a newspaper after the printing has been started.

stopwatch *n* a watch which can be stopped instantly for exact timing of a sporting event.

storage *n* **1** the act of storing or the state of being stored. **2** space for storing. **3** *Computers* the process of storing information in a computer.

storage device *n* a piece of computer equipment, such as a magnetic tape or a disk in or on which information can be stored.

storage heater *n* an electric device that accumulates and radiates heat generated by cheap off-peak electricity.

store *vb* **storing, stored 1** to keep, set aside, or gather (things) for future use. **2** to place furniture or other possessions in a warehouse for safekeeping. **3** to supply or stock (certain goods). **4** *Computers* to enter or keep (information) in a storage device. *~n* **5** a shop (in Britain usually a large one). **6** a large supply or stock kept for future use. **7** short for **department store. 8** a storage place, such as a warehouse. **9** *Computers chiefly Brit* same as **memory** (sense 7). **10 in store** about to happen; forthcoming: *you've got a treat in store.* **11 set great store by something** to value something as important. ~See also **stores.**

storehouse *n* **1** a building where goods are stored. **2** a collection of things or ideas: *a storehouse of memories.*

storeroom *n* a room in which things are stored.

stores *pl n* supply or stock of food and other essentials for a journey.

storey *or esp US* **story** *n, pl* **-reys** *or* **-ries** a floor or level of a building.

stork *n* a large wading bird with very long legs, a long bill, and white-and-black feathers.

storm *n* **1** a violent weather condition of strong winds, rain, hail, thunder, lightning, etc. **2** a violent disturbance or quarrel: *a storm of protest from the opposition.* **3** (usually foll. by *of*) a heavy discharge of bullets or missiles. **4 take a place by storm a** to capture or overrun a place by a violent attack. **b** to surprise people, but receive their praise, by being extremely successful at something. *~vb* **5** to attack or capture (a place) suddenly and violently. **6** to shout angrily. **7** to move or rush violently or angrily: *she stormed into the study.*

storm centre *n* **1** the centre of a storm, where pressure is lowest. **2** the centre of any disturbance or trouble.

storm door *n* an additional door outside an ordinary door, providing extra protection against wind, cold, and rain.

storm trooper *n* a member of the paramilitary wing of the Nazi Party.

stormy *adj* **stormier, stormiest 1** (of weather) violent with dark skies, heavy rain or snow, and strong winds. **2** involving violent emotions: *a stormy affair.*

stormy petrel *or* **storm petrel** *n* **1** a small sea bird with dark feathers and paler underparts. **2** a person who brings trouble.

story[1] *n, pl* **-ries 1** a description of a chain of events told or written in prose or verse. **2** Also called: **short story** a piece of fiction, shorter and usually less detailed than a novel. **3** Also called: **story line** the plot of a book or film. **4** a news report. **5** the event or material for such a report. **6** *Informal* a lie.

story[2] *n, pl* **-ries** *Chiefly US* same as **storey.**

storybook *n* **1** a book containing stories for children. *~adj* **2** better or happier than in real life: *a storybook romance.*

stoup *or* **stoop** (**stoop**) *n* a small basin in a church for holy water.

stoush *Austral & NZ slang ~vb* **1** to hit or punch (someone). *~n* **2** fighting or violence.

stout *adj* **1** solidly built or fat. **2** strong and sturdy: *stout footwear.* **3** brave or determined: *they were held up by unexpectedly stout resistance. ~n* **4** strong dark beer. **stoutly** *adv*

THESAURUS

stoppage **5.** cessation, conclusion, discontinuation, end, finish, halt, standstill **6.** depot, destination, halt, stage, station, termination, terminus

stopgap improvisation, makeshift, resort, shift, substitute, temporary expedient

stoppage abeyance, arrest, close, closure, cutoff, deduction, discontinuance, halt, hindrance, lay-off, shutdown, standstill, stopping

store *vb.* **1.** accumulate, deposit, garner, hoard, husband, keep, keep in reserve, lay by *or* in, lock away, put aside, put aside for a rainy day, put by, put in storage, reserve, salt away, save, stash (*informal*), stock, stockpile *~n.* **2.** chain store, department store, emporium, market, mart, outlet, shop, supermarket **3.** abundance, accumulation, cache, fund, hoard, lot, mine, plenty, plethora, provision, quantity, reserve, reservoir, stock, stockpile, supply, wealth **4.** depository, repository, storehouse, storeroom, warehouse **5.** **set great store by** appreciate, esteem, hold in high regard, prize, think highly of, value

storm *n.* **1.** blast, blizzard, cyclone, gale, gust, hurricane, squall, tempest, tornado, whirlwind **2.** agitation, anger, clamour, commotion, disturbance, furore, hubbub, outbreak, outburst, outcry, passion, roar, row, rumpus, stir, strife, tumult, turmoil, violence **3.** assault, attack, blitz, blitzkrieg, offensive, onset, onslaught, rush *~vb.* **4.** assail, assault, beset, charge, rush, take by storm **5.** bluster, complain, fly off the handle (*informal*), fume, rage, rant, rave, scold, thunder **6.** flounce, fly, rush, stalk, stamp, stomp (*informal*)

stormy blustering, blustery, boisterous, dirty, foul, gusty, inclement, raging, rough, squally, tempestuous, turbulent, wild, windy

story **1.** account, anecdote, chronicle, fictional account, history, legend, narration, narrative, novel, recital, record, relation, romance, tale, urban legend, version, yarn **2.** article, feature, news, news item, report, scoop **3.** *informal* falsehood, fib, fiction, lie, pork pie (*Brit. slang*), porky (*Brit. slang*), untruth, white lie

stout **1.** big, bulky, burly, corpulent, fat, fleshy, heavy, obese, on the large *or* heavy side, overweight, plump, portly, rotund, substantial, tubby **2.** able-bodied, athletic, beefy (*informal*), brawny, hardy, hulking, husky (*informal*), lusty, muscular, robust, stalwart, strapping, strong, sturdy, substantial, thickset, tough, vigorous **3.**

stouthearted *adj Old-fashioned* determined or brave.

stove[1] *n* **1** same as **cooker** (sense 1). **2** any apparatus for heating, such as a kiln.

stove[2] *vb* a past tense and past participle of **stave.**

stovepipe *n* a pipe that takes fumes and smoke away from a stove.

stow *vb* (often foll. by *away*) to pack or store (something).

stowage *n* **1** space, room, or a charge for stowing goods. **2** the act of stowing.

stowaway *n* **1** a person who hides aboard a ship or aircraft in order to travel free. *~vb* **stow away 2** to travel in such a way.

strabismus *n Pathol* same as **squint** (sense 3).

straddle *vb* **-dling, -dled 1** to have one leg or part on each side of (something). **2** *US & Canad informal* to be in favour of both sides of (an issue).

Stradivarius *n* a violin manufactured in Italy by Antonio Stradivari (?1644–1737) or his family.

strafe *vb* **strafing, strafed** to machine-gun (an enemy) from the air.

straggle *vb* **-gling, -gled 1** to spread out in an untidy and rambling way: *the town straggled off to the east.* **2** to linger behind or wander from a main line or part. **straggler** *n* **straggly** *adj*

straight *adj* **1** continuing in the same direction without bending; not curved or crooked. **2** even, level, or upright. **3** in keeping with the facts; accurate. **4** outright or candid: *a straight rejection.* **5** in continuous succession. **6** (of an alcoholic drink) undiluted. **7** not wavy or curly: *straight hair.* **8** in good order. **9** (of a play or acting style) straightforward or serious. **10** honest, respectable, or reliable. **11** *Slang* heterosexual. **12** *Slang* conventional in views, customs, or appearance. **13** *Informal* no longer owing or being owed something: *if you buy the next round we'll be straight.* *~adv* **14** in a straight line or direct course. **15** immediately; at once: *get straight back here.* **16** in a level or upright position: *he sat up straight.* **17** continuously; uninterruptedly: *we waited for three hours straight.* **18** (often foll. by *out*) frankly; candidly: *she asked me straight out.* **19 go straight** *Informal* to reform after having been a criminal. **20 straight away** *or* **straightaway** at once. *~n* **21** a straight line, form, part, or position. **22** *Brit* a straight part of a racetrack.

straighten *vb* (sometimes foll. by *up* or *out*) **1** to make or become straight. **2** to make (something) neat or tidy.

straighten out *vb* to make (something) less complicated or confused.

straight face *n* a serious facial expression which hides a desire to laugh. **straight-faced** *adj*

straight fight *n* a contest between two candidates only.

straightforward *adj* **1** (of a person) honest, frank, and open. **2** *Chiefly Brit* (of a task) easy to do.

straight man *n* an actor who acts as the butt of a comedian's jokes.

strain[1] *n* **1** tension or tiredness resulting from overwork or worry. **2** tension between people or organizations: *there are signs of strain between the economic super-powers.* **3** an intense physical or mental effort. **4** the damage resulting from excessive physical exertion. **5** a great demand on the emotions, strength, or resources. **6** a way of speaking: *he would have gone on in this strain for some time.* **7** *Physics* the change in dimension of a body caused by outside forces. **8** **strains** *Music* a theme, melody, or tune. *~vb* **9** to subject (someone) to mental tension or stress. **10** to make an intense effort: *the rest were straining to follow the conversation.* **11** to use (resources) to, or beyond, their limits. **12** to injure or damage (oneself or a part of one's body) by overexertion: *he appeared to have strained a muscle.* **13** to pour (a substance) through a sieve or filter. **14 strain at** to push, pull, or work with violent effort (on something). **15** to draw (something) taut or be drawn taut.

strain[2] *n* **1** a group of animals or plants within a species or variety, distinguished by one or more minor characteristics. **2** a trace or streak: *a strain of ruthlessness in their play.*

strained *adj* **1** (of an action, expression, etc.) not

THESAURUS

bold, brave, courageous, dauntless, doughty, fearless, gallant, intrepid, lion-hearted, manly, plucky, resolute, valiant, valorous

straggle drift, lag, loiter, ramble, range, roam, rove, spread, stray, string out, trail, wander

straight *adj.* **1.** aligned, erect, even, horizontal, in line, level, perpendicular, plumb, right, smooth, square, true, upright, vertical **2.** blunt, candid, downright, forthright, frank, honest, outright, plain, point-blank, straightforward, unqualified, upfront (*informal*) **3.** consecutive, continuous, nonstop, running, solid, successive, sustained, through, uninterrupted, unrelieved **4.** neat, pure, unadulterated, undiluted, unmixed **5.** above board, accurate, authentic, decent, equitable, fair, fair and square, honest, honourable, just, law-abiding, reliable, respectable, trustworthy, upright **6.** *slang* bourgeois, conservative, conventional, orthodox, square (*informal*), traditional *~adv.* **7.** as the crow flies, at once, directly, immediately, instantly **8.** *often with* **out** candidly, frankly, honestly, in plain English, point-blank, pulling no punches (*informal*), with no holds barred

straight away at once, directly, immediately, instantly, now, on the spot, right away, straightway (*archaic*), there and then, this minute, without any delay, without more ado

straighten *sometimes with* **up** *or* **out** arrange, neaten, order, put in order, set *or* put to rights, smarten up, spruce up, tidy (up)

straighten out become clear, clear up, correct, disentangle, put right, rectify, regularize, resolve, settle, sort out, unsnarl, work out

straightforward **1.** above board, candid, direct, forthright, genuine, guileless, honest, open, sincere, truthful, upfront (*informal*) **2.** *chiefly Brit.* clear-cut, easy, elementary, routine, simple, uncomplicated, undemanding

strain[1] *n.* **1.** anxiety, burden, pressure, stress, tension **2.** effort, exertion, force, injury, pull, sprain, struggle, tautness, tension, tensity (*rare*), wrench **3.** *often plural Music* air, lay, measure (*poetic*), melody, song, theme, tune *~vb.* **4.** bend over backwards (*informal*), break one's neck (*informal*), bust a gut (*informal*), do one's damnedest (*informal*), endeavour, give it one's all (*informal*), give it one's best shot (*informal*), go all out for (*informal*), go for broke (*slang*), go for it (*informal*), knock oneself out (*informal*), labour, make an all-out effort (*informal*), make a supreme effort, rupture oneself (*informal*), strive, struggle **5.** drive, exert, fatigue, injure, overexert, overtax, overwork, pull, push to the limit, sprain, tax, tear, tire, twist, weaken, wrench **6.** filter, percolate, purify, riddle, screen, seep, separate, sieve, sift **7.** distend, draw tight, extend, stretch, tauten, tighten

strain[2] *n.* **1.** ancestry, blood, descent, extraction, family, lineage, pedigree, race, stock **2.** streak, suggestion, suspicion, tendency, trace, trait

strained artificial, awkward, constrained, difficult,

natural or spontaneous. **2** (of an atmosphere, relationship, etc.) not relaxed; tense.

strainer *n* a sieve used for straining sauces, vegetables, or tea.

strait *n* **1** (*often pl*) a narrow channel of the sea linking two larger areas of sea. **2 straits** a position of extreme difficulty: *in desperate straits.*

straitened *adj* **in straitened circumstances** not having much money.

straitjacket *n* **1** a strong canvas jacket with long sleeves used to bind the arms of a violent person. **2** anything which holds back or restricts development or freedom: *exporters are wrapped in a straitjacket of regulations.*

strait-laced *or* **straight-laced** *adj* having a strict code of moral standards; puritanical.

strand[1] *vb* **1** to leave or drive (ships or fish) ashore. **2** to leave (someone) helpless, for example without transport or money. *~n* **3** *Chiefly poetic* a shore or beach.

strand[2] *n* **1** one of the individual fibres of string or wire that form a rope, cord, or cable. **2** a single length of string, hair, wool, or wire. **3** a string of pearls or beads. **4** a part of something; element: *the many disparate strands of the Anglican Church.*

stranded *adj* stuck somewhere and unable to leave.

strange *adj* **1** odd or unexpected. **2** not known, seen, or experienced before; unfamiliar. **3 strange to** inexperienced (in) or unaccustomed (to): *they are in some degree strange to it.* **strangely** *adv* **strangeness** *n*

stranger *n* **1** any person whom one does not know. **2** a person who is new to a particular place. **3 stranger to** a person who is unfamiliar with or new to something: *Paul is no stranger to lavish spending.*

strangle *vb* **-gling, -gled 1** to kill (someone) by pressing his or her windpipe; throttle. **2** to prevent the growth or development of: *another attempt at strangling national identity.* **3** to stifle (a voice, cry, or laugh) by swallowing suddenly: *the words were strangled by sobs.* **strangler** *n*

stranglehold *n* **1** a wrestling hold in which a wrestler's arms are pressed against his opponent's windpipe. **2** complete power or control over a person or situation.

strangulate *vb* **-lating, -lated 1** *Pathol* to constrict (a hollow organ or vessel) so as to stop the flow of air or blood through it: *a badly strangulated hernia.* **2** same as **strangle. strangulation** *n*

strap *n* **1** a strip of strong flexible material used for carrying, lifting, fastening, or holding things in place. **2** a loop of leather or rubber, hanging from the roof in a bus or train for standing passengers to hold on to. **3** short for **shoulder strap. 4 the strap** a beating with a strap as a punishment. *~vb* **strapping, strapped 5** to tie or bind (something) with a strap.

straphanger *n Informal* a passenger in a bus or train who has to travel standing and holding on to a strap.

strapless *adj* (of women's clothes) without straps over the shoulders.

strapped *adj* **strapped for** *Slang* badly in need of: *strapped for cash.*

strapping *adj* tall, strong, and healthy-looking: *a strapping young lad.*

strata *n* the plural of **stratum.**

stratagem *n* a clever plan to deceive an enemy.

strategic (strat-**ee**-jik) *adj* **1** planned to achieve an advantage; tactical. **2** (of weapons, esp. missiles) directed against an enemy's homeland rather than used on a battlefield. **strategically** *adv*

strategy *n, pl* **-gies 1** a long-term plan for success, such as in politics or business. **2** the art of the planning and conduct of a war. **strategist** *n*

strath *n Scot* a flat river valley.

strathspey *n* **1** a Scottish dance with gliding steps, slower than a reel. **2** music for this dance.

stratified *adj* **1** (of rocks) formed in horizontal layers of different materials. **2** *Sociol* (of a society) divided into different classes or groups. **stratification** *n*

stratocumulus (strat-oh-**kew**-myew-luss) *n, pl* **-li** (-lie) *Meteorol* an unbroken stretch of dark grey cloud.

stratosphere *n* the atmospheric layer between about 15 and 50 km above the earth.

stratum (**strah**-tum) *n, pl* **-ta** (-ta) **1** any of the distinct layers into which certain rocks are divided. **2** a layer of ocean or atmosphere marked off naturally or decided arbitrarily by man. **3** a social class.

stratus (**stray**-tuss) *n, pl* **-ti** (-tie) a grey layer cloud.

straw *n* **1** dried stalks of threshed grain, such as wheat or barley. **2** a single stalk of straw. **3** a long thin hollow paper or plastic tube, used for sucking up liquids into the mouth. **4 clutch at straws** to turn in desperation to something with little chance of success. **5 draw the short straw** to be the person chosen to perform an unpleasant task. *~adj* **6** made of straw: *straw baskets.*

strawberry *n, pl* **-ries** a sweet fleshy red fruit with small seeds on the outside.

strawberry blonde *adj* **1** (of hair) reddish-blonde. *~n* **2** a woman with such hair.

THESAURUS

embarrassed, false, forced, laboured, put on, self-conscious, stiff, tense, uncomfortable, uneasy, unnatural, unrelaxed

strait *n.* **1.** *often plural* channel, narrows, sound **2.** *plural* crisis, difficulty, dilemma, distress, embarrassment, emergency, extremity, hardship, hole (*slang*), mess, panic stations (*informal*), pass, perplexity, plight, predicament, pretty *or* fine kettle of fish (*informal*)

strait-laced moralistic, narrow, narrow-minded, of the old school, old-maidish (*informal*), overscrupulous, prim, proper, prudish, puritanical, strict, Victorian

strand *n.* fibre, filament, length, lock, rope, string, thread, tress, twist, wisp

stranded aground, ashore, beached, cast away, grounded, marooned, wrecked

strange 1. abnormal, astonishing, bizarre, curious, eccentric, exceptional, extraordinary, fantastic, funny, irregular, marvellous, mystifying, odd, oddball (*informal*), off-the-wall (*slang*), out-of-the-way, outré, peculiar, perplexing, queer, rare, remarkable, rum (*Brit. slang*), singular, unaccountable, uncanny, uncommon, unheard of, weird, wonderful **2.** alien, exotic, foreign, new, novel, outside one's experience, remote, unexplored, unfamiliar, unknown, untried **3.** *with* **to** a stranger to, ignorant of, inexperienced, new to, unaccustomed, unpractised, unseasoned, unused, unversed in

stranger alien, foreigner, guest, incomer, new arrival, newcomer, outlander, unknown, visitor

strangle 1. asphyxiate, choke, garrotte, smother, strangulate, suffocate, throttle **2.** gag, inhibit, repress, stifle, suppress

strap 1. *n.* belt, leash, thong, tie **2.** *vb.* bind, buckle, fasten, lash, secure, tie, truss

stratagem artifice, device, dodge, feint, intrigue, manoeuvre, plan, plot, ploy, ruse, scheme, subterfuge, trick, wile

strawberry mark *n* a red birthmark.
straw-coloured *adj* pale yellow: *straw-coloured hair.*
straw poll *or* **vote** *n* an unofficial poll or vote taken to find out the opinion of a group or the public on some issue.
stray *vb* **1** to wander away from the correct path or from a given area. **2** to move away from the point or lose concentration. **3** to fail to live up to certain moral standards: *her man had strayed.* ~*n* **4** a domestic animal that has wandered away from its home. **5** *Old-fashioned* a lost or homeless child. ~*adj* **6** (of a domestic animal) having wandered away from its home. **7** random or separated from the main group of things of their kind: *stray bombs and rockets.*
streak *n* **1** a long thin stripe or trace of some contrasting colour. **2** (of lightning) a sudden flash. **3** a quality or characteristic: *a nasty streak.* **4** a short stretch of good or bad luck: *a losing streak.* **5** *Informal* an instance of running naked through a public place. ~*vb* **6** to mark (something) with a streak or streaks: *sweat streaking the grime of his face.* **7** to move quickly in a straight line. **8** *Informal* to run naked through a public place. **streaked** *or* **streaky** *adj* **streaker** *n*
stream *n* **1** a small river. **2** any steady flow of water or other liquid. **3** something that resembles a stream in moving continuously in a line or particular direction: *the stream of traffic.* **4** a fast and continuous flow of speech: *the constant stream of jargon.* **5** *Brit, Austral, & NZ* a class of school children grouped together because of similar ability. ~*vb* **6** to pour in a continuous flow: *rain streamed down her cheeks.* **7** (of a crowd of people or traffic or a herd of animals) to move in unbroken succession. **8** to float freely or with a waving motion: *a flimsy pink dress that streamed out behind her.* **9** *Brit* to group (school children) in streams. **streaming** *n* **streamlet** *n*
streamer *n* **1** a long coiled ribbon of coloured paper that unrolls when tossed. **2** a long narrow flag.
streamline *vb* **-lining, -lined 1** to improve (something) by removing the parts that are least useful or profitable. **2** to make (an aircraft, boat, or vehicle) less resistant to flowing air or water by improving its shape. **streamlined** *adj*
street *n* **1** a public road that is usually lined with buildings, esp. in a town: *Sauchiehall Street.* **2** the part of the road between the pavements, used by vehicles. **3** the people living in a particular street. **4 on the streets** homeless. **5 right up one's street** *Informal* just what one knows or likes best. **6 streets ahead of** *Informal* superior to or more advanced than.
streetcar *n US & Canad* a tram.
street credibility *or* **cred** *n* a command of the styles, knowledge, etc., associated with urban youngsters who are respected by their contemporaries: *having children was the quickest way to lose your street cred.*
street value *n* the price that would be paid for goods, esp. illegal ones such as drugs, by the final user: *cocaine with a street value of £2.5m was seized at Heathrow airport.*
streetwalker *n* a prostitute who tries to find customers in the streets.
streetwise *adj* knowing how to survive or succeed in poor and often criminal sections of big cities.
strength *n* **1** the state or quality of being physically or mentally strong. **2** the ability to withstand great force, stress, or pressure. **3** something regarded as valuable or a source of power: *his chief strength is rocketry.* **4** potency or effectiveness, such as of a drink or drug. **5** power to convince: *the strength of this argument.* **6** degree of intensity or concentration of colour, light, sound, or flavour: *a strong cheese.* **7** the total number of people in a group: *at full strength; 50 000 men below strength.* **8 go from strength to strength** to have ever-increasing success. **9 on the strength of** on the basis of or relying upon.
strengthen *vb* to make (something) stronger or become stronger.
strenuous *adj* requiring or involving the use of great energy or effort. **strenuously** *adv*
streptococcus (strep-toe-**kok**-uss) *n, pl* **-cocci** (-**kok**-eye) a bacterium occurring in chains and including many species that cause disease.
streptomycin *n Med* an antibiotic used in the treatment of tuberculosis and other bacterial infections.
stress *n* **1** mental, emotional, or physical strain or tension. **2** special emphasis or significance. **3** emphasis placed upon a syllable by pronouncing it more loudly than those that surround it. **4** *Physics* force producing a change in shape or volume. ~*vb* **5** to give

THESAURUS

strategic calculated, deliberate, diplomatic, planned, politic, tactical
strategy approach, grand design, manoeuvring, plan, planning, policy, procedure, programme, scheme
stray *vb.* **1.** be abandoned *or* lost, drift, err, go astray, lose one's way, meander, range, roam, rove, straggle, wander **2.** deviate, digress, diverge, get off the point, get sidetracked, go off at a tangent, ramble ~*adj.* **3.** abandoned, homeless, lost, roaming, vagrant **4.** accidental, chance, erratic, freak, odd, random, scattered
streak *n.* **1.** band, dash, element, layer, line, slash, smear, strain, strip, stripe, stroke, touch, trace, vein ~*vb.* **2.** band, daub, fleck, slash, smear, striate, stripe **3.** dart, flash, fly, hurtle, move like greased lightning (*informal*), speed, sprint, sweep, tear, whistle, whizz (*informal*), zoom
stream 1. *n.* bayou (*in the southern U.S.*), beck (*in N England*), brook, burn (*Scot.*), course, creek (*U.S., Canad., Austral. & N.Z.*), current, drift, flow, freshet, outpouring, rill, river, rivulet, run, rush, surge, tide, torrent, tributary, undertow **2.** *vb.* cascade, course, emit, flood, flow, glide, gush, issue, pour, run, shed, spill, spout
streamlined efficient, modernized, organized, rationalized, sleek, slick, smooth, smooth-running, time-saving, well-run
street 1. avenue, boulevard, lane, road, roadway, row, terrace, thoroughfare **2. right up one's street** *informal* acceptable, compatible, congenial, familiar, one's cup of tea (*informal*), pleasing, suitable, to one's liking, to one's taste
strength 1. backbone, brawn, brawniness, courage, firmness, fortitude, health, lustiness, might, muscle, robustness, sinew, stamina, stoutness, sturdiness, toughness **2.** advantage, anchor, asset, mainstay, security, strong point, succour, tower of strength **3.** cogency, concentration, effectiveness, efficacy, energy, force, intensity, potency, power, resolution, spirit, vehemence, vigour
strengthen animate, augment, bolster, brace, brace up, build up, buttress, confirm, consolidate, corroborate, encourage, enhance, establish, fortify, give a boost to, give new energy to, harden, hearten, heighten, increase, intensify, invigorate, justify, nerve, nourish, reinforce, rejuvenate, restore, steel, stiffen, substantiate, support, toughen
strenuous arduous, demanding, exhausting, hard, Herculean, laborious, taxing, toilsome (*literary*), tough, tough going, unrelaxing, uphill

emphasis to (a point or subject): *she stressed how difficult it had been.* **6** to pronounce (a word or syllable) more loudly than those surrounding it. **stressful** *adj*

stressed-out *adj Informal* suffering from anxiety or tension.

stretch *vb* **1 stretch over** *or* **for** to extend or spread over (a specified distance): *the flood barrier stretches for several miles.* **2** to draw out or extend (something) or to be drawn out or extended in length or area. **3** to distort or lengthen (something) or to be distorted or lengthened permanently. **4** to extend (the limbs or body), for example when one has just woken up. **5** (often foll. by *out, forward,* etc.) to reach or hold out (a part of one's body). **6** to reach or suspend (a rope, etc.) from one place to another. **7** to draw (something) tight; tighten. **8** (usually foll. by *over*) to extend in time: *a dinner which stretched over three consecutive evenings.* **9** to put a great strain upon (one's money or resources). **10** to make do with (limited resources): *the Walkers decided to stretch their budget.* **11** to extend (someone) to the limit of his or her abilities. **12** to extend (someone) to the limit of his or her tolerance. **13 stretch a point** to make an exception not usually made. *~n* **14** the act of stretching. **15** a large or continuous expanse or distance: *this stretch of desert.* **16** extent in time. **17** a term of imprisonment. **18 at a stretch** *Chiefly Brit* **a** with some difficulty; by making a special effort. **b** at one time: *for hours at a stretch they had no conversation.* *~adj* **19** (of clothes) able to be stretched without permanently losing shape: *a stretch suit.* **stretchy** *adj*

stretcher *n* a frame covered with canvas, on which an ill or injured person is carried.

stretcher-bearer *n* a person who helps to carry a stretcher.

strew *vb* **strewing, strewed, strewn** to scatter (things) over a surface.

strewth *interj Informal* an expression of surprise or alarm.

stria (strye-a) *n, pl* **striae** (strye-ee) *Geol* a scratch or groove on the surface of a rock crystal.

striation *n* **1** an arrangement or pattern of striae. **2** same as **stria. striated** *adj*

stricken *adj* badly affected by disease, pain, grief, etc.: *flood-stricken areas.*

strict *adj* **1** severely correct in attention to behaviour or morality: *a strict disciplinarian.* **2** following carefully and exactly a set of rules: *she is a strict vegetarian.* **3** (of a rule or law) very precise and requiring total obedience: *a strict code of practice.* **4** (of a meaning) exact: *this is not, in the strictest sense, a biography.* **5** (of a punishment, etc.) harsh or severe. **6** complete; absolute: *strict obedience.* **strictly** *adv* **strictness** *n*

stricture *n Formal* a severe criticism.

stride *n* **1** a long step or pace. **2** the length of such a step. **3** a striding walk. **4** progress or development: *he has made great strides in regaining his confidence.* **5** a regular pace or rate of progress: *it put me off my stride.* **6 take something in one's stride** to do something without difficulty or effort. *~vb* **striding, strode, stridden 7** to walk with long steps or paces. **8 stride over** *or* **across** to cross (over a space or an obstacle) with a stride.

strident *adj* **1** (of a voice or sound) loud and harsh. **2** loud, persistent, and forceful: *a strident critic of the establishment.* **stridency** *n*

strife *n* angry or violent struggle; conflict.

strike *vb* **striking, struck 1** (of employees) to stop work collectively as a protest against working conditions, low pay, etc. **2** to hit (someone). **3** to cause (something) to come into sudden or violent contact with something. **4 strike at** to attack (someone or something). **5** to cause (a match) to light by friction. **6** to sound (a specific note) on a musical instrument. **7** (of a clock) to indicate (a time) by the sound of a bell. **8** to affect (someone) deeply in a particular way: *he never struck me as the supportive type.* **9** to enter the mind of: *a brilliant thought struck me.* **10** (of a poisonous snake) to injure by biting. **11** (*past participle* **struck** *or* **stricken**) to change into (a different state): *struck blind.* **12** to be noticed by; catch: *the heavy smell of incense struck my nostrils.* **13** to arrive at (something) suddenly or unexpectedly: *to strike on a solution.* **14** to afflict (someone) with a disease: *she has been struck down by breast cancer.* **15** to discover a source of (gold, oil, etc.). **16** to reach (something) by agreement: *to strike a deal.* **17** to take up (a posture or an attitude). **18** to take apart or pack up: *to strike camp.* **19** to make (a coin) by stamping it. **20 strike home** to achieve the desired effect. **21 strike it rich** *Informal* to have an unexpected financial success. *~n* **22** a stopping of work, as a protest against working conditions, low pay, etc.: *a one-day strike.* **23** an act or instance of striking. **24** a military attack, esp. an air attack on a target on land or at sea: *a pre-emptive strike.* **25** *Baseball* a pitched ball swung at and missed by the batter. **26** *Tenpin bowling* the knocking down of all the pins with one bowl. **27** the discovery of a source of gold, oil, etc. ~See also **strike off, strike out, strike up.**

strikebreaker *n* a person who tries to make a strike

THESAURUS

stress *n.* **1.** anxiety, burden, hassle (*informal*), nervous tension, oppression, pressure, strain, tautness, tension, trauma, worry **2.** emphasis, force, importance, significance, urgency, weight **3.** accent, accentuation, beat, emphasis *~vb.* **4.** accentuate, belabour, dwell on, emphasize, harp on, lay emphasis upon, point up, repeat, rub in, underline, underscore

stretch *vb.* **1. stretch over** *or* **for** cover, extend, put forth, reach, spread, unfold, unroll **2.** distend, draw out, elongate, expand, inflate, lengthen, pull, pull out of shape, rack, strain, swell, tighten *~n.* **3.** area, distance, expanse, extent, spread, sweep, tract **4.** bit, period, run, space, spell, stint, term, time

strict 1. austere, authoritarian, firm, harsh, no-nonsense, rigid, rigorous, severe, stern, stringent **2.** accurate, close, exact, faithful, meticulous, particular, precise, religious, scrupulous, true **3.** absolute, complete, perfect, total, utter

strident clamorous, clashing, discordant, grating, harsh, jangling, jarring, rasping, raucous, screeching, shrill, unmusical, vociferous

strife animosity, battle, bickering, clash, clashes, combat, conflict, contention, contest, controversy, discord, dissension, friction, quarrel, rivalry, row, squabbling, struggle, warfare, wrangling

strike 1. down tools, mutiny, revolt, walk out **2.** bang, beat, box, buffet, chastise, chin (*slang*), clobber (*slang*), clout (*informal*), clump (*slang*), cuff, deck (*slang*), hammer, hit, knock, lambast(e), lay a finger on (*informal*), lay one on (*slang*), pound, punch, punish, slap, smack, smite (*archaic, Biblical*), sock (*slang*), thump, wallop (*informal*) **3.** be in collision with, bump into, clash, collide with, come into contact with, dash, hit, knock into, run into, smash into, touch **4. strike at** affect, assail, assault, attack, deal a blow to, devastate, fall upon, hit, invade, set upon, smite (*archaic, Biblical*) **5.** affect, come to, come to the mind of, dawn on *or* upon, hit, impress, make an impact on, occur to, reach, register (*informal*), seem **6.** come

fail by working or by taking the place of those on strike.

strike off *vb* to remove the name of (a doctor or lawyer who has done something wrong) from an official register, preventing him or her from practising again.

strike out *vb* **1** to score out (something written). **2** to start out or begin: *I'm going to strike out for town.*

strike pay *n* money paid to strikers by a trade union.

striker *n* **1** a person who is on strike. **2** *Soccer* an attacking player.

strike up *vb* **1** to begin (a conversation or friendship). **2** (of a band or an orchestra) to begin to play.

striking *adj* **1** attracting attention; impressive: *her striking appearance.* **2** very noticeable: *a striking difference.* **strikingly** *adv*

Strine *n* a humorous transliteration of Australian pronunciation, as in *Gloria Soame* for *glorious home.*

string *n* **1** thin cord or twine used for tying, hanging, or binding things. **2** a group of objects threaded on a single strand: *a string of pearls.* **3** a series of things or events: *a string of wins.* **4** a tightly stretched wire or cord on a musical instrument, such as the guitar, violin, or piano, that produces sound when vibrated. **5 the strings** *Music* **a** violins, violas, cellos, and double basses collectively. **b** the section of an orchestra consisting of such instruments. **6** a group of characters that can be treated as a unit by a computer program. **7 with no strings attached** (of an offer) without complications or conditions. **8 pull strings** *Informal* to use one's power or influence, esp. secretly or unofficially. *~adj* **9** composed of stringlike strands woven in a large mesh: *a string bag.* *~vb* **stringing, strung 10** to hang or stretch (something) from one point to another. **11** to provide (something) with a string or strings. **12** to thread (beads) on a string. **13** to extend in a line or series: *towns strung out along the valley.* **stringlike** *adj*

string along *vb Informal* **1 string along with** to accompany: *I'll string along with you.* **2** to deceive (someone) over a period of time: *she had only been stringing him along.*

string bean *n* same as **runner bean.**

string course *n Archit* an ornamental projecting band along a wall.

stringed *adj* (of musical instruments) having strings.

stringent (**strin**-jent) *adj* requiring strict attention to rules or detail. **stringency** *n*

stringer *n* **1** *Archit* a long horizontal timber beam that connects upright posts. **2** a journalist employed by a newspaper on a part-time basis to cover a particular town or area.

string quartet *n Music* **1** a group of musicians consisting of two violins, one viola, and one cello. **2** a piece of music composed for such a group.

string up *vb Informal* to kill (a person) by hanging.

stringy *adj* **stringier, stringiest 1** thin and rough: *stringy hair.* **2** (of meat or other food) tough and fibrous.

strip[1] *vb* **stripping, stripped 1** to take (the covering or clothes) off (oneself, another person, or thing). **2 a** to undress completely. **b** to perform a striptease. **3** to empty (a building) of all furniture. **4** to take something away from (someone): *they were stripped of their possessions.* **5** to remove (paint) from (a surface or furniture): *she stripped the plaster from the kitchen walls.* **6** (often foll. by *down*) to dismantle (an engine or a mechanism) into individual parts. *~n* **7** the act or an instance of undressing or of performing a striptease.

strip[2] *n* **1** a long narrow piece of something. **2** short for **airstrip. 3** the clothes a football team plays in.

strip cartoon *n* a sequence of drawings in a newspaper or magazine, telling an amusing story or an adventure.

strip club *n* a club in which striptease performances take place.

stripe[1] *n* **1** a long band of colour that differs from the surrounding material. **2** a chevron or band worn on a uniform to indicate rank. *~vb* **striping, striped 3** to mark (something) with stripes. **striped, stripy,** *or* **stripey** *adj*

stripe[2] *n* a stroke from a whip, rod, or cane.

strip lighting *n* a method of electric lighting that uses fluorescent lamps in long glass tubes.

stripling *n* a teenage boy or young man.

stripper *n* **1** a person who performs a striptease. **2** a tool or liquid for removing paint or varnish.

strip-searching *n* the practice by police or customs officials of stripping a prisoner or suspect naked and searching him or her for drugs or smuggled goods.

striptease *n* an entertainment in which a person gradually undresses to music.

strive *vb* **striving, strove, striven** to make a great effort: *to strive for a peaceful settlement.*

strobe *n* short for **strobe lighting** or **stroboscope.**

strobe lighting *n* a flashing beam of very bright light produced by a perforated disc rotating in front of a light source.

stroboscope *n* an instrument producing a very bright flashing light which makes moving people appear stationary.

strode *vb* the past tense of **stride.**

stroganoff *n* a dish of sliced beef cooked with onions and mushrooms, served in a sour-cream sauce. Also called: **beef stroganoff**

stroke *vb* **stroking, stroked 1** to touch or brush lightly or gently. *~n* **2** a light touch or caress with the fingers. **3** *Pathol* rupture of a blood vessel in the brain resulting in loss of consciousness, often followed by paralysis and damage to speech. **4** a blow, knock, or hit. **5** an action or occurrence of the kind specified: *a fantastic stroke of luck; a stroke of intuition.* **6 a** the

THESAURUS

upon *or* across, discover, encounter, find, happen *or* chance upon, hit upon, light upon, reach, stumble upon *or* across, turn up, uncover, unearth **7.** achieve, arrange, arrive at, attain, effect, reach

striking astonishing, conspicuous, dazzling, extraordinary, forcible, impressive, memorable, noticeable, out of the ordinary, outstanding, stunning (*informal*), wonderful

string *n.* **1.** cord, fibre, twine **2.** chain, file, line, procession, queue, row, sequence, series, strand, succession **3. pull strings** *informal* influence, use one's influence *~vb.* **4.** festoon, hang, link, loop, sling, stretch, suspend, thread **5.** disperse, extend, fan out, lengthen, protract, space out, spread out, straggle

stringent binding, demanding, exacting, inflexible, rigid, rigorous, severe, strict, tight, tough

strip[1] **1.** bare, denude, divest, peel, skin **2.** disrobe, unclothe, uncover, undress

strip[2] band, belt, bit, fillet, piece, ribbon, shred, slip, swathe, tongue

stripling adolescent, boy, fledgling, lad, shaver (*old-fashioned*), young fellow, youngster, youth

strive attempt, bend over backwards (*informal*), compete, contend, do all one can, do one's best, do one's damnedest (*informal*), do one's utmost, endeavour, exert oneself, fight, give it one's all (*informal*), give it one's best shot (*informal*), go all out (*informal*), go for it (*informal*), knock oneself out (*informal*), la-

striking of a clock. **b** the hour registered by this: *at the stroke of twelve.* **7** a mark made by a pen or paintbrush. **8** same as **solidus:** used esp. when dictating or reading aloud. **9** the hitting of the ball in sports such as golf or cricket. **10** any one of the repeated movements used by a swimmer. **11** a particular style of swimming, such as the crawl. **12** a single pull on the oars in rowing. **13 at a stroke** with one action. **14 not a stroke (of work)** no work at all.

stroll *vb* **1** to walk about in a leisurely manner. *~n* **2** a leisurely walk.

strong *adj* **stronger, strongest 1** having physical power. **2** not easily broken or injured; solid or robust. **3** great in degree or intensity; not faint or feeble: *a strong voice; a strong smell of explosive.* **4** (of arguments) supported by evidence; convincing. **5** concentrated; not weak or diluted. **6** having a powerful taste or smell: *strong perfume.* **7** (of language) using swear words. **8** (of a person) self-confident: *a strong personality.* **9** committed or fervent: *a strong believer in free trade.* **10** important or having a lot of power or influence: *a strong pro-Europe faction in the party.* **11** very competent at a particular activity: *they sent a very strong team to the Olympics.* **12** containing or having a specified number: *the 700-strong workforce.* **13** (of an accent) distinct and indicating where the speaker comes from. **14** (of a relationship) stable and likely to last. **15** having an extreme or drastic effect: *strong discipline.* **16** (of a colour) very bright and intense. **17** (of a wind, current, or earthquake) moving fast or intensely. **18** (of an economy, an industry, a currency, etc.) growing, successful, or increasing in value. *~adv* **19 come on strong** *Informal* **a** to show blatantly that one is sexually attracted to someone. **b** to make a forceful or exaggerated impression. **20 going strong** *Informal* working or performing well; thriving. **strongly** *adv*

strong-arm *adj Informal* involving physical force or violence: *strong-arm tactics.*

strongbox *n* a box in which valuables are locked for safety.

strong drink *n* alcoholic drink.

stronghold *n* **1** an area in which a particular belief is shared by many people: *a Labour stronghold.* **2** a place that is well defended; fortress.

strong-minded *adj* not easily persuaded to change beliefs or opinions.

strong point *n* something at which one is very good: *diplomacy wasn't his strong point.*

strongroom *n* a specially designed room in which valuables are locked for safety.

strontium *n Chem* a soft silvery-white metallic element: the radioactive isotope **strontium-90** is used in nuclear power sources and is a hazardous nuclear fallout product. Symbol: Sr

strop *n* a leather strap for sharpening razors.

stroppy *adj* **-pier, -piest** *Brit informal* bad-tempered or deliberately awkward.

strove *vb* the past tense of **strive.**

struck *vb* a past of **strike.**

structural *adj* **1** of or having structure or a structure. **2** of or forming part of the structure of a building. **3** *Chem* of or involving the arrangement of atoms in molecules: *a structural formula.* **structurally** *adv*

structuralism *n* an approach to social sciences and to literature which sees changes in the subject as caused and organized by a hidden set of universal rules. **structuralist** *n, adj*

structure *n* **1** something that has been built or organized. **2** the way the individual parts of something are made, built, or organized into a whole. **3** the pattern of interrelationships within an organization, society, etc. **4** an organized method of working, thinking, or behaving. **5** *Chem* the arrangement of atoms in a molecule of a chemical compound. **6** *Geol* the way in which a rock is made up of its component parts. *~vb* **-turing, -tured 7** to arrange (something) into an organized system or pattern: *a structured school curriculum.*

strudel *n* a thin sheet of filled dough rolled up and baked: *apple strudel.*

struggle *vb* **-gling, -gled 1** to work or strive: *the old regime struggled for power; he struggled to keep the conversation flowing.* **2** to move about violently in an attempt to escape from something restricting. **3** to fight with someone, often for possession of something. **4** to go or progress with difficulty. **5 struggle on** to manage to do (something) with difficulty. *~n* **6** something requiring a lot of exertion or effort to achieve. **7** a fight or battle. **struggling** *adj*

THESAURUS

bour, leave no stone unturned, make an all-out effort (*informal*), make every effort, strain, struggle, toil, try, try hard

stroke *vb.* **1.** caress, fondle, pat, pet, rub *~n.* **2.** *Pathol.* apoplexy, attack, collapse, fit, seizure, shock **3.** blow, hit, knock, rap, thump

stroll 1. *vb.* amble, make one's way, mooch (*slang*), mosey along *or* on (*informal*), promenade, ramble, saunter, stretch one's legs, take a turn, toddle, wander **2.** *n.* airing, breath of air, constitutional, excursion, promenade, ramble, turn, walk

strong 1. athletic, beefy (*informal*), brawny, burly, capable, hale, hardy, healthy, Herculean, lusty, muscular, powerful, robust, sinewy, sound, stalwart, stout, strapping, sturdy, tough, virile **2.** durable, hard-wearing, heavy-duty, on a firm foundation, reinforced, sturdy, substantial, well-armed, well-built, well-protected **3.** clear, clear-cut, cogent, compelling, convincing, distinct, effective, formidable, great, marked, overpowering, persuasive, potent, redoubtable, sound, telling, trenchant, unmistakable, urgent, weighty, well-established, well-founded **4.** biting, concentrated, heady, highly-flavoured, highly-seasoned, hot, intoxicating, piquant, pungent, pure, sharp, spicy, undiluted **5.** aggressive, brave, courageous, determined, feisty (*informal, chiefly U.S. & Canad.*), firm in spirit, forceful, hard as nails, hard-nosed (*informal*), high-powered, plucky, resilient, resolute, self-assertive, steadfast, stouthearted, tenacious, tough, unyielding **6.** acute, dedicated, deep, deep-rooted, eager, fervent, fervid, fierce, firm, intense, keen, severe, staunch, vehement, violent, zealous **7.** Draconian, drastic, extreme, forceful, severe **8.** bold, bright, brilliant, dazzling, glaring, loud, stark

stronghold bastion, bulwark, castle, citadel, fastness, fort, fortress, keep, refuge

strong-minded determined, firm, independent, iron-willed, resolute, strong-willed, unbending, uncompromising

structure *n.* **1.** building, construction, edifice, erection, pile **2.** arrangement, configuration, conformation, construction, design, fabric, form, formation, interrelation of parts, make, make-up, organization *~vb.* **3.** arrange, assemble, build up, design, organize, put together, shape

struggle *vb.* **1.** bend over backwards, do one's damnedest (*informal*), exert oneself, give it one's all (*informal*), give it one's best shot (*informal*), go all out (*informal*), go for broke (*slang*), go for it (*informal*), labour, make an all-out effort (*informal*), make every effort, strain, strive, toil, work, work like a Trojan **2.** battle, compete, contend, fight, grapple, lock horns, scuffle, wrestle *~n.* **3.** effort, exertion, grind (*infor-*

strum *vb* **strumming, strummed 1** to play (a stringed instrument) by sweeping the thumb or a plectrum across the strings. **2** to play (a tune) in this way.

strumpet *n Archaic* a prostitute or promiscuous woman.

strung *vb* the past of **string.**

strung up *adj Informal* tense or nervous: *you sound a bit strung up.*

strut *vb* **strutting, strutted 1** to walk in a stiff proud way with head high and shoulders back; swagger. *~n* **2** a piece of wood or metal that forms part of the framework of a structure.

strychnine (**strik**-neen) *n* a very poisonous drug used in small quantities as a stimulant.

Stuart *adj* of or relating to the royal house that ruled Scotland from 1371 to 1714 and England from 1603 to 1714.

stub *n* **1** a short piece remaining after something has been used: *a cigarette stub.* **2** the section of a ticket or cheque which the purchaser keeps as a receipt. *~vb* **stubbing, stubbed 3** to strike (one's toe or foot) painfully against a hard surface. **4 stub out** to put out (a cigarette or cigar) by pressing the end against a surface.

stubble *n* **1** the short stalks left in a field where a crop has been harvested. **2** the short bristly hair on the chin of a man who has not shaved for a while. **stubbly** *adj*

stubble-jumper *n Canad slang* a prairie grain farmer.

stubborn *adj* **1** refusing to agree or give in. **2** persistent and determined. **3** difficult to handle, treat, or overcome: *the most stubborn dandruff.* **stubbornly** *adv* **stubbornness** *n*

stubby *adj* **-bier, -biest** short and broad.

STUC Scottish Trades Union Congress.

stucco *n* **1** plaster used for coating or decorating outside walls. *~vb* **-coing, -coed 2** to apply stucco to (a building).

stuck *vb* **1** the past of **stick**[2]. *~adj* **2** *Informal* baffled by a problem or unable to find an answer to a question. **3 stuck on** *Slang* feeling a strong attraction (to); infatuated with. **4 get stuck in** *Informal* to perform a task with determination.

stuck-up *adj Informal* proud or snobbish.

stud[1] *n* **1** a small piece of metal attached to a surface for decoration. **2** a fastener consisting of two discs at either end of a short bar, usually used with clothes. **3** one of several small round objects attached to the sole of a football boot to give better grip. *~vb* **studding, studded 4** to decorate or cover (something) with or as if with studs: *apartment houses studded with satellite dishes.*

stud[2] *n* **1** a male animal, esp. a stallion kept for breeding. **2** Also: **stud farm** a place where animals are bred. **3** the state of being kept for breeding purposes. **4** *Slang* a virile or sexually active man.

student *n* **1** a person following a course of study in a school, college, or university. **2** a person who makes a thorough study of a subject: *a keen student of opinion polls.*

studied *adj* carefully practised or planned: *studied calm.*

studio *n, pl* **-dios 1** a room in which an artist, photographer, or musician works. **2** a room used to record television or radio programmes or to make films or records. **3 studios** the premises of a radio, television, record, or film company.

studio couch *n* a backless couch that can be converted into a double bed.

studio flat *n* a flat with one main room and, usually, a small kitchen and bathroom. Also called: **studio apartment**

studious (**styoo**-dee-uss) *adj* **1** serious, thoughtful, and hard-working. **2** precise, careful, or deliberate. **studiously** *adv*

study *vb* **studies, studying, studied 1** to be engaged in the learning or understanding of (a subject). **2** to investigate or examine (something) by observation and research. **3** to look at (something or someone) closely; scrutinize. *~n, pl* **studies 4** the act or process of studying. **5** a room used for studying, reading, or writing. **6** (*often pl*) work relating to a particular area of learning: *environmental studies.* **7** an investigation and analysis of a particular subject. **8** a paper or book produced as a result of study. **9** a work of art, such as a drawing, done for practice or in preparation for another work. **10** a musical composition designed to develop playing technique.

stuff *n* **1** substance or material. **2** any collection of unnamed things. **3** the raw material of something. **4** subject matter, skill, etc.: *this journalist knew his stuff.* **5** woollen fabric. **6 do one's stuff** *Informal* to do what is expected of one. *~vb* **7** to pack or fill (something) completely; cram. **8** to force, shove, or squeeze (something somewhere): *I stuffed it in my briefcase.* **9** to fill (food such as poultry or tomatoes) with a seasoned mixture. **10** to fill (a dead animal's skin) with

THESAURUS

mal), labour, long haul, pains, scramble, toil, work **4.** battle, brush, clash, combat, conflict, contest, encounter, hostilities, skirmish, strife, tussle

strut *vb.* parade, peacock, prance, stalk, swagger

stub *n.* butt, counterfoil, dog-end (*informal*), end, fag end (*informal*), remnant, stump, tail, tail end

stubborn bull-headed, contumacious (*literary*), dogged, dour, fixed, headstrong, inflexible, intractable, mulish, obdurate, obstinate, opinionated, persistent, pig-headed, recalcitrant, refractory, self-willed, stiff-necked, tenacious, unbending, unmanageable, unshakable, unyielding, wilful

stuck 1. *informal* at a loss, at a standstill, at one's wits' end, baffled, beaten, bereft of ideas, nonplussed, stumped, up against a brick wall (*informal*) **2. stuck on** *slang* crazy about, for, *or* over (*informal*), enthusiastic about, hung up on (*slang*), infatuated, keen, mad, obsessed with, wild about (*informal*) **3. get stuck in** *informal* get down to, make a start on, set about, tackle

stud *vb.* bejewel, bespangle, dot, fleck, ornament, spangle, speckle, spot, sprinkle

student apprentice, disciple, learner, observer, pupil, scholar, trainee, undergraduate

studied calculated, conscious, deliberate, intentional, planned, premeditated, purposeful, well-considered, wilful

studio atelier, workshop

studious academic, assiduous, attentive, bookish, careful, diligent, eager, earnest, hard-working, intellectual, meditative, reflective, scholarly, sedulous, serious, thoughtful

study *vb.* **1.** apply oneself (to), bone up on (*informal*), burn the midnight oil, cogitate, con (*archaic*), consider, contemplate, cram (*informal*), examine, go into, hammer away at, learn, meditate, mug up (*Brit. slang*), ponder, pore over, read, read up, swot (up) (*Brit. informal*) **2.** analyse, deliberate, examine, investigate, look into, peruse, research, scrutinize, survey, work over *~n.* **3.** academic work, application, book work, cramming (*informal*), learning, lessons, reading, re-

material so as to restore the shape of the live animal. **11 get stuffed!** *Brit slang* an exclamation of anger or annoyance with someone. **12 stuff oneself** *or* **one's face** to eat a large amount of food.

stuffed shirt *n Informal* a pompous or old-fashioned person.

stuffed-up *adj* having the passages of one's nose blocked with mucus.

stuffing *n* **1** a mixture of ingredients with which poultry or meat is stuffed before cooking. **2** the material used to fill and give shape to soft toys, pillows, furniture, etc.; padding.

stuffy *adj* **-ier, -iest 1** lacking fresh air. **2** old-fashioned and very formal: *she was glad to escape stuffy Victorian England.* **stuffiness** *n*

stultify *vb* **-fies, -fying, -fied** to dull (the mind) by boring routine. **stultifying** *adj*

stumble *vb* **-bling, -bled 1** to trip and almost fall while walking or running. **2** to walk in an unsteady or unsure way. **3** to make mistakes or hesitate in speech. **4 stumble across, on** *or* **upon** to encounter or discover (someone or something) by accident. *~n* **5** an act of stumbling.

stumbling block *n* any obstacle that prevents something from taking place or progressing.

stump *n* **1** the base of a tree trunk left standing after the tree has been cut down or has fallen. **2** the part of something, such as a tooth or limb, that remains after a larger part has been removed. **3** *Cricket* any of three upright wooden sticks that, with two bails laid across them, form a wicket. *~vb* **4** to baffle or confuse (someone). **5** *Cricket* to dismiss (a batsman) by breaking his wicket with the ball. **6** *Chiefly US & Canad* to campaign or canvass (an area), by political speech-making. **7** to walk with heavy steps; trudge.

stump up *vb Brit informal* to give (the money required).

stumpy *adj* **stumpier, stumpiest** short and thick like a stump; stubby.

stun *vb* **stunning, stunned 1** to shock or astonish (someone) so that he or she is unable to speak or act. **2** (of a heavy blow or fall) to make (a person or an animal) unconscious.

stung *vb* the past of **sting.**

stunk *vb* a past of **stink.**

stunner *n Informal* a person or thing of great beauty.

stunning *adj Informal* very attractive or impressive. **stunningly** *adv*

stunt[1] *vb* to prevent or slow down (the growth or development) of a plant, animal, or person. **stunted** *adj*

stunt[2] *n* **1** an acrobatic or dangerous piece of action in a film or television programme. **2** anything spectacular or unusual done to gain publicity. *~adj* **3** of or relating to acrobatic or dangerous pieces of action in films or television programmes: *a stunt man.*

stupefaction *n* the state of being unable to think clearly because of tiredness or boredom.

stupefy *vb* **-pefies, -pefying, -pefied 1** to make (someone) feel so bored and tired that he or she is unable to think clearly. **2** to confuse or astound (someone). **stupefying** *adj*

stupendous *adj* very large or impressive. **stupendously** *adv*

stupid *adj* **1** lacking in common sense or intelligence.

THESAURUS

search, school work, swotting (*Brit. informal*), thought **4.** analysis, attention, cogitation, consideration, contemplation, examination, inquiry, inspection, investigation, perusal, review, scrutiny, survey

stuff *n.* **1.** belongings, bits and pieces, clobber (*Brit. slang*), effects, equipment, gear, goods and chattels, impedimenta, junk, kit, luggage, materials, objects, paraphernalia, possessions, tackle, things, trappings **2.** fabric, material, raw material **3.** essence, matter, pith, quintessence, staple, substance *~vb.* **4.** compress, cram, crowd, fill, force, jam, load, pack, pad, push, ram, shove, squeeze, stow, wedge **5. stuff oneself** *or* **one's face** gobble, gorge, gormandize, guzzle, make a pig of oneself (*informal*), overindulge, pig out (*slang*), sate, satiate

stuffing 1. forcemeat **2.** filler, kapok, packing, quilting, wadding

stuffy 1. airless, close, fetid, frowsty, fuggy, heavy, muggy, oppressive, stale, stifling, suffocating, sultry, unventilated **2.** conventional, deadly, dreary, dull, fusty, humourless, musty, old-fashioned, old-fogeyish, pompous, priggish, prim, prim and proper, staid, stilted, stodgy, strait-laced, uninteresting

stumble 1. blunder about, come a cropper (*informal*), fall, falter, flounder, hesitate, lose one's balance, lurch, reel, slip, stagger, trip **2.** falter, fluff (*informal*), stammer, stutter **3. stumble across, on,** *or* **upon** blunder upon, chance upon, come across, discover, encounter, find, happen upon, light upon, run across, turn up

stump *vb.* **1.** baffle, bewilder, bring (someone) up short, confound, confuse, dumbfound, flummox, foil, mystify, nonplus, outwit, perplex, puzzle, stop, stymie **2.** clomp, clump, lumber, plod, stamp, stomp (*informal*), trudge

stump up *Brit. informal* chip in (*informal*), come across with (*informal*), contribute, cough up (*informal*), donate, fork out (*slang*), hand over, pay, shell out (*informal*)

stun amaze, astonish, astound, bewilder, confound, confuse, daze, dumbfound, flabbergast (*informal*), knock out, knock (someone) for six (*informal*), overcome, overpower, shock, stagger, strike (someone) dumb, stupefy, take (someone's) breath away

stunning *informal* beautiful, brilliant, dazzling, devastating (*informal*), gorgeous, great (*informal*), heavenly, impressive, lovely, marvellous, out of this world (*informal*), ravishing, remarkable, sensational (*informal*), smashing (*informal*), spectacular, striking, wonderful

stunt *n.* act, deed, exploit, feat, feature, tour de force, trick

stunted diminutive, dwarfed, dwarfish, little, small, tiny, undersized

stupefaction amazement, astonishment, awe, wonder, wonderment

stupefy amaze, astound, bewilder, confound, daze, dumbfound, knock senseless, numb, shock, stagger, stun

stupendous amazing, astounding, breathtaking, brilliant, colossal, enormous, fabulous (*informal*), fantastic (*informal*), gigantic, huge, marvellous, mega (*slang*), mind-boggling (*informal*), out of this world (*informal*), overwhelming, phenomenal, prodigious, sensational (*informal*), staggering, stunning (*informal*), superb, surpassing belief, surprising, tremendous (*informal*), vast, wonderful, wondrous (*archaic or literary*)

stupid 1. brainless, cretinous, deficient, dense, dim, doltish, dopey (*slang*), dozy (*Brit. informal*), dull, dumb (*informal*), foolish, gullible, half-witted, moronic, naive, obtuse, simple, simple-minded, slow, slow on the uptake (*informal*), slow-witted, sluggish, stolid, thick, thickheaded, unintelligent, witless **2.** asinine, crackbrained, daft (*informal*), futile, half-baked (*informal*), idiotic, ill-advised, imbecilic, inane, indiscreet, irrelevant, irresponsible, laughable, ludicrous,

2 trivial, silly, or childish: *we got into a stupid quarrel.* 3 unable to think clearly; dazed: *stupid with tiredness.* **stupidity** *n* **stupidly** *adv*

stupor *n* a state of near unconsciousness in which a person is unable to behave normally or think clearly.

sturdy *adj* **-dier, -diest 1** (of a person) healthy, strong, and unlikely to tire or become injured. **2** (of a piece of furniture, shoes, etc.) strongly built or made. **sturdily** *adv*

sturgeon *n* a bony fish from which caviar is obtained.

stutter *vb* **1** to speak (a word or phrase) with involuntary repetition of initial consonants. *~n* **2** the tendency to involuntarily repeat initial consonants while speaking. **stuttering** *n*

sty[1] *n, pl* **sties** a pen in which pigs are kept.

sty[2] *or* **stye** *n, pl* **sties** *or* **styes** inflammation of a gland at the base of an eyelash.

Stygian (**stij**-jee-an) *adj Chiefly literary* dark or gloomy.

style *n* **1** a form of appearance, design, or production: *I like that style of dress.* **2** the way in which something is done: *a new style of command.* **3** elegance or refinement of manners and dress: *he has bags of style.* **4** a distinctive manner of expression in words, music, painting, etc.: *a painting in the Expressionist style.* **5** popular fashion in dress and looks: *the old ones had gone out of style.* **6** a fashionable or showy way of life: *the newly rich could dine in style.* **7** the particular kind of spelling, punctuation, and design followed in a book, journal, or publishing house. **8** *Bot* the stemlike part of a flower that bears the stigma. *~vb* **styling, styled 9** to design, shape, or tailor: *neatly styled hair.* **10** to name or call: *Walsh, who styled himself the Memory Man.*

styling mousse *n* a light foam applied to the hair before styling in order to hold the style.

stylish *adj* smart, fashionable, and attracting attention. **stylishly** *adv*

stylist *n* **1** a hairdresser who styles hair. **2** a person who performs, writes, or acts with great attention to the particular style he or she employs.

stylistic *adj* of the techniques used in creating or performing a work of art: *there are many stylistic problems facing the performers of Baroque music.* **stylistically** *adv*

stylized *or* **-ised** *adj* conforming to an established stylistic form.

stylus *n* a needle-like device in the pick-up arm of a record player that rests in the groove in the record and picks up the sound signals.

stymie *vb* **-mieing, -mied 1** to hinder or foil (someone): *the President was stymied by a reluctant Congress.* *~n, pl* **-mies 2** *Golf* (formerly) a situation in which an opponent's ball is blocking the line between the hole and the ball about to be played.

styptic *adj* **1** used to stop bleeding: *a styptic pencil.* *~n* **2** a styptic drug.

suave (**swahv**) *adj* (esp. of a man) smooth, confident, and sophisticated. **suavely** *adv*

sub *n* **1** short for **subeditor, submarine, subscription** or **substitute. 2** *Brit informal* an advance payment of wages or salary. Formal term: **subsistence allowance** *~vb* **subbing, subbed 3** to act as a substitute.

sub- *or before r* **sur-** *prefix* used with many main words to mean: **1** situated under or beneath: *subterranean.* **2** secondary in rank; subordinate: *sublieutenant; surrogate.* **3** falling short of; less than or imperfectly: *subarctic; subhuman.* **4** forming a subdivision or less important part: *subcommittee.*

subaltern *n* any commissioned army officer below the rank of captain.

subaqua *adj* of or relating to underwater sport: *subaqua swimming.*

subatomic *adj Physics* of, relating to, or being one of the particles making up an atom.

subcommittee *n* a small committee consisting of members of a larger committee and which is set up to look into a particular matter.

subconscious *adj* **1** happening or existing without one's awareness. *~n* **2** *Psychol* the part of the mind that contains memories and motives of which one is not aware but which can influence one's behaviour. **subconsciously** *adv*

subcontinent *n* a large land mass that is a distinct part of a continent, such as India is of Asia.

subcontract *n* **1** a secondary contract by which the main contractor for a job puts work out to another company. *~vb* **2** to let out (work) on a subcontract. **subcontractor** *n*

subculture *n* a group of people within a society or class with a distinct pattern of behaviour, beliefs, and attitudes.

subcutaneous (sub-cute-**ayn**-ee-uss) *adj Med* beneath the skin.

subdivide *vb* **-viding, -vided** to divide (a part of something) into smaller parts. **subdivision** *n*

THESAURUS

meaningless, mindless, nonsensical, pointless, puerile, rash, senseless, short-sighted, trivial, unintelligent, unthinking **3.** dazed, groggy, in a daze, insensate, punch-drunk, semiconscious, senseless, stunned, stupefied

stupidity 1. asininity, brainlessness, denseness, dimness, dopiness (*slang*), doziness (*Brit. informal*), dullness, dumbness (*informal*), feeble-mindedness, imbecility, lack of brain, lack of intelligence, naivety, obtuseness, puerility, simplicity, slowness, thickheadedness, thickness **2.** absurdity, fatuity, fatuousness, folly, foolhardiness, foolishness, futility, idiocy, inanity, indiscretion, irresponsibility, ludicrousness, lunacy, madness, pointlessness, rashness, senselessness, silliness

sturdy athletic, brawny, built to last, determined, durable, firm, flourishing, hardy, hearty, lusty, muscular, powerful, resolute, robust, secure, solid, stalwart, staunch, steadfast, stouthearted, substantial, thickset, vigorous, well-built, well-made

stutter *vb.* falter, hesitate, speak haltingly, splutter, stammer, stumble

style *n.* **1.** appearance, category, characteristic, cut, design, form, genre, hand, kind, manner, pattern, sort, spirit, strain, technique, tenor, tone, type, variety **2.** approach, custom, manner, method, mode, technique, way **3.** chic, cosmopolitanism, dash, dressiness (*informal*), élan, elegance, fashionableness, flair, grace, panache, polish, refinement, savoir-faire, smartness, sophistication, stylishness, taste, urbanity **4.** diction, expression, mode of expression, phraseology, phrasing, treatment, turn of phrase, vein, wording **5.** fashion, mode, rage, trend, vogue **6.** affluence, comfort, ease, elegance, gracious living, grandeur, luxury *~vb.* **7.** adapt, arrange, cut, design, dress, fashion, shape, tailor **8.** address, call, christen, denominate, designate, dub, entitle, label, name, term

stylish à la mode, chic, classy (*slang*), dapper, dressy (*informal*), fashionable, in fashion, in vogue, modish, natty (*informal*), polished, smart, snappy, snazzy (*informal*), trendy (*Brit. informal*), urbane, voguish, well turned out

subdue *vb* **-duing, -dued 1** to overcome and bring (a person or people) under control by persuasion or force. **2** to make (feelings, colour, or lighting) less intense.

subeditor *n* a person who checks and edits text for a newspaper or other publication.

subgroup *n* a small group that is part of a larger group.

subheading *n* the heading of a subdivision of a piece of writing.

subhuman *adj* lacking the intelligence or decency expected of a human being.

subject *n* **1** the person, thing, or topic being dealt with or discussed. **2** any branch of learning considered as a course of study. **3** a person, object, idea, or scene portrayed in a work of art. **4** *Grammar* a word or phrase that represents the person or thing performing the action of the verb in a sentence; for example, *the cat* in the sentence *The cat catches mice.* **5** a person or thing that undergoes an experiment or treatment. **6** a person under the rule of a monarch or government: *Zambian subjects.* ~*adj* **7** being under the rule of a monarch or government: *a subject race.* **8 subject to a** showing a tendency towards: *they are expensive and subject to over-runs in cost and time.* **b** exposed or vulnerable to: *subject to ridicule.* **c** conditional upon: *pay is subject to negotiation.* ~*adv* **9 subject to** under the condition that something takes place: *my visit was agreed subject to certain conditions.* ~*vb* (sub-**ject**) **10 subject to a** to cause (someone) to experience (something unpleasant): *they were subjected to beatings.* **b** to bring under the control or authority (of): *to subject a soldier to discipline.* **subjection** *n*

subjective *adj* **1** of or based on a person's emotions or prejudices. ~*n* **2** *Grammar* the grammatical case in certain languages that identifies the subject of a verb. **subjectively** *adv*

sub judice (sub **joo**-diss-ee) *adj* before a court of law: *he declined to comment on the case saying it was sub judice.*

subjugate *vb* **-gating, -gated** to bring (a group of people) under one's control. **subjugation** *n*

subjunctive *Grammar* ~*adj* **1** denoting a mood of verbs used when the content of the clause is being doubted, supposed, or feared true, for example *were* in the sentence *I'd be careful if I were you.* ~*n* **2** the subjunctive mood.

sublet *vb* **-letting, -let** to rent out (property which one is renting from someone else).

sublieutenant *n* a junior officer in a navy.

sublimate *vb* **-mating, -mated** *Psychol* to direct the energy of (a strong desire, esp. a sexual one) into activities that are socially more acceptable. **sublimation** *n*

sublime *adj* **1** causing deep emotions and feelings of wonder or joy. **2** without equal; supreme. **3** of great moral, artistic, or spiritual value. ~*n* **4 the sublime** something that is sublime. ~*vb* **-liming, -limed 5** *Chem, physics* to change directly from a solid to a vapour without first melting. **sublimely** *adv*

subliminal *adj* resulting from or relating to mental processes of which the individual is not aware: *the subliminal message.*

sub-machine-gun *n* a portable automatic or semi-automatic gun with a short barrel.

submarine *n* **1** a vessel which can operate below the surface of the sea. ~*adj* **2** existing or located below the surface of the sea: *submarine cables.* **submariner** *n*

submerge *vb* **-merging, -merged 1** to put or go below the surface of water or another liquid. **2** to involve totally: *she submerged herself in her work.* **submersion** *n*

submersible *adj* **1** capable of operating under water. ~*n* **2** a small vessel designed to operate under water.

submission *n* **1** an act or instance of submitting. **2** something submitted, such as a proposal. **3** the state in which someone has to accept the control of another person.

submissive *adj* showing quiet obedience. **submissively** *adv* **submissiveness** *n*

submit *vb* **-mitting, -mitted 1** to accept the will of another person or a superior force. **2** to send (an application or proposal) to someone for judgment or consideration. **3** to be voluntarily subjected (to medical or psychiatric treatment).

subnormal *adj* **1** less than the normal: *subnormal white blood cells.* **2** *No longer in technical use* having a lower than average intelligence. ~*n* **3** *No longer in technical use* a subnormal person.

subordinate *adj* **1** of lesser rank or importance. ~*n* **2** a person or thing that is of lesser rank or importance. ~*vb* **-nating, -nated 3** (usually foll. by *to*) to regard (something) as less important than another: *the*

THESAURUS

subconscious *adj.* hidden, inner, innermost, intuitive, latent, repressed, subliminal, suppressed

subdue 1. beat down, break, conquer, control, crush, defeat, discipline, gain ascendancy over, get the better of, get the upper hand over, get under control, humble, master, overcome, overpower, overrun, put down, quell, tame, trample, triumph over, vanquish **2.** check, control, mellow, moderate, quieten down, repress, soften, suppress, tone down

subject *n.* **1.** affair, business, field of inquiry *or* reference, issue, matter, object, point, question, subject matter, substance, theme, topic **2.** case, client, guinea pig (*informal*), participant, patient, victim **3.** citizen, dependant, national, subordinate, vassal ~*adj.* **4.** answerable, bound, dependent, inferior, subjugated, subordinate, subservient **5.** *with* **to a** at the mercy of, disposed, exposed, in danger of, liable, open, prone, susceptible, vulnerable **b** conditional, contingent, dependent ~*vb.* **6.** *with* **to** expose, lay open, make liable, put through, submit, treat

subjective biased, emotional, idiosyncratic, instinctive, intuitive, nonobjective, personal, prejudiced

sublime elevated, eminent, exalted, glorious, grand, great, high, imposing, lofty, magnificent, majestic, noble, transcendent

submerge deluge, dip, drown, duck, dunk, engulf, flood, immerse, inundate, overflow, overwhelm, plunge, sink, swamp

submission 1. acquiescence, assent, capitulation, giving in, surrender, yielding **2.** entry, handing in, presentation, submitting, tendering **3.** argument, contention, proposal **4.** compliance, deference, docility, meekness, obedience, passivity, resignation, submissiveness, tractability, unassertiveness

submissive abject, accommodating, acquiescent, amenable, biddable, compliant, deferential, docile, dutiful, humble, ingratiating, lowly, malleable, meek, obedient, obeisant, obsequious, passive, patient, pliant, resigned, subdued, tractable, uncomplaining, unresisting, yielding

submit 1. accede, acquiesce, agree, bend, bow, capitulate, comply, defer, endure, give in, knuckle under, put up with (*informal*), resign oneself, stoop, succumb, surrender, throw in the towel, toe the line, tolerate, yield **2.** commit, hand in, present, proffer, put forward, refer, table, tender

army's interests were subordinated to those of the air force. **subordination** *n*

subordinate clause *n Grammar* a clause that functions as an adjective, an adverb, or a noun rather than one that functions as a sentence in its own right.

suborn *vb Formal* to bribe or incite (a person) to commit a wrongful act.

subplot *n* a secondary plot in a novel, play, or film.

subpoena (sub-**pee**-na) *n* **1** a legal document requiring a person to appear before a court of law at a specified time. *~vb* **-naing, -naed 2** to summon (someone) with a subpoena.

sub-post office *n* (in Britain) a post office which is run by a self-employed agent for the Post Office.

sub rosa (sub **rose**-a) *adv Literary* in secret.

subroutine *n* a section of a computer program that is stored only once but can be used at several different points in the program.

subscribe *vb* **-scribing, -scribed 1** (usually foll. by *to*) to pay (money) as a contribution (to a charity, for a magazine, etc.) at regular intervals. **2 subscribe to** to give support or approval: *I do not subscribe to this view.* **subscriber** *n*

subscriber trunk dialling *n Brit* a system allowing telephone users to obtain trunk calls by dialling direct without the help of an operator.

subscript *Printing ~adj* **1** (of a character) written or printed below the line. *~n* **2** a subscript character.

subscription *n* **1** a payment for issues of a publication over a specified period of time. **2** money paid or promised, such as to a charity or the fund raised in this way. **3** *Chiefly Brit* the membership fees paid to a society. **4** an advance order for a new product.

subsection *n* any of the smaller parts into which a section may be divided.

subsequent *adj* occurring after; succeeding. **subsequently** *adv*

subservient *adj* **1** overeager to carry out someone else's wishes. **2** of less importance or rank: *the subservient role of women in society.* **subservience** *n*

subset *n* a mathematical set contained within a larger set.

subside *vb* **-siding, -sided 1** to become less loud, excited, or violent. **2** to sink to a lower level. **3** (of the surface of the earth) to cave in; collapse. **subsidence** *n*

subsidiarity *n* the principle of taking political decisions at the lowest practical level.

subsidiary *n, pl* **-aries 1** Also called: **subsidiary company** a company which is at least half owned by another company. **2** a person or thing that is of lesser importance. *~adj* **3** of lesser importance; subordinate.

subsidize *or* **-dise** *vb* **-dizing, -dized** *or* **-dising, -dised** to aid or support (an industry, a person, a public service, or a venture) with money.

subsidy *n, pl* **-dies 1** financial aid supplied by a government, for example to industry, or for public welfare. **2** any financial aid, grant, or contribution.

subsist *vb* **subsist on** to manage to live: *to subsist on a diet of sausage rolls.* **subsistence** *n*

subsistence farming *n* a type of farming in which most of the produce is consumed by the farmer and his family.

subsoil *n* the layer of soil beneath the surface soil.

subsonic *adj* being or moving at a speed below that of sound.

substance *n* **1** the basic matter of which a thing consists. **2** a specific type of matter with definite or fairly definite chemical composition: *a fatty substance.* **3** the essential meaning of a speech, thought, or written article. **4** important or meaningful quality: *the only evidence of substance against him.* **5** material possessions or wealth: *a woman of substance.* **6 in substance** with regard to the most important points.

substandard *adj* below an established or required standard.

substantial *adj* **1** of a considerable size or value: *a substantial amount of money.* **2** (of food or a meal) large and filling. **3** solid or strong: *substantial brick pillars.* **4** *Formal* available to the senses; real: *substantial evidence.* **5** of or relating to the basic material substance of a thing. **substantially** *adv*

substantiate *vb* **-ating, -ated** to establish (a story) as genuine. **substantiation** *n*

substantive *n* **1** *Grammar* a noun or pronoun used

THESAURUS

subordinate 1. *adj.* dependent, inferior, junior, lesser, lower, minor, secondary, subject, subservient **2.** *n.* aide, assistant, attendant, dependant, inferior, junior, second, subaltern, underling

subordination inferiority, inferior *or* secondary status, servitude, subjection, submission

subscribe 1. *usually with* **to** chip in (*informal*), contribute, donate, give, offer, pledge, promise **2. subscribe to** acquiesce, advocate, agree, consent, countenance, endorse, support

subscription annual payment, contribution, donation, dues, gift, membership fee, offering

subsequent after, consequent, consequential, ensuing, following, later, succeeding, successive

subsequently afterwards, at a later date, consequently, in the aftermath (of), in the end, later

subside 1. abate, decrease, de-escalate, diminish, dwindle, ease, ebb, lessen, let up, level off, melt away, moderate, peter out, quieten, recede, slacken, wane **2.** cave in, collapse, decline, descend, drop, ebb, lower, settle, sink

subsidence 1. abatement, decrease, de-escalation, diminution, easing off, lessening, slackening **2.** decline, descent, ebb, settlement, settling, sinking

subsidiary *adj.* aiding, ancillary, assistant, auxiliary, contributory, cooperative, helpful, lesser, minor, secondary, serviceable, subordinate, subservient, supplemental, supplementary, useful

subsidize finance, fund, promote, put up the money for, sponsor, support, underwrite

subsidy aid, allowance, assistance, contribution, financial aid, grant, help, stipend, subvention (*informal*), support

subsist be, continue, eke out an existence, endure, exist, keep going, last, live, make ends meet, remain, stay alive, survive, sustain oneself

subsistence aliment, existence, food, keep, livelihood, living, maintenance, provision, rations, support, survival, sustenance, upkeep, victuals

substance 1. body, element, fabric, material, stuff, texture **2.** burden, essence, gist, import, main point, matter, meaning, pith, significance, subject, sum and substance, theme **3.** actuality, concreteness, entity, force, reality **4.** affluence, assets, estate, means, property, resources, wealth

substantial 1. ample, big, considerable, generous, goodly, important, large, significant, sizable, tidy (*informal*), worthwhile **2.** bulky, durable, firm, hefty, massive, solid, sound, stout, strong, sturdy, well-built **3.** *formal* actual, existent, material, positive, real, true, valid, weighty

substantially essentially, in essence, in essentials, in

in place of a noun. *~adj* **2** having importance or significance: *substantive negotiations between management and staff.* **3** of or being the essential element of a thing.

substitute *vb* **-tuting, -tuted 1** (often foll. by *for*) to take the place of or put in place of another person or thing. **2** *Chem* to replace (an atom or group in a molecule) with (another atom or group). *~n* **3** a person or thing that takes the place of another, such as a player who takes the place of a team-mate. **substitution** *n*

substitution reaction *n Chem* the replacing of an atom or group in a molecule by another atom or group.

substructure *n* **1** a structure that forms a part of anything. **2** a structure that forms a foundation or framework for a building.

subsume *vb* **-suming, -sumed** *Formal* to include (something) under a larger classification or group: *an attempt to subsume fascism and communism under a general concept of totalitarianism.*

subtenant *n* a person who rents property from a tenant. **subtenancy** *n*

subtend *vb Geom* to be opposite (an angle or side).

subterfuge *n* a trick or deception used to achieve an objective.

subterranean *adj* **1** found or operating below the surface of the earth. **2** existing or working in a concealed or mysterious way: *the resistance movement worked largely by subterranean methods.*

subtitle *n* **1 subtitles** *Films* a written translation at the bottom of the picture in a film with foreign dialogue. **2** a secondary title given to a book or play. *~vb* **-tling, -tled 3** to provide subtitles for (a film) or a subtitle for (a book or play).

subtle *adj* **1** not immediately obvious: *a subtle change in his views.* **2** (of a colour, taste, or smell) delicate or faint: *the subtle aroma.* **3** using shrewd and indirect methods to achieve an objective. **4** having or requiring the ability to make fine distinctions: *a subtle argument.* **subtly** *adv*

subtlety *n* **1** (*pl* **-ties**) a fine distinction. **2** the state or quality of being subtle.

subtract *vb* **1** *Maths* to take (one number or quantity) away from another. **2** to remove (a part of something) from the whole. **subtraction** *n*

subtropical *adj* of the region lying between the tropics and temperate lands.

suburb *n* a residential district on the outskirts of a city or town.

suburban *adj* **1** of, in, or inhabiting a suburb. **2** *Mildly disparaging* conventional and unexciting.

suburbanite *n* a person who lives in a suburb.

suburbia *n* suburbs or the people living in them considered as a distinct community or class in society.

subvention *n Formal* a grant or subsidy, for example one from a government.

subversion *n* the act or an instance of attempting to weaken or overthrow a government or an institution.

subversive *adj* **1** intended or intending to weaken or overthrow a government or an institution. *~n* **2** a person engaged in subversive activities.

subvert *vb* to bring about the downfall of (something existing by a system of law, such as a government).

subway *n* **1** *Brit* an underground passage for pedestrians to cross a road or railway. **2** an underground railway.

subzero *adj* lower than zero: *subzero temperatures.*

succeed *vb* **1** to achieve an aim. **2** to turn out satisfactorily: *Grandfather's plan succeeded.* **3** to do well in a specified field: *how to succeed in show biz.* **4** to come next in order after (someone or something): *the first shock had been succeeded by a different kind of gloom.* **5** to take over (a position) from (someone): *Henry VIII succeeded to the throne in 1509; Clinton succeeded Bush as President.* **succeeding** *adj*

success *n* **1** the achievement of something attempted. **2** the attainment of wealth, fame, or position. **3** a person or thing that is successful: *I've got to be a success.*

THESAURUS

substance, in the main, largely, materially, to a large extent

substantiate affirm, attest to, authenticate, bear out, confirm, corroborate, establish, prove, support, validate, verify

substitute 1. *vb. often with* **for** act for, be in place of, change, commute, cover for, deputize, double for, exchange, fill in for, hold the fort for, interchange, relieve, replace, stand in for, swap, switch, take over **2.** *n.* agent, deputy, equivalent, expedient, locum (*chiefly Brit.*), makeshift, proxy, relief, replacement, representative, reserve, stand-by, stopgap, sub, supply, surrogate, temp (*informal*), temporary

substitution change, exchange, interchange, replacement, swap, switch

subterfuge artifice, deception, deviousness, dodge, duplicity, evasion, excuse, machination, manoeuvre, ploy, pretence, pretext, quibble, ruse, shift, stall, stratagem, trick

subtle 1. delicate, faint, implied, indirect, insinuated, slight, understated **2.** artful, astute, crafty, cunning, designing, devious, intriguing, keen, Machiavellian, scheming, shrewd, sly, wily **3.** deep, delicate, discriminating, ingenious, nice, penetrating, profound, refined, sophisticated

subtlety 1. delicacy, fine point, intricacy, nicety, refinement **2.** artfulness, astuteness, craftiness, cunning, deviousness, guile, slyness, wiliness **3.** acumen, acuteness, cleverness, discernment, discrimination, finesse, penetration, sagacity, skill, sophistication

subtract deduct, detract, diminish, remove, take away, take from, take off, withdraw

suburbs dormitory area (*Brit.*), environs, neighbourhood, outskirts, precincts, purlieus (*literary*), residential areas, suburbia

subversive 1. *adj.* destructive, incendiary, inflammatory, insurrectionary, overthrowing, perversive, riotous, seditious, treasonous, underground, undermining **2.** *n.* deviationist, dissident, fifth columnist, insurrectionary, quisling, saboteur, seditionary, seditionist, terrorist, traitor

subvert demolish, destroy, invalidate, overturn, raze, ruin, sabotage, undermine, upset, wreck

succeed 1. arrive (*informal*), be successful, come off (*informal*), crack it (*informal*), cut it (*informal*), do the trick (*informal*), flourish, gain one's end, get to the top, make good, make it (*informal*), prosper, thrive, triumph, turn out well, work **2.** be subsequent, come next, ensue, follow, result, supervene **3.** accede, assume the office of, come into, come into possession of, enter upon, inherit, replace, take over

succeeding ensuing, following, next, subsequent, successive

success 1. ascendancy, eminence, fame, favourable outcome, fortune, happiness, hit (*informal*), luck, prosperity, triumph **2.** best seller, big name, celebrity, hit (*informal*), market leader, megastar (*informal*), sensation, smash (*informal*), somebody, star, VIP, winner

successful acknowledged, at the top of the tree,

successful *adj* 1 having a favourable outcome. 2 having attained fame, wealth, or position. **successfully** *adv*

succession *n* 1 a number of people or things following one another in order. 2 the act or right by which one person succeeds another in a position. 3 **in succession** one after another: *the third time in succession.*

successive *adj* following another or others without interruption: *eleven successive victories.* **successively** *adv*

successor *n* a person or thing that follows another, esp. a person who takes over another's job or position.

succinct *adj* brief and clear: *a succinct answer to this question.* **succinctly** *adv*

succour *or US* **succor** *n* 1 help in time of difficulty. ~*vb* 2 to give aid to (someone in time of difficulty).

succubus *n, pl* **-bi** a female demon fabled to have sex with sleeping men.

succulent *adj* 1 (of food) juicy and delicious. 2 (of plants) having thick fleshy leaves or stems. ~*n* 3 a plant that can exist in very dry conditions by using water stored in its fleshy tissues. **succulence** *n*

succumb *vb* **succumb to a** to give way to the force of or desire for (something). **b** to die of (a disease).

such *adj* 1 of the sort specified or understood: *such places.* 2 so great or so much: *such a mess.* ~*adv* 3 extremely: *such a powerful friend.* ~*pron* 4 a person or thing of the sort specified or understood: *such is the law of the land; fruitcakes and puddings and such.* 5 **as such** in itself or themselves: *the Nordic countries are not lifting sanctions as such.* 6 **such as** for example: *other socialist groups, such as the Fabians.*

such and such *adj* 1 specific, but not known or named: *such and such a percentage.* ~*n* 2 a specific, but not known or named, person or thing: *you have not taken such and such into account.*

suchlike *n* 1 such or similar things: *shampoos, talcs, and suchlike.* ~*adj* 2 of such a kind; similar: *astrology and suchlike nonsense.*

suck *vb* 1 to draw (a liquid) into the mouth through pursed lips. 2 to take (something) into the mouth and moisten, dissolve, or roll it around with the tongue: *suck a mint.* 3 to extract liquid from (a solid food): *he sat sucking orange segments.* 4 to draw in (fluid) as if by sucking: *the mussel sucks in water.* 5 to drink milk from (a mother's breast); suckle. 6 (often foll. by *down, in,* etc.) to draw (a thing or person somewhere) with a powerful force. ~*n* 7 a sucking.

sucker *n* 1 *Slang* a person who is easily deceived or swindled. 2 *Slang* a person who cannot resist something: *he's a sucker for fast cars.* 3 *Zool* a part of the body of certain animals that is used for sucking or sticking to a surface. 4 a rubber cup-shaped device attached to objects allowing them to stick to a surface by suction. 5 *Bot* a strong shoot coming from a mature plant's root or the base of its main stem.

suck into *vb* to draw (someone) into (a situation) by using a powerful pressure or inducement: *to be sucked into a guerrilla war.*

suckle *vb* **-ling, -led** to give (a baby or young animal) milk from the breast or udder or (of a baby or young animal) to suck milk from its mother's breast or udder.

suckling *n* a baby or young animal that is still sucking milk from its mother's breast or udder.

suck up to *vb Informal* to flatter (a person in authority) in order to get something, such as praise or promotion.

sucrose (**soo**-kroze) *n Chem* sugar.

suction *n* 1 the act or process of sucking. 2 the force produced by drawing air out of a space to make a vacuum that will suck in a substance from another space.

Sudanese *adj* 1 of the Sudan. ~*n, pl* **-nese** 2 a person from the Sudan.

sudden *adj* 1 occurring or performed quickly and without warning. ~*n* 2 **all of a sudden** without warning; unexpectedly. **suddenly** *adv* **suddenness** *n*

sudden death *n Sport* an extra period of play to decide the winner of a tied competition: the first player or team to go into the lead is the winner.

sudden infant death syndrome *n* same as **cot death.**

sudorific (syoo-dor-**if**-ik) *adj* 1 causing sweating. ~*n* 2 a drug that causes sweating.

suds *pl n* the bubbles on the surface of water in which soap or detergent has been dissolved; lather.

sue *vb* **suing, sued** to start legal proceedings (against): *we want to sue the council; he sued for custody of the three children.*

suede *n* a leather with a fine velvet-like surface on one side.

suet *n* a hard fat obtained from sheep and cattle and used for making pastry and puddings.

suffer *vb* 1 to undergo or be subjected to (physical pain or mental distress). 2 **suffer from** to be badly affected by (an illness): *he was suffering from severe depression.* 3 to become worse in quality; deteriorate: *his work suffered during their divorce.* 4 to tolerate:

THESAURUS

best-selling, booming, efficacious, favourable, flourishing, fortunate, fruitful, lucky, lucrative, moneymaking, out in front (*informal*), paying, profitable, prosperous, rewarding, thriving, top, unbeaten, victorious, wealthy

successfully famously (*informal*), favourably, in triumph, swimmingly, victoriously, well, with flying colours

succession **1.** chain, continuation, course, cycle, flow, order, procession, progression, run, sequence, series, train **2.** accession, assumption, elevation, entering upon, inheritance, taking over **3. in succession** consecutively, one after the other, one behind the other, on the trot (*informal*), running, successively

successive consecutive, following, in a row, in succession, sequent, succeeding

succinct brief, compact, compendious, concise, condensed, gnomic (*literary*), laconic, pithy, summary, terse, to the point

succour **1.** *n.* aid, assistance, comfort, help, relief, support **2.** *vb.* aid, assist, befriend, comfort, encourage, foster, help, minister to, nurse, relieve, render assistance to, support

succulent juicy, luscious, lush, mellow, moist, mouthwatering, rich

succumb **a** capitulate, fall, give in, give way, go under, knuckle under, submit, surrender, yield **b** die, fall victim to

sucker *slang* butt, cat's paw, dupe, easy game *or* mark (*informal*), fool, mug (*Brit. slang*), nerd *or* nurd (*slang*), pushover (*slang*), sap (*slang*), sitting duck (*informal*), victim

sudden abrupt, hasty, hurried, impulsive, quick, rapid, rash, swift, unexpected, unforeseen, unusual

suddenly abruptly, all at once, all of a sudden, on the spur of the moment, out of the blue (*informal*), unexpectedly, without warning

sue bring an action against (someone), charge, have the law on (someone) (*informal*), indict, institute legal proceedings against (someone), prefer charges against

he suffers no fools. **5** to be set at a disadvantage: *the strongest of them suffers by comparison.* **sufferer** *n* **suffering** *n*

sufferance *n* **on sufferance** tolerated with reluctance: *I was there on sufferance and all knew it.*

suffice (suf-**fice**) *vb* **-ficing, -ficed 1** to be enough or satisfactory for a purpose. **2 suffice it to say ...** it is enough to say ...: *suffice it to say that AIDS is on the increase.*

sufficiency *n, pl* **-cies** an adequate amount.

sufficient *adj* enough to meet a need or purpose; adequate. **sufficiently** *adv*

suffix *Grammar ~n* **1** a letter or letters added to the end of a word to form another word, such as *-s* and *-ness* in *dogs* and *softness.* ~*vb* **2** to add (a letter or letters) to the end of a word to form another word.

suffocate *vb* **-cating, -cated 1** to kill or die through lack of oxygen, such as by blockage of the air passage. **2** to feel uncomfortable from heat and lack of air. **suffocating** *adj* **suffocation** *n*

suffragan *n* a bishop appointed to assist an archbishop.

suffrage *n* the right to vote in public elections.

suffragette *n* (in Britain at the beginning of the 20th century) a woman who campaigned militantly for women to be given the right to vote in public elections.

suffragist *n* (in Britain at the beginning of the 20th century) a person who campaigned for women to be given the right to vote in public elections.

suffuse *vb* **-fusing, -fused** to spread through or over (something): *the dawn suffused the sky with a cold grey wash.* **suffusion** *n*

sugar *n* **1** a sweet carbohydrate, usually in the form of white or brown crystals, which is found in many plants and is used to sweeten food and drinks. **2** *Informal, chiefly US & Canad* a term of affection. ~*vb* **3** to add sugar to (food or drink) to make it sweet. **4** to cover with sugar: *sugared almonds.* **5 sugar the pill** to make something unpleasant more tolerable by adding something pleasant. **sugared** *adj*

sugar beet *n* a beet grown for the sugar obtained from its roots.

sugar cane *n* a tropical grass grown for the sugar obtained from its tall stout canes.

sugar daddy *n* an elderly man who gives a young woman money and gifts in return for her company.

sugaring off *n Canad* the boiling down of maple sap to produce sugar, traditionally a social event in early spring.

sugar loaf *n* a large cone-shaped mass of hard refined sugar.

sugar maple *n* a North American maple tree, grown as a source of sugar, which is extracted from the sap.

sugary *adj* **1** of, like, or containing sugar. **2** (of behaviour or language) very pleasant but probably not sincere: *sugary sentiment.* **sugariness** *n*

suggest *vb* **1** to put forward (a plan or an idea) for consideration: *he didn't suggest a meeting.* **2** to bring (a person or thing) to the mind by the association of ideas: *a man whose very name suggests blandness.* **3** to give a hint of: *her grey eyes suggesting a livelier mood than usual.*

suggestible *adj* easily influenced by other people's ideas.

suggestion *n* **1** something that is suggested. **2** a hint or indication: *the entire castle gave no suggestion of period.* **3** *Psychol* the process whereby the presentation of an idea to a receptive individual leads to the acceptance of that idea.

suggestive *adj* **1** (of remarks or gestures) causing people to think of sex. **2 suggestive of** communicating a hint of.

suicidal *adj* **1** wanting to commit suicide. **2** likely to lead to danger or death: *a suicidal attempt to rescue her son.* **3** likely to destroy one's own career or future: *it would be suicidal for them to ignore public opinion.*

suicide *n* **1** the act of killing oneself deliberately: *he tried to commit suicide.* **2** a person who kills himself or herself intentionally. **3** the self-inflicted ruin of one's own career or future: *such a cut would be political suicide.*

suit *n* **1** a set of clothes of the same material designed to be worn together, usually a jacket with matching trousers or skirt. **2** an outfit worn for a specific purpose: *a diving suit.* **3** a legal action taken against someone; lawsuit. **4** any of the four types of card in a pack of playing cards: spades, hearts, diamonds, or clubs. **5 follow suit** to act in the same way as someone else. **6 strong suit** *or* **strongest suit** something one excels in. ~*vb* **7** to be fit or appropriate for: *that colour suits you.* **8** to be acceptable to (someone). **9 suit oneself** to do what one wants without considering other people. **suited** *adj*

THESAURUS

(someone), prosecute, summon, take (someone) to court

suffer 1. ache, agonize, be affected, be in pain, be racked, experience, feel, feel wretched, go through, go through a lot (*informal*), grieve, have a thin *or* bad time, hurt, undergo **2.** bear, endure, put up with (*informal*), tolerate **3.** appear in a poor light, be handicapped, be impaired, deteriorate, fall off, show to disadvantage

suffering *n.* affliction, agony, anguish, discomfort, distress, hardship, martyrdom, misery, ordeal, pain, torment, torture

suffice answer, be sufficient (adequate, enough), content, do, fill the bill (*informal*), meet requirements, satisfy, serve

sufficient adequate, competent, enough, satisfactory

suffocate asphyxiate, choke, smother, stifle, strangle

suffuse bathe, cover, flood, imbue, infuse, mantle, overspread, permeate, pervade, spread over, steep, transfuse

suggest 1. advise, advocate, move, offer a suggestion, prescribe, propose, put forward, recommend **2.** bring to mind, connote, evoke, put one in mind of **3.** hint, imply, indicate, insinuate, intimate, lead one to believe

suggestion 1. motion, plan, proposal, proposition, recommendation **2.** breath, hint, indication, insinuation, intimation, suspicion, trace, whisper

suggestive 1. bawdy, blue, immodest, improper, indecent, indelicate, off colour, provocative, prurient, racy, ribald, risqué, rude, smutty, spicy (*informal*), titillating, unseemly **2.** *with* **of** evocative, expressive, indicative, redolent, reminiscent

suit *n.* **1.** clothing, costume, dress, ensemble, habit, outfit **2.** action, case, cause, industrial tribunal, lawsuit, proceeding, prosecution, trial **3. follow suit** accord with, copy, emulate, run with the herd, take one's cue from ~*vb.* **4.** agree, agree with, answer, be acceptable to, become, befit, be seemly, conform to, correspond, do, go with, gratify, harmonize, match, please, satisfy, tally

suitability appropriateness, aptness, fitness, opportuneness, rightness, timeliness

suitable acceptable, applicable, apposite, appropriate, apt, becoming, befitting, convenient, cut out for,

suitable *adj* appropriate for a particular function or occasion; proper. **suitability** *n* **suitably** *adv*
suitcase *n* a large portable travelling case for clothing.
suite *n* **1** a set of connected rooms in a hotel. **2** a matching set of furniture, for example two armchairs and a settee. **3** *Music* a composition of several movements in the same key.
suitor *n* **1** *Old-fashioned* a man who wants to marry a woman. **2** *Law* a person who starts legal proceedings against someone; plaintiff.
Sukkoth (**sook**-oat) *n* an eight-day Jewish harvest festival, commemorating the period when the Israelites lived in the wilderness.
sulk *vb* **1** to be silent and moody as a way of showing anger or resentment: *I went home and sulked for two days.* ~*n* **2** a mood in which one shows anger or resentment by being silent and moody: *he was just in a sulk.*
sulky *adj* **sulkier, sulkiest** moody or silent because of anger or resentment. **sulkily** *adv* **sulkiness** *n*
sullen *adj* unwilling to talk or be sociable; sulky. **sullenly** *adv* **sullenness** *n*
sully *vb* **-lies, -lying, -lied 1** to ruin (someone's reputation). **2** to spoil or make dirty: *the stream had been sullied by the smelter's pollution.*
sulpha *or US* **sulfa drug** *n Pharmacol* any of a group of sulphonamides that prevent the growth of bacteria: used to treat bacterial infections.
sulphate *or US* **sulfate** *n Chem* a salt or ester of sulphuric acid.
sulphide *or US* **sulfide** *n Chem* a compound of sulphur with another element.
sulphite *or US* **sulfite** *n Chem* any salt or ester of sulphurous acid.
sulphonamide *or US* **sulfonamide** (sulf-**on**-a-mide) *n Pharmacol* any of a class of organic compounds that prevent the growth of bacteria.
sulphur *or US* **sulfur** *n Chem* a light yellow, highly inflammable, nonmetallic element used in the production of sulphuric acid, in the vulcanization of rubber, and in medicine. Symbol: S **sulphuric** *or US* **sulfuric** *adj*
sulphur dioxide *n Chem* a strong-smelling colourless soluble gas, used in the manufacture of sulphuric acid and in the preservation of foodstuffs.
sulphureous *or US* **sulfureous** (sulf-**yoor**-ee-uss) *adj* same as **sulphurous** (sense 1).
sulphuric acid *n Chem* a colourless dense oily corrosive liquid used in the manufacture of fertilizers and explosives.
sulphurize *or* **-rise** *or US* **sulfurize** (**sulf**-yoor-rise) *vb* **-rizing, -rized** *or* **-rising, -rised** *Chem* to combine with or treat (something) with sulphur or a sulphur compound.
sulphurous *or US* **sulfurous** *adj Chem* **1** of or resembling sulphur. **2** containing sulphur, esp. with a valence of four.
sultan *n* the sovereign of a Muslim country.
sultana *n* **1** the dried fruit of a small white seedless grape. **2** a sultan's wife, mother, daughter, or concubine.
sultanate *n* **1** the territory ruled by a sultan. **2** the office or rank of a sultan.
sultry *adj* **-trier, -triest 1** (of weather or climate) very hot and humid. **2** suggesting hidden passion: *a sultry brunette.*
sum *n* **1** the result of the addition of numbers or quantities. **2** one or more columns or rows of numbers to be added, subtracted, multiplied, or divided. **3** a quantity of money: *they can win enormous sums.* **4 in sum** as a summary; in short: *in sum, it's been a bad week for the government.* ~*adj* **5** complete or final: *the sum total.* ~*vb* **summing, summed 6** See **sum up.**
summarize *or* **-rise** *vb* **-rizing, -rized** *or* **-rising, -rised** to give a short account of (something).
summary *n, pl* **-maries 1** a brief account giving the main points of something. ~*adj* **2** performed quickly, without formality or attention to details: *a summary judgment.* **summarily** *adv*
summation *n* **1** a summary of what has just been done or said. **2** the process of working out a sum; addition. **3** the result of such a process.
summer *n* **1** the warmest season of the year, between spring and autumn. **2** *Literary* a time of youth, success, or happiness. **summery** *adj*
summerhouse *n* a small building in a garden, used for shade in the summer.
summer school *n* an academic course held during the summer.
summer solstice *n* the time, about June 21, at which the sun is at its northernmost point in the sky.
summertime *n* the period or season of summer.
summing-up *n* **1** a summary of the main points of an argument, speech, or piece of writing. **2** concluding statements made by a judge to the jury before they retire to consider their verdict.
summit *n* **1** the highest point or part of a mountain or hill. **2** the highest possible degree or state; peak or climax: *the summit of success.* **3** a meeting of heads of governments or other high officials.
summon *vb* **1** to order (someone) to come. **2** send for (someone) to appear in court. **3** to call upon (someone) to do something: *the authorities had*

THESAURUS

due, fit, fitting, in character, in keeping, opportune, pertinent, proper, relevant, right, satisfactory, seemly, suited
suite apartment, collection, furniture, rooms, series, set
suitor *old-fashioned* admirer, beau (*chiefly U.S.*), swain (*archaic or poetic*), wooer (*old-fashioned*), young man
sulk be in a huff, be put out, brood, have the hump (*Brit. informal*), look sullen, pout
sulky aloof, churlish, cross, disgruntled, huffy, ill-humoured, moody, morose, perverse, petulant, put out, querulous, resentful, sullen, vexed
sullen brooding, cheerless, cross, dismal, dull, gloomy, glowering, heavy, moody, morose, obstinate, out of humour, perverse, silent, sombre, sour, stubborn, surly, unsociable
sultry 1. close, hot, humid, muggy, oppressive, sticky, stifling, stuffy, sweltering **2.** amorous, come-hither (*informal*), erotic, passionate, provocative, seductive, sensual, sexy (*informal*), voluptuous
sum aggregate, amount, entirety, quantity, reckoning, score, sum total, tally, total, totality, whole
summarily arbitrarily, at short notice, expeditiously, forthwith, immediately, on the spot, peremptorily, promptly, speedily, swiftly, without delay, without wasting words
summarize abridge, condense, encapsulate, epitomize, give a rundown of, give the main points of, outline, précis, put in a nutshell, review, sum up
summary 1. *n.* abridgment, abstract, compendium, digest, epitome, essence, extract, outline, précis, recapitulation, résumé, review, rundown, summing-up, synopsis **2.** *adj.* arbitrary, brief, compact, compendi-

summoned the relatives to be available. **4** to convene (a meeting). **5** (often foll. by *up*) to call into action (one's strength, courage, etc.); muster.

summons *n, pl* **-monses 1** a call or an order to attend a specified place at a specified time. **2** an official order requiring a person to attend court, either to answer a charge or to give evidence. *~vb* **3** to order (someone) to appear in court.

sumo *n* the national style of wrestling of Japan, in which two contestants of great height and weight attempt to force each other out of the ring.

sump *n* **1** a container in an internal-combustion engine into which oil can drain. **2** same as **cesspool. 3** *Mining* a hollow at the bottom of a shaft where water collects.

sumptuary *adj* controlling expenditure or extravagant use of resources.

sumptuous *adj* magnificent and very expensive; splendid: *sumptuous decoration.*

sum up *vb* **1** to give a short account of (the main points of an argument, speech, or piece of writing). **2** to form a quick opinion of: *how well you have summed me up!*

sun *n* **1** the star that is the source of heat and light for the planets in the solar system. **2** any star around which a system of planets revolves. **3** the heat and light received from the sun; sunshine. **4 catch the sun** to become slightly sun-tanned. **5 under the sun** on earth; at all: *there are no free lunches under the sun. ~vb* **sunning, sunned 6 sun oneself** to lie, sit, or walk in the sunshine on a warm day. **sunless** *adj*

Sun. Sunday.

sunbathe *vb* **-bathing, -bathed** to lie or sit in the sunshine, in order to get a suntan. **sunbather** *n* **sunbathing** *n*

sunbeam *n* a ray of sunlight.

sunburn *n* painful reddening of the skin caused by overexposure to the sun. **sunburnt** *or* **sunburned** *adj*

sundae *n* ice cream topped with a sweet sauce, nuts, whipped cream, and fruit.

Sunday *n* the first day of the week and the Christian day of worship.

Sunday best *n* a person's best clothes, sometimes regarded as those most suitable for wearing at church.

Sunday school *n* a school for teaching children about Christianity, usually held in a church on Sunday.

sundial *n* a device used for telling the time during the hours of sunlight, consisting of a pointer that casts a shadow onto a surface marked in hours.

sundown *n US* sunset.

sundries *pl n* several things of various sorts.

sundry *adj* **1** several or various; miscellaneous. *~pron* **2 all and sundry** everybody.

sunfish *n, pl* **-fish** *or* **-fishes** a large sea fish with a rounded body.

sunflower *n* **1** a very tall plant with large yellow flowers. **2 sunflower seed oil** the oil extracted from sunflower seeds, used as a salad oil and in margarine.

sung *vb* the past participle of **sing.**

sunglasses *pl n* glasses with darkened lenses that protect the eyes from bright sunlight.

sun-god *n* the sun considered as a god.

sunk *vb* a past tense and past participle of **sink.**

sunken *vb* **1** a past participle of **sink.** *~adj* **2** (of a person's cheeks, eyes, or chest) curving inward due to old age or bad health. **3** situated at a lower level than the surrounding or usual one: *the sunken garden.* **4** situated under water; submerged: *sunken ships.*

sun lamp *n* a lamp that gives off ultraviolet rays, used for muscular therapy or for giving people an artificial suntan.

sunlight *n* the light that comes from the sun. **sunlit** *adj*

sun lounge *or US* **sun parlor** *n* a room with large windows designed to receive as much sunlight as possible.

sunny *adj* **-nier, -niest 1** full of or lit up by sunshine. **2** cheerful and happy: *a sunny nature.*

sunrise *n* **1** the daily appearance of the sun above the horizon. **2** the time at which the sun rises.

sunrise industry *n* any of the fast-developing high-technology industries, such as electronics.

sunroof *n* a panel in the roof of a car that may be opened to let in air or sunshine.

sunset *n* **1** the daily disappearance of the sun below the horizon. **2** the time at which the sun sets.

sunshade *n* anything used to shade people from the sun, such as a parasol or awning.

sunshine *n* **1** the light and warmth from the sun. **2** *Brit* a light-hearted term of address.

sunspot *n* **1** *Informal* a sunny holiday resort. **2** a dark cool patch on the surface of the sun.

sunstroke *n* a condition caused by spending too much time exposed to intensely hot sunlight and producing high fever and sometimes loss of consciousness.

suntan *n* a brownish colouring of the skin caused by exposure to the sun or a sun lamp. **suntanned** *adj*

sup[1] *vb* **supping, supped 1** to take (liquid) by swallowing a little at a time. *~n* **2** a sip.

sup[2] *vb* **supping, supped** *Archaic* to have supper.

super *Informal ~adj* **1** very good or very nice: *they had a super holiday. ~n* **2** *Austral & NZ informal*

THESAURUS

ous, concise, condensed, cursory, hasty, laconic, perfunctory, pithy, succinct

summit acme, apex, crest, crown, crowning point, culmination, head, height, peak, pinnacle, top, zenith

summon 1. arouse, assemble, bid, call, call together, cite, convene, convoke, invite, rally, rouse, send for **2.** *often with* **up** call into action, draw on, gather, invoke, mobilize, muster

sumptuous costly, dear, de luxe, expensive, extravagant, gorgeous, grand, lavish, luxurious, magnificent, opulent, plush (*informal*), posh (*informal, chiefly Brit.*), rich, ritzy (*slang*), splendid, splendiferous (*facetious, old-fashioned*), superb

sum up 1. close, conclude, put in a nutshell, recapitulate, review, summarize **2.** estimate, form an opinion of, get the measure of, size up (*informal*)

sun *vb.* **sun oneself** bake, bask, sunbathe, tan

sunburnt bronzed, brown, brown as a berry, burnt, like a lobster, peeling, red, ruddy, scarlet, tanned

sundry assorted, different, miscellaneous, several, some, varied, various

sunken 1. concave, drawn, haggard, hollow, hollowed **2.** at a lower level, below ground, buried, depressed, immersed, lower, recessed, submerged

sunless bleak, cheerless, cloudy, dark, depressing, gloomy, grey, hazy, overcast, sombre

sunny 1. bright, brilliant, clear, fine, luminous, radiant, summery, sunlit, sunshiny, unclouded, without a cloud in the sky **2.** beaming, blithe, buoyant, cheerful, cheery, chirpy (*informal*), genial, happy, joyful, light-hearted, optimistic, pleasant, smiling

superannuation. 3 *Austral & NZ informal* superphosphate.

super- *prefix* used with many main words to mean: 1 above or over: *superscript.* 2 outstanding: *superstar.* 3 of greater size, extent, or quality: *supermarket.*

superabundant *adj* existing in very large numbers or amount. **superabundance** *n*

superannuated *adj* 1 discharged with a pension, owing to age or illness. 2 too old to be useful; obsolete.

superannuation *n* **a** a regular payment made by an employee into a pension fund. **b** the pension finally paid.

superb *adj* extremely good or impressive. **superbly** *adv*

Super Bowl *n American football* the championship game held annually between the best team of the American Football Conference and that of the National Football Conference.

supercharge *vb* **-charging, -charged** 1 to increase the power of (an internal-combustion engine) with a supercharger. 2 to charge (the atmosphere, a remark, etc.) with an excess amount of (tension, emotion, etc.). 3 to apply pressure to (a fluid); pressurize.

supercharger *n* a device that increases the power of an internal-combustion engine by forcing extra air into it.

supercilious *adj* behaving in a superior and arrogant manner. **superciliously** *adv* **superciliousness** *n*

superconductivity *n Physics* the ability of certain substances to conduct electric current with almost no resistance at very low temperatures. **superconducting** *adj* **superconductor** *n*

superego *n, pl* **-gos** *Psychoanal* that part of the unconscious mind that governs a person's ideas concerning what is right and wrong.

supererogation *n* the act of doing more work than is required.

superficial *adj* 1 not careful or thorough: *a superficial analysis.* 2 only outwardly apparent rather than genuine or actual: *those are merely superficial differences.* 3 (of a person) lacking deep emotions or serious interests; shallow. 4 of, near, or forming the surface: *the gash was superficial.* **superficiality** *n* **superficially** *adv*

superfluous (soo-per-flew-uss) *adj* more than is sufficient or required. **superfluity** *n*

superglue *n* an extremely strong and quick-drying glue.

supergrass *n* an informer who names a large number of people as terrorists or criminals, esp. one who gives this information in order to avoid being put on trial.

superhuman *adj* beyond normal human ability or experience: *a superhuman effort.*

superimpose *vb* **-posing, -posed** to set or place (something) on or over something else.

superintend *vb* to supervise (a person or an activity).

superintendent *n* 1 a senior police officer. 2 a person who directs and manages an organization or office.

superior *adj* 1 greater in quality, quantity, or usefulness. 2 higher in rank, position, or status: *he was reprimanded by a superior officer.* 3 believing oneself to be better than others. 4 of very high quality or respectability: *superior merchandise.* 5 *Formal* placed higher up: *damage to the superior surface of the wing.* 6 *Printing* (of a character) written or printed above the line. *~n* 7 a person of greater rank or status. 8 See **mother superior. superiority** *n*

superlative (soo-per-lat-iv) *adj* 1 of outstanding quality; supreme. 2 *Grammar* denoting the form of an adjective or adverb that expresses the highest degree of quality. *~n* 3 the highest quality. 4 *Grammar* the superlative form of an adjective or adverb.

superman *n, pl* **-men** any man with great physical or mental powers.

supermarket *n* a large self-service shop selling food and household goods.

supermodel *n* a famous and highly-paid fashion model.

supernatural *adj* 1 of or relating to things that cannot be explained by science, such as clairvoyance,

THESAURUS

sunrise aurora (*poetic*), break of day, cockcrow, dawn, daybreak, daylight, sunup

sunset close of (the) day, dusk, eventide, gloaming (*Scot. poetic*), nightfall, sundown

superb admirable, breathtaking, brill (*informal*), choice, excellent, exquisite, fine, first-rate, gorgeous, grand, magnificent, marvellous, mega (*slang*), splendid, splendiferous (*facetious*), superior, unrivalled, world-class

supercilious arrogant, condescending, contemptuous, disdainful, haughty, high and mighty (*informal*), hoity-toity (*informal*), imperious, insolent, lofty, lordly, overbearing, patronizing, proud, scornful, snooty (*informal*), stuck-up (*informal*), toffee-nosed (*slang, chiefly Brit.*), uppish (*Brit. informal*), vainglorious

superficial 1. casual, cosmetic, cursory, desultory, hasty, hurried, inattentive, nodding, passing, perfunctory, sketchy, slapdash 2. apparent, evident, ostensible, outward, seeming 3. empty, empty-headed, frivolous, lightweight, shallow, silly, trivial 4. exterior, external, on the surface, peripheral, shallow, skin-deep, slight, surface

superficiality emptiness, lack of depth, lack of substance, shallowness, triviality

superficially apparently, at first glance, externally, on the surface, ostensibly, to the casual eye

superfluous excess, excessive, extra, in excess, left over, needless, on one's hands, pleonastic (*Rhetoric*), redundant, remaining, residuary, spare, superabundant, supererogatory, supernumerary, surplus, surplus to requirements, uncalled-for, unnecessary, unneeded, unrequired

superhuman herculean, heroic, phenomenal, prodigious, stupendous, valiant

superintend administer, control, direct, handle, inspect, look after, manage, overlook, oversee, run, supervise

superintendent administrator, chief, conductor, controller, director, governor, inspector, manager, overseer, supervisor

superior *adj.* 1. better, grander, greater, higher, more advanced (expert, extensive, skilful), paramount, predominant, preferred, prevailing, surpassing, unrivalled 2. airy, condescending, disdainful, haughty, lofty, lordly, patronizing, pretentious, snobbish, stuck-up (*informal*), supercilious 3. a cut above (*informal*), admirable, choice, de luxe, distinguished, excellent, exceptional, exclusive, fine, first-class, first-rate, good, good quality, high-calibre, high-class, of the first order, world-class *~n.* 4. boss (*informal*), chief, director, manager, principal, senior, supervisor

superiority advantage, ascendancy, excellence, lead, predominance, pre-eminence, preponderance, prevalence, supremacy

superlative *adj.* consummate, crack (*slang*), excellent, greatest, highest, magnificent, matchless, of the

ghosts, etc. *~n* 2 **the supernatural** forces, occurrences, and beings that cannot be explained by science.

supernova *n, pl* **-vae** *or* **-vas** a star that explodes, and for a few days, becomes one hundred million times brighter than the sun.

supernumerary *adj* 1 exceeding the required or regular number; extra. 2 employed as a substitute or assistant. *~n, pl* **-aries** 3 a person or thing that exceeds the required or regular number. 4 a substitute or assistant. 5 an actor who has no lines to say.

superphosphate *n* a chemical fertilizer, esp. one made by treating rock phosphate with sulphuric acid.

superpower *n* a country of very great military and economic power, such as the US.

superscript *Printing ~adj* 1 (of a character) written or printed above the line. *~n* 2 a superscript character.

supersede *vb* **-seding, -seded** 1 to take the place of (something old-fashioned or less appropriate): *cavalry was superseded by armoured vehicles.* 2 to replace (someone) in function or office.

supersonic *adj* being, having, or capable of a speed greater than the speed of sound.

superstar *n* an extremely popular and famous entertainer or sportsperson.

superstition *n* 1 irrational belief in magic and the powers that supposedly bring good luck or bad luck. 2 a belief or practice based on this. **superstitious** *adj*

superstore *n* a large supermarket.

superstructure *n* 1 any structure or concept built on something else. 2 *Naut* any structure above the main deck of a ship.

supertanker *n* a very large fast tanker.

supertax *n* an extra tax on incomes above a certain level.

supervene *vb* **-vening, -vened** to happen as an unexpected development. **supervention** *n*

supervise *vb* **-vising, -vised** 1 to direct the performance or operation of (an activity or a process). 2 to watch over (people) so as to ensure appropriate behaviour. **supervision** *n* **supervisor** *n* **supervisory** *adj*

supine (**soo**-pine) *adj Formal* lying on one's back.

supper *n* an evening meal.

supplant *vb* to take the place of (someone or something).

supple *adj* 1 (of a person) moving and bending easily and gracefully. 2 (of a material or object) soft and bending easily without breaking. **suppleness** *n*

supplement *n* 1 an addition designed to make something more adequate. 2 a magazine distributed free with a newspaper. 3 a section added to a publication to supply further information or correct errors. 4 (of money) an additional payment to obtain special services. *~vb* 5 to provide an addition to (something), esp. in order to make up for an inadequacy: *a Saturday job to supplement her grant.* **supplementary** *adj*

supplementary benefit *n* (in Britain) an earlier form of income support.

supplicant *n Formal* a person who makes a humble request.

supplication *n Formal* a humble request for help.

supply *vb* **-plies, -plying, -plied** 1 to provide with something required: *Nigeria may supply them with oil.* *~n, pl* **-plies** 2 the act of providing something. 3 an amount available for use; stock: *electricity supply.* 4 **supplies** food and equipment needed for a trip or military campaign. 5 *Econ* the amount of a commodity that producers are willing and able to offer for sale at a specified price: *supply and demand.* 6 a person who acts as a temporary substitute. *~adj* 7 acting as a temporary substitute: *supply teachers.* **supplier** *n*

support *vb* 1 to carry the weight of (a thing or person). 2 to provide the necessities of life for (a family or person). 3 to give practical or emotional help to (someone). 4 to give approval to (a cause, idea, or political party). 5 to take an active interest in and be loyal to (a particular football or other sport team). 6 to establish the truthfulness or accuracy of (a theory or statement) by providing new facts. 7 to speak in a debate in favour of (a motion). 8 (in a concert) to perform earlier than (the main attraction). 9 *Films, theatre* to play a less important role to (the leading actor or actress). *~n* 10 the act of supporting or the condition of being supported. 11 a thing that bears the weight of an object from below. 12 a person who gives someone practical or emotional help. 13 the means of

THESAURUS

first water, of the highest order, outstanding, peerless, supreme, surpassing, transcendent, unparalleled, unrivalled, unsurpassed

supernatural *adj.* abnormal, dark, ghostly, hidden, miraculous, mysterious, mystic, occult, paranormal, phantom, preternatural, psychic, spectral, supranatural, uncanny, unearthly, unnatural

supervise administer, be on duty at, be responsible for, conduct, control, direct, handle, have *or* be in charge of, inspect, keep an eye on, look after, manage, oversee, preside over, run, superintend

supervision administration, auspices, care, charge, control, direction, guidance, instruction, management, oversight, stewardship, superintendence, surveillance

supervisor administrator, boss (*informal*), chief, foreman, gaffer (*informal, chiefly Brit.*), inspector, manager, overseer, steward, superintendent

supervisory administrative, executive, managerial, overseeing, superintendent

supplant displace, oust, overthrow, remove, replace, supersede, take over, take the place of, undermine, unseat

supple bending, elastic, flexible, limber, lissom(e), lithe, loose-limbed, plastic, pliable, pliant

supplement 1. *n.* added feature, addendum, addition, add-on, appendix, codicil, complement, extra, insert, postscript, pull-out, sequel 2. *vb.* add, augment, complement, extend, fill out, reinforce, supply, top up

supplementary accompanying, additional, add-on, ancillary, auxiliary, complementary, extra, secondary, supplemental

supplication *formal* appeal, entreaty, invocation, petition, plea, pleading, prayer, request, solicitation, suit

supply *vb.* 1. afford, cater to *or* for, come up with, contribute, endow, fill, furnish, give, grant, minister, outfit, produce, provide, purvey, replenish, satisfy, stock, store, victual, yield *~n.* 2. cache, fund, hoard, quantity, reserve, reservoir, source, stock, stockpile, store 3. **supplies** equipment, food, foodstuff, items, materials, necessities, provender, provisions, rations, stores

support *vb.* 1. bear, bolster, brace, buttress, carry, hold, hold up, prop, reinforce, shore up, sustain, underpin, uphold 2. buoy up, cherish, encourage, finance, foster, fund, keep, look after, maintain, nourish, provide for, strengthen, subsidize, succour, sustain, take care of, underwrite 3. advocate, aid, assist, back, boost (someone's) morale, champion, defend, espouse, forward, go along with, help, promote, second, side with, stand behind, stand up for, stick up for (*informal*), take (someone's) part, take up the cudgels for, uphold 4. attest to, authenticate, bear out, con-

providing the necessities of life for a family or person. **14** a band or entertainer not topping the bill. **supportive** *adj*

supporter *n* a person who supports a sports team, politician, etc.

suppose *vb* **-posing, -posed 1** to presume (something) to be true without certain knowledge: *I suppose it will be in the papers.* **2** to consider (something) as a possible suggestion for the sake of discussion: *suppose you're arrested on a misdemeanour.* **3** (of a theory) to depend on the truth or existence of: *this scenario supposes that he would do so.*

supposed *adj* **1 supposed to** expected to: *spies aren't supposed to be nice.* **2** presumed to be true without certain knowledge; doubtful: *the supposed wonders of drug therapy.* **supposedly** *adv*

supposition *n* **1** an idea or a statement believed or assumed to be true. **2** the act of supposing: *much of it is based on supposition.*

suppositious *adj* deduced from an idea or statement believed or assumed to be true; hypothetical.

suppository *n, pl* **-ries** *Med* a medicine in solid form that is inserted into the vagina or rectum and left to dissolve.

suppress *vb* **1** to put an end to (something) by physical or legal force. **2** to prevent the circulation or publication of (information or books). **3** to hold (an emotion or a response) in check; restrain: *he could barely suppress a groan.* **4** *Electronics* to reduce or eliminate (interference) in a circuit. **suppression** *n*

suppressant *n* a drug that suppresses an action: *a cough suppressant.*

suppurate *vb* **-rating, -rated** *Pathol* (of a wound or sore) to produce or leak pus.

supremacy *n* **1** supreme power; dominance. **2** the state or quality of being superior.

supreme *adj* **1** of highest status or power: *the Supreme Council.* **2** of highest quality or importance: *a supreme player.* **3** greatest in degree; extreme: *supreme happiness.* **supremely** *adv*

supremo *n, pl* **-mos** *Brit informal* a person in overall authority.

sur-[1] *prefix* over; above; beyond: *surcharge; surrealism.*

sur-[2] *prefix* See **sub-**.

surcharge *n* **1** a charge in addition to the usual payment or tax. **2** an excessive sum charged, often unlawfully. *~vb* **-charging, -charged 3** to charge (someone) an additional sum or tax. **4** to overcharge (someone) for something.

surd *Maths ~n* **1** an irrational number. *~adj* **2** of or relating to a surd.

sure *adj* **1** free from doubt or uncertainty (in regard to a belief): *she was sure that she was still at home; I am sure he didn't mean it.* **2 sure of** having no doubt, such as of the occurrence of a future state or event: *sure of winning the point.* **3** reliable or accurate: *a sure sign of dry rot.* **4** bound inevitably (to be or do something); certain: *his aggressive style is sure to please the American fans.* **5 sure of** *or* **about** happy to put one's trust in (someone): *I'm still not quite sure about her.* **6 sure of oneself** confident in one's own abilities and opinions. **7** not open to doubt: *sure proof.* **8** bound to be or occur; inevitable: *victory is sure.* **9** physically secure: *a sure footing.* **10 be sure** to be careful or certain: *be sure to label each jar.* **11 for sure** without a doubt. **12 make sure** to make certain: *make sure there is no-one in the car.* **13 sure enough** *Informal* in fact: *sure enough, this is happening.* **14 to be sure** it has to be acknowledged; admittedly. *~adv* **15** *US & Canad informal* without question; certainly: *it sure is bad news.* *~interj* **16** *US & Canad informal* willingly; yes. **sureness** *n*

sure-fire *adj Informal* certain to succeed: *a sure-fire cure.*

sure-footed *adj* **1** unlikely to fall, slip, or stumble. **2** unlikely to make a mistake.

surely *adv* **1** am I not right in thinking that?; I am sure

THESAURUS

firm, corroborate, document, endorse, lend credence to, substantiate, verify *~n.* **5.** aid, approval, assistance, backing, blessing, championship, comfort, encouragement, espousal, friendship, furtherance, help, loyalty, moral support, patronage, promotion, protection, relief, succour, sustenance **6.** abutment, back, brace, foundation, lining, pillar, post, prop, shore, stanchion, stay, stiffener, underpinning **7.** backbone, backer, comforter, mainstay, prop, second, stay, supporter, tower of strength **8.** keep, livelihood, maintenance, subsistence, sustenance, upkeep

supporter adherent, advocate, ally, apologist, champion, co-worker, defender, fan, follower, friend, helper, henchman, patron, protagonist, sponsor, upholder, well-wisher

suppose 1. assume, believe, conclude, conjecture, dare say, expect, guess (*informal, chiefly U.S. & Canad.*), imagine, infer, judge, opine, presume, presuppose, surmise, take as read, take for granted, think **2.** conceive, conjecture, consider, fancy, hypothesize, imagine, postulate, pretend

supposed 1. *with* **to** expected, meant, obliged, ought, required **2.** accepted, alleged, assumed, hypothetical, presumed, presupposed, professed, putative, reputed, rumoured

supposedly allegedly, at a guess, avowedly, by all accounts, hypothetically, ostensibly, presumably, professedly, purportedly, theoretically

supposition conjecture, doubt, guess, guesswork, hypothesis, idea, notion, postulate, presumption, speculation, surmise, theory

suppress 1. beat down, check, clamp down on, conquer, crack down on, crush, drive underground, extinguish, overpower, overthrow, put an end to, quash, quell, quench, snuff out, stamp out, stop, subdue, trample on **2.** censor, conceal, contain, cover up, curb, hold in *or* back, hold in check, keep secret, muffle, muzzle, repress, restrain, silence, smother, stifle, withhold

suppression check, clampdown, crackdown, crushing, dissolution, elimination, extinction, inhibition, prohibition, quashing, smothering, termination

supremacy absolute rule, ascendancy, dominance, domination, dominion, lordship, mastery, paramountcy, predominance, pre-eminence, primacy, sovereignty, supreme authority, sway

supreme cardinal, chief, crowning, culminating, extreme, final, first, foremost, greatest, head, highest, incomparable, leading, matchless, paramount, peerless, predominant, pre-eminent, prevailing, prime, principal, sovereign, superlative, surpassing, top, ultimate, unsurpassed, utmost

sure 1. assured, certain, clear, confident, convinced, decided, definite, free from doubt, persuaded, positive, satisfied **2.** accurate, dependable, effective, foolproof, honest, indisputable, infallible, never-failing, precise, reliable, sure-fire (*informal*), tried and true, trustworthy, trusty, undeniable, undoubted, unerring, unfailing, unmistakable, well-proven **3.** assured, bound, guaranteed, ineluctable, inescapable, inevitable, irrevocable **4.** fast, firm, fixed, safe, secure, solid, stable, staunch, steady

that: *surely you can see that?* **2** without doubt: *without support they will surely fail.* **3 slowly but surely** gradually but noticeably. *~interj* **4** *Chiefly US & Canad* willingly; yes.

surety *n, pl* **-ties 1** a person who takes legal responsibility for the fulfilment of another's debt or obligation. **2** security given as a guarantee that an obligation will be met.

surf *n* **1** foam caused by waves breaking on the shore or on a reef. *~vb* **2** to take part in surfing. **surfer** *n*

surface *n* **1** the outside or top of an object. **2** the size of such an area. **3** material covering the surface of an object. **4** the outward appearance as opposed to the real or hidden nature of something: *on the surface the idea seems attractive.* **5** *Geom* **a** the complete boundary of a solid figure. **b** something that has length and breadth but no thickness. **6** the uppermost level of the land or sea. **7 come to the surface** to become apparent after being hidden. *~vb* **-facing, -faced 8** to become apparent or widely known. **9** to rise to the surface of water. **10** to give (an area) a particular kind of surface. **11** *Informal* to get up out of bed.

surface tension *n Physics* a property of liquids, caused by molecular forces, that leads to the apparent presence of a surface film and to rising and falling in contact with solids.

surfboard *n* a long narrow board used in surfing.

surfeit *n Formal* **1** an excessive amount. **2** excessive eating or drinking. **3** an uncomfortably full or sickened feeling caused by eating or drinking too much.

surfing *n* the sport of riding towards shore on the crest of a wave by standing or lying on a surfboard.

surge *n* **1** a sudden powerful increase: *a surge in spending.* **2** a strong rolling movement of the sea. **3** a heavy rolling motion or sound: *a great surge of people.* *~vb* **surging, surged 4** to move forward strongly and suddenly. **5** (of the sea) to rise or roll with a heavy swelling motion.

surgeon *n* a medical doctor who specializes in surgery.

surgery *n, pl* **-geries 1** medical treatment in which a person's body is cut open by a surgeon in order to treat or remove the problem part. **2** *Brit* a place where, or time when, a doctor or dentist can be consulted. **3** *Brit* a time when an MP or councillor can be consulted.

surgical *adj* involving or used in surgery. **surgically** *adv*

surgical spirit *n* methylated spirit used medically for cleaning wounds and sterilizing equipment.

surly *adj* **-lier, -liest** bad-tempered and rude.

surmise *vb* **-mising, -mised 1** to guess (something) from incomplete or uncertain evidence. *~n* **2** a conclusion based on incomplete or uncertain evidence.

surmount *vb* **1** to overcome (a problem). **2** to be situated on top of (something): *the island is surmounted by a huge black castle.* **surmountable** *adj*

surname *n* a family name as opposed to a Christian name.

surpass *vb* **1** to be greater in extent than or superior in achievement to (something or someone). **2 surpass oneself** *or* **expectations** to go beyond the limit of what was expected.

surplice *n* a loose knee-length garment with wide sleeves, worn by clergymen and choristers.

surplus *n* **1** a quantity or amount left over in excess of what is required. **2** *Accounting* an excess of income over spending. *~adj* **3** being in excess; extra: *surplus to requirements.*

surprise *n* **1** the act of taking someone unawares: *the element of surprise.* **2** a sudden or unexpected event, gift, etc.: *this is a nice surprise.* **3** the feeling of being surprised; astonishment: *to our great surprise.* **4 take someone by surprise** to capture someone unexpectedly or catch someone unprepared. *~adj* **5** causing surprise: *a surprise attack.* *~vb* **-prising, -prised 6** to cause (someone) to feel amazement or wonder. **7** to come upon or discover (someone) unexpectedly or suddenly. **8** to capture or attack (someone) suddenly and without warning. **9 surprise into** to provoke (someone) to unintended action by a trick or deception. **surprised** *adj* **surprising** *adj* **surprisingly** *adv*

surreal *adj* very strange or dreamlike; bizarre.

surrealism *n* a movement in art and literature in the 1920s, involving the combination of images that would not normally be found together, as if in a dream. **surrealist** *n, adj* **surrealistic** *adj*

surrender *vb* **1** to give oneself up physically to an enemy after defeat. **2** to give (something) up to another, under pressure or on demand: *the rebels surrendered their arms.* **3** to give (something) up vol-

THESAURUS

surely assuredly, beyond the shadow of a doubt, certainly, come what may, definitely, doubtlessly, for certain, indubitably, inevitably, inexorably, undoubtedly, unquestionably, without doubt, without fail

surface 1. *n.* covering, exterior, facade, face, facet, outside, plane, side, skin, superficies (*rare*), top, veneer **2.** *vb.* appear, come to light, come up, crop up (*informal*), emerge, materialize, rise, transpire

surfeit *formal* excess, glut, overindulgence, plethora, satiety, superabundance, superfluity

surge 1. *n.* billow, breaker, efflux, flood, flow, gush, intensification, outpouring, roller, rush, swell, uprush, upsurge, wave **2.** *vb.* billow, eddy, gush, heave, rise, roll, rush, swell, swirl, tower, undulate, well forth

surly brusque, churlish, crabbed, cross, crusty, curmudgeonly, grouchy (*informal*), gruff, ill-natured, morose, perverse, sulky, sullen, testy, uncivil, ungracious

surmise 1. *vb.* come to the conclusion, conclude, conjecture, consider, deduce, fancy, guess, hazard a guess, imagine, infer, opine, presume, speculate, suppose, suspect **2.** *n.* assumption, conclusion, conjecture, deduction, guess, hypothesis, idea, inference, notion, possibility, presumption, speculation, supposition, suspicion, thought

surmount conquer, exceed, master, overcome, overpower, overtop, pass, prevail over, surpass, triumph over, vanquish

surpass beat, best, eclipse, exceed, excel, go one better than (*informal*), outdo, outshine, outstrip, override, overshadow, top, tower above, transcend

surplus 1. *n.* balance, excess, remainder, residue, superabundance, superfluity, surfeit (*informal*) **2.** *adj.* excess, extra, in excess, left over, odd, remaining, spare, superfluous, unused

surprise *n.* **1.** bolt from the blue, bombshell, eye-opener (*informal*), jolt, revelation, shock, start (*informal*) **2.** amazement, astonishment, bewilderment, incredulity, stupefaction, wonder *~vb.* **3.** amaze, astonish, astound, bewilder, bowl over (*informal*), confuse, disconcert, flabbergast (*informal*), leave open-mouthed, nonplus, stagger, stun, take aback **4.** burst in on, catch in the act *or* red-handed, catch napping, catch unawares *or* off-guard, come down on like a bolt from the blue, discover, spring upon, startle

surprised amazed, astonished, at a loss, caught on the hop (*Brit. informal*), caught on the wrong foot (*informal*), disconcerted, incredulous, nonplussed, open-mouthed, speechless, startled, taken aback, taken by surprise, thunderstruck, unable to believe one's eyes

surprising amazing, astonishing, astounding,

untarily to another: *he was surrendering his own chance for the championship.* **4** to give in to a temptation or an influence. *~n* **5** the act or instance of surrendering.

surreptitious *adj* done in secret or without permission: *surreptitious moments of bliss.* **surreptitiously** *adv*

surrogate *n* **1** a person or thing acting as a substitute. *~adj* **2** acting as a substitute: *a surrogate father.*

surrogate mother *n* a woman who gives birth to a child on behalf of a couple who cannot have a baby themselves, usually by artificial insemination. **surrogate motherhood** *or* **surrogacy** *n*

surround *vb* **1** to encircle or enclose (something or someone). **2** to exist around (someone or something): *the family members who surround him.* *~n* **3** *Chiefly Brit* a border, such as the area of uncovered floor between the walls of a room and the carpet. **surrounding** *adj*

surroundings *pl n* the area and environment around a person, place, or thing.

surtax *n* an extra tax on incomes above a certain level.

surveillance *n* close observation of a person suspected of being a spy or a criminal.

survey *vb* **1** to view or consider (something) as a whole: *she surveyed her purchases anxiously.* **2** to make a detailed map of (an area of land) by measuring or calculating distances and height. **3** *Brit* to inspect (a building) to assess its condition and value. **4** to make a detailed investigation of the behaviour, opinions, etc., of (a group of people). *~n* **5** a detailed investigation of the behaviour, opinions, etc., of a group of people. **6** the act of making a detailed map of an area of land by measuring or calculating distance and height. **7** *Brit* an inspection of a building to assess its condition and value. **surveying** *n* **surveyor** *n*

survival *n* **1** the condition of having survived something. **2** a person or thing that continues to exist in the present despite being from an earlier time, such as a custom. *~adj* **3** of, relating to, or assisting the act of surviving: *survival suits.*

survive *vb* **-viving, -vived 1** to continue to live or exist after (a passage of time or a difficult or dangerous experience). **2** to live after the death of (another). **survivor** *n*

susceptibility *n, pl* **-ties 1** the quality or condition of being easily affected or influenced by something. **2** **susceptibilities** emotional feelings.

susceptible *adj* **1 susceptible to a** giving in easily to: *susceptible to political pressure.* **b** vulnerable to (a disease or injury): *susceptible to pneumonia.* **2** easily affected emotionally; impressionable.

sushi (soo-shee) *n* a Japanese dish consisting of small cakes of cold rice with a topping of raw fish.

suspect *vb* **1** to believe (someone) to be guilty without having any proof. **2** to think (something) to be false or doubtful: *he suspected her intent.* **3** to believe (something) to be the case; think probable: *I suspect he had another reason.* *~n* **4** a person who is believed guilty of a specified offence. *~adj* **5** not to be trusted or relied upon: *her commitment to the cause has always been suspect.*

suspend *vb* **1** to hang (something) from a high place. **2** to cause (something) to remain floating or hanging: *a huge orange sun suspended above the horizon.* **3** to cause (something) to stop temporarily: *the discussions have been suspended.* **4** to remove (someone) temporarily from a job or position, usually as a punishment.

suspended animation *n* a state in which the body's functions are slowed down to a minimum for a period of time, such as by freezing or hibernation.

suspended sentence *n* a sentence of imprisonment that is not served by an offender unless he or she commits a further offence during a specified time.

suspender belt *n* a belt with suspenders hanging from it for holding up women's stockings.

suspenders *pl n* **1** *Brit* **a** elastic straps attached to a belt or corset, with fasteners for holding up women's stockings. **b** similar fasteners attached to garters for holding up men's socks. **2** *US & Canad* braces.

suspense *n* **1** a state of anxiety or uncertainty: *Sue and I stared at each other in suspense.* **2** excitement felt at the approach of the climax of a book, film, or play: *action and suspense abound in this thriller.* **suspenseful** *adj*

suspension *n* **1** the delaying or stopping temporarily of something: *the suspension of the talks.* **2** temporary removal from a job or position, usually as a punishment. **3** the act of suspending or the state of being suspended. **4** a system of springs and shock absorbers

THESAURUS

extraordinary, incredible, marvellous, remarkable, staggering, startling, unexpected, unlooked-for, unusual, wonderful

surrender *vb.* **1.** capitulate, give in, give oneself up, give way, lay down arms, quit, show the white flag, submit, succumb, throw in the towel, yield **2.** abandon, cede, concede, deliver up, forego, give up, part with, relinquish, renounce, resign, waive, yield *~n.* **3.** capitulation, delivery, relinquishment, renunciation, resignation, submission, yielding

surreptitious clandestine, covert, fraudulent, furtive, secret, sly, sneaking, stealthy, unauthorized, underhand, veiled

surround close in on, encircle, enclose, encompass, envelop, environ, fence in, girdle, hem in, ring

surrounding nearby, neighbouring

surroundings background, environment, environs, location, milieu, neighbourhood, setting

surveillance care, control, direction, inspection, observation, scrutiny, superintendence, supervision, vigilance, watch

survey *vb.* **1.** contemplate, examine, eye up, inspect, look over, observe, recce (*slang*), reconnoitre, research, review, scan, scrutinize, study, supervise, view **2.** appraise, assess, estimate, eye up, measure, plan, plot, prospect, size up, take stock of, triangulate *~n.* **3.** examination, inquiry, inspection, overview, perusal, random sample, review, scrutiny, study

survive be extant, endure, exist, hold out, last, live, live on, outlast, outlive, pull through, remain alive, subsist

susceptibility liability, predisposition, proneness, propensity, responsiveness, sensitivity, suggestibility, vulnerability, weakness

susceptible **1.** *with* **to** disposed, given, inclined, liable, open, predisposed, prone, subject, vulnerable **2.** alive to, easily moved, impressionable, receptive, responsive, sensitive, suggestible, tender

suspect *vb.* **1.** distrust, doubt, harbour suspicions about, have one's doubts about, mistrust, smell a rat (*informal*) **2.** believe, conclude, conjecture, consider, fancy, feel, guess, have a sneaking suspicion, hazard a guess, speculate, suppose, surmise, think probable *~adj.* **3.** dodgy (*Brit., Austral., & N.Z. informal*), doubtful, dubious, fishy (*informal*), iffy (*informal*), open to suspicion, questionable

suspend **1.** append, attach, dangle, hang, swing **2.** adjourn, arrest, cease, cut short, debar, defer, delay, discontinue, hold off, interrupt, lay aside, pigeonhole, postpone, put off, shelve, stay, withhold

that supports the body of a vehicle. **5** a device, usually a wire or spring, that suspends or supports something, such as the pendulum of a clock. **6** *Chem* a mixture in which fine solid or liquid particles are suspended in a fluid.

suspension bridge *n* a bridge suspended from cables that hang between two towers and are secured at both ends.

suspicion *n* **1** the act or an instance of suspecting; belief without sure proof that something is wrong. **2** a feeling of mistrust. **3** a slight trace: *the merest suspicion of a threat.* **4 above suspicion** not possibly guilty of anything, through having a good reputation. **5 under suspicion** suspected of doing something wrong.

suspicious *adj* **1** causing one to suspect something is wrong: *suspicious activities.* **2** unwilling to trust: *I'm suspicious of his motives.* **suspiciously** *adv*

suss out *vb Brit & NZ slang* to work out (a situation or a person's character), using one's intuition.

sustain *vb* **1** to maintain or continue for a period of time: *I managed to sustain a conversation.* **2** to keep up the strength or energy of (someone): *one mouthful of water to sustain him; the merest drop of comfort to sustain me.* **3** to suffer (an injury or loss): *he sustained a spinal injury.* **4** to support (something) from below. **5** to support or agree with (a decision or statement): *objection sustained.* **sustained** *adj*

sustained-release *adj* (of a pill or tablet) coated with a chemical substance that controls the dosage released into a patient's system.

sustenance *n* means of maintaining health or life; food and drink.

suture (**soo**-tcher) *n Surgery* a stitch made with catgut or silk thread, to join the edges of a wound together.

suzerain *n* **1** a state or sovereign that has some degree of control over a dependent state. **2** (formerly) a person who had power over many people. **suzerainty** *n*

svelte *adj* attractively or gracefully slim; slender.

SW **1** southwest(ern). **2** short wave.

swab *n* **1** *Med* a small piece of cotton wool used for applying medication or cleansing a wound. *~vb* **swabbing, swabbed** **2** to clean or apply medication to (a wound) with a swab. **3** to clean (the deck of a ship) with a mop.

swaddle *vb* **-dling, -dled** to wrap (a baby) in swaddling clothes.

swaddling clothes *pl n* long strips of cloth formerly wrapped round a newborn baby.

swag *n* **1** *Slang* stolen property. **2** *Austral & NZ informal* a swagman's pack containing personal belongings.

swagger *vb* **1** to walk or behave in an arrogant manner. *~n* **2** an arrogant walk or manner.

swagger stick *n* a short cane carried by army officers.

swagman *n, pl* **-men** *Austral & NZ informal* a tramp who carries his possessions on his back.

Swahili (swah-**heel**-ee) *n* a language of E Africa that is an official language of Kenya and Tanzania.

swain *n Archaic or poetic* **1** a male lover or admirer. **2** a young man from the countryside.

swallow[1] *vb* **1** to pass (food, drink, etc.) through the mouth and gullet to the stomach. **2** *Informal* to believe (something) trustingly: *I was supposed to swallow the lie.* **3** not to show: *I believe they should swallow their pride.* **4** to make a gulping movement in the throat, such as when nervous. **5** to put up with (an insult) without answering back. **6 be swallowed up** to be taken into and made a part of something: *the old centre was being swallowed up by new estates.* *~n* **7** the act of swallowing. **8** the amount swallowed at any single time; mouthful.

swallow[2] *n* a small migratory bird with long pointed wings and a forked tail.

swallow dive *n* a dive in which the legs are kept straight and the arms outstretched while in the air, with entry into the water made headfirst.

swallowtail *n* **1** a butterfly with a long tail-like part on each hind wing. **2** the forked tail of a swallow or similar bird.

swam *vb* the past tense of **swim.**

swami (**swah**-mee) *n* a Hindu religious teacher.

swamp *n* **1** an area of permanently waterlogged land; bog. *~vb* **2** *Naut* to cause (a boat) to sink or fill with water. **3** to overwhelm (a person or place) with more than can be dealt with or accommodated. **swampy** *adj*

THESAURUS

suspense anticipation, anxiety, apprehension, doubt, expectancy, expectation, indecision, insecurity, irresolution, tension, uncertainty, wavering

suspension abeyance, adjournment, break, breaking off, deferment, delay, disbarment, discontinuation, interruption, moratorium, postponement, remission, respite, stay

suspicion **1.** conjecture, guess, gut feeling (*informal*), hunch, idea, impression, notion, supposition, surmise **2.** bad vibes (*informal*), chariness, distrust, doubt, dubiety, funny feeling (*informal*), jealousy, lack of confidence, misgiving, mistrust, qualm, scepticism, wariness **3.** glimmer, hint, shade, shadow (soupçon), strain, streak, suggestion, tinge, touch, trace **4. above suspicion** above reproach, blameless, honourable, pure, sinless, unimpeachable, virtuous

suspicious **1.** dodgy (*Brit., Austral., & N.Z. informal*), doubtful, dubious, fishy (*informal*), funny, irregular, of doubtful honesty, open to doubt *or* misconstruction, queer, questionable, shady (*informal*), suspect **2.** apprehensive, distrustful, doubtful, jealous, leery (*slang*), mistrustful, sceptical, suspecting, unbelieving, wary

sustain **1.** continue, keep alive, keep going, keep up, maintain, prolong, protract **2.** aid, assist, comfort, foster, help, keep alive, nourish, nurture, provide for, relieve **3.** bear, bear up under, endure, experience, feel, suffer, undergo, withstand **4.** bear, carry, keep from falling, keep up, support, uphold **5.** approve, confirm, ratify

sustained constant, continuous, nonstop, perpetual, prolonged, steady, unremitting

sustenance **1.** livelihood, maintenance, subsistence, support **2.** comestibles, daily bread, eatables, edibles, food, nourishment, provender (*old-fashioned*), provisions, rations, refreshments, victuals (*old-fashioned*)

swagger **1.** *vb.* bluster, boast, brag, bully, hector, parade, prance, show off (*informal*), strut, swank (*informal*) **2.** *n.* arrogance, bluster, display, ostentation, pomposity, show, showing off (*informal*), swank (*informal*), swashbuckling

swallow *vb.* **1.** absorb, consume, devour, down (*informal*), drink, eat, gulp, ingest, swig (*informal*), swill, wash down **2.** *informal* accept, believe, buy (*slang*), fall for **3.** choke back, hold in, repress

swamp *n.* **1.** bog, fen, marsh, mire, morass, moss (*Scot. & northern English*), quagmire, slough *~vb.* **2.** *Naut.* capsize, drench, engulf, flood, inundate, overwhelm, sink, submerge, swallow up, upset, wash over,

swan *n* 1 a large, usually white, water bird with a long neck. ~*vb* **swanning, swanned 2 swan around** *or* **about** *Informal* to wander about without purpose, but with an air of superiority.

swank *Informal* ~*vb* 1 to show off or boast. ~*n* 2 showing off or boasting. **swanky** *adj*

swan song *n* the last public act of a person before retirement or death.

swap *or* **swop** *vb* **swapping, swapped** 1 to exchange (something) for something else. ~*n* 2 an exchange.

SWAPO *or* **Swapo** South-West Africa People's Organization.

sward *n* a stretch of turf or grass.

swarm[1] *n* 1 a group of bees, led by a queen, that has left the hive to make a new home. 2 a large mass of insects or other small animals. 3 a moving mass of people. ~*vb* 4 to move quickly and in large numbers. 5 to be overrun: *the place is swarming with cops.*

swarm[2] *vb* **swarm up** to climb (a ladder or rope) by gripping it with the hands and feet: *the boys swarmed up the rigging.*

swarthy *adj* **swarthier, swarthiest** having a dark complexion.

swash (**swosh**) *n* the rush of water up a beach following each break of the waves.

swashbuckling *adj* having the exciting manner or behaviour of pirates, esp. those depicted in films. **swashbuckler** *n*

swastika *n* 1 a primitive religious symbol in the shape of a Greek cross with the ends of the arms bent at right angles. 2 this symbol with clockwise arms as the emblem of Nazi Germany.

swat *vb* **swatting, swatted** 1 to hit sharply: *swatting the ball with confidence.* ~*n* 2 a sharp blow.

swatch *n* 1 a sample of cloth. 2 a collection of such samples.

swath (**swawth**) *n* same as **swathe.**

swathe *vb* **swathing, swathed** 1 to wrap a bandage, garment, or piece of cloth around (a person or part of the body). ~*n* 2 a long strip of cloth wrapped around something. 3 the width of one sweep of a scythe or of the blade of a mowing machine. 4 the strip cut in one sweep. 5 the quantity of cut crops left in one sweep. 6 a long narrow strip of land.

sway *vb* 1 to swing to and fro: *red poppies swayed in the faint breeze.* 2 to lean to one side and then the other: *entire rows swayed in time.* 3 to be unable to decide between two or more opinions. 4 to influence (someone) in his or her opinion or judgment. ~*n* 5 power or influence. 6 a swinging or leaning movement. 7 **hold sway** to have power or influence.

swear *vb* **swearing, swore, sworn** 1 to use words considered obscene or blasphemous. 2 to promise solemnly on oath; vow: *Sally and Peter swore to love and cherish each other.* 3 **swear by** to have complete confidence in (something). 4 to state (something) earnestly: *I swear he was all right.* 5 to give evidence on oath in a law court.

swear in *vb* to make (someone) take an oath when taking up an official position or entering the witness box to give evidence in court: *a new federal president was sworn in.*

swear off *vb* to promise to give up: *I lived with memories of the gooey sundaes I've sworn off.*

swearword *n* a word considered rude or blasphemous.

sweat *n* 1 the salty liquid that comes out of the skin's pores during strenuous activity in excessive heat or when afraid. 2 the state or condition of sweating: *he worked up a sweat.* 3 *Slang* hard work or effort: *climbing to the crest of Ward Hill was a sweat.* 4 **in a sweat** *Informal* in a state of worry. 5 **no sweat** *Slang* no problem. ~*vb* **sweating, sweat** *or* **sweated** 6 to have sweat come through the skin's pores, as a result of strenuous activity, excessive heat, nervousness, or fear. 7 *Informal* to suffer anxiety or distress. 8 **sweat blood** *Informal* **a** to work very hard. **b** to be filled with anxiety. ~See also **sweats. sweaty** *adj*

sweatband *n* a piece of cloth tied around the forehead or around the wrist to absorb sweat during strenuous physical activity.

sweater *n* a warm knitted piece of clothing covering the upper part of the body.

sweat off *vb Informal* to get rid of (weight) by doing exercises.

sweat out *vb* **sweat it out** *Informal* to endure an unpleasant situation for a time, hoping for an improvement.

sweats *pl n* sweatshirts and sweat suit trousers collectively.

sweatshirt *n* a long-sleeved casual top made of knitted cotton or cotton mixture.

sweatshop *n* a workshop where employees work long hours in poor conditions for low pay.

sweat suit *n* a suit worn by athletes for training, consisting of a sweatshirt and trousers made of the same material.

THESAURUS

waterlog 3. beset, besiege, deluge, flood, inundate, overload, overwhelm, snow under

swampy boggy, fenny, marish (*obsolete*), marshy, miry, quaggy, waterlogged, wet

swap, swop *vb.* bandy, barter, exchange, interchange, switch, trade, traffic

swarm *n.* **1.** army, bevy, concourse, crowd, drove, flock, herd, horde, host, mass, multitude, myriad, shoal, throng ~*vb.* **2.** congregate, crowd, flock, mass, stream, throng **3.** abound, be alive (infested, overrun), bristle, crawl, teem

swarthy black, brown, dark, dark-complexioned, dark-skinned, dusky, tawny

swashbuckling bold, daredevil, dashing, flamboyant, gallant, mettlesome, roisterous, spirited, swaggering

swathe bandage, bind, bundle up, cloak, drape, envelop, enwrap, fold, furl, lap, muffle up, sheathe, shroud, swaddle, wrap

sway *vb.* **1.** bend, fluctuate, incline, lean, lurch, oscillate, rock, roll, swing, wave **2.** affect, control, direct, dominate, govern, guide, induce, influence, persuade, prevail on, win over ~*n.* **3.** ascendency, authority, clout (*informal*), command, control, dominion, government, influence, jurisdiction, power, predominance, rule, sovereignty **4. hold sway** predominate, prevail, reign, rule, run

swear 1. be foul-mouthed, blaspheme, curse, cuss (*informal*), imprecate, utter profanities **2.** affirm, assert, asseverate, attest, avow, declare, depose, give one's word, pledge oneself, promise, state under oath, take an oath, testify, vow, warrant **3. swear by** depend on, have confidence in, rely on, trust

sweat *n.* **1.** exudation, perspiration **2.** *slang* backbreaking task, chore, drudgery, effort, labour, toil ~*vb.* **3.** break out in a sweat, exude moisture, glow, perspire **4.** *informal* agonize, be on pins and needles (*informal*), be on tenterhooks, chafe, fret, lose sleep over, suffer, torture oneself, worry

swede *n* a round root vegetable with a purplish-brown skin and yellow flesh.

Swede *n* a person from Sweden.

Swedish *adj* 1 of Sweden. ~*n* 2 the language of Sweden.

sweep *vb* **sweeping, swept** 1 to clean (a floor or chimney) with a brush. 2 (often foll. by *up*) to remove or collect (dirt or rubbish) with a brush. 3 to move smoothly and quickly: *the car swept into the drive.* 4 to spread rapidly across or through (a place): *the wave of democracy that had swept through Eastern Europe.* 5 to move in a proud and majestic fashion: *the boss himself swept into the hall.* 6 to direct (one's eyes, line of fire, etc.) over (a place or target). 7 **sweep away** *or* **off** to overwhelm (someone) emotionally: *I've been swept away by my fears.* 8 to brush or lightly touch (a surface): *the dress swept along the ground.* 9 to clear away or get rid of (something) suddenly or forcefully: *these doubts were quickly swept aside; bridges have been swept away by the floods.* 10 to stretch out gracefully or majestically, esp. in a wide circle: *the hills swept down into the green valley.* 11 to win overwhelmingly in an election: *the umbrella party which swept these elections.* 12 **sweep the board** to win every event or prize in a contest. ~*n* 13 the act or an instance of sweeping. 14 a swift or steady movement: *the wide sweep of the shoulders.* 15 a wide expanse: *the whole sweep of the bay.* 16 any curving line or contour, such as a driveway. 17 short for **sweepstake.** 18 *Chiefly Brit* same as **chimney sweep.** 19 **make a clean sweep** to win an overwhelming victory.

sweeper *n* 1 a device used to sweep carpets, consisting of a long handle attached to a revolving brush. 2 *Informal soccer* a defensive player usually positioned in front of the goalkeeper.

sweeping *adj* 1 affecting many people to a great extent: *sweeping financial reforms.* 2 (of a statement) making general assumptions about an issue without considering the details. 3 decisive or overwhelming: *to suffer sweeping losses.* 4 taking in a wide area: *a sweeping view of the area.*

sweepstake *or esp US* **sweepstakes** *n* 1 a lottery in which the stakes of the participants make up the prize. 2 a horse race involving such a lottery.

sweet *adj* 1 tasting of or like sugar. 2 kind and charming: *that was really sweet of you.* 3 attractive and delightful: *a sweet child.* 4 (of a sound) pleasant and tuneful: *sweet music.* 5 (of wine) having a high sugar content; not dry. 6 fresh, clear, and clean: *sweet water; sweet air.* 7 **sweet on someone** fond of or infatuated with someone. ~*n* 8 *Brit* a shaped piece of confectionery consisting mainly of sugar. 9 *Brit* a dessert. **sweetly** *adv* **sweetness** *n*

sweet-and-sour *adj* (of food) cooked in a sauce made from sugar and vinegar and other ingredients.

sweetbread *n* the meat obtained from the pancreas of a calf or lamb.

sweetbrier *n* a wild rose with sweet-smelling leaves and pink flowers.

sweet corn *n* 1 a kind of maize with sweet yellow kernels, eaten as a vegetable when young. 2 the sweet kernels removed from the maize cob, cooked as a vegetable.

sweeten *vb* 1 to make (food or drink) sweet or sweeter. 2 to be nice to (someone) in order to ensure cooperation. 3 to make (an offer or a proposal) more acceptable.

sweetener *n* 1 a sweetening agent that does not contain sugar. 2 *Slang* a bribe.

sweetheart *n* 1 an affectionate name to call someone. 2 *Old-fashioned* one's boyfriend or girlfriend. 3 *Informal* a lovable or generous person.

sweetie *n Informal* 1 an affectionate name to call someone. 2 *Brit* same as **sweet** (sense 8). 3 *Chiefly Brit* a lovable or generous person.

sweetmeat *n Old-fashioned* a small delicacy preserved in sugar.

sweet pea *n* a climbing plant with sweet-smelling pastel-coloured flowers.

sweet pepper *n* the large bell-shaped fruit of the pepper plant, which is eaten unripe (**green pepper**) or ripe (**red pepper**) as a vegetable.

sweet potato *n* a root vegetable, grown in the tropics, with pinkish-brown skin and yellow flesh.

sweet-talk *Informal* ~*vb* 1 to persuade (someone) by flattery: *I thought I could sweet-talk you into teaching me.* ~*n* **sweet talk** 2 insincere flattery intended to persuade.

sweet tooth *n* a strong liking for sweet foods.

sweet william *n* a garden plant with clusters of white, pink, red, or purple flowers.

swell *vb* **swelling, swelled; swollen** *or* **swelled** 1 (of a part of the body) to grow in size as a result of injury or infection: *his face swelled and became pale.* 2 to increase in size as a result of being filled with air or liquid: *a balloon swells if you force in more air.* 3 to grow or cause (something) to grow in size, numbers, amount, or degree: *Israel's population is swelling.* 4 (of an emotion) to become more intense: *his anger swelled within him.* 5 (of the seas) to rise in waves. 6 (of a sound) to become gradually louder and then die away. ~*n* 7 the waving movement of the surface of the open sea. 8 an increase in size, numbers, amount, or degree. 9 a bulge. 10 *Old-fashioned, informal* a person who is wealthy, upper class, and fashionably dressed.

THESAURUS

sweat out **sweat it out** *informal* endure, see (something) through, stay the course, stick it out (*informal*)

sweaty clammy, drenched (bathed, soaked) in perspiration, glowing, perspiring, sticky, sweating

sweep *vb.* **1.** brush, clean, clear, remove **2.** career, flounce, fly, glance, glide, hurtle, pass, sail, scud, skim, tear, zoom ~*n.* **3.** arc, bend, curve, gesture, move, movement, stroke, swing **4.** compass, extent, range, scope, span, stretch, vista

sweeping 1. all-embracing, all-inclusive, bird's-eye, broad, comprehensive, extensive, global, radical, thoroughgoing, wide, wide-ranging **2.** across-the-board, blanket, exaggerated, indiscriminate, overdrawn, overstated, unqualified, wholesale

sweepstake draw, lottery, raffle, sweep

sweet *adj.* **1.** cloying, honeyed, luscious, melting, saccharine, sugary, sweetened, syrupy, toothsome, treacly **2.** affectionate, agreeable, amiable, appealing, attractive, beautiful, charming, cute, delightful, engaging, fair, gentle, kind, likeable, lovable, sweet-tempered, taking, tender, unselfish, winning, winsome **3.** dulcet, euphonic, euphonious, harmonious, mellow, melodious, musical, silver-toned, silvery, soft, sweet-sounding, tuneful **4.** aromatic, balmy, clean, fragrant, fresh, new, perfumed, pure, redolent, sweet-smelling, wholesome **5. sweet on** enamoured of, gone on (*slang*), head over heels in love with, infatuated by, in love with, keen on, obsessed *or* bewitched by, taken with, wild *or* mad about (*informal*) ~*n.* **6.** *Brit.* bonbon, candy (*chiefly U.S. & Canad.*), sweetie, sweetmeat (*old-fashioned*) **7.** *Brit.* afters (*Brit. informal*), dessert, pudding, sweet course

sweeten 1. honey, sugar, sugar-coat **2.** alleviate, appease, mollify, pacify, soften up, soothe, sugar the pill

sweetheart admirer, beau (*chiefly U.S.*), beloved, boyfriend, darling, dear, girlfriend, inamorata (*liter-*

11 *Music* an increase in sound followed by an immediate dying away. *~adj* **12** *Slang, chiefly US* excellent or fine.

swelling *n* an enlargement of a part of the body as the result of injury or infection.

swelter *vb* **1** to feel uncomfortable under extreme heat. *~n* **2** a hot and uncomfortable condition: *they left the city swelter for the beach.*

sweltering *adj* uncomfortably hot: *a sweltering summer.*

swept *vb* the past of **sweep.**

swerve *vb* **swerving, swerved 1** to turn aside from a course sharply or suddenly. *~n* **2** the act of swerving.

swift *adj* **1** moving or able to move quickly; fast. **2** happening or performed quickly or suddenly: *a swift glance this way.* **3 swift to** prompt to (do something): *swift to retaliate.* *~n* **4** a small fast-flying insect-eating bird with long wings. **swiftly** *adv* **swiftness** *n*

swig *Informal ~n* **1** a large swallow or deep drink, esp. from a bottle. *~vb* **swigging, swigged 2** to drink (some liquid) in large swallows, esp. from a bottle.

swill *vb* **1** to drink large quantities of (an alcoholic drink). **2** (often foll. by *out*) *Chiefly Brit* to rinse (something) in large amounts of water. *~n* **3** a liquid mixture containing waste food, fed to pigs. **4** a deep drink, esp. of beer.

swim *vb* **swimming, swam, swum 1** to move along in water by movements of the arms and legs, or (in the case of fish) tail and fins. **2** to cover (a stretch of water) in this way: *to swim the English Channel.* **3** to float on a liquid: *flies swimming on the milk.* **4** to be affected by dizziness: *his head was swimming.* **5** (of the objects in someone's vision) to appear to spin or move around: *the faces of the nurses swam around her.* **6** (often foll. by *in* or *with*) to be covered or flooded with liquid: *a steak swimming in gravy.* *~n* **7** the act, an instance, or a period of swimming. **8 in the swim** *Informal* fashionable or active in social or political activities. **swimmer** *n* **swimming** *n*

swimming bath *n* an indoor swimming pool.

swimming costume *or* **bathing costume** *n* *Chiefly Brit* same as **swimsuit.**

swimmingly *adv* successfully, effortlessly, or well: *everything went swimmingly.*

swimming pool *n* a large hole in the ground, tiled and filled with water for swimming in.

swimsuit *n* a woman's swimming garment that leaves the arms and legs bare.

swindle *vb* **-dling, -dled 1** to cheat (someone) out of money. **2** to obtain (money) from someone by fraud. *~n* **3** an instance of cheating someone out of money. **swindler** *n*

swine *n* **1** a mean or unpleasant person. **2** (*pl* **swine**) same as **pig. swinish** *adj*

swing *vb* **swinging, swung 1** to move backwards and forwards; sway. **2** to pivot or cause (something) to pivot from a fixed point such as a hinge: *the door swung open.* **3** to move in a sweeping curve: *the headlights swung along the street.* **4** to alter one's opinion or mood suddenly. **5** to hang so as to be able to turn freely. **6** *Old-fashioned, slang* to be hanged: *you'll swing for this!* **7** *Informal* to manipulate or influence successfully: *it may help to swing the election.* **8** (often foll. by *at*) to hit out with a sweeping motion. **9** *Old-fashioned* to play (music) in the style of swing. **10** *Old-fashioned, slang* to be lively and modern. *~n* **11** the act of swinging. **12** a sweeping stroke or punch. **13** a seat hanging from two chains or ropes on which a person may swing back and forth. **14** popular dance music played by big bands in the 1930s and 1940s. **15** *Informal* the normal pace at which an activity, such as work, happens: *I'm into the swing of things now.* **16** a sudden or extreme change, for example in some business activity or voting pattern. **17 go with a swing** to go well; be successful. **18 in full swing** at the height of activity.

swingboat *n* a boat-shaped carriage for swinging in at a fairground.

swing bridge *n* a bridge that can be swung open to let ships pass through.

swingeing (**swin**-jing) *adj Chiefly Brit* severe or causing hardship: *swingeing spending cuts.*

swipe *vb* **swiping, swiped 1** *Informal* to try to hit (someone or something) with a sweeping blow: *he swiped at a boy who ran forward.* **2** *Slang* to steal (something). **3** to pass (a credit or debit card) through a machine which electronically interprets the information stored in the card. *~n* **4** *Informal* a hard blow.

THESAURUS

ary), inamorato (*literary*), love, lover, steady (*informal*), suitor, swain (*archaic or poetic*), sweetie (*informal*), truelove, valentine

swell *vb.* **1.** balloon, become bloated *or* distended, become larger, be inflated, belly, billow, bloat, bulge, dilate, distend, enlarge, expand, extend, fatten, grow, increase, protrude, puff up, rise, round out, tumefy, well up **2.** add to, aggravate, augment, enhance, heighten, intensify, mount, surge *~n.* **3.** billow, rise, surge, undulation, wave **4.** *old-fashioned informal* beau (*chiefly U.S.*), coxcomb (*informal*), dandy, fop, nob (*slang, chiefly Brit.*), toff (*Brit. slang*)

swelling blister, bruise, bulge, bump, dilation, distension, enlargement, inflammation, lump, protuberance, puffiness, tumescence

swerve *vb.* bend, deflect, depart from, deviate, diverge, incline, sheer off, shift, skew, stray, swing, turn, turn aside, veer, wander, wind

swift abrupt, expeditious, express, fast, fleet, fleet-footed, flying, hurried, nimble, nippy (*informal*), prompt, quick, quickie (*informal*), rapid, ready, short, short-lived, spanking, speedy, sudden, winged

swiftly apace, (at) full tilt, double-quick, fast, hotfoot, hurriedly, nippily (*informal*), posthaste, promptly, pronto (*informal*), rapidly, speedily, without losing time

swiftness alacrity, celerity, dispatch, expedition, fleetness, promptness, quickness, rapidity, speed, speediness, velocity

swill *vb.* **1.** bevvy (*dialect*), consume, drain, drink (down), gulp, guzzle, imbibe, quaff, swallow, swig (*informal*), toss off **2.** *often with* **out** *chiefly Brit.* drench, flush, rinse, sluice, wash down, wash out *~n.* **3.** hogwash, mash, mush, pigswill, scourings, slops, waste

swindle 1. *vb.* bamboozle (*informal*), bilk (of), cheat, con, cozen (*literary*), deceive, defraud, diddle (*informal*), do (*slang*), dupe, fleece, overcharge, pull a fast one (on someone) (*informal*), put one over on (someone) (*informal*), rip (someone) off (*slang*), rook (*slang*), skin (*slang*), sting (*informal*), take (someone) for a ride (*informal*), take to the cleaners (*informal*), trick **2.** *n.* con trick (*informal*), deceit, deception, double-dealing, fiddle (*Brit. informal*), fraud, imposition, knavery (*old-fashioned*), racket, rip-off (*slang*), roguery, scam (*slang*), sting (*informal*), swizz (*Brit. informal*), trickery

swindler charlatan, cheat, confidence man, con man (*informal*), fraud, imposter, knave (*archaic*), mountebank, rascal, rogue, shark, sharper, trickster

swing *vb.* **1.** fluctuate, oscillate, rock, sway, vary, veer, vibrate, wave **2.** curve, pivot, rotate, swivel, turn, turn on one's heel, wheel **3.** be pendent, be suspended,

swirl *vb* **1** to turn round and round with a twisting motion. *~n* **2** a twisting or spinning motion. **3** a twisting shape. **swirling** *adj*

swish *vb* **1** to move with or cause (something) to make a whistling or hissing sound. *~n* **2** a hissing or rustling sound or movement: *she turned with a swish of her skirt.* *~adj* **3** *Informal, chiefly Brit* smart and fashionable.

Swiss *adj* **1** of Switzerland. *~n, pl* **Swiss 2** a person from Switzerland.

swiss roll *n* a sponge cake spread with jam or cream and rolled up.

switch *n* **1** a device for opening or closing an electric circuit. **2** a sudden quick change. **3** an exchange or swap. **4** a flexible rod or twig, used for punishment. **5** *US & Canad* a pair of movable rails for diverting moving trains from one track to another. *~vb* **6** to change quickly and suddenly. **7** to exchange (places) or swap (something for something else). **8** *Chiefly US & Canad* to transfer (rolling stock) from one railway track to another. **9** See **switch off, switch on.**

switchback *n* a steep mountain road, railway, or track with very sharp bends.

switchboard *n* the place in a telephone exchange or office building where telephone calls are connected.

switch off *vb* **1** to cause (a device) to stop operating by moving a switch or lever: *she switched off the television.* **2** *Informal* to become bored and stop paying attention: *when the conversation turned to house prices I switched off.*

switch on *vb* **1** to cause (a device) to operate by moving a switch or lever. **2** *Informal* to produce (a certain type of behaviour or emotion) suddenly or automatically: *she was good at switching on the charm.*

swither *Scot ~vb* **1** to hesitate or be indecisive. *~n* **2** a state of hesitation or uncertainty.

swivel *vb* **-elling, -elled** *or US* **-eling, -eled 1** to turn on or swing round on a central point. *~n* **2** a coupling device which allows an attached object to turn freely.

swivel chair *n* a chair, whose seat is joined to the legs by a swivel, enabling it to be spun round.

swizz *n Brit informal* a swindle or disappointment.

swizzle stick *n* a small stick used to stir cocktails.

swollen *vb* **1** a past participle of **swell.** *~adj* **2** enlarged by swelling.

swoon *vb* **1** *Literary* to faint because of shock or strong emotion. **2** to be deeply affected by passion for (someone): *you've swooned over a string of rotten men.* *~n* **3** *Literary* a faint. **swooning** *adj*

swoop *vb* **1** (usually foll. by *down*) to move quickly through the air in a downward curve: *an owl swooped down from its perch.* **2** (usually foll. by *on*) to move suddenly and quickly towards (a place) in order to attack, arrest, or question the people inside: *Inland Revenue officials swooped on the UK offices of the bankrupt tycoon.* *~n* **3** the act of swooping.

swoosh *vb* **1** to make a swirling or rustling sound when moving or pouring out. *~n* **2** a swirling or rustling sound or movement.

swop *vb* **swopping, swopped,** *n* same as **swap.**

sword *n* **1** a weapon with a long sharp blade and a short handle. **2 the sword a** military power. **b** death; destruction: *we will put them to the sword.* **3 cross swords** to have a disagreement with someone.

sword dance *n* a dance in which the performer dances over swords on the ground.

swordfish *n, pl* **-fish** *or* **-fishes** a large fish with a very long upper jaw that resembles a sword.

Sword of Damocles (**dam**-a-kleez) *n* a disaster that is about to take place.

swordplay *n* the action or art of fighting with a sword.

swordsman *n, pl* **-men** a person who is skilled in the use of a sword. **swordsmanship** *n*

swordstick *n* a hollow walking stick that contains a short sword.

swore *vb* the past tense of **swear.**

sworn *vb* **1** the past participle of **swear.** *~adj* **2** bound by or as if by an oath: *a sworn enemy.*

swot[1] *Brit informal ~vb* **swotting, swotted 1** (often foll. by *up*) to study (a subject) very hard, esp. for an exam; cram. *~n* **2** a person who works or studies hard.

swot[2] *vb* **swotting, swotted,** *n* same as **swat.**

swum *vb* the past participle of **swim.**

swung *vb* the past of **swing.**

sybarite (**sib**-bar-ite) *n* **1** a lover of luxury and pleasure. *~adj* **2** luxurious or sensuous. **sybaritic** *adj*

sycamore *n* **1** a tree with five-pointed leaves and two-winged fruits. **2** *US & Canad* an American plane tree.

sycophant *n* a person who uses flattery to win favour from people with power or influence. **sycophancy** *n* **sycophantic** *adj*

syllabic *adj* of or relating to syllables.

syllabify *vb* **-fies, -fying, -fied** to divide (a word) into syllables. **syllabification** *n*

syllable *n* **1** a part of a word which is pronounced as a unit, which contains a single vowel sound, and which may or may not contain consonants: for example, "paper" has two syllables. **2** the least mention: *without a syllable about what went on.* **3 in words of one syllable** simply and plainly.

syllabub *n Brit* a dessert made from milk or cream beaten with sugar, wine, and lemon juice.

syllabus (**sill**-lab-buss) *n, pl* **-buses** *or* **-bi** (-bye) **a** the subjects studied for a particular course. **b** a list of these subjects.

➤ The usual plural is *syllabuses.*

syllogism *n* a form of reasoning consisting of two premises and a conclusion, for example *some temples are in ruins; all ruins are fascinating; so some temples are fascinating.* **syllogistic** *adj*

sylph *n* **1** a slender graceful girl or young woman. **2** an imaginary creature believed to live in the air. **sylphlike** *adj*

sylvan *or* **silvan** *adj Chiefly poetic* of or consisting of woods or forests.

symbiosis *n* **1** *Biol* a close association of two differ-

THESAURUS

dangle, hang, move back and forth, suspend *~n.* **4.** fluctuation, oscillation, stroke, sway, swaying, vibration **5. in full swing** animated, at its height, lively, on the go (*informal*), under way

swirl *vb.* agitate, boil, churn, eddy, spin, surge, twirl, twist, whirl

switch 1. *n.* about-turn, alteration, change, change of direction, exchange, reversal, shift, substitution, swap **2.** *vb.* change, change course, deflect, deviate, divert, exchange, interchange, rearrange, replace by, shift, substitute, swap, trade, turn aside

swollen bloated, distended, dropsical, enlarged, inflamed, oedematous *or* edematous (*Pathol.*), puffed up, puffy, tumescent, tumid

swoop 1. *vb. usually with* **down** descend, dive, pounce, rush, stoop, sweep **2.** *n.* descent, drop, lunge, plunge, pounce, rush, stoop, sweep

sword 1. blade, brand (*archaic*), trusty steel **2. the sword a** arms, military might **b** butchery, death, mas-

ent animal or plant species living together to their mutual benefit. 2 a similar relationship between different individuals or groups: *the symbiosis of the coal and railway industries.* **symbiotic** *adj*

symbol *n* **1** something that represents or stands for something else, usually an object used to represent something abstract. **2** a letter, figure, or sign used in mathematics, music, etc., to represent a quantity, operation, function, etc.

symbolic *adj* **1** of or relating to a symbol or symbols. **2** being a symbol of something. **symbolically** *adv*

symbolism *n* **1** the representation of something by the use of symbols. **2** an art movement involving the use of symbols to express mystical or abstract ideas. **symbolist** *adj, n*

symbolize *or* **-ise** *vb* **-izing, -ized** *or* **-ising, -ised 1** to be a symbol of (something). **2** to represent with a symbol. **symbolization** *or* **-isation** *n*

symmetry *n, pl* **-tries 1** the state of having two halves that are mirror images of each other. **2** beauty resulting from a balanced arrangement of parts. **symmetrical** *adj* **symmetrically** *adv*

sympathetic *adj* **1** feeling or showing kindness and understanding. **2** (of a person) likeable and appealing: *the film's only sympathetic character.* **3 sympathetic to** showing agreement with or willing to lend support to: *sympathetic to the movement.* **sympathetically** *adv*

sympathize *or* **-thise** *vb* **-thizing, -thized** *or* **-thising, -thised sympathize with a** to feel or express sympathy for: *I sympathized with this fear.* **b** to agree with or support: *Pitt sympathized with these objectives.* **sympathizer** *or* **-thiser** *n*

sympathy *n, pl* **-thies 1** (often foll. by *for*) understanding of other people's problems; compassion. **2 sympathy with** agreement with someone's feelings or interests: *we have every sympathy with how she felt.* **3** (*often pl*) feelings of loyalty or support for an idea or a cause: *was this where her sympathies lay?* **4** mutual affection or understanding between two people or a person and an animal.

symphony *n, pl* **-nies 1** a large-scale orchestral composition with several movements. **2** an orchestral movement in a vocal work such as an oratorio. **3** short for **symphony orchestra. 4** anything that has a pleasing arrangement of colours or shapes: *the garden was a symphony of coloured bunting.* **symphonic** *adj*

symphony orchestra *n Music* a large orchestra that performs symphonies.

symposium *n, pl* **-sia** *or* **-siums 1** a conference at which experts or academics discuss a particular subject. **2** a collection of essays on a particular subject.

symptom *n* **1** *Med* a sign indicating the presence of an illness or disease. **2** anything that is taken as an indication that something is wrong: *a growing symptom of grave social injustice.* **symptomatic** *adj*

synagogue *n* a building for Jewish religious services and religious instruction.

sync *or* **synch** *Films, television, computers informal* ~*vb* **1** to synchronize. ~*n* **2** synchronization: *the film and sound are in sync.*

synchromesh *adj* **1** (of a gearbox) having a system of clutches that synchronizes the speeds of the gearwheels before they engage. ~*n* **2** a gear system having these features.

synchronism *n* the quality or condition of occurrence at the same time or rate.

synchronize *or* **-nise** *vb* **-nizing, -nized** *or* **-nising, -nised 1** (of two or more people) to perform (an action) at the same time: *a synchronized withdrawal of Allied forces.* **2** to cause (two or more clocks or watches) to show the same time. **3** *Films* to match (the soundtrack and the action of a film) precisely. **synchronization** *or* **-nisation** *n*

synchronous *adj* occurring at the same time and rate.

syncline *n Geol* a downward slope of stratified rock in which the layers dip towards each other from either side.

syncopate *vb* **-pating, -pated** *Music* to stress the weak beats in (a rhythm or a piece of music) instead of the strong beats. **syncopation** *n*

syncope (**sing**-kop-ee) *n* **1** *Med* a faint. **2** *Linguistics* the omission of sounds or letters from the middle of a word, as in *ne'er* for *never.*

syndic *n Brit* a business or legal agent of some universities or other institutions.

syndicalism *n* a movement advocating seizure of economic and political power by the industrial working class by means of industrial action, esp. general strikes. **syndicalist** *n*

syndicate *n* **1** a group of people or firms organized to undertake a joint project. **2** an association of individuals who control organized crime. **3** a news agency that sells articles and photographs to a number of newspapers for simultaneous publication. ~*vb* **-cating, -cated 4** to sell (articles and photographs) to several newspapers for simultaneous publication. **5** to form a syndicate of (people). **syndication** *n*

syndrome *n* **1** *Med* a combination of signs and symptoms that indicate a particular disease. **2** a set of

THESAURUS

sacre, murder, slaying (*archaic or literary*) **3. cross swords** argue, come to blows, dispute, fight, spar, wrangle

syllabus course of study, curriculum

symbol badge, emblem, figure, image, logo, mark, representation, sign, token, type

symbolic allegorical, emblematic, figurative, representative, significant, token, typical

symbolize betoken, connote, denote, exemplify, mean, personify, represent, signify, stand for, typify

symmetrical balanced, in proportion, proportional, regular, well-proportioned

symmetry agreement, balance, correspondence, evenness, form, harmony, order, proportion, regularity

sympathetic 1. affectionate, caring, commiserating, compassionate, concerned, condoling, feeling, interested, kind, kindly, pitying, responsive, supportive, tender, understanding, warm, warm-hearted **2. sympathetic to** agreeable, approving, encouraging, favourably disposed, friendly, in sympathy with, pro, well-disposed

sympathetically appreciatively, feelingly, kindly, perceptively, responsively, sensitively, understandingly, warm-heartedly, warmly, with compassion, with feeling, with interest

sympathize *with* **with a** bleed for, commiserate, condole, empathize, feel for, feel one's heart go out to, grieve with, have compassion, offer consolation, pity, share another's sorrow **b** agree, be in accord, be in sympathy, go along with, identify with, side with, understand

sympathizer condoler, fellow traveller, partisan, protagonist, supporter, well-wisher

sympathy 1. *often with* **for** commiseration, compassion, condolence(s), empathy, pity, tenderness, thoughtfulness, understanding **2.** *with* **with** affinity, agreement, congeniality, correspondence, fellow feeling, harmony, rapport, union, warmth

characteristics indicating the existence of a particular condition or problem.

synecdoche (sin-**neck**-dock-ee) *n* a figure of speech in which a part is substituted for a whole or a whole for a part, as in *50 head of cattle* for *50 cows*.

synergy *n* the potential ability for individuals or groups to be more successful working together than on their own.

synod *n* a special church council which meets regularly to discuss church affairs.

synonym *n* a word that means the same as another word, such as *bucket* and *pail*.

synonymous *adj* **synonymous with a** having the same meaning. **b** closely associated with: *a family whose name had been synonymous with fine jewellery*.

synopsis (sin-**op**-siss) *n, pl* **-ses** (-seez) a brief review or outline of a subject; summary.

synoptic *adj* **1** of or relating to a synopsis. **2** *Bible* of or relating to the Gospels of Matthew, Mark, and Luke. **synoptically** *adv*

synovia (sine-**oh**-vee-a) *n Med* a clear thick fluid that lubricates the body joints. **synovial** *adj*

syntax *n* the grammatical rules of a language and the way in which words are arranged to form phrases and sentences. **syntactic** *or* **syntactical** *adj*

synthesis (**sinth**-iss-siss) *n, pl* **-ses** (-seez) **1** the process of combining objects or ideas into a complex whole. **2** the combination produced by such a process. **3** *Chem* the process of producing a compound by one or more chemical reactions, usually from simpler starting materials.

synthesize *or* **-sise** *vb* **-sizing, -sized** *or* **-sising, -sised 1** to combine (objects or ideas) into a complex whole. **2** to produce (a compound) by synthesis.

synthesizer *n* a keyboard instrument in which speech, music, or other sounds are produced electronically.

synthetic *adj* **1** (of a substance or material) made artificially by chemical reaction. **2** not sincere or genuine: *synthetic compassion*. *~n* **3** a synthetic substance or material. **synthetically** *adv*

syphilis *n* a sexually transmitted disease that causes sores on the genitals and eventually on other parts of the body. **syphilitic** *adj*

syphon *n, vb* same as **siphon.**

Syrian *adj* **1** of Syria. *~n* **2** a person from Syria.

syringa *n* same as **mock orange** or **lilac.**

syringe *n* **1** *Med* a device used for withdrawing or injecting fluids, consisting of a hollow cylinder of glass or plastic, a tightly fitting piston, and a hollow needle. *~vb* **-ringing, -ringed 2** to wash out, inject, or spray with a syringe: *a harmless blue dye is syringed into the uterus*.

syrup *n* **1** a solution of sugar dissolved in water and often flavoured with fruit juice: used for sweetening fruit, etc. **2** a thick sweet liquid food made from sugar or molasses: *maple syrup*. **3** a liquid medicine containing a sugar solution: *cough syrup*.

syrupy *adj* **1** (of a liquid) thick or sweet. **2** excessively sentimental: *a soundtrack of syrupy violins*.

system *n* **1** a method or set of methods for doing or organizing something: *a new system of production or distribution*. **2** orderliness or routine; an ordered manner: *there is no system in his work*. **3** the manner in which an institution or aspect of society has been arranged: *the Scottish legal system*. **4 the system** the government and state regarded as exploiting, restricting, and repressing individuals. **5** the manner in which the parts of something fit or function together; structure: *disruption of the earth's weather system*. **6** any scheme or set of rules used to classify, explain, or calculate: *the Newtonian system of physics*. **7** a network of communications, transportation, or distribution. **8** *Biol* an animal considered as a whole. **9** *Biol* a set of organs or structures that together perform some function: *the immune system*. **10** one's physical or mental constitution: *the intrusion of the ME virus into my system; to get the hate out of my system*. **11** an assembly of electronic or mechanical parts forming a self-contained unit: *an alarm system*.

systematic *adj* following a fixed plan and done in an efficient and methodical way: *a systematic approach to teaching*. **systematically** *adv*

systematize *or* **-tise** *vb* **-tizing, -tized** *or* **-tising, -tised** to arrange (information) in a system. **systematization** *or* **-tisation** *n*

systemic *adj Biol* (of a poison, disease, etc.) affecting the entire animal or body. **systemically** *adv*

systems analysis *n* the analysis of the requirements of a task and the expression of these in a form that enables a computer to perform the task. **systems analyst** *n*

systole (**siss**-tol-ee) *n Physiol* contraction of the heart, during which blood is pumped into the arteries. **systolic** *adj*

THESAURUS

symptom expression, indication, mark, note, sign, syndrome, token, warning

symptomatic characteristic, indicative, suggestive

synthesis 1. amalgamation, coalescence, combination, integration, unification, welding **2.** amalgam, blend, combination, composite, compound, fusion, meld, union

synthetic artificial, ersatz, fake, man-made, manufactured, mock, pseudo (*informal*), sham, simulated

system 1. fixed order, frame of reference, method, methodology, modus operandi, practice, procedure, routine, technique, theory, usage **2.** definite plan, logical process, method, methodicalness, orderliness, regularity, systematization **3.** arrangement, classification, combination, coordination, organization, scheme, setup (*informal*), structure

systematic businesslike, efficient, methodical, orderly, organized, precise, standardized, systematized, well-ordered

T

t *or* **T** *n, pl* **t's, T's,** *or* **Ts 1** the 20th letter of the English alphabet. **2 to a T a** in every detail: *that's her to a T.* **b** perfectly: *that dress suits you to a T.*

t tonne(s).

T 1 *Chem* tritium. **2** tera-.

t. 1 temperature. **2** ton(s).

ta *interj Brit informal* thank you.

Ta *Chem* tantalum.

TA (in Britain) Territorial Army.

tab[1] *n* **1** a small flap of material, esp. one on a garment for decoration or for fastening to a button. **2** any similar flap, such as a piece of paper attached to a file for identification. **3** *Chiefly US & Canad* a bill, esp. for a meal or drinks. **4 keep tabs on** *Informal* to keep a watchful eye on.

tab[2] *n* short for **tabulator.**

tabard *n* **1** a sleeveless jacket, esp. one worn by a medieval knight over his armour. **2** a short coat bearing the coat of arms of the sovereign, worn by a herald.

Tabasco *n Trademark* a very hot red sauce made from peppers.

tabby *n, pl* **-bies 1** a cat whose fur has dark stripes or wavy markings on a lighter background. *~adj* **2** having dark stripes or wavy markings on a lighter background.

tabernacle *n* **1 the Tabernacle** *Bible* the portable sanctuary in which the ancient Israelites carried the Ark of the Covenant. **2** any place of Christian worship that is not called a church. **3** *RC Church* a receptacle in which the Blessed Sacrament is kept.

tabla *n, pl* **-bla** *or* **-blas** one of a pair of Indian drums played with the hands.

table *n* **1** a piece of furniture consisting of a flat top supported by legs: *a coffee table.* **2** a set of facts or figures arranged in rows and columns: *a league table.* **3** a group of people sitting round a table for a meal, game, etc.: *the whole table laughed.* **4** *Formal* the food provided at a meal or in a particular house: *he keeps a good table.* **5 turn the tables** to cause a complete reversal of circumstances. *~vb* **-bling, -bled 6** *Brit* to submit (a motion) for discussion by a meeting. **7** *US* to suspend discussion of (a proposal) indefinitely.

tableau (**tab**-loh) *n, pl* **-leaux** (-loh) a silent motionless group of people arranged to represent a scene from history, legend, or literature.

tablecloth *n* a cloth for covering the top of a table, esp. during meals.

table d'hôte (**tah**-bla **dote**) *adj* **1** (of a meal) consisting of a set number of courses with a limited choice of dishes offered at a fixed price. *~n, pl* **tables d'hôte** (**tah**-bla **dote**) **2** a table d'hôte meal or menu.

tableland *n* a flat area of high ground; plateau.

table licence *n* a licence permitting the sale of alcohol with meals only.

tablespoon *n* **1** a spoon, larger than a dessertspoon, used for serving food. **2** Also called: **tablespoonful** the amount contained in such a spoon. **3** a unit of capacity used in cooking, equal to half a fluid ounce.

tablet *n* **1** a pill consisting of a compressed medicinal substance. **2** a flattish cake of some substance, such as soap. **3** a slab of stone, wood, etc., used for writing on before the invention of paper. **4** an inscribed piece of stone, wood, etc., that is fixed to a wall as a memorial: *a tablet in memory of those who died.*

table tennis *n* a game resembling a miniature form of tennis played on a table with bats and a small light ball.

table wine *n* **1** fairly cheap wine for everyday drinking with meals. **2** ordinary wine, as opposed to fortified wine such as sherry or port.

tabloid *n* a newspaper with fairly small pages, usually with many photographs and a concise and often sensational style.

taboo *or* **tabu** *n, pl* **-boos** *or* **-bus 1** a restriction or prohibition resulting from social or other conventions. **2** a ritual prohibition, esp. of something that is considered holy or unclean. *~adj* **3** forbidden or disapproved-of: *a taboo subject.*

tabor *n* a small drum used esp. in the Middle Ages, struck with one hand while the other held a pipe.

tabular *adj* arranged in parallel columns so as to form a table.

tabulate *vb* **-lating, -lated** to arrange (information) in rows and columns. **tabulation** *n*

tabulator *n* a key on a typewriter or word processor that sets stops so that data can be arranged in columns.

tachograph *n* a device that measures the speed of a vehicle and the distance that it covers, and produces a record (**tachogram**) of its readings.

tachometer *n* a device for measuring speed, esp. that of a revolving shaft.

tacit (**tass**-it) *adj* understood or implied without actually being stated: *tacit support.*

taciturn (**tass**-it-turn) *adj* habitually silent, reserved, or uncommunicative. **taciturnity** *n*

tack[1] *n* **1** a short sharp-pointed nail with a large flat head. **2** *Brit* a long loose temporary stitch used in dressmaking. *~vb* **3** to fasten (something) with a tack or tacks: *the carpet needs to be tacked down.* **4** *Brit* to sew (something) with long loose temporary stitches. ~See also **tack on.**

tack[2] *n* **1** *Naut* the course of a boat sailing obliquely into the wind, expressed in terms of the side of the boat against which the wind is blowing: *on the port tack.* **2** a course of action or a policy: *telling her to get off my back hadn't worked, so I took a different tack.*

THESAURUS

table *n.* **1.** bench, board, counter, slab, stand **2.** chart, diagram, graph, index, inventory, list, record, register, roll, synopsis, tabulation **3.** *formal* board, diet, fare, food, spread (*informal*), victuals *~vb.* **4.** *Brit.* enter, move, propose, put forward, submit, suggest

tableau picture, representation, scene, spectacle

taboo 1. *n.* ban, interdict, prohibition, proscription, restriction **2.** *adj.* banned, beyond the pale, disapproved of, forbidden, frowned on, not allowed, not permitted, outlawed, prohibited, proscribed, ruled out, unacceptable, unmentionable, unthinkable

tabulate arrange, catalogue, categorize, chart, classify, index, list, order, range, systematize

tacit implicit, implied, inferred, silent, taken for granted, undeclared, understood, unexpressed, unspoken, unstated, wordless

taciturn close-lipped, distant, quiet, reserved, reticent, silent, tight-lipped, uncommunicative, unforthcoming, withdrawn

~*vb* **3** *Naut* to steer (a boat) on a zigzag course, so as to make progress against the wind.

tack[3] *n* riding harness for horses, including saddles and bridles.

tackies *or* **takkies** *pl n, sing* **tacky** *S African informal* tennis shoes or plimsolls.

tackle *vb* **-ling, -led 1** to deal with (a problem or task) in a determined way. **2** to confront (someone) about something: *I intend to tackle both management and union on this issue.* **3** to attack and fight (a person or animal). **4** *Sport* to attempt to get the ball away from (an opposing player). ~*n* **5** *Sport* an attempt to get the ball away from an opposing player. **6** the equipment required for a particular sport or occupation: *fishing tackle.* **7** a set of ropes and pulleys for lifting heavy weights. **8** *Naut* the ropes and other rigging aboard a ship.

tack on *vb* to attach or add (something) to something that is already complete: *an elegant mansion with a modern extension tacked on at the back.*

tacky[1] *adj* **tackier, tackiest** slightly sticky. **tackiness** *n*

tacky[2] *adj* **tackier, tackiest** *Informal* **1** vulgar and tasteless: *tacky commercialism.* **2** shabby or shoddy: *tacky streets.* **tackiness** *n*

tact *n* **1** a sense of the best and most considerate way to deal with people so as not to upset them. **2** skill in handling difficult situations. **tactful** *adj* **tactfully** *adv* **tactless** *adj* **tactlessly** *adv* **tactlessness** *n*

tactic *n* a move or method used to achieve an aim or task: *he has perfected dissent as a tactic to further his career.* See also **tactics.**

tactical *adj* **1** of or employing tactics: *a tactical advantage.* **2** (of missiles, bombing, etc.) for use in limited military operations. **tactically** *adv*

tactical voting *n* (in an election) the practice of voting for a candidate or party one would not normally support in an attempt to prevent an even less acceptable candidate or party being elected.

tactics *n* **1** *Mil* the science of the detailed direction of forces in battle to achieve an aim or task. ~*pl n* **2** the plans and methods used to achieve a particular short-term aim. **tactician** *n*

tactile *adj* of or having a sense of touch: *the tactile sense.*

tadpole *n* the aquatic larva of a frog or toad, which develops from a limbless tailed form with external gills into a form with internal gills, limbs, and a reduced tail.

taffeta *n* a thin shiny silk or rayon fabric used esp. for women's clothes.

taffrail *n Naut* a rail at the back of a ship or boat.

tag[1] *n* **1** a piece of paper, leather, etc., for attaching to something as a mark or label: *the price tag.* **2** a point of metal or plastic at the end of a cord or lace. **3** a brief trite quotation. **4** an electronic device worn by a prisoner under house arrest so that his or her movements can be monitored. ~*vb* **tagging, tagged 5** to mark with a tag. ~See also **tag along, tag on.**

tag[2] *n* **1** a children's game in which one player chases the others in an attempt to touch one of them, who will then become the chaser. ~*vb* **tagging, tagged 2** to catch and touch (another child) in the game of tag. ~Also: **tig**

Tagalog (tag-**gah**-log) *n* a language spoken in the Philippines.

tag along *vb* to accompany someone, esp. when uninvited: *I tagged along behind the gang.*

tag end *n* the last part of something: *at the tag end of the Ice Age.*

tagetes (taj-**eat**-eez) *n, pl* **-tes** any of a genus of plants with yellow or orange flowers, including the French and African marigolds.

tagliatelle (tal-yat-**tell**-ee) *n* a form of pasta made in narrow strips.

tag on *vb* to add at the end of something: *a throwaway remark, tagged on at the end of a casual conversation.*

tahini (tah-**hee**-nee) *n* a paste made from ground sesame seeds, used esp. in Middle Eastern cookery.

t'ai chi (tie **chee**) *n* a Chinese system of exercises and self-defence characterized by slow rhythmic movements.

taiga (**tie**-ga) *n* the belt of coniferous forest extending across much of subarctic North America, Europe, and Asia.

tail[1] *n* **1** the rear part of an animal's body, usually forming a long thin flexible part attached to the trunk. **2** any long thin part projecting or hanging from the back or end of something: *the waiter produced menus from beneath the tail of his coat.* **3** the last part: *the tail of the procession.* **4** the rear part of an aircraft. **5** *Astron* the luminous stream of gas and dust particles driven from the head of a comet when it is close to the sun. **6** *Informal* a person employed to follow and spy upon another. **7 turn tail** to run away. **8 with one's tail between one's legs** completely defeated and demoralized. ~*adj* **9** at the back: *tail feathers.* ~*vb* **10** *Infor-*

THESAURUS

tack[1] *n.* **1.** drawing pin (*Brit.*), nail, pin, staple, thumbtack (*U.S.*), tintack ~*vb.* **2.** affix, attach, fasten, fix, nail, pin, staple **3.** *Brit.* baste, stitch

tack[2] *n.* **1.** *Naut.* bearing, course, direction, path, way **2.** approach, line, method, plan, procedure, tactic, way

tackle *vb.* **1.** apply oneself to, attempt, begin, come *or* get to grips with, deal with, embark upon, engage in, essay, get stuck into (*informal*), have a go at (*informal*), have a stab at (*informal*), set about, take on, try, turn one's hand to, undertake, wade into **2.** *Sport* block, bring down, challenge, clutch, grab, grasp, halt, intercept, seize, stop, take hold of ~*n.* **3.** *Sport* block, challenge, stop **4.** accoutrements, apparatus, equipment, gear, implements, outfit, paraphernalia, rig, rigging, tools, trappings

tact consideration, delicacy, diplomacy, discretion, finesse, judgment, perception, savoir-faire, sensitivity, skill, thoughtfulness, understanding

tactful careful, considerate, delicate, diplomatic, discreet, judicious, perceptive, polite, politic, prudent, sensitive, subtle, thoughtful, understanding

tactic approach, course, device, line, manoeuvre, means, method, move, ploy, policy, scheme, stratagem, tack, trick, way

tactical adroit, artful, clever, cunning, diplomatic, foxy, politic, shrewd, skilful, smart, strategic

tactician campaigner, coordinator, director, general, mastermind, planner, strategist

tactics 1. *n. Mil.* campaign, generalship, manoeuvres, strategy **2.** *pl. n.* manoeuvres, plans, strategy

tactless blundering, boorish, careless, clumsy, discourteous, gauche, impolite, impolitic, imprudent, inconsiderate, indelicate, indiscreet, injudicious, insensitive, rude, thoughtless, uncivil, undiplomatic, unfeeling, unkind, unsubtle

tail *n.* **1.** appendage, end, extremity, rear end **2.** conclusion, end, tailpiece, train **3. turn tail** cut and run, escape, flee, hook it (*slang*), make off, retreat, run away, run for it (*informal*), run off, scarper (*Brit.*

mal to follow (someone) stealthily. ~See also **tail off, tails. tailless** *adj*

tail[2] *n Law* the limitation of an estate or interest to a person and his or her descendants.

tailback *n* a queue of traffic stretching back from an obstruction.

tailboard *n* a removable or hinged rear board on a lorry or trailer.

tail coat *n* a man's black coat which stops at the hips at the front and has a long back split into two below the waist.

tailgate *n* **1** same as **tailboard. 2** a door at the rear of a hatchback vehicle.

tail-light *or* **tail-lamp** *n US & Canad* a red light, usually one of a pair, attached to the rear of a vehicle.

tail off *or* **away** *vb* **1** to decrease gradually: *orders tailed off.* **2** (of someone's voice) to become gradually quieter and then silent.

tailor *n* **1** a person who makes, repairs, or alters outer garments, esp. menswear. ~*vb* **2** to cut or style (a garment) to satisfy specific requirements. **3** to adapt (something) so as to make it suitable: *activities are tailored to participants' capabilities.* **tailored** *adj*

tailorbird *n* a tropical Asian warbler that builds a nest by sewing together large leaves using plant fibres.

tailor-made *adj* **1** (of clothing) made by a tailor to fit exactly. **2** perfect for a particular purpose: *I'm tailor-made for the role.*

tailpiece *n* **1** a piece added at the end of something, for example a report. **2** a decorative design at the end of a chapter. **3** a piece of wood to which the strings of a stringed musical instrument are attached at its lower end.

tailpipe *n* a pipe from which exhaust gases are discharged, esp. in a motor vehicle.

tailplane *n* a small horizontal wing at the tail of an aircraft to help keep it stable.

tails *pl n* **1** *Informal* same as **tail coat.** ~*interj, adv* **2** with the side of a coin uppermost that does not have a portrait of a head on it.

tailspin *n* **1** *Aeronautics* same as **spin** (sense 9). **2** *Informal* a state of confusion or panic.

tailwind *n* a wind blowing from behind an aircraft or vehicle.

taint *vb* **1** to spoil or contaminate by an undesirable quality: *tainted by corruption.* ~*n* **2** a defect or flaw. **3** a trace of contamination or infection. **tainted** *adj*

take *vb* **taking, took, taken 1** to remove from a place, usually by grasping with the hand: *he took a fifty-dollar note from his wallet.* **2** to accompany or escort: *he took me home.* **3** to use as a means of transport: *we took a taxi.* **4** to conduct or lead: *that road takes you to Preston.* **5** to obtain possession of (something), often dishonestly: *they had taken everything most precious to us.* **6** to seize or capture: *her husband had been taken by the rebels.* **7** (in games such as chess or cards) to win or capture (a piece, trick, etc.). **8** to choose or select (something to use or buy): *I'll take the green one, please.* **9** to put an end to: *he took his own life.* **10** to require (time, resources, or ability): *this would have taken years to set up.* **11** to use as a particular case: *take a friend of mine for example.* **12** to find and make use of (a seat, flat, etc.). **13** to accept the duties of: *two days after Mr Major took office.* **14** to receive in a specified way: *my mother took it calmly.* **15** to receive and make use of: *she took the opportunity to splash her heated face.* **16** to eat or drink: *all food substances are toxic if taken in excess.* **17** to perform (an action, esp. a beneficial one): *she took a deep breath.* **18** to accept (something that is offered or given): *she took a job as a waitress.* **19** to put into effect: *taking military action simply.* **20** to make (a photograph). **21** to write down or copy: *taking notes.* **22** to work at or study: *taking painting lessons.* **23** to do or sit (a test, exam, etc.). **24** to begin to experience or feel: *he took an interest in psychoanalysis.* **25** to accept (responsibility, blame, or credit). **26** to accept as valid: *I take your point.* **27** to stand up to or endure: *I can't take this harassment any more.* **28** to wear a particular size of shoes or clothes: *what size of shoes do you take?* **29** to have a capacity of or room for: *the Concert Hall can take about 2500 people.* **30** to ascertain by measuring: *she comes after breakfast to take her pulse and temperature.* **31** to subtract or deduct: *take seven from eleven.* **32** to aim or direct: *he took a few steps towards the door.* **33** (of a shop, club, etc.) to make (a specified amount of money) from sales, tickets, etc.: *we can take over £5000 on a good night.* **34** to have or produce the intended effect: *the dye hasn't taken on your shoes.* **35** (of seedlings) to start growing successfully. **36 take account of** *or* **take into account** See **account** (sense 9). **37 take advantage of** See **advantage** (sense 4). **38 take care** See **care** (sense 10). **39 take care of** See **care** (sense 11). **40 take it** to assume or believe: *I take it that means they don't want to leave.* **41 take part in** See **part** (sense 17). **42 take place** See **place** (sense 20). **43 take upon oneself** to assume the right or duty (to do something). **44 take your time** use as much time as you need. ~*n* **45** *Films, music* one of a series of recordings from which the best will be selected. ~See also **take after, take against,** etc.

take after *vb* to resemble in appearance or character: *he takes after his grandfather.*

take against *vb Informal* to start to dislike, esp. for no good reason: *I took against her right from the start.*

take apart *vb* **1** to separate (something) into its component parts: *once I'd taken the clock apart I*

THESAURUS

slang), show a clean pair of heels, skedaddle (*informal*), take off (*informal*), take to one's heels ~*vb.* **4.** *informal* dog the footsteps of, follow, keep an eye on, shadow, stalk, track, trail

tail off *or* **away** decrease, die out, drop, dwindle, fade, fall away, peter out, wane

tailor 1. *n.* clothier, costumier, couturier, dressmaker, garment maker, outfitter, seamstress **2.** *vb.* accommodate, adapt, adjust, alter, convert, cut, fashion, fit, modify, mould, shape, style, suit

taint *vb.* **1.** besmirch, blacken, blemish, blight, blot, contaminate, corrupt, damage, defile, dirty, disgrace, dishonour, foul, infect, poison, pollute, ruin, shame, smear, smirch, soil, spoil, stain, stigmatize, sully, tarnish ~*n.* **2.** black mark, blemish, blot, blot on one's escutcheon, defect, demerit, disgrace, dishonour, fault, flaw, shame, smear, smirch, spot, stain, stigma **3.** contagion, contamination, infection, pollution

take *vb.* **1.** accompany, bring, conduct, escort, guide, lead, usher **2.** abstract, appropriate, blag (*slang*), carry off, filch, misappropriate, nick (*slang, chiefly Brit.*), pinch (*informal*), pocket, purloin, run off with, steal, swipe (*slang*), walk off with **3.** abduct, arrest, capture, carry off, catch, gain possession of, get, get hold of, lay hold of, obtain, secure, seize, win **4.** book, buy, engage, hire, lease, pick, purchase, rent, reserve, select **5.** call for, demand, necessitate, need, require **6.** accept, adopt, assume, enter upon, undertake **7.** consume, drink, eat, imbibe, ingest, swallow **8.** do, effect, execute, have, make, perform **9.** abide, bear, brave, brook, endure, go through, put up with (*informal*), stand, stomach, submit to, suffer, swallow, thole (*Scot. & Northern English*), tolerate, undergo, weath-

couldn't fit the bits together again. **2** *Informal* to criticize severely.

take away *vb* **1** to remove or subtract: *the lymph glands are taken away and examined under a microscope.* **2** to detract from or lessen the value of (something): *the fact that he beat his wife doesn't take away from his merits as a writer.* ~*prep* **3** minus: *six take away two is four.* ~*adj* **takeaway 4** *Brit, Austral, & NZ* sold for consumption away from the premises: *takeaway food.* ~*n* **takeaway** *Brit, Austral, & NZ* **5** a shop or restaurant that sells such food. **6** a meal sold for consumption away from the premises.

take back *vb* **1** to retract or withdraw (something said or promised): *I take back what I said about him.* **2** to regain possession of. **3** to return for exchange or a refund: *shopkeepers are often reluctant to take back unsatisfactory goods.* **4** to accept (someone) back into one's home, affections, etc.: *I'll only take you back if you promise to behave.* **5** to remind (one) of the past: *this takes me back to my childhood.*

take down *vb* **1** to record in writing. **2** to dismantle or remove. **3** to reduce (someone) in power or arrogance: *I do think he needed taking down a peg or two.*

take for *vb Informal* to consider or suppose to be, esp. mistakenly: *what kind of mug do you take me for?*

take-home pay *n* the remainder of one's pay after income tax and other compulsory deductions have been made.

take in *vb* **1** to understand: *I was too tired to take in all of what was being said.* **2** *Informal* to cheat or deceive: *don't be taken in by his charming manner.* **3** to include: *this tour takes in the romance and history of Salzburg, Vienna, and Munich.* **4** to receive into one's house: *his widowed mother lived by taking in boarders.* **5** to make (clothing) smaller by altering the seams. **6** *US* to go to: *taking in a movie.*

taken *vb* **1** the past participle of **take**. ~*adj* **2 taken with** enthusiastically impressed by.

take off *vb* **1** to remove (a garment). **2** (of an aircraft) to become airborne. **3** *Informal* to set out on a journey: *taking off for the Highlands.* **4** *Informal* to become successful or popular: *the record took off after being used in a film.* **5** to deduct (an amount) from a price or total. **6** to withdraw or put an end to: *the bus service has been taken off because of lack of demand.* **7** *Informal* to mimic (someone). ~*n* **takeoff 8** the act or process of making an aircraft airborne. **9** *Informal* an act of mimicry.

take on *vb* **1** to employ or hire. **2** to assume or acquire: *his eyes took on a strange intensity.* **3** to agree to do: *he took on the job of treasurer.* **4** to compete against: *we must take on our foreign competitors.*

take out *vb* **1** to remove (something) from a place: *she took a comb out of her bag.* **2** to obtain: *she took out American citizenship in 1937.* **3** to escort or go out with (someone) on a social trip: *can I take you out for a meal some time?* **4** *Informal* to kill, destroy, or maim: *most of the enemy's air defences have been taken out.* **5 take it** *or* **a lot out of** *Informal* to sap the energy or vitality of. **6 take it out on** *Informal* to vent one's anger on. ~*adj, n* **takeout 7** *US & Canad* same as **takeaway** (senses 4, 5, 6).

take over *vb* **1** to gain control or management of. **2** to become responsible for (a job) after another person has stopped doing it: *I'll take over the driving if you want a break.* **3 take over from** to become more successful or important than (something), and eventually replace it: *CDs have more or less taken over from records.* ~*n* **takeover 4** the act of gaining control of a company by buying its shares. **5** the act of seizing and taking control of something: *the rebel takeover in Ethiopia.*

taker *n* a person who agrees to take something that is offered: *there's only one sweet left – any takers?*

take to *vb* **1** to form a liking for. **2** to start using or doing (something) as a habit: *I took to studying the published records of his life.*

take up *vb* **1** to occupy or fill (space or time): *looking after the baby takes up most of my time.* **2** to adopt the study, practice, or activity of: *I took up architecture.* **3** to shorten (a garment). **4** to accept (an offer): *I'd like to take up your offer of help.* **5 take up on a** to accept what is offered by (someone): *I might just take you up on that offer.* **b** to discuss (something) further with (someone): *I'd like to take you up on that last point.* **6 take up with a** to discuss (an issue) with (someone): *take up the matter with the District Council more seriously.* **b** to begin to be friendly and spend time with (someone): *he's already taken up with the woman he would marry.*

taking *adj* charming, fascinating, or intriguing.

takings *pl n* receipts; earnings.

THESAURUS

er, withstand **10.** accept, accommodate, contain, have room for, hold **11.** deduct, eliminate, remove, subtract **12.** be efficacious, do the trick (*informal*), have effect, operate, succeed, work

take back 1. disavow, disclaim, recant, renege, renounce, retract, unsay, withdraw **2.** get back, recapture, reclaim, reconquer, regain, repossess, retake **3.** accept back, exchange, give one a refund for

take down 1. make a note of, minute, note, put on record, record, set down, transcribe, write down **2.** demolish, disassemble, dismantle, level, raze, take apart, take to pieces, tear down **3.** deflate, humble, humiliate, mortify, put down (*slang*)

take in 1. absorb, assimilate, comprehend, digest, grasp, understand **2.** *informal* bilk, cheat, con (*informal*), cozen (*literary*), deceive, do (*slang*), dupe, fool, gull (*archaic*), hoodwink, mislead, pull the wool over (someone's) eyes (*informal*), stiff (*slang*), swindle, trick **3.** comprise, contain, cover, embrace, encompass, include **4.** accommodate, admit, let in, receive

take off 1. discard, divest oneself of, doff, drop, peel off, remove, strip off **2.** become airborne, leave the ground, lift off, take to the air **3.** *informal* abscond, beat it (*slang*), decamp, depart, disappear, go, hit the road (*slang*), hook it (*slang*), leave, set out, slope off, split (*slang*), strike out **4.** *informal* caricature, hit off, imitate, lampoon, mimic, mock, parody, satirize, send up (*Brit. informal*), spoof (*informal*), take the piss (out of) (*taboo slang*), travesty

takeoff 1. departure, launch, liftoff **2.** *informal* caricature, imitation, lampoon, parody, satire, send-up (*Brit. informal*), spoof (*informal*), travesty

take on 1. employ, engage, enlist, enrol, hire **2.** acquire, assume, come to have **3.** accept, address oneself to, agree to do, have a go at (*informal*), tackle, undertake **4.** compete against, contend with, face, fight, match oneself against, oppose, pit oneself against, vie with

take over assume control of, become leader of, come to power, gain control of, succeed to, take command of

take to 1. become friendly, be pleased by, be taken with, conceive an affection for, get on with, like, warm to **2.** have recourse to, make a habit of, resort to

take up 1. absorb, consume, cover, extend over, fill, occupy, use up **2.** adopt, assume, become involved in, engage in, start

taking *adj.* attractive, beguiling, captivating, charming, compelling, delightful, enchanting, engaging, fas-

talc *or* **talcum** *n* **1** same as **talcum powder. 2** a soft mineral, consisting of magnesium silicate, used in the manufacture of ceramics, paints, and talcum powder.

talcum powder *n* a powder made of purified talc, usually scented, used to dry or perfume the body.

tale *n* **1** a report, account, or story: *everyone had their own tale to tell about the flood.* **2** a malicious piece of gossip. **3 tell tales a** to tell fanciful lies. **b** to report malicious stories or trivial complaints, esp. to someone in authority. **4 tell a tale** to reveal something important. **5 tell its own tale** to be self-evident.

talent *n* **1** a natural ability to do something well: *the boy has a real talent for writing.* **2** a person or people with such ability: *he is the major talent in Italian fashion.* **3** *Informal* attractive members of the opposite sex collectively: *there's always lots of talent in that pub.* **4** any of various ancient units of weight and money. **talented** *adj*

talent scout *n* a person whose occupation is the search for talented people, such as sportsmen or performers, for work as professionals.

talisman *n, pl* **-mans** a stone or other small object, usually inscribed or carved, believed to protect the wearer from evil influences. **talismanic** *adj*

talk *vb* **1** to express one's thoughts or feelings by means of spoken words. **2** to exchange ideas or opinions about something: *they were talking about where they would go on holiday.* **3** to give voice to; utter: *he was talking rubbish.* **4** to discuss: *the political leaders were talking peace.* **5** to reveal information: *she was ready to talk.* **6** to be able to speak (a language or style) in conversation: *the ferry was full of people talking French.* **7** to spread rumours or gossip. **8** to be effective or persuasive: *money talks.* **9** to get into a particular condition or state of mind by talking: *I had talked myself hoarse.* **10 now you're talking** *Informal* at last you're saying something agreeable. **11 you can** *or* **can't talk** *Informal* you are in no position to comment or criticize. ~*n* **12** a speech or lecture: *a talk on local government reform.* **13** an exchange of ideas or thoughts: *we had a talk about our holiday plans.* **14** idle chatter, gossip, or rumour. **15** (*often pl*) a conference, discussion, or negotiation. ~See also **talk back, talk down,** etc. **talker** *n*

talkative *adj* given to talking a great deal.

talk back *vb* to answer (someone) rudely or cheekily.

talk down *vb* **1 talk down to** to speak to (someone) in a patronizing manner. **2** to give instructions to (an aircraft) by radio to enable it to land.

talkie *n Informal* an early film with a soundtrack.

Talking Book *n Trademark* a recording of a book, designed to be used by the blind.

talking head *n* (on television) a person, shown only from the shoulders up, who speaks without illustrative material.

talking point *n* something that causes discussion or argument: *his appointment as manager was a major talking point in football circles.*

talking-to *n Informal* a scolding or telling-off.

talk into *vb* to persuade (someone) to do something by talking to him or her: *don't let anyone talk you into buying things you don't want.*

talk out *vb* **1** to resolve (a problem) by talking: *we won't reach a compromise unless we can talk out our differences.* **2** *Brit* to block (a bill) in parliament by discussing it for so long that there is no time to vote on it. **3 talk out of** to dissuade (someone) from doing something by talking to him or her.

talk round *vb* **1** to persuade (someone) to agree with one's opinion or suggestion: *he didn't want to go, but I talked him round.* **2** to discuss (a subject) without coming to a conclusion.

tall *adj* **1** of greater than average height. **2** having a specified height: *five feet tall.*

tallboy *n* a high chest of drawers made in two sections placed one on top of the other.

tall order *n Informal* a difficult or unreasonable request.

tallow *n* a hard fatty animal fat used in making soap and candles.

tall ship *n* a large square-rigged sailing ship.

tall story *n Informal* an unlikely and probably untrue tale.

tally *vb* **-lies, -lying, -lied 1** to agree with or be consistent with something else: *this description didn't seem to me to tally with what we saw.* **2** to keep score. ~*n, pl* **-lies 3** any record of debit, credit, the score in a game, etc. **4** an identifying label or mark. **5** a stick used (esp. formerly) as a record of the amount of a debt according to the notches cut in it.

tally-ho *interj* the cry of a participant at a hunt when the quarry is sighted.

Talmud *n Judaism* the primary source of Jewish religious law. **Talmudic** *adj* **Talmudist** *n*

talon *n* a sharply hooked claw, such as that of a bird of prey.

tamarillo *n, pl* **-los** a shrub with a red oval edible fruit.

THESAURUS

cinating, fetching (*informal*), intriguing, likable *or* likeable, pleasing, prepossessing, winning

takings earnings, gain, gate, income, pickings, proceeds, profits, receipts, returns, revenue, yield

tale account, anecdote, fable, fiction, legend, narration, narrative, report, romance, saga, short story, story, urban legend, yarn (*informal*)

talent ability, aptitude, bent, capacity, endowment, faculty, flair, forte, genius, gift, knack, power

talented able, artistic, brilliant, gifted, well-endowed

talk *vb.* **1.** articulate, chat, chatter, communicate, converse, express oneself, gab (*informal*), give voice to, gossip, natter, prate, prattle, rap (*slang*), say, speak, spout, utter, verbalize **2.** chew the rag *or* fat (*slang*), confabulate, confer, have a confab (*informal*), hold discussions, negotiate **3.** blab, crack, give the game away, grass (*Brit. slang*), inform, reveal information, shop (*slang, chiefly Brit.*), sing (*slang, chiefly U.S.*), spill one's guts (*slang*), spill the beans (*informal*), squeak (*informal*), squeal (*slang*), tell all ~*n.* **4.** address, discourse, disquisition, dissertation, lecture, oration, sermon, speech **5.** chat, chatter, chitchat, conversation, gab (*informal*), gossip, jaw (*slang*), natter, rap (*slang*) **6.** colloquy, conclave, confab (*informal*), confabulation, conference, congress, consultation, dialogue, discussion, meeting, negotiation, parley, seminar, symposium

talkative big-mouthed (*slang*), chatty, effusive, gabby (*informal*), garrulous, gossipy, long-winded, loquacious, mouthy, prolix, verbose, voluble, wordy

talker conversationalist, lecturer, orator, speaker, speechmaker

talking-to *informal* criticism, dressing-down (*informal*), lecture, rap on the knuckles, rebuke, reprimand, reproach, reproof, row, scolding, slating (*informal*), telling-off (*informal*), ticking-off (*informal*), wigging (*Brit. slang*)

tall big, elevated, giant, high, lanky, lofty, soaring, towering

tally *vb.* **1.** accord, agree, coincide, concur, conform,

tamarind *n* a tropical evergreen tree with fruit whose acid pulp is used as a food and to make beverages and medicines.

tamarisk *n* a tree or shrub of the Mediterranean region and S Asia, with scalelike leaves, slender branches, and feathery flower clusters.

tambour *n* an embroidery frame, consisting of two hoops over which the fabric is stretched while being worked.

tambourine *n Music* a percussion instrument consisting of a single drum skin stretched over a circular wooden frame with pairs of metal discs that jingle when it is struck or shaken.

tame *adj* **1** (of an animal) **a** changed by humans from a wild state into a domesticated state. **b** not afraid of or aggressive towards humans. **2** (of a person) tending to do what one is told without questioning or criticizing it. **3** mild and unexciting: *the love scenes are fairly tame by modern standards.* ~*vb* **taming, tamed 4** to make (an animal) tame, domesticate. **5** to bring under control; make less extreme or dangerous: *many previously deadly diseases have been tamed by antibiotics.*

Tamil *n* **1** (*pl* **-ils** *or* **-il**) a member of a people of S India and Sri Lanka. **2** the language of the Tamils. ~*adj* **3** of the Tamils.

tam-o'-shanter *n* a Scottish brimless woollen cap with a bobble in the centre.

tamp *vb* to force or pack (something) down by tapping it several times: *he tamped the bowl of his pipe.*

tamper *vb* (foll. by *with*) **1** to interfere or meddle with without permission: *someone has been tampering with the locks.* **2** to attempt to influence someone, esp. by bribery: *an attempt to tamper with the jury.*

tampon *n* an absorbent plug of cotton wool inserted into the vagina during menstruation.

tan[1] *n* **1** a brown coloration of the skin caused by exposure to ultraviolet rays, esp. those of the sun. ~*vb* **tanning, tanned 2** (of a person or his or her skin) to go brown after exposure to ultraviolet rays. **3** to convert (a skin or hide) into leather by treating it with a tanning agent. **4** *Slang* to beat or flog. ~*adj* **5** yellowish-brown.

tan[2] *Maths* tangent.

tandem *n* **1** a bicycle with two sets of pedals and two saddles, arranged one behind the other for two riders. **2 in tandem** together or in conjunction: *the two drugs work in tandem to combat the disease.* ~*adv* **3** one behind the other: *Jim and Ruth arrived, riding tandem.*

tandoor *n* a type of Indian clay oven.

tandoori *adj* cooked in a tandoor: *tandoori chicken.*

tang *n* **1** a strong sharp taste or smell: *we could already smell the tang of the distant sea.* **2** a trace or hint of something: *there was a tang of cloves in the apple pie.* **3** the pointed end of a tool, such as a knife or chisel, which fits into the handle. **tangy** *adj*

tangent *n* **1** a line, curve, or plane that touches another curve or surface at one point but does not cross it. **2** (in trigonometry) the ratio of the length of the opposite side to that of the adjacent side of a right-angled triangle. **3 go off at a tangent** suddenly take a completely different line of thought or action. ~*adj* **4** of or involving a tangent. **5** touching at a single point.

tangential *adj* **1** only having an indirect or superficial relevance: *Hitler's vegetarianism only has a tangential link with the policies of the Nazis.* **2** of or being a tangent: *a street tangential to the market square.* **tangentially** *adv*

tangerine *n* **1** the small orange-like fruit, with a sweet juicy flesh, of an Asian tree. ~*adj* **2** reddish-orange.

tangi (**tang**-ee) *n NZ* **1** a Maori funeral ceremony. **2** *Informal* a lamentation.

tangible *adj* **1** able to be touched; material or physical. **2** real or substantial: *tangible results.* **tangibility** *n* **tangibly** *adv*

tangle *n* **1** a confused or complicated mass of things, such as hair or fibres, knotted or coiled together. **2** a complicated problem or situation. ~*vb* **-gling, -gled 3** to twist (things, such as hair or fibres) together in a confused mass. **4** to come into conflict: *the last thing she wanted was to tangle with the police.* **5** to catch or trap in a net, ropes, etc.: *the string of the kite had got tangled in the branches.* **tangled** *adj*

tango *n, pl* **-gos 1** a Latin-American dance characterized by long gliding steps and sudden pauses. **2** music for this dance. ~*vb* **-going, -goed 3** to perform this dance.

tank *n* **1** a large container for storing liquids or gases. **2** an armoured combat vehicle moving on tracks and armed with guns. **3** Also called: **tankful** the quantity contained in a tank.

tankard *n* a large one-handled beer-mug, sometimes fitted with a hinged lid.

tanked up *adj Slang, chiefly Brit* very drunk.

tanker *n* a ship or lorry for carrying liquid in bulk: *an oil tanker.*

tank farming *n* same as **hydroponics. tank farmer** *n*

tannery *n, pl* **-neries** a place or building where skins and hides are tanned.

tannic *adj* of, containing, or produced from tannin or tannic acid.

tannie (**tun**-nee) *n S African* a title of respect used to refer to an elderly woman.

tannin *n* a yellowish compound found in many plants, such as tea and grapes, and used in tanning and dyeing. Also called: **tannic acid**

THESAURUS

correspond, fit, harmonize, match, parallel, square, suit **2.** compute, count up, keep score, mark, reckon, record, register, total ~*n.* **3.** count, mark, reckoning, record, running total, score, total

tame *adj.* **1.** amenable, broken, disciplined, docile, domesticated, gentle, obedient, tractable **2.** fearless, unafraid, used to human contact **3.** compliant, docile, manageable, meek, obedient, submissive, unresisting **4.** bland, boring, dull, flat, humdrum, insipid, lifeless, prosaic, tedious, unexciting, uninspiring, uninteresting, vapid ~*vb.* **5.** break in, domesticate, house-train, make tame, train **6.** mitigate, mute, soften, soft-pedal (*informal*), subdue, temper, tone down, water down

tamper 1. fiddle (*informal*), fool about (*informal*), interfere, intrude, meddle, mess about, monkey around, muck about (*Brit. slang*), poke one's nose into (*informal*), tinker **2.** bribe, corrupt, fix (*informal*), get at, influence, manipulate, rig

tangible 1. concrete, corporeal, material, palpable, physical, solid, substantial, tactile, touchable **2.** actual, definite, discernible, evident, manifest, perceptible, positive, real

tangle *n.* **1.** coil, confusion, entanglement, jam, jungle, knot, mass, mat, mesh, snarl, twist, web **2.** complication, entanglement, fix (*informal*), imbroglio, labyrinth, maze, mess, mix-up ~*vb.* **3.** coil, confuse, entangle, interlace, interlock, intertwist, interweave, jam, knot, mat, mesh, ravel, snarl, twist **4.** *often with* **with** come into conflict, come up against, contend, contest, cross swords, dispute, lock horns **5.** catch, enmesh, ensnare, entangle, entrap

tangled 1. entangled, jumbled, knotted, knotty, mat-

Tannoy *n Trademark* a type of public-address system.

tansy *n, pl* **-sies** a plant with yellow flowers in flat-topped clusters.

tantalize *or* **-lise** *vb* **-lizing, -lized** *or* **-lising, -lised** to tease or make frustrated, for example by tormenting (someone) with the sight of something that he or she wants but cannot have. **tantalizing** *or* **-lising** *adj* **tantalizingly** *or* **-lisingly** *adv*

tantalum *n Chem* a hard greyish-white metallic element that resists corrosion. Symbol: Ta

tantalus *n Brit* a case in which bottles of wine and spirits may be locked with their contents tantalizingly visible.

tantamount *adj* **tantamount to** equivalent in effect to: *the raid was tantamount to a declaration of war.*

tantrum *n* a childish outburst of bad temper.

Taoiseach (**tee**-shack) *n* the Prime Minister of the Irish Republic.

Taoism (rhymes with **Maoism**) *n* a Chinese system of religion and philosophy advocating a simple honest life and noninterference with the course of natural events. **Taoist** *n, adj*

tap[1] *vb* **tapping, tapped 1** to knock lightly and usually repeatedly: *she tapped gently on the door.* **2** to make a rhythmic sound with the hands or feet by lightly and repeatedly hitting a surface with them: *he was tapping one foot to the music.* ~*n* **3** a light blow or knock, or the sound made by it. **4** the metal piece attached to the toe or heel of a shoe used for tap-dancing. **5** same as **tap-dancing.**

tap[2] *n* **1** *Chiefly Brit* a valve by which the flow of a liquid or gas from a pipe can be controlled. Usual US word: **faucet 2** a stopper to plug a cask or barrel. **3** a concealed listening or recording device connected to a telephone. **4** *Med* the withdrawal of fluid from a bodily cavity: *a spinal tap.* **5 on tap a** *Informal* ready for use. **b** (of drinks) on draught rather than in bottles. ~*vb* **tapping, tapped 6** to listen in on (a telephone conversation) secretly by making an illegal connection. **7** to obtain something useful or desirable from (something): *a new way of tapping the sun's energy.* **8** to withdraw liquid from (something) as if through a tap: *to tap a cask of wine.* **9** to cut into (a tree) and draw off sap from it. **10** *Brit informal* to obtain (money or information) from (someone).

tapas (**tap**-ass) *pl n* (in Spanish cookery) light snacks or appetizers, usually eaten with drinks.

tap-dancing *n* a style of dancing in which the performer wears shoes with metal plates at the heels and toes that make a rhythmic sound on the stage as he or she dances. **tap-dancer** *n* **tap dance** *n*

tape *n* **1** a long thin strip of cotton or linen used for tying or fastening: *a parcel tied with pink tape.* **2 a** short for **magnetic tape. b** a spool or cassette containing magnetic tape, and used for recording or playing sound or video signals: *he put a tape into his stereo.* **c** the music, speech, or pictures which have been recorded on a particular cassette or spool of magnetic tape. **3** a narrow strip of plastic which has one side coated with an adhesive substance and is used to stick paper, etc., together: *sticky tape.* **4** a string stretched across the track at the end of a race course. **5** short for **tape measure.** ~*vb* **taping, taped 6** Also: **tape-record** to record (speech, music, etc.) on magnetic tape. **7** to bind or fasten with tape. **8 have a person** *or* **situation taped** *Brit informal* to have full understanding and control of a person *or* situation.

tape deck *n* **1** the part of a tape recorder which supports the spools or cassettes, and contains the motor and the playback, recording, and erasing heads. **2** the unit in a hi-fi system which fulfils the same function.

tape drive *n* a machine for storing or transferring information from a computer onto tape.

tape measure *n* a tape or length of metal marked off in centimetres or inches, used for measuring.

taper *vb* **1** to become narrower towards one end. **2 taper off** to become gradually less: *treatment should be tapered off gradually.* ~*n* **3** a long thin fast-burning candle. **4** a narrowing.

tape recorder *n* an electrical device used for recording and reproducing sounds on magnetic tape.

tape recording *n* **1** the act of recording sounds on magnetic tape. **2** the magnetic tape used for this: *a tape recording of the interview.* **3** the sounds so recorded.

tapestry *n, pl* **-tries 1** a heavy woven fabric, often in the form of a picture, used for wall hangings or furnishings. **2** same as **needlepoint** (sense 1). **3** a colourful and complicated situation that is made up of many different kinds of things: *the rich tapestry of London life.*

tapeworm *n* a long flat parasitic worm that inhabits the intestines of vertebrates, including man.

tapioca *n* a beadlike starch made from cassava root, used in puddings.

tapir (**tape**-er) *n* a piglike mammal of South and Central America and SE Asia, with a long snout, three-toed hind legs, and four-toed forelegs.

tappet *n* a short steel rod in an engine which moves up and down transferring movement from one part of the machine to another.

taproom *n Old-fashioned* the public bar in a hotel or pub.

taproot *n* the main root of plants such as the dandelion, which grows straight down and bears smaller lateral roots.

tar[1] *n* **1** a dark sticky substance obtained by distilling organic matter such as coal, wood, or peat. **2** same as **coal tar.** ~*vb* **tarring, tarred 3** to coat with tar. **4 tar and feather** to cover (someone) with tar and feathers as a punishment. **5 tarred with the same brush** having, or regarded as having, the same faults. **tarry** *adj*

tar[2] *n Informal* a seaman.

tarakihi (**tarr**-a-kee-hee) *or* **terakihi** (**terr**-a-kee-hee) *n* a common edible sea fish of New Zealand waters.

THESAURUS

ted, messy, scrambled, snarled, tousled, twisted **2.** complex, complicated, confused, convoluted, involved, knotty, messy, mixed-up

tantalize frustrate, keep (someone) hanging on, lead on, make (someone's) mouth water, provoke, taunt, tease, titillate, torment, torture

tantamount to as good as, commensurate with, equal to, equivalent to, synonymous with, the same as

tantrum fit, flare-up, hysterics, ill humour, outburst, paddy (*Brit. informal*), paroxysm, storm, temper

tap[1] **1.** *vb.* beat, drum, knock, pat, rap, strike, touch **2.** *n.* beat, knock, light blow, pat, rap, touch

tap[2] *n.* **1.** *chiefly Brit.* faucet (*U.S.*), spigot, spout, stopcock, valve **2.** bung, plug, stopper **3.** bug (*informal*), listening device **4. on tap a.** *informal* at hand, available, in reserve, on hand, ready **b.** on draught ~*vb.* **5.** bug (*informal*), eavesdrop on, listen in on **6.** draw on, exploit, make use of, milk, mine, put to use, turn to account, use, utilize **7.** bleed, drain, draw off, siphon off

taramasalata *n* a creamy pale pink pâté, made from the eggs of fish, esp. smoked cod's roe, and served as an hors d'oeuvre.

tarantella *n* **1** a peasant dance from S Italy. **2** music for this dance.

tarantula *n* **1** a large hairy spider of tropical America with a poisonous bite. **2** a large hairy spider of S Europe.

tarboosh *n* a felt or cloth brimless cap, usually red and often with a silk tassel, formerly worn by Muslim men.

tardy *adj* **-dier, -diest 1** occurring later than it is expected to or than it should: *he spent the weekend writing tardy thank-you letters.* **2** slow in progress, growth, etc.: *we made tardy progress across the ice.* **tardily** *adv* **tardiness** *n*

tare[1] *n* **1** the weight of the wrapping or container in which goods are packed. **2** the unladen weight of a vehicle.

tare[2] *n* **1** any of various vetch plants of Eurasia and N Africa. **2** *Bible* a weed, thought to be the darnel.

target *n* **1** the object or person that a weapon, ball, etc., is aimed at: *the station was an easy target for an air attack.* **2** an object at which an archer or marksman aims, usually a round flat surface marked with circles. **3** a fixed goal or objective: *our sales figures are well below target.* **4** a person or thing at which criticism or ridicule is directed: *the Chancellor has been the target of much of the criticism.* ~*vb* **-geting, -geted 5** to direct: *an advertising campaign targeted at gay men.* **6** to aim (a missile).

tariff *n* **1 a** a tax levied by a government on imports or occasionally exports. **b** a list of such taxes. **2** a list of fixed prices, for example in a hotel. **3** *Chiefly Brit* a method of charging for services such as gas and electricity by setting a price per unit.

Tarmac *n* **1** *Trademark* a paving material made of crushed stone bound with a mixture of tar and bitumen, used for a road or airport runway. **2 the tarmac** the area of an airport where planes wait, taxi, and take off or land: *we had to wait for an hour on the tarmac.* ~*vb* **tarmac, -macking, -macked 3** to apply Tarmac to (a surface).

tarn *n* a small mountain lake.

tarnish *vb* **1** (of a metal) to become stained or less bright, esp. by exposure to air or moisture. **2** to damage or taint: *the affair could tarnish the reputation of the prime minister.* ~*n* **3** a tarnished condition, surface, or film on a surface. **tarnished** *adj*

taro *n, pl* **-ros** an Asian plant with a large edible rootstock.

tarot (**tarr**-oh) *n* **1** a special pack of cards, now used mainly for fortune-telling. **2** a card in a tarot pack with a distinctive symbolic design.

tarpaulin *n* **1** a heavy waterproof canvas coated with tar, wax, or paint. **2** a sheet of this canvas, used as a waterproof covering.

tarragon *n* a European herb with narrow leaves, which are used as seasoning in cooking.

tarry *vb* **-ries, -rying, -ried** *Old-fashioned* **1** to delay or linger: *I have no plans to tarry longer than necessary.* **2** to stay briefly: *most people tarried only a few hours before moving on.*

tarsal *Anat* ~*adj* **1** of the tarsus or tarsi. ~*n* **2** a tarsal bone.

tarseal *n NZ* **1** the bitumen surface of a road. **2 the tarseal** the main highway.

tarsier *n* a small nocturnal primate of the E Indies, which has very large eyes.

tarsus *n, pl* **-si 1** the bones of the ankle and heel collectively. **2** the corresponding part in other mammals and in amphibians and reptiles.

tart[1] *n* **1** *Chiefly Brit* a pastry case, often having no top crust, with a sweet filling, such as jam or custard. **2** *Chiefly US* a small open pie with a fruit filling.

tart[2] *adj* **1** (of a flavour) sour or bitter. **2** sharp and hurtful: *he made a rather tart comment.* **tartly** *adv* **tartness** *n*

tart[3] *n Informal* a sexually provocative or promiscuous woman. See also **tart up.**

tartan *n* **1** a design of straight lines, crossing at right angles to give a chequered appearance, esp. one associated with a Scottish clan. **2** a fabric with this design.

tartar[1] *n* **1** a hard deposit on the teeth. **2** a brownish-red substance deposited in a cask during the fermentation of wine.

tartar[2] *n* a fearsome or formidable person.

Tartar *or* **Tatar** *n* **1** a member of a Mongoloid people who established a powerful state in central Asia in the 13th century, now scattered throughout Russia and central Asia. ~*adj* **2** of the Tartars.

tartaric *adj* of or derived from tartar or tartaric acid.

tartaric acid *n* a colourless crystalline acid which is found in many fruits.

tartar sauce *n* a mayonnaise sauce mixed with chopped herbs and capers, served with seafood.

tartrazine (**tar**-traz-zeen) *n* an artificial yellow dye used as a food additive.

tart up *vb Brit informal* **1** to decorate in a cheap and flashy way: *the shops were tarted up for Christmas.* **2** to try to make (oneself) look smart and attractive.

Tarzan *n Informal, often ironical* a man with great physical strength, agility, and virility.

task *n* **1** a specific piece of work required to be done.

THESAURUS

tape *n.* **1.** band, ribbon, strip ~*vb.* **2.** record, tape-record, video **3.** bind, seal, secure, stick, wrap

taper 1. come to a point, narrow, thin **2.** *with* **off** decrease, die away, die out, dwindle, fade, lessen, reduce, subside, thin out, wane, weaken, wind down

target 1. bull's-eye, goal, mark **2.** aim, ambition, end, goal, intention, object, objective **3.** butt, quarry, scapegoat, victim

tariff 1. assessment, duty, excise, levy, rate, tax, toll **2.** bill of fare, charges, menu, price list

tarnish *vb.* **1.** darken, dim, discolour, dull, lose lustre *or* shine, rust **2.** befoul, blacken, blemish, blot, drag through the mud, smirch, soil, spot, stain, sully, taint ~*n.* **3.** blemish, blot, discoloration, rust, spot, stain

tarry *old-fashioned* abide, bide, dally, dawdle, delay, hang around (*informal*), linger, loiter, pause, remain, rest, stay, take one's time, wait

tart[1] *n. chiefly Brit.* pastry, pie, tartlet

tart[2] *adj.* **1.** acerbic, acid, acidulous, astringent, bitter, piquant, sharp, sour, tangy, vinegary **2.** acrimonious, astringent, barbed, biting, caustic, cutting, harsh, mordant, nasty, scathing, sharp, short, snappish, testy, trenchant, vitriolic, wounding

tart[3] *n. informal* call girl, fallen woman, *fille de joie,* floozy (*slang*), harlot, hooker (*U.S. slang*), loose woman, prostitute, scrubber (*Brit. & Austral. slang*), slag (*Brit. slang*), slut, streetwalker, strumpet, trollop, whore, woman of easy virtue, working girl (*facetious slang*)

task 1. assignment, business, charge, chore, duty, employment, enterprise, exercise, job, labour, mission, occupation, toil, undertaking, work **2. take to task** bawl out (*informal*), blame, blast, carpet (*informal*), censure, chew out (*U.S. & Canad. informal*), criticize, give a rocket (*Brit. & N.Z. informal*), lambast(e), lec-

2 an unpleasant or difficult job or duty. **3 take to task** to criticize or rebuke.

task force *n* **1** a temporary grouping of military units formed to undertake a specific mission. **2** any organization set up to carry out a continuing task.

taskmaster *n* a person who enforces hard or continuous work.

Tasmanian devil *n* a small ferocious flesh-eating marsupial of Tasmania.

Tass *n* (formerly) the principal news agency of the Soviet Union.

tassel *n* a tuft of loose threads secured by a knot or knob, used to decorate a cushion, piece of clothing, etc.

taste *n* **1** the sense by which the flavour of a substance is distinguished by the taste buds. **2** the sensation experienced by means of the taste buds. **3** a small amount eaten, sipped, or tried on the tongue. **4** a brief experience of something: *a taste of the planter's life.* **5** a liking for something: *a taste for puns.* **6** the ability to appreciate what is beautiful and excellent: *she's got very good taste in clothes.* **7** a person's typical preferences as displayed by what they choose to buy, enjoy, etc.: *the film was good but a bit violent for my taste.* **8** the quality of not being offensive or bad-mannered: *that remark was in rather poor taste.* ~*vb* **tasting, tasted 9** to distinguish the taste of (a substance) by means of the taste buds: *I've got a stinking cold and can't taste anything.* **10** to take a small amount of (a food or liquid) into the mouth, esp. in order to test the flavour. **11** to have a flavour or taste as specified: *the pizza tastes delicious.* **12** to have a brief experience of (something): *they have tasted democracy and they won't let go.*

taste bud *n* any of the cells on the surface of the tongue, by means of which the sensation of taste is experienced.

tasteful *adj* having or showing good social or aesthetic taste: *tasteful decor.* **tastefully** *adv*

tasteless *adj* **1** lacking in flavour: *the canteen serves cold, tasteless pizzas.* **2** lacking social or aesthetic taste: *a room full of tasteless ornaments; a tasteless remark.* **tastelessly** *adv* **tastelessness** *n*

taster *n* **1** a person employed to test the quality of food or drink by tasting it. **2** a sample of something intended to indicate what the entire thing is like: *the entrance hall was filled with flowers, giving a taster of the splendours in the main exhibition.*

tasty *adj* **tastier, tastiest** having a pleasant flavour.

tat *n* tatty or tasteless articles.

ta-ta *interj Brit informal* goodbye.

Tatar *n, adj* same as **Tartar.**

tater *n Dialect* a potato.

tattered *adj* **1** ragged or torn: *a tattered old book.* **2** wearing ragged or torn clothing: *the tattered refugees.*

tatters *pl n* **1** torn ragged clothing. **2 in tatters a** (of clothing) torn in several places. **b** (of an argument, plan, etc.) completely destroyed.

tatting *n* **1** an intricate type of lace made by looping a thread of cotton or linen with a hand shuttle. **2** the work of producing this.

tattle *vb* **-tling, -tled 1** to gossip or chatter. ~*n* **2** gossip or chatter. **tattler** *n*

tattletale *n Chiefly US & Canad* a scandalmonger or gossip.

tattoo[1] *n, pl* **-toos 1** a picture or design made on someone's body by pricking small holes in the skin and filling them with indelible dye. ~*vb* **-tooing, -tooed 2** to make pictures or designs on (a person's skin) by pricking and staining it with indelible colours. **tattooed** *adj* **tattooist** *n*

tattoo[2] *n, pl* **-toos 1** (formerly) a signal by drum or bugle ordering soldiers to return to their quarters. **2** a military display or pageant. **3** any drumming or tapping.

tatty *adj* **-tier, -tiest** *Chiefly Brit* worn out, shabby, or unkempt.

taught *vb* the past of **teach.**

taunt *vb* **1** to tease or provoke (someone) with jeering remarks. ~*n* **2** a jeering remark. **taunting** *adj*

Taurus *n Astrol* the second sign of the zodiac; the Bull.

taut *adj* **1** stretched tight: *the cable must be taut.* **2** showing nervous strain: *he was looking taut and anxious.* **3** (of a film or piece of writing) having no unnecessary or irrelevant details: *a taut thriller.*

tauten *vb* to make or become taut.

tautology *n, pl* **-gies** the use of words which merely repeat something already stated, as in *reverse back.* **tautological** *or* **tautologous** *adj*

tavern *n* **1** *Old-fashioned* a pub. **2** *US, Canad, & NZ* a place licensed for the sale and consumption of alcoholic drink.

tawdry *adj* **-drier, -driest** cheap, showy, and of poor quality: *tawdry Christmas decorations.*

tawny *adj* brown to brownish-orange.

THESAURUS

ture, read the riot act, reprimand, reproach, reprove, scold, tear into (*informal*), tear (someone) off a strip (*Brit. informal*), tell off (*informal*), upbraid

taste *n.* **1.** flavour, relish, savour, smack, tang **2.** bit, bite, dash, drop, morsel, mouthful, nip, sample, sip, *soupçon*, spoonful, swallow, titbit, touch **3.** appetite, bent, desire, fancy, fondness, inclination, leaning, liking, palate, partiality, penchant, predilection, preference, relish **4.** appreciation, cultivation, culture, discernment, discrimination, elegance, grace, judgment, perception, polish, refinement, sophistication, style **5.** correctness, decorum, delicacy, discretion, nicety, politeness, propriety, restraint, tact, tactfulness ~*vb.* **6.** differentiate, discern, distinguish, perceive **7.** nibble, sample, savour, sip, test, try **8.** have a flavour of, savour of, smack of **9.** come up against, encounter, experience, feel, have knowledge of, know, meet with, partake of, undergo

tasteful aesthetically pleasing, artistic, beautiful, charming, cultivated, cultured, delicate, discriminating, elegant, exquisite, fastidious, graceful, handsome, harmonious, in good taste, polished, refined, restrained, smart, stylish

tasteless 1. bland, boring, dull, flat, flavourless, insipid, mild, watered-down, weak **2.** cheap, coarse, crass, crude, flashy, garish, gaudy, graceless, gross, impolite, improper, indecorous, indelicate, indiscreet, inelegant, low, naff (*Brit. slang*), rude, tacky (*informal*), tactless, tawdry, uncouth, unseemly, vulgar

tasty appetizing, delectable, delicious, flavourful, flavoursome, full-flavoured, good-tasting, luscious, palatable, savoury, scrumptious (*informal*), toothsome, yummy (*slang*)

taunt 1. *vb.* deride, flout, insult, jeer, jibe, mock, provoke, ridicule, sneer at, take the piss (out of) (*taboo slang*), tease, torment **2.** *n.* barb, derision, dig, gibe, insult, jeer, provocation, ridicule, teasing

taut flexed, rigid, strained, stressed, stretched, tense, tight

tavern *old-fashioned* alehouse (*archaic*), bar, boozer (*Brit., Austral., & N.Z. informal*), hostelry, inn, pub (*in-*

tawny owl *n* a European owl having a reddish-brown plumage and a round head.

tawse *n Scot* a leather strap with one end cut into thongs, formerly used by schoolteachers to hit children who had misbehaved.

tax *n* **1** a compulsory payment to a government to raise revenue, levied on income, property, or goods and services. *~vb* **2** to levy a tax on (people, companies, etc.). **3** to make heavy demands on: *the task taxed his ingenuity and patience.* **4 tax someone with** to accuse someone of: *he was taxed with parochialism and meanness.* **taxable** *adj* **taxing** *adj*

taxation *n* the levying of taxes or the condition of being taxed.

tax avoidance *n* reduction of tax liability by lawful methods.

tax-deductible *adj* legally deductible from income or wealth before tax assessment.

tax disc *n* (in Britain) a small disc of paper which must be displayed on a vehicle to show that the tax due on it for that year has been paid.

tax evasion *n* reduction of tax liability by illegal methods.

tax-free *adj* not needing to have tax paid on it: *a tax-free lump sum.*

tax haven *n* a country or state having a lower rate of taxation than elsewhere.

taxi *n, pl* **taxis 1** Also called: **cab, taxicab** a car that may be hired, along with its driver, to carry passengers to any specified destination. *~vb* **taxiing, taxied 2** (of an aircraft) to move along the ground, esp. before takeoff and after landing.

taxidermy *n* the art of preparing, stuffing, and mounting animal skins so that they have a lifelike appearance. **taxidermist** *n*

taximeter *n* a meter fitted to a taxi to register the fare, based on the length of the journey.

taxi rank *n* a place where taxis wait to be hired.

taxonomy *n* **1** the branch of biology concerned with the classification of plants and animals into groups based on their similarities and differences. **2** the science or practice of classification. **taxonomic** *adj* **taxonomist** *n*

taxpayer *n* a person or organization that pays taxes.

tax relief *n* a reduction in the amount of tax a person or company has to pay.

tax return *n* a declaration of personal income used as a basis for assessing an individual's liability for taxation.

tax year *n* a period of twelve months used by a government as a basis for calculating taxes.

Tb *Chem* terbium.

TB tuberculosis.

T-bone steak *n* a large choice steak cut from the sirloin of beef, containing a T-shaped bone.

tbs. *or* **tbsp.** tablespoon(ful).

Tc *Chem* technetium.

te *n Music* (in tonic sol-fa) the seventh note of any ascending major scale.

Te *Chem* tellurium.

tea *n* **1 a** a drink made by infusing the dried chopped leaves of an Asian shrub in boiling water: *would you like a cup of tea?* **b** the dried chopped leaves of an Asian shrub used to make this drink: *could you get some tea at the grocer's?* **c** the Asian shrub on which these leaves grow. **2** *Brit, Austral, & NZ* the main evening meal. **3** *Chiefly Brit* a light meal eaten in mid-afternoon, usually consisting of tea and cakes, sometimes with sandwiches. **4** a drink like tea made from other plants: *mint tea.*

tea bag *n* a small bag containing tea leaves, infused in boiling water to make tea.

tea ball *n Chiefly US* a perforated metal ball filled with tea leaves, used to make tea.

teacake *n Brit* a flat bun, usually eaten toasted and buttered.

teach *vb* **teaching, taught 1** to tell or show (someone) how to do something. **2** to give instruction or lessons in (a subject) to (students). **3** to cause to learn or understand: *life has taught me to seize the day.* **4 teach someone a lesson** to warn or punish someone: *there are occasions when a bully has to be taught a lesson.* **teachable** *adj*

teacher *n* a person whose job is to teach others, esp. children.

tea chest *n* a large light wooden box used for exporting tea or storing things in.

teaching *n* **1** the art or profession of a teacher. **2 teachings** the ideas and principles taught by a person, school of thought, etc.: *the teachings of the Catholic Church.*

teaching hospital *n* a hospital attached to a medical school, in which students are taught and given supervised practical experience.

tea cloth *n* same as **tea towel.**

tea cosy *n* a covering for a teapot to keep the contents hot.

teacup *n* **1** a cup out of which tea may be drunk. **2** Also called: **teacupful** the amount a teacup will hold.

teahouse *n* a restaurant, esp. in Japan or China, where tea and light refreshments are served.

teak *n* the hard yellowish-brown wood of an East Indian tree, used for furniture making.

teal *n, pl* **teals** *or* **teal** a small freshwater duck related to the mallard.

tea leaves *pl n, sing* **tea leaf** the dried and shredded leaves of the tea shrub, esp. those left behind in a cup or teapot after tea has been made and drunk.

team *n* **1** a group of players forming one of the sides in a sporting contest. **2** a group of people organized to work together: *a team of scientists.* **3** two or more animals working together: *a sledge pulled by a team of dogs.* *~vb* **4 team up with** to join with (someone) in

THESAURUS

formal, chiefly Brit.), public house, taproom, watering hole (*facetious slang*)

tawdry cheap, cheap-jack (*informal*), flashy, gaudy, gimcrack, naff (*Brit. slang*), plastic (*slang*), showy, tacky (*informal*), tasteless, tinselly, vulgar

tax *n.* **1.** assessment, charge, contribution, customs, duty, excise, levy, rate, tariff, tithe, toll, tribute *~vb.* **2.** assess, charge, demand, exact, extract, impose, levy a tax on, rate, tithe **3.** burden, drain, enervate, exhaust, load, make heavy demands on, overburden, push, put pressure on, sap, strain, stretch, try, weaken, wear out, weary, weigh heavily on **4.** *with* **with** accuse, arraign, blame, charge, impeach, impugn, incriminate, lay at one's door

taxing burdensome, demanding, enervating, exacting, heavy, onerous, punishing, sapping, stressful, tiring, tough, trying, wearing, wearisome

teach advise, coach, demonstrate, direct, discipline, drill, edify, educate, enlighten, give lessons in, guide, instil, instruct, school, show, train, tutor

teacher coach, don, educator, guide, guru, handler, instructor, lecturer, master, mentor, mistress, pedagogue, professor, schoolmaster, schoolmistress, schoolteacher, trainer, tutor

team *n.* **1.** line-up, side, squad **2.** band, body, bunch,

order to work together. **5 team with** to match (something) with something else: *navy skirts teamed with various coloured blouses.*

team-mate *n* a fellow member of a team.

team spirit *n* willingness to cooperate as part of a team.

teamster *n* **1** *US & Canad* a truck driver. **2** (formerly) a driver of a team of horses.

teamwork *n* the cooperative work done by a team.

teapot *n* a container with a lid, spout, and handle, in which tea is made and from which it is served.

tear[1] *n* **1** Also called: **teardrop** a drop of salty fluid appearing in and falling from the eye. **2 in tears** weeping.

tear[2] *vb* **tearing, tore, torn 1** to rip a hole in (something): *I tore my jumper on a nail.* **2** to pull apart or to pieces: *eagles have powerful beaks for tearing flesh.* **3** to hurry or rush. **4** to remove or take by force: *the sacred things torn from the temples of Inca worshippers.* **5 tear at someone's heartstrings** to cause someone distress or anguish. **6** to injure (a muscle or ligament) by moving or twisting it violently. *~n* **7** a hole or split. ~See also **tear away, tear down, tear into.**

tear away *vb* **1** to persuade (oneself or someone else) to leave: *she stood and watched, unable to tear herself away from the room.* *~n* **tearaway 2** *Brit* a wild or unruly person.

tear down *vb* to destroy or demolish: *it will be cheaper to tear down the old house and build a new one than to repair it.*

tear duct *n* a short tube in the inner corner of the eyelid, through which tears drain into the nose.

tearful *adj* weeping or about to weep. **tearfully** *adv*

tear gas *n* a gas that stings the eyes and causes temporary blindness, used in warfare and to control riots.

tearing *adj* very urgent: *I had been in a tearing hurry to leave the camp.*

tear into *vb Informal* to attack vigorously and damagingly.

tear-jerker *n Informal* an excessively sentimental film or book.

tearoom *n Brit* a restaurant where tea and light refreshments are served.

tease *vb* **teasing, teased 1** to make fun of (someone) in a provocative and often playful manner. **2** to arouse sexual desire in (someone) with no intention of satisfying it. **3** to raise the nap of (a fabric) with a teasel. *~n* **4** a person who teases. **5** a piece of teasing behaviour. See also **tease out. teaser** *n* **teasing** *adj*

teasel, teazel, *or* **teazle** *n* **1** a plant of Eurasia and N Africa, with prickly heads of yellow or purple flowers. **2** the dried flower head of a teasel, used, esp. formerly, for raising the nap of cloth.

tease out *vb* **1** to comb (hair, flax, or wool) so as to remove any tangles. **2** to extract information with difficulty: *it's not easy to tease out the differences between anxiety and depression.*

teaspoon *n* **1** a small spoon used for stirring tea or coffee. **2** Also called: **teaspoonful** the amount contained in such a spoon. **3** a unit of capacity used in cooking etc., equal to 5 ml.

teat *n* **1** the nipple of a breast or udder. **2** something resembling a teat such as the rubber mouthpiece of a feeding bottle.

tea towel *or* **tea cloth** *n* a towel for drying dishes.

tech *n Informal* a technical college.

tech. 1 technical. **2** technology.

technetium (tek-**neesh**-ee-um) *n Chem* a silvery-grey metallic element, produced artificially, esp. by the fission of uranium. Symbol: Tc

technical *adj* **1** of or specializing in industrial, practical, or mechanical arts and applied sciences: *a technical school.* **2** skilled in practical activities rather than abstract thinking. **3** relating to a particular field of activity: *technical jargon.* **4** according to the letter of the law: *a last-minute penalty awarded to the Irish for a technical offence.* **5** showing technique: *technical perfection.* **technically** *adv*

technical college *n Brit* an institution for further education that provides courses in art and technical subjects.

technical drawing *n* drawing done by a draughtsman with compasses, T-squares, etc.

technicality *n, pl* **-ties 1** a petty formal point arising from a strict interpretation of the law or a set of rules: *the case was dismissed on a legal technicality.* **2** a detail of the method used to do something: *the technicalities of making a recording.*

technical knockout *n Boxing* a judgment of a knockout given when a boxer is, in the referee's opinion, too badly beaten to continue without risk of serious injury.

technician *n* a person skilled in a particular technical field: *oil technicians.*

Technicolor *n Trademark* a process of producing colour film for the cinema by superimposing synchronized films of the same scene, each having a different colour filter.

technique *n* **1** a method or skill used for a particular task: *modern management techniques.* **2** proficiency in a practical or mechanical skill: *he lacks the technique to be a good player.*

techno *n* a type of very fast disco music, using electronic sounds and having a strong technological influence.

techno- *combining form* of or relating to technology: *technocrat.*

technocracy *n, pl* **-cies** government by scientists, engineers, and other experts. **technocrat** *n* **technocratic** *adj*

technology *n, pl* **-gies 1** the application of practical or mechanical sciences to industry or commerce. **2** the scientific methods or devices used in a particular field: *the latest aircraft technology.* **technological** *adj* **technologist** *n*

THESAURUS

company, crew, gang, group, posse (*informal*), set, squad, troupe **3.** pair, span, yoke *~vb.* **4. team up** band together, cooperate, couple, get together, join, link, unite, work together, yoke

tear[1] **in tears** blubbering, crying, distressed, sobbing, visibly moved, weeping, whimpering

tear[2] *vb.* **1.** claw, lacerate, mangle, mutilate, rend, rip, rupture, scratch, split **2.** divide, pull apart, sever, shred, sunder **3.** barrel (along) (*informal, chiefly U.S. & Canad.*), belt (*slang*), bolt, career, charge, dart, dash, fly, gallop, hurry, race, run, rush, shoot, speed, sprint, zoom **4.** grab, pluck, pull, rip, seize, snatch, wrench, wrest, yank *~n.* **5.** hole, laceration, mutilation, rent, rip, run, rupture, scratch, split

tearful blubbering, crying, in tears, lachrymose, sobbing, weeping, weepy (*informal*), whimpering

tease aggravate (*informal*), annoy, badger, bait, bedevil, bother, chaff, goad, jibe, lead on, mock, needle (*informal*), pester, plague (*informal*), provoke, rag (*Brit. informal*), rib (*informal*), ridicule, take the piss (out of) (*taboo slang*), tantalize, taunt, torment, vex, wind up (*Brit. slang*), worry

technique 1. approach, course, fashion, manner, means, method, mode, modus operandi, procedure,

tectonics *n Geol* the study of the earth's crust and the forces that produce changes in it.

ted[1] *vb* **tedding, tedded** to shake out (hay), so as to dry it.

ted[2] *n Informal* short for **teddy boy.**

teddy[1] *n, pl* **-dies** short for **teddy bear.**

teddy[2] *n, pl* **-dies** a woman's one-piece undergarment incorporating a camisole top and French knickers.

teddy bear *n* a stuffed toy bear.

teddy boy *n* (in Britain, esp. in the mid-1950s) a youth who wore mock Edwardian fashions.

Te Deum (tee **dee**-um) *n Christianity* an ancient Latin hymn beginning Te Deum Laudamus (we praise thee, O God).

tedious *adj* boring and uninteresting. **tediously** *adv* **tediousness** *n*

tedium *n* the state of being bored or the quality of being boring: *the tedium of a nine-to-five white-collar job.*

tee *n* **1** a support for a golf ball, usually a small wooden or plastic peg, used when teeing off. **2** an area on a golf course from which the first stroke of a hole is made. **3** a mark used as a target in certain games such as curling and quoits. ~See also **tee off.**

tee-hee *or* **te-hee** *interj* an exclamation of mocking laughter.

teem[1] *vb* **teem with** to have a great number of: *the woods were teeming with snakes and bears.*

teem[2] *vb* (of rain) to pour down in torrents.

teen *adj Informal* same as **teenage.**

teenage *adj* **1** (of a person) aged between 13 and 19. **2** typical of or designed for people aged between 13 and 19: *teenage fashions.*

teenager *n* a person between the ages of 13 and 19.

teens *pl n* **1** the years of a person's life between the ages of 13 and 19. **2** all the numbers that end in *-teen.*

teeny *adj* **-nier, -niest** extremely small.

teenybopper *n Old-fashioned slang* a young teenager, usually a girl, who is a keen follower of fashion and pop music.

tee off *vb* **teeing, teed** *Golf* to hit (the ball) from a tee at the start of a hole.

teepee *n* same as **tepee.**

teeter *vb* to wobble or move unsteadily.

teeth *n* **1** the plural of **tooth. 2** the power to produce a desired effect: *resolution 672 had no teeth.* **3 armed to the teeth** very heavily armed. **4 get one's teeth into** to become engrossed in. **5 in the teeth of** in spite of: *trying to run a business in the teeth of the recession.*

teethe *vb* **teething, teethed** (of a baby) to grow his or her first teeth.

teething ring *n* a hard ring on which babies may bite while teething.

teething troubles *pl n* problems arising during the early stages of a project.

teetotal *adj* never drinking alcohol. **teetotaller** *n*

TEFL Teaching of English as a Foreign Language.

Teflon *n Trademark* a substance used for nonstick coatings on saucepans etc.

te-hee *interj* same as **tee-hee.**

tel. telephone.

tele- *combining form* **1** at or over a distance: *telecommunications.* **2** television: *telegenic.* **3** via telephone or television: *teleconference.*

telecast *vb* **-casting, -cast** *or* **-casted 1** to broadcast by television. ~*n* **2** a television broadcast. **telecaster** *n*

telecommunications *n* communications using electronic equipment, such as telephones, radio, and television.

telegram *n* (formerly) a message transmitted by telegraph.

telegraph *n* **1** (formerly) a system by which information could be transmitted over a distance, using electrical signals sent along a cable. ~*vb* **2** (formerly) to send (a message) by telegraph. **3** to give advance notice of (something), esp. unintentionally: *the twist in the plot was telegraphed long in advance.* **4** *Canad informal* to cast (a vote) illegally by impersonating a registered voter. **telegraphist** *n* **telegraphic** *adj*

telegraphy *n* (formerly) the science or use of a telegraph.

telekinesis *n* movement of a body by thought or willpower, without the application of a physical force. **telekinetic** *adj*

Telemessage *n Brit trademark* a message sent by telephone or telex and delivered in printed form.

telemetry *n* the use of electronic devices to record or measure a distant event and transmit the data to a receiver. **telemetric** *adj*

teleology *n* **1** *Philosophy* the doctrine that there is evidence of purpose or design in the universe. **2** *Biol* the belief that natural phenomena have a predetermined purpose and are not determined by mechanical laws. **teleological** *adj* **teleologist** *n*

telepathy *n* the direct communication of thoughts and feelings between minds without the need to use normal means such as speech, writing, or touch. **telepathic** *adj* **telepathically** *adv*

telephone *n* **1** a piece of equipment for transmitting speech, consisting of a microphone and receiver mounted on a handset: *the telephone was ringing.* **2** the worldwide system of communications using telephones: *reports came in by telephone.* ~*vb* **-phoning, -phoned 3** to call or talk to (a person) by telephone. ~*adj* **4** of or using a telephone: *a telephone call.* **telephonic** *adj*

telephone box *n* a soundproof enclosure from which a paid telephone call can be made.

telephone directory *n* a book listing the names, addresses, and telephone numbers of subscribers in a particular area.

THESAURUS

style, system, way **2.** adroitness, art, artistry, craft, craftsmanship, facility, knack, know-how (*informal*), performance, proficiency, skill, touch

tedious annoying, banal, boring, deadly dull, drab, dreary, dull, fatiguing, ho-hum (*informal*), humdrum, irksome, laborious, lifeless, long-drawn-out, mind-numbing, monotonous, prosaic, soporific, tiring, unexciting, uninteresting, vapid, wearisome

tedium banality, boredom, deadness, drabness, dreariness, dullness, ennui, lifelessness, monotony, routine, sameness, tediousness

teem *with* **with** abound, bear, be crawling with, be full of, be prolific, brim, bristle, burst at the seams, overflow, produce, swarm

teenager adolescent, boy, girl, juvenile, minor, youth

telegram cable, telegraph, wire (*informal*)

telegraph 1. *n.* cable, telegram, wire (*informal*) **2.** *vb.* cable, send, transmit, wire (*informal*)

telepathy mind-reading, sixth sense, thought transference

telephone 1. *n.* blower (*informal*), handset, line, phone **2.** *vb.* buzz (*informal*), call, call up, dial, get on the blower (*informal*), give (someone) a bell (*Brit. slang*), give (someone) a buzz (*informal*), give (some-

telephonist *n Brit* a person who operates a telephone switchboard.

telephony *n* a system of telecommunications for the transmission of speech or other sounds.

telephoto lens *n* a lens fitted to a camera to produce a magnified image of a distant object.

teleprinter *n* an apparatus, similar to a typewriter, by which typed messages are sent and received by wire.

Teleprompter *n Trademark* a device for displaying a script under a television camera, so that a speaker can read it while appearing to look at the camera.

telesales *n* the selling of a commodity or service by telephone.

telescope *n* **1** an optical instrument for making distant objects appear closer by use of a combination of lenses. **2** See **radio telescope.** *~vb* **-scoping, -scoped 3** to shorten (something) while still keeping the important parts: *a hundred years of change has been telescoped into five years.* **telescopic** *adj*

telescopic sight *n* a sight on a rifle, etc., consisting of a telescope, used for aiming at distant objects.

Teletext *n Trademark* a Videotex service in which information is broadcast by a television station and received on a specially equipped television set.

Teletype *n Trademark* a type of teleprinter.

televangelist *n US* an evangelical preacher who appears regularly on television, preaching the gospel and appealing for donations from viewers.

televise *vb* **-vising, -vised** to show (a programme or event) on television.

television *n* **1** the system or process of producing a moving image with accompanying sound on a distant screen. **2** Also called: **television set** a device for receiving broadcast signals and converting them into sound and pictures. **3** the content of television programmes: *some people think that television is too violent nowadays.* *~adj* **4** of or relating to television: *a television interview.* **televisual** *adj*

telex *n* **1** an international communication service which sends messages by teleprinter. **2** a teleprinter used in such a service. **3** a message sent by telex. *~vb* **4** to transmit (a message) by telex.

Telidon *n Trademark* a Canadian interactive viewdata service.

tell *vb* **telling, told 1** to make known in words; notify: *I told her what had happened.* **2** to order or instruct (someone to do something): *he had been told to wait.* **3** to give an account (of an event or situation): *the President had been told of the developments.* **4** to communicate by words: *he was woken at 5 a.m. to be told the news.* **5** to discover, distinguish, or discern: *she could tell that he was not sorry.* **6** to have or produce an impact or effect: *the pressure had begun to tell on him.* **7** *Informal* to reveal secrets or gossip. **8 tell the time** to read the time from a clock. **9 you're telling me** *Slang* I know that very well.

tell apart *vb* to distinguish between: *they're different colours, otherwise how would you tell them apart?*

teller *n* **1** a narrator. **2** a bank cashier. **3** a person appointed to count votes.

telling *adj* having a marked effect or impact: *to inflict telling damage on the enemy.*

tell off *vb Informal* to reprimand or scold (someone). **telling-off** *n*

telltale *n* **1** a person who tells tales about others. *~adj* **2** giving away information: *examining the hands for telltale signs of age.*

tellurian *adj* of the earth.

tellurium *n Chem* a brittle silvery-white nonmetallic element. Symbol: Te

telly *n, pl* **-lies** *Informal, chiefly Brit* short for **television.**

temerity (tim-**merr**-it-tee) *n* boldness or audacity.

temp *Informal ~n* **1** a person, esp. a secretary, employed on a temporary basis. *~vb* **2** to work as a temp.

temp. **1** temperature. **2** temporary.

temper *n* **1** a sudden outburst of anger: *she stormed out in a temper.* **2** a tendency to have sudden outbursts of anger: *you've got a temper all right.* **3** a mental condition of moderation and calm: *he lost his temper.* **4** a person's frame of mind: *he was in a bad temper.* *~vb* **5** to modify so as to make less extreme or more acceptable: *past militancy has been tempered with compassion and caring.* **6** to reduce the brittleness of (a hardened metal) by reheating it and allowing it to cool. **7** *Music* to adjust the frequency differences between the notes of a scale on (a keyboard instrument).

tempera *n* a painting medium for powdered pigments, consisting usually of egg yolk and water.

temperament *n* a person's character or disposition.

temperamental *adj* **1** (of a person) tending to be moody and have sudden outbursts of anger. **2** *Informal* working erratically and inconsistently; unreliable: *the temperamental microphone.* **3** of or relating to a

THESAURUS

one) a call, give (someone) a ring (*informal, chiefly Brit.*), give someone a tinkle (*Brit. informal*), phone, put a call through to, ring (*informal, chiefly Brit.*)

telescope **1.** *n.* glass, spyglass **2.** *vb.* abbreviate, abridge, capsulize, compress, condense, contract, curtail, cut, shorten, shrink, tighten, trim, truncate

television gogglebox (*Brit. slang*), idiot box (*slang*), receiver, small screen (*informal*), telly (*Brit. informal*), the box (*Brit. informal*), the tube (*slang*), TV, TV set

tell *vb.* **1.** acquaint, announce, apprise, communicate, confess, disclose, divulge, express, impart, inform, let know, make known, mention, notify, proclaim, reveal, say, speak, state, utter **2.** authorize, bid, call upon, command, direct, enjoin, instruct, order, require, summon **3.** chronicle, depict, describe, give an account of, narrate, portray, recount, relate, report **4.** comprehend, discern, discover, make out, see, understand **5.** carry weight, count, have *or* take effect, have force, make its presence felt, register, take its toll, weigh

telling considerable, decisive, effective, effectual, forceful, forcible, impressive, influential, marked, potent, powerful, significant, solid, striking, trenchant, weighty

temper *n.* **1.** anger, bad mood, bate (*Brit. slang*), fit of pique, fury, gall, ill humour, paddy (*Brit. informal*), passion, rage, tantrum, wax (*informal, chiefly Brit.*) **2.** calm, calmness, composure, cool (*slang*), coolness, equanimity, good humour, moderation, self-control, tranquillity **3.** attitude, character, constitution, disposition, frame of mind, humour, mind, mood, nature, temperament, tenor, vein *~vb.* **4.** abate, allay, assuage, calm, lessen, mitigate, moderate, mollify, palliate, restrain, soften, soft-pedal (*informal*), soothe, tone down **5.** anneal, harden, strengthen, toughen

temperament bent, cast of mind, character, complexion, constitution, disposition, frame of mind, humour, make-up, mettle, nature, outlook, personality, quality, soul, spirit, stamp, temper, tendencies, tendency

temperamental **1.** capricious, easily upset, emotional, erratic, excitable, explosive, fiery, highly strung, hot-headed, hypersensitive, impatient, mercurial, moody, neurotic, passionate, sensitive, touchy, volatile **2.** *informal* erratic, inconsistent, inconstant,

person's temperament: *we discussed temperamental and developmental differences.* **temperamentally** *adv*

temperance *n* **1** restraint or moderation, esp. in yielding to one's appetites or desires. **2** abstinence from alcoholic drink.

temperate *adj* **1** of a climate which is never extremely hot or extremely cold. **2** mild or moderate in quality or character: *try to be more temperate in your statements.*

Temperate Zone *n* those parts of the earth's surface lying between the Arctic Circle and the tropic of Cancer and between the Antarctic Circle and the tropic of Capricorn.

temperature *n* **1** the hotness or coldness of something, as measured on a scale that has one or more fixed reference points. **2** *Informal* an abnormally high body temperature. **3** the strength of feeling among a group of people: *his remarks are likely to raise the political temperature considerably.*

tempest *n Literary* a violent wind or storm.

tempestuous *adj* **1** violent or stormy. **2** extremely emotional or passionate: *a tempestuous relationship.* **tempestuously** *adv*

template *n* a wood or metal pattern, used to help cut out shapes accurately.

temple[1] *n* a building or place used for the worship of a god or gods.

temple[2] *n* the region on each side of the head in front of the ear and above the cheek bone.

tempo (**tem**-po) *n, pl* **-pi** (-pee) *or* **-pos 1** rate or pace: *the slow tempo of change in an overwhelmingly rural country.* **2** the speed at which a piece of music is played or meant to be played.

temporal[1] *adj* **1** of or relating to time. **2** of secular as opposed to spiritual or religious affairs: *in the Middle Ages the Pope had temporal as well as spiritual power.* **3** not permanent or eternal: *a temporal view of drugs as the No. 1 social problem.*

temporal[2] *adj Anat* of or near the temple or temples.

temporal bone *n* either of two compound bones forming the sides of the skull.

temporary *adj* lasting only for a short time; not permanent: *temporary accommodation.* **temporarily** *adv*

temporize *or* **-rise** *vb* **-rizing, -rized** *or* **-rising, -rised 1** to delay, act evasively, or protract a negotiation in order to gain time or avoid making a decision: *"Well," I temporized, "I'll have to ask your mother".* **2** to adapt oneself to circumstances, as by temporary or apparent agreement.

tempt *vb* **1** to entice (someone) to do something, esp. something morally wrong or unwise: *can I tempt you to have another whisky?* **2** to allure or attract: *she was tempted by the glamour of a modelling career.* **3 be tempted** to want to do something while knowing it would be wrong or inappropriate to do so: *many youngsters are tempted to experiment with drugs.* **4 tempt fate** *or* **providence** to take foolish or unnecessary risks. **tempter** *n* **temptress** *fem n*

temptation *n* **1** the act of tempting or the state of being tempted. **2** a person or thing that tempts.

tempting *adj* attractive or inviting: *it's tempting to say I told you so.* **temptingly** *adv*

ten *n* **1** the cardinal number that is the sum of one and nine. **2** a numeral, 10 or X, representing this number. **3** something representing or consisting of ten units. *~adj* **4** amounting to ten: *ten years.* **tenth** *adj, n*

tenable *adj* **1** able to be upheld or maintained: *a tenable strategy.* **2** (of a job) intended to be held by a person for a particular length of time: *the post will be tenable for three years in the first instance.* **tenability** *n* **tenably** *adv*

tenacious *adj* **1** holding firmly: *a tenacious grasp.* **2** stubborn or persistent: *tenacious support.* **tenaciously** *adv* **tenacity** *n*

tenancy *n, pl* **-cies 1** the temporary possession or use of lands or property owned by somebody else, in return for payment. **2** the period of holding or occupying such property.

tenant *n* **1** a person who pays rent for the use of land or property. **2** any holder or occupant.

tenant farmer *n* a person who farms land rented from somebody else.

tenantry *n Old-fashioned* tenants collectively.

THESAURUS

undependable, unpredictable, unreliable **3.** congenital, constitutional, inborn, ingrained, inherent, innate, natural

temperance 1. continence, discretion, forbearance, moderation, restraint, self-control, self-discipline, self-restraint **2.** abstemiousness, abstinence, sobriety, teetotalism

temperate 1. agreeable, balmy, calm, clement, cool, fair, gentle, mild, moderate, pleasant, soft **2.** calm, composed, dispassionate, equable, even-tempered, mild, moderate, reasonable, self-controlled, self-restrained, sensible, stable

tempest *literary* cyclone, gale, hurricane, squall, storm, tornado, typhoon

tempestuous 1. agitated, blustery, boisterous, breezy, gusty, inclement, raging, squally, stormy, turbulent, windy **2.** agitated, boisterous, emotional, excited, feverish, flaming, furious, heated, hysterical, impassioned, intense, passionate, stormy, turbulent, uncontrolled, violent, wild

temple church, holy place, place of worship, sanctuary, shrine

temporarily briefly, fleetingly, for a little while, for a moment, for a short time, for a short while, for the moment, for the nonce, for the time being, momentarily, pro tem

temporary brief, ephemeral, evanescent, fleeting, fugitive, here today and gone tomorrow, impermanent, interim, momentary, passing, pro tem, *pro tempore,* provisional, short-lived, transient, transitory

tempt 1. coax, entice, inveigle, invite, lead on, lure, seduce **2.** allure, appeal to, attract, draw, make one's mouth water, tantalize, whet the appetite of, woo

temptation allurement, appeal, attraction, attractiveness, blandishments, coaxing, come-on (*informal*), draw, enticement, inducement, invitation, lure, pull, seduction, tantalization

tempting alluring, appetizing, attractive, enticing, inviting, mouthwatering, seductive, tantalizing

tenable arguable, believable, defendable, defensible, justifiable, maintainable, plausible, rational, reasonable, sound, viable

tenacious 1. clinging, fast, firm, forceful, immovable, iron, strong, tight, unshakable **2.** adamant, determined, dogged, firm, immovable, inflexible, intransigent, obdurate, obstinate, persistent, pertinacious, resolute, staunch, steadfast, stiff-necked, strong-willed, stubborn, sure, unswerving, unyielding

tenacity 1. fastness, firmness, force, forcefulness, power, strength **2.** application, determination, diligence, doggedness, firmness, inflexibility, intransigence, obduracy, obstinacy, perseverance, persistence, pertinacity, resoluteness, resolution, resolve, staunchness, steadfastness, strength of purpose, strength of will, stubbornness

tench *n* a European freshwater game fish of the carp family.

Ten Commandments *pl n Bible* the commandments given by God to Moses on Mount Sinai, summarizing the basic obligations of people towards God and their fellow humans.

tend[1] *vb* to be inclined (to take a particular kind of action or to be in a particular condition) as a rule: *she tends to be rather absent-minded.*

tend[2] *vb* **1** to take care of: *it is she who tends his wounds.* **2 tend to** to attend to: *excuse me, I have to tend to the other guests.*

tendency *n, pl* **-cies 1** an inclination to act in a particular way. **2** the general course or drift of something. **3** a faction, esp. within a political party.

tendentious *adj* expressing a particular viewpoint or opinion, esp. a controversial one, in very strong terms: *a somewhat tendentious reading of French history.* **tendentiously** *adv*

tender[1] *adj* **1** (of cooked food) having softened and become easy to chew or cut. **2** gentle and kind: *tender loving care.* **3** vulnerable or sensitive: *at the tender age of 9.* **4** painful when touched: *his wrist was swollen and tender.* **tenderly** *adv* **tenderness** *n*

tender[2] *vb* **1** to present or offer: *he tendered his resignation.* **2** to make a formal offer or estimate for a job or contract: *contractors tendering for government work.* ~*n* **3** a formal offer to supply specified goods or services at a stated cost or rate: *the government invited tenders to run television and radio services.* **tenderer** *n* **tendering** *n*

tender[3] *n* **1** a small boat that brings supplies to larger vessels in a port. **2** a wagon attached to the rear of a steam locomotive that carries the fuel and water.

tenderfoot *n, pl* **-foots** *or* **-feet** a newcomer to a particular activity.

tenderize *or* **-ise** *vb* **-izing, -ized** *or* **-ising, -ised** to make (meat) tender, by pounding it or adding a substance to break down the fibres. **tenderizer** *or* **-iser** *n*

tenderloin *n* a tender cut of pork from between the sirloin and ribs.

tendon *n* a band of tough tissue that attaches a muscle to a bone.

tendril *n* a threadlike leaf or stem by which a climbing plant attaches itself to a support.

tenement *n* a large building divided into several different flats.

tenet (ten-nit) *n* a principle on which a belief or doctrine is based.

tenfold *adj* **1** having ten times as many or as much. **2** composed of ten parts. ~*adv* **3** by ten times as many or as much.

ten-gallon hat *n* (in the U.S.) a cowboy's broad-brimmed felt hat with a very high crown.

tenner *n Informal* **1** a ten-pound or ten-dollar note. **2** the sum of ten pounds or ten dollars: *it's worth a tenner at least.*

tennis *n* a game played between two players or pairs of players who use a racket to hit a ball to and fro over a net on a rectangular court. ~See also **lawn tennis, real tennis, table tennis.**

tennis elbow *n* inflammation of the elbow, typically caused by exertion in playing tennis.

tenon *n* a projecting end of a piece of wood, formed to fit into a corresponding slot in another piece.

tenor *n* **1 a** the second highest male voice, between alto and baritone. **b** a singer with such a voice. **c** a saxophone, horn, or other musical instrument between the alto and baritone or bass. **2** a general meaning or character: *it was clear from the tenor of the meeting that the chairman's actions are very unpopular.* ~*adj* **3** denoting a musical instrument between alto and baritone: *a tenor saxophone.* **4** of or relating to the second highest male voice: *his voice lacks the range needed for the tenor role.*

tenpin bowling *n* a game in which players try to knock over ten skittles by rolling a ball at them.

tense[1] *adj* **1** having, showing, or causing mental or emotional strain: *the tense atmosphere.* **2** stretched tight: *tense muscles.* ~*vb* **tensing, tensed 3** Also: **tense up** to make or become tense. **tensely** *adv* **tenseness** *n*

tense[2] *n Grammar* the form of a verb that indicates whether the action referred to in the sentence is located in the past, the present, or the future: *"ate" is the past tense of "to eat".*

tensile *adj* of or relating to tension or being stretched: *the addition of linseed oil improved the tensile strength of the cricket bat.*

tensile strength *n* a measure of the ability of a material to withstand lengthwise stress, expressed as the greatest stress that the material can stand without breaking.

tension *n* **1** a situation or condition of hostility, suspense, or uneasiness: *a renewed state of tension between old enemies.* **2** mental or emotional strain: *nervous tension.* **3** a force that stretches or the state or degree of being stretched tight: *keep tension on the line until the fish comes within range of the net.* **4**

THESAURUS

tenancy holding, lease, occupancy, occupation, possession, renting, residence

tenant holder, inhabitant, leaseholder, lessee, occupant, occupier, renter, resident

tend[1] be apt, be biased, be disposed, be inclined, be liable, be likely, gravitate, have a leaning, have an inclination, have a tendency, incline, lean, trend

tend[2] **1.** attend, care for, keep, keep an eye on, look after, maintain, manage, minister to, nurse, nurture, protect, watch, watch over **2. tend to** attend to, cater to, look after, see to, serve, take care of, wait on

tendency 1. bent, disposition, inclination, leaning, liability, partiality, penchant, predilection, predisposition, proclivity, proneness, propensity, readiness, susceptibility **2.** bearing, bias, course, direction, drift, drive, heading, movement, purport, tenor, trend, turning

tender[1] **1.** affectionate, amorous, benevolent, caring, compassionate, considerate, fond, gentle, humane, kind, loving, merciful, pitiful, sentimental, softhearted, sympathetic, tenderhearted, warm, warm-hearted **2.** aching, acute, bruised, inflamed, irritated, painful, raw, sensitive, smarting, sore

tender[2] **1.** *vb.* extend, give, hand in, offer, present, proffer, propose, put forward, submit, suggest, volunteer **2.** *n.* bid, estimate, offer, proposal, submission, suggestion

tenderness 1. affection, amorousness, attachment, benevolence, care, compassion, consideration, devotion, fondness, gentleness, humaneness, humanity, kindness, liking, love, mercy, pity, sentimentality, softheartedness, sympathy, tenderheartedness, warm-heartedness, warmth **2.** ache, aching, bruising, inflammation, irritation, pain, painfulness, rawness, sensitiveness, sensitivity, smart, soreness

tense *adj.* **1.** anxious, apprehensive, edgy, fidgety, jittery (*informal*), jumpy, keyed up, nerve-racking, nervous, on edge, overwrought, restless, strained, stressful, strung up (*informal*), twitchy (*informal*), under pressure, uptight (*informal*), wired (*slang*), worrying,

Physics a force that tends to produce an elongation of a body or structure. **5** *Physics* voltage, electromotive force, or potential difference.

tent *n* **1** a portable shelter made of canvas or other fabric supported on poles, stretched out, and fastened to the ground by pegs and ropes. **2** See **oxygen tent.**

tentacle *n* **1** a flexible organ that grows near the mouth in many invertebrates and is used for feeding, grasping, etc. **2 tentacles** the unseen methods by which an organization or idea, esp. a sinister one, influences people and events: *the tentacles of the secret police.* **tentacled** *adj*

tentative *adj* **1** provisional or unconfirmed: *a tentative agreement.* **2** hesitant, uncertain, or cautious: *their rather tentative approach.* **tentatively** *adv* **tentativeness** *n*

tenterhooks *pl n* **on tenterhooks** in a state of tension or suspense.

tenth *adj, n* See **ten.**

tenuous *adj* insignificant or flimsy: *there is only the most tenuous evidence for it.* **tenuously** *adv*

tenure *n* **1** the holding of an office or position. **2** the length of time an office or position lasts. **3** the holding of a teaching position at a university on a permanent basis. **4** the legal right to live in a place or to use land or buildings for a period of time.

tepee *or* **teepee** (**tee**-pee) *n* a cone-shaped tent of animal skins, formerly used by American Indians.

tepid *adj* **1** slightly warm. **2** lacking enthusiasm: *tepid applause.* **tepidity** *n* **tepidly** *adv*

tequila *n* a Mexican alcoholic spirit distilled from the agave plant.

tera- *combining form* denoting one million million (10^{12}): *terameter.*

terbium *n Chem* a soft, silvery-grey element of the lanthanide series of metals. Symbol: Tb

tercentenary *or* **tercentennial** *adj* **1** marking a 300th anniversary. ~*n, pl* **-tenaries** *or* **-tennials 2** a 300th anniversary.

teredo (ter-**ree**-doh) *n, pl* **-dos** *or* **-dines** (-din-eez) a marine mollusc that bores into and destroys submerged timber.

tergiversate (**tur**-jiv-verse-ate) *vb* **-sating, -sated** *Formal* **1** to be evasive or ambiguous. **2** to change sides or loyalties. **tergiversation** *n* **tergiversator** *n*

term *n* **1** a word or expression, esp. one used in a specialized field of knowledge: *he coined the term "inferiority complex".* **2** a period of time: *a four-year prison term.* **3** one of the periods of the year when a school, university, or college is open or a lawcourt holds sessions. **4** the period of pregnancy when childbirth is imminent. **5** *Maths* any distinct quantity making up a fraction or proportion, or contained in a sequence, series, etc. **6** *Logic* any of the three subjects or predicates occurring in a syllogism. **7 full term** the end of a specific period of time: *the agony of carrying the child to full term.* ~*vb* **8** to name, call, or describe as being: *social workers tend to be termed lefties.* ~See also **terms.**

termagant *n Literary* an unpleasant, aggressive, and overbearing woman.

terminable *adj* capable of being terminated: *his terminable interest in the property.* **terminability** *n*

terminal *adj* **1** (of an illness) ending in death. **2** situated at an end, terminus, or boundary: *the terminal joints of the fingers.* **3** *Informal* extreme or severe: *terminal boredom.* ~*n* **4** a place where vehicles, passengers, or goods begin or end a journey: *the ferry terminal.* **5** a point at which current enters or leaves an electrical device. **6** *Computers* a device, usually a keyboard and a visual display unit, having input/output links with a computer. **terminally** *adv*

terminal velocity *n Physics* the maximum velocity reached by a body falling under gravity through a liquid or gas, esp. the atmosphere.

terminate *vb* **-nating, -nated 1** to bring or come to an end: *his flying career was terminated by this crash.* **2** to put an end to (a pregnancy) by inducing an abortion. **3** (of the route of a train, bus, etc.) to stop at a particular place and not go any further: *this train terminates at Leicester.* **termination** *n*

terminology *n, pl* **-gies** the specialized words and expressions relating to a particular subject. **terminological** *adj* **terminologist** *n*

terminus (**term**-in-nuss) *n, pl* **-ni** (-nye) *or* **-nuses** the station or town at one end of a railway line or bus route: *Vienna's Westbahnhof is the terminus for trains to France.*

termite *n* a whitish antlike insect of warm and tropical regions that destroys timber.

terms *pl n* **1** the actual language or mode of presentation used: *the test is carried out in plain non-engineering terms.* **2** the conditions of an agreement. **3** mutual relationship or standing of a specified nature: *he is on first-name terms with many of the directors.* **4 come to terms with** to learn to accept (an unpleasant or difficult situation). **5 in terms of** as expressed by; with regard to: *he is the best cricketer we have got in fact in terms of pure ability.*

THESAURUS

wound up (*informal*), wrought up **2.** rigid, strained, stretched, taut, tight ~*vb.* **3.** brace, flex, strain, stretch, tauten, tighten

tension 1. anxiety, apprehension, edginess, hostility, ill feeling, nervousness, pressure, restlessness, strain, stress, suspense, the jitters (*informal*), unease **2.** pressure, rigidity, stiffness, straining, stress, stretching, tautness, tightness

tentative 1. conjectural, experimental, indefinite, provisional, speculative, unconfirmed, unsettled **2.** cautious, diffident, doubtful, faltering, hesitant, timid, uncertain, undecided, unsure

tepid 1. lukewarm, slightly warm, warmish **2.** apathetic, cool, half-arsed (*slang*), half-assed (*U.S. & Canad. slang*), half-hearted, indifferent, lukewarm, unenthusiastic

term *n.* **1.** appellation, denomination, designation, expression, locution, name, phrase, title, word **2.** duration, interval, period, season, space, span, spell, time, while **3.** course, session ~*vb.* **4.** call, denominate, designate, dub, entitle, label, name, style

terminal *adj.* **1.** deadly, fatal, incurable, killing, lethal, mortal **2.** bounding, concluding, extreme, final, last, limiting, ultimate, utmost ~*n.* **3.** depot, end of the line, station, terminus

terminate abort, axe (*informal*), bring *or* come to an end, cease, close, complete, conclude, cut off, discontinue, end, expire, finish, issue, lapse, put an end to, result, run out, stop, wind up

termination abortion, cessation, close, completion, conclusion, cut-off point, discontinuation, effect, end, ending, expiry, finale, finis, finish, issue, result, wind-up

terminology argot, cant, jargon, language, lingo (*informal*), nomenclature, patois, phraseology, terms, vocabulary

terminus depot, end of the line, garage, last stop, station

terms 1. language, manner of speaking, phraseology, terminology **2.** conditions, particulars, premises (*Law*), provisions, provisos, qualifications, specifica-

tern *n* a gull-like sea bird with a forked tail and long narrow wings.

ternary *adj* **1** consisting of three items or groups of three items. **2** *Maths* (of a number system) to the base three.

Terpsichorean (turp-sick-or-**ee**-an) *adj Often used facetiously* of or relating to dancing.

Terr. 1 terrace. 2 territory.

terrace *n* **1** a row of houses, usually identical and joined together by common dividing walls, or the street onto which they face. **2** a paved area alongside a building. **3** a horizontal flat area of ground, often one of a series in a slope. **4 the terraces** *or* **terracing** *Brit* a tiered area in a stadium where spectators stand. *~vb* **-racing, -raced 5** to make into terraces.

terraced house *n Brit* a house that is part of a terrace.

terracotta *n* **1** a hard unglazed brownish-red earthenware used for pottery. *~adj* **2** made of terracotta. **3** brownish-orange.

terra firma *n* the ground, as opposed to the sea.

terrain *n* an area of ground, esp. with reference to its physical character: *mountainous terrain.*

terra incognita (**terr**-a in-**kog**-nit-a) *n* an unexplored region.

terrapin *n* a small turtle-like reptile of N America that lives in fresh water and on land.

terrarium *n* **1** an enclosed area or container where small land animals are kept. **2** a glass container in which plants are grown.

terrazzo *n, pl* **-zos** a floor made by setting marble chips into a layer of mortar and polishing the surface.

terrestrial *adj* **1** of the planet earth. **2** of the land as opposed to the sea or air. **3** (of animals and plants) living or growing on the land. **4** *Television* denoting or using a signal sent over land from a transmitter on land, rather than by satellite.

terrible *adj* **1** very serious or extreme: *war is a terrible thing.* **2** *Informal* very bad, unpleasant, or unsatisfactory: *terrible books.* **3** causing fear. **terribly** *adv*

terrier *n* any of several small active breeds of dog, originally trained to hunt animals living underground.

terrific *adj* **1** very great or intense: *a terrific blow on the head.* **2** *Informal* very good; excellent: *a terrific book.* **terrifically** *adv*

terrify *vb* **-fies, -fying, -fied** to frighten greatly. **terrified** *adj* **terrifying** *adj* **terrifyingly** *adv*

terrine (terr-**reen**) *n* **1** an oval earthenware cooking dish with a tightly fitting lid. **2** the food cooked or served in such a dish, esp. pâté.

territorial *adj* **1** of or relating to a territory or territories. **2** of or concerned with the ownership and control of an area of land or water: *a territorial dispute.* **3** (of an animal or bird) establishing and defending an area which it will not let other animals or birds into: *the baboon is a territorial species.* **4** of or relating to a territorial army. **territorially** *adv* **territoriality** *n*

Territorial *n* a member of a Territorial Army.

Territorial Army *n* (in Britain) a reserve army whose members are not full-time soldiers but undergo military training in their spare time so that they can be called upon in an emergency.

territorial waters *pl n* the part of the sea near to a country's coast, which is under the control of the government of that country.

territory *n, pl* **-ries 1** any tract of land; district: *mountainous territory.* **2** the geographical area under the control of a particular government: *the islands are Japanese territory.* **3** an area inhabited and defended by a particular animal or pair of animals. **4** an area of knowledge or experience: *all this is familiar territory to readers of her recent novels.* **5** a country or region under the control of a foreign country: *a French Overseas Territory.* **6** a region of a country, esp. of a federal state, that enjoys less autonomy and a lower status than most constituent parts of the state.

terror *n* **1** very great fear, panic, or dread. **2** a person or thing that inspires great dread. **3** *Informal* a troublesome person, esp. a child.

terrorism *n* the systematic use of violence and intimidation to achieve political ends. **terrorist** *n, adj*

terrorize *or* **-ise** *vb* **-izing, -ized** *or* **-ising, -ised 1** to control or force (someone) to do something by violence, fear, threats, etc.: *he was terrorized into withdrawing his accusations.* **2** to make (someone) very frightened. **terrorization** *or* **-isation** *n* **terrorizer** *or* **-iser** *n*

THESAURUS

tions, stipulations **3.** footing, position, relations, relationship, standing, status **4. come to terms with** be reconciled to, learn to live with

terrible 1. bad, dangerous, desperate, extreme, serious, severe **2.** *informal* abhorrent, abysmal, awful, bad, beastly (*informal*), dire, dreadful, duff (*Brit. informal*), foul, frightful, godawful (*slang*), hateful, hellacious (*U.S. slang*), hideous, loathsome, obnoxious, obscene, odious, offensive, poor, repulsive, revolting, rotten (*informal*), shitty (*taboo slang*), unpleasant, vile **3.** appalling, awful, dread, dreaded, dreadful, fearful, frightful, gruesome, harrowing, horrendous, horrible, horrid, horrifying, monstrous, shocking, terrifying, unspeakable

terribly awfully (*informal*), decidedly, desperately, exceedingly, extremely, gravely, greatly, much, seriously, thoroughly, very

terrific 1. awful, dreadful, enormous, excessive, extreme, fearful, fierce, gigantic, great, huge, intense, severe, terrible, tremendous **2.** *informal* ace (*informal*), amazing, boffo (*slang*), breathtaking, brill (*informal*), brilliant, chillin' (*U.S. slang*), cracking (*Brit. informal*), excellent, fabulous (*informal*), fantastic (*informal*), fine, great (*informal*), jim-dandy (*slang*), magnificent, marvellous, mean (*slang*), outstanding, sensational (*informal*), smashing (*informal*), sovereign, stupendous, super (*informal*), superb, topping (*Brit. slang*), very good, wonderful

terrified alarmed, frightened, frightened out of one's wits, horrified, horror-struck, intimidated, panic-stricken, petrified, scared, scared shitless (*taboo slang*), scared stiff, scared to death, shit-scared (*taboo slang*), shocked, terror-stricken

terrify alarm, fill with terror, frighten, frighten out of one's wits, horrify, intimidate, make one's blood run cold, make one's flesh creep, make one's hair stand on end, petrify, put the fear of God into, scare, scare to death, shock, terrorize

territory 1. area, country, district, land, region, terrain, tract, zone **2.** bailiwick, domain, province, sector, state **3.** domain, patch, turf (*U.S. slang*)

terror 1. alarm, anxiety, dread, fear, fear and trembling, fright, horror, intimidation, panic, shock **2.** bogeyman, bugbear, devil, fiend, monster, scourge

terrorize 1. browbeat, bully, coerce, intimidate, menace, oppress, strong-arm (*informal*), threaten **2.** alarm, fill with terror, frighten, frighten out of one's wits, horrify, inspire panic in, intimidate, make one's blood run cold, make one's flesh creep, make one's hair stand on end, petrify, put the fear of God into, scare, scare to death, shock, strike terror into, terrify

terse 1. aphoristic, brief, clipped, compact, concise,

terry *n* a fabric covered on both sides with small uncut loops, used for towelling and nappies.

terse *adj* **1** neatly brief and concise. **2** curt or abrupt. **tersely** *adv* **terseness** *n*

tertiary (**tur**-shar-ee) *adj* **1** third in degree, order, etc. **2** (of education) at university or college level. **3** (of an industry) involving services, such as transport and financial services, as opposed to manufacture.

Tertiary *adj Geol* of the period of geological time lasting from about 65 million years ago to 600 000 years ago.

Terylene *n Trademark* a synthetic polyester fibre or fabric.

TESL Teaching of English as a Second Language.

TESSA (in Britain) Tax Exempt Special Savings Account.

tessellated *adj* paved or inlaid with a mosaic of small tiles.

tessera *n, pl* **-serae** a small square tile used in mosaics.

test[1] *vb* **1** to try (something) out to ascertain its worth, safety, or endurance: *the company has never tested its products on animals.* **2** to carry out an examination on (a substance, material, or system) in order to discover whether a particular substance, component, or feature is present: *baby foods are regularly tested for pesticides.* **3** to make heavy demands on: *his behaviour really tests my patience.* **4** to achieve a result in a test which indicates the presence or absence of something: *he tested positive for cocaine.* *~n* **5** a method, practice, or examination designed to test a person or thing. **6** a series of questions or problems designed to test a specific skill or knowledge. **7** a chemical reaction or physical procedure for testing the composition or other qualities of a substance. **8** *Sport* short for **Test match. 9 put to the test** to use (something) in order to gauge its usefulness or effectiveness. **testable** *adj* **testing** *adj*

test[2] *n* the hard outer covering of certain invertebrates.

testa (**tess**-ta) *n, pl* **-tae** (-tee) the hard outer layer of a seed.

testaceous (test-**ay**-shuss) *adj Biol* of or having a hard continuous shell.

testament *n* **1** something which provides proof of a fact about someone or something: *the size of the audience was an immediate testament to his appeal.* **2** *Law* a formal statement of how a person wants his or her property to be disposed of after his or her death: *last will and testament.* **testamentary** *adj*

Testament *n* either, of the two main parts of the Bible, the Old Testament or the New Testament.

testate *Law ~adj* **1** having left a legally valid will at death. *~n* **2** a person who dies and leaves a legally valid will. **testacy** *n*

testator (test-**tay**-tor) *or fem* **testatrix** (test-**tay**-triks) *n Law* a person who has made a will, esp. one who has died testate.

test card *n* a complex pattern used to test the characteristics of a television transmission system.

test case *n* a legal action that serves as a precedent in deciding similar succeeding cases.

testicle *n* either of the two male reproductive glands, in most mammals enclosed within the scrotum, that produce spermatozoa.

testify *vb* **-fies, -fying, -fied 1** *Law* to declare or give evidence under oath, esp. in court. **2 testify to** to be evidence of: *a piece of paper testifying to their educational qualifications.*

testimonial *n* **1** a recommendation of the character or worth of a person or thing. **2** a tribute given for services or achievements. *~adj* **3** of a testimony or testimonial: *a testimonial match.*

➤ A *testimonial* is an open letter of recommendation about someone. A *reference* is a confidential report that is not read by the person who is the subject.

testimony *n, pl* **-nies 1** a declaration of truth or fact. **2** *Law* evidence given by a witness, esp. in court under oath. **3** evidence proving or supporting something: *that they are still talking is a testimony to their 20 year friendship.*

testis *n, pl* **-tes** same as **testicle.**

Test match *n* (in various sports, esp. cricket) any of a series of international matches.

testosterone *n* a steroid male sex hormone secreted by the testes.

test paper *n* **1** the question sheet of a test. **2** *Chem* paper impregnated with an indicator for use in chemical tests.

test pilot *n* a pilot who flies aircraft of new design to test their performance in the air.

test tube *n* a cylindrical round-bottomed glass tube open at one end, which is used in scientific experiments.

test-tube baby *n* **1** a fetus that has developed from an ovum fertilized in an artificial womb. **2** a baby conceived by artificial insemination.

testy *adj* **-tier, -tiest** irritable or touchy. **testily** *adv* **testiness** *n*

tetanus *n* an acute infectious disease in which toxins released from a bacterium cause muscular spasms and convulsions.

tetchy *adj* **tetchier, tetchiest** cross, irritable, or touchy. **tetchily** *adv* **tetchiness** *n*

tête-à-tête *n, pl* **-têtes** *or* **-tête 1** a private conversation between two people. *~adv* **2** together in private: *they dined tête-à-tête.*

tether *n* **1** a rope or chain for tying an animal to a fence, post, etc., so that it cannot move away from a particular place. **2 at the end of one's tether** at the limit of one's patience or endurance. *~vb* **3** to tie with a tether.

tetra- *combining form* four: *tetrapod.*

tetrad *n* a group or series of four.

tetraethyl lead *n* a colourless oily insoluble liquid used in petrol to prevent knocking.

tetragon *n* a shape with four angles and four sides. **tetragonal** *adj*

tetrahedron (tet-ra-**heed**-ron) *n, pl* **-drons** *or* **-dra** a

THESAURUS

condensed, crisp, epigrammatic, laconic, neat, pithy, sententious, short, succinct, summary, to the point **2.** abrupt, brusque, curt, short, snappy

test 1. *vb.* analyse, assay, assess, check, examine, experiment, investigate, prove, put to the proof, put to the test, research, try, try out, verify, work over **2.** *n.* analysis, assessment, attempt, check, evaluation, examination, investigation, probation, proof, research, trial

testament 1. attestation, demonstration, evidence, exemplification, proof, testimony, tribute, witness **2.** last wishes, will

testify affirm, assert, attest, bear witness, certify, corroborate, declare, depose (*Law*), give testimony, show, state, swear, vouch, witness

testimonial certificate, character, commendation, credential, endorsement, recommendation, reference

testimony 1. affidavit, affirmation, attestation, avowal, confirmation, corroboration, declaration,

solid figure with four triangular plane faces. **tetrahedral** *adj*

tetralogy *n, pl* **-gies** a series of four related books, dramas, operas, etc.

tetrameter (tet-**tram**-it-er) *n* **1** *Prosody* a line of verse consisting of four metrical feet. **2** verse consisting of such lines.

Teuton (**tew**-tonn) *n* **1** a member of an ancient Germanic people of N Europe. **2** a member of any people speaking a Germanic language, esp. a German. *~adj* **3** Teutonic.

Teutonic (tew-**tonn**-ik) *adj* **1** characteristic of or relating to the Germans. **2** of the ancient Teutons.

Tex-Mex *adj* **1** combining elements of Texan and Mexican culture. *~n* **2** Tex-Mex music or cooking.

text *n* **1** the main body of a printed or written work as distinct from items such as notes or illustrations. **2** any written material, such as words displayed on a visual display unit. **3** the written version of the words of a speech, broadcast or recording: *an advance text of the remarks the president will deliver tonight.* **4** a short passage of the Bible used as a starting point for a sermon. **5** a book required as part of a course of study: *shelves full of sociology texts.*

textbook *n* **1** a book of facts about a subject used by someone who is studying that subject. *~adj* **2** perfect or exemplary: *a textbook example of an emergency descent.*

textile *n* **1** any fabric or cloth, esp. a woven one. *~adj* **2** of or relating to fabrics or their production: *the world textile market.*

textual *adj* of, based on, or relating to, a text or texts. **textually** *adv*

texture *n* **1** the structure, appearance, and feel of a substance: *curtains of many textures and colours.* **2** the overall sound of a piece of music, resulting from the way the different instrumental parts in it are combined: *a big orchestra weaving rich textures.* *~vb* **-turing, -tured 3** to give a distinctive texture to (something). **textural** *adj*

TGV *n* (in France) a high-speed passenger train.

TGWU Transport and General Workers Union.

Th *Chem* thorium.

Thai *adj* **1** of Thailand. *~n* **2** (*pl* **Thais** *or* **Thai**) a person from Thailand. **3** the main language of Thailand.

thalidomide (thal-**lid**-oh-mide) *n* a drug formerly used as a sedative and hypnotic but withdrawn from use when found to cause abnormalities in developing fetuses.

thallium *n Chem* a soft highly toxic white metallic element. Symbol: Tl

than *conj, prep* **1** used to introduce the second element of a comparison, the first element of which expresses difference: *men are less observant than women and children.* **2** used to state a number, quantity, or value in approximate terms by contrasting it with another number, quantity, or value: *temperatures lower than 25 degrees.* **3** used after the adverbs *rather* and *sooner* to introduce a rejected alternative: *fruit is examined by hand, rather than by faster but less fussy machines.*

thane *n* **1** (in Anglo-Saxon England) a nobleman who held land from the king or from a superior nobleman in return for certain services. **2** (in medieval Scotland) a person of rank holding land from the king.

thank *vb* **1** to convey feelings of gratitude to: *he thanked the nursing staff for saving his life.* **2** to hold responsible: *he has his father to thank for his familiarity with the film world.* **3 thank you** a polite response or expression of gratitude. **4 thank goodness, thank heavens** *or* **thank God** an exclamation of relief.

➤ When *thank you* is used to express gratitude it should be written as two words: *Thank you for the gift.* When it is used as an adjective, use a hyphen: *a thank-you note.*

thankful *adj* grateful and appreciative. **thankfully** *adv*

thankless *adj* unrewarding or unappreciated: *she took on the thankless task of organizing the office Xmas lunch.* **thanklessly** *adv* **thanklessness** *n*

thanks *pl n* **1** an expression of appreciation or gratitude. **2 thanks to** because of: *the birth went very smoothly, thanks to the help of the GHQ medical officer.* *~interj* **3** *Informal* an exclamation expressing gratitude.

thanksgiving *n* a formal public expression of thanks to God.

Thanksgiving Day *n* (in North America) an annual holiday celebrated on the fourth Thursday of November in the United States and on the second Monday of October in Canada.

that *adj* **1** used preceding a noun that has been mentioned or is already familiar: *he'd have to give up on that idea.* **2** used preceding a noun that denotes something more remote: *that book on the top shelf.* *~pron* **3** used to denote something already mentioned or understood: *that's right.* **4** used to denote a more remote person or thing: *is that him over there?* **5** used to introduce a restrictive relative clause: *a problem that has to be overcome.* **6 and all that** *or* **and that** *Informal* and similar or related things: *import cutting and all that.* **7 that is a** to be precise. **b** in other words. **8 that's that** there is no more to be said or done. *~conj* **9** used to introduce a noun clause: *he denied that the country was suffering from famine.* **10** used, usually after *so,* to introduce a clause of purpose: *he turns his face away from her so that she shall not see his tears.* **11** used to introduce a clause of result: *a scene so sickening and horrible that it is impossible to describe it.* *~adv* **12** Also: **all that** *Informal* very or particularly: *the fines imposed have not been that large.*

➤ The relative pronoun *that* may often be used interchangeably with *which* in defining clauses: *the coat that/which you bought.* Some people, however, prefer to reserve *which* for the type of clause (called nondefining) that contains explanations and amplifications and is divided by a comma from the rest of the sentence: *he found the book, which was a start.*

thatch *n* **1** Also called: **thatching** a roofing material that consists of straw or reeds. **2** a roof made of such a material. **3** a mass of thick untidy hair on someone's

THESAURUS

deposition, evidence, information, statement, submission **2.** corroboration, demonstration, evidence, indication, manifestation, proof, support, verification

text 1. body, contents, main body, matter **2.** wording, words **3.** lesson, paragraph, passage, reading, sentence, verse **4.** reader, reference book, source, textbook

texture character, composition, consistency, constitution, fabric, feel, grain, make, quality, structure, surface, tissue, weave

thank express gratitude, say thank you, show gratitude, show one's appreciation

thankful appreciative, beholden, grateful, indebted, obliged, pleased, relieved

thankless fruitless, unappreciated, unprofitable, unrewarding

head. ~*vb* **4** to cover with thatch. **thatched** *adj* **thatcher** *n*

thaw *vb* **1** to melt or cause to melt: *snow thawing in the gutter.* **2** (of frozen food) to become or cause to become unfrozen; defrost. **3** (of weather) to be warm enough to cause ice or snow to melt: *it's not freezing, it's thawing again.* **4** to become more relaxed or friendly: *only with Llewelyn did he thaw, let his defences down.* ~*n* **5** the act or process of thawing. **6** a spell of relatively warm weather, causing snow or ice to melt.

the[1] *adj (definite article)* **1** used preceding a noun that has been previously specified or is a matter of common knowledge: *those involved in the search.* **2** used to indicate a particular person or object: *the man called Frank turned to look at it.* **3** used preceding certain nouns associated with one's culture, society, or community: *to comply with the law.* **4** used preceding an adjective that is functioning as a collective noun: *the unemployed.* **5** used preceding titles and certain proper nouns: *the Middle East.* **6** used preceding an adjective or noun in certain names or titles: *Alexander the Great.* **7** used preceding a noun to make it refer to its class as a whole: *cultivation of the coca plant.* **8** used instead of *my, your, her,* etc., with parts of the body: *swelling of tissues in the brain.* **9** the best or most remarkable: *it's THE place in town for good Mexican food.*

the[2] *adv* used in front of each of two things which are being compared to show how they increase or decrease in relation to each other: *the smaller the baby, the lower its chances of survival.*

theatre *or US* **theater** *n* **1** a building designed for the performance of plays, operas, etc. **2** a large room or hall with tiered seats for an audience: *a lecture theatre.* **3** a room in a hospital equipped for surgical operations. **4 the theatre** drama and acting in general. **5** a region in which a war or conflict takes place: *a potential theatre of war close to Russian borders.* **6** *US, Austral, & NZ* same as **cinema** (sense 1).

theatrical *adj* **1** of or relating to the theatre or dramatic performances. **2** exaggerated and affected in manner or behaviour. **theatricality** *n* **theatrically** *adv*

theatricals *pl n* dramatic performances, esp. as given by amateurs.

thee *pron Old-fashioned* the objective form of **thou**[1].

theft *n* **1** the act or an instance of stealing: *he reported the theft of his passport.* **2** the crime of stealing: *he had a number of convictions for theft.*

their *adj* of or associated with them: *owning their own land; two girls on their way to school.*

➤ Be careful not to confuse *their* with *there. Their* is used for possession: *their new baby. There* indicates place and has a similar "-ere" spelling pattern to *here* and *where.*

theirs *pron* **1** something or someone belonging to or associated with them: *it was his fault, not theirs.* **2 of theirs** belonging to them.

theism (**thee**-iz-zum) *n* **1** belief in one God as the creator of everything in the universe. **2** belief in the existence of a God or gods. **theist** *n, adj* **theistic** *adj*

them *pron (objective)* refers to things or people other than the speaker or people addressed: *I want you to give this to them.*

➤ *Them* may be used after a singular to avoid the clumsy *him or her: If you see a person looking lost, help them.*

theme *n* **1** the main idea or topic in a discussion or lecture. **2** (in literature, music, or art) an idea, image, or motif, repeated or developed throughout a work or throughout an artist's career. **3** *Music* a group of notes forming a recognizable melodic unit, used as the basis of part or all of a composition. **4** a short essay, esp. one set as an exercise for a student. **thematic** *adj* **thematically** *adv*

theme park *n* an area planned as a leisure attraction in which all the displays and activities are based on a particular theme, story, or idea: *a Wild West theme park.*

theme tune *or* **theme song** *n* a tune or song used to introduce or identify a television or radio programme or performer.

themselves *pron* **1 a** the reflexive form of *they* or *them: two men barricaded themselves into a cell.* **b** used for emphasis: *among the targets were police officers themselves.* **2** their normal or usual selves: *they don't seem themselves these days.*

then *adv* **1** at that time: *he was then at the height of his sporting career.* **2** after that: *let's eat first and then we can explore the town.* **3** in that case: *then why did he work for you?* ~*pron* **4** that time: *since then the list of grievances has steadily grown.* ~*adj* **5** existing or functioning at that time: *the then Defence Minister.*

thence *adv Formal* **1** from that place: *the train went south into Switzerland, and thence on to Italy.* **2** for that reason; therefore.

thenceforth *or* **thenceforward** *adv Formal* from that time on.

theocracy *n, pl* **-cies** **1** government by a god or by priests. **2** a community under such government. **theocrat** *n* **theocratic** *adj* **theocratically** *adv*

theodolite (thee-**odd**-oh-lite) *n* an instrument used in surveying for measuring horizontal and vertical angles.

theologian *n* a person versed in the study of theology.

theology *n, pl* **-gies** **1** the systematic study of religions and religious beliefs. **2** a specific system, form, or branch of this study: *Muslim theology.* **theological** *adj* **theologically** *adv*

theorem *n* a proposition, esp. in maths, that can be proved by reasoning from the basic principles of a subject.

theoretical *or* **theoretic** *adj* **1** based on or concerned with the ideas and abstract principles relating to a particular subject rather than its practical uses: *theoretical physics.* **2** existing in theory but perhaps not in reality: *the secret service is under the theoretical control of the government.* **theoretically** *adv*

theoretician *n* a person who develops or studies the theory of a subject rather than its practical aspects.

theorize *or* **-rise** *vb* **-rizing, -rized** *or* **-rising,**

THESAURUS

thanks **1.** acknowledgment, appreciation, Brownie points, credit, gratefulness, gratitude, recognition, thanksgiving **2. thanks to** as a result of, because of, by reason of, due to, owing to, through

thaw defrost, dissolve, liquefy, melt, soften, unfreeze, warm

theatrical **1.** dramatic, Thespian **2.** actorly, actressy, affected, artificial, camp (*informal*), ceremonious, dramatic, exaggerated, hammy (*informal*), histrionic, mannered, melodramatic, overdone, showy, stagy, unreal

theft embezzlement, fraud, larceny, pilfering, purloining, rip-off (*slang*), robbery, stealing, swindling, thievery, thieving

theme **1.** argument, burden, idea, keynote, matter, subject, subject matter, text, topic **2.** leitmotiv, motif, recurrent image, unifying idea **3.** composition, dissertation, essay, exercise, paper

theological divine, doctrinal, ecclesiastical, religious

-rised to produce or use theories; speculate. **theorist** *n*

theory *n, pl* **-ries** **1** a set of ideas, based on evidence and careful reasoning, which offers an explanation of how something works or why something happens, but has not been completely proved: *the theory of cosmology.* **2** the ideas and abstract knowledge relating to something: *political theory.* **3** an idea or opinion: *it's only a theory, admittedly, but I think it's worth pursuing.* **4 in theory** in an ideal or hypothetical situation: *in theory, the tax is supposed to limit inflation.*

theosophy *n* a religious or philosophical system claiming to be based on an intuitive insight into the divine nature. **theosophical** *adj* **theosophist** *n*

therapeutic (ther-rap-**pew**-tik) *adj* of or relating to the treatment and cure of disease. **therapeutically** *adv*

therapeutics *n* the branch of medicine concerned with the treatment of disease.

therapy *n, pl* **-pies** the treatment of physical, mental, or social disorders or disease. **therapist** *n*

there *adv* **1** in, at, or to that place or position: *he won't be there.* **2** in that respect: *you're right there.* **3 there and then** immediately and without delay: *he walked out there and then.* ~*adj* **4 not all there** *Informal* mentally defective or silly. ~*pron* **5** that place: *to return from there.* **6** used as a grammatical subject when the true subject follows the verb, esp. the verb "to be": *there are no children in the house.* **7 so there!** an exclamation, used esp. by children, that usually follows a declaration of refusal or defiance: *you can't come, so there!* **8 there you are** *or* **go a** an expression used when handing a person something. **b** an exclamation of satisfaction or vindication. ~*interj* **9** an expression of sympathy, for example when consoling a child: *there, there, pet!*

➤ Be careful not to confuse *there* with *their. There* indicates place and has a similar "-ere" spelling pattern to *here* and *where. Their* indicates possession: *their new baby.*

thereabouts *or US* **thereabout** *adv* near that place, time, amount, etc.: *meet me at three o'clock or thereabouts.*

thereafter *adv Formal* from that time onwards.

thereby *adv Formal* by that means or consequently.

therefore *adv* for that reason: *the training is long, and therefore expensive.*

therein *adv Formal* in or into that place or thing.

thereof *adv Formal* of or concerning that or it.

thereto *adv Formal* **1** to that or it. **2** Also: **thereunto** in addition to that.

thereupon *adv Formal* immediately after that; at that point.

therm *n Brit* a unit of heat equal to $1.055\ 056 \times 10^8$ joules.

thermal *adj* **1** of, caused by, or generating heat. **2** hot or warm: *thermal springs.* **3** (of garments) specially made so as to have exceptional heat-retaining qualities: *thermal underwear.* ~*n* **4** a column of rising air caused by uneven heating of the land surface, and used by gliders and birds to gain height.

thermionic valve *or esp US & Canad* **thermionic tube** *n* an electronic valve in which electrons are emitted from a heated rather than a cold cathode.

thermistor (therm-**mist**-or) *n Physics* a metal-oxide rod whose resistance falls as temperature rises, used in electronic circuits and as a thermometer.

thermocouple *n* a device for measuring temperature, consisting of a pair of wires of different metals joined at both ends.

thermodynamics *n* the branch of physical science concerned with the relationship between heat and other forms of energy.

thermoelectric *or* **thermoelectrical** *adj* of or relating to the conversion of heat energy to electrical energy.

thermometer *n* an instrument used to measure temperature, esp. one in which a thin column of liquid, such as mercury, expands and contracts within a sealed tube marked with a temperature scale.

thermonuclear *adj* **1** (of a nuclear reaction) involving a nuclear fusion reaction of a type which occurs at very high temperatures. **2** (of a weapon) giving off energy as the result of a thermonuclear reaction. **3** involving thermonuclear weapons.

thermoplastic *adj* **1** (of a material, esp. a synthetic plastic) becoming soft when heated and rehardening on cooling. ~*n* **2** a synthetic plastic or resin, such as polystyrene.

Thermos *or* **Thermos flask** *n Trademark* a type of stoppered vacuum flask used to preserve the temperature of its contents.

thermosetting *adj* (of a material, esp. a synthetic plastic) hardening permanently after one application of heat and pressure.

thermostat *n* a device which automatically regulates the temperature of central heating, an oven, etc., by switching it off or on when it reaches or drops below a particular temperature. **thermostatic** *adj* **thermostatically** *adv*

thesaurus (thiss-**sore**-uss) *n, pl* **-ruses** *or* **-ri** a book containing lists of synonyms and related words.

these *adj, pron* the plural of **this**.

thesis (**theess**-siss) *n, pl* **-ses** (-seez) **1** a written work resulting from original research, esp. one submitted for a higher degree in a university. **2** an opinion supported by reasoned argument: *it is the author's thesis that Britain has yet to come to terms with the loss of its Empire.* **3** *Logic* an unproved statement put forward as a premise in an argument.

Thespian *n* **1** *Often facetious* an actor or actress. ~*adj* **2** of or relating to drama and the theatre.

they *pron* (*subjective*) refers to: **1** people or things other than the speaker or people addressed: *they both giggled.* **2** people in general: *they say he beats his wife.* **3** *Informal* an individual person, whose sex is either not known or not regarded as important: *someone could have a nasty accident if they tripped over that.*

➤ *They* may be used after a singular to avoid the clumsy *he or she: If a person is born gloomy, they cannot help it.*

thiamine *or* **thiamin** *n* vitamin B_1, a vitamin found

THESAURUS

theorem deduction, dictum, formula, hypothesis, principle, proposition, rule, statement

theoretical **1.** abstract, academic, ideal, pure **2.** conjectural, hypothetical, notional, speculative

theory **1.** assumption, conjecture, guess, hypothesis, presumption, speculation, supposition, surmise, thesis **2.** philosophy, plan, proposal, scheme, system

therapeutic beneficial, corrective, curative, good, healing, remedial, restorative, salubrious, salutary

therapy cure, healing, remedial treatment, remedy, treatment

therefore accordingly, as a result, consequently, ergo, for that reason, hence, so, then, thence, thus, whence

thesis **1.** composition, disquisition, dissertation,

in the outer coat of rice and other grains, a deficiency of which leads to nervous disorders and to beriberi.

thick *adj* **1** having a relatively great distance between opposite surfaces: *thick slices.* **2** having a specified distance between opposite surfaces: *fifty metres thick.* **3** having a dense consistency: *thick fog.* **4** consisting of a lot of things grouped closely together: *thick forest.* **5** (of clothes) made of heavy cloth or wool: *a thick jumper.* **6** *Informal* stupid, slow, or insensitive. **7** (of an accent) very noticeable: *each word was pronounced in a thick Dutch accent.* **8** Also: **thick as thieves** *Informal* very friendly. **9 a bit thick** *Brit informal* unfair or unreasonable: *£2 an hour, that's a bit thick!* **10 thick with a** covered with a lot of: *glass panels thick with dust.* **b** (of a voice) throaty and hard to make out: *his voice was thick with emotion.* ~*adv* **11** in order to produce something thick: *the machine sliced the potatoes too thick.* **12 lay it on thick** *Informal* **a** to exaggerate a story. **b** to flatter someone excessively. **13 thick and fast** quickly and in large numbers: *theories were flying thick and fast.* ~*n* **14 the thick** the most intense or active part: *in the thick of the fighting.* **15 through thick and thin** in good times and bad. **thickly** *adv*

thicken *vb* **1** to make or become thick or thicker. **2** to become more complicated: *the plot thickens.* **thickener** *n*

thickening *n* **1** something added to a liquid to thicken it. **2** a thickened part or piece.

thicket *n* a dense growth of small trees or shrubs.

thickhead *n Slang* a stupid or ignorant person. **thickheaded** *adj*

thickness *n* **1** the state or quality of being thick. **2** the dimension through an object, as opposed to length or width. **3** a layer: *several thicknesses of brown paper.*

thickset *adj* **1** stocky in build. **2** planted or placed close together.

thick-skinned *adj* insensitive to criticism or hints; not easily upset.

thief *n, pl* **thieves** a person who steals something from another. **thievish** *adj*

thieve *vb* **thieving, thieved** to steal other people's possessions. **thieving** *adj*

thigh *n* the part of the human leg between the hip and the knee.

thighbone *n* same as **femur.**

thimble *n* a small metal or plastic cap used to protect the end of the finger from the needle when sewing.

thin *adj* **thinner, thinnest 1** having a relatively small distance between opposite surfaces: *a thin mattress.* **2** much narrower than it is long: *push a thin stick up the pipe in order to clear it.* **3** (of a person or animal) having no excess body fat. **4** made up of only a few, widely separated, people or things: *thin hair.* **5** not dense: *a thin film of dust.* **6** unconvincing because badly thought out or badly presented: *the evidence against him was extremely thin.* **7** (of a voice) high-pitched and not very loud: *a thin squeaky voice.* ~*adv* **8** in order to produce something thin: *roll the dough very thin.* ~*vb* **thinning, thinned 9** to make or become thin or sparse. **thinly** *adv* **thinness** *n*

thine *Old-fashioned* ~*adj* **1** (*preceding a vowel*) of or associated with you (thou): *if thine eye offend thee, pluck it out!* ~*pron* **2** something belonging to you (thou): *the victory shall be thine.*

thing *n* **1** any physical object that is not alive: *there are very few jobs left where people actually make things.* **2** an object, fact, circumstance, or concept considered as being a separate entity: *that would be a terrible thing to do.* **3** an object or entity that cannot or need not be precisely named: *squares and circles and things.* **4** *Informal* a person or animal: *pretty little thing, isn't she?* **5** a possession, article of clothing, etc.: *have you brought your swimming things?* **6** *Informal* a preoccupation or obsession: *they have this thing about policemen.* **7 do one's own thing** to engage in an activity or mode of behaviour satisfying to one's personality. **8 make a thing of** to exaggerate the importance of. **9 the thing** the latest fashion.

thingumabob *or* **thingamabob** *n Informal* a per-

THESAURUS

essay, monograph, paper, treatise **2.** contention, hypothesis, idea, line of argument, opinion, proposal, proposition, theory, view **3.** assumption, postulate (*formal*), premise, proposition, statement, supposition, surmise

thick *adj.* **1.** broad, bulky, deep, fat, solid, substantial, wide **2.** close, clotted, coagulated, compact, concentrated, condensed, crowded, deep, dense, heavy, impenetrable, opaque **3.** abundant, brimming, bristling, bursting, chock-a-block, chock-full, covered, crawling, frequent, full, numerous, packed, replete, swarming, teeming **4.** *informal* blockheaded, braindead (*informal*), brainless, dense, dim-witted (*informal*), dopey (*slang*), dozy (*Brit. slang*), dull, moronic, obtuse, slow, slow-witted, stupid, thickheaded **5.** broad, decided, distinct, marked, pronounced, rich, strong **6.** *informal* buddy-buddy (*slang, chiefly U.S. & Canad.*), chummy (*informal*), close, confidential, devoted, familiar, friendly, hand in glove, inseparable, intimate, matey *or* maty (*Brit. informal*), on good terms, pally (*informal*), palsy-walsy (*informal*), well in (*informal*) **7. a bit thick** *Brit. informal* excessive, over the score (*informal*), too much, unfair, unjust, unreasonable ~*n.* **8. the thick** centre, heart, middle, midst

thicken cake, clot, coagulate, condense, congeal, deepen, gel *or* jell, set

thickset 1. beefy (*informal*), brawny, bulky, burly, heavy, muscular, powerfully built, stocky, strong, stubby, sturdy, well-built **2.** closely packed, dense, densely planted, solid, thick

thick-skinned callous, hard-boiled (*informal*), hardened, impervious, insensitive, stolid, tough, unfeeling, unsusceptible

thief bandit, burglar, crook (*informal*), embezzler, housebreaker, larcenist, mugger (*informal*), pickpocket, pilferer, plunderer, purloiner, robber, shoplifter, stealer, swindler

thieve blag (*slang*), embezzle, filch, knock off (*slang*), lift (*informal*), misappropriate, nick (*slang, chiefly Brit.*), peculate (*literary*), pilfer, pinch (*informal*), plunder, poach, purloin, rip off (*slang*), rob, run off with, snitch (*slang*), steal, swindle, swipe (*slang*)

thin *adj.* **1.** attenuated, fine, narrow, threadlike **2.** bony, emaciated, lank, lanky, lean, meagre, scraggy, scrawny, skeletal, skinny, slender, slight, slim, spare, spindly, thin as a rake, undernourished, underweight **3.** deficient, meagre, scanty, scarce, scattered, skimpy, sparse, wispy **4.** dilute, diluted, rarefied, runny, watery, weak **5.** feeble, flimsy, inadequate, insufficient, lame, poor, scant, scanty, shallow, slight, superficial, unconvincing, unsubstantial, weak ~*vb.* **6.** attenuate, cut back, dilute, diminish, prune, rarefy, reduce, refine, trim, water down, weaken, weed out

thing 1. article, item, object, something **2.** act, deed, event, eventuality, feat, happening, incident, occurrence, phenomenon, proceeding **3.** *usually plural* baggage, belongings, bits and pieces, clobber (*Brit. slang*), clothes, effects, equipment, gear, goods, impedimenta, luggage, odds and ends, paraphernalia, possessions,

son or thing the name of which is unknown, temporarily forgotten, or deliberately overlooked. Also: **thingumajig, thingamajig,** *or* **thingummy**

think *vb* **thinking, thought 1** to consider, judge, or believe: *I think that it is scandalous.* **2** to make use of the mind, for example in order to make a decision: *I'll need to think about what I'm going to do.* **3** to engage in conscious thought: *that made me think.* **4** to be considerate enough or remember (to do something): *no other company had thought to bring high tech down to the user.* **5 think much** *or* **a lot of** to have a favourable opinion of: *I don't think much of the new design.* **6 think of a** to remember or recollect: *I couldn't think of your surname.* **b** to conceive of or formulate: *for a long time he couldn't think of a response.* **7 think twice** to consider something carefully before making a decision. *~n* **8** *Informal* a careful open-minded assessment: *she had a long hard think.* **thinker** *n*

thinking *n* **1** opinion or judgment: *contrary to all fashionable thinking.* **2** the process of thought. *~adj* **3** using intelligent thought: *the thinking man's sport.*

think over *vb* to ponder or consider.

think-tank *n Informal* a group of experts employed to study specific problems.

think up *vb* to invent or devise.

thinner *n* a solvent, such as turpentine, added to paint or varnish to dilute it.

thin-skinned *adj* sensitive to criticism or hints; easily upset.

third *adj* **1** of or being number three in a series. **2** rated, graded, or ranked below the second level. **3** denoting the third lowest forward gear in a motor vehicle. *~n* **4** one of three equal parts of something. **5** the fraction equal to one divided by three ($\frac{1}{3}$). **6** the third lowest forward gear in a motor vehicle. **7** *Brit* an honours degree of the third and usually the lowest class. **8** *Music* the interval between one note and the note four semitones (**major third**) or three semitones (**minor third**) higher or lower than it. *~adv* **9** Also: **thirdly** in the third place.

third class *n* **1** the class or grade next in value, rank, or quality to the second. *~adj* **third-class 2** of the class or grade next in value, rank, or quality to the second.

third degree *n Informal* torture or bullying, esp. as used to extort confessions or information.

third-degree burn *n* a burn in which both the surface and the underlying layers of the skin are destroyed.

third man *n Cricket* a fielding position on the off side, near the boundary behind the batsman's wicket.

third party *n* **1** a person who is involved in an event, legal proceeding, agreement, or other transaction only by chance or indirectly. *~adj* **2** *Insurance* providing protection against liability caused by accidental injury or death of other people: *third-party cover.*

third person *n* the form of a pronoun or verb used to refer to something or someone other than the speaker or the person or people being addressed.

third-rate *adj* mediocre or inferior.

Third Reich *n* See **Reich.**

Third World *n* the developing countries of Africa, Asia, and Latin America collectively.

thirst *n* **1** a desire to drink, accompanied by a feeling of dryness in the mouth and throat. **2** a craving or yearning: *a thirst for knowledge.* *~vb* **3** to feel a thirst.

thirsty *adj* **thirstier, thirstiest 1** feeling a desire to drink. **2** causing thirst: *morris dancing is thirsty work.* **3 thirsty for** feeling an eager desire for: *thirsty for information.* **thirstily** *adv*

thirteen *n* **1** the cardinal number that is the sum of ten and three. **2** a numeral, 13 or XIII, representing this number. **3** something representing or consisting of thirteen units. *~adj* **4** amounting to thirteen: *thirteen people.* **thirteenth** *adj, n*

thirty *n, pl* **-ties 1** the cardinal number that is the product of ten and three. **2** a numeral, 30 or XXX, representing this number. **3** something representing or consisting of thirty units. *~adj* **4** amounting to thirty: *thirty miles.* **thirtieth** *adj, n*

Thirty-nine Articles *pl n* a set of formulas defining the doctrinal position of the Church of England.

this *adj* **1** used preceding a noun referring to something or someone that is closer: *on this side of the Channel.* **2** used preceding a noun that has just been mentioned or is understood: *this text has two chief goals.* **3** used to refer to something about to be mentioned: *NPR's Anne Garrels has this report.* **4** used to refer to the present time or occasion: *this week's edition of the newspaper.* **5** *Informal* used instead of *a* or *the* in telling a story: *see, it's about this bird who fancies you.* *~pron* **6** used to denote a person or thing that is relatively close: *black coral like this.* **7** used to denote something already mentioned or understood: *this didn't seem fair to me.* **8** used to denote something about to be mentioned: *just say this: collect Standish from the top of the fire escape.* **9** the present time or occasion: *after this it was impossible to talk to him*

THESAURUS

stuff **4.** *informal* attitude, bee in one's bonnet, fetish, fixation, hang-up (*informal*), *idée fixe,* mania, obsession, phobia, preoccupation, quirk

think *vb.* **1.** believe, conceive, conclude, consider, deem, esteem, estimate, guess (*informal, chiefly U.S. & Canad.*), hold, imagine, judge, reckon, regard, suppose, surmise **2.** brood, cerebrate (*usually facetious*), chew over (*informal*), cogitate, consider, contemplate, deliberate, have in mind, meditate, mull over, muse, ponder, reason, reflect, revolve, ruminate, turn over in one's mind, weigh up **3. think much** *or* **a lot of** admire, attach importance to, esteem, have a high opinion of, hold in high regard, rate (*slang*), respect, set store by, think highly of, value **4. think of** call to mind, recall, recollect, remember *~n.* **5.** *informal* assessment, consideration, contemplation, deliberation, look, reflection

thinker intellect (*informal*), mastermind, philosopher, sage, theorist, wise man

thinking 1. *n.* assessment, conclusions, conjecture, idea, judgment, opinion, outlook, philosophy, position, reasoning, theory, thoughts, view **2.** *adj.* contemplative, cultured, intelligent, meditative, philosophical, rational, reasoning, reflective, sophisticated, thoughtful

think over chew over (*informal*), consider, consider the pros and cons of, contemplate, give thought to, mull over, ponder, reflect upon, turn over in one's mind, weigh up

think up come up with, concoct, contrive, create, devise, dream up, imagine, improvise, invent, manufacture, visualize

thin-skinned easily hurt, hypersensitive, quick to take offence, sensitive, soft, susceptible, tender, touchy, vulnerable

third-rate bad, cheap-jack, chickenshit (*U.S. slang*), duff (*Brit. informal*), indifferent, inferior, low-grade, mediocre, of a sort *or* of sorts, poor, poor-quality, ropy *or* ropey (*Brit. informal*), shoddy

thirst *n.* **1.** craving to drink, dryness, thirstiness **2.** appetite, craving, desire, eagerness, hankering, hunger, keenness, longing, lust, passion, yearning, yen (*informal*)

about his feelings. **10 this and that** various unspecified and trivial events or facts.

thistle *n* a plant with prickly-edged leaves, dense flower heads, and feathery hairs on the seeds. **thistly** *adj*

thistledown *n* the mass of feathery plumed seeds produced by a thistle.

thither *adv Formal* to or towards that place.

tho *or* **tho'** *conj, adv US or poetic* same as **though.**

thole[1] *or* **tholepin** *n* one of a pair of wooden pins set upright in the gunwale on either side of a rowing boat to serve as a fulcrum in rowing.

thole[2] *vb* **tholing, tholed** *Scot & N English* to bear or put up with.

thong *n* **1** a thin strip of leather or other material. **2** *US, Canad, & Austral* same as **flip-flop. 3** a skimpy article of beachwear consisting of thin strips of leather or cloth attached to a piece of material that covers the genitals while leaving the buttocks bare.

thorax (**thaw**-racks) *n, pl* **thoraxes** *or* **thoraces** (**thaw**-rass-seez) **1** the part of the human body enclosed by the ribs. **2** the part of an insect's body between the head and abdomen. **thoracic** *adj*

thorium *n Chem* a silvery-white radioactive metallic element. It is used in electronic equipment and as a nuclear power source. Symbol: Th

thorn *n* **1** a sharp pointed woody projection from a stem or leaf. **2** any of various trees or shrubs having thorns, esp. the hawthorn. **3 a thorn in one's side** *or* **flesh** a source of irritation: *he was sufficiently bright at school to become a thorn in the side of his maths teacher.* **thornless** *adj*

thorny *adj* **thornier, thorniest 1** covered with thorns. **2** difficult or unpleasant: *a thorny issue.*

thorough *adj* **1** carried out completely and carefully: *he needs a thorough checkup by the doctor.* **2** (of a person) painstakingly careful: *he is very thorough if rather unimaginative.* **3** great in extent or degree; utter: *a thorough disgrace.* **thoroughly** *adv* **thoroughness** *n*

thoroughbred *adj* **1** obtained through successive generations of selective breeding: *thoroughbred horses.* ~*n* **2** a pedigree animal, esp. a horse.

thoroughfare *n* a way through from one place to another: *the great thoroughfare from the Castle to the Palace of Holyrood.*

thoroughgoing *adj* **1** extremely thorough. **2** absolute or complete: *a thoroughgoing hatred.*

those *adj, pron* the plural of **that.**

thou[1] *pron Old-fashioned* same as **you:** used when talking to one person.

thou[2] *n, pl* **thou** *Informal* **1** one thousandth of an inch. **2** a thousand.

though *conj* **1** despite the fact that: *he was smiling with relief and happiness though the tears still flowed down his cheeks.* ~*adv* **2** nevertheless or however: *he can't dance – he sings well, though.*

thought *vb* **1** the past of **think.** ~*n* **2** the act or process of thinking. **3** a concept or idea. **4** ideas typical of a particular time or place: *the development of Western intellectual thought.* **5** detailed consideration: *he appeared to give some sort of thought to the question.* **6** an intention, hope, or reason for doing something: *his first thought was to call the guard and have the man arrested.*

thoughtful *adj* **1** considerate in the treatment of other people. **2** showing careful thought: *a thoughtful and scholarly book.* **3** quiet, serious, and deep in thought: *she looked thoughtful.* **thoughtfully** *adv* **thoughtfulness** *n*

thoughtless *adj* not considerate of the feelings of other people. **thoughtlessly** *adv* **thoughtlessness** *n*

thousand *n, pl* **-sands** *or* **-sand 1** the cardinal number that is the product of ten and one hundred. **2** a numeral, 1000 or 10^3, representing this number. **3** a very large but unspecified number: *thousands of bees swarmed out of the hive.* **4** something representing or consisting of 1000 units. ~*adj* **5** amounting to a thousand: *a thousand members.* **thousandth** *adj, n*

thrall *n* the state of being completely in the power of, or spellbound by, a person or thing: *he was held in thrall by her almost supernatural beauty.*

thrash *vb* **1** to beat (someone), esp. with a stick or whip. **2** to defeat totally: *the All Blacks thrashed Eng-*

THESAURUS

thirsty thirsty for athirst, avid, burning, craving, desirous, dying, eager, greedy, hankering, hungry, itching, longing, lusting, thirsting, yearning

thorn 1. barb, prickle, spike, spine **2. thorn in one's side** *or* **flesh** affliction, annoyance, bane, bother, curse, hassle (*informal*), irritant, irritation, nuisance, pest, plague, scourge, torment, torture, trouble

thorny 1. barbed, bristling with thorns, bristly, pointed, prickly, sharp, spiky, spinous, spiny **2.** awkward, difficult, harassing, hard, irksome, problematic(al), sticky (*informal*), ticklish, tough, troublesome, trying, unpleasant, upsetting, vexatious, worrying

thorough 1. all-embracing, all-inclusive, assiduous, careful, complete, comprehensive, conscientious, efficient, exhaustive, full, in-depth, intensive, leaving no stone unturned, meticulous, painstaking, scrupulous **2.** absolute, arrant, complete, deep-dyed (*usually derogatory*), downright, entire, out-and-out, outright, perfect, pure, sheer, total, unmitigated, unqualified, utter

thoroughbred *adj.* blood, full-blooded, of unmixed stock, pedigree, pure-blooded, purebred

thoroughfare avenue, highway, passage, passageway, road, roadway, street, way

thoroughly 1. assiduously, carefully, completely, comprehensively, conscientiously, efficiently, exhaustively, from top to bottom, fully, inside out, intensively, leaving no stone unturned, meticulously, painstakingly, scrupulously, through and through, throughout **2.** absolutely, completely, downright, entirely, perfectly, quite, totally, to the full, utterly, without reservation

though 1. *conj.* albeit, allowing, although, despite the fact that, even if, even supposing, even though, granted, notwithstanding, tho' (*U.S. or poetic*), while **2.** *adv.* all the same, for all that, however, nevertheless, nonetheless, notwithstanding, still, yet

thought 1. brainwork, cerebration (*usually facetious*), cogitation, consideration, contemplation, deliberation, introspection, meditation, musing, reflection, regard, rumination, thinking **2.** assessment, belief, concept, conception, conclusion, conjecture, conviction, estimation, idea, judgment, notion, opinion, thinking, view **3.** attention, consideration, heed, regard, scrutiny, study **4.** aim, design, idea, intention, notion, object, plan, purpose

thoughtful 1. attentive, caring, considerate, helpful, kind, kindly, solicitous, unselfish **2.** astute, canny, careful, cautious, circumspect, deliberate, discreet, heedful, mindful, prudent, wary, well thought-out **3.** contemplative, deliberative, in a brown study, introspective, lost in thought, meditative, musing, pensive, rapt, reflective, ruminative, serious, studious, thinking, wistful

thoughtless impolite, inconsiderate, indiscreet, in-

land 24-3. **3** to move about in a wild manner: *his legs stuck and he fell sideways, thrashing about wildly.* **4** same as **thresh.** ~*n* **5** *Informal* a party. ~See also **thrash out.**

thrashing *n* a severe beating.

thrash out *vb* to discuss (a problem or difficulty) fully in order to come to an agreement or decision about it: *we must arrange a meeting to thrash out the details of the scheme.*

thread *n* **1** a fine strand or fibre of some material. **2** a fine cord of twisted yarns, esp. of cotton, used in sewing or weaving. **3** something acting as the continuous link or theme of a whole: *the thread of the story.* **4** the spiral ridge on a screw, bolt, or nut. **5** a very small amount (of something): *there was a thread of nervousness in his voice.* **6** a very thin seam of coal or vein of ore. ~*vb* **7** to pass thread through the eye of (a needle) before sewing with it. **8** to string together: *plastic beads threaded on lengths of nylon line.* **9** to make (one's way) through a crowd of people or group of objects: *she threaded and pushed her way through the crowds.* **threadlike** *adj*

threadbare *adj* **1** (of cloth, clothing, or a carpet) having the nap worn off so that the threads are exposed. **2** having been used or expressed so often as to be no longer interesting: *threadbare ideas.* **3** wearing shabby worn-out clothes.

threadworm *n* a small threadlike worm that is a parasite of humans.

threat *n* **1** a declaration of an intention to inflict harm: *they carried out their threat to kill the hostages.* **2** a strong possibility of something dangerous or unpleasant happening: *the wet weather will bring a threat of flooding.* **3** a person or thing that is regarded as dangerous and likely to inflict harm: *unemployment is a serious threat to the social order.*

threaten *vb* **1** to express a threat to (someone): *he threatened John with the sack.* **2** to be a threat to: *he was worried about anything that might threaten the health of his child.* **3** to be a menacing indication of (something): *the early summer threatened drought.* **threatening** *adj* **threateningly** *adv*

three *n* **1** the cardinal number that is the sum of one and two. **2** a numeral, 3 or III, representing this number. **3** something representing or consisting of three units. ~*adj* **4** amounting to three: *three days.*

three-decker *n* **1** a warship with guns on three decks. **2** anything that has three levels, layers, or tiers.

three-dimensional *or* **3-D** *adj* **1** having three dimensions. **2** lifelike: *all the characters are three-dimensional.*

threefold *adj* **1** having three times as many or as much. **2** composed of three parts. ~*adv* **3** by three times as many or as much.

three-legged race *n* a race in which pairs of competitors run with their adjacent legs tied together.

three-ply *adj* made of three thicknesses, layers, or strands.

three-point turn *n* a complete turn of a motor vehicle using forward and reverse gears alternately, and completed after only three movements.

three-quarter *adj* **1** amounting to three out of four equal parts of something. **2** being three quarters of the normal length: *a three-quarter-length coat.* ~*n* **3** *Rugby* one of the four players between the fullback and the halfbacks, whose role is mainly to run with the ball when it is passed to them.

three Rs *pl n* reading, writing, and arithmetic regarded as the three fundamental skills to be taught in primary schools.

threescore *adj Archaic* sixty.

threesome *n* a group of three people.

threnody *n, pl* **threnodies** *Formal* a lament for the dead. **threnodic** *adj* **threnodist** *n*

thresh *vb* **1** to beat (stalks of ripe corn, rice, etc.), either with a hand tool or by machine to separate the grain from the husks and straw. **2 thresh about** to toss and turn.

thresher *n* any of a genus of large sharks occurring in tropical and temperate seas. They have a very long whiplike tail.

threshold *n* **1** the lower horizontal part of an entrance or doorway, esp. one made of stone or hardwood. **2** any doorway or entrance: *he had never been over the threshold of a pub before.* **3** the starting point of an experience, event, or venture: *she was on the threshold of a glorious career.* **4** the point at which something begins to take effect or be noticeable: *the threshold for basic rate tax; he has a low boredom threshold.*

threw *vb* the past tense of **throw.**

thrice *adv Literary* **1** three times: *he was thrice mayor of Birmingham.* **2** three times as big, much, etc.: *his vegetables are thrice the size of mine.*

thrift *n* **1** wisdom and caution with money. **2** a low-

THESAURUS

sensitive, rude, selfish, tactless, uncaring, undiplomatic, unkind

thrash 1. beat, belt (*informal*), birch, cane, chastise, clobber (*slang*), flagellate, flog, give (someone) a (good) hiding (*informal*), hide (*informal*), horsewhip, lambast(e), leather, lick (*informal*), paste (*slang*), scourge, spank, take a stick to, tan (*slang*), whip **2.** beat, beat (someone) hollow (*Brit. informal*), blow out of the water (*slang*), clobber (*slang*), crush, defeat, hammer (*informal*), lick (*informal*), overwhelm, paste (*slang*), rout, run rings around (*informal*), slaughter (*informal*), tank (*slang*), trounce, wipe the floor with (*informal*) **3.** flail, heave, jerk, plunge, squirm, thresh, toss, toss and turn, writhe

thrashing beating, belting (*informal*), caning, flogging, hiding (*informal*), lashing, pasting (*slang*), tanning (*slang*), whipping

thrash out argue out, debate, discuss, have out, resolve, settle, solve, talk over

thread *n.* **1.** cotton, fibre, filament, line, strand, string, yarn **2.** course, direction, drift, motif, plot, story line, strain, tenor, theme, train of thought ~*vb.* **3.** ease, inch, pass, pick (one's way), squeeze through, wind

threadbare 1. down at heel, frayed, old, ragged, scruffy, shabby, tattered, tatty, used, worn, worn-out **2.** clichéd, cliché-ridden, common, commonplace, conventional, corny (*slang*), familiar, hackneyed, overused, stale, stereotyped, stock, tired, trite, well-worn

threat 1. intimidatory remark, menace, threatening remark, warning **2.** foreboding, foreshadowing, omen, portent, presage, warning, writing on the wall **3.** danger, hazard, menace, peril, risk

threaten 1. browbeat, bully, cow, intimidate, lean on (*slang*), make threats to, menace, pressurize, terrorize, warn **2.** endanger, imperil, jeopardize, put at risk, put in jeopardy **3.** be imminent, be in the air, be in the offing, forebode, foreshadow, hang over, impend, loom over, portend, presage, warn

threatening 1. bullying, intimidatory, menacing, terrorizing **2.** baleful, forbidding, grim, inauspicious, ominous, sinister

threesome triad, trilogy, trinity, trio, triple, triplet, triumvirate

threshold 1. door, doorsill, doorstep, doorway, entrance, sill **2.** beginning, brink, dawn, inception, open-

growing plant of Europe, W Asia, and North America, with narrow leaves and round heads of pink or white flowers. **thriftless** *adj*

thrifty *adj* **thriftier, thriftiest** not wasteful with money. **thriftily** *adv* **thriftiness** *n*

thrill *n* **1** a sudden sensation of excitement and pleasure: *he felt a thrill of excitement.* **2** a situation producing such a sensation: *all the thrills of rafting the meandering Dordogne.* **3** a sudden trembling sensation caused by fear or emotional shock. *~vb* **4** to feel or cause to feel a thrill. **5** to vibrate or quiver. **thrilling** *adj*

thriller *n* a book, film, or play depicting crime, mystery, or espionage in an atmosphere of excitement and suspense.

thrips *n, pl* **thrips** a small slender-bodied insect with piercing mouthparts that feeds on plant sap.

thrive *vb* **thriving; thrived** *or* **throve; thrived** *or* **thriven** **1** to do well; be successful: *Munich has thrived as a centre of European commerce.* **2** to grow strongly and vigorously: *the vine can thrive in the most unlikely soils.*

thro' *or* **thro** *prep, adv Informal* same as **through.**

throat *n* **1** the passage from the mouth and nose to the stomach and lungs. **2** the front part of the neck. **3 at each other's throats** quarrelling or fighting with each other. **4 cut one's own throat** to bring about one's own ruin. **5 cut someone's throat** to kill someone. **6 ram** *or* **force something down someone's throat** to insist that someone listen to or accept something. **7 stick in one's throat** to be hard to accept: *his arrogance really sticks in my throat.*

throaty *adj* **throatier, throatiest** **1** hoarse and suggestive of a sore throat: *a throaty 40 fags-a-day bark.* **2** deep, husky, or guttural: *she gives a deliciously throaty laugh.*

throb *vb* **throbbing, throbbed** **1** to pulsate or beat repeatedly, esp. with abnormally strong force: *her eardrums were throbbing with pain.* **2** (of engines, drums, etc.) to have a strong rhythmic vibration or beat. *~n* **3** the act or sensation of throbbing: *he felt a throb of fear; the throb of the engines.* **throbbing** *adj, n*

throes *pl n* **1** violent pangs, pain, or convulsions: *an animal in its death throes.* **2 in the throes of** struggling to cope with (something difficult or disruptive): *in the throes of a civil war.*

thrombosis (throm-**boh**-siss) *n, pl* **-ses** (-seez) coagulation of the blood in the heart or in a blood vessel, forming a blood clot.

throne *n* **1** the ceremonial seat occupied by a monarch or bishop on occasions of state. **2** the rank or power of a monarch: *she came to the throne after her father was murdered.*

throng *n* **1** a great number of people or things crowded together. *~vb* **2** to gather in or fill (a place) in large numbers: *the streets were thronged with shoppers.*

throstle *n Poetic* a song thrush.

throttle *n* **1** a device that controls the fuel-and-air mixture entering an engine. *~vb* **-tling, -tled** **2** to kill or injure (someone) by squeezing his or her throat. **3** to suppress or censor: *the government is trying to throttle dissent.*

throttle back *vb* to reduce the speed of a vehicle or aircraft by reducing the quantity of fuel entering the engine: *throttling back the engine failed to bring the plane under control.*

through *prep* **1** going in at one side and coming out at the other side of: *he drove through the West of the city.* **2** occupying or visiting several points scattered around in (an area): *a journey through the Scottish Highlands.* **3** as a result of: *diminished responsibility through temporary insanity.* **4** during: *driving for five hours through the night.* **5** for all of (a period): *it rained all through that summer.* **6** *Chiefly US* up to and including: *from Monday through Saturday.* *~adj* **7** finished: *I'm through with history.* **8** having completed a specified amount of an activity: *he tried to stop the investigation halfway through.* **9** (on a telephone line) connected. **10** no longer able to function successfully in some specified capacity: *they are through, they haven't got a chance.* **11** (of a train, plane flight, etc.) going directly to a place, so that passengers do not have to change: *there's no through train from Edinburgh to Sheffield.* *~adv* **12** through a thing, place, or period of time: *the script gives up around halfway through.* **13** extremely or absolutely: *I'm soaked through.* **14 through and through** to the greatest possible extent: *the boards are rotten through and through.*

throughout *prep* **1** through the whole of (a place or a period of time): *radio stations throughout the UK.* *~adv* **2** throughout a place or a period of time: *I led both races throughout.*

THESAURUS

ing, outset, start, starting point, verge **3.** lower limit, minimum

thrift carefulness, economy, frugality, good husbandry, prudence, saving, thriftiness

thrifty careful, economical, frugal, provident, prudent, saving, sparing

thrill *n.* **1.** buzz (*slang*), charge (*slang*), flush of excitement, glow, kick (*informal*), pleasure, sensation, stimulation, tingle, titillation **2.** flutter, fluttering, quiver, shudder, throb, tremble, tremor, vibration *~vb.* **3.** arouse, electrify, excite, get a charge (*slang*), get a kick (*informal*), glow, move, send (*slang*), stimulate, stir, tingle, titillate **4.** flutter, quake, quiver, shake, shudder, throb, tremble, vibrate

thrilling **1.** electrifying, exciting, gripping, hair-raising, rip-roaring (*informal*), riveting, rousing, sensational, sexy (*informal*), stimulating, stirring **2.** quaking, shaking, shivering, shuddering, trembling, vibrating

thrive advance, bloom, boom, burgeon, develop, do well, flourish, get on, grow, grow rich, increase, prosper, succeed, wax

thriving blooming, booming, burgeoning, developing, doing well, flourishing, going strong, growing, healthy, prosperous, successful, wealthy, well

throb **1.** *vb.* beat, palpitate, pound, pulsate, pulse, thump, vibrate **2.** *n.* beat, palpitation, pounding, pulsating, pulse, thump, thumping, vibration

throng **1.** *n.* assemblage, concourse, congregation, crowd, crush, horde, host, jam, mass, mob, multitude, pack, press, swarm **2.** *vb.* bunch, congregate, converge, cram, crowd, fill, flock, herd, jam, mill around, pack, press, swarm around

throttle *vb.* **1.** choke, garrotte, strangle, strangulate **2.** control, gag, inhibit, silence, stifle, suppress

through *prep.* **1.** between, by, from end to end of, from one side to the other of, in and out of, past **2.** as a consequence *or* result of, because of, by means of, by virtue of, by way of, using, via, with the help of **3.** during, in, in the middle of, throughout *~adj.* **4.** *with* **with** at the end of, done, finished, having completed, having had enough of **5.** done, finished, washed up (*informal*) *~adv.* **6. through and through** altogether, completely, entirely, fully, thoroughly, totally, to the core, unreservedly, utterly, wholly

throughout **1.** *prep.* all over, all through, during the whole of, for the duration of, over the length and

throughput *n* the amount of material processed in a given period, esp. by a computer.

throve *vb* a past tense of **thrive.**

throw *vb* **throwing, threw, thrown 1** to hurl (something) through the air, esp. with a rapid motion of the arm. **2** to put or move suddenly, carelessly, or violently: *she threw her arms round his neck.* **3** to bring into a specified state or condition, esp. suddenly: *the invasion threw the region into turmoil.* **4** to move (a switch or lever) so as to engage or disengage a mechanism. **5** to cause (someone) to fall: *I'm riding the horse that threw me.* **6 a** to tip (dice) out onto a flat surface. **b** to obtain (a specified number) in this way: *one throws a 3 and the other throws a 5.* **7** to shape (pottery) on a potter's wheel. **8** to give (a party). **9** *Informal* to confuse or disconcert: *the question threw me.* **10** to direct or cast (a look, light, etc.): *the lamp threw a shadow on the ceiling.* **11** to project (the voice) so as to make it appear to come from somewhere else. **12** *Informal* to lose (a contest) deliberately. **13 throw a punch** to strike, or attempt to strike, someone with one's fist. **14 throw oneself at** to behave in a way which makes it clear that one is trying to win the affection of (someone). **15 throw oneself into** to involve oneself enthusiastically in. **16 throw oneself on** to rely entirely upon (someone's goodwill, etc.): *the president threw himself on the mercy of the American people.* ~*n* **17** the act or an instance of throwing. **18** the distance thrown. **19** (in sports such as wrestling or judo) a move which causes one's opponent to fall to the floor. **20 a throw** each: *we drank our way through a couple of bottles of claret at £12.50 a throw.* ~See also **throwaway, throwback,** etc.

throwaway *adj* **1** *Chiefly Brit* said or done incidentally: *a throwaway line.* **2** designed to be discarded after use: *throwaway cups.* ~*vb* **throw away 3** to get rid of or discard: *try to recycle glass bottles instead of simply throwing them away.* **4** to fail to make good use of: *she threw away the chance of a brilliant career when she got married.*

throwback *n* **1** a person or thing that is like something that existed or was common long ago: *his ideas were a throwback to old colonial attitudes.* ~*vb* **throw back 2** to remind someone of (something he or she said or did previously) in order to upset him or her: *he threw back at me everything I'd said the week before.*

throw in *vb* **1** to add at no additional cost: *he'd got good at bargaining them down, making them throw in variations for free.* **2** to contribute (a remark) in a discussion. **3 throw in the towel** *Informal* to give in; accept defeat. ~*n* **throw-in 4** *Soccer etc* the act of putting the ball back into play when it has gone over one of the sidelines, by throwing it over one's head with both hands.

throw off *vb* **1** to take off (clothing) hurriedly. **2** *Literary* to free oneself of: *Vietnamese farmers threw off their dependency on European seed potatoes.*

throw out *vb* **1** to discard or reject: *the House of Lords threw out the proposed reforms.* **2** to expel or dismiss, esp. forcibly: *her parents threw her out when they discovered she was pregnant.*

throw over *vb* *Old-fashioned* to leave or reject (a lover).

throw together *vb* **1** to assemble (something) hurriedly. **2** (of a set of circumstances) to cause (people) to meet and get to know each other.

throw up *vb* **1** *Informal* to vomit. **2** to give up or abandon: *he would threaten to throw up his job.* **3** to construct (a building or structure) hastily. **4** to produce: *these links are throwing up fresh opportunities.*

thru *prep, adv, adj* *Chiefly US* same as **through.**

thrum *vb* **thrumming, thrummed 1** to strum rhythmically but without expression on (a musical instrument). **2** to make a low beating or humming sound: *the air conditioner thrummed.* ~*n* **3** a repetitive strumming.

thrush[1] *n* any of a large group of songbirds, esp. one having a brown plumage with a spotted breast, such as the mistle thrush and song thrush.

thrush[2] *n* **1** a fungal disease, esp. of infants, in which whitish spots form on the mouth, throat, and lips. **2** a vaginal infection caused by the same fungus.

thrust *vb* **thrusting, thrust 1** to push (someone or something) with force: *he took him by the arm and thrust him towards the door.* **2** to force (someone) into some condition or situation: *the unemployed have been thrust into the frontline of politics.* **3** to force (one's way) through a crowd, forest, etc.: *Edward thrust his way towards them.* **4** to stick out or up: *she thrust out her lower lip.* ~*n* **5** a forceful drive, push, stab, or lunge: *the thrust of his spear.* **6** a force, esp. one that produces motion. **7** the propulsive force produced by the pressure of air and gas forced out of a jet engine or rocket engine. **8** the essential or most forceful part: *the main thrust of the report.* **9** *Physics* a continuous pressure exerted by one part of an object against another. **10** *Informal* intellectual or emotional drive; forcefulness: *thanks to the ingenuity and enterprising thrust of this company.*

thrusting *adj* ambitious and having great drive: *a thrusting young executive.*

thud *n* **1** a dull heavy sound. **2** a blow or fall that causes such a sound. ~*vb* **thudding, thudded 3** to make or cause to make such a sound.

thug *n* a tough and violent man, esp. a criminal. **thuggery** *n* **thuggish** *adj*

thulium *n* *Chem* a silvery-grey element of the lanthanide series. Symbol: Tm

THESAURUS

breadth of, right through, through the whole of **2.** *adv.* all the time, everywhere, from beginning to end, from end to end, from start to finish, from the start, the whole time

throw *vb.* **1.** cast, chuck (*informal*), fling, heave, hurl, launch, lob (*informal*), pitch, project, propel, put, send, shy, sling, toss **2.** bring down, dislodge, fell, floor, hurl to the ground, overturn, unseat, upset **3.** *informal* astonish, baffle, confound, confuse, disconcert, dumbfound, faze, put one off one's stroke, throw off, throw one off one's stride, throw out ~*n.* **4.** cast, fling, heave, lob (*informal*), pitch, shy, sling, toss

throw away 1. axe (*informal*), bin (*informal*), cast off, chuck (*informal*), discard, dispense with, dispose of, ditch (*slang*), dump (*informal*), get rid of, jettison, junk (*informal*), reject, scrap, throw out **2.** blow (*slang*), fail to exploit, fritter away, lose, make poor use of, squander, waste

throw off cast off, discard, drop

throw out 1. bin (*informal*), cast off, chuck (*informal*), discard, dispense with, ditch (*slang*), dump (*informal*), get rid of, jettison, junk (*informal*), kiss off (*slang, chiefly U.S. & Canad.*), reject, scrap, throw away, turn down **2.** dismiss, eject, evict, expel, get rid of, give the bum's rush (*slang*), kick out (*informal*), oust, reject, relegate, show one the door, turf out (*Brit. informal*)

thrust *vb.* **1.** butt, drive, force, impel, jam, plunge, poke, press, prod, propel, push, ram, shove, urge **2.** jab, lunge, pierce, stab, stick ~*n.* **3.** drive, lunge, poke, prod, push, shove, stab **4.** impetus, momentum, motive force, motive power, propulsive force

thumb *n* **1** the short thick finger of the hand set apart from the others. **2** the part of a glove shaped to fit the thumb. **3 all thumbs** very clumsy. **4 thumbs down** an indication of refusal or disapproval. **5 thumbs up** an indication of encouragement or approval. **6 under someone's thumb** completely under someone else's control. *~vb* **7** to touch, mark, or move with the thumb: *he thumbed the volume switch to maximum.* **8** to attempt to obtain (a lift in a motor vehicle) by signalling with the thumb: *he thumbed a lift to the station.* **9 thumb one's nose at** to behave in a way that shows one's contempt or disregard for: *her mother had always thumbed her nose at convention.* **10 thumb through** to flip the pages of (a book or magazine) in order to glance at the contents.

thumb index *n* a series of notches cut into the fore-edge of a book to facilitate quick reference.

thumbnail *n* **1** the nail of the thumb. *~adj* **2** concise and brief: *a thumbnail sketch.*

thumbscrew *n* (formerly) an instrument of torture that pinches or crushes the thumbs.

thump *n* **1** the sound of something heavy hitting a comparatively soft surface. **2** a heavy blow with the hand. *~vb* **3** to place (something) on or bang against (something) with a loud dull sound: *thumping the table is aggressive.* **4** to hit or punch (someone): *stop that at once or I'll thump you!* **5** to throb or beat violently: *he could feel his heart thumping.*

thumping *adj Slang* huge or excessive: *a thumping majority.*

thunder *n* **1** a loud cracking or deep rumbling noise caused by the rapid expansion of atmospheric gases that are suddenly heated by lightning. **2** any loud booming sound: *the thunder of heavy gunfire.* **3 steal someone's thunder** to lessen the effect of someone's idea or action by anticipating it. *~vb* **4** to make a loud noise like thunder: *an explosion thundered through the shaft.* **5** to speak in a loud, angry manner: *"Get out of here this instant!" he thundered.* **6** to move fast, heavily, and noisily: *a lorry thundered by.* **thundery** *adj*

thunderbolt *n* **1** a flash of lightning accompanying thunder. **2** something sudden and unexpected: *his career has been no thunderbolt.* **3** *Myth* a weapon thrown to earth by certain gods. **4** *Sport* a very fast-moving shot or serve.

thunderclap *n* **1** a loud outburst of thunder. **2** something as violent or unexpected as a clap of thunder.

thundercloud *n* a large dark electrically charged cloud associated with thunderstorms.

thundering *adj, adv Old-fashioned slang* extreme or extremely: *a thundering disgrace; thundering good music.*

thunderous *adj* **1** resembling thunder in loudness: *thunderous applause.* **2** threatening or angry: *a thunderous scowl.*

thunderstorm *n* a storm with thunder and lightning and usually heavy rain or hail.

thunderstruck *adj* amazed or shocked.

thurible (**thyoor**-rib-bl) *n* same as **censer.**

Thurs. Thursday.

Thursday *n* the fifth day of the week.

thus *adv* **1** as a result or consequence: *the platforms provided a new floor and thus improved and enlarged the premises.* **2** in this manner: *I sat thus for nearly half an hour.* **3** to such a degree: *the competition has been almost bereft of surprise thus far.*

thwack *vb* **1** to beat with something flat. *~n* **2 a** a blow with something flat. **b** the sound made by it.

thwart *vb* **1** to prevent or foil: *they inflicted such severe losses that they thwarted the invasion.* *~n* **2** the seat across a boat where the rower sits.

thy *adj Old-fashioned* belonging to or associated in some way with you (thou): *love thy neighbour.*

thyme (**time**) *n* a small shrub with white, pink, or red flowers and scented leaves used for seasoning food.

thymol *n* a white crystalline substance obtained from thyme, used as a fungicide and an antiseptic.

thymus (**thigh**-muss) *n, pl* **-muses** *or* **-mi** (-my) *Anat* a small gland situated near the base of the neck.

thyroid *Anat ~adj* **1** of or relating to the thyroid gland. **2** of or relating to the largest cartilage of the larynx, which forms the Adam's apple in men. *~n* **3** the thyroid gland.

thyroid gland *n Anat* an endocrine gland that secretes hormones that control metabolism and body growth.

thyself *pron Archaic* the reflexive form of **thou**[1].

ti *n Music* same as **te.**

Ti *Chem* titanium.

tiara *n* **1** a semicircular jewelled headdress worn by

THESAURUS

thud *n./vb.* clump, clunk, crash, knock, smack, thump, wallop (*informal*)

thug bruiser (*informal*), bully boy, heavy (*slang*), hooligan, ruffian, tough

thumb *n.* **1.** pollex **2. all thumbs** butterfingered (*informal*), cack-handed (*informal*), clumsy, ham-fisted (*informal*), inept, maladroit **3. thumbs down** disapproval, negation, no, rebuff, refusal, rejection **4. thumbs up** acceptance, affirmation, approval, encouragement, go-ahead (*informal*), green light, O.K. *or* okay (*informal*), yes *~vb.* **5.** hitch (*informal*), hitchhike **6. thumb one's nose at** be contemptuous of, cock a snook at, deride, flout, jeer at, laugh at, laugh in the face of, mock, ridicule, show contempt for, show disrespect to **7. thumb through** browse through, flick through, flip through, glance at, leaf through, riffle through, run one's eye over, scan the pages of, skim through, turn over

thump **1.** *n.* bang, blow, clout (*informal*), clunk, crash, knock, punch, rap, smack, thud, thwack, wallop (*informal*), whack **2.** *vb.* bang, batter, beat, belabour, chin (*slang*), clobber (*slang*), clout (*informal*), crash, deck (*slang*), hit, knock, lambast(e), lay one on (*slang*), pound, punch, rap, smack, strike, thrash, throb, thud, thwack, wallop (*informal*), whack

thumping *slang* colossal, elephantine, enormous, excessive, exorbitant, gargantuan, gigantic, great, huge, humongous (*U.S. slang*), mammoth, massive, monumental, terrific, thundering (*slang*), titanic, tremendous, whopping (*informal*)

thunder *n.* **1.** boom, booming, cracking, crash, crashing, detonation, explosion, pealing, rumble, rumbling *~vb.* **2.** blast, boom, clap, crack, crash, detonate, explode, peal, resound, reverberate, roar, rumble **3.** bark, bellow, declaim, roar, shout, yell

thunderous booming, deafening, ear-splitting, loud, noisy, resounding, roaring, tumultuous

thunderstruck aghast, amazed, astonished, astounded, bowled over (*informal*), dazed, dumbfounded, flabbergasted (*informal*), floored (*informal*), flummoxed, gobsmacked (*Brit. slang*), knocked for six (*informal*), left speechless, nonplussed, open-mouthed, paralysed, petrified, rooted to the spot, shocked, staggered, struck dumb, stunned, taken aback

thus **1.** accordingly, consequently, ergo, for this reason, hence, on that account, so, then, therefore **2.** as

some women on formal occasions. **2** the triple-tiered crown sometimes worn by the pope.

tibia (tib-ee-a) *n, pl* **tibiae** (tib-ee-ee) *or* **tibias** the inner and thicker of the two bones of the human leg below the knee; shinbone. **tibial** *adj*

tic *n* a spasmodic muscular twitch.

tick[1] *n* **1** a mark (√) used to check off or indicate the correctness of something. **2** a recurrent metallic tapping or clicking sound, such as that made by a clock. **3** *Brit informal* a moment or instant: *won't be a tick.* ~*vb* **4** to mark or check with a tick. **5** to produce a recurrent tapping sound or indicate by such a sound: *the clock ticked away.* **6 what makes someone tick** *Informal* the basic motivation of a person. ~See also **tick off, tick over.**

tick[2] *n* a small parasitic creature typically living on the skin of warm-blooded animals and feeding on the blood and tissues of their hosts.

tick[3] *n Brit informal* account or credit: *a spending spree that was financed on tick.*

ticker *n Slang* the heart.

ticker tape *n* (formerly) a continuous paper tape on which current stock quotations were printed by machine.

ticket *n* **1** a printed piece of paper or cardboard showing that the holder is entitled to certain rights, such as travel on a train or bus or entry to a place of public entertainment. **2** a label or tag attached to an article showing information such as its price and size. **3** an official notification of a parking or traffic offence. **4** the declared policy of a political party. **5 that's (just) the ticket** *Informal* that's the right or appropriate thing. ~*vb* **-eting, -eted 6** to issue or attach a ticket or tickets to.

tickets *pl n S African informal* death or ruin; the end.

ticking *n* a strong cotton fabric, often striped, used esp. for mattress and pillow covers.

tickle *vb* **-ling, -led 1** to touch or stroke (someone), so as to produce laughter or a twitching sensation. **2** to itch or tingle. **3** to amuse or please. **4 tickled pink** *or* **to death** *Informal* greatly pleased. **5 tickle someone's fancy** to appeal to or amuse someone. ~*n* **6** a sensation of light stroking or itching: *a tickle in the throat.* **7** the act of tickling. **8** *Canad* (in the Atlantic Provinces) a narrow strait.

ticklish *adj* **1** sensitive to being tickled. **2** delicate or difficult: *a ticklish problem.*

tick off *vb* **1** to mark with a tick, esp. to show that an item on a list has been dealt with. **2** *Informal, chiefly Brit* to reprimand or scold (someone). **ticking-off** *n*

tick over *vb* **1** *Brit* (of an engine) to run at low speed with the transmission disengaged. **2** to run smoothly without any major changes: *the business is just ticking over.*

ticktack *n Brit* a system of sign language, mainly using the hands, by which bookmakers transmit their odds to each other at race courses.

ticktock *n* a ticking sound made by a clock.

tidal *adj* **1** (of a river, lake, or sea) having tides. **2** of or relating to tides: *a tidal surge.*

tidal wave *n* **1** *Not in technical use* same as **tsunami. 2** an unusually large incoming wave, often caused by high winds and spring tides. **3** a forceful and widespread movement in public opinion, action, etc.: *a tidal wave of scandals and embezzlement.*

tiddler *n Brit informal* **1** a very small fish, esp. a stickleback. **2** a small child.

tiddly[1] *adj* **-dlier, -dliest** *Brit* very small.

tiddly[2] *adj* **-dlier, -dliest** *Informal, chiefly Brit* slightly drunk.

tiddlywinks *n* a game in which players try to flick discs of plastic into a cup.

tide *n* **1** the alternate rise and fall of sea level caused by the gravitational pull of the sun and moon. **2** the current caused by these changes in level: *I got caught by the tide and almost drowned.* **3** a widespread tendency or movement: *the rising tide of nationalism.* **4** *Literary or old-fashioned* a season or time: *Yuletide.*

tideline *n* the mark or line left by the tide when it retreats from its highest point.

tidemark *n* **1** a mark left by the highest or lowest point of a tide. **2** *Chiefly Brit* a line of dirt left round a bath after the water has been drained away. **3** *Informal, chiefly Brit* a dirty mark on the skin, indicating the extent to which someone has washed.

tide over *vb* **tiding, tided** to help (someone) to get through a period of difficulty or distress: *they need some form of Social Security to tide them over.*

tidings *pl n* information or news.

tidy *adj* **-dier, -diest 1** neat and orderly. **2** *Informal* quite large: *a tidy sum of money.* ~*vb* **-dies, -dying, -died 3** to put (things) in their proper place; make neat: *I've tidied up the toys under the bed.* ~*n, pl* **-dies 4** a small container for odds and ends. **tidily** *adv* **tidiness** *n*

THESAURUS

follows, in this fashion (manner, way), like so, like this, so

thwart baffle, balk, check, defeat, foil, frustrate, hinder, impede, obstruct, prevent, stop, stymie

tick[1] *n.* **1.** dash, mark, stroke **2.** clack, click, clicking, tap, tapping, ticktock **3.** *Brit. informal* flash, half a mo (*Brit. informal*), instant, jiffy (*informal*), minute, moment, sec (*informal*), second, shake (*informal*), split second, trice, twinkling, two shakes of a lamb's tail (*informal*) ~*vb.* **4.** check off, choose, indicate, mark, mark off, select **5.** clack, click, tap, ticktock **6. what makes someone tick** drive, motivation, motive, *raison d'être*

tick[2] *Brit. informal* account, credit, deferred payment, the slate (*Brit. informal*)

ticket 1. card, certificate, coupon, pass, slip, token, voucher **2.** card, docket, label, marker, slip, sticker, tab, tag

tickle amuse, delight, divert, entertain, excite, gratify, please, thrill, titillate

ticklish awkward, critical, delicate, difficult, risky, sensitive, thorny, touchy, tricky, uncertain, unstable, unsteady

tick off 1. check off, mark off, put a tick at **2.** *informal, chiefly Brit.* bawl out (*informal*), berate, carpet (*informal*), censure, chew out (*U.S. & Canad. informal*), chide, give a rocket (*Brit. & N.Z. informal*), haul over the coals (*informal*), lecture, read the riot act, rebuke, reprimand, reproach, reprove, scold, take to task, tear into (*informal*), tear (someone) off a strip (*Brit. informal*), tell off (*informal*), upbraid

tide 1. course, current, ebb, flow, stream, tideway, undertow **2.** course, current, direction, drift, movement, tendency, trend

tide over aid, assist, bridge the gap, help, keep one going, keep one's head above water, keep the wolf from the door, see one through

tidings bulletin, communication, gen (*Brit. informal*), information, intelligence, latest (*informal*), message, news, report, word

tidy *adj.* **1.** businesslike, clean, cleanly, methodical, neat, ordered, orderly, shipshape, spick-and-span, spruce, systematic, trim, well-groomed, well-kept, well-ordered **2.** *informal* ample, considerable, fair,

tie *vb* **tying, tied 1** to fasten or be fastened with string, rope, etc. **2** to make a knot or bow in (something): *hang on while I tie my laces.* **3** to restrict or limit: *they had children and were consequently tied to the school holidays.* **4** to equal the score of a competitor or fellow candidate: *three players tied for second place.* ~*n* **5** a long narrow piece of material worn, esp. by men, under the collar of a shirt, tied in a knot close to the throat with the ends hanging down the front. **6** a bond or link: *he still has close ties to the town where he grew up.* **7** a string, wire, etc., with which something is tied. **8** *Brit sport* a match in a knockout competition: *whoever wins the tie will play Australia in the semifinals.* **9 a** a result in a match or competition in which the scores or times of some of the competitors are the same: *a tie for second place.* **b** the match or competition in which the scores or results are equal. **10** a regular commitment that limits a person's freedom: *it's a bit of a tie having to visit my mother every day.* **11** something which supports or links parts of a structure. **12** *US & Canad* a sleeper on a railway track. **13** *Music* a curved line connecting two notes of the same pitch indicating that the sound is to be prolonged for their joint time value. ~See also **tie in, tie up.**

tie beam *n* a horizontal beam that holds two parts of a structure together, such as one that connects two corresponding rafters in a roof.

tie-break *or* **tie-breaker** *n* an extra game or question that decides the result of a contest that has ended in a draw.

tied *adj Brit* **1** (of a public house) allowed to sell beer from only one particular brewery. **2** (of a house) rented out to the tenant for as long as he or she is employed by the owner.

tie-dye, tie-dyed, *or* **tie and dye** *adj* (of a garment or fabric) dyed in a pattern by tying sections of the cloth together so that they will not absorb the dye: *a tie-dye T-shirt.*

tie in *vb* **1** to have or cause to have a close link or connection: *there's no evidence to tie this killing in with the murder of Mrs McGowan.* ~*n* **tie-in 2** a link or connection. **3** a book or other product that is linked with a film or TV programme.

tiepin *n* an ornamental pin used to pin the two ends of a tie to a shirt.

tier *n* one of a set of rows placed one above and behind the other, such as theatre seats.

tie up *vb* **1** to bind (someone or something) securely with string or rope. **2** to moor (a vessel). **3** to commit (money etc.) so that it is unavailable for other uses: *people don't want to tie up their savings for a long period.* ~*n* **tie-up 4** a link or connection.

tiff *n* a minor quarrel.

tiffin *n* (in India) a light meal, esp. at midday.

tiger *n* **1** a large Asian mammal of the cat family which has a tawny yellow coat with black stripes. **2** a dynamic, forceful, or cruel person.

tiger lily *n* a lily of China and Japan with black-spotted orange flowers.

tiger moth *n* a moth with conspicuously striped and spotted wings.

tight *adj* **1** stretched or drawn taut: *loosening-up of tight muscles.* **2** closely fitting: *wearing a jacket that was too tight for him.* **3** made, fixed, or closed firmly and securely: *a tight band.* **4** constructed so as to prevent the passage of water, air, etc.: *watertight.* **5** cramped and allowing very little room for movement: *they squeezed him into the tight space.* **6** unyielding or stringent: *tight security.* **7** (of a situation) difficult or dangerous. **8** allowing only the minimum time or money for doing something: *a tight schedule.* **9** *Informal* mean or miserly. **10** (of a match or game) very close or even. **11** *Informal* drunk. **12** (of a corner or turn) turning through a large angle in a short distance: *the boat skidded round in a tight turn.* ~*adv* **13** in a close, firm, or secure way: *they held each other tight.* **tightly** *adv* **tightness** *n*

tighten *vb* to make or become tight or tighter.

tightfisted *adj* unwilling to spend money; mean.

tightknit *adj* closely integrated: *a tightknit community.*

tight-lipped *adj* **1** unwilling to give any information; secretive: *the Minister remained tight-lipped when it came to answering the press's questions.* **2** with the lips pressed tightly together, as through anger: *tight-lipped determination.*

tightrope *n* a rope stretched taut on which acrobats perform.

tights *pl n* a one-piece clinging garment covering the body from the waist to the feet, worn by women and also by acrobats, dancers, etc.

tigress *n* **1** a female tiger. **2** a fierce, cruel, or passionate woman.

tike *n* same as **tyke.**

tiki (tee-kee) *n* a Maori greenstone neck ornament in the form of a fetus.

THESAURUS

generous, good, goodly, handsome, healthy, large, largish, respectable, sizable, substantial ~*vb.* **3.** clean, groom, neaten, order, put in order, put in trim, put to rights, spruce up, straighten

tie *vb.* **1.** attach, bind, connect, fasten, join, knot, lash, link, make fast, moor, rope, secure, tether, truss, unite **2.** bind, confine, hamper, hinder, hold, limit, restrain, restrict **3.** be even, be neck and neck, draw, equal, match ~*n.* **4.** affiliation, affinity, allegiance, bond, connection, kinship, relationship **5.** band, bond, connection, cord, fastening, fetter, joint, knot, ligature, link, rope, string **6.** *Brit.* contest, fixture, game, match **7.** dead heat, deadlock, draw, stalemate **8.** encumbrance, hindrance, limitation, restraint, restriction

tier bank, file, layer, level, line, order, rank, row, series, storey, stratum

tie up 1. bind, pinion, restrain, tether, truss **2.** lash, make fast, moor, rope, secure

tight 1. rigid, stiff, stretched, taut, tense **2.** close, close-fitting, compact, constricted, cramped, fast, firm, fixed, narrow, secure, snug **3.** hermetic, impervious, proof, sealed, sound, watertight **4.** harsh, inflexible, rigid, rigorous, severe, stern, strict, stringent, tough, uncompromising, unyielding **5.** dangerous, difficult, hazardous, perilous, precarious, problematic, sticky (*informal*), ticklish, tough, tricky, troublesome, worrisome **6.** *informal* close, grasping, mean, miserly, niggardly, parsimonious, penurious, sparing, stingy, tight-arse (*taboo slang*), tight-arsed (*taboo slang*), tight as a duck's arse (*taboo slang*), tight-ass (*U.S. taboo slang*), tight-assed (*U.S. taboo slang*), tightfisted **7.** close, even, evenly-balanced, near, well-matched **8.** *informal* bevvied (*dialect*), blitzed (*slang*), blotto (*slang*), bombed (*slang*), drunk, flying (*slang*), half cut (*Brit. slang*), half seas over (*Brit. informal*), inebriated, in one's cups, intoxicated, legless (*informal*), lit up (*slang*), out of it (*slang*), out to it (*Austral. & N.Z. slang*), paralytic (*informal*), pickled (*informal*), pie-eyed (*slang*), pissed (*taboo slang*), plastered (*slang*), smashed (*slang*), sozzled (*informal*), steamboats (*slang*), steaming (*slang*), stewed (*slang*), stoned (*slang*), three sheets in the wind (*slang*), tiddly (*slang, chiefly Brit.*), tipsy, under the influence (*informal*), wasted (*slang*), wrecked (*slang*), zonked (*slang*)

tikka *adj Indian cookery* (of meat) marinated in spices and then dry-roasted: *chicken tikka.*

tilde *n* a mark (˜) used in some languages to indicate that the letter over which it is placed is pronounced in a certain way, as in Spanish *señor.*

tile *n* **1** a thin piece of ceramic, plastic, etc., used with others to cover a surface, such as a floor or wall. **2** a rectangular block used as a playing piece in mah jong and other games. **3 on the tiles** *Informal* out having a good time and drinking a lot. *~vb* **tiling, tiled 4** to cover (a surface) with tiles. **tiled** *adj* **tiler** *n*

tiling *n* **1** tiles collectively. **2** something made of or surfaced with tiles.

till[1] *conj, prep* same as **until.**

till[2] *vb* to cultivate (land) for the raising of crops: *a constant round of sowing, tilling and harvesting.* **tillable** *adj* **tiller** *n*

till[3] *n* a box or drawer into which money taken from customers is put, now usually part of a cash register.

tillage *n* **1** the act, process, or art of tilling. **2** tilled land.

tiller *n Naut* a handle used to turn the rudder when steering a boat.

tilt *vb* **1** to move into a sloping position with one end or side higher than the other: *Dave tilted his chair back on two legs.* **2** to move (part of the body) slightly upwards or to the side: *Marie tilted her head back.* **3** to become more influenced by a particular idea or group: *the party is tilting more and more to the right.* **4** to compete against someone in a jousting contest. *~n* **5** a slope or angle: *a tilt to one side.* **6** the act of tilting. **7** (esp. in medieval Europe) **a** a jousting contest. **b** a thrust with a lance delivered during a tournament. **8** an attempt to do or win something: *a tilt at the world title.* **9 at full tilt** at full speed or force.

tilth *n* **1** the tilling of land. **2** the condition of land that has been tilled.

timber *n* **1** wood as a building material. **2** trees collectively. **3** a wooden beam in the frame of a house, boat, etc. *~adj* **4** made out of timber: *timber houses.* **5** of or involved in the production or sale of wood as a building material: *a timber merchant.* **timbered** *adj* **timbering** *n*

timber limit *n Canad* **1** the area to which rights of cutting timber, granted by a government licence, are limited. **2** same as **timber line.**

timber line *n* the geographical limit beyond which trees will not grow.

timbre (**tam**-bra) *n* the distinctive quality of sound produced by a particular voice or musical instrument.

timbrel *n Chiefly biblical* a tambourine.

Timbuktu *or* **Timbuctoo** (tim-buck-**too**) *n* any distant or outlandish place: *we could run our office from Timbuktu as long as there was a good fax line.*

time *n* **1** the past, present, and future regarded as a continuous whole. **2** *Physics* a quantity measuring duration, measured with reference to the rotation of the earth or from the vibrations of certain atoms. **3** a specific point in time expressed in hours and minutes: *what time are you going?* **4** a system of reckoning for expressing time: *the deadline is 5:00 Eastern Time today.* **5** an unspecified interval; a while: *some recover for a time and then relapse.* **6** an instance or occasion: *when was the last time you saw it?* **7** a sufficient interval or period: *I need time to think.* **8** an occasion or period of specified quality: *they'd had a lovely time.* **9** a suitable moment: *the time has come to make peace.* **10** a period or point marked by specific attributes or events: *in Victorian times.* **11** *Brit* the time at which licensed premises are required by law to stop selling alcoholic drinks. **12** the rate of pay for work done in normal working hours: *you get double time for working on a Sunday.* **13 a** the system of combining beats in music into successive groupings by which the rhythm of the music is established. **b** a specific system having a specific number of beats in each grouping or bar: *duple time.* **14 against time** in an effort to complete something in a limited period. **15 ahead of time** before the deadline. **16 at one time a** once or formerly. **b** simultaneously. **17 at the same time a** simultaneously. **b** nevertheless or however. **18 at times** sometimes. **19 beat time** to indicate the tempo of a piece of music by waving a baton, hand, etc. **20 do time** *Informal* to serve a term in jail. **21 for the time being** for the moment; temporarily. **22 from time to time** at intervals; occasionally. **23 have no time for** to have no patience with. **24 in no time** very quickly. **25 in one's own time a** outside paid working hours. **b** at the speed of one's choice. **26 in time a** early or at the appointed time: *he made it to the hospital in time for the baby's arrival.* **b** eventually: *in time, the children of intelligent parents will come to dominate.* **c** *Music* at a correct metrical or rhythmical pulse. **27 make time** to find an opportunity. **28 on time** at the expected or scheduled time. **29 pass the time** to occupy oneself when there is nothing else to do: *they pass their time watching game shows on television.* **30 pass the time of day** to have a short casual conversation (with someone). **31 time and again** frequently. **32 time of one's life** a memorably enjoyable time. **33 time out of mind** from long before anyone can remember. *~vb* **timing, timed 34** to measure the speed or duration of: *my Porsche was timed at 128 mph.* **35** to set a time for: *the attack was timed for 6 a.m.* **36** to do (something) at a suitable time: *her entry could not have been better timed.* *~adj* **37** operating automati-

THESAURUS

tighten 1. stiffen, stretch, tauten, tense **2.** close, constrict, cramp, fasten, fix, narrow, screw, secure, squeeze

till[1] *vb.* cultivate, dig, plough, turn over, work

till[2] *n.* cash box, cash drawer, cash register

tilt *vb.* **1.** cant, heel, incline, lean, list, slant, slope, tip *~n.* **2.** angle, cant, inclination, incline, list, pitch, slant, slope **3. (at) full tilt** for dear life, full force, full speed, headlong, like a bat out of hell (*slang*), like the clappers (*Brit. informal*)

timber 1. boards, logs, planks **2.** forest, trees, wood **3.** beams

time *n.* **1.** age, chronology, date, duration, epoch, era, generation, hour, interval, period, season, space, span, spell, stretch, term, while **2.** instance, juncture, occasion, point, stage **3.** beat, measure, metre, rhythm, tempo **4. at one time a.** for a while, formerly, hitherto, once, once upon a time, previously **b.** all at once, at the same time, simultaneously, together **5. at times** every now and then, every so often, from time to time, now and then, occasionally, once in a while, on occasion, sometimes **6. for the time being** for now, for the moment, for the nonce, for the present, in the meantime, meantime, meanwhile, pro tem, temporarily **7. from time to time** at times, every now and then, every so often, now and then, occasionally, once in a while, on occasion, sometimes **8. in no time** apace, before one knows it, before you can say Jack Robinson, in an instant, in a trice (flash, jiffy (*informal*), moment), in two shakes of a lamb's tail (*informal*), quickly, rapidly, speedily, swiftly **9. in time a.** at the appointed time, early, in good time, on schedule, on time, with time to spare **b.** by and by, eventually, one day, some day, sooner or later, ultimately **10. on time** in good time, on the dot, punctually **11. time and again** frequently, many times, often, on many occa-

cally at or for a set time: *an electrical time switch.* ~*interj* **38** the word called out by a publican signalling that it is closing time. ~See also **times.**

time and a half *n* a rate of pay one and a half times the normal rate, often offered for overtime work.

time-and-motion study *n* the analysis of work procedures to work out the most efficient methods of operation.

time bomb *n* **1** a bomb containing a timing mechanism that is set so that the bomb will explode at a specified time. **2** something that will have a large, often damaging, effect at a later date: *the decline of the manufacturing industry is a political time bomb.*

time capsule *n* a container holding articles representative of the current age, buried for discovery in the future.

time clock *n* a clock with a device for recording the time of arrival or departure of an employee.

time-consuming *adj* taking up a great deal of time.

time exposure *n* a photograph produced by exposing film for a relatively long period, usually a few seconds.

time-honoured *adj* having been used or done for a long time and established by custom.

timekeeper *n* **1** a person or thing that keeps or records time, for instance at a sporting event. **2** an employee with a record of punctuality as specified: *a poor timekeeper.* **timekeeping** *n*

time lag *n* a gap or delay between one event and a related event that happens after it: *the time lag between the development and the marketing of new products.*

timeless *adj* **1** unaffected by time or by changes in fashion, society, etc.: *the timeless appeal of tailored wool jackets.* **2** eternal and everlasting: *the timeless universal reality behind all religions.* **timelessness** *n*

timely *adj* **-lier, -liest,** *adv* at the right or an appropriate time.

time-out *n* **1** *Sport chiefly US & Canad* an interruption in play during which players rest, discuss tactics, etc. **2 take time out** to take a break from a job or activity.

timepiece *n* a device, such as a clock or watch, which measures and indicates time.

timer *n* a device for measuring time, esp. a switch or regulator that causes a mechanism to operate at a specific time.

times *prep* multiplied by: *ten times four is forty.*

timescale *n* the period of time within which events occur or are due to occur.

time-served *adj* having successfully completed an apprenticeship or period of training: *a time-served electrician.*

timeserver *n* a person who changes his or her views in order to gain support or favour.

time sharing *n* **1** a system of part ownership of a property for use as a holiday home whereby each participant owns the property for a particular period every year. **2** a system by which users at different terminals of a computer can communicate with it at the same time.

time signature *n Music* a sign, usually consisting of two figures placed after the key signature, that indicates the number and length of beats in the bar.

timetable *n* **1** a plan of the times when a job or activity should be done: *the timetable for the Royal Visit.* **2** a list of departure and arrival times of trains or buses: *a timetable hung on the wall beside the ticket office.* **3** a plan of the times when different subjects or classes are taught in a school or college: *a heavy timetable of lectures and practical classes.* ~*vb* **-tabling, -tabled 4** to set a time when a particular thing should be done: *the meeting is timetabled for 3 o'clock.*

time value *n Music* the duration of a note relative to other notes in a composition and considered in relation to the basic tempo.

time warp *n* an imagined distortion of the progress of time, so that, for instance, events from the past seem to be happening in the present.

timeworn *adj* **1** showing the adverse effects of overlong use or of old age: *a timeworn café.* **2** having been used so often as to be no longer interesting: *a timeworn cliché.*

time zone *n* a region throughout which the same standard time is used.

timid *adj* **1** lacking courage or self-confidence: *a timid youth.* **2** indicating shyness or fear: *a timid and embarrassed smile.* **timidity** *n* **timidly** *adv*

timing *n* the ability to judge when to do or say something so as to make the best effect, for instance in the theatre, in playing an instrument, or in hitting a ball in sport.

timorous (**tim**-mor-uss) *adj Literary* lacking courage or self-confidence: *a reclusive timorous creature.* **timorously** *adv*

timpani *or* **tympani** (**tim**-pan-ee) *pl n* a set of kettledrums. **timpanist** *or* **tympanist** *n*

tin *n* **1** a soft silvery white metallic element. Symbol: Sn **2** a sealed airtight metal container used for preserving and storing food or drink: *a cupboard full of packets and tins.* **3** any metal container: *a tin of paint.* **4** the contents of a tin. **5** *Brit, Austral, & NZ* galvanized iron, used to make roofs. ~*vb* **tinning, tinned 6** to put (food) into tins.

tin can *n* a metal food container.

tincture *n* a medicine consisting of a small amount of a drug dissolved in alcohol.

tinder *n* dry wood or other easily-burning material used to start a fire. **tindery** *adj*

tinderbox *n* (formerly) a small box for tinder, esp. one fitted with a flint and steel which could be used to make a spark.

tine *n* a slender prong of a fork or a deer's antler. **tined** *adj*

tinfoil *n* a paper-thin sheet of metal, used for wrapping foodstuffs.

ting *n* a high metallic sound such as that made by a small bell.

ting-a-ling *n* the sound of a small bell.

tinge *n* **1** a slight tint or colouring: *his skin had an unhealthy greyish tinge.* **2** a very small amount: *both goals had a tinge of fortune.* ~*vb* **tingeing** *or* **tinging, tinged 3** to colour or tint faintly: *the sunset tinged the*

THESAURUS

sions, over and over again, repeatedly, time after time ~*vb.* **12.** clock, control, count, judge, measure, regulate, schedule, set

timeless abiding, ageless, ceaseless, changeless, deathless, endless, enduring, eternal, everlasting, immortal, immutable, imperishable, indestructible, lasting, permanent, persistent, undying

timely appropriate, at the right time, convenient, judicious, opportune, prompt, propitious, punctual, seasonable, suitable, well-timed

timetable agenda, calendar, curriculum, diary, list, order of the day, programme, schedule

timid afraid, apprehensive, bashful, cowardly, diffident, faint-hearted, fearful, irresolute, mousy, nervous, pusillanimous (*formal*), retiring, shrinking, shy, timorous

lake with pink. **4 tinged with** having a small amount of a particular quality: *the victory was tinged with sadness.*

tingle *vb* **-gling, -gled 1** to feel a mild prickling or stinging sensation, as from cold or excitement. *~n* **2** a mild prickling or stinging feeling. **tingling** *adj* **tingly** *adj*

tin god *n* a self-important person.

tinker *n* **1** (esp. formerly) a travelling mender of pots and pans. **2** *Scot & Irish* a Gypsy. **3** a mischievous child. *~vb* **4 tinker with** to try to repair or improve (something) by making lots of minor adjustments.

tinker's damn *or* **cuss** *n* **not give a tinker's damn** *or* **cuss** *Slang* not to care at all.

tinkle *vb* **-kling, -kled 1** to ring with a high tinny sound like a small bell. *~n* **2** a high clear ringing sound. **3** *Brit informal* a telephone call. **tinkly** *adj*

tinned *adj* (of food) preserved by being sealed in a tin.

tinny *adj* **-nier, -niest 1** (of a sound) high, thin, and metallic: *the tinny sound of a transistor radio.* **2** cheap or shoddy: *a tinny East European car.*

tin-opener *n* a small tool for opening tins.

Tin Pan Alley *n* the popular music industry, esp. the more commercial aspects of it.

tin plate *n* thin steel sheet coated with a layer of tin to protect it from corrosion.

tinpot *adj Brit informal* worthless or unimportant: *a tinpot dictator.*

tinsel *n* **1** a decoration consisting of a piece of metallic thread with thin strips of metal foil attached along its length. **2** anything cheap, showy, and gaudy: *all their tinsel and show counts for nothing.* *~adj* **3** made of or decorated with tinsel. **4** cheap, showy, and gaudy. **tinselly** *adj*

Tinseltown *n Informal* Hollywood, the centre of the US film industry.

tinsmith *n* a person who works with tin or tin plate.

tint *n* **1** a shade of a colour, esp. a pale one: *his eyes had a yellow tint.* **2** a colour that is softened by the addition of white: *a room decorated in pastel tints.* **3** a dye for the hair. *~vb* **4** to give a tint to (something, such as hair).

tintinnabulation *n* the ringing or pealing of bells.

tiny *adj* **tinier, tiniest** very small.

tip[1] *n* **1** a narrow or pointed end of something: *the northern tip of Japan.* **2** a small piece attached to the end or bottom of something: *boot tips keep boots from getting scuffed.* *~vb* **tipping, tipped 3** to make or form a tip on: *the long strips that hang down are tipped with silver cones.* **tipped** *adj*

tip[2] *n* **1** an amount of money given to someone, such as a waiter, in return for service. **2** a helpful hint or warning: *here are some sensible tips to help you avoid sunburn.* **3** a piece of inside information, esp. in betting or investing. *~vb* **tipping, tipped 4** to give a tip to.

tip[3] *vb* **tipping, tipped 1** to tilt: *he tipped back his chair.* **2 tip over** to tilt so as to overturn or fall: *the box tipped over and the clothes in it spilled out.* **3** *Brit* to dump (rubbish). **4** to pour out (the contents of a container): *he tipped the water from the basin down the sink.* *~n* **5** *Brit* a rubbish dump.

tip-off *n* **1** a warning or hint, esp. one given confidentially and based on inside information. *~vb* **tip off 2** to give a hint or warning to: *the police had been tipped off about the robbery.*

tippet *n* a scarflike piece of fur, often made from a whole animal skin, worn, esp. formerly, round a woman's shoulders.

tipple *vb* **-pling, -pled 1** to drink alcohol regularly, esp. in small quantities. *~n* **2** an alcoholic drink. **tippler** *n*

tipstaff *n* **1** a court official. **2** a metal-tipped staff formerly used as a symbol of office.

tipster *n* a person who sells tips to people betting on horse races or speculating on the stock market.

tipsy *adj* **-sier, -siest** slightly drunk. **tipsiness** *n*

tiptoe *vb* **-toeing, -toed 1** to walk quietly with the heels off the ground. *~n* **2 on tiptoe** on the tips of the toes or on the ball of the foot and the toes.

tiptop *adj, adv* of the highest quality or condition.

tip-up *adj* able to be turned upwards around a hinge or pivot: *tip-up seats.*

TIR International Road Transport.

tirade *n* a long angry speech or denunciation.

tire[1] *vb* **tiring, tired 1** to reduce the energy of, as by exertion: *she could still do things that would tire women half her age.* **2** to become wearied or bored: *he simply stopped talking when he tired of my questions.* **tiring** *adj*

tire[2] *n US* same as **tyre.**

tired *adj* **1** weary or exhausted: *they were tired after their long journey.* **2** bored of or no longer interested in something: *I'm tired of staying in watching TV every*

THESAURUS

timorous *literary* afraid, apprehensive, bashful, cowardly, diffident, faint-hearted, fearful, frightened, irresolute, mousy, nervous, pusillanimous (*formal*), retiring, shrinking, shy, timid, trembling

tinge *n.* **1.** cast, colour, dye, shade, stain, tincture, tint, wash **2.** bit, dash, drop, pinch, smack, smattering, *soupçon*, sprinkling, suggestion, touch, trace *~vb.* **3.** colour, dye, shade, stain, tinge, tint

tingle 1. *vb.* have goose pimples, itch, prickle, sting, tickle **2.** *n.* goose pimples, itch, itching, pins and needles (*informal*), prickling, stinging, thrill, tickle, tickling

tinker *vb. with* **with** dabble, fiddle (*informal*), meddle, mess about, monkey, muck about (*Brit. slang*), play, potter, toy

tint *n.* **1.** cast, colour, hue, shade, tone **2.** dye, rinse, stain, tincture, tinge, wash *~vb.* **3.** colour, dye, rinse, stain, tincture, tinge

tiny diminutive, dwarfish, infinitesimal, insignificant, Lilliputian, little, microscopic, mini, miniature, minute, negligible, petite, pint-sized (*informal*), puny, pygmy, slight, small, teensy-weensy, teeny-weeny, trifling, wee

tip[1] **1.** *n.* apex, cap, crown, end, extremity, head, peak, point, summit, top **2.** *vb.* cap, crown, finish, surmount, top

tip[2] *n.* **1.** baksheesh, gift, gratuity, perquisite, *pourboire* **2.** hint, pointer, suggestion, word, word of advice **3.** clue, forecast, gen (*Brit. informal*), hint, information, inside information, warning *~vb.* **4.** remunerate, reward

tip[3] *vb.* **1.** cant, capsize, incline, lean, list, overturn, slant, spill, tilt, topple over, upend, upset **2.** *Brit.* ditch (*slang*), dump, empty, pour out, unload *~n.* **3.** *Brit.* dump, midden (*dialect*), refuse heap, rubbish heap

tip-off *n.* clue, forecast, gen (*Brit. informal*), hint, information, inside information, warning

tip off *vb.* advise, caution, forewarn, give a clue, give a hint, suggest, tip (someone) the wink (*Brit. informal*), warn

tipple 1. *vb.* bend the elbow (*informal*), bevvy (*dialect*), drink, imbibe, indulge (*informal*), quaff, swig, take a drink, tope **2.** *n.* alcohol, booze (*informal*), drink, liquor, poison (*informal*)

tire drain, droop, enervate, exhaust, fag (*informal*),

night. **3** having been used so often as to be no longer interesting: *you haven't fallen for that tired old line, have you?* **tiredness** *n*

tireless *adj* energetic and determined: *a tireless worker for charity.* **tirelessly** *adv*

tiresome *adj* boring and irritating.

'tis *Poetic or dialect* it is.

tissue *n* **1** a group of cells in an animal or plant with a similar structure and function: *muscular tissue forms 42% of the body tissue.* **2** a thin piece of soft absorbent paper used as a disposable handkerchief, towel, etc. **3** short for **tissue paper. 4** an interwoven series: *a tissue of lies.*

tissue paper *n* very thin soft delicate paper used esp. to wrap breakable goods.

tit[1] *n* any of various small European songbirds, such as the bluetit, that feed on insects and seeds.

tit[2] *n* **1** *Slang* a female breast. **2** a teat or nipple.

titan *n* a person of great strength, importance, or size: *one of the titans of the computer industry.*

titanic *adj* having or requiring colossal strength: *a titanic struggle.*

titanium *n Chem* a strong white metallic element used in the manufacture of strong lightweight alloys, esp. aircraft parts. Symbol: Ti

titbit *or esp US* **tidbit** *n* **1** a tasty small piece of food. **2** a pleasing scrap of scandal: *an interesting titbit of gossip.*

titfer *n Old-fashioned, Brit slang* a hat.

tit-for-tat *adj* done in return or retaliation for a similar act: *a spate of tit-for-tat killings.*

tithe *n* **1** one tenth of one's income or produce paid to the church as a tax. **2** a tenth or very small part of anything: *he had accomplished only a tithe of his great dream.* ~*vb* **tithing, tithed 3** to demand a tithe from. **4** to pay a tithe or tithes. **tithable** *adj*

tithe barn *n* a large barn where, formerly, the agricultural tithe of a parish was stored.

Titian (**tish**-un) *adj* (of hair) reddish-yellow.

titillate *vb* **-lating, -lated** to arouse or excite pleasurably, esp. in a sexual way. **titillating** *adj* **titillation** *n*

titivate *vb* **-vating, -vated** to make smarter or neater. **titivation** *n*

title *n* **1** the distinctive name of a book, film, record, etc.: *his first album bore the title "Safe as Milk".* **2** a descriptive name or heading of a section of a book, speech, etc. **3** a book or periodical: *publishers were averaging a total of 500 new titles annually.* **4** a name or epithet signifying rank, office, or function: *the job bears the title Assistant Divisional Administrator.* **5** a formal designation, such as *Mrs* or *Dr.* **6** *Sport* a championship: *the British heavyweight title.* **7** *Law* the legal right to possession of property.

titled *adj* having a title such as "Lady" or "Sir" which indicates a high social rank.

title deed *n* a document containing evidence of a person's legal right or title to property, esp. a house or land.

titleholder *n* a person who holds a title, esp. a sporting championship.

title page *n* the page in a book that gives the title, author, publisher, etc.

title role *n* the role of the character after whom a play or film is named.

titmouse *n, pl* **-mice** same as **tit**[1].

titrate (**tite**-rate) *vb* **-trating, -trated** *Chem* to measure the volume or concentration of (a solution) by titration.

titration *n Chem* an operation in which a measured amount of one solution is added to a known quantity of another solution until the reaction between the two is complete. If the concentration of one solution is known, that of the other can be calculated.

titter *vb* **1** to snigger, esp. derisively or in a suppressed way. ~*n* **2** a suppressed laugh or snigger.

tittle *n* a very small amount: *it doesn't matter one jot or tittle what you think.*

tittle-tattle *n* **1** idle chat or gossip. ~*vb* **-tattling, -tattled 2** to chatter or gossip.

tittup *vb* **-tupping, -tupped** *or US* **-tuping, -tuped 1** to prance or frolic. ~*n* **2** a caper.

titular *adj* **1** in name only: *titular head of state.* **2** of or having a title.

tizzy *n, pl* **-zies** *Informal* a state of confusion or excitement.

T-junction *n* a junction where one road joins another at right angles but does not cross it.

Tl *Chem* thallium.

Tm *Chem* thulium.

TN Tennessee.

TNT *n* 2,4,6-trinitrotoluene: a type of powerful explosive.

to *prep* **1** used to indicate the destination of the subject or object of an action: *he went to the theatre.* **2** used to introduce the indirect object of a verb: *talk to him.* **3** used to introduce the infinitive of a verb: *I'm going to lie down.* **4** as far as or until: *from September 11 to October 25.* **5** used to indicate that two things have an equivalent value: *there are 16 ounces to the pound.* **6** against or onto: *I put my ear to the door.* **7** before the hour of: *17 minutes to midnight.* **8** accompanied by: *dancing to a live band.* **9** as compared with: *four goals to nil.* **10** used to indicate a resulting condition: *burnt to death.* **11** working for or employed by:

THESAURUS

fail, fatigue, flag, jade, knacker (*slang*), sink, take it out of (*informal*), wear down, wear out, weary

tired 1. all in (*slang*), asleep *or* dead on one's feet (*informal*), clapped out (*Austral. & N.Z. informal*), dead beat (*informal*), dog-tired (*informal*), done in (*informal*), drained, drooping, drowsy, enervated, exhausted, fagged (*informal*), fatigued, flagging, jaded, knackered (*slang*), ready to drop, sleepy, spent, weary, whacked (*Brit. informal*), worn out, zonked (*slang*) **2.** *with* **of** annoyed with, bored with, exasperated by, fed up with, irked by, irritated by, pissed off with (*taboo slang*), sick of, weary of **3.** clichéd, conventional, corny (*slang*), familiar, hackneyed, old, outworn, stale, stock, threadbare, trite, well-worn

tireless determined, energetic, indefatigable, industrious, resolute, unflagging, untiring, unwearied, vigorous

tiresome annoying, boring, dull, exasperating, flat, irksome, irritating, laborious, monotonous, tedious, trying, uninteresting, vexatious, wearing, wearisome

tiring arduous, demanding, exacting, exhausting, fatiguing, laborious, strenuous, tough, wearing, wearying

tissue 1. fabric, gauze, mesh, structure, stuff, texture, web **2.** paper, paper handkerchief, wrapping paper **3.** accumulation, chain, collection, combination, concatenation, conglomeration, fabrication, mass, network, pack, series, web

titbit *bonne bouche*, choice item, dainty, delicacy, goody, morsel, scrap, snack, treat

title *n.* **1.** appellation, denomination, designation, epithet, handle (*slang*), moniker (*slang*), name, nickname, nom de plume, pseudonym, sobriquet, term **2.** caption,

Chaplain to the Nigerian Chaplaincy in Britain. **12** in commemoration of: *a memorial to the victims of the disaster.* ~*adv* **13** towards a closed position: *push the door to.*

toad *n* **1** an amphibian which resembles a frog, but has a warty skin and spends more time on dry land. **2** a loathsome person.

toadflax *n* a plant with narrow leaves and yellow-orange flowers.

toad-in-the-hole *n Brit* a dish made of sausages baked in a batter.

toadstool *n* any of various poisonous funguses consisting of a caplike top on a stem.

toady *n, pl* **toadies 1** a person who flatters and ingratiates himself or herself in a fawning way. ~*vb* **toadies, toadying, toadied 2** to fawn on and flatter (someone). **toadyism** *n*

to and fro *adv, adj also* **to-and-fro 1** back and forth: *he moved his head to and fro as if dodging blows.* **2** from one place to another then back again: *the ferry sailed to and fro across the river.* **toing and froing** *n*

toast[1] *n* **1** sliced bread browned by exposure to heat. ~*vb* **2** to brown (bread) under a grill or over a fire. **3** to warm or be warmed: *toasting his feet at the fire.*

toast[2] *n* **1** a proposal of health or success given to a person or thing and marked by people raising glasses and drinking together. **2** a person or thing that is honoured: *his success made him the toast of the British film industry.* ~*vb* **3** to propose or drink a toast to (a person or thing).

toaster *n* an electrical device for toasting bread.

toastmaster *n* a person who introduces speakers and proposes toasts at public dinners.

tobacco *n, pl* **-cos** *or* **-coes** an American plant with large leaves which are dried for smoking, or chewing, or made into snuff.

tobacconist *n Chiefly Brit* a person or shop that sells tobacco, cigarettes, pipes, etc.

-to-be *adj* about to be; future: *the bride-to-be.*

toboggan *n* **1** a long narrow sledge used for sliding over snow and ice. ~*vb* **2** to ride on a toboggan.

toby *n, pl* **-bies** *NZ* a water stopcock at the boundary of a street and house section.

toby jug *n* a beer mug or jug in the form of a stout seated man wearing a three-cornered hat and smoking a pipe.

toccata (tok-**kah**-ta) *n* a piece of fast music for the organ, harpsichord, or piano, usually in a rhythmically free style.

Toc H *n* a society formed after World War I to encourage Christian comradeship.

tocsin *n* **1** a warning signal. **2** an alarm bell.

tod *n* **on one's tod** *Brit slang* by oneself; alone.

today *n* **1** this day, as distinct from yesterday or tomorrow. **2** the present age: *in today's world.* ~*adv* **3** during or on this day: *I hope you're feeling better today.* **4** nowadays: *this is one of the most reliable cars available today.*

toddle *vb* **-dling, -dled 1** to walk with short unsteady steps, like a young child. **2 toddle off** *Jocular* to depart: *he toddled off to bed.* ~*n* **3** the act or an instance of walking with short unsteady steps.

toddler *n* a young child who has only just learned how to walk.

toddy *n, pl* **-dies** a drink made from spirits, esp. whisky, hot water, sugar, and usually lemon juice.

to-do *n, pl* **-dos** a commotion, fuss, or quarrel.

toe *n* **1** any one of the digits of the foot. **2** the part of a shoe or sock covering the toes. **3 on one's toes** alert. **4 tread on someone's toes** to offend a person, esp. by trespassing on his or her field of responsibility. ~*vb* **toeing, toed 5** to touch or kick with the toe. **6 toe the line** to conform to expected attitudes or standards.

toecap *n* a reinforced covering for the toe of a boot or shoe.

toehold *n* **1** a small space on a rock, mountain, etc., which can be used to support the toe of the foot in climbing. **2** any means of gaining access or advantage: *the French car industry has lost its last toehold in America.*

toenail *n* a thin hard clear plate covering part of the upper surface of the end of each toe.

toerag *n Brit slang* a contemptible or despicable person.

toff *n Brit slang* a well-dressed or upper-class person.

toffee *n* **1** a sticky chewy sweet made by boiling sugar with water and butter. **2 can't (do something) for toffee** *Informal* is not competent or talented at (doing something): *she couldn't dance for toffee.*

toffee-apple *n* an apple fixed on a stick and coated with a thin layer of toffee.

toffee-nosed *adj Slang, chiefly Brit* snobbish or conceited.

tofu *n* a food with a soft cheeselike consistency made from unfermented soya-bean curd.

tog *n* unit for measuring the insulating power of duvets.

toga (**toe**-ga) *n* a garment worn by citizens of ancient Rome, consisting of a piece of cloth draped around the body. **togaed** *adj*

together *adv* **1** with cooperation between people or organizations: *we started a company together.* **2** in or into contact with each other: *he clasped his hands together.* **3** in or into one place: *the family gets together to talk.* **4** at the same time: *"Disgusting," said Julie and Alice together.* **5** considered collectively: *together the two estates are likely to be worth more than £2.5 billion.* **6** *Old-fashioned* continuously: *working for eight hours together.* **7 together with** in addition to. ~*adj* **8** *Slang* self-possessed, competent, and well-organized.
➤ Two nouns linked by *together with* do not make a

THESAURUS

heading, inscription, label, legend, name **3.** *Law* claim, entitlement, ownership, prerogative, privilege, right

titter chortle (*informal*), chuckle, giggle, laugh, snigger, tee-hee

toady 1. *n.* apple polisher (*U.S. slang*), ass-kisser (*U.S. & Canad. taboo slang*), bootlicker (*informal*), brown-noser (*taboo slang*), crawler (*slang*), creep (*slang*), fawner, flatterer, hanger-on, lackey, sycophant, yes man **2.** *vb.* be obsequious to, bow and scrape, brown-nose (*taboo slang*), butter up, crawl, creep, cringe, curry favour with, fawn on, flatter, grovel, kiss (someone's) ass (*U.S. & Canad. taboo slang*), kiss the feet of, kowtow to, lick (someone's) boots, pander to, suck up to (*informal*)

toast[1] *vb.* brown, grill, heat, roast, warm

toast[2] *n.* **1.** compliment, drink, health, pledge, salute, tribute **2.** darling, favourite, hero, heroine ~*vb.* **3.** drink to, drink (to) the health of, pledge, salute

together *adv.* **1.** as a group, as one, cheek by jowl, closely, collectively, hand in glove, hand in hand, in a body, in concert, in cooperation, in unison, jointly, mutually, shoulder to shoulder, side by side **2.** all at once, as one, at one fell swoop, at the same time, concurrently, contemporaneously, en masse, in unison, simultaneously, with one accord **3.** *old-fashioned* consecutively, continuously, in a row, in succession, one after the other, on end, successively, without a break,

plural subject so the following verb must be singular: *Jones, together with his partner, has had great success.*

togetherness *n* a feeling of closeness to and affection for other people.

togged up *adj Informal* dressed up in smart clothes. Also: **togged out**

toggle *n* **1** a bar-shaped button inserted through a loop for fastening coats etc. **2** *Computers* a key on a keyboard which, when pressed, will turn a function or feature on if it is currently off, and turn it off if it is currently on. **3** short for **toggle switch** (sense 1).

toggle switch *n* **1** an electric switch with a projecting lever that is moved in a particular way to open or close a circuit. **2** same as **toggle** (sense 2).

togs *pl n Informal* clothes.

toheroa (toe-a-**roe**-a) *n* a large edible mollusc of New Zealand with a distinctive flavour.

tohunga (**toe**-hung-a) *n NZ* a Maori priest.

toil *n* **1** hard or exhausting work: *hours of toil beneath the Catalan sun.* ~*vb* **2** to work hard: *workers toiling in the fields to produce tea for westerners to drink.* **3** to move slowly and with difficulty, for instance because of exhaustion or the steepness of a slope: *Joanna toiled up the steps to the church.*

toilet *n* **1 a** a bowl fitted with a water-flushing device and connected to a drain, for receiving and disposing of urine and faeces. **b** a room with such a fitment. **2** the act of dressing and preparing oneself.

toilet paper *n* thin absorbent paper used for cleaning oneself after defecation or urination.

toilet roll *n* a long strip of toilet paper wound around a cardboard tube.

toiletry *n, pl* **-ries** an object or cosmetic used in making up, dressing, etc.

toilette (twah-**let**) *n* same as **toilet** (sense 2).

toilet water *n* liquid perfume lighter than cologne.

toilsome *adj Literary* requiring hard work: *a most toilsome job.*

token *n* **1** a symbol, sign, or indication of something: *as a token of respect.* **2** a gift voucher that can be used as payment for goods of a specified value. **3** a metal or plastic disc, such as a substitute for currency for use in a slot machine. **4 by the same token** in the same way as something mentioned previously. ~*adj* **5** intended to create an impression but having no real importance: *as a token gesture of goodwill.*

tokenism *n* the practice of making only a token effort or doing no more than the minimum, esp. in order to comply with a law. **tokenist** *adj*

token strike *n* a brief stoppage of work intended to convey strength of feeling on a disputed issue.

told *vb* the past of **tell.**

tolerable *adj* **1** able to be put up with; bearable. **2** *Informal* fairly good. **tolerably** *adv*

tolerance *n* **1** the quality of accepting other people's rights to their own opinions, beliefs, or actions. **2** capacity to endure something, esp. pain or hardship. **3** the ability of a substance to withstand heat, stress, etc., without damage. **4** *Med* the capacity to endure the effects of a continued or increasing dose of a drug, poison, etc. **5** an acceptable degree of variation in a measurement or value: *the bodywork of the car is precision-engineered with a tolerance of 0.01 millimetres.*

tolerant *adj* **1** accepting of the beliefs, actions, etc., of other people. **2 tolerant of** able to withstand (heat, stress, etc.) without damage.

tolerate *vb* **-ating, -ated 1** to allow something to exist or happen, even although one does not approve of it: *you must learn to tolerate opinions other than your own.* **2** to put up with (someone or something): *he found the pain hard to tolerate.* **toleration** *n*

toll[1] *vb* **1** to ring (a bell) slowly and regularly. **2** to announce by tolling: *the bells tolled the Queen's death.* ~*n* **3** the slow regular ringing of a bell.

toll[2] *n* **1** a charge for the use of certain roads and bridges. **2** loss or damage from a disaster: *the annual death toll on the roads is about 4500.* **3 take a** *or* **its toll** to have a severe and damaging effect: *the continued stress had taken a toll on her health.*

tollgate *n* a gate across a toll road or bridge at which travellers must pay.

THESAURUS

without interruption ~*adj.* **4.** *slang* calm, composed, cool, stable, well-adjusted, well-balanced, well-organized

toil 1. *n.* application, donkey-work, drudgery, effort, elbow grease (*informal*), exertion, graft (*informal*), hard work, industry, labour, pains, slog, sweat, travail (*literary*) **2.** *vb.* bend over backwards (*informal*), break one's neck (*informal*), bust a gut (*informal*), do one's damnedest (*informal*), drudge, give it one's all (*informal*), give it one's best shot (*informal*), go for broke (*slang*), go for it (*informal*), graft (*informal*), grind (*informal*), knock oneself out (*informal*), labour, make an all-out effort (*informal*), push oneself, rupture oneself (*informal*), slave, slog, strive, struggle, sweat (*informal*), work, work like a dog, work like a Trojan, work one's fingers to the bone

toilet 1. bathroom, bog (*slang*), can (*U.S. & Canad. slang*), closet, convenience, crapper (*taboo slang*), gents (*Brit. informal*), john (*slang, chiefly U.S. & Canad.*), khazi (*slang*), ladies' room, latrine, lavatory, little boys' room (*informal*), little girls' room (*informal*), loo (*Brit. informal*), outhouse, *pissoir,* powder room, privy, urinal, washroom, water closet, WC **2.** ablutions, bathing, dressing, grooming, toilette

token 1. *n.* badge, clue, demonstration, evidence, expression, index, indication, manifestation, mark, note, proof, representation, sign, symbol **2.** *adj.* hollow, minimal, nominal, perfunctory, superficial, symbolic

tolerable 1. acceptable, allowable, bearable, endurable, sufferable, supportable **2.** *informal* acceptable, adequate, all right, average, fair, fairly good, fair to middling, good enough, indifferent, mediocre, middling, not bad (*informal*), O.K. *or* okay (*informal*), ordinary, passable, run-of-the-mill, so-so (*informal*), unexceptional

tolerance 1. broad-mindedness, charity, forbearance, indulgence, lenity, magnanimity, open-mindedness, patience, permissiveness, sufferance, sympathy **2.** endurance, fortitude, hardiness, hardness, resilience, resistance, stamina, staying power, toughness **3.** fluctuation, play, swing, variation

tolerant broad-minded, catholic, charitable, easy-going, easy-oasy (*slang*), fair, forbearing, free and easy, indulgent, latitudinarian, lenient, liberal, magnanimous, open-minded, patient, permissive, sympathetic, unbigoted, understanding, unprejudiced

tolerate 1. abide, accept, admit, allow, brook, condone, countenance, indulge, permit, put up with (*informal*), sanction, turn a blind eye to, wink at **2.** bear, endure, put up with (*informal*), stand, stomach, submit to, suffer, swallow, take, thole (*Scot. & northern English*)

toleration acceptance, allowance, endurance, indulgence, permissiveness, sanction, sufferance

toll[1] *vb.* **1.** chime, clang, knell, peal, ring, sound, strike **2.** announce, call, signal, warn ~*n.* **3.** chime, clang, knell, peal, ring, ringing, tolling

tolu (tol-**loo**) *n* a sweet-smelling balsam obtained from a South American tree, used in medicine and perfume.

toluene *n* a flammable liquid obtained from petroleum and coal tar and used as a solvent and in the manufacture of dyes, explosives, etc.

tom *n* **1** a male cat. *~adj* **2** (of an animal) male: *a tom turkey.*

tomahawk *n* a fighting axe used by the North American Indians.

tomato *n, pl* **-toes 1** a red fleshy juicy fruit with many edible seeds, eaten in salads, as a vegetable, etc. **2** the plant, originally from South America, on which this fruit grows.

tomb *n* **1** a place for the burial of a corpse. **2** a monument over a grave. **3 the tomb** *Poetic* death.

tombola *n Brit* a type of lottery, in which tickets are drawn from a revolving drum.

tomboy *n* a girl who behaves or dresses like a boy.

tombstone *n* a gravestone.

tome *n* a large heavy book.

tomfoolery *n* foolish behaviour.

Tommy *n, pl* **-mies** *Brit old-fashioned, informal* a private in the British Army.

Tommy gun *n* a type of light sub-machine-gun.

tommyrot *n Old-fashioned, informal* utter nonsense.

tomorrow *n* **1** the day after today: *tomorrow's meeting has been cancelled.* **2** the future: *the struggle to build a better tomorrow.* *~adv* **3** on the day after today: *the festival starts tomorrow.* **4** at some time in the future: *they live today as millions more will live tomorrow.*

tomtit *n Brit* a small European bird that eats insects and seeds.

tom-tom *n* a long narrow drum beaten with the hands.

ton[1] *n* **1** *Brit* a unit of weight equal to 2240 pounds or 1016.046 909 kilograms. **2** *US & Canad* a unit of weight equal to 2000 pounds or 907.184 kilograms. **3** See **metric ton. 4 come down on someone like a ton of bricks** to scold someone very severely. *~adv* **5 tons** a lot: *I've got tons of things to do before going on holiday.*

ton[2] *n Slang, chiefly Brit* a hundred miles per hour.

tonal *adj* **1** *Music* written in a key. **2** of or relating to tone or tonality.

tonality *n, pl* **-ties 1** *Music* the presence of a musical key in a composition. **2** the overall scheme of colours and tones in a painting.

tone *n* **1** sound with reference to its pitch, timbre, or volume. **2** *US & Canad* same as **note** (sense 6). **3** *Music* an interval of two semitones, such as that between doh and ray in tonic sol-fa. **4** the quality or character of a sound: *her tone was angry.* **5** general aspect, quality, or style: *the tone of the conversation made him queasy.* **6** high quality or style: *my car with its patches of rust lowered the tone of the neighbourhood.* **7** the quality of a given colour, as modified by mixture with white or black; shade or tint. **8** *Physiol* the natural firmness of the tissues and normal functioning of bodily organs in health. *~vb* **toning, toned 9** to be of a matching or similar tone. **10** to give a tone to or correct the tone of. **toneless** *adj* **tonelessly** *adv*

tone-deaf *adj* unable to distinguish subtle differences in musical pitch.

tone down *vb* to moderate in tone: *I sensed some reserve in his manner, so I toned down my enthusiasm.*

tone poem *n Music* an extended orchestral composition based on nonmusical material, such as a work of literature or a fairy tale.

toner *n* **1** a cosmetic applied to the skin to reduce oiliness. **2** a powdered chemical that forms the image produced by a photocopier.

tone up *vb* to make or become more vigorous, healthy, etc.: *muscle tissue can be toned up.*

tong *n* (formerly) a secret society of Chinese Americans.

tongs *pl n* a tool for grasping or lifting, consisting of two long metal or wooden arms, joined with a hinge or flexible metal strip at one end.

tongue *n* **1** a movable mass of muscular tissue attached to the floor of the mouth, used for tasting, eating, and speaking. **2** a language, dialect, or idiom: *the Scots tongue.* **3** the ability to speak: *taken aback, she could not find her tongue.* **4** a manner of speaking: *a sharp tongue.* **5** the tongue of certain animals used as food. **6** a narrow strip of something that extends outwards: *a narrow tongue of flame shot from between the logs.* **7** a flap of leather on a shoe. **8** the clapper of a bell. **9** a projecting strip along an edge of a board that is made to fit a groove in another board. **10 hold one's tongue** to keep quiet. **11 on the tip of one's tongue** about to come to mind. **12 with (one's) tongue in one's cheek** with insincere or ironical intent.

tongue-tie *n* a congenital condition in which movement of the tongue is limited as the result of the fold of skin under the tongue extending too close to the front of the tongue.

tongue-tied *adj* speechless, esp. with embarrassment or shyness.

tongue twister *n* a sentence or phrase that is difficult to say clearly and quickly, such as *the sixth sick sheikh's sixth sheep's sick.*

tonguing *n* a technique of playing a wind instrument by obstructing and uncovering the air passage through the lips with the tongue.

tonic *n* **1** a medicine that improves the functioning of the body or increases the feeling of wellbeing. **2** anything that enlivens or strengthens: *his dry humour was a stimulating tonic.* **3** Also called: **tonic water** a carbonated beverage containing quinine and often mixed with alcoholic drinks: *gin and tonic.* **4** *Music* the first

THESAURUS

toll[2] **1.** assessment, charge, customs, demand, duty, fee, levy, payment, rate, tariff, tax, tribute **2.** cost, damage, inroads, loss, penalty

tomb burial chamber, catacomb, crypt, grave, mausoleum, sarcophagus, sepulchre, vault

tombstone gravestone, headstone, marker, memorial, monument

tome book, title, volume, work

tomfoolery buffoonery, childishness, clowning, fooling around (*informal*), foolishness, horseplay, idiocy, larks (*informal*), messing around (*informal*), shenanigans (*informal*), silliness, skylarking (*informal*), stupidity

tone *n.* **1.** force, inflection, intonation, modulation, pitch, stress, timbre, tonality, volume **2.** air, approach, aspect, attitude, character, drift, effect, feel, frame, grain, manner, mood, note, quality, spirit, style, temper, tenor, vein **3.** cast, colour, hue, shade, tinge, tint *~vb.* **4.** blend, go well with, harmonize, match, suit

tone down dampen, dim, mitigate, moderate, modulate, play down, reduce, restrain, soften, soft-pedal (*informal*), subdue, temper

tongue 1. argot, dialect, idiom, language, lingo (*informal*), parlance, patois, speech, talk, vernacular **2.**

note of a major or minor scale and the tonal centre of a piece composed in a particular key. ~*adj* **5** having an invigorating or refreshing effect: *a tonic bath.* **6** *Music* of the first note of a major or minor scale.

tonic sol-fa *n* a method of teaching music, by which syllables are used as names for the notes of the major scale in any key.

tonight *n* **1** the night or evening of this present day: *tonight's programme examines the rise of poverty in the 1990s.* ~*adv* **2** in or during the night or evening of this day: *I want to go out dancing tonight.*

toning table *n* an exercise table parts of which move mechanically to exercise specific parts of the body of the person lying on it.

tonnage *n* **1** the capacity of a merchant ship expressed in tons. **2** the weight of the cargo of a merchant ship. **3** the total amount of shipping of a port or nation.

tonne (**tunn**) *n* a unit of mass equal to 1000 kg or 2204.6 pounds.

tonsil *n* either of two small oval lumps of spongy tissue situated one on each side of the back of the mouth. **tonsillar** *adj*

tonsillectomy *n, pl* **-mies** surgical removal of the tonsils.

tonsillitis *n* inflammation of the tonsils, causing a sore throat and fever.

tonsorial *adj Often facetious* of a barber or his trade.

tonsure *n* **1** (in certain religions and monastic orders) **a** the shaving of the head or the crown of the head only. **b** the part of the head left bare by shaving. ~*vb* **-suring, -sured 2** to shave the head of. **tonsured** *adj*

too *adv* **1** as well or also: *I'll miss you, too.* **2** in or to an excessive degree: *it's too noisy in here.* **3** extremely: *you're too kind.* **4** *US & Canad informal* used to emphasize contradiction of a negative statement: *You didn't! – I did too!*

took *vb* the past tense of **take.**

tool *n* **1 a** an implement, such as a hammer, saw, or spade, that is used by hand to help do a particular type of work. **b** a power-driven instrument: *machine tool.* **2** the cutting part of such an instrument. **3** a person used to perform dishonourable or unpleasant tasks for another: *the government is acting as a tool of big business.* **4** any object, skill, etc., used for a particular task or in a particular job: *a skilled therapist can use photographs as tools.* ~*vb* **5** to work, cut, or form (something) with a tool.

tool-maker *n* a person who specializes in the production or reconditioning of machine tools. **toolmaking** *n*

tool-pusher *n* a person who supervises drilling operations on an oil rig.

toot *n* **1** a short hooting sound. ~*vb* **2** to give or cause to give a short blast, hoot, or whistle: *motorists tooted their car horns.*

tooth *n, pl* **teeth 1** one of the bonelike projections in the jaws of most vertebrates that are used for biting, tearing, or chewing. **2** one of the sharp projections on the edge of a comb, saw, zip, etc. **3 long in the tooth** old or ageing. **4 a sweet tooth** a liking for sweet food. **5 tooth and nail** with great vigour and determination: *the union would oppose compulsory redundancies tooth and nail.* ~See also **teeth.**

toothache *n* a pain in or near a tooth.

toothbrush *n* a small brush with a long handle, for cleaning the teeth.

toothless *adj* **1** having no teeth. **2** having no real power: *the proposed Commission will not be as toothless as scoffers suggest.*

toothpaste *n* a paste used for cleaning the teeth, applied with a toothbrush.

toothpick *n* a small wooden or plastic stick used for extracting pieces of food from between the teeth.

tooth powder *n* a powder used for cleaning the teeth, applied with a toothbrush.

toothsome *adj* delicious or appetizing in appearance, flavour, or smell.

toothy *adj* **toothier, toothiest** having or showing numerous, large, or prominent teeth: *a toothy grin.*

tootle *vb* **-tling, -tled 1** to hoot softly or repeatedly. ~*n* **2** a soft hoot or series of hoots.

top[1] *n* **1** the highest point or part of anything: *the top of the stairs.* **2** the most important or successful position: *at the top of the agenda.* **3** a lid or cap that fits on to one end of something, esp. to close it: *he unscrewed the top from a quart of ale.* **4** the highest degree or point: *the two people at the top of the Party.* **5** the most important person or people in an organization: *the top of the military establishment.* **6** the loudest or highest pitch: *she cheered and sang at the top of her voice.* **7** a garment, esp. for a woman, that extends from the shoulders to the waist or hips. **8** the part of a plant that is above ground: *nettle tops.* **9** same as **top gear. 10 off the top of one's head** without previous preparation or careful thought. **11 on top of a** in addition to: *the average member of staff will get 25% on top of salary.* **b** *Informal* in complete control of: *we're on top of our costs and expenses and looking for other opportunities.* **12 over the top a** lacking restraint or a sense of proportion: *you went over the top when you called her a religious maniac.* **b** *Mil* over the edge of a trench. ~*adj* **13** at, of, or being the top: *men still hold most of the top jobs in industry.* ~*vb* **topping, topped 14** to put on top of (something): *top your salad with a mild dressing.* **15** to reach or pass the top of. **16** to be at the top of: *her biggest hit topped the charts for six weeks.* **17** to exceed or surpass: *his estimated fortune tops £2 billion.* ~See also **top off, top out, tops,** etc.

THESAURUS

articulation, speech, utterance, verbal expression, voice

tongue-tied at a loss for words, dumb, dumbstruck, inarticulate, mute, speechless, struck dumb

tonic boost, bracer (*informal*), cordial, fillip, livener, pick-me-up (*informal*), refresher, restorative, shot in the arm (*informal*), stimulant

too 1. also, as well, besides, further, in addition, into the bargain, likewise, moreover, to boot **2.** excessively, exorbitantly, extremely, immoderately, inordinately, over-, overly, unduly, unreasonably, very

tool *n.* **1.** apparatus, appliance, contraption, contrivance, device, gadget, implement, instrument, machine, utensil **2.** cat's-paw, creature, dupe, hireling, lackey, minion, pawn, puppet, stooge (*slang*) **3.** agency, agent, intermediary, means, medium, vehicle, wherewithal ~*vb.* **4.** chase, cut, decorate, ornament, shape, work

top *n.* **1.** acme, apex, apogee, crest, crown, culmination, head, height, high point, meridian, peak, pinnacle, summit, vertex, zenith **2.** cap, cork, cover, lid, stopper **3.** first place, head, highest rank, lead **4. over the top** a bit much (*informal*), excessive, going too far, immoderate, inordinate, over the limit, too much, uncalled-for ~*adj.* **5.** best, chief, crack (*informal*), dominant, elite, finest, first, foremost, greatest, head, highest, lead, leading, pre-eminent, prime, principal, ruling, sovereign, superior, topmost, upper, uppermost ~*vb.* **6.** cap, cover, crown, finish, garnish, roof, tip **7.** ascend, climb, crest, reach the top of, scale, surmount **8.**

top[2] *n* **1** a toy that is spun on its pointed base. **2 sleep like a top** to sleep very soundly.

topaz (**toe**-pazz) *n* a hard glassy yellow, pink, or colourless mineral used in making jewellery.

top brass *pl n* the most important or high-ranking officials or leaders.

topcoat *n* **1** an overcoat. **2** a final coat of paint applied to a surface.

top dog *n Informal* the leader or chief of a group.

top drawer *n Old-fashioned, informal* people of the highest social standing.

top dressing *n* a layer of fertilizer or manure spread on the surface of land. **top-dress** *vb*

tope[1] *vb* **toping, toped** to drink (alcohol), usually in large quantities. **toper** *n*

tope[2] *n* a small grey shark of European coastal waters.

topee *or* **topi** (**toe**-pee) *n* same as **pith helmet.**

top-flight *adj* of very high quality.

topgallant *n* **1** a mast or sail above a topmast. ~*adj* **2** of or relating to a topgallant.

top gear *n* the highest forward ratio of a gearbox in a motor vehicle.

top hat *n* a man's hat with a tall cylindrical crown and narrow brim, now only worn for some formal occasions.

top-heavy *adj* unstable through being overloaded at the top.

topiary (**tope**-yar-ee) *n* **1** the art of trimming trees or bushes into artificial decorative shapes. **2** trees or bushes trimmed into decorative shapes. ~*adj* **3** of or relating to topiary. **topiarist** *n*

topic *n* a subject of a speech, book, conversation, etc.

topical *adj* of or relating to current affairs. **topicality** *n* **topically** *adv*

topknot *n* a crest, tuft, decorative bow, etc., on the top of the head.

topless *adj* of or relating to women wearing costumes that do not cover the breasts: *topless bars.*

top-level *adj* of, involving, or by those with the highest level of influence or ability: *a top-level meeting.*

topmast *n* the mast next above a lower mast on a sailing vessel.

topmost *adj* at or nearest the top.

topnotch *adj Informal* excellent or superb: *topnotch entertainment.*

top off *vb* to finish or complete, esp. with some decisive action.

topography *n, pl* **-phies 1** the surface features of a region, such as its hills, valleys, or rivers: *the islands are fragile, with a topography constantly changed by wind and wave.* **2** the study or description of such surface features. **3** the representation of these features on a map. **topographer** *n* **topographical** *adj*

topology *n* a branch of geometry describing the properties of a figure that are unaffected by continuous distortion. **topological** *adj*

top out *vb* to place the highest stone on (a building).

topper *n Informal* a top hat.

topping *n* a sauce or garnish for food.

topple *vb* **-pling, -pled 1** to fall over or cause (something) to fall over, esp. from a height: *he staggered back against the railing and toppled over into the river.* **2** to overthrow or oust: *few believe the scandal will topple the government.*

tops *Slang* ~*n* **1 the tops** a person or thing of top quality. ~*adj* **2** excellent: *Pacino's no-holds-barred performance is tops.*

topsail *n* a square sail carried on a yard set on a topmast.

top-secret *adj* (of military or government information) classified as needing the highest level of secrecy and security.

topside *n Brit & NZ* a lean cut of beef from the thigh containing no bone.

topsoil *n* the surface layer of soil.

topsy-turvy *adj* **1** upside down. **2** in a state of confusion. ~*adv* **3** in a topsy-turvy manner.

top up *Brit* ~*vb* **1** to refill (a container), usually to the brim: *I topped up his glass.* **2** to add to (an amount) in order to make it sufficient: *the grant can be topped up by a student loan.* ~*n* **top-up 3** another serving of a drink in the glass that was used for the first one: *anyone want a top-up?* ~*adj* **top-up 4** serving to top something up: *a top-up loan.*

toque (**toke**) *n* **1** a woman's small round brimless hat. **2** *Canad* a knitted cap with a round tassel on top.

tor *n* a high hill, esp. a bare rocky one.

Torah *n* the whole body of traditional Jewish teaching, including the Oral Law.

torch *n* **1** a small portable electric lamp powered by batteries. **2** a wooden shaft dipped in wax or tallow and set alight. **3** anything regarded as a source of enlightenment, guidance, etc.: *a torch of hope.* **4 carry a torch for** to be in love with (someone), esp. unrequitedly. ~*vb* **5** *Informal* to deliberately set (a building) on fire.

tore *vb* the past tense of **tear**[2].

toreador (**torr**-ee-a-dor) *n* a bullfighter, esp. one on horseback.

torero (tor-**air**-oh) *n, pl* **-ros** a bullfighter, esp. one on foot.

torment *vb* **1** to cause (someone) great pain or suffering. **2** to tease or pester (a person or animal) in an annoying or cruel way. ~*n* **3** physical or mental pain. **4** a source of pain or suffering. **tormentor** *n*

tormentil *n* a creeping plant with yellow four-petalled flowers.

torn *vb* **1** the past participle of **tear**[2]. ~*adj* **2** split or

THESAURUS

be first, be in charge of, command, head, lead, rule **9.** beat, best, better, eclipse, exceed, excel, go beyond, outdo, outshine, outstrip, surpass, transcend

topic issue, matter, point, question, subject, subject matter, text, theme, thesis

topical contemporary, current, newsworthy, popular, up-to-date, up-to-the-minute

topmost dominant, foremost, highest, leading, loftiest, paramount, principal, supreme, top, upper, uppermost

topple 1. capsize, collapse, fall, fall headlong, fall over, keel over, knock down, knock over, overbalance, overturn, tip over, totter, tumble, upset **2.** bring down, bring low, oust, overthrow, overturn, unseat

topsy-turvy chaotic, confused, disarranged, disorderly, disorganized, inside-out, jumbled, messy, mixed-up, untidy, upside-down

torment *vb.* **1.** afflict, agonize, crucify, distress, harrow, pain, rack, torture **2.** aggravate (*informal*), annoy, bedevil, bother, harass, harry, hassle (*informal*), hound, irritate, nag, persecute, pester, plague, provoke, tease, trouble, vex, worry ~*n.* **3.** agony, anguish, distress, hell, misery, pain, suffering, torture **4.** affliction, annoyance, bane, bother, harassment, hassle (*informal*), irritation, nag, nagging, nuisance, pain in the neck (*informal*), persecution, pest, plague, provocation, scourge, thorn in one's flesh, trouble, vexation, worry

torn *adj.* **1.** cut, lacerated, ragged, rent, ripped, slit,

cut. **3** divided or undecided, as in preference: *torn between two lovers.*

tornado *n, pl* **-dos** *or* **-does** a rapidly whirling column of air, usually characterized by a dark funnel-shaped cloud causing damage along its path.

torpedo *n, pl* **-does 1** a cylindrical self-propelled weapon carrying explosives that is launched from aircraft, ships, or submarines and follows an underwater path to hit its target. *~vb* **-doing, -doed 2** to attack or hit (a ship) with one or a number of torpedoes. **3** to destroy or wreck: *the Prime Minister warned his party against torpedoing the bill.*

torpedo boat *n* (formerly) a small high-speed warship for torpedo attacks.

torpid *adj* **1** sluggish or dull: *he has a rather torpid intellect.* **2** (of a hibernating animal) dormant.

torpor *n* drowsiness and apathy.

torque (**tork**) *n* **1** a force that causes rotation around a central point such as an axle. **2** an ancient Celtic necklace or armband made of twisted metal.

torr *n, pl* **torr** a unit of pressure equal to one millimetre of mercury (133.3 newtons per square metre).

torrent *n* **1** a fast or violent stream, esp. of water. **2** a rapid flow of questions, abuse, etc.

torrential *adj* (of rain) very heavy.

torrid *adj* **1** (of weather) so hot and dry as to parch or scorch. **2** (of land) arid or parched. **3** highly charged emotionally: *a torrid affair.*

torsion *n* the twisting of a part by equal forces being applied at both ends but in opposite directions. **torsional** *adj*

torso *n, pl* **-sos 1** the trunk of the human body. **2** a statue of a nude human trunk, esp. without the head or limbs.

tort *n Law* a civil wrong or injury, for which an action for damages may be brought.

tortilla *n Mexican cookery* a kind of thin pancake made from corn meal.

tortoise *n* a land reptile with a heavy dome-shaped shell into which it can withdraw its head and legs.

tortoiseshell *n* **1** the horny yellow-and-brown mottled shell of a sea turtle, used for making ornaments and jewellery. **2** a domestic cat with black, cream, and brownish markings. **3** a butterfly which has orange-brown wings with black markings. *~adj* **4** made of tortoiseshell.

tortuous *adj* **1** twisted or winding: *a tortuous route.* **2** devious or cunning: *months of tortuous negotiations.*

torture *vb* **-turing, -tured 1** to cause (someone) extreme physical pain, esp. to extract information, etc.: *suspects were regularly tortured and murdered by the secret police.* **2** to cause (someone) mental anguish. *~n* **3** physical or mental anguish. **4** the practice of torturing a person. **5** something which causes great mental distress: *she was going through the torture of a collapsing marriage.* **tortured** *adj* **torturer** *n* **torturous** *adj*

Tory *n, pl* **-ries 1** a member of the Conservative Party in Great Britain or Canada. **2** *History* a member of the English political party that supported the Church and Crown and traditional political structures and opposed the Whigs. *~adj* **3** of or relating to a Tory or Tories. **Toryism** *n*

toss *vb* **1** to throw (something) lightly. **2** to fling or be flung about, esp. in an violent way: *the salty sea breeze tossing the branches of the palms.* **3** to coat (food) with a dressing by gentle stirring or mixing: *her technique for tossing Caesar salad.* **4** (of a horse) to throw (its rider). **5** to move (one's head) suddenly backwards, as in impatience. **6** to throw up (a coin) to decide between alternatives by guessing which side will land uppermost. **7 toss and turn** to be restless when trying to sleep. *~n* **8** the act or an instance of tossing. **9** the act of deciding between alternatives by throwing up a coin and guessing which side will land uppermost: *Essex won the toss and decided to bat first.* **10 argue the toss** to waste time and energy arguing about an unimportant point. **11 not give a toss** *Informal* not to care at all.

toss off *vb* **1** to do or produce (something) quickly and easily: *the tales my sister tossed off so lightly over the dusting.* **2** to finish (a drink) in one swallow.

toss up *vb* **1** to spin (a coin) in the air in order to decide between alternatives by guessing which side will land uppermost. *~n* **toss-up 2** an instance of tossing up a coin. **3** *Informal* an even chance or risk: *if it's a toss-up for a top position, he gives it to the woman.*

tot *n* **1** a very young child. **2** a small drink of spirits.

total *n* **1** the whole, esp. regarded as the sum of a number of parts. **2 in total** overall: *the company employs over 700 people in total.* *~adj* **3** complete: *a total ban on alcohol.* **4** being or related to a total: *the total number of deaths.* *~vb* **-talling, -talled** *or US* **-taling, -taled 5** to amount to: *the firm's losses totalled more than $2 billion.* **6** to add up: *purchases are totalled with a pencil and a notepad.* **totally** *adv*

totalitarian *adj* of a political system in which there is only one party, which allows no opposition and attempts to control everything: *a totalitarian state.* **totalitarianism** *n*

THESAURUS

split **2.** divided, in two minds (*informal*), irresolute, split, uncertain, undecided, unsure, vacillating, wavering

tornado cyclone, gale, hurricane, squall, storm, tempest, twister (*U.S. informal*), typhoon, whirlwind, windstorm

torpor apathy, dormancy, drowsiness, dullness, inactivity, indolence, inertia, inertness, languor, laziness, lethargy, listlessness, numbness, passivity, sloth, sluggishness, somnolence, stagnancy, stupor

torrent cascade, deluge, downpour, effusion, flood, flow, gush, outburst, rush, spate, stream, tide

tortuous 1. bent, circuitous, convoluted, crooked, curved, indirect, meandering, serpentine, sinuous, twisted, twisting, winding, zigzag **2.** ambiguous, complicated, convoluted, cunning, deceptive, devious, indirect, involved, misleading, roundabout, tricky

torture 1. *vb.* afflict, agonize, crucify, distress, harrow, martyr, pain, persecute, put on the rack, rack, torment **2.** *n.* affliction, agony, anguish, distress, hell, martyrdom, misery, pain, pang(s), persecution, rack, suffering, torment

toss *vb.* **1.** cast, chuck (*informal*), fling, flip, hurl, launch, lob (*informal*), pitch, project, propel, shy, sling, throw **2.** agitate, disturb, jiggle, joggle, jolt, rock, roll, shake, thrash, tumble, wriggle, writhe *~n.* **3.** cast, fling, lob (*informal*), pitch, shy, throw

tot *n.* **1.** ankle-biter (*Austral. slang*), baby, child, infant, little one, mite, rug rat (*slang*), sprog (*slang*), toddler, wean (*Scot.*) **2.** dram, finger, measure, nip, shot (*informal*), slug, snifter (*informal*)

total 1. *n.* aggregate, all, amount, entirety, full amount, mass, sum, totality, whole **2.** *adj.* absolute, all-out, arrant, complete, consummate, deep-dyed (*usually derogatory*), downright, entire, full, gross, out-and-out, outright, perfect, sheer, thorough, thoroughgoing, unconditional, undisputed, unmitigated, unqualified, utter, whole **3.** *vb.* add up, amount to, come to, mount up to, reach, reckon, sum up, tot up

totality *n, pl* **-ties 1** the whole amount. **2** the state of being total.

totalizator, totalizer, *or* **totalisator, totaliser** *n* a machine to operate a system of betting on a racecourse in which money is paid out to the winners in proportion to their stakes.

tote[1] *vb* **toting, toted** *Informal* **1** to carry or wear (a gun). **2** to haul or carry.

tote[2] *n* **the tote** *Informal* short for **totalizator.**

tote bag *n* a large handbag or shopping bag.

totem *n* **1** (esp. among North American Indians) an object or animal symbolizing a clan or family. **2** a representation of such an object. **totemic** *adj* **totemism** *n*

totem pole *n* a pole carved or painted with totemic figures set up by certain North American Indians as a tribal symbol.

totter *vb* **1** to move in an unsteady manner. **2** to sway or shake as if about to fall. **3** to be failing, unstable, or precarious: *the world was tottering on the edge of war.*

tot up *vb* **totting, totted** *Chiefly Brit* to add (numbers) together: *I'll just tot up what you owe me.*

toucan *n* a tropical American fruit-eating bird with a large brightly coloured bill.

touch *vb* **1** to cause or permit a part of the body to come into contact with (someone or something): *the baking tin is too hot to touch.* **2** to tap, feel, or strike (someone or something): *he touched me on the shoulder.* **3** to come or bring (something) into contact with (something else): *the plane's wheels touched the runway.* **4** to move or disturb by handling: *we shouldn't touch anything before the police arrive.* **5** to have an effect on: *millions of people's lives had been touched by the music of the Beatles.* **6** to produce an emotional response in: *the painful truth of it touched her.* **7** to eat or drink: *she hardly ever touched alcohol.* **8** to compare to in quality or attainment; equal or match: *when Clough and Taylor were in tandem no-one could touch them.* **9** *Slang* to ask (someone) for a loan or gift of money. **10** to fondle in a sexual manner: *I wouldn't let him touch me unless I was in the mood.* **11** to strike, harm, or molest: *I never touched him!* **12 touch on** *or* **upon** to allude to briefly or in passing: *these two issues may be touched upon during the talks.* ~*n* **13** the sense by which the texture and other qualities of objects can be experienced when they come in contact with a part of the body surface, esp. the tips of the fingers. **14** the feel or texture of an object as perceived by this sense: *she enjoyed the touch of the damp grass on her feet.* **15** the act or an instance of something coming into contact with the body: *he remembered the touch of her hand.* **16** a gentle push, tap, or caress: *the switch takes only the merest touch to operate.* **17** a small amount; trace: *a touch of luxury.* **18** a particular manner or style of doing something: *his songs always reveal his keen melodic touch.* **19** a detail of some work: *final touches were now being put to the plans.* **20** a slight attack: *a touch of dysentery.* **21** (in sports such as football or rugby) the area outside the lines marking the side of the pitch: *he kicked the ball into touch.* **22** the technique of fingering a keyboard instrument. **23 a touch** slightly or marginally: *it's nice, but a touch expensive.* **24 in touch a** regularly speaking to, writing to, or visiting someone. **b** having up-to-date knowledge or understanding of a situation or trend. **25 lose touch a** to gradually stop speaking to, writing to, or visiting someone. **b** to stop having up-to-date knowledge or understanding of a situation or trend. **26 out of touch a** no longer speaking to, writing to, or visiting someone. **b** no longer having up-to-date knowledge or understanding of a situation or trend. ~See also **touchdown, touch off, touch up.**

touch and go *adj* risky or critical: *it was touch and go whether the mission would succeed.*

touchdown *n* **1** the moment at which a landing aircraft or spacecraft comes into contact with the landing surface. **2** *American football* a scoring move in which an attacking player takes the ball into the area behind his opponents' goal. ~*vb* **touch down 3** (of an aircraft or spacecraft) to land.

touché (too-shay) *interj* **1** an acknowledgment that a remark or witty reply has been effective. **2** an acknowledgment of a scoring hit in fencing.

touched *adj* **1** moved to sympathy or emotion: *I was touched by her understanding.* **2** slightly mad: *she's a bit touched.*

touching *adj* **1** arousing tender feelings. ~*prep* **2** relating to or concerning: *she might talk about matters touching both of them.*

touch judge *n* one of the two linesmen in rugby.

touchline *n* either of the lines marking the side of the playing area in certain games, such as rugby.

touch off *vb* to cause (a disturbance, violence, etc.) to begin: *the death of a teenager in police custody touched off a night of riots.*

touchpaper *n* a fuse of dark blue paper on a firework.

touchstone *n* a standard by which judgment is made: *this restaurant is the touchstone for genuine Italian cookery in Leeds.*

THESAURUS

totalitarian authoritarian, despotic, dictatorial, monolithic, one-party, oppressive, tyrannous, undemocratic

totally absolutely, completely, consummately, entirely, fully, perfectly, quite, thoroughly, unconditionally, unmitigatedly, utterly, wholeheartedly, wholly

totter 1. lurch, stagger, stumble, walk unsteadily **2.** falter, quiver, reel, rock, shake, sway, teeter, tremble, waver

tot up add up, calculate, count up, reckon, sum (up), tally, total

touch *vb.* **1.** brush, caress, contact, feel, finger, fondle, graze, handle, hit, lay a finger on, palpate, pat, push, strike, stroke, tap **2.** abut, adjoin, be in contact, border, brush, come together, contact, converge, graze, impinge upon, meet **3.** affect, disturb, get through to, get to (*informal*), have an effect on, impress, influence, inspire, make an impression on, mark, melt, move, soften, stir, strike, upset **4.** consume, drink, eat, partake of **5.** be a match for, be in the same league as, be on a par with, come near, come up to, compare with, equal, hold a candle to (*informal*), match, parallel, rival **6. touch on** *or* **upon** allude to, bring in, cover, deal with, mention, refer to, speak of ~*n.* **7.** feel, feeling, handling, palpation, physical contact, tactility **8.** blow, brush, caress, contact, fondling, hit, pat, push, stroke, tap **9.** bit, dash, detail, drop, hint, intimation, jot, pinch, smack, small amount, smattering, *soupçon*, speck, spot, suggestion, suspicion, taste, tincture, tinge, trace, whiff **10.** approach, characteristic, handiwork, manner, method, style, technique, trademark, way

touchiness bad temper, crabbedness, fretfulness, grouchiness (*informal*), irascibility, irritability, peevishness, pettishness, petulance, surliness, testiness, tetchiness, ticklishness

touching affecting, emotive, heartbreaking, melting, moving, pathetic, piteous, pitiable, pitiful, poignant, sad, stirring, tender

touch-type *vb* **-typing, -typed** to type without looking at the keyboard. **touch-typist** *n*

touch up *vb* to enhance, renovate, or falsify (a picture) by adding extra touches to.

touchwood *n* something, esp. dry wood, used as tinder.

touchy *adj* **touchier, touchiest 1** easily upset or irritated: *he is a touchy and quick-tempered man.* **2** requiring careful and tactful handling: *a touchy subject.* **touchiness** *n*

tough *adj* **1** strong and difficult to break, cut, or tear: *this fabric is tough and water-resistant.* **2** (of meat or other food) difficult to cut and chew; not tender. **3** physically or mentally strong and able to cope with hardship: *a tough uncompromising woman, unwilling to take no for an answer.* **4** rough or violent: *a tough and ruthless mercenary.* **5** strict and firm: *the country's tough drugs laws.* **6** difficult or troublesome to do or deal with: *a tough task.* **7 tough luck!** *Informal* an expression of lack of sympathy for someone else's problems. *~n* **8** a rough, vicious, or violent person. *~vb* **9 tough it out** *Informal* to endure a difficult situation until it improves: *criticism of his performance has reinforced his desire to tough it out.* **toughness** *n*

toughen *vb* to make or become tough or tougher.

toupee (**too**-pay) *n* a hairpiece worn by men to cover a bald place.

tour *n* **1** an extended journey visiting places of interest along the route. **2** a trip, by a band, theatre company, etc., to perform in several places. **3** an overseas trip made by a cricket team, rugby team, etc., to play in several places. **4** *Mil* a period of service, esp. in one place: *the regiment has served several tours in Northern Ireland.* *~vb* **5** to make a tour of (a place).

tour de force *n, pl* **tours de force** a masterly or brilliant stroke or achievement.

tourism *n* tourist travel, esp. when regarded as an industry.

tourist *n* **1** a person who travels for pleasure, usually sightseeing and staying in hotels. **2** a member of a sports team which is visiting a country to play a series of matches: *the tourists were bowled out for 135.* **3** the lowest class of accommodation on a passenger ship. *~adj* **4** of or relating to tourists or tourism: *a popular tourist attraction.* **5** of the lowest class of accommodation on a passenger ship or aircraft.

touristy *adj Informal, often disparaging* full of tourists or tourist attractions.

tourmaline *n* a hard crystalline mineral used in jewellery and electrical equipment.

tournament *n* **1** a sporting competition in which contestants play a series of games to determine an overall winner. **2** Also: **tourney** *Medieval history* a contest in which mounted knights fought for a prize.

tournedos (**tour**-ned-doh) *n, pl* **-dos** (-doze) a thick round steak of beef.

tourniquet (**tour**-nick-kay) *n Med* a strip of cloth tied tightly round an arm or leg to stop bleeding from an artery.

tousle (rhymes with **arousal**) *vb* **-sling, -sled** to make (hair or clothes) ruffled and untidy. **tousled** *adj*

tout (rhymes with **shout**) *vb* **1** to seek (business, customers, etc.) or try to sell (goods), esp. in a persistent or direct manner: *he went from door to door touting for business.* **2** to put forward or recommend (a person or thing) as a good or suitable example or candidate: *the plant was once touted as a showcase factory.* *~n* **3** a person who sells tickets for a heavily booked event at inflated prices.

tow[1] *vb* **1** to pull or drag (a vehicle), esp. by means of a rope or cable. *~n* **2** the act or an instance of towing. **3 in tow** *Informal* in one's company or one's charge or under one's influence: *she had an older man in tow.* **4 on tow** (of a vehicle) being towed.

tow[2] *n* fibres of hemp, flax, jute, etc., prepared for spinning.

towards *or US* **toward** *prep* **1** in the direction of: *towards the lake.* **2** with regard to: *hostility towards the President.* **3** as a contribution to: *the profits will go towards three projects.* **4** just before: *towards evening.* ➤ *Towards* is usual. The form *toward* is chiefly American.

towbar *n* a rigid metal bar attached to the back of a vehicle, from which a trailer or caravan can be towed.

towel *n* **1** a piece of absorbent cloth or paper used for drying things. **2 throw in the towel** See **throw in** (sense 3). *~vb* **-elling, -elled** *US* **-eling, -eled 3** to dry or wipe with a towel.

towelling *or US* **toweling** *n* a soft, fairly thick fabric used to make towels and dressing gowns.

tower *n* **1** a tall, usually square or circular structure, sometimes part of a larger building and usually built

THESAURUS

touchstone criterion, gauge, measure, norm, par, standard, yardstick

touch up brush up, enhance, fake (up), falsify, give a face-lift to, gloss over, improve, patch up, polish up, renovate, retouch, revamp, titivate

touchy bad-tempered, captious, crabbed, cross, easily offended, grouchy (*informal*), grumpy, irascible, irritable, oversensitive, peevish, pettish, petulant, querulous, quick-tempered, ratty (*Brit. informal*), splenetic, surly, testy, tetchy, thin-skinned, ticklish

tough *adj.* **1.** cohesive, durable, firm, hard, inflexible, leathery, resilient, resistant, rigid, rugged, solid, stiff, strong, sturdy, tenacious **2.** brawny, fit, hard as nails, hardened, hardy, resilient, seasoned, stalwart, stout, strapping, strong, sturdy, vigorous **3.** hard-bitten, pugnacious, rough, ruffianly, ruthless, vicious, violent **4.** adamant, callous, exacting, firm, hard, hard-boiled (*informal*), inflexible, intractable, merciless, obdurate, obstinate, refractory, resolute, severe, stern, strict, stubborn, unbending, unforgiving, unyielding **5.** arduous, baffling, difficult, exacting, exhausting, hard, intractable, irksome, knotty, laborious, perplexing, puzzling, strenuous, thorny, troublesome, uphill **6. tough luck!** *informal* hard cheese (*Brit. slang*), hard lines (*Brit. informal*), too bad (*informal*) *~n.* **7.** bravo, bruiser (*informal*), brute, bully, bully boy, heavy (*slang*), hooligan, rough (*informal*), roughneck (*slang*), rowdy, ruffian, thug

tour *n.* **1.** excursion, expedition, jaunt, journey, outing, peregrination (*formal*), progress, trip **2.** circuit, course, round *~vb.* **3.** explore, go on the road, go round, holiday in, journey, sightsee, travel round, travel through, visit

tourist excursionist, globetrotter, holiday-maker, journeyer, sightseer, traveller, tripper, voyager

tournament 1. competition, contest, event, match, meeting, series **2.** *Also* **tourney** *Medieval history* joust, the lists, tourney

tow *vb.* drag, draw, haul, lug, pull, trail, trawl, tug

towards *or U.S* **toward 1.** en route for, for, in the direction of, in the vicinity of, on the road to, on the way to, to **2.** about, concerning, for, regarding, with regard to, with respect to **3.** almost, close to, coming up to, getting on for, just before, nearing, nearly, not quite, shortly before

tower 1. *n.* belfry, castle, citadel, column, fort, fortification, fortress, keep, obelisk, pillar, refuge, skyscraper, steeple, stronghold, turret **2.** *vb.* **tower over**

for a specific purpose. **2 tower of strength** a person who supports or comforts someone else at a time of difficulty. *~vb* **3 tower over** to be much taller than: *sheer walls of limestone towered over us.*

tower block *n* a very tall building divided into flats or offices.

towering *adj* **1** very tall. **2** very impressive or important: *his towering presence on stage.* **3** very intense: *in a towering rage.*

towheaded *adj* having blonde or yellowish hair.

town *n* **1** a large group of houses, shops, factories, etc., smaller than a city and larger than a village. **2** the nearest town or the chief town of an area: *people from town rarely went out to the farm.* **3** the central area of a town where most of the shops and offices are: *we're going to a pub in town tonight.* **4** the people of a town: *the town is split over the plans for a bypass.* **5** built-up areas in general, as opposed to the countryside: *migration from the country to the town.* **6 go to town** to make a supreme or unrestricted effort. **7 on the town** visiting nightclubs, restaurants, etc.: *we'd a night on the town to celebrate her promotion.*

town clerk *n* (in Britain until 1974) the chief administrative officer of a town.

town crier *n* (formerly) a person employed to make public announcements in the streets.

town hall *n* a large building in a town often containing the council offices and a hall for public meetings.

town house *n* **1** a terraced house in an urban area, esp. an up-market one. **2** a person's town residence as distinct from his or her country residence.

townie *or* **townee** *n Informal, often disparaging* a resident in a town, esp. as distinct from country dwellers.

town planning *n* the comprehensive planning of the physical and social development of a town.

township *n* **1** a small town. **2** (in South Africa) a planned urban settlement of Black Africans or Coloureds. **3** (in the US and Canada) a small unit of local government, often consisting of a town and the area surrounding it. **4** (in Canada) a land-survey area, usually 36 square miles (93 square kilometres).

townsman *n, pl* **-men** an inhabitant of a town. **townswoman** *fem n*

townspeople *or* **townsfolk** *pl n* the people who live in a town.

towpath *n* a path beside a canal or river, formerly used by horses pulling barges.

towrope *n* a rope or cable used for towing a vehicle or vessel.

toxaemia *or US* **toxemia** (tox-**seem**-ya) *n* **1** a form of blood poisoning caused by toxins released by bacteria at a wound or other site of infection. **2** a condition in pregnant women characterized by high blood pressure. **toxaemic** *or US* **toxemic** *adj*

toxic *adj* **1** poisonous: *toxic fumes.* **2** caused by poison: *toxic effects.* **toxicity** *n*

toxicology *n* the branch of science concerned with poisons and their effects. **toxicological** *adj* **toxicologist** *n*

toxin *n* **1** any of various poisonous substances produced by microorganisms and causing certain diseases. **2** any other poisonous substance of plant or animal origin.

toy *n* **1** an object designed for children to play with, such as a doll or model car. **2** an object that adults use for entertainment rather than for a serious purpose: *I do use my computer: it's not just a toy.* *~adj* **3** being an imitation or model of something for children to play with: *a toy aeroplane.* **4** (of a dog) of a variety much smaller than is normal for that breed: *a toy poodle.*

toy boy *n* the much younger male lover of an older woman.

toy-toy *or* **toyi-toyi** *S African* *~n* **1** a dance expressing defiance and protest. *~vb* **2** to dance in this way.

toy with *vb* **1** to consider an idea without being serious about it or being able to decide about it: *I've been toying with the idea of setting up my own firm.* **2** to keep moving (an object) about with one's fingers, esp. when thinking about something else: *Jessica sat toying with her glass.*

trace *vb* **tracing, traced 1** to locate or work out (the cause or source of something): *he traced the trouble to a faulty connection.* **2** to find (something or someone that was missing): *the police were unable to trace her missing husband.* **3** to discover or describe the progress or development of (something): *throughout the 19th century we can trace the development of more complex machinery.* **4** to copy (a design, map, etc.) by putting a piece of transparent paper over it and following the lines which show through the paper with a pencil. **5** to make the outline of (a shape or pattern): *his index finger was tracing circles on the arm of the chair.* *~n* **6** a mark, footprint, or other sign that shows that a person, animal, or thing has been in a particular place: *the police could find no trace of the missing van.* **7** an amount of something so small that it is barely noticeable: *I detected a trace of jealousy in her voice.* **8** a remnant of something: *traces of an Iron-Age fort remain visible.* **9** a pattern made on a screen or a piece of paper by a device that is measuring or detecting something: *a baffling radar trace.* **traceable** *adj*

trace element *n* a chemical element that occurs in very small amounts in soil, water, etc. and is essential for healthy growth.

tracer *n* **1** a projectile that can be observed when in flight by the burning of chemical substances in its base. **2** *Med* an element or other substance introduced into the body to study metabolic processes.

tracer bullet *n* a round of small-arms ammunition containing a tracer.

tracery *n, pl* **-eries 1** a pattern of interlacing lines, esp. one in a stained glass window. **2** any fine lacy pattern resembling this.

traces *pl n* **1** the two side straps that connect a horse's harness to the vehicle being pulled. **2 kick over the traces** to escape or defy control.

trachea (track-**kee**-a) *n, pl* **-cheae** (-**kee**-ee) *Anat, zool* the tube that carries inhaled air from the throat to the lungs.

tracheotomy (track-ee-**ot**-a-mee) *n, pl* **-mies** surgical incision into the trachea, as performed when the air passage has been blocked.

trachoma (track-**oh**-ma) *n* a chronic contagious dis-

THESAURUS

ascend, be head and shoulders above, dominate, exceed, loom, mount, overlook, overtop, rear, rise, soar, surpass, top, transcend

toxic deadly, harmful, lethal, noxious, pernicious, pestilential, poisonous, septic

toy 1. doll, game, plaything **2.** bauble, knick-knack, trifle, trinket

trace *vb.* **1.** ascertain, detect, determine, discover, ferret out, find, follow, hunt down, pursue, search for, seek, shadow, stalk, track, trail, unearth **2.** chart, copy, delineate, depict, draw, map, mark out, outline, record, show, sketch *~n.* **3.** footmark, footprint, footstep, path, slot, spoor, track, trail **4.** bit, dash, drop, hint, iota, jot, shadow, soupçon, suggestion, suspicion,

ease of the eye characterized by inflammation of the inner surface of the lids and the formation of scar tissue.

tracing *n* **1** a copy of something, such as a map, made by tracing. **2** a line traced by a recording instrument.

track *n* **1** a rough road or path: *a farm track.* **2** the mark or trail left by something that has passed by: *the fox didn't leave any tracks.* **3** a rail or pair of parallel rails on which a vehicle, such as a train, runs. **4** a course for running or racing on: *a running track.* **5** a separate song or piece of music on a record, tape, or CD: *Dolphy switches back to bass clarinet for the final track.* **6** a course of action, thought, etc.: *I don't think you're on the right track at all.* **7** an endless band on the wheels of a tank, bulldozer, etc. to enable it to move across rough ground. **8 keep** *or* **lose track of** to follow *or* fail to follow the course or progress of. **9 off the beaten track** in an isolated location: *the village where she lives is a bit off the beaten track.* ~*vb* **10** to follow the trail of (a person or animal). **11** to follow the flight path of (a satellite etc.) by picking up signals transmitted or reflected by it. **12** *Films* to follow (a moving object) while filming. ~See also **tracks. tracker** *n*

track down *vb* to find (someone or something) by tracking or pursuing.

tracker dog *n* a dog specially trained to search for missing people.

track event *n* a competition in athletics, such as sprinting, that takes place on a running track.

track record *n Informal* the past record of the accomplishments and failures of a person or organization.

tracks *pl n* **1** marks, such as footprints, left by someone or something that has passed. **2 in one's tracks** on the very spot where one is standing: *those words stopped her in her tracks.* **3 make tracks** to leave or depart: *it was time to start making tracks.*

track shoe *n* a light running shoe fitted with steel spikes for better grip.

tracksuit *n* a warm loose-fitting suit worn by athletes etc., esp. during training.

tract[1] *n* **1** a large area, esp. of land: *an extensive tract of moorland.* **2** *Anat* a system of organs or glands that has a particular function: *the urinary tract.*

tract[2] *n* a pamphlet, esp. a religious one.

tractable *adj Formal* easy to control, manage, or deal with: *he could easily manage his tractable and worshipping younger brother.* **tractability** *n*

traction *n* **1** pulling, esp. by engine power: *the increased use of electric traction.* **2** *Med* the application of a steady pull on an injured limb using a system of weights and pulleys or splints: *he was in traction for weeks following the accident.* **3** the grip that the wheels of a vehicle have on the ground: *four-wheel drive gives much better traction in wet or icy conditions.*

traction engine *n* a heavy steam-powered vehicle used, esp. formerly, for drawing heavy loads along roads or over rough ground.

tractor *n* a motor vehicle with large rear wheels, used to pull heavy loads, esp. farm machinery.

trade *n* **1** the buying and selling of goods and services. **2** a person's job, esp. a craft requiring skill: *he's a plumber by trade.* **3** the people and practices of an industry, craft, or business. **4** amount of custom or commercial dealings: *a brisk trade in second-hand weapons.* **5** a specified market or business: *the wool trade.* **6 trades** the trade winds. ~*vb* **trading, traded 7** to buy and sell (goods). **8** to exchange: *he traded a job in New York for a life as a cowboy.* **9** to engage in trade. **10** to deal or do business (with). **tradable** or **tradeable** *adj* **trading** *n* **trader** *n*

trade-in *n* **1** a used article given in part payment for the purchase of a new article. ~*vb* **trade in 2** to give (a used article) as part payment for a new article.

trademark *n* **1 a** the name or other symbol used by a manufacturer to distinguish his or her products from those of competitors. **b Registered Trademark** one that is officially registered and legally protected. **2** any distinctive sign or mark of a person or thing: *the designer bars which have become the trademark of the city.*

trade name *n* **1** the name used by a trade to refer to a product or range of products. **2** the name under which a commercial enterprise operates in business.

trade-off *n* an exchange, esp. as a compromise: *there is often a trade-off between manpower costs and computer costs.*

trade on *vb* to exploit or take advantage of: *a demanding woman who traded on her poor health to get her own way.*

tradescantia (trad-dess-**kan**-shee-a) *n* a widely cultivated plant with striped leaves.

trade secret *n* a secret formula, technique, or process known and used to advantage by only one manufacturer.

tradesman *n, pl* **-men 1** a skilled worker, such as an electrician or painter. **2** a shopkeeper. **tradeswoman** *fem n*

Trades Union Congress *n* the major association

THESAURUS

tincture, tinge, touch, trifle, whiff **5.** evidence, indication, mark, record, relic, remains, remnant, sign, survival, token, vestige

track *n.* **1.** path, pathway, road, way **2.** footmark, footprint, footstep, mark, path, scent, slipstream, slot, spoor, trace, trail, wake **3.** line, permanent way, rail, rails **4. keep track of** follow, keep an eye on, keep in sight, keep in touch with, keep up to date with, keep up with, monitor, oversee, watch **5. lose track of** lose, lose sight of, misplace ~*vb.* **6.** chase, dog, follow, follow the trail of, hunt down, pursue, shadow, stalk, tail (*informal*), trace, trail

track down apprehend, bring to light, capture, catch, dig up, discover, expose, ferret out, find, hunt down, run to earth, sniff out, trace, unearth

tracks 1. footprints, impressions, imprints, tyremarks, tyreprints, wheelmarks **2. make tracks** beat it (*slang*), depart, disappear, get going, get moving, go, head off, hit the road (*slang*), leave, set out, split (*slang*), take off (*informal*)

tract[1] area, district, estate, expanse, extent, lot, plot, quarter, region, stretch, territory, zone

tract[2] booklet, brochure, disquisition, dissertation, essay, homily, leaflet, monograph, pamphlet, treatise

tractable *formal* amenable, biddable, compliant, controllable, docile, governable, manageable, obedient, persuadable, submissive, tame, willing, yielding

traction adhesion, drag, draught, drawing, friction, grip, haulage, pull, pulling, purchase, resistance

trade *n.* **1.** barter, business, buying and selling, commerce, dealing, exchange, traffic, transactions, truck **2.** avocation, business, calling, craft, employment, job, line, line of work, metier, occupation, profession, pursuit, skill ~*vb.* **3.** bargain, barter, buy and sell, deal, do business, exchange, have dealings, peddle, traffic, transact, truck **4.** barter, exchange, swap, switch

of British trade unions, which includes all the larger unions.

trade union *or* **trades union** *n* a society of workers formed to protect and improve their working conditions, pay, etc. **trade unionism** *or* **trades unionism** *n* **trade unionist** *or* **trades unionist** *n*

trade wind *n* a wind blowing steadily towards the equator either from the northeast in the N hemisphere or the southeast in the S hemisphere.

trading estate *n Chiefly Brit* a large area in which a number of commercial or industrial firms are situated.

tradition *n* **1** the handing down from generation to generation of customs, beliefs, etc. **2** the unwritten body of beliefs, customs, etc. handed down from generation to generation. **3** a custom or practice of long standing. **4 in the tradition of** having many features similar to those of a person or thing in the past: *a thriller writer in the tradition of Chandler.*

traditional *adj* of, relating to, or being a tradition. **traditionally** *adv*

traditionalist *n* a person who supports established customs or beliefs. **traditionalism** *n*

traduce *vb* **-ducing, -duced** *Formal* to speak badly of (someone). **traducement** *n* **traducer** *n*

traffic *n* **1** the vehicles travelling on roads. **2** the movement of vehicles or people in a particular place or for a particular purpose: *air traffic.* **3** trade, esp. of an illicit kind: *drug traffic.* **4** the exchange of ideas between people or organizations: *a lively traffic in ideas.* ~*vb* **-ficking, -ficked 5** to carry on trade or business, esp. of an illicit kind: *he confessed to trafficking in gold and ivory.* **trafficker** *n*

traffic island *n* a raised area in the middle of a road designed as a guide for traffic flow and to provide a stopping place for pedestrians crossing.

traffic light *n* one of a set of coloured lights placed at a junction to control the flow of traffic.

traffic warden *n Brit* a person employed to supervise road traffic and report traffic offences.

tragedian (traj-**jee**-dee-an) *or fem* **tragedienne** (traj-jee-dee-**enn**) *n* **1** an actor who specializes in tragic roles. **2** a writer of tragedy.

tragedy *n, pl* **-dies 1** a shocking or sad event. **2** a serious play, film, or opera in which the main character is destroyed by a combination of a personal failing and adverse circumstances.

tragic *adj* **1** sad and distressing because it involves death or suffering: *she was blinded in a tragic accident.* **2** of or like a tragedy: *a tragic hero.* **3** sad or mournful: *a tragic melody.* **tragically** *adv*

tragicomedy *n, pl* **-dies** a play or other written work having both comic and tragic elements. **tragicomic** *adj*

trail *n* **1** a rough path across open country or through a forest. **2** a route along a series of roads or paths that has been specially planned to let people see or do particular things: *a nature trail through the woods.* **3** a print, mark, or scent left by a person, animal, or object: *a trail of blood was found down three flights of stairs.* **4** something that trails behind: *a vapour trail.* **5** a sequence of results from an event: *a trail of mishaps.* ~*vb* **6** to drag or stream along the ground or through the air behind someone or something: *part of her sari trailed behind her on the floor.* **7** to lag behind (a person or thing): *Max had arrived as well, trailing behind the others.* **8** to follow or hunt (an animal or person), usually secretly, by following the marks or tracks he, she, or it has made: *the police had trailed him the length and breadth of the country.* **9** to be falling behind in a race, match or competition: *they trailed 2-1 at half-time.* **10** to move wearily or slowly: *we spent the afternoon trailing round the shops.*

trail away *or* **off** *vb* to become fainter, quieter, or weaker: *his voice trailed away.*

trailblazer *n* a pioneer in a particular field. **trailblazing** *adj, n*

trailer *n* **1** a road vehicle, usually two-wheeled, towed by a motor vehicle and used for carrying goods, transporting boats, etc.: *ahead of us was a tractor, drawing a trailer laden with dung.* **2** the rear section of an articulated lorry. **3** an extract or series of extracts from a film, TV or radio programme, used to advertise it. **4** *US & Canad* same as **caravan** (sense 1).

trailing *adj* (of a plant) having a long stem which spreads over the ground or hangs loosely: *trailing ivy.*

train *vb* **1** to instruct (someone) in a skill: *soldiers are trained to obey orders unquestioningly.* **2** to learn the skills needed to do a particular job or activity: *she was training to be a computer programmer.* **3** to do exercises and prepare for a specific purpose: *he was training for a marathon.* **4** to focus on or aim at (something): *the warship kept its guns trained on the trawler.* **5** to discipline (an animal) to obey commands or perform tricks. **6** to tie or prune (a plant) so that it grows in a particular way: *he had trained the roses to grow up the wall.* ~*n* **7** a line of railway coaches or wagons coupled together and drawn by a engine. **8** a sequence or series: *following an earlier train of thought.* **9** the long back section of a dress that trails along the floor. **10 in its train** as a consequence: *economic mismanagement brought unemployment*

THESAURUS

trader broker, buyer, dealer, marketer, merchandiser, merchant, purveyor, seller, supplier

tradesman 1. artisan, craftsman, journeyman, skilled worker, workman **2.** dealer, merchant, purveyor, retailer, seller, shopkeeper, supplier, vendor

tradition convention, custom, customs, established practice, folklore, habit, institution, lore, praxis, ritual, unwritten law, usage

traditional accustomed, ancestral, conventional, customary, established, fixed, folk, historic, long-established, old, oral, time-honoured, transmitted, unwritten, usual

traffic *n.* **1.** coming and going, freight, movement, passengers, transport, transportation, vehicles **2.** barter, business, buying and selling, commerce, communication, dealing, dealings, doings, exchange, intercourse, peddling, relations, trade, truck ~*vb.* **3.** bargain, barter, buy and sell, deal, do business, exchange, have dealings, have transactions, market, peddle, trade, truck

tragedy adversity, affliction, calamity, catastrophe, disaster, grievous blow, misfortune

tragic anguished, appalling, awful, calamitous, catastrophic, deadly, dire, disastrous, dismal, doleful, dreadful, fatal, grievous, heartbreaking, heart-rending, ill-fated, ill-starred, lamentable, miserable, mournful, pathetic, pitiable, ruinous, sad, shocking, sorrowful, unfortunate, woeful, wretched

trail *n.* **1.** beaten track, footpath, path, road, route, track, way **2.** footprints, footsteps, mark, marks, path, scent, slipstream, spoor, trace, track, wake **3.** appendage, stream, tail, train ~*vb.* **4.** dangle, drag, draw, droop, extend, hang, hang down, haul, pull, straggle, stream, tow **5.** bring up the rear, dawdle, drag oneself, fall behind, follow, hang back, lag, linger, loiter, straggle, traipse (*informal*) **6.** chase, follow, hunt, pursue, shadow, stalk, tail (*informal*), trace, track

train *vb.* **1.** coach, discipline, drill, educate, guide, im-

and inflation in its train. **11 in train** actually happening or being done: *the programme of reforms set in train by the new government.* ~*adj* **12** of or by a train: *the long train journey North.*

trainbearer *n* an attendant who holds up the train of a dignitary's robe or bride's gown.

trainee *n* **1** a person undergoing training. ~*adj* **2** (of a person) undergoing training: *a trainee journalist.*

trainer *n* **1** a person who coaches a person or team in a sport. **2** a person who trains racehorses. **3** an aircraft used for training pilots. **4** a flat-soled sports shoe of the style used by athletes when training.

training *n* the process of bringing a person to an agreed standard of proficiency by practice and instruction.

train spotter *n* a person who collects the numbers of railway locomotives.

traipse *Informal* ~*vb* **traipsing, traipsed 1** to walk heavily or tiredly. ~*n* **2** a long or tiring walk.

trait *n* a characteristic feature or quality of a person or thing.

traitor *n* a person who betrays friends, country, a cause, etc. **traitorous** *adj* **traitress** *fem n*

trajectory *n, pl* **-ries** the path described by an object moving in air or space, esp. the curved path of a projectile.

tram *n* an electrically driven public transport vehicle that runs on rails laid into the road and takes its power from an overhead cable.

tramlines *pl n* **1** the tracks on which a tram runs. **2** the outer markings along the sides of a tennis or badminton court.

trammel *vb* **-elling, -elled** *or US* **-eling, -eled 1** to hinder or restrict: *trammelled by family responsibilities.* ~*n* **2 trammels** things that hinder or restrict someone: *the trammels of social respectability.*

tramp *vb* **1** to walk long and far; hike. **2** to walk heavily or firmly across or through (a place): *she tramped slowly up the beach.* ~*n* **3** a homeless person who travels about on foot, living by begging or doing casual work. **4** a long hard walk; hike: *we went for a long tramp over the downs.* **5** the sound of heavy regular footsteps: *we could hear the tramp of the marching soldiers.* **6** a small cargo ship that does not run on a regular schedule. **7** *Slang, chiefly US & Canad* a promiscuous woman.

tramping *n NZ* the leisure activity of walking in the bush. **tramper** *n*

trample *vb* **-pling, -pled 1** Also: **trample on** to tread on and crush: *three children were trampled to death when the crowd panicked and ran.* **2 trample on** to treat (a person or his or her rights or feelings) with disregard or contempt.

trampoline *n* **1** a tough canvas sheet suspended by springs or cords from a frame, which acrobats, gymnasts, etc., bounce on. ~*vb* **-lining, -lined 2** to exercise on a trampoline.

trance *n* **1** a hypnotic state resembling sleep in which a person is unable to move or act of his or her own will. **2** a dazed or stunned state.

tranche (**trahnsh**) *n* an instalment or portion of something large, esp. a sum of money: *the new shares will be offered in four tranches around the world.*

trannie *or* **tranny** *n, pl* **-nies** *Informal, chiefly Brit* a transistor radio.

tranquil *adj* calm, peaceful, or quiet. **tranquilly** *adv*

tranquillity *or US sometimes* **tranquility** *n* a state of calmness or peace.

tranquillize, -lise *or US* **tranquilize** *vb* **-lizing, -lized** *or* **-lising, -lised 1** to make or become calm or calmer. **2** to give (someone) a drug to make them calm or calmer. **tranquillization, -lisation,** *or US* **tranquilization** *n* **tranquillizing, -lising,** *or US* **tranquilizing** *adj*

tranquillizer, -liser *or US* **tranquilizer** *n* a drug that calms someone suffering from anxiety, tension, etc.

trans. **1** transitive. **2** translated.

trans- *prefix* **1** across, beyond, crossing, or on the other side of: *transnational.* **2** changing thoroughly: *transliterate.*

transact *vb* to do, conduct, or negotiate (a business deal).

transaction *n* **1** something that is transacted, esp. a business deal. **2 transactions** the records of the proceedings of a society etc.: *an article on land use in the Niagara area taken from the "Transactions of the Royal Canadian Institute".*

THESAURUS

prove, instruct, prepare, rear, rehearse, school, teach, tutor **2.** exercise, improve, prepare, work out **3.** aim, bring to bear, direct, focus, level, line up, point ~*n.* **4.** caravan, column, convoy, file, procession **5.** chain, concatenation, course, order, progression, sequence, series, set, string, succession **6.** appendage, tail, trail

trainer coach, handler

training coaching, discipline, education, exercise, grounding, guidance, instruction, practice, preparation, schooling, teaching, tuition, tutelage, upbringing

trait attribute, characteristic, feature, idiosyncrasy, lineament, mannerism, peculiarity, quality, quirk

traitor apostate, back-stabber, betrayer, deceiver, defector, deserter, double-crosser, fifth columnist, informer, Judas, miscreant, quisling, rebel, renegade, snake in the grass (*informal*), turncoat

trajectory course, flight, flight path, line, path, route, track

tramp *vb.* **1.** footslog, hike, march, ramble, range, roam, rove, slog, trek, walk **2.** march, plod, stamp, stump, toil, traipse (*informal*), trudge, walk heavily ~*n.* **3.** bag lady, bum (*informal*), derelict, dosser (*Brit. slang*), down-and-out, drifter, hobo (*chiefly U.S. & Canad.*), vagabond, vagrant **4.** hike, march, ramble, slog, trek **5.** footfall, footstep, stamp, tread

trample 1. *Also* **trample on** crush, flatten, run over, squash, stamp, tread, walk over **2. trample on** do violence to, encroach upon, hurt, infringe, ride roughshod over, show no consideration for, violate

trance abstraction, daze, dream, ecstasy, hypnotic state, muse, rapture, reverie, spell, stupor, unconsciousness

tranquil at peace, calm, composed, cool, pacific, peaceful, placid, quiet, restful, sedate, serene, still, undisturbed, unexcited, unperturbed, unruffled, untroubled

tranquillity *or U.S. sometimes* **tranquility** calm, calmness, composure, coolness, equanimity, hush, imperturbability, peace, peacefulness, placidity, quiet, quietness, quietude, repose, rest, restfulness, sedateness, serenity, stillness

tranquillize, tranquillise *or U.S.* **tranquilize** calm, compose, lull, pacify, quell, quiet, relax, sedate, settle one's nerves, soothe

tranquillizer, tranquiliser *or U.S.* **tranquilizer** barbiturate, bromide, downer (*slang*), opiate, sedative

transact accomplish, carry on, carry out, conclude, conduct, discharge, do, enact, execute, handle, manage, negotiate, perform, prosecute, see to, settle, take care of

transaction 1. action, affair, bargain, business, coup, deal, deed, enterprise, event, matter, negotia-

transalpine *adj* beyond the Alps, esp. as viewed from Italy.

transatlantic *adj* **1** on or from the other side of the Atlantic. **2** crossing the Atlantic.

transceiver *n* a combined radio transmitter and receiver.

transcend *vb* **1** to go above or beyond what is expected or normal: *a vital party issue that transcends traditional party loyalties.* **2** to overcome or be superior to: *to transcend all difficulties.*

transcendent *adj* **1** above or beyond what is expected or normal. **2** *Theol* (of God) having existence outside the created world. **transcendence** *n*

transcendental *adj* **1** above or beyond what is expected or normal. **2** *Philosophy* based on intuition or innate belief rather than experience. **3** supernatural or mystical. **transcendentally** *adv*

transcendentalism *n* any system of philosophy that seeks to discover the nature of reality by examining the processes of thought rather than the things thought about, or that emphasizes intuition as a means to knowledge. **transcendentalist** *n, adj*

transcendental meditation *n* a technique, based on Hindu traditions, for relaxing and refreshing the mind and body through the silent repetition of a special formula of words.

transcribe *vb* **-scribing, -scribed 1** to write, type, or print out (a text) fully from a speech or notes. **2** to make an electrical recording of (a programme or speech) for a later broadcast. **3** *Music* to rewrite (a piece of music) for an instrument other than that originally intended. **transcriber** *n*

transcript *n* **1** a written, typed, or printed copy made by transcribing. **2** *Chiefly US & Canad* an official record of a student's school progress.

transcription *n* **1** the act of transcribing. **2** something transcribed.

transducer *n* any device, such as a microphone or electric motor, that converts one form of energy into another.

transect *n Biol* a sample strip of land used to monitor plant distribution and animal populations within a given area.

transept *n* either of the two shorter wings of a cross-shaped church.

transfer *vb* **-ferring, -ferred 1** to change or move from one thing, person, place, etc., to another: *he was transferred from prison to hospital.* **2** to move (money or property) from the control of one person or organization to that of another: *£10 000 has been transferred into your account.* **3** (of a football club) to sell or release (a player) to another club: *he was transferred to Norwich in 1988.* **4** to move (a drawing or design) from one surface to another. ~*n* **5** the act, process, or system of transferring, or the state of being transferred. **6** a person or thing that transfers or is transferred. **7** a design or drawing that is transferred from one surface to another. **8** the moving of (money or property) from the control of one person or organization to that of another. **transferable** *or* **transferrable** *adj* **transference** *n*

transfiguration *n* a transfiguring or being transfigured.

Transfiguration *n* **1** *New Testament* the change in the appearance of Christ on the mountain. **2** the Church festival held in commemoration of this on August 6.

transfigure *vb* **-uring, -ured 1** to change or cause to change in appearance. **2** to become or cause to become more exalted.

transfix *vb* **-fixing, -fixed** *or* **-fixt 1** to make (someone) motionless, esp. with horror or shock: *they stood transfixed and revolted by what they saw.* **2** to pierce (a person or animal) through with a pointed object: *the Pharaoh is shown transfixing enemies with arrows from a moving chariot.*

transform *vb* **1** to change completely in form or function: *the last forty years have seen the country transformed from a peasant economy to a major industrial power.* **2** to change so as to make better or more attractive: *most religions claim to be able to transform people's lives.* **3** to convert (one form of energy) to another. **4** *Maths* to change the form of (an equation, expression, etc.) without changing its value. **5** to change (an alternating current or voltage) using a transformer. **transformation** *n*

transformer *n* a device that transfers an alternating current from one circuit to one or more other circuits, usually with a change of voltage.

transfuse *vb* **-fusing, -fused 1** to inject (blood or other fluid) into a blood vessel. **2** *Literary* to transmit or instil.

transfusion *n* **1** the injection of blood, blood plasma, etc., into the blood vessels of a patient. **2** the act of transferring something: *a transfusion of new funds.*

transgress *vb Formal* **1** to break (a law or rule). **2** to

THESAURUS

tion, occurrence, proceeding, undertaking **2. transactions** affairs, annals, doings, goings-on (*informal*), minutes, proceedings, record

transcend eclipse, exceed, excel, go above, go beyond, leave behind, leave in the shade (*informal*), outdo, outrival, outshine, outstrip, outvie, overstep, rise above, surpass

transcendent consummate, exceeding, extraordinary, incomparable, matchless, peerless, pre-eminent, second to none, sublime, superior, transcendental, unequalled, unique, unparalleled, unrivalled

transcribe 1. copy out, engross, note, reproduce, rewrite, set out, take down, transfer, write out **2.** record, tape, tape-record

transcript carbon, carbon copy, copy, duplicate, manuscript, note, notes, record, reproduction, transcription, translation, transliteration, version

transfer 1. *vb.* carry, change, consign, convey, displace, hand over, make over, move, pass on, relocate, remove, shift, translate, transmit, transplant, transport, transpose, turn over **2.** *n.* change, displacement, handover, move, relocation, removal, shift, transference, translation, transmission, transposition

transfix 1. engross, fascinate, halt *or* stop in one's tracks, hold, hypnotize, mesmerize, paralyse, petrify, rivet the attention of, root to the spot, spellbind, stop dead, stun **2.** fix, impale, pierce, puncture, run through, skewer, spear, spit, transpierce

transform alter, change, convert, make over, metamorphose, reconstruct, remodel, renew, revolutionize, transfigure, translate, transmogrify (*jocular*), transmute

transformation alteration, change, conversion, metamorphosis, radical change, renewal, revolution, revolutionary change, sea change, transfiguration, transmogrification (*jocular*), transmutation

transgress *formal* be out of order, break, break the law, contravene, defy, disobey, do *or* go wrong, encroach, err, exceed, fall from grace, go astray, go beyond, infringe, lapse, misbehave, offend, overstep, sin, trespass, violate

transgression *formal* breach, contravention, crime, encroachment, error, fault, infraction, infringement, iniquity, lapse, misbehaviour, misdeed, misdemeanour, offence, peccadillo, sin, trespass, violation, wrong, wrongdoing

overstep (a limit): *he had never before been known to transgress the very slowest of walks.* **transgression** *n* **transgressor** *n*

transient *adj* **1** lasting for a short time only: *she had a number of transient relationships with fellow students.* **2** (of a person) not remaining in a place for a long time: *the transient population of the inner city.* ~*n* **3** a transient person or thing. **transience** *n*

transistor *n* **1** a semiconductor device used to amplify and control electric currents. **2** *Informal* a small portable radio containing transistors.

transistorized *or* **-ised** *adj* (of an electronic device) using transistors.

transit *n* **1** the moving or carrying of goods or people from one place to another. **2** a route or means of transport: *transit by road.* **3** *Astron* the apparent passage of a celestial body across the meridian. **4 in transit** while travelling or being taken from one place to another: *in transit the fruit can be damaged.* ~*adj* **5** indicating a place or building where people wait or goods are kept between different stages of a journey: *a transit lounge for passengers who are changing planes.*

transit camp *n* a camp in which refugees, soldiers, etc., live temporarily.

transition *n* **1** the process of changing from one state or stage to another: *the transition from dictatorship to democracy.* **2** *Music* a movement from one key to another. **transitional** *adj*

transition element *or* **metal** *n Chem* any element belonging to one of three series of elements with atomic numbers between 21 and 30, 39 and 48, and 57 and 80 (**transition series**). They tend to have more than one valency and to form complexes.

transitive *adj Grammar* denoting a verb that requires a direct object.

transitory *adj* lasting only for a short time.

translate *vb* **-lating, -lated 1 a** to change (something spoken or written in one language) into another. **b** to be capable of being changed from one language into another: *puns do not translate well.* **2** to express (something) in a different way, for instance by using a different measurement system or less technical language: *the temperature is 30° Celsius, or if we translate into Fahrenheit, 86°.* **3** to transform or convert, for instance by putting an idea into practice: *cheap crops translate into lower feed prices.* **4** to interpret the significance of (a gesture, action, etc.): *I gave him what I hoped would be translated as a thoughtful look.* **5** to act as a translator: *I had to translate for a party of visiting Greeks.* **translatable** *adj* **translator** *n*

translation *n* **1** a piece of writing or speech that has been translated into another language. **2** the act of translating something. **3** the expression of something in a different way or form: *the book's plot was radically altered during its translation to film.* **4** *Maths* a transformation in which the origin of a coordinate system is moved to another position so that each axis retains the same direction. **translational** *adj*

transliterate *vb* **-ating, -ated** to write or spell (a word etc.) into corresponding letters of another alphabet. **transliteration** *n*

translucent *adj* allowing light to pass through, but not transparent. **translucency** *or* **translucence** *n*

transmigrate *vb* **-grating, -grated** (of a soul) to pass from one body into another at death. **transmigration** *n*

transmission *n* **1** the sending or passing of something, such as a message or disease from one place or person to another. **2** something that is transmitted, esp. a radio or television broadcast. **3** a system of shafts and gears that transmits power from the engine to the driving wheels of a motor vehicle.

transmit *vb* **-mitting, -mitted 1** to pass (something, such as a message or disease) from one place or person to another. **2 a** to send out (signals) by means of radio waves. **b** to broadcast (a radio or television programme). **3** to allow the passage of (particles, energy, etc.): *water transmits sound better than air.* **4** to transfer (a force, motion, etc.) from one part of a mechanical system to another: *the chain of the bike transmits the motion of the pedals to the rear wheel.* **transmittable** *adj*

transmitter *n* **1** a piece of equipment used for broadcasting radio or television programmes. **2** a person or thing that transmits something.

transmogrify *vb* **-fies, -fying, -fied** *Jocular* to change or transform (someone or something) into a different shape or appearance, esp. a grotesque or bizarre one. **transmogrification** *n*

transmute *vb* **-muting, -muted** to change the form or nature of: *self-contempt is transmuted into hatred of others.* **transmutation** *n*

transom *n* **1** a horizontal bar across a window. **2** a horizontal bar that separates a door from a window over it.

transparency *n, pl* **-cies 1** the state of being trans-

THESAURUS

transgressor *formal* criminal, culprit, delinquent, evildoer, felon, lawbreaker, malefactor, miscreant, offender, sinner, trespasser, villain, wrongdoer

transient brief, ephemeral, evanescent, fleeting, flying, fugacious, fugitive, here today and gone tomorrow, impermanent, momentary, passing, short, short-lived, short-term, temporary, transitory

transit 1. carriage, conveyance, crossing, motion, movement, passage, portage, shipment, transfer, transport, transportation, travel, traverse **2. in transit** during passage, en route, on the journey, on the move, on the road, on the way, while travelling

transition alteration, change, changeover, conversion, development, evolution, flux, metamorphosis, metastasis (*Pathol.*), passage, passing, progression, shift, transit, transmutation, upheaval

transitional changing, developmental, fluid, intermediate, passing, provisional, temporary, unsettled

transitory brief, ephemeral, evanescent, fleeting, flying, here today and gone tomorrow, impermanent, momentary, passing, short, short-lived, short-term, temporary, transient

translate 1. construe, convert, decipher, decode, interpret, paraphrase, render, transcribe, transliterate **2.** elucidate, explain, make clear, paraphrase, put in plain English, simplify, spell out, state in layman's language **3.** alter, change, convert, metamorphose, transfigure, transform, transmute, turn

translation 1. construction, decoding, gloss, interpretation, paraphrase, rendering, rendition, transcription, transliteration, version **2.** elucidation, explanation, paraphrase, rephrasing, rewording, simplification **3.** alteration, change, conversion, metamorphosis, transfiguration, transformation, transmutation

translator interpreter, linguist

transmission 1. broadcasting, carriage, communication, conveyance, diffusion, dispatch, dissemination, putting out, relaying, remission, sending, shipment, showing, spread, transfer, transference, transport **2.** broadcast, programme, show

transmit 1. bear, carry, communicate, convey, diffuse, dispatch, disseminate, forward, hand down, hand on, impart, pass on, remit, send, spread, take, transfer, transport **2.** broadcast, disseminate, put on the air, radio, relay, send, send out

parent. **2** a positive photograph on transparent film, usually mounted in a frame or between glass plates, which can be viewed with the use of a slide projector.

transparent *adj* **1** able to be seen through; clear. **2** easy to understand or recognize; obvious: *transparent honesty.* **transparently** *adv*

transpire *vb* **-spiring, -spired 1** to come to light; become known. **2** *Not universally accepted* to happen or occur. **3** *Physiol* to give off (water or vapour) through the pores of the skin, etc. **transpiration** *n*

➤ *Transpire* is so often used for "happen" or "occur" that the objection that it should be used only for "become known" is no longer valid.

transplant *vb* **1** *Surgery* to transfer (an organ or tissue) from one part of the body or from one person to another. **2** to remove or transfer (esp. a plant) from one place to another. *~n* **3** *Surgery* **a** the procedure involved in transferring an organ or tissue. **b** the organ or tissue transplanted. **transplantation** *n*

transponder *n* a type of radio or radar transmitter-receiver that transmits signals automatically when it receives predetermined signals.

transport *vb* **1** to carry or move (people or goods) from one place to another, esp. over some distance. **2** *History* to exile (a criminal) to a penal colony. **3** to have a strong emotional effect on: *transported by joy.* *~n* **4** the business or system of transporting goods or people: *public transport.* **5** *Brit* freight vehicles generally. **6** a vehicle used to transport troops. **7** a transporting or being transported. **8** ecstasy or rapture: *transports of delight.* **transportable** *adj*

transportation *n* **1** a means or system of transporting. **2** the act of transporting or the state of being transported. **3** *History* deportation to a penal colony.

transport café *n Brit* an inexpensive eating place on a main road, used mainly by long-distance lorry drivers.

transporter *n* a large vehicle used for carrying cars from the factory to garages for sale.

transpose *vb* **-posing, -posed 1** to change the order of (letters, words, or sentences). **2** *Music* to play (notes, music, etc.) in a different key. **3** *Maths* to move (a term) from one side of an equation to the other with a corresponding reversal in sign: *transposing 3 in* $x - 3 = 6$ *gives* $x = 6 + 3$. **transposition** *n*

transsexual *n* a person who has had medical treatment to alter his or her sexual characteristics to those of the opposite sex.

transship *vb* **-shipping, -shipped** to transfer or be transferred from one ship or vehicle to another. **transshipment** *n*

transubstantiation *n Christianity* the doctrine that the bread and wine consecrated in Communion changes into the substance of Christ's body and blood.

transuranic (tranz-yoor-**ran**-ik) *adj Chem* (of an element) having an atomic number greater than that of uranium.

transverse *adj* crossing from side to side: *the transverse arches in the main hall of the college.*

transvestite *n* a person, esp. a man, who seeks sexual pleasure from wearing clothes of the opposite sex. **transvestism** *n*

trap *n* **1** a device or hole in which something, esp. an animal, is caught. **2** a plan for tricking a person into being caught unawares. **3** a situation from which it is difficult to escape: *the poverty trap.* **4** a bend in a pipe that contains standing water to prevent the passage of gases. **5** a boxlike stall in which greyhounds are enclosed before the start of a race. **6** a device that hurls clay pigeons into the air to be fired at. **7** See **trap door.** **8** a light two-wheeled carriage: *a pony and trap.* **9** *Slang* the mouth: *shut your trap!* *~vb* **trapping, trapped 10** to catch (an animal) in a trap. **11** to catch (someone) by a trick: *the police trapped the drug dealers by posing as potential customers.* **12** to hold or confine in an unpleasant situation from which it is difficult to escape: *trapped in the rubble of collapsed buildings.* ~See also **trap out.**

trap door *n* a hinged door in a ceiling, floor, or stage.

trapeze *n* a horizontal bar suspended from two ropes, used by circus acrobats.

trapezium *n, pl* **-ziums** *or* **-zia 1** a quadrilateral having two parallel sides of unequal length. **2** *Chiefly US & Canad* a quadrilateral having neither pair of sides parallel. **trapezial** *adj*

trapezoid (**trap**-piz-zoid) *n* **1** a quadrilateral having neither pair of sides parallel. **2** *US & Canad* same as **trapezium** (sense 1).

trap out *vb* **trapping, trapped** to dress or adorn.

trapper *n* a person who traps animals, esp. for their furs or skins.

trappings *pl n* **1** the accessories that symbolize a condition, office, etc.: *the trappings of power.* **2** ceremonial harness for a horse or other animal.

Trappist *n* a member of an order of Christian monks who follow a rule of strict silence.

trash *n* **1** foolish ideas or talk; nonsense. **2** *Chiefly US & Canad* unwanted objects; rubbish. **3** *Chiefly US &*

THESAURUS

transparency 1. clarity, clearness, diaphanousness, filminess, gauziness, limpidity, limpidness, pellucidity, pellucidness, sheerness, translucence, translucency, transparence **2.** apparentness, distinctness, explicitness, obviousness, patentness, perspicuousness, plainness, unambiguousness, visibility **3.** photograph, slide

transparent 1. clear, crystal clear, crystalline, diaphanous, filmy, gauzy, limpid, lucent, lucid, pellucid, see-through, sheer, translucent **2.** apparent, as plain as the nose on one's face (*informal*), distinct, easy, evident, explicit, manifest, obvious, patent, perspicuous, plain, recognizable, unambiguous, understandable, undisguised, visible

transpire 1. become known, be disclosed, be discovered, be made public, come out, come to light, emerge **2.** *not universally accepted* arise, befall, chance, come about, come to pass (*archaic*), happen, occur, take place, turn up

transplant displace, relocate, remove, resettle, shift, transfer, uproot

transport *vb.* **1.** bear, bring, carry, convey, fetch, haul, move, remove, run, ship, take, transfer **2.** *History* banish, deport, exile, sentence to transportation **3.** captivate, carry away, delight, electrify, enchant, enrapture, entrance, move, ravish, spellbind *~n.* **4.** conveyance, transportation, vehicle **5.** carriage, conveyance, removal, shipment, shipping, transference, transportation **6.** bliss, cloud nine (*informal*), delight, ecstasy, enchantment, euphoria, happiness, heaven, rapture, ravishment, seventh heaven

transpose alter, change, exchange, interchange, move, rearrange, relocate, reorder, shift, substitute, swap, switch, transfer

transverse athwart, crossways, crosswise, diagonal, oblique

trap *n.* **1.** ambush, gin, net, noose, pitfall, snare, springe, toils **2.** ambush, artifice, deception, device, ruse, stratagem, subterfuge, trick, wile *~vb.* **3.** catch, corner, enmesh, ensnare, entrap, snare, take **4.** ambush, beguile, deceive, dupe, ensnare, inveigle, trick

trappings accoutrements, adornments, decorations,

Canad a worthless person or group of people. *~vb* **4** *Slang* to attack or destroy maliciously: *we've never trashed a hotel room.* **trashy** *adj*

trattoria (trat-or-ee-a) *n* an Italian restaurant.

trauma (**traw**-ma) *n* **1** *Psychol* an emotional shock that may have long-lasting effects. **2** *Pathol* any bodily injury or wound. **traumatic** *adj* **traumatically** *adv* **traumatize** *or* **-ise** *vb*

travail *n Literary* painful or exceptionally hard work.

travel *vb* **-elling, -elled** *or US* **-eling, -eled 1** to go or move from one place to another. **2** to go or journey through or across (an area, region, etc.): *Margaret travelled widely when she was in New Zealand.* **3** to go at a specified speed or for a specified distance: *the car was travelling at 30 mph.* **4** to go from place to place as a salesman. **5** (of perishable goods) to withstand a journey: *not all wines travel well.* **6** (of light or sound) to be transmitted or carried from one place to another: *sound travels a long distance in these conditions.* **7** (of a machine or part) to move in a fixed path. **8** (of a vehicle) *Informal* to move rapidly. *~n* **9** the act or a means of travelling: *air travel has changed the way people live.* **10** a tour or journey: *his travels took him to Dublin.* **11** the distance moved by a mechanical part, such as the stroke of a piston.

travel agency *n* an agency that arranges flights, hotel accommodation, etc., for tourists. **travel agent** *n*

traveller *n* **1** a person who travels, esp. habitually. **2** a travelling salesman. **3** a Gypsy.

traveller's cheque *n* a cheque sold by a bank, travel agency, etc., which the buyer signs on purchase and can cash abroad by signing it again.

travelling salesman *n* a salesman who travels within an assigned area in order to sell goods or get orders for the company he or she represents.

travelogue *or US* **travelog** *n* a film or lecture on travels and travelling.

travel sickness *n* nausea or vomiting caused by riding in a car or other moving vehicle. **travel-sick** *adj*

traverse *vb* **-ersing, -ersed 1** to move over or back and forth over; cross: *he once traversed San Francisco harbour in a balloon.* **2** to reach across. **3** to walk, climb, or ski diagonally up or down a slope. *~n* **4** something being or lying across, such as a crossbar. **5** the act or an instance of traversing or crossing. **6** a path or road across. *~adj* **7** being or lying across. **traversal** *n*

travesty *n, pl* **-ties 1** a grotesque imitation or mockery: *a travesty of justice.* *~vb* **-ties, -tying, -tied 2** to make or be a travesty of.

travois (trav-**voy**) *n, pl* **-vois** (-**voyz**) *Canad* a sled used for dragging logs.

trawl *n* **1** a large net, usually in the shape of a sock or bag, dragged at deep levels behind a fishing boat. *~vb* **2** to fish using such a net.

trawler *n* a ship used for trawling.

tray *n* **1** a flat board of wood, plastic, or metal, usually with a rim, on which things can be carried. **2** an open receptacle for office correspondence.

treacherous *adj* **1** disloyal and untrustworthy: *he was cruel, treacherous, and unscrupulous.* **2** unreliable or dangerous, esp. because of sudden changes: *the tides here can be very treacherous.* **treacherously** *adv*

treachery *n, pl* **-eries** the act or an instance of wilful betrayal.

treacle *n Brit* a thick dark syrup obtained during the refining of sugar. **treacly** *adj*

tread *vb* **treading, trod; trodden** *or* **trod 1** to set one's foot down on or in something: *he trod on some dog's dirt.* **2** to crush or squash by treading (on): *treading on a biscuit.* **3** to walk along (a path or road). **4** **tread carefully** *or* **warily** to proceed in a delicate or tactful manner. **5** **tread water** to stay afloat in an upright position by moving the legs in a walking motion. *~n* **6** a way of walking or the sound of walking: *he walked, with a heavy tread, up the stairs.* **7** the top surface of a step in a staircase. **8** the pattern of grooves in the outer surface of a tyre that helps it grip the road. **9** the part of a shoe that is generally in contact with the ground.

treadle (**tred**-dl) *n* a lever operated by the foot to turn a wheel.

treadmill *n* **1** (formerly) an apparatus turned by the weight of men or animals climbing steps on a revolv-

THESAURUS

dress, equipment, finery, fittings, fixtures, fripperies, furnishings, gear, livery, ornaments, panoply, paraphernalia, raiment (*archaic or poetic*), things, trimmings

trash 1. balderdash, balls (*taboo slang*), bilge (*informal*), bosh (*informal*), bullshit (*taboo slang*), bunkum, cobblers (*Brit. taboo slang*), crap (*slang*), drivel, eyewash (*informal*), foolish talk, garbage (*informal*), guff (*slang*), hogwash (*informal*), hokum (*slang, chiefly U.S. & Canad.*), hot air (*informal*), inanity, moonshine, nonsense, pap, piffle (*informal*), poppycock (*informal*), rot, rubbish, shit (*taboo slang*), tommyrot (*old-fashioned, informal*), tripe (*informal*), twaddle **2.** *chiefly U.S. & Canad.* dregs, dross, garbage, junk (*informal*), litter, refuse, rubbish, sweepings, waste

trashy catchpenny, cheap, cheap-jack (*informal*), crappy (*slang*), flimsy, inferior, of a sort *or* of sorts, poxy (*slang*), rubbishy, shabby, shoddy, tawdry, thrown together, tinsel, worthless

traumatic agonizing, damaging, disturbing, hurtful, injurious, painful, scarring, shocking, upsetting, wounding

travel *vb.* **1.** cross, go, journey, make a journey, make one's way, move, proceed, progress, ramble, roam, rove, take a trip, tour, traverse, trek, voyage, walk, wander, wend **2.** be transmitted, carry, get through, move *~n.* **3.** excursion, expedition, globetrotting, journey, movement, passage, peregrination, ramble, tour, touring, trip, voyage, walk, wandering

traveller 1. excursionist, explorer, globetrotter, Gypsy, hiker, holiday-maker, journeyer, migrant, nomad, passenger, tourist, tripper, voyager, wanderer, wayfarer (*old-fashioned*) **2.** agent, commercial traveller, rep, representative, salesman, travelling salesman

traverse bridge, cover, cross, cut across, go across, go over, make one's way across, negotiate, pass over, ply, range, roam, span, travel over, wander

travesty 1. *n.* burlesque, caricature, distortion, lampoon, mockery, parody, perversion, send-up (*Brit. informal*), sham, spoof (*informal*), takeoff (*informal*) **2.** *vb.* burlesque, caricature, deride, distort, lampoon, make a mockery of, make fun of, mock, parody, pervert, ridicule, send up (*Brit. informal*), sham, spoof (*informal*), take off (*informal*)

treacherous 1. deceitful, disloyal, double-crossing (*informal*), double-dealing, duplicitous, faithless, false, perfidious, recreant (*archaic*), traitorous, treasonable, unfaithful, unreliable, untrue, untrustworthy **2.** dangerous, deceptive, hazardous, icy, perilous, precarious, risky, slippery, slippy (*informal or dialect*), tricky, unreliable, unsafe, unstable

treachery betrayal, disloyalty, double-cross (*informal*), double-dealing, duplicity, faithlessness, infidelity, perfidiousness, perfidy, stab in the back, treason

ing cylinder or wheel. **2** a dreary routine: *the treadmill of housework.* **3** an exercise machine that consists of a continuous moving belt on which to walk or jog.

treason *n* **1** betrayal of one's sovereign or country, esp. by attempting to overthrow the government. **2** any treachery or betrayal. **treasonable** *adj* **treasonous** *adj*

treasure *n* **1** a collection of wealth, esp. in the form of money, precious metals, or gems. **2** a valuable painting, ornament, or other object: *the museum has many art treasures.* **3** *Informal* a person who is highly valued: *she can turn her hand to anything, she's a perfect treasure.* ~*vb* **-uring, -ured 4** to cherish (someone or something).

treasure hunt *n* a game in which players act upon successive clues to find a hidden prize.

treasurer *n* a person appointed to look after the funds of a society or other organization.

treasure-trove *n Law* any articles, such as coins or valuable objects found hidden and without any evidence of ownership.

treasury *n, pl* **-uries 1** a storage place for treasure. **2** the revenues or funds of a government or organization.

Treasury *n* (in various countries) the government department in charge of finance.

treat *vb* **1** to deal with or regard in a certain manner: *her love for a man who treats her abominably.* **2** to attempt to cure or lessen the symptoms of (an illness or injury or a person suffering from it): *the drug is prescribed to treat asthma.* **3** to subject to a chemical or industrial process: *the wood should be treated with a preservative.* **4** to provide (someone) with something as a treat: *I'll treat you to an ice cream.* **5 treat of** to deal with (something) in writing or speaking: *this book treats of a most abstruse subject.* ~*n* **6** a celebration, entertainment, gift, or meal given for or to someone and paid for by someone else. **7** any delightful surprise or specially pleasant occasion. **treatable** *adj*

treatise (**treat**-izz) *n* a formal piece of writing that deals systematically with a particular subject.

treatment *n* **1** the medical or surgical care given to a patient. **2** a way of handling a person or thing: *the party has had unfair treatment in the press.*

treaty *n, pl* **-ties 1** a formal written agreement between two or more states, such as an alliance or trade arrangement: *the Treaty of Rome established the Common Market.* **2** an agreement between two parties concerning the purchase of property.

treble *adj* **1** three times as much or as many. **2** of or denoting a soprano voice or part or a high-pitched instrument. ~*n* **3** a soprano voice or part or a high-pitched instrument. **4** of the highest range of musical notes: *these loudspeakers give excellent treble reproduction.* ~*vb* **-bling, -bled 5** to make or become three times as much or as many: *sales have trebled in three years.* **trebly** *adv*

treble chance *n* a method of betting in football pools in which the chances of winning are related to the number of draws and the number of home and away wins forecast by the competitor.

treble clef *n Music* the clef that establishes G a fifth above middle C as being on the second line of the staff.

tree *n* **1** any large woody perennial plant with a distinct trunk and usually having leaves and branches. **2** See **family tree, shoetree, saddletree. 3 at the top of the tree** in the highest position of a profession. **treeless** *adj*

tree creeper *n* a small songbird of the N hemisphere that creeps up trees to feed on insects

tree fern *n* any of numerous large tropical ferns with a trunklike stem.

tree line *n* same as **timber line.**

tree-lined *adj* (of a road) having trees on either side of it: *a pleasant tree-lined avenue in Bristol.*

tree surgery *n* the treatment of damaged trees by filling cavities, applying braces, etc. **tree surgeon** *n*

tree tomato *n* same as **tamarillo.**

treetop *n* the highest part of a tree, where the leaves and branches are: *monkeys swung through the treetops.*

trefoil (**tref**-foil) *n* **1** a plant, such as clover, with leaves divided into three smaller leaves. **2** *Archit* a carved ornament with a shape like such leaves. **trefoiled** *adj*

trek *n* **1** a long and often difficult journey, esp. on foot. **2** *S African* a journey or stage of a journey, esp. a migration by ox wagon. ~*vb* **trekking, trekked 3** to make a trek.

trellis *n* a frame made of vertical and horizontal strips of wood, esp. one used to support climbing plants. **trelliswork** *n*

tremble *vb* **-bling, -bled 1** to shake with short slight movements: *her hands trembled uncontrollably; he felt the ground trembling beneath him.* **2** to experience fear or anxiety: *his parents trembled with apprehension about his future.* **3** (of the voice) to sound uncer-

THESAURUS

tread *vb.* **1.** hike, march, pace, plod, stamp, step, stride, tramp, trudge, walk **2.** crush underfoot, squash, trample ~*n.* **3.** footfall, footstep, gait, pace, step, stride, walk

treason disaffection, disloyalty, duplicity, lese-majesty, mutiny, perfidy, sedition, subversion, traitorousness, treachery

treasonable disloyal, false, mutinous, perfidious, seditious, subversive, traitorous, treacherous, treasonous

treasure *n.* **1.** cash, fortune, funds, gold, jewels, money, riches, valuables, wealth **2.** *informal* apple of one's eye, darling, gem, jewel, nonpareil, paragon, pearl, precious, pride and joy, prize ~*vb.* **3.** adore, cherish, dote upon, esteem, hold dear, idolize, love, prize, revere, value, venerate, worship

treasury **1.** bank, cache, hoard, repository, store, storehouse, vault **2.** assets, capital, coffers, exchequer, finances, funds, money, resources, revenues

treat *vb.* **1.** act towards, behave towards, consider, deal with, handle, look upon, manage, regard, use **2.** apply treatment to, attend to, care for, doctor, medicate, nurse **3.** buy for, entertain, feast, foot *or* pay the bill, give, lay on, pay for, provide, regale, stand (*informal*), take out, wine and dine **4. treat of** be concerned with, contain, deal with, discourse upon, discuss, go into, touch upon ~*n.* **5.** banquet, celebration, entertainment, feast, gift, party, refreshment **6.** delight, enjoyment, fun, gratification, joy, pleasure, satisfaction, surprise, thrill

treatise disquisition, dissertation, essay, exposition, monograph, pamphlet, paper, study, thesis, tract, work, writing

treatment **1.** care, cure, healing, medication, medicine, remedy, surgery, therapy **2.** action towards, behaviour towards, conduct, dealing, handling, management, manipulation, reception, usage

treaty agreement, alliance, bargain, bond, compact, concordat, contract, convention, covenant, entente, pact

trek **1.** *n.* expedition, footslog, hike, journey, long haul, march, odyssey, safari, slog, tramp **2.** *vb.* foot-

tain or unsteady, for instance through pain or emotion. ~*n* **4** the act or an instance of trembling. **trembling** *adj*

tremendous *adj* **1** very large or impressive: *a tremendous amount of money.* **2** very exciting or unusual: *a tremendous feeling of elation.* **3** very good or pleasing: *my wife has given me tremendous support.* **tremendously** *adv*

tremolo *n, pl* **-los** *Music* **1** (in playing the violin or other stringed instrument) the rapid repetition of a note or notes to produce a trembling effect. **2** (in singing) a fluctuation in pitch.

tremor *n* **1** an involuntary shudder or vibration: *the slight tremor of excitement.* **2** a minor earthquake.

tremulous *adj Literary* trembling, as from fear or excitement: *I managed a tremulous smile.* **tremulously** *adv*

trench *n* **1** a long narrow ditch in the ground, such as one for laying a pipe in. **2** a long deep ditch used by soldiers for protection in a war: *my grandfather fought in the trenches in the First World War.* ~*adj* **3** of or involving military trenches: *trench warfare.*

trenchant *adj* **1** keen or incisive: *a trenchant screenplay.* **2** vigorous and effective: *the prime minister's trenchant adoption of this issue.* **trenchancy** *n*

trench coat *n* a belted raincoat similar in style to a military officer's coat.

trencher *n History* a wooden board on which food was served or cut.

trencherman *n, pl* **-men** a person who enjoys food; hearty eater.

trench warfare *n* a type of warfare in which opposing armies face each other in entrenched positions.

trend *n* **1** general tendency or direction: *an accelerating trend towards the use of mobile phones.* **2** fashionable style: *she set a trend for wearing lingerie as outer garments.* ~*vb* **3** to take a certain trend.

trendsetter *n* a person or thing that creates, or may create, a new fashion. **trendsetting** *adj*

trendy *Brit informal* ~*adj* **trendier, trendiest 1** consciously fashionable: *a flat in Glasgow's trendy West End.* ~*n, pl* **trendies 2** a trendy person: *a media trendy.* **trendily** *adv* **trendiness** *n*

trepidation *n Formal* a state of fear or anxiety.

trespass *vb* **1** to go onto somebody else's property without permission. ~*n* **2** the act or an instance of trespassing. **3** *Old-fashioned* a sin or wrong-doing. **trespasser** *n*

trespass on *or* **upon** *vb Formal* to take unfair advantage of (someone's friendship, patience, etc.): *I won't trespass upon your hospitality any longer.*

tresses *pl n* a woman's long flowing hair.

trestle *n* **1** a support for one end of a table or beam, consisting of two rectangular frameworks or sets of legs which are joined at the top but not the bottom. **2** Also called: **trestle table** a table consisting of a board supported by a trestle at each end.

trews *pl n Chiefly Brit* close-fitting trousers of tartan cloth.

tri- *combining form* **1** three or thrice: *trilingual.* **2** occurring every three: *triweekly.*

triad *n* **1** a group of three. **2** *Music* a three-note chord consisting of a note and the third and fifth above it. **triadic** *adj*

Triad *n* a Chinese secret society involved in criminal activities, such as drug trafficking.

trial *n* **1** *Law* an investigation of a case in front of a judge to decide whether a person is innocent or guilty of a crime by questioning him or her and considering the evidence. **2** the act or an instance of trying or proving; test or experiment: *the new drug is undergoing clinical trials.* **3** an annoying or frustrating person or thing: *young children can be a great trial at times.* **4** **trials** a sporting competition for individual people or animals: *horse trials.* **5** **on trial a** undergoing trial,

THESAURUS

slog, hike, journey, march, plod, range, roam, rove, slog, traipse (*informal*), tramp, trud

tremble 1. *vb.* oscillate, quake, quiver, rock, shake, shake in one's shoes, shiver, shudder, teeter, totter, vibrate, wobble **2.** *n.* oscillation, quake, quiver, shake, shiver, shudder, tremor, vibration, wobble

tremendous 1. appalling, awesome, awful, colossal, deafening, dreadful, enormous, fearful, formidable, frightful, gargantuan, gigantic, great, huge, immense, mammoth, monstrous, prodigious, stupendous, terrible, terrific, titanic, towering, vast, whopping (*informal*) **2.** ace (*informal*), amazing, brill (*informal*), brilliant, cracking (*Brit. informal*), excellent, exceptional, extraordinary, fabulous (*informal*), fantastic (*informal*), great, incredible, jim-dandy (*slang*), marvellous, mean (*slang*), sensational (*informal*), sovereign, super (*informal*), terrific (*informal*), wonderful

tremor 1. agitation, quaking, quaver, quiver, quivering, shake, shaking, shiver, tremble, trembling, trepidation, vibration, wobble **2.** earthquake, quake (*informal*), shock

trench channel, cut, ditch, drain, earthwork, entrenchment, excavation, fosse, furrow, gutter, pit, trough, waterway

trenchant 1. acerbic, acid, acidulous, acute, astringent, biting, caustic, cutting, hurtful, incisive, keen, mordacious, mordant, penetrating, piquant, pointed, pungent, sarcastic, scathing, severe, sharp, tart, vitriolic **2.** driving, effective, effectual, emphatic, energetic, forceful, potent, powerful, strong, vigorous

trend *n.* **1.** bias, course, current, direction, drift, flow, inclination, leaning, tendency **2.** craze, fad (*informal*), fashion, look, mode, rage, style, thing, vogue ~*vb.* **3.** bend, flow, head, incline, lean, run, stretch, swing, tend, turn, veer

trepidation *formal* agitation, alarm, anxiety, apprehension, blue funk (*informal*), butterflies (*informal*), cold feet (*informal*), cold sweat (*informal*), consternation, dismay, disquiet, disturbance, dread, emotion, excitement, fear, fright, jitters (*informal*), nervousness, palpitation, perturbation, quivering, shaking, the heebie-jeebies (*slang*), trembling, tremor, uneasiness, worry

trespass *vb.* **1.** encroach, infringe, intrude, invade, obtrude, poach ~*n.* **2.** encroachment, infringement, intrusion, invasion, poaching, unlawful entry, wrongful entry **3.** *old-fashioned* breach, crime, delinquency, error, evildoing, fault, infraction, iniquity, injury, misbehaviour, misconduct, misdeed, misdemeanour, offence, sin, transgression, wrongdoing

trespasser 1. infringer, interloper, intruder, invader, poacher, unwelcome visitor **2.** *old-fashioned* criminal, delinquent, evildoer, malefactor, offender, sinner, transgressor, wrongdoer

tresses curls, locks, ringlets

triad threesome, trilogy, trinity, trio, triple, triplet, triptych, triumvirate

trial *n.* **1.** *Law* contest, hearing, industrial tribunal, judicial examination, litigation, tribunal **2. a.** attempt, crack (*informal*), effort, endeavour, go (*informal*), shot (*informal*), stab (*informal*), try, venture, whack (*informal*) **b.** assay, audition, check, dry run (*informal*), examination, experience, experiment, probation, proof, test, testing, test-run **3.** bane, bother, drag (*in-*

esp. before a court of law. **b** being tested, for example before a commitment to purchase: *I only have the car out on trial.* ~*adj* **6** on a temporary basis while being tried out or tested: *a trial run.*

trial and error *n* a method of discovery based on practical experiment and experience rather than on theory: *raising her children has been a matter of trial and error.*

trial balance *n Book-keeping* a statement of all the debit and credit balances in the double-entry ledger.

triangle *n* **1** a geometric figure with three sides and three angles. **2** any object shaped like a triangle: *a triangle of streets running up from the river.* **3** *Music* a percussion instrument that consists of a metal bar bent into a triangular shape, played by striking it with a metal stick. **4** any situation involving three people or points of view: *a torrid sex triangle.* **triangular** *adj*

triangulate *vb* **-lating, -lated** to survey (an area) by dividing it into triangles.

triangulation *n* a method of surveying in which an area is divided into triangles, one side (the base line) and all angles of which are measured and the lengths of the other lines calculated by trigonometry.

Triassic *adj Geol* of the period of geological time about 230 million years ago.

triathlon *n* an athletic contest in which each athlete competes in three different events: swimming, cycling, and horse riding. **triathlete** *n*

tribalism *n* loyalty to a tribe, esp. as opposed to a modern political entity such as a state.

tribe *n* **1** a group of families or clans believed to have a common ancestor. **2** *Informal* a group of people who do the same type of thing: *a tribe of German yachtsmen bound for the Mediterranean.* **tribal** *adj*

tribesman *n, pl* **-men** a member of a tribe.

tribulation *n* great distress: *the tribulations of a deserted wife.*

tribunal *n* **1** (in Britain) a special court or committee that is appointed to deal with a particular problem: *an industrial tribunal investigating allegations of unfair dismissal.* **2** a court of justice.

tribune *n* **1** a person who upholds public rights. **2** (in ancient Rome) an officer elected by the plebs to protect their interests.

tributary *n, pl* **-taries** **1** a stream or river that flows into a larger one: *Frankfurt lies on the River Main, a tributary of the Rhine.* **2** a person, nation, or people that pays tribute. ~*adj* **3** (of a stream or river) flowing into a larger stream. **4** paying tribute: *Egypt was formerly a tributary province of the Turkish Empire.*

tribute *n* **1** something given, done, or said as a mark of respect or admiration. **2** a payment by one ruler or state to another, usually as an acknowledgment of submission. **3** something that shows the merits of a particular quality of a person or thing: *the car's low fuel consumption is a tribute to the quality of its engine.*

trice *n* **in a trice** in a moment: *she was back in a trice.*

triceps *n* the muscle at the back of the upper arm.

trichology (trick-**ol**-a-jee) *n* the branch of medicine concerned with the hair and its diseases. **trichologist** *n*

trichromatic *adj* **1** having or involving three colours. **2** of or having normal colour vision. **trichromatism** *n*

trick *n* **1** a deceitful or cunning action or plan: *she was willing to use any dirty trick to get what she wanted.* **2** a joke or prank: *he loves playing tricks on his sister.* **3** a clever way of doing something, learnt from experience: *an old campers' trick is to use three thin blankets rather than one thick one.* **4** an illusory or magical feat or device. **5** a simple feat learned by an animal or person. **6** a deceptive illusion: *a trick of the light.* **7** a habit or mannerism: *she had a trick of saying "oh dear".* **8** *Cards* a batch of cards played in turn and won by the person playing the highest card. **9 do the trick** *Informal* to produce the desired result. **10 how's tricks?** *Slang* how are you? ~*vb* **11** to defraud, deceive, or cheat (someone). **trickery** *n*

trickle *vb* **-ling, -led** **1** to flow or cause to flow in a thin stream or drops: *tears trickled down her cheeks.* **2** to move slowly or in small groups: *voters trickled to the polls.* ~*n* **3** a thin, irregular, or slow flow of something: *a trickle of blood.*

trick out *vb* to dress up: *tricked out in chauffeur's rig.*

trickster *n* a person who deceives or plays tricks.

tricky *adj* **trickier, trickiest** **1** involving snags or difficulties: *a tricky task.* **2** needing careful handling: *a*

THESAURUS

formal), hassle (*informal*), irritation, nuisance, pain in the arse (*taboo informal*), pain in the neck (*informal*), pest, plague (*informal*), thorn in one's flesh, vexation ~*adj.* **4.** experimental, exploratory, pilot, probationary, provisional, testing

tribe blood, caste, clan, class, division, dynasty, ethnic group, family, gens, house, people, race, seed (*chiefly Bible*), sept, stock

tribulation adversity, affliction, bad luck, blow, burden, care, cross to bear, curse, distress, grief, hardship, hassle (*informal*), heartache, ill fortune, misery, misfortune, ordeal, pain, reverse, sorrow, suffering, trial, trouble, unhappiness, vexation, woe, worry, wretchedness

tribunal bar, bench, court, hearing, industrial tribunal, judgment seat, judicial examination, trial

tribute **1.** accolade, acknowledgment, applause, commendation, compliment, encomium, esteem, eulogy, gift, gratitude, honour, laudation, panegyric, praise, recognition, respect, testimonial **2.** charge, contribution, customs, duty, excise, homage, impost, offering, payment, ransom, subsidy, tax, toll

trick *n.* **1.** artifice, canard, con (*informal*), deceit, deception, device, dodge, feint, fraud, gimmick, hoax, imposition, imposture, manoeuvre, ploy, ruse, scam (*slang*), sting (*informal*), stratagem, subterfuge, swindle, trap, wile **2.** antic, caper, device, feat, frolic, gag (*informal*), gambol, jape, joke, juggle, legerdemain, leg-pull (*Brit. informal*), practical joke, prank, put-on (*slang*), sleight of hand, stunt **3.** art, command, craft, device, expertise, gift, hang (*informal*), knack, know-how (*informal*), secret, skill, technique **4.** characteristic, crotchet, foible, habit, idiosyncrasy, mannerism, peculiarity, practice, quirk, trait **5. do the trick** *informal* be effective *or* effectual, have effect, produce the desired result, work ~*vb.* **6.** bamboozle (*informal*), cheat, con (*informal*), deceive, defraud, delude, dupe, fool, have (someone) on, hoax, hoodwink, impose upon, kid (*informal*), mislead, pull the wool over (someone's) eyes, put one over on (someone) (*informal*), sting (*informal*), swindle, take in (*informal*), trap

trickery cheating, chicanery, con (*informal*), deceit, deception, dishonesty, double-dealing, fraud, funny business, guile, hanky-panky (*informal*), hoax, hokum (*slang, chiefly U.S. & Canad.*), imposture, jiggery-pokery (*informal, chiefly Brit.*), monkey business (*informal*), pretence, skulduggery (*informal*), swindling

trickle **1.** *vb.* crawl, creep, dribble, drip, drop, exude, ooze, percolate, run, seep, stream **2.** *n.* dribble, drip, seepage

tricky **1.** complicated, delicate, difficult, knotty, problematic, risky, sticky (*informal*), thorny, ticklish,

tricky situation. **3** sly or wily: *a tricky customer.* **trickily** *adv* **trickiness** *n*

tricolour *or US* **tricolor** (**trick**-kol-lor) *n* a flag with three equal stripes in different colours, esp. the French or Irish national flags.

tricycle *n* a three-wheeled cycle. **tricyclist** *n*

trident *n* a three-pronged spear.

tried *vb* the past of **try.**

triennial *adj* occurring every three years. **triennially** *adv*

trier *n* a person or thing that tries.

trifle[1] *n* **1** a thing of little or no value or significance. **2** *Brit* a cold dessert made of sponge cake spread with jam or fruit, soaked in sherry, covered with custard and cream. **3 a trifle** to a small extent or degree; slightly: *he is a trifle eccentric.*

trifle[2] *vb* **trifling, trifled trifle with** to treat (a person or his or her feelings) with disdain or disregard.

trifling *adj* insignificant, petty, or frivolous: *a trifling misunderstanding.*

trig. trigonometry.

trigger *n* **1** a small lever that releases a catch on a gun or machine. **2** any event that sets a course of action in motion: *his murder was the trigger for a night of rioting.* ~*vb* **3** Also: **trigger off** to set (an action or process) in motion: *various factors can trigger off a migraine.*

trigger-happy *adj Informal* too ready or willing to use guns or violence: *trigger-happy border guards.*

trigonometry *n* the branch of mathematics concerned with the relations of sides and angles of triangles, which is used in surveying, navigation, etc.

trig point *n* a point on a hilltop etc., used for triangulation by a surveyor.

trike *n Informal* a tricycle.

trilateral *adj* having three sides.

trilby *n, pl* **-bies** a man's soft felt hat with an indented crown.

trill *n* **1** *Music* a rapid alternation between a note and the note above it. **2** a shrill warbling sound made by some birds: *the canary's high trills.* ~*vb* **3** (of a bird) to make a shrill warbling sound. **4** (of a person) to talk or laugh in a high-pitched musical voice.

trillion *n* **-lions** *or* **-lion 1** (in Britain, France, and Germany) the number represented as one followed by eighteen zeros (10^{18}); a million million million. **2** (in the U.S. and Canada) the number represented as one followed by twelve zeros (10^{12}); a million million. ~*adj* **3** amounting to a trillion: *a trillion dollars.* **trillionth** *n, adj*

➤ A *trillion* is what British speakers used to call "a billion".

trillium *n* a plant of Asia and North America that has three leaves at the top of the stem with a single white, pink, or purple three-petalled flower.

trilobite (**trile**-oh-bite) *n* a small prehistoric marine arthropod, found as a fossil.

trilogy (**trill**-a-jee) *n, pl* **-gies** a series of three books, plays, etc., which form a related group but are each complete works in themselves.

trim *adj* **trimmer, trimmest 1** neat and spruce in appearance: *trim lace curtains.* **2** attractively slim: *his body was trim and athletic.* ~*vb* **trimming, trimmed 3** to make (something) neater by cutting it slightly without changing its basic shape: *his white beard was neatly trimmed.* **4** to adorn or decorate (something, such as a garment) with lace, ribbons, etc.: *a cotton camisole neatly trimmed with lace.* **5 a** to adjust the balance of (a ship or aircraft) by shifting cargo etc. **b** to adjust (a ship's sails) to take advantage of the wind. **6** to reduce or lower the size of: *the company has trimmed its pretax profits forecast by $2.3 million.* **7** to alter (a plan or policy) by removing parts which seem unnecessary or unpopular: *the government would rather trim its policies than lose the election.* **8 trim off** *or* **away** to cut so as to remove: *trim off most of the fat before cooking the meat.* ~*n* **9** a decoration or adornment: *a black suit with scarlet trim.* **10** the upholstery and decorative facings of a car's interior. **11** good physical condition: *he had always kept himself in trim.* **12** a haircut that neatens but does not alter the existing hairstyle.

trimaran (**trime**-a-ran) *n* a boat with one smaller hull on each side of the main hull.

trimming *n* **1** an extra piece added to a garment for decoration: *a pink nightie with lace trimming.* **2 trimmings** usual or traditional accompaniments: *bacon and eggs with all the trimmings.*

Trinitarian *n* **1** a person who believes in the doctrine of the Trinity. ~*adj* **2** of or relating to the Trinity. **Trinitarianism** *n*

trinitrotoluene *n* the full name for **TNT.**

trinity *n, pl* **-ties** a group of three people or things.

Trinity *n Christianity* the union of three persons, the Father, Son, and Holy Spirit, in one God.

trinket *n* a small or worthless ornament or piece of jewellery.

trio *n, pl* **trios 1** a group of three people or things. **2** a group of three instrumentalists or singers. **3** a piece of music for three performers.

trip *n* **1** a journey to a place and back, esp. for pleasure: *they took a coach trip round the island.* **2** a false step; stumble. **3** the act of causing someone to stumble or fall by catching his or her foot with one's own. **4**

THESAURUS

touch-and-go **2.** artful, crafty, cunning, deceitful, deceptive, devious, foxy, scheming, slippery, sly, subtle, wily

trifle 1. bagatelle, bauble, child's play (*informal*), knick-knack, nothing, plaything, toy, triviality **2.** bit, dash, drop, jot, little, pinch, spot, touch, trace

trifling empty, frivolous, idle, inconsiderable, insignificant, measly, minuscule, negligible, paltry, petty, piddling (*informal*), puny, shallow, silly, slight, small, tiny, trivial, unimportant, valueless, worthless

trigger *or* **trigger off** activate, bring about, cause, elicit, generate, give rise to, produce, prompt, provoke, set in motion, set off, spark off, start

trim *adj.* **1.** compact, dapper, natty (*informal*), neat, nice, orderly, shipshape, smart, soigné *or fem.* soignée, spick-and-span, spruce, tidy, well-groomed, well-ordered, well turned-out **2.** fit, shapely, sleek, slender, slim, streamlined, svelte, willowy ~*vb.* **3.** barber, clip, crop, curtail, cut, cut back, dock, even up, lop, pare, prune, shave, shear, tidy **4.** adorn, array, beautify, bedeck, deck out, decorate, dress, embellish, embroider, garnish, ornament, trick out **5.** adjust, arrange, balance, distribute, order, prepare, settle ~*n.* **6.** adornment, border, decoration, edging, embellishment, frill, fringe, garnish, ornamentation, piping, trimming **7.** condition, fettle, fitness, form, health, order, repair, shape (*informal*), situation, state **8.** clipping, crop, cut, pruning, shave, shearing, tidying up, trimming

trimming 1. adornment, border, braid, decoration, edging, embellishment, festoon, frill, fringe, garnish, ornamentation, piping **2. trimmings** accessories, accompaniments, appurtenances, extras, frills, garnish, ornaments, paraphernalia, trappings

trinity threesome, triad, trilogy, trio, triple, triplet, triptych, triumvirate

Informal a hallucinogenic drug experience. **5** a catch on a mechanism that acts as a switch. *~vb* **tripping, tripped 6** Also: **trip up** to stumble or cause (someone) to stumble. **7** Also: **trip up** to trap or catch (someone) in a mistake. **8** to walk lightly and quickly, with a dancelike motion: *I could see Amelia tripping along beside him.* **9** *Informal* to experience the effects of a hallucinogenic drug.

tripartite *adj* involving or composed of three people or parts. **tripartism** *n*

tripe *n* **1** the stomach lining of a cow or pig used as a food. **2** *Informal* nonsense or rubbish.

Tripitaka (trip-it-**tah**-ka) *n* the three collections of books making up the Buddhist scriptures.

triple *adj* **1** made up of three parts or things: *a triple murder.* **2** (of musical time or rhythm) having three beats in each bar. **3** three times as great or as much: *a triple brandy.* *~vb* **-pling, -pled 4** to make or become three times as much or as many: *the company has tripled its sales over the past five years.* *~n* **5** something that is, or contains, three times as much as normal. **6** a group of three. **triply** *adv*

triple jump *n* an athletic event in which the competitor has to perform a hop, a step, and a jump in a continuous movement.

triple point *n Chem* the temperature and pressure at which a substance can exist as a solid, liquid, and gas.

triplet *n* **1** one of three children born at one birth. **2** a group of three musical notes played in the time that two would normally take. **3** a group or set of three similar things.

triplicate *adj* **1** triple. *~vb* **-cating, -cated 2** to multiply or be multiplied by three. *~n* **3 in triplicate** written out three times: *my request to interview the commander had to be made in triplicate.* **triplication** *n*

tripod (**tripe**-pod) *n* **1** a three-legged stand to which a camera can be attached to hold it steady. **2** a three-legged stool, table, etc.

tripos (**tripe**-poss) *n Brit* the final honours degree examinations at Cambridge University.

tripper *n Chiefly Brit* a tourist.

triptych (**trip**-tick) *n* a set of three pictures or panels, usually hinged together and often used as an altarpiece.

trireme (**try**-ream) *n* an ancient Greek warship with three rows of oars on each side.

trismus *n Pathol* the state of being unable to open the mouth because of sustained contractions of the jaw muscles, caused by tetanus. Nontechnical name: **lockjaw**

triste (**treest**) *adj Old-fashioned* sad.

trite *adj* (of a remark or idea) commonplace and unoriginal.

tritium *n* a radioactive isotope of hydrogen. Symbol: T or ^{3}H

triumph *n* **1** the feeling of great happiness resulting from a victory or major achievement. **2** an outstanding success, achievement, or victory: *the concert was a musical triumph.* **3** (in ancient Rome) a procession held in honour of a victorious general. *~vb* **4** to gain control or success: *triumphing over adversity.* **5** to rejoice over a victory. **triumphal** *adj*

triumphant *adj* **1** feeling or displaying triumph: *her smile was triumphant.* **2** celebrating a victory or success: *the general's triumphant tour round the city.* **triumphantly** *adv*

triumvir (try-**umm**-vir) *n* (esp. in ancient Rome) a member of a triumvirate.

triumvirate (try-**umm**-vir-rit) *n* **1** a group of three people in joint control of something: *the triumvirate of great orchestras which dominates classical music in Europe.* **2** (in ancient Rome) a board of three officials jointly responsible for some task.

trivalent *adj Chem* **1** having a valency of three. **2** having three valencies. **trivalency** *n*

trivet (**triv**-vit) *n* **1** a three-legged stand for holding a

THESAURUS

trinket bagatelle, bauble, bibelot, knick-knack, ornament, piece of bric-a-brac, toy, trifle

trio threesome, triad, trilogy, trinity, triple, triplet, triptych, triumvirate

trip *n.* **1.** errand, excursion, expedition, foray, jaunt, journey, outing, ramble, run, tour, travel, voyage **2.** bloomer (*Brit. informal*), blunder, boob (*Brit. slang*), error, fall, false move, false step, faux pas, indiscretion, lapse, misstep, slip, stumble *~vb.* **3.** *Also* **trip up** blunder, boob (*Brit. slang*), err, fall, go wrong, lapse, lose one's balance, lose one's footing, make a false move, make a faux pas, miscalculate, misstep, slip, slip up (*informal*), stumble, tumble **4.** *Also* **trip up** catch out, confuse, disconcert, put off one's stride, throw off, trap, unsettle **5.** caper, dance, flit, frisk, gambol, hop, skip, spring, tread lightly **6.** *informal* get high (*informal*), get stoned (*slang*), take drugs

tripe balderdash, balls (*taboo slang*), bilge (*informal*), bosh (*informal*), bullshit (*taboo slang*), bunkum, claptrap (*informal*), cobblers (*Brit. taboo slang*), crap (*slang*), drivel, eyewash (*informal*), foolish talk, garbage (*informal*), guff (*slang*), hogwash, hokum (*slang, chiefly U.S. & Canad.*), hot air (*informal*), inanity, moonshine, nonsense, pap, piffle (*informal*), poppycock (*informal*), rot, rubbish, shit (*taboo slang*), tommyrot (*old-fashioned, informal*), trash, twaddle

triple 1. *adj.* threefold, three times as much, three-way, tripartite **2.** *vb.* increase threefold, treble, triplicate **3.** *n.* threesome, triad, trilogy, trinity, trio, triplet, triumvirate

triplet threesome, triad, trilogy, trinity, trio, triple, triumvirate

tripper *chiefly Brit.* excursionist, holiday-maker, journeyer, sightseer, tourist, voyager

trite banal, clichéd, common, commonplace, corny (*slang*), dull, hack, hackneyed, ordinary, pedestrian, routine, run-of-the-mill, stale, stereotyped, stock, threadbare, tired, uninspired, unoriginal, worn

triumph *n.* **1.** elation, exultation, happiness, joy, jubilation, pride, rejoicing **2.** accomplishment, achievement, ascendancy, attainment, conquest, coup, feat, hit (*informal*), mastery, sensation, smash (*informal*), smash-hit (*informal*), success, tour de force, victory, walkover (*informal*) *~vb.* **3.** best, carry the day, come out on top (*informal*), dominate, flourish, get the better of, overcome, overwhelm, prevail, prosper, subdue, succeed, take the honours, thrive, vanquish, win **4.** celebrate, crow, drool, exult, gloat, glory, jubilate, rejoice, revel, swagger

triumphant boastful, celebratory, cock-a-hoop, conquering, dominant, elated, exultant, glorious, jubilant, proud, rejoicing, successful, swaggering, triumphal, undefeated, victorious, winning

trivia details, minutiae, petty details, trifles, trivialities

trivial commonplace, everyday, frivolous, incidental, inconsequential, inconsiderable, insignificant, little, meaningless, minor, negligible, paltry, petty, puny, slight, small, trifling, trite, unimportant, valueless, worthless

triviality 1. frivolity, inconsequentiality, insignifi-

pot, kettle, etc., over a fire. **2** a short metal stand on which hot dishes are placed on a table.

trivia *n* petty and unimportant things or details.

trivial *adj* of little importance: *a trivial matter.* **triviality** *n* **trivially** *adv*

trivialize *or* **-ise** *vb* **-izing, -ized** *or* **-ising, -ised** to make (something) seem less important or complex than it is.

trochee (**troke**-ee) *n Prosody* a metrical foot of one long and one short syllable. **trochaic** *adj*

trod *vb* the past tense and a past participle of **tread.**

trodden *vb* a past participle of **tread.**

troglodyte *n* a person who lives in a cave.

troika *n* **1** a Russian coach or sleigh drawn by three horses abreast. **2** a group of three people in authority: *a troika of European foreign ministers.*

Trojan *adj* **1** of ancient Troy or its people. *~n* **2** a person from ancient Troy. **3** a hard-working person.

Trojan Horse *n* **1** *Greek myth* the huge wooden hollow figure of a horse used by the Greeks to enter Troy. **2** a trap or trick intended to undermine an enemy.

troll[1] *n* (in Scandinavian folklore) a supernatural dwarf or giant that dwells in a cave or mountain.

troll[2] *vb Angling* to fish by dragging a baited hook through the water.

trolley *n* **1** a small table on casters used for carrying food or drink. **2** *Chiefly Brit* a wheeled cart or stand used for moving heavy items, such as shopping in a supermarket or luggage at a railway station. **3** *Brit* See **trolley bus. 4** *US & Canad* See **trolley car. 5** a device, such as a wheel that collects the current from an overhead wire, to drive the motor of an electric vehicle. **6** *Chiefly Brit* a low truck running on rails, used in factories, mines, etc.

trolley bus *n* a bus powered by electricity from two overhead wires but not running on rails.

trolley car *n US & Canad* same as **tram.**

trollop *n Derogatory* a promiscuous or slovenly woman.

trombone *n* a brass musical instrument with a sliding tube which is moved in or out to alter the note played. **trombonist** *n*

trompe l'oeil (tromp **luh**-ee) *n, pl* **trompe l'oeils** (tromp **luh**-ee) **1** a painting etc. giving a convincing illusion that the objects represented are real. **2** an effect of this kind.

troop *n* **1** a large group: *a troop of dogs.* **2 troops** soldiers: *British troops in Northern Ireland.* **3** a subdivision of a cavalry or armoured regiment. **4** a large group of Scouts made up of several patrols. *~vb* **5** to move in a crowd: *we trooped into the room after her.* **6** *Mil, chiefly Brit* to parade (a flag or banner) ceremonially: *trooping the colour.*

trooper *n* **1** a soldier in a cavalry regiment. **2** *US & Austral* a mounted policeman. **3** *US* a state policeman. **4** a cavalry horse. **5** *Informal, chiefly Brit* a troopship.

troopship *n* a ship used to transport military personnel.

trope *n* a word or expression used in a figurative sense.

trophy *n, pl* **-phies 1** a cup, shield, etc., given as a prize. **2** a memento of success, esp. one taken in war or hunting: *stuffed animal heads and other hunting trophies.*

tropic *n* **1** either of the lines of latitude at about 23½°N (**tropic of Cancer**) and 23½°S (**tropic of Capricorn**) of the equator **2 the tropics** that part of the earth's surface between the tropics of Cancer and Capricorn.

tropical *adj* belonging to, typical of, or located in, the tropics: *tropical rainforests.* **tropically** *adv*

tropism *n* the tendency of a plant or animal to turn or curve in response to an external stimulus.

troposphere *n* the lowest layer of the Earth's atmosphere, about 18 kilometres (11 miles) thick at the equator to about 6 km (4 miles) at the Poles.

trot *vb* **trotting, trotted 1** (of a horse) to move in a manner faster than a walk but slower than a gallop, in which diagonally opposite legs come down together. **2** (of a person) to move fairly quickly, with small quick steps. *~n* **3** a medium-paced gait of a horse, in which diagonally opposite legs come down together. **4** a steady brisk pace. **5 on the trot** *Informal* one after the other: *ten years on the trot.* **6 the trots** *Slang* diarrhoea.

Trot *n Informal* a follower of Trotsky.

troth (rhymes with **growth**) *n Archaic* **1** a pledge of fidelity, esp. a betrothal. **2 in troth** truly.

trot out *vb Informal* to repeat (old information or ideas) without fresh thought: *the government trots out the same excuse every time.*

Trotskyist *or* **Trotskyite** *adj* **1** of the theories of Leon Trotsky (1879–1940), Russian Communist, which call for a worldwide revolution by the proletariat. *~n* **2** a supporter of Trotsky or his theories. **Trotskyism** *n*

trotter *n* **1** the foot of a pig. **2** a horse that is specially trained to trot fast.

troubadour (**troo**-bad-oor) *n* a travelling poet and singer in S France or N Italy from the 11th to the 13th century who wrote chiefly on courtly love.

trouble *n* **1** difficulties or problems: *I'd trouble finding somewhere to park.* **2** a cause of distress, disturbance, or pain: *we must be sensitive to the troubles of other people.* **3** disease or a problem with one's health: *ear trouble.* **4** a state of disorder, ill-feeling, or unrest: *the police had orders to intervene at the first sign of trouble.* **5** effort or exertion to do something: *they didn't even take the trouble to see the film before banning it.* **6** a personal weakness or cause of annoyance: *his trouble is that he's constitutionally jealous.* **7 in trouble a** likely to be punished for something one has done: *in trouble with the public prosecutor.* **b** pregnant when not married. **8 more trouble than it's worth** involving a lot of time or effort for very little reward: *making your own pasta is more trouble than it's worth.* *~vb* **-bling, -bled 9** to cause trouble to. **10** to make an effort or exert oneself: *he dismissed the*

THESAURUS

cance, littleness, meaninglessness, negligibility, paltriness, pettiness, slightness, smallness, triteness, unimportance, valuelessness, worthlessness **2.** detail, no big thing, no great matter, nothing, petty detail, technicality, trifle

troop *n.* **1.** assemblage, band, bevy, body, bunch (*informal*), company, contingent, crew (*informal*), crowd, drove, flock, gang, gathering, group, herd, horde, multitude, pack, posse (*informal*), squad, swarm, team, throng, unit **2. troops** armed forces, army, fighting men, men, military, servicemen, soldiers, soldiery *~vb.* **3.** crowd, flock, march, parade, stream, swarm, throng, traipse (*informal*)

trophy award, bays, booty, cup, laurels, memento, prize, souvenir, spoils

tropical hot, humid, lush, steamy, stifling, sultry, sweltering, torrid

trot *vb.* **1.** canter, go briskly, jog, lope, run, scamper *~n.* **2.** brisk pace, canter, jog, lope, run **3. on the trot** *informal* consecutively, in a row, in succession, one after the other, without a break, without interruption

trot out *informal* bring forward, bring up, come out

letters as forgeries without troubling to examine them. **11** to cause inconvenience or discomfort to: *sorry to trouble you!* **troubled** *adj*

troublemaker *n* a person who causes trouble, esp. between people. **troublemaking** *adj, n*

troubleshooter *n* a person employed to locate and deal with faults or problems. **troubleshooting** *n, adj*

troublesome *adj* causing trouble.

trouble spot *n* a place where there is frequent fighting or violence: *the Balkans have long been one of the major European trouble spots.*

troublous *adj Literary* unsettled or agitated.

trough (**troff**) *n* **1** a long open container, esp. one for animals' food or water. **2** a narrow channel between two waves or ridges. **3** a low point in a pattern that has regular high and low points: *the trough of the slump in pupil numbers was in 1985.* **4** *Meteorol* a long narrow area of low pressure. **5** a narrow channel or gutter.

trounce *vb* **trouncing, trounced** to defeat (someone) utterly.

troupe (**troop**) *n* a company of actors or other performers.

trouper *n* **1** a member of a troupe. **2** an experienced person.

trouser *adj* of or relating to trousers: *trouser legs.*

trousers *pl n* a garment that covers the body from the waist to the ankles or knees with a separate tube-shaped section for each leg.

trousseau (**troo**-so) *n, pl* **-seaux** (-so) the clothes, linen, and other possessions collected by a bride for her marriage.

trout *n, pl* **trout** *or* **trouts** any of various game fishes related to the salmon and found chiefly in fresh water in northern regions.

trove *n* See **treasure-trove.**

trowel *n* **1** a hand tool resembling a small spade with a curved blade, used by gardeners for lifting plants, etc. **2** a similar tool with a flat metal blade, used for spreading cement or plaster on a surface.

troy weight *or* **troy** *n* a system of weights used for precious metals and gemstones in which one pound equals twelve ounces.

truant *n* **1** a pupil who stays away from school without permission. **2 play truant** to stay away from school without permission. *~adj* **3** being or relating to a truant: *a truant schoolkid.* **truancy** *n*

truce *n* a temporary agreement to stop fighting or quarrelling.

truck[1] *n* **1** *Brit* a railway wagon for carrying freight. **2** *Chiefly US, Canad, Austral, & NZ* a lorry. **3** any wheeled vehicle used to move goods. *~vb* **4** *Chiefly US* to transport goods in a truck.

truck[2] *n* **1** *History* the payment of wages in goods rather than in money. **2 have no truck with** to refuse to be involved with: *the opposition will have no truck with the planned cut in pensions.*

truckle *vb* **-ling, -led** to yield weakly or give in: *he accused the government of truckling to the right-wing press.*

truckle bed *n* a low bed on wheels, stored under a larger bed.

truculent (**truck**-yew-lent) *adj* defiantly aggressive or bad-tempered. **truculence** *n* **truculently** *adv*

trudge *vb* **trudging, trudged 1** to walk or plod heavily or wearily. *~n* **2** a long tiring walk.

true *adj* **truer, truest 1** in accordance with the truth or facts; factual: *not all of the stories about her are true.* **2** real or genuine: *he didn't want to reveal his true feelings.* **3** faithful and loyal: *a true friend.* **4** accurate or precise: *he looked through the telescopic sight until he was convinced his aim was true.* **5** (of a compass bearing) according to the earth's geographical ra-

THESAURUS

with, drag up, exhibit, recite, rehearse, reiterate, relate, repeat

trouble *n.* **1.** bother, concern, danger, difficulty, dilemma, dire straits, hassle (*informal*), hot water (*informal*), mess, nuisance, pest, pickle (*informal*), predicament, problem, scrape (*informal*), spot (*informal*), tight spot **2.** agitation, annoyance, anxiety, disquiet, distress, grief, hardship, hassle (*informal*), heartache, irritation, misfortune, pain, sorrow, suffering, torment, tribulation, vexation, woe, worry **3.** ailment, complaint, defect, disability, disease, disorder, failure, illness, malfunction, upset **4.** agitation, bother (*informal*), commotion, discontent, discord, disorder, dissatisfaction, disturbance, hassle (*informal*), row, strife, tumult, unrest **5.** attention, bother, care, effort, exertion, inconvenience, labour, pains, struggle, thought, work *~vb.* **6.** afflict, agitate, annoy, bother, discompose, disconcert, disquiet, distress, disturb, faze, fret, grieve, harass, hassle (*informal*), inconvenience, pain, perplex, perturb, pester, plague, sadden, torment, upset, vex, worry **7.** exert oneself, go to the effort of, make an effort, take pains, take the time **8.** be concerned, bother, burden, discomfort, discommode, disturb, impose upon, incommode, inconvenience, put out

troublemaker *agent provocateur,* agitator, firebrand, incendiary, instigator, meddler, mischief-maker, rabble-rouser, stirrer (*informal*), stormy petrel *or* storm petrel

troublesome 1. annoying, arduous, bothersome, burdensome, demanding, difficult, harassing, hard, importunate, inconvenient, irksome, irritating, laborious, oppressive, pestilential, taxing, tiresome, tricky, trying, upsetting, vexatious, wearisome, worrisome, worrying **2.** disorderly, insubordinate, rebellious, recalcitrant, refractory, rowdy, turbulent, uncooperative, undisciplined, unruly, violent

trough 1. crib, manger, water trough **2.** canal, channel, depression, ditch, duct, flume, furrow, gully, gutter, trench, watercourse

trounce beat, clobber (*slang*), crush, defeat heavily *or* utterly, give a hiding (*informal*), give a pasting (*slang*), hammer (*informal*), lick (*informal*), make mincemeat of, overwhelm, paste (*slang*), rout, run rings around (*informal*), slaughter (*informal*), tank (*slang*), thrash, walk over (*informal*), wipe the floor with (*informal*)

troupe band, cast, company

trouper actor, artiste, entertainer, performer, player, theatrical, thespian

truancy absence, absence without leave, malingering, shirking, skiving (*Brit. slang*)

truant *n.* **1.** absentee, delinquent, deserter, dodger, malingerer, runaway, shirker, skiver (*Brit. slang*), straggler **2. play truant** absent oneself, desert, dodge, go missing, malinger, play truant, run away, shirk, skive (*Brit. slang*) *~adj.* **3.** absent, absent without leave, AWOL, missing, skiving (*Brit. slang*)

truce armistice, break, ceasefire, cessation, cessation of hostilities, intermission, interval, let-up (*informal*), lull, moratorium, peace, respite, rest, stay, treaty

truculent aggressive, antagonistic, bad-tempered, bellicose, belligerent, combative, contentious, cross, defiant, fierce, hostile, ill-tempered, itching *or* spoiling for a fight (*informal*), obstreperous, pugnacious, scrappy (*informal*), sullen, violent

trudge 1. *vb.* clump, drag oneself, footslog, hike,

ther than magnetic poles: *true north.* **6 come true** to actually happen: *fortunately his gloomy prediction didn't come true.* **7 in** *or* **out of true** in *or* not in correct alignment. ~*adv* **8** truthfully or rightly: *I'd like to move to Edinburgh, true, but I'd need to get a job there first.*

true-blue *adj* **1** staunchly loyal. ~*n* **true blue 2** *Chiefly Brit* a staunch royalist or Conservative.

true-life *adj* taken directly from reality: *true-life TV horror stories.*

truelove *n* the person that one loves.

true north *n* the direction from any point along a meridian towards the North Pole.

truffle *n* **1** a round fungus which grows underground and is regarded as a delicacy. **2** Also called: **rum truffle** *Chiefly Brit* a sweet flavoured with chocolate or rum.

trug *n* a long shallow basket for carrying garden tools, flowers, etc.

truism *n* a statement that is clearly true and well known.

truly *adv* **1** in a true, just, or faithful manner. **2** really: *a truly awful poem.*

trump[1] *n* **1** same as **trump card.** ~*vb* **2** *Cards* to beat a card by playing a card which belongs to a suit which outranks it. **3** to outdo or surpass: *she trumped his news by announcing that she had been picked for the Olympic team.* ~See also **trumps.**

trump[2] *n Archaic or literary* **1** a trumpet or the sound produced by one. **2 the last trump** the final trumpet call on the Day of Judgment.

trump card *n* **1** any card from the suit that ranks higher than any other suit in one particular game. **2** an advantage, weapon, etc., that is kept in reserve until needed: *the President hoped to use his experience of foreign affairs as a trump card in the election.* Also called: **trump**

trumped up *adj* (of charges, excuses, etc.) made up in order to deceive.

trumpery *n, pl* **-eries 1** something useless or worthless. ~*adj* **2** useless or worthless.

trumpet *n* **1** a valved brass musical instrument consisting of a narrow tube ending in a flare. **2** a loud sound such as that of a trumpet: *the elephant gave a loud trumpet.* **3 blow one's own trumpet** to boast about one's own skills or good qualities. ~*vb* **-peting, -peted 4** to proclaim or state forcefully: *almost every one of the party's loudly trumpeted election claims is untrue.* **5** (of an elephant) to make a loud cry. **trumpeter** *n*

trumps *pl n* **1** *Cards* any one of the four suits that outranks all the other suits for the duration of a deal or game. **2 turn up trumps** (of a person) to bring about a happy or successful conclusion, esp. unexpectedly.

truncate *vb* **-cating, -cated** to shorten by cutting. **truncated** *adj* **truncation** *n*

truncheon *n Chiefly Brit* a small club carried by a policeman.

trundle *vb* **-dling, -dled** to move heavily on or as if on wheels: *a bus trundled along the drive.*

trundler *n NZ* **1** a golf or shopping trolley. **2** a child's pushchair.

trunk *n* **1** the main stem of a tree. **2** a large strong case or box used to contain clothes when travelling and for storage. **3** a person's body excluding the head, neck, and limbs; torso. **4** the long nose of an elephant. **5** *US* the boot of a car. ~See also **trunks.**

trunk call *n Chiefly Brit* a long-distance telephone call.

trunk line *n* **1** a direct link between two distant telephone exchanges or switchboards. **2** the main route or routes on a railway.

trunk road *n Brit* a main road, esp. one maintained by the central government.

trunks *pl n* shorts worn by a man for swimming.

truss *vb* **1** to tie or bind (someone) up. **2** to bind the wings and legs of (a fowl) before cooking. ~*n* **3** *Med* a device for holding a hernia in place. **4** a framework of wood or metal used to support a roof, bridge, etc. **5** a cluster of flowers or fruit growing at the end of a single stalk.

trust *vb* **1** to believe that (someone) is honest and means no harm: *my father warned me never to trust strangers.* **2** to feel that (something) is safe and reliable: *I don't trust those new gadgets.* **3** to entrust (someone) with important information or valuables: *she's not somebody I would trust with this sort of secret.* **4** to believe that (someone) is likely to do something safely and reliably: *I wouldn't trust anyone else to look after my child properly.* **5** to believe (a story, account, etc.). **6** to expect, hope, or suppose: *I trust*

THESAURUS

lumber, march, plod, slog, stump, traipse (*informal*), tramp, trek, walk heavily **2.** *n.* footslog, haul, hike, march, slog, traipse (*informal*), tramp, trek

true *adj.* **1.** accurate, actual, authentic, bona fide, correct, exact, factual, genuine, legitimate, natural, precise, pure, real, right, truthful, valid, veracious, veritable **2.** confirmed, constant, dedicated, devoted, dutiful, faithful, fast, firm, honest, honourable, loyal, pure, reliable, sincere, staunch, steady, true-blue, trustworthy, trusty, unswerving, upright **3.** accurate, correct, exact, on target, perfect, precise, proper, spot-on (*Brit. informal*), unerring **4. come true** become reality, be granted, be realized, come to pass, happen, occur ~*adv.* **5.** honestly, rightly, truthfully, veraciously, veritably

truism axiom, bromide, cliché, commonplace, platitude, stock phrase, trite saying

truly 1. accurately, authentically, beyond doubt, beyond question, correctly, exactly, factually, genuinely, in actuality, in fact, in reality, in truth, legitimately, precisely, really, rightly, truthfully, veraciously, veritably, without a doubt **2.** confirmedly, constantly, devotedly, dutifully, faithfully, firmly, honestly, honourably, loyally, sincerely, staunchly, steadily, with all one's heart, with dedication, with devotion **3.** exceptionally, extremely, greatly, indeed, of course, really, to be sure, verily, very

trumped up concocted, contrived, cooked-up (*informal*), fabricated, fake, false, falsified, invented, made-up, manufactured, phoney *or* phony (*informal*), untrue

trumpery 1. *n.* bagatelle, bauble, gewgaw, kickshaw, knick-knack, toy, trifle, trinket **2.** *adj.* cheap, flashy, meretricious, nasty, rubbishy, shabby, shoddy, tawdry, trashy, trifling, useless, valueless, worthless

trumpet *n.* **1.** bugle, clarion, horn **2.** bay, bellow, call, cry, roar **3. blow one's own trumpet** boast, brag, crow, sing one's own praises, vaunt ~*vb.* **4.** advertise, announce, broadcast, crack up (*informal*), extol, noise abroad, proclaim, publish, shout from the rooftops, sound loudly, tout (*informal*)

truncate abbreviate, clip, crop, curtail, cut, cut short, dock, lop, pare, prune, shorten, trim

truncheon *chiefly Brit.* baton, club, cudgel, staff

trunk 1. bole, stalk, stem **2.** bin, box, case, casket, chest, coffer, crate, locker, portmanteau **3.** body, torso **4.** proboscis, snout

truss *vb.* **1.** bind, bundle, fasten, make fast, pack, pin-

you've made your brother welcome here. ~*n* **7** confidence in the truth, worth, reliability, etc., of a person or thing; faith: *he knew that his father had great trust in him.* **8** the obligation of someone in a responsible position: *he was in a position of trust as her substitute father.* **9 a** a legal arrangement whereby one person looks after property, money, etc., on another's behalf. **b** property that is the subject of such an arrangement. **10** (in Britain) a self-governing hospital, group of hospitals, or other body that operates as an independent commercial unit within the National Health Service. **11** *Chiefly US & Canad* a group of companies joined together to control the market for any commodity. ~*adj* **12** of or relating to a trust or trusts: *trust status.*

trustee *n* **1** a person who administers property on someone else's behalf. **2** a member of a board that manages the affairs of an institution or organization.

trustful *or* **trusting** *adj* characterized by a readiness to trust others. **trustfully** *or* **trustingly** *adv*

trust fund *n* money, securities, etc., held in trust.

trustworthy *adj* (of a person) honest, reliable, or dependable.

trusty *adj* **trustier, trustiest 1** faithful or reliable: *his trusty steed.* ~*n, pl* **trusties 2** a trustworthy convict to whom special privileges are granted.

truth *n* **1** the quality of being true, genuine, or factual: *there is no truth in the allegations.* **2** something that is true: *he finally learned the truth about his parents' marriage.* **3** a proven or verified fact, principle, etc.: *some profound truths about biology have come to light.*

truthful *adj* **1** telling the truth; honest. **2** true; based on facts: *a truthful answer.* **truthfully** *adv* **truthfulness** *n*

try *vb* **tries, trying, tried 1** to make an effort or attempt: *you must try to understand.* **2** to sample or test (something) to see how enjoyable, good, or useful it is: *I tried smoking once but didn't like it.* **3** to put strain or stress on (someone's patience). **4** to give pain, affliction, or vexation to: *sometimes when I've been sorely tried, my temper gets a little out of hand.* **5 a** to investigate (a case) in a court of law. **b** to hear evidence in order to determine the guilt or innocence of (a person). ~*n, pl* **tries 6** an attempt or effort. **7** *Rugby* a score made by placing the ball down behind the opposing team's goal line.

➤ The idiom *try to* can be used at any time. The alternative *try and* is less formal and often signals a "dare": *Just try and stop me!*

trying *adj* upsetting, difficult, or annoying.

try on *vb* **1** to put on (a garment) to find out whether it fits. **2 try it on** *Informal* to attempt to deceive or fool someone. ~*n* **try-on 3** *Brit informal* something done to test out a person's tolerance etc.

try out *vb* **1** to test (something), esp. to find out how good it is. ~*n* **tryout 2** *Chiefly US & Canad* a trial or test, for example of an athlete or actor.

trysail *n* a small fore-and-aft sail set on a sailing vessel to help keep her head to the wind in a storm.

tryst *n Archaic or literary* **1** an arrangement to meet, esp. secretly. **2** a meeting, esp. a secret one with a lover, or the place where such a meeting takes place.

tsar *or* **czar** (**zahr**) *n* (until 1917) the emperor of Russia. Also: **tzar tsarist** *or* **czarist** *n*

tsarevitch *or* **czarevitch** (**zahr**-rev-itch) *n* the eldest son of a Russian tsar.

tsarina *or* **czarina** (zahr-**een**-a) *n* the wife of a Russian tsar.

tsetse fly *or* **tzetze fly** (**tset**-see) *n* a bloodsucking African fly whose bite transmits disease, esp. sleeping sickness.

T-shirt *or* **tee-shirt** *n* a short-sleeved casual shirt or top.

tsotsi (**tsot**-see) *n S African* a Black street thug or gang member.

tsp. teaspoon.

T-square *n* a T-shaped ruler used for drawing horizontal lines and to support set squares when drawing vertical and inclined lines.

tsunami *n* a large, often destructive, sea wave, usually caused by an earthquake under the sea.

THESAURUS

ion, secure, strap, tether, tie ~*n.* **2.** *Medical* bandage, support **3.** beam, brace, buttress, joist, prop, shore, stanchion, stay, strut, support

trust *vb.* **1.** bank on, believe, count on, depend on, have faith in, lean on, pin one's faith on, place confidence in, place one's trust in, place reliance on, rely upon, swear by, take at face value **2.** assign, command, commit, confide, consign, delegate, entrust, give, put into the hands of, sign over, turn over **3.** assume, believe, expect, hope, presume, suppose, surmise, think likely ~*n.* **4.** assurance, belief, certainty, certitude, confidence, conviction, credence, credit, expectation, faith, hope, reliance **5.** duty, obligation, responsibility **6.** care, charge, custody, guard, guardianship, protection, safekeeping, trusteeship

trustful *or* **trusting** confiding, credulous, gullible, innocent, naive, optimistic, simple, unguarded, unsuspecting, unsuspicious, unwary

trustworthy dependable, ethical, honest, honourable, level-headed, mature, principled, reliable, reputable, responsible, righteous, sensible, staunch, steadfast, to be trusted, true, trusty, truthful, upright

trusty dependable, faithful, firm, honest, reliable, responsible, solid, staunch, steady, straightforward, strong, true, trustworthy, upright

truth 1. candour, constancy, dedication, devotion, dutifulness, faith, faithfulness, fidelity, frankness, honesty, integrity, loyalty, naturalism, realism, uprightness **2.** accuracy, actuality, exactness, fact, factuality, factualness, genuineness, legitimacy, precision, reality, truthfulness, validity, veracity, verity **3.** axiom, certainty, fact, law, maxim, proven principle, reality, truism, verity

truthful accurate, candid, correct, exact, faithful, forthright, frank, honest, literal, naturalistic, plain-spoken, precise, realistic, reliable, sincere, straight, straightforward, true, trustworthy, upfront (*informal*), veracious, veritable

try *vb.* **1.** aim, attempt, bend over backwards (*informal*), do one's best, do one's damnedest (*informal*), endeavour, essay, exert oneself, give it one's all (*informal*), give it one's best shot (*informal*), go for it (*informal*), have a go (crack (*informal*), shot (*informal*), stab (*informal*), whack (*informal*)) (*informal*), knock oneself out (*informal*), make an all-out effort (*informal*), make an attempt, make an effort, seek, strive, struggle, undertake **2.** appraise, check out, evaluate, examine, experiment, inspect, investigate, prove, put to the test, sample, taste, test **3.** afflict, annoy, inconvenience, irk, irritate, pain, plague, strain, stress, tax, tire, trouble, upset, vex, weary **4.** adjudge, adjudicate, examine, hear ~*n.* **5.** attempt, crack (*informal*), effort, endeavour, essay, go (*informal*), shot (*informal*), stab (*informal*), whack (*informal*)

trying aggravating (*informal*), annoying, arduous, bothersome, difficult, exasperating, fatiguing, hard, irksome, irritating, stressful, taxing, tiresome, tough, troublesome, upsetting, vexing, wearisome

try out appraise, check out, evaluate, experiment

TT 1 teetotal. 2 teetotaller. 3 tuberculin-tested.

tub *n* **1** a low wide, usually round container. **2** a small plastic or cardboard container for ice cream etc. **3** *Chiefly US* same as **bath** (sense 1). **4** Also called: **tubful** the amount a tub will hold. **5** a slow and uncomfortable boat or ship.

tuba (tube-a) *n* a low-pitched brass musical instrument with valves.

tubby *adj* **-bier, -biest** (of a person) fat and short. **tubbiness** *n*

tube *n* **1** a long hollow cylindrical object, used for the passage of fluids or as a container. **2** a flexible cylinder of soft metal or plastic closed with a cap, used to hold substances such as toothpaste. **3** *Anat* any hollow cylindrical structure: *the Fallopian tubes.* **4 the tube** *Brit* the underground railway system in London. **5** *Electronics* See **cathode-ray tube. 6** *Slang, chiefly US* a television set. **tubeless** *adj*

tuber (tube-er) *n* a fleshy underground root of a plant such as a potato.

tubercle (tube-er-kl) *n* **1** a small rounded swelling. **2** any abnormal hard swelling, esp. one characteristic of tuberculosis.

tubercular (tube-**berk**-yew-lar) *or* **tuberculous** *adj* **1** of or symptomatic of tuberculosis. **2** of or relating to a tubercle.

tuberculin (tube-**berk**-yew-lin) *n* a sterile liquid prepared from cultures of the tubercle bacillus and used in the diagnosis of tuberculosis.

tuberculin-tested *adj* (of milk) produced by cows that have been certified as free of tuberculosis.

tuberculosis (tube-berk-yew-**lohss**-iss) *n* an infectious disease characterized by the formation of tubercles, esp. in the lungs.

tuberous (tube-er-uss) *adj* (of plants) forming, bearing, or resembling a tuber or tubers.

tubing (tube-ing) *n* **1** a length of tube. **2** a system of tubes.

tub-thumper *n* a noisy or ranting public speaker. **tub-thumping** *adj, n*

tubular (tube-yew-lar) *adj* **1** having the shape of a tube or tubes. **2** of or relating to a tube or tubing.

tubule (tube-yewl) *n* any small tubular structure, esp. in an animal or plant.

TUC (in Britain) Trades Union Congress.

tuck *vb* **1** to push or fold into a small space or between two surfaces: *she tucked the letter into her handbag.* **2** to thrust the loose ends or sides of (something) into a confining space, so as to make it neat and secure: *he tucked his shirt back into his trousers.* **3** to make a tuck or tucks in (a garment). ~*n* **4** a pleat or fold in a part of a garment, usually stitched down. **5** *Brit informal* food, esp. cakes and sweets.

tuck away *vb Informal* **1** to eat (a large amount of food). **2** to store (something) in a safe place: *we knew he had some money tucked away somewhere.* **3** to have a quiet, rarely disturbed or visited location: *the chapel is tucked away in a side street.*

tucker *n* **1** a detachable yoke of lace, linen, etc., formerly worn over the breast of a low-cut dress. **2 one's best bib and tucker** *Informal* one's best clothes.

tuckered *adj* **tuckered out** *Informal, chiefly US & Canad* exhausted.

tuck in *vb* **1** to put (someone) to bed and make him or her snug. **2** to thrust the loose ends or sides of (something) into a confining space: *tuck in the bedclothes.* **3** *Informal* to eat, esp. heartily.

tuck shop *n Chiefly Brit* a shop in or near a school, where cakes and sweets are sold.

Tudor *adj* **1** of or in the reign of the English royal house ruling from 1485 to 1603. **2** denoting a style of architecture characterized by half-timbered houses.

Tues. Tuesday.

Tuesday *n* the third day of the week.

tufa (tew-fa) *n* a porous rock formed of calcium carbonate deposited from springs.

tuff *n Geol* a porous rock formed from volcanic dust or ash.

tuffet *n* a small mound or low seat.

tuft *n* a bunch of feathers, grass, hair, threads, etc., held together at the base. **tufted** *adj* **tufty** *adj*

tug *vb* **tugging, tugged 1** to pull or drag with a sharp or powerful movement: *she tugged at my arm.* **2** to tow (a ship or boat) by means of a tug. ~*n* **3** a strong pull or jerk. **4** Also called: **tugboat** a boat with a powerful engine, used for towing barges, ships, etc.

tug of love *n* a conflict over the custody of a child between divorced parents or between the child's natural parents and its foster or adoptive parents.

tug of war *n* **1** a contest in which two people or teams pull opposite ends of a rope in an attempt to drag the opposition over a central line. **2** any hard struggle between two people or two groups.

tuition *n* **1** instruction, esp. that received individually or in a small group. **2** the payment for instruction, esp. in colleges or universities.

tulip *n* **1** a plant which produces bright cup-shaped flowers in spring. **2** the flower or bulb.

tulip tree *n* a North American tree with tulip-shaped greenish-yellow flowers and long conelike fruits.

tulle (tewl) *n* a fine net fabric of silk, rayon, etc., used to make evening dresses.

tumble *vb* **-bling, -bled 1** to fall or cause to fall, esp. awkwardly or violently: *chairs tumbled over.* **2** to roll or twist, esp. in playing: *they rolled and tumbled as wild beasts.* **3** to decrease in value suddenly: *interest rates tumbled.* **4** to move in a quick and uncontrolled manner: *the crowd tumbled down the stairs.* **5** to disturb, rumple, or toss around: *she was all tumbled by the fall.* **6** to perform leaps or somersaults. ~*n* **7** a fall, esp. an awkward or violent one: *he took a tumble down the stairs.* **8** a somersault. **tumbled** *adj*

tumbledown *adj* (of a building) falling to pieces; dilapidated.

tumble dryer *n* an electrically-operated machine that dries wet laundry by rotating it in warmed air inside a metal drum.

tumbler *n* **1 a** a flat-bottomed drinking glass with no

THESAURUS

with, inspect, put into practice, put to the test, sample, taste, test

tsar, czar autocrat, despot, emperor, head, leader, overlord, ruler, sovereign, tyrant

tuck *vb.* **1.** fold, gather, insert, push ~*n.* **2.** fold, gather, pinch, pleat **3.** *Brit. informal* comestibles, food, grub (*slang*), nosh (*slang*), scoff (*slang*), victuals

tuck in 1. bed down, enfold, fold under, make snug, put to bed, swaddle, wrap up **2.** *informal* eat heartily, get stuck in (*informal*)

tug 1. *vb.* drag, draw, haul, heave, jerk, lug, pull, tow, wrench, yank **2.** *n.* drag, haul, heave, jerk, pull, tow, traction, wrench, yank

tuition education, instruction, lessons, schooling, teaching, training, tutelage, tutoring

tumble 1. *vb.* drop, fall, fall end over end, fall headlong, fall head over heels, flop, lose one's footing, pitch, plummet, roll, stumble, topple, toss, trip up **2.** *n.* collapse, drop, fall, flop, headlong fall, plunge, roll, spill, stumble, toss, trip

handle or stem. **b** the amount a tumbler will hold. **2** a person who performs somersaults and other acrobatic feats. **3** a part of the mechanism of a lock.

tumble to *vb* to understand or become aware of: *how did he tumble to this?*

tumbril *n* a farm cart that tilts backwards to empty its load, which was used to take condemned prisoners to the guillotine during the French Revolution.

tumescent (tew-**mess**-ent) *adj* swollen or becoming swollen.

tumid (**tew**-mid) *adj Rare* **1** (of an organ or part of the body) enlarged or swollen. **2** pompous or fulsome in style: *a tumid tome.* **tumidity** *n*

tummy *n, pl* **-mies** an informal or childish word for **stomach.**

tumour *or US* **tumor** (**tew**-mer) *n Pathol* **a** any abnormal swelling. **b** a mass of tissue formed by a new growth of cells. **tumorous** *adj*

tumult (**tew**-mult) *n* **1** a loud confused noise, such as one produced by a crowd. **2** a state of confusion and excitement: *a tumult of emotions.*

tumultuous (tew-**mull**-tew-uss) *adj* **1** exciting, confused, or turbulent: *this week's tumultuous events.* **2** unruly, noisy, or excited: *a tumultuous welcome.*

tumulus (**tew**-myew-luss) *n, pl* **-li** (-lie) *Archaeol no longer in technical usage* a burial mound.

tun *n* a large beer cask.

tuna (**tune**-a) *n, pl* **-na** *or* **-nas** **1** a large marine spiny-finned fish. **2** the flesh of this fish, often tinned for food.

tundra *n* a vast treeless Arctic region with permanently frozen subsoil.

tune *n* **1** a melody, esp. one for which harmony is not essential. **2** the correct musical pitch: *many of the notes are out of tune.* **3 call the tune** to be in control of the proceedings. **4 change one's tune** to alter one's attitude or tone of speech. **5 in** *or* **out of tune with** in *or* not in agreement or sympathy with: *in tune with public opinion.* **6 to the tune of** *Informal* to the amount or extent of. *~vb* **tuning, tuned 7** to adjust (a musical instrument) so each string, key, etc., produces the right note. **8** to make small adjustments to (an engine, machine, etc.) to obtain the proper or desired performance. **9** to adjust (a radio or television) to receive a particular station or programme: *the radio in the kitchen was tuned to Radio Two.* **tuner** *n*

tuneful *adj* having a pleasant tune. **tunefully** *adv*

tune in *vb* **1** to adjust (a radio or television) to receive (a station or programme). **2 tuned in to** *Slang* aware of or knowledgeable about: *tuned in to European cinema.*

tuneless *adj* having no melody or tune.

tune up *vb* **1** to adjust (a musical instrument) to a particular pitch. **2** to adjust the engine of a car, etc., to improve its performance.

tungsten *n Chem* a hard greyish-white metallic element. Symbol: W

tunic *n* **1** a close-fitting jacket forming part of some uniforms. **2** a loose-fitting knee-length garment.

tuning fork *n* a two-pronged metal fork that when struck produces a pure note of constant specified pitch.

tunnel *n* **1** an underground passageway, esp. one for trains or cars. **2** any passage or channel through or under something: *the carpal tunnel.* *~vb* **-nelling, -nelled** *or US* **-neling, -neled 3** to make one's way through or under (something) by digging a tunnel: *ten men succeeded in tunnelling out of the prisoner-of-war camp.* **4** to dig a tunnel (through or under something): *the idea of tunnelling under the English Channel has been around for a long time.*

tunnel vision *n* **1** a condition in which a person is unable to see things that are not straight in front. **2** narrowness of viewpoint resulting from concentration on only one aspect of a subject or situation.

tunny *n, pl* **-nies** *or* **-ny** same as **tuna.**

tup *n Chiefly Brit* a male sheep.

tupik (**too**-pick) *n* a tent of seal or caribou skin used for shelter by the Inuit in summer.

tuppence *n Brit* same as **twopence. tuppenny** *adj*

tuque (rhymes with **fluke**) *n* (in Canada) a knitted cap with a long tapering end.

turban *n* **1** a head-covering worn by a Muslim, Hindu, or Sikh man, consisting of a long piece of cloth wound round the head. **2** any head-covering resembling this. **turbaned** *adj*

turbid *adj Literary* (of water or air) full of mud or dirt, and frequently swirling around: *the turbid stream of the Loire.* **turbidity** *n*

turbine *n* a machine in which power is produced by a stream of water, air, etc., that pushes the blades of a wheel and causes it to rotate.

turbocharger *n* a device that increases the power of an internal-combustion engine by using the exhaust gases to drive a turbine. **turbocharged** *adj*

turbofan *n* a type of engine in which a large fan driven by a turbine forces air rearwards to increase the propulsive thrust.

turbojet *n* **1** a gas turbine in which the exhaust gases provide the propulsive thrust to drive an aircraft. **2** an aircraft powered by turbojet engines.

turboprop *n* a gas turbine for driving an aircraft propeller.

turbot *n, pl* **-bot** *or* **-bots** a European flatfish, highly valued as a food fish.

THESAURUS

tumbledown crumbling, decrepit, dilapidated, disintegrating, falling to pieces, ramshackle, rickety, ruined, shaky, tottering

tumour cancer, carcinoma, growth, lump, sarcoma (*Pathol.*), swelling

tumult ado, affray (*Law*), agitation, altercation, bedlam, brawl, brouhaha, clamour, commotion, din, disorder, disturbance, excitement, fracas, hubbub, hullabaloo, outbreak, pandemonium, quarrel, racket, riot, row, ruction (*informal*), stir, strife, turmoil, unrest, upheaval, uproar

tumultuous agitated, boisterous, clamorous, confused, disorderly, disturbed, excited, fierce, hectic, irregular, lawless, noisy, obstreperous, passionate, raging, restless, riotous, rowdy, rumbustious, stormy, turbulent, unrestrained, unruly, uproarious, violent, vociferous, wild

tune *n.* **1.** air, melody, melody line, motif, song, strain, theme **2. call the tune** be in charge (command, control), call the shots (*slang*), command, dictate, govern, lead, rule, rule the roost **3. change one's tune** change one's mind, do an about-face, have a change of heart, reconsider, take a different tack, think again *~vb.* **4.** adapt, adjust, attune, bring into harmony, harmonize, pitch, regulate

tuneful catchy, consonant, easy on the ear (*informal*), euphonic, euphonious, harmonious, mellifluous, melodic, melodious, musical, pleasant, symphonic

tuneless atonal, cacophonous, clashing, discordant, dissonant, harsh, unmelodic, unmelodious, unmusical

tunnel 1. *n.* burrow, channel, hole, passage, passageway, shaft, subway, underpass **2.** *vb.* burrow, dig, dig one's way, excavate, mine, penetrate, scoop out, undermine

turbulence *n* **1** a state or condition of confusion, movement, or agitation. **2** *Meteorol* instability in the atmosphere causing gusty air currents.

turbulent *adj* **1** involving a lot of sudden changes and conflicting elements: *the city has had a turbulent history.* **2** (of people) wild and unruly: *a harsh mountain land inhabited by a score of turbulent tribes.* **3** (of water or air) full of violent unpredictable currents: *the turbulent ocean.*

turd *n Taboo* **1** a piece of excrement. **2** *Slang* a contemptible person.

tureen *n* a large deep dish with a lid, used for serving soups.

turf *n, pl* **turfs** *or* **turves** **1** a layer of thick even grass with roots and soil attached: *a short turf rich in wild flowers.* **2** a piece cut from this layer: *we spent the afternoon digging turves.* **3** *Informal* **a** the area where a person lives and feels at home: *my boyhood turf of east Cork.* **b** a person's area of knowledge or influence: *when Kate is at work, she's on her own turf.* **4 the turf a** a track where horse races are run. **b** horse racing as a sport or industry. **5** same as **peat.** *~vb* **6** to cover (an area of ground) with pieces of turf.

turf accountant *n Brit* same as **bookmaker.**

turf out *vb Brit informal* to throw (someone or something) out: *the residents fear a new landlord might push up rents and turf them out of their homes.*

turgid (tur-jid) *adj* **1** (of language) pompous, boring, and hard to understand. **2** (of water or mud) unpleasantly thick and brown. **turgidity** *n*

Turk *n* a person from Turkey.

turkey *n, pl* **-keys** *or* **-key** **1** a large bird of North America bred for its meat. **2** *Informal, chiefly US & Canad* something, esp. a theatrical production, that fails. **3 cold turkey** *Slang* a method of curing drug addiction by abrupt withdrawal of all doses. **4 talk turkey** *Informal, chiefly US & Canad* to discuss, esp. business, frankly and practically.

Turkic *n* a family of Asian languages including Turkish and Azerbaijani.

Turkish *adj* **1** of Turkey. *~n* **2** the language of Turkey.

Turkish bath *n* **1** a type of bath in which the bather sweats freely in a steam room, is then washed, often massaged, and has a cold plunge or shower. **2 Turkish baths** an establishment for such baths.

Turkish coffee *n* very strong black coffee.

Turkish delight *n* a jelly-like sweet flavoured with flower essences, usually cut into cubes and covered in icing sugar.

turmeric *n* **1** a tropical Asian plant with yellow flowers and an aromatic underground stem. **2** a yellow spice obtained from the root of this plant.

turmoil *n* disorder, agitation, or confusion: *a period of political turmoil and uncertainty.*

turn *vb* **1** to move to face in another direction. **2** to rotate or move round. **3** to operate (a switch, key, etc.) by twisting it. **4** to aim or point (something) in a particular direction: *they turned their guns on the crowd.* **5** to change in course or direction: *the van turned right into Victoria Road.* **6** (of a road, river, etc.) to have a bend or curve in it. **7** to perform or do (something) with a rotating movement: *a small boy was turning somersaults.* **8** to change so as to become: *he turned pale.* **9** to reach, pass, or progress beyond in age, time, etc.: *she had just turned fourteen.* **10** to find (a particular page) in a book: *turn to page 78.* **11** to look at the other side of: *turning the pages of a book.* **12** to shape (wood, metal, etc.) on a lathe. **13** (of leaves) to change colour in autumn. **14** to make or become sour: *the milk is starting to turn.* **15** to affect or be affected with nausea or giddiness: *that would turn the strongest stomach.* **16** (of the tide) to start coming in or going out. **17 turn against** to stop liking (something or someone one previously liked): *people turned against her because she became so dictatorial.* **18 turn into** to become or change into: *my mother turned our house into four apartments.* **19 turn loose** to set (an animal or a person) free. **20 turn someone's head** to affect someone mentally or emotionally. **21 turn to a** to direct or apply (one's attention or thoughts) to. **b** to stop doing or using one thing and start doing or using (another): *I turned to photography from writing.* **c** to appeal or apply to (someone) for help, advice, etc. *~n* **22** the act of turning. **23** a movement of complete or partial rotation: *a turn of the dial.* **24** a change of direction or position. **25** same as **turning** (sense 1). **26** the right or opportunity to do something in an agreed order or succession: *it was her turn to play next.* **27** a change in something that is happening or being done: *events took an unhappy turn.* **28** a period of action, work, etc. **29** a short walk, ride, or excursion. **30** natural inclination: *a liberal turn of mind.* **31** distinctive form or style: *she'd a nice turn of phrase.* **32** a deed that helps or hinders someone: *I'm trying to do you a good turn.* **33** a twist, bend, or distortion in shape. **34** a slight attack of an illness: *she's just having one of her turns.* **35** *Music* a melodic ornament that alternates the main note with the notes above and below it, beginning with the note above, in a variety of sequences. **36** a short theatrical act: *tonight's star turn.* **37** *Informal* a shock or surprise: *you gave me rather a turn.* **38 done to a turn** *Infor-*

THESAURUS

turbulence agitation, boiling, commotion, confusion, disorder, instability, pandemonium, roughness, storm, tumult, turmoil, unrest, upheaval

turbulent 1. agitated, anarchic, boisterous, disorderly, insubordinate, lawless, mutinous, obstreperous, rebellious, refractory, riotous, rowdy, seditious, tumultuous, unbridled, undisciplined, ungovernable, unruly, uproarious, violent, wild **2.** agitated, blustery, boiling, choppy, confused, disordered, foaming, furious, raging, rough, tempestuous, tumultuous, unsettled, unstable

turf 1. clod, divot, grass, green, sod, sward **2. the turf** horse-racing, racecourse, racetrack, racing, the flat

turmoil agitation, bedlam, brouhaha, bustle, chaos, commotion, confusion, disarray, disorder, disturbance, ferment, flurry, hubbub, noise, pandemonium, row, stir, strife, trouble, tumult, turbulence, upheaval, uproar, violence

turn *vb.* **1.** circle, go round, gyrate, move in a circle, pivot, revolve, roll, rotate, spin, swivel, twirl, twist, wheel, whirl **2.** change course, change position, go back, move, return, reverse, shift, swerve, switch, veer, wheel **3.** arc, come round, corner, go round, negotiate, pass, pass around, take a bend **4.** adapt, alter, become, change, convert, divert, fashion, fit, form, metamorphose, mould, mutate, remodel, shape, transfigure, transform, transmute **5.** fashion, make, mould, shape **6.** become rancid, curdle, go bad, go off (*Brit. informal*), go sour, make rancid, sour, spoil, taint **7.** nauseate, sicken, upset **8. turn to** appeal, apply, approach, go, have recourse, look, resort *~n.* **9.** bend, change of course, change of direction, curve, departure, deviation, shift **10.** bend, change, circle, curve, cycle, gyration, pivot, reversal, revolution, rotation, spin, swing, turning, twist, whirl **11.** chance, crack (*informal*), fling, go, opportunity, period, round, shift, shot (*informal*), spell, stint, succession, time, try, whack (*informal*) **12.** airing, circuit, constitutional, drive, excursion, jaunt, outing, promenade, ride, saunter, spin (*informal*), stroll, walk **13.** affinity, aptitude,

mal cooked perfectly. **39 turn and turn about** one after another; alternately. ~See also **turn down, turn in,** etc. **turner** *n*

turnaround *or* **turnabout** *n* a complete change or reversal: *a turnaround in the fortunes of South Wales.*

turncoat *n* a person who deserts one cause or party to join an opposing one.

turn down *vb* **1** to reduce (the volume, brightness, or temperature of something): *turn the heat down.* **2** to reject or refuse: *the invitation was turned down.* **3** to fold down (sheets, etc.).

turn in *vb Informal* **1** to go to bed for the night. **2** to hand in: *turning in my essay.* **3** to hand (a suspect or criminal) over to the police: *his own brother turned him in.*

turning *n* **1** a road, river, or path that turns off the main way. **2** the point where such a way turns off. **3** the process of turning objects on a lathe.

turning circle *n* the smallest circle in which a vehicle can turn.

turning point *n* a moment when a decisive change occurs.

turnip *n* a vegetable with a large yellow or white edible root.

turnkey *n Old-fashioned* a jailer.

turn off *vb* **1** to leave (a road or path): *turning off the main road.* **2** (of a road or path) to lead away from (another road or path): *a main street with alleys twisting and turning off it.* **3** to cause (something) to stop operating by turning a knob, pushing a button, etc. **4** *Informal* to cause disgust or disinterest in (someone): *keeping kids from getting turned off by mathematics.* ~*n* **turn-off 5** a road or other way branching off from the main thoroughfare. **6** *Informal* a person or thing that causes dislike.

turn on *vb* **1** to cause (something) to operate by turning a knob, pushing a button, etc. **2** to attack (someone), esp. without warning: *the Labrador turned on me.* **3** *Informal* to produce suddenly or automatically: *turning on that bland smile.* **4** *Slang* to arouse emotionally or sexually. **5** to depend or hinge on: *the match turned on three double faults by Sampras.* ~*n* **turn-on 6** *Slang* a person or thing that causes emotional or sexual arousal.

turn out *vb* **1** to cause (something, esp. a light) to stop operating by moving a switch. **2** to produce or create: *turning out two hits a year.* **3** to force (someone) out of a place or position: *turned out of office.* **4** to empty the contents of (something): *the police ordered him to turn out his pockets.* **5** to be discovered or found (to be or do something): *he turned out to be a Finn.* **6** to end up or result: *how interesting to see how it all turned out!* **7** to dress and groom: *she is always very well turned out.* **8** to assemble or gather: *crowds turned out to see him.* ~*n* **turnout 9** a number of people attending an event: *there was an 82% turnout of members.* **10** the quantity or amount produced.

turn over *vb* **1** to change position, esp. so as to reverse top and bottom. **2** to shift position, for instance by rolling onto one's side: *he turned over and went straight to sleep.* **3** to consider carefully: *as I walked, I turned her story over.* **4** to give (something) to someone who has a right to it or to the authorities: *the police ordered him to turn over the files to them.* **5** (of an engine) to start or function correctly: *when he pressed the starter button, the engine turned over at once.* **6** *Slang* to rob: *the house had been turned over while they were out.* ~*n* **turnover 7 a** the amount of business done by a company during a specified period. **b** the rate at which stock in trade is sold and replenished. **8** a small pastry case filled with fruit or jam: *an apple turnover.* **9** the number of workers employed by a firm in a given period to replace those who have left.

turnpike *n* **1** *History* a barrier across a road to prevent vehicles or pedestrians passing until a charge (toll) had been paid. **2** *US* a motorway for use of which a toll is charged.

turnstile *n* a mechanical barrier with arms that are turned to admit one person at a time.

turntable *n* **1** the circular platform in a record player that rotates the record while it is being played. **2** a circular platform used for turning locomotives and cars.

turn up *vb* **1** to arrive or appear: *few people turned up.* **2** to find or discover or be found or discovered: *a medical checkup has only turned up a sinus infection.*

THESAURUS

bent, bias, flair, gift, inclination, knack, leaning, propensity, talent **14.** cast, fashion, form, format, guise, make-up, manner, mode, mould, shape, style, way **15.** act, action, deed, favour, gesture, service **16.** bend, distortion, twist, warp **17.** *informal* fright, scare, shock, start, surprise **18. to a turn** correctly, exactly, just right, perfectly, precisely **19. turn and turn about** alternately, by turns, in succession, one after another, reciprocally

turn down 1. diminish, lessen, lower, muffle, mute, quieten, reduce the volume of, soften **2.** abstain from, decline, rebuff, refuse, reject, repudiate, say no to, spurn, throw out

turn in *informal* **1.** go to bed, go to sleep, hit the sack (*slang*), retire for the night **2.** deliver, give back, give up, hand in, hand over, return, submit, surrender, tender

turning bend, crossroads, curve, junction, side road, turn, turn-off

turning point change, climacteric, crisis, critical moment, crossroads, crux, decisive moment, moment of decision, moment of truth

turn off 1. branch off, change direction, depart from, deviate, leave, quit, take another road, take a side road **2.** cut out, kill, put out, shut down, stop, switch off, turn out, unplug **3.** *informal* alienate, bore, disenchant, disgust, displease, irritate, lose one's interest, nauseate, offend, put off, repel, sicken

turn on 1. activate, energize, ignite, kick-start, put on, set in motion, start, start up, switch on **2.** assail, assault, attack, fall on, lose one's temper with, round on **3.** *slang* arouse, arouse one's desire, attract, excite, please, stimulate, thrill, titillate, work up **4.** balance, be contingent on, be decided by, depend, hang, hinge, pivot, rest

turn out 1. put out, switch off, turn off, unplug **2.** bring out, fabricate, finish, make, manufacture, process, produce, put out **3.** axe (*informal*), banish, cashier, cast out, deport, discharge, dismiss, dispossess, drive out, drum out, evict, expel, fire (*informal*), give one the sack (*informal*), kick out (*informal*), oust, put out, relegate, sack (*informal*), show one the door, throw out, turf out (*Brit. informal*), unseat **4.** clean out, clear, discharge, empty, take out the contents of **5.** become, come about, come to be, come to light, develop, emerge, end up, eventuate, evolve, happen, prove to be, result, transpire (*informal*), work out **6.** accoutre, attire, clothe, dress, fit, outfit, rig out **7.** appear, assemble, attend, be present, come, gather, go, put in an appearance, show up (*informal*), turn up

turnover 1. business, flow, output, outturn (*rare*), production, productivity, volume, yield **2.** change, coming and going, movement, replacement

turn up 1. appear, arrive, attend, come, put in an ap-

3 to increase the flow, volume, etc., of: *he turned up the radio.* ~*n* **turn-up** 4 *Brit* the turned-up fold at the bottom of some trouser legs. **5 a turn-up for the books** *Informal* an unexpected happening.

turpentine *n* **1** a strong-smelling colourless oil distilled from the resin of some coniferous trees, and used for thinning paint, for cleaning, and in medicine. **2** a semisolid mixture of resin and oil obtained from various conifers, which is the main source of commercial turpentine. **3** *Not in technical usage* any one of a number of thinners for paints and varnishes, consisting of fractions of petroleum.

turpitude *n Formal* depravity or wickedness: *newspapers owned by proprietors whose moral turpitude far exceeded anything chronicled in their pages.*

turps *n Brit* short for **turpentine** (senses 1, 3).

turquoise *adj* **1** greenish-blue. ~*n* **2** a greenish-blue precious stone.

turret *n* **1** a small tower that projects from the wall of a building, esp. a castle. **2** (on a tank or warship) a rotating structure on which guns are mounted. **3** (on a machine tool) a turret like steel structure with tools projecting from it that can be rotated to bring each tool to bear on the work. **turreted** *adj*

turtle *n* **1** an aquatic reptile with a flattened shell enclosing the body and flipper-like limbs adapted for swimming. **2 turn turtle** (of a boat) to capsize.

turtledove *n* an Old World dove noted for its soft cooing and devotion to its mate.

turtleneck *n* a round high close-fitting neck on a sweater or a sweater with such a neck.

Tuscan *adj* of a style of classical architecture characterized by unfluted columns.

tusk *n* a long pointed tooth in the elephant, walrus, and certain other mammals. **tusked** *adj*

tussle *n* **1** an energetic fight, struggle, or argument: *the chief executive resigned following a protracted boardroom tussle.* ~*vb* **-sling, -sled 2** to fight or struggle energetically.

tussock *n* a dense tuft of grass or other vegetation. **tussocky** *adj*

tut *interj, n, vb* **tutting, tutted** short for **tut-tut.**

tutelage (tew-till-lij) *n Formal* **1** instruction or guidance, esp. by a tutor. **2** the state of being supervised by a guardian or tutor.

tutelary (tew-till-lar-ee) *adj Literary* **1** having the role of guardian or protector. **2** of a guardian.

tutor *n* **1** a teacher, usually one instructing individual pupils. **2** (at a college or university) a member of staff responsible for the teaching and supervision of a certain number of students. ~*vb* **3** to act as a tutor to (someone). **tutorship** *n*

tutorial *n* **1** a period of intensive tuition given by a tutor to an individual student or to a small group of students. ~*adj* **2** of or relating to a tutor.

tutti *adj, adv Music* to be performed by the whole orchestra, choir, etc.

tutti-frutti *n, pl* **-fruttis** an ice cream or other sweet food containing small pieces of candied or fresh fruits.

tut-tut *interj* **1** an exclamation of mild reprimand, disapproval, or surprise. ~*vb* **-tutting, -tutted 2** to express disapproval by the exclamation of "tut-tut". ~*n* **3** the act of tut-tutting: *his bright red tennis shorts provoked a few tut-tuts from the traditionalists.*

tutu *n* a very short skirt worn by ballerinas, made of projecting layers of stiffened material.

tu-whit tu-whoo *interj* an imitation of the sound made by an owl.

tuxedo *n, pl* **-dos** *US & Canad* a dinner jacket.

TV television.

TVEI *Brit* technical and vocational educational initiative: a national educational scheme in which pupils gain practical experience in technology and industry, often through work placement.

twaddle *n* **1** silly, trivial, or pretentious talk or writing. ~*vb* **-dling, -dled 2** to talk or write in a silly or pretentious way.

twain *adj, n Archaic* two.

twang *n* **1** a sharp ringing sound produced by or as if by the plucking of a taut string. **2** a strongly nasal quality in a person's speech: *he spoke with a high-pitched Texas twang.* ~*vb* **3** to make or cause to make a twang: *a bunch of angels twanging harps.* **twangy** *adj*

twat *n Taboo slang* **1** the female genitals. **2** a foolish person.

tweak *vb* **1** to twist or pinch with a sharp or sudden movement: *she tweaked his ear.* ~*n* **2** the act of tweaking.

twee *adj Informal* excessively sentimental, sweet, or pretty.

tweed *n* **1** a thick woollen cloth produced originally in Scotland. **2 tweeds** a suit made of tweed.

tweedy *adj* **tweedier, tweediest 1** of, made of, or resembling tweed. **2** showing a fondness for a hearty outdoor life, often associated with wearers of tweeds.

tweet *interj* **1** an imitation of the thin chirping sound made by small birds. ~*vb* **2** to make this sound.

tweeter *n* a loudspeaker used in high-fidelity systems for the reproduction of high audio frequencies.

tweezers *pl n* a small pincer-like tool used for tasks such as handling small objects or plucking out hairs.

twelfth *adj* **1** of or being number twelve in a series. ~*n* **2** number twelve in a series. **3** one of twelve equal parts of something.

Twelfth Day *n* Jan 6, the twelfth day after Christmas and the feast of the Epiphany.

twelfth man *n* a reserve player in a cricket team.

Twelfth Night *n* **a** the evening of Jan 5, the eve of Twelfth Day. **b** the evening of Twelfth Day itself.

twelve *n* **1** the cardinal number that is the sum of ten and two. **2** a numeral, 12 or XII, representing this number. **3** something representing or consisting of twelve units. ~*adj* **4** amounting to twelve: *twelve months.*

twelvemonth *n Archaic, chiefly Brit* a year.

twelve-tone *adj* of or denoting the type of serial music which uses as its musical material a sequence of notes containing all 12 semitones of the chromatic scale.

twenty *n, pl* **-ties 1** the cardinal number that is the

THESAURUS

pearance, show (*informal*), show one's face, show up (*informal*) **2.** appear, become known, be found, bring to light, come to light, come to pass, come up with, crop up (*informal*), dig up, disclose, discover, expose, find, pop up, reveal, transpire, unearth **3.** amplify, boost, enhance, increase, increase the volume of, intensify, make louder, raise

tussle 1. *n.* battle, bout, brawl, competition, conflict, contention, contest, fight, fracas, fray, punch-up (*Brit. informal*), scrap (*informal*), scrimmage, scuffle, set-to (*informal*), shindig (*slang*), shindy (*slang*), struggle **2.** *vb.* battle, brawl, contend, fight, grapple, scrap (*informal*), scuffle, struggle, vie, wrestle

tutor 1. *n.* coach, educator, governor, guardian, guide, guru, instructor, lecturer, master, mentor, preceptor, schoolmaster, teacher **2.** *vb.* coach, direct, discipline, drill, edify, educate, guide, instruct, lecture, school, teach, train

product of ten and two. **2** a numeral, 20 or XX, representing this number. **3** something representing or consisting of twenty units. *~adj* **4** amounting to twenty: *twenty minutes.* **twentieth** *adj, n*

twerp *or* **twirp** *n Informal* a silly, stupid, or contemptible person.

twice *adv* **1** two times; on two occasions or in two cases. **2** double in degree or quantity: *twice as big.*

twiddle *vb* **-dling, -dled 1** to twirl or fiddle, often in an idle way: *twiddling the knobs of a radio.* **2 twiddle one's thumbs a** to rotate one's thumbs around one another, when bored or impatient. **b** to be bored, with nothing to do. *~n* **3** an unnecessary decoration, esp. a curly one.

twig[1] *n* a small branch or shoot of a tree. **twiggy** *adj*

twig[2] *vb* **twigging, twigged** *Brit informal* to realize or understand: *I should have twigged it earlier.*

twilight *n* **1** the soft dim light that occurs when the sun is just below the horizon after sunset. **2** the period in which this light occurs: *soon after twilight we started marching again.* **3** a period in which strength, importance, etc., is gradually declining: *the twilight of his political career.* *~adj* **4** of or relating to twilight. **5** of or being a period of decline: *he spent most of his twilight years working on a history of France.* **twilit** *adj*

twilight zone *n* any indefinite or intermediate condition or area: *the twilight zone between sleep and wakefulness.*

twill *n* a fabric woven to produce an effect of parallel diagonal lines or ribs in the cloth.

twin *n* **1** one of a pair of people or animals conceived at the same time. **2** one of a pair of people or things that are identical or very similar. *~vb* **twinning, twinned 3** to pair or be paired together.

twin bed *n* one of a pair of matching single beds.

twin-bedded *adj* (of a room in a hotel etc.) containing two single beds.

twine *n* **1** string or cord made by twisting fibres together. *~vb* **twining, twined 2** to twist or wind together: *she twined the flowers into a garland.* **3 twine round** *or* **around** to twist or wind around: *she twined her arms around her neck.*

twin-engined *adj* (of an aeroplane) having two engines.

twinge *n* **1** a sudden brief darting or stabbing pain. **2** a sharp emotional pang: *a twinge of conscience.*

twinkle *vb* **-kling, -kled 1** to shine brightly and intermittently; sparkle. **2** (of the eyes) to sparkle, esp. with amusement or delight. *~n* **3** a flickering brightness; sparkle.

twinkling *n* **in the twinkling of an eye** in a very short time.

twinset *n Brit* a matching jumper and cardigan.

twin town *n Brit* a town that has cultural and social links with a foreign town: *Nuremberg is one of Glasgow's twin towns.*

twirl *vb* **1** to move around rapidly and repeatedly in a circle. **2** to twist, wind, or twiddle, often idly: *twirling the glass in her hand.* *~n* **3** a whirl or twist. **4** a written flourish.

twist *vb* **1** to turn one end or part while the other end or parts remain still or turn in the opposite direction: *never twist or wring woollen garments.* **2** to distort or be distorted. **3** to wind or twine: *the wire had been twisted twice.* **4** to force or be forced out of the natural form or position: *I twisted my knee.* **5** to change the meaning of; distort: *he'd twisted the truth to make himself look good.* **6** to revolve or rotate: *he twisted the switch to turn the radio off.* **7** to wrench with a turning action: *he twisted the wheel sharply.* **8** to follow a winding course: *the road twisted as it climbed.* **9** to dance the twist. **10 twist someone's arm** to persuade or coerce someone. *~n* **11** the act of twisting: *she gave a dainty little twist to her parasol.* **12** something formed by or as if by twisting: *there's a twist in the cable.* **13** a decisive change of direction, aim, meaning, or character: *the latest revelations give a new twist to the company's boardroom wranglings.* **14** an unexpected development in a story, play, or film. **15** a bend: *a twist of the mountain road.* **16** a distortion of the original shape or form. **17** a jerky pull, wrench, or turn. **18 the twist** a dance popular in the 1960s, in which dancers vigorously twist the hips. **19 round the twist** *Brit slang* mad or eccentric.

twisted *adj* (of a person) cruel or perverted.

twister *n Brit* a swindling or dishonest person.

twit[1] *vb* **twitting, twitted** to poke fun at (someone).

twit[2] *n Informal, chiefly Brit* a foolish or stupid person.

THESAURUS

tutorial 1. *n.* individual instruction, lesson, seminar **2.** *adj.* coaching, guiding, instructional, teaching

tweak *vb./n.* jerk, nip, pinch, pull, squeeze, twist, twitch

twig branch, offshoot, shoot, spray, sprig, stick, withe

twilight *n.* **1.** dimness, dusk, evening, gloaming (*Scot. poetic*), half-light, sundown, sunset **2.** decline, ebb, last phase *~adj.* **3.** crepuscular, darkening, dim, evening **4.** declining, dying, ebbing, final, last

twin 1. *n.* clone, corollary, counterpart, double, duplicate, fellow, likeness, lookalike, match, mate, ringer (*slang*) **2.** *vb.* couple, join, link, match, pair, yoke

twine *n.* **1.** cord, string, yarn *~vb.* **2.** braid, entwine, interlace, interweave, knit, plait, splice, twist, twist together, weave **3. twine round** *or* **around** bend, coil, curl, encircle, loop, meander, spiral, surround, twist, wind, wrap, wreathe

twinge bite, gripe, pain, pang, pinch, prick, sharp pain, spasm, stab, stitch, throb, tic, tweak, twist, twitch

twirl *vb.* **1.** gyrate, pirouette, pivot, revolve, rotate, spin, turn, turn on one's heel, twiddle, twist, wheel, whirl, wind *~n.* **2.** gyration, pirouette, revolution, rotation, spin, turn, twist, wheel, whirl **3.** coil, spiral, twist

twist *vb.* **1.** coil, corkscrew, curl, encircle, entwine, intertwine, screw, spin, swivel, twine, weave, wind, wrap, wreathe, wring **2.** contort, distort, screw up **3.** rick, sprain, turn, wrench **4.** alter, change, distort, falsify, garble, misquote, misrepresent, pervert, warp **5. twist someone's arm** bully, coerce, force, persuade, pressurize, talk into *~n.* **6.** coil, curl, spin, swivel, twine, wind **7.** braid, coil, curl, hank, plug, quid, roll **8.** change, development, revelation, slant, surprise, turn, variation **9.** arc, bend, convolution, curve, meander, turn, undulation, zigzag **10.** defect, deformation, distortion, flaw, imperfection, kink, warp **11.** jerk, pull, sprain, turn, wrench **12. round the twist** *Brit. slang* barmy (*slang*), batty (*slang*), bonkers (*slang, chiefly Brit.*), crazy, cuckoo (*informal*), daft (*informal*), insane, loopy (*informal*), mad, not all there, not right in the head, nuts (*slang*), nutty (*slang*), off one's rocker (*slang*), off one's trolley (*slang*), out to lunch (*informal*), up the pole (*Brit., Austral., & N.Z. informal*)

twister *Brit.* cheat, con man (*informal*), crook (*informal*), deceiver, fraud, rogue, swindler, trickster

twit *informal, chiefly Brit.* airhead (*slang*), ass, berk (*Brit. slang*), blockhead, charlie (*Brit. informal*), chump (*informal*), clown, dickhead (*slang*), dipstick (*Brit. slang*), divvy (*Brit. slang*), dope (*informal*), fool, halfwit, idiot, jerk (*slang, chiefly U.S. & Canad.*), nerd (*slang*), nincompoop, ninny, nitwit (*informal*), numbskull, oaf, pillock (*Brit. slang*), plank (*Brit. slang*),

twitch *vb* **1** (of a person or part of a person's body) to move in a jerky spasmodic way: *his left eyelid twitched involuntarily.* **2** to pull (something) with a quick jerky movement: *she twitched the curtains shut.* ~*n* **3** a sharp jerking movement, esp. one caused by a nervous condition.

twitcher *n Informal* a bird-watcher who tries to spot as many rare varieties as possible.

twitchy *adj* **twitchier, twitchiest** nervous, worried, and ill-at-ease: *he was twitchy with anticipation.*

twitter *vb* **1** (esp. of a bird) to utter a succession of chirping sounds. **2** to talk rapidly and nervously in a high-pitched voice. ~*n* **3** the act or sound of twittering. **4 in a twitter** in a state of nervous excitement. **twittering** *n* **twittery** *adj*

two *n* **1** the cardinal number that is the sum of one and one. **2** a numeral, 2 or II, representing this number. **3** something representing or consisting of two units. **4 in two** in or into two parts: *cut the cake in two and take a bit each.* **5 put two and two together** to reach an obvious conclusion by considering the evidence available. **6 that makes two of us** the same applies to me. ~*adj* **7** amounting to two: *two years.*

two-dimensional *adj* **1** having two dimensions. **2** somewhat lacking in depth or complexity: *a modern audience is unable to tolerate two-dimensional characters.*

two-edged *adj* **1** (of a remark) having both a favourable and an unfavourable interpretation, such as *she looks nice when she smiles.* **2** (of a knife, saw, etc.) having two cutting edges.

two-faced *adj* deceitful or hypocritical: *he's a two-faced liar and opportunist.*

twofold *adj* **1** having twice as many or as much. **2** composed of two parts. ~*adv* **3** by twice as many or as much.

two-handed *adj* **1** requiring the use of both hands. **2** requiring the participation of two people: *a two-handed transatlantic yacht race.*

twopence *or* **tuppence** (**tup**-pence) *n Brit* **1** the sum of two pennies. **2** the slightest amount: *I don't care twopence who your father is.*

twopenny *or* **tuppenny** (**tup**-pen-ee) *adj Chiefly Brit* **1** cheap or tawdry. **2** worth or costing two pence. **3 not care a twopenny damn** to not care at all.

two-piece *adj* **1** consisting of two separate parts, usually matching, such as a woman's suit or swimsuit. ~*n* **2** such an outfit.

two-ply *adj* made of two thicknesses, layers, or strands.

two-sided *adj* **1** having two sides: *two-sided paper.* **2** having two aspects or interpretations: *an ambivalent two-sided event.*

twosome *n* a group of two people.

two-step *n* **1** an old-time dance in duple time: *the next dance was the Military Two-Step.* **2** music for this dance.

two-stroke *adj* of an internal-combustion engine whose piston makes two strokes for every explosion.

Two Thousand Guineas *n* **the Two Thousand Guineas** an annual horse race for three-year-olds, run at Newmarket.

two-time *vb* **-timing, -timed** *Informal* to deceive (a lover) by having an affair with someone else. **two-timer** *n*

two-way *adj* **1** moving in, or allowing movement in, two opposite directions: *two-way traffic.* **2** involving mutual involvement or cooperation: *two-way communication.* **3** (of a radio or transmitter) capable of both transmission and reception of messages.

TX Texas.

tycoon *n* a businessman of great wealth and power.

tyke *or* **tike** *n* **1** *Informal* a small or cheeky child. **2** *Brit dialect* a rough ill-mannered person.

tympani *pl n* same as **timpani.**

tympanic membrane *n Anat* the thin membrane separating the external ear from the middle ear; eardrum.

tympanum *n, pl* **-nums** *or* **-na 1** *Anat* **a** the cavity of the middle ear. **b** same as **tympanic membrane. 2** *Archit* the recessed space between the arch and the lintel above a door. **tympanic** *adj*

Tynwald (**tin**-wold) *n* the Parliament of the Isle of Man.

type *n* **1** a kind, class, or category of things, all of which have something in common. **2** a subdivision of a particular class; sort: *it is more alcoholic than most wines of this type.* **3** the general characteristics distinguishing a particular group: *the old-fashioned type of nanny.* **4** *Informal* a person, esp. of a specified kind: *a seagoing type.* **5** a block with a raised character on it used for printing. **6** text printed from type; print. ~*vb* **typing, typed 7** to write using a typewriter or word processor. **8** to be a symbol of or typify. **9** to decide the type of; classify.

typecast *vb* **-casting, -cast** to cast (an actor or actress) in the same kind of role continually.

typeface *n* the size and style of printing used in a book, magazine, etc.

typescript *n* any typewritten document.

typeset *vb* **-setting, -set** *Printing* to set (text for printing) in type.

typesetter *n* a person who sets type; compositor.

typewriter *n* a machine which prints a letter or other character when the appropriate key is pressed.

typewritten *adj* typed on a typewriter or word processor.

typhoid *Pathol* ~*n* **1** short for **typhoid fever.** ~*adj* **2** of or relating to typhoid fever: *typhoid vaccines.*

typhoid fever *n* an acute infectious disease characterized by high fever, spots, abdominal pain, etc. It is spread by contaminated food or water.

typhoon *n* a violent tropical storm, esp. one in the China Seas or W Pacific.

typhus *n* an acute infectious disease transmitted by lice or mites and characterized by high fever, skin rash, and severe headache.

typical *adj* **1** being or serving as a representative example of a particular type; characteristic: *a typical working day.* **2** considered to be an example of some

THESAURUS

plonker (*slang*), prat (*slang*), prick (*slang offensive*), silly-billy (*informal*), simpleton, twerp *or* twirp (*informal*), wally (*slang*)

twitch 1. *vb.* blink, flutter, jerk, jump, pluck, pull, snatch, squirm, tug, yank **2.** *n.* blink, flutter, jerk, jump, pull, spasm, tic, tremor, twinge

two-edged ambiguous, ambivalent, backhanded, double-edged, equivocal

two-faced deceitful, deceiving, dissembling, double-dealing, duplicitous, false, hypocritical, insincere, perfidious, treacherous, untrustworthy

tycoon baron, big cheese (*slang*), capitalist, captain of industry, financier, industrialist, magnate, mogul, plutocrat, potentate, wealthy businessman

type 1. breed, category, class, classification, form, genre, group, ilk, kidney, kind, order, sort, species, stamp, strain, subdivision, variety **2.** case, characters, face, fount, print, printing

undesirable trait: *it was typical that he should start talking almost before he was inside the room.* **typically** *adv*

typify *vb* **-fies, -fying, -fied 1** to be typical of or characterize: *the beers made here typify all that is best about the independent brewing sector.* **2** to symbolize or represent: *a number of dissident intellectuals, typified by Andrei Sakharov.*

typing *n* **1** the work or activity of using a typewriter or word processor. **2** the skill of using a typewriter quickly and accurately.

typist *n* a person who types letters, reports, etc., esp. for a living.

typo *n, pl* **-pos** *Informal* a typographical error.

typography *n* **1** the art or craft of printing. **2** the style or quality of printing and layout in a book, magazine, etc. **typographical** *adj* **typographically** *adv*

tyrannical *adj* of or like a tyrant unjust and oppressive.

tyrannize *or* **-ise** *vb* **-nizing, -nized** *or* **-nising, -nised** to rule or exercise power (over) in a cruel or oppressive manner: *he dominated and tyrannized his younger brother.*

tyrannosaurus *or* **tyrannosaur** (tirr-ran-oh-**sore**-uss) *n* a large two-footed flesh-eating dinosaur common in North America in Cretaceous times.

tyranny *n, pl* **-nies 1 a** government by a tyrant. **b** oppressive and unjust government by more than one person. **2** the condition or state of being dominated or controlled by something that makes unpleasant or harsh demands: *the tyranny of fashion drives many women to diet although they are not overweight.* **tyrannous** *adj*

tyrant *n* **1** a person who governs oppressively, unjustly, and arbitrarily. **2** any person who exercises authority in a tyrannical manner.

tyre *or US* **tire** *n* a ring of rubber, usually filled with air but sometimes solid, fitted round the rim of a wheel of a road vehicle to grip the road.

tyro *n, pl* **-ros** a novice or beginner.

tzar *n* same as **tsar.**

tzatziki (tsat-**see**-kee) *n* a Greek dip made from yogurt, chopped cucumber, and mint.

tzetze fly *n* same as **tsetse fly.**

THESAURUS

typhoon cyclone, squall, storm, tempest, tornado, tropical storm

typical archetypal, average, characteristic, classic, conventional, essential, illustrative, in character, indicative, in keeping, model, normal, orthodox, representative, standard, stock, true to type, usual

typify characterize, embody, epitomize, exemplify, illustrate, incarnate, personify, represent, sum up, symbolize

tyrannical absolute, arbitrary, authoritarian, autocratic, coercive, cruel, despotic, dictatorial, domineering, high-handed, imperious, inhuman, magisterial, oppressive, overbearing, overweening, peremptory, severe, tyrannous, unjust, unreasonable

tyranny absolutism, authoritarianism, autocracy, coercion, cruelty, despotism, dictatorship, harsh discipline, high-handedness, imperiousness, oppression, peremptoriness, reign of terror, unreasonableness

tyrant absolutist, authoritarian, autocrat, bully, despot, dictator, martinet, oppressor, slave-driver

tyro apprentice, beginner, greenhorn, initiate, learner, neophyte, novice, novitiate, pupil, student, trainee

U

U 1 (in Britain) universal (used to describe a film certified as suitable for viewing by anyone). 2 *Chem* uranium. *adj* 3 *Brit informal* (of language or behaviour) characteristic of the upper class.

UB40 *n* (in Britain) 1 a registration card issued to an unemployed person. 2 *Informal* a person registered as unemployed.

ubiquitous (yew-**bik**-wit-uss) *adj* being or seeming to be everywhere at once. **ubiquity** *n*

U-boat *n* a German submarine.

uc *Printing* upper case.

UCAS (in Britain) Universities and Colleges Admissions Service.

UCCA (formerly, in Britain) Universities Central Council on Admissions.

udder *n* the large baglike milk-producing gland of cows, sheep, or goats, with two or more teats.

UDI Unilateral Declaration of Independence.

UEFA Union of European Football Associations.

UFO unidentified flying object.

ugh (**uhh**) *interj* an exclamation of disgust, annoyance, or dislike.

ugli *n, pl* **-lis** *or* **-lies** *Trademark* a yellow citrus fruit: a cross between a tangerine, grapefruit, and orange.

ugly *adj* **uglier, ugliest** 1 so unattractive as to be unpleasant to look at. 2 very unpleasant and involving violence or aggression: *an ugly incident in which one man was stabbed.* 3 repulsive or displeasing: *ugly rumours.* 4 bad-tempered or sullen: *an ugly mood.* **ugliness** *n*

ugly duckling *n* a person or thing, initially ugly or unpromising, that becomes beautiful or admirable.

UHF *Radio* ultrahigh frequency.

UHT ultra-heat-treated (milk or cream).

UK United Kingdom.

ukase (yew-**kaze**) *n* (in imperial Russia) a decree from the tsar.

Ukrainian *adj* 1 of the Ukraine. ~*n* 2 a person from the Ukraine. 3 the language of the Ukraine.

ukulele *or* **ukelele** (yew-kal-**lay**-lee) *n* a small four-stringed guitar.

ulcer *n* an open sore on the surface of the skin or a mucous membrane.

ulcerated *adj* made or becoming ulcerous. **ulceration** *n*

ulcerous *adj* of, like, or characterized by ulcers.

ulna *n, pl* **-nae** *or* **-nas** the inner and longer of the two bones of the human forearm or of the forelimb in other vertebrates. **ulnar** *adj*

ulster *n* a man's heavy double-breasted overcoat.

Ulsterman *or fem* **Ulsterwoman** *n, pl* **-men** *or* **-women** a person from Ulster.

ult. ultimo.

ulterior (ult-**ear**-ee-or) *adj* (of an aim, reason, etc.) concealed or hidden: *an ulterior motive.*

ultimate *adj* 1 final in a series or process: *his ultimate destination was Luton.* 2 highest, supreme, or unchallengeable: *he has the ultimate power to dismiss the Prime Minister.* 3 fundamental or essential: *a believer in the ultimate goodness of man.* 4 most extreme: *genocide is the ultimate abuse of human rights.* 5 final or total: *an ultimate cost of over twenty million pounds.* ~*n* 6 **the ultimate in** the best example of: *the ultimate in luxury holidays.* **ultimately** *adv*

ultimatum (ult-im-**may**-tum) *n* a final warning to someone that they must agree to certain conditions or requirements, or else action will be taken against them: *Britain declared war after the Nazis rejected the ultimatum to withdraw from Poland.*

ultimo *adv Now rare except when abbreviated to ult. in formal correspondence* in or during the previous month: *your communication of the 1st ultimo.*

ultra *n* a person who has extreme or immoderate beliefs or opinions.

ultra- *prefix* 1 beyond a specified extent, range, or limit: *ultrasonic.* 2 extremely: *ultraleftist.*

ultraconservative *adj* 1 highly reactionary. ~*n* 2 a reactionary person.

ultrahigh frequency *n* a radio frequency between 3000 and 300 megahertz.

ultramarine *n* 1 a blue pigment originally made from lapis lazuli. ~*adj* 2 vivid blue.

ultramodern *adj* extremely modern.

ultramontane *adj* 1 on the other side of the mountains, usually the Alps, from the speaker or writer. 2 of a movement in the Roman Catholic Church which favours supreme papal authority. ~*n* 3 a person from beyond the Alps. 4 a member of the ultramontane party of the Roman Catholic Church.

ultrasonic *adj* of or producing sound waves with higher frequencies than humans can hear. **ultrasonically** *adv*

ultrasonics *n* the branch of physics concerned with ultrasonic waves.

ultrasound *n* ultrasonic waves, used in echo sounding, medical diagnosis, and therapy.

ultrasound scan *n* an examination of an internal bodily structure by the use of ultrasonic waves, esp. for diagnosing abnormality in a fetus.

ultraviolet *n* 1 the part of the electromagnetic spectrum with wavelengths shorter than light but longer than x-rays. ~*adj* 2 of or consisting of radiation lying in the ultraviolet: *ultraviolet light.*

ultra vires (ult-ra **vire**-eez) *adv, adj* beyond the legal power of a person or organization.

THESAURUS

ubiquitous all-over, ever-present, everywhere, omnipresent, pervasive, universal

ugly **1.** hard-favoured, hard-featured, homely (*chiefly U.S.*), ill-favoured, misshapen, no oil painting (*informal*), not much to look at, plain, unattractive, unlovely, unprepossessing, unsightly **2.** baleful, dangerous, forbidding, menacing, ominous, sinister, threatening **3.** disagreeable, disgusting, distasteful, frightful, hideous, horrid, monstrous, objectionable, obscene, offensive, repugnant, repulsive, revolting, shocking, terrible, unpleasant, vile **4.** angry, bad-tempered, dark, evil, malevolent, nasty, spiteful, sullen, surly

ulcer abscess, boil, fester, gathering, gumboil, peptic ulcer, pustule, sore

ulterior concealed, covert, hidden, personal, secondary, secret, selfish, undisclosed, unexpressed

ultimate *adj.* **1.** conclusive, decisive, end, eventual, extreme, final, furthest, last, terminal **2.** extreme, greatest, highest, maximum, most significant, paramount, superlative, supreme, topmost, utmost **3.** basic, elemental, fundamental, primary, radical ~*n.* **4.** culmination, epitome, extreme, greatest, height, peak, perfection, summit, the last word

ululate (**yewl**-yew-late) *vb Literary* **-lating, -lated** to howl or wail. **ululation** *n*

umbel *n* a type of compound flower in which the flowers arise from the same point in the main stem and have stalks of the same length, to give a cluster with the youngest flowers at the centre. **umbellate** *adj*

umbelliferous *adj* of or denoting a plant with flowers in umbels, such as fennel, parsley, carrot, or parsnip.

umber *n* **1** a type of dark brown earth containing ferric oxide (rust). *~adj* **2** dark brown to reddish-brown.

umbilical (um-**bill**-ik-kl) *adj* of or like the navel or the umbilical cord.

umbilical cord *n* the long flexible cordlike structure that connects a fetus to the placenta.

umbilicus (um-**bill**-ik-kuss) *n Anat* the navel.

umbra *n, pl* **-brae** *or* **-bras** a shadow, usually the shadow cast by the moon onto the earth during a solar eclipse.

umbrage *n* **take umbrage** to take offence.

umbrella *n* **1** a portable device used for protection against rain, consisting of a light canopy supported on a collapsible metal frame mounted on a central rod. **2** a single organization, idea, etc., that contains or covers many different organizations or ideas. **3** anything that has the effect of a protective screen or general cover: *under the umbrella of the Helsinki security conference.* *~adj* **4** containing or covering many different organizations, ideas, etc.: *an umbrella group of nationalists and anti-communists.* **umbrella-like** *adj*

umiak, oomiak, *or* **oomiac** (**oo**-mee-ak) *n* a large open boat made of stretched skins, used by Eskimos.

umlaut (**oom**-lout) *n* **1** the mark (¨) placed over a vowel, esp. in German, indicating change in its sound. **2** (esp. in Germanic languages) the change of a vowel brought about by the influence of a vowel in the next syllable.

umlungu (oom-**loong**-goo) *n S African* a White man: used esp. as a term of address.

umpire *n* **1** an official who ensures that the people taking part in a game follow the rules; referee. *~vb* **-piring, -pired 2** to act as umpire in a game.

umpteen *adj Informal* very many: *the centre of umpteen scandals.* **umpteenth** *n, adj*

UN United Nations.

un-[1] *prefix* (*freely used with adjectives, participles, and their derivative adverbs and nouns: less frequently used with certain other nouns*) not; contrary to; opposite of: *uncertain; untidiness; unbelief; untruth.*

un-[2] *prefix forming verbs* **1** denoting reversal of an action or state: *uncover; untie.* **2** denoting removal from, release, or deprivation: *unharness.*

unabashed *adj* not ashamed or embarrassed.

unabated *adv* without any reduction in force: *the storm continued unabated.*

unable *adj* **unable to** not having the power, ability, or authority to; not able to.

unabridged *adj* (of a book or text) complete and not shortened or condensed.

unacceptable *adj* too bad to be accepted; intolerable.

unaccompanied *adj* **1** not having anyone with one: *unaccompanied female travellers should take care.* **2** (of singing or a musical instrument) not being accompanied by musical instruments.

unaccountable *adj* **1** without any sensible explanation: *for some unaccountable reason I got on the wrong bus.* **2** not having to justify or answer for one's actions to other people: *the secret service remains unaccountable to the public.* **unaccountably** *adv*

unaccounted *adj* **unaccounted for** unable to be found or traced: *four people were killed in the floods, and eleven remain unaccounted for.*

unaccustomed *adj* **1 unaccustomed to** not used to: *unaccustomed to such behaviour.* **2** not familiar: *moments of unaccustomed freedom.*

unacknowledged *adj* **1** ignored or not accepted as true or existing. **2** not officially recognized as being important.

unacquainted *adj* **unacquainted with** not knowing about; unfamiliar with.

unadopted *adj Brit* (of a road) not maintained by a local authority.

unadorned *adj* not decorated; plain.

unadulterated *adj* **1** completely pure, with nothing added: *fresh unadulterated spring water.* **2** (of an emotion) not mixed with anything else: *a look of unadulterated terror.*

unadventurous *adj* not taking chances or trying anything new.

unaffected[1] *adj* unpretentious, natural, or sincere.

unaffected[2] *adj* not influenced or changed.

unafraid *adj* not frightened or nervous.

unaided *adv* without any help or assistance; inde-

THESAURUS

ultimately after all, at last, basically, eventually, finally, fundamentally, in due time, in the end, sooner or later

umbrage anger, chagrin, displeasure, grudge, high dudgeon, huff, indignation, offence, pique, resentment, sense of injury

umbrella 1. brolly (*Brit. informal*), gamp (*Brit. informal*) **2.** aegis, agency, cover, patronage, protection

umpire 1. *n.* adjudicator, arbiter, arbitrator, judge, moderator, ref (*informal*), referee **2.** *vb.* adjudicate, arbitrate, call (*Sport*), judge, mediate, moderate, referee

unabashed blatant, bold, brazen, confident, unawed, unblushing, unconcerned, undaunted, undismayed, unembarrassed

unable impotent, inadequate, incapable, ineffectual, no good, not able, not equal to, not up to, powerless, unfit, unfitted, unqualified

unabridged complete, full-length, uncondensed, uncut, unexpurgated, unshortened, whole

unacceptable disagreeable, displeasing, distasteful, improper, inadmissible, insupportable, objectionable, offensive, undesirable, unpleasant, unsatisfactory, unwelcome

unaccompanied a cappella (*Music*), alone, by oneself, lone, on one's own, solo, unescorted

unaccountable 1. baffling, incomprehensible, inexplicable, inscrutable, mysterious, odd, peculiar, puzzling, strange, unexplainable, unfathomable, unintelligible **2.** clear, exempt, free, not answerable, not responsible, unliable

unaccustomed 1. unaccustomed to a newcomer to, a novice at, green, inexperienced, not given to, not used to, unfamiliar with, unpractised, unused to, unversed in **2.** new, out of the ordinary, remarkable, special, strange, surprising, uncommon, unexpected, unfamiliar, unprecedented, unusual, unwonted

unaffected artless, genuine, honest, ingenuous, naive, natural, plain, simple, sincere, straightforward, unassuming, unpretentious, unsophisticated, unspoilt, unstudied, without airs

unaffected aloof, impervious, not influenced, proof,

pendently: *he could not walk unaided for months after the accident.*

unalienable *adj Law* same as **inalienable.**

unalike *adj* not similar; different.

unalloyed *adj Literary* not spoiled by being mixed with anything else.

unalterable *adj* not able to be changed.

unambiguous *adj* having a clear meaning which can only be interpreted in one way.

un-American *adj* **1** not in accordance with the aims, ideals, or customs of the US. **2** against the interests of the US. **un-Americanism** *n*

unanimous (yew-**nan**-im-uss) *adj* **1** in complete agreement. **2** characterized by complete agreement: *unanimous approval.* **unanimity** *n* **unanimously** *adv*

unannounced *adv* without warning: *she turned up unannounced.*

unanswerable *adj* **1** having no possible answer. **2** so obviously correct that disagreement is impossible.

unappealing *adj* unpleasant or off-putting.

unappetizing *adj* tasting, looking, or smelling unpleasant to eat.

unappreciated *adj* not given the respect or recognition that is deserved.

unapproachable *adj* discouraging friendliness; aloof.

unarguable *adj* so obviously correct that disagreement is impossible.

unarmed *adj* **1** not carrying any weapons: *they were shooting unarmed peasants.* **2** not using any weapons: *unarmed combat.*

unashamed *adj* not embarrassed, esp. when doing something some people might find offensive: *unashamed greed.* **unashamedly** *adv*

unasked *adv* **1** without being asked to do something: *he opened the door unasked.* ~*adj* **2** (of a question) not asked, although sometimes implied.

unassailable *adj* not able to be destroyed or overcome: *an unassailable lead.*

unassisted *adj* without help from anyone else.

unassuming *adj* modest or unpretentious.

unattached *adj* **1** not connected with any specific body or group. **2** not engaged or married.

unattainable *adj* not able to be achieved; impossible.

unattended *adj* not being watched or looked after: *unattended baggage.*

unattractive *adj* not attractive or appealing.

unauthorized *or* **-ised** *adj* done or made without official permission.

unavailable *adj* not able to be met, obtained, or contacted.

unavailing *adj* useless or futile.

unavoidable *adj* unable to be avoided or prevented. **unavoidably** *adv*

unaware *adj* **1** not aware or conscious: *unaware of my surroundings.* ~*adv* **2** *Not universally accepted* same as **unawares.**

➤ Note the difference between the adjective *unaware,* usually followed by *of* or *that,* and the adverb *unawares.*

unawares *adv* **1** by surprise: *death had taken him unawares.* **2** without knowing: *had he passed her, all unawares?*

unbalanced *adj* **1** lacking balance. **2** mentally deranged. **3** biased; one-sided: *his unbalanced summing-up.*

THESAURUS

unaltered, unchanged, unimpressed, unmoved, unresponsive, unstirred, untouched

unafraid confident, daring, dauntless, fearless, intrepid, unfearing, unshakable

unalterable fixed, immovable, immutable, invariable, permanent, steadfast, unchangeable, unchanging

unanimity accord, agreement, assent, chorus, concert, concord, concurrence, consensus, harmony, like-mindedness, one mind, unison, unity

unanimous agreed, agreeing, at one, common, concerted, concordant, harmonious, in agreement, in complete accord, like-minded, of one mind, united

unanimously by common consent, unitedly, unopposed, with one accord, without exception, without opposition

unanswerable **1.** insoluble, insolvable, unascertainable, unexplainable, unresolvable **2.** absolute, conclusive, incontestable, incontrovertible, indisputable, irrefutable, unarguable, undeniable

unappetizing distasteful, insipid, off-putting (*Brit. informal*), tasteless, unappealing, unattractive, uninteresting, uninviting, unpalatable, unpleasant, unsavoury, vapid

unapproachable aloof, chilly, cool, distant, frigid, offish (*informal*), remote, reserved, standoffish, unfriendly, unsociable, withdrawn

unarmed assailable, defenceless, exposed, helpless, open, open to attack, unarmoured, unprotected, weak, weaponless, without arms

unasked off one's own bat, of one's own accord, voluntarily, without prompting

unassailable impregnable, invincible, invulnerable, secure, well-defended

unassuming diffident, humble, meek, modest, quiet, reserved, retiring, self-effacing, simple, unassertive, unobtrusive, unostentatious, unpretentious

unattached **1.** autonomous, free, independent, nonaligned, unaffiliated, uncommitted **2.** a free agent, available, by oneself, footloose and fancy-free, not spoken for, on one's own, single, unengaged, unmarried

unattended abandoned, disregarded, ignored, left alone, not cared for, unguarded, unwatched

unauthorized illegal, unapproved, unconstitutional, under-the-table, unlawful, unofficial, unsanctioned, unwarranted

unavailing abortive, bootless, fruitless, futile, idle, ineffective, ineffectual, of no avail, pointless, to no purpose, unproductive, unsuccessful, useless, vain

unavoidable bound to happen, certain, compulsory, fated, ineluctable, inescapable, inevitable, inexorable, necessary, obligatory, sure

unaware heedless, ignorant, incognizant, oblivious, unconscious, unenlightened, uninformed, unknowing, unmindful, unsuspecting

unawares **1.** aback, abruptly, by surprise, off guard, on the hop (*Brit. informal*), suddenly, unexpectedly, unprepared, without warning **2.** accidentally, by accident, by mistake, inadvertently, mistakenly, unconsciously, unintentionally, unknowingly, unwittingly

unbalanced **1.** asymmetrical, irregular, lopsided, not balanced, shaky, unequal, uneven, unstable, unsymmetrical, wobbly **2.** barking (*slang*), barking mad (*slang*), crazy, demented, deranged, disturbed, eccentric, erratic, insane, irrational, loopy (*informal*), lunatic, mad, *non compos mentis,* not all there, not the full shilling (*informal*), off one's trolley (*slang*), out to lunch (*informal*), touched, unhinged, unsound, unstable, up the pole (*informal*) **3.** biased, inequitable, one-sided, partial, partisan, prejudiced, unfair, unjust

unbearable *adj* not able to be endured. **unbearably** *adv*
unbeatable *adj* not able to be bettered.
unbecoming *adj* **1** unattractive or unsuitable: *unbecoming garments.* **2** not proper or appropriate to a person or position: *acts unbecoming of university students.*
unbeknown *adv* (foll. by *to*) without the knowledge of (a person): *unbeknown to her family she had acquired modern ways.* Also (esp. Brit.): **unbeknownst**
unbelievable *adj* **1** too unlikely to be believed. **2** extremely impressive; marvellous. **3** *Informal* terrible or shocking. **unbelievably** *adv*
unbeliever *n* a person who does not believe in a religion.
unbend *vb* **-bending, -bent** to become less strict or more informal in one's attitudes or behaviour.
unbending *adj* rigid or inflexible: *an unbending routine.*
unbiased *adj* not having or showing prejudice or favouritism; impartial.
unbidden *adj Literary* not ordered or asked; voluntary or spontaneous: *unbidden thoughts came into Catherine's mind.*
unbind *vb* **-binding, -bound 1** to set free from bonds or chains. **2** to unfasten or untie.
unblemished *adj* not spoiled, damaged or marked.
unblinking *adj* looking at something without blinking.
unblock *vb* to remove a blockage from; clear or free.
unblushing *adj* immodest or shameless.
unbolt *vb* to unfasten a bolt of a door.
unborn *adj* not yet born.
unbosom *vb* to relieve oneself of secrets or feelings by telling someone.
unbounded *adj* having no boundaries or limits.
unbowed *adj* not giving in or submitting: *the battered but as yet unbowed general secretary.*
unbreakable *adj* not able to be broken; indestructible.
unbridled *adj* (of feelings or behaviour) not restrained or controlled in any way: *unbridled passion.*
unbroken *adj* **1** complete or whole. **2** continuous: *I slept for eight unbroken hours.* **3** not disturbed or upset: *an unbroken night.* **4** (of a record) not improved upon. **5** (of animals, esp. horses) not tamed.
unburden *vb* to relieve one's mind or oneself of a worry or trouble by telling someone about it.
uncalled-for *adj* unnecessary or unwarranted: *uncalled-for comments.*
uncanny *adj* **1** weird or mysterious: *an uncanny silence.* **2** beyond what is normal: *an uncanny eye for detail.* **uncannily** *adv* **uncanniness** *n*
uncared-for *adj* not cared for; neglected.
uncaring *adj* showing no concern for other people's suffering and hardship.
unceasing *adj* continuing without a break; never stopping.
unceremonious *adj* **1** relaxed and informal: *she greeted him with unceremonious friendliness.* **2** abrupt or rude: *the answer was an unceremonious "no".* **unceremoniously** *adv*
uncertain *adj* **1** not able to be accurately known or predicted: *an uncertain future.* **2** not definitely decid-

THESAURUS

unbearable insufferable, insupportable, intolerable, oppressive, too much (*informal*), unacceptable, unendurable
unbeatable indomitable, invincible, more than a match for, unconquerable, unstoppable, unsurpassable
unbecoming discreditable, ill-suited, improper, inappropriate, incongruous, indecorous, indelicate, offensive, tasteless, unattractive, unbefitting, unfit, unflattering, unseemly, unsightly, unsuitable, unsuited
unbelievable astonishing, beyond belief, far-fetched, implausible, impossible, improbable, inconceivable, incredible, outlandish, preposterous, questionable, staggering, unconvincing, unimaginable, unthinkable
unbeliever agnostic, atheist, disbeliever, doubting Thomas, infidel, sceptic
unbending firm, inflexible, intractable, reserved, resolute, rigid, stiff, stubborn, tough, uncompromising, unyielding
unbiased disinterested, dispassionate, equitable, even-handed, fair, impartial, just, neutral, objective, open-minded, unprejudiced
unbidden free, spontaneous, unasked, unforced, uninvited, unprompted, unwanted, unwelcome, voluntary, willing
unbind free, loosen, release, set free, unbridle, unchain, undo, unfasten, unfetter, unloose, unshackle, untie, unyoke
unblemished flawless, immaculate, impeccable, perfect, pure, spotless, unflawed, unmarked, unspotted, unstained, unsullied, untarnished
unborn awaited, embryonic, expected, *in utero*
unbounded absolute, boundless, endless, immeasurable, infinite, lavish, limitless, unbridled, unchecked, unconstrained, uncontrolled, unlimited, unrestrained, vast
unbreakable armoured, durable, indestructible, infrangible, lasting, nonbreakable, resistant, rugged, shatterproof, solid, strong, toughened
unbridled excessive, intemperate, licentious, rampant, riotous, unchecked, unconstrained, uncontrolled, uncurbed, ungovernable, ungoverned, unrestrained, unruly, violent, wanton
unbroken 1. complete, entire, intact, solid, total, unimpaired, whole **2.** ceaseless, constant, continuous, endless, incessant, progressive, serried, successive, uninterrupted, unremitting **3.** deep, fast, profound, sound, undisturbed, unruffled, untroubled **4.** unbowed, unsubdued, untamed
unburden come clean (*informal*), confess, confide, disclose, get (something) off one's chest (*informal*), lay bare, make a clean breast of, reveal, spill one's guts about (*slang*), tell all, unbosom
uncalled-for gratuitous, inappropriate, needless, undeserved, unjust, unjustified, unnecessary, unprovoked, unwarranted, unwelcome
uncanny 1. creepy (*informal*), eerie, eldritch (*poetic*), mysterious, preternatural, queer, spooky (*informal*), strange, supernatural, unearthly, unnatural, weird **2.** astonishing, astounding, exceptional, extraordinary, fantastic, incredible, inspired, miraculous, prodigious, remarkable, singular, unheard-of, unusual
unceasing ceaseless, constant, continual, continuing, continuous, endless, incessant, never-ending, nonstop, perpetual, persistent, unending, unfailing, unremitting
uncertain 1. ambiguous, chancy, conjectural, doubtful, iffy (*informal*), incalculable, indefinite, indeterminate, indistinct, questionable, risky, speculative, undetermined, unforeseeable, unpredictable **2.** ambivalent, doubtful, dubious, hazy, in two minds, irresolute, unclear, unconfirmed, undecided, undetermined, unfixed, unresolved, unsettled, unsure, up in the air, vac-

ed: *they are uncertain about the date.* **3** not to be depended upon: *an uncertain career.* **4** changeable: *an uncertain sky.* **uncertainty** *n*

unchallenged *adj, adv* done or accepted without being challenged: *seventy years of unchallenged rule; her decisions went unchallenged.*

unchangeable *adj* not able to be altered.

unchanged *adj* remaining the same.

uncharacteristic *adj* not typical. **uncharacteristically** *adv*

uncharitable *adj* unkind or harsh. **uncharitably** *adv*

uncharted *adj* **1** (of an area of sea or land) not having had a map made of it, esp. because it is unexplored. **2** unknown or unfamiliar: *a whole uncharted universe of emotions.*

unchecked *adj* **1** not prevented from continuing or growing: *unchecked population growth.* **2** not examined or inspected. *~adv* **3** without being stopped or hindered: *the virus could spread unchecked.* **4** without being examined or inspected: *the drugs passed unchecked through airport security.*

unchristian *or* **un-Christian** *adj* not in accordance with Christian principles.

uncial (**un**-see-al) *adj* **1** of or written in letters that resemble modern capitals, as used in Greek and Latin manuscripts of the third to ninth centuries. *~n* **2** an uncial letter or manuscript.

uncivil *adj* impolite, rude or bad-mannered. **uncivilly** *adv*

uncivilized *or* **-ised** *adj* **1** (of a tribe or people) not yet civilized. **2** lacking culture or sophistication.

unclassified *adj* **1** not arranged in any specific order or grouping. **2** (of official information) not secret.

uncle *n* **1** a brother of one's father or mother. **2** the husband of one's aunt. **3** a child's term of address for a male friend of its parents. **4** *Slang* a pawnbroker.

unclean *adj* lacking moral, spiritual, or physical cleanliness.

unclear *adj* confusing or hard to understand.

Uncle Sam *n* a personification of the government of the United States.

Uncle Tom *n Informal, offensive* a Black person whose behaviour towards White people is regarded as servile.

unclothed *adj* not wearing any clothes; naked.

uncluttered *adj* not containing anything unnecessary; austere and simple.

uncoil *vb* to unwind or untwist.

uncomfortable *adj* **1** not physically relaxed: *he was forced to sit in an uncomfortable cross-legged position.* **2** not comfortable to be in or use: *an uncomfortable chair.* **3** causing discomfort or unease: *the uncomfortable truth.* **uncomfortably** *adv*

uncommitted *adj* not bound to a specific opinion, course of action, or cause.

uncommon *adj* **1** not happening or encountered often. **2** in excess of what is normal: *an uncommon amount of powder.*

uncommonly *adv* **1** in an unusual manner or degree. **2** extremely: *an uncommonly good humour.*

uncommunicative *adj* disinclined to talk or give information.

uncomplaining *adj* doing or tolerating something unpleasant or difficult without complaint.

uncomplicated *adj* simple and straightforward.

uncomplimentary *adj* not expressing respect or praise; insulting.

uncomprehending *adj* not understanding what is happening or what has been said.

uncompromising *adj* not prepared to compromise; inflexible. **uncompromisingly** *adv*

unconcealed *adj* not hidden or disguised: *a look of unconcealed hatred.*

unconcern *n* apathy or indifference.

unconcerned *adj* **1** not interested in something and

THESAURUS

illating, vague **3.** changeable, erratic, fitful, hesitant, iffy (*informal*), inconstant, insecure, irregular, precarious, unpredictable, unreliable, vacillating, variable, wavering

uncertainty ambiguity, bewilderment, confusion, dilemma, doubt, dubiety, hesitancy, hesitation, inconclusiveness, indecision, irresolution, lack of confidence, misgiving, mystification, perplexity, puzzlement, qualm, quandary, scepticism, state of suspense, unpredictability, vagueness

unchangeable changeless, constant, fixed, immovable, immutable, inevitable, invariable, irreversible, permanent, stable, steadfast, strong, unalterable

uncharitable cruel, hardhearted, harsh, insensitive, mean, merciless, stingy, unchristian, unfeeling, unforgiving, unfriendly, ungenerous, unkind, unsympathetic

uncharted not mapped, strange, undiscovered, unexplored, unfamiliar, unknown, unplumbed, virgin

uncivil bad-mannered, bearish, boorish, brusque, churlish, discourteous, disrespectful, gruff, ill-bred, ill-mannered, impolite, rude, surly, uncouth, unmannerly

uncivilized 1. barbarian, barbaric, barbarous, illiterate, primitive, savage, wild **2.** beyond the pale, boorish, brutish, churlish, coarse, gross, philistine, uncouth, uncultivated, uncultured, uneducated, unmannered, unpolished, unsophisticated, vulgar

unclean contaminated, corrupt, defiled, dirty, evil, filthy, foul, impure, nasty, polluted, scuzzy (*slang, chiefly U.S.*), soiled, spotted, stained, sullied, tainted

uncomfortable awkward, causing discomfort, cramped, disagreeable, hard, ill-fitting, incommodious, irritating, painful, rough, troublesome

uncommitted floating, free, free-floating, neutral, nonaligned, nonpartisan, not involved, (sitting) on the fence, unattached, uninvolved

uncommon 1. bizarre, curious, few and far between, infrequent, novel, odd, out of the ordinary, peculiar, queer, rare, scarce, singular, strange, unfamiliar, unusual **2.** distinctive, exceptional, extraordinary, incomparable, inimitable, notable, noteworthy, outstanding, rare, remarkable, singular, special, superior, unparalleled, unprecedented

uncommonly exceptionally, extremely, particularly, peculiarly, remarkably, strangely, unusually, very

uncommunicative close, curt, guarded, reserved, reticent, retiring, secretive, short, shy, silent, taciturn, tight-lipped, unforthcoming, unresponsive, unsociable, withdrawn

uncompromising decided, die-hard, firm, hard-line, inexorable, inflexible, intransigent, obdurate, obstinate, rigid, steadfast, stiff-necked, strict, stubborn, tough, unbending, unyielding

unconcern aloofness, apathy, detachment, indifference, insouciance, lack of interest, nonchalance, remoteness, uninterestedness

unconcerned 1. aloof, apathetic, cool, detached, dispassionate, distant, incurious, indifferent, oblivious, uninterested, uninvolved, unmoved, unsympathetic **2.** blithe, callous, carefree, careless, easy, insouciant, nonchalant, not bothered, relaxed, serene, unperturbed, unruffled, untroubled, unworried

not wanting to become involved. **2** not worried or troubled. **unconcernedly** (un-kon-**sern**-id-lee) *adv*

unconditional *adj* without conditions or limitations: *an unconditional ceasefire.* **unconditionally** *adv*

unconfirmed *adj* not yet proved to be true: *unconfirmed reports of a major accident.*

uncongenial *adj* (of a place or condition) unpleasant and unfriendly.

unconnected *adj* not linked to each other: *a series of unconnected incidents.*

unconscionable *adj* **1** unscrupulous or unprincipled: *an unconscionable charmer.* **2** excessive in amount or degree: *unconscionable number of social obligations.*

unconscious *adj* **1** unable to notice or respond to things which one would normally be aware of through the senses; insensible or comatose. **2** not aware of one's actions or behaviour: *unconscious of his failure.* **3** not realized or intended: *unconscious duplicity.* **4** coming from or produced by the unconscious: *unconscious mental processes.* ~*n* **5** *Psychoanal* the part of the mind containing instincts, impulses, and ideas that are not available for direct examination. **unconsciously** *adv* **unconsciousness** *n*

unconstitutional *adj* forbidden by the rules or laws which state how an organization or country must function.

uncontrollable *adj* **1** unable to be restrained or prevented: *a fit of uncontrollable giggles.* **2** (of a person) wild and unmanageable in behaviour: *he became violent and uncontrollable.* **uncontrollably** *adv*

unconventional *adj* not conforming to accepted rules or standards.

unconvinced *adj* not certain that something is true or right: *I remained unconvinced by his arguments.*

unconvincing *adj* (of a reason, argument, etc.) not good enough to convince people that something is true or right.

uncooked *adj* raw.

uncooperative *adj* not willing to help other people with what they are trying to do.

uncoordinated *adj* **1** not joining or functioning together properly to form a whole. **2** (of a person) not able to control his or her movements properly; clumsy.

uncork *vb* to remove the cork from a bottle.

uncorroborated *adj* not supported by other evidence or proof.

uncountable *adj* existing in such large numbers that it is impossible to say how many there are.

uncouple *vb* **-pling, -pled** to disconnect or become disconnected.

uncouth *adj* lacking in good manners, refinement, or grace.

uncover *vb* **1** to remove the cover or top from. **2** to reveal or disclose: *they have uncovered a plot to overthrow the government.* **uncovered** *adj*

uncritical *adj* not making a judgment about the merits or morality of something.

uncrowned *adj* **1** having the powers, but not the title, of royalty. **2** (of a king or queen) not yet crowned.

unction *n* **1** *Chiefly RC & Eastern Churches* the act of anointing with oil in sacramental ceremonies. **2** oily charm. **3** an ointment. **4** anything soothing.

unctuous *adj* pretending to be kind and concerned but obviously not sincere.

uncultured *adj* not knowing much about art, literature, etc.

uncut *adj* **1** not shortened or censored. **2** not cut. **3** (of precious stones) not having shaped and polished surfaces.

undamaged *adj* not spoilt or damaged; intact.

undaunted *adj* not put off, discouraged, or beaten.

undeceive *vb* **-ceiving, -ceived** to reveal the truth to someone previously misled or deceived.

undecided *adj* **1** not having made up one's mind. **2** (of an issue or problem) not agreed or decided upon.

THESAURUS

unconditional absolute, arrant, categorical, complete, downright, entire, explicit, full, out-and-out, outright, plenary, positive, thoroughgoing, total, unlimited, unqualified, unreserved, unrestricted, utter

uncongenial antagonistic, antipathetic, disagreeable, discordant, displeasing, distasteful, incompatible, not one's cup of tea (*informal*), unharmonious, uninviting, unpleasant, unsuited, unsympathetic

unconnected detached, disconnected, divided, independent, not related, separate, unrelated

unconscionable 1. amoral, criminal, unethical, unfair, unjust, unprincipled, unscrupulous **2.** excessive, exorbitant, extravagant, extreme, immoderate, inordinate, outrageous, preposterous, unreasonable

unconscious 1. blacked out (*informal*), comatose, dead to the world (*informal*), insensible, knocked out, numb, out, out cold, senseless, stunned **2.** blind to, deaf to, heedless, ignorant, in ignorance, lost to, oblivious, unaware, unknowing, unmindful, unsuspecting **3.** accidental, inadvertent, unintended, unintentional, unpremeditated, unwitting **4.** automatic, gut (*informal*), inherent, innate, instinctive, involuntary, latent, reflex, repressed, subconscious, subliminal, suppressed, unrealized

uncontrollable beside oneself, carried away, frantic, furious, irrepressible, irresistible, like one possessed, mad, strong, ungovernable, unmanageable, unruly, violent, wild

unconventional atypical, bizarre, bohemian, different, eccentric, far-out (*slang*), freakish, idiosyncratic, individual, individualistic, informal, irregular, nonconformist, odd, oddball (*informal*), offbeat, off-the-wall (*slang*), original, out of the ordinary, outré, uncustomary, unorthodox, unusual, wacko (*slang*), way-out (*informal*)

unconvincing dubious, feeble, fishy (*informal*), flimsy, hard to believe, implausible, improbable, inconclusive, lame, questionable, specious, suspect, thin, unlikely, unpersuasive, weak

uncoordinated all thumbs, awkward, bumbling, bungling, butterfingered (*informal*), clodhopping (*informal*), clumsy, graceless, heavy-footed, inept, lumbering, maladroit, ungainly, ungraceful

uncouth awkward, barbaric, boorish, clownish, clumsy, coarse, crude, gawky, graceless, gross, ill-mannered, loutish, lubberly, oafish, rough, rude, rustic, uncivilized, uncultivated, ungainly, unrefined, unseemly, vulgar

uncover 1. bare, lay open, lift the lid, open, show, strip, take the wraps off, unwrap **2.** blow wide open (*slang*), bring to light, disclose, discover, divulge, expose, lay bare, make known, reveal, unearth, unmask

uncritical easily pleased, indiscriminate, undiscerning, undiscriminating, unexacting, unfussy, unperceptive, unselective, unthinking

undeceive be honest with, correct, disabuse, disillusion, enlighten, open (someone's) eyes (to), put (someone) right, set (someone) straight, shatter (someone's) illusions

undecided 1. ambivalent, dithering (*chiefly Brit.*), doubtful, dubious, hesitant, in two minds, irresolute, swithering (*Scot.*), torn, uncertain, uncommitted, un-

undeclared *adj* not acknowledged for tax purposes.
undemanding *adj* not difficult to do or deal with: *an undemanding task.*
undemonstrative *adj* not showing emotions openly or easily.
undeniable *adj* **1** unquestionably true. **2** of unquestionable excellence: *of undeniable character.* **undeniably** *adv*
under *prep* **1** directly below; on, to, or beneath the underside or base of: *under the bed.* **2** less than: *in just under an hour.* **3** lower in rank than: *under a general.* **4** subject to the supervision, control, or influence of: *under communism for 45 years.* **5** in or subject to certain circumstances or conditions: *the bridge is still under construction; under battle conditions.* **6** in (a specified category): *he had filed Kafka's "The Trial" under crime stories.* **7** known by: *under their own names.* **8** planted with: *a field under corn.* **9** powered by: *under sail.* ~*adv* **10** below; to a position underneath
under- *prefix* **1** below or beneath: *underarm; underground.* **2** insufficient or insufficiently: *underemployed.* **3** of lesser importance or lower rank: *undersecretary.* **4** indicating secrecy or deception: *underhand.*
underachieve *vb* **-achieving, -achieved** to fail to achieve a performance appropriate to one's age or talents. **underachiever** *n*
underactive *adj* less active than is normal or desirable: *an underactive thyroid gland.*
underage *adj* below the required or standard age, usually below the legal age for voting or drinking.
underarm *adj* **1** *Sport* denoting a style of throwing, bowling, or serving in which the hand is swung below shoulder level. **2** below the arm. ~*adv* **3** in an underarm style.
underbelly *n, pl* **-lies 1** the part of an animal's belly nearest the ground. **2** a vulnerable or unprotected part, aspect, or region.
underbrush *n US, Canad, & Austral* same as **undergrowth.**
undercarriage *n* **1** the wheels, shock absorbers, and struts that support an aircraft on the ground and enable it to take off and land. **2** the framework supporting the body of a vehicle.
undercharge *vb* **-charging, -charged** to charge too little for something.
underclass *n* a class beneath the usual social scale consisting of the most disadvantaged people, such as the long-term unemployed.
underclothes *pl n* same as **underwear.** Also called: **underclothing**
undercoat *n* **1** a coat of paint applied before the top coat. **2** *Zool* a layer of soft fur beneath the outer fur of animals such as the otter. ~*vb* **3** to apply an undercoat to a surface.
undercook *vb* to cook for too short a time or at too low a temperature.
undercover *adj* done or acting in secret: *an undercover investigation.*
undercurrent *n* **1** a current that is not apparent at the surface. **2** an underlying opinion or emotion.
undercut *vb* **-cutting, -cut 1** to charge less than a competitor in order to obtain trade. **2** to undermine or render less effective: *the latest fighting undercuts diplomatic attempts to find a peaceful solution.* **3** to cut away the under part of something.
underdeveloped *adj* **1** immature or undersized. **2** (of a country or its economy) lacking the finance, industries, and organization necessary to advance.
underdog *n* a person or team in a weak or underprivileged position.
underdone *adj* insufficiently or lightly cooked.
underemployed *adj* not fully or adequately employed.
underestimate *vb* **-mating, -mated 1** to make too low an estimate of: *the trust had underestimated the cost of work.* **2** to not be aware or take account of the full abilities or potential of: *the police had underestimated him.* ~*n* **3** too low an estimate. **underestimation** *n*
underexpose *vb* **-posing, -posed** *Photog* to expose (a film, plate, or paper) for too short a time or with insufficient light. **underexposure** *n*
underfed *adj* not getting enough food to be healthy.
underfelt *n* thick felt laid under a carpet to increase insulation.
underfoot *adv* **1** underneath the feet; on the ground. **2 trample** *or* **crush underfoot a** to damage or destroy by stepping on. **b** to treat with contempt.
undergarment *n* a garment worn under clothes.
undergo *vb* **-going, -went, -gone** to experience, endure, or sustain: *he underwent a three-hour operation.*
undergraduate *n* a person studying in a university for a first degree.
underground *adj, adv* **1** occurring, situated, used, or going below ground level. **2** secret or secretly: *an underground organization; several political parties had to operate underground for many years.* **3** (of art, film, music, etc.) avant-garde, experimental, or subversive.

THESAURUS

sure, wavering **2.** debatable, iffy (*informal*), indefinite, in the balance, moot, open, pending, tentative, unconcluded, undetermined, unsettled, up in the air, vague
undemonstrative aloof, cold, contained, distant, formal, impassive, reserved, restrained, reticent, stiff, stolid, unaffectionate, uncommunicative, unemotional, unresponsive, withdrawn
undeniable beyond (a) doubt, beyond question, certain, clear, evident, incontestable, incontrovertible, indisputable, indubitable, irrefutable, manifest, obvious, patent, proven, sound, sure, unassailable, undoubted, unquestionable
under *prep.* **1.** below, beneath, on the bottom of, underneath **2.** directed by, governed by, inferior to, junior to, reporting to, secondary to, subject to, subordinate to, subservient to **3.** belonging to, comprised in, included in, subsumed under ~*adv.* **4.** below, beneath, down, downward, lower, to the bottom
underclothes lingerie, smalls (*informal*), underclothing, undergarments, underlinen, underthings, underwear, undies (*informal*), unmentionables (*humorous*)
undercover clandestine, concealed, confidential, covert, hidden, hush-hush (*informal*), intelligence, private, secret, spy, surreptitious, underground
undercurrent 1. crosscurrent, rip, rip current, riptide, tideway, underflow, undertow **2.** atmosphere, aura, drift, feeling, flavour, hidden feeling, hint, murmur, overtone, sense, suggestion, tendency, tenor, tinge, trend, undertone, vibes (*slang*), vibrations
undercut 1. sell at a loss, sell cheaply, undercharge, underprice, undersell **2.** cut away, cut out, excavate, gouge out, hollow out, mine, undermine
underdog fall guy (*informal*), little fellow (*informal*), loser, victim, weaker party
underestimate belittle, hold cheap, minimize, miscalculate, misprize, not do justice to, rate too low, sell short (*informal*), set no store by, think too little of, underrate, undervalue

~*n* **4** a movement dedicated to overthrowing a government or occupation forces. **5** (often preceded by *the*) an electric passenger railway operated in underground tunnels.

undergrowth *n* small trees and bushes growing beneath taller trees in a wood or forest.

underhand *adj also* **underhanded 1** sly, deceitful, and secretive. **2** *Sport* same as **underarm.** ~*adv* **3** in an underhand manner or style.

underinsured *adj* not insured for enough money to cover the replacement value of the goods covered.

underlay *n* felt or rubber laid under a carpet to increase insulation and resilience.

underlie *vb* **-lying, -lay, -lain 1** to lie or be placed under. **2** to be the foundation, cause, or basis of: *the basic unity which underlies all religion.*

underline *vb* **-lining, -lined 1** to put a line under. **2** to emphasize.

underling *n Derogatory* a subordinate.

underlying *adj* **1** not obvious but detectable: *the deeper and underlying aim of her travels.* **2** fundamental; basic: *an underlying belief.* **3** lying under: *the underlying layers of the skin.*

undermanned *adj* not having enough staff to function properly.

undermentioned *adj* mentioned below or later.

undermine *vb* **-mining, -mined 1** to weaken gradually or insidiously: *morphia had undermined his grasp of reality.* **2** (of the sea or wind) to wear away the base of cliffs.

underneath *prep, adv* **1** under or beneath. ~*adj* **2** lower. ~*n* **3** a lower part or surface.

undernourished *adj* lacking the food needed for health and growth. **undernourishment** *n*

underpaid *adj* not paid as much as the job deserves.

underpants *pl n* a man's undergarment covering the body from the waist or hips to the thighs.

underpass *n* **1** a section of a road that passes under another road or a railway line. **2** a subway for pedestrians.

underpay *vb* **-paying, -paid** to pay someone insufficiently. **underpayment** *n*

underpin *vb* **-pinning, -pinned 1** to give strength or support to: *the principles that underpin his political convictions.* **2** to support from beneath with a prop: *to underpin a wall.* **underpinning** *n*

underplay *vb* to achieve (an effect) by deliberate lack of emphasis.

underprivileged *adj* **1** lacking the rights and advantages of other members of society; deprived. ~*n* **2 the underprivileged** underprivileged people regarded as a group.

underrate *vb* **-rating, -rated** to not be aware or take account of the full abilities or potential of. **underrated** *adj*

underscore *vb* **-scoring, -scored** same as **underline.**

undersea *adj, adv* below the surface of the sea.

underseal *Brit* ~*n* **1** a special coating applied to the underside of a motor vehicle to prevent corrosion. ~*vb* **2** to apply such a coating to a motor vehicle.

undersecretary *n, pl* **-taries** a senior civil servant or junior minister in a government department.

undersell *vb* **-selling, -sold** to sell at a price lower than that of another seller.

undersexed *adj* having weaker sexual urges than is considered normal.

undershirt *n US & Canad* a vest.

undershoot *vb* **-shooting, -shot** *Aviation* to land an aircraft short of a runway.

underside *n* the bottom or lower surface.

undersigned *n* **the undersigned** the person or people who have signed at the foot of a document, statement, or letter.

undersized *adj* smaller than normal.

underskirt *n* a skirtlike garment worn under a skirt or dress; petticoat.

understaffed *adj* not having enough staff to function properly.

understand *vb* **-standing, -stood 1** to know and comprehend the nature or meaning of: *I understand what you are saying.* **2** to know what is happening or why it is happening: *in order to understand the problems that can occur.* **3** to assume, infer, or believe: *I understand he is based in this town.* **4** to know how to translate or read: *don't you understand Russian?* **5** to be sympathetic to or compatible with: *she needed him to understand her completely.* **understandable** *adj* **understandably** *adv*

THESAURUS

undergo bear, be subjected to, endure, experience, go through, stand, submit to, suffer, sustain, weather, withstand

underground *adj.* **1.** below ground, below the surface, buried, covered, subterranean **2.** clandestine, concealed, covert, hidden, secret, surreptitious, undercover **3.** alternative, avant-garde, experimental, radical, revolutionary, subversive ~*n.* **4.** partisans, the Maquis, the Resistance **5.** the metro, the subway, the tube (*Brit.*)

undergrowth bracken, brambles, briars, brush, brushwood, scrub, underbrush, underbush, underwood

underhand clandestine, crafty, crooked (*informal*), deceitful, deceptive, devious, dishonest, dishonourable, fraudulent, furtive, secret, secretive, sly, sneaky, stealthy, surreptitious, treacherous, underhanded, unethical, unscrupulous

underline 1. italicize, mark, rule a line under, underscore **2.** accentuate, bring home, call *or* draw attention to, emphasize, give emphasis to, highlight, point up, stress

underling flunky, hireling, inferior, lackey, menial, minion, nonentity, retainer, servant, slave, subordinate

underlying 1. concealed, hidden, latent, lurking, veiled **2.** basal, basic, elementary, essential, fundamental, intrinsic, primary, prime, radical, root

undermine 1. debilitate, disable, impair, sabotage, sap, subvert, threaten, weaken **2.** dig out, eat away at, erode, excavate, mine, tunnel, undercut, wear away

underprivileged badly off, deprived, destitute, disadvantaged, impoverished, in need, in want, needy, poor

underrate belittle, discount, disparage, fail to appreciate, not do justice to, set (too) little store by, underestimate, undervalue

undersized atrophied, dwarfish, miniature, pygmy *or* pigmy, runtish, runty, small, squat, stunted, teensy-weensy, teeny-weeny, tiny, underdeveloped, underweight

understand 1. appreciate, apprehend, be aware, catch on (*informal*), comprehend, conceive, cotton on (*informal*), discern, fathom, follow, get, get the hang of (*informal*), get to the bottom of, grasp, know, make head or tail of (*informal*), make out, penetrate, perceive, realize, recognize, savvy (*slang*), see, take in, tumble to (*informal*), twig (*Brit. informal*) **2.** assume, be informed, believe, conclude, gather, hear, infer,

understanding *n* **1** the ability to learn, judge, or make decisions. **2** personal opinion or interpretation of a subject: *my understanding of what he said.* **3** a mutual agreement, usually an informal or private one. *~adj* **4** kind, sympathetic, or tolerant towards people.

understate *vb* **-stating, -stated 1** to describe or portray something in restrained terms, often to obtain an ironic effect. **2** to state that something, such as a number is less than it is. **understatement** *n*

understood *vb* **1** the past of **understand.** *~adj* **2** implied or inferred. **3** taken for granted.

understudy *n, pl* **-studies 1** an actor who studies a part so as to be able to replace the usual actor if necessary. **2** anyone who is trained to take the place of another if necessary. *~vb* **-studies, -studying, -studied 3** to act as an understudy to.

undertake *vb* **-taking, -took, -taken 1** to agree to or commit oneself to something or to do something: *I undertook the worst job in gardening.* **2** to promise to do something.

undertaker *n* a person whose job is to look after the bodies of people who have died and to organize funerals.

undertaking *n* **1** a task or enterprise. **2** an agreement to do something.

undertone *n* **1** a quiet tone of voice. **2** something which suggests an underlying quality or feeling: *an undertone of anger.*

undertow *n* a strong undercurrent flowing in a different direction from the surface current, such as in the sea.

undervalue *vb* **-valuing, -valued** to value a person or thing at less than the true worth or importance.

underwater *adj* **1** situated, occurring, or for use under the surface of the sea, a lake, or a river. *~adv* **2** beneath the surface of the sea, a lake, or a river.

under way *adj* **1** in progress; taking place: *this test is already under way.* **2** *Naut* in motion in the direction headed.

underwear *n* clothing worn under other garments, usually next to the skin.

underweight *adj* weighing less than is average, expected, or healthy.

underwent *vb* the past tense of **undergo.**

underworld *n* **1** criminals and their associates. **2** *Greek & Roman myth* the regions below the earth's surface regarded as the abode of the dead.

underwrite *vb* **-writing, -wrote, -written 1** to accept financial responsibility for a commercial project or enterprise. **2** to sign and issue an insurance policy, thus accepting liability. **3** to support. **underwriter** *n*

undeserved *adj* not earned or deserved.

undesirable *adj* **1** not desirable or pleasant; objectionable. *~n* **2** a person considered undesirable.

undetected *adj* not having been discovered: *an undetected cancer.*

undeterred *adj* not put off or dissuaded.

undeveloped *adj* **1** not yet mature or adult. **2** (of land) not built on or used for commercial or agricultural purposes.

undies *pl n Informal* women's underwear.

undignified *adj* foolish or embarrassing.

undiluted *adj* **1** (of a liquid) not having any water added to it; concentrated. **2** not mixed with any other feeling or quality: *undiluted hatred.*

undiminished *adj* not lessened or decreased: *his admiration for her remained undiminished.*

undine (un-dean) *n* a female water spirit.

undisciplined *adj* behaving badly, with a lack of self-control.

undisguised *adj* shown openly; not concealed: *undisguised curiosity.*

THESAURUS

learn, presume, suppose, take it, think **3.** accept, appreciate, be able to see, commiserate, show compassion for, sympathize with, tolerate

understanding *n.* **1.** appreciation, awareness, comprehension, discernment, grasp, insight, intelligence, judgment, knowledge, penetration, perception, sense **2.** belief, conclusion, estimation, idea, interpretation, judgment, notion, opinion, perception, view, viewpoint **3.** accord, agreement, common view, gentlemen's agreement, meeting of minds, pact *~adj.* **4.** accepting, compassionate, considerate, discerning, forbearing, forgiving, kind, kindly, patient, perceptive, responsive, sensitive, sympathetic, tolerant

understood 1. implicit, implied, inferred, tacit, unspoken, unstated **2.** accepted, assumed, axiomatic, presumed, taken for granted

understudy *n.* double, fill-in, replacement, reserve, stand-in, sub, substitute

undertake agree, bargain, commit oneself, contract, covenant, engage, guarantee, pledge, promise, stipulate, take upon oneself

undertaker funeral director, mortician (*U.S.*)

undertaking 1. affair, attempt, business, effort, endeavour, enterprise, game, operation, project, task, venture **2.** agreement, assurance, commitment, pledge, promise, solemn word, vow, word, word of honour

undertone 1. low tone, murmur, subdued voice, whisper **2.** atmosphere, feeling, flavour, hint, suggestion, tinge, touch, trace, undercurrent, vibes (*slang*)

undervalue depreciate, hold cheap, look down on, make light of, minimize, misjudge, misprize, set no store by, underestimate, underrate

underwater submarine, submerged, sunken, undersea

under way afoot, begun, going on, in motion, in operation, in progress, started

underwear lingerie, smalls (*informal*), underclothes, underclothing, undergarments, underlinen, underthings, undies (*informal*), unmentionables (*humorous*)

underweight anorexic, bulimic, emaciated, half-starved, puny, skin and bone (*informal*), skinny, undernourished, undersized

underworld 1. criminal element, criminals, gangland (*informal*), gangsters, organized crime **2.** abode of the dead, Hades, hell, infernal region, nether regions, nether world, the inferno

underwrite 1. back, finance, fund, guarantee, insure, provide security, sponsor, subsidize **2.** countersign, endorse, initial, sign, subscribe **3.** agree to, approve, consent, O.K. *or* okay (*informal*), sanction, support

undesirable disagreeable, disliked, distasteful, dreaded, objectionable, obnoxious, offensive, out of place, repugnant, to be avoided, unacceptable, unattractive, unpleasing, unpopular, unsavoury, unsuitable, unwanted, unwelcome, unwished-for

undeveloped embryonic, immature, inchoate, in embryo, latent, potential, primordial (*Biol.*)

undignified beneath one, beneath one's dignity, improper, inappropriate, indecorous, inelegant, infra dig (*informal*), lacking dignity, unbecoming, ungentlemanly, unladylike, unrefined, unseemly, unsuitable

undisciplined disobedient, erratic, fitful, obstreperous, uncontrolled, unpredictable, unreliable, unrestrained, unruly, unschooled, unsteady, unsystematic, untrained, wayward, wild, wilful

undismayed *adj* not upset about something; undaunted.
undisputed *adj* unquestionably true or accurately described: *Mao became undisputed leader of China.*
undistinguished *adj* not particularly good or bad; mediocre.
undisturbed *adj* **1** quiet and peaceful: *an undisturbed village.* **2** uninterrupted: *three hours' undisturbed work.* **3** not touched, moved, or used by anyone: *the wreck has lain undisturbed for centuries.*
undivided *adj* **1** total and whole-hearted: *her undivided attention.* **2** not separated into different parts or groups.
undo *vb* **-doing, -did, -done 1** to open, unwrap or untie. **2** to reverse the effects of: *all the work of the congress would be undone.* **3** to cause the downfall of.
undoing *n* **1** ruin; downfall. **2** the cause of someone's downfall: *his confidence was his undoing.*
undone[1] *adj* not done or completed; unfinished.
undone[2] *adj* **1** ruined; destroyed. **2** unfastened; untied.
undoubted *adj* beyond doubt; certain or indisputable. **undoubtedly** *adv*
undreamed *or* **undreamt** *adj* (often foll. by *of*) not thought of or imagined.
undress *vb* **1** to take off the clothes of oneself or another. *~n* **2 in a state of undress** naked or nearly naked. **3** informal or ordinary working clothes or uniform. **undressed** *adj*
undue *adj* greater than is reasonable; excessive: *undue attention.*
undulate *vb* **-lating, -lated 1** to move gently and slowly from side to side or up and down. **2** to have a wavy shape or appearance. **undulation** *n*
unduly *adv* excessively.
undying *adj* never ending; eternal.
unearned *adj* **1** not deserved. **2** not yet earned.
unearned income *n* income from property or investments rather than work.
unearth *vb* **1** to discover by searching. **2** to dig up out of the earth.
unearthly *adj* **1** strange, unnatural, or eerie: *unearthly beauty.* **2** ridiculous or unreasonable: *the unearthly hour of seven in the morning.* **unearthliness** *n*
unease *n* **1** anxiety or nervousness: *my unease grew when she was not back by midnight.* **2** dissatisfaction or tension: *unease about the government's handling of the affair.*
uneasy *adj* **1** (of a person) anxious or apprehensive. **2** (of a condition) precarious or insecure: *an uneasy peace.* **3** (of a thought or feeling) disquieting. **uneasily** *adv* **uneasiness** *n*
uneatable *adj* (of food) so rotten or unattractive as to be unfit to eat.
uneconomic *adj* not producing enough profit.

THESAURUS

undisguised blatant, complete, evident, explicit, genuine, manifest, obvious, open, out-and-out, overt, patent, thoroughgoing, transparent, unconcealed, unfeigned, unmistakable, utter, wholehearted
undisputed accepted, acknowledged, beyond question, certain, conclusive, freely admitted, incontestable, incontrovertible, indisputable, irrefutable, not disputed, recognized, sure, unchallenged, uncontested, undeniable, undoubted, unquestioned
undistinguished commonplace, everyday, indifferent, mediocre, no great shakes (*informal*), nothing to write home about (*informal*), ordinary, pedestrian, prosaic, run-of-the-mill, so-so (*informal*), unexceptional, unexciting, unimpressive, unremarkable
undisturbed 1. calm, peaceful, placid, quiet, sedate, serene, tranquil **2.** uninterrupted, without interruption **3.** not moved, quiet, untouched
undivided combined, complete, concentrated, concerted, entire, exclusive, full, solid, thorough, unanimous, undistracted, united, whole, wholehearted
undo 1. disengage, disentangle, loose, loosen, open, unbutton, unfasten, unlock, untie, unwrap **2.** annul, cancel, invalidate, neutralize, nullify, offset, reverse, wipe out **3.** bring to naught, defeat, destroy, impoverish, invalidate, mar, overturn, quash, ruin, shatter, subvert, undermine, upset, wreck
undoing 1. collapse, defeat, destruction, disgrace, downfall, humiliation, overthrow, overturn, reversal, ruin, ruination, shame **2.** affliction, blight, curse, fatal flaw, misfortune, the last straw, trial, trouble, weakness
undone incomplete, left, neglected, not completed, not done, omitted, outstanding, passed over, unattended to, unfinished, unfulfilled, unperformed
undoubted acknowledged, certain, definite, evident, incontrovertible, indisputable, indubitable, obvious, sure, undisputed, unquestionable, unquestioned
undoubtedly assuredly, beyond a shadow of (a) doubt, beyond question, certainly, definitely, doubtless, of course, surely, undeniably, unmistakably, unquestionably, without doubt
undreamed of astonishing, inconceivable, incredible, miraculous, undreamt, unexpected, unforeseen, unheard-of, unimagined, unsuspected, unthought-of
undress 1. *vb.* disrobe, divest oneself of, peel off (*slang*), shed, strip, take off one's clothes **2.** *n.* disarray, dishabille, nakedness, nudity
undue disproportionate, excessive, extravagant, extreme, immoderate, improper, inordinate, intemperate, needless, overmuch, too great, too much, uncalled-for, undeserved, unnecessary, unseemly, unwarranted
unduly disproportionately, excessively, extravagantly, immoderately, improperly, inordinately, out of all proportion, overly, overmuch, unjustifiably, unnecessarily, unreasonably
undying constant, continuing, deathless, eternal, everlasting, immortal, imperishable, indestructible, inextinguishable, infinite, perennial, permanent, perpetual, undiminished, unending, unfading
unearth 1. bring to light, discover, expose, ferret out, find, reveal, root up, turn up, uncover **2.** dig up, disinter, dredge up, excavate, exhume
unearthly 1. eerie, eldritch (*poetic*), ethereal, ghostly, haunted, heavenly, nightmarish, not of this world, phantom, preternatural, spectral, spooky (*informal*), strange, sublime, supernatural, uncanny, weird **2.** abnormal, absurd, extraordinary, ridiculous, strange, ungodly (*informal*), unholy (*informal*), unreasonable
uneasiness agitation, alarm, anxiety, apprehension, apprehensiveness, disquiet, doubt, dubiety, misgiving, nervousness, perturbation, qualms, suspicion, trepidation, worry
uneasy 1. agitated, anxious, apprehensive, discomposed, disturbed, edgy, ill at ease, impatient, jittery (*informal*), nervous, on edge, perturbed, restive, restless, troubled, twitchy (*informal*), uncomfortable, unsettled, upset, wired (*slang*), worried **2.** awkward, constrained, insecure, precarious, shaky, strained, tense, uncomfortable, unstable **3.** bothering, dismaying, disquieting, disturbing, troubling, upsetting, worrying
uneconomic loss-making, nonpaying, non-profit-making, nonviable, unprofitable

uneconomical *adj* not economical; wasteful.
uneducated *adj* not educated well or at all.
unemotional *adj* (of a person) not displaying any emotion.
unemployable *adj* unable or unfit to keep a job.
unemployed *adj* **1** without paid employment; out of work. **2** not being used; idle. *~pl n* **3** people who are out of work: *the long-term unemployed.*
unemployment *n* **1** the condition of being unemployed. **2** the number of unemployed workers: *unemployment rose again last month.*
unemployment benefit *n* (in the British National Insurance scheme) a regular payment to an unemployed person.
unencumbered *adj* not hindered or held back: *unencumbered by the responsibilities of childcare.*
unending *adj* not showing any signs of ever stopping.
unendurable *adj* too unpleasant to bear.
unenthusiastic *adj* not keen about or interested in (something). **unenthusiastically** *adv*
unenviable *adj* (of a task) so difficult, dangerous, or unpleasant that one is glad not to have to do it oneself: *the unenviable task of phoning the parents of the dead child.*
unequal *adj* **1** not equal in quantity, size, rank, or value. **2 unequal to** inadequate for: *he felt unequal to the job.* **3** not offering all people or groups the same opportunities and privileges: *the unequal distribution of wealth.* **4** (of a contest) having competitors of different ability. **unequally** *adv*
unequalled *or US* **unequaled** *adj* greater, better, or more extreme than anything else of the same kind.
unequivocal *adj* completely clear in meaning; unambiguous. **unequivocally** *adv*
unerring *adj* never mistaken; consistently accurate.
UNESCO United Nations Educational, Scientific, and Cultural Organization.
unethical *adj* morally wrong.
uneven *adj* **1** (of a surface) not level or flat. **2** not consistent in quality: *an uneven performance.* **3** not parallel, straight, or horizontal. **4** not fairly matched: *the uneven battle.*
uneventful *adj* ordinary, routine, or quiet. **uneventfully** *adv*
unexampled *adj* without precedent.
unexceptionable *adj* not likely to be criticised or objected to.
unexceptional *adj* usual, ordinary, or normal.
unexciting *adj* slightly dull and boring.
unexpected *adj* surprising or unforeseen. **unexpectedly** *adv*
unexplained *adj* strange or unclear because the reason for it is not known.
unexpurgated *adj* (of a piece of writing) not censored by having allegedly offensive passages removed.
unfailing *adj* continuous or reliable: *his unfailing enthusiasm.* **unfailingly** *adv*
unfair *adj* **1** unequal or unjust. **2** dishonest or unethical. **unfairly** *adv* **unfairness** *n*
unfaithful *adj* **1** having sex with someone other than one's regular partner. **2** not true to a promise or vow. **unfaithfulness** *n*
unfamiliar *adj* **1** not known; strange: *an unfamiliar American accent.* **2 unfamiliar with** not acquainted

THESAURUS

uneducated ignorant, illiterate, unlettered, unread, unschooled, untaught
unemotional apathetic, cold, cool, impassive, indifferent, listless, passionless, phlegmatic, reserved, undemonstrative, unexcitable, unfeeling, unimpressionable, unresponsive
unemployed idle, jobless, laid off, on the dole (*Brit. informal*), out of a job, out-of-work, redundant, resting (*of an actor*), workless
unending ceaseless, constant, continual, endless, eternal, everlasting, incessant, interminable, never-ending, perpetual, unceasing, unremitting
unendurable insufferable, insupportable, intolerable, unbearable
unenthusiastic apathetic, blasé, bored, half-hearted, indifferent, lukewarm, neutral, nonchalant, unimpressed, uninterested, unmoved, unresponsive
unenviable disagreeable, painful, thankless, uncomfortable, undesirable, unpleasant
unequal 1. different, differing, disparate, dissimilar, not uniform, unlike, unmatched, variable, varying **2. unequal to** found wanting, inadequate, insufficient, not up to **3.** disproportionate, ill-matched, irregular, unbalanced, uneven
unequalled beyond compare, incomparable, inimitable, matchless, nonpareil, paramount, peerless, pre-eminent, second to none, supreme, transcendent, unmatched, unparalleled, unrivalled, unsurpassed, without equal
unequivocal absolute, certain, clear, clear-cut, decisive, definite, direct, evident, explicit, incontrovertible, indubitable, manifest, plain, positive, straight, unambiguous, uncontestable, unmistakable
unethical dirty, dishonest, dishonourable, disreputable, illegal, immoral, improper, shady (*informal*), underhand, under-the-table, unfair, unprincipled, unprofessional, unscrupulous, wrong
uneven 1. bumpy, not flat, not level, not smooth, rough **2.** broken, changeable, fitful, fluctuating, intermittent, irregular, jerky, patchy, spasmodic, unsteady, variable **3.** asymmetrical, lopsided, not parallel, odd, out of true, unbalanced **4.** disparate, ill-matched, one-sided, unequal, unfair
uneventful boring, commonplace, dull, ho-hum (*informal*), humdrum, monotonous, ordinary, quiet, routine, tedious, unexceptional, unexciting, uninteresting, unmemorable, unremarkable, unvaried
unexceptional common or garden (*informal*), commonplace, conventional, insignificant, mediocre, normal, ordinary, pedestrian, run-of-the-mill, undistinguished, unimpressive, unremarkable, usual
unexpected abrupt, accidental, astonishing, chance, fortuitous, not bargained for, out of the blue, startling, sudden, surprising, unanticipated, unforeseen, unlooked-for, unpredictable
unfailing bottomless, boundless, ceaseless, certain, constant, continual, continuous, dependable, endless, faithful, inexhaustible, infallible, loyal, never-failing, persistent, reliable, staunch, steadfast, sure, tried and true, true, unflagging, unlimited
unfair 1. arbitrary, biased, bigoted, discriminatory, inequitable, one-sided, partial, partisan, prejudiced, unequal, unjust **2.** crooked (*informal*), dishonest, dishonourable, uncalled-for, unethical, unprincipled, unscrupulous, unsporting, unwarranted, wrongful
unfaithful 1. adulterous, faithless, fickle, inconstant, two-timing (*informal*), unchaste, untrue **2.** deceitful, disloyal, faithless, false, false-hearted, perfidious, traitorous, treacherous, treasonable, unreliable, untrustworthy
unfamiliar 1. alien, curious, different, little known, new, novel, out-of-the-way, strange, unaccustomed,

with: *anyone who is unfamiliar with the language.* **unfamiliarity** *n*

unfashionable *adj* not popular or in vogue.

unfasten *vb* to undo, untie, or open or become undone, untied, or opened.

unfathomable *adj* too strange or complicated to be understood.

unfavourable *or US* **unfavorable** *adj* **1** making a successful or positive outcome unlikely: *unfavourable weather conditions.* **2** disapproving: *an unfavourable opinion.* **unfavourably** *or US* **unfavorably** *adv*

unfeeling *adj* without sympathy; callous.

unfettered *adj* not limited or controlled: *unfettered competition.*

unfinished *adj* **1** incomplete or imperfect. **2** (of paint) without an applied finish.

unfit *adj* **1** unqualified for or incapable of a particular role or task: *an unfit mother; he was unfit to drive.* **2** unsuitable: *this meat is unfit for human consumption.* **3** in poor physical condition.

unfitted *adj* unsuitable: *unused to and unfitted for any form of manual labour.*

unflappable *adj Informal* (of a person) not easily upset. **unflappability** *n*

unfledged *adj* **1** (of a young bird) not having developed adult feathers. **2** immature and inexperienced.

unflinching *adj* not shrinking from danger or difficulty.

unfold *vb* **1** to open or spread out from a folded state. **2** to reveal or be revealed: *a terrible truth unfolds.* **3** to develop or be developed: *the novel unfolds through their recollections.*

unforeseen *adj* surprising because not expected.

unforgettable *adj* making such a strong impression that it is impossible to forget. **unforgettably** *adv*

unforgivable *adj* too bad or cruel to be excused.

unforgiving *adj* unwilling to forgive other people's mistakes or wrongdoings.

unformed *adj* in an early stage of development; not fully developed or thought out.

unforthcoming *adj* not inclined to speak, explain, or communicate.

unfortunate *adj* **1** caused or accompanied by bad luck: *an unfortunate coincidence.* **2** having bad luck: *my unfortunate daughter.* **3** regrettable or unsuitable: *an unfortunate choice of phrase.* ~*n* **4** an unlucky person. **unfortunately** *adv*

unfounded *adj* (of ideas, fears, or allegations) not based on facts or evidence.

unfreeze *vb* **-freezing, -froze, -frozen 1** to thaw or cause to thaw. **2** to relax restrictions or controls on (trade, the transfer of money, etc.): *Congress is considering unfreezing US aid to Jordan.*

unfriendly *adj* **-lier, -liest** not friendly; hostile.

unfrock *vb* to deprive a person in holy orders of the status of a priest.

unfulfilled *adj* not satisfied.

unfurl *vb* to unroll or spread out (an umbrella, flag, or sail) or (of an umbrella, flag, or sail) to be unrolled or spread out.

unfurnished *adj* not containing any furniture.

ungainly *adj* **-lier, -liest** lacking grace when moving. **ungainliness** *n*

ungenerous *adj* **1** mean or overly thrifty. **2** (of a remark or thought) unfair or harsh.

ungodly *adj* **-lier, -liest 1** wicked or sinful. **2** *Infor-*

THESAURUS

uncommon, unknown, unusual **2. unfamiliar with** a stranger to, inexperienced in, unaccustomed to, unacquainted with, unconversant with, uninformed about, uninitiated in, unpractised in, unskilled at, unversed in

unfashionable antiquated, behind the times, dated, obsolete, old-fashioned, old hat, out, outmoded, out-of-date, out of fashion, passé, square (*informal*), unpopular

unfasten detach, disconnect, let go, loosen, open, separate, uncouple, undo, unlace, unlock, untie

unfathomable abstruse, baffling, deep, esoteric, impenetrable, incomprehensible, indecipherable, inexplicable, profound, unknowable

unfavourable inauspicious, inopportune, ominous, threatening, unlucky, unpromising, unpropitious, unseasonable, untimely, untoward

unfeeling apathetic, callous, cold, cruel, hardened, hardhearted, heartless, inhuman, insensitive, pitiless, stony, uncaring, unsympathetic

unfinished 1. deficient, half-done, imperfect, incomplete, in the making, lacking, unaccomplished, uncompleted, undone, unfulfilled, wanting **2.** bare, crude, natural, raw, rough, sketchy, unpolished, unrefined, unvarnished

unfit 1. ill-equipped, inadequate, incapable, incompetent, ineligible, no good, not cut out for, not equal to, not up to, unprepared, unqualified, untrained, useless **2.** ill-adapted, inadequate, inappropriate, ineffective, not designed, not fit, unsuitable, unsuited, useless **3.** debilitated, decrepit, feeble, flabby, in poor condition, out of shape, out of trim, unhealthy

unflappable calm, collected, composed, cool, impassive, imperturbable, level-headed, not given to worry, self-possessed, unfazed (*informal*), unruffled

unflinching bold, constant, determined, firm, immovable, resolute, stalwart, staunch, steadfast, steady, unfaltering, unshaken, unshrinking, unswerving, unwavering

unfold 1. disentangle, expand, flatten, open, spread out, straighten, stretch out, undo, unfurl, unravel, unroll, unwrap **2.** clarify, describe, disclose, divulge, explain, illustrate, make known, present, reveal, show, uncover **3.** bear fruit, blossom, develop, evolve, expand, grow, mature

unforeseen abrupt, accidental, out of the blue, startling, sudden, surprise, surprising, unanticipated, unexpected, unlooked-for, unpredicted

unforgettable exceptional, extraordinary, fixed in the mind, impressive, memorable, never to be forgotten, notable, striking

unforgivable deplorable, disgraceful, indefensible, inexcusable, shameful, unjustifiable, unpardonable, unwarrantable

unfortunate 1. adverse, calamitous, disastrous, ill-fated, ill-starred, inopportune, ruinous, unfavourable, untoward **2.** cursed, doomed, hapless, hopeless, luckless, out of luck, poor, star-crossed, unhappy, unlucky, unprosperous, unsuccessful, wretched **3.** deplorable, ill-advised, inappropriate, infelicitous, lamentable, regrettable, unbecoming, unsuitable

unfounded baseless, fabricated, false, groundless, idle, spurious, trumped up, unjustified, unproven, unsubstantiated, vain, without basis, without foundation

unfriendly aloof, antagonistic, chilly, cold, disagreeable, distant, hostile, ill-disposed, inhospitable, not on speaking terms, quarrelsome, sour, surly, uncongenial, unneighbourly, unsociable

ungainly awkward, clumsy, gangling, gawky, inelegant, loutish, lubberly, lumbering, slouching, uncoordinated, uncouth, ungraceful

ungodly 1. blasphemous, corrupt, depraved, godless, immoral, impious, irreligious, profane, sinful, vile,

mal unreasonable or outrageous: *at this ungodly hour.* **ungodliness** *n*

ungovernable *adj* **1** (of an emotion) not able to be controlled or restrained: *an ungovernable rage.* **2** (of a country or area) not able to be effectively governed, esp. because of unrest or violence: *years of religious conflict had made much of the island ungovernable.*

ungracious *adj* not polite or friendly, esp. when being offered praise or thanks.

ungrammatical *adj* not following the rules of grammar.

ungrateful *adj* not showing or offering thanks for a favour or compliment.

unguarded *adj* **1** unprotected. **2** open or frank: *one unguarded briefing.* **3** incautious or careless: *an unguarded moment.*

unguent (**ung**-gwent) *n Literary* an ointment.

ungulate (**ung**-gyew-lit) *n* a hoofed mammal.

unhallowed *adj* **1** not consecrated or holy: *unhallowed ground.* **2** sinful or wicked.

unhand *vb Old-fashioned or literary* to release from one's grasp.

unhappy *adj* **-pier, -piest 1** sad or depressed. **2** unfortunate or wretched. **unhappily** *adv* **unhappiness** *n*

unharmed *adj* not hurt or damaged in any way.

unhealthy *adj* **-healthier, -healthiest 1** likely to cause illness or poor health: *Scottish eating habits are very unhealthy.* **2** not very fit or well. **3** caused by or looking as if caused by poor health: *a thin unhealthy look about him.* **4** morbid or unwholesome: *an unhealthy interest in computer fraud.* **unhealthiness** *n*

unheard *adj* not listened to; unheeded: *all my warnings went unheard.*

unheard-of *adj* **1** without precedent: *an unheard-of phenomenon.* **2** highly offensive: *unheard-of behaviour.*

unheeded *adj* noticed but ignored: *their protests went unheeded.*

unhelpful *adj* doing nothing to improve a situation.

unheralded *adj* not announced beforehand.

unhindered *adj* **1** not prevented or obstructed: *unhindered access.* ~*adv* **2** without being prevented or obstructed: *he was able to go about his work unhindered.*

unhinge *vb* **-hinging, -hinged** to make a person mentally deranged or unbalanced. **unhinged** *adj*

unholy *adj* **-lier, -liest 1** immoral or wicked. **2** *Informal* outrageous or unnatural: *this unholy mess.* **unholiness** *n*

unhook *vb* **1** to unfasten the hooks of a garment. **2** to remove something from a hook.

unhurried *adj* done at a leisurely pace, without any rush or anxiety.

unhurt *adj* not injured in an accident, attack, etc.

unhygienic *adj* dirty and likely to cause disease or infection.

uni *n Informal* short for **university.**

uni- *combining form* of, consisting of, or having only one: *unilateral.*

unicameral *adj* of or having a single legislative chamber: *Denmark's unicameral parliament, known as the Folketing.*

UNICEF United Nations Children's Fund.

unicellular *adj* (of organisms) consisting of a single cell.

unicorn *n* a legendary creature resembling a white horse with one horn growing from its forehead.

unicycle *n* a one wheeled vehicle driven by pedals, used in a circus. **unicyclist** *n*

unidentified *adj* **1** not able to be recognized; unknown: *unidentified gunmen.* **2** anonymous or unnamed: *the house of an unidentified Scottish businessman.* **unidentifiable** *adj*

uniform *n* **1** a special identifying set of clothes for the members of an organization, such as soldiers. ~*adj* **2** regular and even throughout: *uniform consistency.* **3** alike or like: *uniform green metal filing cabinets.* **uniformity** *n* **uniformly** *adv*

THESAURUS

wicked **2.** *informal* dreadful, horrendous, intolerable, outrageous, unearthly, unholy (*informal*), unreasonable, unseemly

ungovernable rebellious, refractory, uncontrollable, unmanageable, unrestrainable, unruly, wild

ungracious bad-mannered, churlish, discourteous, ill-bred, impolite, offhand, rude, uncivil, unmannerly

ungrateful heedless, selfish, thankless, unappreciative, unmindful, unthankful

unguarded 1. defenceless, open to attack, undefended, unpatrolled, unprotected, vulnerable **2.** artless, candid, direct, frank, guileless, open, straightforward **3.** careless, foolhardy, heedless, ill-considered, impolitic, imprudent, incautious, indiscreet, rash, thoughtless, uncircumspect, undiplomatic, unthinking, unwary

unhappy 1. blue, crestfallen, dejected, depressed, despondent, disconsolate, dispirited, down, downcast, gloomy, long-faced, melancholy, miserable, mournful, sad, sorrowful **2.** cursed, hapless, ill-fated, ill-omened, luckless, unfortunate, unlucky, wretched

unharmed in one piece (*informal*), intact, safe, safe and sound, sound, undamaged, unhurt, uninjured, unscarred, unscathed, untouched, whole, without a scratch

unhealthy 1. deleterious, detrimental, harmful, insalubrious, insanitary, noisome, noxious, unwholesome **2.** ailing, delicate, feeble, frail, infirm, in poor health, invalid, poorly (*informal*), sick, sickly, unsound, unwell, weak **3.** bad, baneful (*archaic*), corrupt, corrupting, degrading, demoralizing, morbid, negative, undesirable

unheard-of 1. inconceivable, never before encountered, new, novel, singular, unbelievable, undreamed of, unexampled, unique, unprecedented, unusual **2.** disgraceful, extreme, offensive, outlandish, outrageous, preposterous, shocking, unacceptable, unthinkable

unhinge confound, confuse, craze, derange, disorder, distemper (*archaic*), drive out of one's mind, madden, unbalance, unsettle

unholy 1. base, corrupt, depraved, dishonest, evil, heinous, immoral, iniquitous, irreligious, profane, sinful, ungodly, vile, wicked **2.** *informal* appalling, awful, dreadful, horrendous, outrageous, shocking, unearthly, ungodly (*informal*), unnatural, unreasonable

unhurried calm, deliberate, easy, easy-going, leisurely, sedate, slow, slow and steady, slow-paced

unidentified anonymous, mysterious, nameless, unclassified, unfamiliar, unknown, unmarked, unnamed, unrecognized, unrevealed

unification alliance, amalgamation, coalescence, coalition, combination, confederation, federation, fusion, merger, union, uniting

uniform *n.* **1.** costume, dress, garb, habit, livery, outfit, regalia, regimentals, suit ~*adj.* **2.** consistent, constant, equable, even, regular, smooth, unbroken, unchanging, undeviating, unvarying **3.** alike, equal, identical, like, same, selfsame, similar

unify *vb* **-fies, -fying, -fied** to make or become one; unite. **unification** *n*
unilateral *adj* made or done by only one person or group: *unilateral action.* **unilateralism** *n*
unimaginable *adj* so unusual, great, or extreme that it is difficult to imagine or understand: *the unimaginable vastness of space.*
unimaginative *adj* not having or showing much imagination.
unimpeachable *adj* completely honest and reliable.
unimpeded *adj* not stopped or disrupted by anything.
unimportant *adj* trivial or insignificant.
uninhabitable *adj* not able to support human life: *an uninhabitable wasteland.*
uninhabited *adj* having no people living in or on it: *an uninhabited island.*
uninhibited *adj* behaving freely and naturally, without worrying what other people will think.
uninitiated *pl n* **the uninitiated** people who have no special knowledge or experience: *much contemporary art is baffling to the uninitiated.*
uninspired *adj* not particularly good or exciting.
uninspiring *adj* not likely to make people interested or excited.
unintelligible *adj* impossible to make out or understand; incomprehensible: *an unintelligible London accent.*
unintended *adj* (of an action or its consequences) not planned or intended: *the unintended consequences of German reunification.*
unintentional *adj* (of an action) not done deliberately; accidental: *unintentional discrimination.* **unintentionally** *adv*
uninterested *adj* having or showing no interest in someone or something.
uninteresting *adj* boring or dull.
uninterrupted *adj* continuous, with no breaks or interruptions.
uninvited *adj* **1** not having been asked: *uninvited guests.* ~*adv* **2** without having been asked: *he sat down uninvited on the side of the bed.*
union *n* **1** the act of merging two or more things to become one, or the state of being merged in such a way. **2** short for **trade union. 3** an association of individuals or groups for a common purpose: *the Scripture Union.* **4 a** an association or society: *the Students' union.* **b** the buildings of such an organization. **5** marriage or sexual intercourse. **6** *Maths* a set containing all the members of two given sets. **7** (in 19th-century England) a workhouse maintained by a number of parishes. ~*adj* **8** of a trade union.
unionism *n* **1** the principles of trade unions. **2** adherence to the principles of trade unions. **unionist** *n, adj*
Unionist *n* a supporter of union between Britain and Northern Ireland.
unionize *or* **-ise** *vb* **-izing, -ized** *or* **-ising, -ised** to organize workers into a trade union. **unionization** *or* **-isation** *n*
Union Jack *or* **Union flag** *n* the national flag of the United Kingdom, combining the crosses of Saint George, Saint Andrew, and Saint Patrick.
unique (yew-**neek**) *adj* **1** being the only one of a particular type. **2 unique to** concerning or belonging to a particular person, thing, or group: *certain dishes are unique to this restaurant.* **3** without equal or like. **4** *Informal* remarkable. **uniquely** *adv*
➤ Because of its meaning, avoid using *unique* with modifiers like *very* and *rather.*
unisex *adj* (of clothing, a hairstyle, or hairdressers) designed for both sexes.
unisexual *adj* **1** of one sex only. **2** (of an organism) having either male or female reproductive organs but not both.
unison *n* **1 in unison** at the same time as another person or other people: *smiling and nodding in unison.*

THESAURUS

uniformity constancy, evenness, homogeneity, invariability, regularity, sameness, similarity
unify amalgamate, bind, bring together, combine, confederate, consolidate, federate, fuse, join, merge, unite
unimaginable beyond one's wildest dreams, fantastic, impossible, inconceivable, incredible, indescribable, ineffable, mind-boggling (*informal*), unbelievable, unheard-of, unthinkable
unimaginative banal, barren, commonplace, derivative, dry, dull, hackneyed, lifeless, matter-of-fact, ordinary, pedestrian, predictable, prosaic, routine, tame, uncreative, uninspired, unoriginal, unromantic, usual
unimpeachable above reproach, beyond criticism, beyond question, blameless, faultless, impeccable, irreproachable, perfect, unassailable, unblemished, unchallengeable, unexceptionable, unquestionable
unimportant immaterial, inconsequential, insignificant, irrelevant, low-ranking, minor, nickel-and-dime (*U.S. slang*), not worth mentioning, nugatory, of no account, of no consequence, of no moment, paltry, petty, slight, trifling, trivial, worthless
uninhabited abandoned, barren, desert, deserted, desolate, empty, unoccupied, unpopulated, unsettled, untenanted, vacant, waste
uninhibited candid, frank, free, free and easy, informal, instinctive, liberated, natural, open, relaxed, spontaneous, unrepressed, unreserved, unselfconscious
uninspired banal, commonplace, dull, humdrum, indifferent, ordinary, prosaic, stale, stock, unexciting, unimaginative, uninspiring, uninteresting, unoriginal
unintelligent braindead (*informal*), brainless, dense, dozy (*Brit. informal*), dull, dumb, empty-headed, foolish, gormless (*Brit. informal*), obtuse, slow, stupid, thick, unreasoning, unthinking
unintelligible double Dutch (*Brit. informal*), illegible, inarticulate, incoherent, incomprehensible, indecipherable, indistinct, jumbled, meaningless, muddled, unfathomable
unintentional accidental, casual, fortuitous, inadvertent, involuntary, unconscious, undesigned, unintended, unpremeditated, unthinking, unwitting
uninterested apathetic, blasé, bored, distant, impassive, incurious, indifferent, listless, unconcerned, uninvolved, unresponsive
uninteresting boring, commonplace, drab, dreary, dry, dull, flat, ho-hum (*informal*), humdrum, mind-numbing, monotonous, tedious, tiresome, unenjoyable, uneventful, unexciting, uninspiring, wearisome
uninterrupted constant, continual, continuous, nonstop, peaceful, steady, sustained, unbroken, undisturbed, unending
uninvited not asked, not invited, unasked, unbidden, unwanted, unwelcome
union 1. amalgam, amalgamation, blend, combination, conjunction, fusion, junction, mixture, synthesis, uniting **2.** alliance, association, coalition, confederacy, confederation, federation, league **3.** coition, coitus, copulation, coupling, intercourse, marriage, matrimony, nookie (*slang*), rumpy-pumpy (*slang*), the other (*informal*), wedlock
unique 1. lone, one and only, only, single, solitary, sui

2 complete agreement: *to act in unison.* 3 *Music* a style, technique, or passage in which all the performers sing or play the same notes at the same time.

Unison *n* a British trade union consisting mainly of council and hospital workers.

unit *n* 1 a single undivided entity or whole. 2 a group or individual regarded as a basic element of a larger whole: *the clan was the basic unit of Highland society.* 3 a mechanical part or small device that does a particular job: *a waste disposal unit.* 4 a team of people that performs a specific function, and often also their buildings and equipment: *a combat unit.* 5 a standard amount of a physical quantity, such as length or energy, used to express magnitudes of that quantity: *the year as a unit of time.* 6 *Maths* the digit or position immediately to the left of the decimal point. 7 a piece of furniture designed to be fitted with other similar pieces: *bedroom units.* 8 *Austral & NZ* short for **home unit.**

Unitarian *n* 1 a person who believes that God is one being and rejects the Trinity. *~adj* 2 of Unitarians or Unitarianism. **Unitarianism** *n*

unitary *adj* 1 consisting of a single undivided whole: *a unitary state.* 2 of a unit or units.

unit cost *n* the actual cost of producing one article.

unite *vb* **uniting, united** 1 to make or become an integrated whole: *conception occurs when a sperm unites with the egg.* 2 to form an association or alliance: *the opposition parties united to fight against privatisation.* 3 to possess (a combination of qualities) at the same time: *he manages to unite charm and ruthlessness.*

united *adj* 1 produced by two or more people or things in combination: *a united effort.* 2 in agreement: *we are united in our opposition to these proposals.* 3 in association or alliance.

United Kingdom *n* a kingdom of NW Europe, consisting of the island of Great Britain together with Northern Ireland.

United Nations *n* an international organization of independent states, formed to promote peace and international security.

unit price *n* the price charged per unit.

unit trust *n Brit* an investment trust that issues units for public sale and invests the money in many different businesses.

unity *n, pl* **-ties** 1 the state of being one. 2 mutual agreement: *unity of intention.* 3 the state of being a single thing that is composed of separate parts, organizations, etc.: *moves towards church unity.* 4 *Maths* the number or numeral one.

Univ. University.

univalent *adj Chem* same as **monovalent.**

universal *adj* 1 of or relating to everyone in the world or everyone in a particular place or society: *the introduction of universal primary education.* 2 of, relating to, or affecting the entire world or universe: *the universal laws of physics.* 3 true and relevant at all times and in all situations: *there may be no single universal solution.* *~n* 4 something which exists or is true in all places and all situations: *universals such as beauty and justice.* **universality** *n* **universally** *adv*

universal joint *or* **coupling** *n* a form of coupling between two rotating shafts allowing freedom of movement in all directions.

universe *n* 1 the whole of all existing matter, energy, and space. 2 the world.

university *n, pl* **-ties** 1 an institution of higher education with authority to award degrees. 2 the buildings, members, staff, or campus of a university.

Unix (**yew**-nicks) *n Trademark* an operating system found on many types of computer.

unjust *adj* not fair or just.

unjustifiable *adj* inexcusably wrong or unfair.

unjustified *adj* not necessary or reasonable.

unkempt *adj* 1 (of the hair) uncombed or dishevelled. 2 untidy or slovenly: *an unkempt appearance.*

unkind *adj* unsympathetic or cruel. **unkindly** *adv* **unkindness** *n*

unknowing *adj* unaware or ignorant: *unknowing victims of fraud.*

unknown *adj* 1 not known, understood, or recognized. 2 not famous: *a young and then unknown actor.* 3 **unknown quantity** a person or thing whose action or effect is unknown or unpredictable. *~n* 4 an unknown person, quantity, or thing. *~adv* 5 **unknown to someone** without someone being aware: *unknown to him, the starboard engine had dropped off.*

unlawful *adj* not permitted by law; illegal.

unleaded *adj* (of petrol) containing less tetraethyl lead, in order to reduce environmental pollution.

unlearn *vb* **-learning, -learnt** *or* **-learned** to try to

THESAURUS

generis 2. incomparable, inimitable, matchless, nonpareil, peerless, unequalled, unexampled, unmatched, unparalleled, unrivalled, without equal

unison accord, accordance, agreement, concert, concord, cooperation, harmony, unanimity, unity

unit 1. assembly, detachment, entity, group, section, system, whole 2. component, constituent, element, item, member, module, part, piece, portion, section, segment 3. measure, measurement, module, quantity

unite 1. amalgamate, blend, coalesce, combine, confederate, consolidate, couple, fuse, incorporate, join, link, marry, meld, merge, unify, wed 2. ally, associate, band, close ranks, club together, cooperate, join forces, join together, league, pool, pull together

united 1. affiliated, allied, banded together, collective, combined, concerted, in partnership, leagued, pooled, unified 2. agreed, in accord, in agreement, like-minded, of like mind, of one mind, of the same opinion, one, unanimous

unity 1. entity, integrity, oneness, singleness, undividedness, unification, union, wholeness 2. accord, agreement, assent, concord, concurrence, consensus, harmony, peace, solidarity, unanimity, unison

universal all-embracing, catholic, common, ecumenical, entire, general, omnipresent, total, unlimited, whole, widespread, worldwide

universality all-inclusiveness, completeness, comprehensiveness, entirety, generality, generalization, totality, ubiquity

universally always, everywhere, in all cases, in every instance, invariably, uniformly, without exception

universe cosmos, creation, everything, macrocosm, nature, the natural world

unjust biased, inequitable, one sided, partial, partisan, prejudiced, undeserved, unfair, unjustified, unmerited, wrong, wrongful

unjustifiable indefensible, inexcusable, outrageous, unacceptable, unforgivable, unjust, unpardonable, unwarrantable, wrong

unkind cruel, hardhearted, harsh, inconsiderate, inhuman, insensitive, malicious, mean, nasty, spiteful, thoughtless, uncaring, uncharitable, unchristian, unfeeling, unfriendly, unsympathetic

unknown 1. alien, concealed, dark, hidden, mysterious, new, secret, strange, unrecognized, unrevealed, untold 2. humble, little known, obscure, undistinguished, unfamiliar, unheard-of, unrenowned, unsung

forget something learnt or to discard accumulated knowledge.

unlearned (un-**lurn**-id) *adj* ignorant or uneducated.

unlearnt *or* **unlearned** *adj* **1** denoting knowledge or skills innately present rather than learnt. **2** not learnt or taken notice of: *unlearnt lessons.*

unleash *vb* to set loose or cause (something bad): *to unleash war.*

unleavened (un-**lev**-vend) *adj* (of bread) made without yeast or leavening.

unless *conj* except under the circumstances that; except on the condition that: *you can't get in unless you can prove you're over eighteen.*

unlettered *adj* uneducated or illiterate.

unlike *adj* **1** not similar; different. *~prep* **2** not like or typical of: *unlike his elder brother, he did not go to Oxford.* **unlikeness** *n*

unlikely *adj* not likely; improbable. **unlikeliness** *n*

unlimited *adj* **1** apparently endless: *there was unlimited coffee.* **2** not restricted or limited: *unlimited access to the rest of the palace.*

unlisted *adj* **1** not entered on a list. **2** (of securities) not quoted on a stock exchange.

unlit *adj* **1** (of a fire, cigarette, etc.) not lit and therefore not burning. **2** (of a road) not having any streetlights switched on.

unload *vb* **1** to remove cargo from a ship, lorry, or plane. **2** to express worries or problems by telling someone about them. **3** to remove the ammunition from a gun.

unlock *vb* **1** to unfasten a lock or door. **2** to release or let loose: *the revelation unlocked a flood of tears.*

unlooked-for *adj* unexpected or unforeseen.

unloose *or* **unloosen** *vb* **-loosing, -loosed** *or* **-loosening, -loosened** to set free or release.

unlovable *adj* too unpleasant or unattractive to be loved.

unloved *adj* not loved by anyone.

unlovely *adj* unpleasant in appearance or character.

unlucky *adj* **1** having bad luck or misfortune: *an unlucky man.* **2** caused by bad luck or misfortune: *an unlucky coincidence.* **3** regarded as likely to bring about bad luck: *an unlucky number.* **unluckily** *adv*

unmade *adj* **1** (of a bed) with the bedclothes not smoothed and tidied. **2** (of a road) not surfaced with tarmac. **3** not yet made.

unmake *vb* **-making, -made** to undo or destroy.

unman *vb* **-manning, -manned 1** to cause to lose courage or nerve. **2** to make effeminate.

unmanageable *adj* difficult to use, deal with, or control, esp. because it is too big.

unmanly *adj* **1** not masculine or virile. **2** cowardly or dishonourable.

unmanned *adj* **1** having no personnel or crew: *the border posts were unmanned.* **2** (of an aircraft or spacecraft) operated by automatic or remote control.

unmannerly *adj* lacking manners; discourteous. **unmannerliness** *n*

unmarked *adj* **1** having no signs of damage or injury. **2** not having any identifying signs or markings: *an unmarked police car.*

unmarried *adj* not married.

unmask *vb* **1** to remove the mask or disguise from. **2** to expose or reveal the true nature or character of.

unmatched *adj* **1** not equalled or surpassed: *his pace is unmatched by any other modern player.* **2** not coordinated or forming a set with anything else: *three unmatched chairs.*

unmentionable *adj* unsuitable as a topic of conversation.

unmercifully *adv* excessively and relentlessly: *the young boy is hounded unmercifully.*

unmistakable *or* **unmistakeable** *adj* clear or unambiguous. **unmistakably** *or* **unmistakeably** *adv*

unmitigated *adj* **1** not reduced or lessened in severity or intensity. **2** total and complete: *unmitigated boredom.*

THESAURUS

unlawful actionable, against the law, banned, criminal, forbidden, illegal, illegitimate, illicit, outlawed, prohibited, unauthorized, under-the-table, unlicensed

unlettered ignorant, illiterate, uneducated, unlearned, unschooled, untaught, untutored

unlike contrasted, different, dissimilar, distinct, divergent, diverse, ill-matched, incompatible, not alike, opposite, unequal, unrelated

unlikely doubtful, faint, improbable, not likely, remote, slight, unimaginable

unlimited 1. boundless, countless, endless, extensive, great, illimitable, immeasurable, immense, incalculable, infinite, limitless, unbounded, vast **2.** absolute, all-encompassing, complete, full, total, unconditional, unconstrained, unfettered, unqualified, unrestricted

unload disburden, discharge, dump, empty, lighten, off-load, relieve, unburden, unlade, unpack

unlock free, let loose, open, release, unbar, unbolt, undo, unfasten, unlatch

unlooked-for chance, fortuitous, out of the blue, surprise, surprising, unanticipated, undreamed of, unexpected, unforeseen, unhoped-for, unpredicted, unthought-of

unloved disliked, forsaken, loveless, neglected, rejected, spurned, uncared-for, uncherished, unpopular, unwanted

unlucky 1. cursed, disastrous, hapless, luckless, miserable, unfortunate, unhappy, unsuccessful, wretched **2.** doomed, ill-fated, ill-omened, ill-starred, inauspicious, ominous, unfavourable, untimely

unmanageable awkward, bulky, cumbersome, difficult to handle, inconvenient, unhandy, unwieldy

unmannerly badly behaved, bad-mannered, discourteous, disrespectful, ill-bred, ill-mannered, impolite, misbehaved, rude, uncivil, uncouth

unmarried bachelor, celibate, maiden, single, unattached, unwed, unwedded, virgin

unmask bare, bring to light, disclose, discover, expose, lay bare, reveal, show up, uncloak, uncover, unveil

unmatched beyond compare, consummate, incomparable, matchless, paramount, peerless, second to none, supreme, unequalled, unparalleled, unrivalled, unsurpassed

unmentionable disgraceful, disreputable, forbidden, frowned on, immodest, indecent, obscene, scandalous, shameful, shocking, taboo, unspeakable, unutterable

unmistakable *or* **unmistakeable** blatant, certain, clear, conspicuous, decided, distinct, evident, glaring, indisputable, manifest, obvious, palpable, patent, plain, positive, pronounced, sure, unambiguous, unequivocal

unmitigated 1. grim, harsh, intense, oppressive, persistent, relentless, unabated, unalleviated, unbroken, undiminished, unmodified, unqualified, unredeemed, unrelieved **2.** absolute, arrant, complete, consummate, deep-dyed (*usually derogatory*), downright,

unmolested *adv* without disturbance or interference: *the enemy aircraft passed overhead unmolested.*
unmoved *adj* not affected by emotion; indifferent.
unmoving *adj* still and motionless.
unmusical *adj* **1** (of a person) unable to appreciate or play music. **2** (of a sound) harsh and unpleasant.
unnamed *adj* **1** not mentioned by name; anonymous: *an unnamed government spokesman.* **2** not known or described clearly enough to be named: *unnamed fears.*
unnatural *adj* **1** strange and slightly frightening because it is not usual; abnormal: *an unnatural silence.* **2** not in accordance with accepted standards of behaviour: *an unnatural relationship.* **3** affected or forced: *a determined smile which seemed unnatural.* **4** inhuman or monstrous: *unnatural evils.* **unnaturally** *adv*
unnecessary *adj* not essential, or more than is essential. **unnecessarily** *adv*
unnerve *vb* **-nerving, -nerved** to cause to lose courage, confidence, or self-control. **unnerving** *adj*
unnil- *prefix Chem* denoting an element with an atomic number greater than 100, for example **unnilquadium** is element 104.
unnoticed *adj* without being seen or noticed.
unnumbered *adj* **1** countless; too many to count. **2** not counted or given a number.
UNO United Nations Organization.
unobtainable *adj* impossible to get.
unobtrusive *adj* not drawing attention to oneself or itself; inconspicuous.
unoccupied *adj* **1** (of a building) without occupants. **2** unemployed or idle. **3** (of an area or country) not overrun by foreign troops.
unofficial *adj* **1** not authorized or approved by the relevant organization or person: *an unofficial strike.* **2** not confirmed officially: *unofficial reports of the minister's resignation.*
unorganized *or* **-nised** *adj* **1** not arranged into an organized system. **2** (of workers) not unionized.
unorthodox *adj* **1** (of ideas, methods, etc.) unconventional and not generally accepted. **2** (of a person) not conventional in beliefs, behaviour, etc.
unpack *vb* **1** to remove the packed contents of a case. **2** to take something out of a packed container.
unpaid *adj* **1** without a salary or wage: *unpaid overtime.* **2** still to be paid: *unpaid bills.*
unpalatable *adj* **1** (of food) unpleasant to taste. **2** (of a fact, idea, etc.) unpleasant and hard to accept.
unparalleled *adj* not equalled; supreme.
unpardonable *adj* unforgivably wrong or rude.
unparliamentary *adj* not consistent with parliamentary procedure or practice.
unperson *n* a person whose existence is officially denied or ignored.
unpick *vb* to undo the stitches of a piece of sewing.
unpin *vb* **-pinning, -pinned 1** to remove a pin or pins from. **2** to unfasten by removing pins.
unplanned *adj* not intentional or deliberate.
unplayable *adj Sport* **1** (of a ball) thrown too fast or too skilfully to be hit. **2** (of a pitch or course) too badly affected by rain or frost to be used.
unpleasant *adj* not pleasant or agreeable. **unpleasantly** *adv* **unpleasantness** *n*
unplug *vb* **-plugging, -plugged** to disconnect a piece of electrical equipment by taking the plug out of the socket.
unplumbed *adj* **1** not measured. **2** not understood in depth.
unpolished *adj* **1** not polished. **2** not elegant or refined.
unpopular *adj* generally disliked or disapproved of. **unpopularity** *n*

THESAURUS

out-and-out, outright, perfect, rank, sheer, thorough, thoroughgoing, total, utter
unmoved cold, dry-eyed, impassive, indifferent, unaffected, unfeeling, unimpressed, unresponsive, unstirred, untouched
unnatural 1. bizarre, extraordinary, freakish, outlandish, queer, strange, supernatural, unaccountable, uncanny **2.** aberrant, abnormal, anomalous, irregular, odd, perverse, perverted, unusual **3.** affected, artificial, assumed, contrived, factitious, false, feigned, forced, insincere, laboured, mannered, phoney *or* phony (*informal*), self-conscious, stagy, stiff, stilted, strained, studied, theatrical **4.** brutal, callous, cold-blooded, evil, fiendish, heartless, inhuman, monstrous, ruthless, savage, unfeeling, wicked
unnecessary dispensable, expendable, inessential, needless, nonessential, redundant, supererogatory, superfluous, surplus to requirements, uncalled-for, unneeded, unrequired, useless
unnerve confound, daunt, demoralize, disarm, disconcert, discourage, dishearten, dismay, dispirit, faze, fluster, frighten, intimidate, psych out (*informal*), rattle (*informal*), shake, throw off balance, unhinge, unman, upset
unnoticed disregarded, ignored, neglected, overlooked, undiscovered, unheeded, unobserved, unperceived, unrecognized, unremarked, unseen
unobtrusive humble, inconspicuous, keeping a low profile, low-key, meek, modest, quiet, restrained, retiring, self-effacing, subdued, unassuming, unnoticeable, unostentatious, unpretentious
unoccupied 1. empty, tenantless, uninhabited, untenanted, vacant **2.** at leisure, disengaged, idle, inactive, unemployed
unofficial informal, personal, private, unauthorized, unconfirmed, wildcat
unorthodox abnormal, heterodox, irregular, off-the-wall (*slang*), unconventional, uncustomary, unusual, unwonted
unpaid 1. honorary, unsalaried, voluntary **2.** due, not discharged, outstanding, overdue, owing, payable, unsettled
unpalatable bitter, disagreeable, displeasing, distasteful, horrid, offensive, repugnant, unappetizing, unattractive, uneatable, unpleasant, unsavoury
unparalleled beyond compare, consummate, exceptional, incomparable, matchless, peerless, rare, singular, superlative, supreme, unequalled, unique, unmatched, unprecedented, unrivalled, unsurpassed, without equal
unpardonable deplorable, disgraceful, indefensible, inexcusable, outrageous, scandalous, shameful, unforgivable, unjustifiable
unpleasant abhorrent, bad, disagreeable, displeasing, distasteful, horrid, ill-natured, irksome, nasty, objectionable, obnoxious, repulsive, troublesome, unattractive, unlikable *or* unlikeable, unlovely, unpalatable
unpopular avoided, detested, disliked, not sought out, out in the cold, out of favour, rejected, shunned, unattractive, undesirable, unloved, unwanted, unwelcome
unprecedented abnormal, exceptional, extraordinary, freakish, new, novel, original, remarkable, singu-

unpractised *or US* **unpracticed** *adj* not experienced or skilled: *an unpractised surgical technique.*

unprecedented *adj* never having happened before; unparalleled.

unpredictable *adj* not easy to predict or foresee.

unprejudiced *adj* free from bias; impartial.

unprepared *adj* surprised or put at a disadvantage by something because you are not ready to deal with it.

unprepossessing *adj* not very attractive or appealing.

unpretentious *adj* modest, unassuming, and down-to-earth.

unprincipled *adj* lacking moral principles; unscrupulous.

unprintable *adj* unsuitable for printing for reasons of obscenity, libel, or indecency.

unproductive *adj* not producing any worthwhile results.

unprofessional *adj* not behaving according to the standards expected of a member of a particular profession.

unprofitable *adj* 1 not making a profit. 2 not producing any worthwhile results: *an unprofitable line of thinking.*

unpromising *adj* not likely to turn out well.

unprompted *adj* doing without being urged by anyone else; spontaneous.

unpronounceable *adj* (of a name or word) too difficult to say.

unprotected *adj* not defended or protected from harm.

unprovoked *adj* carried out without any cause or reason: *an unprovoked attack.*

unpunished *adj* without suffering or resulting in a penalty: *the guilty must not go unpunished; such crimes should not remain unpunished.*

unputdownable *adj* (of a book, usually a novel) so gripping that one wants to read it at one sitting.

unqualified *adj* **1** lacking the necessary qualifications. **2** having no conditions or limitations: *an unqualified denial.* **3** total or complete: *unqualified admiration.*

unquestionable *adj* not to be doubted; indisputable. **unquestionably** *adv*

unquestioned *adj* accepted by everyone without doubt or disagreement: *an engineer of unquestioned genius.*

unquestioning *adj* accepting a belief or order without thinking about or doubting it in any way: *unquestioning obedience.* **unquestioningly** *adv*

unquiet *adj Chiefly literary* anxious or uneasy.

unquote *interj* an expression used to indicate the end of a quotation that was introduced with the word "quote".

unravel *vb* **-elling, -elled** *or US* **-eling, -eled 1** to separate something knitted or woven into individual strands. **2** to become separated into individual strands. **3** to explain or solve: *we unravelled the secrets.*

unread *adj* **1** (of a book or article) not yet read. **2** (of a person) having read little.

unreadable *adj* **1** unable to be read or deciphered; illegible. **2** too difficult or dull to read.

unreal *adj* **1** existing only in the imagination or giving the impression of doing so: *an unreal quality.* **2** insincere or artificial. **unreality** *n*

unrealistic *adj* **1** not accepting the facts of a situation and not dealing with them in a practical way: *he had unrealistic expectations of his son.* **2** not true to life: *an unrealistic portrayal of Scottish life.* **unrealistically** *adv*

unreasonable *adj* **1** unfair and excessive: *an unreasonable request.* **2** refusing to listen to reason. **unreasonably** *adv*

THESAURUS

lar, unexampled, unheard-of, unparalleled, unrivalled, unusual

unpredictable chance, changeable, doubtful, erratic, fickle, fluky (*informal*), iffy (*informal*), inconstant, random, unforeseeable, unreliable, unstable, variable

unprejudiced balanced, even-handed, fair, fair-minded, impartial, just, nonpartisan, objective, open-minded, unbiased, uninfluenced

unprepared caught napping, caught on the hop (*Brit. informal*), surprised, taken aback, taken off guard, unaware, unready, unsuspecting

unpretentious down-to-earth, homely, honest, humble, modest, plain, simple, straightforward, unaffected, unassuming, unimposing, unobtrusive, unostentatious, unspoiled

unprincipled amoral, corrupt, crooked, deceitful, devious, dishonest, immoral, tricky, unconscionable, underhand, unethical, unprofessional, unscrupulous

unproductive bootless, fruitless, futile, idle, ineffective, inefficacious, otiose, unavailing, unprofitable, unremunerative, unrewarding, useless, vain, valueless, worthless

unprofessional amateur, amateurish, cowboy (*informal*), improper, incompetent, inefficient, inexperienced, inexpert, lax, negligent, slapdash, slipshod, unethical, unfitting, unseemly, untrained, unworthy

unpromising adverse, discouraging, doubtful, gloomy, inauspicious, infelicitous, ominous, unfavourable, unpropitious

unprotected defenceless, exposed, helpless, naked, open, open to attack, pregnable, unarmed, undefended, unguarded, unsheltered, unshielded, vulnerable

unqualified **1.** ill-equipped, incapable, incompetent, ineligible, not equal to, not up to, unfit, unprepared **2.** categorical, downright, outright, unconditional, unmitigated, unreserved, unrestricted, without reservation **3.** absolute, arrant, complete, consummate, deep-dyed (*usually derogatory*), downright, out-and-out, outright, thorough, thoroughgoing, total, utter

unquestionable absolute, beyond a shadow of doubt, certain, clear, conclusive, definite, faultless, flawless, incontestable, incontrovertible, indisputable, indubitable, irrefutable, manifest, patent, perfect, self-evident, sure, undeniable, unequivocal, unmistakable

unravel **1.** disentangle, extricate, free, separate, straighten out, undo, unknot, untangle, unwind **2.** clear up, explain, figure out (*informal*), get straight, get to the bottom of, interpret, make out, puzzle out, resolve, solve, suss (out) (*slang*), work out

unreadable **1.** crabbed, illegible, undecipherable **2.** badly written, dry as dust, heavy going, turgid

unreal **1.** chimerical, dreamlike, fabulous, fanciful, fictitious, hypothetical, illusory, imaginary, immaterial, impalpable, insubstantial, intangible, make-believe, mythical, nebulous, phantasmagoric, storybook, visionary **2.** artificial, fake, false, insincere, mock, ostensible, pretended, seeming, sham

unrealistic **1.** half-baked (*informal*), impracticable, impractical, improbable, quixotic, romantic, starry-eyed, theoretical, unworkable **2.** non-naturalistic, unauthentic, unlifelike, unreal

unreasonable **1.** excessive, exorbitant, extortion-

unreasoning *adj* not controlled by reason; irrational.
unrecognizable *or* **-isable** *adj* changed or damaged so much that it is hard to recognize.
unrecognized *or* **-ised** *adj* not properly identified or acknowledged: *her talents went unrecognized during her lifetime.*
unregenerate *adj* unrepentant or unreformed.
unrelated *adj* not connected with each other: *a series of unrelated mishaps.*
unrelenting *adj* **1** refusing to relent or take pity. **2** not diminishing in determination, effort, or force.
unreliable *adj* not able to be trusted or relied on.
unremitting *adj* never slackening or stopping.
unrepentant *adj* not ashamed of one's beliefs or actions.
unrequited *adj* (of love) not returned.
unreserved *adj* **1** complete and without holding back any doubts: *unreserved support.* **2** open and forthcoming in manner. **3** not booked or not able to be booked: *all the seats are unreserved.* **unreservedly** (un-riz-**zerv**-id-lee) *adv*
unresolved *adj* not satisfactorily solved or concluded: *the mystery of her death remains unresolved.*
unresponsive *adj* not reacting or responding.
unrest *n* **1** a rebellious state of discontent. **2** an uneasy or troubled state.
unrestrained *adj* not controlled or limited: *the unrestrained use of state power.*
unrestricted *adj* not limited by any laws or rules.
unrewarding *adj* not giving any satisfaction.
unrighteous *adj* sinful or wicked.
unripe *adj* not fully matured.
unrivalled *or US* **unrivaled** *adj* having no equal; matchless.
unroll *vb* **1** to open out or unwind: *I unrolled the map.* **2** (of a series of events or period of time) to happen or be revealed or remembered one after the other.
unruffled *adj* **1** calm and unperturbed. **2** smooth and still: *unruffled ponds.*
unruly *adj* **-lier, -liest** difficult to control or organize; disobedient or undisciplined. **unruliness** *n*
unsaddle *vb* **-dling, -dled 1** to remove the saddle from a horse. **2** to cause to fall or dismount from a horse.
unsafe *adj* dangerous.
unsaid *adj* not said or expressed.
unsaleable *adj* unable to be sold.
unsatisfactory *adj* not good enough.
unsaturated *adj* **1** *Chem* (of an organic compound) containing a double or triple bond and therefore capable of combining with other substances. **2** (of a fat, esp. a vegetable fat) containing a high proportion of fatty acids with double bonds.
unsavoury *or US* **unsavory** *adj* objectionable or distasteful.
unscathed *adj* not harmed or injured.
unscheduled *adj* not planned or intended.
unscramble *vb* **-bling, -bled 1** to sort out something confused or disorderly. **2** to restore a scrambled message to an intelligible form. **unscrambler** *n*
unscrew *vb* **1** to loosen a screw or lid by turning it. **2** to unfasten something by removing the screws which fasten it: *the mirror had been unscrewed and removed.*
unscripted *adj* spoken without a previously prepared text.
unscrupulous *adj* prepared to act in a dishonest or immoral manner.
unseasonable *adj* **1** (of the weather) inappropriate for the season. **2** inappropriate or unusual for the time of year: *an unseasonable dip in the sea.*
unseat *vb* **1** to throw or displace from a seat or saddle. **2** to depose from office or position.
unseeded *adj* (of a player in a sport) not given a top player's position in the opening rounds of a tournament.

THESAURUS

ate, extravagant, immoderate, steep (*informal*), too great, uncalled-for, undue, unfair, unjust, unwarranted **2.** arbitrary, biased, blinkered, capricious, erratic, headstrong, inconsistent, opinionated, quirky
unregenerate godless, impious, profane, sinful, unconverted, unreformed, unrepentant, wicked
unrelated different, dissimilar, not kin, not kindred, not related, unconnected, unlike
unreliable deceptive, delusive, disreputable, erroneous, fake, fallible, false, implausible, inaccurate, irresponsible, mistaken, not conscientious, specious, treacherous, uncertain, unconvincing, undependable, unsound, unstable, untrustworthy
unrepentant abandoned, callous, hardened, impenitent, incorrigible, not contrite, obdurate, shameless, unregenerate, unremorseful, unrepenting
unreserved 1. absolute, complete, entire, full, total, unconditional, unlimited, unqualified, wholehearted, without reservation **2.** demonstrative, extrovert, forthright, frank, free, open, open-hearted, outgoing, outspoken, uninhibited, unrestrained, unreticent
unresolved doubtful, moot, open to question, pending, problematical, unanswered, undecided, undetermined, unsettled, unsolved, up in the air, vague, yet to be decided
unrest 1. agitation, disaffection, discontent, discord, dissatisfaction, dissension, protest, rebellion, sedition, strife, tumult, turmoil, upheaval **2.** agitation, anxiety, disquiet, distress, perturbation, restlessness, trepidation, uneasiness, worry
unrestrained abandoned, boisterous, free, immoderate, inordinate, intemperate, natural, unbounded, unbridled, unchecked, unconstrained, uncontrolled, unhindered, uninhibited, unrepressed
unrestricted absolute, free, free-for-all (*informal*), freewheeling (*informal*), open, unbounded, uncircumscribed, unhindered, unlimited, unregulated
unrivalled beyond compare, incomparable, matchless, nonpareil, peerless, supreme, unequalled, unexcelled, unmatched, unparalleled, unsurpassed, without equal
unruly disobedient, disorderly, fractious, headstrong, insubordinate, intractable, lawless, mutinous, obstreperous, rebellious, refractory, riotous, rowdy, turbulent, uncontrollable, ungovernable, unmanageable, wayward, wild, wilful
unsafe dangerous, hazardous, insecure, perilous, precarious, risky, threatening, treacherous, uncertain, unreliable, unsound, unstable
unsaid left to the imagination, tacit, undeclared, unexpressed, unspoken, unstated, unuttered, unvoiced
unsatisfactory deficient, disappointing, displeasing, inadequate, insufficient, mediocre, not good enough, not up to par, not up to scratch (*informal*), pathetic, poor, unacceptable, unsuitable, unworthy, weak
unsavoury distasteful, nasty, objectionable, obnoxious, offensive, repellent, repugnant, repulsive, revolting, unpleasant
unscrupulous conscienceless, corrupt, crooked (*informal*), dishonest, dishonourable, exploitative, immoral, improper, knavish, roguish, ruthless, unconscientious, unconscionable, unethical, unprincipled

unseeing *adj* not noticing or looking at anything: *staring with unseeing eyes.*

unseemly *adj* not according to expected standards of behaviour. **unseemliness** *n*

unseen *adj* **1** hidden or invisible: *an unseen organist was practising.* **2** mysterious or supernatural: *unseen powers.* ~*adv* **3** without being seen; unnoticed: *the thief entered unseen.* ~*n* **4** a passage which is given to students for translation without them having seen it in advance.

unselfish *adj* concerned about other people's wishes and needs rather than one's own. **unselfishly** *adv* **unselfishness** *n*

unsettle *vb* **-tling, -tled 1** to change or become changed from a fixed or settled condition. **2** to confuse or agitate a person or the mind.

unsettled *adj* **1** lacking order or stability: *an unsettled time.* **2** disturbed and restless: *your child will feel unsettled and insecure.* **3** constantly changing or moving from place to place: *his wandering unsettled life.* **4** (of an argument or dispute) not resolved. **5** (of a debt or bill) not yet paid.

unshakable *or* **unshakeable** *adj* (of beliefs) utterly firm and unwavering.

unshaken *adj* (of faith or feelings) not having been weakened.

unshaven *adj* (of a man who does not have a beard) having stubble on his chin because he has not shaved recently.

unsheathe *vb* **-sheathing, -sheathed** to pull a weapon from a sheath.

unshockable *adj* not likely to be upset by anything seen, heard, or read.

unsightly *adj* unpleasant to look at; ugly. **unsightliness** *n*

unsigned *adj* (of a letter etc.) anonymous.

unskilled *adj* not having or requiring any special skill or training.

unsociable *adj* (of a person) not fond of the company of other people.

unsocial *adj* **1** not fond of the company of other people. **2** (of the hours of work of a job) falling outside the normal working day.

unsolicited *adj* given or sent without being asked for: *unsolicited advice; unsolicited junk mail.*

unsophisticated *adj* **1** (of a person) lacking experience or worldly wisdom. **2** lacking refinement or complexity: *unsophisticated fighter aircraft.*

unsound *adj* **1** unhealthy or unstable: *of unsound mind.* **2** based on faulty ideas: *unsound judgment.* **3** not firm: *unsound foundations.* **4** not financially reliable: *his business plan was unsound.*

unsparing *adj* **1** very generous; lavish. **2** harsh or severe. **unsparingly** *adv*

unspeakable *adj* **1** incapable of expression in words: *unspeakable gratitude.* **2** indescribably bad or evil: *unspeakable atrocities.* **unspeakably** *adv*

unspoiled *adj* **1** not damaged or harmed. **2** (of a place) attractive and not having changed for a long time.

unspoken *adj* not openly expressed: *unspoken fears; an unspoken agreement.*

unsporting *adj* not following the principles of fair play.

unstable *adj* **1** not firmly fixed and likely to wobble or fall: *an unstable pile of books.* **2** likely to change

THESAURUS

unseat 1. throw, unhorse, unsaddle **2.** depose, dethrone, discharge, dismiss, displace, oust, overthrow, remove

unseemly discreditable, disreputable, improper, inappropriate, indecorous, indelicate, in poor taste, out of keeping, out of place, unbecoming, unbefitting, undignified, unrefined, unsuitable

unseen concealed, hidden, invisible, lurking, obscure, undetected, unnoticed, unobserved, unobtrusive, unperceived, veiled

unselfish altruistic, charitable, devoted, disinterested, generous, humanitarian, kind, liberal, magnanimous, noble, self-denying, selfless, self-sacrificing

unsettle agitate, bother, confuse, discompose, disconcert, disorder, disturb, faze, fluster, perturb, rattle (*informal*), ruffle, throw (*informal*), throw into confusion (disorder, uproar), throw off balance, trouble, unbalance, unnerve, upset

unsettled 1. disorderly, insecure, shaky, unstable, unsteady **2.** agitated, anxious, confused, disturbed, flustered, on edge, perturbed, restive, restless, shaken, tense, troubled, uneasy, unnerved, wired (*slang*) **3.** changeable, changing, inconstant, uncertain, unpredictable, variable **4.** debatable, doubtful, moot, open, undecided, undetermined, unresolved **5.** due, in arrears, outstanding, owing, payable, pending

unshakable *or* **unshakeable** absolute, constant, firm, fixed, immovable, resolute, staunch, steadfast, sure, unassailable, unswerving, unwavering, well-founded

unshaken calm, collected, composed, impassive, unaffected, unalarmed, undaunted, undismayed, undisturbed, unfazed (*informal*), unmoved, unperturbed, unruffled

unsightly disagreeable, hideous, horrid, repulsive, revolting (*informal*), ugly, unattractive, unpleasant, unprepossessing

unskilled amateurish, cowboy (*informal*), inexperienced, uneducated, unprofessional, unqualified, untalented, untrained

unsociable chilly, cold, distant, hostile, inhospitable, introverted, reclusive, retiring, standoffish, uncongenial, unforthcoming, unfriendly, unneighbourly, unsocial, withdrawn

unsolicited free-will, gratuitous, spontaneous, unasked for, uncalled-for, unforced, uninvited, unrequested, unsought, unwelcome, voluntary, volunteered

unsophisticated 1. artless, childlike, guileless, inexperienced, ingenuous, innocent, naive, natural, unaffected, untutored, unworldly **2.** plain, simple, straightforward, uncomplex, uncomplicated, uninvolved, unrefined, unspecialized

unsound 1. ailing, defective, delicate, deranged, diseased, frail, ill, in poor health, unbalanced, unhealthy, unhinged, unstable, unwell, weak **2.** defective, erroneous, fallacious, false, faulty, flawed, ill-founded, illogical, invalid, shaky, specious, unreliable, weak **3.** flimsy, insecure, not solid, rickety, shaky, tottering, unreliable, unsafe, unstable, unsteady, wobbly

unspeakable 1. beyond description, beyond words, inconceivable, indescribable, ineffable, inexpressible, overwhelming, unbelievable, unimaginable, unutterable, wonderful **2.** abominable, appalling, awful, bad, dreadful, evil, execrable, frightful, heinous, hellacious (*U.S. slang*), horrible, loathsome, monstrous, odious, repellent, shocking, too horrible for words

unspoiled intact, perfect, preserved, unaffected, unblemished, unchanged, undamaged, unharmed, unimpaired, untouched

unspoken assumed, implicit, implied, left to the imagination, not put into words, not spelt out, tacit,

suddenly and create difficulties or danger: *the unstable political climate.* **3** (of a person) having abrupt changes of mood or behaviour. **4** *Chem, physics* readily decomposing.

unsteady *adj* **1** not securely fixed: *unsteady metal posts.* **2** (of a manner of walking, standing, or holding) shaky or staggering. **unsteadily** *adv* **unsteadiness** *n*

unstinting *adj* generous and gladly given: *unstinting praise.*

unstoppable *adj* impossible to prevent from continuing or developing.

unstrap *vb* **-strapping, -strapped** to undo the straps fastening (something) in position.

unstructured *adj* without formal or systematic organization.

unstuck *adj* **1** freed from being stuck, glued, or fastened. **2 come unstuck** to suffer failure or disaster.

unstudied *adj* natural or spontaneous: *her unstudied elegance.*

unsubstantial *adj* **1** lacking weight or firmness. **2** having no material existence.

unsubstantiated *adj* not yet confirmed or proved to be true: *unsubstantiated rumours.*

unsuccessful *adj* not achieving success.

unsuitable *adj* not right or appropriate for a particular purpose.

unsuited *adj* **1** not appropriate for a particular task or situation: *a likeable man unsuited to a military career.* **2** (of a couple) having different personalities or tastes and unlikely to form a lasting relationship: *they are totally unsuited to each other.*

unsung *adj* not appreciated or honoured: *an unsung hero.*

unsure *adj* **1** lacking assurance or self-confidence. **2** uncertain or undecided: *he was unsure who was really in charge.*

unsurpassed *adj* better or greater than anything else of its kind.

unsuspected *adj* **1** not known to exist: *an unsuspected talent.* **2** not under suspicion.

unsuspecting *adj* having no idea of what is happening or about to happen.

unsweetened *adj* having no sugar or other sweetener added.

unswerving *adj* not turning aside; constant.

unsympathetic *adj* **1** not feeling or showing sympathy. **2** unpleasant and unlikeable. **3** (foll. by *to*) opposed or hostile to.

untamed *adj* not brought under human control; wild: *an untamed wilderness.*

untangle *vb* **-gling, -gled** to free from tangles or confusion.

untapped *adj* not yet used or exploited: *untapped mineral reserves.*

untaught *adj* **1** without training or education. **2** acquired without instruction.

untenable *adj* (of a theory, idea, etc.) impossible to defend in an argument.

unthinkable *adj* **1** so shocking or unpleasant that one cannot believe it to be true. **2** unimaginable or inconceivable.

unthinking *adj* **1** thoughtless and inconsiderate. **2** done or happening without careful consideration: *an unthinking reflex.* **unthinkingly** *adv*

untidy *adj* **-dier, -diest** not neat; messy and disordered. **untidily** *adv* **untidiness** *n*

untie *vb* **-tying, -tied** to unfasten or free something that is tied.

until *conj* **1** up to a time that: *he lifted the wire until it was taut.* **2** before (a time or event): *until the present crisis, they weren't allowed into the country.* ~*prep* **3** (often preceded by *up*) in or throughout the period be-

THESAURUS

taken for granted, undeclared, understood, unexpressed, unstated

unstable 1. insecure, not fixed, precarious, rickety, risky, shaky, tottering, unsettled, unsteady, wobbly 2. capricious, changeable, erratic, fitful, fluctuating, inconsistent, inconstant, irrational, temperamental, unpredictable, unsteady, untrustworthy, vacillating, variable, volatile

unsteady infirm, insecure, precarious, reeling, rickety, shaky, tottering, treacherous, unsafe, unstable, wobbly

unsubstantial 1. airy, flimsy, fragile, frail, inadequate, light, slight, thin 2. dreamlike, fanciful, illusory, imaginary, immaterial, impalpable, visionary

unsubstantiated open to question, unattested, unconfirmed, uncorroborated, unestablished, unproven, unsupported

unsuccessful abortive, bootless, failed, fruitless, futile, ineffective, unavailing, unproductive, useless, vain

unsuitable improper, inapposite, inappropriate, inapt, incompatible, incongruous, ineligible, infelicitous, out of character, out of keeping, out of place, unacceptable, unbecoming, unbefitting, unfitting, unseasonable, unseemly, unsuited

unsure 1. insecure, lacking in confidence, unassured, unconfident 2. distrustful, doubtful, dubious, hesitant, in a quandary, irresolute, mistrustful, sceptical, suspicious, uncertain, unconvinced, undecided

unsurpassed consummate, exceptional, incomparable, matchless, nonpareil, paramount, peerless, second to none, superlative, supreme, transcendent, unequalled, unexcelled, unparalleled, unrivalled, without an equal

unsuspecting confiding, credulous, gullible, inexperienced, ingenuous, innocent, naive, off guard, trustful, trusting, unconscious, unsuspicious, unwarned, unwary

unswerving constant, dedicated, devoted, direct, firm, resolute, single-minded, staunch, steadfast, steady, true, undeviating, unfaltering, unflagging, untiring, unwavering

unsympathetic apathetic, callous, cold, compassionless (*rare*), cruel, hard, harsh, heartless, indifferent, insensitive, soulless, stony-hearted, uncompassionate, unconcerned, unfeeling, unkind, unmoved, unpitying, unresponsive

untamed barbarous, feral, fierce, not broken in, savage, unbroken, uncontrollable, undomesticated, untameable, wild

untangle clear up, disentangle, explain, extricate, solve, straighten out, unravel, unsnarl

untenable fallacious, flawed, groundless, illogical, indefensible, insupportable, shaky, unreasonable, unsound, unsustainable, weak

unthinkable beyond belief, beyond the bounds of possibility, implausible, inconceivable, incredible, insupportable, unbelievable, unimaginable

unthinking 1. blundering, inconsiderate, insensitive, rude, selfish, tactless, thoughtless, undiplomatic 2. careless, heedless, impulsive, inadvertent, instinctive, mechanical, negligent, oblivious, rash, senseless, unconscious, unmindful, vacant, witless

untidy bedraggled, chaotic, cluttered, disarrayed, disorderly, higgledy-piggledy (*informal*), jumbled, littered, messy, muddled, muddly, rumpled, shambolic,

fore: *up until then I'd never thought about having kids.* **4** before: *Baker does not get to Israel until Sunday.*

untimely *adj* **1** occurring before the expected or normal time: *his untimely death.* **2** inappropriate to the occasion or time: *an untimely idea to raise at the United Nations.* **untimeliness** *n*

unto *prep Archaic* to.

untold *adj* **1** incapable of description: *untold misery.* **2** incalculably great in number or quantity: *untold millions.* **3** not told.

untouchable *adj* **1** above criticism, suspicion or punishment. **2** unable to be touched. *~n* **3** a member of the lowest class in India, whose touch was formerly regarded as defiling to the four main castes.

untouched *adj* **1** not changed, moved, or affected: *a sleepy backwater untouched by mass tourism.* **2** not injured or harmed: *the Cathedral survived the war untouched.* **3** (of food or drink) not eaten or consumed. **4** emotionally unaffected: *he was untouched by the news of his uncle's death.*

untoward *adj* **1** causing misfortune or annoyance. **2** unfavourable: *untoward reactions.* **3** out of the ordinary; out of the way: *nothing untoward had happened.*

untrained *adj* without formal or adequate training or education.

untrammelled *adj* able to act freely and without restrictions.

untried *adj* **1** not yet used, done, or tested. **2** (of a prisoner) not yet put on trial.

untroubled *adj* calm and unworried.

untrue *adj* **1** incorrect or false. **2** disloyal or unfaithful.

untrustworthy *adj* unreliable and not able to be trusted.

untruth *n* a statement that is not true; lie.

untruthful *adj* **1** (of a person) given to lying. **2** (of a statement) not true. **untruthfully** *adv*

untutored *adj* **1** without formal education. **2** lacking sophistication or refinement.

unusable *adj* not in good enough condition to be used.

unused *adj* **1** not being or never having been used. **2** (foll. by *to*) not accustomed to.

unusual *adj* uncommon or extraordinary. **unusually** *adv*

unutterable *adj* incapable of being expressed in words. **unutterably** *adv*

unvarnished *adj* not elaborated upon; plain: *an unvarnished account of literary life.*

unvarying *adj* always staying the same; unchanging.

unveil *vb* **1** to ceremonially remove the cover from a new picture, statue, plaque, etc. **2** to make public a secret. **3** to remove the veil from one's own or another person's face.

unveiling *n* **1** a ceremony involving the removal of a veil covering a statue. **2** the presentation of something for the first time.

unvoiced *adj* **1** not expressed or spoken. **2** *Phonetics* voiceless.

unwaged *adj* (of a person) not having a paid job.

unwanted *adj* not wanted or welcome.

unwarranted *adj* not justified or necessary.

THESAURUS

slatternly, slipshod, sloppy (*informal*), slovenly, topsy-turvy, unkempt

untie free, loosen, release, unbind, unbridle, undo, unfasten, unknot, unlace

untimely awkward, badly timed, early, ill-timed, inappropriate, inauspicious, inconvenient, inopportune, mistimed, premature, unfortunate, unseasonable, unsuitable

untold 1. indescribable, inexpressible, undreamed of, unimaginable, unspeakable, unthinkable, unutterable **2.** countless, incalculable, innumerable, measureless, myriad, numberless, uncountable, uncounted, unnumbered **3.** hidden, private, secret, undisclosed, unknown, unpublished, unrecounted, unrelated, unrevealed

untouched 1. intact, safe and sound, undamaged, unharmed, unhurt, uninjured, unscathed, without a scratch **2.** dry-eyed, indifferent, unaffected, unconcerned, unimpressed, unmoved, unstirred

untoward 1. annoying, awkward, disastrous, ill-timed, inconvenient, inimical, irritating, troublesome, unfortunate, vexatious **2.** adverse, contrary, inauspicious, inopportune, unfavourable, unlucky, untimely **3.** improper, inappropriate, indecorous, out of place, out of the ordinary, out of the way, unbecoming, unfitting, unseemly, unsuitable

untrained amateur, green, inexperienced, raw, uneducated, unpractised, unqualified, unschooled, unskilled, untaught, untutored

untroubled calm, composed, cool, peaceful, placid, sedate, serene, steady, tranquil, unagitated, unconcerned, undisturbed, unfazed (*informal*), unflappable (*informal*), unflustered, unperturbed, unruffled, unstirred, unworried

untrue 1. deceptive, dishonest, erroneous, fallacious, false, inaccurate, incorrect, lying, misleading, mistaken, sham, spurious, untruthful, wrong **2.** deceitful, disloyal, faithless, false, forsworn, inconstant, perfidious, traitorous, treacherous, two-faced, unfaithful, untrustworthy

untrustworthy capricious, deceitful, devious, dishonest, disloyal, fair-weather, faithless, false, fickle, fly-by-night (*informal*), not to be depended on, slippery, treacherous, tricky, two-faced, undependable, unfaithful, unreliable, untrue, untrusty

untruth deceit, fabrication, falsehood, falsification, fib, fiction, lie, pork pie (*Brit. slang*), porky (*Brit. slang*), prevarication, story, tale, trick, whopper (*informal*)

untruthful crooked (*informal*), deceitful, deceptive, dishonest, dissembling, false, fibbing, hypocritical, lying, mendacious

unusual abnormal, atypical, bizarre, curious, different, exceptional, extraordinary, notable, odd, out of the ordinary, phenomenal, queer, rare, remarkable, singular, strange, surprising, uncommon, unconventional, unexpected, unfamiliar, unwonted

unutterable beyond words, extreme, indescribable, ineffable, overwhelming, unimaginable, unspeakable

unvarnished bare, candid, frank, honest, naked, plain, pure, pure and simple, simple, sincere, stark, straightforward, unadorned, unembellished

unveil bare, bring to light, disclose, divulge, expose, lay bare, lay open, make known, make public, reveal, uncover

unwanted *de trop*, going begging, outcast, rejected, superfluous, surplus to requirements, unasked, undesired, uninvited, unneeded, unsolicited, unwelcome, useless

unwarranted gratuitous, groundless, indefensible, inexcusable, uncalled-for, unjust, unjustified, unprovoked, unreasonable, wrong

unwary careless, hasty, heedless, imprudent, incautious, indiscreet, rash, reckless, thoughtless, uncircumspect, unguarded, unwatchful

unwavering consistent, dedicated, determined, im-

unwary *adj* not careful or cautious and therefore likely to be harmed. **unwarily** *adv* **unwariness** *n*

unwavering *adj* (of a feeling or attitude) remaining firm and never weakening.

unwelcome *adj* unpleasant and unwanted.

unwell *adj* not healthy; ill.

unwept *adj* not wept for or lamented.

unwholesome *adj* **1** harmful to the body or mind: *unwholesome food.* **2** morally harmful: *unwholesome dreams.* **3** unhealthy-looking. **4** (of food) of inferior quality.

unwieldy *adj* too heavy, large, or awkward to be easily handled.

unwilling *adj* **1** reluctant. **2** done or said with reluctance. **unwillingly** *adv* **unwillingness** *n*

unwind *vb* **-winding, -wound 1** to slacken, undo, or unravel: *Paul started to unwind the bandage.* **2** to relax after a busy or tense time: *we go out to unwind after work.*

unwise *adj* foolish; not sensible. **unwisely** *adv*

unwitting *adj* **1** not intentional. **2** not knowing or conscious. **unwittingly** *adv*

unwonted *adj* out of the ordinary; unusual.

unworkable *adj* impractical and certain to fail: *unworkable proposals for reform.*

unworldly *adj* **1** not concerned with material values or pursuits. **2** lacking sophistication; naive.

unworn *adj* **1** not having deteriorated through use or age. **2** (of a garment) never having been worn.

unworried *adj* not bothered or perturbed.

unworthy *adj* **1** not deserving or meriting: *a person deemed unworthy of membership.* **2** (often foll. by *of*) beneath the level considered befitting (to): *unworthy of a prime minister.* **3** lacking merit or value. **unworthiness** *n*

unwrap *vb* **-wrapping, -wrapped** to remove the wrapping from something or (of something wrapped) to have the covering removed.

unwritten *adj* **1** not printed or in writing. **2** operating only through custom: *an unwritten code of conduct.*

unyielding *adj* remaining firm and determined.

unzip *vb* **-zipping, -zipped** to unfasten the zip of a garment or (of a zip or a garment with a zip) to become unfastened.

up *prep* **1** indicating movement to a higher position: *go up the stairs.* **2** at a higher or further level or position in or on: *a shop up the road.* ~*adv* **3** to an upward, higher, or erect position: *the men straightened up from their digging.* **4** indicating readiness for an activity: *up and about.* **5** indicating intensity or completion of an action: *he tore up the cheque.* **6** to the place referred to or where the speaker is: *a man came up to me.* **7 a** to a more important place: *up to the city.* **b** to a more northerly place: *up to Orkney.* **c** to or at university. **8** above the horizon: *the sun came up.* **9** appearing for trial: *up before the judge.* **10** having gained: *ten pounds up on the deal.* **11** higher in price: *beer has gone up again.* **12 all up with someone** *Informal* over for or hopeless for someone. **13 something's up** *Informal* something strange is happening. **14 up against** having to cope with: *look what we're up against now.* **15 up for** being a candidate or applicant for: *he's up for the job.* **16 up to a** occupied with; scheming: *she's up to no good.* **b** dependent upon: *the decision is up to you.* **c** equal to or capable of: *are you up to playing in the final?* **d** as far as: *up to his neck in mud.* **e** as many as: *up to two years' credit.* **f** comparable with: *not up to my usual standard.* **17 what's up?** *Informal* **a** what is the matter? **b** what is happening? ~*adj* **18** of a high or higher position. **19** out of bed: *aren't you up yet?* **20** (of a period of time) over or completed: *the examiner announced that their time was up.* **21** of or relating to a train going to a more important place: *the up platform.* ~*vb* **upping, upped 22** to increase or raise. **23 up and** *Informal* to do something suddenly: *he upped and left her.* ~*n* **24** a high point: *every couple has ups and downs.* **25 on the up and up a** trustworthy or honest. **b** *Brit* on an upward trend: *our firm's on the up and up.*

up-and-coming *adj* likely to be successful in the future; promising.

upbeat *adj* **1** *Informal* cheerful and optimistic. ~*n* **2** *Music* **a** an unaccented beat. **b** the upward gesture of a conductor's baton indicating this.

upbraid *vb* to scold or reproach.

upbringing *n* the education of a person during his or her formative years.

THESAURUS

movable, resolute, single-minded, staunch, steadfast, steady, undeviating, unfaltering, unflagging, unshakable, unshaken, unswerving, untiring

unwelcome disagreeable, displeasing, distasteful, excluded, rejected, thankless, unacceptable, undesirable, uninvited, unpleasant, unpopular, unwanted, unwished for

unwell ailing, ill, indisposed, in poor health, off colour, out of sorts, poorly (*informal*), sick, sickly, under the weather (*informal*), unhealthy

unwholesome 1. deleterious, harmful, insalubrious, junk (*informal*), noxious, poisonous, tainted, unhealthy, unnourishing **2.** bad, corrupting, degrading, demoralizing, depraving, evil, immoral, maleficent, perverting, wicked **3.** anaemic, pale, pallid, pasty, sickly, wan

unwieldy awkward, bulky, burdensome, clumsy, cumbersome, hefty, inconvenient, massive, ponderous, ungainly, unhandy, unmanageable, weighty

unwilling averse, demurring, disinclined, grudging, indisposed, loath, not in the mood, opposed, reluctant, resistant, unenthusiastic

unwind 1. disentangle, slacken, uncoil, undo, unravel, unreel, unroll, untwine, untwist **2.** calm down, let oneself go, loosen up, quieten down, relax, sit back, slow down, take a break, take it easy, wind down

unwise asinine, foolhardy, foolish, ill-advised, ill-considered, ill-judged, impolitic, improvident, imprudent, inadvisable, inane, indiscreet, injudicious, irresponsible, rash, reckless, senseless, short-sighted, silly, stupid

unwitting 1. accidental, chance, inadvertent, involuntary, undesigned, unintended, unintentional, unmeant, unplanned **2.** ignorant, innocent, unaware, unconscious, unknowing, unsuspecting

unworldly 1. nonmaterialistic, religious, spiritual **2.** green, idealistic, inexperienced, innocent, naive, raw, trusting, unsophisticated

unworthy 1. ineligible, not deserving of, not fit for, not good enough, not worth, undeserving **2.** *often with* **of** beneath the dignity of, improper, inappropriate, out of character, out of place, unbecoming, unbefitting, unfitting, unseemly, unsuitable **3.** base, contemptible, degrading, discreditable, disgraceful, dishonourable, disreputable, ignoble, shameful

unwritten 1. oral, unrecorded, vocal, word-of-mouth **2.** accepted, conventional, customary, tacit, traditional, understood, unformulated

unyielding adamant, determined, firm, hardline, immovable, inexorable, inflexible, intractable, obdurate, obstinate, relentless, resolute, rigid, staunch, stead-

upcountry *adj* 1 of or from the interior of a country. ~*adv* 2 towards or in the interior of a country.
update *vb* **-dating, -dated** to bring up to date.
upend *vb* to turn or set or become turned or set on end.
upfront *adj* 1 open and frank. ~*adv, adj* 2 (of money) paid out at the beginning of a business arrangement.
upgrade *vb* **-grading, -graded** 1 to promote a person or job to a higher rank. 2 to raise in value, importance, or esteem.
upheaval *n* a strong, sudden, or violent disturbance.
uphill *adj* 1 sloping or leading upwards. 2 requiring a great deal of effort: *an uphill struggle.* ~*adv* 3 up a slope.
uphold *vb* **-holding, -held** 1 to maintain or defend against opposition. 2 to give moral support to. **upholder** *n*
upholster *vb* to fit chairs or sofas with padding, springs, and covering. **upholstered** *adj* **upholsterer** *n*
upholstery *n* the padding, springs, and covering of a chair or sofa.
upkeep *n* 1 the act or process of keeping something in good repair. 2 the cost of maintenance.
upland *adj* of or in an area of high or relatively high ground: *an upland wilderness.*
uplands *pl n* an area of high or relatively high ground: *the limestone uplands of Yorkshire.*
uplift *vb* 1 to raise or lift up. 2 to raise morally or spiritually. 3 *Scot* to collect or pick up. ~*n* 4 the act or process of bettering moral, social, or cultural conditions. ~*adj* 5 (of a bra) designed to lift and support the breasts. **uplifting** *adj*
up-market *adj* expensive and of superior quality.
upon *prep* 1 on. 2 up and on: *they climbed upon his lap for comfort.*
upper *adj* 1 higher or highest in physical position, wealth, rank, or status. 2 **Upper** *Geol* denoting the late part of a period or formation: *Upper Cretaceous.* ~*n* 3 the part of a shoe above the sole. 4 **on one's uppers** very poor; penniless.
upper-case *adj* denoting capital letters as used in printed or typed matter.
upper class *n* 1 the highest social class; aristocracy. ~*adj* **upper-class** 2 of the upper class.
upper crust *n Informal* the upper class.
uppercut *n* a short swinging upward punch delivered to the chin.
upper hand *n* the position of control: *the hardliners have gained the upper hand.*
Upper House *n* the smaller and less representative chamber of a two-chamber parliament, for example the House of Lords or a Senate.
uppermost *adj* 1 highest in position, power, or importance. ~*adv* 2 in or into the highest place or position.
uppish *adj Brit informal* uppity.
uppity *adj Informal* snobbish, arrogant, or presumptuous.
upright *adj* 1 vertical or erect. 2 honest or just. ~*adv* 3 vertically or in an erect position. ~*n* 4 a vertical support, such as a post. 5 short for **upright piano.** 6 the state of being vertical. **uprightness** *n*
upright piano *n* a piano which has a rectangular vertical case.
uprising *n* a revolt or rebellion.
up-river *adj, adv* nearer the source of a river: *we sailed slowly up-river; the village of Juffure, four days up-river.*
uproar *n* 1 a commotion or disturbance characterized by loud noise and confusion. 2 angry public criticism or debates: *the decision to close the railway led to an uproar.*
uproarious *adj* 1 very funny. 2 (of laughter) loud and boisterous.
uproot *vb* 1 to pull up by or as if by the roots. 2 to displace (a person or people) from their native or usual surroundings. 3 to remove or destroy utterly: *we must uproot all remnants of feudalism.*
ups and downs *pl n* alternating periods of good and bad luck or high and low spirits.
upset *adj* 1 emotionally or physically disturbed or

THESAURUS

fast, stiff-necked, stubborn, tough, unbending, uncompromising, unwavering
upbringing breeding, bringing-up, care, cultivation, education, nurture, raising, rearing, tending, training
upgrade advance, ameliorate, better, elevate, enhance, improve, promote, raise
upheaval cataclysm, disorder, disruption, disturbance, eruption, overthrow, revolution, turmoil, violent change
uphill *adj.* 1. ascending, climbing, mounting, rising 2. arduous, difficult, exhausting, gruelling, hard, laborious, punishing, strenuous, taxing, tough, wearisome
uphold advocate, aid, back, champion, defend, encourage, endorse, hold to, justify, maintain, promote, stand by, stick up for (*informal*), support, sustain, vindicate
upkeep 1. conservation, keep, maintenance, preservation, repair, running, subsistence, support, sustenance 2. expenditure, expenses, oncosts (*Brit.*), operating costs, outlay, overheads, running costs
uplift *vb.* 1. elevate, heave, hoist, lift up, raise 2. advance, ameliorate, better, civilize, cultivate, edify, improve, inspire, raise, refine, upgrade ~*n.* 3. advancement, betterment, cultivation, edification, enhancement, enlightenment, enrichment, improvement, refinement
upper elevated, eminent, greater, high, higher, important, loftier, superior, top, topmost
upper-class aristocratic, blue-blooded, highborn, high-class, noble, patrician, top-drawer, well-bred
upper hand advantage, ascendancy, control, dominion, edge, mastery, superiority, supremacy, sway, whip hand
uppermost chief, dominant, foremost, greatest, highest, leading, loftiest, main, most elevated, paramount, predominant, pre-eminent, primary, principal, supreme, top, topmost, upmost
uppish affected, arrogant, cocky, conceited, high and mighty (*informal*), hoity-toity (*informal*), overweening, presumptuous, putting on airs, self-important, snobbish, stuck-up (*informal*), supercilious, toffee-nosed (*slang, chiefly Brit.*), uppity (*informal*)
upright 1. erect, on end, perpendicular, straight, vertical 2. above board, conscientious, ethical, faithful, good, high-minded, honest, honourable, incorruptible, just, principled, righteous, straightforward, true, trustworthy, unimpeachable, virtuous
uprising disturbance, insurgence, insurrection, mutiny, outbreak, putsch, rebellion, revolt, revolution, rising, upheaval
uproar brawl, brouhaha, clamour, commotion, confusion, din, furore, hubbub, hullabaloo, hurly-burly, mayhem, noise, outcry, pandemonium, racket, riot, ruckus (*informal*), ruction (*informal*), rumpus, turbulence, turmoil
uproarious 1. convulsive (*informal*), hilarious, hys-

distressed. *~vb* **-setting, -set 2** to turn or tip over. **3** to disrupt the normal state or progress of: *bad weather upset their plans.* **4** to disturb mentally or emotionally. **5** to make physically ill: *it still seems to upset my stomach.* *~n* **6** an unexpected defeat or reversal, as in a contest or plans. **7** a disturbance or disorder of the emotions, mind, or body. **upsetting** *adj*

upset price *n Chiefly Scot, US, & Canad* the lowest price acceptable for something that is for sale by auction, usually a house.

upshot *n* the final result or conclusion; outcome.

upside down *adj* **1** with the bottom where the top would normally be; inverted. **2** *Informal* confused or jumbled. *~adv* **3** in an inverted fashion. **4** in a chaotic manner or into a chaotic state: *recent events have changed many peoples lives upside down.*

upsides *adv Informal, chiefly Brit* (foll. by *with*) equal or level with, as through revenge.

upstage *adv* **1** on, at, or to the rear of the stage. *~adj* **2** at the back half of the stage. *~vb* **-staging, -staged 3** to move upstage of another actor, forcing him or her to turn away from the audience. **4** *Informal* to draw attention to oneself and away from someone else.

upstairs *adv* **1** to or on an upper floor of a building. **2** *Informal* to or into a higher rank or office. *~n* **3** an upper floor. *~adj* **4** situated on an upper floor: *an upstairs bedroom.*

upstanding *adj* **1** of good character. **2** upright and vigorous in build.

upstart *n* a person who has risen suddenly to a position of power and behaves arrogantly.

upstream *adv, adj* in or towards the higher part of a stream; against the current.

upsurge *n* a rapid rise or swell.

upswing *n* **1** *Econ* a recovery period in the trade cycle. **2** any increase or improvement.

upsy-daisy *or* **upsadaisy** *interj* an expression of reassurance, usually used to a child, e.g. when it stumbles or is being lifted up.

uptake *n* **1 quick** *or* **slow on the uptake** *Informal* quick *or* slow to understand or learn. **2** the use or consumption of something by a machine or part of the body: *the uptake of oxygen into the blood.*

upthrust *n* **1** an upward push. **2** *Geol* a violent upheaval of the earth's surface.

uptight *adj Informal* **1** nervously tense, irritable, or angry. **2** unable to express one's feelings.

up-to-date *adj* modern or fashionable: *an up-to-date kitchen.*

up-to-the-minute *adj* the latest or most modern possible: *up-to-the-minute news about what's on in town.*

upturn *n* **1** an upward trend or improvement. *~vb* **2** to turn or cause to turn over or upside down.

upward *adj* **1** directed or moving towards a higher place or level. *~adv also* **upwards 2** from a lower to a higher place, level, or condition. **3 upward** *or* **upwards of** more than (the stated figure): *a crowd estimated at upward of one hundred thousand people.*

upward mobility *n* movement from a lower to a higher economic and social status.

upwind *adv* **1** into or against the wind. **2** towards or on the side where the wind is blowing. *~adj* **3** going against the wind. **4** on the windward side.

uranium (yew-**rain**-ee-um) *n Chem* a radioactive silvery-white metallic element of the actinide series. It is used chiefly as a source of nuclear energy by fission of the radioisotope **uranium 235**. Symbol: U

Uranus *n* **1** *Greek myth* a god; the personification of the sky. **2** the seventh planet from the sun.

urban *adj* of or living in a city or town.

urbane *adj* polite, elegant, and sophisticated in manner.

urbanity *n* the quality of being urbane.

urbanize *or* **-ise** *vb* **-izing, -ized** *or* **-ising, -ised** to make a rural area more industrialized and urban. **urbanization** *or* **-isation** *n*

urchin *n* **1** a mischievous child. **2** See **sea urchin.**

Urdu (**oor**-doo) *n* an Indic language of the Indo-European family which is an official language of Pakistan and is also spoken in India.

urea (yew-**ree**-a) *n* a white soluble crystalline compound found in urine.

ureter (yew-**reet**-er) *n* the tube that carries urine from the kidney to the bladder.

urethra (yew-**reeth**-ra) *n* the tube that in most mammals carries urine from the bladder out of the body.

urethritis (yew-rith-**rite**-iss) *n* inflammation of the urethra causing a discharge and painful urination.

urge *n* **1** a strong impulse, inner drive, or yearning. *~vb* **urging, urged 2** to plead with or press someone

THESAURUS

terical, killing (*informal*), rib-tickling, rip-roaring (*informal*), screamingly funny, side-splitting, very funny **2.** boisterous, gleeful, loud, rollicking, unrestrained

upset *adj.* **1.** agitated, bothered, confused, disconcerted, dismayed, disquieted, distressed, disturbed, frantic, gippy (*slang*), grieved, hassled (*informal*), hurt, ill, overwrought, poorly (*informal*), put out, queasy, ruffled, sick, troubled, worried *~vb.* **2.** capsize, knock over, overturn, spill, tip over, topple over **3.** change, disorder, disorganize, disrupt, disturb, mess up, mix up, put out of order, spoil, turn topsy-turvy **4.** agitate, bother, discompose, disconcert, dismay, disquiet, distress, disturb, faze, fluster, grieve, hassle (*informal*), perturb, ruffle, throw (someone) off balance, trouble, unnerve *~n.* **5.** defeat, reverse, shake-up (*informal*), sudden change, surprise **6.** agitation, bother, bug (*informal*), complaint, discomposure, disorder, disquiet, distress, disturbance, hassle (*informal*), illness, indisposition, malady, queasiness, shock, sickness, trouble, worry

upshot conclusion, consequence, culmination, end, end result, event, finale, issue, outcome, payoff (*informal*), result, sequel

upside down 1. bottom up, inverted, on its head, overturned, upturned, wrong side up **2.** *informal* chaotic, confused, disordered, higgledy-piggledy (*informal*), in confusion (chaos, disarray, disorder), jumbled, muddled, topsy-turvy

upstanding 1. ethical, good, honest, honourable, incorruptible, moral, principled, true, trustworthy, upright **2.** firm, hale and hearty, hardy, healthy, robust, stalwart, strong, sturdy, upright, vigorous

upstart arriviste, nobody, *nouveau riche,* parvenu, social climber, status seeker

up-to-date à la mode, all the rage, contemporary, current, fashionable, happening (*informal*), in, in vogue, modern, newest, now (*informal*), stylish, trendy (*Brit. informal*), up-to-the-minute, with it (*informal*)

urban city, civic, inner-city, metropolitan, municipal, town

urbane civil, civilized, cosmopolitan, courteous, cultivated, cultured, debonair, elegant, mannerly, polished, refined, smooth, sophisticated, suave, well-bred, well-mannered

urbanity charm, civility, courtesy, culture, elegance, grace, mannerliness, polish, refinement, sophistication, suavity, worldliness

to do something: *he urged his readers to do the same.* **3** to advocate earnestly and persistently: *I have long urged this change.* **4** to force or hasten onwards: *something very powerful urged him on.*

urgent *adj* **1** requiring speedy action or attention: *an urgent inquiry.* **2** earnest and forceful: *she heard loud urgent voices in the corridor.* **urgency** *n* **urgently** *adv*

uric (**yew**-rik) *adj* of or derived from urine.

uric acid *n* a white odourless crystalline acid present in the blood and urine.

urinal *n* **1** a sanitary fitting, used by men for urination. **2** a room containing urinals.

urinary *adj Anat* of urine or the organs that secrete and pass urine.

urinary bladder *n* a membranous sac that can expand in which urine excreted from the kidneys is stored.

urinate *vb* **-nating, -nated** to excrete urine. **urination** *n*

urine *n* the pale yellow fluid excreted by the kidneys, containing waste products from the blood. It is stored in the bladder and discharged through the urethra.

urinogenital (yew-rin-oh-**jen**-it-al) *adj* same as **urogenital.**

urn *n* **1** a vaselike container, usually with a foot and a rounded body. **2** a vase used as a container for the ashes of the dead. **3** a large metal container, with a tap, used for making and holding tea or coffee.

urogenital (yew-roh-**jen**-it-al) *or* **urinogenital** *adj* of the urinary and genital organs and their functions. Also: **genitourinary**

urology (yew-**rol**-a-jee) *n* the branch of medicine concerned with the urinary system and its diseases.

ursine *adj* of or like a bear.

us *pron* (*objective*) **1** refers to the speaker or writer and another person or other people: *the bond between us.* **2** refers to all people or people in general: *this table shows us the tides.* **3** *Informal* me: *give us a kiss!* **4** *Formal* same as **me:** used by monarchs.

U.S. *or* **US** United States.

U.S.A. *or* **USA** United States of America.

usable *adj* able to be used. **usability** *n*

usage *n* **1** regular or constant use: *a move to reduce pesticide usage.* **2** the way in which a word is actually used in a language. **3** a particular meaning or use that a word can have.

use *vb* **using, used 1** to put into service or action; employ for a given purpose: *use a garden fork to mix them together.* **2** to choose or employ regularly: *what sort of toothpaste do you use?* **3** to take advantage of; exploit: *I used Jason and he used me.* **4** to consume or expend: *a manufacturing plant uses 1000 tonnes of steel a month.* ~*n* **5** the act or fact using or being used: *large-scale use of pesticides.* **6** the ability or permission to use. **7** need or opportunity to use: *the Colombian government had no use for them.* **8** usefulness or advantage: *there is no use in complaining.* **9** the purpose for which something is used. **10 have no use for a** to have no need of. **b** to have a contemptuous dislike for. **11 make use of a** to employ; use. **b** to exploit (a person). ~See also **use up. user** *n*

used *adj* second-hand: *it was a used car.*

used to *adj* **1** accustomed to: *I am used to being a medical guinea pig.* ~*vb* **2** used as an auxiliary to express habitual or accustomed actions or states taking place in the past but not continuing to be the case in the present: *he used to vanish into his studio for days.*

➤ In the negative there are two common combinations: *didn't use to* and *used not to.* The abbreviated form is *usedn't to.*

useful *adj* **1** able to be used advantageously or for several purposes. **2** *Informal* commendable or capable: *a useful hurdler.* **usefully** *adv* **usefulness** *n*

useless *adj* **1** having no practical use. **2** *Informal* ineffectual, weak, or stupid: *I'm useless at most things.* **uselessly** *adv* **uselessness** *n*

user-friendly *adj* easy to familiarize oneself with, understand, and use.

use up *vb* to finish a supply of something completely.

U-shaped valley *n* a steep-sided valley caused by glacial erosion.

usher *n* **1** an official who shows people to their seats, as in a church. **2** a person who acts as doorkeeper in a court of law. ~*vb* **3** to conduct or escort. **4** (foll. by *in*)

THESAURUS

urchin brat, gamin, guttersnipe, mudlark (*slang*), ragamuffin, street Arab (*offensive*), waif, young rogue

urge *n.* **1.** compulsion, desire, drive, fancy, impulse, itch, longing, thirst, wish, yearning, yen (*informal*) ~*vb.* **2.** appeal to, beg, beseech, entreat, exhort, implore, plead, press, solicit **3.** advise, advocate, champion, counsel, insist on, push for, recommend, support **4.** compel, constrain, drive, egg on, encourage, force, goad, hasten, impel, incite, induce, instigate, press, prompt, propel, push, spur, stimulate

urgency exigency, extremity, gravity, hurry, imperativeness, importance, importunity, necessity, need, pressure, seriousness, stress

urgent 1. compelling, critical, crucial, immediate, imperative, important, instant, not to be delayed, pressing, top-priority **2.** clamorous, earnest, forceful, importunate, insistent, intense, persistent, persuasive

urinate leak (*slang*), make water, micturate, pass water, pee (*slang*), piddle (*informal*), piss (*taboo slang*), spend a penny (*Brit. informal*), tinkle (*Brit. informal*), wee (*informal*), wee-wee (*informal*)

usable at one's disposal, available, current, fit for use, functional, in running order, practical, ready for use, serviceable, utilizable, valid, working

usage control, employment, handling, management, operation, regulation, running, treatment, use

use *vb.* **1.** apply, avail oneself of, bring into play, employ, exercise, exert, find a use for, make use of, operate, ply, practise, profit by, put to use, turn to account, utilize, wield, work **2.** act towards, behave towards, deal with, exploit, handle, manipulate, misuse, take advantage of, treat **3.** consume, exhaust, expend, run through, spend, waste ~*n.* **4.** application, employment, exercise, handling, operation, practice, service, treatment, usage, wear and tear **5.** advantage, application, avail, benefit, good, help, mileage (*informal*), point, profit, service, usefulness, utility, value, worth **6.** call, cause, end, necessity, need, object, occasion, point, purpose, reason

used cast-off, hand-me-down (*informal*), nearly new, not new, reach-me-down (*informal*), second-hand, shopsoiled, worn

used to accustomed to, at home in, attuned to, familiar with, given to, habituated to, hardened to, in the habit of, inured to, tolerant of, wont to

useful advantageous, all-purpose, beneficial, effective, fruitful, general-purpose, helpful, of help, of service, of use, practical, profitable, salutary, serviceable, valuable, worthwhile

useless 1. bootless, disadvantageous, fruitless, futile, hopeless, idle, impractical, ineffective, ineffectual, of no use, pointless, profitless, unavailing, unproductive, unworkable, vain, valueless, worthless **2.** *informal* hopeless, incompetent, ineffectual, inept, no good, stupid, weak

to happen immediately before something or cause it to happen; herald: *the French Revolution ushered in a new age.*

usherette *n* a woman assistant in a cinema, who shows people to their seats.

USSR Union of Soviet Socialist Republics: a former state in E Europe and N Asia, covering the area now composed of Russia, the Ukraine, Kazakhstan and a number of smaller states.

usual *adj* **1** of the most normal, frequent, or regular type: *the usual assortment of stories.* ~*n* **2** ordinary or commonplace events: *the dirt was nothing out of the usual.* **3 as usual** as happens normally. **4 the usual** *Informal* the habitual or usual drink. **usually** *adv*

usurp (yewz-**zurp**) *vb* to seize a position or power without authority. **usurpation** *n* **usurper** *n*

usury (**yewz**-yoor-ree) *n, pl* **-ries** *Old-fashioned* **1** the practice of loaning money at an exorbitant rate of interest. **2** an unlawfully high rate of interest. **usurer** *n*

UT Utah.

utensil *n* a tool or container for practical use: *cooking utensils.*

uterine *adj* of or affecting the womb.

uterus (**yew**-ter-russ) *n, pl* **uteri** (**yew**-ter-rye) *Anat* a hollow muscular organ in the pelvic cavity of female mammals, which houses the developing fetus; womb.

utilidor (yew-**till**-lid-or) *n Canad* above-ground insulated casing for pipes carrying water in permafrost regions.

utilitarian *adj* **1** useful rather than beautiful. **2** of utilitarianism. ~*n* **3** an advocate of utilitarianism.

utilitarianism *n Ethics* the doctrine that the right thing to do is that which brings about the greatest good for the greatest number.

utility *n, pl* **-ties 1** usefulness. **2** something useful. **3** a public service, such as water or electricity. ~*adj* **4** designed for use rather than beauty: *utility fabrics.*

utility room *n* a room used for large domestic appliances and equipment.

utility truck *n Austral & NZ* a small truck with an open body and low sides.

utilize *or* **-lise** *vb* **-lizing, -lized** *or* **-lising, -lised** to make practical or worthwhile use of. **utilization** *or* **-lisation** *n*

utmost *adj* **1** of the greatest possible degree or amount: *the utmost seriousness.* **2** at the furthest limit: *the utmost point.* ~*n* **3** the greatest possible degree or amount: *I was doing my utmost to comply.*

Utopia (yew-**tope**-ee-a) *n* any real or imaginary society, place, or state considered to be perfect or ideal. **Utopian** *adj*

utter[1] *vb* **1** to express something in sounds or words: *she hadn't uttered a single word.* **2** *Criminal law* to put counterfeit money or forged cheques into circulation.

utter[2] *adj* total or absolute: *utter amazement.* **utterly** *adv*

utterance *n* **1** something expressed in speech or writing. **2** the expression in words of ideas, thoughts, or feelings.

uttermost *adj, n* same as **utmost.**

U-turn *n* **1** a turn, made by a vehicle, in the shape of a U, resulting in a reversal of direction. **2** a complete change in policy.

UV ultraviolet.

UV-A *or* **UVA** *n* ultraviolet radiation with a range of 320-380 nanometres.

UV-B *or* **UVB** *n* ultraviolet radiation with a range of 280-320 nanometres.

uvula (**yew**-view-la) *n* the small fleshy part of the soft palate that hangs in the back of the throat. **uvular** *adj*

uxorious (ux-**or**-ee-uss) *adj* excessively fond of or dependent on one's wife.

THESAURUS

use up absorb, burn up, consume, deplete, devour, drain, exhaust, finish, fritter away, run through, squander, swallow up, waste

usher *n.* **1.** attendant, doorkeeper, escort, guide, usherette ~*vb.* **2.** conduct, direct, escort, guide, lead, pilot, show in *or* out, steer **3.** *with* **in** bring in, herald, inaugurate, initiate, introduce, launch, open the door to, pave the way for, precede, ring in

usual accustomed, common, constant, customary, everyday, expected, familiar, fixed, general, habitual, normal, ordinary, regular, routine, standard, stock, typical, wonted

usually as a rule, as is the custom, as is usual, by and large, commonly, for the most part, generally, habitually, in the main, mainly, mostly, most often, normally, on the whole, ordinarily, regularly, routinely

utility advantageousness, avail, benefit, convenience, efficacy, fitness, point, practicality, profit, service, serviceableness, use, usefulness

utilize appropriate, avail oneself of, employ, have recourse to, make the most of, make use of, profit by, put to use, resort to, take advantage of, turn to account, use

utmost *adj.* **1.** chief, extreme, greatest, highest, maximum, paramount, pre-eminent, supreme **2.** extreme, farthest, final, last, most distant, outermost, remotest, uttermost ~*n.* **3.** best, greatest, hardest, highest, most

utter *vb.* articulate, declare, divulge, enunciate, express, give expression to, make known, proclaim, promulgate, pronounce, publish, put into words, reveal, say, speak, state, verbalize, vocalize, voice

utter *adj.* absolute, arrant, complete, consummate, deep-dyed (*usually derogatory*), downright, entire, out-and-out, outright, perfect, sheer, stark, thorough, thoroughgoing, total, unmitigated, unqualified

utterly absolutely, completely, entirely, extremely, fully, perfectly, thoroughly, totally, to the core, wholly

V

V 1 *Chem* vanadium. **2** volt. **3** the Roman numeral for five.

v. 1 verb. **2** verse. **3** versus. **4** volume.

VA Virginia.

vac *n Brit informal* short for **vacation.**

vacancy *n, pl* **-cies 1** an unoccupied job or position: *he had heard of a vacancy for a librarian.* **2** an unoccupied room in a hotel or guesthouse: *the last hotel we tried had a vacancy.* **3** the state of being unoccupied.

vacant *adj* **1** (of a toilet, room, etc.) unoccupied or not being used: *I sat down in a vacant chair.* **2** (of a job or position) unfilled at the present time. **3** having or suggesting a lack of interest or understanding: *he sat there staring at me with a vacant look.* **4** (of a period of time) not set aside for any particular activity: *two slots in his programme have been left vacant.* **vacantly** *adv*

vacate *vb* **-cating, -cated 1** to cause (something) to be empty by leaving: *do you wish us to vacate the room?* **2** to give up (a job or position).

vacation *n* **1** *Chiefly Brit* a time of the year when the universities or law courts are closed. **2** *US & Canad* same as **holiday** (sense 2).

vaccinate *vb* **-nating, -nated** to inject (someone) with a vaccine in order to protect them against a disease. **vaccination** *n*

vaccine *n Med* a substance made from the germs that cause a disease which is given to people to prevent them getting the disease.

vacillate (**vass**-ill-late) *vb* **-lating, -lated** to keep changing one's mind or opinions about something: *he vacillated between republican and monarchist sentiments.* **vacillation** *n*

vacuity *n* an absence of intelligent thought or ideas: *I suggested to one of his advisers that his vacuity was a handicap in these debates.*

vacuous *adj* **1** lacking in intelligent ideas. **2** showing no sign of intelligence or understanding: *her smile was vacuous but without malice.*

vacuum *n, pl* **vacuums** *or* **vacua 1** a space which contains no air or other gas. **2** a vacant place or position that needs to be filled by someone or something else: *the army moved in to fill the power vacuum.* **3** short for **vacuum cleaner.** *~vb* **4** to clean (something) with a vacuum cleaner.

vacuum cleaner *n* an electric machine which sucks up dust and dirt from carpets and upholstery. **vacuum cleaning** *n*

vacuum flask *n* a double-walled flask with a vacuum between the walls that keeps drinks hot or cold.

vacuum-packed *adj* (of food) packed in an airtight container in order to preserve freshness.

vacuum tube *or* **valve** *n* same as **valve** (sense 3).

vade mecum (**vah**-dee **make**-um) *n* a handbook carried for immediate use when needed.

vagabond *n* a person who travels from place to place and has no fixed home or job.

vagary (**vaig**-a-ree) *n, pl* **-garies** an unpredictable change in a situation or in someone's behaviour: *I was unused to the vagaries of the retailer's world.*

vagina (vaj-**jine**-a) *n* the passage in most female mammals that extends from the neck of the womb to the external genitals. **vaginal** *adj*

vagrant (**vaig**-rant) *n* **1** a person who moves from place to place and has no regular home or job. *~adj* **2** wandering about. **vagrancy** *n*

vague *adj* **1** not expressed or explained clearly: *he thought of his instructions, so vague and imprecise.* **2** deliberately withholding information: *he was rather vague about the whole deal.* **3** (of a sound or shape) unable to be heard or seen clearly: *he heard some vague sound from downstairs.* **4** (of a person) not concentrating or thinking clearly: *she was mumbling to herself in a vague way.* **5** not clearly established or known: *it was a vague rumour which would fade away and be forgotten.* **vaguely** *adv* **vagueness** *n*

vain *adj* **1** excessively proud of one's appearance or achievements. **2** senseless or unsuccessful: *he made a vain attempt to lighten the atmosphere.* *~n* **3 in vain** without achieving the desired effects or results: *the old man searched in vain for his son.* **vainly** *adv*

vainglorious *adj* boastful or proud: *his vainglorious posturing had earned him numerous powerful enemies.*

valance (**val**-lenss) *n* a short piece of decorative material hung round the edge of a bed or above a window.

vale *n Literary* a valley.

THESAURUS

vacancy job, opening, opportunity, position, post, room, situation

vacant 1. available, empty, free, idle, not in use, to let, unemployed, unengaged, unfilled, unoccupied, untenanted, void **2.** absent-minded, abstracted, blank, dreaming, dreamy, expressionless, idle, inane, incurious, thoughtless, unthinking, vacuous

vacuum emptiness, free space, gap, nothingness, space, void

vagabond bag lady (*chiefly U.S.*), beggar, bum (*informal*), down-and-out, hobo (*U.S.*), itinerant, knight of the road, migrant, nomad, outcast, rascal, rover, tramp, vagrant, wanderer, wayfarer

vagrant 1. *n.* bag lady (*chiefly U.S.*), beggar, bird of passage, bum (*informal*), hobo (*U.S.*), itinerant, person of no fixed address, rolling stone, tramp, wanderer **2.** *adj.* itinerant, nomadic, roaming, rootless, roving, unsettled, vagabond

vague 1. fuzzy, generalized, hazy, ill-defined, imprecise, indefinite, indeterminate, nebulous, obscure, unclear, unspecified, woolly **2.** amorphous, blurred, dim, fuzzy, hazy, ill-defined, indistinct, nebulous, obscure, shadowy, unclear **3.** doubtful, uncertain, unclear, unknown

vaguely 1. imprecisely, in a general way, obscurely **2.** evasively **3.** dimly, obscurely **4.** absent-mindedly, vacantly

vagueness ambiguity, impreciseness, inexactitude, lack of preciseness, looseness, obscurity, undecidedness, woolliness

vain 1. arrogant, bigheaded (*informal*), cocky, conceited, egotistical, inflated, ostentatious, overweening, pleased with oneself, proud, self-important, stuck-up (*informal*), swaggering, swanky (*informal*), swollen-headed (*informal*), vainglorious **2.** abortive, empty, fruitless, futile, hollow, idle, nugatory, pointless, senseless, time-wasting, trifling, trivial, unavailing, unimportant, unproductive, unprofitable, useless, worthless **3. in vain** bootless, fruitless(ly), ineffectual(ly),

valediction (val-lid-**dik**-shun) *n* a farewell speech. **valedictory** *adj*

valence (**vale**-enss) *n Chem* the ability of atoms and chemical groups to form compounds.

valency *or esp US & Canad* **valence** *n, pl* **-cies** *or* **-ces** *Chem* the number of atoms of hydrogen that an atom or chemical group is able to combine with in forming compounds.

valentine *n* **1** a card sent as an expression of love on Saint Valentine's Day. **2** the person to whom one sends such a card.

valerian *n* a plant with small white or pinkish flowers and a medicinal root.

valet *n* **1** a male servant employed to look after another man. *~vb* **-eting, -eted 2** to act as a valet (for). **3** to clean the bodywork and interior of (a car) as a professional service.

valetudinarian (val-lit-yew-din-**air**-ee-an) *n* **1** a person who is chronically sick. **2** a person who continually worries about his or her health. **valetudinarianism** *n*

Valhalla *n Norse myth* the great hall of Odin where warriors who die as heroes in battle dwell eternally.

valiant *adj* very brave: *it was a valiant attempt to rescue the struggling victim.* **valiantly** *adv*

valid *adj* **1** based on sound reasoning: *I think that's a very valid question.* **2** legally acceptable: *she must produce a valid driving licence.* **3** important or serious enough to say or do: *religious broadcasting has a valid purpose.* **validity** *n*

validate *vb* **-dating, -dated 1** to prove (a claim or statement) to be true or correct. **2** to give legal force or official confirmation to. **validation** *n*

valise (val-**leez**) *n Old-fashioned* a small suitcase.

Valium *n Trademark* a drug used as a tranquillizer.

Valkyrie (val-**keer**-ee) *n Norse myth* any of the beautiful maidens who take the dead heroes to Valhalla.

valley *n* a long stretch of land between hills, often with a river flowing through it.

valour *or US* **valor** *n Literary* great bravery, esp. in battle. **valorous** *adj*

valuable *adj* **1** worth a large amount of money: *his house was furnished with valuable antique furniture.* **2** of great use or importance: *the investigations will provide valuable information.* *~n* **3 valuables** valuable articles of personal property, such as jewellery.

valuation *n* **1** a formal assessment of how much something is worth: *they will arrange a valuation on your house.* **2** the price arrived at by the process of valuing.

value *n* **1** the desirability of something, often in terms of its usefulness or exchangeability. **2** an amount of money considered to be a fair exchange for something: *50 kilos of cocaine with an approximate street value of £5 000 000.* **3** something worth the money it cost: *the set meal was value for money.* **4 values** the moral principles and beliefs of a person or group. **5** *Maths* a particular number or quantity represented by a figure or symbol. **6** *Music* short for **time value.** *~vb* **-uing, -ued 7** to assess the worth or desirability of (something). **8** to hold (someone or something) in high regard. **valued** *adj* **valueless** *adj* **valuer** *n*

value-added tax *n* See **VAT.**

value judgment *n* a personal opinion about something based on an individual's beliefs and not on facts which can be checked or proved.

valve *n* **1** a part attached to a pipe or tube which controls the flow of gas or liquid. **2** *Anat* a small flap in a hollow organ, such as the heart, that controls the flow and direction of blood. **3** a closed tube through which electrons move in a vacuum. **4** *Zool* one of the hinged shells of an oyster or clam. **5** *Music* a device on some brass instruments by which the effective length of the tube may be varied.

valvular *adj* of or relating to valves: *valvular heart disease.*

vamoose *vb* **-moosing, -moosed** *Slang, chiefly US* to leave a place hurriedly.

vamp[1] *Informal ~n* **1** a sexually attractive woman who seduces men. *~vb* **2** (of a woman) to seduce (a man).

vamp[2] *vb* **vamp up** to make (a story, piece of music, etc.) seem new by inventing additional parts.

vampire *n* (in European folklore) a corpse that rises nightly from its grave to drink the blood of living people.

vampire bat *n* a bat of Central and South America that feeds on the blood of birds and mammals.

van[1] *n* **1** a road vehicle with a roof and no side windows used to transport goods. **2** *Brit* a closed railway wagon used to transport luggage, goods, or mail.

van[2] *n* short for **vanguard.**

vanadium *n Chem* a silvery-white metallic element used to toughen steel. Symbol: V

Van Allen belt *n* either of two belts of charged particles which surround the Earth.

vandal *n* someone who deliberately causes damage to personal or public property. **vandalism** *n*

vandalize *or* **-ise** *vb* **-izing, -ized** *or* **-ising, -ised** to cause damage to (personal or public property) deliberately.

Van der Hum *n S African* a liqueur made from tangerines.

Vandyke beard *n* a short pointed beard.

vane *n* **1** one of the blades forming part of the wheel

THESAURUS

to no avail, to no purpose, unsuccessful(ly), useless(ly), vain(ly), wasted, without success

valedictory *adj.* farewell, final, parting

valiant bold, brave, courageous, dauntless, doughty, fearless, gallant, heroic, indomitable, intrepid, lionhearted, plucky, redoubtable, stouthearted, valorous, worthy

valid 1. acceptable, binding, conclusive, convincing, efficacious, efficient, good, just, logical, powerful, sound, substantial, telling, weighty, well-founded, well-grounded **2.** authentic, bona fide, genuine, in force, lawful, legal, legally binding, legitimate, official

validity 1. force, foundation, grounds, point, power, soundness, strength, substance, weight **2.** authority, lawfulness, legality, legitimacy, right

valley coomb, cwm (*Welsh*), dale, dell, depression, dingle, glen, hollow, strath (*Scot.*), vale

valuable *adj.* **1.** costly, dear, expensive, high-priced, precious **2.** beneficial, cherished, esteemed, estimable, held dear, helpful, important, prized, profitable, serviceable, treasured, useful, valued, worthwhile, worthy *~n.* **3.** *plural* heirlooms, treasure(s)

value *n.* **1.** advantage, benefit, desirability, help, importance, merit, profit, serviceableness, significance, use, usefulness, utility, worth **2.** cost, equivalent, market price, monetary worth, rate **3. values** code of behaviour, ethics, (moral) standards, principles *~vb.* **4.** account, appraise, assess, compute, estimate, evaluate, price, put a price on, rate, set at, survey **5.** appreciate, cherish, esteem, hold dear, hold in high regard *or* esteem, prize, regard highly, respect, set store by, treasure

of a windmill, a screw propeller, etc. **2** short for **weather vane.**

vanguard *n* **1** the leading division or units of an army. **2** the most advanced group or position in scientific research, a movement, etc.: *a distinguished architect in the vanguard of his profession.*

vanilla *n* **1** a flavouring for food such as ice cream, which comes from the pods of a tropical plant. **2** a flavouring extract prepared from the beans of this plant and used in cooking. *~adj* **3** flavoured with vanilla: *vanilla essence.*

vanish *vb* **1** to disappear suddenly: *the choppers vanished from radar screens at dawn yesterday.* **2** to cease to exist: *our favourite landmarks had vanished.*

vanishing cream *n Old-fashioned* a cosmetic cream that is colourless once applied.

vanishing point *n* the point in the distance where parallel lines appear to meet.

vanity *n* **1** a feeling of pride about one's appearance or ability. **2** (*pl* **-ties**) something about which one is vain: *it's one of my vanities that I can guess scents.*

vanity case *n* a small bag for holding cosmetics.

vanity unit *n* a hand basin built into a surface, usually with a cupboard below it.

vanquish *vb Literary* to defeat (someone) in a battle, contest, or argument.

vantage *n* a state, position, or opportunity offering advantage.

vantage point *n* a position that gives one an overall view of a scene or situation.

vapid *adj* dull and uninteresting: *their publications were vapid and amateurish.* **vapidity** *n*

vapor *n US* same as **vapour.**

vaporize *or* **-ise** *vb* **-izing, -ized** *or* **-ising, -ised** (of a liquid or solid) to change into vapour. **vaporization** *or* **-isation** *n*

vaporous *adj* resembling or full of vapour.

vapour *or US* **vapor** *n* **1** a mass of tiny drops of water or other liquids in the air, which appear as a mist. **2** the gaseous form of a substance that is usually a liquid or a solid. **3 the vapours** *Old-fashioned* a feeling of faintness, dizziness, and depression.

variable *adj* **1** likely to change at any time: *variable weather.* **2** *Maths* having a range of possible values. *~n* **3** something that is subject to variation. **4** *Maths* an expression that can be assigned any of a set of values. **variability** *n* **variably** *adv*

variance *n* **at variance** not in agreement: *the results of the UK poll were at variance with the overall EU findings.*

variant *adj* **1** differing from a standard or type: *variant spellings.* *~n* **2** something that differs from a standard or type.

variation *n* **1** something presented in a slightly different form: *his books are all variations on a basic theme.* **2** a change in level, amount, or quantity: *there was a variation in the figures.* **3** *Music* the repetition of a simple tune with the addition of new harmonies or a change in rhythm.

varicoloured *or US* **varicolored** *adj* having many colours.

varicose *adj* of or resulting from varicose veins: *a varicose ulcer.*

varicose veins *pl n* veins, usually in the legs, which have become knotted, swollen, and sometimes painful.

varied *adj* of different types, sizes, or quantities: *these young men and women would be of varied backgrounds.*

variegated *adj* having patches or streaks of different colours: *variegated holly.* **variegation** *n*

variety *n, pl* **-ties 1** the state of being diverse or various. **2** different things of the same kind: *I'm cooking the mince with a variety of vegetables.* **3** a particular type of something in the same general category: *this variety of pear is extremely juicy.* **4** *Taxonomy* a race whose distinct characters do not justify classification as a separate species. **5** a type of entertainment consisting of short unrelated acts, such as singing, dancing, and comedy.

various *adj* **1** several different: *there are various possible answers to this question.* **2** of different kinds: *the causes of high blood pressure are various and complicated.* **variously** *adv*

varlet *n Old-fashioned* **1** a menial servant. **2** a rascal.

varmint *n Informal* an irritating or obnoxious person or animal.

varnish *n* **1** a liquid painted onto a surface to give it a hard glossy finish. **2** a smooth surface, coated with or as if with varnish. **3** an artificial, superficial, or decep-

THESAURUS

valued cherished, dear, esteemed, highly regarded, loved, prized, treasured

valueless miserable, no good, of no earthly use, of no value, unsaleable, useless, worthless

vanguard advance guard, cutting edge, forefront, forerunners, front, front line, front rank, leaders, spearhead, trailblazers, trendsetters, van

vanish become invisible, be lost to sight, die out, disappear, disappear from sight *or* from the face of the earth, dissolve, evanesce, evaporate, exit, fade (away), melt (away)

vanity affected ways, airs, arrogance, bigheadedness (*informal*), conceit, conceitedness, egotism, narcissism, ostentation, pretension, pride, self-admiration, self-love, showing off (*informal*), swollen-headedness (*informal*)

vanquish beat, blow out of the water (*slang*), clobber (*slang*), conquer, crush, defeat, get the upper hand over, lick (*informal*), master, overcome, overpower, overwhelm, put down, put to flight, put to rout, quell, reduce, repress, rout, run rings around (*informal*), subdue, subjugate, tank (*slang*), triumph over, undo, wipe the floor with (*informal*)

vapour breath, dampness, exhalation, fog, fumes, haze, miasma, mist, smoke, steam

variable capricious, changeable, fickle, fitful, flexible, fluctuating, inconstant, mercurial, mutable, protean, shifting, temperamental, uneven, unstable, unsteady, vacillating, wavering

variance at variance at loggerheads, at odds, at sixes and sevens (*informal*), conflicting, in disagreement, in opposition, out of harmony, out of line

variant 1. *adj.* alternative, derived, different, divergent, exceptional, modified **2.** *n.* alternative, derived form, development, modification, sport (*Biol.*), variation

variation alteration, break in routine, change, departure, departure from the norm, deviation, difference, discrepancy, diversification, diversity, innovation, modification, novelty, variety

varied assorted, different, diverse, heterogeneous, manifold, miscellaneous, mixed, motley, sundry, various

variety 1. change, difference, discrepancy, diversification, diversity, many-sidedness, variation **2.** array, assortment, collection, cross section, intermixture, medley, miscellany, mixture, multiplicity, range **3.** brand, breed, category, class, kind, make, order, sort, species, strain, type

various assorted, different, differing, disparate, dis-

tively pleasing manner or appearance: *those who aspired to become civil servants acquired a varnish of university education.* 4 *Chiefly Brit* short for **nail varnish.** ~*vb* 5 to apply varnish to. 6 to try to make (something unpleasant) appear more attractive: *when did we start equivocating, camouflaging, varnishing the truth?*

varsity *n, pl* **-ties** *Brit & NZ old-fashioned & informal* short for **university.**

vary *vb* **varies, varying, varied 1** to change in appearance, character, or form. **2** to be different or cause to be different: *the age of appearance of underarm and body hair varies greatly from person to person.* **3** to give variety to: *you can vary the type of exercise you do.* **4** to change in accordance with another variable: *an individual's calorie requirement varies with age, sex, and physical activity.* **varying** *adj*

vas *n, pl* **vasa** *Anat, zool* a vessel or tube that carries a fluid.

vascular *adj Biol, anat* of or relating to the vessels that conduct and circulate body fluids such as blood or sap: *the vascular system.*

vas deferens *n, pl* **vasa deferentia** *Anat* either of the two ducts that convey sperm from the testicles to the penis.

vase *n* a glass or pottery jar used as an ornament or for holding cut flowers.

vasectomy *n, pl* **-mies** surgical removal of all or part of the vas deferens as a method of contraception.

Vaseline *n Trademark* petroleum jelly, used as an ointment or a lubricant.

vassal *n* **1** (in feudal society) a man who gave military service to a lord in return for protection and often land. **2** a person, nation, or state dominated by another. **vassalage** *n*

vast *adj* unusually large in size, degree, or number. **vastly** *adv* **vastness** *n*

vat *n* a large container for holding or storing liquids.

VAT (in Britain) value-added tax: a tax levied on the difference between the cost of materials and the selling price of a commodity or service.

Vatican *n* **1** the Pope's palace, in Rome. **2** the authority of the Pope.

vaudeville *n* variety entertainment consisting of short acts such as song-and-dance routines and comic turns.

vault[1] *n* **1** a secure room where money and other valuables are stored safely. **2** an underground burial chamber. **3** an arched structure that forms a roof or ceiling. **4** a cellar for storing wine.

vault[2] *vb* **1** to jump over (something) by resting one's hands on it or by using a long pole. ~*n* **2** the act of vaulting. **vaulter** *n*

vaulted *adj* being or having an arched roof: *an atmospheric vaulted dining-room.*

vaulting[1] *n* the arrangement of ceiling vaults in a building.

vaulting[2] *adj* excessively confident: *a vaulting ambition for the highest political office.*

vaunt *vb* **1** to describe or display (one's success or possessions) boastfully. ~*n* **2** a boast. **vaunted** *adj*

vb verb.

VC 1 Vice Chancellor. **2** Victoria Cross. **3** *History* Vietcong: the Communist-led guerrilla force of South Vietnam.

VCR video cassette recorder.

VD venereal disease.

VDU visual display unit.

veal *n* the meat from a calf, used as food.

vector *n* **1** *Maths* a variable quantity, such as force, that has magnitude and direction. **2** *Pathol* an animal, usually an insect, that carries a disease-producing microorganism from person to person.

Veda (vay da) *n* any or all of the most ancient sacred writings of Hinduism. **Vedic** *adj*

veer *vb* **1** to change direction suddenly: *the plane veered off the runway and careered through the perimeter fence.* **2** to change from one position or opinion to another: *her feelings veered from tenderness to sudden spurts of genuine love.* ~*n* **3** a change of course or direction.

veg *n Informal* a vegetable or vegetables.

vegan (vee-gan) *n* a person who does not eat meat, fish, or any animal products such as cheese, butter, etc.

vegeburger *or* **veggieburger** *n* a flat cake of chopped vegetables or pulses that is grilled or fried.

vegetable *n* **1** a plant, such as potato or cauliflower, with parts that are used as food. **2** *Informal* someone who is unable to move or think, as a result of brain damage. ~*adj* **3** of or like plants or vegetables.

vegetable marrow *n* a long green vegetable which can be cooked and eaten.

vegetable oil *n* any of a group of oils that are obtained from plants.

vegetal *adj* of or relating to plant life.

vegetarian *n* **1** a person who does not eat meat or fish. ~*adj* **2** excluding meat and fish: *a vegetarian diet.* **vegetarianism** *n*

vegetate *vb* **-tating, -tated** to live in a dull and boring way with no mental stimulation.

vegetation *n* plant life as a whole.

vegetative *adj* **1** of or relating to plant life or plant growth. **2** (of reproduction) characterized by asexual processes.

THESAURUS

tinct, divers (*archaic*), diverse, diversified, heterogeneous, manifold, many, many-sided, miscellaneous, several, sundry, varied, variegated

varnish *vb.* adorn, decorate, embellish, gild, glaze, gloss, japan, lacquer, polish, shellac

vary alter, alternate, be unlike, change, depart, differ, disagree, diverge, diversify, fluctuate, intermix, modify, permutate, reorder, transform

varying changing, different, distinct, distinguishable, diverse, fluctuating, inconsistent

vast astronomical, boundless, colossal, elephantine, enormous, extensive, gigantic, ginormous (*informal*), great, huge, humongous (*U.S. slang*), illimitable, immeasurable, immense, limitless, mammoth, massive, measureless, mega (*slang*), monstrous, monumental, never-ending, prodigious, sweeping, tremendous, unbounded, unlimited, voluminous, wide

vault[1] *n.* **1.** depository, repository, strongroom **2.** catacomb, cellar, crypt, mausoleum, tomb **3.** arch, ceiling, roof, span

vault[2] *vb.* bound, clear, hurdle, jump, leap, spring

vaunt boast about, brag about, crow about, exult in, flaunt, give oneself airs about, make a display of, make much of, parade, prate about, show off, talk big about (*informal*)

veer be deflected, change, change course, change direction, sheer, shift, swerve, tack, turn

vegetate be inert, deteriorate, exist, go to seed, idle, languish, loaf, moulder, stagnate, veg out (*slang, chiefly U.S.*)

veggie *Informal* ~*n* **1** a vegetable. **2** a vegetarian. ~*adj* **3** vegetarian: *a veggie cookbook.*

veggieburger *n* same as **vegeburger.**

vehement *adj* **1** expressing strong feelings or opinions. **2** (of actions or gestures) performed with great force or energy. **vehemence** *n* **vehemently** *adv*

vehicle *n* **1** a machine such as a bus or car for transporting people or goods. **2** something used to achieve a particular purpose or as a means of expression: *the newspaper was a vehicle for explaining government policies.* **3** *Pharmacol* an inactive substance mixed with the active ingredient in a medicine. **4** a liquid, such as oil, in which a pigment is mixed before it is applied to a surface. **vehicular** *adj*

veil *n* **1** a piece of thin cloth, usually as part of a hat or headdress, used to cover a woman's face. **2** something that conceals the truth: *a veil of secrecy.* **3 take the veil** to become a nun. ~*vb* **4** to cover or conceal with or as if with a veil.

veiled *adj* (of a comment or remark) presented in a disguised form: *it was a thinly veiled criticism.*

vein *n* **1** any of the tubes that carry blood to the heart. **2** a thin line in a leaf or in an insect's wing. **3** a clearly defined layer of ore or mineral in rock. **4** an irregular streak of colour in marble, wood, or cheese. **5** a distinctive trait or quality in speech or writing: *critics have exposed a strong vein of moralism in the poem.* **6** a temporary mood: *we're in a very humorous vein tonight.* **veined** *adj*

Velcro *n Trademark* a type of fastening consisting of one piece of fabric with tiny hooked threads and another with a coarse surface that sticks to it.

veld *or* **veldt** *n* the open country of South Africa including landscapes which are grassy, bushy, or thinly forested.

veleta (vel-**lee**-ta) *n* an old-time dance in triple time.

vellum *n* **1** a fine calf, kid, or lamb parchment. **2** a strong good-quality paper that resembles vellum.

velocipede (vel-**loss**-sip-peed) *n* an early form of bicycle.

velocity (vel-**loss**-it-ee) *n, pl* **-ties** the speed at which something is moving in a particular direction.

velour *or* **velours** (vel-**loor**) *n* a silk or cotton cloth similar to velvet.

velskoen (**fell**-skoon) *n S African* a sturdy ankle boot.

velvet *n* **1** a fabric with a thick close soft pile on one side. **2** the furry covering of the newly formed antlers of a deer. ~*adj* **3** made of velvet. **4** soft or smooth like velvet. **5 an iron hand in a velvet glove** determination concealed by a gentle manner. **velvety** *adj*

velveteen *n* a cotton fabric that resembles velvet.

venal (**vee**-nal) *adj* **1** willing to accept bribes in return for acting dishonestly: *venal politicians.* **2** associated with corruption or bribery: *venal greed.* **venality** *n*

vend *vb* to sell (goods).

vendetta *n* **1** a long-lasting quarrel between people or organizations in which they attempt to harm each other: *it's an inexplicable vendetta against the firm and its directors.* **2** a private feud between families in which members of one family kill members of the other family in revenge for earlier murders.

vending machine *n* a machine that automatically dispenses food, drinks, or cigarettes when money is inserted.

vendor *n* **1** a person who sells goods such as newspapers or hamburgers from a stall or cart. **2** *Chiefly law* a person who sells property.

veneer *n* **1** a thin layer of wood or plastic used to cover the surface of something made of cheaper material. **2** a deceptive but convincing appearance: *nobody penetrated his veneer of modest charm.*

venerable *adj* **1** (of a person) entitled to respect because of great age or wisdom. **2** (of an object) impressive because it is old or important historically. **3** *RC Church* a title given to a dead person who is going to be declared a saint. **4** *Church of England* a title given to an archdeacon.

venerate *vb* **-ating, -ated** to hold (someone) in deep respect. **venerator** *n*

veneration *n* a feeling of awe or great respect: *George Gershwin is worthy of the veneration accorded his classical counterparts.*

venereal (vin-**ear**-ee-al) *adj* **1** transmitted by sexual intercourse: *venereal infections.* **2** of the genitals: *venereal warts.*

venereal disease *n* a disease, such as syphilis, transmitted by sexual intercourse.

Venetian *adj* **1** of Venice, a port in NE Italy. ~*n* **2** a person from Venice.

Venetian blind *n* a window blind made of thin horizontal slats.

vengeance *n* **1** the act of killing, injuring, or harming someone for revenge. **2 with a vengeance** to a much greater extent or with much greater force than expected: *my career was beginning to take off with a vengeance.*

vengeful *adj* wanting revenge.

venial (**veen**-ee-al) *adj* easily excused or forgiven: *venial sins.*

venison *n* the flesh of a deer, used as food.

THESAURUS

vehemence ardour, eagerness, earnestness, emphasis, energy, enthusiasm, fervency, fervour, fire, force, forcefulness, heat, impetuosity, intensity, keenness, passion, verve, vigour, violence, warmth, zeal

vehement ardent, eager, earnest, emphatic, enthusiastic, fervent, fervid, fierce, flaming, forceful, forcible, impassioned, impetuous, intense, passionate, powerful, strong, violent, zealous

vehicle apparatus, channel, means, means of expression, mechanism, medium, organ

veil **1.** *n.* blind, cloak, cover, curtain, disguise, film, mask, screen, shade, shroud **2.** *vb.* cloak, conceal, cover, dim, disguise, hide, mantle, mask, obscure, screen, shield

veiled concealed, covert, disguised, hinted at, implied, masked, suppressed

vein **1.** blood vessel **2.** lode, seam, stratum **3.** streak, stripe **4.** dash, hint, strain, streak, thread, trait **5.** attitude, bent, character, faculty, humour, mode, mood, note, style, temper, tenor, tone, turn

venal bent (*slang*), corrupt, corruptible, crooked (*informal*), dishonourable, mercenary, rapacious, sordid, unprincipled

vendetta bad blood, blood feud, feud, quarrel

veneer *n.* appearance, façade, false front, finish, front, gloss, guise, mask, pretence, semblance, show

venerable august, esteemed, grave, honoured, respected, revered, reverenced, sage, sedate, wise, worshipped

venerate adore, esteem, hold in awe, honour, look up to, respect, revere, worship

veneration adoration, awe, deference, esteem, respect, reverence, worship

vengeance **1.** an eye for an eye, avenging, reprisal, requital, retaliation, retribution, revenge, settling of scores **2. with a vengeance** and no mistake, extreme-

Venn diagram *n Maths* a drawing which uses circles to show the relationships between different sets.

venom *n* **1** a feeling of great bitterness or anger towards someone. **2** the poison that certain snakes and scorpions inject when they bite or sting. **venomous** *adj* **venomously** *adv*

venous (vee-nuss) *adj* of or relating to veins.

vent[1] *n* **1** a small opening in something through which fresh air can enter and fumes can be released. **2** the shaft of a volcano through which lava and gases erupt. **3** the anal opening of a bird or other small animal. **4 give vent to** to release (an emotion) in an outburst: *she gave vent to her misery and loneliness.* ~*vb* **5** to release or express freely: *consumers vented their anger on the group by boycotting its products.* **6** to make vents in.

vent[2] *n* a vertical slit in the lower hem of a jacket.

ventilate *vb* **-lating, -lated 1** to let fresh air into (a room or building). **2** to discuss (ideas or feelings) openly: *ultra-rightists ventilated anti-Semitic sentiments.* **ventilation** *n*

ventilator *n* an opening or device, such as a fan, used to let fresh air into a room or building.

ventral *adj* relating to the front part of the body. **ventrally** *adv*

ventricle *n Anat* **1** a chamber of the heart that pumps blood to the arteries. **2** any one of the four main cavities of the brain. **ventricular** *adj*

ventriloquism *n* the ability to speak without moving the lips so that the words appear to come from another person or from another part of the room. **ventriloquist** *n*

venture *n* **1** a project or activity that is risky or of uncertain outcome. **2** a business operation in which there is the risk of loss as well as the opportunity for profit. ~*vb* **-turing, -tured 3** to do something that involves risk or danger: *I thought it wise to venture into foreign trade.* **4** to dare to express (an opinion). **5** to go to an unknown or dangerous place. **6** to dare (to do something): *you have asked me so often to come to your place that I ventured to drop in.* **venturer** *n*

Venture Scout *or* **Venturer** *n Brit* a member of the senior branch of the Scouts.

venturesome *adj* willing to take risks.

venue *n* a place where an organized gathering, such as a concert or a sporting event, is held.

Venus *n* **1** the Roman goddess of love. **2** the planet second nearest to the sun.

Venus's flytrap *or* **Venus flytrap** *n* a plant that traps and digests insects between hinged leaves.

veracious *adj* habitually truthful.

veracity *n* **1** habitual truthfulness. **2** accuracy.

verandah *or* **veranda** *n* **1** an open porch attached to a house. **2** *NZ* a continuous overhead canopy that gives shelter to pedestrians.

verb *n* a word that is used to indicate the occurrence or performance of an action or the existence of a state, for example *run, make,* or *do.*

verbal *adj* **1** of or relating to words: *verbal skills.* **2** spoken rather than written: *a verbal agreement.* **3** *Grammar* of or relating to a verb. **verbally** *adv*

verbalism *n* an exaggerated emphasis on the importance of words.

verbalize *or* **-ise** *vb* **-izing, -ized** *or* **-ising, -ised** to express (an idea or feeling) in words.

verbal noun *n Grammar* a noun derived from a verb, for example *smoking* in the sentence *smoking is bad for you.*

verbatim (verb-**bait**-im) *adv, adj* using exactly the same words: *a verbatim account of events.*

verbena *n* a plant with red, white, or purple sweet-smelling flowers.

verbiage *n* the excessive use of words.

verbose (verb-**bohss**) *adj* using more words than is necessary. **verbosity** *n*

verdant *adj Literary* covered with green vegetation.

verdict *n* **1** the decision made by a jury about the guilt or innocence of a defendant. **2** an opinion formed after examining the facts.

verdigris (ver-dig-reess) *n* a green or bluish coating which forms on copper, brass, or bronze that has been exposed to damp.

verdure *n Literary* flourishing green vegetation.

verge[1] *n* **1** a grass border along a road. **2 on the verge of** having almost reached (a point or condition). **3** an edge or rim. ~*vb* **verging, verged 4 verge on** to be near to: *she was verging on hysteria.*

verge[2] *vb* **verging, verged** to move in a specified direction: *verging towards the Irish Sea.*

verger *n Chiefly Church of England* **1** a church official who acts as caretaker. **2** an official who carries the rod of office before a bishop or dean in ceremonies and processions.

verify *vb* **-fies, -fying, -fied 1** to check the truth of (something) by investigation. **2** to prove (something) to be true. **verifiable** *adj* **verification** *n*

THESAURUS

ly, forcefully, furiously, greatly, to the full, to the utmost, vehemently, violently, with no holds barred

venial allowable, excusable, forgivable, insignificant, minor, pardonable, slight, trivial

venom 1. acidity, acrimony, bitterness, gall, grudge, hate, ill will, malevolence, malice, maliciousness, malignity, rancour, spite, spitefulness, spleen, virulence **2.** bane, poison, toxin

venomous 1. baleful, hostile, malicious, malignant, rancorous, savage, spiteful, vicious, vindictive, virulent **2.** baneful (*archaic*), noxious, poison, poisonous, toxic, virulent

vent 1. *n.* aperture, duct, hole, opening, orifice, outlet, split **2.** *vb.* air, come out with, discharge, emit, empty, express, give expression to, give vent to, pour out, release, utter, voice

ventilate air, bring out into the open, broadcast, debate, discuss, examine, make known, scrutinize, sift, talk about

venture *n.* **1.** adventure, chance, endeavour, enterprise, fling, gamble, hazard, jeopardy, project, risk, speculation, undertaking ~*vb.* **2.** chance, endanger, hazard, imperil, jeopardize, put in jeopardy, risk, speculate, stake, wager **3.** advance, dare, dare say, hazard, make bold, presume, stick one's neck out (*informal*), take the liberty, volunteer

verbal literal, oral, spoken, unwritten, verbatim, word-of-mouth

verbally by word of mouth, orally

verbatim exactly, precisely, to the letter, word for word

verbose diffuse, garrulous, long-winded, prolix, tautological, windy, wordy

verbosity long-windedness, loquaciousness, prolixity, rambling, verbiage, verboseness, wordiness

verdict adjudication, conclusion, decision, finding, judgment, opinion, sentence

verge 1. *n.* border, boundary, brim, brink, edge, extreme, limit, lip, margin, roadside, threshold **2.** *vb.* **verge on** approach, border, come near

verification authentication, confirmation, corroboration, proof, substantiation, validation

verily *adv Literary* truly: *for verily, this was their destiny.*

verisimilitude *n* the appearance of truth or reality.

veritable *adj* rightly called; real: *a veritable mine of information.* **veritably** *adv*

verity *n, pl* **-ties** a true statement or principle.

vermicelli (ver-me-**chell**-ee) *n* **1** very fine strands of pasta. **2** tiny chocolate strands used as a topping for cakes or ice cream.

vermiform *adj* shaped like a worm.

vermiform appendix *n Anat* same as **appendix.**

vermilion *adj* **1** orange-red. ~*n* **2** mercuric sulphide, used as an orange-red pigment; cinnabar.

vermin *pl n* **1** small animals collectively, such as insects and rodents, that spread disease and damage crops. **2** unpleasant people. **verminous** *adj*

vermouth (**ver**-muth) *n* a wine flavoured with herbs.

vernacular (ver-**nak**-yew-lar) *n* **1** the commonly spoken language or dialect of a particular people or place. ~*adj* **2** in or using the vernacular.

vernal *adj* of or occurring in spring. **vernally** *adv*

vernier (**ver**-nee-er) *n* a small movable scale in certain measuring instruments such as theodolites, used to obtain a fractional reading of one of the divisions on the main scale.

veronica *n* a plant with small blue, pink, or white flowers.

verruca (ver-**roo**-ka) *n Pathol* a wart, usually on the sole of the foot.

versatile *adj* having many different skills or uses. **versatility** *n*

verse *n* **1** a division of a poem or song. **2** poetry as distinct from prose. **3** one of the short sections into which chapters of the books of the Bible are divided. **4** a poem.

versed *adj* **versed in** knowledgeable about or skilled in.

versify *vb* **-fies, -fying, -fied 1** to put (something) into verse. **2** to write in verse. **versification** *n* **versifier** *n*

version *n* **1** a form of something, such as a piece of writing, with some differences from other forms. **2** an account of something from a certain point of view: *so far there's been no official version of the incident.* **3** an adaptation, for example of a book or play into a film.

verso *n, pl* **-sos 1** the left-hand page of a book. **2** the back of a sheet of printed paper.

versus *prep* **1** (in a sporting competition or lawsuit) against. **2** in opposition to or in contrast with: *man versus machine.*

vertebra (**ver**-tib-bra) *n, pl* **-brae** (-bree) one of the bony segments of the spinal column. **vertebral** *adj*

vertebrate *n* **1** an animal with a backbone, such as a fish, amphibian, reptile, bird, or mammal. ~*adj* **2** having a backbone.

vertex (**ver**-tex) *n, pl* **-tices** (-tiss-seez) **1** the highest point. **2** *Maths* **a** the point on a geometric figure where the sides form an angle. **b** the highest point of a triangle.

vertical *adj* **1** at right angles to the horizon: *the vertical cliff.* **2** straight up and down: *a vertical cut.* **3** *Econ* of or relating to associated or consecutive, though not identical, stages of industrial activity: *the purchase of a chain of travel agents by a leading tour operator will increase vertical integration in the holiday industry.* ~*n* **4** a vertical line or direction. **vertically** *adv*

vertiginous *adj* producing dizziness.

vertigo *n Pathol* a sensation of dizziness felt because one's balance is disturbed, sometimes experienced when looking down from a high place.

vervain *n* a plant with long slender spikes of purple, blue, or white flowers.

verve *n* great enthusiasm or liveliness.

very *adv* **1** used to add emphasis to adjectives and adverbs that are able to be graded: *I'm very happy; he'll be home very soon.* ~*adj* **2** used with nouns to give emphasis or exaggerated intensity: *the very end of his visit.*

very high frequency *n* a radio-frequency band lying between 300 and 30 megahertz.

Very light *n* a coloured flare for signalling at night.

vesicle *n Biol* **1** a small sac or cavity, esp. one filled with fluid. **2** a blister.

vespers *n* an evening service in some Christian churches.

vessel *n* **1** a ship or large boat. **2** an object used as a container for liquid. **3** *Biol* a tubular structure in animals and plants that carries body fluids, such as blood and sap.

vest *n* **1** *Brit* an undergarment covering the top half of the body. **2** *US, Canad, & Austral* a waistcoat. ~*vb* **3** **vest in** to settle (power or property) on: *by the power vested in me, I pronounce you man and wife.* **4** **vest with** to bestow on: *the sponsorship has vested these matches with a new interest.*

vestal *adj* **1** chaste or pure. ~*n* **2** a chaste woman.

vestal virgin *n* (in ancient Rome) one of the virgin priestesses dedicated to the goddess Vesta and to maintaining the sacred fire in her temple.

vested *adj Property law* having an existing right to the immediate or future possession of property.

vested interest *n* **1** a strong personal interest

THESAURUS

verify attest, attest to, authenticate, bear out, check, confirm, corroborate, prove, substantiate, support, validate

vernacular **1.** *n.* argot, cant, dialect, idiom, jargon, native language, parlance, patois, speech, vulgar tongue **2.** *adj.* colloquial, common, indigenous, informal, local, mother, native, popular, vulgar

versatile adaptable, adjustable, all-purpose, all-round, flexible, functional, handy, many-sided, protean, resourceful, variable

versed **versed in** accomplished, acquainted, competent, conversant, experienced, familiar, knowledgeable, practised, proficient, qualified, seasoned, skilled, well informed, well up in (*informal*)

version **1.** design, form, kind, model, style, type, variant **2.** account, adaptation, exercise, interpretation, portrayal, reading, rendering, side, translation

vertical erect, on end, perpendicular, upright

vertigo dizziness, giddiness, light-headedness, loss of equilibrium, swimming of the head

verve animation, dash, élan, energy, enthusiasm, force, get-up-and-go (*informal*), gusto, life, liveliness, pep, punch (*informal*), sparkle, spirit, vigour, vim (*slang*), vitality, vivacity, zeal, zip (*informal*)

very **1.** *adv.* absolutely, acutely, awfully (*informal*), decidedly, deeply, eminently, exceedingly, excessively, extremely, greatly, highly, jolly (*Brit.*), noticeably, particularly, profoundly, really, remarkably, superlatively, surpassingly, terribly, truly, uncommonly, unusually, wonderfully **2.** *adj.* actual, appropriate, exact, express, identical, perfect, precise, real, same, selfsame, unqualified

vessel **1.** barque (*poetic*), boat, craft, ship **2.** container, pot, receptacle, utensil

someone has in a matter because he or she might benefit from it. **2** *Property law* an existing right to the immediate or future possession of property.

vestibule *n* a small entrance hall.

vestige (**vest-ij**) *n* **1** a small amount or trace. **2** *Biol* an organ or part that is a small nonfunctional remnant of a functional organ in an ancestor.

vestigial (**vest-ij-ee-al**) *adj* remaining after a larger or more important thing has gone: *a strong seam of vestigial belief.*

vestments *pl n* **1** ceremonial clothes worn by the clergy at religious services. **2** robes that show authority or rank.

vestry *n, pl* **-tries** a room in a church used as an office by the priest or minister.

vet[1] *n* **1** short for **veterinary surgeon.** *~vb* **vetting, vetted 2** *Chiefly Brit* to make a careful check of (a person or document) for suitability: *guests have to be vetted and vouched for.*

vet[2] *n US & Canad* short for **veteran.**

vetch *n* **1** a climbing plant with blue or purple flowers. **2** the beanlike fruit of the vetch, used as fodder.

veteran *n* **1** a person who has given long service in some capacity. **2** a soldier who has seen a lot of active service. **3** *US & Canad* a person who has served in the military forces.

veteran car *n Brit* a car built before 1919, esp. before 1905.

veterinarian *n US & Canad* a veterinary surgeon.

veterinary *adj* relating to veterinary science.

veterinary medicine *or* **science** *n* the branch of medicine concerned with the treatment of animals.

veterinary surgeon *n Brit* a person qualified to practise veterinary medicine.

veto (**vee-toe**) *n, pl* **-toes 1** the power to prevent legislation or action proposed by others: *no single state has a veto.* **2** the exercise of this power. *~vb* **-toing, -toed 3** to refuse consent to (a proposal, such as a government bill). **4** to prohibit or forbid: *the Sports Minister vetoed the appointments.*

vex *vb* to cause (someone) to feel annoyance or irritation. **vexing** *adj* **vexation** *n*

vexatious *adj* vexing.

vexed *adj* **1** annoyed and puzzled. **2** much debated: *the vexed question of pay.*

VHF *or* **vhf** *Radio* very high frequency.

VHS *Trademark* Video Home System: a video cassette recorder system using half-inch magnetic tape.

VI Vancouver Island.

via *prep* **1** by way of; through: *he fled to London via Crete.* **2** by means of: *working from home and keeping in touch with office life via a video link-up.*

viable *adj* **1** able to be put into practice: *a viable alternative.* **2** (of seeds or eggs) capable of growth. **3** (of a fetus) sufficiently developed to survive outside the uterus. **viability** *n*

viaduct *n* a bridge for carrying a road or railway across a valley.

vial *n* same as **phial.**

viands *pl n Old-fashioned* food.

viaticum *n, pl* **-ca** *or* **-cums** *Christianity* Holy Communion given to a person dying or in danger of death.

vibes *pl n Informal* **1** the emotional reactions between people. **2** the atmosphere of a place. **3** short for **vibraphone.**

vibrant (**vibe-rant**) *adj* **1** full of energy and enthusiasm. **2** (of a voice) rich and full of emotion. **3** (of a colour) strong and bright. **vibrancy** *n*

vibraphone *n* a musical instrument with metal bars that resonate electronically when hit.

vibrate *vb* **-brating, -brated 1** to move backwards and forwards rapidly. **2** to have or produce a quivering or echoing sound. **3** *Physics* to undergo or cause to undergo vibration. **vibratory** *adj*

vibration *n* **1** a vibrating. **2** *Physics* **a** a periodic motion about an equilibrium position, such as in the production of sound. **b** a single cycle of such a motion.

vibrato *n, pl* **-tos** *Music* a slight rapid fluctuation in the pitch of a note.

vibrator *n* a device for producing a vibratory motion, used for massage or as a sex aid.

viburnum (**vie-burn-um**) *n* a subtropical shrub with white flowers and berry-like fruits.

Vic. Victoria (Australian state).

vicar *n* **1** *Church of England* a priest who is in charge

THESAURUS

vest *vb.* *with* **in** *or* **with** authorize, be devolved upon, bestow, confer, consign, empower, endow, entrust, furnish, invest, lodge, place, put in the hands of, settle

vestibule anteroom, entrance hall, foyer, hall, lobby, porch, portico

vestige evidence, glimmer, hint, indication, relic, remainder, remains, remnant, residue, scrap, sign, suspicion, token, trace, track

vet *vb.* appraise, check, check out, examine, give (someone *or* something) the once-over (*informal*), investigate, look over, pass under review, review, scan, scrutinize, size up (*informal*)

veteran master, old hand, old stager, old-timer, past master, past mistress, pro (*informal*), trouper, warhorse (*informal*)

veto 1. *n.* ban, boycott, embargo, interdict, nonconsent, prohibition **2.** *vb.* ban, boycott, disallow, forbid, give the thumbs down to, interdict, kill (*informal*), negative, prohibit, put the kibosh on (*slang*), refuse permission, reject, rule out, turn down

vex afflict, aggravate (*informal*), agitate, annoy, bother, bug (*informal*), displease, distress, disturb, exasperate, fret, gall, get on one's nerves (*informal*), grate on, harass, hassle (*informal*), irritate, molest, nark (*Brit., Austral., & N.Z. slang*), needle (*informal*), nettle, offend, peeve (*informal*), perplex, pester, pique, plague, provoke, put out, rile, tease, torment, trouble, upset, worry

vexation aggravation (*informal*), annoyance, displeasure, dissatisfaction, exasperation, frustration, irritation, pique

vexatious afflicting, aggravating (*informal*), annoying, bothersome, burdensome, disagreeable, disappointing, distressing, exasperating, harassing, irksome, irritating, nagging, provoking, teasing, tormenting, troublesome, trying, unpleasant, upsetting, worrisome, worrying

vexed 1. afflicted, aggravated (*informal*), agitated, annoyed, bothered, confused, displeased, distressed, disturbed, exasperated, fed up, hacked (off) (*U.S. slang*), harassed, irritated, miffed (*informal*), nettled, out of countenance, peeved (*informal*), perplexed, pissed off (*taboo slang*), provoked, put out, riled, ruffled, tormented, troubled, upset, worried **2.** contested, controversial, disputed, moot, much debated

viable applicable, feasible, operable, practicable, usable, within the bounds of possibility, workable

vibrant alive, animated, colourful, dynamic, electrifying, full of pep (*informal*), responsive, sensitive, sparkling, spirited, vivacious, vivid

vibrate fluctuate, judder (*informal*), oscillate, pulsate, pulse, quiver, resonate, reverberate, shake, shiver, sway, swing, throb, tremble, undulate

of a parish. **2** *RC Church* a church officer acting as deputy to a bishop. **vicarial** *adj*

vicarage *n* the house where a vicar lives.

vicar apostolic *n RC Church* a clergyman with authority in missionary countries.

vicar general *n, pl* **vicars general** an official appointed to assist the bishop in his administrative duties.

vicarious (vik-**air**-ee-uss) *adj* **1** felt indirectly by imagining what another person experiences: *vicarious satisfaction.* **2** undergone or done as the substitute for another: *vicarious adventures.* **3** delegated: *vicarious power.* **vicariously** *adv*

Vicar of Christ *n RC Church* the Pope as Christ's representative on earth.

vice[1] *n* **1** an immoral or evil habit or action: *greed is only one of their vices.* **2** a habit regarded as a weakness in someone's character: *one of his few vices is cigars.* **3** criminal activities involving sex, drugs, or gambling.

vice[2] *or US* **vise** *n* a tool with a pair of jaws for holding an object while work is done on it.

vice[3] *adj* serving in the place of; being next in importance to: *the vice chairman.*

vice admiral *n* a senior commissioned officer in certain navies.

vice chancellor *n* the chief executive or administrator at some British universities.

vicegerent *n* a person appointed to exercise all or some of the authority of another.

vice president *n* an officer ranking immediately below a president and serving as his or her deputy. **vice-presidency** *n*

viceregal *adj* **1** of a viceroy. **2** *Chiefly Austral & NZ* of a governor or governor general.

viceroy *n* a governor of a colony or country who represents the monarch.

vice squad *n* a police division responsible for the enforcement of gaming and prostitution laws.

vice versa *adv* the other way round: *there were attacks on northerners by southerners and vice versa.*

Vichy water (**vee**-shee) *n* a natural mineral water from Vichy in France which is supposed to be good for the health.

vicinity (viss-**in**-it-ee) *n* the area immediately surrounding a place.

vicious *adj* **1** cruel or violent: *vicious attacks.* **2** forceful or ferocious: *she gave the chair a vicious jerk.* **3** intended to cause hurt or distress: *vicious letters.* **4** (of an animal) fierce or hostile. **viciously** *adv* **viciousness** *n*

vicious circle *n* a situation in which an attempt to resolve one problem creates new problems that recreate the original one.

vicissitudes (viss-**iss**-it-yewds) *pl n* changes in circumstance or fortune.

victim *n* **1** a person or thing that suffers harm or death. **2** a person who is tricked or swindled. **3** a living person or animal sacrificed in a religious rite.

victimize *or* **-ise** *vb* **-izing, -ized** *or* **-ising, -ised** to punish or discriminate against (someone) selectively or unfairly. **victimization** *or* **-isation** *n*

victor *n* **1** a person or nation that has defeated an enemy in war. **2** the winner of a contest or struggle.

victoria *n* **1** a large sweet red-and-yellow plum. **2** a light four-wheeled horse-drawn carriage with a folding hood.

Victoria Cross *n* the highest decoration for bravery in battle awarded to the British and Commonwealth armed forces.

Victorian *adj* **1** of or in the reign of Queen Victoria of Great Britain and Ireland (1837–1901). **2** characterized by prudery or hypocrisy. *~n* **3** a person who lived during the reign of Queen Victoria.

Victoriana *pl n* objects of the Victorian period.

victorious *adj* **1** having defeated an enemy or opponent: *the victorious allies.* **2** of or characterized by victory: *a victorious smile.*

victory *n, pl* **-ries 1** the winning of a war or battle. **2** success attained in a contest or struggle.

victual *vb* **-ualling, -ualled** *or US* **-ualing, -ualed** *Old-fashioned* to supply with or obtain victuals. **victualler** *or US* **-ualer** *n*

victuals (**vit**-tals) *pl n Old-fashioned* food and drink.

vicuna (vik-**kew**-na) *n* **1** a S American mammal like the llama. **2** the fine cloth made from its wool.

vide (**vie**-dee) see: used to direct a reader to a specified place in a text or in another book.

videlicet (vid-**deal**-ee-set) *adv* namely: used to specify items.

video *n, pl* **-os 1** the recording and showing of films and events using a television set, video tapes, and a video recorder. **2** short for **video cassette. 3** short for **video cassette recorder.** *~vb* **videoing, videoed 4** to record (a television programme or an event) on video. *~adj* **5** relating to or used in producing televised images.

video cassette *n* a cassette containing video tape.

video cassette recorder *n* a tape recorder for recording and playing back television programmes and films.

video frequency *n* the frequency of a signal conveying the image and synchronizing pulses in a television broadcasting system.

video game *n* a game that can be played by using an

THESAURUS

vibration juddering (*informal*), oscillation, pulsation, pulse, quiver, resonance, reverberation, shaking, throb, throbbing, trembling, tremor

vice 1. blemish, defect, failing, fault, imperfection, shortcoming, weakness **2.** corruption, degeneracy, depravity, evil, evildoing, immorality, iniquity, profligacy, sin, turpitude, venality, wickedness

vicinity area, district, environs, locality, neck of the woods (*informal*), neighbourhood, precincts, propinquity, proximity

vicious 1. abhorrent, atrocious, barbarous, cruel, dangerous, diabolical, ferocious, fiendish, foul, heinous, monstrous, savage, vile, violent **2.** backbiting, bitchy (*informal*), cruel, defamatory, malicious, mean, rancorous, slanderous, spiteful, venomous, vindictive

viciousness 1. cruelty, ferocity, savagery **2.** bitchiness (*slang*), malice, rancour, spite, spitefulness, venom

victim 1. casualty, fatality, injured party, martyr, sacrifice, scapegoat, sufferer **2.** dupe, easy prey, fall guy (*informal*), innocent, sitting duck (*informal*), sitting target, sucker (*slang*)

victimize discriminate against, have a down on (someone) (*informal*), have it in for (someone) (*informal*), have one's knife into (someone), persecute, pick on

victor champ (*informal*), champion, conquering hero, conqueror, first, prizewinner, top dog (*informal*), vanquisher, winner

victorious champion, conquering, first, prizewinning, successful, triumphant, vanquishing, winning

victory conquest, laurels, mastery, success, superiority, the prize, triumph, win

electronic control to move symbols on the screen of a visual display unit.

video nasty *n* a film, usually specially made for video, that is explicitly horrific and pornographic.

videophone *n* a communications device by which people can both see and speak to each other.

video recorder *n* short for **video cassette recorder.**

video tape *n* **1** magnetic tape used mainly for recording the video-frequency signals of a television programme or film. *~vb* **video-tape, -taping, -taped 2** to record (a film or programme) on video tape.

video tape recorder *n* a tape recorder for visual signals, using magnetic tape on open spools: used in television broadcasting.

videotex *n* same as **viewdata.**

videotext *n* a means of providing a written or graphical representation of computerized information on a television screen.

vie *vb* **vying, vied** to compete (with someone): *the sisters vied with each other to care for her.* **vying** *adj, n*

Vietnamese *adj* **1** of Vietnam. *~n* **2** (*pl* **-ese**) a person from Vietnam. **3** the language of Vietnam.

view *n* **1** opinion, judgment, or belief: *in my view that doesn't really work.* **2** an understanding of or outlook on something: *a specific view of human history.* **3** everything that can be seen from a particular place or in a particular direction: *there was a beautiful view from the window.* **4** vision or sight, esp. range of vision: *as they turned into the drive, the house came into view.* **5** a picture of a scene. **6** the act of seeing or observing. **7 in view of** taking into consideration. **8 on view** exhibited to the public. **9 take a dim** *or* **poor view of** to regard (something) unfavourably. **10 with a view to** with the intention of. *~vb* **11** to consider in a specified manner: *they viewed the visit with hardly disguised apprehension.* **12** to examine or inspect (a house or flat) carefully with a view to buying it. **13** to look at. **14** to watch (television).

viewdata *n Trademark* a videotext service linking users to a computer by telephone, enabling shopping, ticket booking, etc., to be done from home.

viewer *n* **1** a person who views something, esp. television. **2** a hand-held device for looking at photographic slides.

viewfinder *n* a device on a camera that lets the user see what will be included in the photograph.

viewpoint *n* **1** a person's attitude towards something. **2** a place from which one gets a good view.

vigil (**vij**-ill) *n* **1** a night-time period of staying awake to look after a sick person, pray, etc. **2** *RC Church, Church of England* the eve of certain major festivals.

vigilance *n* careful attention.

vigilance committee *n* (in the U.S.) a self-appointed body of citizens organized to maintain order.

vigilant *adj* on the watch for trouble or danger.

vigilante (vij-ill-**ant**-ee) *n* a person who takes it upon himself or herself to enforce the law.

vignette (vin-**yet**) *n* **1** a short description of the typical features of something. **2** a small decorative illustration in a book. **3** a photograph or drawing with edges that are shaded off.

vigorous *adj* **1** having physical or mental energy. **2** displaying or performed with vigour: *vigorous exercise.* **vigorously** *adv*

vigour *or US* **vigor** *n* **1** physical or mental energy. **2** forcefulness: *the vigour of his invective astonished MPs.* **3** strong healthy growth.

Viking *n* any of the Scandinavians who raided by sea most of N and W Europe from the 8th to the 11th centuries.

vile *adj* **1** morally wicked: *a vile regime.* **2** disgusting: *the vile smell of the man.* **3** unpleasant or bad: *a vile day at work.* **vilely** *adv*

vilify (vill-if-fie) *vb* **-fies, -fying, -fied** to speak very badly of (someone). **vilification** *n*

villa *n* **1** a large house with gardens. **2** a house rented to holiday-makers.

THESAURUS

victuals bread, eats (*slang*), food, grub (*slang*), meat, nosebag (*slang*), nosh (*slang*), provisions, rations, stores, supplies, tack (*informal*), viands

view *n.* **1.** *Sometimes plural* attitude, belief, conviction, feeling, impression, judgment, notion, opinion, point of view, sentiment, thought, way of thinking **2.** aspect, landscape, outlook, panorama, perspective, picture, prospect, scene, spectacle, vista **3.** range *or* field of vision, sight, vision **4.** contemplation, display, examination, inspection, look, recce (*slang*), scan, scrutiny, sight, survey, viewing **5. with a view to** in order to, in the hope of, so as to, with the aim *or* intention of *~vb.* **6.** consider, deem, judge, look on, regard, think about **7.** behold, check, check out (*informal*), clock (*Brit. slang*), contemplate, examine, explore, eye, eyeball (*U.S. slang*), gaze at, get a load of (*informal*), inspect, look at, observe, recce (*slang*), regard, scan, spectate, stare at, survey, take a dekko at (*Brit. slang*), watch, witness

viewer observer, one of an audience, onlooker, spectator, TV watcher, watcher

viewpoint angle, frame of reference, perspective, point of view, position, slant, stance, standpoint, vantage point, way of thinking

vigilant alert, attentive, careful, cautious, circumspect, keeping one's eyes peeled *or* skinned (*informal*), on one's guard, on one's toes, on the alert, on the lookout, on the watch, sleepless, unsleeping, wakeful, watchful, wide awake

vigorous active, brisk, dynamic, effective, efficient, energetic, enterprising, flourishing, forceful, forcible, full of energy, hale, hale and hearty, hardy, healthy, intense, lively, lusty, powerful, red-blooded, robust, sound, spanking, spirited, strenuous, strong, virile, vital, zippy (*informal*)

vigorously all out, eagerly, energetically, forcefully, hammer and tongs, hard, like mad (*slang*), lustily, strenuously, strongly, with a vengeance, with might and main

vigour activity, animation, balls (*taboo slang*), brio, dash, dynamism, energy, force, forcefulness, gusto, health, liveliness, might, oomph (*informal*), pep, power, punch (*informal*), robustness, soundness, spirit, strength, verve, vim (*slang*), virility, vitality, zip (*informal*)

vile 1. abandoned, abject, appalling, bad, base, coarse, contemptible, corrupt, debased, degenerate, degrading, depraved, despicable, disgraceful, evil, humiliating, ignoble, impure, loathsome, low, mean, miserable, nefarious, perverted, shocking, sinful, ugly, vicious, vulgar, wicked, worthless, wretched **2.** disgusting, foul, horrid, loathsome, nasty, nauseating, noxious, obscene, offensive, repellent, repugnant, repulsive, revolting, sickening, yucky *or* yukky (*slang*)

vilify abuse, berate, calumniate, debase, decry, defame, denigrate, disparage, knock (*informal*), malign, pull to pieces (*informal*), revile, rubbish (*informal*), run down, slag (off) (*slang*), slander, smear, speak ill of, traduce

village *n* **1** a small group of houses in a country area. **2** the inhabitants of such a community. **villager** *n*

villain *n* **1** a wicked or evil person. **2** the main wicked character in a novel or play.

villainous *adj* of or like a villain.

villainy *n, pl* **-lainies** evil or vicious behaviour.

villein (**vill**-an) *n* (in medieval Europe) a peasant who was directly subject to his lord, to whom he paid dues and services in return for his land. **villeinage** *n*

villus *n, pl* **villi** *Zool, anat* any of the numerous finger-like projections of the mucous membrane lining the small intestine of many vertebrates.

vim *n Informal* vigour and energy.

vinaigrette *n* salad dressing made from oil and vinegar with seasonings.

vindicate *vb* **-cating, -cated 1** to clear (someone) of guilt or suspicion. **2** to provide justification for: *the arrests may vindicate the strong-arm tactics.* **vindication** *n*

vindictive *adj* **1** maliciously seeking revenge. **2** characterized by spite or ill will. **vindictively** *adv* **vindictiveness** *n*

vine *n* **1** a plant, such as the grapevine, with long flexible stems that climb by clinging to a support. **2** the stem of such a plant. **viny** *adj*

vinegar *n* **1** a sour-tasting liquid made by fermentation of beer, wine, or cider, used for salad dressing or for pickling. **2** bad temper or spitefulness: *the vinegar in her pen is often a welcome seasoning to duller news.* **vinegary** *adj*

vineyard (**vinn**-yard) *n* an area of land where grapes are grown.

vingt-et-un (**van**-tay-**uhn**) *n* same as **pontoon**[2].

viniculture *n* the process or business of growing grapes and making wine. **viniculturist** *n*

vino (**vee**-noh) *n, pl* **-nos** *Informal* wine.

vinous (**vine**-uss) *adj* of or characteristic of wine.

vintage *n* **1** the wine obtained from a particular harvest of grapes. **2** the harvest from which such a wine is obtained. **3** a time of origin: *an open-necked shirt of uncertain vintage.* ~*adj* **4** (of wine) of an outstandingly good year. **5** representative of the best and most typical: *a vintage Saint Laurent dress.*

vintage car *n Chiefly Brit* a car built between 1919 and 1930.

vintner *n* a wine merchant.

vinyl (**vine**-ill) *n* **1** any of various strong plastics made by the polymerization of vinyl compounds, such as PVC. **2** conventional records made of vinyl as opposed to compact discs. ~*adj* **3** *Chem* of or containing the monovalent group of atoms CH_2CH–: *vinyl chloride.* **4** of or made of vinyl: *vinyl tiles.*

viol (**vie**-oll) *n* a stringed musical instrument that preceded the violin.

viola[1] (vee-**oh**-la) *n* a bowed stringed instrument of the violin family, slightly larger and lower in pitch than the violin.

viola[2] (**vie**-ol-la) *n* a variety of pansy.

viola da gamba (vee-**oh**-la da **gam**-ba) *n* the second largest and lowest member of the viol family.

violate *vb* **-lating, -lated 1** to break (a law or agreement). **2** to disturb rudely or improperly: *these men who were violating her privacy.* **3** to treat (a sacred place) disrespectfully. **4** to rape. **violation** *n* **violator** *n*

violence *n* **1** the use of physical force, usually intended to cause injury or destruction. **2** great force or strength in action, feeling, or expression.

violent *adj* **1** using or involving physical force with the intention of causing injury or destruction: *violent clashes with government supporters.* **2** very intense: *I took a violent dislike to him.* **3** sudden and forceful: *a violent explosion.* **violently** *adv*

violet *n* **1** a plant with bluish-purple flowers. ~*adj* **2** bluish-purple.

violin *n* a musical instrument, the highest member of the violin family, with four strings played with a bow.

violinist *n* a person who plays the violin.

violist (vee-**oh**-list) *n* a person who plays the viola.

violoncello (vie-oll-on-**chell**-oh) *n, pl* **-los** same as **cello**.

VIP very important person.

viper *n* a type of poisonous snake.

virago (vir-**rah**-go) *n, pl* **-goes** *or* **-gos** an aggressive woman.

viral (**vie**-ral) *adj* of or caused by a virus.

virgin *n* **1** a person, esp. a woman, who has never had sexual intercourse. ~*adj* **2** not having had sexual intercourse. **3** fresh and unused: *he found a scrap of virgin*

THESAURUS

villain 1. blackguard, criminal, evildoer, knave (*archaic*), libertine, malefactor, miscreant, profligate, rapscallion, reprobate, rogue, scoundrel, wretch **2.** antihero, baddy (*informal*)

villainous atrocious, bad, base, blackguardly, criminal, cruel, debased, degenerate, depraved, detestable, diabolical, evil, fiendish, hateful, heinous, ignoble, infamous, inhuman, mean, nefarious, outrageous, sinful, terrible, thievish, vicious, vile, wicked

villainy atrocity, baseness, crime, criminality, delinquency, depravity, devilry, iniquity, knavery, rascality, sin, turpitude, vice, wickedness

vindicate 1. absolve, acquit, clear, defend, do justice to, exculpate, excuse, exonerate, free from blame, justify, rehabilitate **2.** advocate, assert, establish, maintain, support, uphold

vindication apology, assertion, defence, excuse, exoneration, justification, maintenance, plea, rehabilitation, substantiation, support

vindictive full of spleen, implacable, malicious, malignant, rancorous, relentless, resentful, revengeful, spiteful, unforgiving, unrelenting, vengeful, venomous

vintage 1. *n.* collection, crop, epoch, era, generation, harvest, origin, year **2.** *adj.* best, choice, classic, mature, prime, rare, ripe, select, superior, venerable

violate 1. break, contravene, disobey, disregard, encroach upon, infringe, transgress **2.** abuse, befoul, defile, desecrate, invade, outrage, pollute, profane **3.** assault, debauch, dishonour, outrage, rape, ravish

violation 1. abuse, breach, contravention, encroachment, infringement, transgression, trespass **2.** defilement, desecration, profanation, sacrilege, spoliation

violence 1. bestiality, bloodshed, bloodthirstiness, brutality, brute force, cruelty, destructiveness, ferocity, fierceness, fighting, force, frenzy, fury, murderousness, passion, rough handling, savagery, strong-arm tactics (*informal*), terrorism, thuggery, vehemence, wildness **2.** abandon, acuteness, fervour, force, harshness, intensity, power, raging, roughness, severity, sharpness, turbulence, wildness

violent 1. berserk, bloodthirsty, brutal, cruel, destructive, fiery, flaming, forcible, furious, headstrong, homicidal, hot-headed, impetuous, intemperate, maddened, maniacal, murderous, passionate, powerful, raging, riotous, rough, savage, strong, tempestuous, uncontrollable, ungovernable, unrestrained, vehement, vicious, wild **2.** acute, agonizing, biting, excruciating,

paper in a sea of memoranda. **4** not yet cultivated, explored, or exploited by people: *virgin territory.*

Virgin *n* **1** **the Virgin** same as **Virgin Mary. 2** a statue or picture of the Virgin Mary.

virginal[1] *adj* **1** like a virgin. **2** extremely pure or fresh.

virginal[2] *n* an early keyboard instrument like a small harpsichord.

Virgin Birth *n Christianity* the doctrine that Jesus Christ was conceived solely by the direct intervention of the Holy Spirit so that Mary remained a virgin.

Virginia creeper *n* a climbing plant with leaves that turn red in autumn.

virginity *n* the condition or fact of being a virgin.

Virgin Mary *n* **the Virgin Mary** *Christianity* Mary, the mother of Christ.

Virgo *n Astrol* the sixth sign of the zodiac; the Virgin.

virile *adj* **1** having the traditional male characteristics of physical strength and a high sex drive. **2** forceful and energetic: *a virile Highland fling.* **virility** *n*

virology *n* the branch of medicine concerned with the study of viruses. **virological** *adj*

virtual *adj* **1** having the effect but not the appearance or form of: *the investigation has now come to a virtual standstill.* **2** *Computers* designed so as to extend the potential of a finite system beyond its immediate limits: *virtual memory.* **3** of or relating to virtual reality.

virtually *adv* almost or nearly: *he is virtually a prisoner in his own palace.*

virtual reality *n* a computer-generated environment that seems real to the user.

virtue *n* **1** moral goodness. **2** a positive moral quality: *the virtue of humility.* **3** an advantage or benefit: *the added virtue of being harmless.* **4** chastity, esp. in women. **5 by virtue of** by reason of; because of: *they escaped execution by virtue of their high rank.*

virtuoso *n, pl* **-si** *or* **-sos 1** a person with exceptional musical skill. **2** a person with exceptional skill in any area. *~adj* **3** showing exceptional skill or brilliance: *a virtuoso performance.* **virtuosity** *n*

virtuous *adj* **1** morally good. **2** (of a woman) chaste. **virtuously** *adv*

virulent (vir-yew-lent) *adj* **1** extremely bitter or hostile. **2 a** (of a microorganism) very infectious. **b** (of a disease) having a violent effect. **3** extremely poisonous or harmful: *the most virulent poison known.* **virulence** *n*

virus *n* **1** a microorganism that is smaller than a bacterium and can cause disease in humans, animals, or plants. **2** *Informal* a disease caused by a virus. **3** *Computers* an unsanctioned and self-replicating program which, when activated, corrupts a computer's data and disables its operating system.

visa *n* an official stamp in a passport permitting its holder to travel into or through the country of the government issuing it.

visage (viz-zij) *n Chiefly literary* **1** face. **2** appearance.

vis-à-vis (veez-ah-vee) *prep* in relation to.

viscera (viss-er-a) *pl n Anat* the large internal organs of the body collectively.

visceral *adj* **1** of or affecting the viscera. **2** instinctive rather than rational: *visceral hatred of the neighbours.*

viscid (viss-id) *adj* sticky.

viscose *n* **1** a sticky solution obtained by dissolving cellulose. **2** rayon made from this material.

viscosity *n, pl* **-ties 1** the state of being viscous. **2** *Physics* the extent to which a fluid resists a tendency to flow.

viscount (vie-count) *n* (in the British Isles) a nobleman ranking below an earl and above a baron. **viscountcy** *n*

viscountess (vie-count-iss) *n* **1** a woman holding the rank of viscount. **2** the wife or widow of a viscount.

viscous *adj* (of liquids) thick and sticky.

vise *n US* same as **vice**[2].

visibility *n* **1** the range or clarity of vision: *visibility was good, despite rain.* **2** the condition of being visible.

visible *adj* **1** able to be seen. **2** able to be perceived by the mind: *a visible and flagrant act of aggression.* **visibly** *adv*

vision *n* **1** the ability to see. **2** a vivid mental image produced by the imagination: *I kept having visions of him being tortured.* **3** a hallucination caused by divine inspiration, madness, or drugs: *visions of God.* **4** great perception of future developments: *what he had in-*

THESAURUS

extreme, harsh, inordinate, intense, outrageous, painful, severe, sharp

virgin *n.* **1.** damsel (*archaic*), girl, maid (*archaic*), maiden (*archaic*), vestal *~adj.* **2.** chaste, immaculate, maidenly, modest, pure, uncorrupted, undefiled, unsullied, vestal, virginal **3.** fresh, immaculate, new, pristine, unsullied, untouched, unused

virile forceful, lusty, macho, male, manlike, manly, masculine, potent, red-blooded, robust, strong, vigorous

virility machismo, manhood, masculinity, potency, vigour

virtual essential, implicit, implied, in all but name, indirect, potential, practical, tacit, unacknowledged

virtually as good as, effectually, for all practical purposes, in all but name, in effect, in essence, nearly, practically, to all intents and purposes

virtue 1. ethicalness, excellence, goodness, high-mindedness, incorruptibility, integrity, justice, morality, probity, quality, rectitude, righteousness, uprightness, worth, worthiness **2.** advantage, asset, attribute, credit, good point, good quality, merit, plus (*informal*), strength **3.** chastity, honour, innocence, morality, purity, virginity **4. by virtue of** as a result of, by dint of, by reason of, in view of, on account of, owing to, thanks to

virtuosity brilliance, craft, expertise, finish, flair, mastery, panache, polish, skill

virtuoso 1. *n.* artist, genius, grandmaster, maestro, magician, master, master hand **2.** *adj.* bravura (*Music*), brilliant, dazzling, masterly

virtuous 1. blameless, ethical, excellent, exemplary, good, high-principled, honest, honourable, incorruptible, moral, praiseworthy, pure, righteous, squeaky-clean, upright, worthy **2.** celibate, chaste, clean-living, innocent, pure, spotless, virginal

virulent 1. acrimonious, bitter, hostile, malevolent, malicious, rancorous, resentful, spiteful, splenetic, venomous, vicious, vindictive **2.** baneful (*archaic*), deadly, infective, injurious, lethal, malignant, pernicious, poisonous, septic, toxic, venomous

visible anywhere to be seen, apparent, clear, conspicuous, detectable, discernible, discoverable, distinguishable, evident, in sight, in view, manifest, not hidden, noticeable, observable, obvious, palpable, patent, perceivable, perceptible, plain, to be seen, unconcealed, unmistakable

vision 1. eyes, eyesight, perception, seeing, sight, view **2.** castle in the air, concept, conception, daydream, dream, fantasy, idea, ideal, image, mental picture, pipe dream **3.** apparition, chimera, delusion, ghost, hallucination, illusion, mirage, phantasm, phan-

stead of charisma was vision. **5** the image on a television screen. **6** a person or thing of extraordinary beauty.

visionary *adj* **1** showing foresight: *a visionary statesman.* **2** idealistic but impractical. **3** given to having visions. **4** of or like visions. *~n, pl* **-aries 5** a visionary person.

visit *vb* **-iting, -ited 1** to go or come to see (a person or place). **2** to stay with (someone) as a guest. **3** *Old-fashioned* (of a disease or disaster) to afflict. **4 visit on** *or* **upon** to inflict (punishment) on. **5 visit with** *US informal* to chat with (someone). *~n* **6** the act or an instance of visiting. **7** a professional or official call. **8** a stay as a guest.

visitant *n* **1** a ghost or apparition. **2** a migratory bird temporarily resting in a particular region.

visitation *n* **1** an official visit or inspection. **2** a punishment or reward from heaven. **3** an appearance of a supernatural being.

Visitation *n* **a** the visit made by the Virgin Mary to her cousin Elizabeth (Luke 1: 39–56). **b** the Church festival commemorating this, held on July 2.

visiting hours *pl n* the times when visitors are allowed to see someone in a hospital or other institution: *many prisoners' wives complain about the short visiting hours.*

visitor *n* a person who visits a person or place.

visitor's passport *n* a British passport, valid for one year, that grants access to some countries, usually for a restricted period.

visor (**vize**-or) *n* **1** a transparent flap on a helmet that can be pulled down to protect the face. **2** a small movable screen attached above the windscreen in a vehicle, used as protection against the glare of the sun. **3** a peak on a cap.

vista *n* **1** an extensive view. **2** a wide range of possibilities or future events: *the vista of opportunity.*

visual *adj* **1** done by or used in seeing. **2** capable of being seen. **visually** *adv*

visual aids *pl n* objects to be looked at that help the viewer to understand or remember something.

visual display unit *n Computers* a device with a screen for displaying data held in a computer.

visualize *or* **-ise** *vb* **-izing, -ized** *or* **-ising, -ised** to form a mental image of (something not at that moment visible). **visualization** *or* **-isation** *n*

vital *adj* **1** essential or highly important: *marriage isn't such a vital part of his life.* **2** energetic or lively: *the epitome of vital youthful manhood.* **3** necessary to maintain life: *the vital organs.* *~n* **4 vitals** the bodily organs, such as the brain and heart, that are necessary to maintain life. **vitally** *adv*

vitality *n* physical or mental energy.

vitalize *or* **-ise** *vb* **-izing, -ized** *or* **-ising, -ised** to fill with life or vitality. **vitalization** *or* **-isation** *n*

vital statistics *pl n* **1** population statistics, such as the numbers of births, marriages, and deaths. **2** *Informal* the measurements of a woman's bust, waist, and hips.

vitamin *n* one of a group of substances that occur naturally in certain foods and are essential for normal health and growth.

vitiate (**vish**-ee-ate) *vb* **-ating, -ated 1** to spoil or weaken the effectiveness of (something). **2** to destroy the legal effect of (a contract). **vitiation** *n*

viticulture *n* the cultivation of grapevines.

vitreous *adj* **1** of or like glass. **2** of or relating to the vitreous humour.

vitreous humour *or* **body** *n* a transparent gelatinous substance that fills the eyeball between the lens and the retina.

vitrify *vb* **-fies, -fying, -fied** to change into glass or a glassy substance. **vitrification** *n*

vitriol *n* **1** language expressing bitterness and hatred. **2** sulphuric acid.

vitriolic *adj* (of language) severely bitter or harsh.

vituperative (vite-**tyew**-pra-tiv) *adj* bitterly abusive. **vituperation** *n*

viva[1] *interj* long live (a specified person or thing).

viva[2] *Brit ~n* **1** an examination in the form of an interview. *~vb* **vivaing, vivaed 2** to examine (a candidate) in a spoken interview.

vivace (viv-**vah**-chee) *adj Music* to be performed in a lively manner.

vivacious *adj* full of energy and enthusiasm.

vivacity *n* the quality of being vivacious.

vivarium *n, pl* **-iums** *or* **-ia** a place where live animals are kept under natural conditions.

THESAURUS

tom, revelation, spectre, wraith **4.** breadth of view, discernment, farsightedness, foresight, imagination, insight, intuition, penetration, prescience **5.** dream, feast for the eyes, perfect picture, picture, sight, sight for sore eyes, spectacle

visionary *adj.* **1.** chimerical, delusory, fanciful, fantastic, ideal, idealized, illusory, imaginary, impractical, speculative, unreal, unrealistic, unworkable, utopian **2.** dreaming, dreamy, idealistic, quixotic, romantic, starry-eyed, with one's head in the clouds *~n.* **3.** daydreamer, Don Quixote, dreamer, enthusiast (*archaic*), idealist, mystic, prophet, romantic, seer, theorist, Utopian, zealot

visit *vb.* **1.** be the guest of, call in, call on, drop in on (*informal*), go to see, inspect, look (someone) up, pay a call on, pop in (*informal*), stay at, stay with, stop by, take in (*informal*) **2.** afflict, assail, attack, befall, descend upon, haunt, smite, trouble **3.** *with* **on** *or* **upon** bring down upon, execute, impose, inflict, wreak *~n.* **4.** call, sojourn, stay, stop

visitation 1. examination, inspection, visit **2.** bane, blight, calamity, cataclysm, catastrophe, disaster, infliction, ordeal, punishment, scourge, trial

visitor caller, company, guest

visual 1. ocular, optic, optical **2.** discernible, observable, perceptible, visible

visualize conceive of, conjure up a mental picture of, envisage, imagine, picture, see in the mind's eye

vital 1. basic, cardinal, essential, fundamental, imperative, indispensable, necessary, radical, requisite **2.** animated, dynamic, energetic, forceful, full of the joy of living, lively, spirited, vibrant, vigorous, vivacious, zestful **3.** critical, crucial, decisive, important, key, life-or-death, significant, urgent

vitality animation, brio, energy, exuberance, go (*informal*), life, liveliness, lustiness, pep, robustness, sparkle, stamina, strength, vigour, vim (*slang*), vivaciousness, vivacity

vitriolic acerbic, acid, bitchy (*informal*), bitter, caustic, destructive, dripping with malice, envenomed, sardonic, scathing, venomous, virulent, withering

vituperation abuse, blame, castigation, censure, fault-finding, flak (*informal*), invective, obloquy, rebuke, reprimand, reproach, scurrility, tongue-lashing, vilification

vivacious animated, bubbling, cheerful, chirpy (*informal*), ebullient, effervescent, frolicsome, full of life, gay, high-spirited, jolly, light-hearted, lively, merry,

viva voce (vive-a **voh**-chee) *adv, adj* **1** by word of mouth. ~*n* **2** same as **viva**[2] (sense 1).
vivid *adj* **1** very bright: *a vivid blue sky.* **2** very clear and detailed: *vivid memories.* **3** easily forming lifelike images: *a vivid imagination.* **vividly** *adv* **vividness** *n*
vivify *vb* **-fies, -fying, -fied 1** to bring to life. **2** to make more vivid or striking.
viviparous (viv-**vip**-a-russ) *adj* giving birth to living offspring, as most mammals do.
vivisection *n* the performing of experiments on living animals, involving cutting into or dissecting the body. **vivisectionist** *n*
vixen *n* **1** a female fox. **2** *Informal* a spiteful woman.
viz *adv* namely: used to specify items: *I had only one object, viz, to beat the Germans.*
vizier (viz-**zeer**) *n* a high official in certain Muslim countries.
vizor *n* same as **visor.**
VLF *or* **vlf** *Radio* very low frequency.
V neck *n* **a** a neck on a garment that comes down to a point, like the letter V. **b** a sweater with a neck like this. **V-neck** *or* **V-necked** *adj*
vocab *n* short for **vocabulary.**
vocable *n Linguistics* a word regarded simply as a sequence of letters or spoken sounds.
vocabulary *n, pl* **-laries 1** all the words that a person knows. **2** all the words contained in a language. **3** the specialist terms used in a given subject. **4** a list of words in another language with their translations. **5** a range of symbols or techniques as used in any of the arts or crafts: *the building's vocabulary of materials, textures, and tones.*
vocal *adj* **1** of or relating to the voice: *vocal pitch.* **2** expressing one's opinions clearly and openly: *a vocal minority with racist views.* ~*n* **3 vocals** the singing part of a piece of jazz or pop music. **vocally** *adv*
vocal cords *pl n* either of two pairs of membranous folds in the larynx, of which the lower pair can be made to vibrate and produce sound by forcing air from the lungs over them.
vocalist *n* a singer with a pop group.
vocalize *or* **-ise** *vb* **-izing, -ized** *or* **-ising, -ised 1** to express with or use the voice. **2** to make vocal or articulate: *vocalize your discontent.* **3** *Phonetics* to articulate (a speech sound) with voice. **vocalization** *or* **-isation** *n*
vocation *n* **1** a specified profession or trade. **2 a** a special urge to a particular calling or career, esp. a religious one. **b** such a calling or career.
vocational *adj* directed towards a particular profession or trade: *vocational training.*
vocative *n Grammar* a grammatical case used in some languages when addressing a person or thing.
vociferate *vb* **-ating, -ated** to exclaim or cry out about (something) noisily. **vociferation** *n*
vociferous *adj* loud and forceful: *a vociferous minority.* **vociferously** *adv*
vodka *n* a clear alcoholic spirit originating in Russia, made from potatoes or grain.
voetsak *or* **voetsek** (**foot**-sak) *interj S African offensive, informal* an expression of dismissal or rejection.
vogue *n* **1** the popular style at a given time. **2 in vogue** fashionable. ~*adj* **3** fashionable: *a vogue word.* **voguish** *adj*
voice *n* **1** the sound made by the vibration of the vocal cords, esp. when modified by the tongue and mouth. **2** a distinctive tone of the speech sounds characteristic of a particular person: *he can recognize her voice.* **3** the ability to speak or sing: *he had at last found his voice.* **4** the condition or quality of a person's voice: *her voice was kind.* **5** the musical sound of a singing voice: *what I have is a good voice and a great love of lyrics.* **6** the expression of feeling or opinion: *there was a chorus of dissenting voices.* **7** a right to express an opinion: *the party should now move towards a system which will give every member an equal voice.* **8** *Grammar* a category of the verb that expresses whether it is active or passive. **9** *Phonetics* the sound characterizing the articulation of several speech sounds, that is produced when the vocal cords are vibrated by the breath. **10 with one voice** unanimously. ~*vb* **voicing, voiced 11** to express verbally: *anyone with an objection has a chance to voice it.* **12** to articulate (a speech sound) with voice.
voiced *adj Phonetics* articulated with accompanying vibration of the vocal cords, for example "b" in English.
voiceless *adj* **1** without a voice. **2** *Phonetics* articulated without accompanying vibration of the vocal cords, for example "p" in English.
voice-over *n* the voice of an unseen commentator heard during a film.
void *n* **1** a feeling or condition of loneliness or deprivation. **2** an empty space or area. ~*adj* **3** having no official value or authority, because the terms have been broken or have not been fulfilled: *the race was declared void and rerun.* **4** *Old-fashioned or literary* empty: *behold, the tomb is void!* **5 void of** devoid of

THESAURUS

scintillating, sparkling, sparky, spirited, sportive, sprightly, upbeat (*informal*), vital
vivacity animation, brio, ebullience, effervescence, energy, gaiety, high spirits, life, liveliness, pep, quickness, sparkle, spirit, sprightliness
vivid 1. bright, brilliant, clear, colourful, glowing, intense, rich **2.** distinct, dramatic, graphic, highly-coloured, lifelike, memorable, powerful, realistic, sharp, sharply-etched, stirring, strong, telling, true to life **3.** active, lively, quick, strong, vigorous
vixen ballbreaker (*slang*), bitch (*slang*), fury, harpy, harridan, scold, shrew, spitfire, termagant (*rare*), virago, Xanthippe
vocabulary dictionary, glossary, language, lexicon, wordbook, word hoard, words, word stock
vocal *adj.* **1.** articulate, articulated, oral, put into words, said, spoken, uttered, voiced **2.** articulate, blunt, clamorous, eloquent, expressive, forthright, frank, free-spoken, noisy, outspoken, plain-spoken, strident, vociferous
vocation business, calling, career, employment, job, life's work, life work, métier, mission, office, post, profession, pursuit, role, trade
vociferous clamant, clamorous, loud, loudmouthed (*informal*), noisy, obstreperous, outspoken, ranting, shouting, strident, uproarious, vehement, vocal
vogue 1. *n.* craze, custom, fashion, last word, mode, style, the latest, the rage, the thing (*informal*), trend, way **2.** *adj.* fashionable, in, modish, now (*informal*), popular, prevalent, trendy (*Brit. inf.*), up-to-the-minute, voguish, with it (*informal*)
voice *n.* **1.** articulation, language, power of speech, sound, tone, utterance, words **2.** decision, expression, part, say, view, vote, will, wish ~*vb.* **3.** air, articulate, assert, come out with (*informal*), declare, divulge, enunciate, express, give expression *or* utterance to, put into words, say, utter, ventilate
void *n.* **1.** blank, blankness, emptiness, gap, lack, opening, space, vacuity, vacuum, want ~*adj.* **2.** dead, ineffective, ineffectual, inoperative, invalid, nonviable,

or without: *the fact of being punished becomes void of all moral significance.* ~*vb* **6** to make ineffective or invalid. **7** to empty. **8** to discharge the contents of (the bowels or bladder).

voile (**voyl**) *n* a light semitransparent dress fabric.

vol. volume.

volatile (**voll**-a-tile) *adj* **1** (of circumstances) liable to sudden change. **2** (of people) liable to sudden changes of mood and behaviour. **3** (of a substance) changing quickly from a solid or liquid form to a vapour. **volatility** *n*

volatilize *or* **-lise** *vb* **-lizing, -lized** *or* **-lising, -lised** to change from a solid or liquid to a vapour. **volatilization** *or* **-lisation** *n*

vol-au-vent (**voll**-oh-von) *n* a very light puff pastry case with a savoury filling.

volcanic *adj* **1** of or relating to volcanoes: *volcanic ash.* **2** displaying sudden violence or anger: *their boisterous and often volcanic behaviour.*

volcano *n, pl* **-noes** *or* **-nos 1** an opening in the earth's crust from which molten lava, ashes, dust, and gases are ejected from below the earth's surface. **2** a mountain formed from volcanic material ejected from a vent.

vole *n* a small rodent with a stocky body and a short tail.

volition *n* **1** the ability to decide things for oneself. **2 of one's own volition** through one's own choice. **volitional** *adj*

volley *n* **1** the simultaneous firing of several weapons. **2** the bullets fired. **3** a burst of questions or critical comments. **4** *Sport* a stroke or kick at a moving ball before it hits the ground. ~*vb* **5** to fire (weapons) in a volley. **6** *Sport* to hit or kick (a moving ball) before it hits the ground.

volleyball *n* a game in which two teams hit a large ball backwards and forwards over a high net with their hands.

volt *n* the SI unit of electric potential; the potential difference between two points on a conductor carrying a current of 1 ampere, when the power dissipated between these points is 1 watt.

voltage *n* an electromotive force or potential difference expressed in volts.

voltaic *adj* same as **galvanic** (sense 1).

volte-face (volt-**fass**) *n, pl* **volte-face** a reversal of opinion.

voltmeter *n* an instrument for measuring voltage.

voluble *adj* talking easily and at length. **volubility** *n* **volubly** *adv*

volume *n* **1** the magnitude of the three-dimensional space enclosed within or occupied by something. **2** an amount or total: *the volume of trade between the two countries; the volume of military traffic.* **3** loudness of sound. **4** the control on a radio etc., for adjusting the loudness of sound. **5** a book: *a slim volume.* **6** one of several books that make up a series. **7** a set of issues of a magazine over a specified period.

volumetric *adj* of or using measurement by volume: *a simple volumetric measurement.*

voluminous *adj* **1** (of clothes) large and roomy. **2** (of writings) extensive and detailed.

voluntary *adj* **1** done or undertaken by free choice: *voluntary repatriation.* **2** done or maintained without payment: *voluntary work.* **3** (of muscles) having their action controlled by the will. ~*n, pl* **-taries 4** *Music* a composition, usually for organ, played at the beginning or end of a church service. **voluntarily** *adv*

volunteer *n* **1** a person who offers voluntarily to do something. **2** a person who freely undertakes military service. ~*vb* **3** to offer (oneself or one's services) by choice and without being forced. **4** to enlist voluntarily for military service. **5** to give (information) willingly. **6** to offer the services of (another person).

voluptuary *n, pl* **-aries** a person devoted to luxury and sensual pleasures.

voluptuous *adj* **1** (of a woman) sexually alluring because of the fullness of her figure. **2** pleasing to the senses: *voluptuous yellow peaches.* **voluptuously** *adv* **voluptuousness** *n*

volute *n* a spiral or twisting shape or object, such as a carved spiral scroll on an Ionic capital.

vomit *vb* **-iting, -ited 1** to eject (the contents of the stomach) through the mouth. **2** to eject or be ejected forcefully. ~*n* **3** the partly digested food and drink ejected in vomiting.

voodoo *n* **1** a religion involving ancestor worship and witchcraft, practised by Black people in the West Indies, esp. in Haiti. ~*adj* **2** of or relating to voodoo: *a voodoo curse.*

THESAURUS

nugatory, null and void, unenforceable, useless, vain, worthless **3.** bare, clear, drained, emptied, empty, free, tenantless, unfilled, unoccupied, vacant **4.** *with* **of** destitute, devoid, lacking, without ~*vb.* **5.** cancel, invalidate, nullify, rescind **6.** discharge, drain, eject, eliminate (*Physiol.*), emit, empty, evacuate

volatile airy, changeable, erratic, explosive, fickle, flighty, gay, giddy, inconstant, lively, mercurial, sprightly, temperamental, unsettled, unstable, unsteady, up and down (*informal*), variable, whimsical

volition choice, choosing, determination, discretion, election, free will, option, preference, purpose, resolution, will

volley *n.* barrage, blast, bombardment, burst, cannonade, discharge, explosion, fusillade, hail, salvo, shower

volubility fluency, gift of the gab, glibness, loquaciousness, loquacity

voluble articulate, blessed with the gift of the gab, fluent, forthcoming, glib, loquacious, talkative

volume 1. aggregate, amount, body, bulk, capacity, compass, cubic content, dimensions, mass, quantity, total **2.** book, publication, title, tome, treatise

voluminous ample, big, billowing, bulky, capacious, cavernous, copious, full, large, massive, prolific, roomy, vast

voluntarily by choice, freely, of one's own accord, of one's own free will, on one's own initiative, willingly, without being asked, without prompting

voluntary discretional, discretionary, free, gratuitous, honorary, intended, intentional, optional, spontaneous, uncompelled, unconstrained, unforced, unpaid, volunteer, willing

volunteer *vb.* advance, let oneself in for (*informal*), need no invitation, offer, offer one's services, present, proffer, propose, put forward, put oneself at (someone's) disposal, step forward, suggest, tender

voluptuous 1. ample, buxom, curvaceous (*informal*), enticing, erotic, full-bosomed, provocative, seductive, shapely, well-stacked (*Brit. slang*) **2.** luxurious, sensual, sybaritic

voluptuousness 1. curvaceousness (*informal*), seductiveness, shapeliness **2.** sensuality

vomit *vb.* barf (*U.S. slang*), belch forth, be sick, bring up, chuck (up) (*slang, chiefly U.S.*), chunder (*slang, chiefly Austral.*), disgorge, do a technicolour yawn (*slang*), eject, emit, heave, puke (*slang*), regurgitate, retch, sick up (*informal*), spew out *or* up, throw up

voorkamer (**foor**-kahm-er) *n S African* the front room of a house.

voracious *adj* **1** eating or craving great quantities of food. **2** very eager or insatiable in some activity: *a voracious collector.* **voraciously** *adv* **voracity** *n*

vortex (**vor**-tex) *n, pl* **-tices** (-tiss-seez) **1** a whirling mass or motion, such as a whirlpool or whirlwind. **2** a situation which draws people into it against their will: *the vortex of other people's problems.* **vortical** *adj*

votary *n, pl* **-ries 1** *RC Church, Eastern Churches* a person who has dedicated himself or herself to religion by taking vows. **2** a person devoted to a cause. **votaress** *fem n*

vote *n* **1** a choice made by a participant in a shared decision, esp. in electing a candidate. **2** the right to vote. **3** the total number of votes cast. **4** the opinion of a group of people as determined by voting: *the draft should be put to the vote at a meeting of the Council.* **5** a body of votes or voters collectively: *the youth vote.* ~*vb* **voting, voted 6** to make a choice by vote. **7** to authorize or allow by voting: *the organizing committee voted itself controversial new powers.* **8** to declare oneself as being (something or in favour of something) by voting: *I've always voted Labour.* **9** *Informal* to declare by common opinion: *he was voted hotelier of the year.*

vote down *vb* to decide against or defeat in a vote: *a proposed British resolution was voted down.*

voter *n* a person who can or does vote.

votive *adj* done or given to fulfil a vow.

vouch *vb* **vouch for a** to give personal assurance about: *I can vouch for the man, he's a relative by marriage.* **b** to give supporting evidence for or be proof of: *his presence alone vouches for the political nature of the trip.*

voucher *n* **1** *Brit* a ticket or card used instead of money to buy specified goods: *a gift voucher.* **2** a document recording a financial transaction.

vouchsafe *vb* **-safing, -safed 1** *Old-fashioned* to give or grant: *she has powers vouchsafed to few.* **2** to offer assurances about; guarantee: *he absolutely vouchsafed your integrity.*

vow *n* **1** a solemn and binding promise. **2 take vows** to enter a religious order and commit oneself to its rule of life by the vows of poverty, chastity, and obedience. ~*vb* **3** to promise or decide solemnly: *she vowed to fight on; I solemnly vowed that some day I would return to live in Europe.*

vowel *n* **a** a voiced speech sound made with the mouth open and the stream of breath unobstructed by the tongue, teeth, or lips, for example *a* or *e*. **b** a letter representing this.

vox pop *n* interviews with members of the public on a radio or television programme.

vox populi *n* public opinion.

voyage *n* **1** a long journey by sea or in space. ~*vb* **-aging, -aged 2** to go on a voyage: *in this story he voyages to Ireland.* **voyager** *n*

voyageur (voy-ahzh-**ur**) *n* (in Canada) a woodsman, guide, trapper, boatman, or explorer, esp. in the North.

voyeur *n* a person who obtains sexual pleasure from watching people undressing or having sexual intercourse. **voyeurism** *n* **voyeuristic** *adj*

VPL *Jocular* visible panty line.

vrou (**froh**) *n S African* an Afrikaner woman, esp. a married woman.

vs versus.

V-sign *n* **1** (in Britain) an offensive gesture made by sticking up the index and middle fingers with the palm of the hand inwards. **2** a similar gesture with the palm outwards meaning victory or peace.

VSO Voluntary Service Overseas.

VSOP very special (*or* superior) old pale: used of brandy or port.

VT Vermont.

VTOL vertical takeoff and landing.

VTR video tape recorder.

vulcanite *n* a hard black rubber produced by vulcanizing natural rubber with sulphur.

vulcanize *or* **-ise** *vb* **-izing, -ized** *or* **-ising, -ised** to treat (rubber) with sulphur under heat and pressure to improve elasticity and strength. **vulcanization** *or* **-isation** *n*

vulgar *adj* **1** showing lack of good taste, decency, or refinement: *vulgar tabloid sensationalism.* **2** denoting a form of a language spoken by the ordinary people, rather than the literary form. **vulgarly** *adv*

vulgar fraction *n* same as **simple fraction.**

vulgarian *n* a vulgar person, usually one who is rich.

vulgarism *n* a coarse or obscene word or phrase.

vulgarity *n, pl* **-ties 1** the condition of being vulgar. **2** a vulgar action or phrase.

vulgarize *or* **-ise** *vb* **-izing, -ized** *or* **-ising, -ised 1** to make vulgar. **2** to make (something little known or difficult to understand) popular. **vulgarization** *or* **-isation** *n*

Vulgar Latin *n* any of the dialects of Latin spoken in the Roman Empire other than classical Latin.

Vulgate *n* the fourth-century Latin version of the Bible.

vulnerable *adj* **1** able to be physically or emotionally hurt. **2** easily influenced or tempted. **3** *Mil* exposed to attack. **4** financially weak and likely to fail: *this company could be vulnerable in a prolonged economic slump.* **5** *Bridge* (of a side that has won one game towards rubber) subject to increased bonuses or penalties. **vulnerability** *n*

THESAURUS

(*informal*), toss one's cookies (*U.S. slang*), upchuck (*U.S. slang*)

voracious avid, devouring, gluttonous, greedy, hungry, insatiable, omnivorous, prodigious, rapacious, ravening, ravenous, uncontrolled, unquenchable

vote *n.* **1.** ballot, franchise, plebiscite, poll, referendum, right to vote, show of hands, suffrage ~*vb.* **2.** ballot, cast one's vote, elect, go to the polls, opt, return **3.** *informal* declare, judge, pronounce, propose, recommend, suggest

vouch *Usually with* **for** affirm, answer for, assert, asseverate, attest to, back, certify, confirm, give assurance of, go bail for, guarantee, stand witness, support, swear to, uphold

vouchsafe accord, cede, condescend to give, confer, deign, favour (someone) with, grant, yield

vow 1. *n.* oath, pledge, promise, troth (*archaic*) **2.** *vb.* affirm, consecrate, dedicate, devote, pledge, promise, swear, undertake solemnly

voyage *n.* crossing, cruise, journey, passage, travels, trip

vulgar 1. blue, boorish, cheap and nasty, coarse, common, crude, dirty, flashy, gaudy, gross, ill-bred, impolite, improper, indecent, indecorous, indelicate, low, nasty, naughty, off colour, ribald, risqué, rude, suggestive, tasteless, tawdry, uncouth, unmannerly, unrefined **2.** general, native, ordinary, unrefined, vernacular

vulgarity bad taste, coarseness, crudeness, crudity, gaudiness, grossness, indelicacy, lack of refinement, ribaldry, rudeness, suggestiveness, tastelessness, tawdriness

vulpine *adj* **1** of or like a fox. **2** clever and cunning.
vulture *n* **1** a very large bird of prey that feeds on flesh of dead animals. **2** a person who profits from the misfortune and weakness of others.
vulva *n* the external genitals of human females.

THESAURUS

vulnerable accessible, assailable, defenceless, exposed, open to attack, sensitive, susceptible, tender, thin-skinned, unprotected, weak, wide open

W

W *Cricket* **a** wicket. **b** wide.
W 1 *Chem* tungsten. **2** watt. **3** West(ern).
WA 1 Washington (state). **2** Western Australia.
wacky *adj* **wackier, wackiest** *Slang* odd, eccentric, or crazy: *a wacky idea.* **wackiness** *n*
wad *n* **1** a small mass of soft material, such as cotton wool, used for packing or stuffing. **2** a roll or bundle of banknotes or papers.
wadding *n* a soft material used for padding or stuffing.
waddle *vb* **-dling, -dled 1** to walk with short steps, rocking slightly from side to side. *~n* **2** a swaying walk.
wade *vb* **wading, waded 1** to walk slowly and with difficulty through water or mud. **2 wade in** *or* **into** to begin doing (something) in an energetic way: *wading into the fray.* **3 wade through** to proceed with difficulty through: *a stack of literature to wade through.*
wader *n* a long-legged bird, such as the heron or stork, that lives near water and feeds on fish. Also called: **wading bird**
waders *pl n* long waterproof boots which completely cover the legs, worn by anglers for standing in water.
wadi **(wod-dee)** *n, pl* **-dies** a river in N Africa or Arabia, which is dry except in the rainy season.
wafer *n* **1** a thin crisp sweetened biscuit, often served with ice cream. **2** *Christianity* a round thin piece of unleavened bread used at Communion. **3** *Electronics* a small thin slice of germanium or silicon that is separated into numerous individual components or circuits.
wafer-thin *adj* very thin: *wafer-thin meat.*
waffle[1] *n* a square crisp pancake with a gridlike pattern.
waffle[2] *Informal, chiefly Brit ~vb* **-fling, -fled 1** to speak or write in a vague and wordy manner. *~n* **2** vague and wordy speech or writing.
waft *vb* **1** to move gently through the air as if being carried by the wind: *the scent of summer flowers gently wafting through my window. ~n* **2** a scent carried on the air.
wag[1] *vb* **wagging, wagged 1** to move rapidly and repeatedly from side to side or up and down. *~n* **2** an instance of wagging.
wag[2] *n Old-fashioned* a humorous or witty person. **waggish** *adj*
wage *n* **1** Also: **wages** the money paid in return for a person's work, esp. when paid weekly or daily rather than monthly: *a campaign for higher wages. ~vb* **waging, waged 2** to engage in (a campaign or war).
wager *n* **1** a bet on the outcome of an event or activity. *~vb* **2** to bet (something, esp. money) on the outcome of an event or activity.
waggle *vb* **-gling, -gled** to move with a rapid shaking or wobbling motion.
wagon *or* **waggon** *n* **1** a four-wheeled vehicle used for carrying heavy loads, sometimes pulled by a horse or tractor. **2** *Brit* an open railway freight truck. **3** a lorry. **4 on the wagon** *Informal* abstaining from alcoholic drink. **wagoner** *or* **waggoner** *n*
wagtail *n* a small songbird of Eurasia and Africa with a very long tail that wags up and down when it walks.
wahine (wah-**hee**-nee) *n NZ* a Maori woman.
waif *n* a person, esp. a child, who is, or who looks as if he or she might be, homeless or neglected.
wail *vb* **1** to utter a prolonged high-pitched cry of pain or sorrow. *~n* **2** a prolonged high-pitched cry of pain or sorrow. **wailing** *n, adj*
wain *n Poetic* a farm cart.
wainscot *n* a wooden covering on the lower half of the walls of a room. Also: **wainscoting**
waist *n* **1** *Anat* the narrow part of the body between the ribs and the hips. **2** the part of a garment covering the waist.
waistband *n* a band of material sewn on to the waist of a garment to strengthen it.
waistcoat *n* a sleeveless upper garment which buttons up the front and is usually worn by men over a shirt and under a jacket.
waistline *n* **1** an imaginary line around the body at the narrowest part of the waist. **2** the place where the upper and lower part of a garment are joined together.
wait *vb* **1** to stay in one place or remain inactive in expectation of something: *the delegates have to wait for a reply.* **2** to be temporarily delayed: *the celebrations can wait.* **3** (of a thing) to be ready or be in store: *waiting for her on the library table was the latest Jilly Cooper novel. ~n* **4** the act or a period of waiting. **5 lie**

THESAURUS

wad ball, block, bundle, chunk, hunk, lump, mass, plug, roll
wadding filler, lining, packing, padding, stuffing
waddle rock, shuffle, sway, toddle, totter, wobble
wade 1. ford, paddle, splash, walk through **2. wade in** *or* **into** assail, attack, get stuck in (*informal*), go for, launch oneself at, light into (*informal*), set about, tackle, tear into (*informal*) **3. wade through** drudge, labour, peg away, plough through, toil, work one's way
waffle *informal, chiefly Brit.* **1.** *vb.* blather, jabber, prate, prattle, rabbit (on) (*Brit. informal*), verbalize, witter on (*informal*) **2.** *n.* blather, jabber, padding, prating, prattle, prolixity, verbiage, verbosity, wordiness
waft 1. *vb.* bear, be carried, carry, convey, drift, float, ride, transmit, transport **2.** *n.* breath, breeze, current, draught, puff, whiff
wag 1. *vb.* bob, flutter, nod, oscillate, quiver, rock, shake, stir, vibrate, waggle, wave, wiggle **2.** *n.* bob, flutter, nod, oscillation, quiver, shake, toss, vibration, waggle, wave, wiggle
wage 1. *n. Also* **wages** allowance, compensation, earnings, emolument, fee, hire, pay, payment, recompense, remuneration, reward, stipend **2.** *vb.* carry on, conduct, engage in, practise, proceed with, prosecute, pursue, undertake
wager 1. *n.* bet, flutter (*Brit. informal*), gamble, pledge, punt (*chiefly Brit.*), stake, venture **2.** *vb.* bet, chance, gamble, hazard, lay, pledge, punt (*chiefly Brit.*), put on, risk, speculate, stake, venture
waggle flutter, oscillate, shake, wag, wave, wiggle, wobble
waif foundling, orphan, stray
wail 1. *vb.* bawl, bemoan, bewail, cry, deplore, grieve, howl, keen, lament, ululate, weep, yowl **2.** *n.* complaint, cry, grief, howl, keen, lament, lamentation, moan, ululation, weeping, yowl
wait 1. *vb.* abide, bide one's time, cool one's heels, dally, delay, hang fire, hold back, hold on (*informal*),

in wait for a to prepare an ambush for. **b** to be ready or be in store for. ~See also **wait on, wait up.**

waiter *n* a man who serves people with food and drink in a restaurant.

waiting game *n* **play a waiting game** to postpone taking action or making a decision in order to gain an advantage.

waiting list *n* a list of people waiting for something that is not immediately available: *hospital waiting lists.*

waiting room *n* a room in which people can wait, for example at a railway station or doctor's surgery.

wait on *vb* **1** to serve (people) with food and drink in a restaurant. **2** to look after the needs of: *they were waited on by a manservant.* ~*interj* **3** *NZ* stop! hold on! Also (for senses 1, 2): **wait upon**

waitress *n* **1** a woman who serves people with food and drink in a restaurant. ~*vb* **2** to work as a waitress.

wait up *vb* to delay going to bed in order to wait for someone or something: *when he's late, she waits up for him.*

waive *vb* **waiving, waived** to refrain from enforcing or claiming (a rule or right).

waiver *n* the act or an instance of voluntary giving up a claim or right.

wake[1] *vb* **waking, woke, woken 1** Also: **wake up** to become conscious again or bring (someone) to consciousness again after a sleep. **2 wake up** to make (someone) more alert after a period of inactivity. **3 wake up to** to become aware of: *the world did not wake up to this tragedy until many people had died.* **4 waking hours** the time when a person is awake: *he often used his waking hours to write music.* ~*n* **5** a watch or vigil held over the body of a dead person during the night before burial.

wake[2] *n* **1** the track left by a ship moving through water. **2 in the wake of** following soon after: *visiting Toxteth in the wake of the 1981 riots.*

wakeful *adj* **1** unable to sleep. **2** without sleep: *wakeful nights.* **3** alert: *wakeful readiness.* **wakefulness** *n*

waken *vb* to become conscious again or bring (someone) to consciousness again after a sleep.

walk *vb* **1** to move on foot at a moderate rate with at least one foot always on the ground. **2** to pass through, on, or over on foot: *to walk a short distance.* **3** to walk somewhere with (a person or a dog). **4 walking on air** very happy and excited. **5 walk the streets** to wander about, esp. when looking for work or when homeless. ~*n* **6** a short journey on foot, usually for pleasure. **7** the action of walking rather than running. **8** a manner of walking: *a proud slow walk.* **9** a place or route for walking. **10 walk of life** social position or profession: *people from all walks of life were drawn to her.* ~See also **walk into, walk out,** etc. **walker** *n*

walkabout *n* an occasion when royalty, politicians, or other celebrities walk among and meet the public.

walkie-talkie *n* a small combined radio transmitter and receiver that can be carried around by one person.

walking stick *n* a stick or cane carried in the hand to assist walking.

walk into *vb* to encounter unexpectedly: *the troop reinforcements had walked into a trap.*

Walkman *n Trademark* a small portable cassette player with headphones.

walk-on *adj* (of a part in a film or play) small and not involving speaking.

walk out *vb* **1** to leave suddenly and without explanation, usually in anger. **2** (of workers) to go on strike. **3 walk out on** *Informal* to abandon or desert. ~*n* **walkout 4** a strike by workers.

walkover *n* **1** *Informal* an easy victory. ~*vb* **walk over 2** to mistreat or bully; take advantage of: *if you don't make your mark early, people will walk all over you.*

walkway *n* **1** a path designed for use by pedestrians. **2** a passage or pathway between two buildings.

wall *n* **1** a vertical structure made of stone, brick, or wood, with a length and height much greater than its thickness, used to enclose, divide, or support. **2** anything that suggests a wall in function or effect: *a wall of elm trees; a wall of suspicion.* **3** *Anat* any lining or membrane that encloses a bodily cavity or structure: *cell walls.* **4 drive someone up the wall** *Slang* to make someone angry or irritated. **5 go to the wall** *Informal* to be financially ruined. **6 have one's back to the wall** *Informal* to be in a very difficult situation, with no obvious way out of it. ~*vb* **7** to surround or enclose

THESAURUS

linger, mark time, pause, remain, rest, stand by, stay, tarry **2.** *n.* delay, halt, hold-up, interval, pause, rest, stay

waiter attendant, server, steward, stewardess

wait on *Also* **wait upon** attend, minister to, serve, tend

waive abandon, defer, dispense with, forgo, give up, postpone, put off, refrain from, relinquish, remit, renounce, resign, set aside, surrender

waiver abandonment, abdication, disclaimer, giving up, relinquishment, remission, renunciation, resignation, setting aside, surrender

wake[1] *vb.* **1.** *Also* **wake up** arise, awake, awaken, bestir, come to, get up, rouse, rouse from sleep, stir **2. wake up** activate, animate, arouse, awaken, enliven, excite, fire, galvanize, kindle, provoke, quicken, rouse, stimulate, stir up ~*n.* **3.** deathwatch, funeral, vigil, watch

wake[2] backwash, path, slipstream, track, trail, train, wash, waves

wakeful 1. insomniac, restless, sleepless, unsleeping **2.** alert, alive, attentive, heedful, observant, on guard, on the alert, on the lookout, unsleeping, vigilant, wary, watchful

waken activate, animate, arouse, awake, awaken, be roused, come awake, come to, enliven, fire, galvanize, get up, kindle, quicken, rouse, stimulate, stir

walk *vb.* **1.** advance, amble, foot it, go, go by shanks's pony (*informal*), go on foot, hike, hoof it (*slang*), march, move, pace, perambulate, promenade, saunter, step, stride, stroll, traipse (*informal*), tramp, travel on foot, trek, trudge **2.** accompany, convoy, escort, take ~*n.* **3.** constitutional, hike, march, perambulation (*formal*), promenade (*old-fashioned*), ramble, saunter, stroll, traipse (*informal*), tramp, trek, trudge, turn **4.** carriage, gait, manner of walking, pace, step, stride **5.** aisle, alley, avenue, esplanade, footpath, lane, path, pathway, pavement, promenade, sidewalk, trail **6. walk of life** area, arena, calling, career, course, field, line, metier, profession, sphere, trade, vocation

walker footslogger, hiker, pedestrian, rambler, wayfarer

walk out 1. flounce out, get up and go, leave suddenly, storm out, take off (*informal*) **2.** down tools, go on strike, stop work, strike, take industrial action, withdraw one's labour **3. walk out on** *informal* abandon, chuck (*informal*), desert, forsake, jilt, leave, leave in the lurch, pack in (*informal*), run away from, throw over

walkout industrial action, protest, stoppage, strike

walkover *informal* breeze (*U.S. & Canad. informal*), cakewalk (*informal*), child's play (*informal*), cinch (*slang*), doddle (*Brit. slang*), easy victory, picnic (*in-

(an area) with a wall. **8 wall in** *or* **up** to enclose (someone or something) completely in a room or place. **walled** *adj*

wallaby *n, pl* **-bies** a marsupial of Australia and New Guinea that resembles a small kangaroo.

wallah (**woll**-a) *n Informal* a person involved with or in charge of a specified thing: *rickshaw wallahs.*

wall bars *pl n* a series of horizontal bars attached to a wall and used in gymnastics.

wallet *n* a small folding case, usually of leather, for holding paper money and credit cards.

walleyed *adj* having eyes with an abnormal amount of white showing because of a squint.

wallflower *n* **1** a plant grown for its clusters of yellow, orange, red, or purple fragrant flowers. **2** *Informal* a woman who does not join in the dancing at a party or dance because she has no partner.

Walloon (wol-**loon**) *n* **1** a French-speaking person from S Belgium or the neighbouring part of France. **2** the French dialect of Belgium. *~adj* **3** of the Walloons.

wallop *Informal ~vb* **1** to hit hard. *~n* **2** a hard blow.

walloping *Informal ~n* **1** a severe physical beating. *~adj* **2** large or great: *a walloping amount of sodium.*

wallow *vb* **1** to indulge oneself in some emotion: *they wallow in self-pity.* **2** to lie or roll about in mud or water for pleasure. *~n* **3** the act or an instance of wallowing. **4** a muddy place where animals wallow.

wallpaper *n* **1** a printed or embossed paper for covering the walls of a room. *~vb* **2** to cover (walls) with wallpaper.

wall-to-wall *adj* (of carpeting) completely covering a floor.

wally *n, pl* **-lies** *Slang* a stupid or foolish person.

walnut *n* **1** an edible nut with a hard, wrinkled, light brown shell. **2** a tree on which walnuts grow. **3** the light brown wood of a walnut tree, used for making furniture.

walrus *n, pl* **-ruses** *or* **-rus** a mammal of cold northern seas, with two tusks that hang down from the upper jaw, tough thick skin, and coarse whiskers.

waltz *n* **1** a ballroom dance in triple time in which couples spin round as they progress round the room. **2** music for this dance. *~vb* **3** to dance a waltz. **4** *Informal* to move in a relaxed and confident way: *he waltzed over to her table to say hello.*

wampum (**wom**-pum) *n* (formerly) money used by North American Indians, made of shells strung or woven together.

wan (rhymes with **swan**) *adj* **wanner, wannest** very pale, as a result of illness or unhappiness. **wanly** *adv*

wand *n* a rod used by a magician when performing a trick or by a fairy when casting a spell.

wander *vb* **1** to walk about in a place without any definite purpose or destination. **2** to leave a place where one is supposed to stay: *kids wander off.* **3** (of the mind) to lose concentration. *~n* **4** the act or an instance of wandering. **wanderer** *n* **wandering** *adj, n*

wanderlust *n* a great desire to travel.

wane *vb* **waning, waned 1** to decrease gradually in size, strength, or power: *the influence of the extremists is waning.* **2** (of the moon) to show a gradually decreasing area of brightness from full moon until new moon. *~n* **3 on the wane** decreasing in size, strength, or power: *his fame was on the wane.* **waning** *adj*

wangle *vb* **-gling, -gled** *Informal* to get (something) by cunning or devious methods: *I've wangled you both an invitation.*

wanigan (**wonn**-ig-an) *n Canad* **1** a lumberjack's chest or box. **2** a cabin or houseboat.

wank *Taboo slang ~vb* **1** (of a man) to masturbate. *~n* **2** an instance of masturbating.

wanker *n Taboo slang* a worthless or stupid person.

wannabe *or* **wannabee** *adj* **1** wanting to be, or be like, a particular person or thing: *a wannabe actress.* *~n* **2** a person who wants to be, or be like, a particular person or thing.

want *vb* **1** to feel a need or longing for: *I want a job.* **2** to wish or desire (to do something): *we did not want to get involved.* **3** *Chiefly Brit* to have need of or require (doing or being something): *what will you do when it wants cleaning?* **4** *Informal* should or ought (to do something): *the last person you want to hire is someone who is desperate for a job.* **5 want for** to be lacking or deficient in: *they were convinced I was wealthy and wanted for nothing.* *~n* **6** something that is needed, desired, or lacked: *attempts to satisfy a*

THESAURUS

formal), piece of cake (*informal*), pushover (*slang*), snap (*informal*)

wall 1. barricade, barrier, block, breastwork, bulwark, divider, embankment, enclosure, fence, fortification, hedge, impediment, obstacle, obstruction, palisade, panel, parapet, partition, rampart, screen, stockade **2. drive up the wall** *slang* aggravate (*informal*), annoy, dement, derange, drive crazy (*informal*), drive insane, exasperate, get on someone's nerves (*informal*), infuriate, irritate, madden, piss someone off (*taboo slang*), send off someone's head (*slang*), try **3. go to the wall** *informal* be ruined, collapse, fail, fall, go bust (*informal*), go under

wallet case, holder, notecase, pocketbook (*chiefly U.S.*), pouch, purse

wallow 1. bask, delight, glory, indulge oneself, luxuriate, relish, revel, take pleasure **2.** lie, roll about, splash around, tumble, welter

wan anaemic, ashen, bloodless, cadaverous, colourless, discoloured, ghastly, livid, pale, pallid, pasty, sickly, washed out, waxen, white

wand baton, rod, stick

wander *vb.* **1.** cruise, drift, knock about *or* around, meander, mooch around (*slang*), peregrinate (*formal*), ramble, range, roam, rove, straggle, stray, stroll, traipse (*informal*) **2.** depart, deviate, digress, divagate (*rare*), diverge, err, get lost, go astray, go off at a tangent, go off course, lapse, lose concentration, lose one's train of thought, lose one's way, swerve, veer *~n.* **3.** cruise, excursion, meander, peregrination (*formal*), ramble, traipse (*informal*)

wanderer bird of passage, drifter, Gypsy, itinerant, nomad, rambler, ranger, rolling stone, rover, stroller, traveller, vagabond, vagrant, voyager

wandering drifting, homeless, itinerant, migratory, nomadic, peripatetic, rambling, rootless, roving, strolling, travelling, vagabond, vagrant, voyaging, wayfaring

wane 1. *vb.* abate, atrophy, decline, decrease, die out, dim, diminish, draw to a close, drop, dwindle, ebb, fade, fade away, fail, lessen, sink, subside, taper off, weaken, wind down, wither **2.** *n.* **on the wane** at its lowest ebb, declining, dropping, dwindling, dying out, ebbing, fading, lessening, obsolescent, on its last legs, on the decline, on the way out, subsiding, tapering off, weakening, withering

want *vb.* **1.** covet, crave, desire, eat one's heart out over, feel a need for, hanker after, have a fancy for, have a yen for (*informal*), hope for, hunger for, long for, need, pine for, require, thirst for, wish, yearn for **2.** *chiefly Brit.* be able to do with, be deficient in, be short of, be without, call for, demand, fall short in, have need of, lack, miss, need, require, stand in need

number of wants. **7** a lack, shortage, or absence: *for want of opportunity.* **8 in want of** needing or lacking: *the Chinese peasant farmer may be in want of a roof, a job, a doctor nearby.*

wanted *adj* being searched for by the police in connection with a crime that has been committed.

wanting *adj* **1** lacking: *I would be wanting in charity if I did not explain the terms.* **2** not meeting requirements or expectations: *she compares herself to her sister and finds herself wanting.*

wanton *adj* **1** without motive, provocation, or justification: *sheer wanton destruction.* **2** (of a person) maliciously and unnecessarily cruel. **3** *Old-fashioned* (of a woman) sexually unrestrained or immodest. *~n* **4** *Old-fashioned* a sexually unrestrained or immodest woman.

wapiti (**wop**-pit-tee) *n, pl* **-tis** a large North American deer, now also found in New Zealand.

war *n* **1** open armed conflict between two or more countries or groups: *this international situation led to war.* **2** a particular armed conflict: *the American war in Vietnam.* **3** any conflict or contest: *a trade war.* **4 have been in the wars** *Informal* to look as if one has been in a fight. *~adj* **5** relating to war or a war: *the war effort; a war correspondent. ~vb* **warring, warred 6** to conduct a war. **warring** *adj*

warble *vb* **-bling, -bled** to sing in a high-pitched trilling voice.

warbler *n* any of various small songbirds.

war crime *n* a crime committed in wartime in violation of the accepted customs, such as ill-treatment of prisoners. **war criminal** *n*

war cry *n* **1** a rallying cry used by combatants in battle. **2** a slogan used to rally support for a cause.

ward *n* **1** a room in a hospital for patients requiring similar kinds of care: *the maternity ward.* **2** one of the districts into which a town, parish, or other area is divided for administration or elections. **3** *Law* Also called: **ward of court** a person, especially a child whose parents are dead, who is placed under the control or protection of a guardian or of a court. ~See also **ward off. wardship** *n*

-ward *suffix* **1** (*forming adjectives*) indicating direction towards: *a backward step.* **2** (*forming adverbs*) *Chiefly US & Canad* same as **-wards.**

warden *n* **1** a person who is in charge of a building, such as a youth hostel, and its occupants. **2** a public official who is responsible for the enforcement of certain regulations: *a game warden.* **3** the chief officer in charge of a prison.

warder *or fem* **wardress** *n Chiefly Brit* a prison officer.

ward off *vb* to prevent (something unpleasant) from happening or from causing harm: *to ward off the pangs of hunger; to ward off cancer cells.*

wardrobe *n* **1** a tall cupboard, with a rail or hooks on which to hang clothes. **2** the total collection of articles of clothing belonging to one person. **3** the collection of costumes belonging to a theatre or theatrical company.

wardrobe mistress *n* the woman in charge of the costumes in a theatre or theatrical company. **wardrobe master** *masc n*

wardroom *n* the quarters assigned to the officers of a warship, apart from the captain.

-wards *or* **-ward** *suffix forming adverbs* indicating direction towards: *a step backwards.*

ware *n* articles of the same kind or material: *crystal ware.* See also **wares.**

warehouse *n* a place where goods are stored prior to their sale or distribution.

wares *pl n* goods for sale.

warfare *n* **1** the act of conducting a war. **2** a violent or intense conflict of any kind: *class warfare.*

war game *n* **1** a tactical exercise for training military commanders, in which no military units are actually deployed. **2** a game in which model soldiers are used to create battles in order to study tactics.

warhead *n* the front section of a missile or projectile that contains explosives.

THESAURUS

of *~n.* **3.** appetite, craving, demand, desire, fancy, hankering, hunger, longing, necessity, need, requirement, thirst, wish, yearning, yen (*informal*) **4.** absence, dearth, default, deficiency, famine, insufficiency, lack, paucity, scantiness, scarcity, shortage

wanting 1. absent, incomplete, lacking, less, missing, short, shy **2.** defective, deficient, disappointing, faulty, imperfect, inadequate, inferior, leaving much to be desired, not good enough, not up to expectations, not up to par, patchy, poor, sketchy, substandard, unsound

wanton *adj.* **1.** arbitrary, cruel, evil, gratuitous, groundless, malevolent, malicious, motiveless, needless, senseless, spiteful, uncalled-for, unjustifiable, unjustified, unprovoked, vicious, wicked, wilful **2.** *old-fashioned* abandoned, dissipated, dissolute, fast, immoral, lecherous, lewd, libertine, libidinous, licentious, loose, lustful, of easy virtue, promiscuous, rakish, shameless, unchaste *~n.* **3.** *old-fashioned* debauchee, harlot (*literary*), libertine, loose woman, profligate, prostitute, scrubber (*offensive slang*), slag (*Brit. slang*), slut, strumpet (*archaic*), tart (*informal*), trollop (*derogatory*), voluptuary, whore, woman of easy virtue

war 1. *n.* armed conflict, battle, bloodshed, combat, conflict, contention, contest, enmity, fighting, hostilities, hostility, strife, struggle, warfare **2.** *vb.* battle, campaign against, carry on hostilities, clash, combat, conduct a war, contend, contest, fight, make war, strive, struggle, take up arms, wage war

war cry battle cry, rallying cry, slogan, war whoop

ward 1. apartment, cubicle, room **2.** area, district, division, precinct, quarter, zone **3.** *Law Also* **ward of court** charge, dependant, minor, protégé *or fem.* protégée

warden administrator, caretaker, curator, custodian, guardian, janitor, keeper, ranger, steward, superintendent, warder, watchman

warder *or fem.* **wardress** *chiefly Brit.* custodian, gaoler, guard, jailer, keeper, prison officer, screw (*slang*), turnkey (*old-fashioned*)

ward off avert, avoid, beat off, block, deflect, fend off, forestall, keep at arm's length, keep at bay, parry, repel, stave off, thwart, turn aside, turn away

wardrobe 1. closet, clothes cupboard, clothes-press **2.** apparel, attire, clothes, collection of clothes, outfit

warehouse depository, depot, stockroom, store, storehouse

wares commodities, goods, lines, manufactures, merchandise, produce, products, stock, stuff

warfare armed conflict, armed struggle, arms, battle, blows, campaigning, clash of arms, combat, conflict, contest, discord, fighting, hostilities, passage of arms, strategy, strife, struggle, war

warily cagily (*informal*), carefully, cautiously, charily, circumspectly, distrustfully, gingerly, guardedly, suspiciously, vigilantly, watchfully, with care

wariness alertness, attention, caginess (*informal*), care, carefulness, caution, circumspection, discretion,

warhorse *n* **1** (formerly) a horse used in battle. **2** *Informal* a veteran soldier or politician.

warlike *adj* **1** of or relating to war: *warlike stores and equipment.* **2** hostile and eager to have a war: *a warlike nation.*

warlock *n* a man who practises black magic.

warlord *n* a military leader of a nation or part of a nation.

warm *adj* **1** feeling or having a moderate degree of heat. **2** giving heat: *warm clothing.* **3** (of colours) predominantly red or yellow in tone. **4** kindly or affectionate: *warm embraces.* **5** *Informal* near to finding a hidden object or guessing facts, for example in a children's game. ~*vb* **6** to make warm. **7 warm to a** to become fonder of: *I warmed to him when he defended me.* **b** to become more excited or enthusiastic about: *he had warmed to his theme.* ~See also **warm up. warmly** *adv* **warmness** *n*

warm-blooded *adj* **1** (of an animal, such as a mammal or a bird) having a constant body temperature, usually higher than the surrounding temperature. **2** having a passionate nature. **warm-bloodedness** *n*

war memorial *n* a monument to people who have died in a war, esp. local people.

warm front *n Meteorol* the boundary between a warm air mass and the cold air it is replacing.

warm-hearted *adj* kind, affectionate, or sympathetic.

warming pan *n* a long-handled pan filled with hot coals, formerly pulled over the sheets to warm a bed.

warmonger *n* a person who encourages warlike ideas or advocates war. **warmongering** *n*

warmth *n* **1** the state of being warm. **2** affection or cordiality: *the warmth of their friendship.*

warm up *vb* **1** to make or become warm or warmer. **2** to prepare for a race, sporting contest, or exercise routine by doing gentle exercises immediately beforehand. **3** (of an engine or machine) to be started and left running until the working temperature is reached. **4** to become more lively: *wait until things warm up.* **5** to reheat (food that has already been cooked). ~*n* **warm-up 6** a preparatory exercise routine.

warn *vb* **1** to make (someone) aware of a possible danger or problem. **2** to inform (someone) in advance: *you'd better warn your girlfriend that you'll be working at the weekend.* **3 warn off** to advise (someone) to go away or not to do something.

warning *n* **1** a hint, threat, or advance notice of a possible danger or problem. **2** advice not to do something. ~*adj* **3** giving or serving as a warning: *warning signs.* **warningly** *adv*

warp *vb* **1** (esp. of wooden objects) to be twisted out of shape, for example by heat or damp. **2** to distort or influence in a negative way: *love warps judgment.* ~*n* **3** a fault or an irregularity in the shape or surface of an object. **4** a fault or deviation in someone's character. **5** See **time warp. 6** the yarns arranged lengthways on a loom through which the weft yarns are woven. **warped** *adj*

war paint *n* **1** paint applied to the face and body by certain North American Indians before battle. **2** *Informal* cosmetics.

warpath *n* **on the warpath a** preparing to engage in battle. **b** *Informal* angry and looking for a fight or conflict.

warrant *n* **1** an official authorization for some action or decision: *Scotland Yard today issued a warrant for the arrest of this man.* **2** a document that certifies or guarantees something, such as a receipt or licence. ~*vb* **3** to make necessary: *we've no hard evidence to warrant a murder investigation.*

warrant officer *n* an officer in certain armed services with a rank between those of commissioned and noncommissioned officers.

Warrant of Fitness *n NZ* a six-monthly certificate required for a motor vehicle certifying that it is mechanically sound.

warrantor *n* a person or company that provides a warranty.

warranty *n, pl* **-ties** a guarantee or assurance that goods meet a specified standard or that the facts in a legal document are as stated.

warren *n* **1** a series of interconnected underground tunnels in which rabbits live. **2** an overcrowded building or area of a city with many narrow passages or streets: *a mountainous concrete warren of apartments.*

warrior *n* a person who is engaged in or experienced in war.

warship *n* a ship designed for naval warfare.

wart *n* **1** a firm abnormal growth on the skin caused by a virus. **2 warts and all** including faults: *she loves him warts and all.* **warty** *adj*

wart hog *n* a wild African pig with heavy tusks, wartlike lumps on the face, and a mane of coarse hair.

wartime *n* **1** a time of war. ~*adj* **2** of or in a time of war: *the wartime coalition.*

wary (**ware**-ree) *adj* **warier, wariest** cautious or on

THESAURUS

distrust, foresight, heedfulness, mindfulness, prudence, suspicion, vigilance, watchfulness

warlike aggressive, bellicose, belligerent, bloodthirsty, combative, hawkish, hostile, inimical, jingoistic, martial, militaristic, military, pugnacious, sabre-rattling, unfriendly, warmongering

warm *adj.* **1.** balmy, heated, lukewarm, moderately hot, pleasant, sunny, tepid, thermal **2.** affable, affectionate, amiable, amorous, cheerful, congenial, cordial, friendly, genial, happy, hearty, hospitable, kindly, likable *or* likeable, loving, pleasant, tender ~*vb.* **3.** heat, heat up, melt, thaw, warm up

warm-blooded ardent, earnest, emotional, enthusiastic, excitable, fervent, impetuous, lively, passionate, rash, spirited, vivacious

warm-hearted affectionate, compassionate, cordial, generous, kind-hearted, kindly, loving, sympathetic, tender, tender-hearted

warmonger belligerent, hawk, jingo, militarist

warmth 1. heat, hotness, warmness **2.** affability, affection, amorousness, cheerfulness, cordiality, happiness, heartiness, hospitableness, kindliness, love, tenderness

warn admonish, advise, alert, apprise, caution, forewarn, give fair warning, give notice, inform, make (someone) aware, notify, put one on one's guard, summon, tip off

warning 1. *n.* admonition, advice, alarm, alert, augury, caution, caveat, foretoken, hint, notice, notification, omen, premonition, presage, sign, signal, threat, tip, tip-off, token, word **2.** *adj.* admonitory, cautionary, monitory, ominous, premonitory, threatening

warrant 1. *n.* assurance, authority, authorization, carte blanche, commission, guarantee, licence, permission, permit, pledge, sanction, security, warranty **2.** *vb.* approve, authorize, call for, commission, demand, deserve, empower, entail, entitle, excuse, give ground for, justify, license, necessitate, permit, require, sanction

warrior champion, combatant, fighter, fighting man, gladiator, man-at-arms, soldier

wary alert, attentive, cagey (*informal*), careful, cau-

one's guard: *be wary of hitchhikers.* **warily** *adv* **wariness** *n*

was *vb* (used with *I, he, she, it* and with singular nouns) the past tense of **be.**

wash *vb* **1** to clean (oneself, part of one's body, or a thing) with soap or detergent and water. **2** (of a garment or fabric) to be capable of being washed without damage or loss of colour. **3** to move or be moved in a particular direction by water: *houses may be washed away in floods.* **4** (of waves) to flow or sweep against or over (a surface or object), often with a lapping sound. **5** *Informal, chiefly Brit* to be acceptable or believable: *the masculine pride argument won't wash now when so many women go out to work.* ~*n* **6** the act or process of washing. **7** all the clothes etc. to be washed together on one occasion. **8** a thin layer of paint or ink: *a pale wash of blue.* **9** the disturbance in the air or water produced at the rear of an aircraft, boat, or other moving object: *we were hit by the wash of a large vessel.* **10 come out in the wash** *Informal* to become known or apparent in the course of time. ~See also **wash down, wash out, wash up. washable** *adj*

washbasin *n* a small sink in a bathroom, used for washing the face and hands. Also: **wash-hand basin**

wash down *vb* **1** to have a drink with or after (food or medicine): *a large steak, washed down with coffee.* **2** to wash from top to bottom: *she washed down the staircase.*

washed out *adj* **1** exhausted and lacking in energy. **2** faded or colourless.

washed up *adj Informal, chiefly US, Canad, & NZ* no longer as successful or important as previously: *she stands discredited, her career probably washed up.*

washer *n* **1** a flat ring of rubber, felt, or metal used to provide a seal under a nut or bolt or in a tap or valve. **2** *Informal* a washing machine. **3** a person who washes things, esp. as a job: *chief cook and bottle washer.*

washerwoman *n, pl* **-women** a woman who washes clothes as a job.

washing *n* all the clothes etc. to be washed together on one occasion.

washing machine *n* a machine for washing clothes and bed linen in.

washing soda *n* crystalline sodium carbonate, used as a cleansing agent.

washing-up *n Brit* the act of washing used dishes and cutlery after a meal.

wash out *vb* **1** Also: **wash off** to remove or be removed by washing: *the rain washes the red dye out of the cap.* **2** to wash the inside of (a container). ~*n* **washout 3** *Informal* a total failure or disaster.

washroom *n US & Canad* a toilet.

washstand *n* a piece of furniture designed to hold a basin for washing the face and hands in.

wash up *vb* **1** *Chiefly Brit* to wash used dishes and cutlery after a meal. **2** *US & Canad* to wash one's face and hands.

washy *adj* **washier, washiest 1** overdiluted or weak. **2** lacking intensity of colour: *a washy blend of pale brown and pale grey.*

wasn't was not.

wasp *n* a common stinging insect with a slender black-and-yellow striped body.

Wasp *or* **WASP** *n US & Canad usually offensive* a White Anglo-Saxon Protestant.

waspish *adj* bad-tempered or spiteful: *waspish comments.*

wasp waist *n* a very narrow waist. **wasp-waisted** *adj*

wassail *n* **1** (formerly) a toast drunk to a person during festivities. **2** a festivity involving a lot of drinking. **3** hot spiced beer or mulled wine drunk at such a festivity. ~*vb* **4 go wassailing** to go from house to house singing carols at Christmas.

wastage *n* **1** the act of wasting something or the state of being wasted: *wastage of raw materials.* **2** reduction in the size of a workforce by retirement, redundancy, etc.

waste *vb* **wasting, wasted 1** to use up thoughtlessly, carelessly, or unsuccessfully. **2** to fail to take advantage of: *let's not waste an opportunity to see the children.* **3 be wasted on** to be too good for; not be appreciated by: *fine brandy is wasted on you.* **4 waste away** to lose one's strength or health: *wasting away from unrequited love.* ~*n* **5** the act of wasting something or the state of being wasted: *a waste of time.* **6** something that is left over because it is in excess of requirements. **7** rubbish: *toxic waste.* **8** *Physiol* matter discharged from the body as faeces or urine. **9 wastes** a region that is wild or uncultivated. ~*adj* **10** rejected as being useless, unwanted, or worthless: *waste products.* **11** not cultivated or productive: *waste ground.* **12** *Physiol* discharged from the body as faeces or urine: *waste matter.* **13 lay waste** *or* **lay waste to** to devastate or destroy: *the Bikini atoll, laid waste by nuclear tests.*

wasted *adj* **1** unnecessary or unfruitful: *wasted effort.* **2** pale, thin, and unhealthy: *the hunched shoulders and the wasted appearance of his body.*

THESAURUS

tious, chary, circumspect, distrustful, guarded, heedful, leery (*slang*), on one's guard, on the lookout, prudent, suspicious, vigilant, watchful, wide-awake

wash *vb.* **1.** bath, bathe, clean, cleanse, launder, moisten, rinse, scrub, shampoo, shower, wet **2.** bear away, carry off, erode, move, sweep away, wash off **3.** *informal, chiefly Brit.* bear scrutiny, be convincing, be plausible, carry weight, hold up, hold water, stand up, stick ~*n.* **4.** ablution, bath, bathe, cleaning, cleansing, laundering, rinse, scrub, shampoo, shower, washing **5.** coat, coating, film, layer, overlay, screen, stain, suffusion

washed out 1. all in (*informal*), clapped out (*Austral. & N.Z. informal*), dead on one's feet (*informal*), dog-tired (*informal*), done in (*informal*), drained, drawn, exhausted, fatigued, haggard, knackered (*slang*), pale, spent, tired-out, wan, weary, worn-out, zonked (*slang*) **2.** blanched, bleached, colourless, etiolated, faded, flat, lacklustre, matt, pale

washout *informal* disappointment, disaster, dud (*informal*), failure, fiasco, flop (*informal*), mess

waspish bad-tempered, cantankerous, captious, crabbed, crabby, cross, crotchety (*informal*), fretful, grumpy, ill-tempered, irascible, irritable, liverish, peevish, peppery, pettish, petulant, ratty (*Brit. informal*), snappish, splenetic, testy, tetchy, touchy

waste *vb.* **1.** blow (*slang*), dissipate, fritter away, lavish, misuse, run through, squander, throw away **2.** **waste away** atrophy, consume, corrode, crumble, debilitate, decay, decline, deplete, disable, drain, dwindle, eat away, ebb, emaciate, enfeeble, exhaust, fade, gnaw, perish, sap the strength of, sink, undermine, wane, wear out, wither ~*n.* **3.** dissipation, expenditure, extravagance, frittering away, loss, lost opportunity, misapplication, misuse, prodigality, squandering, unthriftiness, wastefulness **4.** debris, dregs, dross, garbage, leavings, leftovers, litter, offal, offscourings, refuse, rubbish, scrap, sweepings, trash **5. wastes** desert, solitude, void, wasteland, wild, wilderness ~*adj.* **6.** leftover, superfluous, supernumerary, unused, unwanted, useless, worthless **7.** bare, barren, desolate, devastated, dismal, dreary, empty, uncultivated, unin-

wasteful *adj* causing waste: *wasteful expenditure.* **wastefully** *adv*
wasteland *n* **1** a barren or desolate area of land. **2** something that is considered spiritually, intellectually, or aesthetically barren: *the TV wasteland.*
wastepaper basket *n* a container for paper discarded after use.
waster *n Informal* a lazy or worthless person.
wasting *adj* reducing the vitality and strength of the body: *a pernicious wasting illness.*
wastrel *n Literary* a lazy or worthless person.
watap (wat-**tahp**) *n* a stringy thread made by American Indians from the roots of conifers.
watch *vb* **1** to look at or observe closely and attentively. **2** to look after (a child or a pet). **3** to maintain a careful interest in or control over: *it reminds me to watch my diet.* **4 watch for** to be keenly alert to or cautious about: *the vigilant night watchman hired to watch for thieves.* **5 watch it!** be careful! ~*n* **6** a small portable timepiece worn strapped to the wrist or in a waistcoat pocket. **7** the act or an instance of watching. **8** *Naut* any of the periods, usually of four hours, during which part of a ship's crew are on duty. **9 keep a close watch on** to maintain a careful interest in or control over: *he keeps a close watch on party opinion.* **10 keep watch** to be keenly alert to danger; keep guard. **11 on the watch** on the lookout. ~See also **watch out, watch over. watcher** *n*
watchable *adj* interesting, enjoyable, or entertaining: *watchable films.*
watchdog *n* **1** a dog kept to guard property. **2** a person or group that acts as a guard against inefficiency or illegality.
watchful *adj* **1** carefully observing everything that happens. **2 under the watchful eye of** being closely observed by. **watchfully** *adv* **watchfulness** *n*
watchmaker *n* a person who makes or mends watches and clocks.
watchman *n, pl* **-men** a man employed to guard buildings or property.
watch-night service *n* (in Protestant churches) a service held on the night of December 31, to mark the passing of the old year.
watch out *vb* to be careful or on one's guard.
watch over *vb* to look after or supervise: *her main ambition is still to watch over the family.*
watchstrap *n* a strap attached to a watch for fastening it round the wrist. Also called (US and Canad.): **watchband**
watchtower *n* a tower on which a sentry keeps watch.
watchword *n* a slogan or motto: *quality, not quantity, is the watchword.*
water *n* **1** a clear colourless tasteless liquid that is essential for plant and animal life, that falls as rain, and forms seas, rivers, and lakes. **2** any area of this liquid, such as a sea, river, or lake. **3** the surface of such an area of water: *four-fifths of an iceberg's mass lies below water.* **4** the level of the tide: *at high water.* **5** *Physiol* **a** any fluid discharged from the body, such as sweat, urine, or tears. **b waters** the fluid surrounding a fetus in the womb. **6 hold water** (of an argument or idea) to be believable or reasonable. **7 of the first water** of the highest quality or the most extreme degree: *he's a scoundrel of the first water.* **8 pass water** to urinate. **9 water under the bridge** events that are past and done with. ~*vb* **10** to moisten or soak with water: *keep greenhouse plants well watered.* **11** to give (an animal) water to drink. **12** (of the eyes) to fill with tears: *our eyes were watering from the fumes.* **13** (of the mouth) to fill with saliva in anticipation of food. ~See also **water down. waterless** *adj*
water bed *n* a waterproof mattress filled with water.
water biscuit *n* a thin crisp unsweetened biscuit, usually eaten with butter or cheese.
water buffalo *n* a large black oxlike draught animal of S Asia, with long backward-curving horns.
water cannon *n* a machine that pumps a jet of water through a nozzle at high pressure, used to disperse crowds.
water chestnut *n* the edible tuber of a Chinese plant, used in Oriental cookery.
water closet *n Old-fashioned* a toilet. Abbrev.: **WC**
watercolour *or US* **watercolor** *n* **1** a kind of paint that is applied with water rather than oil. **2** a painting done in watercolours.
water-cooled *adj* (of an engine) kept from overheating by a flow of water circulating in a casing.
watercourse *n* the channel or bed of a river or stream.
watercress *n* a plant that grows in ponds and streams, with strong-tasting leaves that are used in salads and as a garnish.
water cycle *n Geol* the circulation of the earth's water, in which water from the sea evaporates, forms

THESAURUS

habited, unproductive, wild **8. lay waste** despoil, destroy, devastate, pillage, rape, ravage, raze, ruin, sack, spoil, wreak havoc upon
wasteful extravagant, improvident, lavish, prodigal, profligate, ruinous, spendthrift, thriftless, uneconomical, unthrifty
wastrel *literary* drone, good-for-nothing, idler, layabout, loafer, loser, malingerer, ne'er-do-well, shirker, skiver (*Brit. slang*), waster
watch *vb.* **1.** clock (*Brit. slang*), contemplate, eye, gaze at, get a load of (*informal*), look, look at, look on, mark, note, observe, pay attention, peer at, regard, see, stare at, take a dekko at (*Brit. slang*), view **2.** guard, keep, look after, mind, protect, superintend, take care of, tend ~*n.* **3.** chronometer, clock, pocket watch, timepiece, wristwatch **4.** alertness, attention, eye, heed, inspection, lookout, notice, observation, supervision, surveillance, vigil, vigilance, watchfulness **5. keep watch** attend, be on the alert, be on the lookout, be vigilant, be wary, be watchful, keep an eye open (*informal*), look out, take heed, wait
watchdog 1. guard dog **2.** custodian, guardian, inspector, monitor, protector, scrutineer
watcher looker-on, lookout, observer, onlooker, spectator, spy, viewer, witness
watchful alert, attentive, circumspect, guarded, heedful, observant, on one's guard, on the lookout, on the watch, suspicious, vigilant, wary, wide awake
watchman caretaker, custodian, guard, security guard, security man
watch out be alert, be careful, be on one's guard, be on the alert, be on (the) watch, be vigilant, be watchful, have a care, keep a sharp lookout, keep a weather eye open, keep one's eyes open, keep one's eyes peeled *or* skinned (*informal*), look out, mind out, watch oneself
watch over defend, guard, keep safe, look after, preserve, protect, shelter, shield, stand guard over
water *n.* **1.** aqua, H_2O **2. hold water** bear examination *or* scrutiny, be credible (logical, sound), make sense, pass the test, ring true, work **3. of the first water** excellent, of the best, of the best quality, of the

clouds, falls as rain or snow, and returns to the sea by rivers.

water diviner *n Brit* a person who can locate the presence of water underground with a divining rod.

water down *vb* **1** to weaken (a drink or food) with water. **2** to make (a story, plan, or proposal) weaker and less controversial. **watered-down** *adj*

waterfall *n* a cascade of falling water where there is a vertical or almost vertical step in a river.

waterfowl *n, pl* **-fowl** a bird that swims on water, such as a duck or swan.

waterfront *n* the area of a town or city next to an area of water, such as a harbour or dockyard.

waterhole *n* a pond or pool in a desert or other dry area, used by animals as a drinking place.

water ice *n* ice cream made from frozen fruit-flavoured syrup.

watering can *n* a container with a handle and a spout with a perforated nozzle, used to sprinkle water over plants.

watering hole *n Facetious slang* a pub.

watering place *n* **1** a place where people or animals can find drinking water. **2** *Brit* a spa or seaside resort.

water jump *n* a ditch or brook over which athletes or horses must jump in a steeplechase.

water level *n* **1** the level reached by the surface of an area of water. **2** same as **water line.**

water lily *n* a plant with large leaves and showy flowers that float on the surface of an area of water.

water line *n* the level to which a ship's hull will be immersed when afloat.

waterlogged *adj* **1** saturated with water: *waterlogged meadows.* **2** (of a boat) having taken in so much water as to be likely to sink.

water main *n* a principal supply pipe in an arrangement of pipes for distributing water to houses and other buildings.

watermark *n* **1** a mark impressed on paper during manufacture, visible when the paper is held up to the light. **2** a line marking the level reached by an area of water.

water meadow *n* a meadow that remains fertile by being periodically flooded by a stream.

watermelon *n* a large round melon with a hard green rind and sweet watery reddish flesh.

water pistol *n* a toy pistol that squirts a stream of water.

water polo *n* a game played in water by two teams of seven swimmers in which each side tries to throw a ball into the opponents' goal.

water power *n* the power of flowing or falling water to drive machinery or generate electricity.

waterproof *adj* **1** not allowing water to pass through: *waterproof trousers.* *~n* **2** *Chiefly Brit* a waterproof garment, such as a raincoat. *~vb* **3** to make waterproof: *the bridge is having its deck waterproofed.*

water rat *n* same as **water vole.**

water rate *n* a charge made for the public supply of water.

water-resistant *adj* (of a fabric or garment) having a finish that resists the absorption of water.

watershed *n* **1** the dividing line between two adjacent river systems, such as a ridge. **2** an important period or factor that serves as a dividing line: *a watershed in European history.*

waterside *n* the area of land beside a river or lake.

water-ski *n* **1** a type of ski used for gliding over water. *~vb* **-skiing, -skied** *or* **-ski'd** **2** to ride over water on water-skis while holding a rope towed by a speedboat. **water-skier** *n* **water-skiing** *n*

water softener *n* a device or substance that removes the minerals that make water hard.

waterspout *n* a tornado occurring over water, which forms a column of water and mist.

water table *n* the level below which the ground is saturated with water.

watertight *adj* **1** not letting water through: *watertight compartments.* **2** without loopholes or weak points: *a watertight system.*

water tower *n* a storage tank mounted on a tower so that water can be distributed at a steady pressure.

water vapour *n* water in a gaseous state, esp. when due to evaporation at a temperature below the boiling point.

water vole *n* a small ratlike animal that can swim and lives on the banks of streams and ponds.

waterway *n* a river, canal, or other navigable channel used as a means of travel or transport.

water wheel *n* a large wheel with vanes set across its rim, which is turned by flowing water to drive machinery.

water wings *pl n* an inflatable rubber device shaped like a pair of wings, which is placed under the arms of a person learning to swim.

waterworks *n* **1** an establishment for storing, purifying, and distributing water for community supply. *~pl n* **2** *Brit informal, euphemistic* the urinary system. **3** **turn on the waterworks** *Informal* to begin to cry deliberately, in order to attract attention or gain sympathy.

watery *adj* **1** of, like, or containing water: *a watery discharge.* **2** (of eyes) filled with tears. **3** insipid, thin, or weak: *a watery sun had appeared.*

watt (**wott**) *n* the SI unit of power, equal to the power dissipated by a current of 1 ampere flowing across a potential difference of 1 amp.

wattage *n* the amount of electrical power, expressed in watts, that an appliance uses or generates.

wattle (**wott**-tl) *n* **1** a frame of rods or stakes interwoven with twigs or branches used to make fences. **2** a loose fold of brightly coloured skin hanging from the throat of certain birds and lizards. **3** an Australian acacia tree with spikes of small brightly coloured flowers. *~adj* **4** made of, formed by, or covered with wattle: *a wattle fence.*

wattle and daub *n* a building material consisting of interwoven twigs plastered with a mixture of clay and water.

wave *vb* **waving, waved** **1** to move (one's hand) to and fro as a greeting. **2** to direct (someone) to move in a particular direction by waving: *I waved him on.* **3** to hold (something) up and move it from side to side in order to attract attention. **4** to move freely to and fro: *flowers waving in the wind.* *~n* **5** one of a sequence of ridges or undulations that moves across the surface of

THESAURUS

finest quality, of the highest degree, of the highest grade *~vb.* **4.** damp, dampen, douse, drench, flood, hose, irrigate, moisten, soak, souse, spray, sprinkle

water down **1.** add water to, adulterate, dilute, put water in, thin, water, weaken **2.** adulterate, mitigate, qualify, soften, tone down, weaken

waterfall cascade, cataract, chute, fall, force

watertight **1.** sound, waterproof **2.** airtight, firm, flawless, foolproof, impregnable, incontrovertible, sound, unassailable

watery **1.** aqueous, damp, fluid, humid, liquid, marshy, moist, soggy, squelchy, wet **2.** rheumy, tear-

the sea or a lake. **6** a curve in the hair. **7** a sudden rise in the frequency or intensity of something: *a wave of sympathy.* **8** a widespread movement that advances in a body: *a new wave of refugees.* **9** a prolonged spell of some particular type of weather: *a heat wave.* **10** the act or an instance of waving. **11** *Physics* an energy-carrying disturbance travelling through a medium or space by a series of vibrations without any overall movement of matter. **12 make waves** to cause trouble.

waveband *n* a range of wavelengths or frequencies used for a particular type of radio transmission.

wave down *vb* to signal to (the driver of a vehicle) to stop.

wavelength *n* **1** *Physics* the distance between two points of the same phase in consecutive cycles of a wave. **2** the wavelength of the carrier wave used by a particular broadcasting station. **3 on the same wavelength** *Informal* having similar views, feelings, or thoughts.

waver *vb* **1** to hesitate between possibilities; be indecisive. **2** to swing from one thing to another: *she wavered between annoyance and civility.* **3** (of a voice or stare) to become unsteady. **4** to move back and forth or one way and another: *the barrel of the gun began to waver.* **wavering** *adj*

wavey *n Canad* a snow goose or other wild goose.

wavy *adj* **wavier, waviest** having curves: *wavy hair; a wavy line.*

wax[1] *n* **1** a solid fatty or oily substance used for making candles and polish, which softens and melts when heated. **2** short for **beeswax** or **sealing wax. 3** *Physiol* a brownish-yellow waxy substance secreted by glands in the ear. ~*vb* **4** to coat or polish with wax. **waxed** *adj* **waxy** *adj*

wax[2] *vb* **1** to increase gradually in size, strength, or power: *trading has waxed and waned with the economic cycle.* **2** (of the moon) to show a gradually increasing area of brightness from new moon until full moon. **3** to become: *he waxed eloquent on the disadvantages of marriage.*

waxed paper *or* **wax paper** *n* paper treated or coated with wax or paraffin to make it waterproof.

waxen *adj* **1** resembling wax in colour or texture: *his face is waxen and pale.* **2** made of, treated with, or covered with wax: *a waxen image.*

waxeye *n* a small New Zealand bird with a white circle round its eye.

waxwork *n* a life-size lifelike wax figure of a famous person.

waxworks *n* a museum or exhibition of wax figures.

way *n* **1** a manner, method, or means: *a new way of life; a tactful way of finding out.* **2** a characteristic style or manner: *we are all special in our own way.* **3 ways** habits or customs: *he had a liking for British ways.* **4** an aspect or detail of something: *the tourist industry is in many ways a success story.* **5** a choice or option, for example in a vote: *he thought it could go either way.* **6** a route or direction: *the shortest way home.* **7** a journey: *you could buy a magazine to read on the way.* **8** distance: *they are a long way from Paris.* **9** space or room for movement or activity: *you won't be in his way.* **10 by the way** incidentally: *by the way, I've decided to leave.* **11 by way of a** serving as: *by way of explanation.* **b** by the route of: *I went by way of my family home.* **12 get one's own way** to have things exactly as one wants them to be. **13 give way a** to collapse or break. **b** to yield or concede: *I tried to make him understand but he did not give way an inch.* **14 give way to a** to be replaced by: *my first feelings of dismay have given way to comparative complacency.* **b** to show (an emotion) unrestrainedly. **c** to slow down or stop when driving to let (another driver) pass. **15 go out of one's way** to take considerable trouble: *he had gone out of his way to reassure me.* **16 have it both ways** to enjoy two things that would normally be mutually exclusive. **17 in a bad way** *Informal* in a poor state of health or a poor financial state. **18 in a way** in some respects. **19 in no way** not at all. **20 make one's way** to proceed or go: *he decided to make his way back in the dark.* **21 on the way out** *Informal* becoming unfashionable. **22 out of the way a** removed or dealt with so as to be no longer a hindrance. **b** remote. **23 under way** having started moving or making progress. ~*adv* **24** *Informal* far or by far: *that is way out of line.*

waybill *n* a document stating the nature, origin, and destination of goods being transported.

wayfarer *n Old-fashioned* a traveller.

waylay *vb* **-laying, -laid 1** to lie in wait for and attack. **2** to intercept (someone) unexpectedly.

way-out *adj Old-fashioned, informal* extremely unconventional.

ways and means *pl n* **1** the methods and resources for accomplishing something. **2** the money and the methods of raising the money needed for the functioning of a political unit.

wayside *adj* **1** *Old-fashioned* situated by the side of a road: *wayside shrines.* ~*n* **2 fall by the wayside** to be unsuccessful or stop being successful: *thousands of*

THESAURUS

filled, tearful, weepy **3.** adulterated, dilute, diluted, flavourless, insipid, runny, tasteless, thin, washy, watered-down, weak, wishy-washy (*informal*)

wave *vb.* **1.** beckon, direct, gesticulate, gesture, indicate, sign, signal **2.** brandish, flap, flourish, flutter, move to and fro, oscillate, quiver, ripple, shake, stir, sway, swing, undulate, wag, waver, wield ~*n.* **3.** billow, breaker, comber, ridge, ripple, roller, sea surf, swell, undulation, unevenness **4.** current, drift, flood, groundswell, movement, outbreak, rash, rush, stream, surge, sweep, tendency, trend, upsurge

waver 1. be indecisive, be irresolute, be unable to decide, be unable to make up one's mind, blow hot and cold (*informal*), dither (*chiefly Brit.*), falter, fluctuate, hesitate, hum and haw, seesaw, shillyshally (*informal*), swither (*Scot.*), vacillate **2.** flicker, fluctuate, quiver, reel, shake, sway, totter, tremble, undulate, vary, wave, weave, wobble

wax *vb.* become fuller, become larger, develop, dilate, enlarge, expand, fill out, get bigger, grow, increase, magnify, mount, rise, swell

way 1. approach, course of action, fashion, manner, means, method, mode, plan, practice, procedure, process, scheme, system, technique **2.** characteristic, conduct, custom, habit, idiosyncrasy, manner, nature, personality, practice, style, trait, usage, wont **3.** aspect, detail, feature, particular, point, respect, sense **4.** access, avenue, channel, course, direction, highway, lane, path, pathway, road, route, street, thoroughfare, track, trail **5.** distance, journey, length, stretch, trail **6.** elbow room, opening, room, space **7. by the way** by the bye, en passant, incidentally, in parenthesis, in passing **8. give way a.** break down, cave in, collapse, crack, crumple, fall, fall to pieces, give, go to pieces, subside **b.** accede, acknowledge defeat, acquiesce, back down, concede, make concessions, withdraw, yield **9. under way** afoot, begun, going, in motion, in progress, moving, on the go (*informal*), on the move, started

wayfarer *old-fashioned* globetrotter, Gypsy, itinerant,

new diets are dreamed up yearly – many fall by the wayside.

wayward *adj* erratic, selfish, or stubborn. **waywardness** *n*

Wb *Physics* weber.

WC *or* **wc** *n* a toilet.

we *pron* (*used as the subject of a verb*) **1** the speaker or writer and another person or other people: *we arrived in Calais.* **2** all people or people in general: *it's an unfair world we live in.* **3** *Formal* same as **I**: used by monarchs and editors.

weak *adj* **1** lacking in physical or mental strength. **2** (of a part of the body) not functioning as well as is normal: *a weak heart.* **3** liable to collapse or break: *weak bridges.* **4** lacking in importance, influence, or strength: *a weak government.* **5** (of a currency or shares) falling in price or characterized by falling prices. **6** lacking in moral strength; easily influenced. **7** not convincing: *weak arguments.* **8** lacking strength or power: *his voice was weak.* **9** not having a strong flavour: *weak coffee.* **weakly** *adv*

weaken *vb* to become or make weak or weaker.

weak-kneed *adj Informal* lacking strength, courage, or resolution.

weakling *n* a person who is lacking in physical or mental strength.

weak-minded *adj* **1** lacking willpower. **2** of low intelligence; foolish.

weakness *n* **1** the state of being weak. **2** a failing in a person's character: *his weakness is his impetuosity.* **3** a self-indulgent liking: *a weakness for gin.*

weal[1] *n* a raised mark on the skin produced by a blow.

weal[2] *n Old-fashioned* prosperity or wellbeing: *the public weal.*

wealth *n* **1** the state of being rich. **2** a large amount of money and valuable material possessions: *redistribution of wealth.* **3** a great amount or number: *a wealth of detail.*

wealthy *adj* **wealthier, wealthiest 1** having a large amount of money and valuable material possessions. **2 wealthy in** having a great amount or number of: *a continent exceptionally wealthy in minerals.*

wean *vb* **1** to start giving (a baby or young mammal) food other than its mother's milk. **2** to cause (oneself or someone else) to give up a former habit: *they are unable to wean themselves from the tobacco habit.* **weaning** *n*

weapon *n* **1** an object used in fighting, such as a knife or gun. **2** anything used to get the better of an opponent: *having a sense of humour is a weapon of self-defence.*

weaponry *n* weapons regarded collectively.

wear *vb* **wearing, wore, worn 1** to carry or have (a garment or jewellery) on one's body as clothing or ornament. **2** to have (a particular facial expression): *she wore a scowl of frank antagonism.* **3** to style (the hair) in a particular way: *she wears her hair in a braid.* **4** to deteriorate or cause to deteriorate by constant use or action. **5** *Brit informal* to accept: *he won't be given a top job – the Party wouldn't wear it.* **6 wear thin** to lessen or become weaker: *his patience began to wear thin.* **7 wear well** to remain in good condition for a long time. ~*n* **8** clothes that are suitable for a particular time or purpose: *evening wear; beach wear.* **9** deterioration from constant or normal use. **10** the quality of resisting the effects of constant use. ~See also **wear down, wear off, wear out. wearable** *adj* **wearer** *n*

wear and tear *n* damage or loss resulting from ordinary use.

wear down *vb* **1** to make shorter by long or constant wearing or rubbing: *the back of his heels were worn*

THESAURUS

journeyer, nomad, rover, traveller, trekker, voyager, walker, wanderer

wayward capricious, changeable, contrary, contumacious, cross-grained, disobedient, erratic, fickle, flighty, froward, headstrong, inconstant, incorrigible, insubordinate, intractable, mulish, obdurate, obstinate, perverse, rebellious, refractory, self-willed, stubborn, undependable, ungovernable, unmanageable, unpredictable, unruly, wilful

weak 1. anaemic, debilitated, decrepit, delicate, effete, enervated, exhausted, faint, feeble, fragile, frail, infirm, languid, puny, shaky, sickly, spent, tender, unsound, unsteady, wasted, weakly **2.** deficient, faulty, inadequate, lacking, pathetic, poor, substandard, under-strength, wanting **3.** cowardly, impotent, indecisive, ineffectual, infirm, irresolute, namby-pamby, pathetic, powerless, soft, spineless, timorous, weak-kneed (*informal*) **4.** feeble, flimsy, hollow, inconclusive, invalid, lame, pathetic, shallow, slight, unconvincing, unsatisfactory **5.** distant, dull, faint, imperceptible, low, muffled, poor, quiet, slight, small, soft **6.** diluted, insipid, milk-and-water, runny, tasteless, thin, under-strength, waterish, watery, wishy-washy (*informal*)

weaken abate, adulterate, cut, debase, debilitate, depress, diminish, droop, dwindle, ease up, enervate, fade, fail, flag, give way, impair, invalidate, lessen, lower, mitigate, moderate, reduce, sap, sap the strength of, soften up, temper, thin, thin out, tire, undermine, wane, water down

weakling coward, doormat (*slang*), drip (*informal*), milksop, mouse, sissy, wet (*Brit. informal*), wimp (*informal*)

weakness 1. debility, decrepitude, enervation, faintness, feebleness, fragility, frailty, impotence, infirmity, irresolution, powerlessness, vulnerability **2.** Achilles heel, blemish, chink in one's armour, defect, deficiency, failing, fault, flaw, imperfection, lack, shortcoming **3.** fondness, inclination, liking, partiality, passion, penchant, predilection, proclivity, proneness, soft spot

wealth 1. affluence, assets, big money, capital, cash, estate, fortune, funds, goods, lucre, means, money, opulence, pelf (*contemptuous*), possessions, pretty penny (*informal*), property, prosperity, resources, riches, substance, tidy sum (*informal*) **2.** abundance, bounty, copiousness, cornucopia, fullness, plenitude, plenty, profusion, richness, store

wealthy affluent, comfortable, filthy rich, flush (*informal*), in the money (*informal*), loaded (*slang*), made of money (*informal*), moneyed, opulent, prosperous, quids in (*slang*), rich, rolling in it (*slang*), stinking rich (*slang*), well-heeled (*informal*), well-off, well-to-do

wear *vb.* **1.** bear, be clothed in, be dressed in, carry, clothe oneself, don, dress in, have on, put on, sport (*informal*) **2.** display, exhibit, show **3.** abrade, consume, corrode, deteriorate, erode, fray, grind, impair, rub, use, wash away, waste **4.** *Brit. informal* accept, allow, brook, countenance, fall for, permit, put up with (*informal*), stand for, stomach, swallow (*informal*), take **5. wear well** bear up, be durable, endure, hold up, last, stand up ~*n.* **6.** apparel, attire, clothes, costume, dress, garb, garments, gear (*informal*), habit, outfit, things **7.** abrasion, attrition, corrosion, damage, depreciation, deterioration, erosion, friction, use, wear and tear **8.** employment, mileage (*informal*), service, use, usefulness, utility

wear down 1. abrade, consume, corrode, erode, grind down, rub away **2.** chip away at (*informal*), fight a war of attrition against, overcome gradually, reduce, undermine

down. **2** to overcome gradually by persistent effort: *to wear down the enemy.*

wearing *adj* causing exhaustion and sometimes irritation.

wearisome *adj* causing fatigue and irritation.

wear off *vb* to have a gradual decrease in effect or intensity: *the cocaine injection was beginning to wear off.*

wear out *vb* **1** to make or become unfit for use through wear: *my red trousers are worn out.* **2** *Informal* to exhaust: *the afternoon's races and games had worn him out.*

weary *adj* **-rier, -riest 1** very tired; lacking energy. **2** caused by or suggestive of weariness: *he managed a weary smile.* **3** causing exhaustion: *a long weary struggle.* **4 weary of** discontented or bored with: *he was weary of the war.* ~*vb* **-ries, -rying, -ried 5** to make weary. **6 weary of** to become discontented or bored with: *he seems to have wearied of her possessiveness.* **wearily** *adv* **weariness** *n* **wearying** *adj*

weasel *n, pl* **-sel** *or* **-sels** a small meat-eating mammal with reddish-brown fur, a long body and neck, and short legs.

weather *n* **1** the day-to-day atmospheric conditions, such as temperature, cloudiness, and rainfall, affecting a specific place. **2 make heavy weather of** *Informal* to carry out (a task) with great difficulty or needless effort. **3 under the weather** *Informal* feeling slightly ill. ~*vb* **4** to undergo or cause to undergo changes, such as discoloration, due to the action of the weather. **5** to come safely through (a storm, problem, or difficulty).

weather-beaten *adj* **1** tanned by exposure to the weather: *a crumpled weather-beaten face.* **2** worn or damaged as a result of exposure to the weather.

weatherboard *n* a timber board that is fixed with others in overlapping horizontal rows to form an exterior cladding on a wall or roof. **weatherboarded** *adj*

weathercock *n* a weather vane in the shape of a cock.

weather eye *n* **keep a weather eye on** to keep a careful watch on: *keep a weather eye on your symptoms.*

weathering *n* the breakdown of rocks by the action of the weather.

weatherman *n, pl* **-men** a man who forecasts the weather on radio or television. **weather girl** *fem n*

weatherproof *adj* able to withstand exposure to weather without deterioration: *a weatherproof roof.*

weather vane *n* a metal object on a roof that indicates the direction in which the wind is blowing.

weave *vb* **weaving, wove** *or* **weaved, woven** *or* **weaved 1** to form (a fabric) by interlacing yarn on a loom. **2** to make (a garment or a blanket) by this process. **3** to construct (a basket or fence) by interlacing cane or twigs. **4** to compose (a story or plan) by combining separate elements into a whole. **5** to move from side to side while going forward: *to weave in and out of lanes.* **6 get weaving** *Informal* to hurry. ~*n* **7** the structure or pattern of a woven fabric: *the rough weave of the cloth.* **weaver** *n* **weaving** *n*

web *n* **1** a mesh of fine tough threads built by a spider to trap insects. **2** anything that is intricately formed or complex: *a web of relationships.* **3** a membrane connecting the toes of some water birds and water-dwelling animals such as frogs. **webbed** *adj*

webbing *n* a strong fabric that is woven in strips and used under springs in upholstery or for straps.

weber (**vay**-ber) *n* the SI unit of magnetic flux (the strength of a magnetic field over a given area).

web-footed *or* **web-toed** *adj* (of certain animals or birds) having webbed feet that aid swimming.

wed *vb* **wedding, wedded** *or* **wed 1** *Old-fashioned* to take (a person) as a husband or wife; marry. **2** to unite closely: *to wed folklore and magic.*

Wed. Wednesday.

wedded *adj* **1** of marriage: *wedded bliss.* **2** firmly in support of an idea or institution: *wedded to the virtues of capitalism.*

wedding *n* **1** a marriage ceremony. **2** a special wed-

THESAURUS

weariness drowsiness, enervation, exhaustion, fatigue, languor, lassitude, lethargy, listlessness, prostration, tiredness

wearing exasperating, exhausting, fatiguing, irksome, oppressive, taxing, tiresome, tiring, trying, wearisome

wearisome annoying, boring, bothersome, burdensome, dull, exasperating, exhausting, fatiguing, humdrum, irksome, mind-numbing, monotonous, oppressive, pestilential, prosaic, tedious, troublesome, trying, uninteresting, vexatious, wearing

wear off abate, decrease, diminish, disappear, dwindle, ebb, fade, lose effect, lose strength, peter out, subside, wane, weaken

wear out 1. become useless, become worn, consume, deteriorate, erode, fray, impair, use up, wear through **2.** *informal* enervate, exhaust, fag out (*informal*), fatigue, frazzle (*informal*), knacker (*slang*), prostrate, sap, tire, weary

weary *adj.* **1.** all in (*informal*), asleep *or* dead on one's feet (*informal*), clapped out (*Austral. & N.Z. informal*), dead beat (*informal*), dog-tired (*informal*), done in (*informal*), drained, drooping, drowsy, enervated, exhausted, fagged (*informal*), fatigued, flagging, jaded, knackered (*slang*), ready to drop, sleepy, spent, tired, wearied, whacked (*Brit. informal*), worn out, zonked (*slang*) **2.** arduous, enervative, irksome, laborious, taxing, tiresome, tiring, wearing, wearisome **3. weary of** bored, browned-off (*informal*), discontented, fed up, impatient, indifferent, jaded, sick (*informal*), sick and tired (*informal*) ~*vb.* **4.** burden, debilitate, drain, droop, enervate, fade, fag (*informal*), fail, fatigue, grow tired, sap, take it out of (*informal*), tax, tire, tire out, wear out **5. weary of** annoy, become bored, bore, exasperate, have had enough, irk, jade, make discontented, plague, sicken, try the patience of, vex

weather *n.* **1.** climate, conditions **2. under the weather** *informal* ailing, below par, ill, indisposed, nauseous, not well, off-colour, out of sorts, poorly (*informal*), seedy (*informal*), sick ~*vb.* **3.** expose, harden, season, toughen **4.** bear up against, brave, come through, endure, get through, live through, make it (*informal*), overcome, pull through, resist, ride out, rise above, stand, stick it out (*informal*), suffer, surmount, survive, withstand

weave 1. blend, braid, entwine, fuse, incorporate, interlace, intermingle, intertwine, introduce, knit, mat, merge, plait, twist, unite **2.** build, construct, contrive, create, fabricate, make, make up, put together, spin **3.** crisscross, move in and out, weave one's way, wind, zigzag **4. get weaving** *informal* get a move on, get going, get one's finger out (*Brit. informal*), get under way, hurry, make a start, shake a leg (*slang*), start

web 1. cobweb, spider's web **2.** interlacing, lattice, mesh, net, netting, network, screen, tangle, toils, weave, webbing

wed 1. *old-fashioned* become man and wife, be married to, espouse, get hitched (*slang*), get married, join, make one, marry, splice (*informal*), take as one's husband, take as one's wife, take to wife, tie the knot (*informal*), unite **2.** ally, blend, coalesce, combine, com-

ding anniversary, esp. the 25th (**silver wedding**) or 50th (**golden wedding**).

wedding breakfast *n* the meal usually served after a wedding ceremony or just before the bride and bridegroom leave for their honeymoon.

wedding cake *n* a rich iced fruit cake, with one, two, or more tiers, which is served at a wedding reception.

wedding ring *n* a plain ring, usually made of a precious metal, worn to indicate that one is married.

wedge *n* **1** a block of solid material, esp. wood or metal, that is shaped like a narrow V in cross section and can be pushed or driven between two objects or parts of an object in order to split or secure them. **2** a slice shaped like a wedge: *a wedge of quiche.* **3** *Golf* a club with a wedge-shaped face, used for bunker or pitch shots. **4 drive a wedge between** to cause a split between (people or groups). **5 the thin end of the wedge** anything unimportant in itself that implies the start of something much larger. *~vb* **wedging, wedged 6** to secure (something) with a wedge. **7** to squeeze into a narrow space: *a book wedged between the bed and the table.*

Wedgwood *n Trademark* a type of fine pottery with applied decoration in white on a coloured background.

wedlock *n* **1** the state of being married. **2 born out of wedlock** born when one's parents are not legally married.

Wednesday *n* the fourth day of the week.

wee[1] *adj* small or short.

wee[2] *Informal, chiefly Brit ~n* **1** an instance of urinating. *~vb* **weeing, weed 2** to urinate. Also: **wee-wee**

weed *n* **1** any plant that grows wild and profusely, esp. among cultivated plants. **2** *Slang* **a** marijuana. **b the weed** *or* **the evil weed** tobacco. **3** *Informal* a thin weak person. *~vb* **4** to remove weeds from (a garden).

weedkiller *n* a chemical or hormonal substance used to kill weeds.

weed out *vb* to separate out, remove, or eliminate (an unwanted element): *to weed out the thugs.*

weedy *adj* **weedier, weediest 1** *Informal* thin or weak: *sick and weedy children.* **2** full of weeds: *weedy patches of garden.*

week *n* **1** a period of seven consecutive days, esp. one beginning with Sunday. **2** a period of seven consecutive days from a specified day: *a week from today.* **3** the period of time within a week that is spent at work.

weekday *n* any day of the week other than Saturday or Sunday.

weekend *n* Saturday and Sunday.

weekly *adj* **1** happening once a week or every week: *a weekly column.* **2** determined or calculated by the week: *weekly earnings.* *~adv* **3** once a week or every week: *report to the police weekly.* *~n, pl* **-lies 4** a newspaper or magazine issued every week.

weeny *adj* **-nier, -niest** *Informal* very small; tiny.

weep *vb* **weeping, wept 1** to shed tears; cry. **2** to ooze liquid: *the skin cracked and wept; the label is weeping black ink in the rain.* *~n* **3** a spell of weeping: *together we had a good weep.*

weeping willow *n* a willow tree with graceful drooping branches.

weepy *Informal ~adj* **weepier, weepiest 1** liable or tending to weep. *~n, pl* **weepies 2** a sentimental film or book.

weevil *n* a beetle with a long snout that feeds on plants.

wee-wee *n, vb* **-weeing, -weed** *Informal, chiefly Brit* same as **wee**[2].

weft *n* the yarns woven across the width of the fabric through the lengthways warp yarns.

weigh *vb* **1** to have weight as specified: *he must weigh a good seventeen stone.* **2** to measure the weight of. **3** to consider carefully: *the President now has to weigh his options.* **4** to be influential: *the authorities did not enter my mind or weigh with me.* **5 weigh anchor** to raise a ship's anchor. **6 weigh out** to measure out by weight. ~See also **weigh down, weigh in,** etc.

weighbridge *n* a machine for weighing vehicles by means of a metal plate set into a road.

weigh down *vb* **1** (of a heavy load) to impede the movements of. **2** (of a problem or difficulty) to worry (someone) a great deal.

weigh in *vb* **1** (of a boxer or jockey) to be weighed to check that one is of the correct weight for the contest. **2** *Informal* to contribute to a discussion or conversation: *he weighed in with a few sharp comments.* *~n* **weigh-in 3** *Sport* the occasion of checking the competitors' weight before a boxing match or a horse race.

weigh on *vb* to be oppressive or burdensome to: *the expectations that weigh so heavily on diplomats' wives.*

weight *n* **1** the heaviness of an object, substance, or person. **2** *Physics* the vertical force experienced by a mass as a result of gravitation. **3 a** a system of units used to express weight: *metric weight.* **b** a unit used to measure weight: *the kilogram is the weight used in the metric system.* **4 a** an object of known heaviness used for weighing objects, substances, or people. **b** an object of known heaviness used in weight training or weightlifting to strengthen the muscles. **5** any heavy load: *with a weight of fish on their backs.* **6** force, importance, or influence: *they want their words to carry weight.* **7** an oppressive force: *the weight of expectation.* **8 pull one's weight** *Informal* to do one's full share of a task. **9 throw one's weight about** *Infor-*

THESAURUS

mingle, dedicate, fuse, interweave, join, link, marry, merge, unify, unite, yoke

wedding espousals, marriage, marriage ceremony, nuptial rite, nuptials, wedlock

wedge 1. *n.* block, chock, chunk, lump, wodge (*Brit. informal*) **2.** *vb.* block, cram, crowd, force, jam, lodge, pack, ram, split, squeeze, stuff, thrust

wedlock marriage, matrimony

weed out dispense with, eliminate, eradicate, extirpate, get rid of, remove, root out, separate out, shed, uproot

weekly by the week, every week, once a week

weep bemoan, bewail, blub (*slang*), blubber, boohoo, complain, cry, greet (*Scot.*), keen, lament, moan, mourn, shed tears, snivel, sob, ululate, whimper, whinge (*informal*)

weigh 1. have a weight of, measure the weight of, put on the scales, tip the scales at (*informal*) **2.** consider, contemplate, deliberate upon, evaluate, examine, eye up, give thought to, meditate upon, mull over, ponder, reflect upon, study, think over **3.** be influential, carry weight, count, cut any ice (*informal*), have influence, impress, matter, tell **4. weigh out** apportion, deal out, dole out, measure

weigh down bear down, burden, depress, get down, oppress, overburden, overload, press down, trouble, weigh upon, worry

weight *n.* **1.** avoirdupois, burden, gravity, heaviness, heft (*informal*), load, mass, poundage, pressure, tonnage **2.** ballast, heavy object, load, mass **3.** authority, bottom, clout (*informal*), consequence, consideration, efficacy, emphasis, impact, import, importance, influence, moment, persuasiveness, power, significance,

mal to act in an aggressive authoritarian manner. *~vb* **10** to add weight to; make heavier. **11** to slant (a system) so that it favours one side rather than another.

weighting *n* an allowance paid to compensate for higher living costs: *salary: £23 500 per year (including Inner London weighting).*

weightless *adj* **1** seeming to have very little weight or no weight at all. **2** seeming not to be affected by gravity, as in the case of astronauts in an orbiting spacecraft. **weightlessness** *n*

weightlifting *n* the sport of lifting barbells of specified weights in a prescribed manner. **weightlifter** *n*

weight training *n* physical exercise using light or heavy weights in order to strengthen the muscles.

weighty *adj* **weightier, weightiest 1** important or serious: *weighty matters.* **2** very heavy.

weigh up *vb* to make an assessment of (a person or situation).

weir *n* **1** a low dam that is built across a river to divert the water or control its flow. **2** a fencelike trap built across a stream for catching fish in

weird *adj* **1** strange or bizarre. **2** suggestive of the supernatural; uncanny. **weirdly** *adv* **weirdness** *n*

weirdo *n, pl* **-dos** *Informal* a person who behaves in a bizarre or eccentric manner.

welch *vb* same as **welsh.**

welcome *vb* **-coming, -comed 1** to greet the arrival of (a guest) cordially. **2** to receive or accept (something) gladly: *I would welcome a chance to speak to him.* *~n* **3** the act of greeting or receiving someone or something in a specified manner: *the President was given a warm welcome.* *~adj* **4** gladly received or admitted: *I wouldn't want to stay where I'm not welcome.* **5** encouraged or invited: *you are welcome to join us at one of our social events.* **6** bringing pleasure: *a welcome change.* **7 you're welcome** an expression used to acknowledge someone's thanks. **welcoming** *adj*

weld *vb* **1** to join (two pieces of metal or plastic) by softening with heat and hammering or by fusion. **2** to unite closely: *the diverse ethnic groups had been welded together by the anti-Fascist cause.* *~n* **3** a joint formed by welding. **welder** *n*

welfare *n* **1** health, happiness, prosperity, and general wellbeing. **2** financial and other assistance given, usually by the government, to people in need.

welfare state *n* a system in which the government undertakes responsibility for the wellbeing of its population, through unemployment insurance, old age pensions, and other social-security measures.

well[1] *adv* **better, best 1** satisfactorily or pleasingly: *well proportioned.* **2** skilfully: *I played well for the last six holes.* **3** thoroughly: *make sure the chicken is well cooked.* **4** comfortably or prosperously: *he has lived well from his various nautical exploits.* **5** suitably or fittingly: *you can't very well refuse.* **6** intimately: *darling Robert, I know him so well.* **7** favourably: *it will go down very well with all the people who support him.* **8** by a considerable margin: *well over half; she left well before tea.* **9** very likely: *the claim may well be true.* **10** *Informal* extremely: *well cool.* **11 all very well** used ironically to express discontent or annoyance: *that's all very well, but I'm left to pick up the pieces.* **12 as well a** in addition. **b** with equal effect: used to express indifference or reluctance: *I might as well go out.* **13 as well as** in addition to. **14 just as well** fortunate or appropriate: *it's just as well I didn't spend all my money.* *~adj* **15** in good health: *I'm not feeling well.* **16** satisfactory or acceptable: *all was well in the aircraft.* *~interj* **17 a** an expression of surprise, indignation, or reproof: *well, what a cheek!* **b** an expression of anticipation in waiting for an answer or remark: *well, what do you think?*

well[2] *n* **1** a hole or shaft bored into the earth to tap a supply of water, oil, or gas. **2** an open shaft through the floors of a building, used for a staircase. *~vb* **3** to flow upwards or outwards: *tears welled up into my eyes.*

we'll we will *or* we shall.

well-advised *adj* prudent or sensible: *you would be well-advised to cooperate with me.*

well-appointed *adj* (of a room or building) equipped or furnished to a high standard.

well-balanced *adj* sensible and emotionally stable.

well-behaved *adj* having good manners; not causing trouble or mischief.

wellbeing *n* the state of being contented and healthy.

THESAURUS

substance, value **4.** burden, load, millstone, oppression, pressure, strain *~vb.* **5.** add weight to, ballast, charge, freight, increase the load on, increase the weight of, load, make heavier **6.** bias, load, unbalance

weighty 1. consequential, considerable, critical, crucial, forcible, grave, important, momentous, portentous, serious, significant, solemn, substantial **2.** burdensome, cumbersome, dense, heavy, hefty (*informal*), massive, ponderous

weird bizarre, creepy (*informal*), eerie, eldritch (*poetic*), far-out (*slang*), freakish, ghostly, grotesque, mysterious, odd, outlandish, queer, spooky (*informal*), strange, supernatural, uncanny, unearthly, unnatural

welcome *vb.* **1.** accept gladly, bid welcome, embrace, greet, hail, meet, offer hospitality to, receive, receive with open arms, roll out the red carpet for, usher in *~n.* **2.** acceptance, entertainment, greeting, hospitality, reception, salutation *~adj.* **3.** acceptable, accepted, appreciated, gladly received, wanted **4.** at home, free, invited, under no obligation **5.** agreeable, delightful, desirable, gratifying, pleasant, pleasing, pleasurable, refreshing

welfare advantage, benefit, good, happiness, health, interest, profit, prosperity, success, wellbeing

well[1] *adv.* **1.** agreeably, capitally, famously (*informal*), happily, in a satisfactory manner, nicely, pleasantly, satisfactorily, smoothly, splendidly, successfully **2.** ably, adeptly, adequately, admirably, conscientiously, correctly, effectively, efficiently, expertly, proficiently, properly, skilfully, with skill **3.** accurately, attentively, carefully, closely **4.** comfortably, flourishingly, prosperously **5.** correctly, easily, fairly, fittingly, in all fairness, justly, properly, readily, rightly, suitably **6.** closely, completely, deeply, fully, intimately, personally, profoundly, thoroughly **7.** approvingly, favourably, glowingly, graciously, highly, kindly, warmly **8.** abundantly, amply, completely, considerably, fully, greatly, heartily, highly, substantially, sufficiently, thoroughly, very much **9. as well** also, besides, in addition, into the bargain, to boot, too **10. as well as** along with, at the same time as, in addition to, including, over and above *~adj.* **11.** able-bodied, fit, hale, healthy, hearty, in fine fettle, in good health, robust, sound, strong, up to par **12.** agreeable, bright, fine, fitting, flourishing, fortunate, good, happy, lucky, pleasing, profitable, proper, prudent, right, satisfactory, thriving, useful

well[2] **1.** *n.* bore, fount, fountain, hole, mine, pit, pool, repository, shaft, source, spring, waterhole, wellspring **2.** *vb.* exude, flow, gush, jet, ooze, pour, rise, run, seep, spout, spring, spurt, stream, surge, trickle

well-balanced judicious, level-headed, rational, reasonable, sane, sensible, sober, sound, together (*slang*), well-adjusted

well-bred civil, courteous, courtly, cultivated, cul-

well-born *adj* belonging to a noble or upper-class family.
well-bred *adj* having good manners; polite.
well-built *adj* strong and well-proportioned.
well-connected *adj* having influential or important relatives or friends.
well-disposed *adj* inclined to be sympathetic, kindly, or friendly towards a person or idea.
well-done *adj* **1** made or accomplished satisfactorily. **2** (of food, esp. meat) cooked very thoroughly.
well-founded *adj* having a sound basis in fact: *a well-founded fear of persecution.*
well-groomed *adj* having a smart tidy appearance.
well-grounded *adj* having a sound basis in fact: *well-grounded suspicions.*
wellhead *n* **1** the source of a well or stream. **2** a source, fountainhead, or origin.
well-heeled *adj Informal* wealthy.
wellies *pl n Brit informal* Wellington boots.
well-informed *adj* knowing a lot about a great variety of subjects or about one particular subject.
Wellington boots *or* **wellingtons** *pl n Brit* long rubber boots, worn in wet or muddy conditions.
well-intentioned *adj* having good or kindly intentions, usually with unfortunate results.
well-known *adj* widely known; famous.
well-meaning *adj* having or indicating good intentions, usually with unfortunate results.
well-nigh *adv* almost: *a well-nigh impossible task.*
well-off *adj* **1** moderately wealthy. **2** in a fortunate position: *some people don't know when they are well-off.*
well-preserved *adj* not showing signs of ageing: *amazingly well-preserved for a man of 70.*
well-read *adj* having read and learned a lot.
well-rounded *adj* **1** desirably varied: *his well-rounded team.* **2** rounded in shape or well developed: *a voluptuous well-rounded lady.*
well-spoken *adj* having a clear, articulate, and socially acceptable accent and way of speaking.
wellspring *n* a source of abundant supply: *the wellspring of truth.*
well-thought-of *adj* liked and respected.
well-to-do *adj* moderately wealthy.
well-versed *adj* knowing a lot about a particular subject.
well-wisher *n* a person who shows benevolence or sympathy towards a person or cause.
well-worn *adj* **1** (of a word or phrase) having lost its meaning or force through being overused. **2** having been used so much as to show signs of wear: *well-worn leather.*
welsh *or* **welch** *vb* **welsh on** to fail to pay (a debt) or fulfil (an obligation).
Welsh *adj* **1** of Wales. *~n* **2** a Celtic language spoken in some parts of Wales. *~pl n* **3 the Welsh** the people of Wales.
Welshman *or fem* **Welshwoman** *n, pl* **-men** *or* **-women** a person from Wales.
Welsh rarebit *n* melted cheese, sometimes mixed with milk or seasonings, served on hot toast. Also called: **Welsh rabbit**
welt *n* **1** a raised mark on the skin produced by a blow. **2** a raised or strengthened seam in a garment.
welter *n* a confused mass or jumble: *a welter of facts.*
welterweight *n* a professional boxer weighing up to 147 pounds (66.5 kg) or an amateur boxer weighing up to 67 kg.
wen *n Pathol* a cyst on the scalp.
wench *n Old-fashioned* **1** *Facetious* a girl or young woman. **2** a prostitute or female servant.
wend *vb* to make (one's way) in a particular direction: *it's time to wend our way back home.*
Wendy house *n* a small toy house for a child to play in.
wensleydale *n* a white cheese with a flaky texture.
went *vb* the past tense of **go.**
wept *vb* the past of **weep.**
were *vb* the form of the past tense of **be** used after *we, you, they,* or a plural noun, or as a subjunctive in conditional sentences.
we're we are.
weren't were not.
werewolf *n, pl* **-wolves** (in folklore) a person who can turn into a wolf.
west *n* **1** one of the four cardinal points of the compass, at 270° clockwise from north the direction along a line of latitude towards the sunset. **2 the west** any area lying in or towards the west. *~adj* **3** situated in, moving towards, or facing the west. **4** (esp. of the wind) from the west. *~adv* **5** in, to, or towards the west.
West *n* **1 the West a** the western part of the world contrasted historically and culturally with the East. **b** (esp. formerly) the non-Communist countries of Europe and America contrasted with the Communist states of the East. *~adj* **2** of or denoting the western part of a country or region.
westbound *adj* going towards the west.
westerly *adj* **1** of or in the west. *~adv, adj* **2** towards the west. **3** from the west: *a westerly wind.*
western *adj* **1** situated in or towards the west. **2** facing or moving towards the west. **3** (*sometimes cap*) of or characteristic of the west or West. *~n* **4** a film or book about cowboys in the western states of the US in the 19th century. **westernmost** *adj*
Western *adj* (esp. formerly) of or characteristic of the Americas and the parts of Europe not under Communist rule.
Westerner *n* a person from the west of a country or region.
western hemisphere *n* the half of the globe that contains the Americas.
westernize *or* **-ise** *vb* **-izing, -ized** *or* **-ising, -ised** to influence or make familiar with the customs or practices of the West. **westernization** *or* **-isation** *n*
West Indian *adj* **1** of the West Indies. *~n* **2** a person from the West Indies.
Westminster *n* the British Houses of Parliament.

THESAURUS

tured, gallant, genteel, gentlemanly, ladylike, mannerly, polished, polite, refined, sophisticated, urbane, well-brought-up, well-mannered
well-groomed dapper, neat, smart, soigné *or fem.* soignée, spruce, tidy, trim, well-dressed, well turned out
well-heeled *informal* affluent, flush (*informal*), moneyed, prosperous, rich, wealthy, well-off, well-to-do
well-known celebrated, familiar, famous, illustrious, notable, noted, popular, renowned, widely known
well-nigh all but, almost, just about, more or less, nearly, next to, practically, virtually
well-off **1.** affluent, comfortable, flush (*informal*), loaded (*slang*), moneyed, prosperous, rich, wealthy, well-heeled (*informal*), well-to-do **2.** comfortable, flourishing, fortunate, lucky, successful, thriving

westward *adj, adv also* **westwards 1** towards the west. ~*n* **2** the westward part or direction.

wet *adj* **wetter, wettest 1** moistened, covered, or soaked with water or some other liquid. **2** not yet dry or solid: *wet paint.* **3** rainy: *the weather was cold and wet.* **4** *Brit informal* feeble or foolish. **5 wet behind the ears** *Informal* immature or inexperienced. ~*n* **6** rainy weather. **7** *Brit informal* a feeble or foolish person. **8** *Brit informal* a Conservative politician who supports moderate policies. ~*vb* **wetting, wet** *or* **wetted 9** to make wet: *wet the brush before applying the paint.* **10** to urinate in (one's clothes or bed). **11 wet oneself** to urinate in one's clothes. **wetly** *adv* **wetness** *n*

wet blanket *n Informal* a person whose low spirits or lack of enthusiasm have a depressing effect on others.

wet dream *n* an erotic dream accompanied by an emission of semen.

wether *n* a male sheep, esp. a castrated one.

wetland *n* an area of marshy land.

wet nurse *n* (esp. formerly) a woman hired to breast-feed another woman's baby.

wet suit *n* a close-fitting rubber suit used by skin-divers and yachtsmen to retain body heat.

W. Glam West Glamorgan.

whack *vb* **1** to hit hard: *that lad whacked him over the head with a bottle.* ~*n* **2** a hard blow or the sound of one: *a whack with a blunt instrument.* **3** *Informal* a share: *he took his whack of that money.* **4 have a whack** to make an attempt. **5 out of whack** *Informal* out of order or out of condition: *my body is just a little out of whack.*

whacked *adj Brit informal* completely exhausted.

whacking *n* **1** *Old-fashioned* a severe beating. ~*adv* **2** *Informal, chiefly Brit* extremely: *a whacking great elm.*

whale *n* **1** a very large fishlike sea mammal that breathes through a blowhole on the top of its head. **2 have a whale of a time** *Informal* to enjoy oneself very much.

whalebone *n* a thin strip of a horny material that hangs from the upper jaw of some whales, formerly used for stiffening corsets.

whalebone whale *n* any whale with a double blowhole and strips of whalebone between the jaws instead of teeth, including the right whale and the blue whale.

whaler *n* **1** a ship used for hunting whales. **2** a person whose job is to hunt whales.

whaling *n* the activity of hunting and killing whales for food or oil.

wham *interj Informal* an expression indicating suddenness or forcefulness: *suddenly, wham! you are caught up right in the middle of it.*

whammy *n, pl* **-mies** *Informal, chiefly US* a devastating setback.

wharepuni (**for**-rep-poon-ee) *n NZ* (in a Maori community) a tall carved building used as a guesthouse.

wharf *n, pl* **wharves** *or* **wharfs** a platform along the side of a waterfront for docking, loading, and unloading ships.

wharfie *n Austral & NZ* a dock labourer.

what *pron* **1** used in requesting further information about the identity or categorization of something: *what was he wearing?; I knew what would happen.* **2** the person, thing, people, or things that: *all was not what it seemed.* **3** used in exclamations to add emphasis: *what a creep!* **4 what for?** for what reason? **5 what have you** other similar or related things: *qualifications, interests, profession, what have you.* ~*adj* **6** used with a noun in requesting further information about the identity or categorization of something: *what difference can it make now?* **7** to any degree or in any amount: *they provided what financial support they could.*

whatever *pron* **1** everything or anything that: *I can handle whatever comes up.* **2** no matter what: *whatever you do, keep your temper.* **3** *Informal* other similar or related things: *a block of wood, rock, or whatever.* **4** an intensive form of *what,* used in questions: *whatever gave you that impression?* ~*adj* **5** an intensive form of *what: I can take whatever actions I deem necessary.* **6** at all: *there is no foundation whatever for such opinions.*

whatnot *n Informal* other similar or related things: *groceries, wines, and whatnot.*

whatsoever *adj* at all: used for emphasis after a noun phrase that uses words such as *none* or *any: there is nothing whatsoever wrong with your heart; it can be used at any time and under any circumstances whatsoever.*

wheat *n* **1** a kind of grain used in making flour and pasta. **2** the plant from which this grain is obtained.

wheatear *n* a small northern songbird with a white rump.

wheaten *adj* made from the grain or flour of wheat: *wheaten bread.*

wheat germ *n* the vitamin-rich middle part of a grain of wheat.

wheatmeal *n* a brown flour intermediate between white flour and wholemeal flour.

wheedle *vb* **-dling, -dled 1** to try to persuade (someone) by coaxing or flattery: *wheedling you into giving them their way.* **2** to obtain (something) in this way: *she wheedled money out of him.* **wheedling** *adj, n*

wheel *n* **1** a circular object mounted on a shaft around which it can turn, fixed under vehicles to enable them to move. **2** anything like a wheel in shape or function: *the steering wheel; a spinning wheel.* **3** something that is repeated in cycles: *the wheel of fashion would turn, and the clothes would be back in style.* **4 at** *or* **behind the wheel** driving a vehicle. ~*vb* **5** to push (a bicycle, wheelchair, or pram) along. **6** to turn

THESAURUS

well-to-do affluent, comfortable, flush (*informal*), loaded (*slang*), moneyed, prosperous, rich, wealthy, well-heeled (*informal*), well-off

wet *adj.* **1.** aqueous, damp, dank, drenched, dripping, humid, moist, moistened, saturated, soaked, soaking, sodden, soggy, sopping, waterlogged, watery, wringing wet **2.** clammy, dank, drizzling, humid, misty, pouring, raining, rainy, showery, teeming **3.** *Brit. informal* effete, feeble, foolish, ineffectual, irresolute, namby-pamby, nerdy *or* nurdy (*slang*), silly, soft, spineless, timorous, weak, weedy (*informal*) **4. wet behind the ears** *informal* born yesterday, callow, green, immature, inexperienced, innocent, naive, new, raw ~*n.* **5.** damp weather, drizzle, rain, rains, rainy season, rainy weather **6.** *Brit. informal* drip (*informal*), milksop, weakling, weed (*informal*), wimp (*informal*) ~*vb.* **7.** damp, dampen, dip, douse, drench, humidify, irrigate, moisten, saturate, soak, splash, spray, sprinkle, steep, water

wharf dock, jetty, landing stage, pier, quay

wheedle butter up, cajole, charm, coax, court, draw, entice, flatter, inveigle, persuade, talk into, worm

wheel *n.* **1.** circle, gyration, pivot, revolution, roll, rotation, spin, turn, twirl, whirl **2. at** *or* **behind the wheel** at the helm, driving, in charge, in command, in

in a circle. **7 wheel and deal** to operate shrewdly and sometimes unscrupulously in order to advance one's own interests. **8 wheel round** to change direction or turn round suddenly. ~See also **wheels.**

wheelbarrow *n* a shallow open box for carrying small loads, with a wheel at the front and two handles.

wheelbase *n* the distance between the front and back axles of a motor vehicle.

wheelchair *n* a special chair on large wheels, for use by people who cannot walk properly.

wheel clamp *n* a device fixed onto one wheel of an illegally parked car to prevent the car being driven off.

wheelhouse *n* an enclosed structure on the bridge of a ship from which it is steered.

wheelie *n* a manoeuvre on a cycle or skateboard in which the front wheel or wheels are raised off the ground.

wheelie bin *n* a large container for household rubbish, mounted on wheels so that it can be moved more easily.

wheeling and dealing *n* shrewd and sometimes unscrupulous moves made in order to advance one's own interests. **wheeler-dealer** *n*

wheels *pl n* **1** *Informal* a car. **2** the main force and mechanism of an organization or system: *the wheels of the economy.* **3 wheels within wheels** a series of intricately connected events or plots.

wheelwright *n* a person whose job is to make and mend wheels.

wheeze *vb* **wheezing, wheezed 1** to breathe with a rasping or whistling sound. ~*n* **2** a wheezing breath or sound. **3** *Brit old-fashioned slang* a trick or plan: *a glorious tax wheeze.* **wheezy** *adj*

whelk *n* an edible sea creature with a strong snail-like shell.

whelp *n* **1** a young wolf or dog. **2** *Offensive* a youth. ~*vb* **3** (of an animal) to give birth.

when *adv* **1** at what time?: *when are they leaving?* ~*conj* **2** at the time at which: *he was twenty when the war started.* **3** although: *he drives when he could walk.* **4** considering the fact that: *how did you pass the exam when you hadn't studied for it?* ~*pron* **5** at which time: *she's at the age when girls get interested in boys.*

➤ Some people dislike the use of *when* in definitions: *famine is when food runs low,* but it is very common in informal usage. More formally, write *...a situation/condition in which...* .

whence *conj Old-fashioned or poetic* from what place, cause, or origin: *he would then ask them whence they came.*

whenever *conj* **1** at every or any time that: *the filly was trained to stop whenever a jockey used a whip.* ~*adv* **2** no matter when: *I am eager to come whenever you suggest.* **3** *Informal* at an unknown or unspecified time: *the 16th, 17th, or whenever.* **4** an intensive form of *when,* used in questions: *if we can't exercise restraint now, whenever can we?*

where *adv* **1** in, at, or to what place, point, or position?: *where are we going?; I know where he found it.* ~*pron* **2** in, at, or to which place: *he found a sandwich bar where he could get a snack.* ~*conj* **3** in the place at which: *he should have stayed where he was doing well.*

➤ *Where* includes the ideas *to* and *at* so avoid the use of these prepositions: *where was it?* (not *where was it at?*).

whereabouts *pl n* **1** the place, esp. the approximate place, where a person or thing is: *investigating the whereabouts of American servicemen missing since the Vietnam War.* ~*adv* **2** approximately where: *whereabouts will you go?*

whereas *conj* but by contrast: *she was crazy about him, whereas for him it was just another affair.*

whereby *pron* by or because of which: *the process whereby pests become resistant to pesticides.*

wherefore *n* **1 the whys and wherefores** the reasons or explanation: *the whys and wherefores of the war.* ~*conj* **2** *Old-fashioned or formal* for which reason.

wherein *Old-fashioned or formal* ~*adv* **1** in what place or respect?: *wherein lies the truth?* ~*pron* **2** in which place or thing: *the mirror wherein he had been gazing.*

whereof *Old-fashioned or formal* ~*adv* **1** of what or which person or thing? ~*pron* **2** of which person or thing: *I know whereof I speak.*

whereupon *conj* at which point: *they sentenced him to death, whereupon he fainted.*

wherever *pron* **1** at, in, or to every place or point which: *I got a wonderful reception wherever I went.* ~*conj* **2** in, to, or at whatever place: *wherever they went, the conditions were harsh.* ~*adv* **3** no matter where: *we're going to find him, wherever he is.* **4** *Informal* at, in, or to an unknown or unspecified place: *the jungles of Borneo or wherever.* **5** an intensive form of *where,* used in questions: *wherever have you been?*

wherewithal *n* **the wherewithal** the necessary funds, resources, or equipment: *the wherewithal for making chemical weapons.*

whet *vb* **whetting, whetted 1 whet someone's appetite** to increase someone's desire for or interest in something: *she gave him just enough information to whet his appetite.* **2** *Old-fashioned* to sharpen (a knife or other tool).

whether *conj* **1** used to introduce an indirect question: *he asked him whether he had seen the hunter.* **2** used to introduce a clause expressing doubt or choice: *you are entitled to the assistance of a lawyer, whether or not you can afford one; we learn from experience, whether good or bad.*

whetstone *n* a stone used for sharpening knives or other tools.

whew *interj* an exclamation of relief, surprise, disbelief or weariness.

whey (**way**) *n* the watery liquid that separates from the curd when milk is clotted, for example in making cheese.

which *adj* **1** used with a noun in requesting that the particular thing being referred to is further identified or distinguished: *which way had he gone?; a questionnaire to find out which shops local consumers use.* **2** any out of several: *you have to choose which goods and services you want.* ~*pron* **3** used in requesting that the particular thing being referred to is further identified or distinguished: *which of these occupations would be suitable for you?* **4** used in relative clauses referring to a thing rather than a person: *a discovery which could have lasting effects.* **5** and that: *her books*

THESAURUS

control, in the driving seat, steering ~*vb.* **3.** circle, gyrate, orbit, pirouette, revolve, roll, rotate, spin, swing, swivel, turn, twirl, whirl

wheeze *vb.* **1.** breathe roughly, catch one's breath, cough, gasp, hiss, rasp, whistle ~*n.* **2.** cough, gasp, hiss, rasp, whistle **3.** *Brit. old-fashioned* expedient, idea, plan, ploy, ruse, scheme, stunt, trick

whereabouts location, position, site, situation

wherewithal capital, equipment, essentials, funds, means, money, ready (*informal*), ready money, resources, supplies

were all over the dining table, which meant we had to eat in the kitchen.

whichever *adj* **1** any out of several: *choose whichever line you feel more comfortable with.* **2** no matter which: *whichever bridge you take, pause mid-stream for a look up and down the river.* ~*pron* **3** any one or ones out of several: *delete whichever is inapplicable.* **4** no matter which one or ones: *whichever you choose, you must be consistent throughout.*

whiff *n* **1** a passing odour: *I got a whiff of her perfume.* **2** a trace or hint: *the first whiff of jealousy.*

Whig *n* **1** a member of a British political party of the 18th–19th centuries that sought limited political and social reform and provided the core of the Liberal Party. ~*adj* **2** of or relating to Whigs. **Whiggism** *n*

while *conj* **1** at the same time that: *anti-inflammatory remedies may be used to alleviate the condition while background factors are investigated.* **2** at some point during the time that: *her father had died while she was gone.* **3** although or whereas: *while she tossed and turned, he fell into a dreamless sleep.* ~*n* **4** a period of time: *I'd like to stay a while.*

while away *vb* **whiling, whiled** to pass (time) idly but pleasantly.

whilst *conj Chiefly Brit* same as **while.**

whim *n* a sudden, passing, and often fanciful idea.

whimper *vb* **1** to cry, complain, or say (something) in a whining plaintive way. ~*n* **2** a soft plaintive whine.

whimsical *adj* unusual, playful, and fanciful: *a whimsical story.* **whimsically** *adv*

whimsy *n* **1** (*pl* **-sies**) a fanciful or playful idea: *they thought sparing the rod a foolish whimsy.* **2** capricious or playful behaviour: *sudden flights of whimsy.*

whin *n* same as **gorse.**

whine *n* **1** a long high-pitched plaintive cry or moan. **2** a peevish complaint. ~*vb* **whining, whined 3** to utter a whine. **whining** *adj, n*

whinge *Informal* ~*vb* **whingeing, whinged 1** to complain in a moaning manner. ~*n* **2** a complaint.

whinny *vb* **-nies, -nying, -nied 1** (of a horse) to neigh softly or gently. ~*n, pl* **-nies 2** a gentle or low-pitched neigh.

whip *n* **1** a piece of leather or rope attached at one end to a stiff handle, used for hitting people or animals. **2 a** a member of a political party who is responsible for urging members to attend Parliament to vote on an important issue. **b** a notice sent to members of a political party by the whip, urging them to attend Parliament to vote in a particular way on an important issue. **3** a dessert made from egg whites or cream beaten stiff: *raspberry whip.* ~*vb* **whipping, whipped 4** to hit with a whip. **5** to hit sharply: *strands of hair whipped across her cheeks.* **6** *Informal* to move or go quickly and suddenly: *machine-gun bullets whipped past him.* **7** to beat (cream or eggs) with a whisk or fork until frothy or stiff. **8** to rouse (someone) into a particular condition: *politicians and businessmen have whipped themselves into a panic about never-ending recession.* **9** *Informal* to steal (something). ~See also **whip out, whip-round, whip up. whipping** *n*

whip hand *n* **the whip hand** an advantage or dominating position: *buyers have the whip hand over estate agents.*

whiplash *n* **1** a quick lash of a whip. **2** short for **whiplash injury.**

whiplash injury *n* an injury to the neck resulting from the head being suddenly thrust forward and then snapped back, for example in a car crash.

whip out *or* **off** *vb* to take (something) out or off quickly and suddenly: *she whipped off her glasses.*

whipper-in *n, pl* **whippers-in** a huntsman's assistant who manages the hounds.

whippersnapper *n Old-fashioned* a young impertinent overconfident person.

whippet *n* a small slender dog similar to a greyhound.

whipping boy *n* a person who is expected to take the blame for other people's mistakes or incompetence.

whip-round *n Informal, chiefly Brit* an impromptu collection of money.

whipstock *n* the handle of a whip.

whip up *vb* **1** to excite or arouse: *to get people all whipped up about something; to whip up enthusiasm.* **2** *Informal* to prepare quickly: *she had whipped up a rich sauce.*

whir *n, vb* **whirring, whirred** same as **whirr.**

whirl *vb* **1** to spin or turn round very fast. **2** to seem to spin from dizziness or confusion: *my mind whirled with half-formed thoughts.* ~*n* **3** the act or an instance of whirling: *he grasps her by the waist and gives her a whirl.* **4** a round of intense activity: *the social whirl of Paris.* **5** a confused state: *my thoughts are in a whirl.* **6** **give something a whirl** *Informal* to try something new.

THESAURUS

whet 1. *as in* **whet someone's appetite** animate, arouse, awaken, enhance, excite, incite, increase, kindle, pique, provoke, quicken, rouse, stimulate, stir **2.** *old-fashioned* edge, file, grind, hone, sharpen, strop

whiff aroma, blast, breath, draught, gust, hint, niff (*Brit. slang*), odour, puff, scent, smell, sniff

whim caprice, conceit, craze, crotchet, fad (*informal*), fancy, freak, humour, impulse, notion, passing thought, quirk, sport, sudden notion, urge, vagary, whimsy

whimper 1. *vb.* blub (*slang*), blubber, cry, grizzle (*informal, chiefly Brit.*), mewl, moan, pule, snivel, sob, weep, whine, whinge (*informal*) **2.** *n.* moan, snivel, sob, whine

whimsical capricious, chimerical, crotchety, curious, droll, eccentric, fanciful, fantastic, fantastical, freakish, funny, mischievous, odd, peculiar, playful, quaint, queer, singular, unusual, waggish, weird

whine *n.* **1.** cry, moan, plaintive cry, sob, wail, whimper **2.** beef (*slang*), complaint, gripe (*informal*), grouch (*informal*), grouse, grumble, moan ~*vb.* **3.** beef (*slang*), bellyache (*slang*), bleat, carp, complain, cry, gripe (*informal*), grizzle (*informal, chiefly Brit.*), grouch (*informal*), grouse, grumble, moan, sob, wail, whimper, whinge (*informal*)

whip *n.* **1.** birch, bullwhip, cane, cat-o'-nine-tails, crop, horsewhip, knout, lash, rawhide, riding crop, scourge, switch, thong ~*vb.* **2.** beat, birch, cane, castigate, flagellate, flog, give a hiding (*informal*), lambast(e), lash, leather, lick (*informal*), punish, scourge, spank, strap, switch, tan (*slang*), thrash **3.** *informal* dart, dash, dive, flit, flounce, fly, rush, shoot, tear, whisk **4.** beat, whisk

whip out *or* **off** exhibit, flash, jerk, produce, pull, remove, seize, show, snatch, whisk

whipping beating, birching, caning, castigation, flagellation, flogging, hiding (*informal*), lashing, leathering, punishment, spanking, tanning (*slang*), the strap, thrashing

whirl *vb.* **1.** circle, gyrate, pirouette, pivot, reel, revolve, roll, rotate, spin, swirl, turn, twirl, twist, wheel **2.** feel dizzy, reel, spin ~*n.* **3.** circle, gyration, pirouette, reel, revolution, roll, rotation, spin, swirl, turn, twirl, twist, wheel **4.** flurry, merry-go-round, round, series, succession **5.** confusion, daze, dither (*chiefly Brit.*), flurry, giddiness, spin **6.** **give something a**

whirligig *n* **1** a spinning toy, such as a top. **2** same as **merry-go-round. 3** anything that whirls.

whirlpool *n* a powerful circular current of water, into which objects floating nearby are drawn.

whirlwind *n* **1** a column of air whirling violently upwards in a spiral. *~adj* **2** done or happening much more quickly than usual: *a whirlwind tour of France.*

whirr *or* **whir** *n* **1** a prolonged soft whizz or buzz: *the whirr of the fax machine.* *~vb* **whirring, whirred 2** to produce a prolonged soft whizz or buzz. **whirring** *n, adj*

whisk *vb* **1** to move or take somewhere swiftly: *I was whisked away in a police car.* **2** to brush away lightly: *the waiter whisked the crumbs away with a napkin.* **3** to beat (cream or eggs) with a whisk or fork until frothy or stiff. *~n* **4** the act or an instance of whisking: *a whisk of a scaly tail.* **5** a utensil for beating cream or eggs until frothy or stiff.

whisker *n* **1** any of the long stiff hairs that grow out from the sides of the mouth of a cat or other mammal. **2** any of the hairs growing on a man's face, esp. on the cheeks or chin. **3 by a whisker** by a very small distance or amount: *we missed him by a whisker.* **whiskered** *or* **whiskery** *adj*

whiskey *n* Irish or American whisky.

whisky *n, pl* **-kies** a strong alcoholic drink made by distilling fermented cereals, esp. in Scotland.

whisky-jack *n Canad* same as **Canada jay.**

whisper *vb* **1** to speak or say (something) very softly, using the breath instead of the vocal cords. **2** to make a low soft rustling sound: *the leaves whispered.* *~n* **3** a low soft voice: *her voice sank to a whisper.* **4** *Informal* a rumour: *I just picked up a whisper on this killing.* **5** a low soft rustling sound: *a whisper of breeze in the shrubbery.* **whispered** *adj*

whist *n* a card game for two pairs of players.

whist drive *n* a social gathering where whist is played.

whistle *vb* **-tling, -tled 1** to produce a shrill sound by forcing breath between pursed lips. **2** to produce (a tune) by making a series of such sounds. **3** to signal (to) by whistling or blowing a whistle: *the doorman whistled a cruising cab.* **4** to move with a whistling sound: *a shell whistled through the upper air.* **5** (of a kettle or train) to produce a shrill sound caused by steam being forced through a small opening. **6** (of a bird) to give a shrill cry. **7 whistle in the dark** to try to keep up one's confidence in spite of being afraid. *~n* **8** the act or sound of whistling: *he gave a whistle of astonishment.* **9** a metal instrument that is blown down its end to produce a tune, signal, or alarm: *he played the tin whistle; the referee's whistle.* **10** a device in a kettle or a train that makes a shrill sound by means of steam under pressure. **11 blow the whistle on** *Informal* to reveal and put a stop to (wrongdoing or a wrongdoer): *to blow the whistle on corrupt top-level officials.* **12 wet one's whistle** *Informal* to have a drink.

whistle for *vb Informal* to expect in vain: *he could whistle for his vote in the future.*

whistle-stop *adj* denoting a tour, esp. a campaign tour by a political candidate, in which short stops are made at many different places.

whit *n* **not a whit** not at all: *it does not matter a whit.*

Whit *n* **1** short for **Whitsuntide.** *~adj* **2** of Whitsuntide: *Whit Monday.*

white *adj* **1** having no hue, owing to the reflection of all or almost all light; of the colour of snow. **2** pale, because of illness, fear, shock, or another emotion: *white with rage.* **3** (of hair) having lost its colour, usually from age. **4** (of coffee or tea) with milk or cream. **5** (of wine) made from pale grapes or from black grapes separated from their skins. **6** denoting flour, or bread made from flour, that has had part of the grain removed. *~n* **7** the lightest colour; the colour of snow. **8** the clear fluid that surrounds the yolk of an egg. **9** *Anat* the white part of the eyeball. **10** anything white, such as white paint or white clothing: *a room decorated all in white.* ~See also **whites. whiteness** *n* **whitish** *adj*

White *n* **1** a member of a light-skinned race. *~adj* **2** of or relating to a White or Whites.

whitebait *n* the young of herrings, sprats, or pilchards, cooked and eaten whole.

white blood cell *n* same as **leucocyte.**

whitecaps *pl n* waves with white broken crests.

white-collar *adj* denoting workers employed in professional and clerical occupations.

white dwarf *n* a small, faint, very dense star.

white elephant *n* a possession that is unwanted by its owner.

white feather *n* a symbol of cowardice.

white fish *n* a sea fish with white flesh that is used for food, such as cod or haddock.

white flag *n* a signal of surrender or to request a truce.

whitefly *n, pl* **-flies** a tiny whitish insect that is harmful to greenhouse plants.

White Friar *n* a Carmelite friar.

white gold *n* a white lustrous hard-wearing alloy containing gold together with platinum or other metals, used in jewellery.

white goods *pl n* large household appliances, such as refrigerators and cookers.

white heat *n* **1** intense heat that produces a white light. **2** *Informal* a state of intense emotion: *the white heat of hate.*

white hope *n Informal* a person who is expected to accomplish a great deal: *the great white hope of English fast bowling.*

white horses *pl n* same as **whitecaps.**

white-hot *adj* **1** at such a high temperature that white light is produced. **2** *Informal* in a state of intense emotion: *white-hot agony.*

White House *n* the US president and the executive branch of the US government: *the White House reviewed the report.*

THESAURUS

whirl *informal* attempt, have a bash (crack (*informal*), go (*informal*), shot (*informal*), stab (*informal*), whack (*informal*)) (*informal*), try

whirlwind 1. *n.* tornado, waterspout **2.** *adj.* hasty, headlong, impetuous, impulsive, lightning, quick, quickie (*informal*), rapid, rash, short, speedy, swift

whisk *vb.* **1.** burn rubber (*informal*), dart, dash, fly, hasten, hurry, race, rush, shoot, speed, sweep, tear **2.** brush, flick, sweep, whip, wipe **3.** beat, fluff up, whip *~n.* **4.** brush, flick, sweep, whip, wipe **5.** beater

whisky bourbon, malt, rye, Scotch, whiskey (*US & Irish*)

whisper *vb.* **1.** breathe, murmur, say softly, speak in hushed tones, utter under the breath **2.** hiss, murmur, rustle, sigh, sough (*literary*), swish *~n.* **3.** hushed tone, low voice, murmur, soft voice, undertone **4.** *informal* buzz, dirt (*informal*), gossip, innuendo, insinuation, report, rumour, word **5.** hiss, murmur, rustle, sigh, sighing, soughing (*literary*), swish

white 1. ashen, bloodless, ghastly, grey, pale, pallid,

white lie *n* a small lie, usually told to avoid hurting someone's feelings.

white light *n* light that contains all the wavelengths of the visible spectrum, such as sunlight.

white matter *n* the whitish tissue of the brain and spinal cord, consisting mainly of nerve fibres.

white meat *n* meat, such as chicken or pork, that is light in colour when cooked.

whiten *vb* to make or become white or whiter. **whitener** *n* **whitening** *n*

white noise *n* noise that has a wide range of frequencies of uniform intensity.

whiteout *n* an atmospheric condition in which blizzards or low clouds make it very difficult to see.

white paper *n* an official government report which sets out the government's policy on a specific matter.

white pepper *n* a hot seasoning made from the seeds of the pepper plant with the husks removed.

White Russian (formerly) *adj* **1** of Byelorussia, an administrative division of the W Soviet Union: now Belarus. *~n* **2** a person from Byelorussia. **3** the language of Byelorussia.

whites *pl n* white clothes, as worn for playing cricket.

white sauce *n* a thick sauce made from flour, butter, seasonings, and milk or stock.

white slave *n* a girl or woman forced or sold into prostitution. **white slavery** *n*

white spirit *n* a colourless liquid obtained from petroleum and used as a substitute for turpentine.

White supremacy *n* the theory or belief that White people are superior to people of other races. **White supremacist** *n, adj*

white tie *n* **1** a white bow tie worn as part of a man's formal evening dress. *~adj* **white-tie** **2** denoting an occasion when formal evening dress should be worn.

whitewash *n* **1** a mixture of lime or chalk in water, for whitening walls and other surfaces. **2** an attempt to conceal the unpleasant truth: *the report was a whitewash.* *~vb* **3** to cover with whitewash. **4** to conceal the unpleasant truth about. **whitewashed** *adj*

whitewood *n* a light-coloured wood often prepared for staining.

whither *conj Old-fashioned or poetic* to what place or for what purpose: *they knew not whither they went.*

whiting (**white-ing**) *n* a white-fleshed food fish of European seas.

whitlow *n* an inflamed sore on the end of a finger or toe.

Whitsun *n* **1** short for **Whitsuntide**. *~adj* **2** of Whit Sunday or Whitsuntide.

Whit Sunday *n* the seventh Sunday after Easter.

Whitsuntide *n* the week that begins with Whit Sunday.

whittle *vb* **-tling, -tled** **1** to make (an object) by cutting or shaving pieces from (a piece of wood) with a small knife. **2 whittle down** *or* **away** to reduce in size or effectiveness gradually: *my self-confidence had been whittled away to almost nothing.*

whizz *or* **whiz** *vb* **whizzing, whizzed** **1** to move with a loud humming or buzzing sound: *the bullets whizzed overhead.* **2** *Informal* to move or go quickly: *we whizzed across the King's Road.* *~n, pl* **whizzes** **3** a loud humming or buzzing sound. **4** *Informal* a person who is extremely good at something: *he's a whizz on finance.*

whizz kid *or* **whiz kid** *n Informal* a person who is outstandingly able and successful for his or her age.

who *pron* **1** which person: *who are you?; he didn't know who had started it.* **2** used at the beginning of a relative clause referring to a person or people already mentioned: *he is a man who can effect change.*

WHO World Health Organization.

whoa *interj* a command used to stop horses or to slow down someone who is moving or talking too fast.

whodunnit *or* **whodunit** (hoo-**dun**-nit) *n Informal* a novel, play, or film about the solving of a murder mystery.

whoever *pron* **1** the person or people who: *whoever bought it for you has to make the claim.* **2** no matter who: *I pity him, whoever he is.* **3** *Informal* other similar or related people or person: *your best friend, your neighbours, or whoever.* **4** an intensive form of *who,* used in questions: *whoever thought of such a thing?*

whole *adj* **1** constituting or referring to all of something: *I'd spent my whole allowance by Saturday afternoon.* **2** unbroken or undamaged. *~adv* **3** in an undivided or unbroken piece: *truffles are cooked whole.* **4** *Informal* completely or entirely: *a whole new theory of treatment.* *~n* **5** all there is of a thing: *the whole of my salary.* **6** a collection of parts viewed together as a unit: *taking Great Britain as a whole.* **7 on the whole a** taking all things into consideration: *on the whole he has worked about one year out of twelve.* **b** in general: *on the whole they were not successful.* **wholeness** *n*

wholefood *n* **1** food that has been refined or processed as little as possible. *~adj* **2** of or relating to wholefood: *a wholefood diet.*

wholehearted *adj* done or given with total sincerity or enthusiasm: *wholehearted support.* **wholeheartedly** *adv*

wholemeal *adj Brit* **1** (of flour) made from the entire wheat kernel. **2** made from wholemeal flour: *wholemeal bread.*

whole number *n Maths* a number that does not contain a fraction, such as 0, 1, or 2.

wholesale *adj, adv* **1** of or by the business of selling goods in large quantities and at lower prices to retailers for resale: *wholesale prices; we buy fruit and vegetables wholesale.* **2** on a large scale or indiscriminately: *the wholesale destruction of forests; they were*

THESAURUS

pasty, wan, waxen, wheyfaced **2.** grey, grizzled, hoary, silver, snowy

white-collar clerical, executive, nonmanual, office, professional, salaried

whiten blanch, bleach, etiolate (*Bot.*), fade, go white, pale, turn pale

whitewash **1.** *n.* camouflage, concealment, cover-up, deception, extenuation **2.** *vb.* camouflage, conceal, cover up, extenuate, gloss over, make light of, suppress

whole *adj.* **1.** complete, entire, full, in one piece, integral, total, unabridged, uncut, undivided **2.** faultless, flawless, good, in one piece, intact, inviolate, mint, perfect, sound, unbroken, undamaged, unharmed, unhurt, unimpaired, uninjured, unmutilated, unscathed, untouched *~adv.* **3.** in one, in one piece *~n.* **4.** aggregate, all, everything, lot, sum total, the entire amount, total **5.** ensemble, entirety, entity, fullness, piece, totality, unit, unity **6. on the whole a.** all in all, all things considered, by and large, taking everything into consideration **b.** as a rule, for the most part, generally, in general, in the main, mostly, predominantly

wholehearted committed, complete, dedicated, determined, devoted, earnest, emphatic, enthusiastic, genuine, heartfelt, hearty, real, sincere, true, unfeigned, unqualified, unreserved, unstinting, warm, zealous

being hunted without mercy and slaughtered wholesale. **wholesaler** *n*

wholesome *adj* **1** physically beneficial: *wholesome food.* **2** morally beneficial: *a wholesome attitude of the mind.*

whole-wheat *adj US & Canad* same as **wholemeal.**

wholly *adv* completely or totally.

whom *pron* the objective form of *who*: *whom will you tell?; he was devoted to his wife, whom he married in 1960.*

whomever *pron* the objective form of *whoever*: *this law limits an employer's right to employ whomever he wants.*

whoop *vb* **1** to cry out in excitement or joy. **2 whoop it up** *Informal* to indulge in a noisy celebration. *~n* **3** a loud cry of excitement or joy.

whoopee *Old-fashioned, informal ~interj* **1** an exclamation of joy or excitement. *~n* **2 make whoopee a** to indulge in a noisy celebration. **b** to make love.

whooping cough *n* an acute infectious disease mainly affecting children, that causes coughing spasms ending with a shrill crowing sound on breathing in.

whoops *interj* an exclamation of mild surprise or of apology.

whopper *n Informal* **1** an unusually large or impressive example of something: *Deauville's beach is a whopper.* **2** a big lie.

whopping *Informal ~adj* **1** unusually large: *a whopping 40 per cent.* *~adv* **2** extremely: *it's a whopping great gamble.*

whore (**hore**) *n* a prostitute or promiscuous woman: often a term of abuse.

whorehouse *n Informal* a brothel.

whorl *n* **1** *Bot* a circular arrangement of leaves or flowers round the stem of a plant. **2** *Zool* a single turn in a spiral shell. **3** anything shaped like a coil.

who's who is *or* who has.

whose *pron* **1** of whom? belonging to whom?: used in direct and indirect questions: *whose idea was it?; I wondered whose it was.* **2** of whom or of which: used as a relative pronoun: *Gran had sympathy for anybody whose life had gone wrong.*

whosoever *pron Old-fashioned or formal* same as **whoever.**

why *adv* **1** for what reason?: *why did he marry her?; she avoided asking him why he was there.* *~pron* **2** for or because of which: *you can think of all kinds of reasons why you should not believe it.* *~n, pl* **whys 3 the whys and wherefores** See **wherefore** (sense 1). *~interj* **4** an exclamation of surprise, indignation, or impatience: *why, I listen to you on the radio twice a week.*

WI **1** Wisconsin. **2** (in Britain) Women's Institute.

wick *n* **1** a cord through the middle of a candle, through which the fuel reaches the flame. **2 get on someone's wick** *Brit slang* to annoy someone.

wicked *adj* **1** morally bad: *the wicked queen in "Snow White".* **2** playfully mischievous or roguish: *let's be wicked and go skinny-dipping.* **3** dangerous or unpleasant: *there was a wicked cut over his eye.* **4** *Slang* very good. **wickedly** *adv* **wickedness** *n*

wicker *adj* made of wickerwork: *a wicker chair.*

wickerwork *n* a material consisting of slender flexible twigs woven together.

wicket *n Cricket* **1** either of two sets of three stumps stuck in the ground with two wooden bails resting on top, at which the batsman stands. **2** the playing space between these. **3** the act or instance of a batsman being got out.

wicketkeeper *n Cricket* the fielder positioned directly behind the wicket.

wide *adj* **1** having a great extent from side to side: *the wide main street.* **2** having a specified extent from side to side: *three metres wide.* **3** covering or including many different things: *a wide range of services.* **4** covering a large distance or extent: *the proposal was voted down by a wide margin.* **5** (of eyes) opened fully. *~adv* **6** to a large or full extent: *he swung the door wide.* **7 far and wide** See **far** (sense 7). *~n* **8** *Cricket* a ball bowled outside the batsman's reach, which scores a run for the batting side. **widely** *adv*

wide-angle lens *n* a lens on a camera which can cover a wider angle of view than an ordinary lens.

wide-awake *adj* fully awake.

wide-eyed *adj* **1** innocent or naive. *~adv, adj* **2** surprised or frightened: *wide-eyed astonishment.*

widen *vb* to make or become wide or wider.

wide open *adj* **1** open to the full extent: *the main door was wide open.* **2** exposed or vulnerable: *he was leaving himself wide open to problems.*

wide-ranging *adj* covering or including many different things or subjects: *a wide-ranging review.*

THESAURUS

wholesale all-inclusive, broad, comprehensive, extensive, far-reaching, indiscriminate, mass, sweeping, wide-ranging

wholesome 1. beneficial, good, healthful, health-giving, healthy, helpful, hygienic, invigorating, nourishing, nutritious, salubrious, salutary, sanitary, strengthening **2.** clean, decent, edifying, ethical, exemplary, honourable, improving, innocent, moral, nice, pure, respectable, righteous, squeaky-clean, uplifting, virtuous, worthy

wholly all, altogether, completely, comprehensively, entirely, fully, heart and soul, in every respect, one hundred per cent (*informal*), perfectly, thoroughly, totally, utterly

whore call girl, courtesan, demimondaine, fallen woman (*old-fashioned*), harlot (*literary*), hooker (*slang*), lady of the night, loose woman, prostitute, scrubber (*offensive slang*), slag (*Brit. slang*), streetwalker, strumpet (*archaic*), tart (*informal*), trollop (*derogatory*), woman of easy virtue, woman of ill repute

wicked 1. abandoned, abominable, amoral, atrocious, bad, black-hearted, corrupt, debased, depraved, devilish, dissolute, egregious, evil, fiendish, foul, guilty, heinous, immoral, impious, iniquitous, irreligious, maleficent, nefarious, scandalous, shameful, sinful, unprincipled, unrighteous, vicious, vile, villainous, worthless **2.** arch, impish, incorrigible, mischievous, naughty, rascally, roguish **3.** acute, agonizing, awful, bothersome, crashing, destructive, difficult, distressing, dreadful, fearful, fierce, galling, harmful, injurious, intense, mighty, offensive, painful, severe, terrible, troublesome, trying, unpleasant

wide 1. *adj.* ample, broad, catholic, comprehensive, distended, encyclopedic, expanded, expansive, extensive, far-reaching, general, immense, inclusive, large, sweeping, vast **2.** *adv.* as far as possible, completely, fully, right out, to the furthest extent

wide-awake conscious, fully awake, roused, wakened

wide-eyed credulous, green, impressionable, ingenuous, innocent, naive, simple, trusting, unsophisticated, unsuspicious, wet behind the ears (*informal*)

widen broaden, dilate, enlarge, expand, extend, open out *or* up, open wide, spread, stretch

wide open 1. fully extended, fully open, gaping, out-

widespread *adj* affecting an extensive area or a large number of people: *widespread damage; widespread public support.*

widgeon *n* same as **wigeon.**

widow *n* a woman whose husband has died and who has not remarried. **widowhood** *n*

widowed *adj* denoting a person, usually a woman, whose spouse has died and who has not remarried.

widower *n* a man whose wife has died and who has not remarried.

widow's weeds *pl n Old-fashioned* the black mourning clothes traditionally worn by a widow.

width *n* **1** the extent or measurement of something from side to side. **2** the distance across a rectangular swimming bath, as opposed to its length.

wield *vb* **1** to handle or use (a weapon or tool). **2** to exert or maintain (power or influence).

wife *n, pl* **wives** the woman to whom a man is married. **wifely** *adj*

wig *n* an artificial head of hair.

wigeon *or* **widgeon** *n* a wild marshland duck.

wigging *n Brit old-fashioned slang* a reprimand.

wiggle *vb* **-gling, -gled 1** to move with jerky movements from side to side or up and down: *she wiggled her toes in the cool water.* ~*n* **2** a wiggling movement or walk.

wigwam *n* a North American Indian's tent, made of animal skins.

wilco *interj* an expression in signalling and telecommunications, indicating that a message just received will be complied with.

wild *adj* **1** (of animals or birds) living in natural surroundings; not domesticated or tame. **2** (of plants) growing in a natural state; not cultivated. **3** uninhabited and desolate: *wild country.* **4** living in a savage or uncivilized way: *a wild mountain man.* **5** lacking restraint or control: *a wild party.* **6** stormy or violent: *a wild windy October morning.* **7** in a state of extreme emotional intensity: *wild with excitement.* **8** without reason or substance: *wild accusations.* **9 wild about** *Informal* very enthusiastic about: *his colleagues aren't all that wild about him.* ~*adv* **10 run wild** to behave without restraint: *she was allowed to run completely wild.* ~*n* **11 the wild** a free natural state of living: *creatures of the wild.* **12 the wilds** a desolate or uninhabited region: *the wilds of Africa.* **wildly** *adv* **wildness** *n*

wild card *n* **1** *Sport* a player or team that is allowed to take part in a competition despite not having met the normal qualifying requirements. **2** *Computers* a character that can be substituted for any other in a file.

wildcat *n, pl* **-cats** *or* **-cat 1** a wild European cat that looks like a domesticated cat but is larger and has a bushy tail. **2** *Informal* a quick-tempered person. ~*adj* **3** *Chiefly US* risky and financially unsound: *a wildcat operation.*

wildcat strike *n* a strike begun by workers spontaneously or without union approval.

wildebeest *n, pl* **-beests** *or* **-beest** same as **gnu.**

wilderness *n* **1** a wild uninhabited uncultivated region. **2** a confused mass or tangle: *a wilderness of long grass and wild flowers.* **3** a state of being no longer in a prominent position: *a long spell in the political wilderness.*

wildfire *n* **spread like wildfire** to spread very quickly or uncontrollably.

wild flower *n* any flowering plant that grows in an uncultivated state.

wildfowl *pl n* wild birds, such as grouse and pheasants, that are hunted for sport or food.

wild-goose chase *n* a search that has little or no chance of success.

wildlife *n* wild animals and plants collectively.

wild rice *n* the dark-coloured edible grain of a North American grass that grows on wet ground.

Wild West *n* the western US during its settlement, esp. with reference to its lawlessness.

wiles *pl n* artful or seductive tricks or ploys.

wilful *or US* **willful** *adj* **1** determined to do things in one's own way: *a wilful and insubordinate child.* **2** deliberate and intentional: *wilful misconduct.* **wilfully** *adv*

will[1] *vb, past* **would** used as an auxiliary: **1** to make the future tense: *he will go on trial on October 7th.* **2**

THESAURUS

spread, outstretched, splayed, spread **2.** at risk, defenceless, exposed, in danger, in peril, open, susceptible, unprotected, vulnerable

widespread broad, common, epidemic, extensive, far-flung, far-reaching, general, pervasive, popular, prevalent, rife, sweeping, universal, wholesale

width breadth, compass, diameter, extent, girth, measure, range, reach, scope, span, thickness, wideness

wield 1. brandish, employ, flourish, handle, manage, manipulate, ply, swing, use **2.** apply, be possessed of, command, control, exercise, exert, have, have at one's disposal, hold, maintain, make use of, manage, possess, put to use, utilize

wife better half (*humorous*), bride, helpmate *or* helpmeet, her indoors (*Brit. slang*), mate, old lady (*informal*), old woman (*informal*), partner, spouse, (the) missis *or* missus (*informal*), woman (*informal*)

wild *adj.* **1.** feral, ferocious, fierce, savage, unbroken, undomesticated, untamed **2.** free, indigenous, native, natural, uncultivated **3.** desert, deserted, desolate, empty, godforsaken, trackless, uncivilized, uncultivated, uninhabited, unpopulated, virgin **4.** barbaric, barbarous, brutish, ferocious, fierce, primitive, rude, savage, uncivilized **5.** boisterous, chaotic, disorderly, impetuous, lawless, noisy, riotous, rough, rowdy, self-willed, turbulent, unbridled, uncontrolled, undisciplined, unfettered, ungovernable, unmanageable, unrestrained, unruly, uproarious, violent, wayward **6.** blustery, choppy, furious, howling, intense, raging, rough, tempestuous, violent **7.** at one's wits' end, berserk, beside oneself, crazed, crazy, delirious, demented, excited, frantic, frenzied, hysterical, irrational, mad, maniacal, rabid, raving **8.** extravagant, fantastic, flighty, foolhardy, foolish, giddy, ill-considered, impracticable, imprudent, madcap, outrageous, preposterous, rash, reckless **9. wild about** *informal* agog, avid, crazy (*informal*), daft (*informal*), eager, enthusiastic, excited, mad (*informal*), nuts (*slang*), potty (*Brit. informal*) ~*adv.* **10. run wild** abandon all restraint, cut loose, go on the rampage, kick over the traces, rampage, run free, run riot, stray ~*n.* **11. the wilds** back of beyond (*informal*), desert, middle of nowhere (*informal*), uninhabited area, wasteland, wilderness

wilderness 1. desert, jungle, waste, wasteland, wild **2.** clutter, confused mass, confusion, congeries, jumble, maze, muddle, tangle, welter

wildlife flora and fauna

wiles artifices, contrivances, devices, dodges, impositions, lures, manoeuvres, ploys, ruses, stratagems, subterfuges, tricks

wilful *or U.S* **willful 1.** adamant, bull-headed, determined, dogged, froward, headstrong, inflexible, intractable, intransigent, mulish, obdurate, obstinate, persistent, perverse, pig-headed, refractory, self-willed, stiff-

to express resolution: *they will not consider giving up territories.* **3** to express a polite request: *will you please calm Mummy and Daddy down.* **4** to express ability: *many essential oils will protect clothing from moths.* **5** to express probability or expectation: *his followers will be relieved to hear that.* **6** to express customary practice: *boys will be boys!* **7** to express desire: *go in very small steps, if you will.*

➤ *Will* is normal for discussing the future. The use of *shall* with *I* and *we* is a matter of preference, not of rule. *Shall* is commonly used for questions in Southern England but less often in the North and Scotland.

will² *n* **1** a strong determination: *a fierce will to survive.* **2** desire or wish: *a referendum to determine the will of the people.* **3** a document setting out a person's wishes regarding the disposal of his or her property after death. **4 at will** when and as one chooses: *customers can withdraw money at will.* ~*vb* **willing, willed 5** to try to make (something) happen by wishing very hard for it: *she willed herself not to cry.* **6** to wish or desire: *if he wills it, we will meet again.* **7** to leave (property) in one's will: *the farm had been willed to her.*

willie *or* **willy** *n, pl* **-lies** *Brit informal* a childish or jocular word for **penis.**

willies *pl n* **give someone the willies** *Slang* to make someone nervous or frightened.

willing *adj* **1** favourably disposed or inclined: *I'm willing to hear what you have to say.* **2** keen and obliging: *willing volunteers.* **willingly** *adv* **willingness** *n*

will-o'-the-wisp *n* **1** someone or something that is elusive or deceptively alluring: *their freedom was just a will-o'-the-wisp.* **2** a pale light that is sometimes seen over marshy ground at night.

willow *n* a tree that grows near water, with thin flexible branches used in weaving baskets and wood used for making cricket bats.

willowherb *n* a plant with narrow leaves and purplish flowers.

willow pattern *n* a pattern in blue on white china, depicting a Chinese landscape with a willow tree, river, bridge, and figures.

willowy *adj* slender and graceful.

willpower *n* strong self-disciplined determination to do something.

willy-nilly *adv* whether desired or not.

wilt *vb* **1** (of a flower or plant) to become limp or drooping. **2** (of a person) to lose strength or confidence.

Wilts Wiltshire.

wily *adj* **wilier, wiliest** sly or crafty.

wimp *Informal* ~*n* **1** a feeble ineffective person. ~*vb* **2 wimp out of** to fail to do (something) through lack of courage. **wimpish** *or* **wimpy** *adj*

WIMP *Computers* windows, icons, menus (or mice), pointers: denoting a type of user-friendly screen display used on small computers.

wimple *n* a piece of cloth draped round the head to frame the face, worn by women in the Middle Ages and now by some nuns.

win *vb* **winning, won 1** to achieve first place in (a competition or race). **2** to gain (a prize or first place) in a competition or race. **3** to gain victory in (a battle, argument, or struggle). **4** to gain (sympathy, approval, or support). ~*n* **5** *Informal* a success, victory, or triumph: *three consecutive wins.* ~See also **win over. winnable** *adj*

wince *vb* **wincing, winced 1** to draw back slightly, as if in sudden pain. ~*n* **2** the act of wincing.

winch *n* **1** a lifting or hauling device consisting of a rope or chain wound round a barrel or drum. ~*vb* **2** to haul or lift using a winch: *two men were winched to safety by a helicopter.*

wind¹ *n* **1** a current of air moving across the earth's surface. **2** a trend or force: *the chill wind of change.* **3** the power to breathe normally, esp. during or after physical exercise: *if you feel tired during the exercise, persevere – you'll soon get a second wind.* **4** gas in the stomach or intestines. **5** *Informal* foolish or empty talk: *political language is designed to give an appearance of solidity to pure wind.* **6 break wind** to release intestinal gas through the anus. **7 get wind of** *Informal* to find out about: *the media finally got wind of her disappearance.* ~*adj* **8** *Music* of or relating to wind instruments: *the wind section.* ~*vb* **winding, winded 9** to cause (someone) to be short of breath: *he fell with a thud that left him winded.* **10** to cause (a baby) to bring up wind after feeding. **windless** *adj*

wind² *vb* **winding, wound 1** to twist (something flexible) round some object: *a sweatband was wound*

THESAURUS

necked, stubborn, uncompromising, unyielding **2.** conscious, deliberate, intended, intentional, purposeful, volitional, voluntary, willed

will *n.* **1.** aim, determination, intention, purpose, resolution, resolve, willpower **2.** choice, decision, decree, desire, fancy, inclination, mind, pleasure, preference, wish **3.** declaration, last wishes, testament **4. at will** as one pleases, as one thinks fit, as one wishes, at one's desire (discretion, inclination, pleasure, whim, wish) ~*vb.* **5.** bid, bring about, cause, command, decree, determine, direct, effect, ordain, order, resolve **6.** choose, desire, elect, opt, prefer, see fit, want, wish **7.** bequeath, confer, give, leave, pass on, transfer

willing agreeable, amenable, compliant, consenting, content, desirous, disposed, eager, enthusiastic, favourable, game (*informal*), happy, inclined, in favour, in the mood, nothing loath, pleased, prepared, ready, so-minded

willingly by choice, cheerfully, eagerly, freely, gladly, happily, of one's own accord, of one's own free will, readily, voluntarily, with all one's heart, without hesitation, with pleasure

willingness agreeableness, agreement, consent, desire, disposition, enthusiasm, favour, goodwill, inclination, volition, will, wish

willpower determination, drive, firmness of purpose *or* will, fixity of purpose, force *or* strength of will, grit, resolution, resolve, self-control, self-discipline, single-mindedness

wilt 1. become limp *or* flaccid, droop, sag, shrivel, wither **2.** diminish, dwindle, ebb, fade, fail, flag, languish, lose courage, melt away, sag, sink, wane, weaken, wither

wily arch, artful, astute, cagey (*informal*), crafty, crooked, cunning, deceitful, deceptive, designing, fly (*slang, chiefly Brit.*), foxy, guileful, intriguing, scheming, sharp, shifty, shrewd, sly, tricky, underhand

win *vb.* **1.** achieve first place, achieve mastery, be victorious, carry all before one, carry the day, come first, conquer, finish first, gain victory, overcome, prevail, succeed, take the prize, triumph **2.** accomplish, achieve, acquire, attain, bag (*informal*), catch, collect, come away with, earn, gain, get, net, obtain, pick up, procure, receive, secure **3.** allure, attract, bring *or* talk round, carry, charm, convert, convince, disarm, induce, influence, persuade, prevail upon, sway ~*n.* **4.** *informal* conquest, success, triumph, victory

wince 1. *vb.* blench, cower, cringe, draw back, flinch, quail, recoil, shrink, start **2.** *n.* cringe, flinch, start

wind¹ *n.* **1.** air, air-current, blast, breath, breeze, cur-

round his head. **2** to tighten the spring of (a clock or watch) by turning a key or knob. **3** to follow a twisting course: *a narrow path wound through the shrubbery.* ~See also **wind down, wind up. winding** *n*

windbag *n Slang* a person who talks a lot but says little of interest.

windblown *adj* blown about by the wind: *windblown hair.*

windbreak *n* a fence or a line of trees that gives protection from the wind by breaking its force.

windcheater *n* a warm jacket with a close-fitting knitted neck, cuffs, and waistband.

wind chill *n* the serious chilling effect of wind and low temperature.

wind down *vb* **1** to move downwards by turning a handle: *he wound down the rear window.* **2** (of a clock or watch) to slow down before stopping completely. **3** to relax after a stressful or tiring time: *I have not had a chance to wind down from a busy day.* **4** to diminish gradually: *trading wound down for the day.*

winded *adj* temporarily out of breath after physical exercise or a blow to the stomach.

windfall *n* **1** a piece of unexpected good fortune, esp. financial gain. **2** a fruit blown off a tree by the wind.

wind farm *n* a large group of wind-driven generators for electricity supply.

wind gauge *n* same as **anemometer.**

winding sheet *n* a sheet in which a dead person is wrapped before being buried.

wind instrument *n* a musical instrument, such as a flute, that is played by having air blown into it.

windjammer *n History* a large merchant sailing ship.

windlass *n* a machine for lifting heavy objects by winding a rope or chain round a barrel or drum driven by a motor.

windmill *n* **1** a building containing machinery for grinding corn or for pumping, driven by sails that are turned by the wind. **2** *Brit* a toy consisting of a stick with plastic vanes attached, which revolve in the wind.

window *n* **1** an opening in a building or a vehicle containing glass within a framework, which lets in light and enables people to see in or out. **2** the display area behind a glass window in a shop. **3** a transparent area in an envelope which reveals the address on the letter inside. **4** an area on a computer screen that can be manipulated separately from the rest of the display area, for example so that two or more files can be displayed at the same time. **5** a period of unbooked time in a diary or schedule.

window box *n* a long narrow box, placed on a windowsill, in which plants are grown.

window-dressing *n* **1** the art of arranging goods in shop windows in such a way as to attract customers. **2** an attempt to make something seem better than it is by stressing only its attractive features: *do you think that the president's calling for an investigation is window-dressing, or do you think he actually means to do something?* **window-dresser** *n*

windowpane *n* a sheet of glass in a window.

window seat *n* **1** a seat below a window. **2** a seat beside a window in a bus, train, or aircraft.

window-shopping *n* looking at goods in shop windows without intending to buy anything.

windowsill *n* a shelf at the bottom of a window, either inside or outside a room.

windpipe *n* a nontechnical name for **trachea.**

windscreen *n Brit* the sheet of glass that forms the front window of a motor vehicle.

windscreen wiper *n Brit* an electrically operated blade with a rubber edge that wipes a windscreen clear of rain.

windshield *n US & Canad* same as **windscreen.**

windsock *n* a cloth cone mounted on a mast, used at airports to indicate wind direction.

windsurfing *n* the sport of riding on water using a surfboard steered and propelled by an attached sail. **windsurfer** *n*

windswept *adj* **1** exposed to the wind: *the vast windswept plains.* **2** blown about by the wind: *his hair was looking a bit windswept.*

wind tunnel *n* a chamber through which a stream of air is forced, in order to test the effects of wind on aircraft.

wind up *vb* **1** to bring to a conclusion: *we want to wind this conflict up as quickly as possible.* **2** *Informal* to dissolve (a company) and divide its assets among creditors. **3** to tighten the spring of (a clockwork mechanism) by turning a key or knob. **4** to move (a car window) upwards by turning a handle. **5** *Informal* to end up: *to wind up in the hospital.* **6** *Informal* to make nervous or tense: *as crisis after crisis broke, I became increasingly wound up.* **7** *Brit slang* to tease or annoy: *that really used to wind my old man up something rotten.* ~*adj* **wind-up 8** operated by clockwork: *a wind-up toy.* ~*n* **wind-up 9** the act of winding someone or something up.

windward *Chiefly naut* ~*adj* **1** of or in the direction from which the wind blows. ~*n* **2** the windward direction. ~*adv* **3** towards the wind.

windy *adj* **windier, windiest 1** denoting a time or conditions in which there is a strong wind: *a windy day.* **2** exposed to the wind: *the windy graveyard.* **3** long-winded or pompous: *his speeches are long and windy.* **4** *Old-fashioned slang* frightened.

wine *n* **1 a** an alcoholic drink produced by the fermenting of grapes with water and sugar. **b** an alcoholic drink produced in this way from other fruits or flowers: *dandelion wine.* ~*adj* **2** dark purplish-red. ~*vb* **wining, wined 3 wine and dine** to entertain (someone) with wine and fine food.

wine bar *n* a bar that specializes in serving wine and usually food.

wine box *n* a cubic carton containing wine, with a tap for dispensing it.

wine cellar *n* **1** a cellar where wine is stored. **2** the stock of wines stored there.

THESAURUS

rent of air, draught, gust, zephyr **2.** breath, puff, respiration **3.** flatulence, flatus, gas **4.** *informal* babble, blather, bluster, boasting, empty talk, gab (*informal*), hot air, humbug, idle talk, talk, verbalizing

wind[2] *vb.* **1.** coil, curl, encircle, furl, loop, reel, roll, spiral, turn around, twine, twist, wreathe **2.** bend, curve, deviate, meander, ramble, snake, turn, twist, zigzag

winded breathless, gasping for breath, out of breath, out of puff, panting, puffed, puffed out

windfall bonanza, find, godsend, jackpot, manna from heaven, stroke of luck

winding bend, convolution, curve, meander, turn, twist, undulation

wind up 1. bring to a close, close, close down, conclude, end, finalize, finish, liquidate, settle, terminate, wrap up **2.** *informal* be left, end one's days, end up, find oneself, finish up **3.** *informal* excite, make nervous, make tense, put on edge, work up

windy 1. blowy, blustering, blustery, boisterous, breezy, gusty, inclement, squally, stormy, tempestu-

wineglass *n* a glass for wine, usually with a small bowl on a stem with a flared base.

wing *n* **1** one of the limbs or organs of a bird, bat, or insect that are used for flying. **2** one of the two wing-like supporting parts of an aircraft. **3** a projecting part of a building: *converting the unused east wing into a suitable habitation.* **4** a faction or group within a political party or other organization: *the youth wing of the African National Congress.* **5** *Brit* the part of a car body surrounding the wheels. **6** *Sport* **a** either of the two sides of the pitch near the touchline. **b** same as **winger. 7 wings** *Theatre* the space offstage to the right or left of the acting area. **8 in the wings** ready to step in when needed. **9 on the wing** flying. **10 spread one's wings** to make fuller use of one's abilities by trying new experiences: *he increasingly spread his wings abroad.* **11 take someone under one's wing** to look after someone. **12 take wing** to fly away. *~vb* **13** to fly: *a lone bird winging its way from the island.* **14** to move through the air: *sending a shower of loose gravel winging towards the house.* **15** to shoot or wound in the wing or arm. **16** to provide with wings. **winged** *adj* **wingless** *adj*

wing chair *n* an easy chair with side pieces extending forward from a high back.

wing commander *n* a middle-ranking commissioned officer in an air force.

winger *n Sport* a player positioned on a wing.

wing nut *n* a threaded nut with two flat projections which allow it to be turned by the thumb and forefinger.

wingspan *n* the distance between the wing tips of a bird, insect, bat, or aircraft.

wink *vb* **1** to close and open one eye quickly as a signal. **2** (of a light) to shine brightly and intermittently; twinkle. *~n* **3** the act or an instance of winking, esp. as a signal. **4** a twinkling of light. **5** *Informal* the smallest amount of sleep: *I didn't sleep a wink last night.* **6 tip someone the wink** *Brit informal* to give someone a hint or warning.

winkle *n* **1** an edible shellfish with a spirally coiled shell. *~vb* **-kling, -kled 2 winkle out** *Informal, chiefly Brit* **a** to obtain (information) from someone who is not willing to provide it: *try to winkle the real problem out of them.* **b** to coax or force out: *he somehow managed to winkle him out of his room.*

winkle-pickers *pl n Old-fashioned* shoes with very pointed narrow toes.

winner *n* **1** a person or thing that wins. **2** *Informal* a person or thing that seems sure to be successful.

winning *adj* **1** gaining victory: *the winning side.* **2** charming or attractive: *her winning smiles.*

winnings *pl n* the money won in a competition or in gambling.

winnow *vb* **1** to separate (grain) from (chaff) by a current of air. **2** to separate out (an unwanted element): *the committee will need to winnow out the nonsense.*

wino (**wine**-oh) *n, pl* **winos** *Informal* a destitute person who habitually drinks cheap wine.

win over *vb* to gain the support or consent of: *I was hoping to win Father over once he realized I was determined to marry Tom.*

winsome *adj Literary* charming or attractive: *a winsome smile.*

winter *n* **1** the coldest season of the year, between autumn and spring. *~vb* **2** to spend the winter in a specified place: *wintering in Rome.*

wintergreen *n* an evergreen shrub from which is obtained a pleasant-smelling oil that is used medicinally and for flavouring.

winter solstice *n* the time, about December 22, at which the sun is at its southernmost point in the sky.

winter sports *pl n* sports held on snow or ice, such as skiing and skating.

wintertime *n* the period or season of winter.

wintry *adj* **-trier, -triest 1** of or characteristic of winter: *a cold wintry day.* **2** cold or unfriendly: *a wintry smile.*

wipe *vb* **wiping, wiped 1** to rub (a surface or object) lightly with a cloth or the hand, in order to remove dirt or liquid from it. **2** to remove by wiping: *she made a futile attempt to wipe away her tears.* **3** to erase a recording from (a video or audio tape). *~n* **4** the act or an instance of wiping: *a quick wipe.*

wipe out *vb* to destroy or get rid of completely: *a hail storm wipes out a wheat crop in five minutes.*

wiper *n* short for **windscreen wiper.**

wire *n* **1** a slender flexible strand of metal. **2** a length of this used to carry electric current in a circuit. **3** a long continuous piece of wire or cable connecting points in a telephone or telegraph system. **4** *Old-fashioned informal* a telegram. *~vb* **wiring, wired 5** to fasten with wire. **6** to equip (an electrical system, circuit, or component) with wires. **7** *Informal* to send a telegram to. **8** to send by telegraph: *they wired the money for a train ticket.*

wired *adj Slang* excitable or edgy, usually from stimulant intake: *I don't want coffee, I'm wired enough as it is.*

wire-haired *adj* (of a dog) having a rough wiry coat.

wireless *n Old-fashioned, chiefly Brit* same as **radio.**

wire netting *n* a net made of wire, used for fencing.

wiretapping *n* the practice of making a connection to a telegraph or telephone wire in order to obtain information secretly.

wireworm *n* a destructive wormlike beetle larva.

THESAURUS

ous, wild, windswept **2.** boastful, bombastic, diffuse, empty, garrulous, long-winded, loquacious, meandering, pompous, prolix, rambling, turgid, verbose, wordy **3.** *old-fashioned slang* afraid, chicken (*slang*), cowardly, fearful, frightened, nervous, scared, timid

wing *n.* **1.** organ of flight, pinion (*chiefly poetic*) **2.** adjunct, annexe, ell, extension **3.** arm, branch, cabal, circle, clique, coterie, faction, group, grouping, schism, section, segment, set, side *~vb.* **4.** fly, glide, soar **5.** clip, hit, nick, wound

wink *vb.* **1.** bat, blink, flutter **2.** flash, gleam, glimmer, sparkle, twinkle *~n.* **3.** blink, flutter, nictation **4.** flash, gleam, glimmering, sparkle, twinkle

winkle out dig out, dislodge, draw out, extract, extricate, force out, prise out, smoke out, worm out

winner champ (*informal*), champion, conquering hero, conqueror, first, master, vanquisher, victor

winning 1. conquering, successful, triumphant, victorious **2.** alluring, amiable, attractive, bewitching, captivating, charming, cute, delectable, delightful, disarming, enchanting, endearing, engaging, fascinating, fetching, likable *or* likeable, lovely, pleasing, prepossessing, sweet, taking, winsome

winnings booty, gains, prize(s), proceeds, profits, spoils, takings

winnow comb, cull, divide, fan, part, screen, select, separate, separate the wheat from the chaff, sift, sort out

wintry chilly, cold, freezing, frosty, frozen, harsh, hibernal, hiemal, icy, snowy

wipe *vb.* **1.** brush, clean, dry, dust, mop, rub, sponge, swab **2.** clean off, erase, get rid of, remove, rub off, take away, take off *~n.* **3.** brush, lick, rub, swab

wiring *n* the network of wires used in an electrical system, device, or circuit.

wiry *adj* **wirier, wiriest 1** (of a person) slim but strong. **2** coarse and stiff: *wiry grass.*

wisdom *n* **1** the ability to use one's experience and knowledge to make sensible decisions or judgments. **2** accumulated knowledge or learning: *the wisdom of Asia and of Africa.*

wisdom tooth *n* any of the four molar teeth, one at the back of each side of the jaw, that are the last of the permanent teeth to come through.

wise[1] *adj* **1** possessing or showing wisdom: *a wise move.* **2 none the wiser** knowing no more than before: *I left the conference none the wiser.* **3 wise to** *Informal* aware of or informed about: *they'll get wise to our system; he put him wise to the rumour.* **wisely** *adv*

wise[2] *n Old-fashioned* way, manner, or respect: *in no wise.*

-wise *adv suffix* **1** indicating direction or manner: *crabwise.* **2** with reference to: *moneywise.*

➤ The ending *-wise* can frequently be replaced by *-ways: sidewise/sideways; lengthways/lengthwise.* Adding *-wise* to a noun to create the meaning "in respect of", as in: *Defencewise, Scotland are strong,* is generally unacceptable except in very informal usage.

wiseacre *n* a person who wishes to seem wise.

wisecrack *Informal* ~*n* **1** a clever, amusing, sometimes unkind, remark. ~*vb* **2** to make such remarks. **wisecracking** *adj*

wise guy *n Informal* a person who likes to give the impression of knowing more than other people.

wise up to *vb* **wising, wised** *Slang, chiefly US & Canad* to become aware of or informed about.

wish *vb* **1** to want or desire (something impossible or improbable): *he wished he'd kept quiet.* **2** to desire or prefer to be or do something: *the next person who wished to speak.* **3** to feel or express a hope concerning the welfare, health, or success of: *we wished him well.* **4** to greet as specified: *I wished her a Merry Christmas.* ~*n* **5** a desire, often for something impossible or improbable: *a desperate wish to succeed as a professional artist.* **6** something desired or wished for: *your wishes will come true.* **7** the expression of a hope for someone's welfare, health, or success: *give him our best wishes.*

wishbone *n* the V-shaped bone above the breastbone of a chicken or turkey.

wishful *adj* desirous or longing: *she seemed wishful of prolonging the discussion.*

wishful thinking *n* an interpretation of the facts as one would like them to be, rather than as they are: *was it wishful thinking, or had the enemy lost heart?*

wish on *vb* to want (something unpleasant) to be experienced by: *I wouldn't wish a wretched childhood on anyone.*

wishy-washy *adj Informal* lacking in character, force, or colour.

wisp *n* **1** a thin, delicate, or filmy piece or streak: *little wisps of cloud.* **2** a small untidy bundle, tuft, or strand: *a wisp of hair.* **3** a slight trace: *a wisp of a smile.*

wispy *adj* **wispier, wispiest** thin, fine, or delicate: *grey wispy hair.*

wisteria *n* a climbing plant with large drooping clusters of blue, purple, or white flowers.

wistful *adj* sadly wishing for something lost or unobtainable. **wistfully** *adv* **wistfulness** *n*

wit[1] *n* **1** the ability to use words or ideas in a clever, amusing, and imaginative way. **2** a person possessing this ability. **3** practical intelligence: *do credit me with some wit.* ~See also **wits.**

wit[2] *vb* **to wit** (used to introduce a statement or explanation) that is to say; namely.

witblits (vit-blits) *n S African* an illegally distilled strong alcoholic drink.

witch *n* **1** (in former times) a woman believed to possess evil magic powers. **2** a person who practises magic or sorcery, esp. black magic. **3** an ugly or wicked old woman.

witchcraft *n* the use of magic, esp. for evil purposes.

witch doctor *n* a man in certain tribal societies who is believed to possess magical powers, which can be used to cure sickness or to harm people.

witch hazel *n* a medicinal solution made from the bark and leaves of a N American shrub, which is put on the skin to treat bruises and inflammation.

witch-hunt *n* a rigorous campaign to expose and discredit people considered to hold unorthodox views on the pretext of safeguarding the public welfare.

with *prep* **1** accompanying; in the company of: *the captain called to the sergeant to come with him.* **2** using; by means of: *unlocking the padlock with a key.* **3** possessing or having: *a woman with black hair; the patient with angina.* **4** concerning or regarding: *be gentle with me.* **5** in a manner characterized by: *I know you will handle it with discretion.* **6** as a result of: *his voice was hoarse with nervousness.* **7** following the line of thought of: *are you with me so far?* **8** having the same opinions as; supporting: *are you with us or against us?*

withdraw *vb* **-drawing, -drew, -drawn 1** to take out

THESAURUS

wipe out annihilate, blot out, destroy, efface, eradicate, erase, expunge, exterminate, extirpate, kill to the last man, massacre, obliterate, take out (*slang*)

wiry 1. lean, sinewy, strong, tough **2.** bristly, kinky, stiff

wisdom astuteness, circumspection, comprehension, discernment, enlightenment, erudition, foresight, insight, intelligence, judgment, judiciousness, knowledge, learning, penetration, prudence, reason, sagacity, sapience, sense, sound judgment, understanding

wise aware, clever, clued-up (*informal*), discerning, enlightened, erudite, informed, intelligent, judicious, knowing, perceptive, politic, prudent, rational, reasonable, sagacious, sage, sapient, sensible, shrewd, sound, understanding, well-advised, well-informed

wisecrack *informal* **1.** *n.* barb, funny (*informal*), gag (*informal*), jest, jibe, joke, pithy remark, quip, sardonic remark, smart remark, witticism **2.** *vb.* be facetious, jest, jibe, joke, quip, tell jokes

wish *vb.* **1.** aspire, covet, crave, desire, hanker, hope, hunger, long, need, set one's heart on, sigh for, thirst, want, yearn **2.** bid, greet with ~*n.* **3.** aspiration, desire, hankering, hope, hunger, inclination, intention, liking, longing, thirst, urge, want, whim, will, yearning

wistful contemplative, disconsolate, dreaming, dreamy, forlorn, longing, meditative, melancholy, mournful, musing, pensive, reflective, sad, thoughtful, yearning

wit 1. badinage, banter, drollery, facetiousness, fun, humour, jocularity, levity, pleasantry, raillery, repartee, wordplay **2.** card (*old-fashioned informal*), comedian, epigrammatist, humorist, joker, punster, wag **3.** acumen, brains, cleverness, common sense, comprehension, discernment, ingenuity, insight, intellect, judgment, mind, nous (*old-fashioned, slang*), perception, practical intelligence, reason, sense, understanding, wisdom

witch crone, enchantress, magician, necromancer, occultist, sorceress

or remove: *he withdrew an envelope from his pocket.* **2** to remove (money) from a bank account or savings account. **3** to leave one place to go to another, usually quieter, place: *he withdrew into his bedroom.* **4** (of troops) to leave or be pulled back from the battleground. **5** to take back (a statement) formally. **6 withdraw from** to give up: *they withdrew from the competition.*

withdrawal *n* **1** the act or an instance of withdrawing. **2** the period that a drug addict goes through after stopping using drugs, during which he or she may experience symptoms such as tremors, sweating, and vomiting. *~adj* **3** of or relating to withdrawal from an addictive drug: *withdrawal symptoms.*

withdrawn *vb* **1** the past participle of **withdraw.** *~adj* **2** extremely reserved or shy.

wither *vb* **1** to make or become dried up or shrivelled: *the leaves had withered but not fallen.* **2** to fade or waste: *deprived of the nerve supply the muscles wither.* **3** to humiliate (someone) with a scornful look or remark. **withered** *adj*

withering *adj* (of a look or remark) extremely scornful.

withers *pl n* the highest part of the back of a horse, between the shoulders.

withhold *vb* **-holding, -held** to keep back (information or money).

within *prep* **1** in or inside: *within the hospital grounds.* **2** before (a period of time) has passed: *within a month.* **3** not beyond: *within the confines of a low budget; he positioned a low table within her reach.* *~adv* **4** *Formal* inside or internally: *a glimpse of what was hidden within.*

without *prep* **1** not accompanied by: *I can't imagine going through life without him.* **2** not using: *our Jeep drove without lights.* **3** not possessing or having: *four months without a job; a lot of them came across the border without shoes.* **4** in a manner showing a lack of: *without reverence.* **5** while not or after not: *she sat without speaking for some while.* *~adv* **6** *Formal* outside: *seated on the graveyard without.*

withstand *vb* **-standing, -stood** to resist or endure successfully: *our ability to withstand stress.*

witless *adj* **1** *Formal* lacking intelligence or sense. **2 scared witless** extremely frightened.

witness *n* **1** a person who has seen or can give first-hand evidence of some event: *the only witness to a killing.* **2** a person who gives evidence in a court of law: *a witness for the defence.* **3** a person who confirms the genuineness of a document or signature by adding his or her own signature. **4** evidence proving or supporting something: *the Church of England, that historic witness to the power of the Christian faith.* **5 bear witness to** to be evidence or proof of: *the high turn-out bore witness to the popularity of the contest.* *~vb* **6** to see, be present at, or know at first hand: *I have witnessed many motor-racing accidents.* **7** to be the scene or setting of: *the 1970s witnessed an enormous increase in international lending.* **8** to confirm the genuineness of (a document or signature) by adding one's own signature. **9 witness to** *Formal* to confirm: *our aim is to witness to the fact of the empty tomb.*

witness box *or esp US* **witness stand** *n* the place in a court of law where witnesses stand to give evidence.

wits *pl n* **1** the ability to think and act quickly: *when he was sober his wits were razor-sharp.* **2 at one's wits' end** at a loss to know what to do. **3 have one's wits about one** to be able to think and act quickly. **4 live by** *or* **on one's wits** to gain a livelihood by craftiness rather than by hard work. **5 scared out of one's wits** extremely frightened.

witter *vb Informal* to chatter or babble pointlessly or at unnecessary length.

witticism *n* a witty remark.

wittingly *adv* intentionally and knowingly.

witty *adj* **-tier, -tiest** clever and amusing. **wittily** *adv*

wives *n* the plural of **wife.**

wizard *n* **1** a man in fairy tales who has magic pow-

THESAURUS

witchcraft enchantment, incantation, magic, necromancy, occultism, sorcery, sortilege, spell, the black art, the occult, voodoo, wizardry

withdraw 1. draw back, draw out, extract, pull out, remove, take away, take off **2.** absent oneself, back out, cop out (*slang*), depart, detach oneself, disengage, drop out, fall back, go, leave, make oneself scarce (*informal*), pull back, pull out, retire, retreat, secede **3.** abjure, disavow, disclaim, recall, recant, rescind, retract, revoke, take back, unsay

withdrawal 1. extraction, removal **2.** departure, disengagement, exit, exodus, retirement, retreat, secession **3.** abjuration, disavowal, disclaimer, recall, recantation, repudiation, rescission, retraction, revocation

withdrawn aloof, detached, distant, introverted, quiet, reserved, retiring, shrinking, shy, silent, taciturn, timorous, uncommunicative, unforthcoming

wither 1. blast, blight, decay, decline, desiccate, disintegrate, droop, dry, fade, languish, perish, shrink, shrivel, wane, waste, wilt **2.** abash, blast, humiliate, mortify, put down, shame, snub

withering blasting, blighting, devastating, humiliating, hurtful, mortifying, scornful, snubbing

withhold check, conceal, deduct, hide, hold back, keep, keep back, keep secret, refuse, repress, reserve, resist, restrain, retain, sit on (*informal*), suppress

withstand bear, brave, combat, confront, cope with, defy, endure, face, grapple with, hold off, hold *or* stand one's ground, hold out, hold out against, oppose, put up with (*informal*), remain firm, resist, stand, stand fast, stand firm, stand up to, suffer, take, take on, thwart, tolerate, weather

witness *n.* **1.** beholder, bystander, eyewitness, looker-on, observer, onlooker, spectator, viewer, watcher **2.** attestant, corroborator, deponent, testifier **3. bear witness to** attest to, bear out, be evidence of, be proof of, betoken, confirm, constitute proof of, corroborate, demonstrate, evince, prove, show, testify to, vouch for *~vb.* **4.** attend, be present at, look on, mark, note, notice, observe, perceive, see, view, watch **5.** countersign, endorse, sign **6. witness to** *formal* attest, authenticate, bear out, bear witness, confirm, corroborate, depone, depose, give evidence, give testimony, testify

wits 1. acumen, astuteness, brains (*informal*), cleverness, comprehension, faculties, ingenuity, intelligence, judgment, nous (*old-fashioned, slang*), reason, sense, understanding **2. at one's wits' end** at a loss, at the end of one's tether, baffled, bewildered, in despair, lost, stuck (*informal*), stumped

witticism bon mot, clever remark, epigram, one-liner (*informal*), play on words, pleasantry, pun, quip, repartee, riposte, sally, witty remark

witty amusing, brilliant, clever, droll, epigrammatic, facetious, fanciful, funny, gay, humorous, ingenious, jocular, lively, original, piquant, sparkling, waggish, whimsical

wizard 1. conjuror, enchanter, magician, magus, necromancer, occultist, shaman, sorcerer, warlock, witch **2.** ace (*informal*), adept, buff (*informal*), expert,

ers. 2 a person who is outstandingly gifted in some specified field: *a financial wizard.*

wizardry *n* 1 magic or sorcery. 2 outstanding skill or accomplishment in some specified field: *technological wizardry.*

wizened (**wiz**-zend) *adj* shrivelled, wrinkled, or dried up with age.

woad *n* a blue dye obtained from a European plant, used by the ancient Britons as a body dye.

wobble *vb* **-bling, -bled** 1 to move or sway unsteadily. 2 to shake: *she was having difficulty in controlling her voice, which wobbled about.* ~*n* 3 a wobbling movement or sound.

wobbly *adj* **-blier, -bliest** 1 unsteady. 2 trembling. ~*n* 3 **throw a wobbly** *Slang* to become suddenly angry or upset.

wodge *n Brit informal* a thick lump or chunk: *my wodge of Kleenex was a sodden ball.*

woe *n* 1 *Literary* intense grief. 2 **woes** misfortunes or problems: *economic woes.* 3 **woe betide someone** someone will or would experience misfortune: *woe betide anyone who got in his way.*

woebegone *adj* sad in appearance.

woeful *adj* 1 extremely sad. 2 pitiful or deplorable: *a woeful lack of understanding.* **woefully** *adv*

wok *n* a large bowl-shaped metal Chinese cooking pot, used for stir-frying.

woke *vb* the past tense of **wake**[1].

woken *vb* the past participle of **wake**[1].

wold *n* a large area of high open rolling country.

wolf *n, pl* **wolves** 1 a predatory doglike wild animal which hunts in packs. 2 *Old-fashioned informal* a man who habitually tries to seduce women. 3 **cry wolf** to give false alarms repeatedly: *if you cry wolf too often, people will take no notice.* ~*vb* 4 **wolf down** to eat quickly or greedily: *wolfing down their dinner.*

wolfhound *n* a very large dog, formerly used to hunt wolves.

wolf whistle *n* 1 a whistle produced by a man to express admiration of a woman's appearance. ~*vb* **wolf-whistle, -whistling, -whistled** 2 to produce such a whistle.

wolverine *n* a large meat-eating mammal of Eurasia and North America with very thick dark fur.

wolves *n* the plural of **wolf.**

woman *n, pl* **women** 1 an adult female human being. 2 adult female human beings collectively: *the very image of woman pared of the trappings of "femininity".* 3 an adult female human being with qualities associated with the female, such as tenderness or maternalism: *she's more woman than you know.* 4 a female servant or domestic help. 5 *Informal* a wife or girlfriend. ~*adj* 6 female: *a woman doctor.*

womanhood *n* 1 the state of being a woman: *young girls approaching womanhood.* 2 women collectively: *Asian womanhood.*

womanish *adj* (of a man) looking or behaving like a woman.

womanizer *or* **-iser** *n* a man who has casual affairs with many women.

womanizing *or* **-ising** *n* (of a man) the practice of indulging in casual affairs with women.

womankind *n* all women considered as a group.

womanly *adj* possessing qualities generally regarded as typical of, or appropriate to, a woman.

womb *n* the nontechnical name for **uterus.**

wombat *n* a furry heavily-built plant-eating Australian marsupial.

women *n* the plural of **woman.**

womenfolk *pl n* 1 women collectively. 2 a group of women, esp. the female members of one's family.

Women's Liberation *n* a movement promoting the removal of inequalities based upon the assumption that men are superior to women. Also called: **women's lib**

won *vb* the past of **win.**

wonder *vb* 1 to think about something with curiosity or doubt: *I wonder why she did that.* 2 to be amazed: *I did wonder at her leaving valuable china on the shelves.* ~*n* 3 something that causes surprise or awe: *it's a wonder she isn't speechless with fright.* 4 the feeling of surprise or awe caused by something strange: *the wonder of travel.* 5 **do** *or* **work wonders** to achieve spectacularly good results. 6 **no** *or* **small wonder** it is not surprising: *no wonder you're going*

THESAURUS

genius, hotshot (*informal*), maestro, master, prodigy, star, virtuoso, whizz (*informal*), whizz kid (*informal*), wiz (*informal*)

wizened dried up, gnarled, lined, shrivelled, shrunken, withered, worn, wrinkled

wobble 1. *vb.* quake, rock, seesaw, shake, sway, teeter, totter, tremble, vibrate, waver 2. *n.* quaking, shake, tremble, tremor, unsteadiness, vibration

woe *literary* adversity, affliction, agony, anguish, burden, curse, dejection, depression, disaster, distress, gloom, grief, hardship, heartache, heartbreak, melancholy, misery, misfortune, pain, sadness, sorrow, suffering, trial, tribulation, trouble, unhappiness, wretchedness

woeful 1. afflicted, agonized, anguished, calamitous, catastrophic, cruel, deplorable, disastrous, disconsolate, dismal, distressing, doleful, dreadful, gloomy, grieving, grievous, harrowing, heartbreaking, heart-rending, lamentable, miserable, mournful, pathetic, piteous, pitiable, pitiful, plaintive, sad, sorrowful, tragic, unhappy, wretched 2. abysmal, appalling, awful, bad, deplorable, disappointing, disgraceful, dreadful, duff (*Brit. informal*), feeble, godawful (*slang*), hopeless, inadequate, lousy (*slang*), mean, miserable, paltry, pathetic, pitiable, pitiful, poor, rotten (*informal*), shitty (*taboo slang*), shocking, sorry, terrible, wretched

wolf 1. *n. old-fashioned informal* Casanova, Don Juan, lady-killer, lecher, Lothario, philanderer, seducer, womanizer *or* womaniser 2. *vb.* **wolf down** bolt, cram, devour, gobble, gollop, gorge, gulp, pig out (*slang*), scoff (*slang*), stuff

woman 1. bird (*slang, chiefly Brit.*), chick (*slang*), dame (*slang*), female, gal (*old-fashioned, slang*), girl, lady, lass, lassie (*Scot. & N. English informal*), maid (*archaic or literary*), maiden (*archaic or literary*), miss (*informal*), she, wench (*old-fashioned, facetious*) 2. chambermaid, char (*informal*), charwoman, domestic, female servant, handmaiden, housekeeper, lady-in-waiting, maid, maidservant 3. *informal* bride, girl, girlfriend, mate, mistress, old lady (*informal*), partner, spouse, sweetheart, wife

womanizer, womaniser Casanova, Don Juan, lady-killer, lecher, Lothario, philanderer, seducer, wolf (*old-fashioned informal*)

womanly female, feminine, ladylike, matronly, motherly, tender, warm

wonder *vb.* 1. ask oneself, be curious, be inquisitive, conjecture, doubt, inquire, meditate, ponder, puzzle, query, question, speculate, think 2. be amazed (astonished, awed, dumbstruck), be flabbergasted (*informal*), boggle, gape, gawk, marvel, stand amazed, stare ~*n.* 3. curiosity, marvel, miracle, nonpareil, phenomenon, portent, prodigy, rarity, sight, spectacle, won-

broke. ~*adj* **7** causing surprise or awe because of spectacular results achieved: *a new wonder drug.* **wonderingly** *adv* **wonderment** *n*

wonderful *adj* **1** extremely fine; excellent: *I've been offered a wonderful job.* **2** causing surprise, amazement, or awe: *a strange and wonderful phenomenon.* **wonderfully** *adv*

wonderland *n* **1** an imaginary land of marvels or wonders. **2** an actual place of great or strange beauty: *the apartment was a wonderland of design and colour.*

wondrous *adj Old-fashioned or literary* causing surprise or awe; marvellous.

wonky *adj* **-kier, -kiest** *Brit slang* **1** shaky or unsteady: *wonky wheelbarrows; wonky knees.* **2** insecure or unreliable: *his marriage is looking a bit wonky.*

wont (rhymes with **don't**) *Old-fashioned* ~*adj* **1** accustomed: *most murderers, his police friends were wont to say, were male.* ~*n* **2** a usual practice: *she waded straight in, as was her wont.*

won't will not.

woo *vb* **wooing, wooed 1** to coax or urge: *he's trying to woo the middle class back to the Democratic Party.* **2** *Old-fashioned* to attempt to gain the love of (a woman). **wooing** *n*

wood *n* **1** the hard fibrous substance beneath the bark in trees and shrubs, which is used in building and carpentry and as fuel. **2** an area of trees growing together that is smaller than a forest: *a track leading into a wood.* **3** *Golf* a long-shafted club with a wooden head. ~*adj* **4** made of, using, or for use with wood: *wood fires.* ~See also **woods.**

wood alcohol *n* same as **methanol.**

woodbine *n* a wild honeysuckle with sweet-smelling yellow flowers.

woodcarving *n* **1** a work of art produced by carving wood. **2** the act or craft of carving wood.

woodcock *n* a large game bird with a long straight bill.

woodcut *n* a print made from a block of wood with a design cut into it.

woodcutter *n* a person who cuts down trees or chops wood.

wooded *adj* covered with woods or trees.

wooden *adj* **1** made of wood. **2** lacking spirit or animation: *the man's expression became wooden.* **woodenly** *adv*

wooden spoon *n* a booby prize, esp. in sporting contests.

woodland *n* **1** land that is mostly covered with woods or trees. ~*adj* **2** living in woods: *woodland birds.*

woodlouse *n, pl* **-lice** a very small grey creature with many legs that lives in damp places.

woodpecker *n* a bird with a strong beak with which it bores into trees for insects.

wood pulp *n* pulp made from wood fibre, used to make paper.

woodruff *n* a plant with small sweet-smelling white flowers and sweet-smelling leaves.

woods *pl n* closely packed trees forming a forest or wood.

woodsman *n, pl* **-men** a person who lives in a wood or who is skilled at woodwork or carving.

woodwind *Music* ~*adj* **1** of or denoting a type of wind instrument, such as the oboe. ~*n* **2** the woodwind instruments of an orchestra.

woodwork *n* **1** the parts of a room or house that are made of wood, such as the doors and window frames: *stark white walls and blue woodwork.* **2** the art or craft of making objects from wood. **3 crawl out of the woodwork** to appear suddenly and in large numbers: *intellectuals and environmentalists crawled out of the woodwork.*

woodworm *n* **1** a beetle larva that bores into wooden furniture or beams. **2** the damage caused to wood by these larvae.

woody *adj* **woodier, woodiest 1** (of a plant) having a very hard stem. **2** (of an area) covered with woods or trees.

woof[1] *n* same as **weft.**

woof[2] *n* an imitation of the bark of a dog.

woofer *n* a loudspeaker used in high-fidelity systems for the reproduction of low audio frequencies.

wool *n* **1** the soft curly hair of sheep and some other animals. **2** yarn spun from this, used in weaving and knitting. **3** cloth made from this yarn. **4 pull the wool over someone's eyes** to deceive someone.

woolgathering *n* idle or absent-minded daydreaming.

woollen *or US* **woolen** *adj* **1** made of wool or of a mixture of wool and another material. **2** relating to wool: *woollen mills.* ~*n* **3 woollens** woollen clothes, esp. knitted ones.

woolly *or US* **wooly** *adj* **-lier, -liest 1** made of or like wool. **2** confused or indistinct: *woolly ideas.* ~*n, pl* **-lies 3** a woollen garment, such as a sweater.

woolshed *n Austral & NZ* a large building in which sheep shearing takes place.

woozy *adj* **woozier, wooziest** *Informal* feeling slightly dizzy.

Worcester sauce (**wooss**-ter) *or* **Worcestershire sauce** *n* a sharp-tasting sauce, made from soy sauce, vinegar, and spices.

THESAURUS

derment **4.** admiration, amazement, astonishment, awe, bewilderment, curiosity, fascination, stupefaction, surprise, wonderment

wonderful 1. ace (*informal*), admirable, brill (*informal*), brilliant, cracking (*Brit. informal*), excellent, fabulous (*informal*), fantastic (*informal*), great (*informal*), magnificent, marvellous, mean (*slang*), outstanding, sensational (*informal*), smashing (*informal*), sovereign, stupendous, super (*informal*), superb, terrific, tiptop, tremendous **2.** amazing, astonishing, astounding, awe-inspiring, awesome, extraordinary, fantastic, incredible, marvellous, miraculous, odd, peculiar, phenomenal, remarkable, staggering, startling, strange, surprising, unheard-of, wondrous (*archaic or literary*)

woo *old-fashioned* chase, court, cultivate, importune, pay court to, pay one's addresses to, pay suit to, press one's suit with, pursue, seek after, seek the hand of, seek to win, solicit the goodwill of, spark (*rare*)

wood 1. planks, timber **2.** coppice, copse, forest, grove, thicket, trees, woodland

wooded forested, sylvan *or* silvan (*chiefly poetic*), timbered, tree-clad, tree-covered, woody

wooden 1. ligneous, made of wood, of wood, timber, woody **2.** blank, colourless, deadpan, dull, emotionless, empty, expressionless, glassy, lifeless, spiritless, unemotional, unresponsive, vacant

wool 1. fleece, hair, yarn **2. pull the wool over someone's eyes** bamboozle (*informal*), con (*slang*), deceive, delude, dupe, fool, hoodwink, kid (*informal*), lead (someone) up the garden path (*informal*), pull a fast one (on someone) (*informal*), put one over on (*slang*), take in (*informal*), trick

woolly *or U.S.* **wooly 1.** fleecy, flocculent, hairy,

Worcs Worcestershire.

word *n* **1** the smallest single meaningful unit of speech or writing. **2** a brief conversation: *I would like a word with you.* **3** a brief statement: *a word of warning.* **4** news or information: *let me know if you get word of my wife.* **5** a solemn promise: *he had given his word as a rabbi.* **6** a command or order: *he had only to say the word and they'd hang him.* **7** *Computers* a set of bits used to store, transmit, or operate upon an item of information in a computer. **8 by word of mouth** by spoken rather than by written means: *their reputation spreads by word of mouth.* **9 in a word** briefly or in short: *in a word, we've won.* **10 my word!** Also: **upon my word!** *Old-fashioned* an exclamation of surprise or amazement. **11 take someone at his** *or* **her word** to accept that someone really means what he or she says: *they're willing to take him at his word when he says he'll change.* **12 take someone's word for it** to believe what someone says. **13 the last word** the closing remark of a conversation or argument, often regarded as settling an issue. **14 the last word in** the finest example of: *the last word in comfort.* **15 word for word** using exactly the same words: *he repeated almost word for word what had been said.* **16 word of honour** a solemn promise. ~*vb* **17** to state in words: *the questions have to be carefully worded.* ~See also **words.**

Word *n* **the Word** the message and teachings contained in the Bible.

word game *n* any game involving the discovery, formation, or alteration of a word or words.

wording *n* the way in which words are used to express something: *the exact wording of the regulation has still not been worked out.*

word-perfect *adj* able to repeat from memory the exact words of a text one has learned.

word processing *n* the storage and organization of text by electronic means, esp. for business purposes.

word processor *n* an electronic machine for word processing, consisting of a keyboard, a VDU incorporating a microprocessor, and a printer.

words *pl n* **1** the text of a song, as opposed to the music. **2** the text of an actor's part. **3 have words** to have an argument or disagreement. **4 in other words** expressing the same idea in a different, more understandable, way. **5 put into words** to express in speech or writing: *she was reluctant to put her thoughts into words.*

wordy *adj* **wordier, wordiest** using too many words, esp. long words: *wordy explanations.*

wore *vb* the past tense of **wear.**

work *n* **1** physical or mental effort directed to doing or making something. **2** paid employment at a job, trade, or profession. **3** duties or tasks: *I had to delegate as much work as I could.* **4** something done or made as a result of effort: *a work by a major artist.* **5** the place where a person is employed: *accidents at work.* **6** *Physics old-fashioned* the transfer of energy occurring when a force is applied to move a body. **7 at work** working or in action: *the social forces at work in society.* ~*adj* **8** of or for work: *work experience.* ~*vb* **9** to do work; labour: *no-one worked harder than Arnold.* **10** to be employed: *she worked as a waitress.* **11** to make (a person or animal) labour. **12** to operate (a machine or a piece of equipment). **13** (of a machine or a piece of equipment) to function, esp. effectively: *he doesn't have to know how things work.* **14** (of a plan or system) to be successful. **15** to cultivate (land). **16** to move gradually into a specific condition or position: *he picked up the shovel, worked it under the ice, and levered.* **17** to make (one's way) with effort: *he worked his way to the top.* **18** *Informal* to manipulate to one's own advantage: *they could see an angle and they'd know how to work it.* ~See also **work off, works,** etc.

workable *adj* **1** able to operate efficiently: *a workable solution.* **2** able to be used: *a workable mine.*

workaday *adj* commonplace or ordinary: *workaday surroundings.*

workaholic *n* a person who is obsessed with work.

workbench *n* a heavy table at which a craftsman or mechanic works.

worker *n* **1** a person who works in a specified way: *a hard worker.* **2** a person who works at a specific job: *a government worker.* **3** an employee, as opposed to an employer. **4** a sterile female bee, ant, or wasp, that works for the colony.

work ethic *n* a belief in the moral value of work.

workforce *n* **1** the total number of workers employed by a company. **2** the total number of people available for work: *the local workforce.*

workhorse *n* a person or thing that does a lot of work, esp. dull or routine work: *this plane is the workhorse of most short-haul airlines.*

workhouse *n* (formerly, in England) a public institu-

THESAURUS

made of wool, shaggy, woollen **2.** blurred, clouded, confused, foggy, fuzzy, hazy, ill-defined, indefinite, indistinct, muddled, nebulous, unclear, vague

word *n.* **1.** expression, locution, name, term, vocable **2.** brief conversation, chat, chitchat, colloquy, confab (*informal*), confabulation, consultation, discussion, talk, tête-à-tête **3.** brief statement, comment, declaration, expression, remark, utterance **4.** account, advice, bulletin, communication, communiqué, dispatch, gen (*Brit. informal*), information, intelligence, intimation, latest (*informal*), message, news, notice, report, tidings **5.** affirmation, assertion, assurance, guarantee, oath, parole, pledge, promise, solemn oath, solemn word, undertaking, vow, word of honour **6.** command, go-ahead (*informal*), green light, order, signal **7. in a word** briefly, concisely, in a nutshell, in short, succinctly, to put it briefly, to sum up **8. the last word** final say, finis, summation, ultimatum ~*vb.* **9.** couch, express, phrase, put, say, state, utter

words lyrics, text

wordy diffuse, discursive, garrulous, long-winded, loquacious, pleonastic, prolix, rambling, verbose, windy

work *n.* **1.** drudgery, effort, elbow grease (*facetious*), exertion, grind (*informal*), industry, labour, slog, sweat, toil, travail (*literary*) **2.** business, calling, craft, duty, employment, job, line, livelihood, metier, occupation, office, profession, pursuit, trade **3.** assignment, chore, commission, duty, job, stint, task, undertaking **4.** achievement, composition, creation, handiwork, opus, performance, piece, production ~*vb.* **5.** drudge, exert oneself, labour, peg away, slave, slog (away), sweat, toil **6.** be employed, be in work, do business, earn a living, have a job **7.** act, control, direct, drive, handle, manage, manipulate, move, operate, ply, use, wield **8.** function, go, operate, perform, run **9.** cultivate, dig, farm, till **10.** force, make one's way, manoeuvre, move, progress **11.** *informal* arrange, bring off, contrive, exploit, fiddle (*informal*), fix (*informal*), handle, manipulate, pull off, swing (*informal*)

workable doable, feasible, possible, practicable, practical, viable

workaday common, commonplace, everyday, familiar, humdrum, mundane, ordinary, practical, prosaic, routine, run-of-the-mill

tion where very poor people did work in return for food and accommodation.

working *adj* 1 having a job: *the working mother.* 2 concerned with, used in, or suitable for work: *working conditions.* 3 capable of being operated or used: a *working mechanism.* ~*n* 4 a part of a mine or quarry that is or has been used. 5 **workings** the way that something works: *the workings of the human brain.*

working capital *n* the amount of capital that a business has available to meet the day-to-day cash requirements of its operations.

working class *n* 1 the social group that consists of people who earn wages, esp. as manual workers. ~*adj* **working-class** 2 of or relating to the working class: a *working-class neighbourhood.*

working day *or esp US & Canad* **workday** *n* 1 a day when people normally go to work: *the last working day of the week.* 2 the part of the day allocated to work: *the long working day of twelve to fourteen hours.*

working party *n* a committee established to investigate a problem.

workload *n* the amount of work to be done, esp. in a specified period: *a heavy workload.*

workman *n, pl* **-men** a man who is employed to do manual work.

workmanlike *adj* skilfully done: *a neat workmanlike job.*

workmanship *n* the degree of skill with which an object is made: *shoddy workmanship.*

workmate *n Informal* a person who works with another person; fellow worker.

work of art *n* 1 a piece of fine art, such as a painting or sculpture. 2 an object or a piece of work that has been exceptionally skilfully made or produced: *the doll was truly a work of art.*

work off *vb* to get rid of, usually by effort: *he went along to the tennis club and worked off his pique there.*

work on *vb* to try to persuade or influence (someone).

work out *vb* 1 to solve, find out, or plan by reasoning or calculation: *working out a new budget.* 2 to happen in a particular way: *he decided to wait and see how things worked out.* 3 to be successful or satisfactory: *the dates never worked out.* 4 to take part in physical exercise. 5 **work out at** to be calculated at (a certain amount): *the return on capital works out at 15 per cent.* ~*n* **workout** 6 a session of physical exercise for training or to keep fit.

work over *vb Slang* to give (someone) a severe beating: *whoever worked her over did a thorough job.*

works *n* 1 a place where something is manufactured: *a chemical works.* ~*pl n* 2 the sum total of a writer's or artist's achievements considered together: *the works of Goethe.* 3 **the works** *Slang* everything associated with a particular subject or thing: *traditional Indian music, sitars, the works.*

workshop *n* 1 a room or building where manufacturing or other manual work is carried on. 2 a group of people engaged in intensive study or work in a creative or practical field: *a writers' workshop.*

workshy *adj* not inclined to work; lazy.

work station *n* 1 an area in an office where one person works. 2 *Computers* a component of an electronic office system consisting of a VDU and keyboard.

worktable *n* a table at which writing, sewing, or other work may be done.

worktop *n* a surface in a kitchen, usually the top of a fitted kitchen unit, which is used for food preparation. Also: **work surface**

work-to-rule *n* a form of industrial action in which employees keep strictly to their employers' rules, with the result of reducing the work rate.

work up *vb* 1 to make angry, excited, or upset: *he worked himself up into a rage.* 2 to build up or develop: *I'd worked up a thirst.* 3 to work on (something) in order to improve it: *there was enough material to be worked up into something publishable.* 4 **work one's way up** to make progress: *he worked his way up in the catering trade.* 5 **work up to** to develop gradually towards: *the fete worked up to a climax around lunch time.*

world *n* 1 the earth as a planet. 2 the human race; people generally: *providing food for the world.* 3 any planet or moon, esp. one that might be inhabited. 4 a particular group of countries or period of history, or its inhabitants: *the Arab world; the post-Cold War world.* 5 an area, sphere, or realm considered as a complete environment: *the art world; the world of nature.* 6 the total circumstances and experience of a person that make up his or her life: *there may not ever be a place for us in your world.* 7 **bring into the world** to deliver or give birth to (a baby). 8 **come into the world** to be born. 9 **for all the world** exactly or very much: *they looked for all the world like a pair of newly-weds.* 10 **in the world** used to emphasize a statement: *she didn't have a worry in the world.* 11 **man** *or* **woman of the world** a man or woman who is experienced in social or public life. 12 **worlds apart**

THESAURUS

worker artisan, craftsman, employee, hand, labourer, proletarian, tradesman, wage earner, working man, working woman, workman

working *adj.* **1.** active, employed, in a job, in work, labouring **2.** effective, functioning, going, operative, practical, running, useful, viable ~*n.* **3.** diggings, excavations, mine, pit, quarry, shaft **4. workings** action, functioning, manner, method, mode of operation, operation, running

workman employee, hand, journeyman, labourer, mechanic, operative, tradesman, worker

workmanlike adept, careful, efficient, expert, masterly, painstaking, professional, proficient, satisfactory, skilful, skilled, thorough

workmanship art, artistry, craft, craftsmanship, execution, expertise, handicraft, handiwork, manufacture, skill, technique, work

work out **1.** arrange, calculate, clear up, construct, contrive, develop, devise, elaborate, evolve, figure out, find out, form, formulate, plan, put together, puzzle out, resolve, solve, suss (out) (*slang*) **2.** come out, develop, evolve, go, happen, pan out (*informal*), result, turn out **3.** be effective, flourish, go as planned, go well, prosper, prove satisfactory, succeed **4.** do exercises, drill, exercise, practise, train, warm up **5. work out at** add up to, amount to, come to, reach, reach a total of

works **1.** *n.* factory, mill, plant, shop, workshop **2.** *pl. n.* canon, output, productions, writings

workshop **1.** atelier, factory, mill, plant, shop, studio, workroom, works **2.** class, discussion group, seminar, study group

work up agitate, animate, arouse, enkindle, excite, foment, generate, get (someone) all steamed up (*slang*), incite, inflame, instigate, move, rouse, spur, stir up, wind up (*informal*)

world **1.** earth, earthly sphere, globe **2.** everybody, everyone, humanity, humankind, human race, man, mankind, men, the public, the race of man **3.** heavenly body, planet, star **4.** age, days, epoch, era, period, times **5.** area, domain, environment, field, kingdom,

very different from each other: *this man and I are worlds apart.* ~*adj* **13** of or concerning the entire world: *the world championship.*

world-class *adj* being as good as anyone else in the world in a particular field: *he has the makings of a world-class batsman.*

World Cup *n* an international football championship competition held every four years between national teams.

worldly *adj* **-lier, -liest 1** not spiritual; earthly or temporal: *as a simple monk he had no interest in politics and other worldly affairs.* **2** of or relating to material things: *all his worldly goods.* **3** wise in the ways of the world; sophisticated: *a suave worldly charming Frenchman.* **worldliness** *n*

worldly-wise *adj* wise in the ways of the world; sophisticated.

world music *n* popular music of a variety of ethnic origins and styles.

world-shaking *adj* of enormous significance; momentous: *world-shaking events.*

World War I *n* the war (1914–18) between the Allies (principally France, Russia, Britain, Italy, Australia, Canada, and the US) and the Central Powers (principally Germany, Austria-Hungary, and Turkey). Also: **First World War**

World War II *n* the war (1939–45) between the Allies (Britain, France, Australia, Canada, the US, and the Soviet Union) and the Axis (Germany, Italy, and Japan). Also: **Second World War**

world-weary *adj* no longer finding pleasure in life.

worldwide *adj* applying or extending throughout the world.

worm *n* **1** an small invertebrate animal with a long thin body and no limbs. **2** an insect larva that looks like a worm. **3** a despicable or weak person. **4** a slight trace: *a worm of doubt.* **5** a shaft on which a spiral thread has been cut, for example in a gear arrangement in which such a shaft drives a toothed wheel. ~*vb* **6** to rid (an animal) of worms in its intestines. **7 worm one's way a** to go or move slowly and with difficulty: *I had to worm my way out sideways from the bench.* **b** to get oneself into a certain situation or position gradually: *worming your way into my good books.* **8 worm out of** to obtain (information) from someone who is not willing to provide it: *it took me weeks to worm the facts out of him.* ~See also **worms.**

WORM *n Computers* write once read many (times): an optical disk which enables users to store their own data.

wormcast *n* a coil of earth or sand that has been excreted by a burrowing worm.

worm-eaten *adj* eaten into by worms: *worm-eaten beams.*

wormhole *n* a hole made by a worm in timber, plants, or fruit.

worms *n* a disease caused by parasitic worms living in the intestines.

wormwood *n* a plant from which a bitter oil formerly used in making absinthe is obtained.

wormy *adj* **wormier, wormiest** infested with or eaten by worms.

worn *vb* **1** the past participle of **wear.** ~*adj* **2** showing signs of long use or wear: *the worn soles of his boots.* **3** looking tired and ill: *that worn pain-creased face.*

worn-out *adj* **1** worn or used until threadbare, valueless, or useless. **2** completely exhausted: *worn out by their exertions.*

worried *adj* concerned and anxious about things that may happen. **worriedly** *adv*

worrisome *adj Old-fashioned* causing worry.

worry *vb* **-ries, -rying, -ried 1** to be or cause to be anxious or uneasy. **2** to annoy or bother: *don't worry yourself with the details.* **3** (of a dog) to frighten (sheep or other animals) by chasing and trying to bite them. **4 worry away at** to struggle with or work on (a problem). ~*n, pl* **-ries 5** a state or feeling of anxiety: *he was beside himself with worry.* **6** a cause for anxiety: *a resurgence of inflation is not now a worry.* **worrier** *n*

worry beads *pl n* a string of beads that supposedly relieves nervous tension when fingered or played with.

worrying *adj* causing concern and anxiety.

worse *adj* **1** the comparative of **bad. 2 none the worse for** not harmed by (adverse events or circumstances). **3 the worse for wear** *Informal* in a poor condition; not at one's best: *returning the worse for wear from the pub.* ~*n* **4 for the worse** into a worse condition: *taking a turn for the worse.* ~*adv* **5** the comparative of **badly. 6 worse off** in a worse condition, esp. financially.

worsen *vb* to make or become worse. **worsening** *adj, n*

worship *vb* **-shipping, -shipped** *or US* **-shiping, -shiped 1** to show profound religious devotion to (one's god), for example by praying. **2** to have intense love and admiration for (a person). ~*n* **3** religious ado-

THESAURUS

province, realm, sphere, system **6. for all the world** exactly, in every respect, in every way, just as if, just like, precisely, to all intents and purposes

worldly 1. carnal, earthly, fleshly, lay, mundane, physical, profane, secular, sublunary, temporal, terrestrial **2.** avaricious, covetous, grasping, greedy, materialistic, selfish, worldly-minded **3.** blasé, cosmopolitan, experienced, knowing, politic, sophisticated, urbane, worldly-wise

worldwide general, global, international, omnipresent, pandemic, ubiquitous, universal

worn 1. frayed, ragged, shabby, shiny, tattered, tatty, the worse for wear, threadbare **2.** careworn, drawn, exhausted, fatigued, haggard, jaded, lined, pinched, played-out (*informal*), spent, tired, tired out, wearied, weary, wizened, worn-out

worn-out 1. broken-down, clapped out (*Brit., Austral., & N.Z. informal*), decrepit, done, frayed, motheaten, on its last legs, ragged, run-down, shabby, tattered, tatty, threadbare, used, used-up, useless, worn **2.** all in (*informal*), clapped out (*Austral. & N.Z. informal*), dog-tired (*informal*), done in (*informal*), exhausted, fatigued, fit to drop, knackered (*slang*), played-out, prostrate, spent, tired, tired out, weary, zonked (*slang*)

worried afraid, anxious, apprehensive, bothered, concerned, distracted, distraught, distressed, disturbed, fearful, fretful, frightened, ill at ease, nervous, on edge, overwrought, perturbed, tense, tormented, troubled, uneasy, unquiet, upset, wired (*slang*)

worry *vb.* **1.** agonize, annoy, badger, be anxious, bother, brood, disquiet, distress, disturb, feel uneasy, fret, harass, harry, hassle (*informal*), hector, importune, irritate, make anxious, perturb, pester, plague, tantalize, tease, torment, trouble, unsettle, upset, vex **2.** attack, go for, harass, harry ~*n.* **3.** annoyance, anxiety, apprehension, care, concern, disturbance, fear, irritation, misery, misgiving, perplexity, torment, trepidation, trouble, unease, vexation, woe **4.** annoyance, bother, care, hassle (*informal*), irritation, pest, plague, problem, torment, trial, trouble, vexation

worsen aggravate, damage, decay, decline, degener-

ration or devotion. **4** formal expression of religious adoration, for example by praying. **5** intense love or devotion to a person. **worshipper** *n*

Worship *n* **Your, His** *or* **Her Worship** *Chiefly Brit* a title for a mayor or magistrate.

worshipful *adj* feeling or showing reverence or adoration.

worst *adj, adv* **1** the superlative of **bad** or **badly**. *~n* **2** the least good or the most terrible person, thing, or part: *the worst is yet to come.* **3 at one's worst** in the worst condition or aspect of a thing or person: *the British male is at his worst in July and August.* **4 at worst** in the least favourable interpretation or conditions: *all the questions should ideally be answered "no", or at worst "sometimes".* *~vb* **5** *Old-fashioned* to defeat or beat.

worsted (**wooss**-tid) *n* a close-textured woollen fabric used to make jackets and trousers.

worth *prep* **1** having a value of: *the fire destroyed property worth $200 million.* **2** worthy of; meriting or justifying: *if a job is worth doing, it's worth doing well.* **3 worth one's weight in gold** extremely useful or helpful; very highly valued. **4 worth one's while** worthy of spending one's time or effort on something: *they needed a wage of at least £140 a week to make it worth their while returning to work.* *~n* **5** monetary value: *the corporation's net worth.* **6** high quality; value: *the submarine proved its military worth during the Second World War.* **7** the amount of something that can be bought for a specified price: *$10 billion worth of property.*

worthless *adj* **1** without value or usefulness: *worthless junk bonds.* **2** without merit: *he sees himself as a worthless creature.* **worthlessness** *n*

worthwhile *adj* sufficiently important, rewarding, or valuable to justify spending time or effort on it.

worthy *adj* **-thier, -thiest 1** deserving of admiration or respect: *motives which were less than worthy.* **2 worthy of** deserving of: *he would practise extra hard to be worthy of such an honour.* *~n, pl* **-thies 3** *Often facetious* an important person. **worthily** *adv* **worthiness** *n*

would *vb* used as an auxiliary: **1** to form the past tense or subjunctive mood of **will**[1].: *he asked if she would marry him; that would be delightful.* **2** to express a polite offer or request: *would you like some lunch?* **3** to describe a habitual past action: *sometimes at lunch time I would choose a painting to go and see.*

would-be *adj* wanting or pretending to be: *would-be brides.*

wouldn't would not.

wound[1] *n* **1** an injury to the body such as a cut or a gunshot injury. **2** an injury to one's feelings or reputation. *~vb* **3** to cause an injury to the body or feelings of. **wounding** *adj*

wound[2] *vb* the past of **wind**[2].

wove *vb* a past tense of **weave.**

woven *vb* a past participle of **weave.**

wow *interj* **1** an exclamation of admiration or amazement. *~n* **2** *Slang* a person or thing that is amazingly successful: *he would be an absolute wow on the chat shows.* *~vb* **3** *Slang* to be a great success with: *the new Disney film wowed festival audiences.*

wowser *n Austral & NZ slang* **1** a fanatically puritanical person. **2** a teetotaller.

wp word processor.

WPC (in Britain) woman police constable.

wpm words per minute.

WRAC (in Britain) Women's Royal Army Corps.

wrack[1] *n* same as **rack**[2].

wrack[2] *n* seaweed that is floating in the sea or has been washed ashore.

WRAF (in Britain) Women's Royal Air Force.

wraith *n Literary* a ghost. **wraithlike** *adj*

wrangle *vb* **-gling, -gled 1** to argue noisily or angrily. *~n* **2** a noisy or angry argument.

wrap *vb* **wrapping, wrapped 1** to fold a covering round (something) and fasten it securely: *a small package wrapped in brown paper.* **2** to fold or wind (something) round a person or thing: *she wrapped a handkerchief around her bleeding palm.* **3** to fold, wind, or coil: *she wrapped her arms around her mother.* *~n* **4** *Old-fashioned* a garment worn wrapped round the shoulders. **5 keep something under wraps** to keep something secret.

wraparound *adj* **1** (of a skirt) designed to be worn

THESAURUS

ate, deteriorate, exacerbate, get worse, go downhill (*informal*), go from bad to worse, retrogress, sink, take a turn for the worse

worship 1. *vb.* adore, adulate, deify, exalt, glorify, honour, idolize, laud, love, praise, pray to, put on a pedestal, respect, revere, reverence, venerate **2.** *n.* adoration, adulation, deification, devotion, exaltation, glorification, glory, homage, honour, laudation, love, praise, prayer(s), regard, respect, reverence

worst *vb. old-fashioned* beat, best, clobber (*slang*), conquer, crush, defeat, gain the advantage over, get the better of, lick (*informal*), master, overcome, overpower, overthrow, run rings around (*informal*), subdue, subjugate, undo, vanquish

worth 1. cost, price, rate, valuation, value **2.** excellence, goodness, importance, merit, quality, usefulness, utility, value, worthiness

worthless 1. futile, ineffectual, insignificant, inutile, meaningless, measly, miserable, no use, nugatory (*formal*), paltry, pointless, poor, poxy (*slang*), rubbishy, trashy, trifling, trivial, unavailing, unimportant, unusable, useless, valueless, wretched **2.** abandoned, abject, base, contemptible, depraved, despicable, good-for-nothing, ignoble, useless, vile

worthwhile beneficial, constructive, expedient, gainful, good, helpful, justifiable, productive, profitable, useful, valuable, worthy

worthy 1. *adj.* admirable, commendable, creditable, decent, dependable, deserving, estimable, excellent, good, honest, honourable, laudable, meritorious, praiseworthy, reliable, reputable, respectable, righteous, upright, valuable, virtuous, worthwhile **2.** *n. often facetious* big shot (*informal*), bigwig (*informal*), dignitary, luminary, notable, personage

wound *n.* **1.** cut, damage, gash, harm, hurt, injury, laceration, lesion, slash **2.** anguish, distress, grief, heartbreak, injury, insult, offence, pain, pang, sense of loss, shock, slight, torment, torture, trauma *~vb.* **3.** cut, damage, gash, harm, hit, hurt, injure, irritate, lacerate, pierce, slash, wing **4.** annoy, cut (someone) to the quick, distress, grieve, hurt, hurt the feelings of, mortify, offend, pain, shock, sting, traumatize

wrangle 1. *vb.* altercate, argue, bicker, brawl, contend, disagree, dispute, fall out (*informal*), fight, have words, quarrel, row, scrap, spar, squabble **2.** *n.* altercation, angry exchange, argy-bargy *or* argie-bargie (*Brit. informal*), barney (*informal*), bickering, brawl, clash, contest, controversy, dispute, falling-out (*informal*), quarrel, row, set-to (*informal*), slanging match (*Brit.*), squabble, tiff

wrap 1. *vb.* absorb, bind, bundle up, cloak, cover, encase, enclose, enfold, envelop, fold, immerse, muffle,

wrapped round the body. **2** extending in a curve from the front round to the sides: *wraparound shades.*

wrapper *n* a paper, foil, or plastic cover in which a product is wrapped.

wrapping *n* a piece of paper, foil, or other material used to wrap something in.

wrap up *vb* **1** to fold paper, cloth, or other material round (something). **2** to put warm clothes on: *remember to wrap up warmly on cold or windy days.* **3** *Informal* to finish or settle: *he will need 60 to 90 days to wrap up his current business dealings.* **4** *Slang* to stop talking. **5 wrapped up in** giving all one's attention to: *wrapped up in her new baby.*

wrasse *n* a brightly coloured sea fish.

wrath (**roth**) *n Old-fashioned or literary* intense anger. **wrathful** *adj*

wreak *vb* **1 wreak havoc** to cause chaos or damage: *this Australian sun will wreak havoc with your complexions.* **2 wreak vengeance on** to take revenge on.

wreath *n, pl* **wreaths 1** a ring of flowers or leaves, placed on a grave as a memorial or worn on the head as a garland or a mark of honour. **2** anything circular or spiral: *a wreath of smoke.*

wreathe *vb* **wreathing, wreathed** *Literary* **1 wreathed in a** surrounded by: *wreathed in pipe smoke.* **b** surrounded by a ring of: *wreathed in geraniums.* **2 wreathed in smiles** smiling broadly.

wreck *vb* **1** to break, spoil, or destroy completely. **2** to cause the accidental sinking or destruction of (a ship) at sea. ~*n* **3** something that has been destroyed or badly damaged, such as a crashed car or aircraft. **4** a ship that has been sunk or destroyed at sea. **5** a person in a poor mental or physical state.

wreckage *n* the remains of something that has been destroyed or badly damaged, such as a crashed car or aircraft.

wrecker *n* **1** a person who destroys or badly damages something: *a marriage wrecker.* **2** (formerly) a person who lured ships on to the rocks in order to plunder them. **3** *Chiefly US & Canad* a person whose job is to demolish buildings or dismantle cars. **4** *US & Canad* a breakdown van.

wren *n* a very small brown songbird.

Wren *n Informal* a member of the Women's Royal Naval Service.

wrench *vb* **1** to twist or pull (something) violently, for example to remove it from something to which it is attached: *he grabbed the cable and wrenched it out of the wall socket.* **2** to move or twist away with a sudden violent effort: *she wrenched free of his embrace.* **3** to injure (a limb or joint) by a sudden twist. ~*n* **4** a violent twist or pull. **5** an injury to a limb or joint, caused by twisting it. **6** a feeling of sadness experienced on leaving a person or place: *it would be a wrench to leave Essex after all these years.* **7** a spanner with adjustable jaws.

wrest *vb* **1** to take (something) away from someone with a violent pull or twist. **2** to seize forcibly by violent or unlawful means: *the army has wrested control from the resistance.*

wrestle *vb* **-tling, -tled 1** to fight (someone) by grappling and trying to throw or pin him or her to the ground, often as a sport. **2 wrestle with** to struggle hard with (a person, problem, or thing): *I have wrestled with my conscience all week.* **wrestler** *n*

wrestling *n* a sport in which each contestant tries to overcome the other either by throwing or pinning him or her to the ground or by forcing a submission.

wretch *n Old-fashioned* **1** a despicable person. **2** a person pitied for his or her misfortune.

wretched (**retch-id**) *adj* **1** in poor or pitiful circumstances: *a vast wretched slum.* **2** feeling very unhappy. **3** of poor quality: *the wretched state of the cabbages.* **4** *Informal* undesirable or displeasing: *what a wretched muddle.* **wretchedly** *adv* **wretchedness** *n*

wriggle *vb* **-gling, -gled 1** to twist and turn with quick movements: *he wriggled on the hard seat.* **2** to move along by twisting and turning. **3 wriggle out of** to avoid (doing something that one does not want to

THESAURUS

pack, package, roll up, sheathe, shroud, surround, swathe, wind **2.** *n. old-fashioned* cape, cloak, mantle, shawl, stole

wrapper case, cover, envelope, jacket, packaging, paper, sheath, sleeve, wrapping

wrap up 1. bundle up, enclose, enwrap, giftwrap, pack, package **2.** dress warmly, muffle up, put warm clothes on, wear something warm **3.** *informal* bring to a close, conclude, end, finish off, polish off, round off, terminate, tidy up, wind up **4.** *slang* be quiet, be silent, button it (*slang*), button one's lip (*slang*), hold one's tongue, put a sock in it (*Brit. slang*), shut one's face (*Brit. slang*), shut one's mouth (*slang*), shut one's trap (*slang*), shut up

wrath *old-fashioned or literary* anger, choler, displeasure, exasperation, fury, indignation, ire, irritation, passion, rage, resentment, temper

wrathful *old-fashioned or literary* angry, beside oneself with rage, displeased, enraged, furious, incensed, indignant, infuriated, irate, on the warpath (*informal*), raging, wroth (*old-fashioned or literary*)

wreath band, chaplet, coronet, crown, festoon, garland, loop, ring

wreck *vb.* **1.** blow (*slang*), break, cock up (*Brit. slang*), dash to pieces, demolish, destroy, devastate, mar, play havoc with, ravage, ruin, screw up (*informal*), shatter, smash, spoil, total (*slang*), trash (*slang*), undo **2.** founder, go *or* run aground, run onto the rocks, shipwreck, strand ~*n.* **3.** derelict, hulk, shipwreck, sunken vessel

wreckage debris, fragments, hulk, pieces, remains, rubble, ruin, wrack

wrench *vb.* **1.** force, jerk, pull, rip, tear, tug, twist, wrest, wring, yank **2.** distort, rick, sprain, strain ~*n.* **3.** jerk, pull, rip, tug, twist, yank **4.** sprain, strain, twist **5.** ache, blow, pain, pang, shock, upheaval, uprooting **6.** adjustable spanner, shifting spanner, spanner

wrestle battle, combat, contend, fight, grapple, scuffle, strive, struggle, tussle

wretch *old-fashioned* **1.** arsehole (*taboo*), bad egg (*old-fashioned informal*), bastard (*offensive*), blackguard, bugger (*taboo slang*), cur, good-for-nothing, miscreant, outcast, profligate, rascal, rat (*informal*), rogue, rotter (*slang, chiefly Brit.*), ruffian, scoundrel, scumbag (*slang*), shit (*taboo slang*), swine, turd (*taboo slang*), vagabond, villain, worm **2.** poor thing, unfortunate

wretched 1. base, calamitous, contemptible, crappy (*slang*), deplorable, despicable, inferior, low, low-down (*informal*), mean, miserable, paltry, pathetic, poor, poxy (*slang*), scurvy, shabby, shameful, sorry, vile, worthless **2.** abject, brokenhearted, cheerless, comfortless, crestfallen, dejected, deplorable, depressed, disconsolate, dismal, distressed, doleful, downcast, forlorn, funereal, gloomy, hapless, hopeless, melancholy, miserable, pathetic, pitiable, pitiful, poor, sorry, unfortunate, unhappy, woebegone, woeful, worthless

wriggle *vb.* **1.** jerk, jiggle, squirm, turn, twist, wag, waggle, wiggle, writhe **2.** crawl, slink, snake, twist and

do): *he wriggled out of donating blood.* ~*n* **4** a wriggling movement or action.

wring *vb* **wringing, wrung 1** Also: **wring out** to squeeze water from (a cloth or clothing) by twisting it tightly. **2** to twist (a neck) violently. **3** to clasp and twist (one's hands) in anguish. **4** to grip (someone's hand) vigorously in greeting. **5** to obtain by forceful means: *to wring concessions from the army.* **6 wring someone's heart** to make someone feel sorrow or pity.

wringer *n* same as **mangle**[2] (sense 1).

wringing *adv* **wringing wet** extremely wet.

wrinkle *n* **1** a slight ridge in the smoothness of a surface, such as a crease in the skin as a result of age. ~*vb* **-kling, -kled 2** to develop or cause to develop wrinkles. **wrinkled** *or* **wrinkly** *adj*

wrist *n* **1** the joint between the forearm and the hand. **2** the part of a sleeve that covers the wrist.

wristwatch *n* a watch worn strapped round the wrist.

writ *n* a formal legal document ordering a person to do or not to do something.

write *vb* **writing, wrote, written 1** to draw or mark (words, letters, or numbers) on paper or a blackboard with a pen, pencil, or chalk. **2** to describe or record (something) in writing: *he began to write his memoirs.* **3** to be an author: *he still taught writing, but he didn't write.* **4** to write a letter to or correspond regularly with someone: *don't forget to write!* **5** *Informal, chiefly US & Canad* to write a letter to (someone): *I wrote him several times.* **6** to say or communicate in a letter or a book: *in a recent letter a friend wrote that everything costs more in Russia now.* **7** to fill in the details for (a cheque or document). **8** *Computers* to record (data) in a storage device. **9 write down** to record in writing: *write it down if you find it too embarrassing to talk about.*

write off *vb* **1** *Accounting* to cancel (a bad debt) from the accounts. **2** to dismiss from consideration: *he wrote her off as a tense woman.* **3** to send a written request (for something): *he wrote off for leaflets on the subject.* **4** *Informal* to damage (a vehicle) beyond repair. ~*n* **write-off 5** *Informal* a vehicle that is damaged beyond repair.

write out *vb* **1** to put into writing or reproduce in full form in writing. **2** to remove (a character) from a television or radio series: *another actress is to be written out of the BBC soap.*

writer *n* **1** a person whose job is writing; author. **2** the person who has written something specified: *the writer of this letter is pretty dangerous.*

write up *vb* **1** to describe fully, complete, or bring up to date in writing: *she would write up her diary in bed.* ~*n* **write-up 2** a published account of something, such as a review in a newspaper or magazine: *I see the Herald didn't give you a very good write-up.*

writhe *vb* **writhing, writhed** to twist or squirm in pain: *writhing in agony.*

writing *n* **1** something that has been written: *the writing on the outer flap was faint.* **2** written form: *permission in writing.* **3** short for **handwriting. 4** a kind or style of writing: *creative writing.* **5** the work of a writer: *Wilde never mentioned chess in his writing.*

written *vb* **1** the past participle of **write.** ~*adj* **2** recorded in writing: *written permission.*

WRNS Women's Royal Naval Service.

wrong *adj* **1** not correct or accurate: *the wrong answers.* **2** acting or judging in error; mistaken: *do correct me if I'm wrong.* **3** not in accordance with correct or conventional rules or standards; immoral: *this group argues that even gently slapping a child is wrong.* **4** not intended or appropriate: *I ordered the wrong things; you've picked the wrong time to ask such questions.* **5** being a problem or trouble: *come on, I know when something's wrong.* **6** not functioning properly: *there's something wrong with the temperature sensor.* **7** denoting the side of cloth that is worn facing inwards. ~*adv* **8** in a wrong manner: *I guessed wrong.* **9 get someone wrong** to misunderstand someone: *don't get me wrong, I'm not making threats.* **10 get something wrong** to make a mistake about something: *he had got his body language wrong.* **11 go wrong a** to turn out badly or not as intended. **b** to make a mistake. **c** (of a machine) to stop functioning properly: *pilots must be able to react instantly if the automatic equipment suddenly goes wrong.* ~*n* **12**

THESAURUS

turn, worm, zigzag **3. wriggle out of** dodge, extricate oneself, manoeuvre, sneak, talk one's way out, worm ~*n.* **4.** jerk, jiggle, squirm, turn, twist, wag, waggle, wiggle

wring coerce, extort, extract, force, screw, squeeze, twist, wrench, wrest

wrinkle 1. *n.* corrugation, crease, crinkle, crow's-foot, crumple, fold, furrow, gather, line, pucker, rumple **2.** *vb.* corrugate, crease, crinkle, crumple, fold, furrow, gather, line, pucker, ruck, rumple

writ court order, decree, document, summons

write commit to paper, compose, copy, correspond, create, draft, draw up, indite, inscribe, jot down, pen, put down in black and white, put in writing, record, scribble, set down, take down, tell, transcribe

write off 1. cancel, cross out, disregard, forget about, give up for lost, score out, shelve **2.** *informal* crash, damage beyond repair, destroy, smash up, trash (*slang*), wreck

writer author, columnist, essayist, hack, man of letters, novelist, penman, penpusher, scribbler, scribe, wordsmith

writhe contort, distort, jerk, squirm, struggle, thrash, thresh, toss, twist, wiggle, wriggle

writing 1. book, composition, document, letter, opus, publication, title, work **2.** *see* HANDWRITING

wrong *adj.* **1.** erroneous, fallacious, false, faulty, inaccurate, incorrect, in error, mistaken, off (the) beam (*informal*), off target, out, unsound, untrue, wide of the mark **2.** bad, blameworthy, criminal, crooked, dishonest, dishonourable, evil, felonious, illegal, illicit, immoral, iniquitous, reprehensible, sinful, under-the-table, unethical, unfair, unjust, unlawful, wicked, wrongful **3.** funny, improper, inappropriate, inapt, incongruous, incorrect, indecorous, infelicitous, malapropos, not done, unacceptable, unbecoming, unconventional, undesirable, unfitting, unhappy, unseemly, unsuitable **4.** amiss, askew, awry, defective, faulty, not working, out of commission, out of order **5.** inside, inverse, opposite, reverse ~*adv.* **6.** amiss, askew, astray, awry, badly, erroneously, inaccurately, incorrectly, mistakenly, wrongly **7. go wrong a.** come to grief (*informal*), come to nothing, fail, fall through, flop (*informal*), miscarry, misfire **b.** boob (*Brit. slang*), err, go astray, make a mistake, slip up (*informal*) **c.** break down, cease to function, conk out (*informal*), fail, go kaput (*informal*), go on the blink (*slang*), go phut (*informal*), malfunction, misfire ~*n.* **8.** abuse, bad *or* evil deed, crime, error, grievance, immorality, inequity, infraction, infringement, iniquity, injury, injustice, misdeed, offence, sin, sinfulness, transgression, trespass, unfairness, wickedness **9. in the wrong** at fault, blameworthy, guilty, in error, mistaken, off (the) beam (*informal*), off course, off target, to be blamed ~*vb.* **10.** abuse, cheat, discredit, dishonour, harm, hurt, ill-treat,

something bad, immoral, or unjust: *how can such a wrong be redressed?* **13 in the wrong** mistaken or guilty. ~*vb* **14** to treat (someone) unjustly. **15** to think or speak unfairly of (someone). **wrongly** *adv*

wrongdoing *n* immoral or illegal behaviour. **wrongdoer** *n*

wrong-foot *vb* **1** *Sport* to play a shot in such a way as to catch (an opponent) off-balance: *his pass completely wrong-footed the England defence.* **2** to gain an advantage over (someone) by doing something unexpected: *China wrong-footed Vietnam by supporting the peace plan.*

wrongful *adj* unjust or illegal: *wrongful imprisonment.* **wrongfully** *adv*

wrong-headed *adj* constantly and stubbornly wrong in judgment.

wrote *vb* the past tense of **write.**

wroth *adj Old-fashioned or literary* angry.

wrought (**rawt**) *vb* **1** *Old-fashioned* a past of **work.** ~*adj* **2** *Metallurgy* shaped by hammering or beating: *wrought copper and brass.*

wrought iron *n* a pure form of iron with a low carbon content, often used for decorative work.

wrung *vb* the past of **wring.**

WRVS Women's Royal Voluntary Service.

wry *adj* **wrier, wriest** *or* **wryer, wryest 1** drily humorous; sardonic: *wry amusement.* **2** (of a facial expression) produced by twisting one's features to denote amusement or displeasure: *a small wry smile twisted the corner of his mouth.* **wryly** *adv*

wrybill *n* a New Zealand plover whose bill is bent to one side enabling it to search for food beneath stones.

wryneck *n* a woodpecker that has a habit of twisting its neck round.

wt. weight.

WV West Virginia.

WWI World War One.

WWII World War Two.

WY Wyoming.

wych-elm *or* **witch-elm** *n* a Eurasian elm with long pointed leaves.

WYSIWYG *n, adj Computers* what you see is what you get: referring to what is displayed on the screen being the same as what will be printed out.

THESAURUS

ill-use, impose upon, injure, malign, maltreat, misrepresent, mistreat, oppress, take advantage of

wrongdoer criminal, culprit, delinquent, evildoer, lawbreaker, malefactor, miscreant, offender, sinner, transgressor, trespasser (*old-fashioned*), villain

wrongful blameworthy, criminal, dishonest, dishonourable, evil, felonious, illegal, illegitimate, illicit, immoral, improper, reprehensible, under-the-table, unethical, unfair, unjust, unlawful, wicked

wry droll, dry, ironic, mocking, mordacious, sarcastic, sardonic

X

x *Maths* **1** (along with *y* and *z*) an unknown quantity. **2** the multiplication symbol.

X **1** indicating an error, a choice, or a kiss. **2** indicating an unknown, unspecified, or variable factor, person, or thing: *Miss X.* **3** the Roman numeral for ten. **4** (formerly) indicating a film that may not be publicly shown to anyone under 18: since 1982 replaced by symbol 18.

X-chromosome *n* the sex chromosome that occurs in pairs in the females of many animals, including humans, and as one of a pair with the Y-chromosome in males.

Xe *Chem* xenon.

xenon *n Chem* a colourless odourless gas found in minute quantities in the air. Symbol: Xe

xenophobia (zen-oh-**fobe**-ee-a) *n* hatred or fear of foreigners or strangers. **xenophobic** *adj*

xerography (zeer-**og**-ra-fee) *n* a photocopying process in which an image of the written or printed material is electrically charged on a surface and attracts oppositely charged dry ink particles which are then fixed by heating. **xerographic** *adj*

Xerox (**zeer**-ox) *n Trademark* **1** a machine for copying printed material. **2** a copy made by a Xerox machine. *~vb* **3** to produce a copy of (a document) using such a machine.

Xhosa (**kawss**-a) *n* **1** (*pl* **-sa** *or* **-sas**) a member of a Black people living in the Republic of South Africa. **2** the language of this people. **Xhosan** *adj*

Xmas (**eks**-mass) *n Informal* short for **Christmas.**

x-ray *or* **X-ray** *n* **1** a stream of electromagnetic radiation of short wavelength that can pass through some solid materials. **2** a picture produced by exposing photographic film to x-rays: used in medicine as a diagnostic aid, since parts of the body, such as bones, absorb x-rays and so appear as opaque areas on the picture. *~vb* **3** to photograph, treat, or examine using x-rays.

x-ray diffraction *n Physics* the scattering of x-rays on contact with matter, resulting in changes in radiation intensity, which is used for studying atomic structure.

xylem (**zile**-em) *n Bot* a plant tissue that conducts water and mineral salts from the roots to all other parts.

xylene (**zile**-lean) *n Chem* a hydrocarbon existing in three isomeric forms, all three being colourless flammable volatile liquids used as solvents and in the manufacture of synthetic resins, dyes, and insecticides.

xylophone (**zile**-oh-fone) *n Music* a percussion instrument consisting of a set of wooden bars played with hammers. **xylophonist** *n*

THESAURUS

X-rays Röntgen rays (*old name*)

Y

y *Maths* (along with *x* and *z*) an unknown quantity.

Y 1 an unknown, unspecified, or variable factor, number, person, or thing. **2** *Chem* yttrium.

yacht (yott) *n* **1** a large boat with sails or an engine, used for racing or pleasure cruising. ~*vb* **2** to sail or cruise in a yacht. **yachting** *n, adj*

yachtsman *or fem* **yachtswoman** *n, pl* **-men** *or* **-women** a person who sails a yacht.

yack *n, vb* same as **yak**[2].

yah *interj* **1** *Informal* same as **yes. 2** an exclamation of derision or disgust.

yahoo *n, pl* **-hoos** a crude, brutish, or obscenely coarse person.

yahweh *or* **yahveh** *n Bible* a personal name of god

yak[1] *n* a Tibetan ox with long shaggy hair.

yak[2] *Slang* ~*n* **1** noisy, continuous, and trivial talk. ~*vb* **yakking, yakked 2** to talk continuously about unimportant matters.

Yale lock *n Trademark* a type of cylinder lock using a flat serrated key.

yam *n* **1** a twining plant of tropical and subtropical regions, cultivated for its starchy roots which are eaten as a vegetable. **2** the sweet potato.

yammer *Informal* ~*vb* **1** to whine in a complaining manner. ~*n* **2** a yammering sound. **3** nonsense or jabber.

Yang *n* See **Yin and Yang.**

yank *vb* **1** to pull (someone or something) with a sharp movement. ~*n* **2** a sudden pull or jerk.

Yank *n Slang* a person from the United States.

Yankee *n* **1** *Slang* same as **Yank. 2** a person from the Northern United States. ~*adj* **3** of or characteristic of Yankees.

yap *vb* **yapping, yapped 1** to bark with a high-pitched sound. **2** *Informal* to talk at length in an annoying or stupid way. ~*n* **3** a high-pitched bark. **4** *Slang* annoying or stupid speech. **yappy** *adj*

yarborough *n Bridge, whist* a hand in which no card is higher than nine.

yard[1] *n* **1** a unit of length equal to 3 feet (0.9144 metre). **2** *Naut* a spar slung across a ship's mast to extend the sail.

yard[2] *n* **1** a piece of enclosed ground, often adjoining or surrounded by a building or buildings. **2** an enclosed or open area where a particular type of work is done: *a shipbuilding yard.* **3** *US & Canad* the garden of a house. **4** *US & Canad* the winter pasture of deer, moose, and similar animals.

Yard *n* **the Yard** *Brit informal* short for **Scotland Yard.**

yardarm *n Naut* the outer end of a ship's yard.

yardstick *n* **1** a measure or standard used for comparison: *there's no yardstick for judging a problem of this sort.* **2** a graduated measuring stick one yard long.

yarmulke (yar-mull-ka) *n* a skullcap worn by Jewish men.

yarn *n* **1** a continuous twisted strand of natural or synthetic fibres, used for knitting or making cloth. **2** *Informal* a long involved story. **3 spin a yarn** *Informal* to tell such a story.

yarrow *n* a wild plant with flat clusters of white flowers.

yashmak *n* a veil worn by a Muslim woman to cover her face in public.

yaw *vb* **1** (of an aircraft or ship) to turn to one side or from side to side while moving. ~*n* **2** the act or movement of yawing.

yawl *n* **1** a two-masted sailing boat. **2** a ship's small boat.

yawn *vb* **1** to open one's mouth wide and take in air deeply, often when sleepy or bored. **2** to be open wide as if threatening to engulf someone or something: *the doorway yawned blackly open at the end of the hall.* ~*n* **3** the act or an instance of yawning. **yawning** *adj*

yaws *n* an infectious disease of tropical climates characterized by red skin eruptions.

Yb *Chem* ytterbium.

Y-chromosome *n* the sex chromosome that occurs as one of a pair with the X-chromosome in the males of many animals, including humans.

yd yard (measure).

YDT Yukon Daylight Time.

ye[1] (yee) *pron Old-fashioned or dialect* you.

ye[2] *adj* (*definite article*) *Old-fashioned or jocular* the: *ye olde Rose and Crown pub.*

yea *interj* **1** *Old-fashioned* yes. ~*adv* **2** *Old-fashioned or literary* indeed or truly: *they wandered about the church, yea, even unto the altar.*

yeah *interj Informal* same as **yes.**

year *n* **1** the time taken for the earth to make one revolution around the sun, about 365 days. **2** the twelve months from January 1 to December 31. **3** a period of twelve months from any specified date. **4** a specific period of time, usually occupying a definite part or parts of a twelve-month period, used for some particular activity: *the financial year.* **5** a group of people who have started an academic course at the same time. **6 year in, year out** regularly or monotonously, over a long period. **7 years a** a long time: *the legal case could take years to resolve.* **b** age, usually old age: *a man of his years.*

yearbook *n* a reference book published once a year containing details of events of the previous year.

yearling *n* an animal that is between one and two years old.

yearly *adj* **1** occurring, done, or appearing once a year or every year. **2** lasting or valid for a year: *the yearly cycle.* ~*adv* **3** once a year.

yearn *vb* **1** to have an intense desire or longing: *he often yearned for life in a country town.* **2** to feel tenderness or affection: *they secretly yearned for the gentleman in question.* **yearning** *n, adj*

yeast *n* a yellowish fungus used in fermenting alcoholic drinks and in raising dough for bread. **yeasty** *adj*

THESAURUS

yank *vb./n.* hitch, jerk, pull, snatch, tug, wrench

yardstick benchmark, criterion, gauge, measure, par, standard, touchstone

yarn *n.* **1.** fibre, thread **2.** *informal* anecdote, cock-and-bull story (*informal*), fable, story, tale, tall story

yawning cavernous, chasmal, gaping, vast, wide, wide-open

yearly annual, annually, every year, once a year, per annum

yearn ache, covet, crave, desire, eat one's heart out

yell *vb* **1** to shout, scream, or cheer in a loud or piercing way. ~*n* **2** a loud piercing cry of pain, anger, or fear.

yellow *n* **1** the colour of a lemon or an egg yolk. **2** anything yellow, such as yellow clothing or yellow paint: *painted in yellow.* ~*adj* **3** of the colour yellow; of the colour of a lemon or an egg yolk. **4** *Informal* cowardly or afraid. **5** having a yellowish complexion. ~*vb* **6** to make or become yellow or yellower. **yellowish** *or* **yellowy** *adj*

yellow-belly *n, pl* **-bellies** *Slang* a coward. **yellow-bellied** *adj*

yellow card *n Soccer* a piece of yellow pasteboard raised by a referee to indicate that a player has been booked for a serious violation of the rules.

yellow fever *n* an acute infectious tropical disease causing fever and jaundice, caused by certain mosquitoes.

yellowhammer *n* a European songbird with a yellowish head and body.

Yellow Pages *pl n Trademark* a telephone directory that lists businesses under the headings of the type of business or service they provide.

yellow streak *n Informal* a cowardly or weak trait.

yelp *vb* **1** to utter a sharp or high-pitched cry of pain. ~*n* **2** a sharp or high-pitched cry of pain.

yen[1] *n, pl* **yen** the standard monetary unit of Japan.

yen[2] *Informal* ~*n* **1** a longing or desire. ~*vb* **yenning, yenned 2** to have a longing.

yeoman (**yo**-man) *n, pl* **-men** *History* a farmer owning and farming his own land.

yeoman of the guard *n* a member of the ceremonial bodyguard (**Yeomen of the Guard**) of the British monarch.

yeomanry *n* **1** yeomen collectively. **2** (in Britain) a former volunteer cavalry force.

yep *interj Informal* same as **yes.**

yes *interj* **1** used to express consent, agreement, or approval, or to answer when one is addressed. **2** used to signal someone to speak or keep speaking, enter a room, or do something. ~*n* **3** an answer or vote of *yes.* **4** a person who answers or votes *yes.*

yes man *n* a person who always agrees with his or her superior in order to gain favour.

yesterday *n* **1** the day before today. **2** the recent past. ~*adv* **3** on or during the day before today. **4** in the recent past.

yesteryear *Formal or literary* ~*n* **1** last year or the past in general. ~*adv* **2** during last year or the past in general.

yet *conj* **1** nevertheless or still: *I'm too tired to work, yet I have to go on.* ~*adv* **2** up until then or now: *this may be her most rewarding book yet.* **3** still: *yet more work to do.* **4** now (as contrasted with later): *not ready for that yet.* **5** eventually in spite of everything: *I'll break your spirit yet!* **6 as yet** up until then or now.

yeti *n* same as **abominable snowman.**

yew *n* an evergreen tree with needle-like leaves, red berries, and fine-grained elastic wood.

Y-fronts *pl n Trademark* men's or boys' underpants that have a front opening within an inverted Y shape.

YHA Youth Hostels Association.

yid *n Slang, offensive* a Jew.

Yiddish *n* **1** a language derived from High German, spoken by Jews in Europe and elsewhere by Jewish emigrants, and usually written in the Hebrew alphabet. ~*adj* **2** of this language.

yield *vb* **1** to produce or bear. **2** to give as a return: *some of his policies have yielded large savings.* **3** to give up control of; surrender. **4** to give way, submit, or surrender, through force or persuasion: *the players finally yielded to the weather.* **5** to agree (to): *governments too weak to say no repeatedly yielded to petitions for charters.* **6** to grant or allow: *to yield right of way.* ~*n* **7** the amount produced.

yielding *adj* **1** compliant or submissive. **2** soft or flexible: *he landed on a yielding surface rather than rock or board.*

Yin and Yang *n* two complementary principles of Chinese philosophy: Yin is negative, dark, and feminine, Yang is positive, bright, and masculine.

yippee *interj* an exclamation of joy, pleasure, or anticipation.

YMCA Young Men's Christian Association.

yo *interj* an expression used as a greeting or to attract someone's attention.

yob *or* **yobbo** *n, pl* **yobs** *or* **yobbos** *Brit slang* a bad-mannered aggressive youth. **yobbish** *adj*

yodel *vb* **-delling, -delled** *or US* **-deling, -deled 1** to sing with abrupt changes back and forth between the normal voice and falsetto, as in folk songs of the Swiss Alps. ~*n* **2** the act or sound of yodelling. **yodeller** *or US* **yodeler** *n*

yoga *n* **1** a Hindu system of philosophy aiming at spiritual, mental, and physical wellbeing by means of deep meditation, prescribed postures, and controlled breathing. **2** a system of exercising involving such meditation, postures, and breathing.

yogi *n* a person who practises or is a master of yoga.

yogurt, yoghurt, *or* **yoghourt** *n* a slightly sour custard-like food made from milk curdled by bacteria, often sweetened and flavoured with fruit.

yoke *n, pl* **yokes** *or* **yoke 1** a wooden frame with a bar put across the necks of two animals to hold them together so that they can be worked as a team. **2** a pair of animals joined by a yoke. **3** a frame fitting over a person's shoulders for carrying buckets. **4** an oppressive force or burden: *the yoke of English tyranny.* **5** a fitted part of a garment to which a fuller part is at-

THESAURUS

over, hanker, have a yen for (*informal*), hunger, itch, languish, long, lust, pant, pine, set one's heart upon

yell 1. *vb.* bawl, holler (*informal*), howl, scream, screech, shout, shriek, squeal **2.** *n.* cry, howl, scream, screech, shriek, whoop

yet *conj.* **1.** however, nevertheless, notwithstanding, still ~*adv.* **2.** as yet, so far, thus far, until now, up to now **3.** additionally, as well, besides, further, in addition, into the bargain, moreover, over and above, still, to boot **4.** already, just now, now, right now, so soon

yield *vb.* **1.** afford, bear, bring forth, bring in, earn, furnish, generate, give, net, pay, produce, provide, return, supply **2.** abandon, abdicate, admit defeat, bow, capitulate, cave in (*informal*), cede, cry quits, give in, give up the struggle, give way, knuckle under, lay down one's arms, part with, raise the white flag, relinquish, resign, resign oneself, submit, succumb, surrender, throw in the towel **3.** accede, agree, allow, bow, comply, concede, consent, go along with, grant, permit ~*n.* **4.** crop, harvest, output, produce

yielding 1. accommodating, acquiescent, biddable, compliant, docile, easy, flexible, obedient, pliant, submissive, tractable **2.** elastic, pliable, quaggy, resilient, soft, spongy, springy, supple, unresisting

yoke *n.* **1.** bond, chain, coupling, ligament, link, tie **2.** bondage, burden, enslavement, helotry, oppression, serfdom, service, servility, servitude, slavery, vassalage ~*vb.* **3.** bracket, connect, couple, harness, hitch, join, link, tie, unite

tached. *~vb* **yoking, yoked 6** to put a yoke on. **7** to unite or link.

yokel *n Disparaging* a person who lives in the country, esp. one who is simple and old-fashioned.

yolk *n* the yellow part in the middle of an egg that provides food for the developing embryo.

Yom Kippur *n* an annual Jewish holiday celebrated as a day of fasting, with prayers of penitence.

yon *adj* **1** *Chiefly Scot & N English dialect* that: *yon dog.* *~adv* **2** yonder: *he flicked glances hither and yon.* *~pron* **3** that person or thing: *yon was a pretty sight.*

yonder *adv* **1** over there. *~adj* **2** situated over there: *a tree at yonder waterfall.*

yonks *pl n Informal* a very long time: *he must have been planning this for yonks.*

yoo-hoo *interj* a call to attract a person's attention.

yore *n* **of yore** a long time ago: *in days of yore.*

yorker *n Cricket* a ball bowled so as to pitch just under or just beyond the bat.

Yorkist *English history ~n* **1** a supporter of the royal House of York, esp. during the Wars of the Roses. *~adj* **2** of or relating to the supporters or members of the House of York.

Yorks. Yorkshire.

Yorkshire pudding *n Chiefly Brit* a baked pudding made from a batter of flour, eggs, and milk, often served with roast beef.

you *pron* refers to: **1** the person or people addressed: *can I get you a drink?* **2** an unspecified person or people in general: *stick to British goods and you can't go wrong.* *~n* **3** *Informal* the personality of the person being addressed: *that hat isn't really you.*

you'd you had *or* you would.

you'll you will *or* you shall.

young *adj* **1** having lived or existed for a relatively short time. **2** having qualities associated with youth: *their innovative approach and young attitude appealed to him.* **3** of or relating to youth: *he'd been a terrorist himself in France in his young days.* **4** of a group representing the younger members of a larger organization: *Young Conservatives.* *~n* **5** young people in general: *that never seems very important to the young.* **6** offspring, esp. young animals: *a deer suckling her young.* **youngish** *adj*

youngster *n* a young person.

your *adj* **1** of, belonging to, or associated with you: *ask your doctor to make the necessary calls.* **2** of, belonging to, or associated with an unspecified person or people in general: *it is not right to take another baby to replace your own.* **3** *Informal* used to indicate all things or people of a certain type: *these characters are not your average housebreakers.*

you're you are.

yours *pron* **1** something belonging to you: *my reputation is better than yours.* **2** your family: *a blessed Christmas to you and yours.* **3** used in closing phrases at the end of a letter: *yours sincerely; yours faithfully.* **4 of yours** belonging to you: *that husband of yours.*

yourself *pron, pl* **-selves 1 a** the reflexive form of *you.* **b** used for emphasis: *you've stated publicly that you yourself use drugs.* **2** your normal self: *you're not yourself today.*

yours truly *pron Informal* I *or* me.

youth *n* **1** the period between childhood and maturity. **2** the quality or condition of being young, immature, or inexperienced: *his youth told against him in the contest.* **3** a young man or boy. **4** young people collectively: *there is still hope for today's youth.* **5** the freshness, vigour, or vitality associated with being young.

youth club *n* a club that provides leisure activities for young people.

youthful *adj* **1** vigorous or active: *the intermediate section was won by a youthful grandmother.* **2** of, relating to, possessing, or associated with youth: *youthful good looks.* **youthfully** *adv* **youthfulness** *n*

youth hostel *n* an inexpensive lodging place for young people travelling cheaply.

you've you have.

yowl *vb* **1** to produce a loud mournful wail or cry. *~n* **2** a wail or howl.

yo-yo *n, pl* **-yos 1** a toy consisting of a spool attached to a string, the end of which is held while it is repeatedly spun out and reeled in. *~vb* **yo-yoing, yo-yoed 2** to change repeatedly from one position to another.

yrs 1 years. **2** yours.

YST Yukon Standard Time.

YT Yukon Territory.

YTS (in Britain) Youth Training Scheme.

ytterbium (it-**terb**-ee-um) *n Chem* a soft silvery element that is used to improve the mechanical properties of steel. Symbol: Yb

yttrium (it-ree-um) *n Chem* a silvery metallic element used in various alloys and in lasers. Symbol: Y

yuan *n, pl* **-an** the standard monetary unit of the People's Republic of China.

yucca *n* a tropical plant with spiky leaves and white flowers.

yucky *or* **yukky** *adj* **yuckier, yuckiest** *or* **yukkier, yukkiest** *Slang* disgusting or nasty.

Yugoslav *adj* **1** of the former Yugoslavia. *~n* **2** a person from the former Yugoslavia.

Yule *n Literary or old-fashioned* Christmas or the Christmas season: *Yuletide.*

yummy *Slang ~adj* **-mier, -miest 1** delicious or attractive: *yummy sauces.* *~interj* **2** Also: **yum-yum** an exclamation indicating pleasure or delight, as in anticipation of delicious food.

Yuppie *n* **1** a young highly-paid professional person, esp. one who has a fashionable way of life. *~adj* **2** typical of or reflecting the values of Yuppies.

YWCA Young Women's Christian Association.

THESAURUS

yokel *disparaging* boor, bucolic, (country) bumpkin, countryman, hick (*informal, chiefly U.S. & Canad.*), hillbilly (*usually disparaging*), peasant, rustic

young *adj.* **1.** adolescent, callow, green, growing, immature, infant, in the springtime of life, junior, juvenile, little, unfledged, youthful **2.** at an early stage, early, fledgling, new, newish, not far advanced, recent, undeveloped *~n.* **3.** babies, brood, family, issue, litter, little ones, offspring, progeny

youngster boy, cub, girl, juvenile, kid (*informal*), lad, lass, shaver (*old-fashioned*), teenager, teenybopper (*old-fashioned slang*), urchin, young adult, young hopeful, young person, youth

youth 1. adolescence, boyhood, early life, girlhood, immaturity, juvenescence, salad days, young days **2.** adolescent, boy, kid (*informal*), lad, shaver (*old-fashioned*), stripling, teenager, young man, youngster **3.** teenagers, the rising generation, the young, younger generation, young people

youthful 1. active, fresh, spry, vigorous, young at heart, young looking **2.** boyish, childish, girlish, immature, inexperienced, juvenile, pubescent, puerile, young

Z

z *or* **Z** *n, pl* **z's, Z's,** *or* **Zs 1** the 26th and last letter of the English alphabet. **2 from A to Z** See **a** (sense 3).
z *Maths* (along with *x* and *y*) an unknown quantity.
Z *Chem* atomic number.
zabaglione (zab-al-**lyoh**-nee) *n* a dessert made of egg yolks, sugar, and wine, whipped together.
zany (**zane**-ee) *adj* **zanier, zaniest** comical in an endearing way.
zap *vb* **zapping, zapped** *Slang* **1** to kill, esp. by shooting. **2** to change television channels rapidly by remote control. **3** to move quickly.
zeal *n* great enthusiasm or eagerness, esp. for a religious movement.
zealot (**zel**-lot) *n* a fanatic or an extreme enthusiast. **zealotry** *n*
zealous (**zel**-luss) *adj* extremely eager or enthusiastic. **zealously** *adv*
zebra *n, pl* **-ras** *or* **-ra** a black-and-white striped African animal of the horse family.
zebra crossing *n Brit* a pedestrian crossing marked by broad black and white stripes: once on the crossing the pedestrian has right of way.
zebu (**zee**-boo) *n* a domesticated ox of Africa and Asia, with a humped back and long horns.
zed *n* the British spoken form of the letter *z.*
zee *n* the US spoken form of the letter *z.*
Zeitgeist (**tsite**-guyst) *n* the spirit or general outlook of a specific time or period.
Zen *n* a Japanese form of Buddhism that concentrates on learning through meditation and intuition.
Zend-Avesta *n* the Zoroastrian scriptures (the **Avesta**), together with the traditional interpretive commentary known as the **Zend.**
zenith *n* **1** the point in the sky directly above an observer. **2** the highest or most successful point of anything: *he was at the zenith of his military career.* **zenithal** *adj*
zephyr (**zef**-fer) *n* a soft gentle breeze.
Zeppelin *n* a large cylindrical rigid German airship of the early 20th century.
zero *n, pl* **-ros** *or* **-roes 1** the cardinal number between +1 and −1. **2** the symbol, 0, representing this number. **3** the line or point on a scale of measurement from which the graduations commence. **4** the lowest point or degree: *my credibility is down to zero.* **5** nothing or nil. **6** the temperature, pressure, etc., that registers a reading of zero on a scale. *~adj* **7** amounting to zero: *zero inflation.* **8** *Meteorol* (of visibility) limited to a very short distance. *~vb* **-roing, -roed 9** to adjust (an instrument or scale) so as to read zero.
zero gravity *n* the state of weightlessness.
zero hour *n* **1** *Mil* the time set for the start of an operation. **2** *Informal* a critical time, usually at the beginning of an action.
zero in on *vb* **1** to aim a weapon at (a target). **2** to concentrate one's attention on.
zero-rated *adj* denoting goods on which the buyer pays no value-added tax.
zest *n* **1** invigorating or keen excitement or enjoyment: *he has a zest for life and a quick intellect.* **2** added interest, flavour, or charm: *he said that she would provide a new zest for his government.* **3** the peel of an orange or lemon, used as flavouring. **zestful** *adj*
ziggurat *n* (in ancient Mesopotamia) a temple in the shape of a pyramid.
zigzag *n* **1** a line or course having sharp turns in alternating directions. *~adj* **2** formed in or proceeding in a zigzag. *~adv* **3** in a zigzag manner. *~vb* **-zagging, -zagged 4** to move in a zigzag.
zilch *n Slang, chiefly US & Canad* nothing.
zillion *n, pl* **-lions** *or* **-lion** (*often pl*) *Informal* an extremely large but unspecified number: *there are zillions of beautiful spots to visit.*
Zimmer *n Trademark* a tubular frame with rubber feet, used as a support to help disabled or infirm people walk.
zinc *n Chem* a brittle bluish-white metallic element that is used in alloys such as brass, to form a protective coating on metals, and in battery electrodes. Symbol: Zn
zinc ointment *n* a medicinal ointment consisting of zinc oxide, petroleum jelly, and paraffin.
zinc oxide *n Chem, pharmacol* a white insoluble powder used as a pigment and in making zinc ointment.
zing *n* **1** *Informal* the quality in something that makes it lively or interesting. **2** a short high-pitched buzzing sound, like the sound of a bullet or vibrating string.
zinnia *n* a plant of tropical and subtropical America, with solitary heads of brightly coloured flowers.
Zion *n* **1** the hill on which the city of Jerusalem stands. **2 a** the modern Jewish nation. **b** Israel as the national home of the Jewish people. **3** *Christianity* heaven.
Zionism *n* a political movement for the establishment and support of a national homeland for Jews in what is now Israel. **Zionist** *n, adj*
zip *n* **1** Also called: **zip fastener** a fastener with two parallel rows of metal or plastic teeth, one on either side of a closure, which are interlocked by a sliding tab. **2** *Informal* energy or vigour. **3** a short sharp whizzing sound, like the sound of a passing bullet. *~vb* **zipping, zipped 4** (often foll. by *up*) to fasten with a zip. **5** to move with a sharp whizzing sound: *bullets zipped and ricocheted all around us.* **6** to hurry or rush.
zip code *n* the US equivalent of **postcode.**
zipper *n US & Canad* same as **zip** (sense 1).
zippy *adj* **-pier, -piest** *Informal* full of energy.

THESAURUS

zeal ardour, devotion, eagerness, earnestness, enthusiasm, fanaticism, fervency, fervour, fire, gusto, keenness, militancy, passion, spirit, verve, warmth, zest
zealot bigot, enthusiast, extremist, fanatic, fiend (*informal*), maniac, militant
zealous ardent, burning, devoted, eager, earnest, enthusiastic, fanatical, fervent, fervid, impassioned, keen, militant, passionate, rabid, spirited
zenith acme, apex, apogee, climax, crest, height, high noon, high point, meridian, peak, pinnacle, summit, top, vertex
zero 1. cipher, naught, nil, nothing, nought **2.** bottom, lowest point *or* ebb, nadir, nothing, rock bottom
zero hour *informal* appointed hour, crisis, moment of decision, moment of truth, turning point, vital moment

zircon *n Mineral* a hard mineral consisting of zirconium silicate, used as a gemstone and in industry.

zirconium *n Chem* a greyish-white metallic element, occurring chiefly in zircon, that is exceptionally corrosion-resistant. Symbol: Zr

zit *n Slang* a spot or pimple.

zither *n* a musical instrument consisting of numerous strings stretched over a flat box and plucked to produce notes. **zitherist** *n*

Zn *Chem* zinc.

zodiac *n* **1** an imaginary belt in the sky within which the sun, moon, and planets appear to move, and which is divided into 12 equal areas called **signs of the zodiac,** each named after the constellation which once lay in it. **2** *Astrol* a diagram, usually circular, representing this belt. **zodiacal** *adj*

zombie *or* **zombi** *n, pl* **-bies** *or* **-bis** **1** a person who appears to be lifeless, apathetic, or totally lacking in independent judgment. **2** a corpse brought to life by witchcraft.

zone *n* **1** a region, area, or section characterized by some distinctive feature or quality: *a demilitarized zone.* **2** *Geog* one of the divisions of the earth's surface according to temperature. **3** a section on a transport route. **4** *Maths* a portion of a sphere between two parallel lines intersecting the sphere. **5** *NZ* a catchment area for a specific school. *~vb* **zoning, zoned 6** to divide (a place) into zones for different uses or activities. **zonal** *adj* **zoning** *n*

zonked *adj Slang* **1** highly intoxicated with drugs or alcohol. **2** exhausted.

zoo *n, pl* **zoos** a place where live animals are kept, studied, bred, and exhibited to the public.

zooid (**zoh**-oid) *n* **1** any independent animal body, such as an individual of a coral colony. **2** a cell or body, produced by an organism and capable of independent motion, such as a gamete.

zool. 1 zoological. 2 zoology.

zoological garden *n* the formal term for **zoo.**

zoology *n* the study of animals, including their classification, structure, physiology, and history. **zoological** *adj* **zoologist** *n*

zoom *vb* **1** to move very rapidly: *the first rocket zoomed into the sky.* **2** to increase or rise rapidly: *stocks zoomed on the American exchange.* **3** to move with or make a continuous buzzing or humming sound. *~n* **4** the sound or act of zooming. **5** a zoom lens.

zoom in *or* **out** *vb Photog, films, television* to increase or decrease rapidly the magnification of the image of a distant object by means of a zoom lens.

zoom lens *n* a lens system that can make the details of a picture larger or smaller while keeping the picture in focus.

zoophyte (**zoh**-a-fite) *n* any animal resembling a plant, such as a sea anemone.

Zoroastrianism (zorr-oh **ass** troo an iz zum) *or* **Zoroastrism** *n* the religion founded by the ancient Persian prophet Zoroaster, based on the concept of a continuous struggle between good and evil. **Zoroastrian** *adj, n*

zounds *interj Old-fashioned* a mild oath indicating surprise or indignation.

Zr *Chem* zirconium.

zucchetto (tsoo-**ket**-toe) *n, pl* **-tos** *RC Church* a small round skullcap worn by clergymen and varying in colour according to the rank of the wearer.

zucchini (zoo-**keen**-ee) *n, pl* **-ni** *or* **-nis** *Chiefly US, Canad, & Austral* a courgette.

Zulu *n* **1** (*pl* **-lus** *or* **-lu**) a member of a tall Black people of Southern Africa. **2** the language of this people.

zygote *n* the cell resulting from the union of an ovum and a spermatozoon.

THESAURUS

zest 1. appetite, delectation, enjoyment, gusto, keenness, relish, zeal, zing (*informal*) **2.** charm, flavour, interest, kick (*informal*), piquancy, pungency, relish, savour, smack, spice, tang, taste

zone area, belt, district, region, section, sector, sphere

Classical and Foreign Words and Phrases

Abbreviations – L. Latin; G. Greek; F. French; It. Italian; Ger. German

à bas [F.] down with.
ab initio [L.] from the beginning.
ab ovo [L.] from the beginning.
absit omen [L.] may there be no ill omen.
accouchement [F.] childbirth, confinement.
à cheval [F.] on horseback, astride.
à deux [F.] of, for two persons.
ad hoc [L.] for this special object.
ad hominem [L.] to the man.
ad infinitum [L.] to infinity.
ad interim [L.] in the meanwhile.
ad majorem Dei gloriam [L.] for the greater glory of God.
ad nauseam [L.] to the point of disgust.
ad referendum [L.] for consideration.
ad rem [L.] to the point.
adsum [L.] I am here: present!
affaire d'amour [F.] a love affair.
affaire d'honneur [F.] an affair of honour, a duel.
affaire du coeur [F.] an affair of the heart.
a fortiori [L.] with stronger reason.
agent provocateur [F.] a police or secret service spy.
aide mémoire [F.] memorandum; summary.
à la carte [F.] picking from the bill of fare; *see* **table d'hote**.
à la française [F.] in the French style.
à la mode [F.] in the fashion.
al dente [It.] cooked so as to be firm when eaten.
al fresco [It.] in the open air.
alma mater [L.] benign mother; the term is used by former students in referring to their university.
alter ego [L.] another self, a close friend.
alto relievo [It.] high relief.
amende honorable [F.] apology.
amor patriae [L.] love of country.
amour propre [F.] self-esteem.
ancien régime [F.] the old order.
anglice [L.] in English.
anno Domini [L.] in the year of our Lord.
anno regni [L.] in the year of the reign.
anno urbis conditae [L.] (**A.U.C.**) in the year from the time of the building of the City (Rome).
annus mirabilis [L.] year of wonder.
ante meridiem [L.] before noon.
aperçu [F.] summary; insight.
à propos [F.] to the point.
arrière-pensée [F.] mental reservation.
arrivederci [It.] goodbye.
au contraire [F.] on the contrary.
au courant [F.] fully acquainted (with).
au fait [F.] fully informed; expert.
au fond [F.] fundamentally; essentially.
au naturel [F.] naked; uncooked or plainly cooked.
au revoir [F.] good-bye, till we meet again.
auf Wiedersehen [Ger.] good-bye, till we meet again.
auto da fé [Portuguese] act of faith, the public burning of heretics.

beau geste [F.] noble or gracious act.
beau idéal [F.] ideal excellence, imagined state of perfection.
beau monde [F.] fashionable world.
bel esprit [F.] a man of wit.
bête noire [F.] an object of special detestation, pet aversion.
billet doux [F.] a love-letter.
blitzkrieg [Ger.] lightning war.
bona fide [L.] in good faith.
bonhomie [F.] good nature.
bonjour [F.] good-morning, good-day.
bon marché [F.] cheaply.
bonne bouche [F.] titbit.
bonsoir [F.] good-evening, good-night.
bon ton [F.] good breeding.

carpe diem [L.] enjoy the present day.
carte blanche [F.] full powers.
casus belli [L.] something which involves war.
cause célèbre [F.] famous lawsuit or controversy.
ça va sans dire [F.] that is a matter of course.
caveat emptor [L.] let the buyer beware.
cave canem [L.] beware of the dog.
c'est la vie [F.] that's life.
ceteris paribus [L.] other things being equal.
chacun à son gout [F.] every one to his taste.
chef-d'oeuvre [F.] masterpiece.
cherchez la femme [F.] look for the woman; there is a woman at the bottom of the business.
che sarà, sarà [It.] what will be, will be.
ciao [It.] hello, goodbye.
ci-devant [F.] former.
cogito, ergo sum [L.] I think, therefore I am.
comme il faut [F.] as it should be.
compos mentis [L.] sane.
compte rendu [F.] a report.

con amore [It.] with love, earnestly.
concierge [F.] a porter or doorkeeper.
coram populo [L.] in the presence of the people, openly.
corpus delicti [L.] the substance of the offence; the body of the victim of murder.
corrigenda [L.] things to be corrected.
coup d'état [F.] a stroke of policy, a sudden decisive political move, an abuse of authority.
coup de foudre [F.] sudden amazing event.
coup de grâce [F.] a finishing blow.
coup de théâtre [F.] a theatrical effect, a sudden change in a situation.
cui bono? [L.] for whose benefit is it? (i.e. the crime – in a law-case).
cum grano salis [L.] with a grain of salt, with reservation.

de facto [L.] actually, in fact.
Dei gratia [L.] by the grace of God.
de jure [L.] in law, by right.
de mortuis nil nisi bonum [L.] say nothing but good about the dead.
de novo [L.] anew.
Deo gratias [L.] thanks to God.
Deo volente [L.] (**D.V.**) God willing.
de profundis [L.] out of the depths. (The first words of the Latin version of Psalm 130.)
de rigueur [F.] indispensable, obligatory.
dernier cri [F.] latest fashion.
de trop [F.] superfluous, intrusive.
deus ex machina [L.] literally, a god out of the (theatrical) machine, i.e. a too obvious device in the plot of a play or story.
dies non [L.] a day on which judges do not sit.
Dieu et mon droit [F.] God and my right; motto of the British crown.
disjecta membra [L.] the scattered remains.
distingué [F.] of distinguished appearance.
distrait [F.] absent-minded.
dolce far niente [It.] pleasant idleness.
double entendre [F.] double meaning.
douceur [F.] a tip, a bribe.
dramatis personae [L.] the characters in a drama.

ecce homo! [L.] behold the man! (Spoken by Pilate; St. John, c.19, v.5.)
embarras de richesses [F.] perplexing wealth.
emeritus [L.] retired from office.
éminence grise [F.] person who wields power unofficially or behind the scenes.
en famille [F.] with one's family; at home informally.
enfant terrible [F.] literally, "a terrible child."
en fête [F.] on holiday, in a state of festivity.
en masse [F.] in a body.
en passant [F.] in passing, by the way.
en rapport [F.] in sympathy with.
en règle [F.] in due order.
en route [F.] on the way; march!
entente cordiale [F.] friendly understanding between two nations.
entre nous [F.] between ourselves.
e pluribus unum [L.] one out of many. (Motto of the U.S.A.)
erratum (*pl.* **errata**) [L.] error.
esprit de corps [F.] team-spirit.
eureka! (heureka) [G.] I have found it! (The exclamation of Archimedes.)
ex cathedra [L.] from the chair of office, hence, authoritatively.
exeat [L.] literally, "let him go out"; formal leave of absence.
exempli gratia [L.] (e.g.) for example.
exeunt omnes [L.] all go out.
exit [L.] goes out.
ex libris [L.] from the books ... (followed by the name of the owner).
ex officio [L.] by virtue of his office.
ex parte [L.] on one side, partisan.

facile princeps [L.] an easy first.
fait accompli [F.] a thing done.
faute de mieux [F.] for lack of anything better.
faux pas [F.] a false step, a mistake.
felo de se [L.] a suicide, literally, a "felon of himself."
femme fatale [F.] seductive woman.
festina lente [L.] hasten slowly.
fête champêtre [F.] a rural festival.
feu de joie [F.] a bonfire; gun salute.
fiat lux [L.] let there be light.
fidei defensor [L.] defender of the faith.
fille de joie [F.] prostitute.
fin de siècle [F.] end of the 19th century; decadent.
finis [L.] the end.
flagrante delicto [L.] in the very act, red-handed.
folie de grandeur [F.] delusions of grandeur.
fons et origo [L.] the source and origin.

gaudeamus igitur [L.] let us then rejoice.
gendarme [F.] one of the *gendarmerie*, a body of armed police in France.

haute couture [F.] high fashion.
haute cuisine [F.] high-class cooking.
hic jacet [L.] here lies.
honi soit qui mal y pense [Old F.] shame to him who thinks ill of it.
horribile dictu [L.] horrible to relate.
hors de combat [F.] out of condition to fight.

ibidem (abbreviated as **ib**, or **ibid**;) [L.] in the same place.
ich dien [Ger.] I serve.
idée fixe [F.] an obsession, monomania.
id est [L.] (usually **i.e.**) that is.
idem [L.] the same.
ignis fatuus [L.] a will-o'-the-wisp.
imprimatur [L.] literally, "let it be printed", a licence to print, sanction.
in camera [L.] in a (judge's private) room.
in extremis [L.] at the point of death.
infra dignitatem [L.] (**infra dig.**) below one's dignity.
in loco parentis [L.] in the place of a parent.
in medias res [L.] into the midst of things.
in memoriam [L.] to the memory of.
in perpetuum [L.] for ever.
in re [L.] in the matter of.
in situ [L.] in its original position.
in statu quo [L.] in the former state.
inter alia [L.] among other things.
in toto [L.] entirely.
in vino veritas [L.] in wine the truth (comes out).
ipse dixit [L.] "he himself said it"; his unsupported word.
ipsissima verba [L.] the very words.
ipso facto [L.] by the fact itself.

je ne sais quoi [F.] "I don't know what", a something or other.
jeu d'esprit [F.] a witticism.
joie de vivre [F.] joy of living; ebullience.

laissez faire [F.] policy of inaction.
lapsus linguae [L.] a slip of the tongue.
lares et penates [L.] household gods.
leitmotif [Ger.] a theme used to indicate a person, idea, etc. in opera, etc.
lèse-majesté [F.] high treason.
l'état, c'est moi [F.] I am the state. (Saying of Louis XIV).
lettre de cachet [F.] a sealed letter; a royal warrant for imprisonment.
locum tenes [L.] "one occupying the place", a deputy or substitute.

magnum opus [L.] a great work.
mal à propos [F.] ill-timed.
mal de mer [F.] sea-sickness.
malentendu [F.] a misunderstanding.
manqué [F.] potential; would-be.
mariage de convenance [F.] a marriage from motives of interest rather than love.
mauvaise honte [F.] false modesty, bashfulness.
mauvais quart d'heure [F.] a brief unpleasant experience.
mea culpa [L.] by my fault.
memento mori [L.] remember death.
ménage à trois [F.] sexual arrangement involving a married couple and the lover of one of them.
mens sana in corpore sano [L.] a sound mind in a sound body.
mésalliance [F.] marriage with someone of lower social status.
meum et tuum [L.] mine and thine.
mirabile dictu [L.] wonderful to relate.
mise en scène [F.] scenic setting.
modus operandi [L.] manner of working.
mot juste [F.] the exact right word.
moue [F.] a disdainful or pouting look.
multum in parvo [L.] much in little.
mutatis mutandis [L.] with the necessary changes.

née [F.] "born", her maiden name being; e.g. *Mrs. Brown née Smith*.
nemine contradicente [L.] (often as **nem.con.**) without opposition.
nemo me impune lacessit [L.] no one hurts me with impunity.
ne plus ultra [L.] nothing further; the uttermost point.
nihil obstat [L.] there is no obstacle.
nil desperandum [L.] despair of nothing.
noblesse oblige [F.] nobility imposes obligations.
nolens volens [L.] whether he will or not.
noli me tangere [L.] don't touch me.
nom de guerre [F.] an assumed name. (**nom de plume** is hardly used in French.)
non compos mentis [L.] insane.
non sequitur [L.] it does not follow.
nota bene [L.] (**N.B.**) note well.
nous avons changé tout cela [F.] we have changed all that.
nouveau riche [F.] one newly enriched, an upstart.
nulli secundus [L.] second to none.

obiit [L.] he (or she) died.
obiter dictum [L.] (*pl.* **obiter dicta**) something said by the way.

on dit [F.] they say; a rumour.
ora pro nobis [L.] pray for us.
O tempora! O mores! [L.] literally, "O the times! O the manners!"; what dreadful times and doings.

pace [L.] by leave of.
par avion [F.] by aeroplane (of mail sent by air).
par excellence [F.] pre-eminently.
pari passu [L.] with equal pace; together.
passim [L.] here and there, everywhere.
pax vobiscum [L.] peace be with you.
peccavi [L.] I have sinned.
per ardua ad astra [L.] through difficulties to the stars.
persona non grata [L.] unacceptable or unwelcome person.
post hoc, ergo propter hoc [L.] after this, therefore because of this (a fallacy in reasoning.)
pour encourager les autres [F.] in order to encourage the others.
prima facie [L.] at a first view.
primus inter pares [L.] first among equals.
pro patria [L.] for one's country.
pro tempore [L.] for the time being.

quis custodiet ipsos custodes? [L.] who will guard the guards?
qui vive? [F.] who goes there?
quod erat demonstrandum [L.] **(Q.E.D.)** which was to be proved.
quot homines, tot sententiae [L.] as many men as there are opinions.
quo vadis? [L.] whither goest thou?

rara avis [L.] a rare bird, something prodigious.
reductio ad absurdum [L.] a reducing to the absurd.
répondez s'il vous plait [F.] **(R.S.V.P.)** please reply.
requiescat in pace [L.] **(R.I.P.)** may he (or she) rest in peace.
rus in urbe [L.] the country in the town.

sans peur et sans reproche [F.] without fear and without reproach.
sans souci [F.] without care.
sauve qui peut [F.] save himself who can – the cry of disorderly retreat.
semper fidelis [L.] always faithful.
seriatim [L.] in order.
sic [L.] thus. Often used to call attention to some quoted mistake.
sic transit gloria mundi [L.] so passes the glory of the world.
sine die [L.] without date, indefinitely postponed.
si monumentum requiris, circumspice [L.] if you seek (his) monument, look around you. (The inscription on the architect Wren's tomb in St. Paul's.)
sine qua non [L.] an indispensable condition.
soi-disant [F.] so-called; self-styled.
status quo [L.] "the state in which", the pre-existing state of affairs.
stet [L.] let it stand.
Sturm und Drang [Ger.] storm and stress.
sub judice [L.] under consideration.
sub rosa [L.] "under the rose", secretly.
sub voce [L.] under that heading.
sursum corda [L.] lift up your hearts (to God).

table d'hôte [F.] general guest-table, meal at a fixed price.
tant mieux [F.] so much the better.
tant pis [F.] so much the worse.
tempore [L.] in the time of.
tempus fugit [L.] time flies.
terra firma [L.] solid earth.
terra incognita [L.] unexplored land or area of study.
tour de force [F.] a feat of strength or skill.
tout de suite [F.] at once.
tout ensemble [F.] the whole taken together, the general effect.
tout le monde [F.] all the world, everyone.

ubique [L.] everywhere.
ultima Thule [L.] the utmost boundary or limit.
ultra vires [L.] beyond one's powers.

vade in pace [L.] go in peace.
vade mecum [L.] go with me; a constant companion, work of reference.
vale [L.] farewell.
veni, vidi, vici [L.] I came, I saw, I conquered.
ventre à terre [F.] belly to the ground; at high speed.
verbum sapienti satis [L.] **(verb.sap.)** a word is enough for a wise man.
via media [L.] a middle course.
videlicet [L.] **(viz.)** namely, to wit.
volente Deo [L.] God willing.

Weltschmerz [Ger.] world-weariness; sentimental pessimism.

Zeitgeist [Ger.] the spirit of the times.

Group Names and Collective Nouns

barren of mules
bevy of quails
bevy of roes
brace or lease of bucks
brood or covey of grouse
brood of hens or chickens
building or clamour of rooks
bunch, company or knob of wigeon (in the water)
bunch, knob or spring of teal
cast of hawks
cete of badgers
charm of goldfinches
chattering of choughs
clowder of cats
colony of gulls (breeding)
covert of coots
covey of partridges
cowardice of curs
desert of lapwings
dopping of sheldrakes
down or husk of hares
drove or herd of cattle (kine)
exaltation of larks
fall of woodcocks
field or string of racehorses
flight of wigeon (in the air)
flight or dule of doves
flight of swallows
flight of dunlins
flight, rush, bunch or knob of pochards
flock or flight of pigeons
flock of sheep
flock of swifts
flock or gaggle of geese
flock, congregation, flight or volery of birds
gaggle of geese (on the ground)
gang of elk
haras (stud) of horses
herd of antelopes
herd of buffaloes
herd, sedge or siege of cranes
herd of curlews
herd of deer
herd of giraffes
herd or tribe of goats
herd or pod of seals
herd or bevy of swans
herd of ponies
herd of swine
hill of ruffs
host of sparrows
kindle of kittens
labour of moles
leap of leopards
litter of cubs
litter of pups or pigs
litter of whelps
murmuration of starlings
muster of peacocks
nest of rabbits
nye or nide of pheasants
pace or herd of asses
pack of grouse
pack, mute or cry of hounds
pack, rout or herd of wolves
paddling of ducks
plump, sord or sute of wildfowl
pod of whiting
pride or troop of lions
rag of colts
richesse of martens
run of poultry
school or run of whales
school or gam of porpoises
sedge or siege of bitterns
sedge or siege of herons
shoal or glean of herrings
shoal, draught, haul, run or catch of fish
shrewdness of apes
skein of geese (in flight)
skulk of foxes
sloth of bears
sord or sute of mallards
sounder of boars
sounder or dryft of swine
stand or wing of plovers
stud of mares
swarm of insects
swarm or grist of bees, or flies
swarm or cloud of gnats
tok of capercailzies
team of ducks (in flight)
troop of kangaroos
troop of monkeys
walk or wisp of snipe
watch of nightingales
yoke, drove, team or herd of oxen

Signs of the Zodiac

Aquarius · Aries · Cancer · Capricorn · Gemini · Leo
Libra · Pisces · Sagittarius · Scorpio · Taurus · Virgo

Characters in Classical Mythology

Achilles	Cupid	Hydra	Pandora
Actaeon	Cybele	Icarus	Paris
Adonis	Cyclopes	Iris	Pegasus
Aeneas	Daedalus	Janus	Penelope
Agamemnon	Demeter	Jason	Persephone
Ajax	Diana	Jocasta	Perseus
Amazons	Dido	Juno	Phoebus
Andromeda	Dionysus	Jupiter	Pleiades
Antigone	dryads	Leda	Pluto
Aphrodite	Echidna	Mars	Poseidon
Apollo	Electra	Medea	Priam
Arachne	Eros	Medusa	Prometheus
Ares	Eurydice	Mercury	Psyche
Argonauts	Galatea	Midas	Pygmalion
Ariadne	Ganymede	Minerva	Remus
Artemis	Gorgons	Minotaur	Romulus
Atalanta	griffin / gryphon	Muses	Saturn
Athena / Athene	Hades	Narcissus	satyrs
Atlas	hamadryads	Nemesis	Selene
Aurora	Harpies	Neptune	sibyl
Bacchus	Hebe	Nereids	Sirens
Bellona	Hecate	Niobe	Sisyphus
Boreas	Hector	Oceanids	Sphinx
Cassandra	Hecuba	Odysseus	Tantalus
Cassiopeia	Helen	Oedipus	Tiresias
centaurs	Hephaestus	oreads	Titans
Charon	Hera	Orestes	Triton
Charybdis	Heracles / Hercules	Orion	Uranus
Chimaera	Hermaphroditus	Orpheus	Venus
Circe	Hermes	Pallas	Vulcan
Cronus		Pan	Zeus

Months in the French Revolutionary Calendar

Brumaire · Floréal · Frimaire · Fructidor · Germinal · Messidor
Nivôse · Pluviôse · Prairial · Thermidor · Vendémiaire · Ventôse

Months in the Hebrew Calendar

Adar · Av · Elul · Heshvan · Iyar · Kislev
Nisan · Shevat · Sivan · Tammuz · Tevet · Tishri

Planets of the Solar System

Earth · Jupiter · Mars · Mercury · Neptune
Pluto · Saturn · Uranus · Venus

Chemical Elements

actinium
aluminium
americium
antimony
argon
arsenic
astatine
barium
berkelium
beryllium
bismuth
bohrium
boron
bromine
cadmium
caesium
calcium
californium
carbon
cerium
chlorine
chromium
cobalt
copper
curium
dubnium
dysprosium
einsteinium
erbium
europium
fermium
fluorine
francium
gadolinium
gallium
germanium
gold
hafnium
hassium
helium
holmium
hydrogen
indium
iodine
iridium
iron
krypton
lanthanum
lawrencium
lead
lithium
lutetium
magnesium
manganese
meitnerium
mendelevium
mercury
molybdenum
neodymium
neon
neptunium
nickel
niobium
nitrogen
nobelium
osmium
oxygen
palladium
phosphorus
platinum
plutonium
plonium
potassium
praseodymium
promethium
protactinium
radium
radon
rhenium
rhodium
rubidium
ruthenium
rutherfordium
samarium
scandium
seaborgium
selenium
silicon
silver
sodium
strontium
sulphur
tantalum
technetium
tellurium
terbium
thallium
thorium
thulium
tin
titanium
tungsten
uranium
vanadium
xenon
ytterbium
yttrium
zinc
zirconium

Books of the Bible (including the Apocrypha)

Acts of the Apostles
Amos
Baruch
Chronicles
Colossians
Corinthians
Daniel
Daniel and Susanna
Daniel, Bel, and the Snake
Deuteronomy
Ecclesiastes
Ecclesiasticus
Ephesians
Esdras
Esther
Exodus
Ezekiel
Ezra
Galatians
Genesis
Habbakuk
Haggai
Hebrews
Hosea
Isaiah
James
Jeremiah
Job
Joel
John
Jonah
Joshua
Jude
Judges
Judith
Kings
Lamentations
Leviticus
Luke
Maccabees
Malachi
Manasseh
Mark
Matthew
Micah
Nahum
Nehemiah
Numbers
Obadiah
Peter
Philemon
Philippians
Proverbs
Psalms
Revelations
Romans
Ruth
Samuel
Solomon
Song of Songs
Song of the Three
Thessalonians
Timothy
Titus
Tobit
Zechariah
Zephaniah

WEDDING ANNIVERSARIES

Year	Traditional	Modern
1st	Paper	Clocks
2nd	Cotton	China
3rd	Leather	Crystal, glass
4th	Linen (silk)	Electrical Appliances
5th	Wood	Silverware
6th	Iron	Wood
7th	Wool (copper)	Desksets
8th	Bronze	Linen, lace
9th	Pottery (china)	Leather
10th	Tin (aluminium)	Diamond jewellery
11th	Steel	Fashion jewellery; accessories
12th	Silk	Pearls or coloured jewels
13th	Lace	Textiles, furs
14th	Ivory	Gold jewellery
15th	Crystal	Watches
20th	China	Platinum
25th	Silver	Sterling silver
30th	Pearl	Diamond
35th	Coral (jade)	Jade
40th	Ruby	Ruby
45th	Sapphire	Sapphire
50th	Gold	Gold
55th	Emerald	Emerald
60th	Diamond	Diamond

Language In Action

Supplement

TABLE OF CONTENTS

INTRODUCTION

Throughout life you often need to communicate your thoughts and feelings in writing. Writing concise and effective letters, speeches, and emails is easy, once you know exactly what you want to say. This supplement covers the basic rules of style and form to follow, whether you are writing a business letter or a text message to a friend. Whatever you need to write, however, the two most important rules for expressing yourself through language are simple, but often ignored:

✔ Be clear

Choose words that occur to you naturally and convey exactly what you mean. If you have a choice between a basic word and a showy one, choose the basic one. Do not repeat yourself, exaggerate, or stray from your main topic. To find the best words to express your thoughts, particularly on difficult or complex subjects, refer to this dictionary and a good thesaurus. Check that each sentence flows easily, and sends a clear message.

✔ Think of your audience

When writing to or for someone, think of that specific person's position, interests, and relationship to you. What information does he or she need from you? How can you persuade him or her to do what you ask? What language would this person best understand? When writing to strangers or business contacts, write in a polite and formal style. When writing to close friends, you are free to use more casual and personal language, including slang. People always respond better to letters that show regard for who they are and what matters to them.

This guide outlines everything you should need to know to communicate effectively and clearly through writing in all areas of life. It shows examples of good letters for work, school, money matters, and social situations. It covers basic rules of etiquette for emails, and text messaging language. It also includes advice for writing and delivering confident and memorable speeches.

Every section of this supplement provides practical answers to frequently asked questions (FAQs) about the format and words required for a particular situation. This guide also suggests useful phrases that you might include in your writing. For each topic and situation, it gives useful tips and examples, and advice regarding how and when to approach a particular subject.

Think through what you want to say. Then use this supplement to write it down in a style that will smoothly communicate your message to your audience.

JOB APPLICATIONS

FAQ

Q. *Should my letter be typed or handwritten?*
A. It should be typed on A4 paper. Only the signature should be handwritten.

Q. *To whom should I address my letter?*
A. If you do not know the name of the person who would deal with your application, call the company to find out their name.

Q. *Is it OK to send out the same letter to all those companies I'm interested in?*
A. No. Try to avoid generalisable letters. Find out as much as you can about the company, and tailor your letter accordingly.

Q. *Should I mention salary in my accompanying letter?*
A. It is usually best not to touch on the subject of salary at this stage, unless requested in the advertisement.

Useful phrases

First of all, identify the job you are applying for:

- I would like to inquire as to whether there are any openings for junior telesales operators in your company.
- I am writing to apply for the post of senior marketing manager.
- I would like to apply for the position of online learning co-ordinator, as advertised on your website.
- I am writing to apply for the above post, as advertised in *the Guardian* of 8 August 2003.

Next, give some examples of personal achievements:

- I have gained experience in several major aspects of publishing.
- I co-ordinated the change-over from one accounting system to another.
- I developed designs for a new range of knitwear.
- I have supervised a team of telesales operators on several projects.
- I contributed to the development of our new database software.

Then outline your personal qualities:

- I see myself as systematic and meticulous in my approach to work.
- I am a fair and broad-minded person, with an ability to get on well with people from all walks of life.
- I am hardworking and business minded, and I tend to thrive under pressure.

Explain why you want this job:

- I am now keen to find a post with more responsibility.
- I now wish to find a more permanent full-time position.
- I would like to further my career in the field of production.
- I feel that your company's activities most closely match my own values and interests.

Express your willingness to attend an interview.

• Application for an advertised post

✓ When applying for an advertised post, ensure that you head the letter with the exact name of the post, quoting any reference number given.

45 Fairways
Little Fordnam
Northumberland
N21 3RS

30 June 2003

Mrs F Reid
Recruitment Officer
Affinity Development Projects
3 Albion Court
Newcastle
N4 7JS

Dear Mrs Reid

application for post of Community Development Officer: post no: 513/6

I am writing in response to your advertisement in the June edition of *Community Now*, and am enclosing my CV for your review.

As you will see, I have gained valuable experience in working with Black and Asian communities, and have a strong understanding of community development. I am self-motivating, and can work as an effective leader of a team.

In my current position at the Northumberland Renewal Programme, I have initiated a strategic framework for obtaining funding and attaining targets.

I am at present completing a distance-learning course on Equality and Diversity Policy Development, and am now looking for a post which gives me an opportunity to use my new skills.

I look forward to having the opportunity to discuss this further with you.

Yours sincerely

Brian Hanlan

Brian Hanlan

• A speculative job application

✓ When applying for a job on a speculative basis, try to speak to the person responsible for recruitment in the appropriate department beforehand. This way, you will have a specific person to write to, as well as having established a relationship with them.

34 St Dunstan's Way
Hove
BN13 5HY

19 July 2003

Ms D Wallis
Youngs Accountancy and Finance
19 Lockwood Road
Brighton
BN2 6HM

Dear Ms Wallis

post of software development co-ordinator

Thank you very much for taking the time to speak to me yesterday about the possibility of a position as software development co-ordinator with your company.

Please find attached a CV which highlights my prior professional experience, and the qualities which I feel make me suited to this position. You will see that I have a strong interest in, and knowledge of, staff management, and have gained extensive experience in handling large development projects and meeting deadlines.

I see myself as being well-organized and self-motivated, and have excellent communication skills. I am keen to develop my career with Youngs Accountancy and Finance, and so would very much appreciate the opportunity to discuss further my suitability for the post.

Please feel free to contact me, either by email: smitchell@netserve.com, or by leaving a message on 01783 639012. I look forward to speaking to you soon.

Yours sincerely

D Gorman

Deborah Gorman

WRITING A CV

FAQ

Q. *How should a CV be presented?*

A. It should be constructed on a word-processor, well laid out and printed on a good quality printer. Do not use too many different font types and sizes. Use bullets or similar to start sub-sections or lists.

Q. *I usually send the same CV out to all potential employers. But should I be tailoring it to different jobs?*

A. Yes, you should. Consider carefully how your skills, education, and experience compare with the skills that the job requires. Ask for more detail if needed. Spend time researching the employer - their structure, products and approach.

Q. *What details do I need to include in my CV?*

A. You should include the following:

personal details: name, home address, phone number, email address, URL of your own web page if you have one, date of birth.

education: Give places of education where you have studied, with most recent first.

work experience: List your most recent experience first. Give the name of your employer, job title, and what you actually did and achieved in that job. Make sure all time periods are accounted for.

interests: If you are just entering the work force, and have little employment experience, an employer will be particularly interested in activities where you have leadership or responsibility, or which involve you in relating to others in a team.

skills: Ability in other languages, computing experience, or possession of a driving licence should be included.

references: Usually give two names. Make sure that referees are willing to give you a reference. If you do not wish to name them on your CV, it is perfectly acceptable to write 'on request'.

Q. *How long should my CV be?*

A. Keep it as short and relevant as possible. One page is ideal. It should not normally be longer than three pages.

Q. *I've heard people talk about writing a 'personal objective statement' at the top of a CV. Is this expected/appropriate?*

A. It can be a good idea to start with a personal objective statement. This is a short overview of your skills, qualities, hopes and plans. If you are replying to a specific job advertisement, review what key words and tasks were used. Which of these words apply to you? Use these words in your statement. But if you do not feel confident about doing this, there is no obligation to include one.

WRITING A CV

• Basic graduate CV

CV

Kate Maxwell

Date of birth	29.02.75
Address	19, The Poplars Bristol B10 2JU
Telephone	0117 123 4567
Email	katemaxwell@atlantic.net
Nationality	British

Education

1994–1998	**BA Hons in Modern Languages, University of Exeter** (final grade 2.1)
1992–1994	**Clifton Road Secondary School**: 3 'A' levels - French (A) German (A) History (B)
1987–1992	**Clifton Road Secondary School**: 8 GCSEs including Maths and English

Employment history

1994–1995	**Sales Assistant, Langs Bookshop, Bristol** I was responsible for training and supervising weekend and holiday staff.
1995–1996	**English Assistant, Lycée Benoit, Lyons** I taught conversational English to pupils aged 12-18, preparing the older students for both technical and more academic qualifications. I organized an educational trip to the UK for fourth-year pupils.

Positions of responsibility held

1995–1996	**Entertainments Officer for University Student Social Society** I organized and budgeted for entertainment for a student society with over 1000 members.
1994 – present	**Captain of the university women's netball team** I was in charge of training, organizing and motivating the women's team from 1995 to date.

Other skills

Fluent French and German

Extensive knowledge of Microsoft Word, Excel and Access

I hold a clean driving licence

References

on request

• CV for experienced candidate

CV

Andrew Baird
134 Newton Road, Lincoln, LI5 6HB
tel: 01453 678234
email: abaird@coms.net
date of birth: 8 September 1965

Work experience

1995 to present

Coogan and Kidd Web Design Ltd, Lincoln – Website Developer

- Development of company website
- Responsible for team of 8 staff
- Project management: have led several projects providing web design and support for a number of leading insurance companies
- Training: overseeing development of technical training programmes
- Customer support: following up and advising customers on website management
- Quality assurance
- Information architecture

1990–1995

Centaur Software Development, Cambridge – Computer Programmer

- programming
- database design: set up database for network of travel companies
- software design: assisted in the design of financial management application for use by financial advisers

Programming languages

C, C++, Java, Perl, Visual Basic, VBScript, JavaScript

Applications

Visual Interdev, Dreamweaver

Servers

Apache, IIS

Other skills

clean driving licence held

Education

1999 – Microsoft Certified Systems Engineer+Internet
1990 – MSc Multimedia Design
1988 – BSc Computer Science (2.1)

References

on request

• Writing business letters

FAQ

Q. *Is there a particular style I should use?*

A. Most companies have their own way of doing things. They have a 'house style' for layout and punctuation so if you are unsure or new to a company, look back in the filing to find out which style has been used as the house style.

Q. *What do I need to include in a business letter?*

A. You should include: the company letterhead; the letter reference; date; addressee's name and address; salutation(opening); subject heading, body of the letter; subscription (closing); signature or signatory.

Tips

- Keep letters short and to the point.
- The subject heading indicates the subject of the letter for quick reference and should only be two or three words.
- Make sure you open with a statement of intent and close with a request or promise of action.
- Avoid using ambiguous words or phrases. If there is any chance of a misunderstanding, find an alternative way to say it.
- Think out your letter before you start to compose it. Make notes if it helps to organize the information in a logical order.
- Remember that the standard method of closing before the signature depends on the opening at the start of the letter. If you opened with 'Dear Sir', you should close with 'Yours faithfully', if you opened with 'Dear Mr....' you should close with 'Yours sincerely'.
- All parts of a letter are designed to give important information. If your letters give accurate information, you will increase efficiency.
- If you can amend a standard or similar letter to say what you need to say, do so. It will save you time.
- If the sender is not available to sign, the letter can be signed *per procurationem* ('for and on behalf of') by another person (the signatory). This is indicated by the abbreviation 'pp' written or typed before the signatory.
- Always proofread your letters for spelling errors and other details. Don't rely on your computer spell-check facility.
- If the letter has been marked 'Personal', 'Private' or 'Confidential', ensure that the envelope has been marked in the same way. Private means personal, confidential means sensitive.

Useful phrases

- Thank you for your letter/email …
- With regard to … I am writing to …
- Further to our recent telephone conversation …
- Further to your recent email …
- If you require further information please don't hesitate to get in touch.

Ms R. Aitchison
124, Raven Road
HARROGATE
HG2 8OP

27th January, 2003

Dear Ms Aitchison

I am writing to thank you for coming down to Oxford yesterday so that we could discuss the possibility of our company taking over responsibility for publishing *The Big Book of Yo-Yos*. This is an exciting opportunity for us and I hope that we are able to reach a mutually beneficial agreement.

I will present this title to my sales and marketing team at our regular meeting midweek, and will then take the proposal to the more formal acquisitions meeting early next week. I have sounded my marketing director out already and he is as enthusiastic as I am to publish your book, so I am not anticipating too many problems getting a positive response from the sales team.

I will also look at the financial side of the project, and you are kindly going to send me a copy of your current contract, detailing royalty rates. I have requested a copy of our standard author contract from the legal department and will forward this to you as soon as it arrives.

I enjoyed meeting you on Friday and hope that this is the start of a fruitful relationship. I will of course keep you up to date with progress.

Yours sincerely

James Nichols

James Nichols
Publishing Manager

• Writing memoranda

FAQ

Q. *What is a memorandum?*

A. A memorandum (or memo) is a short letter or note sent to a particular in-house member of staff or circulated to groups of people.

Q. *Can I send a memo to someone in another company?*

A. Memos are not usually sent out of house.

Q. *What information does a memo usually contain?*

A. A memo usually contains: the sender's name and department; the addressee's name and department; date; and the subject.

Q. *Can memos be used for confidential information and do they need a signature?*

A. They are not normally used for confidential information, but if they are they should be placed in a sealed envelope marked 'Confidential'. Memos are not usually signed, but if they contain financial information it may be usual for the sender to add initials as confirmation.

Q. *Do I need to keep a copy?*

A. Always keep and file copies of all memoranda, as with other forms of correspondence.

To: Amy Wall
Publishing Production

From: Lorna Gilmour
Editorial Department

23/01/03

THE BIG BOOK OF YO-YOS
TEXT PRINTING COPY

Amy,
With regard to passing the book for press, I enclose the text printing copy:
- complete set of text pages, with book pages marked and margins ruled up for all prelims.
- pagination and margins list.
- sheet showing book pages and their content.

Please pass this and request a full set of proofs from the printer for checking.

Cover copy for this edition already passed.

Thanks,
Lorna

Writing business reports

FAQ

Q. *How do I start?*

A. You will find it much easier to write if you have a clear idea in your mind of the line of argument you want to take before you begin to write. Begin by making a note of all the evidence you have amassed and decide on a line of argument. Group together the evidence under various headings and gradually the argument will begin to take shape.

Q. *What should a report contain?*

A. Reports should include: a heading; a reason for the report; an argument; and a conclusion or recommendation.

Q. *How do I persuade the reader to accept my proposal?*

A. The golden rule is to find out what the priorities of your reader are, and then write the report from that point of view.

Tips

- Aim to be accurate, concise and brief.
- Never use words that you don't understand. Keep jargon to a minimum, but use technical words accurately.
- Reports on meetings should be written in the third person: 'It was decided', 'A proposal was put forward'. Individual reports can be written in the first person: 'I looked into the cost of …'
- Think about whether or not you need to include graphics or illustrations (such as pie charts, bar graphs, line graphs or flow charts) in your report and choose the ones that are best suited to your purpose.
- Decide whether you want to use paragraph numbering or headings. Paragraph numbering is often much clearer than using headings and allows you to refer back and forward to specific paragraphs by number. It also reduces the need for page numbering. If you do decide to use headings, make sure that the hierarchy is consistent.
- Also think about the general layout. Do you want the text to be justified or unjustified? Where are you going to position the page numbers, if you use them? Are you going to include footnotes and a bibliography?
- To make sure you've included everything, ask yourself four questions:
  - Have I included all the information that may be needed for the reader to make a decision?

- Have I covered all the possible options and made a convincing case for the alternative that I am recommending?
- Have I explained my proposal adequately and proved that it is better than alternatives?
- Have I successfully put myself in the reader's shoes, and presented the problem and the solutions with his or her priorities in mind?

- Always pay attention to:
  - consistency in headings or numbering.
  - accuracy of information in graphics, tables, footnotes, etc.
  - spelling, punctuation and grammar.
  - overall order of the argument.
  - length: is the report too long?

• Asking for increased salary

FAQ

Q. *Isn't this usually done verbally?*

A. Yes, but you may be asked to follow up in writing. The advantage of putting your request in writing is that it enables you to set down your thoughts clearly, and gives your supervisor something concrete to use when negotiating with upper management on your behalf.

Q. *Is it a good idea to threaten to leave as a way of getting a pay increase?*

A. Generally not. Your boss is likely to call your bluff, and you may have problems further down the line if you need to ask him or her for a reference. However, if you have genuinely been offered another job with a higher salary, but are reluctant to leave your current job, it may be worth mentioning this.

Q. *Whom should I address my letter to?*

A. Check with your supervisor, but it is a good idea to address it to your supervisor, and to copy in his or her manager and the human resource manager if there is one.

Tips

- Open by telling your recipient how much you enjoy being a part of the team at your company, mentioning specific skills that you have.
- Let your recipient know how valuable you are to them, by listing some accomplishments, especially in terms of revenue you have brought in to the company or money saved.
- Finish off by saying that you would like to continue being a valuable asset to the firm and that you appreciate their serious

consideration of your request for an increase.

- Be realistic in the amount that you ask for: find out how much others make in comparable jobs.
- You could also attach an updated copy of your CV, which should show all of your accomplishments in your current position as well as those for your previous jobs.

Useful phrases

- I am writing to ask if you could consider the question of my salary.
- I enjoy my work with … very much.
- Since joining PGL, I have greatly enjoyed being a member of the I.T. department.
- During my time with PGL I have made several valuable contributions to the company's success: …
- Many responsibilities have been added to my work over the last year.
- I am therefore requesting a salary increase of £… per annum.
- I would like to continue being a valuable asset to the firm and I appreciate your serious consideration of my request.
- Please find attached an updated copy of my CV, which details my skills and accomplishments.
- I should appreciate the opportunity to discuss this with you further.
- If you would like to discuss this matter further, please do not hesitate to contact me to arrange a meeting at your convenience.

48 Ashgate Drive
Preston
Lancs
PR3 6NZ

14 April 2003

Mr A Williamson
Head of I.T.
Planet Insurance Ltd
Henderson Way
Preston
Lancs
PR1 4TG

Dear Mr Williamson

request for increased salary

In the three years that I have been working for Planet Insurance, I have greatly enjoyed being a member of the I.T. department, combining my programming knowledge with my communication and people skills.

I feel that during this time, I have not only benefitted greatly from the experience, but that I have also made certain accomplishments that have been of benefit to the company. In 2001, for example, I wrote a computer program which greatly reduced the time spent on certain backup procedures, and in July 2002 I was responsible for the successful introduction of the online account management system.

With these points in mind, I would like to request a salary increase of £2000 per annum.

I am very keen to continue being a valuable asset to the firm and I appreciate your serious consideration of my request.

Please find attached an updated copy of my CV, which details my skills and accomplishments, both in my current work at Planet Insurance and in my previous jobs.

If you would like to discuss this matter further, please do not hesitate to arrange a meeting at your convenience.

Yours sincerely

Patrick Evans

Patrick Evans

• Giving notification of maternity leave

✓ You are required by law to give your employer 21 days' notice in writing of your intention to take maternity leave. You must tell them the date you intend to stop work, the week the baby is due, and whether you intend to return to your job. This protects your right to maternity pay and return to work. ***You must give at least 21 days' notice, in writing, of the date on which you intend to return to work.***

6 Dudley Avenue
Livingston
Edinburgh EH14 5TY

15 July 2003

Mr C McLeod
Cardrona Housing Association
3 Victoria Road
Edinburgh EH3 5WD

Dear Mr McLeod

maternity leave notification

I am writing to notify you that I am pregnant, the expected date of delivery being 24 September 2003. Please find attached a copy of form MAT B1, which confirms this date. I plan to begin my maternity leave on 27 August 2003.

I intend to return to work in April 2004, and will give you at least 21 days' notice of the exact date of my return.

Yours sincerely

Linda Allen

Linda Allen

6 Dudley Avenue
Livingston
Edinburgh EH14 5TY

15 July 2003

Mr C McLeod
Cardrona Housing Association
3 Victoria Road
Edinburgh EH3 5WD

Dear Mr McLeod

notification of return to work

I am writing to notify you that I intend to return to work on 4 April 2004.

I am looking forward to taking up my post with you again after maternity leave.

Yours sincerely
Linda Allen
Linda Allen

• Asking for holiday entitlement

✓ It may not be necessary to write a letter when asking for holiday entitlement. An email is often considered satisfactory.

Dear George
I would like to take two weeks of my holiday entitlement from 25 April 2003–7 March 2003.

I have checked schedules, and feel confident that my work on the first stage of the current web project will be completed by then.

I hope these dates will be convenient.

Kind regards
Jack Lyons

• Asking for unpaid leave

> Dear George
> I would like to request permission to be absent from work from 6–10 June 2004. My mother will be undergoing an operation on 3 June, and she will be requiring assistance with daily chores on her return home.
> I hope you will give my request consideration. I realize that I would not be paid for this week's leave.
> Kind regards
> *Sandra Greene*
> Sandra Greene

• Writing a letter of resignation

Tips

- Keep it simple.
- If giving your reason for leaving, try to avoid indirectly criticizing the company or your co-workers: you may wish to use your employer as a reference at a later date.
- Thank the recipient for any help or support you feel they have given you during your time at the company.
- Show that you are willing to make the transfer as easy as possible.

Useful phrases

- I have decided that it is time to move on and I have accepted a position elsewhere.
- This is to inform you that an opportunity has presented itself that will enable me to work in the area of …
- Please accept this letter as my formal resignation as Systems Administrator for DAL publishing, to become effective as of …
- I am tendering my resignation from your company and wish to advise you that … will be my last day of employment.
- As required by my contract of employment, I hereby give you 4 weeks' notice of my intention to leave my position as …
- I am confident that my new role will help me to move towards some of the goals I have for my career.
- I believe this position will offer me more opportunity for advancement, and allow me to broaden my own experience and knowledge.
- I want to take this opportunity to thank you for your time and

efforts in my training and advancement during the past three years.

- The support shown by you and the rest of the management team has been greatly appreciated.
- My experience with FTL has been very rewarding.
- Thank you for your time and consideration, and I wish you all the best in the future.
- Please be assured that I will do all I can to assist in the smooth transfer of my responsibilities before leaving.

16 Lonsdale Crescent
Betchworth
Surrey
RH10 7KM

4 April 2003

Mr K Robertson
Managing Director
Geode Publishing
3-5 Guildford Road
Dorking
Surrey
RH7 4GL

Dear Keith

resignation

I am writing to inform you that I have decided it is time to move on, and I have accepted a position at Topline Publishing in Croydon, starting on 5 April 2003. I believe this position will offer me more opportunity for advancement, and allow me to broaden my own experience and knowledge.

I want to take this opportunity to thank you for your time and effort in my training during the past three years, and wish you all the best for continued success in the future.

Please be assured that I will do all I can to assist in the smooth transfer of my responsibilities before leaving.

Yours sincerely

James Payne

James Payne

FAQ

Q. *Whom should I address my letter to?*

A. For straightforward matters such as homework and absences, write to your child's class teacher. For more serious issues or complaints, address your letter to the headteacher. If you are not satisfied with the response, you local education authority will be able to tell you whom to contact next.

Q. *How can I find out about legal issues regarding bullying, truancy, exclusion, etc?*

A. The Advisory Centre for Education (ACE) publishes booklets outlining your rights on these matters. The material can also be read on their website.

• Explaining a child's absence from school

16 Newstead Road
Bournemouth
BO3 6HM

12 Jan 2003

Dear Mr Dobson

Stephen was unable to attend school yesterday as he was suffering from a 24-hour stomach bug. He seems to be well enough to come in today.

Please advise us of any work he should be doing to make up for lost time.

Thank you.

Yours

Lesley Allen

• Excusing a child from school

✓ Your letter is more likely to receive a positive response if you phrase it as a request rather than as a *fait accompli*. Ensure that the educational value of the arrangement is stressed. Express willingness to make up for any missed work.

39 Kayside Cottages
Perth
PE2 5GK
16 Jan 2003

Mrs H Ross
Headteacher
St Mary's High School
Perth
PE3 5RA

Dear Mrs Ross

request for absence from school

On 1 Feb 2003, my employer, the NHS, will be observing 'Take your child to work day'. The purpose of this event is to introduce children aged 8 to 16 to the world of work, and to encourage them to consider a career in medicine. The programme will include many educational activities, including workshops, tours and demonstrations. I feel sure that the experience will prove to be rewarding for all children concerned.

I am therefore writing to request that my daughter, Isobel, be excused from school that day. She will, of course, make every effort to catch up on any vital school or homework that she will be forced to miss.

I look forward to hearing from you. If you wish to discuss the matter further, please do not hesitate to call me on 01252 568356.

Yours sincerely
Irene Marchant
Irene Marchant

• Notifying school of bullying

✓ Attach a report giving details of exactly where and when the incident(s) took place, who was responsible, what happened, and how your child was affected by this. Be sure to ask for details of the school's anti-bullying strategy. (The headteacher must by law have measures in place to deal with bullying among pupils.)

Useful phrases

- I wish to inform you of a serious situation involving …
- I am writing to express my deep concern about …
- My daughter has recently been experiencing …
- I have spoken to … but the situation has not improved.
- He has spoken to his class teacher, who has reprimanded those concerned. However, …
- My daughter is usually able to look after herself, but …
- As you can imagine, this problem is causing him great anxiety.
- I am anxious to resolve this problem as soon as possible.
- Please find attached a report of the series of incidents in question.
- I would like to request a meeting to discuss a resolution to this problem.

19 Fairfield Drive
Hornslea
Bucks.
RD15 6YS

25 March 2003

Mr D Fitzgerald
Headteacher
Hornslea Primary School
Hornslea
Bucks
RD15 7JA

Dear Mr Fitzgerald

For the last three days my daughter, Hannah Moore, has been arriving home in tears, due to continual name-calling from a small group of girls in her class. I have mentioned it to her class teacher, who has spoken to those concerned, but it has only made the problem worse. As you can imagine, this problem is causing Helen great anxiety, and now she is becoming fearful of going to school.

I understand that the school and the LEA have a duty of care towards my child, and so I would like to request a meeting at your earliest convenience to discuss this.

I look forward to hearing from you.

Yours sincerely,

Katherine Moore

Katherine Moore (Mrs)

56 Holmes Drive
Reigate
Surrey
RH2 5GD

25 February 2003

Mr R Thomson
Headteacher
Croydon High School
Selsdon Road
Croydon
SE14 6YE

Dear Mr Thomson

change of school

I would like to inform you that my daughter, Emma Dixon, will be leaving Croydon High School at the end of this term.

My husband has taken a new job in Scotland, and we will therefore be moving to Edinburgh at the end of April. Emma has a place at James Gillespie's School in Marchmont, which I am told has an excellent academic record.

I would like to take this opportunity to thank you for all the help and encouragement you and your staff have given Emma over the last three years.

Yours sincerely

Pauline Dixon

Pauline Dixon

• Excusing a child from religious instruction

67 Langley Avenue
Crawley
W. Sussex
RH8 3FX

12 July 2003

Mrs J Wilson
Langley Green Secondary School
Langley Drive
Crawley
RH8 4WA

Dear Mrs Wilson

religious instruction

My son, Aashir, will be attending your school from the beginning of next term, and I am writing to ask that he be excused from religious education classes.

He is being raised in the Muslim faith, and receives his religious instruction outside school.

Thank you very much for your understanding.

Yours sincerely

Mahira Pandit

Mahira Pandit (Mrs)

• Non-completion of homework

Dear Mr Mitchell
John was unable to finish his essay that was due to be handed in today, as he was suffering from a severe migraine for most of yesterday evening.
He will make every effort to complete it tonight and hand it in tomorrow.
Thank you for your understanding.
Yours sincerely
Helen Maxwell

• To a landlord concerning outstanding repairs

✓ In the first instance, simply list the repairs required, and ask the landlord to contact you so that a time may be arranged for them to be carried out.

56 Kayside Close
Redditch
Worcs.
RD14 7NX

4 April 2003

Dear Mr Fairchild

I am writing to notify you that the following repairs to 56 Kayside Close require attention:

There are several loose tiles on the roof.
The kitchen tap is leaking.
The sealant round the bath needs replacing.

I would appreciate it if you would contact me as soon as possible to arrange a time to have these problems taken care of. Thank you very much.

Yours sincerely

Matthew Chalmers

Matthew Chalmers

✓ If repairs are not forthcoming within a reasonable amount of time, write again, once more itemizing the repairs, and reminding the recipient how long you have been waiting. This time you might want to give the landlord a deadline, and show that you are aware of your rights in law.

Useful phrases

- Further to my previous correspondence, the following repairs to the above address remain outstanding: …
- I have been waiting for a considerable amount of time to have these repairs completed.
- By law, a landlord is responsible for providing and maintaining residence in a good state of repair.
- Please contact me immediately so that we may resolve this problem.
- I would be glad if you could see that the matter is resolved as soon as possible.

56 Kayside Close
Redditch
Worcs.
RD14 7NX

1 May 2003

Dear Mr Fairchild

In my previous correspondence to you I requested repairs to be completed to 56 Kayside Close. The following items remain outstanding:

There are several loose tiles on the roof.
The kitchen tap is leaking.
The sealant round the bath needs replacing.

I have been waiting for a considerable amount of time to have these repairs completed. I would ask you to take care of this matter within one week of receipt of this letter.

I remind you that by law, a landlord is responsible for providing and maintaining residence in a good state of repair, and for complying with housing and maintenance standards.

Please contact me immediately so that we may resolve this problem.

Yours sincerely

Matthew Chalmers

Matthew Chalmers

• Letter to a housing advice centre regarding unfair rent

✓ If your landlord/landlady is trying to put the rent up and you don't agree to the increase, it may be worth negotiating with them. They may agree to a lower rent increase in return rather than having to relet the property. Alternatively, they may agree to increase the rent in stages over a period of time.

45 Victoria Street
Headley
Northants.
NO3 7FS

16 April 2003

The Rents Adviser
Headley Housing Advice
4 The Row
Headley
Northants.
NO2 4TY

Dear Sir/Madam

unfair rent query

I am writing to request your advice on an issue regarding what I consider to be an unfair increase in rent.

My landlord has recently increased my rent from £300 a month to £360 a month. Not only do I find this amount unreasonable, but I am also having difficulty sustaining the payments. Furthermore, there are several outstanding repairs to be attended to in the house.

I would be grateful if you could inform me of my rights, and let me know what, if anything, I can do to challenge this increase.
I look forward to hearing from you.

Yours faithfully

Katherine Gulliver

Katherine Gulliver

• Letter to a housing advice centre regarding eviction

✓ Most private tenants can only be evicted if their landlord gets a possession order from the court. If your landlord has evicted you without following the correct procedure this may be illegal.

34 Tadworth Court
Duckbury
Berkshire
RD7 4GN

3 June 2003

Dear Sir/Madam

eviction query

I am writing to request advice from you regarding a matter of urgency.

My landlord has just issued me with an eviction notice, due to come into force on 4 July 2003. His justification for this action is that I have not paid my rent for the last two months.

I am a single mother with two young children, and I have been unable to pay the rent due to the fact that my ex-husband has not kept up regular maintenance payments over the last four months.

Could you please inform me of my rights, and advise me on how I should proceed?

I look forward to hearing from you. If you wish to speak to me directly, please call me on 01456 783219.

Thank you in advance.

Yours faithfully

Sally Nettles

Sally Nettles

• letter to planning authority inquiring as to whether planning permission is needed

✓ Some minor developments (such as certain extensions to domestic property, or changes in the way a building is used) may not need express planning permission. With buildings that are listed for preservation, it is generally best to consult with the local planning authority before any changes are made. If you are unsure as to whether or not your development requires planning permission, you should contact your local planning authority.

19 Limes Avenue
Cambridge
CB12 4LA
tel: 01356 721673

17 June 2003

The Planning Department
Cambridge District Council
University Road
Cambridge
CB2 7KS

Dear Sir/Madam

inquiry re. necessity of planning permission

I am writing to inquire as to whether I will need to apply for planning permission for a proposed development I wish to undertake at the above address.

The specifications of the development are as follows:

description:
garage
location:
side of property
use:
car storage
dimensions:
floor surface area: 6m x 3.5m
height: 2.5m

If you require any further information, please do not hesitate to contact me at the telephone number above. I look forward to hearing from you.

Yours faithfully
Harriet Yates
Harriet Yates (Mrs)

• Objecting to a planning permission application

FAQ

Q. *What sort of objection is considered valid, and what is not?*

A. Objections should be confined to such issues as:

design, appearance and general impact
significant overlooking or overshadowing
traffic impact
noise, smell or other pollutants
harm to local landmarks or public views

Objections which cannot normally be considered include:

loss of a personal view from a particular property
loss of property value

Tips

- Write to the Director of Planning at your local district council.
- Refer to the application number and the site address.
- Clearly outline the reasons why you wish to object to the proposal.

Useful phrases

- I wish to object to the above planning permission application for …
- I am writing to register my objection to the planning application detailed above.
- I am seriously concerned that the noise and the smell from the plant would be detrimental to my health.
- The increase in traffic caused by the development would significantly affect the character of the area.
- This building would significantly affect my family's quality of life.
- I request that you take this into account when considering this application.
- I urge you to give my objection serious consideration.
- I urge you to reject this application.

7 Fallowfield Terrace
Fordham
Hants
SO12 5AZ

19 May 2003

The Director of Planning and Technical Services
Fordham District Council
Riverside House
Fordham
Hants
SO13 5HB

Dear Sir/Madam

Planning application no: 00006721 45793

I wish to object to the above planning permission application for 5 Fallowfield Terrace.

This extension, if constructed, would significantly affect the amount of light reaching the back rooms of my house, as well as compromising my family's privacy and quality of life.

I request that you take this into account when considering this application and urge you to reject it.

Yours faithfully

Malcolm Skinner

Malcolm Skinner

• Objecting to the proposed erection of a mobile phone mast

FAQ

Q. *To whom should I address my letter?*

A. Write to the council's planning department and copy it to your local councillor and the landowner. You could also write to your MP about the application and contact the local press.

Q. *How should I formulate my objection?*

A. Some ideas for formulating your objection are:

Have the regulations been followed? To find out the details of

regulations affecting mobile phone masts, visit your local library, or find an appropriate site on the World Wide Web.
Is it necessary?
Are there alternative sites, and if so, is the application accompanied by evidence that they were considered?

Tips

- Identify the deadline date for objections.
- Different regions have different policies on the erection of mobile phone masts.
- Find out what your council's policy is before writing your letter.

45 Hopetoun Gardens
Hopetoun, West Lothian
LV4 7NX

3 April 2003

Mr R. McKinnon
Chief Planning Officer
Hopetoun District Council
Hopetoun, West Lothian
LV2 4GY

Dear Mr McKinnon

Re: planning application no. 39100921/000128

I am writing in objection to the proposed erection of a telecommunication mast on land situated at Hopetoun Park, West Lothian. My objection is based on the following grounds:

As you will be aware, there are a large number of conflicting academic reports on the dangers of irradiation emitted from base stations. The proposed mast would be situated only 30 metres away from a residential area. With no clear evidence showing that such masts are safe, particularly with regard to children's health, I feel that this is proximity is unacceptable.

The mast is unnecessary, since the signal for the network concerned is adequate in this area.

With these points in mind, I urge you to reject this application.

Yours sincerely

Roger Hall

Roger Hall

• letter to a lender advising of difficulty in mortgage payment

Tips

- Identify the deadline date for objections.
- If you are having trouble with your mortgage payments, or if you can see that you are going to have problems, contact your lender as soon as possible.
- In your letter, show that you are willing to negotiate with the lender. Most will help you explore your options.
- Make it clear to your lender that you are keen to keep paying as much as you can afford.

Useful phrases

- I am writing to inform you that I am anticipating having some difficulty in continuing to meet my mortgage payments.
- I am currently finding it hard to meet all my financial commitments.
- My employers went into liquidation two months ago.
- I have recently been made redundant.
- I am suffering from a long-term illness, and am no longer entitled to sickness pay.
- I was wondering if it would be possible to reduce my monthly payments.
- I would like to request that my mortgage payments be reduced from July.
- I am keen to continue paying as much as possible.
- I would be pleased to come into your office and discuss this matter further with you.
- Would it be possible to arrange an interview with you, so that we may come to some sort of arrangement?
- I do hope that you will give sympathetic consideration to my situation, and look forward to hearing from you.

92 Lockwood Avenue
Leadingham
Bucks
GR2 9TN

15 May 2003

Mr J McVee
Senior Credit Controller
Castle Building Society
2 York Road
Leeds
N. Yorks
LE3 3RA

Dear Mr McVee

request for reduction in mortgage payments

I am writing to inform you that, due to my recent redundancy, I am anticipating having some difficulty in continuing to meet my mortgage payments.

I am making every attempt to find work elsewhere, but if I am unsuccessful, I would like to request that my mortgage payments be temporarily reduced from July, and the terms of my mortgage extended accordingly.

I am keen to continue paying as much as possible, and am currently in consultation with my financial adviser to calculate how much money I can reasonably afford each month.

Would it be possible to arrange an interview with you, so that we may come to some sort of arrangement?

I do hope that you will give sympathetic consideration to my situation, and look forward to hearing from you.

Yours sincerely

Jack Everett

Jack Everett

• letter to an insurance company advising of an accident

Ken Howland
2 Rowlands Ave
Birmingham
B6 7PL

25 July 2003

The Claims Officer
Hotline Insurance
3 Castle Court
London
W1 5HT

Dear Sir/Madam

Policy No: 0000931 45621

I am writing to notify you that I wish to make a claim under the provisions of the insurance policy detailed above.

The loss came about on 12 July 2003 as a result of an accident between the insured vehicle and another vehicle at the intersection of Channel Street and Caddonfoot Road in Pitlochry, Perthshire. As a result, the insured vehicle suffered damage to the rear bumper and the lights.

Please contact me at the address shown above, so that a formal claim according to your company's procedures may be made.

Thank you for your attention to this matter.

Yours faithfully

Kenneth Howland

Kenneth Howland

• letter to an insurance company advising of a home burglary

Patrick Norton
23 Lucas Rd
Kingston-Upon-Thames
Surrey
KT6 2PL

25 July 2003

The Claims Officer
UK Assured Ltd
6 West Gorton Rd
Lincoln
LI4 9TZ

Dear Sir/Madam

Policy No: 12409745 000002

I am writing to inform you that I have suffered a loss to the above-named property, insured with you, and I would like to make a claim under the provisions of the insurance policy named above.

The loss came about on 23 July 2003, as a result of a burglary. I sustained losses of jewellery believed to have a value of £2000, a television with a value of £350, and damage to the home which will cost £500 to repair.

I would be grateful if you could contact me at the address shown above, so that a formal claim according to your company's procedures may be made.

Thank you for your attention to this matter.

Yours faithfully

Patrick Norton

Patrick Norton

LETTERS OF COMPLAINT

FAQ

Q. *Is it OK to send a complaint by email?*

A. On the whole, it is advisable to send your complaint in the form of a letter, rather than an email.

Q. *To whom should I address the letter?*

A. For a large company, direct your letter in the first instance to the Customer Relations Manager.
For a small company, you should write directly to the Managing Director.

Q. *What is the best way to ensure a speedy reply and get the desired result?*

A. Collect together all the relevant facts, then calmly set them down in a logical sequence. If you have a reference number that will help to identify the purchase or invoice in question, quote this in the subject heading of the letter. Show that you are a reasonable person by making reference to positive aspects of your contact with the company. Finally, specify a time limit (usually 14 days) within which you expect to hear from the company, stating the action you wish to be taken.

Q. *What sort of tone should I use? Is an angry tone more likely to get results?*

A. A letter that is polite and firm, and that sticks to the facts is far more effective than one written in a fit of temper.

Q. *What do I need to know about my legal rights?*

A. It often helps if you know the basics of the Sale of Goods Act, and to make this fact known to your recipient. Unless you are really sure about particular laws, though, it is best just to suggest that you know your legal rights and will use them if reasonable action is not taken.

Q. *How should I respond if I just get a bland, non-committal reply?*

A. Contact the managing director of the company, explaining your problem again. If you still do not get results, try contacting a Citizens' Advice Bureau to get legal help.

Useful phrases

- I am writing to express my dissatisfaction with the service I received from your …
- At the time of booking it was agreed that …
- However, on our arrival, we discovered that …
- I recently bought …(include colour, model and price) in your shop in …
- When I tried to use this item, I discovered that …
- I have contacted you by telephone three times and each time you have promised to visit and put the faults right.
- To date these problems have not been resolved.

- Under the terms of your guarantee, I would like to request a full reimbursement of the amount paid.
- I am withholding payment of the above invoice until I have heard your response to the points outlined above.
- Under the Goods and Services Act 1982, I am entitled to expect work to be carried out using due care and skill.
- If I do not hear from you within 14 days, I will have no choice but to take the matter further.
- Because of these faults I now consider you to be in breach of contract.

• letter of complaint regarding unsatisfactory holiday accommodation

16 Hopeside Crescent
East Sussex
EG13 6HJ

24 August 2002

The Customer Relations Manager
Sunkiss Holidays
58-60 East Preston Street
Manchester
M2 9LP

Dear Sir

Re. booking reference number 610004367

I am writing to express my dissatisfaction at the standard of holiday accommodation my family and I were forced to accept at the above holiday apartment in Ibiza last week.

At the time of booking, I requested a three-bedroomed apartment with living room and fully-equipped kitchen. However, on our arrival, we discovered that the third 'bedroom' consisted of a sofa-bed in the living area, and the kitchen was small, dirty and in a very bad state of repair. I enclose photos.

Under the Supply of Goods and Services Act 1982, I am entitled to expect the accommodation provided to be of a satisfactory standard, and for it to be as described in your brochure. I look forward to an offer of compensation within 14 days.

Yours faithfully

Charles MacLennan

Charles MacLennan (Mr)

• letter of complaint regarding a faulty appliance

41 Selwood Avenue
Kingston-upon-Hull
East Yorks
HU7 4DS

4 May 2003

Ms Jane Andrews
Customer Relations Officer
Stewarts Electrics
Electra House
Foxton High Road
London
SW3 6BZ

Dear Ms Andrews

Re: faulty appliance: Giolaggio Express A261

I recently bought a chrome 'Giolaggio Express' A261 espresso machine (£129.99) from your store in Middleham. When I tried to use it, I discovered that the element was faulty, and that the resulting coffee was lukewarm.

I have returned to your store in Middleham on several occasions, firstly requesting a replacement appliance, and subsequently, due to an extended delay, requesting a refund. The latter has not been forthcoming, and I have been advised by the shop manager to take my complaint to you.

Under the Sale of Goods Act 1979, purchased items should be of satisfactory quality and fit for their purpose. Since neither of these criteria are met, I would like to request a full reimbursement of the amount paid.

I look forward to your reply within 14 days, and hope this matter can be resolved quickly.

Yours sincerely,

A. Fraser

Anne Fraser (Mrs)

LETTERS OF COMPLAINT

Complaining about public transport

✓ If your letter of complaint is triggered by a series of problems that have been experienced in relation to a particular service, it is important that your letter should not become a long and verbose essay. It can be easy to get carried away with all the negative implications of each error, in the misguided belief that you will arouse your recipient's sympathy. Instead, list your complaint clearly and succinctly. If you are using a computer, you could separate the items with bullet points.

35 Fairways Drive
Penicuik
Midlothian
EH17 4KC

4 October 2002

The Customer Relations Manager
Scotbus
Burns House
McGowan Road
Glasgow
G4 7JY

Dear Sir/Madam

Re: Route 95, Penicuik to Edinburgh, 2 October 2002

I am writing to complain about the bus journey I undertook yesterday on the number 95 bus from Penicuik to Edinburgh. I had scheduled a meeting for lunchtime, and gave myself ample time, choosing to take the 11.15 service. I was dissatisfied with the service in the following ways:

The bus arrived 20 minutes late.

The bus finally left the bus station 30 minutes late.

The temperature inside the bus was about 35 degrees Centigrade. I asked the driver if he could turn the heating off, but he explained that it had to be switched on, as it formed part of the bus's cooling system.

Being nearly 7 months' pregnant, I found this journey very uncomfortable, and by the end, quite distressing.

I would be interested to hear your comments on this, and any offer of compensation you may consider appropriate.

Yours faithfully

P. Holmes

Patricia Holmes

LETTERS OF COMPLAINT

• Shoddy workmanship

Tips

- Discuss the problem with the tradesperson first, and give them a chance to put it right. If this doesn't work, put your complaint in writing giving a deadline. Send it to the head office if there is one.
- Keep copies of all letters sent and received and make a note of conversations.
- If you chose a contractor that belongs to a trade association, they may offer a conciliation or arbitration service to settle your dispute.

77 Bishop Road
Newport
Gwent
NP3 5NQ

31 October 2002

The Customer Services Manager
L. Smart & Co. Contractors
17 Trevellyan Road
Cardiff
CA4 5GT

Dear Sir/Madam

Re: estimate 700003412

I am writing to express my dissatisfaction with the service I received from one of your builders recently.

Before accepting your estimate for the job, I was assured that the work would be completed by 10 October. Three weeks later, the work is still incomplete. Moreover, the work that has been done is defective. The new door that was fitted is not flush with the frame, and the lock is consequently very stiff.

If the work is not completed and the defect rectified within 14 days, I shall consider our contract to be at an end. I shall then instruct another firm to complete the work, and deduct the cost from your original price.

Yours faithfully

Douglas Fairburn

Douglas Fairburn

Complaining to a health authority

Tips

- Address your letter to the Complaints Manager of the Local Health Authority
- Give name of doctor, GP or practitioner concerned.
- Give a brief background to case.
- State the problem. If your complaint consists of a catalogue of errors, itemize them clearly and succinctly.
- Note that it is one of the NHS's officially stated core principles that it is committed to shaping its services around the needs and preferences of individual patients, their families and carers.

7 Oaklands
Horley RH6 2QT

17 November 2002

The Complaints Manager
East Surrey Local Health Authority
5 Market Street
Redhill
RH1 4GA

Dear Sir

I am writing to express my concern about the treatment that my elderly mother, Mrs Grace Harding, is currently undergoing. Her GP is Dr Middleton at the Longwood Surgery, Horley.

In 2001, my mother was diagnosed as suffering from shingles. Since that time she has experienced continual pain down the sides of her body.

However, she recently received a letter informing her that she would no longer be able to attend the pain clinic at this surgery. She has been given no explanation as to the reasons for this decision from the health authority or from her doctor.

Since it is one of the NHS's officially stated core principles that it is committed to shaping its services around the needs and preferences of individual patients, I feel that you have a duty to ensure that she enjoys this later period of her life.

I would be glad to hear your comments on this case.

Yours faithfully

G. Glover

Gillian Glover

Complaining about financial services

Tips

- You must complain to the firm before you go to the ombudsman.
- Remember to include important details like your customer number or your policy or account number. Put these details at the top of your letter.
- Remember to enclose copies of any relevant documents that you believe back up your case.
- Keep a copy of any letters between you and the firm. You may need to refer to them later.

4 Hove Lane
Newhaven
W Sussex BN12 6JL

24 October 2002

The Customer Relations Manager
Castle Building Society
Grove Street
Derby
DB5 4FY

Dear Sir/Madam

Complaint: savings acc. no. 9450001992

I wish to register my dissatisfaction with the service that I have received from the staff at your Brighton branch.

I opened a savings account, and arranged for a monthly standing order of £150 a month to be made from my current account, held at another bank. However, the last time I asked for a mini-statement, I noticed that there had not been a credit to my savings account for the previous two months, despite the fact that the money had been debited from my current account. Enclosed are copies of both the relevant statements. I brought this to the attention of your Brighton staff, but they dismissed the problem as being outside their remit.

I am therefore appealing to you for a thorough investigation into this matter, and look forward to hearing from you.

Yours faithfully

Patrick Horton

Patrick Horton

Formal invitations

Tips

- Use good quality stationery that reflects your personal style, and the nature of the occasion.
- Issue your invitation well in advance of the occasion, so that the recipient will be able to make space in his or her calendar for your event.
- Include details of the nature of the event, the address, date and time, and indicate whether or not food and drink will be provided if the time is near to a usual meal time. If a dress code or special parking arrangements are required, give these details in as clear and brief a manner as possible.
- Include the line "RSVP" with a telephone number or address, so that guests can tell you whether or not they will be able to attend. You may want to include an RSVP card for the recipient's use.

A wedding invitation

John and Angela Shaw
are delighted to invite
Jeremy Kempton and Kay Whitcroft
to the wedding of their daughter
Catharine
to
Matthew Tibbits
on Saturday 5th April 2003
at 2pm
at Hemel Methodist Church, Bristol
and afterwards to a
Reception
at Austen Place, Keynsham

RSVP
Cathy Shaw
89 Caird Drive
Brighton
BN1 9TQ

• Refusing invitations

Tips

- Begin by thanking the person for the invitation.
- Then show regret and give reasons.
- Finally, express desire to see them at a future date.

Useful phrases

- Thank you so much for the invitation to …
- Many thanks for your invitation to …
- I'm afraid I'm not going to be able to come.
- Unfortunately we're not going to be able to make it.
- Unfortunately I already have something arranged for that day.
- It's our 30th wedding anniversary, and we're going out for a meal that night.
- It's the day we get back from our holiday, so I don't know if we'll be home in time.
- Harry's got his school concert that night.
- What a shame!
- I'm really sorry, as I'd have loved to see you all.
- I hope we can get together soon, though.
- I hope you all have a really great time.

• Declining a formal invitation to a wedding

✓ Use the same style as that used in the invitation.

25 Dean Avenue
Yeovil
Somerset
YO3 8LR

23 March 2003

Mr and Mrs K Forbes thank Mr and Mrs O'Neill for their kind invitation to their daughter's wedding, and to the reception afterwards, but regret that a prior engagement prevents them from attending.

• Declining a formal invitation to dinner

8 Holmes Close
Eskbank
Midlothian
EH16 3BV

14 May 2003

Dear Caroline

Many thanks for your kind invitation to dinner on 1st August. Unfortunately, Jeff is away on business that week, and I've arranged to go and visit Jackie and the children, so I'm afraid we won't be able to be with you.

We are both very sorry, and hope to see you soon.

Thank you again.

Fiona

• An informal letter or email declining an invitation

67 Hawthornevale
Gosforth
Newcastle
N7 5GD

24 April 2003

Dear Nicola

Thanks ever so much for the invitation to Gordon's party, but I'm afraid I'm not going to be able to make it. It's our 30th wedding anniversary that day, and we're going out for a meal in the evening. What a shame! I hope we'll be able to get together again soon.

Hope you all have a great time.

love,

Teresa

xxx

SOCIAL CORRESPONDENCE

• Writing a letter of apology

Tips

- Make it clear from the start that you are apologizing, and state what you are apologizing for.
- Explain how the mistake came about, accepting responsibility if you are at fault.
- Think about how you can put the problem right, and suggest your solution tentatively.
- At the end of the letter, reiterate your apology.

Useful phrases

- I am writing to apologize for …
- I've just realized that …
- I can't tell you how sorry I am.
- I am sorry that …
- Due to …, I was unable to …
- I know it's no excuse, but …
- Unfortunately …
- I hope you will accept …
- Can I suggest …?
- Would you agree to …?
- Again, please accept my apologies (for …).
- In the meantime, many apologies again.

• Letters wishing a speedy recovery

FAQ

Q. *What sort of tone should I use?*

A. It is acceptable to use a fairly informal tone if you know that the person will recover quickly. If the illness is serious, you will need to use a slightly more formal tone.

Q. *Should I send a card or a letter?*

A. For informal wishes, a card is most appropriate. For more formal wishes, or if the illness is serious, you may like to write a letter.

• Informal wishes (card)

Useful phrases

- Hoping you get well very soon.
- Wishing you a speedy recovery.
- Sorry to hear you're not well. We're thinking of you.

• Formal wishes (letter)

Useful phrases

- I was very sorry to hear of …
- Please accept my sympathies …
- … and best wishes for a speedy recovery.
- It must be an anxious time for you.
- You have our deepest sympathy.
- Is there any way in which we can help?
- If there's anything I can do, please don't hesitate to let me know.
- We hope and trust you will soon be better.
- We are feeling for you.

• Formal letter wishing someone a speedy recovery

Upper Steading, 17 June, 2003

Dear Mr Grierson

We were very sorry to hear of your wife's sudden illness. Please accept our sympathies and give her our best wishes for a speedy recovery.

It must be a very anxious time for you. If there's anything we can do, please don't hesitate to let us know. In the meantime, we are thinking of you both.

Yours sincerely

Mary Fawkes

✓ If the recipient is unlikely to make a full recovery, it is unwise to suggest that this might be the case.

• Letters of condolence

FAQ

Q. *What form should a letter of condolence take?*

A. A letter of condolence should normally be handwritten. However, you need to use your own discretion, depending on your relationship with the recipient.

Q. *I never know what to say at such times. Don't letters of condolence require flowery language and literary turns of phrase?*

A. No. Try to express yourself simply, and speak from the heart.

Q. *Should I make reference to God and religion?*

A. Only if you know that your recipient shares your beliefs.

Tips

A simple and effective structure for a condolence letter might be as follows:

- Express your shock or regret and the person's death.
- Briefly point out the deceased's qualities, and any achievements you may want to mention.
- Say how much the deceased will be missed.
- Offer any help that you are genuinely willing to give.

An informal letter of condolence

Useful phrases

- We were very sad to hear of ...'s death.
- It came as a terrible shock to us all.
- Everyone who knew him found him a warm and affectionate person.
- She was such a good friend to us.
- We will all miss him terribly.
- We're thinking of you all.
- Please don't hesitate to call on us at any time.
- Is there anything we can do to help?

Littleton, 24 March 2003

Dear Pat,

We were terribly sad to hear the tragic news of Ken's death. It 's been a great shock, and we want you to know that you are in our thoughts.

Everyone who knew Ken found him an exceptional person, with his great talent for painting and his kindness and warmth. We will miss him greatly.

You know that you can call on us any time. Please don't hesitate if there is anything we can do to help.

All our love

Leonie and Andrew

A more formal letter of condolence

Useful phrases

- I was deeply saddened to hear of …'s death last …
- I have just heard of the sad death of …
- It has come to us as a great shock.
- Please accept my sincerest condolences.
- I am sure you know how much he was liked and respected by everyone.
- We will all miss him greatly.
- He will be greatly missed.
- It must be a comfort to you to know that …

Taunton, 14 April 2003

Dear Mrs Morrison

I was very sad to hear of your husband's death last week, and I write to offer sincere condolences to you and your family.

I am sure you know how much Mr Morrison was liked and respected in the community. We will all miss him greatly.

If there is anything I can do to help, please don't hesitate to get in touch.

Kindest regards

Yvonne Tullis

Writing your speech

Tips

- When writing your speech, if you're unsure of what to say, look at other people's speeches in books and on websites. Reading what others have said can help you decide what's appropriate for you.
- Think about who will be in the audience. What would *they* appreciate? How formal is the setting? What kind of jokes are likely to go down well?
- Brainstorm on topics.
- Select topic(s).
- Gather your material.
- Organize your material.
- Draft your speech.
- Practise your delivery.

Delivering your speech

FAQ

Q. *Is It OK to read my speech or should I try to memorize it?*
A. It's best not to trust everything to memory. Try to thoroughly familiarise yourself with your speech and then reduce it to a set of brief notes on cue cards. This way your speech will not sound as if it is being read word for word.
Q. *Should I practise my speech, or might too much practice make it sound contrived?*
A. You should rehearse it, then rehearse it again. And then again, until you have had enough of it. Get a friend or family member to help by listening and ask them to tell you honestly how your voice sounds.
Q. *I tend to gabble when I'm nervous. How can I avoid this?*
A. Always pause to let your points sink in and wait for the laughs you want. Take your time. What will seem like an age to you will really only be a few seconds to your audience. Use pauses to gather your thoughts, glance at your notes and breathe in and out. Don't give in to the urge to speed up.
Q. *Is it advisable to have a few drinks beforehand?*
A. Don't drink too much before speaking. You might think it helps, but your audience won't.
Q. *How can I give an impression of confidence, even when I'm nervous?*
A. When delivering your speech, be conscious of your body language from the start. Stand with your weight equal on both feet, and look around at your audience for a few seconds before you start to speak. Try to make eye contact with the audience. Try to make everyone feel included.

• Wedding speeches

There are three main speeches that are usually given at a wedding reception. They are:

- the bride's father's speech
- the bridegroom's speech
- the best man's speech

Other speeches are possible. For example, the bridegroom's father may give a short speech of thanks to the host and hostess for the occasion, or the bride may wish to give a speech. Here, though, we will look at the three principal speeches.

✓ *Tips*

- Once you have completed all the formalities, you may wish to expand your speech a little. When drafting your speech, start by considering some of the following points:
- When did you first meet the bride/groom?
- Who brought you together? (for bridegroom only)
- How did she/he come across to you then?
- Can you remember anything unusual that happened when you first met?
- What are her/his best qualities?
- Think of three words describing the way you feel about him/her.
- Do you have any plans or wishes for your future together? (for bridegroom only)

• The bride's father

The bride's father is called upon by the best man to propose a toast of health and happiness to the bride and bridegroom.
Before doing so, he should welcome the groom's parents, and the relatives of both families. He should say a few words about his daughter, and then the groom, welcoming him into the family.

Useful phrases

- On behalf of (name of wife) and myself, I would like to start by saying what a pleasure it is to welcome, on this very happy occasion (names of groom's parents), (named close relatives), together with all relatives and friends of both families.
- As father of the bride, it is my privilege to make the first speech, and I would like to start by …
- First I would like to welcome everybody here today to join (bride) and (groom) on this special day.
- To (name of officiator), our thanks for officiating at the ceremony,

and to his 'boss' for keeping the weather at bay.

- I know some people have travelled quite some distance, and I would like to express our gratitude and thanks for the effort they have made.
- I would like to thank (bride) and (groom) for organizing such a splendid occasion. I am sure you will agree that it is a tremendous success.
- I'd like to take this opportunity to thank especially, (wife), for not only being a tolerant wife but more importantly an outstanding mother.
- (Groom) is attentive, caring, hard-working, intelligent, and informed on most subjects, except football (he supports ……). I am very pleased and proud to welcome him as a son-in-law.
- During the time we've known him, we've come to realize how special he is to her. I would like to welcome my new son-in-law into our family.
- (Bride's name) and (groom's name),

  Here's to the past
  Here's to the present
  And here's to the future, for all that you can look forward to together.
- Ladies and gentlemen, please be upstanding, and raise your glasses to (bride) and (groom).
- The bride and groom.
- Thank you.
- It is now my pleasant duty to propose a toast to the happy couple. Please join me in wishing them a long and happy life together. Ladies and Gentlemen fill your glasses and join in the toast to the happy couple, (bride) and (groom).

• The bridegroom

The bridegroom replies on behalf of himself and his bride, thanking his parents for their love and care, and for the start they gave him in life.
He will also take this opportunity to thank all those present for their gifts.
Any members of the family who could not attend the wedding because of illness should be mentioned and wished a speedy recovery.
He would normally then say a few words about his new wife.
The bridegroom should propose a toast to the bridesmaids, and thank them for doing such a good job.

Useful phrases

- I'd like to thank (bride's father) for those kind words, I am very proud to be your son-in-law; I hope I can live up to your expectations.
- I would sincerely like to thank you and (bride's mother) for welcoming me into your family.
- Thank you again to (bride's father) and (bride's mother) for your daughter's hand. Julia is the most special person I've ever known, and I promise I'll take good care of her.
- To our parents, thank you for your love and support over the years, for the advice you have given us, for putting up with us and pointing us in the right direction.
- On behalf of my new wife and myself, I would like to say thank you to a few people:
- Firstly, to (bride)'s parents and to my own parents … We could never thank you enough for all your very generous help and the tremendous love and support you've always given us, but in particular in the last few months.
- To our two lovely bridesmaids for taking such good care of (bride) and getting her to the church on time.
- To my ushers, (names), for looking after me so well today.
- To (name of Master of Ceremonies), for keeping us all in line today as Master of Ceremonies.
- To my best man (name), for calming my nerves on the run-up to the wedding and for looking after me so well today.
- To everybody for all your cards, kind thoughts and presents. We've been quite staggered by your generosity.
- I would like to say thanks very much for all of you for sharing this special day with us.
- It's been an amazing day and having you all here has helped to make this the most memorable and happiest day of our lives.
- In conclusion, I would also like to thank my best friend for agreeing to marry me today.
- The one person in this room to which I owe the most thanks is (bride), my wife. I am sure you will all agree how stunning she looks today.
- She is beautiful, intelligent, hard-working – the list is endless, but unfortunately I can't read her handwriting …

• The best man

It is the best man's duty to respond to this toast on behalf of the bridesmaids. His speech should be light-hearted and fun.

Useful phrases

- Firstly on behalf of the bridesmaid(s), (names), I'd like to thank (groom) for his kind words. I'm sure you'd agree with me that they look beautiful and that they have done an excellent job today.
- Firstly on behalf of the bridesmaid(s), (bridesmaids' names), I would like to thank (groom) for his kind words.
- I am sure you will all agree she does/they do look marvellous.
- The bride, well, we all agree how wonderful she looks today, and (groom) scrubs up well himself …
- I must say she is one of the nicest people you could ever wish to meet.
- On a serious note, can you all be up standing and charge your glasses while I propose a toast:
- To the bride – may she share everything with her husband, including the housework!
- To the bride and groom – may the roof above you never fall in and may you both never fall out!
- Please stay upstanding and join me in a toast to the bride and groom's parents … and those who were sadly unable to be here today.
- It gives me great pleasure to invite you to all stand and raise your glasses in a toast for (bride) and (groom). We wish them well for the future and hope they enjoy a long and happy marriage together.

• Writing a eulogy

FAQ

Q. *What sort of tone should I adopt when writing a eulogy?*

A. Generally, a eulogy should be written in an informal, conversational tone. Humour is acceptable if it fits the personality of the deceased. When delivering your eulogy, talk to the audience as though you were talking to a friend.

Q. *Should I just speak about my own experiences of the deceased, or should I try to include other people's experiences?*

A. A eulogy should convey the feelings and experiences of the person giving it. Don't try to objectively summarize the person's life or speak for all present. Having said that, it can be a good idea to write about memories that the audience can remember, and to get the audience involved in what you are saying.

Q. *How long should I speak for?*

A. Keep it brief. Five to ten minutes is the norm, but it's a good idea to verify that with the officiator.

WRITING SPEECHES

Tips

- Be yourself.
- Be honest, and focus on the person's positive qualities.
- You may want to include the deceased's favourite poems, book passages, scripture verses, quotes, expressions or lines from songs.
- You could interview family and friends when preparing your draft.
- Some of the simplest thoughts are deeply touching and easy for those congregated to identify with. For example, 'I'll miss her laughter' is just as good as 'I admired her courage.'
- Here are some questions to ask yourself:
- How did you and the deceased become close?
- Is there a humorous or touching event that represents the essence of the deceased?
- What did you and others love and admire about the deceased?
- What will you miss most about him or her?

Useful phrases

- When I think of …, I think of laughter and love.
- I can remember …ing with …
- One time …
- … even made it into the newspaper about it.
- … taught me how to …
- … was involved in so many activities; she/he was very popular.
- I can see her/him now: …ing, …ing and …
- … was like a ray of sunshine.
- … gave me so much wisdom.
- She/he always showed loyalty, courtesy and consideration for others.
- I am so lucky to have had … as a friend.
- And in spirit she/he joins us today.
- I will miss her/him very much.

WRITING SPEECHES

• Leaving and retirement speeches

Tips

- Remember that your approach may be slightly different depending on whether the employee is leaving under happy or more regrettable circumstances.
- Make sure you get your facts right, for example how long the employee has been working for the company.
- Remember that your main aim is to thank the employee and to praise them for any achievements you want to mention.
- On the whole, this kind of speech should be short, as people are usually standing at such occasions.
- Even if your relationship with the employee was not very warm, try to concentrate on their good points.
- Try to think of at least one anecdote, humorous if possible, that you can recount about the person who is leaving.

Useful phrases

- This is both a time to look back and a time to look forward.
- Some people here may remember the time when …
- When Jack first arrived at the company, there was … Now, there are …
- Thank you for all your hard work, especially …
- You have certainly made my job easier.
- The company has a lot to thank you for.
- We respect the decision you have made, and wish you all the best in your future career.
- We are sorry you had to leave under these circumstances, but we wish you every success in the future.
- Your future is looking very exciting, and we wish you great happiness in your new job.
- We are all going to miss you very much, and hope that the rest will do you the good your deserve.
- Everyone joins me in wishing you well.
- Please accept this gift as a mark of our respect and gratitude for all you have done.

EMAILS

Tips

The rules of polite behaviour for email conversation are known as 'netiquette'. Some rules of netiquette are:

- Do not write in capital letters. This is considered to be the equivalent of shouting in speech.
- Use asterisks (*) before and after a word if you want to emphasize it.
- Be careful about using irony or sarcasm. Readers cannot see facial expressions or hear the tone of voice, and so statements intended as jokes may be taken seriously.
- Jokes can be shown by using a 'smiley' or 'emoticon' such as :-). On the other hand, do not use too many of these.
- Avoid 'flames'. A flame is an angry response to a message, especially on a newsgroup. An exchange of flames or a 'flame war' can be very annoying for other newsgroup readers.
- Always include the subject of a message in the subject line.
- Messages should be relatively short and to the point.
- Do not forward other people's messages without the author's permission.
- Include the parts of the message being responded to in new emails or posts to newsgroups.

• Emoticons

Emoticons or 'smileys' are often used to indicate tone. These symbols are read with the head tilted on the left shoulder. The basic smiley is :-). It may mean 'I'm happy to hear from you', or it may be used after a jokey statement. Tongue-in-cheek remarks might use a winking smiley ;-). Below is a list of emoticons in common use, both in email and text messaging:

o:-)	angel
;/	confused
>:-)	devil
:-%	Get lost!
:-s	I'm not making sense.
:-p	naughty
:@)	pig
:-(	sad
:-O	shouting
:o	surprised
:-@!	swearing
;&	tongue-tied

EMAILS

• Net abbreviations

Net abbreviations have developed to shorten messages and speed up typing. It is best to avoid using them if you are not sure that your recipient will understand them. Some of the more common ones are:

AFK	away from keyboard
BAK	back at keyboard
BTW	by the way
FAQ	frequently asked question(s) (or a web page containing frequently asked questions)
FWIW	for what it's worth
FYI	for your information
FUA	frequently used acronym
IAE	in any event
IMO	in my opinion
IMCO	in my considered opinion
IMHO	in my humble opinion
IOW	in other words
NRN	no reply necessary
OTOH	on the other hand
ROFL	rolling on the floor laughing
RSN	real soon now (often used ironically)
SITD	still in the dark
TIA	thanks in advance
TIC	tongue in cheek
TLA	three letter acronym

Useful phrases

Generally, email avoids the use of the more formal opening and closing conventions used in traditional letter writing. Below are the most common ones used:

more formal

Dear George	All the best
Dear Mr Thomas	Best wishes
	Kind regards
	Regards

more informal

Hi Jenny
Jenny
Hi there!

See you soon
All the best
Best wishes
Take care
Love
Lots of love

EMAILS

• A more formal email

To: frankcollins@planet.co.uk, viviankaye@planet.co.uk
Cc: robertwestwood@planet.co.uk
Bcc:
Subject: sales review meeting
Attachments: salesfigures_jan_to_march2003.doc

Dear Frank, Vivian

I've just been looking at the sales figures for the last quarter, and I think it would be beneficial for us all to get together to discuss them.

I'm attaching a copy of the document, and would be grateful for any comments you may have, especially with regard to the post-Christmas sale period.

Would Thursday afternoon suit you both, say, 2.30pm? Please let me know if this is not convenient. Thanks.

Regards

Brian

• An informal email

To: jennymartin@viking.net
Cc:
Bcc:
Subject: Friday night
Attachments:

Hi Jenny

How're things? Hope all's well, and that you had a riveting time last night at the committee meeting ;-)

I was wondering what you and Will are up to on Friday? We're thinking of going out for something to eat – maybe an Indian. Do you fancy coming too?

BTW, I've just heard that Kate's taken that new job. IMHO it's not going to be an easy job, but good for her anyway.

Let us know what you think about Friday night.

Lots of love

Tamsin xxx

EMAILS

• Response to an informal email

To: tforbes@pgl.com
Cc:
Bcc:
Subject: Re: Friday night
Attachments:

Hi Tamsin

You wrote:

>Hope all's well, and that you had a riveting time last night at the >committee meeting ;-)

I nearly died of boredom, as you can well imagine!

>I was wondering what you and Will are up to on Friday? We're thinking of going out for >something to eat – maybe an Indian. Do you fancy coming too?

Sounds great! I'll have been paid by then, so I'll be up for a big night :-)

>BTW, I've just heard that Kate's taken that new job. IMHO it's not going to be an easy >job, but good for her anyway.

I'm amazed, but I suppose our Kate's always up for a challenge. Rather her than me though …

Looking forward to seeing you. Will give you a ring about meeting up on Friday.

Love

Jenny

xx

• Text messaging

Since most mobile phones do not have keyboards, senders of messages have to key through the letters marked on the numeric keypad. This can be tedious, and so text messages tend to be short, using a large number of short cuts. As with email, emoticon are also used. Some of the more common abbreviations are listed below:

1CE	once
2DAY	today
2MOR	tomorrow
2NITE	tonight
ASAP	as soon as possible
B	be
BCNU	be seeing you
BRB	be right back
BTDT	been there, done that
BTW	by the way
C	see
CID	consider it done
COZ	because
CU	see you
DA	the
EZ	easy
F2T	free to talk
FOTFLOL	falling on the floor, laughing out loud
GAL	get a life
GR8	great
GTG	got to go
H8	hate
K	okay
L8	late
L8ER	later
LOL	laughing out loud *or* loads of love
LV	love
M8	mate
MMFU	my mate fancies you
NE	any
NE1	anyone
NETHING	anything
NO1	no one
NP	no problem
OIC	oh, I see
OMG	oh, my God
PLS	please
PPL	people
R	are
RTFM	read the flippin' manual
RU	are you
RUOK	are you okay
SOZ	sorry
STFU	shut up
SUM1	someone
THANQ	thank you
THX	thanks
TMB	text me back
TTYL	talk to you later
TXT BAC	text back
TYVM	thank you very much
U	you
W/O	without
WAN2	want to
WBS	write back soon
WIV	with
WKND	weekend
WUD?	what you doing?
XLNT	excellent
Y	why
YR	your
YYSSW	yeah yeah sure whatever